READERS' GUIDE TO PERIODICAL LITERATURE

An Author and Subject Index

MARCH 1977—FEBRUARY 1978

Edited by
ZADA LIMERICK

Assistant Editor
JEAN M. MARRA

Indexers
DOROTHY A. HARRINGTON
MARIA L. KOCYLOWSKY
ALICE P. ORDIERS
BARBARA SCHREIBER
ROSEMARY STRAMMIELI
MARIAN J. WESTON

THE H. W. WILSON COMPANY
NEW YORK 1978

International Standard Serial Number 0034-0464

Library of Congress Catalog Card No. (6-8232)

PRINTED IN THE UNITED STATES OF AMERICA

ACKNOWLEDGMENTS

In addition to the staff members whose names appear on the title page we wish to acknowledge the contributions of Ann F. Dietz who indexed for this volume.

Z. L.

PREFATORY NOTE

The READERS' GUIDE TO PERIODICAL LITERATURE is a cumulative author subject index to periodicals of general interest published in the United States.

The main body of the Index consists of subject and author entries to periodical articles arranged in one alphabet. In addition there is an author listing of citations to book reviews following the main body of the Index.

The Committee on Wilson Indexes of the American Library Association's Reference and Adult Services Division advises the publisher on indexing and editorial policy by means of in-depth contents studies conducted at intervals of several years.

Suggestions for additions or deletions of titles should be brought to the attention of the Committee in care of The H. W. Wilson Company.

SUGGESTIONS FOR THE USE OF THE READERS' GUIDE TO PERIODICAL LITERATURE

Arrangement

Authors and subjects are arranged in one alphabet. Under authors and subjects, titles are arranged also in alphabetical order by the first word, initial articles being disregarded. Under personal names titles *by* author precede those *about* him. Subdivisions of a subject are arranged alphabetically under the subject. Geographical subheads follow the other subdivisions in a separate alphabet.

Book Reviews

For citations of reviews of individual books, see book review section following main body of the Index.

Cross References

See references are made from various forms of personal names and subject headings to the most generally accepted forms, appearing in the first issue, after made, and thereafter in but one quarterly issue, until the annual volume. They are also made from titles of dramas and operas to names of dramatists and composers.

See also references are made from a subject to related subjects under which additional material may be found.

Dramas

Dramas are indexed under the dramatist's name with a *see* reference from the title of the drama; titles are also listed under the heading Drama reviews—Single works.

Fiction

Short stories are indexed under the author's name; titles are listed under the heading Short stories with a *see* reference to the author's name. Subject entries are made for selected types of fiction, e.g. Historical fiction; Christmas stories; etc.

Motion Pictures

Motion pictures are indexed under the headings Motion picture reviews—Single works or Motion pictures, Documentary—Reviews—*Single works*. No title references are made.

Musical comedies, revues, etc.

Musical comedies, revues, etc. are indexed under the heading Musical comedy, revue, etc. —Reviews—*Single works* with a *see* reference from the title of the work.

Operas, Operettas

Operas, Operettas are indexed under the composer's name with a *see* reference from the title of the opera or operetta; titles are also listed under the headings Opera reviews—Single works or Operetta reviews—Single works.

Television programs

Television programs are indexed under the headings Television program reviews—Single works or Television programs. Documentary—Reviews—*Single works*. No title references are made.

For those unfamiliar with form of reference used in the entries, the following explanation is given.

Sample subject entry: ANDALUSIA, Spain
Love letter to Andalusia. J. Winslow. il Holiday 58:36-8+ S '77

An illustrated article on the subject ANDALUSIA, Spain entitled "Love letter to Andalusia," by J. Winslow, will be found in volume 58 of Holiday, pages 36-8 (continued on later pages of the same issue) the September 1977 number

Sample name entry: SEVAREID, Eric
Eric Sevareid on today's morals, TV, war or peace, prosperity; interview. pors U.S. News 83:60-2 D 26 '77

about

Sign-off for Sevareid. il pors Time 110:111 D 12 '77 *

An article *by* Eric Sevareid, with portraits will be found in volume 83 of U.S. News & World Report, pages 60-2 the December 26, 1977 number.

An article about Eric Sevareid will be found in volume 110 of Time, page 111, the December 12, 1977 number.

The asterisk is a printer's device used following a name entry to facilitate the filing of articles *by* a person from articles *about* a person. This device does not affect usage of Readers' Guide in any way.

ABBREVIATIONS OF PERIODICALS INDEXED

For full information, consult pages xi-xiv

Aging—Aging
Am Artist—American Artist
Am City & County—American City & County
Am Educ—American Education
Am For—American Forests
*__Am Heritage__—American Heritage
Am Hist Illus—American History Illustrated
Am Hist R—American Historical Review
Am Home—American Home
Am Imago—American Imago
Am Lib—American Libraries
Am Rec G—American Record Guide
(Publication suspended with D '72 issue; resumed N '76)
Am Scholar—American Scholar
Am West—American West
America—America
American City. See American City & County
Américas—Américas
Ann Am Acad—Annals of the American Academy of Political and Social Science
Antiques—Antiques
Archit Rec—Architectural Record
Art in Am—Art in America
Art N—Art News
*__Atlantic__—Atlanic
Audubon—Audubon
Aviation W—Aviation Week & Space Technology

*__Bet Hom & Gard__—Better Homes and Gardens
BioScience—BioScience
Bull Atom Sci—Bulletin of the Atomic Scientists
Bus W—Business Week

Camp Mag—Camping Magazine
Car & Dr—Car and Driver
Ceram Mo—Ceramics Monthly
*__Changing T__—Changing Times
Chemistry—Chemistry
Chr Cent—Christian Century
Chr Today—Christianity Today
Clearing H—Clearing House
Commentary—Commentary
Commonweal—Commonweal
Cong Digest—Congressional Digest
Conservationist—Conservationist (Albany)
*__Consumer Rep__—Consumer Reports
*__Consumers Res Mag__—Consumers' Research Magazine
Craft Horiz—Craft Horizons
Cur Hist—Current History
Current—Current

Dance Mag—Dance Magazine
Dept State Bull—Department of State Bulletin
Design (US)—Design (United States)
Duns R—Dun's Review

*__Ebony__—Ebony
Educ Digest—Education Digest
Engl J—English Journal
Environment—Environment
Esquire—Esquire

Fam Health—Family Health incorporating Today's Health
*__Farm J__—Farm Journal
Field & S—Field & Stream
Film Q—Film Quarterly
Flying—Flying
Focus—Focus
*__For Affairs__—Foreign Affairs
Forbes—Forbes
*__Fortune__—Fortune

*__Good H__—Good Housekeeping

Harp Baz—Harper's Bazaar
*__Harpers__—Harper's
Harvard Bus R—Harvard Business Review
*__Hi Fi__—High Fidelity and Musical America
Hobbies—Hobbies
Holiday—Holiday
Incorporated in Travel, N '77
*__Horizon__—Horizon
Horn Bk—Horn Book Magazine
Horticulture—Horticulture
Hot Rod—Hot Rod
House & Gard—House & Garden incorporating Living for Young Homemakers
House B—House Beautiful

Int Wildlife—International Wildlife
Intellect—Intellect

*__Ladies Home J__—Ladies' Home Journal
Lib J—Library Journal
Liv Wildn—Living Wilderness

MH—MH
M Labor R—Monthly Labor Review
McCalls—McCall's
Mademoiselle—Mademoiselle
Mech Illus—Mechanix Illustrated
Mod Phot—Modern Photography
Motor B & S—Motor Boating & Sailing
Motor T—Motor Trend
Ms—Ms.
*__Mus Q__—Musical Quarterly

N Y Times Mag—New York Times Magazine
***Nat Geog**—National Geographic Magazine
Nat Parks & Con Mag—National Parks & Conservation Magazine
***Nat R**—National Review (48p issue only, pub. in alternate weeks)
Nat Wildlife—National Wildlife
Nation—Nation
Nations Bus—Nation's Business
***Natur Hist**—Natural History
Negro Hist Bull—Negro History Bulletin
New Cath World—New Catholic World
New Repub—New Republic
New Yorker—New Yorker
***Newsweek**—Newsweek

Oceans—Oceans
Opera N—Opera News
Org Gard & Farm—Organic Gardening and Farming
Outdoor Life—Outdoor Life

Parents Mag—Parents' Magazine
Parks & Rec—Parks & Recreation
Phys Today—Physics Today
Plays—Plays
Poetry—Poetry
Pop Electr—Popular Electronics
***Pop Mech**—Popular Mechanics
Pop Phot—Popular Photography
Pop Sci—Popular Science
Progressive—Progressive
Psychol Today—Psychology Today
Pub W—Publishers Weekly

Radio-Electr—Radio-Electronics
***Read Digest**—Reader's Digest
Redbook—Redbook
***Ret Liv**—Retirement Living

SLJ—SLJ/School Library Journal
Sat Eve Post—Saturday Evening Post
***Sat R**—Saturday Review
Sch Arts—School Arts
***Sci Am**—Scientific American
Sci Digest—Science Digest
Sci N—Science News
Science—Science
Science and Public Affairs. See Bulletin of the Atomic Scientists
Sea Front—Sea Frontiers
***Seventeen**—Seventeen
Sky & Tel—Sky and Telescope
Smithsonian—Smithsonian
Society—Society
Space World—Space World
***Sports Illus**—Sports Illustrated
Sr Schol—Senior Scholastic including World Week (Scholastic Teacher's edition)
Suc Farm—Successful Farming (Midwest edition)
Sunset—Sunset (Central edition)

Time—Time
Todays Educ—Today's Education
Trav/Holiday—Travel incorporating Holiday
Travel—Travel

UN Chron—UN Chronicle
UNESCO Courier—UNESCO Courier
***U.S. News**—U.S. News & World Report

Vital Speeches—Vital Speeches of the Day
Vogue—Vogue

Weatherwise—Weatherwise
Wilson Lib Bull—Wilson Library Bulletin
World Week. See Senior Scholastic
***Writer**—Writer
Writers Digest—Writer's Digest

Yachting—Yachting
Yale R—Yale Review

* Available for blind and other physically handicapped readers on talking books, in braille, or on magnetic tape. For information address Division for the Blind and Physically Handicapped, Library of Congress, Washington, D.C. 20542

PERIODICALS INDEXED

March 1977—February 1978

All data as of latest issue received

Aging–$5.05. m (bi-m F-Mr, My-Je, Jl-Ag, D-Ja) Aging, Superintendent of Documents, U.S. Government Printing Office, Washington, D.C. 20402

America–$14. w (except Ja 1, and alternate Saturdays in Jl and Ag) America Press, 106 W 56th St, New York, N.Y. 10019

American Artist–$15. m American Artist, 1 Color Court, Marion, Ohio 43302

The American City. See The American City & County

The American City & County–$20. m Morgan-Grampian Publishing Co, Berkshire Common, Pittsfield, Mass. 01201

American Education–$13.50. m (bi-m Ja-F, Ag-S) American Education, Superintendent of Documents, U.S. Government Printing Office, Washington, D.C. 20402

American Forests–$8.50. m American Forestry Association, 1319 18th St, NW, Washington, D.C. 20036

***American Heritage**–$24. bi-m American Heritage, 383 W Center St, Marion, Ohio 43302

The American Historical Review–$35. free to members of the American Historical Association. 5 times a yr (O, D, F, Ap, Je) American Historical Association, 400 A St, SE, Washington, D.C. 20003

American History Illustrated–$10. m (except Mr, S) The National Historical Society, 3300 Walnut St, Boulder, Colo. 80302

American Home–$5.94. m American Home, P.O. Box 4568, Des Moines, Ia. 50306

American Imago–$12. q Wayne State Univ. Press, 5980 Cass Ave, Detroit, Mich. 48202

American Libraries–available only to members. m (bi-m Jl-Ag) American Library Association, 50 E Huron St, Chicago, Ill. 60611

American Record Guide–$7.50. m American Record Guide, Box 812, Melville, N.Y. 11746
(Publication suspended with D '72; resumed N '76)

The American Scholar–$8. q United Chapters of Phi Beta Kappa, 1811 Q St, NW, Washington, D.C. 20009

The American West–$12. bi-m American West Pub. Co. 20380 Town Center Lane, Cupertino, Calif. 95014

Américas–$10. m (bi-m Je-Jl, N-D) General Secretariat of the Organization of American States, Washington, D.C. 20006

The Annals of the American Academy of Political and Social Science–$15. free to members. bi-m American Academy of Political and Social Science, 3937 Chestnut St, Philadelphia, Pa. 19104

Antiques–$24. m Straight Enterprises, Inc, 551 5th Ave, New York, N.Y. 10017

Architectural Record–$17. m (semi-m My, Ag, O) Architectural Record, P.O. Box 430, Hightstown, N.J. 08520

Art in America–$17.95. bi-m Art in America, 542 Pacific Ave, Marion, Ohio 43302

Art News–$18. m (q Je-Ag) Art News, P.O. Box 969, Farmingdale, N.Y. 11737

***The Atlantic**–$13. m Atlantic, P.O. Box 1857, Greenwich, Conn. 06830

Audubon–$13. bi-m National Audubon Society, 950 3rd Ave, New York, N.Y. 10022

Aviation Week & Space Technology–$30. w Aviation Week, P.O. Box 430, Hightstown, N.J. 08520

***Better Homes and Gardens**–$8. m Better Homes and Gardens, 1716 Locust St, Des Moines, Ia. 50336

BioScience–$32. m BioScience, 1401 Wilson Blvd, Arlington, Va. 22209

Bulletin of the Atomic Scientists–$18. m (S-Je) Bulletin of the Atomic Scientists, 1020-24 E 58th St, Chicago, Ill. 60637

Business Week–$26. w (except for one issue in Ja) Business Week, P.O. Box 506, Hightstown, N.J. 08520

Camping Magazine–$10. free to members of the American Camping Association. m (Ja, F, Mr, Ap, My, Je) bi-m (S-O) Camping Magazine, Bradford Woods, Martinsville, Ind. 46151

Car and Driver–$9.98. m Car and Driver, P.O. Box 2770, Boulder, Colo. 80323

Ceramics Monthly–$10. m (S-Je) Ceramics Monthly, P.O. Box 12448, Columbus, Ohio 43212

***Changing Times**–$9. m Changing Times, The Kiplinger Magazine, Editors Park, Md. 20782

Chemistry–$8. m (bi-m Ja-F, Jl-Ag) American Chemical Society, P.O. Box 3337, Columbus, Ohio 43210

The Christian Century–$15. w (bi-w the first 2 weeks in Ja and F, and from the 2nd week in Je through the 2nd week in S) Christian Century Foundation, 407 S Dearborn St, Chicago, Ill. 60605

Christianity Today–$15. (plus .60 for postage) semi-m Christianity Today, Circulation Office, P.O. Box 3800, Greenwich, Conn. 06830

The Clearing House–$15. m (S-My) Heldref Publications, 4000 Albemarle St, NW, Washington, D.C. 20016

Commentary–$20. m American Jewish Committee, 165 E 56th St, New York, N.Y. 10022

Commonweal–$17. bi-w Commonweal Pub. Co, Inc, 232 Madison Ave, New York, N.Y. 10016

Congressional Digest–$18. m (bi-m Je-Jl, Ag-S) Congressional Digest Corp, 3231 P St, NW, Washington, D.C. 20007

Conservationist (Albany)—$3.50. bi-m The New York State Environmental Conservationist, Circulation Dept, New York State Conservation Department, Albany, N.Y. 12233

***Consumer Reports**—$11. m Consumer Reports, P.O. Box 1000, Orangeburg, N.Y. 10962

***Consumers' Research Magazine**—$10. m Consumers' Research, Inc, Washington, N.J. 07882

Craft Horizons—$18. bi-m American Crafts Council, 44 W 53rd St, New York, N.Y. 10019

Current—$15. m (bi-m My-Je, Jl-Ag) Current, 4000 Albemarle St, NW, Washington, D.C. 20016

Current History—$14.50. m (bi-m My-Je, Jl-Ag) Current History, Inc, 4225 Main St, Philadelphia, Pa. 19127

Dance Magazine—$15. m Dance Magazine, 10 Columbus Circle, New York, N.Y. 10019

The Department of State Bulletin—$42.50. w Department of State Bulletin, Superintendent of Documents, U.S. Government Printing Office, Washington, D.C. 20402

Design (United States)—$7. 6 times a yr Design Magazine, 1100 Waterway Blvd, Indianapolis, Ind. 46206

Dun's Review—$12. m Dun's Review Corp, 666 5th Ave, New York, N.Y. 10019

***Ebony**—$12. m Ebony, 820 S Michigan Ave, Chicago, Ill. 60605

The Education Digest—$10. m (S-My) Prakken Publications, Inc, 416 Longshore Drive, Ann Arbor, Mich. 48107

English Journal—$20. m (S-My) National Council of Teachers of English, 1111 Kenyon Road, Urbana, Ill. 61801

Environment—$17.50. m (bi-m Ja-F, Jl-Ag) Environment, P.O. Box 3066, St Louis, Mo. 63130

Esquire—$16. m Esquire, 1255 Portland Pl, Boulder, Colo. 80302

Family Health incorporating Today's Health—$6.95. m Family Health Magazine, Portland Pl, Boulder, Colo. 80302

***Farm Journal**—$5. m (semi-m F-Mr) bi-m (Je-Jl) Farm Journal, Inc, 230 W Washington Sq, Philadelphia, Pa. 19105

Field & Stream—$7.95. m Field & Stream, 383 Madison Ave, New York, N.Y. 10017

Film Quarterly—$6. q University of California Press, Berkeley, Calif. 94702

Flying—$14. m Flying, P.O. Box 2772, Boulder, Colo. 80323

Focus—$8. bi-m (S-Je) American Geographical Society, Broadway at 156th St, New York, N.Y. 10032

Forbes—$18. semi-m Forbes, 60 Fifth Ave, New York, N.Y. 10011

***Foreign Affairs**—$12. q Foreign Affairs, P.O. Box 1891, Baltimore, Md. 21203

***Fortune**—$20. m Fortune, 541 N Fairbanks Court, Chicago, Ill. 60611

***Good Housekeeping**—$8.97. m Good Housekeeping, P.O. Box 10055, Des Moines, Ia. 50350

***Harper's**—$9.98. m Harper's, 1255 Portland Pl, Boulder, Colo. 80323

Harper's Bazaar—$12. m Harper's Bazaar, P.O. Box 552, New York, N.Y. 10019

Harvard Business Review—$21. bi-m Harvard Business Review, P.O. Box 9730, Greenwich, Conn. 06830

***High Fidelity and Musical America**—$18. m High Fidelity, 1 Sound Ave, Marion, Ohio 43302

Hobbies—$7. m Lightner Pub. Corp, 1006 S Michigan Ave, Chicago, Ill. 60605

Holiday—incorporated in Travel, N 77

***Horizon**—$21.75. m Horizon, 381 W Center St, Marion, Ohio 43302

The Horn Book Magazine—$12. bi-m Horn Book, Inc, Park Square Building, 31 St James Ave, Boston, Mass. 02116

Horticulture—$10. m Horticulture, 125 Garden St, Marion, Ohio 43302

Hot Rod—$9. m Petersen Pub. Co, 8490 Sunset Blvd, Los Angeles, Calif. 90069

House & Garden incorporating Living for Young Homemakers—$10. m House & Garden, Box 5202, Boulder, Colo. 80323

House Beautiful—$10. m House Beautiful, P.O. Box 10083, Des Moines, Ia. 50340

Intellect—$17.50. m The Society for the Advancement of Education, Inc, 1860 Broadway, New York, N.Y. 10023

International Wildlife—$7.50. bi-m National Wildlife Federation, 1412 16th St, NW, Washington, D.C. 20036

***Ladies Home Journal**—$6.99. m Ladies' Home Journal, P.O. Box 1697, Des Moines, Ia. 50306

Library Journal—$19. semi-m (m Jl, Ag) Library Journal, R. R. Bowker Co, P.O. Box 67, Whitinsville, Mass. 01588

The Living Wilderness—$10. q The Wilderness Society, 1901 Pennsylvania Ave, NW, Washington, D.C. 20006

MH—$10. q National Association for Mental Health, 49 Sheridan Ave, Albany, N.Y. 12210

McCall's—$8.95. m McCall's, P.O. Box 5261, Des Moines, Ia. 50340

Mademoiselle—$10. m Mademoiselle, P.O. Box 5204, Boulder, Colo. 80323

The Magazine Antiques. See Antiques

Mechanix Illustrated—$6.95. m 1 Fawcett Place, Greenwich, Conn. 06830

Modern Photography—$9. m Modern Photography, 1 Picture Place, Marion, Ohio 43302

Monthly Labor Review—$16. m Monthly Labor Review, Box 353, La Plata, Md. 20646

Motor Boating & Sailing—$10. m Motor Boating & Sailing, P.O. Box 10075, Des Moines, Ia. 50340

Motor Trend—$9. m Motor Trend, P.O. Box 3290, Los Angeles, Calif. 90028

Ms.—$10. m Ms. Magazine, 123 Garden St, Marion, Ohio 43302

Musical America. See High Fidelity and Musical America

***The Musical Quarterly**—$14. q G. Schirmer, Inc, 48-02 48th Ave, Woodside, N.Y. 11377

The Nation—$21. w (except for the first week in Ja, and bi-w Jl, Ag) Nation Associates, Inc, 333 6th Ave, New York, N.Y. 10014

***National Geographic Magazine**—$10. m The Secretary, National Geographic Society, Washington, D.C. 20036

National Parks & Conservation Magazine—$6.50. m National Parks and Conservation Association, 1701 18th St, NW, Washington, D.C. 20009

*National Review—$19. bi-w (48p issue) National Review, 150 E 35th St, New York, N.Y. 10016

National Wildlife—$7.50. bi-m National Wildlife Federation, 1412 16th St, NW, Washington, D.C. 20036

Nation's Business—$49.75. (3 yrs) m Chamber of Commerce of the U.S, 1615 H St, NW, Washington, D.C. 20062

***Natural History**—$10. m (bi-m Je-Jl, Ag-S) American Museum of Natural History, Central Park W at 79th St, New York, N.Y. 10024

The Negro History Bulletin—$8. bi-m Association for the Study of Negro Life and History, Inc, 1401 14th St, NW, Washington, D.C. 20005

New Catholic World—$7. bi-m New Catholic World, 545 Island Road, Ramsey, N.J. 07446

The New Republic—$24. w (47 issues a yr) New Republic, 205 W Center St, Marion, Ohio 43302

The New York Times Magazine—$64.80. w (complete Sunday ed; not sold separately) New York Times, Times Bldg, 229 W 43rd St, New York, N.Y. 10036

The New Yorker—$20. w New Yorker Magazine, Inc, 25 W 43rd St, New York, N.Y. 10036

***Newsweek**—$26. w Newsweek, The Newsweek Building, Livingston, N.J. 07039

Oceans—$12. bi-m Oceanic Society, P.O. Box 65, Uxbridge, Mass. 01569

Opera News—$20. m (Jl, Ag, S, O, N, My, Je) w (D 3-24, Ja 28-Ap 8) bi-w (Ja 7-21) The Metropolitan Opera Guild, Inc, 1865 Broadway, New York, N.Y. 10023

Organic Gardening and Farming—$7.85. m Rodale Press, Inc, 33 E Minor St, Emmaus, Pa. 18049

Outdoor Life—$7.94. m Outdoor Life, Boulder, Colo. 80302

Parents' Magazine—$9.95. m Parents' Magazine, Bergenfield, N.J. 07621

Parks & Recreation—$10. m National Recreation and Park Association, 1601 N Kent St, Arlington, Va. 22209

Physics Today—$24. m American Institute of Physics, Inc, 335 E 45th St, New York, N.Y. 10017

Plays—$12. m (O-My) Plays, Inc, 8 Arlington St, Boston, Mass. 02116

Poetry—$18. m Modern Poetry Association, 1228 N Dearborn Parkway, Chicago, Ill. 60610

Popular Electronics—$12. m Popular Electronics, P.O. Box 2774, Boulder, Colo. 80302

***Popular Mechanics**—$7.97. m Popular Mechanics, P.O. Box 10064, Des Moines, Ia. 50350

Popular Photography—$9.98. m Popular Photography, P.O. Box 2775, Boulder, Colo. 80323

Popular Science—$7.94. m Popular Science, Boulder, Colo. 80302

The Progressive—$17. m The Progressive, 408 W Gorham St, Madison, Wis. 53703

Psychology Today—$12. m Psychology Today, P.O. Box 2990, Boulder, Colo. 80323

Publishers Weekly—$30. w (bi-w year-end issue) R. R. Bowker Co, P.O. Box 67, Whitinsville, Mass. 01588

Radio-Electronics—$8.75. m Radio-Electronics, P.O. Box 2520, Boulder, Colo. 80322

***Reader's Digest**—$7.97. (plus .84 for postage) m (Available in a special Large-Type Edition at $12.95.) Reader's Digest Association, Inc, Pleasantville, N.Y. 10570

Redbook—$7.95. m Redbook, P.O. Box 5225, Des Moines, Ia. 50340

***Retirement Living**—$7.95. m Retirement Living, 99 Garden St, Marion, Ohio 43302

SLJ/School Library Journal—$13. m (S-My) SLJ/School Library Journal, P.O. Box 67, Whitinsville, Mass. 01588

The Saturday Evening Post—$12. m (bi-m Ja-F, My-Je, Jl-Ag) The Saturday Evening Post, 1100 Waterway Blvd, Indianapolis, Ind. 46202

***Saturday Review**—$14. bi-w Saturday Review, P.O. Box 10010, Des Moines, Ia. 50340

School Arts—$11. m (S-Je) School Arts, 50 Portland St, Worcester, Mass. 01608

Science—$60. w (except year-end issue, extra issue on the fourth Tuesday in September) American Association for the Advancement of Science, 1515 Massachusetts Ave, NW, Washington, D.C. 20005

Science and Public Affairs. See Bulletin of the Atomic Scientists

Science Digest—$7.97. m Science Digest, P.O. Box 10076, Des Moines, Ia. 50340

Science News—$12.50. w (bi-w year end issue) Science Service, Inc, 231 W Center St, Marion, Ohio 43302

***Scientific American**—$18. m Scientific American, 415 Madison Ave, New York, N.Y. 10017

Sea Frontiers—$15. bi-m International Oceanographic Foundation, 3979 Rickenbacker Causeway, Virginia Key, Miami, Fla. 33149

Senior Scholastic including World Week (Scholastic Teacher's edition)—$7. bi-w during the school year Scholastic Magazines, 902 Sylvan Ave, Englewood Cliffs, N.J. 07632

***Seventeen**—$10.50. m Seventeen, Radnor, Pa. 19088

Sky and Telescope—$10. m Sky Pub. Corp, 49-50-51 Bay State Road, Cambridge, Mass. 02138

Smithsonian—$12. m Smithsonian Institution, P.O. Box 5300, Greenwich, Conn. 06830

Society—$15. bi-m Society, Box A, Rutgers—The State University, New Brunswick, N.J. 08903

Space World—$10. m Space World, Amherst, Wis. 54406

***Sports Illustrated**—$20. w (except one issue at year end) Sports Illustrated, 541 N Fairbanks Court, Chicago, Ill. 60611

Successful Farming (Midwest edition)—$5. m (semi-m F, Mr) bi-m (Je-Jl) Successful Farming, 1716 Locust St, Des Moines, Ia. 50336

Sunset (Central edition)—$8. in Calif, Ore, Wash, Idaho, Ariz, Nev, Utah, Hawaii, Alaska. $11. in other states m Sunset Magazine, Menlo Park, Calif. 94025

Time—$26. w Time, 541 N Fairbanks Court, Chicago, Ill. 60611

Today's Education—available only to members. 4 times a yr (S-O, N-D, Ja-F, Mr-Ap) National Education Association of the United States, 1201 16th St, NW, Washington, D.C. 20036

Today's Health. See Family Health

Travel—continued as Travel incorporating Holiday—$10. m Travel, Travel Bldg, Floral Park, N.Y. 11001

UN Chronicle—$9.50. m (bi-m Ag-S) United Nations Publications, Room LX-2300, New York, N.Y. 10017

The UNESCO Courier—$6.75. (28 French francs) m (bi-m Ag-S) Unipub, Box 433, Murray Hill Station, New York, N.Y. 10016

*__U.S. News & World Report__—$18. w (except one issue at year end) U.S. News & World Report, P.O. Box 2860, Greenwich, Conn. 06830

Vital Speeches of the Day—$12. semi-m City News Pub. Co, Inc, Box 606, Southold, N.Y. 11971

Vogue—$12. m Vogue, Box 5201, Boulder, Colo. 80302

Weatherwise—$8. bi-m Weatherwise, 4000 Albemarle St, NW, Washington, D.C. 20016

Wilson Library Bulletin—$14. m (S-Je) The H. W. Wilson Co, 950 University Ave, Bronx, N.Y. 10452

World Week. See Senior Scholastic

*__The Writer__—$10. m The Writer, Inc, 8 Arlington St, Boston, Mass. 02116

Writer's Digest—$12. m Writer's Digest, 9933 Alliance Road, Cincinnati, Ohio 45242

Yachting—$12. m Yachting Pub. Corp, 50 W 44th St, New York, N.Y. 10036

The Yale Review—$10. q Yale Review, 250 Church St, 1902A Yale Station, New Haven, Conn. 06520

* Available for blind and other physically handicapped readers on talking books, in braille, or on magnetic tape. For information address Division for the Blind and Physically Handicapped, Library of Congress, Washington, D.C. 20542.

ABBREVIATIONS

*	following name entry, a printer's device
+	continued on later pages of same issue
Abp	Archbishop
abr	abridged
Ag	August
Ap	April
arch	architect
Assn	Association
Aut	Autumn
Ave	Avenue
Bart	Baronet
bibl	bibliography
bibl f	bibliographical footnotes
bi-m	bimonthly
bi-w	biweekly
bldg	building
Bp	Bishop
Co	Company
comp	compiled, compiler
cond	condensed
cont	continued
Corp	Corporation
D	December
Dept	Department
ed	edited, edition, editor
F	February
Hon	Honorable
il	illustrated, illustration, illustrator
Inc	Incorporated
introd	introduction, introductory
Ja	January
Je	June
Jl	July
Jr	Junior
jt auth	joint author
Ltd	Limited
m	monthly
Mr	March
My	May
N	November
no	number
O	October
por	portrait
pseud	pseudonym
pt	part
pub	published, publisher, publishing
q	quarterly
rev	revised
S	September
sec	section
semi-m	semimonthly
Soc	Society
Spr	Spring
Sq	Square
Sr	Senior
St	Street
Summ	Summer
supp	supplement
supt	superintendent
tr	translated, translation, translator
v	volume
w	weekly
Wint	Winter
yr	year

READERS' GUIDE TO PERIODICAL LITERATURE

MARCH 1977—FEBRUARY 1978

A&M Records (firm) See Phonograph record industry
A&P Company. See Great Atlantic & Pacific Tea Company
A-10 (airplane) See Airplanes, Military—United States
A. Zito Bakery, New York City. See Bakers and bakeries
AAA. See American Automobile Association
AAAS. See American Association for the Advancement of Science
AACR (Anglo-American cataloging rules) See Cataloging
AAE. See Alliance for Arts Education
AALS. See Association of American Library Schools
AAP. See Association of American Publishers
AAPT. See American Association of Physics Teachers
AASL. See American Library Association—American Association of School Librarians
AAUP. See Association of American University Presses
AAVSO. See American Association of Variable Star Observers
ABA. See American Bar Association; American Booksellers Association
ABC. See American Broadcasting Companies
ABM (anti-ballistic missiles) See Guided missiles—Defenses
ABT. See American Ballet Theatre
ACA. See American Camping Association
ACC. See American Crafts Council
ACDA. See United States—Arms Control and Disarmament Agency
AChE. See Acetylcholinesterase
ACLU. See American Civil Liberties Union
ACP. See Associated Church Press (organization)
ACT. See American College Testing program
ACTH
β-Endorphin and adrenocorticotropin are secreted concomitantly by the pituitary gland. R. Guillemin and others. bibl il Science 197:1367-9 S 30 '77
Synchronized ultradian cortisol rhythms in monkeys: persistence during corticotropin infusion. J. W. Holaday and others. bibl il Science 198: 56-8 O 7 '77
ADA. See American for Democratic Action (organization)
ADAMHA. See United States—Alcohol, Drug Abuse, and Mental Health Administration
ADF (automatic direction finders) See Radio direction finders
ADT. See American District Telegraph Company
AEA Investors Inc. See Small business investment companies
AEC. See United States—Atomic Energy Commission
AECT. See National Education Association—Association for Educational Communication and Technology
AFA. See American Forestry Association
AFGE. See American Federation of Government Employees
AFL-CIO. See American Federation of Labor and Congress of Industrial Organizations
AFSC. See American Friends Service Committee
AFSCME. See American Federation of State, County, and Municipal Employees
AFT. See American Federation of Teachers
AG-Land Fund 1. See Real estate investment trusts
AGA. See American Gas Association
AGC. See Associated General Contractors of America
AI. See Artificial insemination
AIA. See American Institute of Architects
AIA-Sunset Western Home Awards. See Western Home Awards
AIBS. See American Institute of Biological Sciences
AICPA. See American Institute of Certified Public Accountants
AID. See United States—Agency for International Development
AIM. See Accuracy in Media (organization); American Indian Movement
AIP. See American Institute of Physics
AIR Galleries. See New York (city)—Galleries and museums
AJC. See American Jewish Committee
ALA. See American Library Association
ALCOA. See Aluminum Company of America
ALPA. See Air Line Pilots Association, International
ALSEP (Apollo Lunar Surface Experiment Packages) See Moon—Exploration—Equipment
AM Hercules. See Stars, Eclipsing binary
AM radio broadcasting. See Radio broadcasting
AMA. See American Medical Association
AMC. See American Motors Corporation
AMCA International Corporation-Amtel, Inc merger. See Corporations—Acquisitions and mergers
AMP. See Adenosine monophosphate
AMSA (American Music Scholarship Association) Competition. See Music—Competitions
AMST (advanced medium STOL transport) See Airplanes, Military transport
AN Ursae Majoris. See Stars, Eclipsing binary
ANSI. See American National Standards Institute
AOA. See United States—Aging, Administration on
APA. See American Psychiatric Association; American Psychological Association
APHIS. See United States—Agriculture, Department of—Animal and Plant Health Inspection Service
APL Corporation
APL's big acquisition plans. por Bus W p92+ S 19 '77
APL Corporation-Pabst Brewing Company merger. See Corporations—Acquisitions and mergers
APS. See American Physical Society
ARBA. See United States—American Revolution Bicentennial Administration
ARCO. See Atlantic Richfield Company
ARL. See Association of Research Libraries
ASAT (anti-satellite interceptor) See Artificial satellites—Military use
ASC. See American Security Council
ASCE. See American Society of Civil Engineers
ASEAN. See Association of Southeast Asian Nations
ASLA. See American Library Association—Association of State Library Agencies
ASOL. See American Symphony Orchestra League
ASPC. See American Sheep Producers Council
ASTP (Apollo-Soyuz Test Project) See Space flight—Manned flights—Apollo-Soyuz flight, 1975
AT & T. See American Telephone & Telegraph Company
ATI. See Appropriate Technology International (organization)
ATIS (automatic transmitter identification system) See Radio transmitters—Identification
AWACS (airborne warning and control system) See Airplanes, Military—Radar equipment
AWWA. See American Water Works Association
AAMODT, Kim
(ed) Book notes and reviews. See issues of Yachting
AARON, Evalyn
Sumi painting. bibl il Am Artist 41:40-5+ S '77
AARON, Sam
Grapes of autumn. il Sat R 4:32 Ag 6 '77

ABAEV, Vasily Ivanovich
Ossetes: Scythians of the 20th century. il UNESCO Courier 29:48-9 D '76
ABALONES
Hydrogen peroxide induces spawning in mollusks, with activation of prostaglandin endoperoxide synthetase. D. E. Morse and others. bibl il Science 196:298-300 Ap 15 '77
Oriental art of abalone scrimshaw. R. D. Ono. il Sea Front 23:16-19 Ja '77
ABANDONED buildings. See Buildings, Abandoned
ABANO TERME, Italy
Luxury of mud. M. Denhof. il House & Gard 149:70+ My '77
ABARBANEL, Karin
Is a relapse ahead for minority medical education? Educ Digest 42:24-7 Mr '77
ABBA (rock group) See Rock groups
ABBEBE, Berhanou
Painted churches of Lake Tana. il UNESCO Courier 30:13-17 F '77
ABBETT, Robert
Robert Abbett; interview, ed by N. Meglin. il por Am Artist 41:46-9 Jl '77
ABBEY, Edward
Desert love affair; excerpt from The journey home. il Read Digest 111:39+ O '77
Last oasis. il Harpers 254:8+ Mr '77
ABBEYS
In King Arthur country, the Glastonbury ruins. il Sunset 158:66 Ap '77
See also
Mont Saint Michel, France
ABBOTT, C. B.
Living together; what are your rights? Am Home 80:36+ O '77
Uncommon scents. il Am Home 80:65+ N '77
ABBOTT, William
Work in the year 2001. Current 193:31-9 My '77
ABBOUD, Alfred Robert
Banking the Abboud way. M. Ruby and C. J. Harper. por Newsweek 90:63 Jl 25 '77 *
ABDUL-JABBAR, Kareem
Walton up on high. P. Axthelm. il pors Newsweek 89:75 My 23 '77 *
ABDUL KHAALIS, Khalifa Hamaas
Allah was on our side. J. T. Clemons. Chr Cent 94:319-20 Ap 6 '77 *
Behind the siege of terror in Washington. il map U.S. News 82:19-21+ Mr 21 '77 *
Civil war in Islamic America. A. Muhammad. Nation 224:721-4 Je 11 '77 *
From faith to faith. Chr Today 21:48-9 Ap 1 '77 *
I fear only Allah. D. M. Alpern and others. il por Newsweek 89:21 Mr 21 '77 *
Seizing hostages: scourge of the '70s. T. Mathews. il por Newsweek 89:16-20+ Mr 21 '77 *
38 hours: trial by terror. il pors map Time 109:14-20 Mr 21 '77 *
Why two sects are at odds. il por U.S. News 82:22 Mr 21 '77 *
ABEL, Elie
Who started the cold war? il pors Am Heritage 28:8-23 Ag '77
ABEL, Ernest L.
When tobacco was king. il Am Hist Illus 11:10-19 F '77
ABEL, I. W.
Struggle in steel. K. Bode. New Repub 176:10-13 F 5 '77 *
ABELE, Lawrence G. and Gilchrist, Sandra
Homosexual rape and sexual selection in acanthocephalan worms. bibl Science 197:81-3 Jl 1 '77
ABELL, Creed W. See Shen, R. S. jt auth
ABELSON, John
Recombinant DNA: examples of present-day research. bibl il Science 196:159-60 Ap 8 '77
ABENAKI Indians. See Abnaki Indians
ABERCROMBIE, Thomas J.
Egypt. il Nat Geog 151:312-43 Mr '77
ABERCROMBIE & Fitch Company
Abercrombie's shuts its doors. il Time 110:97 N 28 '77
ABILITY
Enkephalins: more than just pain killers; effect on learning ability. J. Arehart-Treichel. il Sci N 112:59+ Jl 23 '77
See also
Creative ability
Efficiency
Great men and women
Learning, Psychology of
Mathematical ability
Success
ABILITY grouping in education
Grouping for instruction: 1965, 1975, 1985. G. B. Helton and others. Educ Digest 43:53-6 D '77
Student classification and legal implications for administrators. M. Fellows. bibl Clearing H 51:80-5 O '77
ABINGDON Press. See Publishers and publishing—Religious literature

ABLON, Ralph E.
Financing of the corporate structure for the 1980s; address, March 25, 1977. Vital Speeches 43:398-401 Ap 15 '77
ABNAKI Indians
Rock art and the power of shamans. D. R. Snow. Natur Hist 86:42-9 bibl(p 100) F '77
ABNORMALITIES (animals)
Congenital anomalies induced in hamster embryos with ribavirin. L. Kilham and V. H. Ferm. bibl il Science 195:413-14 Ja 28 '77
ABNORMALITIES (man) See Deformities
ABOLITIONISTS
Martyrdom of Elijah P. Lovejoy. D. W. Blight. il Am Hist Illus 12:20-7 N '77
See also
Remond, C. L.
ABOMINABLE snowman. See Animals, Mythical
ABORN, Carlene Mello
Multi-image productions are magical motivators. bibl il por SLJ 23:33-7 Ap '77
ABORTION
Abortion alert. G. Steinem. Ms 6:118 N '77
Abortion and child abuse; excerpt from Death before birth. H. O. J. Brown. Chr Today 22:34 O 7 '77
Between guilt and gratification: abortion doctors reveal their feelings. N. Rosen. il N Y Times Mag p70-1+ Ap 17 '77
Countdown to an abortion. T. Ashford. America 136:128-30 F 12 '77
Essay on the unfairness of life. L. Morrow. Horizon 20:34-7 D '77
Legal abortion. C. Tietze and S. Lewit. il maps Sci Am 236:21-7 bibl(p 132) Ja '77
Tying abortion to the death penalty; study by Paul Cameron. J. Horn. Psychol Today 11:43+ N '77

Laws and legislation

Debating abortion. J. Garn. Nat R 29:1299+ N 11 '77
Never again! Never again? Can we lose our right to abortion? R. B. Gratz. il Ms 6:54-5 Jl '77
What I learned marching with N.O.W. J. M. Shutt. por Farm J 101:F1 D '77
Why a constitutional convention is needed; human life amendment. E. J. McMahon. America 137:12-14 Jl 2 '77

Italy

We did it for the women. il Time 109:32 Ja 31 '77

Moral and religious aspects

Another double standard; Call to Concern campaign. America 137:274 O 29 '77
Born and the unborn alike; position of the Catholic Church. A. Bernard. America 136:270-2 Mr 26 '77
Demystification of life. R. J. Henle. Commonweal 104:457-60 Jl 22 '77
Grievous moral mischief. J. A. Tetlow. America 137:359 N 19 '77
Performing abortions; excerpt from In necessity and sorrow: life and death in an abortion hospital. M. Denes. discussion. Commentary 62:4+ D '76; 63:18+ Ja; 22+ F '77
Real dialogue in Los Angeles; Los Angeles Roman Catholic-Jewish Respect Life Committee. America 137:324 N 12 '77
Religious tension in Saint Cloud; refusal of United Way funds to agencies making abortion referrals. J. M. Wall. Chr Cent 94:1019-20 N 9 '77
Welcome prepared. E. Schaeffer. Chr Today 21:28-9 Ap 1 '77

Psychological aspects

Abortion and men; excerpt from The ambivalence of abortion. L. B. Francke. il Esquire 89:58-60 Ja '78
Are you sorry you had an abortion? interviews, ed by M. Rockmore. il Good H 185:120-1+ Jl '77

State aid

Abortion and fairness. Progressive 41:9 S '77
Abortion double standard; medicaid vs health insurance coverage. New Repub 177:12 O 15 '77
Abortion funding. Chr Today 22:40 D 30 '77
Abortion: the debate goes on; limiting medicaid funds for abortions. America 137:2 Jl 2 '77
Abortion: who pays? Supreme Court decision on state funds. S. Fraker and others. il Newsweek 90:12-13 Jl 4 '77
Carter and abortion. C. Tucker. Sat R 4:64 S 17 '77
Cruelty of morality; abortion views of J. Carter. Nation 225:68 Jl 23 '77
Danse macabre; Hyde amendment. M. Kinsley. New Repub 177:13+ N 19 '77
Debating abortion. J. Garn. Nat R 29:1299+ N 11 '77
Fight over abortions—heating up again. il U.S. News 83:68 D 19 '77

* Printer's device

ABORTION—State aid—*Continued*
Intelligent woman's guide to sex; Supreme Court's decision on use of medicaid for abortions. J. Coburn. Mademoiselle 83:136+ S '77
New abortion debate; Supreme Court decision on medicaid funding. Commonweal 104:451-2 Jl 22 '77
New abortion rulings (what they really mean) L. Prinz. McCalls 105:111 O '77
New limits on abortion. il Time 110:12-13 D 19 '77
Of abortion and the unfairness of life; Time essay. L. Morrow. Time 110:49 Ag 1 '77
Politics of abortion; Supreme Court decision on medicaid funding. P. Steinfels. Commonweal 104:456 Jl 22 '77
Punitive and tragic; decision to deny public funds for abortion. Nation 225:3-4 Jl 2 '77
Supreme Court ignites a fiery abortion debate. il Time 110:6-8 Jl 4 '77
Unborn and the born again; Supreme Court decision on use of state funds to cover abortion costs. New Repub 177:5-6+ Jl 2 '77

ABORTION decisions. See United States—Supreme Court—Decisions—Abortion decisions

ABPLANALP, Robert H.
Precision Valve: spray it again, Bob. por Duns R 110:14-15 Ag '77 *

ABRAHAM, George, and Abraham, Katy
Cold-weather survival guide for houseplants. il Org Gard & Farm 25:166-71 Ja '78

ABRAHAM, Katy. See Abraham, G. jt. auth

ABRAHAM, Lynne
Good healthy eyes for good. Harp Baz 110:112+ Ag '77

ABRAHAM, Molly
Dining out in Detroit. il Lib J 102:1148-51 My 15 '77

ABRAHAMS, Roger D.
Inaugural square dance. New Repub 176:21-2 F 26 '77

ABRAHAMSEN, David
Kicking Nixon around the couch. il por Time 109:29-30 Ap 18 '77 *

ABRAHAMSON, David
Dream diver. il Motor B & S 140:73-5+ Ag '77
For your information. See issues of Car and driver

ABRAMS, Doug
Marshes; Freezes; Credences the saplings know; poems. Poetry 130:131-3 Je '77

ABRAMS, Floyd
Press, privacy and the Constitution. il N Y Times Mag p 11-13+ Ag 21 '77; Same with title What of the privacy explosion? Current 196:7-17 O '77

ABRAMS, H. Leon, Jr
Beware of coffee, tea, and cola beverages if you value good health. Consumers Res Mag 60:21-2+ My '77

ABRAMS, Nancy Ellen, and Berry, R. S.
Mediation: a better alternative to science courts. Bull Atom Sci 33:50-3 Ap '77

ABRASIVES
PS guide to sandpaper and other coated abrasives. R. Hill. il Pop Sci 211:106-9 Jl '77

ABSAROKA-Beartooth Wilderness Area (proposed)
See Wilderness areas—Western States

ABSENT friends; drama. See Ayckbourn, A.

ABSENTEEISM
Absence from work—measuring the hours lost. J. N. Hedges. bibl M Labor R 100:16-23 O '77
Job absence and turnover: a new source of data. M. G. Miner. il M Labor R 100:24-31 O '77
Pay for no work; Volvo. il Time 109:67-8 F 21 '77

ABSORBANTS
Super-slurper soaks up awards; Association for the Advancement of Invention and Innovation. il Sci Digest 81:82-3 Ap '77

ABSORPTION (physiology)
1,25-Dihydroxycholecalciferol and parathormone: effects on isolated osteoclast-like and osteoblast-like cells. G. L. Wong and others. bibl il Science 197:663-5 Ag 12 '77
Direct resorption of bone by human monocytes. G. R. Mundy and others. bibl il Science 196: 1109-11 Je 3 '77
Folate conjugase: two separate activities in human jejunum. A. M. Reisenauer and others. bibl il Science 198:196-7 O 14 '77

ABSTINENCE. See Fasting

ABSTRACT art. See Art, Abstract

ABSTRACT expressionism
In the vein of abstract expressionism. L. J. Miller. il Sch Arts 77:14-15 N '77
Pollock paints a picture; excerpt from The art world; ed by B. Diamonstein. R. Goodnough. il pors Art N 76:162+ N '77
Surrealism's automatic painting lesson. J. Wechsler. il Art N 76:44-7 Ap '77
Trouble in paradise; The Natural Paradise exhibition at the Museum of Modern Art. S. Schwartz. il Art in Am 65:103-5 Ja '77

ABT, Helmut A.
Companions of sunlike stars; with biographical sketch. il Sci Am 236:20, 96-104 bibl(p 148) Ap '77

ABU Daoud
Abu Daoud and the law. S. E. Rapoport. Commentary 63:70-2 Mr '77; Reply. S. Liskofsky. 63:10-11 My '77 *
L'affaire Daoud: too hot to handle. il por Time 109:29-31 Ja 24 '77 *
Arch-terrorist who went scot-free. D. Reed. Read Digest 111:114-18 S '77 *
French recipe for cowardice. Nation 224:98-9 Ja 29 '77 *
Mind of Abu Daoud. R. Carroll. il Newsweek 89:45 Ja 24 '77 *
Moral message from La Grande France. Art N 76:31 Mr '77 *
Terrorist cross fire. A. Deming and others. il por Newsweek 89:43+ Ja 24 '77 *

ABUNDANCES of elements. See Chemical elements

ABZUG, Bella
Bella Abzug and the future of American women; interview. ed D. Davis. por Am Home 80:88-9 N '77
Excerpts from debate on Federal Elections Campaign Act Amendments, April 1, 1976. Cong Digest 56:88+ Mr '77

about

Abzug: rage and asphalt glamour. L. I. Barrett. il pors Time 110:12-14 Jl 18 '77 *
Beame's scenario: how to beat Bella. M. Carroll. il pors N Y Times Mag p32-5+ Je 26 '77 *
In search of Bella Abzug. C. Winfrey. il pors N Y Times Mag p 14-16+ Ag 21 '77 *
Political update: New York's finest—Bella, Ronnie, & Carol. L. Sherr. il pors Ms 6:60-1 S '77 *

ABZUG, Charles. See Winson, J. jt auth

ACADEMIC achievements. See Student achievements

ACADEMIC freedom
Academics in New York and California fight disclosure policies. B. J. Culliton. Science 196: 37-8 Ap 1 '77
Censorship and the classroom teacher. A. A. Glatthorn. Engl J 66:12-15 F '77; Same abr. Educ Digest 43:54-6 S '77
Censorship, the law, and the teacher of English; symposium. A. A. Glatthorn. bibl il Engl J 66:12-25 F '77
Giving Yale to Connecticut; excerpt from God and man at Yale. W. F. Buckley, Jr. il Harpers 255:43-8+ N '77
N.Y. State United Teachers to vote on academic freedom resolution. SLJ 23:65 Mr '77

ACADEMIC research. See Colleges and universities—Research

ACADEMY Awards (motion pictures)
Conspirator in Berlin. P. Bogdanovich. Esquire 88:96+ D '77
Night of the cuckoo; L. Hellman at Oscar Awards ceremony. W. F. Buckley, Jr. Nat R 29:513 Ap 29 '77
Rocky KO's Hollywood. M. Kasindorf. il pors Newsweek 89:70-2+ Ap 11 '77
Television; Academy Award telecasts. C. Gilbert. il Am Home 80:19 Mr '77

Anecdotes, facetiae, satire, etc.

. . . And what are we trying to tell Hollywood? now for the envelopes they didn't open. S. Braudy. il Ms 5:50-2 Ap '77
Gold and dross. G. Ace. Sat R 4:3 Je 25 '77

ACADEMY for Contemporary Problems, Columbus, Ohio
Declining interest rates forecast; study. il Am City & County 92:34 S '77
Land use battles on the way out? study. Am City & County 92:37 Ap '77

ACADEMY of Motion Picture Arts and Sciences
See also
Academy Awards (motion pictures)

ACADEMY of Music, Brooklyn
Chekhov in Brooklyn; BAM Theatre Company. G. Rogoff. Sat R 4:50-1 Jl 9 '77

ACADEMY of Sciences of the USSR
Four Ukrainian archaeologists present their latest finds; Scythian burial mound excavations by Institute of Archaeology of the Academy of Sciences of the Ukrainian S.S.R. il UNESCO Courier 29:17-22 D '76

ACADEMY of the Elevated Ones, Florence. See Music schools—History

ACADIA National Park
Park service capitulates, plans Isle au Haut giveaway. Nat Parks & Con Mag 51:22-3 D '77

ACAPULCO, Mexico
Acapulco: what the snobs are missing. S. Birnbaum. Esquire 87:60+ Je '77
Arango house, Acapulco. il Archit Rec 161:64-7 mid-My '77

ACCADEMIA Chigiana festival, Siena, Italy. See Music festivals—Italy

ACCADEMIA degli Elevati, Florence. See Music schools—History

ACCELERATION of particles. See Particles (nuclear physics)—Acceleration

ACCELERATORS (electrons, etc)

And the neutrons go round and round; neutron storage ring. il Sci N 112:407 D 17 '77

Budget includes three centers for synchrotron radiation. G. B. Lubkin. il Phys Today 30:17-19 Mr '77

Carbon-14: direct detection at natural concentrations; use of Van de Graaff accelerator. D. E. Nelson and others. bibl il Science 198:507-8 N 4 '77

Casting light on material structures; synchrotron radiation. D. E. Thomsen. il Sci N 112:426-7 D 24 '77

Electron storage ring from Cornell synchrotron? M. S. Rothenberg. Phys Today 30:20 Ag '77

400-GeV experiments begin at Geneva. il Sci N 111:70 Ja 29 '77

New accelerators: Cornell gets an electron storage ring. A. L. Robinson. Science 198:480 N 4 '77

New accelerators making end runs. W. D. Metz. Science 198:710 N 18 '77

Particle refrigerator; proton-antiproton storage rings. Sci Am 236:58+ Ap '77

Radiocarbon dating using electrostatic accelerators: negative ions provide the key. C. L. Bennett and others. bibl il Science 198:508-10 N 4 '77

Radioisotope dating with a cyclotron. R. A. Muller. bibl il Science 196:489-94 Ap 29 '77

Sandweiss panel urges construction of Isabelle at BNL. G. B. Lubkin. il Phys Today 30:93-4 N '77

Synchrotron radiation: large demand spurs new facilities. A. L. Robinson. il Science 197:148 Jl 8 '77

Uses of synchrotron radiation. E. M. Rowe and J. H. Weaver. il Sci Am 236:32-41 bibl(p 142) Je '77

Wide-ranging experiments at Los Alamos meson factory. G. B. Lubkin. il Phys Today 30:17+ F '77

See also

National Accelerator Laboratory

History

Atom smashers—50 years; exhibit at the National Museum of History and Technology. D. E. Thomsen. il Sci N 112:410-11 D 17 '77

International aspects

World-class accelerator. D. E. Thomsen. Sci N 111:316 My 14 '77

ACCENTS and accentuation

See also

English language—Accents and accentuation

ACCEPTANCES

Why loan demand has fuzzy figures. Bus W p 138 F 14 '77

ACCESSORIES, Dress. See Dress accessories

ACCESSORIES, Fireplace. See Fireplaces

ACCESSORIES, Household. See Household furnishings

ACCESSORY tables (machine work) See Machinery—Stands, tables, etc.

ACCIDENT survival. See Survival after airplane accidents, shipwrecks, etc.

ACCIDENTS

Children's emergencies; injuries and illnesses. W. Seed. Harp Baz 110:88-9 Jl '77

See also

Ambulance service
Burns and scalds
Drowning
Fires
First aid in illness and injury
Ice accidents
Rescue work
Shipwrecks
Traffic accidents

also subhead Accidents or Accidents and injuries under various subjects, e.g. Subways —Accidents

Prevention

Blood sports. D. E. Beauchamp. Chr Cent 94:237-8 Mr 9 '77

Caution play it safe. M. Weisinger. il Fam Health 9:44-5+ Je '77

Give your home a safety checkup. Changing T 31:45-7 Ag '77

How to make your household safe for the holidays. Bet Hom & Gard 55:82+ D '77

How to prevent accidents. J. Wang. Harp Baz 110:100-1+ Ap '77

Parents' special section on home safety. il Parents Mag 52:42-3+ My '77

Safety begins at home. S. Mennear-Dubas. Fam Health 9:31 S '77

See also

United States—Consumer Product Safety Commission

also subhead Safety devices and measures under various subjects, e.g. Tank ships —Safety devices and measures

Psychological aspects

Accident prone? Harp Baz 110:101 Ap '77

ACCIDENTS, Industrial

See also

Insurance, Workmens compensation

Statistics

Factors in more costly accidents drawn from compensated cases. H. J. Hilaski. il M Labor R 100:41-3 Ag '77

Work injuries and earnings of partially disabled men in California. W. Vroman. il M Labor R 100:58-60 Ap '77

ACCIDENTS, Liability for. See Liability (law)

ACCLIMATIZATION

Cell membrane sodium pump as a mechanism for increasing thermogenesis during cold acclimation in rats. D. L. Guernsey and E. D. Stevens. bibl il Science 196:908-10 My 20 '77

ACCOUNTABILITY. See Responsibility

ACCOUNTABILITY (education)

Malpractice in the schools. J. C. Baratz and T. W. Hartle. Progressive 41:33-4 Je '77

Suing the teacher. Newsweek 90:101 O 3 '77

ACCOUNTANTS

Accountants—cleaning up America's mystery profession. C. E. Mayer. il U.S. News 83:39-42 D 19 '77

CPAs agree to audit a federal agency—free; ACTION. Bus W p43-4 My 16 '77

Name game; Price Waterhouse. Forbes 120:94 O 1 '77

Sue the consultant? West German court ruling against Peat, Marwick, Mitchell & Company. Forbes 120:36 D 1 '77

To merge or not to merge, that is the question. il Forbes 120:58-9 D 1 '77

U.S. newest glamour job; certified public accountants. L. Minard and B. McGlynn. il Forbes 120:32-6 S 1 '77

White House likes its accounting freebie; ACTION audit. Bus W p36-7 Ag 15 '77

See also

Government investigations—Accountants

ACCOUNTING

See also

American Institute of Certified Public Accountants
Corporations—Accounting
Disclosure in accounting
Financial statements
Fuel industry—Accounting
Petroleum industry—Accounting
Steel industry—Accounting
Telephone companies—Accounting

Mechanical aids

See also

Computers—Business use

Standards

Accountants—cleaning up America's mystery profession. C. E. Mayer. il U.S. News 83:39-42 D 19 '77

CPAs suggest the watchdogs they want; written statements presented to the Senate Subcommittee on Reports, Accounting, and Management. il Bus W p94+ My 23 '77

FASB: a single oil standard. Bus W p50 Ag 1 '77

FASB moves to close a loophole; bank accounting procedure. il Bus W p76 F 21 '77

FASB ruling hurts oil exploration; successful-efforts accounting for oil and gas companies. Bus W p41-2 O 10 '77

Figures don't lie, but. . .: auditing the auditors; FASB. J. Thackray. Nation 224:582-4 My 14 '77

Global snares for corporate accountants; International Accounting Standards Committee. Bus W p 162+ Jl 25 '77

It's tough to fill an FASB vacancy. Bus W p28 Ja 24 '77

New rules on troubled debt; FASB bank accounting standards. Bus W p70+ F 7 '77

Pressuring the FASB to broaden its reach. R. Mims. il Bus W p96 N 28 '77

Who needs external audits? por Forbes 120:110 D 1 '77

Who shall set accounting standards? address, February 22, 1977. J. C. Biegler. Vital Speches 43:347-9 Mr 15 '77

Why everybody's jumping on the accountants these days. il Forbes 119:37-40+ Mr 15 '77

See also

Government investigations—Accountants

ACCOUNTING—*Continued*

Germany, West

Sue the consultant? court ruling against Peat, Marwick, Mitchell & Company. Forbes 120:36 D 1 '77

Great Britain

Who needs external audits? por Forbes 120:110 D 1 '77
Why Britain still lacks inflation accounting. il Bus W p 102+ O 31 '77

Japan

Japan's accounting shake-up. il Bus W p 112+ Ap 25 '77

ACCOUNTING ethics
Business and accounting: address, January 21, 1977. W. S. Kanaga. Vital Speeches 43:274-8 F 15 '77
Tangling with an IRS code for professionals; rules of conduct for lawyers and accountants arguing tax cases. Bus W p84 F 14 '77

ACCOUNTS, Collecting of. See Collecting of accounts

ACCOUNTS, Household. See Budget, Household

ACCREDITATION, College. See Colleges and universities—Accreditation

ACCREDITATION Committee (American Library Association) See American Library Association —Accreditation, Committee on

ACCREDITATION of library schools. See Library schools and education

ACCREDITATION of medical colleges. See Medical colleges—Accreditation

ACCULTURATION
Our world gets smaller and smaller. il U.S. News 83:24-5 Jl 18 '77
See also
Assimilation (sociology)

ACCURACY in Media (organization)
Tariff on truth; AIM criticism of article on Cuba. M. J. Sobran, Jr. Nat R 29:564-5 My 13 '77

ACE, Goodman
Top of my head. See occasional issues of Saturday review
about
Profiles. M. Singer. por New Yorker 53:41-6+ Ap 4 '77 *

ACE Books, Inc. See Publishers and publishing—Paperback books

ACERRANO, Anthony J.
Spinning for trout. il Field & S 85:50-1+ D '77

ACETAMINOPHEN. See Paracetamol

ACETATES
Moth mating: role of diet challenged. Sci N 111:37 Ja 15 '77

ACETYLCHOLINE
Response to acetylcholine. H. A. Lester. il Sci Am 236:106-16+ F '77

ACETYLCHOLINE receptors. See Receptors, Neural

ACETYLCHOLINESTERASE
Induction of acetylcholinesterase activity by β-ecdysone in a drosophila cell line. P. Cherbas and others. bibl il Science 197:275-7 Jl 15 '77

ACETYLENE
Heaviest (99) space molecule yet; cyanotriacetylene. Sci N 111:260-1 Ap 23 '77

ACETYLSALICYLIC acid. See Aspirin

ACHEAMPONG, Ignatius
Decline of Ghana's military government. J. Kraus. il Cur Hist 73:214-17+ D '77 *

ACHEBE, Chinua
Arrow of God. R. Patterson. Engl J 66:64-5 Mr '77 *

ACHEE, Bonnie
Living in space. il Sci Digest 81:8-12 Ap '77

ACHIEVEMENT. See Success

ACHIEVEMENT tests
Looking-glass world of testing. E. F. Taylor. il Todays Educ 66:39-42+ Mr '77

ACHIEVEMENTS, Student. See Student achievements

ACHTENBERG, Ben
(ed) See Van Dongen, H. Helen Van Dongen: an interview

ACID rain. See Rain and rainfall

ACID soils. See Soil acidity

ACIDOSIS
25-Hydroxycholecalciferol to 1,25-dihydroxycholecalciferol: conversion impaired by systemic metabolic acidosis. S. W. Lee and others. bibl il Science 195:994-6 Mr 11 '77

ACIDS
See also names of acids and acid groups, e.g. Nucleic acid

ACIDS, Fatty
Fatty acids and their prostaglandin derivatives: inhibitors of proliferation in aortic smooth muscle cells. J. J. Huttner and others. bibl il Science 197:289-91 Jl 15 '77

ACKERMAN, James Sloss
On architecture. il Art N 76:111 N '77

ACKERMANN-BLOUNT, Joan
Keeper of the bees. Atlantic 240:85-8 Ag '77

ACKLEY, Gardner
Economy. See alternate issues of Dun's review

ACKLEY, Helen Herdman
Our haunted house on the Hudson. il Read Digest 110:217-19+ My '77

ACNE
Acne: all the facts. J. Gerston. Seventeen 36:36+ Jl '77
Bazaar's anti-acne guide. L. A. Schoen. Harp Baz 110:54-5+ Jl '77
Breakthrough! Doctors find improved acne treatments; interview, ed by N. Simon. S. Hurwitz. Vogue 167:389+ S '77
Clearer days on the acne scene. Mademoiselle 83:147 My '77

ACORNS
From little acorns grow. L. Line. Field & S 82:36 O '77

ACOUSTIC insulators. See Audio systems—Equipment

ACOUSTIC surface wave devices
New technologies for signal processing. R. W. Brodersen and R. M. White. bibl il Science 195:1216-22 Mr 18 '77

ACOUSTICAL engineering. See Audio engineering

ACOUSTICAL Society of America
Greenspan and Jeffress win ASA silver medals. pors Phys Today 30:67 D '77
Stephens wins Acoustical Society gold medal. por Phys Today 30:65 Je '77

ACOUSTICS. See Music—Acoustics and physics

ACOUSTICS, Architectural
House that hi-fi built; Avery Fisher Hall. R. Hodges. il Pop Electr 11:20+ Mr '77
Yes plugs in at the Garden: equipment. M. Lobel. il Hi Fi 27:29-31 D '77

ACQUISITION of Latin American Library Materials, Seminar on the. See Library institutes and workshops

ACQUISITIONS, College library. See College libraries—Acquisitions

ACQUISITIONS, Library. See Libraries—Acquisitions

ACQUISITIONS and mergers. See Corporations—Acquisitions and mergers

ACREE, Vernon Darrell
Tricks that smugglers use—and how they get caught; interview. il por U.S. News 82:52-4 Mr 14 '77

ACRIDINES
Bifunctional intercalators: relationship of antitumor activity of diacridines to the cell membrane. R. M. Fico and others. bibl il Science 198:53-6 O 7 '77

ACRODERMATITIS enteropathica
Zinc binding: a difference between human and bovine milk. C. D. Eckhert and others. bibl il Science 195:789-90 F 25 '77

ACROPOLIS. See Athens, Greece—Acropolis

ACRYLIC painting. See Painting

ACT; musical comedy. See Musical comedy, revue, etc.—Reviews—Single works

ACTING
See also
Dramatization in education
Motion picture acting

Anecdotes, facetiae, satire, etc.

Living it up; excerpt. G. Burns. il pors Sat Eve Post 249:14-15 Mr '77

Study and teaching

Spotlight on books. See issues of Plays

ACTINOMYCIN
Stimulation of in vitro translation of messenger RNA by actinomycin D and cordycepin. L. Leinwand and F. H. Ruddle. bibl il Science 197:381-3 Jl 22 '77

ACTION Corps. See United States—ACTION

ACTION in art
Jim Jonson. M. Tinkelman. il por Am Artist 41:74-7 Jl '77
See also
Kinetic art
Mobiles
Sports in art

ACTION potentials. See Electrophysiology

ACTIONS and defenses
Case closed; New York City's suit against G. Willig for climbing World Trade Center. New Yorker 53:28-30 Je 13 '77
Chilling impact of litigation. il Bus W p58-62+ Je 6 '77
Class actions shift to the state courts. Bus W p53-4 Ja 24 '77
Disaster damages; international airline-disaster litigation. J. K. Footlick and others. il Newsweek 89:111 Ap 18 '77
End of the great engine flap; settlement of suit against GM for use of Chevrolet engines in other cars. Time 111:66 Ja 2 '78
Litigations; publishing. Pub W 211:43 Je 6; 28 Je 20 '77

ACTIONS and defenses—*Continued*
MCA vs. Sony; suit to prevent manufacture of Betamax video tape system. L. Marcus. Hi Fi 27:4 Ap '77
Nepotism question at General Motors; lawsuits charging E. M. Estes with furthering his sons' careers. por Bus W p41 S 19 '77
Notes and comment; case of M. Halperin. New Yorker 53:19-21 Ag 22 '77
Taking DES to court. il Time 109:44 My 9 '77
Those cases that go on and on. il Time 109:40+ Je 27 '77
Tribulations for Christian ads; lawsuits against business directories for born-again Christians. il Bus W p 148 S 19 '77
We've got too much law! J. K. Footlick. Read Digest 110:96-100 My '77
See also
Civil procedure
Damages
Injunctions
Libel and slander
ACTORS, Animal. See Animals as actors
ACTORS and actresses
American actor. D. B. Wilmeth. Intellect 106:258 D '77
Autographs. K. V. Hostick. Hobbies 82:154-5+ Ap '77
Headliner couples. il Ladies Home J 94:76+ N '77
See also
British Actors' Equity Association
Children as actors and actresses
Motion picture actors and actresses
Theatrical agencies
also names of actors and actresses, e.g. R. De Niro
ACTRESSES. See Actors and actresses; Motion picture actors and actresses
ACUÑA, Héctor R.
PAHO at 75. il Américas 29:2-4 N '77
ACUÑA, Isidoro Vázquez de. See Vázquez de Acuña, I.
ACUPUNCTURE
Can acupuncture help you lose weight? Stop smoking? R. Blackmon and S. Sheppard. Vogue 167:148+ Mr '77
Medical mailbox; C. Chung and the Acupuncture Research Clinic of Taipei. C. SerVaas. il Sat Eve Post 249:138-9 D '77
ADAGES. See Proverbs
ADAIR, Anne, and Adair, Mike
Hang it all! RC paper quick dried efficiently. il Mod Phot 41:112 My '77
—See Adair, M. jt auth
ADAIR, Mike, and Adair, Anne
Load film on the go. il Mod Phot 41:139 O '77
—See Adair, A. jt auth
ADAIR, Paul Neal
Red, boots, coots and toots. K. Willenson and N. C. Proffitt. il por Newsweek 89:50 My 9 '77 *
ADAMO, Salvatore J.
Catholic press today. Commonweal 104:176-7, 274-5, Mr 18, Ap 29 '77
ADAMS, Alice
Beautiful girl; story. New Yorker 53:23-6 Ag 1 '77
For good; story. Mademoiselle 83:80 Mr '77
Girl across the room; story. New Yorker 53:40-3 O 10 '77
ADAMS, Billye-Lee
Samuel Powel House in Philadelphia. il Antiques 112:1156-63 D '77
ADAMS, Brockman
Coming soon: gasoline at a dollar a gallon; interview. il pors U.S. News 83:43-5 Ag 15 '77
about
Adams and the bag. T. Nicholson and J. B. Copeland. il por Newsweek 90:64 Jl 11 '77 *
Brock Adams—mystery man. T. Orme. Motor T 29:6+ Mr '77 *
Green light for air bags. il Time 110:51 Jl 11 '77 *
What to expect from the new man at DOT. B. Yates. Car & Dr 22:14+ Ap '77 *
ADAMS, Ed
Testing the gate start. Yachting 141:48+ Je '77
ADAMS, Fred
461 you are over! Yachting 141:142-5 Je '77
ADAMS, Henry
Clover and Henry Adams—a most unusual love story. O. Friedrich. il pors Smithsonian 8: 58-64+ bibl(p 146-7) Ap '77 *
ADAMS, J. A. S. and others
Wood versus fossil fuel as a source of excess carbon dioxide in the atmosphere: a preliminary report. bibl il Science 196:54-6 Ap 1 '77
ADAMS, James E.
Missouri's compromise. Chr Cent 94:709-10 Ag 17 '77
ADAMS, James Ring
Reshaping secondary education. Educ Digest 43:2-4 D '77
ADAMS, Janis L.
What's new (cont) MH 60:16-17 Wint; 61:12-13 Spr '77
ADAMS, John, 1735-1826
Quasi-War. A. DeConde. il Am Hist Illus 12: 4-9+ Ap '77 *
ADAMS, John E.
Spiny lobster fishing in the Grenadines. il map Sea Front 23:322-30 N '77
ADAMS, Junius
Think thin and get thin. Read Digest 110:113-16 Ap '77
ADAMS, Marian (Hooper)
Clover and Henry Adams—a most unusual love story. O. Friedrich. il pors Smithsonian 8: 58-64+ bibl(p 146-7) Ap '77 *
ADAMS, Muriel J.
Going by bus. Seventeen 36:124 Jl '77
ADAMS, Nathan M.
America's newest crime syndicate—the Mexican Mafia. Read Digest 111:97-102 N '77
New kings of heroin. Read Digest 110:117-21 Ap '77
Tracing of Beretta A47469. il Read Digest 112: 203-6+ Ja '78
ADAMS, Phoebe-Lou
PLA. See issues of Atlantic
ADAMS, Sherman
Inoperative recollection. il por Time 109:22 My 16 '77 *
ADAMS Cup race. See Rowing
ADAMSON, Joy
Elsa the lioness. il Sat Eve Post 249:51 Jl '77 *
ADAPTATION (biology)
See also
Acclimatization
ADAPTATION (botany)
Annual plants: adaptations to desert environments. T. W. Mulroy and P. W. Rundel. bibl BioScience 27:109-14 F '77
Coadapted competitors: the flowering seasons of hummingbird-pollinated plants in a tropical forest. F. G. Stiles. bibl il Science 198:1177-8 D 16 '77
ADAPTATIONS, Motion picture. See Motion picture adaptations
ADAPTATIONS, Television. See Television adaptations
ADDICTS, Drug. See Narcotic addicts
ADDITIONS, Building. See Buildings, Remodeled
ADDITIONS, House. See Houses, Remodeled
ADDITIVES. See Food additives
ADDOMS, Samuel D.
Taming the cattle cycle. il Forbes 119:81+ Ap 15 '77 *
ADDRESSOGRAPH Multigraph Corporation
Addressograph gets the Roy Ash treatment. il Bus W p36 Mr 21 '77
Addressograph jumps into word processing. Bus W p 19-20 Jl 4 '77
ADE, Ginny
Disposable camping. il Mech Illus 73:112+ Mr '77
ADELIE penguins. See Penguins
ADELPHI Dance Theatre. See Dance companies
ADELSON, Alan
Tragedy of Joanne Bashold. il pors Good H 184: 124-5+ Mr '77
ADENEY, David H.
Church in China: praise amid persecution. Chr Today 22:10-13 N 18 '77
ADENINE
Adenine and adenosine are toxic to human lymphoblast mutants defective in purine salvage enzymes. M. E. Hershfield and others. bibl il Science 197:1284-7 S 23 '77
ADENINE arabinoside. See Vidarabine
ADENOSINE
Adenine and adenosine are toxic to human lymphoblast mutants defective in purine salvage enzymes. M. S. Hershfield and others. bibl il Science 197:1284-7 S 23 '77
ADENOSINE monophosphate
Axial bending in the early chick embryo by a cyclic adenosine monophosphate source. A. Robertson and A. R. Gingle. bibl il Science 197:1078-9 S 9 '77
Dibutyryl cyclic AMP mimics ovariectomy: nuclear protein phosphorylation in mammary tumor regression. S. C. C. Yoon and B. H. Redler. bibl il Science 197:272-5 Jl 15 '77
Localization of cyclic GMP and cyclic AMP in cardiac and skeletal muscle: immunocytochemical demonstration. S. H. Ong and A. L. Steiner. bibl il Science 195:183-5 Ja 14 '77
Second messengers in the brain. J. A. Nathanson and P. Greengard. il Sci Am 237:108-19 bibl(p 140) Ag '77
ADENOSINE triphosphatase
Membrane adenosinetriphosphatase: a digitalis receptor? T. Akera. bibl il Science 198:569-74 N 11 '77
ADENYLATE cyclase. See Enzymes
ADHESION
How bacteria stick. J. W. Costerton and others. il Sci Am 238:86-95 Ja '78
ADHESIVES
Consumer's guide to adhesives. il Mech Illus 73:100 O '77

ADHESIVES—*Continued*
Household cements. il Consumers Res Mag 60: 23-7 S '77
Primer on household glues. il Consumer Rep 42: 576-80 O '77
We try a new contact cement. il Mech Illus 73:104 F '77
See also
Cement
Epoxy adhesives
Glue
Loctite Corporation
ADIOS (race) See Harness racing
ADIPOSE tissues
Adipose tissue regeneration following lipectomy. I. M. Faust and others. bibl il Science 197: 391-3 Jl 22 '77
Beauty/New focus . . . body; cellulite; ideas of P. R. Alper. il Vogue 167:210-11 Mr '77
Surgical removal of adipose tissue alters feeding behavior and the development of obesity in rats. I. M. Faust and others. bibl il Science 197:393-6 Jl 22 '77
ADIRONDACK Mountains
Adirondack guide. R. F. Hall. por Conservationist 31:48 Ja '77
ADJUSTMENT, Social
Moving; period of adjustment. J. D. Bucher. il Redbook 149:60+ Jl '77
See also
Aged—Adjustment problems
High school students—Adjustment
Maturity
Normality
School children—Adjustment
Widows—Adjustment
ADKINS, Lynn
Dun's extends Midwest coverage with new bureau. por Duns R 110:3 Ag '77 *
ADLER, Alan J.
Sailing yacht symposium. il Yachting 141:118+ Ap '77
ADLER, Bill
(comp) Great soap opera fan letters; excerpt from Letters from soap opera fans. Good H 184:76+ Mr '77
(comp) Kids' letters to President Carter; excerpt. il McCalls 105:165+ N '77
ADLER, David
Amorphous-semiconductor devices; with biographical sketch. il Sci Am 236:13, 36-48 bibl(p 146) My '77
ADLER, Frederick R.
Advantage, Adler! il por Forbes 119:66-7 Ja 15 '77 *
ADLER, Irving, and Zelman, B. M.
Aftermath of a witch hunt. Nation 224:434-6 Ap 9 '77
ADLER, Jacob Pavlovitch
Yiddish idol; excerpt from Bright star of exile: Jacob Adler and the Yiddish theater. L. Rosenfeld. il pors N Y Times Mag p32-3+ Je 12 '77 *
ADLER, Lawrence R.
Toward a new professionalism; the master teacher. Clearing H 50:248-50 F '77
ADLER, Mortimer Jerome
Debating in the groves of Aspen. il pors Time 110:57 Jl 25 '77 *
Great books. il Time 109:65-6 Mr 7 '77 *
Great treasury of western thought. J. S. Allen. Sat R 4:26 S 3 '77 *
ADMINISTRATION, Public. See Public administration
ADMINISTRATION of justice. See Justice, Administration of
ADMINISTRATIVE efficiency. See Efficiency, Administrative
ADMINISTRATORS, College. See College officials
ADMIRAL'S Cup Race. See Yacht racing
ADNI, Daniel
Daniel Adni, piano; performance at the 92nd Street YMHA. Hi Fi 27:MA28 Je '77 *
ADOBE buildings. See Building, Adobe
ADOLESCENCE
Adolescent in the house; teen-age daughter. J. Geniesse. McCall 104:31+ Jl '77
Culture and youth. J. L. Wood. bibl Clearing H 50:240-1 F '77
Family ecology; studies by J. F. Kett and the Carnegie Council on Children. J. W. Donohue. America 137:456-9 D 24 '77
High school years. J. W. Donohue. il America 136:107-9 F 5 '77
See also
Boys
High school students
Youth
ADOLESCENCE in literature. See Literature—Themes
ADOLESCENT counseling. See Counseling
ADOLESCENT drinking. See Alcohol and youth
ADOLESCENT literature. See Young adults literature
ADOLESCENT mothers, Unmarried. See Mothers, Unmarried
ADOLESCENTS. See Youth
ADONIS (asteroid) See Asteroids
ADOPTED children. See Children, Adopted
ADOPTION
Adopting a child today. Changing T 31:42-4 Ap '77
Assortative mating by unwed biological parents of adopted children. R. Plomin and others. bibl il Science 196:449-50 Ap 22 '77
Constitutional nonsense; NYCLU adoption suit. D. Oliver. Nat R 29:1493 D 23 '77
Lingering pain of surrendering a child. A. Baran and others. il Psychol Today 11:58-60+ Je '77
McCall's family lobby; Opportunities for adoption bill. A. O'Shea. McCalls 104:74 Ag '77
Mixed families: white parents and black children; excerpt from Mixed families: adopting across racial boundaries. J. A. Ladner. bibl il Society 14:70-8 S '77
New approach to adopting children? il U.S. News 83:67 Ag 29 '77
Should whites adopt black children? M. Burgen. il Ebony 33:63-4+ D '77
Welcome prepared. E. Schaeffer. Chr Today 21: 28-9 Ap 1 '77
See also
Children, Adopted
ADOUM, Jorge Enrique
Communities in crisis. il UNESCO Courier 30: 46-50 Ag '77
ADRENALIN
Homeostasis during hypoglycemia: central control of adrenal secretion and peripheral control of feeding. E. M. Stricker and others. bibl il Science 196:79-81 Ap 1 '77
ADRENOCORTICOTROPIN. See ACTH
ADRIAMYCIN
Adriamycin: the role of lipid peroxidation in cardiac toxicity and tumor response. C. E. Myers and others. bibl il Science 197:165-7 Jl 8 '77
ADRIANA Lecouvreur; opera. See Cilea, F.
ADRIEN, Pierre-Marie, and Baumgardner, M. F.
Landsat, computers, and development projects. bibl il Science 198:466-70 N 4 '77
ADS. See Advertising
ADSORPTION
Geometry of adsorbates on solid surfaces; angle-resolved photoemission spectroscopy. E. W. Plummer and T. Gustafsson. bibl il Science 198:165-70 O 14 '77
Molecular metal clusters; insights to chemisorption. E. L. Muetterties. bibl il Science 196:839-48 My 20 '77
Surface science: an X-ray probe for adsorbed molecules. A. L. Robinson. Science 197:34-6 Jl 1 '77
See also
Adhesion
ADULT-child relationship. See Child-adult relationship
ADULT communities. See Retirement communities
ADULT education
Adult continuing education growth: no time for complacency. S. J. Drazek. bibl il Intellect 106: 49-51 Ag '77
Adult students breathe new life into education. il U.S. News 82:70-2 Mr 28 '77
Applying the gray matter. il Time 110:92 O 3 '77
Back to the ablative absolute. M. Greenfield. Newsweek 90:112 S 12 '77
Changing stages of learning; address, October 26, 1977. G. M. Ambach. Vital Speeches 44: 150-3 D 15 '77
Colleges learn the hard sell. il Bus W p92+ F 14 '77
Future of the community college. E. J. Gleazer, Jr. il Intellect 106:152-4 O '77
Going back to school at 35 and over. A. M. Young. il M Labor R 100:43-5 Jl '77
Night campus; creative writing class. M. Schreiber. il Todays Educ 66:65-6 S '77
OASES in Oklahoma; Open Access Satellite Education Services, a joint project of the Oklahoma County Libraries System and the South Oklahoma City Junior College. P. L. Little and J. R. Gilliland. pors Lib J 102: 1458-61 Jl '77
Self-renewal takes new directions in hobbies, culture, back-to-school. il U.S. News 82:64-9 My 23 '77
See also
Aged—Education
Chautauqua Institution, Chautauqua, N.Y.
Education of women
Executives—Education
Illiteracy
Self culture
University extension
ADULT vocational counseling centers. See Vocational guidance
ADULT-youth relationship. See Youth-adult relationship

ADULTERY
Infidelity: a sympton, not a solution of problems. W. C. Nichols. Parents Mag 52:42 N '77
Marriage-law controversy in Kenya. R. Mann. Chr Cent 94:457 My 11 '77
My husband was unfaithful. il Good H 184:28+ F '77
Psychiatrist's notebook. T. I. Rubin. Ladies Home J 94:70 N '77
Unfaithful husband. L. Wolfe. Ladies Home J 94:69+ Ag '77
Why some husbands stay faithful. N. Lobsenz. Read Digest 111:98-101 O '77
Why some marriages can survive an affair and others can't; with questions and answers. M. Lasswell and N. Lobsenz. McCalls 105:50+ N '77

ADULTHOOD. See Maturity

ADULTS and children. See Child-adult relationship

ADVANCED Micro Devices, Inc-Siemens Ag (firm) merger. See Electronic industries—Acquisitions and mergers

ADVENT
Advent meditation:
Christmas letter. A. M. Miller. Chr Cent 94:1157 D 14 '77
Divine inhabitant. R. Goetz. Chr Cent 94:1085 N 23 '77
Making ready the way; excerpt from Meditations on hope and love. K. Rahner. Chr Cent 94:1110-11 N 30 '77
We are all forerunners; excerpt from Meditations on hope and love. K. Rahner. Chr Cent 94:1134 D 7 '77
Ashes in our mouths. J. A. Tetlow. America 137:402 D 3 '77
Christmas in Advent. G. L. Rygh. Chr Cent 94:1133 D 7 '77
Christmas is coming. M. L. Dodds. Chr Today 22:17-18 N 18 '77
Deep down, around hope. J. P. Parkes. America 137:444 D 17 '77
See also
Second Advent

ADVENT calendars. See Calendars

ADVENTURE playgrounds. See Playgrounds

ADVENTURE stories
See also
Science fiction

ADVENTURES, Joint. See Joint adventures

ADVENTURES of Tom Sawyer; dramatization. See Olfson, L.

ADVERTISEMENTS. See Advertising

ADVERTISING
Art director who has a way with words also has a book coming from Abrams; publication of The art of advertising; interview, ed by R. Dahlin. G. Lois. Pub W 211:55+ Ja 17 '77
Giving impact to ideas; address, October 11, 1977. L. T. Hagopian. Vital Speeches 44:154-7 D 15 '77
News behind the ads. See alternate issues of Changing times
Preaching in the marketplace. America 136:457 My 21 '77
Selling it. Consumer Rep 42:385, 458, 635 Jl-Ag, N '77
See also
Photography in advertising
Religious advertising
Television advertising
Women in advertising
also subhead Advertising under various subjects, e.g. Books—Advertising

Awards, prizes, etc.
Saturday review's 23rd annual Advertising Awards. C. Tucker. il Sat R 4:34-5 Jl 23 '77

Laws and regulations
Crackdown ahead on advertising: what the government plans next; interview. M. Pertschuk. pors U.S. News 83:70-2 O 17 '77
FTC broadens its attack on ads. Bus W p27-8 Je 20 '77

Moral aspects
See Advertising ethics

Psychological aspects
Art of implying more than you say; work of Richard Harris. S. Bush. Psychol Today 10:36+ My '77
Genderisms; reinforcement of sex role stereotypes. E. Goffman. il Psychol Today 11:60-3 Ag '77

Rates
Challenge to ad discounts; effect on small retailers of rate structure used in newspaper and magazine advertising. il Bus W p 146 S 19 '77
Drop in TV viewing, but not in ad pricing. il Bus W p33-4 Ja 16 '78

Testimonials
Big scorers in the ad game; endorsements by athletes. M. Ludtke. Sports Illus 47:50 N 7 '77
Bruce's bowl; truth-in-advertising suit against General Mills. il pors Time 110:36 D 5 '77
Do you know Barney's? W. F. Buckley, Jr. Nat R 29:959 Ag 19 '77
Notes and comment. New Yorker 53:23-4 F 28 '77
Playing the endorsement game; big-name athletes. N. Howard. il Duns R 110:43-6 Ag '77

ADVERTISING, Classified
Love among the brains; personal ads in New York review of books. M. Barton. Nat R 29:840-1 Jl 22 '77
Singles scene: poetic Germans, bargain-hunting Americans; comparing personals. N. Napp. Psychol Today 10:94 F '77

History
18th century limited; newspaper ads and notices. il Sat Eve Post 249:26 Jl '77

ADVERTISING, Comparison
Battle over comparative ads. N. Howard. il Duns R 110:60-2 N '77

ADVERTISING, Direct mail
Privacy group recommends direct-mail measures. S. Wagner. Pub W 212:47-8 Ag 1 '77
Whiff of things to come; scented fliers. B. Coffman. Farm J 101:H4 Ja '77
Why so much mail? Chr Today 22:22 N 18 '77

ADVERTISING, Magazine
Why the black ink is spurting at magazines. il Bus W p 142+ D 12 '77

Rates
See Advertising—Rates

ADVERTISING, Mail. See Advertising, Direct mail

ADVERTISING, Newspaper
Advertising integrity and the newspapers. Chr Today 22:32-3 O 7 '77
All the ads fit to print; ban on advertising of pornographic movies in newspapers. il Time 110:80 S 12 '77
See also
Advertising, Classified

Rates
See Advertising—Rates

ADVERTISING, Outdoor
See also
Billboards

ADVERTISING, Personal. See Advertising, Classified

ADVERTISING, Political
Prince maker strikes again; D. Garth. il por Time 110:19-20 N 21 '77

ADVERTISING, Window. See Show windows

ADVERTISING agencies
Advertising: the best one-liners; Peter Rogers Associates. il por Time 111:66 Ja 2 '78
Controversial ad consultants. N. Howard. il Duns R 110:112-13+ O '77
Datsun switches; William Esty Co. L. Langway and M. Resse. il Newsweek 89:73 Je 27 '77
Madison Avenue likes showbiz. il Bus W p 120 D 5 '77
Now ad agencies are going private. il Bus W p76-7 Ja 24 '77
Sussman & Sugar resigns Grove Press account. M. Reuter. Pub W 212:24+ Jl 4 '77
Testy topic; Ogilvy and Mather International. Forbes 119:80 Ap 1 '77
West Coast agencies lose out. il Bus W p 121-2 My 23 '77

ADVERTISING awards. See Advertising—Awards, prizes, etc.

ADVERTISING campaigns
Coordinated advertising campaign to combat environmental pollution. B. A. Jones. il Sch Arts 76:30-1 Ap '77
Crying Wurf; advertising campaign attacking city of Atlanta and Mayor M. Jackson. K. Bode. New Repub 177:14-17 Jl 2 '77

Anecdotes, facetiae, satire, etc.
Likely story. S. N. Judy. Engl J 66:7-8 D '77

ADVERTISING cards
Baseball card investors. il Time 110:54-5 Ag 22 '77

ADVERTISING characters
Marlboro man; D. Winfield. M. Smith. il pors Sports Illus 46:58-62+ Ja 17 '77

ADVERTISING copy
And now a few words on writing for radio. R. Jacobs. Writers Digest 57:15-19 Ap '77

ADVERTISING ethics
Publisher's letter; question of advertising ethics in nursery mailorder business. R. J. Fibkins. Horticulture 55:96 F '77
Really socking it to women; misogyny. il Time 109:58-9 F 7 '77

ADVERTISING mediums

Motion pictures

Tonight at the movies; the latest national ads. Bus W p39 O 24 '77

Pamphlets

Way I see it. B. Catton. por Am Heritage 28:63 Je '77

ADVERTISING posters. See Posters

ADVERTISING rates. See Advertising—Rates

ADVERTISING research

Reinforcing the impact of TV commercials. il Bus W p40-1 Jl 18 '77

ADVERTISING signs. See Billboards

ADVICE columns. See Newspapers—Advice columns

AEGEAN Islands

See also

Siphnos (island)
Thera (island)

AEGEAN Sea Region

Antiquities

Paleogeographic reconstructions of coastal Aegean archaeological sites. J. C. Kraft and others. bibl il maps Science 195:941-7 Mr 11 '77

AEQUORIN

Aequorin luminescence: relation of light emission to calcium concentration—a calcium-independent component. D. G. Allen and others. bibl il Science 195:996-8 Mr 11 '77

AERATION of sewage. See Sewage purification—Aeration

AERIAL mapping. See Mapping, Aerial

AERIAL photography. See Photography, Aerial

AERIAL reconnaissance

Strategic reconnaissance. H. F. York and G. A. Greb. bibl il Bull Atom Sci 33:33-42 Ap '77
Time of the angel: the U-2, Cuba, and the CIA. D. Moser. il Am Heritage 28:4-15 O '77

See also

Artificial satellites—Military use

AERIAL target drones. See Airplanes, Drone

AERIAL warfare. See Air warfare

AERIE, Edward, pseud

Defense miscalculations. Nation 225:78-81 Jl 23 '77

AEROBATIC airplanes. See Airplanes, Aerobatic

AEROBICS. See Exercise

AERODYNAMICS

See also

Lift (aerodynamics)

AEROFLOT (airline) See Airlines—Russia

AEROFOIL boats. See Air cushion vehicles

AERONAUTIC instruments

Controller improved for VTOL studies. B. M. Elson. il Aviation W 107:63-4 Jl 18 '77
FAA intensifies windshear R&D effort. K. J. Stein. il Aviation W 107:66-7 S 12 '77
Onboard windshear monitor developed. W. C. Wetmore. il Aviation W 107:59-62 Ag 22 '77
Stormscope. R. L. Collins. il Flying 100:61-2+ Je '77

See also

Air navigation—Aids and devices
Detectors, Infrared
Inertial guidance systems

Display systems

Cockpit traffic displays studied. Aviation W 107:25 S 12 '77
Head-up display concept under development. il Aviation W 106:55-6 My 16 '77
Head-up display systems evaluated. R. R. Ropelewski. il Aviation W 106:70-3+ Ja 10 '77
Navy expands simpler cockpit displays. B. M. Elson. il Aviation W 107:59-61+ Jl 11 '77
Navy studies helmet-mounted display. B. Miller. il Aviation W 106:52-3 My 16 '77
Pilot display program set; F-16. D. A. Brown. il Aviation W 106:129-30 My 2 '77
Versatile displays stressed at Reading. K. J. Stein. il Aviation W 106:85+ Je 27 '77

AERONAUTIC meteorology. See Meteorology, Aeronautic

AERONAUTIC museums

See also

Smithsonian Institution—National Air and Space Museum

AERONAUTIC research

General aviation research pushed. E. Kozicharow. Aviation W 107:38-9 O 10 '77
Greater government R&D urged to spur advances. Aviation W 107:35-6 S 12 '77
Laurels for 1977; people who made contributions to the aerospace world. R. Hotz. Aviation W 108:9 Ja 2 '77
Research effort seeks better reliability, V/STOL base. il Aviation W 106:118-19+ Ja 31 '77
Transport technology gains stressed. Aviation W 106:223 Je 6 '77

AERONAUTICS

See also

Airships
Aviation

History

Breakthroughs: critical checkpoints in the course of aircraft development. J. W. Olcott. il Flying 101:282+ S '77
DH and his marvelous Moths. J. Gilbert. il Flying 100:82-90+ My '77
Dreamers who dared. T. Satrom. il Sat Eve Post 249:64-5+ My '77
First flight; symposium. il Flying 101:66-98+ S '77
Flight at fifty; symposium, ed by H. Sutton. il Sat R 4:6-10 Ap 16 '77
Iron Annie; Junkers Ju 52. M. Caidin. il Flying 101:305-8 S '77
Lindbergh alone; condensation. B. Gill. il pors Read Digest 110:225-8+ My '77
Living legends:
- Gordon Israel. G. C. Larson. il por Flying 100:62-3+ Ap '77
- Max Conrad. D. Mosteller. Flying 101:50-1+ N '77

Lucky Lindy. il por Sr Schol 109:10-11 My 5 '77
Milestones:
- Beech's brilliant biplane. R. Munson. il Flying 101:74-81+ Jl '77

Pilot in command. T. J. Watson. il Flying 101:309+ S '77
Turbulent decade; postwar years. F. K. Smith. il Flying 101:200-5+ S '77

See also

Airplane industry—United States—History
Airplane racing—History
Airplanes in business—History
Airships—History
Aviation—Stunt flying—History
Aviation—Transatlantic flights—History
Aviation records—History
Private flying—History

Study and teaching

See also

Air pilots—Training
Aviation schools

AERONAUTICS, Commercial

See also

Air freight service
Air travel
Airlines
Airports
International Civil Aviation Organization

History

Air commerce. P. Trenner. il Flying 101:90-1 S '77

See also

Airlines—History
Airlines—United States—History

Arab countries

Mideast nations move slowly to self-support in aviation. il Aviation W 106:327-9 Je 6 '77

Canada

See also

Okanagan Helicopters Ltd

United States

Air transportation leadership; excerpts from address. H. L. Lawrence. Aviation W 106:11 My 23 '77

AERONAUTICS, Military

Future flight: military. R. Tuttle. il Flying 101:356-7 S '77

See also

Air warfare
Helicopters—Military use

History

Centerfold; Blackburn Firebrand. S. Wilkinson. il Flying 100:110 Je '77
Zero; Messerschmitt. P. Garrison. Flying 101:275 S '77

See also

Korean War, 1950-1953—Aerial operations
United States—Army—Air Corps
World War, 1914-1918—Aerial operations
World War, 1939-1945—Aerial operations

United States

See also

United States—Air Force

AEROSAT system. See Artificial satellites—Air traffic control use

AEROSOL packaging. See Pressure packaging

AEROSOL pump sprayer. See Pressure packaging

AEROSOLS

Dust concentration in the atmosphere of the equatorial North Atlantic: possible relationship to the Sahelian drought. J. M. Prospero and R. T. Nees. bibl il Science 196:1196-8 Je 10 '77
Planetary radiation balance as a function of atmospheric dust: climatological consequences. S. B. Idso and A. J. Brazel. bibl il Science 198:731-3 N 18 '77

AEROSOLS—*Continued*
Release of particles containing metals from vegetation into the atmosphere. W. Beauford and others. bibl il Science 195:571-3 F 11 '77
Sulfate aerosol: its geographical extent in the midwestern and southern United States. R. J. Weiss and others. bibl il Science 195:979-81 Mr 11 '77
Virus transfer from surf to wind. E. R. Baylor and others. bibl il Science 198:575-80 N 11 '77
See also
Pressure packaging

AEROSPACE industries
Laurels for 1977; people who made contributions to the aerospace world. R. Hotz. Aviation W 108:9 Ja 2 '78
See also
Airplane industry
Collective labor agreements—Aerospace industries
Guided missile industries

Employees

See also
International Association of Machinists and Aerospace Workers
Strikes—United States—Aerospace industries

Export-import trade

Aerospace exports to top $8 billion. il Aviation W 106:35-6 Mr 21 '77
Casualties of a cut in arms sales abroad; Middle East sales. il Bus W p34-5 Ap 25 '77
Major 1978 aerospace gain foreseen. H. J. Coleman. il Aviation W 108:15-16 Ja 9 '78
Moves on Latin America impact on export market. Aviation W 106:18 Mr 7 '77
Special report: new trends reshaping global export market; with editorial comment. il Aviation W 106:37, 82-5+ Je 6 '77
Special rules for the Shah; proposed AWACS sale to Iran. New Repub 177:10 Jl 30 '77

Finance

Aerospace & defense. il Forbes 121:61-2+ Ja 9 '78
Military spending pushes sales of aerospace past $30 billion. W. H. Gregory. Aviation W 106:8-9 Mr 21 '77

Social aspects

Slow awakening. R. Hotz. Aviation W 107:9 Ag 15 '77

Europe, Western

Europe gains in aerospace. Aviation W 107:101+ S 26 '77
Germans ponder industry consolidation; MBB and VFW-Fokker. R. R. Ropelewski. Aviation W 107:18-19 Ag 15 '77
Strength of Europe's industry stressed. il Aviation W 106:163+ Je 6 '77
VFW-Fokker discontinues output of 614 transport. R. R. Ropelewski. Aviation W 108:29-30 Ja 2 '78
Why VFW-Fokker may have to split up. il Bus W p37-8 Mr 28 '77

France

Exports buoy aerospace for French. R. R. Ropelewski. il Aviation W 106:47+ Mr 21 '77
French aerospace exports rise slightly. il Aviation W 106:50-1 Mr 7 '77
Profit picture colors French takeover. R. R. Ropelewski. Aviation W 107:22-3 Ag 1 '77

Germany, West

Military aircraft spur German industry. il Aviation W 106:51+ Mr 21 '77
See also
Messerschmitt-Boelkow-Blohm (firm)

Great Britain

British Aerospace Corp. outlook mixed. D. A. Brown. Aviation W 106:15-17 My 9 '77
British industry braced for nationalization move. D. A. Brown. il Aviation W 106:42-3+ Mr 21 '77
British industry changes raise doubts. D. A. Brown. il Aviation W 106:156-7+ Je 6 '77

Japan

Economic, political factors key to Japan's aerospace outlook. Aviation W 106:55 Mr 21 '77

United States

Case for private industry. R. V. Paolucci. Aviation W 107:7 Jl 25; 7 Ag 1 '77
Outlook for 1977. R. Hotz. Aviation W 106:7 Ja 10 '77
See also
Collective bargaining—Aerospace industries
Grumman Corporation
Lockheed Aircraft Corporation
Rockwell International Corporation
Rohr Industries, Inc
Strikes—United States—Aerospace industries
United Technologies Corporation

AEROSPATIALE Group of France Helicopter Division. See Helicopter industry—France

AESCHYLUS
Agamemnon. Reviews
America 136:528 Je 11 '77 *
Nation 224:701-2 Je 4 '77
New Repub 177:24 Jl 9 '77 *
New Yorker 53:84 My 30 '77 *
Newsweek 89:89 My 30 '77 *
Time 109:76 My 30 '77 *

AESTHETICS
How to find more beauty in your life. C. Seebohm. il House & Gard 149:66+ Jl '77
One hundred metronomes; art, artists and works of art. E. T. Cone. Am Scholar 46:443-57 Aut '77
See also
Architecture—Philosophy
Harmony (aesthetics)

AFARS and the Issas, French Territory of
Note:
For material after June 1977, see heading Djibouti
France asked to implement plan for independence by summer this year; with text of resolution. UN Chron 14:34-5, 100-1 Ja '77

AFFECTION. See Love

AFFILIATE Artists, Inc
San Francisco/Affiliate Artists Opera Program. Hi Fi 27:MA38 Jl '77

AFFILIATED Hospitals Center. See Boston—Hospitals

AFFIRMATIVE action. See Discrimination

AFFIRMATIVE action in employment. See Discrimination in employment

AFFLICTION. See Suffering

AFFORESTATION. See Forest planting

AFGHANISTAN
High adventure in ancient Afghanistan. C. Lucas. il Read Digest 111:184-90 Ag '77

AFGHANS (coverlets)
One man's afghan, another man's purl. E. A. Yeager. il pors Ret Liv 17:43 Ap '77

AFLATOXIN. See Toxins and antitoxins

AFRICA
Africa in transition; symposium, ed by M. E. Wolfgang. bibl f Ann Am Acad 432:1-119 Jl '77
Africa, 1977; symposium. bibl f il Cur Hist 73:193-229+ map(inside back cover) D '77
See also
Agriculture—Africa
Children—Africa
Communism—Africa
Crime and criminals—Africa
Ecology—Africa
Economic assistance, American—Africa
Education—Africa
Hunting—Africa
Iron age—Africa
Marriage customs and rites—Africa
Military assistance, Cuban—Africa
Military assistance, Russian—Africa
Political prisoners—Africa
Theater—Africa
Zoology—Africa

Antiquities

See also
Carthage, Africa

Bibliography

Book reviews. Cur Hist 73:223 D '77

Civilization

Changing face of Africa; symposium. il UNESCO Courier 30:4-33 My '77

Colonization

Organization of African Unity and decolonization: present and future trends. G. L. Binaisa. bibl f Ann Am Acad 432:52-69 Jl '77

Commerce

United States

See United States—Commerce—Africa

Drought

See Droughts

Economic conditions

Air transport can help strengthen Africa's economy, ICAO study finds. UN Chron 14:30-1 Mr '77
Developing states of Africa. R. S. Morgenthau. bibl f Ann Am Acad 432:80-95 Jl '77
See also
United Nations—Economic Commission for Africa

Foreign relations

Arab Countries

See Arab Countries—Foreign relations—Africa

China

See China—Foreign relations—Africa

Russia

See Russia—Foreign relations—Africa

United States

See United States—Foreign relations—Africa

AFRICA—*Continued*

History

Bibliography

Reviews of books: Africa. See issues of American historical review

Industries

See also

Motion picture industry—Africa

Languages

See also

Bantu languages
Swahili language

Maps

Map section. Sr Schol 110:29 O 20 '77

Native races

See also

Pygmies

Politics and government

Political transition in urban Africa; Mushin sector of Lagos, Nigeria. S. T. Barnes. bibl f Ann Am Acad 432:26-41 Jl '77

See also

Organization of African Unity

Religious institutions and affairs

Church in Africa: from adolescence to maturity; interview, ed by H. Lindsell. G. B. Osei-Mensah. por Chr Today 21:17-19 Ja 7 '77

Reappraisal of polygamy in Africa. P. Bock. bibl il Intellect 105:435-6 Je '77

See also

Catholic Church in Africa
Christians in Africa
Church and state in Africa
Lutheran Church in Africa
Missions—Africa
Religious conferences—Africa

Social conditions

Crime and development in Africa. L. Sesay. Ann Am Acad 432:42-51 Jl '77

AFRICA, Central

See also

Central African Empire
Gabon
Uganda
Zaïre

Population

Trends and prospects of population in tropical Africa. E. Van De Walle. bibl f Ann Am Acad 432:1-11 Jl '77

AFRICA, East

See also

Afars and the Issas, French Territory of
Airlines—Africa, East
Djibouti
Education—Africa, East
Ethiopia
Kenya
Lamu (island and town)
Mozambique
Tanzania
Wildlife management—Africa, East

AFRICA, North

North Africa: the eye of the storm. W. H. Lewis. Cur Hist 73:196-8+ D '77

See also

Morocco
Sahara Desert
Tunisia
United States—History—Tripolitan War, 1801-1805

Foreign relations

United States

See United States—Foreign relations—Africa, North

AFRICA, Northwest

Foreign relations

Russia

See Russia—Foreign relations—Africa, Northwest

AFRICA, Southern

See also

Civil rights—Africa, Southern
Industry and state—Africa, Southern
Investments, American—Africa, Southern
Military assistance—Africa, Southern
Railroads—Africa, Southern
Rhodesia
South Africa
United Nations—Africa, Southern
Visitors, Foreign—Africa, Southern

Antiquities

Ecology of early man in southern Africa. R. G. Klein. bibl il map Science 197:115-26 Jl 8 '77

Economic relations

Activities of foreign economic interests, military bases condemned. UN Chron 14:12-14 Ag '77
Southern Africa: trade feeds on interdependence. map Bus W p66-7 F 14 '77

United States

See United States—Economic relations—Africa, Southern

Foreign relations

Assembly condemns collaboration with southern Africa racist régimes. UN Chron 14:61 Ja '77

United States

See United States—Foreign relations—Africa, Southern

Native races

See also

Bushmen

Politics and government

African front-line states: forcing the pace. J. Marcum. map Nation 225:492-5 N 12 '77
Does the Carter administration have a strategy for Southern Africa? G. W. Shepherd, Jr. il Chr Cent 94:782-6 S 14 '77
Nyerere: how much war? interview, ed by L. Griggs. J. Nyerere. por Time 109:25 Mr 14 '77
Peace possibilities in Southern Africa. Chr Today 21:27-8 Ja 21 '77
Shattering effect of tribal allegiances. Bus W p76 F 14 '77

Race question

African-American manifesto; Black Leadership Conference on southern Africa, September 25, 1976. Current 190:43-50 F '77
Assembly condemns collaboration with southern Africa racist régimes. UN Chron 14:61 Ja '77
Growing peril of race war in southern Africa. D. B. Richardson. il map U.S. News 82:22+ F 7 '77
How long can Africa's whites hold out? S. Topping. il N Y Times Mag p37-9+ N 13 '77
Southern Africa at grips with racism; symposium. il maps UNESCO Courier 30:4-32 N '77
Southern Africa: race conflict or third world war? Otto. il Sat Eve Post 249:68-9 S '77
Vorster's crocodile. F. Willey and others. il Newsweek 90:37-8 Ag 22 '77

Religious institutions and affairs

African impatience for change; meeting at Bergamo East Conference Center. C. E. Brewster. il Chr Cent 94:382-4 Ap 20 '77

See also

Catholics in Africa, Southern

AFRICA, Southwest

See also

Angola

AFRICA, Sub-Saharan

See also

Agriculture—Africa, Sub-Saharan
Paleontology—Africa, Sub-Saharan

Civilization

Challenge of cultural transition in Sub-Saharan Africa. V. C. Uchendu. bibl f Ann Am Acad 432:70-9 Jl '77

AFRICA, West

See also

Ghana
Ivory Coast
Togo
Visitors, Foreign—Africa, West

Native races

Africa—American style; Oyotunji; South Carolina village; Yoruba culture. M. Popp. il Ebony 33:86-8+ Ja '78

Religious institutions and affairs

English-speaking West Africa. J. R. W. Stott. Chr Today 22:38-9 D 9 '77

AFRICAN art. See Art, African

AFRICAN dancing. See Dancing, African

AFRICAN Development Bank

Administration supports increased U.S. contributions to the African Development Fund; statement, April 18, 1977. Dept State Bull 76:471-4 My 9 '77

AFRICAN Development Fund. See African Development Bank

AFRICAN folk music. See Folk music, African

AFRICAN literature

Study and teaching

Teaching African literature: the case of Zimbabwe. K. Phaswana. bibl f il Engl J 66:46-8 Mr '77

AFRICAN names. See Names, African

AFRICAN pottery. See Pottery, African

AFRICAN proverbs. See Proverbs, African

AFRICAN sculpture. See Sculpture, African

AFRICAN sleeping sickness. See Trypanosomiasis

AFRICAN wild dogs. See Wild dogs

AFRICANO, Lillian. See Sloan, D. jt auth

AFRICANS in literature

Arrow of God; C. Achebe's novel. R. Patterson. Engl J 66:64-5 Mr '77

AFRIKANER Broederbond. See Secret societies—South Africa

AFRIKANERS. See South Africans

AFRO-AMERICANS. See Blacks

AFRO-CUBAN poetry. See Cuban poetry

AFTER images
Comparison of Fourier analysis and feature analysis in pattern-specific color aftereffects. M. A. Green and others; discussion. bibl il Science 198:207-10 O 14 '77
Phantom-motion aftereffect. N. Weisstein and others. bibl il Science 198:955-8 D 2 '77

AFTERLIFE. See Future life

AFTERNOON teas. See Teas

AGAMEMNON; drama. See Aeschylus

AGAPANTHUS
South Africa's love flower. I. Zucker. Horticulture 55:2-3+ Je '77

AGASSIZ, Jean Louis. See Agassiz, L.

AGASSIZ, Louis
American adventure of Louis Agassiz. D. McCullough. il por Audubon 79:2-17 Ja '77 *
Faces of slavery. E. Reichlin. il Am Heritage 28:4-11 Je '77 *

AGATHA, Saint
Witness of St Agatha. M. E. Marty. Chr Cent 94:183 F 23 '77 *

AGAVES
See also
Tequila

AGE
Profile of an aging America. il U.S. News 83:54 Ag 8 '77
See also
Aging
Longevity
Old age

AGE (animals)
Levodopa, fertility, and longevity. G. C. Cotzias and others. bibl il Science 196:549-51 Ap 29 '77
When animals grow older; aging pets. M. W. Fox. McCalls 105:86+ Ja '78

AGE (psychology)
Acting your age. T. Griffith. Atlantic 239:20+ Mr '77
Don't be adultish! interview, ed by D. Goleman. A. Montagu. il Psychol Today 11:46-7+ Ag '77
Is a woman over the hill at 40? V. M. Grosvenor. il por Ebony 32:144-6+ Ag '77

AGE and employment
Finding my niche—at 61. S. Gorsky. McCalls 104:56+ Mr '77
Too old or not too old. B. Rosen and T. H. Jerdee. il Harvard Bus R 55:97-106 N '77
Unlucky generation. P. A. Samuelson. Newsweek 90:100 O 10 '77
See also
Aged—Employment
Children—Employment
Retirement

AGED
First Lady hosts discussion on the Nation's elderly; NCOA conference provides forum for national leaders; Washington D.C. il por Aging 272:3-5 Je '77
Gift of life; excerpt. J. L. Kenigsberg. por Sr Schol 109:24 My 5 '77
Graying of America. A. Mayer and others. il Newsweek 89:50-2+ F 28 '77; Same abr. Read Digest 111:173-4+ Jl '77
Major proposals before Congress affecting the elderly: June 30, 1977. Aging 274:38 Ag '77
Mayors form task force on urban elderly. Aging 268:7-8 F '77
Not ready for the rocking chair:
- Buckminster Fuller, optimist on tomorrow. E. Berger. il pors Ret Liv 17:30-2 O '77
- Don't buy it if you can build it or repair it. E. Morris. il por Ret Liv 17:45 Ap '77
- George Horn, motorman. S. Fischler and D. Rubenstein. il por Ret Liv 17:33-4+ F '77
- H. Gordon playhouse impresario and M. Elias amateur film maker. Ret Liv 17:31-3 Ag '77
- Nimble grandma in Santa's workshop. M. Baughman. il Ret Liv 16:36-7 D '76
- No retiring for Christmas; D. Rankin's personal story. H. S. Davenport. il por Ret Liv 17:32-4 D '77
- Once again it was up, up, and away; Ivan Carlson. S. Carlson. il por Ret Liv 17:14+ Je '77
- 13 is his lucky number; T. Mumby. J. R. Hanley. il por Ret Liv 17:40-1 Jl '77
- Varoom! Goes the preacher; Stan George. D. Kloss. il Ret Liv 17:42+ Mr '77

Old people and public policy. A. Etzioni. Current 192:21-34 Ap '77
Rural aged. E. G. Youmans. bibl f il Ann Am Acad 429:81-91 Ja '77
Sunny Florida: foreshadowing our future? J. R. Wooten. map U.S. News 84:34-5 Ja 9 '78
Trends in American marriage, childbirth, and retirement; excerpts from addresses. W. J. Cohen; C. F. Westoff. por Intellect 106:93-5 S '77
Writing for the aged: new vistas for the old. H. Alpert. Writers Digest 57:15+ Mr '77
See also
Aging
Centenarians
National Association of Area Agencies on Aging
National Council of Senior Citizens
Old age
Retirement
Retirement income
Sports for the aged
Television and the aged

Activities

And the band played on; senior band in Hot Springs, Ark. J. Wallworth. il Ret Liv 17:46-8 My '77
Candlelight and vintage years; Sarasota, Fla. M. H. Freedman. Aging 274:11 Ag '77
Do it yourself: Texas gardeners grow bumper crop; Amarillo Senior Citizens Assn. il Aging 274:15 Ag '77
Old bakery used as marketplace for Texas seniors. il Aging 275:29-31 S '77
Retirement gardening; symposium. il Org Gard & Farm 24:104-12 My '77
Senior citizen cultural revolution; New York City. F. R. Jankovitz. il Aging 270:12-16 Ap '77
Supporting the life style of retired men through community service: a two-way street; Fix-it Workshop and Handyman Projects. M. Goodman and B. Soloman. il Aging 266:7 D '76
25 things to do this summer. R. Hemming and H. Alpert. il Ret Liv 17:22-5 Je '77
See also
Aged—Political activities
Gray Panthers (pressure group)
Volunteer service

Adjustment problems

As your parents grow older; excerpt from When your parents grow old. J. Otten and F. D. Shelley. il Parents Mag 52:42+ Je '77

Anecdotes, facetiae, satire, etc.

Gray chic. J. Otten. por Newsweek 90:13 D 5 '77

Attitudes

Old age: facts and fancies; excerpt from A good age. A. Comfort. Sat Eve Post 249:45 Mr '77

Bibliography

Publications. See issues of Aging

Care and hygiene

Caring for the elderly in your family. il Bus W p83-5+ F 7 '77
Goal, a program and a community; Areawide Council on Aging of Broward County, Inc, Fort Lauderdale, Fla. E. H. Sluyter. il por Aging 272:13-17 Je '77
New York training program treats psychiatric disorders; Daughters of Jacob Geriatric Center in the Bronx. Aging 274:25 Ag '77
Over 60? Exercise! il Sci Digest 81:87 F '77
Q&A about health. M. A. Hinrichs. See issues of Retirement living
Sleep clinic's experts say most older people need less sleep than younger adults. il Ret Liv 17:11-12 F '77
Start planning early to cushion the hardships of age; interview. J. Otten. por U.S. News 83:57-8 O 3 '77
Taking time to care. A. L. Molberg. il MH 60:19-23 Wint '77
See also,
Aged—Housing
Aged—Medical care
Cardinal Ritter Institute, St Louis, Mo.
Home care services
Nursing homes
Physical education for the aged

Caricatures and cartoons

Build a classy chassis from the vintage stars. il Sat Eve Post 249:70-1 Mr '77

Clubs and societies

National organizations form Ad Hoc Coalition on Aging. Aging 270:5 Ap '77

Conduct of life

Growing old happy. K. L. Woodward. il Newsweek 89:56-7 F 28 '77

Economic conditions

Energy costs: large portion of elderly's bill. Aging 274:13+ Ag '77
Gentle art of poverty: how to live in southern California on $2000 a year. J. Brooke. il Atlantic 240:62-8 O '77
Politics and the aged. D. Edwards. il Intellect 106:181 N '77

Education

Festival of education for older people; University of Nebraska at Omaha. S. Francke and B. Horacek. il Aging 275:24-5 S '77
Lifetime learning and the arts—a new priority. S. Timmermann. Educ Digest 43:40-2 S '77

AGED—Education—*Continued*
Many institutions offering programs for elderly, survey shows. Aging 268:12 F '77
Mother and daughter back in school; University of Wisconsin-Whitewater's Live In and Learn Program. il Aging 266:6 D '76
Retirement, no—back to college, yes! M. R. Koller. bibl il Intellect 106:52-4 Ag '77
So you'd like to go back to college? I. M. Ahern. il Ret Liv 17:32-3+ Ja '77
Taking senior citizens off the shelf; Santa Rosa Senior Skills Center. S. Brown. Educ Digest 42:45-7 My '77

Employment

Flexitime, flexiwork, flexijobs, & retiree job-sharing. H. Alpert. il Ret Liv 17:22-5 My '77
Old folks at work; Fertl, Inc. S. T. Atlas and M. Reese. il por Newsweek 90:64 S 26 '77
One way to get good workers; older people as temporary employees. R. Ross. Nations Bus 65:39-40 S '77

Family relationships

As your parents grow older; excerpt from When your parents grow old. J. Otten and F. D. Shelley. il Parents Mag 52:42+ Je '77
Older Americans in the family context. C. Tibbitts. Aging 270:6-11 Ap '77
Two older adult generations under one roof; aging parent and single, middle-aged daughter. M. Odmark. il Ret Liv 17:27-8 Ja '77

Federal aid

See Old age assistance

Health and hygiene

See Aged—Care and hygiene

Housing

Building types study: housing the aging. il Archit Rec 161:123-38 My '77
Maryland pioneers new concept in housing; sheltered housing for elderly. D. F. Thomas. il Aging 268:21-4 F '77
Money & your home. C. Carlson; J. M. Guttentag. il Ret Liv 17:34-9+ Ja '77
Recycled tannery provides historical and spatial amenities for elderly near Boston; The Tannery, Peabody. il Archit Rec 162:124-6 S '77
University professor urges community-centered housing. Aging 275:33 S '77
See also
Retirement communities

International aspects

Aging around the world. See issues of Aging

Legal assistance

See Legal assistance to the aged

Legal status, laws, etc.

Missouri sponsors Silver Haired Legislation Project. il Aging 268:15-17 F '77

Medical care

Q&A about health. M. A. Hinrichs. See issues of Retirement living
Treating the old and sick. M. Clark and M. Gosnell. il Newsweek 89:64-5 F 28 '77

Mental hygiene

See Aged—Care and hygiene

Nutrition

Nutrition: special section. il Aging 274:3-15 Ag '77

Periodicals

Golden oldies. H. Alpert and B. Hillman. il Writers Digest 57:16-17 Mr '77

Personality

See Aged—Psychology

Photographs

After ninety; excerpts. M. Mitchell; I. Cunningham. por Pop Phot 81:126-35+ O '77

Poetry

Green winter; excerpt from Green winter: celebration of old age. E. Maclay. il Read Digest 110:106-9 Mr '77
Pursuing a gray-haired muse. il por Time 109:52 Ap 4 '77

Political activities

As older folks gain more—a backlash from young? J. Mann. il U.S. News 83:59 D 5 '77
90 seniors get close-up of Capitol Hill; Congressional internship program. il Ret Liv 17:40 Ag '77
Working on the campaign trail. C. R. Arrington. il por Ret Liv 17:38+ O '77
See also
Gray Panthers (pressure group)

Psychology

Change of scene can be fatal; nursing-home patients. S. Bush. Psychol Today 10:32 F '77
Whenever somebody says I'm too old. W. E. Lindau. Ret Liv 17:37+ Ap '77

Recreation

Happy hour lives up to its name in Boston experiment. Aging 272:5-6 Je '77
Needs of the elderly: an overview of the research. L. H. McAvoy. bibl il Parks & Rec 12:31-4+ Mr '77
New leisure class: gray but not blue. G. Cross. il Parks & Rec 12:32-5+ Je '77
Planning for the elderly. Am City & County 92:41 N '77
Psychomotor approach in the nursing home; dancing programs for the aged. L. R. Schoenfeld. il Dance Mag 51:82-4 O '77
Spanish-speaking seniors provide music for Oklahoma elderly. il Aging 272:18-19 Je '77
See also
Sports for the aged

Sexual behavior

Sex after sixty-five; excerpt from Human sexual inadequacy. W. H. Masters and V. E. Johnson. il Sat Eve Post 249:48-52 Mr '77
Sexual activity of the elderly. J. Brier and D. Rubenstein. Intellect 105:383-5 My '77
Sexual lives of women over 60. C. Tavris. Ms 6:62-5 Jl '77
Staying young longer; views of A. Comfort. C. Seebohm. il House & Gard 149:131+ Mr '77

Social security

See Social security

State aid

See Old age assistance

Transportation

Transportation projects face insurance coverage problems. Aging 275:11-12 S '77

Travel

Senior savings; foreign travel bargains. K. Simmon. il Travel 147:60-3+ Mr '77

Volunteer service

See Volunteer service

Europe

Europe's bumper crop of old people. J. Horn. Psychol Today 10:91-2 F '77

Great Britain

Being old in Britain. A. Perkins. Chr Cent 94:540-1 Je 1 '77

Puerto Rico

Puerto Rico holds first Governor's Conference on Aging. il Aging 266:14-15 D '76
Puerto Rico honors its older citizens. il Aging 275:23 S '77

Russia

Yogurt & the fountain of youth; filming of Dannon commercial in Soviet Georgia. C. Turgeon. il Sat Eve Post 249:18+ O '77

United States

See Aged

AGED and children. See Child-adult relationship
AGED in childrens literature. See Childrens literature—Themes
AGED volunteers in education. See Volunteer workers in education
AGED-youth relationship. See Youth-adult relationship
AGEE, Jane M.
Realities of college composition courses. Engl J 66:58-60 N '77
AGEE, Joel
Is Dinu Lipatti beyond reproach? Harpers 255:69-73 S '77
Succurrere vitae. il Harpers 225:88-90+ D '77
AGEE, Philip
Cuba's role in Jamaica. A. De Borchgrave. il por Newsweek 89:37-8 F 28 '77 *
England revives the star chamber. R. Clark. Nation 224:261-3 Mr 5 '77 *
AGEE, William C.
American art 1910-1940: a neglected vision. B. Forgey. il Art N 76:66-8 O '77 *
AGEE, William McReynolds
Early arrival of a happy family man. por Fortune 95:17 F '77 *
Room at the top. por Time 109:68 F 21 '77 *
William M. Agee of Bendix: careful campaigner. por Forbes 119:93 F 15 '77 *
AGEL, Jerome
If you had three wishes. . . N Y Times Mag p84+ My 15 '77
AGENCIES, Advertising. See Advertising agencies
AGENCIES, Federal. See United States—Executive departments
AGENCIES, Regulatory. See Independent regulatory commissions
AGENCIES, Travel. See Travel agencies and agents
AGENCY for Consumer Advocacy (proposed) See United States—Agency for Consumer Advocacy (proposed)

AGENCY for International Development. See United States—Agency for International Development
AGENT Orange. See Herbicides
AGENTS, Insurance. See Insurance agents
AGENTS, Literary. See Literary agents
AGENTS, Manufacturers. See Manufacturers agents
AGENTS, Photographers. See Photographers agents
AGENTS, Press. See Press agents
AGENTS, Real estate. See Real estate agents
AGENTS, Talent. See Theatrical agencies
AGENTS provocateurs
Investigative asymmetry; proposed reestablishment of House Internal Security Committee. M. S. Evans. Nat R 29:997 S 2 '77
AGGLUTININS
See also
Lectins
AGGREGATES (building materials)
Short course on exposed aggregate; concrete sidewalk. il Parks & Rec 12:49-51 My '77
AGGRESSIVENESS (psychology)
Is it our culture, not our genes, that makes us killers? excerpt from Origins. R. E. Leakey and R. Lewin. il por Smithsonian 8:56-8+ bibl (p 160) N '77
One of the best: the lionhearted editor. G. E. Vaillant. Psychol Today 11:40 S '77
Temporal lobe aggression in rats. J. P. J. Pinel and others. bibl il Science 197:1088-9 S 9 '77
See also
Assertiveness (psychology)
Violence
AGGREY, James Emman Kwegyir
Professor James Emman Kwegyir Aggrey's personality. D. C. Yancey. bibl Negro Hist Bull 40:722-4 Jl '77 *
AGHAJANIAN, George K. See Wang, R. Y. jt auth
AGING
Getting older and loving it; symposium. il Sat Eve Post 249:45-59+ Mr '77
Testing the commitment theory of cellular aging. R. Holliday and others. bibl il Science 198: 366-72 O 28 '77
See also
Gerontological Society
National Council on the Aging

Conferences

See Gerontology—Conferences

Psychology

See Aged—Psychology

Research

Biology of aging. L. Hayflick. Natur Hist 86:22+ bibl(p 116) Ag '77
Can we live forever? E. K. Pye. por Sat Eve Post 249:35+ Mr '77; Same abr. Sci Digest 82:14-15 S '77
How does vitamin E prevent aging? Sci N 111: 341 My 28 '77
Octopus's life; aging process impeded by optic gland removal. il Newsweek 90:81 D 12 '77
Why you age. S. M. Bailey. Sci Digest 82:50-2 Jl '77
See also
United States—National Institute on Aging
United States—National Institutes of Health—Gerontology Research Center

Study and teaching

Schools take a new look at old people. S. Moramarco. McCalls 105:80 N '77
AGING, Administration on. See United States—Aging, Administration on
AGING, Select Committee on. See United States—Congress—House—Aging, Select Committee on
AGING, Special Committee on. See United States—Congress—Senate—Aging, Special Committee on
AGINS, Stephen M.
Nairobi: a city safari. il Travel 148:52-5 Jl '77
AGNEW, Harold Melvin
Plan to lessen suspicions. Bull Atom Sci 33:6-7 Mr '77; Same with title Truth in verification. Aviation W 106:7 My 16 '77
Primer on enhanced radiation weapons. Bull Atom Sci 33:6-8 D '77
AGORAPHOBIA. See Phobias
AGRANOFF, Bernard William. See Heacock, A. M. jt auth
AGRARIAN reform. See Land reform
AGREEMENTS, Collective labor. See Collective labor agreements
AGRICULTURAL administration
Roots of hunger. D. Morgan. Natur Hist 86: 118-21 O '77
World of extremes; address, April 27, 1977. M. Fribourg. Vital Speeches 43:527-9 Je 15 '77
See also
Farm produce—Prices
Land reform

Brazil

Shaky price floor under coffee beans. il Bus W p52-3+ O 10 '77

Canada

Canadian agriculture today. T. S. Veeman and M. M. Veeman. bibl f Cur Hist 72:162-5 Ap '77

Europe, Western

Europe's farmers—tougher competitors than you think. R. C. Black. il Farm J 101:K1+ Ja '77

United States

Behind the unrest on America's farms; Parity: what strike is all about. il U.S. News 83:69-70 D 26 '77
Bergland's new farm policy. L. Smith. por Duns R 109:70-2 Ap '77
Blessings and problems of 1977's bumper crops. il U.S. News 83:32-4 S 19 '77
Bumper crop of controversy. il Bus W p48-9 Jl 25 '77
Bumper crop of controversy over farm aid. il Bus W p 110-11+ Ap 18 '77
Carter and the farmers. New Repub 178:5-6 Ja 7 '78
Carter's guide on crop cutbacks. il Bus W p44-5 S 12 '77
Don't expect 85% of parity; price support legislation. C. S. Machan. Farm J 101:Dairy 7 Ja '77
Echoes of OPEC in Bergland's commodity pricing scheme. il Bus W p76 Mr 14 '77
Ends and beginnings. F. Getlein. Commonweal 105:4-5 Ja 6 '78
Farm-price pinch: Carter to the rescue. il U.S. News 83:72-3 S 12 '77
Farm program we can endorse. Farm J 101:44 My '77
Farmer plea: fair profit; no excess regulation. il Suc Farm 75:no3 28-9+ F '77
Farmers and consumers can work together. F. Richmond. Farm J 101:14 Ja '77
Farmers disenchanted with Carter farm policy. il Farm J 101:B2 Ag '77
Farmers to government: leave us alone but stay close by. il Suc Farm 75:no3 8-9 F '77
Furious farmers. Time 110:17 D 19 '77
Get set for wheat allotments this fall. R. D. Wennblom. il Farm J 101:20A+ Je '77
Great Treasury raid of 1977; new farm subsidy bill. J. Berry. Forbes 120:26-7 Ag 15 '77
How to handle taxes on money you get from Uncle Sam. L. Lane. il Farm J 101:30-1+ N '77
New farm bill. il Farm J 101:13+ S '77
New farm bill—a mixed bag. Farm J 101:44 S '77
New farm bill ties targets to cost of production. R. D. Wennblom. Farm J 101:9 mid-F '77
Opinion. See issues of Farm journal
Paying farmers not to work. J. Solkoff. New Repub 177:19-21 S 17 '77
Plant not, want not. Newsweek 90:90+ S 12 '77
Plowshares into swords; price support controversy. il Time 110:28+ O 24 '77
Reversing agricultural priorities; Southern Regional Council report. Society 14:5 S '77
65% loan rate can help. D. Howe. Farm J 101:9 Mr '77
65% loan rate can hurt wheat. Farm J 101:44 mid-F '77
Sugar's anguished plea for more Federal aid. il Bus W p60-1 Ag 8 '77
Swollen silos, edgy farmers. il map Time 110: 16-18 S 12 '77
These government benefits will help. R. D. Wennblom. Farm J 101:21 N '77
Toward a sane food policy. Progressive 41:8-9 Ap '77
Tractor rebellion. T. Nicholson and others. il Newsweek 90:57 D 19 '77
Two milk duds; question of increase in milk price supports. E. Yoffe. New Repub 177:9 Jl 23 '77
Washington. See issues of Farm journal
Washington report. See issues of Successful farming
Washington report; interview, ed by J. Harms. B. Bergland. Suc Farm 75:no2 6 F '77
We don't need handouts. C. Machan. Farm J 101:Dairy 28 Ja '77
What farmers want in the new farm bill. L. Palmer. Farm J 101:16+ mid-F '77
What to expect from your new Secretary of Agriculture. R. D. Wennblom. pors Farm J 101:23-5 Ja '77
What will the higher supports do to you? C. S. Machan. Farm J 101:Dairy 6 My '77
What's in the administration's new farm bill. R. Wennblom. il Farm J 101:15-17 My '77
Wheat growers ask for loans at 65%. G. Lorang. Farm J 101:32A Mr '77
Why Farm Bureau endorsed target prices. R. D. Wennblom. Farm J 101:33 Mr '77
Why farmers are up in arms; interview. B. Bergland. il por U.S. News 83:57-8+ O 31 '77
You, me and the government. il Farm J 101: Dairy 12 My '77
See also
United States—Agriculture, Department of
United States—Congress—House—Agriculture, Committee on

AGRICULTURAL administration—United States—*Continued*

History

How the Department got its start; early agricultural administration by the Patent Office. S. B. Sutton. il Horticulture 55:33-7 Ap '77

AGRICULTURAL airplanes. See Airplanes in agriculture

AGRICULTURAL chemicals

EPA lists restricted farm chemicals. Farm J 101:A4 Je '77

Restricted-use chemicals: new list. Suc Farm 75:46 Je '77

See also

Herbicides

Pesticides

Spraying and dusting

AGRICULTURAL clubs. See Agricultural societies

AGRICULTURAL colleges

Back to the soil; enrollment. A. Wolff. Sat R 4:48 My 14 '77

Graduates

Good jobs for ag school graduates. J. Gillies. il Farm J 101:55-7 O '77

Good way to hire help; campus interviews. Farm J 101:D4 Je '77

AGRICULTURAL consultants

Would you hire a management consultant? S. Torgerson. il Farm J 101:C1-2 mid-F '77

AGRICULTURAL contracts. See Contracts, Agricultural

AGRICULTURAL cooperatives. See Agriculture, Cooperative

AGRICULTURAL credit

Bumper crop of loans to farmers. il Bus W p82-4 F 28 '77

Famine in cash flow. il Bus W p71-2+ D 19 '77

His bank meets margin calls; swine contract hedging at First American Bank, Canton, S.D. D. Seim. il Farm J 101:Hog 7 + Je '77

Lenders tell how farmers are surviving the money crunch. R. C. Black. il Farm J 101: 28-30 Ag '77

Making farms affordable for young people; state guaranteed loans. R. Blobaum. il Org Gard & Farm 24:76-9 O '77

More credit available to livestock producers. W. Kester. Farm J 101:Beef 18 Ag '77

New systemwide bond to finance your farm credit. Farm J 101:P1 N '77

SBA can lend you money now. C. Bickers. Farm J 101:A8 O '77

SBA no! Time 110:28+ N 14 '77

These farmers outgrew hometown banking. Suc Farm 75:no5 8 Mr '77

You're welcome at the bank in '77. J. D. Boyd. il Farm J 101:33+ Ja '77

See also

United States—Agriculture, Department of—Commodity Credit Corporation

United States—Agriculture, Department of—Farmers Home Administration

AGRICULTURAL economics. See Agriculture—Economic aspects

AGRICULTURAL education

See also

Agricultural colleges

AGRICULTURAL forecasting

EPA official looks ahead at farming; views of William C. Holmberg. Farm J 101:A1 Je '77

Farm outlook for 1978. R. D. Wennblom. Farm J 101:17+ D '77

Farmcast. See issues of Farm journal

What we see for century 3. Farm J 100:44 D '76

Will drouth ease in 1977? D. Seim. il Farm J 101:17+ F '77

Your '77 outlook: steady to strong. R. D. Wennblom. Farm J 100:13 D '76

See also

Crop reporting services

AGRICULTURAL journalism. See Journalism, Agricultural

AGRICULTURAL land. See Land

AGRICULTURAL laws and legislation

Down on the farm; regulations preventing ownership of more than 160 acres of federally watered land. A. J. Mayer and others. il Newsweek 90:67-8 S 5 '77

Fairness for farmers; question of enforcing limit on ownership of federally watered land. New Repub 177:2+ N 12 '77

Farmers vs. agribusiness: the new winning of the West; controversy over enforcement of the National Reclamation Law. M. E. Leary. Nation 225:646-50 D 17 '77

Food and Agriculture Act of 1977. il Suc Farm 75:8-9 D '77

Homestead Act hits home. il Time 110:20 O 17 '77

New farm bill: how will it work out? D. Paarlberg. por Farm J 101:28+ O '77

New set of rules for your marketing game. G. Lepper. il Suc Farm 75:32-3 D '77

Populist Doc; attempts to cut off federal irrigation water to large farms. por Forbes 120:190 N 15 '77

Sanitation laws squeeze out small producers. W. Berry and G. Logsdon. il Org Gard & Farm 24:43-6+ O '77

U.S. Interior Department moves to enforce the law to break up big farms. Farm J 101:14 O '77

AGRICULTURAL machinery

Machinery management. G. Lepper and L. Reichenberger. See issues of Successful farming

Machinery parade; photographs. See issues of Farm journal

Machinery preview for '77. G. W. Wormley. il Farm J 101:26-32 Ja '77

Machines get bigger down on the farm. R. Wolkomir. il Mech Illus 73:74+ S '77

See also

Augers

Cultivators

Harvesting machinery

Irrigation machinery

Planters (farm machines)

Plows

Spraying apparatus

Tractors

Cost of operation

Neat way to figure fuel and lubrication costs. Suc Farm 75:K8 Ap '77

History

Strange monsters of farm and field. E. Shrum. il Hobbies 82:113-15+ Jl '77

Leasing and renting

Put a young man in the driver's seat. W. Waltner and E. Waltner. il Farm J 101:H4 Mr '77

Purchasing

Inside look at machinery investment; a Successful farming survey. G. Lepper. Suc Farm 75:no2 31-41 F '77

More buyers shopping early for machinery. B. Fogarty. Farm J 101:B2 N '77

Stretch your machinery dollars. il Suc Farm 75: 38 D '77

Storage

See also

Sheds

AGRICULTURAL machinery industry

Farm equipment sales go slow. il Bus W p49-50 Jl 25 '77

J. I. Case's optimism about Brazil's future. Bus W p76 D 5 '77

See also

Deere and Company

International Harvester Company

Tractor industry

Export-import trade

Red tractors in the Midwest. il Time 110:44-5 Ag 22 '77

Canada

See also

Massey-Ferguson, Ltd

AGRICULTURAL museums

Way we were—see it on your vacation. il Farm J 101:A6-8 Ap '77

AGRICULTURAL pests

See also

Birds, Injurious and beneficial

Slugs

AGRICULTURAL photography. See Photography, Agricultural

AGRICULTURAL policy. See Agricultural administration

AGRICULTURAL production. See Production, Agricultural

AGRICULTURAL research

Agriculture and behavioral science: emerging orientations. W. S. Saint and E. W. Coward, Jr. bibl Science 197:733-7 Ag 19 '77

Beltsville scientists await new congressional priorities. E. M. Leeper. il por BioScience 27: 85-8 F '77; Discussion. 27:382 Je '77

Carter on agricultural research. J. Carter. Science 195:967 Mr 11 '77

NASA tackles a down-to-earth job. E. M. Leeper. il BioScience 27:223 Mr '77

Remote-sensing of crop yields. S. B. Idso and others. bibl il Science 196:19-25 Ap 1 '77

Research reports from field days. Suc Farm 75: no3 B14 F '77

Researchers take a new look at organic farming. J. Goldstein. Org Gard & Farm 24:68-71 Je '77

Searching for new methods. R. Rodale. il Org Gard & Farm 24:52-6 Ag '77

Where the research action's at. BioScience 27: 143-4 F '77

World food crisis will be back. G. Reynolds. Farm J 101:40 Ja '77

See also

Corn—Field experiments

Plant breeding

Federal aid

Seed money. Sci Am 237:100-1 S '77

AGRICULTURAL schools
See also
Agricultural colleges

AGRICULTURAL societies
Concerned Farm Wives; promotional visit to New York City. New Yorker 53:41-2 N 5 '77
Good feed from petroleum; annual meeting of the American Society of Animal Science. J. Russell. Farm J 101:Hog 21-2 S '77
Midwestern farmers expect $1.75 corn this fall; annual meeting of the National Corn Growers Association. G. Reynolds. Farm J 101:G4 S '77
People and places (cont of) Meetings and farm groups. See issues of Organic gardening and farming
United front for agriculture; American Agri-Women. L. Lane. il Farm J 101:K8 Ja '77
Wheat women convoy wheat to barge point; protest by WIFE (Women Involved in Farm Economics) Farm J 101:F4 Ag '77
See also
American Farm Bureau Federation
4-H Clubs
National Cattlemen's Association
National Farmers Organization

AGRICULTURAL subsidies. See Agricultural administration—United States

AGRICULTURAL surplus products. See Surplus products, Agricultural

AGRICULTURAL trade. See Produce trade

AGRICULTURAL workers. See Farm labor

AGRICULTURE
Food and agriculture: symposium; discussion. Sci Am 236:8+ Ja '77
See also
Airplanes in agriculture
Aquaculture
Artificial satellites—Agricultural use
Botany, Economic
Citizens band radio in agriculture
Cold frames
Computers—Agricultural use
Crops
Double cropping
Dry farming
Electricity on the farm
Electronics in agriculture
Food and Agriculture Organization of the United Nations
Food supply
Hill farming
Homesteads
Irrigation
Land
Organic farming
Rotation of crops
Seeds
Telephone in agriculture
Terraces (agriculture)
Tillage
Viticulture
also headings beginning Farm; Soil

Conferences

Hill land farming: how the experts view its future; International Hill Land Symposium. W. Berry. il Org Gard & Farm 24:68-71 Ap '77

Economic aspects

Another losing year; plight of D. Yokum. por Time 110:30 O 24 '77
Behind the unrest on America's farms: Parity: what strike is all about. il U.S. News 83:69-70 D 26 '77
Bountiful crops—so why are farmers and bankers worried? ed by K. Sheets. P. Racer and others. il U.S. News 82:23-5 Je 27 '77
Bumper crop of controversy over farm aid. il Bus W p 110-11+ Ap 18 '77
Can you ride it out? il Farm J 101:19-21 N '77
Farmcast. See issues of Farm journal
15 ways to control risk. Suc Farm 75:8 Ja '77
How the family farm can harvest millions. il Bus W p68-70 Jl 4 '77
How U.S. farmers became specialists-in cash and debts; excerpt from The American farm. M. Conrat and R. Conrat. il Smithsonian 7:48-55 Mr '77
Lush crop of discontent. il Time 109:76 Je 20 '77
Money management. L. Kruse and S. Cain. See issues of Successful farming
National cheap food policy #1; plan of the Exploratory Project for Economic Alternatives. Farm J 101:52 Ap '77
Risk capital. G. L. Vincent. il Suc Farm 75: 32-3+ Ja '77
Uneven squeeze on the U.S. farmer. il Bus W p70-1 D 19 '77
Up the economic ladder with a spade and hoe. J. Goldstein. il Org Gard & Farm 24:30+ Jl '77
Why farmers are up in arms; interview. B. Bergland. il por U.S. News 83:57-8+ O 31 '77
See also
Agricultural administration
Agricultural credit
Contracts, Agricultural
Farm corporations
Farm produce—Prices
Farms, Size of
Land reform
Land values
Produce trade
Truck farming—Economic aspects

Federal aid

See Agricultural administration—United States

Fuel requirements

Energy conservation in Amish agriculture. W. A. Johnson and others. bibl il Science 198: 373-8 O 28 '77

History

See also
Corn—History

Information services

See also
Crop reporting services
United States—Agriculture, Department of

Periodicals

Farm markets. B. J. Hillman. Writers Digest 57:28-30 Ag '77

Public relations

Farmers blitz the Big Apple. D. Braun. il Farm J 101:J1+ mid-Mr '77
Hear me. Farm J 101:14 Ja; 9 Mr; B4 S '77
Just when farmers are squeezed they're calling you millionaires. il Farm J 101:19+ Ag '77
So they know we're out there; Lake Crystal Farm Forum, Lake Crystal, Minn. S. Torgerson. il Farm J 101:L5 Ap '77

Study and teaching

See also
Agricultural colleges

Africa

Operation tsetse fly; livestock vs wildlife in United Nations tsetse fly control project. N. Myers. il Int Wildlife 7:33-5 My '77

Africa, Sub-Saharan

Smallholder agriculture in Africa—constraints and potential. K. G. V. Krishna. Ann Am Acad 432:12-25 Jl '77

Brazil

See also
Agricultural administration—Brazil

California

Drought fails to wilt California's harvest. Bus W p40 O 24 '77
San Diego's greenbelt; San Pasqual. M. E. Trussell. il maps Am For 83:26-30 O '77
Scorched earth; San Joaquin Valley. P. Brinkley-Rogers. il Newsweek 89:40 Ap 11 '77
Tough tomatoes; mechanical harvesting. P. Barnett. Progressive 41:32-6 D '77
With this California co-op . . . 12 salesmen sell your hay; San Joaquin Valley Hay Growers Association. D. Braun. Farm J 101:J4 Ag '77

History

What about the Okies? California migrations during the Depression. G. Haslam. il Am Hist Illus 12:28-39 Ap '77

Central America

Interplanting helps increase Central American food supply. T. Black and S. Black. il Org Gard & Farm 24:132-4+ Jl '77

Colorado

Bone-dry west prospects for snow; Colorado's emergency cloud-seeding program. Bus W p33-4 F 21 '77

England

Our far-flung correspondents. C. Trillin. New Yorker 53:149-52+ N 21 '77

Europe, Western

See also
Agricultural administration—Europe, Western

Florida

Florida grits and bears it. T. Nicholson and A. Jaffe. il Newsweek 89:56-7 F 7 '77
Price impact of Florida's freeze. il Bus W p30-1 F 7 '77

Great Britain

Drought. Audubon 79:150-1 Ja '77

Michigan

Michigan episode; PBB contamination of feed. N. Cousins. Sat R 4:4 Mr 19 '77
Reports & comment: Michigan; PBB feed contamination. E. Chen. il Atlantic 240:12+ Ag '77
Ron Thomas' horror story: my family was poisoned! E. Keiffer. il Good H 185:64+ Ag '77
Somebody simply goofed; PBB contamination of feed. W. Chapman. Progressive 41:30-2 My '77

AGRICULTURE—*Continued*

Middle Western States

Spreading impact of worst drought in decades. il map U.S. News 82:55-7 Mr 7 '77

Minnesota

Confrontation on the prairie; farmers' opposition to power lines. P. D. Wellstone and L. Tarbox. Progressive 41:41-3 D '77
Great energy standoff; opposition to high-voltage transmission lines crossing Minnesota farms. L. P. Gerlach. Natur Hist 87:22+ Ja '78

Montana

New grassroots reform movement checks the great raid on Montana's resources. T. Judge. Horticulture 55:12+ Ag '77

New England

History

Self-reliance and hard work. M. Franz. Org Gard & Farm 24:138-41 My '77

Peru

Farming the edge of the Andes. S. B. Brush. il Natur Hist 86:32-41 bibl(p94) My '77

Russia

Russia's harvest: a battle against the elements. il U.S. News 38:60 O 31 '77
Soviet agriculture and United States-Soviet relations. D. G. Johnson. Cur Hist 73:118-22+ O '77
Soviet grain harvests: CIA study pessimistic on effects of weather. D. Shapley. Science 195:377-8 Ja 28 '77
Soviets expand meat complexes, need more grain. Farm J 101:B2 S '77
Why Russia will continue to buy our farm products. R. Krumme. map Suc Farm 75:27 O '77

South Dakota

McGovern vs. the farmers: South Dakota's water showdown; Oahe Irrigation Project. H. Gardner. il Nation 224:456-61 Ap 16 '77

Southern States

Just trying to survive; Southeast drought. il map Time 110:30+ Jl 11 '77
Sun Belt wears a corn buckle. L. Kruse and others. il Suc Farm 75:30-1 S '77

United States

Farmcast. See issues of Farm journal
Food for peace or food for power? M. Marchino and R. K. Musil. il Chr Cent 94:714-18 Ag 17 '77
New era for agriculture. R. C. Black. Farm J 101:21 Mr '77
Place of U.S. food in eliminating world hunger. G. E. Brandow. bibl f il Ann Am Acad 429:1-11 Ja '77
U.S. agriculture: muscle in reserve. Suc Farm 75:no3 F16 F '77
U.S. agripower and a hungry world. D. Morgan. Current 191:30-7 Mr '77
See also
Agricultural administration—United States
Poultry industry

History

How U.S. farmers became specialists-in cash and debts; excerpt from The American farm. M. Conrat and R. Conrat. il Smithsonian 7:48-55 Mr '77

West Virginia

Agriculture in Appalachia is looking brighter. D. O. Cunnion. Org Gard & Farm 24:149-51 D '77

Western States

Coping with today's drought—scenes from a parched land. il U.S. News 82:48-50 Ap 4 '77
Dry threat to the West. L. Langway and W. J. Cook. il Newsweek 89:72 F 14 '77
Spreading impact of worst drought in decades. il map U.S. News 82:55-7 Mr 7 '77

Wisconsin

How dairymen differ on promotion. il Farm J 101:Dairy 12+ O '77

AGRICULTURE, Committee on. See United States—Congress—House—Agriculture, Committee on

AGRICULTURE, Cooperative
Billion-dollar farm co-ops nobody knows. il Bus W p54-8+ F 7 '77
Farmer cooperatives. R. E. Torgerson. bibl f il Ann Am Acad 429:91-102 Ja '77
Farmers who market together make it together. L. Kruse. il Suc Farm 75:30-1 D '77
Pooling assets builds investment power; swine co-op in North Dakota. S. Retka. il Farm J 101:Hog 14-15+ S '77
Tale of two sow co-ops. G. Johnston. il Suc Farm 75:no3 H12-13 F '77
Will new marketing pools get more for your grain? G. Lorang and G. Reynolds. il Farm J 101:24-5+ F '77
With this California co-op . . . 12 salesmen sell your hay; San Joaquin Valley Hay Growers Association. D. Braun. Farm J 101:J4 Ag '77
Yes, we have no undue enhancement; USDA investigating dairy co-op price enhancement. Farm J 101:Dairy 19 F '77
See also
Community gardens

AGRICULTURE, Department of. See United States—Agriculture, Department of

AGRICULTURE and climate. See Plants, Effect of climate on

AGRICULTURE and state. See Agricultural administration

AGUADO, Deborah
Plastic/leather. il Craft Horiz 37:17 Je '77

AGUAYO, Albert J.
Schwann cells: mixing and matching. Sci N 112:356-7 N 26 '77 *

AHERN, Ida Mae
So you'd like to go back to college? il Ret Liv 17:32-3+ Ja '77

AHERN, James F.
Clay feet in Connecticut. K. McAuliffe. Progressive 41:43-4 N '77 *

AHERN, John
La un-dolce vita. Commonweal 104:521-8 Ag 19 '77

AHMED, M. Basheeruddin, and Birenbaum, Arnold
Paraprofessionals in a multiservice community mental health center. il Intellect 106:149-51 O '77

AHRENS, Thomas J. See O'Keefe, J. D. jt auth

AHYI, Paul
Art that explains the universe; excerpt from The present significance of the creative arts in Africa and their influence outside Africa. il UNESCO Courier 30:21 My '77

AIDA; opera. See Verdi, G.

AIDES, Teachers. See Teachers aides

AIDOO, Ama Ata. See Aidoo, C. A. A.

AIDOO, Christina Ama Ata
Reflections from a black-eyed squint; story. Ms 6:66-9 Ag '77

AIDS in teaching. See Teaching—Aids and devices

AIKEN, George David
Man from Putney. H. N. Muller, 3d. il por Am For 83:18-21+ S '77 *

AIKEN, William
Room at the top. pors Forbes 120:34 S 1 '77 *

AILEY, Alvin
Alvin Ailey: total dance theater. L. F. Rosen. Progressive 41:36-7 Ag '77 *

AIMS in education. See Education—Aims and objectives

AIR bags. See Automobiles—Safety devices and measures

AIR bases
Space shuttle and Vandenberg Air Force Base. R. C. Henry and A. B. Sloan. bibl il pors map Space World N-2-158:29-36 F '77

AIR bladders (in fishes) See Fishes—Anatomy

AIR cleaners. See Air filters

AIR conditioning
Air-conditioning: stay cool and save energy, too. il Changing T 31:21-3 My '77
See also
Automobiles—Air conditioning

AIR conditioning equipment
Cashing in on cooling. J. S. King. Am Home 80:80+ My '77
Ceramic air cooler. Z. Kujundzic. il Ceram Mo 25:56-7 S '77
Cooling the home. il Consumers Res Mag 60:178-82 O '77
High-efficiency air-conditioners. il Consumer Rep 42:417-23 Jl '77
High efficiency window air conditioners of 1977. il Consumers Res Mag 60:7-11 Je '77
Ice-block house—winter's heating creates summer cooling; ACES concept. V. E. Smay. il Pop Sci 210:82-4+ F '77
Other story on solar air conditioning. C. Seymour. il Mech Illus 73:40-1+ Jl '77
Solar nexus: library pioneers in tapping the sun's energy. il Am Lib 8:188-90 Ap '77
See also
Dehumidifiers
Heat pumps
Humidifiers

Installation

How to build in a room airconditioner. M. McClintock. il Pop Mech 147:114-15 Ap '77
Remodeling notebook; central air conditioning. J. H. Ingersoll. House B 119:44+ Ap '77

AIR conditioning industry
Profiting from misery. Time 110:35 Ag 1 '77
Who says concept stocks are dead? Rovac Corp. P. Berman. il por Forbes 120:30-1 Ag 15 '77
See also
Carrier Corporation

AIR coolers. See Air conditioning equipment

AIR currents. See Winds

AIR cushion vehicles
Air cushion vehicle readied for testing. B. M. Elson. il Aviation W 106:53+ My 23 '77
Here comes the 100-mile-an-hour Navy! surface effect ships. J. G. Hubbell. il Read Digest 111:112-16 Ag '77
Leading int'l. surface effect vehicles; tables. Aviation W 106:125 Mr 21 '77
New English fun: hovercrafting. G. Wilkins. il Mech Illus 73:62+ F '77
PM tests a new kit-built hovercraft. B. Mc-Keown. il Pop Mech 149:73+ Ja '78
Ram-wing X-114 floats, skims, and flies. B. Kocivar. il Pop Sci 211:70-3 D '77
2 new hovercraft. il Mech Illus 73:167 My '77

AIR defenses
Aircraft detection system advances. B. Miller. Aviation W 106:22-3 Je 20 '77
See also
Russia—Defenses

AIR engines
Cam-action air motor develops full torque at rest. D. Scott. il Pop Sci 210:102+ Mr '77

AIR filters
Electronic air cleaner slips into place. E. Powell. il Pop Sci 210:150-1 My '77
Filter sentinel tells you when to clean. E. Powell. il Pop Sci 210:168 Mr '77
See also
Automobile engines—Filters

AIR Force Academy. See United States Air Force Academy, Colorado Springs

AIR France. See Airlines—France

AIR freight service
Breathing under water; Federal Express Corp. R. J. Flaherty. il por Forbes 119:36-8 Mr 1 '77
Cargo service cuts criticized; Airborne Freight Corp. Aviation W 106:33 Mr 28 '77
Forwarder authority extended by CAB. Aviation W 107:26 Jl 4 '77
See also
Flying Tiger Corporation

Export-import trade

Freight carriers track trade restraints. J. M. Lenorovitz. il Aviation W 106:331-4 Je 6 '77

Laws and regulations

Deregulation arrives for cargo flights. Bus W p55-6 N 21 '77
Price, service, capacity gains forecast in cargo deregulation. D. R. Griffiths. Aviation W 107:29 D 19 '77

AIR guns
It's a Daisy. E. B. Mann. il Field & S 82:64-9 O '77

AIR-launched cruise missiles. See Guided missiles —Launching from airplanes

AIR Line Pilots Association, International
Logan procedures spark pilots' threat. Aviation W 106:69 Ap 25 '77

AIR Liquide (firm) See Gas industry—France

AIR Malta. See Airlines—Malta

AIR navigation
Shorted out. T. Whorton. il Flying 100:32-3 Je '77
Way-out wonders. G. C. Larson. il Flying 100:50-4+ F '77

Aids and devices

A-10 pilots stress navaid requirement. D. A. Brown. Aviation W 107:52-3 S 19 '77
Wide usage seen for helicopter navaid; Doppler navigation system. P. J. Klass. il Aviation W 106:62-3 Ja 17 '77
See also
Inertial guidance systems

AIR pilots
Corporate pilot: man on the run. J. W. Olcott. il Flying 100:64-6+ Ap '77
Hijacking proposal; pilots' boycott of countries harboring terrorists. W. F. Buckley, Jr. Nat R 29:1384 N 25 '77
It's all in your head; simulated emergency. T. H. Block. il Flying 101:14-15 Ag '77
Once again it was up, up, and away; Ivan Carlson. S. Carlson. il Ret Liv 17:14+ Je '77
People who fly:
  Robert Murray. S. Wilkinson. il pors Flying 100:54-5+ Je '77
  Tom Peterson. G. Baxter. il por Flying 100:65-6+ My '77
Pilot recalls, hirings on rise. D. M. North. Aviation W 106:45-8 Ap 25 '77
Pilots talk about air crashes; excerpt from Final approach: the crash of Eastern 212. W. Stockton. il N Y Times Mag p41-2+ Ap 10 '77
Pro's nest. T. H. Block. See issues of Flying
See also
Air Line Pilots Association, International
Airplane crews
Airplanes—Piloting
Aviation—Physiological aspects
Black air pilots
Women air pilots

Psychology

Attachments. T. M. Block. il Flying 100:23-4 F '77
Penalty play; aftermath of small plane crash in football stadium. R. L. Collins. Flying 100:39 Mr '77
Your own worst enemy. P. Garrison. il Flying 101:82+ N '77

Selection

New United pilot hiring plan stresses minorities, females. J. M. Lenorovitz. Aviation W 107:30-1 O 10 '77

Testing

FAA proficiency proposal hit. D. M. North. Aviation W 107:23-4 S 12 '77
Overrated; ATP exam. H. Morland. il Flying 101:23+ Jl '77

Training

Business aircraft pilot training stressed. Aviation W 107:46 O 10 '77
Learning to fly. L. Collins; J. R. Hunt. Flying 101:301 S '77
Realism enhanced in combat tests. B. Miller. il Aviation W 106:63+ Je 20 '77
Up, up and away! Flight Safety International. por Forbes 120:36 N 1 '77
What's wrong with flight training? J. W. Olcott. Flying 101:74-5 O '77
See also
Airplanes, Training
Aviation schools

AIR plants
See also
Bromeliads

AIR pollution
Kitchen smog. Chemistry 50:5 Jl '77
Mercury emissions from geothermal power plants. D. E. Robertson and others. bibl il Science 196:1094-7 Je 3 '77
See also
Asphalt plants—Environmental aspects
Automobiles—Environmental aspects
Chemical plants—Environmental aspects
Coke plants—Environmental aspects
Electric plants—Environmental aspects
Petroleum refineries—Environmental aspects
Smog
Steel works—Environmental aspects

Control

EPA gets tough with air polluters. il Am City & County 92:10 Ja '77
See also
Automobiles—Pollution control devices
Refuse incinerators—Pollution control devices

Laws and legislation

Changing the mix of clean air rules. il Bus W p36-7 Je 13 '77
Cheyennes drive for clean-air rights; redesignating air quality status to prevent industrial development. il Bus W p29 Ap 4 '77
Clean Air Act Amendments: fresh air for the national parks. Nat Parks & Con Mag 51:21-5 N '77
Cleaner air: it'll be slow, expensive; Clean Air Act. il U.S. News 83:17 Ag 15 '77
Cleaning the Air; amendments. Time 110:80 Jl 11 '77
Debating a clean-air timetable; 1977 Senate version of amendments to the Clean Air Act. il Bus W p80 F 28 '77
Detroit and Congress: eyeball to eyeball. J. A. Briggs. il Forbes 119:33-6+ F 15 '77
MMT backfires as an octane booster; manganese additives. il Bus W p34 Ap 4 '77
Washington report; Clean Air climax. T. Orme. Motor T 29:7-8 N '77
When the public will buy a parking ban; implementing transportation control plans. il Bus W p58 Ag 22 '77

Measurement

Downwind; SO_2 transport and transformation processes. K. H. Hohenemser. il Environment 19:2-4 Ap '77

Physiological effects

Ammonia in the human airways: neutralization of inspired acid sulfate aerosols. T. V. Larson and others. bibl il Science 197:161-3 Jl 8 '77
Indoor smog. Newsweek 89:78 My 30 '77
Rx travel and play. C. SerVaas. Holiday 58:8 Mr '77

Atlantic Coast

Estimate of the contribution of biologically produced dimethyl sulfide to the global sulfur cycle. P. J. Maroulis and A. R. Bandy. bibl il map Science 196:647-8 My 6 '77

Connecticut

Dust still falls on Derby despite a tough new law; pollution by Derby Sand and Gravel's asphalt plant. D. Starr. Audubon 79:136-8 S '77

Greece

See also
Athens, Greece—Air pollution

AIR pollution—*Continued*

Maryland

Asbestos hazard on U.S. roads? use of asbestos-carrying crushed stone in Montgomery County. il Am City & County 92:36 Ag '77
Asbestos: trouble in the air from Maryland rock quarry. L. J. Carter. map Science 197:237-40 Jl 15 '77
Environmental asbestos pollution related to use of quarried serpentine rock. A. N. Rohl and others. bibl il Science 196:1319-22 Je 17 '77; Reply with rejoinder. J. T. Hack. 197:716+ Ag 19 '77

Minnesota

Stillness (however brief) at Silver Bay; Reserve Mining Company. J. G. Mitchell. il Audubon 79:129-34 S '77

Missouri

See also
St Louis—Air pollution

New York (state)

See also
New York (city)—Air pollution

Ohio

In search of a final SO_2 plan. il Bus W p78+ S 26 '77

Pennsylvania

High noon at Clairton. J. G. Mitchell. Audubon 79:128-36 Ja '77
PennDOT curbs cutback asphalt use; EPA emissions offset ruling. il Am City & County 92:30 Ag '77
Pollution may kill VW's Rabbit plant; EPA ruling. il Bus W p26 Mr 7 '77

Utah

Son of a gun, it's son of Kaiparowits! P. L. Fradkin. Audubon 79:146-8 My '77
Utah proposes blueprint for industrial development. Nat Parks & Con Mag 51:22+ Ap '77

AIR pressure. See Atmospheric pressure
AIR races. See Airplane racing
AIR raid shelters
See also
Atomic bomb shelters
AIR rifles. See Air guns
AIR rights. See Airspace (law)
AIR routes. See Airlines—United States—Routes; Airways
AIR safety. See Aviation—Safety devices and measures
AIR-sea interaction. See Ocean-atmosphere interaction
AIR ships. See Airships
AIR shows. See Aviation—Exhibitions
AIR shuttle service. See Airlines—Shuttle service
AIR space (international law) See Airspace (international law)
AIR space (law) See Airspace (law)
AIR stewardesses. See Airlines—Flight attendants
AIR-supported roofs. See Roofs
AIR traffic. See Airlines—Traffic
AIR traffic control
Collision insurance. R. L. Collins. Flying 101:44 Ag '77
More pilot aid in traffic control urged. E. Kozicharow. Aviation W 106:34 Je 27 '77
On top; GAO study of FAA's development of an air traffic control system. R. L. Collins. Flying 100:17-18+ Ap '77

International aspects

MLS faces key decision in Montreal. P. J. Klass. Aviation W 106:19-21 Ja 10 '77

Spain

Spain studies traffic control system. D. A. Brown. il Aviation W 107:38-9 D 12 '77

AIR traffic controllers (persons)
Assertiveness training. T. H. Block. il Flying 101:40 O '77
NTSB, pilots' chief criticize controllers in Georgia crash. Aviation W 106:31 My 9 '77
Sweaty palms in the control tower; Chicago's O'Hare field. D. Martindale. bibl il por Psychol Today 10:70-2+ F '77
See also
Collective bargaining—Air traffic controllers (persons)
Strikes—United States—Air traffic controllers (persons)
AIR traffic controllers (persons) strike (Great Britain) See Strikes—Great Britain
AIR travel
Exotic vacations: inexpensive and accessible; One-Stop Tour Charter trips. B. Mack. il Harp Baz 110:184 F '77
Survival tips for long distance travelers. M. R. C. Berg. il Mademoiselle 83:142-3 My '77
See also
Airlines
Private flying

Anecdotes, facetiae, satire, etc.

Transatlantic cheap. S. L. Vernando. Nat R 29:1298 N 11 '77

History

How Mombasa became the new place. C. Stinnett. il Sat R 4:11-12+ Ap 16 '77

Physiological aspects

See Aviation—Physiological aspects

Russia

Christening the Concordski; Soviet Tu-144. M. Clark. il Time 110:41 N 14 '77

AIR travel, Fear of. See Phobias
AIR travel with pets. See Travel with pets
AIR warfare
Future air warfare; excerpts from address. J. M. Keck. Aviation W 106:7 F 21 '77
AIRBORNE Warning and Control System. See Airplanes, Military—Radar equipment
AIRBUS Industrie (firm) See Airplane industry—Europe, Western
AIRBUSES. See Airplanes, Jet
AIRCRAFT
See also
Airplanes
Airships
Balloons
Gliders (aeronautics)
Helicopters
AIRCRAFT carriers
Carriers face Congress fight. K. Johnsen. Aviation W 106:12-13 My 9 '77
House stifles smaller carrier plans of Navy. Aviation W 106:20-1 My 30 '77
New mini flattop flies like a plane. L. Wood. il Pop Mech 149:62-3+ Ja '78
AIRLIFT, Berlin. See Berlin Airlift
AIRLINE flight attendants. See Airlines—Flight attendants
AIRLINE liability. See Liability (law)
AIRLINE monitor receivers. See Radio receivers
AIRLINE Passengers Association
Pan Am, American win popularity poll. L. Doty. Aviation W 107:38 S 19 '77
AIRLINE pilots. Se Air pilots
AIRLINE schedules. See Airlines—Management
AIRLINE stocks. See Airlines—Securities
AIRLINE strikes (France) See Strikes—France
AIRLINE ticket fraud. See Fraud
AIRLINES
Five worst hassles in air travel. Changing T 31:41-4 Ag '77
Foreign airlines: the family tree; chart. Flying 101:238-9 S '77
Future flight: airlines. R. S. Goodman. Flying 101:354-5 S '77
Ticket to anywhere. W. W. Parrish. il Sat R R 4:16+ Ap 16 '77
See also
Helicopter airlines
International Air Transport Association

Automation

See also
Computers—Airline use

Baggage handling

See Airlines—Luggage handling

Beverage and food service

How to feast and fast in flight; minimizing jet lag. B. Dubivsky. N Y Times Mag p28 S 4 '77

Communication systems

Two carriers plan automatic data link. P. J. Klass. il Aviation W 106:36+ My 23 '77

Emergency passenger briefings

See Aviation—Safety devices and measures

Employees

See also
Airlines—Flight attendants

Salaries, allowances, etc.

Pilot study of pilots' earnings and other scheduled airline pay. M Labor R 100:49-50 N '77

Equipment and supplies

CAB to hear oral arguments on intercarrier equipment talks. Aviation W 107:30 Ag 15 '77
McDonnell Douglas, Eastern oppose Boeing on carrier talks. Aviation W 107:35 O 10 '77
New aircraft plans still unresolved. Aviation W 106:22-3 Ja 10 '77

Fares

Air fares: what you need to know to get the best deals. Bet Hom & Gard 55:58 My '77
Airline eyes more lower fares; Texas International Airlines. Aviation W 106:25 F 21 '77
American fare bid draws fire. L. Doty. Aviation W 106:24 F 21 '77

AIRLINES—Fares—*Continued*

Bargains ahead for U.S. air travelers. il U.S. News 82:55-6 Mr 21 '77

Carriers mull discount policies. R. K. Ellingsworth. Aviation W 106:62-3 Je 6 '77

Cautious approach set in Midway case. R. K. Ellingsworth. Aviation W 106:32 My 23 '77

Champ of the cheap flight; F. Laker. G. Sereny. il pors N Y Times Mag p 14+ S 4 '77

Chicago-Los Angeles fare cut requested. Aviation W 106:65 Je 6 '77

Delta offers New York-Miami low fare. L. Dunkelberg. il Aviation W 107:31 S 26 '77

Discount mania hits the airlines. Bus W p26-7 Ag 8 '77

Dogfight over the Atlantic: six airlines are chasing Laker to London. il Time 110:54 Ag 29 '77

Expansion of low fares on North Atlantic urged. Aviation W 107:29 S 5 '77

Fare fights. L. Langway and B. Graustark. Newsweek 90:64-5 Ag 15 '77

Free flights; CAB and regulation of intrastate airlines. Nat R 29:779 Jl 8 '77

Hasty fare approval confuses travelers. Aviation W 107:29 S 26 '77

IATA stand-by fare approved; budget, super-apex bids denied. Aviation W 107:34 S 19 '77

IATA turmoil in rates continues. Aviation W 107:21-2 N 21 '77

IATA unit studies plans to meet Laker challenge. Aviation W 107:29 Jl 18 '77

I'm Freddie, fly me. A. J. Mayer and A. Collings. il Newsweek 90:92+ O 10 '77

Laker's cut-rate fares trigger retaliation. il Bus W p58 Jl 25 '77

Latest on cut-rate air fares—. il U.S. News 83:66 O 10 '77

Latest on the bargains in air travel. il U.S. News 83:40 Ag 29 '77

Latest plans for cheaper air fares. il U.S. News 82:67 Je 27 '77

London for only $236; Laker Airways Skytrain plan. il Time 109:63 Je 27 '77

Lowered fare feasibility claimed in study by GAO. Aviation W 106:38 Mr 7 '77

Major slash in some transatlantic air fares set to begin this month. il Ret Liv 17:61 S '77

Midway case may reveal Carter policy. R. K. Ellingsworth. Aviation W 106:30 F 7 '77

More airlines join in transatlantic fare reductions. il Ret Liv 17:50-1 O '77

New York-London budget fare may face predatory charge. Aviation W 107:33 Ag 22 '77

Nothing to lose but their chains; United Airlines stand in favor of deregulation. Forbes 120:42 Ag 15 '77

Peanut fares planned for new markets; Texas International. il Aviation W 106:30 F 14 '77

Price war in the sky; lowering prices on regularly scheduled transcontinental flights. D. Pauly and J. B. Copeland. il Newsweek 89:68 F 28 '77

Real ferment in low-fare flying. Bus W p58 S 26 '77

Shifts in fare standards seen. R. K. Ellingsworth. Aviation W 107:24-5 Ag 29 '77

Shifts urged in discount tests. R. K. Ellingsworth. Aviation W 107:24-5 Ag 15 '77

Sky wars over North America. il Time 110:49 S 12 '77

Skytrain spurs IATA fares reduction. Aviation W 107:32 Ag 22 '77

Standby fare spurs challenges. L. Doty. Aviation W 107:27+ O 17 '77

Standing by for London; Pan Am's cut-rate service. P. L. Abraham. il Newsweek 90:65 S 26 '77

Super Apex negotiations seen dominating IATA conference. Aviation W 107:29 O 3 '77

TWA discount approval spurs quick response by competitors. Aviation W 107:27 Jl 18 '77

Texas International files for Baltimore; peanut fare discount. Aviation W 107:38 D 19 '77

To London for 4¢ a mile. il Time 110:67-8 O 10 '77

Utilization key to Worlds fare plan. Aviation W 106:34 Je 20 '77

Why price-cutting backfires in the airline industry. B. Welling, Jr. il Bus W p 116+ O 10 '77

Federal aid

DOT proposes new trust fund to aid noise curb compliance. Aviation W 106:30 Ja 24 '77

Finance

Airline costs rise in all operating areas. L. Doty. Aviation W 107:35 Ag 29 '77

Airline economic influence; excerpts from address. W. T. Seawell. Aviation W 107:9 Jl 4 '77

Airline income, expense; tables (cont) Aviation W 106:35 Ja 3; 34 My 9; 107:39 Jl 11; 37 S 19; 42 D 12 '77

Airline operating revenues; Airline operating expenses; tables. Aviation W 106:42-3 My 23 '77

Airline reequipment financing studied. W. H. Gregory. il Aviation W 107:26-9 Jl 11 '77

Airlines' capital challenge; excerpts from address. G. W. James. Aviation W 107:9 N 28 '77

Airlines' costly glide into the equity market. Bus W p54 Je 6 '77

Fleet financing outlook clouded. R. G. O'Lone. Aviation W 106:29-30 My 23 '77

Flood of travelers boosts airline profits. il Bus W p36-7 N 28 '77

House bill perils aircraft financing; proposed bankruptcy law changes. W. H. Gregory. Aviation W 106:14 Mr 7 '77

IATA carriers' profits increase. R. R. Ropelewski. Aviation W 107:26 Jl 25 '77

See also

Airlines—Securities

Flight attendants

Pilot recalls, hirings on rise. D. M. North. Aviation W 106:45-8 Ap 25 '77

Winged woman. J. Feldman. il Sat R 4:36+ Ap 16 '77

Food service

See Airlines—Beverage and food service

Freight service

See Air freight service

Fuel requirements

Airline fuel conservation effort hit in GAO report. Aviation W 107:36 S 12 '77

Airlines fly more people on less fuel. Aviation W 106:30 Mr 7 '77

Computers' role grows in fuel planning. K. J. Stein. Aviation W 107:28-9 N 21 '77

Shortage of jet fuel stimulates contingency planning by airlines. Aviation W 106:25-6 F 7 '77

History

Foreign airlines. W. W. Parrish. il Flying 101:236-7 S '77

Hostesses

See Airlines—Flight attendants

Insurance

See Insurance, Aviation

International services

Politics complicate international outlook. L. Doty. il Aviation W 106:157-9 Mr 21 '77

European-Asiatic

British expected to resume Concorde effort in Malaysia. Aviation W 108:30 Ja 2 '78

North America

Mexico presses its baggage rule. Aviation W 107:24 N 28 '77

Transatlantic

Braniff London award sparks criticism. D. R. Griffiths. il Aviation W 108:27-9 Ja 2 '78

British Caledonian sets date for London-Houston service. Aviation W 107:31 Jl 4 '77

British government not to appeal Laker ruling; Skytrain service. Aviation W 106:25 F 21 '77

CAB expands carrier access to Europe. R. K. Ellingsworth. Aviation W 107:29 S 19 '77

Charters cloud growth forecasts. L. Doty. Aviation W 106:20-1 My 16 '77

Concordes begin service to N.Y. il Aviation W 107:14-15 N 28 '77

Delta readies for Atlanta-London route. D. M. North. il Aviation W 107:30-2 D 5 '77

Dogfight over the Atlantic: six airlines are chasing Laker to London. il Time 110:54 Ag 29 '77

Extended Paris-Miami authority pushed. R. K. Ellingsworth. Aviation W 107:30-1 Jl 11 '77

Fare fights. L. Langway and B. Graustark. Newsweek 90:64-5 Ag 15 '77

I'm Freddie, fly me. A. J. Mayer and A. Collings. il Newsweek 90:92+ O 10 '77

Laker seeks Los Angeles route. Aviation W 107:27 D 19 '77

Laker's cut-rate fares trigger retaliation. il Bus W p58 Jl 25 '77

London for only $236; Laker Airways Skytrain plan. il Time 109:63 Je 27 '77

Major slash in some transatlantic air fares set to begin this month. il Ret Liv 17:61 S '77

More airlines join in transatlantic fare reductions. il Ret Liv 17:50-1 O '77

National mounts intense Paris marketing. R. K. Ellingsworth. il Aviation W 107:35-6 Jl 18 '77

Pan Am Paris route reopening planned. Aviation W 107:30 D 19 '77

Playing politics with airlines; J. Carter's dispersal of routes. map Time 111:46 Ja 16 '78

Real ferment in low-fare flying. Bus W p58 S 26 '77

Sing a song of Skytrain. S. Birnbaum. Esquire 88:17-18 Jl '77

Skytrain spurs IATA fares reduction. Aviation W 107:32 Ag 22 '77

Skytrain start set in September. Aviation W 106:28-9 Je 20 '77

AIRLINES—International services—Transatlantic —*Continued*
Standing by for London; Pan Am's cut-rate service. P. L. Abraham. il Newsweek 90:65 S 26 '77
To London for 4¢ a mile. il Time 110:67-8 O 10 '77
Too many looks spoil the route. il Forbes 119:23 F 1 '77
Try me; inaugural Skytrain flight. New Yorker 53:38-9 O 10 '77
U.S. and U.K. initial new air services agreement; statement; with department announcement, June 22, 1977. J. Carter. Dept State Bull 77:83-4 Jl 18 '77
What a little competition can do; Pan Am and TWA New York to London experiments. il Time 110:48+ Jl 25 '77

Transpacific

CAB proposes Continental for South Pacific. Aviation W 106:31 My 16 '77
Continental readies South Pacific push. J. M. Lenorovitz. Aviation W 107:31-3+ D 19 '77
Continental readying Pacific service. J. M. Lenorovitz. map Aviation W 107:36-7 S 5 '77
Landing rights clouding Continental Pacific route. Aviation W 107:30 Ag 1 '77

Laws and regulations

See Aviation—Laws and regulations

Local service

Airline eyes more lower fares; Texas International Airlines. Aviation W 106:25 F 21 '77
Cautious approach set in Midway case. R. K. Ellingsworth. Aviation W 106:32 My 23 '77
Commuter beginning Dash 7 service; Rocky Mountain Airways. B. A. Smith. il Aviation W 108:35-6 Ja 2 '78
Free flights; CAB and regulation of intrastate airlines. Nat R 29:779 Jl 8 '77
Intrastates eye regulatory reform. map Aviation W 106:28-30 Ap 11 '77
New pacts reflect commuter success. L. Doty. Aviation W 106:38 Ap 4 '77
Peanut fares planned for new markets; Texas International. il Aviation W 106:30 F 14 '77
Six Midway routes urged for new airline operation. Aviation W 107:32 D 12 '77
Texas International files for Baltimore; peanut fare discount. Aviation W 107:38 D 19 '77
Two carriers plan automatic data link; Piedmont Airline. P. J. Klass. il Aviation W 106:36+ My 23 '77
See also
Southwest Airlines

Luggage handling

Mexico presses its baggage rule. Aviation W 107:24 N 28 '77
New baggage regulations. H. W. Shane. Trav/Holiday 149:21 Ja '78
What every traveler should know about the new international luggage regulations. il House & Gard 149:108+ N '77

Management

U.S. eases its position on multiple designation of U.S. carriers on routes serving the U.K. Aviation W 106:28 Mr 7 '77

Non-scheduled operations

Air charters for price-conscious travelers. il Bet Hom & Gard 55:123 My '77
Air-tour packagers fight for their lives. il Bus W p28-9 F 28 '77
Bargains ahead for U.S. air travelers. il U.S. News 82:55-6 Mr 21 '77
Charter growth sparks concern. R. K. Ellingsworth. Aviation W 106:29-30 F 28 '77
Charters cloud growth forecasts. L. Doty. Aviation W 106:20-1 My 16 '77
Consumer watch; beat the charter cancellation blues. J. Carper. Am Home 80:16 Je '77
Exotic vacations: inexpensive and accessible; One-Stop Tour Charter trips. B. Mack. il Harp Baz 110:18+ F '77
Going places, finding things: how to choose a charter. N. Richardson. il House & Gard 149:74+ Ap '77
Know your ABC. D. McPherson. il Sat Eve Post 249:90+ My '77
Latest on the bargains in air travel. il U.S. News 83:40 Ag 29 '77
Magna charter: an airline pilot flies general aviation's routes. T. H. Block. il Flying 100:29 Ap '77
Off-route charter proposal stirs supplementals storm. Aviation W 106:38 My 2 '77
Pay now, go later—and cheaper. il Time 109:36-7 Ja 31 '77
Price war in the sky. D. Pauly and J. B. Copeland. il Newsweek 89:68 F 28 '77
TIA emphasizes long-range operations. W. H. Gregory. il Aviation W 106:40-1+ F 7 '77
Two sides of charter travel: big savings, but headaches, too. il U.S. News 83:42 N 7 '77
Update on charter travel. il Changing T 31:29-30 F '77
Utilization key to World's fare plan. Aviation W 106:34 Je 20 '77
Way to fly. D. Pauly and others. il Newsweek 89:76+ Je 20 '77
When your charter flight lets you down; where to complain. H. Hyans. il McCalls 104:54 S '77

Passenger service

Current cinema; motion pictures on airplanes. P. Gilliatt. New Yorker 53:65-7 Ag 29 '77
Fitness in flight; Lufthansa's program. Time 110:53 Ag 1 '77
Skytrain ground plan approved over Port Authority objections; Laker Airways' proposal. Aviation W 107:25 Ag 29 '77

Anecdotes, facetiae, satire, etc.

Tidying up after an act of God. C. Stinnett. Atlantic 239:23-4 F '77

Passenger traffic

See Airlines—Traffic

Passengers

See also
Airline Passengers Association

Rates

See Airlines—Fares

Reservation systems

CAB plans new overbooking proposal. Aviation W 107:30 Ag 8 '77
Overbook plan reactions mixed. D. R. Griffiths. Aviation W 107:26+ D 12 '77

Routes

See Airlines—International services; Airways

Safety devices and measures

See Aviation—Safety devices and measures

Schedules

See Airlines—Management

Securities

Fly me, I'm sad sack. il Forbes 120:92 D 1 '77

Security measures

See also
Airplane hijacking—Prevention

Shuttle service

Long-term Eastern shuttle growth seen. Aviation W 107:34 O 10 '77
Shuttle serves as economic barometer. L. Doty. il Aviation W 106:26-8 F 14 '77

Smoking problem

See Smoking on airplanes

Statistics

Airline traffic; tables (cont) Aviation W 106:67 Ja 10; 39 F 7; 35 Mr 7; 30 Mr 14; 34 Mr 28; 43 My 2; 8 Je 6; 107:34 Jl 11; 36 Ag 1; 34 S 5; 34 S 26; 34 O 24; 32 N 28 '77
North Atlantic air passenger load factors; tables. Aviation W 107:36-7 Jl 25 '77
North Atlantic passenger traffic; tables (cont) Aviation W 106:26 Ja 3; 41 F 7; 28 F 14; 70 Ap 25; 30 My 9; 107:36 Jl 18; 30 Ag 29; 44 S 26; 32 O 3; 34 O 24; 32 N 28 '77; 108:37 Ja 2 '78
Operating and cost data 747, DC-10 and L-1011; tables (cont) Aviation W 106:36-7 Ja 3; 34-5 My 16; 107:32-3 Jl 18; 46-7 S 26; 40-1 D 12 '77
Operating and cost data—727, 737, DC-9, BAC III; tables (cont) Aviation W 106:48-9 Je 13 '77
U.S. airline participation in selected markets; table. Aviation W 107:41 S 12 '77

Traffic

Clear weather patterns boost U.S. carriers' holiday results. Aviation W 106:23-4 Ja 10 '77
Delta offers New York-Miami low fare. L. Dunkelberg. il Aviation W 107:31 S 26 '77
Domestic trunk traffic in U.S. to rise 6-7% over last year. Aviation W 107:25 N 21 '77
European passenger traffic increased in 1976. Aviation W 106:39 Mr 7 77
European traffic slowed by strikes, slowdowns. R. R. Ropelewski. Aviation W 107:25-6 S 5 '77
Fall traffic figures top predictions. L. Dunkelberg. Aviation W 107:28-9 O 24 '77
Holiday traffic gains strongly. D. R. Griffiths. Aviation W 108:27 Ja 9 '78
June traffic gains mixed but future seen brighter. Aviation W 107:26-7 Jl 18 '77
Local-service traffic outgains trunks. D. M. North. Aviation W 107:31-2 Jl 25 '77
Traffic gains spur optimism. D. M. North. Aviation W 106:26-7 Ap 18 '77

AIRLINES—Traffic—*Continued*
Traffic growth declines in May. W. H. Gregory. Aviation W 106:37 Je 13 '77
Traffic rebounds on N.Y/L.A. il Aviation W 107:33 N 28 '77
Traffic rises despite weather problems. D. M. North. Aviation W 106:26-7 Mr 7 '77

Africa, East

East African nations ponder airline future. Aviation W 106:25 F 14 '77

Alaska

Wien, pilots at impasse in strike over Boeing 737 crew size. Aviation W 106:70 Je 6 '77

Arab countries

Airports' lag slows Arab carriers. L. Doty. Aviation W 107:30 N 21 '77
Arab carriers edge toward closer ties. L. Doty. Aviation W 107:34 D 5 '77

Belgium

Sabena expanding combi quick change. L. Dunkelberg. il Aviation W 107:37+ S 26 '77

Canada

Industry poised for recession recovery. R. G. O'Lone. il Aviation W 107:33-5 Ag 1 '77
Pacific Western seeks area dominance. R. G. O'Lone. il Aviation W 107:33-5 Ag 8 '77
Wardair plans technological advances. R. G. O'Lone. il Aviation W 107:28-30 Ag 29 '77

Europe, Western

European passengers voice complaints. Aviation W 106:160 Mr 21 '77
European traffic slowed by strikes, slowdowns. R. R. Ropelewski. Aviation W 107:25-6 S 5 '77

France

Air France leaning to DC-9, 737. R. R. Ropelewski. Aviation W 106:23-4 Ap '11 '77
Boeing brings off a French coup; Air France purchase of planes. il Bus W p31-2 My 9 '77
Concorde proved operationally. il Aviation W 106:22-6 My 30 '77
Concordes begin service to N.Y. il Aviation W 107:14-15 N 28 '77
Concordes spur strong traffic, losses. Aviation W 106:23 Ja 31 '77
N.Y.-Dulles air link offered by Air France for Concorde. Aviation W 107:26 Ag 29 '77
Way clearing for Air France 737 lease. R. R. Ropelewski. Aviation W 108:28-9 Ja 9 '78

Germany, West

How a terrorist threat is wounding Lufthansa. il Bus W p37 N 28 '77
Lufthansa computerizing maintenance. Aviation W 107:35 S 19 '77
Lufthansa reequipping its fleet. D. A. Brown. il Aviation W 107:27-8 S 26 '77
Mogadishu's aftermath; Lufthansa's security measures. il Time 110:56 N 28 '77
We shall blow up a plane; Lufthansa. A. J. Mayer and others. il Newsweek 90:93 N 28 '77

Great Britain

British Caledonian sets date for London-Houston service. Aviation W 107:31 Jl 4 '77
British government not to appeal Laker ruling; Skytrain service. Aviation W 106:25 F 21 '77
Champ of the cheap flight; F. Laker. G. Sereny. il pors N Y Times Mag p 14+ S 4 '77
I'm Freddie, fly me. A. J. Mayer and A. Collings. il Newsweek 90:92+ O 10 '77
Laker authorized to operate Skytrain from Gatwick Airport. Aviation W 107:34 S 19 '77
Laker moves to counter IATA fare cuts. Aviation W 107:33 Ag 22 '77
Laker seeks Los Angeles route. Aviation W 107:27 D 19 '77
Laker seeks to allay early concerns. L. Dunkelberg. Aviation W 107:28-9 O 3 '77
London for only $236; Laker Airways Skytrain plan. il Time 109:63 Je 27 '77
Sing a song of Skytrain. S. Birnbaum. Esquire 88:17-18 Jl '77
Skytrain faces market limits. L. Doty. Aviation W 107:28-30 O 10 '77
Skytrain ground plan approved over Port Authority objections; Laker Airways' proposal. Aviation W 107:25 Ag 29 '77
Skytrain: I'm Freddie. Fly me; Laker Airways. il por Time 109:37 Ja 31 '77
Swashbuckler in the sky; F. Laker. H. Sutton. il por Sat R 4:50+ Mr 19 '77
To London for 4¢ a mile; Laker's Skytrain. il Time 110:67-8 O 10 '77
Try me; inaugural Skytrain flight. New Yorker 53:38-9 O 10 '77
See also
British Airways

India

Indian Airlines hopes to acquire added capacity. il Aviation W 106:38-41 F 14 '77

Japan

Short-field version of DC-9 designed. D. E. Fink. il Aviation W 106:63+ Ap 25 '77

Malta

Air Malta's leased fleet shows profit. L. Doty. il Aviation W 107:37-8 D 19 '77

Russia

Aeroflot orders 200 short-haul Yak-42s. W. C. Wetmore. il Aviation W 106:39-41 Je 20 '77
Tempest over Russia's airline. U.S. News 82:56 Mr 21 '77

Scandinavia

See also
Scandinavian Airlines System

Sweden

SAS buying A-300s; orders 747s, DC-9s. Aviation W 107:31 Jl 4 '77

United States

Airbus pushes hard for U.S. customers. il Bus W p34-5 Je 13 '77
Genealogy of United States airlines; chart. Flying 101:216-19 S '77
More regulation or deregulation of the airlines? nationalization may be the answer for the future; address, December 8, 1976. C. C. Tillinghast. Vital Speeches 43:206-9 Ja 15 '77
See also
Aeronautics, Commercial—United States
Government investigations—Airlines
Strikes—United States—Airlines
also names of airlines, e.g. Delta Air Lines

History

America's airlines. R. J. Serling. il Flying 101:223-30 S '77

Routes

747SP enhances route restructuring. L. Doty. il Aviation W 106:32-3 Je 27 '77
See also
Airlines—International services

AIRLINES, Local service. See Airlines—Local service
AIRPLANE accidents. See Aviation—Accidents
AIRPLANE crews
Debate on crew size reheats. Aviation W 107:24-5 S 5 '77
AIRPLANE engines
Powerplants: prime movers for aviation's progress. J. W. Olcott. il Flying 101:281+ S '77
Prop-fan powerplant studies evolve. W. C. Wetmore. il Aviation W 106:46-50 Ja 3 '77
Rotary engines: should we give them a whirl? S. Wilkinson. il Flying 100:46-8+ Mr '77

Cooling

Liquid-cooled engines are coming back. G. C. Larson. il Flying 101:60-5+ Jl '77

Fuel

See also
Gasoline

Fuel consumption

Every drop counts. R. L. Collins. Flying 101:54-5+ Ag '77
Only fools run out of fuel. L. Morgan. il Flying 101:56-7+ O '77
See also
Airlines—Fuel requirements
Airplane engines, Jet—Fuel consumption

Maintenance and repair

Airlines push engine refurbishment. Aviation W 106:71+ Je 6 '77
Does it sound a little funny to you? R. L. Collins. il Flying 100:38-9+ F '77

Specifications

U.S. reciprocating engines; tables. Aviation W 106:124-5 Mr 21 '77

Superchargers

Beefy Cherokee: Rajay's turbo Lance. G. C. Larson. il Flying 100:27 Je '77
How those wastegates work. S. Wilkinson. il Flying 100:58 My '77
Running the traps in a Turbo Arrow. G. C. Larson. il Flying 101:58-61 O '77

AIRPLANE engines, Jet
Hypersonic propulsion milestone passed. il Aviation W 106:49-51 My 9 '77
New engine development adds to Japan's technology base; FJR 710 turbofan engine. il Aviation W 106:207-8 Je 6 '77
New TF30 version nears production use. Aviation W 106:26 F 28 '77
Refanned JT8D aimed at retrofits. W. C. Wetmore. il Aviation W 107:26+ S 12 '77
Rolls-Royce leaves JT10D turbofan development program. Aviation W 106:17 My 16 '77
Two new engines offered for DC-8. J. M. Lenorovitz. il Aviation W 106:22-4 My 16 '77

AIRPLANE engines, Jet—*Continued*

Blades

Tests explore turbine blade failures. Aviation W 106:64 F 28 '77

Failure

Tests explore turbine blade failures. Aviation W 106:64 F 28 '77

Fuel consumption

Fuel-saving computer system studied. B. M. Elson. il Aviation W 106:40-1+ Mr 7 '77

Maintenance and repair

Canada's Rolls pushing overhaul effort. K. J. Stein. il Aviation W 107:71-2+ S 26 '77

Manufacture

F-16 engine partnership plans nearing completion. W. C. Wetmore. il Aviation W 106:115+ My 2 '77

Specifications

Leading international gas turbines; tables. Aviation W 106:134-5 Mr 21 '77
U.S. gas turbine engines; tables. Aviation W 106: 132-3 Mr 21 '77

AIRPLANE factories
Fighter program prompts plant update; USAF plant 4 at Ft Worth, Tex. il Aviation W 106: 103-4 My 2 '77

AIRPLANE fares. See Airlines—Fares

AIRPLANE hijacking
Commandos thwart hijackers rescue of 85 hostages on Lufthansa 737 in Somalia. R. R. Ropelewski. il Aviation W 107:14-16 O 24 '77
Detour to Dubai; Lufthansa 737. M. R. Benjamin and P. Martin. il Newsweek 90:62 O 24 '77
Encouraging pattern. R. Hotz. Aviation W 107:9 O 24 '77
German Entebbe; Mogadishu. Nat R 29:1285-6 N 11 '77
Is the tide turning against terrorists? West German rescue of hostages in Mogadishu, Somalia. il U.S. News 83:22-4 O 31 '77
New war on terrorism; rescue of hostages by German commandos in Mogadishu, Somalia. A. Deming and others. il map Newsweek 90: 48-50+ O 31 '77
No more extensions; skyjacking of Lufthansa Flight 181. il por Time 110:53 O 24 '77
Notes while being hijacked. R. Brockman. Read Digest 110:15-18+ Je '77
Red Army's coup; Japanese hijacking in Bangladesh. A. Deming and T. Clifton. il Newsweek 90:48 O 10 '77
Skyjacker in exile; R. Minichiello. E. Keerdoja. Newsweek 89:18 Ap 18 '77
Soviets pressing for return of Aeroflot An-24 hijackers. Aviation W 107:28 O 31 '77
Terror and triumph at Mogadishu; New breed of commando. il map Time 110:42-4 O 31 '77

Anecdotes, facetiae, satire, etc.

Transatlantic cheap. S. L. Varnando. Nat R 29:1298 N 11 '77

Prevention

Happy landings? F. Willey. Newsweek 90:56 O 31 '77
Hijacking proposal; pilots' boycott of countries harboring terrorists. W. F. Buckley, Jr. Nat R 29:1384 N 25 '77
Mogadishu's aftermath; Lufthansa's security measures. il Time 110:56 N 28 '77
We shall blow up a plane; Lufthansa. A. J. Mayer and others. il Newsweek 90:93 N 28 '77
Why U.S. skyjackings are fewer: tight airport security—and no ransom. il U.S. News 83:24 O 31 '77

AIRPLANE industry
See also
Helicopter industry

Export-import trade

Business jet competition intensifies. D. A. Brown. il Aviation W 106:57-9+ Je 27 '77
Cessna starts factory support programs to aid foreign sales. E. J. Bulban. Aviation W 107: 85-6 D 12 '77
Concerted European export policy urged. Aviation W 108:59 Ja 9 '78
Europe seen weighing F-16 import duty snag. R. R. Ropelewski. Aviation W 107:22-3 O 3 '77
New export sales areas emerge. il Aviation W 106:14-15 Je 13 '77
Proposed sales of military equipment to Egypt; statement, September 15, 1977. A. L. Atherton, Jr. Dept State Bull 77:650-2 N 7 '77
Rabin sees no change possible in block of Kfirs for Ecuador. Aviation W 106:24 Mr 14 '77
Senate gets assurances on MiG repair. Aviation W 107:22-3 S 26 '77
Senate unit schedules hearings on Coast Guard buy of Falcon. il Aviation. W 106:23-4 Ja 3 '77
Transport sales continue surge in Mideast, African regions. Aviation W 106:38-9 Mr 7 '77
White House authorizes F-18L export discussions. C. Brownlow. Aviation W 106:22 Je 27 '77
See also
Airplanes, Military—Marketing

Finance

General aviation group expects additional sales gains in 1977. Aviation W 106:22 Ja 17 '77
$100 billion shoot-out; fighter planes. il U.S. News 84:54-6 Ja 9 '78

International aspects

Boeing cools on cooperative effort for next new transport program. R. G. O'Lone. il Aviation W 106:216-17+ Je 6 '77
Canadian CP-140 offset sets precedent. B. Miller. il Aviation W 106:145+ Je 6 '77
Challenge from Europe; excerpts from address. G. C. Klapwijk. Aviation W 107:9 O 31 '77
Civil transport collaboration pushed. il Aviation W 106:31-3 Je 13 '77
F-16 buyers seek offset assurances. R. R. Ropelewski. Aviation W 106:28 Ja 24 '77
F-16 engine partnership plans nearing completion. W. C. Wetmore. il Aviation W 106:115+ My 2 '77
Fighter contract tied to jobs; Canadian plane contract. Bus W p42 S 12 '77
Fighter effort tests collaboration concepts. E. H. Kolcum. il Aviation W 106:44-5+ My 2 '77
Five-nation coproduction under way; the F-16. R. R. Ropelewski. il Aviation W 106:59+ My 2 '77
General Dynamics struggles to build a plane for all nations; F-16. L. Kraar. il Fortune 95:180-4+ Mr '77
International management team sets quick response time goal. Aviation W 106:93 My 2 '77
Need seen for U.S. role in Europe consortiums. il Aviation W 106:15-19 Je 13 '77
Offset deal pivotal for Canadian fighter selection. C. A. Robinson, Jr. il Aviation W 106:124-5+ Je 6 '77
Results mixed in engine collaboration; JT10D turbofan. il Aviation W 106:213-16 Je 6 '77
World airline industry; interview. K. Hammarskjöld. il por U.S. News 82:56+ Mr 21 '76

Statistics

Business & utility aircraft shipments; tables (title varies) Aviation W 106:55 Ja 3; 67 F 7; 65 F 28; 76-7 Ap 4; 59 Ap 11; 62 My 9; 52 My 30; 91 Je 27; 107:67 Ag 1; 57 S 5; 55 S 26; 77 N 21; 65 D 5 '77; 108:51 Ja 2 '78

Brazil

Brazil seeking new aircraft markets; Embraer. il Aviation W 106:63+ Je 27 '77

Canada

In this corner. . .Fat Albert; Canadair Ltd. por Forbes 120:106 D 1 '77
King Lear? partnership with Canadair Ltd. il por Forbes 119:74 Mr 1 '77

Europe, Western

Airbus pushes hard for U.S. customers. il Bus W p34-5 Je 13 '77
Blow to Europe's Airbus; effect of Western Air Line's non-purchase decision on Airbus Industries. Bus W p99 F 14 '77
French approve Transall restart. il Aviation W 106:21-2 Ja 3 '77
Multinational European effort in aircraft development urged. Aviation W 106:28 Mr 28 '77
Past and present: the leading foreign airframe and engine manufacturers. J. Fricker. il Flying 101:262-71 S '77
Tightened rules fail to restrict Europe's general aviation rise. Aviation W 106:190 Mr 21 '77

France

Aerospatiale, Dassault vie for helicopter role. Aviation W 108:21 Ja 2 '78
Corvette windup seen; losses at $190 million. Aviation W 107:22-3 Ag 22 '77
Leftists eye Dassault nationalization. Aviation W 108:18 Ja 9 '78
Moving in on Dassault. il Time 109:78-9 Je 20 '77

Great Britain

U.K. firm uses U.S. experience to break into other markets; Dowty Aviation Div. il Aviation W 106:159-60 Je 6 '77
See also
Rolls-Royce, Ltd.

History

When the British almost won the battle for the sky; De Havilland Comet. L. Smith. il Duns R 110:18+ Jl '77

India

India's aircraft industry grows. D. A. Brown. il Aviation W 106:14-16 Ja 17 '77

AIRPLANE industry—*Continued*

Spain

CASA C-101 trainer prototype assembly under way; Construcciones Aeronauticas. W. H. Gregory. il Aviation W 107:60-2 D 12 '77

United States

Clearing skies for the planemakers. T. J. Murray. il Duns R 109:39-41 Ja '77
General aviation backlog strong. E. J. Bulban. il Aviation W 106:183+ Mr 21 '77
Record sales build hefty backlog into 1980; business aircraft. E. J. Bulban. il Aviation W 107:48-9+ S 26 '77
Revamped jet confounds the plane makers; DC-9 Super 80. il Bus W p95+ N 14 '77
See also names of airplane manufacturing companies, e.g. McDonnell Douglas Corporation

History

Roots of America's current major airframe and engine manufacturers. D. Mosteller. il Flying 101:240-7 S '77

AIRPLANE instruments. See Aeronautic instruments

AIRPLANE models

Engines

3 control-line fighters to make. F. L. Wolff. il Pop Mech 147:192-4 F '77

AIRPLANE monitor receivers. See Radio receivers

AIRPLANE parts

Inquiry on unapproved parts for Boeing transports broadens. Aviation W 106:29 F 21 '77

AIRPLANE pilots. See Air pilots

AIRPLANE propellers. See Airplanes—Propellers

AIRPLANE racing

Great Australian air race; Benson and Hedges Australian Air Race of 1976. E. F. Ball. il por map Sat Eve Post 249:22-3+ My '77

History

When air racing was king. G. Baxter. il Flying 101:175-8 S '77

AIRPLANE seats. See Airplanes—Seats

AIRPLANE speed records

Speed dash in a homemade jet; D. Greenamyer's F-104 Starfighter. R. L. Emerson. il Pop Mech 147:102+ Je '77

AIRPLANE travel. See Air travel

AIRPLANE wakes. See Atmospheric turbulence

AIRPLANE wings. See Airplanes—Wings

AIRPLANES

Editors' choice: aircraft hall of fame. il Flying 101:283-7 S '77
Offbeat new planes from the Paris air show. B. Kocivar. il Pop Sci 211:94-7 D '77
See also
Aviation
Helicopters
Salvage (airplanes)
Seaplanes

Accidents

See Aviation—Accidents

Cabins

See also
Airplanes, Military—Cabins

Chartering

See Airplanes—Leasing and renting

Control

See also
Airplanes, Jet—Control

Design

No more frontiers; C. L. Johnson. il por Forbes 120:118 N 1 '77

Detection

USAF, Navy cooperate tracking Soviet Bears along east coast. Aviation W 108:23-4 Ja 9 '78

Electronic equipment

IFR on a budget. G. C. Larson. il Flying 101:53+ N '77
Survey 800 miles per day by prospecting from the air; Britten Norman Trislander. B. Kocivar. il Pop Sci 212:48 Ja '78
See also
Aeronautic instruments
Airplanes, Jet—Electronic equipment

Engines

See Airplane engines

Environmental aspects

FAA official claims new data minimize aircraft ozone impact. Aviation W 107:28 Ag 8 '77
See also
Airplanes, Supersonic—Environmental aspects

Equipment

Jumbo loading ramp flies anywhere. E. Bendall. il Pop Sci 210:32 Mr '77

Escape devices

GAO hits F-18 ejection seat selection. E. Kozicharow. Aviation W 106:24-5 Ap 18 '77

Fires and fire prevention

FAA takes unified look at cabin fires. Aviation W 107:40 S 26 '77

Fuel consumption

See Airplane engines—Fuel consumption; Airplane engines, Jet—Fuel consumption

History

See Aeronautics—History

Ice protection

Flying techniques: iceman. R. L. Collins. Flying 100:53+ Mr '77

Instruments

See Aeronautic instruments

Landing

Adoption of landing aid stymied. Aviation W 106:24-5 F 7 '77
British landing system tested in Switzerland; Doppler microwave landing system. Aviation W 108:30 Ja 9 '78
Doppler/scanning beam tests pushed. D. A. Brown. il Aviation W 107:53-5+ O 3 '77
Flying techniques:
Landing at a jetport. R. L. Collins. il Flying 100:64-5+ Je '77
ICAO moves toward landing system choice. Aviation W 107:21 Jl 4 '77
ILS with eyes. T. H. Block. il Flying 100:40 Je '77
Last word on landing. R. L. Collins. il Flying 101:50-3+ Jl '77
MLS faces key decision in Montreal. P. J. Klass. Aviation W 106:19-21 Ja 10 '77
Magic marker; visual descent point. T. H. Block. Flying 100:38 My '77
Pilot error:
No glideslope. R. L. Collins. Flying 100:38+ Je '77
Scanning-beam landing aid wins vote. P. J. Klass. Aviation W 106:26-7 Mr 28 '77
Short subject. T. H. Block. il Flying 100:30+ Mr '77
Swing votes key to landing aid choice. P. J. Klass. il Aviation W 106:46-8 F 21 '77
U.K. challenges U.S. landing system. Aviation W 107:23 Jl 18 '77
U.K. landing system test set for Brussels airport. Aviation W 106:30-1 My 9 '77
U.S. rejects British MLS challenge. P. J. Klass. Aviation W 107:60-1 Ag 1 '77
U.S.-sponsored MLS tested at Kennedy; microwave landing system. K. J. Stein. Aviation W 107:34 D 12 '77

Landing gear

Murphy wins again. J. A. Slocum. il Flying 100:68+ F '77
Stress test mishap damages F-16 unit. Aviation W 106:17 My 16 '77

Laws and regulations

See Aviation—Laws and regulations

Leasing and renting

Bay area aerial tour; chartering a small plane. il Sunset 159:26+ N '77
Corporate pilot: man on the run. J. W. Olcott. il Flying 100:64-6+ Ap '77

Maintenance and repair

Temptation to tinker. G. C. Larson. il por Flying 101:16-17+ Jl '77
See also
Airplane engines—Maintenance and repair

Manufacture

See also
Airplane factories
Airplanes, Military—Manufacture

Marketing

Airbus pushes hard for U.S. customers. il Bus W p34-5 Je 13 '77
Cessna criticizes dumping practices. E. J. Bulban. il Aviation W 107:72-4 N 21 '77
See also
Airplanes, Business—Marketing
Airplanes, Military—Marketing

Materials

Fuel efficiency improvements described. D. R. Griffiths. Aviation W 107:26 N 21 '77

Noise

Airport operator noise plans, surcharge on tickets proposed. Aviation W 106:28 Mr 14 '77
DOT proposes new trust fund to aid noise curb compliance. il Aviation W 106:30 Ja 24 '77
House unit eases noise rule deadline. R. K. Ellingsworth. Aviation W 107:26 Jl 4 '77

AIRPLANES—Noise—*Continued*
Noise to drive you crazy—jets and mental hospitals; study by W. C. Meecham and H. G. Smith. N. Napp. Psychol Today 11:33 Je '77
Two new engines offered for DC-8. J. M. Lenorovitz. il Aviation W 106:22-4 My 16 '77
See also
Airplanes, Supersonic—Noise

Parts

See Airplane parts

Passenger service

See Airlines—Passenger service

Performance

Demonstration flights deliver message. A. W. Bedford. il Aviation W 107:36-9+ N 21 '77

Piloting

Combat fatigue. S. Wilkinson. il Flying 101:104 Ag '77
Flying techniques:
Communications breakdown. R. L. Collins. Flying 101:56-7 N '77
Every drop counts. R. L. Collins. Flying 101:54-5+ Ag '77
Fly by night. R. L. Collins. il Flying 100:50-1+ My '77
How to stay healthy in a twin. R. L. Collins. il Flying 100:76-8+ Ap '77
Iceman. R. L. Collins. Flying 100:53+ Mr '77
Landing at a jetport. R. L. Collins. il Flying 100:64-5+ Je '77
Flying the three-holer. L. Morgan. il Flying 101:68-73+ O '77
I learned about flying from that. See issues of Flying
Pilot error:
Center, is that weather heavy? R. L. Collins. Flying 100:34+ Mr '77
Chance encounter. R. L. Collins. Flying 100:96+ My '77
Fuel crisis. R. L. Collins. Flying 100:38+ Ap '77
No glideslope. R. L. Collins. Flying 100:38+ Je '77
Pilot in command. T. J. Watson. il Flying 101:309+ S '77
Running the traps in a Turbo Arrow. G. C. Larson. il Flying 101:58-61 O '77
Silent night. R. Young. il Flying 101:23+ Ag '77
Time machine; flying an American Airlines flagship. S. Wilkinson. il pors Flying 101:210-15 S '77
See also
Air navigation
Airplanes, Military—Piloting
Aviation—Instrument flying

Pressurization

How pressurization works. J. W. Olcott. il Flying 101:44-5 N '77

Propellers

Why the Fanliner has a fan. J. W. Olcott. il Flying 100:49 Mr '77

Racing

See Airplane racing

Radar equipment

Side-looking airborne radar. H. Jensen and others. il Sci Am 237:84-95 bibl(p 152) O '77
See also
Radar meteorology

Radio equipment

Heavenly voices. P. Garrison. il Flying 100:80-2 Mr '77
See also
Radio direction finders
Radiotelephone on aircraft

Repossession

See Possession (law)

Safety devices and measures

FAA cuts collision avoidance options. P. J. Klass. il Aviation W 106:57-9 My 9 '77
FAA hit on regulatory reforms safety role, collision avoidance. Aviation W 107:31-2 D 12 '77
See also
Airplanes—Escape devices

Seats

Seat sized for narrow-body aircraft. W. H. Gregory. il Aviation W 108:34 Ja 2 '78

Specifications

Leading international aircraft; tables. Aviation W 106:98-101 Mr 21 '77
Leading multinational aircraft programs; tables. Aviation W 106:104 Mr 21 '77
Leading turbine-powered business aircraft; tables. Aviation W 106:119 Mr 21 '77
USSR military and civil aircraft; tables. Aviation W 106:90 Mr 21 '77
U.S. and Canadian V/STOL aircraft; U.S. and Canadian STOL aircraft; tables. Aviation W 106:115 Mr 21 '77
U.S. business, personal and utility aircraft; tables. Aviation W 106:117 Mr 21 '77
U.S. commercial transports; tables. Aviation W 106:95 Mr 21 '77
U.S. military aircraft; tables. Aviation W 106:81-2 Mr 21 '77
U.S. remotely piloted vehicles & target drones; tables. Aviation W 106:120-1 Mr 21 '77

Speed records

See Airplane speed records

Stability and stabilizers

707 tail inspection tightened. Aviation W 107:29 Jl 11 '77

Stalling

P&W believes fixes solve F100 stagnation stall problem. il Aviation W 106:119-20 My 2 '77
Top priority given solution of F100's problems with stall. Aviation W 106:28 F 28 '77

Standards

U.S. sets pattern for fatigue standards. Aviation W 106:32 Mr 28 '77
See also
Airplanes, Business—Standards
Airplanes, Jet—Standards

Take-off

See also
Airplanes, Military—Take-off

Testing

See also
Airplanes, Business—Testing
Airplanes, Military—Testing
Airplanes, Military transport—Testing

Tracking

See Airplanes—Detection

Transportation

Piggyback planes. R. Dempewolff. il Pop Mech 148:90-1 D '77

Weight

Airbus faces weight limitations. W. H. Gregory. Aviation W 107:25-6 O 31 '77

Wings

Dangerous wake turbulence finally is defeated... with winglets. D. Berliner. il Sci Digest 82:72-5 N '77
Free-wing, free-canard concept tested; photographs. Aviation W 107:63 Ag 8 '77
How a wing works. J. W. Olcott. il Flying 100:52-4+ Ap '77
New Sabreliner uses supercritical wing. J. M. Lenorovitz. il Aviation W 107:66-7+ Jl 18 '77
Scissor wings to snip the sonic boom. W. D. Siuru, Jr. il Mech Illus 73:41-3 My '77

AIRPLANES, Aerobatic
Aerobatic Yak-50 seen in Soviet display; photographs. Aviation W 106:67 Je 27 '77

AIRPLANES, Amphibious
Japanese pushing flying boat designs. R. G. O'Lone. il Aviation W 106:45-7 My 16 '77

AIRPLANES, Business
Citation Eagle production rollout nears. il Aviation W 108:48 Ja 2 '78
Ducted-fan Islander undergoing tests; photographs. Aviation W 107:56 S 26 '77
FAA relaxation on Challenger sought. C. Covault. il Aviation W 106:67+ Ap 4 '77
High-flying business machines. P. Lancaster. il Fortune 96:90-5 Jl '77
Hustler 400 prototype assembly begun. D. E. Fink. il Aviation W 106:53+ My 30 '77
Modifications developed for Citation. E. J. Bulban. il Aviation W 107:41+ O 10 '77
New Sabreliner uses supercritical wing. J. M. Lenorovitz. il Aviation W 106:66-7+ Jl 18 '77
New twin-turbofan aircraft planned. il Aviation W 106:57+ My 16 '77
9¢-a-mile executive jet. S. Bronson. il Pop Sci 211:38 O '77
Piper moves to bolster turboprop market stance. D. M. North. il Aviation W 107:18-19 O 3 '77
Reengined Cessnas nearing flight. E. J. Bulban. il Aviation W 108:76-7 Ja 9 '78
What has three engines and flies? Fairey Britten-Norman Trislander. R. L. Collins. il Flying 101:18+ N '77

Marketing

No fear of flying; Learjet saleswoman. M. Mead. J. Lelyveld. il por N Y Times Mag p 131 My 1 '77
U.S. faces business turbine challenge. E. J. Bulban. il Aviation W 106:242-3+ Je 6 '77

Specifications

See Airplanes—Specifications

AIRPLANES, Business—*Continued*

Standards

Conquest certification review planned. D. M. North. Aviation W 107:19 N 28 '77

Testing

Aviation week pilot report:
Falcon 50 raises range, performance. D. M. North. il Aviation W 107:40-3 O 31 '77
Pilot report:
Commander 690B: hot and heady. R. L. Collins. il Flying 101:56-9+ Jl '77
421C: Cessna's blast from the past. G. C. Larson. il Flying 100:54-7+ Mr '77
King Air C90: trusty turboprop. R. L. Collins. il Flying 101:62-5 Ag '77
Mitsubishi MU-2P. T. H. Block. il Flying 100:68-70 My '77

AIRPLANES, Convertible
Quick-change Commander tests planned. il Aviation W 106:95+ Ja 10 '77
Sabena expanding combi quick change. L. Dunkelberg. il Aviation W 107:37+ S 26 '77

AIRPLANES, Drone
Army emerges as lead RPV proponent. P. J. Klass. il Aviation W 106:81+ Je 20 '77
Compass Cope seen in anti-tank role. R. G. O'Lone. il map Aviation W 106:60-2 Je 13 '77
D-21 drone features similar to SR-71. il Aviation W 107:48-9 O 31 '77
GAO urges tighter scrutiny of RPV programs. Aviation W 106:50 Mr 7 '77
Navy upgrading aerial target drones. B. Miller. il Aviation W 106:52-3+ F 21 '77
RPV technology development pressed. il Aviation W 106:176+ Ja 31 '77
Streaker target production increasing; photographs. Aviation W 106:56 My 9 '77
Target drone design simulates cruise missile. il Aviation W 107:17-18 N 28 '77
Tooling begins for research vehicles; unmanned Highly Maneuverable Aircraft Technology vehicles. J. M. Lenorovitz. il Aviation W 106:36-9 F 21 '77

Specifications

See Airplanes—Specifications

Testing

Experimental RPV tested successfully. P. J. Klass. il Aviation W 106:60-1 F 7 '77

AIRPLANES, Experimental
Varieze: also vary fast, vary efficient. P. Garrison. il Flying 100:33 My '77
See also
Experimental Aircraft Association

AIRPLANES, Freight
See also
Air freight service
Airplanes, Convertible

AIRPLANES, Government
Getting there is half the fun; Air Force One. il U.S. News 82:23 My 16 '77

AIRPLANES, Hijacking of. See Airplane hijacking

AIRPLANES, Jet
Aeroflot orders 200 short-haul Yak-42s. W. C. Wetmore. il Aviation W 106:39-41 Je 20 '77
Boeing edging toward transport design decision. W. H. Gregory. Aviation W 106:28 Ap 18 '77
Boeing offering carriers 747SP Combi. Aviation W 106:26 Ja 31 '77
Boeing studies 707 powered by CFM56. il Aviation W 106:26 F 21 '77
British again propose new transport. D. A. Brown. il Aviation W 106:31+ F 28 '77
Civil transport collaboration pushed. il Aviation W 106:31-3 Je 13 '77
DC-9-55 development aid sought. B. Miller. Aviation W 106:24 Ap 4 '77
DC-9-Super 80 stretch gets go-ahead. D. E. Fink. il Aviation W 107:26-7 O 24 '77
Eastern lease, new sales bolster Airbus prospects. il Aviation W 106:234-5+ Je 6 '77
Eastern to pay no lease fee for Airbus A-300s. J. M. Lenorovitz. Aviation W 106:28-9 My 30 '77
Europe debates new transport designs. R. P. Ropelewski. il Aviation W 106:221+ Je 6 '77
L-1011 derivatives under study. il Aviation W 106:194-7 Mr 21 '77
Lockheed studies twin Hercules market. il Aviation W 106:51 F 14 '77
Market data for smaller Airbus studied. Aviation W 107:35 N 21 '77
New Boeing transport family seen as 7N7/7X7 compromise. Aviation W 107:30 Ag 22 '77
New European aircraft decision nears. D. A. Brown. Aviation W 107:23+ D 19 '77
Now, the poor man's jumbo jet; A300 Airbus. il Time 110:56+ O 17 '77
Revamped jet confounds the plane makers; DC-9 Super 80. il Bus W p95+ N 14 '77
Sabreliner aerodynamics modified. Aviation W 106:56 Ja 17 '77
747SP enhances route restructuring. L. Doty. il Aviation W 106:32-3 Je 27 '77
Short-field version of DC-9 designed. D. E. Fink. il Aviation W 106:63+ Ap 25 '77
Soviets pressing Il-86 service start. il Aviation W 106:22-4 Je 13 '77
Soviets roll out, fly new Llyushin-86; photographs. Aviation W 106:27 Ja 10 '77
Stretched European 737 studied. D. A. Brown. Aviation W 107:29-30 Ag 22 '77
Swedish carrier gets Fokker Mk. 4000s; photographs. Aviation W 106:32 Ja 10 '77
Transport designs taking shape. il Aviation W 106:141+ Mr 21 '77
Way clearing for Air France 737 lease. R. R. Ropelewski. Aviation W 108:28-9 Ja 9 '78
West Europeans study 737 derivative. Aviation W 107:32 O 3 '77
See also
Airplanes, Business
Airplanes, Convertible

Control

L-1011 active control system tested. J. M. Lenorovitz. il Aviation W 107:26-8 S 19 '77

Cost of operation

Operating and cost data 747, DC-10 and L-1011; tables (cont) Aviation W 106:36-7 Ja 3; 34-5 My 16; 107:32-3 Jl 18; 46-7 S 26; 40-1 D 12 '77
Operating and cost data—727, 737, DC-9, BAC III; tables (cont) Aviation W 106:48-9 Je 13 '77

Design

Economics key to new Mercure design. D. E. Fink. il Aviation W 106:46-7+ F 7 '77
Lockheed refining new aircraft plans. D. E. Fink. il Aviation W 106:49-51 Mr 28 '77
Stretched DC-10 concept being studied. J. M. Lenorovitz. il Aviation W 107:49-51 Jl 11 '77
Transport construction costs studied. il Aviation W 107:68-70 D 12 '77

Electronic equipment

Monitor devices offer air carrier gains. K. J. Stein. il Aviation W 106:169-70+ Mr 21 '77

Engines

See Airplane engines, Jet

Fuel consumption

See Airplane engines, Jet—Fuel consumption

Manufacture

VFW-Fokker discontinues output of 614 transport. R. R. Ropelewski. Aviation W 108:29-30 Ja 2 '78

Noise

See Airplanes—Noise

Piloting

See Airplanes—Piloting

Seats

See Airplanes—Seats

Standards

Boeing bolsters fail-safe data. R. G. O'Lone. il Aviation W 108:24-6 Ja 2 '78
British seek airworthiness standards. D. A. Brown. Aviation W 107:23-4 N 21 '77

Weight

See Airplanes—Weight

AIRPLANES, Light
Beech's brilliant biplane. R. Munson. il Flying 101:74-81+ Jl '77
Cessna's pressurized Centurion: the compleat single. R. L. Collins. il Flying 101::42-3+ N '77
Cougar: return of the light twin. R. L. Collins. il Flying 101:48-55+ O '77
Country cousin; Cessna 180. P. Garrison. il Flying 100:70-4 Ap '77
Cycling in the sky; man powered flight competition. P. Gwynne and D. Gram. il Newsweek 90:76-7 Ag 1 '77
Dream of wings—via feet; B. Allen wins man-powered flight contest. il Sci N 112:149 S 3 '77
First really promising U.S. man-powered aircraft. P. Wahl. il Pop Sci 211:122-3 O '77
Flight of the Gossamer Condor. M. E. Long. il por Nat Geog 153:130-40 Ja '78
Flying bike that won $86,000; Henry Kremer Prize. il por U.S. News 83:92 O 31 '77
Gossamer wings. il Sci Am 237:74+ O '77
Human-powered flight: Californians claim Kremer Prize. A. L. Robinson. il Science 197:1171 S 16 '77
IAR-823 nears certification in Canada; photographs. Aviation W 106:73 Je 27 '77
I pedaled the mile to aviation's big prize; ed by J. Joseph. B. Allen. il por Pop Mech 148:100-2+ D '77
King Kong singles. J. W. Olcott. il Flying 100:44-9 F '77
Man-powered aircraft shatters flight records. P. Wahl. il Pop Sci 210:16 My '77
Mooney the efficiency expert. J. A. Slocum. il Flying 101:62-7 O '77

AIRPLANES, Light—*Continued*
New homebuilts: classy looks with a dash of the old days. S. M. Gallager and H. Levy. il Pop Mech 149:54-6+ Ja '78
New 152. S. Wilkinson. il Flying 100:44-9+ My '77
On Gossamer wings, one of those things; P. MacCready's man-powered airplane. S. Moses. il por Sports Illus 47:19-21 Ag 1 '77
On top; Mooney 201. R. L. Collins. Flying 100:12+ Mr '77
PZL 104 WILGA: how the Pole vaults. G. C. Larson. il Flying 101:42 Jl '77
Pilot report:
Great Lakes. P. Garrison. il Flying 100:80-4 F '77
Poles demonstrate turbofan biplane. W. C. Wetmore. il Aviation W 106:69-70 Je 27 '77
Secret of the straight-tail 150. G. C. Larson. il Flying 100:103 My '77
They fly what they build. S. M. Gallager and H. Levy. il Pop Mech 147:72-3 F '77
Tinkerer's toys; Piper PA-12 Super Cruiser N4229M. A. Davis. il Flying 100:126 Ap '77
Wankel Fanliner. B. Kocivar. il Pop Sci 210:87-9 Mr '77
The winner; P. MacCready wins Kremer Prize for man-powered planes. P. Wahl. il por Pop Sci 212:56-8+ Ja '78
See also
Experimental Aircraft Association

Marketing

See Airplanes—Marketing

Piloting

See Airplanes—Piloting

Specifications

See Airplanes—Specifications

Testing

Fokker's Fanliner fantasy. P. Garrison. il Flying 100:42-5 Mr '77
Pilot report:
Aerostar 601P. R. L. Collins. il Flying 101:58-60+ N '77
Aztec F. J. W. Olcott. il Flying 100:57-60 Je '77
Beech Sierra. R. L. Collins. il Flying 100:58-60 Mr '77
Cessna's middleweight champ; Skylane II. R. L. Collins. il Flying 100:32-7+ F '77
Grumman American Tiger. il Flying 101:66-8 Jl '77
Mix-and-match Baron. J. W. Olcott. il Flying 100:55-60 Ap '77
P337. T. H. Block. il Flying 101:76-9 O '77
Piper Warrior II. S. Wilkinson. il Flying 101:66-8 Ag '77
Turbo Arrow III. J. W. Olcott. il Flying 100:52-7+ My '77
Workhawk: Cessna Hawk XP. G. C. Larson. il Flying 100:66-9 Je '77
Prototype report: Bellanca Aries T-250. R. L. Collins. il Flying 100:44-51 Ap '77

AIRPLANES, Military
Aileron control rods for Harrier checked. Aviation W 107:26 O 10 '77
F-16 survivability reassessment urged. Aviation W 106:19-20 Ap 11 '77
GAO wary of multinational F-16 pace. E. Kozicharow. Aviation W 107:20-1 Ag 22 '77
General Dynamics struggles to build a plane for all nations; F-16. L. Kraar. il Fortune 95:180-4+ Mr '77
Need for West's fighters put at 6,000. il Aviation W 106:73+ My 2 '77
New attack aircraft proposed; joint Brazil/Italy project. il Aviation W 106:26 Je 13 '77
Special report: F-16 multinational fighter program. Aviation W 106:44-5+ My 2 '77
Two-place A-10 offered to Australia. H. J. Coleman. il Aviation W 106:41+ F 28 '77
War spurred lightweight fighter effort. il Aviation W 106:71-2 My 2 '77
See also
Airplanes, Training

Accidents

See Aviation—Accidents

Armaments

USAF launches bomber weapon study. K. Johnsen. Aviation W 106:94-5+ Je 20 '77

Astronomical use

See Airplanes in astronomy

Bomb delivery systems

Nuclear bomb delivery system tested by USAF. E. J. Bulban. il Aviation W 108:12-15 Ja 9 '78

Cabins

Airborne command post interior shown: photographs. Aviation W 106:23 F 21 '77

Cost

B-1 stretchout, inflation factor could boost costs $1.9 billion. Aviation W 106:203 Mr 21 '77
B-52s, B-1s, FB-111Hs, B-Xs: the Air Force never forgets. R. C. Aldridge. Nation 225:592-3 D 3 '77
Carriers face Congress fight. K. Johnsen. Aviation W 106:12-13 My 9 '77

Design

Fighter integrates advanced concepts; F-16. Aviation W 106:79+ My 2 '77
Improved fighter capabilities sought. D. E. Fink. il Aviation W 107:56-8+ Jl 4 '77
Meeting the press; B-49 Flying Wing; interview, ed by R. B. Parke. J. K. Northrop. il por Flying 101:4 Jl '77

Electronic equipment

Diagnostic system developed for F100. K. J. Stein. il Aviation W 107:49+ S 5 '77
E-4A communications features detailed. il Aviation W 106:61 F 28 '77
EF-111A to begin full flight tests. K. J. Stein. il Aviation W 106:65+ Je 13 '77
Equipment reliability factors studied. il Aviation W 106:56-8 Mr 28 '77
F-16 electronic warfare system depends on proved technology. il Aviation W 106:125-6 My 2 '77
Pave Penny laser identification pods to equip 1,300 aircraft. Aviation W 106:22 Mr 28 '77
Smooth B-1 avionics transition sought. B. M. Elson. Aviation W 106:86 Ap 25 '77
Some B-1 avionics may be salvaged. Aviation W 107:20-1 Jl 11 '77
Target sensor expands A-6E capability; TRAM system. D. M. North. il Aviation W 106:91+ Ja 31 '77

Testing

Target acquisition system tested on Jaguar fighter. il Aviation W 107:54 S 19 '77

Escape devices

See Airplanes—Escape devices

History

See Aeronautics, Military—History

Landing gear

See Airplanes—Landing gear

Maintenance and repair

Broad logistics support plan evolves. Aviation W 106:114-15 My 2 '77
F-14 overhaul done at Norfolk facility; Alameda base specializes in missile, flight controls. il Aviation W 106:56-7 Mr 7 '77
GAO hits British support for Harriers. H. J. Coleman. Aviation W 106:23 Ja 17 '77
Naval rework unit stresses versatility. il Aviation W 106:52-3+ Mr 7 '77
Navy utilizes airline maintenance gains. il Aviation W 106:244-5 Ja 31 '77

Manufacture

Europe prepares for F-16 production; photographs. Aviation W 107:20-1 S 19 '77
Europeans ready production tooling. il Aviation W 106:94+ My 2 '77
Studies pinpoint cost-saving F-16 manufacturing techniques. E. J. Bulban. il Aviation W 106:81-2+ My 2 '77

Marketing

Casualties of a cut in arms sales abroad; Middle East sales. il Bus W p34-5 Ap 25 '77
Early warning battle intensifies. Aviation W 106:50 Je 6 '77

Piloting

A-10 pilots stress navaid requirement. D. A. Brown. Aviation W 107:52-3 S 19 '77
Flying the F4U. W. Langewiesche. Flying 100:53+ Je '77
Kerosene toys; de Havilland DH 100 Vampire jet fighters. G. C. Larson. il por Flying 100:40-1 My '77

Radar equipment

AWACS plan tests NATO cooperation. il Aviation W 106:88-9+ Je 6 '77
Airborne warning crucial alliance issue. C. A. Robinson, Jr. il map Aviation W 107:39+ Ag 22 '77
Carter withdraws notice of AWACS sale to Iran. Aviation W 107:18 Ag 1 '77
Carter's way with Congress; sale of AWACS aircraft to Iran. G. Rushford. Nation 225:270 S 24 '77
Common development sought for AWACS. Aviation W 106:23 My 23 '77
Congressional criticism mounts against AWACS sale to Iran. Aviation W 107:22 Jl 18 '77
Decision on AWACS purchase expected to be delayed again. Aviation W 106:201 Mr 21 '77
E-3A expands USAF defense capabilities. B. M. Elson. il Aviation W 106:49+ Ap 18 '77
French air force chief opposes AWACS. Aviation W 106:33 Ap 25 '77

AIRPLANES, Military—Radar equipment—*Cont.*
French assess AWACS favorably. Aviation W 106:14 Ap 11 '77
GAO criticizes AWACS sale to Iran on justification basis. Aviation W 107:24-5 Jl 25 '77
Iran AWACS sale returned to Congress. Aviation W 107:18-19 S 12 '77
Multimission radar adds F-16 combat capabilities. P. J. Klass. Aviation W 106:120-1+ My 2 '77
NATO unit agrees to common AWACS. D. A. Brown. Aviation W 107:17 D 12 '77
Proposed sale of AWACS to Iran; statement, July 28, 1977. C. R. Vance. Dept State Bull 77:245-7 Ag 22 '77
Radar coproduction agreement required extensive negotiation. il Aviation W 106:123-5 My 2 '77
Special rules for the Shah; proposed AWACS sale to Iran. New Repub 177:10 Jl 30 '77
Those controversial planes for Iran. . . il U.S. News 83:36 Ag 15 '77
Versatility, cost keys to radar choice; F-16. il Aviation W 106:127-8 My 2 '77

Safety devices and measures

Safety factors begin in design phase. il Aviation W 106:247+ Ja 31 '77

Specifications

See Airplanes—Specifications

Speed records

See Airplane speed records

Stalling

See Airplanes—Stalling

Take-off

Harrier ski jump takeoff ramp tested. D. A. Brown. il Aviation W 107:39-41 D 5 '77
Piggyback planes. R. Dempewolff. il Pop Mech 148:90-1 D '77

Testing

Aviation week pilot report:
Alphajet evaluated at Paris air show. R. R. Ropelewski. il Aviation W 107:46+ Jl 4 '77
YC-14 designed to cut pilot workload. D. M. North. il Aviation W 106:41+ Jl 18 '77
Full flight test program advancing; F-16. D. E. Fink. il Aviation W 106:105-6+ My 2 '77
PS aviation editor takes a ride in the F-14. B. Kocivar. il Pop Sci 211:88-90+ Jl '77
PS editor flies the new STOL's. B. Kocivar. il Pop Sci 211:78-80 N '77
XFV-12A ground tests 90% completed. C. Covault. il Aviation W 107:48+ S 12 '77
See also
Military maneuvers
United States—Naval Air Test Center

Transportation

See Airplanes—Transportation

Canada

Bids on new fighter sought by Canadians. Aviation W 106:14 Ap 4 '77
Fighter contract tied to jobs. Bus W p42 S 12 '77
Offset deal pivotal for Canadian fighter selection. C. A. Robinson, Jr. il Aviation W 106:124-5+ Je 6 '77

Egypt

Egyptian MiG flown with Smiths HUD. Aviation W 107:22 O 24 '77
Proposed sales of military equipment to Egypt; statement, September 15, 1977. A. L. Atherton, Jr. Dept State Bull 77:650-2 N 7 '77
Senate gets assurances on MiG repair. Aviation W 107:22-3 S 26 '77

Europe, Western

Europe seen weighing F-16 import duty snag. R. R. Ropelewski. Aviation W 107:22-3 O 3 '77
Formal European F-16 contract expected. Aviation W 106:13 Ja 10 '77
Grumman's chance to bag a NATO plane; E-2C Hawkeye. il Bus W p49+ Ap 18 '77
U.S. proposes NATO buy fewer E-3As. Aviation W 106:21 Mr 28 '77

France

Mirage 2000 to be prime French fighter. R. R. Ropelewski. Aviation W 106:33-4 Ap 25 '77

Great Britain

British order Nimrod AEW development. D. S. Brown. Aviation W 106:15 Ap 4 '77
Debate seen on British A-10 buy. Aviation W 107:21 Jl 18 '77
Harrier starts takeoff tests on ski jump; photographs. Aviation W 107:25 S 26 '77
Nimrod early warning version pushed. D. A. Brown. il Aviation W 106:47+ Mr 14 '77

Iran

Iranian F-14s displayed in flyby for the Shah; photographs. Aviation W 106:54-5 My 9 '77

Israel

Litton's Israel sale awaiting Defense Dept. approval. Aviation W 106:204 Mr 21 '77

Japan

Japanese doubts rising over F-15, P-3C. il Aviation W 106:201-3+ Je 6 '77

Russia

Airborne warning crucial alliance issue. C. A. Robinson, Jr. il map Aviation W 107:39+ Ag 22 '77
Design details of Flagon fighter shown; photographs. Aviation W 107:17 Jl 4 '77
Soviets test two-seat MiG-25 version. D. M. North. Aviation W 106:17-18 Mr 28 '77
USSR military and civil aircraft; tables. Aviation W 106:90 Mr 21 '77

Sweden

Viggen recon versions being delivered; photographs. Aviation W 107:52 O 3 '77

United States

A-10 survivability in attack role shown during simulated combat. D. E. Fink. il Aviation W 106:88-9+ Je 20 '77
AV-8B pivotal in naval aviation fight. C. A. Robinson, Jr. il Aviation. W 107:18-20 O 31 '77
Advanced Harrier pushed for fleet use. il Aviation W 107:55+ N 28 '77
Advances stretch service life of A-7. D. M. North. il Aviation W 106:87-9 Ja 31 '77
After the B-1. Nation 225:66-8 Jl 23 '77
Agencies quick to blunt GAO impact on F-16. Aviation W 106:23 Ap 18 '77
Air Force gets first operational E-3A. B. M. Elson. il Aviation W 106:19-21 Mr 28 '77
B-1 cost-effectiveness claimed; study by Rockwell on B-1 cruise missile launchers. D. E. Fink. il Aviation W 107:14-16 D 12 '77
B-1 for cruise missiles urged. E. Kozicharow. Aviation W 107:14-15 S 19 '77
B-1 halt generates wild impact. Aviation W 107:12 Jl 11 '77
B-1 no, cruise yes. S. Fraker and others. il por Newsweek 90:14-17 Jl 11 '77
B-1 R&D decision expected. Aviation W 107:16 Jl 18 '77
Carter and the B-1 bomber. R. Freund. Chr Cent 94:53-4 Ja 26 '77
Carter and the big bomber; B-1 supersonic bomber. S. Fraker and others. il Newsweek 89:30+ Je 20 '77
Carter blocks production of B-1. il Aviation W 107:14-16 Jl 4 '77
Carter's B-1 shocker. il U.S. News 83:13-14 Jl 11 '77
Carter's big decision: down goes the B-1, here comes the cruise. il por Time 110:8-12 Jl 11 '77
Death of the B-1: the events behind Carter's decision. N. Wade. il Science 197:536-9 Ag 5 '77
Down in flames; rejection of B-1. F. Getlein. Commonweal 104:484-6 Ag 5 '77
Dump the B-1. S. Chapman. New Repub 176:16-18 My 28 '77
E-2C cements early warning role with other pilots. D. M. North. il Aviation W 106:108-9 Ja 31 '77
E-4B seen meeting time and cost goals. B. M. Elson. Aviation W 107:54-5 Ag 1 '77
EC-130 fleet nearing full strength. W. C. Wetmore. il Aviation W 106:38-9 F 28 '77
F-14A fighter performance upgraded. il Aviation W 106:82-3 Ja 31 '77
F-18 blends advanced fighter concepts. D. E. Fink. il Aviation W 107:38-41+ S 5 '77
FB-111H proposal cites survivability, low cost. E. Kozicharow. il Aviation W 107:20-2 O 10 '77
Good news and bad; decision to exchange cruise missiles for B-1. B. T. Feld. Bull Atom Sci 33:10-11 S '77
Harrier breaks path in Navy V/STOL. C. Covault. il Aviation W 106:99-101+ Ja 31 '77
High-spying U-2. E. Keerdoja and W. J. Cook. il por Newsweek 89:11+ F 28 '77
House deletes FB-111H study funding. E. Kozicharow. Aviation W 107:21 O 17 '77
How the B-1 bomber was brought down; work of Clergy and Laity Concerned and American Friends Service Committee. J. Robison. Chr Cent 94:711-12 Ag 17 '77
Inter-service weapons rivalry. R. F. Coulam. bibl il Bull Atom Sci 33:25-36 Je '77
Jimmy's weapons choice; B-1 decision. R. Hotz. Aviation W 107:7 Jl 11 '77
Marines' bad luck plane; Harriers. il Time 110:15-16 Ag 15 '77
Marines emphasize night air capability. il Aviation W 106:61-3 Ja 31 '77
Marines to press for AV-8B in spite of opposition, accidents. Aviation W 107:25 S 19 '77
Navy conceptual design work centers on eight new aircraft types, half V/STOL. il Aviation W 106:110-11+ Ja 31 '77

AIRPLANES, Military—United States—*Continued*
Navy restudies carrier options. C. A. Robinson, Jr. Aviation W 107:14-16 S 5 '77
Navy to seek design proposals for new V/STOLs. C. A. Robinson, Jr. il Aviation W 107:34-5+ N 28 '77
Of weapons and strategy; B-1 decision. Nat R 29:815-16 Jl 22 '77
$100 billion shoot-out; fighter planes. il U.S. News 84:54-6 Ja 9 '78
Other story about the controversial B-1. J. Schefter. il Pop Sci 210:109-12+ My '77
Rockwell designers define new derivatives of B-1. D. E. Fink. il Aviation W 107:22-3 O 10 '77
Rockwell seeks funding to complete two B-1s. D. E. Fink. il Aviation W 107:20-1 S 26 '77
Rockwell's bombshell; loss of the B-1 bomber program. D. Pauly and D. Gram. il Newsweek 90:61-2 Jl 11 '77
SALT: a bargaining chip; FB-111H. M. R. Benjamin and S. Sullivan. il Newsweek 90:44-5 O 3 '77
Search for the missing tomcat; F-14 retrieved in North Atlantic. D. Reed. il Read Digest 110:79-83 Mr '77
Sold to the highest bidder; controversy over manufacture of F-14 and F-18 fighter planes. Nat R 29:766-7 Jl 8 '77
Stacking the B-1 deck; evaluation committee. C. Miller. Progressive 41:7-8 Mr '77
Stretched FB-111 version urged. E. Kozicharow. il Aviation W 107:18-19 S 26 '77
Support for B-1 decision seen mixed in Congress. K. Johnsen. Aviation W 107:21-2 Jl 11 '77
Time of the angel: the U-2, Cuba, and the CIA. D. Moser. il Am Heritage 28:4-15 O '77
U-2: the original bear in the air. J. Joss. il Flying 100:36 My '77
Ugliest plane in the Air Force; A-10 tank-killer. M. Rubenstein. il Mech Illus 73:64-5+ F '77
Uncertainties stalk aircraft advances. D. M. North. il Aviation W 106:27+ Mr 21 '77
V/STOL design emphasizes simplicity. D. M. North. il Aviation W 106:17-18 F 7 '77
V/STOL design stresses composites. il Aviation W 107:52-3 O 10 '77
V/STOL technology advances expected. il Aviation W 106:70-1+ Ja 31 '77
Vought, Navy discuss twin-engine A-7. E. J. Bulban. il Aviation W 107:50+ N 21 '77
What Carter will do with the B-1 money. Bus W p21-2 Jl 18 '77
See also
United States—Air Force—Civil Reserve Air Fleet

AIRPLANES, Military transport
AMST competitors vie at Paris show; photographs. Aviation W 106:20-1 Je 13 '77
AMST engineering proposals awaited. D. E. Fink. il Aviation W 107:55-7 O 10 '77
Air force studies AMST procurement. D. E. Fink. il Aviation W 106:60-1 My 9 '77
DC-10 selected for tanker/cargo role. il Aviation W 108:17 Ja 2 '78
STOL may lose out in the budget battle. Bus W p37-8 N 28 '77
Stretched Air Force C-141 rolled out; photographs . Aviation W 106:14 Ja 10 '77

Testing

YC-14 flight test program accelerating; AMST prototype evaluation. D. E. Fink. il Aviation W 106:36-7+ My 16 '77
YC-15 enters new flight test series; photographs. Aviation W 106:27 F 21 '77

AIRPLANES, Private
Waiting for the pressurized turbo Cardinal RG. R. L. Collins. Flying 100:12+ Je '77
See also
Private flying

AIRPLANES, Remodeled
Modifiers. J. A. Slocum. il Flying 101:259 S '77
Pilot report:
Machen Magnum 300. P. Garrison. il Flying 100:71-2 Je '77
Radial chic; Douglas A-26 conversion. G. C. Larson. il Flying 100:61+ Ap '77

AIRPLANES, Short take-off and landing
Aussie STOL is rugged performer. B. Kulkopf. il Pop Mech 147:53 Mr '77
Aviation week pilot report:
DHC-7 performance, low noise stressed. D. M. North. il Aviation W 106:40-1+ Je 13 '77
Commuter beginning Dash 7 service. B. A. Smith. il Aviation W 108:35-6 Ja 2 '78
Russians test STOL twin-engine AN-28. il Aviation W 106:41-2 Je 20 '77
Soviet AN-32 STOL transport displayed. il Aviation W 106:25-6 Je 13 '77
See also
Airplanes, Military transport

Specifications

See Airplanes—Specifications

AIRPLANES, Supersonic
Around City Hall; Concorde controversy. A. Logan. New Yorker 53:91-8 Ap 4; 86-90 Je 27 '77
Beautiful but dumb. Nation 225:453-4 N 5 '77
British expected to resume Concorde effort in Malaysia. Aviation W 108:30 Ja 2 '78
Carriers sign new Concorde service pact. Aviation W 107:28 O 31 '77
Carter's Concorde strategy. New Repub 177:8 O 8 '77
Concorde ban termed discriminatory. Aviation W 106:38 Je 13 '77
Concorde in New York. L. Langway. il Newsweek 90:67 O 31 '77
Concorde JFK approval drive mounted. Aviation W 106:34 F 7 '77
Concorde JFK service to begin Nov. 22. W. C. Wetmore. il Aviation W 107:30-2 O 24 '77
Concorde landing rights court hearing postponed. Aviation W 106:202 Mr 21 '77
Concorde proved operationally. il Aviation W 106:22-6 My 30 '77
Concorde rumbling may continue. Sci N 112:212 O 1 '77
Concorde: yes. il Time 110:82 O 3 '77
Court action nears on Concorde rights. R. K. Ellingsworth. Aviation W 106:29 Ap 18 '77
Court requests U.S. role in Concorde entry case. Aviation W 106:63+ Je 6 '77
Court ruling awaited in Concorde case; Kennedy Airport landing rights. W. H. Gregory. Aviation W 106:24+ My 9 '77
Europeans react to Concorde decision; most candidate cities cool to Concorde. Aviation W 107:30-1 O 3 '77
Fair Concorde decision. R. Hotz. Aviation W 107:11 O 3 '77
Federal judge lifts ban on Concorde. Aviation W 107:34 Ag 22 '77
First landing; Kennedy Airport. New Yorker 53:31-2 O 31 '77
Flights of folly. Nation 224:644 My 28 '77
La grande crise over Concorde. il Time 109:40 Mr 21 '77
Holding pattern over New York; the Concorde. New Repub 176:9-10 My 28 '77
NASA advances supersonic technology. C. Covault. Aviation W 106:16-17 Ja 10 '77
NASA to end manned hypersonic effort. Aviation W 107:24 S 26 '77
N.Y.-Dulles air link offered by Air France for Concorde. Aviation W 107:26 Ag 29 '77
Nerve war in the sky; Concorde landing rights decision. A. J. Mayer and others. il Newsweek 89:68-9 Mr 21 '77
New York ban on Concorde continued. Aviation W 107:24 Jl 11 '77
New York's Concorde stall. R. Hotz. Aviation W 106:9 Mr 14 '77
Port Authority delay attacked. Aviation W 107:24 Jl 18 '77
Problems pare Soviet Tu-144 flight service; photographs. Aviation W 107:25 N 28 '77
Putting up with the ugly duckling; Time essay. B. Y. Pines. Time 109:41 Mr 21 '77
SST technology readiness studied. C. Covault. il Aviation W 107:33-4 O 17 '77
Security curtain charged during Concorde hearing. Aviation W 107:24-5 S 12 '77
Shaky lift-off for Concordski; TU-144. il Bus W p58 D 12 '77
Smooth landing for the birds. il Time 110:36 D 5 '77
Sound and the fury. Newsweek 89:20 My 23 '77
Sounding off at two airports. il Time 109:49 My 23 '77
U.K. France ponder JFK Concorde action. Aviation W 106:29 Je 20 '77
See also
Sonic boom

Anecdotes, facetiae, satire, etc.

Time of your life. R. Baker. N Y Times Mag p 12 N 6 '77

Environmental aspects

Vapor emission termed greater ozone threat. R. G. O'Lone. Aviation W 108:38-9 Ja 2 '78
Wounded bird; Concorde. Nat R 29:373-4 Ap 1 '77

Noise

Concorde curfew urged at Heathrow. Aviation W 106:52 Ap 25 '77
FAA monitors find Concorde quieter at Kennedy than Dulles. Aviation W 107:30 D 19 '77
Ground laid for Concorde noise parley; British, French erupt over Concorde delay. Aviation W 106:9 Mr 14 '77
It's not only Concorde that ruffles people. il U.S. News 83:53 O 3 '77
Port Authority chastised for noise standard delay. Aviation W 107:30 S 26 '77
U.K. noise study assesses Concorde operations impact. Aviation W 106:34 My 2 '77

Wings

See Airplanes—Wings

AIRPLANES, Theft of
See also
Airplane hijacking

AIRPLANES, Training
Beech plans T-34C tests. Aviation W 106:48 Ja 24 '77
Beech trainer stresses commonality; photographs. Aviation W 107:75 N 21 '77
CASA C-101 trainer prototype assembly under way; Construcciones Aeronauticas. W. H. Gregory. il Aviation W 107:60-2 D 12 '77
Czech L-39 aimed at Warsaw Pact role. il Aviation W 106:71-2 Je 27 '77
European training aircraft for USAF, Navy face obstacles. D. M. North. il Aviation W 106: 268-9+ Je 6 '77
Light, 4-seat twin trainer under development by Britten. Aviation W 106:98 Je 20 '77
MB-339 offers low-cost jet trainer. R. R. Ropelewski. il Aviation W 106:38-9+ Ja 3 '77
New single-engine trainer developed. il Aviation W 106:63 Je 13 '77
The 150 as a teaching tool: good because it's bad. J. A. Slocum. Flying 100:101-2 My '77
Piper counts on new trainer to boost market identification. D. M. North. il Aviation W 107:21-2 O 24 '77
Spanish C-101 jet trainer in first flight; photographs. Aviation W 107:43 S 19 '77
T-34C planning to continue. Aviation W 107:19 Ag 15 '77
Trainers perform in Paris flights; photographs. Aviation W 106:71 Je 20 '77

AIRPLANES, Vertical take-off and landing
VTOLs studied for offshore support. E. J. Bulban. Aviation W 106:93-4 Ja 10 '77
See also
Airplanes, Military

Specifications

See Airplanes—Specifications

AIRPLANES in agriculture
Agricultural aircraft sales rise foreseen. D. M. North. il Aviation W 107:85+ S 26 '77
How we see crop prospects. B. Coffman. il Farm J 101:20-1 Ag '77
NASA spurs agricultural aircraft effort. E. Kozicharow. il Aviation W 107:80+ S 26 '77
Poles demonstrate turbofan biplane. W. C. Wetmore. il Aviation W 106:69-70 Je 27 '77
U.S. agricultural aircraft; tables. Aviation W 106:104 Mr 21 '77

AIRPLANES in astronomy
Cosmic snooping; U-2 flights. P. Gwynne and S. Begley. il Newsweek 90:88 N 28 '77
U-2 stability aided scientists in new study of earth origins. R. G. O'Lone. Aviation W 107: 19-20 N 21 '77

AIRPLANES in business
Business flying boom continues. R. Hotz. Aviation W 107:13 S 26 '77
Fuel supply, cost worrying operators. E. J. Bulban. Aviation W 106:62-3 F 7 '77
See also
National Business Aircraft Association

History

Traveling salesmen. L. Collins. Flying 101:162-3+ S '77

AIRPLANES in motion pictures. See Aviation in motion pictures

AIRPLANES in narcotics control
Border wars: busting the dope trade. G. C. Larson. il Flying 101:62-9+ N '77
Combat on the border; Customs department Night rider patrol on U.S.-Mexican border. il pors Ebony 32:104-6+ Ap '77

AIRPLANES in patrol work
Coast Guard buy challenges Falcon Jet. E. J. Bulban. il Aviation W 107:53-8 Ag 29 '77
Customs plans turbine aircraft buy. E. J. Bulban. il Aviation W 106:57-8 Ap 11 '77
See also
Airplanes in narcotics control

AIRPLANES in prospecting
Survey 800 miles per day by prospecting from the air; Britten Norman Trislander. B. Kocivar. il Pop Sci 212:48 Ja '78

AIRPLANES in television. See Aviation in television

AIRPLANES in the petroleum industry
VTOLs studied for offshore support. E. J. Bulban. Aviation W 106:93-4 Ja 10 '77

AIRPORT buildings
Eastern to get new terminal for air shuttle. il Aviation W 107:29 D 5 '77
Logan Airport: the new South Terminal. il Archit Rec 162:105-10 S '77
Soviets expand terminals for Olympics; photographs. Aviation W 107:29 Ag 8 '77

AIRPORT Development Aid Program. See Airports—Federal aid

AIRPORT Parking Company of America. See Automobile parking

AIRPORTS
Home is where the airport is. T. H. Block. Flying 101:80 N '77
Ideal airport. C. Schwalberg. Mademoiselle 83: 42+ F '77
Rating the world's airports. il Time 109:35 Ap 11 '77
Time's guide to airports: jet lag on the ground. Time 110:82-5 Jl 18 '77

Automobile rental services

See Automobiles—Leasing and renting

Buildings

See Airport buildings

Federal aid

Airport aid of $355 million approved. Aviation W 106:32 Ap 18 '77
Airport programs in 29 states receive allocations from FAA. Aviation W 106:39 Mr 7 '77
FAA approves $211 million for airports. Aviation W 107:33 S 12 '77
$3.3 million for airport planning approved. Aviation W 106:31 Ja 10 '77
Transportation Dept. cuts airport grants. Aviation W 106:22-3 Ja 24 '77

Fires and fire prevention

Foaming out air-crash fires; airport fire trucks. C. Haas. il Mech Illus 73:120 O '77

Noise

Airport operator noise plans, surcharge on tickets proposed. Aviation W 106:28 Mr 14 '77
Bill would curtail airport noise liability. Aviation W 106:25 Ap 4 '77
It's not only Concorde that ruffles people. il U.S. News 83:53 O 3 '77
Logan procedures spark pilots' threat. Aviation W 106:69 Ap 25 '77
Port Authority publishes new N.Y. noise rule. Aviation W 107:31 O 17 '77

Safety devices and measures

Black star airports; International Federation of Air Line Pilots Associations list. F. Wiley. Newsweek 89:53 Ap 11 '77

Security measures

See also
Airplane hijacking—Prevention

Stores

Bringing back the goods. S. Birnbaum. Esquire 87:42+ Ap '77

Traffic control

Pork-barrel tower do you read? R. L. Collins. Flying 101:40 N '77

Transportation problems

Don't drive to the S.F. airport? map Sunset 159:38+ D '77

California

See also
Los Angeles—Airports
San Francisco—Airports

Great Britain

See also
London—Airports

Illinois

See also
Chicago—Airports

India

Airport improvements pushed in India. Aviation W 106:40 F 14 '77

Japan

See also
Tokyo—Airports

Massachusetts

See also
Boston—Airports

New York (state)

See also
New York (city)—Airports

Oregon

See also
Portland, Ore.—Airports

United States

Why U.S. skyjackings are fewer: tight airport security—and no ransom. il U.S. News 83:24 O 31 '77

AIRSHIPS
Big boom in gas bags. B. Allen. bibl il Pop Mech 148:64-7+ Jl '77
Dirigibles: a comeback? J. Kornfeld. il Sci Digest 81:38-42 My '77
Flogging the good ship Columbia; Goodyear blimp; with editorial comment. J. McGraw. il Hot Rod 30:5-6, 28-32 F '77
New age of airships may dawn. K. R. Stehling. il Smithsonian 8:123-33 Ap '77
Takeoff for disaster; plans for imperial airship fleet. J. Morris. il Horizon 19:24-33 Ja '77

AIRSHIPS—*Continued*

History

Honoring the Shenandoah. Hobbies 82:155 S '77
Lighter than air. J. Gilbert. il Flying 101:84-5 S '77

AIRSPACE (international law)
Soviet arms airlift to Ethiopia violates air space of Pakistan. Aviation W 107:17 D 19 '77
Viet overflight charges spur airline concern. Aviation W 107:31 Jl 11 '77

AIRSPACE (law)
Uptown parks and air rights. W. Theobald. bibl Parks & Rec 12:31-3+ Ag '77

AIRWAYS
Viet overflight charges spur airline concern. Aviation W 107:31 Jl 11 '77
See also
Airlines—International services

Traffic control

See Air traffic control

AIRWORTHINESS certification of jet airplanes. See Airplanes, Jet—Standards

AIST, James R.
Mechanically induced wall appositions of plant cells can prevent penetration by a parasitic fungus. bibl il Science 197:568-71 Ag 5 '77

AJAMI, Fouad
Human rights: sermons or substance. Nation 224:389-90 Ap 2 '77

AKA, Tanoé. See Tanoe-Aka

AKABAS, Sheila H. and Bellinger, Susan
Programming mental health care for the world of work. il MH 61:4-8 Spr '77

AKERA, Tai
Membrane adenosinetriphosphatase: a digitalis receptor? bibl il Science 198:569-74 N 11 '77

AKERMAN, Chantal
Reflections on Jeanne Dielman. M. Kinder. il Film Q 30:2-8 Summ '77 *

AKERS, Adela
Adela Akers: the loomed plane; interview, ed by P. Scheinman. il Craft Horiz 37:24-5+ F '77

AKERT, Robin M. See Archer, D. jt auth

AKHMADULINA, Bella
Tale about rain in several episodes; poem; excerpt from Fever and other new poems; tr by G. Dutton and I. Mezhakoff-Koriakin. Vogue 167:113+ Jl '77
about
Bella: Russian best. O. Carlisle. por Vogue 167:110-11+ Jl '77 *
Why Russian poets? J. Brodsky. Vogue 167:112 Jl '77 *

AKI (Biennial of New Music, Cleveland) See Music festivals—Ohio

AKINS, James E.
OPEC: where does the balance of power lie? interview. il por Forbes 120:34-6 O 1 '77

AKSEN, Gerald
Debate over consolidation of arbitration proceedings is enlivened by a recent New York case. Archit Rec 162:59 O '77

AKZIN, Benjamin
Palestinian issue: anatomy of a slogan. Intellect 106:198-200 D '77

AL-FAISAL, Saud, Prince of Saudi Arabia. See Saud al Faisal

AL FATAH (organization) See Palestine Liberation Organization

AL-HAMAD, Abdlatif-. See Hamad, A.

AL-KADDOUMI, Farouk. See Kaddoumi, F.

AL-QADDAFI, Muammar. See Qaddafi, M.

ALABAMA
See also
Architecture—Alabama
Architecture, Domestic—Alabama
Crime and criminals—Alabama
Criminal justice, Administration of—Alabama
Historic houses, sites, etc.—Alabama
Hunting—Alabama
Libraries—Alabama
Opera—Alabama
Police—Alabama
Tombigbee River

ALABAMA Regional Library for the Blind and Physically Handicapped (proposed) See Libraries—Alabama

ALADDIN strikes it rich; drama. See Cheatham, V. R.

ALAERTS, Leo, and others
Primordial noble gases in chondrites: the abundance pattern was established in the solar nebula. bibl il Science 198:927-30 D 2 '77

ALAMEDA County, Calif.

Water supply

See Water supply—California

ALAMIA, Leticia V. See Valdez, R. jt auth

ALAN Wood Steel Company. See Steel industry—United States

ALANI
Ossetes: Scythians of the 20th century. V. I. Abaev. il UNESCO Courier 29:48-9 D '76

ALARM pheromones. See Pheromones

ALARMS
See also
Electronic alarm systems

ALASKA
See also
Barrow
Bristol Bay
Conservation of resources—Alaska
Cruising—Alaska
Environmental movement—Alaska
Eskimos
Finance—Alaska
Fishing—Alaska
Forests and forestry—Alaska
Gas, Natural—Alaska
Hunting—Alaska
Indians of North America—Alaska
Katmai National Monument
Lakes—Alaska
Land tenure—Alaska
Mines and mineral resources—Alaska
Mount McKinley National Park
National parks and reserves—Alaska
Newspapers—Alaska
Noatak River
Petroleum pipelines—Alaska
Pribilof Islands
Public lands—Alaska
Salmon River (Alaska)
Sheenjek River
Valdez
Water pollution—Alaska
Wilderness areas—Alaska
Wildlife conservation—Alaska
Wildlife management—Alaska
Yukon
Zoology—Alaska

Capital

Alaska: capital formation. S. Fraker. il map Newsweek 91:27 Ja 16 '78
Brasilia for the North. il map Time 110:50+ D 26 '77

Description and travel

Reporter at large; excerpt from Coming into the country. J. McPhee. New Yorker 53:47-8+ My 2; 88+ My 9 '77; Same abr with title Encircled river. il por map Liv Wildn 41:44-60 Jl '77
Southeast Alaska. R. Callahan. il Travel 148: 62-7 Ag '77
Summer with Alex; father and son's trip to Alaska. P. L. Fradkin. il por Audubon 79: 36-41 My '77
Two different worlds; American Forestry Association tour of Alaska and Japan. R. Pardo. il Am For 83:14-17+ Ap '77

Economic conditions

Alaska's oil flows south; with interview with E. L. Patton. K. M. Chrysler. il map U.S. News 82:35-8 Je 20 '77

Fish and Game, Department of

Where have all the *tuttu* gone? with editorial comment. J. G. Mitchell. il Audubon 79:inside cover, 2-15 Mr '77

Industries

See also
Lumber industry—Alaska

Photographs

Images of Alaska. J. P. Milton. Liv Wildn 41: 24-9 Jl '77

Restaurants

See Restaurants—United States

Social conditions

Taming of Alaska. R. Rau; discussion. Nat Wildlife 15:17 Ap '77

ALASKA National Interest Lands Conservation Act. See Land utilization—Laws and regulations

ALASKA. University, Fairbanks

Kuskokwim Community College

Community college that would not freeze. H. D. Masden. Educ Digest 42:34-5 Ap '77

ALASKAN brown bear hunting. See Bear hunting

ALASKAN brown bears. See Bears

ALBANY, N.Y.

Buildings

Space age comes to the Empire state; Albany Mall. P. Goldberger. il Horizon 19:60-71 Jl '77

City planning

Albany's first city planner; P. Byrne. il por map Conservationist 31:34-7 Ja '77

Street traffic

Bringing order to Albany streets. il Am City & County 92:30 N '77

ALBANY campus. See New York (state). State University—Albany campus

ALBEDA, Wil
Between harmony and conflict: industrial democracy in the Netherlands. Ann Am Acad 431:74-82 My '77
ALBEE, Edward
Counting the ways. Reviews
Newsweek il 89:69 F 14 '77 *
Sat R 4:36 Ap 2 '77 *
Listening. Reviews
Newsweek il 89:69 F 14 '77 *
Sat R 4:36 Ap 2 '77 *
ALBEMARLE County, Va.
Jefferson's country. D. A. Tice. il por Am For 83:24-7 My '77
ALBERDI, Juan Bautista
Détente, then and now. G. H. Watson. il pors Américas 29:2-7 Ja '77 *
ALBERT, Frankie
Melding of men all suited to a T. R. Fimrite. il Sports Illus 47:90-100 S 5 '77 *
ALBERT, John. See Dwyer, J. jt auth
ALBERT, Leo N.
Albert reports on Peking visit, coming book exhibit. M. Reuter. il Pub W 212:19-20 O 17 '77 *
Bernstein and Albert testify on censorship, currency. S. Wagner. Pub W 211:39+ Je 6 '77 *
ALBERT, Rollin'
Gusty goat to the rescue; drama. Plays 36:69-72 Ap '77
ALBERT, Sherri, pseud
Day I found my father. Good H 184:158+ Je '77
ALBERT and Mary Lasker Foundation
Lasker awards to five Europeans. Sci N 112:359 N 26 '77
To Stockholm, with love. il Time 110:78 N 28 '77
ALBERTA Gas Trunk Line Company. See Pipeline companies
ALBERTI, Charles E.
Due process in discipline. bibl Clearing H 51:12-14 S '77
ALBERTI, Giorgio. See Whyte, W. F. jt auth
ALBERTSON, Marge
Seven choices of delivery. Good H 186:68+ Ja '78
ALBERTSON'S Inc
Home-baked bread, anyone? TV sets? Blue jeans? Skaggs-Albertson's combination stores. il Forbes 119:144+ My 15 '77
Skaggs-Albertson's amicable separation; dissolution of joint venture. Bus W p39+ F 14 '77
ALBINONI, Tommaso
Aria structure and ritornello form in the music of Albinoni. J. E. Solie. bibl f il Mus Q 63:31-47 Ja '77 *
ALBINOS and albinism
Rare albino turtle. J. R. Fletemeyer. il Sea Front 23:233 Jl '77
ALBINSKI, Henry S.
Currents in Canadian politics. Cur Hist 72: 158:61+ Ap '77
ALBION, Mich.
Where HEW money brings help—and growing frustration. U.S. News 82:45 My 16 '77
ALBRECHT, Marcus J.
Off the force. Progressive 41:42 My '77
ALBRECHT, Susanne
Hit women. K. Willenson and T. Nater. il pors Newsweek 90:30 Ag 15 '77 *
Red roses from Roter Morgen. pors Time 110:30 Ag 15 '77 *
ALBRIGHT, Ivan Le Lorraine
Ivan Albright: more than meets the eye. J. Van Der Marck. bibl il por Art in Am 65:92-9 N '77 *
ALBRIGHT, Thomas
California art since the modern dawn. il Art N 76:68-72 Ja '77
San Francisco. See issues of Art news
(ed) See Irwin, R. Robert Irwin: everything I've done in the last five years doesn't exist
ALBUM covers, Phonograph record. See Phonograph record covers
ALBUMINS
Reduced warfarin binding of albumin variants. G. Wilding and others. bibl il Science 195: 991-4 Mr 11 '77
See also
Blood—Proteins
ALBUQUERQUE, N.Mex.
Albuquerque. R. W. Armstrong. il Trav/Holiday 149:34-9 Ja '78
Albuquerque closes water-wastewater cycle. il Am City & County 92:60 Jl '77

Police

See also
Strikes—United States—Police
ALCAN Aluminium Ltd
Alcan's latest cliff-hanger. il Forbes 120:83-4 N 1 '77
ALCAN pipeline. See Gas, Natural—Pipelines
ALCAN Pipeline Company. See Pipeline companies
ALCINDOR, Lewis. See Abdul-Jabbar, K.
ALCOHOL
Chemical relevance—a heuristic approach. A. Mancott. Chemistry 50:26 Ap; 28 My '77

Physiological effects

Alcohol: a heart disease preventive? Sci N 112: 102-3 Ag 13 '77
Alcohol tolerance in a cholinergic nerve terminal: relation to the membrane expansion-fluidization theory of ethanol action. M. Curran and P. Seeman. bibl il Science 197:910-11 Ag 26 '77
Baldness experiment; Bowery bums and baldness. G. De Leon. il por Psychol Today 11: 62-3+ O '77
Drug tolerance in biomembranes: a spin label study of the effects of ethanol. J. H. Chin and D. B. Goldstein. bibl il Science 196:684-5 My 6 '77
Happy hour lives up to its name in Boston experiment. Aging 272:5-6 Je '77
Is there a safe way to drink? excerpt from Why drinking can be good for you. M. Chafetz. Read Digest 111:100-3 Jl '77
ALCOHOL and the clergy
Alcohol addiction: priests and prelates. J. H. Fichter. America 137:258-60 O 22 '77
Spirituality, religiosity and alcoholism: clergy. J. H. Fichter. America 136:458-61 My 21 '77; Discussion. 136:513 Je 11 '77
ALCOHOL and traffic accidents. See Drinking and traffic accidents
ALCOHOL and women
Alcohol; women alcoholics. J. C. Wang. Harp Baz 110:87+ Je '77
Causes of female alcoholism. E. S. Gomberg. il Intellect 105:213 Ja '77
Shocking facts about women and alcohol. A. Rosenblum. il Good H 185:207-8 S '77
Women drinking: stigma and sickness. G. M. Anderson. America 137:434-7 D 17 '77
ALCOHOL and youth
Minnie's story; the story of a teenage alcoholic; interview, excerpt from ABC news closeup. Sr Schol 110:12-13 O 6 '77
Mounting a counterattack against child alcoholism. il U.S. News 83:33-4 Jl 11 '77
Sexes equal in alcohol, drug use. Sci N 111:277-8 Ap 30 '77
Teenage drinking; Horace Greeley High School; Chappaqua, N.Y. L. G. Holmes. il Good H 184:58+ F '77
Teenagers & alcohol; quiz. il Sr Schol 110:14-15 O 6 '77
ALCOHOL as fuel
Alcohol: a Brazilian answer to the energy crisis. A. L. Hammond. il Science 195:564-6 F 11 '77
Alcohol comes back to power your car. K. Ludvigsen. il Mech Illus 74:46+ Ja '78
Alcohol for gasoline. J. Schinto. Progressive 41: 46-9 N '77
Fill'er up—with gasohol. W. H. Spencer. il Pop Mech 147:46 Ap '77
They turn to alcohol to cut oil imports. Farm J 101:49 Ja '77
ALCOHOL, Drug Abuse, and Mental Health Administration. See United States—Alcohol, Drug Abuse, and Mental Health Administration
ALCOHOLIC beverages
Drinks: chill-chasers; Drink it hot time. A. Gold and R. Fizdale. Vogue 167:130+, 210+ D '77
Great white spirits. D. Tobias. il House & Gard 149:182+ O '77
Hot & spicy: drinks to warm a winter traveler. L. B. Downs. House B 119:110 Mr '77
Movable drinks. D. Tobias. il House & Gard 149:136+ Je '77
Nothing fancy. D. Bauer. il Esquire 87:101-3 My '77
Social Sundays; party drink recipes. A. Fraser. Mademoiselle 83:116 O '77
Summer favorites. il Redbook 149:122-3+ Jl '77
Sweet spirits. il Time 109:58 Je 6 '77
Tea teasers. H. McNulty. il House & Gard 149: 121+ F '77
Tips for mixing low-calorie drinks. D. Tobias. il House & Gard 149:114+ Jl '77
Wonderful offbeat whiskey drinks. H. McNulty. il House & Gard 149:154+ S '77
See also
Beer
Cocktails
Punch (beverage)
Wine
ALCOHOLICS
Fair play for drunks; Labor Department's proposal of affirmative action for alcoholics and drug addicts. E. Marshall. New Repub 177:7 Jl 23 '77
Impaired MDs now recognized as a peril to patients. M. Grosswirth. il Sci Digest 81:8-11+ Je '77
Menace of drunken doctors. D. Robinson. Ladies Home J 94:94+ Ap '77
Test detects liver damage in alcoholics. Sci N 112:55+ Jl 23 '77
See also
Children of alcoholics

ALCOHOLICS—*Continued*

Rehabilitation

See Alcoholism—Therapy

ALCOHOLISM
Alcohol drinking: abnormal intake caused by tetrahydropapaveroline in brain. R. D. Myers and C. L. Melchior. bibl il Science 196:554-6 Ap 29 '77
Carol Burnett & Dick Van Dyke: what alcoholism did to their lives. L. Fosburgh. pors Ladies Home J 94:34+ S '77
Chemical cause of alcoholism; THP in brain. Sci N 111:327 My 21 '77
Diazepam maintenance of alcohol preference during alcohol withdrawal. J. A. Deutsch and N. Y. Walton. bibl il Science 198:307-9 O 21 '77
How to prevent a drinking problem. J. Chan. McCalls 104:81-2 Je '77
Ratio of plasma alpha amino-*n*-butyric acid to leucine as an empirical marker of alcoholism: diagnostic value. M. Y. Morgan and others. il Science 197:1183-5 S 16 '77
Tranquilizers may sustain alcoholism. Sci N 112: 277-8 O 29 '77
See also
Alcohol—Physiological effects
Alcohol and the clergy
Alcohol and women
Alcohol and youth
Alcoholics
Liquor problem

Personal narratives

Behavior: habit-kicking; excerpt from Turnabout: help for a new life. J. Kirkpatrick. Vogue 167:186+ N '77
I only drank when I needed it. Rachel L. McCalls 104:112+ Ag '77

Therapy

Alcoholics on the school staff. J. Cramer. Educ Digest 43:38-40 N '77
Interview with an alcoholic. C. H. Folsom, Jr. il MH 61:6-9 Summ '77
Sensory deprivation helps social drinkers cut down; work of G. David Cooper and others. D. Cohen. Psychol Today 11:46+ N '77

ALCOHOLS
See also
Triacontanol

ALDEHYDE oxidase. See Oxidases

ALDER, Caine
Unknown recordings of Vladimir Horowitz. pors Hi Fi 28:69-74 Ja '78

ALDERMAN, Karen C. See Levitan, S. A. jt auth

ALDI-Benner (firm) See Supermarkets

ALDOMET. See Methyldopa

ALDOSE reductase. See Reductases

ALDRICH, George H.
Department testifies on East Timor; statement, July 19, 1977. Dept State Bull 77:324-6 S 5 '77

ALDRICH, Peter C. and Upton, King
Real estate investment for pension funds. Harvard Bus R 55:14+ My '77

ALDRICH, Robert S.
Now that's a laugh. Writers Digest 57:27-31 O '77

ALDRIDGE, John W.
State of the novel. Commentary 64:44-52 O '77

ALDRIDGE, Robert C.
B-52s, B-1, FB-111Hs, B-Xs. Nation 225:592-3 D 3 '77
First-strike capability. Nation 224:360-4 Mr 26 '77
Hideout for Trident. Progressive 41:11 F '77
Pentagon is working on it. Nation 224:711-14 Je 11 '77

ALECHINSKY, Pierre
God and the painter. il Horizon 20:56 O '77 *

ALEIXANDRE, Vicente
Spain coming into her own: Aleixandre's Nobel Prize. A. Josephs. il por New Repub 177:25-7 D 24 '77 *

ALEJANDRO, Reynaldo
Contemporary dance in the Philippines. il Dance Mag 51:99 Jl '77

ALEMAN, Harry, murder trial. See Trials (murder)

ALEUTS
Green eggs by the thousands; collecting murre eggs on Walrus Island. V. B. Scheffer. il Audubon 79:112-13 S '77

ALEXANDER, Clifford L. 1933-
Secretary of the Army Clifford Alexander . . . wants you; interview, ed by J. Landman. il por Sr Schol 110:16-17+ N 3 '77

about

Boss man of the Army. il pors Ebony 32:33-6+ Je '77 *

ALEXANDER, Cosmo John
Cosmo Alexander's travels and patrons in America. P. M. Geddy. bibl il Antiques 112:972-7 N '77 *

ALEXANDER, D. E. Stuart-. See Stuart-Alexander, D. E.

ALEXANDER, George
Our changing weather. il maps Pop Sci 211:90-4 S; 100-3+ O '77
Viking science: tantalizing Viking scientists; cautious. il Space World N-6-162:9-17 Je '77

ALEXANDER, John
Get fit, trim, slim—and grin. il Sat Eve Post 249:70-1 O '77
Margaret Sanger. il por Sat Eve Post 249:10-11+ My '77

ALEXANDER, Judd H.
Truth and consequences; address, May 17, 1977. Vital Speeches 43:565-9 Jl 1 '77

ALEXANDER, Kay
Meet the masters! il Sch Arts 76:16-17 F '77

ALEXANDER, Richard D. and Sherman, P. W.
Local mate competition and parental investment in social insects. bibl Science 196:494-500 Ap 20 '77

ALEXANDER, Tom
Deceptive allure of national planning. il Fortune 95:148-52+ Mr '77
Industry can save energy without stunting its growth. il Fortune 95:186-9+ My '77
Why the breeder reactor is inevitable. il Fortune 96:122-8+ S '77

ALEXANDER CITY, Ala.

Crime

See Crime and criminals—Alabama

ALEXANDER Hamilton (steamboat) See Steamships and steamboats

ALEXANDRIA, Va.

Historic houses, sites, etc.

See Historic houses, sites, etc.—Virginia

ALEXEEV, Dmitri
Brahms: Three intermezzi. D. M. Garvelmann. il por Am Rec G 40:24-6 S '77 *

ALFA Romeo (automobile) See Automobiles, Foreign

ALFALFA
Alfalfa yields a mystery chemical that spurs plant growth, even in the dark; triacontanol. E. Driscoll. il por Horticulture 55:8+ Ag '77
Can we recover more protein from alfalfa? N. Reeder. il Farm J 101:F1 N '77
Treat alfalfa as a cash crop. D. Allen. Suc Farm 75:no3 F40 F '77
Triacontanol: a new naturally occurring plant growth regulator. S. K. Ries and others. bibl il Science 195:1339-41 Mr 25 '77

Disease and pest resistance

New alfalfa variety resists blue aphid. C. Bickers. Farm J 100:K4 D '76

Marketing

Strong market for dehy alfalfa will continue. Farm J 101:H2 My '77

Seeding

Direct seeding passes the time test. R. Brunoehler. il Farm J 101:E1 mid-Mr '77

ALFORD, Albert L.
Education amendments of 1976. Am Educ 13: 6-11 Ja '77

ALFRED I. duPont trust. See Trusts and trustees

ALFVEN, Kerstin
Conversation. il Bull Atom Sci 33:43-4 My '77

ALGAE
Gas vacuoles of blue-green algae. A. E. Walsby. il Sci Am 237:90-7 bibl(p 140) Ag '77
Photosynthetic unit of hydrogen evolution; chlorella vulgaris. E. Greenbaum. bibl il Science 196:879-80 My 20 '77
See also
Dinoflagellates
Euglena
Seaweed
Water bloom

ALGAE, Fossil
Figtree fossils: oldest algae yet. il Sci N 112: 245 O 15 '77

ALGAL bloom. See Water bloom

ALGARIN, Miguel
(tr) See Neruda, P. So is my life

ALGER, Horatio, 1832-1899
Novels that boys of a century ago couldn't put down. B. Blackbeard. il por Smithsonian 8:122-4+ bibl(p 162) N '77 *

ALGERIA
See also
Cities and towns—Algeria
Geology—Algeria
Investments, Foreign—Algeria
Investments, German—Algeria

Commerce

France

See France—Commerce—Algeria

Foreign relations

Morocco

U.S. walks a tightrope in the Sahara. S. W. Sanders. il Bus W p47 Ja 16 '78

ALGONQUIAN Indians
See also
Abnaki Indians
Cree Indians

ALGONQUIN Hotel. See New York (city)—Hotels, restaurants, etc.

ALGONQUIN Round Table. See Literary clubs and societies

ALGORITHMS
Algorithms. D. E. Knuth. il Sci Am 236:63-6+ bibl(p 148) Ap '77
Efficiency of algorithms. H. R. Lewis and C. H. Papadimitriou. il map Sci Am 238:96-109 bibl(p 138+) Ja '78

ALI, Belinda. See Ali, K.

ALI, Khalilah
Khalilah Ali: karate disciplines her new life. R. Kisner. il por Ebony 32:78-80+ S '77 *

ALI, Muhammad
These sporting poets; Marianne Moore's meeting with Muhammad Ali; interview, ed by G. Plimpton. il pors Harpers 254:76-9+ My '77
about
Hyperbole's child. A. B. Giamatti. Harpers 225:117-18+ D '77 *
I am the greatest! condensation. R. Lipsyte. il pors Read Digest 110:211-18+ Mr '77 *
Once more to the well. P. Putnam. il pors Sports Illus 47:20-3 O 10 '77 *
Who is Veronica Porche? S. D. Lewis. il pors Ebony 32:60-2+ Jl '77 *
You gotta have heart. P. Bonventre. il pors Newsweek 90:77 O 10 '77 *

ALI, Veronica (Porche)
Who is Veronica Porche? S. D. Lewis. il pors Ebony 32:60-2+ Jl '77 *

ALICE in Wonderland; dramatization. See Hill, R.

ALIEN and Sedition Laws, 1798
Ragged Mat, the Democrat; case of M. Lyon. L. Gragg. il Am Hist Illus 12:20-5 My '77

ALIEN animals. See Animal introduction

ALIEN labor
Apple picker blues; question of importing Jamaican pickers. D. McGhee. New Repub 177: 15-16 O 29 '77
As Jamaican as apple pie; apple harvest workers in Virginia. J. Egerton. Progressive 41:37-40 D '77
Doubly difficult apple to pluck; foreign pickers. il Time 110:28 N 7 '77
Illegal aliens: refugees from hunger. G. M. Anderson. America 136:68-72 Ja 29 '77
Immigrants, employers, and exclusion. B. W. Parlin. Society 14:23-6 S '77
Labor functions of illegal aliens. A. Portes. bibl il Society 14:31-7 S '77
North of the border—who needs whom? J. Flanigan. il Forbes 119:37-41 Ap 15 '77
Rumblings in the volcano. New Repub 177:2+ Jl 30 '77
Undocumented worker; address, May 13, 1977. R. Marshall. Vital Speeches 43:551-3 Jl 1 '77
What illegal aliens cost the economy. il Bus W p86-8 Je 13 '77

Germany, West

They wish us to hell. il Time 110:58 O 10 '77

ALIENATION (social psychology)
Contemporary look at Kafka: illustrations for four stories of alienation. A. Cober. il Horizon 20:74-7 D '77

ALIENS
Alienating the aliens; plan for illegal immigrants. il Time 110:26 S 26 '77
Amnesty for aliens? R. Steele and E. Clift. il Newsweek 90:16+ Jl 4 '77
Border crisis: illegal aliens out of control. O. Kelly. il U.S. News 82:33-8+ Ap 25 '77
Camp of the saints. Nat R 29:1096 S 30 '77
Carter's plan for illegal aliens: meaning for business, workers, consumers. il U.S. News 83:19-20 Ag 15 '77
Coping with illegals. M. Stone. U.S. News 82: 80 My 30 '77
Department testifies on undocumented aliens; statement, September 14, 1977. R. G. Arellano. Dept State Bull 77:592-4 O 31 '77
Earnings gap. C. McWilliams. Nation 224:356 Mr 26 '77
Foreign nationals and American law. D. E. La Voy. bibl Society 15:58-64 N '77
Generous, fair and flexible immigration. America 136:409 My 7 '77
Getting their slice of paradise. il Time 109: 26-7+ My 2 '77
Guarding the border; sham marriages with illegal aliens. New Repub 176:2+ Mr 12 '77
Manzo raid: sweeping up the aliens. M. Day. Nation 224:146-8 F 5 '77
My fake husband: notes on a very strange marriage. Ms 5:60-1+ Mr '77
New curbs on illegal aliens? G. R. Rosen. il por Duns R 110:49 Jl '77
Problem at home and abroad; illegal aliens in the United States and race problems in South Africa. Sat Eve Post 249:32 S '77
Recent immigration and current data collection. R. Warren. bibl il M Labor R 100:36-41 O '77
Special report; illegal Mexican immigrants in the United States. il map U.S. News 83:27-34 Jl 4 '77
TRB from Washington; reports of the Domestic Council Committee on Illegal Aliens. New Repub 176:2+ F 26 '77
This month's feature: controversy in Congress over proposed amnesty for illegal aliens. Cong Digest 56:225-56 O '77
Undocumented aliens; remarks and message to Congress, August 4, 1977. J. Carter. Dept State Bull 77:315-20 S 5 '77
U.S.-Mexican border problems. A. Paredes and others. Intellect 106:98 S '77
Wetback scapegoats; indictment of workers at the Manzo Area Council. Nation 224:357 Mr 26 '77
See also
Alien labor
Citizenship
Self determination, National

ALIGNMENT of automobile wheels. See Automobiles—Wheels

ALIMONY
Alimony: the short goodbye. R. Williams. il por Psychol Today 11:70-2+ Jl '77

ALIOTO, Joe
Talking tuna. R. Vaughan. il por Motor B & S 139:66-9+ Je '77 *

ALISKY, Marvin
Mexico's population pressures. bibl f Cur Hist 72:106-10+ Mr '77

ALKALI metals
Anions of the alkali metals. J. L. Dye. il Sci Am 237:92-6+ bibl(p 154) Jl '77

ALKALOIDS
Pyrrolizidine alkaloids: their occurence in honey from tansy ragwort (senecio jacobaea L.) M. L. Deinzer and others. bibl il Science 195: 497-9 F 4 '77
See also
Veatchine

ALKIRE, Leland G. Jr
Sand dunes, sagebrush. . .and sails? Yachting 141:199-203 My '77

ALKYD paint. See Paint

ALKYLATION
Bioactivation as a model for drug design bioreductive alkylation. H. W. Moore. bibl il Science 197:527-32 Ag 5 '77

ALL Africa Conference of Churches. See Religious conferences—Africa

ALL-America cities
All-American City awards reflect citizen involvement and interest. il Am City & County 92:30+ S '77

ALL-America Rose Selections. See Plants—All-America Selections

ALL-America Skeet Teams. See Trap shooting

ALL-American football players. See Football players

ALL-England Lawn Tennis Group Ltd. See Sports clubs

ALL-fabric bleaches. See Bleaching materials

ALL for love: drama. See Dryden, J.

ALL-India Congress of Mission and Evangelization. See Religious conferences—India

ALL terrain vehicles. See Motor vehicles, All terrain

ALL year schools. See School year

ALLAN, Mea
Overlooked link: Darwin and his flowers; excerpt from Darwin and his flowers. il por Horticulture 55:12-21 O '77

ALLARD, William Albert
Chief Joseph. il por map Nat Geog 151:408-34 Mr '77

ALLEGHANY Corporation-Investors Diversified Services, Inc merger. See Corporations—Acquisitions and mergers

ALLEGHENY Airlines
I'm Allegheny—fly me. il Forbes 119:63 Mr 1 '77
New pacts reflect commuter success. L. Doty. Aviation W 106:38 Ap 4 '77

ALLEGHENY County, Pa.
Steel grid bridge deck outlives concrete. il Am City & County 92:45 Ja '77

Manpower Department

Offside in Pittsburgh? investigation of football players for possible involvement in fraud. S. Fraker and S. Lesher. pors Newsweek 89:40 My 9 '77

ALLEGHENY Ludlum Industries, Inc
Allegheny Ludlum: breaking the rules to grow. por Bus W p74+ Jl 18 '77

ALLEGHENY Ludlum Industries, Inc-Chemetron Corporation merger. See Corporations—Acquisitions and mergers

ALLEGHENY Ludlum Industries, Inc-Wilkinson Match, Ltd merger. See Corporations—Acquisitions and mergers—International aspects

ALLEGHENY Portage Railroad National Historic Site. See Historic houses, sites, etc.—Pennsylvania

ALLEGORIES
See also
Parables
ALLELOMORPHISM
Marek's disease: effects of B histocompatibility alloalleles in resistant and susceptible chicken lines. W. E. Briles and others. bibl il Science 195:193-5 Ja 14 '77
ALLEMAN, Richard
Riviera in our own backyard. map Vogue 167: 210+ O '77
San Diego—the city that's still too good to be true. il Vogue 167:236+ N '77
ALLEN, Barbara
On-the-run make-up and fashion plans. il pors Harp Baz 110:100-5 Mr '77 *
ALLEN, Bryan
I pedaled the mile to aviation's big prize; ed. by J. Joseph. il por Pop Mech 148:100-2+ D '77
about
Dream of wings—via feet. il Sci N 112:149 S 3 '77 *
ALLEN, David A.
Astronomer's impressions of ancient Egypt. il map Sky & Tel 54:15-19 Jl '77
ALLEN, David G. and others
Aequorin luminescence: relation of light emission to calcium concentration—a calcium-independent component. bibl il Science 195:996-8 Mr 11 '77
ALLEN, Dick
To the wall. Poetry 130:342-52 S '77
ALLEN, Donna
Tell it to Allen. K. Barker. por Ms 65:20-1 F '77 *
ALLEN, Douglas
Douglas Allen: echoes of the Brandywine. B. Silverstein. il por Am Artist 41:44-9+ N '77 *
ALLEN, Durward L.
Proposal: Great Plains National Park; adaptation of address, November, 1976. il Nat Parks & Con Mag 51:4-9 Ag '77; Same with title Great Plains National Park. Current 197:13-17 N '77
ALLEN, Elizabeth
Understanding heart; story. Good H 184:136-7 My '77
ALLEN, Ethan, 1738-1789
Ethan Allen and the Green Mountain Boys. D. B. Sabine. il pors Am Hist Illus 11:8-15 Ja '77 *
ALLEN, Fred T.
Winning and holding employee loyality; interview. pors Nations Bus 65:40-2+ Ap '77
ALLEN, Garland E.
Lorenz observed. il Natur Hist 86:78-82+ Je '77
ALLEN, Irving
Mighty monolith? bibl Society 15:11+ N '77
ALLEN, James Browning
Excerpts from debate on U.S. African policy, June 25, 1976. Cong Digest 56:13+ Ja '77
ALLEN, James Sloan
Great treasury of western thought. Sat R 4:26 S 3 '77
ALLEN, Jennifer
Harriet Houdini. Seventeen 36:60+ My '77
On female macho. Mademoiselle 83:88+ N '77
ALLEN, John
Education of John Allen; excerpt from Assault with a deadly weapon: the autobiography of a street criminal, ed by P. Heymann and D. Kelly; with comments by O. Coombs. il Psychol Today 11:96-7+ O '77
ALLEN, John Milton
I killed your cat. Read Digest 110:69-70 Ap '77
Reaching for the Reader's digest. Writer 90: 26-8+ Ap '77
ALLEN, Linda
Olympic hopeful pays dues. il pors Ebony 32:44-5+ Je '77 *
ALLEN, Mel
Teen taxidermist. il por Seventeen 36:19+ Ag '77
(ed) See King, S. Witches and aspirin
ALLEN, Ray
Too close for comfort. D. Wallace. il pors Hot Rod 30:22-3 D '77 *
ALLEN, Robert
Margin of life. il Int Wildlife 7:20-9 Mr '77
ALLEN, Robert Thomas
Once upon a dime. Read Digest 110:29-33+ Mr '77
ALLEN, Sally J. and Foreman, D. I.
Can values be evaluated? Todays Educ 66:66-7 Ja '77
ALLEN, Tom
Tom Allen. N. Meglin. il por Am Artist 41:52-5 Jl '77 *
ALLEN, W. H, Publishers Inc-Hawthorn Books, Inc merger. See Publishers and publishing—Acquisitions and mergers
ALLEN, William McPherson
Allen. P. Garrison. por Flying 101:253 S '77 *
ALLEN, Woody
Condemned. New Yorker 53:57-9 N 21 '77
Kugelmass episode. il New Yorker 53:34-9 My 2 '77
Lunatic's tale. New Repub 176:17-19 Ap 23 '77
UFO menace. New Yorker 53:31-3 Je 13 '77
about
Woody Allen: schlemiel as sex maniac. R. Wetzsteon. il pors Ms 6:14-15 N '77 *
Woody Allen, theologian. J. Dart. bibl il por Chr Cent 94:585-9 Je 22 '77 *
Woody Allen wipes the smile off his face. F. Rich. por Esquire 87:72-6+ My '77 *
ALLENDE, Laura
Letter from a Chilean exile. Chr Cent 94:79-80 F 2 '77
ALLERGIC encephalitis, Experimental. See Immunologic diseases
ALLERGY
Allergic reaction to insect sting. A. Frank and S. Frank. Mademoiselle 83:134 S '77
Allergy in infancy: early care can prevent future problems. M. A. Wessel. il Parents Mag 52:18 D '77
Can't stop sneezing? H. Alpert. il Ret Liv 17: 24-6+ Jl '77
Coping with allergies. J. Rodgers. Ladies Home J 94:44+ O '77
Cosmetics; what you should know to use them safely. L. Lambert. Bet Hom & Gard 55: 26+ Ap '77
Do-it-yourself guide for allergy sufferers. M. P. Scott. Bet Hom & Gard 55:46+ Ag '77
Fighting hives; reports given at allergists conference in New York City. M. Clark and D. Shapiro. il Newsweek 89:65-6 Ap 11 '77
Getting your baby off to a good start. J. Chan. McCalls 105:83 N '77
What to do about seasonal allergies; discomfort for children. P. S. Papageorgiou. por Intellect 106:12-13 Jl '77
See also
Food allergy
Hay fever
Poison ivy
ALLFORD, Ernest E.
Underbench tool center. il Mech Illus 73:142+ My '77
ALLIANCE Against Sexual Coercion. See Sex in business
ALLIANCE for Arts Education
On education; Arts Education Advocacy project. C. B. Fowler. Hi Fi 27:MA9+ F '77
ALLIANCE for Displaced Homemakers. See Vocational guidance
ALLIANCES
See also
Nato
ALLIED Chemical Corporation
Risk rewarded. il por Forbes 119:101-2 Mr 15 '77
ALLIED intervention, 1918-1920. See Russia—History—Allied intervention, 1918-1920
ALLIED Military Currency. See World War, 1939-1945—Military currency
ALLIGATOR poaching. See Poaching
ALLIGATORS
Alligator protections loosened. C. Holden. Science 195:561 F 11 '77
Alligator revealed. L. D. Garrick and J. W. Lang. il Natur Hist 86:54-61 bibl(p92-3) Je '77
Return of 'gators—a double-edged triumph. U.S. News 83:30 D 19 '77
See also
Crocodiles
ALLILUEVA, Svetlana. See Stalina, S. I.
ALLISON, Bobby
Hot blood down in Dixie; excerpts from King Richard, ed by B. Libby. il pors Sports Illus 46:64-6 F 21 '77
ALLISON, John
Gardening; poem. Esquire 88:34 N '77
Night animal; poem. Poetry 131:88-9 N '77
ALLIUMS
Here are onions to appreciate but not bite into. il Sunset 159:244-5 N '77
ALLMAN, Gregg
Gregg Allman: the fink has soul. L. Baines. por Hi Fi 27:110 Ag '77 *
ALLMAN, T. D.
America's innocence abroad. il Harpers 255:57-60+ N '77
Britain's inexhaustible complacence. Harpers 254:18+ My '77
Calcutta's bounty. Harpers 255:12-16 S '77
Influence game. New Repub 176:25-7 Mr 26 '77
Rebirth of Eldridge Cleaver. il pors N Y Times Mag p 10-11+ Ja 16 '77
San Francisco blues. New Repub 175:11-13 D 4 '76; 176:39-40 Ja 29 '77
Why we can't stay married. il Am Home 80: 66+ F '77
ALLON, Yigal
Secretary Vance meets at London with Israeli foreign minister; remarks, May 11, 1977. Dept State Bull 76:607-9 Je 6 '77
ALLOWANCES, Childrens. See Childrens allowances

ALLOWAY, Lawrence
Art. See occasional issues of Nation
Art books 1977. Nation 225:661-5 D 17 '77
Artist count: in praise of plenty. bibl il Art in Am 65:105-9 S '77
ALLOYS
Bell Labs reports manmade single-crystal monolayer alloys. G. B. Lubkin. il Phys Today 30:17-18 F '77
Interstitial compounds; heat resistant refractory metals; adaptation of address, March 1976. L. H. Bennett and others. bibl il Phys Today 30:34-6+ S '77
ALLSTATE Insurance Company
Meanwhile. . .back at Allstate. il Forbes 119:29 Je 15 '77
Tale of two giants. Consumer Rep 42:384 Jl '77
ALMANACS
Almanackery. L. Taylor. Writers Digest 57:39 My '77
Wonderful world of women; excerpt from Good housekeeping woman's almanac. il Good H 185:248-9 O '77
ALMAVIVA, Count (operatic character) See Characters in opera
ALMEIDA, Arminda de. See Villa-Lobos, A.
ALMLI, W. Thomas
Low-cost bookshelves you can build in a hurry. il Pop Mech 149:88-9 Ja '78
ALMON, Vera
Sexual liberation, V.D. and our children. America 137:169-72 S 24 '77
ALMOND, Ann Merriol
One-day hospital stay for children. Parents Mag 53:41+ Ja '78
ALMOND, Gabriel A.
Redistribution of wealth means bloody politics; excerpts from address. por Intellect 105:205-6 Ja '77
ALMOST perfect person; drama. See Ross, J.
ALOFF, Mindy
Portland, Oregon: braving the new world. Dance Mag 51:124-5 My '77
ALONSO, Alicia
Glimpses of Alonso; interview, ed by T. Tobias. il pors Dance Mag 52:38-41 Ja '78
ALONSO Castro Dance Theatre. See Dance companies
ALONSO PIÑEIRO, Armando
When Argentina conquered California. il por Américas 29:34-7 Je '77
ALPER, Philip R.
Beauty/New focus. . .body. il Vogue 167:210-11 Mr '77 *
ALPEROVITZ, Gar, and Faux, Jeff
Building a democratic economy. Progressive 41:15-19 Jl '77; Same with title Changing American economy. Current 195:18-27 S '77
ALPERT, Helen
Can't stop sneezing? il Ret Liv 17:24-6+ Jl '77
Coping with the credit crunch. il Ret Liv 17:22-4+ F '77
Fishing for compliments . . . the frozen way. il Ret Liv 17:46-8 Ap '77
What you eat today can decide your health tomorrow. il Ret Liv 17:26-30 S '77
Why you need a will. il Ret Liv 17:26-9 Mr '77
Writing for the aged: new vistas for the old. Writers Digest 57:15+ Mr '77
—and Hillman, B. J.
Golden oldies. il Writers Digest 57:16-17 Mr '77
—and Miller, Steven
50 Christmas gifts for under $10. il Ret Liv 17:38-41 N '77
—See Hemming, R. jt auth
ALPERT, Herb
Independent that could: A&M records. T. Everett. il pors Hi Fi 27:132-4 Ap '77 *
ALPERT, Jonathan L.
Q&A about the law (cont) por Ret Liv 17:56-7 F; 18 D '77
ALPERT, Richard. See Ram Dass
ALPINE climbing. See Mountaineering
ALPINE County, Calif.
Four high passes in Alpine County. il map Sunset 159:74-7 S '77
ALPINE Lakes Wilderness. See Wilderness areas —Washington (state)
ALPS
Our far-flung correspondents. J. Bernstein. New Yorker 53:106-20 S 26 '77
ALTAI Mountains

Antiquities

Pazyrk; Altaian tombs excavated. M. P. Zavitukhina. il UNESCO Courier 29:30-3+ D '76
ALTAZIMUTH telescopes. See Telescopes
ALTER, Robert
New York and/or Jerusalem. Commentary 64:50-6 Ag '77
Poet of exile. Commentary 63:49-55 F '77
ALTERNATIVE (periodical)
God and man in Bloomington. il por Time 109:93-4 Mr 7 '77
ALTERNATIVE lifestyles. See Counterculture
ALTERNATIVE schools. See Schools, Experimental

ALTITUDE, Influence of
Going up: heights disease. M. Weber. Vogue 167:174 Mr '77
ALTMAN, Robert
Altman returns to the labyrinth. J. Crist. il Sat R 4:51-2 Ap 16 '77 *
Altman's Three women. K. Turan. Progressive 41:37-8 Jl 77 *
Master of images. L. Quart. Intellect 106:159 O '77 *
ALTRUISM
Altruism versus New York City; address, May 17, 1977. M. N. Buechner. Vital Speeches 43:629-34 Ag 1 '77
Child altruism: saving Johnny not mommy. Sci N 112:358-9 N 26 '77
Enormous party. L. Thomas. il House & Gard 149:86-9+ D '77
See also
Helping behavior
ALTSCHUL, Siri von Reis
Exploring the herbarium; with biographical sketch. il Sci Am 236:15+, 96-104 bibl(146+) My '77
ALTSCHULER, H. H. See Charp, S. jt auth
ALUMINA
Lithium-sodium beta alumina: first of a family of co-ionic conductors? W. L. Roth and G. C. Farrington. bibl il Science 196:1332-4 Je 17 '77
ALUMINUM

Prices

Case for another aluminum price rise; Kaiser Aluminum & Chemical Corp. announcement. il Bus W p25-6 Je 27 '77
ALUMINUM boats. See Boats—Materials
ALUMINUM Company of America
Aluminum accords comparable to steel settlement. L. Bornstein and others. M Labor R 100:52-3 Ag '77
Doing it by the numbers. por Forbes 119:71 F 15 '77
ALUMINUM Company of Canada. See Alcan Aluminium Ltd
ALUMINUM in automobiles. See Automobiles—Materials
ALUMINUM in the body
Aluminum absorption and distribution: effect of parathyroid hormone. G. H. Mayor and others. bibl il Science 197:1187-9 S 16 '77
ALUMINIUM industry
See also
Collective labor agreements—Aluminum industry

Fuel requirements

Belgium hits Badger for shutting an office. Bus W p30+ Mr 28 '77

International aspects

Cartel that never was; effect of International Bauxite Association on aluminum industry. il Forbes 119:30-2 Mr 1 '77

Canada

See also
Alcan Aluminium Ltd

United States

Paradise lost; effect of Bonneville Power Administration's forthcoming power shortage on the aluminum industry. il Forbes 119:32 F 1 '77
See also
Aluminum Company of America
Kaiser Aluminum and Chemical Corporation
Reynolds Metal Company
ALUMINUM light poles. See Street lighting fixtures
ALUMINUM siding. See Siding (building)
ALUMNI, College. See College graduates
ALVAREZ, Luis Echeverría-. See Echeverría Alvarez, L.
ALVIN Ailey American Dance Theater
Alvin Ailey: Blood memories; December season at the New York City Center. J. Maskey. il Hi Fi 27:MA11 Mr '77
Art of ballezz; City Center performances May 4-22. S. Banes. il Dance Mag 51:42-4 S '77
Gumdrops; December presentations. R. Baker. il Dance Mag 51:20-2+ F '77
ALWIN Nikolais Dance Theatre
Dance; troupes of Alwin Nikolais and Murray Louis at the Beacon Theater. J. Maskey. il Hi Fi 27:MA12-13 Je '77
Murray and Nik; peformances at New York's Beacon Theater. H. Saal. il Newsweek 89:43 F 21 '77
Musical theatre. D. Diether. il Am Rec G 40:52-3 N '76
Nik and Murray at the Beacon. L. Small. il Dance Mag 51:22-3+ My '77
Nik: movement, shape, sound, and color. W. Terry. il Sat R 4:37-8 F 19 '77
ALWYN, William
All about Alwyn. R. Tiedman. il por Am Rec G 40:4+ S '77

ALYESKA Pipeline Service Company. See Pipeline companies
ALYWARD, David
200-mile limit: showdown at sea. S. Kimber. il pors Int Wildlife 7:41-5 S '77 *
ALZADO, Lyle
No end with this end. S. Pileggi. il pors Sports Illus 47:32-4+ D 12 '77 *
ALZHEIMER'S disease. See Brain—Diseases
AMADO, Jorge
Where gods and men have mingled. il UNESCO Courier 30:18-19 Ag '77
AMALGAMATED Clothing and Textile Workers Union
Labor victory; unionizing of J. P. Stevens and Co. F. Gaillard. Progressive 41:8 N '77
New tactics in the textile war. D. Freedman. il Nation 225:618-21 D 10 '77
Organizing J. P. Stevens. F. Gaillard. Progressive 41:37 F '77
Recidivist; question of unionization at J. P. Stevens. New Repub 177:2+ S 17 '77
Stevens digs its heels in deeper; boycott to force unionization. il Bus W p29 Mr 14 '77
Textile workers fight on: the battle against J.P. Stevens. A. Fishel. Ms 6:22 D '77
Touch of civil rights fervor; actions taken against J. P. Stevens and Co. il Time 109:44 Mr 14 '77
Trouble looming; J.P. Stevens' anti-union strategy. P. D. Wellstone. New Repub 176:14-15 Mr 12 '77
U.S. injunction against Stevens? il Time 110:76 D 12 '77
When a union goes all out in a boycott drive—. il U.S. News 82:71-2 Je 20 '77
AMALGAMATED Clothing Workers of America—Textile Workers Union of America merger. See Trade unions—Acquisitions and mergers
AMALGAMATED Meat Cutters and Butcher Workmen of North America
She's a fighter on three fronts; A. Wyatt. por Ebony 32:70 Ag '77
AMALRIK, Andrei Alekseevich
Future of the Soviet Union. Intellect 106:3+ Jl '77
AMAN, Reinhold
Insult artistry. Time 111:64-5 Ja 9 '78 *
AMANA Refrigeration, Inc. See Household appliances industry
AMAR, Wesley F.
My son, the musical administrator. Clearing H 51:142 N '77
AMARANTHS
Amaranth: a comeback for the food of the Aztecs? J. L. Marx. Science 198:40 O 7 '77
Amaranth secrets of the Aztecs. D. Early. il Org Gard & Farm 24:69-73 D '77
Chinese spinach: hot-weather greens that won't quit. J. Ruttle. il Org Gard & Farm 24:153-5 Ap '77
Closer look at amaranth. J. C. McCullagh. Org Gard & Farm 24:57-8 O '77
AMARILLO, Tex.
Do it yourself: Texas gardeners grow bumper crop; Amarillo Senior Citizens Assn. il Aging 274:15 Ag '77
Gazetteer. il Ret Liv 17:39+ S '77
AMARYLLIS
Classic amaryllis. House & Gard 149:92+ O '77
How to grow an amaryllis. Bet Hom & Gard 55:253 N '77
See also
Kafir lilies
AMATEUR architecture. See Architecture, Amateur
AMATEUR art. See Art, Amateur
AMATEUR astronomers. See Astronomers, Amateur
AMATEUR Astronomers Association (New York) See Astronomical societies
AMATEUR motion pictures. See Motion pictures, Amateur
AMATEUR photographers. See Photographers
AMATEUR radio operators. See Radio operators
AMATEURISM (sports)
See also
Government investigations—Amateurism (sports)
AMAX Inc
Moly's baby-sitter takes on the whole family. por Fortune 95:33+ Je '77
AMAYA, Mario
Dante Gabriel Rossetti and the double work of art. il Art in Am 65:90-3 Mr '77
AMAZON Jungle. See Rain forests
AMAZON River
Timely reprieve or a death sentence for the Amazon. R. Campbell. il Smithsonian 8:100-11 bibl(p 160-1) O '77
AMAZON River Region
See also
Petroleum—Amazon River Region
AMAZON Valley
Remote sensing: Brazil explores its Amazon wilderness; Project Radam. A. L. Hammond. il map Science 196:513-15 Ap 29 '77
See also
Botany—Amazon Valley

AMBACH, Gordon M.
Changing stages of learning; address, October 26, 1977. Vital Speeches 44:150-3 D 15 '77
about
Ambach aids librarians; state mandate restored. por SLJ 24:10 D '77 *
AMBASSADORS
Ambassadors are no joke. Nation 224:613 My 21 '77
Courtesy calls; briefings of American ambassadors by the Business Council for International Understanding. Nation 224:709 Je 11 '77
New ambassadors. il pors Newsweek 90:69-70 N 21 '77
Son-in-law also rises; appointment of P. Jay as Britain's ambassador to Washington. K. Willenson and M. MacPherson. il por Newsweek 89:30 My 23 '77
See also
Diplomatic privileges and immunities
United Nations—Delegates
United States—Diplomatic and Consular Service
United States—Presidential Advisory Board on Ambassadorial Appointments
also names of ambassadors, e.g. K. Brewster
AMBER
Golden window on the past. P. A. Zahl. il Nat Geog 152:422-35 S '77
AMBERG, John W.
Among the pork and beans. il Engl J 66:37-40 D '77
AMBOSELI National Park. See National parks and reserves—Kenya
AMBROGGI, Robert P.
Underground reservoirs to control the water cycle; with biographical sketch. il map Sci Am 236:15, 21-7 My '77
AMBROTYPES
Collectors beware! Which of these ambrotypes are fake? R. Busch. il Pop Phot 80:110-11+ My '77
AMBULANCE service
Nursing an ambulance and a county; San Jacinto County, Tex. D. Lampe. il pors Fam Health 9:28-30 Je '77
Sea rescue; work of Connecticut's Star of Life I. S. Mennear-Dubas. il Fam Health 9:40-3 Ag '77
AMBULANCES
Ambulances and rescue vehicles. il Am City & County 92:95-8 O '77
New shape for ambulances. il Mech Illus 73:76 Mr '77
AMCENA Corporation-Miller-Wohl Company merger. See Chain stores—Acquisitions and mergers
AMDAHL, Gene Myron
Gene Amdahl takes aim at I.B.M. B. Uttal. il por Fortune 96:106-10+ S '77 *
AMDAHL Corporation. See Computer industry
AMDUR, Harry
Such good friends. R. Wolters. Writers Digest 57:16+ D '77 *
AMEBAS
Pathogenic amoebas from brackish and ocean sediments, with a description of acanthamoeba hatchetti, n. sp. T. K. Sawyer and others. bibl il Science 196:1324-5 Je 17 '77
AMEBIC meningoencephalitis. See Encephalitis
AMEN, Carol
Rewards of nostalgia. Writer 91:29-31 Ja '78
AMEND, Paul
Broker profile; interview. por Motor B & S 140:176 S '77
AMENDMENTS to the Constitution. See United States—Constitution—Amendments
AMENTA, Allan
Audiovisual writing: a world beyond words. Writers Digest 57:19-25 Je '77
AMERADA Hess Corporation
Playing for high stakes in the Virgin Islands. T. Szulc. il Forbes 120:53-5 Ag 1 '77
AMERICA
Our America; special section, ed by A. J. Lowe. il maps Américas 29:16-49 N '77

Antiquities

See also
Paleo-Indians

Commerce

Reach for the New World. M. Peterson. il Nat Geog 152:724-67, supp(folded map) D '77

Discovery and exploration

St Brendan's fantastic voyage; re-enactment of voyage described in Navigatio Sancti Brendani. G. Schomp. il map Am Hist Illus 12:22-7 Ap '77
Terror of the wilderness; spread of Western civilization; excerpt from The cost of living. F. Turner. il Am Heritage 28:58-65 F '77
Who really discovered America? ideas of B. Fell. T. Fleming. il Read Digest 110:69-73 F '77
AMERICA (periodical)
Of many things. J. O'Hare. America 136:inside cover Je 25 '77

AMERICAN Academy and Institute of Arts and Letters
Awards, and still more awards. J. B. Breslin. America 136:507 Je 4 '77
See also
National Book Awards

AMERICAN Academy of Family Physicians
Convention. J. Lelyveld. il N Y Times Mag p 110 O 30 '77

AMERICAN Academy of Political and Social Science
Bicentennial conference on the United States Constitution: the shaping of public policy—issues and questions for discussion; ed by E. B. Staats. Ann Am Acad 432:121-31 Jl '77

AMERICAN Agri-Women (organization) See Agricultural societies

AMERICAN Airlines
American fare bid draws fire. L. Doty. Aviation W 106:24 F 21 '77
Pan Am, American win popularity poll. L. Doty. Aviation W 107:38 S 19 '77
Two carriers plan automatic data link. P. J. Klass. il Aviation W 106:36+ My 23 '77

AMERICAN Alliance for Health, Physical Education and Recreation. See Physical education and training

AMERICAN antelope hunting. See Pronghorn hunting

AMERICAN antelopes. See Pronghorns

AMERICAN Antiquarian Society, Worcester, Mass.
American Antiquarian Society show. S. B. Sherrill. il Antiques 111:662+ Ap '77

AMERICAN architecture. See Architecture, American

AMERICAN art. See Art, American

AMERICAN Art-Union. See Art clubs and societies

AMERICAN artist (periodical)
American artist at forty; symposium. il Am Artist 4119-38 F '77
Cover. M. Schiller. Am Artist 41:6+ Ja '77; Correction. 41:5 Mr '77

AMERICAN artists. See Artists, American

AMERICAN Association for the Advancement of Science
AAAS annual elections. il Science 197:859-82 Ag 26 '77
AAAS annual elections: preliminary announcement. Science 196:1078-81 Je 3 '77
AAAS news. See occasional issues of Science
AAAS officers, staff, committees, and representatives for 1977. Science 196:345-9 Ap 15 '77
Amendments to the AAAS constitution and bylaws: 1977 election results. Science 198:916-17 D 2 '77
Dispute over Jensen election as fellow flares in council. P. M. Boffey. Science 195:965 Mr 11 '77
Handicapped resource group members work for barrier elimination. il Science 195:475-6 F 4 '77
Human rights; Subcommittee on Infringements of Scientific Freedom in Foreign Countries. J. Edsall and J. Primack. Science 195:245-6 Ja 21 '77
Jensen's AAAS fellowship; letters. Science 196: 831-2+ My 20 '77
New directions for AAAS. W. D. Carey. Science 195:539 F 11 '77
1976 report to the Association. W. D. Carey. il Science 196:337-41 Ap 15 '77
Science digest interviews new AAAS president; ed by W. K. Stuckey. E. M. Daddario. por Sci Digest 81:back cover, 80 Mr '77

Meetings

AAAS annual meeting, Washington; meeting program. il Science 198:910-15, 1137-41, 1240-5 D 2, D 16-23 '77
AAAS Council meeting, 1977. C. Borras. Science 196:342-4 Ap 15 '77
AAAS meeting: drought was the topic of the week. P. M. Boffey. Science 195:964+ Mr 11 '77
Science and technology: new tools, new dimensions; annual meeting, Washington, 12-17 February 1978; with preliminary program. A. Herschman. il map Science 198:487-95 N 4 '77
Science at the AAAS. Sci N 111:152 Mr 5 '77
Sociobiology symposium highlights AAAS Pacific Division annual meeting. Science 197:547-9 Ag 5 '77

AMERICAN Association for the Advancement of the Humanities
Humanists on the move. C. Holden. Science 198: 902 D 2 '77

AMERICAN Association of Library Schools. See Association of American Library Schools

AMERICAN Association of Physics Teachers
APS—AAPT meet in Chicago. B. C. Carr. il Phys Today 30:23-6 Ja '77

AMERICAN Association of School Librarians. See American Library Association—American Association of School Librarians

AMERICAN Association of Variable Star Observers
Variable Star Observers meet on Nantucket. il Sky & Tel 54:484-5 D '77

AMERICAN Astronomical Society
Astronomy. D. E. Thomsen. Sci N 112:11 Jl 2 '77
Shu and Hall win Astronomical Society prizes. F. H. S. Shu; D. N. B. Hall. pors Phys Today 30:95 My '77
Space sciences; summaries of papers. Sci N 111: 72 Ja 29 '77

AMERICAN Automobile Association
Mexico agrees to AAA plan to provide more tourist safety. il Ret Liv 17:18 Je '77

AMERICAN Ballet Theatre
ABT's star system. L. F. Rosen. Progressive 41: 51-2 Ap '77
American Ballet Theatre; performance of Coppélia and Giselle. R. A. Thom. il Dance Mag 51:91 Ap '77
American Ballet Theatre; season at the Metropolitan Opera House. D. Vaughan. il Dance Mag 51:71-4 O '77
Ballet for all seasons; Coppélia. il Sat R 4:50 Mr 5 '77
Celebration; television production of ABT's Nutcracker. T. Tobias. il pors Dance Mag 51:50-3 D '77
Dance:
Firebird. N. Goldner. Nation 224:637-8 My 21 '77
The sleeping beauty. N. Goldner. Nation 224: 666-8 My 28 '77
Dance; new productions of Firebird and Voluntaries. J. Maskey. il Hi Fi 27:MA12-14 Ag '77
Dancing:
Beyond Ballet Theatre. A. Croce. New Yorker 53:69-70 Jl 4 '77
Firebird. New Yorker 53:79-80 My 16 '77
Giselle. A. Croce. New Yorker 52:102+ F 14 '77
Nutcracker and Sleeping beauty. A. Croce. il New Yorker 52:94-6 Ja 17 '77
Firebird: a hop into history. M. Duffy. il Time 109:63 My 9 '77
Grown-up Nutcracker; M. Baryshnikov's production. J. Maskey. il por Hi Fi 27:MA8-10 S '77
Two ballet theatres. B. H. Haggin. New Repub 177:28-31 Ag 6 '77

AMERICAN Baptist Churches in the U.S.A. See Baptists in the United States

AMERICAN Bar Association
ABA misses the mark on advertising. J. K. Lieberman. Bus W p74 Ag 29 '77
More trouble for doctors and lawyers; Advisory Committee on Accreditation & Institutional Eligibility. il Bus W p 102 Ap 25 '77

AMERICAN bison. See Bison, American

AMERICAN Booksellers Association
ABA: around the booths; exhibitors. Pub W 211: 173-80+ My 23 '77
ABA fever grips publishers in the West. P. Holt. Pub W 211:40-1 Ap 18 '77
ABA in Denver presents a new kind of regionalism. P. Holt. il Pub W 212:47-8+ N 21 '77
ABA 1977; symposium, ed by D. Maryles. il Pub W 211:72-3 Je 27 '77
ABA regional in Washington, D.C: low turnout, high spirits. J. Giusto. il Pub W 212:66-8 O 17 '77
ABA's 77th annual convention: San Francisco, May 28-31. Pub W 211:164-6+ My 23 '77
Notes on the trade; San Francisco meeting. Colophon. Pub W 211:8 Je 13 '77
San Francisco ABA may be biggest yet. D. Maryles. Pub W 211:86 Mr 7 '77
San Francisco diarist; convention report. New Repub 176:46 Je 18 '77

AMERICAN Brands Inc-Franklin Life Insurance Company merger. See Corporations—Acquisitions and mergers

AMERICAN Broadcasting Companies
ABC gets the feel of TV's no. 1 spot. il Bus W p33 My 9 '77
ABC-TV's new raiding game. Bus W p27+ Mr 28 '77
ABC's wider world of news; appointment of R. Arledge. il por Time 109:79-80 My 16 '77
Black eye for TV boxing. P. Bonventre. pors Newsweek 89:81-2 My 2 '77
Giving ABC news athletic support. K. E. Meyer. Sat R 5:47 N 12 '77
King-size scandal in the ring; United States Boxing Championships. por Time 109:64 My 2 '77
Man with the golden gut; F. Silverman. il pors Time 110:46-7+ S 5 '77
Modest proposal. W. Welch. il Forbes 120:37-8 N 15 '77
New ABC's of news. D. M. Alpern and B. Carter. il por Newsweek 90:62 Ag 22 '77
Revving up the television news. T. Griffith. por Time 110:58+ Ag 22 '77
Roone at the top; excerpts from interview, ed by H. F. Waters. R. Arledge. por Newsweek 89: 103-4 My 16 '77

AMERICAN Broadcasting Companies—*Continued*
Some very wrong numbers; ABC's suspension of D. King's United States Championship boxing tournament. R. H. Boyle. il por Sports Illus 46:22-7 My 2 '77
Technological strike at ABC. il Bus W p67+ Ag 8 '77
AMERICAN buffalo; drama. See Mamet, D.
AMERICAN businessmen. See Businessmen
AMERICAN businessmen in foreign countries. See Americans in foreign countries
AMERICAN Camping Association
ACA national convention at Disneyland. il Camp Mag 50:8-9 S '77
Board adopts first $1 million budget. il Camp Mag 49:8-9 Mr '77
OBIS and ACA—the impossible equation does match. D. Buller. il Camp Mag 49:10-11 Ap '77
AMERICAN Can Company
Controller expands his territory; L. N. Sterling. por Bus W p90 Ag 15 '77
AMERICAN Cancer Society
New cancer weapons; Sarasota, Fla. seminar. M. Clark. il Newsweek 89:67-8 Ap 18 '77
AMERICAN Catholicism. See Catholic Church in the United States
AMERICAN Catholics. See Catholics in the United States
AMERICAN Ceramic Society
Don Pilcher; 1976 Ceramic Art Award. il por Ceram Mo 25:37-9 Mr '77
AMERICAN Chemical Society
Chemistry; summaries of papers. Sci N 111:220 Ap 2 '77
AMERICAN chestnut trees. See Chestnut trees
AMERICAN citizenship. See Citizenship—United States
AMERICAN city and county (periodical)
Man of the Year; interview. D. C. Tillman. il pors Am City & County 92:27-9 Ja '77
AMERICAN Civil Liberties Union
Auction time at the ACLU. W. F. Buckley, Jr. Nat R 29:845 Jl 22 '77
Can Chuck Morgan keep Jimmy Carter honest? T. Branch. Esquire 87:14+ F '77
Constitutional nonsense; NYCLU adoption suit. D. Oliver. Nat R 29:1493 D 23 '77
Constitutionality of book ban challenged by NYCLU: suit filed by the New York Civil Liberties Union against Island Trees School District. Lib J 102:530+ Mr 1 '77
Down memory lane with the ACLU. New Repub 176:20 Mr 12 '77
Purging of the ACLU. Nation 225:130-1 Ag 20 '77
AMERICAN coins. See Coins
AMERICAN College Testing program
How are English teachers reacting to declining college entrance scores? C. Tibbetts and A. M. Tibbetts. Engl J 66:13-16 D '77
I passed my A*C*T test. J. W. Ney. Engl J 66:10-12 D '77
AMERICAN Communist Party. See Communist Party (United States)
AMERICAN composers. See Composers, American
AMERICAN Composers Alliance. See Musical societies
AMERICAN Consulting Engineers Council
ACEC will tighten discipline to fight corruption scandals. W. Hickman. Archit Rec 162:35+ N '77
AMERICAN Convention on Human Rights
President Carter signs American Convention on Human Rights; remarks, with text of convention, June 1, 1977. J. Carter. Dept State Bull 77:28-38 Jl 4 '77
AMERICAN cookery. See Cookery, American
AMERICAN correspondents in foreign countries. See Foreign correspondents
AMERICAN Crafts Council
ACC news. Craft Horiz 37:38-9 Ag; 34-5 O; 42-3 D '77
ACC's eighth National Conference at Winston-Salem. il Craft Horiz 37:46-7+ Ag '77
ACC's National Conference to hail U.S. craft history and traditions. Craft Horiz 37:7 Ap '77
Fellows hailed at Winston-Salem fête. Craft Horiz 37:41+ Je '77
Staccato notes: a day in the life of Research and Education. Craft Horiz 37:43+ Je '77
Wyckoff resigns to seek new interests. Craft Horiz 37:8 F '77
See also
Craft horizon (periodical)
AMERICAN culture. See United States—Civilization
AMERICAN Cyanamid Company
Opportunities missed, opportunities miffed. Forbes 120:113-14 N 1 '77
AMERICAN deserts. See Deserts
AMERICAN designers. See Costume designers
AMERICAN Distilling Company. See Liquor industry
AMERICAN District Telegraph Company
Fiery debate over smoke-alarm efficiency; controversy surrounding claims made by Gillette and ADT concerning their photoelectric detectors. il Bus W p95-6+ S 26 '77
Where crime pays. il Forbes 120:126 O 15 '77
AMERICAN drama
See also
Dramatists, American
AMERICAN economic assistance. See Economic assistance, American
AMERICAN Enterprise Institute for Public Policy Research
Conservative's think tank. il Bus W p80-1 My 2 '77
Other think tank. Time 110:79 S 19 '77
Professors, politics, and palaver. C. Holden. Science 197:742 Ag 19 '77
Rewards of enterprise. T. Bethell. New Repub 177:17-19 Jl 9 '77
AMERICAN espionage. See Espionage, American
AMERICAN Express Company
American Express. il Bus W p56-9+ D 19 '77
American Express Operations Center. il Archit Rec 162:93-6 N '77
Young Atlantan for American Express. por Bus W p31-2 Mr 14 '77
AMERICAN Family Life Assurance Company. See Insurance companies
AMERICAN Farm Bureau Federation
Why Farm Bureau endorsed target prices. R. D. Wennblom. Farm J 101:33 Mr '77
AMERICAN Federation of Arts

International Exhibitions Committee

Sending the best of America abroad. F. Ferretti. il Art N 76:62-5 Summ '77
AMERICAN Federation of Government Employees
Let soldiers join labor unions? interviews. K. Blaylock; R. Beard. pors U.S. News 82:51-2 Mr 28 '77
Union of soldiers. M. Uhl and T. Ensign. Progressive 41:46-8 Mr '77
Unorganizing GIs. T. Ensign and M. Uhl. Progressive 41:8-9 D '77
AMERICAN Federation of Labor and Congress of Industrial Organizations
AFL-CIO rebuffed on shoe imports, situs picketing. L. Bornstein and others. M Labor R 100:64 Je '77
AFL-CIO: set to bargain hard with Congress. il Bus W p68+ Mr 7 '77
AFL-CIO's growing troubles. B. J. Widick. Nation 225:168-71 S 3 '77
Annual sunbath: organized labor comes to terms with Jimmy Carter. New Repub 176:12 Mr 12 '77
Auto Workers' return to AFL-CIO hits a snag; with interview with D. A. Fraser. il U.S. News 82:68-9 My 30 '77
Big labor's big defeat; common-situs picketing bill. T. Nicholson and others. il Newsweek 89:54+ Ap 4 '77
Big union blues: labor caught in Meany's grip. B. J. Widick. Nation 226:10-13 Ja 7 '78
Business fights union power grab; proposed reforms of National Labor Relations Act. il Nations Bus 65:21-4+ S '77
Can labor's tired leaders deal with a troubled movement? N. Kotz. il por N Y Times Mag p8-11+ S 4 '77
Carter's detente; proposed reforms of the National Labor Relations Act. T. Nicholson and J. B. Copeland. Newsweek 90:64+ Jl 25 '77
Emancipation from Meany: new life for the unions. B. J. Widick. Nation 224:368-72 Mr 26 '77
Impact of U.S. pullout from ILO. il U.S. News 83:102-3 N 14 '77
Labor reform faces potent opposition. Bus W p34+ My 2 '77
Labor's call on Carter. T. Nicholson and T. Joyce. il por Newsweek 89:60-1 Mr 7 '77
Labor's new push for protection. il Bus W p31-2 D 26 '77
Labor's new southern strategy; AFL-CIO support of Labor Reform Act of 1977. il map Bus W p28-9 F 7 '77
Meany and business vs. the ILO: will we pick up our marbles? B. Koeppel. Nation 225:429-31 O 29 '77
Meany draws up his shopping list; with report on Bal Harbour, Fla. executive council meeting by P. Taubman. il por Time 109:43-4 Mr 7 '77
Meany faction. C. McWilliams. Nation 224:165 F 12 '77
Meany rejects prenotification of wage increases; meeting of Executive Council in Bal Harbour, Fla. L. Bornstein and others. M Labor R 100:84 Ap '77
Meany the meanie. il Time 109:38-9 Ja 31 '77
Mellowed Bridges talks of reconciliation; International Longshoremen's and Warehousemen's Union. por Bus W p40+ My 9 '77
More jobs at any cost: organized labor's top goal for 1977. il Nations Bus 65:23-6 F '77

AMERICAN Federation of Labor and Congress of Industrial Organizations—*Continued*
New challenge for world labor. J. Holland and P. J. Henriot. America 137:209-12 O 8 '77
New union drive for one-sided labor law. il Nations Bus 65:18-21 Jl '77
No entangling alliances; proposed reaffiliation of the United Auto Workers Union and the AFL-CIO. B. J. Widick. Nation 225:388 O 22 '77
Peace with Jimmy, war on the Hill. il Time 110:47-8 Jl 25 '77
Rapid decline in political clout. il Time 109:55+ Ap 11 '77
Storm brews over union demands on Congress. il U.S. News 82:88-9 Mr 7 '77
Unions divided; question of Bakke case. K. Bode. New Repub 177:20-2 O 15 '77
Unions go all out for tougher curbs on imports. il U.S. News 83:83-4 D 19 '77
Unions hit the comeback trail in Congress. U.S. News 83:112+ O 17 '77
Unions' sweet hopes turn sour. F. W. Frailey. U.S. News 82:93 Ap 11 '77
Waiting for Meany; question of support for Chilean unions. Nation 225:644-5 D 17 '77
What situs taught the unions. il Bus W p 100 Ap 11 '77
Women and unions. G. Steinem. Progressive 41:34 Jl '77

AMERICAN Federation of State, County and Municipal Employees
AFSCME: public employees in trouble. M. Levinson. Nation 225:208-10 S 10 '77
Crying Wurf; advertising campaign attacking city of Atlanta and Mayor M. Jackson. K. Bode. New Repub 177:14-17 Jl 2 '77
NEA, State employees union reach accord. L. Bornstein and others. M Labor R 100:89 F '77
Strikes used to save money, AFSCME charges. Am City & County 92:13 Ap '77

AMERICAN Federation of Teachers
Unions on the brink: death wish among the teachers. L. Weiner. Nation 225:276-7 S 24 '77

AMERICAN fiction
Authors without fear or shame. J. Simon. Esquire 88:22+ Jl '77
Books: Washington, D.C. political novels. J. Kraft. New Yorker 53:140-6+ D 19 '77
Flirting with guilt and tyranny. E. Larsen. il Harpers 225:95-8+ D '77; Reply. G. Lyons. Nation 226:24-6 Ja 7 '78
Picture of success. N. Mills. Yale R 66:347-63 Mr '77
State of the novel. J. W. Aldridge. Commentary 64:44-52 O '77

Study and teaching

Twain and Vonnegut. M. Bobkoff. Engl J 66:55 S '77

AMERICAN Film Festival. See Motion picture festivals

AMERICAN Financial Corporation
Carl Lindner's singular financial empire. C. J. Loomis. il pors Fortune 95:126-30+ Ja '77

AMERICAN flag. See Flags—United States

AMERICAN folk art. See Folk art

AMERICAN folk songs. See Folk songs, American

AMERICAN Folklife, Festival of. See Festivals—Washington, D.C.

AMERICAN Forestry Association
AFA annual meeting. J. Westenberger. por Am For 83:20 Jl '77
AFA honors. . .Humphrey, Bazan, Clepper, Craig. il Am For 83:8-9 D '77
California—here we come! R. Pardo. il Am For 83:32-3 Ap '77
What's new at AFA. W. E. Towell. See issues of American forests

AMERICAN forests (periodical)
Man with roots; retirement of editor J. B. Craig. W. E. Towell. por Am For 83:inside back cover O '77

AMERICAN Friends Service Committee
How the B-1 bomber was brought down. J. Robison. Chr Cent 94:711-12 Ag 17 '77
Swords and plowshares; project in Calif. area to sway companies from military contracts. S. H. Day, Jr. Bull Atom Sci 33:4-5 N '77

AMERICAN furniture. See Furniture, American

AMERICAN Gas Association
They're giving us gas, all right: gas industry efforts to force deregulation through inaccurate reports of reserves. J. N. Miller. New Repub 176:15-17 F 12 '77

AMERICAN General Insurance Company-Richmond Corporation merger. See Insurance companies—Acquisitions and mergers

AMERICAN Geophysical Union
Geophysical sciences. Sci N 111:378-9 Je 11 '77

AMERICAN glass. See Glassware

AMERICAN goldfinches. See Goldfinches

AMERICAN heritage (periodical)
American heritage announces the presentation of the 1977 Samuel Eliot Morison Award to Joseph P. Lash for Roosevelt and Churchill. il por Am Heritage 28:96-7 O '77

AMERICAN house decoration. See House decoration, American

AMERICAN Indian Movement
Skyhorse and Mohawk: more than a murder trial. D. Blackburn. il Nation 225:682-6 D 24 '77

AMERICAN Institute of Architects
AIA bestows honor awards on 17 buildings in its 29th annual program. il Archit Rec 161:41-3 Je '77
AIA Gold Medal goes to Neutra; International Style. W. Marlin. por Archit Rec 161:37 Ap '77
Advertising and AIA ethics: for all the activity, no early resolution is in sight. A. T. Kornblut. Archit Rec 161:73 My '77
Architecture; 1977 awards. J. H. Kay. Nation 225:90-2 Jl 23 '77
First awards program of Rhode Island AIA honors four buildings for distinctive design. il Archit Rec 162:41 S '77
On the 25th anniversary of its honor awards program, the Seattle Chapter, AIA, commends 11 buildings. il Archit Rec 161:45 Mr '77
Six winners in AIA awards program in Puerto Rico. il Archit Rec 161:42-3 Ap '77
6 winners; residences selected by the New York Chapter. P. Goldberger. il N Y Times Mag p66-9 Mr 13 '77
Two messages from AIA President McGinty. W. F. Wagner, Jr. Archit Rec 162:13 N '77
When architects pick America's best buildings. il U.S. News 83:52-4 Ag 15 '77

Meetings

News reports: 1977 AIA convention. J. Nairn and W. F. Wagner, Jr. il Archit Rec 162:26-7 Jl '77
Some random thoughts on the San Diego convention. W. F. Wagner, Jr. Archit Rec 162:13 Jl '77

AMERICAN Institute of Biological Sciences
AIBS report (cont) BioScience 27:192-5, 283, 552, 680-1, 746, 810 Mr-Ap, Ag, O-D '77
AIBS state public responsibilities representatives. BioScience 27:503 Jl '77
Annual AIBS meeting. See issues of BioScience
Awards for excellence. BioScience 27:699 O '77
Botanists capture distinguished service awards. pors BioScience 27:346 My '77
Great Lakes odyssey keynotes 28th annual meeting. E. M. Leeper. BioScience 27:651-2 O '77
New officers stress building membership. por BioScience 27:41 Ja '77

AMERICAN Institute of Certified Public Accountants
CPAs are trying to outrace Congress. Bus W p58-9 S 26 '77

AMERICAN Institute of Graphic Arts Fifty Books of the Year exhibit. See Book exhibits

AMERICAN Institute of Physics
AIP in 1976. il Phys Today 30:45-7+ Jl '77
AIP will ask authors to transfer copyright under new law; with editorial comment. B. C. Carr. Phys Today 30:85-7, 104 S '77
Corporate associates meeting stresses industrial physics. G. B. Lubkin. il Phys Today 30:93-6 Ja '77

AMERICAN Institute of Real Estate Appraisers
Attempt to control thought; Justice Dept. complaint. J. J. Kilpatrick. Nations Bus 65:11-12 O '77

AMERICAN Jewish Committee
Graham: feted by Jews; first national interreligious award. A. H. Matthews. Chr Today 22:49-50 N 18 '77

AMERICAN Jews. See Jews in the United States

AMERICAN Jumping Derby. See Horsemanship

AMERICAN Land Trust. See Land trusts

AMERICAN legends. See Legends, American

AMERICAN Legion

Pennsylvania convention. Philadelphia, 1976

Casebook of the medical detective; work of H. Friedman of Philadelphia's Children's Hospital in attempting to diagnose Legionnaire's disease (cont) D. Russell. Fam Health 9:40-1+ Ja '77

AMERICAN libraries (periodical)
Couple's article wins first $1,000 prize; Ruth and Lawrence McCrank. il Am Lib 8:293 Je '77
Library manuscripts wanted: $1,000 prize article competition. Am Lib 8:237 My '77

AMERICAN Library Association
ALA election results. SLJ 24:31 S '77
ALA general news. See issues of American libraries.
ALA 1977 election results; ALA and other 1977 library awards, an alphabetical guide. il Wilson Lib Bull 52:43-4 S '77
Awards 1977. il Am Lib 8:495-7 O '77
Changing ALA's structure: membership input sought. Lib J 102:1996-7 O 1 '77
Controversy continues over ALA's The speaker. SLJ 24:10 N '77

AMERICAN Library Association—*Continued*
If elected I will. . . ; responses of candidates for the presidency of ALA to questions from the editors. D. Broderick; R. Shank; F. W. Summers. il por Lib J 102:880-7 Ap 15 '77
Jones asks for panel to review The speaker. SLJ 24:9 D '77
Liberating, not repressive: ALA President views the Racism/Sexism Resolution. C. S. Jones. Am Lib 8:244-5 My '77
Library Bill of Rights vs. the Racism and Sexism Awareness Resolution. Z. Horn. Lib J 102: 1254-5 Je 1 '77
Moonshine; question of rights of the young to access to information. E. Moon; L. N. Gerhardt. SLJ 24:9 S; 5 N '77
Nominating Committee report. il Am Lib 8:507-8 O '77
Orphans without a home; question of indifference to individual librarian members. E. Hodgin. Lib J 102:1722 S 1 '77
Resolution on Racism & Sexism Awareness revisited. E. J. Josey. Wilson Lib Bull 51:727-8 My '77
Russell Shank wins presidency; twenty-five councilors elected; bylaw amendments passed. Am Lib 8:365-8 Jl '77
Son of Speaker; with comments by readers. D. Broderick. Am Lib 8:502-5 O '77
State of the Association; views of R. Wedgeworth. il Am Lib 8:380 Jl '77
Technology & the catalog; tradition vs. the new wave; ALA institute. Lib J 102:666 Mr 15 '77
Walk away talk at ALA. L. N. Gerhardt. SLJ 23:55 Mr '77
Where have all the leaders gone? ALA's democracy produces chaos. W. Brahm. Am Lib 8:423-4 S '77

Meetings, 1977

ALA Midwinter Meeting '77. L. N. Gerhardt and others. il SLJ 23:110-19 Mr '77
ALA-Midwinter preview. Lib J 102:150 Ja 15 '77
ALA program highlights. SLJ 23:18 My '77
Complete coverage of ALA's 96th annual conference; symposium. il Am Lib 8:370-90 Jl '77
Conference preview; with editorial comment. Lib J 102:1081, 1154-9 My 15 '77
Debate nobody won; The speaker; criticism of the film; with editorial comment. J. Berry. il Lib J 102:1543, 1573-80 Ag '77; Discussion. 102: 2289-90 N 15 '77
Editor's Midwinter gleanings. A. Plotnik. il Am Lib 8:192-3 Ap '77
Editors' Midwinter notebook. il Am Lib 8:108 Mr '77
Head-on collision: ALA in Motor City. W. R. Eshelman and others. il Wilson Lib Bull 52: 30-42 S '77
Issues, arguments, actions: ALA in Detroit. L. N. Gerhardt and others. SLJ 24:26-37 S '77
It all boiled down to money; Midwinter Meeting; with editorial comment. il Lib J 102: 651, 682-91 Mr 15 '77
Key word was access; with editorial comment. il Lib J 102:1543, 1555-72 Ag '77
Late notes on conference programs. Lib J 102: 1332-4 Je 15 '77
Media at Midwinter—surreal impressions. D. Boyle. il Am Lib 8:209 Ap '77
1977 ALA Midwinter Meeting. il Wilson Lib Bull 51:582-92 Mr '77
Unmissable meetings in Motown: highlights of ALA's 101st-year conference. il Am Lib 8:329-30 Je '77

Meetings, 1978

ALA Midwinter meeting. Am Lib 8:629-31 D '77
1978 ALA Midwinter meeting. il Am Lib 8: 493-4 O '77

Accreditation, Committee on

Schools do the judging: evaluating the Accreditation Committee. R. E. Bidlack. Am Lib 8:442-3 S '77

American Association of School Librarians

AECT, AASL, and school librarians. B. M. Cheatham. SLJ 24:45 S '77
ALA testifies on school library/media aid. E. D. Cooke and H. W. Sprouse. Wilson Lib Bull 52:305+ D '77
A few new projects. . . ; annual meeting. N. Horrocks. Lib J 102:688-9 Mr 15 '77
Teeth for the professionally nameless; views of F. Henne. L. N. Gerhardt. SLJ 24:7 D '77

Association of State Library Agencies

Co-op options, $$ roles debated at ASLA. N. Savage. Lib J 102:1104+ My 15 '77

Black Caucus

Black Caucus vetoes patching; The speaker stands as is. Am Lib 8:405-6 S '77

Children's Services Division

Add your voice to CSD. il SLJ 23:50 F '77
CSD selects Notable books. SLJ 23:94-5 Mr '77
IFC/CSD documents in question. L. N. Gerhardt and others. SLJ 23:118-19 Mr '77

Council

Council determines ALA stand on current issues. A. G. Bushman. il Am Lib 8:377-8 Jl '77

Executive Board

ALA ExecBoard delays distribution of film. W. R. Eshelman. Wilson Lib Bull 51:794-5+ Je '77
ALA Executive Board meeting. K. Nyren. il Lib J 102:157-9 Ja 15 '77
ALA Executive Board's fall meeting. W. R. Eshelman. Wilson Lib Bull 52:290-2 D '77
Board takes business step by step. E. P. Mitchell. Am Lib 8:382 Jl '77
High drama, high rise in fall Board meeting. il Am Lib 8:628-9 D '77
Rites and wrongs of a Board in springtime. Am Lib 8:336-9 Je '77

History

Wayward bookman; question of embezzlement by Milwaukee public librarian and ALA president K. A. Linderfelt. W. A. Wiegand. bibl il Am Lib 8:134-7, 197-200 Mr-Ap '77

Information Science and Automation Division

ALA/ISAD institute on the national network. K. Nyren. il Lib J 102:761-3 Ap 1 '77

Intellectual Freedom Committee

ALA ExecBoard delays distribution of film; The speaker. W. R. Eshelman. Wilson Lib Bull 51:794-5 Je '77
Debate nobody won; The speaker; criticism of the film; with editorial comment. J. Berry. il Lib J 102:1543, 1573-80 Ag '77; Discussion. 102: 2289-90 N 15 '77
Freedom of speech for The speaker. A. Plotnik. il Am Lib 8:337 Je '77
IFC/CSD documents in question. L. N. Gerhardt and others. SLJ 23:118-19 Mr '77
Reflections on The speaker. C. S. Jones. il Wilson Lib Bull 52:51-5 S '77
Speaker: step or misstep into filmmaking? symposium. il Am Lib 8:371-6 Jl '77
Whimper for freedom; controversy surrounding the film, The speaker. J. Berry. Lib J 102: 1227 Je 1 '77

Notable Books Council

See American Library Association—Reference and Adult Services Division

Office for Intellectual Freedom

See also
Freedom to Read Foundation

Public Library Association

Mission statement for public libraries: guidelines for public library service; excerpt from text; with comments of librarians. Am Lib 8:615-20 D '77
New public library mission. J. Berry. Lib J 102: 2379 D 1 '77
PLA drafts new public library mission. Lib J 102:2460-1 D 15 '77

Reference and Adult Services Division

ALA issues booklist, Notable books for adults. Lib J 102:668 Mr 15 '77

Young Adult Services Division

Best books for whom; or, Where have all the grown-ups gone? L. L. Shapiro. Wilson Lib Bull 51:803-4+ Je '77
Best books for YAs. SLJ 23:95 Mr '77; Same. Todays Educ 66:82-4+ S '77
Still alive: the best of the best, 1960-1974. Todays Educ 66:97-101 Ja '77

AMERICAN lions. See Pumas

AMERICAN literature
But what'll I read? Clearing H 50:265-7 F '77
Conspiracy of silence. J. Epstein. il Harpers 255: 77-80+ N '77
See also
American fiction
American poetry
Black literature

Jewish authors

Laughter without joy: the burlesque of our secular age. D. B. Lockerbie. Chr Today 22: 14-16 O 7 '77
Poet of exile; C. Reznikoff's objectivist poetry. R. Alter. Commentary 63:49-55 F '77
Strangers. I. Howe. Yale R 66:481-500 Je '77

Study and teaching

American nonfiction: dreams and nightmares; utopian thought. D. Rosen. Engl J 66:54 S '77
Focus: multicultural literature; symposium. il Engl J 66:24-52 Mr '77
Hang-ups. P. O. Tierney. Engl J 66:61-2 S '77

Aids and devices

Hollywood and American literature: the American novel on the screen. H. Jay. Engl J 66: 82-6 Ja '77

AMERICAN lithographs. See Lithographs
AMERICAN Lutheran Church. See Lutheran Church in the United States
AMERICAN Medical Association
AMA digs in against ads; FTC case. Bus W p45+ S 19 '77
AMA vs. HMOs. E. Marshall. New Repub 177:9-11 O 29 '77
AMA's health plan. R. E. Palmer. por Newsweek 89:11 Je 6 '77
FTC sues AMA over code of ethics. R. J. Smith. Science 197:1346 S 30 '77
Impaired MDs now recognized as a peril to patients. M. Grosswirth. il Sci Digest 81:8-11+ Je '77
More trouble for doctors and lawyers; Advisory Committee on Accreditation & Institutional Eligibility. il Bus W p 102 Ap 25 '77
Rationed care; address, June 19, 1977. R. E. Palmer. Vital Speeches 43:700-2 S 1 '77
AMERICAN messianism. See Messianism, American
AMERICAN military assistance. See Military assistance, American
AMERICAN minorities. See Minorities
AMERICAN Motors Corporation
AMC struggles to pull its cars out of a skid. il Bus W p39-40 S 12 '77
American Motors hangs in there. il Time 109:51 F 14 '77
Danger—cash needs ahead. M. King. il Forbes 119:53-5 Je 15 '77
New driver for the laggard; chief executive G. C. Meyers. il por Time 110:113 N 7 '77
Nice guys and where I'd like to see them finish. D. E. Davis, Jr. Car & Dr 22:7 F '77
Searching for hope at struggling AMC. Bus W p30-1 My 2 '77
AMERICAN Museum of Natural History, New York
Animal rights: NIH cat sex study brings grief to New York museum. N. Wade; discussion. Science 195:131 Ja 14 '77
Hall of Reptiles and Amphibians. F. Hartmann. il Natur Hist 86:98-101 N '77
AMERICAN music. See Music, American
AMERICAN Music Scholarship Association competition. See Music—Competitions
AMERICAN National Cattlemen's Association. See National Cattlemen's Association
AMERICAN National Cattlemen's Association-National Livestock Feeders Association merger. See Cattle industry—Consolidations and mergers
AMERICAN National Standards Institute
New ANSI standards on barrier-free design expected in 1978. W. Hickman. Archit Rec 162:63 D '77
AMERICAN Nazi Party. See Nazis in the United States
AMERICAN Opera Center. See Lincoln Center for the Performing Arts, New York—Juilliard School
AMERICAN painting. See Painting, American
AMERICAN people. See Americans
AMERICAN Physical Society
APS—AAPT meet in Chicago. B. C. Carr. il Phys Today 30:23-6 Ja '77
APS awards annual prizes in nuclear and surface physics. il Phys Today 30:61 Ap '77
APS news. See issues of Physics today
APS tests computer system for publishing operations. il Phys Today 30:75 D '77
Career opportunities will be APS summer conference topic. il Phys Today 30:75 Je '77
March meeting in San Diego. B. C. Carr. il Phys Today 30:43-6 Mr '77
New bylaws join recently revised constitution. il Phys Today 30:79 Ja '77
New guidelines clarify POPA—Council interactions. Phys Today 30:65 F '77
Physics in 1976—a personal account. W. A. Fowler. il Phys Today 30:33-8+ Ap '77
Should rank of fellow in the APS be discontinued? symposium. Phys Today 30:9+ S '77
AMERICAN poetry
Poetry of apocalypse. J. F. Cotter. America 136:295-7 Ap 2 '77

Bibliography

Harold Bloom on poetry. H. Bloom. il New Repub 177:24-6 N 26 '77

Jewish authors

See American literature—Jewish authors

Translations into Spanish

Through a Spanish looking glass: Williams' poetry in translation. J. Felstiner. Américas 29:5-8 N '77
AMERICAN portraits. See Portraits, American
AMERICAN pottery. See Pottery, American
AMERICAN prints. See Prints
AMERICAN Professional Slo-pitch League. See Softball
AMERICAN Psychiatric Association
Behavior; summaries of papers. J. Greenberg. Sci N 111:312 My 14 '77
Legitimizing homosexuality. M. Spector. bibl il Society 14:52-6 Jl '77
AMERICAN Psychological Association
Behavior; summaries of papers. J. Greenberg. Sci N 112:232 O 8 '77
Psychologists back women, chuck magazine, gear up for NHI. C. Holden. Science 197:1168 S 16 '77
Report: PT goes to the APA. P. Horn. Psychol Today 11:14+ D '77
AMERICAN public opinion. See Public opinion—United States
AMERICAN record guide (periodical)
ARG and how she grew; reprint from 30th anniversary issue; And an update. P. L. Miller. il Am Rec G 40:7-9 N '76
Bouquets and brickbats. il Am Rec G 40:4-5 My '77
Results of the survey. Am Rec G 40:4-5 D '76
Statement of intent. Am Rec G 40:3 N '76
AMERICAN Revolution. See United States—History—Revolution, 1775-1783
AMERICAN Revolution Bicentennial Administration. See United States—American Revolution Bicentennial Administration
AMERICAN Safety Razor Company
Scraping along. D. Pauly and E. Shannon. il Newsweek 90:83 N 7 '77
AMERICAN Safety Razor Company-Bic Pen Corporation merger. See Corporations—Acquisitions and mergers
AMERICAN sculpture. See Sculpture, American
AMERICAN Security Council
Hair-raising brass propaganda; American Security Council film, The price of peace and freedom. A. Kanegis. Nation 225:486-7 N 12 '77
AMERICAN Sheep Producers Council
Sheep don't believe in supply and demand. Suc Farm 75:9 My '77
AMERICAN Siberian expedition, 1918-1920. See Russia—History—Allied intervention, 1918-1920
AMERICAN Society for Cell Biology
Biology. J. A. Miller. Sci N 112:377 D 3 '77
AMERICAN Society for Information Science
SLA/ASIS Janus meet: costs of information scrutinized. N. Savage. Lib J 102:540-1 Mr 1 '77
AMERICAN Society for Microbiology
Microbiology; summaries of papers. J. Arehart-Treichel. Sci N 111:328 My 21 '77
AMERICAN Society of Animal Science. See Agricultural societies
AMERICAN Society of Civil Engineers
Troubled BART takes 1977 ASCE award. il Am City & County 92:39 My '77
AMERICAN songs. See Songs, American
AMERICAN spectator (periodical)
Talking back. M. J. Sobran, Jr. Nat R 29:1506 D 23 '77
AMERICAN Standards Association. See American National Standards Institute
AMERICAN Stock Exchange. See Stock exchanges—American Exchange
AMERICAN students in foreign countries
See also
Foreign study
AMERICAN students in France. See Foreign students in France
AMERICAN students in Great Britain. See Foreign students in Great Britain
AMERICAN students in Rumania. See Foreign students in Rumania
AMERICAN students in the Netherlands. See Foreign students in the Netherlands
AMERICAN Symphony Orchestra
Amer. Sym: Filipino composers; concert at Carnegie Hall on April 6. Hi Fi 27:MA24-5 Ag '77
AMERICAN Symphony Orchestra League
ASOL Festival of Youth Orchestras; Washington, D.C. L. Sears. il Hi Fi 27:MA24-6 D '77
AMERICAN Telephone & Telegraph Company
AT&T's stock sale has investors puzzled. D. G. Santry. Bus W p92 N 7 '77
Antitrust suit against Bell winds onward. D. Shapley. Science 198:278 O 21 '77
Communications dog fight. G. R. Rosen. il Duns R 109:48-53 Je '77
Cracks in AT&T's monopoly: Ma Bell shows her teeth. L. Light. Nation 225:690-2 D 24 '77
Freak-proof computer arms Ma Bell against toll cheats. R. Field. Sci Digest 82:86-7 S '77
How courts will treat IBM, AT&T. A. Hershman. por Duns R 110:76-7+ D '77
How Ma Bell is training women for management. G. Cravens. il N Y Times Mag p 12-13+ My 29 '77
Ma Bell faces life. P. Gibson. il Forbes 120:47-50+ N 1 '77
Ma Bell, firebug. F. Warner. Nation 224:684-8 Je 4 '77
Phone calls and philandering; Southwestern Bell scandal. il pors Time 110:32-3 S 5 '77
Planning and policy: keys to our telephone network; address, February 4, 1977. G. L. Hough. Vital Speeches 43:344-7 Mr 15 '77

AMERICAN Telephone & Telegraph Company —*Continued*
Sponsor as star. por Forbes 119:66 F 1 '77
Telephone industry; address, August 9, 1977. C. L. Brown. Vital Speeches 43:764-7 O 1 '77
Who won? FCC decision on Western Electric and AT&T. Forbes 119:46 My 1 '77
Whole new way to figure AT&T's rates. il Bus W p86-8+ F 14 '77
See also
Bell Telephone Laboratories
AMERICAN tourists. See Travelers
AMERICAN Vacuum Society
Vacuum Society meets in Boston. B. C. Carr. il Phys Today 30:52-4 O '77
AMERICAN visitors in foreign countries. See Visitors, Foreign
AMERICAN Water Works Association
Three cities earn AWWA awards. Am City & County 92:40 Je '77
AMERICAN women. See Women—United States
AMERICAN Zoetrope (firm) See Motion picture industry—United States
AMERICANA
Historical goodies crammed in old camelback trunks; West Virginia Heritage Trunk project. D. Sherwood. il Smithsonian 8:106+ Je '77
Treasury of Americana by special invitation; top floor of the State Department. il U.S. News 83:69-70 O 24 '77
AMERICANS
American characters:
Aimee Semple McPherson. W. B. Hamilton. il por Am Heritage 28:62-3 O '77
Emily Post. E. Oettinger. por Am Heritage 28:38-9 Ap '77
John McLoughlin. D. Lavender. por Am Heritage 28:64-5 Je '77
Nikola Tesla. N. Brandt. il por Am Heritage 28:44-5 Ag '77
Englishman's affection for Americans sparks a book and a television series; interview. ed by P. Dahlin. D. Wilcox. il Pub W 213:55 O 17 '77
God's almost chosen people. M. E. Marty. il Am Heritage 28:4-7 Ag '77
Going our own way—at 65 m.p.h; Time essay. F. Trippett. Time 110:95 N 21 '77
How America lives. Ladies Home J 94:65-73 Mr '77
See also
Finnish Americans
Georgians
German Americans
Greek Americans
Irish Americans
Italian Americans
Mexican Americans
Polish Americans
Texans

Anecdotes, facetiae, satire, etc.

Conversation with a patriot. R. Rosenblatt. New Repub 176:37-8 Mr 12 '77
AMERICANS abroad. See Americans in foreign countries
AMERICANS for Democratic Action (organization)
Feeling left out. E. Marshall. New Repub 176:12-13 My 21 '77
Liberals and Carter. Progressive 41:5-6 Jl '77
AMERICANS in Argentina
Despite kidnapings and murder, Americans are returning to Argentina. U.S. News 83:26 N 21 '77
AMERICANS in Bolivia
C.I.A. and the funny men. C. L. Bach. America 137:142-5 S 17 '77
AMERICANS in Canada
Transfer of sanctions treaties with Mexico and Canada; American prisoners in foreign jails; statement, July 13, 1977. B. M. Watson. Dept State Bull 77:208-10 Ag 15 '77
AMERICANS in Chile
What happened to Horman? Nation 225:453 N 5 '77
AMERICANS in Europe
See also
United States—Armed Forces—Forces in Europe
AMERICANS in foreign countries
Department discusses consular services for Americans abroad; statements, July 14, 1977. B. M. Watson; W. P. Stedman, Jr. il Dept State Bull 77:248-65 Ag 22 '77
See also
United States—Armed Forces—Forces in foreign countries

Taxation

Corporate expatriates fight a U.S. tax law. Bus W p44+ Ap 11 '77
Expatriates may keep a tax break; efforts of Tax Equity for Americans Abroad. il Bus W p31 O 31 '77
Uproar over taxing Americans who work abroad; How taxes force Americans to leave a key Arab region. il U.S. News 83:73-4 S 19 '77
AMERICANS in France
Why where you from has replaced what's your sign; black woman in Paris. V. Smart-Grosvenor. Mademoiselle 83:96-7+ Jl '77
AMERICANS in Germany, West
See also
United States—Army—Forces in Germany, West
AMERICANS in Ghana
Retired teachers share skills as Peace Corps volunteers in Ghana. il por Aging 268:18-20 F '77
AMERICANS in Hong Kong
On knowing when to come home. D. Lee. Mademoiselle 83:34+ Jl '77
AMERICANS in Iran
No wreath for Mr Baskerville: America in cahoots with the Shah. R. Baraheni. Nation 224:307-8 Mr 12 '77
AMERICANS in Israel
See also
Jerusalem—Foreign population
AMERICANS in Japan
Family's affair with Japan. A. H. Malcolm. il N Y Times Mag p36-8 Jl 10 '77; Same abr. Read Digest 111:145-8 D '77
AMERICANS in Korea, South
See also
United States—Army—Forces in Korea, South
AMERICANS in Latin America
Department discusses consular services for Americans abroad; statements, July 14, 1977. W. P. Stedman. il Dept State Bull 77:259-65 Ag 22 '77
AMERICANS in Mexico
Busted in Mexico; Americans. D. Harris. il pors N Y Times Mag p26-30+ My 1 '77
Mexican jailbirds. Nation 225:645 D 17 '77
Mexican prison swap. D. Holt and others. il Newsweek 90:35-6 D 19 '77
Mexican transfer; treaty to return American prisoners. P. Meyer. Harpers 255:26+ N '77
Transfer of sanctions treaties with Mexico and Canada; American prisoners in foreign jails; statement, July 13, 1977. B. M. Watson. Dept State Bull 77:208-10 Ag 15 '77
Yankees come home; transfer of convicts. il Time 110:25 D 19 '77
Young Americans in Mexican jails. C. J. Migdail. il U.S. News 82:31-2 Je 27 '77
AMERICANS in Paris. See Americans in France
AMERICANS in Rhodesia
Smith's Yankee recruits. A. De Borchgrave. il Newsweek 90:40 S 12 '77
Why Americans are fighting on Rhodesia's front lines. S. Hempstone. il map U.S. News 82:31-2 My 23 '77
AMERICANS in Russia
Message from Moscow; arrest and interrogation of R. Toth. A. Deming and others. il por Newsweek 89:14-16 Je 27 '77
AMERICANS in Saudi Arabia
Americans in Arabia: keys to the Kingdom. J. Miller. map Progressive 41:44-7 Ap '77
AMERICANS in the Panama Canal Zone
It's a spooky atmosphere. U.S. News 82:30 My 2 '77
Panic in a tropical playground. il Time 110:18 Ag 22 '77
AMERICANS in the United Arab Emirates
How taxes force Americans to leave a key Arab region. D. Mullin. il map U.S. News 83:75-6 S 19 '77
AMERICANS in Uganda
Amin's purge. A. Deming and others. il por Newsweek 89:25-6 Mr 14 '77
Retreat from a collision course. il por Time 109:24 Mr 14 '77
AMERICANS United for Separation of Church and State (organization)
Americans United: advocacy role; National Conference on Church and State in San Diego. R. Chandler. Chr Today 21:47 Mr 4 '77
AMERICA'S Cup race. See Yacht racing
AMERICIUM
Caution: smoke detectors may be dangerous to your health; use of americium. M. C. Olson. Progressive 41:22-5 Ag '77
Retention of plutonium and americium by rock. S. Fried and others. bibl il Science 196:1087-9 Je 3 '77
Riddled by isotopes. M. Clark and P. S. Greenberg. il por Newsweek 89:49 Mr 21 '77
AMES, B. Charles
Reliance's route to steady growth. por Bus W p86-7 Mr 7 '77 •
AMES, Lois
(ed) See Sexton, A. Uncensored poet
AMES, Michael M.
Tovil: exorcism by white magic; with biographical sketch. il Natur Hist 87:4, 42-9 bibl(p 108) Ja '78
AMES, Wilmer
Body building. il Sports Illus 47:91-2+ D 5 '77
AMEX. See Stock exchanges—American Exchange
AMFAC, Inc
Why Amfac got rid of Joseph Magnin. Bus W p 19 Jl 4 '77
AMFT, M. J.
Art of larks; story. Seventeen 36:152-3 N '77
AMICUS, Inc. See Volunteer service
AMIEL, Barbara
Canadian couple look to American market. R. Fulford. pors Pub W 212:48 O 24 '77 •

AMIN DADA, Idi
Quotations from President Amin. Newsweek 89:31 Mr 7 '77

about

Ace to issue its first instant title on Amin. M. Reuter. Pub W 212:74+ Jl 18 '77 *
America's shaky truce with Amin. map U.S. News 82:28 Mr 14 '77 *
Amin plays possum. il por Newsweek 90:58 S 19 '77 *
Amin steals the OAU show. R. Carroll and J. Pringle. por Newsweek 90:30+ Jl 18 '77 *
Amin: the wild man of Africa. il pors map Time 109:18-22+ Mr 7 '77 *
Amin's purge. A. Deming and others. il por Newsweek 89:25-6 Mr 14 '77 *
Big Daddy in books. il pors Time 110:46 S 19 '77 *
Coup or con job? il por Time 110:28 Jl 4 '77 *
Dealing with Dada. New Repub 176:5-6+ Mr 19 '77 *
Helping Ugandans. Chr Today 21:38-9 Ag 12 '77 *
Henry Kyemba awaits the end of Idi Amin; interview, ed by G. Stuttaford. H. Kyemba. por Pub W 212:44 O 3 '77 *
Idi Amin: more cunning than crazy. T. H. Snitch. il Intellect 105:410-11 Je '77 *
Idi Amin's holy war. R. Carroll and C. Harrison. il por Newsweek 89:35-6 F 28 '77 *
Idi Amin's rule of blood. A. Deming and others. il pors map Newsweek 89:28-30+ Mr 7 '77 *
Idi's latest adventure. R. Watson and others. il Newsweek 90:43-4 Jl 4 '77 *
Learning from Idi Amin. M. Greenfield. il Newsweek 89:100 Mr 14 '77 *
Limits of morality. R. Steele and others. il por Newsweek 89:14-15 Mr 7 '77 *
Over lake & turf with Big Daddy. J. Osman. Time 109:20-1 Mr 7 '77 *
Power of irresponsibility. Nation 224:292-3 Mr 12 '77 *
Retreat from a collision course. il por Time 109:24 Mr 14 '77 *
Uganda: a helpless world wrings its hands. il por U.S. News 82:36 Mr 7 '77 *
Uganda after Idi Amin. W. P. Wood. America 137:51-3 Jl 30 '77 *

AMINES
From joy to depression: new insights into the chemistry of moods. M. Scarf. il N Y Times Mag p30-4+ Ap 24 '77; Same abr. with title What makes our moods? Read Digest 111:45-7+ Ag '77
See also
Phenylethanolamine

AMINO acid dating
Amino acid dating: now it has teeth. Sci N 111: 196 Mr 26 '77
Isoleucine epimerization for dating marine sediments: importance of analyzing monospecific foraminiferal samples. K. King and C. Neville. bibl il Science 195:1333-5 Mr 25 '77

AMINO acid transport. See Biological transport

AMINO acids
Deuterolysis of amino acid precursors: evidence for hydrogen cyanide polymers as protein ancestors. C. Matthews and others. bibl il Science 198:622-5 N 11 '77
Diet and uptake of aldomet by the brain: competition with natural large neutral amino acids. D. C. Markovit and J. D. Fernstrom. bibl il Science 197:1014-15 S 2 '77
Hyperphenylalanemia: effect on brain polyribosomes can be partially reversed by other amino acids. J. V. Hughes and T. C. Johnson. bibl il Science 195:402-4 Ja 28 '77
Posttranslational covalent modification of proteins. R. Uy and F. Wold. bibl il Science 198: 890-6 D 2 '77
See also
Arginine
Canavanine
Leucine
Proline

AMINOPEROXY radical. See Radicals (chemistry)

AMISH. See Mennonites

AMITE County, Miss.

Education

See Education—Mississippi

AMMETERS
Accurate milliammeters on a budget. D. Corbin. il Pop Electr 11:67-8 Je '77
How to use split-core ammeters. E. Powell. il Pop Sci 211:150+ N '77

AMMONIA
ACA—zinc additive for anhydrous ammonia. B. Gergen. il Suc Farm 75:no3 F32 F '77
Anhydrous ammonia for corn silage. J. R. Borcherding and L. Reichenberger. il Suc Farm 75:24-7 Ag '77
Anhydrous ammonia: the miracle of crop production. G. Vincent. il Suc Farm 75:36-7 O '77
Apply nitrogen this fall? using N-Serve with anhydrous. N. Reeder. il Farm J 101:22-3 N '77
Cold-flo ammonia: an alternative to conventional ammonia application. B. Gergen. il Suc Farm 75:no3 F5 F '77
Don't wait to fertilize wheat; the time to apply anhydrous. Suc Farm 75:39 D '77
How hot is Cold-flo ammonia? L. Reichenberger. il Suc Farm 75:28-9 O '77

AMMONIA in the body
Ammonia in the human airways: neutralization of inspired acid sulfate aerosols. T. V. Larson and others. bibl il Science 197:161-3 Jl 8 '77

AMMONS, A. R.
Man's nature; poem. Yale R 66:399 Mr '77
Perfect journey is; On walks I go a long way along; poems; excerpt from The snow poems. Mademoiselle 83:54 Je '77
Significances; poem. Nation 224:342 Mr 19 '77

AMMUNITION
See also
Cartridges

AMNESTY for draft resisters. See Military service, Compulsory—Draft resisters

AMNESTY for military deserters. See United States—Armed Forces—Desertion

AMNESTY International (organization)
For human rights; recording of benefit concert. J. R. Oestreich. il Am Rec G 40:12-15 My '77
Two Peace Prizes from Oslo. il pors Time 110:54 O 24 '77
World's conscience. Newsweek 90:61 O 24 '77

AMNIOCENTESIS
Women: the next endangered species? use in sex selection. P. K. Lynch. bibl Mademoiselle 83: 32+ My '77

AMOEBAS. See Amebas

L'AMORE dei tre re; opera. See Montemezzi, I.

AMORPHOUS semiconductors. See Semiconductors

AMORY, Cleveland
Blue bloods. il Sat Eve Post 249:84 Jl '77
Curmudgeon-at-large. See alternate issues of Saturday review to March 19, 1977
Stutz massage parlor. il Esquire 88:141-3 Jl '77

AMOS, John B.
Heck of a sales force. B. McMennamin. por Forbes 119:53-5 Mr 1 '77 *

AMOS, William H.
Unseen life of a mountain stream. il Nat Geog 151:562-80 Ap '77

AMPEX Corporation
High fidelity pathfinders; A. M. Poniatoff. N. Eisenberg. il por Hi Fi 27:72-3 S '77

AMPHETAMINES
Behavioral history as a determinant of the effects of *d*-amphetamine on punished behavior. J. E. Barrett. bibl il Science 198:67-9 O 7 '77
Cocaine, alcohol & amphetamines: thrillers or killers? J. C. Wang. Harp Baz 110:87+ Je '77
Paradoxical effects of amphetamine on preweanling and postweanling rats. B. A. Campbell and P. J. Randall. bibl il Science 195: 888-91 Mr 4 '77
Speed heals; combining morphine with amphetamine. Newsweek 89:65 Ap 11 '77

AMPHIBIA
See also
Embryology—Amphibia
Eye (amphibia)
Frogs
Salamanders
Toads

AMPHIBIANS, Hall of. See American Museum of Natural History, New York

AMPHIBIOUS landing craft. See Landing craft

AMPHIPRION. See Damselfishes

AMPLIFIERS
Amplifier kits: good sound with built-in savings. A. Santoni. il Pop Mech 147:82-3+ F '77
Better than MOS; RCA CA3140 family of operational amplifiers. L. Garner. il Pop Electr 11: 66-9+ Ap '77
Classes of audio amplifiers. L. Feldman. il Pop Electr 11:74-6 Mr '77
Heath's Module I; it's more than just a preamp. Pop Mech 147:166 F '77
Hi-fi: at the frontier. H. Fantel. Opera N 42:32-3 D 17 '77
IC audio preamplifiers. L. Garner. il Pop Electr 12:85-7+ S '77
New, practical OP AMP circuits. S. D. Prensky. il Pop Electr 11:47-8 F '77
Operational amplifier quiz. W. E. Parker. il Pop Electr 11:111 Mr '77
Pair of high quality amplifiers. C. Graham. Am Rec G 40:53-5 Je '77
Preamplifier for long distance reception. G. Sante. il Radio-Electr 48:70-1+ My '77
Pulse-width modulation for hi-fi. L. Feldman. il Radio-Electr 48:59-61 S '77
Stereo amp adapts for 4 channels. J. Free. il Pop Sci 210:72 Je '77
Telephone amplifiers. Consumers Res Mag 60:33 S '77
Two years of the power rule; FTC amplifier power rule. Hi Fi 27:33 N '77

Design

Class-H variproportional amplifier. L. Feldman. il Radio-Electr 48:53-5+ O '77

AMPLIFIERS—*Continued*

Noise

IHF sensitivity—what it really means. L. Feldman. il Radio-Electr 48:62-4 N '77
TIM distortion—how it affects your system. L. Feldman. il Radio-Electr 48:47-9 Jl '77

Testing

Dynamic crosstalk. J. Hirsch. il Pop Electr 12:32-3+ N '77
Equipment reports:
Heathkit AA-1640 power amplifier. il Radio-Electr 48:28-9+ Ap '77
Julian Hirsch audio reports:
Mitsubishi model DA-P10 preamplifier and model DA-A15 basic power amplifier. J. Hirsch. il Pop Electr 12:32-3+ N '77
Ortofon Model MC20 phono cartridge and Model MCA-76 preamplifier. J. Hirsch. il Pop Electr 12:35-6 Ag '77
Listening room; Dynaco and Health preamplifier and amplifiers. C. Graham. il Am Rec G 40:50-1 D '76
New equipment reports:
Another rare bird from Nakamichi; 630 tuner/preamplifier. il Hi Fi 28:45-7 Ja '78
Distinctly unconventional preamp from Philips; Philips AH-572. il Hi Fi 27:56+ N '77
Dynaco's stereo 300 amplifier—muscle and lots of moves. il Hi Fi 27:62+ Mr '77
Hegeman Probe: probity for low-level inputs. Hi Fi 27:44 Ag '77
Kenwood's KA-9100 is cool—and more. il Hi Fi 27:27-9 D '77
Loaded V-FET amp from Sony. il Hi Fi 27:39-40 My '77
Nikko Beta 1: smart looks and a dandy phono stage. il Hi Fi 27:35-6 D '77
Onkyo's A-7 integrated amp: virtue in reticence. il Hi Fi 27:63-4 N '77
Pioneer Spec-4, an amp for persnickety ears. il Hi Fi 28:56+ Ja '78
Pro styling, features in an integrated Scott. il Hi Fi 27:61-2 Jl '77
Specs plus in Pioneer Spec-2. il Hi Fi 27:45-6 Ap '77
Superb amplifier from Sansui. il Hi Fi 27:65-6 S '77
Yamaha's C-2, a preamp for purists. il Hi Fi 27:55-7 Mr '77
Radio-electronics tests:
Dynaco SCA-50. L. Feldman. il Radio-Electr 48:60-2 O '77
Epicure PR-4 preamplifier. il Radio-Electr 48:68-9+ S '77
Health AP-1615 preamplifier. il Radio-Electr 48:58-9+ My '77
Kenwood KA-8300. L. Feldman. il Radio-Electr 48:62-3+ S '77
Nakamichi 610 preamplifier. il Radio-Electr 48:49-50 Mr '77
Nikko TRM-750 integrated amplifier. L. Feldman. il Radio-Electr 48:56-8 My '77
Sansui AU-717 amplifier. il Radio-Electr 49:60-1 Ja '78
Sherwood HP-2000 amplifier. il Radio-Electr 48:59+ Je '77
Spectro-acoustics 101B preamp. il Radio-Electr 48:67-8 N '77
Sorting out amp and preamp specs. E. J. Foster. il Hi Fi 27:60-3 D '77

AMPLITUDE modulation radio broadcasting. See Radio broadcasting

AMPUTATION
When the patient says no; refusing permission to amputate; case of O. Simmons. Newsweek 89:77 Ja 24 '77

AMSEL, Abram, and others
Ultrasound emission in infant rats as an indicant of arousal during appetitive learning and extinction. bibl il Science 197:786-8 Ag 19 '77

AMSTERDAM, Anthony Guy
Capital punishment; address, Jule 8, 1977. Vital Speeches 43:677-82 S 1 '77
Dying institution. C. McWilliams. Nation 225:611-12 D 10 '77

AMSTERDAM, Netherlands

Art

Amsterdam (cont) G. Schwartz. Art N 76:99-102 My '77

Description

Touch of the Dutch. J. Ferri. il Holiday 58:44-7+ Ja '77

Jewish population

See Jews in the Netherlands

Music

See also
Opera—Netherlands

AMTEL, Inc-AMCA International Corporation merger. See Corporations—Acquisitions and mergers

AMTRAK. See National Railroad Passenger Corporation

AMUSEMENT parks
Family fun in the big-time theme parks. il Changing T 31:12-14 Je '77
Pop Xanadus of fun and fantasy. M. Demarest. il Time 110:32-4 Jl 4 '77
Theme parks: the profits in pleasure. R. Levy. il Duns R 109:88-91+ Ap '77
Utah's past in Pioneer Village. il Sunset 159:32 Ag '77
Vagabond camera; Carowinds amusement park. R. H. Rufa. il Travel 147:64-5+ Je '77

Equipment

See also
Roller coasters

Management

Ride is getting scarier for theme park owners. B. Uttal. il map Fortune 96:166-72+ D '77

AMUSEMENTS
See also
Circus
Games
Literary recreations
Mathematical recreations
Motion pictures
Play
Puzzles

AMUZEGAR, Jahangir
Requiem for the North-South conference. bibl f For Affairs 56:136-59 O '77

AMYGDALA. See Brain

ANABLE, Gloria
Nature preservers. B. Delatiner. McCalls 104:69 Jl '77 •

ANABOLIC steroids. See Steroids

ANAEROBIOSIS
Anaerobiosis and a theory of growth line formation. R. A. Lutz and D. C. Rhoads. bibl il Science 198:1222-7 D 23 '77

ANALEPTICS
See also
Pentylenetetrazole

ANALGESIA
Analgesia: how the body inhibits pain perception. J. L. Marx. Science 195:471-3 F 4 '77; Reply. R. Hayes and others. bibl 196:600 My 6 '77
New look at heroin could spur better medical use of narcotics. C. Holden. Science 198:807-9 N 25 '77
Pain relief by electrical stimulation of the central gray matter in humans and its reversal by naloxone. Y. Hosobuchi and others. bibl il Science 197:183-6 Jl 8 '77

ANALGESICS
See also
Aspirin
Enkephalins
Morphine

ANALOG to digital converters. See Digital electronics

ANALYSIS, Mathematical. See Mathematical analysis

ANAMORPHOSIS
Secrets of anamorphic art. S. Ferris. il Horizon 19:16-23 Ja '77

ANANIA, Michael
Aesthetique du râle; poem. Poetry 129:337-9 Mr '77

ANANTHANAYAGAM, Rosalia
In between; poem. Seventeen 36:38 S '77

ANARCHISM and anarchists
Breaking the shame barrier. B. Levin. il Horizon 19:88-9 Mr '77

ANASAZI culture. See Pueblo Indians

ANATOMICAL gifts. See Donation of organs, tissues, etc.

ANATOMY
See also
Homology (biology)
Women—Anatomy and physiology
also names of organs and regions of the body, e.g. Heart

ANATOMY, Artistic
Surrealistic anatomy studies. A. N. Sponzilli. il por Sch Arts 77:24-5 N '77

ANCESTRY. See Genealogy

ANCHORAGE
It's 10 p.m. Do you know where your anchor is? J. Cartwright. il Motor B & S 140:10+ D '77
See also
Marinas

Anecdotes, facetiae, satire, etc.

Anchor to leeward. D. Bradley. il Motor B & S 140:10+ N '77

ANCHORAGE, Alaska

Restaurants

See Restaurants—United States

ANCHORAGE daily news. See Newspapers—Alaska

ANCHORAGE times. See Newspapers—Alaska

ANCHORING. See Anchorage

ANCHORS
All about anchors; excerpt from Anchors and anchoring. R. D. Ogg. il Motor B & S 140: 45-6 Ag '77
How many ways to stow an anchor? B. Robinson. il Yachting 141:96-7 Ap '77
ANCHOVIES
Chain of events. Sci Am 237:60+ Jl '77
ANCIENT astronomy. See Astronomy, Ancient
ANCIENT libraries. See Libraries—History
ANCIENT records. See Records, Ancient
ANCRAM, N.Y.

Historic houses, sites, etc.

See Historic houses, sites, etc.—New York (state)
ANDALUSIA, Spain
Love letter to Andalusia. J. Winslow. il Holiday 58:36-8+ S '77
ANDERS, Edward, and Owen, Tobias
Mars and earth: origin and abundance of volatiles. bibl il Science 198:453-65 N 4 '77
ANDERS, William A.
Excerpts from testimony on nuclear reactor safety, March 2, 1976. Cong Digest 56:50+ F '77
ANDERSEN, Christopher
Name game. il Time 110:65 S 26 '77 *
ANDERSEN, Hans Christian
Fir tree; story. Sat Eve Post 249:68-71+ D '77
Tin soldier; story. Sat Eve Post 249:28-9 Jl '77
Wonderful world of Hans Christian Andersen; dramatization. See Newman, D.
ANDERSEN, Judith C. See Tan, H. K. jt auth
ANDERSEN, Juel. See Bauer, C. jt auth
ANDERSON, Alan, Jr
Managing headache. il N Y Times Mag p48+ My 8 '77
ANDERSON, Alexandra C.
Gifts: for the season. Vogue 167:93-4+ D '77
ANDERSON, Bernard E.
Make a larger investment in training programs; interview. por U.S. News 82:59 F 21 '77
ANDERSON, Bernhard W.
Herberg as theologian of Christianity. por Nat R 29:884-5 Ag 5 '77
ANDERSON, Bette
Customs reorganization and modernization; address, May 17, 1977. Vital Speeches 43:621-3 Ag 1 '77
ANDERSON, C. Wilson
Status of welfare reform in the United States. bibl Intellect 106:137-40 O '77
ANDERSON, Curtiss
(ed) See Hartman, D. Nice man to wake up to
ANDERSON, Dave
O. J. Simpson's run to glory. Read Digest 111: 217-18+ N '77
ANDERSON, David C.
Contract services stretch sewer maintenance budget. il Am City & County 92:53 F '77
ANDERSON, David E. See McClellan, J. jt auth
ANDERSON, Don L. and others
Earth as a seismic absorption band. bibl il Science 196:1104-6 Je 3 '77
ANDERSON, Garth R. and Matovcik, L. M.
Expression of murine sarcoma virus genes in uninfected rat cells subjected to anaerobic stress. bibl il Science 197:1371-4 S 30 '77
ANDERSON, George M.
Child abuse. America 136:478-82 My 28 '77
Illegal aliens: refugees from hunger. America 136:68-72 Ja 29 '77
Prostitution: old problem, new conflicts. America 136:350-4 Ap 16 '77
Wives, mothers and victims. America 137:46-50 Jl 30 '77
Women drinking: stigma and sickness. America 137:434-7 D 17 '77
ANDERSON, Gordon B. Jr
Oregon's forest conservation laws. il por Am For 83:16-19+ Mr; 19-21+ Ap '77
ANDERSON, Howard L.
Dispelling a highway safety myth; excerpt from address, December 1976. il Am City & County 92:109 My '77
ANDERSON, J. G. and others
Atomic chlorine and the chlorine monoxide radical in the stratosphere: three in situ observations. bibl il Science 198:501-3 N 4 '77
ANDERSON, J. N. See Dryden G. L. jt auth
ANDERSON, Jack
Dancing in a January world: Winnipeg's Contemporary Dancers. il por Dance Mag 51:44-9 Mr '77
Glorious unpredictability of George Balanchine. il Dance Mag 51:75-8 O '77
ANDERSON, Jack, 1922-
Regulating Congress. Current 189:11-16 Ja '77
ANDERSON, James D.
Black conjugations. Am Scholar 46:384+ Summ '77
ANDERSON, Jean
Azores; Madeira. il Sat R 5:30-1 O 29 '77
ANDERSON, Jervis
Reporter at large (cont) New Yorker 53:81-2+ N 14 '77
ANDERSON, Kay D.
Before the baby comes. il Parents Mag 52:20 My; 26 Jl; 28 Ag; 15 S; 31 N '77; 53:21 Ja '78
ANDERSON, Marian
Voice one hears once in a hundred years; interview, ed by B. Klaw. il pors Am Heritage 28:50-7 F '77
ANDERSON, Nancy
(ed) See Presley, V. Elvis
ANDERSON, Odin W.
Are national health services systems converging? Predictions for the United States. bibl f Ann Am Acad 434:24-38 N '77
ANDERSON, Peter A. V. and Mackie, G. O.
Electrically coupled, photosensitive neurons control swimming in a jelly-fish. bibl il Science 197:186-8 Jl 8 '77
ANDERSON, Philip W.
1977 Nobel Prize in physics. M. L. Cohen and L. M. Falicov. bibl pors Science 198:713-15 N 18 '77 *
Nobel prizes: seven in '77. pors Sci N 112:260-1 O 22 '77 *
Physicists share in Nobel Prizes in three disciplines. G. B. Lubkin. pors Phys Today 30:77-8 D '77 *
ANDERSON, Robert Orville
Under Observation. D. K. Shah and A. Collings. il por Newsweek 90:102-3 D 19 '77 *
ANDERSON, Robin L.
Brazil: walking the tightrope. bibl f Cur Hist 72:53-6+ F '77
ANDERSON, Roger E.
Financing the future; address, March 7, 1977. Vital Speeches 43:408-11 Ap 15 '77
Improving U.S. prospects in global competition. por Nations Bus 65:66-8 My '77
ANDERSON, Roy A.
Anderson to succeed Haack as Lockheed's chief executive. Aviation W 107:24 Ag 8 '77 *
Can Roy Anderson make people forget Lockheed's problems? il por Bus W p74-7+ O 10 '77 *
Lockheed's great dilemma. il por Time 110:40+ Ag 22 '77 *
ANDERSON, Sally
Norway's reindeer Lapps. il map Nat Geog 152: 364-79 S '77
ANDERSON, Sparky
Cincinnati Kid. R. Kahn. il pors Time 109:78 Ap 11 '77 *
ANDERSON, Terryl L.
Angles and angels; poem. Chr Cent 94:1162 D 14 '77
Ballad of the church bazaar. Chr Cent 94:397 Ap 27 '77
ANDERSON, Walter Inglis
Southern gentleman and Pope's Homer. R. S. Sugg, Jr. il por Smithsonian 7:125-30+ F '77 *
ANDERSON, Wendell R.
5 freshman senators who are moving into the spotlight. pors U.S. News 82:24-5 F 7 '77 *
ANDERSON, William T.
William T. Anderson: army officer, doctor, minister, and writer. F. R. Levstik. il Negro Hist Bull 40:662-3 Ja '77 *
ANDERSON, Clayton & Company-Gerber Products Company merger. See Food industry—Acquisitions and mergers
ANDERSSON, Stikken
Beatle beaters. G. Smith. por Forbes 120:78 Jl 15 '77 *
ANDES, Charles L.
Bicentennial era; address, October 27, 1976. Vital Speeches 43:194-6 Ja 15 '77
ANDRAE Crouch and the Disciples (gospel singers) See Singers
ANDRE, Carl
Indentations in space; interview. New Yorker 53:51-2 N 21 '77

about

Andre's square one. Vasari. il Art N 76:29 N '77 *
Connecticut rocks; Stone Field Sculpture in Hartford. il por Horizon 20:59 N '77 *
ANDRE, Constance G. and others
Lunar surface chemistry: a new imaging technique. bibl il map Science 197:986-9 S 2 '77
ANDREA, Marianne
Finding the path; poem. Sat Eve Post 249:110 Mr '77
ANDREA Chénier; opera. See Giordano, U.
ANDREASEN, Alan R. and Best, Arthur
Consumers complain—does business respond? il Harvard Bus R 55:93-101 Jl '77
ANDREE, Robert G.
Teacher rights in a changing society. Clearing H 50:398-401 My '77
ANDREJEVIC, Helen B.
Books for boys and girls. See issues of Parents' magazine & better homemaking
ANDREOTTI, Giulio
First-hand appraisal of Communist threat in Italy; interview, ed by D. B. Richardson. por U.S. News 83:30-1 Ag 1 '77
Prime Minister Andreotti of Italy visits Washington; exchange of remarks, December 6, 1976. Dept State Bull 76:13-14 Ja 3 '77

ANDREOTTI, Giulio—*Continued*

Visit to the United States, 1976

Prime Minister Andreotti of Italy visits Washington; exchange of remarks, December 6, 1976. G. R. Ford; G. Andreotti. Dept State Bull 76: 12-14 Ja 3 '77

Visit to the United States, 1977

Prime Minister Andreotti of Italy visits Washington; statement, July 27, 1977. Dept State Bull 77:224-6 Ag 22 '77

ANDRETTI, Mario
Andretti's comeback. P. Bonventre and J. Lowell. il por Newsweek 89:63 My 30 '77 *
Man with a mission. J. Scalzo. il pors Motor T 29:114-16+ Mr '77 *
Suddenly Mario is the magician again; Monte Carlo Grand Prix. S. Moses. il por Sports Illus 46:22-3 My 30 '77 *

ANDREW, Brother
I am not anti-Communist; excerpt from Battle for Africa. Chr Today 22:28-30 D 9 '77

ANDREWS, Frank Emerson
Special report: as others see us. Wilson Lib Bull 52:124-7 O '77

ANDREWS, Joseph
Europe's scenic train rides. il Travel 147:54-9 Mr '77

ANDREWS, Larry
Responses to literature: enlarging the range. Engl J 66:60-2 F '77

ANDREWS, Paul
Sacramental color of a fire engine. Chr Cent 94:549-50 Je 1 '77

ANDREWS, Peter
Birth of the talkies. Sat R 5:40+ N 12 '77
Boring the audience is unforgivable. il pors Horizon 20:58-65 O '77
Coffee table books, demitasse size. il Sat R 5:32+ N 26 '77
Edward Gorey onstage. il pors Horizon 20:12-15 N '77
Famous last apothegms. il Horizon 19:96 Ja '77
Rarest of birds. il pors Horizon 21:56-61 Ja '78
Totally freaked out on music. il pors Horizon 20:10-16 D '77

ANDREWS, Roy Chapman
Bound for glory. Sat Eve Post 249:19 Jl '77

ANDREWS, Sheryl B.
Second look:
Glass slipper. Horn Bk 53:193-4 Ap '77

ANDREWS, Weston, and Miller, D. L.
Instant pictures. See issues of Modern photography

ANDRISANI, Paul J. and Kohen, A. I.
Effects of collective bargaining as measured for men in blue-collar jobs. bibl il M Labor R 100: 46-9 Ap '77

ANDROGENS
Androgen concentration in motor neurons of cranial nerves and spinal cord. M. Sar and W. E. Stumpf. bibl il Science 197:77-9 Jl 1 '77
Pheromonally induced sexual maturation in females: regulation by the social environment of the male: house mice. J. R. Lombardi and J. G. Vandenbergh. bibl il Science 196:545-6 Ap 29 '77

ANDROIDS. See Automatons

ANDRONIKOS, Manolis Leonidas
Athenian democracy's grand design. il UNESCO Courier 30:20-3 O '77

about

Treasures from a golden tomb. N. Gage and J. Gage. il por map N Y Times Mag p 14-19+ D 25 '77 *

ANDROSCH, Hannes
Austerity: a way to avoid devaluation. il por Bus W p32-3 Ja 9 '78 *

ANDRUS, Cecil D.
Audubon talks with Andrus; interview, ed by G. Reiger. Audubon 79:148-50 My '77
Commitment for recreation. por Parks & Rec 12:15 Jl '77
Energy, water, environment—a top official looks ahead; interview. il por U.S. News 82:62-4 Je 27 '77
Federal feedback. por Nat Parks & Con Mag 51: 21 Je '77

about

From symbolism to substance. J. B. Craig. Am For 83:23 My '77 *
Inside the Interior's superior. T. Trueblood. il por Field & S 82:16+ My '77 *
Interior Department: Andrus promises sweeping changes. L. J. Carter. por Science 196:507-10 Ap 29 '77 *
Interior redesign. R. Boeth and others. il por Newsweek 90:22 Ag 8 '78 *
New environment at Interior. J. Shepherd. il por N Y Times Mag p36+ My 8 '77 *
New man at Interior. E. A. Bauer. por Outdoor Life 159:106+ Mr '77 *
Secretary of the Interior Andrus. Am For 83:14 F '77 *

ANECDOTES
See also
Last words

ANEMIA
Anemia epidemic; correcting iron deficiency in women by diet. J. C. Wang. Harp Baz 110: 91+ Je '77
Hereditary hemolytic anemia with increased red cell adenosine deaminase (45- to 70-fold) and decreased adenosine triphosphate. W. N. Valentine and others. bibl il Science 195:783-5 F 25 '77
Theta-sensitive cell and erythropoiesis: identification of a defect in W/Wv anemic mice. W. Wiktor-Jedrzejczak. bibl il Science 196: 313-15 Ap 15 '77
See also
Sickle cell anemia

ANEMOMETER
Vortex sensor measures wind speed with no moving parts. J. Free. il Pop Sci 210:53 Mr '77

ANEMONE fish. See Damselfishes

ANEMONES, Sea. See Sea anemones

ANESTHESIA
Statistics and ethics in surgery and anesthesia. J. P. Gilbert and others. bibl il Science 198: 684-9 N 18 '77
What patients should know about anesthesia. W. A. Nolen. McCalls 104:36+ Mr '77

ANGEL, Daniel Duane
Product liability; address, September 22, 1977. Vital Speeches 44:49-52 N 1 '77

ANGEL, John Lawrence
Breathing life into dry bones. M. Kernan. il por Smithsonian 7:116-18+ bibl(p 156) F '77 *

ANGEL dust (drug) See Phencyclidine hydrochloride

ANGELICA Press. See Printing industry

ANGELL, Roger
Greetings, friends! poem. New Yorker 53:25 D 26 '77
Sporting scene (cont) New Yorker 53:103-4+ Ap 25; 48-54+ N 14 '77

ANGELOPOULOS, Theodor
Reviews: O Thiasos. H. Koning. il Film Q 30: 46-50 Spr '77 *

ANGELOU, Maya
Cicely Tyson: reflections on a lone black rose. il pors Ladies Home J 94:40-1+ F '77
Maya Angelou: in search of self; interview, ed by J. M. Elliot. por Negro Hist Bull 40:694-5 My '77

ANGER
Control your temper. L. David. Seventeen 36: 116-17+ F '77
How to control your anger; interview. J. P. Comer. il por U.S. News 83:53-4 O 10 '77
How to deal with anger. M. Lasswell and N. Lobsenz. McCalls 105:127+ O '77
Seven deadly sins today; excerpt. H. Fairlie. il New Repub 177:18-21 S 24 '77
Why it's good to get good and mad. M.-E. Banashek. Mademoiselle 83:126-7+ Je '77

ANGERMUELLER, Hans H.
Commercial vs. investment bankers. il Harvard Bus R 55:132-44 S '77

ANGINO, Ernest E.
High-level and long-lived radioactive waste disposal. bibl il Science 198:885-90 D 2 '77

ANGIOGRAPHY
New medical techniques from space technology; vascular image processing. D. H. Blankenhorn. Intellect 106:189 N '77

ANGIOSPERMS
Ecology and evolution of flowering plant dominance. P. J. Regal. bibl Science 196:622-9 My 6 '77
See also
Flagellaria

ANGIOSPERMS, Fossil
Chemistry of still-green fossil leaves. Sci N 111:391 Je 18 '77
Flavonoids and other chemical constituents of fossil miocene zelkova (ulmaceae) K. J. Niklas and D. E. Giannasi. bibl il Science 196:877-8 My 20 '77

ANGIOTENSIN
Angiotensin injected into the neostriatum after learning disrupts retention performance. J. M. Morgan and A. Routtenberg. bibl il Science 196: 87-9 Ap 1 '77
Angiotensin: physiological role in water-deprivation—induced thirst of rats. R. L. Malvin and others. bibl il Science 197:171-3 Jl 8 '77

ANGIOTENSIN converting enzyme. See Peptidases

ANGLE of repose; opera. See Imbrie, A. W.

ANGLE-resolved photoemission spectroscopy. See Spectrum analysis

ANGLICAN Church. See Church of England

ANGLICAN Church in Australia. See Church of England in Australia

ANGLICAN Church in North America. See Church of England in America

ANGLICAN Church in Uganda. See Church of England in Uganda

ANGLICAN Church of Canada. See Church of England in Canada
ANGLING. See Fishing
ANGLO-AMERICAN cataloging rules. See Cataloging
ANGLO AMERICAN Corporation of South Africa, Ltd
Closer to the top at Anglo American. il Bus W p38-9 Je 27 '77
ANGOLA
Africa, Soviet imperialism & the retreat of American power. B. Rustin and C. Gershman. Commentary 64:33-43 O '77
See also
Guerrillas—Angola
United Nations—Angola
ANGRIST, Stanley W.
Commodities. See issues of Forbes
ANGUS, Robert
Those old-time voices are big-time again. il Ret Liv 16:40-2 D '76
What test reports don't tell you about blank cassettes. il Hi Fi 27:58-63 F '77
ANH, Le Thi
New Vietnam. Nat R 29:487-8 Ap 29 '77
ANHYDROUS ammonia. See Ammonia
ANIFIED field theories. See Field theory (physics)
ANIKULAPO-KUTI, Fela
Nigeria's dissident superstar. J. Darton. il pors N Y Times Mag p 10-12+ Jl 24 '77 *
ANIMAL actors. See Animals as actors
ANIMAL and Plant Health Inspection Service. See United States—Agriculture, Department of—Animal and Plant Health Inspection Service
ANIMAL behavior. See Animals—Habits and behavior
ANIMAL calling
Bugle your elk. C. J. Farmer. il Field & S 82:40-1+ N '77
See also
Bird calling
ANIMAL communication
Almost human; training methods. P. Gwynne and others. il Newsweek 89:70-1+ Mr 7 '77
Pursuit of reason. H. T. P. Hayes. il pors N Y Times Mag p21-3+ Je 12 '77; Reply. B. DeMott. Atlantic 240:86+ S '77
Smell signals in fox scavenging. J. Arehart-Treichel. il Sci N 112:348-9 N 19 '77
Social communication in canids: evidence for the evolution of a stereotyped mammalian display. M. Bekoff. bibl il Science 197:1097-9 S 9 '77
See also
Animal sounds
ANIMAL defenses. See Defense mechanisms (biology)
ANIMAL electricity. See Electrophysiology
ANIMAL experimentation
Of rats and men. A. Wolff. N Y Times Mag p88+ My 15 '77
Primate model for long-term study of intraventricularly or intrathecally administered drugs and intracranial pressure. J. H. Wood and others. bibl il Science 195:499-501 F 4 '77
See also
Laboratory animals
Stimulation (physiology)
Laws and legislation
Creative penmanship in animal testing prompts FDA controls; Good Laboratory Practice regulations. R. J. Smith. Science 198:1227-9 D 23 '77
ANIMAL genetics
Genetic predisposition and stress-induced hypertension. R. Friedman and J. Iwai; reply with rejoinder. M. Peters. bibl Science 198:80 O 7 '77
Paternity and genetic heterogeneity in the polygynous bat, phyllostomus hastatus. G. F. McCracken and J. W. Bradbury. bibl il Science 198:303-6 O 21 '77
ANIMAL habitat. See Zoology—Ecology
ANIMAL introduction
Carolina haven for red wolf; introduction in Cape Romain National Wildlife Refuge. P. Laurie. Audubon 79:152 Ja '77
In South Carolina, another transplant runs into trouble; death of transplanted red wolf in Cape Romain National Wildlife Refuge. M. A. T. Neville. il Nat Wildlife 15:10-11 Ag '77
Wildlife roulette. G. Laycock. il Outdoor Life 159:34+ F '77
See also
Fish introduction
ANIMAL language. See Animal communication
ANIMAL learning
Angiotensin injected into the neostriatum after learning disrupts retention performance. J. M. Morgan and A. Routtenberg. bibl il Science 196:87-9 Ap 1 '77
Classical conditioning with auditory discrimination of the eye blink in decerebrate cats. R. J. Norman and others. bibl il Science 196:551-3 Ap 29 '77
Odor-aversion learning in neonatal rats. J. W. Rudy and M. D. Cheatle. bibl il Science 198:845-6 N 25 '77
Selective vocal learning in a sparrow. P. Marler and S. Peters. bibl il Science 198:519-21 N 4 '77
Suckling as incentive to instrumental learning in preweanling rats. J. T. Kenny and E. M. Blass. bibl il Science 196:898-9 My 20 '77
See also
Memory
ANIMAL locomotion
Electrically coupled, photosensitive neurons control swimming in a jellyfish. P. A. V. Anderson and G. O. Mackie. bibl il Science 197:186-8 Jl 8 '77
Leap; fishes. J. Gibbs. il Outdoor Life 160:67-71+ N '77
Pulmonary metabolism during diving; conditioning blood for the brain. P. W. Hochachka and others. bibl il Science 198:831-4 N 25 '77
Terrestrial locomotion in penguins: it costs more to waddle. B. Pinshow and others. bibl il Science 195:592-4 F 11 '77
ANIMAL lore
Bambi factor; animal symbolism. B. Nietschmann. Natur Hist 86:84+ Ag '77
Cult of the wild; excerpt. B. Rensberger. il Sci Digest 82:56-61 N '77
ANIMAL luminescence. See Bioluminescence
ANIMAL models of human diseases. See Diseases—Animal models
ANIMAL painting and illustration. See Animals in art
ANIMAL populations
See also
Fish populations
Population genetics
Control
See also
Wildlife management
ANIMAL sculpture
Wood masterpieces: China and Japan. J. Brzostoski. il Craft Horiz 37:46-9+ Ap '77
ANIMAL sounds
Call of the duck. G. Gottlieb. Natur Hist 86:40+ O '77
Layman's guide to animal sounds abroad. il Int Wildlife 7:50 N '77
Nepotism and the evolution of alarm calls. P. W. Sherman. bibl il Science 197:1246-53 S 23 '77
See also
Fish sounds
Insect sounds
ANIMAL symbolism. See Animal lore
ANIMAL temperature. See Temperature, Animal and human
ANIMAL training. See Animals—Training
ANIMAL traps. See Traps
ANIMALS
See also
Desert fauna
Feral animals
Game
Hybridization
Livestock
Mammals
Pets
Photography of animals
Pregnancy in animals
Rare animals
Wildlife
Zoology
also names of animals and classes of animals, e.g. Monkeys
Anecdotes, facetiae, satire, etc.
Beaver at the door. R. Rosenblatt. New Repub 176:36-7 Je 4 '77
Breeding
See Breeding
Capture
Confessions of an animal trafficker; excerpt from The animal connection. J.-Y. Domalain. il Natur Hist 86:54-67 bibl(p94+) My '77
Classification
See Zoology—Classification
Coloration
See Color of animals
Diseases and pests
See also
Veterinary medicine
also subhead Diseases and pests under names of animals, e.g. Dogs—Diseases and pests
Ear
See Ear (animals)
Ecology
See Zoology—Ecology
Economic value
See Zoology, Economic

ANIMALS—*Continued*

Export-import trade

See also
Animal introduction

Eyes

See Eye (animals)

Food and feeding

Bugging the bugs. A. Odum. il Int Wildlife 8:18-19 Ja '78
Deadly harvests and wildlife. J. V. Dennis. il por Conservationist 31:26-7 My '77
Feeding behavior and predator avoidance in heterospecific groups. D. H. Morse. bibl BioScience 27:332-9 My '77
Fighting the white death; winter feeding. R. Halverson. Outdoor Life 161:69+ Ja '78
To catch a fish. A. Odum. il Int Wildlife 7:18-19 Jl '77
See also
Game—Food and feeding
Monkeys—Food and feeding
Rats—Food and feeding
Reptiles—Food and feeding
Salt licks

Habits and behavior

Call of the duck. G. Gottlieb. Natur Hist 86:40+ O '77
Can animals anticipate earthquakes? E. Shaw. Natur Hist 86:14+ N '77
Caring groups and selfish genes; theories of V. C. Wynne-Edwards and R. Dawkins. S. J. Gould. Natur Hist 86:20+ D '77
Compressional and surface waves in sand: used by desert scorpions to locate prey. P. H. Brownell. bibl il Science 197:479-82 Jl 29 '77
How to avoid shark attack (if you happen to be a Hawaiian monk seal) L. R. Taylor and G. Naftel. il Oceans 10:21-3 N '77
How to keep your pet from running your life; dog problems; excerpts from Your pet isn't sick (he just wants you to think so) H. Tanzer and N. Lyons. Redbook 149:254+ My '77
How to prevent dog bites. J. E. Rodgers. il Ladies Home J 94:199-200 N '77
Human drama in a small cage. A. Roiphe. il N Y Times Mag p52-3 Je 26 '77
If pandas scream, an earthquake is coming. P. Magida. il Int Wildlife 7:36-9 S '77
Law of the jungle (revised): do you know that the king of beasts is a permissive father? C. Moss. il Ms 6:65-7 Ja '78
Lindberghs liberate monkeys from constraints; Verlhiac Primate Center. R. Chelminski. il pors Smithsonian 7:58-65 bibl(p 126) Mr '77
Lorenz observed. G. E. Allen. il Natur Hist 86:78-82+ Je '77
Monogamous mammals: variations on a scheme. M. G. Riegel. il Sci N 112:76-8 Jl 30 '77
Rat societies. R. Lore and K. Flannelly. il Sci Am 236:106-11+ My '77
Sketch book looks at territories. W. Trimm. il Conservationist 32:inside back cover Jl '77
Smell signals in fox scavenging. J. Arehart-Treichel. il Sci N 112:348-9 N 19 '77
Social behavior in hatching green iguanas: life at a reptile rookery. G. M. Burghardt and others. bibl il Science 195:689-91 F 18 '77
Successful whitetail hunting; habits of deer. B. W. Dalrymple. il Field & S 82:43-5 D '77
Who loves you? work of S. J. Suomi on the emotional development of rhesus monkeys. J. Greenberg. il por Sci N 112:139+ Ag 27 '77
Why animals develop emotional problems. M. W. Fox. il McCalls 104:88+ F '77
See also
Behavior genetics
Biotelemetry
Birds—Habits and behavior
Defense mechanisms (biology)
Fishes—Habits and behavior
Hibernation
Licking (animals)
Sexual behavior—Animals

Language

See Animal communication

Protection

See Conservation associations; Wildlife conservation; Wildlife sanctuaries

Sterilization

See Sterilization, Sexual—Animals

Stories

All things wise and wonderful; excerpt. J. Herriot. il Read Digest 111:233-42+ O '77
Encounters in a winter wilderness; excerpt from The living wilderness. E. W. Hunt. il Read Digest 112:124-8 Ja '78
See also
Cats—Stories
Dogs—Stories
Passenger pigeons—Stories

Temperature

See Temperature, Animal and human

Training

Animal lover finds ideal career; M. Robinson. il pors Ebony 32:104+ O '77
Greatest showman on earth; circus animal trainer G. Gebel-Williams. C. Kirkpatrick. il pors Sports Illus 47:82-6+ S 26 '77
See also
Animals as actors
Cats—Training
Elephants—Training

Treatment

Humane education: a forgotten mandate. P. J. Quinn. Educ Digest 43:60-1 S '77
See also
Hunting—Ethical aspects
Trapping

Vision

See Vision (animals)

ANIMALS, Abnormalities of. See Abnormalities (animals)

ANIMALS, Effect of salt on
Lure of the salt lick. P. Magida. il Int Wildlife 7:37 Mr '77

ANIMALS, Extinct
See also
Dinosaurs
Plesiosaurs

ANIMALS, Food habits of. See Animals—Food and feeding

ANIMALS, Fossil. See Paleontology

ANIMALS, Injurious and beneficial. See Zoology, Economic

ANIMALS, Mythical
Bigfoot is back. R. Boeth and E. Sciolino. il Newsweek 90:40 O 31 '77
See also
Loch Ness monster
Sea serpents

Anecdotes, facetiae, satire, etc.

Nessie no, but Yeti yes: an abominable abdomen. M. Hamman. il Smithsonian 7:132 Mr '77

ANIMALS, Predatory
Enemies of gamebirds. C. Elliott. il Outdoor Life 160:74-7+ S '77
See also
Foxes
Hyenas
Wolves

ANIMALS, Rare. See Rare animals

ANIMALS, Stuffed. See Toys

ANIMALS, Treatment of. See Animals—Treatment

ANIMALS and children. See Children and animals

ANIMALS and civilization
Cult of the wild; excerpt. B. Rensberger. il Sci Digest 82:56-61 N '77

ANIMALS as actors
Hello, doggy! Sandy of Annie. A. Quindlen. il N Y Times Mag p38-9 My 15 '77

ANIMALS in art
Animals and men: love, admiration and outright war; excerpt from Animals and men. K. Clark. il Smithsonian 8:52-61 bibl(p 130) S '77
Art of shooting and the shooting arts; Ducks Unlimited Midwest Wildlife Art Show. B. Tarrant. il Field & S 81:144-8 F '77
Balth and the beasts. S. Butchkes. il pors Craft Horiz 37:28-31 Ag '77
Bison in art and history; excerpt from The bison in art. L. Barsness. il Am West 14:10-21 Mr '77
Button collecting: bears. D. F. Brown. il Hobbies 82:138-9 O '77
Canadian sketchbook. A. Odum. il Int Wildlife 7:42-3 Mr '77
Charles Livingston Bull. D. L. Tuttle. il por Conservationist 32:8-13 Jl '77
Douglas Allen: echoes of the Brandywine. B. Silverstein. il por Am Artist 41:44-9+ N '77
Flap of vultures. B. Kuhn. il Audubon 79:56-7 N '77
International sketchbook (cont) A. Odum. il Int Wildlife 7:18-19 My; 18-19 Jl; 22-3 N '77; 8:18-19 Ja '78
Maynard Reece paints—memories on canvas. G. H. Harrison. il pors Am For 83:24-7 Jl '77
Painted as they are. G. Coheleach. il Read Digest 111:168-73 Ap '77
Robert Abbett; painting hunting dogs; interview, ed by N. Meglin. R. Abbett. il por Am Artist 41:46-9 Jl '77
Scythians: nomad goldsmiths of the open steppes; symposium. il UNESCO Courier 29:4-49 D '76
See also
Animal sculpture
Horses in art

Exhibitions

In praise of beasts: round-the-world museum observance. M. Green. il Smithsonian 8:108-14 bibl(p 162) N '77

ANIMALS in literature
See also
Animal lore

ANIMALS in religion, folklore, etc. See Animal lore
ANIMATED cartoons. See Motion pictures—Animated cartoons
ANIONS. See Ions
ANIS. See Cuckoos
ANISOMYCIN. See Antibiotics
ANKNEY, Carol
Night before graduation. il McCalls 104:128-9+ Je '77
ANKYLOSING spondylitis. See Spondylitis
ANN ARBOR, Mich.

Education

Charting the grandperson galaxy; Teaching-Learning Communities Project. M. Mehta. Educ Digest 42:22-5 Ja '77

Municipal improvement

Ann Arbor neighborhood preserves its history; Old West Side. K. Grover. il Am City & County 92:64-5 Mr '77
ANNA Christie; drama. See O'Neill, E. G.
ANNAPOLIS, Md.
Annapolis. M. C. Hurley. il Travel 147:40-5 Je '77
Antiques; special issue; ed by W. Garrett. bibl il maps Antiques 111:144-200 Ja '77

Education

See Education—Maryland

Historic houses, sites, etc.

See Historic houses, sites, etc.—Maryland
ANNAPOLIS Naval Academy. See United States Naval Academy, Annapolis
ANNAPOLIS-Newport Race. See Yacht racing
ANNAU, Zoltan. See Fechter, L. D. jt auth
ANNELIDS
Vision in annelid worms. G. Wald and R. Stephen. bibl il Science 196:1434-9 Je 24 '77
ANNENBERG, Walter Hubert
Annenberg controversy. G. Glueck. por Art N 76:63-4 My '77 *
Annenberg *interruptus.* por Time 109:64 Mr 28 '77 *
Hoving years; interview, ed by M. N. Carter. T. P. F. Hoving. pors Art N 76:37-40 Ja '77 *
ANNEXATION (municipal government)
Octopus; Houston's expansion. il Newsweek 89: 27 Je 13 '77
ANNIE; musical comedy. See Musical comedy, revue, etc.—Reviews—Single works
ANNOBON (island) See Pigalu (island)
ANNUAL meetings, Stockholders. See Stockholders meetings
ANNUAL reports, Corporate. See Corporation reports
ANNUALS (plants)
Annual plants: adaptations to desert environments. T. W. Mulroy and P. W. Rundel. bibl BioScience 27:109-14 F '77
Nostalgic annuals to start from seed. Bet Hom & Gard 55:261 My '77
ANNUITIES
Annuity with a new twist. il Changing T 31:43-5 N '77
Stodgy old annuities take on a fresh allure. il U.S. News 83:91-2 O 10 '77
ANNULMENT of marriage (canon law) See Marriage—Annulment (canon law)
ANORECTIC drugs. See Weight reducing preparations
ANOREXIA nervosa
Anorexia nervosa: the dieting disease. W. A. Nolen. McCalls 104:72+ Je '77
Girl who wouldn't grow up; case of S. Parsons. J. P. Blank. il Read Digest 111:199-202+ O '77
ANOXEMIA
Hepatic regeneration and erythropoietin production in the rat. B. A. Naughton and others. bibl il Science 196:301-2 Ap 15 '77
Reversal of cardiopulmonary failure during active sleep in hypoxic kittens: implications for sudden infant death. T. L. Baker and D. J. McGinty. bibl il Science 198:419-21 O 28 '77
ANSELMO, Sandra
Parent involvement in the schools. bibl Clearing H 50:297-9 Mr '77
ANSKY, S. pseud
Dybbuk. Reviews
New Yorker 53:47-8 Ja 2 '78 *
ANSON, John S.
Clouds; I know the star; Early frost; Mothwings; poems. Poetry 131:145-6 D '77
ANT lions
Pit and the antlion. H. Topoff. il Natur Hist 86: 64-71 bibl(p 100-1) Ap '77
ANTARCTIC exploration
Endurance: the epic of Ernest Shackleton. N. Rosa. il por Oceans 10:31-5 My '77
Penguins and their neighbors; M. S. Lindblad Explorer wildlife odyssey. R. T. Peterson. il map Nat Geog 152:236-55 Ag '77
Scott's last voyage; ed by A. Savours. R. F. Scott. il por Sat Eve Post 249:42-3+ N '77
Stonington Island: America's most southerly ghost town; the United States Antarctic Service Expedition and the Ronne Antarctic Research Expedition. J. H. Lipps. il Oceans 10:42-5 My '77
This accursed land; excerpt from Mawson's will. L. Bickel. il por map Read Digest 111: 199-202+ Jl '77
ANTARCTIC Ocean
Antarctic marine flora: uniquely devoid of kelps. R. L. Moe and P. C. Silva. bibl il Science 196: 1206-8 Je 10 '77
Antarctic soft-bottom benthos in oligotrophic and eutrophic environments. P. K. Dayton and J. S. Oliver. bibl il map Science 197:55-8 Jl 1 '77
ANTARCTIC Regions
Antarctica; symposium. il Oceans 10:12-59 My '77
It's like entering another world. J. F. McWethy. il U.S. News 82:67-8 F 28 '77
See also
Antarctic exploration
Natural resources—Antarctic Regions
Scotia Sea
South Georgia (island)
Stonington Island
Zoology—Antarctic Regions
ANTARCTIC research
Antarctica: rich around the edges. R. Burton. il Sea Front 23:287-95 S '77
Antarctica's icy assets. P. Gwynne and others. il Newsweek 90:92-3+ O 3 '77
Get ready Antarctica. . . here comes the boom! P. Gwynne. il Int Wildlife 7:4-11 N '77
Life beneath the Antarctic ice; Ross-Ice Shelf Project. il Sci N 112:421 D 24 '77
Meteorite on ice. Newsweek 91:50 Ja 16 '78
Rise and fall of Antarctic ice: the rest of the iceberg. I. Ashkenazy. il Oceans 10:26-30 My '77
ANTARCTIC Seals Conservation Agreement. See Marine mammals—Laws and legislation
ANTARCTIC Treaty, 1959
Antarctica's icy assets. P. Gwynne and others. il Newsweek 90:92-3+ O 3 '77
Parties to Antarctic Treaty meet in London; statement, September 19, 1977. R. C. Brewster. Dept State Bull 77:738-40 N 21 '77
Recommendation to protect Antarctic environment; statement, September 12, 1977. R. C. Brewster. Dept State Bull 77:576-7 O 24 '77
Science in Europe: moratorium set on Antarctic oil at October meeting. N. Hawkes. il map Science 198:709-12 N 18 '77
ANTELMAN, Seymour M. and Caggiula, A. R.
Norepinephrine-dopamine interactions and behavior. bibl Science 195:646-53 F 18 '77
ANTELOPE hunting
See also
Pronghorn hunting
ANTELOPES
See also
Pronghorns
ANTENNAS (electronics)
NASA planning Spacelab/antenna test. B. M. Elson. il Aviation W 107:54-5+ O 31 '77
See also
Radio antennas
Television antennas
ANTHOLOGIES
Why is poem a four-letter word? childrens poetry anthologies. M. Lewis. bibl SLJ 23:38-9 My '77
ANTHONY, Carolyn Additon
Questions, anyone? Am Educ 13:13-18 O '77
ANTHONY, Earl
$100,000 bowling machine. R. Bongartz. il pors Sports Illus 46:66-9+ Mr 7 '77 *
ANTHONY, John
John Anthony gives a party. il por Harp Baz 110:210-11+ S '77 *
ANTHONY Scally, Sister. See Scally, A.
ANTHROPOLOGICAL museums
See also
British Columbia. University, Vancouver—Museum of Anthropology
ANTHROPOLOGISTS
Social anthropologists learn to be scientific. G. B. Kolata. Science 195:770 F 25 '77; Discussion. 196:372+ Ap 22 '77
See also
Angel, J L.
Castaneda, C.
Douglas-Hamilton, I.
Leakey, R. E. F.
Mead, M.
ANTHROPOLOGY
See also
Anthropometry
Ethnology
Man, Prehistoric
ANTHROPOLOGY, Philosophical. See Philosophical anthropology
ANTHROPOMETRY
Breathing life into dry bones. M. Kernan. il por Smithsonian 7:116-18+ bibl(p 156) F '77

ANTHROPOMORPHISM
Anthropomorphism. D. R. Griffin. bibl BioScience 27:445-6 Jl '77

ANTIBACTERIAL activity. See Bactericidal action

ANTI-BALLISTIC missile system. See Guided missiles—Defenses

ANTIBIOTIC feed supplements
Antibiotics in feed: the first punch has been thrown. J. Russell. Farm J 101:Hog 20 Je '77
Drive to limit the antibiotics in animal feed. il Bus W p55-6 Ja 16 '78
FDA to limit drugs in animal feeds. B. J. Culliton. Science 196:510 Ap 29 '77
What an antibiotic ban will mean. J. Rohlf. Farm J 101:Beef 12 Je '77
What if you lose feed drugs? K. Daly. Farm J 101:Hog 16 Ag '77

ANTIBIOTICS
Monomeric forms of the acid ionophore lasalocid A (X-537A) from polar solvents. C. C. Chiang and I. C. Paul. bibl il Science 196:1441-3 Je 24 '77
Neuronal circadian rhythm: phase shifting by a protein synthesis inhibitor; anisomycin. J. W. Jacklet. bibl il Science 198:69-71 O 7 '77
Reverse banding on chromosomes produced by a guanosine-cytosine specific DNA binding antibiotic: olivomycin. J. H. Van De Sande and others. bibl il Science 195:400-2 Ja 28 '77
Stimulation of in vitro translation of messenger RNA by actinomycin D and cordycepin. L. Leinwand and F. H. Ruddle. bibl il Science 197:381-3 Jl 22 '77
See also
Adriamycin
Bacteria—Resistance and sensitivity
Cycloheximide

ANTIBODIES. See Antigens and antibodies

ANTICOAGULANTS
Psychochemical treatment counteracts senility. Sci N 111:292 My 7 '77
See also
Warfarin

ANTI-COLLISION systems. See Automobiles—Safety devices and measures

ANTI-COMMUNIST movements
On the screen: Joe McCarthyoid; Tail Gunner Joe. M. J. Sobran, Jr. il Nat R 29:335-6 Mr 18 '77
Tail Gunner Joe; career of J. McCarthy. W. F. Buckley, Jr. Nat R 29:350 Mr 18 '77
See also
Committee on the Present Danger
Loyalty investigations
United States—Foreign relations—Anti-Communist measures

History

Incomplete candor; Harvard's policy toward ex-Communist faculty members in the 1950s. K. L. Woodward. pors Newsweek 90:77 Jl 25 '77
Tears of ivory towers: California libraries during the McCarthy era. W. E. Benemann. bibl il Am Lib 8:305-9 Je '77
Trial of the 1950s; J. Scales. M. Pinsky. Progressive 41:36-7 F '77

Trade unions

See Trade unions and communism

ANTI-DEFAMATION League. See B'nai B'rith—Anti-Defamation League

ANTIDEPRESSANTS
And now, Gerovital. . . Newsweek 89:89 My 30 '77
Strange case of the anti-aging drug; gerovital H3. S. J. Sansweet. McCalls 105:79-80 N '77

ANTIDOTES
Antidote kits save poisoned livestock; Wisconsin program. Farm J 101:G3 S '77
Rx for poisoning; antidotes. J. Carper. il Am Home 80:20 F '77

ANTI-FREEZE solutions
Consumer's guide to antifreeze for your car. il Mech Illus 73:26 N '77

ANTI-FREEZE testers. See Testing instruments

ANTIGENS and antibodies
Antibody binding measurements with hapten-selective membrane electrodes. M. Meyerhoff and G. A. Rechnitz. bibl il Science 195:494-5 F 4 '77
Antibody combining site. J. D. Capra and A. B. Edmundson. il Sci Am 236:50-9 bibl(p 132) Ja '77
Antigen-antibody reactions in rat brain sites induce transient changes in drinking behavior. C. A. Williams, Jr and N. Schupf. bibl il Science 196:328-30 Ap 15 '77
Australia antigen and the biology of hepatitis B; Nobel prize lecture, December 13, 1976. B. S. Blumberg. bibl il Science 197:17-25 Jl 1 '77
Autoantibodies to zona pellucida: a possible cause for infertility in women. C. A. Shivers and B. S. Dunbar. bibl il Science 197:1082-4 S 9 '77
CEA: puzzling new information about a useful marker. T. H. Maugh. Science 197:544 Ag 5 '77
Feline oncornavirus-associated cell membrane antigen: expression in transformed nonproducer mink cell. A. H. Sliski and others. bibl il Science 196:1336-9 Je 17 '77
H-Y antigen and the genetics of sex determination. S. S. Wachtel. bibl Science 198:797-9 N 25 '77
H-Y antigen: behavior and function. W. K. Silvers and S. S. Wachtel. bibl il Science 195:956-60 Mr 11 '77
H-Y antigen: expression in human subjects with the testicular feminization syndrome. G. C. Koo and others. bibl il Science 196:655-6 My 6 '77
Healy sisters—clues to diabetes. W. Stockton. il N Y Times Mag p88+ Je 12 '77
Hepatitis B "e" antigen: an apparent association with lactate dehydrogenase isozyme-5. G. N. Vyas and others. bibl il Science 198:1068-70 D 9 '77
Making sure about sex; testing for H-Y antigen; work of S. S. Wachtel and others. il por Time 110:57 D 5 '77
Sperm autoantibodies in vasectomized rats of different inbred strains. P. E. Bigazzi and others. bibl il Science 197:1282-3 S 23 '77
Structure and function of histocompatibility antigens. B. A. Cunningham. il Sci Am 237:96-107 bibl(p 152) O '77
Synthetic galactocerebrosides evoke myelination-inhibiting antibodies. S. Hruby and others. bibl il Science 195:173-5 Ja 14 '77
Tumor antigen and human chorionic gonadotropin in CaSki cells: a new epidermoid cervical cancer cell line. R. A. Pattillo and others. bibl il Science 196:1456-8 Je 24 '77
See also
Complements (immunity)
Immunofluorescence
Immunoglobulins
Immunological tolerance

ANTIGUA (island)
Antigua: sailing, tennis relaxing. S. Hart. il Harp Baz 110:12+ My '77

ANTIGUA Sailing Week. See Yacht racing

ANTIHISTAMINES
Ulcer pains? possible relief with cimetidine. Time 110:67 Ag 29 '77

ANTIHYPERTENSIVE agents
See also
Methyldopa

ANTILIPEMIC agents
Three hypolipidemic drugs increase hepatic palmitoy-coenzyme A oxidation in the rat. P. B. Lazarow. bibl il Science 197:580-1 Ag 5 '77

ANTILLES. See West Indies

ANTIMALARIALS
Malaria drugs: new ones are available, but little used. T. H. Maugh. Science 196:415 Ap 22 '77

ANTIOCH, Tenn.

Historic houses, sites, etc.

See Historic houses, sites, etc.—Tennessee

ANTIPOV, Yuri

Anecdotes, facetiae, satire, etc.

Comrade Yuri. D. K. Mano. Nat R 29:1313+ N 11 '77

ANTIPROTON beams. See Particle beams

ANTIQUE automobiles. See Automobiles, Antique

ANTIQUE automobiles in art. See Automobiles in art

ANTIQUE dealers
See also
Sotheby Parke Bernet Group, Ltd

ANTIQUE dolls. See Dolls

ANTIQUE furniture. See Furniture

ANTIQUE motorcycles. See Motorcycles, Antique

ANTIQUE tools. See Tools

ANTIQUES
Antiques. M. D. Schwartz. See issues of Art news to Summer, 1977
Antiques: questions from readers. M. D. Schwartz. See issues of American home
Clues and footnotes. E. H. Gustafson. See issues of Antiques
Great finds! antiques; with excerpts from Living places and Made with oak. il Good H 184:134-9+ Je '77
I decorated this room at auctions: learn from a master the winning techniques. P. R. Jackson. il House & Gard 149:132-5+ Ap '77
It fit together like a jigsaw puzzle; home of C. Barnes in Winston-Salem, N.C. M. Gough and J. Macurdy. il por House B 119:104-13 N '77

ANTIQUES—*Continued*
Living with antiques:
The Bernard Constantine house in Savannah. il Antiques 111:1210-15 Je '77
The Hays-Kiser house, Antioch, Tennessee. J. Kiser. il Antiques 111:526-9 Mr '77
In Alexandria, Virginia. S. B. Sherrill. il Antiques 111:1002-5 My '77
The Manhattan apartment of Mr and Mrs Robert Lee Gill. E. D. Garrett. il Antiques 111:990-1001 My '77
Marshall-Hixon house in Mobile. M. R. Ingate. il Antiques 112:492-5 S '77
Mobile residence of Dr and Mrs Charles Rutherford Jr. M. R. Ingate. il Antiques 112:476-81 S '77
Old Richmond, the Houston guest cottage of Mr and Mrs Fred T. Couper Jr. E. D. Garrett. il Antiques 112:514-21 S '77
Questions and answers: antiques. L. A. Boger. See issues of House & garden incorporating Living for young homemakers
See also
Americana
Heirlooms

Bibliography

Books about antiques. See issues of Antiques
Books reviewed. See issues of Hobbies

Collectors and collecting

Classics and collectibles: American antiques as history and art. C. F. Montgomery. il Art N 76:126-9+ N '77
Collect anything—for fun and profit; excerpt from Antiques for amateurs on a shoestring budget. M. Brunner. il Read Digest 110:49-52+ Ap '77
With diligence, you may find a treasure amid the junk. J. Dixon. House B 119:54-5+ Ap '77

Anecdotes, facetiae, satire, etc.

Rationale for collecting. K. Haueisen. House B 119:46+ Mr '77

Exhibitions

Calendar of shows. Antiques 111:589-90 Mr '77
Conservative definition; 23rd annual Winter Antiques Show, East Side House. M. D. Schwartz. il Art N 76:124+ Mr '77
Current and coming. S. B. Sherrill. See issues of Antiques
Fairs, fleas and historic houses. M. D. Schwartz. Art N 76:144 Summ '77
Hobbies magazine salutes a continuous advertiser in Hobbies magazine for 40 years; New Haven Antiques Show. il Hobbies 82:116 Ap '77

Expertising

Detecting fraudulent antiques. R. Field. il Sci Digest 81:89-91 F '77

ANTIQUES, Forged. See Forgery of antiques

ANTIQUING of furniture. See Furniture—Finishing

ANTIQUITIES
See also
Bible—Antiquities
also subhead Antiquities under names of continents, countries, states, etc, e.g. Europe—Antiquities

ANTIQUITIES, Pillage of. See Pillage

ANTI-SATELLITE interceptor. See Artificial satellites—Military use

ANTI-SEMITISM
British anti-Semitism, then and now; controversy surrounding David Pryce-Jones's Unity Mitford: a quest. D. R. Katz. New Repub 176:21 F 5 '77
Get out, Jews; Argentina. K. Bird and R. Moreau. il Newsweek 90:31 Ag 15 '77
Jews and leftists tremble: anti-Semitism in Argentina. H. Maurer. Nation 224:170-3 F 12 '77
Script trouble at Oberammergau. il Time 110:74 Ag 29 '77
See also
World War, 1939-1945—Jews

ANTISERUMS. See Serums

ANTI-SLAVERY Society for the Protection of Human Rights
Slave trade. D. Katz. New Repub 176:19-21 Je 4 '77

ANTI-SUBMARINE warfare
Advanced sensors major anti-submarine warfare goal. il Aviation W 106:134-5+ Ja 31 '77
Pentagon is working on it. R. C. Aldridge. Nation 224:711-14 Je 11 '77

ANTI-TANK missiles. See Guided missiles

ANTITRUST Division. See United States—Justice, Department of—Antitrust Division

ANTITRUST legislation. See Trusts, Industrial—Law

ANTITRYPSIN. See Serums

ANTITUMOR substances. See Cancer inhibiting substances

ANTIVIRAL agents. See Viruses—Inactivation

ANTIVIRAL proteins. See Interferon

ANTLIONS. See Ant lions

ANTOINE, Tex
Giggling newscasters. M. Kempton. Progressive 41:52 Mr '77 *

ANTONIONI, Michelangelo
De interpretatione, or the difficulty of being Marco Polo (on the occasion of Antonioni's China film); tr by C. Leefeldt. U. Eco. Film Q 30:8-12 Summ '77 *

ANTROBUS, Edmund
Britain's brave bells. il Am For 83:42-5+ Mr '77
Treasure of Tobermory Bay. il map Am For 83:20-3+ Je '77

ANTS
Competition between seed-eating rodents and ants in desert ecosystems. J. H. Brown and D. W. Davidson. bibl il Science 196:880-2 My 20 '77
Fire ants. R. E. Arnold. Field & S 82:87 Jl '77
Interspecific hybridization and caste specificity of protein in fire ant. A. C. F. Hung and S. B. Vinson. bibl il Science 196:1458-60 Je 24 '77
Odor gives home team ants early lead. il Sci N 111:356-7 Je 4 '77
Sexual calling behavior in primitive ants. B. Hölldobler and C. P. Haskins. bibl il Science 195:793-4 F 25 '77
Weaver ants. B. K. Hölldobler and E. O. Wilson. il Sci Am 237:146-8+ D '77
Weaver ants: social establishment and maintenance of territory. B. Hölldobler and E. O. Wilson. bibl il Science 195:900-2 Mr 4 '77

ANTWERP, Belgium
Rubens year: carnival in Flanders. R. Dobson. il por Art N 76:176+ Summ '77

Historic houses, sites, etc.

Mansion for a master; Rubens' house. il UNESCO Courier 30:8-9 Je '77

ANXIETY
Anxiety, stress, tension: how to turn them into creative energy; interview, ed by A. Gross. R. Suinn. Mademoiselle 83:164+ My '77
Good to the last drop—but not for some patients; caffeine; study by John Greden and others. J. Gaylin. Psychol Today 11:50+ N '77
Handling your anxieties; with exercises. J. Segal and Z. Segal. il Seventeen 36:146-7+ Mr '77
Intimate terrorism. M. V. Miller. bibl il por Psychol Today 10:78-80+ Ap '77
What single women fear the most. J. Lynch. Harp Baz 110:93+ Mr '77
See also
Worry

AOYAGI, Akiko. See Shurtleff, W. jt auth

APACHE Indians
Apache capitalism; Jicarilla tribe. Forbes 120:105 Ag 15 '77

APARTHEID. See South Africa—Race question

APARTMENT houses
Apartments of the year. il Archit Rec 161:109-26 mid-My '77
Building types study: high density housing; with introd by J. Nairn. il Archit Rec 162:111-26 S '77
Pulitzer for Mildred A. Pappas; apartment house newsletter, Ontario bulletin. N. Ephron. Esquire 87:18+ Mr '77

Condominium plan ownership

See Condominium (housing)

Cooperative ownership

Hanging bookshelves on tax brackets. A. Tobias. Esquire 88:42+ Jl '77

APARTMENT houses, Remodeled
High-density apartment conversion in New York City affords special design amenities; 240 East 26th Street. il Archit Rec 162:122-3 S '77
Recycled tannery provides historical and spatial amenities for elderly near Boston; The Tannery, Peabody. il Archit Rec 162:124-6 S '77
Transformation of office tower to apartments creates luxurious living space in New York City; Turtle Bay Towers. il Archit Rec 162:112-15 S '77

APARTMENT life (periodical)
Bidding for an elusive market. il Bus W p72 N 7 '77

APARTMENTS
American hurrah! Rustic in town; apartment of George E. Schoellkopf. il House & Gard 149:78-81 F '77
Apartment living. il Am Home 80:54-5 Mr; 58-9 Ap; 46-7, 56 My; 96-7 Je; 60-3 Ag '77
Barefoot in New York; apartment of Jo and Joel Grey. L. Davis. il pors Vogue 167:158-61+ Je '77
Bold! A designer's personal mix; Manhattan duplex. R. Weil. il House B 119:78-83 F '77
Boldly elegant; New York apartment of Pano de Hoyos. il House B 119:80-2 Ap '77
Bringing home Art Deco; Richard Gillette apartment, New York City. N. Skurka. il N Y Times Mag p74-5 Ap 3 '77

APARTMENTS—*Continued*
Chez Kenzo, chez Karl. M. Russell. il pors N Y Times Mag p 130-1 N 27 '77
Chosen few; home of Juan Montoya. il House B 119:114-15 O '77
City apartment with a greenhouse for a heart; decoration by Renée Graubart. il House & Gard 149:68-73 Jl '77
Comfort gets a glow on; apartment of Mrs S. Joseph Tankoos, Jr. il House & Gard 149:90-3 F '77
Country in the city; New York City apartment of John and Mary Emmerling. il Mademoiselle 83:152-7 Je '77
Cozy grand; apartment decorated by Robert Denning and Vincent Fourcade. il Vogue 167: 180-3 F '77
Decorating with imagination, not money. Harp Baz 110:52+ Je '77
Environmental eloquence; Manhattan apartment designed by Chvotzkin. R. Weil. il House B 119:94-103 N '77
Everything you always wanted to know about finding/moving into an apartment. Mademoiselle 83:80+ O '77
For joyful living; interview, ed by R. Weil and J. Macurdy. H. G. Brown and D. Brown. il pors House B 119:118-25 My '77
Grand romance; New York City apartment of Mrs Patricia Harmsworth. il por House & Gard 150:66-9 Ja '78
Great ideas from apartment living. il House & Gard 149:124-43 O '77
Holiday at home; New York apartment of Cathy and Alessandro di Montezemolo. il House & Gard 149:52-7 Ag '77
Home and office; bridging the gap; Milan apartment of G. Aulenti. R. Reif. il por N Y Times Mag p64-5 F 13 '77
How they share space & entertaining; New York City apartments of Gail Joy and Michael Wiles. il Mademoiselle 83:206-7+ S '77
Inner city provincial; apartment of Joe Allen. J. Macurdy. il House B 119:74-9 Mr '77
Invisible kitchen; apartment of Pamela Kane. il por House & Gard 150:96-9 Ja '78
Living alone & loving it; New York City apartment of S. Martine. il por Mademoiselle 83: 202-3+ S '77
Living big in one room: 3 designers' terrific solutions. il Mademoiselle 83:208-11 Ag '77
Living swell; apartment of K. Unger. K. Ungar. il por Mademoiselle 83:158-61 F '77
Luxe alive! Jackie Machado Macedo's Paris apartment. il Vogue 167:120-3 Jl '77
9 lives in 1 room. il Seventeen 36:134-5 F '77
No-care apartment; Francesca Paolozzi's apartment. il Harp Baz 110:128+ Ag '77
Place of your own. il Redbook 149:136-7+ My '77
Problem with noise in an apartment; excerpt from Quieting: a practical guide to noise control. Consumers Res Mag 60:25 F '77
Renter's survival guide. T. Vellela. Am Home 80:36 N '77
See your apartment in a new light. J. R. Cary. House B 119:83-4+ D '77
Setting the stage; Manhattan co-op apartment of M. McFadden. N. Skurka. il N Y Times Mag p68-9+ Mr 6 '77
Splitting a one-bedroom apartment two ways; M. O'Connor. il pors Mademoiselle 83:204-5+ S '77
Trade secrets; New York City apartment of Tom O'Toole. J. Macurdy. il House B 119:146-9 S '77
Trends in decorating; interviews, ed by J. Lynch. il Harp Baz 110:112+ S '77
Who needs a kitchen really? communal kitchens in apartments. R. Sokolov. il Am Home 80:9 F '77

Anecdotes, facetiae, satire, etc.

Personal: alone is best. M. Wolynski. Vogue 167:183-4+ N '77

Leasing and renting

Before you go apartment hunting. il Sr Schol 109:12+ My 5 '77

APARTMENTS, Remodeled
California recycle; studio-apartment complex in Venice, Calif. il Mademoiselle 83:218-19 Ap '77
Fixturing up a loft; New York apartments. N. Skurka. il N Y Times Mag p82-3 F 6 '77
From classrooms to living rooms. A. M. Miller. McCalls 105:84 N '77
Loft living: big spaces, fresh images. il Archit Rec 162:97-100 Jl '77
Magic is the balance of creativity & useability; converted garment-factory loft in Manhattan's SoHo; interview, ed by M. Gough and others. B. Van Allen. il por House B 119:140-5+ S '77

APATITE
Fibrous apatite grown on modified collagen. E. Banks and others. bibl il Science 198:1164-6 D 16 '77

APE men. See Man, Prehistoric

APECO Corporation
Why Apeco preferred filing for bankruptcy. Bus W p25-6 N 7 '77

APERITIF wines. See Wine

APES
Almost human; training methods. P. Gwynne and others. il Newsweek 89:70-1+ Mr 7 '77
See also
Gorillas
Orangutans

APEXES (botany) See Shoot apexes

APHIDS. See Plant lice

APHRODISIAMANIA; ballet. See Ballet reviews—Single works

APICULTURE. See Bee culture

APLYSIA. See Sea hares

APOLLO 11 flight. See Space flight to the moon—Manned flights—Apollo 11 flight

APOLLO 15 flight. See Space flight to the moon—Manned flights—Apollo 15 flight

APOLLO Lunar Science Experiment Packages. See Moon—Exploration—Equipment

APOLLO-Soyuz flight, 1975. See Space flight—Manned flights—Apollo-Soyuz flight, 1975

APOLOGETICS
At the beginning, God; interview, ed by D. E. Kucharsky. C. Van Til. por Chr Today 22:18-22 D 30 '77

APPALACHIAN Mountains
See also
Blue Ridge Mountains
Great Smoky Mountains

APPALACHIAN Region
See also
Arts and crafts—Appalachian Region
Coal mines and mining—Appalachian Region
Education—Appalachian Region
Reclamation of land—Appalachian Region
Strip mining—Appalachian Region

Religious institutions and affairs

Foot-washin' church and the prayer-book church: resisting cultural imperialism in southern Appalachia. L. Johnson; discussion. Chr Cent 94:332-6 Ap 6 '77

Social life and customs

I like to feel free. il Sr Schol 109:16-17 Ja 27 '77

APPALACHIAN State University. See North Carolina. Appalachian State University, Boone

APPALACHIAN Trail
House overwhelmingly approves $90 million to protect Trail from encroaching development. il Nat Parks & Con Mag 51:22-3 D '77
Learning to see things whole. L. Walsh. il Sci Digest 81:51-4 Ap '77

APPARITIONS
See also
Jesus Christ—Apparitions and miracles (modern)

APPEL, Benjamin
Obituary
Pub W 211:38 Ap 25 '77

APPEL, Kenneth, and Haken, Wolfgang
Solution of the four-color-map problem; with biographical sketches. il map Sci Am 237:15, 108-9+ bibl(p 152) O '77

APPELBAUM, Anita
Ending; poem. Ladies Home J 94:120 Ag '77

APPELBAUM, Norman M.
Ask the dentist; questions and answers. See issues of Family health incorporating Today's health to June 1977

APPELBAUM, Richard P.
Future is made, not predicted: technocratic planners vs. public interests. bibl il Society 14:49-53 My '77

APPELSON, Herb, and Wright, Jim
Collage with a message. il Sch Arts 76:28-9 Mr '77

APPENDICITIS
Is it appendicitis? M. P. Scott. Bet Hom & Gard 55:248+ My '77

APPETITE
See also
Anorexia nervosa
Hyperphagia

APPETITE suppressing drugs. See Weight reducing preparations

APPETIZERS
Before dinner the Dutch enjoy hot bites of bitterballen. il Sunset 158:231 My '77
Creamy dips, all are low calorie: tofu or soybean curd. il Sunset 159:146 D '77
Dips for snacking and partying. il Ebony 33:98+ Ja '78
Freeze-ahead appetizers. il Bet Hom & Gard 55:258 My '77
Get fresh; dips. G. Steves. il Am Home 80:69+ Ap '77
Great Texas appetizers. Redbook 150:143-4 D '77
Guacamole—the perfect dip. il Good H 185:48 Jl '77
Guatemalan *boquitas*. il Sunset 159:170-1 N '77
Instant appetizers. G. Steves. Am Home 80:64 D '77
Real Hungarian? cheese spread. il Sunset 158: 244 Ap '77

APPIGNANESI, Richard
(ed) See Wesker, A. Making the case for Shylock

APPLE, Max
Business talk; story. Mademoiselle 83:126 S '77
APPLE cider. See Cider
APPLE desserts. See Desserts
APPLE industry. See Fruit industry
APPLE trees
Bud grafting to make an old-fashioned orchard. K. C. Rhee. il Org Gard & Farm 25:92-6 Ja '78
Unusual and antique apples; century-old varieties. il Sunset 159:260-2 O '77
APPLE trees, Dwarf. See Fruit trees, Dwarf
APPLE worms. See Codling moths
APPLEBEE, Arthur N.
ERIC/RCS report. bibl Engl J 66:81-5 D '77
APPLEMAN, Philip
Comment. J. Parini. Poetry 130:296-7 Ag '77 *
APPLES
See also
Cookery—Fruit

Diseases and pests

Natural steps to beat apple scab. L. Hill. il Org Gard & Farm 24:84-7 Ag '77

Picking

Pick of the crop. Am Home 80:70 O '77
APPLETON, Jane Scovell
Beverly Sills is not like the girl next door. por Am Home 80:80-1 Ap '77
APPLEWHITE, James
Tobacco men; poem. Atlantic 240:69 O '77
APPLIANCE repairmen. See Repairmen
APPLIANCES, Household. See Household appliances
APPLICATIONS for positions
Extent of job search by employed workers. C. Rosenfeld. bibl il M Labor R 100:58-62 Mr '77
15 ways to land a job; ideas of employers. K. R. Gertz. Harp Baz 110:47+ Je '77
How to get a job; special section. il Esquire 88:51-77+ Jl '77
How to land the job you're after. Mademoiselle 83:192-5 Ag '77
How to transplant & survive; getting a job and living in Los Angeles and San Francisco. D. Duke and others. il Mademoiselle 83:205+ Ap '77
How to write a resumé to highlight the skills every homemaker has. M. P. Rowe. Parents Mag 52:24 Jl '77
Job résumés to spotlight that face in the crowd. J. A. Noble, Sr. Writers Digest 57: 32-4 Mr '77
Job search of the unemployed, May 1976. C. Rosenfeld. il M Labor R 100:39-43 N '77
Markets & careers; presentation of a photo portfolio. H. Chapnick. Pop Phot 80:34+ F '77
Promote yourself! advertising for summer jobs on bulletin boards. il Sr Schol 109:26 My 19 '76
Reentry ripoff: one housewife's exposé. E. Zanar. il Ms 6:83-6+ O '77
Resources for a California job hunt. D. Duke. Mademoiselle 83:12+ Ap '77
Your first-job strategy. V. Y. Pellegrino. Harp Baz 110:48+ Je '77
See also
Employment interviewing

Caricatures and cartoons

My résumé is enclosed . . . Changing T 31:32-3 O '77
APPLICATOR pads, Paint. See Painting, Industrial and practical—Equipment and supplies
APPLIQUÉ work
Appliqué methods; excerpt from Designing in stitching and appliqué. N. Belfer. il Sch Arts 77:36-42 N '77
Garden in stitches. il House & Gard 149:140-1+ S '77
Happy holiday appliques. il Redbook 150:141+ D '77
APPORTIONMENT (election law)
Political structure of rural America. D. Knoke and C. Henry. bibl f il Ann Am Acad 429: 51-62 Ja '77
Some are more equal; Supreme Court decisions affecting discrimination in education and political representation. B. Odom. Nat R 29: 1114-15 S 30 '77
See also
Gerrymander
APPRAISAL. See Assessment; Real property—Valuation
APPRAISAL of works of art. See Art—Valuation
APPRECIATION
How will you know unless I tell you? J. Lindstrom. Read Digest 110:43-4+ Ap '77
APPRECIATION of architecture. See Architecture—Appreciation
APPRECIATION of art. See Art—Appreciation
APPRECIATION of music. See Music—Analysis, appreciation

APPRENTICES
Be an apprentice; women and blue collar jobs. L. Luciano. Seventeen 36:55 Ap '77
How to get a blue collar. K. West. il Ms 5:62-5 My '77
See also
Interns (civil service)
APPROPRIATE technology. See Technology
APPROPRIATE Technology International (organization)
Appropriate technology. A. Von Lazar and K. Bode. New Repub 176:11-13 Je 11 '77
APRIL
April's skies. J. Mullaney. il Sci Digest 81:68-9 Ap '77
APRILLE, June R.
Reye's syndrome: patient serum alters mitochondrial function and morphology in vitro. bibl il Science 197:908-10 Ag 26 '77
APRIL'S rebellion; drama. See Marshall, S. L.
APTE, Stu
Grand fish at night: the ultimate action. il Outdoor Life 160:66-7+ Jl '77
APTER, Michael J.
Can computers be programmed to appreciate art? Art N 76:18 Summ '77
APTITUDE tests
See also
College Entrance Examination Board—Scholastic Aptitude Test
AQUACULTURE
Aquaculture: a new frontier for the home producer. G. Logsdon. il Org Gard & Farm 24: 56-61 Mr '77
Aquaculture: newest hope to expand food lifeline; work at International Center for Living Aquatic Resources Management. L. Muhlfeld. il Sci Digest 81:37-9 Ap '77
California's kelp beds flourish again. M. Tennesen. il Nat Wildlife 15:12-16 O '77
Compleat aquaculturist. M. King. il Forbes 120: 44 O 15 '77
Farming giant kelp. L. Wood. il Sea Front 23:159-66 My '77
See also
Fish culture
Shellfish culture
AQUARIUMS
Fish will swim around you; Steinhart Aquarium's Fish Roundabout. il Sunset 158:34 My '77
Shark in miniature: keeping a horn shark in a home aquarium. B. W. Myers. il Oceans 10: 39-41 N '77
Taking the plunge into an aquarium. V. D. Chase. il Mech Illus 73:58-9+ Mr '77
Whale of a time; with list of aquariums in the U.S. R. Langer. il House & Gard 149:62-4+ Ap '77
AQUASOL packaging. See Pressure packaging
AQUATIC games. See Games
AQUATIC insects. See Insects, Aquatic
AQUATIC life. See Fresh water fauna; Marine fauna
AQUATIC plants
August in the garden; plants for a water garden. D. Fell. Horticulture 55:4 Ag '77
Unseen life of a mountain stream. W. H. Amos. il Nat Geog 151:562-80 Ap '77
See also
Algae
Bulrushes
Water hyacinths
AQUATIC sports
Opinion; water sports. R. B. Kauffman. Camp Mag 49:5+ Je '77
See also
Boats and boating
Regattas
Rowing
Sailing
Skin diving
Surf riding
Swimming
AQUATIC weeds
Turning a nuisance into an asset. il BioScience 27:435 Je '77
AQUEDUCTS
Schoharie Aqueduct. A. S. Fick. il por Conservationist 32:16-17 N '77
AQUINAS, Thomas, Saint. See Thomas Aquinas, Saint
AQUINO, Benigno S. Jr
Quality of justice in Manila. America 137:410 D 10 '77 *
ARA-A. See Vidarabine
ARA-C. See Cytosine arabinoside
ARAB countries
Palestinian issue: anatomy of a slogan. B. Akzin. Intellect 106:198-200 D '77
See also
Aeronautics, Commercial—Arab countries
Airlines—Arab countries
Aviation—Arab countries
Contracts, Government—Arab countries
Crime and criminals—Arab countries
Finance—Arab countries
Investments, Arab
Investments, Korean—Arab countries
Money—Arab countries
United Nations—Arab countries

ARAB countries—*Continued*

Commerce

Arab boycott of Israel. N. Turck. bibl f For Affairs 55:472-93 Ap '77

United States

See United States—Commerce—Arab countries

Economic relations

Malta

New gateway to Arab markets. il Bus W p52 Je 13 '77

Foreign opinion

American

Our ugly-Arab complex. M. Greenfield. Newsweek 90:110 D 5 '77

Foreign relations

Goodbye, Arab solidarity. il por Time 110:38-40+ D 12 '77
Hussein: close ranks; excerpts from interview, ed by A. de Borchgrave. Hussein. por Newsweek 90:59-60+ D 12 '77
In the Arab world: alarm—and few cheers—over Sadat's moves. il U.S. News 83:27 N 28 '77
Truth about myth of Arab unity. U.S. News 83:12 D 19 '77
Violent recoil. T. Mathews and others. il Newsweek 90:44 N 28 '77
See also
Cairo conference, 1977

Africa

Pledging a tithe that binds; summit meeting. il Time 109:32-3 Mr 21 '77

United States

See United States—Foreign relations—Arab countries

Industries

See also
Construction industry—Arab countries
Munitions—Arab countries

Israeli occupation, 1967-

Council expresses concern over serious situation in occupied Arab Territories. UN Chron 13:5-11+ D '76
Destruction of Quneitra condemned; Assembly says Syria entitled to full compensation. UN Chron 14:20-6 Ja '77
Human Rights Commission acts on situations in Southern Africa and Israeli-occupied territories. il UN Chron 14:44-8 Ap '77
Israel under Begin: changing horses in the old stream. I. L. Gendzier. Nation 224:742-4 Je 18 '77
Mideast: phase 2. K. Willenson and others. il pors map Newsweek 91:28-31 Ja 9 '78
President Carter meets with President Asad of Syria at Geneva; exchange of remarks and toasts, May 9, 1977. J. Carter and H. Assad. Dept State Bull 76:593-7 Je 6 '77
Sniping at Begin. R. Carroll and M. J. Kubic. il Newsweek 91:31 Ja 9 '78
Two Arab leaders reply to Begin; excerpts from interviews, ed by A. de Borchgrave. Hussein; H. Assad. pors Newsweek 90:30-2 Ag 1 '77
See also
United Nations—Special Committee to Investigate Israeli Practices Affecting the Human Rights of the Population of the Occupied Territories

ARAB-Israel War, 1948-1949. See Israel-Arab War, 1948-1949

ARAB-Israel Wars, 1967-. See Israel-Arab Wars, 1967-

ARAB-Jewish relations. See Jewish-Arab relations

ARAB Satellite Communications Organization. See Communications satellites, Arab

ARABS
One outsider's view of Arabian culture pictured in spring Doubleday book; interview, ed by R. Dahlin. R. De Combray. il Pub W 212:33 N 28 '77
Our ugly-Arab complex. M. Greenfield. Newsweek 90:110 D 5 '77
See also
Bedouins in Jordan
Jewish-Arab relations
Palestinian Arabs

ARABS in the United States
Houston's Arab connection. N. Proffitt. il Newsweek 89:88+ Je 13 '77

ARACHNIDS
See also
Scorpions
Spiders

ARAFAT, Yasir
Arafat: solutions, not theatrics; excerpts from interview, ed by M. Gart and W. Wynn. il por Time 109:33 Mr 21 '77

about

Genius for survival. pors Time 109:28 F 28 '77 *

ARALIAS
Ming aralia and its South Sea cousins. J. U. Crockett. il Horticulture 55:2 F '77

ARANTES DO NASCIMENTO, Edson. See Pelé

ARBATOV, Georgil A.
Dangers of a new Cold War. Bull Atom Sci 33:33-40 Mr '77
Soviet official tells U.S.—don't push the issue too far; interview, ed by R. Knight. il por U.S. News 82:23-4+ Mr 14 '77

ARBER, Carol H.
Keeping women in their place. Nation 225:654-7 D 17 '77

ARBER, Myles
Price of success. E. Keerdoja. il por Newsweek 89:5+ Ja 31 '77 *

ARBITRAGE
Blood in the water at Babcock & Wilcox. Bus W p25-6 Je 6 '77
Killing in Babcock & Wilcox. E. J. Tracy. il por Fortune 96:266-9 O '77
Wall Street's highest rollers. il Time 110:54+ O 17 '77
Wall Street's tender trap. D. Pauly. il Newsweek 89:88 Ap 11 '77

ARBITRATION, Industrial
See also
Collective bargaining

United States

Expedited arbitration: less grief over grievances. L. Stessin; reply. W. T. Lowe, Jr. Harvard Bus R 55:172 My '77
Goodrich proposes binding arbitration plan. L. Bornstein and others. M Labor R 100:59 My '77
How final-offer arbitration affects baseball bargaining. J. B. Dworkin. bibl il M Labor R 100:52-3 Mr '77
Labor: trouble ahead? maritime and coal industries. G. R. Rosen. por Duns R 110:57 S '77

ARBITRATION, International
See also
Disarmament—Conferences
Peace

ARBITRATION and award
Debate over consolidation of arbitration proceedings is enlivened by a recent New York case. G. Aksen. Archit Rec 162:59 O '77

ARBORETUMS
See also
Washington, D.C.—National Arboretum

ARBOVIRUS. See Viruses

ARBORVITAE
Twilight of the great cedars; western red cedar. D. J. Chasan. il Audubon 79:50-5 N '77

ARBUZOV, Aleksei Nikolaevich
Do you turn somersaults? Reviews
Time 110:53 S 5 '77 *

ARCHAEBACTERIA. See Microorganisms

ARCHAEOPTERYX. See Birds, Fossil

ARCHBISHOP's ceiling; drama. See Miller, A.

ARCHEOLOGICAL photography. See Photography in archeology

ARCHEOLOGICAL pillage. See Pillage

ARCHEOLOGISTS, Amateur. See Scientists, Amateur

ARCHEOLOGY
Archaeology. Sci N 111:108 F 12; 112:90 Ag 6 '77
See also
Bible—Antiquities
Cave drawings and paintings
Earthworks (archeology)
Excavations (archeology)
Inscriptions
Iron age
Man—Origin and antiquity
Mummies
Petroglyphs
Stone age
Stone implements and weapons
also subhead Antiquities under names of continents, countries, states, etc, e.g. Europe —Antiquities

Methodology

Archeological asphalts approached analytically. Chemistry 50:21 D '77
Detection and examination of anthrosols by phosphate analysis. R. C. Eidt. bibl il Science 197:1327-33 S 30 '77
Paleogeographic reconstructions of coastal Aegean archaeological sites. J. C. Kraft and others. bibl il maps Science 195:941-7 Mr 11 '77
Thermoluminescent determination of prehistoric heat treatment of chert artifacts. C. L. Melcher and D. W. Zimmerman. bibl il Science 197:1359-62 S 30 '77
See also
Radioactive dating
Radiocarbon dating

ARCHEOLOGY, Submarine
Danger to artifacts on the continental shelf. Intellect 105:304 Mr '77
Earthwatch expeditions are the real thing; search for shipwrecks near Palma de Mallorca. G. Goshgarian. Todays Educ 66:67-9 Mr '77
Greek art from the Atlantic depths; Sir William Hamilton's Greek vases. A. Birchall. il Horizon 19:66-71 Ja '77
Monitor mission. P. Gwynne and E. Clark. il Newsweek 90:54 Ag 15 '77
Wreck at Sheytan Deresi. G. F. Bass. il Oceans 10:34-9 Ja '77
See also
Treasure trove

ARCHER, Dane, and Akert, R. M.
How well do you read body language? bibl il pors Psychol Today 11:68-9+ O '77

ARCHERY
Fastest growing American sport is camp's least understood program. C. Krich. il Camp Mag 49:14-15+ My '77
See also
Hunting with bow and arrow

Equipment

See also
Bow and arrow

ARCHERY ranges. See Shooting ranges

ARCHES National Park
National parks sampler. il Nat Parks & Con Mag 51:21 D '77
Over, under, and through arches. F. Hammond and O. Hammond. il Ret Liv 17:24-6 Ja '77

ARCHIMEDES
Burning question. Sci Am 236:64 Je '77 *

ARCHITECTS
COFPAES meeting indicates support to retain Brooks Law; COFPAES renews its costs and audits argument: Committee on Federal Procurement of Architect-Engineer Services. W. Hickman. Archit Rec 161:34, 75 Ap '77
Case for design quality in today's marketplace: four studies of collaboration between architects and developers that explore the arithmetic of excellence: symposium. il Archit Rec 162:81-128 D '77
Planning your personal financial strategy. M. Pollard. Archit Rec 161:59 Mr; 77 Ap '77
Something borrowed, something new; post-modernism. R. A. M. Stern. il Horizon 20:50-7 D '77
See also
American Institute of Architects
Architectural firms
Architecture as a profession
Women architects
also names of architects, e.g. P. Johnson

Advertising

Advertising and AIA ethics: for all the activity, no early resolution is in sight. A. T. Kornblut. Archit Rec 161:73 My '77
Supreme Court rules that attorneys may advertise, and speculation flourishes among the other professions. W. Hickman. Archit Rec 162:34 Ag '77

Legal status, laws, etc.

Basic guide to pitfalls in foreign contracts. P. F. Purcell. Archit Rec 161:69 Je '77
Legal perspectives. A. T. Kornblut. Archit Rec 161:57 F; 55+ Mr; 67+ Ap; 73 My; 162:63 Ag; 63 N; 53 D '77
See also
Architects—Licenses and registration
Liability (law)

Licenses and registration

Continuing education as a requirement for recertification takes hold in California. B. Lamb. Archit Rec 162:57 O '77
Laymen will outnumber pros on California licensing board. J. Nairn. Archit Rec 161:36 Ja '77
See also
National Council of Architectural Registration Boards

Supply and demand

Britain's economic travails leave a quarter of its architects unemployed and put a third of its private firms out of business. M. Burns and T. Marshall. Archit Rec 161:36 Ja '77

Training

See Architectural education

ARCHITECTS, Professional ethics for
Advertising and AIA ethics: for all the activity, no early resolution is in sight. A. T. Kornblut. Archit Rec 161:73 My '77
In thoughtful debate, AIA rejects ethics changes that would allow general contracting. W. F. Wagner, Jr. Archit Rec 162:26 Jl '77
Some random thoughts on ethics. W. F. Wagner, Jr. Archit Rec 161:13 My '77

ARCHITECTS Collaborative (firm) See Architectural firms

ARCHITECTS contracts. See Building—Contracts and specifications

ARCHITECTURAL acoustics. See Acoustics, Architectural

ARCHITECTURAL articles. See Periodical articles

ARCHITECTURAL competitions. See Architecture—Competitions

ARCHITECTURAL conferences. See Architecture—Conferences

ARCHITECTURAL decoration. See Decoration and ornament, Architectural

ARCHITECTURAL design
Case for design quality in today's marketplace: four studies of collaboration between architects and developers that explore the arithmetic of excellence; symposium. il Archit Rec 162:81-128 D '77
Defining a design methodology. G. Birkerts. il Archit Rec 161:91-4 F '77
GAO criticizes federal procurement agencies for their leniency with A-E errors and omissions; report entitled Procedures used for holding architects and engineers responsible for the quality of their design work. W. Hickman. Archit Rec 162:34 S '77
Maybe this year we can get back to talking about design quality? W. F. Wagner, Jr. Archit Rec 161:13 F '77
Notes from the field: how architects, and their consultants, approach solar design. M. F. Gaskie. il Archit Rec 162:108-13 mid-Ag '77
See also
Architectural drawing

ARCHITECTURAL designs. See Architecture—Designs and plans

ARCHITECTURAL drawing
Art of building on paper; 200 Years of American Architectural Drawing, at the Cooper-Hewitt Museum. P. Goldberger. il N Y Times Mag p74-5+ Je 5 '77

ARCHITECTURAL education
Agency plans fire safety courses for architects; program of the National Academy for Fire Prevention and Control. W. Hickman. Archit Rec 162:33 mid-Ag '77
Continuing education as a requirement for recertification takes hold in California. B. Lamb. Archit Rec 162:57 O '77
NCARB: tough talk on recertification, ethics and the testing of young architects. W. Wagner, Jr. Archit Rec 162:13 Ag '77; Reply with rejoinder. J. M. McGinty. 162:2, 13 N '77
See also
Bauhaus

ARCHITECTURAL engineering. See Structural engineering

ARCHITECTURAL exhibits. See Architecture—Exhibitions

ARCHITECTURAL firms
Brash, young and post-modern: Hardy Holzman Pfeiffer Associates P. Goldberger. il N Y Times Mag p18-20+ F 20 '77
Design for orderly living; Gwathmey & Siegel. P. Goldberger. il N Y Times Mag p 146-8+ D 11 '77
Johns-Manville world headquarters building—a winner for J-M and TAC; work of The Architects Collaborative. M. F. Schmertz. il Archit Rec 162:89-100 S '77
Managing your marketing communications program; excerpt from Creative communications for a successful design practice. S. A. Kliment. il Archit Rec 161:77-9 My '77
News release as marketing tool. S. A. Kliment. Archit Rec 162:55 Jl '77
Recycling architectural masterpieces—and other buildings not so great; Hardy Holzman Pfeiffer Associates; ed by M. Holzman and N. Pfeiffer; with introd by M. F. Schmertz. H. Hardy. il Archit Rec 162:81-92 Ag '77
Trojan connection; James M. Sink Associates. il Forbes 119:116 Je 15 '77
What's a high-style design firm like Gwathmey-Siegel doing designing speculative office buildings along freeways and in office campuses? W. F. Wagner, Jr. il Archit Rec 162:108-15 D '77
Writing for marketing impact: letters, brochures, proposals. S. A. Kliment. Archit Rec 161:71+ Je '77
See also
Site, Inc

ARCHITECTURAL lighting. See Lighting, Architectural and decorative

ARCHITECTURAL news
News reports. See issues of Architectural record

ARCHITECTURAL plans. See Architecture—Designs and plans

ARCHITECTURAL record (periodical)
Apartments of the year. il Archit Rec 161:109-26 mid-My '77
Building types study as a not-too-clouded crystal ball; with introd by M. F. Schmertz. C. K. Hoyt. il Archit Rec 161:117, 138-46 Ap '77
Building types study: Record interiors of 1977; with introd by B. Gordon. il Archit Rec 161:101-28 Ja '77

ARCHITECTURAL record (periodical)—*Continued*
Magic nostalgia and a hint of greatness in the workaday world of the Building types study; analysis of 40 years of Architectural record's Building types studies; with introd by M. F. Schmertz. C. W. Moore and R. B. Oliver. Archit Rec 161:117-37 Ap '77
Record houses of 1977; with introd by B. F. Gordon. il Archit Rec 161:49-108 mid-My '77

ARCHITECTURAL sculpture. See Decoration and ornament, Architectural

ARCHITECTURAL societies
See also
American Institute of Architects

ARCHITECTURAL space. See Space (architecture)

ARCHITECTURAL specifications. See Building—Contracts and specifications

ARCHITECTURE
Architecture. W. Von Eckardt. il New Repub 177:31-3 Ag 6; 26-9 Ag 20; 26-8 N 5; 25-6 D 17 '77
Buildings in the news. See issues of Architectural record
See also
Airport buildings
Architects
Barns and stables
Building
Building materials
Church architecture
College architecture
Computers—Architectural use
Concrete construction
Courthouses
Environmental design
Environmental engineering (buildings)
Glass construction
Greenhouses
Hillside architecture
Hospitals—Architecture
Hotels, motels, etc.—Architecture
Industrial buildings
Laboratories—Architecture
Library architecture
Museums—Architecture
Naval architecture
Navy yards and naval stations
Office buildings
Photography of buildings and structures
Public buildings
Recreation centers
Remodeling (architecture)
Restaurants—Architecture
Skyscrapers
Steel construction
Stores
Theater buildings

Appreciation

On architecture. J. Ackerman. il Art N 76:111 N '77
On getting the public involved and interested in architecture; proposals for public education founded by the National Endowment for the Arts. W. F. Wagner, Jr. il Archit Rec 162:13 S '77

Awards, prizes, etc.

1977 Reynolds prize goes to Richard Meier. il Archit Rec 161:35 Je '77
U.S. Navy and the AIA honor architecture at Annapolis and at naval bases around the country. il Archit Rec 161:39 F '77
See also
Western Home Awards

Bibliography

Architectural book marks (cont) J. H. Kay. Nation 224:408-9 Ap 2 '77
Books on architecture. J. H. Kay. Nation 225:665 D 17 '77
Required reading. See issues of Architectural record

Caricatures and cartoons

Great moments in architecture; excerpt. D. Macaulay. il Atlantic 240:71-6 D '77

Climatic factors

See Architecture and climate

Competitions

Parkin wins Canadian National Gallery competition. il Archit Rec 162:39 S '77

Conferences

Calendar. See issues of Architectural record
See also
American Institute of Architects—Meetings

Conservation and restoration

Acropolis in danger. A. M. M'Bow. il por UNESCO Courier 30:4-6 F '77
Anchors aweigh on Chicago's latest amenity; Navy Pier restoration. W. Marlin. il Archit Rec 161:107-14 Mr '77
Architecture; question of downtown renovations. J. H. Kay. Nation 225:635-6 D 10 '77
East Germany restores Gropius's Bauhaus workshop for its 50th anniversary. il Archit Rec 161:35 Je '77
Historic preservation in Annapolis. C. Wright. bibl il Antiques 111:152-7 Ja '77
Historic preservation in Natchez, Mississippi. R. W. Miller. il Antiques 111:538-45 Mr '77
Hostal Nicolás de Ovando; two houses restored as a hotel in Santo Domingo. G. de Zéndegui. il Américas 29:21-8 Ag '77
How the Acropolis can be saved. C. Bouras. il UNESCO Courier 30:4-11 O '77
Preserving a neighborhood. T. H. Watkins. il Am Heritage 28:106-9 Je '77
Reconstruction, recreation, restoration: the preservation of historic theatre buildings. D. B. Wilmeth. Intellect 105:269 F '77
Recycling of Boston. J. H. Kay. il Sat R 4:38-40 F 5 '77
Recycling the city. C. Wiseman. il Horizon 21:43-9 Ja '78
Report from Chicago: restoration of the Trading Room; Louis Sullivan's Chicago Stock Exchange Trading Room. F. Schulze. il Art in Am 65:58-9 N '77
Saving old Orleans; architect protects the Vieux Carré. P. Brooks. il por Ms 6:21 Ag '77
1765 mill grinds into action; restoration of Rest Place Mill, High Falls, N.Y. by Tang and Jane Hansen. B. Russell. il House & Gard 149:36+ Je '77
Shahn's Bronx P.O. murals: the perils of public art. C. Baldwin. il Art in Am 65:15-16+ My '77
Sleeping beauty in the Canadian West; the Orpheum Theater, Vancouver. R. Gelatt. il Sat R 4:36-7 My 28 '77
Texas Supreme Court ruling jeopardizes historic buildings. L. Smith. il Archit Rec 162:37 O '77
Yesterday is here in Petaluma; restoration of mill and Lan Mart building. il Sunset 158:71 Ap '77
You can have your city's past and use it too. A. L. Huxtable. Vogue 167:222 Mr '77
See also
Historic houses, sites, etc.
Houses, Restored
National Trust for Historic Preservation

Designs and plans

Continuity in a framework of change. M. Breuer. il Archit Rec 162:105-12 Ag '77
Mapping and remapping: four projects by R. M. Kliment and F. Halsband; with introd by G. Allen. il Archit Rec 161:103-10 F '77
Minimizing defects in plans and specifications. M. Stokes. Archit Rec 162:49 Jl '77
See also
Architectural drawing
Architecture, Domestic—Designs and plans

Exhibitions

Architecture; Women in American Architecture: A History and Contemporary Perspective, exhibition. J. H. Kay. Nation 224:474-6 Ap 16 '77
Art of building on paper; 200 Years of American Architectural Drawing, at the Cooper-Hewitt Museum. P. Goldberger. il N Y Times Mag Mag p74-5+ Je 5 '77
Designing women; Brooklyn Museum exhibition, Women in American Architecture. D. Davis. il Newsweek 89:79-80 Mr 7 '77
Most influential architect in history; A. Palladio exhibit at New York's Cooper-Hewitt Museum. A. L. Huxtable. il N Y Times Mag p22-5 Jl 17 '77
Palladio's splendid creations; exhibition at the Cooper-Hewitt Museum. F. Schulze. il por Art N 76:70-1 O '77
Proletarian ideologies and visionary alternatives; Alternative Architecture at the Louisiana Museum of Modern Art, Humlebaek, Denmark. J. Gruen. il Art N 76:105-6 O '77
Three in one; Andrea Palladio Exhibition at the Cooper-Hewitt Museum. New Yorker 53:23 Jl 4 '77
Women design space; Brooklyn Museum exhibition, Women in American Architecture. il Ms 5:62-7 Mr '77

International aspects

Human settlements: world news. See issues of Architectural record

Periodicals

See also
Architectural record (periodical)

Philosophy

Architecture for people and not for things; excerpt from The architect as devoloper. J. Portman. il Archit Rec 161:133-40 Ja '77
Defining a design methodology. G. Birkerts. il Archit Rec 161:91-4 F '77
Juxtapositions; reconciling new architecture with old. B. C. Brolin. il Harpers 256:55-8 Ja '78
Possibilities in architecture. R. Geddes. il Archit Rec 162:103-8 N '77

ARCHITECTURE—*Continued*

Reconstruction

See Architecture—Conservation and restoration

Social aspects

Architecture for people and not for things; excerpt from The architect as developer. J. Portman. il Archit Rec 161:133-40 Ja '77
Buildings may be hazardous to your health. C. W. Taylor. Intellect 106:101-2 S '77
Death of the moderns. W. Von Eckardt. il New Repub 177:31-3 Ag 6; 26-9 Ag 20 '77
Possibilities in architecture. R. Geddes. il Archit Rec 162:103-8 N '77

Specifications

See Building—Contracts and specifications

Study and teaching

Houses children dream up; projects devised by Nancy Renfro. B. Russell. il House & Gard 149:42+ Je '77
See also
Architectural education
Architecture—Appreciation

Alabama

Transition and adaptation in Mobile architecture. E. B. Gould. il Antiques 112:466-75 S '77

California

Continuing education as a requirement for recertification takes hold in California. B. Lamb. Archit Rec 162:57 O '77
Great architect looks at California architecture. C. W. Moore. il Mademoiselle 83:100-1+ Ap '77
Laymen will outnumber pros on California licensing board. J. Nairn. Archit Rec 161:36 Ja '77
System of energy codes will govern California building. J. Nairn. Archit Rec 162:33 mid-Ag '77

Colorado

Notes from the field: how architects, and their consultants, approach solar design. M. F. Gaskie. il Archit Rec 162:108-13 mid-Ag '77

England

See also
Historic houses, sites, etc.—England

Florida

Spiraling arches shape a great space; Temple Beth El in West Palm Beach. il Archit Rec 161:111-14 F '77
See also
Miami Beach, Fla.—Architecture

France

See also
Cathedrals—France

Indiana

Showplace on the prairie; Columbus. il Time 110:68-9 D 5 '77

Louisiana

See also
New Orleans—Architecture

Massachusetts

See also
Boston—Architecture

New Hampshire

History in towns: Orford, New Hampshire. A. D. Hodgson. il Antiques 112:712-25 O '77

New York (state)

Doodles on the landscape: barn decorations in central New York. N. C. Hage. il Conservationist 31:42-3 N '76
See also
New York (city)—Architecture

Nigeria

Nigeria's Court of Appeals will have six regional centers. il Archit Rec 161:41 Mr '77

Puerto Rico

Six winners in new AIA awards program in Puerto Rico. il Archit Rec 161:42-3 Ap '77

Rhode Island

First awards program of Rhode Island AIA honors four buildings for distinctive design. il Archit Rec 162:41 S '77

United States

Buildings in the news. See issues of Architectural record
Buildings of the future—as a noted architect sees them; interview. E. D. Stone. il por U.S. News 83:55-6 Ag 15 '77
See also
Architecture, American
National Institute of Building Sciences
also subhead Architecture under names of cities, e.g. New Orleans—Architecture

History

Building types study as a not-too-clouded crystal ball; with introd by M. F. Schmertz. C. K. Hoyt. il Archit Rec 161:117, 138-46 Ap '77
Magic, nostalgia and a hint of greatness in the workaday world of the Building types study; analysis of 40 years of Architectural record's Building types studies; with introd by M. F. Schmertz. C. W. Moore and R. Oliver. Archit Rec 161:117-37 Ap '77

ARCHITECTURE, Amateur

Patchwork architecture. S. Ferris. il Horizon 19:24-31 Mr '77

ARCHITECTURE, American

Many-sided splendors; American polygonal architecture. R. Taylor. il House & Gard 149:58+ My '77
Unbuilt buildings. A. L. Huxtable. il N Y Times Mag p44-5+ Ja 30 '77

ARCHITECTURE, Ancient

See also
Cliff dwellers and cliff dwellings

ARCHITECTURE, Buddhist

See also
Borobudur, Java

ARCHITECTURE, Domestic

Rustic with class; house designed for Arthur Williams. il House & Gard 149:72-7 F '77
Shotgun houses. J. Vlach. il Natur Hist 86:50-7 bibl(p 100-1) F '77
Space alive; house by Peter Eisenman. il House & Gard 150:70-5 Ja '78
Transformation of the tract home. R. Nilsen. il Org Gard & Farm 24:178-81 Ag '77
See also
Apartment houses
Apartment houses, Remodeled
Apartments
Beach architecture
City houses
Cottages
Country houses
Decks, patios, terraces, etc.
Environmental engineering (buildings)
Farmhouses
Garages
Halls
Hillside architecture
Historic houses, sites, etc.
House construction
Houses
Houses, Prefabricated
Houses, Remodeled
Housing
Housing projects
Sod houses
Solar houses
Swimming pools, Home
Vacation houses

Designs and plans

Easy living; vacation houses. B. Niles. il Am Home 80:46-9+ Je '77
PS leisure home of the month:
  Atrium house—you build it in stages for progressive privacy. A. Lees. il Pop Sci 211:124-5+ O '77
  Cool house for a hot climate. R. Gannon. il Pop Sci 212:90-3+ Ja '78
  Fireproof retreat. A. Lees. il Pop Sci 211:106-7 S '77
  Hex cluster. il Pop Sci 210:144 Ap '77
  King-post pagoda. A. Lees. il Pop Sci 210:122 My '77
  Octagon on piers. A. Lees. il Pop Sci 210:132 F '77
  Peak house on stilts. il Pop Sci 211:91+ Jl '77
  Skewed-prow two-story. A. Lees. il Pop Sci 210:113+ Mr '77
  Split-level twin shed. A. Lees. il Pop Sci 211:123 Ag '77
  Sun cottage for all seasons. A. Lees. il Pop Sci 211:93 D '77
  Sun trap. A. Lees. il Pop Sci 211:118-19 N '77
  Two-phase split pavilions. A. Lees. il Pop Sci 210:102-3 Je '77
Record houses of 1977; with introd by B. F. Gordon. il Archit Rec 161:49-108 mid-My '77
Sensational barn of your own; prefabricated house. il House & Gard 149:122-7 Je '77
Sneak peek at our new idea houses. K. L. Petersen. il Bet Hom & Gard 55:86-7 O '77
Solar with style; house designed by Antoine Predock in New Mexico. il House & Gard 149:130-3 S '77
To surreal with love; houses by S. Tigerman. W. Marlin. il Archit Rec 162:89-94 O '77

Alabama

Living with antiques: the Mobile residence of Dr and Mrs Charles Rutherford Jr. M. R. Ingate. il Antiques 112:476-81 S '77

Arizona

Bruder residence, New River, Arizona; desert house. il Archit Rec 161:104-5 mid-My '77
Hospitality, southwestern style; house of William Joffroy family. B. Niles and N. Williams. il Am Home 80:52-9 N '77
Only $10+ per square foot; Bruder house, Phoenix. il Sunset 159:74-5 Jl '77

ARCHITECTURE, Domestic—*Continued*

Belgium

Farmhouse for art; home of P. Culot near Brussels. N. Skurka. il por N Y Times Mag p42-3 Ag 14 '77

California

At home with Helen Reddy. il por Good H 186: 102-5 Ja '78
Country house, California style; Marin County. J. Friedman-Weiss and H. H. Wise. il McCalls 104:104-6 S '77
Decorating—let yourself go. il House & Gard 150:88-91 Ja '78
Delightful weekend retreat at the Sea Ranch. il Archit Rec 161:147-50 Ja '77
Earth, Wind & Fire members build their dream homes. il pors Ebony 33:154-6+ D '77
Family living—open house. il House & Gard 150:84-7 Ja '78
Garden within; house of Maxine Smith. il House & Gard 149:98-103 Je '77
Gray residence, Santa Barbara, California. il Archit Rec 161:100-3 mid-My '77
House in the hill; Alexander house near Santa Barbara. P. Goldberger. il N Y Times Mag p42-4 Ag 7 '77
It all fits together; home of Sandy Gallin, Beverly Hills. R. Weil. il House B 119:72-9 Je '77
Large house of varied spaces and surprises; with introd by J. Nairn. il Archit Rec 161:113-16 Ap '77
Most creative house in America; home of the Wolfman family. P. Sadowsky. il Am Home 80:34-9 Ag '77
Natural connection; house of John and Eleanor McGuire. il House & Gard 149:86-91 Je '77
One-room hideaway; F. Lyman home in Malibu. il Am Home 80:52-3 Je '77
Tall pipes of water heat and cool award-winning house; solar houses. il Sunset 159:112-15 N '77
Theatrical Santa Monica house; Leland S. Burns. il Sunset 158:116-19 Ap '77
Tomorrow's house? Sea Ranch, Calif. solar house. il Sunset 158:132-4 Ap '77
22 energy-miser tricks that cut your living costs. R. F. Dempewolff. il Pop Mech 148:88-91+ Jl '77
Unusual semicircle house hangs on its central tower. il Sunset 158:119 F '77
Venetian Gardens, Stockton, California. il Archit Rec 161:120-1 mid-My '77
Whalers' Cove Apartments, Foster City, California. il Archit Rec 161:124-6 mid-My '77
Year-round sanctuary; Chew house designed by C. C. Calvin; Santa Barbara. il Am Home 80:48-9 Je '77
See also
Sacramento, Calif.—Architecture
San Francisco—Architecture

Canada

Chiu residence, Vancouver, British Columbia. il Archit Rec 161:72-3 mid-My '77
See also
Toronto—Architecture

Connecticut

Good life, country style; house of Martha Stewart. il House & Gard 149:92-7 Je '77
House as sculptural object; the Frank house designed by P. Eisenman. P. Goldberger. il N Y Times Mag p74-6+ Mr 20 '77
Motherwell atelier; Greenwich. A. A. Cohen. il por Vogue 167:230-3+ Mr '77
One-of-a-kind country look; farmhouse of the Bill Crofut family. B. Niles. il pors Am Home 80:46-9 S '77

England

Conrans in the country. E. Brown. il por N Y Times Mag p74-5 O 30 '77

Fire Island

Quick and easy decorating for a holiday haven; Fire Island home. J. Macurdy and K. Mahoney. il House B 119:66-71 Ag '77
Weekend escape house; Fire Island beach house. N. Skurka. il N Y Times Mag p84-5 My 1 '77

Florida

For maximal living; family home of designer D. Singer. S. G. Lewin. il House B 119:74-9 Ag '77
Private residence, northern Florida. il Archit Rec 161:106-8 mid-My '77
See also
Miami, Fla.—Architecture

France

Weekend wonderplace: the Antenor Patiños French country house; remodeled seventeenth-century mill near Fontainebleau. il Vogue 167: 166-9 Ap '77

Hawaii

Hawaii's Energy House. il Sunset 158:142 Ap '77

Illinois

For ever & today; interior of Wiliamsburg house designed by Chuck Winslow in Aurora, Ill. J. Macurdy. il House B 119:62-73 Ap '77
To surreal with love; houses by S. Tigerman. W. Marlin. il Archit Rec 162:89-94 O '77
See also
Chicago—Architecture

Italy

Renaissance of a villa. N. Skurka. il N Y Times Mag p46-7 Ag 28 '77

Japan

How to keep warm for pennies . . . Japanese style. W. Shurtleff. il Org Gard & Farm 24: 120-2+ Mr '77

Long Island

Carefree cube; home in Amagansett. B. Niles. il Am Home 80:46-7 Je '77
Chapell residence, eastern Long Island. il Archit Rec 161:76-7 mid-My '77
Come up to comfort; weekend house. il House & Gard 149:86-9 Ag '77
Design for orderly living; Kislevitz house in Westhampton Beach. P. Goldberger. il N Y Times Mag p 146-8+ D 11 '77
House on the beach, eastern Long Island. il Archit Rec 161:86-9 mid-My '77
Preserving the rustic life; Mascheroni family. il House & Gard 149:154-7 Ap '77
Private residence, eastern Long Island; weekend house. il Archit Rec 161:54-5 mid-My '77
See also
Architecture, Domestic—Fire Island

Maine

Imagination, country style; house of S. Parish. il House & Gard 149:110-15 D '77

Martha's Vineyard

Bridge to nature. il House & Gard 149:174-7 N '77

Maryland

House in Maryland, by Hartman-Cox; with introd by J. Nairn. il Archit Rec 161:119-22 My '77
Residential remodeling and addition, Chevy Chase, Maryland. il Archit Rec 161:82-3 mid-My '77

Massachusetts

Catch the sun; house designed by Leland Cott. il House & Gard 149:84-7 Jl '77
Private residence, Weston, Massachusetts. il Archit Rec 161:56-9 mid-My '77
Recycled tannery provides historical and spatial amenities for elderly near Boston; The Tannery, Peabody. il Archit Rec 162:124-6 S '77
Winter into summer; D. Daniels' snow belt house. New Yorker 53:19-22 Ja 9 '78
See also
Architecture, Domestic—Martha's Vineyard

Mexico

Arango house, Acapulco. il Archit Rec 161:64-7 mid-My '77
Welcome into private homes in Yucatan; Mérida. il Sunset 159:76 O '77

Michigan

Solar home in the Northland; Stevensville. J. Mueller. il Mech Illus 74:36-7+ Ja '78

Nebraska

Ball residence, Omaha, Nebraska. il Archit Rec 161:90-3 mid-My '77

History

Shelters on the plains. R. Welsch. il Natur Hist 86:48-53 bibl(p94) My '77

New England

Serenity was their goal. S. G. Lewin. il House B 119:80-5 Je '77

New Jersey

Cottage industry; interior of hillside retreat designed by C. Winslow and G. Lajeski. J. Macurdy. il House B 119:134-9 My '77

New Mexico

A-frame energy saver; Taos. il Mech Illus 73:70 O '77
Home in an adobe; home of F. Scholder; Galisteo. R. Kent. il pors N Y Times Mag p46-7+ Ja 23 '77
Private residence, Albuquerque, New Mexico; desert house. il Archit Rec 161:60-1 mid-My '77
Solar with style; house designed by Antoine Predock. il House & Gard 149:130-3 S '77
Stay in touch with the land; adobe house. il House & Gard 149:66-9 Ag '77
Two-story greenhouse is three-way heater for this Santa Fe adobe. il Sunset 158:146+ My '77

ARCHITECTURE, Domestic—*Continued*

New York (state)

Classic purity; home of the Volney Righters. C. R. Smith. il N Y Times Mag p70-1 Ap 10 '77
Joyful place of light and color; interview, ed by R. Weil. P. Duchin and C. Duchin. il House B 119:28-35 Ag '77
Landings near Buffalo, New York. il Archit Rec 161:118-19 mid-My '77
Lieto residence, Westchester, New York. il Archit Rec 161:78-81 mid-My '77
More than meets the eye. P. Goldberger. il N Y Times Mag p46-7+ Ja 16 '77
Phased growth; interior of upstate home designed by J. Crissman and S. Soloman. S. G. Lewin. il House B 119:126-33 My '77
Private residence, New York State. il Archit Rec 161:94-7 mid-My '77
Private residence, Westchester, New York. il Archit Rec 161:68-71 mid-My '77
6 winners; residences selected by the New York Chapter of the American Institute of Architects. P. Goldberger. il N Y Times Mag p66-9 Mr 13 '77
Two houses by Charles Moore. M. F. Schmertz. il Archit Rec 161:109-16 Je '77
See also
Architecture, Domestic—Fire Island
Architecture, Domestic—Long Island

North America

Patchwork architecture. S. Ferris. il Horizon 19:24-31 Mr '77

North Carolina

It fit together like a jigsaw puzzle; home of C. Barnes in Winston-Salem, N.C. M. Gough and J. Macurdy. il por House B 119:104-13 N '77

Ohio

Erdos residence northern Ohio. il Archit Rec 161:62-3 mid-My '77

Oregon

Built for rugged living; Oregon ranch by Saul Zaik. il House & Gard 149:82-5 F '77
Crest Apartments, St. Helens, Oregon. il Archit Rec 161:116-17 mid-My '77
Embarcadero Condominiums, Newport, Oregon. il Archit Rec 161:114-15 mid-My '77
Small is more. il Sunset 158:84-7 Mr '77
See also
Portland, Ore.—Architecture

Pennsylvania

Maxey residence, Wayne County, Pennsylvania. il Archit Rec 161:74-5 mid-My '77

Rhode Island

See also
Providence, R.I.—Architecture

South Carolina

Space age home; C. J. Williams' home in Orangeburg. il pors Ebony 32:86-8+ Je '77

Southern States

Along the Natchez Trace. E. Cheatham and P. Cheatham. il Travel 148:52-7+ O '77

Texas

Tour of the LBJ ranch. J. Egan. il por Good H 185:112-17+ O '77

United States

Americans at home; excerpt from Good lives. J. Friedman-Weiss and H. H. Wise. il McCalls 104:98-100+ S '77
Home sweet dome; geodesic domes. il Time 109:34-5 Mr 14 '77

Vermont

Butternut Hill Condominiums, Waitsfield, Vermont; vacation condominiums. il Archit Rec 161:110-11 mid-My '77

Virginia

Lattice house life. il House & Gard 149:126-9 Mr '77
Private residence, Arlington, Virginia. il Archit Rec 161:84-5 mid-My '77

Washington, D.C.

Classic town house in the Nation's Capital; Georgetown. J. Friedman-Weiss and H. H. Wise. il McCalls 104:98-100+ S '77
We wanted the new house to have the same flavor as the old; remodeled Victorian house. il House & Gard 149:142-5 My '77

Washington (state)

Vacation house, Puget Sound. il Archit Rec 161:98-9 mid-My '77

Western States

See also
Western Home Awards

Yucatan

See Architecture, Domestic—Mexico

ARCHITECTURE, Ecclesiastical. See Church architecture
ARCHITECTURE, English
Museum of old buildings is established in England; Avoncroft Museum of Buildings. M. Burns. il Archit Rec 161:34 My '77
ARCHITECTURE, Greek revival
Acropolomania. il UNESCO Courier 30:28 O '77
ARCHITECTURE, Hillside. See Hillside architecture
ARCHITECTURE, Hotel. See Hotels, motels, etc.—Architecture
ARCHITECTURE, Italian
Most influential architect in history; A. Palladio. A. L. Huxtable. il N Y Times Mag p22-5 Jl 17 '77
Palladio's splendid creations. F. Schulze. il por Art N 76:70-1 O '77
ARCHITECTURE, Mexican
Arresting view to the south; the Mexican embassy in Brasilia and the Colegio de Mexico in Mexico City. il Archit Rec 162:81-8 O '77
See also
Indians of Mexico—Architecture
ARCHITECTURE, Modern
AIA Gold Medal goes to Neutra; International Style. W. Marlin. por Archit Rec 161:37 Ap '77
Death of the moderns. W. Von Eckardt. il New Repub 177:31-3 Ag 6; 26-9 Ag 20 '77
House that modernism built; Corbusian revival. N. Silver il Harpers 255:77+ Ag '77
Juxtapositions; reconciling new architecture with old. B. C. Brolin. il Harpers 256:55-8 Ja '78
On architecture. J. Ackerman. il Art N 76:111 N '77
Something borrowed, something new; postmodernism. R. A. M. Stern. il Horizon 20:50-7 D '77
See also
Art déco
Bauhaus
ARCHITECTURE, Naval. See Naval architecture
ARCHITECTURE, Neo-Greek. See Architecture, Greek revival
ARCHITECTURE, Synagogue. See Synagogues
ARCHITECTURE and climate
Bruder residence, New River, Arizona; desert house. il Archit Rec 161:104-5 mid-My '77
Private residence, Albuquerque, New Mexico; desert house. il Archit Rec 161:60-1 mid-My '77
ARCHITECTURE and the blind
More than meets the eye. P. Goldberger. il N Y Times Mag p46-7+ Ja 16 '77
Two houses by Charles Moore. M. F. Schmertz. il Archit Rec 161:109-16 Je '77
ARCHITECTURE and the handicapped
Helping the handicapped. il Time 110:34 D 5 '77
New ANSI standards on barrier-free design expected in 1978. W. Hickman. Archit Rec 162:63 D '77
Opening minds and entryways at cultural centers. R. D. MacNeil. bibl il Parks & Rec 12:41-4 N '77
ARCHITECTURE as a profession
Careers in art. P. Savino. il Sch Arts 76:10 Ap '77
ARCHITECTURE/Environmental Arts Program. See United States—National Foundation on the Arts and the Humanities
ARCHITECTURE in art
Architecture and scratchboard. M. A. Stafford. il Design (US) 78:30 mid-Wint '77
ARCHIVES
See also
Public officers—Archives

Czechoslovakia

Secrets from the Prague spring; documents in K. Kaplan's possession. il Time 109:38 My 9 '77

Spain

Key to the past; archival collections in Madrid relating to Latin American history. J. Luján Muñoz. il Américas 29:42-3 O '77

United States

Designs and documents; preservation of papers of F. L. Olmsted. J. H. Kay. Sat R 4:27 My 14 '77
Now it's a wave of thefts in historic documents. il U.S. News 83:51-2 S 5 '77
See also
Rockefeller Archive Center
ARCINIEGAS, Germán
Anita and Giuseppe Garibaldi: a love story on two continents. il pors Américas 29:2-7 My '77
ARCOSANTI, Ariz.
Visionary doing inspires Arcosanti. J. Springwater. Craft Horiz 37:9 F '77
ARCTIC Enterprises Inc. See Snowmobile industry
ARCTIC Regions
See also
Cruising—Arctic Regions
Eskimos
Greenland
Ice—Polar Regions
Lapps

ARTIC Regions—See also—*Continued*
Mackenzie River (Canada)
Northwest Passage
Northwest Territories, Canada
Petroleum—Arctic Regions
Wrangel Island
Yukon

ARCTIC research
ONR/AIBS sponsor symposium on Arctic environment. il BioScience 27:415-16 Je '77

ARD, Roger H.
Why the conservatives won in Miami. Chr Cent 94:677-9 Ag 3 '77

ARDAYNE, Julia Collins
Stranger in a crowd; poem. Ladies Home J 94: 78 Ap '77

ARDEN, Harvey
America's little mainstream. il Nat Geog 151: 344-59 Mr '77

ARDEN-Mayfair, Inc
Arden-Mayfair's fifth turnaround try. il Bus W p30 Mr 14 '77

ARDISIA
Ardisia: a colorful plant for Christmas. Horticulture 55:44+ D '77

ARDMORE, Jane
Like father, like son. pors Good H 184:52+ F '77
Special kind of love. il pors Fam Health 9:28-31 F '77
(ed) See Ireland, J. I love being Mrs Charles Bronson, but . . .
(ed) See Thomas, M. Marlo Thomas: men, marriage & me

ARDOIN, John
Love-hate relationship. il por Opera N 42:10-11 D 17 '77
One of a kind. il por Opera N 42:18-23 D 3 '77
Three masterpieces return. il Hi Fi 17:MA30-2 D '77

ARDURA, Ernesto
Transcendentalism and the expectation of dawn: Emerson and Thoreau. il pors Américas 29: 36-41 Ag '77

AREHART-TREICHEL, Joan
[Articles on medical science] See issues of Science news
Laetrile: the science behind the controversy. il Sci N 112:92-5 Ag 6 '77

ARELLANO, Richard G.
Department testifies on undocumented aliens; statement, September 14, 1977. Dept State Bull 77:592-4 O 31 '77

ARENA di Verona. See Opera—Italy

ARENAL, Electa
Muñoz of Barcelona. il Craft Horiz 37:58-61+ D '77

ARENAS, Sports. See Stadiums

ARENDT, Hannah
Reflections. New Yorker 53:65-8+ N 21; 114+ N 28; 135-42+ D 5 '77

ARGENTINA
See also
Americans in Argentina
Buenos Aires
Civil rights—Argentina
Fishing—Argentina
Government ownership—Argentina
Jews in Argentina
Paleontology—Argentina
Patagonia
Political prisoners—Argentina

Economic policy

Show of confidence in economic recovery. Bus W p40 My 30 '77

Foreign relations

History

Détente, then and now; J. B. Alberdi and H. Kissinger. G. H. Watson. il pors Américas 29: 2-7 Ja '77

History

When Argentina conquered California; naval battles fought by Argentine ship on voyage around the world. A. Alonso Piñeiro. il por Américas 29:34-7 Je '77

Politics and government

Argentina today; address, June 28, 1977. R. C. Hill. Vital Speeches 43:612-15 Ag 1 '77
Argentina's military government. D. C. Jordan. bibl f Cur Hist 72:57-60+ F '77
Hope from a clockwork coup. J. R. Videla. il por Time 109:45-6 Ap 11 '77
Juntas of Chile and Argentina: studies in government by terror. R. O'Mara. por Sat R 4:13-16 Ap 2 '77
Murder in Argentina; death of E. Käsemann. E. Magalis. Chr Cent 94:1030-3 N 9 '77
Reports & comment: Argentina: a state of fear. J. B. Treaster. Atlantic 240:16+ N '77
Repression in Argentina. R. F. Drinan. Commonweal 104:103-4 F 18 '77
Revolution that wasn't; press coverage. T. Powers. Commonweal 104:19-20 Ja 7 '77
Self-liquidating junta. E. Galbraith. Nat R 29: 1494 D 23 '77

ARGENTINE fiction
Poem of the pampas; gaucho theme of R. Güiraldes' Don Segundo Sombra. E. A. Echevarria. il Americas 29:2-5 Ap '77

ARGENTINE poetry

Translations into English

Brunanburh, A.D. 937; tr. by A. Reid. J. L. Borges. New Yorker 53:42 Ap 18 '77
Hengist wants men; tr by A. Reid. J. L. Borges. New Yorker 53:34 Je 20 '77
Palace; poem; tr by A. Reid. J. L. Borges. New Yorker 53:38 S 26 '77
Talismans; tr by A. Reid. J. L. Borges. New Yorker 53:26 Ag 8 '77
To the nightingale; tr. by A. Reid. J. L. Borges. New Yorker 53:42 My 9 '77

ARGENTINE scientists. See Scientists, Argentine

ARGENTO, Dominick
Water bird talk. Reviews
New Yorker 53:108+ Je 6 '77 *

ARGININE
Arginyl residues: anion recognition sites in enzymes. J. F. Riordan and others. bibl il Science 195:884-6 Mr 4 '77

ARGO Merchant shipwreck. See Shipwrecks

ARGONNE, Battle of the, 1918. See World War, 1914-1918—Campaigns and battles

ARGUESO, Stephanie
Real looks: how four young women dress for job/home/night. il pors Mademoiselle 83:176-81 S '77 *

ARGYRIS, Chris
Double loop learning in organizations. il Harvard Bus R 55:115-25 S '77

ARIAS
Aria structure and ritornello form in the music of Albinoni. J. E. Solie. bibl f il Mus Q 63:31-47 Ja '77

ARID Lands Ecology Reserve. See Natural areas —Washington (state)

ARID regions
Precarious balance upset; increase in aridification. V. A. Kovda. il map UNESCO Courier 30:11-14 Jl '77
See also
Desert vegetation
Deserts
Dry farming

ARIEL, Gideon
Computer readout translates body language into skills. P. Garfinkel. il Sci Digest 81:12-14 Mr '77 *
Gideon Ariel and his magic machine. K. Moore. il por Sports Illus 47:52-60 Ag 22 '77 *

ARIETI, Silvano
How to read how-to books. Psychol Today 11: 142+ O '77

ARISTA Records (firm) See Phonograph record industry

ARISTIDES, pseud
Greetings and salutations. Am Scholar 47:16+ Wint '77
It's so hard to be good under capitalism. Am Scholar 46:290+ Summ '77
Life and letters. . . Am Scholar 46:432+ Aut '77
Observing the Sabbath. Am Scholar 46:159-63 Spr '77

ARISTOTLE
Aristotle. C. Despotopoulos. por UNESCO Courier 30:31-3 O '77 *
Aristotle's biology. L. P. Coonen. bibl BioScience 27:733-8 N '77 *

ARITHMETIC
Unprovable problem in arithmetic. Sci N 111: 373-4 Je 11 '77

ARITHMETIC ability. See Mathematical ability

ARIYOSHI, George Ryoichi
Paradise closed? il Forbes 120:98-9 N 15 '77 *
Rotten system. T. Mathews and G. C. Lubenow. il pors Newsweek 90:47 N 14 '77 *

ARIZONA
See also
Architecture, Domestic—Arizona
Colorado Plateau
Crime and criminals—Arizona
Education—Arizona
Fishing—Arizona
Grand Canyon
Grand Canyon National Park
Hunting—Arizona
Irrigation—Arizona
Paleontology—Arizona
Petrified Forest National Park
Powell, Lake
Sonoran Desert
Water supply—Arizona

Antiquities

Intaglios-ancient earth paintings. il Sunset 158: 61-2 Ap '77

Description and travel

Bird watching in Arizona canyons. il map Sunset 158:104-6 Je '77
Few hot licks on Arizona. H. Sutton. il Sat R 4:54-6 Jl 9 '77

ARIZONA republic (newspaper) See Phoenix, Ariz.—Newspapers
ARIZONA-Sonora Desert Museum. See Natural history museums
ARK, Noah's. See Noah's Ark
ARKANSAS
See also
Buffalo National River
Cache River
Education—Arkansas
Organic farming—Arkansas
Ozark Mountains
ARKANSAS. University

Little Rock campus

Wonderful product; Puppet Opera. B. Thebom. il por Opera N 42:40-1 N '77
ARKES, Hadley
Idea whose time is passing? Nat R 29:1108-10+ S 30 '77
ARKSEY, Laura
Library of Assurbanipal, King of the world. bibl il Wilson Lib Bull 51:832-40 Je '77
ARLEDGE, Roone Pinckney
Roone at the top; excerpts from interview, ed by H. F. Waters. por Newsweek 89:103-4 My 16 '77
about
ABC's wider world of news. il por Time 109:79-80 My 16 '77 *
Black eye for TV boxing. P. Bonventre. il pors Newsweek 89:81-2 My 2 '77 *
New ABC's of news. D. M. Alpern and B. Carter. il por Newsweek 90:62 Ag 22 '77 *
Revving up the television news. T. Griffith. por Time 110:58+ Ag 22 '77 *
ARLEN, Michael J.
The air (cont) New Yorker 53:115-18+ O 3; 104+ O 17; 119-27 O 31; 167-8+ N 14; 166-73 N 28 '77
ARLEN Realty and Development Corporation
Arlen's dream versus Korvettes' reality. P. Blustein. il por Forbes 119:85+ Ap 15 '77
Arlen's switch to a stress on earnings. il Bus W p86 Mr 14 '77
ARLES workshop. See Photography—Study and teaching
ARLINGTON, Mass.

Education

See Education—Massachusetts
ARLINGTON, Va.
Pentagon City is a family affair; new development project of Rose Associates Inc. il Bus W p25 Mr 7 '77
ARLINGTON Heights, Ill.

Housing

See Housing—Illinois
ARMADILLOS
Unloved and unloving, the armadillo blunders on. D. Lampe. il Nat Wildlife 15:34-7 F '77
ARMAMENT industries. See Munitions
ARMAMENTS
Armament decade. Sci Am 237:70 N '77
Armed camp. Sci Am 236:52-3 My '77
More weapons for what? J. Burnham. Nat R 29:140 F 4 '77
See also
Airplanes, Military—Armaments
Disarmament
Militarism
Munitions
United Nations Group of Experts on the Economic and Social Consequences of the Arms Race and of Military Expenditures
ARMATRADING, Joan
Joan Armatrading; interview. New Yorker 53:38 D 5 '77
ARMBRISTER, Trevor
Anatomy of a boondoggle. il Read Digest 111: 133-6 Ag '77
Behind those soaring coffee prices. Read Digest 110:65-6+ My '77
ARMBRUSTER, Frank E.
The more we spend, the less children learn; excerpt from Our children's crippled future: how American education has failed. il N Y Times Mag p9-11+ Ag 28 '77; Same abr. with title Why American education is failing. Read Digest 112:106-9 Ja '78
ARMCO Steel Corporation
Diversification that offsets the slack in steel. il por Bus W p99+ D 12 '77
PR man helps select author of book on pollution case. L. J. Carter. Science 195:468 F 4 '77
ARMED Forces
See also subhead Armed Forces under names of countries, e.g. Sweden—Armed Forces

Appropriations and expenditures

See also
United Nations Group of Experts on the Economic and Social Consequences of the Arms Race and of Military Expenditures

Anecdotes, facetiae, satire, etc.

Late, great earth. New Repub 177:2+ Jl 2 '77

ARMIES
See also subhead Army under names of countries, e.g. Rhodesia—Army
ARMISTICE Day. See Veterans Day
ARMOIRES
Furniture of the river road plantations in Louisiana. J. J. Poesch. bibl il Antiques 111: 1184-8 Je '77
ARMOR, David J.
Dangers of forced integration. bibl il Society 14:41-4 My '77
ARMORED vessels
Admiral Yi and the turtle boats; ironclad warships in sixteenth century Asian war. B. I. Wiley. il por Am Hist Illus 12:44-8 Je '77
ARMORY Show of 1913. See Art, Modern—Exhibitions
ARMOUR, Richard
Throwing some light on light verse. Writer 90:15-18 O '77
ARMOUR, Robert
Poetry and film for the classroom. Engl J 66: 88-91 Ja '77
ARMS, Coats of. See Heraldry
ARMS control. See Disarmament
ARMS Control and Disarmament Agency. See United States—Arms Control and Disarmament Agency
ARMS race. See Armaments
ARMS trade. See Munitions—Export-import problems
ARMSTRONG, David G. and Pinney, R. E.
Practitioner's guide to machete-swinging in the paperwork jungle: record keeping and individualized instruction. il Clearing H 50:196-9 Ja '77
ARMSTRONG, DeWitt C. 3d
Why we should leave Panama. por Newsweek 90:32-3 N 28 '77
ARMSTRONG, Frank Harris
Jobs for youth. il Am For 83:30-3+ N '77
ARMSTRONG, Herbert W.
Armstrong's Worldwide Church of God: musical chairs of change. J. M. Hopkins. Chr Today 21:20-3 Ap 1; 22-4 Ap 15 '77 *
ARMSTRONG, James
In contact with Mangrove. il Dance Mag 51:42-5 D '77
ARMSTRONG, James, Bp
Conversation with Castro. Chr Cent 94:743-4 Ag 31 '77
James Armstrong: an address that sets a new tone. Chr Cent 94:6-7 Ja 5 '77
ARMSTRONG, Karen A. and others
Gene cloning and containment properties of plasmid col E1 and its derivatives. bibl il Science 196:172-4 Ap 8 '77
ARMSTRONG, Louis
Indigenous music. N. Hentoff. Nation 224:414 Ap 2 '77 *
Jazz. W. Balliett. New Yorker 53:84 Ap 4 '77 *
ARMSTRONG, O. K.
Railroad fights its way into the 20th century. il Nations Bus 65:58-61+ Jl '77
ARMSTRONG, Peter B.
Cellular positional stability and intercellular invasion. bibl il BioScience 27:803-9 D '77
ARMSTRONG, Robert A. and Gilpin, M. E.
Evolution in a time-varying environment. bibl il Science 195:591-2 F 11 '77
ARMSTRONG, Ruth W.
Albuquerque. il Trav/Holiday 149:34-9 Ja '78
ARMSTRONG-JONES, Antony Charles Robert, 1st Earl of Snowdon. See Snowdon, A. C. R. A.-J.
ARMY Air Corps. See United States—Army—Air Corps
ARMY Electronics Command. See United States —Army Electronics Command
ARMY engineers. See United States—Army—Corps of Engineers
ARMYTAGE, Stephen Green-. See Green-Armytage, S.
ARNESON, Howard D.
Economic diary (cont) il Bus W p20+ Ap 18; p 16+ S 5 '77
ARNESON, Howard M.
Success with a mind-boggling invention. P. Schwab. il por Nations Bus 65:92 D '77 *
ARNOLD, Becky
Reviews. M. Robertson. Dance Mag 51:34-5 D '77 *
ARNOLD, Eberhard
Bruderhof: living God's word. R. H. Bainton. Chr Cent 94:569-70 Je 8 '77 *
ARNOLD, Glenn
(ed) See Jackson, J. L. You can pray if you want to
ARNOLD, H. J. P.
Earth from space: reality & promise. il maps Space World N-11-167:20-9 N '77
ARNOLD, James R.
Studying near-earth resources. Aviation W 107: 9 S 19 '77
ARNOLD, Robert E.
Poison! See issues of Field & stream
—and Pearce, Laer
Burgeoning cult of wild food nourishes fatal misconceptions. il Smithsonian 8:48-55 My '77

ARNOLD, Roland R. and others
Bactericidal effect for human lactoferrin. bibl il Science 197:263-5 Jl 15 '77

ARNOLD, Sally, pseud
Consciousness-raising; truth and consequences. il Ms 6:101-4+ Jl; 12-13 N '77

ARNOLD, Stevan J.
Polymorphism and geographic variation in the feeding behavior of the garter snake thamnophis elegans. bibl il Science 197:676-8 Ag 12 '77

ARNOLD, William P. and others
Cigarette smoke activates guanylate cyclase and increases guanosine 3',5-monophosphate in tissues. bibl il Science 198.934-6 D 2 '77

ARNOLD Schoenberg Institute, Los Angeles
Commentary. H. Heinsheimer. Mus Q 63:428-33 Jl '77
Schoenberg is alive! V. Perlis. il Hi Fi 27:MA19-21 Ag '77

ARNSTEIN, George E.
Fighting fraud in education. il Am Educ 13:27-30 Ap '77

ARNY, T. and Valeriani, G.
Five College Radio Astronomy Observatory. il Sky & Tel 53:431-5 Je '77

AROCHI, Luis Enrique
Visit of the plumed serpent. il Américas 29:32-5 Ag '77

AROMATIC compounds
Azaarenes in recent marine sediments. M. Blumer and others. bibl il Science 195:283-4 Ja 21 '77

AROMATIC hydrocarbons. See Hydrocarbons

ARONOW, Don
Racy retirement. S. Reier. il por Forbes 120:98 Ag 15 '77 *

ARONS, Stephen
Friends of the Court. . .and the man who started it all. Sat R 5:12-13 O 15 '77
—and Katsh, Ethan
How TV cops flout the law. il Sat R 4:10-14+ Mr 19 '77

ARONSON, James
Chou En-Lai's cortege. Nation 224:165-6 F 12 '77

ARONSON, Jonathan, and Stein, Elliot, Jr
Bankers milk the third world. Progressive 41:49-51 O '77

ARONSON, Len
Ibex in Israel; with biographical sketch. il por Natur Hist 87:4, 50-5 bibl(p 108) Ja '78

AROSTEGUI, Martin. See Moss, R. jt auth

AROUND the world tours. See World tours

ARP, Robert C. Jr
Build: digital clock for your car. il Radio-Electr 48:61-3+ F '77

ARP and Friend, Inc. See Music trade

ARPINO, Gerald
Movement with meaning. R. Philp. Dance Mag 51:92 Jl '77 *

ARRANGEMENT of flowers. See Flowers, Arrangement of

ARRANGEMENT of furniture. See Furniture, Arrangement of

ARREST
Pinch must really sting; study by the Institute for Law and Social Research. il Time 110:59-60 S 26 '77
We've been asked about making a citizen's arrest. U.S. News 83:56 D 12 '77
See also
Bail

ARRINGTON, Chris Rigby
Working on the campaign trail. il por Ret Liv 17:38+ O '77

ARROYO, Antonio M. Stevens-. See Stevens-Arroyo, A. M.

ARSON
Arson for hate and profit. il Time 110:22-3+ O 31 '77
Business battles the arsonist. il Bus W p64+ F 28 '77
Fastest-growing crime. S. Fraker and others. il Newsweek 89:38 Ja 24 '77
New tactics in the battle against fires for profit. il U.S. News 83:31-2 S 5 '77
Torches for sale. S. T. Atlas. il Newsweek 90: 89-90 S 12 '77

ART
Art. J. E. Canaday. il New Repub 177:28-9 O 1; 25-6+ N 12; 22-4 D 10 '77; 178:25-7 Ja 7 '78
See also
Action in art
Aesthetics
Anatomy, Artistic
Art déco
Art nouveau
The Arts
Arts and crafts
Arts and crafts movement
Assemblage (art)
Booksellers and bookselling—Art
Bronzes
Caricatures and cartoons
Childrens art
Christian art and symbolism
Computers—Art use
Decoration and ornament
Design
Design, Decorative
Drawing
Engraving
Etching
Folk art
Graphic arts
Illumination of books and manuscripts
Illustration
Impressionism (art)
Landscape painting
Lasers—Art use
Light in art
Line (art)
Lithographs
Miniature painting
Mobiles
Multiple art
Mural painting and decoration
Pastel drawing
Photography, Artistic
Post-impressionism (art)
Posters
Prints
Publishers and publishing—Art
Realism in art
Reproductions of works of art
Sculpture
Symbolism in art
United States—Centennial celebrations, etc.—Art
Video art
Water color painting

Anecdotes, facetiae, satire, etc.

Ad Reinhardt, where are you now that we really need you? P. Plagens. Art in Am 65:10-11 S '77

Appreciation

Art appreciation: a practical approach; a volunteer program in Monmouth County, N.J. schools. C. K. Sills. il Sch Arts 76:44+ Mr '77
Art market: what is its future? pro and con discussion. J. Solomon; A. Rosenberg. pors Am Artist 41:12-13 Ap '77
Brickbats and favorites; Art news poll of most overrated and underrated artists of the 20th century. il Horizon 21:34 Ja '78
Can computers be programmed to appreciate art? M. J. Apter. Art N 76:18 Summ '77
Far-from-last judgments; or, Who's overrated now? And underrated; views of art historians, museum directors, curators and critics; ed by J. Gruen. il Art N 76:106-20 N '77
How to keep your students from yawning at art museums. J. C. Vitale. Design (US) 79: 10-11 Fall '77
How to read a painting. J. C. Vitale. il Sch Arts 77:44-6 N '77
Looking at paintings. B. Dunstan. See issues of American artist
20th-century artists most admired by other artists; views of nearly 100 artists; ed by G. Glueck. il Art N 76:78-103 N '77

Attribution

See Art—Expertising

Bibliography

Art books. See issues of American artist
Art books 1977. L. Alloway. Nation 225:661-5 D 17 '77
Book reviews. See issues of Design (US)
Books. See issues of Art news
John Canaday on art books. J. Canaday. il New Repub 177:29-30+ N 26 '77
Many faces of art. J. R. Mellow. il Sat R 5:38-40 N 26 '77
New art books for spring. Am Artist 41:22+ Ap '77
Resource materials. B. Wasserman. See issues of School arts
Review of books. See issues of Art in America

Collections

See Art—Private collections; Art galleries and museums

Collectors and collecting

Decentralized collectors. B. Chamberlain. Am Artist 41:28 Je '77
Panhandle pop; S. Marsh. J. Lelyveld. il por N Y Times Mag p94 My 8 '77
Post-war collecting: the emergence of phase III; the American contemporary art market. A. Kuhn. Art in Am 65:110-11+ S '77
See also
Art as an investment
Costakis, G.

Competitions

Art; painting awards of the Creative Artists Public Service Program. L. Alloway. Nation 225:508-9 N 12 '77
1977 Scholastic Awards. il Sr Schol 109:9-12+ My 19 '77

ART—*Continued*

Conservation and restoration

Conservation queries. R. Mayer. Am Artist 41:43 F '77
Have laser, will travel; cleaning industrial pollutants; work of J. Asmus. C. Panati and D. Gram. por Newsweek 89:87 Mr 28 '77
Maryhill Museum: a case history of cultural abuse. P. Failing. il Art N 76:83-90 Mr '77
See also
Italy—Istituto Centrale del Restauro
Mural painting and decoration—Conservation and restoration
Paintings—Conservation and restoration
Photographs—Conservation and restoration

Copyright

See Copyright—Art

Critics and criticism

See Art critics and criticism

Education

See Art education

Exhibitions

Art. L. Alloway. See occasional issues of Nation
Art. B. Rose. See issues of Vogue
Art for joy's sake; Rubens, Cézanne and Matisse exhibitions. B. Rose. il Vogue 167:170-5 D '77
Art of shooting and the shooting arts; Ducks Unlimited Midwest Wildlife Art Show. B. Tarrant. il Field & S 81:144-8 F '77
Art world (cont) H. Rosenberg. New Yorker 53: 108+ Ap 11; 123-8 My 16; 98-102 Je 20; 83-6 Ag 22; 155-8 O 24; 42-5 D 26 '77
Artist calendar. See issues of Design (US)
Bulletin board. See issues of American artist
Current and coming. S. B. Sherrill. See issues of Antiques
Exhibitions in sight (cont) B. Wasserman. il Sch Arts 76:58-61 F; 48-51 Ap; 77:34-7 D '77
Fine arts. K. Kuh. il Sat R 4:52-4+ Ag 6 '77
Four current exhibitions. J. Canaday. il New Repub 177:22-4 D 10 '77
Goings on about town. See issues of New Yorker
Nation. See issues of Art news
New York reviews. See issues of Art news
Quartet of spectaculars. il Horizon 19:11-29 My '77
Review of exhibitions. See issues of Art in America
Seattle's rolling art galleries. il Sunset 159:46 D '77
Sending the best of America abroad; American involvement in the Venice Biennale. F. Ferretti. il Art N 76: 62-5 Summ '77
Summer travel guide; United States and Canada. il Art N 76:77-8+ Summ '77
Where and when to exhibit (cont) Art N 76:112 Ja; 112 F; 130 Mr; 114 Ap; 140 S; 236 N '77
World. See issues of Art news
See also
Animals in art—Exhibitions
Art, African—Exhibitions
Art, American—Exhibitions
Art, British—Exhibitions
Art, Canadian—Exhibitions
Art, Chinese—Exhibitions
Art, Egyptian—Exhibitions
Art, European—Exhibitions
Art, French—Exhibitions
Art, German—Exhibitions
Art, Japanese—Exhibitions
Art, Russian—Exhibitions
Art, Thracian—Exhibitions
Art galleries and museums
Arts and crafts—Exhibitions
Folk art—Exhibitions
Indians of North America—Art—Exhibitions
Paintings—Exhibitions
Photography—Exhibitions
Pottery—Exhibitions

Expertising

By George, a Stuart! painting found in New Bedford, Mass. por Time 110:24+ N 28 '77
Programmed connoisseurship; theories of M. van Dantzig. G. Schwartz. Art N 76:99-102 My '77

Federal aid

See Art and state

Finance

Squandered funds. B. Chamberlain. Am Artist 41:20+ N '77
Tax support for visual arts. B. Chamberlain. Am Artist 41:14-15 Ap '77

Galleries and museums

See Art galleries and museums

History

Study and teaching

My name is not Kevin. . .it's Michelangelo! M. L. Elliott. il Sch Arts 77:21 N '77

Laws and regulations

Arts bills: pluses and minuses. A. Elsen. il por Art N 76:52-4 O '77
See also
Artists contracts
Artists rights
Copyright—Art

Periodicals

See also
American artist (periodical)
Art news (periodical)
Ceramics monthly (periodical)
Craft horizons (periodical)

Philosophy

Malraux mystery. G. Hartman. New Repub 176: 27-30 Ja 29 '77
Sol LeWitt: the look of thought. D. B. Kuspit; rejoinder. Art in Am 65:5+ Ja '77
See also
Architecture—Philosophy

Prices

Hirshhorn waltz. Vasari. Art N 76:27-8 Ja '77

Private collections

American paintings from the collection of John J. McDonough. E. J. Bullard. il Antiques 112:946-53 N '77
Due West: the Costakis collection comes out. D. Davis. il Art in Am 65:122-3+ N '77
For Russia, with love; donation of bulk of George Costakis collection to the Soviet government. Vasari. il por Art N 76:22+ My '77
Great collection of tiny artistry—how it was made; Arthur Gilbert's micromosaics. M. Zucker. il Smithsonian 8:84-91 My '77
Greening of a collector; Alice Kaplan. il Sat R 4:44+ Jl 9 '77
Momentous happening in Moscow; Costakis collection. il por Time 109:75-6 Ap 11 '77
Recent arrival in the ranks of great collectors; Jackson and Mary Burke collection. M. Murase. il Smithsonian 8:84-91 Je '77
See also
Art in the home
Frick Collection, New York

Psychology

See also
Art therapy

Registration

Art burglars beware. B. Chamberlain. Am Artist 41:36+ O '77

Scholarships and fellowships

NEA grants go to 156 craftsmakers and artists. Craft Horiz 37:37+ Ag '77

Social aspects

See Art and society

State aid

See Art and state

Study and teaching

Children meet artists; field trips to artists' studios by Los Angeles students. E. Levin. il Sch Arts 76:20-2 Je '77
Clipboard. V. G. Timmons. See issues of School arts
Evaluating teaching and learning in art. G. A. Mittler. il Clearing H 50:252-5 F '77
Meet the masters! K. Alexander. il Sch Arts 76:16-17 F '77
Planning for successful teaching. G. F. Horn. il Sch Arts 77:4-5 O '77
Reading improvement through art; success story from the Big Apple. S. K. Corwin; reply. I. Seidenberg. Sch Arts 77:66 S '77
See also
Art—Appreciation
Art—History—Study and teaching
Art education
Art schools
Art teachers
Artists as teachers
Colleges and universities—Departments of art
also Sculpture—Study and teaching and similar headings

Materials

See also
Papier-mâché

Projects

Animation. G. Bregman. il Sch Arts 77:20-1 D '77
Artistic self-discovery through group reflection. R. Sarnoff. il Sch Arts 77:30-3 O '77
Boilers can be beautiful. M. Reay. il Sch Arts 77:10-11 N '77
Bottle fantasy. G. Dostal. il Sch Arts 76:47 F '77
Breaking the frame barrier. R. Boneno. il Design (US) 78:2-4 Spr '77
Directed creativity; art project for deaf and brain damaged children. J. W. Bell. il Sch Arts 76:78-9 F '77
Old wheel takes a new turn; art class carousel. R. Reinke. il Sch Arts 76:6 Mr '77

ART—Study and teaching—Projects—*Continued*
Sign that took three years to build; Stadley Rough School, Danbury, Conn. R. Farrell. il Sch Arts 76:46-7 Ap '77
Three basic methods to approach art, creatively. M. K. Gerstman. il Design (US) 78:14-17 mid-Wint '77
See also
Assemblage (art)
Block printing
Calendars
Collage
Masks (sculpture)
Montage
Mosaics
Mural painting and decoration
Mural painting and decoration, Exterior
Paper sculpture
Paper work
Plaster work (craft)
Prints—Technique
Puppets and puppet plays
Weaving

Taxation

See Taxation of works of art

Technique

See also
Painting—Technique

Themes

See also
Animals in art
Architecture in art
Astronomy in art
Automobiles in art
Birds in art
Brazil in art
Country life in art
Dancing in art
Death in art
Fishing in art
Head in art
Horror in art
Horses in art
Human figure in art
Hunting in art
Indians (American) in art
Insanity in art
Machinery in art
Music in art
Mythology in art
Nature in art
Pottery—Themes
Prints—Themes
Sports in art
United States in art
War in art
Western States in art
Women in art

Therapeutic use

See Art therapy

Valuation

Appraising your treasures. E. V. Warren. il House B 119:10+ Ag '77
Gems among your junk? Sotheby Parke Bernet's Heirloom Discovery Days. B. H. Schneider. McCalls 105:110 O '77
Treasure or trash? Sotheby Parke Bernet's Heirloom Discovery Day. M. Kasindorf. il Newsweek 89:10 Mr 14 '77

Brazil

Early visions of imperial Brazil; illustrations produced by cultural and scientific missions. I. A. Striker. il Américas 29:S1-12 Ja '77

California

Art ramble at UC Santa Cruz. il Sunset 159:22 D '77
Artists put their colorful stamp on Santa Cruz. il map Sunset 159:36-8 Ag '77
California art since the modern dawn. A. Albright. il Art N 76:68-72 Ja '77
California royalty bill: milestone or mistake? pro and con discussion. J. H. Merryman; H. Sandison. pors Am Artist 41:60-1 F '77
California's art resale law: the failure of innocence. A. Elsen. Art in Am 65:15-16 Mr '77
Far West's 20th-century art in East Coast review; Painting and Sculpture in California: the Modern Era, exhibition. J. Tarshis. il Smithsonian 8:56-61 My '77
Five footnotes to modern art history. M. Wortz. il Art N 76:73-5 Ja '77
Legislating royalties for artists. S. Hochfield; reply. B. K. Brill. Art N 76:34 Ap '77
Matters of state and local coordination. B. Chamberlain. Am Artist 41:16-17 F '77
70 years of California modernism in 340 works by 200 artists. P. Plagens. il Art in Am 65:63-9 My '77
Tenacious figure; Works on Paper, 1900-1960, From Southern California Collections. M. Wortz. il Art N 76:106+ D '77

Canada

Banking art in Ottawa; the Art Bank. R. Bongartz. il Art N 76:80-2+ Ap '77
Summer travel guide. il Art N 76:138-40+ Summ '77
See also
Montreal—Art

Colorado

Art on the range; Boulder. J. Heath. il Ms 5:43+ My '77

France

See also
Art and state—France
Paris—Art

Great Britain

See also
London—Art

Indiana

Patient art of grantsmanship; the Driftwood Valley Arts Council, Columbus. M. N. Carter. il Art N 76:34-5 My '77

Israel

See also
Jerusalem—Art

Italy

Art is long, tax suits short; controversy surrounding Italian claims to a Greek statue in the J. Paul Getty Museum. il Time 110:22 D 12 '77

Netherlands

Haarlem. G. Schwartz. il Art N 76:96-7 F '77
See also
Amsterdam, Netherlands—Art

New England

Boston; WPA art projects in New England. J. H. Kay. Art N 76:116-18 D '77

New Mexico

Epilogue: those who followed; Taos artists. M. C. Nelson. il Am Artist 42:68-73+ Ja '78
New Mexico: open land and psychic elbow room. C. Moser. il Art N 76:74-8 D '77
See also
Taos Society of Artists

Russia

Larry Rivers and George Segal: back in the U.S.S.R.; interview, ed by E. C. Baker. L. Rivers; G. Segal. il por Art in Am 65:104-12 N '77
See also
Art and state—Russia
Moscow—Art

Spain

See also
Art and state—Spain

Switzerland

Art; exhibition of European paintings from Swiss collections at the Museum of Modern Art. L. Alloway. Nation 224:91-2 Ja 22 '77

United States

Nation. See issues of Art news
Review of exhibitions. See issues of Art in America
Summer travel guide. il Art N 76:77-8+ Summ '77
See also
Federal Art Project
also subhead Art under names of cities, e.g. Philadelphia—Art

Western States

One percent for art idea; funding for public art. il Sunset 159:272 N '77

ART, Abstract
Art; pattern painting. L. Alloway. Nation 225:698-9 D 24 '77
Charles Biederman's abstract analogues of nature. D. B. Kuspit. bibl il Art in Am 65:80-3 My '77
Color, format and abstract art: an interview with Kenneth Noland; ed by D. Waldman. K. Noland. il por Art in Am 65:99-105 My '77
Corcoran Bienmal: a generational split. B. F. Forgey. il Art N 76:106+ My '77
Kenneth Noland: independence in the face of conformity. S. Polcari. il por Art N 76:153-5 Summ '77
See also
Abstract expressionism

Exhibitions

Art; exhibition, Tenth Steet Days; the Co-ops of the 50s. L. Alloway. Nation 226:30 Ja 7 '78

ART, African
Art that explains the universe; excerpt from The present significance of the creative arts in Africa and their influence outside Africa. P. Ahyi. il UNESCO Courier 30:21 My '77
See also
Scupture, African

Exhibitions

African clay; exhibition of art from Detroit collections. F. J. Cummings. il Ceram Mo 25:28-31 D '77

ART, Amateur
Armenian Grandma Moses. P. J. Thomajan. il por Ret Liv 17:50 My '77
Grass roots art. C. Carlson. il Ms 6:64-8 O '77
Painting as a pastime; excerpt from The art world; ed by B. Diamonstein. W. S. Churchill. Art N 76:162 N '77
Victor Hugo: the painter. C. Barth. il Design (US) 78:6-9 mid-Summ '77
When you wish upon a star . . .; work of A. Battles. M. Battles. il Design (US) 79:2-5 Fall '77
See also
Folk art

ART, American
Arts in Mobile. S. A. Smith. il Antiques 112: 482-91 S '77
Gallery (cont) il Ms 5:33-5 F; 43+ My '77
Post-war collecting: the emergence of phase III; the American contemporary art market. A. Kuhn. Art in Am 65:110-11+ S '77
See also
American Federation of Arts
Art, Black
Artists, American
Indians of North America—Art
Painting, American
Pottery, American
Sculpture, American
Whitney Museum of American Art, New York

Anecdotes, facetiae, satire, etc.

Vemler's Elm Street group. J. Kaplan. il New Yorker 53:29-30 F 28 '77

Exhibitions

American art 1890 to 1910; Whitney Museum of American Art. S. B. Sherrill. il Antiques 112:46+ Jl '77
American drawings: a salute; exhibition of American Master Drawings and Watercolors. K. Kuh. il Sat R 4:43-5 Mr 5 '77
Art; 35th Biennial Exhibition at the Corcoran Gallery of Art and 76th Exhibition by Artists of Chicago and Vicinity at the Chicago Art Institute. L. Alloway. Nation 224:349-50 Mr 19 '77
Art: Turn-of-the-Century America, exhibit at the Whitney. L. Alloway. Nation 225:124-5 Ag 6 '77
Art; Turn-of-the-century America; paintings, graphics, photographs, 1890-1910. il House B 119:24+ N '77
New England schoolgirl art; exhibitions in old Sturbridge Village. S. B. Sherrill. il Antiques 111:430+ Mr '77
1970s at the Whitney; the Whitney Biennial. R. Smith. il Art in Am 65:91-3 My '77
Paris-New York: a continuing romance. G. Henry. il Art N 76:60-2 D '77
Realism, past and present; Eight Contemporary American Realists. A. Jarmusch. il Art N 76: 194-5 N '77
Spanish America in today's New Mexico; Santa Fe's Museum of International Folk Art. il map Sunset 158:94-9 My '77
Versatile Maine artists; exhibitions at the William A. Farnsworth Library and Art Museum in Rockland, Me. S. B. Sherrill. il Antiques 112:36+ Jl '77
Whitney Biennial. B. Forgey. il Art N 76:120-1 Ap '77

ART, Asian
See also
Art, Buddhist

ART, Automatic. See Automatism

ART, Baroque
Extravaganza of baroque; Latin American art and architecture. il UNESCO Courier 30:56-7 Ag '77

ART, Black
Not so black; American artists. R. Berenson. Nat R 29:896-7 Ag 5 '77

Exhibitions

Art; Two Centuries of Black American Art. L. Alloway. Nation 225:94 Jl 23 '77
Being outside; Two Centuries of Black American Art. H. Rosenberg. New Yorker 53:83-6 Ag 22 '77
Two Centuries of Black American Art. L. Robinson. il Ebony 32:33-6+ F '77

ART, British
See also
Pottery, English
Yale University—Center for British Art

Exhibitions

Ritual complaints, tepid memories; Hayward Annual. W. Feaver. il Art N 76:106+ O '77

ART, Buddhist

Photographs

Ken Domon: a documentary pilgrimage. K. Domon. il Mod Phot 41:85-92 Mr '77

ART, Canadian
Canada's restive nationalism. R. Fulford. il Art N 76:76-8 Ap '77
Report from Toronto & Montreal. A. Goldin. il Art in Am 65:35-45+ Mr '77

Exhibitions

Canada—a new national vision; Group of Seven at the Phillips Collection and 14 Canadians: a Critic's Choice at the Hirshhorn Museum, Washington, D.C. B. Forgey. il Art N 76:70-2+ Ap '77

ART, Celtic
Celts. M. Severy. il Nat Geog 151:582-630, supp(folded map) My '77

ART, Chinese
See also
Painting, Chinese
Pottery, Chinese

Exhibitions

Pleasant art of peasant art. M. Loke. il N Y Times Mag p46-9 D 11 '77
Proletarian ideologies and visionary alternatives; Peasant Paintings from Huhsien County at the Louisiana Museum of Modern Art, Humlebaek, Denmark. J. Gruen. il Art N 76:105-6 O '77

ART, Christian. See Christian art and symbolism

ART, Classical

Exhibitions

Between Olympus and Golgotha; Age of Spirituality exhibit at the Metropolitan Museum. R. Hughes. il Time 111:70-1 Ja 2 '78
Contest for men's souls; Age of Spirituality exhibition. L. Casson. il Horizon 21:78-84 Ja '78

ART, Commercial
See also
Illustration
Push Pin Studios, Inc

ART, Decorative. See Decoration and ornament

ART, Dutch
Dutch Republic in John Adams' day; exhibition. S. B. Sherrill. il Antiques 111:26 Ja '77

ART, Egyptian
Treasures of King Tut; discovery of tomb by H. Carter. S. Flythe, Jr. il Sat Eve Post 249:68-71+ My '77

Exhibitions

Art; Treasures of Tutankhamun. E. V. Warren. il House B 119:34 Ap '77
Craft of King Tut's jewels. J. A. Black. il Craft Horiz 37:20-3 F '77
Dazzling legacy of an ancient quest; King Tut's gold. A. J. Hall. il Nat Geog 151:292-311 Mr '77
King Tut rises again. il Horizon 19:12-15 My '77
Nefertiti graffiti; visitors' comments at the Brooklyn Museum's 1973 Akhenaten and Nefertiti exhibition. Vasari. Art N 76:21+ Summ '77
Treasures of a teenage god-king. il Sr Schol 109: 8-10 Ap 7 '77
Tut lives. C.-G. McDaniel. Progressive 41:35-6 Jl '77
Tut-o-mania. S. C. Cowley and others. il Newsweek 89:94-5 My 9 '77
Tutankhamun adventure. J. Warren. Chr Cent 94:409-10 Ap 27 '77
View from the castle; contemplating Tut's treasures. S. D. Ripley. Smithsonian 7:6 F '77
Waiting to see King Tut. T. Benfey. Chemistry 50:2 Je '77
Wonderful things; Treasures of Tutankhamun. S. Hochfield. il Art N 76:54-7 Ja '77
Young King Tut. L. Prothro. il Nat R 29:211 F 18 '77

ART, English. See Art, British

ART, Ethiopian
See also
Painting, Ethiopian

ART, European

Exhibitions

Common Market politics at Rosc '77. K. Moffett. il Art N 76:215-16+ N '77
Life wasn't a cabaret; Trends of the Twenties exhibition. S. Spender. il N Y Times Mag p20-1+ O 30 '77
Trends of the Twenties; Council of Europe's exhibition. W. S. Lieberman. il Art N 76:39-44 O '77
Trends of the Twenties; exhibition in Berlin. R. Hughes. il Time 110:104-5 O 10 '77
23 European artists; show called Europe in the seventies. il Horizon 20:80 O '77

ART, Fantastic
Fantastic voyages. M. Rourke. il Newsweek 90: 49-50 Jl 11 '77
Incredible paintings of Frank Frazetta. D. Newlove. il por Esquire 87:86-94+ Je '77
Lovely monsters of Brian Froud. il Esquire 88: 179-83 D '77

ART, Flemish
See also
Painting, Flemish

ART, French
See also
Pottery, French
Exhibitions
Paris-New York: a continuing romance. G. Henry. il Art N 76:60-2 D '77

ART, German
See also
Pottery, German
Exhibitions
Art; exhibition, Realistic Tendencies, at the New School art center. L. Alloway. Nation 224:476 Ap 16 '77
Whose Berlin? Berlin Now exhibition sponsored by Goethe House in New York. R. Berenson. Nat R 29:565-6 My 13 '77

ART, Gothic
See also
Sculpture, Gothic

ART, Graphic. See Graphic arts

ART, Greek
See also
Sculpture, Greek
Vases, Greek

ART, Indian (American) See Indians of North America—Art

ART, Indian (East Indian)
Redeeming Indian culture; Asian Christian art. W. A. Dyrness. il Chr Today 21:26-7 Mr 18 '77
See also
Painting, Indian (East Indian)

ART, Irish
See also
Art, Celtic
Exhibitions
Early Irish art. J. Brzostoski. il Craft Horiz 37:50-3 D '77
Early Irish art. S. B. Sherrill. il Antiques 112:658+ O '77
Gold from the Dark Ages. R. Hughes. il Time 110:52-3 N 14 '77
Ireland's golden age; Metropolitan Museum of Art exhibit. M. Stevens. il Newsweek 90:91-2 N 7 '77
Out of the bogs; Metropolitan Museum show. New Yorker 53:32 O 31 '77
Wonders of Irish art; exhibit at the Metropolitan. C. R. Baldwin. il N Y Times Mag p34-7+ O 9 '77

ART, Islamic
Islam goes to England; World of Islam Festival in London. A. Goldin. bibl il Art in Am 65:106-13 Ja '77

ART, Japanese
See also
Art, Buddhist
Painting, Japanese
Pottery, Japanese
Exhibitions
Recent arrival in the ranks of great collectors; Jackson and Mary Burke collection. M. Murase. il Smithsonian 8:84-91 Je '77

ART, Jewish. See Jewish art and symbolism

ART, Kinetic. See Kinetic art

ART, Latin American
Art. See issues of Américas
Art and politics: from protest to myth. J. Canaday. il New Repub 178:25-7 Ja 7 '78
Extravaganza of baroque. il UNESCO Courier 30:56-7 Ag '77
Museum of Modern Art of Latin America. A. J. Lowe. il Américas 29:S1-S12 Mr '77
Out of the tropics, an avant-garde art. A. Uslar-Pietri. il UNESCO Courier 30:30-8+ Ag '77
Exhibitions
Roots and visions; traveling exhibition of Hispanic art. V. G. Stoddart. il Américas 29:13-16 O '77

ART, Mexican
Fiesta of death. il UNESCO Courier 30:28-9 Ag '77
See also
Painting, Mexican
Pottery, Mexican

ART, Modern
Brickbats and favorites; Art news poll of most overrated and underrated artists of the 20th century. il Horizon 21:34 Ja '78
Far-from-last judgments; or, Who's overrated now? And underrated; views of art historians, museum directors, curators and critics; ed by J. Gruen. il Art N 76:106-20 N '77
Out in front; N. Graves and D. Rockburne. B. Rose. pors Vogue 167:152-3+ Je '77
Pop! goes the sickle; works of Warhol, Segal and Dine. R. Berenson. Nat R 29:342 Mr 18 '77
Pop's master of cheesecake; M. Ramos. T. Albright. Art N 76:208+ N '77
Post-war collecting: the emergence of phase III; the American contemporary art market. A. Kuhn. Art in Am 65:110-11+ S '77
Present tense: new art and the New York museum. A. Goldin and R. Smith. Art in Am 65:92-104 S '77
Robert Irwin: everything I've done in the last five years doesn't exist; interview, ed by T. Albright. R. Irwin. il Art N 76:49-54 Summ '77
20th-century artists most admired by other artists; views of nearly 100 artists; ed by G. Glueck. il Art N 76:78-103 N '77
What is pop art? interview, ed by G. R. Swenson; excerpt from The art world; ed by B. Diamonstein. J. Johns. il Art N 76:170+ N '77
See also
Abstract expressionism
Art déco
Dadaism
Environment (art)
Museum of Modern Art, New York
Surrealism
Exhibitions
Ambroise Vollard—impresario. G. Needham. il por Art N 76:78-80+ S '77
Art; 35th Biennial Exhibition at the Corcoran Gallery of Art and 76th Exhibition by Artists of Chicago and Vicinity at the Chicago Art Institute. L. Alloway. Nation 224:349-50 Mr 19 '77
Bomb from the blue; the International Exhibition of Modern Art (Armory Show of 1913) excerpt from The art world; ed by B. Diamonstein. J. B. Townsend. il Art N 76:142-3 N '77
Botch of an epic theme; Paris—New York show at the Pompidou Center. R. Hughes. il Time 110:74-5 Jl 11 '77
Documenta 6: the medium was the message. J. A. Thwaites. il Art N 76:46-9 S '77
Earthbound and sublime; exhibition, Modern Portraits: the Self and Others. K. Evett. New Repub 176:30-1 Mr 5 '77
Genius disguised as a sloth; survey of A. Vollard's work as impresario on view at Museum of Modern Art. R. Hughes. il por Time 109:68-9 Je 20 '77
Holy foolishness; Documenta art festival, Kassel, Germany. M. Stevens. il Newsweek 90:82-3 Ag 8 '77
Out of nowhere, he became the top art dealer in Paris; A. Vollard exhibition at the Museum of Modern Art. J. Russell. bibl (p 101) il por Smithsonian 8:68-75 Jl '77
Paris' contemporary art fair; the FIAC, International Fair of Contemporary Art in Paris. M. Gibson. il Art N 76:92 S '77
Paris: tale of two cities; Paris-New York exhibit at the Beaubourg. J. Gruen. il Art N 76:109-11 S '77
Put your money where the talent is; A. Vollard. B. Rose. il pors Vogue 167:146-7+ Ag '77
Report from Kassel Documenta VI. E. C. Baker. Art in Am 65:44-5 S '77
Rooms with a point of view; alternative spaces. K. Larson. il Art N 76:32-8 O '77
70 years of California modernism in 340 works by 200 artists. P. Plagens. il Art in Am 65:63-9 My '77
Six art institutes: on the long lonesome road of the avant-garde. K. Larson. il Art N 76:50-4 D '77
Tale of two cities; Paris-New York exhibit at the Beaubourg. E. Peer. il Newsweek 89:64-5 Je 13 '77
Vollard: dealer for the demigods; exhibition at the Museum of Modern Art. H. Kramer. il pors N Y Times Mag p28-30+ Je 5 '77

ART, Municipal
Houston's new cultural decision makers. C. Moser. il Art N 76:74-6 F '77

ART, Mythology in. See Mythology in art

ART, Oriental
See also
Art, Chinese
Art, Japanese
Pottery, Oriental

ART, Peruvian
Exhibitions
Great golden art of the ancient Peruvian artisans; at New York's Museum of Natural History. T. Belcher and E. Belcher. il Smithsonian 8:84-91 bibl(p 135) D '77

ART, Pre-Columbian
See also
Art, Peruvian

ART, Primitive
See also
Cave drawings and paintings

ART, Religious. See Christian art and symbolism; Jewish art and symbolism

ART, Romantic. See Romanticism in art

ART, Russian
Due West: the Costakis collection comes out. D. Davis. il Art in Am 65:122-3+ N '77
Imperial Russia's glittering legacy. il Nat Geog 153:24-33 Ja '78
See also
Painting, Russian

ART, Russian—*Continued*

Exhibitions

Art on the line: New York Moscow New York Moscow. M. A. Tighe. il New Repub 176:24-6 Ap 16 '77

Paris; Sixty Years of Soviet Art. il Art N 76:104 O '77

Soviet unofficial art in the U.S. A. Hilton and N. Dodge. bibl il Art in Am 65:113-19 N '77

ART, Scythian

Scythians: nomad goldsmiths of the open steppes: symposium. il UNESCO Courier 29:4-49 D '76

ART, Spanish

On the Spanish easel. M. L. Lieberthal. il Sat R 5:24-5 O 29 '77

ART, Spanish American. See Art, Latin American

ART, Thracian

Exhibitions

Rich and rugged Thracian life seen in a glittering show; Thracian Treasures from Bulgaria. T. Prideaux. il Smithsonian 8:42-51 Je '77

Thracians; exhibit at the Metropolitan Museum. New Yorker 53:21-2 Jl 11 '77

Treasures of Thrace. J. Brozostoski. il Craft Horiz 37:32+ O '77

ART and architecture

See also

Decoration and ornament, Architectural

ART and children

Encouraging children's interest in art. H. Hoffa. il Intellect 105:304 Mr '77

ART and industry

Crafts in industry: five jewelers join skills with Reed & Barton; ed by A. Gold. A. Fisch. il por Craft Horiz 37:10-15 Ag '77

Scramble for museum sponsors: is curatorial independence for sale? L. Rosenbaum. il Art in Am 65:10-14 Ja '77

See also

Art patronage

Business in the Arts Awards

ART and literature

Dante Gabriel Rossetti and the double work of art. M. Amaya. il Art in Am 65:90-3 Mr '77

Hemingway the painter. A. Kazin. por New Repub 176:21-8 Mr 19 '77

Object as Poet; exhibition at the Renwick Gallery of the National Collection of Fine Arts, Smithsonian Institution. R. Slivka. il Craft Horiz 37:26-39+ F '77

Picture of success; characters in American fiction. N. Mills. Yale R 66:347-63 Mr '77

ART and music

See also

Music in art

ART and photography

Lumigraphic print process; combination of drawing and photographic printing processes. M. Sapiro. bibl il Sch Arts 77:28-35 S '77

Painting and photography: the two-way street; influence on Degas. B. Rose. il Vogue 167:236-7+ My '77

See also

Photography, Artistic

Photography of works of art

ART and poetry. See Art and literature

ART and politics

Art and freedom. R. Squirru. il Américas 29:2-5 F '77

Art and politics: from protest to myth. J. Canaday. il New Repub 178:25-7 Ja 7 '78

Art & politics '77. N. Marmer. il Art in Am 65:64-6 Jl '77

Common Market politics at Rosc '77. K. Moffett. il Art N 76:215-16+ N '77

Skirmish over Guernica; Museum of Modern Art's refusal to return painting. P. Nobile. il Harpers 254:15+ Mr '77

ART and psychoanalysis. See Psychoanalysis and art

ART and society

American artist from loner to lobbyist; Open to New Ideas: a Collection of New Art for Jimmy Carter. C. Ratcliff. il Art in Am 65:10-12 Mr '77

Art and freedom. R. Squirru. il Américas 29:2-5 F '77

Leonardo and the stain. E. Genauer. por Newsweek 90:27 D 12 '77

Manhattan seven. H. Herrera. bibl il Art in Am 65:50-63 Jl '77

Murray Stern: social surrealist. A. Sanders. il por Am Artist 41:76-83+ F '77

ART and state

Government's subtle censorship. B. Chamberlain. Am Artist 41:26-7+ S '77

In what ways can the government assist American artists? J. Mondale. il por Am Artist 41:12 S '77

More on government support of the arts; pro and con discussion. P. Svenson. S. L. Sheppard. pors Am Artist 41:16-17 N '77

One percent for art idea; funding for public art by Western States. il Sunset 159:272 N '77

Other voices, other rooms: the rise of the alternative space. P. Patton. il Art in Am 65:80-9 Jl '77

Squandered funds. B. Chamberlain. Am Artist 41:20+ N '77

State arts budgets for '77. il Craft Horiz 37:37 O '77

See also

Art and society

Federal Art Project

United States—National Foundation on the Arts and the Humanities

France

Moral message from La Grande France; boycott of Pompidou Center in protest to release of Abu Daoud. Art N 76:31 Mr '77

Russia

Ars brevis for a Soviet painter; cancellation of I. Glazunov's exhibition in Moscow. il Time 110:35+ Jl 11 '77

Capitalist decadent? ed by A. Newman. G. Segal. Art N 76:36 F '77

Defiant Russian painter; I. Glazunov. F. Willey and F. Coleman. il Newsweek 89:44 Je 6 '77

Dissidence as a way of art; Russian artists V. Komar and A. Melamid. G. Glueck. il pors N Y Times Mag p33-5 My 8 '77

For Russia, with love; donation of bulk of George Costakis collection to the Soviet government. Vasari. il por Art N 76:22+ My '77

Politics of Soviet art. E. Kornetchuk. bibl il Bull Atom Sci 33:32-7 O '77

Reliable Soviet citizen; cancellation of I. Glazunov's exhibition in Moscow. J. E. Bowlt. Art N 76:109-11 O '77

Soviet painter poses a question; I. Glazunov. S. F. Starr. il por Smithsonian 8:101-4+ bibl(p 135) D '77

Soviet unofficial art in the U.S. A. Hilton and N. Dodge. bibl il Art in Am 65:113-19 N '77

Spain

Guernica will hang in the Prado as Picasso wished. G. Marzorati. il por Art N 76:65-7 My '77

Spanish acquisition? Guernica. E. Keerdoja. il Newsweek 90:16 O 31 '77

ART and war

See also

Spain—History—Civil War, 1936-1939—Art and the war

ART appreciation. See Art—Appreciation

ART as a profession

Art on the wild side; interview, ed by M. Berges. B. A. Bengston. il por Design (US) 78:6-9 Spr '77

Career potentials. B. Chamberlain. Am Artist 41:28+ Ag '77

Careers in art. P. Savino. il Sch Arts 76:4-5 F; 8-9 Mr; 10-11 Ap '77

Problems, prospects of production craft; adaptation of address, September 1976. A. Fisch. Craft Horiz 37:10+ F '77

Should the art school curriculum include professional job training? pro and con discussion. J. Brodsky; N. Harrison. il Am Artist 41:16-17 O '77

Sources of job information. B. Chamberlain. Am Artist 41:14+ Jl '77

ART as an investment

Exotica: the appeal of tangible objects. il Bus W p 146-8 D 26 '77

ART as recreation. See Recreation—Activities

ART associations. See Art clubs and societies

ART auctions. See Art sales

ART Bank, Canada. See Art—Canada

ART books. See Art literature

ART Center College of Design, Los Angeles. See Art schools

ART centers

Hoosuck: a community story; Windsor Mill art center in remodeled textile mill. M. Flad and H. Flad. il Craft Horiz 37:20-1+ Ap '77

Singapore Handicraft Centre. A. Hullett. il Trav/Holiday 148:32-5 N '77

ART clubs and societies

American Art-Union; exhibition. S. B. Sherrill. il Antiques 112:844+ N '77

Exhibition/sale—how does it happen? annual event of the potters' association Clay. J. Lincoln. il Ceram Mo 25:44-6 D '77

Group improvement. B. Chamberlain. Am Artist 41:16 D '77

Matters of state and local coordination. B. Chamberlain. Am Artist 41:16-17 F '77

See also

American Ceramic Society

American Federation of Arts

Taos Society of Artists

ART collecting. See Art—Collectors and collecting

ART collectors. See Art—Collectors and collecting

ART colonies. See Artists and authors colonies

ART competitions. See Art—Competitions

ART critics and criticism
Art criticism of Pushkin, Gogol, Dostoevsky and Tolstoy. J. E. Bowlt. il Art N 76:86-8+ My '77
Artist count: in praise of plenty. L. Alloway. bibl il Art in Am 65:105-9 S '77
Need for ceramics criticism; adaptation of address, July 1977. G. Clark. Ceram Mo 25:17+ O '77
See also
Photography—Criticism, interpretation, etc.

ART dealers
See also
Castelli, L.
Christie's (firm)
Lakeside Studio (firm)
Marlborough Gallery, Inc.
Sotheby Parke Bernet Group, Ltd
Vollard, A.

ART dealers-artists contracts. See Artists contracts

ART déco
Bringing home Art deco; Richard Gillette apartment, New York City. N. Skurka. il N Y Times Mag p74-5 Ap 3 '77
Those were the days, my friend; art déco architecture and design. H. Sutton. il Sat R 5:66-7 D 10 '77

ART déco jewelry. See Jewelry

ART education
Art education and career education. F. Bedogne. bibl il Sch Arts 77:42-5 D '77
Art education, art therapy, art. H. McConeghey. bibl il Sch Arts 77:52-5 S '77
Art educators' odyssey, USSR. A. Hurwitz. il Sch Arts 76:56-8+ Ap '77
Art program and the metric system. T. A. Hatfield. il Sch Arts 76:60-1 Mr '77
Centering as a process for children's imaging. R. B. Kent. bibl il Sch Arts 77:18-30 N '77
Measurement of affective art objectives. J. M. Cook. il Sch Arts 77:14-17 O '77
Research or plagiarize? B. Chamberlain. Am Artist 41:18-19 Mr '77
See also
Art—Study and teaching
Art schools
Colleges and universities—Department of art

Television programs

See Television programs—Educational programs

ART exhibitions. See Art—Exhibitions

ART fairs. See Arts and crafts—Exhibitions

ART films. See Motion pictures—Art films

ART Foods (restaurant) See New York (city)—Hotels, restaurants, etc.

ART forgeries. See Forgery of works of art

ART galleries and museums
How to keep your students from yawning at art museums. J. C. Vitale. Design (US) 79:10-11 Fall '77
Rooms with a point of view; alternative spaces. K. Larson. il Art N 76:32-8 O '77
Six art institutes: on the long lonesome road of the avant-garde. K. Larson. il Art N 76:50-4+ D '77
Summer travel guide; United States and Canada. il Art N 76:77-8+ Summ '77
See also
Museum stores
Museums and schools
also subhead Galleries and museums under names of cities; e.g. Jacksonville, Fla.—Galleries and museums; *also* names of galleries and museums, e.g. National Gallery of Art, Washington, D.C.

Acquisitions

Museum accessions. E. H. Gustafson. See issues of Antiques

Architecture

See Museums—Architecture

Contracts with artists

See Artists contracts

Directors

See Museum directors

Finance

Portland's starving grande dame; financial crisis at the Portland Art Museum. P. Failing. il Art N 76:85-8 O '77
Scramble for museum sponsors: is curatorial independence for sale? L. Rosenbaum. il Art in Am 65:10-14 Ja '77
Slapping wrists; question of Pennsylvania Academy of the Fine Arts' admission fee policy and use of Pennsylvania Bicentennial Commission grant. A. Jarmusch. Art N 76:170+ Summ '77

Management

Who should manage museums? with views of museum administrators. P. M. Kadis. il por Art N 76:46-51 O '77
See also
Art galleries and museums—Trustees, boards, committees, etc.

Remodeled buildings

See Buildings, Remodeled

Trustees, boards, committees, etc.

Are museum trustees and the law out of step? excerpt from The art world; ed by B. Diamonstein. J. H. Merryman. Art N 76:174 N '77
Growing number of women trustees. T. Trucco. il Art N 76:54-5 F '77

Work with children

Art museum and the school. B. Y. Newsom. il Am Educ 13:12-16 D '77

Work with the blind

Touch; Metropolitan Museum's exhibition. New Yorker 53:22 S 5 '77

Australia

Pollock and politics. A. Levy. Art N 76:96+ My '77

California

From bad to worse in California; proposed bill exempting state museums from taxation of purchased or donated works of art. A. Elsen. por Art N 76:53 O '77

Denmark

Proletarian ideologies and visionary alternatives; the Louisiana Museum of Modern Art, Humlebaek, Denmark. J. Gruen. il Art N 76:105-6 O '77

Great Britain

Fallacies of hope; question of establishing a special gallery for display of J. M. W. Turner's art. Vasari. Art N 76:23+ Summ '77

New York (state)

David Smith's art is best revealed in natural settings; Storm King Art Center. J. Russell. il por Smithsonian 7:68-75 bibl(p 126-7) Mr '77
Far Eastern art in New York collections. il Ceram Mo 25:19-25 S '77

Texas

Texas' small museums discovering each other. J. Kutner. il Art N 76:77-80+ F '77

Washington (state)

Maryhill investigation. P. Failing. Art N 76:128-30+ S '77
Maryhill Museum: a case history of cultural abuse. P. Failing. il Art N 76:83-90 Mr '77

Western States

Western history today. Am West 14:54 Ja; 54 Mr; 56+ My; 48+ Jl; 54 S '77

ART history. See Art—History

ART in motion. See Kinetic art

ART in public buildings
Art will be considered just as important as the bricks; J. Solomon and GSA's Art-in-Architecture program. J. A. Lewis. il por Art N 76:56-8 D '77
Jack Beal's history of American labor; murals in the new Labor Department building. B. Forgey. il Art N 76:38 Ap '77
Labor Department mural: a complicated voyage; J. Beal's murals. B. Carter. il por Art N 76:40-1 My '77
Modern Medici for public art. J. A. Lewis. il Art N 76:36-7+ Ap '77
One percent for art idea; funding for public art by Western States. il Sunset 159:272 N '77
Shahn's Bronx P.O. murals: the perils of public art. C. Baldwin. il Art in Am 65:15-16+ My '77
Taking care of the government's public art. T. Crawford. Art in Am 65:19+ My '77

ART in the home
Farmhouse for art; home of P. Culot near Brussels. N. Skurka. il por N Y Times Mag p42-3 Ag 14 '77
Good art you can afford; fine prints or original prints. Changing T 31:37-9 O '77
House that Joan Mondale decorated. S. B. Conroy. il por Art N 76:56-7+ Summ '77
Setting the stage; Manhattan co-op apartment of M. McFadden. N. Skurka. il N Y Times Mag p68-9+ Mr 6 '77

ART in the school
Children's museum and art carnival. H. C. Rose. il Sch Arts 76:62-3 F '77

ART Institute of Chicago. See Chicago Art Institute

ART literature
Artist's book goes public. L. R. Lippard. il Art in Am 65:40-1 Ja '77
Pleasure principle: where is it in kids' art books? S. M. Wilton. il SLJ 23:44-5 F '77
See also
Art—Bibliography
Arts and crafts—Bibliography

Collectors and collecting

Art reference books can be collectors' items, too. W. Rodger. Hobbies 82:152-3 Ja '78

ART loans
Russian paintings at the Met: an inside look at museum diplomacy. J. E. Bowlt. il Art in Am 65:74-9 My; 120-1 N '77
ART market. See Art sales; Art trade
ART materials. See Artists materials
ART metal work
American metalwork. il Sch Arts 76:39-46 F '77
Chicago metalsmiths, 1840-1970; exhibition at Chicago Historical Society. il Hobbies 82:153+ Ag '77
Copper, Brass, and Bronze; exhibition. A. Wingate. il Craft Horiz 37:16-19 Ag '77
Metalsmith. B. Cortright. il Craft Horiz 37:32 9 Ap '77
See also
Cloisonné
Goldsmithing
Ironwork
Jewelry
Metal etching
Metal sculpture
ART museum directors. See Museum directors
ART museums. See Art galleries and museums
ART news
Art on TV: an unhappy marriage. B. Matusow. Art N 76:26+ F '77
Artworld; comp by L. Rosenbaum. See issues of Art in America
ART news (periodical)
Art world: a seventy-five year treasury of ARTnews; excerpts; ed by B. Diamonstein. il Art N 76:141-4+ N '77
First 75 years. M. Esterow. Art N 76:77 N '77
ART nouveau
Gallé: transcendence in glass and wood. H. Littleton. il Craft Horiz 37:32-6+ Ag '77
ART objects
See also
Art in the home
Ivory carving
Miniature objects

Conservation and restoration

See Art—Conservation and restoration

Copyright

See Copyright—Art
ART objects, Chinese
Rediscovering Chinese export in America; Museum of the American China Trade (Forbes House) Milton, Mass. C. Seebohm. il House & Gard 149:48+ My '77
Riches from the China trade; Museum of the American China Trade (Forbes House) Milton, Mass. il House & Gard 149:160-3 My '77
ART objects, Reproductions of. See Reproductions of works of art
ART objects as an investment. See Art as an investment
ART organizations. See Art clubs and societies
ART patronage
Big business: photography's newest patron; sponsorship of exhibitions. M. R. Weiss. il Sat R 4:44-5+ Jl 23 '77
Can the show go on? role of business R. Brustein. il N Y Times Mag p8-9+ Jl 10 '77; Discussion. p50-1 Ag 7 '77
Glenys Barton at Wedgwood. J. Mallet. il Ceram Mo 25:28-30 O '77
Right to raze; question of Renault's right to destroy commissioned work by J. Dubuffet. Vasari. il por Art N 76:19 S '77
Sculpture cut to your taste; commissioning art work for a garden ornament. A. Ogden. House B 119:10+ Ap '77
Spring forecast: business support. B. Chamberlain. Am Artist 41:15+ My '77
What makes Exxon give? R. Gelatt. il Sat R 4:34 Je 25 '77
ART prices. See Art—Prices
ART Project, Federal. See Federal Art Project
ART publishing. See Publishers and publishing—Art
ART rooms, School. See Classrooms
ART sales
Art market. il Art N 76:124 My; 113-14 O '77
Arts bills: pluses and minuses; question of federal resale royalty bill. A. Elsen. il por Art N 76:52-4 O '77
Auction crowd. S. Birmingham. il N Y Times Mag p38-40+ Mr 6 '77
Auctions. L. Rosenbaum. Art in Am 65:33+ S '77
California royalty bill: milestone or mistake? pro and con discussion. J. H. Merryman; H. Sandison. pors Am Artist 41:60-1 F '77
California's art resale law: the failure of innocence. A. Elsen. Art in Am 65:15-16 Mr '77
Exhibition/sale—how does it happen? annual event of the potters' association Clay. J. Lincoln. il Ceram Mo 25:44-6 D '77
Greening of the black-and-white:
At the auctions. M. R. Weiss. il Sat R 4:32-4+ Ap 2 '77
How to buy—and how not to buy—prints. J. Goldman. Vogue 167:58 N '77

Anecdotes, facetiae, satire, etc.

Buying Van Goghs for a song; excerpt from The art world; ed by B. Diamonstein. Art N 76:172 N '77
ART schools
Crafty vacations. E. O'Bryan. Am Home 80:42+ Ap '77
Joseph Henninger; the artist as teacher; career at Art Center College of Design, Los Angeles. D. C. Hines. il por Am Artist 41:52-7+ My '77
1977 American artist directory of art schools and workshops; ed by S. Ward and others. Am Artist 41:D1-40 Mr '77
Potter of Penland. N. Schulman. il Craft Horiz 37:23-7 Je '77
Visionary doing inspires Arcosanti; second session of Haystack at Arcosanti. J. Springwater. Craft Horiz 37:9 F '77
See also
Colleges and universities—Department of art
Idyllwild School of Music and the Arts
ART shows. See Art—Exhibitions
ART societies. See Art clubs and societies
ART studios. See Artists studios
ART teachers
Profiles; R. B. Hale. P. Hamburger. il New Yorker 53:41-2+ Je 13 '77
ART thefts
Agent OO-art; FBI art crime agent; interview, ed by Vasari. D. Mason. por Art N 76:20+ Ja '77
Art burglars beware. B. Chamberlain. Am Artist 41:36+ O '77
Burglary was for the birds; theft of Audubon folios. R. Cantwell. il Sports Illus 47:20-3+ Jl 11 '77
Call to halt illicit traffic in works of art. UN Chron 14:69+ Ja '77
Purloined pedigree. Vasari. Art N 76:24-5 S '77
Would you like to buy 118 stolen Picassos? Vasari. Art N 76:22+ Ja '77
See also
Library thefts
ART therapy
Art education, art therapy, art. H. McConeghey. bibl il Sch Arts 77:52-5 S '77
ART trade
Art market: what is its future? pro and con discussion. J. Solomon; A. Rosenberg. pors Am Artist 41:12-13 Ap '77
Business of crafts; opening a craft store; ed by J. Coyne. J. Farrell. Ceram Mo 25:19+ My '77
Call to halt illicit traffic in works of art. UN Chron 14:69+ Ja '77
Economics; marketing crafts. E. P. McGuire. Craft Horiz 37:17 F; 9 Ag '77
Economics; order handling techniques for craftspeople. E. P. McGuire. Craft Horiz 37:13 Ap '77
Giving birth to a business; arts and crafts shop. R. A. Petit. il por Redbook 148:57+ F '77
Old bakery used as marketplace for Texas seniors. il Aging 275:29-31 S '77
Post-war collecting: the emergence of phase III; the American contemporary art market. A. Kuhn. Art in Am 65:110-11+ S '77
Purloined pedigree; trade in stolen art. Vasari. Art N 76:24-5 S '77
Special section: reproducibles; symposium. Art in Am 65:31-43 Ja '77
Winter Market; a crafts fair and trade show at Civic Center Baltimore. J. W. Rousuck. il Craft Horiz 37:44-5+ Ap '77
See also
Art galleries and museums
Art sales
Pottery—Marketing
ARTERIES
Coronary tone modulation: formation and actions of prostaglandins, endoperoxides, and thromboxanes. P. Needleman and others. bibl il Science 195:409-12 Ja 28 '77
Rapid brain cooling in exercising dogs; function of the carotid rete. M. A. Baker and L. W. Chapman. bibl il Science 195:781-3 F 25 '77
See also
Pulse

Radiography

See Angiography

Surgery

See Blood vessels—Surgery
ARTERIOSCLEROSIS
Arteriosclerosis: is stress-induced immune suppression a risk factor? E. C. Lattime and H. R. Strausser. bibl il Science 198:302-3 O 21 '77
Case of the smoking baboons. il Sci Digest 82:14-15 Ag '77
Endothelial damage and thrombocyte adhesion in pigeon atherosclerosis. J. C. Lewis and B. A. Kottke. bibl il Science 196:1007-9 My 27 '77

ARTERIOSCLEROSIS—*Continued*
Fat-containing uterine smooth muscle cells in toxemia: possible relevance to atherosclerosis? M. D. Haust and others. bibl il Science 195: 1353-4 Mr 25 '77
Origin of atherosclerosis. E. P. Benditt. il Sci Am 236:74-6+ bibl(p 138) F '77

Diagnosis

See also
Angiography

ARTHRITIS
Arthritis update. R. Winter. Ladies Home J 94:76+ Mr '77
Collagense production by rheumatoid synovial cells: stimulation by a human lymphocyte factor. J.-M. Dayer and others. bibl il Science 195:181-3 Ja 14 '77
Diagnosing Lyme's malady. il Time 109:56 Je 13 '77
Erythema chronicum migrans and Lyme arthritis: cryoimmunoglobulins and clinical activity of skin and joints. A. C. Steere and others. bibl il Science 196:1121-2 Je 3 '77
Genetic markers may point to cause of RA. Sci N 112:215 O 1 '77
Mrs Murray's mystery disease; Lyme arthritis discovered. E. Keiffer. il por Good H 184:80+ Mr '77
3 new studies link arthritis with viruses. il Ret Liv 17:16 Mr '77
See also
Spondylitis

Surgery

Surgical replacement of the human knee joint; spherocentric prosthesis. D. A. Sonstegard and others. il Sci Am 238:44-51 bibl(p 138) Ja '78

ARTHROPODS, Fossil
Arthropod invasion of land during late Silurian and Devonian times. L. Størmer. bibl il Science 197:1362-4 S 30 '77

ARTHUR, Jay
Learning to make records at Eastman. il por Hi Fi 27:MA18-20 Je '77

ARTHUR Rubinstein International Piano Master Competition. See Music—Competitions

ARTICHOKE thistles. See Cardoons

ARTICLES for periodicals. See Periodical articles

ARTIFACTS, Indian (American) See Indians of North America—Antiquities

ARTIFICIAL body parts. See Prosthesis

ARTIFICIAL flowers. See Flowers, Artificial

ARTIFICIAL insemination
A.I. without heat detection; cow breeding. C. S. Machan. il Farm J 101:Dairy 1-2 S '77
New ways to get heifers bred earlier. W. Kester il Farm J 100:LK3 D '76
Prostaglandins can make AI work better. il Suc Farm 75:no4 D2-3 Mr '77
See also
Ova—Transplantation

ARTIFICIAL insemination, Human
Kim Casali's miracle baby. D. deH. Cayzer. il pors Good H 185:90+ N '77

ARTIFICIAL intelligence
See also
Computers

ARTIFICIAL islands
Sand island—heavy-duty structure for the seas. V. E. Smay. il Pop Sci 211:74 Jl '77

ARTIFICIAL joints. See Joints, Artificial

ARTIFICIAL light gardening
Plants around the house: gardening by lights. R. Langer. il House & Gard 150:32+ Ja '78

ARTIFICIAL pacemaker (heart) See Pacemaker, Artificial (heart)

ARTIFICIAL pancreas. See Pancreas, Artificial

ARTIFICIAL respiration. See Respiration, Artificial

ARTIFICIAL satellites
Economical multi-mission spacecraft for the shuttle era. J. S. Marino. il Space World N-3-159:20-3 Mr '77
From golf balls to box cars, NORAD keeps track of what's awhirl above. il Sci Digest 82:79-80 Ag '77
Looking in on us. D. Jordan. il Environment 19:6-11 Ag '77; Same with title Surveilling the earth. Current 198:34-41 D '77
Satellite report; tables. See issues of Space world
Special report: satellite technology serving earth; with editorial comment. il maps Aviation W 107:9, 40-2+ O 17 '77
See also
Space stations

Accidents

See Space flight—Accidents

Agricultural use

Eye-in-the-sky: satellites add confidence to world crop estimates; Large Area Crop Inventory Experiment. Suc Farm 75:no2 50 F '77
Satellite crop inventory tests evaluated. C. Covault. il Aviation W 106:74-5+ Je 20 '77

Air traffic control use

Aerosat bill facing hurdles in Congress. Aviation W 106:49 F 21 '77

Astronomical use

Backup gyros weighed for astronomy flight. Aviation W 107:54 Jl 11 '77
Design phase of space telescope nears. B. M. Elson. il Aviation W 107:54-5+ Ag 8 '77
GAO space telescope study disputed. Aviation W 106:47 My 23 '77
HEAO: one up and two to go. il Sci N 112:119 Ag 20 '77
HEAO raises X-ray source score. Sci N 112: 406 D 17 '77
HEAO satellite makes major findings. C. Covault. Aviation W 107:20-1 D 5 '77
HEAO-A awaits long-delayed launching. il Sci N 112:38 Jl 16 '77
HEAO-A launch. il Sky & Tel 53:252 Ap '77
Helios mission provides new solar data. B. M. Elson. il Aviation W 106:46-9 F 14 '77
Lockheed wins contract to build NASA'S space telescope. il Space World N-11-167:32-3 N '77
Mission to expand X-ray source study. C. Covault. il Aviation W 106:36-7+ Ap 11 '77
Survey satellite to map high-energy sources. F. C. Bennett. il Phys Today 30:20 My '77
Telescope research openings announcement by NASA nears. Aviation W 106:15 F 7 '77
2.4-meter telescope could orbit in 1983. G. B. Lubkin. il Phys Today 30:18-19 Ap '77
Ultraviolet spectroscopy with Copernicus. T. P. Snow, Jr. il Sky & Tel 54:371-4 N '77

Atomic power plants

See Space vehicles—Atomic power plants

Biological use

Soviets invite additional U.S. space cooperation. Aviation W 107:12-13 D 19 '77
U.S, Soviets to discuss more biosat missions. R. G. O'Lone. il Aviation W 107:95+ S 26 '77
See also
Artificial satellites—Cosmos missions

Communication use

See Communications satellites

Cosmos missions

Biosputnik hauls Yankee rats, fruit flies; Cosmos 936. il Sci N 112:230 O 8 '77
Killer satellite tests pop-up; Cosmos 918. Aviation W 107:19 Jl 4 '77
Russian biology satellite carries U.S. experiments. Space World N-11-167:33 N '77
Soviet UFO due to secret launch; Cosmos-995 spy satellite. Sci N 112:230-1 O 8 '77
Soviets make new intercept in space, fourth in 1976. Aviation W 106:22-3 Ja 3 '77

Earth sciences use

Budget revision to cover additional Landsat vehicle. Aviation W 106:23 F 28 '77
ESA, to have responsibility for resource satellite effort. Aviation W 106:20 Ja 3 '77
Earth from space: reality & promise. H. J. P. Arnold. il maps Space World N-11-167:20-9 N '77
Earth resources benefits to expand. il Aviation W 107:42+ O 17 '77
Geological Survey hits thematic mapper. C. Covault. Aviation W 107:20-1 Ag 8 '77
God's eye view; Landsat. J. A. Ralph. il Commonweal 104:587-8 S 16 '77
Landsat, computers, and development projects. P.-M. Adrien and M. F. Baumgardner. bibl il Science 198:466-70 N 4 '77
Landsat data pressed for western U.S. Aviation W 106:47 Ap 4 '77
Landsat data use urged to aid developing nations. Aviation W 108:24-5 Ja 9 '78
Landsat satellites. il Space World N-1-157:23-6 Ja '77
Landsats moved to boost data return. Aviation W 106:15 Ja 10 '77
Major European satellite: low but going; Geos. Sci N 111:325 My 21 '77
Meteorite impact crater discovered in central Alaska with Landsat imagery; Sithylemenkat Lake. P. J. Cannon. il Science 196:1322-4 Je 17 '77
Microwave spectroscopic imagery of the earth. D. H. Staelin and others. bibl il Science 197: 991-3 S 2 '77
Multispectral scanner urged for Landsat D. Aviation W 107:49 D 5 '77
New techniques spur Landsat data use. il Aviation W 107:48-56+ O 17 '77
Operational Landsat due further study. P. J. Klass. Aviation W 107:53-5 Jl 11 '77
Operational Landsat tied to added users' interest. Aviation W 106:91+ Je 13 '77
RCA environmental satellites to play major role in study to predict water supply availability. il Space World N-11-167:34 N '77
Remote sensing commitments urged. C. Covault. Aviation W 106:48-9+ My 16 '77

ARTIFICIAL satellites—Earth sciences use—*Cont.*
Remote sensing: Landsat takes hold in South America. A. L. Hammond. il Science 196:511-12 Ap 29 '77
Remote-sensing of crop yields. S. B. Idso and others. bibl il Science 196:19-25 Ap 1 '77
Resources unit studies space sensing. W. H. Gregory. il Aviation W 106:264-8 Je 6 '77
Seasat use boosts Satellite Service bid. Aviation W 106:55 F 7 '77
Space tracking network measures earth crust movements. il Space World N-2-158:2 F '77
Techniques tomorrow; Landsat. B. Sherman. il Mod Phot 41:49+ S '77
User aid sought on operational Landsat. Aviation W 106:21 F 14 '77
Users reassured on thematic mapper. C. Covault. il Aviation W 106:46-7 Mr 7 '77

Electronic equipment

Satellite vulnerability fixes emphasized. P. J. Klass. Aviation W 107:58-9+ O 24 '77

Insurance

See Insurance, Space flight

International aspects

See also
Artificial satellites—Cosmos missions

Leasing and renting

See also
Communications satellites—Leasing and renting

Meteorological use

Dust storm tracked across U.S. il Space World N-11-167:32 N '77
First Japanese weather satellite launched. il Space World N-11-167:15-19 N '77
Future European weather satellite efforts uncertain. il Aviation W 107:146-7+ O 17 '77
Geos returning data despite orbit. C. Covault. il Aviation W 106:44-5 My 23 '77
ISEE satellites set for launch. Aviation W 107:23 S 26 '77
ISEE: staking out earth's magnetosphere. il Sci N 112:276 O 29 '77
International Sun-Earth Explorer: a three-spacecraft program. K. W. Ogilvie and others. bibl il Science 198:131-8 O 14 '77
NOAA, Space Agency defining weather satellite system for deployment by 1985. il Aviation W 107:140-1+ O 17 '77
Soviets test scanners, weather sensors on Meteor-2. il Aviation W 107:66-7+ O 17 '77
Super lightning detected by satellite. Sci N 112:15 Jl 2 '77
Survey of the United States meteorological satellite program. A. Schnapf. il Weatherwise 30:180-91+ O '77
TIROS I satellite transmitted first weather picture from space 17 years ago. il Space World N-12-168:33-4 D '77
Unusual trajectories set for sun-earth explorers. C. Covault. il Aviation W 107:38-41 O 3 '77

Military use

Killer satellite tests pop-up; Cosmos 918. Aviation W 107:19 Jl 4 '77
Now a new arms race in space: Soviet satellite killer. il U.S. News 83:28 N 14 '77
Satellite vulnerability fixes emphasized. P. J. Klass. Aviation W 107:58-9+ O 24 '77
Soviet geodetic mission ends 26-day space hiatus. Aviation W 107:59 D 12 '77
Strategic reconnaissance. H. F. York and G. A. Greb. bibl il Bull Atom Sci 33:33-42 Ap '77
Surveillance satellite for all. A. Chayes and others. Bull Atom Sci 33:7 Ja '77
Targeting a hunter-killer; anti-satellite interceptor (ASAT) il Time 110:10 O 17 '77
USAF defining shuttle sensor payload. J. M. Lenorovitz. il Aviation W 106:44-6 Mr 14 '77
USAF pushes satellite survivability. B. Miller. il Aviation W 106:52-5 Mr 28 '77
Will the next war be fought in space? E. Hymoff. il Pop Mech 148:47-51+ Jl '77
See also
Artificial satellites—Cosmos missions
Communications satellites—Military use

Navigational use

GAO cites NavStar slippage. Aviation W 106:22 Mr 14 '77
Navigation satellite carries atomic clock. il Sci N 112:6 Jl 2 '77
NavStar achieves goals in first test of concept. Aviation W 107:159 O 17 '77
Navstar delays begin to force launching conflicts with NASA. Aviation W 107:105 S 26 '77
NavStar development to be restructured. Aviation W 106:28 F 28 '77
Transit navigation. J. West. il Motor B & S 139:66 My '77
USAF advancing NavStar positioning. B. Miller. il Aviation W 106:71+ Je 13 '77

Oceanographic use

Commercial value early Seasat target. il Aviation W 107:150-1+ O 17 '77
Long waves in the eastern equatorial Pacific Ocean; a view from a geostationary satellite. R. Legeckis. bibl il Science 197:1179-81 S 16 '77
NESS: National Environmental Satellite Service. J. C. Fine. il Sea Front 23:198-203 Jl '77
Seasat user program organized. C. Covault. Aviation W 106:14-16 Mr 14 '77
Seasat-A could spur operational plan. B. M. Elson. il Aviation W 107:51+ D 12 '77

Orbits

Europeans working to salvage Geos data in unplanned orbit. Aviation W 106:44 Ap 25 '77
Landsats moved to boost data return. Aviation W 106:15 Ja 10 '77

Propulsion systems

See Space vehicles—Propulsion systems

Rescue work

See Space rescue work

Solar energy use

Energy from outer space. R. F. Dempewolff. il Pop Mech 147:98-101+ Je '77
Industry seeks stronger effort in solar power. Aviation W 106:54-5 F 28 '77
Solar power from satellites; adaptation of address, October 1976. P. E. Glaser. bibl il Phys Today 30:30-2+ F '77; Discussion. 30:9+ Jl '77
Space-based solar power study near completion. B. M. Elson. il Aviation W 107:58-9+ S 19 '77
Space prospect: factories and electric power. R. S. Lewis. il Smithsonian 8:94-9 D '77
Space solar power—an available energy source. S. Ferdman and R. L. Kline. il Space World M-12-156:4-17 D '76

Use in tracking and trailing

Satellite boat watch makes for safe sailing. S. Renner-Smith. map Pop Sci 211:89 O '77
Watchful eye guides craft thru Triangle. il map Sci Digest 82:50-2 Ag '77

ARTIFICIAL satellites, European
Geos returning data despite orbit. C. Covault. il Aviation W 106:44-5 My 23 '77

ARTIFICIAL satellites, French
French spacecraft launched by Soviets; photographs. il Aviation W 107:57 Jl 18 '77

ARTIFICIAL satellites, Japanese
First Japanese weather satellite launched. il Space World N-11-167:15-19 N '77
Japan expands technology program. il Aviation W 107:104-5+ O 17 '77
Japanese geosynchronous satellite. Sci N 111:168 Mr 12 '77

ARTIFICIAL satellites, Russian
Now a new arms race in space; Soviet satellite killer. il U.S. News 83:28 N 14 '77
Soviets pass 1,000 space launch mark. Aviation W 106:31 My 2 '77
Soviets test another killer satellite; Cosmos 970. Aviation W 108:21 Ja 2 '78
Soviets test scanners, weather sensors on Meteor-2. il Aviation W 107:66-7+ O 17 '77
Targeting a hunter-killer; anti-satellite interceptor (ASAT) il Time 110:10 O 17 '77
Why of Sputnik. bibl f il por map Space World N-12-168:4-15 D '77

ARTIFICIAL sweeteners. See Sugar substitutes

ARTIFICIAL trees. See Trees, Artificial

ARTIS, John
American travesty. J. B. Lieber. por Nation 224:393-400 Ap 2 '77 *

ARTISANS
Craftsmen in business: taxes; excerpt from Craftsmen in business: a guide to financial management and taxes. H. W. Connaughton. Ceram Mo 25:40-4 Mr '77
Health issues; ed by J. Waller and L. Whitehead; excerpts from De morbis artificum. B. Ramazzini. Craft Horiz 37:8+ O '77
Reviving nearly lost crafts. B. H. Schneider. House B 119:12+ Je '77
Taxes for the craftsman (title varies) (cont) E. Marcum. Craft Horiz 37:12+ F '77
See also
Potters

ARTISTIC anatomy. See Anatomy, Artistic

ARTISTIC photography. See Photography, Artistic

ARTISTS
Brickbats and favorites; Art news poll of most overrated and underrated artists of the 20th century. il Horizon 21:34 Ja '78
Far-from-last judgments: or, Who's overrated now? And underrated; views of art historians, museum directors, curators and critics; ed by J. Gruen. il Art N 76:106-20 N '77
Leonardo was a southpaw; left-handed artists. Vasari. il Art N 76:22-3 Ap '77
Meet the masters! comments about artists by students. K. Alexander. il Sch Arts 76:16-17 F '77

ARTISTS—*Continued*
New York reviews. See issues of Art news
20th-century artists most admired by other artists; views of nearly 100 artists; ed by G. Glueck. il Art N 76:78-103 N '77
See also
Illustrators
Potters
Printmakers
Prisoners as artists
Women artists

Health and hygiene
Anthrax: the deadly fruit of the loom. G. Hokanson. Craft Horiz 37:9+ F '77
Hazards in arts and crafts; chemical dangers reported by Badi M. Boulos and Michael McCann. Consumers Res Mag 60:16-17 Jl '77
Health issues (title varies) J. Waller and L. Whitehead. Craft Horiz 37:56+ Je; 8+ D '77

Political activities
American artist from loner to lobbyist; Open to New Ideas: a Collection of New Art for Jimmy Carter. C. Ratcliff. il Art in Am 65:10-12 Mr '77
Moral message from La Grande France; boycott of Pompidou Center in protest to release of Abu Daoud. Art N 76:31 Mr '77

Salaries, allowances, etc.
See also
Artists—Taxation

Taxation
Artists and taxes. J. A. Mondale. il Ceram Mo 25:73-5 O '77
Artists' tax bills. B. Chamberlain. Am Artist 42:18+ Ja '78
Is the Internal Revenue Service unfair to artists? pro and con discussion. Am Artist 41:8-9 Mr '77
Little bit of haven; tax free Ireland. il Time 110:115-16 O 10 '77
Money matters: business at home. G. Krefetz. Craft Horiz 37:49+ D '77
Special tax problem: no profits. P. Schwab. il por Nations Bus 65:100 N '77

ARTISTS, American
Art; opening of New York artists' studio to public. L. Alloway. Nation 224:669-70 My 28 '77
Manhattan seven. H. Herrera. bibl il Art in Am 65:50-63 Jl '77
New York today: some artists comment; interviews, ed by D. B. Kuspit and others. il Art in Am 65:78-85 S '77
Second Lady's lunch. New Yorker 53:30-1 My 30 '77
See also
Allen, D.
Bearden, R.
Berman, W.
Biederman, C.
Bull, C. L.
Chicago, J.
Christo
Conner, B.
Dow, A. W.
Federal Art Project
Fisher, V.
Fuller, M. V. W.
Graves, N.
Hare, D.
Heinecken, R.
Henninger, J.
Hudson, G. C.
Irwin, R.
James, J.
Kelly, E.
LaVerdiere, B.
LeWitt, S.
Lichtenstein, R.
Markowski, E.
Max, P.
Morton, R.
Murphy, E.
Peterson, R. T.
Pitz, H. C.
Price, J.
Rattner, A.
Ray, M.
Rivers, L.
Rockburne, D.
Schapiro, M.
Schwebler, Y.
Soyer, R.
Stahl, B
Vogel, M.
Whistler, J. A. M.

Photographs
Younger generation: a cross section. il Art in Am 65:86-91 S '77

ARTISTS, Belgian
See also
Culot, P.
Dotremont, C.
Ensor, J.

ARTISTS, British
See also
Haden, F. S.

ARTISTS, French
See also
Daumier, H.
Degas, E.
Gallé, E.
Gaudier-Brzeska, H.
Lalanne, C.
Lepère, A. L.
Leuquet, P.
Matisse, H.
Steinlen, T. A.

ARTISTS, German
See also
Klinger, M.

ARTISTS, Italian
See also
Crivelli, C.

ARTISTS, Japanese
See also
Yokoi, T.

ARTISTS, Norwegian
See also
Munch, E.

ARTISTS, Puerto Rican
See also
Ferrer, R.

ARTISTS, Russian
On the Russian avant-garde. D. Sarabyanov. il Art N 76:116-17 N '77
See also
Chagall, M.
Komar, V.
Melamid, A.

ARTISTS, Spanish
See also
Miró, J.
Muñoz, A.
Tàpies, A.

ARTISTS and authors colonies
Fine print. D. Grumbach. Sat R 5:33 O 15 '77
Where artists do as they please—and mostly, work; Yaddo and MacDowell colonies. W. F. Claire. il Smithsonian 8:44-51 Jl '77
See also
MacDowell Colony, Peterboro, N.H.

ARTISTS as authors
Artist's book goes public. L. R. Lippard. il Art in Am 65:40-1 Ja '77

ARTISTS as teachers
Conversation with Marshall Joyce; interview, ed by C. Movalli. M. Joyce. il por Am Artist 41:90-5+ F '77
Conversation with Ted Göerschner; interview, ed by C. Movalli. T. Göerschner. il por Am Artist 41:52-7+ S '77
Duane Wakeham: sharing a way of seeing; interview, ed by J. McCord. D. Wakeham. il por Am Artist 41:60-5 N '77
Joseph Henninger: the artist as teacher. D. C. Hines. il por Am Artist 41:52-7+ My '77

ARTISTS contracts
Artist-gallery contracts: scenes from a marriage. L. Rosenbaum. Art in Am 65:10-14 Jl '77

ARTISTS in Schools program. See United States—National Foundation on the Arts and the Humanities

ARTISTS materials
Art mart. See issues of American artist
Christmas shopping guide. il Am Artist 41:21-30 D '77
Clipboard. V. G. Timmons. See issues of School arts
Constructing your own slab roller; excerpt from Getting into pots, a basic pottery manual. G. Wettlaufer and N. Wettlaufer. il Ceram Mo 25:30-2 F '77
Hazards in arts and crafts; chemical dangers reported by Badi M. Boulos and Michael McCann. Consumers Res Mag 60:16-17 Jl '77
Health issues (title varies) J. Waller and L. Whitehead. Craft Horiz 37:56+ Je; 8+ D '77
Leonardo and the stain. E. Genauer. por Newsweek 90:27 D 12 '77
New sources, new materials. See issues of Art news
Quick tips. See occasional issues of American artist
Technical page; questions and answers. R. Mayer. See issues of American artist
What's new. See issues of Design (US)
See also
Clay
Paint
Paper

ARTISTS rights
Arts bills: pluses and minuses; question of federal resale royalty bill. A. Elsen. il por Art N 76:52-4 O '77
Bernard Buffet's Refrigerator and the integrity of the work of art. J. H. Merryman. il Art N 76:38-42 F '77
California royalty bill: milestone or mistake? pro and con discussion. J. H. Merryman; H. Sandison. pors Am Artist 41:60-1 F '77

ARTISTS rights—*Continued*
California's art resale law: the failure of innocence. A. Elsen. Art in Am 65:15-16 Mr '77
Legislating royalties for artists. S. Hochfield; reply. B. K. Brill. Art N 76:34 Ap '77
Taking care of the government's public art. T. Crawford. Art in Am 65:19+ My '77
See also
Copyright—Art

ARTISTS studios
Art; opening of New York artists' studio to public. L. Alloway. Nation 224:669-70 My 28 '77
Children meet artists; field trips to artists' studios by Los Angeles students. E. Levin. il Sch Arts 76:20-2 Je '77

ARTNER, Alan G.
Chicago. il Art N 76:93-5 Mr; 92+ Ap; 158-9 Summ '77

ARTNEWS (periodical) See Art news (periodical)

ARTOBOLEVSKY, Ivan I.
Soviet leader considers it mutually advantageous. por Sci Digest 81:30-1+ Je '77

ARTPARK, Lewiston, N.Y. See New York (state) —Parks and reserves

The ARTS
Against the grain: why the arts have jumped the tracks. B. Levin. il Horizon 19:90-2 Ja '77
Artsletter. R. Gelatt. See issues of Saturday review
Very special autumn; special issue. ed by H. Sutton. il Sat R 4:11-14+ Ag 6 '77
See also
Performing arts
Video art
Violence in the arts
Women in the arts

Federal aid

See The Arts and state

Finance

Beggar's opera; fund raising by cultural institutions. L. H. Lapham. Harpers 255:16+ O '77
Climate for creativity. D. B. Wilmeth. Intellect 106:82 Ag '77
Viewpoint. R. Jacobson. Opera N 42:6 S '77
Why is New York called the Big Apple? Because everything about it is appealing. Vasari. Art N 76:26 Ap '77

International aspects

American culture takes the world by storm. il U.S. News 82:54-6 Je 27 '77

Scholarships and fellowships

See also
Arts and crafts—Scholarships and fellowships
Music—Scholarships and fellowships

Study and teaching

Arts are for learning; Seattle. J. B. Gaines. il Todays Educ 66:72-4 N '77
Arts-In! What is it? J. Schultz. il Sch Arts 76:18-21 Ap '77
Career guides for the arts and humanities; guidebooks produced by the Technical Education Research Center. E. B. Roth. il Am Educ 13:14-15 Je '77
Coming to our senses: arts education and American popular entertainment; report on Coming to our senses: the significance of the arts for American education. D. B. Wilmeth. Intellect 106:174 O '77
Community school movement; instruction in music and the arts. C. B. Fowler. il Hi Fi 27:MA12-13 Jl '77
From the echoes of Chautaqua; Creative Education Program and the Children's Experimental Workshop at Glen Echo Park in Maryland. M. Travaglini. il Am Educ 13:17-21 My '77
Industry without art; question of the report Coming to our senses: the significance of the arts for American education. R. Rosenblatt. New Repub 177:41-2 Jl 2 '77
Lifetime learning and the arts—a new priority. S. Timmermann. Educ Digest 43:40-2 S '77
More arts for the handicapped; programs for children. il Hi Fi 27:MA9-11 Je '77
NEA'S low marks in self-assessment; Artists in Schools program. M. N. Carter. il Art N 76:44-5 My '77; Reply. P. H. Bihler. 76:34 S '77
On education; recommendations and other aspects of the Rockefeller panel report entitled Coming to our senses: the significance of the arts for American education. C. B. Fowler. il Hi Fi 27:MA13-15 S '77
Project ARTS; public school program in Montgomery County, Md. C. B. Fowler. il Hi Fi 27:MA12-13+ My '77
Special treatment for the gifted; program for gifted and talented children of the Riverside Center for the Arts, Harrisburg, Pa. C. B. Fowler. il Hi Fi 27:MA14-15 Ap '77
Statement to Congress. P. Cooper. il por Hi Fi 27:MA16-18+ O '77
Why children should draw: the surprising link between art and learning. R. M. Williams. il Sat R 4:10-16 S 3 '77
See also
Alliance for Arts Education

China

Now it's China's cultural thaw. H. E. Salisbury. il pors N Y Times Mag p49+ D 4 '77

Latin America

Blacks in Latin America; Africa's imprint on the arts. A. Carpentier. il UNESCO Courier 30:8-12 Ag '77

Mexico

Sunday afternoon in Mexico City. C. Hartman. il Holiday 57:32-3 N '76

Spain

After Franco's forty years: the popular arts in Spain. S. Meisler. il Nation 224:461-4 Ap 16 '77

United States

Bits (cont of) Show biz, arts, etc. M. Latour. See issues of Mademoiselle
Cross country. il Horizon 20:4 S; 4 O; 4 N; 4 D '77; 21:4+ Ja '78
Culture boom. il U.S. News 83:50-3 Ag 8 '77
Little man at Chehaw Station: the American artist and his audience. R. Ellison. Am Scholar 47:25-48 Wint '77
Star trekking. J. Kroll. il Newsweek 90:48 D 26 '77
To artist Jamie Wyeth, U.S. is moving again. J. Wyeth. il pors U.S. News 82:90 My 16 '77
What's going on; special section. M. Latour and A. Gross. il Mademoiselle 83:40+ O '77
See also
American Academy and Institute of Arts and Letters

The ARTS, Black
Elma Lewis: keeping African culture alive in Boston; Elma Lewis School of Fine Arts. S. Quinn. il por Ms 5:14-15+ My '77

ARTS, Graphic. See Graphic arts

ARTS and crafts
Get inspired! P. Sadowsky. il Am Home 80:29-33 Ag '77
Keep those film cans! L. O. Rexrode. il Pop Phot 81:258 D '77
See also
Appliqué work
Batik
Block printing
Christmas projects
Collage
Folk art
Ironwork
Ivory carving
Jewelry making
Leather work
Montage
Mosaics
Needlework
Paper work
Papier-mâché
Plaster work (craft)
Plastics work
Pottery
Stencil work
Tapestry
Weaving
Wood carving
Woodworking
World Crafts Council

Bibliography

Book reviews. See issues of Design (US)
Books (cont) Craft Horiz 37:18-19+ F; 14 Ap; 10-11 O; 10+ D '77
Resource materials. B. Wasserman. See issues of School arts

Exhibitions

Artists put their colorful stamp on Santa Cruz. il map Sunset 159:36-8 Ag '77
Booth design at Northeast Craft Fair. il Ceram Mo 25:62-3 My '77
Booth design; design of Winter Market booth. J. Yesberger and M. Saffer. il Craft Horiz 37:57 Je '77
Calendar. See issues of Craft horizons
California crafts. il Ceram Mo 25:35 O '77
Craftsmanship of Lancaster County, Pennsylvania. S. B. Sherrill. il Antiques 112:592+ O '77
Exhibitions. See issues of Craft horizons
Indian arts and crafts from Phoenix; Heard Museum exhibit of Mexican Indian crafts. il Sunset 158:68-9 My '77
Itinerary. See issues of Ceramics monthly
May Show. il Ceram Mo 25:53 O '77
New peak at Timberline. R. Griffin. il Craft Horiz 37:14-17 O '77
Object as Poet; exhibition at the Renwick Gallery of the National Collection of Fine Arts, Smithsonian Institution. R. Slivka. il Craft Horiz 37:26-39+ F '77

ARTS and crafts—Exhibitions—*Continued*
Style: the craft of being you; The craft of joyful eating. il Craft Horiz 37:12-15 D '77
Where to show. Ceram Mo 25:8+ S; 8+ O; 15+ N; 13+ D '77
Where to show. See issues of Craft horizons
Winter Market; a crafts fair and trade show at Civic Center, Baltimore. J. W. Rousuck. il Craft Horiz 37:44-5+ Ap '77
Young Americans: fiber/wood/plastic/leather. il Craft Horiz 37:14-19+ Je '77
See also
Pottery—Exhibitions
Tapestry—Exhibitions
Textile crafts—Exhibitions
Weaving—Exhibitions

Scholarships and fellowships

Grants, deadlines, and '77 guidelines (cont) Craft Horiz 37:6 F '77
Green grow the grants, oh! Funds for fertile programs. Craft Horiz 37:38 Ag '77
NEA craft grants to workshops, exhibits. Craft Horiz 37:8 Ap '77
NEA grants go to 156 craftsmakers and artists. Craft Horiz 37:37+ Ag '77
Nancy Hanks on craft grants; excerpt from address. N. Hanks. Craft Horiz 37:6 F '77

Study and teaching

Arts & crafts ideas. S. Sundick. See issues of Design (US)
Illinois training program treats crafts seriously. D. Owen. il Aging 275:26-7 S '77
Learn-to-do-something-new vacations: arts & crafts. B. Humeston. il Bet Hom & Gard 55:199-200+ Ap '77
Preschool craft activities. M. I. Lane. il SLJ 23:43 My '77
Travel and study abroad 1977. Craft Horiz 37: 16-17+ Ap '77
Workshops. See issues of Craft horizons
See also
Art schools

Appalachian Region

Appalachia revisited. G. Mendes. il Craft Horiz 37:28-40+ Je '77

Ghana

Arts of Ghana coming to UCLA. il Sunset 159: 78 O '77

United States

Crafts renaissance. bibl il Am Home 80:15 Ag '77
New craft era. R. Slivka. Craft Horiz 37:9 Je '77
Our legacy of crafts; address, June 1977. J. Melchert. Craft Horiz 37:45 Ag '77
White House showcase for crafts. J. B. Reiter and J. Macurdy. il pors House B 119:116-19 O '77
See also
American Crafts Council

ARTS and crafts as a profession. See Art as a profession

ARTS and crafts centers. See Art centers

ARTS and crafts movement
Arts and crafts movement in New England; exhibition. S. B. Sherrill. il Antiques 111:254+ F '77

ARTS and crafts schools. See Art schools

ARTS and crafts trade. See Art trade

The **ARTS and industry**
Boulevard to a fuller life. M. Wellemeyer. il Fortune 96:125-6+ O '77
See also
Art patronage
Business Committee for the Arts

ARTS and Letters, American Academy and Institute of. See American Academy and Institute of Arts and Letters

The **ARTS and politics**
Jimmy Carter: a big grin for culture. P. M. Kadis. il por Art N 76:50-4 My '77

The **ARTS and state**
Artists versus bureaucracy. D. Davis. Newsweek 89:11 Mr 21 '77
CETA funds—a boon to North Carolina; employment programs for artists and musicians. C. B. Fowler. il Hi Fi 27:MA16-18 D '77
Can the Commerce Department revolutionize federal policy on the arts? L. Wiener. por Am Artist 41:12 D '77
Cultural tithe. T. Bethell. Harpers 255:18-19+ Ag '77
Government and the arts. C. C. Mark. por Am Artist 41:4+ Je '77
Jimmy Carter: a big grin for culture. P. M. Kadis. il por Art N 76:50-4 My '77
Money for art's sake. E. Munro. il Atlantic 239:75-8 Ap '77
National arts policy. J. Brademas. por Am Artist 42:16+ Ja '78
See also
Alliance for Arts Education
United States—National Foundation on the Arts and the Humanities

The **ARTS as recreation.** See Recreation—Activities

ARTS education. See The Arts—Study and teaching

ARTS Education Advocacy project. See Alliance for Arts Education

ARTS festivals. See Festivals

ARTSAY, Alda Favia-. See Favia-Artsay, A.

AS is; ballet. See Ballet reviews—Single works

AS to the meaning of words; drama. See Eichman, M.

ASA, Warren
King-sized cleanup pan. il Org Gard & Farm 24:95 Ap '77
Syringing: a simple, workable insect control. il Org Gard & Farm 24:134+ My '77
Vigorous, productive vine. Org Gard & Farm 24:160 Ag '77
When to pick a perfect vegetable. Horticulture 55:24+ Jl '77

ASAKAWALKER Dance Company. See Dance companies

ASARCO Inc. See Metal industry

ASBESTOS
Asbestos, maple trees, and Mounties. R. Paehlke. Environment 19:3-4 Ja '77

ASBESTOS-cement water pipes. See Water pipes

ASBESTOS pollution of the air. See Air pollution

ASBESTOS workers
Who is responsible for workplace safety? J. S. Shaw. Bus W p42 D 26 '77

ASBURY, Barbara N. See Galvin, H. R. jt auth

ASBURY, Joseph G. and Mueller, R. O.
Solar energy and electric utilities: should they be interfaced? bibl il Science 195:445-50 F 4 '77

ASCIU, Niculae
Pictures without words. il por Horizon 21:96 Ja '78

ASCORBIC acid. See Vitamins—Vitamin C

ASH, Roy Lawrence
Addressograph gets the Roy Ash treatment. il Bus W p36 Mr 21 '77 *

ASH, Volcanic. See Volcanic ash, tuff, etc.

ASH glazes. See Glazes and glazing (ceramics)

ASHBERY, John
Collective dawns; poems. New Yorker 53:34 F 21 '77
Fantasia on The nut-brown maid; poem. Poetry 130:260-75 Ag '77
Lament upon the waters; poem. New Yorker 53: 42 Je 6 '77
Saying it to keep it from happening; Other tradition; poems. Sat R 4:36 S 17 '77
Syringa; Blue sonata; Ice-cream wars; poems. Poetry 130:4-9 Ap '77
Two deaths; And *ut pictura poesis* is her name; poems; excerpt from Houseboat days. Mademoiselle 83:96 S '77
Wrong kind of insurance; poem. New Yorker 53: 31 Je 27 '77
about
Robert Lowell and John Ashbery: the difference between poets. A. Kazin. il Esquire 89:20+ Ja '78 *

ASHBROOK, John Milan
Excerpt from remarks on amnesty for illegal aliens, July 13, 1977. Cong Digest 56:245+ O '77

ASHBROOK, Joseph
Astronomical scrapbook. See issues of Sky and telescope

ASHBROOK, William
Love and revolution. Opera N 41:14-15 Mr 26 '77
Of prayers and curses. il Opera N 41:28-9 Mr 12 '77
Saint-Saëns et Dalila. il Opera N 41:26-7 Ap 16 '77

ASHBY, Gene
Reaching out to orphans. M. McDonald. por Outdoor Life 159:140 My '77 *

ASHBY, Neal
Does your quirk irk you . . . and others, too? Fam Health 9:40-3 Mr '77

ASHE, Arthur, 1943-
Arthur Ashe: on politics & sports; interview, ed by E. Dowling. il por Sr Schol 110:4-6+ S 22 '77
about
Arthur Ashe: defeat doesn't scare him. il por Sr Schol 110:7 S 22 '77 *

ASHER, Peter
Peter Asher—producer power & a touch of class. S. Sutherland. il por Hi Fi 27:107-10 Je '77 *

ASHES
Ten uses for wood ashes. C. Jabs. Org Gard & Farm 24:130-1 N '77

ASHES; drama. See Rudkin, D.

ASHES as fertilizer. See Fertilizers and manures

ASHFORD, Thomas, pseud
Countdown to an abortion. America 136:128-30 F 12 '77

ASHKENAZY, Irvin
Rise and fall of Antarctic ice: the rest of the iceberg. il Oceans 10:26-30 My '77

ASHLAND, Ore. Shakespeare Festival. See Shakespeare festivals
ASHLAND Oil, Inc
Crude-poor Ashland Oil: prototype of the future. il Bus W p98-9+ Ja 31 '77
ASHLAND Oil, Inc.-Commonwealth Oil Refining Company merger. See Petroleum industry—Acquisitions and mergers
ASHLEY, James
Phone calls and philandering. il pors Time 110: 32-3 S 5 '77 *
ASHLEY, Nova Trimble
How do I love thee? poem. Ladies Home J 94: 170 D '77
ASHLEY, Thomas William Ludlow
All it needs is Lud. T. Mathews and others. il por Newsweek 89:24 My 9 '77 *
ASHRAM (resort) Calabasas, Calif. See Health resorts, watering places, etc.
ASHTON, Sir Frederick
Dance. N. Goldner. Nation 225:568-9 N 26 '77 *
ASHWORTH, William
Hells Canyon. il map Am Heritage 28:12-23 Ap '77
ASIA
See also
Education—Asia
Evangelistic work—Asia
Far East
Public opinion—Asia
Siberia

Defenses

See also
United States—Armed Forces—Forces in Asia

Economic conditions

See also
United Nations—Economic and Social Commission for Asia and the Pacific

Foreign relations

Russia

See Russia—Foreign relations—Asia

United States

See United States—Foreign relations—Asia

History

Bibliography

Reviews of books: Asia and the East. See issues of American historical review

Maps

Map section. Sr Schol 110:30 O 20 '77

Politics and government

Danger spots in the Far East. D. N. Rowe. il Nat R 29:829-30 Jl 22 '77
In Asia—a reservoir of good will for Americans. L. Hansen. il U.S. News 83:25-6 S 5 '77

Religious institutions and affairs

Asian views of dialogue. S. R. Athyal. Chr Today 21:44+ Je 17 '77
See also
Christians in Asia

Social conditions

See also
United Nations—Economic and Social Commission for Asia and the Pacific
ASIA, Central
See also
Afghanistan
Altai Mountains
Ladakh
ASIA, Southeastern
Stability in Southeast Asia: a lot depends on U.S. leadership. il U.S. News 83:43-4 O 31 '77
See also
Association of Southeast Asian Nations
Crime and criminals—Asia, Southeastern
Economic assistance, American—Asia, Southeastern
Hotels, motels, etc.—Asia, Southeastern
Indochina
Mekong River
Thailand
Visitors, Foreign—Asia, Southeastern

Defenses

See also
United States—Armed Forces—Forces in Southeast Asia

Economic relations

United States

See United States—Economic relations—Asia, Southeastern

Foreign relations

See also
Cambodian-Vietnamese conflict, 1977-
ASIA, Southern
Nation, region, and welfare: ethnicity, regionalism, and development politics in south Asia. J. Das Gupta. bibl f il Ann Am Acad 433:125-36 S '77
See also
Economic assistance, American—Asia, Southern
ASIA, Southwestern
See also
United Nations—Economic Commission for Western Asia
ASIA and the United States
See also
United States—Foreign opinion—Asian
ASIADOLLAR market
Asiadollar market starts to sprout. Bus W p44 Jl 11 '77
ASIAN musk shrews. See Shrews
ASIANS in South Africa
Apartheid's other victims. il Time 110:40+ O 3 '77
ASIMOV, Isaac
Collapsing universe; excerpt. por Sci Digest 81: 12-16+ Je '77
Gene scene. il Sat Eve Post 249:12+ S '77
Isaac Asimov advises the President. il Sci Digest 81:8-12 F '77
Nightmare life without fuel. Time 109:33 Ap 25 '77; Same abr. with title Life without fuel. Read Digest 111:126-8 Ag '77
Salt of the earth. il Int Wildlife 7:30-6 Mr '77
Story machine; drama. Plays 36:24, 61-70 My '77
20 ways the world could end. il Pop Mech 147:86-9+ Mr '77

about

Asimov, the human writing machine. J. L. Collier. por Read Digest 111:123-6 Ag '77 *
Backward, march! por Forbes 119:74 Ap 1 '77 *
ASIR, Saudi Arabia
Money is no object. por Forbes 120:97 Jl 1 '77
ASKIN, Frank
Is reverse discrimination justified? interview. pors U.S. News 83:39-40 O 3 '77
ASLEEP at the Wheel (band) See Bands (music)
ASMUS, John F.
Have laser, will travel. C. Panati and D. Gram. por Newsweek 89:87 Mr 28 '77 *
ASOLO Opera Theatre. See Opera—Florida
ASPARAGUS
Ornamental asparagus—unthirsty, easy to propagate. il Sunset 158:210+ Je '77
See also
Cookery—Vegetables
ASPEN, Colo.
Land of Peter Pan. S. Moses. Sports Illus 47: 34-6+ O 10 '77
ASPEN Music Festival. See Music festivals—Colorado
ASPERGILLUS
Aspergillus oryzae (NRRL strain 1988) L. Stoloff and others. bibl Science 196:1353 Je 17 '77
ASPHALT
Archeological asphalts approached analytically. Chemistry 50:21 D '77
PennDOT curbs cutback asphalt use; EPA emissions offset ruling. il Am City & County 92:30 Ag '77
ASPHALT driveways. See Driveways
ASPHALT pavements. See Pavements
ASPHALT plants

Environmental aspects

Dust still falls on Derby despite a tough new law; pollution by Derby Sand and Gravel's asphalt plant in Connecticut. D. Starr. Audubon 79:136-8 S '77
ASPHYXIA
See also
Respiration, Artificial
ASPIC
Party pâté; duck aspic and pâté. C. Claiborne and P. Franey. il N Y Times Mag p 141+ D 11 '77
ASPIDISTRA
Two old houseplant toughies: aspidistra and sanseviera. G. R. Robinson. il Org Gard & Farm 24:170-3 O '77
ASPIN, Les
Burden of generosity. il Harpers 253:22-4 D '76; 254:6+ F '77
ASPIRIN
AMIS trial: can aspirin prevent heart attacks? J. L. Marx. Science 196:1075 Je 3 '77
Aspirin. il Sci Digest 82:54-7 S '77
Consumer watch. J. Carper. Am Home 80:28 O '77
FDA urges new caveats for aspirin users. Ret Liv 17:60 S '77
No, all aspirin and pain remedies are not alike. M. Rubenstein. il Ret Liv 17:30-2+ Mr '77
Pained Bayer cries foul; ad refuting Tylenol's claims. il Bus W p 142 Jl 25 '77
Painkiller war. L. Langway and J. Whitmore. il Newsweek 90:79-80 Jl 18 '77
Relieving the analgesic headache; FDA study. il Time 110:70 Ag 1 '77

ASSAD, Hafez
Assad: Sadat's folly; excerpts from interview, ed by A. de Borchgrave. il pors Newsweek 91:41-2+ Ja 16 '78
Peace, but not this year; excerpts from interview, ed by W. Wynn. por Time 109:32+ Ja 24 '77
President Carter meets with President Asad of Syria at Geneva; exchange of remarks and toasts, May 9, 1977. Dept State Bull 76:594-5+ Je 6 '77
Two Arab leaders reply to Begin; excerpts from interview, ed by A. de Borchgrave. pors Newsweek 90:30-2 Ag 1 '77
about
For Syria: a growing role in Middle East drama. D. Mullin. il por map U.S. News 82:79-80 Ap 18 '77 *
Pressures mount on Syria's Assad—. D. Mullin. il por U.S. News 84:25-6 Ja 9 '78 *
Syria's Assad: walking a tightrope. por U.S. News 83:22 D 12 '77 *

ASSASSINATION
See also
Jumblatt, K.—Assassination
Kennedy, R. F.—Assassination
Lincoln, A.—Assassination
United States—Congress—House—Assassinations, Select Committee on

ASSASSINATIONS, Select Committee on. See United States—Congress—House—Assassinations, Select Committee on

ASSASSINS
Assassins! J. W. Booth and L. H. Oswald. B. Z. Spencer. il por Sat Eve Post 249:72 Jl '77

ASSAY, Biological. See Biological assay

ASSEMBLAGE (art)
Imaginary creatures. P. Schneider. il Sch Arts 76:35 Je '77
Leonardo and the stain. E. Genauer. por Newsweek 90:27 D 12 '77
Lipstick cases, typewriter parts melded into motorcycle art. S. Parker. il por Design (US) 79:14-16 Fall '77
Name of the game: boxes. R. V. Schoenborn. il Sch Arts 77:36-7 S '77

ASSEMBLERS (computers) See Computers—Input-output equipment

ASSEMBLIES of God
Assemblies of God: a leader upheld. E. E. Plowman. Chr Today 21:64-9 S 9 '77

ASSEMBLY line methods
See also
Automobile factories

ASSERTIVENESS (psychology)
Speak for yourself! quiz. M. E. Mihaly. Seventeen 36:142-3+ O '77

ASSES and mules
See also
Burros

ASSESSMENT
Dead trees, dying communities; real property reassessment in Buffalo. J. F. Keenan. America 137:265-8 O 22 '77
How to fight that property tax assessment. Changing T 31:7-9 O '77

ASSETS (accounting) See Corporations—Accounting

ASSIMILATION (sociology)
Assimilationist dilemma: Ambassador Morgenthau's story; adaptation of address, December 1976. B. W. Tuchman. Commentary 63:58-62 My '77; Discussion. 64:12+ Ag '77
Bring back the melting pot. M. Stone. U.S. News 83:92 D 5 '77
Communities in crisis, Indians of South America. J. E. Adoum. il UNESCO Courier 30:46-50 Ag '77

ASSISTANCE in emergencies
Bystanders' creed: don't meddle in family fights; study by R. Lance Shotland and Margret K. Straw. J. Gaylin. il Psychol Today 10:29-30 F '77
Mobilizing eyewitnesses to crime: the use of radios and rewards. J. P. Levine. bibl il Intellect 105:254-7 F '77
See also
Disaster relief

ASSOCIATED Church Press (organization)
Praying editors. Chr Today 21:37 Je 3 '77

ASSOCIATED General Contractors of America
Business, too, tests reverse discrimination. il Bus W p40-1 N 14 '77

ASSOCIATION (biology) See Symbiosis

ASSOCIATION for Educational Communication and Technology. See National Education Association—Association for Educational Communication and Technology

ASSOCIATION for the Advancement of Creative Musicians festival. See Music festivals—New York (state)

ASSOCIATION for the Study of Afro-American Life and History
More ASALH projects, black American representation in national parks. J. R. Picott. Negro Hist Bull 40:736-7 S '77
Thoughts about the ASALH 1978 program. J. R. Picott. Negro Hist Bull 40:714-15 Jl '77
Woodson and the genesis of ASALH. A. Scally. il por Negro Hist Bull 40:653-5 Ja '77

ASSOCIATION of American Library Schools
AALS meets in Denver: accreditation study preview. Lib J 102:1325 Je 15 '77
Day at the Assn. of American Library Schools. W. R. Eshelman. Wilson Lib Bull 51:563-4 Mr '77

ASSOCIATION of American Publishers
AAP acts on four fronts dealing with postal matters. S. Wagner. il Pub W 211:25+ Ja 17 '77
AAP & authors clash over copy fee scheme. Lib J 102:1083 My 15 '77
AAP cautions Senate on pending obscenity law. S. Wagner. Pub W 212:29+ Jl 25 '77
AAP launches the 1977 Books as Gifts campaign in nine major book markets. D. Maryles. il Pub W 212:40 N 28 '77
AAP pleads for loans to small publishers. S. Wagner. Pub W 212:22 D 26 '77
AAP protests proposed solid waste tax on paper. S. Wagner. Pub W 213:13 Ja 2 '78
AAP seeks bids to run copy payments center. S. Wagner. Pub W 212:28 Jl 11 '77
AAP spells out clearinghouse plan for photocopying at CONTU meeting. S. Wagner. Pub W 211:28 Ap 11 '77
AAP to present plan for photocopying fees. S. Wagner. Pub W 211:27-8 Mr 28 '77
AAP urges end to Arab book boycott. M. Reuter. Pub W 212:22-3 Ag 8 '77
ACLU, AAP oppose lobbying law dues disclosure. S. Wagner. Pub W 212:14 Ag 22 '77
Books as Gifts test results are in; AAP to vote on $400,000 budget for 1977. D. Maryles. il Pub W 211:24 My 9 '77; Correction. 211:17 My 30 '77
Obscenity: new High Court ruling, AAP on Flynt. S. Wagner. Pub W 211:41-2 Mr 14 '77
Seventh annual AAP meeting. M. Reuter and S. Wagner. il Pub W 211:54-9 Je 20 '77

College Division
Western College group looks at rapidly changing market. P. Holt. Pub W 212:27-8 D 26 '77

Education for Publishing Committee
AAP group submits two-year report; proposes publishing education center. M. Reuter. Pub W 211:22 My 9 '77

International Freedom to Publish Committee
AAP aids Iranian writers in plea for association. M. Reuter. Pub W 212:16+ Ag 15 '77
AAP protests to Soviet on Shcharansky's arrest. M. Reuter. Pub W 211:14 My 30 '77

School Division
Educational publishers plan campaign to boost national spending on materials. P. D. Doebler. il Pub W 211:66-7 F 28 '77

Technical, Scientific and Medical Division
TSM publishers peer at the future—and find it bright; annual meeting. P. D. Doebler. Pub W 211:24+ My 2 '77

ASSOCIATION of American University Presses
Annual AAUP meeting focuses on two identity problems. M. Reuter. il Pub W 212:56-60 Ag 1 '77
Temple University hosts regional AAUP meeting. C. B. Grannis. Pub W 211:34 Ap 18 '77

ASSOCIATION of Evangelical Lutheran Churches. See Lutheran Church in the United States

ASSOCIATION of Evangelicals of Africa and Madagascar conference. See Religious conferences—Africa

ASSOCIATION of Professional Color Laboratories. See Photography—Societies

ASSOCIATION of Research Libraries
Academic librarians share their know-how; the Systems and Procedures Exchange Center. M. Sitts. Am Lib 8:570 N '77
Research libraries buy fewer books, more serials. Wilson Lib Bull 51:632 Ap '77

ASSOCIATION of Southeast Asian Nations
United States and ASEAN hold economic consultations in Manila; statement, transcript of joint press conference, and text of press release, September 8, 10, 1977. R. N. Cooper; C. P. Romulo. Dept State Bull 77:595-605 O 31 '77

ASSOCIATION of State Library Agencies. See American Library Association—Association of State Library Agencies

ASSOCIATIONS, institutions, etc.
Help! How to cope with it all; national and governmental organizations. J. L. Barkas. Redbook 149:81-8 O '77
See also
International agencies
National Association for the Advancement of Colored People
United Nations—Council Committee on Nongovernmental Organizations

ASSUMPTION of the Virgin Mary. See Mary, Virgin
ASSURBANIPAL, King of Assyria
Library of Assurbanipal, King of the world. L. Arksey. bibl il Wilson Lib Bull 51:832-40 Je '77 *
ASSYRIAN library of Assurbanipal. See Libraries —History
ASSYRIAN tablets (paleography) See Tablets (paleography)
ASTERIX (comic strip) See Comics (books, strips, etc)
ASTEROIDS
Adonis recovered. Sky & Tel 53:243 Ap '77
Asteroid families: observational evidence for common origins. J. Gradie and B. Zellner. bibl il Science 197:254-5 Jl 15 '77
Diameters of minor planets. D. Morrison. il Sky & Tel 53:181-3 Mr '77
Mining the Apollo and Amor asteroids. B. O'Leary. bibl il Science 197:363-6 Jl 22 '77
New Apollo asteroids. Sci N 111:325 My 21 '77
Return of Adonis: an asteroid refound. Sci N 111:183 Mr 19 '77
Studying near-earth resources. J. R. Arnold. Aviation W 107:9 S 19 '77
Taking the measure of Vesta. Sci N 111:279 Ap 30 '77
ASTHMA
Breathe easy! S. H. Young. il Parents Mag 52: 23+ Jl '77
ASTIN, Alexander W.
New realists. il por Psychol Today 11:50-1+ S '77; Same with title New mood on campus. Current 197:7-12 N '77
ASTON Martin. See Automobiles, Foreign
ASTOR, Gerald
Theory vs. marketable skills: what do we teach the neophyte? il por Pub W 212:30-2 S 5 '77
ASTRACHAN, Anthony
Obsession with unity. New Repub 177:21-3 Ag 20 '77; Same. Current 196:46-52 O '77
ASTROCHEMISTRY
Organic chemistry in space. R. D. Johnson. bibl il Chemistry 50:17-22 O '77
Strange xenon, extinct superheavy elements, and the solar neutrino puzzle. O. K. Manuel; D. D. Sabu; R. S. Lewis and others. bibl Science 195:208-10 Ja 14 '77
See also
Matter, Interstellar
ASTROLOGERS
See also
Godillo, S.
ASTROLOGY
Astrology can cause more mischief than good. G. Belson. por Seventeen 36:94 Mr '77
Horoscope. M. E. Crummere. See issues of Vogue
Horoscopes. Aurora. See issues of Harper's bazaar
Starcast. M. L. Fiel. See issues of Mademoiselle
Writer in his heavenly house. W. H. Scheib. Writer 90:27-9 Ja '77
Your horoscope. See issues of McCall's
See also
Zodiac
ASTRONAUTS
Astronauts & UFOs—the whole story! J. E. Oberg. il por Space World N-2-158:4-28 F '77
NASA begins selection of new astronaut group. Aviation W 107:20 Jl 4 '77
Soyuz cosmonaut portrait gallery. il Space World N-7-163:32-6 Jl '77
See also
Women astronauts
also names of astronauts, e.g. D. K. Slayton

Clothing

Shuttle suit shows advances on Apollo. C. Covault. il Aviation W 107:37-40 Ag 15 '77

Training

See also
Space flight simulators
ASTRONOMERS
See also
Menzel, D. H.
Brahe, T.
Ptolemy, C.
ASTRONOMERS, Amateur
Amateur astronomers. See issues of Sky and telescope
Gleaning for ATM's; ed by R. E. Cox and R. W. Sinnott. See issues of Sky and telescope

Societies

See Astronomical societies
ASTRONOMICAL charts. See Astronomy—Charts, diagrams, etc.
ASTRONOMICAL conferences. See Astronomy—Conferences
ASTRONOMICAL distances
Mobile lunar laser ranging station; University of Texas McDonald Observatory. il Intellect 105:300-1 Mr '77
ASTRONOMICAL instruments
Low light level detectors for astronomy. P. B. Boyce. bibl Science 198:145-8 O 14 '77
Observing equipment for amateurs. Sky & Tel 54:355 N '77
See also
Spectroscopes
Telescopes
ASTRONOMICAL observations. See Astronomy—Observations
ASTRONOMICAL observatories
Five College Radio Astronomy Observatory. T. Arny and G. Valeriani. il Sky & Tel 53:431-5 Je '77
Large observatory for amateurs in the Northwest; Goldendale Observatory. il Sky & Tel 53:276-7 Ap '77
Let there be darkness; light pollution near observatory sites. S. P. Maran. Natur Hist 86:88+ Ap '77
Mobile lunar laser ranging station; University of Texas McDonald Observatory il Intellect 105:300-1 Mr '77
Panorama of observatories. il Sky & Tel 53:332-8 My '77

Chile

Big astronomy in Chile: the southern observatories come of age. A. L. Hammond. il Science 198:1235-9 D 23 '77
First light for the ESO 3.6-meter telescope. S. Laustsen. il Sky & Tel 53:96-103 F '77
Wise men from the south peer toward what may be limits of the universe; Cerro Las Campanas Observatory. S. Seagrave. il Smithsonian 8:40-7 bibl (p 146) Ap '77

Ireland

W. E. Wilson and the Daramona observatory. B. Warner. il Sky & Tel 53:108-10 F '77
ASTRONOMICAL photography
Computer-enhanced photographs of galaxies. il Sky & Tel 53:170-2 Mr '77
Make your own astrophotographs. D. Healy. il Pop Phot 81:110-11+ O '77
Photographing the moon's shadow. D. Di Cicco. il Sky & Tel 53:322-3 Ap '77
Photography project for the 1977-78 school year; Mars. R. C. Victor il Sky & Tel 54:215 S '77
Structure of the interstellar medium; synthetic photography from radio wavelengths of interstellar gases. C. Heiles. Sci Am 238:74-84 Ja '78
Super-wide-angle photographs of the Milky Way. T. Schmidt-Kaler and W. Schlosser. il Sky & Tel 53:436-9 Je '77
See also
Moon—Photographs
Space photography

Apparatus and supplies

Camera mount for projection photography. D. A. Harbour. il Sky & Tel 54:63-4 Jl '77
On the road to better astronomical photographs. B. D. Wallis and R. W. Provin. il por Sky & Tel 53:314-18, 399-405, 484-91 Ap-Je '77

Competitions

Some astrophotos to enjoy. il Sky & Tel 54: 283-7 O '77

Conferences

Astrophotographers meet in California. P. Townsend. il Sky & Tel 53:362-3 My '77
ASTRONOMICAL radio programs. See Radio programs—Science programs
ASTRONOMICAL research
Recent astronomical research in China. T. Kiang. il map Sky & Tel 54:260-3 O '77
See also
Artificial satellites—Astronomical use
Monterey Institute for Research in Astronomy
ASTRONOMICAL societies
Coming astronomical gatherings in 1977. il Sky & Tel 53:278-9 Ap '77
Double-double; Amateur Astronomers Association. New Yorker 53:28 S 19 '77
NASA is host to Northern California convention. D. Berger. il Sky & Tel 54:487 D '77
See also
American Association of Variable Star Observers
American Astronomical Society
ASTRONOMICAL spectroscopy
Companions of sunlike stars. H. A. Abt. il Sci Am 236:96-104 bibl(p 148) Ap '77
Far-ultraviolet rocket survey of Orion. G. R. Carruthers and C. B. Opal. il Sky & Tel 53: 270-5 Ap '77
Ultraviolet spectroscopy with Copernicus. T. P. Snow, Jr. il Sky & Tel 54:371-4 N '77
See also
Spectrum, Solar
ASTRONOMY
Astronomy (cont) Sci N 111:88, 185, 222, 249, 361; 112:41, 153, 216, 376 F 5, Mr 19, Ap 2, 16, Je 4, Jl 16, S 3, O 1, D 3 '77
Calculator programs. Sky & Tel 54:292 O '77
[Month] stars. J. Stokley. See fourth issue of each month of Science news to December 24, 1977

ASTRONOMY—*Continued*
Sky reporter. See issues of Natural history
Wise men from the south peer toward what may be limits of the universe. S. Seagrave. il Smithsonian 8:40-7 bibl (p 146) Ap '77
See also
Airplanes in astronomy
Asteroids
Astrophysics
Black holes (astronomy)
Chronology
Computers—Astronomical use
Constellations
Cosmology
Eclipses
Eclipses, Lunar
Eclipses, Solar
Electronics in astronomy
Galaxies
Halos (meteorology)
Infrared astronomy
Lasers—Astronomical use
Life on other planets
Meteorites
Meteors
Milky Way
Nebulae
Occultations
Planetariums
Planets
Quasars
Radar in astronomy
Rockets—Astronomical use
Satellites
Sky
Solar system
Space astronomy
Stars—Evolution
Telescopes
Tides
Ultraviolet astronomy
Universe
X ray astronomy

Awards, prizes, etc.

Some student projects in astronomy. il Sky Tel 54:171-3 S '77

Bibliography

Books and the sky. See issues of Sky and telescope
Science books. R. Berendzen. Am Scholar 46: 514+ Aut '77

Charts, diagrams, etc.

Celestial events. T. D. Nicholson. See issues of Natural history
Looking south from Siding Spring. C. A. Federer, Jr. il Sky & Tel 53:186-9 Mr '77
Southern stars. See issues of Sky and telescope
Stars for [the month] G. Lovi. See issues of Sky & telescope
Winter sky. C. Bain. il Conservationist 31:26-7 Ja '77

Conferences

Amateur progress seen at Boulder; National Amateur Astronomers Convention. il Sky & Tel 54:278-82 O '77
Coming astronomical gatherings in 1977. Sky & Tel 53:198 Mr; 278-9 Ap '77
Ninth Riverside convention. A. McDermott and D. DiCicco. il pors Sky & Tel 54:100-4 Ag '77
Some highlights of Stellafane. R. W. S. Sinnott. il Sky & Tel 54:328-31+ O '77

History

Asaph Hall finds the moons of Mars. J. Ashbrook. il por Sky & Tel 54:20-1 Jl '77
Astronomical scrapbook. J. Ashbrook. See issues of Sky and telescope
Case of the missing sunspots; the Maunder minimum. J. A. Eddy. il Sci Am 236:80-8 My '77
Mars centennial; work of C. Flammarion. K. L. Franklin. il Sci Digest 82:66-9 S '77
Ptruth about Ptolemy; charges by R. R. Newton. Time 110:116 N 28 '77
Thomas Clap and the terrestrial comets. H. A. Smith. il Sky & Tel 53:420-2 Je '77
Tycho Brahe and the great comet of 1577. O. Gingerich. il Sky & Tel 54:452-8 D '77
W. E. Wilson and the Daramona Observatory. B. Warner. il Sky & Tel 53:108-10 F '77

Observations

Observer's page. See issues of Sky and telescope
Puzzle in the sky; Object-Kowal. map Newsweek 90:141 N 21 '77
Tenth planet? C. Kowal's finding. Time 110:98 N 21 '77
See also
Planets—Observations
Venus (planet)—Observations

Study and teaching

Summer science program; Thacher School, Ojai, Calif. D. A. Pierce. il Sky & Tel 53:175-7 Mr '77

China

Recent astronomical research in China. T. Kiang. il map Sky & Tel 54:260-3 O '77

Poland

Amateur astronomy in Poland. D. Trombino. il Sky & Tel 53:195+ Mr '77

ASTRONOMY, Ancient
Once and future stars. P. Gwynne and S. Begley. il Newsweek 90:98-100 D 19 '77
ASTRONOMY, Indian (American)
Astronomy, architecture, and adaptation at Pueblo Bonito. J. E. Reyman; reply with rejoinder. R. A. Williamson. bibl Science 197: 618-20 Ag 12 '77
ASTRONOMY, Oriental
Ancient astronomical records from the Orient. F. R. Stephenson and D. H. Clark. il map Sky & Tel 53:84-91 F '77
ASTRONOMY in art
About an astronomical woodcut. J. Ashbrook. il Sky & Tel 53:356-7+ My '77
Solar eclipses and ancient artistic motifs; letter. R. M. Sinclair. bibl Science 196:715-17 My 13 '77
ASTRONOMY on postage stamps. See Postage stamps
ASTROPHOTOGRAPHY. See Astronomical photography
ASTROPHYSICS
Concept opening way to a scientific world of fantasy; white holes. J. Gribbin. il Smithsonian 8:100-7 bibl(p 161-2) N '77
See also
Black holes (astronomy)
Cosmic rays
Magnetic fields (cosmic physics)
Quasars
Stars—Evolution
ASYLUM, Right of
American political asylum: not for victims of our friends. C. Hanson. Nation 224:527-30 Ap 30 '77
See also
United Nations Conference of Plenipotentiaries on Territorial Asylum
ASYMMETRY. See Symmetry (biology)
ATAKA and Company. See Trading companies—Japan
ATALLA, Jorge Wolney
Brazil's coffee with sugar billionaire. A. M. Louis. il pors Fortune 96:82-8 Jl '77 *
ATCHISON, Wayne
Lonely stillhunter. il Outdoor Life 160:118+ S '77
ATGET, Eugène
Images from the Paris Salon. R. Martinez. il Pop Phot 81:134-7+ D '77 *
ATHAYDE, Roberto
Miss Margarida's way. Reviews
America 137:243 O 15 '77 *
Nation 225:286 S 24 '77 *
New Yorker 53:91 O 10 '77 *
Sat R 5:51 O 29 '77 *
Time il 110:108 O 10 '77 *
ATHEISM
Bob and Madalyn's fight to the finish; B. Harrington-M. M. O'Hair debates. J. C. Hefley and E. E. Plowman. il por Chr Today 21: 34-5 Ag 26 '77
Combat zone. Chr Today 22:50-1 N 18 '77
On tour; M. M. O'Hair vs B. Harrington. Chr Today 22:58-9 O 7 '77
Soul mates; debates between M. M. O'Hair and B. Harrington. M. Montagno and F. Maier. pors Newsweek 90:72 S 19 '77
ATHEISM in literature. See Religion in literature
ATHENEUM Publishers. See Publishers and publishing—United States
ATHENS, Ga.
New confidence. il U.S. News 82:31-2 Je 13 '77
ATHENS, Greece

Acropolis

Acropolis in danger. A. M. M'Bow. il por UNESCO Courier 30:4-6 F '77
Acropolis in peril; symposium. UNESCO Courier 30:4-33 O '77
Ceremony; UNESCO appeal for funds to save the Acropolis. New Yorker 52:22-3 Ja 31 '77
Parthenon is shrinking. E. Vermeule. il Atlantic 239:82-4+ My '77
See also
Parthenon

Air pollution

Parthenon is shrinking. E. Vermeule. il Atlantic 239:82-4+ My '77

Antiquities

See also
Athens, Greece—Acropolis
Parthenon
ATHENSTAEDT, Herbert. See Lang, S. B. jt auth
ATHEROSCLEROSIS. See Arteriosclerosis

ATHERTON, Alfred Leroy, 1921-
Department discusses U.S. efforts in search for Middle East peace; statement, June 8, 1977. Dept State Bull 77:25-7 Jl 4 '77
Israeli settlements in occupied territories; statement, October 19, 1977. Dept State Bull 77:828-9 D 5 '77
Middle East; remarks, November 21, 1977. Dept State Bull 77:891-4 D 19 '77
Proposed sales of military equipment to Egypt; statement, September 15, 1977. Dept State Bull 77:650-2 N 7 '77

ATHLETES
Big scorers in the ad game. M. Ludtke. Sports Illus 47:50 N 7 '77
On the other hand. . ; left-handed athletes. J. Kirshenbaum. il Sports Illus 46:60-3+ Ja 24 '77
Secret lives of the super jocks. J. Durso. il Sat Eve Post 249:40-1+ Mr '77
Their way. P. Axthelm. Newsweek 90:63+ D 26 '77
See also
Baseball players
Basketball players
Black athletes
Football players
Golfers
Hockey players
Women athletes

Anecdotes, facetiae, satire, etc.
There'll never be another. il Sat Eve Post 249: 36-8 Jl '77

Health and hygiene
Science and the athlete:
Ability plus science equal world's best. L. Bortstein. il Sci Digest 81:10-11 Mr '77
Computer readout translates body language into skills. P. Garfinkel. il Sci Digest 81: 12-14 Mr '77
Train your eyes; better your score. P. Martin. il Sci Digest 81:7-9 Mr '77

Names
Dedicated to Fair Hooker, wherever he is. Esquire 87:46+ Mr '77

Nutrition
They hunger for success. J. D. Reed. il Sports Illus 46:64-8+ F 28 '77

Photographs
Speaking of youth. Sports Illus 47:52-6 D 19 '77

Political activities
Poll ball game. B. Weber. il Sr Schol 109:29 Ja 13 '77

Psychology
This half, go out there and make statements! R. Blount, Jr. Esquire 87:44+ Ap '77
What do you do when you grow up? problems of amateurs. J. Kaplan. il pors Sports Illus 47:30-2+ Jl 4 '77

Recruiting
Ethics, due process, diversity, and balance; address, March 25, 1977. S. Horn. Vital Speeches 43:463-8 My 15 '77

Religious life
Training for pros. W. Spoelstra. Chr Today 21: 53 Mr 18 '77
Winners; Dodgers and Yankees attend pre-game chapel services. Chr Today 22:50 N 4 '77
See also
Athletes in Action (organization)

Salaries, pensions, etc.
One treasurer's report. Time 110:63 S 12 '77
What inflation is doing to the world of sports. il U.S. News 82:53-6 My 16 '77

Training
Pricking up their ears; lactic acid blood testing to determine most efficient training pace. J. Kirshenbaum. il por Sports Illus 47:94+ O 31 '77

ATHLETE'S foot (disease)
How to stamp out athlete's foot. Bet Hom & Gard 55:100+ Jl '77

ATHLETES in Action (organization)
Athletes in Action; game against Moscow Red Army. Chr Today 21:53-4 Ap 15 '77
Hallelujah, what a team! Athletes in Action vs college teams. J. Jares. il Sports Illus 46:41-2 F 7 '77

ATHLETIC clubs. See Sports clubs

ATHLETIC fields
Coping with a water shortage; care of grass in recreation facilities. J. R. Watson. il Parks & Rec 12:54-5+ Jl '77
Greening of a ball field. R. Thomas. il Parks & Rec 12:26-7+ My '77

ATHLETIC locker rooms. See Locker rooms

ATHLETIC scholarships. See Scholarships and fellowships

ATHLETICS
See also
Athletes
College athletics
Gymnastics
Olympic Games
School athletics
Sports
Track athletics

Medical aspects
See Sports medicine

ATHYAL, Saphir P.
Asian views of dialogue. Chr Today 21:44+ Je 17 '77
Emergence of Asian theologies. Chr Today 21: 70+ S 23 '77
Indian evangelicals: some issues in mission. Chr Today 21:60-1 Mr 18 '77

ATIKOKAN Generating Station (proposed) See Electric plants—Canada

ATKINS, Eileen
Forceful magistrate. il por Horizon 20:84 D '77 *

ATKINS, Robert Coleman
Low-low-carbohydrate diet; interview. il por Good H 185:294+ N '77

ATKINSON, George
Walk on the sordid side. W. O. Johnson. il por Sports Illus 47:10-15 Ag 1 '77 *

ATKINSON, Joan L.
Developing statewide services for young adults. SLJ 24:96 O '77

ATKINSON, Richard C.
Atkinson sees good relationship between NSF and White House; interview. por BioScience 27:447-50+ Jl '77
about
New director forecasts fresh commitments for NSF. F. C. Bennett. por Phys Today 30:77+ Jl '77 *
Psychologist Atkinson to head NSF. Sci N 111:215 Ap 2 '77 *

ATLANTA

Architecture
Architecture for people and not for things; excerpt from The architect as developer. J. Portman. il Archit Rec 161:133-40 Ja '77

Banks
Bert Lance's bind; National Bank of Georgia. M. Rudy and others. il por Newsweek 90:69-70+ Jl 18 '77
For budget chief: a money problem all his own; B. Lance's National Bank of Georgia. il por U.S. News 83:65 Jl 25 '77
Gap narrows between Atlanta's top banks; First National Bank of Atlanta and Citizens & Southern National Bank. il Bus W p98+ N 28 '77
Going to bat for beleaguered Bert; B. Lance's National Bank of Georgia stock. il por Time 110:26+ Jl 25 '77
Good old boy network; Atlanta bank loans to J. Carter campaign; with White House response by J. Powell, R. Reeves and B. M. Hager. New Repub 177:6+ S 10 '77
Is Bert Lance losing his clout? il por U.S. News 83:21 Ag 8 '77
Lance alone; memo linking personal loan to correspondent relationship between Manufacturers and National Bank of Georgia. D. M. Alpern and others. por Newsweek 90:14-15 Ag 15 '77
Lance on the carpet; National Bank of Georgia-First Chicago relationship. M. Ruby and R. Thomas. il por Newsweek 90:57-8 Ag 1 '77
Lance's mysterious rescuer; G. Pharaon's offer to buy National Bank of Georgia stock. il por Time 111:45 Ja 9 '78
Little Georgia bank with the big headlines; National Bank of Georgia. Bus W p24-5 Ag 29 '77
Send Lance back to banking: questionable loans incurred as head of National Bank of Georgia. por New Repub 177:10-12 Ag 6 '77
Sharpening battle over Bert Lance. il por Time 110:6-8 Ag 1 '77
Still a good old boy; sale of National Bank of Georgia stock to the Saudi Research and Development Corporation. Nation 225:707-8 D 31 '77
Surprising turn in saga of Bert Lance; purchase of National Bank of Georgia stock by G. Pharaon. pors U.S. News 84:36 Ja 9 '78

Buildings
Picking the bones of Colony Square; division of assets by Prudential Insurance Co. and Chase Manhattan Mortgage & Realty Trust. Bus W p39+ Ja 31 '77

Clubs
Clubs Griffin Bell had to quit; Piedmont Driving Club. S. Birmingham. il N Y Times Mag p20-1+ F 6 '77

Description
Atlanta. Bet Hom & Gard 55:239-40 O '77

ATLANTA—*Continued*

Hotels, restaurants, etc.

Where football comes to a head; Manuel's Tavern. R. Blount, Jr. il Sports Illus 47:37 S 5 '77

Parks and playgrounds

Playscapes sculpture-playground in Atlanta. A. Bledsoe. il Sch Arts 76:22-5 Ap '77

Politics and government

Crying Wurf; advertising campaign attacking city of Atlanta and Mayor M. Jackson. K. Bode. New Repub 177:14-17 Jl 2 '77

Restaurants

See Atlanta—Hotels, restaurants, etc.

Sports

See Sports—United States

Stores

Bromeliad boys at Nature's Way. C. Seagraves. il pors Horticulture 55:36-7 D '77

Strikes

See also
Strikes—United States—Sanitation workers

ATLANTA Ballet
Critic-at-large; Atlanta Ballet's Nutcracker. D. Hering. Dance Mag 51:30+ Mr '77

ATLANTA 500. See Automobile racing

ATLANTA Public Library
Call the shots yourself. C. C. Rochell. Am Lib 8:574-5 N '77

ATLANTIC CITY
Atlantic City gambles on casinos. D. Schlossberg. il Travel 148:50-1+ O '77
Atlantic City: soon to be Las Vegas of the East. D. L. Battle. il U.S. News 83:40-1 Ag 22 '77
Big gamble. D. Pauly and M. Reese. il Newsweek 90:66-7 Ag 8 '77
Trouble in Las Vegas East. il Time 111:14-15 Ja 16 '78

Hotels, restaurants, etc.

Big spender hits Atlantic City; Bally Mfg. Corp. il Bus W p47 Ap 18 '77

ATLANTIC Coast
Shoreline forms and shoreline dynamics. R. Dolan and others. bibl il maps Science 197:49-51 Jl 1 '77
See also
Air pollution—Atlantic Coast

ATLANTIC flights. See Aviation—Transatlantic flights

ATLANTIC OCEAN
Dust concentration in the atmosphere of the equatorial North Atlantic: possible relationship to the Sahelian drought. J. M. Prospero and R. T. Nees. bibl il Science 196:1196-8 Je 10 '77
Interstitial nitrate profiles and oxidation of sedimentary organic matter in the eastern equatorial Atlantic. M. L. Bender. bibl il Science 198:605-9 N 11 '77
North Atlantic ice-rafting: a major change at 75,000 years before the present. W. F. Ruddiman. bibl il maps Science 196:1208-11 Je 10 '77
See also
Grand Banks (submarine plateau)
Gulf Stream
Pigalu (island)
Sargasso Sea

ATLANTIC Richfield Company
Oil to the rescue; purchase of The Observer by ARCO. B. D. Nossiter. Progressive 41:38-9 Mr '77
Under Observation. D. K. Shah and A. Collings. il por Newsweek 90:102-3 D 19 '77

ATLANTIC States
See also
Fishing—Atlantic States

Description and travel

Revisiting America's canals. S. McCoy. il Travel 148:60-5 Jl '77

ATLAS, David
Paradox of hail suppression. bibl il Science 195:139-45 Ja 14 '77

ATLAS, Jacobs
(ed) See Fonda, J. Will the real Jane Fonda please stand up

ATLASES
See also
Booksellers and bookselling—Reference books

ATMOSPHERE
Anthropogenic CO emissions: implications for the atmospheric CO-OH-CH_4 cycle. N. D. Sze. bibl Science 195:673-5 F 18 '77
Carbon dioxide question. G. M. Woodwell. il map Sci Am 238:34-43 Ja '78
Desert greenhouse; fossil fuels and climate. il maps Environment 19:14-20 N '77
History of the earth's atmosphere. il Sky & Tel 53:266+ Ap '77
Implications of solar evolution from the earth's early atmosphere. M. J. Newman and R. T. Rood. bibl il Science 198:1035-7 D 9 '77
Mars and earth; origin and abundance of volatiles. E. Anders and T. Owen. bibl il Science 198:453-65 N 4 '77
See also
Atmospheric pressure
Biosphere
Planets—Atmosphere
Winds

ATMOSPHERE, Upper
Atomic chlorine and the chlorine monoxide radical in the stratosphere: three in situ observations. J. G. Anderson and others. bibl il Science 198:501-3 N 4 '77
Energetic oxygen ions stream up to magnetosphere. W. A. Flanagan. bibl il Phys Today 30:17-19 N '77

ATMOSPHERE-ocean interaction. See Ocean-atmosphere interaction

ATMOSPHERIC aerosols. See Aerosols

ATMOSPHERIC carbon dioxide. See Carbon dioxide

ATMOSPHERIC electricity
Meteorological consequences of atmospheric Krypton-85. W. L. Boeck; reply with rejoinder. H. L. Gjorup. Science 196:380-1+ Ap 22 '77
See also
Auroras
Lightning
Thunderstorms

ATMOSPHERIC pressure
Weather course: atmospheric pressure. il Motor B & S 140:56-7+ D '77

Physiological effects

See also
Decompression sickness

ATMOSPHERIC research
Concorde sonic booms as an atmospheric probe. N. K. Balachandran and others. bibl il map Science 197:47-9 Jl 1 '77
See also
Artificial satellites—Meteorological use

ATMOSPHERIC temperature
See also
Global temperature changes

ATMOSPHERIC turbulence
Clear air turbulence: detection by infrared observations of water vapor. P. Kuhn and others. bibl il Science 196:1099-100 Je 3 '77
Dangerous wake turbulence finally is defeated . . . with winglets. D. Berliner. il Sci Digest 82:72-5 N '77
Wake vortex sensing efforts advance. P. J. Klass. il Aviation W 106:92-3+ Ap 25 '77
See also
Mountain waves

ATOCHA (ship) See Treasure trove

ATOMIC absorption spectroscopy. See Spectrum analysis

ATOMIC bomb shelters
Whatever happened to: fallout shelters: dwindling interest. il U.S. News 82:74 Mr 14 '77

ATOMIC bombs
Making nuclear bombs the quick, dirty way. Sci N 112:357-8 N 26 '77
See also
Neutron bombs

History

I am become death. . .; the agony of J. R. Oppenheimer. R. Rhodes. il pors Am Heritage 28:70-83 O '77
Science and defense policy; physicist E. Teller, father of the hydrogen bomb. J. Marsh. Commentary 63:67-70 Ap '77

Manufacture

Homebuilt atomic bomb? il Mech Illus 73:156+ N '77

Physiological effects

See Radioactivity—Physiological effects

Testing

Halting Pretoria's A-test. Newsweek 90:36 S 5 '77

Testing, Underground

Death by incompetence: the blowout at Yucca Flat; exposure to radiation after underground test accident. J. Harris. Nation 226:18-20 Ja 7 '78
Progress and problems in arms control negotiations; address, September 19, 1977. P. C. Warnke. Dept State Bull 77:772-7 N 28 '77
Ratification recommended for treaties with U.S.S.R. restricting nuclear testing; statements, July 28, 1977. P. C. Warnke; P. C. Habib. Dept State Bull 77:310-14 S 5 '77

ATOMIC bombs in motion pictures. See Motion pictures—Plots, themes, etc.

ATOMIC clocks
And now, atomic clocks. J. Fincher. Read Digest 111:34+ N '77
Navigation satellite carries atomic clock. il Sci N 112:6 Jl 2 '77

ATOMIC energy. See Atomic power
ATOMIC Energy Agency. See International Atomic Energy Agency
ATOMIC Energy Commission. See United States —Atomic Energy Commission
ATOMIC fuels. See Nuclear fuels
ATOMIC insurance. See Insurance, Atomic hazards
ATOMIC nuclei

Fission

See Nuclear fission

Spin

Second back bend helps explain nuclear band crossing. H. R. Leuchtag. il Phys Today 30:17-19 S '77

ATOMIC power
Campaigning for an embattled cause. il Time 109:73 Mr 21 '77
Carter & the plutonium economy. J. J. Berger. Nation 224:101-4 Ja 29 '77
Carter's frustrations on nuclear policy. Bus W p62+ S 26 '77
Carter's nuclear policy: running into trouble. J. McWethy. il U.S. News 83:51-2 Jl 4 '77
Carter's nuclear switch. D. M. Alpern and others. il Newsweek 89:22-4 Ap 18 '77
Critical mass. New Repub 176:2+ My 28 '77
Department testifies on nonproliferation and nuclear export policies; statement, May 6, 1977. J. S. Nye, Jr. Dept State Bull 76:558-64 My 30 '77
Distrust of nuclear power. C. Hohenemser and others. bibl il Science 196:25-34 Ap 1 '77
Distrust of nuclear power. K. H. Hohenemser. il Environment 19:48-50 Je '77
For energy solution: Teller gives us 5 years. J. E. Persico. por Sci Digest 82:37-9 Jl '77
Ford-MITRE study: nuclear power yes, plutonium no. W. D. Metz. Science 196:41 Ap 1 '77
How to have nuclear power without weapons proliferation. R. Wilson. bibl il por Bull Atom Sci 33:39-44 N '77
Letter from Washington. R. Rovere. New Yorker 53:54-8 Ja 2 '78
News conference of Secretary Vance and Secretary Blumenthal, May 8. C. R. Vance and W. M. Blumenthal. Dept State Bull 76:586-93 Je 6 '77
Nuclear energy. G. Present. il Sci Digest 82:20-5 O '77
Nuclear energy: paradise deferred; symposium. il Sat R 4:6-10+ Ja 22 '77; Discussion. 4:5 Mr 19 '77
Nuclear moratorium: study claims that effects would be modest, foresees low growth rate for total energy demand. A. L. Hammond. Science 195:156-7 Ja 14 '77; Discussion. 195:634-6 F 18 '77
Nuclear power policy issues; recommendations of the Nuclear Energy Policy Study Group, Ford Foundation. K. H. Hohenemser. Environment 19:3-5 Ag '77
Nuclear power: promise or peril? il Sr Schol 109:3-5+ Ja 27 '77
Nuclear power without nuclear proliferation; address, October 3, 1977. J. S. Nye, Jr. Dept State Bull 77:666-71 N 14 '77
Power play. G. Hill; discussion. Nat Wildlife 15:38-9 F '77
President Carter announces decisions on nuclear power policy; statement, and remarks, with transcript of question and answer session, April 7, 1977. J. Carter. Dept State Bull 76:429-33 My 2 '77
Putting brakes on the fast breeder; J. Carter's policy on plutonium recycling. il Time 109:57 Ap 18 '77
Science in Europe: Carter nuclear policy finds few friends. N. Hawkes. Science 196:1067 Je 3 '77
Selling the nuclear faith; campaign by Edison Electric Institute. Progressive 41:22 S '77
Six views of atomic energy; symposium. bibl il pors Bull Atom Sci 33:59-69 Mr '77
Time to plan for the next generation of nuclear technology. J. S. Nye. il Bull Atom Sci 33:38-41 O '77
U.S. nuclear power may be on the wrong track. D. Ediger and A. Parisi. il Bus W p 142-3 Ap 18 '77
United States policy on nuclear technology: combining energy and security; address, May 2, 1977. J. S. Nye, Jr. Dept State Bull 76:550-4 My 30 '77
Unreal thinking about energy. J. Selbin. Bull Atom Sci 33:54-5 S '77
War against the atom. S. McCracken. bibl f Commentary 64:33-47 S '77; Discussion. 64:4+ D '77
We must move forward with all deliberate speed; report of the IAEA director-general. S. Eklund. il Bull Atom Sci 33:42-7 O '77
Why the nagging doubts about atomic power. J. McWethy. il U.S. News 83:88 S 19 '77
See also
Nuclear fuels
Nuclear fusion
Nuclear reactors
Underdeveloped areas—Atomic power

Bibliography

Battle of the books. W. Likely. Sat R 4:31 Ja 22 '77

Economic aspects

Nuclear energy on the dole. B. L. Welch. Nation 224:231-5 F 26 '77

Environmental aspects

Mind control, the Edison Electric way. M. Zeldin. Audubon 79:115-17 Jl '77
Nuclear game; Energy-Environment Game distributed by Edison Electric Institute. il Progressive 41:10 N '77

Insurance

See Insurance, Atomic hazards

International aspects

Carter's nuclear policy: running into trouble. J. McWethy. il U.S. News 83:51-2 Jl 4 '77
Fizzle in Carter's anti-atom blast. Bus W p30 My 23 '77
How the genie got out of the bottle. T. Szulc. Forbes 119:89-91 My 15 '77
Nuclear proliferation: prospects, problems, and proposals; symposium, ed by J. I. Coffey. il Ann Am Acad 430:1-174 Mr '77
Promise and the curse. T. C. Schelling. il Sat R 4:16-20 Ja 22 '77
Reasons U.S. may not be no. 1 in nuclear energy much longer. J. McWethy. il map U.S. News 83:52-4+ Jl 11 '77
Third World's critical mass. K. Bird and D. Berick. Nation 224:236-8 F 26 '77
U.S. Canada exchange notes on nuclear cooperation; November 15, 1977. Dept State Bull 77:857 D 12 '77
Why Pakistan is uneasy about U.S. as an ally; with interview with Z. A. Bhutto, ed by J. N. Wallace. il map U.S. News 82:70-2 Mr 14 '77
See also
International Atomic Energy Agency

International control

Reducing the incentives to proliferation. G. H. Quester. Ann Am Acad 430:70-81 Mr '77
Safeguards against diversion of nuclear material: an overview. R. Imai. Ann Am Acad 430:58-69 Mr '77

Laws and regulations

Nonproliferation Act: a vote for apple pie. Sci N 112:231 O 8 '77
Nuclear cost of regulatory delay; controversy surrounding construction of power plant in Seabrook, N.H. il Bus W p22-3 Ja 24 '77
Nuclear energy and the ballot. J. N. Barkenbus. il Bull Atom Sci 33:4-5 Ap '77
Nuclear licensing: promised reform miffs all sides of nuclear debate. W. D. Metz. Science 198:590-3 N 11 '77
Paralysis on the Potomac. J. C. Sawhill. Sat R 4:19-20 Ja 22 '77
Program to contain nuclear knowhow. Bus W p31 Ap 11 '77
Speeding up the nuclear plants; Nuclear Regulatory Reform Act. il Time 110:30-1 S 5 '77
States OK nuclear power, but. . . Sci Digest 81:86 F '77
Unlimited nuclear risk; liability limits set by the Price-Anderson Act. A. S. Miller. Progressive 41:8-9 Jl '77

Security measures

Nuclear power: will it produce a world of Saturday night specials? address, June 30, 1977. C. B. Yulish. Vital Speeches 43:645-8 Ag 15 '77
Real nuclear terrorists; a study by the NRC. Progressive 41:7 Ap '77

Terminology

Nuclear primer. W. Likely. Sat R 4:8 Ja 22 '77

Brazil

Brazil's nuclear program: Carter's nonproliferation policy backfires. A. L. Hammond. Science 195:657-9 F 18 '77

Canada

Why nuclear energy! address, June 17, 1977. R. F. Shaw. Vital Speeches 43:648-51 Ag 15 '77

Europe, Western

Anti-nuclear ferment in Europe. W. Hines. Progressive 41:19-21 S '77
Crusading against the atom. il Time 109:48+ Ap 25 '77
Europe's nuclear disappointment. D. Yergin. New Repub 178:13-16 Ja 7 '78
Opposition to nuclear power in Europe. W. Sweet. bibl f il map Bull Atom Sci 33:40-7 D '77
Science in Europe: the antinuclear movement takes hold. N. Hawkes. Science 197:1167-9 S 16 '77
Waste, plutonium, breeders—three ways Europe is moving ahead. il U.S. News 83:55 Jl 11 '77

ATOMIC power—*Continued*

France

Clash at Super Phénix. il Time 110:31 Ag 15 '77
France gains on US in nuclear-power generation and trade. H. L. Davis. il Phys Today 30:101+ Mr '77
French antinuclear forces get rough. il Bus W p64 Jl 25 '77
Giscard's quandary. R. Chelminski. Sat R 4:28-9 Ja 22 '77
Reprocessing race. il Time 111:22 Ja 9 '78

Germany, West

Case of the bugged physicist; Verfassungsschutz' bugging of K. R. Traube's home. il por Time 109:28 Mr 14 '77

Great Britain

Are nukes cricket? B. Wicker. Commonweal 104:708-10 N 11 '77
Nuclear underground. W. C. Patterson. Environment 19:20+ My '77
Science in Europe: Mr Justice Parker and plutonium. N. Hawkes. Science 197:141-3 Jl 8 '77

India

Underappreciated India. N. Eberstadt. New Repub 176:14-16 Ja 15 '77

Israel

Mystery of Israel's bomb: investigation of missing uranium from processing plant in Apollo, Pa. D. Martin. il por Newsweek 91:26-7 Ja 9 '78

Japan

Made in Japan. D. Kirk. Sat R 4:24 Ja 22 '77

South Africa

Friend in need; Israeli cooperation. K. Willenson and others. il Newsweek 90:44 S 12 '77
Halting Pretoria's A-test. Newsweek 90:36 S 5 '77

ATOMIC power in motion pictures. See Motion pictures—Plots, themes, etc.

ATOMIC power industry

Boom gone bust. A. J. Mayer and W. J. Cook. il Newsweek 90:65-6 O 31 '77
Industry hides from the sun. H. Wasserman. il Nation 224:263-6 Mr 5 '77
Nuclear power—where do we go from here? P. W. Sturm. Forbes 119:91-2 My 15 '77
Persistent shortage of reactor orders. Bus W p62+ D 12 '77
See also
Reactor fuel reprocessing

Export-import trade

Nuclear exporters cartel. M. Mandelbaum. bibl il Bull Atom Sci 33:42-50 Ja '77
Secretary Vance discusses antiboycott legislation and nuclear nonproliferation; statement, March 1, 1977. C. R. Vance. Dept State Bull 76:267-71 Mr 21 '77
U.S. nuclear exports to South Africa; statement, July 12, 1977. J. S. Nye, Jr. Dept State Bull 77:236-41 Ag 22 '77

Federal aid

Nuclear energy on the dole. B. L. Welch. Nation 224:231-5 F 26 '77
Reactors that can sub for the fast breeder. il Bus W p24 Ag 8 '77

Germany, West

West Germany: twin clouds over the nuclear industry. il Bus W p36 Mr 7 '77

Great Britain

Setback for plutonium; British Nuclear Fuels, Limited. W. C. Patterson. Environment 19:41-3 Mr '77

ATOMIC power plants

Lead times. Sci Am 237:56 Jl '77
Mystery of Israel's bomb; investigation of missing uranium from processing plant in Apollo, Pa. D. Martin. il por Newsweek 91:26-7 Ja 9 '78
Nuclear energy expert; C. Reed. il pors Ebony 32:64-6+ Je '77
Nuclear partners: adversity breeds trouble between Dow and utility. L. J. Carter. Science 195:162-3 Ja 14 '77
Nuclear power plants: why do some work better than others? D. Shapley. Science 195:1311-13 Mr 25 '77
Offshore reactors: where not to put the nuke. L. Light. il Nation 225:205-8 S 10 '77
Outrageous Mr Cherry and the underachieving nukes; controversy surrounding construction of nuclear power plant in Midland, Mich. F. Graham, Jr. il por Audubon 79:50-67 S '77; Discussion. 79:128-30 N '77
Seabrook stalemate. H. Wasserman. Progressive 41:41 My '77
War against the atom. S. McCracken. bibl f Commentary 64:33-47 S '77; Discussion. 64:4+ D '77
See also
Radioactive waste disposal

Accidents

Unlimited nuclear risk; liability limits set by the Price-Anderson Act. A. S. Miller. Progressive 41:8-9 Jl '77

Anecdotes, facetiae, satire, etc.

Johnny Carson sets us straight; excerpt from monologue. J. Carson. Nation 224:746 Je 18 '77

Environmental aspects

Public health hazards from electricity-producing plants. J. Neyman. bibl il Science 195:754-8 F 25 '77

Laws and regulations

See Atomic power—Laws and regulations

Location

Indiana Dunes: another border to defend; proposed location of the Bailly nuclear power plant. T. L. Erwin. il map Nat Parks & Con Mag 51:4-7 O '77
Nuclear cost of regulatory delay; controversy surrounding construction of power plant in Seabrook, N.H. il Bus W p22-3 Ja 24 '77
Second chance for floating reactors; Offshore Power Systems. map Bus W p31+ Ap 25 '77

Protests, demonstrations, etc. against

Anti-nuclear ferment in Europe. W. Hines. Progressive 41:19-21 S '77
Clamshell Alliance: getting it together; Seabrook plant. H. Wasserman. Progressive 41:14-18 S '77
Clamshell reaction; protest against atomic power plant at Seabrook, N.H. by Clamshell Alliance. H. Wasserman. Nation 224:744-9 Je 18 '77
Clash at Super Phénix. il Time 110:31 Ag 15 '77
Confrontation at Seabrook; Clamshell Alliance. H. Wasserman. Progressive 41:11-12 Jl '77
Counterattack for Seabrook. il Time 110:80 Jl 11 '77
Fault at Diablo Canyon. T. W. Speers and P. von Loewenfeldt. Nation 225:333-6 O 8 '77
France kills its first protester; Malville actions. A. Gyorgy. Nation 225:330-3 O 8 '77
French antinuclear forces get rough. il Bus W p64 Jl 25 '77
Hiroshima remembered. H. Wasserman. Progressive 41:8 O '77
No-nuke movement. D. A. Williams and others. il Newsweek 89:25-6 My 23 '77
Opposition to nuclear power in Europe. W. Sweet. bibl f il map Bull Atom Sci 33:40-7 D '77
Resistance nears a critical mass. H. Wasserman. Nation 225:328-30 O 8 '77
Seabrook saga; Clamshell Alliance. E. Keerdoja and P. Malamud. Newsweek 91:5 Ja 2 '78
Siege of Seabrook. il Time 109:59 My 16 '77

Safety devices and measures

Massing at the grass roots. R. M. Williams. Sat R 4:14+ Ja 22 '77
Special report: the dangers of nuclear power. R. Nader; reply with rejoinder. B. L. Cohen. Fam Health 9:52-3 Ja '77

Security measures

Nuclear sabotage. M. Flood; reply J. Penkrot. Bull Atom Sci 33:6 Ja '77

France

France kills its first protester; Malville actions. A. Gyorgy. Nation 225:330-3 O 8 '77

ATOMIC power plants (space vehicles) See Space vehicles—Atomic power plants

ATOMIC powered submarine boats. See Submarine boats, Atomic powered

ATOMIC powered warships. See Warships, Atomic powered

ATOMIC research

Europe, Western

See also
European Organization for Nuclear Research

ATOMIC research laboratories

Converting the weapons labs; U.C. Weapons Lab Conversion Project. S. H. Day, Jr. Bull Atom Sci 33:27 Ja '77
ERDA laboratories: Los Alamos attracts some special attention. J. Walsh. Science 196:743-5 My 13 '77
Nuclear weapons labs; Los Alamos and Lawrence Livermore laboratories. S. H. Day, Jr. il Bull Atom Sci 33:21-6 Ap '77
See also
National Accelerator Laboratory

ATOMIC security measures. See Atomic power—Security measures

ATOMIC submarines. See Submarine boats, Atomic powered

ATOMIC warfare

Aposematic statement on nuclear war: ultraviolet radiation in the postattack environment. E. E. Koslow. bibl BioScience 27:409-13 Je '77

ATOMIC warfare—*Continued*
Farewell. S. H. Day, Jr. Bull Atom Sci 33:4-5 D '77
Have we learned to think in a new way? M. A. Markov. il Bull Atom Sci 33:20-3 N '77
Monologue on an unpopular theme. K. C. Turkisher. Bull Atom Sci 33:48-51 F '77
Mounting prospects of nuclear war. F. Barnaby. il Bull Atom Sci 33:10-20 Je '77
Nuclear dilemma revisited. B. T. Feld. Bull Atom Sci 33:7 F '77
Nuclear proliferation: prospects, problems, and proposals; symposium, ed by J. I. Coffey. il Ann Am Acad 430:1-174 Mr '77
Obsession with nuclear strategy. A. Wolfe. Nation 225:265-8 S 24 '77
Some nuclear explosions will be necessary. B. Stewart. Bull Atom Sci 33:51-4 O '77
Surprise attack by Russia: still unthinkable? with interview with H. Brown. R. Kelly. il U.S. News 83:18-24 S 5 '77
See also
Civil defense

Defenses

Brown on deterrence; excerpts from address, March 1975. H. Brown. Science 195:465 F 4 '77
Dangerous delusion. E. R. Zumwalt, Jr. il pors Sat Eve Post 249:12-14 N '77
U.S. strategic forces; address, March 16, 1977. R. E. Dougherty. Vital Speeches 43:584-90 Jl 15 '77
Why the Soviet Union thinks it could fight and win a nuclear war. R. E. Pipes. bibl f Commentary 64:21-34 Jl '77; Discussion. 64:4+ S '77
See also
Russia—Defenses
United States—Defenses

Ethical aspects

Lest we forget:
Challenge of the century. A. Kastler. por Bull Atom Sci 33:20-2 S '77
New morality for a new world. S. MacBride. por Bull Atom Sci 33:22-3 S '77
Peace or oblivion? P. J. Noel-Baker. por Bull Atom Sci 33:18-20 S '77

ATOMIC wastes. See Radioactive wastes

ATOMIC weapons
Arsenal of democracy; excerpt from Arsenal for democracy: a catalogue of American weapons. T. Gervasi. il Harpers 254:68-9 Je '77
Carter and the new weapons. Nat R 29:868 Ag 5 '77
Congress unit urges shift in European nuclear arms. E. Kozicharow. Aviation W 106:18 Ja 17 '77
Hiroshima echo. W. G. Kelsey. il Progressive 41:28-30 N '77
Mounting prospects of nuclear war. F. Barnaby. il Bull Atom Sci 33:10-20 Je '77
Nine nuclear weapons devices scheduled for U.S. production. Aviation W 106:97 Je 20 '77
Nuclear power: will it produce a world of Saturday night specials? address, June 30, 1977. C. B. Yulish. Vital Speeches 43:645-8 Ag 15 '77
Of weapons and strategy. Nat R 29:815-16 Jl 22 '77
Time to bury deterrence. W. Epstein. Bull Atom Sci 33:6-7 Je '77
Toward nuclear stability. E. C. Ravenal. Atlantic 240:35-41 S '77
Western alliance seeks to update nuclear capability. D. A. Brown. il maps Aviation W 107:12-15 Ag 1 '77
See also
Guided missiles

International control

See Atomic weapons and disarmament

Protests, demonstrations, etc. against

Dan Berrigan in Santa Cruz. C. Fager. Chr Cent 94:654-7 Jl 20 '77

Testing, Suspension of

Anti-test-ban coalition. J. Pomerance. bibl Bull Atom Sci 33:51-4 Ja '77
Banning the test bomb. Sci Am 236:52 Ap '77
Carter appointments: fresh moves on sea law, arms control. D. Shapley. Science 195:560-2 F 11 '77
Congress concerned by test ban talks. Aviation W 108:54+ Ja 9 '78
Display of anniversary amity; Russian test ban treaty proposal. il Time 110:34-5 N 14 '77
Half a loaf can be worse; question of limited test ban. Progressive 41:5-6 My '77
Hidden issues behind a nuclear-test ban. R. K. Bennett. Read Digest 111:124-8 S '77
Nuclear test ban: a dangerous anachronism. S. T. Cohen and W. R. Van Cleave. Nat R 29:770-5 Jl 8 '77
Nuclear test halt under study. C. A. Robinson, Jr. Aviation W 106:12-13 F 21 '77
Progress and problems in arms control negotiations; address, September 19, 1977. P. C. Warnke. Dept State Bull 77:772-7 N 28 '77
Test ban talks scrutiny urged. E. Kozicharow. Aviation W 107:12-13 N 21 '77
Why not stop testing? J. C. Hopkins. por Bull Atom Sci 33:30-1 Ap '77

ATOMIC weapons and disarmament
Arms and the man; views of H. Brown. M. Greenfield. Newsweek 89:88 Mr 28 '77
Arms race: a call to action. Bull Atom Sci 33:6 N '77
Arms race: a primer. S. Lens. Progressive 41:37-42 O '77; Same. il Current 197:50-61 N '77
Can Carter stop the arms race? special report. W. Laqueur; R. Barnet; G. C. Smitn. N Y Times Mag p 15-19+ F 27 '77
Carter and Brezhnev: the game begins. il por Time 109:40-2 F 7 '77
Defense planning and arms control; address, April 13, 1977. H. Brown. Vital Speeches 43:460-3 My 15 '77
Disarmament scoreboard. H. A. Jack. Bull Atom Sci 33:54-8 Mr '77
$49.50 cruise missile and another moratorium. Nat R 29:1097 S 30 '77
Hard-nosed idealism: a model for disarmament. G. S. Weigel, Jr. America 137:186-8 O 1 '77
Have we learned to think in a new way? M. A. Markov. il Bull Atom Sci 33:20-3 N '77
Heroine among the last survivors; A. Myrdal. C. L. Mee, Jr. il por Horizon 19:90-2 Mr '77
Hope and a goal; views of J. Carter. Nation 224:130 F 5 '77
How to have nuclear power without weapons proliferation. R. Wilson. bibl il por Bull Atom Sci 33:39-44 N '77
Human rights: conflicts among our ideals; excerpts from address, June 5, 1977. D. Riesman. Commonweal 104:711-15 N 11 '77
Lest we forget:
Challenge of the century. A. Kastler. por Bull Atom Sci 33:20-2 S '77
New morality for a new world. S. MacBride. por Bull Atom Sci 33:22-3 S '77
Peace or oblivion? P. J. Noel-Baker. por Bull Atom Sci 33:18-20 S '77
Limits of non-proliferation. T. C. Schelling. New Repub 176:38-40 Ja 22 '77
Mutual deterrence: the need for a new definition. B. G. Lall. Bull Atom Sci 33:10-11 D '77
Nuclear arms control and disarmament; report of Pugwash Conference. Bull Atom Sci 33:33-4 D '77
Nuclear arms reduction; address, October 4, 1977. J. Carter. Vital Speeches 44:2-5 O 15 '77; Same. Dept State Bull 77:547-52 O 24 '77
Nuclear issue and international security. K. Subrahmanyam. il Bull Atom Sci 33:17-21 F '77
Nuclear nonproliferation policy act of 1977 transmitted to the Congress; message, with White House fact sheet, April 27, 1977. Dept State Bull 76:477-80 My 16 '77
Nuclear proliferation: prospects, problems, and proposals; symposium, ed by J. I. Coffey. il Ann Am Acad 430:1-174 Mr '77
Nuclear South Pacific: can it be averted? J. F. McCahon and M. K. Robertson. il Bull Atom Sci 33:26-7 Ap '77
Planning a safeguardable nuclear future; address, June 30, 1977. J. S. Nye, Jr. Dept State Bull 77:183-90 Ag 8 '77
Politics of arms control: President Carter's proposals. R. J. Bresler. Intellect 105:392-3 Je '77
President Carter interviewed by AP and UPI correspondents; excerpts from transcript of interview, January 23, 1977. J. Carter. Dept State Bull 76:123-5 F 14 '77
President Carter's news conference of February 8. J. Carter. Dept State Bull 76:157-60 F 28 '77
President signs Latin America nuclear free zone treaty; Tlatelolco treaty; remarks, May 26, 1977. Dept State Bull 77:10 Jl 4 '77
Proposed modifications to nonproliferation legislation; statement, September 13, 1977. S. M. Keeny, Jr. Dept State Bull 77:671-3 N 14 '77
Prospects for human rights; adaptation of address, June 5, 1977. D. Riesman. bibl il Society 15:28-33 N '77
Review conference calls for consideration of further measures to halt arms race on sea-bed. il UN Chron 14:18-19 Jl '77
Russians are coming—again. G. McGovern. Progressive 41:17-23 My '77
Secretary Vance discusses antiboycott legislation and nuclear nonproliferation; statement, March 1, 1977. C. R. Vance. Dept State Bull 76:267-71 Mr 21 '77
Signal to the Soviets—and to Carter; excerpts from interview. P. Warnke. il por Time 109:28 Mr 21 '77
Slowing the arms race. H. Scoville, Jr. Bull Atom Sci 33:4-5 S '77
Terrifying prospect: atomic bombs everywhere. D. Yergin. il Atlantic 239:46-9+ Ap '77
U.S.-U.S.S.R. communique on antiballistic missile systems; treaty review, November 21, 1977. Dept State Bull 77:856 D 12 '77

ATOMIC weapons and disarmament—*Continued*
Way to begin is to stop. B. T. Feld. Bull Atom Sci 33:9 Mr '77
Why weapons make poor bargaining chips. R. C. Gray and R. J. Bresler. Bull Atom Sci 33:8-9 S '77
See also
Atomic weapons—Testing, Suspension of
Strategic Arms Limitation Talks
United States—Arms Control and Disarmament Agency

History

Reporter at large. E. Drew. New Yorker 53:99-117 Ap 4 '77

ATOMIC weapons in motion pictures. See Motion pictures—Plots, themes, etc.

ATOMS
See also
Neutrons

ATONEMENT
Brokenness and wholeness; Jesus Christ. E. Schaeffer. Chr Today 21:27+ Mr 4 '77

ATRIUM houses. See Architecture, Domestic

ATRIUMS
Impressive new government center around a grand atrium space; Hennepin County Government Center, Minneapolis. il Archit Rec 161:101-6 Mr '77

ATTACK dogs. See Watchdogs

ATTACK on Pearl Harbor. See Pearl Harbor, Attack on, 1941

ATTENTION
Why fun is fun; flow experience. W. B. Furlong. Read Digest 110:140-2 My '77
See also
Listening

ATTIC insulation. See Insulation (heat)

ATTIC ventilators. See Ventilators

ATTICA prison. See Prisons—New York (state)

ATTICS
Super scheme for attic storage. T. H. Jones. il Mech Illus 73:70+ Ap '77

Caricatures and cartoons

Cleaning the attic. S. Berenstain and J. Berenstain. il Good H 185:168+ S '77

ATTITUDE change
Energy behavior. P. C. Stern and E. M. Kirkpatrick. bibl il Environment 19:10-15 D '77
So, you don't change your mind . . . much? attitudes of Americans toward other nations. il Sr Schol 109:18 Mr 10 '77

ATTITUDES
See also
Aged—Attitudes
Black women—Attitudes
Children—Attitudes
College teachers—Attitudes
Employees—Attitudes
Farmers—Attitudes
Political attitudes
Public opinion
Stereotype (psychology)
Students—Attitudes
Women—Attitudes
Youth—Attitudes

Testing

See Psychological tests

ATTMORE, Toni
How we got started in the herb business. il por Org Gard & Farm 24:85-7 N '77

ATTORNEYS. See Lawyers

ATTRACTING of birds. See Birds, Attracting of

ATTUCKS, Crispus, Memorial Monument. See Boston—Monuments, statues, etc.

ATWOOD, Cap
Bear of a man. B. Brady. il por Outdoor Life 159:88-9+ My '77 *

ATWOOD, John Leland
Atwood-Kindelberger. J. A. Slocum. il Flying 101:251 S '77 *

ATWOOD, Margaret
Once I could move; poem. Mademoiselle 83:142 Jl '77

ATWOOD, R. K.
Plug-in remote ringer. il Radio-Electr 48:45-8 N '77

AUBURN (historic house) Natchez. See Historic houses, sites, etc.—Mississippi

AUBURN Dam (proposed) See Dams

AUCTIONS
Auction time at the ACLU. W. F. Buckley, Jr. Nat R 29:845 Jl 22 '77
Bluegrass auctions for bluebloods; Keeneland and Fasig-Tipton Select Summer Yearling Sales. il Time 110:68-9 Ag 1 '77
Bluegrass dreams; race horse sales. P. Axthelm. il Newsweek 90:66-7 Ag 1 '77
Breeding stock demand reflects new optimism; National Western cattle auction. W. Kester. il Farm J 101:LK2-3 Ap '77
Carnations from Kenya . . .; flower auctions in Holland. il Forbes 120:115-16 N 15 '77
Death of a salesman; auctioning off the contents of all Robert Hall outlets. L. Langway and M. Reese. il Newsweek 90:64 Ag 15 '77
Finding bargains at auctions & flea markets. T. Pyle. il Mech Illus 73:76-8 Ag '77
Going, going. . ; condominium auction. il por Forbes 119:74 Ja 15 '77
How to buy at a farm auction. K. P. Maize. il Org Gard & Farm 24:114-18 My '77
I decorated this room at auctions: learn from a master the winning techniques. P. R. Jackson. il House & Gard 149:132-5+ Ap '77
Navajo rug auction in New Mexico. il Sunset 159:48 N '77
Not-so-simple case of larceny; automobile auctions fraud. R. J. Gottlieb. Motor T 29:64-5 Mr '77
Sell livestock on big screen; videotaped cattle auction. il Farm J 100:LK2 D '76
Souvenirs; pier auction of surplus equipment, New York City. New Yorker 53:29-30 Ap 25 '77
Telephone feeder pig auction: a marketing hot line. R. Brunoehler. il Suc Farm 75:47 D '77
Up: record auction prices. il Horizon 19:39 My '77
View point; photographic auctioneer and dealer; interview, ed by J. Deschin. D. Stulz. il por Pop Phot 81:117+ Ag '77
See also
Art sales

AUDEN, Wystan Hugh
Auden and W. B. Yeats. E. T. Callan. pors Commonweal 104:298-303 My 13 '77 *
Comment. D. Lehman. Poetry 131:159-64 D '77 *

AUDI (automobile) See Automobiles, Foreign

AUDIENCES
At last, opera makes it big with U.S. audiences. il U.S. News 82:64-6 Ap 18 '77
From the inside: on curtain time; audience's enjoyment of a performance. M. Louis. Dance Mag 51:102-3 Ap '77
Little man at Chehaw Station: the American artist and his audience. R. Ellison. Am Scholar 47:25-48 Wint '77
See also
Television audiences

AUDIO amplifiers. See Amplifiers

AUDIO distortion. See Audio systems—Noise

AUDIO engineering
In the loudspeaker testing lab; measurement techniques. E. Torick. il Hi Fi 27:69-73 O '77
See also
Computers—Audio engineering use
Sound—Recording and reproducing

Study and teaching

Careers in audio: choosing a course. S. Traiman. il Hi Fi 27:134-7 Jl '77

AUDIO equipment industry

Germany, West

Mysterious West. R. Hodges. il Pop Electr 12:20+ D '77

United States

Audio sales make store owners hum. il Bus W p42 Ag 15 '77
Boston: hub city of American audio. M. Riggs. il Hi Fi 27:79-83 Mr '77
Super-speaker; AudioPlate produced by Barcus-Berry, Inc. T. Nicholson and others. il Newsweek 89:71-2 Je 6 '77
Why Maremont is going after Pemcor; success of Pemcor's Jensen Sound Laboratories. Bus W p94 Ag 29 '77
See also
Harman International Industries, Inc

History

High fidelity pathfinders. See issues of High fidelity and Musical America

AUDIO generators. See Signal generators

AUDIO Plate speakers. See Loudspeakers

AUDIO systems
Audio '78. H. A. Rodgers and R. Long. il Hi Fi 27:74-84 S '77
From bits into pieces; digital technology and audio systems. I. Berger. il Sat R 4:32-3 Jl 23 '77
Hi-fi components that think. L. Feldman. il Esquire 88:122-4+ N '77
How to match hi-fi components. il Pop Electr 11:66-8+ My '77
Julian Hirsch audio reports. J. Hirsch. See issues of Popular electronics including Electronics world
Sea sounds; shipboard stereo. il Motor B & S 140:75-7 O '77
Special focus on audio. il Pop Electr 12:57-72 S '77
Stereo scene. R. Hodges. See issues of Popular electronics including Electronics world
What next in high fidelity? J. Hirsch. il Pop Electr 12:23-4+ D '77
See also names of audio system components, e.g. Loudspeakers

AUDIO systems—*Continued*

Control

Loudness control—boon or bane? J. Hirsch. il Pop Electr 13:24-6 Ja '78

Equipment

Build AM/FM frequency display. G. McClellan. il Radio-Electr 49:21-4+ Ja '78
Build the hi-fi/tv audio-minder. C. Kobylarz. il Pop Electr 11:41-4 Ap '77
Build the Phlanger for dramatic music effects. M. Jones. il Radio-Electr 48:42-5+ O '77
Equipment in the news. See issues of High fidelity and Musical America
Gadgets that turn your hi-fi off for you. W. Kanner. il Pop Mech 147:48 Mr '77
IC multiplex decoder improves stereo FM performance. M. Meyer. il Pop Electr 12:67-71 S '77
New equipment reports:
Audio-Technica acoustic insulators. il Hi Fi 27:53 Ap '77
New products at half time. R. Long and H. A. Rodgers. il Hi Fi 27:60-5 My '77
1/2-octave real time audio analyzer. B. Jones and R. Marsh. il Pop Electr 12:47-54 S; 66-9 O '77
Shape of sounds to come. C. Graham. il Am Rec G 40:48 N '76; 56-7 Mr '77
Soundwise. C. Graham. See issues of American record guide
To reduce unwanted sounds; Acousti-Mount Speaker-pods. il Am Rec G 40:53-4 O '77
Upgrade your aging stereo; replacing old components. Changing T 32:11-12 Ja '78

Exhibitions

Hi-fi: fair values. H. Fantel. Opera N 42:66-7 S '77
1977 Multi-Track Expo. J. Woram. il Hi Fi 27:109 Ag '77

Noise

Dynamic noise reduction systems and expanders. W. S. Gordon. il Pop Electr 12:60-2 S '77
Get the noise out of your system. R. Long and H. A. Rodgers. il Hi Fi 27:64-9 Jl '77
Most improbable noise suppressor; Transient Noise Suppressor. Hi Fi 27:27 Ag '77
Much ado about noise (title varies) C. Graham. il Am Rec G 40:52+ Mr; 44-6 Ag '77
New equipment reports:
Crosswinds' rumble filter. Hi Fi 27:52-3 Ap '77
Smart black box from Heath: AD-1304 Active Audio Processor. il Hi Fi 28:54 Ja '78
Noise filtering for hi-fi. J. Hirsch. il Pop Electr 12:32-3 Jl '77
Noise reduction: choosing your options. J. Woram. Hi Fi 27:110 My '77

Purchasing

Basics of buying hi-fi components. il Pop Electr 12:57-9 S '77
Hi fi: sound dollar '77. H. Fantel. il Opera N 42:64-5 N '77
Shopping guide for hi-fi components. il Consumer Rep 42:207-15 D '77
Stereo, hi-fi. Consumers Res Mag 60:183-93 O '77
Upgrade your aging stereo; replacing old components. Changing T 32:11-12 Ja '78

Terminology

Glossary of audio terms. Consumer Rep 42:211-12 D '77

Testing

Compact stereo systems. il Consumer Rep 42:265-9 My '77
New equipment reports. See issues of High fidelity and Musical America

Tuning

Hi-fi: at the frontier. H. Fantel. Opera N 42:32-3 D 17 '77

AUDIO systems, Portable
Quality portables for vacation entertainment. S. Traiman. il Hi Fi 27:66-70 My '77

AUDIO technicians. See Electronic technicians

AUDIO-visual equipment
Students teach teachers. C. Buchanan. SLJ 24:39 D '77

Purchasing

Purchase AV equipment with care. H. Deutsch. SLJ 23:48 Ap '77

AUDIO-visual instruction
See also
School libraries and audio-visual materials
Video recorders and recording—Educational use

AUDIO-visual materials
Earth's greatest hits; audio-visual record on Voyager. A. Druyan and T. Ferris. N Y Times Mag p 12-13 S 4 '77
Resource materials. B. Wasserman. See issues of School arts
World on a record; audio-visual recording on Voyager flights. J. Eberhart. il Sci N 112:124-5 Ag 20 '77
See also
Filmstrips
Filmstrips in religious education
Instructional materials centers
Language arts—Study and teaching—Aids and devices
Libraries and audio-visual materials
Motion pictures in education

AUDIO-visual materials, Bibliographical control of. See Bibliographical control

AUDIO-visual script authorship
Audiovisual writing: a world beyond words. A. Amenta. Writers Digest 57:19-25 Je '77

AUDIOMETRY
Auditory evoked potentials as probes of hemispheric differences in cognitive processing. D. W. Shucard and others. bibl il Science 197:1295-8 S 23 '77

AUDITING
See also
Disclosure in accounting
Tax auditing
United States—General Accounting Office

AUDITIONS, Opera. See Singing—Competitions

AUDITORIUMS
See also
Concert halls

AUDITORY system (animals) See Hearing (animals)

AUDITORY system (birds) See Hearing (birds)

AUDUBON, John James
Bird watcher nonpareil. il Sat Eve Post 249:16 Jl '77

about

Audubon on the wing; with reproductions of paintings. D. Jeffery. il por Nat Geog 151:148-77 F '77 *
Maria Martin: the brush behind Audubon's birds. M. Williams and P. Elliott. il Ms 5:14-15+ Ap '77 *

AUDUBON (periodical)
For reporting excellence—again. Audubon 79:146 Jl '77

AUDUBON Mobile Environmental Education Project. See Environmental education

AUDUBON prints. See Birds in art

AUDUBON societies
See also
Michigan Audubon Society
National Audubon Society

AUERBACH, Red
Dreams of Celtic pride. P. Axthelm. il por Newsweek 90:79 N 28 '77

AUERBACH, Robert
How to clean & care for your skin; interview. Mademoiselle 83:174-7 Ag '77

AUERBACH, Stevanne
All about day care. il Parents Mag 52:40-1+ Ap '77
Preschool push to independence. il por Parents Mag 52:33+ D '77

AUERBACH, Sylvia
More than money. See issues of American home

AUERHAHN shooting. See Grouse shooting

AUFDERHEIDE, Karl J.
Saltatory motility of uninserted trichocysts and mitochondria in paramecium tetraurelia. bibl il Science 198:299-300 O 21 '77

AUGERS
Auger ideas for versatile grain handling. il Suc Farm 75:50 D '77
3 augers that take the backwork out of moving grain. il Farm J 101:D4 Mr '77

AUGUST
August '77; back-to-school calendar. il Seventeen 36:222-3 Ag '77

AUGUSTA National Golf Club course. See Golf courses

AUGUSTA Opera Company. See Opera—Georgia

AUGUSTINE, Saint
St Augustine: the Confessions. L. S. Cunningham. Chr Cent 94:166 F 23 '77; Reply. G. Eldredge. 94:547-9 Je 1 '77

AUKS
Green eggs by the thousands; collecting murre eggs on Walrus Island. V. B. Scheffer. il Audubon 79:112-13 S '77

AULENTI, Gae
Home and office: bridging the gap. R. Reif. il por N Y Times Mag p64-5 F 13 '77 *

AULETTA, Ken
Reporter at large. New Yorker 53:28-30+ Ag 1; 138 O 3 '77

AUMONT, Jean Pierre
Grace Kelly broke my heart; excerpt from Sun and shadow. Vogue 167:166+ My '77

AURORA, pseud
Horoscopes. See issues of Harper's bazaar

AURORA, Colo.

Recreation

See Recreation—Colorado

AURORA borealis. See Auroras

AURORAS
Aurora borealis: the greatest light show on earth. T. A. Potemra. il Smithsonian 7:64-70 bibl(p 152+) F '77
Auroras. C. Bain. il Conservationist 31:24-5 Ja '77
Auroras. R. G. Roble. il Natur Hist 86:60-7 bibl(p 122) O '77

AUSCHWITZ Concentration Camp. See Concentration camps—Germany

AUSTER, Albert
(ed) See Price, R. Studs Lonigan in the Bronx

AUSTIN, Debbie
If at first you don't succeed. B. McDermott. il por Sports Illus 47:80-1 Ag 29 '77 *

AUSTIN, Donald F. See Enstrom, J. E. jt auth

AUSTIN, Gerard
God's love for us. New Cath World 220:38 Ja '77

AUSTIN, James H.
How to make your luck work for you; excerpt from Chase, chance and creativity, the lucky art of novelty. il House & Gard 149:172+ N '77

AUSTIN, John Paul
Carter's chum from Coke. T. Nicholson and others. il por Newsweek 89:57-8 F 7 '77 *

AUSTIN, Michael. See Betten, N. jt auth

AUSTIN, Richard Cartwright
Three axioms for land use. il Chr Cent 94:910-11+ O 12 '77

AUSTIN, Tracy
First she curtsied, then she bowed. C. Kirkpatrick. il por Sports Illus 47:49-51 Jl 4 '77 *
Little Miss Ace. P. Axthelm. il por Newsweek 90:57 Jl 4 '77 *
90-pound net threat. K. Gilman. por Vogue 167:28+ Je '77 *
Tracy Austin: is she tennis' next Chris Evert? J. Kaplan. il pors Seventeen 36:176-7+ Ap '77 *

AUSTIN, Tex.

Crime

See Crime and criminals—Texas

Music

See Music—Texas

AUSTRALIA
See also
Art galleries and museums—Australia
Booksellers and bookselling—Australia
Bridges—Australia
Finance companies—Australia
Fishing—Australia
Geology—Australia
Music—Australia
Opera—Australia
Paleontology—Australia
Papua New Guinea
Publishers and publishing—Australia
Restaurants—Australia
Sydney, Australia
Telephone—Australia
Torres Strait

Anecdotes, facetiae, satire, etc.

Future doesn't work. B. Sloan. por Newsweek 90:15 S 19 '77

Description and travel

Australia. K. Boys. il Trav/Holiday 148:40+ D '77
Australia: Down Under is up. S. Train. il por map Vogue 167:284+ S '77

Economic conditions

Reports & comment: Australia: running out of luck. D. Warner. il Atlantic 240:26-31 O '77

Foreign relations

From Whitlam to Fraser. T. B. Millar. For Affairs 55:854-72 Jl '77

Industries

See also
Gas industry—Australia
Uranium industry—Australia

Nationalism

Republican sentiment in Australia. R. Mathias Chr Cent 94:630 Jl 6 '77

Politics and government

Reports & comment: Australia: running out of luck. D. Warner. il Atlantic 240:26-31 O '77
See also
Elections—Australia

Religious institutions and affairs

Passing of the old imperialisms. C. Northcott. Chr Cent 94:268-9 Mr 23 '77
See also
Church of England in Australia
Uniting Church in Australia

AUSTRALIAN Opera Company. See Opera—Australia

AUSTRIA
See also
Ballet—Austria
Civil service—Austria
Hunting—Austria
Music festivals—Austria
Opera—Austria
Publishers and publishing—Austria

Economic policy

Austerity: a way to avoid devaluation. il por Bus W p32-3 Ja 9 '78
See also
Wage-price policy—Austria

History

See also
Maria Theresa, Empress of Austria

Social conditions

Aging gracefully. C. Fenyvesi. New Repub 176:11-12 F 19 '77

Social life and customs

Great Austrian true-blue, down-on-the-farm Epiphany celebrations. K. Cure. il Holiday 57:22-3 N '76

AUTHORITY
Idea of authority in the West. L. Krieger. bibl f Am Hist R 82:249-70 Ap '77

AUTHORITY (religion)
See also
Bible—Evidence, authority, etc.
Catholic Church—Authority

AUTHORS
Biolines. il por Writers Digest 57:40-1 F; 30-1 Mr '77
Dead writers: a parable. S. Maloff. Commonweal 104:307-9 My 13 '77
From typographer to novelist: one man's experience in switching keyboards. E. Cantor. il Pub W 213:44+ Ja 2 '78
PW interviews. See issues of Publishers weekly
Portrait of the artist as an old man. L. Edel. Am Scholar 47:52-68 Wint '77
Why writers need islands. C. N. Parkinson. il Sat R 5:33-4 Ja 7 '78
Writer in his heavenly house. W. H. Scheib. Writer 90:27-9 Ja '77
Writer on the road. J. D. Vickery. il por Writers Digest 57:20 Ap '77
See also
Artists as authors
Authorship
Black authors
Copyright
Literary agents
Literature
Novelists
PEN Club
Poets
Prisoners as authors
Royalties
Women authors

Childrens literature

New generation of writers and artists brings fresh vision to children's books. J. F. Mercier. Pub W 211:99-100 F 28 '77

Civil rights

See Authors rights

Conferences

See Authors conferences

Photographs

Woman behind the credit: photo by Jill Krementz. D. K. Mano. il Esquire 87:16+ F '77

Psychology

Can a complete s.o.b. be a good writer? M. Cowley. il Esquire 88:120-1+ N '77

Salaries, allowances, etc.

See also
Authors—Taxation

Taxation

Authors League protests tax reform act inequities. S. Wagner. Pub W 212:19 D 5 '77
Little bit of haven; tax free Ireland. il Time 110:115-16 O 10 '77
Rates of spring. P. A. Fox. Writers Digest 57:20-1 Mr '77

Writing equipment

See Writing—Materials and instruments

AUTHORS, American
American writers: who's up, who's down? il Esquire 88:77-81 Ag '77
Questions they never asked me. W. Percy. il pors Esquire 88:170-2+ D '77
When writers meet; Soviet-American conference. N. Cousins. il Sat R 4:8-9+ S 17 '77
See also
American literature
Asimov, I
Beattie, A
Bellow, S.

AUTHORS, American—See also—*Continued*
Biggers, E. D.
Black authors
Capote, T.
Cheever, J.
Clemens, S. L.
Coolidge, D.
Dick, P. K.
Dramatists, American
Emerson, R. W.
Faulkner, W.
Fox, P.
Gifford, T.
Grey, Z.
Hemingway, E.
Irving, W.
Jackson, J. T.
Kotlowitz, R.
Lardner, R.
London, J.
Mano, D. K.
Mencken, H. L.
O'Connor, F.
Percy, W.
Rawlings, M. K.
Rhodes, E. M.
Sendak, M.
Southern, T.
Taylor, M. D.
Thoreau, H. D.
Tunis, J. R.
Vidal, G.
Williams, J.
Wilson, E.
Wolfe, T. K.

AUTHORS, Canadian
See also
Amiel, B.

AUTHORS, Czech
Writing on the party's terms. C. Sawyer. il Harpers 256:25+ Ja '78
See also
Kafka, F.

AUTHORS, English
See also
Carroll, L. pseud
English literature
Garner, A.
Greene, G.
Irving, D. J. C.
Johnson, S.
Lewis, C. S.
Nicholson, W.
Potter, B.
Richardson, S.
Sayers, D. L.
Tolkien, J. R. R.
Wilde, O.
Woolf, V. S.

AUTHORS, French
See also
Claudel, P.
Malraux, A.
Murger, H.
Weil, S.

AUTHORS, German
See also
Grass, G.
Mann, T.

AUTHORS, Hungarian
See also
Balázs, B.

AUTHORS, Iranian
AAP aids Iranian writers in plea for association. M. Reuter. Pub W 212:16+ Ag 15 '77

AUTHORS, Irish
See also
Joyce, J.
Yeats, W. B.

AUTHORS, Italian
See also
Casanova de Seingalt, G. G.

AUTHORS, Jewish
See also
Babel', I. E.
Weil, S.

AUTHORS, Latin American
See also
Latin American literature

AUTHORS, Russian
Art criticism of Pushkin, Gogol, Dostoevsky and Tolstoy. J. E. Bowlt. il Art N 76:86-8+ My '77
Exiles' silent world. C. D. May. pors Newsweek 89:51 Ap 4 '77
When writers meet; Soviet-American conference. N. Cousins. il Sat R 4:8-9+ S 17 '77
See also
Babel', I. E.
Dostoevskii, F. M.
Russian literature
Tolstoi, L. N.

AUTHORS, South African
See also
Schreiner, O.

AUTHORS, Women. See Women authors

AUTHORS agents. See Literary agents

AUTHORS and editors
Bennett Cerf; excerpt from At Random. B. Cerf. il por Pub W 212:28-31 Ag 15 '77
Editor; policy affecting manuscripts. D. E. Petzal. Field & S 82:6 D '77
Getting published: an unraveled mystery; excerpt from Creative communications for a successful design practice. S. A. Kliment. Archit Rec 161:59+ F '77
Martin Levin: the good humor man; interview, ed by L. Taylor. M. Levin. por Writers Digest 57:29 O '77
Neatness counts. A. Spikol. Writers Digest 57:12+ Ap '77
Reaching for the Reader's Digest. J. M. Allen. Writer 90:26-8+ Ap '77
Tears before the mast; submitting work to periodical editors. A. Spikol. Writers Digest 57:14+ F '77
Ten ways to build article sales. K. Cruzic. Writer 90:30-1 D '77
Theory of the silver bullet. L. S. Bernstein. Writer 90:28-9 Ag '77
Timing the submission. A. S. Harris, Jr. Writer 90:19-21+ Mr '77
Write a query—get an assignment! magazine writers and editors. S. W. Olds. Writer 90:15-19 Ag '77
Writers vs. editors. A. Spikol. Writers Digest 57:14-15 S '77

AUTHORS and libraries. See Libraries and authors

AUTHORS and publishers
AAP & authors clash over copy fee scheme. Lib J 102:1083 My 15 '77
Bennett Cerf; excerpt from At Random. B. Cerf. il por Pub W 212:28-31 Ag 15 '77
Book contracts: trial and terror. D. Waitley. Writers Digest 57:49-50 S '77
Cave of the winds. L. H. Lapham. Nat R 29:1055-8+ S 16 '77
Getting published: an unraveled mystery; excerpt from Creative communications for a successful design practice. S. A. Kliment. Archit Rec 161:59+ F '77
Historian and publisher; S. E. Morison. A. A. Knopf. pors Am Heritage 28:100-6 Ap '77
How to submit a book manuscript. Writer 90:31 Jl '77
Life and letters. . . Aristides. Am Scholar 46:432+ Aut '77
Make a big name with little markets. T. Schwarz. Writers Digest 57:21-2 Ap '77
Market newsletter. See issues of Writer
Market update; ed by D. Sandhage. See issues of Writer's digest
Markets. See issues of Writer's digest
New York newsletter. J. P. Hayes. See issues of Writer's digest
On one who wrote not wisely but to sell; magazine freelancing. M. Malone. Nation 224:597-8 My 14 '77
Paperback historical romance (title varies) J. A. Glass and Y. MacManus. Writer 90:33-5 Ap; 18 My '77
Special tabloid issue; writing for the tabloid press; symposium. il Writers Digest 57:19-28 Jl '77
Subsidy publishing: stigma or sesame? N. Richardson. il Writers Digest 57:44-8 Jl '77
Ways to publish what you write. Changing T 31:15-17 Mr '77
What's ahead for writers? comments by leading authors and editors. Writer 90:20-2 Ap '77
Where to sell manuscripts. See issues of Writer
Where to sell op-ed articles. Writer 90:23-4 My '77
Writing for the hidden markets; fund-raising groups. A. R. Blackburn. Writers Digest 57:41-3 Jl '77
See also
Literary agents

AUTHORS clubs and societies. See Literary clubs and societies

AUTHORS colonies. See Artists and authors colonies

AUTHORS conferences
Talking writing; Bread Loaf Writers Conference. il Time 110:40-1 S 5 '77
What do you learn at a writers conference? M. Costigan. Writer 90:16-18+ D '77
When writers meet; Soviet-American conference. N. Cousins. il Sat R 4:8-9+ S 17 '77
Workshop trio. P. D. Boles. Writer 90:15-17 My '77
Writers conferences 1977. Writer 90:25-33 My '77
Writers conferences/77. R. Adkins. il Writers Digest 57:42-8+ My '77

AUTHORS Guild. See Authors League of America, Inc—Authors Guild

AUTHORS League of America, Inc
Authors League protests tax reform act inequities. S. Wagner. Pub W 212:19 D 5 '77
Writers blast copyright registration concept. S. Wagner. Pub W 212:35 O 24 '77

AUTHORS League of America, inc—*Continued*

Authors Guild

Authors Guild asks U.S. to block BOMC purchase by Time. M. Reuter; S. Wagner. Pub W 212:16 Ag 15 '77

Authors Guild asks U.S. to halt sinister merger trend. S. Wagner. Pub W 211:21-2 Je 20 '77; Reply. A. Hatcher. 212:7 Ag 15 '77

AUTHORS markets. See Authors and publishers

AUTHORS offices. See Offices

AUTHORS promotion tours. See Books—Advertising

AUTHORS rights

P.E.N. lists 606 writers as victims of repression. M. Reuter. Pub W 212:18 N 14 '77

See also

Copyright

AUTHORSHIP

Adventures of a consultant writer; freelance business consultant. C. S. Blinderman. Writers Digest 57:25-6 My '77

And having writ, wrote on. C. Stinnett. Atlantic 239:20 Je '77

Creative cycle. S. Grafton. Writer 90:11-15 D '77

Day in the life of Joan Didion; interview, ed by S. Braudy. J. G. Dunne and J. Didion. Ms 5: 65-8+ F '77

Gee, I've always wanted to write; interviews, ed by C. Calvert. Mademoiselle 83:96+ N '77

Liberal artist at work; staff writing. R. Bayan. Nat R 29:156-7 F 4 '77

Maybe you should write a book; excerpt. R. Daigh. Writer 90:19-22 S; 19-21 O '77

Ned Bobkoff and me. J. T. Jackson. il pors Writers Digest 57:16-18+ F '77

Nonfiction books: the new bestsellers. T. Thompson. por Writers Digest 57:18-21 Ag '77

Off the cuff. L. Conger. See issues of Writer

On changing jobs: from fulltime to freelance. H. Brubach. Mademoiselle 83:72-4 D '77

On writing well. R. S. Wolper. Nation 224:345-6 Mr 19 '77

What Dick Powell taught me about writing. W. J. Slattery. Writers Digest 57:4-5 Mr '77

Writing life. See issues of Writer's digest

See also

Advertising copy
Audio-visual script authorship
Authors
Biography
Childrens literature—Authorship
Creative writing
Detective and mystery stories—Authorship
Drama—Technique
Fiction—Authorship
Fiction—Technique
Historical fiction—Authorship
Humor—Authorship
Journalism—Authorship
Literary research
Motion picture authorship
Pamphlets—Authorship
Periodical articles
Plots (drama, novel, etc)
Poetics
Poetry—Authorship
Prose literature
Science fiction—Authorship
Short story
Technical writing
Television authorship
Young adults literature—Authorship

Anecdotes, facetiae, satire, etc.

Beating writer's block. il Time 110:101 O 31 '77

Bibliography

Writer's library (cont) Writer 90:46 F; 46 Mr '77

Collaboration

Equal credit for ghosts. R. Reeves. Esquire 88: 40-1 Ag '77

Meyer and Kaplan: two into one will go; interviews with authors of novel Black orchid; ed by R. Dahlin. B. J. Kaplan; N. Meyer. il pors Pub W 212:46 N 21 '77

Copy preparation

Neatness counts. A. Spikol. Writers Digest 57: 12+ Ap '77

AUTISM

Autism: insights into the causes. Sci N 111:167 Mr 12 '77

Mother-to-be's anxiety linked to autism. Sci N 112:374 D 3 '77

Special kind of love; J. Woodward's work with autistic children. J. Ardmore. il pors Fam Health 9:28-31 F '77

AUTO Expo/New York. See Automobiles—Exhibitions

AUTOBIOGRAPHY

Hidden Presidents: looking through their memoirs for involuntary truth. F. M. Brodie. il Harpers 254:61-6+ Ap '77; Discussion. 254:4+ Je '77

See also

Diaries

AUTOCROSSING. See Automobile racing

AUTOGRAPHS

Collectors and collecting

Autographs:

American prince; cardinals. R. C. Weekes. Hobbies 82:156 N '77

Famous physicians & medical researchers. W. Rodger. Hobbies 82:156+ D '77

Handwriting of history's celebrities. W. Rodger. Hobbies 82:138-9 Ja '78

Kings and their English. W. Rodger. Hobbies 82:154-5+ My '77

Men of the cloth. W. Rodger. il Hobbies 81:154-5+ F '77

On the road to rarity. K. V. Hostick. Hobbies 82:141-3 Jl '77

Queen Isabella I. K. V. Hostick. Hobbies 82: 142 O '77

Rarity in autographs! How and why? K. V. Hostick. Hobbies 82:142 S '77

Signatures from the silver screen. W. Rodger. Hobbies 82:154-5+ Ap '77

Some really rare autographs. W. Rodger. Hobbies 82:154-5+ Je '77

Some thoughts on starting an autograph collection. W. Rodger. Hobbies 82:154-5+ Mr '77

In search of a real John Hancock. E. James. il Sat Eve Post 249:12-13+ My '77

$20,000 for a hat? C. Massey. il por Ret Liv 17:44 Ap '77

AUTOIMMUNE diseases. See Immunologic diseases

AUTOMATED radio. See Computers—Radio broadcasting use

AUTOMATIC coffee makers. See Coffee pots, percolators, etc.

AUTOMATIC control

See also

Electronic control

AUTOMATIC direction finders. See Radio direction finders

AUTOMATIC drafting. See Computer graphics

AUTOMATIC painting. See Automatism

AUTOMATIC pens. See Signature writing machines

AUTOMATIC pilot (boats)

Electronic helmsmen. O. Moore. il Motor B & S 140:104-5 O '77

AUTOMATIC signature writers. See Signature writing machines

AUTOMATIC timers. See Photography, Time-lapse

AUTOMATIC transmission. See Automobiles—Transmission

AUTOMATIC turntables. See Phonograph—Turntables

AUTOMATION

See also

Automobile factories—Automation
College libraries—Automation
Libraries—Automation
Sewage disposal plants—Automation
Systems engineering

AUTOMATISM

Surrealism's automatic painting lesson. J. Wechsler. il Art N 76:44-7 Ap '77

AUTOMATONS

Is there a robot in your future? Yes, there is. At least in a Harvest/HBJ spring paperback; interview, ed by R. Dahlin. R. Malone. il Pub W 212:30 D 5 '77

Parapeople; androids. il Horizon 20:75 N '77

Robots are here! W. B. Hendrickson, Jr. il Sci Digest 82:21-6 N '77

AUTOMOBILE accidents. See Traffic accidents

AUTOMOBILE auctions. See Auctions

AUTOMOBILE batteries. See Storage batteries

AUTOMOBILE battery chargers. See Storage battery chargers

AUTOMOBILE boat trailers

Boatkeeper trailering handbook. J. Gribbins. il Motor B & S 139:115-22 My '77

Trailering techniques. F. M. Paulson. il Field & S 82:126+ Ag '77

See also

Yachts—Automobile trailer combination

Maintenance and repair

New life for an old trailer. F. M. Paulson. il Field & S 82:176-7+ Je '77

Trailer maintenance. B. Matlack. Yachting 142: 128-30 D '77

AUTOMOBILE body work. See Automobiles—Maintenance and repair

AUTOMOBILE brakes. See Brakes, Automobile

AUTOMOBILE buying. See Automobiles—Purchasing

AUTOMOBILE cleaners. See Cleaning compositions

AUTOMOBILE clubs

Sizing up auto clubs. il Changing T 31:24-5 Jl '77

Suiting the enthusiast to a 'T'. R. J. Gottlieb. Motor T 29:63-4+ My '77

AUTOMOBILE cylinder heads. See Automobile engines—Cylinders

AUTOMOBILE dealers

CU readers rate dealer service. il Consumer Rep 42:239 Ap '77

Dealers are thinking spring. il Bus W p35-6 F 14 '77

From Wall Street to auto sales—a success story; F. Weinberg and M. Holden. V. Louviere. il pors Nations Bus 65:76 S '77

Getting used to the used-car business again. B. McCall. Car & Dr 22:22-3 Je '77

How to deal with the dealer this year. il Consumer Rep 42:192-4 Ap '77

New-car dealers experience long-term gains in productivity. J. Duke. bibl il M Labor R 100: 29-33 Mr '77

Oh, the advantage of owning a Ferrari dealership. il Car & Dr 22:74 Mr '77

See also

Automobile salesmen

AUTOMOBILE decoration

50 golden goodies; vinyl tape stripping. J. McCraw. il Hot Rod 30:101-4+ Ap '77

Von Dutch: machine age gypsy; interview, ed by T. Kramer. V. Dutch. il por Hot Rod 30: 44-8+ Mr '77

AUTOMOBILE drivers

Becoming a Saab Man—the liberal conversion. P. Bedard. il Car & Dr 22:16 F '77

Driving tips for experienced drivers. R. A. Dickelman. Bet Hom & Gard 55:236 My '77

See also

Taxicab drivers

Anecdotes, facetiae, satire, etc.

Auto fantasies. G. Millstein. N Y Times Mag p80-1 Je 26 '77

AUTOMOBILE driving

Getting into gear for winter driving. R. Taylor and J. Taylor. il pors House & Gard 149:72+ D '77

How to beat the odds when you drive at night. B. Hampton. il Pop Mech 147:75-7+ Mr '77

How to drive a small car. T. Swan. il Esquire 88:110-12+ O '77

How to drive on ice. . .when it's too slippery to walk. S. F. Wilder. il Pop Mech 148:92-5+ N '77

How to go in snow! E. D. Fales, Jr. il Pop Mech 148:82-5 D '77

Mercedes-Benz odyssey: new cars and old castles, memories and wine; driving new cars. D. E. Davis, Jr and others. il Car & Dr 22:50-3+ Mr '77

Night glasses for safer highway driving. Sci N 112:85 Ag 6 '77

Nighttime driving accidents and selective visual degradation; letter. H. W. Leibowitz and D. A. Owens. bibl Science 197:422-3 Jl 29 '77

Safe-driving rules that work. il Changing T 31:13-14 D '77

Take this wintertime safe-driving quiz. J. L. Lippert. il Good H 184:221 F '77

When your car acts up or breaks down. A. M. Miller. McCalls 104:56 S '77

You auto take this test. J. Brewer. il Sat Eve Post 249:6+ N '77

See also

Automobile drivers

Storm hazards

How to survive being buried alive; blizzard conditions. E. D. Fales, Jr. il Pop Mech 149:58-61 Ja '78

Study and teaching

Gentlemen, your brakes; Jim Russell International Racing Drivers School. il por Time 110: 69 Ag 1 '77

How P.J. became A.J. in just five days; Bob Bondurant School of High Performance Driving. P. J. O'Rourke. il por Esquire 87:58-62+ F '77

Think slow; police safety instructor. R. Turner. Time 110:63 N 7 '77

Stunt driving

Man who loved stunt driving. K. Snedaker. il por Car & Dr 23:108-9 Jl '77

California

Freeway driving. A. K. Dukes. Mademoiselle 83:105 Ap '77

France

Going places and ducking bills. B. Yates. Car & Dr 23:14 N '77

AUTOMOBILE emission standards. See Automobiles—Environmental aspects

AUTOMOBILE engines

All-new lightweight; Chevy's new aluminum small block engine. C. J. Baker. il Hot Rod 30:42-3 S '77

Baseball, hot dogs, apple pie & Chevrolet; small-block V8. C. J. Baker. il Hot Rod 30:93 N '77

Budget-building V8S:

Building a better mousetrap. G. Baskerville. il Hot Rod 30:61-3 Ap '77

501/302. R. McGonegal. il Hot Rod 30:64+ Ap '77

Summer Lark. N. Mayersohn. il Hot Rod 30:68+ Ap '77

Buick's even-firing V-6. J. Ethridge. il Motor T 29:78-9 Jl '77

Choice pickings from the year of the engineer. D. Sherman. il Car & Dr 23:46+ O '77

Different strokes for all the folks; variable displacement. A. Stockton. il Motor T 29:44-6 Jl '77

Editorially speaking; future engines. J. Dianna. il Hot Rod 30:7 O '77

End of the great engine flap; settlement of suit against GM for use of Chevrolet engines in other cars. Time 111:66 Ja 2 '78

Engine that might; Wankel rotary engine. E. Keerdoja. il Newsweek 89:16 My 16 '77

Engine trouble; use of Chevrolet engines in Oldsmobiles. Time 109:66 My 9 '77

Engines will be different, but not revolutionary. C. G. Burck. il Fortune 96:116 Jl '77

Even-firing V6 smoothed out for GM's small cars. R. Ceppos. il Pop Sci 211:13 Jl '77

How's your new Chevrobile? engine switch in GM cars. Nation 224:549 My 7 '77

Numbers game; engine dimensions and weights. il Hot Rod 30:77 O '77

An Otto for the automobile. A. W. Reitze, Jr. bibl il Environment 19:32-42 My '77

Playing it straight: why six in a row beats three in a vee. L. J. K. Setright. Car & Dr 23:142 D '77

Pontiac's 2.5 liter four: yesterday's engine tomorrow. D. Sherman. il Car & Dr 22:68 F '77

Porsche power to the small-car people. D. Sherman. il Car & Dr 22:105-6 My '77

Shoo-in; V8 Vega kits. G. Baskerville. il Hot Rod 30:77-9 D '77

Speed and the single rotor. B. Hartford. il por Pop Mech 147:198 Mr '77

Street & strip machines: recycled performance for the street. il Hot Rod 30:76-9 F '77

Take a minute and tell me why, exactly, it's bad to lug an engine? P. Bedard. Car & Dr 22:26 My '77

See also

Automobiles—Cams
Automobiles, Racing—Engines
Carburetors
Diesel engines, Automotive
Manifolds
Piston rings
Tachometers

Air supply

Fresh air is free horsepower for those who catch the wind. D. Wallace. il Hot Rod 30:39-41 N '77

See also

Automobile engines—Superchargers

Belts

How to check (and replace) drive belts. il Bet Hom & Gard 55:269 O '77

Cooling

Care 'n' feeding of your cooling system. W. Woron. il Motor T 29:83-7 My '77

Cooling system. il Pop Mech 147:178+ My '77

Your cooling system; all you need to know about it. M. Schultz. il Pop Mech 148:99-101+ Ag; 106-8+ S '77

Cylinders

Clamp down. . .on big block Chevy head leaks. il Hot Rod 30:47-8 Ap '77

Driving a car with 4, 5, 6, 7 or 8 cylinders. S. F. Wilder. il Pop Mech 148:68+ N '77

Littlest porcupine; Chevrolet aluminum cylinder heads. C. J. Baker. il Hot Rod 30:42 Je '77

Offset stud; high-lift rocker arms. C. J. Baker. il Hot Rod 30:54 Je '77

Design

Fireball V-6: super-motor of the future. D. Sherman. il Car & Dr 23:67-9+ Jl '77

Stalled; question of developing low-emission vehicles. A. W. Reitze, Jr. bibl il Environment 19:39-42 Ag '77

Distributors

See Automobile engines—Ignition

Electronic equipment

See Automobiles—Electronic equipment

Exhaust

Exhaust system. il Pop Mech 147:187+ My '77

Incredible thinking engines; Lambda-sonde sensor system. K. Ludvigsen. il Motor T 29: 77-80 F '77

Muscle makers. C. J. Baker. il Hot Rod 30:85-9 Ap '77

See also

Automobiles—Environmental aspects

AUTOMOBILE engines—*Continued*

Filters

Car filters—what to know, how to change them. W. O. Koehler. il Pop Sci 210:128+ Mr '77
Gimmick or godsend? Monroe filter plus. G. Witzenburg. il Motor T 29:95-6+ Mr '77

Fuel

Around the Mall and beyond; alternative energy engines. E. Park. Smithsonian 7:18-20+ Mr '77
Hydrogen engine that looks practical. D. Francis. il Mech Illus 73:42-3 Jl '77
See also
Alcohol as fuel
Gasoline
Methanol

Fuel consumption

Behind the uproar over those gas-mileage ratings. il U.S. News 83:32 S 26 '77
Car-models and gas-mileage. il Sr Schol 110:8-9 S 8 '77
Economy tests: Chevy vs Ford vs Plymouth. R. G. Beason. il Mech Illus 73:46-7+ Mr '77
Expensive widget that tells MPG—sometimes; Autocomp. il Consumer Rep 42:622 N '77
Gas-saving baby cars. R. Taylor and J. Taylor. il pors House & Gard 149:104+ O '77
MCA jet system; Dodge Colt/Plymouth Arrow engines. C. Nerpel. il Motor T 29:82-3 O '77
More miles per gallon. Sci Am 236:43+ Ja '77
Numbers game; EPA estimates. il Newsweek 90:83 O 3 '77
What do we do until the well runs dry? T. Orme. Motor T 29:7-8+ Ap '77
What this country needs is a good 20-mpg speed limit. P. Bedard. il Car & Dr 23:37-8 N '77

Fuel feeding

Bosch's K-Jetronic: fuel injection made easy. D. Sherman. il Car & Dr 22:65 Mr '77
Fuel system. il Pop Mech 147:198+ My '77
Fuel vaporizer heats the mix to cut emissions. D. Scott. il Pop Sci 210:28 Ap '77
Your fuel system: all you need to know about it. M. Schultz. il Pop Mech 148:120-3+ N '77

Hoses

Braided beauty. C. J. Baker. il Hot Rod 30:78+ O '77
How to handle the hose problem. T. Tappett. il Mech Illus 73:102+ Mr '77

Ignition

Equipment reports:
Tiger cub breakerless ignition. il Radio-Electr 48:22+ N '77
How to get more power and mpg by installing electronic ignition. E. F. Lindsley. il Pop Sci 210:118-19+ Je '77
How to use a timing light. W. Koehler. il Pop Sci 210:123-4+ My '77
Ignition and electrical. il Pop Mech 147:169+ My '77
Key to ignition basics; distributors. C. J. Baker. il Hot Rod 30:35-7 F '77
See also
Spark plugs

Lubrication

See Automobiles—Lubrication

Maintenance and repair

Backyard bonus. See issues of Hot rod
Build this easy auto circuit checker. R. F. Graf and G. F. Whalen. il Pop Mech 147:184 Mr '77
C. J. talks tech. C. J. Baker. See issues of Hot rod
Engine. il Pop Mech 147:166-7+ My '77
How to check vacuum systems. W. O. Koehler. il Pop Sci 212:106+ Ja '78
How to do that engine overhaul yourself! M. Schultz. il Pop Mech 147:110-12+ Je '77
How to stop hesitation. M. Schultz. il Pop Mech 147:102-3+ F '77
How to tune your car to save fuel. T. Tappett. il Mech Illus 73:96+ Ag '77
Re-engined: your car as good as new? questions and answers. J. Joseph. il Motor T 29:105-9 Je '77
16 pages money saving backyard how-tos. C. J. Baker. il Hot Rod 30:82-4+ My '77
Special section: backyard tech tips. il Hot Rod 30:77-8+ O '77
When you're faced with major repairs . . . T. Tappett. il Mech Illus 73:96+ Jl '77
See also
Anti-freeze solution
Automobiles, Racing—Engines—Maintenance and repair
Midas-International Corporation

Parts

See Automobile parts

Repairing

See Automobile engines—Maintenance and repair

Starting

See Automobiles—Starting

Superchargers

Adventures in turboland. S. Thompson. Car & Dr 23:14-15 O '77
Buick Regal Sport Coupe. D. Sherman. il Car & Dr 23:64+ S '77
Buick turbocharged V-6. J. Ethridge. il Motor T 29:104-5 O '77
Buick's turbocharged V6: is it the engine of the '80's? E. F. Lindsley il Pop Sci 211:84-6 S '77
Building a BMW berserker. M. Jordan and D. Sherman. il Car & Dr 23:72+ O '77
Driving Buick's turbocharged V6. R. Lund. il Pop Mech 148:40+ S '77
Goodol' toy; turbocharged Chevrolet Vega. F. M. H. Gregory. il Motor T 29:57-8+ Mr '77
Mythstakes . . . or how to avoid the traps that surround turbocharging. G. Baskerville. il Hot Rod 30:60+ Mr '77
1978 Buick Regal Turbo: the royal blast. J. McCraw. il Hot Rod 30:88+ S '77
Project turbo-in-every-garage: blower Granada, believe it or not. P. Bedard. il Car & Dr 23:72-5 S '77
Roots. G. Baskerville. il Hot Rod 30:100+ N '77
Saab Turbo. P. Bedard. il Car & Dr 23:65-70 O '77
Turbo potpourri. il Hot Rod 30:80-2+ S '77
Turbos come to Grand Prix racing; Renault Elf. R. A. Cutter. il Mech Illus 73:140-2 O '77
VW's 60-mpg turbo-diesel safety car. J. Dunne. il Pop Sci 211:104-5 O '77
We test the new turbo Saab. R. G. Beason. il Mech Illus 74:60-1+ Ja '78

Testing

See also
Diesel engines, Automotive—Testing

Valves

5-in-1 engine. E. F. Lindsley. il Pop Sci 211:72-3+ Jl '77

AUTOMOBILE equipment. See Automobiles—Equipment

AUTOMOBILE equipment industry
Souped-up cars bump into emissions curbs. il Bus W p26-7 D 19 '77
See also
Budd Company
Harman International Industries, Inc

Export-import trade

Shift in imported auto parts. il Bus W p 106 Ja 31 '77

Germany, West

Germany's Bosch adds to its U.S. string. il Bus W p72-3 Ag 29 '77

Great Britain

There's a lot of G.K.N. in Europe's cars. R. Ball. il por Fortune 95:156-61+ Ja '77

AUTOMOBILE factories
Humanizing mass production jobs; Volvo plant; excerpts from address. P. Gyllenhammar. il Intellect 105:380-1 My '77

Automation

Technology and labor in automobile production. R. V. Critchlow. il M Labor R 100:32-5 O '77

Management

See Factory management

AUTOMOBILE financing. See Instalment plan

AUTOMOBILE frauds. See Fraud

AUTOMOBILE industry
For your information. D. Abrahamson. See issues of Car and driver
International report. See issues of Motor trend
See also
Automobile dealers
Automobile factories
Collective bargaining—Automobile industry

Acquisitions and mergers

Volvo, Saab talk merger. Motor T 29:96 Jl '77
Why Volvo and Saab are joing forces. Bus W p42+ My 23 '77

Advertising

Bob Jones speaks, General Motors listens; canceling sponsorship of television program, Jesus of Nazareth. J. M. Wall Chr Cent 94:291 Mr 30 '77
Datsun switches; William Esty Co. L. Langway and M. Reese. il Newsweek 89:73 Je 27 '77
We're No. 3! Opel campaign. il Newsweek 89:58 Ap 4 '77

Antitrust cases

You're damned if you do. . . il Forbes 121:33-6 Ja 9 '78

Awards, prizes, etc.

See also
Motor Trend Awards

Costs

Launching a car company: finances are the hard part. D. C. Smith. il Car & Dr 23:40 Jl '77

AUTOMOBILE industry—*Continued*

Finance

Auto makers play an expensive new game. il Bus W p72-6+ O 24 '77

Regulation

See Automobiles—Laws and regulations

Europe, Western

Europe: U.S. parents cash in on an auto boom. il Bus W p40 F 21 '77
Unexpected boom in sales of new cars. Bus W p48 D 26 '77
Why the foot on the gas pedal will stay mine. Car & Dr 22:140 Je '77

France

Peugeot-Citroen: the odd pair. il Bus W p 112+ Mr 28 '77
Right to raze; question of Renault's right to destroy commissioned work by J. Dubuffet. Vasari. il por Art N 76:19 S '77
See also
Strikes—France

Germany, West

Persuasive man who drives Mercedes; J. Zahn of Daimler-Benz AG. R. Ball. il pors Fortune 96:136-40+ D '77
Pollution may kill VW's Rabbit plant; EPA ruling. il Bus W p26 Mr 7 '77
Preemptive jawboning astonishes business. il Bus W p36-7 Mr 28 '77
Volkswagen moves into Pennsylvania: start of a wholesale migration? New Stanton. il U.S. News 83:41 O 31 '77
Volkswagen's Herr Fix-it; T. Schmücker. il por Time 109:66+ My 16 '77

Great Britain

British labor problems dim Chrysler's hopes. il Bus W p53-4 N 21 '77
Chrysler U.K.'s uphill struggle for profits. Bus W p42+ Je 20 '77
See also
British Leyland Motor Corporation, Ltd
Ford Motor Company Ltd

Italy

Lancia: the gem of Turin. K. Ludvigsen. il Motor T 29:60-2+ Je '77
What Fiat will do with Libya's money. Bus W p97+ Mr 14 '77

Japan

Can Honda factories keep up with demand? il Bus W p27-8 My 23 '77
Toyota: two breathtaking decades. Motor T 30:37+ Ja '78

Mexico

Why the auto makers are taking a beating. Bus W p41+ My 2 '77

Russia

Russia finally takes to the highways. R. Knight. il map U.S. News 82:52-5 Ja 31 '77

Sweden

How Volvo adapts work to people; excerpt from People at work. P. G. Gyllenhammar. il Harvard Bus R 55:102-13 Jl '77
Humanizing mass production jobs; Volvo plant; excerpts from address. P. Gyllenhammar. il Intellect 105:380-1 My '77
Pay for no work; Volvo. il Time 109:67-8 F 21 '77
Volvo: half-century of Swedish quality. K. Ludvigsen. il Motor T 29:94-101 Jl '77
Volvo way: efficiency without pain; views of Pehr Gyllenhammar. J. Gaylin. Psychol Today 11:45 O '77
Why Volvo and Saab are joining forces. Bus W p42+ My 23 '77

United States

Auto sale: high but no records. U.S. News 83:24 N 14 '77
Autos: sales down, optimism up. il Time 110:42 D 26 '77
Big cars boom—is it the last gasp? il U.S. News 82:51 F 14 '77
Dangers in the auto sales slowdown. S. Zucker. Bus W p32 Ja 16 '78
Detroit battles back; small car sales. il Newsweek 90:62+ Jl 11 '77
Detroit fights back. K. K. Wiegner. il Forbes 120:36-41 Jl 15 '77
Detroit listening post. R. Lund. See issues of Popular mechanics
Detroit on the spot; energy policy taxes. T. Nicholson and J. C. Jones. il Newsweek 89:29 My 2 '77
Detroit overview: going our way at last. D. E. Davis, Jr. il Car & Dr 23:40-1 O '77
Detroit report. See issues of Motor trend
Detroit report. J. Dunne. See issues of Popular science
Detroit takes EV seriously, but output on large scale is at least decade away. B. Posner. Sci Digest 82:78-9 S '77
Detroit's minicars threaten the imports. il Bus W p24-5 Ap 4 '77
Detroit's response to the energy problem. il Bus W p 100+ My 23 '77
Future shock in Detroit. T. Nicholson and J. C. Jones. il Newsweek 90:68+ Ag 8 '77
Got a lemon? how to get the drop on Detroit. R. Lund. il Pop Mech 149:84-5+ Ja '78
How they stage the sneakiest of the sneak previews. R. Lund. il Pop Mech 147:80-1+ Je '77
Introducing the 1979 DeLorean—the car and the company. K. Ludvigsen. il por Motor T 29:44-9+ S '77
John DeLorean builds a sports car: the DMC-12. P. Bedard. il Car & Dr 23:37-9+ Jl '77
Password for '78 downsize. il Time 110:32+ Ag 1 '77
Plastics take the pole in the light-car race. C. G. Burck. il Fortune 96:114-15+ Jl '77
Puzzling rush to buy cars. il Bus W p23-4 Je 6 '77
Shift to midsize cars. il Bus W p26-7 Mr 14 '77
Sizing up a key industry. J. Fraser. U.S. News 83:84 S 12 '77
Slowing market scares Detroit. il Bus W p38-40 Ja 9 '78
Sudden softening in Detroit. il Bus W p25-6 D 19 '77
Talisman/Ford 1930 Model A. D. Sherman. il por Car & Dr 23:81-4 O '77
Tempered optimism for 1978 auto sales. il Bus W p53-4 S 26 '77
Washington report. T. Orme. See issues of Motor trend
What America makes; question of energy policy taxes and rebates. New Repub 176:5-6 Je 4 '77
When better cars are built, will Detroit build them? Consumer Rep 42:187 Ap '77
Worries behind Detroit's rosy figures. Bus W p50 N 14 '77
See also
American Motors Corporation
Checker Motors Corporation
Chrysler Corporation
Ford Motor Company
General Motors Corporation
United Automobile, Aerospace and Agricultural Implement Workers of America

AUTOMOBILE industry workers strike (France) See Strikes—France

AUTOMOBILE industry workers strike (Great Britain) See Strikes—Great Britain

AUTOMOBILE insurance. See Insurance, Automobile

AUTOMOBILE insurance companies. See Insurance companies

AUTOMOBILE laws and regulations. See Automobiles—Laws and regulations

AUTOMOBILE license plates. See Automobiles—License plates

AUTOMOBILE literature
Authoritative automotive almanac to hit the road for Scribners. R. Dahlin. il Pub W 211:67 Mr 21 '77

AUTOMOBILE loans. See Loans, Personal

AUTOMOBILE magazines. See Automobiles—Periodicals

AUTOMOBILE mechanics (persons)
Classic career choices; repairmen for antique cars. R. J. Gottlieb. Motor T 29:88+ Jl '77
It's not worth a damn if it doesn't run. B. Kilpatrick. Field & S 82:106+ N '77
See also
Schmidt, H.
Weis, F.

AUTOMOBILE models
Road racing sets. il Consumer Rep 42:104-9 F '77

AUTOMOBILE museums
See also
Harrah's Automobile Collection, Reno, Nev.

AUTOMOBILE ownership
Car ownership: how to take the low-cost road. il Pop Mech 147:128-30+ My '77
If you think you've got it bad . . .; owning a car in Japan. B. Hall. il Motor T 29:90-1 Ag '77
See also
Automobiles—Purchasing
Automobiles—Selling

AUTOMOBILE parking
Parallel parking? It's easy. J. L. Lippert. Good H 184:219 Je '77
Parking-lot king; Airport Parking Co. of America. por Forbes 119:78 Ap 1 '77
See also
Garages
Garages, Municipal
Parking meters

Laws and regulations

Parking ticket gives Denver new headache. il Am City & County 92:30 My '77
When the public will buy a parking ban; implementing transportation control plans. il Bus W p58 Ag 22 '77

AUTOMOBILE parts
ABC's of fiberglass. il Hot Rod 30:80-90+ Mr '77
Bracket racing secrets: packaged power. Hot Rod 30:88-91 Jl '77
Consumer's guide to auto parts. il Mech Illus 73:30 S '77
Hard core: an exclusive preview of special parts; racing parts. il Hot Rod 30:27-30 Mr '77
Used parts for the car—good and cheap. il Changing T 31:23-4 Mr '77
When suppliers stop supplying and start deciding. L. J. K. Setright. or Car & Dr 22:132 My '77
AUTOMOBILE parts industry. See Automobile equipment industry
AUTOMOBILE pools
Commuter vans catch on at corporations; test program in Los Angeles. il Bus W p54-5 F 28 '77
Van pooling: an alternative for some commuters? Consumer Rep 42:528-9 S '77
AUTOMOBILE race tracks. See Speedways
AUTOMOBILE racing
A. J, you're amazing; Indianapolis 500. S. Moses. il por Sports Illus 46:16-19 Je 6 '77
Beyond miniature golf: tacos, pinball machines and tiny race cars; miniracers. M. Jordan. il Car & Dr 23:115-16+ N '77
Bull's-eye for the black dart; U.S. Grand Prix West. S. Moses. il Sports Illus 46:28-9 Ap 11 '77
Competition. See issues of Motor trend
Dateline Daytona. C. J. Baker. il Hot Rod 30: 39-42 My '77
Day at the races—Southern style. pors Forbes 119:106+ Mr 15 '77
Daytona 500 & them good ol' boys. M. Spiegel. il Mech Illus 73:74+ F '77
Double-teaming the Talladega jinx. S. Moses. il Sports Illus 47:12-13 Ag 15 '77
Driving a NASCAR stocker: take the high groove! P. Bedard. il Car & Dr 23:79-84+ Ja '78
Fastest Indy ever! G. Howell. il Pop Mech 147: 89-91+ My '77
Foyt stands alone in Indy history. A. J. Foyt. il por Motor T 29:118-19 Ag '77
Great globe trot; National Car Rental/Pontiac Global Record Run (cont) C. Nerpel. il Motor T 28:58-60+ D '76
He packed his title and split; United States Grand Prix. S. Moses. Sports Illus 47:108 O 10 '77
High-speed voices; use of two-way radios in auto racing. J. Scalzo. il Motor T 30:64+ Ja '78
Hot blood down in Dixie; excerpt from King Richard, ed by B. Libby. R. Petty; D. Pearson; B. Allison. il pors Sports Illus 46:58-62+ F 21 '77
Hot dogging it in the bullring. B. Kilpatrick. il Pop Mech 147:78-81+ F '77
Le Mans for the masses; Malibu Grand Prix minitrack racing. il Time 110:91 S 19 '77
Life in the fast lane; Atlanta 500. J. Scalzo. il Hot Rod 30:48-50 Je '77
Nothin' could be finah; Daytona 500. S. Moses. il Sports Illus 46:16-19 F 28 '77
On the pit road stands an Eagle. K. Tesoriere. il Car & Dr 22:61-4+ My '77
Outsider looks in; 1976 Indianapolis 500. J. Cole. il Sports Illus 46:40-2+ My 16 '77
Playing at the racing game; racing on mini tracks. R. Bauman. il Mech Illus 73:36 O '77
Running fast and furious; Pocono 500. S. Moses. il por Sports Illus 47:52-3 Jl 4 '77
Special section: International Race of Champions. il Car & Dr 23:81-2+ S '77
Sport. P. Bedard. See issues of Car and driver
Suddenly Mario is the magician again; Monte Carlo Grand Prix. S. Moses. il por Sports Illus 46:22-3 My 30 '77
Teaching them a lesson in timing; breaking the 200-mph mark at Indianapolis. S. Moses. il Sports Illus 46:30-1 My 23 '77
3rd annual Monterey Historic Car Races; canter for auld crocks. J. Christy. il Motor T 28:68-71 D '76
Turmoil in Texas; autocrossing; National SCCA Solo II Championship. A. Hurvitz. il Car & Dr 23:75-8 Ja '78
Why economy driving is dangerous. L. J. K. Setright. Car & Dr 23:122 O '77
See also
Automobile rallies
Automobile speed records
Automobiles, Racing
Drag racing
Speedways

Economic aspects

Foyt, Fangio and the sponsor's ego. D. E. Davis, Jr. Car & Dr 23:7 O '77

History

Grand Prix racing in the thirties: when an Englishman drove for the Germans. J. Dugdale. il pors Car & Dr 23:105-6+ N '77
Peter Helck. M. Tinkelman. il por Am Artist 41:40-5 Jl '77
Woman we would have loved to love; Golden age of motor racing. B. Yates. Car & Dr 22: 18-19 Mr '77

Photographs

Breathtaking ride through the autumn countryside; United States Grand Prix at Watkins Glen; with report by B. Yates. S. Green-Armytage. il Sports Illus 47:28-33 O 3 '77
Countdown to a pot of gold; Indianapolis 500; with report by S. Posey. L. Stewart. il pors Sports Illus 46:34-9 My 16 '77

France

Down a dark hall at 185 m.p.h. S. Posey. il Read Digest 110:93-6 Mr '77

Great Britain

See also
Automobile rallies—Great Britain
AUTOMOBILE racing drivers
Barney Oldfield; one of the first racing drivers. R. F. Snow. il por Am Heritage 28:66-7 F '77
Competition. See issues of Motor trend
Honor isn't hollow; competition for NASCAR's Rookie of the Year. S. Moses. por Sports Illus 47:100+ N 14 '77
Ladies and gentlemen, start your engines. J. Lowe. il Seventeen 36:100+ Ap '77
Tommy Ivo's silver anniversary; drag racing, ed by A. Scalzo. T. Ivo. il pors Hot Rod 30: 22-4 S '77
See also
Andretti, M.
Beadle, R.
Cheever, E.
Fangio, J. M.
Foyt, A. J.
Greenwood, J.
Hunt, J.
Johncock, G.
Lauda, N.
Muldowney, S.
Mullins, J.
Pearson, D.
Petty, R.
Prudhomme, D.
Rutherford, J.
Waltrip, D.
AUTOMOBILE radios. See Automobiles—Radio equipment
AUTOMOBILE rallies
Classic comments; Bay to L.A. Run. R. J. Gottlieb. il Motor T 29:86-8 Ag '77
Fender-splitting fun in the winter wonderland; Pirelli/Lancia/Wonder Muffler Marquette 1000. D. Sherman. il Car & Dr 22:53-4+ F '77

Great Britain

Sputtering run to Brighton; Brighton Veteran Car Run. J. A. Maxtone Graham. il Pop Mech 147:86-8+ Je '77
AUTOMOBILE ramps. See Ramps
AUTOMOBILE renting. See Automobiles—Leasing and renting
AUTOMOBILE research
See also
Automobiles, Experimental
AUTOMOBILE safety belts. See Automobiles—Safety belts
AUTOMOBILE salesmen
Selling Joe Girard. por Forbes 120:120 N 1 '77
Yes, you would buy a car from this man! L. Mandel. il Car & Dr 22:45-6+ F '77
You too can be an ace car salesman. L. Mandel. il Car & Dr 22:50-2 F '77
See also
Automobile dealers
AUTOMOBILE service stations
How to fill'er up yourself. Bet Hom & Gard 55:108 S '77
Now, the no-service station. il Time 110:43 Ag 22 '77

Chain and franchise operations

Franchisers tune in to tune-ups. il Bus W p 136 Jl 25 '77
AUTOMOBILE shows. See Automobiles—Exhibitions
AUTOMOBILE speed records
Fastest woman on earth; K. O'Neil .P. Bowie. il pors Sat Eve Post 249:42-3+ Mr '77
Flat-out in Ohio! D. Sherman. il Car & Dr 23: 40-2+ N '77
Rocket ride to glory and gloom; women's land speed record broken by K. O'Neil. C. Phinizy. il por Sports Illus 46:26-31 Ja 17 '77
AUTOMOBILE starting. See Automobiles—Starting
AUTOMOBILE stealing. See Automobiles, Theft of
AUTOMOBILE stickers. See Labels
AUTOMOBILE styling. See Automobiles—Design
AUTOMOBILE telephones. See Radiotelephone on automobiles
AUTOMOBILE test instruments. See Testing instruments

AUTOMOBILE thefts. See Automobiles, Theft of
AUTOMOBILE tires. See Tires, Automobile
AUTOMOBILE tools. See Tools
AUTOMOBILE touring
Home on wheels. R. Magruder and M. Magruder. il Travel 147:58-63 Je '77
Light-hearted I take to the open road. S. Jones. il Holiday 58:54-6 Ap '77
See also
American Automobile Association

California

Bountiful Coachella Valley for a midwinter holiday. il map Sunset 159:82-5 D '77

California, Lower

Now you can loop the top of Baja. il map Sunset 158:122-5 Ap '77

Mexico

Mexico agrees to AAA plan to provide more tourist safety. il Ret Liv 17:13 Je '77
See also
Automobile touring—California, Lower

United States

Edie in trailerland. E. B. Campaigne and J. G. Campaigne. il Sat Eve Post 249:34-7 My; 38-9+ S; 36-7+ O '77
Firms that find a driver for your car. . . or a car for you to drive; driveaway companies. Changing T 31:29-30 N '77
Hamburgers turn gray when halted on a slanting street; touring the United States in a motor home. R. Bongartz. il Sat Eve Post 249:22+ Ap '77
If people cut back on driving. . .how business will deal with it. il U.S. News 82:29-30 Je 6 '77
On the road. il Mademoiselle 83:110-12+ Mr '77
Truck story: San Francisco-New York trip. New Yorker 53:38-40 D 12 '77

Anecdotes, facetiae, satire, etc.

Roadside America. D. K. Mano. Nat R 29:1064+ S 16 '77

Utah

Natural Bridges . . . new paving makes it an easy Utah detour. il map Sunset 159:56 O '77

Western States

Away from Interstate 5; attractions in California, Oregon and Washington. il maps Sunset 158:80-9 Je '77
Roads not taken; retracing the Oregon Trail by car. il map Sat Eve Post 249:90-3 Ap '77
AUTOMOBILE touring with children. See Travel with children
AUTOMOBILE trailer hitches. See Automobiles—Equipment
AUTOMOBILE trailers
Bringing it all back home; race car trailers. il Hot Rod 30:105-7 Je '77
Edie in trailerland. E. B. Campaigne and J. G. Campaigne. il Sat Eve Post 249:34-7 My; 38-9+ S; 36-7+ O '77
Life in a trailer caravan. W. Thoms. il Mech Illus 73:92+ D '77
Low-profile folding trailer. E. H. Arctander. il Pop Sci 210:24 My '77
No-frill campers. H. Schuldiner. il Pop Sci 210:106-9 Mr '77
RV roundup towables; camping trailers. B. Behme. il Field & S 81:122+ Mr '77
Tent on wheels. il Sunset 158:68+ Mr '77
See also
Automobile boat trailers

Storage

Storing the trailer behind a removable fence. il Sunset 159:107 S '77
AUTOMOBILE trips. See Automobile touring
AUTOMOBILE wheels. See Automobiles—Wheels
AUTOMOBILE wrecking industry. See Automobiles—Wrecking
AUTOMOBILES
AMC for '78—a V8 for the Pacer, and now there's the Concord. R. Ceppos. il Pop Sci 211:98 O '77
About autos. il Consumer Rep 42:86 F '77
Auto suggestions. M. E. Falter. House & Gard 149:54+ My '77
Auto suggestions. R. Taylor and J. Taylor. il pors House & Gard 149:57-8+ S; 56+ N; 72+ D '77
Automobiles and accessories. il Consumers Res Mag 60:206-14 O '77
Big cars boom—is it the last gasp? il U.S. News 82:51 F 14 '77
Big changes ahead in '78 cars. il U.S. News 82:34-7 My 9 '77
Buick Regal—new turbocharged V6 in a smaller intermediate. J. Dunne. il Pop Sci 211:87 S '77
Cars. R. A. Dickelman. See issues of Better homes and gardens
Cars for 78. il Ebony 33:44-6+ Ja '78
Chrysler starts building its minis at home. il Bus W p25 D 19 '77
Chrysler's new-look minis. il Newsweek 90:58 D 19 '77
Classic comments; convertibles. R. J. Gottlieb. Motor T 29:122-3 Ap '77
Comeback of the convertible. B. Hartford. il Pop Mech 147:76-7 Ap '77
Convertibles: on a new age dawning. J. Williams. il Esquire 87:76-80 Ap '77
Detroit report. See issues of Motor trend
Detroit's diesel; Oldsmobile 88. il Time 110:74 S 19 '77
First of the '78 cars. il Mech Illus 73:45-7 S '77
For your information. D. Abrahamson. See issues of Car and driver
Future shock in Detroit. T. Nicholson and J. C. Jones. il Newsweek 90:68+ Ag 8 '77
GM for '78—the intermediates are smaller. J. Dunne. il Pop Sci 211:92-5 O '77
Gas-saving baby cars. R. Taylor and J. Taylor. il pors House & Gard 149:104+ O '77
International report. See issues of Motor trend
Look at the cars of 1985. il Time 109:61 My 16 '77
Minis are coming. T. Nicholson and J. C. Jones. il Newsweek 89:79 F 21 '77
More luxury from Detroit; Cadillacs. il Mech Illus 73:58 N '77
Nash Metropolitan. B. McCall. il Car & Dr 22:103-4+ Ap '77
New cars '78; special section. il Car & Dr 23:40-2+ O '77
New cars: trimmer, slimmer and smaller. L. McKirgan. il U.S. News 83:29-31 S 26 '77
New Lincoln Versailles. R. Lund. il Pop Mech 147:112 Ap '77
1977 cars. il Consumer Rep 42:201-38 Ap '77
1977 convertibles—they're for real! M. Schultz. il Pop Mech 147:78-9+ Ap '77
1977½ Dodge Charger limited edition. Motor T 29:54+ Mr '77
1977½ Pontiac Phoenix. il Motor T 29:68 Mr '77
1978 cars—preview of tomorrow. Changing T 31:4 Ag '77
1978 GM intermediates. il Motor T 29:34-6 Mr '77
1978 Pontiac Grand Am. B. Hall. il Motor T 29:103-4 Ag '77
PM owners report:
Buick Skyhawk. M. Lamm. il Pop Mech 148:92-3+ Ag '77
Dodge Charger. M. Lamm. il Pop Mech 148:58-9 Jl '77
Dodge Diplomat and Chrysler LeBaron. il Pop Mech 149:82-3+ Ja '78
Ford Mustang II. M. Lamm. il Pop Mech 148:110-11 S '77
Ford Thunderbird. M. Lamm. il Pop Mech 147:104-5+ Je '77
Lincoln Continental Mark V. M. Lamm. il Pop Mech 147:110-12+ Ap '77
1977 Chevrolet. M. Lamm. il Pop Mech 147:90-1+ Ap '77
Oldsmobile Cutlass. M. Lamm. il Pop Mech 147:88-9+ F '77
Plymouth Fury. M. Lamm. il Pop Mech 147:90-1+ Je '77
Pontiac Grand Prix. M. Lamm. il Pop Mech 148:66-7 Ag '77
Password for '78: downsize. il Time 110:32+ Ag 1 '77
'78 AMC, Chrysler, GM. il Motor T 29:27-40+ O '77
'78 cars. J. Dunne. il Pop Sci 210:76-8 Je '77
'78 cars; symposium. il Pop Mech 148:100-11+ O '77
'78 Chryslers—goodbye to big cars. R. Ceppos. il Pop Sci 211:96-7 O '77
'78 Fords—new leaders in the economy-compact race? J. Dunne. il Pop Sci 211:80-3 S '77
Shift to midsize cars. il Bus W p26-7 Mr 14 '77
Short take:
Chevrolet Caprice Classic. D. Abrahamson. il Car & Dr 23:84+ Ag '77
Mercury Cougar XR-7. P. Bedard. il Car & Dr 22:114 My '77
Oldsmobile Cutlass S 4-4-2. D. Abrahamson. il Car & Dr 22:38 Mr '77
Pontiac Can-Am. D. Abrahamson. il Car & Dr 22:36 Je '77
Pontiac Phoenix. D. E. Davis, Jr. il Car & Dr 23:82 Ag '77
Sneak preview of the 1978 cars. B. Tripolsky. il Mech Illus 73:52-4+ Jl '77
Target: Seville: Lincoln Versailles, Chrysler LeBaron and Dodge Diplomat take aim. M. Jordan. il Car & Dr 22:49-50+ My '77
Thrill is back; cars for 1978. il Hot Rod 30:62-5 O '77
What's new in the new cars. il Mech Illus 73:74+ O '77
See also
Jeep automobiles
Sports cars
Station wagons
Trucks

Accessories

See Automobiles—Equipment

Accidents

See Traffic accidents

AUTOMOBILES—*Continued*

Advertising

See Automobile industry—Advertising

Air conditioning

Aftermarket air. E. Orr. il Motor T 29:81-5 Je '77
Cooling system. il Pop Mech 147:178+ My '77
How to service auto air conditioners. T. Tappett. il Mech Illus 73:108+ Je '77

Anecdotes, facetiae, satire, etc.

Fables, plots, shams, hoaxes and other oft-fold untruths. B. McCall. Car & Dr 23:16 O '77
Unveiling a future of non-happenings. B. McCall. Car & Dr 23:21 Ja '78
Why shouldn't my daughter like cars? L. Mandel. Car & Dr 22:24 My '77

Batteries

See Storage batteries

Bearings

Inspecting and servicing wheel bearings. A. Hughes. il Pop Sci 210:164-6 F '77

Bibliography

Book reviews. See issues of Car and driver

Bodies

Cars you can build from kits. W. Thoms. il Mech Illus 73:62+ Mr '77
Do-it-yourself auto body kits. il Consumer Rep 42:97-101 F '77

Brakes

See Brakes, Automobile

Camping equipment

See also
Automobile trailers

Cams

Fine tuning. C. J. Baker. il Hot Rod 30:42-3+ F '77
Magic mushrooms; mushroom camshaft technology. C. J. Baker. il Hot Rod 30:70-1 Jl '77

Carburetors

See Carburetors

Care

See Automobiles—Maintenance and repair

Chassis

Plans of action. il Hot Rod 30:61-4+ F '77

Cleaning

Car body. il Pop Mech 147:182-4 My '77
How to wash your car. M. Lamm. il Pop Mech 147:116-17+ Mr '77
Rx for your paint and brightwork. W. Woron. il Motor T 29:103-7 Jl '77
Spring cleaning your car. A. K. Dukes. Mademoiselle 83:20+ Mr '77
Target: your car's interior. W. Woron. il Motor T 29:97-102 Ag '77

Clutches

Forbidden island. C. J. Baker. il Hot Rod 30: 50-2+ Mr '77

Collectors and collecting

Art of collecting vintage cars. il Bus W p77-81 Ag 22 '77
Can't-miss system to make money on old cars. R. Taylor. il Car & Dr 22:80+ Mr '77
See also
Harrah's Automobile Collection, Reno, Nev.

Cost of operation

Car ownership: how to take the low-cost road. il Pop Mech 147:128-30+ My '77
How much does auto upkeep really cost? il Bet Hom & Gard 54:28+ Ag '76

Decoration

See Automobile decoration

Defects

Got a lemon? how to get the drop on Detroit. R. Lund. il Pop Mech 149:84-5+ Ja '78

Depreciation

See Depreciation

Design

Another way to do it . . . il Mech Illus 73:54 Jl '77
Designer's designer; W. L. Mitchell. G. Witzenburg. il pors Motor T 29:72-4+ Jl '77
Designing the Car of the Year. il Motor T 29: 40-1+ F '77
Detroit's response to the energy problem. il Bus W p 100+ My 23 '77
Motor Trend Man of the Year Awards to Thomas A. Murphy and E. M. "Pete" Estes. pors Motor T 29:34+ F '77
Rolling sculpture. il Car & Dr 23:53-6 O '77
View from the castle; re-creation of the Philadelphia Centennial Exposition of 1876. S. D. Ripley. il Smithsonian 8:6 Jl '77
X-raying Chrysler's Omni & Horizon. K. Ludvigsen. il Motor T 30:29-34 Ja '78
See also
Sports cars—Design

History

History of the Airflow car. H. S. Irwin. il Sci Am 237:98-104+ bibl(p 140) Ag '77; Reply. P. Caviness. 237:6+ N '77
Turning off the annual model change. K. Ludvigsen. il Motor T 29:71-2+ Ag '77

Driving

See Automobile driving

Electric equipment

Don't electrocute your car battery. J. Sandler. il Pop Mech 148:68+ O '77

Electric wiring

Dealing with the socket; troubleshooting electrical circuits. T. Tappett. il Mech Illus 73:118+ S '77
How to troubleshoot electrical-accessory failures. K. Jensen. il Pop Sci 211:124-5+ Ag '77
More about wires. Sci Digest 81:87 My '77

Electronic equipment

Build a silencer; squelches operating radio or tape player when CB signal begins. R. Miles. il Pop Electr 11:57-60 Mr '77
Build: digital clock for your car. R. C. Arp. il Radio-Electr 48:61-3+ F '77
Cadillac's cockpit copilot: Tripmaster. K. Ludvigsen. il Motor T 29:106-7 O '77
Detroit's new appetite for electronic controls; engine control microprocessor. il Bus W p64 Ag 29 '77
Digital clock kits for your car. F. Blechman. il Radio-Electr 48:35-9 O; 41-4 N; 45-7 D '77
Some recent and future automotive electronic developments. T. O. Jones. bibl il Science 195:1156-60 Mr 18 '77
See also
Automobiles—Security measures
Computers—Automotive use

Environmental aspects

Big gamble for emissions standards; amendments to the 1976 Clean Air Act. Motor T 29: 4+ F '77
Cleaner air: it'll be slow, expensive. il U.S. News 83:17 Ag 15 '77
Control of automobile emissions. P. H. Abelson. Science 197:517 Ag 5 '77
Debating a clean-air timetable; 1977 Senate version of amendments to the Clean Air Act. il Bus W p80+ F 28 '77
Detroit and Congress: eyeball to eyeball. J. A. Briggs. il Forbes 119:33-6+ F 15 '77
Driving the Lambda Sond Volvo. B. Hartford. il Pop Mech 148:57+ Jl '77
Emissions control: the impossible standards that could have been met. Consumer Rep 24:190-2 Ap '77
Reprieve for auto makers? antipollution standards. U.S. News 82:47 Mr 14 '77
Reprieve on emission rules. il Bus W p27 Ag 8 '77
Souped-up cars bump into emissions curbs. il Bus W p26-7 D 19 '77
Stalled; question of developing low-emission vehicles. A. W. Reitze, Jr. bibl il Environment 19:39-42 Ag '77
Sulfuric acid from cars: a problem that never materialized. T. H. Maugh, 2d. Science 198: 280-4 O 21 '77
Washington report; Clean Air climax. T. Orme. Motor T 29:7-8 N '77
Washington won't fight: Detroit's chemical warfare. P. J. Bernstein. Nation 224:422-5 Ap 9 '77

Equipment

All the comforts of home. W. Woron. il Motor T 29:102-5 D '77
Choosing options: which extras are worth buying? Consumer Rep 42:194-7 Ap '77
New products. See issues of Motor trend
New stuff. See issues of Hot rod
PM garage. See issues of Popular mechanics
Rod carrier for quick-draw fishing. S. Stall. il Pop Mech 148:103 Jl '77
Roof-rack system carries skis, bikes, luggage. E. C. Bendall. il Pop Sci 210:164 Je '77
Stepped trailer hitch puts you on the level. S. Stall and M. Stall. il Pop Sci 210:156 Mr '77
Trailer hitching. C. Edwards. il Consumers Res Mag 60:18-20 Jl '77
See also
Automobiles—Safety devices and measures
Speedometers
Sports cars—Equipment
Tires, Automobile

AUTOMOBILES—*Continued*

Exhibitions

Auto Expo; foreign car exhibit. New Yorker 53:35 Ap 18 '77
Classic comments: judging the judges; antique car shows. R. J. Gottlieb. il Motor T 29:67+ S '77
Concours: the ultimate car-care contest. W. A. Wyss. il Pop Mech 147:82-4+ Mr '77
Good times at Pebble Beach; Concours d'Elegance. T. Swan il Motor T 28:91-2 D '76
How they stage the sneakiest of the sneak previews. R. Lund. il Pop Mech 147:80-1+ Je '77

Export-import trade

Auto imports go on the defensive. il Bus W p90+ D 12 '77
Detroit fights back. K. K. Wiegner. il Forbes 120:36-41 Jl 15 '77
Detroit's minicars threaten the imports. il Bus W p24-5 Ap 4 '77
U.S. seeks an auto cartel. Bus W p46+ My 16 '77

Fenders

Flared out. il Hot Rod 30:93-5 Mr '77

Front wheel drive

1980 front-wheel-drive GM compacts. L. Mead. il Motor T 29:47-50 Mr '77
X-raying Chrysler's Omni & Horizon. K. Ludvigsen. il Motor T 30:29-34 Ja '78

Fuel

See Automobile engines—Fuel

Fuel systems

See Automobile engines—Fuel feeding

Gas mileage

See Automobile engines—Fuel consumption

Gearing

See also
Automobiles—Steering gear
Automobiles—Transmission

History

History of the Airflow car. H. S. Irwin. il Sci Am 237:98-104+ bibl(p 140) Ag '77; Reply. P. Caviness. 237:6+ N '77
Retrospect:
 1932 Austro Daimler ADR 8. O. Zipper. il Motor T 29:93-6+ F '77
 1942 Nash 600 Coupe. R. J. Gottlieb. il Motor T 29:109-12+ Ap '77
That fabulous mix of metal and miracle—the car. T. Hyde. il Sat Eve Post 249:48-51 N '77
What year was that? il Ret Liv 17:31 S '77
See also
Automobiles, Antique

Ignition

See Automobile engines—Ignition

Insurance

See Insurance, Automobile

Laws and regulations

Harnessing the auto. A. W. Reitze, Jr. bibl il Environment 19:6-15 Ap '77
Washington report. T. Orme. See issues of Motor trend
We are losing the freedom to decide; address, August 6, 1977. T. A. Murphy. Vital Speeches 43:714-17 S 15 '77
What to expect from the new man at DOT; B. Adams. B. Yates. Car & Dr 22:14+ Ap '77
See also
Automobile parking—Laws and regulations
Traffic regulations
Traffic violations

Leasing and renting

Enquiry concerning the principles of car rental; with fly/drive information. N. Benezra. Holiday 58:24-5 Mr '77
Leasing vs. buying a car. M. E. Falter. House & Gard 149:54 My '77
Mr Rent-a-wreck. M. Lamm. il pors Pop Mech 147:85+ Mr '77
Will the car of your dreams belong to somebody else? A. Burns. Pop Mech 148:78-9+ Ag '77
See also
Avis, Inc
Hertz Corporation

License plates

X-rated license plates; Minnesota. T. Westover. il McCalls 104:87 Je '77

Lubrication and lubricants

Engine oil. il Pop Mech 147:173-4+ My '77
15-30,000-mile oils. R. T. Trites. Pop Sci 212:46+ Ja '78
How to give your car's body a lube job. R. A. Dickelman. Bet Hom & Gard 55:18 O '77
Oil analysis for your car; use of spectroscopic analysis. C. P. Gilmore. il Pop Sci 211:82-4+ Ag '77
Return of the home grease job. T. Tappett. il Mech Illus 73:94+ F '77

Maintenance and repair

Auto-maintenance basics:
 Car filters—what to know, how to change them. W. O. Koehler. il Pop Sci 210:128+ Mr '77
 Checking and maintaining fluid levels. H. Carrier. il Pop Sci 210:166+ Ap '77
 How to troubleshoot electrical-accessory failures. K. Jensen. il Pop Sci 211:124-5+ Ag '77
 How to use a dwell tach. R. Hill. il Pop Sci 211:160+ S '77
 Inspecting and repairing your car's brakes. R. Hill. il Pop Sci 211:138+ N '77
 Inspecting and servicing wheel bearings. A. Hughes. il Pop Sci 210:164-6 F '77
 Pro tells you how to make body repairs. R. Hill. il Pop Sci 211:104-7 D '77
Backyard bonus. See issues of Hot rod
Basics of do-it-yourself car care. il Mech Illus 73:77-80+ My '77
C.J. talks tech. C. J. Baker. See issues of Hot rod
Car care. See issues of Motor trend
Car care. T. Tappett. See issues of Mechanix illustrated
Car care guide. il Pop Mech 147:121+ My '77
Car clinic; questions and answers. M. Schultz. See issues of Popular mechanics
Coil springs at the Union Dime; seminar conducted by R. Joyce. New Yorker 53:32-4 My 16 '77
Detroit's war on car corrosion. G. Stone. il Pop Sci 212:84-7 Ja '78
Do-it-yourself auto body kits. il Consumer Rep 42:97-101 F '77
Do-it-yourself bodywork. R. A. Dickelman. il Bet Hom & Gard 55:192 Je '77
Fighting rust, the perennial foe. T. Tappett. il Mech Illus 73:112+ N '77
Frequency-of-repair 1972-1976 models. il Consumer Rep 42:390-8 D '77
Frequency-of-repair records, 1972-76. il Consumer Rep 42:230-8 Ap '77
Getting into gear for winter driving. R. Taylor and J. Taylor. il pors House & Gard 149:72+ D '77
High cost of auto damage repair; study by American Mutual Insurance Alliance. Society 15:8 N '77
How to crack impossible nuts. D. Richmond. il Pop Mech 148:116-17+ O '77
How to protect your car against the cold. M. Schultz. il Pop Mech 148:109-11 D '77
Make sure the car will keep going; winterizing. Changing T 31:11-12 N '77
Preparing your car for a trip. M. E. Falter. House & Gard 149:56+ My '77
Saturday mechanic. See issues of Popular mechanics
Say, Smokey; questions and answers. S. Yunick. See issues of Popular science
Smokey's guide to troubleshooting your car. S. Yunick. il por Pop Sci 210:121-2+ Je '77
Special section; backyard tech tips. il Hot Rod 30:77-8+ O '77
Taking care of your car. R. Ceppos. See issues of Popular science
Ten car noises you can't live with. R. R. Olney. il Pop Mech 147:84-6+ Ap '77
See also
Automobile engines—Maintenance and repair
Automobile mechanics (persons)
Automobile service stations
Automobiles, Restored—Maintenance and repair

Anecdotes, facetiae, satire, etc.

Fix it yourself. R. Lipez. Progressive 41:50 Jl '77

Manufacture

See also
Automobile factories

Materials

ABC's of fiberglass; building parts. il Hot Rod 30:80-90+ Mr '77
Perils—and profits—of pioneering; use of Reynolds aluminum in automobiles. il Forbes 119:41 Ja 15 '77
Plastics take the pole in the light-car race. C. G. Burck. il Fortune 96:114-15+ Jl '77

AUTOMOBILES—*Continued*

Noise

Noise and the home mechanic; effects of California law. Mech Illus 73:120 Ag '77
Ten car noises you can't live with. R. R. Olney. il Pop Mech 147:84-6+ Ap '77

Options

See Automobiles—Equipment

Painting

See also
Automobile decoration

Parking

See Automobile parking

Parts

See Automobile parts

Periodicals

How to read up with the media heavies. B. Yates. Car & Dr 23:18-19 Ag '77
See also
Car and driver (periodical)

Photographs

Hot rod gallery. G. Baskerville. il Hot Rod 30:44-50+ F; 40 Mr; 126 My '77
See also
Sports cars—Photographs

Pollution control devices

Catalytic converters—protection or peril? Chemistry 50:22 D '77
Emissions control: the impossible standards that could have been met. Consumer Rep 42:190-2 Ap '77
Exhaust system; catalytic converters. il Pop Mech 147:187+ My '77

Prices

'77 cars: dealer cost vs. list price. il Consumer Rep 42:202-3 Ap '77

Purchasing

Buying a new car. Consumer Rep 42:369-74 D '77
How to deal with the dealer this year. il Consumer Rep 42:192-4 Ap '77
See also
Automobiles, Antique—Purchasing
Automobiles, Used—Purchasing

Caricatures and cartoons

It's all in the family; new car. S. Berenstain and J. Berenstain. il Good H 184:124-5 Je '77

Radar equipment

What's the story on radar detectors? il Mech Illus 73:34+ N '77

Radio antennas

See Radio antennas

Radio equipment

What's what in car sound systems? R. A. Dickelman. il Bet Hom & Gard 55:6 Mr '77
See also
Radiotelephone on automobiles

Recall

How to handle a recall. R. A. Dickelman. Bet Hom & Gard 55:166+ Jl '77

Repairing

See Automobiles—Maintenance and repair

Roofs

Let the sun shine in. J. Scagnetti. il Motor T 29:82-6+ Jl '77

Safety belts

Buckle up or be ready to check out. P. Bedard. Car & Dr 23:20 Jl '77
Case for mandatory buckling up. W. J. Hampton. Bus W p20 Jl 4 '77

Safety devices and measures

Adams and the bag. T. Nicholson and J. B. Copeland. il por Newsweek 90:64 Jl 11 '77
Air bag anticlimax. T. Orme. Motor T 30:9-10 Ja '78
Air-bag controversy: passive action on passive restraints. Consumer Rep 42:188-9 Ap '77
Air bags—a non-decision. T. Orme. Motor T 29:5+ Mr '77
Air bags. Motor T 29:21 N '77
Airbags: an insider explains why the DOT should demur. M. Wright. Car & Dr 23:24 S '77
Are air bags worth the trouble? interviews. J. Claybrook; B. Shuster. il pors U.S. News 83:33-4 S 26 '77
Auto safety dialogue; tough gap to narrow; interviews, ed by J. Norris. J. Claybrook; E. M. Estes. pors Motor T 29:13-14 O '77
Big cars safer than small? New study says so. Consumer Rep 42:312 Je '77
Brock Adams—mystery man. T. Orme. Motor T 29:6+ Mr '77
Car safety restraints for children. il Consumer Rep 42:314-17 Je '77
Green light for air bags. il Time 110:51 Jl 11 '77
Green light for air bags if Congress goes along. Consumer Rep 42:500 S '77
Hopes for the airbag on the rise. C. Holden. Science 195:968 Mr 11 '77
How Coleman sold Detroit on airbags. por Bus W p36 Ja 31 '77
How to design automotive anti-collision systems. M. B. Weinstein. il Radio-Electr 48:44-6 Jl; 52-3+ Ag '77
Ralph's wrath; R. Nader's attack on J. B. Claybrook over air bag decision. il pors Newsweek 90:90+ D 12 '77
Safety with a bang! Airbags: the great statistical inflation. M. Jordan. il Car & Dr 23:62-5 N '77
See also
Brakes, Automobile
Reflectors (safety devices)

Scrapping

See Automobiles—Wrecking

Security measures

Foil car thieves with Digistart, the electronic security lock. J. Fortuna. il Pop Electr 11:48-9 Ap '77
Stop thief! Security for your car. W. Woron. il Motor T 29:115-20+ N '77

Selling

Sell your car the way a dealer would. il Changing T 31:11-12 F '77

Shock absorbers

Aftershock. M. Davis. il Hot Rod 30:66+ My '77
Are your shocks in shape? R. A. Dickelman. Bet Hom & Gard 55:90 F '77
Mission: control. il Hot Rod 30:58+ My '77
Shopping for shock (cont) F. J. Furrer. il Motor T 29:82-4 F; 76-8+ Mr '77
Wheels afield; Gabriel's new carefree SL. B. Kovacik. il Motor T 29:91-3 Jl '77

Shows

See Automobiles—Exhibitions

Social aspects

Automobile as social cohesion. L. Bogart. il Society 14:10-15 Jl '77
Automobiles: the driving force. il Forbes 120: P111-18 S 15 '77
City life's automotive pleasures; automobile usage in New York City. W. Weith. Car & Dr 22:20 Mr '77
Hell on wheels. F. Getlein. Commonweal 104: 420-2 Jl 8 '77
Russia finally takes to the highways. R. Knight. il map U.S. News 82:52-5 Ja 31 '77
War against the automobile. P. Bedard. il Car & Dr 23:31-3 Ja '78
What the next generation is coming to; reaction of college students to old Excalibur automobile. L. Mandel. il Car & Dr 22:12+ Mr '77

Anecdotes, facetiae, satire, etc.

Burying the special-interest caste system. S. Thompson. il Car & Dr 22:14-15 Je '77

Societies

See Automobile clubs

Specifications

Facts and figures '78. il Motor T 29:95-6+ N '77
Mechanical specifications. il Consumer Rep 42: 222-6 Ap '77

Speed

From the drivers' log. P. Bedard and others. il Car & Dr 23:46+ N '77
Take it to the limit one more time. L. J. K. Setright. Car & Dr 23:104 Ja '78
See also
Automobile speed records
Speed indicators
Speedometers

Speed limits

See Traffic regulations

Springs and suspension

Bracket racing suspension basics. il Hot Rod 30:110+ Jl '77
Suspension and steering. il Pop Mech 147:160+ My '77

Starting

Cold-weather starting tips the service stations use. R. A. Dickelman. il Bet Hom & Gard 55: 46+ N '77
Spray cans for cold starts. P. Weissler. il Mech Illus 74:16 Ja '78
Starting system. il Pop Mech 147:149-50+ My '77

AUTOMOBILES—*Continued*

Steering gear

Suspension and steering. il Pop Mech 147:160+ My '77

Styling

See Automobiles—Design

Tape equipment

Choosing portable & mobile tape recorders. J. R. Hortsman. il Pop Electr 12:43-5 Ag '77
What's what in car sound systems? R. A. Dickelman. il Bet Hom & Gard 55:6 Mr '77

Taxation

Detroit on the spot; energy policy taxes. T. Nicholson and J. C. Jones. il Newsweek 89:29 My 2 '77
What America makes; question of energy policy taxes and rebates. New Repub 176:5-6 Je 4 '77

Testing

At last, a U.S.-made minicar; Dodge Omni and Plymouth Horizon. R. Ceppos. il Pop Sci 212:37 Ja '78
Brief test:
Comparison Granada and Monarch. J. Ethridge. il Motor T 29:70-2+ Mr '77
1977 Gremlin X 4-cylinder. J. Norris. il Motor T 29:51-2+ F '77
1977 Mustang II T-Top. J. Ethridge. il Motor T 29:67-9 F '77
Buick turbocharged V-6. J. Ethridge. il Motor T 29:104-5 O '77
CU judges the 1977 cars. Consumer Rep 42:211-38 Ap '77
Chevrolet Caprice Classic. il Consumers Res Mag 60:16-19 Mr '77
Chevrolet Nova, Plymouth Fury, Plymouth Volaré. il Consumers Res Mag 60:7-12 Ap '77
Closer look at today versus the good old days. B. Yates. Car & Dr 23:22 D '77
Compact cars; Chevrolet Concours, Buick Skylark, Plymouth Volare, Ford Granada. il Consumer Rep 42:137-43 Mr '77
Comparison test: Camaro Z/28 vs. Firebird Trans-Am. il Car & Dr 22:39-42+ Ap '77
Driving Buick's turbocharged V6. R. Lund. il Pop Mech 148:40+ S '77
Driving impression:
Continental Mark V. M. Knepper. il Motor T 28:81-2+ D '76
Mercury Zephyr. B. Hall. il Motor T 29:80-1 O '77
Driving the Diesel Oldsmobile; Delta 88. R. Lund. il Pop Mech 148:84-5 Jl '77
Driving the Dodge Diplomat and Chrysler LeBaron. M. Lamm. il Pop Mech 147:44+ My '77
Driving the Dodge Omni and Plymouth Horizon. R. Lund. il Pop Mech 149:64-5+ Ja '78
Driving the new 30-mpg Gremlin. M. Lamm. il Pop Mech 147:87+ F '77
First test flight: even-firing Buick Skyhawk. D. Sherman. il Car & Dr 23:70 Jl '77
Ford Fairmont. D. Sherman. il Car & Dr 23:27-9+ S '77
Four economy subcompacts: Chevette, Colt, Subaru, Gremlin. il Consumer Rep 42:396-402 Jl '77
Four specialty cars: Pontiac Grand Prix, Chevrolet Monte Carlo, Chrysler Cordoba, Ford Thunderbird. il Consumer Rep 42:270-6 My '77
Four subcompacts: Volkswagen Rabbit, Pontiac Sunbird, Toyota Corolla, Ford Mustang II. il Consumer Rep 42:335-41 Je '77
Fuel-saving cars for 1978. R. Taylor and J. Taylor. il pors House & Gard 149:57-8+ S '77
Has the tow car lost its pull? testing the '77 Buick Limited. il Motor T 29:59-62+ F '77
Hot rod road test:
Half-breed; Pontiac Can Am. il Hot Rod 30:100-1+ Mr '77
How CU tests and rates its cars. il Consumer Rep 42:204-5 Ap '77
Large cars. il Consumer Rep 42:81-7 F '77
1977 automobile test reports. il Consumers Res Mag 60:14-19 F '77
1978 Buick Regal Turbo: the royal blast. J. McCraw. il Hot Rod 30:88+ S '77
1978 cars—smaller, lighter, roomier. il Changing T 32:24-9 Ja '78
1978 Detroit model review. R. Huntington. il Consumers Res Mag 60:12-16 N '77
1978 Ford; offerings for the coming model year. J. Ethridge. Motor T 29:28-9+ S '77
Oldsmobile Diesel: PS 10,000-mile test. R. Ceppos. il Pop Sci 212:80-2+ Ja '78
PS car test & driving report:
Economy subcompacts; Ford Fiesta challenges Gremlin and Chevette. J. Dunne and R. Ceppos. il Pop Sci 211:30+ Jl '77
Intermediate coupes. J. Dunne and R. Hill. il Pop Sci 210:34+ F '77
Intermediate sedans; Malibu, Monaco LTD II. J. Dunne and R. Ceppos. il Pop Sci 212:30+ Ja '78
Mini-"muscle" cars. J. Dunne and R. Hill. il Pop Sci 210:32+ Ap '77
Super-luxury compacts. J. Dunne and R. Ceppos. il Pop Sci 211:32+ Ag '77
Preview test:
Dodge Omni and Plymouth Horizon. D. Sherman. il Car & Dr 23:44+ Ja '78
Road test:
AMC Gremlin X. il Car & Dr 22:103-4 My '77
AMC Hornet AMX. il Car & Dr 22:35-7+ F '77
AMC Matador Barcelona II. B. Hall. il Motor T 29:107-9 Ag '77
Bird of prey; Buick Skyhawk. J. McCraw. il Hot Rod 30:109-10+ Je '77
Buick LeSabre Sport Coupe. il Car & Dr 22:75-81 My '77
Buick Regal Sport Coupe. D. Sherman. il Car & Dr 23:64+ S '77
Cadillac Seville. J. Ethridge. il Motor T 29:44-6 Je '77
Chevrolet Caprice. J. Christy. il Motor T 29:29-32 F '77
Chevrolet Chevelle Malibu. J. Ethridge. il Motor T 29:61-2+ Jl '77
Chevrolet Monte Carlo. T. Cook. il Car & Dr 23:70-4 Ja '78
Chrysler LeBaron. J. Ethridge. il Motor T 29:81+ Ag '77
Dodge Colt Mileage Maker. il Car & Dr 22:79-80+ Ap '77
Firebird Formula. J. Ethridge. il Motor T 29:63-4+ Ap '77
Healthy Aspen. il Hot Rod 30:66-8 F '77
Lincoln Continental Mark V. il Car & Dr 22:59-62+ Je '77
Lincoln Versailles. J. Ethridge. il Motor T 29:32-4+ My '77
1977½ Chevrolet Camaro Z-28. B. Hall. il Motor T 29:55-6+ My '77
Oldsmobile Cutlass Salon. il Car & Dr 22:73-4+ Ap '77
Oldsmobile Cutlass Salon. B. Hall. il Motor T 29:113-15 Ag '77
Oldsmobile Diesel. D. Sherman. il Car & Dr 23:55-8 D '77
Pontiac Astre. il Car & Dr 22:65-8+ F '77
Pontiac Can Am. J. Ethridge. il Motor T 29:105-9 My '77
Pontiac Grand Am. S. Thompson. il Car & Dr 23:85-6+ N '77
Pontiac Phoenix. B. Hall. il Motor T 29:77+ S '77
Resurrection of Z; Z/28 Camaro. J. McCraw. il Hot Rod 30:52-4+ Ap '77
Roadmaster; Buick's Century Sport Coupe. il Hot Rod 30:88-90 N '77
Sunbird reflections. Motor T 29:38-40+ Mr '77
Zephyr cross-country. J. Ethridge. il Motor T 29:42-4+ N '77
Rod test:
Meet the king; Mustang King Cobra. il Hot Rod 30:66+ O '77
Seville vs. Versailles. J. Ethridge. il Motor T 29:48 Je '77
Test drives: Chevrolet's Chevette and Ford's Fiesta. A. K. Dukes. Mademoiselle 83:94 S '77
Testing the Car of the Year nominees. il Motor T 30:49+ Ja '78
3,000-mi. travel test of the shrunken Caddy. B. Brender. il Mech Illus 73:104+ My '77
Top ten economy cars. R. G. Beason. il Mech Illus 73:30+ Ap '77
Truth-in-testing department: doing it by the numbers. D. Sherman. il Car & Dr 22:87-8+ Ap '77
Two wheels against four! Kawasaki KZ1000 vs. Firebird Trans-Am. S. Thompson. il Car & Dr 23:35-6+ Ag '77
We test:
Buick's new Turbo Regal. B. Tripolsky. il Mech Illus 73:78+ S '77
Chevy's resized intermediate; Malibu. il Mech Illus 73:74-5+ N '77
Chrysler's new little car; Le Baron. B. Tripolsky. il Mech Illus 73:94+ Je '77
Chrysler's new mini; Plymouth Horizon. B. Tripolsky. il Mech Illus 74:34-5+ Ja '78
Dodge's all-new Magnum. B. Tripolsky. il Mech Illus 73:98-9 O '77
Dodge's new little Monaco. B. Tripolsky. il Mech Illus 73:84+ Mr '77
Ford's all-new Fairmont. B. Tripolsky. il Mech Illus 73:64+ S '77
Ford's Maverick. F. Mackerodt. il Mech Illus 73:50-1+ F '77
Mercury's Cougar. B. Tripolsky. il Mech Illus 73:82+ N '77
New AMC Concord. B. Tripolsky. il Mech Illus 73:48-9+ D '77
New shrunken Lincoln. A. Laidlaw. il Mech Illus 73:120+ Ap '77
Olds Diesel. B. Tripolsky. il Mech Illus 73:43-5 O '77
Year in review; five dozen 1977 cars. il Car & Dr 23:39 O '77
See also
Automobiles, Foreign—Testing
Sports cars—Testing

Tires

See Tires, Automobile

AUTOMOBILES—*Continued*

Trailers

See Automobile trailers

Transmission

Car that can store power; Inertial Storage Transmission. W. Thoms. il Mech Illus 73:60+ N '77

Drive train. il Pop Mech 147:155-6+ My '77

Swifter shifter. il Hot Rod 30:127-8+ Je '77

What went wrong; automatic transmission failure symptoms. C. J. Baker. il Hot Rod 30: 84-7 O '77

Transportation

Firms that find a driver for your car. . .or a car for you to drive; driveaway companies. Changing T 31:29-30 N '77

Washing

See Automobiles—Cleaning

Wheel bearings

See Automobiles—Bearings

Wheels

Replacing the irreplaceable; wheels for 1914 Detroit Electric Roadster. R. J. Gottlieb. il Motor T 28:106+ D '76

Straight talk about front-end alignment. R. A. Dickelman. il Bet Hom & Gard 55:216 Ap '77

Wheel balancing for home mechanics. T. Tappett. il Mech Illus 74:108+ Ja '78

Windshields

How to keep your windshield clean. P. Bryan. il Pop Mech 147:108-9+ Ap '77

Wrecking

From the shredder file: junk. C. Fox. il Car & Dr 23:79+ D '77

Insider's guide to Junkerdom. B. McCall. il Car & Dr 22:22 Mr '77

Scrap dealers see red over salvage bill; Texas regulation of automobile salvage business. Am City & County 92:28 Ap '77

AUTOMOBILES, Antique

Classic comments; Bay to L.A. Run. R. J. Gottlieb. il Motor T 29:86-8 Ag '77

Concours: the ultimate car-care contest. W. A. Wyss. il Pop Mech 147:82-4+ Mr '77

De Soto of my dreams—and why it will stay that way. B. McCall. Car & Dr 22:20 Ap '77

Improving the breed can spoil the original. R. J. Gottlieb. il Motor T 29:106+ D '77

Landau ahead. il Hot Rod 30:47+ Jl '77

Little red hen; '51 Ford. G. Baxter. il Car & Dr 22:92-4 Mr '77

Retrospect:

1929 Cadillac 341 B roadster; excerpt from Survivors. H. Rasmussen. il Motor T 29: 51-4 S '77

1931 Packard Deluxe 8 Model 840. J. P. Kennedy. il Motor T 29:55-8 Jl '77

1934 La Salle. M. Lamm. il Motor T 29:66+ O '77

1941 Cadillac 60-Special. M. Lamm. il Motor T 29:119-23 Je '77

Sputtering run to Brighton; Brighton Veteran Car Run. J. A. Maxtone Graham. il Pop Mech 147:86-8+ Je '77

Talisman/Ford 1930 Model A. D. Sherman. il por Car & Dr 23:81-4 O '77

Anecdotes, facetiae, satire, etc.

Fine piece of machinery. E. Greenbaum. il Sat Eve Post 249:56-7+ N '77

Collectors and collecting

Art of collecting vintage cars. il Bus W p77-81 Ag 22 '77

Old cars in southern California. il Sunset 158: 55-6 My '77

Profiteers, bad laws are old-car collectors' worst foes. R. J. Gottlieb. Motor T 29:116+ Je '77

Real boom in older cars lies ahead. R. J. Gottlieb. Motor T 30:35-6 Ja '78

Suiting the enthusiast to a 'T'. R. J. Gottlieb. Motor T 29:63-4+ My '77

See also

Harrah's Automobile Collection, Reno, Nev.

Exhibitions

See Automobiles—Exhibitions

Maintenance and repair

See also

Automobile mechanics (persons)

Purchasing

Smart shoppers can save. R. J. Gottlieb. il Motor T 29:70+ F '77

Testing

Driving a legend; 1927 Bugatti. C. Fox. il Car & Dr 23:92-3+ S '77

AUTOMOBILES, Care of. See Automobiles—Maintenance and repair

AUTOMOBILES, Defective. See Automobiles—Defects

AUTOMOBILES, Electric

Electric car you can build. R. Q. Riley. il Mech Illus 73:45-7 F '77

Electric vehicles (EV's) in your future. . . N. Gluckin. il Sci Digest 82:7-13+ S '77

Electrics get federal recharge. T. Orme. il Motor T 29:6+ Je '77

Future car's future. il Forbes 120:12+ O 15 '77

Homebuilts and conversions. M. Lamm and R. Lund. il Pop Mech 147:93+ Mr '77

How ERDA is spending your money. C. A. Miller. il Mech Illus 73:48+ N '77

PM owners report: electric cars; Sebring-Vanguard Citicars. M. Lamm. il Pop Mech 147: 90-2 Mr '77

Short take:

Sebring Vanguard Citicar. T. Cook. il Car & Dr 23:126 N '77

History

Classic comments. R. J. Gottlieb. il pors Motor T 29:83-5 N '77

Testing

Editorially speaking; driving the Sears XDH-1. J. Dianna. il Hot Rod 30:4+ D '77

Reddy Kilowatt was my co-pilot; XDH-1 by Sears. P. Bedard. Car & Dr 23:12 Ja '78

AUTOMOBILES, Experimental

VW's 60-mpg turbo-diesel safety car. J. Dunne. il Pop Sci 211:104-5 O '77

Whatever happened to our safety cars? experimental research safety vehicles. P. M. Eckstein. il Mech Illus 73:16 Ap '77

AUTOMOBILES, Foreign

Air-cushioned Mercedes. J. Dunne. il Pop Sci 211:77 Ag '77

Behind the surge in foreign-car sales. il U.S. News 82:54 Je 13 '77

Cars and bikes together: a shopper's sampler. M. Jordan. il Car & Dr 23:40+ Ag '77

Driver's seat: on location. D. E. Davis, Jr. il Car & Dr 23:5-6 Ja '78

First look at new foreign cars. il U.S. News 83:39-41 O 31 '77

Fit for a king; Volvo's 264 TE limousine. il Motor T 29:62 Mr '77

Floodtide for imports. il Time 109:77 Je 20 '77

For your information. D. Abrahamson. See issues of Car and driver

Ford's Fiesta: $800 million bet. J. Ross-Skinner. il Duns R 110:62-4 Ag '77

Ford's Fiesta makes a big sales splash. il Bus W p38-9 Ag 22 '77

Hypertourers: Ferrari 4000 Auto, Bristol 412 and Aston Martin Lagonda. L. J. K. Setright. il Car & Dr 22:106-8+ Je '77

Import car buyer's guide. il Motor T 29:82-4+ Ap; 92-4+ My '77

International report. See issues of Motor trend

Lagonda: a fitting revival. J. Blunsden. il Motor T 29:44-6+ F '77

Lancia: the gem of Turin. K. Ludvigsen. il Motor T 29:60-2+ Je '77

Letting loose the dogs of wear. L. J. K. Setright. Car & Dr 23:116 Ag '77

Maneuverable mini-Mazda GLC has outstanding handling. R. Ceppos. il Pop Sci 210:120 Je '77

Mercedes-Benz odyssey: new cars and old castles, memories and wine; driving new cars. D. E. Davis, Jr. and others. il Car & Dr 22:50-3+ Mr '77

Mercedes-Benz 6.9. J. Christy. il Motor T 29:67-70 Jl '77

New car in town; Fiesta. il Newsweek 90:62+ Ag 29 '77

New from Mercedes. M. Knepper. il Motor T 28:76-8 D '76

Other imported cars share Honda's success. Bus W p28 My 23 '77

Over there. D. E. Davis, Jr. Car & Dr 23:9-10 Jl '77

PM owners report:

Opel Isuzu. M. Lamm. il Pop Mech 147:112-13+ Mr '77

Rolls-Royce Silver Shadow II. R. Ceppos. il Pop Sci 211:99 O '77

Sayonara, Volkswagen. J. Seelye. il New Repub 177:27-9 O 8 '77

Short take:

Alfa Romeo 2000 Spider Veloce. D. Abrahamson. il Car & Dr 23:32 N '77

Datsun 280-Z 2+2 five-speed. M. Jordan. il Car & Dr 23:60 O '77

Honda Accord. M. Jordan. il Car & Dr 22:73 My '77

Jaguar XJ6L. D. Abrahamson. il Car & Dr 23:92 Ag '77

Mazda Cosmo. P. Bedard. il Car & Dr 22:98 Ap '77

Mazda GLC. P. Bedard. il Car & Dr 22:30 F '77

Mazda RX-3SP. S. Thompson. il Car & Dr 23:62 D '77

Plymouth Arrow 160 GT. P. Bedard. il Car & Dr 23:30 N '77

Renault 12 GTL. M. Jordan. il Car & Dr 22:104 F '77

Saab 99 EMS Lambda-Sond. M. Jordan. il Car & Dr 23:103-4 Jl '77

Volvo 262 GT. D. E. Davis, Jr. il Car & Dr 22:32 F '77

AUTOMOBILES, Foreign—*Continued*
Silver Shadow II; new model. il Motor T 29:93 Je '77
Stutz massage parlor. C. Amory. il Esquire 88: 141-3 Jl '77
See also
Sports cars
Station wagons, Foreign

Anecdotes, facetiae, satire, etc.

Olaf the lazy goes off to college. W. Weith. Car & Dr 23:22 Jl '77

Awards, prizes, etc.

See also
Motor Trend Awards

Collectors and collecting

Retrospect:
Survivors; H. Ramussen's collection. F. M. H. Gregory. il Motor T 28:101-4 D '76

Engines

See Automobile engines

Exhibitions

See Automobiles—Exhibitions

History

Mercedes milestones. K. Ludvigsen. il Motor T 29:46-8 Ap '77
Retrospect:
1932 Aston Martin Le Mans tourer prototype. W. S. Jackson. il Motor T 29:59-62+ Ag '77
1966 Sunbeam Tiger and 1967 Sunbeam Tiger II. W. S. Jackson. il Motor T 29:103-6+ Mr '77
Volvo: half-century of Swedish quality. K. Ludvigsen. il Motor T 29:94-101 Jl '77

Manufacture

Off the beaten-panel path: little men with hammers. L. J. K. Setright. il Car & Dr 23:86+ O '77

Testing

And the Fiesta. . . il Mech Illus 73:66 S '77
Datsun B-210, Honda Accord, Toyota Corolla, Volkswagen Rabbit. il Consumers Res Mag 60: 12-20 Je '77
Double take: Peugeot 504D and Mercedes 240/300D. il Car & Dr 22:103-5 Je '77
Driving Ford's Fiesta, the newest minicar. il Changing T 31:13-15 S '77
Driving impression:
Audi 5000. C. Nerpel. il Motor T 29:83-5 S '77
Datsun 200-SX Turbo. B. Hall. il Motor T 29:68-9 Ag '77
Return of the 510! Datsun. B. Hall. il Motor T 29:54-5 N '77
Saab blows up a storm. J. Christy. il Motor T 28:87-9 D '76
Toyota Corona. P. Frey. il Motor T 29:91-2 S '77
Driving Mazda's new piston-packin' GLC. B. Hartford. il Pop Mech 147:197-8 Mr '77
Driving the Datsun 510. M. Lamm. il Pop Mech 149:87+ Ja '78
Driving the Diesel Rabbit. M. Lamm. il Pop Mech 148:82-3 Jl '77
Driving the five-cylinder Audi. B. Hartford. il Pop Mech 148:106-7 N '77
Driving the Ford Fiesta. M. Lamm. il Pop Mech 148:54-6 Jl '77
Driving the Mercedes-Benz 6.9. B. Hartford. il Pop Mech 148:83+ S '77
Driving the new Datsun 200SX and 810. M. Lamm. il Pop Mech 147:23-4+ Je '77
Fastest European sedan: Mercedes-Benz unleashes the potent 6.9! D. E. Davis, Jr. il Car & Dr 23:55-6+ Jl '77
Five super-economy subcompacts: VW Rabbit Diesel, Ford Fiesta, Mazda GLC, Datsun B210 5-Speed, Honda Civic 5-Speed. il Consumer Rep 43:32-41 Ja '78
Foreign cars: facts & figures on the favorites. il Changing T 31:24-9 Ap '77
Four economy subcompacts: Chevette, Colt, Subaru, Gremlin. il Consumer Rep 42:396-402 Jl '77
Four expensive imports: VW Dasher, Datsun 810, BMW 320i, Mazda RX-4. il Consumer Rep 42:469-75 Ag '77
Four subcompacts: Volkswagen Rabbit, Pontiac Sunbird, Toyota Corolla, Ford Mustang II. il Consumer Rep 42:335-41 Je '77
4000-mile test of the new Ford Fiesta. R. Ceppos. il Pop Sci 211:76-7+ Jl '77
Luxotouring: starring the Jaguar XJ-S, Mercedes-Benz 450SLC and BMW 630CSi. S. Thompson and others. il Car & Dr 23:64-7+ D '77
1977 Motor Trend Import Car of the Year Award; testing the nominees. J. Christy. il Motor T 29:44-6 Mr '77
PM owners report:
Honda Accord. M. Lamm. il Pop Mech 147: 114-15+ My '77
PS car test & driving report:
Diesel Rabbit. J. Dunne and R. Ceppos. il Pop Sci 211:34+ S '77
Economy subcompacts; Ford Fiesta challenges Gremlin and Chevette. J. Dunne and R. Ceppos. il Pop Sci 211:30+ Jl '77
Subcompact sports coupes; Honda Accord, Toyota Celica GT Liftback, Datsun 200 SX. J. Dunne and R. Ceppos. il Pop Sci 211:26+ D '77
Road test:
Alfa Romeo trio. J. Christy. il Motor T 29: 61-6 S '77
Aston Martin V-8. il Car & Dr 22:53-4+ Ap '77
Audi 5000. D. Sherman. il Car & Dr 23:107-8+ D '77
Audi Fox automatic. J. Christy. il Motor T 29:58+ O '77
BMW 630CSi. K. Ludvigsen. il Motor T 29: 52-4+ Je '77
BMW 630CSI; with editorial comment. il Car & Dr 22:8, 41-8 My '77
Datsun 200-SX. il Car & Dr 22:85-8 My '77
Datsun 510. P. Bedard. il Car & Dr 23: 120+ D '77
Datsun 810. il Car & Dr 22:117-18+ Je '77
Dodge Challenger. D. Sherman. il Car & Dr 23:72+ N '77
Fiat Xl/9. P. Bedard. il Car & Dr 23:59-61+ Ja '78
Ford Fiesta. B. Hall. il Motor T 29:35-6+ Ag '77
Ford Fiesta S. il Car & Dr 23:91-5 Jl '77
Mazda Cosmo. B. Hall. il Motor T 29:111-12+ Je '77
Mazda GLC. D. Sherman. il Car & Dr 23: 77-80 Ag '77
Mazda GLC Sport. B. Hall. il Motor T 29: 71-2+ D '77
Mercedes-Benz 280E. il Car & Dr 22:62-6+ Mr '77
Mercedes Benz 280E. J. Christy. il Motor T 29:41-4+ Ap '77
Mercedes-Benz 300CD. J. Christy. il Motor T 29:45-9 D '77
Mercedes-Benz 450SEL 6.9. J. Christy.. il Motor T 29:43-4+ Ag '77
Peugeot 604 SL. il Car & Dr 23:47-51 Ag '77
Peugeot 694 SL. J. Christy. il Motor T 29: 39-42 My '77
Saab EMS. J. Christy. il Motor T 29:74-6+ My '77
Saab Turbo. P. Bedard. il Car & Dr 23:65-70 O '77
TVR 2500M. il Car & Dr 22:91-2+ My 77
Toyota Celica GT Liftback. M. Jordan. il Car & Dr 23:51+ Ja '78
Two new Datsuns: Datsun 810 and 200-SX. B. Hall. il Motor T 29:96-8+ Ap '77
Volkswagen Convertible. M. Jordan. il Car & Dr 23:95-7+ O '77
Volkswagen Rabbit Diesel. il Car & Dr 22: 87-8+ Je '77
Test drives: Chevrolet's Chevette and Ford's Fiesta. A. K. Dukes. Mademoiselle 83:94 S '77
Top ten economy cars. R. G. Beason. il Mech Illus 73:30+ Ap '77
Toyota Celica GT Liftback: testing the Import Car of the Year. B. Hall. il Motor T 30:26-8 Ja '78
VW Diesel Rabbit. il Consumers Res Mag 60:28-31+ D '77
Viewpoint: Volvo 242 GT. D. E. Davis, Jr. il Car & Dr 23:47-8+ D '77
We test:
Mazda's new small car. B. Tripolsky. il Mech Illus 73:44-5 My '77
New Turbo Saab. R. G. Beason. il Mech Illus 74:60-1+ Ja '78
Plush new Peugeot 604. G. Wilkins. il Mech Illus 73:116-17 Mr '77
VW's new Diesel Rabbit. G. Wilkins. il Mech Illus 73:46-7 Ap '77
Year in review; five dozen 1977 cars. il Car & Dr 23:39 O '77

AUTOMOBILES, Miniature. See Automobile models

AUTOMOBILES, Police
Art of the states: a civilian bear-spotter's guide. D. Abrahamson. il Car & Dr 23:99-102 D '77
Patrol car logs cut speeding accidents; tachographic recording devices; Hawthorne, Calif. il Am City & County 92:96 My '77

Testing

Fastest American sedan: Dodge Monaco Police Pursuit. il Car & Dr 23:47-50+ Jl '77
Road test:
Chevrolet's Eurosedan supercars. J. Christy. il Motor T 29:57-8+ N '77

AUTOMOBILES, Racing
Back from the ashes; F. Mazi's Opel. il Hot Rod 30:102-3 O '77
Bracket racing America: [state] G. Baskerville and D. Wallace. il Hot Rod 30:35-8 S '77
Bracket racing America: [state] D. Wallace. il Hot Rod 30:28-32 Ag; 29-32 O; 35-8 N; 32-6 D '77
Chrysler's custom coupes. J. Norris. il Motor T 29:38-41 N '77

AUTOMOBILES, Racing—*Continued*

Crazy bird; Trans Am. il Hot Rod 30:58-9 O '77

Editorially speaking; Hot rod magazine's convertible racer. J. Dianna. il Hot Rod 30:7-8 Jl '77

Fleetwood black; bracket Camaro. il Hot Rod 30:68-70 Ag '77

Gang that shoots straight; Performance East Corvettes. R. McGonegal. il Hot Rod 30:54-7 D '77

Handle with care: the next generation of Greenwood Corvettes. B. Yates. il Car & Dr 23:108 O '77

Homemade hummer; racing go-karts. il Hot Rod 30:108-9 Jl '77

Horse of a different color; Monroe Handler Mustang II (title varies) il Hot Rod 30:118-22+ Je; 43-4+ Ag; 44+ S '77

Identicars; Camaro IROC racer. il Car & Dr 23:85-7 S '77

King of the road; R. Petty's immaculate Dodge Charger. J. Scalzo. il Hot Rod 30:96-7 Jl '77

Men who make the Blue Max run; funny car of H. Schmidt and R. Beadle. J. Scalzo. il pors Hot Rod 30:24-6+ Ag '77

Mopar bracket guide. D. Wallace. il Hot Rod 30:42-4+ D '77

Motivatin' down the line; B. Meyer's SMT Motivator. il Hot Rod 30:80-1 My '77

Mustang magic. il Hot Rod 30:52-3 Je '77

Necessary evil; B. Mitchell's Corvette Econo altered. R. McGonegal. il Hot Rod 30:108-10 My '77

Ragged edge of racing technology. M. Jordan. il Car & Dr 22:74-6+ F '77

Rally GLC: chained lightning. P. Frey. il Motor T 29:70 D '77

Roddin' at random. See issues of Hot rod

Straight arrow; Pro Stock Plymouth Arrow. il Hot Rod 30:56-7 O '77

Survivor Vette; L-88 C-48. T. Swan. il Motor T 28:40-2 D '76

Tequila Sunrise. il Hot Rod 30:120-1 Ap '77

Those amazing radial racers. P. Bedard. il Car & Dr 23:134-5 D '77

Triple threat; Hot rod's 3-in-1 Chevy II. J. Dianna. il por Hot Rod 30:56-7+ Ag; 26-8+ S; 36-7+ O '77

True confessions; R. Butler's technique for planning and building a drag race car. C. J. Baker. il pors Hot Rod 30:32-3+ Mr '77

Years of the snake; Cobra project. W. Wyss. il por Hot Rod 30:31-4+ Je '77

Brakes

See Brakes, Automobile

Engines

Budget Buick buildup; 455 engine. C. J. Baker. il Hot Rod 30:56-8 Jl '77

500-HP, blown small-block buildup. M. Davis. il Hot Rod 30:70-1+ O '77

Indy has a new boy in town. R. A. Cutter. il Mech Illus 73:126+ My '77

Maxi-mouse; building the small-block Chevy engine. J. McCraw. il Hot Rod 30:35-7+ Ag '77

Southern fried Ford; how to build a racing engine. M. Rossi. il Hot Rod 30:98+ Je; 80+ Jl '77

Turbos come to Grand Prix racing; Renault Elf. il Mech Illus 73:140-2 O '77

Maintenance and repair

Basic machining guide. C. J. Baker. il Hot Rod 30:48-50+ Jl '77

History

Retrospect:
 1910 12-litre Grand Prix Itala. E. Eves. il Motor T 30:66-8 Ja '78
 1965 Shelby GT 350 5R001 Competition. W. S. Jackson. il Motor T 29:86+ N '77

Maintenance and repair

See also
Automobiles, Racing—Engines—Maintenance and repair

Models

See Automobile models

Parts

See Automobile parts

Photographs

Hot rod gallery. il Hot Rod 30:47 My; 46+ Je; 60+ Jl; 54+ Ag; 41+ S; 54 O '77

Hot rod gallery. G. Baskerville. il Hot Rod 30:44-50+ F '77

Springs and suspension

See Automobiles—Springs and suspension

Testing

Hot rod magazine rod test:
 Built to boogie; 1937 Buick. G. Baskerville. il Hot Rod 30:50-2 Ag '77
 Horseradish; Boss 429 Mustang. R. McGonegal. il Hot Rod 30:120-3 My '77
 Little spruce coupe; 1934 Ford. il Hot Rod 30:56-8 Mr '77
 Silent springer; AMC Hornet. G. Baskerville. il Hot Rod 30:96-7 S '77
 Snake bit: 427 Cobra. G. Baskerville. il Hot Rod 30:67-9 Je '77

Journalist's ultimate track test; Elf Tyrrell P34. J. Rosinski. il por Motor T 29:92-5 Ag '77

Road test:
 Pace-setter; Datsun 200-SX. il Hot Rod 30:72-4+ Jl '77

Trailers

See Automobile trailers

AUTOMOBILES, Remodeled

Auto stretch; custom limousines. il Sci Digest 81:18-19 Mr '77

Building a BMW berserker. M. Jordan and D. Sherman. il Car & Dr 23:72+ O '77

Do-it-yourself GT dept: project super Seville. D. Sherman. il Car & Dr 23:61-3+ Ag '77

Fantastic fomopar; '32 Chrysler. il Hot Rod 30:90-1 F '77

Hit or miss? G. Baskerville. il Hot Rod 30:26-9 My '77

How to build a repro street rod. G. Baskerville. il Hot Rod 30:47-51 O; 30-3 N; 28-31 D '77

Junkyard jamboree; locating and using parts for rods and vans. il Hot Rod 30:70-4+ F '77

Just a passing dream; building around a Kelmar GT kit. il Hot Rod 30:52-3 O '77

Master plan. C. J. Baker. il Hot Rod 30:24-6 D '77

Monza Mirage. B. Hall. il Motor T 28:56 D '76

One man's ultimate Corvette: big banana. C. Nerpel. il Motor T 28:52-3+ D '76

Short take:
 Daytona MiGi. P. Bedard. il Car & Dr 22:111-13 My '77
 Herb Adams Firebird Trans-Am. P. Bedard. il Car & Dr 23:105-6 Jl '77

Summer Lark; 1976 Buick. N. Mayersohn. il Hot Rod 30:76-8 Mr '77

See also
Automobiles, Racing

Engines

See Automobile engines

Photographs

Best of Ford pictorial review. il Hot Rod 30:78-81 Je '77

Body & soul. G. Baskerville. Hot Rod 30:63-9 D '77

Hot rod gallery. See issues of Hot rod, May 1977-

Testing

Hot rod magazine rod test:
 Bold, the bad and the beautiful; 1955 Bel Air. G. Baskerville. il Hot Rod 30:81-3 D '77
 Mighty hybrid; Porschev. G. Baskerville. il Hot Rod 30:24-5+ O '77
 Newstalgia; 1948 remodeled Ford. G. Baskerville. il Hot Rod 30:39+ Jl '77
 Simply superb; 1928 Ford Highboy. G. Baskerville. il Hot Rod 30:45-7+ N '77
 Sudden death; Mustang II. G. Baskerville. il Hot Rod 30:28-30 Ap '77

AUTOMOBILES, Restored

Maintenance and repair

This law is tough but necessary. R. J. Gottlieb. il Motor T 29:88+ O '77

AUTOMOBILES, Steam

Running out of steam. A. W. Reitze, Jr. bibl il Environment 19:34-40 Je '77

AUTOMOBILES, Theft of

Steal-to-order biz: is your car next? K. Snedaker. il Car & Dr 22:47-8+ Ap '77

See also
Automobiles—Security measures

AUTOMOBILES, Three wheel

Return of the three-wheeler. R. G. Beason. il Mech Illus 73:138-9 Ap '77

Two's a motorcycle, three's a. . .very strange car. M. Lamm. il pors Pop Mech 148:102-4+ N '77

We test a 3-wheel car. R. G. Beason. il Mech Illus 73:48-9+ Ag '77

AUTOMOBILES, Used

Pre-owned racers. B. Oursler. il Car & Dr 22:125-6 My '77

Purchasing

Buying a used car. A. K. Dukes. Mademoiselle 83:50+ Jl '77

Buying a used car. il Consumer Rep 42:374-89 D '77

Can't-miss system to make money on old cars. R. Taylor. il Car & Dr 22:80+ Mr '77

Checklist for used-car buyers. Changing T 31:4 O '77

AUTOMOBILES, Used—Purchasing—*Continued*
Good bets in used cars; Some used car models to avoid. Consumer Rep 42:240 Ap '77
Used car buyer's guide. J. Joseph. il Motor T 29:95-6+ Je '77
Wheeling and dealing; used-car capitalism in Warsaw. Time 109:40 Je 6 '77

Selling

See Automobiles—Selling

AUTOMOBILES in art
Cars had faces then. J. Flint. il Esquire 88:111-15 N '77
Life and art of Peter Helck. W. S. Jackson. il Motor T 29:72-5 F '77

AUTOMOTIVE diesel engines. See Diesel engines, Automotive

AUTOMOTIVE electronics. See Automobiles—Electronic equipment

AUTOMOTIVE industries
See also
Automobile industry
Bus industry
Truck industry

Finance

Automotive. il Forbes 121:54+ Ja 9 '78

AUTOMOTIVE transportation. See Transportation, Automotive

AUTONOMY
Global separatism: nations coming unglued? Sr Schol 109:13 F 10 '77
Institution design and the separatist impulse: Quebec and the antebellum American South. M. V. Levine. bibl f Ann Am Acad 433:60-72 S '77

AUTOPENS. See Signature writing machines

AUTORADIOGRAPHY
Scintillator distribution in high-speed autoradiography. L. Goldgefter and V. Toder; B. G. M. Durie. Science 195:208 Ja 14 '77

AUTUMN
Autumn ought-to's. S. Mennear-Dubas. il Fam Health 9:28-31 S '77
Season for hymning and hawing. F. Trippett. il Time 110:100 S 19 '77
See also
October

Photographs

Splendor of autumn. A. Eisenstaedt. Horticulture 55:36-43 S '77
Upstate autumn. Conservationist 32:34-5 S '77

AUTUMN leaves, Color of. See Color of leaves

AUXINS
Managing your house plant's hormones. J. G. Greene. il Horticulture 55:18-20 N '77

AVAILABLE-light photography. See Photography—Light

AVALANCHES
Colorado's avalanche warning program. A. Judson. bibl il map Weatherwise 29:268-77 D '76
Unusual weather: the Alta snow slide story. il Weatherwise 29:286-7 D '77

AVANT-garde art. See Art, Modern

AVANT-garde motion pictures. See Motion pictures, Experimental

AVANT-garde music. See Music, Experimental

AVANT-garde phonograph records. See Phonograph records—Music, Experimental

AVANT-garde theater. See Theater, Experimental

AVARICE
Money talks. G. McCauley. America 137:137 S 10 '77
Seven deadly sins today; excerpt. H. Fairlie. New Repub 177:23-5 O 1 '77

AVCO Corporation
Avco gets its act together—for profit. por Bus W p 115-16 O 3 '77

AVEDON, Richard
Phony photographer. R. Boeth and others. il por Newsweek 90:43 S 19 '77 *
You ought to be in pictures. R. Rosenblatt. New Repub 177:45-6 O 1 '77 *

AVERAGE
Stein's paradox in statistics. B. Efron and C. Morris. il map Sci Am 236:119-27 bibl(p 148) My '77

AVERAGES, Stock. See Stocks—Price indexes and averages

AVERMAETE, Roger
Rubens: a portrait of the artist as a universal man. UNESCO Courier 30:6-18+ Je '77

AVERRE, Marlene
Grow your own rootstock. il Org Gard & Farm 25:82-3 Ja '78

AVERY, David
Case for shock therapy. Psychol Today 11:104 Ag '77

AVERY Fisher Award Concerts. See Concerts

AVERY Fisher Hall. See Lincoln Center for the Performing Arts, New York—Avery Fisher Hall

AVIATION
Flying in 2002. I. Asimov. il Flying 101:372 S '77
Future choice. E. G. Thripp. il Flying 101:428 S '77
Future flight: general aviation. J. W. Olcott. il Flying 101:352-4 S '77
See also
Air navigation
Air travel
Airlines
Airports
Airships
Airways
Balloon ascensions
Gliding and soaring
Private flying
also headings beginning Aeronautic, Aeronautics, Airplane, Airplanes

Accident investigation

See also
United States—National Transportation Safety Board

Accident prevention

See Aviation—Safety devices and measures

Accidents

A-10 crashes at Le Bourget; A-10 program unaffected by crash at Paris show. il Aviation W 106:34-6 Je 13 '77
After the holocaust; crash of Pan Am and KLM jets on Tenerife runway. S. Drake and others. il Newsweek 90:10+ S 26 '77
Air-safety challenge. M. E. Long. il Nat Geog 152:206-35 Ag '77
Bird ingestion cited in DC-10 accident. il Aviation W 107:61-3 Jl 25 '77
Board assays Alaska runway overrun. Aviation W 107:64-6 Ag 22 '77
Board cites ATC in Spokane near miss. Aviation W 106:59+ Mr 28 '77
Board probes crash of Rockwell 690A. Aviation W 106:64-6 Ja 17 '77
Board reports on near miss at Spokane. Aviation W 106:57+ Mr 14 '77
Cause of 707 crash at Tahiti eludes French investigating unit. il Aviation W 106:30 My 30 '77
Clawed by the hook in the sky; crash of Southern Airways DC-9. il Time 109:19 Ap 18 '77
Collision course; runway crash of KLM and Pan Am jets at Tenerife airport, Canary Islands. R. Carroll and others. il Newsweek 89:49-51+ Ap 11 '77
Conclusions reached in 727 accident; Harry S. Truman Airport, Charlotte Amalie, St Thomas, Virgin Islands, Apr. 27, 1976. Aviation W 106:66-7 My 23 '77
Conquest certification review planned. D. M. North. Aviation W 107:19 N 28 '77
Crash investigation focuses on tapes; Pan Am-KLM collision at Tenerife. D. M. North. il Aviation W 106:33+ Ap 4 '77
Disaster damages; international airline-disaster litigation. J. K. Footlick and others. il Newsweek 89:111 Ap 18 '77
Downtrend in aviation accidents spurs caution on 1977 outlook. Aviation W 106:28 Ja 17 '77
Great Yosemite gold rush; crash of airplane carrying thousands of pounds of marijuana. G. Rowell. Audubon 79:135 S '77
Holiday eve disasters; crash of the University of Evansville basketball team's plane. il Time 110:16 D 26 '77
Investigators continue search for cause of Air-India crash. Aviation W 108:25 Ja 9 '78
Jet Avia crashes claim six lives. Aviation W 106:26 Ja 17 '77
Landing maneuver cited in 727 crash; American Airlines at Charlotte Amalie, St Thomas, Virgin Islands, April 27, 1976. il Aviation W 106:63+ My 9 '77
Marines' bad luck plane; Harriers. il Time 110:15-16 Ag 15 '77
Marines seek Harrier solutions. Aviation W 107:19 S 12 '77
NTSB analyzes cargo aircraft crash; 1975 crash of Aerotransportes Entre Rios at Miami. Aviation W 108:52-3+ Ja 2 '78
NTSB analyzes factors in 727 crash. Aviation W 107:59-62 O 3 '77
NTSB analyzes Virgin Islands accident. Aviation W 106:60-1+ My 16 '77
NTSB cites approach in 727 crash. Aviation W 107:62-3 O 10 '77
NTSB cites heavy load in DHC-2 crash; Ketchum Air Service accident, September 12, 1975. Aviation W 108:78-9 Ja 9 '78
NTSB, pilots' chiefs criticize controllers in Georgia crash. Aviation W 106:31 My 9 '77
NTSB studies Alaska runway accident. il Aviation W 107:70-2 S 19 '77
New questions about air safety; with views on Canary Islands collision. il U.S. News 82:35+ Ap 11 '77
ONA crash analysis procedure detailed. Aviation W 107:73-5 Ag 8 '77

AVIATION—Accidents—*Continued*

Pilot error:

Center, is that weather heavy? R. L. Collins. Flying 100:34+ Mr '77

Chance encounter. R. L. Collins. Flying 100: 96+ My '77

Fuel crisis. R. L. Collins. Flying 100:38+ Ap '77

No glideslope. R. L. Collins. Flying 100: 38+ Je '77

Pilot judgment cited in 727 accident; American Airlines Boeing 727 at Harry S. Truman Airport, Charlotte Amalie, St Thomas, Virgin Islands, April 27, 1976. Aviation W 106:102-3 Ap 25 '77

Pilot selection, training altered as crashes of AV-8A mount. Aviation W 107:24-5 Ag 1 '77

Recommendations made in ONA crash. Aviation W 107:61+ Ag 15 '77

Rescue from the heart of a typhoon; crew of downed bomber saved by nuclear subs. C. Barton. il map Pop Mech 148:73-6+ D '77

Safety board investigates blade separation incident; Puerto Rico International Airlines incident, July 11, 1975, at Puerto Rico International Airport. Aviation W 106:56-9 Ja 24 '77

Safety board studies takeoff accident; Sept 20, 1975, accident of Airlift International McDonnell Douglas DC-8-63F at John F. Kennedy International Airport. Aviation W 106: 56-7+ Ja 3 '77

Tenerife case may alter liability rules. il Aviation W 106:32 Ap 4 '77

Tenerife collision still baffles. Aviation W 106: 34 My 2 '77

Terrible Tenerife. L. Morgan. Flying 100: 30 Je '77

Weather eyed in DC-9 crash. Aviation W 106:25 Ap 11 '77

. . . What's he doing? He'll kill us all; Canary Islands crash. il Time 109:22-8 Ap 11 '77; Same abr. with title Tragedy at Tenerife. il Read Digest 111:90-5 S '77

See also

Bermuda Triangle

Helicopters—Accidents

Salvage (airplanes)

Altitude flying

Ozone irritation problem sparks various solutions. Aviation W 106:33 Ap 18 '77

Plague of ozone. L. Langway and others. Newsweek 89:97-8 My 16 '77

Clubs

See Aviation clubs

Cold weather conditions

See Aviation—Winter flying

Competitions

Cycling in the sky; man powered flight competition. P. Gwynne and D. Gram. il Newsweek 90:76-7 Ag 1 '77

Dream of wings—via feet; B. Allen wins man-powered flight contest. il Sci N 112:149 S 3 '77

Flight of the Gossamer Condor. M. E. Long. il por Nat Geog 153:130-40 Ja '78

Flying bike that won $86,000; Henry Kremer Prize. il por U.S. News 83:92 O 31 '77

Gossamer wings; Henry Kremer Prize. Sci Am 237:74+ O '77

I pedaled the mile to aviation's big prize; ed by J. Joseph. B. Allen. il por Pop Mech 148:100-2+ D '77

Judgment days. R. L. Collins. il Flying 101:17 O '77

The winner; P. MacCready wins Kremer Prize for man-powered planes. P. Wahl. il por Pop Sci 212:56-8+ Ja '78

See also

Airplane racing

Conferences

Calendar. See issues of Flying

Economic aspects

See also

Airlines—Fares

Exhibitions

Attendance, sales records shattered at Paris Air Show. il Aviation W 106:20-1 Je 20 '77

Barometer of Le Bourget. R. Hotz. Aviation W 106:7 Je 27 '77

Calendar. See issues of Flying

NASA to stress space, aircraft in Paris. Aviation W 106:53 F 28 '77

New business aircraft pace show flight line; static display at Hobby Airport in Houston. il Aviation W 107:36-9 O 31 '77

Paris Air Show: air display future clouded by controls; with editorial comment. R. R. Ropelewski. il Aviation W 106:9, 14-20 Je 20 '77

Paris Air Show; photographs. Aviation W 106: 71-3 Je 20 '77

Paris show to attract record number of exhibitors. R. R. Ropelewski. il Aviation W 106:74-5+ Ap 25 '77

Paris underscores battle for exports. il Aviation W 106:42-9 Je 6 '77

Reading show emphasizes customers over spectators. K. J. Stein. Aviation W 106:27 Je 20 '77

Special photo report: Paris show in color. il Aviation W 106:35-42 Je 27; 107:38-45 Jl 4; 40-3 Jl 11 '77

Special report: Paris Air Show; with editorial comment. il Aviation W 106:7, 14-26+ Je 13 '77

U.S. helicopters get Paris exposure. il Aviation W 106:53-5 Je 27 '77

Weekenders in the air. il Flying 101:310-15 S '77

Fog hazards

Goosed. J. Moore. il Flying 100:18+ My '77

Fuel requirements

Carter energy proposal holds far-reaching aviation impact. Aviation W 106:48 Ap 25 '77

Fuel line. R. L. Collins. il Flying 100:42 Ap '77

Future tense. F. Zarb. Flying 101:371 S '77

See also

Airlines—Fuel requirements

History

See Aeronautics—History

Hot weather conditions

See Aviation—Summer flying

Instrument flying

Instrument flying made simple. S. Wilkinson. il Flying 101:52+ N '77

International aspects

Bermuda pact provisions backed. D. R. Griffiths. Aviation W 107:23-4 D 5 '77

Bermuda pact sparks opposition. R. K. Ellingsworth. Aviation W 107:26-7 Ag 1 '77

British victory; Bermuda agreement. Time 110:64 Jl 4 '77

CAB delays foreign permits. Aviation W 106:27 Ja 3 '77

Civil aviation parleys with USSR produce mixed results. Aviation W 106:36-7 Mr 7 '77

Closing the gaps in air-service talks; Bermuda agreement. il Bus W p32-3 My 9 '77

Compromise marks bilateral pact; Bermuda treaty replacement. D. A. Brown. Aviation W 106:26-7 Je 27 '77

Dissenter's view; Bermuda agreement. C. Tillinghast, Jr. Aviation W 106:7 My 30 '77

Ford overturns Atlantic decision. R. K. Ellingsworth. Aviation W 106:25 Ja 3 '77

Italians urge firmness in U.S. bilateral talks. L. Doty. Aviation W 107:26-7 O 31 '77

Japan displays firmness on capacity limitations. L. Doty. Aviation W 106:30 Ap 18 '77

Japan's turn to haggle over airline routes. Bus W p39-40 O 17 '77

Liberal bilaterals favored by Swissair. Aviation W 106:28 Ja 17 '77

Nerve war in the sky. A. J. Mayer and others. il Newsweek 89:68-9 Mr 21 '77

Pact seen dangerous precedent; U.S./U.K. air bilateral. Aviation W 107:25-6 Jl 18 '77

Saipan authority clouds Japanese bilateral talks. L. Doty. Aviation W 106:27-8 My 30 '77

That elusive U.S.-British air agreement; Bermuda agreement. il Bus W p46+ Mr 28 '77

U.S. carriers seek unified Bermuda position. Aviation W 106:34 F 7 '77

U.S. eases its position on multiple designation; U.S. carriers on routes serving the U.K. Aviation W 106:28 Mr 7 '77

U.S. holds firm on Japanese bilateral. L. Doty. Aviation W 107:38 Jl 25 '77

U.S. readies stiffer international policy. Aviation W 107:29 S 12 '77

U.S. readying solid Bermuda parley position. Aviation W 106:31 Ja 10 '77

U.S. sets June 2 target in British talks. D. A. Brown. Aviation W 106:26-7 My 30 '77

U.S.-U.K. service cut warned. Aviation W 106: 30 My 16 '77

U.S./U.K. talks still face tough issues. R. K. Ellingsworth. Aviation W 106:51 Ap 25 '77

White paper confirms gap on bilateral. L. Doty. Aviation W 106:26-7 Ja 3 '77

See also

Airlines—International services

Airspace (international law)

International Air Transport Association

International Civil Aviation Organization

Warsaw Convention

Laws and regulations

Airline regulatory reform seen federal bellwether. Aviation W 108:37 Ja 9 '78

Basic reform tenets emerging; Federal Aviation Act. R. K. Ellingsworth. Aviation W 106:29+ Mr 28 '77

Carriers urge cautious reform effort. R. K. Ellingsworth. Aviation W 106:25-6 Ap 4 '77

Carter backs reform bill; final form still in doubt. Aviation W 106:30 Je 27 '77

Commanding voice in airline reform; M. M. Schuman. por Bus W p 170+ N 14 '77

Commuter operators assessing proposed regulation changes. Aviation W 107:30 S 5 '77

AVIATION—Laws and regulations—*Continued*
Deregulation mess. W. H. Gregory. Aviation W 107:7 N 21 '77
Environment and business aviation; excerpts from address. F. B. McIntosh. Aviation W 107:11 O 10 '77
Final reform bill reflects compromises. R. K. Ellingsworth. Aviation W 106:30 Ja 17 '77
Fleet financing outlook clouded. R. G. O'Lone. Aviation W 106:29-30 My 23 '77
Industry seeks expedited Part 23 rulemaking. Aviation W 107:31 O 10 '77
Intrastates eye regulatory reform. map Aviation W 106:28-30 Ap 11 '77
Legislation on aviation faces mixed prospects in Congress. Aviation W 107:32 O 31 '77
Let's do it; more competition into the domestic airline industry. por Forbes 120:98 Jl 1 '77
Mirage of deregulation. R. Hotz. Aviation W 106:7 Ap 4 '77
More regulation or deregulation of the airlines? nationalization may be the answer for the future; address, December 8, 1976. C. C. Tillinghast. Vital Speeches 43:206-9 Ja 15 '77
New regulatory bill to ease transition. D. M. North. Aviation W 106:33-4 Je 20 '77
Odds look good for less airline regulation. il Bus W p 156+ Mr 21 '77
Pan Am chief favors capacity rules; Carriers get domestic fill-up rights. R. G. O'Lone. Aviation W 106:32-3 My 9 '77
Rapid markup of reform bill no assurance of fast passage. Aviation W 107:32 Jl 25 '77
Reform bill hits new deadlock. R. K. Ellingsworth. Aviation W 107:26-8 Ag 8 '77
Reform with caution; excerpts from address, February 17, 1977. F. Lorenzo. Aviation W 106:9 Mr 28 '77
Regulatory reform accelerated. D. M. North. Aviation W 107:25 Jl 4 '77
Senate hearing may spur revisions in reform bill. R. K. Ellingsworth. Aviation W 106:24-5 Ap 11 '77
Should airline rules be loosened? interviews. H. W. Cannon and F. Borman. il U.S. News 82:75-6 My 9 '77
U.S. hit on open skies policy. D. R. Griffiths. Aviation W 107:23 N 28 '77
United supports reforms for more flexible pricing. Aviation W 106:197+ Mr 21 '77
Westerlies; Part 135 Regulatory Review Conference. G. C. Larson. Flying 100:26+ Mr '77
See also
Air freight service—Laws and regulations
Air traffic control
Airspace (international law)
United States—Civil Aeronautics Board
United States—Federal Aviation Administration
Warsaw Convention

Meteorological aspects

See Meteorology, Aeronautic

Night flying

Fly by night. R. L. Collins. il Flying 100:50-1+ My '77

Periodicals

See also
Aviation week & space technology (periodical)
Flying (periodical)

Physiological aspects

How to feast and fast in flight; minimizing jet lag. B. Dubivsky. N Y Times Mag p28 S 4 '77
Ozone irritation problem sparks various solutions. Aviation W 106:33 Ap 18 '77
Plague of ozone. L. Langway and others. Newsweek 89:97-8 My 16 '77
What can we do about jet lag. V. Goldberg. bibl il Psychol Today 11:68-9+ Ag '77

Records

See Aviation records

Safety devices and measures

Air-safety challenge. M. E. Long. il Nat Geog 152:206-35 Ag '77
Braking the record. R. L. Collins. Flying 101:48 Jl '77
Constant quest for safety. il Time 109:28+ Ap 11 '77
Drive pushed to extend safety gains. D. M. North. Aviation W 106:26 Ja 10 '77
FAA safety role seen boosted with airline regulatory reform. D. M. North. Aviation W 107:31 S 19 '77
Future flight: safe flight. W. B. Todd, Jr. Flying 101:370 S '77
New questions about air safety; with views on Canary Islands collision. il U.S. News 82:35+ Ap 11 '77
Passenger emergency briefing improvements urged in hearings. Aviation W 107:30 Ag 1 '77
Pilots talk about air crashes; excerpt from Final approach: the crash of Eastern 212. W. Stockton. il N Y Times Mag p41-2+ Ap 10 '77
Zero-zero-stupid-stupid. C. S. Osborn. Flying 101:42+ O '77
See also
United States—Federal Aviation Administration—Flight Service Stations

Social aspects

Thirty-three hours that changed the world. E. K. Gann. il por Sat R 4:7-10 Ap 16 '77

Storm hazards

Center, am I inverted? R. L. Collins. Flying 101:22+ N '77
Clawed by the hook in the sky; crash of Southern Airways DC-9. il Time 109:19 Ap 18 '77
Double jeopardy. R. L. Collins. Flying 101:88+ O '77
FAA intensifies windshear R&D effort. K. J. Stein. il Aviation W 107:66-7 S 12 '77
It only hurts for a little while. S. Wilkinson. Flying 101:118 O '77
Onboard windshear monitor developed. W. C. Wetmore. il Aviation W 107:59-62 Ag 22 '77
One-way street; a nest of thunderstorms. R. L. Collins. Flying 101:37+ Ag '77
Pilot error:
Center, is that weather heavy? R. L. Collins. Flying 100:34+ Mr '77
Unpadded cell. G. Baxter. Flying 100:18+ Je '77

Stunt flying

Demonstration flights deliver message. A. W. Bedford. il Aviation W 107:36-9+ N 21 '77
Riding high; wing-riding. G. Baxter. il Flying 101:38 O '77

History

Barnstorming. N. Slepyan. il Flying 101:86-9+ S '77

Summer flying

Summertime, and the flyin' ain't easy. P. Garrison. il Flying 101:95-6+ Jl '77

Taxation

Surcharges urged for noise compliance. Aviation W 106:32 My 9 '77

Transatlantic flights

History

Flight on N-X-211. P. Garrison. il Flying 101:152-5 S '77
Flight that opened an era: a master stroke of skill, daring. L. D. Lyman. il Sci Digest 81:32-3 My '77
Flight to remember; Lindbergh flight. R. F. Dempewolff. il por map Pop Mech 147:81-3+ My '77
Lindbergh alone; condensation. B. Gill. il pors Read Digest 110:225-8+ My '77
Lucky Lindy. il por Sr Schol 109:10-11 My 5 '77

Wind hazards

See Aviation—Storm hazards

Winter flying

Traffic rises despite weather problems. D. M. North. Aviation W 106:26-7 Mr 7 '77

Arab countries

Arab airline, government unity sought. L. Doty. Aviation W 107:26-7 N 28 '77

Bahamas

Bax seat. G. Baxter. Flying 100:19-20 Mr '77

Great Britain

Takeoff for disaster; plans for imperial airship fleet. J. Morris. il Horizon 19:24-33 Ja '77

South America

Around Cape Horn the easy way. E. K. Gann. il por map Flying 101:69-72+ Jl; 56-9+ Ag '77

United States

Underdog; general aviation. M. Karant. il Flying 101:206-7 S '77

Western States

Westerlies. G. C. Larson. See issues of Flying to April, 1977

AVIATION, Commercial. See Aeronautics, Commercial

AVIATION and health. See Aviation—Physiological aspects

AVIATION and state
Air transport fundamentals; excerpts from address, April 18, 1977. E. H. Boullioun. Aviation W 106:11 Ap 18 '77
Aviation policy position clouded. R. K. Ellingsworth. Aviation W 106:25-6 Mr 14 '77
Court clears Concorde JFK service. W. C. Wetmore. Aviation W 106:29 My 16 '77
Court requests U.S. role in Concorde entry case. Aviation W 106:63+ Je 6 '77
Court ruling awaited in Concorde case; Kennedy Airport landing rights. W. H. Gregory. Aviation W 106:24+ My 9 '77

AVIATION and state—*Continued*
Future flight: flight control. R. L. Collins. Flying 101:359-60+ S '77
Playing politics with airlines; J. Carter's dispersal of routes. map Time 111:46 Ja 16 '78
See also
United States—Civil Aeronautics Board
United States—Federal Aviation Administration

France

French adopt new civil aviation policy. Aviation W 106:32 Je 13 '77
AVIATION associations
Aerospace calendar. See issues of Aviation week & space technology
Calendar. See issues of Flying
See also
Experimental Aircraft Association
International Air Transport Association
National Aeronautic Association
AVIATION clubs
They take to the sky; Bessie Coleman Aviators. il Ebony 32:88-90+ My '77
AVIATION education
See also
Air pilots—Training
Aviation schools
AVIATION in motion pictures
Chairborne aviator at the flicks. J. Crist. il Sat R 4:24+ Ap 16 '77
AVIATION in television
Corsair: old hose-nose becomes a TV star. G. Baxter. il Flying 100:46-51+ Je '77
AVIATION insurance. See Insurance, Aviation
AVIATION policy. See Aviation and state
AVIATION records

History

Other flights. D. Mosteller. il Flying 101:156-60 S '77
AVIATION research. See Aeronautic research
AVIATION schools
Aeronautical university plans expansion; Embry-Riddle. il Aviation W 107:55+ D 5 '77
Getting your water wings is easy even if you live in Ohio. J. A. Slocum; K. A. Leibell. Flying 101:50-1 Ag '77
AVIATION week & space technology (periodical)
Charged debate erupts over Russian beam weapon. N. Wade. Science 196:957-9 My 27 '77
Message for our readers. R. Hotz. Aviation W 107:7 D 19 '77
Whole new ball game? announcement of Russian particle beam weapon. Nat R 29:596-7 My 27 '77
AVINERI, Shlomo
Israel's dilemma. Commentary 64:47-50 D '77
AVIONICS
Avionics effort keyed to Soviet threats. il Aviation W 106:201-3+ Ja 31 '77
Avionics standardization is sought. Aviation W 106:208-9 Ja 31 '77
Future avionics trends emerge. P. J. Klass. il Aviation W 106:163+ Mr 21 '77
Inexpensive advanced avionics concepts being sought. B. M. Elson il Aviation W 107:62-3+ Ag 1 '77
Standard power-supply units emerge. P. J. Klass. il Aviation W 107:59-61 Jl 18 '77
USAF advancing NavStar positioning. B. Miller. il Aviation W 106:71+ Je 13 '77
Use of large-scale microcircuits pushed. P. J. Klass. il Aviation W 107:49-51 Ag 29 '77
See also
Airplanes, Military—Electronic equipment
Helicopters—Electronic equipment
United States—Naval Air Systems Command—Naval Avionics Facility
AVIONICS industry

Export-import trade

Export efforts seek turnkey programs. K. J. Stein. il Aviation W 106:281-3+ Je 6 '77

International aspects

Joint avionics interest rises in USSR. P. J. Klass. Aviation W 106:16-17 Je 27 '77
AVIONS Marcel Dassault-Breguet Aviation (firm) See Airplane industry—France
AVIOPHOBIA. See Phobias
AVIS, Inc
Avis: back on the main road, gathering speed. por Duns R 109:18-19 Ja '77
Moving in; move to New York City. New Yorker 53:38-40 D 5 '77
AVIS, Inc mergers. See Corporations—Acquisitions and mergers
AVOCADOS
How to treat thirsty avocados in a water-short year. il Sunset 158:287 Ap '77
See also
Cookery—Fruit
AVON, Anthony Eden, 1st Earl of
Eden: a memoir. H. Mitgang. Nation 224:100-1 Ja 29 '77 *
Eden: the loyal adjutant. il pors Time 109:40-1 Ja 24 '77 *

AVON Books (firm) See Publishers and publishing—Paperback books
AVON Products, Inc
Calling on Avon; spokeswoman S. Griffin. M. R. Carter. Mademoiselle 83:72 Je '77
AVONCROFT Museum of Buildings. See Museums—Great Britain
AVRIL, Joan
Parade. New Yorker 53:39-40 O 17 '77 *
AWARDS. See Rewards, prizes, etc.
AX, Emanuel
Musician of the month: Emanuel Ax. S. Clark. por Hi Fi 27:MA5+ O '77 *
AXELROD, Julius. See Paul, S. M. jt auth
AXELSEN, Donald F.
Art in Westbrook. il Sch Arts 76:34 Je '77
AXELSON, Kenneth Strong
Axelson's gaffe. D. Pauly and R. Thomas. por Newsweek 89:70 Mr 21 '77 *
AXTELL, James
Who invented scalping? il Am Heritage 28:96-9 Ap '77
AXTHELM, Pete
Pssst! Wanna tip on a hot horse? il Esquire 87:92-3 Ap '77
Voice of the South. pors Newsweek 89:25 Ja 31 '77
AYCKBOURN, Alan
Absent friends. Reviews
Time il 110:62 Jl 25 '77 *
AYENSU, Edward S.
Eucalyptus bark; with biographical sketch. il Natur Hist 86:6, 36-9 D '77
AYERS, Thomas G.
CommEd: tomorrow's utility today. il por Bus W p58+ O 24 '77 *
AYERST Laboratories. See Drug industry
AYMOND, Alphonse H.
Who's in charge here? Forbes 119:60 Mr 1 '77 *
AYRES, William
Father Bill and the voices of the night. T. Ichniowski. America 136:50-2 Ja 22 '77 *
AZAARENES. See Aromatic compounds
AZEVEDO, Alfonso Llambias de. See Llambias de Azevedo, A.
AZORES
Azores. J. Anderson. il Sat R 5:30-1 O 29 '77
See also
Cruising—Azores
AZTECS
Enigma of Aztec sacrifice. M. Harner. il map Natur Hist 86:46-51 bibl(p 100) Ap '77; Discussion. 86:20+ My '77
AZZIYE, Lebanon. See Villages—Lebanon

B

B. Dalton Bookseller (firm) See Booksellers and bookselling—United States
B. Dalton Bookseller (firm). New York City. See Booksellers and bookselling—New York (state)
B-1 (airplane) See Airplanes, Military—United States
BART (Bay Area Rapid Transit) See San Francisco Bay Region—Transit systems
BB guns. See Air guns
BBC. See British Broadcasting Corporation
BCA. See Business Committee for the Arts
BCIU. See Business Council for International Understanding
B. F. Goodrich Company. See Goodrich, B. F. Company
BHT. See Butylated hydroxytoluene
BISAC. See Book Industry Systems Advisory Committee
BL Lacertae objects. See Radio sources (astronomy)
BLM. See United States—Land Management, Bureau of
BLS. See United States—Labor Statistics, Bureau of
BMI. See Book Manufacturers' Institute
BMW (automobile) See Automobiles, Foreign
BOR. See United States—Outdoor Recreation, Bureau of
BP Company. See British Petroleum Company
BWCA (Boundary Waters Canoe Area) See Quetico-Superior Region
BAADER, Andreas
Guilty as charged. Time 109:43 My 9 '77 *
BAADER-Meinhof gang. See Terrorists, German
BABAEV, Agadjhan Geldievitch, and Orlovsky, N. S.
Winning battle against destruction. il UNESCO Courier 30:18-22 Jl '77
BABCOCK, Charles L.
Tutankhamun and Star trek; address, July 29, 1977. Vital Speeches 43:744-7 O 1 '77

BACTERIA—*Continued*

Culture

In vitro growth of mycobacterium lepraemurium, an obligate intracellular microbe. A. M. Dhople and J. H. Hanks. bibl il Science 197: 379-81 Jl 22 '77

Growth

See Growth (bacteria)

Metabolism

Circulation of H^+ and K^+ across the plasma membrane is not obligatory for bacterial growth. F. M. Harold and J. Van Brunt. bibl il Science 197:372-3 Jl 22 '77

Resistance and sensitivity

Conjugal transfer of the gonococcal penicillinase plasmid. B. I. Eisenstein and others. bibl il Science 195:998-1000 Mr 11 '77

Naturally occurring plasmid carrying genes for enterotoxin production and drug resistance. C. L. Gyles and others. bibl il Science 198:198-9 O 14 '77

BACTERIA, Luminous

Luminous bacterium that emits yellow light; photobacterium fischeri. E. G. Ruby and K. H. Nealson. bibl il Science 196:432-4 Ap 22 '77

BACTERIA, Nitrogen fixing

Intergeneric transfer of genes involved in the rhizobium-legume symbiosis. P. E. Bishop and others. bibl il Science 198:938-40 D 2 '77

Nitrogen fixation in grasses inoculated with spirillum lipoferum. R. L. Smith and others; reply with rejoinder. A. C. Rogerson. Science 195: 1362 Mr 25 '77

See also

Rhizobium

BACTERIA, Pathogenic

Legion disease; culprit caged. il Sci N 111:69-70 Ja 29 '77

Mystery bacterium; Legionnaire's disease. M. Clark. il Newsweek 90:98 S 19 '77

Philadelphia disease story; Legionnaire's disease. Chemistry 50:22 Mr '77

See also

Neisseria

BACTERIAL chemotaxis. See Chemotaxis

BACTERIAL conjugation. See Conjugation (biology)

BACTERIAL control of oil spills. See Oil pollution of rivers, harbors, etc.—Control

BACTERIAL genetics. See Microbial genetics

BACTERIAL growth. See Growth (bacteria)

BACTERIAL plasmids. See Plasmids

BACTERIAL viruses. See Bacteriophages

BACTERICIDAL action

Bactericidal effect for human lactoferrin. R. R. Arnold and others. bibl il Science 197:263-5 Jl 15 '77

BACTERIOLYSIS

Plasmid detection and sizing in single colony lysates. W. M. Barnes. bibl il Science 195:393-4 Ja 28 '77

BACTERIOPHAGES

Bacteriophages in live virus vaccines: lack of evidence for effects on the genome of rhesus monkeys. J. B. Milstien and others. bibl il Science 197:469-70 Jl 29 '77

Charon phages: safer derivatives of bacteriophage lambda for DNA cloning. F. R. Blattner and others. bibl il Science 196:161-9 Ap 8 '77

Construction of chimeric phages and plasmids containing the origin of replication of bacteriophage lambda. D. D. Moore and others. bibl il Science 198:1041-6 D 9 '77

EK2 derivatives of bacteriophage lambda useful in the cloning of DNA from higher organisms: the λgtWES system. P. Leder and others. bibl il Science 196:175-7 Ap 8 '77

Effects of escherichia coli and yeast DNA insertions on the growth of lambda bacteriophage. J. R. Cameron and R. W. Davis. bibl il Science 196:212-15 Ap 8 '77

Full gene sequence of DNA virus solved. il Sci N 111:148-9 Mr 5 '77

Genetic structure of the replication origin of bacteriophage lambda. M. E. Furth and others. bibl il Science 198:1046-51 D 9 '77

Physical structure of the replication origin of bacteriophage lambda. K. Denniston-Thompson and others. bibl il Science 198:1051-6 D 9 '77

Screening λgt recombinant clones by hybridization to single plaques in situ. W. D. Benton and R. W. Davis. bibl il Science 196:180-2 Ap 8 '77

BACTERIORHODOPSIN. See Pigments (biology)

BADACZEWSKI, Dennis

Where will our future English teachers come from? Educ Digest 42:54-5 Mr '77

BADEA, Christian

Artist life. D. J. Soria. pors Hi Fi 27:MA9 D '77 *

BADGER Company, Inc. See Engineering construction companies—Belgium

BADGERS

Sure, it looks cute. W. Curtis. il Nat Wildlife 16: 36-9 D '77

BADILLO, Herman

Excerpt from remarks on amnesty for illegal aliens, March, 2, 1977. Cong Digest 56:240+ O '77

Excerpts from the debate on Federal Elections Campaign Act Amendments, April 1, 1976. Cong Digest 56:80-1+ Mr '77

BAENSCH, Robert E.

Robert E. Baensch: the global man at Harper & Row; interview, ed by H. R. Lottman. il por Pub W 212:87+ S 19 '77

BAER, Jean. See Fensterheim, H. jt auth

BAER, John M.

Housing and community development. Nation 224:274-6 Mr 5 '77

BAER, Walter S. and others

Government-sponsored demonstrations of new technologies. bibl il Science 196:950-7 My 27 '77

BAEYENS, Gill

Adventureland: the Himalayas. il Vogue 167: 180+ My '77

BAG cells. See Nerve cells

BAGDIKIAN, Ben Haig

Woodstein U. il Atlantic 239:80-92 Mr; 32 My '77

BAGGAGE. See Luggage

BAGGE, Carl E.

Coal: the once and future king; address, August 26, 1977. Vital Speeches 44:9-15 O 15 '77

Too much of a good thing? por Forbes 119:66 My 1 '77 *

BAGGETT, James R.

Let us now praise the lowly onion. il Horticulture 55:24-7 Ap '77

BAGS

Fold-and-stash shopping tote. il Bet Hom & Gard 55:185 N '77

Handy pouch for the bedtime reader. il Sunset 159:166 O '77

Now everything goes in gear bags. J. Campbell. il Sports Illus 47:50-1+ Jl 18 '77

Stitch-'em up bags to pack with pride. N. Lindemeyer and C. Vaughan. il Bet Hom & Gard 55:98-9 Ag '77

Tote bag opens out to a table setting for four. il Sunset 158:109 Je '77

See also

Handbags

BAHAMAS

See also

Aviation—Bahamas

Cruising—Bahamas

Fishing—Bahamas

BAHER, Constance Whitman

The life you save. . . il N Y Times Mag p82+ My 1 '77

BAHR, Robert

How to make your kids smarter. il Am Home 80: 44-5+ Je '77

New ethical question: head transplants? il Sci Digest 81:76-8 My '77

Regeneration: a potential for cancer aid is seen in research; excerpt from reprint from Smithsonian, January 1977. il Sci Digest 81: 42-4 Ap '77

BAHRAIN. See Bahrein

BAHREIN

For the U.S. Navy, a strategic setback in the Persian Gulf. D. Mullin. il map U.S. News 82:43-4 Je 6 '77

Weighing anchor. W. E. Schmidt. il map Newsweek 90:33 Jl 11 '77

BAIC, Dusan. See Gans, C. jt auth

BAIL

Bail debate. J. K. Footlick and others. il Newsweek 89:40 My 23 '77

BAILAR, Benjamin Franklin

Leave Postal Service as it is. il U.S. News 82: 53:4 Ap 25 '77

Mail service: better, but—excerpts from address, February 7, 1977. por U.S. News 82:81 F 14 '77

about

Still trying to make the post office work. il por Bus W p 133+ Mr 21 '77 *

BAILEY, Angela

Prisoners; poem. Chr Cent 94:1031 N 9 '77

BAILEY, Anthony

Profiles; Queen Elizabeth II. New Yorker 53: 42-4+ Ap 11; 51-2+ Ap 18 '77

Reporter at large. New Yorker 53:158+ N 21 '77

BAILEY, Bruce H.

Ball lightning. bibl il Weatherwise 30:99-105 Je '77

BAILEY, Francis Lee

Watch out for trial lawyers. por Newsweek 91:7 Ja 2 '78

BAILEY, Herbert Smith, 1921-

Traditional book in the electronic age; address, November 10, 1977. il pors Pub W 212:24-9 D 5 '77

BAILEY, James E. and others

Characterization of bacterial growth by means of flow microfluorometry. bibl il Science 198: 1175-6 D 16 '77

BAILEY, Jim
Batteries: should you charge or chuck 'em? il Mod Phot 41:20+ Mr '77
Phototronics. il Mod Phot 41:70+ D '77
Thermometers: how do they measure up? il Mod Phot 41:84-7+ Ag '77
What's ahead in batteries? il Mod Phot 41:73-4+ S '77

BAILEY, John
John Bailey: keeper of the faith. B. Tarrant. il pors Field & S 82:168-72 O '77 *

BAILEY, Martin
Namibia spells uranium. Nation 224:525-7 Ap 30 '77

BAILEY, Maurice
Checklist for survival. il Motor B & S 139:70-1+ Mr '77

BAILEY, Norman
Instinctive artist; interview, ed by G. Movshon. pors Opera N 41:24-7 F 19 '77

BAILEY, Pearl
United States calls for support for UNRWA; statement, November 2, 1976. Dept State Bull 75:755-6 D 27 '76
about
23rd annual Traveler of the Year Award. por Travel 148:66-7 Jl '77 *

BAILEY, Renée
Growing up in Harlem. Seventeen 36:138-9+ N '77

BAILEY, S. M.
Why you age. Sci Digest 82:50-2 Jl '77

BAILEY, William H.
Bill Bailey's Rhode Island blues. il por Time 109:70 Mr 21 '77 *

BAILEY, Wilma A.
Foreign language and area research program. Am Educ 13:26-7 N '77

BAILLY nuclear power plant (proposed) See Atomic power plants

BAIN, Christine A.
Aurora. il Conservationist 31:24-5 Ja '77
Winter sky. il Conservationist 31:26-7 Ja '77

BAINBRIDGE, John
Our far-flung correspondents. New Yorker 53:141-8+ D 12 '77

BAINE, Reginald
Take us as we are. il Sat Eve Post 249:94-5 O '77

BAIRD, Andrew
At a Confederate cemetery near Resaca, Georgia; poem. New Repub 177:27 S 3 '77

BAIRD, George H.
Getting economic basics across to children. V. Louviere. il Nations Bus 65:57 Ag '77 *

BAIRD, Peter. See McCaughan, E. jt auth

BAISINGER, Grace
Parents' PTA page. por Parents Mag 52:25 Je; 12 S '77

BAIT
Bassing with bait. B. Dalrymple. il Outdoor Life 159:78-81 Je '77
Day the pike put the move on Herman; use of suckerfish when pike ice fishing in Michigan. R. Rau. il Sports Illus 46:38-40+ F 28 '77
Stripers and bait; Atlantic States. N. Bryant. il Field & S 82:42-6 Ag '77
See also
Earthworms

BAITS, Bird. See Bird baits and repellents

BAITS, Deer. See Deer baits and repellents

BAKAL, Carl
Linda's haunting vision. il por Read Digest 110:68-72 Mr '77

BAKALAR, James B. See Grinspoon, L. jt auth

BAKAN, David
Unmanifest. New Yorker 53:28-9 Ap 4 '77 *

BAKER, Bob
Harbor-hopping the Pacific coast. il Motor B & S 140:68-9+ S '77
Lessons of a long-distance cruiser. il Motor B & S 141:122-4+ Ja '78
North to Alaska. il Motor B & S 140:40-3+ D '77
When the going gets tough. il Motor B & S 140:54-5+ Jl '77

BAKER, Bobby Gene
Bobby Baker. E. Keerdoja. il por Newsweek 89:12 My 30 '77 *

BAKER, C. J.
C. J. talks tech. See issues of Hot rod
Road test. il Hot Rod 30:58+ D '77

BAKER, D. Philip
Exemplary media programs; excerpt from School and public library media programs for children and young adults. il por SLJ 23:23-7 My '77
Mediacentric. Wilson Lib Bull 52:308-9 D '77

BAKER, Elizabeth C.
(ed) See Rivers, L. Larry Rivers and George Segal: back in the U.S.S.R.
(ed) See Segal, G. Larry Rivers and George Segal: back in the U.S.S.R.

BAKER, Herman
Herman Baker: a dynamic midwest retailer-publisher. il por Pub W 212:67-9 S 26 '77 *

BAKER, Howard Henry, 1925-
Dying party? interview. pors U.S. News 83:23 Ag 29 '77
about
Baker does the hustle. T. Mathews and J. J. Lindsay. il pors Newsweek 90:14-15 Jl 4 '77 *
Path to 1980. J. Lelyveld. il pors N Y Times Mag p 110 O 2 '77 *

BAKER, James T.
Prophetic minority. Commonweal 104:550-1 S 2 '77
Red-Haired saint. il Chr Cent 94:328-32 Ap 6 '77

BAKER, James Wesley
Imprisonment of Lafayette. il Am Heritage 28:86-91 Je '77

BAKER, Janet
Sense and sensibility; interview, ed by S. Wadsworth. il pors Opera N 42:8-13 Jl '77

BAKER, John C.
Are corporate executives overpaid? bibl f Harvard Bus R 55:51-6 Jl '77

BAKER, John F.
(ed) PW interviews. See issues of Publishers weekly to May 16, 1977
Some criticism, some faint praise—but still struggling along. il Pub W 211:32-4 My 2 '77
Talking with Ved Mehta. Sat R 4:35 Ja 22 '77

BAKER, Josephine
Not for entertainment only. G. H. Hudson. bibl f por Negro Hist Bull 40:682-3 Mr '77 *

BAKER, Kenneth
William Tucker: meaning vs. matter. il Art in Am 65:102-3 N '77

BAKER, Laurin M.
From Little River to Georgetown: South Carolina's Grand Strand. il Travel 147:54-7 Je '77

BAKER, Lucinda
Every writer needs a turquoise horse. Writer 90:14-17 Je '77

BAKER, M. A. and Chapman, L. W.
Rapid brain cooling in exercising dogs. bibl il Science 195:781-3 F 25 '77

BAKER, Nancy C.
Tough love: new way to help teens in trouble. il Parents Mag 52:43+ Jl '77

BAKER, Philip John Noel-. See Noel-Baker, P. J.

BAKER, Ross K.
Alleviating the research famine. bibl Society 14:10-11 My '77
Entry of women into federal job world—at a price. il Smithsonian 8:82-4+ Jl '77

BAKER, Russell
Role models. Am Home 80:8 N '77
Sunday observer. See issues of New York times magazine

BAKER, Seth H.
How Los Angeles magazine thrives on rivalry. por Bus W p38 Mr 7 '77 *

BAKER, Theodore L. and McGinty, D. J.
Reversal of cardiopulmonary failure during active sleep in hypoxic kittens: implications for sudden infant death. bibl il Science 198:419-21 O 28 '77

BAKER, Timothy S. and others
Ribulose bisphosphate carboxylase: a two-layered, square-shaped molecule of symmetry 422. bibl il Science 196:293-5 Ap 15 '77

BAKER, W. Lowell
Sawdust injection firing. il pors Ceram Mo 25:45-7 S '77

BAKER, Walter Charles
Classic comments. R. J. Gottlieb. il pors Motor T 29:83-5 N '77 *

BAKER, William Oliver, and others
Computers and research. bibl il Science 195:1134-9 Mr 18 '77

BAKER and Taylor Companies
Baker & Taylor program will bring librarians and publishers together; New Books Showcase. D. Maryles. Pub W 211:56-7 Ja 10 '77
Major shifts planned for Baker & Taylor Texas facility; interview, ed by J. Giusto. D. Kutner. Pub W 212:55 O 10 '77

BAKER/Beech-Nut Corporation. See Food industry

BAKER Book House (bookstore) See Booksellers and bookselling—Michigan

BAKER International Corporation
Baker: calling the shots—and booming. por Duns R 110:22-3 O '77

BAKER Sanctuary. See Wildlife sanctuaries—Michigan

BAKERS and bakeries
Great Italian bread from a real bread expert; A. Zito's and Sons, New York City. S. P. Torpey. il Bet Hom & Gard 55:62-3+ F '77
Someone's in the kitchen besides the Entenmanns. il Forbes 119:48+ Mr 15 '77
See also
ITT Continental Baking Company
Nabisco, Inc

BAKFARK, Bálint
Complete works for solo lute. J. Warren. Am Rec G 40:10-11 Je '77 *

BAKING
Bake it in the oven. E. W. Manning. il Farm J 101:32-3+ S '77
See also
Bread
Cake
Coffee cake
Cookies
Desserts
Dough
Flour
Pastry
Pie

BAKING contests. See Cookery—Competitions

BAKING industry. See Bakers and bakeries

BAKING pans. See Kitchen utensils and appliances

BAKKE, Allan, case
Bakke battle. J. K. Footlick and D. Camper. il Newsweek 90:45-6 O 24 '77
Bakke brief. N. Lewin. New Repub 177:17-18 O 1 '77
Bakke brief; Justice Department preparatory brief. J. K. Footlick and D. Camper. Newsweek 90:97 S 19 '77
Bakke case: affirmative distraction. S. A. Cleverdon. Progressive 41:26-9 D '77
Bakke case: are racial quotas defensible? C. Lawrence, 3d. il Sat R 5:10-16 O 15 '77; Same. Current 198:3-11 D '77; Discussion. Sat R 5:5 D 10 '77
Bakke case: how to argue about reverse discrimination. S. Pottinger. Ms 6:59-60 Ja '78
Bakke case; just the beginning. N. Cousins. Sat R 5:4 N 26 '77
Bakke case: question of special minority admissions programs. J. Walsh. Science 197:25-7 Jl 1 '77; Reply. C. S. Ralston. 197:514 Ag 5 '77
Bakke case: testing the liberal alliance. P. Delaney. Nation 225:498-9 N 12 '77
Bakke conundrum. Nation 225:322-4 O 8 '77
Bakke vs. University of California. J. H. Bunzel. Commentary 63:59-64 Mr '77; Discussion. 64:8+ Jl '77
Courts v. self-government; A. Cox. P. H. Connolly. Nat R 29:1225-8 O 28 '77
Disadvantaged groups, individual rights. Current 198:11-16 D '77
Essay on the unfairness of life. L. Morrow. Horizon 20:34-7 D '77
Fateful court test; with legal arguments and briefs and editorial comment. il U.S. News 83: 21-2, 94-6, 112 O 24 '77
Furor over reverse discrimination. J. K. Footlick and others. il Newsweek 90:52-5+ S 26 '77
High court turns to landmark race-quota case. por U.S. News 83:39 S 26 '77
How to resolve the Bakke case. M. Greenfield. Newsweek 90:128 O 24 '77
Issue before the court: who gets ahead in America? M. Bundy. Atlantic 240:41-50+ N '77; Discussion. 241:75-80 Ja '78
Meritocracy and its discontents; symposium. New Repub 177:5-9+ O 15 '77
Must principles collide? charges of reverse discrimination in Bakke v. Regents of the University of California. America 137:121 S 10 '77
Parable of the talents. B. L. Martin. il Harpers 256:12+ Ja '78
Racial quotas at med school. W. F. Buckley, Jr. Nat R 29:904-5 Ag 5 '77
Reverse discrimination. J. K. Footlick. il Newsweek 89:66 Mr 7 '77
Supreme Court and quotas. J. S. Fuerst and R. Petty. il Chr Cent 94:948-52 O 19 '77
Unequal but fair. D. C. Maguire. Commonweal 104:647-52 O 14 '77; Discussion. 105:29+ Ja 6 '78
What rights for whites? il por Time 110:95+ O 24 '77
White/Caucasian—and rejected. R. Lindsey. il pors N Y Times Mag p42-7+ Ap 3 '77

BAKKER, Jim
If Christ were alive today. por Ladies Home J 94:68+ D '77

BALABAN, John
Opening Le Ba Khon's dictionary; poem. Am Scholar 46:212 Spr '77

BALABAN-MALENBAUM, Gloria, and Gilbert, Fred
Double minute chromosomes and the homogeneously staining regions in chromosomes of a human neuroblastoma cell line. bibl il Science 198:739-41 N 18 '77

BALACHANDRAN, Nambath K. and others
Concorde sonic booms as an atmospheric probe. bibl il map Science 197:47-9 Jl 1 '77

BALANCE in ballet. See Ballet—Technique

BALANCE of nature. See Ecology

BALANCE of payments
Global scapegoats. Nat R 29:1161+ O 14 '77
International monetary system; statement, September 23, 1977. P. H. Boeker. Dept State Bull 77:704-7 N 14 '77
NASA cites balance-of-payments gains. Aviation W 106:51-2 F 28 '77
Stoking the West's economic locomotive. E. Mervosh. Bus W p29 Jl 11 '77
Worse is better. il Forbes 119:125 Je 15 '77

United States

Why so few are worried about huge trade deficit. A. Rossi. il U.S. News 82:29 Je 27 '77

BALANCE of power
Military leaders clash on Soviet threat. Aviation W 106:16 F 7 '77
New assessment put on Soviet threat; address. G. J. Keegan Jr. il por Aviation W 106:38-43+ Mr 28 '77
Perils of détente. W. Laqueur. N Y Times Mag p 16+ F 27 '77
Practical power use urged on planners. H. J. Coleman. il Aviation W 107:18-21 Jl 18 '77
Time to bury deterrence. W. Epstein. Bull Atom Sci 33:6-7 Je '77
U.S.-Soviet strategic balance assayed. E. Kozicharow. Aviation W 106:16 My 16 '77
What was Kissinger saying? farewell appearance before the National Press Club. Nat R 29:134 F 4 '77
See also
World politics

BALANCE of trade

United States

Backlash from U.S. growth. il Bus W p 16-17 Jl 4 '77
Dangerous U.S. trade deficit. G. R. Rosen. il map Duns R 110:62-5+ O '77
Dollar slump. A. J. Mayer. il Newsweek 90:60 Ag 8 '77
Face-off on dollar strategy. il por Bus W p20-1 Ag 8 '77
Flare-up at yawning gap. il Time 110:66-7 Ag 8 '77
Help wanted with the trade deficit. B. France and J. Pearson. Bus W p46 My 16 '77
Lower dollar may be a plus. il Bus W p 100+ Ag 15 '77
Propping the dollar at last. il Time 111:38-40 Ja 16 '78
Rising interest rates revive the dollar. il Bus W p35-6 O 17 '77
Rumbles over a wider gap. il Time 110:50-1 Jl 11 '77
Saving the sick dollar. M. Ruby and others. il Newsweek 91:62+ Ja 16 '78
Trade gap puts a strain on Carter. S. H. Wildstrom. Bus W p54 D 12 '77

BALANCE sheets. See Financial statements

BALANCED diet. See Diet

BALANCHINE, George
Antic arts. C. Hughes. Holiday 57:12 N '76*
Ballet is Balanchine. R. Garis. New Repub 177: 29-31 Ag 20 '77 *
Glorious unpredictability of George Balanchine; spring performances by the New York City Ballet. J. Anderson. il Dance Mag 51:75-8 O '77 *

BALASEK, Jerry
In the boondocks. il por Outdoor Life 160:90-1 S '77

BALATSOS, Dimitris Nikolas
Confidence in the future versus government spending. por Nations Bus 65:64-6 F '77

BALÁZS, Béla
Béla Balázs in German exile. J. Ralmon. bibl il por Film Q 30:12-19 Spr '77 *

BALCH School, Providence, R.I. See Private schools

BALCONY gardens, roof gardens, etc.
Back to the land on a terrace. il Bus W p89 My 2 '77
Consider the lilies of the terrace. A. Green. il Horticulture 55:44-5 N '77
Garden in the sky in San Francisco. il Sunset 159:86-7 S '77
Gardening without land. H. Olkowski and W. Olkowski. il Horticulture 55:34-6 F '77
Living high in the sky. N. Skurka. il N Y Times Mag p42-3 Jl 10 '77
Sky gardens—the greening of the city. il Am Home 80:96-7 Je '77
Wall Street garden. New Yorker 53:31-2 My 30 '77

BALD eagles. See Eagles

BALDERSTON, F. E. and others
Computers in banking and marketing. bibl Science 195:1115-19 Mr 18 '77

BALDERSTON, John Lloyd, and Deane, Hamilton
Dracula; dramatization of novel by B. Stoker. Reviews
America 137:334 N 12 '77 *
N Y Times Mag p40-2+ O 16 '77 *
New Yorker 53:115 O 31 '77 *
Newsweek il 90:74-5+ O 31 '77 *
Time 110:93 O 31 '77 *

BALDNESS
Baldness experiment; Bowery bums and baldness. G. De Leon. il por Psychol Today 11: 62-3+ O '77
Hair-raising tale. N. Benezra. il por Fam Health 9:25-9 D '77

BALDRIGE, Letitia
Who says manners are out of style? Seventeen 36:142-3 My '77

BALDWIN, Carl R.
Shahn's Bronx P.O. murals: the perils of public art. il Art in Am 65:15-16+ My '77
Wonders of Irish art. il N Y Times Mag p34-7+ O 9 '77
BALDWIN, D. H. Company-United Corporation merger. See Corporations—Acquisitions and mergers
BALDWIN, Faith
My crabbèd age. Read Digest 110:31-2 My '77
BALDWIN, James
Twin urges of James Baldwin. W. Sheed. por Commonweal 104:404-7 Je 24 '77 *
BALDWIN, Robert Hayes Burns
Frustration in the formation of investment capital; address, February 23, 1977. Vital Speeches 43:405-8 Ap 15 '77
BALDWIN, Roger
Norman Thomas: successful failure. Nation 224: 85 Ja 22 '77
BALEARIC Islands
Balearics. M. Gough. Sat R 5:31+ O 29 '77
BALI
Island of the gods. C. Lucas. il map Read Digest 110:188-9+ F '77
BALIN, Robert P.
RC circuit quiz. il Pop Electr 12:26 Jl '77
BALINESE dancing. See Dancing, Balinese
BALINESE music. See Music, Balinese
BALIOTTI, Dan
You can't beat this game with a stick; photographs. Sports Illus 46:34-8 Ap 25 '77
BALKY bike; drama. See Miller, H. L.
BALL, Aimee Lee
Fooling around with the Fonz. il por Redbook 148:107+ Mr '77
BALL, Angela
To my brother, hardly born; poem. Mademoiselle 83:144 O '77
BALL, Armand B. Jr
On the ball. See issues of Camping magazine —See Stolz, A. J. jt auth
BALL, Edmund F.
Great Australian air race. il por map Sat Eve Post 249:22-3+ My '77
BALL, Edward
Fight to control a $2 billion estate. D. G. Santry. il por Bus W p 108 S 26 '77 *
No rest at 89. por Time 110:69-71 O 10 '77 *
Strange case of Ed Ball. P. Berman. il por Forbes 119:63-6 F 15 '77 *
BALL, George Wildman
Asking for trouble in South Africa. Atlantic 240:43-51 O '77; Same abr. Read Digest 112: 59-63 Ja '78
How to save Israel in spite of herself. For Affairs 55:453-71, 889-90; 56:224-5 Ap-O '77
Middle East is the most urgent problem that we face. por U.S. News 82:46 Je 27 '77

about

Right again? por Forbes 119:76 Mr 1 '77 *
South Africa: what is to be done. C. Ferguson and W. R. Cotter. bibl f For Affairs 56:253-74 Ja '78 *
BALL, John
Four tests for a paragraph. Writer 90:15-16+ Ja '77
BALL, Karlene. See Sekuler, R. jt auth
BALL, Lucille
Comedienne Lucille Ball on the mess in television land. il pors U.S. News 83:58 S 26 '77

about

House where Lucille Ball lives! il pors Good H 185:132-5 S '77 *
BALL, Robert (editor)
Dangerous left turn ahead in France. il Fortune 96:130-3+ Ag '77
Insurance companies' insurance company. il Fortune 95:154-9 Je '77
Persuasive man who drives Mercedes. il pors Fortune 96:136-40+ D '77
There's a lot of G.K.N. in Europe's cars. il por Fortune 95:156-61+ Ja '77
What North Sea oil won't do for Britain. il Fortune 95:138-42+ Ap '77
BALL, Travis, Jr
(ed) More sources of free and inexpensive material. Engl J 66:100-6 Ja '77
BALL lightning. See Lightning
BALL-point pens. See Pens
BALLAD opera
Eastman School-Lib. of Congress: The disappointment; performance of the first American ballad opera. il Hi Fi 27:MA14-15+ Mr '77
BALLANTINE, Betty
Ballantine Books at quarter century: founders; interview, ed by T. Weyr. il pors Pub W 212: 30-3 D 12 '77
BALLANTINE, Christopher
Towards an aesthetic of experimental music. bibl f Mus Q 63:224-46 Ap '77

BALLANTINE, Ian
Ballantine Books at quarter century: founders; interview, ed by T. Weyr. il pors Pub W 212: 30-3 D 12 '77
Kathy Larkin of Kroch's & Brentano's: total enthusiasm for the customer. il por Pub W 212:83-4 Jl 18 '77
BALLANTINE Books, inc. See Publishers and publishing—Paperback books
BALLARD, Lockett Ford, Jr
Paintings of Ralph Earl at the Litchfield Historical Society. il Antiques 112:959-63 N '77
BALLARD, Robert D. See Corliss, J. B. jt auth
BALLES, John J.
Inflation, interest rates and the Fed; address, July 26, 1977. Vital Speeches 43:741-4 O 1 '77
BALLET
Calendar of summer dance events 1977. il Dance Mag 51:52-7 My '77
Dance. J. Maskey. See issues of High fidelity and Musical America
Dance. W. Terry. Sat R 4:50 Ag 6 '77
Dance floors: their selection and preparation. R. Gelabert. il Dance Mag 51:94-5 Mr '77
Editor's log. W. Como. Dance Mag 52:23 Ja '78
Perspectives. See issues of Dance magazine
Presstime news. See issues of Dance magazine
Reviews. See issues of Dance magazine
See also
Choreography
Motion pictures—Dance films

Accidents and injuries

Myth of dance-induced pain. R. Gelabert. il Dance Mag 51:96-7 My '77
Stage injuries. R. Gelabert. il Dance Mag 51:86-7 Jl; 30-1 Ag '77

Benefit performances

See Dancing—Benefit performances

Bibliography

Book briefs (title varies) Dance Mag 51:98 Jl; 26-9 Ag; 100 S; 41 O; 74-6 N '77; 52:96 Ja '78

Injuries

See Ballet—Accidents and injuries

Study and teaching

Children of Theatre Street; film of dancers at the Kirov School. N. M. Stoop. il Dance Mag 51: 63-5 S '77
Dancers and teachers. R. Gelabert. il Dance Mag 51:72-3 S '77
Ecole de ballet, changeless and secure; Paris Opéra. W. Terry. il Sat R 4:48-9 Ja 22 '77
Education briefs. H. Von Obenauer. See issues of Dance magazine
Myth of dance-induced pain. R. Gelabert. il Dance Mag 51:96-7 My '77
Rosin: its use and abuse; treatment of dance floors. R. Gelabert. Dance Mag 51:88 Ap '77
Turning out. R. Gelabert. il Dance Mag 51:86-7 F '77
Volkova: pedagogical prima. W. Terry. por Sat R 4:43 Ap 2 '77

Technique

Pas de deux; finding the point of balance; excerpt from Pas de deux or duet dance. tr by E. Kraft. N. Serebrennikov. il Dance Mag 52:76-7 Ja '78

Austria

John Neumeier's new tour de force: Legend of Joseph; Vienna State Opera Ballet. H. Koegler. il Dance Mag 51:89 Je '77

Canada

See also
National Ballet of Canada
Royal Winnipeg Ballet

China

Dancing; Shanghai Ballet. A. Croce. New Yorker 53:104-6 Je 13 '77
Perspectives; performance of The white-haired girl by the Shanghai Ballet Company in Toronto. G. B. Strauss. Dance Mag 51:102-4 O '77

France

Ecole de ballet, changeless and secure; Paris Opéra. W. Terry. il Sat R 4:48-9 Ja 22 '77
Ivan the Terrible at the Paris Opera. B. Fitzgerald. il Dance Mag 51:122 Mr '77

Germany, West

Hamburg's stylish dream of A dream; Hamburg State Opera Ballet. H. Koegler. il pors Dance Mag 51:48-50 N '77
See also
Stuttgart Ballet

Great Britain

Perspectives:
Performance of Romeo and Juliet by London Festival Ballet. J. Percival. Dance Mag 51:82+ N '77
See also
Ballet Rambert

BALLET—*Continued*

Hungary

Story of the migrating Magyar; I. Nagy. W. Terry. il por Sat R 4:50-1 Ag 6 '77

Israel

Reviews:
Israel Ballet's United States debut. M. Robertson. Dance Mag 52:31-2 Ja '78

Italy

Reviews: performances during the first six months of 1977. V. Ottolenghi. Dance Mag 51: 80 D '77

Netherlands

Dutch National Ballet; New York debut. J Maskey. il Hi Fi 27:MA10-11 Mr '77

Philippines

Contemporary dance in the Philippines. R. Alejandro. il Dance Mag 51:99 Jl '77

Russia

See also
Kirov Ballet

United States

Alicia Markova: her appearances in America. A. Fay. il pors Dance Mag 51:47-55 Je '77
Dance. D. Diether. il Am Rec G 40:52-3 N; 59-62 D '76; 56 Je; 49-51 O '77
Holiday habit: Nutcracker. il Horizon 20:72 D '77
Viewpoint; ballet at the New York Metropolitan Opera. R. Jacobson. Opera N 41:7 Je '77
See also
National Association for Regional Ballet

History

From Pavlova to ABT. W. Terry. il pors Opera N 41:10-14 Je '77

Venezuela

Ballet International de Caracas and two of its dancers; Z. Rodriguez and Z. Wilson. N. M. Stoop. il pors Dance Mag 52:51-66 Ja '78

Yugoslavia

Dance in Yugoslavia. O. Maynard. il map Dance Mag 51:67-82 My '77

BALLET companies
Alfonso Figueroa and the Birmingham Ballet; interview, ed by L. Small. A. Figueroa. Dance Mag 52:73-4 Ja '78
Ballet West's Don Quixote. J. Anderson. il Dance Mag 51:36-8 Jl '77
Bruce Marks and Toni Lander: breaking ground at Ballet West. J. Cumming. il pors Dance Mag 51:62-5 D '77
Dancers, dances and images; Dennis Wayne's Dancers. J. Pikula. Dance Mag 51:93-4 Jl '77
Dancing:
Les Ballets Trockadero de Monte Carlo. A. Croce. New Yorker 53:136-7 My 2 '77
Romeo and Juliet performed by the Maryland Ballet. A. Croce. il New Yorker 53: 135 My 2 '77
For Dennis Wayne the emphasis is on Dancers. L. Draegin. il pors Dance Mag 51:36-9 N '77
Ohio Ballet: Poll's ensemble tackles Taylor. J Pikula. il Dance Mag 51:39-40 Jl '77
On the road with dance and dancers; Les Ballets Jazz and the Connecticut Ballet Company. W. Terry. il Sat R 4:40-1 My 14 '77
Portland, Oregon: braving the new world; Portland Dance Theater and the Portland Ballet Company. M. Aloff. il Dance Mag 51:124-5 My '77
Reviews:
Bernhard Ballet's performance November 5 at Westport County Playhouse. H. Robertson. Dance Mag 52:33-4 Ja '78
Hartford Ballet debut in Hackensack. J. Anderson. Dance Mag 51:29-30 F '77
Houston Ballet's Swan Lake. L. Draegin. Dance Mag 51:78 D '77
Maryland Ballet's Romeo and Juliet. Z. Cameron. il Dance Mag 51:80+ D '77
Southwest Ballet Center performances. L. Small. il Dance Mag 51:76-7 D '77
Upstate New York: performances by Syracuse Ballet Theatre. H. M. Simpson. Dance Mag 51:23-4 N '77
See also
American Ballet Theatre
Atlanta Ballet
Ballet Rambert
Ballets Russes (ballet companies)
Cincinnati Ballet Company
City Center Joffrey Ballet
Dance Theatre of Harlem
Eglevsky Ballet Company
Eliot Feld Ballet
Maurice Béjart's Ballet of the 20th Century
Metropolitan Opera Ballet
New York City Ballet
Pennsylvania Ballet
Pittsburgh Ballet Theatre
Royal Winnipeg Ballet
San Francisco Ballet
Stuttgart Ballet

BALLET costume. See Costume, Theatrical
BALLET dancers. See Dancers
BALLET exercises. See Exercise
BALLET festivals. See Dance festivals
BALLET International de Caracas. See Ballet—Venezuela
BALLET music
See also
Phonograph records—Ballet music
BALLET of the 20th Century. See Maurice Béjart's Ballet of the 20th Century
BALLET Rambert
Reviews:
Seven works premiered in London. J. Percival. il Dance Mag 52:71 Ja '78
BALLET reviews

Single works

Aphrodisiamania
Nation 225:700-1 D 24 '77
As is
Nation 225:507-8 N 12 '77
Blood memories
Horizon 19:38-9 My '77
Bournonville divertissements
Hi Fi 27:MA11 My '77
Nation 224:251-2 F 26 '77
New Yorker 53:95-7 F 21 '77
Coppélia
Dance Mag il 51:91 Ap '77
Sat R il 4:50 Mr 5 '77
Don Quixote
Dance Mag 51:36-8 Jl '77
La fille mal gardée
Dance Mag 51:112+ Mr '77
Dance Mag il 51:71-3 N '77
Firebird
Dance Mag il 51:71-4 O '77
Hi Fi il 27:MA12-13 Ag '77
Nation 224:637-8 My 21 '77
New Yorker 53:79-80 My 16 '77
Time il 109:63 My 9 '77
Footstep of air
Nation 224:413-14 Ap 2 '77
Giselle
Dance Mag il 51:91 Ap '77
Dance Mag il 52:38-41 Ja '78
New Yorker 52:102+ F 14 '77
Happily ever after
New Repub 176:19-20 F 12 '77
Ivan the Terrible
Dance Mag il 51:122 Mr '77
Legend of Joseph
Dance Mag il 51:89 Je '77
Midsummer night's dream
Dance Mag il 51:48-50 N '77
Le Molière imaginaire
Dance Mag il 51:50-5 Ap '77
Notre Faust
Hi Fi il 27:MA10-11 Jl '77
Nutcracker
Dance Mag 51:30+ Mr '77
Dance Mag 51:50-3 D '77
Hi Fi il 27:MA8-10 S '77
New Yorker 52:94-6 Ja 17 '77
Sat R il 4:49-50 Mr 5 '77
Les patineurs
Nation 225:569-70 N 26 '77
Prodigal son
Nation 225:28-30 Jl 2 '77
Quarry
New Yorker 52:79 Ja 24 '77
Requiem
Dance Mag il 51:56-8 Ap '77
Dance Mag il 51:67-70 N '77
Romeo and Juliet
Dance Mag 51:82+ N '77
Dance Mag 51:80+ D '77
Dance Mag il 51:78-9 D '77
New Yorker 53:135 My 2 '77
Sat R 5:60 D 10 '77
Sleeping beauty
Dance Mag il 51:67-70 N '77
Hi Fi 27:MA12-13 N '77
Nation 224:666-8 My 28 '77
New Yorker 52:96-7 Ja 17 '77
Solo
Nation 224:187 F 12 '77
Sounddance
Nation 224:187 F 12 '77
Swan lake
Dance Mag 51:78 D '77
Dance Mag il 51:71-4 O '77
Travelogue
Nation 224:187-8 F 12 '77
Variations on America
Dance Mag 51:63-5 Je '77
Nation 224:412-13 Ap 2 '77
Time il 109:88 Mr 21 '77
Vienna waltzes
Hi Fi il 27:MA9+ O '77
Nation 225:88+ Jl 23 '77
Newsweek il 90:53 Jl 4 '77
La vivandière
Nation 225:506-7 N 12 '77
White-haired girl
Dance Mag 51:102-4 O '77
BALLET Russe de Monte Carlo. See Ballets Russes (ballet companies)

BALLET West (ballet company) See Ballet companies

Les **BALLETS Jazz (ballet company)** See Ballet companies

BALLETS Russes (ballet companies)
Belle of the Ballets Russes: Alexandra Danilova. A. Fay. il pors Dance Mag 51:55-70 O '77

BALLHAUS, William Francis
Tax that is killing investment. J. Cobbs. il Bus W p 14+ Ja 16 '78 *

BALLIETT, Whitney
Jazz (cont) New Yorker 53:98-104 F 21; 84-90 Ap 4; 94-8+ Ap 25; 120-2+ Je 6; 92-7 Je 20; 80-6+ Jl 18; 118+ S 12 '77; 60-9 Ja 9 '78
Our local correspondents (cont) New Yorker 53:80-6 S 5; 100-1+ O 31; 33-4+ D 26 '77
Profiles; H. Panassié and C. Delaunay. pors New Yorker 52:43-6+ F 14 '77
Profiles; H. Shannon. por New Yorker 52:36-42 Ja 17 '77
Profiles; B. Wilber. por New Yorker 53:45-8+ My 9 '77

BALLIOL College. See Oxford. University

BALLOON ascensions
Adirondack Hot-Air Balloon Festival 1977. W. Grishkot. il Conservationist 32:30-1 S '77
Balloon is a moon. R. Blount, Jr. Esquire 88:46+ D '77
Fire near the sun. J. Gardey. il Sci Digest 82:8-10 N '77
Longest manned balloon flight; Silver Fox. E. Yost. il por Nat Geog 151:208-17 F '77
Sailing the skies of summer. il Time 110:62-3 Ag 29 '77
Sky sports: the thrill of flight. T. Crawford. Harp Baz 110:85+ My '77
Totally at the whim of the elements; excerpt from The complete ballooning book. W. Hayes. il Sci Digest 82:11-14 N '77
Up, up, and away. il pors Ebony 32:88-90+ Jl '77

History

Balloon to cross the ocean in 1859: the Atlantic. D. M. Ludlum. il por Weatherwise 30:154-7 Ag '77

BALLOON racing
Balloons over Iowa; National Hot Air Balloon Championship. il Sat Eve Post 249:50-1 My '77

BALLOON television relay system. See Television relay systems

BALLOONS
Build a balloon—a 3-D project that flies. R. F. Salzberg. il Design (US) 78:10-12 Spr '77
See also
Balloon ascensions

History

Gas bags. il Chemistry 50:8-9 O '77

Research use

Balloons and modern science. il Chemistry 50:10-12 O '77
Vast balloons create confusion. D. Lampe. Sci Digest 82:33-5 Jl '77

BALLOONS, Kite
Inflation; inflating balloons for Macy's Thanksgiving Day parade. New Yorker 53:40-1 D 12 '77

BALLOONS in ship loading and unloading. See Loading and unloading

BALLROOM dancing. See Dancing

BALLS
See also
Baseballs
Tennis balls

BALLY, C. F, Ltd. See Shoe industry—Switzerland

BALLY Manufacturing Corporation. See Gambling machines—Manufacture

BALOGUN, Ola
Decoding the message of African sculpture. il UNESCO Courier 30:12-15+ My '77

BALSHONE, Bruce L.
Community maintenance for city parks. il Parks & Rec 12:34-6 Ag '77

BALTH, Charles
Balth and the beasts. S. Butchkes. il pors Craft Horiz 37:28-31 Ag '77 *

BALTHASAR, Hans Urs von
New voice for American theology. J. M. McDermott. America 137:374-6 N 26 '77 *

BALTHUS
Connoisseur of eros; exhibition at the Pierre Matisse Gallery in New York. M. Stevens. il Newsweek 90:93-4 D 5 '77 *
Nymphets of Balthus; show at Manhattan's Pierre Matisse Gallery. R. Hughes. il Time 110:101 N 28 '77 *

BALTIC Region
See also
Cruising—Baltic Region

BALTIMORE

Bookstores

See Booksellers and bookselling—Maryland

City planning

What is reviving Baltimore. il Bus W p 122-3 Ag 15 '77

Education

Group painting project; Thomas Johnson Elementary School. il Sch Arts 76:49 Mr '77

Galleries and museums

See also
Baltimore Museum of Art

Hospitals

It's an emergency! Maryland Institute for Emergency Medical Services. P. Bonventre and others. il Newsweek 90:105+ N 21 '77

Music

See also
Baltimore Symphony Orchestra
Opera—Maryland

Streets

Mobile concrete batchers save time, manpower and money. S. Cortese. il Am City & County 92:51-2 F '77

BALTIMORE County, Md.
How Baltimore County keeps its residents high and dry. J. D. Seyffert. il por Am City & County 92:78-80 S '77

BALTIMORE Museum of Art
It's like love, a one-to-one relationship between a human being and a work of art; director T. Freudenheim. R. Bongartz. il por Art N 76:78-80+ My '77

BALTIMORE Opera Company. See Opera—Maryland

BALTIMORE Symphony Orchestra
Musician of the month: Sergiu Comissiona. C. Suttoni. por Hi Fi 27:MA8-9 My '77

BALZER, Robert Lawrence
Bordeaux is for wine lovers . . . and other romantics. il Holiday 58:32-3+ Ja '77
8 paradise islands called Hawaii. il Trav/Holiday 149:48-9+ Ja '78
International chef. Trav/Holiday 148:13 N '77
Rosellini's Other Place. il por Holiday 57:40-1+ N '76

BAMBOO
Bamboo as lumber—for stakes, fences, other uses. il Sunset 158:212+ Mr '77
Jungle gems: bamboo and palm. R. Langer. il House & Gard 149:82+ Ap '77
120-year bamboo clock. S. J. Gould. Natur Hist 86:8+ Ap '77

BANANAS
Bananamania. R. Sokolov. il Natur Hist 86:80-3 My '77
See also
Cookery—Fruit

Anecdotes, facetiae, satire, etc.

But yes we had bananas—coming out of our ears. W. Breisky. il Smithsonian 7:96-102 Mr '77

BANASHEK, Mary-Ellen
Being single: how to stop waiting and start living. Mademoiselle 83:95+ Jl '77
(ed) Two-career couples: how they make it work; interviews. il Mademoiselle 83:168-9+ S '77
VD: the disease of the year. Mademoiselle 83:52+ Mr '77
Why it's good to get good and mad. Mademoiselle 83:126-7+ Je '77

BANCAL Tri-State Corporation
Who is kidding whom? BanCal Tri-State Corp's refusal of tender offer for Bank of California. il Forbes 119:30 Mr 15 '77

The **BAND (rock group)** See Rock groups

BANDARANAIKE, Sirimavo
End of a dynasty. K. Willenson and B. Came. il por Newsweek 90:33-4 Ag 1 '77 *

BANDEEN, Robert Angus
Idea is good. por Forbes 119:68 My 1 '77 *

BANDELIER National Monument
Hide-and-seek in New Mexico; attempts to capture wild burros. R. Cantwell. Sports Illus 47:48-9 Ag 1 '77

BANDI, W. R.
Second phases in steel. bibl il Science 196:136-42 Ap 8 '77

BANDING, Bird. See Bird banding

BANDS (music)
And the band played on; senior band in Hot Springs, Ark. J. Wallworth. il Ret Liv 17:46-8 My '77
Ban and the big bands. G. Lees. Hi Fi 27:28+ N '77
Big bands. G. Lees. Hi Fi 27:24-6 S '77
Indigenous music; Asleep at the Wheel band. N. Hentoff. Nation 225:30 Jl 2 '77
Swing era; jazz music of the big bands. G. Lees. Hi Fi 27:19-20 Ag '77

BANDY, Alan R. See Maroulis, P. J. jt auth

BANDY, Way
Transforming faces; interview, ed by A. Penny. il N Y Times Mag p 129-31 S 25 '77
Way Bandy's makeup book; excerpt from Designing your face. il Good H 185:121-5 O '77

BANES, Sally
Art of ballezz. il Dance Mag 51:42-4 S '77

BANGKOK
Passing of the old imperialisms. C. Northcott. Chr Cent 94:268-9 Mr 23 '77

Description and travel

Bangkok (cont) C. D. B. Bryan. il Holiday 57: 34-5+ N '76

Hotels, restaurants, etc.

Grand old hotels of the Orient; The Oriental. G. Plimpton. il Holiday 58:42-3+ Mr '77

BANGLADESH
See also
Civil rights—Bangladesh
Terrorism—Bangladesh

Foreign relations
India

See India—Foreign relations—Bangladesh

Politics and government

Voting with their guns: mutiny in Bangladesh. K. Bird. Nation 225:650-3 D 17 '77

Religious institutions and affairs

Bangladesh update. P. Parshall Chr Today 21: 35 Ag 12 '77

BANGOR Naval Submarine Base. See Navy yards and naval stations

BANGOR Punta Corporation-Canadian Pacific, Ltd merger. See Corporations—Acquisitions and mergers—International aspects

BANISHMENT. See Exiles

BANISTER, Judith
Wine and spirit labels in Harvey's Wine Museum. il Antiques 112:278-81 Ag '77

BANK acceptances. See Acceptances

BANK accounting. See Banks and banking—Accounting

BANK boards of directors. See Banks and banking—Directors

BANK credit cards. See Credit cards

BANK deposits
See also
Banks and banking—Overdrafts
Certificates of deposit
Custodianship accounts

BANK deposits, Foreign
Central bank boost for foreign borrowing; Brazil. il Bus W p56 S 12 '77

BANK directors. See Banks and banking—Directors

BANK ethics. See Business ethics

BANK failures
Bank regulation: the reforms we really need. S. Rose. il Fortune 96:122-4+ D '77
Biggest liquidator of them all; Federal Deposit Insurance Corp. il Forbes 119:55+ F 15 '77
In the shade of the FDIC: the tax-shelter farmers: failure of the U.S. National Bank in San Diego. R. B. Taylor. Nation 224:590-4 My 14 '77

BANK fees. See Banks and banking—Service charges

BANK holding companies
Fight to control a $2 billion estate; A. I. duPont trust's 24% interest in Florida National. D. G. Santry. il por Bus W p 108 S 26 '77
History, not fads; Harris Bankcorp. por Forbes 120:102 O 1 '77
Now, mom-and-pop coal mines; Citizens Fidelity and First Kentucky National. S. Chace. il Forbes 120:69+ Jl 1 '77
Texas: enough to go around. il Forbes 120:71-2 Jl 1 '77
Turncoat banker? First Banc Group of Ohio. P. Sturm. por Forbes 120:80 Jl 15 '77
See also
BanCal Tri-State Corporation
BankAmerica Corporation
Chase Manhattan Corporation
Citicorp
Continental Illinois Corporation

Acquisitions and mergers

Trying to make Texas a major money center. il Bus W p 105 Jl 25 '77

Finance

Hoards of bonds pay off for banks. Bus W p57-8 Ja 24 '77

Leasing business

See Banks and banking—Leasing business

Statistics

100 largest bank holding companies: a statistical profile. Forbes 120:64-7 Jl 1 '77

BANK leasing subsidiaries. See Banks and banking—Leasing business

BANK loans. See Loans, Bank

BANK management
Choosing strategies for business success; interview. G. Hauge. pors Nations Bus 65:32-5 Je '77
Painful job: turning bankers into managers. il Bus W p49+ Mr 7 '77

BANK notes
How do you replace a wild card? B. Weberman. Forbes 120:110 O 1 '77
Why a money-maker is making more money; Britain's De La Rue Co. Bus W p58 Ag 8 '77

BANK of America. See Bank of America National Trust and Savings Association

BANK of America National Trust and Savings Association
Imasco buys a slice of Hardee's Food. Bus W p42+ F 14 '77

BANK of British Columbia. See Banks and banking—Canada

BANK of California. See Banks and banking—California

BANK of England
Bank of England's fall from grace. il Bus W p60-4+ Mr 14 '77

BANK of the Commonwealth. See Detroit—Banks

BANK overdrafts. See Banks and banking—Overdrafts

BANK rates. See Interest (economics)

BANK robberies. See Robberies and assaults

BANK Secrecy Act. See Banks and banking—Laws and regulations

BANK statements. See Banks and banking—Accounting

BANK stocks. See Banks and banking—Securities

BANKAMERICA Corporation
Excerpt from statement on mandatory retirement policy, February 14, 1977. G. A. Skoglund. Cong Digest 56:267+ N '77

BANKERS acceptances. See Acceptances

BANKERS Life and Casualty Company
Excerpt from statement on retirement age policy, March 16, 1977. G. L. Maguire. Cong Digest 56: 278+ N '77

BANKING. See Banks and banking

BANKNOTES. See Bank notes

BANKRUPTCY
House bill perils aircraft financing; proposed bankruptcy law changes. W. H. Gregory. Aviation W 106:14 Mr 7 '77
Pound of flesh? proposed legislation to affect consumer bankruptcy. L. Minard. il Forbes 119:94+ Je 15 '77
Updating bankruptcy rules. U.S. News 83:66 S 26 '77
See also
Bank failures
Business failures

BANKS, Dennis J.
Dennis Bank's extradition fight. H. Rubin. il Chr Cent 94:691-2 Ag 3 '77 *
Legal history of an Indian. H. Rubin. por Nation 225:113-15 Ag 6 '77 *

BANKS, E. and others
Fibrous apatite grown on modified collagen. bibl il Science 198:1164-6 D 16 '77

BANKS, Gordon
He's still holding the Fort. C. Gammon. il Sports Illus 47:59-60 Jl 11 '77 *

BANKS, Russell
Little fish eats big fish. por Forbes 119:67 My 15 '77 *

BANKS, William Nathaniel
River road plantations of Louisiana. bibl il Antiques 111:1170-83 Je '77

BANKS, Coin
Old mechanical banks. F. H. Griffith. See issues of Hobbies

BANKS and banking
Banks. B. Weberman. Forbes 120:110 O 1 '77
See also
Acceptances
Agricultural credit
Bank failures
Computers—Banking use
Credit
Custodianship accounts
Development banks
Interest (economics)
Loans, Bank
Mortgage banks
Savings and loan associations
Supermarkets—Banking services

Accounting

FASB moves to close a loophole. il Bus W p76 F 21 '77
Gauging bank profits by one bottom line; SEC's plan for bank income statements. il Bus W p56-7 Jl 4 '77
New rules on troubled debt. Bus W p70+ F 7 '77

BANKS and banking—*Continued*

Acquisitions and mergers

Closer watch on bank takeovers. por Bus W p29 Ag 22 '77
Who is kidding whom? BanCal Tri-State Corp's refusal of tender offer for Bank of California. il Forbes 119:30 Mr 15 '77
See also
Investment banking—Acquisitions and mergers

Advertising

Bank ads attacked for misleading come-ons by consumer study group. Ret Liv 17:16 My '77

Branch banking

See also
Banks and banking—Foreign business

Central banks

Monetary policy instrumentation and the relationship of central banks and governments. J. T. Woolley. bibl f il Ann Am Acad 434:151-73 N '77

Checking accounts

Fewer fetters for the banks. il Bus W p26-7 My 23 '77
Interest on checking accounts: what it would mean to you; NOW accounts. il U.S. News 82:68-9 Je 27 '77
Keeping your bank records. il Sr Schol 110:26-7 N 17 '77
NOW arrives at Capitol Hill. il Bus W p96-7 Je 27 '77
Time is NOW; interest-bearing checking accounts. il Forbes 120:61-2 Jl 1 '77
Writing a check. il Sr Schol 110:18-19 N 3 '77
See also
Checks

Correspondent banks

Bert, I'm proud of you. il pors Time 110:8-10 Ag 29 '77
Lance's contribution to tough banking laws; proposed ban on loans from correspondent banks. Bus W p28-9 S 5 '77
Personal loans and bank ethics. Time 110:49-50 Ag 29 '77

Credit services

See Banks and banking—Services

Deposit services

See Banks and banking—Services

Directors

Liabilities of sitting on a bank board. il Bus W p86-7 S 26 '77

Finance

Billion-dollar banks go on the watch list; FDIC list. Bus W p23-4 Mr 28 '77
Finance. il Forbes 121:119-22 Ja 9 '78
Loan demand leaves bankers still flush. il Bus W p26 Ja 9 '78
Rating the banks. il Forbes 120:63 Jl 1 '77
Second mortgages entice the big banks. il Bus W p49 My 9 '77

Float

Money fund extends the float; Capital Preservation Fund Inc. Bus W p 118 Mr 21 '77

Foreign branches

See Banks and banking—Foreign business

Foreign business

Bankers close ranks against the foreigners; Spain. Bus W p39+ D 19 '77
Banking on New York. S. T. Atlas and P. L. Abraham. il Newsweek 90:93 S 19 '77
Canada's banking crackdown. il Bus W p63 Ja 16 '78
Door may open to foreign banks; in Spain. il Bus W p40-1 S 5 '77
Germany's drive to be the no. 2 banker. il Bus W p53+ D 5 '77
Japan cracks down on foreign banks. Bus W p40 Je 13 '77
Why foreign banks like Houston so much. il Bus W p39+ D 5 '77

Government ownership

See Government ownership

Holding companies

See Bank holding companies

Investment services

See Banks and banking—Services

Investments

Small Texas bank's high-powered porfolio; U.S. National Bank of Galveston. il Bus W p 102 S 19 '77
See also
Banks and banking—Leasing business

Laws and regulations

Bank reform loses a lot of momentum. il por Bus W p43 O 3 '77
Bank regulation: the reforms we really need. S. Rose. il Fortune 96:122-4+ D '77
Big snoop strikes again; Bank Secrecy Act. C Twight. Nat R 29:269 Mr 4 '77
Closer watch on bank takeovers. por Bus W p29 Ag 22 '77
Fewer fetters for the banks. il Bus W p26 My 23 '77
High tide for bank reform. M. Ruby and others. il Newsweek 90:85-7 S 12 '77
How bankers view Bert. Time 110:16+ S 19 '77
Interest on checking accounts: what it would mean to you; NOW accounts. il U.S. News 82:68-9 Je 27 '77
Lance's contribution to tough banking laws; proposed ban on loans from correspondent banks. Bus W p28-9 S 5 '77
Merrill Lynch's dual assault on the banks. il Bus W p23-4 Jl 4 '77
NOW arrives at Capitol Hill. il Bus W p96-7 Je 27 '77
Suddenly everybody is looking at the way banks do business. U.S. News 83:51-3 S 12 '77
Tougher banking laws? G. R. Rosen. por Duns R 110:81 O '77
What the report says; Comptroller Heimann's report on B. Lance. M. Ruby and others. il Newsweek 90:18-19 Ag 29 '77

Leasing business

Banks cash in on capital-equipment leasing. il Bus W p62-3 Ag 8 '77

Location

See Location in business and industry

Management

See Bank management

Overdrafts

We've been asked: about the rules on overdrafts. U.S. News 83:82 O 3 '77

Savings departments

See also
Savings deposits

Securities

Investor fears still haunt bank stocks. il Bus W p90 Ap 25 '77
Why investors pick Chase over Citicorp. il Bus W p46-7 Jl 4 '77

Securities handling

How the bond balloon burst at Chase. C. J. Loomis. Fortune 96:78-9 Jl '77
Merrill Lynch's dual assault on the banks. il Bus W p23-4 Jl 4 '77

Service charges

Fewer strings on bank loans. Bus W p 103 F 21 '77
Nudging bankers to unbundle prices. Bus W p44 F 14 '77

Services

AoA and Treasury launch joint project on direct deposit. Aging 275:5-6 S '77
Banking services. Mech Illus 73:20 Je '77
Banks cash in on collecting student loans. il Bus W p97 O 10 '77
Commercial vs. investment bankers. H. H. Angermueller; M. A. Taylor. il Harvard Bus R 55:132-44 S '77
Direct deposit of social security faltering as interest slackens. Ret Liv 17:47-8 D '77
Medium-sized companies: outflank the hungry bankers. P. S. Nadler. Harvard Bus R 55:8+ My '77
Paying bills by telephone. il Changing T 31:15-17 Je '77
Why your bank is making eyes at you. Changing T 31:37-40 N '77

Social aspects

Bank's drive to rescue neighborhoods; Chemical Bank's program in New York city. V. Louviere. il Nations Bus 65:43 F '77

Statistics

Annual survey of bank performance. il Bus W p97-8+ Ap 18 '77
Fifty largest commercial-banking companies. il Fortune 96:162-3 Jl '77

Trust departments

Going where the money is; bank trust operations. Forbes 119:62 Mr 15 '77

Brazil

Central bank boost for foreign borrowing. il Bus W p56 S 12 '77

BANKS and banking—*Continued*

California

Banks help the cities rebuild. il Bus W p 124+ N 21 '77
California may become a banker. Bus W p46 O 3 '77
Who is kidding whom? BanCal Tri-State Corp's refusal of tender offer for Bank of California. il Forbes 119:30 Mr 15 '77
See also
San Diego, Calif.—Banks

Canada

Canada's banking crackdown. il Bus W p63 Ja 16 '78
Renegade bank feels the heat; Bank of British Columbia. il Bus W p 138+ S 19 '77

Chile

Chile fights for its credit rating; government takeover of banks. il Bus W p 104 F 14 '77

Colorado

Banking challenge to margin checking; complaint against Merrill Lynch. Bus W p56 D 12 '77

France

Bank looks to Case to rescue a borrower; Poclain's proposed merger helping Credit du Nord's profit picture. il Bus W p42 Ap 11 '77
French banks turn traders. il Bus W p 148 N 21 '77

Georgia

Embezzler; B. L. Campbell of the Calhoun First National Bank. S. Fraker and others. por Newsweek 90:27 S 19 '77
See also
Atlanta—Banks

Germany, West

Big bank loses a powerful personality; J. Ponto of Dresdner Bank. por Bus W p48+ Ag 15 '77
German bankers win a big one; Dresdner Bank. il Bus W p33 Je 20 '77
Germany's drive to be the no. 2 banker. il Bus W p53+ D 5 '77
Hard-liner takes over at the Bundesbank; O. Emminger. il por Bus W p94+ Je 20 '77
West Germany: banks band together in a new credit card; Eurocard. il Bus W p44+ Ap 25 '77

Great Britain

See also
Bank of England
London—Banks

Illinois

See also
Chicago—Banks

Iowa

Iowa and Nebraska: critical testing grounds; electronic banking. Bus W p83 Ap 18 '77

Italy

Britain: a real estate flop embarrasses Labor; effect of financial problems of Italian International Bank Ltd on Labor Party Properties Ltd. Bus W p42+ F 7 '77
Industrial giants need salvaging again. il Bus W p68 S 26 '77
Salvage job to stave off a banking crisis. il Bus W p40 My 2 '77

Japan

Japan cracks down on foreign banks. Bus W p40 Je 13 '77
See also
Tokyo—Banks

Kentucky

See also
Louisville—Banks

Latin America

Workers' banks in Latin America. M. Frankenfeld. il Américas 29:2-6 Ag '77

Louisiana

See also
New Orleans—Banks

Michigan

See also
Detroit—Banks

Nebraska

Iowa and Nebraska: critical testing grounds; electronic banking. Bus W p83 Ap 18 '77

New York (state)

Banking without cash a reality; electronic fund transfer on Long Island's North Shore. il U.S. News 83:81-2 D 26 '77
See also
New York (city)—Banks

Pennsylvania

See also
Philadelphia—Banks

South Dakota

His bank meets margin calls; swine contract hedging at First American Bank, Canton. D. Seim. il Farm J 101:Hog 7+ Je '77

Spain

Bankers close ranks against the foreigners. Bus W p39+ D 19 '77
Door may open to foreign banks. il Bus W p40-1 S 5 '77

Switzerland

Are secret Swiss accounts in jeopardy? E. Mervosh. Bus W p73 Jl 18 '77
Dirty money, dirty hands; Swiss Credit Bank. D. Pauly and others. il Newsweek 89:67-8 My 30 '77
Less go-go in Switzerland. il Time 110:74+ Jl 18 '77
Oh, those impetuous Swiss; Swiss Bank Corp. por Forbes 119:68 F 1 '77
Suicide in Switzerland. Time 109:72 My 23 '77
Swiss shuffle; Italian border branch of Swiss Credit Bank. D. Pauly. il Newsweek 89:81 My 9 '77
Why Swiss banks need a housecleaning. il Bus W p 102+ Je 6 '77

Tennessee

See also
Nashville, Tenn.—Banks

Texas

How a Texas maverick lost one of his banks; First State Bank & Trust Co. il por Bus W p84+ Ja 24 '77
Small Texas bank's high-powered portfolio; U.S. National Bank of Galveston. il Bus W p 102 S 19 '77
Texas: enough to go around. il Forbes 120:71-2 Jl 1 '77
Texas piggy bank; misapplication of funds at Citizens State Bank of Carrizo Springs. D. Pauly and S. McGuire. il por Newsweek 90:86-7 S 12 '77
Trying to make Texas a major money center. il Bus W p 105 Jl 25 '77
See also
Houston, Tex.—Banks

United States

Banks. B. Weberman. Forbes 120:110 O 1; 128 N 1; 98 D 1 '77
1977 annual banking survey. il Forbes 120:61-76 Jl 1 '77
Problems, perspectives and responsibilities; address, March 15, 1977. D. Rockefeller. Vital Speeches 43:357-60 Ap 1 '77
Retreat from the cashless society. il map Bus W p80-3+ Ap 18 '77
See also
Chase Manhattan Bank
Federal Deposit Insurance Corporation
Federal Reserve banks
Manufacturers Hanover Trust Company
National Association of Bank Women
United States—Federal Reserve System
United States Trust Company of New York
also subhead Banks under names of cities, e.g. Atlanta—Banks

BANKS and banking, Cooperative
See also
Credit unions

BANKS and banking, International
Falling-out among City partners; London's consortium bankers. Bus W p48-9 O 24 '77
Fifty largest commercial-banking companies outside the U.S; with introd by S. Spencer. il Fortune 96:238-9 Ag '77
Germany's drive to be the no. 2 banker. il Bus W p53+ D 5 '77
See also
Asiadollar market
Banks and banking—Foreign business
Eurobond market
Export-Import Bank of the United States of America
International Bank for Reconstruction and Development

BANNING, Margaret Culkin
Absorbing reality into fiction. Writer 90:12-14+ O '77

BANNON, Barbara A.
(ed) PW forecasts. See issues of Publishers weekly
(ed) See Clark, E. PW interviews
(ed) See Fleming, T. PW interviews
(ed) See Household, G. PW interviews
(ed) See Jong, E. PW interviews
(ed) See Kliban, B. PW interviews
about
PW names Brandt and Bannon to top posts. M. Reuter. Pub W 212:23 D 26 '77 *

BANQUETS. See Dinners and dining

BANTA, Ruth Fark. See Noland, H. W. jt auth

BANTAM Books, Inc-Bertelsmann Publishing Group (firm) merger. See Publishers and publishing—Acquisitions and mergers

BANTLE, Louis F.
U.S. Tobacco: everything but cigarettes. por Duns R 110:26-8 N '77 *

BANTU languages
Spread of the Bantu language. D. W. Phillipson. il maps Sci Am 236:106-14 bibl(p 148) Ap '77

BANVILLE, Thomas G.
Hyperactivity or chocolate milk? Educ Digest 42:48-9 My '77
BANZER SUAREZ, Hugo
Bolivia: Andean power shift. J. Kohl. map Progressive 41:39-42 F '77 *
BANZHAF, Peter G.
Market trends (cont) por Forbes 120:76 F 1; 307 My 15; 227-8 S 15; 210 N 15 '77
BAPTISM
Baptists and baptism. G. T. Sparkman. Chr Cent 94:349-50 Ap 13 '77
Good baptism is not an end in itself. A. T. Kachel. Chr Cent 94:500-1 My 25 '77
BAPTIST colleges and universities. See Church colleges and universities
BAPTISTS
Baptists and baptism. G. T. Sparkman. Chr Cent 94:349-50 Ap 13 '77
BAPTISTS in Great Britain
British Baptists. Chr Today 21:38 Je 3 '77
BAPTISTS in Rumania
Believers in Romania: divided they stand. E. E. Plowman. il pors Chr Today 21:18-21 My 20 '77
Romanian Baptists: notes of triumph. A. Scarfe. Chr Today 21:54-5 Mr 18 '77
BAPTISTS in Russia
Soviet crackdown on Baptists—a special meaning for Carter. il U.S. News 82:26+ Ap 18 '77
BAPTISTS in the United States
American Baptists: now more inclusive. E. S. Parsons. Chr Cent 94:721 Ag 17 '77
Carter and the church. N. King. il Nat R 29:384-5+ Ap 1 '77
Easing the pains in Plains; J. Carter's visit to Plains Baptist and Maranatha Baptist. Chr Today 21:37 Ag 26 '77
Emboldened Baptists: bidding for the world; Southern Baptist Convention. W. L. Molton. Chr Cent 94:616-17 Jl 6 '77
Jackson: keeping it cool; National Baptist Convention, U.S.A. Chr Today 22:63 O 7 '77
Minister's farewell to Plains, Georgia; B. Edwards ousted as head of Plains Baptist Church. V. Cadden. il por McCalls 104:115+ Jl '77
Pilgrimage to Plains. L. Sandon, Jr. Chr Cent 94:145-6 F 16 '77
Plains Baptists. E. Keerdoja and H. Camp. il Newsweek 90:12 O 17 '77
Schism in Plains; ousting B. Edwards from pastorship of Plains Baptist Church. M. Montagno and others. il por Newsweek 89:76 Mr 7 '77
Selling of Jesus; Baptist General Convention of Texas evangelical ad campaign. M. Montagno and J. Huck. il Newsweek 89:48+ F 28 '77
Southern Baptists: tensions and togetherness: Which way, American Baptists? J. C. Hefley and R. Chandler. Chr Today 21:32-4 Jl 29 '77
Strain in Plains. il Time 109:51 Je 27 '77
To the lions; B. Edwards' resignation as pastor of Plains Baptist Church. Time 109:14 Mr 7 '77
BAR-AM, Micha
Israel journal: 1972-1976: reflections on a troubled people; photographs. Sat R 4:8-16+ F 5 '77
BAR associations
See also
American Bar Association
BARAM, Tallie, and others
Gonadotropin-releasing hormone in milk. bibl il Science 198:300-2 O 21 '77
BARAHENI, Reza
No wreath for Mr Baskerville. Nation 224:307-8 Mr 12 '77
BARAN, Annette, and others
Lingering pain of surrendering a child. il Psychol Today 11:58-60+ Je '77
BARAN, Paul. See Farber, D. jt auth
BARANSON, Branley Allan
Changing bowls. bibl il Environment 19:25-30 Ap '77
BARASH, David P.
Sociobiology of rape in mallards anas platyrhynchos: responses of the mated male. bibl Science 197:788-9 Ag 19 '77
BARATZ, Joan C. and Hartle, T. W.
Malpractice in the schools. Progressive 41:33-4 Je '77
BARBADOS
Danse macabre in Barbados. A. N. Forde. il Américas 29:29-31 My '77
BARBAGELATA, John J.
Grudge match. C. J. Harper and G. C. Lubenow. por Newsweek 90:22 Ag 1 '77 *
BARBARELLO, James
Build Cabonga an electronic percussion synthesizer. il Pop Electr 12:39-42 Ag; 76-80 S '77
Build the V-4 VCO for electronic music. il Pop Electr 11:42-4 Mr '77
To the electronic races! il Pop Electr 12:52-5 D '77
BARBARO, Fred
Role of interest groups in educational politics. bibl il Clearing H 51:136-42 N '77
BARBARY Wars. See United States—History—Tripolitan War, 1801-1805
BARBASH, Jack
Forces working to reshape collective bargaining. bibl M Labor R 100:60-1 F '77
BARBEAU, Anne T.
Lest I steal: the morality of theft. bibl Intellect 105:281-2 F '77
BARBECUE cookery
BBQ rib review. il Bet Hom & Gard 55:38-9 My '77
Backyard brochettes. C. Clairborne and P. Franey. il N Y Times Mag p38+ Jl 24 '77
Barbecue innovations with less-expensive beef. il Sunset 159:80-2 Jl '77
Barbecue '77—Journal men on the grill. il Ladies Home J 94:90-1+ Jl '77
Barbecue time. G. Steves. il Am Home 80:60-1+ Je '77
Barbecued spareribs. il Good H 184:42 Je '77
Budget BBQ for a crowd. il Bet Hom & Gard 55:158 Ag '77
Cooking on a skewer—the easy way. il McCalls 104:104+ Je '77
Grill it Greek-style: BBQ for a bunch. S. P. Torpey. il Bet Hom & Gard 55:128-31+ Jl '77
Juicy inside and crispy outside is how duck on the barbecue turns out. il Sunset 159:118-19 Ag '77
Stick cookery. il Ladies Home J 94:102+ Ag '77
Tandoori mixed grill. il Sunset 159:122-3 S '77
U.S. journal: Kentucky: stalking the barbecued mutton. C. Trillin. New Yorker 52:70+ F 7 '77
BARBECUE grills
Barbecue grills from $2.50 to $400. D. Sawyer. il Good H 184:146+ Ap '77
Barbecue with charcoal all year round. il McCalls 105:138+ Ja '78
Build a cook-out pole; compact barbecue center. R. Capotosto. il Pop Sci 211:123-5+ S '77
Converting from charcoal to electric. J. Toy. il Mech Ilus 73:38 Ag '77
Gas barbecue grills. il Consumer Rep 42:386-90 Jl '77
Indoor grill promises outdoor flavor—for $100. il Consumer Rep 42:66 F '77

Manufacture

Backyard bonanza; Weber grills. il por Time 109:78 Je 20 '77
BARBED wire
Hooked on barbed wire; antique wire collecting. E. P. Oubre. Sat Eve Post 249:14-15 My '77
BARBER, A. Richard
On to the Manhathalon. N Y Times Mag p4 S 4 '77
BARBER, Arthur L. Jr
Four seconds to eternity. Yachting 141:180-3 My '77
BARBER, Lynn E. See Evans, H. J. jt auth
BARBER, Ralph W.
Organizing clusters in a traditional building. Clearing H 50:314-15 Mr '77
BARBER of Seville; opera. See Rossini, G.
BARBER shop quartets. See Singing
BARBERS and barber shops
H.C. Haynes: barber & inventor. G. Gray. bibl il Negro Hist Bull 40:751-2 S '77
Il **BARBIERE di Siviglia; opera.** See Rossini, G.
BARBIERI, Fedora
Old pros: Tajo & Barbieri; interview, ed by C. Faria. il pors Opera N 41:8-13 F 26 '77
BARBOSA, Roberto
Bishop of São Félix. Chr Cent 94:422-3 My 4 '77
Brazil expels a missionary. Chr Cent 94:710-11 Ag 17 '77
Chile's image designed for export. Chr Cent 94:283-4 Mr 23 '77
New hope for Paraguay's prisoners. Chr Cent 94:301-2 Mr 30 '77
BARBOUR, William Rinehart, 1922-
William R. Barbour, Jr, Revell president, talks about getting our books out there where the unbeliever action is; interview. pors Pub W 211:55-8 Mr 14 '77
BARCELÓ, Carlos Romero-. See Romero Barceló, C.
BARCELONA
Homage to Barcelona. A. Burgess. il N Y Times Mag p44-5+ D 4 '77

Galleries and museums

Homage to Catalonia; Center for the study of Contemporary Art/Joan Miró Foundation; with introd by M. F. Schmertz. il Archit Rec 161:85-92 Mr '77

Music

See also
Opera—Spain
BARCIA, Roberto Caldeyro-, See Caldeyro-Barcia, R.
BARCLAY, Richard L.
ILL policy directory: making sharing easier. Lib J 102:2322-3 N 15 '77
BARCUS-Berry, Inc. See Audio equipment industry—United States
BARDEEN, John
John Bardeen: a study in the elusive nature of genius. por Sci Digest 81:55-7 Ap '77 *
BARDEN, William, Jr
Computer corner. il Radio-Electr 48:78-9 N; 72-3 D '77; 49:68-9 Ja '78

BARDO thödol (Tibetan book of the dead) See Buddhist literature
BAREBOAT chartering. See Yachts—Leasing and renting
BARETTA, Alberto
Wandering gaucho. A. J. Lowe. il pors Américas 29:26 Ja '77 *
BARGE Canal. See Canals—New York (state)
BARGE cruising. See Cruising
BARGES
Hundred years' war; controversy between barge and railroad transportation in Mississippi Valley. Forbes 119:54 Ja 15 '77
BARGHOORN, Elso S.
—See Knoll, A. H. jt auth

about

Figtree fossils: oldest algae yet. il Sci N 112: 245 O 15 '77 *
BARGMAN, Abraham
United Nations, the superpowers, and proliferation. Ann Am Acad 430:122-32 Mr '77
BARISHNIKOV, Mikhail
Dance; dancing of The prodigal son. N. Goldner. Nation 225:28-30 Jl 2 '77 *
Dancing (cont) A. Croce. por New Yorker 52: 94-6 Ja 17 '77 *
Grown-up Nutcracker. J. Maskey. il por Hi Fi 27:MA8-10 S '77 *
BARITEAU, Corinne Adria
Full circle; poem. McCalls 104:220 F '77
BARK
Eucalyptus bark. E. S. Ayensu. il Natur Hist 86:36-9 D '77
BARKAN, Alexander Elias
Myth of voter apathy. por Newsweek 89:9 Ja 24 '77
BARKAS, J. L.
Help! How to cope with it all. Redbook 149:81-8 O '77
BARKENBUS, Jack N.
Nuclear energy and the ballot. Bull Atom Sci 33:4-5 Ap '77
BARKER, Frank Granville-. See Granville-Barker, F.
BARKER, Philip A.
Canyon maple—a colorful mountaineer. il Am For 83:22-5 D '77
BARKER, Rodney
Whooper rally; with biographical sketch. il map Natur Hist 86:4, 22-4+ bibl(p96) Mr '77
BARKER, Sue
New stars of the court. P. Axthelm and J. B. Cumming, Jr. pors Newsweek 89:95 Ap 11 '77 *
BARKIN, Solomon
European union agreements provide framework for public policies. M Labor R 100:62-4 Ja '77
BARKLEY, David S. and others
Huntington's disease: delayed hypersensitivity in vitro to human central nervous system antigens. bibl il Science 195:314-16 Ja 21 '77
BARKLEY, Richard L.
N-boat standoff. map Nat R 29:660-2 Je 10 '77
BARLEY
Salty irrigation: bringing in the sheaves. il Sci N 112:53 Jl 23 '77
Seawater-based crop production: a feasibility study. E. Epstein and J. D. Norlyn. bibl il Science 197:249-51 Jl 15 '77
BARLOW, Robert B. Jr, and others
Efferent optic nerve fibers mediate circadian rhythms in the limulus eye. bibl il Science 197:86-9 Jl 1 '77
BARMORE, Judith M. and Morse, P. S.
Developing lifelong readers in the middle schools. Engl J 66:57-61 Ap '77
BARN decoration. See Decoration and ornament, Architectural
BARN murals. See Mural painting and decoration, Exterior
BARN owls. See Owls
BARNABY, Frank C.
Continuing body count at Hiroshima and Nagasaki. il Bull Atom Sci 33:48-51+ D '77
How states can go nuclear. il Ann Am Acad 430:29-43 Mr '77
Mounting prospects of nuclear war. il Bull Atom Sci 33:10-20 Je '77
BARNARD, Christiaan Neethling
Baboon heart. J. Seligmann and P. Young-Husband. il por Newsweek 90:60 Jl 4 '77 *
Christiaan Barnard: South Africa's premier surgeon; interview, ed by W. Bradley. il pors Sat Eve Post 249:62-4 Mr '77
BARNES, Bob, family
Natchez tradition at home. A. Scharffenberger. il pors Am Home 80:40-1 Mr '77
BARNES, C. A. and others
Circadian rhythm of synaptic excitability in rat and monkey central nervous system. bibl il Science 197:91-2 Jl 1 '77
BARNES, Carl
It fit together like a jigsaw puzzle. M. Gough and J. Macurdy. il por House B 119:104-13 N '77 *
BARNES, Jim
Elegy for the girl who drowned at Goats Bluff. Nation 224:600 My 14 '77
Letter to a poet; poem. Nation 225:630 D 10 '77
Midwinter; poem. Nation 224:728 Je 11 '77
Return to La Plata, Missouri; poem. Nation 225: 534 N 19 '77
BARNES, Leroy. See Barnes, N.
BARNES, Marvin
This time the News is good. J. Papanek. por Sports Illus 47:72 O 24 '77 *
BARNES, Nicky
Bad, bad Leroy Barnes. il por Time 110:21 D 12 '77 *
Mister Untouchable. F. Ferretti. il pors N Y Times Mag p 15-17+ Je 5 '77 *
BARNES, Sandra T.
Political transition in urban Africa. bibl f Ann Am Acad 432:26-41 Jl '77
BARNES, Wayne M.
Plasmid detection and sizing in single colony lysates. bibl il Science 195:393-4 Ja 28 '77
BARNES & Noble bookstore. See Booksellers and bookselling—New York (state)
BARNET, Richard Joseph
Behind the SALT fiasco. Progressive 41:6-7 Je '77
Carter's patchwork doctrine. Harpers 255:27-30+ Ag '77
Promise of disarmament. N Y Times Mag p 17+ F 27 '77
What U.S. stand on human rights? Current 193: 12-15 My '77
BARNETT, Arthur Doak
Military-security relations between China and the United States; excerpt from China policy: Old problems and new challenges. bibl f For Affairs 55:584-97 Ap '77
BARNETT, Mary
Midwives vs. doctors. Nation 225:10-12 Jl 2 '77
BARNETT, Paul
Tough tomatoes. Progressive 41:32-6 D '77
BARNETT, Richard S.
Grammar barrier. Nat R 29:210 F 18 '77
BARNETT, T. P.
An allegory. Bull Atom Sci 33:39 F '77
BARNHILL, William
(ed) See Upton, A. C. Talk with the new head of the NCI
BARNHOUSE, Ruth Tiffany
Sex roles and how children learn them. il New Cath World 220:280-3 N '77
BARNITZ, Albert, and Barnitz, J. P.
Campaigning with Custer; excerpt from Life in Custer's cavalry: diaries and letters of Albert and Jennie Barnitz, 1867-68, ed by R. M. Utley. il pors Am West 14:4-9+ Jl '77
BARNITZ, Jennie (Platt) See Barnitz, A. jt auth
BARNS, Converted. See Houses, Remodeled
BARNS and stables
Investment credit on confinement units: in pursuit of a decision. il Suc Farm 75:9 S '77
National Park Service stable by architects Hartman-Cox; in Washington, D.C.'s Rock Creek Park. il Archit Rec 161:120-1 F '77
See also
Milking parlors

Sanitation

But officer, it's just fertilizer! C. Bickers. Farm J 101:Dairy 15 S '77
Can your cattle pay for confinement? W. Kester. il Farm J 101:Beef 10-11 O '77
Low calf mortality without a big price. il Farm J 101:Dairy 12 Ag '77
Zero run-off system for $20 a cow. W. Kester. il Farm J 101:Dairy 6-8 O '77
BARNSTABLE, Mass.

Education

See Education—Massachusetts
BARNSTEAD, William A.
Let's limit the length of Congressional service. il por Duns R 110:101+ D '77
BARNSTONE, Willis
Eye which sees heaven; Easter Island. il Holiday 58:44-6+ Mr '77
Portugal: poet kings and the sea. il Sat Eve Post 249:70-1 N '77
BARNSTORMING. See Aviation—Stunt flying
BARNUM, Phineas Taylor
Selling the Swedish Nightingale. R. Hume. il pors Am Heritage 28:98-107 O '77 *
BARNWELL, William H.
Pedestrian-idealist's approach to education. Chr Cent 94:944-8 O 19 '77
BARNWELL family
Barnwell coat-of-arms. H. K. Eilers. Hobbies 82:146-7 Ap '77
BARON, Joan. See Rogers, V. R. jt auth
BARON, Virginia Olsen
Journal from Northern Ireland. Chr Cent 94: 757-9, 820-4 Ag 31, S 21 '77
BAROQUE art. See Art, Baroque
BARR, Browne
Finding the good at Garden Grove. il por Chr Cent 94:424-7 My 4 '77

BARR, James Clayton
Ship that hunted itself. C. Simpson. il pors map Read Digest 111:188-92+ S '77
BARR, Lou
Helgoland diary: sixteen days under the North Atlantic. il Oceans 10:16-21 Ja '77
BARR, Thomas D.
IBM's high-flying legal eagle. por Forbes 119: 74 Ap 1 '77 *
BARRACKS
See also
United States—Army—Barracks and quarters
BARRACLOUGH, William G.
International reactions to the problems of steel trade; statement, September 20, 1977. Dept State Bull 77:742-50 N 21 '77
BARRE, Mohamed Siad
Young is misinformed; excerpts from interview, ed by A. De Borchgrave. il Newsweek 89:45-6 Je 27 '77
about
Crossed wires. A. De Borchgrave. il por Newsweek 90:42-3 S 26 '77 *
Ivan, go home. il U.S. News 83:76 S 26 '77 *
BARRE, Raymond
Tough policy to stabilize France; interview, ed by R. Dorang. por Bus W p64-6 Mr 7 '77
about
Professor's gamble. il por Time 110:72+ O 24 '77 *
Visit to the United States, 1977
French Prime Minister Barre visits the United States; statement, September 16, 1977. Dept State Bull 77:566-8 O 24 '77
BARRET, Ann
Story behind the books: two unusual mysteries from the U. of Chicago press. Pub W 212:62 O 17 '77
BARRETT, Ellen
Lesbian priest. por Time 109:58 Ja 24 '77 *
BARRETT, Harrison H. See Swindell, W. jt auth
BARRETT, James E.
Behavioral history as a determinant of the effects of *d*-amphetamine on punished behavior. bibl il Science 198:67-9 O 7 '77
BARRETT, M. Edgar
Case of the tangled transfer price. il Harvard Bus R 55:20-2+ My '77
—and Fraser, L. B. 3d
Conflicting roles in budgeting for operations. il Harvard Bus R 55:137-46 Jl '77
BARRETT, Peter
Magic 40 degree mark. il por Field & S 82:76-7+ My '77
Malarkey flies. il Field & S 82:50+ O '77
Outdoors. See issues of Mechanix illustrated
Terrible-tempered ox. il Field & S 82:48-50+ N '77
BARRICK, D. E. and others
Ocean surface currents mapped by radar. bibl il Science 198:138-44 O 14 '77
BARRIER Islands
Shoreline forms and shoreline dynamics. R. Dolan and others. bibl il maps Science 197:49-51 Jl 1 '77
See also
Sea Islands
BARRINGTON, Carol Bisbee
Isla Mujeres: Mexico's sleeping island. il Travel 148:52-7 S '77
BARRON, John
Espionage: the dark side of détente. Read Digest 112:78-82 Ja '78
Soviet-American trade: trick or treat? Read Digest 111:67-8+ O '77
—and Paul, Anthony
Murder of a gentle land; condensation. il map Read Digest 110:227-34+ F '77
BARRON, Neil
Launching the SF collection. Wilson Lib Bull 52:56-60 S '77
BARROW, Alaska
Alaskan tragedy. B. Lopez. map Harpers 255:30-3 S '77
BARROWS, Anita
Salt and lemon; poem. Nation 224:565 My 7 '77
BARRY, Ann
(ed) See Guion, P. Diary of a 19th-century lass
BARRY, John
John Barry, fighting Irishman. B. Everett. il pors map Am Hist Illus 12:18-25 D '77 *
BARRY, Rick
Splendid Warrior who knows his onions. R. Fimrite. il por Sports Illus 46:63-5 My 9 '77
BARRY, Tim
Komputer korner (cont) il Radio-Electr 48:22+ Mr '77
BARRY, William H. and others
Measurement of the human magnetic heart vector. bibl il Science 198:1159-62 D 16 '77
BARS and barrooms
Nothing fancy; Cardinal Inn, Prairie City, Iowa. D. Bauer. il Esquire 87:101-3 My '77
Watering holes; reproductions of paintings; with report by R. Blount, Jr. B. Fuchs. Sports Illus 47:32-7 S 5 '77
See also
Atlanta—Hotels, restaurants, etc.
BARS for the home
Emergency party bar. D. Tobias. il Am Home 80:69 N '77
BARSHAY, Stephen S. See Prinn, R. G. jt auth
BARSNESS, Larry
Bison in art and history; excerpt from The bison in art. il Am West 14:10-21 Mr '77
BARSUKOV, L. I. See Bergelson, L. D. jt auth
BART, Muriel
Special report: the bilingual library. il por Wilson Lib Bull 51:475-6 F '77
BARTELL, Ernest
Higher education and government; address, January 18, 1977. Vital Speeches 43:389-94 Ap 15 '77
BARTER
Backyard barter: the best things in life are (almost) free. il Org Gard & Farm 24:130-5 Ap '77
Bartering gets to be a business in the billions. il U.S. News 82:47-8 Mr 21 '77
How to barter for what you want. R. A. Barnett. il Mech Illus 73:8+ S '77
Trading game. B. Graustark. il Newsweek 90: 62+ Ag 1 '77
BARTH, Catherine
French ceramist. il por Ceram Mo 25:48-50 N '77
Pottery by Japanese masters. il Design (US) 78: 18-20 Spr '77
Victor Hugo: the painter. il Design (US) 78:6-9 mid-Summ '77
BARTH, Howard G.
Separations using liquid chromatography. bibl il por Chemistry 50:11-13 S '77
BARTH, Rodney J.
ERIC/RCS report (cont) Engl J 66:68-72 Ja '77
BARTHELME, Donald
Cortes and Montezuma; story. New Yorker 53 25-6 Ag 22 '77
Crisis; story. New Yorker 53:42-3 O 24 '77
King of jazz; story. New Yorker 52:31-2 F 7 '77
On the steps of the Conservatory; story. New Yorker 53:33-5 F 21 '77
Question party; story. New Yorker 52:32-4 Ja 17 '77
Tales of the Swedish Army; story. New Yorker 53:23-4 D 26 '77
Zombies; story. New Yorker 53:35-5 Ap 25 '77
BARTHES, Roland
Segmentation. B. Henderson. Film Q 31:57-65 Fall '77 *
BARTHOLDI, Frédéric Auguste
He built the Statue of Liberty. N. Poulain. il Read Digest 110:27-32 Ap '77 *
BARTHOLOMEW, George A. and Casey, T. M.
Endothermy during terrestrial activity in large beetles. bibl il Science 195:882-3 Mr 4 '77
BARTLETT, Laile E.
What do we really know about psychic phenomena? Read Digest 111:82-7 Ag '77
BARTLETT, Lu
John Shaw, cabinetmaker of Annapolis. bibl il Antiques 111:362-77 F '77
BARTLEY, Letha Wolfe, and Wolfe, S. J.
Meadowlark sang. il Am West 14:34-7 Mr '77
BARTÓK, Béla
Six string quartets. D. W. Moore. il Am Rec G 40:12-14 Ap '77 *
Wooden Prince; Boulez recording. W. Botsford. Am Rec G 40:16 Jl '77 *
BARTON, Bob
Racing clinic, offshore. il Yachting 141:56+ Mr '77
BARTON, Charles
Missing plane they had to find. il Pop Mech 147: 69-73+ Je '77
Navy's natural divers: United States Navy Marine Mammal Training Program. il Oceans 10:34-9 Jl '77
Rescue from the heart of a typhoon. il map Pop Mech 148:73-6+ D '77
Spruce Goose; pterodactyl of World War II. il Pop Mech 148:83+ N '77
BARTON, Glenys
Glenys Barton at Wedgwood. J. Mallet. il Ceram Mo 25:28-30 O '77 *
BARTON, Michael
Love among the brains. Nat R 29:840-1 Jl 22 '77
Up from the DAR. Nat R 29:1252-3 O 28 '77
BARTÓN, Paulé
Honey seller; poem; tr by H. A. Norman. Nation 225:700 D 24 '77
BARTRAM, John
Colonial botanist, self-taught, filled European gardens; excerpt from A species of eternity. J. Kastner. il Smithsonian 8:122-9 bibl(p 161) O '77 *
BARWOOD, Hal, and others
MacArthur; excerpt from screenplay. il pors map Sr Schol 110:14-17 D 15 '77
BARYSHNIKOV, Mikhail. See Barishnikov, M.
BARZINI, Luigi
Certain complications; excerpt from O America. Am Heritage 28:64-7 Ap '77
BASALT
Unique volcanic subsea specimens. Sci N 111: 102 F 12 '77

BASCH, Buddy
New England's islands. il Travel 147:44-9 Ap '77

BASEBALL
Baseball in the mind. R. Rabinowitz. New Repub 177:24-5 Jl 23 '77
Perfect beauty of a ninety-foot field. W. Smith. il Horizon 19:92-3 Mr '77
See also
Batting (baseball)
Softball

History

Way I see it. B. Catton. por Am Heritage 28:107 Ap '77

Cuba

In Cuba, it's viva el grand old game. R. Fimrite. il Sports Illus 46:68-72+ Je 6 '77

BASEBALL, Childrens
Little League lunacy. J. Farmer. il Org Gard & Farm 24:120+ My '77
Tying one on for Taiwan; Little League World Series. R. Reid. il Sports Illus 47:78-9 S 5 '77

Umpiring

Ump. L. Sheehan. il Atlantic 240:83-4 S '77

BASEBALL, College
He's a one-man Hurricane; R. Fraser, University of Miami coach. J. Underwood. il pors Sports Illus 46:46+ My 30 '77
They had a devil of a time; College World Series. P. Gammons. Sports Illus 46:47 Je 27 '77

BASEBALL, Professional
At the other end of the rainbows; R. Buhrke's catching of home runs hit out of Wrigley Field. R. Telander. il por Sports Illus 46: 50-2 Ap 25 '77
Baseball 1977. Sports Illus 46:36-46+ Ap 11 '77
Baseball '77: National League; title predictions. Sr Schol 109:34 Ap 21 '77
Behind baseball's comeback: it's an island of stability. il U.S. News 83:56-7 S 19 '77
Boom! Boston Red Sox. K. Hannon. il Sports Illus 47:10-15 Jl 4 '77
Chi, oh my! White Sox and Cubs. P. Gammons. il Sports Illus 47:8-13 Jl 25 '77
Conversation with Fingers. E. Istomin. il pors N Y Times Mag p56-7+ O 9 '77
Cubs join the club—maybe. P. Gammons. il Sports Illus 46:19 My 30 '77
Devil of a time for the Angels. L. Keith. il Sports Illus 47:16-17 Ag 1 '77
Dodgers: no longer seeing Red. il Time 109:90-1 My 23 '77
Encountering the Yankees. R. Kahn. il Time 109: 79 Je 6 '77
Fan's notes; Chicago Cubs. G. F. Will. il Newsweek 89:84 Je 27 '77
Good old days revisited; minor league ball in Jersey City. il Sports Illus 46:52+ Je 13 '77
His biggest pitch is yet to come; M. Stone, Boston's batting practice hurler. P. Gammons. il por Sports Illus 47:37-9 Ag 22 '77
How the Franchise went West; T. Seaver trade. il por Time 109:49 Je 27 '77
In L.A. it's up, up, and away with Cey. L. Keith. il por Sports Illus 46:24-8+ My 16 '77
Indian tomahawked; firing of managr F. Robinson. J. Jares. il por Sports Illus 47:40+ Jl 4 '77
It turned into a Royal occasion; American League West. il Sports Illus 47:20-4+ S 5 '77
It's hard to pass the Bucs; Pittsburgh Pirates. W. Bingham. il Sports Illus 46:16-19 My 30 '77
Lessons in defeat; American League contenders. P. Axthelm. il Newsweek 90:50 S 5 '77
Long green. R. Angell. New Yorker 53:103-4+ Ap 25 '77
Lot of person; D. Kaye, owner of the Seattle Mariners. R. Fimrite. il pors Sports Illus 46: 76-80+ Ap 4 '77
Minny gets the max from a minimum. L. Keith. il Sports Illus 46:22-3 Je 20 '77
Notes and comment; trading T. Seaver to the Cincinnati Reds. New Yorker 53:19 Jl 4 '77
Now there is one, maybe; American League East pennant race. P. Gammons. il Sports Illus 47:62+ S 26 '77
Octopus; Los Angeles Dodgers. P. Bonventre and D. Gram. il Newsweek 89:77 My 16 '77
Off on a rampage; Philadelphia Phillies. L. Keith. il Sports Illus 47:14-17 Ag 29 '77
Old uniforms, new Sox; Chicago White Sox. P. Gammons. il por Sports Illus 46:53-4 My 16 '77
Reds are singing the blues. R. Fimrite. il Sports Illus 47:16-19 Ag 22 '77
Revival and survival; Oriole-Yankee series. L. Keith. il Sports Illus 47:16-19 Ag 8 '77
Rigors of spring; reproductions of paintings; with report by L. Keith. J. McMullan. il Sports Illus 46:32-7 Mr 7 '77
Runs, hits and dollars. P. Axthelm. il Newsweek 89:95 Ap 18 '77
Script written by God; Dodgers vs Phillies for National League title. R. Fimrite. il Sports Illus 47:21-3 O 17 '77
Series full of flip-flops; Yankees vs Royals for American League title. L. Keith. il Sports Illus 47:18-21 O 17 '77
Several stories with sudden endings. R. Angell. New Yorker 53:48-54+ N 14 '77
Somebody old and somebody new; Oakland A's. L. Keith. il Sports Illus 46:30-1 Ap 18 '77
Spring training; Boston Red Sox. T. Murray. il Sat Eve Post 249:72-3+ Ap '77
There goes the franchise; T. Seaver trade. P. Axthelm. il pors Newsweek 89:62-4 Je 27 '77
They kept cool during a cold streak; New York Yankees. L. Keith. il Sports Illus 46:30-2+ My 2 '77
They're beginning to sound like a broken record; attendance at Los Angeles Dodgers' games. il Sports Illus 47:36-41 S 26 '77
Tip of the hat, cut of the bat; Toronto Blue Jays. R. Fimrite. Sports Illus 46:24-5 Ap 25 '77
Tom Terrific arms the Red arsenal. L. Keith. il por Sports Illus 46:22-4+ Je 27 '77
True tests of talent; Philadelphia-Los Angeles and New York-Kansas City playoff pairings. L. Keith. il Sports Illus 47:18-21 O 3 '77
Week; baseball. H. Weiskopf. See issues of Sports illustrated published during the baseball season
See also
Baseball players
National Baseball Hall of Fame and Museum

Advertising

Bananas in the bushes; J. Paul's promotions work for the El Paso Diablos. P. Putnam. il por Sports Illus 47:32-5 S 12 '77
Of frogs and hats and bats; promotional days; photographs; with report by L. Keith. R. Mackson. Sports Illus 47:36-41 Jl 18 '77

Anecdotes, facetiae, satire, etc.

Memories of a left fielder. J. G. Dunne. Esquire 88:27+ S '77

Economic aspects

Brains vs. bucks. P. Axthelm. il por Newsweek 89:65 My 30 '77
Playoff for the Red Sox. il Bus W p59+ N 21 '77
So, you want to own a ball club. A. B. Block. il Forbes 119:37-40 Ap 1 '77
There's a rub in the Hub; bidding for the Boston Red Sox. P. Gammons. il Sports Illus 47:83+ N 14 '77
Toronto's profitable new passion; Blue Jays. il Bus W p37 O 24 '77

Ethical aspects

Fighting side of baseball. R. Blount, Jr. Esquire 88:30+ Jl '77

History

Confessions of a gunkball artist; excerpt from Whitey and Mickey, ed by J. Durso. W. Ford. il pors N Y Times Mag p38-41 Ap 3 '77
Everybody knew me Al; excerpt from Ring, a biography of Ring Lardner. J. Yardley. il Sports Illus 47:82-6+ Ag 29 '77
Fastest start of them all; 1955 Brooklyn Dodgers. W. Bingham. Sports Illus 46:28 My 16 '77
Life with Casey Stengel; excerpt from Whitey and Mickey, ed by J. Durso, W. Ford and M. Mantle. il Sat Eve Post 249:44-5+ My '77
Spalding's baseball tour. C. Davidson. il Am Heritage 28:46-9 O '77

Organization and administration

Benched from the bench; Braves owner T. Turner. K. Hannon. il por Sports Illus 46:67-8 My 23 '77
Bill Veeck: the happy hustler; owner of the Chicago White Sox. Time 109:90 Ap 25 '77
Bowie's bean ball; failure to arrange US-Cuba game. Nation 224:420 Ap 9 '77
Management kingpin of the Atlanta Braves; W. Lucas of the Atlanta Braves. il pors Ebony 32:52-4+ Jl '77
Miles high in Mile High City; move of Oakland A's to Denver. Time 110:70-1 D 26 '77
So, you want to own a ball club. A. B. Block. il Forbes 119:37-40 Ap 1 '77
Yankee Clipper; owner G. Steinbrenner. R. Fimrite. il pors Sports Illus 47:122-6+ O 10 '77

Radio broadcasting

See Radio broadcasting—Sports

Television broadcasting

See Television broadcasting—Sports

World Series

Baseball 1977: the American league; World Series predictions. B. Weber. Sr Schol 109:39 Ap 7 '77
Brave new World Series; Yankees and Dodgers. P. Axthelm. il Newsweek 90:105-6 O 24 '77
Good guys against the bad guys; Yankees vs Dodgers. R. Fimrite. il Sports Illus 47:18-25 O 24 '77

BASEBALL, Professional—World Series—*Cont.*
Nice guys always finish. . . ? Yankees vs Dodgers. il Time 110:110-12 O 24 '77
Now for a long, hot winter; Yankee's victory. il Time 110:81 O 31 '77
Reg-gie. P. Axthelm. il por Newsweek 90:45+ O 31 '77
Reg-gie! Reg-gie!! Reg-gie!!! R. Fimrite. il pors Sports Illus 47:28-30+ O 31 '77
Several stories with sudden endings. R. Angell. New Yorker 53:48-54+ N 14 '77

History

Black Sox scandal. D. Smith. il por Am Hist Illus 11:16-24 Ja '77
Crack! Roar! It's World Series time! W. Schulz. il Read Digest 111:189-90+ O '77
World Series. il Sports Illus 47:61-2+ O 10 '77

Japan

Move over for Oh-san. F. Deford. il pors Sports Illus 47:58-64+ Ag 15 '77

BASEBALL cards. See Advertising cards

BASEBALL coaches
See also
Fraser, R.

BASEBALL Hall of Fame. See National Baseball Hall of Fame and Museum

BASEBALL managers
Lasorda's mates in the class of '77; new National League managers. J. Kaplan. Sports Illus 46:41 Mr 14 '77
See also
Anderson, S.
Lasorda, T.
Martin, B.
Robinson, F.

BASEBALL players
Annual baseball roundup. il Ebony 32:153-6+ Je '77
Bargain, and bye-bye basement; Montreal Expos' outfield. B. Dunn. il Sports Illus 47:42-4+ Ag 8 '77
Bumper crop of boys from the farm; rookies. P. Gammons. il Sports Illus 46:24-6 Mr 28 '77
Chaws. R. Blount, Jr. il Sports Illus 47:54-9+ Jl 4 '77
High-risk hurlers; relievers. P. Axthelm. il Newsweek 90:43 Ag 15 '77
Hitters can be ranked. H. Weiskopf. il Sports Illus 47:24-5 Jl 18 '77
Those Golden boys; ex-Oakland A's. P. Bonventre. il Newsweek 89:76-7 Ap 4 '77
See also
Brock, L.
Carew, R.
Carlton, S.
Cedeno, C.
Cey, R.
Denny, J.
Fidrych, M.
Foster, G.
Guidry, R.
Henderson, S.
Jackson, R.
Kennedy, T.
McCovey, W.
McLain, D.
Maris, R.
National Baseball Hall of Fame and Museum
Niekro, P.
Oh, S.
Parker, W.
Plummer, B.
Randle, L.
Robinson, B.
Rozema, D.
Scott, G.
Seaver, T.
Singleton, K.
Tanana, F.
Templeton, G.
Wilson, H.
Zisk, R.

Caricatures and cartoons

There's surprise in every package. R. Grossman. il Sports Illus 46:38-43 Ap 11 '77

Recruiting

Is it daft—or deft—to draft? L. Keith. il Sports Illus 47:30-2+ N 7 '77

Salaries, pensions, etc.

How much is a ball player worth? il Ebony 32:153-6+ Je '77
See also
Collective bargaining—Baseball, Professional

BASEBALL records. See Sports records

BASEBALL scouting
Scout: sports' indefatigable spy. B. Surface. il Read Digest 111:53-4+ D '77

BASEBALLS
Going, going, gone! P. Bonventre. il Newsweek 89:66 Je 13 '77
Sometimes the ball just takes a funny bounce. R. Blount, Jr. il Esquire 88:17-18 Ag '77
They're knocking the stuffing out of it. L. Keith. il Sports Illus 46:22-5+ Je 13 '77

BASEMENTS and cellars
Convert your basement into a cold cellar. R. Weinsteiger. il Org Gard & Farm 24:112-13 S '77
Low-cost root cellar solves winter storage problems. I. Haidenthaller. il Org Gard & Farm 24:114-16 S '77
Remodeling: smart ways to make a basement more inviting. D. Haupert. il Bet Hom & Gard 55:128-31 My '77
Stocking the cold cellar. R. B. Yepsen, Jr. il Org Gard & Farm 24:109-10+ S '77
Super basement: do 1 or 2 or 3 rooms! il Mech Illus 73:64-6 Je '77
See also
Dampness in buildings

BASES, Military. See Military bases

BASHAM, Ray
Anchor watch. Yachting 141:194-6 My '77
How to heave-to. il Yachting 142:123-5 D '77

BASHEVKIN, Joy
Dear Barbara Walters; poem. Redbook 150:64 D '77

BASHFULNESS
How to overcome shyness; excerpt from Shyness: what it is, what to do about it. P. G. Zimbardo. Ladies Home J 94:62+ My '77
Shyness—the people phobia. P. Zimbardo. Todays Educ 66:47-9 Ja '77
Therapy for the shy; views of P. Zimbardo. M. Clark and P. S. Greenberg. il por Newsweek 89:72 Je 13 '77

BASHLINE, Jim
[Column] See issues of Field & stream

BASHLINE, Sylvia
[Column] See issues of Field & stream

BASHOLD, Joanne
Tragedy of Joanne. R. Severo. il pors Sr Schol 109:23-6+ Mr 24 '77 *
Tragedy of Joanne Bashold. A. Adelson. il pors Good H 184:124-5+ Mr '77 *

BASIC Educational Opportunity Grant. See Student aid

BASIC training of Pavlo Hummel; drama. See Rabe, D.

BASIL, Robert A.
Strengthening NATO ties; excerpts from address. Aviation W 107:7 Ag 29 '77

BASIL
See also
Cookery—Herbs

BASKERVILLE, Gray
Hot rod gallery. il Hot Rod 30:44-50+ F; 40 Mr; 126 My '77
Hot rod magazine rod test. See issues of Hot Rod
How to build a repro street rod. il Hot Rod 30:47-51 O; 30-3 N; 28-31 D '77

—and Wallace, Dave
Bracket racing America: [state] il Hot Rod 30:35-8 S '77

BASKET making
Make-ahead presents: work a woven basket. il Seventeen 36:130-1 N '77

BASKETBALL
Hooping it up; women's basketball. B. Weber. Sr Schol 109:27 Ja 27 '77
Our men in Havana. E. Sciolino. il Newsweek 89:45+ Ap 18 '77

Equipment

Grid to backstop the backboard. il Sunset 158:160 Ap '77

Tournaments

City game, country style; Western Invitational Tourney. R. Telander. il Sports Illus 46:38-43 Mr 21 '77
Hooping it up big in the Cornbelt; women's high school championships in Iowa. il Time 109:84-5 Mr 28 '77
Now for the all-star wars; Amateur Athletic Union's Youth National Championship. B. McDermott. il Sports Illus 47:50-2 Jl 11 '77

BASKETBALL, College
Big change in the affairs of State; Ohio State coach E. Miller. L. Keith. il por Sports Illus 47:24-6+ D 12 '77
College basketball 1977-78. il Sports Illus 47:34-44+ N 28 '77
Color for the Orange is gray; Syracuse team. B. McDermott. il Sports Illus 46:47-8 Mr 7 '77
Coming to the Point; Princeton-West Point women's game. New Yorker 52:26-7 Ja 24 '77
Dons were wan; Notre Dame vs San Francisco. K. Hannon il Sports Illus 46:44+ Mr 14 '77
Dunkers are strutting their stuffs. B. McDermott. il Sports Illus 46:20-2+ Mr 14 '77
Hallelujah, what a team! Athletes in Action vs college teams. J. Jares. il Sports Illus 46:41-2 F 7 '77
Heels are really clicking; North Carolina. L. Keith. il Sports Illus 46:40-1 Ja 17 '77
Macy had the goods in every department; Kentucky vs Notre Dame. L. Keith. il Sports Illus 48:12-13 Ja 9 '78
On the trip to the pit the Bruins got bit; Oregon vs UCLA. L. Keith. il Sports Illus 46:20-1 F 28 '77

BASKETBALL, College—*Continued*
School of hard Knoxville; University of Tennessee. L. Keith. il Sports Illus 46:48-9 Ja 24 '77
Streaks of San Francisco. B. McDermott. il Sports Illus 46:26-9 Ja 31 '77
Sub was the rub; Kansas vs Kansas State. K. Hannon. il Sports Illus 48:72-3 Ja 9 '78
That trip to Vegas was no honeymoon; Nevada-Las Vegas vs Louisville. B. McDermott. il Sports Illus 46:22-3+ F 21 '77
Three applications for one vacancy; Michigan in Big Ten race L. Keith. il Sports Illus 46:20-1 F 14 '77
Uncourtly Dons; University of San Francisco team. P. Bonventre. il Newsweek 89:84 Mr 7 '77
Week; college basketball. H. Weiskopf. See issues of Sports illustrated published during the basketball season
Winning is the order of the day; Virginia Military Institute. K. Hannon. il Sports Illus 46:38+ F 14 '77
Wizard's disciple; G. Cunningham, coach of UCLA. J. Jares. il por Sports Illus 47:81-2 D 5 '77
Year of the superstuffers. il Time 109:61-2 Mr 21 '77

History

Magic numbers were 6 and 60; University of San Francisco basketball teams of the mid-1950s. L. Keith. Sports Illus 46:28 Ja 31 '77

Television broadcasting

See Television broadcasting—Sports

Tournaments

Al, you went out in style; NCAA championship. B. McDermott. il por Sports Illus 46:20-3 Ap 4 '77
Dance on his face, Flenoil! National Junior College Basketball Tournament. B. Newman. il Sports Illus 46:53-4 Mr 28 '77
Off and running toward Atlanta; NCAA regionals; symposium. B. McDermott. il Sports Illus 46:16-21 Mr 28 '77
Sixteen sweetest fight for a kiss; NCAA tournament. B. McDermott. il Sports Illus 46:28-9 Mr 21 '77
Smaller stood taller; Association for Intercollegiate Athletics for Women national championships. B. Gilbert. il Sports Illus 46:59+ Ap 4 '77

BASKETBALL, Professional
Add super to the Sonics. J. Papanek. il por Sports Illus 48:81-2+ Ja 9 '78
All for one sure beats one for all; Portland vs Philadelphia for NBA title. C. Kirkpatrick. il Sports Illus 46:30-2+ Je 13 '77
At full into the playoffs. C. Kirkpatrick. il Sports Illus 46:32-4+ Ap 18 '77
Bearing of the green; Boston Celtics' playoff victories. C. Kirkpatrick. il Sports Illus 46:20-3 Ap 25 '77
Big men the Knicks got, but a team they ain't. J. Papanek. il Sports Illus 47:75+ D 12 '77
Blasting off in Houston. C. Kirkpatrick. il Sports Illus 46:16-17 Ja 17 '77
Couple of babes in the woods; Portland vs Denver in the semifinal playoffs of the NBA Western Conference. C. Kirkpatrick. il Sports Illus 46:22-3 My 9 '77
Dreams of Celtic pride. P. Axthelm. il por Newsweek 90:79 N 28 '77
Fight team, fight, fight, fight! Detroit Pistons il Time 109:65 F 28 '77
Good, but why not the best? Philadelphia 76ers. C. Kirkpatrick. il Sports Illus 46:22-5 Mr 21 '77
Heavy truckin' on Bourbon Street; New Orleans Jazz. J. Papanek. il pors Sports Illus 47:26-7 D 5 '77
It's a wild West show; Los Angeles Lakers. C. Kirkpatrick. il Sports Illus 46:14-17 F 14 '77
L.A. couldn't move the mountain; Portland's victory in NBA Western Conference finals. C. Kirkpatrick. il Sports Illus 46:28-9 My 23 '77
Moaning and winning in Motown; Detroit Pistons. J. Papanek. il Sports Illus 46:62-3 F 28 '77
Pro basketball, 1977-78. il Sports Illus 47:36-44+ O 31 '77
Pro basketball roundup. il Ebony 33:51-2+ Ja '78
Sixers do the hustle; NBA's Eastern Division championship. J. Papanek. il Sports Illus 46:64+ My 16 '77
Storms over the Atlantic; Boston Celtics and Philadelphia 76ers. C. Kirkpatrick. il pors Sports Illus 47:16-19 N 21 '77
There's no place like home court; Portland Trail Blazers vs Philadelphia 76ers in the NBA championships. C. Kirkpatrick. il Sports Illus 46:22-3 Je 6 '77
Toddling team on a rampage; Chicago Bulls. J. Papanek. il por Sports Illus 46:71-2+ Ap 4 '77
Trouble? Call the bomb squad; 76ers vs Trail Blazers. J. Papanek. il Sports Illus 47:24-5 D 19 '77
Walton gang; B. Walton of the Portland Trail Blazers. B. Weber. Sr Schol 110:25 D 1 '77
Walton up on high; Portland Trail Blazers and the Los Angeles Lakers. P. Axthelm. il pors Newsweek 89:75 My 23 '77
You can't buy heart; team play. B. Bradley. il pors Sports Illus 47:102-6+ O 31 '77
See also
Basketball players
National Basketball Association

Accidents and injuries

Low blow in Los Angeles; Kermit Washington's slugging of Rudy Tomjanovich. il Time 110:70 D 26 '77

Ethical aspects

Out of kilter; question of violence. C. McWilliams. Nation 225:709 D 31 '77
Shattered and shaken; NBA violence. C. Kirkpatrick. il Sports Illus 48:46-7 Ja 2 '78

Fiction

Christmas gift for Fort Zack. F. Deford. Sports Illus 47:62-4+ D 19 '77

Organization and administration

See also
National Basketball Association

Television broadcasting

See Television broadcasting—Sports

BASKETBALL coaches
Every Yow has the old know-how; coaching Yow sisters. N. Williamson. il pors Sports Illus 46:42+ F 21 '77
See also
Carril, P.
Cunningham, B.
Cunningham, G.
Lemons, A.
McGuire, A.
Miller, E.
Reed, W.
Snowden, F.
Tarkanian, J.
West, J.
Wilkens, L.

BASKETBALL courts
We had this nice big rectangle. So why not put a painting on it? R. Indiana's design for the basketball court of the Milwaukee Exposition Convention Center Arena. Vasari. il por Art N 76:24 D '77

BASKETBALL players
Nine more good ones; NBA rookies. Sports Illus 46:63 Mr 14 '77
Pro basketball roundup. il Ebony 33:51-2+ Ja '78
Six million dollar man; Bob McAdoo and Julius Erving. B. Weber. il Sr Schol 109:29 F 10 '77
See also
Barnes, M.
Barry, R.
Blazejowski, C.
Buse, D.
Cowens, D.
Criss, C.
Dantley, A.
Frazier, W.
Harris, L.
Havlicek, J.
Hawkins, R.
Jones, E.
King, A.
Long, D.
Maravich, P.
Murphy, C.
Perry, R.
Phegley, R.
Van Lier, N.
Walton, B.

Photographs

Hottest of the hot shots; jump shooters; with report by K. Hannon. Sports Illus 47:38-44+ N 28 '77
When the going gets rough; with report by J. Papanek. il Sports Illus 47:38-44+ O 31 '77

Recruiting

Shark gets a ruling with bite; J. Tarkanian vs NCAA. R. Telander. il por Sports Illus 47:26-7 O 10 '77

BASKETBALL uniforms. See Uniforms, Sports

BASKETRY. See Basket making

BASNEY, Lionel
Nadezhda Mandelstam: memoir as prophecy. Chr Today 21:20-1 Jl 29 '77
Serpico and the voyeurs of the moral war. il Chr Today 21:23-5 Mar 4 '77

BASS, G. H, & Company. See Shoe industry

BASS, George F.
Wreck at Sheytan Deresi. il Oceans 10:34-9 Ja '77

BASS, John T.
Interview with John T. Bass of the Christian Booksellers Association; ed by P. Hewitt. por Pub W 212:69-70 S 26 '77

BASS
Meanmouth; research on hybird bass behavior by W. Childers. K. Schultz. il Field & S 82:84-5+ Je '77
Understanding our bass population. B. D. Shupp. il Conservationist 32:26-9 Jl '77
See also
Cookery—Fish

BASS boats. See Fishing boats

BASS fishing
Bank of the giant sea bass; Uncle Sam Bank, Baja California. C. Garrison. il Field & S 82: 94-5+ My '77
Bass and the worm. K. Schultz. il por Field & S 82:84-9 My '77
Bass boom south of the border. A. Eason. il map Outdoor Life 161:82-4+ Ja '78
Bass when it sizzles; suggestions from 6 experts. il Outdoor Life 160:72-5 Jl '77
Bassin' Mann; interview, ed by P. Miller. T. Mann. il pors Outdoor Life 159:55-7+ Mr '77
Bassing with bait. B. Dalrymple. il Outdoor Life 159:78-81 Je '77
Behold the new fisherperson; FEM, America's oldest women's bass tournament. P. Miller. il Outdoor Life 159:56-9+ F '77
Bionic bassing. T. Drace. il Motors B & S 139: 84-6+ Je '77
Fancy worms for hungry bass. P. Barrett. il Mech Illus 73:10+ Ag '77
First anglers into Cuba. E. A. Bauer. il map Outdoor Life 160:69-73+ S '77
Get more strikes and hookups with these hot new worming systems. J. Gibbs. il Outdoor Life 159:18+ My '77
How experts solve fishing's 5 big problems; interviews, ed by F. Sargeant. il Outdoor Life 159:90-3 My '77
How the bass pros face tough weather; interviews with experts, ed by N. Sisley. il Field & S 82:46-7+ D '77
How to read a bass lake. K. Schultz. il Field & S 81:88-9+ Ap '77
Landlocked striper tops previous record. il Outdoor Life 160:52 Ag '77
Largemouth bass. C. Farmer. il Outdoor Life 159: 66-7 Je '77
Midnight stripers; San Francisco Bay. R. Chatham. il Field & S 81:136-8+ Mr '77
9 up-and-coming lakes. il map Outdoor Life 159:66-73+ Ap '77
Record bass: the quest is getting frantic. P. Miller. il Outdoor Life 160:94-7+ S '77
Secrets from a heartland bass lab; largemouth bass; interview, ed by J. Randolph. A. A. Ciuffa. il por Outdoor Life 160:82-5+ D '77
Secrets of the strike; largemouth bass. J. Gibbs. il Outdoor Life 160:61-5+ Ag '77
Smallmouth bass. H. L. Lawrence. il Outdoor Life 159:68-9 Je '77
Smallmouth bass: facts that can change your fishing; interview, ed by B. J. Gibbs. G. Lau. il pors Outdoor Life 160:86-7+ Jl '77
Stripers and bait; Atlantic States. N. Bryant. il Field & S 82:42-6 Ag '77
Stripers for everybody! B. W. Dalrymple. il Outdoor Life 160:59-61+ Jl '77
Tom Mann's best summer bass bets. K. Schultz. il Field & S 82:48+ Jl '77
Treasure lives; bass fishing in Treasure Lake, Cuba. K. Schultz. il Field & S 82:114-22+ Ag '77
Update: bass; ed by J. Gibbs. il Outdoor Life 160:34 O; 52 N; 52 D '77; 161:44 Ja '78
War and peace in a bass boat; slob guides, kooky clients. J. Weiss; A. Eason. Outdoor Life 160:94-6+ O '77
Winter bass: the cold hard facts. il Outdoor Life 160:78-81+ N '77
You can catch bass after a front. S. Price. il Field & S 82:44-5+ N '77

BASS Islands
Ohio's Erie islands. D. Gleasner and B. Gleasner. il Travel 148:36-9 Jl '77

BASS Masters Classic. See Fishing—Competitions

BASS viol. See Double bass

BASSHAM, James A.
Increasing crop production through more controlled photosynthesis. bibl il Science 197:630-8 Ag 12 '77

BAST, Kim
Five great gardens. il Horticulture 55:28+ Mr '77

BASTOS, Augusto Antonio Roa. See Roa Bastos, A. A.

BASUALTO, Neftalí Ricardo Reyes. See Neruda, P.

BATCOLUMN. See Chicago—Monuments, statues, etc.

BATDORFF, Emerson
Publix, the Cleveland bookstore that could not go out of business, celebrates its 40 years. il pors Pub W 212:347-50 Ag 29 '77

BATEMAN, Jim
Super(market) scriptwriter; interview, ed by N. Levinson. il pors Writers Digest 57:38-9 Ap '77

BATEMAN, Raymond Henry
Political suicide in New Jersey. J. McLaughlin. Nation 225:593-6 D 3 '77 *
Statehouse derby. R. Boeth and others. il pors Newsweek 90:42+ O 17 '77 *
Two tight gubernatorial races. il pors Time 110: 25-6 N 7 '77 *

BATES, Barbara S.
Identifying high interest/low reading level books. bibl il SLJ 24:19-21 N '77

BATES, Harvey
Letters from Ernest; correspondence between E. Becker and H. Bates. il pors Chr Cent 94:217-27 Mr 9 '77

BATESIAN mimicry. See Mimicry (biology)

BATESON, Gregory
Rattling the cage. M. Sheils and others. por Newsweek 90:141 N 21 '77 *

BATH exercises. See Exercise

BATH preparations
Bath bags of herbs, flowers. il Sunset 158:138+ My '77

BATH robes. See Clothing and dress

BATH rooms. See Bathrooms

BATH tubs. See Bathtubs

BATHING. See Baths

BATHING customs
Bed/bath: new exposure. J. O'Reilly. Vogue 167: 245+ D '77

BATHING suits
Bare 'n' beautiful beachwear. il Ebony 33:104-6+ Ja '78
Bold and the beautiful. M. A. Kellogg and L. Whitman. il Newsweek 89:75-7+ Mr 21 '77
New swimsuits: more is less. il Time 110:40-1 Jl 4 '77
Tank heaven for not so little girls; photographs. A. Kane. Sports Illus 46:36-43 Ja 24 '77

BATHROBES. See Clothing and dress

BATHROOM cabinets. See Cabinets (furniture)

BATHROOM fixtures
Hook towel bar, paper holder—all fashioned in oak. il Sunset 158:90 F '77
Weather machine built into your bathroom; synthetic environmental chamber. E. F. Lindsley. il Pop Sci 210:120-1 My '77
See also
Plumbing

BATHROOMS
Add a bath. R. Stepler. il Pop Sci 212:94-6 Ja '78
Antique bathroom updated, but oh, so carefully. il House B 119:74 My '77
Bath designs for elegant relaxation. S. Renner-Smith. il Pop Sci 211:106-9 N '77
Bathroom magic: you do it yourself. il Mech Illus 73:64+ Ap '77
Brightening up the bathroom. il Redbook 149: 138-9+ My '77
Cure a tepid bath. Redbook 148:202 Ap '77; Same. Ladies Home J 94:188+ Ap '77
Diane von Furstenberg's total-spa bathroom. F. De La Renta. il Vogue 167:370-1 S '77
Expand to create a big, comfortable bath-beauty room. il House & Gard 149:142-3 O '77
Garden bath is a remodel. il Sunset 158:166 Ap '77
Make your bath a splash! Ladies Home J 94: 150 S '77; Same. Redbook 149:191-2 S '77
Tub and shower are sculptured in tile. il Sunset 158:170 My '77
Two's company; bathroom/greenhouse. B. Niles and N. Williams. il Am Home 80:42-5 F '77
Your own home spa; bathroom designed by Yann Weymouth and Peter Coan. il House & Gard 149:98-102+ F '77

BATHS
Beauty baths. C. B. Abbott. il Am Home 80: 56-7+ S '77
See also
Bath preparations
Bathing customs
Shower baths
Sun baths

BATHS, Vapor
See also
Sauna

BATHS, Whirlpool
Bubbly balm that's fun. J. H. Ingersoll. il House B 119:12+ Je '77

BATHTUBS
Barrel of fun; hot tubs. M. Chester. il Am Home 80:36-8 Je '77
Come soak with me; hot tubs. il Horizon 21:63 Ja '78
Neat idea: a bath in a box; folding bathtub by Babette Newburger. E. V. Warren. il House B 119:10+ Ap '77

BATIK
Sizzling designs with a soldering iron. V. FitzGibbons. il Design (US) 79:23 Fall '77

BATLINER, Arnold
Need money laundered? Then see Arnold Batliner. J. D. Lewis. il por Ret Liv 17:16-17 Jl '77 *

BATON ROUGE, La.

Parks and playgrounds

Interstate land for municipal parks; Expressway Park. E. A. Young. il Parks & Rec 12:36-8 Ap '77

BATON twirling

Calvin discovers Murphy's law; United States Twirling Association's national championships. C. Kirkpatrick. il por Sports Illus 47:14-15 Ag 15 '77

BATS

Amplitude spectrum representation in the Doppler-shifted-CF processing area of the auditory cortex of the mustache bat. N. Suga. bibl il Science 196:64-7 Ap 1 '77

Carlsbad's famous bats are dying off. M. Gosnell. il Nat Wildlife 15:28-33 Je '77

Echo-detecting characteristic of neurons in inferior colliculus of unanesthetized bats. G. Pollak and others. bibl il Science 196:675-8 My 6 '77

Paternity and genetic heterogeneity in the polygynous bat, phyllostomus hastatus. G. F. McCracken and J. W. Bradbury. bibl il Science 198:303-6 O 21 '77

BATTAGLIA, Carmen L.

How to ask for Federal funding. il Am Educ 13:6-9 Jl '77; Same abr. Educ Digest 43:24-7 D '77

BATTEAU, John M.

Sexual differences: a cultural convention? Chr Today 21:8-10 Jl 8 '77

BATTELLE, Phyllis

(ed) See Johnson, J. A. Patty Hearst: the way it really was—and is

(ed) See Johnson, J. A. Real story of Patty Hearst

BATTEN, William Milfred

Big board strategy for staying alive. W. Robertson. il por Fortune 95:134-41+ Mr '77 *

Skittish investors—what will lure them back to stock market. interview. il por U.S. News 83:89-90 N 28 '77

BATTEN disease. See Metabolism, Disorders of

BATTER frying. See Frying

BATTERIES, Electric. See Electric batteries

BATTERIES, Storage. See Storage batteries

BATTERY chargers. See Storage battery chargers

BATTERY charging. See Electric batteries—Charging; Storage batteries—Charging

BATTERY-operated clocks. See Clocks

BATTING (baseball)

Hitters can be ranked. H. Weiskopf. il Sports Illus 47:24-5 Jl 18 '77

I hope Rod Carew hits .400; ed by J. Underwood. T. Williams. il pors Sports Illus 47:20-3 Jl 18 '77

In batting practice, even you can be Johnny Bench. R. Blount, Jr. il Esquire 87:42-4 My '77

BATTING records. See Sports records

BATTLE, William Cullen

How basic management principles pay off; interview. pors Nations Bus 65:46-8+ Mr '77

BATTLES, Asa

When you wish upon a star. . .M. Battles. il Design (US) 79:2-5 Fall '77 *

BATTLES, Marge

When you wish upon a star. . .il Design (US) 79:2-5 Fall '77

BATTLES

See also

Naval battles

also names of battles, e.g. Lexington, Battle of, 1775; *also* subhead Campaigns and battles under names of wars, e.g. World War, 1914-1918—Campaigns and battles

BATTLES in art. See War in art

BATZINGER, Robert P. and others

Saccharin and other sweeteners: mutagenic properties. bibl il Science 198:944-6 D 2 '77

BAUDOUIN, Frans

Rubens: emissary of peace in strife-torn Europe. il UNESCO Courier 30:23-6 Je '77

BAUER, Cathy, and Andersen, Juel

Try making tofu—you'll like it. il Org Gard & Farm 24:100+ Ap '77

BAUER, Douglas

Nothing fancy. il Esquire 87:101-3 My '77

BAUER, Erwin A.

African wildlife: the end of the game? il Outdoor Life 160:68-73+ D '77

Camping. See issues of Outdoor life

Doughnuts are dandy. il Outdoor Life 159:78-9+ Ap '77

First anglers into Cuba. il map Outdoor Life 160:69-73+ S '77

High-up, way-out ways of a rimrock guide. il Outdoor Life 160:90-2 N '77

No bull moose hunt. il Outdoor Life 160:64-6 N '77

To the elk kingdom. il Outdoor Life 160:80-4 Ag '77

Wild rivers, trout galore. il map Nat Wildlife 15:42-7 Ag '77

World's greatest wildflower show. il Travel 147:148-53 Mr '77

—and others

Cross-country to action. il Outdoor Life 161:66-8 Ja '78

BAUER, Peter T. and Yamey, B. S.

Against the New Economic Order. bibl f Commentary 63:25-31 Ap; 6-7 Jl '77

BAUER, Steven

Stars in Maine; poem. Nation 225:438 O 29 '77

BAUERS, Susan

Postponement; poem. Seventeen 36:70 Mr '77

BAUGHMAN, M. Dale

Teaching as a performing art. Clearing H 51:100 N '77

BAUGHMAN, Michael

Hunting. il Sports Illus 47:66+ O 3 '77

BAUGHMAN, Mildred

Nimble grandma in Santa's workshop. il Ret Liv 16:36-7 D '76

BAUHAUS

East Germany restores Gropius's Bauhaus workshop for its 50th anniversary. il Archit Rec 161:35 Je '77

BAULEKE, Maynard P.

Digging your own clay—a geologist's viewpoint. il Ceram Mo 25:46-9 My '77

BAUM, Joseph

Joe Baum's food machine. R. A. Sokolov. il por N Y Times Mag p64-5+ Mr 6 '77 *

Joe's in his heaven—his Window's on the World. C. Claiborne. il por Holiday 58:32-7+ Je '77 *

BAUM, Patricia

Meet superstar O. J. Simpson: home is always where the heart is. il por Parents Mag 52:42-3+ F '77

BAUM, Ralph

Such good friends. R. Wolters. Writers Digest 57:16+ D '77 *

BAUMAN, Carl

Imports; classical recordings from foreign countries (title varies) See issues of American record guide

BAUMAN, Richard

Diving champ at sixty. por Ret Liv 17:49+ My '77

BAUMANN, Susan

Admission of two; poem. Nation 224:794 Je 25 '77

BAUMGARDNER, Marion F. See Adrien, P.-M. jt auth

BAUMGOLD, Julie

Agoraphobia: life ruled by panic. il N Y Times Mag p46-8+ D 4 '77

BAUMGRAS, George R.

Build programmable frequency divider. il Radio-Electr 48:37-41 My '77

BAUSCH and Lomb, Inc

Shifting channels. P. Berman. il Forbes 119:27-8 My 1 '77

BAVARIA

Description and travel

Other Bavaria: Gothic, gloriously untraveled; Regensburg and vicinity. D. Messinesi. il Vogue 167:243-4+ O '77

BAVARIAN State Opera. See Opera—Germany, West

BAVIER, Robert Newton, 1918-

From the cockpit. See issues of Yachting

BAXLEY, William Joseph

Arrest in Birmingham. R. Boeth and V. E. Smith. il pors Newsweek 90:32+ O 10 '77 *

Law moves at last. B. Cornwell. Nation 225:463-5 N 5 '77 *

Verdict on bloody Sunday. D. A. Williams and J. B. Cumming. Newsweek 90:63 N 28 '77 *

BAXTER, Gordon

Bax seat. See issues of Flying

BAXTER, Jennifer

For my father; poem. Seventeen 36:151 F '77

BAXTER, Patricia J. and Goldstein, Joan

Pine Barrens under pressure. il map Parks & Rec 12:20-3+ O '77

BAXTER, Percival Proctor

As Baxter Park burns, so burns Maine. A. Gauvin. il maps Audubon 79:146-53 S '77; Reply. J. L. Baxter. 79:128 N '77 *

BAXTER, Samuel S.

Public works perspective. See issues of American city & county

BAXTER State Park. See Maine—Parks and reserves

BAXTER Travenol Laboratories, Inc

Miracle of sorts. Forbes 120:106 N 15 '77

BAY, Timothy

Coal. il Sci Digest 82:53-6 O '77

How hypnosis aids in passing over the threshold of consciousness. il por Sci Digest 81:45-8 Je '77

Hypnosis: will medicine recognize its use in therapy? il Sci Digest 81:53-6+ My '77

(ed) Unlikely routes to the top; interviews. Harp Baz 110:48-9+ Je '77

Who (if anyone) is living way out there? Sci Digest 82:64-9 Ag; 46-7 S '77

BAY Area. See San Francisco Bay Region
BAY Area Rapid Transit. See San Francisco Bay Region—Transit systems
BAY of Islands. See Islands, Bay of
BAY of Pigs invasion. See Cuba—History—Invasion, 1961
BAYAN, Richard
Liberal artist at work. Nat R 29:156-7 F 4 '77
BAYANO Dam. See Dams—Panama
BAYER, Ann
Growing up bespectacled. Seventeen 36:138-9+ S '77
Growing up tall. il Seventeen 36:186-7+ Ap '77
Pleasure and pain of that first crush. il Seventeen 36:144-5+ My '77
BAYER, AG. See Chemical industries—Germany, West
BAYER AG-Miles Laboratories, Inc merger. See Corporations—Acquisitions and mergers—International aspects
BAYH, Birch Evans, 1928-
Excerpt from statement on the ERA, April 13, 1977. Cong Digest 56:170+ Je '77
BAYLESS, George
Space scientist launches infrared photo service for farmers. J. D. Boyd. por Farm J 101:K2 F '77 *
BAYLESS, Sandy
Librarianship is a discipline; adaptation of address, December 1976. Lib J 102:1715-17 S 1 '77
BAYLISS, John
Delectable collectibles. il Sat Eve Post 249:30-1 My '77
Happy marriage of mini and max. il Sat Eve Post 249:26-7 Ap '77
BAYLOR, Byrd
Way to start a day; poem. McCalls 104:104 F '77
BAYLOR, D. B.
Ghost story; story. Ladies Home J 94:72-3 Ag '77
BAYLOR, Edward R. and Peters, Virginia
Water-to-air transfer of virus. bibl il Science 197:763-4 Ag 19 '77
—and others
Virus transfer from surf to wind. bibl il Science 198:575-80 N 11 '77
BAYLY, Joseph
Yes, there are semi-evangelicals. Chr Today 21:23 Jl 29 '77
BAYREUTH Festival. See Music festivals—Germany, West
BAYS and gulfs
See also
Bristol Bay
Chesapeake Bay
Magdalena Bay
BAZAARS, Charitable
How to run a bazaar. Bet Hom & Gard 55:72+ S '77
BAZELI, Frank P.
Achievement values reinforcement in public schools. bibl Clearing H 51:78-80 O '77
BEACH, Amy Mary (Cheney)
Foote: Sonata in G minor for violin & piano; Beach: Sonata in A minor for violin & piano. W. Simmons. Am Rec G 40:27-8 O '77 *
Grand, glorious & unknown. D. Garvelmann. Am Rec G 40:17-19 O '77 *
BEACH, Richard W.
Film and television research. bibl Engl J 66:90-3 Mr '77
BEACH architecture
Decorating—let yourself go; California. il House & Gard 150:88-91 Ja '78
House on the beach, eastern Long Island. il Archit Rec 161:86-9 mid-My '77
Private residence, northern Florida. il Archit Rec 161:106-8 mid-My '77
Tatiana von Hessen's summer solace; beach house on Sylt Island in the North Sea. il por Vogue 167:154-7 Ag '77
They ordered a house raising; home of James and Mily Drury of Montauk, N.Y. il House B 119:96 S '77
To live with nature. il House & Gard 149:156-9 O '77
Vacation house, Puget Sound. il Archit Rec 161:98-9 mid-My '77
Weekend escape house; Fire Island beach house. N. Skurka. il N Y Times Mag p84-5 My 1 '77
BEACH Boys (rock group) See Rock groups
BEACH camping. See Camping
BEACH clothes. See Clothing and dress
BEACH photography. See Photography—Marines
BEACHAM, Walton
Against the grain. Nation 224:729-31 Je 11 '77
BEACHCRAFT Boat Company. See Boatbuilding
BEACHES
California litter; question of beach litter. B. E. Bechtol and J. R. Williams. il Natur Hist 86:62-5 bibl(p93) Je '77
Last question of summer; Lucy Vincent Beach on Martha's Vineyard. J. Lelyveld. il N Y Times Mag p47 S 4 '77
Swimsuit optional zone; nude sunbathing at Black's beach in La Jolla, Calif. B. Golden. Progressive 41:41-2 My '77
Walking beach in wild Washington; Olympic National Park. il map Sunset 158:76+ My '77

BEACON Theater. See New York (city)—Theater
BEACONS
See also
Lighthouses
Radio beacons
BEADLE, George Wells
Corn patch Nobel laureate. B. Nelson. Bull Atom Sci 33:48-50 O '77 *
BEADLE, Raymond
Men who make the Blue Max run. J. Scalzo. il pors Hot Rod 30:24-6+ Ag '77 *
BEADS
Your necklace from paper beads. il Sunset 158:158+ Mr '77
BEAGLES (dogs)
Which is the best all-round dog? D. M. Duffey. il Outdoor Life 159:78-81+ My '77

Training

See Hunting dogs—Training
BEAGLEY, Walter K. and Holley, T. L.
Hypothalamic stimulation facilitates contralateral visual control of a learned response. bibl il Science 196:321-2 Ap 15 '77
BEAL, Jack
Jack Beal's history of American labor. B. Forgey. il Art N 76:38 Ap '77 *
Labor Department mural: a complicated voyage. B. Carter. il por Art N 76:40-1 My '77 *
BEALE, Andrew V. and McLeod, A. M.
Facilitating class discussion: another way. Clearing H 51:67-70 O '77
BEALE, Edith (Bouvier)
Alone in Grey Gardens. il por Newsweek 90:10+ Ag 15 '77 *
BEALS, John
Hard water sailing. il Conservationist 31:2-5 Ja '77
BEALS, Margaret
Reviews; two programs at American Theatre Laboratory. A. Smith. Dance Mag 51:78+ Ag '77 *
BEAM, Alex
Helsinki check list: Russia keeps tabs. Nation 224:709-10 Je 11 '77
BEAM, James Michael
(ed) See Graham, B. I can't play God any more
BEAME, Abraham David
Around City Hall (cont) A. Logan. New Yorker 52:101-8 F 7; 53:96-103 My 30; 72-7 Jl 18; 64-72 Ag 15; 71-6+ S 5; 203-11 N 21; 54-6 D 26 '77 *
Bad news for Beame. D. M. Alpern and others. il por Newsweek 90:18-19 S 5 '77 *
Beame's scenario: how to beat Bella. M. Carroll. il pors N Y Times Mag p32-5+ Je 26 '77 *
Embattled Abe. D. A. Williams and S. Agrest. il por Newsweek 89:30 My 30 '77 *
Mob scene in New York. il por Time 110:21-2 S 5 '77 *
BEAMS, Jesse Wakefield
Obituary
Phys Today por 30:74 N '77. J. C. Stret
BEAMS. See Girders
BEAMS, Artificial
Installing decorative beams. McCalls 105:142 Ja '78
BEAMS, Particle. See Particle beams
BEAN, Michael J.
Endangered Species Act under fire. il Nat Parks & Con Mag 51:16-20 Je '77
BEAN sprout industry. See Food industry
BEANS
Almost magical bean; fava bean. M. G. Mullen. il Org Gard & Farm 24:75-7 Ap '77
Beans, the perfect interplant companion. J. Ruttle. il Org Gard & Farm 24:66-8 F '77
Green bean bargain. J. Older. il Org Gard & Farm 24:67-8 Jl '77
Green beans can also be shelley beans. il Sunset 158:234 Mr '77
Green beans; fresh, frozen or canned string beans. il Consumer Rep 42:392-95 Jl '77
Lima as king bean. W. G. Tilsher. il Org Gard & Farm 24:72-5 Ap '77
Reviving the beans of America's past. S. Smyser. il Org Gard & Farm 25:58-62 Ja '78
See also
Cookery—Vegetables
BEAR, Frank. See Bear, J. jt auth
BEAR, Fred
Bowhunter's camp. il por Field & S 82:64-6+ My '77
Hunting the quiet way. il Conservationist 31:17-19+ N '76
BEAR, Joan
Professional mom; interview. il por Am Home 80:24-5+ My '77
BEAR, Joy, and Bear, Frank
Salute to autumn leaves. il pors Conservationist 32:38-9 N '77

BEAR hunting
Bear fever; hunter C. T. Johnson. B. East. por Outdoor Life 160:7 O '77
Results of 1976 deer and bear seasons. il Conservationist 32:22 Jl '77
Stalk for a cannibal brown. L. Francisco. il Outdoor Life 160:68-9+ Jl '77

Anecdotes, facetiae, satire, etc.

B'ar. P. F. McManus. il Field & S 81:73-4+ Mr '77

BEAR Mountain State Park. See New York (state)—Parks and reserves

BEARBERRIES
Manzanita: the ornamental with practical value. J. Jankowiak. il Org Gard & Farm 24:128-30 D '77
Manzanitas come in from the wild. il Sunset 159:236 N '77

BEARD, Allen
Dust still falls on Derby despite a tough new law. Audubon 79:136-8 S '77 *

BEARD, Edward
Blue-collar caucus. M. Kondracke. New Repub 176:18-20 My 28 '77 *

BEARD, James Andrews
Spice is right: James Beard gives new life to diet food. il por House & Gard 149:117+ F '77

about

James Beard's recipe for living. il por House & Gard 149:108-13 F '77 *
Sensuous cook. M. Rourke. il por Newsweek 89: 93 Ap 11 '77 *

BEARD, Peter Hill
This is the end of the game; photographs; excerpt from The end of the game. N Y Times Mag p38-43+ N 6 '77

about

Epitaph on film; elephant photographs at the International Center of Photography. R. Hughes. il Time 110:60 D 12 '77 *
Journalist of the plague years. O. Edwards. il Sat R 5:43-5 Ja 7 '78 *

BEARD, Robin Leo, 1939-
Let soldiers join labor unions? interview. pors U.S. News 82:51-2 Mr 28 '77

BEARDEN, Romare
Artist's plea for harmony; address. il Sch Arts 77:72-3 S '77
Profiles. C. Tomkins. por New Yorker 53:53-8+ N 28 '77 *

BEARDSLEY, Grant L. Jr
Bluefin tuna: vulnerable giant; with biographical sketch. il Sea Front 23:9-15, 62 Ja '77
Marlins; with biographical sketch. il Sea Front 23:273-9, 318 S '77

BEARINGS (machinery)
Slow roller; rolamite. E. Keerdoja. il por Newsweek 90:13+ D 19 '77
See also
Automobiles—Bearings

BEARS
About fishing and bears; encounter with brown bears while salmon fishing in Alaska. B. Brister. il Field & S 82:46-8+ Je '77
Critical crossroads; question of critical habitat of endangered species, using grizzly bear as example. il map Nat Parks & Con Mag 51: 19-22 F '77
Everybody's favorite bear; black bears. G. Laycock. il Audubon 79:6-19 My '77
Great grizzly grapple. C. Cauble. il Natur Hist 86:74-81 bibl(p 117) Ag '77; Discussion. 86:132-3 O '77
Grizzly's rage to live. D. Chadwick. il Sports Illus 47:64-9+ Jl 18 '77; Same abr. with title Outlaw bear. Read Digest 111:162-5 N '77
It's a summer to be especially cautious around bears. il Sunset 158:38 Je '77
Last fight for the grizzly; excerpt from Where the grizzly walks. B. Schneider. il Outdoor Life 161:55-8+ Ja '78
My God, I've gotten too close! grizzly attack. D. Richey. il Outdoor Life 161:58-9+ Ja '78
Uproar over grizzly habitat. G. Laycock. Audubon 79:126 My '77
Ursus horribilis in extremis; grizzly bears. J. G. Mitchell. il Am Heritage 28:16-29 O '77
Will this grizzly attack? B. Schneider. il Nat Wildlife 15:4-9 F '77

BEARS, Photography of. See Photography of animals

BEARS in art. See Animals in art

BEAR'S paw fern. See Ferns

BEART, Sheila
Genetic peril in cattle. Environment 19:2-3 Mr '77

BEARTOOTH-Absaroka Wilderness Area (proposed) See Wilderness areas—Western states

BEASLEY, Ron
How to use dried foods. il Org Gard & Farm 24: 104+ Ag '77

BEATIFICATION
Saints of the classroom; beatification of Francisco Febres Cordero and Louis Joseph Wiaux. America 137:345 N 19 '77

BEATLEMANIA; revue. See Musical comedy, revue, etc.—Reviews—Single works

BEATLES (rock group)
Beatles at the Hollywood Bowl; Beatles live! at the Star Club in Hamburg, Germany; 1962. S. Sutherland. Hi Fi 27:111 Ag '77
I wanna hold your hand—again. il por Time 110: 54-5 Ag 8 '77
Resurrecting the Beatles: Star-Club to stereo; phonograph record made from tape of 1962 Hamburg performance. C. Repka. il Hi Fi 27: 101-3 Ag '77

BEATRICE Foods Company
Beatrice Foods puts it together. por Duns R 110: 55-6+ D '77

BEATTIE, Ann
Distant music; story. New Yorker 53:27-32 Jl 4 '77
Shifting; story. New Yorker 53:38-44 F 21 '77

about

Ann Beattie & the 60's. J. Romano. Commentary 63:62-4 F '77 *

BEATTY, David D. See Tsin, A. T. C. jt auth

BEATTY, Florence
New model me. il Am Educ 13:23-6 Ja '77

BEATTY, Frank
Frank Beatty: the peripatetic pastellist; interview, ed by C. Movalli. il por Am Artist 41: 66-9+ O '77

BEATTY, J. Kelly
Comsat revolution. il Sky & Tel 54:4-8 Jl '77; Same abr. with title Communications satellites: how your voice (or TV show) is routed geosynchronously. Sci Digest 82:53-5+ N '77

BEATTY, John J.
Reconsideration. il New Repub 177:35-8 D 17 '77

BEATY, Barry J. See Thompson, W. H. jt auth

BEAUBOURG Center. See Paris—Georges Pompidou Center

BEAUCARNEA
Easy to grow house plants: beaucarnea recurvata or ponytail plant. E. McDonald. il House B 119:32 Jl '77

BEAUCHAMP, Dan E.
Blood sports. Chr Cent 94:237-8 Mr 9 '77

BEAUDOIN, John T. and Mattlin, Everett
Interface your output with computerese; excerpt from The phrase-dropper's handbook. il Sci Digest 81:43-6 My '77

BEAUFORD, W. and others
Release of particles containing metals from vegetation into the atmosphere. bibl il Science 195:571-3 F 11 '77

BEAUFORT, Sir Francis
Admiral Beaufort charted coasts for ships of the world. A. Friendly. il por map Smithsonian 8:68-70+ bibl(p 101) Ag '77 *

BEAUMARCHAIS, Pierre Augustin Caron de
Beaumarchais: Figaro's playwright. S. Hughes. il Opera N 41:13-15 Mr 5 '77 *
Beyond Figaro. B. Fischer-Williams. il Opera N 41:26-8 Mr 5 '77 *

BEAUMONT, Tex.
Transport efficiency and future economic growth; address, January 12, 1977. A. L. Wilson. Vital Speeches 43:337-9 Mr 15 '77

BEAUMONTIA grandiflora. See Heralds-trumpets

BEAUTICIANS. See Beauty operators

BEAUTIFYING of cities. See Municipal improvement

BEAUTY. See Aesthetics

BEAUTY, Personal
After dark: the big difference. Harp Baz 110: 204-9 S '77
Assignment: White House; beauty report on Judy Woodruff. il pors Redbook 149:116-17+ Jl '77
Autumn beauty trends. M. Lynch. il Ladies Home J 94:90-5 S '77
Beautiful black woman. A. R. Fornay, Jr. il Ebony 32:138-42 F '77
Beauty. il Vogue 167:216-19 D '77
Beauty at every age. M. Lynch. il Ladies Home J 94:128-35 O '77
Beauty bazaar. See issues of Harper's bazaar
Beauty collections. il Vogue 167:280-95 O '77
Beauty is as beauty does. S. Beck. Parents Mag 52:28+ S '77
Beauty journal. See issues of Ladies' home journal
Beauty power; women celebrities. il Harp Baz 111:106-21 N '77
Beauty Q & A (cont of) Vogue answers your beauty questions. See issues of Vogue
Beauty tips for working mothers. S. Beck. Parents Mag 52:16 Ap '77
Beauty today. il Vogue 167:186-93 F '77
California life up close; ideas of four actresses; interviews, ed by M. Cantwell. il Mademoiselle 83:188-99+ Ap '77
Cold-weather beauty. Harp Baz 111:136-7 D '77
Dear beauty editor; questions and answers. See issues of Seventeen
Eat and grow beautiful. M. Weber. il Ladies Home J 94:74+ My '77

BEAUTY, Personal—*Continued*
Expert answers to all your beauty questions. il Harp Baz 110:110-17 Mr '77
Expert beauties. il Harp Baz 110:90-9 Ag '77
Fall beauty makeover. il Seventeen 36:194 Ag '77
50 cool ways to beat the heat. il Harp Baz 110:44-5+ Jl '77
Foot facials and other helpful hints; summer beauty tips. A. Penney. il N Y Times Mag p40-1 Jl 31 '77
45 shortcuts to good looks. il Harp Baz 110:106-7+ Ag '77
42 timesavers & tips from the pros. il Mademoiselle 83:128-9 F '77
Freebies! haircuts, makeup, cosmetics, etc. Seventeen 36:116 Ag '77
Get up and glow. M. Hill. il Am Home 80:54-5 Ap '77
Good looks. See issues of McCall's
Good looks, 1977; special section. il McCalls 105:25-8+ O '77
Good looks through good grooming. il Ebony 32:117-18+ My '77
Great going; staying beautiful while traveling. C. B. Abbott. il Am Home 80:32+ O '77
Herbs for beauty, health and sex. L. Lee. il Am Home 80:19+ My '77
How to get the look that's best for you; four young college women's systems. il Mademoiselle 83:144-73 Ag '77
How you look; symposium, ed by E. L. Gross. Vogue 167:116-18+ Je '77
Let's hear it from the pros; tips from models and beauty experts. il Mademoiselle 83:150-71 O '77
Look at Mariel run. il pors Seventeen 36:124-31 Mr '77
Makeover of the month. See issues of Good housekeeping
New beautiful people; beauty regimen of women athletes. A. Scharffenberger. il Am Home 80:56-8 Je '77
New looks for successful dieters. il McCalls 105:74+ O '77
New ways to create a new image. il Harp Baz 110:74-9 Je '77
Nobody's perfect; seven models. il Seventeen 36:130-3 O '77
Off camera with seven super sales stars. R. Graham. il House B 119:72-3+ Ag '77
On-the-run make-up and fashion plans; routine of B. Allen. il pors Harp Baz 110:100-5 Mr '77
Our Christmas belles: the Walton women. il Good H 185:144-5+ D '77
Outdoor look: three leading athletes talk about their beauty problems. il McCalls 104:134-7 Jl '77
Power of beauty. N. Lande and A. Slade. Harp Baz 111:122+ N '77
Recharge! Make the most of your looks, your time. il Mademoiselle 83:108-13 F '77
Right face for the right job. A. Penney. il N Y Times Mag p 100-1 O 9 '77
Sportsproof beauty. il Seventeen 36:178-85 Ap '77
Summer beauty. S. Beck. Parents Mag 52:32 Ag '77
Summer beauty secrets from New Orleans. il Redbook 149:116-19 Je '77
Sun lover's guide to beauty and health. il McCalls 104:122-5 Je '77
Super makeovers; Nevada City, Calif. il Mademoiselle 83:220-3 Ap '77
Take care of yourself. il Vogue 167:162-7 Je '77
10 beauty changes to make this fall. il Harp Baz 110:126-31 O '77
That California spirit. il Redbook 148:117+ Ap '77
30 ways to stay looking 30 forever; ideas of experts. il Harp Baz 110:138-41+ O '77
Town that grows American beauties; Edina Minn. il Good H 184:138-41 My '77
20 ways to summerize your looks. il Harp Baz 110:98-103 My '77
22 myths & realities about your body. C. Dreifus. il Seventeen 36:125-9+ Je '77
Twin beauty rights and wrongs; Valerie and Vanessa Browne. il Seventeen 36:136-9 Je '77
Winning looks; winners of Seventeen's Losers Take All diet contest. il Seventeen 36:110 Mr '77
Your beauty notebook. See issues of Good housekeeping
See also
Baths
Beauty shops
Charm
Cosmetics
Exercise
Hairdressing
Make-up
Manicuring
Skin

Men

Cosmetic lib for men. J. Kelly. il N Y Times Mag p 119-20+ S 25 '77
On creating a new face through plastic surgery. M. G. Haddad. il Mademoiselle 83:53+ O '77
Vogue beauty report on men; views of experts. il Vogue 167:220-3+ D '77

Anecdotes, facetiae, satire, etc.

Lonely guy's grooming guide. B. J. Friedman. il Esquire 88:116-18+ N '77

BEAUTY contests
Trinidadian crowned Miss Universe. il Américas 29:23-5 O '77

Anecdotes, facetiae, satire, etc.

Miss Universe. C. Sagan. il N Y Times Mag p32+ O 23 '77

BEAUTY operators
Summer in the life of a beauty parlor: the stories of 5 women who work there; excerpt from Pink collar workers. L. K. Howe. Ms 5:52-5+ Mr '77
Tips on tipping. A. Penney. il N Y Times Mag p 150-1 D 4 '77
BEAUTY preparations. See Cosmetics; Toilet preparations
BEAUTY queens. See Beauty contests
BEAUTY resorts. See Health resorts, watering places, etc.
BEAUTY shops
Beauty salon prices from coast to coast. Good H 185:276 N '77
Choosing a salon; New York. A. Penney. il N Y Times Mag p 157-8+ N 6 '77
How to look beautiful in Paris. M. Russell. il N Y Times Mag p 132-3 N 27 '77
New bloom on you. A. Taylor. il N Y Times Mag p84+ Ap 3 '77
Salon facials: where to go. il Seventeen 36:80-1+ Ag '77
Secret sources; stores for cosmetics. A. Penney. il N Y Times Mag p90-1 O 23 '77
See also
Beauty operators
BEAUVAIS, Carol
Why a woman can't be a good boss—because no one will let you. Mademoiselle 83:120+ Jl '77 *
BEAUVOIR, Simone de
Talking to a friend—an interview with Simone de Beauvoir; ed. by A. Schwarzer. por Ms 6:12-13+ Jl '77
BEAVER ponds. See Ponds
BEAVERS
Paddy—orphan of the wild; condensation of Paddy: a naturalist's story of an orphan beaver. R. D. Lawrence. il Read Digest 110:206-16+ Je '77
BEAZLEY, John
Obituary
Pub W 211:34 Mr 28 '77
BEBEY, Francis
Awakening African cinema. il UNESCO Courier 30:30-3 My '77
BECERRA DE JENKINS, Lyll
Aunt Adela; story. Américas 29:41-3 S '77
BECHTEL, Mary K.
Library birthday parties. il SLJ 24:36 N '77
BECHTEL Corporation
Master builder Bechtel. D. Pauly and G. C. Lubenow. il Newsweek 90:60-2 Ag 29 '77
BECHTOL, Bruce E. and Williams, J. R.
California litter; with biographical sketches. il Natur Hist 86:6, 62-5 bibl(p93) Je '77
BECK, Alan M. and Marden, Philip
Street dwellers; with biographical sketches. il Natur Hist 86:8, 78-85 bibl(p 119) N '77
BECK, Earl J.
Ocean thermal gradients—a practical source of energy? bibl Science 195:207 Ja 14 '77
BECK, Eckhardt C.
Water pollution control: an overview of the laws. il Parks & Rec 12:5a-14a F '77
BECK, Henry G. J.
Roman Catholic/Presbyterian-Reformed consultation. il New Cath World 220:202-6 Jl '77
BECK, M. N.
Myth of the self-sufficient man; excerpt from address. Chr Today 21:12-16 S 23 '77
BECK, Ray
Walk 'em up. il Outdoor Life 160:86-9 Ag '77
BECK, Virginia E.
Retrieving overdue materials in court. Lib J 102:2321-2 N 15 '77
BECKENBAUER, Franz
Recovery from *kulturschock*. C. Gammon. il pors Sports Illus 46:28-9 Je 13 '77 *
BECKER, Ernest
Letters from Ernest; correspondence between E. Becker and H. Bates. il pors Chr Cent 94:217-27 Mr 9 '77
BECKER, Stuart
Now aren't you glad you didn't go into a tax shelter? A. Tobias. il Esquire 89:12+ Ja '78 *
BECKER, Verena
Old lady and the terrorists. il Time 109:46 My 16 '77 *
BECKERMAN, Wilfred
St George for growth. por Time 109:63 Je 6 '77
BECKET, Marta
Why stop over in Death Valley Junction? Look. il por Sunset 159:66 N '77 *

BECKETT, Samuel
Beckett piece by piece. J. D. O'Hara. Nation 224: 216-17+ F 19 '77 *
Beckett without angst. J. Romano. Am Scholar 47:95-102 Wint '77 *
Play and other plays. Reviews
Nation 226:28 Ja 7 '78 *
New Yorker 53:49-50 Ja 2 '78 *
Time il 111:59 Ja 2 '78 *
Waiting for Godot. Reviews
New Republic 176:20-1 Ap 23 '77 *

BECKMAN, G. G. See Bridge, B. J. jt auth

BECKMAN, Margaret
Participative management urged as best option. Lib J 102:321-2 F 1 '77 *

BECKMANN, Jacques S. and others
Cloning of yeast transfer RNA genes in escherichia coli. bibl il Science 196:205-8 Ap 8 '77

BECKWITH, Thomas
Dreams and your health. il House & Gard 149:28+ S '77

BECTON, Dickinson & Company
Directors' squabble at Becton Dickinson. il por Bus W p40-1 O 3 '77

BEDARD, Patrick
[Column] Car & Dr 22:16 F; 26 My; 23:11 S; 12 N '77; 12 Ja '78
Sport. See issues of Car and driver

BEDDING
How to get the best buys at white sales. Good H 186:120 Ja '78
See also
Blankets
Coverlets
Mattresses
Quilts
Sheets

BEDDING (horticulture) See Gardening

BEDDING for animals. See Litter (bedding)

BEDDINGTON, J. R. and May, R. M.
Harvesting natural populations in a randomly fluctuating environment. bibl il Science 197: 463-5 Jl 29 '77

BEDFORD, William
Childhood; poem. Nation 225:60 Jl 9 '77

BEDFORD-Stuyvesant. See Brooklyn

BEDOGNE, Frank
Art education and career education. bibl il Sch Arts 77:42-5 D '77

BEDOUINS in Jordan
Last of the Bedouin. P. Iseman. il Horizon 19: 32-9 Mr '77

BEDROOM furniture
Two rooms from one; bed-wall unit. H. Wicks. il Pop Mech 148:96-9+ S '77
See also
Beds

BEDROOMS
Beautiful bedrooms for two. il McCalls 105:96-9 Ja '78
Bed alcoves. A. Lees. il Pop Sci 211:126-7 O '77
Bedroom: place of many moods. il Ladies Home J 94:116-19 Ap '77
Design-a-room kit. il Seventeen 36:166-8 S '77
8 by 8 bedroom that seems big. il Sunset 159: 142 O '77
How to make more of your master bedroom. P. W. Cullison and R. E. Dittmer. il Bet Hom & Gard 55:132-5 N '77
Live-in bedrooms, moveable feasts. il Mademoiselle 83:192-7 O '77
Night before Christmas; holiday bedroom. il Am Home 80:40-3 D '77
Sheets play a dual role; Rita Moreno's decorating. J. Macurdy. il House B 119:58-61 Mr '77
24-hour bedroom. il Redbook 149:118-19+ Jl '77
See also
Childrens rooms
Guest rooms

BEDS
Big bed is practically a room. il Sunset 159: 186 O '77
Canopy beds are back. il Am Home 80:38-9 Mr '77
Compact sleep center you can build. il Bet Hom & Gard 55:267 O '77
Four beds from the lumberyard. il Sunset 158: 176-8+ My '77
Four poster you can make. L. Palmer. il Mech Illus 73:58+ Jl '77
From box to sleep in 15 minutes. S. G. Lewin. il House B 119:14+ My '77
Out-of-sight sleepers. E. Liman. il Am Home 80:13 D '77
Upbeat beds for kids; frames and headboards. il Bet Hom & Gard 55:100 Je '77
See also
Bedding
Boats—Berths
Mattresses

Anecdotes, facetiae, satire, etc.

My adolescent bed. R. Baker. N Y Times Mag p 10 My 8 '77

BEDSPREADS. See Coverlets

BEE culture
Keeper of the bees. J. Ackermann-Blount. Atlantic 240:85-8 Ag '77
Smoking the bee. D. Grant. il Org Gard & Farm 24:146-7 Ap '77
So you want to keep bees. R. Morse. il Conservationist 31:48 My '77

Equipment and supplies

House your bees in a homemade hive. il Org Gard & Farm 24:90-5 Ap '77

BEEBE, William Thomas
Flying high at Delta Air Lines. por Duns R 110:60-1 D '77 *

BEECH, Linda
Looking good. Sr Schol 109:14, 26 Ap 7; 18 Ap 21; 16 My 5; 20 My 19; 110:40 S 22; 18 O 6; 20-1 N 17 '77

BEECH, Olive Ann (Mellor)
Beech. P. Trenner. por Flying 101:260-1 S '77 *
Will Olive Ann marry? il por Time 110:72 Jl 18 '77 *

BEECH
Turkey and the beech. W. W. Betts, Jr. il Nat Wildlife 15:18-23 O '77

BEECH Aircraft Corporation
Beech predicts continued sales growth. E. J. Bulban. il Aviation W 107:45 O 31 '77

BEECH Aircraft Corporation-General Dynamics Corporation merger. See Corporations—Acquisitions and mergers

BEECH-Nut Corporation. See Food industry

BEECHER, H.
(ed) Scorched cowboys: an old Colorado cowhand's tale. il Am West 14:30-1 N '77

BEECHICK, Ruth
Lawrence Kohlberg: why Johnny can be good without being religious. il Chr Today 22:12-14 D 30 '77

BEEF
See also
Cookery—Meat

Advertising

See Meat industry—Advertising

BEEF cattle. See Cattle

BEEF cattle industry. See Cattle industry

BEEF grading. See Meat—Grading

BEEF industry. See Meat industry

BEEF Industry Council. See National Livestock and Meat Board

BEEF jerky. See Meat, Dried

BEEF stew. See Stew

BEEFALOES. See Cattle—Hybrids

BEEHIVES. See Bee culture—Equipment & supplies

BEEKEEPING. See Bee culture

BEEKMAN, Philip E.
Seagram finds no. 3: Colgate's Beekman. por Bus W p26-7 Ja 24 '77 *
Soap? Whiskey? What's the difference? por Forbes 119:67 F 1 ''77 *

BEEPING devices, Radio. See Radio apparatus and instruments, Portable

BEER
Beer: the froth of July. S. Kanfer. il Time 110:44 Jl 4 '77
Small beer; hometown beers. J. Lelyveld. il N Y Times Mag p 110 My 22 '77
See also
Brewing industry
Cookery—Beer

BEER boycott. See Boycott

BEES
Bee gums and long sweet'nin'; hunting for honeybee trees. J. Madson. il Audubon 79:32-7 S '77
Behavioral control of workers by queens in primitively eusocial bees. M. D. Breed and G. J. Gamboa. bibl il Science 195:694-6 F 18 '77
Cleptoparasitism and odor mimetism in bees: do nomada males imitate the odor of andrena females? J. Tengo and G. Bergstrom. bibl il Science 196:1117-19 Je 3 '77
Coevolution of foraging in bombus and nectar dispensing in chilopsis: a last dreg theory. T. G. Whitham. bibl il Science 197:593-6 Ag 5 '77
Game of the bees. B. Heinrich. il Horticulture 55:38-9+ Jl '77
Herb garden for the bees. B. Fisher. il Org Gard & Farm 24:85-7 F '77
Pesticides and pollution. H. M. Caine. bibl il Environment 19:28-33 N '77
Resource partitioning in bumble bees: the role of behavioral factors. D. H. Morse. bibl il Science 197:678-80 Ag 12 '77
Sting; Brazilian or killer bees. R. E. Arnold. Field & S 81:104 Ap '77
See also
Bee culture

BEESTON, Diane
Lady with a camera; photographs. il Yachting 141:76-80 Ap '77

BEETHOVEN, Ludwig van
Again the mighty nine; recording. G. S. Fox and M. Cooper. Am Rec G 40:23-5 F '77 *
Fidelio. Reviews
Hi Fi 27:MA19+ N '77 *
Kubelik and the mighty nine; Beethoven symphonies. G. S. Fox. Am Rec G 40:16-17 D '76 *
Late quartets; performed by Quartetto Italiano. E. Belov. Am Rec G 41:11-12 N '77 *
Missa solemnis, op. 123. P. L. Althouse. Am Rec G 40:13-15 D '76 *
Second thoughts on the performance of Beethoven's trills. R. Winter. bibl f il Mus Q 63: 483-504 O '77 *
Survey for cello & piano. D. W. Moore. Am Rec G 40:19-22 O '77 *
Symphonies (9); Fidelio overture, op. 72c; Philips recording conducted by W. Mengelberg. H. Goldsmith. il por Hi Fi 27:78-80 D '77 *
Symphonies (9); Philips recording. H. Goldsmith. Hi Fi 27:99-100 Jl '77 *
Symphony no. 6 in F major op. 68; Symphony no. 7 in A major op. 92. J. Waxman. Am Rec G 40:15 D '76 *
Symphony no. 7. G. S. Fox. Am Rec G 40:11-12 Je '77 *

BEETLES
Cardiac glycosides in the defensive secretion of chrysomelid beetles: evidence for their production by the insects. J. M. Pasteels and D. Daloze. bibl il Science 197:70-2 Jl 1 '77
Degradation and detoxification of canavanine by a specialized seed predator. G. A. Rosenthal and others. bibl il Science 196:658-60 My 6 '77
Endothermy during terrestrial activity in large beetles. G. A. Bartholomew and T. M. Casey. bibl il Science 195:882-3 Mr 4 '77
Identification of the female Japanese beetle sex pheromone: inhibition of male response by an enantiomer. J. H. Tumlinson and others. bibl il Science 197:789-92 Ag 19 '77
See also
Ladybirds
Larvae
Weevils

BEGELMAN, David
Fallen star. D. Pauly and M. Kasindorf. Newsweek 90:89-90 O 17 '77 *

BEGGIATOA
Interaction of Beggiatoa and rice plant: detoxification of hydrogen sulfide in the rice rhizosphere. M. M. Joshi and J. P. Hollis. bibl il Science 195:179-80 Ja 14 '77

BEGGING and beggars
Panhandling: sharing of resources. J. S. Lockard and others; discussion. bibl Science 198:857-8 N 25 '77

BEGIN, Menachem
Begin autonomy; excerpts from interview, ed by M. J. Kubic. por Newsweek 91:40-1 Ja 16 '78
Everything is open to negotiation; address, November 20, 1977. Vital Speeches 44:105-8 D 1 '77
Palestine state: inconceivable; interview, ed by D. Neff and D. Halevy. il pors Time 109:31-2 My 30 '77
We cannot give up Judea and Samaria; excerpts from interview, ed by M. J. Kubic. il por map Newsweek 89:36-7 My 30 '77

about
Begin in Middle East perspective. I. L. Gendzier. Nation 225:102-4 Ag 6 '77 *
Begin: partner for peace. il por Time 111:14-15 Ja 2 '78 *
Begin the Begin. New Repub 176:5-6+ My 28 '77 *
Begin, the winner. M. Kondracke. New Repub 177:11-13 D 24 '77 *
Begin without smears. E. Breindel. New Repub 176:16-18 Je 18 '77 *
Begin's American bandwagon. D. Sider. il pors Time 110:22-3 S 5 '77 *
Begin's challenge. M. Sheils and others. il por Newsweek 90:38+ Ag 29 '77 *
Begin's strategy and Dayan's tactics: the conduct of Israeli foreign policy. A. Perlmutter. For Affairs 56:357-72 Ja '78 *
Begin's surprise maneuver. il por Time 109:36 Je 6 '77 *
Begin's trouble at home. E. M. Breindel. New Repub 178:10-11 Ja 7 '78 *
Breakthrough in Middle East. il U.S. News 83: 25-7 N 28 '77 *
Christmas summit. K. Willenson and others. il pors Newsweek 91:12-14 Ja 2 '78 *
Getting ready for Begin. J. M. Wall. Chr Cent 94:643-4 Jl 20 '77 *
Governing from intensive care. por Time 110:33 O 17 '77 *
Hawk on a mission of peace. W. E. Farrell. il pors N Y Times Mag p9-11+ Jl 17 '77 *
If peace talks fail war would come quickly. D. Mullin. il por U.S. News 83:17 D 5 '77 *
Israel and the evangelicals. J. M. Wall. Chr Cent 94:1083-4 N 23 '77 *
Israel: Begin takes charge. M. R. Benjamin and M. J. Kubic. il por Newsweek 90:50 Jl 4 '77 *
Israel: day of the hawks. R. Carroll and others. il pors Newsweek 89:32-3+ My 30 '77 *
Israel thumps the Bible. Nation 224:674 Je 4 '77 *
Israel under Begin. I. L. Gendzier. Nation 224: 742-4 Je 18 '77 *
Israeli election and the Begin victory. H. L. Chandler. il por Chr Cent 94:650-4 Jl 20 '77 *
Israelis watch Begin: can he bend or must he go? M. Viorst. Nation 225:686-90 D 24 '77 *
Israel's De Gaulle. A. Perlmutter. il pors Newsweek 90:28-9 Ag 15 '77 *
Israel's election shocker: setback for U.S. peace hopes? il por U.S. News 82:27-8 My 30 '77 *
Israel's hardening line in the Middle East. D. Mullin. il por map U.S. News 83:59-61 Jl 4 '77 *
Israel's soul. M. Kempton. Progressive 41:11 D '77 *
Likud's victory. B. J. Wattenberg. Harpers 255: 14-17 Ag '77 *
Middle Eastern prospects. Commonweal 104: 387-8 Je 24 '77 *
Mideast: what's next. il Newsweek 89:38+ My 30 '77 *
Not-so-odd couple. P. Webb and M. J. Kubic. il pors Newsweek 90:49 N 28 '77 *
Sadat in Israel. R. Steele and others. il pors maps Newsweek 90:36-40+ N 28 '77 *
Sadat in Jerusalem. Nat R 29:1406 D 9 '77 *
Sadat's courage, Begin's desire. New Repub 177:8-9 N 26 '77 *
Sadat's historic trip. J. M. Wall. Chr Cent 94: 1107-8 N 30 '77 *
Sadat's sacred mission. il pors Time 110:28-34+ N 28 '77 *
Sniping at Begin. R. Carroll and M. J. Kubic. il Newsweek 91:31 Ja 9 '78 *
Springing some more surprises. por Time 110: 36+ Ag 29 '77 *
Stormy start for a stylish hard-liner. il por Time 110:14-16 Jl 4 '77 *
Television. P. Sourian. Nation 225:670 D 17 '77 *
Triumph of a superhawk. il por map Time 109: 22-3+ My 30 '77 *
Two Mideast leaders on the hot seat. pors U.S. News 83:28 N 28 '77 *
Warning shot across Begin's bow. por Time 110:34 Jl 11 '77 *
Zealot. A. Deming and M. J. Kubic. il pors Newsweek 89:35 My 30 '77 *

Visit to Egypt, 1977
Mideast: phase 2. K. Willenson and others. il pors map Newsweek 91:28-31 Ja 9 '78
Morning after Ismailia. map Time 111:16-17 Ja 9 '78
Summit: peeks behind the scenes. D. Halevy. il pors Time 111:18 Ja 9 '78
What's holding up peace. il por U.S. News 84: 24-5 Ja 9 '78

Visit to the United States, 1977
Begin brings his plans for peace. il pors Time 110:31-3 Jl 25 '77
Begin's peace plan. T. Mathews and others. il pors Newsweek 90:73-4 D 26 '77
Charmer named Begin. S. Fraker and others. il por Newsweek 90:27-8 Ag 1 '77
Face to face with Israel. R. Steele and others. il por Newsweek 90:32-3 Jl 25 '77
Friendly talk, but outlook for Mideast peace still dim. D. Mullin. il por U.S. News 83:23 Ag 1 '7
From Geneva up to Geneva down. il Time 110: 21-2 Ag 1 '77
Israeli Prime Minister Begin visits Washington; statement, July 19, 1977. Dept State Bull 77:201-2 Ag 15 '77
Jimmy and Menachem. M. Kondracke. New Repub 177:13-15 Jl 30 '77
Letter from Washington. R. Rovere. New Yorker 53:56-8 Ag 1 '77
Media shuttle. Nation 225:706 D 31 '77
Menachem Begin's big blitz. il pors Time 110: 20-4 D 26 '77
Sticking point. Nat R 29:865-6+ Ag 5 '77

BEGONIAS
Begonia beauty—the hollyhock. il Sunset 158: 294 Ap '77

BEHAVIOR (psychology)
Behavior. Sci N 111:30, 44, 58, 125, 172, 222, 248, 281, 299, 346, 360, 392; 112:10, 25, 58, 90, 105, 121, 153, 170, 201, 265, 317, 361, 377, 393 Ja 8-22, F 19, Mr 12, Ap 2, 16, 30-My 7, 28-Je 4, 18, Jl 2-9, 23, Ag 6-20, S 3-10, 24, O 22, N 12, 26 D 3-10 '77
Between freedom and despotism; self government; excerpt from address. B. F. Skinner. il por Psychol Today 11:80-2+ S '77
Borderline behavior; diagnosing emotional or behavioral problems. E. B. Wilson. Harp Baz 110:228-9+ S '77
Do you have a compulsive personality? K. R. Gertz. Harp Baz 110:86+ Ag '77
Does your quirk irk you . . . and others, too? N. Ashby. Fam Health 9:40-3 Mr '77

BEHAVIOR (psychology)—*Continued*
Energy behavior. P. C. Stern and E. M. Kirkpatrick. bibl il Environment 19:10-15 D '77
Listening to B. F. Skinner. J. W. Woelfel. Chr Cent 94:1112-16 N 30 '77
Lorenz observed. G. E. Allen. il Natur Hist 86: 78-82+ Je '77
Manipulation: shortcut to the top. B. Howell. Harp Baz 110:84+ Ag '77
Psychiatry labeling in cross-cultural perspective. J. M. Murphy; discussion. bibl Science 196: 480+ Ap 29 '77
Social scientists and moral theology. S. M. Natale and O. J. Morgan. bibl il New Cath World 220:301-9 N '77
Therapies ministers use; analysis of the work of C. Rogers, F. Perls and E. Berne. J. S. Miller. il Chr Cent 94:504-8 My 25 '77; Discussion. 94:852-4 S 28 '77
Virus-induced behavioral alteration of mice; lymphocytic choriomeningitis. J. Hotchin and R. Seegal. bibl il Science 196:671-4 My 6 '77
See also
Aggressiveness (psychology)
Helping behavior

Bibliography

Behavioral sciences. Am Scholar 46:545-6 Aut '77
Thomas J. Cottle on behavior. T. J. Cottle. New Repub 177:29-30 D 3 '77

BEHAVIOR, Animal. See Animals—Habits and behavior

BEHAVIOR, Organizational. See Organizational behavior

BEHAVIOR genetics
Is it our culture, not our genes, that makes us killers? excerpt from Origins. R. E. Leakey and R. Lewin. il por Smithsonian 8:56-8+ bibl(p 160) N '77
Naked coward. F. Hapgood. Atlantic 240:88-91 Ag '77
You—the gene machine. R. Dawkins. il Vogue 167:234-5+ My '77

BEHAVIOR modification
How I stopped nagging and started teaching my children to behave; excerpt from Positive parenthood. P. S. Graubard. McCalls 104:90+ My '77
How to gear your mind to think yourself slim; interview, ed by C. Seebohm. F. M. Stern. House & Gard 149:22+ Ag '77
Learning to be thin; views of S. Simon. McCalls 105:81-2 O '77
Orchestra conductors would make good porpoise trainers. K. Pryor. il por Psychol Today 10:61+ F '77
People shapers; excerpt. V. Packard. Sat R 4: 33-48 Ag 6 '77
Study faults behavior modification. Sci N 112: 312 N 12 '77
Thinner with Skinner: a food critic's strategy for belly modification. R. Sokolov. il Psychol Today 11:98+ Je '77

BEHAVIOR of animals. See Animals—Habits and behavior

BEHAVIOR problems (children) See Problem children

BEHAVIORAL objectives in education. See Education—Aims and objectives

BEHAVIORAL pharmacology. See Psychopharmacology

BEHME, Bob
Vehicles. See issues of Field & stream

BEHNKE, Robert J.
Trout truths. B. Saile. il por Outdoor Life 160: 86-9 N '77 *

BEHREND, Cathie
Recreation at your doorstep. il Parks & Rec 12: 54-5 Je '77

BEHRENS, Richard
Arabian luster glazes. Ceram Mo 25:46 Je '77
Barium glazes. il por Ceram Mo 25:64-5 My '77
Cone 5 to 8 oxidation glazes. il Ceram Mo 25: 56-7 D '77
Manganese glazes. Ceram Mo 25:64 Mr '77
Vitrified bisque. por Ceram Mo 25:62-3 O '77

BEHRMAN, Daniel
New wave in oceanography. il UNESCO Courier 30:16-17+ Ja '77
What can we do about marine pollution? il UNESCO Courier 30:27-8 Ja '77

BEIM, David Odell
Rescuing the LDCs. For Affairs 55:717-31 Jl '77

BEIRUT
Beirut: better, but not yet well. il map Time 110:42-3 N 14 '77
Lebanon: the chore of getting Beirut back in shape. il Bus W p42 F 28 '77

BEIT-HALLAHMI, Benjamin
Turn of the screw and The exorcist: demoniacal possession and childhood purity. bibl Am Imago 33:296-303 Fall '76

BÉJART, Maurice, Ballet of the 20th Century. See Maurice Béjart's Ballet of the 20th Century

BEKER Industries Corporation. See Fertilizer industry

BEKOFF, Marc
Social communication in canids: evidence for the evolution of a stereotyped mammalian display. bibl il Science 197:1097-9 S 9 '77

BEL Canto Opera Company. See Opera—New York (state)

BELA VISTA (hotel) See Hotels, motels, etc.—Macao

BELCHER, Edith. See Belcher, T. G. jt auth

BELCHER, Taylor Garrison, and Belcher, Edith
Great golden art of the ancient Peruvian artisans. il Smithsonian 8:84-91 bibl(p 135) D '77

BELDING, Robert E.
How PRYO worked for one student. il Am Educ 13:12-13 Ag '77

BELFAST
Buying back Belfast? IRA business activities. M. Dammerman. il Forbes 119:25-7 My 15 '77
Doing business in Belfast. por Forbes 119:6 Mr 15 '77
Journal from Northern Ireland. V. O. Baron. Chr Cent 94:757-9 Ag 31 '77

BELFER, Nancy
Appliqué methods; excerpt from Designing in stitching and appliqué. il Sch Arts 77:36-42 N '77
Hooking, looping and knotting: versatile fiber techniques for rugs and wall hangings; excerpt from Weaving: design and expression. il Sch Arts 77:20-5 S '77
Stitching; excerpt from Designing in stitching and appliqué. il Sch Arts 76:16-21 Mr '77
Tapestry weaving on the frame loom; excerpt from Weaving: design and expression. il Sch Arts 77:48-53 O '77
Tie dye—designing with color; excerpt from Designing in batik and tie dye. il Sch Arts 76:12-17 Ap '77

BELFORD, Lee Archer
Sun Myung Moon and the Unification Church. Intellect 105:336-7 Ap '77

BELFRAGE, Cedric
On political exile. Progressive 41:20-1 Ag '77

BELGIAN waffles. See Pancakes, waffles, etc.

BELGIUM
See also
Airlines—Belgium
Antwerp
Architecture, Domestic—Belgium
Brussels
Gardens—Belgium
Investments, American—Belgium
Investments, Belgian
Opera—Belgium

Description and travel

Travel: Belgium. S. McElwaine. il Vogue 167:150+ D '77

Industries

See also
Engineering construction companies—Belgium
Petroleum industry—Belgium

Politics and government

See also
Decentralization in government—Belgium

Social policy

Toward a multidimensional framework for the analysis of social policy. M. O. Heisler and B. G. Peters. bibl f Ann Am Acad 434:58-70 N '77

BELGRADE summit. See Conference on Security and Cooperation in Europe

BELIEF and doubt
Brain evolution and the biology of belief. H. Hoagland. Bull Atom Sci 33:41-4 Mr '77
See also
Faith

BELIEF in God. See Faith

BELITT, Ben
(tr) See Neruda, P. Tides

BELIZE
See also
Fishing—Belize
United Nations—Belize

Antiquities

Earliest Maya. N. Hammond. il maps Sci Am 236:116-23 bibl(p 150) Mr '77
Oldest dates for Mayans' origins; Cuello excavations. Sci N 112:4 Jl 2 '77

Industries

See also
Fisheries—Belize

BELL, Bob
Study in gray. . .the rifleman's squirrel. il Outdoor Life 160:82-3+ N '77

BELL, Brian J.
Last out; story. New Repub 177:44-6 Jl 30 '77

BELL, Bruce
Where the action isn't; interview. il por Chr Today 22:28-9 O 7 '77

BELL, Carolyn Shaw
Let's get rid of families! por Newsweek 89:19 My 9 '77

BELL, Griffin B.
How Griffin Bell sees his role as Attorney General; interview. il pors U.S. News 82:67-8+ My 16 '77
Plan to cut litigation; interview, ed by J. K. Lieberman and D. B. Moskowitz. por Bus W p60-2+ Je 6 '77

about

Early returns on Griffin Bell. Nation 224:260-1 Mr 5 '77 *
Greening of Griffin Bell. V. S. Navasky. por N Y Times Mag p41-2+ F 27 '77 *
Griffin Bell believes in law. Nation 224:547-8 My 7 '77 *
Griffin Bell opens the doors. P. Goldman and S. Lesher. il por Newsweek 89:20-1 F 28 '77 *
Griffin Bell's dilemma. D. Holt and others. il Newsweek 90:35 D 19 '77 *
New look at old crime problems. il U.S. News 82:48 Ja 31 '77 *
Reflections. C. Trillin. il New Yorker 53:85-8+ Mr 21 '77 *
Trial by Congress? por Time 109:71 My 23 '77 *
When G-men break the law. P. Goldman and N. Horrock. il Newsweek 89:28+ My 30 '77 *

BELL, Janice W.
Directed creativity. il Sch Arts 76:78-9 F '77

BELL, Joseph N.
Family that fought back. il McCalls 104:26+ My '77
(ed) See Black, S. T. Will young people ever have heroes again?
(ed) See Pleshette, S. Suzanne Pleshette

BELL, Marvin
Dew at the edge of a leaf; poem. Nation 224:88 Ja 22 '77

BELL, Pearl K.
Philip Roth: Sonny Boy or Lenny Bruce? Commentary 64:60-3 N '77

BELL, Raymond J.
Quick hex-decimal conversions. il Pop Electr 12:72 D '77

BELL, Ricky
First and foremost for now. J. Marshall. il Sports Illus 47:21 S 26 '77 *

BELL & Howell Company
Don Frey's dilemma. il pors Forbes 120:74-5 D 1 '77

BELL ringing. See Bells

BELL Telephone Laboratories
Bell Labs reports manmade single-crystal monolayer alloys. G. B. Lubkin. il Phys Today 30:17-18 F '77
But what can it do? por Forbes 120:104 O 1 '77
Roots of solid-state research at Bell Labs. L. H. Hoddeson. bibl il Phys Today 30:23-6+ Mr '77

BELL Telephone System. See American Telephone & Telegraph Company

BELLAH, Robert Neelly
Incomplete candor. K. L. Woodward. pors Newsweek 90:77 Jl 25 '77 *

BELLAMY, Carol
New Cinderella for Gotham. por Time 110:23 O 3 '77 *
Political update: New York's finest—Bella, Ronnie, & Carol. L. Sherr. il pors Ms 6:60-1 S '77 *

BELLANCA, Giuseppe Mario
Bellanca. P. Trenner. il Flying 101:110 S '77 *

BELLER, Andrea H.
Effect on women's earnings of enforcement in Title VII cases. bibl il M Labor R 100:56-7 Mr '77

BELLFLOWER. See Campanulas

BELLICO, Russ
On lotteries. il Progressive 41:24-5 Ap '77

BELLINGER, Marcia
Literature from prison. Engl J 66:62-3 S '77

BELLINGER, Susan. See Akabas, S. H. jt auth

BELLINI, Giovanni
Looking at paintings. B. Dunstan. il Am Artist 41:72-3 N '77 *

BELLINI, Vincenzo
Norma. Reviews
Hi Fi 27:14 Je '77 *
Hi Fi por 27:MA26 O '77 *

BELLOCCHIO, Marco
1976 minus one. W. S. Pechter. Commentary 63:75-7 Mr '77 *

BELLOCQ, E. J.
Bellocq's girls; exhibition at New York's Light Gallery. D. Davis. il Newsweek 89:89 Mr 14 '77 *

BELLOW, Saul
Nobel lecture. Am Scholar 46:316-25 Summ '77

about

Epistle of a Gentile to Saul Bellow. H. Fairlie. New Repub 176:18-20+ F 5 '77 *
Great man syndrome: Saul Bellow & me. S. Dworkin. por Ms 5:72-3 Mr '77 *
Human understanding of Saul Bellow. J. W. Sire. Chr Today 21:20+ Ja 21 '77 *
Zeroing in; adaptation of Kirchner's opera Lily from S. Bellow's Henderson, the rain king. H. Heinsheimer. il por Opera N 41:12-15 Ap 16 '77 *

BELLOWS, James G.
Fixit goes west. por Time 110:112+ D 5 '77 *
Star wars. H. F. Waters and J. B. Copeland. por Newsweek 90:129-30 N 28 '77 *

BELLS
Britain's brave bells. E. Antrobus. il Am For 83:42-5+ Mr '77
Miracle of the reborn bells; Our Lady of Good Counsel Church, Bedford-Stuyvesant. C. W. Moodie. il por Read Digest 111:9-12+ N '77

Collectors and collecting

Canadian's bells make the welkin ring; collection of H. Rowland. H. L. Miller. il pors Hobbies 82:118-19 S '77

BELLY dancing. See Dancing, Oriental

BELMONT Stakes. See Horse racing

BELOFF, Nora
Hard pressed. New Repub 177:12-13 S 3 '77

BELSER, Jess L.
Equal opportunity; address, November 21, 1976. Vital Speeches 43:251-3 F 1 '77

BELSON, Abby Avin
Daydream those pounds away. Seventeen 36:234-5+ Ag '77
Little-known diseases. Fam Health 9:42-4+ My '77
New treatments vs. unknown risks. Vogue 167:132-3+ Jl '77
Yogurt—so-so or so good? Vogue 167:140+ Ap '77

BELSON, Gabrielle
Astrology can cause more mischief than good. por Seventeen 36:94 Mr '77
Here at Seventeen. Seventeen 36:59-60 Ap '77

BELT, Forest H.
CB test instruments. il Radio-Electr 48:42-4 D '77
What you need to know about CB test gear. il por Radio-Electr 48:49-61 N '77
What you need to know about tools and handy gadgets. il Radio-Electr 49:33-42 Ja '78

BELTER, John Henry
Patent model by John Henry Belter. R. Roth. bibl il Antiques 111:1038-40 My '77 *

BELTING
See also
Automobile engines—Belts

BELTRANTE, Nick
Supersleuthing: fair means or foul. il por Time 110:18 Jl 18 '77 *

BELZ, Mary, and others
Is there a treatment for terror? il Psychol Today 11:54-6+ O '77

BEMAN, Lewis
Ned Cook in the agonies of corporate confession. il por Fortune 95:340-3+ My '77

BEMISS, Margaret
What do the real clients, the aging, think about the current facilities? Archit Rec 161:137-8 My '77

BEMIS'S HEIGHTS, Battle of, 1777. See Saratoga Campaign, 1777

BEN-AMI, Jacob
Obituary
Nation 225:221-2 S 10 '77. H. Clurman

BENACERRAF, Baruj. See Paul, W. E. jt auth

BENAVIDES, Felipe
How Peru saved Paracas. M. Wexler. il Int Wildlife 7:24-31 S '77 *

BENCH rest shooting. See Target practice

BENCHES
Their fence is a friendly bench. il Sunset 158:273 Ap '77
See also
Work benches

BENCHTOP vises. See Vises

BENDA, Georg
3 concerti for harpsichord. Am Rec G 40:22-3 O '77 *

BENDA, Jiri Antonin. See Benda, G.

BENDEL, Don
Bendel burner. il Ceram Mo 25:48-9 S '77

BENDER, Michael L. and others
Interstitial nitrate profiles and oxidation of sedimentary organic matter in the eastern equatorial Atlantic. bibl il Science 198:605-9 N 11 '77

BENDER, Tom
Passing of the age of affluence. Current 197:23-33 N '77

BENDERSKY, Charles
Ma Bell, firebug. F. Warner. Nation 224:684-8 Je 4 '77 *

BENDITT, Earl P.
Origin of atherosclerosis; with biographical sketch. il Sci Am 236:16, 74-6+ bibl(p 138) F '77

BENDIX, Michael
Shark fishermen of Mexico. il Oceans 10:12-17 N '77

BENDIX Corporation
Early arrival of a happy family man. por Fortune 95:17 F '77
Room at the top; W. M. Agee named chairman. por Time 109:68 F 21 '77
Soviet Union: Bendix breaks ground in trade with Russia. Bus W p49 Ja 31 '77

BENECKE, Mary Beth
Rhythm: ideal and reality. America 137:240-1 O 15 '77

BENEDEK, Yvette E.
(ed) See McGowan, A. Ann McGowan: design in color and black-and-white

BENEDÍ, Claudio F.
Foresight of Félix Varela. il por Américas 29:9-12 Ap '77

BENEDIKT, Michael
Comment. B. Howard. Poetry 130:289-90 Ag '77 *

BENEDUCE, Ann K.
Bologna's children's book fair reflects the changing world of juvenile publishing. il Pub W 211:37-8 My 2 '77

BENEFIT funds (trade unions) See Trade unions—Benefit funds

BENEFIT performances
See also
Dancing—Benefit performances

BENEFITS, Employee. See Non-wage payments

BENELLI, Giovanni, Cardinal
Papabile Cardinal Benelli. D. O'Grady. Commonweal 104:488 Ag 5 '77 *
Red hat for the right-hand man. por Time 109:49 Je 13 '77 *

BENEMANN, William E.
Tears and ivory towers: California libraries during the McCarthy era. bibl il Am Lib 8:305-9 Je '77

BENENSON, Tom
A friend's going to fly my plane. Flying 100:24+ Ap '77

BENET, James
Public TV kills a news winner. Nation 225:588-90 D 3 '77

BENEZRA, Nat
Enquiry concerning the principles of car rental. Holiday 58:24-5 Mr '77
Hair-raising tale. il por Fam Health 9:25-9 D '77
Would you eat your child's school lunch? il Fam Health 9:40-3+ S '77

BENFEY, Theodor
Limits of knowledge; adaptation of address, 1975. Chemistry 50:2-3 Mr '77

BENGIS, Ingrid
TV. il Ms 5:34+ My '77

BENGSTON, Billy Al
Art on the wild side; interview, ed by M. Berges. il por Design (US) 78:6-9 Spr '77

BENIGER, James R.
Legacy of Carter and Reagan: political reality overtakes the myth of the presidential primaries. bibl il Intellect 105:234-7 F '77

BENIN
See also
United Nations—Benin

BENINGER, Richard J. and others
Schedule control of behavior reinforced by electrical stimulation of the brain. bibl il Science 196:547-9 Ap 29 '77

BENITEZ, Jaime
Should Puerto Rico be a state? interview. pors U.S. News 82:47-8 Ap 11 '77

BENITEZ, Wilfredo
Over the ropes is out. C. Gammon. il pors Sports Illus 47:52+ Ag 15 '77 *

BENJAMIN, James M.
Alternative schools: another view. Clearing H 50:312-13 Mr '77
Does occupational education need a different emphasis? Clearing H 50:401-2 My '77

BENJAMIN, Joseph
High fidelity pathfinders. N. Eisenberg. Hi Fi 27:56+ D '77

BENJAMIN, Julia
Satan: alive and well? il Sat Eve Post 249:56-7 Ap '77

BENJAMIN, Randal
Pots from slab and wheel-thrown sections. il Ceram Mo 25:58-61 O '77

BENJAMIN, Roy
Roy Benjamin on premiums, incentives, special sales and copublishing ventures; interview, ed by D. Maryles. il por Pub W 213:26-31 Ja 2 '78

BENJAMIN, Walter
Towards an aesthetic of experimental music. C. Ballantine. bibl f Mus Q 63:224-46 Ap '77 *

BENJAMIN-MURRAY, Betsy
Dye painting with fiber reactive dyes. il Sch Arts 77:22-6 D '77

BENJAMIN Company, Inc. See Publishers and publishing—United States

BENKE, Paul J. and Dittmar, David
Phosphoribosylpyrophosphate synthesis in cultured human cells. bibl il Science 198:1171-3 D 16 '77

BENNE, Mae
Leavening for the youth culture. bibl il por Wilson Lib Bull 52:312-18 D '77

BENNET, Richard Dyer-. See Dyer-Bennet, R.

BENNETT, Alan
Old country. Reviews
New Yorker 53:196-7 N 14 '77 *
Time 110:89 O 3 '77 *

BENNETT, C. L. and others
Radiocarbon dating using electrostatic accelerators: negative ions provide the key. bibl il Science 198:508-10 N 4 '77

BENNETT, John Coleman
Morality and foreign policy; excerpt from U.S. foreign policy and Christian ethics. Chr Cent 94:778-81 S 14 '77

BENNETT, Lawrence H. and others
Interstitial compounds; heat resistant refractory metals; adaptation of address, March 1976. bibl il Phys Today 30:34-6+ S '77

BENNETT, Lerone, Jr
Black man who founded Chicago. il por maps Ebony 33:64-6+ N '77
Great moments in black history (cont) Ebony 32:128-30+ F; 132-6+ My; 54-6+ S '77
Inaugural marks new and undefined era. il Ebony 32:152-4 Mr '77
Last of the great schoolmasters. il pors Ebony 33:72-4+ D '77
No crystal stair: the black woman in history. il Ebony 32:164-5+ Ag '77

BENNETT, Lester W.
Kinky minks. por Forbes 119:106 My 15 '77 *

BENNETT, Margaret, pseud. See Biermann J. and Toohey, B.

BENNETT, Ralph Kinney
Hidden issues behind a nuclear-test ban. Read Digest 111:124-8 S '77
Missile the Russians fear most. il Read Digest 110:129-32 F '77

BENNETT, Richard Rodney
Interview with Richard Rodney Bennett; ed by J. Caps. il por Hi Fi 27:58-62 Je '77

BENNETT, William
Of Mars. . .and realistic goals. Sci Digest 81:20-2 Mr '77

—and Gurin, Joel
Science that frightens scientists: the great debate over DNA. il Atlantic 239:43-50+ F '77; Same abr. with title Public & science regulation. Sci Digest 81:22-4 Je '77

BENNETT, William J.
Let's bring back heroes. por Newsweek 90:3 Ag 15 '77; Same abr. il Read Digest 111:91-2 D '77

BENNETT, William Richards
Government selloff in British Columbia. por Bus W p69-70 S 26 '77 *

BENNETT, William Tapley, 1917-
U.S. supports establishment of U.N. Ad Hoc Committee on Drafting of Convention Against Taking of Hostages; statement, December 15, 1976. Dept State Bull 76:74 Ja 24 '77

BENORE, Charles
Electric utility stocks are shining again; interview, ed by A. Hershman. por Duns R 110:73-5 Ag '77

BENRUS Corporation
Benrus gets out of the watch business—almost. por Duns R 109:20-1 Mr '77

BENSON, Frank
Space age swimming hole. il Parks & Rec 12:24-5+ O '77

BENSON, Sir Frank Robert
The play's still the thing. R. Morley. il Sat R 4:12-13 Je 11 '77 *

BENSON, George
George Benson & Tommy LiPuma: the in flight sessions; interview, ed by D. Heckman. il pors Hi Fi 27:134-6 F '77

about
George Benson: still breezin'. il pors Ebony 33:114-16+ N '77 *
Four faces of Benson. M. Orth. il por Newsweek 89:94-5 My 23 '77 *

BENSON, Gertrude
Painted wood furniture. il Craft Horiz 37:55-7+ Ag '77

BENSON, Harry
When the going gets rough. il Sports Illus 47:38-42 O 31 '77

about
Letter from the publisher. J. Meyers. il por Sports Illus 47:6 O 31 '77 *

BENSON, Kent
Dreams to reality. il por Camp Mag 49:34-5+ Ja '77

BENSON, Lucy Peters (Wilson)
Controlling arms transfers: an instrument of U.S. foreign policy; address, June 27, 1977. Dept State Bull 77:155-9 Ag 1 '77
Department discusses security assistance programs; statement, April 21, 1977. Dept State Bull 76:485-9 My 16 '77

about
Science and technology at State: recognizing the problem. J. Walsh. Science 196:148-50 Ap 8 '77 *

BENSON and Hedges Australian Air Race of 1976. See Airplane racing

BENTHOS
Antarctic soft-botton benthos in oligotrophic and eutrophic environments. P. K. Dayton and J. S. Oliver. bibl il map Science 197:55-8 Jl 1 '77
Deep pastures. Sci Am 237:74-5 N '77
Living sea: life on the Galapagos Rift. il Sci N 111:279 Ap 30 '77
Microbial life in the deep sea. H. W. Jannasch and C. O. Wirsen. il Sci Am 236:42-52 bibl(p 142) Je '77
BENTLEY, David R. See Carlson, J. R. jt auth
BENTLEY, Walter Owen
1925 Bentley 3 litre speed model. W. S. Jackson. il Motor T 29:113-19 My '77 *
BENTLEY, William
Dr William Bentley of Salem, Massachusetts. S. B. Sherrill. il por Antiques 112:26+ Jl '77 *
BENTON, John B.
Electronic funds transfer: pitfalls and payoffs. il Harvard Bus R 55:16-17+ Jl '77
BENTON, W. David, and Davis, R. W.
Screening λgt recombinant clones by hybridization to single plaques in situ. bibl il Science 196:180-2 Ap 8 '77
BENTON-HARRIS, John
John Benton-Harris: Yankee eye on the English. P. Turner. il Mod Phot 41:128-37 O '77 *
BENTSEN, Bill
Have you read your sailing instructions lately? Yachting 141:80-1+ F '77
BENTZEN, Warren R. See Harris, J. J. 3d, jt auth
BENZ, Edward, Jr, and others
Stability of the individual globin genes during erythroid differentiation. bibl il Science 196:1213-14 Je 10 '77
BENZENE
Industry's challenge on benzene; OSHA hearing on benzene links to leukemia. il Bus W p30+ Ag 22 '77
What benzene's link to leukemia will cost; OSHA standard. il Bus W p35 My 9 '77
BENZODIAZEPINE receptors. See Drug receptors
BENZODIAZEPINES. See Tranquilizing drugs
BENZOPYRENE
Benzo [a] pyrene diol epoxides: mechanism of enzymatic formation and optically active intermediates. S. K. Yang. bibl il Science 196:1199-201 Je 10 '77
DNA strand scission by benzo[a]pyrene diol epoxides. H. B. Gamper and others. bibl il Science 197:671-4 Ag 12 '77
BEQUESTS. See Wills
BEQUIA (island)
Whalers of Bequia. E. Kuperschmid. il map Motor B & S 139:40-5 F '77
BEREAVEMENT. See Grief
BERENDT, John
Facing the interview. Esquire 88:57-9 Jl '77
I catch a burglar. il Read Digest 110:109-13 F '77
BERENDZEN, Richard
Science books. Am Scholar 46:514+ Aut '77
BERENSON, Ruth
Art (cont) Nat R 29:565-6, 680-1, 786-7, 896-7, 1124-5, 1378-80; 30:40-1 My 13, Je 10, Jl 8, Ag 5, S 30, N 25 '77, Ja 6 '78
Dance. Nat R 29:155 F 4 '77
BERENSTAIN, Janice. See Berenstain, S. jt auth
BERENSTAIN, Stanley, and Berenstain, Janice
It's all in the family (cont) il Good H 184:118-19 Mr; 124-5 Je; 185:114-15 Ag; 168+ S; 160-1 D '77
BERETTA revolvers. See Revolvers
BERG, Alban
Alban Berg: as I knew him. H. Heinsheimer. il por Opera N 41:10-13 Ap 2 '77 *
Berg's master array of the interval cycles. G. Perle. bibl f il Mus Q 63:1-30 Ja '77 *
Earth spirit; author of the Lulu plays. G. R. Marek. il pors Opera N 41:16-17+ Ap 2 '77 *
Essay in virtuosity; music of Lulu. M. Steinberg. il Opera N 41:32-5 Ap 2 '77 *
Lulu. Reviews
Hi Fi 27:MA26-7+ Jl '77 *
Nat R 29:733-4 Je 24 '77 *
Nation 224:444-5 Ap 9 '77 *
New Yorker 53:125-31 Ap 4 '77 *
Newsweek il 89:105-6 Ap 11 '77 *
Opera N il 41:24+ Ap 2 '77 *
Sat R il 4:37-8 Ap 30 '77 *
Time il 109:96 Mr 28 '77 *
Lulu's last stand: Jack the Ripper. F. Stevenson. Opera N 41:36 Ap 2 '77 *
Met's Lulu. C. L. Osborne. il Hi Fi 27:MA26-7+ Jl '77 *
Real Lulu: Carole Farley; interview, ed by S. Wadsworth. C. Farley. por Opera N 41:14 Ap 2 '77 *
Viewpoint; Lulu. R. Jacobson. Opera N 41:7 Ap 2 '77 *
BERG, Josef
St Luke ch. ens: Berg premieres; performances on November 24 at the 92nd Street Y. il Hi Fi 27:MA14 Mr '77 *
BERG, Kenneth A.
Educational leadership. bibl Clearing H 50:212-14 Ja '77
BERG, Moses David
Children of God: disciples of deception; interviews, ed by J. M. Hopkins, D. Jacks and J. Wasson. il Chr Today 21:18-23 F 18 '77 *
Tracking the Children of God. il pors Time 110:48 Ag 22 '77 *
BERG, Paul
Berg calls gene mapping most important practical benefit. E. M. Leeper. por BioScience 27:369 My '77 *
—See Villarreal, L. P. jt auth
BERG, Stephen
Comment. R. Holland. Poetry 129:285-7 F '77 *
BERGELSON, L. D. and Barsukov, L. I.
Topological asymmetry of phospholipids in membranes. bibl il Science 197:224-30 Jl 15 '77
BERGEN, Candice
Candy Bergen has a question; interview, ed by A. E. Hotchner. por McCalls 104:56-61 Je '77
Four successful women talk about what they want—and can't have. pors Redbook 148:92-3+ F '77
BERGEN, Stanley Silvers, 1929-
Need for caring in medical practice; excerpts from address. por Intellect 105:213-14 Ja '77
BERGER, Alan
Le nouveau regime. New Repub 176:18-20 Je 18 '77
BERGER, Bob
Macau. il Travel 147:32-5+ F '77
BERGER, Celia
Working on the campaign trail. C. R. Arrington. il por Ret Liv 17:38+ O '77 *
BERGER, Eric
Not ready for the rocking chair. il pors Ret Liv 17:30-2 O '77
BERGER, Frank
Seagram antes $40 million. il por Bus W p68 Ag 22 '77 *
BERGER, Ivan
From bits into pieces. il Sat R 4:32-3 Jl 23 '77
BERGER, John J.
Carter & the plutonium economy. Nation 224:101-4 Ja 29 '77
Let the sun shine in. Progressive 41:43-6 F '77
BERGER, Marilyn
Vance and Brzezinski: peaceful coexistence or guerrilla war? il pors N Y Times Mag p 19+ F 13 '77
BERGER, Patricia J. and others
Phenolic plant compounds functioning as reproductive inhibitors in Micrctus montanus. bibl il Science 195:575-7 F 11 '77
—See Negus, N. C. jt auth
BERGER, Peter L.
Are human rights universal? Commentary 64:60-3 S '77
Great revival coming for America's churches; interview. por U.S. News 82:70+ Ap 11 '77
In praise of New York; adaptation of address. Commentary 63:59-62 F '77
about
Caring for the caretakers. H. B. Kuhn. Chr Today 21:41 Ag 12 '77 *
Some semi-tough questions. M. E. Marty. Chr Cent 94:415 Ap 27 '77 *
BERGER, Raoul
Imperial court; excerpt from Government by judiciary. il N Y Times Mag p38+ O 9 '77
about
Berger v. Court. J. K. Footlick. por Newsweek 90:75 N 14 '77 *
Berger's big book. W. F. Buckley, Jr. Nat R 29:1320 N 11 '77 *
Fie on the 14th. Time 110:101-2 N 14 '77 *
BERGER, Terry
Tulipomania was no Dutch treat to gambling burghers. il Smithsonian 8:70-7 Ap '77
BERGER, Theodore W. and Thompson, R. F.
Limbic system interrelations: functional division among hippocampal-septal connections. bibl il Science 197:587-9 Ag 5 '77
BERGER, Thomas Louis
Radical Americanist. B. Landon. Nation 225:151-3 Ag 20 '77 *
Second decade of Little big man. F. Turner. Nation 225:149-51 Ag 20 '77 *
BERGER, Thomas Rodney
Berger report: northern frontier, northern homeland; excerpt from Northern frontier, northern homeland. il por maps Liv Wildn 41:4-33 Ap '77
about
Berger commission brings the North to the South. M. Panitch. Science 195:1310 Mr 25 '77 *
BERGER, Wolfgang H. and Killingley, J. S.
Glacial-Holocene transition in deep-sea carbonates: selective dissolution and the stable isotope signal. bibl il Science 197:563-6 Ag 5 '77
BERGERON, Victor Jules
Hospitality on a budget. il por House & Gard 149:152-3 S '77
How to host (and enjoy) a holiday party. il House B 119:118-20+ D '77 *

BERGES, Mashall
(ed) See Bengston, B. A. Art on the wild side

BERGESEN, Victoria
Despotism is not enough. Nation 224:682-4 Je 4 '77

BERGIN, Ed, and Buchanek, Jack
Push button navigators. il Motor B & S 139: 88-90+ My '77
Push-button piloting. il Motor B & S 140:68-70+ Ag '77

BERGLAND, Bob Selmer
Washington report; interview, ed by J. Harms. Suc Farm 75:no2 6 F '77
Why farmers are up in arms; interview. il por U.S. News 83:57-8+ O 31 '77

about

Bergland to redirect USDA research? L. J. Carter. Science 196:506 Ap 29 '77 *
Bergland's new farm policy. L. Smith. por Duns R 109:70-2 Ap '77 *
Echoes of OPEC in Bergland's commodity pricing scheme. il Bus W p76 Mr 14 '77 *
Real farmer in Carter's Cabinet. H. Sidey. il pors Horticulture 55:28-31 Ap '77 *
Secretary of Agriculture Bergland. Am For 83: 14 F '77 *
What Bergland really said about farm chemicals. Farm J 101:32 N '77 *
What to expect from your new Secretary of Agriculture. R. D. Wennblom. pors Farm J 101:23-5 Ja '77 *

BERGLAND, Bob Selmer, family
Visit to the Bob Bergland farm and family. R. D. Wennblom. il pors Farm J 101:10-11 mid-F '77

BERGLUND, Paavo Allan Engelbert
Sibelius: Symphony no. 1. C. Bauman. Am Rec G 40:55 O '77 *

BERGMAN, Bernard A.
(ed) Lewis, A. H. PW interviews

BERGMAN, David
Actors' equity; poem. Am Scholar 46:440 Aut '77
Rubenesque; poem. Am Scholar 46:158 Spr '77

BERGMAN, Gregory
Other Ireland. Chr Cent 94:1006-7 N 2 '77
You can't talk to the trees! il Ret Liv 17:32-3 Je '77

BERGMAN, Ingmar
Changing; excerpt. L. Ullmann. por McCalls 104:130-1+ F '77 *
Day on the Bergmanstrasse. L. Janos. il por Time 109:78-9 F 14 '77 *
Hour of the wolf: the case of Ingmar B. L. Buntzen and C. Craig. bibl f il por Film Q 30: 23-34 Wint '76 *
Liv Ullmann on love and Bergman; excerpt from Changing. L. Ullmann. il Vogue 167:172-3+ F '77 *
Schemes from a marriage. J. K. Larson. il Chr Cent 94:535-40 Je 1 '77 *
Tight close-up on Ingmar Bergman. R. A. Blake. America 136:202-3 Mr 5 '77 *
When an artist feels anxiety. J. Morris. il pors Horizon 20:16-22 N '77 *

BERGMAN, Jules
From Sputnik to Star Trek. il Flying 101:317-21 S '77

BERGMAN, Maius
Dissent in Czechoslovakia. New Repub 176:12-13 F 26 '77

BERGONZI, Carlo
Carlo Bergonzi sings Verdi: 31 tenor arias from 25 operas. D. Arthur. por Am Rec G 40:41-4 N '76 *

BERGSTEN, C. Fred
Should U.S. curb imports? interview. pors U.S. News 83:25-6 Ag 8 '77
U.S. commodity policy; address, October 3, 1977. Vital Speeches 44:57-61 N 1 '77

BERGSTROM, Gunnar. See Tengö, J. jt auth

BERICK, David. See Bird, K. jt auth

BERINGER, Johannes
Paleontological hoaxes. A. M. Keen. Natur Hist 86:24+ My '77 *

BERIO, Luciano
Nones; Allelujah II; Concerto for two piano; London Symphony Orchestra. J. Ringo. Am Rec G 40:14-15 Ap '77 *

BERKELEY, Norborne, 1922-
Importance of current trade negotiations on U.S. industry; address, October 13, 1977. Vital Speeches 44:75-8 N 15 '77

BERKELEY, Calif.

Bookstores

See Booksellers and bookselling—California

Organic farming

See Organic farming—California

BERKELEY Campus. See California. University—Berkeley campus

BERKMAN, Ted
(ed) See Jimenez, J. Patty Hearst: my prisoner, my friend

BERKOWITZ, Bernard
—See Newman, M. jt auth

about

Celebrity shrinks. S. Edmiston. il pors Esquire 88:53-6+ Ag '77 *

BERKOWITZ, David
David Berkowitz story. Commonweal 104:547-8 S 2 '77 *
The night TV cried wolf. C. Tucker. Sat R 5:56 O 1 '77 *
Notes and comment. New Yorker 53:19-22 S 5 '77 *
Sam told me to do it...Sam is the devil. il pors Time 110:22-3+ Ag 22 '77 *
Sick world of Son of Sam. P. Axthelm and others. il pors Newsweek 90:16-20+ Ag 22 '77 *
Son of Sam, child of God. Chr Today 21:45-6 S 23 '77 *
Son of Sam—the killer who terrorized New York. il por Read Digest 111:155-60 N '77 *
Tale of midnight. T. Powers. il Commonweal 104:594-6 S 16 '77 *
What about the Son of Sam? P. G. Zimbardo. Psychol Today 11:70 N '77 *
Will he stand trial? D. M. Alpern and S. Agrest. il por Newsweek 90:27-8 Ag 29 '77 *

BERKOWITZ, Monroe
Workers' compensation compared with other disability programs. il M Labor R 100:57-8 Ap '77

BERKSON, William
(ed) Thought control in Mao's China; interview with Chinese intellectual. il Nat R 29:1173-7+ O 14 '77

BERLAND, Theodore
Big killers & how to avoid them. Harp Baz 110:94-5+ Ap '77
Physical disorders & how to cope with them. Harp Baz 110:96-7 Ap '77

BERLIN, Mike
Shark attack at the Riviera. H. Weiskopf. por Sports Illus 46:66 My 9 '77 *

BERLIN

Blockade, 1948-1949

See also
Berlin Airlift

History

Life wasn't a cabaret. S. Spender. il N Y Times Mag p20-1+ O 30 '77
Outwitting the final solution; Jews in Berlin. R. Gay. il Horizon 19:42-7 Ja '77

BERLIN (East Berlin)

Music

See also
Opera—Germany, East

Riots

Unrest erupts. Time 110:56+ O 24 '77

BERLIN (West Berlin)
Whose Berlin? Berlin Now exhibition sponsored by Goethe House in New York. R. Berenson. Nat R 29:565-6 My 13 '77

Labor and laboring classes

They wish us to hell; guest workers. il Time 110:58 O 10 '77

Music

See also
Opera—Germany, West

BERLIN Airlift
Bridge across the sky; condensation. R. Collier. il Read Digest 111:258-62+ N '77
Time of eagles. F. L. Harvey. il Flying 101:276-80 S '77

BERLIN Festival. See Music festivals—Germany, West

BERLIN Film Festival. See Motion picture festivals

BERLIN question, 1945-
President Carter attends economic, Berlin, and NATO meetings at London; text of declaration, May 9, 1977. Dept State Bull 76:593 Je 6 '77

BERLIN University. See Colleges and universities—Germany

BERLINER, Don
Dangerous wake turbulence finally is defeated...with winglets. il Sci Digest 82:72-5 N '77
What were those 585 objects the USAF failed to identify—and why the cover-up? il Sci Digest 82:24-8 Ag '77

BERLINERS
Berlin remembers; donations to the American Red Cross by West Berliners. il Time 109:63 Mr 7 '77

BERLINGUER, Enrico
Enrico's encyclical. il por Time 110:51 N 7 '77 *

BERLINRUT, Peter
Talk with Trotsky. Harpers 254:62-3+ F '77

BERLIOZ, Hector
Boulez signs off with Berlioz Damnation. por Hi Fi 27:MA25 S '77 *
Lélio, ou Le Retour à la vie. J. W. Barker. Am Rec G 41:12-14 N '77 *
Requiem, op. 5; two recordings. Hi Fi 27:93-4 Ap '77 *
Te Deum; Columbia recording. J. W. Barker. il Am Rec G 41:21-2 D '77 *

BERLOW, Alan
Undercutting Miranda. Nation 224:498-500 Ap 23 '77
—See Roeder, E. jt auth
BERMAN, Edgar
Warning: your doctor may be hazardous to your health. Harp Baz 110:128+ F '77
BERMAN, Eleanor
How to get your child to help at home. Harp Baz 110:179+ O '77
Paradores: Spain's castle hotels. il Harp Baz 110:12+ Je '77
BERMAN, Jeffrey
Conrad's Lord Jim and the enigma of sublimation. bibl f Am Imago 33:380-402 Wint '76
BERMAN, Lazar
Behind the Berman legend. S. E. Rubin. il pors N Y Times Mag p33+ O 23 '77 *
Music to my ears. I. Kolodin. Sat R 4:52-3 Ap 16 '77 *
BERMAN, Norman, and Pinto, Andrew
Tackle your spackle for ingenious sculpture. il Design (US) 79:18-19 Fall '77
BERMAN, Reuben
Jerusalem. M. Ronnen. il por Art N 76:101 F '77 *
BERMAN, Ronald S.
Track at the middle distance. New Repub 177: 19-21 Jl 23 '77
about
Devolution at NEH. Nat R 29:932-3 Ag 19 '77 *
BERMAN, Sanford
Cataloging *shtik*. bibl Lib J 102:1251-3 Je 1 '77
Getting to it; a guest editorial. Am Lib 8:77 F '77
BERMAN, Wallace
Los Angeles. M. Wortz. Art N 76:202+ N '77 *
BERMUDA
See also
Fishing—Bermuda
United Nations—Bermuda
Description and travel
Bermuda angle. J. Winslow. il Sat Eve Post 249:90-3+ O '77
Bermuda in the pink. H. Sutton. il Sat R 4: 46-7+ S 3 '77
Bermuda throws a party! vacations for college students. D. Byron. il Seventeen 36:162 F '77
Dream isles for night life or quiet beaches; for singles, couples and families. M. Zellers. Redbook 149:196+ O '77
Thurber's Bermuda. A. Pastore and A. Pastore. il Travel 147:32-7 Mr '77
Race question
Root of the problem. V. E. Smith. Newsweek 90:49 D 19 '77
Riots
Bermuda: the fire this time. il Newsweek 90: 69 D 12 '77
BERMUDA agreement. See Aviation—International aspects
BERMUDA Race. See Yacht racing
BERMUDA Triangle
Bermuda Triangle: hypotheses of Soviet scientists. il Oceans 10:58-9 S '77
Satellite boat watch makes for safe sailing. S. Renner-Smith. map Pop Sci 211:89 O '77
Watchful eye guides craft thru Triangle. il map Sci Digest 82:50-2 Ag '77
BERMUDA Triangle mystery; drama. See Murray, J.
BERMÚDEZ, Morales
Peruvian revolution in crisis. D. P. Werlich. Cur Hist 72:61-4+ F '77 *
BERNAC, Pierre
Certain grace. il Opera N 41:28-32 F 5 '77
BERNACKI, Ralph J. and Kim, Untae
Concomitant elevations in serum sialyltransferase activity and sialic acid content in rats with metastasizing mammary tumors. bibl il Science 195:577-80 F 11 '77
BERNARD, Anne
Born and the unborn alike. America 136:270-2 Mr 26 '77
BERNARD, Jessie
Expanding academic competence. Society 14:8-9 My '77
BERNARD Constantine House. See Savannah, Ga.—Historic houses, sites, etc.
BERNARD W. Baker Sanctuary. See Wildlife sanctuaries—Michigan
BERNARDIN, Joseph Louis, Abp
Bishop to bishop; report of address by J. L. Bernardin. America 137:390 D 3 '77 *
Bishops reply. Chr Today 21:31-2 Je 3 '77 *
BERNARDIN (resort) See Seaside resorts—Yugoslavia
BERNAYS, Edward L.
Visionary and a master stylist helped share modern PR. pors Duns R 110:29-30 S '77 *
BERNE, Eric
Therapies ministers use. J. S. Miller. il Chr Cent 94:504-8 My 25 '77; Discussion. 94:852-4 S 28 '77 *

BERNHARD Ballet. See Ballet companies
BERNHARDT, Mary, and Sprague, Bob
Are we depriving our children of healthy teeth? excerpt from The health robbers, ed by S. Barrett and G. Knight. il Fam Health 9:30-3 Ap '77
BERNHARDT, Peter
San Salvador's urban orchids; with biographical sketch. il Natur Hist 86:9, 64-71 D '77
BERNIER, Rosamond
Art talker; interview. New Yorker 52:28-9 F 14 '77
BERNIKOW, Louise
Harlan; poem. Ms 6:62 S '77
BERNINGHAUS, Oscar E.
Oscar E. Berninghaus: modesty and expertise. M. C. Nelson. il por Am Artist 42:42-7 Ja '78 *
BERNSTEIN, Art
America, the mostest. il Am For 83:24-8 Mr '77
BERNSTEIN, Barbara Elaine
Remedial therapy for the lost art of writing. il Engl J 66:49-51 D '77
BERNSTEIN, Barton J.
Franklin D. Roosevelt and the coming of war with Germany. Intellect 105:360-1 Ap '77
BERNSTEIN, Carl
On the edge. por Newsweek 89:39 My 16 '77
about
Working for the Company. il Time 110:60 S 26 '77 *
BERNSTEIN, Carol. See Berthèrat, T. jt auth
BERNSTEIN, Irving
Easing the constraints of time-oriented work. bibl M Labor R 100:58-60 F '77
BERNSTEIN, Jeremy
Our far-flung correspondents. New Yorker 53: 106-20 S 26 '77
Profiles; Y. Chouinard. New Yorker 52:36-40+ Ja 31 '77
Profiles; L. Thomas. por New Yorker 53:27-32+ Ja 2 '78
Scientific cranks. Am Scholar 47:8+ Wint '77
Sky reporter. Natur Hist 86:106-7+ O '77
BERNSTEIN, Leonard
Bernstein in Israel. G. Paz. il por Hi Fi 27: MA32-3 S '77 *
Bloch: Schelomo; Schumann: Cello concerto. L. M. Smoley. Am Rec G 40:21-3 S '77 *
Musical events. A. Porter. New Yorker 53:51-2 Ja 2 '78 *
BERNSTEIN, Leonard S.
Pickle diet. House B 119:161+ O '77
Tell me where all past years are; story. Sat Eve Post 249:30-2 Ap '77
Theory of the silver bullet. Writer 90:28-9 Ag '77
BERNSTEIN, Marvin
DIY ceramic-tile floor. il Pop Sci 211:102-4 Jl '77
BERNSTEIN, Michael
Nerves; what makes you tic? Harp Baz 110:125+ Mr '77
BERNSTEIN, Peter J.
Here come the dredgers! il Nation 225:614-18 D 10 '77
Those rusty tankers. Nation 224:73-7 Ja 22 '77
Washington won't fight. Nation 224:422-5 Ap 9 '77
BERNSTEIN, Peter W.
Pastor Peterson makes a deal with Citicorp. il pors Fortune 96:140-6+ N '77
BERNSTEIN, Robert L.
—and others
California current eddy formation: ship, air, and satellite results. bibl il maps Science 195: 353-9 Ja 28 '77
about
Bernstein and Albert testify on censorship, currency. S. Wagner. Pub W 211:39+ Je 6 '77 *
BERNSTEIN Festival. See Music festivals—Israel
BEROFF, Michel
Messiaen: Vingt regards sur l'enfant Jésus. D. Garvelmann. por Am Rec G 40:21-2 Ag '77 *
BERRIE, Phillip J.
Assessing instructional needs in your district. bibl Clearing H 50:221-3 Ja '77
BERRIED anemones. See Sea anemones
BERRIEN County, Mich.
How business management improves government; career awareness program. Berrien County, Mich. V. Louviere. il Nations Bus 65: 37-8 Ap '77
BERRIES
See also
Cookery—Fruit
also names of berries, e.g. Cranberries
BERRIGAN, Daniel
Bible parables bristle with modern pains—and hopes—in Seabury book by Berrigan; interview, ed by R. Dahlin. Pub W 211:72 Mr 14 '77
Homecoming; Russian prisoner; poems. Chr Cent 94:655-6 Jl 20 '77
Leveling of John McNeill. Commonweal 104:778-83 D 9 '77
about
Dan Berrigan in Santa Cruz. C. Fager. Chr Cent 94:654-7 Jl 20 '77 *

BERRIGAN, Philip
To be accurate and blunt: the activist as a writer; interview, ed by H. J. Cargas. il por Chr Cent 94:532-4 Je 1 '77
BERROCAL, Migual
Mathematical games. M. Gardner. il Sci Am 238: 14-16+ Ja '78
BERRY, Bryan
Incinerator ship deep-sixes poisons. il Pop Sci 211:105 N '77
BERRY, C. M.
What the Chinese told a visiting U.S. banker; interview. il por U.S. News 83:53-4 Ag 22 '77
BERRY, David
G.R. point. Reviews
Time 109:84 Ap 25 '77 *
BERRY, James W. and Shaffer, Peter
We found virus in our drinking water. il Am City & County 92:65-6 Je '77
BERRY, John
There's only one motto; watch your step! Ret Liv 17:22 Jl '77 *
BERRY, John M.
Meet John Berry. por Forbes 120:6 Jl 15 '77 *
BERRY, R. Stephen. See Abrams, N. E. jt auth
BERRY, Wendell
Converse; The wind too; Anniverse; The hidden singer; The watchers; Now; A meeting; The first; poems. Harpers 255:65 S '77
Hill land farming: how the experts view its future. Org Gard & Farm 24:68-71 Ap '77
Life on and off schedule. il Org Gard & Farm 24:44+ Ag '77
PW interviews; ed by A. W. Ehrlich. por Pub W 212:10-11 S 5 '77
Some difficulties to think about before buying a farm. il Org Gard & Farm 24:59-61 Jl '77
—and Logsdon, Gene
Sanitation laws squeeze out small producers. il Org Gard & Farm 24:43-6+ O '77
BERRY-eating birds. See Birds, Injurious and beneficial
BERRYMAN, John
Grace soften my dreams—John Berryman. J. Leax. Chr Today 21:25-6 Ap 1 '77 *
BERRYMAN, Phillip
Cost of coffee. il Environment 19:12-15 Ag '77
BERTELSMANN Publishing Group (firm)-Bantam Books, Inc merger. See Publishers and publishing—Acquisitions and mergers
BERTHERAT, Therese, and Bernstein, Carol
Marvelous new route to total body awareness; excerpt from The body has its reasons. Mademoiselle 83:165+ My '77
BERTHS, Boat. See Boats—Berths
BERTINELLI, Valerie
Valerie loves Elton John and football and Clancy the cat and hats like this. il pors Seventeen 36:138-41 My '77 *
BERTOLUCCI, Bernardo
Messy fight for the final cut. il Time 109: 70-1 My 2 '77 *
Screen. C. L. Westerbeck, Jr. Commonweal 104: 820 D 23 '77; 105:16-18 Ja 6 '78 *
BERTON, Pierre
Joshua Slocum's magnificent voyage; excerpt from My country. il Read Digest 110:218-20+ F '77
BERTRAM, Christoph
View from Europe. por U.S. News 82:48-9 Je 27 '77
BERTRAM, Lenore
High style in Miami. il Motor B & S 140:84 Ag '77
BERTRAND, John
Sailing fast with John Bertrand. D. Rose. il por Yachting 142:38+ Jl '77 *
BERTSCH, Gary K.
Ethnicity and politics in socialist Yugoslavia. bibl f il Ann Am Acad 433:88-99 S '77
BERUBE, Maurice R.
Revolt against college. Commonweal 104:233-6 Ap 15 '77
BERYLLIUM
Occupational cancer: government challenged in beryllium proceeding. D. Shapley. Science 198: 898-9+ D 2 '77
BESANT, Larry X.
Copyright dilemma. Lib J 102:1337-9 Je 15 '77
BESHARSE, Joseph C. and others
Photoreceptor outer segments: accelerated membrane renewal in rods after exposure to light. bibl il Science 196:536-8 Ap 29 '77
BESSERAT, Denise Schmandt-. See Schmandt-Besserat, D.
BESSIE Coleman Aviators Club. See Aviation clubs
BESSO, Michele
Einstein and his closest friend. G. M. Spruch. il pors Phys Today 30:9+ Mr '77 *
BEST, Arthur. See Andreasen, A. R. jt auth
BEST, Connie, and Best, Winfield
Kids afraid to grow up. il Parents Mag 52:58-9+ O '77
BEST, Harold M.
Music: offerings of creativity; interview, ed by C. Forbes. por Chr Today 21:12-15 My 6 '77
BEST, Winfield. See Best, C. jt auth
BEST books. See Books and reading—Best books
BEST present of all; drama. See Sollid, L.
BEST Products Company. See Chain stores
BEST sellers
Computers star in expanded New York times best seller lists. D. Maryles. il Pub W 212:22 S 5 '77
Continuing phenomenon of the religious best seller. G. C. Wharton. Pub W 211:82-3 Mr 14 '77
PW hardcover best sellers. See issues of Publishers weekly
PW paperback best sellers. See issues of Publishers weekly
Publishers report top-selling juveniles. Pub W 211:97-8 F 28 '77
Top-selling children's books. Pub W 212:85-7 Jl 18 '77
Year in review: the best sellers. D. Maryles. Pub W 211:38-40 F 14 '77
Year in review: the paperback scene; Trade paperbacks in 1976. G. Stuttaford. Pub W 211:41-3 F 14 '77
BESTER, Alfred
(ed) See Stinnett, C. PW interviews
BESTON, Henry
Voices of the surf; excerpt from The outermost house. il Read Digest 111:45-8 D '77
BETA-endorphin. See Endorphins
BETENSLEY, Bertha
Buttonhooks combined with various useful items. il Hobbies 82:139+ My '77
BETHE, Hans Albrecht
Need for nuclear power. bibl il por Bull Atom Sci 33:59-63 Mr; 55 S '77
BETHEL, Gar
Pittsburgh center pinpoints the art of the needle; Center for the history of American Needlework. Craft Horiz 37:42 Ag '77
BETHELL, Tom
Darwin's mistake. bibl Chr Today 21:12-15 Je 17 '77
Myth of an adversary press. il Harpers 254:33-40 Ja; 6 Mr '77
Rewards of enterprise. New Repub 177:17-19 Jl 9 '77
Washington's world of style. il Harpers 256:66-9+ Ja '78

about

Media: truth or consequences? M. Novak. Chr Cent 94:317-18 Ap 6 '77 *
BETHLEHEM Steel Corporation
Bethlehem's bind in Johnstown; air pollution moratorium request. il Bus W p40+ Ag 15 '77
BETHUNE, George Amory
Faneuil family silver cruet stand rediscovered. R. Feigenbaum. il Antiques 112:120-1 Jl '77 *
BETJEMAN, Sir John
Comment. R. Howard. Poetry 129:231-2 Ja '77 *
Royal paean. por Time 109:74-5 F 21 '77 *
BETTEN, Neil, and Austin, Michael
Unwanted helping hand. bibl il Environment 19: 13-20+ Ja '77
BETTER Business Bureaus
Role of business self-regulation in a changing world; address, October 11, 1977. W. H. Tankersley. Vital Speeches 44:125-8 D 1 '77
BETTING. See Gambling; Horse race betting
BETTIS, Valerie
Valerie Bettis: looking back; interview, ed by H. M. Simpson. il pors Dance Mag 51:51-66 F '77
BETTS, Henry Brognard
Latest on helping the handicapped; interview. il por U.S. News 82:61-3 Ja 31 '77
BETTS, William J.
Amphibious flycatcher. il Org Gard & Farm 24: 120+ Ap '77
BETTS, William W. Jr
Turkey and the beech. il Nat Wildlife 15:18-23 O '77
BETTY, L. Stafford
Importance of psychical research for religion. bibl Intellect 106:168-70 O '77
BETTY, Maurice Moore-. See Moore-Betty, M.
BETZ, Dorothy
(tr) See Levy, B. H. Trouble in Red City
BEVERAGE containers
Containing waste. E. A. Goldstein. bibl il Environment 19:42-4 O '77
Throwaways. Audubon 79:150 Ja '77

Laws and regulations

Federal label on bottle bills; proposed national deposit law effect on beverage industry. il Bus W p84-5 F 21 '77
Government bans sale of throwaway bottles in parks. Nat Parks & Con Mag 51:22 Jl '77

BEVERAGE industry
Federal label on bottle bills; proposed national deposit law effect on beverage industry. il Bus W p84-5 F 21 '77
See also
Brewing industry
Liquor industry
Soft drink industry
Wine industry

Finance

Food & drink. il Forbes 121:156+ Ja 9 '78

BEVERAGE mixes
Chocolate drink mixes. Consumer Rep 42:83-5 D '77
Orange drink mixes. Consumer Rep 42:68-70 F '77

BEVERAGES
Beware of coffee, tea, and cola beverages if you value good health. H. L. Abrams, Jr. Consumers Res Mag 60:21-2+ My '77
Celebration sippers. S. P. Torpey. il Bet Hom & Gard 55:112-13 D '77
Herb-flavored drinks. il Org Gard & Farm 24:117 N '77
Summer coolers from Mexico. il Sunset 159:130 Jl '77
Switchel—the Yankee haymakers' drink. W. E. Keys. il Org Gard & Farm 24:100-1 Je '77
These summer coolers are two-way treats. L. B. Downs. il House B 119:90 Jl '77
Thirst quenchers. J. Mayer. il Fam Health 9:32-4+ Je '77
See also
Alcoholic beverages
Cider
Coffee
Milkshakes
Punch (beverage)
Tea (beverage)

BEVERLY Hills Supper Club, Southgate, Ky. See Night clubs

BEWLEY, Lois M.
Canadian caution. Lib J 102:1727 S 1 '77

BEYER, Andrew
Days of wine and races. Esquire 87:92-3+ Ap '77

BEYER, Monica M. and others
Unilateral nephrectomy: effect on survival in NZB/NZW mice. bibl il Science 198:511-13 N 4 '77

BHAJAN (yogi)
Yogi Bhajan's synthetic Sikhism. il pors Time 110:70-1 S 5 '77 *

BHUTTO, Zulfikar Ali
Pakistan is being singled out for discrimination by U.S; interview, ed by J. N. Wallace. il por U.S. News 82:71-2 Mr 14 '77

about

Absentee candidate. T. Clifton. Newsweek 90:46 O 3 '77 *
Bhutto gets bounced. R. Steele and others. il por Newsweek 90:27-9 Jl 18 '77 *
Bhutto hangs on, but his troubles grow. il Time 109:38 My 2 '77 *
Bhutto's last card. R. Carroll and T. Clifton. il por Newsweek 89:57+ My 2 '77 *
Bitter victory. por Time 109:42+ Ap 11 '77 *
Evil genius. Time 110:51+ S 19 '77 *
Rioting for a recount. M. Sheils and T. Clifton. il por Newsweek 89:39+ Ap 25 '77 *
Sir, the troops have come. pors Time 110:29-30 Jl 18 '77 *

BIAGGI, Mario
Excerpt from remarks on amnesty for illegal aliens, April 22, 1977. Cong Digest 56:247+ O '77

BIBESCO, H.
Lunch with Uncle Ez. Atlantic 240:55-8 Ag '77

BIBESCO, Marthe Lucie (Lahovary) Princess
Last Tsar. il por Sat Eve Post 249:46-7 Jl '77

BIBLE
See also
Creation
Light and darkness in the Bible
Sex in the Bible

Antiquities

Self-discoveries in the Middle East. J. Swetnam. America 136:292-5 Ap 2 '77
See also
Noah's Ark

Bibliography

Both testaments; key books of '76. C. E. Armerding and W. W. Gasque. Chr Today 21:12-13 Mr 18 '77

Biography

Isaac syndrome. S. G. Shoham. bibl f Am Imago 33:329-49 Wint '76

Chronology

New Testament dating game; views of J. A. T. Robinson. il por Time 109:95 Mr 21 '77

Covenants

See Covenants (theology)

Criticism, interpretation, etc.

Word. G. McCauley. See issues of America

Bibliography

Books about the book, words about the Word. America 137:380-8 N 26 '77

Economic aspects

Sharing the wealth: the church as biblical model for public policy. R. J. Sider. il Chr Cent 94:560-5 Je 8 '77

Evidence, authority, etc.

Battle for the Bible: renewing the inerrancy debate. D. W. Dayton; discussion. Chr Cent 94:198-9 Mr 2 '77
From myth to myth. E. Schaeffer. Chr Today 21:45-6 S 9 '77
Is God as good as his word? G. A. Taylor. Chr Today 21:22-5 F 4 '77
Philosophy: the roots of vain deceit. N. L. Geisler. Chr Today 21:8-12 My 20 '77
Whither biblical inerrancy? J. W. Montgomery. Chr Today 21:40+ Jl 29 '77
See also
International Council on Biblical Inerrancy

Anecdotes, facetiae, satire, etc.

Noninerrancy debate. M. E. Marty. Chr Cent 94:311 Mr 30 '77

Food

Communion as a culinary art. W. H. Willimon. Chr Cent 94:829-30 S 21 '77
See also
Hunger in the Bible

Homosexuality

See Homosexuality in the Bible

Hunger

See Hunger in the Bible

Inerrancy

See Bible—Evidence, authority, etc.

Inspiration

See also
Bible—Evidence, authority, etc.

Literary character

Sanctification of literature. H. Fisch. Commentary 63:63-9 Je '77

Liturgical use

Our apostasy in worship. J. F. White. Chr Cent 94:842-5 S 28 '77

Manuscripts

Books the Bible left out. K. L. Woodward and J. B. Cumming, Jr. il por Newsweek 90:121+ N 28 '77
See also
Book of Durrow

Mineralogy

No salt in the city; church and the ghetto. K. Phillips. il Chr Today 21:12-15 My 20 '77

Music

Christians are singing people. E. Schaeffer. Chr Today 21:24-5 Ja 7 '77
Music: a bridge through time. E. Schaeffer. Chr Today 21:22 Je 17 '77

Publication and distribution

Rembrandt's art illustrates gift edition of The living Bible from Abrams. R. Dahlin. il Pub W 212:118 S 26 '77

Study and teaching

Church teaching: content without context. L. Richards. il Chr Today 21:16-18 Ap 15 '77
Sunday school is a start. Chr Today 21:38-9 Ap 15 '77

Theology

See also
Divorce—Biblical teaching
Justice—Biblical teaching
Wine—Biblical teaching

Translations

See Bible—Versions

Versions

Seven versions of the Bible. il Sat Eve Post 249:68-9 Ap '77
Story behind the book: Good News Bible; interview, ed by R. Dahlin. W. Hutchinson. Pub W 211:78 Mr 14 '77
See also
Wycliffe Bible Translators, Inc

Anecdotes, facetiae, satire, etc.

Much babbling about the Book; Good News Bible. M. E. Marty. Chr Cent 94:23 Ja 5 '77

Old Testament

See also
Commandments, Ten

Bibliography

Old Testament; key books of '76. C. E. Armerding. il Chr Today 21:17-19 Mr 18 '77

BIBLE—Old Testament—*Continued*

Criticisms, interpretation, etc

Bible: a fallible guide. map Time 110:32 Jl 25 '77

Manuscripts

See also
Dead Sea Scrolls

Genesis

See also
Noah's Ark

Job

Suffering of Job. R. A. F. MacKenzie. America 136:242 Mr 19 '77

Jonah

After three days and three nights. . . H. Lindsell. Chr Today 21:14-16 Ap 1 '77

New Testament

See also
Jesus Christ

Bibliography

New Testament: key books of '76. W. W. Gasque. il Chr Today 21:13-16 Mr 18 '77

Chronology

See Bible—Chronology

BIBLE as literature. See Bible—Literary character

BIBLE characters. See Bible—Biography

BIBLE in literature
Argument for Milton's Dalila; Samson Agonistes. J. Colony. Yale R 66:562-75 Je '77

BIBLE Memory Association. See Bible societies

BIBLE societies
Shift at the top; Bible Memory Association. E. E. Plowman. Chr Today 22:43 D 30 '77
See also
International Council on Biblical Inerrancy

BIBLE study. See Bible—Study and teaching

BIBLICAL archeology. See Bible—Antiquities

BIBLICAL inerrancy. See Bible—Evidence, authority, etc.

BIBLIOGRAPHICAL control
NCLIS and ACET conduct Project Mediabase. SLJ 23:14-15 Ap '77
Public libraries, the Library of Congress, and the national bibliographic network; adaptation of address, February 1977. M. J. Freedman. il Lib J 102:2211-15 N 1 '77
Wanted: a minicomputer serials control system. R. De Gennaro. bibl Lib J 102:878-9 Ap 15 '77
Yes, Virginia, is there a national bibliographic network? ALA institute. A. Plotnik. Am Lib 8:176+ Ap '77

BIBLIOGRAPHY
See also subhead Bibliography under various subjects, e.g. Art—Bibliography

BIC Pen Corporation
Gillette after the diversification that failed. il Bus W p58-62 F 28 '77

BIC Pen Corporation-American Safety Razor Company merger. See Corporations—Acquisitions and mergers

BICENTENNIAL celebration (United States) See United States—Centennial celebrations, etc.

BICENTENNIAL Conference on the United States Constitution. See American Academy of Political and Social Science

BICENTENNIAL school projects. See United States—Centennial celebrations, etc.—School projects

BICKEL, Lennard
This accursed land; excerpt from Mawson's will. il por map Read Digest 111:199-202+ Jl '77

BICKERING. See Quarrels

BICKFORD, Edward Davidson
Why government should stay out of steel pricing. il por Nations Bus 65:40-2 Ja '77

BICYCLE industry
Bicycle boom pedals into high gear. il U.S. News 83:69-70 D 19 '77
Court switches franchising signals; Schwinn Bicycle Company ruling. Bus W p30 Jl 11 '77
Huffy puts new spin in the bicycle business. il Bus W p 134 O 10 '77

BICYCLE racing
Another kind of bike racing. B. George. il Mech Illus 73:66-7+ Ag '77
Staying under 55mph (but not by much) International Human Powered Speed Championship. B. Hartford. il Pop Mech 148:104-5 S '77

BICYCLE racks
Bikes get boost from mass transit. il Am City & County 92:48 Ja '77
Space-saver bicycle rack. il Mech Illus 73:152 O '77

BICYCLE routes. See Cycling

BICYCLE seats, Add-on. See Bicycles—Equipment

BICYCLES
Bicycle boom pedals into high gear. il U.S. News 83:69-70 D 19 '77
Bikes. New Yorker 53:34 My 9 '77
Electric bike. D. Scott. il Pop Sci 210:48+ Mr '77
Hang on to that balloon-tire bike! L. Dixon. il Pop Mech 149:52-3+ Ja '78
How to build a bicycle built for two out of two built for one; tandems. E. A. Sloane. il Pop Mech 147:43-5+ Je '77
Pedal power; excerpts. il Org Gard & Farm 24:82-92 Je '77
Ten-speed bikes. Consumer Rep 42:134-40 D '77
See also
Cycling
Mopeds

Design

Bicycles built for speed; racing bikes. R. Bongartz. il Horizon 19:56-9 Jl '77

Equipment

Add-on bike seats for children. Consumer Rep 42:140-1 D '77
Bike hiking. K. Reading. Seventeen 36:68 S '77
11 new add-ons for cycling fun. E. A. Sloane. il Pop Mech 147:258-60 My '77
Rear wheel bicycle adapter: building instructions. D. Branch. il Org Gard & Farm 24:85-7 Je '77
See also
Speedometers

Maintenance and repair

Spring cycle shape-up. S. Schenk. il Seventeen 36:50 Ap '77
Tune-up tips for midsummer bicycling. E. A. Sloane. il Pop Mech 148:161-3 Ag '77

Safety devices and measures

Is your bicycle safe? C. A. Robbins. il McCalls 104:54-5 S '77

Storage

Bike storage unit for city apartments. il House B 119:80 S '77

BICYCLING. See Cycling

BIDDLE, Livingston Ludlow, 1918-
Federal pie. por Horizon 20:72-3 D '77 *
Populism vs. elitism. R. Steele and others. il Newsweek 90:39 O 31 '77 *

BIDLACK, Russell E.
Schools do the judging: evaluating the Accreditation Committee. Am Lib 8:442-3 S '77

BIDNER, Robert
Cars had faces then. J. Flint. il Esquire 88:111-15 N '77 *

BIEDERMAN, Charles Joseph
Charles Biederman's abstract analogues for nature. D. B. Kuspit. bibl il Art in Am 65:80-3 My '77 *

BIEGLER, John Charles
Who shall set accounting standards? address, February 22, 1977. Vital Speeches 43:347-9 Mr 15 '77

BIEGON, Brad
Mars landing: like a final roll of dice. . . il por Space World N-1-157:28 Ja '77

BIEL, Heinz H.
Stock comments. See issues of Forbes

BIELEFELD, Germany

Music

See also
Opera—Germany, West

BIEMILLER, Andrew J.
Excerpts from testimony on the proposed Fair Labor Standards Act, March 9, 1977. Cong Digest 56:152+ My '77

BIENNIAL of New Music, Cleveland. See Music festivals—Ohio

BIERCE, Ambrose
Satan's lexicographer. L. Harris. Am Heritage 28:56-63 Ap '77 *

BIERMAN, Sheldon, and Hunt, G. T.
Geothermal energy. Nation 225:487-9 N 12 '77

BIERMANN, June, and Toohey, Barbara
Big wheels; excerpt from Biking for grownups. il Fam Health 9:50-2 Ag '77

BIERSCHWAL, C. J.
Here's expert advice on calving problems. J. D. Ritchie. il Farm J 101:LK2-3+ Mr '77 *

BIFFLE, Dick
Combat on the border. il pors Ebony 32:104-6+ Ap '77 *

BIG Apple Circus. See Circus

BIG BASIN Redwoods State Park. See California—Parks and reserves

BIG BEND National Park
Big Bend gambusia: . . . and then there were three. J. M. Schlatter. il Nat Parks & Con Mag 51:8-10 N '77

BIG business
See also
Competition
Corporations—Size

BIG CYPRESS National Preserve
Big Cypress: tomorrow has arrived. J. G. Mitchell. il map Audubon 79:20-31 S '77
Putting the Big Cypress together again. M. F. Toner. il map Nat Parks & Con Mag 51:4-9 Mr '77

BIG DIOMEDE Island. See Diomede Islands

BIG game hunting. See Hunting

BIG SKY, Mont (resort) See Resorts

BIG Sky Realty of Montana (firm) See Real estate business

BIG SUR, Calif.
Sleeping space in and near Big Sur. Sunset 159:26 S '77

BIG THICKET
Big Thicket; interviews with residents; excerpt from Big Thicket legacy. il Am Heritage 28: 44-51 Je '77

BIG THICKET National Preserve
Big Thicket, born again. P. A. Y. Gunter. il map Nat Wildlife 15:4-11 Je '77

BIG THOMPSON River flood. See Floods—United States

BIG Three Industries Inc
Hardest decision of them all. por Forbes 120:50 D 1 '77

BIGAZZI, Pierluigi E. and others
Sperm autoantibodies in vasectomized rats of different inbred strains. bibl il Science 197: 1282-3 S 23 '77

BIGFOOT. See Animals, Mythical

BIGGERS, Earl Derr
Murder number one. J. L. Breen. New Repub 177:38-9 Jl 30 '77 *

BIGOTRY. See Prejudice

BIGWOOD, Catherine
Books. Am Home 80:20 Ap; 26 O; 10 D '77

BIKALES, Gerda
Immigration policy: the new environmental battlefield. il Nat Parks & Con Mag 51:13-16 D '77

BIKE routes. See Cycling

BIKEWAYS. See Cycling

BIKING. See Cycling

BIKO, Stephen
Biko on death; excerpts from interview. New Repub 178:11-13 Ja 7 '78
I must keep this country safe; interview, ed by W. McWhirter. J. Kruger. pors Time 110:38 O 17 '77

about

Apartheid Committee pays tribute to deceased young African leader; Mr Biko left deep mark on South African scene, says Secretary-General. UN Chron 14:25-6 O '77 *
Biko's last days. S. Strasser and P. Younghusband. il Newsweek 90:74 N 28 '77 *
Death of a prisoner. por Time 110:35 S 26 '77 *
Inquest into a curious death. il Time 110:53 N 28 '77 *
No-fault verdict. R. Carroll and P. Younghusband. il Newsweek 90:67+ D 12 '77 *
Steve Biko is dead. Nation 225:356-7 O 15 '77 *
Steve Biko is dead. R. Carroll and P. Younghusband. il pors Newsweek 90:41-2 S 26 '77 *
Steve Biko: liberator and martyr. T. W. Jennings. Chr Cent 94:997-9 N 2 '77 *
Tragic turn to terrorism. K. Willenson and P. Younghusband. il por Newsweek 90:50-1 O 10 '77 *

BILALIANS. See Black Muslims

BILANDIC, Michael A.
Arrangement. J. Lelyveld. il por N Y Times Mag p 138 Mr 27 '77 *
Bilandic the bland. R. Steele and F. Maier. Newsweek 89:29-30 Ap 18 '77 *
Janie and the Mayor. D. A. Williams and F. Maier. il pors Newsweek 90:40 D 5 '77 *

BILATERAL air agreements. See Aviation—International aspects

BILD, Richard W. and Wasson, J. T.
Netschaëvo: a new class of chondritic meteorite. bibl il Science 197:58-62 Jl 1 '77

BILDERBACK, Trudy
Students print a calendar. il Sch Arts 77:18-19 D '77

BILE ducts
Fascioliassis: role of proline in bile duct hyperplasia. H. Isseroff and others. bibl il Science 198:1157-9 D 16 '77

BILGORE, Ellen
Games people play. il House & Gard 149:128+ N '77

BILINGUAL collections in libraries. See School libraries—Bilingual collections

BILINGUAL education. See Education, Bilingual

BILL collecting. See Collecting of accounts

BILL of Rights (United States) See United States—Constitution—Bill of Rights

BILL of Rights Day. See Human Rights Day and Week

BILL payment services, Bank. See Banks and banking—Services

BILLBOARDS
Art as big as all outdoors. il Horizon 21:23-9 Ja '78
Low-priced spread. il Forbes 119:64 Ja 15 '77
November street show in S.F; paintings on billboards. il Sunset 159:23-4 N '77
Spectacolor; animated-light billboard in Times Square. New Yorker 52:27-8 F 14 '77
Whatever happened to: billboard removal: states drag their feet. il U.S. News 82:68 F 14 '77

BILLFISH fishing. See Sailfish fishing

BILLIARDS
Easy times the hard way; pool shooter D. DiLiberto. B. McDermott. il Sports Illus 47:54-62+ Ag 8 '77
Hustler meets an artist; Challenge of Champions. M. DelNagro. il pors Sports Illus 46: 52+ Je 27 '77
Minnesota Fats: benefit performance. New Yorker 53:23-4 Jl 4 '77
Poetry in motion on the long green. M. Wellemeyer. il Fortune 95:67+ F '77

BILLING, J. R. and Grouni, H. N.
Elevated guideways can be good neighbors. il Am City & County 92:87-8 S '77

BILLING services, Bank. See Banks and banking—Services

BILLINGS, Roger
Hydrogen. P. Luedtke. por Sci Digest 82:68-72 O '77 *

BILLINGS, Victoria
Breakup: how he feels when it's over. Seventeen 36:94-5 Jl '77

BILLINGTON, James Hadley
Wilson Center immerses scholars in think tank. E. P. Morgan. il pors Smithsonian 8:76-83 Ag '77 *

BILLINGTON, Ray A.
Informal chronicle of the Western History Association. il Am West 14:30-1+ S '77

BILLS (legislation) See Legislation

BILTMORE Hotel. See New York (city)—Hotels, restaurants, etc.

BIMINI Big Game Club Members Tournament. See Fishing—Competitions

BINAISA, Godfrey L.
Organization of African Unity and decolonization: present and future trends. bibl f Ann Am Acad 432:52-69 Jl '77

BINARY stars. See Stars, Double

BINAURAL sound reproduction. See Sound—Recording and reproducing

BINDING (books) See Bookbinding

BING, Elisabeth, and Colman, Libby
Sex during pregnancy; excerpt from Making love during pregnancy. il Redbook 150:89-90+ N '77

BINGHAM, Eula
Critics size up OSHA's new chief. por Bus W p38 F 28 '77 *
Eula Bingham: will she take the nonsense out of OSHA? pors Nations Bus 65:28-32 Ag '77 *

BINGHAM, Jonathan Brewster
Should U.S. do business with Cuba? interview. pors U.S. News 82:73-4 Mr 7 '77 *

BINGHAM, June
Carter, Castro and Reinhold Niebuhr. Chr Cent 94:775-6 S 14 '77

BINGHAM, Walter
Ambush on the comeback trail. il pors Sports Illus 47:34-5 N 14 '77
College football. Sports Illus 47:50+ S 26 '77
Football. il Sports Illus 47:60+ O 10 '77
Isn't it warm, isn't it cozy, side by side. il Sports Illus 47:22-3 D 12 '77
It wasn't all in the cards. il pors Sports Illus 46:22-5 Ap 11 '77
It's hard to pass the Bucs. il Sports Illus 46: 16-19 My 30 '77
Nary a bomb in the rockets' red glare. il Sports Illus 47:20-1 N 21 '77
South America takes it away. il Sports Illus 46:20-1 My 9 '77
Track & field. pors Sports Illus 46:56+ Ap 25 '77

BINGHAMTON, N.Y.

Music

Debuts & reappearances. il Hi Fi 27:MA18 Mr '77

See also

Opera—New York (state)

BINKLEY, Sue, and others
Timekeeping by the pineal gland. bibl il Science 197:1181-3 S 16 '77

BINOCULAR cameras. See Cameras

BINOCULARS. See Field glasses

BINS
Bins that are big enough . . . il Farm J 101: 22-3 Ag '77

BIOASSAY. See Biological assay

BIOCHEMISTRY
From joy to depression: new insights into the chemistry of moods. M. Scarf. il N Y Times Mag p30-4+ Ap 24 '77; Same abr. with title What makes our moods? Read Digest 111:45-7+ Ag '77

See also

Immunochemistry
Neurochemistry

BIOCLIMATOLOGY

See also

Weather—Mental and physiological effects

BIOCRYSTALLOGRAPHY. See Crystallography

BIODEGRADATION
Degradation of DNA by nucleases in intestinal tract of rats. L. Maturin and R. Curtiss, 3d. bibl il Science 196:216-18 Ap 8 '77
Protein degradation: putting the research together. G. B. Kolata. il Science 198:596-8 N 11 '77

BIO-DYNAMIC/French intensive method. See Organic gardening

BIOELECTRICITY. See Electrophysiology

BIOENERGETICS
Energy limits crop improvement. Sci N 111:23 Ja 8 '77
Intravenous self-feeding: long-term regulation of energy balance in rats. S. Nicolaïdis and N. Rowland. bibl il Science 195:589-91 F 11 '77
Nutritional outputs and energy inputs in seafoods. M. Rawitscher and J. Mayer. bibl il Science 198:261-4 O 21 '77
Terrestrial locomotion in penguins: it costs more to waddle. B. Pinshow and others. bibl il Science 195:592-4 F 11 '77
See also
Energy metabolism

BIOENGINEERING
Artificial organs and beyond. J. A. Miller. il Sci N 112:154-6 S 3 '77

BIOETHICS
Scientist and environmental bioethics; symposium. bibl BioScience 27:251-8+ Ap '77
Scientist: trustee for humanity. B. Glass. bibl BioScience 27:277-8 Ap '77
When man becomes as god: the biological prospect. A. Rosenfeld. il Sat R 5:14-20 D 10 '77
See also
Institute of Society, Ethics and Life Sciences
Medical ethics

BIOFEEDBACK training
Biofeedback picture: negative. Sci N 112:22 Jl 9 '77
Biofeedback: what it is and how it can help you; interview. E. Green. il pors U.S. News 82:63-4 Ap 4 '77
Fighting stress. L. Smith. il Duns R 109:59-61 Ja '77
Tuning in on the twilight zone. T. Budzynski. bibl il pors Psychol Today 11:38-9+ Ag '77

BIOGAS as fuel. See Fuel

BIOGEOCHEMICAL cycles
Anthropogenic CO emissions: implications for the atmospheric CO-OH-CH_4 cycle. N. D. Sze. il Science 195:673-5 F 18 '77
Biomethylation of toxic elements in the environment. W. P. Ridley and others. bibl il Science 197:329-32 Jl 22 '77
See also
Carbon cycle (biogeochemistry)
Detritus
Nitrogen—Fixation
Nitrogen cycle

BIOGEOGRAPHY. See Geographical distribution of animals and plants

BIOGRAPHICAL films. See Motion pictures—Biographical films

BIOGRAPHY
History's 50-minute hour; psychobiography. K. L. Woodward and others. il Newsweek 89:96+ Ap 18 '77
Psychobiography of everyday life. R. W. Noland. Nation 224:570-2 My 7 '77
See also
Autobiography
Obituaries

Bibliography

Biography (cont) F. X. J. Homer. America 136:428-30 My 7 '77
Richard Ellmann on biography. R. Ellmann. il New Repub 177:26+ N 26 '77

Study and teaching

Lesson of the master; L. Edel, Vernon Visiting Professorship of Biography. por Time 110:47 Ag 22 '77

BIOLOGICAL apparatus and supplies
New products. See issues of BioScience

BIOLOGICAL assay
Hepatitis B "e" antigen: an apparent association with lactate dehydrogenase isozyme-5. G. N. Vyas and others. bibl il Science 198:1068-70 D 9 '77
Human chorionic gonadotropin-like substance in nonendocrine tissues of normal subjects. Y. Yoshimoto and others. bibl il Science 197:575-7 Ag 5 '77
Medicine: spotlight on hormones. Sci N 112:260 O 22 '77
New way to detect variant hemoglobins. Sci N 111:407 Je 25 '77
1977 Nobel prize in physiology or medicine. J. Meites. il pors Science 198:594-6 N 11 '77
Plasmid detection and sizing in single colony lysates. W. M. Barnes. bibl il Science 195:393-4 Ja 28 '77
Primary bioassay of human tumor stem cells. A. W. Hamburger and S. E. Salmon. bibl il Science 197:461-3 Jl 29 '77
Quantitation of cytoplasmic tubulin by radioimmunoassay. J. L. Morgan and others. bibl il Science 197:578-80 Ag 5 '77
Radioimmunoassay for abnormal hemoglobins. F. A. Garver and others. bibl il Science 196:1334-6 Je 17 '77
Radioimmunoassay for antibodies to cytoplasmic ribosomes in human serum. D. Koffler and others. bibl il Science 198:741-3 N 18 '77
Work for which Dr Yalow won the Nobel Prize; radioimmunoassay. il por Parents Mag 53:39+ Ja '78
Yalow wins half of Nobel Prize in medicine. H. R. Leuchtag. pors Phys Today 30:78-9 D '77

BIOLOGICAL chemistry. See Biochemistry

BIOLOGICAL clocks. See Biology—Periodicity

BIOLOGICAL control of insects. See Insect control—Biological control

BIOLOGICAL control systems
Norepinephrine-dopamine interactions and behavior. S. M. Antelman and A. R. Caggiula. bibl Science 195:646-53 F 18 '77
Oscillation and chaos in physiological control systems. M. C. Mackey and L. Glass. bibl il Science 197:287-9 Jl 15 '77
Phase control of neural pacemakers. A. T. Winfree. bibl il Science 197:761-3 Ag 19 '77
See also
Biofeedback training

BIOLOGICAL laboratories
Recombinant lab for DNA and my 95 days in it; H. Boyer's lab at the University of California's School of Medicine in San Francisco. J. L. Hopson. il pors Smithsonian 8:54-63 Je '77
See also
California. University—Scripps Institution of Oceanography

BIOLOGICAL luminescence. See Bioluminescence

BIOLOGICAL models
To build a brain; electronic models of nerve cells. J. A. Miller. il por Sci N 111:156-7 Mr 5 '77

BIOLOGICAL research
Biology briefs. See issues of BioScience
See also
Brain research
Genetic research

BIOLOGICAL rhythms. See Biology—Periodicity

BIOLOGICAL Sciences Curriculum Study
GAO decision on NSF claim favors curriculum study group. J. Walsh. Science 197:234 Jl 15 '77

BIOLOGICAL societies
See also
American Institute of Biological Sciences
Genetics Society of America
Society for Neuroscience

BIOLOGICAL transport
Adrenergic stimulation of taurine transport by the heart. R. Huxtable and J. Chubb. bibl il Science 198:409-11 O 28 '77
Chloride transport across isolated opercular epithelium of killifish: a membrane rich in chloride cells. K. J. Karnaky, Jr and others. bibl il Science 195:203-5 Ja 14 '77
Transport interaction of cystine and dibasic amino acids in renal brush border vesicles. S. Segal and others. bibl il Science 197:169-71 Jl 8 '77

BIOLOGISTS
Biologist census. R. Trumbull. il BioScience 27:192-5 Mr '77
Biology and developing standard methods; letter. J. Cairns, Jr. BioScience 27:444 Jl '77
Ecofreaks, technofreaks, and one-armed biologists; excerpt from address. W. S. Hillman. BioScience 27:315 My '77
People and places. See issues of BioScience

BIOLOGY
Biology (cont) Sci N 111:40, 89, 153, 202, 266, 410; 112:73, 104, 152, 201, 216, 233, 297, 393 Ja 15, F 5, Mr 5, 26, Ap 23, Je 25, Jl 30, Ag 13, S 3, 24-O 8, N 5, D 10 '77
Revising the facts of life; excerpt from The life science: current ideas of biology. P. Medawar and J. S. Medawar. Harpers 254:41-8+ F '77
See also
Artificial satellites—Biological use
Biochemistry
Bioengineering
Cells
Environment
Eugenics
Evolution
Fresh water biology
Heredity
Hybridization
Marine biology
Microbiology
Molecular biology
Morphogenesis
Mutation (biology)
Natural history
Parthenogenesis

BIOLOGY—See also—*Continued*
Polarity (biology)
Population biology
Regeneration (biology)
Reproduction
Space biology
Symbiosis
Zoology

Bibliography

Books. See issues of BioScience

History

Aristotle's biology. L. P. Coonen. bibl BioScience 27:733-8 N '77
Jefferson: quiet patron of nature and science; excerpt from BioScience, December 1976. L. P. Coonen and C. M. Porter. por Sci Digest 81:40-1 Ap '77

Periodicals

See also
BioScience (periodical)

Periodicity

Biorhythm clock. F. Blechman. il Radio-Electr 48:33-7 N '77
Biorhythm forecast. P. Lutus. il Pop Electr 11: 45-6 Je '77
Biorhythms: a key to your ups and downs. J. Bolch. il Read Digest 111:63-7 S '77
Blind man living in normal society has circadian rhythms of 24.9 hours. L. E. M. Miles and others. bibl il Science 198:421-3 O 28 '77
Circadian organization in lizards: the role of the pineal organ. H. Underwood. bibl il Science 195:587-9 F 11 '77
Circadian rhythm of synaptic excitability in rat and monkey central nervous system. C. A. Barnes and others. bibl il Science 197:91-2 Jl 1 '77
Do body rhythms really make you sick? V. Goldberg. Read Digest 110:181-2+ Je '77
Efferent optic nerve fibers mediate circadian rhythms in the limulus eye. R. B. Barlow, Jr and others. bibl il Science 197:86-9 Jl 1 '77
Estradiol shortens the period of hamster circadian rhythms. L. P. Morin and others. bibl il Science 196:305-7 Ap 15 '77
Hibernation and body weight in dormice: a new type of endogenous cycle. N. Mrosovsky. bibl il Science 196:902-3 My 20 '77
Human rhythms; excerpt from An introduction to biological rhythms. J. D. Palmer. bibl il BioScience 27:93-9 F '77
Hyperalgesia induced by naloxone follows diurnal rhythm in responsivity to painful stimuli. R. C. Frederickson and others. bibl il Science 198:756-8 N 18 '77
Melatonin: daily cycle in plasma cerebrospinal fluid of calves. L. Hedlund and others. bibl il Science 195:686-7 F 18 '77
Neuronal circadian rhythm: phase shifting by a protein synthesis inhibitor. J. W. Jacklet. bibl il Science 198:69-71 O 7 '77
120-year bamboo clock; reproductive periodicity of bamboo and cicadas. S. J. Gould. Natur Hist 86:8+ Ap '77
Refractoriness in female lizard reproduction: a probable circannual clock. H. S. Cuellar and O. Cuellar. bibl il Science 197:495-7 Jl 29 '77
Resetting biological clocks. G. Present. Sci Digest 81:82 Je '77
Suprachiasmatic nuclear lesions do not abolish food-shifted circadian adrenal and temperature rhythmicity. D. T. Krieger and others. bibl il Science 197:398-9 Jl 22 '77
Suprachiasmatic nucleus: use of ^{14}C-labeled deoxyglucose uptake as a functional marker. W. J. Schwartz and H. Gainer. bibl il Science 197:1089-91 S 9 '77
Synchronized ultradian cortisol rhythms in monkeys: persistence during corticotropin infusion. J. W. Holaday and others. bibl il Science 198:56-8 O 7 '77
Timekeeping by the pineal gland. S. Binkley and others. bibl il Science 197:1181-3 S 16 '77
What can we do about jet lag; circadian dysrhythmia. V. Goldberg. bibl il Psychol Today 11:68-9+ Ag '77

Social aspects

Are we born to be good? theories of E. O. Wilson; with editorial comment. N. Calder. il por Horizon 19:42-9 Mr '77
New science of genetic self-interest; interview, ed by S. Morris. I. DeVore. il Psychol Today 10: 42-6+ F '77
Sexual dimorphism and mating systems: how did they evolve? G. B. Kolata. Science 195:382-3 Ja 28 '77
Sociobiology. J. Terrell. Sci Digest 82:58-61 S '77
When man becomes as god: the biological prospect. A. Rosenfeld. il Sat R 5:14-20 D 10 '77
Why you do what you do; sociobiology. il Time 110:54-8+ Ag 1 '77; Same abr. with title Why we do what we do. Read Digest 111:183-4+ D '77

Study and teaching

Chicago teacher makes his classes come alive; E. Hamberlin's biology course at DuSable High School, Chicago. B. Rhoden. il pors Ebony 32:43-6+ Mr '77
Open new doors through biology education. G. A. Gries. BioScience 27:7 Ja '77
Toward a common biology curriculum; proposed study by European Community Biologists Association. BioScience 27:636 S '77
See also
Biological Sciences Curriculum Study

Textbooks

Creationism controversy in Dallas. J. C. Evans. Chr Cent 94:188-9 Mr 2 '77
Unequal time; Indiana biology text case. Sci Am 236:61 Je '77

BIOLUMINESCENCE
Aequorin luminescence: relation of light emission to calcium concentration—a calcium-independent component. D. G. Allen and others. bibl il Science 195:996-8 Mr 11 '77
Bizarre world of undersea lights. G. S. Fichter. il Int Wildlife 8:12-15 Ja '78
See also
Bacteria, Luminous
Electric organs in fishes

BIOMASS energy
And if all else fails: cattails. K. A. Matichek. Sci Digest 82:61 O '77
Biological sources of commercial energy; excerpt from Rays of hope. D. Hayes. bibl BioScience 27:540-6 Ag '77
Modern agrarianism; letter. B. Hannon. bibl Science 197:821-2 Ag 26 '77
Photosynthetic solar energy: rediscovering biomass fuels. A. L. Hammond. Science 197:745-6 Ag 19 '77
Plant crops as a source of fuel and hydrocarbon-like materials. P. E. Nielsen and others. bibl il Science 198:942-4 D 2 '77

BIOME projects. See International biological program

BIOMECHANICS. See Human mechanics

BIOMEDICAL research. See Medical research

BIOMEDICAL Systems Program. See Jet Propulsion Laboratory

BIOMETHYLATION. See Methylation

BIORHYTHM. See Biology—Periodicity

BIOSATS. See Artificial satellites—Biological use

BIOSCIENCE. See Life sciences

BIOSCIENCE (periodical)
Broadening biological communication. J. A. Behnke. BioScience 27:773 D '77
Copyright law dictates new procedures for authors. W. G. Peter. il BioScience 27:829-30 D '77

BIOSPHERE
Gaia: the harmony of our sphere; theories of J. Lovelock and L. Margulis. A. Hapgood. Atlantic 240:100-4 D '77
Interaction of two great rivers helps sustain the earth's vital biosphere. R. Campbell. il Smithsonian 8:38-51 S '77

BIOSPHERE reserves. See Natural areas

BIOSYNTHESIS. See Synthesis

BIOTELEMETRY
Wired rats reveal whereabouts. il BioScience 27: 430 Je '77

BIPHENYL compounds. See Diphenyl compounds

BIPLANES. See Airplanes, Light

BIRCH
Birch trees are the Graces of our wild forests. C. Ogburn. il Smithsonian 8:72-81 bibl(p 134) D '77

BIRCHALL, Ann
Greek art from the Atlantic depths. il Horizon 19:66-71 Ja '77

BIRCHENOUGH, Ernest
Time capsule. Am Rec G 40:8-10 Jl '77

BIRD, Caroline
Ten steps to success; excerpt from The case against college. Parents Mag 52:59+ S '77
What do women want? address, June 4, 1977. Vital Speeches 43:598-601 Jl 15 '77; Same abr. il Sat Eve Post 249:48-9+ O '77

BIRD, Florence
Great decade for Canadian women. Cur Hist 72: 170 2+ Ap '77

BIRD, Kai
Co-opting the third world elites. Nation 224:425-8 Ap 9 '77
Voting with their guns. Nation 225:650-3 D 17 '77
—and Berick, David
Third world's critical mass. Nation 224:236-8 F 26 '77
—and Goldmark, Susan
India's permanent emergency. Progressive 41: 43-6 Mr '77
—and Holland, Max
Human rights in Bangladesh. Progressive 41:48 O '77
—and Teng, F. Y.
Singapore/Malaysia. Nation 225:242-4 S 17 '77
—See Holland, M. jt auth

BIRD, Rose Elizabeth
Another first for California. por Time 109:69 F 28 '77 *
Ms Chief Justice. P. Bonventre and W. J. Cook. il por Newsweek 89:70 F 28 '77 *

BIRD attracting. See Birds, Attracting of

BIRD baits and repellents
Baiting laws are a mess; waterfowl baiting. J. Phillips. il Outdoor Life 159:63-5+ Je '77

BIRD banding
Snow geese are coming! The snow geese are coming! J. H. Phillips. il por Int Wildlife 7:21 N '77

BIRD breeding. See Birds—Breeding

BIRD calling
Calling spring gobblers; tips on turkey calling. A. Martin. il Field & S 81:86-9+ F '77
Two clucks are enough; turkey calling. C. Elliott. il Outdoor Life 159:64-5+ F '77

BIRD calls. See Birds—Song

BIRD census
It's all for the birds! National Audubon Society's Christmas bird count. il Time 111:48 Ja 16 '78
Keeping track of hawks. D. R. Zimmerman. il Audubon 79:2-12 Jl '77

BIRD control
Improve the lot of quail; managing populations. B. Brister. il Field & S 81:109-10+ Ap '77
Uncle Sam says scram! efforts to reduce Canada geese population in Horicon Marsh refuges. B. Gilbert. il maps Audubon 79:42-55 Ja '77

BIRD eggs. See Birds—Eggs

BIRD feeders
My bird problem, and ours. L. Sheehan. il Atlantic 239:84-5 Je '77

BIRD flocks. See Birds—Habits and behavior

BIRD houses
Birdhouses are a gamble. il Sunset 158:138 Mr '77
Build a wood duck nest box. il Outdoor Life 159:164 My '77
Castles in the air. D. Grussing. il Nat Wildlife 15:12-16 F '77
Simple wood duck box. K. Schultz. il Field & S 82:200 N '77

BIRD hunting. See Fowling; Game bird shooting; Water bird shooting

BIRD populations
See also
Bird census

Control

See Bird control

BIRD prints. See Birds in art

BIRD protection. See Birds—Protection

BIRD sanctuaries

California

Now its the Busch Bird Sanctuary. il Sunset 158:74 Mr '77

Idaho

Eagle's fate and mine are one; Snake River Birds of Prey Natural Area. A. Zwinger. il map Audubon 79:50-80+ Jl '77

BIRD shooting. See Fowling; Game bird shooting; Water bird shooting

BIRD songs. See Birds—Song

BIRD study
Alexander Wilson: Father of American Ornithology. D. Maurizi. il pors Conservationist 31:2-7 My '77
Bird study aids camp enrichment. G. R. Dudderar. il Camp Mag 49:6-7 Je '77
Bird watcher nonpareil. J. J. Audubon. il Sat Eve Post 249:16 Jl '77
Bird watching in Arizona canyons. il map Sunset 158:104-6 Je '77
Bird watching near Los Banos. . .here are five places to look. il Sunset 158:59 F '77
Birds of a feather indeed flock together. F. Heppner. il Audubon 79:16-19 S '77
Dean of bird watchers; interview, ed by G. H. Harrison. R. T. Peterson. il por Américas 29:33-9 My '77
Eagle's fate and mine are one. A. Zwinger. il map Audubon 79:50-80+ Jl '77
For the birds. L. Scarbrough. il Seventeen 36:42-3 Mr '77
Irresistible mystery of the birds. M. Wellemeyer. il Fortune 96:41+ S '77
John O'Neill doesn't just paint birds. J. Fisher. il por Int Wildlife 7:30-7 N '77
Making of the world's number one bird watcher. G. H. Harrison. il pors Am For 83:18-21+ F '77
My bird problem, and ours. L. Sheehan. il Atlantic 239:84-5 Je '77
Mystery goose; bird watching; excerpt from To behold a bird. L. Line. il Field & S 81:82+ Mr '77
President goes birding. J. L. Whitehead. il pors Conservationist 31:20-3 My '77
Primer for bird-watchers. N. Smith. il Nat Wildlife 15:22-3 Ap '77
Sighting at Pine Knot. A. A. Lindsey. il Natur Hist 86:40+ N '77
Watching vagrants in Santa Cruz. il Sunset 159:63 S '77
See also
Bird banding
Bird census
Birds—Identification

Bibliography

New books for the bird watcher. Sunset 159:28 S '77

BIRD watching. See Bird study

BIRDHOUSES. See Bird houses

BIRDS
All the smale foweles. J. J. DuPont. il Conservationist 31:1 My '77
See also
Embryology—Birds
Game birds
Hearing (birds)
Rare birds
Sexual behavior—Birds
Water birds
also names of birds, e.g. Sparrows

Accidents and hazards

Wings of winter. H. Borland. Progressive 41:49-50 Mr '77

Banding

See Bird banding

Breeding

Chilean flamingo court and dance. J. Muñoz. il Natur Hist 86:72-8 D '77
In quest of the snatcher; harpy eagles. N. Rettig. il map Audubon 79:26-9 N '77

Caricatures and cartoons

Pterribly ptalkative ptarmigan and other zany birds. P. Shortt. il Int Wildlife 8:32 Ja '78

Control

See Bird control

Diseases and pests

See also
Poultry—Diseases and pests

Ecology

Species turnover rates on islands: dependence on census interval. R. M. May and J. M. Diamond. bibl il Science 197:266-70 Jl 15 '77

Eggs

Altered yolk structure and reduced hatchability of eggs from birds fed single doses of petroleum oils. C. R. Grau and others. bibl il Science 195:779-81 F 25 '77
Green eggs by the thousands; collecting murre eggs on Walrus Island. V. B. Scheffer. il Audubon 79:112-13 S '77

Export-import trade

Bird lovers. E. R. Ricciuti. il Audubon 79:68-72+ S '77

Food and feeding

Birdseed boom. il Nat Wildlife 15:34 Ap '77
Case of the missing thistleseed; question of embargo by India. G. Reiger. Audubon 79:161 N '77
Sketch book visit to a winter bird feeder. W. Trimm. il Conservationist 32:inside back cover N '77
Watch the birds catch more fish. J. Weiss. il Outdoor Life 159:76-81+ F '77
See also
Bird feeders

Habits and behavior

Birds of a feather indeed flock together. F. Heppner. il Audubon 78:16-19 S '77
Night birds. L. Line. il por Field & S 82:42-3 Jl '77
See also
Birds—Food and feeding
Courtship of birds

Identification

Field guide to Roger Tory Peterson. J. Diffily. il por Am Artist 41:28-33+ Ap '77
Track on the beach; efforts to identify birds as either sharp-tailed grouse or heath hens. P. Matthiessen. il Audubon 79:68-9+ Mr '77

Locomotion

See Animal locomotion

Migration

Bird that is loath to fly but roams afar all the same; excerpt from Rails of the world. S. D. Ripley. il Smithsonian 7:88-93 Mr '77

BIRDS—Migration—*Continued*
Convention on Migratory Birds transmitted to Senate; message, July 18, 1977. J. Carter. Dept State Bull 77:326-7 S 5 '77
See also
Bird banding
Orientation

Orientation

See Orientation

Photographs

Boyers' birds; with photographs by P. Boyer. W. Trimm. il pors Conservationist 31:28-32 Mr '77

Poetry

Sparrow hawk resting; poem; excerpt from Another kind of autumn. L. Eiseley. il Audubon 79:48-9 Mr '77

Protection

Endangered birds: tinkering for time; Symposium on Management Techniques for Preserving Endangered Birds. F. Graham, Jr. Audubon 79:137:41 N '77
Too sacred to survive? Japan's red crested cranes, tancho. F. H. Marks. il por Int Wildlife 8:20-5 Ja '78
See also
Birds, Attracting of
Birds of prey—Protection
Game laws
Sea birds—Protection
Water birds—Protection

Song

Bird song; an acoustic flag. R. E. Lemon. bibl BioScience 27:402-8 Je '77
Play it again, Sam. I. Smullen. il Int Wildlife 7:38-40 Mr '77
Selective vocal learning in a sparrow. P. Marler and S. Peters. bibl il Science 198:519-21 N 4 '77
Species identification in the North American cowbird: appropriate responses to abnormal song. A. P. King and M. J. West. bibl il Science 195:1002-4 Mr 11 '77

Study

See Bird study

Vision

See Vision (birds)

Australia

See also
Bowerbirds

Guyana

In quest of the snatcher; harpy eagles. N. Rettig. il map Audubon 79:26-49 N '77

Japan

Too sacred to survive? Japan's red crested cranes, tancho. F. H. Marks. il por Int Wildlife 8:20-5 Ja '78

Long Island

It's all for the birds! National Audubon Society's Christmas bird count. il Time 111:48 Ja 16 '78

Mexico

Un gran pedazo de carne; search for the rare imperial ivory-billed woodpecker. G. Plimpton. il pors Audubon 79:10-25 N '77

New York (state)

See also
Birds—Long Island

New Zealand

Rare birds, bold men; efforts of the New Zealand Wildlife Service. J. Rearden. il Int Wildlife 7:4-11 Mr '77

North America

Song of hope for the bluebird. L. Zeleny. il map Nat Geog 151:854-65 Je '77

Peru

John O'Neill doesn't just paint birds. J. Fisher. il por Int Wildlife 7:30-7 N '77

South America

Dean of bird watchers; interview, ed by G. H. Harrison. R. T. Peterson. il por Américas 29:33-9 My '77

Utah

Splendor at the shore; photographs. C. G. Summers, Jr. Nat Wildlife 15:42-7 Je '77

BIRDS, Attracting of
Attract more birds this winter. G. H. Harrison. il Nat Wildlife 16:40-5 D '77
Gifts that will bring birds to the bird watcher's garden. il Sunset 159:192-3 D '77
See also
Bird feeders

BIRDS, Extinct
See also
Dodos
Heath hens
Passenger pigeons

BIRDS, Fossil
Bone bonanza: early bird and mastodon. il Sci N 112:198 S 24 '77
Pleistocene avifaunas and the overkill hypothesis. D. K. Grayson. bibl Science 195:691-3 F 18 '77
Teeth in Ichthyornis (class: aves) L. D. Martin and J. D. Stewart. bibl il Science 195:1331-2 Mr 25 '77
Telltale wishbone; Archaeopteryx and the question of direct descent of birds from dinosaurs. S. J. Gould. il Natur Hist 86:26+ N '77

BIRDS, Injurious and beneficial
My solution to the feathered berry thieves. R. E. Hampton. Org Gard & Farm 24:156 Je '77
See also
Crows

BIRDS, Nocturnal. See Birds—Habits and behavior

BIRDS, Predatory. See Birds of prey

BIRDS, Rare. See Rare birds

BIRDS in art
Alexander Wilson: Father of American Ornithology. D. Maurizi. il pors Conservationist 31:2-7 My '77
Art print of the year:
  Eastern bluebird. M. Wexler. il Nat Wildlife 15:33 O '77
  Rose-breasted grosbeak. B. Vogt. il Nat Wildlife 15:24 O '77
Audubon on the wing; with reproductions of J. J. Audubon paintings. D. Jeffery. il por Nat Geog 151:148-77 F '77
Boyers' birds; with photographs by P. Boyer. W. Trimm. il pors Conservationist 31:28-32 Mr '77
Burglary was for the birds; theft of Audubon folios. R. Cantwell. il Sports Illus 47:20-2+ Jl 11 '77
Expert's secrets for carving lifelike birds. P. Angell. il por Pop Mech 149:94+ Ja '78
Field guide to Roger Tory Peterson. J. Diffily. il por Am Artist 41:28-33+ Ap '77
First, you've got to know wildlife; interview, ed by B. Strohm. M. Reece il Nat Wildlife 15:48-55 O '77
Fuertes portfolio; birds of prey; reproductions of paintings. L. A. Fuertes. il Conservationist 31:8-15 Ja '77
John O'Neill doesn't just paint birds. J. Fisher. il por Int Wildlife 7:30-7 N '77
Maass vision; game bird paintings. R. Schara. il Outdoor Life 161:74-81 Ja '78
Making of the world's number one bird watcher. G. H. Harrison. il pors Am For 83:18-21+ F '77
Many faces of birds. T. Shortt. il Int Wildlife 7:26-9 My '77
Outdoor prints: a sporting chance for pleasure and profit; game bird prints. P. Miller. il Outdoor Life 159:72-7+ Je '77

BIRDS in religion, folklore, etc.
Sketch book looks at folklore. H. W. Trimm. il Conservationist 32:inside back cover S '77

BIRDS of prey
See also
Eagles
Falcons
Hawks
Owls

Care

Earth log: eagle doctor of Tesuque. J. Neary. il pors Audubon 79:90-2+ Jl '77

Photographs

With curved beak and claw. Audubon 79:13-49 Jl '77

Protection

Fighting beak and claw. D. D. Jackson. il Sports Illus 46:78-82+ My 16 '77
See also
Bird sanctuaries

BIRDS of prey in art. See Birds in art

BIRDSALL, Jim
You never know. New Yorker 53:30-1 Ap 11 '77 *

BIRDSEED. See Birds—Food and feeding

BIRDSFOOT trefoil
Chemotaxis of rhizobium spp. to a glycoprotein produced by birdsfoot trefoil roots. W. W. Currier and G. A. Strobel. bibl il Science 196:434-6 Ap 22 '77

BIRENBAUM, Arnold. See Ahmed, M. B. jt auth

BIRKERTS, Gunnar
Defining a design methodology. il Archit Rec 161:91-4 F '77
about
School for the dance by Gunnar Birkerts; with introd by M. F. Schmertz. il Archit Rec 161:85-90 F '77 *

BIRLEY, Robin
Frontier post in Roman Britain; with biographical sketch. il maps Sci Am 236:16, 38-46 bibl(p 138) F '77

BIRMINGHAM, Frederic A.
Let's have lunch! Holiday 58:31+ Je '77
Mystery ride. il Holiday 58:52-4 S '77
BIRMINGHAM, Stephen
Auction crowd. il N Y Times Mag p38-40+ Mr 6 '77
Clubs Griffin Bell had to quit. il N Y Times Mag p20-1+ F 6 '77
BIRMINGHAM, Ala.
Blacks
Law moves at last: the Birmingham bombing of 1963; indictment of R. E. Chambliss. B. Cornwell. Nation 225:463-5 N 5 '77
Crime
Arrest in Birmingham; charging R. E. Chambliss with 1963 church bombing. R. Boeth and V. E. Smith. il pors Newsweek 90:32+ O 10 '77
Birmingham clears its name; R. Chambliss case. Nation 225:578 D 3 '77
Law moves at last: the Birmingham bombing of 1963; indictment of R. E. Chambliss. B. Cornwell. Nation 225:463-5 N 5 '77
Verdict on bloody Sunday; R. E. Chambliss murder trial. D. A. Williams and J. B. Cumming. Newsweek 90:63 N 28 '77
Music
See also
Opera—Alabama
BIRMINGHAM, Ala, Chamber of Commerce
Chamber of Commerce starts economic protection society. il Am City & County 92:44 My '77
BIRMINGHAM, Mich.
Town that lives in terror; child murders in Oakland County. B. Davidson. il Good H 185:136-7+ S '77
BIRMINGHAM Ballet Company. See Ballet companies
BIRMINGHAM Civic Opera Association. See Opera —Alabama
BIRNBAUM, Karl E.
Human rights and East-West relations. bibl f For Affairs 55:783-99 Jl '77
BIRNBAUM, Norman
French left. Nation 225:424-8 O 29 '77
Left and right in bed together. Nation 225:177-81 S 3 '77
Under the lid of West Germany. Nation 225:520-4 N 19 '77
BIRNBAUM, Stephen
Getting away. See issues of Esquire
Getting there. Esquire 87:42+ Ap '77
Pacific overture. il Esquire 88:85-93 Ag '77
Short guide to guidebooks. il Esquire 87:130+ F '77
Top decks. il Esquire 88:147-51 D '77
Why not the best? il Esquire 88:149-53 N '77
BIRTH. See Childbirth
BIRTH, Multiple
See also
Twins
BIRTH control
Another child? Does it make sense. G. Carro. il Ladies Home J 94:102 My '77
HEW and the sexual revolution: why teenagers get pregnant; contraception programs. M. Castleman. Nation 225:549-52 N 26 '77
Margaret Sanger; pioneer of the future. J. Alexander. il por Sat Eve Post 249:10-11+ My '77
Natural way; fertility awareness. Time 110:51 D 26 '77
Of many things. J. O'Hare. America 136:inside front cover Ap 23 '77
Rhythm: ideal and reality. M. B. Benecke. America 137:240-1 O 15 '77
Sterilizing the poor. S. M. Rothman. bibl Society 14:36-40 Ja '77
See also
Abortion
Childlessness
Contraceptives
Research
Research funding drops as the need rises. J. Gaylin. Psychol Today 10:46a My '77
China
Planned birth program in China. K. I. Chen. bibl Cur Hist 73:73-8 S '77
India
Cobbler's tale. H. Jensen. il Newsweek 89:42 Ap 4 '77
Compulsory sterilization: the change in India's population policy. K. Gulhati. bibl il Science 195:1300-5 Mr 25 '77
Issue that inflamed India. L. Malkin. il Time 109:38-9 Ap 4 '77
Mexico
Mexico's population pressures. M. Alisky. bibl f Cur Hist 72:106-10+ Mr '77
BIRTH control clinics
His body, himself; Men's Reproductive Health Clinic in San Francisco. M. Goodman. Ms 5:21 My '77
BIRTH defects. See Deformities; Heredity of disease
BIRTH order
Birth order and intellectual development: the confluence model in the light of cross-cultural evidence. D. J. Davis and others. bibl il Science 196:1470-2 Je 24 '77
Lastborn speaks out—at last. M. S. Kennedy. por Newsweek 90:22-3 N 7 '77
BIRTH rate
First nations stop population growth; views of L. R. Brown. L. R. Palmer. Farm J 101:J2 mid-Mr '77
See also
Birth control
Population, Increase of
United States
Babies bottom out—a maybe boom. Sci N 112:101 Ag 13 '77
Elusive rise in the American birthrate. C. Gibson. bibl il Science 196:500-3 Ap 29 '77; Reply with rejoinder. J. Sklar and B. Berkov. 197:108+ Jl 8 '77
Trends in American marriage, childbirth, and retirement; excerpts from addresses. W. J. Cohen; C. F. Westoff. por Intellect 106:93-5 S '77
BIRTHPLACES
American hometown; symposium. il Sat R 5:8-14+ N 26 '77
BIRTWISTLE, Harrison
Musical events; Silbury air. A. Porter. New Yorker 53:128 O 31 '77 *
BISBEE, Chester A. and others
Albumin phylogeny for clawed frogs (xenopus) bibl il Science 195:785-7 F 25 '77
BISCAYNE Bay
To a different beat; bonefish fishing. J. Bashline. il Field & S 81:184+ Ap '77
BISCUIT and cracker industry
See also
Nabisco, Inc
Great Britain
Touch of British realism; United biscuits. por Forbes 119:32 Ap 15 '77
BISCUIT ware. See Pottery
BISHOP, Charles E.
Human ecology; address, March 25, 1977. Vital Speeches 43:470-2 My 15 '77
BISHOP, Christine E.
Health employment and the Nation's health. bibl f Cur Hist 72:201-10+ My '77
BISHOP, Claire (Huchet)
Case for The five Chinese brothers. S. G. Lanes. il SLJ 24:90-1 O '77 *
BISHOP, Jim
Journey to faith. Read Digest 111:163-4+ Ag '77
BISHOP, John (dramatist)
Trip back down. Reviews
America 136:60 Ja 22 '77 *
Nation 224:124 Ja 29 '77 *
New Yorker 52:47 Ja 17 '77 *
BISHOP, Jordan
French fact. Commonweal 104:294-6 My 13 '77
BISHOP, Paul E. and others
Intergeneric transfer of genes involved in the rhizobium-legume symbiosis. bibl il Science 198:938-40 D 2 '77
BISHOP, Robert
John S. Blunt. il Antiques 112:964-71 N '77
BISHOPS
Divided shepherds of a restive flock; conflicts within the Catholic Church. T. Fleming. il N Y Times Mag p9+ Ja 16 '77
New chance for the bishops; Call to Action conference in Detroit. P. Steinfels. Commonweal 104:200+ Ap 1 '77
See also
National Conference of Catholic Bishops
Synod of Bishops, 1977
Appointment, call and election
Black bishop for Mississippi; installation of J. L. Howze. G. V. Murry. America 137:32 Jl 16 '77
Anecdotes, facetiae, satire, etc.
New bishop for New York. R. A. Blake. America 137:331-2 N 12 '77
BISON, American
Bison in art and history; excerpt from The bison in art. L. Barsness. il Am West 14:10-21 Mr '77
BISQUE dolls. See Dolls
BISQUE ware. See Pottery
BISSELL, Richard E.
United States policy in Africa. bibl f Cur Hist 73:193-5+ D '77
BISSET, George
(tr) See Gedin, P. Novel in a changing society
BISSET, Jacqueline
Jacqueline Bisset: spunky star of The deep; interview, ed by A. L. Ball. il por Redbook 149:90+ Jl '77
about
Beauty named Bisset. J. Kroll and L. Jenkins. il pors Newsweek 90:68-9+ Jl 11 '77 *
Tale of two Jackies. il pors Ladies Home J 94:28 O '77 *

BISSON, Thomas N.
Organized peace in southern France and Catalonia, ca. 1140-ca. 1233. bibl f map Am Hist R 82:290-311 Ap '77
BISSONETTE, David
Spring spectrum; poem. America 136:275 Mr 26 '77
BISTLINE, Susan
Mexico balks at revised copyright procedures; ed by S. Wagner. Pub W 212:26+ D 12 '77
BISTRITZKY, Leibel
Grocery. New Yorker 53:29-30 My 23 '77 *
BITAUTAS, William
Take off your shoes. il Sch Arts 76:40-1 Je '77
BITES, Dog. See Dog bites
BITES, Insect. See Insect bites and stings
BITNER, Richard
Antennas for 40-channels. il Radio-Electr 48:45-6 F '77
BITO, Laszlo Z.
Inflammatory effects of endotoxin-like contaminants in commonly used protein preparations. bibl il Science 196:83-5 Ap 1 '77
BITS (drilling and boring)
Drill bit sharpening devices. il Consumers Res Mag 60:34-6 My '77
BITTLE, Camilla
To every thing there is a season. . . ; story. Good H 186:78-9 Ja '78
BITTNER, John R.
Day the first amendment died; address, September 16, 1977. Vital Speeches 44:24-8 O 15 '77
BITUMINOUS materials
See also
Asphalt
BITUMINOUS sand. See Oil sands
BIVALVES. See Mollusks
BIZET, Georges
Carmen. Reviews
New Yorker 53:102-5 S 26 '77 *
Connoisseur's Carmen. D. Arthur. Am Rec G 40:19-21 D '76 *
BIZZARRO, Salvatore
Mexico's government in crisis. bibl f Cur Hist 72:102-5+ Mr '77
BJELDANES, L. F. and Chang, G. W.
Mutagenic activity of quercetin and related compounds. bibl il Science 197:577-8 Ag 5 '77
BLACK, Betty L. and Moog, Florence
Goblet cells in embryonic intestine: accelerated differentiation in culture. bibl il Science 197:368-70 Jl 22 '77
BLACK, David
Rummage and loss; story. Harpers 255:60-2 Jl '77
BLACK, Douglas M.
Obituary
Pub W 211:16-17 My 30 '77
BLACK, Hallie
Connecticut's last virgin forest. il Am For 83:24-7+ N '77
BLACK, J. Anderson
Craft of King Tut's jewels. il Craft Horiz 37:20-3 F '77
BLACK, Karen
Four successful women talk about what they want—and can't have. pors Redbook 148:92-3+ F '77
BLACK, Max
Objectivity of science. bibl Bull Atom Sci 33:55-60 F '77
BLACK, Richard Glynn
Bite by bite, count yourself thin. S. Mines. il Read Digest 112:176-8+ Ja '78
BLACK, Robert G.
Boating beat. See issues of Popular science
Cuddy cabins turn runabouts into mini-cruisers. il Pop Sci 210:106-8 F '77
BLACK, Shirley. See Black, T. jt auth
BLACK, Shirley (Temple)
Will young people ever have heroes again? ed by J. N. Bell. il pors Seventeen 36:136-7+ S '77
BLACK, Ted, and Black, Shirley
Interplanting helps increase Central American food supply. il Org Gard & Farm 24:132-4+ Jl '77
BLACK, Theodore M.
Political role of educators. Educ Digest 42:30-2 Mr '77
BLACK, Vicki H.
More than a museum. il Am For 83:12-15 Mr '77
BLACK, Watt L.
Law Focused Education: a new thrust in education. Clearing H 50:304-6 Mr '77
BLACK actors and actresses
See also names of black actors and actresses, e.g. C. Tyson
BLACK admirals
See also
Gravely, S. L. Jr
BLACK air pilots
Black pilots. il Ebony 33:58-60+ Ja '78
See also
Biffle, D.
BLACK art. See Art, Black
BLACK artists
See also
Bearden, R.
Pippin, H.
BLACK arts. See The Arts, Black
BLACK athletes
Black dominance. il Time 109:57-60 My 9 '77; Same abr. with title Growing black dominance in sports. il Read Digest 111:138-41 Ag '77
See also names of black athletes, e.g. L. Allen
BLACK authors
Ned Bobkoff and me. J. T. Jackson. il pors Writers Digest 57:16-18+ F '77
See also
Haley, A.
Jackson, J. T.
Taylor, M. D.
Wright, R.
BLACK bachelors. See Single men
BLACK barbers. See Barbers and barber shops
BLACK bears. See Bears
BLACK business enterprises
Black capitalism runs into tough sledding. il U.S. News 83:26 D 5 '77
Henry G. Parks gives his rules for success. J. Saddler. il pors Ebony 32:100-2+ Mr '77
Quiet success of a talented engineer; H. Henderson of Henderson Industries. H. Johnson. il pors Ebony 32:72-4+ F '77
SBA scandals: whites bilk black fronts. A. Poinsett. il Ebony 32:75-6+ O '77
They are owners, bosses, workers; black women. M. Burgen. il Ebony 32:122-4+ Ag '77
BLACK businesswomen. See Business and professional women
BLACK Caucus (American Library Association)
See American Library Association—Black Caucus
BLACK Caucus. See Caucuses
BLACK celebrities
Class and style; poll of Ebony readers. il Ebony 33:33-6+ N '77
Way they were. il Ebony 32:84-6+ O '77
BLACK Church and Black Community Conference.
See Religious conferences
BLACK colleges and universities
See also
Grambling College, Grambling, La.
BLACK comedians
See also
Cosby, B.
Pryor, R.
BLACK composers
Convocation at the Philharmonic; celebration of black composers. I. Kolodin. il Sat R 5:42-3 O 15 '77
BLACK congresswomen. See Congresswomen
BLACK Creek watershed. See Watersheds
BLACK criminals. See Blacks—Crime
BLACK culture. See Blacks—Culture
BLACK dialects. See Black-English dialects
BLACK diplomats
Washington notebook; serving on the U.S. delegation to the United Nations. S. Booker. Ebony 32:26 Jl '77
BLACK dolls. See Dolls
BLACK education. See Blacks—Education
BLACK educators
See also
Mays, B. E.
BLACK engineers
Push for black engineers. il Bus W p 124+ F 14 '77
See also
Reed, C.
BLACK-English dialects
Cloze procedure and dialect considerations. C. W. Bonds. bibl Clearing H 50:360-2 Ap '77
BLACK entertainers
Children of the stars. il Ebony 33:82-4+ N '77
Money problems of the stars. R. Kisner. il Ebony 32:142-6+ My '77
See also names of black entertainers, e.g. J. Wright
BLACK executives
See also names of black executives, e.g. H. G. Parks, Jr
BLACK family life. See Blacks—Social conditions
BLACK health workers
Janitor and his six daughters prove we can. il por Ebony 32:33-4+ S '77
BLACK HILLS, S.D.
See also
Mount Rushmore National Memorial
BLACK history. See Blacks—History
BLACK holes (astronomy)
Astrophysics: discovery and the ubiquity of black holes. W. D. Metz. Science 195:276-7 Ja 21 '77
Black hole in Messier 15? Sky & Tel 53:172 Mr '77
Black holes. J. Gribbin. Sci Digest 81:45-7 Ap '77
Black holes—the darkest riddle of the universe. J. L. Wilhelm. il Read Digest 111:68-72 S '77
Collapsing universe; excerpt. I. Asimov. por Sci Digest 81:12-16+ Je '77
Continued: the mystery of black holes that warp space/halt time. M. Davidson and N. Ponnamperuma. il Sci Digest 81:57-8 My '77

BLACK holes (astronomy)—*Continued*
Hole in the middle of the galaxy. D. E. Thomsen. il Sci N 111:121+ F 19 '77
Out from under the cosmic censor: Stephen Hawking's black holes. D. Overbye. il por Sky & Tel 54:84-9+ Ag '77
Peering into black holes; theories of S. Hawking. P. Gwynne. por Newsweek 89:78-9 Ja 24 '77
Quantum mechanics of black holes. S. W. Hawking. il Sci Am 236:34-40 bibl(p 132) Ja '77
Science's now cloudy crystal ball; effects of S. W. Hawking's findings. F. R. Haig. America 136:192-3 Mr 5 '77

Anecdotes, facetiae, satire, etc.
Black holes. J. Munves. New Yorker 53:32-3 Ap 11 '77

BLACK journalism. See Black press
BLACK journalists
See also
DuBois, W.E.B.
McKay, C.
BLACK judges
See also
Hastie, W. H.
Thompson, W. S.
BLACK lawyers
See also
McCree, W. H.
Smith, O. M.
BLACK leadership
Edward E. Cooper & 10 greatest Negroes of 1890; contest run by the Indianapolis Freeman. W. B. Gatewood, Jr. bibl por Negro Hist Bull 40:708-10 My '77
Leading black Americans. il U.S. News 82:37 Ap 18 '77
100 most influential black Americans. il Ebony 32:76+ My '77
U.S. black leadership—now going collective. J. Thornton. il U.S. News 83:53-4 Jl 4 '77
Washington notebook. S. Booker. Ebony 33:22 Ja '78
What black leaders want from business. il Bus W p85+ O 10 '77
BLACK librarians
See also
American Library Association—Black Caucus
BLACK literature
Bonsai. G. C. Oden. por Negro Hist Bull 40:716-17 Jl '77
See also
Blacks in literature

Bibliography
Ebony book shelf. See issues of Ebony

Study and teaching
Black literature and changing attitudes: does it do the job? E. R. Page. il bibl f Engl J 66:29-33 Mr '77

BLACK markets
Film pirates. D. Pauly and others. il Newsweek 90:90+ O 17 '77
BLACK marlin fishing. See Marlin fishing
BLACK men and women. See Women and men
BLACK militants
See also
Newton, H. P.
BLACK models. See Models (persons)
BLACK Mormons. See Mormons and Mormonism, Black
BLACK motion pictures
Sidney Poitier tells how to stay on top in Hollywood. L. Robinson. il pors Ebony 33:53-4+ N '77
BLACK Mountain College, North Carolina
Black Mountain College: a golden seed. M. C. Richards. il Craft Horiz 37:21-2+ Je '77
BLACK music
Live from the library; program of the Free Library of Philadelphia's Fleisher Collection. A. Milner. il Am Lib 8:75-6 F '77
See also
Blues (songs, etc)
Jazz music
BLACK musicians
Ebony music poll: the winners for 1977. il Ebony 32:83-4+ Jl '77
See also
Benson, G.
Braxton, A.
Carrington, T.
Gordon, D.
Liston, M.
BLACK Muslims
Civil war in Islamic America. A. Muhammad. Nation 224:721-4 Je 11 '77
Conversion of the Muslims. il por Time 109:59 Mr 14 '77
From faith to faith; Hanafi sect. Chr Today 21:48-9 Ap 1 '77
Second resurrection. K. L. Woodward and N. Davis. por Newsweek 90:67 Ag 22 '77
Seizing hostages: scourge of the '70s; Washington, D.C. siege by Hanafi commandos. T. Mathews. il por Newsweek 89:16-20+ Mr 21 '77
38 hours: trial by terror; Washington, D.C. siege by Hanafi Muslims. il pors map Time 109:14-20 Mr 21 '77

BLACK newspapers. See Black press
BLACK Panther Party
End of the Panther trial. S. Simon. Progressive 41:9 Je '77
Huey Newton come home. P. Goldman and others. il pors Newsweek 90:27 Jl 11 '77
Welcome back, Huey. R. M. Brown. Chr Cent 94:679-80 Ag 3 '77
BLACK periodicals
W.E.B. DuBois: his journalistic career. D. S. Green. bibl f il pors Negro Hist Bull 40:672-7 Mr '77
See also
Liberator (periodical)
BLACK physicians
Dr Myers and Dr Myers. il pors Ebony 33:107-8+ N '77
BLACK poets
See also
Hayden, R.
Matthews, J.
Stuckey, E.
BLACK power
See also
Blacks and politics
BLACK press
Black press: 150 years old. il Ebony 32:112-13 Ap '77
Black press: 150 years old. H. G. La Brie, 3d. bibl il Negro Hist Bull 40:705-7 My '77
Edward E. Cooper & 10 greatest Negroes of 1890; contest run by the Indianapolis Freeman. W. B. Gatewood, Jr. bibl por Negro Hist Bull 40:708-10 My '77
BLACK professional women. See Business and professional women
BLACK public officers
Blacks on the Carter team. il Ebony 32:150-1 Mr '77
See also names of black public officers, e.g. W. H. Hastie
BLACK race
Can blackness prolong life? melanin experiments of L. M. Edelstein. il pors Ebony 32:124-7 Je '77
Frederick Douglass on ethnology: a commencement address at Western Reserve College, 1854. A. McCluskey and J. McCluskey. bibl il por Negro Hist Bull 40:746-9 S '77
BLACK rock groups. See Rock groups
BLACK singers
Ebony music poll: the winners for 1977. il Ebony 32:83-4+ Jl '77
See also
Caesar, S.
Horne, L.
Hunter, A.
Pendergrass, T.
Ross, D.
Summer, D.
Williams, D.
Wonder, S.
BLACK student achievements. See Student achievements
BLACK students
Race still intimidates us; feelings of a black high school student. P. W. Wiggins. Todays Educ 66:67 N '77
See also
Colleges and universities—Desegregation
BLACK students, Women
1977 black college queens: beauty, brains, versatility. il Ebony 32:146-8+ Ap '77
BLACK studies
Roots; using the telecast in black studies course at Miami/Dade Community College, Miami, Fla. M. Rein and J. M. Elliot. il por Negro Hist Bull 40:664-7 Ja '77
BLACK television programs. See Television programs—Black programs
BLACK veterans
Sam Waller: eyewitness to history. M. Jones. il pors Ebony 32:79-80+ F '77
BLACK walnut trees. See Walnut trees
BLACK-white intermarriage. See Interracial marriage
BLACK-white relations. See Race relations
BLACK widow spiders. See Spiders
BLACK women
Bachelorettes for 1977. il Ebony 32:164-6+ My '77
Beautiful black woman. A. R. Fornay, Jr. il Ebony 32:138-42 F '77
Black woman finds her roots. O. Coombs. Redbook 149:56+ O '77
Black woman; special issue; with editorial comment. Ebony 32:24+ Ag '77
Black woman's guide to skin care. G. Pfaeffle. il McCalls 104:140-1+ F '77
Making black hair more beautiful. il McCalls 105:92+ N '77
Second thoughts of a black feminist; adaptation of address, February 1976. J. Jordan. Ms 5:113-15 '77
Why I'm not married. S. D. Lewis. il Ebony 32:120+ S '77

BLACK women—*Continued*

Attitudes

Tomorrow's black woman: independent, smart, feminine. L. Norment. il Ebony 32:44-6+ Ag '77

Bibliography

Ebony book shelf. Ebony 32:24 Ag '77

Employment

Washington notebook. S. Booker. por Ebony 32:50 Ag '77
See also
Black women—Occupations

History

Discovering my foremothers. C. Bovoso. il pors Ms 6:56-9 S '77
No crystal stair: the black woman in history. L. Bennett, Jr. il Ebony 32:164-5+ Ag '77

Occupations

Black women in the professions, 1890-1970. M. Kilson. bibl il M Labor R 100:38-41 My '77
Nine profiles of black womanhood. il Ebony 32:69 Ag '77
What's a nice girl like you doing in a place like this? il Ebony 32:103-4+ Je '77

Poetry

In celebration of black women. il Ebony 32:30 Ag '77

Psychology

Is a woman over the hill at 40? V. M. Grosvenor. il por Ebony 32:144-6+ Ag '77

BLACK women air pilots. See Women air pilots
BLACK women and men. See Women and men
BLACK women athletes. See Women athletes
BLACK women executives. See Women executives
BLACK women in the arts. See Women in the arts
BLACK women mayors. See Women mayors
BLACK women public officers. See Women public officers
BLACK women trade union officials. See Women trade union officials
BLACK womens clubs and societies. See Womens clubs and societies
BLACK youth
Are black youth more romantic about love? J. Wright. il Ebony 32:164-6+ O '77
Growing up in Harlem. R. Bailey. Seventeen 36:138-9+ N '77
Unforgettable Clarence Mathews; leader of black Boy Scout troop. B. N. Butler. il Read Digest 111:139-42 D '77
See also
Black students

Employment

Let's always have hope for future. il Ebony 32:128-9 Je '77

Unemployment

See Unemployment

BLACKBEARD, Bill
Novels that boys of a century ago couldn't put down. il por Smithsonian 8:122-4+ bibl(p 162) N '77
BLACKBERRIES
Blackberry, king of the brambles. L. Riotte. il Org Gard & Farm 24:190-2+ Mr '77
BLACKBIRDS
See also
Grackles
BLACKBODY radiation
Flying through the cosmos. D. E. Thomsen. il Sci N 112:44-5 Jl 16 '77
It moves. Sci Am 237:70+ N '77
BLACKBURN, Alan R.
Writing for the hidden markets. il Writers Digest 57:41-3 Jl '77
BLACKBURN, Dan
Skyhorse and Mohawk. il Nation 225:682-6 D 24 '77
BLACKIE, William
Hall of Fame for Business Leadership. M. Ways. por Fortune 95:122 Ja '77 *
BLACKJACK (game)
Hit me! K. Uston's techniques. T. Schwartz. il por Newsweek 89:58 Je 27 '77
BLACKLEY, James M.
Banking on privacy. il Time 110:59 S 26 '77 *
BLACKLISTING
AAP urges end to Arab boycott. M. Reuter. Pub W 212:22-3 Ag 8 '77
Anti-boycott legislation. E. M. Bronfman. New Repub 176:17-19 Je 4 '77
Arab boycott of Israel. N. Turck. bibl f For Affairs 55:472-93 Ap '77
Fragile pact to beat the Arab boycott; Business Roundtable—B'nai B'rith Anti-Defamation League agreement. Bus W p25-6 Mr 28 '77
How antiboycott law was hammered out. D. C. Bacon. il U.S. News 82:64 Je 20 '77
President Carter discusses boycott issue; remarks, February 9, 1977. J. Carter. Dept State Bull 76:266 Mr 21 '77
President signs 1977 amendments to Export Administration Act; statement, June 22, 1977. J. Carter. Dept State Bull 77:162-3 Ag 1 '77
Push to curb Arab boycott; new legislation. U.S. News 82:66 Ap 25 '77
Secretary Vance discusses antiboycott legislation and nuclear nonproliferation; statement, March 1, 1977. C. R. Vance. Dept State Bull 76:267-71 Mr 21 '77
BLACKLOCK, Les
Encounters in the wild; excerpt from Meet my psychiatrist. il Nat Wildlife 15:25-9 O '77
BLACKMON, Rosemary, and Sheppard, S.
Can acupuncture help you lose weight? Stop smoking? Vogue 167:148+ Mr '77
BLACKOUTS (electric power) See Electric power failures
BLACKS
Annual progress report. A. Poinsett. il Ebony 33:25-8 Ja '78
Getting to it; a guest editorial; Library of Congress' black subject headings. S. Berman. Am Lib 8:77 F '77
Modern black movement and Marxism. M. S. Copeland. bibl il New Cath World 220:134-9 My '77
Those riot-torn cities—a look at progress 10 years later. il U.S. News 83:50-1 Ag 29 '77
See also
Black Muslims
National Urban League
Race relations
Slavery—United States

Bibliography

Keeping up; a checklist; black reference books. A. S. Meyers. Am Lib 8:77 F '77

Caricatures and cartoons

Strictly for laughs. See issues of Ebony

Civil rights

Inaugural marks new and undefined era. L. Bennett, Jr. il Ebony 32:152-4 Mr '77
Where blacks have it good: Soweto looks at the U.S. A. Silk. Nation 225:144-7 Ag 20 '77
See also
Civil rights demonstrations
People United to Save Humanity (organization)
Race relations

History

Last of the great schoolmasters; B. E. Mays. L. Bennett, Jr. il pors Ebony 33:72-4+ D '77
Reflections: remembrance of moderates past. C. Trillin. il New Yorker 58:85-8+ Mr 21 '77
Woman who changed the South; a memory of Fannie Lou Hamer. E. H. Norton. por Ms 6:51+ Jl '77

Clubs, societies, etc.

See also
Association for the Study of Afro-American Life and History
National Association for the advancement of Colored People
National Urban League

Crime

Education of John Allen; excerpt from Assault with a deadly weapon: the autobiography of a street criminal, ed by P. Heymann and D. Kelly; with comments by O. Coombs. J. Allen. il Psychol Today 11:96-7+ O '77

Culture

Africa—American style; Oyotunji; South Carolina village. M. Popp. il Ebony 33:86-8+ Ja '78
Crisis of the black spirit. L. Bennett, Jr. il Ebony 32:142-4 O '77
Interview with Alex Haley; ed by W. McGuire and M. S. Clayton. A. Haley. Todays Educ 66:46-7 S '77
Merry Kwanza! S. C. Cowley and M. Lord. il Newsweek 90:103 D 19 '77

Study and teaching

Elma Lewis: keeping African culture alive in Boston; Elma Lewis School of Fine Arts. S. Quinn. il por Ms 5:14-15+ My '77

Economic conditions

Black progress myth and ghetto reality. J. Dreyfuss. il Progressive 41:21-5 N '77
Economic gains of black workers; excerpts from address. R. Freeman. Intellect 106:102-3 S '77
How racial bias and social status affect the earnings of young men. G. D. Jud and J. L. Walker. bibl M Labor R 100:44-6 Ap '77
What black leaders want from business. il Bus W p85+ O 10 '77

Education

Eliminating black cultural oppression in the school curriculum. J. L. Colquit. Educ Digest 42:21-3 Mr '77
Sources of school-community conflict in black communities. T. Monteiro. il Intellect 106:155-6 O '77

BLACKS—Education—*Continued*
Washington notebook; views of D. S. MacNaughton. S. Booker. Ebony 33:25 D '77
Westside story; M. Collins, founder of Westside Preparatory School, Chicago. il por Time 110: 39 D 26 '77
See also
Black students
Catholic schools—Desegregation
Colleges and universities—Desegregation
Public schools—Desegregation
Socially handicapped children—Education

Conferences

See Education—Conferences

Employment

Equality in industry for U.S. blacks. E. D. Jackson. por Nations Bus 65:91 D '77
Maybe things haven't really changed. il Ebony 32:112-13 F '77
See also
Black youth—Employment

Food

See Blacks—Nutrition

Health and hygiene

Is your doctor ripping you off? T. E. Evans. Ebony 32:45-6+ S '77
On the health of black Americans. T. E. Evans. por Ebony 32:112 Mr '77
Ten worst things you can do to your health. B. Rhoden. il Ebony 33:30+ Ja '78

History

Great moments in black history:
Day race relations changed forever; Brown v. Board of Education; school desegregation decision. L. Bennett, Jr. il Ebony 32:132-6+ My '77
Day the black revolution began; Montgomery bus boycott, 1955. L. Bennett, Jr. il pors Ebony 32:54-6+ S '77
Day they didn't march. L. Bennett, Jr. il Ebony 32:128-30+ F '77
My search for roots; excerpt. A. Haley. il por Read Digest 110:148-52 Ap '77
Roots; condensation; reprint of 1974 article. A. Haley. il Read Digest 110:153-79 Ap; 145-68 My '77
See also
Association for the Study of Afro-American Life and History
Slavery—United States

Study and teaching

See also
Black studies

Housing

Town that refused to panic; integration of Laurelton section of Queens, N.Y. J. Cook. McCalls 104:71 Jl '77
See also
Housing—Desegregation

Income

See Blacks—Economic conditions

Intelligence

See Intelligence levels—Blacks

Language

See also
Black-English dialects

Names

What's in a name? S. S. Walker. il Ebony 32: 74-6+ Je '77

Nutrition

Why where you from has replaced what's your sign; black woman in Paris. V. Smart-Grosvenor. Mademoiselle 83:96-7+ Jl '77

Occupations

Speaking of people. See issues of Ebony
See also
Black health workers

Photographs

Faces of slavery. E. Reichlin. il Am Heritage 28:4-11 Je '77

Political activities

See Blacks and politics

Psychology

Black women/black men: has something gone wrong between them? interviews. A. Poussaint; A. A. Poussaint. il pors Ebony 32:160-2 Ag '77

Religious life

Black theology: raising the questions; conference on Black Church and Black Community: Unity and Education for Action in Atlanta. G. S. Wilmore. Chr Cent 94:645-6 Jl 20 '77
Views of a regenerate radical; interview, ed by J. S. Tinney. E. Cleaver. il pors Chr Today 21:14-15 Jl 8 '77
See also
Catholic Church—Blacks
Church and race problems
Mormons and Mormonism, Black
National Black Evangelical Association

Segregation

Cities' secret: heading toward apartheid. I. Howe. New Repub 176:55-7 Ja 22 '77
See also
Catholic schools—Desegregation
Church and race problems
Public schools—Desegregation
Segregation in education

Segregation, Resistance to

Day the black revolution began; Montgomery bus boycott, 1955. L. Bennett, Jr. il pors Ebony 32:54-6+ S '77
See also
Civil rights demonstrations

Social conditions

American family, Duffy family of Arkansas. J. P. Blank. il Read Digest 111:107-12 Jl '77
Black conjugations; Black family in slavery and freedom, 1750-1925. J. D. Anderson. Am Scholar 46:384+ Summ '77
Crisis of the black spirit. L. Bennett, Jr. il Ebony 32:142-4 O '77
See also
Blacks—Segregation

Unemployment

See Unemployment

Alabama

See also
Birmingham, Ala.—Blacks
Montgomery, Ala.—Blacks

Delaware

Underground railroad in Delaware. J. E. Newton. bibl il Negro Hist Bull 40:702-3 My '77

Florida

Booker T. Washington: a visit to Florida. R. C. Potter. por Negro Hist Bull 40:744-5 S '77

Georgia

Reflections: remembrance of moderates past. C. Trillin. il New Yorker 58:85-8+ Mr 21 '77

Louisiana

See also
New Orleans—Blacks

Montana

Stagecoach Mary; M. Fields; ed by M. Crawford. G. Cooper. il pors Ebony 32:96-8+ O '77

New Jersey

See also
Newark, N.J.—Blacks

New York (state)

See also
New York (city)—Harlem

South Carolina

Africa—American style; Oyotunji; South Carolina village. M. Popp. il Ebony 33:86-8+ Ja '78

Southern States

Woman who changed the South; a memory of Fannie Lou Hamer. E. H. Norton. por Ms 6: 51+ Jl '77

BLACKS and Indians of North America. See Indians of North America and blacks

BLACKS and Jews. See Jews and blacks

BLACKS and politics

Barbara Jordan—new voice in Washington. I. Ross. por Read Digest 110:148-52 F '77
Black monolith. W. F. Buckley, Jr. Nat R 29: 1452-3 D 9 '77
Black vote; Joint Center for Political Studies survey. Society 14:8 Ja '77
Carter and black Americans. P. Delaney. Nation 225:132-3 Ag 20 '77
Dynamics of black local politics: an interview with G. Lindsay; ed by J. Elliot. G. Lindsay. por Negro Hist Bull 40:718-20 Jl '77
Fallout between friends; J. Carter rebuked by V. Jordan. por Time 110:27-8 Ag 8 '77
Family squabble; V. Jordan's criticism of the Carter administration. P. Goldman and others. il pors Newsweek 90:16-18 Ag 8 '77
Let them eat words. New Repub 177:5-6 S 17 '77
U.S. black leadership—now going collective. J. Thornton. il U.S. News 83:53-4 Jl 4 '77
Washington notebook. S. Booker. See issues of Ebony
See also
Black public officers

BLACKS in Brazil
Afro-Brazilian experiment. G. Freyre. il UNESCO Courier 30:13-18 Ag '77
Where gods and men have mingled. J. Amado. il UNESCO Courier 30:18-19 Ag '77
BLACKS in Cuba
Afro-Cuban poetry. J. A. León. il Américas 29:28-32 S '77
BLACKS in England
Question of fault; race problems in London schools. T. J. Cottle. Progressive 41:34-6 O '77
BLACKS in France
Why where you from has replaced what's your sign; black woman in Paris. V. Smart-Grosvenor. Mademoiselle 83:96-7+ Jl '77
BLACKS in Great Britain
Cost of hope. T. J. Cottle. America 136:125-7 F 12 '77
Jamie Horace Pinkerton. T. J. Cottle. il America 136:370-3 Ap 23 '77
BLACKS in Latin America
Blacks in Latin America. A. Carpentier. il UNESCO Courier 30:8-12 Ag '77
BLACKS in literature
Black boy; R. Wright's novel. K. T. Lund. Engl J 66:59-60 Mr '77
Flying home; R. Ellison's short story. M. W. Mintz. Engl J 66:67-8 Mr '77
Not without laughter; L. Hughes novel. M. J. Moran. Engl J 66:58 Mr '77
Poems on various subjects, religious and moral; P. Wheatley's poetry. K. Holder. Engl J 66:68 Mr '77
Soul brothers and sister Lou; K. Hunter's novel. N. Stimpfle. Engl J 66:61 Mr '77
Uncle Tom's Roots. M. Greenfield. il Newsweek 89:100 F 14 '77
BLACKS in motion pictures
Cine-opsis; searches for roots. J. Varlejs. il Wilson Lib Bull 52:258-9 N 77
BLACKS in poetry. See Blacks in literature
BLACKS in South Africa
See also
South Africa—Race question
BLACKS in Surinam
Bush Negroes carry on tradition of rebel ancestors; A. Counter-D. Evans expeditions. C. M. Turnbull. il Smithsonian 7:78-85 Mr '77
BLACKS in Sweden
Scholar moonlights at T'ai chi ch'uan. il pors Ebony 32:44-6+ Jl '77
BLACKS in the Armed Forces. See United States—Armed Forces—Blacks
BLACKS in Uruguay
Night of nights in Montevideo; Llamadas festival. C. Paez Vilaró. il Américas 29:58-9 N '77
BLACKSMITHING
Art in wrought iron: the collection of James C. Sorber, West Chester, Pennsylvania. L. H. Solis-Cohen. il Antiques 111:782-93 Ap '77
BLACKSMITHS
Get it hot and hit it is blacksmiths' cry. E. Johnson. il Craft Horiz 37:9 F '77
BLACKWELL, Harriet Gray
Lost children; poem. Ladies Home J 94:166 F '77
BLACKWELL, Unita
Lady mayor of Mayersville. il pors Ebony 33:53-6+ D '77 *
BLACKWELL'S Children's Bookshop, Oxford. See Booksellers and bookselling—Great Britain
BLADDER
Cancer
13-cis Retinoic acid: inhibition of bladder carcinogenesis in the rat. M. B. Sporn and others. bibl il Science 195:487-9 F 4 '77
BLADES, Saw. See Saws
BLAFFORD, Antoinette
Yabba-yabba, doodle-doodle; interview. New Yorker 53:55-6 N 21 '77
BLAFFORD, Clem
Yabba-yabba, doodle-doodle; interview. New Yorker 53:55-6 N 21 '77
BLAGOWIDOW, George
PW interviews; ed by J. F. Baker. por Pub W 211:8-10 My 16 '77
BLAIR, Calvin P.
Echeverría's economic policy. bibl f Cur Hist 72:124-7+ Mr '77
BLAIR, John M.
Spanking the sisters. Time 109:47-8 F 28 '77 *
BLAIR, John S.
Tennis on a tank. il Parks & Rec 12:35a F '77
BLAIR, Linda
Close-up; interview, ed by E. Miller. por Seventeen 36:92 Je '77
BLAIR, S. Robert
Man who won the pipeline. por Bus W p88-9 Ag 22 '77 *
BLAKE, Andrea
Enchanted bride; story. Good H 184:163-6 Ap '77
BLAKE, David Leonard
Toussaint; or The aristocracy of the skin. Reviews
New Yorker 53:165-7 O 24 '77
BLAKE, Fay M. and Perlmutter, E. L.
Rush to user fees: alternative proposals. bibl Lib J 102:2005-8 O 1 '77
BLAKE, Richard A.
Dialogue weekend. America 136:105-6 F 5 '77
Films/TV. See issues of America
King's own daughter. America 137:421 D 10 '77
New bishop for New York. America 137:331-2 N 12 '77
Pail of water. America 136:239-40 Mr 19 '77
BLAKEMORE, Colin
Unsolved marvel of memory; excerpt from Mechanics of the mind. il N Y Times Mag p42-6+ F 6 '77
—See Garey, L. J. jt auth
BLANCH DE ALCOLEA, Montserrat. See Soper, C. L. jt auth
BLANCHARD, Florence
High-altitude growing in California. il Org Gard & Farm 25:80-1 Ja '78
BLANCHARD, Gertrude
Christmas tree story; story. Parks & Rec 12:24-5 D '77
BLANCHETTE, Romeo, Bp
Lift up your hearts. New Cath World 220:10 Ja '77
BLANCK, Clarence A.
End taste and odor complaints with granular activated carbon. il por Am City & County 92:89-90 O '77
BLANCO, Hugo
Foggy bottom curtain. Nation 225:260 S 24 '77 *
BLAND, Alexander
Tamerlane of the performing arts. il pors Horizon 20:28-34 S '77
BLANK, Joseph P.
American family. il Read Digest 111:107-12 Jl '77
Girl who wouldn't grow up. il Read Digest 111:199-202+ O '77
I'm gonna miss you. Read Digest 111:233-4+ N '77
Kidnapped! The ordeal that shook Chowchilla. il Read Digest 111:51-5+ S '77
—and Mueller, M. J.
Convict and the boy. il Read Digest 110:135-9 My '77
—See Thomsen, P. M. jt auth
BLANKENHORN, David H.
New medical techniques from space technology. Intellect 106:189 N '77
BLANKETS
Blankets. Consumer Rep 42:319-20 D '77
BLANKETS, rugs, etc, Indian (American) See Indian blankets, rugs, etc (American)
BLANTON, Henry
Profiles. J. Kramer. New Yorker 53:44-6+ My 30; 40-4+ Je 6 '77 *
BLASHFORD-SNELL, John
Man who would be Kipling. H. Sutton. il Sat R 4:44-5 My 28 '77 *
BLASING, Randy
All present; poem. Poetry 130:3 Ap '77
BLASPHEMY
See also
Trails (blasphemy)
BLASS, Elliott M. See Kenny, J. T; Teicher, M. H. jt auths
BLASTING
Blasted ditches—new way to drain land. C. E. Sommers. il Suc Farm 75:no5 58 Mr '77
BLASTOCYSTS
Does blastocyst estrogen initiate implantation? Z. Dickmann and others. bibl Science 195:687-8 F 18 '77
BLASTS. See Explosions
BLATCHLEY, David, and Gove, Clayton
Saying, showing, shaping. il Parks & Rec 12:38-40 N '77
BLATTNER, Frederick R. and others
Charon phages: safer derivatives of bacteriophage lambda for DNA cloning. bibl il Science 196:161-9 Ap 8 '77
BLAUROCK, Allen E. and King, G. I.
Asymmetric structure of the purple membrane. bibl il Science 196:1101-4 Je 3 '77
BLAUSTEIN, Andrew R. See Kuris, A. M. jt auth
BLAUSTEIN, Arthur I.
California still dreaming. il Harpers 254:19-21 Je '77
BLAUSTEIN, John
Just keep your head above water; photographs. Sports Illus 47:24-8 Ag 1 '77
BLAWIS, Michele
Glomar Challenger. il Oceans 10:6-7 N '77
BLAYLOCK, Kenneth
Let soldiers join labor unions? interview. pors U.S. News 82:51-2 Mr 28 '77
BLAZEJOWSKI, Carol
No one is hotter than the Blaze. K. Hannon. il por Sports Illus 48:35-6 Ja 2 '78 *
BLAZER, J. S. pseud. See Scott, Justin
BLEACHES. See Bleaching materials
BLEACHING materials
Detergents, bleaches, softeners—when to use what. il Changing T 31:29-30 My '77
Guide to laundry aids; bleaches and fabric softeners. il Good H 184:216+ My '77
Laundry bleaches; all-fabric bleaches. il Consumer Rep 42:514-15 S '77

BLECHMAN, Fred
Biorhythm clock. il Radio-Electr 48:33-7 N '77
Build this digital on-screen TV clock. il Radio-Electr 48:35-8 Jl '77
Digital clock kits for your car. il Radio-Electr 48:35-9 O; 41-4 N; 45-7 D '77
Easy-to-build digital clocks. il Radio-Electr 48:54-7+ Mr '77

BLECHNER, Mark
Group for Contemporary Music. il Hi Fi 27:MA24-5 N '77

BLEDSOE, Audrey
Playscapes sculpture-playground in Atlanta. il Sch Arts 76:22-5 Ap '77
Preparing teenagers for the world of work. il Parents Mag 52:23-4 My '77

BLEDSOE, Eugene
Teaching about divorce. Todays Educ 66:31 Ja '77

BLEED, Peter
Early flakes from Sozudai, Japan: are they man-made? bibl il Science 197:1357-9 S 30 '77

BLEGEN, Judith
Music to my ears. I. Kolodin. por Sat R 4:43-4 F 5 '77 *
Songs of Strauss and Wolf. C. T. Veilleux. Am Rec G 40:46 Mr '77 *

BLEHL, Vincent Ferrer
Letters of John Henry Newman. America 137:184-6 O 1 '77

BLENDERS. See Kitchen utensils and appliances

BLESSING
Icon tree; excerpt from Irrational season. M. L'Engle. Chr Cent 94:321-4 Ap 6 '77

BLETILLA. See Orchids

BLEY, Carla (Borg)
Indigenous music. N. Hentoff. Nation 225:126 Ag 6 '77 *

BLIGHT, David W.
Bull in the China shop. il pors Am Hist Illus 12:10-19 Ap '77
Martyrdom of Elijah P. Lovejoy. il Am Hist Illus 12:20-7 N '77

BLIMPS. See Airships

BLIND
Blind jurors. Newsweek 90:70 O 10 '77
Blind man living in normal society has circadian rhythms of 24.9 hours. L. E. M. Miles and others. bibl il Science 198:421-3 O 28 '77
On a reef, darkly; conchologist G. Vermeij. K. Brower. il Read Digest 110:125-8 F '77
Second sight; case of C. Sanford. L. David. il por Ladies Home J 94:154+ Jl '77
To every thing there is a season: discrimination against the blind; address, July 7, 1977. K. Jernigan. Vital Speeches 43:666-71 Ag 15 '77
Visual association cortex and vision in man: pattern-evoked occipital potentials in a blind boy. I. Bodis-Wollner and others. bibl il Science 198:629-31 N 11 '77
See also
Architecture and the blind
Art galleries and museums—Work with the blind
Libraries—Services to the blind

Education

David Hartman's impossible dream; graduate of Temple University School of Medicine. A. Rankin. il por Read Digest 110:78-82 Ap '77

Recreation

See also
Camps for the handicapped
Sports for the blind

BLIND, Apparatus for the
Vibrotactile pattern perception: extraordinary observers; use of Optacon. J. C. Craig. bibl il Science 196:450-2 Ap 22 '77

BLIND, Books for the
See also
Talking books

BLIND, Libraries for the
Barrier free; Alabama Regional Library for the Blind and Physically Handicapped. A. G. Bushman. il Am Lib 8:303-4 Je '77
See also
Illinois Regional Library for the Blind and Physically Handicapped, Chicago

BLIND, National Federation of the. See National Federation of the Blind

BLINDERMAN, Charles S.
Adventures of a consultant writer. Writers Digest 57:25-6 My '77

BLINDNESS
Losing sight: a chronicle of affliction; excerpt from Eyes, etc. E. Clark. Commentary 63:36-47 My '77
New ways to save your sight. A. Rosenblum. Good H 184:204 Ap '77
See also
Blind

BLINDS
See also
Shutters

BLINDS (camouflage)
For candid wildlife pictures, build a blind. R. Sheppard. il Pop Phot 81:106-8+ Ag '77
Good blind can be big as a truck or small as your hat; duck blinds. J. O. Cartier. il Outdoor Life 160:74-7+ N '77
Photo blind you can build. H. Engels. il Mech Illus 73:110-11 O '77

BLINK comparators. See Comparators

BLINTZES. See Pancakes, waffles, etc.

BLISS, Charles M.
History, not fads. por Forbes 120:102 O 1 '77 *

BLISS, Edwin C.
Ten tips to help you manage your time; excerpt from Getting things done: the ABC's of time management. Read Digest 110:185-6+ Ap '77

BLISTERS
Blister formation—another test of hypnotic suggestion; research by Theodore Barber and R. F. Q. Johnson. Psychol Today 11:28+ S '77

BLITZSTEIN, Marc
Regina. Reviews
Hi Fi il 28:MA19-20 Ja '78 *
New Yorker 53:162 O 24 '77 *

BLIVEN, Bruce, 1889-1977
Obituary
New Repub 176:8-9 Je 11 '77. M. Cowley

BLIXEN, Karen (Dinesen) Baronesse
Reality in fantasy. D. Grumbach. Sat R 5:54-5 D 10 '77 *

BLIZZARDS. See Snowstorms

BLOAT (cattle) See Cattle—Diseases and pests

BLOBAUM, Roger
Getting started in farming: it's still a hard row to hoe. il Org Gard & Farm 24:69-71 Ag '77
Making farms affordable for young people. il Org Gard & Farm 24:76-9 O '77

BLOCH, Alfred M.
Battered teacher. Todays Educ 66:58-9+ Mr '77

BLOCH, Ernest
Symphony for trombone and orchestra; Suite symphonique. W. Simmons. por Am Rec G 40:22-3 D '76 *

BLOCH, Henry
Independent Schools Orchestra. B. R. Paolucci. il por Hi Fi 27:MA22-5 O '77 *

BLOCK, Jean Libman
Rebirth of Beth Thorne. Good H 185:99+ Jl '77
What the Carters are doing to wipe out divorce in Washington. il Good H 184:109+ Je '77

BLOCK, Julian
Remodeling notebook. House B 119:44 Mr '77
Taxes. See issues of Vogue

BLOCK, Lawrence
Fiction. See occasional issues of Writer's digest

BLOCK, Thomas H.
Pro's nest. See issues of Flying

BLOCK booking. See Motion pictures—Distribution

BLOCK printing
Printed mural. M. Foster. il Sch Arts 77:48-50 D '77
See also
Wood engravings

BLOCKS, Toy. See Toys

BLODGETT, Geoffrey
Comments; ideology and political culture. Am Hist R 82:563-7 Je '77

BLOEMENDAL, Hans
Vertebrate eye lens. bibl il Science 197:127-38 Jl 8 '77

BLOESER, Bonnie, and others
Chitinozoans from the late Precambrian Chuar Group of the Grand Canyon, Arizona. bibl il Science 195:676-9 F 18 '77

BLOOD

Cholesterol content

See Cholesterol

Circulation

See also
Pulse

Cleansing

See Plasmapheresis

Coagulation

Blood clotting: the role of the prostaglandins. J. L. Marx. il Science 196:1072-5 Je 3 '77; Reply. L. S. Wolfe and C. Pace-Asciak. bibl 197:210 Jl 15 '77
Formation of a serine enzyme in the presence of bovine factor VIII (antihemophilic factor) and thrombin. G. A. Vehar and E. W. Davie. bibl il Science 197:374-6 Jl 22 '77
Human factor VIII: morphometric analysis of purified material in solution. H. K. Tan and J. C. Andersen. bibl il Science 198:932-4 D 2 '77
See also
Anticoagulants
Embolism

Collection and preservation

FDA enforcing new standards for blood donations. Ret Liv 17:14 Ja '77

BLOOD—*Continued*

Corpuscles and platelets

See Blood cells

Dialysis

See Hemodialysis

Diseases

See also
Anemia
Leukemia
Piroplasmosis
Sickle cell anemia

Formation

Surface molecules of hematopoietic stem cells: requirement for sialic acid in spleen colony formation. Q. Tonelli and R. H. Meints. bibl il Science 195:897-8 Mr 4 '77

Gas content

Venous gas bubbles: production by transient, deep isobaric counterdiffusion of helium against nitrogen. B. G. D'Aoust and others. bibl il Science 197:889-91 Ag 26 '77

Jurisprudence

See Forensic hematology

Pigments

See also
Hemoglobin

Plasma

Insulin, glucagon, and glucose exhibit synchronous, sustained oscillations in fasting monkeys. C. J. Goodner and others. bibl il Science 195: 177-9 Ja 14 '77

Proteins

Albumin phylogeny for clawed frogs (xenopus) C. A. Bisbee and others. bibl il Science 195: 785-7 F 25 '77
Good v. bad cholesterol; role of lipoproteins. il Time 110:119 N 21 '77
Hepatic binding protein: the protective role of its sialic acid residues. R. J. Stockert and others. bibl il Science 197:667-8 Ag 12 '77
Leukemia fighters in the bloodstream. Sci N 112: 86-7 Ag 6 '77
See also
Immunoglobulins
Properdin

Serum

See Serums

Testing

Pricking up their ears; lactic acid blood testing to determine most efficient training pace for athletes. J. Kirshenbaum. il por Sports Illus 47:94+ O 31 '77
Test detects liver damage in alcoholics. Sci N 112:55+ Jl 23 '77
Test to prevent birth defects; blood test for susceptibility to rubella. M. R. Skrocki. McCalls 104:67 Jl '77

Transfusion

See also
Blood donors
Blood groups

BLOOD banks
See also
Blood donors

BLOOD cells
Blood corpuscles and blood hemoglobins: a possible example of coevolution. G. K. Snyder. bibl il Science 195:412-13 Ja 28 '77
Overlapping platelets: a diffusion barrier in a teleost swimbladder. D. S. Brown and D. E. Copeland. bibl il Science 197:383-4 Jl 22 '77
See also
Erythrocytes
Erythropoiesis
Leukocytes
Lymphocytes

BLOOD clotting. See Blood—Coagulation

BLOOD coagulation factors. See Blood—Coagulation

BLOOD donors
Blood: it's safe to give, but sometimes dangerous to receive. W. Hoffer. il Fam Health 9:36-9 Mr '77
See also
Blood—Collection and preservation

BLOOD groups
Blood-type clues. M. Clark and D. Shapiro. Newsweek 91:70-1 Ja 9 '78

BLOOD memories; ballet. See Ballet reviews—Single works

BLOOD pressure
See also
Hypertension
Sphygomomanometers

BLOOD sugar
Homeostasis during hypoglycemia: central control of adrenal secretion and peripheral control of feeding. E. M. Stricker and others. bibl il Science 196:79-81 Ap 1 '77
Hunger in humans induced by 2-deoxy-D-glucose: glucoprivic control of taste preference and food intake. D. A. Thompson and R. G. Campbell. bibl il Science 198:1065-8 D 9 '77
Insulin, glucagon, and glucose exhibit synchronous, sustained oscillations in fasting monkeys. C. J. Goodner and others. bibl il Science 195: 177-9 Ja 14 '77

BLOOD types. See Blood groups

BLOOD vessels
See also
Arteries

Radiography

See Angiography

Surgery

Preventing strokes; surgical bypass of the internal carotid artery. Newsweek 89:79 Ja 31 '77

BLOODHOUNDS
Bloodhound. R. Caras. il por Sci Digest 82:62-5 N '77

BLOODY Mary (cocktail) See Cocktails

BLOOM, Benjamin S.
Only one-third of children learning. il Intellect 106:184-5 N '77

BLOOM, Elizabeth Gilboy
Elizabeth Bloom: art and nature. E. Medoff. il Am Artist 41:62-7 Je '77 *

BLOOM, Fred A.
Psychotherapy and moral culture: a psychiatrist's field report. Yale R 66:321-46 Mr '77

BLOOM, Harold
Harold Bloom on poetry. il New Repub 177:24-6 N 26 '77

BLOOM, Norman
God and Norman Bloom. C. Sagan. il Am Scholar 46:460-6 Aut '77 *

BLOOMFIELD, Maureen
Morning; Ghosts; Near the end of June; The long ton; Isuprel; poems. Poetry 129:257-62 F '77

BLOOMING of plants. See Plants, Flowering of

BLOOMINGDALE'S stores. See Department stores

BLOOMINGTON, Ind.
Town dilemma; PCB contamination of Bloomington, Ind. sewage. D. Jordan. il map Environment 19:6-15 Mr '77

BLOOMINGTON, Minn.
Make gasoline losses evaporate; computerized control over fuel records for municipal vehicles. H. G. Wurdelman. il Am City & County 92: 39-40 Ja '77

BLOSSOM, Mark
Treadle power in the workshop. il Org Gard & Farm 24:83-5 Je '77

BLOT, William J. and others
Cancer mortality in U.S. counties with petroleum industries. bibl Science 198:51-3 O 7 '77

BLOUGH, Donald S.
Visual search in the pigeon: hunt and peck method. bibl il Science 196:1013-14 My 27 '77

BLOUIN, Michael Thomas
Excerpts from remarks on reorganization powers of the President, February 22, 1977. Cong Digest 56:116+ Ap '77

BLOUNT, Joan Ackermann-. See Ackermann-Blount, J.

BLOUNT, Mel
Football is art. Holding out is life. R. Blount, Jr. Esquire 88:68+ N '77 *

BLOUNT, Roy, Jr
Bear Bryant's stompin' school. Esquire 88:52+ S '77
Chaws. il Sports Illus 47:54-9+ Jl 4 '77
Country's angels. il pors Esquire 87:62-7+ Mr '77
Games (cont) Esquire 87:38+ F; 44+ Ap '77
Losersville, U.S.A. il por Sports Illus 46:74-7+ Mr 21 '77
Love songs of Roy Blount jr. il por Esquire 87:105-7 Ap '77
Sports (title varies) See issues of Esquire

about

Letter from the publisher. J. Meyers. por Sports Illus 46:6 Mr 21 '77 *

BLOUNT, Winton Malcolm
Life after the post office. por Forbes 119:142 Ap 15 '77 *

BLOUNT, Inc. See Construction industry

BLOW dryers. See Hair dryers

BLOWERS, Leaf. See Lawn tools, equipment, and supplies

BLOY, Betsy
How self-hypnosis worked for me. Seventeen 36: 158+ My '77

BLUE, Anthony Dias
ABC of fruit liqueurs. il House & Gard 149:160+ Mr '77
Sugar and spice liqueurs. il House & Gard 149: 136+ D '77

BLUE Bell, Inc
Strong management is always in style at Blue Bell. il Duns R 109:18-19 F '77

BLUE-collar Caucus. See Caucuses

BLUE collar workers. See Labor and laboring classes

BLUE crabs. See Crabs
BLUE Cross-Blue Shield insurance. See Insurance, Health—United States
BLUE Cross plan of law insurance. See Insurance, Litigation
BLUE-green algae. See Algae
BLUE jays. See Jays
BLUE marlin fishing. See Marlin fishing
BLUE Ridge Mountains
Blue Ridge of Georgia. R. Magruder and M. Magruder. il Travel 147:36-41+ F '77
Waste no pity upon these foxes; excerpt from The foxes' union. J. J. Kilpatrick. il Smithsonian 8:85-7 Ag '77
BLUE Shield-Blue Cross insurance. See Insurance, Health—United States
BLUE Shield insurance. See Insurance, Health—United States
BLUE Train. See Railroads—Africa, Southern
BLUE Water Cruising Race. See Yacht racing
BLUEBERRIES
See also
Cookery—Fruit
BLUEBIRDS
Art print of the year: eastern bluebird. M. Wexler. il Nat Wildlife 15:33 O '77
Song of hope for the bluebird. L. Zeleny. il map Nat Geog 151:854-65 Je '77
BLUEFIN tuna. See Tuna fish
BLUEFISH fishing
Tumult on a wild shore; Nantucket. W. Humphrey. il Sports Illus 47:42-4+ N 7 '77
BLUEGILL fishing. See Sunfish fishing
BLUEGRASS music festivals. See Music festivals
BLUES. See Depression, Mental
BLUES (songs, etc)
Foghat: paying dues to the blues; benefit concert for blues collection of New York Public Library. il Sr Schol 110:23 D 1 '77
Rebirth of the blues; A. Hunter. H. Saal. il pors Newsweek 90:101 O 31 '77
BLUHDORN, Charles G.
Blues for Mr Charlie. il por Time 110:71-2 Jl 18 '77 *
Bluhdorn is at it. . .again. por Forbes 119:30-1 Ap 15 '77 *
BLUM, Albert
Labor movement today. Intellect 106:9 Jl '77
BLUM, Arthur F.
Q&A about insurance. Ret Liv 17:48 Je; 16 N '77
BLUM, Etta
As though existence; poem. Nation 225:478 N 5 '77
Olive tree, first pilgrim; poem. New Repub 176:26 F 5 '77
BLUM, Howard
Story behind the book: Wanted! The search for Nazis in America; interview, ed by J. F. Baker. Pub W 211:72 F 7 '77
BLUM, Ralph C. and Solberg, C. E.
Is pavement reinforcing worth its cost? il Am City & County 92:59-61 D '77
BLUM, Stephen
Ives's position in social and musical history. bibl f il Mus Q 63:459-82 O '77
BLUM, Virgil C.
Recent developments in the law; address, January 25, 1977. Vital Speeches 43:296-300 Mr 1 '77
BLUM, Zevi
When god was a woman. il por Horizon 20:82-5 O '77
BLUMBERG, Baruch S.
Australia antigen and the biology of hepatitis B. bibl il Science 197:17-25 Jl 1 '77
BLUMBERG, Bonnie Birtwistle
Rocker; poem. Chr Cent 94:60 Ja 26 '77
BLUMBERG, Paul
An authority tells why status symbols keep changing; interview. por U.S. News 82:41-2 F 14 '77
BLUME, Mary
Cultural colossus of Beaubourg. il Art N 76:36-9 Mr '77
Wine: new panacea. Vogue 167:331-2 N '77
BLUMENAU, Lili
Obituary
Craft Horiz 37:10 F '77. N. Znamierowski
BLUMENFELD, Samuel L.
Motherhood; address, July 16, 1977. Vital Speeches 43:661-6 Ag 15 '77
BLUMENSCHEIN, Ernest Leonard
Ernest L. Blumenschein: intellect and growth. M. C. Nelson. il por Am Artist 42:36-41+ Ja '78 *
BLUMENSON, Martin
Patton in Mexico. il pors Am Hist Illus 12:34-42 O '77
Perspectives on the past. Am Hist Illus 12:50 My; 19 Jl; 48 O '77

BLUMENSTOCK, Robert S.
What is a 12-meter? il Yachting 142:144+ S '77
BLUMENTHAL, Joseph
Finding things to say. New Yorker 53:29-31 S 12 '77 *
BLUMENTHAL, Sidney
Urban aid—banned in Boston. Nation 224:70-2 Ja 22 '77
BLUMENTHAL, Werner Michael
Ahead: at least 3 years of prosperity; interview. por U.S. News 82:31-4 Ap 11 '77
Keynesian moves in as Treasury Secretary; interview. por Bus W p34-5 Ja 31 '77
Message from OPEC; excerpts from interview, ed by R. Thomas. il por Newsweek 90:92 N 14 '77
News conference of Secretary Vance and Secretary Blumenthal, May 8. Dept State Bull 76:586-93 Je 6 '77
Our tax system; address, July 20, 1977. Vital Speeches 43:674-7 S 1 '77
Secretary Vance attends ministerial conference of the Organization for Economic Cooperation and Development; remarks and transcript of joint news conference, June 24, 1977. Dept State Bull 77:109-17 Jl 25 '77
Toward international equilibrium: a strategy for the longer pull; address, May 25, 1977. Dept State Bull 77:13-18 Jl 4 '77
Treasury Secretary Blumenthal testifies on legislation on illicit payments abroad; statement, March 16, 1977. Dept State Bull 76:351-5 Ap 11 '77
about
Face-off on dollar strategy. il por Bus W p20-1 Ag 8 '77 *
He met a payroll. Suetonius. New Repub 176:16-17 Ja 29 '77 *
Jimmy Carter gets mixed marks in economics I. J. Cameron. il pors Fortune 95:98-102+ Je '77 *
Sagging dollar may raise oil prices. il Bus W p42 N 14 '77 *
Spenders vs. savers: split in the Cabinet. W. C. Bryant. il pors U.S. News 82:18 Ap 18 '77 *
Tax package made for stimulus. E. Lewis. Bus W p91 Ja 9 '78 *
Trials of a T-man. T. Mathews and others. il por Newsweek 90:40 O 17 '77 *
Who's calling the economic shots. Bus W p 117 Mr 28 '77 *
BLUMER, Max and others
Azaarenes in recent marine sediments. bibl il Science 195:283-4 Ja 21 '77
BLUNT, John S.
John S. Blunt. R. Bishop. il Antiques 112:964-71 N '77 *
BLY, Robert
Tiny spinning wheel concerto; poem. New Repub 177:28 S 3 '77
Two years after the war; poem. Nation 224:636 My 21 '77
B'NAI B'rith
Anti-Defamation League
Fragile pact to beat the Arab boycott; Business Roundtable—B'nai B'rith Anti-Defamation League agreement. Bus W p25-6 Mr 28 '77
Unglued alliance on the Arab boycott; Business Roundtable and B'nai B'rith Anti-Defamation League. Bus W p43-4 S 12 '77
BOAR hunting. See Wild boar hunting
BOARD of directors meetings. See Corporations—Meetings
BOARD of Trade, Chicago. See Chicago Board of Trade
BOARDS of directors. See Corporations—Directors
BOARDS of directors, Bank. See Banks and banking—Directors
BOARDS of education. See School boards
BOAT accessories. See Boats—Equipment
BOAT building. See Boatbuilding
BOAT buying. See Boats—Purchasing
BOAT camping. See Camping
BOAT clubs
See also
Yacht clubs
BOAT cockpits. See Boats—Cockpits
BOAT covers. See Boats—Equipment
BOAT decoration
Le salon à la mode; yachts. B. O'Donovan. il Motor B & S 140:64-7 Ag '77
New interiors: styling comes to sailboat design. J. Rousmaniere. il Yachting 141:82-5 My '77
Trend to hull graphics. il Motor B & S 140:58-61 N '77
BOAT deliveries. See Boats—Transportation
BOAT docks. See Docks, wharves, etc.
BOAT engines. See Marine engines
BOAT filters. See Marine engines—Filters
BOAT fittings. See Boats—Equipment
BOAT flags. See Flags

BOAT hijacking
Cops & robbers offshore. T. Plate. il map Motor B & S 140:51-3 O '77
Mysterious disappearance of Pirate's Lady. T. Plate. il por Motor B & S 140:57-60+ S '77
Piracy on the low seas. J. Rothchild. il N Y Times Mag p50+ My 22 '77
Piracy update. P. Whittell. Motor B & S 141: 222 Ja '78
BOAT hulls. See Hulls (naval architecture)
BOAT models. See Ship and boat models
BOAT ownership

Anecdotes, facetiae, satire, etc.

Beyond the realm of logic. D. Bradley. il Motor B & S 139:7+ Mr '77
BOAT propellers. See Propellers
BOAT racing
See also
Canoe racing
Hydroplane racing
Motor boat racing
Raft racing
Rowing
Running rapids
Sailboat racing
BOAT radar. See Radar in navigation
BOAT railings. See Boats and boating—Safety devices and measures
BOAT shows. See Boats—Exhibitions
BOAT signals. See Signals and signaling
BOAT speed records
Mighty Magoon rides again; transatlantic crossing. T. West. il por Motor B & S 140:51-3+ Jl '77
Ondine vs. Atlantic; attempt to break transatlantic record. R. Humphreys. Yachting 142: 60-1+ Jl '77
Revved up to ride on an ocean of trouble; R. Magoon in the Citicorp Trans-Atlantic Challenge. R. Kennedy. il por Sports Illus 46:30-2+ Je 27 '77
BOAT thefts. See Boats, Theft of
BOAT toilets. See Boats—Toilet facilities
BOAT trade. See Boating industry
BOAT trailers. See Automobile boat trailers
BOAT varnishing. See Varnish and varnishing
BOAT winches. See Winches
BOAT yards. See Boatyards
BOATBUILDING
Aristocrat of boat builders. A. F. Ehrbar. il por Fortune 95:122-9 Ap '77
Deadly trade in under-built boats; Beachcraft Boat Company. W. P. Coughlin. il Motor B & S 139:61-5+ Ap '77
Modern wooden boat; construction of No go VIII. M. Walker. il Yachting 141:116+ My '77
One for the road; sailboats by MacGregor Yacht Corp. il por Forbes 120:100 O 1 '77
One of a kind; T. Elliott. O. Moore. il pors Motor B & S 140:58-60+ Jl '77
Powering round the globe; building the Wanderlure II. C. M. Heintz. il Motor B & S 139:46-9 Mr '77
See also
Boats—Materials
Hulls (naval architecture)
Keels
BOATING clothes. See Clothing and dress—Sports clothes
BOATING industry
Boating business. M. Lostrom. See issues of Yachting
Joys of boating. T. J. Murray. il Duns R 110: 54-6 Ag '77
BOATING schools. See Boats and boating—Study and teaching
BOATS

Anchoring

See Anchorage

Batteries

See Solar batteries; Storage batteries

Berths

Privacy (and comfort) afloat starts with a basic bed. J. Groene. Yachting 142:78-9 N '77

Cabins

Cuddy cabins turn runabouts into mini-cruisers. R. G. Black. il Pop Sci 210:106-8 F '77
Voyaging with Tristan Jones; accommodation. T. Jones. il Motor B & S 139:10+ Ap '77
See also
Boats—Galleys

Cockpits

As easy as π; cockpit drainage time. J. Cartwright. il Motor B & S 140:10+ Jl '77

Corrosion

See Corrosion and anti-corrosives

Defects

Cuckolded boat owner; dry rot. D. Bradley. il Motor B & S 139:10+ F '77
Designs; ed by J. Smith. See issues of Yachting

Design

Drawing board. See issues of Motor boating & sailing
Styling; work of W. Heintze. J. Gribbins. il por Motor B & S 139:54-7+ Ap '77
See also
Cruisers (pleasure boats)—Design
Fishing boats—Design
Sailboats—Design

Study and teaching

See Naval architecture—Study and teaching

Displacement

See Displacement (ships)

Electric equipment

ABYC's new wiring color code. T. Bottomley. il Motor B & S 139:85-6 F '77
See also
Electric generators, Alternating current

Electronic equipment

Electronic world of Manfred Meisels (cont of) Electronics. M. Meisels. il por Motor B & S 139:20+ My; 18-19+ Je; 140:13+ Jl; 28+ S; 23-4 N '77; 141:25+ Ja '78
Electronics: buying the basics. M. E. Foster. il Motor B & S 139:76-9+ Ap '77
It's new. . .in electronics. il Yachting 141:105 Mr '77
Mariner's guide to marine electronics; symposium. il Motor B & S 140:73-80+ O '77
See also
Automatic pilot (boats)
Boats—Radio equipment
Depth indicators
Electronics in fishing
Navigation—Aids and devices
Radar in navigation

Engines

See Marine engines

Equipment

Best new gear for skippers. B. McKeown. il Pop Mech 147:94-5 F '77
Blue water stern-drive; instrumentation on the Betty Cee. B. O'Donovan. il por Motor B & S 140:71-2+ O '77
Boating: on-water test reports of new gear. R. D. Stearns. See issues of Outdoor life
Choosing the galley stove; excerpt from The galley book. J. Groene. Yachting 141:90-1+ My '77
Convert to a cruiser with canvas. J. Martenhoff. il Pop Mech 147:32+ My '77
Fishing accessories; boat equipment. F. M. Paulson. il Field & S 81:146-50 Ap '77
Flexible couplings. N. Warren. il Motor B & S 141:43-6 Ja '78
Gadgets and gilhickies. J. Smith. See issues of Yachting
Good stove is priceless. M. Greenwald. il Motor B & S 141:104-7+ Ja '78
Good stoves for little boats. A. J. McMasters. il Mech Illus 73:16-17 S '77
Having a galley in a small boat. A. J. McMasters. il Mech Illus 73:10+ My '77
It's new. See issues of Yachting
Living aboard is a state of mind: storing possessions. D. Bradley. Motor B & S 140:10+ Ag '77
New gear for boatmen. il Mech Illus 73:30 Je '77
Proper stemhead fitting. J. Cartwright. il Motor B & S 141:19+ Ja '78
Radar reflector. il Motor B & S 140:64-6 Jl '77
Show stoppers. il Motor B & S 140:74-7 D '77; 141:142-6 Ja '78
Tech section. See issues of Motor boating & sailing
Ten winter covers. G. Cole and others. il Motor B & S 140:113-15 O '77
Three intriguing new gadgets. D. Rose. il Yachting 141:60+ Ap '77
Warm-weather companion slides; screens. B. White. il Motor B & S 140:102-3 Jl '77
What's new. See issues of Motor boating & sailing
Where and how to stow it. B. McPherson. il por Yachting 141:98-9+ My '77
See also
Anchors
Depth indicators
Rope
Sailboats—Equipment
Yachts—Equipment

Exhibitions

Boat show calendar. See issues of Yachting
International in-water boat show. il Motor B & S 140:97-9+ S '77
Rough log; London and Paris boat shows. T. Gibbs. il Yachting 141:112+ Mr '77

Finance

Creative ways to raise the cash. K. C. Kole. il Motor B & S 141:130-1+ Ja '78
See also
Yachts—Finance

BOATS—*Continued*

Fires and fire prevention

Fire; hazards with diesel engines. J. West. il Motor B & S 139:68-9+ Ap '77
Fire extinguishers. B. Behme. il Field & S 82:130+ Je '77
Five pounds of firefighting; Halon gas. M. Griffin. il Motor B & S 140:99-101 Ag '77

Fuel requirements

See Boats and boating—Fuel requirements

Fuel systems

See Marine engines—Fuel feeding

Galleys

Perfect set-up: or, How to go about designing the ideal galley. R. Marshall. il Yachting 141: 86-9 My '77

Gas detectors

See Gas detectors

Handling

See also
Motor boats—Handling
Sailboats—Handling

Heating and ventilation

Making a windsail. J. Smith. il Yachting 142:86 D '77

Hulls

See Hulls (naval architecture)

Instrument panels

Lighting

Night vision. D. Hart. il Motor B & S 140:26+ N '77

Interior decoration

See Boat decoration

Launching

Beach and launch unit lets ships walk on land. S. Renner-Smith. il Pop Sci 210:64 Mr '77
Dry-foot boat launching. D. R. Hart. il Motor B & S 139:12+ My '77

Leasing and renting

See also
Fishing boats—Leasing and renting
Yachts—Leasing and renting

Maintenance and repair

Boatkeeper; ed by J. Gribbins. See issues of Motor boating & sailing
Checklist for confidence. G. Hammond. Motor B & S 140:6 D '77
Notes from the ditty bag. F. M. Paulson. il Field & S 82:150+ N '77
Secrets of successful winter layup. B. Whittier. il Pop Mech 148:116-17+ N '77
See also
Boatyards

Materials

Accepting the materials; use of fiberglass on sailboat Pearson 323. T. Gibbs. il Yachting 141:164-6+ Mr '77
Aluminum hull construction; yachts. il Motor B & S 140:47 Ag '77
Boat you build with plastic planking; sloops. B. McKeown. il Pop Mech 147:106-8 Je '77
Build your own fiberglass sloop. B. Whittier. il Mech Illus 73:109-12+ F '77
Electrolysis: how and why it can affect your boat and what to do about it; metal parts on boats. J. Pazereskis. il Yachting 142:53-5 D '77
Fiberglass refinishing—the easy way; the hard way; excerpts from Fiberglass repairs. P. J. Petrick. il Motor B & S 139:108-11 Ap '77
Foam-cored fiberglass boats. J. L. Conboy. il Yachting 141:98-101 Ap '77
Kevlar boats: say goodbye to fiberglass? A. J. Hand. il Pop Sci 210:99-101 F '77
Laminating fiberglass over wood. A. H. Vaitses; P. J. Petrick. il Motor B & S 140:97-104 D '77
Modern wooden boat; construction of No go VIII. M. Walker. il Yachting 141:116+ My '77
Paint job for fiberglass. A. J. McMasters. il Mech Illus 73:12+ Ap '77

Noise

Boatkeeper noise handbook. D. Hart. il Motor B & S 140:155-62 S '77
Noise source analysis. il Motor B & S 139:62+ My '77

Painting

Paint job for fiberglass. A. J. McMasters. il Mech Illus 73:12+ Ap '77
Spray-painting pros and cons. R. Muff. il Motor B & S 139:111-13 Ap '77

Prices

Price of new boats. J. Hammond. Motor B & S 140:7 O '77

Purchasing

Confessions of a continuous convert; motor vs. sail. D. Bradley. Motor B & S 139:6+ My '77
New boat buyer's guide; symposium. il Motor B & S 140:73-96+ S '77
Small sailboats. Consumer Rep 42:129-31 D '77
10 facts to know before you buy. A. J. McMasters. il Mech Illus 73:16+ N '77
See also
Fishing boats—Purchasing

Radio antennas

See Radio antennas

Radio equipment

Help needed for 2182. M. Meisels. il Motor B & S 140:13+ Jl '77
VHF-FM weather service. G. V. West. il Yachting 142:211-15 S '77
See also
Citizens band radio on ships, boats, etc.
Radio direction finders
Radio in navigation
Radiotelephone on ships, boats, etc.

Refrigerators

See Refrigeration on boats

Sanitation

And some plumbing projects. F. W. Fleischhauer. il Motor B & S 140:98-9 N '77
Protecting the boat's plumbing. E. Osborne. Motor B & S 140:120 O '77
See also
Boats—Toilet facilities

Solar batteries

See Solar batteries

Stability and stabilizers

Make a stabilizer. J. Skrdla. il Motor B & S 140:103 Ag '77
Masthead weight and stability. J. Teale. Motor B & S 141:52+ Ja '78
Roll aids. J. West. il Motor B & S 139:98+ My '77
Trim-tab steering. R. Campoli. il Motor B & S 139:34 F '77

Steering gear

Extra hand at the tiller. F. E. Lane. il Motor B & S 139:88-9 F '77
Phantom helmsman; self-steering. W. D. Teague. il Motor B & S 139:74-5+ Ap '77
What to do when the rudder doesn't. J. Cartwright. il Motor B & S 140:14+ Ag '77

Survival equipment

See Survival and emergency equipment

Testing

See also
Motor boats—Testing
Sailboats—Testing

Toilet facilities

All at sea with MSDs. T. Gibbs. Yachting 141: 54-8 Je '77
Head aches. F. MacLear. il Motor B & S 141: 90-3 Ja '78

Transportation

Canoe caddy—one man can handle. il Sunset 158:145 Mr '77
Special delivery; yacht deliveries. S. Stapleton. il Motor B & S 139:82-3+ My '77
See also
Automobile boat trailers

Ventilation

See Boats—Heating and ventilation

BOATS, Jet
San Francisco launches world's first water-jet ferry. J. Zmuda. il Pop Sci 210:102 Ap '77

BOATS, Remodeled
Fit out for making money. H. Lake. il Pop Mech 147:100 F '77
See also
Sailboats, Remodeled

BOATS, Submarine. See Submarine boats

BOATS, Theft of
Cops & robbers offshore. T. Plate. il map Motor B & S 140:51-3 O '77
Wanted; P. E. Marschner. il pors Motor B & S 140:71-2 Ag '77
See also
Boat hijacking

BOATS and boating
And now. . .an electric boat; Electric Feather. A. Eason. il Mech Illus 73:36 Ag '77
Blow-up boat; inflatables. F. M. Paulson. il Field & S 82:124-6+ S '77
Boaters' wilderness; Lake Powell. il map Sunset 158:102-7 Ap '77
Boating. F. M. Paulson. See issues of Field & stream
Boating beat. R. G. Black. See issues of Popular science
Boating '77. B. McKeown. il Pop Mech 147:90-7+ F '77

BOATS and boating—*Continued*
Boatkeeper; ed by J. Gribbins. See issues of Motor boating & sailing
Boatkeeping below decks and you. il Yachting 141:82-99+ My '77
Boats & boating. A. J. McMasters. See issues of Mechanix illustrated
Buyer's guide. il Motor B & S 141:151-82+ Ja '78
Duck boat you can build. J. Seville. il Mech Illus 73:70-2 N '77
Four-wheel drive for back-country boating. B. McKeown. il Pop Mech 147:102-3 Mr '77
From the cockpit. R. N. Bavier. See issues of Yachting
Fun boats. B. O'Donovan. il Motor B & S 139:84-7+ My '77
Getting the most in inflatable dinghies. T. Gibbs. il Yachting 142:84-7+ N '77
High-seas homesteaders; living abroad. B. O'Donovan. il Motor B & S 140:57-60+ Ag '77
Little boat that folds up; Porta-bote. A. J. Maher. il Mech Illus 73:34+ S '77
New boats. il Motor B & S 139:92-3 Je; 140:86-7 Jl; 86-7 Ag; 42-3 N; 36-7 D '77
New boats & motors for 1978. B. Stearns. il Outdoor Life 161:85-8+ Ja '78
New boats in Yachting. See occasional issues of Yachting
New boats just for fun. B. McKeown. il Pop Mech 148:84-6+ Ag '77
New for '78—more performance, more fun. B. McKeown. il Pop Mech 149:74-5+ Ja '78
New trend—convertible boats. A. J. McMasters. il Mech Illus 74:44-5 Ja '78
Piano aboard: the sound of music on the water D. Hollmann. il Yachting 141:195-7 Ap '77
Tech section. See issues of Motor boating & sailing
10 best west boating spots. R. Burnham. maps Motor B & S 139:91-3+ My '77
Tender trap; dinghies. T. Meisel. il Motor B & S 141:111-13 Ja '78
Tips for better boating; three quick projects for the do-it-yourself skipper. il Pop Mech 147:32 Mr '77
Winter warmers; cold weather boating. A. H. Drummond, Jr. il Motor B & S 140:58-61+ D '77

See also

Boatbuilding
Boating industry
Canoe trips
Canoes and canoeing
Catamarans
Children in boating
Cruisers (pleasure boats)
Cruising
Ferries
Fishing boats
Hydrofoils
Ice boats and ice boating
Kayaks and kayaking
Marinas
Motor boats
Navigation
Rafts
River trips
Running rapids
Sailboats
Sailing
Seamanship
Trimarans
United States Power Squadrons, Inc
Women in boating
Yachts and yachting

Accidents

Four seconds to eternity: the story of a near-miss while racing. A. L. Barber, Jr. Yachting 141:180-3 My '77
From official Coast Guard files: accident report. R. Taylor. Motor B & S 140:60-3 O '77
Hang on for my life; boating accident while steelhead trout fishing. B. Knoll. il Outdoor Life 159:76-7+ My '77
Put the helm over! R. A. Ryan. Yachting 141:182-4+ Ap '77
Sea rescue; work of Connecticut's Star of Life I. S. Mennear-Dubas. il Fam Health 9:40-3 Ag '77

Anecdotes, facetiae, satire, etc.

Sex and the single hull. D. Bradley. il Motor B & S 140:14+ S '77

Bibliography

Book notes and reviews. K. Aamodt. See issues of Yachting

Economic aspects

How to go boating without going broke. A. J. McMasters. il Mech Illus 73:16+ Ag '77
Living aboard; excerpt. B. Moeller and J. Moeller. Yachting 142:143-5 Jl '77
Tax tips to save you money. J. Cameron. Motor B & S 139:82+ Ap '77
What makes yard owners cry uncle. H. D. Whall. il Motor B & S 139:60-1 F '77

Food problems

Maintaining your food supply. D. G. Brown and R. Wyatt. il Motor B & S 140:103-6 Jl '77

See also

Cookery, Marine

Fuel requirements

Fuel in your future; with editorial comment. il Motor B & S 141:8, 94-7 Ja '78

Hurricane hazards

See Boats and boating—Storm hazards

Laws and regulations

Can't they leave us alone? D. Bradley. Motor B & S 140:8 O '77
Washington report. M. P. Crain. See issues of Yachting

Safety devices and measures

Buoyancy in a bottle; triggered foam flotation system. S. Stapleton. il Motor B & S 139:72-4 Mr '77
How to go near the water safely. D. Kendall. il Ret Liv 17:20-3 Jl '77
New rules for gasoline-powered inboards. T. Gibbs. Yachting 141:112-16 F '77
Now hear this about safe boating. Changing T 31:11-13 Jl '77
Proper pushpit for Pipit; boat railings. S. C. Henkel. il Yachting 141:92-4 Ap '77

See also

Life preservers
Lighthouses
Radio beacons

Storm hazards

Anchor watch; Hurricane Agnes. R. Basham. Yachting 141:194-6 My '77
Get up off your old anchor and go. T. Gibbs. Yachting 142:94 Ag '77
When the going gets tough; heavy weather powerboating. B. Baker. il Motor B & S 140:54-5+ Jl '77

Study and teaching

Learning to cruise; Coast Navigation School. T. Gibbs. il Yachting 142:71-3+ Jl '77

See also

Sailing—Study and teaching

BOATYARDS
From the people who brought you full employment; insurance coverage of boatyard and marina workers. B. O'Donovan. il Motor B & S 139:81-3+ Je '77
What makes yard owners cry uncle. H. D. Whall. il Motor B & S 139:60-1+ F '77

BOB Bondurant School of High Performance Driving. See Automobile driving—Study and teaching

BOBICK, Duane
He's not pretty, he's just persistent. D. S. Looney. il pors Sports Illus 46:40-2+ My 9 '77 *
Make him 38 and one. P. Putnam. il pors Sports Illus 46:96+ My 23 '77 *

BOBINCHAK, Edward G.
Beyond efficiency: choosing a Christian life style. America 136:187-9 Mr 5 '77

BOBKOFF, Michael
Twain and Vonnegut. Engl J 66:55 S '77

BOBKOFF, Ned
James Thomas Jackson and me. il pors Writers Digest 57:19 F '77

about

Ned Bobkoff and me. J. T. Jackson. il pors Writers Digest 57:16-18+ F '77 *

BOBOWSKI, Rita Cipalla
Community problem-solver. il Am Educ 13:16-19 Je '77
Education for the public service. il Am Educ 13:31-2 Ap '77
Molding the new breed public officials. il Am Educ 13:22-7 D '77

BOBWHITE shooting. See Quail shooting

BOCARDO, Claire
My job vs my husband's pride. McCalls 105:57+ N '77

BOCK, D. Joleen
Two-year college LRC buildings. il por Lib J 102:2410-11 D 1 '77

BOCK, Gregory R. and Saunders, J. C.
Critical period for acoustic trauma in the hamster and its relation to cochlear development. bibl il Science 197:396-8 Jl 22 '77

BOCK, Hedwig
Women in modern drama. il Intellect 105:388 My '77

BOCK, Paul
Reappraisal of polygamy in Africa. bibl il Intellect 105:435-6 Je '77

BOCKELMAN, Wilfred
Tanzanian socialism. Chr Cent 94:774 S 14 '77

BOCKMÜHL, Klaus
Is there a Christian life-style? Chr Today 21:48-9 My 20 '77
Natural law. Chr Today 22:59-60 N 18 '77
Ten Commandments. Chr Today 21:43 Ag 26 '77
Under the perspective of eternity. Chr Today 21:64-5 F 18 '77

BOCKSTOCE, John R.
Issue of survival: bowhead vs. tradition. Audubon 79:142-5 S '77

BOCUSE, Paul
Food: France's best; ed by A. Gold and R. Fizdale. il Vogue 167:214+ N '77

BODIS-WOLLNER, Ivan, and others
Visual association cortex and vision in man: pattern-evoked occipital potentials in a blind boy. bibl il Science 198:629-31 N 11 '77

BODMER, Karl
Winter at Fort Clark; with reproductions of paintings by K. Bodmer; excerpt from People of the first man, ed by D. Thomas and K. Ronnefeldt. A. P. Maximilian. Am West 14: 36-47 Ja '77 *

BODY, Human
Dancer's physique. R. Gelabert. il Dance Mag 51: 78-80 N '77
See also
Mind and body
Women—Anatomy and physiology

BODY building
Does he or doesn't he? use of anabolic steroids. W. Ames. il Sports Illus 47:91-2+ D 5 '77
Is all this muscle all that healthy? A. Schwarzenegger. E. Kaye. il por Fam Health 9:20-4 D '77

BODY decoration. See Decoration and ornament, Personal

BODY fluids
Fingerprinting body fluids. BioScience 27:370 My '77
See also
Semen

BODY language. See Communication, Nonverbal

BODY painting. See Decoration and ornament, Personal

BODY rhythms. See Biology—Periodicity

BODY searches. See Searches and seizures

BODY size
Minimum size of mammalian homeotherms: role of the thermal environment. C. R. Tracy. bibl il Science 198:1034-5 D 9 '77

BODY weight. See Weight (physiology)

BODY work, Automobile. See Automobiles—Maintenance and repair

BOECK, William L.
Meteorological consequences of atmospheric Krypton-85. bibl il Science 193:195-8; 196:381+ Jl 16 '76, Ap 22 '77

BOEHM, Karl
Interview with Karl Boehm; ed by P. Hertelendy. por Hi Fi 27:MA30-1 My '77

BOEING, William Edward
Boeing. D. Scheuer. Flying 101:253 S '77 *

BOEING Company
Aerospace industry facing serious labor problems. R. G. O'Lone. Aviation W 107:25 O 10 '77
Boeing bolsters fail-safe data. R. G. O'Lone. il Aviation W 108:24-6 Ja 2 '78
Boeing brings off a French coup; Air France purchase of planes. il Bus W p31-2 My 9 '77
Boeing cools on cooperative effort for next new transport program. R. G. O'Lone. il Aviation W 106:216-17+ Je 6 '77
Boeing offering carriers 747SP Combi. Aviation W 106:26 Ja 31 '77
New aircraft plans still unresolved. Aviation W 106:22-3 Ja 10 '77
Wing and a prayer. Forbes 120:31-2 Ag 15 '77

Vertol Division

Tale of two cities; UTTAS contract awarded to Sikorsky. E. Shields. il Time 109:51+ F 14 '77
When Boeing gets into the streetcar business. il Bus W p 127+ S 12 '77

BOEKER, Paul H.
Balance-of-payments assistance for Portugal; statement, June 9, 1977. Dept State Bull 77: 136-8 Jl 25 '77
Department discusses debt situations of developing countries and the role of private banks; statement, April 5, 1977. Dept State Bull 76: 441-4 My 2 '77
Department urges appropriation of funds for international financial institutions; statement, February 16, 1977. Dept State Bull 76:198-201 Mr 7 '77
Developing codes of conduct for multinational enterprises; statement, September 7, 1977. Dept State Bull 77:475-9 O 10 '77
International monetary system; statement, September 23, 1977. Dept State Bull 77:704-7 N 14 '77

BOERUM HILL. See Brooklyn

BOESKY, Ivan Frederick
Killing in Babcock & Wilcox. E. J. Tracy. il pors Fortune 96:266-9 O '77 *

BOG people. See Denmark—Antiquities

BOGART, Leo
Automobile as social cohesion. il Society 14:10-15 Jl '77

BOGDANOVICH, Peter
Hollywood. Esquire 88:96+ D '77; 89:28+ Ja '78

BOGDANOVSKY, Georgy. See Ivanov, B. jt auth

BOGEN, Irving
New logo for American artist. D. Preiss. il Am Artist 41:37-8 F '77 *

BOGEN, Lester H.
Case for negative color. il Mod Phot 41:90-3+ My '77
Turn your color flops into exciting images. il Pop Phot 81:116-17+ Jl '77

BOGER, Louise Ade
Questions & answers: antiques. See issues of House & garden incorporating Living for young homemakers

BOGOTÁ, Colombia

Housing

Colombia will build shell housing with unfinished interiors at a Bogotá condominium. T. Berry. il Archit Rec 161:39 Ja '77

Recreation

Bogota connection; recreology students from University of Ottawa. T. L. Goodale. il Parks & Rec 12:54-7+ S '77

Religious institutions and affairs

In Bogotá, a banquet of hope; Colombian Confederation of Evangelicals. J. C. Hefley. il Chr Today 22:44-6 N 18 '77

BOGS
Cranberry bogs of Long Island. T. Huss. il por Conservationist 32:5-8 N '77

BOHDAN, Carol Lorraine and Volpe, T. M.
Furniture of Gustav Stickley. bibl il por Antiques 111:984-9 My '77

La **BOHÈME**; opera. See Puccini, G.

BOHIGIAN, Valerie
Queen of chaos. il por Redbook 149:102+ My '77

BOHN, Dennis A.
Build a pink noise generator for audio testing. il Pop Electr 12:66 Jl '77

BOHR, Niels Henrik David
J. J. Thomson and the Bohr atom. J. L. Heilbron. il pors Phys Today 30:23-4+ Ap '77 *

BOIKO, Claire
Carry on, Maid Marian! drama. Plays 36:13-22, 42 Ap '77
Cupivac; drama. Plays 36:47-52 F '77
Gracie at the bat; drama. Plays 36:65-9 Mr '77
Hiding Mr Hale; drama. Plays 37:47-52 O '77
Mollie and the invisible giant; dramatization of an English folktale. Plays 37:43-50 N '77
Town that couldn't wake up; drama. Plays 36: 1-14 Mr '77

BOILERS in art. See Machinery in art

BOISE, Idaho
4-mile bike loop unlocks Boise River. il Sunset 158:72 Je '77

Police

See Police—Idaho

BOKASSA, Emperor of Central African Empire
Bokassa's new clothes. L. Jenkins. il pors Newsweek 90:42-4 D 19 '77 *
Mounting a golden throne. il pors Time 110:42-3 D 19 '77 *

BOKASSA, Jean Bedel. See Bokassa, Emperor of Central African Empire

BOLAND, Bridget, and Boland, Maureen
Old wisdom for new gardens; excerpt from Old wives' lore for gardeners. il House & Gard 149:80+ My '77

BOLAND, Maureen. See Boland, B. jt auth

BOLAS spiders. See Spiders

BOLCH, Jennifer
Biorhythms: a key to your ups and downs. il Read Digest 111:63-7 S '77

BOLEN, David B.
Administration supports increased U.S. contributions to the African Development Fund; statement, April 18, 1977. Dept State Bull 76:472-4 My 9 '77
U.S. emphasizes role of international lending institutions in African development; statement, May 3, 1977. Dept State Bull 76:576-9 My 30 '77

BOLES, Paul Darcy
Last romantic; story. McCalls 104:148-9 F '77
Such a lovely light; story. Good H 184:132-3 Je '77
Workshop trio. Writer 90:15-17 My '77

BOLGER, Ray
Ray Bolger: leprechaun of the light fantastic. A. Jones. il Read Digest 110:124-8 Ap '77 *

BOLIN, Bert
Changes of land biota and their importance for the carbon cycle. bibl il Science 196:613-15 My 6 '77

BOLING, William G.
Summer food program: how your camp can join; questions and answers. Camp Mag 49:9+ My '77

BOLÍVAR, Simón
Assembly pays tribute to Simón Bolívar. UN Chron 14:27 Ja '77 *
Bolívar and the Congress of Panama. A. Uslar-Pietri. il por UNESCO Courier 30:28-32 F '77 *

BOLIVIA
See also
Americans in Bolivia
Libraries—Bolivia
Loans, British—Bolivia
Prisons—Bolivia

Foreign relations

United States

See United States—Foreign relations—Bolivia

Industries

See also
Mining industry and finance—Bolivia

Politics and government

Bolivia: Andean power shift. J. Kohl. map Progressive 41:39-42 F '77

BOLIVIAN Yacht Club. See Yacht clubs

BÖLL, Heinrich
German terrorism. J. Deedy. Commonweal 104: 706 N 11 '77 *

BOLLE, Frank
World of electronics. il Pop Electr 12:67 Jl '77

BOLLE, James
Oil of dog. J. Ringo. Am Rec G 40:15 N '76 *

BOLLES, Don F.
Anatomy of a reporter's murder. R. Lindsey. il por N Y Times Mag p 11-14+ F 20 '77 *
Bolles file. il por Newsweek 89:32 Ja 31 '77 *

BOLLIER, David, and Waitzman, Norman
Wage and price stability. il Nation 225:456-8 N 5 '77

BOLLING, Claude
Concerto for classic guitar and jazz piano. J. Ringo. Am Rec G 40:23-5 D '76 *

BOLLMAN, Justus Erich
Imprisonment of Lafayette. J. W. Baker. il Am Heritage 28:86-91 Je '77 *

BOLLWORMS
Controlling the pink bollworm by disrupting sex pheromone communication between adult moths. L. K. Gaston and others. bibl il Science 196:904-5 My 20 '77

BOLOGNA, Italy

Music

See also
Opera—Italy

Politics and government

Big brawl in Bologna; students against Italian Communist Party. il Time 110:47-8 O 3 '77
Trouble in Red City; tr by D. Betz. B. H. Levy. New Repub 177:23 O 8 '77
La Un-dolce vita. J. Ahern. Commonweal 104: 521-8 Ag 19 '77

BOLOGNA (meat) See Sausage

BOLOGNA Children's Book Fair. See Book fairs

BOLSHOI Opera Company. See Opera—Russia

BOLSTER, Warren
All aboard the tunnel express; photographs. Sports Illus 46:32-6 My 30 '77

about

Letter from the publisher. J. A. Meyers. il por Sports Illus 46:4 My 30 '77 *

BOLT, Tommy
Did old Tom throw that club? D. Jenkins. il pors Sports Illus 46:36-8+ Je 20 '77 *

BOLT extractors. See Tools

BOLTS and nuts
How to crack impossible nuts. D. Richmond. il Pop Mech 148:116-17+ O '77
Locking nut that really locks. il Mech Illus 73:128 Ag '77

BOLZ, Frank
Cool-headed cop who saves hostages. B. Gelb. il pors N Y Times Mag p30-3+ Ap 17 '77 *

BOMB delivery systems. See Airplanes, Military—Bomb delivery systems

BOMB shelters. See Atomic bomb shelters

BOMBECK, Erma
Boston straggler is a tour type not to be missed. il Smithsonian 8:128 Je '77
Firmer Erma. il Ladies Home J 94:32 Ag '77
First 12 days of school. il Read Digest 111:81-2 S '77
$500,000 housewife. D. K. Shah. il pors Newsweek 91:60 Ja 2 '78 *
So long, volunteers. Read Digest 110:146 Ap '77
Stow it till the commercial! il Read Digest 111: 120-2 Jl '77

BOMBERS (airplanes) See Airplanes, Military

BOMBESIN. See Peptides

BOMBING, Aerial
See also
Bombing and gunnery ranges

BOMBING, Terrorists. See Terrorism

BOMBING and gunnery ranges
Return of the natives to Kahoolawe; protesting Navy bombing. J. Wilde. il Time 110:32 Ag 8 '77

BOMBS
See also
Atomic bombs

BOMBYX. See Silkworms

BONACICH, Edna, and others
Koreans in business. bibl il Society 14:54-9 S '77

BONANNO, Ellen, and Mechlin, Stuart
Plantable box: a new way to start roses. il Horticulture 55:50-1 My '77

BOND, Langhorne
Bonded. R. L. Collins. por Flying 101:46 O '77 *

BOND, Walter L.
Obituary
Phys Today por 30:79-80 S '77. E. A. Wood

BOND markets. See Bonds

BOND traders. See Brokers

BONDS, Charles W.
Cloze procedure and dialect considerations. bibl Clearing H 50:360-2 Ap '77

BONDS
Active traders move into bonds. il Bus W p79-80 D 26 '77
Arabs breed a new capital market. il Bus W p76 Ap 18 '77
Bond and capital markets. B. Weberman. See issues of Forbes
Bonds: a brighter outlook for longer term investors; interview. A. M. Wojnilower. por U.S. News 83:52-3 D 26 '77
Bonds: false security. J. Train. por Forbes 120: 182 O 15 '77
Exodus begins from long-term bonds. il Bus W p90+ N 7 '77
Why bond rates declined dramatically. il Bus W p76 Jl 11 '77
World comes to Wall Street. il Time 110:65 D 5 '77
See also
Banks and banking—Securities handling
Eurobond market
Mortgage bonds

Marketing

Borrower's market in private placements. Bus W p 106 D 12 '77
Debenture swaps that trim debt. Bus W p54 Jl 4 '77

Private placement

See Bonds—Marketing

Yields

High risks—and rewards—in high-yield bonds; interview, ed by A. Hershman. M. R. Milken. por Duns R 109:121+ Je '77

BONDS, Convertible
Look at convertible bonds. J. Fraser. U.S. News 83:72 Jl 18 '77

BONDS, Government
Bond market falls into a Fed trap; raising the Federal funds rate. il Bus W p 187+ N 14 '77
Look who made it in Wall street! Government bond traders. P. Blustein. il Forbes 119:37-42 F 1 '77
See also
Bonds, Housing authority
Municipal bonds
State bonds

Taxation

See Taxation of bonds, securities, etc.

Great Britain

Glow of gilts warms the pound. il Bus W p 108 F 14 '77

BONDS, Housing authority
Ingenious scheme to help New York; government-insured mortgage-backed bonds. Bus W p28-9 Ag 22 '77
Lazarus bonds; discovery of federally guaranteed New York City Housing Authority bonds by Stoever Glass & Co. Forbes 119:68 F 1 '77

BONDS, Industrial development
Little guy's bond; industrial revenue bond to aid pollution-control problems. Forbes 119:61 Je 15 '77
Now small business can pay its pollution tab. il Bus W p90 N 21 '77

BONDS, Industrial revenue. See Bonds, Industrial development

BONDS, State. See State bonds

BONE, Jan
Peotone fights school failure. il Am Educ 13: 32-5 Ja '77

BONE, L. W. and Shorey, H. H.
Disruption of sex pheromone communication in a nematode. bibl il Science 197:694-5 Ag 12 '77

BONE, Maurice D.
Planning & development. Camp Mag 49:40-1 Ja '77

BONE
See also
Osteopuncture

BONE marrow. See Marrow

BONE resorption. See Absorption (physiology)

BONEFISH fishing
To a different beat; bonefish fishing in Biscayne Bay. J. Bashline. il Field & S 81:184+ Ap '77
Turneffe Islands cornucopia; bonefish off coast of Belize. J. Bashline. il Field & S 82:160-4 N '77

BONENO, Richard N.
Breaking the frame barrier. il Design (US) 78:2-4 Spr '77

BONGARD-LEVIN, Grigory M. and Grantovsky, E. A.
Shamans and shamanism. il UNESCO Courier 29:42-7 D '76

BONGARTZ, Roy
Banking art in Ottawa. il Art N 76:80-2+ Ap '77
Bicycles built for speed. il Horizon 19:56-9 Jl '77
Hamburgers turn gray when halted on a slanting street. il Sat Eve Post 249:22+ Ap '77
It's like love, a one-to-one relationship between a human being and a work of art. il por Art N 76:78-80+ My '77
It's the real thing. il pors Horizon 20:72-81 S '77
$100,000 bowling machine. il pors Sports Illus 46:66-9+ Mr 7 '77

about

Letter from the publisher. J. Meyers. por Sports Illus 46:4 Mr 7 '77 *

BONGO, Omar
Glories of Gabon. J. Pringle. por map Newsweek 90:33 Jl 18 '77 *

BONHAM, Roger D.
Indiana State University. il Ceram Mo 25:28-33 N '77

BONHEUR, Rosa
Art isn't a man's world. W. Rodger. Hobbies 82:148-9 S '77 *

BONHOMME, Susan
(ed) See Davis, P. Paul Davis: a personal vision

BONING of fishes. See Fish as food

BONK, Kathleen, and Gardner, J. E.
Sexism's universal curriculum. il Am Educ 13:15-19 Jl '77

BONNER, Arthur
Heavy manners in Jamaica. Nation 224:80-4 Ja 22 '77

BONNEVILLE Power Administration. See United States—Bonneville Power Administration

BONO, Agostino
Forging economic unity. Commonweal 104:618-20 S 30 '77

BONSAI. See Trees, Dwarf

BONTA, Marcia
Raising Muscovy ducks for the table. il Org Gard & Farm 24:134-6 Je '77

BONUS system
See also
Incentives in industry

BOOK advertising. See Books—Advertising

BOOK awards. See Literary prizes

BOOK Awards, National. See National Book Awards

BOOK binding. See Bookbinding

BOOK clubs
British book clubs brace for Bertelsmann invasion P. Kleinman. Pub W 211:30-1 F 14 '77
Buying hardcover books. il Consumer Rep 42:505-13 S '77
See also
Literary Guild of America

BOOK collecting
Collecting early law books. E. Shrum. il Hobbies 82:80+ My '77
See also
Book rarities
Childrens literature—Collectors and collecting

BOOK covers
Publishers, binders hear analysis of Tyvek production problems, solutions. P. Doebler. Pub W 211:71-2 Mr 7 '77
Type II cover materials demonstrate good test results. P. Doebler. Pub W 212:82 O 3 '77

Anecdotes, facetiae, satire, etc.

Posh bars of Anchorage; book flap literature. R. Rosenblatt. New Repub 176:33-4 Ja 15 '77

BOOK critics and criticism. See Book reviewers and reviewing

BOOK Critics awards. See National Book Critics Circle

BOOK dedications
Page nobody reads. M. Weisinger. Writers Digest 57:19 Mr '77

BOOK design
Alvin Lustig's graphic design draws well at AIGA reprospective exhibit. P. Doebler. il Pub W 211:72 Ap 4 '77
Art director's growing (or fading) role in book graphics debated at clinic. P. Doebler. Pub W 211:77-8 F 7 '77
Book design and manufacturing ed by P. Doebler. See first issue of every month of Publishers weekly
Classic bird monograph done in 19th century tradition; publication of Rails of the world. P. Doebler. il Pub W 211:70 Ap 4 '77
Marketing managers tell AIGA clinic how design influences book sales. P. Doebler. Pub W 211:74-5 Ap 4 '77
Richard Ellis honored for his book designs by Franklin Club. F. Harrington. il por Pub W 212:95-6 Ag 1 '77
See also
Copyright—Book design

BOOK design firms. See Design firms

BOOK Distributors (firm) See Book wholesalers

BOOK editors. See Editors and editing

BOOK exhibits
AIGA redesigns Fifty Books Show format. P. Doebler. Pub W 211:76-7 F 7 '77
Children's Book Council announces titles in this year's Showcase. P. Doebler. Pub W 211:81 Mr 7 '77
Children's books provide the backdrop for department store back-to-school promotion; G. Fox and Company's Show and Tell Book Jamboree. D. Maryles. il Pub W 212:50+ O 10 '77
PW's book show review; special issue. il Pub W 211:61-81 Je 13 '77
See also
Book fairs
Library exhibits

BOOK fairs
AAP queries VAAP delegates on Moscow Book Fair. Pub W 211:27-8 F 21 '77
Albert reports on Peking visit, coming book exhibit. M. Reuter. il Pub W 212:19-20 O 17 '77
Bologna's children's book fair reflects the changing world of juvenile publishing. A. Beneduce. il Pub W 211:37-8 My 2 '77
Book fair in Jerusalem; International Book Fair. R. Casellas. il Américas 29:44-5 S '77
Children's books celebration draws SRO crowds; New England. J. F. Mercier. il Pub W 212:46-8 N 14 '77
Despite aura of censorship, first Moscow Book Fair has positive results. H. R. Lottman. il Pub W 212:46-53 O 3 '77
Frankfurt: the biggest fair ever, yet threatened by growth pains. H. R. Lottman. Pub W 212:40 O 24 '77
From Nigeria, guarded optimism; from Montreal, guarded pessimism; Montreal International Book Fair and Ife Book Fair. B. Slopen; H. Jenkins. Pub W 211:29-30 My 16 '77
International Book Fairs 1978. Pub W 212:98 S 19 '77
London Book Fair 1977: bigger, and still growing. P. Kleinman. il Pub W 212:97 S 19 '77
London Book Fair scores a triumph. il Pub W 212:29 O 31 '77
New York Fair highlights growing interest in books by specialized publishers. R. Kostelanetz. il Pub W 212:28-30 N 14 '77
Ninth Festival du Livre; Nice. H. R. Lottman. il Pub W 211:55-6 Je 13 '77
Opportunities for downright business apparent at successful eighth biennial; Jerusalem International Book Fair. H. R. Lottman. il Pub W 211:20-4 My 30 '77
Planning problem-free book fairs; the school book fair. C. Kline. il SLJ 23:36-40 F '77
Previewing the fairs:
Critical choices ahead as Montreal goes into third year. B. Slopen. Pub W 211:65-6 Mr 21 '77
Jerusalem in 1977 will be the biggest yet. M. Reuter. Pub W 211:66 Mr 21 '77
Publishers assail N.Y. times for Moscow Fair editorial. M. Reuter. Pub W 212:27 Jl 25 '77
Publishers attend briefing for Moscow Book Fair. M. Reuter. Pub W 212:24 Jl 11 '77
Soviets covet U.S. books—but no sales allowed; Moscow International Book Fair. Am Lib 8:474 O '77
10th Cairo Fair: U.S. firms expect business increase. H. R. Lottman. Pub W 212:18 D 5 '77
U.S. not to exhibit at Moscow Book Fair. S. Wagner. Pub W 211:26 Mr 28 '77
Washingtonian's Book Fair—first edition. D. Grumbach. il Pub W 211:56-8 Je 6 '77
What looked like a quiet fair was actually a record-setting event; Frankfurt Book Fair. H. R. Lottman. il Pub W 212:28-35 N 7 '77

BOOK industries
Technologists trace graphic arts trends for AIGA Clinic. P. Doebler. Pub W 211:55-6 My 2 '77
See also
Book fairs
Book wholesalers
Bookbinding
Booksellers and bookselling
Literary agents
Paper industry
Printing
Printing industry
Publishers and publishing

Conferences

Book manufacturers face profit squeeze; report of the Book Manufacturers' Institute Management Conference. S. Wagner. Pub W 211:155+ My 23 '77

BOOK industries—*Continued*

Statistics

American imports and exports; international title output. C. B. Grannis. il Pub W 212: 93-6 S 19 '77
1976 statistics: title counts and average prices per volume; Highlights from the annual AAP report. C. B. Grannis. il Pub W 212:32-6+ Ag 22 '77
Year in review: U.S. book industry statistics: prices, sales, trends. il Pub W 211:52-6 F 14 '77

Germany, West

Germany and the German book business; symposium, ed by H. R. Lottman. il Pub W 212: 9-14+ S 12 '77

Hungary

Hungarians have an appetite for reading—and a rich larder to delve into. T. Weyr. il Pub W 212:26-8 O 31 '77

United States

Book design and manufacturing; ed by P. Doebler. See first issue of every month of Publishers weekly
Book Industry Study Group announces three major projects at first annual meeting. M. Reuter. Pub W 212:49-50 Ag 1 '77
Book Industry Study Group issues five-year forecast. M. Reuter. Pub W 212:17-18 O 31 '77
Eight-year quest for manufacturing method leads to decorators' workbook. P. Doebler. il Pub W 211:72 Mr 7 '77
Enough paper, but prices up in 1977-78, BISG study says; 1979 shortages likely. P. Doebler. Pub W 211:74-6 F 7 '77
PW's annual technology review. P. D. Doebler. Pub W 212:45-7+ D 5 '77
Printers describe systems for quality control before Book Clinic audience. P. Doebler. Pub W 211:78 Mr 7 '77
Pubmart draws publishing people from across the nation. P. D. Doebler. il Pub W 212: 28 Jl 4 '77
Too many books (?) revisited. J. P. Dessauer. Pub W 211:41-3 My 16 '77
Year in review; manufacturing; growing capacity promises keen pricing, but paper situation cloudy. Pub W 211:44-5 F 14 '77
See also
Book Manufacturers' Institute
Publishers and publishing—United States

BOOK Industry Study Group. See Book industries —United States

BOOK Industry Systems Advisory Committee
New Standard data format hastens computer ordering. P. Doebler. Pub W 212:38 D 12 '77

BOOK jobbers. See Book wholesalers

BOOK lists. See Books and reading—Bibliography; Childrens literature—Bibliography; Young adults literature—Bibliography

BOOK Manufacturers' Institute
BMI told to expect long, gradual recovery, rising paper demand; new foreign competition. Pub W 213:41-2 Ja 2 '78

BOOK manufacturing industry. See Book industries

BOOK numbers
See also
Book Industry Systems Advisory Committee

BOOK of changes. See I ching (Book of changes)

BOOK of Durrow
Gold from the Dark Ages. R. Hughes. il Time 110:52-3 N 14 '77
Wonders of Irish art. C. R. Baldwin. il N Y Times Mag p34-7+ O 9 '77

BOOK of Job. See Bible—Old Testament—Job

BOOK of Kells
Gold from the Dark Ages. R. Hughes. il Time 110:52-3 N 14 '77
Great Book of Kells in shining exhibit of ancient Irish art; Metropolitan Museum of Art. A. Friendly. il Smithsonian 8:66-75 bibl(p 160) O '77
Wonders of Irish art. C. R. Baldwin. il N Y Times Mag p34-7+ O 9 '77

BOOK of Mormon. See Mormons and Mormonism —Book of Mormon

BOOK-of-the-Month Club, Inc-Time Inc merger. See Corporations—Acquisitions and mergers

BOOK orders, Library. See Libraries—Acquisitions

BOOK postal rates. See Postal rates—United States

BOOK prices. See Books—Prices

BOOK prizes. See Literary prizes

BOOK producers. See Literary agents

BOOK promotion. See Books—Advertising

BOOK racks. See Bookends and bookracks

BOOK rarities
Guide to literary collectibles. il Bus W p 103-5+ Je 27 '77
New literary appreciation. il Time 109:85-6+ Ap 25 '77
See also
Book of Kells
Booksellers and bookselling—Book rarities

Collections

See College libraries—Special collections

Facsimiles

Historical group recreates Old Christmas; work of Sleepy Hollow Restorations. P. Doebler. il Pub W 212:51 S 5 '77

BOOK reports. See Student themes and reports

BOOK reviewers and reviewing
Beyond book reviewing; announcement of meeting concerning childrens' books at the ALA conference in Detroit. L. N. Gerhardt. SLJ 23:9 My '77
Book reviewing for city newspapers. J. Modert. Writer 90:20-2+ Ja '77
Dead writers: a parable. S. Maloff. Commonweal 104:307-9 My 13 '77
Lehmann-Haupt two three, four. D. K. Mano. Esquire 87:34+ Mr '77
PW interviews; book editor of the Washington post; ed by S. Wagner. W. McPherson. por Pub W 212:10-11 Ag 8 '77
PW interviews; literary critic of the Los Angeles times; ed by J. Kirsch. R. Kirsch. por Pub W 212:10-11 D 12 '77
Picture book as art object: a call for balance reviewing. K. Marantz. il Wilson Lib Bull 52: 148-51 O '77
Shrivel of critics. A. Burgess. Harpers 254:87+ F '77
Unanswered questions on reviewing for YA's. J. Milton. SLJ 23:127 Mr '77
See also
National Book Critics Circle

BOOK reviews
For citations of reviews of individual books, see book review section following main body of the Index
Yes, 'no' counts: the value of negative reviews; comments of readers. SLJ 24:38-9 S '77
See also
Bookviews (periodical)
New York review of books
New York times book review
Times literary supplement, London

BOOK selection
Are we selecting for a generation of skeptics? excerpt from address, November 4, 1976. K. E. Vandergrift. SLJ 23:41-3 F '77
Best books for whom; or, Where have all the grown-ups gone? L. L. Shapiro. Wilson Lib Bull 51:803-4+ Je '77
Beyond book reviewing; announcement of meeting concerning childrens' books at the ALA conference in Detroit. L. N. Gerhardt. SLJ 23:9 My '77
Selection and soapboxes: an ideological primer. E. Fain. Wilson Lib Bull 52:136-9 O '77

BOOK shelves. See Bookcases

BOOK shows. See Book exhibits

BOOK thefts
See also
Library thefts

BOOK tokens. See Books as gifts

BOOK wholesalers
Approaching 50, Bookazine still stresses aggressive wholesaling with the personal touch. R. Smith and J. Giusto. il Pub W 212:73-6 O 3 '77
Bookstore improves net profit via Book Distributors' new ordering service. P. D. Doebler. il Pub W 211:47-8 My 16 '77
North Country Book Express: a mobile service for mountain booksellers (and publishers) il Pub W 211:63-5 Ap 11 '77
Paperback revolution: where has it gone? adaptation of address, October 1977. O. Dystel. por Pub W 212:31-3 N 14 '77
Ray and Mary Jane Surguine retire; paperback wholesalers; interview, ed by P. Holt. R. Surguine. il por Pub W 212:49 N 21 '77
See also
Baker and Taylor Companies

Great Britain

W. H. Smith subsidiary pondering U.S. distribution network. P. Kleinman. Pub W 212:23 Ag 8 '77

BOOKAZINE Company. See Book wholesalers

BOOKBINDING
Binding. P. D. Doebler. Pub W 212:60+ D 5 '77
Book art. D. Evetts. il pors House & Gard 149: 160-1+ O '77
Book of the century: Fuller's Tetrascroll; with introd by P. Lada-Mocarski. R. Minsky and P. Seidler. il pors Craft Horiz 37:18-21+ O '77
Grosset & Dunlap binds trade, children's editions by new paper welding process. P. Doebler. il Pub W 211:59+ Je 6 '77

History

Early bookbindings are majestic art forms. W. Rodger. il Hobbies 82:151-3+ Je '77

BOOKCASES
Low-cost bookshelves you can build in a hurry. W. T. Almli. il Pop Mech 149:88-9 Ja '78
No visible means of support. il Sunset 159:162 N '77
Steel bookstore fixtures—a winning concept; designs of B. Corns; with photographs by E. V. Smith. P. Holt. il por Pub W 212:115-17 S 12 '77

BOOKENDS and bookracks
Desk top file or rack for books. il Sunset 158:106 Mr '77
The pull of paperback displays. H. H. Laskey. il por SLJ 23:31-5 F '77

BOOKER, Simeon
Washington notebook. See issues of Ebony

BOOKLETS. See Pamphlets

BOOKMOBILES
Le$$ costly, more popular; paperback book collections in the Oklahoma County Libraries System. P. Little. il por Lib J 102:451-6 F 15 '77
Special report: director's diary of a crisis; bookmobile budget of the Kearney, Neb. Public Library. R. Norman. il Wilson Lib Bull 51:566-7 Mr '77

BOOKRACKS. See Bookends and bookracks

BOOKS
Traditional book in the electronic age; address, November 10, 1977. H. S. Bailey, Jr. il pors Pub W 212:24-9 D 5 '77
See also
Best sellers
Copyright
Paperback books
Picture books
Royalties

Advertising

AAP launches the 1977 Books as Gifts campaign in nine major book markets. D. Maryles. il Pub W 212:40 N 28 '77
Best friends of bestsellers. B. Harris. Writers Digest 57:26 O '77
Books as Gifts test results are in; AAP to vote on $400,000 budget for 1977. D. Maryles. il Pub W 211:24 My 9 '77; Correction. 211:17 My 30 '77
Frederick Warne's party kits help booksellers celebrate Peter Rabbit's 75th birthday. D. Maryles. il Pub W 212:116-17 Jl 18 '77
Money-saving coupons is the come-on in HBJ's fall trade paperback campaign. Pub W 212:55 Jl 11 '77
O my America; tour promoting A book of common prayer. J. Didion. il Esquire 88:32-4 Ag '77
On the road. A McCarthy. Commonweal 104:489 Ag 5 '77
Paperback potpourri: some major spring campaigns from mass marketers. D. Maryles. il Pub W 211:46-7 My 2 '77
Paperback publishers approach a critical point in their use of broadcast advertising. L. Gaynor. il Pub W 212:36-8 D 5 '77
Paperbacks: getting the giveaways. il SLJ 24:24-5 S '77
Paying $1 million to sell a book; television commercials for The Random House encyclopedia. il Bus W p 102+ S 12 '77
Sussman & Sugar resigns Grove Press account. M. Reuter. Pub W 212:24 Jl 4 '77
Truisms of book advertising; report of ABA panel discussion. D. Maryles. il Pub W 211:80 Je 27 '77
Two-way TV may alter traditional book buying; Qube pay cable system direct response advertising. J. Giusto. Pub W 212:55 D 26 '77

Collectors and collecting

See Book collecting

Design

See Book design

Exhibitions

See Book exhibits

Export-import trade

American imports and exports; international title output. C. B. Grannis. il Pub W 212:93-6 S 19 '77

Manufacture

See Book industries

Marketing

Bookselling and marketing; ed by D. Maryles. See issues of Publishers weekly
British are coming! N. Dunnan. Lib J 102:2311-16 N 15 '77
Marketing managers tell AIGA clinic how design influences book sales. P. Doebler. Pub W 211:74-5 Ap 4 '77
See also
Book wholesalers
Booksellers and bookselling
Paperback books—Marketing

Postal rates

See Postal rates—United States

Prices

1976 statistics: title counts and average prices per volume; Highlights from the annual AAP report. C. B. Grannis. il Pub W 212:32-6+ Ag 22 '77
Prices, printings and profits: how to draw the bottom line; adaptation of address. T. J. McCormack. il Pub W 212:34-41 Ag 15 '77
Year in review: U.S. book industry statistics: prices, sales, trends. il Pub W 211:52-6 F 14 '77

Selection

See Book selection

Statistics

See Book industries—Statistics; Publishers and publishing—Statistics

Storage

See also
Warehouses

Transportation

Soft answers by U.S. Postal Service turn away publishers' wrath. S. Wagner. Pub W 211:43-4 F 21 '77

BOOKS, Filmed. See Motion picture adaptations; Television adaptations

BOOKS, Rare. See Book rarities

BOOKS, Secondhand
See also
Booksellers and bookselling—Secondhand books

BOOKS and reading
Are books an endangered species? B. Greene. por Newsweek 89:9 My 2 '77
Book watch (cont) D. K. Mano. Esquire 87:16+ F; 34+ Mr; 20+ Ap; 54+ My '77
Cave of the winds. L. H. Lapham. Nat R 29:1055-8+ S 16 '77
See also
Biography
Book reviews
Books as gifts
Carter, J. —Reading
Childrens reading
Fiction
Prisoners—Reading
Reference books
Television and reading
Young adults reading
also Religious literature; Scientific literature; etc.

Anecdotes, facetiae, satire, etc.

Classic confrontation. A. Ward. Atlantic 240:97-8 O '77

Best books

ALA issues booklist, Notable Books for Adults. Lib J 102:668 Mr 15 '77
Best bets from publishers' fall lists. M. E. Marty. Chr Cent 94:854+ S 28 '77
Bookmarks. Read Digest 110:124-5 Je '77
Books for a long, hot summer. America 136:417+ My 7 '77
Fall survey of books: story time, the delights of divinity. G. C. Reedy; J. Gaffney. America 137:336+ N 12 '77
Great books; 20th century; views of M. J. Adler. il Time 109:65-6 Mr 7 '77
Pick of the list. B. DeMott. Sat R 4:62-3 Ag 6 '77
University press books. Commonweal 104:343-7 My 27 '77
Year's best. Time 111:76 Ja 2 '78
See also
Best sellers

Bibliography

About books; ed by J. Cox. See issues of Organic gardening and farming
Book review. See issues of Library journal
Book reviews. See issues of Smithsonian
Books. Writers Digest 57:40 Ap; 46 Je; 54 Ag; 58 O '77
Books. See issues of Business week
Books. See issues of Intellect
Books. See issues of Ms.
Books. See occasional issues of House beautiful
Books. C. Bigwood. Am Home 80:20 Ap; 14 Je; 16 Ag; 26 O; 10 D '77
Books. J. Howard. See issues of Mademoiselle
Books. A. Kazin. See issues of Esquire
Books. A. Talmey. See issues of Vogue
Books. R. Todd. See issues of Atlantic
Books in brief. See issues of National review
Books that shape lives. See issues of Christian century
Booktrucking about town (cont) Wilson Lib Bull 51:706-13 My; 52:206-12 N '77
Criticism. See issues of Christian century

BOOKS and reading—Bibliography—*Continued*
Dark horses. M. S. Evans. See issues of National review
Elderly books for youngerly readers (title varies) M. McCue and E. Wilson. See issues of Wilson library bulletin
Fall announcements. il Pub W 212:285-307 Ag 29 '77
Fast food for the summer. Newsweek 89:91-3 Je 20 '77
New fall books. Lib J 102:2022+ O 1 '77
New spring books. Lib J 102:348-50+ F 1 '77; Correction. 102:668 Mr 15 '77
New Yorker lists at this season some books by its contributors published during the year. New Yorker 53:189 D 12 '77
PLA. P.-L. Adams. See issues of Atlantic
PW forecasts; ed by B. A. Bannon. See issues of Publishers weekly
Personal mentions. W. Cole. Sat R 4:64 Ag 6 '77
Reviewers' choices: summer reading. Chr Cent 94:477-9+ My 18 '77
Right of center (cont) J. H. Hillard. Wilson Lib Bull 51:668-9 Ap; 52:74-5 S '77
Saturday evening post book shelf. Sat Eve Post 249:74 Ap '77
Short reviews. See issues of Atlantic
Siftings. D. Grumbach. Sat R 5:41 Ja 7 '78
Spring announcements 1977. Pub W 211:259-81 Ja 24 '77
Summer announcements. Pub W 211:29-39 Ap 4 '77
This week's arrivals. See issues of Christian century
Words with the President; a list of suggestions. R. Rosenblatt. New Repub 176:84-6 Ja 22 '77
Writer's library (cont) Writer 90:46 F; 46 Mr '77
Year's books; symposium. New Repub 177:24-6+ N 26; 21+ D 3 '77

International aspects

See also
United States—Government Advisory Committee on International Book and Library Programs

Reading aloud

Reading; non-stop reading of Gertrude Stein's The making of Americans. New Yorker 52:26-8 Ja 17 '77
Special report: rejoycing at the library; reading of James Joyce's Ulysses at the Ortega Branch of the San Francisco Public Library. G. T. Hooper. il Wilson Lib Bull 51:718-19 My '77

Study and teaching

See Literature—Study and teaching

Namibia

Namibia's freedom fighters chose books, not guns. L. R. Pearson. Am Lib 8:287 Je '77

BOOKS as gifts
Book-giving made easy; sale of book tokens. G. R. Smith. Horn Bk 53:372-3 Je '77
Books for Christmas giving. C. Bigwood. Am Home 80:10 D '77
Books of the season; Christmas gifts. Chr Cent 94:1173-4 D 14 '77
Bound for pleasure; Christmas presents. J. H. Denner. House & Gard 149:60+ D '77
Catchers in the rye, teen-age fiction. C. Michener. il Newsweek 90:85 D 19 '77
Children's books for the trail; Selected list of children's books. E. M. Graves. il Commonweal 104:726-35 N 11 '77
Christmas special. M. Latour. Mademoiselle 83:28+ D '77
Cornucopia of children's books. S. Kanfer. il Time 110:66-7+ N 21 '77
Critics' choices for Christmas. Commonweal 104:794-9 D 9 '77
Diamonds in the kiddie litter. C. Michener. il Newsweek 90:81-2+ D 19 '77
For Christmas giving. Chr Today 22:42 N 4 '77
Gift books. D. Preiss. il Am Artist 41:32-4 D '77
Gift books of special interest. Good H 185:171 D '77
Give books; Christmas gifts. A. Talmey. Vogue 167:97-8 D '77
Holiday gift books. D. Preiss. il Am Artist 41:22+ N '77
Holiday gifts between covers; symposium. il Sat R 5:31-2+ N 26 '77
New readings of the season. il Time 110:82-4+ D 12 '77
Reader's Christmas feast. P. S. Prescott. il Newsweek 90:101-2+ D 12 '77
Sugar and spice mannerly mice. America 137:404-8 D 3 '77

BOOKS from motion pictures. See Motion pictures and literature

BOOKS from television programs. See Television and literature

BOOKSELLERS and bookselling
Book-giving made easy; sale of book tokens. G. R. Smith. Horn Bk 53:372-3 Je '77
See also
Books—Marketing
School bookstores

Advertising

See Books—Advertising

Anecdotes, facetiae, satire, etc.

Notes on the trade. Colophon. Pub W 212:16 D 26 '77
Thanksgiving—for some, it's over. Pub W 212:51 N 21 '77

Art

Art publisher and jobber opens a bookshop in N.Y; Printed Matter bookstore in New York City. J. Giusto. il Pub W 212:54 D 26 '77

Book rarities

Through the looking glass: notes on an antiquarian children's bookshop; Justin G. Schiller, Ltd. J. G. Schiller and R. M. Wapner. il Horn Bk 53:140-6 Ap '77

Childrens literature

Blackwell's Children's Bookshop; Oxford. E. Taylor. il Horn Bk 53:206-8 Ap '77
Bookshop for Boys and Girls; Boston. L. Kingman. il Horn Bk 53:209-14 Ap '77
Children and librarians are encouraged to browse in this successful Toronto shop; The Children's Book Store. B. Slopen. il Pub W 211:110-11 F 28 '77
Children's Book Store in Toronto. H. Sarick and J. Sarick. il Horn Bk 53:202-5 Ap '77
Children's bookshop in New Zealand: one family's enterprise. D. Butler. il Horn Bk 53:128-33 Ap '77
Hathaway House Bookshop; Wellesley, Mass. R. D. Hale. il Horn Bk 53:121-7 Ap '77
Joyful noise: the resurgence of children's bookselling. E. L. Heins. Horn Bk 53:118-19 Ap '77
Kathy Larkin of Kroch's & Brentano's: total enthusiasm for the customer. I. Ballantine. il por Pub W 212:33-4 Jl 18 '77
Magic Fishbone Bookshop: a California story; Carmel. M. R. Bruggeman. il Horn Bk 53:134-9 Ap '77
Publishers report top-selling juveniles. Pub W 211:97-9 F 28 '77
Through the looking glass: notes on an antiquarian children's bookshop; Justin G. Schiller, Ltd. J. G. Schiller and R. M. Wapner. il Horn Bk 53:140-6 Ap '77
Top-selling children's books. Pub W 212:85-7 Jl 18 '77

Equipment and supplies

Steel bookstore fixtures—a winning concept; designs of B. Corns; with photographs by E. V. Smith. P. Holt. il por Pub W 212:115-17 S 12 '77

Finance

U.S. consumer expenditures on books in 1976. J. P. Dessauer. il Pub W 211:39-40 Ap 25 '77

International aspects

International scene at ABA. H. R. Lottman. il Pub W 211:89-93 Je 27 '77
See also
International Community of Booksellers Associations

Maps

Maps, globes and atlases. D. Maryles. il map Pub W 211:57-8 Ap 25 '77

Order processing

Bookstore improves net profit via Book Distributors' new ordering service. P. D. Doebler. Pub W 211:47-8 My 16 '77
New standard data format hastens computer ordering. P. Doebler. Pub W 212:38 D 12 '77

Paperback books

Slugging it out at the retail level. il Bus W p50-1 Jl 4 '77

Phonograph records

Sideline with an added dimension. il Pub W 212:51+ O 24 '77

Publicity

See also
Show windows

Reference books

Maps, globes and atlases. D. Maryles. il map Pub W 211:57-8 Ap 25 '77

Religious literature

See also
Christian Booksellers Association

Remainders

Life and letters. . . ; Marboro Country. Aristides. Am Scholar 46:432+ Aut '77
Remaindering: it's dirty job but somebody has to do it. D. K. Mano. Esquire 87:54+ My '77

Returns policy

Booksellers report conservative buying, hence fewer returns in early 1977. D. Maryles. Pub W 211:59-60+ F 21 '77

BOOKSELLERS and bookselling—*Continued*

Secondhand books

Address book; secondhand book stores. S. Sunderlin. House B 119:16+ Ag '77

Study and teaching

View from here: a publisher's rep attends ABA/NACS booksellers school. H. Hubert. Pub W 211:47-8 My 2 '77

Tape recordings

Sideline with an added dimension. il Pub W 212:51+ O 24 '77

Textbooks

Profits on textbooks: a call for group action by college store managers. H. W. Davis. Pub W 212:37-8 N 28 '77; Reply. I. L. Sanderson. 212:53 D 26 '77

Australia

Australia: Dyer's new best selling zone. il por Pub W 212:40 D 12 '77

California

Bookstores of downtown San Francisco; photographs. E. V. Smith. il Pub W 211:42-3 Ap 18 '77

Cody's Books of Berkeley: after 21 years, the Cody's move on. P. Holt. il pors Pub W 212:48-9+ N 7 '77

Magic Fishbone Bookshop: a California story; Carmel. M. R. Bruggeman. il Horn Bk 53:134-9 Ap '77

PW interviews; owner of Peninsula Bookshop, Palo Alto; ed by P. Holt. A. Lorentz. por Pub W 211:138 My 23 '77

Pickwick's founder reminisces about his early bookselling days; Los Angeles bookstores. L. Epstein. Pub W 211:55-6 Ja 10 '77

Canada

Children and librarians are encouraged to browse in this successful Toronto shop; The Children's Book Store. B. Slopen. il Pub W 211:110-11 F 28 '77

Children's Book Store in Toronto. H. Sarick and J. Sarick. il Horn Bk 53:202-5 Ap '77

See also

Canadian Booksellers Association

Connecticut

Children's books provide the backdrop for department store back-to-school promotion; G. Fox and Company's Show and Tell Book Jamboree. D. Maryles. il Pub W 212:50+ O 10 '77

Russians came to browse in Hartford bookstore; visit of members of the Leningrad Philharmonic. T. Huntington. Pub W 211:62-3 Mr 28 '77

Finland

Scandinavia's biggest bookstore; Academic Book Store in Helsinki. H. R. Lottman. il Pub W 211:48 My 9 '77

France

Eppe's of Paris. W. Saroyan. New Repub 176:23-5 Je 18 '77

Great Britain

BASH, and other bookselling ideas. P. Kleinman. Pub W 211:57 Je 13 '77

Blackwell's Children's Bookshop; Oxford. E. Taylor. il Horn Bk 53:206-8 Ap '77

Booming new way to get books to children in Britain: the school bookstore. S. Paulden. il Pub W 211:95-6 F 28 '77

Letter from England: bookselling in schools; School Bookshop Association. A. Chambers. Horn Bk 53:217-21 Ap '77

Through the looking glass: notes on an antiquarian children's bookshop; Justin G. Schiller, Ltd. J. G. Schiller and R. M. Wapner. il Horn Bk 53:140-6 Ap '77

Illinois

Kathy Larkin of Kroch's & Brentano's: total enthusiasm for the customer. I. Ballantine. il por Pub W 212:83-4 Jl 18 '77

Maryland

Bookstores of Baltimore: Abe's and the Peabody. G. W. Johnson. il New Repub 177:33-6 S 17 '77

Massachusetts

Bookshop for Boys and Girls; Boston. L. Kingman. il Horn Bk 53:209-14 Ap '77

Hathaway House Bookshop; Wellesley. R. D. Hale. il Horn Bk 53:121-7 Ap '77

Moonlighting in a bookstore: learning lessons at first hand; Booksmith Bookstore, Natick. T. Lopopolo. il por Pub W 212:123-5 S 26 '77

Summer business on Martha's Vineyard: how Bunch of Grapes makes it year-round. S. S. Steinberg. il por Pub W 212:44+ S 5 '77

Michigan

Herman Baker: a dynamic midwest retailer-publisher. il por Pub W 212:67-9 S 26 '77

New England

Booksellers flock to 4th annual regional; New England Booksellers Association meeting. R. A. Fort. il Pub W 212:49-50 N 14 '77

New Hampshire

Keep on truckin': two days in the life of publisher as book peddler. P. S. Jennison. il por Pub W 211:66-7 Ap 4 '77

New York (state)

Art publisher and jobber opens a bookshop in N.Y; Printed Matter bookstore in New York City. J. Giusto. il Pub W 212:54 D 26 '77

Compleat strategist: the place for war game aficionados. D. Maryles. il Pub W 211:52 Mr 7 '77

750,000 books: new Barnes & Noble branch. New Yorker 53:12-15 Ag 1 '77

Three aggressive booksellers proliferate into Manhattan's bustling Rockefeller Center area; Barnes & Noble, B. Dalton Bookseller and Classic Bookshop. D. Maryles. il Pub W 211:32-4 My 30 '77

New Zealand

Children's bookshop in New Zealand: one family's enterprise. D. Butler. il Horn Bk 53:128-33 Ap '77

Ohio

Publix, the Cleveland bookstore that could not go out of business, celebrates its 40 years. E. Batdorff. il pors Pub W 212:347-50 Ag 29 '77

United States

B. Dalton, with 350 outlets due by 1979, views its bookselling future with rosy optimism. D. Maryles. il Pub W 212:126-9 S 19 '77

Booksellers choose what books look best under the Christmas tree. D. Maryles and others. il Pub W 212:38+ D 5 '77

Bookselling and marketing; ed by D. Maryles. See issues of Publishers weekly

Buying hardcover books. il Consumer Rep 42:505-13 S '77

Commerce Department review: multiunit firms dominant. C. B. Grannis. Pub W 211:34 My 30 '77

Currents: PW's annual survey of Christmas buying trends. D. Maryles and J. Giusto. Pub W 212:36-7 D 12 '77

Currents: survey of summer bookstore business. D. Maryles. Pub W 212:24-5 Ag 22 '77

Love for bookstores inspires spring valentine to them in Sheed Andrews & McMeel title; interview, ed by R. Dahlin. F. Brady. Pub W 212:45 Ag 8 '77

Notes on trade. Colophon. Pub W 212:10 Jl 11; 6 Ag 15; 8 S 12; 10 O 31; 6 N 28 '77

PW interviews; ed by I. Kropotkin. J. Consolino. il Pub W 212:8-10 Jl 25 '77

Prepare for Christmas. il Pub W 212:66-8+ Ag 1 '77

Selection of games, puzzles and toys: sidelines that educate and entertain. D. Maryles. il Pub W 211:41-52 Mr 7 '77

See also

American Booksellers Association

Washington, D.C.

Rizzoli opens store in Washington, D.C. il Pub W 212:56 O 10 '77

BOOKSHELVES. See Bookcases

BOOKSHOP for Boys and Girls, Boston. See Booksellers and bookselling—Massachusetts

BOOKSMITH Bookstore, Natick. See Booksellers and bookselling—Massachusetts

BOOKSPAN, Martin

Record reviews. Consumer Rep 42:114-15, 172-3, 333, 430, 490, 678 F-Mr, Je-Ag, N '77

Second Arthur Rubinstein Piano Competition. il Hi Fi 27:MA37-8 Ag '77

BOOKSTEIN, Fred L.

Orthogenesis of the hominids: an exploration using biorthogonal grids. bibl il Science 197:901-4 Ag 26 '77

BOOKSTORE windows. See Show windows

BOOKSTORES. See Booksellers and bookselling; School bookstores

BOOKVIEWS (periodical)

Bowker to launch Bookviews, monthly consumer book magazine. M. Reuter. Pub W 211:34 Ap 25 '77

BOONE, Daniel

Daniel Boone's Kentucky. J. Jordon and C. Jordon. il Travel 148:46-51 Jl '77 *

BOORE, David M.

Motion of the ground in earthquakes; with biographical sketch. il map Sci Am 237:10, 68-78 bibl(p 190) D '77

BOOT repairing. See Shoes, boots, rubbers, etc.—Repairing

BOOTH, Donald

After 18 years of searching: we're a family again! E. P. Frank. il pors Good H 185:111+ O '77 *

BOOTH, John Wilkes
Assassins! B. Z. Spencer. il por Sat Eve Post 249:72 Jl '77 *

BOOTH, Philip
Building her; poem. Atlantic 239:85 My '77

about

Comment. R. Siegel. Poetry 130:111-14 My '77 *

BOOTH, Wallace Wray, 1922-
United Brands shifts to a shirtsleeve boss. por Bus W p37 F 14 '77 *

BOOTHE Courier Corporation. See Computer industry

BOOTHS, Exhibition. See Exhibition booths

BOOTLEGGING. See Smuggling

BOOTS. See Shoes, boots, rubbers, etc.

BOOTS Company, Ltd. See Drugstores—Great Britain

BO-Peep cult. See Cults

BOPHUTHATSWANA
Birth of Bophuthatswana. il map Time 110:40 D 19 '77

BORAGE
Borage goes like spinach. J. Jankowiak. il Org Gard & Farm 24:74-5 My '77

BORANES. See Boron hydrides

BORCH, Otto Rose
Cooperation among European nations; excerpts from address. por Intellect 106:97-8 S '77

BORCHERDING, James R.
Dairy management. See issues of Successful farming
(ed) Successful dairy management (cont) il Suc Farm 75:no4 D1-8+ Mr '77

BORDA, Owen M.
It takes more than credentials. Lib J 102:1727 S 1 '77

BORDEAUX
Bordeaux is for wine lovers. . .and other romantics: Le Saint-James. R. L. Balzer. il Holiday 58:32-3+ Ja '77

BORDEAUX wines. See Wine

BORDELON, Bruce V.
Dance funding. See issues of Dance magazine

BORDEN, Inc
Some fun at last. por Forbes 120:112 D 1 '77

BORDER patrols
See also
United States—Border Patrol

BORDERS, William
India's crown prince. il por N Y Times Mag p 13-15+ F 13 '77

BORDES, Marilynn Johnson
Reuben Swift, cabinetmaker of New Bedford. bibl il Antiques 112:750-2 O '77

BORDIER, André
At home with the sweetlips and angelfish. G. Scott. il por Fortune 95:91+ Mr '77 *

BOREDOM
Chasing the blahs away: boredom and how to beat it. S. Keen. il por Psychol Today 10:78-80+ My '77

Anecdotes, facetiae, satire, etc.

There's no such thing as a little boredom. P. Ryan. Smithsonian 8:104 Jl '77

BORELLO, Mary Ann, and Mathias, Elizabeth
Botanicas: Puerto Rican folk pharmacies; with biographical sketches. il Natur Hist 86:4, 64-73 bibl(p 116-17) Ag '77

BORG, Bjorn
Borg's hot hand took all the tricks. C. Kirkpatrick. il pors Sports Illus 46:16-17 Ja 31 '77 *
Wimbledon was never better. C. Kirkpatrick. il pors Sports Illus 47:12-15 Jl 11 '77 *

BORGE, Victor
Theatre. B. Gill. New Yorker 53:93-4 O 17 '77 *

BORGENICHT, Miriam
Many faces of a brownstone. il N Y Times Mag p74-5+ O 9 '77

BORGENS, Richard B.
Skin batteries and limb regeneration; with biographical sketch. il Natur Hist 86:4, 84-9 bibl(p 123) O '77

BORGES, Jorge Luis
Avelino Arredondo; story, tr by N. T. di Giovanni. New Yorker 53:24-5 Jl 11 '77
Brunanburh, A.D. 937; poem; tr. by A. Reid. New Yorker 53:42 Ap 18 '77
Hengist wants men; poem; tr by A. Reid. New Yorker 53:34 Je 20 '77
Keeper; poem, tr by A. Reid. New Yorker 53:26 S 5 '77
Mirror and the mask; story; tr by N. T. di Giovanni. New Yorker 53:33-4 Je 6 '77
Night of the gifts; story, tr by N. T. Di Giovanni. New Yorker 53:27-8 Ag 15 '77
Palace; poem; tr by A. Reid. New Yorker 53:38 S 26 '77
Talismans; poem; tr by A. Reid. New Yorker 53:26 Ag 8 '77
Tankas; Poem of quantity; Milonga of Manuel Flores; Susana Bombal; Elegy; Fifteen coins; poems; excerpts from The gold of the tigers; selected later poems; tr by A. Reid. por New Repub 177:26-8 N 19 '77
To the nightingale; poem, tr by A. Reid. New Yorker 53:42 My 9 '77
Ulrike; story, tr by N. T. Di Giovanni. N Y Times Mag p94 Mr 6 '77
Undr; story; tr by N. T. Di Giovanni. New Yorker 53:18-19 Ag 1 '77

about

Borges in his poetry. A. Reid. New Repub 177:29-30 N 19 '77 *

BORGESE, Elisabeth (Mann)
International Ocean Institute. il Oceans 10:52-7 Ja '77

BORGESON, Lillian
Wild colors, natural dyes. il Nat Wildlife 15:50-3 Ap '77

BORGLUM, Gutzon
Carving the American colossus. E. M. Halliday. il por Am Heritage 28:18-27 Je '77 *

BORGLUM, John Gutzon de la Mothe. See Borglum, G.

BORGSTROM, Georg
Challenging the world food crisis. Intellect 105:322-4 Ap '77

BORGZINNER, Jon
Fishing world of Johnny Harms. il por Motor B & S 139:58-9+ Je '77

BORIS Godunov; opera. See Musorgskiĭ, M. P.

BORKMAN, Raymond F. See Lerman, S. jt auth

BORLAND, Hal
Bashful blue jay. il Audubon 79:2-5 My '77
'Dobe birds. il Audubon 79:16-17 Mr '77
Letter from the valley. Progressive 41:52-3 O '77
Wings of winter. Progressive 41:49-50 Mr '77

BORMAN, Frank
Should airline rules be loosened? interview. por U.S. News 82:75-6 My 9 '77

about

Moon Man turns Eastern around. il pors Time 109:53 F 7 '77

BORMANN, F. Herbert, and Likens, G. E.
Fresh air-clean water exchange; with biographical sketches. il Natur Hist 86:7, 62-71 bibl (p 118) N '77

—and others
Nitrogen budget for an aggrading northern hardwood forest ecosystem. bibl il Science 196:981-3 My 27 '77

BORNINO, Bruno
Black & white of Wild Cherry. il Hi Fi 27:125-6 Mr '77

BORNOFF, George
String training on the Cape. Mrs Conlon-Hoffman. il Hi Fi 28:MA14-15 Ja '78 *

BORNSTEIN, Leon, and others
Developments in industrial relations. See issues of Monthly labor review

BOROBUDUR, Java
Borobudur—Nirvana in central Java. M. Durazzo. il Holiday 58:36-9 Mr '77

BORODIN Quartet. See Quartets, Instrumental

BORON hydrides
Boranes and their relatives; Nobel prize lecture, December 11, 1976. W. N. Lipscomb. il Science 196:1047-55 Je 3 '77

BOROSAGE, Robert L. See Cortright, D. jt auth

BORRAS, Catherine
AAAS Council meeting, 1977. Science 196:342-4 Ap 15 '77

BORROFF, Marie
Floating; poem. New Repub 177:26 S 3 '77
Waves; poem. Yale R 66:403 Mr '77

BORROWING of money. See Credit

BORTLE, John E.
Comet digest. See issues of Sky and telescope, July 1977-

BORTON, Lady
Olivia: a vinyl victory. il Ms 6:68 D '77

BORTSTEIN, Larry
Ability plus science equal world's best. Sci Digest 81:10-11 Mr '77

BOSCH, Orlando
Incident. T. Branch and J. Rothchild. il pors Esquire 87:57 Mr '77 *

BOSCH, Robert, Corporation. See Automobile equipment industry—Germany, West

BOSEMAN and Lena; drama. See Fugard, A.

BOSHER, William J. Jr
JHS/MS teacher: penal, pastural, or preparatory. Engl J 66:64-5 D '77

BOSKIND-LODAHL, Marlene, and Sirlin, Joyce
Gorging-purging syndrome. il Psychol Today 10:50-2+ Mr '77

BOSLEY, Keith
Drought; poem. Nation 224:763 Je 18 '77
Icons; poem. Nation 224:634 My 21 '77

BOSONS. See Particles (nuclear physics)

BOSPHORUS. See Bosporus

BOSPORUS
Bosphorus: with one key opens and closes two worlds, two seas. M. Brooke. il Oceans 10:40-5 Ja '77

BOSS, Caroline A. See Sterrett, F. S. jt auth

BOSS rule
Last hurrah? The perpetual motion of the political machine. T. J. McDonald. Intellect 106:30-2 Ag '77

BOSTON

Airports

Logan Airport: the new South Terminal. il Archit Rec 162:105-10 S '77
Logan procedures spark pilots' threat. Aviation W 106:69 Ap 25 '77

Architecture

Recycling of Boston. J. H. Kay. il Sat R 4:38-40 F 5 '77

Art

Boston (cont) J. H. Kay. il Art N 76:96+ Ja; 98-101 Mr; 115-18 D '77

Bookstores

See Booksellers and bookselling—Massachusetts

Buildings

Eyes on the Tower; John Hancock Tower. il Newsweek 90:18+ O 10 '77
Some reflections on the John Hancock Tower. W. Marlin. il Archit Rec 161:117-26 Je '77
Super-strong trusses cantilever building tower over restricted site; Fiduciary Trust building. E. Moran. il Pop Sci 210:182 Ap '77

Courts

Justice with a different face; appointment of M. A. Burnham to the Boston Municipal Court. H. J. Scarupa. por Ms 6:19 D '77

Description

Boston. il Bet Hom & Gard 55:247-8+ N '77

Education

Ban in Boston? Poem provokes dispute; Chelsea High. L. R. Pearson. Am Lib 8:472 O '77
Boston after Louise Day Hicks: no more mileage in busing. H. Husock. il por Nation 225: 710-12 D 31 '77
Boston desegregation: what went wrong? K. Clark. bibl Clearing H 51:157-9 D '77
Elma Lewis: keeping African culture alive in Boston; Elma Lewis School of Fine Arts. S. Quinn. il pors Ms 5:14-15+ My '77

Galleries and museums

See also
Boston Museum of Fine Arts

Hospitals

Bionic grandmother. N. Hazelton. Nat R 29:953-4 Ag 19 '77
Controlling medical expansion; protesting against Affiliated Hospitals Center's planned destruction of neighborhood housing. H. Waitzkin and J. A. Sharratt. il Society 14:30-5 Ja '77
Great hospital war. E. Marshall. New Repub 176:22-5 My 28 '77

Industries

Boston: hub city of American audio. M. Riggs. il Hi Fi 27:79-83 Mr '77

Libraries

See also
Boston Public Library

Markets

Boston's historic Faneuil Hall Marketplace. M. F. Schmertz. il Archit Rec 162:116-27 D '77

Monuments, statues, etc.

Crispus Attucks monument controversy of 1887. D. P. Ryan. il Negro Hist Bull 40:656-7 Ja '77

Music

Debuts & reappearances. Hi Fi 27:MA24 Je; MA33 Jl '77
See also
Boston Symphony Orchestra
Opera—Massachusetts

Politics and government

Boston after Louise Day Hicks: no more mileage in busing. H. Husock. il por Nation 225: 710-12 D 31 '77

Poor

New confidence. il U.S. News 82:29-30 Je 13 '77

Schools

See Boston—Education

Transit systems

See also
Massachusetts Bay Transportation Authority

BOSTON (rock group) See Rock groups
BOSTON Consulting Group. See Business consultants
BOSTON dance companies. See Dance companies
BOSTON Marathon. See Running
BOSTON Museum of Fine Arts
Museum within a museum. J. H. Kay. Art N 76:115-18 D '77
Seventeenth-and early eighteenth-century decorative motifs in New England; permanent display at the Boston Museum of Fine Arts. S. B. Sherrill. il Antiques 112:180 Ag '77

BOSTON Public Library
Wonderful news in NYC, optimism in Boston. Am Lib 8:231-2 My '77
BOSTON Symphony Orchestra
BSO: Eugene Onegin (Ozawa); concert version at Carnegie Hall. Hi Fi 27:MA31 F '77
BSO: Takemitsu Quatrain. por Hi Fi 27:MA33 Jl '77
BOSTON University
Academic gore; J. Silber. N. Ephron. il por Esquire 88:76-8+ S '77
Texas rawhide in academia. F. J. Pratson. Nat R 29:204-5 F 18 '77
BOSTON University Concert Orchestra. See Orchestras
BOSTON University Orchestra. See Orchestras
BOSVELD, Jane
Dinosaurs. il Sci Digest 82:31-2+ S '77
Geothermal energies. il Sci Digest 82:73-6 O '77
Learning violence via TV. Sci Digest 81:27-30 Mr '77
That old feeling. Sci Digest 81:65-7+ Ap '77
You may be more normal than you think! Sci Digest 81:47-8 My '77
BOSWORTH, Barry P.
Bosworth: firm ideas for a drifting COWPS. por Bus W p28 Jl 11 '77 *
Fight on prices. il por Time 110:54-5 Ag 15 '77 *
BOSWORTH, Stephen W.
Department testifies on Alcan project; statement, October 12, 1977. Dept State Bull 77: 822-6 D 5 '77
BOTANICAL chemistry
See also
Alkaloids
Photosynthesis
BOTANICAL exploration

History

Colonial botanist, self-taught, filled European gardens; J. Bartram; excerpt from A species of eternity. J. Kastner. il Smithsonian 8:122-9 bibl(p 161) O '77
Innocent botanist who herbalized the West; excerpt from A species of eternity. J. Kastner. il por Horticulture 55:44-51 S '77

BOTANICAL gardens
For garden lovers, garden scientists in San Diego County; Quail Botanical Gardens. il Sunset 159:142-3 Jl '77
Jungle walk in San Diego; botanical collection of San Diego Zoo. il Sunset 158:220-2 Je '77
Legacy of Sri Lanka's Royal Botanic Gardens. R. Howard. il Horticulture 55:66 Mr '77
Sri Lanka's Royal Botanic Gardens: a laboratory in a paradise. C. Mydans. il Horticulture 55:58-65 Mr '77
See also
Brooklyn Botanic Garden
BOTANICAL literature
Legacy of Sri Lanka's Royal Botanic Gardens R. Howard. il Horticulture 55:66 Mr '77
BOTANICAL museums
See also
Herbariums
BOTANICAL research
6 scientists working hard on the hardwoods. J. Marks. il Am For 83:16-19+ N '77
Sri Lanka's Royal Botanic Gardens: a laboratory in a paradise; tropical plant research. C. Mydans. il Horticulture 55:58-65 Mr '77
BOTANISTS
See also
Bartram, J.
Carver, G. W.
Nuttall, T.
BOTANY
Botany (cont) Sci N 112:138 Ag 27 '77
See also
Angiosperms
Bark
Clones (botany)
Grasses
Herbariums
Hybridization
Paleobotany
Plants
Pollen
Seeds
Urban flora

Anatomy

See also
Stomata
Tendrils

Ecology

Ecology and evolution of flowering plant dominance. P. J. Regal. bibl Science 196:622-9 My 6 '77
See also
Forest ecology
Plant succession

History

Overlooked link: Darwin and his flowers; excerpt from Darwin and his flowers. M. Allan. il por Horticulture 55:12-21 O '77

Morphology

See also
Phyllotaxis

BOTANY—*Continued*

Nomenclature

Dr Garden's wonderfully scented and almost imaginary namesake; excerpt from Species of eternity. J. Kastner. il Horticulture 55:64 N '77
Houseplant pronunciation guide. Bet Hom & Gard 55:76+ My '77

Periodicity

120-year bamboo clock; reproductive periodicity of bamboo and cicadas. S. J. Gould. Natur Hist 86:8+ Ap '77
See also
Tree rings

Physiology

See also
Dormancy (plants)
Growth (plants)
Photosynthesis
Plants—Reproduction
Roots
Shoot apexes

Study and teaching

See also
Nature study

Amazon Valley

Medical secrets of the Amazon. N. Maxwell. il por Américas 29:2-8 Je '77

California

Vernal pools. D. M. Small. il Am For 83:30-3 My '77

Costa Rica

Flames in the jungle. S. Shaw. il Int Wildlife 7:44-7 N '77
Lives of a tree; the mysterious inner world of tropical plants. D. Perry. il Horticulture 55:30-5 O '77
Poison in a monkey's Garden of Eden. K. E. Glander. il Natur Hist 86:34-41 bibl(p96) Mr '77

Greece

Get with child a mandrake root. J. Eliot. Horticulture 55:12-13+ Je '77

Hawaii

Objects to Bureaucratus delayus; letters. T. Tagawa; F. R. Fosberg. il Nat Parks & Con Mag 51:27-9 F '77

Maine

Of dams and Kate Furbish; threat to Maine's rare plants by proposed Dickey-Lincoln Dams Project. R. Saltonstall, Jr. il por Liv Wildn 40:42-3 Ja '77
Women behind the wildflower that stopped a dam; K. Furbish. J. Cole. il por Horticulture 55:30-5 D '77

Michigan

Geology, vegetation, and vertebrate fauna of Michigan. J. H. Beaman. bibl map BioScience 27:350-2 My '77

Middle Western States

Cornbelt conifers. S. Reardon and D. Dickmann. il por Am For 83:8-10 Ag '77

New York (state)

Roadside beauty. J. Taylor and R. Jenkins. il Conservationist 32:14-21 Jl '77

Northwestern States

Twilight of the great cedars; western red cedar. D. J. Chasan. il Audubon 79:50-5 N '77

Salvador

San Salvador's urban orchids. P. Bernhardt. il Natur Hist 86:64-71 D '77

Texas

Texas natives. D. Snell. il pors Horticulture 55:38-51 Ap '77

Western States

Innocent botanist who herbalized the West; excerpt from A species of eternity. J. Kastner. il por Horticulture 55:44-51 S '77

BOTANY, Economic
Texas natives. D. Snell. il pors Horticulture 55:38-51 Ap '77
See also
Botanical research
Rubber plants

BOTANY, Medical
Belly-my-grizzle; herbal medicine. S. Klaw. il por Am Heritage 28:96-105 Je '77
Herbs for beauty, health and sex. L. Lee. il Am Home 80:19+ My '77
Lore of herbs revived for kitchen and for cures; with views of John Williamson. E. V. Warren. il House B 119:14+ O '77
Medical secrets of the Amazon. N. Maxwell. il por Américas 29:2-8 Je '77
See also
Ginseng

BOTHA, Roelof F.
Why South Africa has a right to exist as a white African nation. por Intellect 106:34-6 Ag '77

BOTHAM, Jane, and Morris, W. C.
Authors & artists as speakers: excerpt from How to do a dozen (and more) odd jobs in library service. il por SLJ 24:27-9 D '77

BOTKIN, Daniel B.
Bits, bytes, and IBP. BioScience 27:385 Je '77
Forests, lakes and the anthropogenic production of carbon dioxide. bibl il BioScience 27:325-31 My '77

BOTRYTISED wines. See Wine

BOTSTEIN, Leon
Are you better off at Harvard? N Y Times Mag p81-6 Ap 17 '77

BOTSWANA
See also
United Nations—Botswana

Foreign relations

Rhodesia

See Rhodesia—Foreign relations—Botswana

BOTTAZZI, Ana Maria Trenchi de
You won't play the piano anymore. R. T. Jones. il por Read Digest 111:103-7 N '77 *

BOTTEL, Helen
Eating disease. Good H 184:176+ My '77
Taking the fear out of hospitals. il Good H 184:232+ Je '77

BOTTLE bills. See Beverage containers—Laws and regulations

BOTTLE feeding. See Infants—Nutrition

BOTTLE house models. See House models

BOTTLED gas. See Liquefied petroleum gas

BOTTLED water. See Water, Bottled

BOTTLENOSED dolphins. See Dolphins (mammals)

BOTTLES
Dewey canteen. M. Wollett and B. Wollett. il Hobbies 82:99 N '77
Teddy Roosevelt figural bottle. M. Wollett and B. Wollett. il Hobbies 82:99 My '77

BOTTLING industry. See Soft drink industry

BOTTO, Louis
Straight from the source. il N Y Times Mag p68+ Je 26 '77

BOTTOMLEY, Thomas R.
ABYC's new wiring color code. il Motor B & S 139:85-6 F '77

BOTTOMS, David
Drunk hunter; Shooting rats at the Bibb County dump; poems. Harpers 254:85 Je '77

BOTULISM
Case of the deadly hot peppers. A. Stark. Read Digest 111:207-8+ N '77

BOUCHAL, Edna L.
Three dimensions in weaving. il Sch Arts 77:65-5 S '77

BOUCHARD, Hypolite
When Argentine conquered California. A. Alonso Piñeiro. il por Américas 29:34-7 Je '77 *

BOUGERE, Marquerite
Non-sexist books. il por Intellect 106:11 Jl '77

BOULANGER, Nadia
Teaching: Nadia Boulanger. S. R. Hoover. Am Scholar 46:496-502 Aut '77 *

BOULDER, Colo.

Art

See Art—Colorado

Industries

Lively publishing scene in Boulder. S. Peckham. il Pub W 211:49-51 Je 6 '77

Music

Colorado Chamber Orchestra. Hi Fi 27:MA18 N '77

BOULDING, Elise
Children's rights. bibl il Society 15:39-43 N '77

BOULET, Richard
Love that the father has lavished on us. New Cath World 220:51 Ja '77

BOULEZ, Pierre
Departure; interview. New Yorker 53:30-2 Je 6 '77

about

Book on Boulez. . .& a discography. B. Pernick. il Am Rec G 40:7-11+ Ag '77 *
Boulez and Mahler. B. H. Haggin. New Repub 176:25-7 Mr 12 '77 *
Boulez' IRCAM: amnesia in Nibelheim. R. McMullen. il por Hi Fi 27:80-4 Ap '77 *
Boulez signs off with Berlioz Damnation. por Hi Fi 27:MA25 S '77 *
Canaveral of sound. H. Saal and J. Friedman. il Newsweek 89:67-8 F 7 '77 *
Most visionary modernist. F. J. Spieler. Harpers 254:86-8 Je '77 *
Music. D. Hamilton. Nation 224:731-2 Je 11 '77 *
Musical events. A. Porter. New Yorker 52:64-8 Ja 31 '77 *

BOULLIOUN, Ernest Herman, 1918-
Air transport fundamentals; excerpts from address, April 18, 1977. Aviation W 106:11 Ap 18 '77
BOUNDARIES
Territorial division: the least-time constraint behind the formation of subnational boundaries. G. E. Stephan. bibl Science 196:523-4 Ap 29 '77
See also
Ethnic barriers
Germany—Boundaries
Israel—Boundaries
Territorial waters
United States—Boundaries
BOUNDARY Waters Canoe Area. See Quetico-Superior Region
BOUQUETIN. See Ibex
BOUQUETS
Flowers for the wedding. il Sunset 158:274-6+ My '77
BOUQUETS, Artificial. See Flowers, Artificial
BOUQUETS, Dried. See Flowers, Dried
BOUQUET'S Expedition, 1763
See also
Pontiac's Conspiracy, 1763-1765
BOURAS, Charalambos
How the Acropolis can be saved. il UNESCO Courier 30:4-11 O '77
BOURDAIN, G. S.
(ed) See Crespin, R. Regine Crespin
BOURDON, David
Critic's diary: the New York art year. il Art in Am 65:67-79 Jl '77
BOURNE, Peter
Peter Bourne: psychiatrist in the White House. C. Holden. por Science 197:539-42 Ag 5 '77 *
BOURNE, Wade L.
Move with 'em or lose 'em. il Outdoor Life 160: 92-3+ S '77
BOURNONVILLE, August
Dance. N. Goldner. Nation 224:250-2 F 26 '77 *
BOURNONVILLE divertissements; ballet. See Ballet reviews—Single works
BOUSH-Tazewell house, Norfolk, Va. See Historic houses, sites, etc.—Virginia
BOUSQUET, Woodward S.
Pond clam. il Conservationist 31:45 N '76
Ram's horn snail. il Conservationist 31:45 My '77
BOUTIQUES. See Specialty stores
BOUTWELL, William D.
Obituary
Pub W 211:34 Mr 28 '77
BOVA, Ben
Character in science fiction; excerpt from Notes to a science fiction writer. Writer 90:17-19+ Ap '77
BOVOSO, Carole
Discovering my foremothers. il pors Ms 6:56-9 S '77
BOW, Clara
Liberated lady. C. L. Westerbeck, Jr. Commonweal 104:790-1 D 9 '77 *
BOW and arrow
New tune on a stringed instrument; compound bow. il Sports Illus 47:77+ O 31 '77
BOW hunting. See Hunting with bow and arrow
BOWDEN, Sally
Reviews. J. Anderson. il Dance Mag 51:21 Ap '77 *
BOWDOIN College Contemporary Music Festival. See Music festivals—Maine
BOWEN, John
Japan's Izu Peninsula. il Travel 147:60-5 F '77
Undiscovered Potomacs. il Travel 148:34-7+ O '77
BOWEN, Murray
Genealogy of the weakest child. il Time 109:85 Ap 11 '77 *
BOWEN, Richard L. Jr
Lamps and candlesticks of the Meriden Britannia Company. bibl il Antiques 111:332-7 F '77
BOWEN, William
(ed) Japanese managers tell how their system works. il Fortune 96:126-32+ N '77
BOWEN, William Gordon
Annals of higher education. E. J. Kahn, Jr. New Yorker 53:88+ My 23 '77 *
BOWEN, William H.
Diet control can prevent decay. il por Parents Mag 52:40-1+ Mr '77
BOWER, Joseph L.
Effective public management. bibl f Harvard Bus R 55:131-40 Mr '77
BOWERBIRDS
Australia's feathered playboy. P. Green. il Nat Geog 152:864-72 D '77
BOWERS, Faubion
Recording that ended World War II. il Hi Fi 27:87-90 O '77
BOWERS, Gordy
Racing clinic; one-design. il por Yachting 141: 60+ Mr '77
BOWERS, John D.
It's easy to write and self-publish a consumer manual. Writers Digest 57:23-4 Ap '77
BOWERS, Randy G.
Pool party: catfish for 600. il Parks & Rec 12:38-40+ Mr '77
BOWERS, William S.
—and Martinez-Pardo, Rafael
Antiallatotropins: inhibition of corpus allatum development. bibl il Science 197:1369-71 S 30 '77
—and others
Sesquiterpene progenitor, germacrene A: an alarm pheromone in aphids. bibl il Science 196:680-1 My 6 '77
about
Aphids foiled by false alarm. il Chemistry 50:23 Jl '77 *
BOWERY bums. See Tramps
BOWHEAD whales. See Whales
BOWIE, Phil
Fastest woman on earth. il pors Sat Eve Post 249:42-3+ Mr '77
BOWIE, Robert R.
Deputies are forever. R. Morris. New Repub 176:15-17 Ap 23 '77 *
BOWL football games. See Football, College
BOWLES, E. A.
Lunatic asylum; excerpt from My garden in spring. Horticulture 55:72-5 F '77
BOWLES, Jane
In the summer house. Reviews
Nation 224:668-9 My 28 '77 *
New Yorker 53:83-4 My 23 '77 *
BOWLES, Samuel
Trilateral Commission: have capitalism and democracy come to a parting of the ways? il Progressive 41:20-3 Je '77
BOWLING
Bowling 'em over; ed by B. Weber. C. Taylor. il por Sr Schol 110:29 N 3 '77
$100,000 bowling machine; E. Anthony. R. Bongartz. il pors Sports Illus 46:66-9+ Mr 7 '77
Shark attack at the Riviera; Firestone Tournament of Champions. H. Weiskopf. por Sports Illus 46:66 My 9 '77

Anecdotes, facetiae, satire, etc.

Why there will never be a great bowling novel. R. Blount, Jr. Esquire 87:38+ F '77

Television broadcasting

See Television broadcasting—Sports
BOWLING exercises. See Exercise
BOWLS
Bowl your students over with coiled clay. T. Dahood. il Design (US) 79:6+ Fall '77
BOWLT, John E.
Art criticism of Pushkin, Gogol, Dostoevsky and Tolstoy. il Art N 76:86-8+ My '77
Crucial room; interview. il New Yorker 53:29-31 My 2 '77
Moscow. Art N 76:109-11 O '77
Russian paintings at the Met: an inside look at museum diplomacy. il Art in Am 65:74-9 My; 120-1 N '77
BOWMAN, Patricia
Marriage and a move: a new chapter in the life of Patricia Bowman. R. Philp. il por Dance Mag 51:133 My '77 *
BOWRING, Dave
For big steelhead only. il Field & S 82:46-7+ S '77
BOWRING, Mary
Dogs in our life; excerpt from The animals come first. il Good H 184:68+ Ap '77
BOWSTRING-hemp. See Sansevieria
BOX assemblage. See Assemblage (art)
BOX lunches. See Lunches
BOX sculpture. See Paper sculpture
BOXERS
See also
Ali, M.
Benitez, W.
Bobick, D.
Fuller, P. D.
Halpern, B.
Monzon, C.
Moore, A.
Norton, K.
Page, G.
Patterson, F.
Shavers, E. B.
Valdes, R.
Young, J.
BOXES, cases, etc.
Cookie art . . . gift boxes that keep. il Ladies Home J 94:98-9+ D '77
Creating a showcase is not an easy task. R. Goldberg. House B 119:74 O '77
Kirigami Christmas boxes. il Design (US) 79: 10 N '77
Playing-card holder. E. Scott. il Pop Mech 147: 276 My '77
See also
Jewelry boxes, cases, etc.
Sewing boxes
Toy chests

BOXING
Amateur night on the Americus plan. R. Kennedy. il Sports Illus 46:32-6+ F 21 '77
Day the gold turned green; professional debut of R. Leonard. P. Putnam. il Sports Illus 46:18-19 F 14 '77
How to get zapped and still be a champ; C. Zarate vs A. Zamora in bantamweight fight. P. Putnam. il pors Sports Illus 46:28-9 My 2 '77
Hyperbole's child; Ali-Shavers fight. A. B. Giamatti. Harpers 225:117-18+ D '77
It's that new college try; National Collegiate Boxing Association championships. R. H. Boyle. il Sports Illus 46:80+ Ap 11 '77
Jeemy Young! Jeemy Young! Jeemy Young! J. Young-G. Foreman fight. P. Putnam. il pors Sports Illus 46:22-3 Mr 28 '77
Make him 38 and one; K. Norton-D. Bobick fight. P. Putnam. il pors Sports Illus 46:96+ My 23 '77
March of the hit paraders. P. Putnam. il Sports Illus 47:22-5 S 26 '77
Once more to the well; M. Ali-E. Shavers bout. P. Putnam. il pors Sports Illus 47:20-3 O 10 '77
Over the ropes is out; W. Benitez-J. Chavez junior welterweight fight. C. Gammon. il pors Sports Illus 47:52+ Ag 15 '77
Star bows out, a star bows in; C. Monzon-R. Valdez middleweight fight. P. Putnam. il pors Sports Illus 47:20-1 Ag 8 '77
Staying at the top of his class; C. Palomino vs M. Muñiz in WBC welterweight championship bout. P. Putnam. il pors Sports Illus 46:20-2 Ja 31 '77
This was the start of something big; L. Spinks and H. Davis in professional boxing debuts. P. Putnam. il pors Sports Illus 46:18-19 Ja 24 '77
Ultimate confrontation (title varies); amateurs vs professionals; excerpt from Shadow box. G. Plimpton. il Sports Illus 47:98-104+ O 17; 38-40+ O 24 '77
Win some, lose some, split the rest; K. Norton-J. Young heavyweight bout. P. Putnam. il pors Sports Illus 47:36-8+ N 14 '77
You gotta have heart; M. Ali-E. Shavers fight. P. Bonventre. il pors Newsweek 90:77 O 10 '77
See also
T'ai chi ch'üan

Accidents and injuries

Three fast rounds in Saginaw; K. Ellison in welterweight Golden Gloves competition after auto accident. R. Rau. il Sports Illus 46:44-6+ Mr 21 '77

Economic aspects

Boxing fits this old boy like a glove; manager G. Kanter. D. Levin. il por Sports Illus 46:46-8+ Ap 4 '77

History

Destruction of a giant; excerpt from Dempsey. J. Dempsey and B. P. Dempsey. il pors Am Heritage 28:72-83 Ap '77
Fight on! And on and on; T. Sayers vs J. C. Heenan in bareknuckle fight; excerpt from The great prize fight. A. Lloyd. il pors Sports Illus 47:54-60+ Jl 25 '77

Television broadcasting

See Television broadcasting—Sports

Tournaments

At sea in a ring; U.S. Boxing Tournament of Champions. il Time 109:51 Ja 31 '77
King-size scandal in the ring; United States Boxing Championships. por Time 109:64 My 2 '77
Some very wrong numbers; ABC's suspension of D. King's United States Championship. R. H. Boyle. il por Sports Illus 46:22-7 My 2 '77

BOY Scouts
Something to strive for. J. Cowle. il Read Digest 111:171-2+ O '77
Unforgettable Clarence Mathews; leader of black Boy Scout troop. B. N. Butler. il Read Digest 111:139-42 D '77
Which future for tomorrow? address, July 20, 1977. W. W. Harman. Vital Speeches 43:696-700 S 1 '77

BOYCE, Christopher
Pyramider spy case. R. Steele and N. Horrock. il por Newsweek 89:29 Ap 18 '77 *
Stealing the company store. il por Time 109:19 My 9 '77 *
To be young, rich—and a spy. R. Lindsey. il pors N Y Times Mag p 18+ My 22 '77 *

BOYCE, Peter B.
Low light level detectors for astronomy. bibl Science 198:145-8 O 14 '77

BOYCOTT
Bitter beercott; dispute over polygraph exams at Adolph Coors Co. il Time 110:15 D 26 '77
Bottle-baby disease; boycott of Nestle products in attempt to stop promotion of infant formula in underdeveloped countries. B. L. Benderly. Ms 6:20 D '77
ERA now? economic boycott in states that have failed to ratify the amendment. il Time 110:28 N 14 '77
Feminists' boycott; support for the ERA. Nation 225:548-9 N 26 '77
Organizing J. P. Stevens. F. Gaillard. Progressive 41:37 F '77
Stevens digs its heels in deeper; boycott by Amalgamated Clothing & Textile Workers to force unionization. il Bus W p29 Mr 14 '77
Touch of civil rights fervor; actions taken against J. P. Stevens and Co. by the Amalgamated Clothing and Textile Workers Union. il Time 109:44 Mr 14 '77
Troubled looming; J. P. Stevens' anti-union strategy. P. D. Wellstone. New Repub 176:14-15 Mr 12 '77
When a union goes all out in a boycott drive—. il U.S. News 82:71-2 Je 20 '77
See also
Blacklisting

BOYD, Andrew
Everywhere but Ireland. il Nation 224:453-6 Ap 16 '77

BOYDTON, Va.
Small town that refuses to die. il U.S. News 83:88-9 N 21 '77

BOYER, David S.
Our wild and scenic rivers. il map Nat Geog 152:30-45 Jl '77

BOYER, Ernest L.
Drive for better schools—what the government plans; interview. il por U.S. News 83:63-4 Jl 11 '77
Energy and the schools; excerpt from address, June 22, 1977. Todays Educ 66:54-5+ S '77

BOYER, Herbert
Recombinant lab for DNA and my 95 days in it. J. L. Hopson. il pors Smithsonian 8:54-63 Je '77 *

BOYER, Martin
Biggest littlest shows on earth. il pors Ebony 32:90-2+ Mr '77 *

BOYER, Mimi
Boyers' birds. W. Trimm. il pors Conservationist 31:28-32 Mr '77 *

BOYER, Phillip
Boyers' birds; photographs. il pors Conservationist 31:28+ Mr '77

BOYER, Robert E.
Family doctor of the year 1977. il pors Good H 185:98+ O '77 *

BOYLAN, Frank T. Jr
Stranded in the merciless sands. il Read Digest 111:77-81 Ag '77

BOYLE, Ann P.
Bringing your grandchildren into your life. il Ret Liv 17:16-18 Ag '77

BOYLE, Deirdre
Media minded. See issues of American libraries

BOYLE, Lisa
Lonely courage of Lisa Boyle. F. Deford. il Seventeen 36:188-9+ Ap '77 *

BOYLE, Robert H.
Boxing (cont) Sports Illus 46:80+ Ap 11 '77
Nature. il Sports Illus 46:54+ F 28 '77
Some very wrong numbers. il por Sports Illus 46:22-7 My 2 '77
Step in and enjoy the turmoil. il pors Sports Illus 46:80-4+ Je 13 '77

BOYLE, T. Coraghessan
Champ; story. Atlantic 241:82-5 Ja '78
We are Norsemen; story. Harpers 255:76-8 S '77

BOYLE, W. S.
Light-wave communications; with biographical sketch. il Sci Am 237:20, 40-8 bibl(p 140) Ag '77

BOYLSTON, Zabdiel
Battling the red death. M. Musser. il por Am Hist Illus 12:30-6 N '77 *

BOYNTON, Robert M. See Tansley, B. W. jt auth

BOYNTON, Searles R.
Pomo Indian portraits of Grace Carpenter Hudson; excerpt from The painter lady. il por Am West 14:20-9 S '77

BOYS, Ken
Australia. il Trav/Holiday 148:40+ D '77

BOYS
Breakup: how he feels when it's over. V. Billings. Seventeen 36:94-5 Jl '77
Raising boys who know how to love. D. Singer and J. L. Singer. il pors Parents Mag 52:32+ D '77
Relating; questions and answers. A. Wood. See issues of Seventeen
Why do boys hide how they feel? Seventeen 36:49 My '77
See also
Sex differences

BOYS camps. See Camps

BOYS clubs
See also
Boy Scouts

BOYS Town, Neb.
Giving and getting taken. Chr Today 22:59-61 D 9 '77

BOYTE, Harry Chatten
New hope for the NAM. Progressive 41:10 O '77

BOZEMAN, Adda Bruemmer
Understating the Communist threat; excerpt from address, July 1977. bibl Society 15:92-6 N '77
BRAASCH, Gary
For love of wilderness. N. Stevens. il Pop Phot 80:86-93 F '77 *
BRABANT, James
Musky fishing. il por Conservationist 31:21-3 Mr '77
BRACELETS, Medic Alert. See Identification tags, bracelets, etc.
BRACES, Orthopedic. See Orthopedic braces
BRACEWELL, Ronald
What to say to the space probe when it arrives. il Horizon 19:48-53 Ja '77
BRACKEN, B. D. See Sieger, R. B. jt auth
BRACKEN, Paul. See Singer, M. jt auth
BRACKET racing. See Drag racing
BRACKET racing cars. See Automobiles, Racing
BRACKETS
What's what in roof brackets. il Bet Hom & Gard 55:80 Je '77
BRADBURY, Jack W. See McCracken, G. F. jt auth
BRADBURY, Ray
The god in science fiction. il Sat R 5:36-8+ D 10 '77
BRADEMAS, John
National arts policy. por Am Artist 42:16+ Ja '78
BRADEN, Joan E. Ridley
Department discusses coffee prices; statement, February 22, 1977. il Dept State Bull 76:301-3 Mr 28 '77
BRADEN, Tom
Birth of the CIA. il Am Heritage 28:4-13 F '77
BRADEN, Waldo W.
In the heads of the listeners; address, September 9, 1977. Vital Speeches 44:42-4 N 1 '77
BRADFIELD, William A.
W. A. Bradfield and his comet seeker. il por Sky and Tel 53:306-11 Ap '77 *
BRADFORD, Allison
On-the-run pizzazz. il pors Seventeen 36:180-1 Ap '77 *
BRADFORD, William, 1663-1752
When New York feared the French. il Am Heritage 28:84-5 O '77 *
BRADLEY, Bill
You can't buy heart. il pors Sports Illus 47:102-6+ O 31 '77
BRADLEY, David G.
Managing against expropriation. il map Harvard Bus R 55:75-83 Jl '77
BRADLEY, Dick
On board with Bradley. See issues of Motor boating & sailing
BRADLEY, Doug
Bad paper vets. Progressive 41:31-3 Ap '77
BRADLEY, William
(ed) See Barnard, C. N. Christiaan Barnard: South Africa's premier surgeon
BRADSHAW, Hank
Fish that takes 1,000 casts. il Outdoor Life 160:80-1+ Jl '77
—and Bradshaw, Vera
Memories of Chopin. il Travel 147:46-9 Je '77
BRADSHAW, Jon
Closing time in the Garden of Eden. il Esquire 88:128-9+ O '77
Elvis. il por Esquire 88:96-8 O '77; Same abr. with title Elvis: the man. Read Digest 112:72-5 Ja '78
The Queen. il Esquire 88:74-6 Ag '77
Reggae way to salvation. il pors N Y Times Mag p24-8+ Ag 14 '77
Savage skulls. il Esquire 87:74-83+ Je '77
BRADSHAW, Thornton Frederick
Government must subsidize tremendous research; interview. por U.S. News 82:43-4 Ap 18 '77
My case for national planning. il por Fortune 95:100-4 F '77
BRADSHAW, Vera. See Bradshaw, H. jt auth
BRADY, Frank
Jackie and Ari; excerpt from Onassis, an extravagant life. il pors Sat Eve Post 249:30+ D '77
Love for bookstores inspires spring valentine to them in Sheed Andrews & McMeel title; interview, ed by R. Dahlin. Pub W 212:45 Ag 8 '77
BRADY, Mathew B.
Hold still—don't move a muscle: you're on Brady's camera! excerpt from Mathew Brady and his world. P. B. Kunhardt, Jr. il Smithsonian 8:58-67 bibl(p 101) Ag '77 *
Images of which history was made bore the Mathew Brady label; excerpts from Mathew Brady and his world. P. B. Kunhardt, Jr. il pors Smithsonian 8:24-35 Jl '77 *
BRAHE, Tyge
Tycho Brahe and the great comet of 1577. O. Gingerich. il Sky & Tel 54:452-8 D '77 *
BRAHM, Walter
Where have all the leaders gone? ALA's democracy produces chaos. Am Lib 8:423-4 S '77
BRAHMS, Johannes
Sonatas for cello and piano: nos. 1 and 2. W. D. Custis. Am Rec G 40:14 Je '77

about

Brahms by Böhm; 4 symphonies; recordings. P. L. Althouse. Am Rec G 40:26-9 F '77 *
Clarinet quintet in B minor, op.115. E. Belov. il Am Rec G 40:19 Ap '77 *
Furtwangler on Brahms; Symphony no. 1 in C minor, op. 68. G. S. Fox. Am Rec G 40:16-17 N '76 *
Piano concerto no. 1. G. S. Fox. Am Rec G 40:23-4 S '77 *
Piano concerto no. 1, in D minor, op. 15. L. Gerber. Am Rec G 40:17 N '76 *
Piano trio, op. 8; Intermezzi, op. 117. D. W. Moore. Am Rec G 40:15 Ap '77 *
Second time around; works by Brahms performed by the Berlin Philharmonic Orchestra conducted by H. von Karajan. P. L. Althouse. il por Am Rec G 40:24-6 O '77 *
Six symphonies and other orchestral works recorded on Vanguard. J. R. Oestreich. Am Rec G 41:22-4 D '77 *
Symphony no. 4 in E minor op. 98. J. Waxman. Am Rec G 40:12-13 Mr '77 *
Three intermezzi, D. Alexeev soloist; Variations and fugue on a theme by Handel, V. Cliburn soloist. D. M. Garvelmann. Am Rec G 40:24-6 S '77 *
BRAIN, Robert
Somebody else should be your own best friend. bibl il por Psychol Today 11:83-4+ O '77
BRAIN
Amygdaloid projections to prefrontal and motor cortex. A. Llamas and others. bibl il Science 195:794-6 F 25 '77
Gating of neuronal transmission in the hippocampus: efficacy of transmission varies with behavioral state. J. Winson and C. Abzug. bibl il Science 196:1223-5 Je 10 '77
Post-human intelligence; excerpt from Until the sun dies. R. Jastrow. Natur Hist 86:12-13+ Je '77
To build a brain; electronic models of nerve cells. J. A. Miller. il por Sci N 111:156-7 Mr 5 '77

See also

Cerebrospinal fluid
Consciousness
Electroencephalography
Hypothalamus
Laterality
Limbic system
Memory
Mind and body
Nervous system
Thalamus

Analysis and chemistry

Adenylate cyclase of brain reflects propensity for breast cancer in mice. G. C. Cotzias and L. C. Tang. bibl il Science 197:1094-6 S 9 '77
Alcohol drinking: abnormal intake caused by tetrahydropapaveroline in brain. R. D. Myers and C. L. Melchior. bibl il Science 196:554-6 Ap 29 '77
Antigen-antibody reactions in rat brain sites induce transient changes in drinking behavior. C. A. Williams, Jr and N. Schupf. bibl il Science 196:328-30 Ap 15 '77
Brain self-stimulation: direct evidence for the involvement of dopamine in the prefrontal cortex. F. Mora and R. D. Myers. bibl il Science 197:1387-9 S 30 '77
Brain's own tranquilizer? il Chemistry 50:26 Jl '77
Chemical cause of alcoholism; THP in brain. Sci N 111:327 My 21 '77
Diet and uptake of aldomet by the brain; competition with natural large neutral amino acids. D. C. Markovitz and J. D. Fernstrom. bibl il Science 197:1014-15 S 2 '77
Dopamine-sensitive adenylate cyclase: location in substantia nigra. K. Gale and others. bibl il Science 195:503-5 F 4 '77
Glia maturation factor: effect on chemical differentiation of glioblasts in culture. R. Lim and others. bibl il Science 195:195-6 Ja 14 '77
Glial-neural interaction demonstrated by the injection of Na^+ and Li^+ into cortical glia. R. G. Grossman and A. Seregin. bibl il Science 195:196-8 Ja 14 '77
Glutamine synthetase: glial localization in brain. A. Martinez-Hernandez and others. bibl il Science 195:1356-8 Mr 25 '77
Hippocampal efferents reach widespread areas of cerebral cortex and amygdala in the rhesus monkey. D. L. Rosene and G. W. Van Hoesen. bibl il Science 198:315-17 O 21 '77
Hyperphenylalanemia: effect on brain polyribosomes can be partially reversed by other amino acids. J. V. Hughes and T. C. Johnson. bibl il Science 195:402-4 Ja 28 '77
Interdependence of the nigrostriatal dopaminergic systems on the two sides of the brain in the cat. A. Nieoullon and others. bibl il Science 198:416-18 O 28 '77

BRAIN—Analysis and chemistry—*Continued*
Localization of nigral dopamine-sensitive adenylate cyclase on neurons originating from the corpus striatum. P. F. Spano and others. bibl il Science 196:1343-5 Je 17 '77
Measuring melanin in the brain. Sci N 112: 6-7 Jl 2 '77
Memory formation: evidence for a specific neurochemical system in the amygdala. M. Gallagher and others. bibl il Science 198:423-5 O 28 '77
Norepinephrine-dopamine interactions and behavior. S. M. Antelman and A. R. Caggiula. bibl Science 195:646-53 F 18 '77
Prolactin-like immunoreactivity: localization in nerve terminals of rat hypothalamus. K. Fuxe and others. bibl il Science 196:899-900 My 20 '77
Second messengers in the brain. J. A. Nathanson and P. Greengard. il Sci Am 237:108-19 bibl(p 140) Ag '77

Diseases

Alzheimer's disease, trisomy 21, and myeloproliferative disorders: associations suggesting a genetic diathesis. L. L. Heston. bibl il Science 196:322-3 Ap 15 '77
Psychochemical treatment counteracts senility. Sci N 111:292 My 7 '77
Senility: more than growing old; Alzheimer's disease. J. Arehart-Treichel. il Sci N 112:218-19+ O 1 '77
Tale of 3 diseases: a common cause? pathological microtubules. Sci N 111:263 Ap 23 '77
See also
Cerebrovascular disease

Innervation

Major innervation of newborn rat cortex by monoaminergic neurons. J. T. Coyle and M. E. Molliver. bibl il Science 196:444-7 Ap 22 '77

Localization of functions

Angiotensin injected into the neostriatum after learning disrupts retention performance. J. M. Morgan and A. Routtenberg. bibl il Science 196:87-9 Ap 1 '77
Bridging a gap between men and monkeys; impairing memory of sound by cutting auditory association cortex. J. H. Dewson; 3d. por Intellect 105:215-16 Ja '77
Classical conditioning with auditory discrimination of the eye blink in decerebrate cats. R. J. Norman and others. bibl il Science 196:551-3 Ap 29 '77
Echo-detecting characteristics of neurons in inferior colliculus of unanesthetized bats. G. Pollak and others. bibl il Science 196:675-8 My 6 '77
Hypothalamic stimulation facilitates contralateral visual control of a learned response. W. K. Beagley and T. L. Holley. bibl il Science 196:321-2 Ap 15 '77
Limbic system interrelations: functional division among hippocampal-septal connections. T. W. Berger and R. F. Thompson. bibl il Science 197:587-9 Ag 5 '77
Physiological evidence for habenula as major link between forebrain and midbrain raphe. R. Y. Wang and G. K. Aghajanian. bibl il Science 197:89-91 Jl 1 '77
Premotor cortical ablations in monkeys: contralateral changes in visually guided reaching behavior. L. Moll and H. G. J. M. Kuypers. bibl il Science 198:317-19 O 21 '77
Selective blockade of hypothalamic hyperphagia and obesity in rats by serotonin-depleting midbrain lesions. D. V. Coscina and H. C. Stancer. bibl il Science 195:416-19 Ja 28 '77
Spatial memory. D. S. Olton. il Sci Am 236:82-4+ bibl(p 142) Je '77
Striatal efferent fibers play a role in maintaining rotational behavior in the rat. J. F. Marshall and U. Ungerstedt. bibl il Science 198: 62-4 O 7 '77
Suprachiasmatic nuclear lesions do not abolish food-shifted circadian adrenal and temperature rhythmicity. D. T. Krieger and others. bibl il Science 197:398-9 Jl 22 '77
Suprachiasmatic nucleus: use of ^{14}C-labeled deoxyglucose uptake as a functional marker. W. J. Schwartz and H. Gainer. bibl il Science 197:1089-91 S 9 '77
Temporal lobe aggression in rats. J. P. J. Pinel and others. bibl il Science 197:1088-9 S 9 '77
Trigeminal substrates of intracrania self-stimulation in the brainstem. D. Van Der Kooy and A. G. Phillips. bibl il Science 196: 447-9 Ap 22 '77
Visual association cortex and vision in man: pattern-evoked occipital potentials in a blind boy. I. Bodis-Wollner and others. bibl il Science 198:629-31 N 11 '77
Visual input to the visuomotor mechanisms of the monkey's parietal lobe. T. C. T. Yin and V. B. Mountcastle. bibl il Science 197:1381-3 S 30 '77
See also
Electronic behavior control

Surgery

Medical wonders of Dr Robert White; experiments in brain cooling and transplants. J. G. Hubbell. por Read Digest 110:138-42 F '77
See also
Psychosurgery

Temperature

See Temperature, Animal and human

Transplantation

Medical wonders of Dr Robert White; experiments in brain cooling and transplants. J. G. Hubbell. por Read Digest 110:138-42 F '77
New ethical question: head transplants? R. Bahr. il Sci Digest 81:76-8 My '77
See also
Head—Transplantation

BRAIN (cetacea)
Cetacean brain. J. C. Lilly. il Oceans 10:4-7 Jl '77

BRAIN catecholamines. See Catecholamines

BRAIN damage
Axon-sparing brain lesioning technique: the use of monosodium-L-glutamate and other amino acids. E. L. Simson and others. bibl il Science 198:515-17 N 4 '77
Progressive brain damage accelerates axon sprouting in the adult rat. S. Scheff and others. bibl il Science 197:795-7 Ag 19 '77
Right brain: surviving retardation. Sci N 112: 229-30 O 8 '77

BRAIN damaged children
Rebirth of Beth Thorne. J. L. Block. Good H 185:99+ Jl '77

BRAIN drain
Brain drain Philippinos. A. J. A. Pido. bibl Society 14:50-3 S '77

BRAIN lesions. See Brain damage

BRAIN research
Medical wonders of Dr Robert White; experiments in brain cooling and transplants. J. G. Hubbell. por Read Digest 110:138-42 F '77
Silent cells: quiet revolution in brain science. il Sci N 112:20-1 Jl 9 '77

BRAIN stimulation. See Stimulation (physiology)

BRAIN surgery. See Brain—Surgery

BRAIN waves
Augmenting mental chronometry: the P300 as a measure of stimulus evaluation time. M. Kutas and others. bibl il Science 197:792-5 Ag 19 '77
See also
Electroencephalography

BRAINARD, John B.
Anti-migraine diet. Harp Baz 111:159+ N '77

BRAINWASHING
Mind-bending disclosures; CIA drug testing. il Time 110:9 Ag 15 '77
Mind bending—latest CIA scandal. U.S. News 83:22 Ag 15 '77
See also
Deprogramming

BRAKEFIELD, Tom
Camera trophies. Field & S 82:20 O '77

BRAKES, Automobile
Gentle art of braking; racing and street cars. L. J. K. Setright. Car & Dr 23:114 Jl '77

Maintenance and repair

Brakes. W. Woron. il Motor T 29:95-100 O '77
Brakes. il Pop Mech 147:185-6 My '77
Inspecting and repairing your car's brakes. R. Hill. il Pop Sci 211:138+ N '77
Plumb crazy; brake line plumbing. C. J. Baker. il Hot Rod 30:88+ O '77

BRAKES, Motorcycle
Anti-skid motorcycle brakes. D. Scott. il Pop Sci 211:58 Jl '77

BRAMLET, Elmer Alton
Another Hoffa case? R. Steele and M. Kasindorf. il por Newsweek 89:23 Mr 14 '77 *
Vegas vanishing act. por Time 109:21 Mr 14 '77 *

BRAN
Time for a bran new diet; South African research. C. SerVaas. il Sat Eve Post 249:72-4 Mr '77

BRAN muffins. See Bread

BRANCH, David R.
Flying nonesuch. il pors Writers Digest 57:41-3 Ag '77

BRANCH, Taylor
New frontiers in American philosophy. il pors N Y Times Mag p 12-14+ Ag 14 '77

—and Rothchild, John
Incident. il pors Esquire 87:55-8+ Mr '77

BRANCH libraries. See Libraries—Branches and stations

BRANCUSI, Constantin
When is a bird not a bird? excerpt from The art world; ed by B. Diamonstein. il Art N 76: 152 N '77 *

BRAND, Don
Diving champ at sixty. R. Bauman. por Ret Liv 17:49+ My '77 *

BRAND, Helena
Shore lines, surf side; poem. Chr Cent 94:752 Ag 31 '77

BRAND, Stuart
Stewart Brand's CoEvolution supplement. por Org Gard & Farm 24:177 Ag '77

BRAND names. See Trade marks and trade names

BRANDED merchandise
Personal products & health care. il Forbes 121: 126-8 Ja 9 '78
See also
Unbranded merchandise

BRANDEIS University, Waltham, Mass.
Name to live up to. M. Sheils and F. V. Boyd. il Newsweek 89:83 My 30 '77

BRANDIES, Monica
Favorite flowers for a cutting garden. il Org Gard & Farm 24:90-1 F '77
Spray day. il Org Gard & Farm 24:90-2 Mr '77
Vegetables in the front yard. Org Gard & Farm 24:124-6 Ap '77

BRANDLI, Henry W. and Johnson, E. I.
America shines. il Environment 19:6-9 D '77

BRANDOW, G. E.
Place of U.S. food in eliminating world hunger. bibl f il Ann Am Acad 429:1-11 Ja '77

BRANDT, Anthony
Lies, lies, lies. Atlantic 240:58-60+ N '77
Views. il Atlantic 240:46-9 Jl '77

BRANDT, Nat
American characters. il por Am Heritage 28: 44-5 Ag '77
Great blizzard of '88. il Am Heritage 28:32-41 F '77
about
PW names Brandt and Bannon to top posts. M. Reuter. Pub W 212:23 D 26 '77 *

BRANDT, Willy
Brandt's plan. S. Strasser and T. Nater. por Newsweek 90:70 D 12 '77 *
In search of an LDC solution. S. W. Sanders. por Bus W p75 D 12 '77 *

BRANDY
Concerning wine & food; cognacs and cordials. R. L. Balzer. Holiday 57:14-15 N '76

BRANFMAN, Fred
California's fight for the sun. Nation 224:749-51 Je 18 '77

BRANIFF Airways, Inc
Braniff London award sparks criticism. D. R. Griffiths. il Aviation W 108:27-9 Ja 2 '78
Braniff seeks Concorde interchange approval. Aviation W 106:27 F 14 '77

BRANIFF International Airways. See Braniff Airways, Inc

BRANSCOME, James
TVA: it ain't what it used to be. il map Am Heritage 28:68-78 F '77

BRANSCOMB, Lewis M.
International conferences and tax reform. Science 196:719 My 13 '77
Science in the White House: a new start: adaptation of address, March 3, 1977. Science 196: 848-52 My 20 '77

BRANSON, Branley Allan
Endangered fish of Kentucky streams; with biographical sketch. il Natur Hist 86:8, 64-9 bibl(p 101) F '77
History on the rocks. il Américas 29:10-14 Ja '77
Pocket of the past: the Great Smokies. il Américas 29:9-15 F '77
Strip mining and the environment. il Nat Parks & Con Mag 51:10-12 Ap '77

BRANTES, Marina de
Cook on the light side. il por House & Gard 149:172-3 O '77 *

BRANTON, Daniel. See Jacobson, B. S. jt auth

BRAS. See Brassieres

BRASS rubbings. See Rubbings

BRASSICA
Cabbage fit for kings; vegetables in genus Brassica. R. Sokolov. il Sat Eve Post 249:100+ My '77
How to treat the common cole. R. Sokolov. Natur Hist 86:22+ F '77
Incompatibility on Brassica stigmas is overcome by treating pollen with cycloheximide. T. E. Ferrari and D. H. Wallace. bibl il Science 196:436-8 Ap 22 '77
Multidisciplinary study of the taxonomy and origin of Brassica crops. J. G. Vaughan. bibl BioScience 27:35-40 Ja '77
See also
Broccoli
Kohlrabi
Turnips

BRASSIERES
Stay well: bustlines. M. Permut. Seventeen 36:55 My '77

BRASWELL, Carol
Substitute teacher; poem. Clearing H 51:75 O '77
We thirst; poem. Clearing H 50:372 Ap '77

BRATCHER, Twila
Ovoviviparous volutes. il Sea Front 23:374-6 N '77

BRATHWAITE, Edward
Comment. J. Silkin. Poetry 130:232 Jl '77 *

BRATISLAVA

Music

See also
Opera—Czechoslovakia

BRATTSTEN, L. B. and Wilkinson, C. F.
Insecticide solvents: interference with insecticidal action. bibl il Science 196:1211-13 Je 10 '77
—and others
Herbivore-plant interactions: mixed-function oxidases and secondary plant substances. bibl il Science 196:1349-52 Je 17 '77

BRAUDEL, Fernand
Master of the Mediterranean. il por Time 109: 77-8 My 23 '77 *

BRAUDY, Susan
Vengeance on $5 a day. il por Esquire 87:105+ Je '77
(ed) See Didion, J. Day in the life of Joan Didion
(ed) See Dunne, J. G. Day in the life of Joan Didion
—and Thom, Mary
(eds) Ms. gazette: news from all over. See issues of Ms.

BRAUN, Armin C.
Cancer as a problem in development. bibl il por Chemistry 50:30-5 Ja '77

BRAUN AG (firm) See Electric industries—Germany, West

BRAUNTHAL, Gerard
West Germany: a balance sheet. Cur Hist 73: 156-9+ N '77

BRAVERMAN, Miriam
Branches, service, and survival. il por Lib J 102: 163-5 Ja 15 '77

BRAVERY. See Courage

Il BRAVO; opera. See Mercadante, S.

BRAXTON, Anthony
Jazz. W. Balliett. il New Yorker 53:84-6 Ap 4 '77 *
Two free spirits. H. Saal. il pors Newsweek 90:52-3 Ag 8 '77 *

BRAY, Charles W. 1933-
Helping Americans understand world affairs; address, June 27, 1977. Dept State Bull 77: 402-4 S 26 '77

BRAY, Howard
Journalists as spooks. Progressive 41:9-10 F '77

BRAY, John Roger
Pleistocene volcanism and glacial initiation. bibl il Science 197:251-4 Jl 15 '77

BRAZEL, Anthony J. See Idso, S. B. jt auth

BRAZELTON, T. Berry
[Column] (cont) il Redbook 148:31+ F; 149:93+ My; 101+ Jl; 150:24+ N '77
Do you have a spoiled child? interview. Harp Baz 110:89+ Jl '77

BRAZIL
See also
Agricultural administration—Brazil
Amazon River
Amazon Valley
Art—Brazil
Atomic power—Brazil
Banks and banking—Brazil
Blacks in Brazil
Energy policy—Brazil
Investments, American—Brazil
Investments, Foreign—Brazil
Investments, Japanese—Brazil
Loans, Bank—Brazil
Opera—Brazil
Photography—Brazil
Power resources—Brazil
Protests, demonstrations, etc.—Brazil
Rio De Janeiro
Science—Brazil

Civilization

Afro-Brazilian experiment. G. Freyre. il UNESCO Courier 30:13-17 Ag '77
Where gods and men have mingled. J. Amado. il UNESCO Courier 30:18-19 Ag '77

Commerce

Brazil's candidacy for major power status: short-term problems and long-term optimism; Brazil: world power 2000? W. A. Selcher and J. M. Young. il Intellect 105:400-9 Je '77

United States

See United States—Commerce—Brazil

Commercial policy

Behind those soaring coffee prices; effect of Brazilian export policy. T. Armbrister. Read Digest 110:65-6+ My '77
Brazil: even components must be Brazilianized. il Bus W p34 Ja 24 '77
Strong soybean price influence from Brazil. Suc Farm 75:C21 D '77

Description and travel

Brazil's wild frontier. L. McIntyre. il map Nat Geog 152:684-719 N '77

Economic conditions

Recompression in Brazil. T. Szulc. il New Repub 176:19-21 My 7 '77

BRAZIL—*Continued*

Economic policy

Austerity turns into political dynamite. Bus W p42+ Je 6 '77
Brazil: walking the tightrope. R. L. Anderson. bibl f Cur Hist 72:53-6+ F '77
Brazilian gamble. il Bus W p72-6+ D 5 '77

Foreign relations

Brazil's candidacy for major power status: short-term problems and long-term optimism; Brazil: world power 2000? W. A. Selcher and J. M. Young. il Intellect 105:400-9 Je '77

United States

See United States—Foreign relations—Brazil

History

Secret war in Brazil; American role in 1964 coup. J. V. Kohl. Progressive 41:33-5 Ag '77

Industries

Brazil: world power 2000? J. M. Young. il Intellect 105:406-9 Je '77
Brazil's coffee with sugar billionaire; J. W. Atalla, head of Copersucar. A. M. Louis. il pors Fortune 96:82-8 Jl '77
See also
Airplane industry—Brazil
Coffee industry—Brazil
Electronic industries—Brazil
Wood pulp industry—Brazil

Politics and government

Brazil: walking the tightrope. R. L. Anderson. bibl f Cur Hist 72:53-6+ F '77
Recompression in Brazil. T. Szulc. il New Repub 176:19-21 My 7 '77

Religious institutions and affairs

See also
Catholic Church in Brazil
Church and state in Brazil
Missions—Brazil
Religious conferences—Brazil

Social policy

Brazilian students spearhead development; Rondon Project. G. Meek. il Américas 29:6-8 F '77

BRAZIL in art
Early visions of imperial Brazil; illustrations produced by cultural and scientific missions. I. A. Striker. il Américas 29:S1-12 Ja '77

BRAZILIAN honey bees. See Bees

BRAZILIAN literature
See also
Publishers and publishing—Brazilian literature

BRAZILIAN music. See Music, Brazilian

BREAD
Anise bread goes back generations. il Sunset 158:132+ F '77
Best breads of 1978. il Good H 186:106-15+ Ja '78
Bran muffins start any day right. il Parents Mag 52:52+ Ap '77
Breakfast news: quick breads with cereals. il Parents Mag 52:90+ N '77
Coffee and popovers. G. Steves. il Am Home 80:72-3+ S '77
From Sweden, Belgium, Russia—three Christmas breads; excerpt from Sunset cook book of breads. il Sunset 159:94-5 D '77
Glorious Easter breads. il McCalls 104:138-9+ Mr '77
Great Italian bread from a real bread expert. S. P. Torpey. il Bet Hom & Gard 55:62-3+ F '77
Great little French breads you can bake; brioches and croissants. E. Connelly. il Good H 184:168 My '77
He cooks! cinnamon popovers. il Bet Hom & Gard 55:194 My '77
He cooks prune nut bread. il Bet Hom & Gard 55:20 Mr '77
Holiday breads. il Bet Hom & Gard 55:159-60 N '77
Homemade breads; symposium. il Org Gard & Farm 25:110+ Ja '78
Honey wheat bread. il McCalls 104:177-8 Ap '77
It's what makes whole grainers enthusiasts; triticale breads. il Sunset 159:210 N '77
Joyful holiday breads; Christmas breads. il Redbook 150:156+ D '77
Let them eat bread. G. Steves. il Am Home 80:70-1+ Mr '77
Men at home: one man's muffins. L. Radwell. Am Home 80:59 Mr '77
1-2-3 bread-baking. il Seventeen 36:156-8+ Mr '77
Picnic in a pocket; pita bread. il Ladies Home J 94:88-9+ Jl '77
Please pass the fiber; bread as diet food. A. Entelis and J. Johnston. Am Home 80:58-9 F '77
Put some bran in your bread? Sunset 158:204 Mr '77
Quick breads. il Good H 185:152-9+ S '77
Rhubarb bread, rhubarb muffins. Sunset 158:174 Je '77
Rolls buttery and garlicky. il Sunset 159:182+ N '77
Sculpture out of the oven. . .the artworks end up as dinner rolls. il Sunset 158:94-5 Mr '77
Shortcut bread making; hurry-up herb bread. il Bet Hom & Gard 55:157 Ag '77
Special preview: the Redbook breadbook; excerpt. il Redbook 149:138-9+ My '77
Three different breads made from homemade frozen dough. P. A. Ward. il Farm J 101:37 My '77
Two bread ideas we brought back from Colombia. il Sunset 158:195-6 My '77
Two famous old breads of old Bath; Sally Lunn and Bath buns. il Sunset 158:114-15 Ap '77
Whole-wheat bread. il Good H 184:28 Ap '77
See also
Dough
Flour
Toast

BREAD dough modeling. See Modeling

BREAD Loaf Writers Conference. See Authors conferences

BREAD trays. See Trays

BREADBOARD circuits. See Electronic circuits—Design

BREAK that record! drama. See Murray, J.

BREAKFAST foods. See Cereal foods

BREAKFASTS
Breakfast way to a better day. R. Molter. il Parents Mag 52:58-60 Mr '77
Eggs for two. il Sunset 158:218 My '77
Fish for breakfast? il Sunset 158:130-1 Ap '77
Hearty, headstart breakfasts and brunches. il Fam Health 9:32-5 S '77
Hearty hurry-up breakfast. il Bet Hom & Gard 55:70 Jl '77
Instant breakfasts nutritious junk food? il Consumer Rep 42:324-7 Je '77
Need for a good breakfast, even when you're dieting. H. McCully. House B 119:52+ Je '77
Sandwich breakfast? Why not. il Sunset 158:172 Je '77
Wake up to the aroma of sizzling meats. il Parents Mag 52:78+ O '77
What you eat today can decide your health tomorrow. H. Alpert. il Ret Liv 17:26-30 S '77
See also
Brunches

BREAM fishing. See Sunfish fishing

BREAST
Do those bust developers really work? Good H 185:152+ Ag '77
A shot—or two or three—in the breast; silicone breast injection. D. Larned. Ms 6:55+ S '77; Discussion. 6:4+ Ja '78
Stay well: bustlines. M. Permut. Seventeen 36:55 My '77
Your breasts. il Vogue 167:194-5+ F '77

Cancer

Adenylate cyclase of brain reflects propensity for breast cancer in mice. G. C. Cotzias and L. C. Tang. bibl Science 197:1094-6 S 9 '77
Antibody-induced antigen redistribution and shedding from human breast cancer cells. R. E. Nordquist and others. bibl il Science 197:366-7 Jl 22 '77
Breast cancer update. J. Arehart-Treichel. il Sci N 111:90-1 F 5 '77
Concomitant elevations in serum sialyltransferase activity and sialic acid content in rats with metastasizing mammary tumors. R. J. Bernacki and U. Kim. bibl il Science 195:577-80 F 11 '77
Human breast cancer: biologically active estrogen receptor in the absence of estrogen? D. T. Zava and others. bibl il Science 196:663-4 My 6 '77
Tanka syndrome; effects of nursing babies on one side only; Chinese boat women study. J. Seligmann. il Newsweek 90:52 S 12 '77

Diagnosis

Are breast X-rays safe? P. Strax. il Parents Mag 52:48-9+ F '77
Breast cancer screening: how, who, when. Sci N 112:197 S 24 '77
Tuning in to breast tumors; use of microwaves. il Time 109:80 Je 20 '77
What every woman should know about breast X-ray; interview, ed by W. S. Ross. B. F. Byrd, Jr. Read Digest 110:116-20 Mr '77
See also
Mammography

Personal narratives

Final victory; connection between the pill and breast cancer. N. S. Greenfield. Good H 184:103+ Ap '77

BREAST—Cancer—*Continued*

Surgery

Breast cancer cures without mastectomy; lumpectomy. M. Lynn. il Parents Mag 52:40-1+ My '77
Emotional pain of mastectomy. J. Gaylin. Psychol Today 10:98+ Ap '77
I didn't feel like a real woman any more. Good H 185:28+ S '77

Therapy

Alternative to mastectomy; interstitial radiation therapy. il Time 109:82 Mr 28 '77
Terpsichore and Artemis: dance as therapy after mastectomy. W. A. Winkler. il Dance Mag 51: 77-8 N '77

BREAST feeding
Breast-feeding and population growth. J. Knodel. bibl il Science 198:1111-15 D 16 '77
Breast or bottle: which way is best for you? G. S. Cranch and S. F. Trien. il Parents Mag 52:49-51+ O '77
Is breast-feeding best for babies? il Consumer Rep 42:152-7 Mr '77
Tanka syndrome; effects of nursing babies on one side only; Chinese boat women study. J. Seligmann. il Newsweek 90:52 S 12 '77
What mothers should know about breast feeding and weaning. B. Spock. Redbook 149:22+ S '77

BREAST implants. See Surgery, Plastic

BREAST surgery, Cosmetic. See Surgery, Plastic

BREAST X-rays. See Mammography

BREATHING. See Respiration

BRECHT, Bertolt
Caucasian chalk circle. Reviews
Sat R 4:36-7 Ap 30 '77 *
Mr Puntila and his chauffeur Matti. Reviews
Nation 224:381 Mr 26 '77 *
Newsweek il 89:85-6 Mr 21 '77 *
Sat R 4:36-7 Ap 30 '77 *
Towards an aesthetic of experimental music. C. Ballantine. bibl f Mus Q 63:224-46 Ap '77 *

BRECKENFELD, Gurney
Business loves the sunbelt and vice versa. map Fortune 95:132-7+ Je '77
It's up to the cities to save themselves. il Fortune 95:194-8+ Mr '77

BRECKENRIDGE, Elizabeth
Mary Lee Hu: high on the wire. il por Craft Horiz 37:40-3+ Ap '77

BRECKENRIDGE, H. L.
Energy management: a crisis in industry. bibl f Intellect 105:352-4 Ap '77

BRECKENRIDGE, Mich.

Public health

See Public health—Michigan

BREECH-loading rifles. See Rifles

BREED, Michael D. and Gamboa, G. J.
Behavioral control of workers by queens in primitively eusocial bees. bibl il Science 195: 694-6 F 18 '77

BREEDER reactors. See Nuclear reactors

BREEDING
View from the castle; breeding programs with rare animals at the National Zoo's Front Royal Va. facility. S. D. Ripley. Smithsonian 7:6 Mr '77
See also
Birds—Breeding
Cattle breeding
Eugenics
Horse breeding
Plant breeding
Reproduction

BREEDS of cattle. See Cattle—Breeds

BREEDS of swine. See Swine—Breeds

BREEN, Jon L.
Murder number one. New Repub 177:38-9 Jl 30 '77
World of mysteries—plus. See alternate issues of Wilson library bulletin

BREER, Carl
History of the Airflow car. H. S. Irwin. il Sci Am 237:98-104+ bibl(p 140) Ag '77 *

BREEZES. See Winds

BREGMAN, Gene R.
Animation. il Sch Arts 77:20-1 D '77

BREILING, Annette
Using parents as teaching partners. Educ Digest 42:50-2 F '77

BREIMYER, Harold F.
Changing American farm. bibl f il map Ann Am Acad 429:12-22 Ja '77

BREINDEL, Eric M.
Begin without smears. New Repub 176:16-18 Je 18 '77
Begin's trouble at home. New Repub 178:10-11 Ja 7 '78

BREINHOLST, Willy
Meet the Vikings. il Holiday 58:42-3, 58+ Ja '77

BREIRA (organization) See Radicalism—Jews

BREISCH, Alvin R.
Dwarf mistletoe. il Conservationist 32:47 N '77

BREISKY, William
But yes, we had bananas—coming out of our ears. il Smithsonian 7:96-102 Mr '77

BRELIS, Dean, and Reader, John
Students immerse selves in foreign living and fun, too il Smithsonian 8:48-55 bibl(p 146) Ap '77

BREM, Steven S. and others
Angiogenesis: a marker for neoplastic transformation of mammary papillary hyperplasia. bibl il Science 195:880-2 Mr 4 '77

BREMER, Michele
Converting to whole grains. Org Gard & Farm 25:128+ Ja '78

BREMER Treuhand (firm) See Construction industry—Germany, West

BRENDAN, Saint
St Brendan's fantastic voyage. G. Schomp. il map Am Hist Illus 12:22-7 Ap '77 *
Voyage of Brendan. T. Severin. il map Nat Geog 152:770-97 D '77

BRENDAN (boat) See Sailboats

BRENDEL, Alfred
Musical events. A. Porter. New Yorker 53:93-4 My 30 '77 *

BRENDER, Brooks
3,000-mi. travel test of the shrunken Caddy. il Mech Illus 73:104+ My '77

BRENNAN, Barbara
Antiques: a family bet that worked. House B 119:48 N '77

BRENNAN, Margaret
Was it not ordained that Christ should suffer and so enter into his glory? New Cath World 220:21 Ja '77

BRENNAN, Patricia
Their (dis)appointed rounds. R. Brookhiser. il Nat R 29:1294-6 N 11 '77 *

BRENNAN, Paul
Intellectuals without influence. Nation 224:229-31 F 26 '77

BRENNAN, Paul, 1948?-
Their (dis)appointed rounds. R. Brookhiser. il Nat R 29:1294-6 N 11 '77 *

BRENNAN, P. H, Hand Delivery Service. See Postal service—United States

BRENNER, Betty
Second coming. Chr Today 21:43-4 Ja 21 '77

BRENNER, Marie
From Berkeley to Jerusalem. il N Y Times Mag p71-3+ Ap 3 '77
What's Robert De Niro hiding? il pors Redbook 149:116+ My '77

BRENNER, Michael J.
Decision making in a nuclear-armed world. Ann Am Acad 430:147-61 Mr '77

BRENNINKMEYER, C&A (firm) See Conglomerate corporations—Netherlands

BRENT, Madeleine
Winds of the morning; story: condensation of Merlin's keep. il Good H 185:225-8 N '77

BRENTON, Myron
Families Anonymous: help for distressed parents. Good H 184:94+ My '77
Runaways. il Todays Educ 66:64-6 Mr '77
What can be done about child abuse? Todays Educ 66:50-2+ S '77

BRESLER, Robert J.
State of the Nation. See alternate issues of Intellect
—See Gray, R. C. jt auth

BRESLIN, Catherine
Lift-line express. il Esquire 87:91-3 F '77
Nun on trial for infanticide; case of Sister Maureen. il por Ms 5:68-71+ Mr '77
Pleasures of sexual freedom. Harp Baz 110:95+ Mr '77
Sister Maureen: not guilty and not free. Ms 6: 22 Jl '77

BRESLIN, John B.
Bookings (cont) America 136:59, 175-6, 258+, 302-3, 403-4, 507 Ja 22, F 26, Mr 19, Ap 2, Ap 30, Je 4 '77
Prayer books and politics. America 136:194-6 Mr 5 '77
Religion. America 136:82-3 Ja 29 '77
Tacking toward Vatican III. America 136:545-7 Je 18 '77
—See McMurray, P. E. jt auth

BRESNAHAN, Robert J.
Charles Fred White: a forgotten black poet. por Negro Hist Bull 40:659-61 Ja '77

BRESSON, Robert
Narrative point of view: the rhetoric of Au hasard, Balthazar. N. Browne. il Film Q 31: 19-31 Fall '77 *

BRETÉCHER, Claire
Cartoon. il Ms 6:110 S '77

BRETT, Richard M.
Different view of the forest. Am For 83:10+ D '77

BRETTON, Elise
Folios. See issues of High fidelity and Musical America

BREUER, Gustl
Theaterblut. pors Opera N 42:14-16 Ja 7 '78

BREUER, Marcel
Continuity in a framework of change. il Archit Rec 162:105-12 Ag '77 *

BREUER, Robert
Meyerbeer revealed: discovering the composer through his own words. il Opera N 41:38-43 Ja 29 '77

BREWER, Jan
You auto take this test. il Sat Eve Post 249: 6+ N '77

BREWER, Richard G.
Coherent optical transients. bibl il Phys Today 30:50-4+ My '77

BREWER, Robert C.
New York State Record Fish Program. il Conservationist 31:29 My '77

BREWERIES
Steam beer—the last brewery; Steam Beer Brewing Company. il Sunset 158:58 Ap '77

BREWERY workers
See also
Strikes—United States—Brewery workers

BREWING industry
After the beer at Chock Full o'Nuts. Bus W p81+ N 7 '77
Heileman Brewing: taking on the big guys. il Duns R 109:20-1 Je '77
Homemade imports. W. J. Schmick Jr. il Forbes 120:33-4 O 15 '77
Let there be light. L. Langway and F. Maier. il Newsweek 89:68 Je 6 '77
Sing no sad songs for Heileman. por Forbes 120:51 O 1 '77
See also
Coors, Adolph, Company
Schlitz, Joseph, Brewing Company

Securities

Why didn't anyone ask about Olympia? S. Cunningham and J. Madrick. il Bus W p91 Ap 11 '77

Japan

Kirin's uphill battle to limit beer sales. Bus W p37-8 Ag 29 '77

BREWSTER, Charles E.
African impatience for change. il Chr Cent 94: 382-4 Ap 20 '77
Israel and its Bloc of Faithful. Chr Cent 94: 174-6 F 23 '77

BREWSTER, Kingman, 1919-
Beggar's opera. L. H. Lapham. Harpers 255:16+ O '77 *
London—mid-Atlantic man. il por Newsweek 90: 69 N 21 '77 *
Once and future King. M. Sheils and P. Malamud. il por Newsweek 89:63 Ap 18 '77 *
Our far-flung correspondents. J. Bainbridge. New Yorker 53:141-8+ D 12 '77 *

BREWSTER, Robert C.
Parties to Antarctic Treaty meet in London; statement, September 19, 1977. Dept State Bull 77:738-40 N 21 '77
Recommendation to protect Antarctic environment; statement, September 12, 1977. Dept State Bull 77:576-7 O 24 '77

BREZHNEV, Leonid Il'ich
International situation; address, January 18, 1977. Vital Speeches 43:262-5 F 15 '77
New draft constitution of the U.S.S.R; address, June 5, 1977. Vital Speeches 43:546-51 Jl 1 '77

about

Brezhnev's purge. F. Willey and F. Coleman. por Newsweek 89:43-4 Je 6 '77 *
Brezhnev's rising sun. il Time 109:41 Je 13 '77 *
Brezhnev's year: politics in the U.S.S.R. R. G. Wesson. Cur Hist 73:109-11+ O '77 *
Carter and Brezhnev: the game begins. il por Time 109:40-2 F 7 '77 *
Carter v. Brezhnev: the SALT standoff. il por Time 109:10-12+ Ap 11 '77 *
Letter to Brezhnev; tr by M. Petrov. B. Rabbot. il pors N Y Times Mag p48+ N 6 '77 *
Russia after Brezhnev: meaning for U.S. il por U.S. News 82:24 Ap 18 '77 *
Secret speech: did Brezhnev come clean? Nat R 29:248+ Mr 4 '77 *
Soviets at 60. R. Carroll and others. il por Newsweek 90:56-7+ N 14 '77 *
Unhitching Podgorny from the Troika. por Time 109:35 Je 6 '77 *
U.S. sets new rules for detente. pors U.S. News 82:24 Ap 4 '77 *

Visit to France, 1977

Brezhnev's bluster. F. Willey and others. il por Newsweek 90:46 Jl 4 '77
Fun and games in Paris. Nat R 29:765 Jl 8 '77
Visit from a rude emperor. il por Time 110:19 Jl 4 '77

BRIAN, Havergal
Name to remember. R. Tiedman. Am Rec G 40:16-18 Je '77 *

BRIAR pipes. See Tobacco pipes

BRIARCLIFF College, Briarcliff Manor, N.Y.
Rest in Pace. M. Sheils and F. V. Boyd. il Newsweek 89:96 Ap 11 '77

BRIBERY
American business bribery shakes the world—can Americans remake it? R. H. Heindel. Intellect 105:312-13 Ap '77
And in Britain, too? Daily mail's charges against British Leyland Motor Corp. il Newsweek 89:74+ My 30 '77
Big rip-off in purchasing. R. Levy. il Duns R 109:76-7+ Mr '77
Bribery and human rights; secret CIA payments. N. Cousins. Sat R 4:4 Ap 2 '77
Businessman and the government; corruption, yesterday and today. J. Brooks. il Am Heritage 28:66-73 Je '77
Canada's flexible bribery standards. Bus W p35 Je 13 '77
Coping with the new rules of conduct. Bus W p76-7 O 10 '77
Developing codes of conduct for multinational enterprises; statement, September 7, 1977. P. H. Boeker. Dept State Bull 77:475-9 O 10 '77
Emersons: dubious payments American-style. A. Hershman. il por Duns R 109:73-5 Mr '77
Ethics of bribery. Nation 224:260 Mr 5 '77
International business and morality; address, March 25, 1977. D. F. Linowes. Vital Speeches 43:475-8 My 15 '77
Is Lockheed's bribery saga over? il Bus W p27 My 30 '77
Kickbacks in living color; charges against Japanese television manufacturers. il Time 109:63 Je 13 '77
Lockheed payments changes approved. Aviation W 106:73 Ap 25 '77
Lockheed report details payments. D. E. Fink. Aviation W 106:50 Je 13 '77
Mining the dossiers; SEC files on corporate payments. il Newsweek 89:71+ My 30 '77
National and multilateral action on corrupt practices; address, April 21, 1977. M. B. Feldman. Dept State Bull 76:554-6 My 30 '77
Payoff; symposium. il Sat R 4:6-12+ Jl 9 '77
Rotten system; bribery case against Honolulu's Mayor F. Fasi. T. Mathews and G. C. Lubenow. il pors Newsweek 90:47 N 14 '77
Taken for a camel ride? Daily mail's charges against British Leyland Motor Corporation. Time 109:67-8 My 30 '77
Teamsters' Watergate connection. il Time 110:28 Ag 8 '77
Treasury Secretary Blumenthal testifies on legislation on illicit payments abroad; statement, March 16, 1977. W. M. Blumenthal. Dept State Bull 76:351-5 Ap 11 '77
U.S. moves to ban overseas payments. Aviation W 106:197-9 Je 6 '77
See also
Politics, Corruption in
United Nations—Ad Hoc Intergovernmental Working Group on the Problem of Corrupt Practices

BRICK, Tim
Price of gas in Texas. Nation 225:559-61 N 26 '77

BRICK construction
See also
Walls, Brick

BRICK pavements. See Pavements

BRICK walls. See Walls, Brick

BRICKER, William
Diamond Shamrock in clover. por Forbes 120: 37 D 15 '77 *

BRICKHAM, Eleanor
Your own space; interview, ed by B. Niles. il por Am Home 80:39-41 My '77

BRICKLAYING
How to dress up your yard with brick. P. Angell. il Pop Mech 147:104-6+ My '77

BRICKLIN, Mark
Gardening: the perfect retirement challenge. il Org Gard & Farm 24:104-6 My '77

BRICKMAN, Marshall
Short history of deedle. New Yorker 53:48-9 N 7 '77

BRICKMAN, Philip
Let the punishment fit the crime. Psychol Today 10:29 My '77

BRIDAL bouquets. See Bouquets

BRIDGE, B. J. and Beckman, G. G.
Slope profiles of cycloidal form. bibl il Science 198:610-12 N 11 '77

BRIDGE, Peter
What parents should know and do about kiddie porn. il Parents Mag 53:42-3+ Ja '78

BRIDGE (game)
Bowl of good cheer; quiz. E. B. Kantar. il Sports Illus 47:92-3+ D 19 '77

Tournaments

It wasn't all in the cards; R. Katz and L. Cohen accused of cheating at the Tribunals in Houston. W. Bingham. il pors Sports Illus 46:22-5 Ap 11 '77

BRIDGE design. See Bridges—Design

BRIDGEMARKET (proposed) See New York (city)—Markets

BRIDGES, Annetta Hereford
Just be ready! Read Digest 111:83-7 O '77

BRIDGES, Harry, 1901-
Harry Bridges. Nat R 29:538 My 13 '77 *
Harry Bridges: then and now. C. McWilliams. Nation 224:580-1 My 14 '77 *
Mellowed Bridges talks of reconciliation. por Bus W p40+ My 9 '77 *
BRIDGES, Lee N.
We'll go on; poem. Negro Hist Bull 40:684 Mr '77
BRIDGES, Linda
Theater. Nat R 29:394-5 Ap 1 '77
BRIDGES, Thomas
(ed) See Vargas Llosa, M. Vargas Llosa, visionary realist
BRIDGES
See also
Drawbridges
New York (city)—Bridges
Passaic River—Bridges
Pittsburgh—Bridges

Design

Bridge with a twist; Ruck-a-Chucky Bridge. R. Stepler. il Pop Sci 210:90-1 Je '77
Hanging a bridge with a bend; Ruck-A-Chucky Bridge. M. Lamm. il Pop Mech 148:94-5 O '77

Floors

Polymer surface revamps bridge; Pittsburgh's Smithfield street bridge. il Am City & County 92:32 Ap '77

Maintenance and repair

Road, bridge repairs to cost $2.8 billion. il Am City & County 92:18 My '77
Sky hook lifts bridge from river; Union Avenue Bridge. il Am City & County 92:46 S '77
Steel grid bridge deck outlives concrete; Allegheny County, Pa. il Am City & County 92:45 Ja '77

Safety devices and measures

Weak bridges: growing hazards on the highways. il U.S. News 84:72 Ja 9 '78

Australia

Over the edge! Tasman Bridge rammed by carrier. S. Johnson. il Read Digest 111:126-30 N '77

BRIDGES, Foot
Steal for small bridges. il Parks & Rec 12:37-8 My '77
BRIDGES, Lift. See Drawbridges
BRIDGES, Natural
See also
Rainbow Bridge National Monument
BRIDGES, Pedestrian. See Bridges, Foot
BRIDGEVILLE, Calif.
Buying a Garden of Eden. il por Time 109:50 Je 27 '77
BRIEFCASES
Brief encounters. il Newsweek 90:90 S 12 '77
BRIER, Herbert S.
Amateur radio. il Pop Elect 11:87 F; 88 Ap '77
BRIGGS, John Danforth
Steel imports; address, September 21, 1977. Vital Speeches 44:73-5 N 15 '77
BRIGGS, Kenneth A.
Episcopal bishops eke out a fragile peace. Chr Cent 94:996 N 2 '77
BRIGGS and Stratton Corporation
Little engine that coins money. il Forbes 120:86 O 1 '77
BRIGHT, Bill. See Bright, W. R.
BRIGHT, William Rohl
Here's life. Chr Today 21:52-5 F 4 '77 *
BRIGHTNESS discrimination
Perceived lightness depends on perceived spatial arrangement. A. L. Gilchrist. bibl il Science 195:185-7 Ja 14 '77
BRIGHTON, Colo.
For results, get citizens involved early. R. A. Hellbusch. Am City & County 92:50 Ja '77
BRIGHTON Beach, N.Y. See Coney Island
BRIGHTON Pavilion. See Palaces
BRIGHTON Veteran Car Run. See Automobile rallies—Great Britain
BRIGS. See Sailing vessels
BRILES, W. Elwood, and others
Marek's disease: effects of B histocompatibility alloalleles in resistant and susceptible chicken lines. bibl il Science 195:193-5 Ja 14 '77
BRILL, Steven
Traffic (legal and illegal) in guns. il Harpers 255:37-44 S '77
BRILL, Thomas B.
Appearance of materials. bibl il por Chemistry 50:6-9 D '77
BRILL, Winston J.
Biological nitrogen fixation; with biographical sketch. il Sci Am 236:22, 68-74+ bibl(p 150) Mr '77
BRIMHALL, E. R.
Principal who cared. A. Morphis. por Clearing H 50:263-5 F '77 *
BRIMMER, Andrew Felton
Why inflation hits some people less than others. il por Nations Bus 65:38-40+ F '77

BRINDISI, Louis J. Jr
Comeback for restricted stock plans. il Harvard Bus R 55:14+ S '77
BRINE
Anoxic, hypersaline basin in the northern Gulf of Mexico. R. F. Shokes and others. bibl il Science 196:1443-6 Je 24 '77
BRINGHURST, Bob
Custom-caught big brown. C. Garrison. il por Field & S 82:76+ Je '77 *
BRINGLE, Cynthia
Potter of Penland. N. Schulman. il Craft Horiz 37:23-7 Je '77 *
BRINGLE, Mary
Christmas memories. il Am Home 80:58-9 D '77
BRINING (food preservation) See Food preservation and preservatives
BRINK, Carol (Ryrie)
Gold mine of experience. Writer 90:11-14 Ag '77
BRINK, Paul E.
African leaders' commitment to justice. Chr Cent 94:1143-6 D 7 '77
BRINK, R. A. and others
Soil deterioration and the growing world demand for food. bibl il Science 197:625-30 Ag 12 '77
BRINK, T. L.
Battle against senility. il MH 61:10-11 Summ '77
BRIOCHE. See Bread
BRISKIN, Bert
Garage sale. J. Briskin. por Writers Digest 57:48+ D '77 *
BRISKIN, Jacqueline
Garage sale. por Writers Digest 57:48+ D '77
BRISSON, Frederick
My wife, Roz. il pors McCalls 104:194-5+ Ap '77
BRISTER, Bob
About fishing and bears. il Field & S 82:46-8+ Je '77
Missing impossible? il Field & S 82:110-12+ O '77
Shooting. Field & S 82:120-4 F; 114-16+ My; 134-9 Je; 102-5 Ag; 112-14+ S; 118-20+ N; 32+ D '77
BRISTOL, England

Museums

See Museums—Great Britain
BRISTOL Bay
Gregarious but contentious walrus; Round Island. F. Bruemmer. il Natur Hist 86:52-61 bibl(p 118) N '77
BRISTON, Richard
Who needs external audits? por Forbes 120:110 D 1 '77 *
BRISTOW, Bill
Alexander Calder: casting seeds into the wind. Chr Today 21:38+ S 9 '77
Andrew Wyeth: oracle of the ordinary. il Chr Today 21:27-8+ F 4 '77
Language of trees. il Chr Today 21:16-17 Je 3 '77
BRITAIN. See Great Britain
BRITAIN (term)
Good-by to Britain, good-by British. J. Morris. il Horizon 19:40-1 Mr '77
BRITANNIA ware
Lamps and candlesticks of the Meriden Britannia Company. R. L. Bowen, Jr. bibl il Antiques 111:332-7 F '77
BRITISH
See also
English
BRITISH Actors' Equity Association
Viewpoint; rejection of American opera singers, Catherine Malfitano and Neil Shicoff. R. Jacobson. Opera N 42:5 Jl '77
BRITISH Aerospace Corporation. See Aerospace industries—Great Britain
BRITISH Airways
British Airways' fiscal gains attributed to record traffic. Aviation W 107:32 Ag 15 '77
Concorde proved operationally. il Aviation W 106:22-6 My 30 '77
Concordes begin service to N.Y. il Aviation W 107:14-15 N 28 '77
Concordes spur strong traffic, losses. Aviation W 106:23 Ja 31 '77
BRITISH art. See Art, British
BRITISH book clubs. See Book clubs
BRITISH Broadcasting Corporation
Televising à la russe; failure of television agreement between BBC and Russia. J. Burnham. Nat R 29:1415 D 9 '77
BRITISH cheese. See Cheese
BRITISH COLUMBIA
See also
Conglomerate corporations—British Columbia
Vancouver
Victoria

Description and travel

North to adventure—following the Yellowhead Highway through British Columbia. il map Sunset 159:40+ Jl '77

Foreign population

See also
Dukhobors

BRITISH COLUMBIA—*Continued*

Politics and government

Socialist tides in Canada. G. Woodcock. Progressive 41:25-8 Jl '77

BRITISH COLUMBIA Resources Development Corporation. See Conglomerate corporations—British Columbia

BRITISH COLUMBIA. University, Vancouver

Museum of Anthropology

Spaces for anthropological art; with introd by M. F. Schmertz. il Archit Rec 161:103-10 My '77

BRITISH Equity. See British Actors' Equity Association

BRITISH fashion. See Fashion

BRITISH Ford. See Ford Motor Company, Ltd

BRITISH GUIANA. See Guyana

BRITISH Honduras. See Belize

BRITISH Land Company Ltd. See Real estate business—Great Britain

BRITISH Leyland Motor Corporation, Ltd
And in Britain, too? Daily mail's charges. il Newsweek 89:74+ My 30 '77
Back to work at Leyland. il Time 109:80 Mr 28 '77
Last chance for Leyland. il por Time 110:82 N 14 '77
New whiz kid at British Leyland; M. O. Edwards. por Bus W p58+ N 14 '77
Taken for a camel ride? Daily mail's charges. Time 109:67-8 My 30 '77

BRITISH Library Association. See Library associations

BRITISH National Oil Corporation. See Petroleum industry—Great Britain

BRITISH Petroleum Company
American chance to buy more of BP. il Bus W p49+ Ap 25 '77
Love unrequited. il Forbes 119:83-5 Mr 15 '77

BRITISH portraits. See Portraits, British

BRITISH propaganda. See Propaganda, British

BRITISH Steel Corporation
Steel losses race toward $1 billion. il Bus W p48 N 28 '77
Stiff upper lip. il por Forbes 120:54+ S 1 '77

BRITTAIN, Alfred, 1922-
Role of foreign investment in the U.S. por Nations Bus 65:54+ Mr '77

BRITTAIN, W. H. Bruce. See Cleveland, H. van B. jt auth

BRITTEN, Benjamin
Benjamin Britten. P. Ramey. por Opera N 41:36-7 F 5 '77 *
Born in exile; composing of Peter Grimes. H. Heinsheimer. il por Opera N 42:16-17 D 10 '77 *
Britten's legacy: to be useful to the living. J. Culshaw. il Hi Fi 27:23 S '77 *
Lump in the throat; Noye's fludde. J. Culshaw. il Hi Fi 27:17 Mr '77 *
Obituary
Chr Today 21:27 Ja 7 '77
Sat R 4:47 Ja 22 '77
Out of The borough; G. Crabbe's poem as the inspiration for B. Britten's opera Peter Grimes. G. Schmidgall. il por Opera N 42:8+ D 10 '77 *
Paul Bunyan. Reviews
New Yorker 53:124-6+ My 2 '77 *
Peter Grimes. Reviews
Opera N il 42:18+ D 10 '77 *
Viewpoint; Peter Grimes. R. Jacobson. Opera N 42:4 D 10 '77 *

BRITTON, Peter
Longwall mining—now there's a better way to get at the coal. il Pop Sci 211:118-21 O '77
World's most advanced solar home. il Pop Sci 211:92-6+ Jl '77

BROAD beans. See Beans

BROADCASTING, Museum of. See New York (city)—Galleries and museums

BROADCASTING-newspaper multiple ownership. See Mass media—Multiple ownership

BROADCASTING-publishing multiple ownership. See Mass media—Multiple ownership

BROADWAY, New York (theater district) See New York (city)—Theater

BROBERG, Fred N. See Watson, D. jt auth

BROCCOLI
Best way I know to grow big broccoli. J. Jankowiak. il Org Gard & Farm 24:77-9 Mr '77
See also
Cookery—Vegetables

BROCHURES. See Pamphlets

BROCK, Juliet Clutton-. See Clutton-Brock, J.

BROCK, Lou
Grand larceny. P. Bonventre. il pors Newsweek 90:78-9 S 12 '77 *
Make way for the Sultan of Swipes. R. Fimrite. il pors Sports Illus 47:24-30 Ag 22 '77 *

BROCK, William Emerson, 1930-
Everyone's second choice. il por Time 109:19 Ja 24 '77 *
Now Republicans map a comeback. por U.S. News 82:56 Ja 31 '77 *

BROCKMAN, James R.
Blood poured out. America 136:328-9 Ap 9 '77
Dilemma in Peru. America 137:148-50 S 17 '77
50-cycle politics. map America 137:484-5 D 31 '77
Our man in Managua. America 136:268-9 Mr 26 '77
Persecution in El Salvador. America 137:10-11 Jl 2 '77

BROCKMAN, Richard
Notes while being hijacked. Read Digest 110:15-18+ Je '77

BRODER, David S.
Canniness of the long-distance runner. il Atlantic 241:35-41 Ja '78

BRODERICK, Dorothy M.
If elected I will. . . il por Lib J 102:880-7 Ap 15 '77
Son of Speaker. Am Lib 8:502-4 O '77

BRODERICK, Jane
I am the mother of eight, a housewife, a feminist—and happy: Jane Broderick's story; interview, ed by J. Lazarre. il por Ms 5:51-5+ My '77

BRODERSEN, Robert W. and White, R. M.
New technologies for signal processing. bibl il Science 195:1216-22 Mr 18 '77

BRODHEAD, William McNulty
Excerpt from remarks on the Kennedy-Corman Health Security Act, March 22, 1976. Cong Digest 56:212+ Ag '77

BRODIE, Fawn M.
Hidden Presidents: looking through their memoirs for involuntary truth. il Harpers 254:61-6+ Ap; 6 Je '77

BRODINSKY, Ben
Back to basics: the movement and its meaning. Educ Digest 42:2-5 My '77

BRODKEY, Harold
Verona: a young woman speaks; story. Esquire 88:88-90 Jl '77

BRODRICK, Bill
Gold ol' toy. F. M. H. Gregory. il Motor T 29:57-8+ Mr '77 *

BRODSKII, Iosif
Elegy: for Robert Lowell. New Yorker 53:38 O 31 '77
Thames at Chelsea; poem; tr by D. Rigsbee. New Yorker 53:56 N 28 '77
Why Russian poets? Vogue 167:112 Jl '77

BRODSKY, Judith
Should the art school curriculum include professional job training? il Am Artist 41:16 O '77

BRODSKY, Louis Daniel
Sky filled with trees; poem. Am Scholar 47:23 Wint '77

BRODY, Benjamin
Psychology and the arts (cont) Psychol Today 10:25 F '77

BRODY, Jane E.
Choosing the right exercise. Read Digest 112:121-3 Ja '78
Drug war on cancer. il N Y Times Mag p48-50+ Ap 3 '77
Link between cancer and nutrition. Am Home 80:41+ Ag '77. Same abr. with title Way to reduce your chances of getting cancer. Read Digest 111:131-4 N '77
Sugar: villain in disguise? Read Digest 111:163-5 O '77

BRODY, Michael
Wonderful world of Disney—its psychological appeal; address, May 1975. bibl Am Imago 33:350-60 Wint '76

BROECKER, Wallace S.
Hazards of coal dependence. il Natur Hist 86:8+ O '77
about
Coal and the coming (?) superinterglacial. Sci N 111:356 Je 4 '77 *

BROEDERBOND. See Secret societies—South Africa

BROEKMEYER, Marius J.
Self-management in Yugoslavia. Ann Am Acad 431:133-40 My '77

BROGAN, Colm
Letter from London. Nat R 29:151-2 F 4 '77
about
Colm Brogan, RIP. W. F. Buckley, Jr. Nat R 29:254-5 Mr 4 '77 *

BROHAUGH, William
Horse markets. il Writers Digest 57:31-3 Ag '77
Humor markets. Writers Digest 57:31-4 O '77
—and others
Religious markets. il Writers Digest 57:25-8+ D '77

BROILER-ovens. See Kitchen utensils and appliances

BROILERS. See Kitchen utensils and appliances

BROKEN homes
See also
Children of divorced parents

BROKEN jug; drama; adaptation. See Nolan, P. T.

BROKERS
Big shake-out. M. Ruby and P. L. Abraham. il Newsweek 90:87+ O 17 '77
Brokers are putting more stock in bonds. Bus W p 106-7 F 14 '77
Fresno raiders; hiring competitors' employees. il Time 109:77 Je 20 '77
Institutional brokers get into retailing. Bus W p58-9 Ja 24 '77
Lazarus bonds; discovery of federally guaranteed New York City Housing Authority bonds by Stoever Glass & Co. Forbes 119:68 F 1 '77
Look who made it in Wall street! Government bond traders. P. Blustein. il Forbes 119:37-42 F 1 '77
Nifty fifty revisited; ratios by Kidder Peabody. il Forbes 120:72-3 D 15 '77
Oppenheimer's plunge into retail brokerage. il Bus W p 106-8 S 26 '77
Quiet one; A. G. Edwards. il Forbes 120:76 O 1 '77
Smith Barney's accurate marksmen. Bus W p84 Mr 28 '77
Stockbroker options. S. Auerbach. il Am Home 80:8+ Jl '77
Thinking of a discount broker? J. Fraser. U.S. News 83:89 D 5 '77
Turmoil in Wall Street. Time 110:46 Ag 29 '77
Who's investing your money? S. Auerbach. Am Home 80:9+ Ag '77
Will brokers continue to manage money? interpreting Section 11(a); amendment to the Securities Exchange Act. D. G. Santry. por Bus W p98 Ag 15 '77
You and your stockbroker. W. Flanagan. Vogue 167:344 O '77
See also
Banks and banking—Securities handling
Foreign exchange brokers
Merrill Lynch, Pierce, Fenner and Smith, Inc
Stock exchanges
Tyrrell, W.

Acquisitions and mergers
Dean Witter buys an army of brokers; Reynolds Securities Inc. il Bus W p37 O 17 '77
Paine Webber buys creative management; Mitchell, Hutchins Inc merger. il Bus W p75-6+ Je 13 '77
Wall Street romances the research houses. il Bus W p89-90 My 23 '77
Wall Street's merger mania. D. Pauly and P. L. Abraham. Newsweek 89:54 My 23 '77

Advertising
Broker uses TV to educate clients; Loewi & Co. of Milwaukee. il Bus W p90 Ap 11 '77
Street is bullish on ad campaigns. il Bus W p 104 O 10 '77

Commissions
How brokers discount underwriting fees. J. Madrick. Bus W p92 Je 20 '77
How to cut costs when you buy or sell stock. il Changing T 31:21-3 F '77
They can get it for you wholesale; discount brokers. E. Dyson. Forbes 119:42+ F 15 '77
Wall Street's discount houses are selling hard. L. Snyder. il Fortune 95:117-18+ Mr '77
Wall Street's taste of freedom. il Bus W p91-3 Ap 4 '77

Finance
Bond dealers take an icy plunge. Bus W p72-3 F 21 '77

BROKERS, Real estate. See Real estate agents
BROKERS, Yacht. See Yacht brokers

BROKHIN, Yuri
Big red machine. il N Y Times Mag p22-4+ My 29 '77

BROLIN, Brent C.
Juxtapositions. il Harpers 256:55-8 Ja '78

BROMATES in sea water. See Marine pollution

BROMELIADS
Bromeliad boys at Nature's Way. C. Seagraves. il pors Horticulture 55:36-7 D '77
Dramatic accents—bromeliads. R. W. Langer. il House & Gard 149:68+ Je '77

BROMFIELD family
Bromfield coat-of-arms. H. K. Eilers. il Hobbies 82:150-1 Ja '78

BRONDFIELD, Jerome
Ever see a worn-out paper clip? Read Digest 111:65-6+ N '77
Explosive Woody Hayes. il Read Digest 111:98-102 S '77

BRONER, E. M. and Nimrod, Naomi
Woman's Passover Haggadah and other revisionist rituals. Ms 5:53-6 Ap '77

BRONFENBRENNER, Urie
American family in decline. Current 189:39-47 Ja '77
Disturbing changes in the American family. Educ Digest 42:22-5 F '77
Nobody home: the erosion of the American family; interview, ed by S. Byrne. il Psychol Today 10:40-3+ My '77

about
Family man. S. Byrne. por Psychol Today 10:42-3 My '77 *

BRONFMAN, Edgar Miles
Anti-boycott legislation. New Repub 176:17-19 Je 4 '77
Cool it, Canada! por Newsweek 90:11 S 26 '77

BRONOWSKI, Jacob
How to encourage your natural creativity. House & Gard 149:173+ N '77

BRONSON, Charles
I love being Mrs Charles Bronson, but. . . ; interview, ed by J. Ardmore. J. Ireland. il pors McCalls 105:28+ N '77 *
Then came Bronson. . . por Time 111:52 Ja 9 '78 *

BRONSON, Susan
Language of scent. . .and you. il Sci Digest 81:59-63 F '77

BRONTOSAURUS; drama. See Wilson, L.

BRONX, N.Y.

Buildings
Living in a work of art; Bronx Developmental Center. M. Stevens. il Newsweek 89:59 My 30 '77
Long-awaited well-respected community center; Webster Community Center. K. Kelly. il Archit Rec 162:95-8 O '77
1977 Reynolds prize goes to Richard Meier; design of the Bronx Developmental Center. il Archit Rec 161:35 Je '77

City planning
Let's go, South Bronx! views of I. D. Robbins. il Time 110:39 N 21 '77

Crime
Savage skulls. J. Bradshaw. il Esquire 87:74-83+ Je '77

Description
Hunts Point. New Yorker 53:22 D 26 '77

Education
Getting involved; La Boheme performed by teenagers at Fieldston School in the Bronx. G. Lipton. il Opera N 42:46-7 N '77
Science High; Bronx High School of Science. J. Lelyveld. il N Y Times Mag p 178 D 4 '77

Fire Department
See New York (city)—Fire Department

Gangs
See Gangs

Historic houses, sites, etc.
Arcadia in the Bronx; Wave Hill sculpture exhibit. il Horizon 20:66-9 N '77

Hotels, restaurants, etc.
Johnny's World Famous. New Yorker 53:34-5 My 16 '77

Housing
Empty houses; study by the Women's City Club of New York. S. T. Atlas. Newsweek 90:100 O 10 '77
New urban pioneers: homesteading in the slums; People's Development Corporation. R. M. Williams. il Sat R 4:8-14 Jl 23 '77
U.S. journal: the Bronx; the Coops. C. Trillin. il New Yorker 53:49-54 Ag 1 '77

Public buildings
Shahn's Bronx P.O. murals: the perils of public art. C. Baldwin. il Art in Am 65:15-16+ My '77

Restaurants
See Bronx, N.Y.—Hotels, restaurants, etc.

BRONX Developmental Center, New York. See Mentally handicapped—Institutional care
BRONX High School of Science. See Bronx, N.Y.—Education
BRONX Opera Company. See Opera—New York (state)

BRONZES
Forgotten (?) sculptures in Golden Gate Park; bronze statues. il Sunset 159:36+ O '77
Great Saddles of the West: an interview with Paul Rossi; ed by K. Mayer. P. Rossi. il Am Artist 41:64-7+ Ag '77

BROOK Farm guest house, Lenox, Mass. See Hotels, motels, etc.—United States
BROOK trout. See Trout
BROOK trout fishing. See Trout fishing

BROOKE, Edward William
PL 94-142—getting the money to make it work. Todays Educ 66:50-2 N '77

BROOKE, John, pseud
Gentle art of poverty. il Atlantic 240:62-8 O '77

BROOKE, Marcus
Bosphorus: with one key opens and closes two worlds, two seas. il Oceans 10:40-5 Ja '77

BROOKES, Warren T.
Think positive? U.S. News 83:116 O 17 '77

BROOKHISER, Richard
Their (dis)appointed rounds. il Nat R 29:1294-6 N 11 '77
BROOKINGS Institution
New set of exiles. por Forbes 119:67 F 1 '77
BROOKLYN
See also
Coney Island

Churches

Miracle of the reborn bells; Our Lady of Good Counsel Church, Bedford-Stuyvesant. C. W. Moodie. il por Read Digest 111:9-12+ N '77

Crime

Going. . .going. . .gone? Time 110:26 N 7 '77

Foreign population

Court docket; gerrymander challenge by Hasidic Jews of Brooklyn; Supreme Court decision. J. K. Footlick. Newsweek 89:97-8 Mr 14 '77

Galleries and museums

See also
Brooklyn Museum

Housing

How a business fights housing blight; Brooklyn Union Gas Co. V. Louviere. il Nations Bus 65:59 Je '77

Municipal improvement

Reporter at large: the making of Boerum Hill. J. Anderson. il New Yorker 53:81-2+ N 14 '77

Music

See also
Brooklyn Philharmonia
Opera—New York (state)

Theater

See also
Academy of Music, Brooklyn
BROOKLYN Academy of Music. See Academy of Music, Brooklyn
BROOKLYN Botanic Garden
Herbs. New Yorker 53:22-3 Ag 15 '77
BROOKLYN College. See New York (city). City University—Brooklyn College
BROOKLYN Museum
Brooklyn Museum. A. Goldin. il Art in Am 65:102-4 S '77
BROOKLYN Philharmonia
Brooklyn Philharmonia: Moderns; concert at the Brooklyn Academy of Music. Hi Fi 27:MA29 Je '77
BROOKLYN Public Library

Branches

Libraries' decay speaks volumes; Park Slope Branch. P. Hamill. il Wilson Lib Bull 52:48-50 S '77
BROOKLYN Union Gas Company. See Gas companies
BROOKS, C. and others
Ancient lithosphere: its role in young continental volcanism. bibl il Science 193:1086-94; 196:1235 S 17 '76, Je 10 '77
BROOKS, John, 1920-
Businessman and the government. il Am Heritage 28:66-73 Je '77
Marts of trade. New Yorker 52:80-90 F 7; 53:48-53 D 26 '77
Sixty years of American business. Forbes 120:69-76+ S 15 '77
BROOKS, Louise
Out of Pandora's box. D. Newlin. por Opera N 41:20+ Ap 2 '77 *
BROOKS, Patricia
Pretty poison. il Fam Health 9:29-32 Jl '77
BROOKS, Paul
Champlain: battleground still. il map Audubon 79:66-77 Ja '77
BROOKS, creeks, etc.
Ten streams of history: how are they now? famous trout streams. J. Gibbs. il Outdoor Life 159:60-5 Mr '77
BROOKS Range Wilderness Area. See Wilderness areas—Alaska
BROOMS
Rustling garden broom from twigs of golden bamboo. il Sunset 159:170 S '77
BROSS, Tom
Santo Domingo. il Trav/Holiday 149:54-7 Ja '78
BROTHERS, Joyce
Do you agree? il por Sr Schol 109:14 F 10 '77
How to decorate with color! il Good H 184:128-33 My '77
Meet the MS Read-a-thon; address, May 23, 1977. Vital Speeches 43:623-6 Ag 1 '77
On being a woman. See issues of Good housekeeping
BROTHERS and sisters. See Siblings
BROUDY, Harry S.
New voice for the schools. Todays Educ 66:28-31 Mr '77
BROUGH, James. See Roosevelt, E. jt auth
BROUMAS, Olga
Artemis; The bite; poems; excerpt from Beginning with O. Mademoiselle 83:107 Ap '77
BROUN, Janice A.
Soviet cure for religion. America 137:26-9 Jl 16 '77
BROUSSARD Camille. See Masse, R. F. jt auth
BROUSSARD, Elsie Rita
Will the child be normal? Ask mother. Sci N 112:213 O 1 '77 *
BROUWER, Arie R.
Tower of Babel. Chr Cent 94:276-9 Mr 23 '77
BROWARD County, Fla.
Goal, a program and a community; Area-wide Council on Aging of Broward County, Inc, Fort Lauderdale, Fla. E. H. Sluyter. il por Aging 272:13-17 Je '77
BROWER, Brock
Bureaucrats redux. map Harpers 254:25-6 Mr '77
Remaking of the Vice President. il pors N Y Times Mag p38+ Je 5 '77; Same abr. Read Digest 111:113-17 D '77
BROWER, Kenneth
On a reef, darkly. il Read Digest 110:125-8 F '77
Urban farm. il Atlantic 241:58-63 Ja '78
BROWER, Lincoln P.
Monarch migration; with biographical sketch. il Natur Hist 86:2, 40-53 bibl(p92) Je '77
BROWER, Robert
Model A Camp Directors Institute. Camp Mag 50:15-17 S '77
BROWN, Alisen
Passage to Hawaii; photographs. Yachting 142:62-5 Ag '77
BROWN, Ann C.
Stock trends. See alternate issues of Forbes
BROWN, Arnold
Discouraging word? address, October 12, 1977. Vital Speeches 44:78-81 N 15 '77
BROWN, Bob
Science myths; or, It ain't necessarily so. il Sci Digest 81:72-5 My '77
BROWN, Bud
Broker profile; interview. il Motor B & S 140:108 Jl '77
BROWN, Butler
Butler Brown: a Jimmy Carter favorite. Vasari. il por Art N 76:20-2+ F '77 *
BROWN, Charles Lee, 1921-
Telephone industry; address, August 9, 1977. Vital Speeches 43:764-7 O 1 '77
BROWN, Chip
Encounter in the Brooks Range. Liv Wildn 41:23 Jl '77
Lake Clark National Park: the Alps of Alaska. il maps Nat Parks & Con Mag 51:4-9 Jl '77
BROWN, Constance
But it's always hot-spring time in the Rockies. il Smithsonian 8:90-7 bibl(p 161) N '77
BROWN, D. Scott, and Copeland, D. E.
Overlapping platelets: a diffusion barrier in a teleost swimbladder. bibl il Science 197:383-4 Jl 22 '77
BROWN, David. See Brown, H. G. jt auth
BROWN, David G. and Wyatt, Ray
Maintaining your food supply. Motor B & S 140:103-6 Jl '77
BROWN, Dee Alexander
Great race; excerpt from Hear that lonesome whistle blow. il Am West 14:4-15+ My '77
Transcontinental railroad; excerpt from Hear that lonesome whistle blow. il Am Heritage 28:14-25 F '77
BROWN, Dorothy Foster
Button collecting. See issues of Hobbies
BROWN, Edith, and Brown, Sam
Vegetables; excerpt from Cooking creatively with natural foods. House B 119:158+ My '77
BROWN, Edmund Gerald, 1938-
Governor Brown speaks out in defense of his state; interview. il por U.S. News 83:43-4 Jl 11 '77

about

Big is beautiful, too. P. Goldman and M. Kasindorf. il por Newsweek 90:25-6 Ag 22 '77 *
Canniness of the long-distance runner. D. S. Broder. il Atlantic 241:35-41 Ja '78 *
Gunning for Brown. C. Wallen, Jr. Nat R 29:1367 N 25 '77 *
Jerry Brown's space program. J. Lelyveld. por N Y Times Mag p55 Jl 17 '77 *
BROWN, Erica
Conrans in the country. il por N Y Times Mag p74-5 O 30 '77
Design. il N Y Times Mag p82-3 Je 12; 166-7 N 20 '77; 52-3 Ja 8 '78
Easy way to a room in a day. il N Y Times Mag p74-6 O 2 '77
Keeping winter green. il N Y Times Mag p86 D 18 '77
BROWN, Frederick Z.
Presidential Commission to visit southeast Asia; statement, February 25, 1977. Dept State Bull 76:258 Mr 21 '77
Provisional limits established for fishery conservation zone; statement, March 1, 1977. Dept State Bull 76:273-4 Mr 21 '77

BROWN, George Scratchley
Armed forces of today; address, February 14, 1977. Vital Speeches 43:324-7 Mr 15 '77
Secretary Vance and other administration officials urge ratification of Panama Canal treaties: statement, September 27, 1977. Dept State Bull 77:620-1 N 7 '77

about

Big mouth. Nation 224:419-20 Ap 9 '77 *
Problem at the Pentagon. S. J. Ungar. por Atlantic 239:6+ F '77 *

BROWN, H. Douglas
Gems and minerals. See issues of Hobbies

BROWN, Harold
Brown comments on beam weapons. Aviation W 106:12 My 30 '77
Brown on deterrence; excerpts from address, March 1975. Science 195:465 F 4 '77
Could Russia blunder into nuclear war? interview. il pors U.S. News 83:21-4 S 5 '77
Defense planning and arms control; address, April 13, 1977. Vital Speeches 43:460-3 My 15 '77
Framework for national security decision-making; remarks, with transcript of question and answer session, July 29, 1977. Dept State Bull 77:297-303 S 5 '77
Secretary Vance and other administration officials urge ratification of Panama Canal treaties; statement, September 27, 1977. Dept State Bull 77:618-20 N 7 '77
To strengthen the American alliance; address, May 11, 1977. Vital Speeches 43:522-5 Je 15 '77

about

Arming for the 21st century. il por Time 109:14:21 My 23 '77 *
Arms and the man. M. Greenfield. Newsweek 89:88 Mr 28 '77 *
Brown vows to maintain military strength of U.S. Aviation W 106:25-6 Ja 17 '77 *
Harold Brown and defense: from scientist to secretary. J. Walsh. por Science 195:463-6 F 4 '77 *
Inside story of battle to control spying. J. Fromm. pors U.S. News 83:27 Ag 8 '77 *
Nimble juggler. T. Mathews and L. H. Norman. il por Newsweek 91:20-1 Ja 9 '78 *
No longer a kid but still a whiz. il pors Time 109:24-5 My 23 '77 *
Science is not enough. Suetonius. New Repub 176:19 Ja 15 '77 *
Scientist triumphant. M. A. Reichek. New Repub 176:16-18+ Ja 15 '77 *
Where Jimmy went wrong. T. Branch. Esquire 87:28+ My '77 *

BROWN, Harold O. J.
Abortion and child abuse; excerpt from Death before birth. Chr Today 22:34 O 7 '77

BROWN, Harrison
Toward a day of reckoning. Current 191:23-9 Mr '77

BROWN, Helen Gurley, and Brown, David
For joyful living; interview, ed by R. Weil and J. Macurdy. il pors House B 119:118-25 My '77

BROWN, Herb
Basketbrawl. P. Bonventre. il Newsweek 89:48 F 28 '77

BROWN, James H. and Davidson, D. W.
Competition between seed-eating rodents and ants in desert ecosystems. bibl il Science 196:880-2 My 20 '77

BROWN, James L.
Recruiting and hiring practices of community college deans of instruction. il Clearing H 51:29-31 S '77

BROWN, James William
Ill-provisioned voyage. il Nation 225:38-41 Jl 9 '77

BROWN, Jerry. See Brown, E. G.

BROWN, Joan
Joan Brown, long-distance painter. S. Schwartz. il Art in Am 65:88-9 Mr '77 *

BROWN, Joan Sayers
Funeral of Henry Clay. il Antiques 112:110-11 Jl '77
William Faris Sr, his sons, and journeymen —Annapolis silversmiths. bibl il Antiques 111:378-85 F '77

BROWN, John Carter
About art museums and the National Gallery; interview, ed by K. Kuh. por Sat R 4:55-6+ Ap 16 '77

about

Moving in on the Met. G. Glueck. il por N Y

BROWN, Joseph E.
Oil spills. Sci Digest 82:36-40 N '77

BROWN, Lester Russell
—See Eckholm, E. P. jt auth

about

First nations stop population growth. L. Palmer. Farm J 101:J2 mid-Mr '77 *

BROWN, Malcolm H.
War and peace. bibl Mus Q 63:297-326 Jl '77

BROWN, Margarette
Teaching LD adolescents; ed by J. Singleton. Todays Educ 66:43-6 N '77

BROWN, Marvin, and others
Bombesin: potent effects on thermoregulation in the rat. bibl il Science 196:998-1000 My 27 '77
Somatostatin: analogs with selected biological activities. bibl il Science 196:1467-9 Je 24 '77

BROWN, Matthew R.
Gerald Manley Hopkins: exploding for Christ. Chr Today 21:20+ Ja 7 '77

BROWN, Max H. and Willems, A. L.
Lifeboat ethics and the first-year teacher. il Clearing H 51:73-5 O '77

BROWN, Nelson E.
Space shuttle safety & rescue. bibl il Space World N-12-168:16-25 D '77

BROWN, Norman B.
Price indexes for 1977: U.S. periodicals and serial services. il Lib J 102:1462-7 Jl '77

BROWN, Paul A.
Why MetPath lost its bid to be no. 2. il por Bus W p27 Ag 22 '77 *

BROWN, Polly
Stingray puts on a show; photographs. Yachting 142:70-1 O '77

BROWN, Ralph Manning, 1915-
Our fragile freedom; address, April 29, 1977. Vital Speeches 43:553-5 Jl 1 '77

BROWN, Ray L. See Suver, J. D. jt auth

BROWN, Raymond E.
Christmas as it was. K. L. Woodward. il por Newsweek 90:89+ D 19 '77 *

BROWN, Reeve (Lindbergh)
Country people; story. McCalls 105:204-5 N '77
Growing up a Lindbergh; interview, ed by A. Whitman. por N Y Times Mag p30 My 8 '77

BROWN, Richard Fargo
How to build a museum with diplomacy, guile and charm. J. Kutner. il Art N 76:87-90 D '77 *

BROWN, Robert McAfee
Welcome back, Huey. Chr Cent 94:679-80 Ag 3 '77

about

Four stories of theology; with editorial comment. T. H. Stahel. America 136:inside cover, 230-3 Mr 19 '77 *

BROWN, Roderick Haig-. See Haig-Brown, R.

BROWN, Rosellen
Angle of vision. Writer 90:15-18+ S '77
Cora Fry; poem; excerpt. Ms 5:81-4 Mr '77

BROWN, Royal S.
Theater and film. See issues of High fidelity and Musical America

BROWN, Russell Richards
Growing feud at American Distilling. D. G. Santry. por Bus W p 106 D 12 '77 *

BROWN, Sam. See Brown, E. jt auth

BROWN, Sam W. Jr
Two new agency heads: study in contrasts. il pors U.S. News 82:60 Mr 14 '77 *

BROWN, Sandra Marie (Senne)
How to make a million before you're 34; interview, ed by D. Kaye and F. Russin. pors Redbook 149:60+ My '77

BROWN, Sara Lou
Room at the top. pors Forbes 120:34 S 1 '77 *

BROWN, Stephen
Taking senior citizens off the shelf. Educ Digest 42:45-7 My '77

BROWN, Tom, Inc. See Fuel industry

BROWN-Forman Distillers Corporation
Brown-Forman: consistency and a sharp eye. il Duns R 110:22-3 O '77
Spend, then earn. il Forbes 120:156 O 15 '77

BROWN bear hunting. See Bear hunting

BROWN bears. See Bears

BROWN lung. See Lungs—Dust diseases

BROWN trout fishing. See Trout fishing

BROWN v Board of Education. See United States —Supreme Court—Decisions

BROWNE, Carl
Coxey's march on Washington, 1894. G. G. Eggert. il pors Am Hist Illus 12:20-31 O '77 *

BROWNE, Jeffrey K. and others
Nucleotide sequences from the rabbit beta globin gene inserted into escherichia coli plasmids. bibl il Science 195:389-91 Ja 28 '77

BROWNE, Juanita
Easter eggs dyed and decorated the natural way. il Org Gard & Farm 24:108+ Mr '77
Making your own natural tree decorations. il Org Gard & Farm 24:106-11 D '77

BROWNE, Leslie
Dancer's life for me! interview, ed by E. Miller. il pors Seventeen 36:134-5+ N '77
Leslie Browne of American Ballet Theatre and The turning point; interview, ed by N. M. Stoop. il pors Dance Mag 51:51-4 O '77

BROWNE, Malcolm W.
Silent fall. il N Y Times Mag p63+ O 23 '77

BROWNE, Nick
Narrative point of view: the rhetoric of Au hasard, Balthazar. il Film Q 31:19-31 Fall '77

BROWNE, Rachel
Dancing in a January world: Winnipeg's Contemporary Dancers. J. Anderson. il por Dance Mag 51:44-9 Mr '77 *

BROWNELL, Morris R.
Ears of an untoward make: Pope and Handel. bibl f il Mus Q 62:554-70 O '76

BROWNELL, Philip H.
Compressional and surface waves in sand: used by desert scorpions to locate prey. bibl il Science 197:479-82 Jl 29 '77

BROWNIES. See Cake

BROWNING, Bob
Odd couple: the building principal and the visiting supervisor. Clearing H 50:352-3 Ap '77

BROWNING, Daphne (Du Maurier) Lady. See Du Maurier, D.

BROWNING, Elizabeth (Barrett)
Ms Browning's spiritual face. Vasari. il Art N 76:34 N '77 *

Drama

Elizabeth. Plays 37:71-7 O '77

BROWNING, Robert
Hamelin pays the piper; dramatization. See Thornton, J. F.

BROWNING (firm)-Fabrique Nationale Herstal SA merger. See Firearms industry—Acquisitions and mergers

BROWNLOW, Kevin
Winstanley; interview, ed by V. Glaessner. il Film Q 30:18-23 Wint '76

BROWNMILLER, Susan
(ed) See Kingston, M. H. Susan Brownmiller talks with Maxine Hong Kingston

BROWNSTEIN, Rachel Mayer
Examplar to her sex: Richardson's Clarissa. Yale R 67:30-47 O '77

BROWNSTONES (houses) See City houses

BROYHILL, James Edgar
From a humble beginning to triumph in business. il pors Nations Bus 65:44-6+ Ja '77

BROZ, Madame Jovanka (Budisavljevic)
Another top red's wife runs afoul of system il pors U.S. News 83:55 N 7 '77 *
Purging of Cinderella. il por Newsweek 90:61 N 7 '77 *

BROZEN, Yale
Road to recovery. il Nat R 29:264-7 Mr 4 '77

BRUBACH, Holly
Adult orthodontics. il Mademoiselle 83:244+ O '77
On changing jobs: from fulltime to freelance. Mademoiselle 83:72-4 D '77
(ed) See Tcherkassky, M. Closeup: Marianna Tcherkassky

BRUCE, Charles J. See Shinkman, P. G. jt auth

BRUCE, Dave
Islands of Indonesia. il map Travel 148:56-61 Ag '77

BRUCE, J. G.
Somali Current: recent measurements during the southwest monsoon. bibl maps Science 197:51-3 Jl 1 '77

BRUCE, Jeannette
Figure skating. Sports Illus 46:53-4 F 14 '77

BRUCELLOSIS in cattle
Bangs! And you're wiped out. C. S. Machan. il Farm J 101:Dairy 7-8 S '77
Brucellosis buyers win damages. Farm J 101: Dairy 11, Beef 13 Ag '77

BRUCKERHOFF, Charles
What do students say about reading instruction? Clearing H 51:104-7 N '77

BRUCKHEIM, Allan H.
Family guide to fitness through fun. por Parents Mag 52:68-9+ N '77

BRUCKNER, Anton
Bruckner tradition moves on; recordings of Symphonies nos. 4, 7, and 8. A. Chipman. il Hi Fi 27:93-4 N '77 *
Magnificent Bruckner Eighth. S. Clark. por Am Rec G 40:6-9 Ap '77 *
Requiem in D minor. J. Diether. Am Rec G 40: 19-20 N '76 *
Symphony no. 3 in D minor. G. S. Fox Am Rec G 40:22-3 Ap '77 *
Symphony no. 4 in E flat major. S. Clark. Am Rec G 40:18-19 Je '77 *
Two settings for the same text; Bruckner: Te Deum: Verdi: Te Deum. P. L. Althouse. Am Rec G 40:19-20 Je '77 *

BRUEGGEMANN, Walter
Biblical perspective on the problem of hunger. il Chr Cent 94:1136-41 D 7 '77

BRUEMMER, Fred
Gregarious but contentious walrus; with biographical sketch. il Natur Hist 86:7, 52-61 bibl(p 118) N '77
Life on a cold rock; with biographical sketch. il map Natur Hist 86:8, 54-65 bibl(p97) Mr '77

BRUGGEMAN, Martha R.
Magic Fishbone Bookshop: a California story. il Horn Bk 53:134-9 Ap '77

BRUGH, Max, Jr
Butylated hydroxytoluene protects chickens exposed to Newcastle disease virus. bibl il Science 197:1291-2 S 23 '77

BRUMLEY, I. Jon
Born again. por Forbes 119:54 Mr 15 '77 *

BRUNCHES
Brunch; with menus for 12 and 25. il Ladies Home J 94:134-6+ N '77
Hearty, headstart breakfasts and brunches. il Fam Health 9:32-5 S '77
Holiday idea—an informal breakfast buffet party. il Sunset 159:134 D '77
Jo and Joel Grey's brunch; recipes. J. Grey and J. Grey. Vogue 167:62+ Je '77
Southern hospitality. . .a Creole brunch. G. Steves. il Am Home 80:68-70+ D '77

BRUNNER, Jacqueline
Exercise: it can be fun keeping fit. il Ret Liv 17:20-1 Ja '77

BRUNNER, Marguerite
Collect anything—for fun and profit; excerpt from Antiques for amateurs on a shoestring budget. il Read Digest 110:49-52+ Ap '77

BRUNO, Brother. See LaVerdiere, B.

BRUNS, Roger
Hoboes told all to 1890s scholar. il por Smithsonian 8:141-2+ N '77

BRUNSWICH Corporation
So whaddya wanna do tonight, Marty? Forbes 119:148 My 15 '77

BRUSH, Stephen B.
Farming the edge of the Andes; with biographical sketch. il Natur Hist 86:4, 32-41 bibl(p94) My '77

BRUSH drawing
See also
Sumie

BRUSH fires
Box-kite blaze; Santa Barbara, Calif. R. Steele and D. Gram. il Newsweek 90:25+ Ag 8 '77
Costly holocaust; Santa Barbara, Calif. il Time 110:29 Ag 8 '77
Weather surrounding the Santa Barbara fire: 26 July 1977. N. E. Graham. il Weatherwise 30:158-9 Ag '77

BRUSHING of teeth. See Teeth—Care and hygiene

BRUSHY Mountain State Prison. See Prisons—Tennessee

BRUSSELS

Description

Brussels. H. Koenig and G. Koenig. il Travel 148:26-31 Ag '77

Hotels, restaurants, etc.

International chef: Chantraine. D. Reynolds. il Travel 148:245 Ag '77

Music

See also
Opera—Belgium

BRUSSELS Opéra National. See Opera—Belgium

BRUSTEIN, Robert
Can the show go on? il N Y Times Mag p8-9+ Jl 10 '77

BRUVERS, Olafs
Eastern bloc voices that won't be silenced. A. H. Matthews. Chr Today 21:44-6 Mr 4 '77 *

BRUZONSKY, Mark A.
Peace in the Middle East. il por Nation 224: 489-92 Ap 23 '77
(ed) See Eliav, A. Tough talk from a dove

BRYAN, C. D. B.
Bangkok (cont) il Holiday 57:34-5+ N '76
On the road to Zihuatanejo. il Holiday 58:32-5 S '77

BRYAN, Dave
Bag trick: carry all in two hands? il Mod Phot 41:95 Ag '77

BRYAN, David H.
To fly like a bird. il Mech Illus 73:74-5 My '77

BRYAN, G. McLeod
Banning of Beyers Naudé. Chr Cent 94:1020-1 N 9 '77

BRYAN, John
Fishing. Sports Illus 47:81-2+ O 17 '77

BRYAN, John H. Jr
John H. Bryan Jr of Consolidated Foods: right place. por Forbes 119:95 F 15 '77 *

BRYAN, Sharon
Making conversation; poem. Nation 225:569 N 26 '77
New kitchen; poem. Nation 225:502 N 12 '77
Sleeping with the light on; poem. Nation 224:535 Ap 30 '77
What to answer; poem. Nation 225:316 O 1 '77

BRYANT, Anita
Anita Bryant is mad about gays. M. Kondracke. New Repub 176:13-15 My 7 '77 *
Anita Bryant on the march. L. Van Gelder. il por Ms 6:75-8+ S '77 *
Anita Bryant's crusade. G. Steinem. Progressive 41:37 Je '77 *
Anita Bryant's crusade. D. A. Williams. por Newsweek 89:39 Ap 11 '77 *
Anita's circle. il por Time 109:76 My 2 '77 *
Battle over gay rights. T. Mathews and others. il por Newsweek 89:16-17+ Je 6 '77 *
Cooler crusader. S. Drake and B. Brubaker. il por Newsweek 90:11-12 O 3 '77 *

BRYANT, Anita—*Continued*
Enough! Enough! Enough! il por Time 109:59-60 Je 20 '77 *
Gay rights showdown in Miami. il por Time 109:20 Je 13 '77 *
Gaycott turns ugly. il por Time 110:33 N 21 '77 *
God's crusader. R. Steele and T. Fuller. il pors Newsweek 89:20-1 Je 6 '77 *
Miami vote: tide turning against homosexuals? il por U.S. News 82:46 Je 20 '77 *
Vengeance is mine, saith Anita. M. E. Marty. Chr Cent 94:1047 N 9 '77 *

BRYANT, Bear
Bear Bryant's stompin' school. R. Blount, Jr. Esquire 88:52+ S '77 *

BRYANT, Carolyn
(comp) Quarterly book-list. See issues of Musical quarterly

BRYANT, Nelson
Behold the hunter. il Atlantic 240:66-70 D '77
Joys of hunting geese. il Field & S 82:28-9+ Je '77
Stripers and bait. il Field & S 82:42-6 Ag '77

BRYANT, Peter J. and others
Biological regeneration and pattern formation; with biographical sketches. il Sci Am 237: 66-76+ bibl(p 154) Jl '77

BRYCE, Mary Charles
Catechesis toward maturity in faith. il por New Cath World 220:96-100 Mr '77
Hopes for the coming Synod. America 137:215-17 O 8 '77

BRYCE-LAPORTE, Roy S.
Visibility of the new immigrants. bibl il Society 14:18-22 S '77

BRYDEN, Ewen L. and Robinson, Toni
Century in the life of Kapiolani Park. bibl il Parks & Rec 12:49-53 Jl '77

BRYN MAWR College, Bryn Mawr, Pa.
Bryn Mawr v. coeducation. Time 109:64 Ja 31 '77

BRYNOLSON, Grace
Gasworks (ugh!) reborn as city park. il Smithsonian 8:116-18+ N '77

BRYSON, Bernarda
Second look: Gilgamesh: man's first story. il Horn Bk 53:74-6 F '77 *

BRYSON, John
Resurrection of Jason Robards. il pors Esquire 89:50-3+ Ja '78

BRZESKA, Henri Gaudier-. See Gaudier-Brzeska, H.

BRZEZINSKI, Zbigniew
Brzezinski details administration's position. il por Aviation W 106:34-5+ Ap 18 '77
New U.S. challenge to Russia; interview. il por U.S. News 82:35-6+ My 30 '77
Presidential assistant Brzezinski interviewed on Face the Nation; transcript of program, October 30, 1977; ed by B. Morton and others. Dept State Bull 77:800-5 D 5 '77
Presidential Assistant Brzezinski's news conference of April 1; transcript of news conference. Z. Brzezinski. Dept State Bull 76:414-21 Ap 25 '77
Talk with Zbig; interview, ed R. Watson and S. Sullivan. por Newsweek 89:58 My 9 '77
Zbig's optimism in a hostile world; interview, ed by S. Cloud. por Time 110:18 Ag 8 '77

about

Brzezinski: role of science in society and foreign policy. N. Wade. Science 195:966-8 Mr 11 '77 *
Life at Brzezinski U. R. Watson and others. il por Newsweek 89:55+ My 9 '77 *
Meaning of Brzezinski: opinions of Kultura; tr by O. Scherer. Nat R 29:612-13 My 27 '77 *
Vance and Brzezinski: peaceful coexistence or guerrilla war? M. Berger. il pors N Y Times Mag p 19+ F 13 '77 *
Zbig and Wolfgang at dawn. H. Sidey. Time 110:17 D 19 '77 *
Zbiggy zpeaks. J. Osborne. New Repub 177:8-9 O 22 '77 *

BRZOSTOSKI, John
Early Irish art. il Craft Horiz 37:50-3 D '77
No robe as perfection. il Craft Horiz 37:22-7 Ag '77
Treasures of Thrace. il Craft Horiz 37:32+ O '77
Wood masterpieces: China and Japan. il Craft Horiz 37:46-9+ Ap '77

BUBACK, Siegfried
Terrorists' revenge? il por Newsweek 89:53 Ap 18 '77 *

BUBBLE gum. See Chewing gum

BUBBLE memory devices (computers) See Computers—Memory systems

BUBEL, Nancy W.
Consumer's guide to winter squash varieties. il Org Gard & Farm 25:69-73 Ja '78
Handling started seedlings. il Org Gard & Farm 24:69-73 Mr '77
Mulching with weeds. il Org Gard & Farm 24: 78-81 Ap '77

BUBER, Martin
Martin Buber: I and Thou. L. S. Cunningham. Chr Cent 94:246-7 Mr 16 '77 *

BUCCANEERS
Campeche: buccaneer's battleground. N. Navarro and R. Bushnell. il Oceans 10:22-5 S '77

BUCH, Siddhartha C.
They speak for the snakes. il pors Int Wildlife 7:16 My '77

BUCHAN, Vivian
Many-splendored thing at any age. il Ret Liv 17:44-5 Jl '77

BUCHANAN, Donald
Update on the status of community education. Parks & Rec 12:70+ My '77

BUCHANAN, Lembi
Ranching Atlantic bluefin: with biographical sketch. il Sea Front 23:172-80 My '77

BUCHANAN, Marlowe J.
Build a transformerless DC-to-DC voltage doubler. il Pop Electr 12:55-6 S '77

BUCHANAN, Patrick Joseph
Lancing the boil. il Newsweek 89:34 My 16 '77

BUCHANAN-DAVIDSON, Dorothy J.
Leukemia breakthrough . . .it can be cured! il Parents Mag 52:22+ N '77

BUCHANEK, Jack. See Bergin, E. jt auth

BUCHBINDER, Rudolf
Haydn: Piano works, v 1. R. Kammerer. Am Rec G 40:36 S '77 *

BUCHER, Glenn R.
Liberation theology. bibl il Intellect 105:278-80 F '77

BUCHER, Judy Darby
Moving. il Redbook 149:60+ Jl '77

BUCHER, Lloyd Mark
Pueblo postscript. E. Keerdoja. il pors Newsweek 91:11 Ja 16 '78 *

BUCHSBAUM, Alan
Loft living: big spaces, fresh images. il Archit Rec 162:97-100 Jl '77 *

BUCHWALD, Art
Have a nice day, Pops; excerpt from Down the Seine and up the Potomac with Art Buchwald. Read Digest 111:108-10 D '77
PW interviews. Pub W 212:6-7 Ag 22 '77
Questions & answers. Horticulture 55:2-3 My '77

BUCK, Pearl (Sydenstricker)
This day to treasure; story. il Good H 185:124-5 D '77

BUCK, Richard A.
Help for salmon. D. Seamans. por Outdoor Life 160:100 Ag '77 *

BUCKHOUT, Robert, and Ellison, K. W.
Line-up: a critical look. bibl il Psychol Today 11:82-4+ Je '77

BUCKI, Michael S.
Tape your interviews for radio. Writers Digest 57:23-5 F '77

BUCKLAND, William
Hammond-Harwood House: a colonial masterpiece. W. H. Pierson, Jr. bibl il Antiques 111:186-93 Ja '77 *

BUCKLER, Ernest
Rarity of June; excerpt from Ox bells and fireflies. il Read Digest 110:114-16 Je '77

BUCKLEY, Francis J.
Whoever sings, prays twice. New Cath World 220:39 Ja '77

BUCKLEY, James L.
Assessing Soviet intentions; excerpts from address. Aviation W 107:7 Ag 22 '77
People's sense of powerlessness; excerpts from address. por Intellect 106:95 S '77

about

After the ball was over: decompression, junior division. C. Buckley; discussion. Nat R 29: 141-2+ F 4 '77 *

BUCKLEY, Jim
Obscenity: who's to say? R. Boeth and E. Sciolino. il por Newsweek 90:53 N 7 '77 *

BUCKLEY, Priscilla L.
Travel. Nat R 29:681-2+ Je 10 '77

BUCKLEY, Robert Joseph
Consumerism and the economic dope habit; address, August 17, 1977. Vital Speeches 44:145-50 D 15 '77

about

Allegheny Ludlum: breaking the rules to grow. por Bus W p74+ Jl 18 '77 *
Allegheny Ludlum diversifies again. por Bus W p 19-20 Ja 9 '78 *
Allegheny Ludlum's coup at Chemetron. por Bus W p54-5 S 26 '77 *

BUCKLEY, Ruth. See Hotchin, J. jt auth

BUCKLEY, Tom
Inside subs. Esquire 87:81-4+ Ap '77
Pinball goes electronic. il N Y Times Mag p30-1 Ja 23 '77
Running short on long underwear. il N Y Times Mag p62-3 F 20 '77

BUCKLEY, William Frank, 1925-
Finding your position; excerpt from Airborne. il Motor B & S 140:67-71+ N '77
Flying at Yale. Flying 101:6+ S '77
Giving Yale to Connecticut; excerpt from God and man at Yale. il Harpers 255:43-8 N '77
Keeping cool in Cozumel. il Motor B & S 139: 37-9+ Mr '77

BUCKLEY, William Frank, 1925- —*Continued*
Notes & asides; replies to letters. See issues of National review
On the right. See issues of National review

about

Fiasco. M. Mayer. Progressive 41:26 F '77 *
Many missions. R. L. Calhoun; A. Ralston; V. Mercier. Harpers 256:6 Ja '78 *
Tortuous exculpation. Nation 225:581 D 3 '77 *

BUCKLEY Amendment. See School reports and records

BUCKNELL University, Lewisburg, Pa.
Bucknell Univ:
Cage, et al; New Music—four views. Hi Fi 27:MA34 Jl '77
New Music; work performed and composed by R. Hannay. por Hi Fi 27:MA20-1 Mr '77

BUCKWALTER, Len
Choosing a CB antenna for the road. il Mech Illus 73:50+ My '77

BUCYRUS-Erie Company
Great expectations. Forbes 119:50 Je 15 '77

BUDAPEST
Hungarian holiday. S. Birnbaum. il Esquire 89:24+ Ja '78

Music

See also
Opera—Hungary

BUDD, James Hodgson
Mexico for retirement? il Ret Liv 17:37-9 Mr '77

BUDD Company
Focusing on people and productivity; interview. G. F. Richards. il pors Nations Bus 65:40-2+ Jl '77

BUDDHA and Buddhism
Buddhism: the middle way. il Sr Schol 109:24-6+ F 24 '77
Tovil: exorcism by white magic; ceremony of Sri Lanka's Buddhists. M. M. Ames. il Natur Hist 87:42-9 bibl(p 108) Ja '78
See also
Monasteries, Buddhist

Study and teaching

Precious master of the mountains; Naropa Institute. il por Time 109:86 F 14 '77

BUDDHISM and Christianity. See Christianity and other religions

BUDDHIST literature
Art of dying; Tibetan book of the dead. D. Goleman. Psychol Today 10:58-9 Ap '77

BUDDHIST monasteries. See Monasteries, Buddhist

BUDGET

Great Britain

Bittersweets for Britain. L. Langway and A. Collings. il por Newsweek 89:87 Ap 11 '77
Britain's turnaround? R. Carroll and A. Collins. il por Newsweek 90:56+ N 7 '77
Early Christmas. il por Time 110:114 N 7 '77

Japan

Japan government seeks rise in defense funding. Aviation W 106:19 Ja 31 '77

Russia

See also
Russia—Armed Forces—Appropriations and expenditures

South Africa

South Africa tightens its grip on capital. Bus W p54 Ap 18 '77

United States

Balancing act. T. Mathews and R. Thomas. Newsweek 89:19-20 F 28 '77
Battle-cry budget. A. J. Mayer and R. Thomas. il Newsweek 89:67-8 Ja 24 '77
Budget deficits year after year and no end in sight. il U.S. News 82:72-5 F 28 '77
Budget shell game. Sat Eve Post 249:30+ O '77
Can Carter ever balance the budget? W. C. Bryant. il U.S. News 83:29 O 3 '77
Carter and the environment: better, but still not good enough. L. S. Clapper. il Nat Wildlife 15:18-19 Je '77
Carter budget gets mixed reviews from local leaders. H. V. Semling. Am City & County 92:26 Ap '77
Carter sets new priorities. il U.S. News 82:15-17 Mr 7 '77
Carter's budget: little biomedical growth; energy conservation pushed; Breeder and other long-term energy projects cut back. B. J. Culliton; L. J. Carter. Science 195:961-2 Mr 11 '77
Deficit could be less than expected. Bus W p33-4 Ja 31 '77
Don't get your hopes up; J. Carter's proposals. il Time 109:15-16 F 28 '77
Ford's farewell budget: science fares quite well. B. J. Culliton. il Science 195:374-6 Ja 28 '77
Full employment and fiscal integrity. T. D. Kane. bibl Intellect 105:246-7 F '77
Hold that line! Forbes 120:42 N 1 '77
Jimmy Carter tells why he will use zero-base budgeting. J. Carter. por Nations Bus 65:24-6 Ja '77
Making it easier for the new man. il por Time 109:14 Ja 24 '77
Making of budget—step by step. il U.S. News 82:63-4 My 9 '77
Money squeeze. D. A. Williams and others. il Newsweek 90:31-2 D 12 '77
OMB director Bert Lance seeks business help; interview, ed by R. L. Lesher. T. B. Lance. il pors Nations Bus 65:18-22+ My '77
Research, development budget up 8%. il Aviation W 106:52-3 F 7 '77
Special report: Fiscal 1978 aerospace budget. il Aviation W 106:12-27 Ja 24 '77
Tests for Carter's balanced-budget plans. Bus W p31-2 Je 13 '77
Transition budget: steady growth for R&D. il Sci N 111:52-4 Ja 22 '77
What it means to build a budget from zero. il Bus W p 160+ Ap 18 '77
What zero-base budgeting is and how Carter wants to use it. U.S. News 82:91-3 Ap 25 '77
Why U.S. will go deeper and deeper in the hole. il U.S. News 82:74-6 Ja 24 '77
Zero-base budgeting: what's wrong with sunset laws. R. Randall. Nation 224:331-4 Mr 19 '77
Zero-based budget to strain Congress. E. Kozicharow. il Aviation W 106:57+ Je 13 '77
See also
United States—Appropriations and expenditures
United States—Congress—Budget Office
United States—Management and Budget, Office of

BUDGET, Business
Conflicting roles in budgeting for operations M. E. Barrett and L. B. Fraser, 3d. il Harvard Bus R 55:137-46 Jl '77
What it means to build a budget from zero. il Bus W p 160+ Ap 18 '77
Where does zero-base budgeting work? J. D. Suver and R. L. Brown. bibl f il Harvard Bus R 55:76-84 N '77

BUDGET, Household
Budgets for retired couples rose moderately in 1976. M. L. McCraw. il M Labor R 100:53-6 O '77
Family budget costs continued to climb in 1976. L. McCraw. il M Labor R 100:35-9 Jl '77
Family money management. M. Daly. See issues of Better homes & gardens
Money: how 35,000 women spend, save and s-t-r-e-t-c-h it; responses to questionnaire. V. Cadden. il McCalls 104:75-80 S '77
More than money. S. Auerbach. See issues of American home
My husband spent all our money on himself. il Good H 186:22+ Ja '78
One family's budgeting plan—it's easy and it works! il Changing T 31:43-9 Jl '77
When your budget signals danger. Changing T 31:33-5 F '77

BUDGET, Library. See Libraries—Finance

BUDGET, Personal
See also
Childrens allowances

BUDGET Committee, Senate. See United States—Congress—Senate—Budget, Committee on the

BUDGET cooking. See Cookery

BUDGET meals. See Meals

BUDGET Office, Congressional. See United States—Congress—Budget Office

BUDGETS, School library. See School libraries—Finance

BUDKER, Gersh Itskovich
Obituary
Phys Today por 30:78-9 S '77. W. K. H. Panofsky

BUDRYS, Algis
Politics of deoxyribonucleic acid. New Repub 176:18-21 Ap 16 '77

BUDWORMS, Spruce. See Spruce budworms

BUDZYNSKI, Thomas
Tuning in on the twilight zone. bibl il pors Psychol Today 11:38-9+ Ag '77

BUECHNER, M. Northrup
Altruism versus New York City; address, May 17, 1977. Vital Speeches 43:629-34 Ag 1 '77

BUECHNER, Thomas Scharman
Coburger Glaspreis 1977. il Craft Horiz 37:16-27 D '77

BUEHLER, Elizabeth W.
Oregon yesterdays; with historic photographs by G. M. Weister. Am West 14:41-53 S '77

BUELL, John, and De Luca, Tom
Let's start talking about socialism. Progressive 41:24-7 Mr '77

BUENOS AIRES

Description

Buenos Aires: a great buy. S. Shevey. il Harp Baz 110:12+ O '77

Popular culture

Tango tangle. C. Fernandez Moreno. il UNESCO Courier 30:60-2 Ag '77

BUFFALO Bill. See Cody, W. F.

BUFFALO, N.Y.
After the thaw. E. Keerdoja. Newsweek 90:7 Jl 25 '77
Blizzard of '77 teaches lessons for '78. il Am City & County 92:61-2 Ag '77
Buffalo: camaraderie and tragedy. M. Knox. il Time 109:11-12 F 14 '77
Buffalo, N.Y.—digging out of the ice age. T. Fuller. il Newsweek 89:27 F 14 '77
How Buffalo dented the Conrail budget. Bus W p32 F 21 '77
What it's like—living in a city drowning in snow. il U.S. News 82:21 F 14 '77

Art
Buffalo (cont) N. T. Willig. Art N 76:195-6+ N '77

Education
Special report: a winning role for the school library; energy technology program at East Senior High School in West Seneca. C. D. Gwitt. bibl il Wilson Lib Bull 52:295-8 D '77

Municipal improvement
Dead trees, dying communities. J. F. Keenan. America 137:265-8 O 22 '77

Music
See also
Opera—New York (state)

Newspapers
Press lord comes to Buffalo; antitrust suit by the Buffalo courier-express against the Buffalo evening news. R. T. Grieves and D. Strack. Nation 225:590-2 D 3 '77

BUFFALO and Erie County Public Library System. See Libraries—New York (state)

BUFFALO Bill Historical Center, Cody, Wyo. See Historical museums

BUFFALO hunting
Terrible-tempered ox; Cape buffalo in Mozambique. P. Barrett. il Field & S 82:48-50+ N '77

BUFFALO National River
America's little mainstream. H. Arden. il Nat Geog 151:344-59 Mr '77

BUFFALOES, American. See Bison, American

BUFFER solutions
See also
Tromethamine

BUFFET meals
Crowd-in-the-kitchen buffet. il Bet Hom & Gard 55:150-1 N '77
Family country lunch; recipes of Gagarin family. il House & Gard 149:132-3+ D '77
Fast feast. R. L. Green. il por N Y Times Mag p 158+ N 20 '77
Get together for a fire-side feast. il Seventeen 36:154-5+ N '77
Halston gives a party; buffet supper. Halston. Harp Baz 110:154-5+ O '77
Holiday idea—an informal breakfast buffet party. il Sunset 159:134 D '77
Oktoberfest; with recipes. il Sunset 159:192-3 O '77
Personalizing the reception—buffet by bride, groom, friends. il Sunset 158:158-9 Je '77
Pub party; with menu and recipes. il Sunset 158:88-9 Mr '77
Ready, set, party! Kitchen buffet. il House & Gard 149:174-5+ O '77
Redbook's Texas holiday cookbook. Redbook 150: 131 D '77
7-salad buffet; vegetable salads. P. Meyers. il pors House & Gard 149:132-3+ Je '77
Spectacular summer buffets; with recipes. il McCalls 104:136-7+ Je '77
Tray-buffet for 24. il Sunset 158:120-1 Ap '77
You start with an eggplant or potato. il Sunset 159:236-7 O '77
See also
Christmas meals

BUFFET tables. See Tables

BUFFETT, Jimmy
Buffett. New Yorker 53:23-5 Ag 15 '77 *
Caribbean country boy. por Time 109:73 Ap 18 '77 *

BUFFETT, Warren Edward
How inflation swindles the equity investor. il por Fortune 95:250-4+ My '77
Press lord comes to Buffalo. R. T. Grieves and D. Strack. Nation 225:590-2 D 3 '77 *

BUGATTI, Ettore Isidoro Arco
Keeping the faith. C. Fox. il pors Car & Dr 23:97-8+ Ag; 89-91 S '77 *

BUGATTI (sports car) See Sports cars

BUGGING. See Electronics in criminal investigation, espionage, etc.

BUGLISI, Jacqulyn
Reviews. J. Dunning. Dance Mag 51:37-8 Ap '77 *

BUHRKE, Rich
At the other end of the rainbows. R. Telander. il por Sports Illus 46:50-2 Ap 25 '77 *

BUIE, Jacqueline
Finding old cookbooks and new friends. House B 119:93+ Jl '77

BUILDING
See also
Architecture and climate
Bricklaying
Concrete construction
Environmental engineering (buildings)
Foundations
Framing (building)
Girders
Glass construction
House construction
Scaffolding
Steel construction
Structural engineering
Systems building
Wood construction

Contracts and specifications
Basic guide to pitfalls in foreign contracts. P. F. Purcell. Archit Rec 161:69 Je '77
Debate over consolidation of arbitration proceedings is enlivened by a recent New York case. G. Aksen. Archit Rec 162:59 O '77
Document A201 strives to clarify—not change—the roles of architect, contractor and owner. A. T. Kornblut. Archit Rec 161:67+ Ap '77
In spite of the controversy, A201 basically reaffirms traditional practices. A. T. Kornblut. Archit Rec 161:55+ Mr '77
In thoughtful debate, AIA rejects ethics changes that would allow general contracting. W. F. Wagner, Jr. Archit Rec 162:26 Jl '77
Minimizing defects in plans and specifications. M. Stokes. Archit Rec 162:49 Jl '77
Responsibility for product innovation: how to be progressive, yet reduce your risk. H. J. Rosen. Archit Rec 162:14 mid-O '77
Snag in Arab contracts. il Bus W p85 Ap 25 '77
Specification writing: a new CSI program provides a one-stop approach to locating references; Construction Specifications Institute. il Archit Rec 162:47 mid-Ag '77
Which contractor and why. S. Auerbach. Am Home 80:21 S '77

Costs
Building costs. il Archit Rec 161:71 Ap; 162:53 Jl; 62-3 S; 63 O '77
See also
Building—Estimates

Estimates
Inexpensive, fast estimating services provide second source costs; Wood and Tower, Inc. il Archit Rec 161:64-5 F '77
Range estimating: a way to predict the accuracy of cost estimates. il Archit Rec 162:62-3 S '77

Finance
Automated project control system aims for improved profitability; Computer-Based Financial Management System. G. N. Harper. il Archit Rec 161:61 Mr '77
See also
Housing finance
Mortgages

Inspection
See Building inspection

Specifications
See Building—Contracts and specifications

Standards
New ANSI standards on barrier-free design expected in 1978. W. Hickman. Archit Rec 162: 63 D '77
See also
Building laws and regulations

Study and teaching
See also
House construction—Study and teaching

BUILDING, Adobe
Home in an adobe; home of F. Scholder; Galisteo, N. Mex. R. Kent. il pors N Y Times Mag p46-7+ Ja 23 '77

BUILDING, Amateur. See Architecture, Amateur

BUILDING and earthquakes. See Earthquakes and building

BUILDING Arts, National Museum of the (proposed) See Washington, D.C.—Galleries and museums

BUILDING blocks, Toy. See Toys

BUILDING climbing. See Stunts

BUILDING codes. See Building laws and regulations

BUILDING contracts and specifications. See Building—Contracts and specifications

BUILDING costs. See Building—Costs

BUILDING estimates. See Building—Estimates

BUILDING finance. See Building—Finance

BUILDING fittings
Address book; stores selling authentic period fixtures and reproductions. S. Sunderlin. House B 119:32+ Ap '77
Product reports. See issues of Architectural record
Product reports 78; special issue. il Archit Rec 162:5-15+ mid-O '77
Manufacture
Still at the helm; Philips Industries. por Forbes 119:72 Ja 15 '77
BUILDING industry. See Construction industry
BUILDING inspection
Private building inspection before you buy? homes. Sunset 159:108+ S '77
BUILDING laws and regulations
Building codes—here is guidance; getting a permit. il Sunset 158:156+ Ap '77
OSHA and the architect: a recent case lessens designer liability; liability for violations of the Construction Safety Standards. A. T. Kornblut. Archit Rec 162:63 N '77
Regulatory codes: one firm's check list for industrial projects. J. E. Compton. Archit Rec 161: 65+ Je '77
System of energy codes will govern California building. J. Nairn. Archit Rec 162:33 mid-Ag '77
See also
Building—Contracts and specifications
BUILDING machinery. See Construction equipment
BUILDING materials
New products to help you build better & waste less. House B 119:84+ S '77
Product reports. See issues of Architectural record
Product reports 78; special issue. il Archit Rec 162:5-15+ mid-O '77
See also
Aggregates (building materials)
Building, Adobe
Concrete blocks
Fireproof construction
Lumber
Plywood
Siding (building)
Prices
Price explosion in building materials. il Bus W p 50 S 12 '77
BUILDING materials industry
Boom too soon; home insulation. S. T. Atlas and J. B. Copeland. il Newsweek 90:68 Ag 15 '77
Fraud in the insulation business. Changing T 32: 4 Ja '78
Home insulation sales are almost too hot. il Bus W p88+ S 26 '77
Running out of insulation. il Time 110:81 N 14 '77
Sweet sound of. . .; Season-all Industries. il por Forbes 119:72 Je 1 '77
See also
Certain-Teed Products Corporation
Johns-Manville Corporation
Finance
Construction. il Forbes 121:88+ Ja 9 '78
Securities
SEC gets slapped for double-dealing; stock fraud investigation of TDA industries, Inc. Bus W p36 Je 20 '77
BUILDING permits. See Building laws and regulations
BUILDING sites
See also
Hillside architecture
BUILDING trades unions. See Trade unions—Construction workers
BUILDINGS
See also
Architecture
Industrial buildings
Office buildings
Public buildings
Skyscrapers
also subhead Buildings under names of cities, e.g. New York (city)—Buildings
Equipment
See Building fittings
Mechanical equipment
See Mechanical equipment of buildings
BUILDINGS, Abandoned
Empty houses; Bronx study by the Women's City Club of New York. S. T. Atlas. Newsweek 90:100 O 10 '77
BUILDINGS, Fireproof. See Fireproof construction
BUILDINGS, Historic. See Historic houses, sites, etc.
BUILDINGS, Moving of. See Moving of structures, etc.
BUILDINGS, Polygonal
Many-sided splendors; American polygonal architecture. R. Taylor. il House & Gard 149:58+ My '77
BUILDINGS, Prefabricated
Prefabricated and portable library units offer quick and easy extension of service. A. G. Bushman. il Am Lib 8:546-8 N '77
See also
Houses, Prefabricated
BUILDINGS, Remodeled
Boom in recycled buildings. il Bus W p 100-1+ Jl 11 '77
Building types study: Record Interiors of 1977; with introd by B. Gordon. il Archit Rec 161: 101:28 Ja '77
Exhibitions in sight; remodeling of the Montreal Museum of Fine Arts. B. Wasserman. il Sch Arts 76:48-51 Ap '77
From shambles to showplace; Chicago Public Library Cultural Center. D. Schabel. il Am Lib 8:602-4 D '77
Hoosuck: a community story; Windsor Mill art center in remodeled textile mill. M. Flad and H. Flad. il Craft Horiz 37:20-1+ Ap '77
Metamorphosis: library emerges from fire station cocoon; Schaumburg Township Public Library, Ill. A. G. Bushman. il Am Lib 8:241-2 My '77
Museum within a museum; new wing for the Boston Museum of Fine Arts. J. H. Kay. Art N 76:115-18 D '77
Recycling Main—a landmark at Vassar; with introd by M. F. Schmertz. il Archit Rec 162: 73-8 Jl '77
Versailles in Indiana limestone; addition to the Frick collection. G. Henry. il Art N 76:117 S '77
See also
Apartment houses, Remodeled
Dormitories, Remodeled
Houses, Remodeled
School buildings, Remodeled
BUILDINGS, Restoration of. See Architecture—Conservation and restoration
BUILDINGS, Round
See also
Geodesic domes
BUILDINGS in art. See Architecture in art
BUILT in furniture. See Furniture, Built in
BUKOVSKY, Vladimir
How a dissident describes human rights in Russia; excerpts from address, February 25, 1977. il U.S. News 82:22 Mr 14 '77
Serbsky treatment; interview, ed by E. F. Torrey. il por Psychol Today 11:38-9+ Je '77
Word is freedom; interview, ed by J. R. Coyne, Jr. il Nat R 29:378-82 Ap 1 '77
about
Mother courage: how Vladimir Bukovsky was saved. L. Thorne. il por N Y Times Mag p38-40+ F 27 '77 *
Prisoner of conscience: the Bukovsky file. L. Elliott. por Read Digest 111:93-7 Ag '77 *
BULB industry
Netherlands
In praise of Darwin, Rembrandt, Mendel and other famous tulips; with photographs by D. Kessel. F. Endt. Horticulture 55:26-39 Ag '77
BULBS
Greenhouse; ordering South African bulbs. J. Kilborn. Horticulture 55:6 Ag '77
How to brighten up your house with an indoor bulb garden. R. Langer. il House & Gard 149: 92 O '77
It's bulb time. il Sunset 159:114-17 O '77
See also
Amaryllis
Forcing (plants)
Narcissus
Tulips
BULBS, Light. See Electric lamps, Incandescent
BULIMAREXIA. See Hyperphagia
BULKLEY, Dwight H.
Innocent victim myth. il Intellect 105:433-4 Je '77
BULL, Charles Livingston
Charles Livingston Bull. D. L. Tuttle. il por Conservationist 32:8-13 Jl '77 *
BULL, Charlotte
Cooking on the trail; excerpt from Wildlife country—how to enjoy it. il Nat Wildlife 15:30-2 Ag '77
BULL, George
(ed) See Philip, Prince Philip: the new battle of Britain. . .and how to win it
BULL, John V. R.
Covering the courts; address, September 23, 1977. Vital Speeches 44:52-4 N 1 '77
BULLARD, E. John
American paintings from the collection of John J. McDonough. il Antiques 112:946-53 N '77
BULLDOZERS (machines)
90-ton Cat. E. F. Lindsley. il Pop Sci 212:88-9 Ja '78
World's largest bulldozer unveiled. il Am City & County 92:54 N '77

BULLER, Dave
OBIS and ACA—the impossible equation does match. il Camp Mag 49:10-11 Ap '77

BULLETIN of the atomic scientists
Farewell; departure of editor. S. H. Day, Jr. Bull Atom Sci 33:4-5 D '77

BULLETS
It all rides on. . .the bullet. J. Wootters. il Field & S 82:100+ O '77
2-stage bullet lets you fire a .22 from a .30-06 rifle. P. Wahl. il Pop Sci 210:59 Ap '77
See also
Cartridges
Shot

BULLFIGHTERS
Lady in the bullring; interview, ed by M. Feiner. B. Trujillo. il pors Américas 29:25-7 S '77

BULLHEAD fishing
Midnight Medusa; fishing in Chataugua Lake, New York State. D. Walrod. il Field & S 81:34+ Mr '77

BULLINS, Ed
Daddy. Reviews
New Yorker 53:89 Je 20 '77 *

BULLOCK, Viola
Black woman finds her roots. O. Coombs. Redbook 149:62+ O '77 *

BULLOUGH, Vern L.
How the FBI spotted me. Nation 225:51-2 Jl 9 '77

BULLS
Performance records and registration
Bull-proving groups: should you join one? C. S. Machan. il Farm J 101:Dairy 12+ S '77
Bulls are better than ever. W. Kester. il Farm J 101:Beef 8-9 F '77
More choice with less grain. W. Kester. il Farm J 101:Beef 8-10 Ja '77
Transportation
Bull; attempting to load bull on airplane at Kennedy Airport, New York. New Yorker 53:26-7 Mr 7 '77
Bull; Gallagher's Pioneer's arrival in Paris. New Yorker 53:30-2 Ap 25 '77

BULLY Hill Vineyards (firm) See Wine industry

BULOVA Watch Company
C.P. Wong makes Bulova tick again. W. Guzzardi, Jr. il por Fortune 95:154-7+ Ap '77
Wong ends his stay at Bulova. il por Bus W p40 N 28 '77

BULRUSHES
Bulrushes thrive on PCB's. BioScience 27:370 My '77

BULYCHEV, Kirill
Talk with Kirill Bulychev, first Russian SF writer to visit U.S; interview, ed by M. Reuter. Pub W 211:34 My 16 '77

BUMBLEBEES. See Bees

BUMP, Robert L.
How to select electrostatic precipitators. il Am City & County 92:76-7 My '77

BUMPER crops. See Crop yields

BUMPER stickers. See Labels

BUMS. See Tramps

BUNAU-VARILLA, Philippe Jean
How the big ditch was dug. il por Time 110:14+ Ag 22 '77 *

BUNCH, Charlotte
Two feminists tell how they work; interview, ed by G. Steinem. pors Ms 6:53+ Jl '77

BUNCH of Grapes (bookstore) See Booksellers and bookselling—Massachusetts

BUNDESBANK. See Banks and banking—Germany, West

BUNDT cake pans. See Kitchen utensils and appliances

BUNDY, McGeorge
Issue before the court: who gets ahead in America? Atlantic 240:41-50+ N '77
about
Incomplete candor. K. L. Woodward. pors Newsweek 90:77 Jl 25 '77 *

BUNDY, William P.
Elements of power. bibl f For Affairs 56:1-26 O '77

BUNGE, Charles Albert
Current reference books. See issues of Wilson library bulletin

BUNKE, Robert W.
Industry's greatest energy / shortage; address, June 6, 1977. Vital Speeches 43:637-40 Ag 1 '77
Learning a lesson from David; address, February 17, 1977. Vital Speeches 43:376-9 Ap 1 '77

BUNKER, Edith (television character) See Women in television

BUNKER, Edward
Let's end the dope war. Nation 224:785-8 Je 25 '77

BUNKER, Ellsworth
Administration officials testify on the Panama Canal treaties; statement, September 8, 1977. Dept State Bull 77:535-7 O 17 '77
New Panama Canal treaties: a negotiator's view. Dept State Bull 77:506-9 O 17 '77
U.S. negotiators brief press on new Panama Canal treaties; transcript of briefing, August 12, 1977. State Dept Bull 77:526-32 O 17 '77
about
Ceding the Canal—slowly. il pors Time 110:8-13 Ag 22 '77 *

BUNKER-Ramo Corporation
Master tinkerer at Bunker Ramo; G. S. Trimble. il por Bus W p 121-2 Ag 15 '77

BUNNELL, Peter C.
Why photography now? New Repub 177:25-7 O 29 '77

BUNTER (television character) See Characters in television

BUNTING, Roger K.
Element number 61. por Chemistry 50:16-18 Je '77

BUNTZEN, Lynda, and Craig, Carla
Hour of the wolf: the case of Ingmar B. bibl f il por Film Q 30:23-34 Wint '76

BUÑUEL, Luis
Profiles. P. Gilliatt. New Yorker 53:53-4+ D 5 '77 *

BUNZEL, John H.
Bakke vs. University of California. Commentary 63:59-64 Mr; 64:11-12 Jl '77

BURCHENAL, Joan Riley. See Burchenal, J. H. jt auth

BURCHENAL, Joseph Holland, and Burchenal, J. R.
Chemotherapy of cancer. bibl il pors Chemistry 50:11-17 Jl '77

BURCHETT, Wilfred Graham
Tokyo Rose in New York. P. Gigot. Nat R 29:1488 D 23 '77 *

BURCK, Charles G.
Place for your boardinghouse reach. il Fortune 95:191-2 F '77
Plastics take the pole in the light-car race. il Fortune 96:114-15+ Jl '77
Surprising changes in American drinking habits. Read Digest 110:163-4+ F '77
Tempest in the sugar pot. il Fortune 95:106-14+ F '77
Whiskey distillers put up their dukes. il Fortune 96:154-8+ S '77
Why the sports business ain't what it used to be. il Fortune 95:294-9+ My '77

BURDEN, Ione
Giving it back to their employer. D. Kirkpatrick. il Ret Liv 17:48-9 N '77 *

BURDEN, Jean
Insomnia; poem. Am Scholar 46:458-9 Aut '77

BURDEN, Steele
Giving it back to their employer. D. Kirkpatrick. il Ret Liv 17:48-9 N '77 *

BURDINES Department Stores. See Federated Department Stores, Inc.

BURDITT, Joyce Rebeta-. See Rebeta-Burditt, J.

BUREAU of Labor Statistics. See United States—Labor Statistics, Bureau of

BUREAU of Land Management. See United States—Land Management, Bureau of

BUREAU of Outdoor Recreation. See United States—Outdoor Recreation, Bureau of

BUREAU of prisons. See United States—Prisons, Bureau of

BUREAUCRACY
Big government; address, June 28, 1977. J. N. Sites. Vital Speeches 43:711-14 S 15 '77
Big government or big brother? J. A. Schnepper. Intellect 105:376 My '77
Bureaucrat's new clothes: a cautionary tale. E. F. Torrey. Psychol Today 11:95 Jl '77
Carter vs the bureaucrats: the interest vested in chaos. R. Jones and P. Woll. Nation 224:402-4 Ap 2 '77
Down among the bureaucrats. N. B. Freeman. Nat R 29:1229 O 28 '77
Fixing up the government (again) S. J. Ungar. Atlantic 240:16+ D '77
Gammon's black holes. M. Friedman. por Newsweek 90:84 N 7 '77
Government bureaucracy: too snarled to untangle? reorganization plans of J. Carter. il Sr Schol 109:6-8+ My 19 '77
Inside look at our runaway bureaucracy; with interview with A. Campbell. J. S. Lang. il U.S. News 83:22-4+ O 3 '77
Need to act. T. Bethell. il Harpers 255:34-6+ N '77
People's sense of powerlessness; excerpts from address. J. L. Buckley. por Intellect 106:95 S '77
President Carter versus Parkinson's law. W. J. Miller. Read Digest 110:59-60 Ap '77
Rage over rising regulation. il Time 111:48+ Ja 2 '78
Requiem for a bureaucrat. J. L. McLucas. Aviation W 106:23 Ap 25 '77
What happened to Carter's pledge to slash red tape? il U.S. News 82:47-9 Je 20 '77
When workers blow whistle on federal waste, fraud. il U.S. News 83:55 D 19 '77
See also
United States—Commission on Federal Paperwork

BUREAUCRACY—*Continued*

Anecdotes, facetiae, satire, etc.

Get rid of the people, and the system runs fine. P. Ryan. Smithsonian 8:140 S '77

BUREAUCRACY, Church. See Church government

BUREAUCRATS. See Public officers

BURG, Dale
Jump your way to health. il Am Home 80:24-5+ Ag '77

BURGEN, Michele
Drastic methods to lose weight. il Ebony 32:124-6+ O '77
How to trace your family tree. il Ebony 32:52-4+ Je '77
Kidney transplant center. il Ebony 32:59-62+ Ap '77
Problems of women bosses. il Ebony 33:94+ N '77
Should whites adopt black children? il Ebony 33:63-4+ D '77
They are owners, bosses, workers. il Ebony 32:122-4+ Ag '77

BURGER, John. See Watkins, E. jt auth

BURGER, Max M. See Meyer, D. I. jt auth

BURGER, Warren Earl
How to break logjam in courts; interview. il pors U.S. News 83:21-4+ D 19 '77

about

Burger vs. Warren: whose Court is better? pors U.S. News 82:58 Mr 7 '77 *
Inside the Burger Court. J. K. Footlick and L. Howard. il pors Newsweek 89:101-2 Je 13 '77 *
Peculiar sense of justice. N. Lewin. por Sat R 4:15-16+ My 28 '77 *

BURGESS, Anthony, pseud
All about Yves. il pors N Y Times Mag p 118-21+ S 11 '77
Homage to Barcelona. il N Y Times Mag p44-5+ D 4 '77
Le mal français: is there a reason for being Cartesian? il N Y Times Mag p46-8+ My 29 '77
Lion's roar. il por Lib J 102:327-9 F 1 '77
Plastic punks. il Psychol Today 11:120+ N '77
Shrivel of critics. Harpers 254:87+ F '77
$200 million erector set. il N Y Times Mag p 14-15+ Ja 23 '77

BURGESS, Robert F.
Guns of Atocha. il Oceans 10:26-9 S '77
Submerged forests. il Oceans 10:46-9 S '77

BURGHARDT, Gordon M. and others
Social behavior in hatchling green iguanas: life at a reptile rookery. bibl il Science 195:689-91 F 18 '77

BURGLAR alarms
Burglar alarms. il Consumer Rep 42:71-7 F '77

BURGLARY and burglars
I catch a burglar; Career Criminal Program. J. Berendt. il Read Digest 110:109-13 F '77
What should you do if you're burgled. J. Wandres. il Ret Liv 17:28-30+ Ap '77
See also
Art thefts

BURGLARY protection
Burglar and fire protection. il Consumers Res Mag 60:156-8 O '77
Home, safe home. Redbook 149:212 S '77; Same. Ladies Home J 94:156+ S '77
How to protect yourself. J. Wilson. Harp Baz 110:93+ Mr '77
Senior home security program aids St Louis elderly. il Aging 266:5 D '76

BURGNER, Jack W.
Printing and evaluation. il Sch Arts 76:36-8+ Je '77

BURGOYNE, John
Decision on the Hudson. A. C. Smith. il por Conservationist 32:23-5 S '77 *
Weather of Independence: Burgoyne's northern campaign (cont) D. M. Ludlum. bibl il maps Weatherwise 29:288-90 D '76 *

BURGOYNE'S invasion, 1777. See Saratoga Campaign, 1777

BURGUNDY, France
Heart of the Burgundy country. il map Sunset 158:42 Mr '77

BURIAL
See also
Catacombs
Funeral rites and ceremonies
Mummies
Undertakers and undertaking

BURIAL grounds. See Cemeteries

BURIAL mounds. See Mounds and mound builders

BURIAL rites. See Funeral rites and ceremonies

BURIED treasure. See Treasure trove

BURITSCH, Linda Anne
Linda's haunting vision. C. Bakal. il por Read Digest 110:68-72 Mr '77 *

BURKE, Derek C.
Status of interferon; with biographical sketch. il Sci Am 236:20, 42-50 bibl(p 148) Ap '77

BURKE, Jackson and Mary, collection. See Art—Private collections

BURKE, Louis
Cremation of Sam McGee and The shooting of Dan McGrew; R. Service's ballads. Engl J 66:69-70 Mr '77

BURKE, Louise
Louise Burke. A. M. Hays. il pors Yachting 142:74-5 Jl '77 *

BURKE, Mary
Women's agenda at Houston. America 137:325-7 N 12 '77

BURKE, Michael
Troubled world of Mike Burke. S. Zion. il pors N Y Times Mag p30-2+ O 9 '77 *

BURKE, Yvonne Brathwaite
Congressional Black Caucus. ed by J. M. Elliot. il pors Negro Hist Bull 40:650-2 Ja '77
Let's play taps for an all male Army! il Sat Eve Post 249:12-13+ O '77

BURKE Mountain Academy. See Skis and skiing—Study and teaching

BURKERT, Nancy Ekholm
Nancy Burkert art featured in two new editions. P. Doebler. il Pub W 212:99-100 Ag 1 '77 *

BURKHALTER, Pamela K.
Quackery. Sci Digest 82:36-7+ S '77

BURKHART, C. J.
Scottsdale, Arizona. il Trav/Holiday 148:58-63+ D '77

BURKHOLZ, Dan
Russian Christianity: conflict and hope. il Chr Cent 94:627-9 Jl 6 '77

BURLEIGH County, N.D.
Coffee shop fertile ground for Dakota meals site. il Aging 274:10-11 Ag '77

BURLEIGH Hill Camp. See Camps—Maine

BURLESQUE

Photographs

Up from the old grind; strippers. Esquire 87:53-7 F '77

BURLINGAME, Carl
Directory of timeshare resorts. Holiday 58:16+ S '77

BURLINGHAM, Bo
Politics under the palms. il pors Esquire 87:47-52+ F '77

BURLINGTON Northern Inc.-St Louis-San Francisco Railway Company merger. See Railroads—Acquisitions and mergers

BURMA

Politics and government

On Burma's heritage. Tran-van-Dinh. Progressive 41:22-3 Mr '77

BURN care units
Burn centers: the new miracle workers; care of G. Schrufer at Crozer-Chester Burn Center. G. Williams, 3d. il Fam Health 9:48-52 Jl '77
Heroic measures—giving the patient a choice; work at Los Angeles County-University of Southern California Medical Center. J. Gaylin. Psychol Today 11:149+ D '77
Medical mailbox: burn care centers and first aid. C. SerVaas. Sat Eve Post 249:106-7 S '77

BURN centers. See Burn care units

BURNERS
Bendel burner. D. Bendel. il Ceram Mo 25:48-9 S '77

BURNERS, Gas. See Gas burners

BURNERS, Oil. See Oil burners

BURNETT, Carol
Carol Burnett & Dick Van Dyke: what alcoholism did to their lives. L. Fosburgh. pors Ladies Home J 94:34+ S '77 *

BURNHAM, James
Protracted conflict. See issues of National review

BURNHAM, Malin
Balance for Lowell. J. Rousmaniere. il pors Yachting 141:69 F '77 *

BURNHAM, Margaret Ann
Justice with a different face. H. J. Scarupa. por Ms 6:19 D '77 *

BURNHAM, Robin
What's new. il Motor B & S 139:48-51 Je; 140:38-9+ Jl; 36-9 Ag; 46-7 S '77

BURNHAM, Sophy
Congresswoman who cares. por McCalls 104:36+ Je '77

BURNING mirrors
Burning question; firing of Roman fleet by burning mirror in Second Punic War. Sci Am 236:64 Je '77

BURNS, Arthur Frank
When Arthur Burns speaks out—. U.S. News 82:45 My 2 '77

about

Adroit switch at money central. il pors Time 111:28-9 Ja 9 '78 *
Arthur Burns: born again at 73. il pors Time 109:53-4+ Je 6 '77 *
Arthur Burns: how good a job? G. R. Rosen. il por Duns R 110:68-71+ D '77 *
Behind tightening bind on federal money managers. R. A. Rossi. U.S. News 83:97 N 28 '77 *

BURNS, Arthur Frank—about—*Continued*
Bill Miller at the Fed—what it adds up to. il pors U.S. News 84:49-50 Ja 9 '78 *
Burns: a tough act to follow. Time 111:33 Ja 9 '78 *
Burns-Carter not-quite fight. por Time 110:108+ N 7 '77 *
Burns on the outside. M. Friedman. por Newsweek 91:52-3 Ja 9 '78 *
Carter gets the message. il Forbes 120:119 D 1 '77 *
Carter, the Fed and confidence. L. C. Thurow. Nation 225:166-8 S 3 '77 *
Fed's sudden tightening: has Burns gone too far? S. H. Wildstrom. por Bus W p43 N 14 '77 *
Fed's view of the economy. S. H. Wildstrom. Bus W p29 Je 6 '77 *
Fire under Burns. M. Ruby and others. il por Newsweek 90:91-2 O 24 '77 *
Here comes the tax cut. il por Time 110:13-14 D 12 '77 *
Importance of being Arthur. H. Sidey. por Time 110:13 D 26 '77 *
King Arthur. E. Marshall. New Repub 177:8-9 D 3 '77 *
Reappoint Burns? P. A. Samuelson. il Newsweek 90:81 N 21 '77 *
Sticking with Burns. Nat R 29:817 Jl 22 '77 *

BURNS, Barbara
Why I decided to go underground. McCalls 104:69+ S '77

BURNS, E. Bradford
Panama: a search for independence. bibl f Cur Hist 72:65-7+ F '77

BURNS, George
Living it up; excerpt. il pors Sat Eve Post 249:14-15 Mr '77

BURNS, Kathryn A. See Krebs, C. T. jt auth

BURNS, Lawrence S.
Noise. il Horizon 20:66-9 S '77

BURNS, Lois. See Burns, S. jt auth

BURNS, Rex
Elements of the police procedural novel. Writer 90:14-17 Jl '77

BURNS, Richard K.
Music LA convention. Lib J 102:870-1 Ap 15 '77

BURNS, Shannon, and Burns, Lois
Ethnic and regional literature: making connections with composition. il Engl J 66:34-6 Mr '77

BURNS and scalds
Convict and the boy; leather brace made for burn victim Kearey Allison by M. Leach. J. P. Blank and M. J. Mueller. il Read Digest 110:135-9 My '77
Medical mailbox; burn care centers and first aid. C. SerVaas. il Sat Eve Post 249:106-7 S '77
Sickest patients you'll see. il Time 109:61-2 Ja 24 '77
See also
Burn care units

BURR, Alex F.
Build this $1 logic probe. il Radio-Electr 48:40-1 Ag '77

BURR, Gray
John P. Bickerly; poem. New Yorker 53:116 Je 20 '77

BURR, James
Highs and lows. por Forbes 120:104 O 1 '77 *

BURR, Robert L.
Certification and competence. Lib J 102:1728-9 S 1 '77

BURRELL, David
Vatican declaration; another view. America 136:289-92; 137:77-8 Ap 2, Ag 13 '77

BURRIS, Carol. See Cornblath-Moshe, N. jt auth

BURROS, Marian
Three restaurants to try in Stowe. House & Gard 149:76+ D '77
(ed) See Carter, R. S. Good Plains cooking from Rosalynn Carter

BURROS
Burro or the bighorn? R. B. Taylor. il Nat Parks & Con Mag 51:10-14 S '77
Hide-and-seek in New Mexico; attempts to capture wild burros at Bandelier National Monument. R. Cantwell. Sports Illus 47:48-9 Ag 1 '77

BURROUGHS, Jeff
Reborn in a Brave new world. il por Sports Illus 46:50+ My 9 '77 *

BURROUGHS, John, 1837-1921
In nature's laboratory. P. W. Metzler. il pors Conservationist 32:30-3+ Jl '77 *

BURROUGHS, Robert
On teaching poetry. il Engl J 66:48-51 F '77

BURROUGHS Corporation
How Ray Macdonald's growth theory created I.B.M.'s toughest competitor. B. Uttal. il pors Fortune 95:94-9+ Ja '77

BURROWAY, Janet
Does genius have a gender? pors Ms 6:57+ D '77

BURROWS, Fredrika A.
Marbles—another fun hobby. Hobbies 82:117 Ap '77

BURROWS, Stephen
Burrows is back—with a little help from his friends. J. Butler. il por N Y Times Mag p72-3+ Je 5 '77 *

BURSTYN, Ellen
Conspirator in Berlin. P. Bogdanovich. Esquire 88:96+ D '77 *

BURT, C. Tyler, and others
Analysis of living tissue by phosphorous-31 magnetic resonance. bibl il Science 195:145-9 Ja 14 '77

BURT, Sir Cyril Lodowic
Burt report: fraud? Society 14:4+ My '77 *
Classic experiment—mistake or deliberate fraud? J. Gaylin. Psychol Today 10:33+ F '77 *
Did Sir Cyril Burt fake his research on heritability of intelligence? O. Gillie; A. R. Jensen. Educ Digest 42:43-5 Mr '77 *
IQ and heredity: suspicion of fraud beclouds classic experiment. N. Wade; discussion. il Science 195:246-8 Ja 21 '77 *

BURT, David R. and others
Antischizophrenic drugs: chronic treatment elevates dopamine receptor binding in brain. bibl il Science 196:326-8 Ap 15 '77

BURTON, Helene
To spank or not to spank? il Parents Mag 52:42-3+ Ag '77

BURTON, John F. Jr
Will workers' compensation standards be mandated by federal legislation? bibl M Labor R 100:55-7 Ap '77

BURTON, LeVar
LeVar Burton's rise to fame. L. Robinson. il pors Ebony 32:146-8+ O '77 *

BURTON, Paul
Broker profile; interview. por Motor B & S 141:237 Ja '78

BURTON, Robert P.
Mating game: it's different if you fly; excerpt from The mating game. il Sci Digest 81:22-6+ Mr '77
about
Catastrophe model: can it see crises? P. P. Luedtke. il por Sci Digest 81:68-70 F '77 *

BURTON, Robin
Antarctica: rich around the edges; with biographical sketch. il Sea Front 23:287-95, 318 S '77
Ever larger propellers; with biographical sketch. il Sea Front 23:144-51, 190 My '77
Suez transformed. il Oceans 10:28-33 Ja '77

BURY, John B.
J. B. Bury's philosophy of history: a reappraisal. D. S. Goldstein. bibl f por Am Hist R 82:896-919 O '77 *

BUS industry
Field shrinks in advanced bus market. il Am City & County 92:13+ Ag '77
GMC puts new bus on the road; price offset controversy. Am City & County 92:19 N '77
U.S. bus builders slow to crawl. il Bus W p32-3 F 7 '77

Federal aid

Drive to subsidize intercity buses. il Bus W p62+ O 3 '77

BUS models
Busman's holiday bus. S. Manning. il Mech Illus 73:140 Mr '77

BUS systems (computers) See Computers—Equipment

BUS travel
Bargain bus fares. Bet Hom & Gard 55:274 My '77
Going by bus. M. J. Adams. Seventeen 36:124 Jl '77
Traveling by bus. K. Jonah. il Ret Liv 17:33-6 O '77

Anecdotes, facetiae, satire, etc.

Hop on a bus, Gus: American package tours through Europe. D. Shaw. il Holiday 58:28-31 Ja '77

BUSBEE, George. See Press, F. jt auth

BUSBEY, Bob
Bob Busbey: long-range planning. E. Horan. il por Yachting 142:44 Ag '77 *

BUSBY, Jack Kemp
Stepping aside. il pors Forbes 119:58 F 1 '77 *

BUSCH, Caroline Leavey
Enjoy the outdoors indoors. il Harp Baz 110:138-9+ Ap '77

BUSCH, Ron
Ballantine Books at quarter century; interview, ed by T. Weyr. il por Pub W 212:44-6 D 26 '77

BUSCH Bird Sanctuary. See Bird sanctuaries—California

BUSCH Memorial Stadium, St Louis. See Stadiums

BUSE, Don
No boo-boos for Boo Boo. J. Papanek. por Sports Illus 46:54+ F 7 '77 *

BUSES
Auto option; bus vs. auto transportation for urban travel. B. Rosenthal. bibl il Environment 19:18-24 Je '77
Buses: no back seat transit mode. il Am City & County 92:37-8 D '77
DOT delays bus specs for more study. il Am City & County 92:22 Ap '77
Transit buses. il Am City & County 92:77-80 Je '77

Small size

Small buses get wide use also. il Am City & County 92:78-9 Je '77

BUSES, Electric
Big battery bus; Townobile in Sydney, Australia. il Mech Illus 73:34 Ag '77

BUSES, Remodeled
Outgrown your motor home? Take the bus! M. Lamm. il Pop Mech 149:70-2 Ja '78

BUSH, Doreen
Volcanes of Hawaii. il Nat Parks & Con Mag 51:10-12 Mr '77

BUSH, Geoffrey
Problem of Li T'ang; story. Atlantic 240:76-82 Ag '77

BUSH, George (editor)
Great springtime vacations along the Gulf of Mexico. il Bet Hom & Gard 55:173-4+ F '77
Vacation discoveries in Canada's national parks. il Bet Hom & Gard 55:212+ My '77
Vacation discoveries in the Florida Keys. il Bet Hom & Gard 55:173-4+ D '77

BUSH, George Herbert Walker
Inside the new Tibet. Newsweek 90:62+ N 7 '77
Where China is headed; interview. il pors U.S. News 83:33-4 N 14 '77

BUSH, Monroe
Reading about resources. See issues of American forests

BUSH, Sherida
Family-help program that really works. il Psychol Today 10:48+ My '77
—See Goleman, D. jt auth

BUSH Negroes. See Blacks in Surinam

BUSHMAN, John H.
Achieving student interaction in creative junior high/middle school programs. il Engl J 66:67-72 Ap '77

BUSHMEN
Life before horticulture; the !Kung San. M. Shostak. il Horticulture 55:38-57 F '77

BUSHMILLS Grand Prix. See Motor boat racing

BUSHNELL, David
Battle of the Kegs. D. H. Cross. il Am Hist Illus 12:40-1 Ap '77 *

BUSHNELL, Philip J. and others
Scotopic vision deficits in young monkeys exposed to lead. bibl il Science 196:333-5 Ap 15 '77

BUSHNELL, Richards. See Navarro, N. jt auth

BUSINESS
See also
Advertising
Capitalism
Christmas business
Competition
Corporations
Entrepreneurs
Financial statements
Free enterprise
Ideas in business
Location in business and industry
Mail order business
Real estate business
Retail trade
Sex in business
Small business
Stock exchanges

Bibliography

Bookshelf (cont) Duns R 109:114+ Je '77
Business books of 1976; comp by S. DiMattia. il Lib J 102:554-9 Mr 1 '77
For the manager's bookshelf. See issues of Harvard business review
Scientific, technical, business and professional books. il Pub W 211:40-4+ Mr 21; 212:27-30+ O 17 '77
Scientific, technical, medical, & business books (cont) Lib J 102:578+, 2227-8+ Mr 1, N 1 '77

History

Bibliography

Business sits for its portrait. R. W. Lovett. Harvard Bus R 55:160+ Jl '77

Information services

See also
Financial services

International aspects

Galbraithian guide to the economic folkways of Americans. J. K. Galbraith. por Fortune 96: 97-8+ Ag '77
International business in Latin America; address, March 1, 1977. W. B. Wolf. Vital Speeches 43:443-7 My 1 '77
See also
Corporations—Foreign business

Periodicals

Business and professional magazines for today's writers; with lists of markets. Writer 90:27-8+ F '77
Three for the money. A. J. Mayer and others. il Newsweek 90:75-6 Ag 1 '77
See also
Business week (periodical)
Dun's review (periodical)
Forbes (periodical)

Political aspects

Bid for votes on Panama. il Bus W p41 S 12 '77
Bridging the gap. M. Ruby and others. Newsweek 90:75-6 N 7 '77
Business and the new Congress—what lies ahead. map Nations Bus 65:16-20 Ja '77
Business vs. Carter: tough breach to heal. W. C. Bryant. U.S. News 83:25 N 14 '77
Business warms up to Carter. A. J. Mayer and others. il Newsweek 89:60-1 Ja 31 '77
Carter: a problem of confidence. il Time 110:68-70+ O 31 '77
Carter and the evolution of liberalism. R. J. Bresler. Intellect 106:22-3 Ag '77
Carter woos in vain. Nation 225:419-20 O 29 '77
Doing business with business. P. Steinfels. Commonweal 104:294-5 My 13 '77
Get involved with government—you can make it better. J. Eckerd. pors Nations Bus 65:61-3 Je '77
Government by what people? P. Steinfels. Commonweal 104:756+ N 25 '77
Is Congress becoming more practical? il Nations Bus 65:30-3 N '77
Keeping them guessing; J. Carter's economic policies. il por Time 110:14-17 N 14 '77
Some praise, growing worry: how business views Carter. il por U.S. News 83:61-4 S 19 '77
Toughest business battles in 1978. R. T. Gray. il Nations Bus 65:22-6+ D '77
Whistling Dixie. Nation 225:322 O 8 '77
See also
Chamber of Commerce of the United States of America
Lobbyists and lobbying

Psychological aspects

See Psychology, Industrial

Public relations

Behind the fronts: phony consumer groups; industry-backed groups. D. H. Rothman. Nation 225:239-42 S 17 '77
Blame not the socialistic college professor. . .; excerpt from address. J. I. Miller. por Forbes 120:48 Ag 1 '77
Bureaucratic Babylon; address, September 23, 1977. W. L. Wearly. Vital Speeches 44:44-9 N 1 '77
Businessman blues. P. A. Samuelson. Newsweek 90:70 Ag 8 '77
Corporations are defending themselves with the wrong weapon. P. H. Weaver. il Fortune 95: 186-7+ Je '77
Giving impact to ideas; address, October 11, 1977. L. T. Hagopian. Vital Speeches 44:154-7 D 15 '77
Growth industry: publicity for top executives. il Bus W p86+ O 24 '77
Make the most of your corporate identity. W. P. Margulies. il Harvard Bus R 55:66-74 Jl '77
Public relations goes public. A. Hershman. il Duns R 110:62-6 S '77
Public trust in business: it's increasing, but—. il U.S. News 82:26-8 Je 27 '77
Visionary and a master stylist helped shape modern PR: E. L. Bernays and B. Sonnenberg. pors Duns R 110:29-30 S '77
What have American writers got against businessmen? J. Leonard. Forbes 119:117-22+ My 15 '77
Why business finds it tough to polish its own image. U.S. News 83:64 S 19 '77
See also
Business and the press
Customer relations
Drug industry—Public relations
Electric utilities—Public relations

Records

See Business records

Reports to government

Merger notification business can live with. Bus W p40 O 17 '77
See also
Cigarette industry—Reports to government
Electric utilities—Reports to government

Security measures

See Industry—Security measures

Small business

See Small business

BUSINESS—*Continued*

Social aspects

Bureaucratic brainstorm: corporate Social Performance Index. M. Stone. U.S. News 84:76 Ja 9 '78
Business looks at health care costs; address, November 18, 1976. J. H. Perkins. Vital Speeches 43:211-15 Ja 15 '77
Corporate social responsibility; address, November 30, 1976. C. G. Eklund. Vital Speeches 43:168-70 Ja 1 '77
End of corporate enterprise? A. Y. Lewin and J. G. Wiles. il pors Duns R 110:129 O '77
Ex cathedra. por Forbes 119:148 Ap 15 '77
Financing of the corporate structure for the 1980s; address, March 25, 1977. R. Ablon. Vital Speeches 43:398-401 Ap 15 '77
Halo game; proposal for corporate social performance lists. Nation 225:516-17 N 19 '77
How to keep big government from growing bigger. R. W. Packwood. por Duns R 110:69-70 Ag '77
It's so hard to be good under capitalism. Aristides. Am Scholar 46:290+ Summ '77
Our fragile freedom; address, April 29, 1977. R. M. Brown, Jr. Vital Speeches 43:553-5 Jl 1 '77
Public responsibility committees of the board; dealing with complex and sensitive social issues. M. L. Lovdal and others. Harvard Bus R 55:40-2+ My '77
Social responsibility of people in business. R. Stuart. por Nations Bus 65:47-8 Ap '77
Thoughts about government and business; address, June 23, 1977. J. M. Kreps. Vital Speeches 43:610-12 Ag 1 '77
What black leaders want from business. il Bus W p85+ O 10 '77
See also
Aerospace industries—Social aspects
Banks and banking—Social aspects
Corporations—Charitable contributions

BUSINESS, Retirement from. See Retirement
BUSINESS airplane industry. See Airplane industry
BUSINESS airplanes. See Airplanes, Business
BUSINESS and art. See Art and industry; Art patronage
BUSINESS and education
Businesses join drive to aid youth in two ways; reading programs to raise money for multiple sclerosis research. V. Louviere. il Nations Bus 65:66 Ja '77
Company helps youngsters launch careers: Rockwell International Corp's Advanced Career Training program. V. Louviere. il Nations Bus 65:60 Je '77
How students react to government regulation; new lecture series at University of Oregon's College of Business Administration. V. Louviere. il Nations Bus 65:64 My '77
How your know-how can save private colleges. R. R. Shinn. por Nations Bus 65:64 O '77
International education: focus for corporate support. J. W. Fulbright. Harvard Bus R 55:137-41 My '77
Involvement of industry with Business and Office; address, August 11, 1977. W. P. Reilly. Vital Speeches 43:756-60 O 1 '77
Path up for women bankers; program designed by Simmons College for the National Association of Bank Women. il Bus W p 105 Je 13 '77
Research crunch. M. Grosswirth. Sci Digest 82:27-9+ N '77
Telling students the truth about business; program at Southern California Gas Co. V. Louviere. il Nations Bus 65:67+ Mr '77
See also
Education, Cooperative

BUSINESS and government. See Industry and state
BUSINESS and libraries. See Libraries—Business services
BUSINESS and politics. See Business—Political aspects
BUSINESS and professional women
Babes in the corporate woods. L. Davis. Vogue 167:105-6 My '77
Bazaar's guide to success on the job; symposium. Harp Baz 110:84-9+ Ag '77
Cooking up a living: catering, cooking schools and food shops. C. Calvert. il Mademoiselle 83:152+ D '77
Do you want $100,000? W. Flanagan. Vogue 167:144+ Jl '77
Game's played that way, lady! il pors Forbes 120:56+ Jl 15 '77
Going up! new rules for women on the job. D. R. Crouch. il Redbook 149:102-3+ Ag '77
Job power: how to get ahead fast. M. Korda. Harp Baz 111:152+ N '77
Leading businesswoman's perspective on management; interview. J. Spain. il pors Nations Bus 65:70-2+ Mr '77
Professional woman: her fields have widened. S. D. Lewis. il Ebony 32:114-16+ Ag '77
Will an MBA make you a VIP? careers of women. R. Shapiro. Harp Baz 110:49+ Je '77
See also
Secretaries
Women entrepreneurs
Women executives
Women scientists

Clothing and dress

See Clothing and dress

BUSINESS and religion
Dissidents gear up for annual meetings. J. Perham. il Duns R 109:74-5+ Ap '77
BUSINESS and society. See Business—Social aspects
BUSINESS and the arts. See The Arts and industry
BUSINESS and the environment. See Industry and the environment
BUSINESS and the Mafia. See Mafia
BUSINESS and the press
Business and the media. L. Smith. il Duns R 109:76-7+ My '77
Business and the press; address, March 14, 1977. A. O. Sulzberger. Vital Speeches 43:426-8 My 1 '77
Taking on big business; S. Hersh's series on Gulf & Western in the New York times. D. M. Alpern and others. il por Newsweek 90:81-2 Ag 8 '77
BUSINESS budget. See Budget, Business
BUSINESS Committee for the Arts
Spring forecast: business support. B. Chamberlain. Am Artist 41:15+ My '77
BUSINESS conditions
Big surge ahead in business; interview. C. L. Schultze. il pors U.S. News 82:23-4 F 28 '77
Business is edgy about the upturn. il Bus W p42-3 Ap 18 '77
Business outlook; ed by W. B. Franklin. See issues of Business week
Business picks up speed again—il U.S. News 83:78-9 O 17 '77
Business roundup. See issues of Fortune
Carter business boom shaping up? with interview with B. Lance. U.S. News 82:15-18 F 7 '77
Cities where business is best. il U.S. News 82:76-9 My 16; 83:72-5 O 24 '77
Economic diary. See issues of Business week
Economy resumes its upward thrust; what business leaders see ahead. il Nations Bus 65:32-4+ Ap '77
How to stop worrying about business and enjoy the year ahead. C. Morgello. por Duns R 110:116 N '77
Lots of life in an aging recovery. il U.S. News 83:82-3 S 26 '77
Patchwork kind of recovery. il Bus W p28-9 O 31 '77
Surge ahead for business—. il U.S. News 82:20-1 Ap 4 '77
Why stock market is going down while business is going up. il U.S. News 83:29-30 S 5 '77
See also
Business depression
Business failures
Business forecasting
Economic conditions
Inflation (finance)
Production
United States—Economic conditions
BUSINESS consolidations and mergers. See Corporations—Acquisitions and mergers
BUSINESS consultants
Ambassador for sale; R. Helms of the Safeer Company. Nation 225:580 D 3 '77
Benefits of doing your own consulting. Bus W p62+ My 16 '77
Big business in credibility; economic consulting. il Bus W p84+ Mr 7 '77
Consultants move to the executive suite. il Bus W p76+ N 7 '77
Easing the pain; out-placement consulting. il Newsweek 90:85 D 5 '77
Flourishing new business of recycling executives; out-placement or dehiring firms. H. E. Meyer. il Fortune 95:328-30+ My '77
Getting management help to the nonprofit sector; Volunteer Urban Consulting Group of New York City. R. A. Mittenthal and B. W. Mahoney. il Harvard Bus R 55:95-103 S '77
Getting your dollar's worth from consultants; advice of Association of Consulting Management Engineers. Nations Bus 65:14 D '77
How to get a good consultant. J. P. Frankenhuis. Harvard Bus R 55:133-9 N '77
New boss for a healthier PRC; Planning Research Corp. il Bus W p28 S 5 '77
Rate yourself as a client. A. Jay. il Harvard Bus R 55:84-92 Jl '77
Should CPAs be management consultants? staff study of the Senate Subcommittee on Reports, Accounting and Management. il Bus W p70+ Ap 18 '77
Ubiquitous news doctors. il Time 110:103 O 24 '77

BUSINESS consultants—*Continued*
Unless you can be a winner, don't play; Boston Consulting Group. il Forbes 120:132 O 15 '77
Upheavals at Planning Research. il Bus W p33 D 5 '77
See also
Investment advisers
Marketing consultants
Public relations consultants

BUSINESS Council for International Understanding
Courtesy calls; briefings of American ambassadors. Nation 224:709 Je 11 '77

BUSINESS crimes. See Commercial crimes

BUSINESS cycles
See also
Business depression

BUSINESS depression
Cure for depression; excerpts from interview, ed by J. de Borchgrave. J. Javits. por Newsweek 90:71 S 26 '77

History

Prelude to the Federal Reserve: the currency panic of 1907. il Duns R 110:21 D '77

BUSINESS depression, 1929-1939
What about the Okies? California migrations. G. Haslam. il Am Hist Illus 12:28-39 Ap '77

BUSINESS directories. See Directories

BUSINESS districts
Architecture; question of downtown renovations. J. H. Kay. Nation 225:635-6 D 10 '77
Business prospects in the inner city. R. N. Farmer. Intellect 105:263-4 F '77
Don't let industry move away. D. J. Springate. il por Am City & County 92:68-9 Ap '77
Midwest gets Main Street Projects. il Am City & County 92:22-3 N '77
Munich; pedestrian malls. W. Von Eckardt. il New Repub 177:25-6 D 17 '77
Pedestrian malls not cure for downtown ills; excerpt from address, September 1976. J. P. Butler, Jr. Am City & County 92:6) Ja '77
New kind of development; four U.S. projects of Mondev International. J. M. Davern. il Archit Rec 162:96-107 D '77
Waiting for the future; Texas Eastern's Houston Center. E. Bailey. il Forbes 120:50+ S 1 '77
See also
Shopping centers

BUSINESS education
Washington notebook; views of D. S. MacNaughton. S. Booker. Ebony 33:25 D '77
See also
Business schools and colleges
Executives—Education

BUSINESS English. See English language—Business English

BUSINESS enterprises
Big bankroll for new business; venture capital. T. J. Murray. il Duns R 109:52-4+ F '77
New companies that beat the odds. G. Bylinsky. il Fortune 96:76-80+ D '77
See also
Minority business enterprises

BUSINESS entertaining
Executive throws a party. il Bus W p87-90+ My 30 '77
Let's have lunch! F. A. Birmingham. Holiday 58:31+ Je '77

Anecdotes, facetiae, satire, etc.

Lunch of champions. R. Baker. il N Y Times Mag p 14 My 1 '77

BUSINESS entertaining deductions. See Income tax—Deductions

BUSINESS ethics
American business bribery shakes the world—can Americans remake it? R. H. Heindel. Intellect 105:312-13 Ap '77
Big rip-off in purchasing. R. Levy. il Duns R 109:76-7+ Mr '77
Bouquet for business. il U.S. News 82:27 Je 27 '77
Businessman and the government: corruption, yesterday and today. J. Brooks. il Am Heritage 28:66-73 Je '77
Developing codes of conduct for multinational enterprises; statement, September 7, 1977. P. H. Boeker. Dept State Bull 77:475-9 O 10 '77
Dissidents gear up for annual meetings. J. Perham. il Duns R 109:74-5+ Ap '77
Emersons: dubious payments American-style. A. Hershman. il por Duns R 109:73-5 Mr '77
Ethics: another kind of oil shortage; individual responsibility; address, January 29, 1977. G. J. Gore. Vital Speeches 43:292-4 Mr 1 '77
High tide for bank reform. M. Ruby and others. il Newsweek 90:85-7 S 12 '77
International business and morality; address, March 25, 1977. D. F. Linowes. Vital Speeches 43:475-8 My 15 '77
Is the ethics of business changing? readers' survey. S. N. Brenner and E. A. Molander; discussion. il Harvard Bus R 55:47+ Mr '77
Multinational corporations. Dept State Bull 77: 707-8 N 14 '77
Payoff; symposium. il Sat R 4:6-12+ Jl 9 '77
Personal loans and bank ethics. il Time 110: 49-50 Ag 29 '77
Pressure to compromise personal ethics; results of studies at Pitney-Bowes and Uniroyal. il Bus W p 107 Ja 31 '77
Profits before ethics; Harvard business review survey. S. Bush. Psychol Today 11:30 Jl '77
Report warns on danger of Iran sales corruption. E. Kozicharow. Aviation W 107:22-3 D 12 '77
Stricter code of ethics; excerpt from address. C. W. Cook. Intellect 106:186 N '77
Suddenly everybody is looking at the way banks do business. U.S. News 83:51-3 S 12 '77
See also
Accounting ethics
Advertising ethics
Better Business Bureaus
Bribery
Trade secrets
United Nations—Ad Hoc Intergovernmental Working Group on the Problem of Corrupt Practices

Anecdotes, facetiae, satire, etc.

Talk with a banker. New Repub 177:2+ O 1 '77

Study and teaching

Ethics in the academy; abolishment of course taught by J. C. O'Brien at California State University, Fresno. R. Kirk. Nat R 29:726 Je 24 '77

BUSINESS executives. See Executives

BUSINESS expenses. See Expense accounts (business)

BUSINESS failures
Alchemist; I. Jones, professional liquidator. E. Dyson. por Forbes 119:34 Ja 15 '77
Death of a salesman; auctioning off the contents of all Robert Hall outlets. L. Langway and M. Reese. il Newsweek 90:64 Ag 15 '77
It's expensive to go broke; legal costs surrounding W. T. Grant bankruptcy case. H. Seneker. Forbes 119:21-2 F 1 '77
Protection from bankrupt packers. R. D. Wennblom. Farm J 100:LK4 D '76
Rancorous bout with Chapter XI; United Merchants & Manufacturers. Bus W p22-3 Ag 1 '77
Sanitas: struggling out of bankruptcy. Bus W p27-8 Ap 4 '77
Spotting hot stocks in bankruptcy court. il Bus W p 103-4 N 21 '77
$3-billion cram-down? L. Minard. il Forbes 119:74+ Ap 15 '77
Why Apeco preferred filing for bankruptcy. Bus W p25-6 N 7 '77

BUSINESS flying. See Airplanes in business

BUSINESS forecasting
Business: a look ahead. G. Heiman. See issues of Nation's business
Business: can we avoid recession? il U.S. News 83:24-6+ D 26 '77
Business outlook now: what Carter is told. il U.S. News 82:29 My 23 '77
Does future look bright for business? It does indeed; interview. J. M. Kreps. pors U.S. News 83:17-19 Ag 1 '77
Even better times coming: as top business economists see it. il U.S. News 82:69-70 Ap 18 '77
Five-year forecast: is there growth after recovery? construction industry. G. A. Christie. il Archit Rec 161:65-6 My '77
How the bellwether industries face 1978; special section. il Bus W p36-40+ Ja 9 '78
Little less push from profits. il Bus W p91-8+ D 26 '77
Long lush summer. A. J. Mayer and others. il Newsweek 89:72-3 Je 20 '77
Managing for an uncertain future; Union Carbide in 1996; address, November 19, 1976. W. S. Sneath. Vital Speeches 43:196-9 Ja 15 '77
Now a search for ways to keep business perking; economists' opinions on five key concerns. il U.S. News 83:23-5 O 24 '77
Outlook for business in '78; latest size-up by experts. U.S. News 83:62 D 19 '77
Outlook now (title varies) il Nations Bus 65: 54-6+ Ja; 32-4+ Ap; 24-6+ Jl; 24-6+ O '77
Trend of American business. See issues of U.S. news and world report
What shifts in population will mean for industry. il map U.S. News 82:60-2 My 30 '77
When experts look to '78—a good year for investors. il U.S. News 83:66-8 D 12 '77
Why inflation worries economists more. S. Zucker. Bus W p28 Ap 25 '77
Why Wall Street is skittish. il Bus W p30-1 My 9 '77

BUSINESS hours
See also
Hours of labor

BUSINESS in fiction. See Business in literature

BUSINESS in literature
Great turn-on. por Forbes 120:92 Jl 1 '77
What have American writers got against businessmen? J. Leonard. il Forbes 119:117-22+ My 15 '77

BUSINESS in motion pictures. See Motion pictures—Plots, themes, etc.
BUSINESS in the Arts Awards
1976 Business in the Arts Awards. il Forbes 120: 94-5 Jl 1 '77
Where art and business meet. il Forbes 119:6 F 1 '77
BUSINESS insurance. See Insurance, Business
BUSINESS intelligence
Business stake in Soviet snooping; phone message interceptions. Bus W p57-8 D 12 '77
BUSINESS journalism. See Journalism, Commercial
BUSINESS Leadership, Hall of Fame for. See Halls of fame
BUSINESS liquidation. See Liquidation
BUSINESS literature
See also
Business—Bibliography
BUSINESS lobby. See Lobbyists and lobbying
BUSINESS lunch deductions. See Income tax—Deductions
BUSINESS machine industry. See Office equipment industry
BUSINESS machines. See Office equipment and supplies
BUSINESS management
Billy Carter: frustrations of the small businessman; interview. B. Carter. il pors Nations Bus 65:28-32+ My '77
Chop the chitchat—save time and money. C. H. Ford. il Nations Bus 65:35-6+ S '77
Emerging solution to corporate governance. R. M. Estes. bibl f Harvard Bus R 55:20-3+ N '77
Executive trends. J. Costello. See issues of Nation's business to December 1977
Film director's approach to managing creativity; A. Penn's Night moves. E. Morley and A. Silver. il por Harvard Bus R 55:59-70 Mr '77
Five best-managed companies. il Duns R 110: 47-52+ D '77
Forbes yardsticks: 1977. il Forbes 121:38-42+ Ja 9 '78
How to stop the buck short of the top; matrix management. il Bus W p82-3 Ja 16 '78
Ideas for action. See issues of Harvard business review
It's a matter of style. T. J. Murray. il Duns R 110:64-6 D '77
Leading businesswoman's perspective on management; interview. J. Spain. il pors Nations Bus 65:70-2+ Mr '77
Learning a lesson from David; address, February 17, 1977. R. W. Bunke. Vital Speeches 43: 376-9 Ap 1 '77
Lessons of leadership. See issues of Nation's business
Managing against expropriation. D. G. Bradley. il map Harvard Bus R 55:75-83 Jl '77
Meeting the greater competition of tomorrow. J. W. Hanley. pors Nations Bus 65:37-40 Mr '77
Power, dependence, and effective management. J. P. Kotter. bibl f Harvard Bus R 55:125-36 Jl '77; Discussion. 55:74 S '77
Thriving in a recession; medium-sized industrials. D. K. Clifford, Jr. il Harvard Bus R 55:57-65 Jl '77
See also
Amusement parks—Management
Art galleries and museums—Management
Bank management
Budget, Business
Business planning
Business records
Communication in management
Computers—Business use
Construction industry—Management
Diversification in industry
Efficiency, Industrial
Executives
Executives—Training
Factory management
Inventories
Location in business and industry
Marketing
Personnel management
Restaurant management
Service industries—Management
Specialty stores—Management

Bibliography

Small business development and management. A. A. Jackson. Harvard Bus R 55:182+ S '77

Case studies

Problems in review. Harvard Bus R 55:20-2+ My '77

Study and teaching

See Business education

Japan

Japanese managers tell how their system works; panel discussion, ed by W. Bowen. il Fortune 96:126-32+ N '77
Japan's ways thrive in the U.S. il Bus W p 156+ D 12 '77
Profit in breaking Japanese traditions; management techniques of U.S. subsidiaries. il Bus W p51-2 F 14 '77
BUSINESS organization. See Business management
BUSINESS patronage of the arts. See Art patronage
BUSINESS planning
Anticipate your long-term foreign exchange risks. H. Hagemann. il Harvard Bus R 55:81-8 Mr '77
Contemporary corporate strategy: a study in change theory. T. W. Zimmerer and P. Preston. bibl Intellect 105:418-19 Je '77
Coupling strategy to operating plans. J. M. Hobbs and D. F. Heany. Harvard Bus R 55: 119-26 My '77
Logistics—essential to strategy. J. L. Heskett. il Harvard Bus R 55:85-96 N '77
Shirt-sleeve approach to long-range plans. R. E. Linneman and J. D. Kennell. bibl f il Harvard Bus R 55:141-50 Mr '77
BUSINESS records
Paper chase; piecing together the business records of T. Park. D. A. Williams and N. Horrock. Newsweek 89:33-4 Je 6 '77
BUSINESS relocation. See Location in business and industry
BUSINESS report writing. See Report writing
BUSINESS risks. See Risk
BUSINESS Roundtable (organization) See Lobbyists and lobbying
BUSINESS schools and colleges
Alaskan original; school operated by B. Smith. S. Auerbach. pors Am Home 80:41-2 S '77
B-school buzzword: creativity. por Bus W p66 Ag 8 '77
Involvement of industry with Business and Office; address, August 11, 1977. W. P. Reilly. Vital Speeches 43:756-60 O 1 '77
Is business school for you. S. Horwitz. Seventeen 36:36 Ap '77
Mystery of the business graduate who can't write; teaching specialized writing courses. il Nations Bus 65:60-2 F '77
Tourney of young tycoons; MBA tournament involving business problem solving. P. Witteman. il Time 109:63 Ja 31 '77
See also
Stanford University, Palo Alto, Calif.—Graduate School of Business

Faculty

See College teachers

Graduates

In hotter pursuit of MBAs. il Bus W p98 F 7 '77
My son, the MBA. il Forbes 119:41-4 Mr 1 '77
New crop of M.B.A.'s goes looking for that fast track. R. Lamb. Fortune 95:160+ Je '77
Will an MBA make you a VIP? careers of women. R. Shapiro. Harp Baz 110:49+ Je '77
BUSINESS secrets. See Trade secrets
BUSINESS security measures. See Industry—Security measures
BUSINESS statistics
Figures of the week. See issues of Business week
BUSINESS success. See Success
BUSINESS travel
Corporate travel revives Cook's. il Bus W p 116+ O 3 '77
How to make that trip abroad more exciting. P. J. Gross. Harvard Bus R 55:14 Mr '77
BUSINESS trips. See Business travel.
BUSINESS week (periodical)
Publisher's memo; a special issue on the investment outlook. R. B. Alexander. il Bus W p 13 D 26 '77
BUSINESS writing. See Authorship
BUSINESSMEN
Businessman blues. P. A. Samuelson. Newsweek 90:70 Ag 8 '77
Businessmen in the news. See issues of Fortune
Faces behind the figures. See issues of Forbes
Galbraithian guide to the economic folkways of Americans. J. K. Galbraith. por Fortune 96: 97-8+ Ag '77
Great businessmen. R. J. Flaherty. il Forbes 120:P14-20+ S 15 '77
Indispensable people. E. Faltermayer. il pors Fortune 96:192-5+ N '77
Money men. See issues of Forbes
People in business. V. Louviere. il Nations Bus 65:64 My; 59 Je; 36-7 Jl; 57-8 Ag; 75 S '77
People in business. P. Schwab. il Nations Bus 65:100 N; 91-2 D '77
They blew it. il Forbes 120:P69-76+ S 15 '77
See also
Entrepreneurs

Clothing and dress

See Clothing and dress—Men

BUSINESSMEN (American) in foreign countries. See Americans in foreign countries
BUSINESSMEN as government consultants. See Government consultants
BUSINESSWOMEN. See Business and professional women
BUSING and integration. See School children—Transportation for integration
BUSING of school children. See School children—Transportation for integration
BUSSEY, Dexter
Detroit's new models. pors Sports Illus 47:91-2+ O 17 '77 *
BUST developers. See Exercising equipment
BUSTANOBY, Andre
How to cope with discouragement. Chr Today 21:28+ Ja 7 '77
Why pastors drop out. Chr Today 21:14-16 Ja 7 '77
BUTCHER block tables. See Tables
BUTCHERS
Tips from the butchers in an old family meat market; Gepperth's Market. il Bet Hom & Gard 55:84-5 O '77
Twice the money for your hogs. D. K. O'Brien. il Farm J 101:Hog 8-10 Je '77
BUTCHKES, Sydney
Balth and the beasts. il pors Craft Horiz 37:28-31 Ag '77
BUTLAR, Stefan Congrat-. See Congrat-Butlar, S.
BUTLER, Ann
Secretary's manifesto. McCalls 105:34+ Ja '78
BUTLER, Broadus Nathaniel
Unforgettable Clarence Mathews. il Read Digest 111:139-42 D '77
BUTLER, Dorothy
Children's bookshop in New Zealand. il Horn Bk 53:128-33 Ap '77
BUTLER, Francis J.
Medicaid fraud: a bitter pill for the Nation's poor. America 136:414-15 My 7 '77
BUTLER, Ian J. See Koslow, S. H. jt auth
BUTLER, Jack
Homage to the first geometer; poem. New Yorker 53:40 S 19 '77
Pain that vision cannot heal; poem. New Yorker 53:46 Ja 2 '78
BUTLER, Jean
Burrows is back—with a little help from his friends. il por N Y Times Mag p72-3+ Je 5 '77
BUTLER, Jerome P. Jr
Pedestrian malls not cure for downtown ills; excerpt from address, September 1976. Am City & County 92:60 Ja '77
BUTLER, Robert Neil
Dr Robert N. Butler issues urgent call for more doctors trained in geriatrics. por Ret Liv 16:14-15 D '76 *
BUTLER, Ron
True confessions. C. J. Baker. il pors Hot Rod 30:32-3+ Mr '77 *
BUTMAN, Hillel I.
Statement by prisoner H. I. Butman to the chief of the Perm administration of corrective labor establishments (ITK-35) il Nat R 29:822-5 Jl 22 '77
BUTNER prison. See Prisons—North Carolina
BUTSCHER, Edward
Fathers and sons. Poetry 130:167-72 Je '77
BUTTER
Butter lamb for the Easter Sunday breakfast table. il Sunset 158:200 Ap '77
BUTTERFIELD, Fox
China: unraveling the new mysteries. il pors N Y Times Mag p32+ Je 19 '77
Improbable welfare state. il map N Y Times Mag p55-6+ N 27 '77
BUTTERFIELD, Jan
Re-placing women artists in history. il Art N 76:40-4 Mr '77
BUTTERFLIES
Its fate is up in the air; protecting the habitat of the El Segundo blue butterfly. R. H. Boyle. il Sports Illus 46:54+ F 28 '77
Monarch migration. L. P. Brower. il Natur Hist 86:40-53 bibl(p92) Je '77
Ovarian dynamics in heliconiine butterflies: programmed senescence versus eternal youth. H. Dunlap-Pianka and others. bibl il Science 197:487-90 Jl 29 '77
BUTTERNUT trees
Make it butternuts for the North. L. Hill. il Org Gard & Farm 24:92-4 S '77
BUTTERWORTHS (firm) See Publishers and publishing—Great Britain
BUTTONHOOKS
Buttonhooks combined with various useful items. B. Betensley. il Hobbies 82:139+ My '77
BUTTONS
Collectors and collecting
Button collecting:
Bears. D. F. Brown. il Hobbies 82:138-9 O '77
Button notes. D. F. Brown. Hobbies 82:138 My '77
Emerald Isle. D. F. Brown. Hobbies 82:139 Mr '77
Expositions. D. F. Brown. il Hobbies 82:138-9 Je '77
Fleur-de-lis. D. F. Brown. il Hobbies 82:138-9 S '77
Heads. D. F. Brown. il Hobbies 81:156-7 F '77
Inlaid buttons. D. F. Brown. il Hobbies 82:138-9 N '77
Paper collectibles. D. F. Brown. il Hobbies 82:156-7 Ja '78
Ship of the desert; camels. D. F. Brown. il Hobbies 82:138-9 Ag '77
Thread backs. D. F. Brown. il Hobbies 82:138-9 D '77
Tortoise-shell. D. F. Brown. il Hobbies 82:138-9 Jl '77
Transfer buttons or decals. D. F. Brown. il Hobbies 82:138-9 Ap '77
Button up! S. B. Madden. SLJ 24:39 N '77
BUTTS, June Dobbs
How to conquer your sexual fears. il Ebony 32:141-2+ Jl '77
Sex education: who needs it? il pors Ebony 32:96-8+ Ap '77
BUTTS, R. Freeman
Education for citizenship. Educ Digest 43:25-7 O '77
BUTWIN, David W.
5 1/2-day mini cruise: a crossing on the QE2. il House & Gard 149:110+ O '77
Making tracks. Am Home 80:39+ Ap '77
BUTYLATED hydroxytoluene
BHT—from preservative to antiviral agent. il Chemistry 50:24-5 N '77
Butylated hydroxytoluene protects chickens exposed to Newcastle disease virus. M. Brugh, Jr. bibl il Science 197:1291-2 S 23 '77
BUTYRIC acid
Ratio of plasma alpha amino-*n*-butyric acid to leucine as an empirical marker of alcoholism: diagnostic value. M. Y. Morgan and others. il Science 197:1183-5 S 16 '77
BUULTJENS, Ralph
China's development efforts and quest for the future. bibl il map Focus 27:1-8 Mr '77; Correction. 27:15 My '77
BUYER protection. See Consumer protection
BUYERS guides. See Consumer education
BUYING. See Shopping and shoppers
BUYOUTS, Business management. See Employee ownership
BUZZARDS Bay
See also
Oil pollution of the sea—Buzzards Bay
BY-products. See Waste products
BYAM, Milton S.
Kiosks and Porta-branches. por Lib J 102:162-3 Ja 15 '77
BYARD, Margaret M.
Poetic responses to the Copernican revolution; with biographical sketch. il Sci Am 236:18, 120-9 bibl(p 142) Je '77
BYERLY, T. C.
Ruminant livestock research and development. bibl il Science 195:450-6 F 4 '77
BYERS, R. B.
Canadian military. bibl f Cur Hist 72:173-5+ Ap '77
BYERS, Stephen W.
Western guest ranching. il Travel 147:54-7+ My '77
BYINGTON, S. John
What the Government can—and cannot—do to protect the public; interview. il por U.S. News 83:33-5 O 24 '77
BYLINSKY, Gene
Big science struggles with the problems of its own success. il Fortune 96:60-6+ Jl '77
Laser alchemy is just around the corner. Fortune 96:186-90 S '77
New companies that beat the odds. il Fortune 96:76-80+ D '77
Preview of the choose your mood society. il Fortune 95:220-4+ Mr '77
Turning your creativity into future success; adaptation of address. il por Sci Digest 81:50-4 Mr '77
BYRD, Benjamin Franklin, 1918-
What every woman should know about breast X-ray; interview, ed by W. S. Ross. Read Digest 110:116-20 Mr '77
BYRD, Larry D. See Gonzalez, F. A. jt auth
BYRD, Martha H.
Battle of the Philippine Sea. il maps Am Hist Illus 12:20-35 Jl '77
Captured by the Americans. il Am Hist Illus 11:24-35 F '77

BYRD, Richard Evelyn
Bound for glory. il Sat Eve Post 249:18-19 Jl '77

BYRD, Robert Carlyle
In defense of Congress. . . il por U.S. News 82: 74 Ap 18 '77

about

Blitz by Fritz. P. Goldman and others. por Newsweek 90:34+ O 17 '77 *
Fiddler. New Repub 177:2+ O 8 '77 *
Filibuster ends, but not the gas war. il por Time 110:10-11+ O 17 '77 *
Jimmy's oracle. T. Mathews and J. J. Lindsay. por Newsweek 90:27 O 3 '77 *
Night of the long winds. il por Time 110:12-14 O 10 '77 *
Senate leader Byrd: no President's man. por U.S. News 83:29 O 17 '77 *
Senator Byrd: more than just a manager. por Bus W p38 O 17 '77 *
Travels with Bobby Byrd. J. Lelyveld. il por N Y Times Mag p47 Jl 31 '77 *

BYRD, Suzanne W.
Treasury of Hispanic lore. il Américas 29:10-13 Mr '77

BYRNE, Brendan T.
Political suicide in New Jersey. J. McLaughlin. Nation 225:593-6 D 3 '77 *
Saving New Jersey. W. F. Buckley, Jr. Nat R 29:1321 N 11 '77 *
Statehouse derby. R. Boeth and others. il pors Newsweek 90:42+ O 17 '77 *
Two tight gubernatorial races. il pors Time 110: 25-6 N 7 '77 *

BYRNE, Donn
Pregnant pause in the sexual revolution. bibl por Psychol Today 11:67-8 Jl '77

BYRNE, Jane
Janie and the Mayor. D. A. Williams and F. Maier. il pors Newsweek 90:40 D 5 '77 *

BYRNE, Kevin
Byrne, as in blazing. A. Verschoth. il por Sports Illus 46:92+ My 23 '77 *

BYRNE, Peggy
Albany's first city planner. il por map Conservationist 31:34-7 Ja '77

BYRNE, Robert
Alternative education: at the crossroads. Clearing H 50:348-9 Ap '77

BYRNE, Susan
(ed) See Bronfenbrenner, U. Nobody home: the erosion of the American family

BYROM, Fletcher Lauman
Going down the drain; excerpts from address. Intellect 105:210 Ja '77

BYRON, Dora
Bermuda throws a party! il Seventeen 36:162 F '77

BYRON, George Gordon Noël Byron, 6th Baron
Scrope's last throw. R. Holmes. Harpers 254:77-9+ Ap '77 *

BYRON, William J.
Ethics of stewardship. il New Cath World 220: 230-2+ S '77
Peanuts, emeralds and the art of giving. America 137:461-3 D 24 '77

BYSSINOSIS. See Lungs—Dust diseases

C

C&A Brenninkmeyer (firm) See Conglomerate corporations—Netherlands

C and O Canal National Historical Park. See Chesapeake and Ohio Canal National Historical Park

CAB. See United States—Civil Aeronautics Board

CALC. See Clergy and Laity Concerned (organization)

CANA (Caribbean News Agency) See News agencies

CAPE. See Council for American Private Education

CASA (Construcciones Aeronauticas, S.A) See Airplane industry—Spain

CAT (computerized axial tomography) See Radiography, Medical

CATV system
Cable-TV industry gets moving again; QUBE system. il Bus W p 154+ N 21 '77
Cable television: diversity or duplication? J. L. Huffman and D. M. Trauth. Intellect 106:157-8 O '77
Extensions downtown; use of pinball machines by Manhattan Cable Television's The game show. New Yorker 53:25-7 F 28 '77
Let's hear it for the cable. D. Davis. por Newsweek 90:29 N 21 '77
Talking to the tube; Qube pay cable system. H. F. Waters and J. C. Jones. il Newsweek 90:107 D 5 '77
Two-way cable TV protects America's safest town; The Woodlands, Tex. D. Lynch. il Pop Sci 211:70-1 Jl '77
Two-way TV may alter traditional book buying; Qube pay cable system direct response advertising. J. Giusto. Pub W 212:55 D 26 '77

CATV system and libraries. See Libraries and television

CB antennas. See Radio antennas

CB radio. See Citizens band radio

CBA. See Christian Booksellers Association

CBGB night club, New York City. See Night clubs

CBS, Inc
As Schorr sees it. H. F. Waters and N. Stadtman. por Newsweek 90:90+ O 31 '77
Behind the executive shake-up at CBS. il por Bus W p57-8+ O 31 '77
Commentaries: on television violence. G. Gerbner; J. A. Schneider. Society 14:8-17 S '77
Dos and don'ts of television news. T. Griffith. Time 110:114 D 5 '77
Excerpt from testimony on retirement age policy, March 16, 1977. G. F. Jankowski. Cong Digest 56:269+ N '77
Herbert's war; ruling in slander suit against CBS. Time 110:103 N 21 '77
Shake-up at CBS. H. F. Waters and B. Carter. il Newsweek 90:83 O 31 '77
Small change at CBS. pors Time 109:62-3 My 2 '77
Strengthening the functions of internal auditors. M. L. Mace. Harvard Bus R 55:46-7 Jl '77

Records Division

CBS records: muscle in the marketplace. B. Ford, Jr. il Hi Fi 27:131-3 Mr '77
Cool conscience of a hot industry; G. Lieberson of Columbia Records. R. Gelatt. il pors Sat R 4:28-9 Jl 23 '77

CCC. See United States—Agriculture, Department of—Community Credit Corporation

CCD (Conference of the Committee on Disarmament) See United Nations—Committee on Disarmament

CCNY. See New York (city). City University—City College

CDs. See Certificates of deposit

CDC. See Control Data Corporation; United States—Public Health Service—Center for Disease Control

CEA. See United States—Council of Economic Advisers

CENTO. See Central Treaty Organization

CEP. See Council on Economic Priorities

CEPEX (Controlled Ecosystem Pollution Experiment) See United States—National Science Foundation

CEQ. See United States—Council on Environmental Quality

CERN (Conseil Européen pour la Recherche Nucleaire) See European Organization for Nuclear Research

CETA (Comprehensive Employment and Training Act) programs. See Unemployment—Relief measures

CF. See Cystic fibrosis

C. F. Bally Ltd. See Shoe industry—Switzerland

C. F. Mueller Company. See Mueller, C. F. Company

CFTC. See United States—Commodity Futures Trading Commission

CIA. See United States—Central Intelligence Agency

CIBC. See Council on Interracial Books for Children

CIIT. See Chemical Industry Institute of Toxicology

CIPEC (Intergovernmental Council of Copper Exporting Countries) See Trusts, Industrial—International trusts

CLA. See California Library Association

CLENE (Continuing Library Education Network and Exchange) See Library schools and education

CLR. See Council on Library Resources, Inc

CMOS circuits. See Electronic circuits, Integrated

CMP. See Cytidine phosphates

CNI (Central Nacional de Informaciónes) See Intelligence service—Chile

COs. See Conscientious objectors

COM (Computer Output Microfilm) See Computers—Input-output equipment

COPS (Communities Organized for Public Service) See Citizens associations

CORVA (Central Ohio River Valley Association for Health Planning and Resource Development) See Health planning

COS. See Central Opera Service

COWPS. See United States—Council on Wage and Price Stability

CPA. See Catholic Press Association

CPB. See Corporation for Public Broadcasting

CPR (cardio-pulmonary resuscitation) See Resuscitation

CPSC. See United States—Consumer Product Safety Commission

CRAF (Civil Reserve Air Fleet) See United States—Air Force—Civil Reserve Air Fleet

CRS. See Catholic Relief Services
CSA. See United States—Community Services Administration
CSD. See American Library Association—Children's Services Division
CT (computerized tomography) See Radiography, Medical
CTS Corporation. See Electronic industries—United States
CU. See Consumers Union of United States
CUNY. See New York (city). City University
CAB drivers. See Taxicab drivers
CABALLÉ, Montserrat
Like singing three Normas; M. Caballé records Donizetti's Gemma di Vergy. R. V. Lucano. il por Am Rec G 40:16-18 My '77 *
CABARETS
What is Montmartre? Nothing! What should it be? Everything! Chat Noir; tr by G. Needham. M. Frèrebeau. il Art N 76:60-2 Mr '77
CABBAGE family. See Brassica
CABINET (United States) See United States—Cabinet
CABINET work
See also
Drawers
Veneers and veneering
Woodworking
CABINETMAKERS
See also
Cleveland, J. C.
Jones, N.
King, W. Jr
Shaw, J.
Swift, R.
True, J.
CABINETS (furniture)
Bathroom cabinets really roomy. il Sunset 159: 182 O '77
Cabinet of real oak. D. DeCristoforo. il Mech Illus 74:76+ Ja '78
Clock in a cabinet. J. Capotosto. il Mech Illus 73:142+ N '77
See also
Kitchen cabinets
CABINS, Boat. See Boats—Cabins
CABLE, Harold
Last stop; drama. Plays 37:29-42 N '77
Way-out Cinderella; drama. Plays 36:19-32 F '77
CABLE television. See CATV system
CABRAL, Alberto
Political murder in Paraguay. il America 136: 376-8 Ap 23 '77
CABRERA INFANTE, Guillermo
Fabulas rasas; tr by A. Reid. il New Repub 177:28-9 D 24 '77
Revelations of a list-maker; tr by A. Reid. New Yorker 53:32-5 S 19 '77
CACHE River
Carter's water projects: pork barrel sellout? B. Vogt. il Outdoor Life 160:34+ N '77
CACTUS
At home with my cactus family. P. Gunn. il Org Gard & Farm 24:160+ D '77
Captivating cacti. R. Langer. il House & Gard 149:32+ Ag '77
Christmas cactus and its relatives: plants that require dry and rainy seasons in your home; crab or lobster cactus. I. Zucker. Horticulture 55:2 Jl '77
Easy to grow house plants. E. McDonald. il House B 119:30 Je; 38 N '77
Saguaro—symbol of the desert; Sonoran Desert. L. Line. il Field & S 82:48 Ag '77
CADDELL, Patrick
Carter's outside insiders. pors Bus W p94+ Je 27 '77 *
Image is substance is image. A. Wolfe. Nation 224:778-81 Je 25 '77 *
Sweet nothings. H. Fairlie. New Repub 176:17-19 Je 11 '77 *
CADDEN, Vivian
Midge Costanza: one door from the Oval Office. il pors Ms 6:48-51+ Ja '78
Minister's farewell to Plains, Georgia. il por McCalls 104:115+ Jl '77
Money: how 35,000 women spend, save and s-t-r-e-t-c-h it. il McCalls 104:75-80 S '77
Murder of President Kennedy. il McCalls 104: 119-20+ Mr '77
CADE, William
Of cricket song and sex; with biographical sketch. il Natur Hist 87:6, 64-73 bibl(p 108-9) Ja '78
CADETS
See also
Women cadets
CADILLAC Motor Division. See General Motors Corporation—Cadillac Motor Division
CADILLAC Ranch, Amarillo, Tex. See Ranches
CADMIUM
Lead and cadmium release; WHO conference on ceramic foodware safety. il Ceram Mo 25:69+ D '77
CADMIUM in the body
Influence of cadmium and other trace metals on human α_1 antitrypsin: an in vitro study. P. Chowdhury and D. B. Louria; reply with rejoinder. C. B. Glaser and others. bibl il Science 196:556-7 Ap 29 '77
CADY, Kent
Coed dorms are the greatest! por Seventeen 36: 66 Ag '77
CADY, Steve
Here comes The Kid! il pors N Y Times Mag p 15-17+ F 20 '77
CAEDMON Company. See Phonograph record industry
CAESAR, Shirley
First lady of gospel. il pors Ebony 32:98-100+ S '77 *
CAESAR and Cleopatra; drama. See Shaw, G. B.
CAESAREAN section. See Cesarean section
CAFFEINE
Beware of coffee, tea, and cola beverages if you value good health. H. L. Abrams, Jr. Consumers Res Mag 60:21-2+ My '77
Good to the last drop—but not for some patients; study by John Greden and others. J. Gaylin. Psychol Today 11:50+ N '77
Got the coffeepot blues? A. Rosenblum. il Good H 184:224 Je '77
CAFFREY, Taylor
Unlikely Flower Gardens; with biographical sketch. il Sea Front 23:242-6, 254 Jl '77
CAGE, John
New music. J. La Barbara. il por Hi Fi 27:MA 10-11 Ag '77 *
CAGES for plants. See Plants, Protection of
CAGGIULA, Anthony R. See Antelman, S. M. jt auth
CAHIER, Bernard
Driving the Porsche 928 in Europe. il por Motor T 29:65-6 Ag '77
CAHILL, Carl
Tyranny in a glass of water. Nation 224:325-6 Mr 19 '77
Well water. Environment 19:46-8 Je '77
CAHN, Robert
Race to save wild Alaska. il Liv Wildn 41:13-19 Jl '77
CAIDIN, Martin
Iron Annie. il Flying 101:305-8 S '77
about
Flying nonesuch. D. R. Branch. il pors Writers Digest 57:41-3 Ag '77 *
Marty's Ju 52 and IRA's air force. R. B. Parke. il Flying 100:4 My '77 *
CAILLEBOTTE, Gustave
Art. L. Alloway. Nation 224:411-12 Ap 2 '77 *
Detached observer. M. S. Young. il Art N 76: 114-15 My '77 *
CAIN, James Mallahan
Obituary
Pub W 212:24 N 7 '77
CAIN, Melanie
People on the cover. por Redbook 149:4 Jl '77
CAIN, Seymour
Syria: daylight in the Middle East? Chr Cent 94:592-3 Je 22 '77
CAIN, Steve. See Kruse, L. jt auth
CAIN, William S.
Differential sensitivity for smell: "noise" at the nose. bibl il Science 195:796-8 F 25 '77
CAINE, Harvey M.
Pesticides and pollination. bibl il Environment 19:28-33 N '77
CAINE, Lynn
Single mothers; excerpt from Lifelines. il Ladies Home J 94:104+ O '77
Widowhood: learning from tragedy. Harp Baz 110:97+ Mr '77
CAINE, Michael
Actor Michael Caine finds marvelous equality in U.S. il pors U.S. News 84:66 Ja 9 '78
CAIRNS, Stephen D.
Deep-water corals; with biographical sketch. il Sea Front 23:84-9, 125-6 Mr '77
CAIRO
Hotels, restaurants, etc.
International chef; Egyptian veal served at the Nile Hilton Hotel. L. Szathmary. Travel 148: 16+ Jl '77
CAIRO conference, 1977
Acceptance front. Nation 225:674-5 O 24 '77
Begin's peace plan. T. Mathews and others. il pors Newsweek 90:73-4 D 26 '77
Conference in Cairo. T. Mathews and others. il por Newsweek 90:20-2 D 19 '77
Goodbye, Arab solidarity. il por Time 110:38-40+ D 12 '77
Israel and Egypt—ready for a separate peace? with editorial comment. U.S. News 83:21-2, 84 D 12 '77
Menachem Begin's big blitz. il pors Time 110: 20-4 D 26 '77
Mideast: on to Cairo? R. Steele and others. il pors Newsweek 90:24-6+ D 5 '77
Next step in Mideast; with report by Dennis Mullin. il por U.S. News 83:16-17 D 5 '77
Rushing toward Cairo. il por map Time 110: 26-8 D 19 '77

CAIRO conference, 1977—*Continued*
Sadat: why Russia balks at peace; interview; ed by D. B. Richardson. A. Sadat. por U.S. News 83:13 D 19 '77
Sadat's stormy wake. R. Steele and others. il Newsweek 90:51+ D 12 '77
Shall I go to Cairo? W. F. Buckley, Jr. Nat R 30:48 Ja 6 '78
Voices of moderation; interviews. A. Sadat; Hussein. pors Newsweek 90:54+ D 12 '77
What role for U.S. in Mideast? il U.S. News 83:11-12 D 19 '77

CAIRO International Book Fair. See Book fairs

CAJUN music. See Music, Popular (songs, etc)

CAKE
Caramel icicles on a nut roll. il Sunset 159:127 Ag '77
Celebrate with cake. R. Motear. il Parents Mag 52:56-8+ F '77
Elegant single-serving cakes: Bundt cake pans. il McCalls 105:179-80+ N '77
Four spice cakes that are blue ribbon winners. P. A. Ward. il Farm J 101:38-9 mid-F '77
Fruitcake show-offs. R. Molter. il Parents Mag 52:42-3+ D '77
Fruitcakes. il Bet Hom & Gard 55:121-2 D '77
House beautiful chef; génoise. J. Pepin. House B 119:86 Ag '77
House beautiful chef: six-layer mocha cake. J. Pepin. il House B 119:142 N '77
It's whole wheat poundcake. il Sunset 159:194 O '77
Light and lemony cake. il McCalls 104:87-8 Mr '77
Search for the perfect brownie. L. Foster. il Am Home 80:62-3+ Ap '77
Special cake roll; lemon roll. il Bet Hom & Gard 55:148 Je '77
Strawberry spectacular; strawberry cream cake. il McCalls 104:167-8 Ap '77
Swedish pudding cake. il Sunset 159:160 D '77
Time is kind to our spicy zucchini fruitcakes. il Sunset 159:146 S '77
Tweed cake—the tweed is chocolate. il Sunset 158:129 F '77
See also
Cheesecake
Coffee cake
Pastry

CAKE, Decorated. See Cookery, Ornamental

CAKE molds and pans. See Kitchen utensils and appliances

CAKE racks. See Kitchen utensils and appliances

CALABRO, Louis
Voyage; Symphony no. 3. W. Simmons. Am Rec G 40:13-14 Mr '77 *

CALAMITIES. See Disasters

CALANDA, Spain
Drums of Calanda. T. Eigeland. il Natur Hist 86:58-63 Ap '77

CALAVERAS skull hoax. See Hoaxes

CALCIFICATION
Fibrous apatite grown on modified collagen. E. Banks and others. bibl il Science 198:1164-6 D 16 '77

CALCIUM
Aequorin luminescence: relation of light emission to calcium concentration—a calcium-independent component. D. G. Allen and others. bibl il Science 195:996-8 Mr 11 '77
See also
Soils—Calcium content

CALCIUM carbonate
Calcium carbonate production of the *mare incognitum*, the upper windward reef slope, at Enewetak Atoll. S. V. Smith and J. T. Harrison. bibl il Science 197:556-9 Ag 5 '77

CALCIUM in the body
Calcium-dependent depression of a late outward current in snail neurons. R. Eckert and H. D. Lux. bibl il Science 197:472-5 Jl 29 '77
Calcium-induced displacement of membrane-associated particles upon aggregation of chromaffin granules. R. Schober and others. bibl il Science 195:495-7 F 4 '77
Calcium: the backbone of minerals. E. R. Trescher. por House & Gard 149:40+ D '77
Internal calcium changes in a bursting pacemaker neuron measured with arsenazo III. M. V. Thomas and A. L. F. Gorman. bibl il Science 196:531-3 Ap 29 '77
Possible cyclic nucleotide regulation of calcium mediating myocardial contraction. A. Schwartz and others. bibl il Science 195:982+ Mr 11 '77

CALCIUM oxalate
Calcium oxalate: occurrence in soils and effect on nutrient and geochemical cycles. W. C. Graustein and others. bibl il Science 198:1252-4 D 23 '77

CALCULATING ability. See Mathematical ability

CALCULATING machines. See Calculators

CALCULATIONS, Numerical. See Numerical calculations

CALCULATOR games. See Mathematical recreations

CALCULATORS
Alarm-clock calculator. R. Chadakoff. il Pop Sci 210:176 Ap '77
Calcu-letter. D. Huff. il Pop Sci 211:23-4 N '77; 212:8 Ja '78
Calculator current predictions; tidal current. E. S. Maloney. il Motor B & S 140:14+ O '77
Calculator navigation. T. Gibbs. il Yachting 141:102-5 Ap '77
Calculator programs. Sky & Tel 54:292 O '77
Desktop calculators that print their results. H. Clark and L. Barandes. il Pop Mech 147:187-9 Ap '77
HP-25 as a digital clock & timer. W. T. Peters. il Pop Electr 12:57-8 Ag '77
Height of tide—by calculator! E. S. Maloney. il Motor B & S 140:16+ Jl '77
How to convert a four banger for stopwatch functions. C. Stanford. il Pop Electr 12:56-7 Ag '77
Printing calculators. K. Lander. il Pop Sci 212:59-61 Ja '78
Programmable calculators use plug-in solid-state memories. J. Free. il Pop Sci 211:130 O '77
Push button navigators. E. Bergin and J. Buchanek. il Motor B & S 139:88-90+ My '77
Push-button piloting. E. Bergin and J. Buchanek. il Motor B & S 140:68-70+ Ag '77
Should your child use a calculator? A. Rosenblum. Good H 184:224 F '77
Some more calculators. il Consumers Res Mag 60:33-6 N '77
Specialized calculators shortcut tough problems. J. Free. il Pop Sci 210:171 Je 77
Those work-saving, time-saving, problem solving programmable calculators. J. Free. il Pop Sci 210:64+ F '77
Two compact calculators with long battery life. Consumer Rep 42:561 O '77
Using hand calculators in schools. E. E. Hopkins. Educ Digest 42:44-5 F '77
See also
Slide rules

CALCUTTA
Jam-packed Calcutta: where unrest lurks. il U.S. News 82:36 Je 27 '77

Social conditions

Calcutta's bounty. T. D. Allman. Harpers 255:12-16 S '77

CALDECOTT Medal
Dillons win Caldecott Medal: Newbery goes to Mildred Taylor. il SLJ 23:65 Mr '77

CALDER, Alexander, 1898-1976
Alexander Calder: casting seeds into the wind. B. Bristow. Chr Today 21:38+ S 9 '77 *
Alexander Calder, 1898-1976. A. Goldin. il por Art in Am 65:70-3 Mr '77 *
Calder: he gave pleasure. il por Horizon 19:20-3 My '77 *
Calder's universe. D. Leder. America 136:298-9 Ap 2 '77 *
Existentialist on mobilist; excerpt from The art world; ed by B. Diamonstein. J. P. Sartre. il por Art N 76:158+ N '77 *
Refrain for Alexander Calder (1898-1976) F. Schulze. por Art N 76:48 Ja '77 *

CALDER, Ethan
Songsmith nobody knows. il por Am Rec G 40:4-7+ Jl '77

CALDER, Nigel
Are we born to be good? il por Horizon 19:42-9 Mr '77
Head south with all deliberate speed: ice may return in a few thousand years. il Smithsonian 8:32-41 bibl(p 114) Ja '78
Key to the universe; excerpt. il Sci Digest 81:58-63+ Je '77

CALDEYRO-BARCIA, Roberto
Houssay Science Prize, 1976. il por Américas 29:32 My '77 *

CALDWELL, Bettye M.
New school plan from toddlers to pre-teens. il Parents Mag 52:56-7+ S '77

CALDWELL, Erskine
Against the grain. W. Beacham. Nation 224:729-31 Je 11 '77 *

CALDWELL, Gilbert H.
Seeking ratifiers. Chr Cent 94:292-3 Mr 30 '77

CALDWELL, Helen
Michio Ito: American pioneer. il por Dance Mag 51:88-91 My '77

CALDWELL, Philip
Ford's new trimotor. T. Nicholson and J. C. Jones. il pors Newsweek 89:65 Ap 25 '77 *
'77 Ford trimotor. il pors Time 109:76-7 Ap 25 '77 *

CALDWELL, Robert
Career education in the English classroom. bibl f il Engl J 66:45-8 N '77

CALDWELL, Sarah
Sarah Caldwell's new idea. H. E. Phillips. il por Hi Fi 27:MA17-19 S '77 *

CALENDAR
See also
Chronology

CALENDARS
Best new calendars. J. L. Lippert. il Good H 186:168 Ja '78
Christmas is coming: count the days with an Advent calendar. il Design (US) 79:4-5 N '77
Christmas tree calendar. il Design (US) 79:16 N '77
Selection of 1978 calendars. il Pub W 212:66-8+ Ag 1 '77
Shopwalk; sports calendars. J. Gilchrist. Sports Illus 47:9 N 21 '77
Students print a calendar. T. Bilderback. il Sch Arts 77:18-19 D '77

CALENDER, June
Playwriting: hints from a first reader. Writer 91:16-17 Ja '78

CALENDULAS
Long lasting new calendula. il Sunset 159:158 Ag '77

CALF barns. See Barns and stables

CALF pens and sheds
Calf pen size—how important? Suc Farm 75:No3 F25 F '77; Same. Suc Farm 75:C3 Ag '77
Cold calf housing idea from Minnesota. il Suc Farm 75:no4 D6 Mr '77
Conversions with calves in mind. il Farm J 101: Dairy 12 F '77
Rollaway calf crates. il Farm J 101:Dairy 6 Je '77

CALF scours. See Calves—Diseases and pests

CALHOUN, George, Jr
Ethnic comparison of juvenile offenses and socioeconomic status. bibl il Clearing H 51:58-9 O '77

CALHOUN, Ga.

Banks

See Banks and banking—Georgia

CALHOUN County, Mich.
Unemployed clean County's drain channels; CETA program. N. Reeder. Farm J 101:K1 O '77

CALHOUN First National Bank. See Banks and banking—Georgia

CALIAN, Carnegie Samuel
Can we expect greatness from the clergy? Chr Cent 94:508-11 My 25 '77

CALIBRATION
Winners: two ways to calibrate a sprayer. G. Lepper. il Suc Farm 75:no4 L22 Mr '77

CALIFANO, Joseph Anthony, 1931-
Cancer research. Chemistry 50:2 Jl '77
Health of our children; address, September 9, 1977. Vital Speeches 44:19-21 O 15 '77
Immunizing our children: the job of every parent. il por Parents Mag 52:66+ N '77
National health care planning; address, October 27, 1977. Vital Speeches 44:112-14 D 1 '77
One more plan to end fraud in welfare; interview. il pors U.S. News 84:41-4 Ja 9 '78
Something less than the millennium; interview, ed by H. Sidey and S. Fentress. por Time 110:7 Ag 15 '77
Straight talk about welfare; adaptation of address, April 27, 1977. Read Digest 111:157-8 S '77
What's wrong with U.S. health care? il Read Digest 111:122-6 O '77

about

Califano under fire. P. Goldman and S. Lesher. por Newsweek 89:24 Ap 4 '77 *
HEW's half-measure. E. Marshall. New Repub 176:8-10 My 7 '77 *
Hot seat. G. F. Will. Newsweek 89:96 Mr 7 '77 *
Mr Califano on quotas. Commonweal 104:291-2 My 13 '77 *
Politics of welfare reform. N. Kotz. New Repub 176:16-21 My 14 '77 *

CALIFORNIA
The Coast. J. Didion. See alternate issues of Esquire to December 1977
The Coast. J. G. Dunne. See alternate issues of Esquire to November 1977
What ever happened to California? Time essay. D. DeVoss. il Time 110:22-3 Jl 18 '77

See also
Agriculture—California
Alpine County
Architecture—California
Architecture, Domestic—California
Art—California
Art galleries and museums—California
Automobile driving—California
Banks and banking—California
Bird sanctuaries—California
Booksellers and bookselling—California
Botany—California
Camps—California
Carquinez Strait
Coachella Valley
Contra Costa County
Courts—California
Crime and criminals—California
Criminal justice, Administration of—California
Eagle Lake
Education—California
Energy policy—California
Environmental movement—California
Environmental policy—California
Festivals—California
Fishing—California
Forests and forestry—California
Gardening—California
Gardens—California
Geology—California
Historic houses, sites, etc.—California
Hospitals—California
Housing—California
Humboldt County
Imperial Valley
Justice, Administration of—California
Kern County
Lakes—California
Land—California
Law—California
Libraries—California
Los Angeles County
Marin County
Morro Bay Region
Muir Woods National Monument
Napa Valley
Opera—California
Orange County
Organic farming—California
Organic gardening—California
Paleontology—California
Point Reyes National Seashore
Police—California
Prisons—California
Recreation areas—California
Redwood National Park
San Bernardino County
San Francisco Bay
San Francisco Bay Region
San Luis Obispo County
Santa Catalina Island
Santa Clara County
School libraries—California
Sequoia National Park
Shasta, Mount
Shore protection—California
Sierra Nevada Mountains
Skis and skiing—California
Sonoma County
Squaw Valley
Sutter Buttes
Tuolumne River
Valley National Monument
Water supply—California
Wilderness areas—California
Wildlife sanctuaries—California
Yosemite National Park

Description and travel

Back road loop detour in the lumber country south of Eureka. il map Sunset 159:46 O '77
California isn't just a great place to live. . .it's a great state to visit. il Mademoiselle 83:144-6+ Ap '77
California's north coast: redwoods, rain, and lots of room. J. Morgan and N. Morgan. il map Nat Geog 152:330-63 S '77
Life on and off schedule. W. Berry. il Org Gard & Farm 24:44+ Ag '77
Mini-holiday; from Los Angeles to San Simeon and back. B. Jeffer. map Holiday 58:10+ Ja '77
Riviera in our own backyard; Orange Coast. R. Alleman. map Vogue 167:210+ O '77

Drought

See Droughts

Economic conditions

California heading for trouble? with interview with E. G. Brown. il U.S. News 83:41-4 Jl 11 '77
California's paradise lost. il Forbes 119:38-40 Ja 15 '77
Dow's pullout haunts California. Bus W p38 F 7 '77

Gas companies

See Gas companies

History

Two hundred years of California earthquakes; excerpt from California quake. L. L. Meyer. il Am West 14:4-9+ Ja '77

Hotels, motels, etc.

See Hotels, motels, etc.—United States

Industries

California heading for trouble? with interview with E. G. Brown. il U.S. News 83:41-4 Jl 11 '77

See also
Citrus fruit industry
Wine industry

CALIFORNIA—*Continued*

Parks and reserves

Bunker Hill Day in Sunol Valley Regional Park. il Sunset 158:40 Je '77
Jack's Peak—behind Monterey; Jack's Peak Regional Park. il Sunset 158:41 Ap '77
Melodramas, surrey rides, air service at old Columbia. il Sunset 159:48 Jl '77
Monte Bello Ridge hike. il Sunset 158:52 Mr '77
Mooney Grove near Visalia—it's a most satisfying trip breaker. il Sunset 159:63 Ag '77
New above Saratoga—walk-in campgrounds; Sanborn-Skyline County Park. il Sunset 159:57 Jl '77
November is a good month to sample the four Valley of the Moon parks; Sonoma County. il map Sunset 159:42-3 N '77
Pioneer conservationist A. P. Hill: he saved the redwoods; early work of the Sempervirens Club. V. T. Olson. il pors Am West 14:32-40 S '77
Pygmies on the fourth terrace, rain forest on the second; ecosystem of new state park north of Mendocino, Calif. il Sunset 159:38-9 Jl '77
Quiet and green Coe Park. il Sunset 159:24 D '77
Redwoods: as the worm turns; with letter by N. B. Livermore, Jr. J. B. Craig. il Am For 83:28-31+ Jl '77; Discussion. 83:4+ O '77
Shinn Ranch is the East Bay's new historic park; Shinn Historical Park. il Sunset 159:[illegible] O '77

Photographs

California. E. Cooper. Am For 83:46-50 O '77

Politics and government

Big is beautiful, too; Space Day gala of J. Brown. P. Goldman and M. Kasindorf. il por Newsweek 90:25-6 Ag 22 '77
California still dreaming. A. I. Blaustein. il Harpers 254:19-21 Je '77
Canniness of the long-distance runner; E. G. Brown. D. S. Broder. il Atlantic 241:35-41 Ja '78
Gunning for Brown. C. Wallen, Jr. Nat R 29:1367 N 25 '77
Port Huron to Santa Barbara; T. Hayden's Campaign for Economic Democracy. K. Lynch. Nat R 29:1112 S 30 '77

Public Utilities Commission

California agency clashes with CAB. Aviation W 106:25 Ja 10 '77

Religious institutions and affairs

Buying a Garden of Eden; Bridgeville, Calif. il por Time 109:50 Je 27 '77
Choice; case of Father J. Dollard of St. Charles Borromeo in Livermore. C. Stephens. Chr Today 21:38 Jl 8 '77
Finding the good at Garden Grove; Robert H. Schuller Institute for Successful Church Leadership. B. Barr. il por Chr Cent 94:424-7 My 4 '77; Discussion. 94:764-5 Ag 31 '77
See also
Missionary Aviation Fellowship

Restaurants

See Restaurants—United States

Social life and customs

East-west blues; a New Yorker goes west. Mademoiselle 83:201+ Ap '77
Keeping fit in California. A. Penney. il N Y Times Mag p58 Ja 8 '78
Semantic spinach; or, Mellowing out in sunny California. C. McFadden. N Y Times Mag p51+ N 20 '77

Theater

See Theater—United States

CALIFORNIA, Gulf of
Diving the Sea of Cortez. L. R. Martin. il Oceans 10:16-19 Mr '77

CALIFORNIA, Lower
See also
Automobile touring—California, Lower
Cruising—California, Lower
Fishing—California, Lower
Magdalena Bay
Wildlife conservation—California, Lower

CALIFORNIA Academy of Sciences, San Francisco
Old Hawaii in San Francisco; Ostheimer collection of Hawaiian antiquities. il Sunset 158:21 Mr '77

CALIFORNIA beaches. See Beaches

CALIFORNIA Computer Products, Inc. See Computer industry

CALIFORNIA cookery. See Cookery, American

CALIFORNIA gold mines. See Gold mines and mining—United States

CALIFORNIA Institute of Technology, Pasadena
See also
Jet Propulsion Laboratory

CALIFORNIA Library Association
California input. J. Berry. il Lib J 102:335-41 F 1 '77
California Library Association's 78th. W. R. Eshelman. il Wilson Lib Bull 51:471-5 F '77

CALIFORNIA, State University, Fresno
Ethics in the academy; abolishment of course taught by J. C. O'Brien. R. Kirk. Nat R 29:726 Je 24 '77

CALIFORNIA. University
Academics in New York and California fight disclosure policies. B. J. Culliton. Science 196:37-8 Ap 1 '77
Rattling the cage; G. Bateson of the regents' board. M. Sheils and others. por Newsweek 90:141 N 21 '77
See also
Bakke, Allan, case

Berkeley campus

Anecdotes, facetiae, satire, etc.

Berkeley memoir. L. Michaels. New Repub 177:13-16 O 22 '77

Libraries

Research library borrows leaf from PL book; loan limits. W. R. Eshelman. Wilson Lib Bull 51:465-6 F '77
Stanford & UC get $$ for broad-gauge co-op. Lib J 102:320 F 1 '77

Davis campus

School of Medicine

Doctored program; case of R. G. Clancy. il por Time 110:89 O 10 '77
Other Bakke; R. G. Clancy case. por Newsweek 90:46 O 24 '77

School of Medicine—Bakke case

See Bakke, Allan, case

Lawrence Radiation Laboratories

Nuclear weapons labs; Los Alamos and Lawrence Livermore laboratories. S. H. Day, Jr. il Bull Atom Sci 33:21-6 Ap '77

Libraries

See also
California. University—Berkeley campus—Libraries

San Francisco campus

School of Medicine

Recombinant lab for DNA and my 95 days in it; H. Boyer's lab. J. L. Hopson. il pors Smithsonian 8:54-63 Je '77

Santa Barbara campus

Center for audio-visual development; the Clark Kerr Learning Resources Hall; with introd by J. Nairn. il Archit Rec 162:85-8 Jl '77

Santa Cruz campus

Art ramble at UC Santa Cruz. il Sunset 159:22 D '77

Scripps Institution of Oceanography

Scripps Institution of Oceanography. E. Golanty. il Oceans 10:2-7 N '77

CALIFORNIANS
What ever happened to California? Time essay. D. DeVoss. il Time 110:22-3 Jl 18 '77

CALISCH, Richard
(ed) Spring poetry festival. Engl J 66:42-60 My '77

CALISHER, Hortense
Head for the—Italian—hills. Vogue 167:108 S '77

CALKINS, Robin
Smaller publishers get together on West Coast. il Pub W 211:24-5 Ap 11 '77

CALLAGHAN, James
British American relations; address, March 11, 1977. Vital Speeches 43:360-3 Ap 1 '77
British Prime Minister Callaghan visits Washington; exchange of remarks, March 10, 1977. Dept State Bull 76:312-13 Ap 4 '77
Pay, inflation and unemployment; address, September 6, 1977. Vital Speeches 44:34-7 N 1 '77

about

Britain: testing a collaboration. R. Carroll and A. Collings. il por Newsweek 89:45-6 Ap 4 '77 *
Callaghan's moment of truth. il por Time 109:38 Mr 28 '77 *
Just wee Geordie for a day. S. Cloud. il Time 109:14-15 My 16 '77 *
Kilt bill. F. Willey and M. MacPherson. il Newsweek 89:43+ Mr 7 '77 *
Letter from London (cont) M. Panter-Downes. New Yorker 53:122 Ap 11 '77 *

Visit to the United States, 1977

British Prime Minister Callaghan visits Washington; exchange of remarks, March 10, 1977. J. Carter; J. Callaghan. Dept State Bull 76:311-13 Ap 4 '77
Making of a state dinner. S. Fraker and J. Whitmore. il por Newsweek 89:30-1 Mr 21 '77

CALLAHAN, Celeste
Uprooted! Seventeen 36:160-1+ Je '77

CALLAHAN, Harry
Reconsideration. S. Rice. New Repub 177:35-7 O 29 '77 *
Seeing pictures. J. Scully. il Mod Phot 41:38-9+ Mr '77 *

CALLAHAN, Rosellen
Southeast Alaska. il Travel 148:62-7 Ag '77

CALLAHAN, Sidney
Abortion and the Supreme Court: anti-abortion view. Current 198:21-3 D '77

CALLAHAN, William E.
Future: energy and wisdom; address, July 14, 1977. Vital Speeches 43:656-9 Ag 15 '77

CALLAN, Edward T.
Auden and W. B. Yeats. pors Commonweal 104: 298-303 My 13 '77

CALLAS, Maria
Callas remembered:
La Divina. W. Legge. pors Opera N 42:8-11+ N '77 *
Greek sorceress; Metropolitan Opera debut and recordings with Angel Records; with discography. D. J. Soria. pors Opera N 42:15-16+ N '77 *
Splendor in the night; seasons at the Lyric Opera of Chicago. C. Casidy. il pors Opera N 42:12-14 N '77 *
La Divina. H. Saal. por Newsweek 90:93 S 26 '77 *
Maria Callas: a personal footnote. J. Culshaw. il por Hi Fi 27:46 D '77 *
Maria Callas remembered. D. J. Soria. por Hi Fi 28:MA4-6 Ja '78 *
Maria Callas: so much done, so much left undone. I. Kolodin. Sat R 5:53 O 29 '77 *
Smoky voice, a fiery lady. il pors Time 110:55-6 S 26 '77 *

CALLAWAY, Howard Hollis
Persecution and character assassination of Howard (Bo) Callaway as performed by inmates of the U.S. Senate under the auspices of the Democratic Party. J. Hougan. Harpers 255:35-42+ Jl '77 *
Price of success. E. Keerdoja. il por Newsweek 89:5+ Ja 31 '77 *

CALLAWAY, Louis M. Jr
Big man at Ford. il pors Ebony 32:62-4+ Mr '77 *

CALLE, Paul
Paul Calle; interview, ed by N. Meglin. il por Am Artist 41:66-9 Jl '77

CALLIGRAPHY
Darling when you read this I shall be alive; work of C. Dotremont. M. Gibson. il Art N 76: 104 O '77
Power of the pen. R. Goldberg. House B 119:80 N '77
Write to the point. J. Glander-Bandyk. il Seventeen 36:50 Ap '77

CALLIGRAPHY, Chinese. See Chinese language—Writing

CALLISON, Charles H.
National outlook. See issues of Audubon to May 1977

CALLOPLESIOPS. See Fishes

CALLS for animals. See Animal calling

CALLS for birds. See Bird calling

CALLS of birds. See Birds—Song

CALORIES, Food. See Diet

CALVARIA
Dodo ecology. Sci Am 237-81-2 O '77
Nature's odd couples; dependency of hermit crabs on whelk shells and Calvaria major on dodos. S. J. Gould. il Natur Hist 87:38-41 Ja '78
Plant-animal mutualism: coevolution with dodo leads to near extinction of plant. S. A. Temple. bibl Science 197:885-6 Ag 26 '77

CALVERT, Catherine
High cost of living safe. Mademoiselle 83:189+ S '77
How to be cheap and keep your self-respect. Mademoiselle 83:32+ Je '77
Persuaders: jobs in publicity. Mademoiselle 83: 214+ O '77
Why a woman can't be a good boss—because no one will let you. Mademoiselle 83:120+ Jl '77

CALVES
Melatonin: daily cycle in plasma and cerebrospinal fluid of calves. L. Hedlund and others. bibl il Science 195:686-7 F 18 '77

Care

Low calf mortality without a big price. il Farm J 101:Dairy 12 Ag '77
New enterprise for crop production units; veal production. il Suc Farm 75:no3 F28 F '77

Diseases and pests

End shipping fever loses? W. Kester. il map Farm J 101:Beef 16+ Ja '77
Sarcocystosis: a clinical outbreak in dairy calves. P. Frelier and others. bibl il Science 195:1341-2 Mr 25 '77
This plan heads off calf scours. Suc Farm 75:D8 D '77

Feeding

University studies say you can wean calves at 50 days. il Suc Farm 75:K10 Ap '77

Pens

See Calf pens and sheds

Transportation

End shipping fever losses? W. Kester. il map Farm J 101:Beef 16+ Ja '77

CALVIN, Melvin
Growing oil. por Forbes 120:64 Ag 1 '77 *

CALVING
Fifteen calving tips from a good herd manager. K. Parker. il Suc Farm 75:no3 B12-13 F '77
Henry Gardiner sees advantages in calving twice a year. il Suc Farm 75:no4 B6 Mr '77
Here's expert advice on calving problems; views of C. J. Bierschwal. J. D. Ritchie. il Farm J 101:Beef 6-7+ F; LK2-3+ Mr '77

CÁMARA, Carlos de la
Invitation to dance. W. Terry. Sat R 5:44+ O 1 '77 *

CÁMARA, Helder Pessôa, Abp
What would St Thomas Aquinas do if faced with Karl Marx? address, 1974. il por New Cath World 220:108-13 My '77

CAMARATA, Peter J.
Hoffa's legacy. J. Lelyveld. il por N Y Times Mag p 142 N 27 '77 *
We're gonna get our asses kicked. R. H. Holden. Nation 225:461-3 N 5 '77 *

CAMBODIA
Transformation in Cambodia. D. P. Chandler. Commonweal 104:207-8+ Ap 1 '77
See also
Civil rights—Cambodia

Foreign relations

Thailand

See also
Cambodian-Vietnamese conflict, 1977-

Vietnam

See also
Cambodian-Vietnamese conflict, 1977-

Politics and government

Communist solution: death of a million Cambodians. J. N. Wallace. il U.S. News 83:33 Ag 8 '77
Distortions at fourth hand. N. Chomsky and E. S. Herman. Nation 224:789-94 Je 25 '77
Exit laughing. Nat R 29:1164 O 14 '77
Horror stories. K. Labich and others. Newsweek 89:50 My 30 '77
How much blood makes a bloodbath? M. Kondracke. New Repub 177:21-2 O 1 '77
Monsters in our footsteps. Nation 224:388 Ap 2 '77
Murder of a gentle land; condensation; with editorial comment. J. Barron and A. Paul. il map Read Digest 110:7-8, 227-34+ F '77
Nation as concentration camp; Khmer Rouge in Cambodia; tr by N. King. S. Groueff. Nat R 29:988-90 S 2 '77
Tales of brave new Kampuchea. D. DeVoss. il Time 110:42 N 21 '77

CAMBODIAN refugees. See Refugees, Cambodian

CAMBODIAN revolutionists. See Revolutionists, Cambodian

CAMBODIAN-Vietnamese conflict, 1977-
Border wars. P. Webb and others. il map Newsweek 91:34 Ja 9 '78
Cambodian border war. H. Jensen. il map Newsweek 90:63 S 19 '77
New Indochina war. K. Willenson and others. il map Newsweek 91:47 Ja 16 '78
When Communists collide. il map Time 111:22-3 Ja 16 '78

CAMBRIAN period. See Geology, Stratigraphic—Cambrian

CAMBRIDGE, Mass.
Gene-splicing: Cambridge citizens OK research but want more safety. N. Wade. il por Science 195:268-9 Ja 21 '77

City planning

See City planning—Massachusetts

Education

See Education—Massachusetts

CAMBRIDGE, Mass. Hyatt Regency. See Hotels, motels, etc.—United States

CAMELLIAS
Come drought or high water, camellias are great favorites. il Sunset 159:230-1 N '77

CAMERA bags, cases, etc.
Bag trick: carry all in two hands? D. Bryan. il Mod Phot 41:95 Ag '77
Nuts & bolts. B. Pierce. il Pop Phot 80:24+ My '77

CAMERA batteries. See Electric batteries
CAMERA buying. See Cameras—Purchasing
CAMERA lenses. See Lenses, Photographic
CAMERA repairmen
Camera collector; Leica repairman. M. Taylor. J. Schneider. il Mod Phot 41:20+ D '77
Get a fix on repairs from pros. Mod Phot 41: 91+ D '77
Shop talk; repairman B. Stimson of the National Geographic Society. N. Goldberg. il Pop Phot 80:10+ Je '77
CAMERA shutters
Shop talk; Foxy shutter and self-timer. N. Goldberg. il Pop Phot 80:20+ Ap '77
View from Kramer. A. Kramer. il Mod Phot 41:51+ O '77

Control

Keppler on the SLR; dual automation. K. Keppler. il Mod Phot 41:12+ S '77
CAMERA supports
Film craft; tripod substitutes. L. Drukker. il por Pop Phot 81:56+ Ag '77
CAMERA tripods
Are medium tripods our ideal? H. Martin. il Mod Phot 41:134-9+ N '77
CAMERAS
Annual guide to 52 top cameras. il Mod Phot 41: 115-70+ D '77
Autofocus, as predicted; Konica C35AF. N. Goldberg. il Pop Phot 81:86+ D '77
Breaking the 110 barrier. N. Rothschild. il Pop Phot 80:104-9+ My '77
Compact 35s. M. Frank. il Pop Phot 81:124+ Jl '77
David Vestal's photo workbook: The camera. D. Vestal. Pop Phot 80:67-8 My '77
Eliot Porter on 35-mm; interview, ed by P. Caulfield. E. Porter. il por Pop Phot 81:108-17+ S '77
First automatic-focus camera; Konica C35AF. S. S. Walton. il Pop Mech 148:66 D '77
Kids and kameras; Snapshooter camera. D. Cyr. il por Pop Phot 80:58+ Mr '77
Large-format cameras. M. Frank. il Pop Phot 80:128+ Je '77
Mini-cameras for the outdoors. J. Tallon. il Field & S 82:40+ D '77
My return to the view camera. L. Jacobs, Jr. il por Pop Phot 81:138-41+ D '77
Nuts & bolts; convenience features on cameras. B. Pierce. il Pop Phot 80:40+ Ap '77
Offbeat; when and when not to use a motor wind. N. Rothschild. il Pop Phot 80:12+ My '77
110s. K. Poli. il Pop Phot 80:95+ Je '77
PS buyer's guide to pocket cameras. P. Wahl. il Pop Sci 211:66-8+ Ag '77
Pocket cameras that pack a punch. W. Kanner. il Pop Mech 147:94-5 Mr '77
Time exposure; binocular cameras. E. S. Lothrop, Jr. il Pop Phot 81:71-2+ O '77
Time exposure; variable format cameras. E. S. Lothrop, Jr. il Pop Phot 80:36+ F '77
View from Kramer:
Galvin 23 view camera. A. Kramer. il Mod Phot 41:50+ N '77
Linhof Master L. A. Kramer. il Mod Phot 41: 26+ F '77
Omega View 45E. A. Kramer. il Mod Phot 41:78+ Je '77
Wista 45. A. Kramer. il Mod Phot 41:102+ Mr '77
What's what. See issues of Modern photography
See also
Camera shutters
Eastman Kodak Company
Motion picture cameras
Motion picture cameras, Instant print

Collectors and collecting

Camera collector:
Aires Automat, Aires 35-V and Fujica Mini. J. Schneider. il Mod Phot 41:41-2+ Jl '77
Argus 35. J. Schneider. il Mod Phot 41:10+ Mr '77
British cameras from the turn-of-the-century. J. Schneider. il Mod Phot 41:20+ F '77
Detrola 400 and the Graphic 35 Electric. J. Schneider. il Mod Phot 41:39+ Ag '77
The Gami. J. Schneider. il Mod Phot 41:24+ O '77
Leica collectors. J. Schneider. il Mod Phot 41:56+ S '77
Mec 16 SB. J. Schneider. il Mod Phot 41:76+ N '77
Mercury cameras. J. Schneider. il Mod Phot 41:62+ My '77
More Argus cameras. J. Schneider. il Mod Phot 41:8+ Ap '77
Vidax press camera. J. Schneider. il Mod Phot 41:61-2+ Je '77

Control

See Camera shutters—Control

Maintenance and repair

See also
Camera repairmen

Mounting

Camera mount for projection photography. D. A. Harbour. il Sky & Tel 54:63-4 Jl '77

Prices

Critical focus. K. Poli. il Pop Phot 80:6+ Je '77

Purchasing

Check before you buy! il Mod Phot 41:169-70+ D '77
Keppler on the SLR. H. Keppler. Mod Phot 41: 6+ F '77
Photographic equipment and supplies. il Consumers Res Mag 60:84-96 O '77
See also
Cameras, Used—Purchasing
Motion picture cameras—Purchasing

Testing

Modern tests:
Widelux F7 panoramic camera. il Mod Phot 41:96-9 Mr '77
New cameras in the 110 and 35mm sizes. il Consumers Res Mag 60:20-3 Mr '77
Pocket cameras. il Consumer Rep 42:666-73 N '77
See also
Motion picture cameras—Testing
CAMERAS, Instant print
First look: 8x10 Polaroid. D. Leavitt. il Pop Phot 81:126-9+ D '77
First look: Polaroid Pronto! RF and SX-70 Alpha 1. M. Frank. il Pop Phot 80:126-7 F '77
Getting the big picture; use of giant Polaroid camera to photograph art works. il Time 110: 82-3 S 26 '77
Instant photography. D. Leavitt. il por Pop Phot 80:62+ My; 66+, 128+ Je; 81:141+ S; 74+ O; 68+ D '77
Instant-picture cameras—news and new models from Polaroid. E. H. Ortner. il Pop Sci 210:63 My '77
Instant pictures. W. Andrews and D. L. Miller. il Mod Phot 41:78-9+ Mr '77
New low-priced Kodak and Polaroid instant-picture cameras. il Consumers Res Mag 60:17-18 S '77
One step vs. The handle: under-$40 instant cameras. G. R. Patton. il Pop Mech 148:84-5 S '77
Snapshot mastery. F. Ritchin. il Horizon 20:75-9 O '77
See also
Motion picture cameras, Instant print

Testing

New Polaroid cameras. il Consumers Res Mag 60:21-2 Je '77
CAMERAS, Single-lens reflex
Buyers guide: incredible new 35mm SLR cameras. P. Wahl. il Pop Sci 210:124-5+ Ap '77
First look:
Asahi Pentax ME & MX. M. Frank. il Pop Phot 80:130-1+ Ap '77
Canon AT-1. N. Rothschild. il Pop Phot 80:130+ Ap '77
Hasselblad 2000FC. M. A. Frank. il Pop Phot 81:108-9 O '77
Leica R3. N. Goldberg. il Pop Phot 80:108-9+ F '77
Minolta XD-11. L. Ericksenn. il Pop Phot 81:96+ D '77
Nikon FM. M. Frank. il Pop Phot 81:52+ Jl '77
Petri MF-1. N. Rothschild. il Pop Phot 81:76 S '77
Rolleiflex SLX. M. Frank. il Pop Phot 81: 134-7 S '77
Keppler on the SLR. H. Keppler. See issues of Modern photography
Modern's inside your camera series:
Bronica ETR. H. Kimata and J. Schneider. il Mod Phot 41:98-9+ Ag '77
Canon AE-1. H. Kimata and J. Schneider. il Mod Phot 41:96-7+ Ap '77
Contax RTS. H. Kimata and J. Schneider. il Mod Phot 41:78-9+ Mr '77
Mamiya RB67 Pro-S. il Mod Phot 41:100-1+ F '77
Olympus OM-2. J. Schneider. il Mod Phot 41:156-7+ N '77
1977 SLR directory. D. L. Miller. il Mod Phot 41:102-13 S '77
SLRs. N. Rothschild. il Pop Phot 80:96-7+ Je '77
SLRs go miniature. W. Kent. il Mech Illus 73:52-3+ S '77

Design

Keppler on the SLR; new Nikon and Hasselblad designs. H. Keppler. il Mod Phot 41: 51+ My '77

Purchasing

See Cameras—Purchasing

CAMERAS, Single-lens reflex—*Continued*

Testing

Lab report:
Canon AE-1. N. Goldberg and others. il Pop Phot 80:116-17+ My '77
Contax RTS. N. Goldberg and others. il Pop Phot 80:78-82+ Mr '77
Konica Autoreflex TC. N. Goldberg and others. il Pop Phot 81:118-21+ Jl '77
Leica R3. N. Goldberg and others. il Pop Phot 81:142-5+ O '77
Yashica FR. N. Goldberg and others. il Pop Phot 81:122-5+ S '77
Modern tests:
Asahi Pentax ME. il Mod Phot 41:115-21 Ap '77
Chinon CE II Memotron. il Mod Phot 41:104-6 F '77
Fujica AZ-1. il Mod Phot 41:164-8 N '77
Hasselblad 500 C/M. il Mod Phot 41:122-7 Je '77
Leica R3. il Mod Phot 41:100-5 Ag '77
Minolta SR-T202. il Mod Phot 41:105-6+ Ag '77
Nikon FM. il Mod Phot 41:142-5 O '77
Pentax MX. il Mod Phot 41:116-17 My '77
Praktica VLC2. il Mod Phot 41:122-5 S '77
Rolleiflex SLX. il Mod Phot 41:100-5+ Jl '77

CAMERAS, Twin-lens
Camera that won't die. J. Wheeler. il Mech Illus 73:22+ D '77

CAMERAS, Used

Purchasing

19 great used camera buys! J. Schneider. il Mod Phot 41:96-7+ Jl '77

CAMERON, Angus
Portland hitch on the Pinware. il Field & S 81:62-4+ Ap '77

CAMERON, John R. and Davis, R. W.
Effects of escherichia coli and yeast DNA insertions on the growth of lambda bacteriophage. bibl il Science 196:212-14 Ap 8 '77

CAMERON, Juan
Carter takes on the budget monster. il Fortune 95:82-7+ Ja '77
Cracking the tanker safety problem. il Fortune 95:150-2 Ap '77
Jimmy Carter gets mixed marks in economics I. il pors Fortune 95:98-102+ Je '77
Nader's invaders are inside the gates. il Fortune 96:252-6+ O '77
Tax tips to save you money. Motor B & S 139: 82+ Ap '77
(ed) See Flittner, G. What your weatherman doesn't tell you

CAMOMILE. See Chamomile

CAMOUFLAGE
See also
Blinds (camouflage)
Mimicry (biology)

CAMP activities. See Camps—Activities

CAMP cookery
Backpacking gourmet; with recipes. J. Condon. Harp Baz 110:88-9+ Ap '77
Backpacking with natural foods. L. Waterman and G. Waterman. il Org Gard & Farm 24: 102+ Je '77
Cooking on the move; backpacking and picnicking. il Bet Hom & Gard 55:118-23+ Je '77
Cooking on the trail; with recipes; excerpt from Wildlife country—how to enjoy it. C. Bull. il Nat Wildlife 15:30-2 Ag '77
Dutch treat; using a cast iron Dutch oven outdoors. S. Bashline. il Field & S 81:178+ Mr '77
Gourmet canoeist. il Bet Hom & Gard 55:124-5+ Je '77
Supermarket: camp cook outfitter; convenience foods. S. Bashline. il Field & S 82:70+ My '77
Winter trail foods. Outdoor Life 161:128 Ja '78
See also
Camps—Food service

CAMP counselors
Director's support key to CIT success. M. Tener. Camp Mag 49:5+ Ap '77
Human relations training. R. Selverstone and W. Hacker. Camp Mag 49:9+ Ap '77
Strong staff: the key ingredient. D. Shellenberger. il Camp Mag 49:6-8+ Ap '77
Successful pre-camp training program instills confidence, helps motivate working team. R. Grundke and R. Vederman. Camp Mag 49: 14-15 Ap '77

Anecdotes, facetiae, satire, etc.

Confessions of a camp counselor. M. Evans. Seventeen 36:140 Jl '77

CAMP David. See Presidents—United States—Homes

CAMP directors
Director's support key to CIT success. M. Tener. Camp Mag 49:5+ Ap '77
Model A Camp Directors Institute. B. Brower. Camp Mag 50:15-17 S '77

CAMP fires
See also
Fire making

CAMP heaters. See Heaters

CAMP lanterns. See Lanterns

CAMP management. See Camps—Administration

CAMP sites, facilities, etc.

Bibliography

Build your own library. B. Behme. Field & S 81:100+ F '77

Directories

Campground guides: picking the best. H. Shuldiner. il Outdoor Life 159:54+ Je '77

CAMP stoves
Camp stoves. il Consumer Rep 42:120-2 D '77
Camping equipment: stoves and catalytic heaters. il Consumers Res Mag 60:26-31 Jl '77
Dutch treat; using a cast iron Dutch oven outdoors. S. Bashline. il Field & S 81:178+ Mr '77
How to set up a safe tent stove; wood stoves. R. Denhardt. il Outdoor Life 159:176 Mr '77

CAMP swimming pools. See Swimming pools, Camp

CAMPAIGN buttons, etc.

Collectors and collecting

Close election of 1876. il Hobbies 81:53-4 F '77

CAMPAIGN funds
Campaign funds: who gave, who got. il Time 109:19 F 28 '77
Democrats' new money man; J. Hay. por Bus W p 128 Mr 21 '77
Fat cats and kitties. Nation 225:708-9 D 31 '78
Good old boy network; Atlanta bank loans to J. Carter campaign; with White House response by J. Powell. R. Reeves and B. M. Hager. New Repub 177:6+ S 10 '77
How to raise a political war chest at $1,000 a crack—or more; J. Carter in Los Angeles. il U.S. News 83:21 O 31 '77
Use tax dollars to elect Congress? interviews. M. K. Udall; L. P. Weicker, Jr. pors U.S. News 82:63-4 Ap 25 '77; Same. Current 194: 3-7 Jl '77

Laws and legislation

Common Cause and campaign financing: reform liberals open up the system. H. Tolley, Jr. il Intellect 106:122-5 O '77
Money for campaigns; proposed federal financing of congressional elections. K. Bode. New Repub 176:8+ F 19 '77
Public financing; address, June 9, 1977. D. Cohen. Vital Speeches 43:692-6 S 1 '77
This month's feature; Federal financing of congressional election campaigns. Cong Digest 56:67-96 Mr '77
Will federal campaign laws make elections more honest? G. D. Webster. por Nations Bus 65: 61-2 Ja '77
See also
United States—Federal Election Commission

CAMPAIGN issues
Promises, promises: home to roost in the White House. A. Clymer. Nation 24:295-8 Mr 12 '77

CAMPAIGN management
After the ball was over: decompression, junior division; J. Buckley campaign. C. Buckley; discussion. Nat R 29:141-2+ F 4 '77

CAMPAIGN workers. See Political campaigns

CAMPAIGNE, Edith B. and Campaigne, J. G.
Edie in trailerland. il Sat Eve Post 249:34-7 My; 38-9+ S; 36-7+ O '77

CAMPAIGNE, Jameson G. See Campaigne, E. B. jt auth

CAMPAIGNS, Advertising. See Advertising campaigns

CAMPAIGNS, Money raising. See Fund raising

CAMPAIGNS, Political. See Political campaigns

CAMPAIGNS, Presidential. See Presidential campaigns

CAMPANULAS
She's hugging Italian bellflower. il Sunset 159: 146 Jl '77

CAMPBELL, Alan Keith
What's right and what's wrong with the federal worker; interview. por U.S. News 83:27-8 O 3 '77

CAMPBELL, Billy Lee
Embezzler. S. Fraker and others. por Newsweek 90:27 S 19 '77 *

CAMPBELL, Byron A. and Randall, P. J.
Paradoxical effects of amphetamine on preweanling and postweanling rats. bibl il Science 195:888-91 Mr 4 '77

CAMPBELL, C. W.
Wild man of Oroville. il por Am Hist Illus 12:18-26+ Je '77

CAMPBELL, D. B. and others
Galilean satellites of Jupiter: 12.6-centimeter radar observations. bibl il Science 196:650-3 My 6 '77

CAMPBELL, John
Publish or perish, library-style. Wilson Lib Bull 52:250 N '77

CAMPBELL, John Coert
Oil power in the Middle East. bibl f For Affairs 56:89-110 O '77
Soviet policy in Africa and the Middle East. bibl f Cur Hist 73:100-4+ O '77

CAMPBELL, John W.
In the gay camp. R. Steele and H. Camp. il por Newsweek 89:19 Je 6 '77 *

CAMPBELL, Joseph
Professor with a thousand faces. D. Newlove. il pors Esquire 88:99-103+ S '77 *

CAMPBELL, Jule
Design for sport. Sports Illus 46:69-70+ Mr 21; 47:50-1 Jl 18 '77

about

Letter from the publisher. J. Meyers. por Sports Illus 46:4 Ja 31 '77 *

CAMPBELL, Patrick
Humorists: in jest or in jail? il Sat R 4:16+ Je 11 '77

CAMPBELL, Robert
Interaction of two great rivers helps sustain the earth's vital biosphere. il map Smithsonian 8:38-51 S '77
Timely reprieve or a death sentence for the Amazon. il Smithsonian 8:100-11 bibl(p 160-1) O '77

CAMPBELL, Robert G. See Thompson, D. A. jt auth

CAMPBELL, Robert K.
Stepping aside. il pors Forbes 119:58 F 1 '77 *

CAMPBELL, William
Mobilizing for a barrier-free zoo. il Parks & Rec 12:30+ My '77 *

CAMPBELL, Ohio
Campbell faces up to hard times. . .again. M. King. il Forbes 120:57-64 N 15 '77

CAMPECHE, Mexico
Campeche: buccaneer's battleground. N. Navarro and R. Bushnell. il Oceans 10:22-5 S '77

CAMPERS (trailers) See Automobile trailers

CAMPERS, Helicopter. See Helicopters, Remodeled

CAMPERS, Truck
Bunkhouse on wheels: a great way to go! J. A. Linkletter. il Pop Mech 147:109 Mr '77
Camper on the beach; motorhomes at the seashore. F. Woolner. il Field & S 82:46+ My '77
Going motorhome full-time. S. Roberson. il Ret Liv 17:27-30 F '77
Going motorhome part-time. J. Favicchio. il Ret Liv 17:31-2 F '77
Hamburgers turn gray when halted on a slanting street; touring the United States in a motor home. R. Bongartz. il Sat Eve Post 249:22+ Ap '77
Happy marriage of mini and max; mini motor homes. J. Bayliss. il Sat Eve Post 249:26-7 Ap '77
Home on wheels. R. Magruder and M. Magruder. il Travel 147:58-63 Je '77
Latest word on the RV scene. F. K. Coffee. il Mech Illus 73:68+ My '77
Minihome you can build. R. Q. Riley. il Mech Illus 73:45-7+ Je '77
Mystery ride; cocktail party in motor home given by Harrison and Sonja Eiteljorg. F. A. Birmingham. il Holiday 58:52-4 S '77
New on-the-go gear for camping. il Pop Mech 147:104-8 Mr '77
New shapes and styles for RV camping. B. McKeown. il Pop Mech 148:98-9 D '77
No-frill campers. H. Shuldiner. il Pop Sci 210:106-9 Mr '77
PM's motor home of the future. B. McKeown. il Pop Mech 148:72-5 Jl '77
Pickup caps: the economy campers. H. Shuldiner. il Outdoor Life 160:32+ Ag '77
RV roundup:
  Self-propelled rigs. B. Behme. il Field & S 81:124+ Ap '77
Super bugger. J. Pashdag. il Motor T 28:96-8 D '76
Why we bought motor homes: three views. il Forbes 119:69-70 Je 15 '77
See also
Vans

Radio equipment

Component stereo on wheels. S. Walton. il Pop Mech 149:68-9 Ja '78

Tape equipment

Component stereo on wheels. S. Walton. il Pop Mech 149:68-9 Ja '78

Testing

Wheels afield:
  GMC motorhome. B. Kovacik. il Motor T 29:77-8 O '77
  Tioga II; motorhomes. B. Kovacik. il Motor T 29:124-5+ Je '77

CAMPERS diet. See Diet

CAMPGROUNDS. See Camp sites, facilities, etc.

CAMPING
ABCs of boat camping. A. J. McMasters. il Mech Illus 73:24+ Je '77
Camper on the beach; motorhomes at the seashore. F. Woolner. il Field & S 82:46+ My '77
Camping. S. Netherby. See issues of Field & stream
Float trip camping. N. Strung. il Field & S 82:52-4+ My '77
Tent camp: perfect base for cold-weather action. P. Nelson. il Outdoor Life 160:78-9+ D '77
Tips on canoe camping. il Mech Illus 73:122+ My '77
See also
Backpacks and backpacking
Camp cookery
Camp sites, facilities, etc.
Camps
Wilderness survival

Anecdotes, facetiae, satire, etc.

My heart doesn't care where the wild goose goes. C. Lavarnway. il Read Digest 110:223-6 Ap '77
Tent traumas. P. F. McManus. Field & S 82:140+ Ag '77

Educational aspects

OBIS and ACA—the impossible equation does match. D. Buller. il Camp Mag 49:10-11 Ap '77

Outfits, supplies, etc.

Camping equipment:
  Lanterns. il Consumers Res Mag 60:22-6 Je '77
  Stoves and catalytic heaters. il Consumers Res Mag 60:26-31 Jl '77
Camping: new equipment & ideas (cont of) Camping: field-use reports of new gear. E. A. Bauer. See issues of Outdoor life
Camping supplies and recreational equipment. il Consumers Res Mag 60:162-8 O '77
Disposable camping. G. Ade. il Mech Illus 73:112+ Mr '77
Go the drop camp way. C. J. Farmer il Outdoor Life 159:68-71+ F '77
Hiking, backpacking & rafting; equipment. J. Condon. Harp Baz 110:88+ Ap '77
New gear for easier camping. B. McKeown. il Pop Mech 148:65 Ag '77
New ways to camp in the cold. J. Elder. il Pop Mech 148:90-1 N '77
Outdoor gear for wilderness wandering. V. E. Smay. il Pop Sci 210:57-8+ Mr '77
Revolution (maybe); lightweight equipment and clothing. S. Netherby. il Field & S 82:40+ My '77
Two built-ins for camper comfort; a catalytic heater and a back-door kitchen. il Pop Mech 147:111 Mr '77
See also
Backpacks and backpacking
Camp cookery
Camp stoves
Sleeping bags
Tents
Trucks—Camping equipment

Canada

Bowhunter's camp; northwest Canada. F. Bear. il por Field & S 82:64-6+ My '77
Camper travel idea. map Outdoor Life 159:173 F '77

Mexico

South of the border on a shoestring. N. Strung. il Field & S 81:158-9+ F '77

Montana

Camping with big game; upper Gallatin River area. B. McRae. il Field & S 82:58-60+ My '77

South Carolina

Home away from home; Ocean Lakes Family Campground, Myrtle Beach. J. B. Cumming, Jr. il Newsweek 90:61+ Jl 18 '77

Southwestern States

Four-wheel drive for back-country boating. B. McKeown. il Pop Mech 147:102-3 Mr '77

United States

Prescription for a beat-up wilderness. B. Scott. il Nat Wildlife 15:12-16 Ap '77

Wyoming

Rocky Mountain high time of your life. V. Landi. il Outdoor Life 159:70-5+ My '77

CAMPING equipment. See Camping—Outfits, supplies, etc.

CAMPING for the handicapped. See Camps for the handicapped

CAMPING outfits. See Camping—Outfits, supplies, etc.

CAMPION, Donald R.
Slumbering Synod. America 137:328-30, 355-8 N 12-19 '77

CAMPION, Elizabeth Q.
Child's art; poem. il Sch Arts 76:42 Je '77

CAMPION, Thomas
Epigrammatum liber primus; Epigrammatum liber secundus; poems. tr by S. Ratcliffe. Poetry 130:90-3 My '77

CAMPOLI, Robert
Trim-tab steering. il Motor B & S 139:34 F '77

CAMPOS-ORTEGA, J. A. See Strausfeld, N. J. jt auth

CAMPS
Buying guide. Camp Mag 49:19-20+ Mr '77
Coed camping—yes! C. B. Rotman and others. il Camp Mag 49:33-4+ Mr '77
Dreams to reality: fame not enough says All-American; sports camp. K. Benson. il pors Camp Mag 49:34-5+ Ja '77
Everybody goes to camp. J. Leo. il Time 110:48 Jl 4 '77
How to pick a camp. R. Flaste. il N Y Times Mag p86+ Mr 20 '77
Let's not all leap on the coed bandwagon; importance of boys' camps. R. W. Patterson, Jr. il Camp Mag 49:36-7+ Ja '77
'77 winter may affect camps. Camp Mag 49:13 Mr '77
Sports camps for kids. il Bet Hom & Gard 55:234+ Ap '77
Time to line up a summer camp for the kids. il Changing T 31:19-20 F '77
See also
American Camping Association

Activities

Bird study aids camp enrichment. G. R. Dudderar. Camp Mag 49:6-7 Je '77
Ceremonies are a part of camping. M. Nagel. Camp Mag 49:35-6+ Mr '77
Fastest growing American sport is camp's least understood program. C. Krich. il Camp Mag 49:14-15+ My '77
Opinion; water sports. R. B. Kauffman. Camp Mag 49:5+ Je '77
Playground blend; adventure playground planned by campers; Forest Acres Camp for Girls in Fryeburg, Me. C. Leigh. il Camp Mag 49:6-8 My '77
Tips for summer photo fun; photograms and sungrams. G. Kolasa. Camp Mag 49:12-13 My '77
Water relays. D. Pick. Camp Mag 49:11+ F '77

Administration

Be specific: standards and roles affect salary administration. il Camp Mag 49:29-32 Mr '77
Planning & development (cont) Camp Mag 49:40-1 Ja; 16-17 F; 38-40 Mr; 17-18 My; 17-18 Je '77
Strong staff: the key ingredient. D. Shellenberger. il Camp Mag 49:6-8+ Ap '77
See also
Camp directors
Fund for Advancement of Camping

Counselors

See Camp counselors

Finance

Cooperative buying—do you save? V. Wolf. Camp Mag 49:18-19 Mr '77

Food service

Summer food program: how your camp can join; questions and answers. W. G. Boling. Camp Mag 49:9+ My '77

Handbooks, manuals, etc.

Good staff handbook should result from director and staff cooperation; Earth Camp One handbook. R. Newman. Camp Mag 49:12-13+ Ap '77

Laws and regulations

Legal advice helps lessen directors' worries. W. Eustis. Camp Mag 49:10-12+ Ja '77
Legislative report. A. J. Stolz and A. B. Ball. See issues of Camping magazine

Maintenance

...helps beautify land; Clean Community System. R. W. Powers. Camp Mag 49:8-9 Je '77

Safety devices and measures

Camp safety; proposed legislation. Chr Today 21:38-9 Je 17 '77
On the ball. A. B. Ball. Camp Mag 49:2+ F '77
Safer summer camps—a new try; camp-safety bill. U.S. News 82:66 Ap 25 '77
Some planning hints for the waterfront safety director. E. Slezak. il Camp Mag 49:12-14+ F '77
Youth camp safety; with pro and con discussion. Camp Mag 50:11-12, 18-20 S '77

Security measures

Camp security. T. Chappelow. Camp Mag 50:12-14 S '77

California

Good staff handbook should result from director and staff cooperation; Earth Camp One handbook. R. Newman. Camp Mag 49:12-13+ Ap '77

Florida

Seacamp: a unique environment for a unique education; Big Pine Key. R. E. Bachert, Jr. il Camp Mag 49:8-10 F '77

Maine

Burleigh Hill sponsors unique fund drive. Camp Mag 49:12 Mr '77
Playground blend; adventure playground planned by campers; Forest Acres Camp for Girls in Fryeburg. C. Leigh. il Camp Mag 49:6-8 My '77

Minnesota

Camp guides deaf teens to informed relationships; Courage North. K. Noling. il Camp Mag 49:10-11+ My '77

Wisconsin

Who can keep up with these kids in the woods? Youth Conservation Corps' camp at Lost Lake. M. Wexler. il Nat Wildlife 15:40-3 F '77

CAMPS for the handicapped
Acorn people. R. Jones. il Psychol Today 11:70-2+ Je '77
Blind teens touch Hawaii via travel camp. N. Kaplan and R. Eskridge. il Camp Mag 49:14-16 Mr '77
Camp guides deaf teens to informed relationships; Courage North in Minn. K. Noling. il Camp Mag 49:10-11+ My '77
Gibson theories applied to integrated camps for mentally retarded. T. Russo and D. Gregory il Camp Mag 49:14-16+ Je '77

CAMPUS, Peter
About faces: the new work of Peter Campus. R. Smith. il Art in Am 65:85-7 Mr '77 *

CAMPUS Crusade for Christ (organization)
Here's life. Chr Today 21:52-5 F 4 '77
Here's life, world. il Chr Today 22:52 D 9 '77
See also
Athletes in Action (organization)

CAMPUS planning
See also
College architecture

CAMPUS police. See Colleges and universities—Security measures

CAMPUS recruiting programs. See Recruiting of employees

CAMS
See also
Automobiles—Cams

CAMUS, Albert
Camus on doublespeak. D. Lazere. Engl J 66:24-6 O '77 *

CAN/Am Hockey School, Guelph, Ont. See Hockey—Study and teaching

CAN openers. See Kitchen utensils and appliances

CANADA
Canada, 1977; symposium. bibl f map Cur Hist 72:145-75+ Ap '77
Canada's time of troubles. B. Hutchison. For Affairs 56:175-89 O '77
See also
Agricultural administration—Canada
Airlines—Canada
Airplanes, Military—Canada
Americans in Canada
Architecture, Domestic—Canada
Art—Canada
Back River
Banks and banking—Canada
Booksellers and bookselling—Canada
Camping—Canada
Colleges and universities—Canada
Conglomerate corporations—Canada
Cruising—Canada
Electric plants—Canada
Electric utilities—Canada
Energy policy—Canada
Environmental movement—Canada
Environmental policy—Canada
Eskimos
Express highways—Canada
Finance—Canada
Fishing—Canada
Football, Professional—Canada
Forests and forestry—Canada
Gas, Natural—Canada
Geology—Canada
Gold mines and mining—Canada
Government ownership—Canada
Hunting—Canada
Hydroelectric plants—Canada
Immigration and emigration—Canada
Investments, American—Canada
Investments, Canadian
Jews in Canada
Journalism—Canada
Labor laws and legislation—Canada
Labor supply—Canada
Land tenure—Canada
Libraries—Canada
Mackenzie River (Canada)
Money—Canada

CANADA—See also—*Continued*
Music festivals—Canada
National parks and reserves—Canada
New Brunswick
Newspaper publishers and publishing—Canada
Northwest Territories
Ontario
Opera—Canada
Periodicals—Canada
Petroleum pipelines—Canada
Prince Edward Island
Quebec (province)
Railroads—Canada
Restaurants—Canada
St Lawrence River
Skis and skiing—Canada
South Nahanni River
Thousand Islands
Trails—Canada
Unemployment—Canada
Villages—Canada
Wilderness areas—Canada
Winnipeg
Yukon
Zoology—Canada

Armed Forces

Canadian military. R. B. Byers. bibl f Cur Hist 72:173-5 Ap '77

Art Bank

See Art—Canada

Climate

Canadian briefs. See issues of Weatherwise

Description and travel

Canada's lively cities. R. S. Kane. il Redbook 149:120+ O '77
Canadian autumn. S. Birnbaum. Esquire 88:46+ O '77
From salt to salt; Dave Halsey's trans-Canada expedition. J. Cassell. Outdoor Life 160:44 Jl '77
Travel: Canada. R. S. Kane. il Vogue 167:97-8+ Ag '77

Economic conditions

Canada's economic squeeze. il map Bus W p60-3+ Mr 28 '77

Economic policy

Controlling inflation in Canada. M. L. Kliman. bibl f Cur Hist 72:166-9 Ap '77
See also
Price regulation by government—Canada
Wage-price policy—Canada

Economic relations

United States

See United States—Economic relations—Canada

Foreign population

See also
Dukhobors

Foreign relations

Canada's foreign policy. P. Regenstreif. Cur Hist 72:150-3+ Ap '77

United States

See United States—Foreign relations—Canada

History

Bibliography

Reviews of books: Canada. See issues of American historical review

Indians

See Indians of North America—Canada

Industries

Canada's flexible bribery standards. Bus W p35 Je 13 '77
See also
Airplane industry—Canada
Coal industry—Canada
Coal mines and mining—Canada
Fisheries—Canada
Forest products industry—Canada
International Nickel Company of Canada
Massey-Ferguson, Ltd
Mining industry and finance—Canada
Petroleum industry—Canada
Photographic industry—Canada
Soft drink industry—Canada
Steel industry—Canada
Telephone apparatus industry—Canada

Languages

See also
Quebec (province)—Languages

Nationalism

Canada's restive nationalism. R. Fulford. il Art N 76:76-8 Ap '77
Editor's page. R. Manning. Atlantic 240:4 D '77
French fact. J. Bishop. Commonweal 104:294-6 My 13 '77
Right again? por Forbes 119:76 Mr 1 '77

Politics and government

Canada and separatism. R. E. Santoni. Progressive 41:10 F '77
Canada: to be or not to be. D. MacDonald. il Read Digest 111:66-70 Ag '77
Cool it, Canada! E. M. Bronfman. por Newsweek 90:11 S 26 '77
Currents in Canadian politics. H. S. Albinski. Cur Hist 72:158-61+ Ap '77
House divided; with interviews with P. E. Trudeau and R. Lévesque. R. Carroll and R. Manning. il Newsweek 90:51+ D 5 '77
Independence for Quebec: the debate gets sharper; with interview with R. Lévesque. il map U.S. News 83:69-72 S 26 '77
Is Canada falling apart? C. W. Gonick. Current 191:38-47 Mr '77
Obsession with unity. A. Astrachan. New Repub 177:21-3 Ag 20 '77; Same. Current 196:46-52 O '77
Quebec and the Canadian political crisis. K. McRoberts. bibl f Ann Am Acad 433:19-31 S '77
See also
Quebec (province)—Politics and government
Socialism—Canada

Race question

Canada has second thoughts about its open door to immigrants. K. M. Chrysler. il U.S. News 83:60+ O 3 '77

Religious institutions and affairs

See also
Church of England in Canada
Evangelical churches in Canada

Royal Canadian Mounted Police

Mountie morass. il Time 110:45 N 14 '77

Royal Commission on the Status of Women in Canada

Great decade for Canadian women. F. Bird. Cur Hist 72:170-2+ Ap '77

Treaties

United States

See United States—Treaties—Canada

CANADA geese. See Geese, Wild

CANADA in literature
Nationalist themes produce a novel success; R. H. Rohmer. por Bus W p66 Mr 28 '77

CANADAIR, Ltd. See Airplane industry—Canada

CANADAY, John E.
Art. il New Repub 177:28-9 O 1; 25-6+ N 12; 22-4 D 10 '77; 178:25-7 Ja 7 '78
John Canaday on art books. il New Repub 177:29-30+ N 26 '77

CANADIAN art. See Art, Canadian

CANADIAN Booksellers Association
Canadian Booksellers Association observes its 25th year with cautious confidence. B. Slopen. Pub W 212:52 Jl 11 '77

CANADIAN communications satellites. See Communications satellites, Canadian

CANADIAN correspondents in foreign countries. See Foreign correspondents

CANADIAN Eskimos. See Eskimos

CANADIAN Javelin, Ltd. See Mining industry and finance—Canada

CANADIAN Library Association
CLA: less form, enough substance. P. Harper. il Wilson Lib Bull 52:68-71 S '77
Increasing CLA effectiveness. N. Horrocks. il por Lib J 102:1732-5 S 1 '77

CANADIAN Mounted Police. See Canada—Royal Canadian Mounted Police

CANADIAN National Railways
Idea is good. por Forbes 119:68 My 1 '77

CANADIAN Opera Company. See Opera—Canada

CANADIAN Pacific, Ltd. See Conglomerate corporations—Canada

CANADIAN Pacific, Ltd-Bangor Punta Corporation merger. See Corporations—Acquisitions and mergers—International aspects

CANAL cruising. See Cruising

CANAL Zone. See Panama Canal Zone

CANALS
See also
Aqueducts
Suez Canal

Europe, Western

New canals for Europe: Russia's invasion path? map U.S. News 82:81 Mr 21 '77

Florida

See also
Cross Florida Barge Canal

New York (state)

Erie Canal; symposium. il Conservationist 32:9-27 N '77
To the Great Lakes; locking through the Barge Canal. P. Ellam. Yachting 141:146+ Je '77

CANALS—*Continued*

Ohio

Opening the locks to the past; use of canals in recreation; Ohio. M. L. Drake. il map Parks & Rec 12:22-7+ Mr '77

Panama

Carter revives dream of a sea-level canal. B. J. Culliton. Science 197:1262-3 S 23 '77

President Carter discusses a new sea-level canal; excerpt from transcript of question and answer session, July 22, 1977. J. Carter. Dept State Bull 77:234 Ag 22 '77

See also

Panama Canal

Russia

Russia's ambitious plans to end its water shortage. map U.S. News 83:80 S 12 '77

United States

Revisiting America's canals. S. McCoy. il Travel 148:60-5 Jl '77

See also

Chesapeake and Ohio Canal National Historical Park

CANALS, Irrigation. See Irrigation canals and ditches

Le **CANARD enchainé (newspaper)** See Newspapers—France

CANARY; opera. See Noda, K.

CANARY grass. See Grasses

CANARY ISLANDS

Canaries. E. McGhee. Sat R 5:35 O 29 '77

Traveler's camera. C. Purcell. il Pop Phot 80:42+ F '77

CANAVANINE

Degradation and detoxification of canavanine by a specialized seed predator. G. A. Rosenthal and others. bibl il Science 196:658-60 My 6 '77

CANAVIER, Elena Karina

White House crafts & craftsmen. il Ceram Mo 25:47-55 D '77

CANAVOR, Natalie

Books. il por Pop Phot 80:72+ My '77

CANBY, Thomas Y.

Rat. il map Nat Geog 152:60-87 Jl '77

Year the weather went wild. il maps Nat Geog 152:798-829 D '77

CANBY, Vincent

Taxi rider. il N Y Times Mag p96-7 Ap 3 '77

CANCER

Cancer and you. P. K. Burkhalter and J. Powell. Sci Digest 82:36-41 S '77

Cancer—the outlaw cell; symposium. bibl il Chemistry 50:2-5+ Ja; 6-11 Ap; 7-21 My; 6-15 Je; 7-17 Jl '77

Cancerphobia. E. M. Whelan. Harp Baz 110:95+ Ap '77

Humphrey's cancer; intestines. por Newsweek 90:27 Ag 29 '77

Moles, cysts and other skin problems; skin cancer. W. A. Nolen. McCalls 105:148+ O '77

New tactics in battle against cancer. il U.S. News 82:81-2 Ap 18 '77

Not-so-terrible truth about cancer. W. A. Nolen. McCalls 104:132+ My '77

President's operation; oral surgery for cancer performed on G. Cleveland. W. W. Keen. il Sat Eve Post 249:106+ Jl '77

Skin cancer: the avoidable killer; interview, ed by D. Robinson. E. Klein. Read Digest 111:123-6 Jl '77

Time to write; J. Graham's column on cancer in the Chicago daily news. il por Time 110:94+ N 14 '77

Transplantable pancreatic carcinoma of the rat. J. K. Reddy and M. S. Rao. bibl il Science 198:78-80 O 7 '77

UN launches cancer survey network. Sci N 111:326 My 21 '77

See also

Bladder—Cancer
Breast—Cancer
Cancer research
Hodgkin's disease
Leukemia
Prostate gland—Cancer
Tumors

Bibliography

Spring books offer cancer prevention hopes and optimism for victims of the disease. R. Dahlin. Pub W 212:50 D 26 '77

Causes

Another saccharin test. M. Clark and others. Newsweek 90:60 Jl 4 '77

Are you a high cancer risk? ideas of P. Cole. E. M. Whelan. Harp Baz 110:127+ F '77

Banning tris; chemically treated nightwear. il Newsweek 89:67 Ap 18 '77

Behind the saccharin uproar. W. Hines and J. Randal. Progressive 41:13-17 Je '77

Bitter reaction to an FDA ban; saccharin. il Time 109:60-1 Mr 21 '77

Cancer and geographic risks; Trace elements and cancer. il Sci N 111:38 Ja 15 '77

Cancer and the environment. S. S. Epstein. bibl il Bull Atom Sci 33:22-30 Mr '77

Cancer-causing chemicals. E. K. Weisburger. bibl il por Chemistry 50:42-8 Ja '77

Cancer-causing radiation. R. L. Ulrich and others. il por Chemistry 50:6-11 Ap '77

Cancer clues from chemical structures. J. A. Miller. il Sci N 111:362-3 Je 4 '77

Cancer mortality in U.S. counties with petroleum industries. W. J. Blot and others. bibl Science 198:51-3 O 7 '77

Carcinogenic risk assessment. J. Cornfield. bibl il Science 198:693-9 N 18 '77

Carcinogens in the workplace: where to start cleaning up. T. H. Maugh, 2d. Science 197:1268-9 S 23 '77

Chasing Chinese chicken cancer. Sci N 112:342-3 N 19 '77

Chemical catastrophes. D. Zwerdling. Progressive 41:15-19 F '77

DES blamed for mothers' cancers. Sci N 112:422 D 24 '77

Environmental cancer. R. E. Train. Science 195:443 F 4 '77

Estrogen-cancer link faces challenge. Sci N 111:294 My 7 '77

FDA proposal to ban saccharin stirs tempest over its testing rules. Ret Liv 17:14-15 Ap '77

Fight over proposed saccharin ban will not be settled for months. B. J. Culliton. Science 196:276-8 Ap 15 '77

Fight starts to beat the ban on saccharin. il U.S. News 82:49 Mr 28 '77

Fill-in-the-blanks standards for carcinogens proposed. D. Shapley. Science 198:278-9 O 21 '77

Fire retardant may pose cancer hazard. Sci N 111:23 Ja 8 '77

Flame-retardant ban dishevels an industry; childrens sleepwear chemical Tris-BP. il Bus W p45-6 Ap 18 '77

Great saccharin snafu. Consumer Rep 42:410-14 Jl '77

Hazards of toxic substances; excerpt from The unfinished agenda: the citizen's policy guide to environmental issues. Nat Parks & Con Mag 51:10-13 Jl '77

How good are the tests? saccharin studies. M. Clark and M. Gosnell. il Newsweek 89:67 Mr 21 '77

How much is enough? saccharin and the law; address, March 24, 1977. S. Gardner. Vital Speeches 43:457-9 My 15 '77

Industry's challenge on benzene; OSHA hearings on benzene links to leukemia. il Bus W p30+ Ag 22 '77

Lesson to be learned from saccharin mess. A. T. Brett. il U.S. News 82:80 Je 6 '77

Metal mutagens and carcinogens affect RNA synthesis rates in a distinct manner. D. J. Hoffman and S. K. Niyogi. bibl il Science 198:513-14 N 4 '77

More on hair dyes. J. Corbett. Ms 5:21 F '77

Neoplastic and possibly related skin lesions in neontenic tiger salamanders from a sewage lagoon. F. L. Rose and J. C. Harshbarger. bibl il Science 196:315-17 Ap 15 '77; Reply with rejoinder. J. G. Windsor, Jr and others. 198:1280-1 D 23 '77

No mad scientists; proposed ban on saccharin. S. Kelman. New Repub 176:8+ Mr 26 '77

Occupational cancer: government challenged in beryllium proceeding. D. Shapley. Science 198:898-9+ D 2 '77

Potential cancer agents from within. Sci N 112:181 S 17 '77

Problems with OSHA's cancer proposal. Bus W p38 O 24 '77

Risks, benefits, and carcinogens; adaptation of address, March 22, 1977. B. Commoner. Chemistry 50:19-20 Je '77

Saccharin: a chemical in search of an identity. B. J. Culliton. Science 196:1179-80+ Je 10 '77; Reply. D. L. Arnold and others. bibl il 197:320 Jl 22 '77

Saccharin and cancer: confounding data. Sci N 112:245-6 O 15 '77

Saccharin and other health scares: what can you believe? N. G. Rollins. Good H 185:201-2 Jl '77

Saccharin ban. L. Langway. il Newsweek 89:65+ Mr 21 '77

Saccharin ban: a sour reception. Sci N 111:182 Mr 19 '77

Saccharin ban: weighing the risks. J. Mayer. il Fam Health 9:38-9+ Jl '77

Saccharin can be sold—for now. il Bus W p38 Ap 25 '77

Screening for cancer; FDA use of the Ames test. M. Weinstock. Environment 19:2-4 D '77

Should saccharin be banned? interviews. G. Nelson; J. G. Martin. pors U.S. News 82:59-60 Ap 4 '77

Split decision; detailed proposals for banning saccharin. Newsweek 89:83 Ap 25 '77

Statistics and the fluoride debate. Sci N 112:262 O 22 '77

CANCER—Causes—*Continued*
Steroid contraceptive use and cervical dysplasia. increased risk of progression. E. Stern and others. bibl il Science 196:1460-2 Je 24 '77
Sweetener problem crystallizes. Sci N 112:388 D 10 '77
Tougher rules to protect workers against cancer. U.S. News 83:115 O 17 '77
Tris—a sleepwear flame retardant banned. Consumers Res Mag 60:4 Je '77
Tris: confusion over another cancer hazard. Consumer Rep 42:415-16 Jl '77
Tris controversy. P. H. Abelson. Science 197:113 Jl 8 '77; Reply. R. H. Harris. bibl 197:1132-3 S 16 '77
Using cancer's rates to track its cause. map Bus W p69-70+ N 14 '77
Well water; illegality of private wells in Chesapeake, Va. C. Cahill. Environment 19:46-8 Je '77
What benzene's link to leukemia will cost; OSHA standard. il Bus W p35 My 9 '77
Why ban saccharin? M. Stone. il U.S. News 82:84 Ap 4 '77
See also
Benzopyrene
Nitrosamines
Sodium nitrite
Stilbestrols

Diagnosis

Biochemical markers: early warning signs of cancer. T. H. Maugh. 2d. Science 197:543-5 Ag 5 '77
Damadian's supermagnet: how he hopes to use it to detect cancer. S. Renner-Smith. il pors Pop Sci 211:76-9+ D '77
Detecting cancer. Chemistry 59:51-2 Ja '77
See also
Breast—Cancer—Diagnosis
Prostate gland—Cancer—Diagnosis

Genetic aspects

Cancer as a problem in development. A. C. Braun. bibl il por Chemistry 50:30-5 Ja '77

Immunological aspects

Antibody-induced antigen redistribution and shedding from human breast cancer cells. R. E. Nordquist and others. bibl il Science 197:366-7 Jl 22 '77
Cancer and the immune response. J. L. Fahey. bibl il por Chemistry 50:6-10 Je '77
Cancer immunization: tempered progress. Sci N 111:341-2 My 28 '77
Cancer immunology. L. J. Old. il Sci Am 236:62-70+ bibl(p 146) My '77
Feline oncornavirus-associated cell membrane antigen: expression in transformed nonproducer mink cells. A. H. Sliski and others. bibl il Science 196:1336-9 Je 17 '77
Rous sarcomas in chickens: enhanced growth coexisting with concomitant immunity. R. McBride and others. bibl Science 197:1079-82 S 9 '77

Nutritional aspects

Cancer and your diet. J. Powell. Sci Digest 82:38-40 S '77
Link between cancer and nutrition. J. E. Brody. Am Home 80:41+ Ag '77; Same abr with title Way to reduce your chances of getting cancer. Read Digest 111:131-4 N '77
Mutagenic activity of nitrite-treated foods: human stomach cancer may be related to dietary factors. H. Marquardt and others. bibl il Science 196:1000-1 My 27 '77
What you eat . . . might prevent cancer—or cause it. A. A. Belson. Vogue 167:234-5+ Mr '77

Personal narratives

Helga's gift; lung cancer victim. P. M. Thomsen and J. P. Blank. il Read Digest 110:72-7 Je '77
We're the lucky ones; case of S. Clark. R. Rooney. il por McCalls 104:28+ S '77
You can't quit. H. H. Humphrey. por Read Digest 111:57-61 Ag '77

Prevention

See also
American Cancer Society
Cancer inhibiting substances

Psychological aspects

After cancer, the tough return to the job; study by the American Cancer Society's California Division. J. Gaylin. Psychol Today 10:30-2 F '77

Statistics

Cancer rate: is it going up or down? Farm J 101:26 mid-Mr '77
Interpreting cancer survival rates. J. E. Enstrom and D. F. Austin. bibl il Science 195:847-51 Mr 4 '77

Therapy

Chemotherapy of cancer. J. H. Burchenal and J. R. Burchenal. bibl il pors Chemistry 50:11-17 Jl '77
Drug war on cancer. J. E. Brody. il N Y Times Mag p48-50+ Ap 3 '77
Immunotherapy of human cancer. L. A. Schafer and E. M. Hersh. bibl il Chemistry 50:11-15 Je '77
Lung cancer: a status report. Sci N 112:294 N 5 '77
New look at heroin could spur better medical use of narcotics. C. Holden. Science 198:807-9 N 25 '77
Radiation therapy. D. F. Nelson and P. Rubin. bibl il pors Chemistry 50:6-10 Jl '77
See also
Laetrile
Leukemia—Therapy

CANCER cells
Control of cell growth in cancer. A. B. Pardee and D. S. Schneider. il pors Chemistry 50:25-9 Ja '77
Inducibility of transferrin receptors on Friend erythroleukemic cells. H. Y. Y. Hu and others. bibl il Science 197:559-61 Ag 5 '77
Localization of the globin gene in the template active fraction of chromatin of Friend leukemia cells. R. B. Wallace and others. bibl il Science 198:1166-8 D 16 '77
Tumor antigen and human chorionic gonadotropin in CaSki cells: a new epidermoid cervical cancer cell line. R. A. Pattillo and others. bibl il Science 196:1456-8 Je 24 '77
Tumor cell collagenase and its inhibition by a cartilage-derived protease inhibitor. K. E. Kuettner and others. bibl il Science 196:653-4 My 6 '77
Tumor growth and spread. I. J. Fidler and M. L. Kripke. bibl il pors Chemistry 50:18-24 Ja '77

CANCER hot lines. See Telephone in medical care

CANCER in children
Home care for children with cancer; Univ. of Minnesota program. K. Leishman. McCalls 105:44-5 Ja '78
Kids with cancer. M. Clark and others. il Newsweek 90:57-9 Ag 15 '77

CANCER inhibiting substances
Antileukemia activity in the oscillatoriaceae: isolation of debromoaplysiatoxin from lyngbya. J. S. Mynderse and others. bibl il Science 196:538-40 Ap 29 '77
Bifunctional intercalators: relationship of antitumor activity of diacridines to the cell membrane. R. M. Fico and others. bibl il Science 198:53-6 O 7 '77
Dibutyryl cyclic AMP mimics ovariectomy: nuclear protein phosphorylation in mammary tumor regression. S. C. C. Yoon and B. H. Redler. bibl il Science 197:272-5 Jl 15 '77
L-dopa: selective toxicity for melanoma cells in vitro. M. M. Wick and others. bibl il Science 197:468-9 Jl 29 '77
Macrophage tumor killings: influence of the local environment. J. B. Hibbs, Jr and others. bibl il Science 197:279-82 Jl 15 '77
Modulation of macrophage tumoricidal capability by components of normal serum: a central role for lipid. H. A. Chapman, Jr and J. B. Hibbs, Jr. bibl il Science 197:282-5 Jl 15 '77
Phospholipid derivative of cytosine arabinoside and its conversion to phosphatidylinositol by animal tissue. C. R. H. Raetz and others. bibl il Science 196:303-5 Ap 15 '77
13-*cis*-Retinoic acid; inhibition of bladder carcinogenesis in the rat. M. B. Sporn and others. bibl il Science 195:487-9 F 4 '77
13-*cis*-Retinoic acid: inhibition of bladder carcinogenesis induced in rats by *N*-butyl-*N*-(4-hydroxylbutyl)nitrosamine. C. J. Grubbs and others. bibl il Science 198:743-4 N 18 '77
Sesquiterpene antitumor agents: inhibitors of cellular metabolism. K. H. Lee and others. bibl il Science 196:533-6 Ap 29 '77
Trace elements and cancer. Sci N 111:38 Ja 15 '77
Tumor cell collagenase and its inhibition by a cartilage-derived protease inhibitor. K. E. Kuettner and others. bibl il Science 196:653-4 My 6 '77
See also
Adriamycin

CANCER producing substances. See Cancer—Causes

CANCER research
Are rats relevant? J. A. Miller. il Sci N 112:12-13 Jl 2 '77
Cancer research. J. A. Califano, Jr. Chemistry 50:2 Jl '77
Cancer unfolding: seeing a cell go bad. il Sci N 111:21 Ja 8 '77
Checkup on medicine. Sci Digest 81:61-5 My '77
Free radical increases in cancer: evidence that there is not a real increase. H. M. Swartz and P. L. Gutierrez. bibl il Science 198:936-8 D 2 '77
Neutron generator aids cancer research. R. Ceppos. il Pop Sci 210:168 Je '77
Of rats and men. A. Wolff. N Y Times Mag p88+ My 15 '77
Regeneration: a potential for cancer aid is seen in research; excerpt from reprint from Smithsonian, January 1977. R. Bahr. il Sci Digest 81:42-4 Ap '77

CANCER research—*Continued*
Relationship of tumor virology to an understanding of nonviral cancers. H. M. Temin. bibl BioScience 27:170-6 Mr '77
Switching cancer cells back to normal. Sci N 111:246 Ap 16 '77
See also
American Cancer Society
Cancer—Causes
Roswell Park Memorial Institute, Buffalo, N.Y.
Sloan-Kettering Institute for Cancer Research, New York
United States—National Cancer Institute

CANCER viruses. See Tumor viruses

CANCUN City (resort) See Seaside resorts—Mexico

CANDIDATES, Political
Trends to watch for in off-year elections. il U.S. News 83:25-6 N 7 '77
See also names of political candidates, e.g. M. Cuomo; *also* subhead Politics and government under names of countries, states and cities, e.g. France—Politics and government

CANDIED fruit. See Confectionery

CANDLE holders. See Candlesticks

CANDLES
Candle power. il Mademoiselle 83:146-9 N '77
Gifts that glow. il Am Home 80:11 D '77

CANDLESTANDS. See Candlesticks

CANDLESTICKS
Adjustable candlestand keeps the light held high. R. Capotosto. il Pop Mech 148:121+ D '77
Candle holder. il Design (US) 79:24 N '77
Iron candlestands: made where, when, and by whom? C. F. Montgomery and G. W. R. Ward. bibl il Antiques 112:282-4 Ag '77
Lamps and candlesticks of the Meriden Britannia Company. R. L. Bowen, Jr. bibl il Antiques 111:332-7 F '77

CANDOR. See Honesty

CANDY
Easter basket treats. il Bet Hom & Gard 55:149 Ap '77
Just-for-fun recipes cooked up by food hobbyists. N. Byal. il Bet Hom & Gard 55:144-5+ O '77
Mexican candies from San Antonio. il Redbook 150:122+ D '77
Milk candies of Latin America. Sunset 158:219 Ap '77
You could call these easy confections health candies. il Sunset 158:202 Je '77

CANDY industry
Pay relationships of candy workers virtually unchanged since 1970. M. S. Sieling. bibl il M Labor R 100:68-70 Mr '77

CANE Pace (race) See Harness racing

CANE weaving
Caning a chair in 7 easy steps. P. Angell. il Pop Mech 147:123-4 Je '77

CANES. See Staffs (canes, sticks, etc)

CANEVARO, Barbara
Tracking the Children of God. il pors Time 110:48 Ag 22 '77 *

CANGIANO, A. and others
Partial denervation affects both denervated and innervated fibers in the mammalian skeletal muscle. bibl il Science 196:542-5 Ap 29 '77

CANIDAE
Social communication in canids: evidence for the evolution of a stereotyped mammalian display. M. Bekoff. bibl il Science 197:1097-9 S 9 '77

CANINE heartworm disease. See Dogs—Diseases and pests

CANING. See Cane weaving

CANISTERS. See Containers

CANIZARO, Joseph
Super Bowl winner. por Forbes 120:78 D 15 '77 *

CANNED food
Canned chili; with recipe for chili con carne. Consumer Rep 42:76-7 D '77
Canned food storage. Bet Hom & Gard 55:151 Je '77

Labeling

See Food—Labeling

CANNES International Film Festival
Catch as catch Cannes. C. Michener. il Newsweek 89:60 Je 6 '77

CANNIBALISM
Enigma of Aztec sacrifice. M. Harner. il map Natur Hist 86:46-51 bibl(p 100) Ap '77; Discussion. 86:20+ My '77

CANNING and preserving
Can do. L. S. Foster. bibl il Am Home 80:56-7+ Ag '77
Canning renaissance; recipes from Ball blue book, the guide to home canning and freezing. C. Taylor. il Sat Eve Post 249:26-9 O '77
Canning together. D. Cunnion. il Org Gard & Farm 24:122-4+ O '77
Ever-improving economics of canning. R. Young. il Org Gard & Farm 24:98-9 Jl '77
Put 'em up! N. Byal. il Bet Hom & Gard 55:104-9+ Ag '77
See also
Jelly, jam, etc.
Pickles and relishes
Vegetables—Preservation

Equipment and supplies

New and better way to preserve juice; use of steam juicer. il Org Gard & Farm 24:96-7 Jl '77
Pressure canners. Consumer Rep 42:31-4 D '77

CANNON, Howard Walter
Should airline rules be loosened? interview. por U.S. News 82:75-6 My 9 '77

CANNON, Maureen
Wedding words; poem. Ladies Home J 94:116 Ag '77

CANNON, P. Jan
Meteorite impact crater discovered in central Alaska with Landsat imagery. il Science 196:1322-4 Je 17 '77

CANNON, Ray
Old man of Cortez dies. C. Garrison. por Field & S 82:81 S '77 *

CANNONS. See Ordnance

CANOE camping. See Camping

CANOE racing
English gate. R. Kauffman. il Camp Mag 49:15+ F '77
See also
Running rapids

CANOE trips
Arctic almost killed me twice! first man to canoe across the Northwest Passage. T. Dauksza. il map Outdoor Life 159:88-91+ Je '77
Canoeing: the Wisconsin Dells. G. Helgeland. il Travel 148:32-5+ Ag '77
Keel of Lake Dickey; St John River; reprint from May 3, 1976 issue of New Yorker; with editorial comment. J. McPhee. il map Liv Wildn 40:3, 4-19+ O '76
New maps & guidos to adventure canoeing. V. Landi. Outdoor Life 160:72+ Ag '77
Our wild and scenic rivers: Noatak. J. M. Kauffmann. il map Nat Geog 152:52-9 Jl '77
Our wild and scenic rivers: the Suwannee. J. Rudloe and A. Rudloe. il map Nat Geog 152:20-9 Jl '77
River that calls to the bold; Back River in the Northwest Territories, Canada. P. Smith. il map Outdoor Life 160:69-73+ Ag '77
See also
Running rapids

Anecdotes, facetiae, satire, etc.

They shoot canoes don't they? P. F. McManus. Field & S 81:68+ Ap '77

History

First crossing: Alexander Mackenzie's quest for the Pacific; excerpt from Winner take all. D. Lavender. il por Am West 14:4-11+ S '77

CANOES

Transportation

See Boats—Transportation

CANOES and canoeing
Opinion. R. B. Kauffman. Camp Mag 49:5+ Je '77
Sailing kit for canoes. B. Nadler. il Mech Illus 73:122 F '77
There's only one motto: watch your step! Ret Liv 17:22 Jl '77
See also
Kayaks and kayaking

CANOL project. See Petroleum pipelines—Canada

CANON law
Canon law after Vatican II: renewal or retreat? R. A. Hill. America 137:298-300 N 5 '77
See also
Marriage—Annulment (canon law)

CANONIZATION
Saint; J. Neumann. New Yorker 53:24-6 Je 27 '77
Saint they almost overlooked; J. Neumann. il por Time 109:70+ Je 20 '77
We have a holy Bishop; J. Neumann. J. W. Donohue. America 136:539-42 Je 18 '77
See also
Beatification

CANONS, fugues, etc.
See also
Phonograph records—Canons, fugues, etc.

CANOPY beds. See Beds

CANOVA, George M.
After the coup at CalComp. por Bus W p35 Ap 25 '77 *

CANS
Explosion-proof gas can. E. C. Bendall. il Pop Sci 210:12 Ap '77
Gas can that won't explode. il Mech Illus 73:102 F '77

CANT, Gilbert
Worrying about ulcers. il N Y Times Mag p70+ N 6 '77

CANTALOUPES. See Melons
CANTATA and cantatas
See also
Phonograph records—Cantatas
CANTEEN Corporation
Canteen's profitable new menu. il Bus W p 134 Ag 15 '77
CANTEENS (flasks) See Bottles
CANTER, Kathleen
Pale is pretty too! por Seventeen 36:64 Jl '77
CANTERBURY, Frederick Donald Coggan, Abp of.
See Coggan, F. D.
CANTON Fair. See Exhibitions
CANTOR, Eli
From typographer to novelist: one man's experience in switching keyboards. il Pub W 213-44+ Ja 2 '78
CANTRELL, Scott
International Congress of Organists. Hi Fi 28: MA26-7 Ja '78
Not-so-bland organs of Britain. il Hi Fi 27:95-6 Jl '77
CANTWELL, Mary
Eat. See issues of Mademoiselle
CANTWELL, Robert, 1908-
Burglary was for the birds. il Sports Illus 47: 20-2+ Jl 11 '77
Cowboy who showed 'em. il pors Sports Illus 46:68-72+ My 9 '77
Fun machines. il Sports Illus 47:24-9 Jl 4 '77
Nature. Sports Illus 47:48-9 Ag 1 '77
Win, place and glow. il Sports Illus 47:32-4+ Ag 29 '77
CANUP, Jan, and Canup, Terry
New generation for High Street. il Ret Liv 17: 35-7+ F '77
CANUP, Terry. See Canup, J. jt auth
CANYON maple. See Maple
CANYONS
Bird watching in Arizona canyons. il map Sunset 158:104-6 Je '77
Last oasis; exploring the Escalante Canyon in Utah. E. Abbey. il Harpers 254:8+ Mr '77
See also
Colorado Plateau
Grand Canyon
Hells Canyon
CAP Skirring, Senegal. See Vacation villages
CAP Trafalgar (ship) See Ocean liners
CAPACITANCE meters. See Electric meters
CAPACITY, Industrial. See Industrial capacity
CAPE BRETON Island
Canada's moth war; efforts to halt spruce budworm spraying program due to increase in Reye's syndrome cases. E. E. May. bibl il map Environment 19:16-24 Ag '77
CAPE buffalo hunting. See Buffalo hunting
CAPE CANAVERAL Space Center. See United States—John F. Kennedy Space Center
CAPE COD
See also
Chatham, Mass.
Environmental movement—Cape Cod
Provincetown, Mass.

Restaurants

See Restaurants—United States
CAPE COD Room, Drake Hotel. See Chicago—Hotels, restaurants, etc.
CAPE cowslips
Greenhouse. J. Kilborn. il Horticulture 55:82-3 Mr '77
CAPE HATTERAS National Seashore
Thirsty developers. Nat Parks & Con Mag 51: 22-3 F '77
CAPE HORN. See Horn, Cape
CAPE OF GOOD HOPE. See Good Hope, Cape of
CAPE ROMAIN National Wildlife Refuge. See Wildlife sanctuaries—South Carolina
CAPE VERDE Islands
See also
United Nations—Cape Verde Islands
CAPE VINCENT Great Lakes Fisheries Research Station. See New York (state)—Environmental Conservation, Department of
CAPES (clothing) See Cloaks
CAPEZIO Ballet Makers (firm)
Capezio Ballet Makers, dancing at ninety. L. Draegin. il Dance Mag 51:110-11 Mr '77
CAPITAL
Capital commitments and the high cost of money. S. L. Hayes, 3d. bibl f Harvard Bus R 55: 155-61 My '77; Discussion. 55:177-8 Jl '77
Capital gap: a big problem for small firms. J. P. Birkelund. Duns R 109:81-2 F '77
Crucial issue of capital to pay for tomorrow. il Nations Bus 65:41-2+ S '77
Financing the future; address, March 7, 1977. R. E. Anderson. Vital Speeches 43:408-11 Ap 15 '77
Japanese connection; address, October 10, 1977. W. F. Rockwell. Vital Speeches 44:61-4 N 1 '77
Lance is rethinking the role of the SEC; possible addition of capital-formation policy planning. Bus W p36+ F 28 '77
CAPITAL, Venture
Advantage, Adler! il por Forbes 119:66-7 Ja 15 '77
Big bankroll for new business. T. J. Murray. il Duns R 109:52-4+ F '77
Venture capital. T. P. Murphy. See second issue of each month of Forbes
CAPITAL Development Fund. See United Nations—Capital Development Fund
CAPITAL formation. See Capital
CAPITAL gains tax. See Income tax—Capital gains tax
CAPITAL investments
Adjusting for risk in business investments. R. F. Dowd. Intellect 105:355-6 Ap '77
Capital spending's elusive boom. il Bus W p38-9 My 16 '77
Caution still pervades capital spending plans. il Bus W p39-40 N 14 '77
Financing the future; address, March 7, 1977. R. E. Anderson. Vital Speeches 43:408-11 Ap 15 '77
Frustration in the formation of investment capital; address, February 23, 1977. R. H. B. Baldwin. Vital Speeches 43:405-8 Ap 15 '77
Glimmer ahead for capital spending. Bus W p38 Mr 14 '77
Keeping business on course: experts tell what's needed. il U.S. News 83:15-16 Ag 1 '77
Kick from capital spending. il Bus W p24-5 Je 27 '77
No animal spirit. il Time 109:62 Ap 11 '77
Slow-investment economy. il Bus W p60-3+ O 17 '77
Steady strength, but no boom, in capital goods. S. Parker and others. il Fortune 95:20+ Je '77
Surprising powers of short-term rates; effects on capital spending. il Bus W p70-1 Ag 22 '77
Tax cuts and federal spending needed to revive economic recovery in 1977. G. A. Christie. Archit Rec 161:83 Ja '77
Ticking time bomb. A. J. Mayer and others. il Newsweek 90:57-8 Ag 29 '77
What it takes to create jobs. Fortune 95:133 Mr '77
Why capital-goods prospects are better than they seem. il Fortune 96:14 D '77
Why inflation worries economists more. S. Zucker. Bus W p28 Ap 25 '77
See also
Investment tax credit

Europe, Western

Britain: a new upbeat mood for investment. Bus W p41-2 F 21 '77
Why capital spending is still sluggish. il Bus W p55 S 19 '77
CAPITAL Preservation Fund Inc. See Investment trusts
CAPITAL punishment
Arguing about death for rape. Time 109:80 Ap 11 '77
Capital punishment; address, July 8, 1977. A. G. Amsterdam. Vital Speeches 43:677-82 S 1 '77
Capital punishment; address, July 15, 1977. E. J. Younger. Vital Speeches 43:682-5 S 1 '77
Capital punishment—or suicide? North Carolina's new legislation. L. Spear. Commonweal 104: 742 N 25 '77
Case against capital punishment. A. Fortas. il N Y Times Mag p8-9+ Ja 23 '77
Death penalty for rape? case of Coker v. Georgia. D. Leavy. Ms 6:20 Jl '77
Death penalty—issue that won't go away. il U.S. News 82:47 Ja 31 '77
Deterrent to the deterrent argument; death penalty. Chr Cent 94:132-3 F 16 '77
Dismantling the cross: a case against capital punishment. L. M. Jendrzejczyk. Chr Cent 94: 296-7 Mr 30 '77
Dying institution; views of A. Amsterdam. C. McWilliams. Nation 225:611-12 D 10 '77
Heard round the world. Nat R 29:133-4 F 4 '77
Horror of death at Eastertime; with views of M. Dees. J. M. Wall. Chr Cent 94:315-16 Ap 6 '77
Injustice of the death penalty; discussion. America 136:41 Ja 22 '77
Not-so-new South: legal aid in the death belt; Team Defense Project. M. Pinsky. il Nation 224:367-8 Mr 26 '77
Rape and death; Supreme Court decision on death penalty in rape cases. il Newsweek 90: 48 Jl 11 '77
Sad footnote; Daniel R. Webster case. J. Deedy. Commonweal 104:772 D 9 '77
Tying abortion to the death penalty; study by Paul Cameron. J. Horn. Psychol Today 11: 43+ N '77
We cannot be sure; death penalty in B. Hauptman case. Nation 224:420 Ap 9 '77
See also
Executions and executioners
CAPITAL sins. See Sin
CAPITAL spending. See Capital investments

CAPITALISM
Capitalism's last gasp. S. Lens. Current 195:27-36 S '77
Capitalist paradox. L. H. Lapham. il Harpers 254:31-4+ Mr '77
Future of capitalism: the intellectual and the businessman; address, February 9, 1977. M. Friedman. Vital Speeches 43:333-7 Mr 15 '77
It's so hard to be good under capitalism. Aristides. Am Scholar 46:290+ Summ '77
Present state of capitalism. R. Marris. New Repub 176:39-41 My 21 '77
Reconsideration. J. Beatty il New Repub 177: 35-8 D 17 '77
Socialism and sin; capitalism vs socialism. B. Douglass; discussion. Chr Cent 94:171-4, 567-9 F 23, Je 8 '77
Trilateral Commission: have capitalism and democracy come to a parting of the ways? S. Bowles. il Progressive 41:20-3 Je '77
See also
Free enterprise
CAPITALISTS and financiers
See also
Eaton, C. S.
CAPITALS (cities)
See also
Alaska—Capital
CAPITOL (United States) See United States—Capitol
CAPITOLA, Calif.
Rediscovery of Capitola. il Sunset 158:72-4 Ap '77
CAPLAN, Frank
(ed) Prepared childbirth; excerpt from The parenting advisor. il Fam Health 9:54-6 Mr '77
CAPLAN, Gerald M.
Why government alone can't end the crime wave. por U.S. News 82:82 Ap 11 '77
CAPLOE, David R.
Is U.S. public opinion shifting? Nation 225:70-2 Jl 23 '77
Prospect with Peres. Nation 224:587-90 My 14 '77
Return to Geneva. Nation 225:359-61 O 15 '77
CAPOEIRA. See Hand-to-hand fighting
CAPOTE, Truman
Guests. il McCalls 104:132-7 F '77
about
Bennett Cerf remembers; excerpt from At Random. B. Cerf. il por Pub W 212:28-31 Ag 15 '77 *
CAPOTOSTO, John
Miter box that's powered! il Mech Illus 73:134-6 Mr '77
Quick & easy window channels. il Mech Illus 73:108+ My '77
CAPOTOSTO, Rosario
ABCs of veneering in easy photo steps. il Mech Illus 73:118 Mr '77
Low-voltage yard lighting. il Pop Sci 210:114-17 Ap '77
Table for routers & sabers. il Mech Illus 73: 162+ My '77
10 shop tricks from a pro; excerpt from The complete book of woodworking. il por Pop Mech 148:110-12 Ag '77
CAPOUYA, Emile
Poetry of M. L. Rosenthal. Nation 225:311-14, 409-11 O 1, 22 '77
CAPP, Al
Dogpatch is ready for Freddie. il Time 110:78 O 17 '77 *
CAPRA, Frank
Mr Smith goes to Philadelphia: Capra and Stallone. L. Quart. Intellect 106:245 D '77 *
CAPRA, Fritjof
Tao of physics: reflections on the cosmic dance. il Sat R 5:21-3+ D 10 '77
CAPRA, J. Donald, and Edmundson, A. B.
Antibody combining site: with biographical sketches. il Sci Am 236:16, 50-9 bibl(p 132) Ja '77
CAPS, John
(ed) See Bennett, R. R. Interview with Richard Rodney Bennett
CAPTURE of animals. See Animals—Capture
CAPUTI, Claudia
Courageous Claudia fights back. il por Time 109:53 Ap 25 '77 *
CAPUTO, Richard S.
Solar power plants: dark horse in the energy stable. bibl il Bull Atom Sci 33:46-8+ My '77
CAR and driver (periodical)
Driver's seat. Car & Dr 22:8 Ap '77
CAR and Driver Readers' Choice Poll
Democracy-in-action dept: Car and Driver 1978 Readers' Choice Poll; nominees. il Car & Dr 23:35-41 D '77
CAR clubs. See Automobile clubs
CAR operating costs. See Automobiles— Cost of operation
CAR telephone. See Radiotelephone on automobiles
CARACCIOLA, Alice Trobek-Hoffmann
Woman we would have loved to love. B. Yates. Car & Dr 22:18-19 Mr '77 *
CARAMANLIS, Constantine
Victory without triumph. il pors Time 110:51 D 5 '77 *
CARAMOOR Festival. See Music festivals—New York (state)
CARANSA, Maurits, kidnapping
$4 million deal. M. Clark. Time 110:41 N 14 '77
Spreading brushfire. il Time 110:45-6 N 7 '77
CARAS, Roger
Bloodhound. il por Sci Digest 82:62-5 N '77
Magic of the snake-stone: does it cure? il Sci Digest 82:53-5 Jl '77
Pet journal (cont) il Ladies Home J 94:148 F; 36 Ap; 156 Je; 128 Ag; 142 S; 198 O; 144 D '77
CARAVANS (trailers) See Automobile trailers
CARAYANNIS, George Pararas-. See Pararas-Carayannis, G.
CARBINES. See Rifles
CARBOHYDRATES
How sugar gets to your skin—and harms it; refined carbohydrates and skin problems; ideas of W. M. Ringsdorf and E. Cheraskin. N. Simon. Vogue 167:108-9 My '77
Spuds; seminar in New York city. il New Yorker 52:25-6 Ja 17 '77
CARBON
See also
Graphite
Isotopes
Carbon-13/carbon-12 ratio is relatively uniform among honeys. L. W. Doner and J. W. White, Jr. bibl il Science 197:891-2 Ag 26 '77
Mechanism of carbon isotope fractionation associated with lipid synthesis. M. J. DeNiro and S. Epstein. bibl il Science 197:261-3 Jl 15 '77
CARBON compounds
See also
Fluorocarbons
CARBON cycle (biogeochemistry)
Changes of land biota and their importance for the carbon cycle. B. Bolin. bibl il Science 196:613-15 My 6 '77
Forests, lakes, and the anthropogenic production of carbon dioxide. D. B. Botkin. bibl il BioScience 27:325-31 My '77
CARBON dioxide
Atmospheric carbon dioxide—NOAA/Scripps data from Mauna Loa Observatory 1958-1977. il Weatherwise 30:207 O '77
CO_2 pollution may change the fuel mix. il Bus W p25 Ag 8 '77
Carbon dioxide and climate: carbon budget still unbalanced. R. A. Kerr. Science 197:1352-3 S 30 '77
Carbon dioxide question. G. M. Woodwell. il map Sci Am 238:34-43 Ja '78
Caution: the greenhouse effect. W. Sullivan. Sci Digest 82:58 O '77
Changes of land biota and their importance for the carbon cycle. B. Bolin. bibl il Science 196:613-15 My 6 '77
Coal and the coming (?) superinterglacial. Sci N 111:356 Je 4 '77
DOE sets interagency CO_2 research priorities. Sci N 112:375 D 3 '77
Desert greenhouse; fossil fuels and climate. il maps Environment 19:14-20 N '77
Forests, lakes, and the anthropogenic production of carbon dioxide. D. B. Botkin. bibl il BioScience 27:325-31 My '77
Hazards of coal dependence. W. S. Broecker. il Natur Hist 86:8+ O '77
Is energy use overheating world? fossil fuels. il U.S. News 83:71 Jl 25 '77
NAS panel is concerned over atmospheric CO_2 buildup. F. C. Bennett. por Phys Today 30: 17-18 O '77
Upsetting the climatic balance. il Chemistry 50:26-7 O '77
Wood versus fossil fuel as a source of excess carbon dioxide in the atmosphere: a preliminary report. J. A. S. Adams and others. bibl il Science 196:54-6 Ap 1 '77
See also
Photosynthesis
CARBON Edge exercise. See Military maneuvers
CARBON filtration. See Filters and filtration
CARBON-14 dating. See Radiocarbon dating
CARBON monoxide
Chemical relevance—a heuristic approach. A. Mancott. Chemistry 50:24 Mr '77
Toxicity of mild prenatal carbon monoxide exposure. L. D. Fechter and Z. Annau. bibl il Science 197:680-2 Ag 12 '77
CARBON tetrachloride
Drinking water: getting rid of the carbon tetrachloride. J. L. Marx. Science 196:632-6 My 6 '77
CARBONATES
Device for detecting carbonates. B. L. Dunicz. il Chemistry 50:27 Ap '77
See also
Calcium carbonate
CARBONIC anhydrase
Erythrocyte carbonic anhydrase I: inherited deficiency in humans. A. G. Kendall and R. E. Tashian. bibl il Science 197:471-2 Jl 29 '77

CARBORUNDUM Company
How Carborundum maintains 15% growth. il Bus W p 117 N 21 '77
CARBORUNDUM Company mergers. See Corporations—Acquisitions and mergers
CARBOXYFLUORESCEIN. See Fluorescein
CARBOXYLASES
Ribulose bisphosphate carboxylase: a two-layered, square-shaped molecule of symmetry 422. T. S. Baker and others. bibl il Science 196:293-5 Ap 15 '77
CARBURETORS
Carburetor. il Pop Mech 147:140+ My '77
Holley's system. G. Witzenburg. il Motor T 29: 73-4+ N '77
How to care for the new carburetors. T. Tappett. il Mech Illus 73:154+ Ap '77
Truth about. . .Holley carb models. C. J. Baker. il Hot Rod 30:47-50+ D '77
Wide open. il Hot Rod 30:89-92+ Je '77
CARCASSES, Cattle. See Cattle—Carcasses
CARCINOEMBRYONIC antigen. See Antigens and antibodies
CARCINOGENS. See Cancer—Causes
CARCINOMA. See Cancer
CARD boxes. See Boxes, cases, etc.
CARD catalogs, Library. See Catalogs, Library
CARDBOARD sculpture. See Paper sculpture
CARDELLICHIO, Thomas C.
School in the middle is not an accordion. Engl J 66:38-41 Ap '77
CARDENOLIDES
See also
Cardiac glycosides
CARDIAC diseases. See Heart—Diseases
CARDIAC glycosides
Cardiac glycosides in the defensive secretion of chrysomelid beetles: evidence for their production by the insects. J. M. Pasteels and D. Daloze. bibl il Science 197:70-2 Jl 1 '77
CARDIAC muscle. See Heart—Muscle
CARDIAC pacemakers. See Pacemaker, Artificial (heart)
CARDIAC rhythm. See Heart beat
CARDIACS
I was given up for dead—twice! D. A. Thompson. Good H 184:1.2+ My '77
CARDIFF, Robert D.
RNA tumor viruses. bibl il por Chemistry 50: 12-16 My '77
CARDIFF, Wales
Cardiff is a good starting point in Wales. il Sunset 159:60 Ag '77
CARDINAL Ritter Institute, St. Louis, Mo.
Cardinal Ritter Institute provides care with flair to St Louis elderly. il Aging 272:8-10 Je '77
CARDINALS
Autographs. R. C. Weekes. Hobbies 82:156 N '77
Pilgrim pope at 80. K. L. Woodward and L. Jenkins. il por Newsweek 90:73-4 O 3 '77
Red hat for the right-hand man; elevation of G. Benelli to College of Cardinals. por Time 109:49 Je 13 '77
CARDIOGRAPHY
Measurement of the human magnetic heart vector. W. H. Barry and others. bibl il Science 198:1159-62 D 16 '77
CARDIOPULMONARY resuscitation. See Resuscitation
CARDIOPULMONARY system

Diseases

Reversal of cardiopulmonary failure during active sleep in hypoxic kittens: implications for sudden infant death. T. L. Baker and D. J. McGinty. bibl il Science 198:419-21 O 28 '77
See also
Heart—Diseases
CARDIOVASCULAR system
See also
Heart
CARDOONS
Cardoon, cardoni—whatever you call it, it's good. J. McDaniel. il Org Gard & Farm 24:148-50 F '77
CARDOZO, Yvette
Ski North Carolina. il Trav/Holiday 148:46-51 D '77
CARDS
Playing cards. D. Powills. See issues of Hobbies
See also
Bridge (game)
Poker (game)
CARDS, Advertising. See Advertising cards
CARDS, Catalog. See Catalog cards
CARDS, Greeting. See Greeting cards
CARDWELL, Walter T. Jr
IC bricklaying for miniature projects. il Radio-Electr 48:58-60 D '77
CAREER counseling. See Vocational guidance
CAREER Criminal Program. See Criminal justice, Administration of—United States
CAREER education. See Technical education; Vocational education
CAREER switching. See Occupational mobility
CAREERS. See Occupations
CAREW, Rod
Baseball's best hitter tries for glory. il pors Time 110:52-3+ Jl 18 '77 *
How Carew does it. P. Bonventre and C. J. Harper. pors Newsweek 90:46-7 Jl 11 '77 *
I hope Rod Carew hits .400; ed by J. Underwood. T. Williams. il pors Sports Illus 47: 20-3 Jl 18 '77 *
CAREY, Hugh L.
Around City Hall (cont) A. Logan. New Yorker 53:96-103 My 30 '77 *
CAREY, Susan, and Diamond, Rhea
From piecemeal to configurational representation of faces. bibl il Science 195:312-14 Ja 21 '77
CAREY, William Daniel
Do not criticize government for all Nation's ills; excerpts from address. por Intellect 105: 290 Mr '77
1976 report to the Association. il Science 196:337-41 Ap 15 '77
CARGAS, Harry James
(ed) See Berrigan, P. To be accurate and blunt: the activist as writer
CARGILL, Inc
Grain marketing for the next decade; address, September 12, 1977. W. B. Saunders. Vital Speeches 44:37-9 N 1 '77
CARGO airlines. See Air freight service
CARGO bill. See Maritime law
CARGO cults. See Cults
CARGO loading and unloading. See Loading and unloading
CARGO planes, Military. See Airplanes, Military transport
CARIBBEAN Development and Cooperation Committee. See United Nations—Economic Commission for Latin America
CARIBBEAN monk seal. See Seals (animals)
CARIBBEAN News Agency. See News agencies
CARIBBEAN Region
See also
Crime and criminals—Caribbean Region
Cruising—Caribbean Region
Fishing—Caribbean Region
Grenada
Investments, American—Caribbean Region
Seaside resorts—Caribbean Region
Trinidad and Tobago
West Indies

Description and travel

Dream isles for night life or quiet beaches; for singles, couples and families. M. Zellers. Redbook 149:196+ O '77

Economic conditions

Crunch in the Caribbean—what hope for these children? with editorial comment. J. Cook. il map Forbes 119:6, 32-6+ My 1 '77

Economic relations

United States

See United States—Economic relations—Caribbean Region
CARIBE. See Piranhas
CARIBOU
Where have all the *tuttu* gone? with editorial comment. J. G. Mitchell. il Audubon 79:inside cover; 2-15 Mr '77
See also
Reindeer
CARICATURES and cartoons
Confessions of a cartoon editor; Saturday review. D. W. Re. il Writers Digest 57:39-41 Je '77
Drawing his own conclusions; work of P. Conrad. H. Lebo. il pors Writers Digest 57:32-3 D '77
In our time. T. Wolfe. il Harpers 255:79 O '77; 256:76 Ja '78
See also
Comics (books, strips, etc)
Motion pictures—Animated cartoons
also subhead Caricatures and cartoons under various subjects, e.g. Electronics—Caricatures and cartoons

Exhibitions

Bill Mauldin: the best gets better; editorial cartoons. H. Mitgang. il Art N 76:92-3 O '77
200 years of the great American freedom to complain; the American Presidency in Political Cartoons: 1776-1976. D. Kunzle. il Art in Am 65:99-105 Mr '77
CARIDE, Vincente J. and Zaret, B. L.
Liposome accumulation in regions of experimental myocardial infarction. bibl il Science 198: 735-8 N 18 '77
CARIES, Dental. See Dental caries
CARINA nebula. See Nebulae
CARL, Ann
New York's gentle industry. il por Conservationist 31:10-15 My '77

CARL, Robert L.
Choosing a new doctor. Ret Liv 17:26-7 Ap '77
CARLBERG, Anita Beth
Science Talent Search 1977. il Chemistry 50:22-3 My '77 *
CARLETON, William G.
Government and health before the New Deal. Cur Hist 72:196-7+ My '77
CARLILE, Henry
Cardinal; poem. New Yorker 53:83 Jl 4 '77
CARLIN, Seth
ISCM World Music Days. il Hi Fi 27:MA30-1+ Ap '77
CARLINSKY, Dan
Can you place the face? Seventeen 36:144-5 Je '77
Who am I? il Seventeen 36:202 My '77
CARLISLE, Madelyn. See Carlisle, N. jt auth
CARLISLE, Norman, and Carlisle, Madelyn
Sitting pretty: science offers 4000 "weighs" it can help you! il Sci Digest 82:43-5 Jl '77
CARLISLE, Olga
Bella: Russian best. por Vogue 167:110-11+ Jl '77
CARLISLE, Thomas Jchn
Flight they took; poem. Chr Cent 94:1164 D 14 '77
Shrinkage; poem. Chr Cent 94:196 Mr 2 '77
CARLISLE, William T.
Slavery and the new history: a guide for the perplexed. bibl il Intellect 106:160-3 O '77
CARLOS (terrorist) See Ramirez Sanchez, I.
CARLSBAD Caverns National Park
Carlsbad's famous bats are dying off. M. Gosnell. il Nat Wildlife 15:28-33 Je '77
CARLSEN, G. Robert, and others
Books for young adults: the 1976 BYA book poll. il Engl J 66:62-7 Ja '77
CARLSEN, Karen L.
Stretch your greenhouse space. il Org Gard & Farm 24:121-5 S '77
Woman's best friend could be her tiller. il Org Gard & Farm 24:81-3 Ag '77
CARLSEN, William D.
Thailand's religious roots. il Chr Today 22:24-7 O 7 '77
CARLSON, Cynthia
How to find a reliable rental tenant. il Ret Liv 17:34-5+ Ja '77
CARLSON, Cynthia J.
Grass roots art. il Ms 6:64-8 O '77
CARLSON, Eric
Habitat plus one: what gives? Archit Rec 161: 37+ Je; 162:29+ Jl '77
CARLSON, Florence, and Shroyer, David
Literature of the interactive education movement. Engl J 66:84-8 Mr '77
CARLSON, Jack Wilson
Excerpt from testimony on the proposed Fair Labor Standards Amendments, March 16, 1977. Cong Digest 56:145+ My '77
Forecasts for the Carter years. por Nations Bus 65:28+ Ja '77
CARLSON, Joseph R. and Bentley, D. R.
Ecdysis: neural orchestration of a complex behavioral performance. bibl il Science 195: 1006-8 Mr 11 '77
CARLSON, Peter
Confessions of a coffee addict. il por Newsweek 89:13 My 16 '77
Killing time on death row. Nation 224:774-5 Je 25 '77
CARLSON, Richard
Sweden's vocational strategy. il Am Educ 13:9-11+ Ag '77
CARLSON, Sue
Once again it was up, up, and away. il por Ret Liv 17:14+ Je '77
CARLTON, Steve
Odd couple, but winning combination. L. Keith. il pors Sports Illus 47:16 Ag 29 '77 *
CARMANIA (ship) See Ocean liners
CARMEL, Calif.

Bookstores

See Booksellers and bookselling—California
CARMELITES
Cloister and the modern world; Carmelite monastery. M. J. S. Smith. il Sat Eve Post 249: 16+ Ap '77
CARMEN; opera. See Bizet, G.
CARMICHAEL, Ian
Ascot and biggin, my Lord? E. Soames. il pors Esquire 88:141-3 D '77 *
CARMICHEL, Jim
Flintlock rifles—new as tomorrow. il Outdoor Life 161:60-3+ Ja '78
Getting the range (cont) il Outdoor Life 159: 144+ F; 146+ Mr '77
Shooting. See issues of Outdoor life
Shotguns & loads: a practical guide. il Outdoor Life 160:86-92+ D '77
Swing. . .swing. . .swing and you'll hit those doves. il Outdoor Life 160:62-3+ Jl '77
Targets (cont) Outdoor Life 159:54+ My '77
CARMODY, Deirdre
Challenging media monopolies. il N Y Times Mag p21-4 Jl 31 '77
CARNATIONS
Carnations from seed—easy. il Sunset 158:218 Mr '77
CARNEGIE Corporation of New York
All our children; report of the Carnegie Council on Children. Time 110:118 S 19 '77
Family ecology; study by the Carnegie Council on Children. J. W. Donohue. America 137:456-9 D 24 '77
Family: it is changing, not breaking up; study by the Carnegie Council on Children. J. Gaylin. Psychol Today 11:36+ O '77
CARNEGIE Council on Children. See Carnegie Corporation of New York
CARNEGIE Foundation for the Advancement of Teaching
Report says colleges too specialized. Sci N 112: 422 D 24 '77
CARNELL, Ron
Clean up the comic book badlands, now. Parents Mag 52:8+ D '77
CARNIVAL
Carnival à la Trinidad and Tobago. C. B. G. London. bibl il Américas 29:19-24 F '77
Farewell to flesh: Rio goes Hollywood; excerpt from Carnival in Rio. A. Goldman. il Esquire 89:66-72+ Ja '78
Joining the crowd for the New Orleans Mardi Gras. B. Hitchings. Bus W p95-6 Ja 16 '78
Run in Mamou; Mardi Gras celebration. H. Camp. Newsweek 89:10 Mr 14 '77
CARNIVALS
Cleaned-up carnivals take over the midways; traveling shows. il U.S. News 83:45 S 5 '77
CARNIVORA
See also
Canidae
CARNIVOROUS plants. See Insectivorous plants
CAROB
See also
Cookery—Organic food
CAROL Reamer, Sister. See Reamer, C.
CAROLINE, Princess of Monaco
Princess Caroline turns twenty. J. Stewart. il por McCalls 104:142-3+ My '77 *
CAROLINE Islands
See also
Palau (islands)
CAROLINGIAN ivories. See Ivories
CAROLS
See also
Christmas carols
CARON, Pierre Augustin. See Beaumarchais, P. A. C. de
CAROTID arteries. See Arteries
CAROUSELS. See Merry-go-rounds
CAROWINDS (amusement park) See Amusement parks
CARPENTER, Charles H. Jr
Nineteenth-century silver in the New York Yacht Club. bibl il Antiques 112:496-505 S '77
CARPENTER, Elizabeth
Here's Texas! il Redbook 150:100-1+ D '77
Rosalynn Carter. il por Redbook 148:68+ Ap '77
CARPENTER, G. Arthur
Overdues overdone. bibl Lib J 102:2137-8 O 15 '77
CARPENTER, Iris
Babel reversed. il Am Educ 13:27-30 Ag '77
CARPENTER, Philip L.
How to commit herbicide. il Horticulture 55:16-21 My '77
CARPENTER, Stanley B.
This princess heals disturbed land. il Am For 83:22-3 Jl '77
CARPENTER, W. L.
The why of liming soils. il Org Gard & Farm 24:143-4 Mr '77
CARPENTER Technology Corporation. See Steel industry—United States
CARPENTERS squares
Using a combination square. H. Wicks. il Pop Mech 148:14 Ag '77
CARPENTIER, Alejo
Blacks in Latin America. il UNESCO Courier 30:8-12 Ag '77
CARPENTRY
Case of the disappearing pipes. T. H. Jones. il Mech Illus 73:104+ Ag '77
See also
Joints (carpentry)
Woodworking

Tools

See Tools
CARPER, Jean
Case for food chemicals. por Newsweek 89:11 Mr 7 '77
Consumer watch. See issues of American home
Health & beauty. Am Home 80:23+ S '77
Rx for poisoning. il Am Home 80:20 F '77
CARPETS. See Rugs and carpets
CARPORTS. See Garages
CARQUINEZ Strait, Calif.
Carquinez Strait—why not some poking around? il map Sunset 158:64-5 My '77

CARR, Bruce C.
APS—AAPT meet in Chicago. il Phys Today 30:23-6 Ja '77
March meeting in San Diego. il Phys Today 30: 43-6 Mr '77
Washington is the site for the sixth CLEA. il Phys Today 30:60-2 My '77
CARR, David Turner
Legalize laetrile as a cancer drug? interview. pors U.S. News 82:51-2 Je 13 '77
CARR, John Dickson
Obituary
Pub W 211:31 Mr 21 '77
CARR, Michael John
Volcanic activity and great earthquakes at convergent plate margins. bibl il map Science 197:655-7 Ag 12 '77
CARR, William Henry
Whitman still walks. il Conservationist 32:23 Jl '77
CARR Square housing project. See St Louis—Housing
CARRAS, Costa
Quartet from far corners. H. Sutton. il por Sat R 4:47 F 5 '77 *
CARREÑO, Mario
Luminous cosmos of Mario Carreño. G. de Zéndegui. il por Américas 29:8-11 My '77 *
CARRERAS, José
Artist life; interview, ed by D. J. Soria. il por Hi Fi 27:MA2+ S '77
CARRIAGE houses, Converted. See Houses, Remodeled
CARRIAGES, Baby. See Baby carriages
CARRICK, Jocelyn
St Francis YC destroyed in fire. il Yachting 141:166 F '77
CARRIER, Herb
Auto-maintenance basics (cont) il Pop Sci 210:166+ Ap '77
CARRIER, Robert
Fresh-from-the-garden cooking. il pors House & Gard 149:151+ Mr '77
CARRIER Corporation
Pumping heat; Carrier Corp's new product. il Forbes 119:75-6 Mr 15 '77
CARRIER Corporation-Inmont Corporation merger. See Corporations—Acquisitions and mergers
CARRIERS, Aircraft. See Aircraft carriers
CARRIERS of infection
See also
Insects as carriers of infection
Mosquitoes as carriers of infection
Swine as carriers of infection
CARRIL, Pete
Blue-collar coach in a button-down league. K. Hannon. il pors Sports Illus 48:26-30 Ja 2 '78 *
CARRILLO, Elisa
Giovanni Battista Franzoni, one year after laicization. il por Chr Cent 94:1093-5 N 23 '77
CARRILLO, Santiago
Quotations from Chairman Carrillo; excerpts from Eurocommunism and the state. por Time 110:32 Jl 11 '77
about
Apostle Carrillo. il por Time 110:47 N 21 '77 *
Carrillo 'neath the elms; speeches at Yale. R. Brookhiser. Nat R 29:1420 D 9 '77 *
Kremlin cracks the whip. M. Ledden. New Repub 177:22-3 Ag 6 '77 *
Not being too beastly to Moscow. il por Time 109:23 Mr 14 '77 *
Parfit gentil knyght. Nat R 29:137 F 4 '77 *
Savaging a comrade. Time 110:19 Jl 4 '77 *
Spain's red Luther. M. R. Benjamin and M. Acoca. por Newsweek 90:38 Jl 11 '77 *
CARRINGTON, Terri
Oooowee, man, that little girl can play! il pors Ebony 32:130-2+ Ap '77 *
CARRO, Geraldine
Mothering. See issues of Ladies' home journal
CARROLL, Chuck
Make the river do the work. B. East. il por Outdoor Life 160:78-81+ O '77 *
CARROLL, Elizabeth
Lord, I believe; help my unbelief. New Cath World 220:35 Ja '77
CARROLL, John
Life on the farm. New Yorker 53:36 Ap 18 '77
CARROLL, John (executive)
6 ways to cut the jobless taxes you pay. Nations Bus 65:64+ Mr '77
CARROLL, Lewis, pseud
Alice in Wonderland; dramatization. See Hill, R.
Wasp in a wig; story. Smithsonian 8:50-7 D '77
about
Suppressed adventure of Alice surfaces after 107 years. il pors Smithsonian 8:50-7 bibl(p 134) D '77 *
Wasp and Tenniel; suppressed chapter of Through the looking glass. il Horizon 19:26 Jl '77 *
CARROLL, Maurice
Beame's scenario: how to beat Bella. il pors N Y Times Mag p32-5+ Je 26 '77
CARROLL, Noël
Mind, medium and metaphor in Harry Smith's Heaven and earth magic. bibl il Film Q 31: 37-44 Wint '77
CARROTS
Growing carrots a new way in a dry year. R. Wolf. il Org Gard & Farm 24:55-6 My '77
CARRUTH, Eleanore
K Mart has to open some new doors on the future. il Fortune 96:144-7+ Jl '77
New arms for an army of insurance agents. Fortune 95:132-4 Ap '77
CARRUTH, Hayden
Appreciation of Robert Lowell. por Harpers 225 110-12 D '77
CARRUTHERS, George R. and Opal, C. B.
Far-ultraviolet rocket survey of Orion. il Sky & Tel 53:270-5 Ap '77
CARRY on, Maid Marian! drama. See Boiko, C.
CARS (automobiles) See Automobiles
CARS, Railroad. See Railroads—Cars
CARSON, Gerald
Marks for the marketplace. il Am Heritage 28: 64-9 O '77
Siege of Paris; with biographical sketch. il Natur Hist 86:2, 68-77 O '77
CARSON, Johnny
Johnny Carson sets us straight; excerpt from monologue. Nation 224:746 Je 18 '77
CARSON-PARKER, John
Commentary. Bus W p82-3 Mr 14 '77
CARTELS, International. See Trusts, Industrial—International trusts
CARTER, Amy Lynn
Amy; interview, ed by L. B. J. Robb. R. Carter. il pors Ladies Home J 94:82+ F '77 *
Amy's immersion. Chr Today 21:47 Mr 4 '77 *
Amy's new teacher. Chr Today 21:38-9 Ja 7 '77 *
Fast start for the first kid. il por Time 109:25 F 7 '77 *
Letters to Amy Carter. por Good H 184:94+ Ap '77 *
My pupil, Amy Carter. V. Meeder. il por McCalls 104:126-7+ Je '77 *
Pumpkin party. il pors Newsweek 90:43 O 31 '77 *
CARTER, Betsy
Jackson Pollock's drawings under analysis; question of psychiatric ethics. il Art N 76:58-60 F '77
Labor Department mural: a complicated voyage. il por Art N 76:40-1 My '77
CARTER, Betty Broadbent
Facing surgery for new sight, new life. il por Ret Liv 16:27-8+ D '76
CARTER, Billy
Billy Carter: frustrations of the small businessman; interview. il pors Nations Bus 65:28-32+ My '77
Billy Carter talks about all the money he's making; interview. il pors U.S. News 83:33-5 Ag 29 '77
Plain talk from brother Billy. il por Newsweek 89:71 My 30 '77
Thoughts of brother Billy; excerpts from Redneck power. por Newsweek 89:16 F 21 '77
about
Brother Billy. P. Axthelm. il pors Newsweek 90: 32-3+ N 14 '77 *
Cashing in on being Billy; Time essay. L. Morrow. il por Time 110:106 O 17 '77 *
People. il pors Time 109:41 Mr 7 '77 *
Prince of Plains. J. Lelyveld. N Y Times Mag p86 Je 26 '77 *

Anecdotes, facetiae, satire, etc.

Brothers in the news. R. Lipez. Progressive 41:66 O '77
CARTER, Caron
White House baby; interview, ed by L. B. J. Robb. il pors Ladies Home J 94:88-9+ S '77
about
Young Carters' crisis. T. B. Feldman. il pors McCalls 105:18+ Ja '78 *
CARTER, Chip
Chip off the Carter block. D. A. Williams and T. M. DeFrank. il por Newsweek 89:28 Ap 4 '77 *
Open-door policy. A. Deming and others. il por Newsweek 89:42 Ap 25 '77 *
Young Carters' crisis. T. B. Feldman. il pors McCalls 105:18+ Ja '78 *
CARTER, David G.
Case against separate schools. bibl Clearing H 51:125-9 N '77
—See Gresson, A. D. jt auth
CARTER, Elliott, 1908-
Milieu of the American composer. por Hi Fi 27:MA16+ S '77
about
Carter's symphony. I. Kolodin. por Sat R 4:37-8 Ap 2 '77 *
Music. D. Hamilton. Nation 224:318 Mr 12 '77 *
Musical events; A symphony of three orchestras. A. Porter. New Yorker 53:101-4 Mr 7 '77 *
N.Y. Phil: Carter premiere. por Hi Fi 27:MA32 Je '77 *

CARTER, Forrest
Little Tree in Forrest; work of F. Carter. D. Davis. por Writers Digest 57:24 My '77 *

CARTER, Harlon B.
Carter/Knox team wins a big one. J. Samson. pors Field & S 82:41+ S '77 *

CARTER, Hodding, 1907-1972
Other Carters. G. Lyons. il pors N Y Times Mag p 14-16+ S 18 '77 *

CARTER, Hodding, 3d
Other Carters. G. Lyons. il pors N Y Times Mag p 14-16+ S 18 '77 *

CARTER, Howard
Treasures of King Tut. S. Flythe, Jr. il Sat Eve Post 249:68-71+ My '77 *

CARTER, James Earl, family
All in the family; 1977 income. il Time 111:15 Ja 9 '78
Christmas with the Carters. R. C. Stapleton. il por Ladies Home J 94:74+ D '77
Miss Lillian: my two sons; interview, ed by G. C. Spann. L. Carter. il por Ladies Home J 94:34+ Ag '77

CARTER, Jimmie, family (of Virginia)
Seven sisters tell you all about good looks, health, energy, their vital lifestyles. il pors Mademoiselle 83:56-71+ Jl '77

CARTER, Jimmy
Address by President Carter to people of other nations; January 20, 1977. Dept State Bull 76:122-3 F 14 '77
Administration recommends Senate approval of Genocide Convention; message, May 23, 1977. Dept State Bull 76:676 Je 27 '77
Alaska natural gas transportation system; text of letter, September 1, 1977. Dept State Bull 77:479 O 10 '77
Amendments to Arms Control and Disarmament Act; statement, August 18, 1977. Dept State Bull 77:413 S 26 '77
As Jimmy sees her; excerpts from interview, ed by E. Clift. Newsweek 89:18 Je 13 '77
Atlantic Treaty Association; text of letter, August 27, 1977. Dept State Bull 77:468 O 10 '77
British Prime Minister Callaghan visits Washington; exchange of remarks, March 10, 1977. Dept State Bull 76:311-12 Ap 4 '77
Carter on agricultural research. Science 195:967 Mr 11 '77
Carter underscores pre-election stand. Am Lib 8:289 Je '77
Carter's blueprint for Europe; excerpts from interviews. U.S. News 82:22 My 16 '77
Carter's impassioned defense of my friend, Bert Lance; excerpts from news conference, September 21, 1977. por U.S. News 83:20-1 O 3 '77
Carter's strategy for dealing with Russia; excerpts from news conference, February 8, 1977. il por U.S. News 82:39 F 21 '77
Convention on Migratory Birds transmitted to Senate; message, July 18, 1977. Dept State Bull 77:326-7 S 5 '77
Crown Prince Fahd of Saudi Arabia visits Washington; exchange of toasts, with remarks, May 24-25, 1977. Dept State Bull 76:670-1+ Je 27 '77
Democratic foreign policy; address, May 22, 1977. Vital Speeches 43:514-17 Je 15 '77; Same with title Foreign policy based on America's essential character. Dept State Bull 76:621-5 Je 13 '77
Editors and news directors interview President Carter; excerpts from question and answer session, August 26, 1977. Dept State Bull 77:397-401 S 26 '77
Editors and news directors interview President Carter; excerpts from transcript, July 15, 1977. Dept State Bull 77:200-1 Ag 15 '77
Editors and news directors interview President Carter; excerpts from transcript, September 16, 1977. Dept State Bull 77:570-2 O 24 '77
Editors and news directors interview President Carter; October 14, 1977. Dept State Bull 77:767-71 N 28 '77
Editors and news directors interview President Carter; remarks, with transcript of question and answer session, July 29, 1977. Dept State Bull 77:304-6 S 5 '77
Fireside chat; address, February 2, 1977. Vital Speeches 43:259-62 F 15 '77; Excerpts. Dept State Bull 76:161 F 28 '77
Foreign aid authorizing bills transmitted to the Congress; text of letters, March 28, 1977. Dept State Bull 76:490-1 My 16 '77
Fourth Sinai Support Mission report transmitted to the Congress; message, October 19, 1977. Dept State Bull 77:787 N 28 '77
I don't intend to lose; excerpts from interview, ed by M. Elfin and others. por Newsweek 89:36-7 My 2 '77
I have learned a lot; interview, ed by H. Grunwald and others. por Time 110:24-5 Ag 8 '77
Inaugural Address of President Carter, January 20, 1977. U.S. News 82:28-9 Ja 31 '77; Same Dept State Bull 76:121-2 F 14 '77; Vital Speeches 43:258-9 F 15 '77; Excerpts. Time 109:10 Ja 31 '77
International broadcasting report transmitted to the Congress; message, March 22, 1977. Dept State Bull 76:423-4 Ap 25 '77
International cooperation to control dangerous drugs; remarks and message to Congress, August 2, 1977. Dept State Bull 77:380-2 S 19 '77
Interview with President Carter by media representatives; April 15, 1977. Dept State Bull 76:459-61 My 9 '77
Interview with President Carter by media representatives; excerpt from transcript of interview, June 24, 1977. Dept State Bull 77:159-62 Ag 1 '77
Jimmy Carter tells why he will use zero-base budgeting. por Nations Bus 65:24-6 Ja '77
King Hussein of Jordan visits Washington; exchange of toasts, with remarks, April 25-26, 1977. Dept State Bull 76:520-1+ My 23 '77
Lt. Gen. Obasanjo of Nigeria visits the United States; exchange of remarks, October 11, 1977. Dept State Bull 77:693-4 N 14 '77
Magazine Publishers Association interviews President Carter; remarks, with excerpt from question and answer session, June 10, 1977. Dept State Bull 77:46-8 Jl 11 '77
Military and political challenges of the 80's; address, May 10, 1977. Vital Speeches 43:482-4 Je 1 '77; Same with title President Carter attends economic, Berlin, and NATO meetings at London. Dept State Bull 76:597-601 Je 6 '77
Moral equivalent of war; address, April 20, 1977. Vital Speeches 43:420-3 My 1 '77
My personal commitment to education. por Todays Educ 66:26-7 Ja '77
National Newspaper Association interviews President Carter; October 28, 1977. Dept State Bull 77:798-9 D 5 '77
New communication agency proposed by President Carter; message to Congress, October 11, 1977. Dept State Bull 77:683-5 N 14 '77
News directors interview President Carter; excerpts from transcript, September 15, 1977. Dept State Bull 77:568-9 O 24 '77
Nuclear arms reduction; address, October 4, 1977. Vital Speeches 44:2-5 O 15 '77; Same. Dept State Bull 77:547-52 O 24 '77; Excerpts. por U.S. News 83:37 O 17 '77
Nuclear nonproliferation policy act of 1977 transmitted to the Congress; message, with White House fact sheet, April 27, 1977. Dept State Bull 76:477-8 My 16 '77
Organizing conference of the International Nuclear Fuel Cycle Evaluation meets in Washington; remarks, October 19, 1977. Dept State Bull 77:659-61 N 14 '77
Peace, arms control, world economic progress, human rights: basic priorities of U.S. foreign policy; address, March 17, 1977. Dept State Bull 76:329-33 Ap 11 '77
President announces measures to control marine oil pollution; message to Congress, March 17, 1977. Dept State Bull 76:422-3 Ap 25 '77
President Carter and General Torrijos sign Panama Canal treaties; remarks, September 7, 1977; with text of treaties. map Dept State Bull 77:481-2 O 17 '77
President Carter announces decisions on nuclear power policy; statement, and remarks, with transcript of question and answer session, April 7, 1977. Dept State Bull 76:429-33 My 2 '77
President Carter announces policy on transfers of conventional arms; statement, May 19, 1977. Dept State Bull 76:625-6 Je 13 '77
President Carter attends economic, Berlin, and NATO meetings at London; remarks, with text of declarations, NATO communique, and question and answer session, May 5, 8-11, 1977. Dept State Bull 76:581-6+ Je 6 '77
President Carter comments on Middle East; exchange of remarks, August 8, 1977. Dept State Bull 77:379-80 S 19 '77
President Carter discusses a new sea-level canal; excerpt from transcript of question and answer session, July 22, 1977. Dept State Bull 77:234 Ag 22 '77
President Carter discusses boycott issue; remarks, February 9, 1977. Dept State Bull 76:266 Mr 21 '77
President Carter discusses Cuba and SALT negotiations; transcript of remarks, May 30, 1977. Dept State Bull 77:9-10 Jl 4 '77
President Carter discusses foreign affairs priorities; remarks, February 16, 1977. Dept State Bull 76:265-6 Mr 21 '77
President Carter discusses Panama Canal treaties; remarks, question and answer session, October 22, 1977. Dept State Bull 77:720-8 N 21 '77
President Carter discusses Strategic Arms Limitation proposals; remarks, with transcript of question and answer session, March 30, 1977. Dept State Bull 76:409-14 Ap 25 '77
President Carter holds bilateral meetings with Western Hemisphere leaders; remarks, September 6-9, 1977. Dept State Bull 77:510+ O 17 '77
President Carter interviewed by ABC news correspondents; excerpt from transcript of program, August 10, 1977; ed by H. Reasoner. Dept State Bull 77:395-6 S 26 '77

CARTER, Jimmy—*Continued*

President Carter interviewed by AP and UPI correspondents; excerpts from transcript of interview, January 23, 1977. Dept State Bull 76:123-5 F 14 '77

President Carter interviewed by European broadcast journalists; transcript of interview, May 2, 1977. Dept State Bull 76:540-8 My 30 '77

President Carter interviewed by European newspaper journalists; transcript of interview, April 25, 1977. Dept State Bull 76:533-9 My 30 '77

President Carter interviewed by media representatives; excerpt from transcript of interview, March 4, 1977. Dept State Bull 76:316-17 Ap 4 '77

President Carter interviewed by newspaper farm editors; excerpt from remarks and question and answer session, September 30, 1977. Dept State Bull 77:681-3 N 14 '77

President Carter meets with President Asad of Syria at Geneva; exchange of remarks and toasts, May 9, 1977. Dept State Bull 76:593-4+ Je 6 '77

President Carter outlines goals of foreign assistance program; message to Congress, March 17, 1977. Dept State Bull 76:340-2 Ap 11 '77

President Carter outlines the U.S.-Soviet relationship; remarks, July 21, 1977. Dept State Bull 77:193-7 Ag 15 '77; Same with title President Carter on the Soviet Union. Cur Hist 73:176-7+ N '77

President Carter signs American Convention on Human Rights; remarks, June 1, 1977. Dept State Bull 77:28-38 Jl 4 '77

President Carter signs covenants on human rights; remarks, October 5, 1977. Dept State Bull 77:586-7 O 31 '77

President Carter signs Security Assistance Act; statement, August 5, 1977. Dept State Bull 77: 361 S 12 '77

President Carter states policy on Northern Ireland; statement, August 30, 1977. Dept State Bull 77:410 S 26 '77

President Carter visits the Department of State; remarks, with excerpts from question and answer session, February 24, 1977. Dept State Bull 76:259-65 Mr 21 '77

President Carter's call-in radio program of March 5; excerpts from transcript of program. Dept State Bull 76:314-16 Ap 4 '77

President Carter's fifth report on Cyprus submitted to Congress; message, October 28, 1977. Dept State Bull 77:787-8 N 28 '77

President Carter's fourth report on Cyprus submitted to Congress; message, August 25, 1977. Dept State Bull 77:445 O 3 '77

President Carter's news conference:
- February 8, 1977. Dept State Bull 76:157-60 F 28 '77
- February 23, 1977. Dept State Bull 76:251-5 Mr 21 '77
- March 9, 1977. Dept State Bull 76:305-9 Ap 4 '77
- March 24, 1977. Dept State Bull 76:357-62 Ap 18 '77
- April 15, 1977. Dept State Bull 76:457-9 My 9 '77
- April 22, 1977. Dept State Bull 76:481-2 My 16 '77
- May 12, 1977. Dept State Bull 76:604-7 Je 6 '77
- May 26, 1977. Dept State Bull 76:653-7 Je 20 '77
- June 13, 1977. Dept State Bull 77:1-4 Jl 4 '77
- June 30, 1977. Dept State Bull 77:146-51 Ag 1 '77
- July 12, 1977. Dept State Bull 77:174-8 Ag 8 '77
- July 28, 1977. Dept State Bull 77:221-4 Ag 22 '77
- August 23, 1977. Dept State Bull 77:376-9 S 19 '77
- September 29, 1977. Dept State Bull 77:584-6 O 31 '77
- October 13, 1977. Dept State Bull 77:630 N 7 '77
- October 27, 1977. Dept State Bull 77:718-20 N 21 '77
- November 10, 1977. Dept State Bull 77:839-40 D 12 '77
- November 30, 1977. Dept State Bull 77:879-84 D 19 '77

President Carter's remarks at Clinton, Mass. town meeting; excerpts from remarks and question and answer session, March 16, 1977. Dept State Bull 76:334-5 Ap 11 '77

President Carter's remarks at Dobbins Air Force Base, Ga; excerpts from transcript of question and answer session, April 8, 1977. Dept State Bull 76:461-2 My 9 '77

President Carter's remarks at Yazoo City, Mississippi; excerpt from transcript of question and answer session, July 21, 1977. Dept State Bull 77:197-200 Ag 15 '77

President Carter's second report on Cyprus submitted to Congress; April 15, 1977. Dept State Bull 76:491-2 My 16 '77

President Carter's third report on Cyprus submitted to Congress; June 22, 1977. Dept State Bull 77:138-9 Jl 25 '77

President discusses Cyprus issue in periodic report to Congress; February 11, 1977. Dept State Bull 76:243 Mr 14 '77

President names new members to Intelligence Oversight Board; statement, May 5, 1977. Dept State Bull 76:658 Je 20 '77

President Pérez of Venezuela visits the United States; exchange of remarks, with texts of joint communiques, June 28, July 1, 1977. Dept State Bull 77:151-2 Ag 1 '77

President Sadat of Egypt visits Washington; exchange of remarks, April 4, 1977. Dept State Bull 76:434-5 My 2 '77

President signs bill restoring embargo on Rhodesian chrome; statement, March 18, 1977. Dept State Bull 76:333-4 Ap 11 '77

President signs 1977 amendments to Export Administration Act; statement, June 22, 1977. Dept State Bull 77:162 Ag 1 '77

President talks tough; interview. il pors U.S. News 82:19-23 Je 6 '77

Presidential Commission visits Vietnam and Laos to seek information on missing Americans; remarks, March 23, 1977. Dept State Bull 76:363-4 Ap 18 '77

President's address at the United Nations; March 17, 1977. Vital Speeches 43:354-6 Ap 1 '77; Excerpts. U.S. News 82:21 Mr 28 '77; UN Chron 14:24-5 Ap '77

President's address on energy problems; November 8, 1977. Vital Speeches 44:98-100 D 1 '77

President's proposed energy policy; address, April 18, 1977. Vital Speeches 43:418-20 My 1 '77

Prime Minister Fraser of Australia visits Washington; exchange of remarks, June 22, 1977. Dept State Bull 77:132-3 Jl 25 '77

Prime Minister Pierre-Elliott Trudeau of Canada visits Washington; exchange of toasts, February 21, 1977. Dept State Bull 76:255-6 Mr 21 '77

Prime Minister Rabin of Israel visits Washington; exchange of remarks, March 7, 1977. Dept State Bull 76:310-11 Ap 4 '77

Reciprocal fisheries agreement with the United Kingdom; message to Senate, October 7, 1977. Dept State Bull 77:708-9 N 14 '77

Report on 1976 U.S. participation in the U.N. transmitted to Congress; message, November 1, 1977. Dept State Bull 77:867-8 D 12 '77

Teachers' feature. por Sr Schol 109:TE15 Ja 13 '77

There's a bit of the Pharisee in us all; excerpt from Why not the best? il por Sat Eve Post 249:36+ Ap '77

Third Sinai Support Mission report transmitted to the Congress; message, April 27, 1977. Dept State Bull 76:639 Je 13 '77

Transfer of defense articles to the Republic of Korea; message, October 21, 1977. Dept State Bull 77:852-4 D 12 '77

Undocumented aliens; remarks and message to Congress, August 4, 1977. Dept State Bull 77: 315-20 S 5 '77

U.S. and U.K. initial new air services agreement; statement, June 22, 1977. Dept State Bull 77: 83 Jl 18 '77

U.S.-Canada agreement on natural gas pipeline; joint statement, message to Congress; September 8, 22, 1977. Dept State Bull 77:610 O 31 '77

U.S.-Canada transit pipeline treaty transmitted to the Senate; message, March 30, 1977. Dept State Bull 76:425 Ap 25 '77

U.S. negotiators brief press on new Panama Canal treaties; remarks, August 12, 1977. Dept State Bull 77:526 O 17 '77

United States' policy toward Latin America; address, April 14, 1977. Vital Speeches 43: 424-6 My 1 '77; Same with title President Carter's Pan American Day address; April 14, 1977. Dept State Bull 76:453-7 My 9 '77

U.S. responsibility toward peace and human rights; address, November 2, 1977. Dept State Bull 77:759-62 N 28 '77

Vice President Mondale visits Europe and Japan; remarks, January 23, 1977. Dept State Bull 76:181 Mr 7 '77

Vice President Mondale visits Europe and meets with South African Prime Minister Vorster; statement, May 3, 1977. Dept State Bull 76: 659-60 Je 20 '77

View from Washington; excerpts from news conference, March 30, 1977. por U.S. News 82: 22 Ap 11 '77

about

Abroad—a sudden respect for Carter. il U.S. News 82:31-2 Ja 31 '77 *

Administration under siege. New Repub 177:5-6 O 22 '77 *

After the B-1. Nation 225:66-8 Jl 23 '77 *

After the pardon. S. Fraker and others. il Newsweek 89:28-9 Ja 31 '77 *

Aid for energy development pledged. Am City & County 92:17-18 Je '77 *

CARTER, Jimmy—about—*Continued*
American Jews and Mr Carter. Commonweal 104:773-4 D 9 '77 *
Ariel versus Caliban; Carter's stand on human rights. Nat R 29:313-14 Mr 18 '77 *
Around City Hall (cont) A. Logan. New Yorker 53:134+ O 31 '77 *
As Carter gets down to brass tacks. il pors U.S. News 82:27-9 F 14 '77 *
Assessing the federal government. Current 191: 3-6 Mr '77 *
B-1 no, cruise yes. S. Fraker and others. il por Newsweek 90:14-17 Jl 11 '77 *
Bad day all around; Lance affair. Nation 225: 290 O 1 '77 *
Battle begins. A. J. Mayer and others. il Newsweek 89:22-4 My 9 '77 *
Bearing witness and human rights. J. P. Dobel. Chr Cent 94:751-3 Ag 31 '77 *
Beat goes on. S. Fraker and others. il por Newsweek 90:17-18 S 5 '77 *
Begin's strategy and Dayan's tactics; the conduct of Israeli foreign policy. A. Perlmutter. For Affairs 56:357-72 Ja '78 *
Bitter battle of the waterways. J. N. Miller. Read Digest 111:83-7 S '77 *
Blowing in the wind. T. Bethell. il Harpers 254: 25-6+ Ap '77 *
Bribery and human rights. N. Cousins. Sat R 4:4 Ap 2 '77 *
Business vs. Carter: tough breach to heal. W. C. Bryant. U.S. News 83:25 N 14 '77 *
Business warms up to Carter. A. J. Mayer and others. il Newsweek 89:60-1 Ja 31 '77 *
Butler Brown: a Jimmy Carter favorite. Vasari. il por Art N 76:20-2+ F '77 *
Campaign's science advisor sees: healthier outlook for creativity. W. K. Stuckey. il Sci Digest 81:12-19 F '77 *
Can Carter afford Lance? Why Jimmy stays loyal. il pors Time 110:8-10 S 12 '77 *
Can Chuck Morgan keep Jimmy Carter honest? T. Branch. Esquire 87:14+ F '77 *
Can Jimmy Carter cope? P. Goldman and others. il por Newsweek 90:36-8 O 24 '77 *
Can Jimmy Carterize foreign policy? Code words from an oracle. il Time 109:24-8 Mr 28 '77 *
Carter: a popular President, but—the way honeymoons compare. il por U.S. News 82:24 My 30 '77 *
Carter: a problem of confidence; views of businessmen. il Time 110:68-70+ O 31 '77 *
Carter after a fortnight. W. F. Buckley, Jr. Nat R 29:222 F 18 '77 *
Carter Agonistes. Nat R 29:1154+ O 14 '77 *
Carter and abortion. C. Tucker. Sat R 4:64 S 17 '77 *
Carter and black Americans. P. Delaney. Nation 225:132-3 Ag 20 '77 *
Carter and Brezhnev: the game begins. il por Time 109:40-2 F 7 '77 *
Carter and compassion. M. Greenfield. Newsweek 90:104 D 19 '77 *
Carter and human rights. S. Karnow. il Sat R 4:6-11 Ap 2 '77; Same. Current 193:3-11 My '77 *
Carter and Israel. S. L. Spiegel. Commentary 64:35-40 Jl '77; Discussion. 64:29-31 S '77 *
Carter and the CIA. A. S. Miller. Progressive 41:9-10 My '77 *
Carter and the Canal. A. Deming and others. il Newsweek 89:43+ F 7 '77 *
Carter and the evolution of liberalism. R. J. Bresler. Intellect 106:22-3 Ag '77 *
Carter and the Kremlin—now a war of nerves. U.S. News 82:23-4 Ap 18 '77 *
Carter and the new weapons. Nat R 29:868 Ag 5 '77 *
Carter & the plutonium economy. J. J. Berger. Nation 224:101-4 Ja 29 '77 *
Carter and the Russians: semi-tough; Just call him Mister. il pors Time 109:10-12 F 21 '77 *
Carter and the union chiefs—will the gulf widen? with interview with R. Marshall. il por U.S. News 82:53-7 Je 6 '77 *
Carter and the worried Jews. R. Steele and others. il por Newsweek 89:21-2 Je 27 '77 *
Carter at home: rising pressure. il por U.S. News 82:21-3 My 23 '77 *
Carter at Notre Dame. W. F. Buckley, Jr. Nat R 29:740 Je 24 '77 *
Carter at sea. Nat R 29:371 Ap 1 '77 *
Carter bears right: social policy. Nation 224:578-80 My 14 '77 *
Carter beginning. Commonweal 104:67-8 F 4 '77 *
Carter blocks production of B-1. il Aviation W 107:14-16 Jl 4 '77 *
Carter: captain or engineer? Commonweal 104: 419-20 Jl 8 '77 *
Carter, Castro and Reinhold Niebuhr. J. Bingham. Chr Cent 94:775-6 S 14 '77 *
Carter complex. E. Randolph. pors Esquire 88: 166-8+ N '77 *
Carter dares his party. il U.S. News 82:19-20 Je 13 '77 *
Carter going slow on national health insurance. B. J. Culliton. Science 195:467 F 4 '77 *
Carter hour. Nat R 29:480 Ap 29 '77 *
Carter in action. Nat R 29:193-4 F 18 '77 *
Carter: man in motion. il pors Time 110:8-9 O 17 '77 *
Carter moves in on Pentagon budgeting. J. Canan. Bus W p55 N 21 '77 *
Carter moves to expand Africa arms sales. Aviation W 107:24 Ag 1 '77 *
Carter on oil & gas. J. F. Flug. Nation 224:652-8 My 28 '77 *
Carter places environment high on agenda. L. J. Carter. Science 196:1065 Je 3 '77 *
Carter remarks provide clues to attitude on science advice. J. Walsh. il por Science 196: 1300-1 Je 17 '77 *
Carter sets a new style in foreign policy. B. France and J. Pearson. Bus W p30 Je 27 '77 *
Carter so far—a puzzle to many. J. W. Mashek. U.S. News 82:19 Ja 31 '77 *
Carter spins the world. il por Time 110:8-12+ Ag 8 '77 *
Carter strikes out in Virginia; gubernatorial race lost by H. Howell. R. Mackenzie. Nat R 29: 1425-6 D 9 '77 *
Carter style—beanies, beer, and Jesus. S. Quinn. Ms 6:106 Ja '78 *
Carter takes on the Russians. U.S. News 82:21-3 Ap 11 '77 *
Carter-talk. W. F. Buckley, Jr. Nat R 29:686 Je 10 '77 *
Carter, the world and the Jews. il por Time 109:8-10 Je 27 '77 *
Carter to propose quick SALT agreement. Aviation W 106:19 F 14 '77 *
Carter unraveling. Nat R 29:1342-3 N 25 '77 *
Carter up close. P. Goldman and others. il por Newsweek 89:32-5+ My 2 '77 *
Carter v. Brezhnev: the SALT standoff. il pors Time 109:10-12+ Ap 11 '77 *
Carter vs the bureaucrats. R. Jones and P. Woll. Nation 224:402-4 Ap 2 '77 *
Carter: will he change course? il pors U.S. News 83:18-21 D 26 '77 *
Carter woos in vain. Nation 225:419-20 O 29 '77 *
Carter's bad start. il por Bus W p96-101 O 31 '77 *
Carter's big decision: down goes the B-1, here comes the cruise. il por Time 110:8-12 Jl 11 '77 *
Carter's blueprint for reorganization. il Bus W p26-7 F 21 '77 *
Carter's chum from Coke. T. Nicholson and others. il por Newsweek 89:57-8 F 7 '77 *
Carter's dog-day afternoons. il pors Time 110: 12-13 S 5 '77 *
Carter's first big test; Jimmy's carrot-and-stick plan; Ninety day wondering. il pors Time 109:8-16 Ap 25 '77 *
Carter's first week. P. Goldman and others. il por Newsweek 89:23-4 F 7 '77 *
Carter's Georgia guru. J. T. Wooten. il pors N Y Times Mag p 14-18 Mr 20 '77 *
Carter's global blitz. R. Steele and others. il map Newsweek 89:16-18 F 28 '77 *
Carter's hard line on the environment. il U.S. News 82:88 Je 6 '77 *
Carter's high-risk move; Panama Canal treaties. U.S. News 83:18-19 S 12 '77 *
Carter's morality play; Skating deftly, but on thin ice. il pors Time 109:10-13 Mr 7 '77 *
Carter's new world order. U.S. News 82:17-18 Je 6 '77 *
Carter's nuclear switch. D. M. Alpern and others. il Newsweek 89:22-4 Ap 18 '77 *
Carter's ocean opportunity. J. J. Logue. Commonweal 104:265-9 Ap 29 '77 *
Carter's own way of running the White House. por U.S. News 82:16-18 Je 27 '77 *
Carter's patchwork doctrine. R. J. Barnet. Harpers 255:27-30+ Ag '77 *
Carter's plain talk. Nation 224:258-9 Mr 5 '77 *
Carter's plan: criticized, but flexible. il Time 109:45-6 Ja 24 '77 *
Carter's pursuit of inconsistent goals. Bus W p56+ D 26 '77 *
Carter's welfare plan: Nixon warmed over? R. Lekachman. Sat R 5:9 D 10 '77 *
Carter's world: too much, too soon? il U.S. News 82:15-17 F 28 '77 *
Caution marks Carter approach. C. Brownlow. Aviation W 106:21 Mr 21 '77 *
Change comes to White House; interview. R. Carter. pors U.S. News 82:31-3 Mr 21 '77 *
Changing of the guard. Sci N 111:21-2 Ja 8 '77 *
Cold war? Nyet. But it's getting chilly; Jimmy woos the Jewish leaders. il por Time 110:10-12 Jl 18 '77 *
Crucial test for Carter as world leader; proposals for the U.N. General Assembly's 32d session. il por U.S. News 83:23-4 S 26 '77 *
Cruelty of morality; abortion views of J. Carter. Nation 225:68-9 Jl 23 '77 *
Crusader's end. Nat R 29:594 My 27 '77 *
Day in the life of the President. il por Read Digest 111:175-6+ S '77 *
Deadly virtue: the willful innocence of Jimmy Carter. L. H. Lapham. Harpers 256:7-8+ Ja '78 *
Democrats in distress. H. Bruno. Newsweek 90:25+ D 19 '77 *

CARTER, Jimmy—about—*Continued*
Dig deeper, Jimmy! Soviet weapon developments. R. Hotz. Aviation W 106:7 My 9 '77 *
Do-it-yourself diplomacy. il por Time 109:26-7 Mr 21 '77 *
Doing business with business. P. Steinfels. Commonweal 104:294-5 My 13 '77 *
Doing it my way; excerpts from interview, ed by J. Whitmore. R. S. Carter. por Newsweek 89:17 Je 13 '77 *
Don't get your hopes up; budget proposals. il Time 109:15-16 F 28 '77 *
Down in flames; rejection of B-1. F. Getlein. Commonweal 104:484-6 Ag 5 '77 *
Down the homestretch; Carter's promises: how many has he kept; with interview with C. H. Kirbo. il por map U.S. News 83:15-20 D 12 '77 *
Editor's page. R. Manning. Atlantic 241:4-5 Ja '78 *
Emerging national consensus on energy policy; address, November 29, 1976. F. X. Gannon. Vital Speeches 43:181-6 Ja 1 '77 *
Emerging under Carter: a Cabinet with real clout. il U.S. News 82:35-6 Mr 14 '77 *
Energy and national will. Nation 224:514 Ap 30 '77 *
Energy brownout. Nation 224:706-8 Je 11 '77 *
Energy program. Progressive 41:5-6 Je '77 *
Energy war. il por Time 109:10-14 My 2 '77 *
Energy: will Americans pay the price? il por U.S. News 82:13-17 My 2 '77 *
Everyone a conservationist. J. B. Craig. Am For 83:6 Je '77 *
Facing the perfectionism backlash. J. M. Wall. Chr Cent 94:835-6 S 28 '77 *
Fallout between friends. por Time 110:27-8 Ag 8 '77 *
Family squabble. P. Goldman and others. il pors Newsweek 90:16-18 Ag 8 '77 *
Feeling left out. E. Marshall. New Repub 176:12-13 My 21 '77 *
First six months. il por U.S. News 83:17-19 Jl 25 '77 *
First small step; pardon of Vietnam draft evaders. Nation 224:131-2 F 5 '77 *
Fizzle in Carter's anti-atom blast. Bus W p30 My 23 '77 *
Flaherty's promise. P. Peckarsky. New Repub 177:9-10 D 10 '77 *
Forecasts for the Carter years. J. Carlson. por Nations Bus 65:28+ Ja '77 *
Freshman year on the job: rough lessons for Carter. J. W. Mashek. U.S. News 83:22-3 D 26 '77 *
Friend at court? J. Deedy. Commonweal 104:2 Ja 7 '77 *
From special-interest groups: a mixed verdict on Carter. il U.S. News 82:20-1 My 30 '77 *
George and Jimmy show. K. Bode. il New Repub 176:28-30+ My 21 '77 *
Getting down to cases on human rights. J. M. Wall. Chr Cent 94:555-6 Je 8 '77 *
Good old boy network. R. Reeves and B. M. Hager. New Repub 177:6+ S 10 '77 *
Government bureaucracy: too snarled to untangle? il Sr Schol 109:6-8+ My 19 '77 *
Government by what people? P. Steinfels. Commonweal 104:756+ N 25 '77 *
Government intervention. il pors Bus W p42-3+ Ap 4 '77 *
Hail-to-the-chiefless chief. M. Greenfield. Newsweek 90:116 N 7 '77 *
Headaches pile up for Carter in Lance affair. il U.S. News 83:25-6 S 19 '77 *
Hit us hard, please, Mr Carter. G. F. Will. Newsweek 89:112 Ap 18 '77 *
Hope and a goal; views on disarmament. Nation 224:130 F 5 '77 *
How Carter is changing us. E. Diamond. por Newsweek 89:21 Ap 11 '77 *
How Carter operates; interview. H. Jordan. il pors U.S. News 82:16-18 F 21 '77 *
How Carter will differ from Ford—an expert's view; interview. M. W. H. Collins, Jr. il por U.S. News 82:17-18 Ja 31 '77 *
How Mondale sees his relationship with Carter; interview. W. F. Mondale. pors U.S. News 82:62-4 Mr 28 '77 *
How we practice arms restraint. M. T. Klare. Nation 225:268-9+ S 24 '77 *
Howard, Hughie and Jimmy. J. Seelye. New Repub 176:23-6 Je 4 '77 *
Human rights as a national policy. J. M. Wall. Chr Cent 94:371-2 Ap 20 '77 *
I voted for a man who. . . P. Fish. Mademoiselle 83:174+ F '77 *
Immodest proposal. P. Steinfels. Commonweal 104:70 F 4 '77 *
Inaugural issue—1977; special issue. il pors New Repub 176:5-6+ Ja 22 '77 *
Is he home free? B. Lance case. P. Goldman and others. il pors Newsweek 90:16-17+ Ag 29 '77 *
Isaac Asimov advises the President. I. Asimov. il Sci Digest 81:8-12 F '77 *
It takes more than 100 days for a president to get a grip. il por U.S. News 82:26-7 My 9 '77 *
Jimmy and Menachem. M. Kondracke. New Repub 177:13-15 Jl 30 '77 *
Jimmy Carter: a big grin for culture. P. M. Kadis. il por Art N 76:50-4 My '77 *
Jimmy Carter and the new reality. S. Lens. il por Chr Cent 94:10-14 Ja 5 '77 *
Jimmy Carter gets mixed marks in economics. I. J. Cameron. il pors Fortune 95:98-102+ Je '77 *
Jimmy Carter revealed: he's a Rockefeller Republican. C. Lydon. Atlantic 240:50-7 Jl '77 *
Jimmy Carter's capital. R. Hotz. Aviation W 106:9 Mr 7 '77 *
Jimmy Carter's Little Rock connection. il pors Bus W p88 Ap 11 '77 *
Jimmy Carter's ruling class. R. Morris. Harpers 255:37-45 O '77 *
Jimmy, the Bible—and Brezhnev. il pors Time 110:12-13 Ag 1 '77 *
Jimmy the engineer. M. Greenfield. Newsweek 89:104 Ap 25 '77 *
Jimmy's music to govern by. il por Time 109:15 Mr 28 '77 *
Judging Carter's judges. il Time 110:76 D 5 '77 *
Keeping fit, Carter style. il pors U.S. News 82:28 Ap 25 '77 *
Keeping them guessing. il por Time 110:14-17 N 14 '77 *
Kicking Carter while he's up. P. Slansky and H. Stein. il pors Esquire 87:59-61 Mr '77 *
Lance and Carter. M. Stone. U.S. News 83:88 S 12 '77 *
Lance, Carter, Babbitt and Gantry. G. F. Will. Newsweek 90:122 S 19 '77 *
Lance: going, going. il pors Time 110:6-10+ S 19 '77 *
Lance heads home—Carter picks up the pieces. il por U.S. News 83:17-20 O 3 '77 *
Lance: wounding Carter. il pors Time 110:14-16 O 3 '77 *
Lancegate: why Carter stuck it out. W. Safire. il pors N Y Times Mag p37-9+ O 16 '77 *
Leading authority sizes up Carter's performance so far; interview. E. C. Hargrove. il pors U.S. News 82:23-4 My 2 '77 *
Learning on the job. Nation 224:226 F 26 '77 *
Legacy of Carter and Reagan: political reality overtakes the myth of the Presidential primaries. J. R. Beniger. bibl il Intellect 105:234-7 F '77 *
Let them eat words. New Repub 177:5-6 S 17 '77 *
Let's put detente back on the rails. S. Pisar. il N Y Times Mag p31-3+ S 25 '77 *
Letter from Washington (cont) R. H. Rovere. New Yorker 52:72-4+ Ja 31; 53:108-14 Mr 7; 129-34 Ap 11; 136-8+ My 9; 108+ Je 13; 56-60 Ag 1; 131-4 S 12; 180+ O 17; 200+ N 14 '77; 54-8 Ja 2 '78 *
Letter to a friend; letter to A. Sakharov. por Time 109:30-1 F 28 '77 *
Liberals and Carter. Progressive 41:5-6 Jl '77 *
Loose talk. J. Osborne. New Repub 176:12-13 Mr 26 '77 *
Lucky president. M. Stone. il U.S. News 83:80 Jl 25 '77 *
Mandate of heaven; open letter to J. Carter. Tran-van-Dinh. Chr Cent 94:29-30 Ja 19 '77 *
Meeting foreign leaders—a whirlwind pace. il pors U.S. News 83:20-2 Ag 1 '77 *
Memo to the White House. G. McGovern. il Harpers 255:33-5 O '77 *
Millions for taxes. Nat R 29:534 My 13 '77 *
Mr Carter's discovery of human rights. W. F. Buckley, Jr. Nat R 29:402 Ap 1 '77 *
My son the President; interview. L. Carter. il pors U.S. News 82:52-4 Mr 7 '77 *
Need to act. T. Bethell. il Harpers 255:34-6+ N '77 *
New Washington; Carterland's fifth estate. il pors Time 109:16-28 F 7 '77 *
Night Carter took over the party; excerpt from Convention. R. Reeves. il pors N Y Times Mag p32-8+ F 20 '77 *
No new dream. R. Hotz. Aviation W 106:7 Ja 24 '77 *
No slip of the tongue. A. de Borchgrave. il Newsweek 89:35 Mr 21 '77 *
Not much cheer for liberals. il Time 109:15-16 My 16 '77 *
Notes and comment (cont) New Yorker 52:23-4 Ja 24; 31-3 My 9 '77 *
Now, back to face the music. il por Time 111:8-9 Ja 16 '78 *
Now, for the substance. il por Time 109:12-15 F 28 '77 *
Now it begins. P. Goldman and others. il pors Newsweek 89:16-17+ Ja 24 '77 *
Of many things. J. O'Hare. America 136:inside cover Mr 12 '77 *
Old gang. R. Baker. il N Y Times Mag p4 Ja 23 '77 *
Old pol takes on the new President. M. Tolchin. il pors N Y Times Mag p6-9+ Jl 24 '77 *
On sources of energy. W. F. Buckley, Jr. Nat R 29:1320-1 N 11 '77 *
Open letter to fellow developer, Jimmy Carter; address, January 28, 1977. R. Nordblom. Vital Speeches 43:290-2 Mr 1 '77 *
Our far-flung correspondents. E. Drew. New Yorker 53:82-8 F 28 '77 *

CARTER, Jimmy—about—*Continued*
Our park system will be restored and protected. il Nat Parks & Con Mag 51:20-1 Mr '77 *
Party of one; $1,000-a-plate assembly at the Waldorf-Astoria. P. Goldman and others. il pors Newsweek 90:13-14 Jl 4 '77 *
Payoff charges on cargo bill. il Time 110:53-4 Ag 15 '77 *
Peace in the Middle East. M. A. Bruzonsky. il por Nation 224:489-92 Ap 23 '77 *
People who fly: Tom Peterson. G. Baxter. il por Flying 100:65-6+ My '77 *
Picking up the pieces. R. Steele and others. il pors map Newsweek 90:22-3+ O 3 '77 *
Plain talk about America's global role. il pors Time 109:8-10 Je 6 '77 *
Plan-of-the-week club. P. Goldman and others. il por Newsweek 89:16-17 My 23 '77 *
Playing politics with airlines. map Time 111:46 Ja 16 '78 *
Point of order. L. H. Lapham. Harpers 254:13-14+ My '77 *
Politics of welfare reform. N. Kotz. New Repub 176:16-21 My 14 '77 *
Power people. R. Steele. il Newsweek 89:23-5 Ja 24 '77 *
Presidency. H. Sidey. See occasional issues of Time *
President at Notre Dame. America 136:494 Je 4 '77 *
President Carter holds meetings with Middle East officials; September 19, 21 and 28, 1977. Dept State Bull 77:634-7 N 7 '77 *
President Carter offers his comprehensive energy program to Congress. W. Hickman. Archit Rec 161:34 Je '77 *
President learning. P. Goldman. por Newsweek 90:26 D 26 '77 *
Problems of a problem solver. H. Smith. il por N Y Times Mag p30+ Ja 8 '78 *
Promised: an overhaul of welfare. il U.S. News 82:68 Ja 24 '77 *
Promises, promises: home to roost in the White House. A. Clymer. Nation 224:295-8 Mr 12 '77 *
Public morality after Bert Lance. J. Castelli. America 137:280-2 O 29 '77 *
Putting brakes on the fast breeder. il Time 109:57 Ap 18 '77 *
Rating Carter; symposium. il por Ms 6:43-60+ Ja '78 *
Real Carter emerges; 100-day benchmark. U.S. News 82:21-2 My 2 '77 *
Rebuffs at home, flak from abroad. Time 110:12+ Jl 11 '77 *
Reflections on the Presidential style. W. F. Buckley, Jr. Nat R 29:512 Ap 29 '77 *
Reporter at large. E. B. Drew. New Yorker 53:112-14+ My 23; 36-8+ Jl 18; 156-62+ O 10 '77 *
Reporter in Washington, D.C. (cont) E. B. Drew. il New Yorker 52:48+ Ja 17 '77 *
Reports & comment: Washington: a town with a memory. W. Just. il Atlantic 241:6+ Ja '78 *
Road show goes West. il pors Time 109:8-9 My 30 '77 *
Rosalynn and Jimmy Carter's Washington. K. Kelley. il por Redbook 149:82+ Je '77 *
S-G confers with President Carter during two-day visit to Washington. K. Waldheim. il pors UN Chron 14:16-17 Mr '77 *
Seeking ratifiers. G. H. Caldwell. Chr Cent 94:292-3 Mr 30 '77 *
Selling Jimmy out; shares in peanut warehouse. D. Pauly and V. E. Smith. il por Newsweek 90:58 Ag 29 '77 *
Shot from Paris. D. Martin and others. il pors Newsweek 90:44 Jl 25 '77 *
Sir, the election is over. M. Stone. U.S. News 82:108 My 9 '77 *
Some praise, growing worry: how business views Carter. il por U.S. News 83:61-4 S 19 '77 *
Sowing seeds of real conflict. Time 109:12-13 Ap 18 '77 *
Stalled abroad;And at home, the Lance case puts Carter on the spot. U.S. News 83:14-15 S 5 '77 *
Strong medicine. New Repub 176:5-6+ Ap 30 '77 *
Sweet nothings. H. Fairlie. New Repub 176:17-19 Je 11 '77 *
Swinging from the floor. Nation 225:418-19 O 29 '77 *
TRB from Washington (cont) New Repub 176:2+ Ja 29; 2+ Mr 19; 2+ Ap 9; 2+ Ap 23; 2 Ap 30; 2+ My 7; 2+ My 14; 2+ Je 11; 177:2+ S 3 '77 *
Thin-skinned Jimmy Carter comes into public view. J. W. Mashek. U.S. News 83:16 Ag 29 '77 *
Time poll. il pors Time 109:12-13 Ap 4; 15-16 Je 13; 110:10-12 D 26 '77 *
Tough talk on energy. D. M. Alpern and others. il Newsweek 89:21-2 Ap 25 '77 *
Tougher tests coming. U.S. News 82:19 Ap 4 '77 *
Transition diary. L. Butler. il por Newsweek 89:26+ Ja 24 '77 *
Trilateral connection. J. Novak. Atlantic 240:57-9 Jl '77 *
Two cheers for Jimmy! M. Stone. U.S. News 82:96 Ap 18 '77 *
Unions tee off on Carter's free trade stand. il U.S. News 82:84-5 Ap 18 '77 *
U.S. and the world new horizons. R. Steele. il por Newsweek 90:37 D 26 '77 *
U.S. sets new rules for detente. pors U.S. News 82:24 Ap 4 '77 *
Uphill road; energy policy. Nation 224:546-7 My 7 '77 *
Verdict from experts on Jimmy Carter's first year. il pors U.S. News 84:16-19 Ja 9 '78 *
Verdict thus far; assessments of performance. il Time 109:20-1 Ap 25 '77 *
Viewing the family from the Oval Office. W. G. Pippert. Chr Today 21:60-1 S 9 '77 *
Viewpoint. R. Jacobson. Opera N 41:6 Ap 16 '77 *
Watershed in Washington. il pors U.S. News 83:23-4 O 10 '77 *
Well begun: Mr Carter passes up some ill-conceived advice. C. Morgello. Duns R 109:88 Ja '77 *
What Carter is up to. T. Mathews and others. il por Newsweek 89:32+ Mr 28 '77 *
What Carter should do now—advice from four political experts. il U.S. News 83:23-4 N 7 '77 *
What damage to Carter? B. Lance affair. R. Steele and others. il pors Newsweek 90:24-6+ S 19 '77 *
What Ford thinks of Carter's style; interview. G. R. Ford. il pors U.S. News 83:20-2 Jl 4 '77 *
What of national "town meetings"? N. R. Peirce. Current 190:21-3 F '77 *
What people expect of Carter; national survey. il U.S. News 82:20-2 Ja 24 '77 *
What price candor? R. Steele and others. il por Newsweek 89:28+ Mr 21 '77 *
What price energy? il por Newsweek 89:12-16 My 2 '77 *
Where Jimmy went wrong. T. Branch. Esquire 87:28+ My '77 *
Whistling Dixie. Nation 225:322 O 8 '77 *
White House watch. J. Osborne. See occasional issues of New republic *
White House woes. il U.S. News 83:20-1 S 26 '77 *
Why Carter is still a mystery. por U.S. News 83:26-8 O 17 '77 *
Why is Jimmy smiling? Why not? il pors Time 109:10-12 Ap 4 '77 *
Why it will be hard to stay just plain folks. il por U.S. News 82:23-5 Ja 24 '77 *
Why Latin Americans are bitter about Carter. il U.S. News 82:33-4 Ap 4 '77 *
Wipe away those tears. il por New Repub 176:5-6+ Ap 16 '77 *
With Jimmy from dawn to midnight. il por Time 109:14-19 Ap 18 '77 *
Word from Washington. F. Getlein. Progressive 41:14-15 D '77 *
Yankee from Georgia. W. L. Miller. il N Y Times Mag p 16-20+ Jl 3 '77 *
Year of the economy. M. Ruby and others. il Newsweek 90:40-1 N 21 '77 *
Zigzagging with the Russians. M. Stone. U.S. News 83:92 N 7 '77 *

Addresses, messages, etc.

Carter at the UN. W. F. Buckley, Jr. Nat R 29:457 Ap 15 '77
Carter environmental message: landmark action plan would shift conservation program into high gear; May 23 message to Congress. Nat Parks & Con Mag 51:26-9 Ag '77
Carter's new world; commencement address at the University of Notre Dame, May 22, 1977. J. Osborne. New Repub 176:8+ Je 4 '77
Editor's page; fireside chats. R. Manning. Atlantic 239:4 F '77
Fireside manner; February 2, 1977. P. Goldman and others. il Newsweek 89:22-4 F 14 '77
From my corner; May 23 message to Congress. C. Hunter. por Liv Wildn 41:39 Ap '77
Kraft flunks Carter; views on June 10 foreign policy statement. Nation 225:4-5 Jl 2 '77
Trouble with loose lingo. H. Sidey. il Time 110:25 N 21 '77
Warm words from Jimmy Cardigan; television address, February 2, 1977. il por Time 109:18 F 14 '77
Washington scene; analysis of environmental message. B. Kravetz. Parks & Rec 12:10+ Jl '77

See also

Carter, J.—Inaugural Address

Anecdotes, facetiae, satire, etc.

Chat. R. Lipez. Progressive 41:66 Ap '77

Anecdotes, facetiae, satire, etc.

Eyes on the White House lawn. S. L. Varnado. Nat R 29:496 Ap 29 '77
I cover Carter. G. W. S. Trow. New Yorker 53:28-9 Jl 25 '77
Jimmy Carter show. R. Baker. N Y Times Mag p 12 D 18 '77
Why President Carter wasn't re-elected. G. F. Will. Newsweek 89:96 F 21 '77

CARTER, Jimmy—*Continued*

Correspondence

Kids' letters to President Carter; excerpt; comp by B. Adler. il McCalls 105:165+ N '77

Inaugural Address

Back where Carter started: Inauguration Day in Des Moines. A. Clymer. Nation 224:133-5 F 5 '77
Carter's inaugural. Nation 224:66 Ja 22 '77
Inauguration Day, 1977: heralding a new spirit D. E. Kucharsky. il por Chr Today 21:50-1 F 4 '77
President walked home. J. M. Wall. Chr Cent 94:75-6 F 2 '77

Inauguration

Bantam to issue official inaugural book January 31. M. Reuter. il por Pub W 211:28 Ja 10 '77
Carter inaugural—pageantry with a populist flavor. il U.S. News 82:18-19 Ja 24 '77
Carter's big day. il pors U.S. News 82:12-16 Ja 31 '77
Clashing symbols. F. Getlein. Commonweal 104: 101-3 F 18 '77
Denim inaugural. S. Fraker and others. il Newsweek 89:21-2 Ja 24 '77
God-language in the inaugural; American civil religion; symposium. Chr Cent 94:3-7 Ja 5 '77
Healed city. New Repub 176:44 Ja 29 '77
Inaugural book is first full-color large-format instant production. P. Doebler. il Pub W 211: 78+ F 7 '77
Inaugural impressions. P. E. McMurray and J. B. Breslin. America 136:102-4 F 5 '77
Inaugural marks new and undefined era. L. Bennett, Jr. il Ebony 32:152-4 Mr '77
Inaugural square dance. R. D. Abrahams. New Repub 176:21-2 F 26 '77
Inauguration. New Yorker 52:25-7 F 7 '77
Inauguration. il pors Ebony 32:139-46+ Mr '77
Inauguration Day, 1977: heralding a new spirit. D. E. Kucharsky. il por Chr Today 21:50-1 F 4 '77
Jimmy's jumbo jamboree. il por Time 109:6-7 Ja 24 '77
Like Sunday morning. H. Sidey. il por Time 109:19 Ja 31 '77
New spirit. T. Mathews and others. il pors Newsweek 89:14-23 Ja 31 '77
Of many things. J. O'Hare. America 136:inside cover F 5 '77
People party. D. M. Alpern and others. il Newsweek 89:24+ Ja 31 '77
Prayers for an inauguration. America 136:91 F 5 '77
President walked home. J. M. Wall. Chr Cent 94:75-6 F 2 '77
Waltzing into office; A nonstop, $3 million bash; Bound for fun and glory. il pors Time 109:8-18 Ja 31 '77

Portraits

First family portraits; reproductions of drawings. R. Templeton. Good H 184:92-3 F '77
From Jamie Wyeth's sketch book; reproduction of drawings. J. Wyeth. New Repub 176:18-19 Ja 22 '77

Press conferences

Biggest rip-off; How big are big oil's profits? attack on petroleum industry. il pors Time 110:24-7 O 24 '77
Breaking the linkage: February 8 press conference. Nation 224:197 F 19 '77
Carter and Helms. J. Osborne. New Repub 177: 10-13 N 19 '77
Carter plan; Mid-East settlement ideas. A. Deming and others. il por map Newsweek 89:32+ Mr 21 '77
Carter's oil war; Big oil's big bucks. A. J. Mayer and others. il Newsweek 90:38-40 O 24 '77
Mr Carter confronts the oil industry. America 137:277 O 29 '77
Please pass the SALT. R. Steele and others. il por Newsweek 89:15-17 F 21 '77
Plus for Carter; February 8, 1977. J. Osborne. New Repub 176:14-15 F 19 '77
TRB from Washington; February 8, 1977. New Repub 176:4+ F 19 '77
Wait a minute. P. Goldman and others. il por Newsweek 90:29 N 7 '77

Press relations

Carter and the press—as Jody Powell sees it; interview. J. L. Powell, Jr. il pors U.S. News 83:25-7 O 10 '77
Fancy rappings; meetings with reporters. Nation 225:228 S 17 '77
Hi, Mr President. W. Wood. Progressive 41:51 O '77
Jimmy One Term and Johnny One Note. Time 110:100 N 7 '77
Jody faces life. D. M. Alpern and others. por Newsweek 90:119-20 S 19 '77
Not-so-cool Jody Powell. C. Mohr. il pors N Y Times Mag p20-1+ My 15 '77
President and press: honeymoon lingers on. il U.S. News 82:44 Ap 11 '77
Press and president. J. Hoge. New Repub 176: 25-6 Ja 22 '77
Reports & comment: Washington. S. J. Ungar. por Atlantic 239:6+ Ap '77
Secrecy lives. New Repub 177:9-10 N 26 '77

Public relations

America gets on the party line. il por Time 109:10-11 Mr 14 '77
Around two worlds in two days. il pors Time 109:12-15 Mr 28 '77
Back home in Dixie. P. Goldman and E. Clift. il pors Newsweek 90:21-2 Ag 1 '77
Carter fights back; trip to the Midwest and California. il pors U.S. News 83:19-21 O 31 '77
Carter on show. J. Osborne. New Repub 176:13-14+ Ap 2 '77
Carter's executive style; staff and public relations. Nat R 29:536 My 13 '77
Dial-a-president. P. Goldman and T. M. DeFrank. il por Newsweek 89:14-16 Mr 14 '77
Down home. J. Osborne. New Repub 177:13-14 Ag 6 '77
Good afternoon, Phyllis; call-in. Nation 224: 323-4 Mr 19 '77
Hearts and minds; reactions to energy proposals. T. Mathews and others. il por Newsweek 89:30 My 2 '77
How Carter spruces up his image. J. W. Mashek. il por U.S. News 82:43-4 Ap 11 '77
How to keep up with the Joneses. R. Steele and E. Clift. il Newsweek 89:14-15 Mr 14 '77
Image is substance is image: reflections on Carter's smile. A. Wolfe. Nation 224:778-81 Je 25 '77
Keeping in touch. H. Flieger. U.S. News 82:88 Ja 24 '77
Launching the energy blitz. il por Time 110: 12-14 O 31 '77
Long-distance runner. P. Goldman and T. M. DeFrank. il pors Newsweek 89:14-16 Mr 28 '77
On the road. R. Boeth and others. il pors Newsweek 90:34-6 O 31 '77
Peace: Mideast solution soon? opinions of senior officials abroad. il por U.S. News 83:38-40 D 26 '77
Pleasures—and perils—of populism. il Time 109: 25-6 Mr 21 '77
Polishing the Carter image. il pors U.S. News 83:15-16 Ag 8 '77
President lends the public an ear; Office of Public Liaison. Bus W p32 F 28 '77
Prime time President. R. Reeves. il por N Y Times Mag p 17-19 My 15 '77
Public writes: run White House as you would your home. U.S. News 82:25 Ja 24 '77
Running in office. New Repub 176:5-6+ Ap 23 '77
Setting the style. P. Goldman and others. il por Newsweek 89:14-15 F 21 '77
Sincerely yours, next. . .Sincerely yours, next. . . M. Friedman. il Sr Schol 109:8-9+ My 5 '77
TRB from Washington; radio call-in, March 5, 1977. New Repub 176:2+ Mr 5 '77
When the President meets the people; town hall meeting in Clinton, Mass. il pors U.S. News 82:20-1 Mr 28 '77
Winging it. J. Osborne. New Repub 177:9-11 N 5 '77
Yazoo City: south toward home. W. Morris. il Time 110:13-14 Ag 1 '77

Anecdotes, facetiae, satire, etc.

Hello. . .Jimmy? proposed radio call-in sessions; Time essay. P. Gray. Time 109:78 F 21 '77
Presidential call-in. W. Goodman. N Y Times Mag p 10 F 27 '77

Reading

Words with the President; a list of suggestions R. Rosenblatt. New Repub 176:84-6 Ja 22 '77

Relations with Congress

Back to the shop. Nation 224:610 My 21 '77
Behind the growing feud. G. Parshall. U.S. News 82:23 My 23 '77
Blitz by Fritz; ending the gas deregulation filibuster. P. Goldman and others. por Newsweek 90:34+ O 17 '77
Burst of energy. A. J. Mayer and others. il Newsweek 89:14-15 Je 13 '77
Can do; energy program. A. J. Mayer and H. W. Hubbard. Newsweek 89:68+ My 30 '77
Carter and Congress. D. M. Alpern and others. il Newsweek 89:18+ Mr 7 '77
Carter and Congress. J. Osborne. New Repub 176:15-17 Mr 5 '77
Carter and Congress: seeds of more discord. U.S. News 83:21-2 N 21 '77
Carter and spyland: meeting with Senate Committee on Intelligence, May 13, 1977. J. Osborne. New Repub 176:9-11 Je 11 '77
Carter, Congress and the Canal. A. Deming and others. il Newsweek 90:49 Jl 4 '77
Carter's waning war with Congress. E. Lewis. Bus W p 137-8 N 28 '77

CARTER, Jimmy—Relations with Congress—*Cont.*
Carter's water projects: pork barrel sellout? B. Vogt. il Outdoor Life 160:34+ N '77
Carter's way with Congress. G. Rushford. Nation 225:270 S 24 '77
Carter's woes—any way out? U.S. News 83:21-2 N 7 '77
Cleaning the in box; legislative proposals. P. Goldman and others. Newsweek 90:16-18 Ag 15 '77
The Club. M. Greenfield. il Newsweek 90:118 O 10 '77
Congress and Carter: who's in charge? J. W. Germond. il por N Y Times Mag p22+ Ja 30 '77
Congress/Carter relations keyed to defense, SALT. E. Kozicharow. Aviation W 106:19-21 Ap 4 '77
Congress gets the message. Fortune 96:59 Jl '77
Congress gives Carter mixed grades on first report card. il U.S. News 82:22-3 Mr 28 '77
Congress plays the Carter game. il Bus W p32 Ag 22 '77
Congress: showdown ahead. il Time 110:18-19 N 7 '77
Defiant Congress. il U.S. News 83:25 O 17 '77
Detente in the Capital. il por U.S. News 82:15-16 Je 27 '77
Energy crisis on the Hill. New Repub 176:5-6 Je 25 '77
Energy talkathon; Senate debate. T. Mathews and others. il por Newsweek 90:28-30 O 10 '77
Fiddler. New Repub 177:2+ O 8 '77
Filibuster ends, but not the gas war. il por Time 110:10-11+ O 17 '77
Flurry in the Capital. il U.S. News 83:15-16 Ag 15 '77
Give-and-take spirit. D. M. Alpern and others. Newsweek 89:17-18 Je 27 '77
Gunfight at the Capitol Hill corral. il por Time 109:11 Je 6 '77
Hard view from the Hill. H. W. Hubbard. Newsweek 90:30 O 10 '77
Home for Christmas. R. Boeth and others. il por Newsweek 90:75-6 D 26 '77
How Congress sizes up Carter as President. il pors U.S. News 83:17-20 Ag 8 '77
How much less is Moore? il por Time 110:15 D 12 '77
In their own words: Congressmen size up the impact; Lance affair. U.S. News 83:19 O 3 '77
Jimmy batties the barons. Time 109:26+ Je 20 '77
Jimmy vs. the liberals. T. Mathews and others. il por Newsweek 89:44 My 16 '77
Jimmy's conciliatory gestures. il Time 110:20 N 21 '77
Jimmy's oracle; R. C. Byrd. T. Mathews and J. J. Lindsay. por Newsweek 90:27 O 3 '77
Letter from Washington. R. Rovere. New Yorker 53:108+ Je 13 '77
Meanwhile, back on the Hill; controversy surrounding decision to stop funding nineteen water-development projects. S. Fraker and J. J. Lindsay. Newsweek 89:16-17 Mr 28 '77
Night of the long winds. il por Time 110:12-14 O 10 '77
Old pol takes on the new President; T. P. O'Neill. M. Tolchin. il pors N Y Times Mag p6-9+ Jl 24 '77
On a collision course. il pors U.S. News 82:14-15 Ap 18 '77
Rebates may drown in a spat over water. Bus W p43-4 Ap 18 '77
Score one for Jimmy; House passage of national energy program. D. M. Alpern and others. il por Newsweek 90:15-16 Ag 15 '77
Shadowboxing. S. Fraker and others. il Newsweek 89:15 Je 6 '77
Some stern tests ahead. il Time 110:13-14 S 12 '77
Spotty scorecard for Carter's lobbyists. il Bus W p88+ N 14 '77
Trojan horse at the FEC. New Repub 177:10-11 N 26 '77
Turning off the water. T. Mathews and M. Lord. il Newsweek 89:26+ Ap 4 '77
War without troops. New Repub 177:2+ D 17 '77
Wasted energy; passage of amendment to deregulate price of natural gas. Nat R 29:1220-1 O 28 '77
Water: a billion dollar battleground. il Time 109:16-17+ Ap 4 '77
Why the energy program is in such a mess. K. R. Sheets. U.S. News 83:28 O 24 '77
Will Congress work with Carter? G. R. Rosen. il Duns R 109:44-5+ Mr '77
Will the liberals buck Carter? G. R. Rosen. por Duns R 110:37 Ag '77

Religion

Carter and the church. N. King. il Nat R 29:384-5 Ap 1 '77
Carter and the religion factor. J. M. Wall. Chr Cent 94:739-40 Ag 31 '77
Carter at Sunday school. W. G. Pippert. Chr Cent 94:446 My 11 '77
Easing the pains in Plains. Chr Today 21:37 Ag 26 '77
New church member in town. E. E. Plowman. Chr Today 21:54-5 F 18 '77
New teacher, pupil at Sunday school. C. Nannes. por Chr Today 21:52-3 Ap 1 '77
Oval office: three models for a Christian. S. V. Monsma. Chr Today 21:28-9 Ja 21 '77
Pilgrimage to Plains. L. Sandon, Jr. Chr Cent 94:145-6 F 16 '77
Sunday school is a start. Chr Today 21:38-9 Ap 15 '77

Salaries, allowances, etc.

See also
Carter, J.—Taxes

Staff

Bleeding for Jimmy. J. Osborne. New Repub 176:11-12 Ja 15 '77
Carter to Cabinet: cut out frills. il U.S. News 82:29 F 14 '77
Carter's executive style; staff and public relations. Nat R 29:536 My 13 '77
Carter's painful reorganization plan. Bus W p52 Jl 25 '77
Carter's shuffle. J. Osborne. New Repub 177:11-13 Jl 30 '77
Georgians on my mind. M. Greenfield. Newsweek 91:88 Ja 16 '78
How Jimmy's staff operates. il Time 109:21-3 Ap 25 '77
Jimmy and the folks. J. Osborne. New Repub 176:8+ Ap 30 '77
Persistent perils of inner-circle vision. H. Sidey. il Time 110:20 S 26 '77
President Carter versus Parkinson's law. W. J. Miller. Read Digest 110:59-60 Ap '77 *
President's boys. il pors Time 109:16-18+ Je 6 '77
President's starting lineup—the new team in Washington. il por U.S. News 82:20-1 Ja 31 '77
Quiet revolutionaries. il Time 109:15 Ja 24 '77
Reports & comment: Washington. S. J. Ungar. por Atlantic 239:6+ Ap 77
Staffing up. J. Osborne. New Repub 176:12-14 Ja 29 '77
Sweetening the pot. il Time 110:18-19 N 28 '77
White House green. S. Fraker and E. Clift. il Newsweek 89:19 My 23 '77
White House is trimming frills, fat. il U.S. News 82:26 Mr 7 '77
White House movers and shakers: what they do, how much they're paid. il U.S. News 82:32-3 My 16 '77
Who's in charge? R. Steele and others. il Newsweek 90:40 O 24 '77
Who's riding high at the White House. il U.S. News 83:20-1 Jl 25 '77
Why Carter is having trouble taking full reins of government. il U.S. News 82:24-5 Mr 21 '77
Zero-based humility. M. Greenfield. Newsweek 89:80 F 28 '77
See also
Clough, S.
Costanza, M.
Eizenstat, S. E.
Jordan, H.
Moore, F.
Rubenstein, D.
Schuman, M. M.

Taxes

Carter's new tax return brings a gift to treasury. U.S. News 83:79 Jl 4 '77
Spotlight on Carter's tax return. il U.S. News 82:73 Je 20 '77
Tax volunteer. il por Time 110:12 Jl 4 '77

Travel

Carter decides to stay home. Time 110:17 N 14 '77
Mr Stay-at-Home. R. Boeth and others. il Newsweek 90:30 N 14 '77

Visit to Great Britain, 1977

Best foot forward. A. Deming and others. il Newsweek 89:29-30 My 23 '77
Carter's crucial summit; London summit. il por U.S. News 82:21-4 My 9 '77
Carter's maiden flight; London summit. A. Deming and others. il por Newsweek 89:43-4 My 9 '77
Carter's triumph in Europe; After summit cheers—real challenges lie ahead; hope for practical results of the London meetings. J. Mashek. il pors U.S. News 82:24-6 My 23 '77
Hey, look me over; London and Geneva conferences. S. Fraker and others. il Newsweek 89:26-8 My 16 '77
Innocent abroad. J. Osborne. New Repub 176:13-14+ My 21 '77
Just wee Geordie for a day; trip to Newcastle. S. Cloud. il Time 109:14-15 My 16 '77
President Carter attends economic, Berlin, and NATO meetings at London; remarks, with text of declarations, NATO communique, and question and answer session, May 5, 8-11, 1977. J. Carter. Dept State Bull 76:581-6+ Je 6 '77

CARTER, Jimmy—Visit to Great Britain, 1977 —*Continued*
Socko performance at the summit. il pors Time 109:12-15 My 16 '77
Summit at Downing Street; seven-nation conference in London. il por Time 109:14-16 My 9 '77
Will Europe follow Carter? il U.S. News 82:19-23 My 16 '77

Visit to seven countries, December 29, 1977-January 6, 1978
Carter on the wing. A. Deming and others. il por Newsweek 91:18-20 Ja 9 '78
Carter's fence-mending mission. il pors U.S. News 84:13-15 Ja 9 '78
Carter's New Year's whirl. T. Mathews and others. il map Newsweek 91:15-16 Ja 2 '78
Grand tour. A. Deming and others. il pors Newsweek 91:18-21+ Ja 16 '78
Jimmy's journey: mostly pluses. il pors Time 111:9-13 Ja 16 '78
Now: a Carter doctrine for the world. il por map U.S. News 83:12-15 D 26 '77
Sadat's confidence restored. il pors Time 111: 24+ Ja 16 '78
Will Carter learn from his trip abroad? S. W. Sanders. il por Bus W p34-5 Ja 9 '78
Winging his way into '78. il pors map Time 111: 8-11 Ja 9 '78

CARTER, Jimmy, family
Carter family scrapbook; with photographs; excerpt from The Carter family scrapbook: an intimate close-up of America's first family. J. Neyland. il Good H 185:100-5+ Jl '77
Changing times in Plains. J. A. Williams. Read Digest 111:133-6 Jl '77
Family at Thanksgiving; reproductions of paintings. T. Utz. Ladies Home J 94:109+ N '77
Family fun in the White House. B. Angelo. il pors Time 110:24-5 Ag 15 '77
Home-style Christmas at the White House. il pors U.S. News 83:58-9 D 26 '77
Magnus Carter: Jimmy's roots. il por Time 110: 20 Ag 22 '77
Meet the first family. il Sr Schol 109:2-4+ Ja 13 '77
Other Carters. J. Osborne. New Repub 176:9-11 F 26 '77
Presidential roots. New Yorker 53:30-2 Mr 14 '77
Private life in the White House—behind the scenes with the Carters. il pors U.S. News 82: 30-2 F 28 '77
Settling in at 1600. T. Mathews and J. Whitmore. il pors Newsweek 89:24-5 F 7 '77
What the Carters are doing to wipe out divorce in Washington. J. L. Block. il Good H 184: 109+ Je '77

CARTER, John Mack
Editor's notebook. See issues of Good housekeeping

CARTER, Joseph C.
Rural life in ancient Italy. il Intellect 106:106-7 S '77

CARTER, Judy (Langford)
Why nice women should speak out for ERA. bibl Redbook 149:118+ O '77
—and Ruffin, F. E.
Making it happen. il Redbook 149:70+ O; 150: 66+ N; 43+ D '77

CARTER, Lillian (Gordy)
Miss Lillian: my two sons; interview, ed by G. C. Spann. il por Ladies Home J 94:34+ Ag '77
My life in the Peace Corps; excerpt from Away from home: letters to my family. il por Good H 184:115-18+ Ap '77
My son the President; interview. il pors U.S. News 82:52-4 Mr 7 '77

about
Carter complex. E. Randolph. pors Esquire 88: 166-8+ N '77 *
Miss Lillian's sentimental journey. il pors Time 109:17 F 28 '77 *

CARTER, Malcolm N.
Impact of the Rothko case. il por Art N 76:78-80 O '77
NEA: will success spoil our biggest patron? il por Art N 76:32-40+ My '77
(ed) See Hoving, T. P. F. Hoving years

CARTER, Mary Randolph
Scent. See issues of Mademoiselle to July 1977

CARTER, Richard, and Nijhout, M. M.
Control of gamete formation (exflagellation) in malaria parasites. bibl il Science 195:407-9 Ja 28 '77

CARTER, Rosalynn (Smith)
Amy; interview, ed by L. B. J. Robb. il pors Ladies Home J 94:82+ F '77
As the delegate from Georgia said. . . .; address, November 19, 1976. MH 60:14 Wint '77
Change comes to White House; interview. pors U.S. News 82:31-3 Mr 21 '77
Doing it my way; excerpts from interview, ed by J. Whitmore. por Newsweek 89:17 Je 13 '77
Good Plains cooking from Rosalynn Carter; interview, ed by M. Burros. il por House & Gard 149:118-19+ F '77
How we entertain in the South. il por McCalls 104:152-3+ F '77
Rosalynn Carter and Margaret Mead: a meeting of minds; interview, ed by M. Mead. pors Redbook 149:123+ O '77
Rosalynn Carter at 50; interview, ed by T. B. Feldman. pors McCalls 104:126-7+ Ag '77
Things I want to do; excerpts from interview, ed by J. Whitmore. il por Newsweek 89:18-19 Ja 24 '77
Toward a more caring society; excerpts from address, August 25, 1977. il por MH 61:3-5 Summ '77

about
As Jimmy sees her; excerpts from interview, ed by E. Clift. J. Carter. Newsweek 89:18 Je 13 '77 *
Carters. Nation 224:740 Je 18 '77 *
Dedicated to a cause. B. Perry, Jr. il por MH 61:14 Spr '77 *
First family portraits; reproductions of drawings. R. Templeton. Good H 184:92-3 F '77 *
First Lady hosts discussion on the Nation's elderly. il por Aging 272:3-5 Je '77 *
Growing up with Rosalynn Carter; excerpt from How Jimmy won. K. Stroud. il pors Good H 185:102-3+ Ag '77 *
Inaugural togs: less is more. il Time 109:69 Ja 24 '77 *
Mrs Carter chairs special White House conference on aging. Ret Liv 17:15 Jl '77 *
Mrs President. M. Greenfield. Newsweek 89:100 Je 20 '77 *
My sister, Rosalynn; interview, ed by P. F. Healy. L. A. S. Wall. il pors Good H 186:76-7+ Ja '78 *
Of many things; First Lady's trip through Latin America. J. O'Hare. America 136:inside cover Je 11 '77 *
Out on her own. P. Goldman and others. il pors Newsweek 89:15-18 Je 13 '77 *
President's closest emissary; R. Carter's visit to Latin America. il pors Time 109:17+ Je 13 '77 *
Rosalynn Carter gets a big hand from 37 craftsmakers at White House luncheon. por Craft Horiz 37:41 Je '77 *
Rosalynn Carter: her toughest challenge. E. Carpenter. il por Redbook 148:8+ Ap '77 *
Rosalynn takes a message home; Latin American trip. il por Time 109:26 Je 20 '77 *
Rosalynn's agenda in the White House. K. Stroud. por N Y Times Mag p 19-20+ Mr 20 '77 *
Rosalynn's turn at diplomacy family style; Latin American trip. por map U.S. News 82:36 Je 6 '77 *
La señora de Carter hits the road. il por map Time 109.10 Je 6 '77 *
Some surprises as First Lady sets a style of her own. P. Avery. il pors U.S. News 83:40-1 N 14 '77 *
White House showcase for crafts. J. B. Reiter and J. Macurdy. il pors House B 119:116-19 O '77 *
Why angry Brazil shaped up as Rosalynn's toughest challenge. J. Benham. il pors map U.S. News 82:44-5 Je 13 '77 *
With Mrs Carter in Latin America. Taurus. New Repub 176:13-14 Je 18 '77 *

CARTER, Rubin, murder trial. See Trials (murder)

CARTER, Sharon. See McCormick, A. G. jt auth

CARTER, Steven A.
Fatal disease. bibl il Environment 19:16-20 Ap '77

CARTER Hawley Hale Stores, Inc
Carter Hawley Hale backs out of Britain; House of Fraser Ltd. Bus W p42+ O 17 '77

CARTER Hawley Hale Stores, Inc-Marshall Field & Company merger. See Department stores—Acquisitions and mergers

CARTHAGE, Africa
Roman Carthage. J. H. Humphrey and J. G. Pedley. il maps Sci Am 238:110-17+ Ja '78
See also
Punic Wars

CARTIER, John O.
(ed) 5-for-5 grouse hunters. il Outdoor Life 160:84-7 O '77
Good blind can be big as a truck or small as your hat. il Outdoor Life 160:74-7+ N '77
So you want to buy a goose hunt. il Outdoor Life 160:76-7+ O '77
We must harvest does or lose our herds. il Outdoor Life 160:61-3+ D '77
What inflation's doing to hunting, fishing. Outdoor Life 160:66+ S '77

CARTMELL, Robert
Roller coaster: king of the park. il Smithsonian 8:44-50 bibl(p 101) Ag '77

CARTOGRAPHY
See also
Computers—Cartographic use
Hydrographic surveying
United Nations Regional Cartographic Conference for Asia and the Pacific

CARTOONISTS
Cartooning. J. Markow. See alternate issues of Writers digest
See also
Capp, A.
Conrad, P.
Goldberg, R.
Hokinson, H. E.
Roth, A.
CARTOONS. See Caricatures and cartoons; Motion pictures—Animated cartoons
CARTRIDGE television. See Video recorders and recording
CARTRIDGES
Magnum seven; rifle cartridges. J. Carmichel. il Outdoor Life 159:112-14+ Je '77
News in ammo; new Federal Premium line. J. Wootters. il Field & S 81:170-2+ Mr '77
Number one: the big 7; 7mm Remington magnum. J. Wootters. il Field & S 82:84-6 Jl '77
CARTRIDGES, Phonograph. See Phonograph—Pickup
CARTRIDGES, Stereo. See Phonograph—Pickup
CARTS
Do-it-yourself garden cart. D. E. Pierce. il Org Gard & Farm 24:142-3 Je '77
They built classroom carts. il Sunset 158:128+ My '77
CARTS, Tea. See Serving carts
CARTWRIGHT, Jerry
Cruising seamanship. See issues of Motor boating & sailing, May 1977-
Design board (cont of) Drawing board. il Motor B & S 139:104-7 My; 52-5 Je; 140:42-5 Jl; 34-5 Ag; 36-9 O; 40-1 N; 32-5 D '77
CARUSO, Enrico
Historical records. A. F. Artsay. il pors Hobbies 81:37+ F '77 *
CARVER, George Washington
Another honor for the peanut man. il pors Ebony 32:102-4+ Jl '77 *
George Washington Carver and the peanut. B. Mackintosh. il pors Am Heritage 28:66-73 Ag '77 *
CARVER, John
Prevention: begin at the beginning. MH 60:7-10 Wint '77
CARVER, Sir Richard Michael Power
Three soldier peacemakers. pors Time 110:40 N 7 '77 *
CARVER, Sally
Picture postcard. See issues of Hobbies
CARVING (art industries)
See also
Ivory carving
Scrimshaw
Wood carving
CARVING (meat, etc)
How to carve cold salmon. J. Pepin. il House B 119:114 Je '77
How to carve the big bird. il Bet Hom & Gard 55:12 N '77
Redbook's competent cook carves the holiday bird. E. Alston. il Redbook 150:160+ N '77
CARVING tools. See Tools
CARVINGS, Mask. See Masks (sculpture)
CARY, Bob
Bass for the shore lunch. il Outdoor Life 159:122 Je '77
CARY, Jane Randolph
See your apartment in a new light. House B 119:83+ D '77
CASADÁLIGA, Pedro, Bp
Bishop of São Félix. R. Barbosa. Chr Cent 94:422-3 My 4 '77 *
CASAGRANDE, Daniel, and Siefert, Kristine
Origins of sulfur in coal: importance of the ester sulfate content of peat. bibl Science 195:675-6 F 18 '77
CASAGRANDE, Joseph B.
Looms of Otavalo; with biographical sketch. il Natur Hist 86:2, 48-59 O '77
CASALI, Kim Grove
Kim Casali's miracle baby. B. deH. Cayzer. il pors Good H 185:90+ N '77 *
CASALS Festival, Mexico. See Music festivals—Mexico
CASANOVA DE SEINGALT, Giacomo Girolamo
Casanova myth. R. Hughes. il Vogue 167:228-9 Mr '77 *
CASAROLI, Agostino, Abp
Vatican's ostpolitik. T. Heneghan. Commonweal 104:137-42 Mr 4 '77 *
CASE, J. I, Company. See Agricultural machinery industry
CASE, J. I, Company-Poclain SA merger. See Corporations—Acquisitions and mergers—International aspects
CASE, Sara
Grants and how to get them: an update. Am Lib 8:556-8 N '77
CASE of the frustrated corpse; drama. See Wallace, R.
CASE of the missing masterpiece; drama. See Huff, B. T.
CASE of the silent dog; drama. See Martens, A. C.
CASE studies
See also
Business management—Case studies
CASE Western Reserve University, Cleveland
Frederick Douglass on ethnology: a commencement address at Western Reserve College, 1854. A. McCluskey and J. McCluskey. bibl il por Negro Hist Bull 40:746-9 S '77
CASELLAS, Roberto
Book fair in Jerusalem. il Américas 29:44-5 S '77
CASES, Photographic. See Photography—Apparatus and supplies
CASEY, Timothy M. See Bartholomew, G. A. jt auth
CASH registers
See also
Cashiers
CASHEN, Jon
Vantastic. il Sat Eve Post 249:20-1+ Ap '77
CASHIERS
Super (market) scriptwriter; interview, ed by N. Levinson. J. Bateman. il pors Writers Digest 57:38-9 Ap '77
CASHMAN, Wayne
Cash was laundered. P. Gammons. il Sports Illus 46:78+ My 2 '77 *
CASHMERE cypress. See Cypress
CASINO gambling. See Gambling
CASINOS
Las Vegas: city built by losers; excerpt from Inside Las Vegas. M. Puzo. il Holiday 58:32-3+ Ap '77

Securities

Gambling stocks are riding a winning streak; hotels and casinos. L. Snyder. il Fortune 96:65-6+ S '77
CASKETS, Burial. See Coffins
CASKI cells. See Cancer cells
CASO, Alfonso
Monte Albán, city of the gods. L. Elliott. il Read Digest 110:202-4+ My '77 *
CASPER, Barry M.
Congress and the cozy triangles: the case of energy. Bull Atom Sci 33:5 My '77
Laser enrichment: a new path to proliferation? bibl il Bull Atom Sci 33:28-41 Ja; 3 Ap; 56 Je '77
Scientists on the Hill. il Bull Atom Sci 33:8-15 N '77
CASSELL, Jay
How to sure-foot your waders. il Outdoor Life 160:158 O '77
Master trout chef. il Outdoor Life 159:164 Mr '77
CASSELL, Kay Ann
Women in print: an update. il Lib J 102:1352-5 Je 15 '77
CASSENTI, Frank
Reviews; Red poster. P. Brunette. il Film Q 31:48-51 Wint '77 *
CASSEROLE cookery
Canned entrees. il Bet Hom & Gard 55:131-2 Je '77
Doubleheader casseroles. il Bet Hom & Gard 55:110 S '77
Great ground beef casseroles. E. W. Manning. il Farm J 101:62-3 O '77
One great casserole makes a party. R. Molter. il Parents Mag 52:48-50+ My '77
Problem-solving casseroles. il Bet Hom & Gard 55:116 O '77
CASSETTE decks. See Tape recorders and recording
CASSETTE recorders. See Tape recorders and recording; Tape recorders and recording, Portable
CASSETTE recorders, Video. See Video recorders and recording
CASSETTES. Magnetic tape. See Tape cartridges, cassettes, etc.
CASSIDY, Claudia
Splendor in the night. il pors Opera N 42:12-14 N '77
CASSIDY, Harold G.
Boundary conditions in energy and ecology. bibl Bull Atom Sci 33:31-2 Mr '77
CASSIDY, Sheila
Prayer under duress. il Nat R 29:826-8 Jl 22 '77
CASSIDY, W. A. and others
Antarctica: a deep-freeze storehouse for meteorites. bibl il map Science 198:727-31 N 18 '77
CASSITY, Turner
Strange case of Dr Jekyll and Dr Jekyll; Two are four; The space between the andirons; poems. Poetry 131:136-7 D '77
CASSON, Lionel
Contest for men's souls. il Horizon 21:78-84 Ja '78
CASSUTT, Michael
Second flight of The Hawk. il Space World N-7-163:36-42 Jl '77
CAST iron
See also
Ironwork
CASTAGNA, Edwin
Will the national inventory lead from the slough of despond to the celestial city? il Am Lib 8:491-2 O '77

CASTANEDA, Carlos
Art of dreaming; excerpt from The second ring of power. il Psychol Today 11:34-6+ D '77
about
Castaneda plot. D. McFerran. America 136:162-4 F 26 '77 *
Don Juan's power trip. S. Keen. il por Psychol Today 11:40-2 D '77 *
CASTAWAYS; musical comedy. See Musical comedy, revue, etc.—Reviews—Single works
CASTELLI, Jim
Draft: service or coercion? America 137:103-5 Ag 27 '77
Priests/nuns/ministers in politics. Commonweal 104:398-400 Je 24 '77
Public morality after Bert Lance. America 137: 280-2 O 29 '77
CASTELLI, Leo
Put your money where the talent is. B. Rose. il pors Vogue 167:146-7+ Ag '77 *
CASTILLO, Leonel J.
Excerpt from address on amnesty for illegal aliens, August 13, 1977. Cong Digest 56:242+ O '77
CASTING (fishing)
How to cast like a champ. P. Barrett. il Mech Illus 73:14+ Mr '77
See also
Fly casting
Salt water fishing
CASTING (sculpture)
New method of metal casting: cold casting with epoxy and metal powders. R. B. Platt. il Am Artist 41:56-61+ Ap '77
See also
Lost wax process
CASTING directors, Motion picture. See Motion picture directors
CASTING rods. See Fishing tackle
CASTLEMAN, Michael. See Lohr, J. F. jt auth
CASTLES
Loire: once over lightly; touring the châteaux. P. L. Buckley. Nat R 29:681-2+ Je 10 '77
Sackville-West's Sissinghurst: a garden of surprising privacies. A. Eliot. bibl il Horticulture 55:12-15 Jl '77
See also
Sand castles
CASTOR, Betty
U.S. journal: Tampa, Florida; discrimination against women at the University Club. C. Trillin. New Yorker 53:101-7 Ap 11 '77 *
CASTRO, Alonso
Reviews: Alonso Castro Dance Theatre. A. Smith. Dance Mag 52:80+ Ja '78 *
CASTRO, Alonso, Dance Theatre. See Dance companies
CASTRO, Fidel
CIA and Cuba. W. F. Buckley, Jr. Nat R 29: 792-3 Jl 8 '77 *
Carter, Castro and Reinhold Niebuhr. J. Bingham. Chr Cent 94:775-6 S 14 '77 *
Conversation with Castro. J. Armstrong. Chr Cent 94:743-4 Ag 31 '77 *
Cuba: no room for naysayers? D. Peerman. il il Chr Cent 94:845-9 S 28 '77 *
JFK, Castro—and controversy. D. Gelman. il pors Newsweek 90:85 Jl 18 '77 *
Talk with Castro. G. S. McGovern. il pors N Y Times Mag p20+ Mr 13 '77 *
Television; B. Moyers' The CIA's secret army. P. Sourian. Nation 225:155-7 Ag 20 '77 *
What Castro risks—and gains—in deal with Carter. C. J. Migdail. U.S. News 82:30 Je 20 '77 *
Why it won't be easy to strike a U.S.-Cuba deal. il por map U.S. News 82:71-2 Mr 7 '77 *
CASUALTY and fire insurance companies. See Insurance companies
CAT food industry. See Pet industries
CATACOMBS
New light on Jewish catacombs; Rome. il Time 109:75 My 23 '77
Unknown catacombs; Jewish catacombs of Rome. M. Ledeen. Commentary 64:64-6 S '77; Discussion. 64:17-18 N '77
CATADIOPTRIC telescopes. See Telescopes
CATALAN cookery. See Cookery, Spanish
CATALDO, Tom
Mini lifesaver. Time 110:57 D 5 '77 *
CATALINA Island. See Santa Catalina Island
CATALOG cards
LC to upgrade catalog card printing system. Lib J 102:1990 O 1 '77
CATALOG houses. See Mail order business
CATALOG showroom securities. See Retail trade —Securities
CATALOG showrooms. See Showrooms
CATALOGING
AACR revision controversy still smouldering. Lib J 102:2105-6 O 15 '77
Cataloging *shtik*. S. Berman. bibl Lib J 102: 1251-3 Je 1 '77; Discussion. 102:1693 S 1 '77
Holograms, putting the third D into the catalog. M. R. D'Alleyrand. bibl il Wilson Lib Bull 51: 746-50 My '77
Laurence Feininger 1909-1976: life, work, legacy; cataloger and transcriber of Catholic Church music. E. E. Lowinsky. bibl il por Mus Q 63:327-66 Jl '77
Public libraries, the Library of Congress, and the national bibliographic network; adaptation of address, February 1977. M. J. Freedman. il Lib J 102:2211-15 N 1 '77
Technology & the catalog; tradition vs. the new wave; ALA institute. Lib J 102:666 Mr 15 '77
See also
Catalogs, Library
CATALOGING, Computerized. See Libraries—Automation
CATALOGS
Bibliography
Dream is only a postage stamp away with autumn's crop of catalogues. R. Dahlin. Pub W 211:60+ Je 27 '77
CATALOGS, Commercial
Barrage of catalogs competes for attention. il Bus W p 122 D 5 '77
Decorate by mail. V. Perlo. il Am Home 80: 62-4 O '77
Gifts: for the season; Christmas gifts from catalogs. A. Anderson. Vogue 167:93-4+ D '77
Shop by mail catalogues. House B 119:56+ S '77
Vogue's holiday preview; a spectacular gift catalogue collection for 1977. Vogue 167:235-8 O '77
Anecdotes, facetiae, satire, etc.
It's the thought; Christmas gifts from catalogs. R. Rosenblatt. New Repub 177:36-7 D 10 '77
CATALOGS, Library
Card catalog to COM. J. North. il Lib J 102: 2132-4 O 15 '77
Exploring catalog country's great divide. D. Peele. bibl il Wilson Lib Bull 52:324-9 D '77
Opening minds to closing catalogs, or, When can we throw out the cards? METRO seminar. A. Plotnik. Am Lib 8:594-5 D '77
See also
United States—Library of Congress—Catalogs
CATALOGS, Literature. See English literature—Catalogs
CATALOGS, Phonograph record. See Phonograph records—Catalogs
CATALOGS, Seed and plant
Horticulture's 1978 garden catalog preview. D. Fell. Horticulture 55:14+ D '77
CATALOGS, Trade. See Catalogs, Commercial
CATALONIA
Homage of sorts. M. Acoca. Newsweek 90:29-30 Jl 18 '77
Homage to Barcelona. A. Burgess. il N Y Times Mag p44-5+ D 4 '77
Organized peace in southern France and Catalonia, ca. 1140-ca. 1233. T. N. Bisson. bibl f map Am Hist R 82:290-311 Ap '77
CATALYSIS
Heterogeneous catalysis: some recent developments. J. H. Sinfelt. bibl il Science 195:641-6 F 18 '77
Perovskite oxides: materials science in catalysis. R. J. H. Voorhoeve and others. bibl Science 195:827-33 Mr 4 '77
CATALYSTS
Intermetallic compounds of the type MNi_5 as methanation catalysts. A. Elattar and others. bibl il Science 196:1093-4 Je 3 '77
CATALYTIC converters. See Automobiles—Pollution control devices
CATALYTIC heaters. See Heaters
CATAMARAN racing. See Sailboat racing
CATAMARANS
How to get started in hot-rod sailing. B. Kocivar. il Pop Sci 210:109-11+ F '77
Multihulls and other manias. D. Bradley. Motor B & S 140:8+ Jl '77
New-fangled cat: a curious case. R. Andrews. il Mech Illus 73:116 F '77
CATARACT surgery. See Eye—Surgery
CATARACTS (eye defect)
Diabetic cataracts and flavonoids. S. D. Varma and others. bibl il Science 195:205-6 Ja 14 '77
Lens cataract formation and reversible alteration in crystallin synthesis in cultured lenses. J. Piatigorsky and T. Shinohara. bibl il Science 196:1345-7 Je 17 '77
Phase separation of a protein-water mixture in cold cataract in the young rat lens. T. Tanaka and others. bibl il Science 197:1010-12 S 2 '77
CATASTROPHE theory. See Topology
CATBIRDS
Dogwood and catbird. W. Trimm. il Conservationist 31:28 My '77
CATCH phrases, Dictionary of. See English language—Dictionaries
CATE, Phillip Dennis
Empathy with the humanity of the streets. il Art N 76:56-9 Mr '77

CATECHETICS
Catholic Church
Display of unity; Synod of Bishops. M. Hammond. Commonweal 104:774-6 D 9 '77
Fiddling in Rome. K. L. Woodward. il Newsweek 90:111 N 7 '77
First sacraments and the Synod on Catechetics. J. L. Cunningham. America 137:212-15 O 8 '77
Hopes for the coming Synod; with editorial comment. M. C. Bryce. America 137:inside cover, 215-17 O 8 '77
How to pass on the faith; International Synod of Bishops. K. L. Woodward and J. Whitmore. il Newsweek 90:69 O 10 '77
Slumbering Synod. D. R. Campion. America 137:328-30, 355-8 N 12-19 '77
Spreading the word of God; Synod of Bishops. America 137:297 N 5 '77
See also
Catholic Church—Catechisms
CATECHISMS
See also
Catholic Church—Catechisms
CATECHOLAMINES
Cardiac pacemaking: an obligatory role of catecholamines? G. H. Pollack. bibl il Science 196:731-8 My 13 '77
Liquid chromatographic analysis of endogenous catecholamine released from brain slices. P. M. Plotsky and others. bibl il Science 197:904-6 Ag 26 '77
See also
Dopamine
Norepinephrine
CATERERS and catering
Who needs a caterer? You do. L. DeMauro. il Am Home 80:50-1+ N '77
CATERING. See Caterers and catering
CATERPILLAR Tractor Company
Auto workers settle with Caterpillar. L. Bornstein and others. M Labor R 100:87 F '77
CATERPILLARS
Why I cared for and fed my garden's caterpillars. J. Dane. il Org Gard & Farm 24:124-5 Je '77
See also
Gypsy moths
Silkworms
CATFISH fishing
Channel cats; two ways. B. W. Dalrymple; C. Elliot. il Outdoor Life 159:84-7+ Ap '77
Pool party: catfish for 600; Pohick Bay Regional Park, Va. R. G. Bowers. il Parks & Rec 12:38-40+ Mr '77
When it's hot. . .it's hot. L. Mueller. il Outdoor Life 160:78-9+ Ag '77
See also
Bullhead fishing
CATHEDRALS
France
Chartres: through a glass darkly. il Time 109:54-5 Ja 31 '77
See also
Paris—Notre Dame (cathedral)
CATHODIC protection. See Corrosion and anticorrosives
CATHOLIC authors
See also
Claudel, P.
Huysmans, J. K.
O'Connor, F.
CATHOLIC Bishops, National Conference of. See National Conference of Catholic Bishops
CATHOLIC Church
Archbishop Lefebvre's religion. M. Hammond. Commonweal 104:422-3 Jl 8 '77; Reply. R. G. Cipolla. 104:610 S 30 '77
Homosexual rights and ordination. America 137:346 N 19 '77; Discussion. 137:409 D 10 '77
Matter preordained. P. Steinfels. Commonweal 104:136 Mr 4 '77
More on Women in the Church. Commonweal 104:109-11 F 18 '77
On the ordination of women. M. Novak. Commonweal 104:425-7 Jl 8 '77; Discussion 104:556-64; 589-91 S 2-16 '77
Paul says no. Newsweek 89:77 F 7 '77
Pope Paul to women: keep out. por Time 109:65 F 7 '77
Schism in the Church. M. B. Martin. Nat R 29:831 Jl 22 '77
Threat of schism; views of M. Lefebvre. America 137:23-4 Jl 16 '77
Tradition vs. traditionalists. Chr Today 21:62 S 9 '77
When an archbishop rebels against the Pope. il por U.S. News 83:62 Jl 25 '77
Women's ordination in the Mother Church. S. Cunneen. Chr Cent 94:256-8 Mr 16 '77
Women's ordination: the future of equality. America 136:118-19 F 12 '77; Discussion. 136:157, 177-8 F 26-Mr 5 '77
See also
Advent
Beatification
Canon law
Canonization
Catechetics—Catholic Church
Ecumenical movement
Fasts and feasts—Catholic Church
Laity—Catholic Church
Lent
Nuns
Pentecost
Religious orders
Saints
Synod of Bishops, 1977
Vatican Council, 2d

Authority
Conscience; theologians and the magisterium. R. A. McCormick. il New Cath World 220:268-71 N '77
Policy changes. G. McCauley. America 136:432-3 My 7 '77
Rome vs. Memphis. Commonweal 104:355-6 Je 10 '77
See also
Popes—Infallibility

Blacks
Black bishop for Mississippi; installation of J. L. Howze. G. V. Murry. America 137:32 Jl 16 '77
Black Catholics. C. Vecsey. Commonweal 104:332-6 My 27 '77

Catechetics
See Catechetics—Catholic Church

Catechisms
National catechetical directory; symposium; with editorial comment. New Cath World 220:54-76+ Mr '77
National catechetical directory: what it is, what it isn't. E. J. McDermott. America 136:76-9 Ja 29 '77

Charities
See also
National Conference of Catholic Charities

Clergy
Widening gyre. Nat R 29:871 Ag 5 '77
See also
Bishops
Cardinals
Deacons
Jesuits
Religious orders

Conferences
See Religious conferences

Discipline
See also
Celibacy
Congregation for the Doctrine of the Faith
Penance

Education
Vatican statement on education; Annuario pontificio 1977. J. W. Donohue. America 137:67-70 Ag 13 '77
Why Johnny can't pray. J. J. DiGiacomo. il America 137:414-18 D 10 '77
See also
Catholic colleges and universities
Catholic schools
Congregation for Catholic Education
Theological seminaries, Catholic

Eucharist
Communion in the hand. A. McCarthy. Commonweal 104:362+ Je 10 '77
Communion in the hand: why the diversity? F. X. Clark. America 136:356-8 Ap 16 '77; Discussion 136:405 My 7 '77
Dual-sex eucharist. M. Novak; reply. H. Cox. Commonweal 104:112-14 F 18 '77
First sacraments and the Synod on Catechetics. J. L. Cunningham. America 137:212-15 O 8 '77
Really present. G. McCauley. America 136: inside back cover Je 4 '77
Rubrics in transition; communion in the hand controversy. America 136:534 Je 18 '77

Infallibility
See also
Popes—Infallibility

Liturgy and ritual
See also
Catholic Church—Eucharist
Confirmation (sacrament)
Mass

Marriage
See Marriage—Catholic Church

Music
See Church music

Parishes
See Parishes

Relations
Christian Church, Disciples of Christ
Disciples of Christ-Roman Catholic dialogue. P. D. Morris. il New Cath World 220:196-201 Jl '77

CATHOLIC Church—Relations—*Continued*

Church of England

Anglican/R. C. agreement. P. Hebblethwaite. Commonweal 104:106-8 F 18 '77
Anglican-Roman Catholic dialogue. H. J. Ryan. il New Cath World 220:168-72 Jl '77
Anglicans and Roman Catholics on authority in the church. H. J. Ryan. America 136:183-6 Mr 5 '77
Dr Coggan and Paul VI. America 136:435 My 14 '77
Nottingham '77: evangelicals eye unity; Coggan, Vatican: has God's time arrived? R. Pulliam. Chr Today 21:44-6 My 20 '77
Pope for Anglicans? il Time 109:44 Ja 31 '77
Power to the Pope; Anglican/Roman Catholic report. K. Woodward. Newsweek 89:56 Ja 31 '77
Reunion's detour; contrasting views in The tablet and The economist. J. Deedy. Commonweal 104:354 Je 10 '77
Third summit: more hurdles. il pors Time 109:80 My 9 '77
Understanding the Church's authority; Joint Anglican Roman Catholic International Commission. T. Beeson. Chr Cent 94:211-12 Mr 9 '77
Word about Rome, Keele, and Nottingham. J. D. Douglas. Chr Today 21:60-1 Ap 1 '77

Eastern Orthodox Church

See also
Ecumenical movement

Jews

Jewish-Catholic relations. J. B. Sheerin. il New Cath World 220:173-8 Jl '77

Lutheran Church

Ambiguity, criticism and promise. C. J. Peter. il New Cath World 220:168-72 Jl '77

Orthodox Eastern Church

Orthodox-Roman Catholic consultation in the U.S.A. E. J. Kilmartin. il New Cath World 220:179-80+ Jl '77

Presbyterian Church

Roman Catholic/Presbyterian-Reformed consultation. H. G. J. Beck. il New Cath World 220:202-6 Jl '77

Protestant churches

Evangelicals and Roman Catholics. J. R. W. Stott. Chr Today 21:30-1 Ag 12 '77
See also
Ecumenical movement

United Methodist Church

Christian mission and spirituality: Roman Catholics and Methodists in dialogue. E. L. Fortin. il New Cath World 220:191-5 Jl '77

Relations (diplomatic)

Europe, Eastern

Vatican's ostpolitik. T. Heneghan. Commonweal 104:137-42 Mr 4 '77

Rites and ceremonies

See also
Exorcism
Ordination

CATHOLIC Church and abortion. See Abortion—Moral and religious aspects
CATHOLIC Church and communism. See Communism and religion
CATHOLIC Church and labor. See Church and labor
CATHOLIC Church and politics. See Church and politics
CATHOLIC Church and sex. See Sex and religion
CATHOLIC Church and social problems. See Church and social problems
CATHOLIC Church and socialism. See Socialism and religion
CATHOLIC Church and women. See Women and religion

CATHOLIC Church in Africa
Trouble in Africa. Chr Today 21:56-7 Ap 15 '77

CATHOLIC Church in Africa, Southern
See also
Catholics in Africa, Southern

CATHOLIC Church in Argentina
Repression in Argentina. R. F. Drinan. Commonweal 104:103-4 F 18 '77

CATHOLIC Church in Brazil
Bishop of São Félix. R. Barbosa. Chr Cent 94:422-3 My 4 '77

CATHOLIC Church in China
Church in China. R. L. Johnston. Commonweal 104:394-5 Je 24 '77

CATHOLIC Church in Ecuador
Ecuadorean Church: new spirit, old believers. J. F. O'Callaghan. America 136:559-62 Je 25 '77
High tension in Latin America; church vs. state. S. R. Sywulka. Chr Today 21:40-1 Ja 7 '77

CATHOLIC Church in El Salvador. See Catholic Church in Salvador

CATHOLIC Church in France
French Catholicism faces the left. P. McCarthy. America 137:350-3 N 19 '77
Requiem for the country priest. America 137:179 O 1 '77
Underground Church. M. Martinez. Nat R 29:944 Ag 19 '77
See also
Catholics in France

CATHOLIC Church in Germany, East
Theology behind the Wall. P. Misner. Commonweal 104:620-2 S 30 '77

CATHOLIC Church in Great Britain
Pastoral strategy. B. Wicker. Commonweal 104:390-1 Je 24 '77

CATHOLIC Church in Hungary
Hungary's Crown. T. Beeson. Chr Cent 94:1158-9 D 14 '77

CATHOLIC Church in Ireland
Death comes for a Cardinal. J. Cooney. Commonweal 104:326-7 My 27 '77
New Archbishop for Armagh; appointment of T. O Fiaich. T. P. O'Mahony. America 137:235-6 O 15 '77
Requiem for a Cardinal. T. P. O'Mahony. America 136:445-6 My 14 '77

CATHOLIC Church in Italy
End of the Concordat? M. Hammond. Commonweal 104:584-5 S 16 '77
Giovanni Battista Franzoni, one year after laicization. E. Carrillo. il por Chr Cent 94:1093-5 N 23 '77
New Concordat in Italy. America 137:372 N 26 '77

CATHOLIC Church in Korea, South
Prophetic minority. J. Baker. Commonweal 104:550-1 S 2 '77

CATHOLIC Church in Latin America
Latin America: Catholics in conflict. S. Sywulka. Chr Today 21:39 Ag 12 '77
Latin America's rebel priests. J. Monahan. Progressive 41:43-6 My '77
Popular religiosity: new wind in Latin America. P. Lernoux. Nation 224:199-205 F 19 '77

CATHOLIC Church in Mexico
Violence in Mexico. America 137:227 O 15 '77

CATHOLIC Church in Paraguay
Paraguayans savor Christian solidarity; visit of Cardinal Paulo Evaristo Arns. M. D. Wilde. Chr Cent 94:302 Mr 30 '77

CATHOLIC Church in Poland
More government pressure. T. Heneghan. Commonweal 104:454-5 Jl 22 '77
Of many things. J. O'Hare. America 136:309 Ap 9 '77

CATHOLIC Church in Rhodesia
Bishop Lamont deported. America 136:312 Ap 9 '77
Of many things. J. O'Hare. America 136:inside cover F 19 '77

CATHOLIC Church in Salvador
Blood poured out; murder of Father R. Grande. J. R. Brockman. America 136:328-9 Ap '77
El Salvador: a test of fire. D. J. Kalke. Chr Cent 94:722-4 Ag 17 '77
El Salvador suppresses the church. P. Lernoux. Nation 225:100-2 Ag 6 '77
Martyrdom in El Salvador. Chr Cent 94:443 My 11 '77
Murder in El Salvador. America 136:264 Mr 26 '77
Of many things. J. O'Hare. America 137: inside cover Jl 16 '77
Persecution in El Salvador. J. R. Brockman. America 137:10-11 Jl 2 '77
Priests in peril. K. L. Woodward. il Newsweek 90:50 Ag 1 '77
Terror in El Salvador. S. R. Sywulka. Chr Today 21:40-1 Je 17 '77
Witness to justice; murder of R. Grande. E. Moran. il America 136:410-14 My 7 '77

CATHOLIC Church in South Africa
Challenging the great white state; desegregation of Catholic schools in South Africa. il Time 109:46 F 7 '77
Church schools in South Africa. America 136:121 F 12 '77
Commitment in South Africa. America 136:206 Mr 12 '77
South Africa's gambling church. America 136:138 F 19 '77
Tortured logic from South Africa; bishops' protest. America 137:371 N 26 '77

CATHOLIC Church in Switzerland
Church is full of wolves; ordination conducted by M. Lefebvre. il por Time 110:64 Jl 11 '77
Lefebvre's defiance. il por Newsweek 90:78 Jl 11 '77

CATHOLIC Church in the Dominican Republic
Married priests: one more try. B. F. McWilliams. America 136:416 My 7 '77

CATHOLIC Church in the Philippines
Church persecution in the Philippines. America 136:159 F 26 '77
Of many things. J. O'Hare. America 136:inside cover F 19; inside cover My 21 '77
Philippine Church: a letter. C. Wilson. America 136:273-4 Mr 26 '77

CATHOLIC Church in the United States
Divided shepherds of a restive flock. T. Fleming. il N Y Times Mag p9+ Ja 16 '77
Gathering of bishops; National Conference of Catholic Bishops. A. P. Klausler. Chr Cent 94:499 My 25 '77
New chance for the bishops; Call to Action conference in Detroit. P. Steinfels. Commonweal 104:200+ Ap 1 '77
No need for the great wait; resolutions of the Detroit Call to Action conference. America 136:227-8 Mr 19 '77
Reconciliation in Memphis. R. R. Holton. Commonweal 104:38-9 Ja 21 '77
Reconciliation in Memphis: a diocese prepared. A. Kirk. America 136:146-8 F 19 '77
Second Call to Action; bishops to address conclusions of Detroit meeting. J. Finn. Commonweal 104:269-72 Ap 29 '77
See also
Catholics in the United States
National Conference of Catholic Bishops

History

Foresight of Felix Varela; establishment of Catholic churches in New York City. C. F. Benedf. il por Americas 29:9-12 Ap '77

CATHOLIC churches. See Church architecture

CATHOLIC colleges and universities
Academic profile; women's Catholic colleges. E. B. Wymard. Commonweal 104:652-7 O 14 '77
America's directory of colleges, 1977. America 137:308-10 N 5 '77
Case for Catholic education. R. P. McBrien. Commonweal 104:41-4 Ja 21 '77; Discussion. 104:242-6 Ap 15 '77
Catholic universities and the Vatican. R. J. Henle. America 136:315-22 Ap 9 '77
Catholic university? Commonweal 104:35-6 Ja 21 '77
Ignatian heritage for today's college; Jesuit colleges. T. S. Healy. America 137:304-6 N 5 '77
Working together: an educational model. W. C. McInnes. America 137:300-3 N 5 '77
See also
Catholic University of America
Detroit. University
Fordham University
Holy Cross College, Worcester, Mass.
Notre Dame. University, Notre Dame, Ind.
Providence College, Providence, R.I.
Theological seminaries, Catholic

CATHOLIC education. See Catholic Church—Education

CATHOLIC laity. See Laity—Catholic Church

CATHOLIC newspapers. See Catholic press

CATHOLIC parishes. See Parishes

CATHOLIC periodicals. See Catholic press

CATHOLIC press
Catholic press today. S. J. Adamo. Commonweal 104:176-7 Mr 18 '77; Discussion. 104:163, 258, 273-5 Ap 29 '77
See also
America (periodical)
Catholic Press Association

Anecdotes, facetiae, satire, etc.

Pail of water. R. A. Blake. America 136:239-40 Mr 19 '77

CATHOLIC Press Association
Praying editors. Chr Today 21:37 Je 3 '77

CATHOLIC Relief Services
Serving under fire. Chr Today 21:39-40 Ja 7 '77

CATHOLIC Scholars, Fellowship of. See Fellowship of Catholic Scholars

CATHOLIC school teachers. See Teachers

CATHOLIC school teachers unions. See Teachers unions

CATHOLIC schools
Bargains at Catholic schools. America 137:158-9 S 24 '77
Board up against the wall; censorship of National Labor Relations Board for union involvement at parochial schools. M Labor R 100:52-3 N '77
Catholic schools. J. Deedy. Commonweal 104:2 Ja S. J. Adamo. Commonweal 104:163, 176-7 Mr 18 7 '77
Commitment to nonpublic schools. America 136: 311 Ap 9 '77
Freedom and parochial schools; NLRB and Catholic schools. R. Kirk. Nat R 29:441-2+ Ap 15 '77
Vatican statement on education; Annuario pontificio 1977. J. W. Donohue. America 137: 67-70 Ag 13 '77

Desegregation

Challenging the great white state; desegregation of Catholic schools in South Africa. il Time 109:46 F 7 '77
Church schools in South Africa. America 136: 121 F 12 '77

Federal aid

Recent developments in the law; Supreme Court cases involving Catholic schools; address, January 25, 1977. V. C. Blum. Vital Speeches 43: 296-300 Mr 1 '77

State aid

Is state aid the saving grace of Catholic education? M. Sherry. America 136:327-8 Ap 9 '77
Saving diversity by distinctions. America 136: 93 F 5 '77

Tax exemption

See Taxation, Exemption from

France

Death by asphyxiation. America 137:256 O 22 '77

CATHOLIC Theological Society of America
Conscience, theologians and the magisterium. R. A. McCormick. il New Cath World 220: 268-71 N '77
It's not official, nor is it right; Human sexuality: new directions in American Catholic thought. Chr Today 21:22 Jl 8 '77
Love and sexuality in Catholic tradition; report. F. X. Meehan. America 137:230-4 O 15 '77
Scriptural response to the report on Human sexuality. G. T. Montague. America 137:284-5 O 29 '77
Sex and the Catholic. K. L. Woodward. Newsweek 90:78-9 Jl 11 '77
Sexual challenge; report. Time 109:49-50 Je 13 '77
Time makes ancient good uncouth: the Catholic report on sexuality. R. R. Ruether. Chr Cent 94:682-5 Ag 3 '77

CATHOLIC University of America

Library

Pope's library is brought to light after 200 years. M. Olmert. il Smithsonian 8:70-7 Ja '78

CATHOLIC Worker Movement
Confronting Dorothy Day. A. McCarthy. Commonweal 104:297+ My 13 '77
Dollar for Dorothy. M. Mayer. por Progressive 41:40-1 N '77

CATHOLICISM
Catholicism: a new vitality emerging out of ferment. il U.S. News 82:63-4+ Ap 11 '77

CATHOLICS in Africa, Southern
Confrontation in Southern Africa; killing of seven Roman Catholic missionaries. Chr Today 21:51 Mr 18 '77

CATHOLICS in France
Catholic vote in France; municipal elections. A. Woodrow. Commonweal 104:261-3 Ap 29 '77

CATHOLICS in Northern Ireland
Conflict and cleavage in Northern Ireland. R. J. Terchek. bibl f Ann Am Acad 433:47-59 S '77

CATHOLICS in the United States
Catholicism: a new vitality emerging out of ferment. il U.S. News 82:63-4+ Ap 11 '77
Empty churches and nonbelievers; report called Catholic life in Yorkville. America 136:161 F 26 '77
Island in the city; Chicago's Catholics; views of J. W. Sanders. J. W. Donohue. America 136:322-4 Ap 9 '77
People's parish; Community of the Living Spirit, Waukesha, Wis. M. True. Commonweal 104: 496-9 Ag 5 '77; Discussion. 104:610-11+ S 30 '77
Update on Leonard Feeney. J. Deedy. Commonweal 104:5-7 Ja 7 '77
Yorkville report. Commonweal 104:131-2 Mr 4 '77
See also
Catholic Worker Movement

Political activities

Friend at court? G. Schneiders and J. Carter. J. Deedy. Commonweal 104:2 Ja 7 '77

CATLIN, George
George Catlin's life amongst the Indians. J. R. Millichap. il pors Am Hist Illus 12:4-9+ Ag '77 *

CATLIN, Hoyt
Old folks at work. S. T. Atlas and M. Reese. il por Newsweek 90:64 S 26 '77 *

CATNIP
Purrfect plant. S. Farlow. Seventeen 36:58 S '77

CATO, pseud
Letter from Washington. See issues of National review

CATS
Cats and commerce. N. B. Todd. il maps Sci Am 237:100-6 bibl(p 163) N '77
Classical nictitating membrane conditioning in the awake, normal, restrained cat. M. M. Patterson and others. bibl il Science 196:1124-6 Je 3 '77
Cortical mechanisms that augment or reduce evoked potentials in cats. J. H. Lukas and J. Siegel. bibl il Science 198:73-5 O 7 '77
I killed your cat. J. M. Allen. Read Digest 110: 69-70 Ap '77
Pets; cats and plants. M. Siegal. House B 119: 80 O '77

CATS—*Continued*
Siamese cats: abnormal responses of retinal ganglion cells. Y. M. Chino and others. bibl il Science 197:173-4 Jl 8 '77
Tracking down a lost animal. M. W. Fox. McCalls 104:63-4+ Ag '77
Working cats. K. Larson. il Ladies Home J 94:72 Jl '77
See also
Lynxes

Anecdotes, facetiae, satire, etc.

Cats I have known and loathed. G. Millstein. il por N Y Times Mag p 110 Mr 13 '77
Feline lib. R. Baker. N Y Times Mag p8 Ap 17 '77

Care

How to help your pet weather winter. B. Humeston. Bet Hom & Gard 55:266+ N '77
How to tell when your cat needs a vet. B. Humeston. Bet Hom & Gard 55:199 F '77

Shedding

See Molting

Stories

Mrs Ainsworth's Christmas cat; story; excerpt from All things wise and wonderful. J. Herriot. Read Digest 111:118-22 D '77

Training

Pets. M. Siegal. House B 119:38+ Jl '77

CATS, Fossil
Cheetah-like cat in the North American Pleistocene. L. D. Martin and others. bibl il Science 195:981-2 Mr 11 '77

CATS vision. See Vision (animals)

CATTAILS
And if all else fails: cattails. K. A. Matichek. Sci Digest 82:61 O '77

CATTELANI, Raúl
Raúl Cattelani, Uruguayan printmaker. A. Llambias De Azevedo. il Américas 29:29-31 Ag '77 *

CATTLE
Beef extra. il Farm J 101:Beef 1-2+ Ja; Beef 1-2+ F; Beef 1-2+ My; Beef 1+ Je; Beef 1-2+ Ag; Beef 1-2+ S; Beef 1-2+ O; Beef 1-2+ D '77
Beef management. B. Eftink. See issues of Successful farming
Lymphocyte-defined loci in cattle. W. R. Usinger and others. bibl il Science 196:1017-18 My 27 '77
See also
Bulls
Calves
Cowboys
Heifers

Breeding

See Cattle breeding

Breeds

Booming new market for longhorns. W. Kester. il Farm J 101:Beef 8-9+ S '77
Don't count the colored breeds out. E. Ainsworth. il Farm J 101:Dairy 5-7 Ag '77
Genetic peril in cattle. S. Beart. Environment 19:2-3 Mr '77

Carcasses

Know what your cattle are worth; USDA's fabricated carcass report. W. Kester. il Farm J 101:Beef 4-5+ Je '77
More choice with less grain. W. Kester. il Farm J 101:Beef 8-10 Ja '77

Care

We need a Red Cross for starving cattle. N. J. Skjold. por Farm J 100:10A-11 D '76

Confinement methods

Can your cattle pay for confinement? W. Kester. il Farm J 101:Beef 10-11 O '77

Diseases and pests

Beat bloat. il Farm J 101:Dairy 7 Je '77
See also
Cows—Diseases and pests
Ticks

Feeding

Beef production efficiency. A. Trenkle and R. L. Willham. bibl il Science 198:1009-15 D 9 '77
Cheapest way to finish quality beef; corn silage rations. C. Bickers. il Farm J 101:Beef 8-9 O '77
Cuts feedlot time in half, boosts profit; grain on grass. V. Ehmke. il Farm J 101:Beef 14+ Ag '77
How to fit NH_3 treated corn silage to beef rations. J. R. Borcherding and L. Reichenberger. il Suc Farm 75:C2 Ag '77
They're bred to make it on grass. il Farm J 101:G4 D '77
This feeding program predicts everything but the market prices; Fox-Black system. N. Reeder. il Farm J 101:Beef 10+ S '77
Whether you feed 150 or 150,000 the basics still apply. il Farm J 101:Beef 17 O '77
See also
Calves—Feeding
Cattle—Preconditioning
Cattle feedlots
Cattle self feeders
Feeds
Grazing

Grading and standardization

Big feedlots make small changes to adjust to new grades. il Suc Farm 75:no3 Y4 F '77

Hormone fattening

For stilbestrol: another round coming up. R. D. Wennblom. Farm J 101:E2 mid-Mr '77
How you implant makes a difference. T. Grandin. il Suc Farm 75:no3 B18-19 F '77

Hybrids

Are beefalo really that good? Farm J 101:Dairy 10 Ag '77
Are bison hybrids really that good? Beefalo. W. Kester. il Farm J 101:Beef 10+ My '77

Marketing

Brucellosis buyers win damages. Farm J 101: Dairy 11, Beef 13 Ag '77
Caught in a one-buyer market. W. Kester. il Farm J 101:Beef 6-7 My '77
Feedlot numbers warn of winter market bulge. il Farm J 101:Beef 12 D '77
How to spot the next numbers build-up. il Farm J 101:Beef 12+ O; LK3-4 N '77
Know what your cattle are worth; USDA's fabricated carcass report. W. Kester. il Farm J 101:Beef 4-5+ Je '77
These steers went to market. B. Eftink. il Suc Farm 75:24-7 D '77
Why didn't we see the glut? J. A. Rohlf. il Farm J 101:Beef 16 F '77

Preconditioning

Backgrounding feeder cattle makes renovation pay. C. Bickers. Farm J 101:N8 Ja '77

Prices

Breeding stock demand reflects new optimism; National Western cattle auction. W. Kester. il Farm J 101:LK2-3 Ap '77
Pricecast (cont) Farm J 101:Beef 1+ Ja; Beef 1+ F; Beef 1+ My; Beef 1+ Je; Beef 1+ Ag; Beef 1+ S; Beef 1+ O; Beef 1+ D '77
There go the cows . . . and there go the prices! Suc Farm 75:no3 A6 F '77
Turnaround in prices. Farm J 101:Beef 7 Ja '77

CATTLE, Beef. See Cattle

CATTLE, Weight and measurements of
Forget about weight gains on heifers? il Farm J 101:Beef 8 My '77
See also
Cattle—Carcasses

CATTLE auctions. See Auctions

CATTLE breeding
A.I. without heat detection; cow breeding. C. S. Machan. il Farm J 101:Dairy 1-2 S '77
Breeding breakthroughs. J. R. Borcherding. il Suc Farm 75:no4 D1-5 Mr '77
Catch cycling cows every time; estrus probes. E. Ainsworth. il Farm J 101:Dairy 1-2, Beef 26 O '77
Embryo transfers practical for more dairymen. C. S. Machan. il Farm J 101:Dairy 16+ Ja '77
45-day breeding season for heifers. V. Ehmke. il Farm J 101:Beef 18 S '77
New help on picking best beef crosses. Farm J 101:Beef 12-13 S '77
Now: calves from frozen embryos. G. Lorang. il Farm J 101:24-6+ Ag '77
Ranchers test their herds' genetics. R. Alleman. il Suc Farm 75:no3 B8+ F '77
See also
Artificial insemination
Cattle—Breeds
Cattle—Hybrids

CATTLE farm management
Bigger, heavier calf crops. il Farm J 101:Beef 24 O; LK5 N '77
How many cows should you run to the acre? il Farm J 101:LK6 Ap '77
How to make expansion work. il Suc Farm 75: no3 B2-3 F '77
Successful beef management (cont) Suc Farm 75:no3 B1-3+ F '77

CATTLE feedlots
Big feedlots make small changes to adjust to new grades. il Suc Farm 75:no3 Y4 F '77
Cattle feeders fatten after three lean years. il Bus W p36 Ja 16 '78
Feedlot numbers warn of winter market bulge. il Farm J 101:Beef 12 D '77
Protect feeding profits with hedges? W. Kester. Farm J 101:Beef 16 S '77
Small feedlot designed for zero pollution. il Suc Farm 75:no4 B2 Mr '77
They built their own custom feedlot. J. Ritchie. il Farm J 101:Beef 7-8 Je '77

CATTLE feedlots—*Continued*
This feeding program predicts everything but the market prices; Fox-Black system. N. Reeder. il Farm J 101:Beef 10+ S '77
Will it pay to have your cattle custom fed? il Suc Farm 75: no4 B4 Mr '77
See also
Monfort of Colorado, Inc

CATTLE industry
Beef production efficiency. A. Trenkle and R. L. Willham. bibl il Science 198:1009-15 D 9 '77
Can cattlemen survive in the merchandising jungle? Tama Beef Producers Marketing Association. E. Ainsworth and W. Kester. il Farm J 101:Beef 7-10 Ag '77
Rancher's revenge. pors Forbes 119:68 Ja 15 '77
Tama Beef: ahead of its time? W. Kester. Farm J 101:Beef 32 O '77
There go the cows . . . and there go the prices! Suc Farm 75:no3 A6 F '77
Your beef business. W. Kester. il Farm J 101: Beef 28 Ja '77
Your beef business (cont) J. A. Rohlf. Farm J 101:Beef 16 F; Beef 16 My; Beef 12 Je; Beef 24 Ag; Beef 24 S; Beef 20 D '77
See also
Monfort of Colorado, Inc

Acquisitions and mergers

Two vital decisions for cattlemen; merger of American National Cattlemen's and National Livestock Feeders Associations. W. Kester. il Farm J 101:Beef 28 Ja '77

Export-import trade

Animal airlift to feed the Japanese. Bus W p28-9 My 23 '77

Fuel requirements

Beef production options and requirements for fossil fuel. G. M. Ward and others. bibl il map Science 198:265-71 O 21 '77

Public relations

How to fight the anti-beef campaign. Farm J 101:Beef 12 Ag '77

CATTLE roundups. See Roundups

CATTLE self feeders
New ways to manage your automatic grain feeders. Suc Farm 75: no4 D7 Mr '77
Newest ways to give high producers extra grain; electronic feeders. C. Tegeder. il Suc Farm 75: no3 Y1 F '77

CATTLE ticks. See Ticks

CATTLEMAN, Michael
HEW and the sexual revolution. Nation 225: 549-52 N 26 '77

CATTLEMEN
See also
Cowboys

CATTON, Bruce
Inspired leak. il Am Heritage 28:44-9 F '77
Way I see it (cont) por Am Heritage 28:79 F; 107 Ap; 63 Je; 97 Ag; 44-5 O '77

CAUBLE, Christopher
Great grizzly grapple; with biographical sketch. il Natur Hist 86:4, 74-81 bibl(p 117) Ag '77

CAUCASIAN chalk circle; drama. See Brecht, B.

CAUCUSES
Balkan Congress. R. Boeth and H. W. Hubbard. il Newsweek 90:40 N 14 '77
Blue-collar Caucus. M. Kondracke. New Repub 176:18-20 My 28 '77
Congressional Black Caucus: an interview with Yvonne Brathwaite Burke; ed by J. M. Elliot. Y. B. Burke. il pors Negro Hist Bull 40:650-2 Ja '77
See also
National Women's Political Caucus

CAUDILL, Harry Monroe
Dead laws and dead men. il Nation 224:492-7 Ap 23 '77

CAULFIELD, Patricia
(ed) See Porter, E. Eliot Porter on 35-mm

CAULKING
Caulking: easy and inexpensive way to save fuel. il McCalls 104:146 S '77
How to caulk it yourself. Bet Hom & Gard 55: 24 Ap '77

CAULKING compounds
Caulking compounds. il Consumers Res Mag 60: 14-16 S '77
Exterior caulking compounds. il Consumer Rep 42:182-6 D '77

CAULKS. See Caulking compounds

CAUSLEY, Charles
Comment. R. B. Shaw. Poetry 129:233-4 Ja '77 *

CAUTHEN, Steve
He looked a tiger in the teeth. W. Leggett. il por Sports Illus 47:16-17 Jl 4 '77 *
Here comes The Kid! il pors N Y Times Mag p 15-17+ F 20 '77 *
King of the bug boys. il por Time 109:50-1 Ja 31 '77 *
Racing's boy wonder. P. Axthelm. il por Newsweek 89:82-4+ F 14 '77; Same abr. with title Horse-racing's boy wonder. Read Digest 110:126-9 Je '77 *
Sportsman of the year. F. Deford. il por Sports Illus 47:38-41+ D 19 '77 *
This could be the start. W. Leggett. il pors Sports Illus 46:16-21 Mr 7 '77 *
Who needs the Derby? R. Kahn. il por Time 109:60 My 9 '77 *

CAVAFY, Constantine Peter
Ithaca; poem; excerpt from The complete poems of Cavafy; tr by R. Dalven. il Ms 5:57 F '77

CAVAGNARO, David
It's a small world. il Nat Wildlife 15:36-41 Ag '77

CAVAIANI, Mabel
Your own family's best-seller cookbook. Ret Liv 16:39 D '76

CAVALLI, Francesco. See Cavalli, P. F.

CAVALLI, Pier Francesco
Musical events; Clarion Opera Group of New York's performance of Giasone. A. Porter. New Yorker 52:74-6 Ja 24 '77 *

CAVALLON, Giorgio
Veiled in a strong white light; retrospective at the Neuberger Museum, Purchase, N.Y. R. Hughes. il Time 109:91 Je 6 '77 *

CAVALRY
See also
United States—Army—Cavalry

CAVANAGH, Gray. See Styles, K. jt auth

CAVANI, Liliana
Cavani's Night porter: a woman's film? T. De Lauretis. Film Q 30:35-8 Wint '76 *

CAVE drawings and paintings
Discovering ancient treasures in Caves of the Thousand Buddhas; Tunhuang cave temples; excerpt from Sir Aurel Stein. J. Mirsky. il por map Smithsonian 8:94-6+ My '77
First hunters. D. Mazonowicz. il Field & S 82: 130+ My '77

CAVERT, Samuel McCrea
Samuel McCrea Cavert: courtly ecumenist. B. Thompson. Chr Cent 94:189-90 Mr 2 '77 *

CAVES
Near Tucson. . .caves to explain desert geology; Arizona-Sonora Desert Museum. il Sunset 159:50 O '77
Researcher as spelunker: driven by danger, rewarded by discovery; Flint Ridge Cave System in Kentucky. R. A. Watson. il Sci Digest 81:48-51 Ap '77
This cave is unreal! man-made cave near Tucson, Ariz. F. Taylor. il Pop Mech 148:103 D '77
See also
Carlsbad Caverns National Park
Mammoth Cave National Park

CAVETT, Dick
Cavett goes public. M. J. Sobran, Jr. Nat R 29:1377-8 N 25 '77 *

CAVITIES, Dental. See Dental caries

CAWELTI, John G.
Murder in the outback. New Repub 177:39-41 Jl 30 '77

CAYMAN Islands
See also
United Nations—Cayman Islands

CAYZER, Bea deHolguin
Kim Casali's miracle baby. il pors Good H 185: 90+ N '77

CECH, Stella Y. and Ignarro, L. J.
Cytidine 3',5'-monophosphate (cyclic CMP) formation in mammalian tissues. bibl il Science 198:1063-5 D 9 '77

CEDAR
Two for the cedar connoisseur; deodars and Cyprus cedars. Sunset 159:184 D '77

CEDAR, Western red. See Arborvitae

CEDAR closets. See Closets

CEDEÑO, Cesar
Cesar's salad days are over. P. Gammons. il por Sports Illus 47:38-9 Ag 1 '77 *

CEEJAY Marina, Provincetown, Mass (proposed)
See Marinas

CEFIS, Eugenio
Italy: Montedison's gamble on raising fresh capital. Bus W p48+ Mr 21 '77 *

CEGLIA, Vincent
Watercolor page. il por Am Artist 41:48-51+ My '77

CEILINGS
Improving your overhead: all about ceilings. Redbook 148:180+ Ap '77; Same. Ladies Home J 94:172+ Ap '77
Look what's up! Redbook 149:200+ S '77
Pro tells how to lay out a suspended ceiling. M. N. Cohen. il Pop Sci 210:146 My '77
See also
Beams, Artificial

CELÂLEDDIN, Rūmī. See Jalāl al-Dīn, R.

CELEBRATIONS
See also
United States—Centennial celebrations, etc.

CELEBRITIES
And away we go; celebrities on the pro-am golf circuit; with photographs by T. Triolo. Sports Illus 48:20-5 Ja 9 '78
Beauty power; women celebrities. il Harp Baz 111:106-21 N '77

CELEBRITIES—*Continued*
Best friends. il Esquire 87:83-6 My '77
Call the next witness; interviews with celebrities. il Sat Eve Post 249:44+ Ap '77
Celebrity shrinks; M. Newman and B. Berkowitz. S. Edmiston. il pors Esquire 88:53-6+ Ag '77
Farrah factor; heroes and heroines of American youth. S Miller. por Ladies Home J 94:34+ Je '77
Friendship survey. Esquire 87:90-1 My '77
GH poll results: the ten most admired women. il Good H 186:28+ Ja '78
Headliner couples. il Ladies Home J 94:76+ N '77
How to survive a heart attack; personal narratives. S. W. Olds. il Fam Health 9:34-7 Ja '77
If you had three wishes... J. Agel. N Y Times Mag p84+ My 15 '77
Maggie and Wilbur; notorious celebrants M. Trudeau and W. Mills. R. Rosenblatt. New Repub 176:37 My 7 '77
Our dinner-party secrets. A. Gold and R. Fizdale. il Vogue 167:248-50+ Mr '77
Our periodic roster of unsatisfactory people. N. B. Freeman. Nat R 29:546-7 My 13 '77
People are talking about... L. Lerman. See issues of Vogue
People perplex. H. F. Waters. il Newsweek 89:89-90 Je 6 '77
Perfectionists; houses of celebrities. P. O'Higgins. House B 119:90-1+ Ap '77
Private lines; settings for five celebrity telephone users. J. Macurdy. il House B 119:38-45 Ag '77
Redbook traveler; where the stars take their romantic vacations; comp by D. Kaye. il Redbook 148:37-9 F '77
Star treatment; excerpts. D. Stelzer. Ladies Home J 94:62+ O '77
Stars in the southern sky; personalities share impressions of Dixie. il Holiday 57:26-7 N '76
Think young; ideas of celebrities. il Sat Eve Post 249:66-7 Mr '77
Wanted: for love and/or money. R. Kent. il Harp Baz 110:142-3 F '77
Wax museums: the Mount Rushmore of pop culture; famous women in wax figures. S. Subtle and R. Reichl. il Ms 6:72-3+ Ja '78
What they're wearing at night. C. Donovan. il N Y Times Mag p83-5 D 18 '77
See also
Black celebrities
Children of celebrities
Great men and women

Anecdotes, facetiae, satire, etc.

Mrs Armand Reef likes to entertain. G. W. S. Trow. New Yorker 53:25-6 Jl 4 '77

Caricatures and cartoons

Build a classy chassis from the vintage stars. il Sat Eve Post 249:70-1 Mr '77

Photographs

Can you place the face? high school photographs of celebrities. D. Carlinsky. il Seventeen 36:144-5 Je '77

Political activities

Washington's world of style. T. Bethell. il Harpers 256:66-9+ Ja '78

CELEBRITY. See Fame
CELESTIAL navigation. See Navigation
CELIBACY
Married priests: one more try. B. F. McWilliams. America 136:416 My 7 '77
Sex and the celibate. B. Häring. il New Cath World 220:272-5 N '77
CELL cycle. See Cells
CELL division
NASA patents cell control method; work of Clarence D. Cone Jr. Sci N 112:134-5 Ag 27 '77
CELL junctions. See Junctions (physiology)
CELL lysis. See Lysis
CELL membranes. See Membranes (biology)
CELL movement. See Cells—Motility
CELL nuclei
Nuclear morphometry during the cell cycle. F. Kendall and others. bibl il Science 196:1106-9 Je 3 '77
CELL organelles
Alzheimer's disease, trisomy 21, and myeloproliferative disorders: associations suggesting a genetic diathesis. L. L. Heston. bibl il Science 196:322-3 Ap 15 '77
Immunofluorescence localization of proteins of high molecular weight along intracellular microtubules. P. Sherline and K. Schiavone. bibl il Science 198:1038-40 D 9 '77
Tale of 3 diseases: a common cause? pathological microtubules. Sci N 111:263 Ap 23 '77
See also
Mitochondria

CELL walls, Plant. See Plant cells and tissues
CELLARS. See Basements and cellars
CELLARS, Wine. See Wine cellars
CELLISTS
See also
Piatigorsky, G.
Rostropovich, M.
CELLO
Bass part in Haydn's early string quartets. J. Webster. bibl il Mus Q 63:390-424 Jl '77
CELLO music
See also
Phonograph records—Cello music
CELLS
Analysis of living tissue by phosphorus-31 magnetic resonance. C. T. Burt and others. bibl il Science 195:145-9 Ja 14 '77
And now, interkingdom fusion: the marriage of plant and animal; hybrid cells. A. Rosenfeld. Sat R 4:38-9 Jl 9 '77
Artificial synthesis of cells. il Sci N 111:197 Mr 26 '77
Biology of aging. L. Hayflick. Natur Hist 86:22+ bibl(p 116) Ag '77
Bone and muscle of cells. J. A. Miller. il Sci N 112:250-1+ O 15 '77
Cell biology experiments conducted in space. G. R. Taylor. bibl BioScience 27:102-8 F '77
Center of life; excerpt. L. L. L. Cudmore. il Sci Digest 82:41-6 N '77
Characterization of a new human diploid cell strain, IMR-90. W. W. Nichols and others. bibl il Science 196:60-3 Ap 1 '77
Chemistry tool probes muscle cells. il Sci N 111:71 Ja 29 '77
Cytoskelton. Sci Am 238:68 Ja '78
Fat-containing uterine smooth muscle cells in toxemia: possible relevance to atherosclerosis? M. D. Haust and others. bibl il Science 195:1353-4 Mr 25 '77
Molecular cell principals. il Chemistry 50:5 Ja '77
Nuclear morphometry during the cell cycle. F. Kendall and others. bibl il Science 196:1106-9 Je 3 '77
See also
Cancer cells
Chromaffin cells
Chromatin
Cytology
Differentiation (biology)
Endoplasmic reticulum
Epithelium
Fibroblasts
Genes
Macrophages
Microsomes
Nerve cells
Plants cells and tissues
Tumor cells

Culture

See Tissues—Culture

Inclusions

Phi bodies: peroxidatic particles that produce crystalloidal cellular inclusions. J. S. Hanker and D. K. Romanovicz. bibl il Science 197:895-8 Ag 26 '77

Motility

Cellular positional stability and intercellular invasion. P. B. Armstrong. bibl il BioScience 27:803-9 D '77
Gold-dust twins; technique for visualizing the tracks of moving cells on a gold-coated glass microscope slide. il Sci Am 237:102+ S '77

Physiology

Calcium-induced displacement of membrane-associated particles upon aggregation of chromaffin granules. R. Schober and others. bibl il Science 195:495-7 F 4 '77
CELLULAR control mechanisms
Pattern regulation in epimorphic fields. V. French and others; reply. L. Glass. Science 198:321-2 O 21 '77
CELLULAR slime molds. See Slime molds
CELLULASES
Cellulases can enhance β glucan synthesis. Y. S. Wong and others. bibl Science 195:679-80 F 18 '77
CELLULITE. See Adipose tissues
CELLULOID dolls. See Dolls
CELLULOSE
Oxygen and hydrogen isotopic ratios in plant cellulose. S. Epstein and others. bibl il Science 198:1209-15 D 23 '77
CELOSIA
Celosia: the annual with many uses. L. Pritzlaff. il Org Gard & Farm 24:84-5 Mr '77
CELTIC art. See Art, Celtic
CELTS
Celtic farmstead in southern Britain. G. Wainwright. il Sci Am 237:156-64+ bibl(p 190) D '77
Celts. M. Severy. il Nat Geog 151:582-630. supp(folded map) My '77

CEMENT
Solidification of cement. D. D. Double and A. Hellawell. il Sci Am 237:82-6+ bibl(p 154) Jl '77
CEMENT adhesives. See Adhesives
CEMENT industry
Cement's bad case of regional softness. Bus W p41-2 N 14 '77
CEMETERIES
Cemetery at Holly Springs. W. D. Miller. America 137:194-5 O 1 '77
Social commentary from the cemetery. E. S. Dethlefsen and K. Jensen. il Natur Hist 86:32-9 bibl(p92) Je '77
See also
Catacombs
National cemeteries
CENOZOIC period. See Geology, Stratigraphic—Cenozoic; Paleontology—Cenozoic
CENSORSHIP
Censorship and the classroom teacher. A. A. Glatthorn. Engl J 66:12-15 F '77; Same abr. Educ Digest 43:54-6 S '77
Censorship, the law, and the teacher of English; symposium. A. A. Glatthorn. bibl il Engl J 66:12-25 F '77
Coming of bold pornography; interviews, ed by W. Goodman. E. Van Den Haag; G. Talese. Current 190:32-8 F '77
Constitutionality of book ban challenged by NYCLU; suit filed by the New York Civil Liberties Union against Island Trees School District. Lib J 102:530+ Mr 1 '77
Four Island Trees students sue book-banning school board. M. Reuter. Pub W 211:29 Ja 10 '77
Students & NYCLU file lawsuit against the Island Trees Board. SLJ 23:17 F '77
Would-be censors of the left; Council on Interracial Books for Children. L. N. Gerhardt; discussion. SLJ 23:3 Ap '77
See also
Freedom of the press
Government and the press
Information Freedom of
Intellectual liberty
Libraries—Censorship
Obscenity (law)
Opera—Censorship
Postal censorship
Radio broadcasting—Censorship
School libraries—Censorship
Television broadcasting—Censorship

Conferences

Censorship conference panelists discuss First Amendment issues; Second Annual Conference of the National Coalition Against Censorship. il SLJ 23:11-12 Ap '77

Chile

Breath of satire in Chile; closing of the play Pages from Parra. F. MacShane. Nation 225: 535-6 N 19 '77

China

Now it's China's cultural thaw. H. E. Salisbury. il pors N Y Times Mag p49+ D 4 '77

Russia

Common censorship. N. Wade. Science 197:646-7 Ag 12 '77

Spain

After Franco's forty years: the popular arts in Spain. S. Meisler. il Nation 224:461-4 Ap 16 '77
CENSORSHIP of mail. See Postal censorship
CENTAC (central tactical units) See United States—Drug Enforcement Administration
CENTENARIANS
Centenarians. A. Wackerle. il Sat Eve Post 249: 68 Mr '77
First U.S. woman governor celebrates her centennial during the bicentennial. il por Aging 268:13-14 F '77
CENTENNIALS
See also
United States—Centennial celebrations, etc.
CENTER for Community Organization and Area Development. See Community development
CENTER for Constructive Alternatives. See Hillsdale College, Hillsdale, Mich—Center for Constructive Alternatives
CENTER for Disease control. See United States—Public Health Service—Center for Disease Control
CENTER for Southern Folklore, Memphis, Tenn. See Folklore—United States
CENTER for the History of American Needlework. See Pittsburgh—Galleries and museums
CENTER for the Study of Contemporary Art/Joan Miró Foundation. See Barcelona—Galleries and museums
CENTER of Concern, Washington, D.C.
Toward a world more human: five years of Concern. J. Coleman. America 136:441-4 My 14 '77
CENTERBOARDS. See Keels
CENTERPIECES. See Table decoration
CENTERS, Mental health. See Mental health centers
CENTERS for the performing arts
See also
John F. Kennedy Center for the Performing Arts, Washington, D.C.
Ottawa—National Arts Centre
Paris—Georges Pompidou Center
Wolf Trap Farm Park for the Performing Arts
CENTO. See Central Treaty Organization
CENTRAL AFRICA. See Africa, Central
CENTRAL AFRICAN EMPIRE
Bokassa's new clothes. L. Jenkins. il pors Newsweek 90:42-4 D 19 '77
Mounting a golden throne. il pors Time 110:42-3 D 19 '77
See also
Government and the press—Central African Empire
CENTRAL AMERICA
See also
Agriculture—Central America
Costa Rica
Guatemala
Honduras
Nicaragua
Salvador
CENTRAL ASIA. See Asia, Central
CENTRAL banks. See Banks and banking—Central banks
CENTRAL City festival. See Music festivals—Colorado
CENTRAL Institute for Restoration. See Italy—Istituto Centrale del Restauro
CENTRAL Intelligence Agency. See United States—Central Intelligence Agency
CENTRAL nervous system. See Nervous system
CENTRAL Ohio River Valley Association for Health Planning and Resource Development. See Health planning
CENTRAL Opera Service
Love-hate relationships; national conference, held in Houston. J. Ardoin. il por Opera N 42:10-11 D 17 '77
CENTRAL Pacific Railroad
Great race; excerpt from Hear that lonesome whistle blow. D. Brown. il Am West 14:4-15+ My '77
CENTRAL Park. See New York (city)—Parks and playgrounds
CENTRAL Treaty Organization
Secretary Vance attends Spanish-U.S. Council meeting at Madrid and CENTO Council of Ministers meeting at Tehran; remarks, with news conference, statement and communiques, May 11-15, 1977. C. R. Vance. Dept State Bull 76:612-18 Je 6 '77
CENTRIFUGATION
Enrichment by centrifugation; gas-centrifuge approach to separating uranium isotopes. Sci Am 237:52+ Ag '77
See also
Plasmapheresis
CENTRIFUGATION in sewage purification. See Sewage purification
CENTS. See Coins
CEPHALOPODS
See also
Squids
CEPPOS, Rich
4000-mile test of the new Ford Fiesta. il Pop Sci 211:76-7+ Jl '77
Maneuverable mini—Mazda GLC has outstanding handling. il Pop Sci 210:120 Je '77
Taking care of your car. See issues of Popular science
—See Dunne, J. jt auth
CERAMIC industries
See also
Clay industries
CERAMIC sculpture
Armature for ceramic sculpture. M. Sapiro. il Ceram Mo 25:42-3 Je '77
Bruno LaVerdiere: clay sculptures. R. Zakin. il Ceram Mo 25:26-7 S '77
Ceramics of Marilyn Levine; interview, ed by S. Peterson. M. Levine. il Craft Horiz 37:40-3+ F '77
Civilizations in clay. il Craft Horiz 37:28-35 D '77
Contemporary Ceramic Sculpture. il Ceram Mo 25:36-7 O '77
David Middlebrook. il Ceram Mo 25:54-5 Mr '77
Glenys Barton at Wedgwood. J. Mallet. il Ceram Mo 25:28-30 O '77
Illusionistic realism. il Ceram Mo 25:59-63 S '77
Jill Crowley. il Ceram Mo 25:36-7 S 77
Karen Gunderman. il Ceram Mo 25:44 S '77
Roy Lichtenstein: ceramic sculpture. C. W. Glenn. il Ceram Mo 25:40-5 My '77
Topsy-turvy or the fright pot. R. F. Eilenberger. il Sch Arts 76:54-7 Mr '77
CERAMIC tile installation. See Tile laying
CERAMICS monthly (periodical)
Comment: recent clay history. S. R. Thompson. Ceram Mo 25:19+ Je '77

CERCOCARPUS. See Mountain mahogany
CEREAL foods
Cereals. Consumer Rep 42:75-6 D '77
See also
Cookery—Grain

Advertising

Battle heats up over sugared cerals. C. Holden. Science 198:902-3 D 2 '77
CEREBELLUM. See Brain
CEREBRAL ischemia. See Cerebrovascular disease
CEREBRAL palsied children

Education

Wesley story. S. C. Sloop. Am Educ 13:19 D '77
CEREBROSIDES
Synthetic galactocerebrosides evoke myelination-inhibiting antibodies. S. Hruby and others. bibl il Science 195:173-5 Ja 14 '77
CEREBROSPINAL fluid
Cerebrospinal fluid production: stimulation by cholera toxin. M. H. Epstein and others. bibl il Science 196:1012-13 My 27 '77
Pineal vasotocin: release into cat cerebrospinal fluid by melanocyte-stimulating hormone release-inhibiting factor. S. Pavel and others. bibl il Science 197:179-80 Jl 8 '77
CEREBROVASCULAR disease
Regions of cerebral ischemia located by pyridine nucleotide fluorescence. F. A. Welsh and others. bibl il Science 198:951-3 D 2 '77
Stroke; excerpt C. C. Dahlberg. il por Psychol Today 11:121-2+ Je '77

Prevention

Preventing strokes; surgical bypass of the internal carotid artery. Newsweek 89:79 Ja 31 '77
CEREMONIES. See Rites and ceremonies
CEREZO DARDÓN, Hugo
Eulogy; story. Américas 29:26-8 O '77
CERF, Bennett
Bennett Cerf remembers; excerpts from At Random. il por Pub W 212:28-31 Ag 15; 26-9 Ag 22 '77
CERF, Steven
Bowdoin's contemporary music festival. il Hi Fi 27:MA28-9 Ap '77
CERGOL, Jack
New HOPE. il Américas 29:17-22 O '77
CERRO Las Campanas Observatory. See Astronomical observatories—Chile
CERRUTI, James
Dominican Republic: Caribbean comeback. il map Nat Geog 152:538-65 O '77
CERTAIN-Teed Products Corporation
Quality certain, satisfaction guaranteed. por Forbes 119:64 My 1 '77
CERTIFICATES of deposit
High yields pull U.S. corporate cash abroad. il Bus W p79-80 Ja 16 '78
How do you replace a wild card? B. Weberman. Forbes 120:110 O 1 '77
CERTIFICATION of librarians. See Librarians—Certification
CERTIFICATION of teachers. See Teachers—Certification
CERTIFIED public accountants. See Accountants
CERVIX

Diseases

Steroid contraceptive use and cervical dysplasia: increased risk of progression. E. Stern and others. bibl il Science 196:1460-2 Je 24 '77
CESAREAN section
Before the baby comes. K. D. Anderson. il Parents Mag 52:26 Jl '77
Caesarean: safer now for mother and child. W. A. Nolen. McCalls 104:80+ F '77
CESSNA Aircraft Company
Cessna starts factory support programs to aid foreign sales. E. J. Bulban. Aviation W 107:85-6 D 12 '77
CETACEA
Cetacea; special issue. il Oceans 10:4-66 Jl '77
See also
Brain (cetacea)
Dolphins (mammals)
Whales

Photographs

King of the boundless sea. Oceans 10:16-21 Jl '77
CETINGOK, Muammer
Alternative to the taxation of gasoline consumption. Intellect 106:46-8 Ag '77
CEY, Ron
In L.A. it's up, up and away with Cey. L. Keith. il por Sports Illus 46:24-8+ My 16 '77 *
Octopus. P. Bonventre and D. Gram. il Newsweek 89:77 My 16 '77 *
CÉZANNE, Paul
Art. L. Alloway. Nation 225:445-6 O 29 '77 *
Cézanne: the autumn years. B. Rose. Sat R 5:44-5 N 26 '77 *
Cézanne's final decade. J. Rewald. il Horizon 20:40-7 O '77 *
Cézanne's revolutionary last decade. K. S. Champa. il Art N 76:20-2 D '77 *
Dialogues with nature; Museum of Modern Art show. M. Stevens. il Newsweek 90:78-9 O 17 '77 *
Quartet and variations; Museum of Modern Art show. R. Berenson. Nat R 30:40-1 Ja 6 '78 *
Triumph of the recluse; exhibition at the Museum of Modern Art. R. Hughes. il Time 110:84-5 O 17 '77 *
CHAADAEV, Peter Iakovlevich
On Lamennais, Chaadaev, and the romantic revolt in France and Russia. N. V. Riasanovsky. bibl f pors Am Hist R 82:1165-86 D '77 *
CHABRIER, Emmanuel
Complete orchestral works. W. Curtis. il Am Rec G 40:18-19 Jl '77 *
Le Roi malgré lui (Reluctant king) Reviews
Hi Fi 27:MA13 Mr '77 *
CHACE, James
America's new strategy of containment. Harpers 256:46-8+ Ja '78
How moral can we get? il N Y Times Mag p38-40+ My 22 '77
CHACE, Susan
Funds. Forbes 121:235-6 Ja 9 '78
CHAD
See also
Political prisoners—Chad
CHADWICK, Douglas H.
Grizzly's rage to live. il Sports Illus 47:64-9+ Jl 18 '77; Same abr. with title Outlaw bear. Read Digest 111:162-5 N '77
Our wild and scenic rivers. il Nat Geog 152:12-19 Jl '77
CHADWICK, George Whitefield
Judith. Reviews
Hi Fi 27:MA20-1 My '77 *
CHAFETZ, Morris E.
Is there a safe way to drink? excerpt from Why drinking can be good for you. Read Digest 111:100-3 Jl '77
CHAGALL, Marc
Chagall at 90: when you have love, you work. That is my life; interview, ed by A. Mosby. il pors Art N 76:44-8 Summ '77

about

Marc Chagall at ninety. A. Werner. Progressive 41:35-7 Je '77 *
CHAIN letters
Great chain robbery. A. Tobias. il Esquire 88:12+ Ag '77
CHAIN saws. See Saws
CHAIN stores
Best Products Company; catalog showrooms designed by SITE, Inc; with introd by G. Allen. il Archit Rec 161:115-7, 124-30 Mr '77
Copycat; Miller-Wohl Co. por Forbes 120:68 S 1 '77
Melville steps into the billion-dollar class. por Bus W p58+ Ap 11 '77
Unlimited Limited. il por Forbes 120:77-80 N 15 '77
See also
Department stores
Drugstores
Grocery trade
Supermarkets

Acquisitions and mergers

Revived Miller-Wohl lures a Dutch bidder; Brenninkmeyers' bid by Amcena. il Bus W p34+ S 5 '77
CHAIR caning. See Cane weaving
CHAIR seats
See also
Cane weaving
CHAIRS
Classic chairs. il Bet Hom & Gard 55:228 Ap '77
Conversation with Charles Eames; ed by O. Gingerich. C. Eames. Am Scholar 46:326-37 Summ '77
Make your own steamer deck chair. T. H. Jones. il Mech Illus 73:98+ Ap '77
Stand-by seating. il Am Home 80:22-3 D '77
Weaving a swing chair. D. Lynde. il Design (US) 78:20-1 mid-Summ '77
See also
Chaise longues
CHAIS, Irving
Moody business. New Yorker 53:17-19 D 26 '77 *
CHAISE longues
Build a redwood chaise. il Pop Mech 147:120-1 Je '77
CHAKRABARTY, Ananda M.
Superstrain of oil-eating microbes. K. Cottrell. il Sea Front 23:28-31 Ja '77 *
CHALCONES
Nonnutritive sweeteners: taste-structure relationships for some new simple dihydrochalcones. G. E. DuBois and others. bibl il Science 195:397-9 Ja 28 '77
CHALFONT, Arthur Gwynne-Jones, Baron
Is it over, over there? il Nat R 29:200-3+ F 18 '77

CHALICE dials. See Sundials
CHALIDZE, Valerii N.
How important is Soviet dissent? tr by G. Daniels. bibl f Commentary 63:57-62 Je '77
CHALONER, Gwen
Court of King Arithmetic; drama. Plays 36:56-62 Ap '77
CHALONES
Lymphocyte and fibroblast chalones: some chemical properties. J. C. Houck and others. bibl il Science 196:896-7 My 20 '77
CHAMBER music
See also
Phonograph records—Chamber music
String quartets
Wind quintets
CHAMBER Music Society of Lincoln Center
Ch. Mus. Soc:
Shostakovich prem: Sonata for viola and piano, op. 147. Hi Fi 27:MA26-7 Ap '77
Music to my ears; performance of last sonata by D. Shostakovich. I. Kolodin. por Sat R 4:43-4 F 5 '77
Musical events:
Performance of F. Lewin's Variations of Greek themes. A. Porter. New Yorker 53:116-20 D 5 '77
CHAMBER of Commerce of the United States of America
Business leaders at work for the enterprise system. il Nations Bus 65:36-8+ N '77
Inspiring public confidence in private enterprise; president of Johnson Wax; interview. W. K. Eastham. il pors Nations Bus 65:50-4+ My '77
Meany and business vs. the ILO: will we pick up our marbles? B. Koeppel. Nation 225:429-31 O 29 '77
Voice of business grows stronger in Washington. il Nations Bus 65:20-7+ Mr '77
CHAMBER orchestras
Colorado Chamber Orchestra; performances in Boulder. Hi Fi 27:MA18 N '77
Contemp. ch. players: Ran prem. por Hi Fi 27:MA20 My '77
Contemporary ch. pl: Shapey; Seventh Quartet. por Hi Fi 27:MA22 Ag '77
Marlboro on the road; Music from Marlboro touring orchestra. B. Paolucci. il Hi Fi 27:MA21-3 D '77
Palo Alto Chamber Orchestra. W. E. Ratliff. il Hi Fi 27:MA31-2+ N '77
Report:
St Luke's Chamber Ensemble's Breakfast at Schlakenwald castle and European tourists. S. Casale. Opera N 41:28-9 F 26 '77
Reviews of records; selected works of J. C. Bach, M. Haydn and W. A. Mozart performed by the St Paul Chamber Orchestra. G. Lazarevich. Mus Q 63:446-50 Jl '77
See also
Quartets, Instrumental
CHAMBERLAIN, Anne
Keeping the reader breathless. Writer 90:20-2+ Ag '77
CHAMBERLAIN, Betty
Professional page. See issues of American artist
CHAMBERLAIN, John
Lindbergh was of the twenties. il por Nat R 29:608-10+ My 27 '77
CHAMBERLAIN, Narcissa G.
History in houses: the Jeremiah Lee Mansion in Marblehead, Massachusetts. bibl il Antiques 112:1164-73 D '77
CHAMBERLIN, Anne
Live show daily at Hamburger Hamlet. il pors Fortune 95:208-15+ Mr '77
CHAMBERLIN, Hal
Computer bits (cont) Pop Electr 11:107-10 Mr; 96-7 My; 12:89-90 Jl; 110-11 S; 88-9 N '77; 13:77-9 Ja '78
CHAMBERLIN, Peter Klotz-. See Klotz-Chamberlin, P.
CHAMBERLIN, Raymond A.
Build this electronic music box. il Radio Electr 48:31-4+ Je '77
CHAMBERS, Aidan
Letter from England. See issues of Horn book magazine
CHAMBERS, Andrea
Calvin Klein's romantic season. il pors N Y Times Mag p46-8 Ja 30 '77
CHAMBERS, Anne
Back-to-basics school created by enterprise. P. Schwab. il por Nations Bus 65:91 D '77 *
CHAMBERS, Anne Cox
Brussels—madame peanut. por Newsweek 90:7? N 21 '77 *
CHAMBERS, M. M.
Durability of reasonable autonomy for state universities. Educ Digest 42:24-7 Ap '77
CHAMBERS of Commerce
See also
Birmingham, Ala. Chamber of Commerce
CHAMBLISS, Robert Edward
Arrest in Birmingham. R. Boeth and V. E. Smith. il pors Newsweek 90:32+ O 10 '77 *
Law moves at last. B. Cornwell. Nation 225:463-5 N 5 '77 *
CHAMBLISS, Robert Edward, murder trial. See Trials (murder)
CHAMOMILE
Chamomile smells like Christmas. il Sunset 158:282-3 Ap '77
CHAMPA, Kermit S.
Cézanne's revolutionary last decade. il Art N 76:70-2 D '77
CHAMPAGNE
Champagne touring in Napa. il Sunset 159:58+ O '77
Society for the prevention of cruelty to champagne. F. J. Prial. il N Y Times Mag p 154+ N 20 '77
CHAMPAGNE Stakes. See Horse racing
CHAMPAIGN County, Ill.
Solid waste disposal needs areawide solutions. H. Paley. por Am City & County 92:63 Mr '77
CHAMPIONSHIP of Champions. See Sailboat racing
CHAMPLAIN, Lake
Champlain: battleground still. P. Brooks. il map Audubon 79:66-77 Ja '77
Ice inevitably wins; Lake Champlain; with photographs. C. H. Smith. Audubon 79:56-65 Ja '77
CHAMPLIN, Charles
Farrah Fawcett-Majors: an unlikely sex symbol. il por McCalls 104:28+ Ap '77
Jaclyn Smith: the cool angel. por McCalls 104:36+ Jl '77
CHANCE
See also
Luck
CHANCELLOR, John William
Hoisting anchor. H. F. Waters and others. il por Newsweek 90:98 D 12 '77 *
CHAND, Prem
Three soldier peacemakers. pors Time 110:40 N 7 '77 *
CHANDLER, Colby H.
At the company that never rests. por Fortune 95:19 Ja '77 *
CHANDLER, Craig
Off the garden path. Horticulture 55:16+ Ap '77
CHANDLER, David L.
Life on Mars. il Atlantic 239:29-34+ Je '77
CHANDLER, David P.
Transformation in Cambodia. Commonweal 104:207-8+ Ap 1 '77
CHANDLER, Dorothy Buffum
Word from Mamma Buff. L. Weymouth. il pors Esquire 88:154-7+ N '77 *
CHANDLER, Edna Walker
Transforming nature's Christmas pretties. il Ret Liv 17:40+ D '77
CHANDLER, Harriette L.
Israeli election and the Begin victory. il por Chr Cent 94:650-4 Jl 20 '77
CHANDLER, Joan M.
TV & sports—wedded with a golden hoop. il por Psychol Today 10:64+ Ap '77
CHANDLER, Otis
Word from Mamma Buff. L. Weymouth. il por Esquire 88:154-7+ N '77 *
CHANDLER, Russell
Americans united: advocacy role. Chr Today 21:47 Mr 4 '77
Fighting cults: the Tucson tactic. il Chr Today 21:57-61 F 4 '77
CHANDOHA, Walter
Remember Swiss chard? il Horticulture 55:22-3 Ap '77
CHANEL, Coco. See Chanel, G.
CHANEL, Gabrielle
Coco Chanel and the Duke of Westminster; excerpt from L'allure de Chanel; tr by A. Foulke. P. Morand. Vogue 167:18+ My '77 *
CHANEY, Ed
Last Idaho land rush: growth at any cost? Audubon 79:154-7 N '77
Phosphate fate will determine Idaho high country's fate. Audubon 79:123-6 Mr '77
CHANEY, Elsa M.
Colombian outpost in New York City. bibl il Society 14:60-4 S '77
CHANG, G. W. See Bjeldanes, L. F. jt auth
CHANG, K. C. and others
Stable semiconductor liquid junction cell with 9 percent solar-to-electrical conversion efficiency. bibl il Science 196:1097-9 Je 3 '77
CHANGE
See also
Educational innovations
Social change
CHANGE (psychology)
How to cope with change at 30. F. F. Flach. Harp Baz 110:133+ O '77
CHANGE of life in women. See Menopause
CHANGE of sex
If the shoe doesn't fit, change the foot. G. Steinem. Ms 5:76+ F '77
Sex switchers. L. Davis. Vogue 167:151+ Ag '77
Transsexual chic: the packaging of Renee Richards. M. Seligson. il Ms 5:74-6+ F '77
Transsexual riddle: an hypothesis. R. J. Trotter. il Sci N 111:236-8 Ap 9 '77

CHANGE of sex surgery. See Generative organs—Surgery
CHANLER family
Step in and enjoy the turmoil. R. H. Boyle. il pors Sports Illus 46:80-4+ Je 13 '77
CHANNEL Islands (English Channel)
Britain's sunny Channel Islands. il map Sunset 158:92 My '77
See also
Guernsey (island)
CHANNELIZATION. See Channels (hydraulic engineering)
CHANNELS (hydraulic engineering)
Make the river do the work; alternative to channelization. B. East. il por Outdoor Life 160:78-81+ O '77
See also
Canals
CHANTEYS. See Sailors songs
CHANTRAINE (restaurant) See Brussels—Hotels, restaurants, etc.
CHANTS (Gregorian, plain, etc)
See also
Phonograph records—Chants (Gregorian, plain, etc)
CHANUKAH. See Hanukkah (Feast of Lights)
CHAOS (theology)
Rage for chaos. C. D. Linton. Chr Today 21:22-5 My 6 '77
CHAPIN, Roy Dikeman, 1915-
Nice guys and where I'd like to see them finish. D. E. Davis, Jr. Car & Dr 22:7 F '77 *
CHAPLAINS
Place to worship; chaplains at Holiday Inns. K. Wilson. il por Sat Eve Post 249:37 Ap '77
CHAPLAINS, Hospital
Go out in joy; condensation. N. L. Herrmann. il Read Digest 110:249-60+ Ap '77
CHAPLIN, Charles, 1889-1977
Exit the tramp, smiling. S. Kanfer. por Time 111:63 Ja 2 '78 *
Farewell to the tramp. il pors Newsweek 91:40-2 Ja 9 '78 *
Washington diarist. H. Fairlie. il por New Repub 178:45 Ja 7 '78 *
CHAPMAN, Bud
Golf's impossible holes. il Read Digest 112:146-50 Ja '78 *
CHAPMAN, Chanler A.
Step in and enjoy the turmoil. R. H. Boyle. il pors Sports Illus 46:80-4+ Je 13 '77 *
CHAPMAN, David S. See Pollack, H. N. jt auth
CHAPMAN, Harold A. Jr, and Hibbs, J. B. Jr
Modulation of macrophage tumoricidal capability by components of normal serum: a central role for lipid. bibl il Science 197:282-5 Jl 15 '77
CHAPMAN, L. W. See Baker, M. A. jt auth
CHAPMAN, Stephen
Big ticket item. New Repub 177:13-14 Jl 9 '77
Dump the B-1. New Repub 176:16-18 My 28 '77
Middle class loophole. New Repub 177:12-14 D 3 '77
Pluralism run amok. New Repub 176:36-9 My 21 '77
Rich get rich, and the poor get lawyers. New Repub 177:9-10+ S 24 '77
CHAPMAN, William
Native Americans' new clout. Progressive 41:30-2 Ag '77
Somebody simply goofed. Progressive 41:30-2 My '77
CHAPMAN, William E. and Ward, P. A.
Babesia rodhaini: requirement of complement for penetration of human erythrocytes. bibl il Science 196:67-70 Ap 1 '77
CHAPNICK, Howard
Markets & careers. See issues of Popular photography
CHAPPAQUA, N.Y.
Teenage drinking; Horace Greeley High School. L. G. Holmes. il Good H 184:58+ F '77
CHAPPELL, John E. Jr
Boys from Buffalo Creek. Progressive 41:11 N '77
CHAPPELL, Suzanne
Taming the steepest slopes. il Org Gard & Farm 24:60-1 Ap '77
CHAPPLE, John V.
American in Greece succeeds as a one-man publisher: meet John Chapple. M. Duggan. por Pub W 211:43-4 Ja 17 '77 *
CHAPRA, Steven C. and Robertson, Andrew
Great Lakes eutrophication: the effect of point source control of total phosphorus. bibl il Science 196:1448-50 Je 24 '77
CHAPTER two: drama. See Simon, N.
CHARACTER
See also
Personality
CHARACTER education. See Moral education
CHARACTERIZATION
Absorbing reality into fiction. M. C. Banning. Writer 90:12-14+ O '77
Birth of a sleuth. N. Marsh. Writer 90:23-5 Ap '77
Building characters from the ground up. G. Owen. Writer 90:17-19 Ja '77
Castings. L. Block. Writers Digest 57:10+ O '77
Character in science fiction; excerpt from Notes to a science fiction writer. B. Bova. Writer 90:17-19+ Ap '77
Likes attract: how to create likeable characters in your fiction. J. Z. Owen. Writers Digest 57:31-2+ Je '77
People, not plot. J. Rikhoff. Writer 90:15-18 Mr '77
Story behind a record-breaking sale; writing The French passion. D. Du Pont. Writer 90:15-17 N '77
CHARACTERS in literature
Conrad's Lord Jim and the enigma of sublimation. J. Berman. bibl f Am Imago 33:308-402 Wint '76
Crime and punishment: matricide and the woman question. D. Kiremidjian. bibl f Am Imago 33:403-33 Wint '76
Horatio Algers of the nightmare; J. Kosinski's characters. E. Stone. il por Psychol Today 11:59-60+ D '77
Joan Didion & her characters. J. Romano. Commentary 64:61-3 Jl '77
Nobel lecture. S. Bellow. Am Scholar 46:316-25 Summ '77
Picture of success; characters in American fiction. N. Mills. Yale R 66:347-63 Mr '77
Welcome back from the raft, Huck honey! K. S. Lynn. Am Scholar 46:338-47 Summ '77
Why of people: the novels of M. E. Kerr. M. Kingsbury. Horn Bk 53:288-95 Je '77
See also
Blacks in literature
Characterization
Shakespeare, W.—Characters
Women in literature
CHARACTERS in motion pictures
Good guys. M. J. Sobran, Jr. Nat R 29:505-6 Ap 29 '77
Technology of Kong. il Sci Digest 81:80 F '77; Reply. A. E. Braun. 81:4-6 Mr '77
See also
Women in motion pictures
CHARACTERS in opera
Beyond Figaro; Almaviva trilogy. B. Fischer-Williams. il Opera N 41:26-8 Mr 5 '77
Don Giovanni as the ideal sensualist; excerpt from Maverick: a director's personal experience in theater and opera. F. Corsaro. por Hi Fi 27:MA6-7 D '77
Lulu's last stand: Jack the Ripper. F. Stevenson. Opera N 41:36 Ap 2 '77
Spirit of the faydit; troubadour-outcasts and Manrico, the hero of Il Trovatore. C. L. Osborne. il Opera N 41:26-8 Ap 9 '77
Woe to the vanquished; Mürger's Vie de Bohème. J. Kestner. il Opera N 41:14-17 Mr 19 '77
See also
Women in opera
CHARACTERS in television
Public believes Kojak; interview, ed by B. Wilkins. T. Savalas. Sat R 4:12 Mr 19 '77
See also
Women in television

Anecdotes, facetiae, satire, etc.

Did Rose live happily ever after? characters from Upstairs, downstairs. A. Cooke. il N Y Times Mag p60-4 My 8 '77
Gentleman's gentlemen; Hudson of Upstairs, downstairs and Bunter of the Peter Wimsey series. R. Baker. N Y Times Mag p6 Ja 30 '77
CHARD
Remember Swiss chard? W. Chandoha. il Horticulture 55:22-3 Ap '77
CHARDIN, Pierre Teilhard de. See Teilhard de Chardin, P.
CHARGE coupled devices (electronics)
CCD: new eye on the sky. J. Eberhart. il Sci N 111:169+ Mr 12 '77
CHARGE transfer devices (electronics)
New technologies for signal processing. R. W. Brodersen and R. M. White. bibl il Science 195:1216-22 Mr 18 '77
CHARGERS, Battery. See Storage battery chargers
CHARISMATIC Renewal in the Christian Churches, Conference on. See Religious conferences
CHARITABLE contributions as tax deductions. See Income tax—Deductions
CHARITABLE remainder trusts. See Trusts and trustees
CHARITIES
Are your favorite charities wasting your money? N. G. Rollins. Good H 184:223-5 My '77
See also
Catholic Worker Movement
Fund raising
National Conference of Catholic Charities
United Way of America (organization)
CHARITY
See also
Love (theology)
CHARLATANS. See Quacks and quackery
CHARLEBOIS, Robert L.
Serving under fire. Chr Today 21:39-40 Ja 7 '77 *

CHARLEMAGNE, King of the Franks
Best of times—the worst of times. P. W. Schmidtchen. il por Hobbies 82:134-6+ Ja '78 *
CHARLES, Prince of Wales
Heir apparent. A. Deming and others. il por Newsweek 89:39-40 Je 13 '77 *
CHARLES Moore Dances and Drums of Africa. See Dancing, African
CHARLES of the Ritz Company. See Cosmetics industry
CHARLESTON, S.C.
Charleston! Charleston! A. Goldman. il Esquire 87:110-13+ Je '77
War of Longitude Lane; cannon hoax. W. Ripley. il Am Hist Illus 11:20-3 F '77

Description

Artist life; Spoleto U.S.A. Festival. D. J. Soria. il Hi Fi 27:MA6-8 O '77
Not going all the way. S. Flythe, Jr. il Holiday 57:24-5+ N '76

Festivals

See Festivals—South Carolina

Historic houses, sites, etc.

See Historic houses, sites, etc.—South Carolina

Siege, 1863

Ethics & armaments. B. Catton. Am Heritage 28:97 Ag '77
CHARLESWORTH, James H.
Books the Bible left out. K. L. Woodward and J. B. Cumming, Jr. il por Newsweek 90:121+ N 28 '77 *
CHARLIP, Remy
R. Charlip's concert at the American Theatre Laboratory. J. Dunning. Dance Mag 51:26+ D '77 *
Remy's imaginative play. J. Maskey. Hi Fi 28: MA10 Ja '78 *
CHARLOTTE, N.C.

Music

See also
Opera—North Carolina
CHARM

Study and teaching

Charm; Ophelia DeVore School of Charm for black women. New Yorker 53:30 Je 6 '77
CHARMS
See also
Evil eye
CHARNEY, Jonathan I.
Law of the sea: breaking the deadlock. bibl f For Affairs 55:598-629 Ap '77
CHARNOCKITES
Charnockite geotherm. S. K. Saxena. bibl il map Science 198:614-17 N 11 '77
CHARP, Sylvia, and Altschuler, H. H.
Decade of usage of the computers for instructional purposes. Educ Digest 42:41-3 F '77
CHARPENTIER, Gustave
Louise. Reviews
New Yorker 53:124-7 Mr 21 '77 *
Louise; recording. D. Arthur. Am Rec G 40: 29-30 F '77 *
New life for Louise. C. L. Osborne. il Hi Fi 27:92-4 F '77 *
CHARPENTIER, Henri
Legendary crepes suzette. C. Claiborne and P. Franey. il N Y Times Mag p66 Mr 6 '77 *
CHARTER airlines. See Airlines—Non-scheduled operations
CHARTER of the United Nations. See United Nations—Charter
CHARTERING of boats. See Fishing boats—Leasing and renting; Sailboats—Leasing and renting
CHARTERING of yachts. See Yachts—Leasing and renting
CHARTRES Cathedral. See Cathedrals—France
CHARTS, Calculating
See also
Nomography (mathematics)
CHARTS, Nautical. See Nautical charts
CHASAN, Daniel Jack
Twilight of the great cedars. il Audubon 79: 50-5 N '77
CHASE, Chevy
Chevy slips into prime time. il pors Time 109:73-4 My 9 '77 *
CHASE, Chris
(ed) See Walters, B. Plot to get Barbara Walters
—See Russell, R. jt auth
CHASE, Francis S.
IGE as a focus for educational reform and renewal. Educ Digest 42:48-50 Mr '77
CHASE, Gordon
Effective public management. J. L. Bower. bibl f Harvard Bus R 55:131-40 Mr '77 *
CHASE, Stuart
Global challenges; excerpt from Bulletin of the atomic scientists, December, 1976. Sci Digest 81:70-2 Ap '77
CHASE, Victor D.
Building how-to's. Am Home 80:87-8+ Ap '77
Owners tell all about life in solar-heated homes. il Pop Mech 148:84-7+ O '77
PM's guide to solar-energy systems. il Pop Mech 147:80-3+ Ap '77
Taking the plunge into an aquarium. il Mech Illus 73:58-9+ Mr '77
CHASE-MARSHALL, Janet
Sex wars: is bed really a battlefield? Mademoiselle 83:167+ S '77
CHASE Manhattan Bank
Three-year deadline at David's bank. C. J. Loomis. il por Fortune 96:70-6+ Jl '77
CHASE Manhattan Corporation
Why investors pick Chase over Citicorp. il Bus W p46-7 Jl 4 '77
CHASE Manhattan Mortgage and Realty Trust. See Real estate investment trusts
CHASES, Police. See Police chases
CHASSIS, Automobile. See Automobiles—Chassis
CHAT Noir (cabaret) See Cabarets
CHAT noir (periodical) See Periodicals—France
CHATEAU Mouton Rothschild (winery) See Wine industry—France
CHÂTEAUX. See Castles
CHATHAM, Russell D.
Midnight stripers. il Field & S 81:136-8+ Mr '77
Outdoors. Esquire 87:16+ Mr '77
CHATHAM, Mass
Portrait of a New England town. F. S. Wight. il Art in Am 65:106-7 My '77
CHATTAHOOCHEE River National Recreation Area (proposed) See Recreation areas—Georgia
CHATTOOGA River
I challenged the Deliverance river—and loved it! J. Janedis. il Redbook 148:55-6 Ap '77
CHAUCER, Daniel
Cooperation. Consumers Res Mag 60:37-8 Jl '77
CHAUCER, Geoffrey
Chaucerian crux. W. Frost. Yale R 66:551-61 Je '77 *
Master storyteller in search of a voice. A. T. Gaylord. Hi Fi 27:74-6 Je '77 *
CHAUTAUQUA Institution, Chautauqua, N.Y.
Chautauqua Institution. il Bet Hom & Gard 55: 200+ Ap '77
CHAVANNES, Pierre Puvis de. See Puvis de Chavannes, P.
CHAVCHAVADZE, David, family
Princesses for ransom: abduction in the grand style. F. MacLean. il pors Horizon 19:82-7 Mr '77
CHÁVEZ, César
Cesar's triumph. T. Nicholson and W. J. Cook. il Newsweek 89:70+ Mr 21 '77 *
Render unto Cesar. il por Time 109:81 Mr 21 '77 *
Trouble with Chavez. M. Yates. por Nation 225:518-20 N 19 '77 *
CHAVEZ, Jose
Over the ropes is out. C. Gammon. il pors Sports Illus 47:52+ Ag 15 '77 *
CHAVIS, Ben
American Gulag. M. Pinsky. Progressive 41:9 N '77 *
CHAWKINS, Steve
Strutting pasta. il Atlantic 239:90-2 F '77
CHAYEFSKY, Paddy
Film. G. Forshey. Chr Cent 94:178-9 F 23 '77 *
Paddy's progress. L. Quart. Intellect 106:78 Ag '77 *
CHAYES, Abram L. and others
Surveillance satellite for all. Bull Atom Sci 33:7 Ja '77
CHAYOTES
Vigorous, productive vine. W. Asa. Org Gard & Farm 24:160 Ag '77
CHEATHAM, Bertha M.
AECT, AASL, and school librarians. SLJ 24:45 S '77
SLJ's 1977 news roundup. il SLJ 24:17-23 D '77
CHEATHAM, Edgar, and Cheatham, Patricia
Along the Natchez Trace. il Travel 148:52-7+ O '77
Hawaiis Kona Coast. il Travel 147:42-7+ F '77
Norfolk & Virginia Beach. il Travel 147:32-7+ Ap '77
North Carolina Piedmont. il Travel 147:48-53+ My '77
CHEATHAM, Patricia. See Cheatham, E. jt auth
CHEATHAM, Val R.
Aladdin strikes it rich; drama. Plays 37:75-80 D '77
Curses! Foiled again! drama. Plays 36:67-70 F '77
Sorcerer's apprentice finds a helping hand; drama. Plays 37:39-46 O '77
CHEATING in school work
Crime of cheating; college students. M. Stone. U.S. News 83:92 S 19 '77
CHEATLE, Martin D. See Rudy, J. W. jt auth
CHECK forgery. See Forgery
CHECK-offs, Promotion. See Meat industry—Advertising

CHECK stealing. See Stealing
CHECKER Motors Corporation
Ed Cole's legacy; new cab design. il Forbes 120:29 Ag 15 '77
CHECKING accounts. See Banks and banking—Checking accounts
CHECKLESS banking. See Computers—Banking use
CHECKS
Banking on privacy; checks printed on red paper. il Time 110:59 S 26 '77
Coping with the credit crunch; cashing checks without backup identification. H. Alpert. il Ret Liv 17:22-4+ F '77
See also
Banks and banking—Float
CHECKS and balances (government) See Separation of powers
CHEERLEADERS. See Cheerleading
CHEERLEADING
Cheerleading doesn't deserve a bad image. G. Norton. por Seventeen 36:64 Je '77
Cowgirls; cheerleaders for the Dallas Cowboys. R. Shaw. il Esquire 88:80-3 O '77
Jeers for cheerleaders. J. Kaplan. Seventeen 36:42 O '77
Sis-Boom-Bah! D. K. Shah and others. il Newsweek 90:87+ N 7 '77
CHEESE
Cheese buymanship. Bet Hom & Gard 55:86 Ag '77
Have a wine & cheese tasting party. il Good H 184:214 My '77
What you should know about cheese. H. P. Schoenberg. il Good H 184:232+ My '77
Whey's and wherefore's of British aristocratic cheeses. D. Waldron. il Holiday 58:38-40+ Je '77
World tour of cheese inside the Cheese Shop. S. P. Torpey. il pors Bet Home & Gard 55:52-3 Ag '77
See also
Cookery—Cheese
CHEESE industry
More money without adding cows. S. Torgerson. il Farm J 101:Dairy 6-7 F '77
CHEESE soufflés. See Soufflés
CHEESE substitutes. See Food substitutes
CHEESECAKE
Best cheesecake. il Good H 185:64 O '77
. . . Something completely different; cheesecake variations. C. Claiborne and P. Franey. il N Y Times Mag p 152+ D 4 '77
CHEEVER, Eddie
Europe uncorks a young Yank. B. Newman. il por Sports Illus 46:56+ Je 20 '77 *
CHEEVER, John
Duet of Cheevers; interview, ed by S. Cheever Cowley. il pors Newsweek 89:68-70+ Mr 14 '77
Falconer; story; excerpt from novel. Ladies Home J 94:115-16 Jl '77
Not only I the narrator, but I John Cheever; interview, ed by E. Munro. il pors Ms 5:74-7+ Ap '77
Talking with John Cheever; interview, ed by J. Firth. il por Sat R 4:22+ Ap 2 '77
about
Cheever's t mph. W. Clemons. il pors Newsweek 89:61-+ Mr 14 '77 *
Redemption according to Cheever. J. Romano. Commentary 63:66-9 My '77 *
CHEEVERS, Gerry
He was a two-time loser. J. Kirshenbaum. il por Sports Illus 46:73-6 My 16 '77 *
CHEFS. See Cooks
CHEKHOV, Anton Pavlovich
Cherry orchard. Reviews
America 136:241 Mr 19 '77 *
Dance Mag 51:37+ My '77 *
Nation 224:313-14 Mr 12 '77 *
New Repub 176:28+ Mr 26 '77
New Yorker 53:54+ F 28 '77 *
Newsweek il 89:78-9 F 28 '77 *
Time il 109:56 F 28 '77 *
Three sisters. Reviews
Nation 224:634-6 My 21 '77 *
New Yorker 53:74 My 16 '77 *
Sat R 4:50-1 Jl 9 '77 *
Time 109:99 My 16 '77 *
CHELMINSKI, Rudolph
Exoskeletal art container is the rage, literally, and the delight of Paris. il Smithsonian 8:20-9 Ag '77
Giscard's quandary. Sat R 4:28-9 Ja 22 '77
Honk, tweet, blare: sounds of the fair. il por Smithsonian 8:78-83 Ja '78
Lindberghs liberate monkeys from constraints. il pors Smithsonian 7:58-65 bibl(p 126) Mr '77
Oh, cuisine! Sat R 5:72 D 10 '77
Pots of wine. Sat R 4:14-15 Jl 9 '77
Reports & comment: Polus Kholodo. il Atlantic 240:4+ O '77
Rubens year—a celebration. il Smithsonian 8:46-55+ bibl(p 160) O '77
CHELSEA, Mass.
Education
See Education—Massachusetts
CHEMETRON Corporation mergers. See Corporations—Acquisitions and mergers
CHEMEY, Ruth
(ed) See Todd, F. S. Adelie and emperor penguins
CHEMICAL additives in food. See Food additives
CHEMICAL Bank. See New York (city)—Banks
CHEMICAL carcinogens. See Cancer—Causes
CHEMICAL compounds
See also
Intermetallic compounds
CHEMICAL contamination of feeds. See Feeds—Contamination by drugs, pesticides, etc.
CHEMICAL elements
Biomethylation of toxic elements in the environment. W. P. Ridley and others. bibl il Science 197:329-32 Jl 22 '77
Mars and earth: origin and abundance of volatiles. E. Anders and T. Owen. bibl il Science 198:453-65 N 4 '77
See also
Transuranium elements
also names of chemical elements, e.g. Carbon
Atomic no. 107
Dubna believes it has produced element 107. G. B. Lubkin. Phys Today 30:19 Ja '77
Atomic no. 126
Element 126—maybe tomorrow. il Chemistry 50:24 Ap '77
Element 126: no evidence. Sci N 111:85 F 5 '77
CHEMICAL evolution. See Evolution
CHEMICAL factories. See Chemical plants
CHEMICAL industries
Against silence; indictments against Velsicol Chemical Corp. in pesticide coverup. Time 110:49 D 26 '77
Careless Kepone; James River contamination. F. S. Sterrett and C. A. Boss. bibl il map. Environment 19:30-6 Mr '77
Little fish eats big fish; Grow Chemical Corp. por Forbes 119:67 My 15 '77
Petrochemicals: the prodigious costs of facing the future. il Bus W p44-7+ Jl 18 '77
Pollution postscripts; Minamata disease and Kepone poisoning. E. Keerdoja. il Newsweek 89:12 Ap 4 '77
Promise and perils of petrochemicals. B. Commoner. N Y Times Mag p38-40+ S 25 '77
Surge of business for independent labs. il Bus W p 116+ Ap 11 '77
White hats and white coats; address, March 9, 1977. J. B. St Clair. Vital Speeches 43:414-16 Ap 15 '77
Why chemical companies are nervous; expansion of ethylene production by oil companies. Forbes 120:68 D 15 '77
See also
Allied Chemical Corporation
American Cyanamid Company
Chemical plants
Chemical workers
Diamond Shamrock Corporation
Dow Chemical Company
Du Pont de Nemours, E. I, and Company
Fertilizer industry
Grace, W. R. & Company
Monsanto Company
Rohm & Haas Company
Union Carbide Corporation
Finance
Cash that does not create capacity; petrochemicals. il Bus W p 108+ O 17 '77
Chemicals. il Forbes 121:74-6 Ja 9 '78
Overcapacity drags down profits. il Bus W p40+ Ja 9 '78
Laws and legislation
See Chemicals—Laws and legislation
Europe, Western
Why petrochemicals face slower growth. il Bus W p48+ N 28 '77
Germany, West
How Bayer is building in the U.S. market. il Bus W p72-3 Ag 1 '77
Italy
Italy: Montedison's gamble on raising fresh capital. Bus W p48+ Mr 21 '77
Montedison: the new chief no one wants; G. Medici. por Bus W p30-1 Ag 1 '77
Surprise get-together for two old rivals; Montedison and SIR Consorzio Industriale. Bus W p41-2 Je 6 '77
Will politics drown a debt-ridden giant? Montedison. il Bus W p72-5+ Jl 25 '77
Japan
Money problems that mercury wrought; compensation paid by Chisso Corp. for Minamata disease. il Bus W p38 Je 27 '77

CHEMICAL industries—*Continued*

Russia

Ready to spend on chemical plants. Bus W p56-7 S 12 '77

Singapore

Welcome injection of petrochemicals; Japanese companies. il Bus W p46 Je 13 '77

CHEMICAL Industry Institute of Toxicology
White hats and white coats; address, March 9, 1977. J. B. St Clair. Vital Speeches 43:414-16 Ap 15 '77

CHEMICAL mimicry. See Mimicry (biology)

CHEMICAL plants

Accidents

Persistent poison; spread of dioxin pollution over Seveso, Italy. E. Keerdoja. map Newsweek 89:10 Je 13 '77
Poison that fell from the sky; dioxin poisoning following factory explosion in Seveso, Italy; condensation. J. G. Fuller. il map Read Digest 111:191-6+ Ag '77
Reporter at large; TCDD explosion at Icmesa chemical plant in Italy. T. Whiteside. New Yorker 53:41+ Jl 25 '77
Seveso—one year later: aftermath of TCDD explosion at Icmesa chemical plant. D. B. Richardson. il U.S. News 83:44-5 Ag 1 '77

Environmental aspects

How are we fixed for toxic clouds? F. Graham, Jr. Audubon 79:137-43 Ja '77

CHEMICAL pollution of rivers, lakes, etc. See Water pollution

CHEMICAL reactions
Mathematics of first-order rate reactions. A. Mancott. il por Chemistry 50:23-4 D '77
See also
Alkylation
Catalysis

CHEMICAL reagents
See also
Isocyanates

CHEMICAL research
Jokichi Takamine (1854-1922); international industrialist and chemical researcher. F. G. Creech. il por Chemistry 50:5-6 My '77
See also
Gordon Research Conferences

CHEMICAL stability
Remarkable replicators: molecular evolution and the law of survival of the stable; excerpt from The selfish gene. R. Dawkins. Natur Hist 86:34+ F '77

CHEMICAL workers
Industrial sterility; chemical workers exposed to DBCP. J. Seligmann and others. il Newsweek 90:69 Ag 29 '77
Sterility scare sends OSHA scurrying. Bus W p45+ S 12 '77

CHEMICALS
Too precious to burn. R. S. Wishart. Conservationist 31:23 N '76
See also
Agricultural chemicals

Laws and legislation

Chemical producers must report to EPA. Sci N 112:423 D 24 '77
Eschewing understatement, United Kingdom's science attaché declares Tosca non grata. C. Holden. Science 196:1182-3 Je 10 '77
Hazards of toxic substances; excerpt from The unfinished agenda: the citizen's policy guide to environmental issues. Nat Parks & Con Mag 51:10-13 Jl '77
How are we fixed for toxic clouds? F. Graham, Jr. Audubon 79:137-43 Ja '77
Problems with OSHA's cancer proposal. Bus W p38 O 24 '77
Saccharin and other health scares: what can you believe? N. G. Rollins. Good H 185:201-2 Jl '77
Secret killers; regulation of chemicals used in industry. D. McGhee. Progressive 41:26 Ag '77
Toxic? To whom? Toxic Substances Control Act J. A. Briggs. Forbes 120:66 S 1 '77
Will EPA do the job? Nat Parks & Con Mag 51:27-8 Jl '77

Physiological effects

Hazards in arts and crafts; chemical dangers reported by Badi M. Boulos and Michael McCann. Consumers Res Mag 60:16-17 Jl '77
New breed of pollutants: the dangers they carry. il U.S. News 82:42-6 F 7 '77
PBBs: more effects and more exposure. il Sci N 112:100-1 Ag 13 '77

Safety regulations

See Chemicals—Laws and legislation

CHEMISORPTION. See Adsorption

CHEMISTRY
Chemistry (cont) Sci N 111:73, 311, 393; 112:171, 316 Ja 29, My 14, Je 18, S 10, N 12 '77
Limits of knowledge; adaptation of address, 1975. T. Benfey. Chemistry 50:2-3 Mr '77
See also
Astrochemistry
Biochemistry
Catalysis
Computers—Chemical use
Immunochemistry
Lasers—Chemical use
Photochemistry
Photographic chemistry
Radicals (chemistry)
Stereochemistry
Transmutation (chemistry)

Conferences

Pittsburgh conference: a special instrumentation report. T. H. Maugh, 2d and A. L. Robinson. Science 195:1314-18+ Mr 25 '77

Experiments

Lab bench. See issues of Chemistry

Periodicals

Prices of physics and chemistry journals. F. F. Clasquin and J. B. Cohen. bibl il Science 197:432-8 Jl 29 '77

CHEMISTRY, Analytic
Lab bench. See issues of Chemistry

CHEMISTRY, Atmospheric. See Atmosphere

CHEMISTRY, Biological. See Biochemistry

CHEMISTRY, Organic
See also
Aromatic compounds
Carbohydrates

CHEMISTRY, Physical and theoretical
See also
Adsorption

CHEMISTRY, Physiological. See Biochemistry

CHEMISTRY, Technical
See also
Alloys
Corrosion and anticorrosives

CHEMORECEPTIVITY
Chemosensory tracking of scent trails by the planktonic shrimp acetes sibogae australis. P. Hamner and W. M. Hamner. bibl il Science 195:886-8 Mr 4 '77

CHEMOTAXIS
Chemotaxis of rhizobium spp. to a glycoprotein produced by birdsfoot trefoil roots. W. W. Currier and G. A. Strobel. bibl il Science 196:434-6 Ap 22 '77
Mutant of paramecium defective in chemotaxis. J. Van Houten. bibl il Science 198:746-8 N 18 '77

CHEMOTHERAPY
Strategy for the chemotherapy of infectious disease. S. S. Cohen. bibl Science 197:431-2 Jl 29 '77
See also
Cancer—Therapy

CHEN, Edwin E.
Model for fraud. Nation 224:242-4 F 26 '77
Reports & comment: Michigan. il Atlantic 240:12+ Ag '77

CHEN, James R. and others
Legionnaires' disease: nickel levels. bibl il Science 196:906-8 My 20 '77

CHEN, Kuan-i
Planned birth program in China. bibl Cur Hist 73:73-8 S '77

CHEN, Lan Bo, and others
Control of a cell surface major glycoprotein by epidermal growth factor. bibl il Science 197:776-8 Ag 19 '77

CHEN, Yung-ping and Chu, K. W.
Future funding of social security and the total dependency ratio. bibl il M Labor R 100:53-5 F '77

CHENEY, Lynne Vincent
You can thank Louis Prang for all those cards. il por Smithsonian 8:120-5 bibl(p 135) D '77

CHENG, Tsai-ying, and Voqui, T. H.
Regeneration of Douglas fir plantlets through tissue culture. bibl il Science 198:306-7 O 21 '77

CHÉNIER, André Marie de
Virtue, weep if I die: the real André Chénier. S. P. Edelman. il por Opera N 41:10-13 Mr 26 '77 *

CHERBAS, Peter, and others
Induction of acetylcholinesterase activity by β-ecdysone in a drosophila cell line. bibl il Science 197:275-7 Jl 15 '77

CHEREMISINOFF, Paul N. and Morresi, A. C.
Energy from wood wastes; excerpt from Energy from solid wastes. il Environment 19:25-31 My '77

CHERLIN, Andrew
No long delay needed. New Repub 177:13-15 D 17 '77

CHERNOW, Burt
Lester Johnson and the kaleidoscopic crowd. il Intellect 105:357-9 Ap '77

CHERNUSH, Kay
Rx for village health. il Américas 29:7-12 S '77
CHEROKEE Indians
Black freedmen of the Cherokee Nation. T. Gammon. bibl il Negro Hist Bull 40:732-5 Jl '77
CHERRY, H. Wendell
Humana's hopes. il por Forbes 120:24-5 S 1 '77 *
CHERRY, Laurence
New vision of dreams. il N Y Times Mag p9-13+ Jl 3 '77; Same abr. with title Why you need to dream. Read Digest 111:139-42 O '77
Solving the mysteries of pain. il N Y Times Mag p 12-13+ Ja 30 '77
CHERRY, Myron M.
Outrageous Mr Cherry and the underachieving nukes. F. Graham, Jr. il por Audubon 79:50-67 S '77; Discussion. 79:128-30 N '77 *
CHERRY desserts. See Desserts
CHERRY orchard; drama. See Chekhov, A. P.
CHESAPEAKE, Va.

Water supply

See Water supply—Virginia
CHESAPEAKE and Ohio Canal National Historical Park
C & O Canal dedicated to Justice Douglas. W. O. Douglas. il por Nat Parks & Con Mag 51:20 Ag '77
CHESAPEAKE Bay
I will survive; duck boat adrift in Chesapeake Bay; ed by B. East. F. W. Stamm. il Outdoor Life 160:80-1+ D '77
Winter comes to the Bay. W. Warner. il Yachting 141:75-7 F '77
See also
Fishing—Chesapeake Bay
Marine pollution—Chesapeake Bay
Oil pollution of the sea—Chesapeake Bay
Smith Island
Tangier Island
CHESAPEAKE Bay oil slicks. See Oil pollution of the sea—Chesapeake Bay
CHESS
Championship season; Vaux Junior High School and Frederick Douglass Elementary School chess teams, Philadelphia. J. Lelyveld. il N Y Times Mag p86 Je 19 '77
Computer chess: easy to play, not easy to beat. J. Curtis. il Pop Mech 148:70 D '77
Good try; chess 4.5. il Sci Am 236:56+ Je '77
Let's go, big beige machine! computer chess championships. J. Kaplan. Sports Illus 47:42 Ag 22 '77
New city game; Philadelphia's Vaux Junior High School team. il Newsweek 90:44 Ag 15 '77
Sorry, wrong number; National Chess League. L. Grossberger. Sports Illus 47:42-4+ Jl 18 '77
Taut duel for two old comrades; B. Spassky vs V. Korchnoi. J. D. Reed. il Sports Illus 47:40-2+ D 12 '77
CHESSON, Frederick W.
How to decipher secret messages. il Radio-Electr 48:48-50 D '77
CHESTER, Arthur Henry
Rig writer. por Forbes 119:78 Mr 1 '77 *
CHESTER, Mark
Barrel of fun. il Am Home 80:36-8 Je '77
CHESTERFIELD, Philip Dormer Stanhope, 4th Earl of
Book of gentlemanly conduct. P. W. Schmidtchen. il Hobbies 82:134-6+ Mr '77 *
CHESTNUT trees
Army offers proving ground for endangered species; American chestnut trees. il Nat Parks & Con Mag 51:26-7 S '77
CHESTNUTS
See also
Cookery—Nuts
CHESTS
Fertility symbols on the Hadley chests. R. L. Greene. bibl il Antiques 112:250-7 Ag '77
See also
Toy chests
CHEVILLOT, Charles
Eating out in New York. L. Prothro. Nat R 29:734-5 Je 24 '77 *
CHEVROLET Motor Division. See General Motors Corporation—Chevrolet Division
CHEWING gum
By gum! Business is bubbling. R. Levy. il Duns R 109:90-1+ Je '77
Over lightly. Seventeen 36:64 S '77
CHEWING of tobacco. See Tobacco chewing
CHEYENNE Indians
Cheyennes drive for clean-air rights; redesignating air quality status to prevent industrial development. il Bus W p29 Ap 4 '77
CHEZ nous; drama. See Nichols, P.
CHIANCIOLA, Ben
Chianciolas of Gloucester. M. King. il por Forbes 120:46 O 15 '77 *
CHIANG, Chian C. and Paul, I. C.
Monomeric forms of the acid ionophore lasalocid A (X-537A) from polar solvents. bibl il Science 196:1441-3 Je 24 '77
CHIANG Ching. See Mao, T. T. Mme
CHIANG, Ching-kuo
Understanding Chiang Ching-kuo. W. F. Buckley, Jr. Nat R 30:48-9 Ja 6 '78 *
CHIANTI. See Wine
CHIARA, Joan
Dollology. See issues of Hobbies
CHIARA, Maria
Chiara's way; interview, ed by L. Rasponi. il pors Opera N 42:33-5 D 24 '77
CHIBANGA, Ernest
African nativity. il Ebony 33:44-6 D '77 *
CHICAGO, Judy
Judy Chicago: china painter. il Ceram Mo 25:34-5 Je '77 *
CHICAGO
Chicago wires 911 into computer. Am City & County 92:38 Ag '77

Airports

Midway case may reveal Carter policy. R. K. Ellingsworth. Aviation W 106:30 F 7 '77
Six Midway routes urged for new airline operation. Aviation W 107:32 D 12 '77
Sweaty palms in the control tower. D. Martindale. bibl il por Psychol Today 10:70-2+ F '77

Anecdotes, facetiae, satire, etc.

Accent on Chicawgo. J. R. Powers. il Holiday 58:46-7+ S '77

Architecture

Remodeling report; home of the Youngren family. J. H. Ingersoll. il House B 119:69-70+ S '77

Architecture, Bureau of

Anchors aweigh on Chicago's latest amenity; Navy Pier restoration. W. Marlin. il Archit Rec 161:107-14 Mr '77

Art

Chicago. A. G. Artner. il Art N 76:93-5 Mr; 92+ Ap; 158-9 Summ '77
See also
Chicago—Monuments, statues, etc.

The Arts

Liberated arts. C. Terry. il Holiday 58:48-9+ S '77

Banks

Banking the Abboud way; First National Bank of Chicago. M. Ruby and C. J. Harper. por Newsweek 90:63 Jl 25 '77
Chicago's great bank heist; First National Bank. Time 110:20 N 28 '77
First Chicago reaches to win Peking's favor. por Bus W p36 O 17 '77
Is Bert Lance losing his clout? il por U.S. News 83:21 Ag 8 '77
Lance on the carpet; National Bank of Georgia-First Chicago relationship. M. Ruby and R. Thomas. il por Newsweek 90:57-8 Ag 1 '77
Outsider escalates a bank's family feud: Sax family control of the Exchange National Bank of Chicago. por Bus W p44-5 N 14 '77
Sharpening battle over Bert Lance. il por Time 110:6-8 Ag 1 '77

Bookstores

See Booksellers and bookselling—Illinois

Buildings

Living in a landmark: Old Colony building. M. E. Marty. Chr Cent 94:1079 N 16 '77
Malls at Water Tower Place. il Archit Rec 162:99-104 O '77
Report from Chicago: restoration of the Trading Room; Louis Sullivan's Chicago Stock Exchange Trading Room. F. Schulze. il Art in Am 65:58-9 N '77
Smoke detectors win Chicago council vote. il Am City & County 92:26 My '77
Urban scene: lost and found cities. M. E. Prior. Am Scholar 46:506-13 Aut '77

City planning

Urban scene: lost and found cities. M. E. Prior. Am Scholar 46:506-13 Aut '77

Crime

Chicago's great bank heist; First National Bank. Time 110:20 N 28 '77
Chop-shop war; Mob murders. R. Steele and C. J. Harper. Newsweek 90:22 Ag 15 '77

Description

Chicago. Bet Hom & Gard 55:243-4 O '77

Docks, wharves, etc.

Anchors aweigh on Chicago's latest amenity; Navy Pier restoration. W. Marlin. il Archit Rec 161:107-14 Mr '77

Education

Basic training; minimum competency standards for elementary school students. M. Sheils and S. Monroe. Newsweek 90:44 Ag 15 '77

CHICAGO—Education—*Continued*
Chicago teacher makes his classes come alive; E. Hamberlin's biology course at DuSable High School. B. Rhoden. il pors Ebony 32:43-6+ Mr '77
Teacher who gets results; L. Lovelace's class at Wendel Phillips High. J. Seligmann and S. Monroe. il por Newsweek 90:67 S 12 '77
Westside story; M. Collins, founder of Westside Preparatory School. il por Time 110:39 D 26 '77
You call us, they'll call you; The Learning Exchange. S. Croteau. Educ Digest 42:16-18 Ap '77

Galleries and museums

See also
Chicago Art Institute

History

Black man who founded Chicago; J. B. P. DuSable. L. Bennett, Jr. il por maps Ebony 33:64-6+ N '77

Hotels, restaurants, etc.

International chef; the Pump Room. L. Szathmary. Travel 147:8+ F '77
Rush Street, that lush street. A. Gold. il Holiday 58:50-1+ S '77
Touch of the ocean on the shores of Lake Michigan; Cape Cod Room in the Drake Hotel. C. A. Whittingham. il Fortune 95:357-8 My '77

Libraries

See also
Chicago Public Library
Illinois Regional Library for the Blind and Physically Handicapped

Monuments, statues, etc.

Chimney stack, upside-down; Batcolumn. il Horizon 19:71 My '77
Fair game; C. Oldenburg's Batcolumn. A. G. Artner. il Art N 76:158-9 Summ '77
Public art's big hit: Oldenburg bats high in Chicago. B. Rose. il por Vogue 167:118-19+ Jl '77

Music

Debuts & reappearances. por Hi Fi 27:MA20 My; MA22 Ag; MA21 S '77
See also
Lyric Opera of Chicago

Newspapers

See also
Chicago daily news
Chicago sun-times

Politics and government

After Daley, what? R. Whitehead, Jr. Commonweal 104:79-82 F 4 '77
Arrangement; M. Bilandic. J. Lelyveld. il por N Y Times Mag p 138 Mr 27 '77
Bilandic the bland. R. Steele and F. Maier. Newsweek 89:29-30 Ap 18 '77
Chicago: A.D (After Daley) S. J. Ungar. il pors Atlantic 239:4+ Mr '77
Chicago without Daley: new cards in the old game. P. Delaney. Nation 224:646-9 My 28 '77
Janie and the Mayor; M. Bilandic's role in cab fare hike. D. A. Williams and F. Maier. il pors Newsweek 90:40 D 5 '77
Kindly omit flowers. K. Bode. New Repub 176: 12-14 Ja 15 '77
Organization man; R. Daley. R. Whitehead, Jr. Am Scholar 46:351-7 Summ '77

Prisons and reformatories

Serving Illinois inmates; Cook County Jail library. J. Morrison. il Wilson Lib Bull 51:522-5 F '77

Protests, demonstrations, etc.

First amendment blues. il Time 110:40 Ag 15 '77
Other convention in Chicago; 1968; interview. ed by L. R. Obst. A. Peck. il N Y Times Mag p92+ N 13 '77

Religious institutions and affairs

Island in the city; Chicago's Catholics; views of J. W. Sanders. J. W. Donohue. America 136:322-4 Ap 9 '77
UCC's covenants for churches in change. Chr Cent 94:1055 N 16 '77

Stores

Malls at Water Tower Place. il Archit Rec 162:99-104 O '77
Why profits shrink at a grand old name; Marshall Field. il Bus W p66-9+ Ap 11 '77

Synagogues

Devotion to stained glass; window created by A. Rattner for the Chicago Loop Synagogue. Vasari. il Art N 76:20+ My '77

Transit systems

Death in the Loop. D. M. Alpern and others. il Newsweek 89:32+ F 14 '77

CHICAGO (rock group) See Rock groups
CHICAGO and North Western Transportation Company
Orphans try harder. Forbes 119:71+ Je 15 '77
Railroads: rags to riches. D. Pauly and F. Maier. il Newsweek 91:50 Ja 2 '78
CHICAGO Art Institute
Report from Chicago: restoration of the Trading Room; Louis Sullivan's Chicago Stock Exchange Trading Room. F. Schulze. il Art in Am 65:58-9 N '77
CHICAGO Board of Trade
Bucketing beans; investigation. il Time 109:65 Je 27 '77
Chicago's booming commodity markets: hotter than Wall Street. il U.S. News 82:81-2 Je 13 '77
State of war in options trading; competition between Chicago Board Options Exchange and the American Stock Exchange. Bus W p60 Mr 7 '77
CHICAGO Board Options Exchange. See Chicago Board of Trade
CHICAGO Call (religious statement) See Evangelicalism
CHICAGO daily news
Hoge gives them Hecht. D. Gelman and others. il por Newsweek 89:52 F 7 '77
Time to write; J. Graham's column on cancer. il por Time 110:94+ N 14 '77
CHICAGO declaration of Christian concern. See Laity—Catholic Church
CHICAGO Lyric Opera. See Lyric Opera of Chicago
CHICAGO Public Library
Chicago library loses its no. 1 friend in Daley. L. R. Pearson. il pors Am Lib 8:60-1 F '77
From shambles to showplace; Chicago Public Library Cultural Center. D. Schabel. il Am Lib 8:602-4 D '77
CHICAGO River
Salmon for Hizzoner. R. Telander. il Sports Illus 46:60+ Mr 28 '77
CHICAGO Stock Exchange building. See Chicago—Buildings
CHICAGO sun-times
Hoge gives them Hecht. D. Gelman and others. il por Newsweek 89:52 F 7 '77
CHICAGO Symphony Orchestra
Musical events:
Carnegie Hall performances. A. Porter. New Yorker 53:88+ My 30 '77
First New York concert of the season. A. Porter. New Yorker 53:180-2 N 14 '77
M. Tippett's Fourth symphony. A. Porter. New Yorker 53:128-30 O 31 '77
CHICAGO. University
Chicago's woman; H. H. Gray. M. Sheils and F. Maier. por Newsweek 90:88 D 19 '77
Mme President; appointment of H. H. Gray. por Time 110:90 D 19 '77
2 learning places by Metz Train Olson & Youngren: a glow on old gothic. W. Marlin. il Archit Rec 162:94-6 Jl '77
CHICAGOANS
Chicago movers and makers; photographs. Holiday 58:56-7 S '77
CHICANOS. See Mexican Americans
CHICHÉN ITZÁ
Visit of the plumed serpent; pyramid of Kukulcán. L. E. Arochi. il Américas 29:32-5 Ag '77
CHICK, William L. and others
Artificial pancreas using living beta cells: effects on glucose homeostasis in diabetic rats. bibl il Science 197:780-2 Ag 19 '77
CHICK embryos. See Embryology—Birds
CHICKEN as food. See Cookery—Poultry
CHICKEN manure. See Fertilizers and manures
CHICKENS. See Poultry
CHIEF executive officers (corporations) See Executives
CHIEFS of Staff. See United States—Joint Chiefs of Staff
CHILD, Julia
From Julia Child's kitchen. See issues of McCall's
White House menu. il N Y Times Mag p55+ Ja 16 '77
CHILD abuse
Abortion and child abuse; excerpt from Death before birth. H. O. J. Brown. Chr Today 22:34 O 7 '77
America discovers child pornography. H. Dudar. Ms 6:45-7+ Ag '77
American scandal: why some parents abuse teens. C. Remsberg and B. Remsberg. Seventeen 36:154-5+ My '77
Battered children. M. Sheils and others. il Newsweek 90:112-13+ O 10 '77
Child abuse. G. M. Anderson. America 136:478-82 My 28 '77
Child abuse: society's symptom of stress. C. A. Frazier. il Chr Today 21:6-8 Je 3 '77
Child abusers: signaling for help. Sci N 111:214-15 Ap 2 '77
Child pornography: outrage starts to stir some action. U.S. News 82:66 Je 13 '77
Child's garden of perversity. il Time 109:55-6 Ap 4 '77; Same abr. with title Kid sex: pornography's all-time low. Read Digest 111:45-8+ Jl '77

CHILD abuse—*Continued*
Exploited children; child pornography. Chr Today 22:23 N 18 '77
New help for battered children, and their parents. J. Gaylin. Psychol Today 11:92+ Je '77
Physical child abuse and its prevention. M. L. Kaul. bibl il Intellect 105:270-2 F '77
Pornography—not sex but the obscene use of power. G. Steinem. Ms 6:43-4 Ag '77
Tragedy of Joanne; J. Bashold's neglect of infant. R. Severo. il pors Sr Schol 109:23-6+ Mr 24 '77
Tragedy of Joanne Bashold; neglect of infant. A. Adelson. il pors Good H 184:124-5+ Mr '77
What can be done about child abuse? M. Brenton. Todays Educ 66:50-2+ S '77
What parents should know and do about kiddie porn; work of F. Osanka. P. Bridge. il Parents Mag 53:42-3+ Ja '78
What pornographers are doing to children: a shocking report. J. Densen-Gerber. Redbook 149:86+ Ag '77
See also
Child molesters

CHILD-adult relationship
As children see old folks. K. Serock and others. il Todays Educ 66:70-3 Mr '77
See also
Parent-child relationship

CHILD care centers. See Day care centers

CHILD care deductions. See Income tax—Deductions

CHILD care tax credit. See Tax credits

CHILD delinquency. See Juvenile delinquency

CHILD Health Assessment Act. See Children—Medical care

CHILD health services. See Children—Medical care

CHILD labor. See Children—Employment

CHILD mental health
Out to protect a vital resource. E. Miller. MH 61:15-17 Spr '77
Problem may lie in the eye of the mother; seeking help for children from mental health professionals. J. Horn. Psychol Today 11:144-5 D '77

CHILD molesters
Incest: sexual abuse begins at home. E. Weber. Ms 5:64-7 Ap '77; Discussion. 6:89-92 S '77
Story of Mary C. J. Stucker. Ms 5:66-7+ Ap '77
Terror of child molestation; with safety quiz for young school children. D. Schultz. il Parents Mag 52:44-5+ F '77
Yes, Virginia, there is a PIE; Paedophile Information Exchange. Nat R 29:1221-2 O 28 '77

CHILD murder. See Murder

CHILD neglect. See Child abuse

CHILD photography. See Photography of children

CHILD placement. See Adoption; Foster home care

CHILD pornography. See Pornography

CHILD psychiatry
Wonderful world of Disney—its psychological appeal; address, May 1975. M. Brody. bibl Am Imago 33:350-60 Wint '76
See also
Child psychotherapy

CHILD psychology
Children of affluence; excerpt from Privileged ones: the well-off and the rich in America. R. Coles. il Atlantic 240:52-8+ S '77
Child's play in Northern Ireland. M. R. Duncan. il Parks & Rec 12:27-30 Ag '77
Cinderella children; urban communes. D. K. Weisberg. bibl il por Psychol Today 10:84-6+ Ap '77
Fantasy trial about a real issue; iatrogenic anguish caused by child psychologists. E. F. Torrey. Psychol Today 10:24 Mr '77
Fascination of freaks; excerpt from Freaks. L. Fiedler. il Psychol Today 11:56-9+ Ag '77
Hormones taken during pregnancy affect the child's personality; study by June Reinisch. J. Gaylin. Psychol Today 11:31-2 O '77
Moving can be fun. S. Bush. Psychol Today 11:28 Jl '77
Mystery of disappearing skills; work of T. G. R. Bower. J. Gaylin. Psychol Today 10:86 My '77
Survey shows children feel loved, have many fears—real and imagined. G. Carro. il Ladies Home J 94:54 Je '77
Torque test for schizophrenia; tendency among youngsters, to draw circles in a clockwise direction. Sci N 112:167 S 10 '77
Understanding rich kids; views of R. Coles. K. L. Woodward and P. Malamud. il por Newsweek 90:51 Ag 29 '77
Vulnerable age—when moving brings special problems; research by Michael Inbar. D. Cohen. il Psychol Today 10:28+ Mr '77
See also
Child mental health
Child psychiatry
Child psychotherapy
Children and death
Infant psychology
Maternal deprivation
Parent-child relationship

CHILD psychotherapy
Should your child be in therapy? L. Salk. Harp Baz 110:231+ S '77

CHILD raising. See Children—Management and training

CHILD study. See Child psychology

CHILD welfare
Children's hour it isn't. R. Rosenblatt. New Repub 177:40 N 19 '77
See also
Adoption
Child abuse
Day care centers
Foster home care
Juvenile courts
Unicef

China

One-fourth of the world's children. R. H. Collins. Educ Digest 43:57-9 S '77

United States

Citizens who need us most; ideas of K. Keniston. C. Tucker. Sat R 5:56 O 15 '77
How not to save a family: a social worker's diary. M. Wagner. Ms 6:25-6+ D '77
More help needed for children. G. J. Hecht. por Parents Mag 52:32+ F '77
Our endangered children: it's a matter of money; National Research Council study. J. Gaylin. Psychol Today 10:94 My '77
Protecting children. . . il McCalls 104:66-7 F '77
Stereotyping child welfare. J. Macaulay. il Society 14:47-51 Ja '77

CHILDBIRTH
All in the family; permitting children to witness birth of siblings at Mendocino Coast Hospital, Fort Bragg, Calif. Newsweek 89:90 My 30 '77
Before the baby comes. il Parents Mag 52:24 F; 26 Jl; 31 N '77
Coping with the threat of premature birth. F. Fuchs. il Parents Mag 52:20 Mr '77
Cost of having a baby, 1978. il Good H 186:170 Ja '78
Easing a baby's way into the world; Danielle Rapoport's follow-up study on children delivered by the Leboyer method. J. Horn. il Psychol Today 10:34 Mr '77
Gap junctions: their presence and necessity in myometrium during parturition. R. E. Garfield and others. bibl il Science 198:958-60 D 2 '77
Great beginnings; V. H. Elkins' classes in the Lamaze method of natural childbirth. K. McLean. il pors Am Home 80:30-2 Mr '77
How women want to have their babies. E. J. Pascoe. McCalls 105:109-10 O '77
Leboyer's babies. R. J. Trotter. il Sci N 111:59 Ja 22 '77
On natural childbirth; criticism of Lamaze method. M. M. Malinovich. Mademoiselle 83: 30-1+ Mr '77
Prepared childbirth; excerpt from The parenting advisor, ed by F. Caplan. il Fam Health 9: 54-6 Mr '77
Same day delivery. C. M. Till. il Parents Mag 52:37-9+ Jl '77
Seven choices of delivery. M. Albertson. Good H 186:68+ Ja '78
What's best for newborns and parents—giving birth in the hospital or at home. M. Newton. por Fam Health 9:19+ Ja '77
When you're having more than one; delivering twins. K. D. Anderson. Parents Mag 52:20 D '77
See also
Cesarean section
Midwives
Pregnancy

CHILDERS, William
Meanmouth. K. Schultz. il Field & S 82:84-5+ Je '77 *

CHILDHOOD. See Children

CHILDHOOD poisoning. See Poisons

CHILDLESSNESS
Choosing a life without children. J. Gaylin. Psychol Today 11:97 Je '77
Pros and cons of parenthood. il Ebony 32:111-12+ Jl '77
See also
National Organization for Non-parents

CHILDREN
Bazaar's guide to having a happy, healthy child; a symposium. il Harp Baz 110:86-91+ Jl '77
Children's exchange (cont) House & Gard 149: 40 Ap; 122+ My; 42+ Je; 51 D '77
See also
Birth order
Boys
Church work with children
Cookery by children
Education of children
Family
Family, Size of
Family life
Fathers
Infants
International Year of the Child, 1979 (proposed)

CHILDREN—See also—*Continued*
Mentally ill children
Mothers
Motion pictures for children
Orphans and orphan asylums
Parents
Presidents—United States—Children
Problem children
School children
Siblings
Single parent families
Television and children
Twins
also headings beginning Child; Childrens

Accidents

See Accidents

Altruism

See Altruism

Anecdotes, facetiae, satire, etc.

Case of the beautiful blonde. E. LeShan. il Parents Mag 52:42+ Jl '77

Attitudes

As children see old folks. K. Serock and others. il Todays Educ 66:70-3 Mr '77
Children's hour; Foundation for Child Development survey. K. L. Woodward. il Newsweek 89:90+ Mr 14 '77
Polling the children; survey by the Foundation for Child Development. Time 109:36 Mr 14 '77
U.S. children give families high marks. Sci N 111:214 Ap 2 '77

Care and hygiene

Ask the pediatrician; questions and answers. See issues of Family health incorporating Today's health
First aid for kids; views of M. Green. S. C. Cowley. il Newsweek 90:48 S 5 '77
Lead poisoning: still a threat to young children. M. A. Wessel. Parents Mag 53:14+ Ja '78
See also
Baby sitters
Child mental health
Child welfare
Children—Growth and development
Children—Medical care
Parent education
Poisons
Sick children

Civil rights

Children's rights. E. Boulding. bibl il Society 15:39-43 N '77
More rights for children—what an expert says; interview. K. Keniston. por U.S. News 83:33 O 31 '77
See also
Mentally handicapped children—Civil rights

Clothing and dress

See Clothing and dress—Children

Day care

All about day care. J. Kagan. il Parents Mag 52:40-1+ Ap '77
Child-care alternatives: good news. J. Curtis. Harp Baz 110:177+ O '77
Day care with a difference; Missoula, Montana's Summer Enrichment Program. L. A. Heywood. il Parks & Rec 12:16-19 Jl '77
See also
Day care centers

Development

See Children—Growth and development

Diseases

Adult diseases children can get. M. L. Schildkraut. Good H 185:252 O '77
See also
Acrodermatitis enteropathica
Allergy
Cancer in children
Heart—Abnormalities and deformities
Hypertension
Prader-Willi syndrome
Reye's syndrome

Preventive inoculation

For childhood diseases: an immunization drive. il U.S. News 82:82 Ap 18 '77
Immunizing our children: the job of every parent. J. A. Califano. il por Parents Mag 52:66+ N '77
Protect your child against these seven deadly diseases. A. Rosenblum. Good H 184:230 My '77
Real victims of the swine-flu fiasco; apathy toward vaccinations against childhood diseases. A. T. Brett. il U.S. News 82:73 Ja 24 '77

Education

See Education of children

Employment

What job for you? age eligibility provisions of the Fair Labor Standards Act. il Sr Schol 110:29 S 22 '77

Food

See Children—Nutrition

Growth and development

Birth order and intellectual development: the confluence model in the light of cross-cultural evidence. D. J. Davis and others. bibl il Science 196:1470-2 Je 24 '77
Children needn't fear bugs and other creepy crawlers. I. Ross. House B 119:163+ O '77
Easing a baby's way into the world; Danielle Rapoport's follow-up study on children delivered by the Leboyer method. J. Horn. il Psychol Today 10:34 Mr '77
Experts/critics discuss children's development. il SLJ 23:25 F '77
From piecemeal to configurational representation of faces. S. Carey and R. Diamond. bibl il Science 195:312-14 Ja 21 '77
How democratic should a family be? B. Spock. Redbook 150:24+ D '77
How to drive your child sane. A. Ginott. il Ladies Home J 94:48+ Ag '77
Learning to live in the real world. M. S. Haram. il por Redbook 149:40+ O '77
Leboyer's babies. R. J. Trotter. il Sci N 111:59 Ja 22 '77
Moral development: implications for pedagogy. R. H. Hersh and D. P. Paolito. Educ Digest 42:13-16 Ja '77
Sex roles and how children learn them. R. T. Barnhouse. il New Cath World 220:280-3 N '77
Trauma of separation: school, divorce, hospital, death. J. Wang. bibl Harp Baz 110:88+ Jl '77
Unspoiling the spoiled child; immature character development. C. R. Partridge. il Todays Educ 66:67-9 S '77
What young children need most in changing society; interview. D. Elkind. il Parents Mag 52:40-1+ Jl '77
Will competitive sports hurt your child? mental and physical demands. L. Mifflin. Harp Baz 110:90+ My '77
See also
Child psychology
Infants—Growth and development
Prader-Willi syndrome

Hairdressing

See Hairdressing

Hospital care

Break for parents of hospitalized children; programs by Chicago's Children's Memorial Hospital and Children's Hospital of Philadelphia. E. J. Pascoe. McCalls 104:83 Je '77
Green-thumb cure for hospital fears; plant therapy. J. Horn. Psychol Today 11:99 Jl '77
Kids with cancer. M. Clark and others. il Newsweek 90:57-9 Ag 15 '77
One-day hospital stay for children. A. M. Almond. Parents Mag 53:41+ Ja '78
$73,000 abandoned babies; boarder babies in New York City hospitals. S. Jacoby. il N Y Times Mag p55-61 Mr 6 '77
Taking the fear out of hospitals. H. Bottel. il Good H 184:232+ Je '77
See also
Children—Surgery
Infants, Newborn—Hospital care

Hospitals

Casebook of the medical detective; work of H. Friedman of Philadelphia's Children's Hospital in attempting to diagnose Legionnaire's disease (cont) D. Russell. il Fam Health 9:40-1+ Ja '77
Hospital that has patience for its patients: a look at Children's Hospital, in Washington, D.C. J. Viorst. il Redbook 148:48+ F '77

Humor

See Humor

Institutional care

See also
Children—Hospital care
Foster home care

Law

See also
Adoption
Children—Civil rights
Children—Employment
Juvenile courts
Juvenile delinquency
Parent and child (law)

Legal aid

See Legal aid

Management and training

Africa's proverbial wit and wisdom; proverbs as guides to raising children. Tanoé-Aka and others. il UNESCO Courier 30:22-5 My '77
Bazaar's guide for every working mother; symposium. Harp Baz 110:176-9+ O '77
Can you work and be a good mother? L. Salk. Harp Baz 110:88-9+ Ag '77

CHILDREN—Management and training—*Continued*
Coping with behavior problems:
Importance of bedtime rituals. R. Galdston. Parents Mag 52:46 Jl '77
One-parent household. R. Galdston. Parents Mag 52:97 O '77
Discipline do's and dont's. E. Leshan. Parents Mag 52:26+ O '77
Do you have a spoiled child? interview. T. B. Brazelton. Harp Baz 110:89+ Jl '77
How I stopped nagging and started teaching my children to behave; excerpt from Positive parenthood. P. S. Graubard. McCalls 104: 90+ My '77
How loving parents can discipline their child. B. Spock. il Redbook 149:22+ Je '77
How to behave when your kids don't: the confessions of a mean mommy. J. Viorst. il Redbook 149:48+ S '77
I am a second-generation lesbian; excerpt from We are everywhere: a celebration of lavender culture. S. Malcolm. Ms 6:13-16 O '77
I mean now the simplest method of raising kids. P. Wood and B. Schwartz. pors Psychol Today 11:113-14+ Jl '77
Preschool push to independence. S. Auerbach. il por Parents Mag 52:33+ D '77
Raising boys who know how to love. D. Singer and J. L. Singer. il pors Parents Mag 52:32+ D '77
Raising your boys to be good men. J. Viorst. il Redbook 149:66+ Je '77
Teaching your child to be responsible. B. Spock. il Redbook 149:42+ My '77
These kids learn farming means business. il Suc Farm 75:no4 8 Mr '77
To spank or not to spank? survey on raising children. H. Burton. il Parents Mag 52:42-3+ Ag '77
What do the experts know about your child? E. LeShan. il Parents Mag 52:40-1+ Je '77
What your one-year-old really needs from you. B. Spock. il Redbook 148:22+ Mr '77
When should you be strict? B. Spock. il Redbook 149:22+ O '77
Will the real Jane Fonda please stand up; interview, ed by J. Atlas. J. Fonda. il pors Parents Mag 52:34-5+ D '77
See also
Child abuse
Child psychology
Childrens allowances
Childrens chores
Corporal punishment
Moral education
Parent-child relationship
Parent education

Anecdotes, facetiae, satire, etc.

French correction. L. Elliott. Read Digest 111: 117-20 Ag '77

Bibliography

Books for parents. P. Pinson. See occasional issues of Parents' magazine

Medical care

Health of our children; proposed Child Health Assessment Act; address, September 9, 1977. J. A. Califano. Vital Speeches 44:19-21 O 15 '77
See also
Children—Medical care

Names

See Names, Personal

Nutrition

Did your mother make you fat? Ebony 32:59-60+ My '77
Diet and disease: breaking the connection. M. Winick. Parents Mag 52:46+ Mr '77
See also
School lunches

Only child problem

Being an only child is terrific! M. Cohen. por Seventeen 36:82 F '77

Photographs

Family of children; excerpts. Read Digest 111: 155-62 O '77
Kids without cliché. Mod Phot 41:86-91 F '77
See also
Photography of children

Psychology

See Child psychology

Recreation

Homemade summer fun. J. M. Stewart. il Bet Hom & Gard 55:74+ Je '77
See also
Christmas projects
Play

Religious life

Christmas is coming. M. L. Dodds. Chr Today 22:17-18 N 18 '77
See also
Catholic Church—Education
Church work with children
Religious education

Sayings

Heard what your grandchildren are saying about you? comp by R. Turner. il Ret Liv 16:29+ D '76

Sexual behavior

When kids explore sex; excerpt from Sex education for today's child. A. S. Uslander and others. il Parents Mag 52:44-5+ Ag '77

Social and economic status

See also
Socially handicapped children

Suicide

See Suicide

Surgery

Twin miracles; open-heart surgery for D'Alessio twins. E. Keiffer. il Good H 186:75+ Ja '78

Psychological aspects

Taking the scare out of childhood surgery. E. Lauter; A. M. Almond. il Parents Mag 53: 40-1+ Ja '78

Training

See Children—Management and training

Travel

See also
Travel with children

Vision

See Vision

Africa

Africa's proverbial wit and wisdom; proverbs as guides to raising children. Tanoé-Aka and others. il UNESCO Courier 30:22-5 My '77

China

See also
Child welfare—China

Great Britain

Enchanted childhood; excerpt from An autobiography. A. Christie. il Ladies Home J 94: 118-19+ O '77

Northern Ireland

Child's play in Northern Ireland. M. R. Duncan. il Parks & Rec 12:27-30 Ag '77

United States

All our children; report of the Carnegie Council on Children. Time 110:118 S 19 '77
Almost half of all children have mothers in the labor force. A. S. Grossman. bibl il M Labor R 100:41-4 Je '77
Family ecology; studies by J. F. Kett and the Carnegie Council on Children. J. W. Donohue. America 137:456-9 D 24 '77
Family: it is changing, not breaking up; study by the Carnegie Council on Children. J. Gaylin. Psychol Today 11:36+ O '77
Montana community honors young children. il SLJ 24:13 S '77
See also
Child welfare—United States

CHILDREN, Adopted
Adoption; work of B. Tizard. D. Cohen. Psychol Today 11:128+ N '77
After 18 years of searching: we're a family again! E. P. Frank. il pors Good H 185:111+ O '77
Greatest gift; a true story about Lorene and Julian Vela. N. Rodgers and E. Lynch. il Good H 185:79-82+ D '77
IQ, culture and adopted children; findings of S. Scarr. Sci N 112:150 S 3 '77
My search for my roots. B. J. Lifton. Seventeen 36:132-3+ Mr '77
Quintana. J. G. Dunne. Esquire 87:8+ Je '77
Search for a stranger. G. S. Livingston. Read Digest 110:85-9 Je '77
What it's like for singles who adopt: four family stories; interviews, ed by G. Kopecky. il Ms 5:45-8+ Je '77
When to tell adopted children: another view; opinions of Anne M. Braff. M. R. Skrocki. McCalls 105:45 Ja '78
Why adoptees search for their parents. B. J. Lifton. il Seventeen 36:145 O '77

CHILDREN, Adoption of. See Adoption

CHILDREN, Deaf. See Deaf

CHILDREN, Delinquent. See Juvenile delinquency

CHILDREN, Exceptional
See also
Children, Gifted
Children, Handicapped
Learning disabilities
Problem children
Slow learning children
Special classes and special schools

CHILDREN, Gifted
Edith Project; raising a child to be a genius. J. McClintock. Harpers 254:21-4 Mr '77
What if your child is gifted. D. A. Sisk. bibl Am Educ 13:23-6 O '77

CHILDREN, Gifted—*Continued*

Education

Gifted, talented child; programs in Texas to help the top 5 percent. M. Wightman. Educ Digest 43:51-3 S '77
In search of the potentially gifted: suggestions for the school administrator. A. D. Gresson and D. G. Carter. bibl Clearing H 50:369-71 Ap '77
Some operational problems in an on-going gifted program. C. W. Humes, 2d. Clearing H 51:163-5 D '77
Special treatment for the gifted; program for gifted and talented children of the Riverside Center for the Arts, Harrisburg, Pa. C. B. Fowler. il Hi Fi 27:MA14-15 Ap '77
Unfavored gifted few. G. I. Maeroff. il N Y Times Mag p 30-2+ Ag 21 '77
See also
United States—Education, Office of—Gifted and Talented, Office for the

CHILDREN, Handicapped
See also
Brain damaged children
Camps for the handicapped
Cerebral palsied children
Hyperactive children
Libraries—Services to the handicapped
Mentally handicapped children
Physical education for the handicapped
School libraries—Services to the handicapped
Socially handicapped children

Education

D-day for the disabled; Education for All Handicapped Children Act. il Time 109:44 My 30 '77
Directed creativity; art project for deaf and brain damaged children. J. W. Bell. il Sch Arts 76:78-9 F '77
From the echoes of Chautauqua; Creative Education Program and the Children's Experimental Workshop at Glen Echo Park in Maryland. M. Travaglini. il Am Educ 13:17-21 My '77
IEP and nonacademic services. Am Educ 13:23-5 N '77
IEP and personnel preparation. Am Educ 13:6-8 O '77
Implementing the IEP concept. Am Educ 13:6-8 Ag '77
Integrating the handicapped; NEA resolution 77-33: education for all handicapped children. J. Ryor. Todays Educ 66:24-6 S '77
Lab classroom: breaking the communication barrier; Horace Mann School. E. Walsh. il Science 196:1425 Je 24 '77
Mediacentric; adaptation of address, April 29, 1977. B. Fast. Wilson Lib Bull 52:133-5 O '77
More arts for the handicapped; programs for children. il Hi Fi 27:MA9-11 Je '77
New Day for the handicapped; mainstreaming. il Time 110:109 S 19 '77
PL 94-142 and teachers. Todays Educ 66:57 N '77
PL 94-142—getting the money to make it work. E. Brooke. Todays Educ 66:50-2 N '77
Washington scene. B. Kravetz. Parks & Rec 12:18 N '77
What the laws and regulations require. Todays Educ 66:54-6 N '77
See also
Cerebral palsied children—Education
Deaf—Education

CHILDREN, Hyperactive. See Hyperactive children
CHILDREN, Mentally handicapped. See Mentally handicapped children
CHILDREN, Mentally ill. See Mentally ill children
CHILDREN, Mentally superior. See Children, Gifted
CHILDREN, Missing. See Missing persons
CHILDREN, Pampering of. See Children—Management and training
CHILDREN, Photography of. See Photography of children
CHILDREN, Retarded. See Mentally handicapped children
CHILDREN, Sick. See Sick children
CHILDREN, Spoiling of. See Children—Management and training
CHILDREN and adults. See Child-adult relationship

CHILDREN and animals
Children needn't fear bugs and other creepy crawlers. I. Ross. House B 119:163+ O '77
Humane education: a forgotten mandate. P. J. Quinn. Educ Digest 43:60-1 S '77
Pets and children. R. Caras. il Ladies Home J 94:198 O '77
Wild creatures and your children. M. W. Fox. McCalls 104:106+ Jl '77
Your child can train his dog. M. S. Pierce. il Parents Mag 52:56-7 Jl '77

CHILDREN and art. See Art and children

CHILDREN and Christmas
Christmas in Mr Rogers' neighborhood; interview, ed by B. White. F. Rogers. por Sat Eve Post 249:24+ D '77
How I found the real Santa Claus. I. Hughes. il Good H 185:60+ D '77
Man who played Santa Claus. J. P. Hayes. il Good H 185:118-19+ D '77
Merry Christmas in your house; merry chaos in mine. P. Mackintosh. il por Redbook 150:80+ D '77
Sharing Christmas with your children. L. Salk. Harp Baz 111:133+ D '77
Yes, there is a Santa Claus. M. I. Levine and J. H. Seligmann. Harp Baz 111:132+ D '77

CHILDREN and death
Go out in joy; condensation. N. L. Herrmann. il Read Digest 110:249-60+ Ap '77
More comfortable death—home care for the dying child. J. Gaylin. Psychol Today 11:30+ Jl '77
When children meet death. J. Koch. bibl il por Psychol Today 11:64-6+ Ag '77
When Wendy's brother died. M. Keyser. Read Digest 111:95-7 Jl '77

CHILDREN and extrasensory perception. See Extrasensory perception
CHILDREN and grandparents. See Grandparents
CHILDREN and insects. See Children and animals

CHILDREN and libraries
See also
Libraries—Services to children

CHILDREN and music. See Music and children
CHILDREN and opera. See Music and children
CHILDREN and parents. See Parent-child relationship
CHILDREN and pets. See Children and animals
CHILDREN and religion. See Children—Religious life
CHILDREN and television. See Television and children

CHILDREN as actors and actresses
Little Orphan Annie lives! C. M. Dobrish. il pors Parents Mag 52:40-1+ Ag '77
New faces on the big screen; interviews, ed by E. Miller. S. Swift; M. Hemingway. pors Seventeen 36:122-3 Mr '77
Starring children; Broadway's theater. J. Maxey. il N Y Times Mag p34-9+ Ag 21 '77
Starring mothers; mothers of cast members of Annie. A. Quindlen. il N Y Times Mag p50-1+ Ag 21 '77
Tatum O'Neal and Jodie Foster: their combined age is 27—what is Hollywood trying to tell us? M. Haskell. il pors Ms 5:49-51 Ap '77

CHILDREN as musicians
Oooowee, man, that little girl can play! il pors Ebony 32:130-2+ Ap '77

CHILDREN as photographers
Kids and kameras (cont) D. Cyr. il por Pop Phot 80:58+ Mr; 38+ Je; 81:51+ Ag; 56+ O '77
Table top photography rediscovered. K. R. Morrison. il Sch Arts 76:28-9 Je '77

CHILDREN as witnesses. See Witnesses

CHILDREN in boating
First-time cruising with the very young. L. Hallenbeck. Yachting 142:20 D '77
Long-distance cruising with children: a second opinion. D. Koontz. il Yachting 142:28+ N '77
Rough log. T. Gibbs. Yachting 141:118 My '77

CHILDREN in motion pictures
From 400 blows to Small change. G. Mast. New Repub 176:23-5 Ap 2 '77
What are they doing to our children? E. P. Frank. il Good H 185:99+ Ag '77

CHILDREN of alcoholics
My father played for me. R. Hohler. il Read Digest 111:156-9 D '77

CHILDREN of celebrities
Children of the stars. il Ebony 33:82-4+ N '77

CHILDREN of divorced parents
Children: sometimes poker chips. M. Goodwin. N Y Times Mag p 15 My 22 '77
Effects of divorce upon school children. R. Theus. bibl Clearing H 50:364-5 Ap '77
How can mom and dad do this to me? A. Sheedy. il Seventeen 36:242-3+ Ag '77
How divorced parents can help their children; views of E. Atkin and E. Rubin. B. Spock. il Redbook 149:22+ Jl '77

CHILDREN of God (movement)
Baiting the hook. J. M. Hopkins. Chr Today 22:40-1 D 30 '77
Children of God; disciples of deception; interviews, ed by J. M. Hopkins. D. Jacks and J. Wasson. il Chr Today 21:18-23 F 18 '77
Tracking the Children of God. il pors Time 110:48 Ag 22 '77

CHILDREN of public officers
Where officials' kids go to school—few follow Amy's example. il U.S. News 82:34 Ja 24 '77

CHILDRENS add-on bicycle seats. See Bicycles—Equipment

CHILDRENS allowances
How to teach your youngsters the value of a dollar. M. Daly. il Bet Hom & Gard 54:10+ Ag '76

Anecdotes, facetiae, satire, etc.

How many dimes make a million dollars? J. Viorst. Read Digest 111:166-8 N '77

CHILDRENS amusements. See Children—Recreation

CHILDRENS art
Children's art into stitchery pillows. il Sunset 159:120 D '77
Is your child gifted? interviews, ed by C. Leon. E. Giobbi and R. Kellogg. House & Gard 149:40 Ap '77
Sandpaper art is easy but you and your oven must help. il Sunset 158:112 Je '77
Showcase 77: presentation of student art; special issue. Sch Arts 76:10-37+ My '77
Student art. See issues of School arts

Exhibitions

Art in Westbrook. D. F. Axelsen. il Sch Arts 76:34 Je '77
Carnival of two centuries; thirty-third Annual Children's Art Exhibition T. Gezari. il Sch Arts 76:52-3 Mr '77
Emphasis: exhibit and display techniques. V. G. Timmons. Sch Arts 76:4 Je '77

CHILDRENS beds. See Beds
CHILDRENS book exhibits. See Book exhibits
CHILDRENS book fairs. See Book fairs
CHILDREN'S Book Store, Toronto. See Booksellers and bookselling—Canada
CHILDRENS books. See Childrens literature
CHILDRENS bookstores. See Booksellers and bookselling—Childrens literature

CHILDRENS chores
How to get your child to help at home. E. Berman. Harp Baz 110:179+ O '77
I hereby resign as keeper of this house. . . love, mom; family housekeeping. S. Roberts. il por Ms 5:56-7 My '77

Anecdotes, facetiae, satire, etc.

How many dimes make a million dollars? J. Viorst. Read Digest 111:166-8 N '77

CHILDRENS clothes. See Clothing and dress—Children
CHILDRENS clothing industry. See Clothing industry
CHILDRENS eating habits. See Food habits
CHILDRENS emotional problems. See Emotional problems of children

CHILDRENS exhibitions
See also
Childrens art—Exhibitions

CHILDREN'S express (periodical) See Childrens periodicals (by children)
CHILDRENS fairs. See Fairs

CHILDRENS fantasies
Yes, there is a Santa Claus. M. I. Levine and J. H. Seligmann. Harp Baz 111:132+ D '77

CHILDRENS fishing. See Fishing
CHILDRENS furniture. See Furniture, Childrens
CHILDRENS games. See Games

CHILDRENS gardens
Garden primer for pre-schoolers. E. Frankenberger. Horticulture 55:48-9 N '77

CHILDRENS hats. See Hats
CHILDREN'S Hospital, Philadelphia. See Children—Hospitals
CHILDREN'S Hospital National Medical Center, Washington, D.C. See Children—Hospitals
CHILDRENS humor. See Humor
CHILDRENS letters (by children) See Letters by children

CHILDRENS librarians
Librarianship—a business or a profession? E. L. Heins. Horn Bk 53:398-9 Ag '77

CHILDRENS lies. See Lying

CHILDRENS literature
Adolescent image in American books for children. M. Lystad. Educ Digest 43:50-2 N '77
Identifying high interest/low reading level books. B. S. Bates. bibl il SLJ 24:19-21 N '77
Is it true boys have more fun? What every parent should know about children's books. S. Scofield. Redbook 149:214+ My '77
PW interviews; ed by M. Freeman. R. Duvoisin and L. Fatio. il pors Pub W 211:54-5 F 28 '77
PW interviews; ed by J. F. Mercier. J. Karl. por Pub W 212:66-7 Jl 18 '77
See also
Art literature
Authors—Childrens literature
Booksellers and bookselling—Childrens literature
Childrens periodicals
Childrens poetry
Childrens stories
Cookbooks for children
Council on Interracial Books for Children
Fairy tales
Historical literature
Libraries—Childrens collections
Nature literature
Picture books for children
Publishers and publishing—Childrens literature
Scientific literature for children
Sex education literature
Story telling

Advertising

See Books—Advertising

Authorship

Any writer who follows anyone else's guidelines ought to be in advertising. N. Hentoff. por SLJ 24:27-9 N '77
Mildred D. Taylor. P. J. Fogelman. por Horn Bk 53:410-14 Ag '77
Newbery Award acceptance; address June 18, 1977. M. D. Taylor. Horn Bk 53:401-9 Ag '77
Notes on the children's book trade. J. Goldthwaite; discussion. SLJ 23:7 F '77; Harpers 254:6-7 Mr '77
Writing for children; excerpts from address. R. Godden. Writer 90:18-19 Jl '77
See also
Authors—Childrens literature

Awards, prizes, etc.

See also
Caldecott Medal
Newbery Medal
Scientific literature for children—Awards, prizes, etc.

Anecdotes, facetiae, satire, etc.

Billy Budd Button & Huckleberry Finn Pin Awards. L. N. Gerhardt. SLJ 23:42-3 Ap '77

Bibliography

Best books for Spring 1977; ed by L. N. Gerhardt and others. il SLJ 23:35-7 My '77
Best books 1977; ed by L. N. Gerhardt and others. il SLJ 24:30-3 D '77
Book review; ed by L. N. Gerhardt and others. See issues of School library journal
Booklist (title varies) E. L. Heins and others. See issues of Horn book magazine
Books for boys and girls. H. B. Andrejevic. See issues of Parents' magazine & better homemaking
Brigitte Weeks on children's books. B. Weeks. New Repub 177:26+ D 3 '77
CSD selects Notable Books. SLJ 23:94-5 Mr '77
Cheer up to here: Christmas books '77. P. D. Pollack. il SLJ 24:86-8 O '77
Children's books: best of the season (cont) W. Cole. il Sat R 4:31-3 My 28; 5:40-2 N 26 '77
Children's books for the trail; Selected list of children's books. E. M. Graves. il Commonweal 104:726-35 N 11 '77
Children's books: the best of the season (cont) W. Cole. il Sat R 4:31-3 My 28 '77
Children's fall books. Pub W 212:88-115 Jl 18 '77
Children's spring books. il Pub W 211:71-94 F 28 '77
Cornucopia of children's books. S. Kanfer. il Time 110:66-7+ N 21 '77
Diamonds in the kiddie litter. C. Michener. il Newsweek 90:81-2+ D 19 '77
For Spanish readers. Y. E. Rivas. Horn Bk 53: 190-2, 686-8 Ap, D '77
For very young dancers: a quickstep through recent books. A. Kellman. il SLJ 24:34-5 D '77
Kids' summer dozen. M. Sheils and F. V. Boyd. il Newsweek 90:92+ Jl 18 '77
Metrics: do the books measure up? S. Weir. il por SLJ 24:30-1 N '77
New fall books for children; religious books. Pub W 212:99-102 S 26 '77
PW forecasts; ed by B. A. Bannon. See issues of Publishers weekly
Sugar and spice and mannerly mice. America 137:404-8 D 3 '77

Book fairs

See Book fairs

Book reviewers and reviewing

See Book reviewers and reviewing

Book reviews

See Book reviews

Book selection

See Book selection

Collectors and collecting

Through the looking glass: notes on an antiquarian children's bookshop; Justin G. Schiller, Ltd. J. G. Schiller and R. M. Wapner. il Horn Bk 53:140-6 Ap '77

Conferences

Loughborough 1978. E. L. Heins. Horn Bk 53: 631 D '77

Anecdotes, facetiae, satire, etc.

Conference notes from all over. J. Donovan. il SLJ 24:22-6 N '77

Exhibitions

See Book exhibits

History and criticism

Cracking open the geode: the fiction of Paula Fox. A. Bach. il Horn Bk 53:514-21 O '77
How you play the game: the novels of John R. Tunis. R. Shereikis. il Horn Bk 53:642-8 D '77

CHILDRENS literature—History and criticism *—Continued*
Novels that boys of a century ago couldn't put down; Horatio Alger books. B. Blackbeard. il por Smithsonian 8:122-4+ bibl(p 162) N '77
Second look:
Clever Bill. S. G. Lanes. il Horn Bk 53:694-6 D '77
Gilgamesh: man's first story. B. F. Harrison. il Horn Bk 53:74-6 F '77
Glass slipper. S. B. Andrews. Horn Bk 53: 193-4 Ap '77
Namesake. S. Long. Horn Bk 53:477-8 Ag '77
Peter Rabbit redux. M. P. Hearn. il Horn Bk 53:563-6 O '77
Yearling. C. McDonnell. Horn Bk 53:344-5 Je '77

Illustration

See Illustration

Study and teaching

Children's literature in the junior high? Of course. D. Mitchell. il Engl J 66:62-4 Ap '77

Technique

Art of the word: significance in stories for young people. P. Neumeyer. bibl Engl J 66:27-30 My '77
Clues to the juvenile mystery. J. L. Nixon. Writer 90:23-6 F '77

Themes

Confronting the ovens: the Holocaust and juvenile fiction. E. A. Kimmel. Horn Bk 53:84-91 F '77
Leavening for the youth culture; theme of old age and grandparents. M. Benne. bibl il por Wilson Lib Bull 52:312-18 D '77
See also
Chinese in literature

Great Britain

Letter from England. A. Chambers. See issues of Horn book magazine

Spain

Heartfelt plea: note on books for children and adolescents from Spain. I. Schon. il Engl J 66: 49-52 Mr '77

CHILDRENS literature, Influence of
Children's literature & mass media. A. P. Nilsen. il por SLJ 23:106-9 Mr '77

CHILDRENS museums
New theaters for learning. il Time 110:56 Jl 25 '77

CHILDRENS parties
Easy-on-you parties for children. Bet Hom & Gard 55:198 N '77

CHILDRENS periodicals
Twenty years of Harper's young people. M. J. Roggenbuck. Horn Bk 53:29-35 F '77

CHILDRENS periodicals (by children)
Ralph Nader reports: child power; Children's express. R. Nader. Ladies Home J 94:72+ N '77

CHILDRENS pets. See Pets

CHILDRENS phonograph records. See Phonograph records—Childrens records

CHILDRENS plays
See also
Christmas plays

Texts

Middle and lower grades. See issues of Plays

CHILDRENS poetry

Authorship

Writing poetry for children. M. C. Livingston. Writer 90:25-8 Je '77

Collections

See Anthologies

CHILDRENS reading
Businesses join drive to aid youth in two ways; reading programs to raise money for multiple sclerosis research. V. Louviere. il Nations Bus 65:66 Ja '77
First R; Reading Is Fundamental. Pub W 211:30-1 Je 13 '77
In (reverent, loving, thankful) praise of books! J. Mills. il Read Digest 111:150-2 O '77
OE allocates funds to Right to Read/RIF; Reading is fundamental. SLJ 23:24 F '77
Talking about reading; back to basics? A. Chambers. Horn Bk 53:567-74, 700-8 O-D '77
To own a book; Inexpensive Book Distribution Program of Reading Is Fundamental, Inc. S. Zuckerman. il Am Educ 13:13-16 N '77
Who reads the Newbery winners? Children's literary needs and reading tastes. J. Shackford. bibl il por SLJ 23:101-5 Mr '77
See also
Childrens literature
Comics (books, strips, etc)
MS Read-a-thon (reading program)

Projects

101 ways to react to books. N. A. Mavrogenes. Engl J 66:64-6 My '77

CHILDRENS rights. See Children—Civil rights

CHILDRENS rooms
Dorm in the basement. il Mech Illus 73:88+ O '77
Rollaway room. B. Niles. il Am Home 80:70 N '77
Two rooms from one. H. Wicks. il Pop Mech 148:96-99+ S '77
See also
Nurseries

CHILDRENS safety seats. See Automobiles—Safety devices and measures

CHILDREN'S Services Division, American Library Association. See American Library Association—Children's Services Division

CHILDRENS sleepwear industry. See Clothing industry

CHILDRENS sports. See Sports for children

CHILDRENS stories
See name of author for full entry
Amazing bone. W. Steig
Fir tree. H. C. Andersen
Girl with the incredible feeling. E. Swados
Half a kingdom. A. McGovern
My brother Steven is retarded. H. L. Sobol
My mother the mail carrier. I. Maury
No jobs for mom. A. Goldwasser
One father, two fathers. J. L. Nixon
Wasp in a wig. L. Carroll
When Judy died. R. I. Lu San
Will it be okay? E. Parsons

CHILDRENS sweaters. See Sweaters

CHILDRENS theater. See Theater, Childrens

CHILDRENS Theatre Company. See Theater, Childrens

CHILDRENS villages
See also
Boys Town, Neb.

CHILE
See also
Americans in Chile
Astronomical observatories—Chile
Banks and banking—Chile
Civil rights—Chile
Copper mines and mining—Chile
Festivals—Chile
Finance—Chile
Intelligence service—Chile
Investments, American—Chile
Investments, Foreign—Chile
Political prisoners—Chile
Santiago
Secret service—Chile
Theater—Chile
Trade unions—Chile

Economic conditions

Once-sick economy grows a lot healthier. il Bus W 64+ Jl 25 '77

Foreign relations

United States

See United States—Foreign relations—Chile

Politics and government

Four years after the fall. T. Szulc. New Repub 177:14-16 S 10 '77
In my own time. C. L. Mee, Jr. por Horizon 19:94-5 Ja '77
Juntas of Chile and Argentina: studies in government by terror. N. E. Roman. por Sat R 4:12+ Ap 2 '77
See also
Referendum—Chile

CHILE peppers. See Peppers

CHILEAN flamingos. See Flamingos

CHILI con carne. See Cookery, Mexican

CHILI peppers. See Peppers

CHILINGIRIAN String Quartet. See String quartets

CHILKOOT Pass climbs. See Mountaineering

CHILOPSIS. See Willow

CHILTON Corporation. See Credit bureaus

CHIMNEY cleaning
Dirty jobs that require more clean sweeps. P. Ryan. Smithsonian 8:176 N '77
Remodeling notebook. J. H. Ingersoll. il House B 119:77 D '77

CHIMNEY sweeps. See Chimney cleaning

CHIMPANZEES
Pursuit of reason. H. T. P. Hayes. il pors N Y Times Mag p21-3+ Je 12 '77; Reply. B. DeMott. Atlantic 240:86+ S '77
Self-awareness: humans are not alone. il Sci N 111:340 My 28 '77

CH'IN Shih-huang-ti, Emperor of China, 259-210 B.C.

Tomb

Clay soldiers: the army of Emperor Ch'in; with editorial comment. A. Topping. il Horizon 19:2, 4-13 Ja '77

CHIN, Frank
Death of a wireman. il por Time 109:19 F 21 '77 •

CHIN, Jane H. and Goldstein, D. B.
Drug tolerance in biomembranes: a spin label study of the effects of ethanol. bibl il Science 196:684-5 My 6 '77

CHIN, Ruth
Yukon Territory. il map Travel 148:56-9+ Jl '77

CHINA
China: unraveling the new mysteries. F. Butterfield and W. Safire. il pors N Y Times Mag p32-4+ Je 19 '77
China's development efforts and quest for the future. R. Buultjens. bibl il map Focus 27:1-8 Mr '77
People's Republic of China, 1977; symposium. bibl il map Cur Hist 73:49-85+ S '77
Where China is headed; interview. G. Bush. il pors U.S. News 83:33-4 N 14 '77
See also
Astronomy—China
Ballet—China
Birth control—China
Censorship—China
Child welfare—China
Christmas—China
Colleges and universities—China
Communism—China
Earthquakes—China
Education—China
Energy policy—China
Lhasa, Tibet
Linhsien
Loans, Bank—China
Power resources—China
Rationing, Consumer—China
Research—China
Restaurants—China
Science—China
Science and state—China
Secret service—China
Space research—China
Taiwan
Visitors, Foreign—China
Women—China
Wuhsien

Air Force

Inside the Air Force; Chinese Commander Fan Yuan-yen's defection to Taiwan. M. Liu. il por Newsweek 90:50 Jl 25 '77

Antiquities

See also
Ch'in Shih-huang-ti—Tomb
Temples—China
Tombs—China

Armed Forces

China's great wall: the People's Liberation Army. H. W. Nelsen. bibl Cur Hist 73:59-62+ S '77

Bibliography

Book reviews. Cur Hist 73:84-5 S '77

Civilization

China's ancient mariners. S. Steiner. il Natur Hist 86:48-63 bibl(p 110) D '77

Commerce

United States

See United States—Commerce—China

Defenses

China's great wall: the People's Liberation Army. H. W. Nelsen. bibl Cur Hist 73:59-62+ S '77

Description and travel

China without gee whiz; Canadian R. H. Munro's journalistic coverage. il por Time 110:99 N 7 '77
Reporter at large. O. Schell. New Yorker 53:40-2+ Mr 7; 74+ Mr 14 '77

Economic conditions

China's economy: big decisions ahead. U.S. News 83:17 S 5 '77

Economic policy

Chinese economy after the Gang of Four. J. S. Prybyla. bibl Cur Hist 73:68-72+ S '77

Foreign relations

Coexistence after Mao. O. E. Clubb. Progressive 41:31-3 F '77
Foreign policy of the People's Republic. D. W. Klein. Cur Hist 73:54-8+ S '77

Africa

China's role in Africa. G. T. Yu. bibl f Ann Am Acad 432:96-109 Jl '77

Russia

See Russia—Foreign relations—China

United States

See United States—Foreign relations—China

History

See also
China—Civilization

1900-

Oral history; interview. W. Koo. il New Yorker 53:32-5 Ap 18 '77
Rise and fall of Mao's Empress. il pors Time 109:42-5 Mr 21 '77

Intellectual life

China's war on the mind; excerpt from Chinese shadows. P. Ryckmans. il Sat R 4:14-16+ Je 25 '77
Flower show. il Time 110:56 D 12 '77
No to Maoism. il Time 110:54 S 19 '77
Thought control in Mao's interview with Chinese intellectual. ed by W. Berkson. Nat R 29:1173-7+ O 14 '77

Kings and rulers

See also
Ch'in Shih-huang-ti

Moral conditions

Back door; illicitly obtained goods and services. Time 111:24 Ja 9 '78
S-e-x. H. Jensen and S. Liu. il Newsweek 91:48-9 Ja 16 '78

Nationalism

Ethnic relations in China. J. T. Dreyer. bibl f Ann Am Acad 433:100-11 S '77

Politics and government

China after Mao. O. E. Clubb. bibl Cur Hist 73:49-53+ S '77
China ends an era. A. Deming and others. il Newsweek 90:32-3+ Ag 29 '77
Comeback for Teng? K. Willenson and others. por Newsweek 89:51 Ja 24 '77
Comeback of a capitalist roader; Teng Hsiao-ping. il por Time 109:31-2 Ja 24 '77
Death wish; denouncement of Chuang Tse-tung. il por Time 110:47 N 21 '77
Eternal China, eternal conspiracies. R. Elegant. il map Nat R 29:1167+ O 14 '77
Legacy of the Gang of Four. Time 110:46 N 7 '77
Reading Chinese tea leaves. S. E. Crane. Commonweal 104:393-7 Je 24 '77
Second comeback for Comrade Teng. il pors Time 110:23-4 Ag 1 '77
Teng: China's real boss. M. Smith. il por Newsweek 90:43-4 S 12 '77
Thought control in Mao's China; interview with Chinese intellectual. ed by W. Berkson. Nat R 29:1173-7+ O 14 '77
Was Chou murdered? F. Willey and others. il por Newsweek 89:49 F 7 '77
Welcome home; T. Hsiao-ping. il por Newsweek 90:34 Ag 1 '77
Wide of the mark. C. Johnson. New Repub 177:12-14 N 26 '77
See also
Communism—China

Anecdotes, facetiae, satire, etc.

News from the China-watchers. M. W. Moseley, Jr. New Yorker 52:29 Ja 17 '77

Religious institutions and affairs

Where have all the churches gone? J. B. Wang. Chr Today 22:12-13 N 18 '77
See also
Catholic Church in China
Christians in China

Social conditions

China behind the guided tour. E. N. Luttwak. Read Digest 110:211-14+ Ap '77
Mao's funeral. B. J. Wattenberg. Harpers 254:31-3 F '77
Seeing China plain. E. N. Luttwak; discussion. Commentary 63:4+ Mr '77
See also
Communism—China
Women—China

Social life and customs

Chinese way of eating A. Y. Dessaint. il Natur Hist 86:94-5+ Ag '77
Roots in China, a first encounter. L. Wong. il por Smithsonian 8:116-20 bibl(p 148) Ap '77

Social policy

Ethnic relations in China. J. T. Dreyer. bibl f Ann Am Acad 433:100-11 S '77

CHINA (People's Republic) See China

CHINA (porcelain) See Pottery

CHINA dolls. See Dolls

CHINA trade art. See Art objects, Chinese

CHINA trade porcelain. See Pottery, Chinese

CHINA-United States cooperative science program. See Science—International aspects

CHINATOWN, New York City. See New York (city)—Chinatown

CHINATOWN, San Francisco. See San Francisco—Chinatown

CHINESE AMERICANS
See also
New York (city)—Chinatown
San Francisco—Chinatown

CHINESE art. See Art, Chinese
CHINESE art objects. See Art objects, Chinese
CHINESE calligraphy. See Chinese language—Writing
CHINESE cookery. See Cookery, Chinese
CHINESE defectors. See Defectors, Political
CHINESE deserts. See Deserts
CHINESE export art. See Art objects, Chinese
CHINESE gooseberries. See Yangtaos
CHINESE greens. See Greens, Edible
CHINESE ground orchid. See Orchids
CHINESE in literature
Case for The five Chinese brothers. S. G. Lanes. il SLJ 24:90-1 O '77
CHINESE in the United States
Changing Chinese. B. L. Sung. bibl il Society 14:44-9 S '77
See also
New York (city)—Chinatown
San Francisco—Chinatown
CHINESE language
Chinese words of science. A. Gottfurcht. il por Chemistry 50:17-19 Mr '77

Writing

Traces of the Brush: the poetry of the painted word; exhibitions of Chinese calligraphy. J. Shaw-Eagle. il Art N 76:84-8 S '77
CHINESE literature
China's war on the mind; excerpt from Chinese shadows. P. Ryckmans. il Sat R 4:14-16+ Je 25 '77
Flower show. il Time 110:56 D 12 '77
CHINESE painting. See Painting, Chinese
CHINESE pottery. See Pottery, Chinese
CHINESE spinach. See Amaranths
CHINESE tablets (paleography) See Tablets (paleography)
CHINESE writing. See Chinese language—Writing
CHINO, Yuzo M. and others
Siamese cats: abnormal responses of retinal ganglion cells. bibl il Science 197:173-4 Jl 8 '77
CHIP circuits. See Electronic circuits, Integrated
CHIPP, Herschel Browning
Skirmish over Guernica. P. Nobile. il Harpers 254:15+ Mr '77 *
CHIPPS, Genie
Liberated love: unmarried, commited & free. Harp Baz 110:120-1+ My '77
—and Jessup, Claudia
How to start a business of your own. bibl Redbook 149:66+ Jl '77
(eds) Overnight success stories; interviews. Harp Baz 110:49+ Je '77
—See Jessup, C. jt auth; jt ed
CHIPS, Wood. See Wood waste
CHIRAC, Jacques
Center holds. il por Time 110:51-2 N 7 '77 *
Duel over city hall. Time 109:31 Ja 31 '77 *
France: a leftist surge. A. Deming and E. Peer. il Newsweek 89:46 Ap 4 '77 *
M. le Maire de Paris. G. Ross. New Repub 176: 17-19 Ap 9 '77 *
Paris is worth a race. K. Willenson and others. pors Newsweek 89:53-4 Ja 31 '77 *
Reporter in Europe. J. Kramer. New Yorker 53:72-81 Jl 4 '77 *
White knight in a graveyard. il pors Time 109: 37-8 Mr 28 '77 *
CHIRAU, J. S.
Chief's plan; interview, ed by A. de Borchgrave. il por Newsweek 90:36 Jl 18 '77
CHIRIBOGA, José R.
Quito. il map Américas 29:S1-3 Ap '77
CHISELS
Chisels and gouges that work where power tools won't. A. J. Hand. il Pop Sci 211:111-13 D '77
Wood chisels. H. Wicks. il Pop Mech 149:93 Ja '78
CHISSO Corporation. See Chemical industries—Japan
CHITAWAN National Park. See National parks and reserves—Nepal
CHITIN
Chitin synthesis inhibitors: new class of insecticides; diflubenzuron. J. L. Marx. il Science 197:1170+ S 16 '77
CHITINOZOA
Chitinozoans from the late Precambrian Chuar Group of the Grand Canyon, Arizona. B. Bloeser and others. bibl il Science 195:676-9 F 18 '77
CHITTENDEN, Eric
Ways to store apple cider. il Org Gard & Farm 24:128-30 O '77
CHITTISTER, Joan
Brotherly love in today's Church. il America 136: 233-6 Mr 19 '77
CHLORELLA. See Algae
CHLORINATION of water. See Water purification
CHLORINE
Atomic chlorine and the chlorine monoxide radical in the stratosphere: three in situ observations. J. G. Anderson and others. bibl il Science 198:501-3 N 14 '77

CHLOROFLUOROCARBONS. See Fluorocarbons
CHLOROFORM
Polyelectrolytes: potential chloroform precursors. K. L. E. Kaiser and J. Lawrence. bibl il Science 196:1205-6 Je 10 '77
CHLOROPLASTS
Cloned ribosomal RNA genes from chloroplasts of euglena gracilis. M. I. Lomax and others. bibl il Science 196:202-5 Ap 8 '77
CHOCK Full o'Nuts Corporation
After the beer at Chock Full o'Nuts. Bus W p81+ N 7 '77
CHOCOLATE
Inflation bites chocolate again. il Bus W p28 Ag 29 '77
See also
Cookery—Chocolate
Hershey Foods Corporation
CHOCOLATE drink mixes. See Beverage mixes
CHOGYAM, Trungpa Tulku
Precious master of the mountains. il por Time 109:86 F 14 '76 *
CHOICE (psychology)
See also
Decision making
Risk taking (psychology)
CHOICE of college. See College, Choice of
CHOIRS
See also
Phonograph records—Choral music
CHOKING
Can you perform this life-saving maneuver? Heimlich maneuver. il Ret Liv 17:44 Je '77
Four minutes to live . . . this maneuver can save you. il por Sci Digest 82:66-7 Jl '77
Hug of life; Heimlich maneuver. E. Keerdoja. il por Newsweek 89:12 My 30 '77
CHOLERA
Ancient scourge strikes again; Middle East. Time 110:62 S 26 '77
Cholera epidemic; Middle East. M. Clark and W. E. Schmidt. il Newsweek 90:94 S 26 '77
CHOLERA toxins. See Toxins and antitoxins
CHOLESTEROL
Cholesterol. . .is just one heart threat. N. Lyon. il Sci Digest 81:28-31 Ap '77
Clinical trials: methods and ethics are debated. G. B. Kolata. Science 198:1127-31 D 16 '77
Failed hypothesis; low-fat, low-cholesterol diet to reduce incidence of coronary heart disease. Sci Am 237:86-7 D '77
Good news about cholesterol. M. L. Schildkraut. Good H 184:217-18 Je '77
Good v. bad cholesterol; role of lipoproteins. il Time 110:119 N 21 '77
Low cholesterol diet: it won't prevent heart attacks. H. J. Johnson. il Duns R 109:93-4+ Mr '77
New technique claims to remove cholesterol while you wait. Ret Liv 16:17 D '76
CHOLINERGIC nerve fibers. See Nerve cells
CHOLINESTERASE
See also
Acetylcholinesterase
CHOLMONDELEY, Hugh N. J.
CANA. il UNESCO Courier 30:10-11 Ap '77
CHOMSKY, Noam
Chomsky on Kripke. N Y Times Mag p20 Ag 14 '77
—and Herman, E. S.
Distortions at fourth hand. Nation 224:789-94 Je 25 '77
CHONDRITES. See Meteorites
CHOPIN, Frédéric François
Memories of Chopin. H. Bradshaw and V. Bradshaw. il Travel 147:46-9 Je '77 *
CHOPPING blocks
Chopping block just slips in. il Sunset 159:168 O '77
CHOPPING of wood. See Wood cutting
CHORAL groups and societies
Bach Aria Group; performance at Alice Tully Hall. Hi Fi 27:MA21-2 My '77
See also
Sacred Music Society of America
CHORAL music
See also
Phonograph records—Choral music
CHOREA, Huntington's. See Huntington's chorea
CHOREOGRAPHY
After Isadora: her art as inspiration. L. Draegin. il por Dance Mag 51:67-71 Jl '77
And taking to the streets. A. Smith. il pors Ms 6:46-9+ D '77
Conversation with Leonide Massine; interview, ed by R. Hardin. L. Massine. il pors Dance Mag 51:68-70 D '77
Dance is climbing the walls; Annabelle Gamson, Phoebe Neville, Dianne McIntyre, and Trisha Brown. J. Dunning. il Ms 6:46-8+ D '77
Dancers and choreographers. R. Gelabert. il Dance Mag 51:84-5 Je '77
Eliot Feld's animated cartoons; Eliot Feld Ballet season at City Center. A. Smith. il por Dance Mag 51:63-5 Je '77
Isadora reexamined. N. Macdonald. il pors Dance Mag 51:51-66 Jl; 42-6 Ag; 60-3 S; 79-81 O '77

CHOREOGRAPHY—*Continued*
Lar Lubovitch: choreographer in search of meaning; interview, ed by J. Gruen. L. Lubovitch. il pors Dance Mag 51:44-7 F '77
Phoebe Neville: going her own way. J. Anderson. il pors Dance Mag 51:40-3 F '77
What a wild idea: Lewitzky and Gernreich design a dance; Inscape. V. H. Swisher. il pors Dance Mag 51:75-7 Mr '77
CHORES, Childrens. See Childrens chores
CHORIOMENINGITIS. See Meningitis
CHORIONIC gonadotropin, Human. See Gonadotropins
CHORMAN, Madeline
Retired teachers share skills as Peace Corps volunteers in Ghana. il por Aging 268:18-20 F '77 *
CHORZEMPA, Daniel
Handel: 16 organ concertos. P Pfunke. por Am Rec G 40:23 Mr '77 *
CHOU, En-lai
Chou En-lai's cortege. J. Aronson. Nation 224: 165-6 F 12 '77 *
Was Chou murdered? F. Willey and others. il por Newsweek 89:49 F 7 '77 *
See also
Peking talks, 1972
CHOUINARD, Yvon
Profiles. J. Bernstein. New Yorker 52:36-40+ Ja 31 '77 *
CHOW, Brian G.
Economic issues of the fast breeder reactor program. bibl il Science 195:551-6 F 11 '77
CHOWCHILLA, Calif.

Crime

See Crime and criminals—California
CHOWDER
Art of the chowder—mixed, clam, fish. il Sunset 159:179 N '77
Skip jack chowder. il Bet Hom & Gard 55:150 O '77
CHOWDHURY, Parimal, and Louria, D. B.
Influence of cadmium and other trace metals on human α_1-antitrypsin: an in vitro study. bibl il Science 191:480-1; 196:556-7 F 6 '76, Ap 29 '77
CHRIST. See Jesus Christ
CHRIST the King, Feast of. See Fasts and feasts —Catholic Church
CHRISTENING of ocean liners. See Ocean liners
CHRISTENSON, Kathryn
Clues to the second coming; poem. Chr Cent 94:254 Mr 16 '77
CHRISTGAU, Georgia
(ed) See McGarrigle, A. Kate and Anna McGarrigle: not afraid to be corny
(ed) See McGarrigle, K. Kate and Anna McGarrigle: not afraid to be corny
CHRISTIAAN (hairdresser)
Beauty/New focus. . .hair. il por Vogue 167:212-15 Mr '77 *
CHRISTIAN, C. N. and others
Synapse formation between two clonal cell lines. bibl il Science 196:995-8 My 27 '77
CHRISTIAN art and symbolism
Painted churches of Lake Tana; Ethiopia. B. Abbebe. il UNESCO Courier 30:13-17 F '77
Redeeming Indian culture; Asian Christian art. W. A. Dyrness. il Chr Today 21:26-7 Mr 18 '77
See also
Church architecture
Jesus Christ—Art

Exhibitions

Between Olympus and Golgotha; Age of Spirituality exhibit at the Metropolitan Museum. R. Hughes. il Time 111:70-1 Ja 2 '78
Contest for men's souls; Age of Spirituality exhibition. L. Casson. il Horizon 21:78-84 Ja '78
CHRISTIAN Booksellers Association
Bookselling as a mission: a visit to the 1977 CBA Caravan. D. Maryles. il Pub W 211:80-2 Mr 14 '77
Interview with John T. Bass of the Christian Booksellers Association; ed by P. Hewitt. J. T. Bass. por Pub W 212:69-70 S 26 '77
Market for ministry. Chr Today 21:20 Ag 12 '77
Record attendance at 28th annual Christian Booksellers Convention. P. F. Hewitt. il Pub W 212:50-2 Ag 15 '77
CHRISTIAN business directories. See Directories
CHRISTIAN century (periodical)
These absorbent pages. M. E. Marty. Chr Cent 94:735 Ag 17 '77
CHRISTIAN Church, Disciples of Christ
Disciples decide; homosexuality issue. Chr Today 22:56-7 N 18 '77
Disciples vote to resume union talks with UCC. H. E. Fey. Chr Cent 94:1021-2 N 9 '77
See also
Catholic Church—Relations—Christian Church, Disciples of Christ
CHRISTIAN colleges. See Church colleges and universities
CHRISTIAN communication. See Communication (theology)
CHRISTIAN converts. See Converts
CHRISTIAN education. See Religious education
CHRISTIAN ethics
Deciding what we deserve; law of recompense. J. Piper. Chr Today 22:12-15 O 21 '77
Natural law. K. Bockmühl. Chr Today 22:59-60 N 18 '77
Social scientists and moral theology. S. M. Natale and O. J. Morgan. bibl il New Cath World 220:301-9 N '77
See also
Commandments, Ten
Forgiveness
Love (theology)
Sin
Stewardship, Christian
CHRISTIAN giving
See also
Stewardship, Christian
CHRISTIAN leadership
Can we expect greatness from the clergy? C. S. Calian. Chr Cent 94:508-11 My 25 '77; Reply. C. E. Bryant. 94:918-19 O 12 '77
Finding the good at Garden Grove; Robert H. Schuller Institute for Successful Church Leadership. B. Barr. il por Chr Cent 94:424-7 My 4 '77; Discussion. 94:764-5 Ag 31 '77
If I were president. . .; Christian editors offering J. Carter advice. Chr Today 21:26-7 Ja 7 '77
CHRISTIAN life
Beyond efficiency: choosing a Christian life style. E. G. Bobinchak. America 136:187-9 Mr 5 '77
Finding sense when it makes no sense; excerpt from On being a Christian, tr by E. Quinn. H. Küng. il Sat Eve Post 249:50-1+ Ap '77
Is there a Christian life-style? K. Bockmuhl. Chr Today 21:48-9 My 20 '77
Personal Christianity. William II. il por Sat Eve Post 249:20 Jl '77
Thinking positively about self. A. A. Hoekema. Chr Today 21:32-3 My 20 '77
Tuning in and turning on; address, September 15, 1977. G. Turbeville. Vital Speeches 43:747-9 O 1 '77
Witness stand. E. Schaeffer. See issues of Christianity today
Word. G. McCauley. See issues of America
See also
Commitment to the church
Faith
Prayer
Spiritual life
Stewardship, Christian

Bibliography

More psychological insights. C. B. Murphey. Chr Today 21:20-5 S 9 '77
Right reading for right actions. D. Tinder. Chr Today 21:26-9 S 9 '77
Sexuality: a new candor in evangelical books. D. Tinder. il Chr Today 21:10-11 Mr 18 '77

Caricatures and cartoons

What if . . . See issues of Christianity today
CHRISTIAN literature
To see life steady and to see it whole. V. S. Owens. il Chr Today 21:18-21 Mr 4 '77
CHRISTIAN love. See Love (theology)
CHRISTIAN missions. See Missions
CHRISTIAN stewardship. See Stewardship, Christian
CHRISTIAN witness. See Witness bearing (Christianity)
CHRISTIANITY
Christianity is Christ. L. Morris. Chr Today 22: 66-7 D 9 '77
Mass media's mythic world: at odds with Christian values. W. F. Fore. bibl Chr Cent 94:32-8 Ja 19 '77
New reformation aborning? Chr Today 22:24 O 21 '77
Spirit of America. M. B. Martin. Nat R 29:615 My 27 '77
Truth and culture; analysis of Holy Shroud. J. Hart. Nat R 29:992-5 S 2 '77
See also
Bible
Catholic Church
Christian ethics
Civilization, Christian
Homosexuality and Christianity
Jesus Christ
Paul, Saint—Teachings
Protestantism
Sunday
Theology
CHRISTIANITY, Primitive. See Church history—Primitive and early church
CHRISTIANITY and communication. See Communication (theology)
CHRISTIANITY and communism. See Communism and religion
CHRISTIANITY and culture
Truth and culture; analysis of Holy Shroud. J. Hart. Nat R 29:992-5 S 2 '77
CHRISTIANITY and ecology. See Religion and ecology

CHRISTIANITY and economics
See also
Church and industry

Biblical teaching

See Bible—Economic aspects

CHRISTIANITY and other religions
Asian views of dialogue. S. R. Athyal. Chr Today 21:44+ Je 17 '77
Church and Israel; views of T. Federici. M. B. Martin. Nat R 29:1435 D 9 '77
Graham: feted by Jews; American Jewish Committee's first national interreligious award. A. H. Matthews. Chr Today 22:49-50 N 18 '77
Let's clear up the fuzziness and still be friends; Christians and Jews. Chr Today 21:29 Mr 18 '77
Should there be a Christian witness to the Jews? I. C. Rottenberg. il Chr Cent 94:352-6 Ap 13 '77; Discussion. 94:631-2 Jl 6 '77
Thailand's religious roots; Christianity and Buddhism. W. D. Carlsen. il Chr Today 22:24-7 O 7 '77

CHRISTIANITY and politics. See Church and politics

CHRISTIANITY and sex. See Sex and religion

CHRISTIANITY and socialism. See Socialism and religion

CHRISTIANITY in literature. See Religion in literature

CHRISTIANITY today (periodical)
Capital flight; moving to Wheaton, Ill. K. L. Woodward and J. Whitmore. il Newsweek 89:77 F 7 '77
Interview on relocation. H. J. Ockenga. Chr Today 21:35 Mr 18 '77
Kenneth Kantzer: a biographical sketch. por Chr Today 21:36-7 S 9 '77
On saying good-bye. C. F. H. Henry. Chr Today 21:47-8 S 9 '77

CHRISTIANS
Taking the world's temperature; interview. B. Graham. pors Chr Today 21:16-19 S 23 '77

Persecutions

See Persecution

CHRISTIANS and Jews. See Christianity and other religions

CHRISTIANS in Africa
Why Christianity is thriving in a turbulent black Africa. J. Worrall. il map U.S. News 82:63-4 My 2 '77

CHRISTIANS in Asia
Emergence of Asian theologies. S. P. Athyal. Chr Today 21:70+ S 23 '77

CHRISTIANS in China
Church in China: praise amid persecution. D. H. Adeney. Chr Today 22:10-13 N 18 '77
Life of Christianity in China; interview, ed by E. L. Stockwell. K. H. Ting and Mrs K. H. Ting. Chr Cent 94:168-71 F 23 '77

CHRISTIANS in Korea, South
Fearless and the humorless. N. Kim. Chr Cent 94:733-4 Ag 17 '77

CHRISTIANS in Latin America
Living the rest to God; dictatorships in Latin America. M. D. Wilde. Chr Cent 94:396-7 Ap 27 '77

CHRISTIANS in Rhodesia
Letter from Zimbabwe. Chr Cent 94:372-3 Ap 20 '77
Trying times for Zimbabwe Christians. J. Shona. Chr Cent 94:1226-7 D 28 '77

CHRISTIANS in Russia
Seeking new sanctuaries. Time 110:77 O 10 '77
Soviet cure for religion. J. A. Broun. America 137:26-9 Jl 16 '77

CHRISTIANS in the United States
Severed roots of American Christianity. P. Williams; rejoinder. Nat R 29:270-1 Mr 4 '77
U.S. Christians and Cuba. D. Kirkpatrick. Chr Cent 94:685-7 Ag 3 '77

CHRISTIANS in Zimbabwe. See Christians in Rhodesia

CHRISTIANSEN, Milo F.
Obituary
Parks & Rec por 12:66 Je '77

CHRISTIE, Dame Agatha
Death in the air; story. Sat Eve Post 249:42-4 O; 33-5 N; 42-6 D '77
Enchanted childhood; excerpt from An autobiography. il Ladies Home J 94:118-19+ O '77
Poirot's first case; excerpt from An autobiography. il por N Y Times Mag p41-2+ S 18 '77

CHRISTIE, George A.
Building financing. il Archit Rec 161:73 Ap; 162:51 Jl; 61 O '77
Dodge/Sweet's construction outlook, 1977: first update. il Archit Rec 161:63+ Mr '77
Five-year forecast: is there growth after recovery? il Archit Rec 161:65-6 My '77
1977 Dodge/Sweet's construction outlook: second update: more gains in architectural work are expected. il Archit Rec 162:55+ Ag '77
Regional activity in 1976 showed the shifts have stabilized. il Archit Rec 161:67 F '77
Tax cuts and federal spending needed to revive economic recovery in 1977. Archit Rec 161:83 Ja '77

CHRISTIE'S (firm)
Auctions: a N.Y.C. wrap-up and a forward look. L. Rosenbaum. Art in Am 65:33+ S '77
Sotheby's and Christie's square off. L. Rosenbaum. Art in Am 65:16+ Mr '77

CHRISTMAS
Family Christmas guide; symposium. il Harp Baz 111:132-40+ D '77
Girl who hated Christmas. K. McAuliffe. il Good H 185:72+ D '77
Of many things. J. O'Hare. America 137:inside cover D 24 '77
See also
Advent
Children and Christmas
Christmas Eve
Jesus Christ—Nativity
Jews and Christmas
Santa Claus

Anecdotes, facetiae, satire, etc.

Yes, North Carolina, there is a Santa Claus. R. Baker. N Y Times Mag p4 D 25 '77

Caricatures and cartoons

Old-fashioned Christmas. S. Berenstain and J. Berenstain. Good H 185:160-1 D '77

China

Memoir of Christmas in China; with recipes. H. McNulty. il House & Gard 149:74+ D '77

Europe, Western

Great Austrian true-blue, down-on-the-farm Epiphany celebrations; other continental Christmastide happenings. K. Cure. Holiday 57:22-3 N '76

France

Family Christmas in France. I. d'Ornano. il por Harp Baz 111:100-1+ D '77

Italy

Festive Roman Christmas. Valentino. il por Harp Baz 111:102-3+ D '77

United States

Ancram's Victorian Christmas. B. Hamilton. il Ret Liv 16:32-4 D '76
Brat's Christmas. C. O'Neill. New Repub 177:43 D 24 '77
Celebrating the season. il Harp Baz 111:104-7 D '77
Christmas in the Southwest; Texas; symposium. il Redbook 150:99-120+ D '77
Christmas is for children of any age. W. Willis. House B 119:72 N '77
Christmas memories. M. Bringle. il Am Home 80:58-9 D '77
Christmas special: a real Christmas love story; Porter and David DeSieyes. M. R. Carter. il Mademoiselle 83:90-7 D '77
Christmas—the coming-together; celebrations in Western States. il Sunset 159:216 D '77
Christmas traditions—is it time to break a few? L. Johnson. il Ret Liv 16:30-1 D '76
Christmas with the Carters. R. C. Stapleton. il por Ladies Home J 94:74+ D '77
Christmases with my father; excerpt from Act one. M. Hart. Redbook 150:63-4 D '77
Home-style Christmas at the White House. il pors U.S. News 83:58-9 D 26 '77
Joy in hard times. B. Gilbert. il Sports Illus 47:100-4+ D 19 '77
Living Christmas in the town park; Twelve Mile, Ind. J. Gillies. il Farm J 101:39-41 D '77
Looking back at Christmas; newspaper editorials and poems. Sat Eve Post 249:18-19+ D '77
Merry Christmas in your house; merry chaos in mine. P. Mackintosh. il por Redbook 150:80+ D '77
New traditions, old innovations. L. Conger. Writer 90:9-10 D '77
Portfolio of Christmases past; Good housekeeping covers. il Good H 185:103-9 D '77
Someday—a real Christmas. D. Lawrence. il U.S. News 83:96+ D 26 '77
This Christmas, their home is your home; symposium. Redbook 150:89+ D '77
Year the Christmas presents didn't come. B Logan. il Good H 185:48+ D '77

CHRISTMAS and Jews. See Jews and Christmas

CHRISTMAS bird count. See Bird census

CHRISTMAS books, Childrens. See Childrens literature

CHRISTMAS boxes. See Boxes, cases, etc.

CHRISTMAS breads. See Bread

CHRISTMAS business
Booksellers choose what books look best under the Christmas tree. D. Maryles and others. il Pub W 212:38+ D 5 '77
Christmas is bringing mixed tidings for toys. il Bus W p59+ D 12 '77
Christmas shoppers: big spenders but picky, too. il U.S. News 83:59-61 N 28 '77
Christmas splurging starts early. il Bus W p24-5 D 19 '77

CHRISTMAS business—*Continued*
Currents: PW's annual survey of Christmas buying trends. D. Maryles and J. Giusto. Pub W 212:36-7 D 12 '77
Deck the halls, clear the shelves. il Time 111: 39 Ja 9 '78
Great toy shortage. L. Langway and P. L. Abraham. il Newsweek 90:58+ D 19 '77
Waiting for some Christmas cheer. Fortune 96: 19+ N '77
Warm afterglow of a Christmas spree. il Bus W p26+ Ja 9 '78

CHRISTMAS cactus. See Cactus

CHRISTMAS candies. See Candles

CHRISTMAS cards
Cards to feel. il Design (US) 79:6-7 N '77
Cards you can make and send for pennies. il Pop Mech 148:110-11+ N '77
Stencil your own cards. il Design (US) 79:33 N '77
Your thumb personalizes these cards. il Sunset 159:130 N '77

History

Prang Christmas cards. L. Freeman. il Hobbies 82:118-19 D '77
You can thank Louis Prang for all those cards. L. Cheney. il por Smithsonian 8:120-5 bibl (p 135) D '77

CHRISTMAS carol; dramatization. See Hackett, W.

CHRISTMAS carols
Christmas in the Ukraine; English translation of Soviet version of Ukrainian Christmas carol Nova radist' stala. Nat R 30:18-19 Ja 6 '78
Tidings of comfort and joy. E. O. Hauser. il Read Digest 111:27-8+ D '77

CHRISTMAS cookery
Entertaining: special holiday recipes by New York's top caterers. il Mademoiselle 83:176-7 D '77
Flaming Christmas feasts. il Harp Baz 111:96-7+ D '77
Foods for holiday festivities. E. W. Manning. il Farm J 100:34-5 D '76
Going home for Christmas. E. W. Manning. il Farm J 101:42-3 D '77
Holiday treats from Fitness House. il Org Gard & Farm 24:100-4 D '77
Indulging without bulging. il Fam Health 9:30-2+ D '77
Many tastes of Christmas. G. Lang. il N Y Times Mag p81+ D 18 '77
Memoir of Christmas in China. H. McNulty. il House & Gard 149:74+ D '77
Redbook's special it's almost Christmas cookbook. il Redbook 150:57-64 N '77
Redbook's Texas holiday cookbook. Redbook 150: 131 D '77
Special sharing of favorite holiday recipes. il Bet Hom & Gard 55:104-11+ D '77
See also
Christmas dinners
Christmas meals
Cookery, Ornamental

CHRISTMAS cookies. See Cookies

CHRISTMAS cribs
African nativity; wooden sculpture by E. Chibanga. il Ebony 33:44-6 D '77
Santons of Provence. R. D. Sullivan. il Hobbies 82:116-17+ D '77

CHRISTMAS decorations
Airy string baubles. il Design (US) 79:38 N '77
Angels, doves, geese got their start as 1¢ paper plates. il Sunset 159:92-3 D '77
Angels from tin-can lids. il Design (US) 79:26-7 N '77
Bazaar's 50 tips for a very enjoyable Christmas. Harp Baz 111:73+ D '77
California hospitality. . .dinner and all the trimmings. il Am Home 80:66-7 D '77
Children's art—fabric ornaments. il Sunset 159: 110 D '77
Christmas canvas of color & candlelight. R. Weil. il House B 119:102-5 D '77
Collector's Christmas. il House B 119:106-7 D '77
Cooperation; standards program for miniature electric Christmas tree lights and decorations. D. Chaucer. Consumers Res Mag 60:37-8 Jl '77
Crafts with a Texas accent. il Redbook 150:110-13+ D '77
Deck the halls. . .colonial style. M. Pulik. il Am Home 80:62-3 D '77
Decorate with natural things. il Farm J 100:J2-3 D '76
Decorate with pompons. il Design (US) 79:19 N '77
Decorations for your Christmas tree from 'round the world. il Pop Mech 148:122-5 D '77
Delight in tradition; Keep it natural. il House & Gard 149:90-7+ D '77
Festivity on a small scale. M. Siple. il House B 119:108-9 D '77
Glad tidings: wreaths of plenty; Deck the halls with roses. il Ladies Home J 94:94-7+ D '77
Holiday ornaments. il Design (US) 79:12-13 N '77
Let it inspire you. il House & Gard 149:100-5 D '77
Magnet pompons. il Design (US) 79:35-7 N '77
Make a Christmas bird. il Design (US) 79:32 N '77
Making your own natural tree decorations. J. Browne. il Org Gard & Farm 24:106-11 D '77
93 enchanting tree ornaments to make. il Good H 185:136-9+ D '77
Open house for holidays. il Good H 185:110-13 D '77
Pattern for a poinsettia garland. il Design (US) 79:9 N '77
Santa in yarn kids can make. il Sunset 159:118 D '77
Shimmering cookies to hang on the Christmas tree. il Sunset 159:168 D '77
Silvery splendor. il Design (US) 79:20 N '77
Snowball ringer; tin-can lid bells. il Design (US) 79:14-15 N '77
Spin and sparkle. il Design (US) 79:34 N '77
Spool Santa; Octopus doll. il Design (US) 79:17 N '77
Stylish nostalgia of a farmhouse Christmas. J. B. Reiter and J. Macurdy. il por House B 119: 90-5 D '77
Trimming the tree. E. Metcalfe. il Sat Eve Post 249:74-7+ D '77
2 simple ideas for recycled decorations. J. Vogel. il Ret Liv 17:35-6 D '77
Warmth of country traditions rekindled in a city apartment. J. B. Reiter. il por House B 119:96-101 D '77
World on your Christmas tree. E. Davis. il Ret Liv 17:37+ D '77
See also
Christmas greens
Christmas tree lights
Christmas trees
Christmas wreaths

CHRISTMAS decorations, Outdoor
15 glorious ways to decorate your doors. il Good H 185:114-17+ D '77

CHRISTMAS depression syndrome. See Depression, Mental

CHRISTMAS desserts. See Desserts

CHRISTMAS dinners
California hospitality. . .dinner and all the trimmings. il Am Home 80:66-7 D '77
Change-of-pace Christmas menu. il Ebony 33: 138+ D '77
Company's coming for a ranch feast; roast turkey dinner Texas style; excerpt from Flavors. il Redbook 150:114-15 D '77
Complete guide to a traditional turkey holiday dinner. il Redbook 150:146+ D '77
Food: Christmas feasting. F. de la Renta. Vogue 167:112+ D '77
Holiday alternative. N. Hazelton. Nat R 30: 42-3 Ja 6 '78
International chef; dinner at Trinidad Hilton. Trav/Holiday 148:20-1+ D '77
No-fuss Christmas feast. S. P. Torpey. il Bet Hom & Gard 55:114-18+ D '77
Put a little glamour in your Christmas feast. C. Turgeon. il Sat Eve Post 249:132-4 D '77

CHRISTMAS entertaining
50 sure-fire, can't-miss, life-of-the-party tips. A. Lovell. Mademoiselle 83:54+ D '77
How to host (and enjoy) a holiday party. il House B 119:118-20+ D '77
Share your home for the holidays; foreign visitors. J. Walker. House B 119:8+ D '77
See also
Christmas meals

CHRISTMAS Eve

Anecdotes, facetiae, satire, etc.

It says here. . . . ; assembling toys on Christmas Eve. A. B. Heath. Nat R 30:30-1 Ja 6 '78

CHRISTMAS gift catalogs. See Catalogs, Commercial

CHRISTMAS gifts
Bazaar's 50 tips for a very enjoyable Christmas. Harp Baz 111:73+ D '77
Best buy gifts. il Consumer Rep 42:651-5 N '77
Christmas presents. il Harp Baz 111:84-90 D '77
Christmas shopping guide; art supplies. il Am Artist 41:21-30 D '77
Dancer's Christmas. il Dance Mag 51:92 D '77
50 Christmas gifts for under $10. H. Alpert and S. Miller. il Ret Liv 17:38-41 N '77
For one who sews, 45 cents and up. il Sunset 159:112 D '77
44 super gifts to make now for next Christmas. il Good H 185:126-9+ Jl '77
Gift ideas for the water miser. il Sunset 159:78-9 D '77
Gift of giving. J. Robinson. Vogue 167:184+ D '77
Gift of you; emotional gifts. D. A. Sugarman. Good H 185:98+ D '77
Gift tools for the baker. il Sunset 159:137 D '77
Gifts. il House B 119:122-7 N '77
Gifts: for the season; Christmas gifts from catalogs. A. Anderson. Vogue 167:93-4+ D '77
Gifts for you & yours. il Redbook 150:122-5 N '77
Gifts from the earth. S. Tait. il Org Gard & Farm 24:119-20 D '77

CHRISTMAS gifts—*Continued*
Gifts that glow. il Am Home 80:11 D '77
Gifts that will bring birds to the bird watcher's garden. il Sunset 159:192-3 D '77
Give:
Collectibles. J. Goldman. Vogue 167:100+ D '77
Sports. K. Gilman. Vogue 167:110 D '77
Video. D. English. Vogue 167:102+ D '77
Great giving. il House & Gard 149:178-93 N '77
Help! For the 11th-hour Santa. Mademoiselle 83:150 D '77
Maps as gifts—wide choices. il Sunset 159:50+ D '77
Merry Christmas, whoever you are. il Esquire 88:156-69 D '77
More love than money. V. Perlo. Am Home 80:8 D '77
One circuit/many gifts. L. Garner. il Pop Electr 12:84-9+ D '77
PM's shop editors pick stocking stuffers. il Pop Mech 148:60+ N '77
Package a gift of unusual teas. il Sunset 159:123 D '77
Pets; gifts for pets and pet owners. M. Siegal. House B 119:42 N '77
Raft of new products for Christmas—or any time. il U.S. News 83:75-6+ N 14 '77
Santa on a shoestring. il House & Gard 149:116-19 D '77
Special Christmas gifts for special people. il Changing T 31:18-20 N '77
201 great gifts for under $25. K. Kent. Good H 185:22+ D '77
Unusual gift. A. Penney. il N Y Times Mag p 157-60 D 4 '77
See also
Books as gifts
Christmas projects
Christmas shopping
Food as gifts
Liquors as gifts
Pets as gifts
Phonograph records as gifts
Plants as gifts
Wrapping of packages

Anecdotes, facetiae, satire, etc.

It's the thought. R. Rosenblatt. New Repub 177:36-7 D 10 '77

CHRISTMAS gifts for children
Sharing Christmas with your children. L. Salk. Harp Baz 111:133+ D '77
Super presents designed to last. J. Gonnet and F. Feighan-Jones. il House & Gard 149:78+ N '77
See also
Books as gifts
Toys

CHRISTMAS gifts for men
Ladies only; gift ideas for sportsmen. B. Tarrant. il Field & S 82:118-19+ D '77
Most-wanted Christmas gifts. il Mech Illus 73:45-7 D '77
Mostly for men. R. L. Green. il N Y Times Mag p 162+ D 4 '77
On and off the avenue. New Yorker 53:75-6+ D 5 '77

CHRISTMAS gifts for the home
Gifts that never leave home. il House B 119:21+ D '77
Here's to the house. M. Davidson. il Parents Mag 52:56-7+ D '77
House gifts. il House & Gard 149:128+ N '77
House presents for the well-tempered cook. B. Portsch and P. R. Jackson. il House & Gard 149:98+ N '77
On and off the avenue. New Yorker 53:87-9+ N 28 '77

CHRISTMAS gifts for women
On and off the avenue. New Yorker 53:188+ N 21 '77

CHRISTMAS greens
Transforming nature's Christmas pretties. E. W. Chandler. il Ret Liv 17:40+ D '77
See also
Christmas trees
Christmas wreaths
Holly

CHRISTMAS lighting. See Christmas decorations

CHRISTMAS literature
See also
Christmas poems

CHRISTMAS literature, Childrens. See Childrens literature

CHRISTMAS meals
Christmas party cookbook. il Good H 185:146-55+ D '77
Company in the kitchen; Christmas desserts and buffet dinner; ideas of Martha Stewart. il Mademoiselle 83:124-7+ D '77
Cross-country Christmas. il Am Home 80:60-4+ D '77
Easy holiday buffets; with menus. il House & Gard 149:134-5 D '77
See also
Christmas dinners

CHRISTMAS music
What you never knew about your favorite Christmas songs; interviews with singers, ed by J. Wilkie. il Good H 185:92+ D '77
See also
Christmas carols

CHRISTMAS parties. See Christmas entertaining

CHRISTMAS plays

Texts

Christmas carol; dramatization of story by C. Dickens. W. Hackett. Plays 37:85-95 D '77
Christmas tale; drama. S. C. Oberacker. Plays 37:73-4 D '77
Nutcracker Prince; drama. L. Mahlmann. Plays 37:81-4 D '77
Red carpet Christmas; drama. H. L. Miller. Plays 37:1-14 D '77
Runaway toys; drama. H. L. Miller. Plays 37:39-44 D '77
Silent night; drama. L. Hollingsworth. Plays 37:45-50, 72 D '77
Year Santa forgot Christmas; drama. S. L. Marshall. Plays 37:51-5 D '77

CHRISTMAS poems
Christmas poetry. America 137:455 D 24 '77
King John's Christmas; poem, execerpt from Now we are six. A. A. Milne. Sat Eve Post 249:17 D '77
Looking back at Christmas; newspaper editorials and poems. Sat Eve Post 249:18-19+ D '77

CHRISTMAS presents. See Christmas gifts

CHRISTMAS projects
Christmas count-down. il Am Home 80:36-9 D '77
Christmas mobile. il Design (US) 79:30-1 N '77
Flying Christmas bird. il Design (US) 79:39 N '77
For a marvelous make-ahead Christmas. il House & Gard 149:146-53+ N '77
Littlest angel; angel-wing chair. P. Sadowsky. il Am Home 80:98-100 O '77
Make-ahead presents:
Cut-and-paste jewelry. il Seventeen 36:128-9 N '77
Decorate with stencils. il Seventeen 36:126-7+ N '77
For all the family. il Seventeen 36:124-5+ N '77
Work a woven basket. il Seventeen 36:130-1 N '77
Make it a Christmas to remember. N. Lindemeyer and C. Vaughan. il Bet Hom & Gard 55:86-103+ D '77
Neighborhood kids' gift-making jamboree. il Sunset 159:88-91 D '77
19 great Christmas gifts you can use. H. Wicks. il Pop Mech 148:131-8+ N '77
Santa Claus hand puppet. il Design (US) 79:28-9 N '77
Santa memo clock. il Design (US) 79:25 N '77
60 glorious gifts to sew, knit, crochet, appliqué, quilt, etc. il Good H 185:164-8+ N '77
Warm hands, warm head, warm feet: lovely presents to knit and crochet for Christmas. il McCalls 105:249-55 N '77
See also
Christmas decorations

CHRISTMAS safety devices and measures. See Accidents—Prevention

CHRISTMAS shopping
Holiday buying tips: are you getting the most for your money? Sr Schol 110:20-1 D 1 '77
Mall; Bergen Mall in Paramus, N.J. New Yorker 53:19 D 26 '77
Sonoma County nurserymen, farmers, craftsmen have Christmas offerings. il map Sunset 159:44 D '77
See also
Christmas business

CHRISTMAS songs. See Christmas music

CHRISTMAS stamps. See Postage stamps

CHRISTMAS stories
See name of author for full entry
Christmas gift for Fort Zack. F. Deford
Christmas tree story. G. Blanchard
Mrs. Ainsworth's Christmas cat. J. Herriot
Pint of judgment. E. Morrow
Right here at Christmas. W. Goyen
Santa Santa. M. Lew
Shepherd. F. Forsyth
Sunshine Christmas. N. Klein
This day to treasure. P. S. Buck
Time of the lamb. L. Wibberley

CHRISTMAS story writing. See Short story

CHRISTMAS table decoration. See Table decoration

CHRISTMAS tale; drama. See Oberacker, S. C.

CHRISTMAS television programs. See Television programs—Christmas programs

CHRISTMAS toys. See Toys

CHRISTMAS travel. See Travel

CHRISTMAS tree lights
Less light this Christmas? il Sunset 159:114 D '77

CHRISTMAS tree ornaments. See Christmas decorations

CHRISTMAS tree stands
Tree stand is a tree stump. il Sunset 159:102 D '77

CHRISTMAS trees
Christmas fruit trees you make yourself. il Sunset 159:74-5 D '77
Littlest tree. V. Perlo. il Am Home 80:44-5 D '77
Taking the tree. J. N. Cole. il Nat Wildlife 16:14-19 D '77
Tree of gold. il Design (US) 79:11 N '77
Year-round Christmas tree; potted Norfolk pine. L. W. Patterson. il Org Gard & Farm 24:144-5 D '77

CHRISTMAS wrappings. See Wrapping of packages

CHRISTMAS wreaths
15 glorious ways to decorate your doors. il Good H 185:114-17+ D '77
Glad tidings: wreaths of plenty; Deck the halls with roses. il Ladies Home J 94:94-7+ D '77
Herbs and peppers into wreaths for the cook. il Sunset 159:194-5 D '77
Holiday wreaths. il Design (US) 79:21-3 N '77
Tiny wreath package decorations. il Design (US) 79:8 N '77

CHRISTO
Fence to remember. E. Keerdoja and L. Burgess. il Newsweek 89:8 F 21 '77 *
Onward and upward with the arts. C. Tomkins. il New Yorker 53:43-6+ Mr 28 '77 *

CHRISTOFFERSON, Rea
High cost of hiring. il por Lib J 102:677-81 Mr 15 '77

CHRISTOPHE, Henri, King of Haiti
Work and discipline. J. Cook. por Forbes 119:40 My 1 '77 *

CHRISTOPHER, Nicholas
Skirting the calm; poem. New Yorker 53:65 D 26 '77

CHRISTOPHER, Robert C.
Communism with little face. il Horizon 20:60-5 D '77

CHRISTOPHER, Warren Minor
Administration recommends Senate approval of Genocide Convention; statement, May 24, 1977. Dept State Bull 76:676-8 Je 27 '77
Deputy Secretary Christopher discusses the Panama Canal treaties; address, November 11, 1977. Dept State Bull 77:835-9 D 12 '77
Human rights: an important concern of U.S. foreign policy; statement, March 7, 1977. Dept State Bull 76:289-91 Mr 28 '77
Human rights: principle and realism; address, August 9, 1977. Dept State Bull 77:269-73 Ag 29 '77
New momentum for Middle East peace; November 22, 1977. Dept State Bull 77:875-9 D 19 '77
Partners in a common enterprise: building for the future; address, June 2, 1977. Dept State Bull 76:681-4 Je 27 '77

—and Reinhardt, J. E.
Reorganizing cultural and informational activities; joint statement, September 1, 1977. Dept State Bull 77:572 O 24 '77

CHRISTOPHERSON, Tina
Overdosing on water. Newsweek 89:46 Mr 14 '77 *

CHRISTY, E. Jennifer, and Weaver, Ken
Ecology interns report—new perspectives gained from Washington experience. il pors BioScience 27:631-3 S '77

CHRISTY, John
Driving impression (cont) il Motor T 28:87-9 D '76
Retrospect. il Motor T 29:77-8+ D '77
Road test. See issues of Motor trend

CHROMAFFIN cells
Calcium-induced displacement of membrane-associated particles upon aggregation of chromaffin granules. R. Schober and others. bibl il Science 195:495-7 F 4 '77

CHROMATIN
Histone occurrence in chromatin from peridinium balticum, a binucleate dinoflagellate. P. J. Rizzo and E. R. Cox. bibl il Science 198:1258-60 D 23 '77
Hydrodynamic evidence in support of spacer regions in chromatin. K. S. Schmitz and B. R. Shaw. bibl il Science 197:661-3 Ag 12 '77
Localization of the globin gene in the template active fraction of chromatin of Friend leukemia cells. R. B. Wallace and others. bibl il Science 198:1166-8 D 16 '77
Reconstitution of chromatin subunits. C. L. F. Woodcock. bibl il Science 195:1350-2 Mr 25 '77
Secondary structure of histones and DNA in chromatin. G. J. Thomas, Jr and others. bibl il Science 197:385-8 Jl 22 '77

CHROMATOGRAPHIC analysis
Ion exchange and liquid chromatography. J. D. Navratil and H. F. Walton. bibl il pors Chemistry 50:18-20 Jl '77
Laser fluorimetry: subpicogram detection of aflatoxins using high-pressure liquid chromatography. G. J. Diebold and R. N. Zare. bibl il Science 196:1439-41 Je 24 '77
Liquid chromatographic analysis of endogenous catecholamine released from brain slices. P. M. Plotsky and others. bibl il Science 197:904-6 Ag 26 '77
Qualitative analysis of some inorganic anions by paper chromatography. D. V. Naik. il por Chemistry 50:27-8 My '77
Separations using liquid chromatography. H. G. Barth. bibl il por Chemistry 50:11-13 S '77

CHROME. See Chromium

CHROMIUM

Export-import trade

Department urges passage of bill to halt importation of Rhodesian chrome; statements, February 10, 1977. J. L. Katz; C. R. Vance. Dept State Bull 76:170-4 F 28 '77
Door is closing on chrome; legislation banning U.S. imports of Rhodesian chrome. Bus W p29-30 F 21 '77
President signs bill restoring embargo on Rhodesian chrome; statement, March 18, 1977. J. Carter. Dept State Bull 76:333-4 Ap 11 '77
Rhodesian chrome. Nat R 29:373 Ap 1 '77

CHROMOSOME mapping
Berg calls gene mapping most important practical benefit. E. M. Leeper. por BioScience 27:369 My '77
Mapping the locus of the H-Y gene on the human Y chromosome. G. C. Koo and others. bibl il Science 198:940-2 D 2 '77
Status of the gene map of the human chromosomes. V. A. McKusick and F. H. Ruddle. bibl il Science 196:390-405 Ap 22 '77

CHROMOSOMES
Chromosomes caught mapping. il Chemistry 50:52-3 Ja '77
Double minute chromosomes and the homogeneously staining regions in chromosomes of a human neuroblastoma cell line. G. Balaban-Malenbaum and F. Gibert. bibl il Science 198:739-41 N 18 '77
Evolution of primate chromosomes. D. A. Miller. bibl il Science 198:1116-24 D 16 '77
Fragile sites on human chromosomes: demonstration of their dependence on the type of tissue culture medium. G. R. Sutherland. bibl il Science 197:265-6 Jl 15 '77
Gene transfer in mammalian cells: mediated by chromosomes. J. L. Marx. il Science 197:146-8 Jl 8 '77
Heteromorphic sex chromosomes in male rainbow trout. G. H. Thorgaard. bibl il Science 196:900-2 My 20 '77
High on XYY. J. Rifkin and T. Howard. Progressive 41:17 D '77
Macronuclear subunits of tetrahymena thermophila are functionally haploid. F. P. Doerder and others. bibl il Science 198:946-8 D 2 '77
Making sure about sex; testing for H-Y antigen; work of S. S. Wachtel and others. il por Time 110:57 D 5 '77
Mouse chromosome translocations: visualization and analysis by electron microscopy of the synaptonemal complex. M. J. Moses and others. bibl il Science 196:892-4 My 20 '77
Reverse banding on chromosomes produced by a guanosine-cytosine specific DNA binding antibiotic: olivomycin. J. H. Van De Sande. bibl il Science 195:400-2 Ja 28 '77
See also
Chromatin
Genes

CHRONOGRAPHS
Connoisseur's guide to chronographs. il Car & Dr 22:84-6+ F '77

CHRONOLOGY
Cosmic calendar; excerpt from The dragons of Eden. C. Sagan. il Read Digest 111:148-9 O '77

CHRONOLOGY, Biblical. See Bible—Chronology

CHRONOMETRY, Mental. See Time perception

CHRYSANTHEMUMS
Blooms almost as big as your head? il Sunset 158:222-3 Mr '77

CHRYSLER Corporation
Autos: sales down, optimism up. il Time 110:42 D 26 '77
Chrysler's plan to head off a cash shortage. por Bus W p83 O 24 '77
History of the Airflow car. H. S. Irwin. il Sci Am 237:98-104+ bibl(p 140) Ag '77; Reply. P. Caviness. 237:6+ N '77

CHRYSLER United Kingdom, Ltd. See Automobile industry—Great Britain

CHRYSOPIDAE. See Lacewings

CHU, Kwang-wen. See Chen, Y. P. jt auth

CHUANG, Tse-tung
Death wish. il por Time 110:47 N 21 '77 *

CHUBB, James. See Huxtable, R. jt auth

CHUBB, Percy
Role of the America's Cup Committee. il Yachting 142:134 Ag '77

CHUCK Davis Dance Company. See Dance companies

CHUCK hunting. See Woodchuck hunting

CHUDNOVSKY, Grigory
Life-or-death case. por Newsweek 90:46 Jl 4 '77 *

CHUM salmon. See Salmon

CHUN, Yolande
Great ways to give money. il Good H 185:212+ D '77

CHUNG, Chieh
Medical mailbox. C. SerVaas. il Sat Eve Post 249:138-9 D '77

CHUNG Trio. See Trios, Instrumental

CHURCH, Frank
Whither wilderness? il por Am For 83:10-12+ Jl '77

CHURCH
See also
Catholic Church
Christianity
Clergy

Anecdotes, facetiae, satire, etc.

Jesus and the tax collectors; defining church. M. E. Marty. Chr Cent 94:343 Ap 6 '77

Authority

See also
Popes—Primacy

CHURCH administration. See Church government

CHURCH and education
Reversal in Zaire; returning administration of public primary and secondary schools to the churches. R. L. Niklaus. Chr Today 21:43 Ja 7 '77
See also
Church colleges and universities
Church schools

CHURCH and homosexuality. See Homosexuality and Christianity

CHURCH and industry
Gospel according to. . . Chr Today 21:58-9 Ap 15 '77

CHURCH and labor
Democracy in the workplace. V. P. Mainelli; reply. J. C. Meisner. America 136:117 F 12 '77

CHURCH and language. See Religion and language

CHURCH and politics
Christian hope and political structures. J. M. Wall. Chr Cent 94:27 Ja 19 '77
Church support for Canal treaties. J. M. Wall. Chr Cent 94:995 N 2 '77
Combating the energy lobbyists. J. M. Wall. Chr Cent 94:395 Ap 27 '77
Divided shepherds of a restive flock; conflicts within the Catholic Church. T. Fleming. il N Y Times Mag p9+ Ja 16 '77
NCC and Carter; supporting the two Panama Canal treaties. Chr Cent 94:1084 N 23 '77
See also
Catholic Church and socialism
Communism and religion

CHURCH and race problems
Plains Baptists. E. Keerodoja and H. Camp. il Newsweek 90:12 O 17 '77
See also
Catholic schools—Desegregation

CHURCH and social problems
Catholics and temperance. J. H. Fichter; discussion. Commonweal 104:62-3 Ja 21 '77
Chicago declaration: barely audible; Evangelicals for Social Action. R. V. Pierard. Chr Today 21:33 Je 3 '77
Churches start facing up to the sexual revolution: abortions, married priests, homosexuals. il U.S. News 83:63-4 S 26 '77
Ethics, medical malpractice and the church. G. L. Haines. Chr Cent 94:1003-5 N 2 '77; Reply. T. E. Daniel. 94:1227-8 D 28 '77
Evangelicals and activities. M. Novak. Chr Cent 94:469-70 My 18 '77
Lobbyists for the people; church support of energy policy. J. M. Wall. Chr Cent 94:467-8 My 18 '77
No salt in the city; church and the ghetto. K. Phillips. il Chr Today 21:12-15 My 20 '77
Sharing the wealth: the church as biblical model for public policy. R. J. Sider. il Chr Cent 94:560-5 Je 8 '77
Works of compassion in Christ's name. Chr Today 22:28-30 D 9 '77
World hunger and Christian conscience. H. B. Kuhn. Chr Today 21:68-9 My 6 '77
See also
Abortion—Moral and religious aspects
Center of Concern, Washington, D.C.
Church and industry
Church and labor
Church and race problems
Church work with homosexuals
Church work with the handicapped
Communism and religion
Liberation theology
Lutheran Social Service
Socialism and religion
Television broadcasting—Moral and religious aspects
Underdeveloped areas—Church and social problems

Honduras

Honduras: did the Church start something it can't stop? Housewives Clubs. M. Peraza and H. Maurer. il Ms 6:12-15 Ag '77

India

Indian evangelicals: some issues in mission; Devlali letter. S. P. Athyal. Chr Today 21:60-1 Mr 18 '77

Latin America

Popular religiosity: new wind in Latin America. P. Lernoux. Nation 224:199-205 F 19 '77

Salvador

El Salvador suppresses the church. P. Lernoux. Nation 225:100-2 Ag 6 '77

CHURCH and state
Bob and Madalyn's fight to the finish; B. Harrington-M. M. O'Hair debates. J. C. Hefley and E. E. Plowman. il por Chr Today 21:34-5 Ag 26 '77
Chile cover-up? alleged covert activities of Jesuit missionary R. Vekemans. Chr Today 21:40-1 Ag 26 '77
More meddling with the wall. Chr Today 21:26 My 20 '77
Mormon Utah: where a church shapes the life of a state; with interview with S. W. Kimball. il U.S. News 83:59-61 D 19 '77
Myth of self-evident truths. W. Muehl. Chr Cent 94:1000-2 N 2 '77
On tour; M. M. O'Hair vs B. Harrington. Chr Today 22:58-9 O 7 '77
Recent developments in the law; Supreme Court cases involving Catholic schools; address, January 25, 1977. V. C. Blum. Vital Speeches 43:296-300 Mr 1 '77
Should this judge be benched? case of H. W. Goodwin. V. Vogelzang and E. E. Plowman. por Chr Today 22:56-7 N 4 '77
Soul mates; debates between M. M. O'Hair and B. Harrington. M. Montagno and F. Maier. pors Newsweek 90:72 S 19 '77
Who defines religion; investigation of the National Commission on Hispanic Affairs. J. M. Wall. Chr Cent 94:523-4 Je 1 '77
See also
Americans United for Separation of Church and State (organization)
Catholic schools
Church schools
Public schools and religion
Religious liberty
Taxation, Exemption from

CHURCH and state in Africa
I am not anti-Communist; excerpt from Battle for Africa. Andrew. Chr Today 22:28-30 D 9 '77
Why Christianity is thriving in a turbulent black Africa. J. Worrall. il map U.S. News 82:63-4 My 2 '77
See also
Catholic Church in Africa

CHURCH and state in Brazil
Brazil expels a missionary. R. Barbosa. Chr Cent 94:710-11 Ag 17 '77
Grass-roots protests in Brazil. R. Barbosa. Chr Cent 94:1119-20 N 30 '77
See also
Catholic Church in Brazil

CHURCH and state in Czechoslovakia
Christianity in Communist Czechoslovakia. K. Winter. Chr Cent 94:919-20 O 12 '77

CHURCH and state in Ecuador
See also
Catholic Church in Ecuador

CHURCH and state in Egypt
See also
Coptic Church

CHURCH and state in Germany, East
East Germany: a vexing issue. R. D. Linder. Chr Today 22:54-5 N 18 '77
See also
Catholic Church in Germany, East

CHURCH and state in Greece
See also
Orthodox Eastern Church in Greece

CHURCH and state in Hungary
See also
Catholic Church in Hungary

CHURCH and state in Italy
See also
Catholic Church in Italy

CHURCH and state in Korea, South
See also
Catholic Church in Korea, South

CHURCH and state in Latin America
See also
Catholic Church in Latin America

CHURCH and state in Latvia
Eastern bloc voices that won't be silenced. A. H. Matthews. Chr Today 21:44-6 Mr 4 '77

CHURCH and state in Mexico
See also
Catholic Church in Mexico

CHURCH and state in Namibia
Namibia: conscience and independence. W. P. Wood. Chr Cent 94:529-31 Je 1 '77

CHURCH and state in Paraguay
See also
Catholic Church in Paraguay

CHURCH and state in Poland
See also
Catholic Church in Poland

CHURCH and state in Rhodesia
Trying times for Zimbabwe Christians. J. Shona. Chr Cent 94:1226-7 D 28 '77
See also
Catholic Church in Rhodesia
CHURCH and state in Rumania
See also
Evangelical churches in Rumania
CHURCH and state in Russia
See also
Christians in Russia
Church and state in Latvia
Orthodox Eastern Church, Russian
CHURCH and state in Salvador
See also
Catholic Church in Salvador
CHURCH and state in South Africa
Banning of Beyers Naudé. G. M. Bryan. Chr Cent 94:1020-1 N 9 '77
Now South Africa's churches press for human rights. il U.S. News 82:29+ Mr 14 '77
South Africa: God and liberation. Chr Today 22:56-7 D 9 '77
South African muzzle: how one of its own got banned; B. Naudé. A. Silk. Nation 225:581-4 D 3 '77
See also
Catholic Church in South Africa
CHURCH and state in the Philippines
See also
Catholic Church in the Philippines
CHURCH and state in the United States. See Church and state
CHURCH and state in Uganda
Chaos in Uganda; views of F. Kivengere. America 136:349 Ap 16 '77
Making headway painfully in Uganda. F. Kivengere. Chr Today 21:20-1 Ap 15 '77
Murder in Uganda. W. P. Wood. America 136: 216-19 Mr 12 '77
CHURCH and state in Zimbabwe. See Church and state in Rhodesia
CHURCH and the press
See also
Vatican and the press
CHURCH architecture
Building types study; religious buildings; with introd by G. Allen. il Archit Rec 162:101-16 Jl '77
Friendly spaces: ecclesiology and the architect; National Interfaith Conference on Religion and Architecture. J. C. Lyles. Chr Cent 94:806-8 S 21 '77
Quito; church architecture and decoration of the colonial period. J. R. Chiriboga; H. Crespo Toral. il map Américas 29:S1-12 Ap '77
See also
Synagogues
CHURCH art. See Christian art and symbolism
CHURCH attendance

Anecdotes, facetiae, satire, etc.

How to succeed at success. M. E. Marty. Chr Cent 94:575 Je 8 '77
CHURCH bells. See Bells
CHURCH bureaucracy. See Church government
CHURCH colleges and universities
College-related church; work of the National Commission on United Methodist Higher Education. J. W. Donohue. America 137:122-5 S 10 '77
No obituary yet for church colleges. Chr Today 21:41-2 Ja 7 '77
Yin and Yang: Baptist and Methodist college surveys. Chr Cent 94:933-5 O 19 '77
You can't tell a school by its name. R. C. Sproul. Chr Today 22:18+ N 4 '77
See also
Catholic colleges and universities
Davidson College, Davidson, N.C.
Toccoa Falls Institute, Toccoa Falls, Ga.
Wheaton College, Wheaton, Ill.

Curriculum

What Christian colleges teach about creation; interview, ed by D. Singer. J. Haas; R. Wright. il Chr Today 21:8-11 Je 17 '77

Finance

Financial crisis that isn't. G. R. Werkema. il por Chr Today 22:22-4 N 4 '77
CHURCH commitment. See Commitment to the church
CHURCH Committee. See United States—Congress—Senate—Select Committee to Study Governmental Operations with Respect to Intelligence Activities
CHURCH conferences. See Religious conferences
CHURCH decoration and ornament
Wood witch; L. Nevelson's sculpture in St Peter's Church in New York City. M. Stevens. il por Newsweek 90:95-6 D 19 '77
CHURCH etiquette. See Etiquette
CHURCH finance
Pluralism and consensus: why mainline church mission budgets are in trouble. R. G. Hutcheson, Jr. Chr Cent 94:618-24 Jl 6 '77; Discussion. 94:955-7 O 19 '77
See also
Evangelistic work—Finance
Fund raising
Taxation, Exemption from
CHURCH government

Anecdotes, facetiae, satire, etc.

Tower of Babel; technical jargon of church bureaucracy. A. R. Brouwer. Chr Cent 94:276-9 Mr 23 '77
CHURCH growth
Developing a climate of trust. D. Gerig. Chr Today 21:30 Ap 15 '77
Intensity of belief: a pragmatic concern for church growth; interviews, ed by D. E. Kucharsky. C. P. Wagner; A. Johnston. pors Chr Today 21:10-14 Ja 7 '77
Should Methodists buy the church growth package? J. C. Lyles. Chr Cent 94:1214-15 D 28 '77
CHURCH history
See also
Bible

Bibliography

Church and how it grew. D. Tinder. Chr Today 21:10-18 S 9 '77

Primitive and early church

Gone with the wind myth; early New Testament church. W. H. Willimon. Chr Cent 94:501-2 My 25 '77
CHURCH leadership. See Christian leadership
CHURCH libraries. See Libraries, Church
CHURCH management
Lifting ministers from the mud. E. R. Dayton. Chr Today 21:10-12 Jl 29 '77
CHURCH manners. See Etiquette
CHURCH membership
See also
Commitment to the church
CHURCH music
Laurence Feininger 1909-1976; life, work, legacy; cataloger and transcriber of Catholic Church music. E. E. Lowinsky. bibl il por Mus Q 63:327-66 Jl '77
See also
Mass (music)
Oratorio
Phonograph records—Church music
Religion and music
Sacred Music Society of America
CHURCH of England
Alison Palmer: upsetting the Anglicans. T. Beeson. Chr Cent 94:1213-14 D 28 '77
Anglican evangelicals: a view from the north. J. D. Douglas. Chr Today 21:41 Jl 8 '77
Anglican evangelicals speak out; Nottingham statement. J. R. W. Stott. Chr Today 21:30-1 Jl 8 '77
His new prayer; Anglican rewording of the Lord's Prayer. W. F. Buckley, Jr. Nat R 29: 1453 D 9 '77
To the rescue; A. Palmer, woman priest, administering communion. Chr Today 22:49-50 N 4 '77
See also
Catholic church—Relations—Church of England

Theological seminaries

See Theological seminaries—Great Britain
CHURCH of England in Australia
Anglican women priests in Australia? R. Mathias. Chr Cent 94:658 Jl 20 '77
Women priests: the door is opening. R. Mathias. Chr Cent 94:1006 N 2 '77
CHURCH of England in Canada
Canadian Anglicans debate life-and-death issues; general synod. J. Hames. Chr Cent 94: 772-3 S 14 '77
CHURCH of England in Uganda
Helping Ugandans. Chr Today 21:38-9 Ag 12 '77
CHURCH of God. See Worldwide Church of God
CHURCH of Jesus Christ of Latter-Day Saints. See Mormons and Mormonism
CHURCH of Scientology. See Scientology
CHURCH of Scotland
Scotland: a path still overgrown. J. D. Douglas. Chr Today 22:70+ O 7 '77
Trouble in the kirk. J. D. Douglas. Chr Today 21:34-5 Jl 8 '77
CHURCH polity. See Church government
CHURCH related colleges. See Church colleges and universities
CHURCH related schools. See Church schools
CHURCH renewal
Unhooked Christians. J. R. W. Stott. Chr Today 22:40-1 O 7 '77

CHURCH schools
Counterattack; controversy over church schools in Kentucky. R. Kirk. Nat R 29:1434 D 9 '77
See also
Catholic schools

Federal aid

See also
Catholic schools—Federal aid

State aid

Aid to nonpublic education; Supreme Court decision. America 137:2-3 Jl 2 '77
Parochial decision; Supreme Court ruling. Newsweek 90:59 Jl 4 '77

Tax exemption

See Taxation. Exemption from

CHURCH union
See also
Ecumenical movement
World Conference on Faith and Order

CHURCH work
See also
Christian leadership

CHURCH work with children
They count, too. C. B. Murphey. Chr Today 22:30-1 O 21 '77

CHURCH work with homosexuals
Set the captives free. J. Gramick. il New Cath World 220:292-5 N '77

CHURCH work with single people
Family church: any place for singles? R. L. Strauss. Chr Today 21:12-14 Jl 29 '77

CHURCH work with the handicapped
Mainstreaming the alienated: the church responds to a new minority. H. H. Wilke. Chr Cent 94:272-5 Mr 23 '77; Reply. G. Maxson. 94:805-6 S 21 '77
Paralytics: strangers in a strange land. K. Cone. il Chr Cent 94:589-92 Je 22 '77

CHURCHES
Why the church roof leaks. M. E. Marty. Chr Cent 94:991 O 26 '77
See also
Church architecture

Management

See Church management

Ecuador

Quito; church architecture and decoration of the colonial period. J. R. Chiriboga; H. Crespo Toral. il map Américas 29:S1-12 Ap '77

England

Britain's brave bells. E. Antrobus. il Am For 83:42-5+ Mr '77

Ethiopia

Painted churches of Lake Tana. B. Abbebe. il UNESCO Courier 30:13-17 F '77

Hawaii

Wayside churches on Kauai. il Sunset 158:32 Ap '77

CHURCHILL, Clementine Ogilvy (Hozier) Spencer, Baroness
Churchill consignments. Art N 76:124 My '77 *
Darling Clemmie. il por Newsweek 90:80 D 26 '77 *

CHURCHILL, Creighton
Wines. See issues of American home

CHURCHILL, Sir Winston Leonard Spencer
Painting as a pastime; excerpt from The art world; ed by B. Diamonstein. Art N 76:162 N '77

about

Churchill and us. E. N. Luttwak. Commentary 63:44-9 Je '77 *
Who started the cold war? C. L. Mee. Jr; W. A. Harriman; E. Abel. il pors Am Heritage 28:8-23 Ag '77 *

CHUSID, Martin
Verdi's early U.S. premieres. il Opera N 42:32-3 Ja 7 '78

CHUTE, Beatrice Joy
What makes a fiction writer? Writer 90:9-11 O '77

La CHUTE de la maison Usher; opera. See Debussy, C.

CHUTNEY. See Pickles and relishes

CHVOTZKIN
Environmental eloquence. R. Weil. il House B 119:94-103 N '77 *

CHWATSKY, Ann Schneider
Sisters. il Good H 185:88+ S '77

CIARDI, John
Manner of speaking. See alternate issues of Saturday review

CICADAS
120-year bamboo clock; reproductive periodicity of bamboo and cicadas. S. J. Gould. Natur Hist 86:8+ Ap '77

CICCHETTI, Charles J.
Still the wrong route. il Environment 19:2-3 Ja '77

CIDER
Ways to store apple cider. E. Chittenden. il Org Gard & Farm 24:128-30 O '77

CIEPLIK, Walt
Jim Murry: king of sports. por Writers Digest 57:23-4 Ag '77

CIGAR industry
Help from Havana? Forbes 120:69 N 15 '77
Meanwhile, U.S. cigar makers are losing customers. A. Stuart. Fortune 95:177 F '77

CIGARETTE industry

Advertising

Notes and comment. New Yorker 53:23-4 Je 27 '77

Marketing

Cigarette makers go all out for low-tar brands. il Bus W p82+ O 31 '77

Reports to government

Cigarette makers balk at the FTC's demands. Bus W p44 My 16 '77

Great Britain

Smokers stub out synthetic cigarettes. Bus W p55 O 3 '77

CIGARETTE smoke
Cigarette smoke activates guanylate cyclase and increases guanosine 3′,5′-monophosphate in tissues. W. P. Arnold and others. bibl il Science 198:934-6 D 2 '77

CIGARETTE smoking. See Smoking

CIGARETTE smuggling. See Smuggling

CIGARETTES

Advertising

See Cigarette industry—Advertising

Taxation

We're not fools! Forbes 119:118 Je 15 '77

CILÈA, Francesco
Adriana Lecouvreur. Reviews
Hi Fi il 27:MA29 S '77 *

CILIATA
See also
Paramecia
Tetrahymena

CILLIÉ, P. J.
Case for Africa's white tribe. il Sat Eve Post 249:90-6+ Mr '77

CIMAROSA, Domenico
Cimarosa's comic masterpiece; DG's recording of Il matrimonio segreto. P. H. Lang. il Hi Fi 27:95-6 N '77 *
Il matrimonio segreto; Deutsche Grammophon recording. G. L. Mayer. il Am Rec G 41:25-7 D '77 *

CIMETIDINE. See Antihistamines

CIMONS, Marlene
For big fish only. New Repub 177:14-15 Jl 9 '77
Occupational health v. civil rights for women. New Repub 176:24 My 21 '77

CINCINNATI

Education

Science and socialization out-of-doors; Doherty School Outing Club. P. D. Dawson. Educ Digest 42:57-9 F '77

Music

Debuts & reappearances. Hi Fi 27:MA24 Ap; MA33-4 Jl; MA21-2 S; MA26 O '77
See also
Cincinnati Symphony Orchestra
Opera—Ohio

Religious institutions and affairs

Kindling fires along the Ohio; B. Graham crusade at Cincinnati's Riverfront Coliseum. A. Toalston. Chr Today 22:47-9 N 18 '77

Social history

Unwanted helping hand; Cincinnati Social Unit. N. Betten and M. Austin. bibl il Environment 19:13-20+ Ja '77

CINCINNATI Ballet Company
From here and there; program at Pace College's Schimmel Center. R. A. Thom. il Dance Mag 51:20-2 Je '77

CINCINNATI Conservatory of Music. See Cincinnati. University—College-Conservatory of Music

CINCINNATI Opera. See Opera—Ohio

CINCINNATI Symphony Orchestra
Cincinnati Sym: Gutchë premiere. Hi Fi 27:MA33-4 Jl '77
Cincinnati Sym: Proto premiere; Three pieces for percussion and orchestra. Hi Fi 27:MA21-2 S '77

CINCINNATI. University

College-Conservatory of Music

College-Conservatory: Stalvey prem; Celebration-sequent II. por Hi Fi 27:MA24 Ap '77

CINDERELLA; dramatization. See Thane, A.

CINEMA. See Motion pictures

CINEMATOGRAPHY. See Motion picture photography

CINNABAR moths. See Moths
CINQUAIN. See Poetry
CIPHERS
Mathematical games. M. Gardner. il Sci Am 237:120-4 Ag '77
CIRCADIAN rhythms. See Biology—Periodicity
CIRCLE, Homer
Look who's fishing now. il Am Home 80:68-9+ Jl '77
CIRCULAR saws. See Saws
CIRCUS
One ring; Big Apple Circus, New York. New Yorker 53:21-2 Ag 22 '77
CIRCUS, Miniature
Biggest littlest shows on earth. il pors Ebony 32:90-2+ Mr '77
CIRCUS animals
See also
Elephants

Training

See Animals—Training
CIRCUS models. See Circus, Miniature
CIRCUS performers
See also
Gebel-Williams, G.
CIRCUS secret; drama. See Paston, B. N. and Tolins, S.
CIRINO, Antonio
Conversation with Antonio Cirino; interview, ed by C. Movalli. il por Am Artist 41:58-63+ Ag '77
CISTERNS
Cistern for the garden. P. Nesbitt. il Org Gard & Farm 24:88-9 Jl '77
CITATION indexes
See also
Science citation index
CITICORP
Citicorp's Australian salvage operation; Industrial Acceptance Corp. Bus W p36 My 2 '77
Glory days are over at Citicorp. il Bus W p64-8+ N 7 '77
Visa-card offensive angers the opposition. il Bus W p31 S 5 '77
Why investors pick Chase over Citicorp. il Bus W p46-7 Jl 4 '77
CITICORP Center. See New York (city)—Buildings
CITIES and towns
Changing city; excerpt; reproductions of paintings, with introd by C. Breslin. Natur Hist 86:86 Je '77
See also
Business districts
City and town life
Education, Urban
Neighborhoods
Playgrounds
Slums
Sociology, Urban
Trees in cities
Urban flora
Urbanization

Finance

See Municipal finance

Growth

Arizona's suburbs of the sun; Phoenix and Tucson. D. Jeffery. il supp (folded map) Nat Geog 152:486-517 O '77
COPS comes to San Antonio. E. D. Yoes, Jr. Progressive 41:33-6 My '77
Craig, Colorado: population unknown, elevation 6,185 feet; energy boom town. P. L. Fradkin. il Audubon 79:118-27 Jl '77
Spaciousness; change in patterns of living space. A. W. Smith. Nat Parks & Con Mag 51:2+ O '77
See also
Annexation (municipal government)
Metropolitan areas
Suburbs

History

Problem of the cities: it's an old refrain; study by Charles Adrian and Ernest Griffith. J. Gaylin. Psychol Today 10:90 Mr '77

Lighting

See also
Street lighting

Planning

See City planning

Recreation

See Recreation

Algeria

Algeria's unearthly cities. U. Wolff. il Travel 147:54-9+ F '77

France

Provincial towns. B. Singer. Am Scholar 46:221-8 Spr '77

Germany, West

Five *wunderbar* German cities. Holiday 58:50 Ja '77

India

India: three historic cities. G. Trotta. il Travel 148:60-3 O '77

Japan

Four fabled cities of Japan. il Mademoiselle 83:134-6+ O '77

Latin America

City planning in the Spanish colonies. G. de Zéndegui. il map Américas 29:S1-12 F '77

Peru

Beyond beautification: cities with souls. J. L. S. Jennings, Jr and N. Sánchez. il Américas 29:50-7 N '77

Russia

Russian paradoxes. R. G. Smith. Intellect 105:373-4 My '77

Spain

Beyond beautification: cities with souls. J. L. S. Jennings, Jr and N. Sánchez. il Américas 29:50-7 N '77

United States

Cities' secret: heading toward apartheid. I. Howe. New Repub 176:55-7 Ja 22 '77
Cities where business is best. il U.S. News 82:76-9 My 16; 83:72-5 O 24 '77
Comeback of the small town. R. Tunley. il Read Digest 111:143-7 O '77
Don't mourn lost military bases; aid to affected communities by the Office of Economic Adjustment. il Am City & County 92:26 S '77
Fresh look at drift from big cities. il U.S. News 82:71 Ap 25 '77
Housing, urban decay challenge Carter; excerpt from address. L. De Moll. Am City & County 92:110+ My '77
Let big cities die? M. Stone. U.S News 83:80 Ag 8 '77
Macro theoretical approaches to public policy analysis: the fiscal crisis of American cities. H. Teune. bibl f Ann Am Acad 434:174-85 N '77
Miniguides: new nightlife; nine cities. Vogue 167:147-8+ N '77
Retiring? a guide to cheapest cities. il U.S. News 83:36 Ag 22 '77
Reviewing the American city; address, March 4, 1977. H. S. Reuss. Vital Speeches 43:401-5 Ap 15 '77
Sportscasters' score the cities. M. J. Gun. il Holiday 58:22-5 Je '77
Why more and more people are coming back to cities. il U.S. News 83:69-71 Ag 8 '77
See also
All-America cities
Metropolitan areas
National League of Cities
United States—Housing and Urban Development, Department of
Urban renewal
CITIES and towns, Models of. See Models of cities, towns, etc.
CITIES and towns, Ruined, extinct, etc.
See also
Chichén Itzá
Pompeii
CITIES and towns in art
See also
New York (city) in art
CITIES and towns in motion pictures
Those mean and dirty streets; City of New York. R. Eder. il Horizon 19:4-10 My '77
CITIES Service Company
Results unrewarded. por Forbes 119:80 F 15 '77
CITIZEN and Shareholders' Rights and Remedies Subcommittee. See United States—Congress—Senate—Judiciary, Committee on the—Citizen and Shareholders' Rights and Remedies Subcommittee
CITIZEN crime commissions. See Crime prevention—Citizen participation
CITIZEN participation in mental health programs. See Mental health care—Citizen participation
CITIZENS and Southern National Bank. See Atlanta—Banks
CITIZENS arrest. See Arrest
CITIZENS associations
COPS comes to San Antonio. E. D. Yoes, Jr. Progressive 41:33-6 My '77
U.S. journal: San Antonio; Communities Organized for Public Service. C. Trillin. il New Yorker 53:92-4+ My 2 '77
See also
Crime prevention—Citizen participation
Pressure groups
CITIZENS band radio
CB & sun spots. J. Walders. il Sci Digest 81:24-7 F '77
CB fiasco. J. Ethridge. Motor T 29:69-70 Ap '77
CB scene. See issues of Popular electronics including Electronics world
CB: uncommon circuits for common problems. R. F. Scott. il Radio-Electr 49:48-50 Ja '78
Europe: the CB craze hits Europeans hard. Bus W p47-8 Mr 21 '77

CITIZENS band radio—*Continued*
Forgotten CB service; Class A. W. Salm. il Pop Electr 12:90-1 N '77
40-channel CB spectacular; symposium. il Radio-Electr 48:39-54 F '77
Special focus on CB radio. il Pop Electr 11:45-60 Mr '77
10-4 for CB? L. Langway and E. Sciolino. il Newsweek 89:68-9 Ja 24 '77

Emergency use

Better emergency services are near. I. Berger. Pop Electr 12:103-5 S '77
Coast Guard will monitor CB. G. West. Yachting 142:126 D '77

Equipment

Build 30-MHz CB frequency counter. G. Santi. il Radio-Electr 48:43-5+ S '77
Build 3 low cost CB test meters. W. E. Osborne. il Radio-Electr 48:40-1+ O '77
Christmas bargains in CB sets. Changing T 31:34 D '77
40 channel CB buyer's guide. M. Davis. il Hot Rod 30:104-7 Jl '77
40-channel CB: PM takes a look at the new sets. A. R. Curtis. il Pop Mech 147:82-5 Je '77
40-channel CB's—lots of new choices. il Pop Sci 210:84-6 My '77
40-channel roundup. F. Petras. il Radio-Electr 48:40-4+ Ja '77
40-channel transceiver directory. il Radio-Electr 48:51-3 F '77
Have more CB fun with these add-ons. A. R. Curtis. il Pop Mech 148:78-9 S '77
How external speakers can improve mobile CB performance. S. R. Davis. il Pop Electr 11:54-7 Mr '77
New CB add-on shows your exact frequency. J. L. Genevicz. il Pop Mech 148:32 N '77
Performance capabilities of 40-channel CB transceivers. B. Scherer. il Pop Electr 11:47-9 Je '77
Preamplifier for long distance reception. G. Sante. il Radio-Electr 48:70-1+ My '77
Pros and cons of CB frequency-generation methods. W. M. Scherer. il Pop Electr 11:46-51 Mr '77
Single sideband: the high-performance CB. G. R. Patton. il Pop Mech 148:100-1+ N '77
Those new 40-channel CBs. il Mech Illus 73:32+ F '77
See also
Microphones
Radio antennas

Noise

Automatic noise blankers—how they work. R. F. Scott. il Radio-Electr 48:60-2 Jl '77
Automatic noise limiters—how they work. R. F. Scott. il Radio-Electr 48:54-6 Je '77

Testing

Hey, good buddy! CU rates CB radios. il Consumer Rep 42:562-7 O '77
Product test reports:
Cobra model 29XLR mobile 40-channel CB transceiver. il Pop Electr 12:85 Jl '77
E.F. Johnson Viking 4360 remote control mobile AM CB transceiver. il Pop Electr 13:74-5 Ja '78
General Electric model 3-5825 AM/SSB CB transceiver. il Pop Electr 12:97-8 S '77
HY-Gain model 2716 mobile AM BC transceiver. il Pop Electr 12:91-3 O '77
Kris model XL-50 40-channel CB mobile transceiver. il Pop Electr 11:94-5 Je '77
President Washington AM/SSB CB base station. il Pop Electr 12:84-5 Ag '77
Realistic model TRC-449 mobile AM/SSB CB transceiver. il Pop Electr 12:85-6 N '77
Sparkomatic model CB 2040 CB AM mobile transceiver. il Pop Electr 12:98-9 D '77
Sharp model CB-800A CB mobile AM transceiver. Pop Electr 11:79+ F '77
Testing CB transceivers. R. J. Constantine. il Radio-Electr 48:51-3+ S '77
What you need to know about CB test gear. F. Belt. il por Radio-Electr 48:49-61 N '77

Exhibitions

CB crossover point; Personal Communications 2-Way Radio Show. A. Salsberg. Pop Electr 11:4 My '77

Illegal use

Really illegal side of citizens band. il Mech Illus 73:48+ Mr '77

Interference

See Radio interference

Laws and regulations

Rules enforcement game plan. G. Garcia. Pop Electr 12:116-17 D '77
See also
United States—Federal Communications Commission

Library use

See Libraries and radio

Testing instruments

See Testing instruments

CITIZENS band radio in agriculture
How to clear up your CB channels. D. O. Hull. il Farm J 101:A4+ mid-F '77

CITIZENS band radio on automobiles
Build a silencer; squelches operating radio or tape player when CB signal begins. R. Miles. il Pop Electr 11:57-60 Mr '77
Build CB switcher for music between calls. G. Sante. il Radio-Electr 48:40-1 D '77
CB radio, Detroit style. L. Buckwalter. il Mech Illus 73:40-1+ O '77
Law and order comes to CB radio. S. Thompson. Car & Dr 23:20 D '77

Security measures

Equipment reports:
Tri-Star Corp Tiger CB Alarm. il Radio-Electr 48:90-1 O '77
How to hide your CB. L. O. Rexrode. il Mech Illus 73:116 N '77

CITIZENS band radio on ships, boats, etc.
Citizens band for mariners. G. West. il Motor B & S 139:28-30 F '77
Coast Guard will monitor CB. G. West. Yachting 142:126 D '77
Marine CB: install one for boating fun and safety. W. J. Hawkins. il Pop Sci 210:56+ F '77

CITIZENS Committee for Broadcasting. See National Citizens Commission for Broadcasting

CITIZENS Communications Center. See Law partnership

CITIZENS complaints. See Complaints

CITIZENS Fidelity Corporation. See Bank holding companies

CITIZENS State Bank, Carrizo Springs, Tex. See Banks and banking—Texas

CITIZENSHIP
See also
Aliens
Self determination, National

United States

America's stepchildren; citizenship claims by Rio Ricans on U.S.-Mexican border. M. Kasindorf. il Newsweek 89:13 Ap 25 '77

CITIZENSHIP, Education for. See Political science—Study and teaching

CITRUS fruit industry
Florida: frost-kissed oranges. R. Rauch. il Time 109:12 F 14 '77
Social history of a singular fruit. T. H. Watkins. il Am Heritage 28:84-7+ Ap '77
Where relief became disaster; south Florida. U.S. News 82:57 Mr 7 '77

Advertising

Crating up the California dream. J. L. Phillips. il Am Heritage 28:88-93 Ap '77

CITRUS fruits
Oranges and their cousins; with recipes. R. Sokolov. il Natur Hist 86:88-91 Je '77
See also
Cookery—Fruit
Lemons

CITTADINO, Mary L. and others
Three computer-based bibliographic retrieval systems for scientific literature. il BioScience 27:739-42 N '77

CITY and country
City people are healthier than their country cousins; study by Leo Srole. S. Bush. Psychol Today 11:26+ Ag '77
Rural-urban differences in attitudes and behavior in the United States. N. D. Glenn and L. Hill, Jr. bibl f il Ann Am Acad 429:36-50 Ja '77
See also
Country life

CITY and town life
Be careful where you aim those binoculars! small town life retirement. R. B. Douglas. il Ret Liv 17:28-9 Je '77
Comeback of the small town. R. Tunley. il Read Digest 111:143-7 O '77
Craig, Colorado: population unknown, elevation 6,185 feet; energy boom town. P. L. Fradkin. il Audubon 79:118-27 Jl '77
Urban pioneers gamble on the inner city. il Bus W p 144+ Jl 25 '77
Urban urge. D. S. Kussmaul. House B 119:66+ N '77
Who wouldn't help a lost child? You, maybe. H. Takooshian and others. bibl il pors Psychol Today 10:67-8+ F '77

CITY Center Joffrey Ballet
Dance:
Les patineurs. N. Goldner. Nation 225:568-9 N 26 '77
Performance of La vivandière. N. Goldner. Nation 225:506-7 N 12 '77
Dancing:
Anthony Dowell in The dream. A. Croce. New Yorker 53:186-7 N 21 '77

CITY Center Joffrey Ballet—*Continued*
Tragical-comical-historical-pastoral; Joffrey Ballet at the City Center 55th Street theater. D. Vaughan. Dance Mag 51:106-7+ Mr '77
Twyla Tharp, in motion; performance of Happily ever after. E. Kendall. New Repub 176: 19-20 F 12 '77

CITY College of New York. See New York (city). City University—City College

CITY councilmen. See Councilmen

CITY employees. See Municipal employees

CITY flora. See Urban flora

CITY gardens
See also
Balcony gardens, roof gardens, etc.
Community gardens

CITY government. See Municipal government

CITY growth. See Cities and towns—Growth

CITY houses
At home with a skyscraper; townhouse of Ame Venema. P. Goldberger. il N Y Times Mag p 106-8 O 23 '77
Classic town house in the Nation's Capital; Georgetown. J. Friedman-Weiss and H. H. Wise. il McCalls 104:98-100+ S '77
Essence of understatement; Halston's Manhattan town house. M. Gough and others. il por House B 119:94-7+ O '77
James Beard's recipe for living; new kitchen in his Greenwich Village town house. il por House & Gard 149:108-13 F '77
Many faces of a brownstone; turn-of-the-century house in New York. M. Borgenicht. il N Y Times Mag p74-5+ O 9 '77
Reporter at large: the making of Boerum Hill; brownstone renovation in Brooklyn. J. Anderson. il New Yorker 53:81-2+ N 14 '77
Toronto townhouse: a year-round garden; home of B. Myers. N. Skurka. il N Y Times Mag p52-3 Ag 21 '77

Condominium plan ownership
See Condominium (housing)

CITY improvement. See Municipal improvement

CITY life. See City and town life

CITY manager plan
Strengthening council and manager relations; views of officials. Am City & County 92:8 F '77

CITY managers
See also
International City Management Association

CITY models. See Models of cities, towns, etc.

CITY planners
See also
Site, Inc

CITY planning
Cities; meeting of New Yorkers to assist in the formation of Federal urban policies. New Yorker 53:38-40 N 14 '77
Global cities of tomorrow. D. A. Heenan. bibl f Harvard Bus R 55:79-92 My '77
Note about cities. A. W. Smith. Nat Parks & Con Mag 51:2+ Jl '77
Urban mayor offers some sensible strategies in searching for a new urban policy; ed by W. F. Wagner, Jr. Archit Rec 161:13 Mr '77
See also
Business districts
Community development
Location in business and industry
Municipal improvement
Rural planning
Suburbs
Urban renewal
Water fronts

History
City planning in the Spanish colonies. G. de Zéndegui. il map Américas 29:S1-12 F '77

California
See also
San Jose, Calif.—City planning

Europe, Western
We can learn from Europe's cities; ICMA European Task Force; address, September 26, 1976. T. Tedesco. Vital Speeches 43:209-11 Ja 15 '77

Germany, West
See also
Munich—City planning

Illinois
See also
Chicago—City planning

Indiana
Showpiece on the prairie; Columbus. il Time 110: 68-9 D 5 '77

Iran
See also
Teheran, Iran—City planning

Israel
See also
Jerusalem—City planning

Massachusetts
Urban aid—banned in Boston; Urban Planning Aid of Cambridge, Mass. S. Blumenthal. Nation 224:70-2 Ja 22 '77

New York (state)
See also
Albany, N.Y.—City planning
Bronx, N.Y.—City planning

Russia
City planning—Soviet style. Y. Shevyakov. Am City & County 92:110 My '77

Texas
See also
San Antonio, Tex.—City planning

Washington, D.C.
See Washington, D.C.—City planning

CITY services. See Municipal services

CITY Stores Company. See Department stores

CITY taxation. See Local taxation

CITY traffic
How the rest of the world copes with traffic jams. il U.S. News 82:31-3 F 7 '77
See also
Albany, N.Y.—Street traffic
Denver—Street traffic
Pedestrians
Washington, D.C.—Street traffic

Automatic control
See also
Computers—Traffic control use
Traffic signals—Control

CITY transit. See Local transit

CITY trees. See Trees in cities

CITY University of New York. See New York (city). City University

CIUDAD BLANCA, Honduras. See Geographical myths

CIUFFA, Anthony A.
Secrets from a heartland bass lab; interview, ed by J. Randolph. il por Outdoor Life 160: 82-5+ D '77

CIVICS. See Political science—Study and teaching

CIVIL Aeronautics Board. See United States—Civil Aeronautics Board

CIVIL Air Patrol. See United States—Civil Air Patrol

CIVIL and Political Rights, International Covenant on. See International Covenant on Civil and Political Rights

CIVIL defense
Planning for the day after doomsday. B. D. Clayton. bibl Bull Atom Sci 33:49-53 S '77
World of survival; planning for aftermath of atomic war. Commonweal 104:739-40 N 25 '77; Reply with rejoinder. D. Berrigan. 105:3+ Ja 6 '78
See also
Atomic bomb shelters

Russia
Congress unit hits significance of Soviet civil defense. E. Kozicharow. il Aviation W 106:50-1 My 30 '77
Russia's bomb shelters. F. Coleman. il Newsweek 89:33 My 23 '77
Soviet civil defense: insiders argue whether strategic balance is shaken. D. Shapley; reply. C. H. Kearny and E. P. Wigner. Science 195:243 Ja 21 '77

CIVIL disobedience. See Government, Resistance to

CIVIL engineering
See also
American Society of Civil Engineers

CIVIL Liberties Union, American. See American Civil Liberties Union

CIVIL liberty. See Liberty

CIVIL procedure
Quicker route to court; speeding pretrial discovery. il Bus W p84+ D 5 '77
See also
Arbitration and award

CIVIL religion. See Religion and sociology

CIVIL Reserve Air Fleet. See United States—Air Force—Civil Reserve Air Fleet

CIVIL rights
Aid, human rights link reappraised. Aviation W 106:18 Ap 11 '77
Are human rights universal? P. L. Berger. Commentary 64:60-3 S '77
Bearing witness and human rights. J. P. Dobel. Chr Cent 94:751-3 Ag 31 '77
Birthright of man; excerpt from Unesco's Medium-Term Plan (1977-1982) il UNESCO Courier 30:14-15 Mr '77
Can Jimmy Carterize foreign policy? il Time 109:24-7 Mr 28 '77
Carter and human rights. S. Karnow. il Sat R 4:6-11 Ap 2 '77; Same. Current 193:3-11 My '77

CIVIL rights—*Continued*
Carter backs off; Belgrade conference on European security and cooperation. C. Whipple and others. Newsweek 90:48+ O 10 '77
Carter's point woman; P. Derian. A. Deming and S. Sullivan. por Newsweek 89:70 My 16 '77
Challenge to the Economic and Social Council: advancing the quality of life in all its aspects; address, April 19, 1977. A. J. Young, Jr. Dept State Bull 76:494-502 My 16 '77
Crusader's end; J. Carter and human rights. Nat R 29:594 My 27 '77
Diplomacy of the possible: the pragmatism of human rights. M. Reisman. Nation 224:554-8 My 7 '77
Getting down to cases on human rights. J. M. Wall. Chr Cent 94:555-6 Je 8 '77
How moral can we get? J. Chace. il N Y Times Mag p38-40+ My 22 '77
Human right to a job. New Repub 177:2+ N 5 '77
Human rights. Commonweal 104:259-60 Ap 29 '77
Human rights. J. Deedy. Commonweal 104:226 Ap 15 '77
Human rights: an important concern of U.S. foreign policy; statement, March 7, 1977. W. Christopher. Dept State Bull 76:289-91 Mr 28 '77
Human rights and foreign policy. T. Buergenthal and others. Intellect 106:179+ N '77
Human rights and foreign policy; address, with question and answer session, April 30, 1977. C. R. Vance. Dept State Bull 76:505-12 My 23 '77
Human rights and wrongs. C. F. H. Henry. Chr Today 21:25 Jl 8 '77
Human rights as a national policy. J. M. Wall. Chr Cent 94:371-2 Ap 20 '77
Human rights: confrontation in Belgrade and another in Grenada. il Time 109:6-8 Je 27 '77
Human-rights dilemma of leaving the ILO. il Bus W p 130+ S 19 '77
Human rights: let's mean what we say; statement, November 24, 1976. W. W. Scranton. Dept State Bull 75:745-9 D 27 '76
Human rights: other violators. il Time 109:10-11 Mr 7 '77
Human rights policy review; statement, October 25, 1977. M. L. Schneider. Dept State Bull 77:829-33 D 5 '77
Human rights: principle and realism; address August 9, 1977. W. M. Christopher. Dept State Bull 77:269-73 Ag 29 '77
Human rights: sermons or substance. F. Ajami. Nation 224:389-90 Ap 2 '77
Issue of human rights. W. Laqueur. Commentary 63:29-35 My '77
Limits of linkage; civil rights and foreign policy. T. Szulc. New Repub 176:17-19 Mr 5 '77
Mr Carter's discovery of human rights. W. F. Buckley, Jr. Nat R 29:402 Ap 1 '77
Mr Schreiber discusses achievements of United Nations in field of human rights; excerpts from address, April 7, 1977. M. Schreiber. il por UN Chron 14:39-40 My '77
Mixed results on rights. Newsweek 89:63-4 My 2 '77
Moral policeman to the world? il U.S. News 82:17-19+ Mr 14 '77
Motherhood, apple pie and human rights. R. Steel. New Repub 176:14-15 Je 4 '77
New hopes for human rights; address, September 9, 1977. C. W. Maynes. Dept State Bull 77:556-61 O 24 '77
Of human rights ... and wrongs. B. Catton. por Am Heritage 28:44-5 O '77
On human rights and social obligations; symposium. bibl il Society 15:26-103 N '77
Politics of human rights. D. P. Moynihan. Commentary 64:19-26 Ag '77; Same abr. Read Digest. 111:229-30+ D '77; Discussion. Commentary 64:4+ O '77
Push for human rights. A. Deming and others. il Newsweek 89:46-8+ Je 20 '77
Report on human rights in the Americas; statement, September 15, 1977. G. W. McGee. Dept State Bull 77:573-5 O 24 '77
Reporter at large; J. Carter's foreign policy. E. B. Drew. New Yorker 53:36-8+ Jl 18 '77
Review meeting of the CSCE opens at Belgrade; statement, with outline, October 6, 1977. A. J. Goldberg. Dept State Bull 77:674-80 N 14 '77
Rights—and wrongs. il Newsweek 89:54-5 Je 20 '77
Risky rhetoric of human rights. M. Greenfield. Newsweek 90:96 Jl 18 '77
Secretary Vance attends OAS General Assembly at Grenada; statements, and transcript of news conference, arrival remarks; with text of resolution, June 14-17, 1977. C. R. Vance. Dept State Bull 77:69-72+ Jl 18 '77
Six senators size up Carter's stand; views on issue of human rights. il U.S. News 82:21 Mr 14 '77
Treating people as equals; views of R. Dworkin. D. Beckwith. il por Time 110:54 S 5 '77
What U.S. stand on human rights? R. J. Barnet. Current 193:12-15 My '77
Zbiggy zpeaks; views of Z. Brzezinski. J. Osborne. New Repub 177:8-9 O 22 '77

See also
American Convention on Human Rights
Blacks—Civil rights
Children—Civil rights
Due process of law
Employees—Civil rights
Free speech
Freedom of the press
Handicapped—Civil rights
Human Rights Day and Week
Information, Freedom of
Intellectual liberty
International Covenant on Economic, Social and Cultural Rights
Liberty
Mentally handicapped—Civil rights
Mentally handicapped children—Civil rights
Mentally ill—Civil rights
Mentally ill children—Civil rights
Minorities—Civil rights
Privacy, Right of
Right to counsel
Scientists—Civil rights
Searches and seizures
Sick, The—Civil rights
Students—Civil rights
Teachers—Civil rights
United Nations—Commission on Human Rights
United Nations—Committee on Human Rights
Universal Declaration of Human Rights
Youth—Civil rights

Africa, Southern

Southern Africa experts hear witnesses on human rights violations. UN Chron 14:44 Ag '77

Argentina

Argentina today; address, June 28, 1977. R. C. Hill. Vital Speeches 43:612-15 Ag 1 '77
Physicist describes oppression of Argentine scientists. F. C. Bennett. Phys Today 30:61-2 Ag '77
Reports & comment: Argentina: a state of fear. J. B. Treaster. Atlantic 240:16+ N '77

Asia, Southeastern

U.S. assistance programs in southeast Asia; statement, March 17, 1977. R. B. Oakley. Dept State Bull 76:342-4 Ap 11 '77

Bangladesh

Human rights in Bangladesh. K. Bird and M. Holland. Progressive 41:48 O '77

Cambodia

Human rights situation in Cambodia; statement, July 26, 1977. R. C. Holbrooke. Dept State Bull 77:323-4 S 5 '77

Chile

Assembly calls on Chile to end torture: reexamine basis of state of siege; with text of resolution. UN Chron 14:62-3, 107-8 Ja '77
Chile's image designed for export. R. Barbosa. Chr Cent 94:283-4 Mr 23 '77
Desaparecidos. H. Fairlie. New Repub 176:10-11 Ap 9 '77
Letter from a Chilean exile. L. Allende. Chr Cent 94:79-80 F 2 '77
Pinochet and human rights. W. F. Buckley, Jr. Nat R 29:350-1 Mr 18 '77

China

Chinese rights. W. F. Buckley, Jr. Nat R 29:1384-5 N 25 '77

Communist countries

Human rights: bridge over troubled waters? il Sr Schol 109:2-5+ Ap 7 '77

Czechoslovakia

Department comments on subject of human rights in Czechoslovakia. Dept State Bull 76:154 F 21 '77
Dissent in Czechoslovakia. M. Bergman. New Repub 176:12-13 F 26 '77
Double standard. Nat R 29:1284 N 11 '77
Dual messages to Washington. il por Time 109:30+ F 14 '77
Spirit of Helsinki, where are you? Time 109:38-9 Ja 24 '77
That slanderous pamphlet; Charter 77. B. Jicinski. Nat R 29:383 Ap 1 '77

Europe, Eastern

Dirty tricks—and worse. F. Willey and others. il Newsweek 89:37+ F 14 '77
Dissent in a cold climate. Nat R 29:196 F 18 '77
Dissidents v. Moscow. il Time 109:20-4+ F 21 '77
How freedom fares in Soviet empire. R. Knight. il map U.S. News 82:19-21 Je 20 '77
Human rights and East-West relations. K. E. Birnbaum. bibl f For Affairs 55:783-99 Jl '77

CIVIL rights—Europe, Eastern—*Continued*
Now a cold war over human rights. U. S. News 82:52 F 14 '77
Silent fall. M. W. Browne. il N Y Times Mag p63+ O 23 '77
To Helsinki, with love. Nat R 29:253 Mr 4 '77
Wave of dissent in Russia's empire. U.S. News 82:35 Mr 7 '77
Writer, swine; complying with the Helsinki accord. F. Willey and others. il Newsweek 89:48+ Ja 24 '77

Great Britain

SS revisited; promotion of book complimentary to the Waffen SS. F. Willey and J. Hopkins. il Newsweek 90:74+ N 28 '77

Indonesia

Human rights in Indonesia; statement, October 18, 1977. R. B. Oakley. Dept State Bull 77: 848-52 D 12 '77

Iran

Human rights in Iran; statement, October 26, 1977. C. W. Naas. Dept State Bull 77:894-6 D 19 '77

Korea, South

New wave of repression in South Korea. Chr Cent 94:420 My 4 '77

Latin America

Human rights in the Americas. A. Orfila. Américas 29:18-20 My '77

Panama

Human rights in Panama; statement, October 11, 1977. W. P. Stedman. Dept State Bull 77: 652-5 N 7 '77

Poland

Polish dissent heats up; Glos manifesto. Time 110:52 O 31 '77

Rumania

Josif Ton's fight for rights. E. E. Plowman. il pors Chr Today 21:40-1 My 20 '77

Russia

AAP protests to Soviet on Shcharansky's arrest. M. Reuter. Pub W 211:14 My 30 '77
Because we care about people; views on Sakharov letter. J. M. Wall. Chr Cent 94:187-8 Mr 2 '77
Carter's plain talk. Nation 224:258-9 Mr 5 '77
Charge of treason; case of A. Shcharansky. F. Willey and F. Coleman. Newsweek 89:42+ Je 13 '77
Daring to talk about human rights; State Department response to statement by A. Sakharov. por Time 109:38 F 7 '77
Détente: the new morality. F. Willey and others. il Newsweek 89:36-7+ F 14 '77
Dissent and repression in the Soviet Union. R. Sharlet. bibl f Cur Hist 73:112-17+ O '77
Dissidents v. Moscow. il Time 109:20-4+ F 21 '77
Dual messages to Washington. il por Time 109: 30+ F 14 '77
Final acts and final solutions; effect of Helsinki agreement on Soviet Jews. W. Korey. bibl il Society 15:81-6 N '77
Forked tongue; Carter administration statements on Russian human rights. New Repub 176:7-8 F 19 '77
From Russia, with dissent. il Read Digest 110: 102-6 Je '77
Future of the Soviet Union. A. Amalrik. Intellect 106:3+ Jl '77
How a dissident describes human rights in Russia; excerpts from address, February 25, 1977. V. Bukovsky. il U.S. News 82:22 Mr 14 '77
How important is Soviet dissent? tr by G. Daniels. V. Chalidze. bibl f Commentary 63:57-62 Je '77
Human rights: conflicts among our ideals; excerpts from address, June 5, 1977. D. Riesman. Commonweal 104:711-15 N 11 '77
Human-rights widows; prisoner families. F. Coleman. il Newsweek 91:28-9 Ja 2 '78
Immoralists. F. Getlein. Commonweal 104:196-8 Ap 1 '77
Impasse at the Soviet embassy. T. Beeson. Chr Cent 94:408-9 Ap 27 '77
Impending political struggle: provisions in new Russian constitution. Nat R 29:703-4 Je 24 '77
Inside the whale. Nat R 29:819 Jl 22 '77
Konstitution. Nation 224:741 Je 18 '77
Kremlin cracks down. F. Coleman. il Newsweek 89:69-70 My 16 '77
Let's put detente back on the rails. S. Pisar. il N Y Times Mag p31-3+ S 25 '77
Letter to a friend: J. Carter's letter to A. Sakharov. por Time 109:30-1 F 28 '77
Life-or-death case; treatment of G. Chudnovsky. por Newsweek 90:46 Jl 4 '77
Loyal opposition. R. Medvedev. il por Newsweek 89:48 Je 20 '77
Now a cold war over human rights. U.S. News 82:52 F 14 '77
Pitfalls of morality. A. Tonelson. New Repub 177:13-15 O 29 '77
Prisoner of conscience: the Bukovsky file. L. Elliott. por Read Digest 111:93-7 Ag '77
Prospects for human rights; adaptation of address, June 5, 1977. D. Riesman. bibl il Society 15:28-33 N '77
Sakharov on human rights; excerpts from interview, ed by F. Coleman. A. D. Sakharov. il por Newsweek 89:31+ Mr 14 '77
Showdown with Russia. U.S. News 82:17-18 Je 20 '77
Soviet official tells U.S.—don't push the issue too far; interview, ed by R. Knight. G. Arbatov. il por U.S. News 82:23-4+ Mr 14 '77
Soviet side. F. Willey and others. il Newsweek 89:30 F 21 '77
Soviet trade. D. Yergin. New Repub 176:16-17 Je 4 '77
Soviets hit back on human rights. il Time 109: 22 Mr 14 '77
Tough talk on human rights—will it scuttle detente? il U.S. News 82:30+ Mr 7 '77

South Africa

Now South Africa's churches press for human rights. il U.S. News 82:29+ Mr 14 '77

Taiwan

Human rights situation in the Republic of China; statement, June 14, 1977. B. Levin. Dept State Bull 77:50-4 Jl 11 '77

Thailand

Department discusses human rights in Thailand; statement, June 30, 1977. R. B. Oakley. Dept State Bull 77:210-13 Ag 15 '77

Uganda

Dealing with Dada. New Repub 176:5-6+ Mr 19 '77
Limits of morality. I. Amin Dada. il por Newsweek 89:14-15 Mr 7 '77

Underdeveloped areas

See Underdeveloped areas—Civil rights

United States

Can Chuck Morgan keep Jimmy Carter honest? T. Branch. Esquire 87:14+ F '77
Civil liberties and national security: the outlook in Congress. I. Shapiro. Intellect 105: 230-3 F '77
Foreign nationals and American law. D. E. La Voy. bibl Society 15:58-64 N '77
Grand juries & human rights. Nation 225:197 S 10 '77
Helsinki check list: Russia keeps tabs. A. Beam. Nation 224:709-10 Je 11 '77
How TV cops flout the law. S. Arons and E. Katsh. il Sat R 4:10-14+ Mr 19 '77
Human rights on Capitol Hill. M. Kondracke. New Repub 176:11+ Ap 9 '77
In Supreme Court: fresh battles over individual rights. U.S. News 83:37 O 3 '77
Just leave it to the states; decisions encouraging state court involvement in protecting civil liberties. Time 109:46 Ap 4 '77
Rights explosion splintering America? D. C. Bacon. il U.S. News 83:29-30+ O 31 '77; Same with title Rights explosion. Current 198:28-33 D '77
Rights of movement. G. L. Houseman. bibl Society 14:16-19 Jl '77
Supreme Court and civil rights. C. H. Falk. Current 191:13-16 Mr '77
When rights collide. A. Etzioni. Psychol Today 11:158 O '77
Your rights with the police; comp by M. Gunther. il Bet Hom & Gard 55:13+ Ap '77
See also
Indians of North America—Civil rights
United States—Commission on Civil Rights
United States—Constitution—Bill of Rights

Vietnam

Human rights and Vietnam. Commonweal 104: 515-16 Ag 19 '77
Of many things. J. O'Hare. America 136:inside cover Ap 30 '77
Vietnam déjà-vu. Nat R 29:1412 D 9 '77
Why I escaped from Vietnam. Nguyen-con-Hoan. por Newsweek 90:24-5 O 31 '77
Winners and losers. Nat R 29:482-3 Ap 29 '77

CIVIL Rights Act of 1964
Effect on women's earnings of enforcement in Title VII cases. A. H. Beller. bibl il M Labor R 100:56-7 Mr '77
Legal cloud over affirmative action. Bus W p40+ D 26 '77

CIVIL Rights Attorney's Fees Awards Act. See Lawyers—Salaries, fees, etc.

CIVIL Rights Commission. See United States—Commission on Civil Rights

CIVIL rights demonstrations
Day they didn't march. L. Bennett, Jr. il Ebony 32:128-30+ F '77
See also
Blacks—Segregation, Resistance to
Coxey's Army, 1894

CIVIL rights organizations
See also
American Civil Liberties Union
Amnesty International (organization)
Anti-slavery Society for the Protection of Human Rights
International League for Human Rights
National Urban League
People United to Save Humanity (organization)

CIVIL service
See also
Bureaucracy
Government employees
Interns (civil service)
Municipal employees
Political patronage
Women in the civil service

Examinations

Getting a job with the government. Sr Schol 109:13 Ja 27 '77

Austria

No longer entitled. Time 110:56 D 12 '77

France

See also
National School of Administration, France

United States

Is civil service outmoded? G. R. Rosen. il Duns R 110:46-50 N '77
Seats at the banquet. N. Lemann. il New Repub 177:16-20 O 29 '77
Why can't do-nothing bureaucrats be fired? E. H. Methvin. Read Digest 111:119-22 N '77

CIVIL service, International. See International officials and employees

CIVIL Service Commission. See United States—Civil Service Commission

CIVIL service pensions
Burden of generosity. L. Aspin; discussion. Harpers 254:4+ F '77
Rising cost of public pensions—can taxpayers afford them? il U.S. News 82:84-6 Ja 24 '77
Washington memo; key Republicans urge merger with Civil Service Retirement Fund to save social security. R. D. Westgate. Ret Liv 17:60-2 N '77
See also
Municipal employees—Pensions

Finance

See Pensions—Finance

CIVIL war
See also
Lebanon—Civil War, 1975-
Spain—History—Civil War, 1936-1939

CIVIL War (United States) See United States—History—Civil War, 1861-1865

CIVILIZATION
Terror of the wilderness; spread of Western civilization; excerpt from The cost of living. F. Turner. il Am Heritage 28:58-65 F '77
Toward a day of reckoning: the poor vs. the rich worlds. H. Brown. Current 191:23-9 Mr '77
Tutankhamun and Star trek; address, July 29, 1977. C. L. Babcock. Vital Speeches 43:744-7 O 1 '77
Visions of futures past; Lindisfarne Association. S. Helgesen. il Harpers 254:80-6 Mr '77
See also
Acculturation
Animals and civilization
History
Popular culture
Renaissance
Social change
Social sciences
Technology and civilization
also subhead Civilization under names of countries, e.g. France—Civilization

Anecdotes, facetiae, satire, etc.

Civilizations in clay. il Craft Horiz 37:28-35 D '77

Philosophy

See also
Philosophical anthropology

CIVILIZATION, Ancient
See also
Mayas

CIVILIZATION, Christian
Without religiosity, a September Morrow title examines Christianity's birth and growth. R. Dahlin. il Pub W 211:28 My 30 '77

CIVILIZATION, Islamic
Islam goes to England; World of Islam Festival in London. A. Goldin. bibl il Art in Am 65:106-13 Ja '77

CIVILIZATION, Medieval
Best of times—the worst of times. P. W. Schmidtchen. il por Hobbies 82:134-6+ Ja '78

CIVILIZATION and computers. See Computers and civilization

CIVILIZATION and technology. See Technology and civilization

CLAIBORNE, Craig
Claiborne on deer and birds. Outdoor Life 160:172 O '77
Joe's in his heaven—his Window's on the World. il por Holiday 58:32-7+ Je '77
—and Franey, Pierre
Food. See issues of New York times magazine

CLAIBORNE, Robert
Great health care rip-off. Sat R 5:10-13+ Ja 7 '78

CLAIBORNE, Sybil
Okinawa's wife; story. New Yorker 53:26-8 Jl 11 '77

CLAIRE, William F.
Where artists do as they please—and, mostly, work. il Smithsonian 8:44-51 Jl '77

CLAIRVOYANCE
See also
Extrasensory perception

CLAMPS
Quick-set woodworker's clamps. H. Wicks. il Pop Mech 148:149 S '77

CLAMS
Centenarians of the mollusk family; quahogs. BioScience 27:832 D '77

CLAMS, Fresh water. See Mussels, Fresh water

CLAMSHELL Alliance. See Pressure groups

CLANCY, Richard G.
Vagabond camera: the beach. il Travel 148:68-9+ Jl '77

CLANCY, Rita Greenwald
Doctored program. il por Time 110:89 O 10 '77 *
Other Bakke. por Newsweek 90:46 O 24 '77 *

CLANCY, Roger
Florida's underwater policemen; with biographical sketch. il Sea Front 23:140-3, 190 My '77

CLANCY, Thomas H.
Lord, it is good for us to be here. New Cath World 220:29 Ja '77

CLANTON, Gordon, and Smith, L. G.
Self-inflicted pain of jealousy; excerpt from Jealousy. il Psychol Today 10:44-7+ Mr '77

CLAP, Thomas
Thomas Clap and the terrestrial comets. H. A. Smith. il Sky & Tel 53:420-2 Je '77 *

CLAPPER, Louis S.
Carter and the environment: better, but still not good enough. il Nat Wildlife 15:18-19 Je '77
—and others
Observations on Alaska. il Am For 83:22-3+ F '77

CLARINETISTS
See also
Goodman, B.

CLARION Music Society, Inc
Musical events:
Performance of Steffani's Niobe. A. Porter. New Yorker 53:182-4+ N 28 '77

CLARION Opera Group of New York. See Opera—New York (state)

CLARISSA Harlowe (literary character) See Women in literature

CLARK, Alfred Alexander Gordon
Murder with manners. C. Strout. il New Repub 177:34-6 Jl 30 '77 *

CLARK, Alvin J. See Crisona, N. J. jt auth

CLARK, Bob
(ed) See Vance, C. R. Secretary Vance interviewed on Issues and answers
—and others
(ed) See Young, A. J. Ambassador Young interviewed on Issues and answers

CLARK, David H. See Stephenson, F. R. jt auth

CLARK, David L. and others
Vestibular stimulation influence on motor development in infants. bibl il Science 196:1228-9 Je 10 '77

CLARK, Dick
Dance goes on; interview, ed by P. Herz. pors Sr Schol 109:29-30 F 10 '77

CLARK, Earnest Hubert, 1926-
Baker: calling the shots—and booming. por Duns R 110:22-3 O '77 *

CLARK, Eleanor
How smartly September comes in. Vogue 167:215-16 S '77
Losing sight; excerpt from Eyes, etc. Commentary 63:36-47 My '77
PW interviews; ed by B. A. Bannon. por Pub W 212:6 O 24 '77
Tidies; excerpt from Eyes, etc. Atlantic 240:60-2 Jl '77
Zoysia grass; story. Yale R 67:57-64 O '77

CLARK, Eugenie
Synagogues & sea fans. il por map Nat Parks & Con Mag 51:13-20 Ap '77

CLARK, Francis X.
Communion in the hand: why the diversity? America 136:356-8 Ap 16 '77

CLARK, George Rogers
George Rogers Clark and the conquest of Illinois. L. H. Harrison. il pors map Am Hist Illus 11:4-7+ F '77 *
George Rogers Clark: bluff over bullets. H. W. Noland and R. F. Banta. il pors map Sat Eve Post 249:54-7 O '77 *

CLARK, George W.
X-ray stars in globular clusters; with biographical sketch. il Sci Am 237:15, 42-55 O '77

CLARK, Howard Longstreth
Young Atlantan for American Express. por Bus W p31-2 Mr 14 '77 *

CLARK, James H. and McCormack, Shirley
Clomid or nafoxidine administered to neonatal rats causes reproductive tract abnormalities. bibl il Science 197:164-5 Jl 8 '77

CLARK, John
Merry yarn: your own kind of story. Camp Mag 49:21 My '77

CLARK, Karen
Boston desegregation: what went wrong? bibl Clearing H 51:157-9 D '77

CLARK, Ken
High-up, way-out of a rimrock guide. E. A. Bauer. il Outdoor Life 160:90-2 N '77 *

CLARK, Kenneth Mackenzie Clark, Baron
Animals and men: love, admiration and outright war; excerpt from Animals and men. il Smithsonian 8:52-61 bibl(p 130) S '77

CLARK, Letti L.
Medicine pots—a motivation operation. il Sch Arts 76:32-3 F '77

CLARK, Marsh
Track & field. Sports Illus 47:48+ Jl 25 '77

CLARK, Michael
Garlic studied as a remedy. il Sci Digest 81:31-2 Ap '77

CLARK, Monte
Party became a lynching. J. Marshall. por Sports Illus 46:68+ Ap 18 '77 *

CLARK, Nancy Carey
Parge away! il Design (US) 78:24-5 mid-Wint '77

CLARK, Nancy Hughes
Birth defects: how to prevent them. Harp Baz 110:86-7+ Jl '77

CLARK, Philip A.
Community education and its major components. Educ Digest 43:58-61 N '77

CLARK, Ramsey
England revives the star chamber. Nation 224: 261-3 Mr 5 '77

CLARK, Scott
We're the lucky ones. R. Rooney. il por McCalls 104:28+ S '77 *

CLARK, Sedgwick
Aspen experience. il Hi Fi 27:MA33-5 D '77
Magnificent Bruckner Eighth. por Am Rec G 40: 6-9 Ap '77

CLARK, Vernon M.
Ron Lyle's last fight? R. Boeth and D. Gram. il pors Newsweek 91:29-30 Ja 16 '78 *

CLARK County, Nev, Library. See Libraries—Nevada

CLARKE, Allen C.
Speaking of people. il por Ret Liv 17:15 Ja '77 *

CLARKE, Norma Taylor
Symphony in sea major. il Sat Eve Post 249:74-5 N '77

CLARKE, Steven
Common death trends in early tribes. Sci N 111:358-9 Je 4 '77 *

CLARK'S Expedition to the Illinois, 1778-1779
George Rogers Clark and the conquest of Illinois. L. H. Harrison. il pors map Am Hist Illus 11:4-7+ F '77

CLARKSON, Kenneth W. and Meiners, R. E.
Inflated unemployment statistics. Intellect 106: 183-4 N '77

CLASQUIN, F. F.
Periodical prices: 1975-77 update. il Lib J 102: 2011-15 O 1 '77
—and Cohen, J. B.
Prices of physics and chemistry journals. bibl il Science 197:432-8 Jl 29 '77

CLASS actions. See Actions and defenses

CLASS distinction. See Discrimination; Social classes

CLASS trips. See School excursions

CLASSIC Bookshop, New York City. See Booksellers and bookselling—New York (state)

CLASSICAL art. See Art, Classical

CLASSICAL education
See also
Latin language—Study and teaching

CLASSICAL music. See Music

CLASSICAL phonograph records. See Phonograph records

CLASSIFICATION
Zoology
See Zoology—Classification

CLASSIFIED advertising. See Advertising, Classified

CLASSIFIED defense information. See Defense information, Classified

CLASSIFIED documents. See Security classification (government documents)

CLASSIFIED government information. See Security classification (government documents)

CLASSROOM management
Classroom behavior problems solved with magic. L. Palmatier. Intellect 106:105 S '77
Extending guidance functions into the classroom. J. Hirt. bibl Clearing H 51:113-17 N '77
How can I best manage my classroom? M. M. McCarthy. Educ Digest 43:20-3 N '77
Principles of classroom discipline: toward a pragmatic synthesis. T. R. McDaniel. bibl Clearing H 51:149-52 D '77
Suggestions for ending classroom conflict. J. C. Stapleton and J. Croft. Educ Digest 42:28-9 Mr '77

CLASSROOMS
Visual order in the art room. C. L. Hallberg. il Sch Arts 77:28-9 N '77
See also
Open plan schools

CLATWORTHY, Nancy Moore
Case against living together; interview, ed by C. Remsberg and B. Remsberg. Seventeen 36: 132-3+ N '77

CLAUDEL, Paul
Claudel reconsidered. P. McCarthy. America 136: 392-3 Ap 30 '77 *

CLAUSSEN, William P.
Selling a service in retailing. P. Schwab. por Nations Bus 65:102 N '77 *

CLAUSTRE, Françoise
End of an ordeal. il por Time 109:38 F 14 '77 *

CLAVER, Francisco F. Bp
Of many things. J. O'Hare. America 136:inside cover My 21 '77; Correction. 136:inside cover My 28 '77

CLAW hammers. See Hammers

CLAWED frogs. See Frogs

CLAY, Belinda (Boyd) See Ali, K.

CLAY, Cassius. See Ali, M.

CLAY, Henry
Funeral of Henry Clay. J. S. Brown. il Antiques 112:110-11 Jl '77 *
Henry Clay's silver urn. il Antiques 112:112 Jl '77 *

CLAY, Katherine, and Dietz, J. J.
Building a human resources file: a model. Clearing H 50:337-40 Ap '77

CLAY, William Caldwell, 1915-
Law and your will; interview. il por U.S. News 82:49-50 My 30 '77

CLAY, William Lacy
Excerpt from remarks on proposal to amend the Hatch Act, January 4, 1977. Cong Digest 56:296+ D '77

CLAY
Bad clay. D. Pilcher. Ceram Mo 25:17+ Mr '77
Desert varnish: the importance of clay minerals. R. M. Potter and G. R. Rossman. bibl il Science 196:1446-8 Je 24 '77
Digging your own clay—a geologist's viewpoint. M. P. Bauleke. il Ceram Mo 25:46-9 My '77
Modeling early evolution with clay. Sci N 112: 277 O 29 '77
Oxidation glazes, slips, stains, and bodies for cone 6. R. Zakin. il Ceram Mo 25:33-43 Ap '77

CLAY (organization) See Art clubs and societies

CLAY industries
Refractories top pay scale in clay products plants. C. B. Barsky. bibl il M Labor R 100: 66-8 Mr '77

CLAY sculpture. See Ceramic sculpture

CLAY whistles. See Whistles

CLAYBIRDS. See Trap shooting

CLAYBROOK, Joan B.
Are air bags worth the trouble? interview. il pors U.S. News 83:33-4 S 26 '77
Auto safety dialogue: tough gap to narrow; interview, ed by J. Norris. pors Motor T 29:13-14 O '77
about
Ralph's wrath. il pors Newsweek 90:90+ D 12 '77 *

CLAYTON, Bruce Douglas
Planning for the day after doomsday. bibl Bull Atom Sci 33:49-53 S '77

CLAYTON, Edward T.
Strange murder of Homer G. Phillips. il pors Ebony 32:160-2+ S '77

CLAYTON, Marian S.
(ed) See Haley, A. Interview with Alex Haley

CLAYTON, Richard
Murder without blood. R. W. Winks. New Repub 177:30-3 Jl 30 '77 *

CLAYTOR, William Graham, 1912-
National strategy considerations in the Pacific Basin; address, June 27, 1977. Vital Speeches 43:706-8 S 15 '77

CLEAN Air Act. See Air pollution—Laws and legislation

CLEAN Community System. See Keep America Beautiful, Inc

CLEAN Water Act of 1972. See Water pollution—Laws and legislation

CLEANERS. See Cleaning compositions

CLEANING
See also
Automobiles—Cleaning
House cleaning

CLEANING compositions
Chemical drain cleaners. il Consumer Rep 42:68-9 D '77
General-purpose household cleaners. il Consumers Res Mag 60:11-15 My '77
Glass cleaners. Consumer Rep 42:318-19 D '77
Innocent packages; fumes from drain cleaners. R. E. Arnold. Field & S 81:104+ Mr '77
Keeping it clean: solutions for record care. H. Fantel. Opera N 41:38-9 Ap 2 '77
Rx for your paint and brightwork. W. Woron. il Motor T 29:103-7 Jl '77
Scouring cleansers. il Consumers Res Mag 60:34-6 Jl '77
Spot removers. il Consumer Rep 42:348-50 Je '77
Target: your car's interior. W. Woron. il Motor T 29:97-102 Ag '77
Toilet bowl cleaners. Consumer Rep 42:316-17 D '77
Waxes, polishes, and cleaning supplies. il Consumers Res Mag 60:78-83 O '77
See also
Bleaching materials
Detergents

CLEANING machinery and appliances
Now! A better, quicker way to clean carpets; steam cleaning machines. il Good H 185:188 N '77
See also
Vacuum cleaners

CLEANING of cities, towns, etc.
See also
Street cleaning

CLEANING of lakes, rivers, etc.
Canoe cleanup campaign; Shenandoah River. B. Gooch. por Outdoor Life 160:30 N '77
Cleanly flows the Thames. T. Fishlock. il Int Wildlife 8:33-5 Ja '78
Cleanup of Lake Winona. R. M. Welch. il map Parks & Rec 12:39-41+ My '77
Fifth-year review of Great Lakes Water Quality Agreement begins. Dept State Bull 76:446 My 2 '77
New life for the Monongahela. P. W. Weiser. il Parks & Rec 12:25a-27a F '77
Thames: new life for a dead river. il U.S. News 83:47 Jl 4 '77

CLEANLINESS. See Hygiene

CLEANUP pans. See Dust pans

CLEAR air turbulence. See Atmospheric turbulence

CLEARCUTTING
Fight for a wildflower haven; proposed clearcutting in the Nantahala National Forest. M. Prince. il Liv Wildn 41:45-7 Ap '77
Logger outcry obscures slow death of ancient park redwoods. il Nat Parks & Con Mag 51:22-3 Je '77

CLEARINGHOUSE for Library and Information Sciences. See Eric

CLEARY, Russell
Sing no sad songs for Heileman. por Forbes 120:51 O 1 '77 *

CLEATH, Robert L.
Schaeffer on film and in person. Chr Today 21:50 Ap 1 '77

CLEAVER, Eldridge
Views of a regenerate radical; interview, ed by J. S. Tinney. il pors Chr Today 21:14-15 Jl 8 '77
about
Convincing case for a pardon. Chr Today 21:36 F 18 '77 *
Party's over. pors Newsweek 90:29 S 5 '77 *
Rebirth of Eldridge Cleaver. T. D. Allman. il pors N Y Times Mag p 10-11+ Ja 16 '77 *

CLEIN, Marvin I.
Ability plus science equal world's best. L. Bortstein. il Sci Digest 81:10-11 Mr '77 *

CLELAND, Max
Two new agency heads: study in contrasts. il pors U.S. News 82:60 Mr 14 '77 *

CLEMATIS
Clematis, the queen of garden climbers. P. Harper. il Horticulture 55:76-81 F '77

CLEMENS, Samuel Langhorne
Adventures of Tom Sawyer; dramatization. See Olfson, L.
Personal habits of the Siamese twins. il por Sat Eve Post 249:24+ Jl '77
Prince and the Pauper; dramatization. See Newman, D.
about
Mark Twain last night. C. Williamson, Jr. Nat R 29:504-5 Ap 29 '77 *
Twain and Vonnegut. M. Bobkoff. Engl J 66:55 S '77 *
Welcome back from the raft, Huck honey! K. S. Lynn. Am Scholar 46:338-47 Summ '77 *

CLEMENT XI, Pope
Pope's library is brought to light after 200 years. M. Olmert. il Smithsonian 8:70-7 Ja '78 *

CLEMENT, Eugene
Resistance to motion. il Motor B & S 141:46+ Ja '78

CLEMENTE, Frank
(ed) New rural America. bibl f il Ann Am Acad 429:1-144 Ja '77
Put limits on the size of our automobiles; interview. por U.S. News 82:42-3 Ap 18 '77

La **CLEMENZA** di Tito; opera. See Mozart, J. C. W. A.

CLEMONS, James T.
Allah was on our side. Chr Cent 94:319-20 Ap 6 '77

CLEPPER, Henry
Pennsylvania Dutch country. il Am For 83:30-5 D '77
Trees and forests in American place names. Am For 83:20-2 Ag '77

CLERGY
Autographs. W. Rodger. il Hobbies 81:154-5+ F '77
Can we expect greatness from the clergy? C. S. Calian. Chr Cent 94:508-11 My 25 '77; Reply. C. E. Bryant. 94:918-19 O 12 '77
Future of the Christian clergy; address, January 7, 1977. J. V. Schall. Vital Speeches 43:271-4 F 15 '77
How to cope with discouragement. A. Bustanoby. Chr Today 21:28+ Ja 7 '77
Polling the preachers. Chr Today 21:36-7 Jl 8 '77
Sacramental color of a fire engine; minister-worker model. P. Andrews. Chr Cent 94:549-50 Je 1 '77
Why pastors drop out. A. Bustanoby. Chr Today 21:14-16 Ja 7 '77
See also
Alcohol and the clergy
Bishops
Catholic Church—Clergy
Deacons
Preaching
Women clergy
Women priests

Anecdotes, facetiae, satire, etc.

Things they didn't tell you at your seminary graduation. Eutychus VIII. Chr Today 21:6 My 20 '77

Education

Freedom for ministry. R. J. Neuhaus. Chr Cent 94:81-6 F 2 '77
Impossible dream: can seminaries deliver? symposium. Chr Today 21:18-21 F 4 '77
See also
Theological education

CLERGY and alcohol. See Alcohol and the clergy

CLERGY and Laity Concerned (organization)
How the B-1 bomber was brought down. J. Robison. Chr Cent 94:711-12 Ag 17 '77

CLERGY conferences
See also
Inter-American Conference of Major Religious Superiors

CLEVELAND, Grover

Health

President's operation; oral surgery for cancer performed on G. Cleveland. W. W. Keen. il Sat Eve Post 249:106+ Jl '77

CLEVELAND, Harold van B. and Brittain, W. H. B.
Are the LDCs in over their heads? il For Affairs 55:732-50 Jl '77

CLEVELAND, Jeremiah Clement
Jeremiah C. Cleveland. K. M. Jones. il Antiques 111:936 My '77 *

CLEVELAND, Pat
Fast-paced ride with the jet set crowd. il pors Ebony 32:72 Ag '77 *

CLEVELAND
Let us now praise Cleveland. J. Damico. por Newsweek 90:18-19 O 17 '77

Art

Cleveland. H. Cullinan. il Art N 76:119-20 D '77
New Deal ceramics: the Cleveland workshop. K. A. Marling. il por Ceram Mo 25:25-31 Je '77

Bookstores

See Booksellers and bookselling—Ohio

Education

Ohio squeeze. M. Sheils. il Newsweek 90:111 O 31 '77

Galleries and museums

See also
Cleveland Museum of Art

Monuments, statues, etc.

Provocative portal; question of steel sculpture by I. Noguchi. Vasari. il Art N 76:30-1 F '77

Moral conditions

Cleveland vs. Mary Hartman; protesting program time. J. H. Kraker. America 136:484-7 My 28 '77

CLEVELAND—*Continued*

Music

See also
Cleveland Institute of Music
Cleveland Orchestra
Opera—Ohio

Politics and government

Dennis the menace; D. Kucinich. D. M. Alpern and J. Lowell. il pors Newsweek 91:20 Ja 2 '78

Water supply

Cathodic protection guards Cleveland water system. R. Klimko. il Am City & County 92:54-5 Mr '77

CLEVELAND, Tex.

Restaurants

See Restaurants—United States

CLEVELAND Institute of Music
Cleveland heritage; recording. J. Ringo. Am Rec G 40:49 F '77

CLEVELAND Museum of Art
Secondhand saint; St Catherine altarpiece found to be a forgery. Vasari. il Art N 76:24+ D '77

CLEVELAND Opera Theater Ensemble. See Opera—Ohio

CLEVELAND Orchestra
Beethoven by Maazel. il Sat R 4:38 Ap 2 '77
Cleveland Orch, Gilels (Maazel) performances in New York in February. il Hi Fi 27:MA29-30 Je '77

CLEVELAND Public Library

Branches

Branches to rebuild cities. M. A. Huttner. por Lib J 102:168-9 Ja 15 '77

CLEVENGER, Mark
North by kicker. il map Motor B & S 139:64-5+ Mr '77

CLEVERDON, Stephanie A.
Bakke case; affirmative distraction. Progressive 41:26-9 D '77

CLIBURN, Van
Brahms: Variation and fugue on a theme by Handel. D. M. Garvelmann. il por Am Rec G 40:24-6 S '77 *

CLIFF dwellers and cliff dwellings
Cliff dwellers of the Mesa Verde; Anasazi Indians. D. Smith. il Am Hist Illus 12:4-9+ O '77

CLIFFORD, Clark McAdams
Exclusive interview with Clark Clifford; ed by B. A. Weisberger. Am Heritage 28:8-11 Ap '77
Recognizing Israel; address, December 28, 1976. pors Am Heritage 28:4-7+ Ap '77

about

Democrats' Mr Fixit. por Time 110:16 S 26 '77 *

CLIFFORD, Donald K. Jr
Thriving in a recession. il Harvard Bus R 55:57-65 Jl '77

CLIFT, Montgomery
Afternoon at the New Yorker. P. Bogdanovich. il Esquire 89:28+ Ja '78 *

CLIMACTERIC
Do men go through menopause, too? M. Newton. por Fam Health 9:20-1 Mr '77

CLIMATE
Energy and climate. P. H. Abelson. Science 197:941 S 2 '77
NASA eyes climate research projects. C. Covault. il Aviation W 107:57-9 N 21 '77
Planetary radiation balance as a function of atmospheric dust: climatological consequences. S. B. Idso and A. J. Brazel. bibl il Science 198:731-3 N 18 '77
Question of climate. J. Norwine. bibl il maps Environment 19:6-13+ N '77
See also
Microclimatology
Paleoclimatology
Plants, Effect of climate on
also subhead Climate under names of continents, countries, cities, etc, e.g. United States—Climate

CLIMATE and architecture. See Architecture and climate

CLIMATE Program Act, National. See Environmental law

CLIMATE-solar relationships. See Sun and meteorology

CLIMATIC changes, Global. See Global temperature changes

CLIMATOLOGY, Phenological. See Phenology

CLIMBING
See also
Mountaineering

CLIMBING plants
See also
Clematis
Ivy
Passionflowers

CLIMBING stunts. See Stunts

CLIMER, G. William
Be specific: standards and roles affect salary administration. il Camp Mag 49:29-31 Mr '77

CLINE, Joel D. and Holmes, M. L.
Submarine seepage of natural gas in Norton Sound, Alaska. bibl il map Science 198:1149-53 D 16 '77

CLINICAL laboratories. See Medical laboratories

CLINICAL research. See Medical research

CLINICS. See Health facilities

CLINICS, Legal. See Legal aid

CLINTON, De Witt
Wedding of the waters. D. Tuttle. il pors Conservationist 32:10-15 N '77 *

CLINTON, George
Chocolate city and beyond. K. Emerson. il por Sat R 5:48-9 N 12 '77 *

CLINTON, Richard Lee
Never-to-be developed countries of Latin America. bibl il Bull Atom Sci 33:19-26 O '77

CLINTON, Mass.
Around two worlds in two days; visit of J. Carter. il pors Time 109:12-15 Mr 28 '77
Long-distance runner; J. Carter's visit. P. Goldman and T. M. DeFrank. il pors Newsweek 89:14-16 Mr 28 '77
When the President meets the people. il U.S. News 82:20-1 Mr 28 '77

CLIVE, Winifred Johnson
Winifred Johnson Clive. J. Opalak. il Design (US) 78:8-11 mid-Wint '77 *

CLIVIA. See Kafir lilies

CLIVUS method. See Sewage purification—Biological treatment

CLOAKS
The cloak; symbol of love, violence, revenge, despair in literature and opera. J. Kestner. il Opera N 41:24-6 F 26 '77

CLOCHE plant covers. See Plants, Protection of

CLOCK cabinets. See Cabinets (furniture)

CLOCK radios
Costly clock radio offers fine radio, mediocre clock. Consumer Rep 42:560 O '77
FM/AM clock radios. il Consumer Rep 42:539-43 S '77
Small radios. il Consumers Res Mag 60:21-6 N '77

CLOCKS
Battery-powered clocks. il Consumers Res Mag 60:7 D '77
On time. O. R. Hagans. See issues of Hobbies
Swinging grandfather clock. T. H. Jones. il Mech Illus 73:50-1+ D '77
See also
Atomic clocks

Collectors and collecting

Old Charter clock collection. O. R. Hagans. See issues of Hobbies to October 1977

CLOCKS, Automobile. See Automobiles—Equipment

CLOCKS, Electronic
Build: digital clock for your car. R. C. Arp. il Radio-Electr 48:61-3+ F '77
Build this digital on-screen TV clock. F. Blechman. il Radio-Electr 48:35-8 Jl '77
Build this no-digit digital wall clock. T. A. Walters il Radio-Electr 48:35-7+ Je '77
Build this 10 function digital clock. J. G. Mazur. il Radio-Electr 48:36-9 Ag; 40-2 S '77
Clock/thermometer sounds time and temperature alarms. J. Free. il Pop Sci 210:180 My '77
Digital clock kits for your car. F. Blechman. il Radio-Electr 48:35-9 O; 41-4 N; 45-7 D '77
Easy-to-build digital clocks. F. Blechman. il Radio-Electr 48:54-7+ Mr '77
HP-25 as a digital clock & timer. W. T. Peters. il Pop Electr 12:57-8 Ag '77
Making digital electronic clocks immune to AC flicker. A. Fraser. il Pop Electr 12:58 N '77
Power your projects with solar energy! B. Green. il Pop Electr 12:41-7 D '77
Self-contained module lets you build your own digital clock. K. Jensen. il Pop Sci 211:123-4 N '77

CLOHERTY, Patricia M.
Businesswomen get a champion at SBA. il pors Nations Bus 65:34-6 D '77 *

CLOISONNÉ
Magic of cloisonne: William Harper. W. Harper. il Craft Horiz 37:54-7 D '77

CLOISTERS (museum) See Metropolitan Museum of Art, New York—Cloisters

CLOMID. See Estrogens

CLONES (biology)
Neuron duplications and deletions in locust clones and clutches. C. S. Goodman. bibl il Science 197:1384-6 S 30 '77

CLONES (botany)
Cloning pine trees. il BioScience 27:832 D '77

CLONING of DNA. See DNA

CLOSE, Charles
Blowing up the closeup; exhibition at New York's Pace Gallery. R. Hughes. il pors Time 109:92 My 23 '77 *
Close up close; New York's Pace Gallery show. M. Stevens. por Newsweek 89:68 My 23 '77 *

CLOSE-up photography. See Photography, Close-up

CLOSETS
Behind neat doors everything in sight; sewing center. il Sunset 159:162 O '77
Boys closet has cubbyholes. il Sunset 158:142 Je '77
Build a freestanding cedar closet. il Pop Mech 147:134 Ap '77
Quick & easy cedar closet. R. Capotosto. il Mech Illus 73:72-3 F '77
Space savers; excerpt from Spacemaker book. E. Liman. il Am Home 80:15 Je '77

CLOSING costs (house buying) See House buying

CLOSTERMANN, Pierre
Dec. 7, 1941; excerpt from Flames in the sky. il Flying 101:186-7 S '77

CLOTH. See Textile fabrics

CLOTHES cupboards. See Armoires

CLOTHES dryers
Automatic washers & dryers. il Changing T 31:16-18 Ap '77
How to buy a washer and dryer. Bet Hom & Gard 55:126 N '77
Portable washers and dryers. Consumer Rep 42:90-6 F '77

CLOTHES horses. See Clothes racks

CLOTHES racks
Clothes horse—the $15 model. il Sunset 159:138 O '77

CLOTHES washing machines. See Washing machines

CLOTHING, Cold weather
Keeping warm when it's cold out. P. Barrett. il Mech Illus 74:22+ Ja '78
100 tips for surviving the cold. il Mademoiselle 83:153-63 N '77
Stave off winter ills. Changing T 31:9-10 N '77
Warm and chic. Time 109:16-17 F 14 '77
Ways to warm up this winter. P. Skalka. il Fam Health 9:40-1 D '77
Winter warmers; cold weather boating. A. H. Drummond, Jr. il Motor B & S 140:58-61+ D '77
See also
Underwear

CLOTHING, Protective
See also
Clothing, Waterproof

CLOTHING, Waterproof
Wet look. il Motor B & S 139:56-8 Mr '77

CLOTHING and dress
Beach dress, beach towel, changing cabaña. il Sunset 159:78-9 Jl '77
Clothing and footwear. il Consumers Res Mag 60:17-24 O '77
Dress for the trip to the top; women executives. S. C. Cowley. il Newsweek 90:76-7 S 26 '77
Going public, coming out on top; camisoles and corselettes. il Time 109:66 My 2 '77
Good looks. See issues of McCall's
How you can update everything you own. il Mademoiselle 83:72-3 Jl '77
Issue of skirting. A. Hollander. il New Repub 177:27 D 17 '77
New York collections: the news and how to shop for it. Vogue 167:295 S '77
Pantsuited pioneer of Women's lib, Dr Mary Walker. A. Lockwood. il pors Smithsonian 7:113-14+ Mr '77
Power dressing; clothes of businesswomen. A. Gross and N. A. Comer. Mademoiselle 83:188-9+ S '77
Warmest bathrobes of all. Good H 185:184 D '77
What they're wearing at night. C. Donovan. il N Y Times Mag p83-5 D 18 '77
See also
Bathing suits
Cloaks
Costume
Costume design
Costume designers
Dress accessories
Fashion
Fashion shows
Hosiery
Pants
Scarves
Shawls
Shoes, boots, rubbers, etc.
Underwear

Care

Life insurance for your wardrobe. P. W. Linck. il pors House & Gard 149:44+ O '77

Children

Boutique Baedeker; childrens clothing stores, New York. A. Skinner. N Y Times Mag p58+ Mr 13 '77
Buying and caring for back-to-school clothes. Good H 185:248 S '77
Kiddie couture. S. C. Cowley and L. Whitman. il Newsweek 90:75-6 D 12 '77
Starring children. J. Maxey. il N Y Times Mag p34-9+ Ag 21 '77
See also
Sweaters

Dancers

Togs for the pros; Protogs made at H. and A. Cherry's Trim-Knits factory. L. Draegin. il Dance Mag 51:88-9 D '77

Men

Ascot and biggin, my Lord? gentlemanly clothes. E. Soames. il pors Esquire 88:141-3 D '77
Dress to succeed; J. T. Molloy's advice for business leaders. il Nations Bus 65:63-6 Ag '77
Elegant comfort: alternatives for after dark. K. M. Fleck. il N Y Times Mag p72-3 O 30 '77
How to shop and care for a suit. il Consumers Res Mag 60:41 F '77
Serving the fashion-conscious male; R. Jackson of J. L. Hudson's menswear department. il pors Ebony 32:99-100+ My '77
See also
Neckties
Shirts

Psychological aspects

Effect of appearance on requests for help in libraries. H. W. Kroll and D. K. Moren. il Am Lib 8:489 O '77

Purchasing

Basics of dressing for less. Changing T 31:11 Ag '77
Dressing better—yet saving money. W. Harter. il Ret Liv 17:32-3 My '77

Size

Touting stout. L. Langway and others. il Newsweek 89:85 Mr 14 '77

Sports clothes

Bright new gear for safer hunting. B. McKeown. il Pop Mech 148:82-3+ O '77
Just an old snow job; ski mountaineering clothing; photographs, with report by J. Campbell. il Sports Illus 47:52-8 D 5 '77
New seaworthies. M. Wiley. il Yachting 141:92-5 My '77
Now this is one way to travel light; Frank Shorter Running Gear. J. Campbell. il por Sports Illus 46:69-70+ Mr 21 '77
What to wear on the tennis court. J. Heldman. Seventeen 36:40+ Je '77
Winter warmers; cold weather boating. A. H. Drummond, Jr. il Motor B & S 140:58-61+ D '77
See also
Uniforms, Sports

Students

Closet crisis: storing clothes in college dormitories. P. Dawson. Seventeen 36:32+ Ag '77

Work clothes

Be a painter! decorating work clothes. il Seventeen 36:200-1+ Ap '77
Overall fun; converting overalls into a jumper. il Seventeen 36:130 Ap '77

CLOTHING factories
New sweatshop; Bronx, N.Y. shop. M. Ruby and J. Concannon. il Newsweek 90:87 D 12 '77

CLOTHING industry
See also
Garment workers
Glove industry

Finance

Household products & apparel. il Forbes 121:162+ Ja 9 '78

Wages and hours

Measuring pay factors in suit and coat fabrication. H. B. Williams. il M Labor R 100:65-7 O '77

Germany, West

Booming market in counterfeit jeans. il Bus W p37-8 Ag 8 '77

United States

Apparel maker who bucked the trend; Marlene Industries Corp. D. G. Santry. il Bus W p 101 O 24 '77
Flame-retardant ban dishevels an industry; childrens sleepwear chemical Tris-BP. il Bus W p45-6 Ap 18 '77
Togs for the pros; Protogs made at H. and A. Cherry's Trim-Knits factory. L. Draegin. il Dance Mag 51:88-9 D '77
Touting stout. L. Langway and others. il Newsweek 89:85 Mr 14 '77
Why Amfac got rid of Joseph Magnin. Bus W p 19 Jl 4 '77
Work Wear tries to be no. 1 again. Bus W p84 N 7 '77
See also
Amalgamated Clothing and Textile Workers Union
Blue Bell, Inc
Capezio Ballet Makers (firm)
Farah Manufacturing Company
Genesco, Inc
Strauss, Levi, and Company

CLOTHING workers. See Garment workers
CLOTURE rule. See United States—Congress—Senate—Rules and practice
CLOUD seeding. See Rain making; Weather control
CLOUDS, Intergalactic. See Matter, Interstellar
CLOUGH, Gene
Youth camp safety—no. Camp Mag 50:19-20 S '77
CLOUGH, Susan
Tennis, folks? White House tennis court. J. Osborne. New Repub 177:11-12 N 26 '77 *
CLOUSE, Bonnidell
Reading, writing, and...right from wrong? Chr Today 22:14-17 D 30 '77
CLOVER
Red clover. N. Reeder. il Farm J 101:A1-2 mid-F '77
CLOWARD, Richard Andrew, and Piven, F. F.
Acquiescence of social work; excerpt from Radical social work. Society 14:55-63 Ja '77
CLOZE tests. See Reading—Testing
CLUB; musical comedy. See Musical comedy, revue, etc.—Reviews—Single works
CLUB Méditerranée. See Vacation villages
CLUBB, Oliver Edmund
China after Mao. bibl Cur Hist 73:49-53+ S '77
Coexistence after Mao. Progressive 41:31-3 F '77
CLUBS
Good food, good company; gourmet dining groups. C. Rufener. Am Home 80:88 D '77
Hobbyist computer clubs. Pop Electr 11:97-8 Ap; 12:91 Jl '77
Should clubs have the right to be exclusive? M. Mead. Redbook 149:31+ Jl '77
Specialties of the house at the great clubs. il Fortune 95:150-5 F '77
See also
Agricultural societies
Art clubs and societies
Atlanta—Clubs
Automobile clubs
Book clubs
Country clubs
Discotheques
Health clubs
London—Clubs
New York (city)—Clubs
Night clubs
Political clubs and associations
Sports clubs
Tampa, Fla.—Clubs
Travel clubs
Womens clubs and societies
Yacht clubs
CLUNIE, Margaret Burke
Joseph True and the piecework system in Salem. bibl il Antiques 111:1006-13 My '77
CLURMAN, Harold
Film festival (cont) Nation 225:378-80, 412-14 O 15-22 '77
Theatre. See issues of Nation
CLUSTER chemistry. See Stereochemistry
CLUTCHES, Automobile. See Automobiles—Clutches
CLUTTON-BROCK, Juliet
Man-made dogs. bibl il Science 197:1340-2 S 30 '77
CLYMER, Adam
Back where Carter started; inauguration day in Des Moines. Nation 224:133-5 F 5 '77
Promises, promises. Nation 224:295-8 Mr 12 '77
COACHELLA Valley, Calif.
Bountiful Coachella Valley for a midwinter holiday. il map Sunset 159:82-5 D '77
COACHES (athletics)
Winning isn't everything; high school coaches. M. Willerman. bibl Clearing H 50:394-7 My '77
See also
Basketball coaches
Football coaches
Moran, R.
Williams, B.
COACHES and coaching
Stagecoach Mary; M. Fields; ed by M. Crawford. G. Cooper. il pors Ebony 32:96-8+ O '77
COAGULATION of blood. See Blood—Coagulation
COAL
Coal. T. Bay. il Sci Digest 82:53-6 O '77
Coal and climate: a yellow light on CO_2. il Sci N 112:68 Jl 30 '77
Coal and the coming (?) superinterglacial. Sci N 111:356 Je 4 '77
Coal: invoking the rule of reason in an energy-environment conflict. L. J. Carter. il Science 198:276-80 O 21 '77
Coal option; General Accounting Office report. Sci Am 238:64 Ja '78
Hazards of coal dependence. W. S. Broecker. il Natur Hist 86:8+ O '77
Second coal age promises to slow our dependence on imported oil. D. Sheridan. il Smithsonian 8:30-7 bibl(p 101) Ag '77
See also
Coke industry
Lignite

Combustion

See Combustion

Desulfurization

See Coal—Sulfur content

Gasification

See Coal gasification

Liquefaction

See Coal liquefaction

Sulfur content

Desulfurization of coal by use of chemical communication. P. H. Howard and R. S. Datta. bibl il Science 197:668-9 Ag 12 '77
Origins of sulfur in coal: importance of the ester sulfate content of peat. D. Casagrande and K. Siefert. bibl Science 195:675-6 F 18 '77
Western coal darkens Ohio's mining future; electric plants threaten switch from high sulfur variety. il Bus W p28 My 2 '77

Transportation

Conversion to coal means a long haul to Texas. J. Walsh. Science 198:587 N 11 '77
Race to carry Carter's coal. map Bus W p78 My 16 '77
See also
Coal pipelines
COAL gasification
Coal-based power cycle. R. Gorman. il Pop Sci 211:102-5 Ag '77
Coal gas: old wine, new bottle. il Sci Digest 81:77 F '77
Double challenge of western coal. Sci N 111:133 F 26 '77
Only way to use coal. A. J. Mayer and W. J. Cook. il Newsweek 90:68+ Jl 4 '77
Underground gasification: an alternate way to exploit coal. T. H. Maugh, 2d. il Science 198:1132-4 D 16 '77
COAL industry
See also
Collective bargaining—Coal industry
Collective labor agreements—Coal industry

Finance

How the coal companies are faring. Bus W p80 N 28 '77
Now, mom-and-pop coal mines. S. Chace. il Forbes 120:69+ Jl 1 '77

Canada

Here comes another Kaiser; Kaiser Resources Ltd. R. Loving, Jr. il pors Fortune 95:156-8+ F '77
Young Kaiser feels his oats; Kaiser Resources Ltd. por Bus W p 131-2 D 5 '77

Great Britain

Britain's new jackpot. il pors Forbes 119:118 Mr 15 '77

United States

All stick and no carrot. il Forbes 119:73-4 Je 1 '77
Coal: a never-never boom. T. Nicholson and others. il Newsweek 89:64+ Ja 31 '77
Coal: Carter and Congress hold the key. G. R. Rosen. il Duns R 109:56-60 F '77
Coal: the once and future king; address, August 26, 1977. C. E. Bagge. Vital Speeches 44:9-15 O 15 '77
Do coal and oil mix? ownership of Consolidation Coal by Continental Oil. J. Cook. il Forbes 120:138+ O 15 '77
From pariah to messiah: recent history of coal; address, February 28, 1977. E. R. Phelps. Vital Speeches 43:366-9 Ap 1 '77
Gloom in coal. il Bus W p76-80+ N 28 '77
Pitfalls of counting too much on coal. il U.S. News 82:75-6+ Ap 25 '77
Too much of a good thing? il por Forbes 119:66 My 1 '77
Why Carter may not meet his coal deadline. il Bus W p31 Jl 11 '77
Wildcatters squeeze the coal supply. il Bus W p29 Ag 29 '77
See also
Collective bargaining—Coal industry
Morrison-Knudsen Company, Inc
Peabody Coal Company
Pittston Company
COAL liquefaction
Ersatz gasoline: forgotten archives yielding secret of how German army ran a war on fuel from low-grade coal. D. Lampe. Sci Digest 82:65-7 O '77
Nazi coal conversion methods reviewed. C. Holden. Science 196:508-9 Ap 29 '77
Recycling Nazi secrets; making petroleum from coal. il Time 109:58 Ap 18 '77
COAL miners
See also
Collective bargaining—Coal industry
Collective labor agreements—Coal industry
Strikes—United States—Coal miners
United Mine Workers of America
Women coal miners

COAL miners—*Continued*

Medical care

Coal and the UMW are still at odds; wildcat coal strike. Bus W p29 Ag 29 '77
Unhealthy state of coalfield health care; 50 clinics. Bus W p38-9 Ag 15 '77
Wildcat strikes: preview of turmoil in coal fields. F. W. Frailey. il U.S. News 83:65-7 S 5 '77

COAL miners strikes (United States) See Strikes—United States—Coal miners

COAL mines and mining
Longwall mining—now there's a better way to get at the coal. P. Britton. il Pop Sci 211:118-21 O '77
See also
Coal miners
Coal supply
Strip mining

Accidents and explosions

Dead laws and dead men; manslaughter in a coal mine; Scotia Coal Company explosions in Oven Fork, Ky. H. M. Caudill. Nation 224:492-7 Ap 23 '77

Laws and legislation

Coal: Carter and Congress hold the key. G. R. Rosen. il Duns R 109:56-60 F '77
Coal: still a disaster area; Federal Coal Mine Health and Safety Act. J. D. McAteer and L. T. Galloway. Nation 225:273-5 S 24 '77

Appalachian Region

In Appalachia: king coal is back, and so are some old problems; with interview with J. D. Rockefeller, 4th. il map U.S. News 82:36-40 My 23 '77

Canada

Okanagan shuttles miners in helicopter operation. R. G. O'Lone. Aviation W 107:25-6 Ag 15 '77

Colorado

Craig, Colorado: population unknown, elevation 6,185 feet; energy boom town. P. L. Fradkin. il Audubon 79:118-27 Jl '77

Great Britain

Early energy crisis and its consequences. J. U. Nef. il map Sci Am 237:140-2+ bibl(p 164) N '77

Montana

New grassroots reform movement checks the great raid on Montana's resources. T. Judge. Horticulture 55:12+ Ag '77

Ohio

Fluid-bed combustion: a sleeper awakes. il Sci N 112:134 Ag 27 '77
Western coal darkens Ohio's mining future; electric plants threaten switch from high sulfur variety. il Bus W p28 My 2 '77

United States

See also
Coal industry—United States

Western States

Losing of the West. D. Whipple. Nation 224:717-20 Je 11 '77
UMW is learning how to lose the West. il Bus W p 128+ Ap 18 '77

Wyoming

Coal on the range; Gillette. A. J. Mayer and J. B. Copeland. il Newsweek 89:67-8 Je 6 '77

COAL mining machinery
Giant miners for a new coal age. B. Kilpatrick. il map Pop Mech 148:77-81+ O '77

COAL pipelines
Flushing coal to market; slurry pipelines. Time 109:61 My 16 '77
West's new range war; slurry systems. A. J. Mayer and others. il Newsweek 89:47-8 My 23 '77

COAL policy. See Coal

COAL slurry pipelines. See Coal pipelines

COAL supply
Coal: no superabundance for USA. A. Bartlett; reply with rejoinder. D. H. Winicur. bibl il Phys Today 30:103-4 My '77
Coal: the new swing fuel? H. H. Landsberg. Science 197:9 Jl 1 '77
Coal: the once and future king; address, August 26, 1977. C. E. Bagge. Vital Speeches 44:9-15 O 15 '77
Pitfalls of counting too much on coal. il U.S. News 82:75-6+ Ap 25 '77
World energy situation would be dominated by oil until end of century but coal likely to make significant comeback. il UN Chron 14:41-3 My '77

COALE, Ansley J.
Population growth and economic development: the case of Mexico. bibl f For Affairs 56:415-29 Ja '78

COALITION of Publishers for Employment, Inc
William Jovanovich delivers keynote address at graduation of publishing workshop. W. Gelles. il Pub W 211:42 Je 27 '77

COAST changes
Mangroves: trees that help build the land. L. E. Jerome. il Oceans 10:38-45 S '77

COAST Guard. See United States—Coast Guard

COAST Guard Academy, United States. See United States Coast Guard Academy, New London, Conn.

COAST Navigation School. See Boats and boating—Study and teaching

COASTAL marshes. See Marshes, Tide

COASTAL protection. See Shore protection

COASTAL Zone Management Act. See Shore protection—Laws and legislation

COASTS
See also
Shore protection

United States

Swept away; danger to coastal communities from hurricanes. B. Funk. il N Y Times Mag p38-40+ S 18 '77

COAT racks. See Clothes racks

COATES, Pat
California co-op cuts bills in half. il por Aging 274:3-5 Ag '77 *

COATS of arms. See Heraldry

COAXIAL connectors. See Electric connectors

COBALAMIN. See Vitamins—Vitamin B_{12}

COBB, Nathan, and others
How your self-image controls your tennis game; excerpt from Love and hate on the tennis court. il Psychol Today 11:46-7+ Je '77

COBER, Alan E.
Contemporary look at Kafka: illustrations for four stories of alienation. il Horizon 20:74-7 D '77

COBRA (sports car) See Sports cars

COBRAS
Cobras. R. E. Arnold. Field & S 82:114 D '77

COBURN, D. L.
Gin game. Reviews
America 137:334 N 12 '77 *
Nation 225:445 O 29 '77 *
New Repub 177:24 N 12 '77 *
New Yorker 53:93 O 17 '77 *
New Yorker 53:36-7 O 24 '77 *
Newsweek il 90:117 O 17 '77 *
Time 110:94 O 17 '77 *

COBURN, Judith
Intelligent woman's guide to sex. See issues of Mademoiselle, August 1977-

COCA-COLA Bottling Company of Los Angeles-MCA, Inc merger. See Corporations—Acquisitions and mergers

COCA-COLA Company
Carter's chum from Coke. T. Nicholson and others. por Newsweek 89:57-8 F 7 '77
India may swallow Coke. il Time 110:44 Ag 22 '77
Sweet stuff; action of the Indian government. Nation 225:228-9 S 17 '77

COCAINE
Acute systemic effects of cocaine in man: a controlled study by intranasal and intravenous routes. R. B. Resnick and others. bibl Science 195:696-8 F 18 '77
Cocaine—a social history; excerpt from Cocaine: a drug and its social evolution. L. Grinspoon and J. B. Bakalar. bibl il pors Psychol Today 10:36-9+ Mr '77
Cocaine, alcohol & amphetamines: thrillers or killers? J. C. Wang. Harp Baz 110:86-7+ Je '77
Cocaine: hazards still unclear. Sci N 112:39 Jl 16 '77
Cocaine scene. R. Steele and others. il Newsweek 89:20-2+ My 30 '77
Coke. Sci Am 237:75 N '77
Getting a kick from cocaine. L. Komisar. il Read Digest 111:103-6 Jl '77
Kick from cocaine. L. Grinspoon and J. B. Bakalar. il Psychol Today 10:41-2+ Mr '77
Pittsburg Fats dodges a silver bullet; football player E. Holmes' trial for possession of cocaine. R. Kennedy. il por Sports Illus 46:24-6+ Mr 7 '77
What the doctors say. M. Clark and D. Shapiro. il Newsweek 89:25 My 30 '77

COCCOLITH plankton. See Plankton

COCHANE, Willard W.
Price of farm products in the future. bibl f Ann Am Acad 429:23-35 Ja '77

COCHRAN, Jacqueline
Cochran. G. Baxter. il por Flying 101:178 S '77 *

COCHRAN, Mary Frances
Kitchen little. il por House & Gard 149:14 F '77 *

COCHRANE, Eric
Science and humanism in the Italian renaissance. bibl f Am Hist R 81:1039-57 D '76

COCHRANE, Louise
Punch and Toby; drama. Plays 36:76-78 My '77

COCK fighting
Cockfighting: an unfashionable view. H. Crews. Esquire 87:8+ Mr '77

COCKBURN, Claud
Pretenders of Fleet Street. Harpers 225:114+ D '77
COCKEYED Tiger; musical comedy. See Musical comedy, revue, etc.—Reviews—Single works
COCKFIGHT; drama. See Jackson, E.
COCKFIGHTING. See Cock fighting
COCKLEBURS
Phyllotaxis in xanthium shoots altered by gibberellic acid. R. Maksymowych and R. O. Erickson. bibl il Science 196:1201-3 Je 10 '77
COCKLIN, Robert F.
Why discriminate against military people? interview. il por U.S. News 83:31-2 Ag 22 '77
COCKPITS, Boat. See Boats—Cockpits
COCKROACH control
How to be your own exterminator. S. George. il Ms 5:27-8+ F '77
COCKROACHES
Cockroaches; plague of boats. F. Seyfarth. il Motor B & S 139:28+ Mr '77
Extermination
See Cockroach control
COCKTAILS
Adventures with wines; wine cocktails. E. Greenberg and M. Greenberg. House B 119:128-9 D '77
Bloody Mary #322. il Esquire 88:91 Jl '77
Drink. A. Fraser. Mademoiselle 83:197-8 F '77
Emergency party bar. D. Tobias. il Am Home 80:69 N '77
Ever-ready party bar; packaged mixes and bottled cocktails. House B 119:129+ N '77
In defense of the martini. H. Sidey. il Time 110:38 O 24 '77
Introducing the cryo-cocktail. il Esquire 87:96-9 Je '77
Let's bring back. . .cocktails; with recipes. L. B. Downs. House B 119:97+ Ap '77
COCOA
See also
Chocolate
COCOA futures. See Commodity exchanges
COCTEAU, Jean
Music critic in Paris in the nineteen-twenties: some personal recollections. R. Myers. il Mus Q 63:524-44 O '77 *
COCUZZA, Phil
Gang that shoots straight. R. McGonegal. il Hot Rod 30:54-7 D '77 *
CODE instruments. See Radio telegraph—Equipment
CODES (ciphers) See Ciphers
CODEX Corporation-Motorola Inc merger. See Electronic industries—Acquisitions and mergers
CODLING moths
To control codling moths. Sunset 158:280 Ap '77
CODONS. See Genetic code
CODY, Fred
Cody's Books of Berkeley: after 21 years, the Codys move on. P. Holt. il pors Pub W 212:48-9+ N 7 '77 *
CODY, Harriet
Marriage contract renewed. pors Ms 6:21 Jl '77
CODY, William Frederick
Buffalo Bill Historical Center. P. H. Hassrick. il Am West 14:16-29 My '77 *
Buffalo Bill story. D. E. Fetzal. il Field & S 82:150-1+ My '77 *
CODY'S Books of Berkeley (bookstore) See Booksellers and bookselling—California
COE, Henry W, State Park. See California—Parks and reserves
COE, Michael D. See Furst, P. T. jt. auth.
COED camps. See Camps
CO-ED dormitories. See Dormitories
COEDUCATION
Bryn Mawr v. coeducation. Time 109:64 Ja 31 '77
COELACANTHS
Old four legs: the living fossil. L. M. Myking. il Sea Front 23:334-41 N '77
COELENTERATES
See also
Corals
Hydra (zoology)
Jellyfish
Nervous system—Coelenterates
Sea anemones
Sponges
COEVOLUTION. See Evolution
COEVOLUTION quarterly
Stewart Brand's CoEvolution supplement. S. Brand. por Org Gard & Farm 24:177 Ag '77
COFFARO, Katherine A. and Hinegardner, R. T.
Immune response in the sea urchin lytechinus pictus. bibl il Science 197:1389-90 S 30 '77
COFFEA. See Coffee trees
COFFEE, Frank K.
Computers move into the kitchen. il Mech Illus 74:38+ Ja '78
Latest word on the RV scene. il Mech Illus 73:68+ My '77
New guide to water filters. il Mech Illus 73:122+ Mr '77
Wedge comes to RVs. il Mech Illus 74:31-3+ Ja '78

COFFEE
Beware of coffee, tea, and cola beverages if you value good health. H. L. Abrams, Jr. Consumers Res Mag 60:21-2+ My '77
Coffee bags: an idea whose time hasn't come. Consumer Rep 43:5-6 Ja '78
Coffee breaks. M. Gunderson. Am Home 80:75 S '77
Confessions of a coffee addict. P. Carlson. il por Newsweek 89:13 My 16 '77
Grounds for delight. R. Sokolov. Natur Hist 87:8+ Ja '78
How to get coffee prices for sugar and vegetable oil. Consumer Rep 42:184-5 Ap '77
Money-saving tips for coffee-lovers. Good H 184:197 Ap '77
Wonders of physics that can be found in a cup of coffee or tea. J. Walker. il Sci Am 237:152+ N '77
See also
Caffeine
Prices
About wild swings in coffee prices. il U.S. News 83:61 Ag 8 '77
Behind those soaring coffee prices; effect of Brazilian export policy. T. Armbrister. Read Digest 110:65-6+ My '77
Brazil cuts and runs on coffee prices. il Bus W p28-9 N 7 '77
Coffee consumption appears stable despite high prices. UN Chron 14:29 Mr '77
Coffee perplex. S. T. Atlas and others. il Newsweek 90:91 N 14 '77
Coffee prices. il Consumer Rep 42:134-6 Mr '77
Coffee producers try salvaging their prices. il Bus W p25-6 Ag 8 '77
Coffee simmers down. Time 109:63 Je 27 '77
Department discusses coffee prices; statements. February 22, 1977. J. L. Katz; J. R. Braden. il Dept State Bull 76:292-303 Mr 28 '77
Falling-out among the coffee exporters. il Bus W p40-1 O 17 '77
Finally, a coffee brake. il Time 110:68 Ag 8 '77
Shaky price floor under coffee beans; Brazil's policy. il Bus W p52-3+ O 10 '77
Take that, el Exigente. il Time 109:79-80 Mr 28 '77
COFFEE cake
He cooks: Daniel W. coffee cake. il Bet Hom & Gard 55:78 D '77
Late summer coffee cake. . . topping is pear, peach, or plum. il Sunset 159:144 S '77
COFFEE desserts. See Desserts
COFFEE industry
Bean bagged; Folger Company. Forbes 119:28 Ap 15 '77
Coffee consumption appears stable despite high prices. UN Chron 14:29 Mr '77
Coffee prices. il Consumer Rep 42:134-6 Mr '77
Export-import trade
Death and coffee in Uganda. J. M. Wall. Chr Cent 94:971-3 O 26 '77
Falling-out among the coffee exporters. il Bus W p40-1 O 17 '77
Marketing
Coffee tries to regain its lost consumers. il Bus W p33-4 D 26 '77
Brazil
Brazil cuts and runs on coffee prices. il Bus W p28-9 N 7 '77
Brazil's coffee with sugar billionaire; J. W. Atalla, head of Copersucar. A. M. Louis. il pors Fortune 96:82-8 Jl '77
Reports & comment: letter from a coffee planter. E. B. Geld. il Atlantic 240:6+ Ag '77
Shaky price floor under coffee beans. il Bus W p52-3+ O 10 '77
Guatemala
Cost of coffee. P. Berryman. il Environment 19:12-15 Ag '77
Latin America
Take that, el Exigente. il Time 109:79-80 Mr 28 '77
COFFEE mills
Consumer's guide to: coffee makers & grinders. il Mech Illus 73:16 F '77
COFFEE pots, percolators, etc.
Consumer's guide to: coffee makers & grinders. il Mech Illus 73:16 F '77
Espresso coffee maker to be used at home. il Consumer Rep 42:374 Jl '77
That automatic pot brews tea, too. R. Field. Sci Digest 81:86-7 My '77
COFFEE substitutes
Coffee alternates: the taste without the cost? Consumer Rep 42:478 Ag '77
Coffee breaks. Time 109:68 My 30 '77
Ersatz brews. L. Langway and others. il Newsweek 89:76 My 30 '77
COFFEE table books. See Picture books
COFFEE tables. See Tables
COFFEE trees
It probably won't grow coffee for you but it is good looking; coffea arabica. il Sunset 158:268 Ap '77

COFFER, Helene Lewis
Ad lib; poem. Good H 185:188 S '77
COFFEY, Joseph I.
(ed) Nuclear proliferation: prospects, problems, and proposals. il Ann Am Acad 430:1-174 Mr '77
Quo vadimus? nuclear proliferation. Ann Am Acad 430:1-13 Mr '77
COFFEY, Rick
Karma is a Chinaman; story. Field & S 81:57-9 Ap '77
COFFIN, William Sloane, 1924-
Leap of faith, a leap of action; excerpt from Once to every man. por Chr Cent 94:938-44 O 19 '77
about
Coffin's midlife memoir. por Horizon 20:58 N '77 *
COFFINS
Bury me not. E. Keerdoja. Newsweek 90:26 N 28 '77
COGENERATION (electric power production) See Electric power production
COGGAN, Frederick Donald, Abp
Coggan, Vatican: has God's time' arrived? R. Pulliam. Chr Today 21:45-6 My 20 '77 *
Dr Coggan and Paul VI. America 136:435 My 14 '77 *
Third summit: more hurdles. il pors Time 109:80 My 9 '77 *
COGGER, B. M. G. See Weatherley, A. H. jt auth
COGNAC. See Brandy
COGSWELL, Elliot P.
He soars through the air. M. Jailer. il por Ret Liv 17:16-17 Ap '77 *
COGSWELL, Jerald M.
Build a solar controller. il Pop Electr 12:69-70 Jl '77
COHABITATION. See Unmarried couples
COHELEACH, Guy
Painted as they are. il Read Digest 111:168-73 Ag '77
COHEN, Arthur
Arlen's dream versus Korvettes' reality. P. Blustein. il por Forbes 119:85+ Ap 15 '77 *
COHEN, Arthur A.
Motherwell atelier. il por Vogue 167:230-3+ Mr '77
COHEN, Benjamin Victor
Fork in the road. E. Yoffe. New Repub 177:21-3 S 17 '77 *
New Deal: born again. T. Mathews and J. Doyle. il pors Newsweek 89:16-17 Mr 14 '77 *
COHEN, Bernard L.
Case for the breeder reactor. Nat R 29:1044-5+, 1206+ S 16, O 28 '77
Disposal of radioactive wastes from fission reactors; with biographical sketch. il Sci Am 236: 18, 21-31 bibl(p 142) Je; 237:10-12 O '77
Special report: the dangers of nuclear power. Fam Health 9:52-3 Ja '77
COHEN, David
Public financing; address, June 9, 1977. Vital Speeches 43:692-6 S 1 '77
COHEN, David, 1946-
Adoption. Psychol Today 11:128+ N '77
COHEN, Dorothy H.
Television and the perception of reality. Educ Digest 42:10-13 Mr '77
COHEN, E. G. D.
Quantum statistics and liquid helium-3—helium-4 mixtures. bibl il Science 197:11-16 Jl 1 '77
COHEN, Jackson B. See Clasquin, F. F. jt auth
COHEN, Joyce
Coed dorms are a nuisance! por Seventeen 36:67 Ag '77
COHEN, Lawrence
It wasn't all in the cards. W. Bingham. il pors Sports Illus 46:22-5 Ap 11 '77 *
COHEN, Lita H. Solis-. See Solis-Cohen, L. H.
COHEN, Lucy M.
Female factor in resettlement. bibl il Society 14: 27-30 S '77
COHEN, Manuel Frederick
Sharper definition of the auditor's job. il por Bus W p55-6 Mr 28 '77 *
COHEN, Marcia
(ed) See Glaser, P. M. Starsky & Hutch
(ed) See Soul, D. Starsky & Hutch
COHEN, Mark
Persistence of vision. K. Poli. il por Pop Phot 80:104-11+ Ap '77
COHEN, Marvin L. and Falicov, L. M.
1977 Nobel prize in physics. bibl pors Science 198:713-15 N 18 '77
COHEN, Meryl
Being an only child is terrific! por Seventeen 36:82 F '77
COHEN, Rosetta
Poet studies herself in the mirror; poem. Mademoiselle 83:139 Ag '77
COHEN, S. T. and Van Cleave, W. R.
Nuclear test ban: a dangerous anachronism. Nat R 29:770-5 Jl 8 '77
COHEN, Seymour S.
Strategy for the chemotherapy of infectious disease. bibl Science 197:431-2 Jl 29 '77
COHEN, Stanley N.
Recombinant DNA: fact and fiction. bibl Science 195:654-7 F 18 '77; Same abr. with little Gene splicing: fact and fantasy. Parents Mag 52: 72-3+ N '77
COHEN, Steve
Interview with two practitioners. il pors Pop Phot 81:104-5+ S '77
COHEN, Stu
South Africa—a police state? Nation 224:143-6 F 5 '77
COHEN, Toby, and Miner, Margaret
Health insurance: how much coverage do you need? Harp Baz 110:87+ Ag '77
COHEN, Wilbur J.
How to pay for social security? interview. pors U.S. News 83:37-8 Jl 4 '77
Trends in American marriage, childbirth, and retirement; excerpts from address. por Intellect 106:93-5 S '77
COHEN, Ze'eva
Reviews. H. M. Simpson. Dance Mag 51:77-8 Je '77 *
COHESION
See also
Adhesion
COHN, Victor. See Mintz, M. jt auth
COHO fishing. See Salmon fishing
COHO salmon. See Salmon
COIN banks. See Banks, Coin
COIN collecting. See Numismatics
COINS
Coin quiz. G. Rayner. See issues of Hobbies
Need money laundered? Then see Arnold Batliner; St Francis Hotel's coin laundry. J. D. Lewis. il por Ret Liv 17:16-17 Jl '77
U.S.A. commemorative coinage. G. Rayner. Hobbies 82:131 Je '77
Will the penny soon be a thing of the past? il U.S. News 83:104-6 N 14 '77
See also
Franklin Mint Corporation

Collectors and collecting

See Numismatics
COINS as an investment
Coin investment of recent times. G. Rayner. Hobbies 82:131 Ja '78
History of the coin investment market. G. Rayner. Hobbies 82:131 O '77
COINTELPRO (Counterintelligence Program) See United States—Federal Bureau of Investigation
COKE industry
Coke and cancer: it's up to the steelworkers. F. Goldsmith and D. Freedman. Nation 224: 113-16 Ja 29 '77
OSHA under fire. S. Kelman. New Repub 176: 18-20+ My 21 '77

Laws and regulations

Safety agency issues coke emission standard. L. Bornstein and others. M Labor R 100:86-7 F '77
COKE plants

Environmental aspects

High noon at Clairton. J. G. Mitchell. Audubon 79:128-36 Ja '77
Republic's struggle to heat up its ovens. Bus W p42+ Ja 31 '77
COLA beverages. See Beverages
COLAMOSCA, Anne
Building business with Africa. map Duns R 109:92-4 My '77
COLD

Physiological effects

Survival: a primer. M. Demarest. il Time 109: 15-17 F 14 '77
See also
Fishes, Effect of temperature on
Hibernation
Hypothermia
Insects, Effect of temperature on

Therapeutic use

Heat and cold for treatment of pain. A. Frank and S. Frank. Mademoiselle 83:46+ F '77
COLD (disease)
Anatomy of a cold. C. Eron. Read Digest 111:110-13 S '77
Colds: 200 strains ache to get you. O. Davies. Sci Digest 81:21-5 Ap '77
Summer colds—allergies in disguise? V. J. Fontana. il Mademoiselle 83:60 Je '77
Winter colds. A. Frank and S. Frank. Mademoiselle 83:80 N '77

Remedies

See Medicines, Patent, proprietary, etc.
COLD acclimatization. See Acclimatization
COLD casting (sculpture) See Casting (sculpture)
COLD cellars. See Basements and cellars

COLD frames
Frames and mulches: self help for vegetables. il House & Gard 149:160-1 Ap '77
Nevada climate challenge. il Sunset 158:290-1 Ap '77
New use for an old device: growing greens in a coldframe for fresh winter salads. K. Kraft and P. Kraft. il Horticulture 55:56-7 S '77

COLD remedies. See Medicines, Patent, proprietary, etc.

COLD storage; drama. See Ribman, R.

COLD storage cellars. See Basements and cellars

COLD war. See World politics

COLD War (United States and Russia) See United States—Foreign relations—Russia

COLD weather
Another frigid winter ahead? What a top authority says; interview. G. P. Cressman. por map U.S. News 83:43-4 N 7 '77
Assessing the cold's damage. Time 109:59 F 21 '77
Bad case of frostbite; weather's effect on economy's performance in the second half. il Bus W p32-3 F 14 '77
Big freeze; Forecast: unsettled weather ahead. il map Time 109:22-8 Ja 31 '77
Chilling cost of winter damage. il Bus W p37 Mr 21 '77
Cold comfort. G. F. Will. Newsweek 89:80 F 7 '77
Cold weather and your skin. L. Lamberg. Bet Hom & Gard 55:59-60 F '77
Cold-weather beauty. Harp Baz 111:136-7 D '77
Congealed traffic waits for the thaw; effect of weather on transportation. il Bus W p33-4 F 14 '77
Deep freeze, drought hit local budgets. il Am City & County 92:13 Mr '77
Deep freeze! Why it's so cold; Winter wasteland. R. Steele. il maps Newsweek 89:34-40+ Ja 31 '77
Feeling the chill. M. Ruby and others. il Newsweek 89:70-1 F 14 '77
Fueling up for winter. Time 110:30 D 5 '77
Great winter hits again; Recovery in a deep freeze. il Time 109:30-2 F 7 '77
How to beat the elements. il Seventeen 36:144-7 N '77
Icy grip tightens. il Time 109:6-11 F 14 '77
Just like the good old days. A. J. Mayer and others. il Newsweek 89:62+ Ja 24 '77
New Hampshire buried under permacurse. J. Skow. New Yorker 53:36-7 F 21 '77
Now, the gas crisis. R. Steele and others. il maps Newsweek 89:14-19 F 7 '77
Old-style winter disrupts the economy. il Bus W p44 Ja 31 '77
100 tips for surviving the cold. il Mademoiselle 83:158-63 N '77
Reports & comment: Polus Kholodo: the coldest place. R. Chelminski. il Atlantic 240:4+ O '77
That awful weather won't slow us down. Fortune 95:9-10 Mr '77
Three fights for survival. V. E. Smith. il Newsweek 89:26 F 14 '77
Weather crisis. il U.S. News 82:11-13 F 7 '77
Winter ahead—not like the last one. map U.S. News 83:40+ D 12 '77
Winter to remember; 1976-77. il U.S. News 82:40-1 Ja 31 '77
Winter's legacy: step-up in search for fuel supplies. il U.S. News 82:19-20 F 21 '77
Winter's tale. R. Steele. il map Newsweek 89:25 F 14 '77
Winter's toll in lost production. Bus W p32-3 F 21 '77
Winter's toll: worse to come. il U.S. News 82:19-20 F 14 '77
See also
Winter

COLD weather and crops. See Plants, Effect of temperature on

COLD weather clothing. See Clothing, Cold weather

COLD weather photography. See Photography—Cold weather conditions

COLDFRAMES. See Cold frames

COLDS. See Cold (disease)

COLE, Charles J.
Value of virgin birth; with biographical sketch. il Natur Hist 87:4, 56-63 bibl(p 108) Ja '78

COLE, Edward N.
Ed Cole was a friend. B. Irvin. por Motor T 29:106 Ag '77 *
Ed Cole's legacy. il Forbes 120:29 Ag 15 '77 *
Measuring Ed Cole's life. J. Norris. il por Motor T 29:105-6 Ag '77 *

COLE, George, and others
Ten winter covers. il Motor B & S 140:113-15 O '77

COLE, George F. and Talarico, S. M.
Rethinking parole. il Intellect 106:143-6 O '77

COLE, Gordon H.
Chains of functional illiteracy. Educ Digest 43:10-13 D '77

COLE, James E.
What to do about violence. Todays Educ 66:58-9 N '77

COLE, John N.
Cold. il N Y Times Mag p71 Ja 30 '77; Same abr. with title Cold comforts. Read Digest 112:157-60 Ja '78
Outsider looks in. il Sports Illus 46:40-2+ My 16 '77
Taking the tree. il Nat Wildlife 16:14-19 D '77
Vanishing tuna. il Read Digest 110:132-5 Mr '77
Woman behind the wildflower that stopped a dam. il por Horticulture 55:30-5 D '77

COLE, Natalie
Daddy's girl makes good; interview, ed by E. Miller. il por Seventeen 36:98-9+ Jl '77
Natalie Cole: producers' puppet, father's daughter, or the new queen of R&B? interview, ed by J. S. Roberts. il pors Hi Fi 27:125+ F '77

COLE, Philip
Are you a high cancer risk? E. M. Whelan. Harp Baz 110:127+ F '77 *

COLE, Roger M. and others
Spiroplasmavirus citri 3: propagation, purification, proteins, and nucleic acid. bibl il Science 198:1262-3 D 23 '77

COLE, Stephen, and others
Peer review and the support of science; with biographical sketches. il Sci Am 237:15, 34-41 O '77

COLE, Thomas
Pic-nic; reproduction of painting; with introd by J. J. DuPont. il Conservationist 32:23-5 Jl '77

COLE, William
Children's books: the best of the season (cont) il Sat R 4:31-3 My 28; 5:40-2 N 26 '77
Trade winds. See issues of Saturday review

COLE family. See Brassica

COLEMAN, A. D.
Practical dreams of Man Ray (1890-1976) il Art N 76:52 Ja '77

COLEMAN, James S.
Population stability and equal rights. il Society 14:34-6 My '77

about
On the use and abuse of data. N. Epstein. Society 14:36-8 My '77 *

COLEMAN, John A.
Suffering, responsibility and ethics: a Lenten reflection. America 136:300-1 Ap 2 '77
Toward a world more human: five years of Concern. America 136:441-4 My 14 '77

COLEMAN, John Royston
College of hard knocks: my life as a garbageman. il pors N Y Times Mag p32-4+ My 1 '77

COLEMAN, William L.
Death they whisper about. Chr Today 21:38-9 S 23 '77

COLEMAN, William Thaddeus, 1920-
How Coleman sold Detroit on airbags. por Bus W p36 Ja 31 '77 *

COLES, Robert
Children of affluence; excerpt from Privileged ones: the well-off and the rich in America. il Atlantic 240:52-8+ S '77
Madness in film. il Horizon 21:18-22 Ja '78
What about moral sensibility? Todays Educ 66:40-2 S '77

about
Understanding rich kids. K. L. Woodward and P. Malamud. il por Newsweek 90:51 Ag 29 '77 *

COLESLAW. See Salads

COLEUS
Coleus grown as a tree. il Sunset 158:280 My '77

COLHOUN, Jack
Discriminatory pardon. Progressive 41:13 My '77
Still the back of the bus. Nation 224:594-6 My 14 '77

COLIN, Patrick L.
Where Puerto Rico meets the sea. il Sea Front 23:350-60 N '77

COLLABORATION, Literary. See Authorship—Collaboration

COLLAGE
Art of cutting up; cloth and paper collages. N. Mandelbaum. il Ladies Home J 94:120-3+ O '77
Carol Wald; interview, ed by M. Tinkelman. C. Wald. il Am Artist 41:78-81 Jl '77
Collage comedy and action; yarn collage. R. Moore. il Sch Arts 76:20-2 F '77
Collage with a message. H. Appelson and J. Wright. il Sch Arts 76:28-9 Mr '77
Mona Lisa, revised; collage at the Red Rocks Campus of the Community College of Denver. T. M. Jenkins. il Design (US) 78:23 Summ '77
Put wallpaper on your walls? J. E. Rutherford. il Sch Arts 76:30-2 Mr '77

COLLAGEN biosynthesis. See Synthesis

COLLAGENASE
Collagenase production by rheumatoid synovial cells: stimulation by a human lymphocyte factor. J. M. Dayer and others. bibl il Science 195:181-3 Ja 14 '77
Tumor cell collagenase and its inhibition by a cartilage-derived protease inhibitor. K. E. Kuettner and others. bibl il Science 196:653-4 My 6 '77
COLLAGRAPH prints. See Prints
COLLARDS. See Kale
COLLECTING. See Collectors and collecting
COLLECTING of accounts
Bill collector always rings twice. Consumer Rep 42:88-9 F '77
We've been asked: about crackdown on bill collectors; Fair Debt Collection Practices Act. il U.S. News 83:48 O 10 '77
When bill collectors play rough—. U.S. News 82:75 My 16 '77
COLLECTING of accounts by banks. See Banks and banking—Services
COLLECTIVE bargaining
Bargaining calendar to be light in 1978. L. W. Bolton. bibl f il M Labor R 100:34-43 D '77
Collective bargaining: the American approach to industrial democracy. M. Derber. bibl f Ann Am Acad 431:83-94 My '77
Cost push of '78 bargaining. il Bus W p52-3 D 12 '77
Effects of collective bargaining as measured for men in blue-collar jobs. P. J. Andrisani and A. I. Kohen. bibl il M Labor R 100:46-9 Ap '77
Forces working to reshape collective bargaining. J. Barbash. bibl M Labor R 100:60-1 F '77
Labor front: a tough year? G. R. Rosen. il Duns R 109:28-32 Ja '77
Organization behavior as an aid to labor impasse resolution. G. Strauss. bibl M Labor R 100:49-52 Ap '77
Process of work restructuring, and its impact on collective bargaining. L. A. Schlesinger and R. E. Walton. M Labor R 100:52-5 Ap '77
Tough talk won't be about wages this time. il U.S. News 83:92-3 D 26 '77
See also
Collective labor agreements

Aerospace industries

Aerospace industry facing serious labor problems. R. G. O'Lone. Aviation W 107:25 O 10 '77
Aerospace is facing a labor showdown. il Bus W p35-6 O 10 '77
Lockheed contract offer rejected by machinists. Aviation W 108:22 Ja 2 '78
Lockheed details offer to machinists. Aviation W 107:21-2 N 28 '77

Air traffic controllers (persons)

Air controllers get restive again. il Bus W p38 N 28 '77

Automobile industry

Job security and reduced work time. R. Wilhelm. Intellect 105:381 My '77

Baseball, Professional

Has collective bargaining altered the salary structure of baseball? J. G. Scoville. bibl il M Labor R 100:51-2 Mr '77

Coal industry

Chaos in coal's labor relations. il Bus W p88+ N 28 '77
Dwindling benefits fuel a UMW strike threat. Bus W p 120+ Jl 25 '77
Hints of compromise in the coal talks. Bus W p32 D 26 '77
How coal's deadlock threatens the economy. il Bus W p30-1 Ja 16 '78
Labor: trouble ahead? G. R. Rosen. por Duns R 110:57 S '77
Separate peace in Western coal. il Bus W p41 D 5 '77
Soft-coal operators take a tough stance. Bus W p30 N 7 '77

College teachers

Faculty collective bargaining: impact on planning. F. E. Crossland. por Intellect 106:67-70 Ag '77

Construction industry

Building trades give some ground. Bus W p48 My 16 '77
Canadian efforts to stabilize collective bargaining in construction. J. B. Rose. bibl M Labor R 100:76-8 Ap '77
Construction works to loosen the rules. il Bus W p32-3 Mr 21 '77

Container industry

Hard line on lifetime security; can-manufacturing industry. il Bus W p33-4 O 31 '77

Faculty

See Collective bargaining—College teachers

Football, Professional

Finding square one. J. Marshall. por Sports Illus 46:63-4 Mr 7 '77

Government employees

Labor relations. A. Leggat. See occasional issues of American city & county
Public employee unions push to catch up. il Bus W p49-50 Ag 1 '77
Public workers and public on a collision course; state and local workers. il U.S. News 82:82 Mr 14 '77

Librarians

Advice for the new trustee negotiator. P. Harris. por Wilson Lib Bull 52:237-40 N '77

Longshoremen

Industry split snarls the ILA talks. Bus W p56 S 26 '77
Labor: trouble ahead? G. R. Rosen. por Duns R 110:57 S '77

Multinational bargaining

Building a counterforce to multinational corporations. H. Rebhan. M Labor R 100:46-7 Mr '77
Problems facing international collective bargaining. B. A. Sharman. M Labor R 100:36-7 Mr '77

Railroads

For railroads, labor—some crucial bargaining. il U.S. News 82:97-8 My 16 '77
Rails aim at crew size again. il Bus W p88 Je 27 '77

Rubber industry

No give on either side in rubber talks. Bus W p43-4 Mr 28 '77

Steel industry

Breaking steel's separate peace; testing the Experimental Negotiating Agreement. il Time 110:55 Ag 15 '77
How lifetime security might work; USW bargaining program. Bus W p28 F 28 '77
Lifetime pay, come what may. Fortune 95:71 Ap '77
Lifetime security in steel? il Time 109:45 F 28 '77
Local issues that threaten steel. Bus W p26 Mr 28 '77
Ore miners threaten steel's labor peace; Experimental Negotiating Agreement. il Bus W p39-40 Ag 15 '77
Steel molds the 1977 pattern. il Bus W p26-7 F 28 '77
Steel strike: another blow for a problem-ridden industry. il U.S. News 83:61-2 Ag 15 '77
Steel's ballooning local issues. il Bus W p24-5 Jl 11 '77
Why a labor pact won't end steel's problems. J. Hoerr. Bus W p56-7 S 26 '77

Teachers

How a mediator can help you bargain. M. Lieberman. Educ Digest 42:29-31 F '77
See also
Collective bargaining—College teachers

Trucking

Three-way split among the carriers. Bus W p 110 O 10 '77
COLLECTIVE bargaining rights. See Labor laws and legislation
COLLECTIVE labor agreements
Developments in industrial relations. L. Bornstein and others. See issues of Monthly labor review
From wage hikes to job security: the unions' new tune. P. Rosenstiel. Nation 225:720-3 D 31 '77
Industrial relations in 1976: highlights of key settlements. L. Bornstein. M Labor R 100:27-35 Ja '77
Labor-management data. See issues of Monthly labor review
Major agreements expiring next month. See issues of Monthly labor review
See also
Collective bargaining
Open and closed shop

Aerospace industries

IAM locals at P&W work under new labor contract. W. C. Wetmore. Aviation W 107:24 D 12 '77
Lockheed employes return to jobs. J. M. Lenorovitz. Aviation W 108:17 Ja 9 '78

Aluminum industry

Aluminum accords comparable to steel settlement. L. Bornstein and others. M. Labor R 100:52-3 Ag '77

Coal industry

UMW is learning how to lose the West. il Bus W p128+ Ap 18 '77

Copper industry

Costly copper pact stuns the industry. Bus W p24-5 Jl 18 '77

COLLECTIVE labor agreements—*Continued*

Government employees

Put more no-strike clout in contracts. A. Leggat. Am City & County 92:83 Ag '77

Longshoremen

What ship lines paid for longshore peace. il Bus W p30-1 D 19 '77

Musicians

Viewpoint; agreement between Metropolitan Opera and its orchestra musicians. R. Jacobson. Opera N 42:6 O '77

Steel industry

How inflationary was the steel settlement? il Forbes 119:97 My 1 '77
Steel industry's expensive settlement. Bus W p28-9 Ap 25 '77
Steelworkers win enhanced employment security. L. Bornstein and others. M Labor R 100:62-3 Je '77

Telephone companies

Telephone accord averts strike. L. Bornstein and others. M Labor R 100:74-5 O '77

Europe, Western

European union agreements provide framework for public policies. S. Barkin. M Labor R 100:62-4 Ja '77

COLLECTIVE settlements
Cinderella children; urban communes. D. K. Weisberg. bibl il por Psychol Today 10:84-6+ Ap '77
How they keep them down on The Farm. K. Wenner. il N Y Times Mag p74+ My 8 '77
Life at Synanon is swinging. il por Time 110:18 D 26 '77
Place called community. P. J. Palmer. Chr Cent 94:252-6 Mr 16 '77
Visions of futures past; Lindisfarne Association. S. Helgesen. il Harpers 254:80-6 Mr '77

Israel

Leisure on the kibbutz. R. Ronen. Parks & Rec 12:56-8 Je '77

United States

See Collective settlements

COLLECTOR, Michael I. See Monjan, A. A. jt auth
COLLECTORS and collecting
Address book. S. Sunderlin. See issues of House beautiful
Antiques' travel guide (cont) Antiques 111:579-86, 1223-30; 112:531-8, 1187-94 Mr, Je, S, D '77
Collecting:
Amish quilts. B. S. Janos. il House B 119:24+ Mr '77
Glass paperweights. N. Mines. il House B 119:28+ S '77
Collecting. J. Goldman. See issues of Vogue
Collecting trouble. J. Train. Forbes 121:232-3 Ja 9 '78
Collectors' notes. K. M. Jones. See issues of Antiques
Delectable collectibles. J. Bayliss. il Sat Eve Post 249:30-1 My '77
See also
Americana
Book collecting
also subhead Collectors and collecting under various subjects, e.g. Engines—Collectors and collecting
COLLEGE, Choice of
Are you better off at Harvard? L. Botstein. N Y Times Mag p81-6 Ap 17 '77
Sensible way to pick the right college. Changing T 31:11-4 O '77
COLLEGE administrators. See College officials
COLLEGE admission. See Colleges and universities—Admission
COLLEGE alumni. See College graduates
COLLEGE and school drama

Texts

Junior and senior high. See issues of Plays
COLLEGE and school journalism
Give them a reason to write: launching the informal school newspaper. E. Strong. Engl J 66:37-40 My '77
Our man at Harvard; writing for The advocate. N. Mailer. il Esquire 87:110-12 Ap '77
See also
Foxfire (periodical)
COLLEGE architecture
Buildings type study: college buildings: the multi-purpose building as an alternative to the sprawling campus; with introd by J. Nairn. il Archit Rec 162:109-24 N '77
Buried bookstore saves energy, saves space, saves the view; Williamson Hall, University of Minnesota. S. J. Marcovich. il Pop Sci 211:96-7 S '77
Center for audio-visual development; the Clark Kerr Learning Resources Hall on the University of California campus in Santa Barbara; with introd by J. Nairn. il Archit Rec 162:85-8 Jl '77
Growing of grids; the Central Building of Tsukuba University; with introd by W. Marlin. il Archit Rec 161:107-12 Ap '77
It's back to school for the systems approach; Stockton State College, Pomona, N.J. il Archit Rec 161:95-102 My '77
New college in Riyadh will train teachers and scientists. il Archit Rec 162:37 N '77
Recycling Main—a landmark at Vassar; with introd by M. F. Schmertz. il Archit Rec 162:73-8 Jl '77
School for the dance by Gunnar Birkerts; with introd by M. F. Schmertz. il Archit Rec 161:85-90 F '77
2 learning places by Metz Train Olson & Youngren. N. Miller and W. Marlin. il Archit Rec 162:89-96 Jl '77
See also
Dormitories, Remodeled
Library architecture
COLLEGE art galleries and museums
See also
Georgia. University, Athens—Georgia Museum of Art
Southern Methodist University, Dallas—Meadows Museum and Sculpture Court
COLLEGE athlete recruiting. See Athletes—Recruiting
COLLEGE athletics
Campus recreation. L. A. Heywood and R. B. Warnick. Educ Digest 42:33-5 Ja '77
School of soft knocks; Pepperdine University. R. Telander. il Sports Illus 46:100-4+ My 23 '77
See also
Baseball, College
Basketball, College
Boxing
Football, College
Hockey, College
Lacrosse
National Collegiate Athletic Association
Rowing
Sailboat racing
Swimming
Tennis
Wrestling

Economic aspects

Color those jerseys red. Time 109:74+ F 28 '77

Ethical aspects

Ethics, due process, diversity, and balance; address, March 25, 1977. S. Horn. Vital Speeches 43:463-8 My 15 '77
COLLEGE attendance. See Colleges and universities—Attendance
COLLEGE bookstore buildings. See College architecture
COLLEGE bookstores
See also
Booksellers and bookselling—Textbooks
National Association of College Stores
COLLEGE buildings. See College architecture
COLLEGE clubs and societies
See also
College sororities
Yale University—Clubs and societies
COLLEGE-Conservatory of Music of Cincinnati. See Cincinnati. University—College-Conservatory of Music
COLLEGE discipline
See also
Student suspension and expulsion
COLLEGE dormitories. See Dormitories
COLLEGE education
100 things every college graduate should know. J. Jones and W. Wilson. il Esquire 88:91-6 S '77
What's going on in schools & colleges. Changing T 31:29-30 S '77
See also
Adult education
Aged—Education
Coeducation
Education, Humanistic
Education of women
Foreign study
Professional education

Aims and objectives

Discouraging word? address, October 13, 1977. A. Brown. Vital Speeches 44:78-81 N 15 '77
Fanaticism and absolutism. S. Hook. il por Intellect 105:387-8 My '77
Intellectual community. R. M. Hutchins. Educ Digest 42:38-41 My '77
What is education? Who is educated? L. Morrow. il Horizon 20:35-9 S '77; Same. Current 196:53-60 O '77
Wide open door to higher education. R. B. Werry. Intellect 105:251-3 F '77

Cost

As colleges search for ways to ease the blow of spiraling costs. il U.S. News 82:37-8 Mr 21 '77
College costs: are middle-income families caught in the middle? il Bet Hom & Gard 55:80+ S '77

COLLEGE education—Cost—*Continued*
Finding $$$ for college. Sr Schol 110:37+ O 20 '77
How can the armed services help cover college costs? M. Daly and E. Sweeney. il Bet Hom & Gard 55:38+ Mr '77
How much will college for your child cost? N. G. Rollins. il Good H 185:247 O '77
How to finance a college education. R. B. Hoey. por Forbes 119:94 Ap 1 '77
How to find money for college. B. Delatiner. il McCalls 104:75 Ag '77
See also
Medical education—Cost

Federal aid

See Colleges and universities—Federal aid

Standards

Onward and downward from the ivory tower. B. DeMott. il por Psychol Today 11:60-2+ S '77

COLLEGE education, Value of
Does it pay to go to college? H. Howe, 2d; R. B. Freeman. pors U.S. News 82:59-60 Ja 24 '77
Is college worthwhile?
Need to know. R. G. Davis. Commonweal 104:236-9 Ap 15 '77
Revolt against college. M. R. Berube. Commonweal 104:233-6 Ap 15 '77
New case for college. Seventeen 36:49 N '77
Value of a college education. Educ Digest 42:19-21 F '77
Value of college education to jobless graduates. M. Wachman. il Intellect 105:210-11 Ja '77
Who needs college? C. Bird; E. Ginzberg. Parents Mag 52:59+ S '77

COLLEGE education and state. See Education and state

COLLEGE enrollment. See Colleges and universities—Attendance

COLLEGE Entrance Examination Board

Scholastic Aptitude Test

Declining SAT scores. J. Ryor. Todays Educ 66:6+ N '77
How are English teachers reacting to declining college entrance scores? C. Tibbetts and A. M. Tibbetts. Engl J 66:13-16 D '77
On further examination: the SAT score decline. il Sci N 112:148-9 S 3 '77
On second thought: reviewing the SAT decline. S. N. Judy. bibl f Engl J 66:5-7 N '77
What's the score on the S.A.T.'s? S. A. Friedman. il McCalls 105:42-3 Ja '78
Why SAT scores decline. M. Sheils. il Newsweek 90:82-3 S 5 '77
Why student test scores are down. il U.S. News 83:55 S 5 '77
Why those falling test scores? il Time 110:40 S 5 '77

COLLEGE entrance requirements. See Colleges and universities—Entrance requirements

COLLEGE essays. See Student themes and reports

COLLEGE facilities

Extended use

Back to school for a vacation. il U.S. News 82:54 My 30 '77
Campus crunch; restriction against college facilities for religious use. M. Allison. Chr Today 22:41-2 O 21 '77
Try a campus vacation. F. Cross. il Read Digest 110:92-5 My '77

COLLEGE graduates
Annals of higher education; conflict between Concerned Alumni of Princeton and the University. E. J. Kahn, Jr. New Yorker 53:88+ My 23 '77
Better students become less competent adults; study by Douglas Heath. J. Horn. Psychol Today 11:29 Ag '77
Let's hear it from the class of '77. il Time 109:42+ Je 13 '77
See also
Agricultural colleges—Graduates
Business schools and colleges—Graduates
College education, Value of

Employment

Brighter job picture for '78 graduates. il U.S. News 84:72 Ja 9 '78
Female college students risking unemployment; excerpts from College women and the job market, 1980. il Intellect 105:211-12 Ja '77
Good news for '77 graduates: more openings, at better pay. il U.S. News 82:65-6 F 21 '77
Jobs for this year's college graduates. il Changing T 31:25-32 Mr '77
Revolt against college. M. R. Berube. Commonweal 104:233-6 Ap 15 '77
What price education? N. Von Hoffman. Progressive 41:55 F '77
When college graduates enter the real world. il U.S. News 82:79-80 Mr 14 '77
Why newly employed college graduates quit. F. S. Endicott. Intellect 106:103 S '77

COLLEGE graduates, Women

Employment

See College graduates—Employment

COLLEGE journalism. See College and school journalism

COLLEGE librarians
One and one-tenth lives of a librarian/scholar; interview, ed by A. Plotnik. D. Kranzler. por Am Lib 8:65 F '77

Qualifications

Publish or perish, library-style. J. Campbell. Wilson Lib Bull 52:250 N '77

Recruiting

High cost of hiring. R. Christofferson. il por Lib J 102:677-81 Mr 15 '77

Supply and demand

See also
College librarians—Recruiting

COLLEGE libraries
See also subhead Libraries or Library under names of colleges and universities, e.g. Columbia University—Libraries

Acquisitions

Pitt study pegs faulty acquisitions patterns. Lib J 102:1438 Jl '77

Administration

See College library administration

Advertising

See College library publicity

Architecture

See Library architecture

Automation

Card catalog to COM; Ryerson Polytechnical Institute, Toronto. J. North. il Lib J 102:2132-4 O 15 '77

Circulation, loans, etc.

Research library borrows leaf from PL book; loan limits. W. R. Eshelman. Wilson Lib Bull 51:465-6 F '77
Special report: book return lag? Try promos; radio promotions. C. Huntley. Wilson Lib Bull 52:294-5 D '77

Conservation and restoration of materials

See College libraries—Technical processes

Finance

How to win the budget battle on campus. C. J. Schmidt. Am Lib 8:569-70 N '77

Instruction in use

Beyond the library tour: those who can, must teach. R. Vuturo. bibl il Wilson Lib Bull 51:736-40 My '77

Manuscript collections

Open letter opens letters; question of access. W. R. Eshelman. il Wilson Lib Bul 51:559-60 Mr '77

Public relations

See also
College library surveys

Return of books

See College libraries—Circulation, loans, etc.

Special collections

Pope's library is brought to light after 200 years; collection at Catholic University. M. Olmert. il Smithsonian 8:70-7 Ja '78
See also
College libraries—Manuscript collections

Statistics

Academic library building in 1977. J. Orne and J. O. Gosling. il Lib J 102:2393-6 D 1 '77
Two-year college LRC buildings. D. J. Bock. il por Lib J 102:2410-11 D 1 '77

Technical processes

Preservation at Harvard: guidelines and goals set. Lib J 102:1230 Je 1 '77

Use studies

See College library surveys

Israel

University libraries in Israel. C. Kurzman. il Wilson Lib Bull 51:824-31 Je '77

COLLEGE library administration
Academic librarians share their know-how; the Systems and Procedures Exchange Center. M. Sitts. Am Lib 8:570 N '77
Participative management urged as best option; views of M. Beckman. Lib J 102:321-2 F 1 '77
Things your boss never told you about library management; excerpt from To know a library. D. Gore. Lib J 102:765-70 Ap 1 '77

COLLEGE library architecture. See Library architecture

COLLEGE library cooperation
Stanford & UC get $$ for broad-gauge co-op. Lib J 102:320 F 1 '77

COLLEGE library instruction. See College libraries—Instruction in use

COLLEGE library publicity
Special report: book return lag? Try promos; radio promotions. C. Huntley. Wilson Lib Bull 52:294-5 D '77

COLLEGE library surveys
Use of a university library collection: a progress report on a Pittsburgh study; with editorial comment. T. J. Galvin and A. Kent. Lib J 102:2295, 2317-20 N 15 '77

COLLEGE museums
See also
British Columbia. University, Vancouver—Museum of Anthropology
Louisiana. State University, Baton Rouge—Rural Life Museum

Architecture

See Museums—Architecture

COLLEGE of Cardinals. See Cardinals

COLLEGE officials
Impolite speculations on higher education. E. L. Galligan. Educ Digest 43:50-2 O '77
Where are the leaders in higher education? F. Reif. Educ Digest 42:25-7 My '77
See also
College presidents

COLLEGE presidents
See also
Mays, B. E.
Silber, J. R.

Selection and appointment

Humanist; A. B. Giamatti appointed president. por Time 111:68 Ja 2 '78
New Haven's presidential search; Help wanted on other campuses. il Time 110:96+ D 5 '77
Renaissance man; A. B. Giamatti Yale University's new president. M. Sheils and P. Malamud. por Newsweek 91:45 Ja 2 '78
Yale's blues; nominations for a new president of Yale University. M. Sheils. il por Newsweek 90:79 D 26 '77

COLLEGE professors and instructors. See College teachers

COLLEGE scholarships. See Scholarships and fellowships

COLLEGE sororities
Going Greek isn't great! S. Megna. por Seventeen 36:28 N '77

COLLEGE sports. See College athletics

COLLEGE student achievements. See Student achievements

COLLEGE student opinion. See Student opinion

COLLEGE student suspension and expulsion. See Student suspension and expulsion

COLLEGE student themes and reports. See Student themes and reports

COLLEGE students
Adult students breathe new life into education. il U.S. News 82:70-2 Mr 28 '77
Great bright hopes. il Esquire 88:80-3 S '77
Imagination gap. A. J. Hansen. por Newsweek 90:9 Jl 25 '77
Let's hear it from the class of '77. il Time 109:42+ Je 13 '77
Tuning in and turning on; address, September 15, 1977. G. Turbeville. Vital Speeches 43:747-9 O 1 '77
See also
Coeducation
Cookery by college students
Student activities
Student militants

Aid

See Student loans

Attitudes

See Students—Attitudes

Cheating

See Cheating in school work

Civil rights

See Students—Civil rights

Clothing

See Clothing and dress—Students

Demonstrations

See Student demonstrations

Employment

See Student employment

Federal aid

See Student aid

Grading

See Grading and marking (students)

Housing

See also
Dormitories

Nutrition

How to avoid freshman weight gain. J. Gerston. Seventeen 36:70 Mr '77
Junk food diet; College survival tipsheet. J. S. Stern. Mademoiselle 83:178-9 Ag '77

Political activities

See also
Students for a Democratic Society (organization)
Young Americans for Freedom (organization)

Psychology

I couldn't cope alone. R. Dale. Seventeen 36:150-1+ N '77

Recruiting

See Colleges and universities—Student recruiting

Religious life

See also
Campus Crusade for Christ (organization)
Colleges and universities—Religious life
Inter-Varsity Christian Fellowship

Sexual behavior

MIT's new coarse guide. Newsweek 89:57 My 30 '77
On female macho; Consumer guide to MIT men. J. Allen. Mademoiselle 83:88+ N '77
Pregnant pause in the sexual revolution. D. Byrne. bibl por Psychol Today 11:67-8 Jl '77
Sexual freedom: is it worth the hassle? G. Kurz. Mademoiselle 83:207 Ag '77

State aid

See Student aid

Suicide

See Suicide

Travel

See Student travel

Volunteer service

See Volunteer service

COLLEGE students, Mentally superior
Smorgasbord for an IQ of 150; Study of Mathematically Precocious Youth program at Johns Hopkins. il Time 109:64 Je 6 '77
Young prodigies take off under special program; Study of Mathematically Precocious Youth at Johns Hopkins. D. Nevin. il por Smithsonian 8:76-81 bibl(p 160) O '77

COLLEGE students, Women
A+ for older college women. E. J. Pascoe. McCalls 104:45 Mr '77
America's homecoming queens. il Good H 185:144-5 O '77
Collegiettes. R. Baker. N Y Times Mag p 13 O 23 '77
See also
Black students, Women
College sororities
Education of women
Sex discrimination in education

COLLEGE students life insurance policies. See Insurance, Life—Policies

COLLEGE teachers
Executives who get into teaching; business school teachers. il Bus W p 123 S 19 '77
Faculty growth contracts. R. Gross. Educ Digest 43:28-31 S '77
Faculty of liberal learning; address, August 22, 1977. F. A. Johnson. Vital Speeches 43:724-31 S 15 '77
Identity crisis in the seminaries. J. T. Laney. Chr Cent 94:95+ F 2 '77
Junior faculty in revolt: reform plans for Berlin University in 1848. E. J. C. Hahn. bibl f il Am Hist R 82:875-95 O '77
See also
Academic freedom
Collective bargaining—College teachers
English teachers
Law teachers
Strikes—United States—College teachers
Women college teachers

Attitudes

Unhappy profs; study by Everett Ladd and Seymour Lipset. Newsweek 90:111-12 O 24 '77

Political activities

Brouhaha in Brooklyn; question of Brooklyn College professor M. Selzer's involvement with the CIA. D. Ravitch. New Repub 176:18-21 Mr 12 '77; Discussion. 176:9 Mr 26; 7-8 Ap 2; 7+ My 7 '77
Cloak, dagger and gown: CIA in academe. J. K. Larson. Chr Cent 94:931-3 O 19 '77
Incomplete candor; Harvard's policy toward ex-Communist faculty members in the 1950s. K. L. Woodward. pors Newsweek 90:77 Jl 25 '77

Retirement

Somewhere over Rainbow Bay. . . R. Wiley. il Ret Liv 17:26-8 Ag '77
Thank you, Mr Chips. P. Bonventre. il Newsweek 89:90-1 Je 6 '77

COLLEGE teachers—*Continued*

Selection and appointment

Recruiting and hiring practices of community college deans of instruction. J. L. Brown. il Clearing H 51:29-31 S '77
Should Dr Kissinger be seated? Columbia's ethical red herring; address, April 26, 1977. M. Teitelman. Nation 224:658 My 28 '77

Sexual behavior

Bod and man at Yale; charges of sex discrimination for tolerating sexual coercion of female students by male teachers. il Time 110:52-3 Ag 8 '77
Women students v. male teachers: sexual harassment at Yale. A. Nelson. Nation 226:7-9 Ja 7 '78

Supply and demand

American dilemma. Sci Am 236:50+ My '77

Tenure

University tenure problem. H. Shull; discussion. Science 195:440-1 F 4 '77

Unions

See Teachers unions

COLLEGE teachers as public officers. See Public officers

COLLEGE tuition. See College education—Cost

COLLEGES and business. See Business and education

COLLEGES and universities
See also
Academic freedom
Agricultural colleges
Business schools and colleges
Catholic colleges and universities
Church colleges and universities
Colleges for women
Community and junior colleges
Medical colleges
also headings beginning College

Accreditation

Path to accreditation; college and university programs in recreation education. I. G. Shapiro. Parks & Rec 12:29-31+ Ja '77
See also
United States—Advisory Committee on Accreditation and Institutional Eligibility

Administration

Contractual relationships between students and universities; University of Texas conference. Intellect 105:297-8 Mr '77
See also
College officials
College presidents

Admission

Entrance examination; U.S. probe into admissions practices of Philadelphia's medical and graduate schools. il por Time 109:14 Je 6 '77
How to help your college-bound teen-ager. B. R. Anderson. House B 119:14+ O '77
Wide open door to higher education. R. R. Werry. Intellect 105:251-3 F '77
See also
Colleges and universities—Entrance requirements
Medical colleges—Admission

Anecdotes, facetiae, satire, etc.

That college countdown. K. Topkins. Seventeen 36:108-9+ F '77

Attendance

Adult students breathe new life into education. il U.S. News 82:70-2 Mr 28 '77

Choice

See College, Choice of

Curriculum

Academic degrees for labor studies—a new goal for unions. L. S. Gray. bibl il M Labor R 100:15-20 Je '77
Behind the push to revive the liberal arts in U.S. colleges. il U.S. News 82:49 My 2 '77
Close-up: what do college students write? special section. Engl J 66:58-69 N '77
Comes the counterrevolution. B. Rice and J. Cramer. il Psychol Today 11:56-7+ S '77
Courses that women can count on; Colleges offering math-anxiety classes. E. J. Pascoe. il McCalls 104:68 Jl '77
Economics gap. H. Flieger. U.S. News 82:76 Ja 31 '77
Pancakes and plumbing; intersession courses. il Time 109:67-8 Ja 24 '77
Report says colleges too specialized; study by Carnegie Foundation for the Advancement of Teaching. Sci N 112:422 D 24 '77
Teaching thinking on paper; work of A. D. Van Nostrand. il por Time 109:74 Ap 18 '77
See also
Education, Humanistic

Anecdotes, facetiae, satire, etc.

In-depth courses in breadth. G. F. Kneller. Intellect 105:351 Ap '77

Departments of art

Fine arts in college: a proposal for redesigning the curriculum. J. W. Strawn. Am Artist 41:64-6 D '77
Should the art school curriculum include professional job training? pro and con discussion. J. Brodsky; N. Harrison. il Am Artist 41:16-17 O '77
See also
New York (city). City University—Brooklyn College—Department of Design

Desegregation

More blacks in colleges; integration order issued by HEW. il U.S. News 83:69 Jl 18 '77

Enrollment

See Colleges and universities—Attendance

Entrance requirements

See also
College Entrance Examination Board

Anecdotes, facetiae, satire, etc.

My college essay; symposium. il pors N Y Times Mag p28-30 Ja 16 '77

Extension

See University extension

Faculty

See College teachers

Federal aid

Notes from the front. R. Kirk. Nat R 29:1179 O 14 '77

Finance

Colleges learn the hard sell. il Bus W p92+ F 14 '77
Petrogrants. M. Sheils. il Newsweek 90:75 Jl 4 '77
See also
College education—Cost

Government regulation

See Education and state

Graduate work

Modernizing advanced degree programs. J. A. Behnke. BioScience 27:159 Mr '77

Graduation requirements

PhD language requirement. O. Gingerich. il Phys Today 30:9+ N '77

Laws and legislation

Road is paved with good intentions; Title IX and sex discrimination; address, January 25, 1977. E. Green. Vital Speeches 43:300-3 Mr 1 '77
Title IX: administrative, legal and constitutional aspects; address, March 10, 1977. D. H. Oaks. Vital Speeches 43:372-6 Ap 1 '77

Publications

See also
University presses

Religious life

Campus crunch; restriction against college facilities for religious use. M. Allison. Chr Today 22:41-2 O 21 '77
DEW Line for the churches. America 137:433 D 17 '77

Research

Academic science: quality decaying. Sci N 111:373 Je 11 '77
Follies of affirmative action; funds for scientific research. E. Loftus. Society 14:21-4 Ja '77
Lab for orphans; medical research at Rockefeller University. Time 110:79 N 28 '77
Overhead headache. H. Shull. Science 195:639 F 18 '77
Report finds US academic research base is endangered. F. C. Bennett. Phys Today 30:61-2+ Ag '77
Research crunch. M. Grosswirth. Sci Digest 82:27-9+ N '77
Science and the law; address, September 20, 1977. W. J. McGill. Vital Speeches 44:28-32 O 15 '77
State of academic science: concern about the vital signs. J. Walsh. Science 196:1184-5 Je 10 '77

Security measures

Officials, students join to combat campus crime. il U.S. News 82:45 Ap 4 '77

Student recruiting

Colleges learn the hard sell. il Bus W p92+ F 14 '77
Colleges turn to the hard sell. il U.S. News 82:63 Ap 18 '77

COLLEGES and universities—*Continued*

Alaska

See also
Alaska. University, Fairbanks

Arkansas

See also
Arkansas University

California

See also
California. State University, Fresno
California. University
Lone Mountain College, San Francisco
Pepperdine University, Malibu
Stanford University, Palo Alto

Canada

Bogota connection; recreology students from University of Ottawa, studying in Colombia, South America. T. L. Goodale. il Parks & Rec 12:54-7+ S '77
Card catalog to COM; Ryerson Polytechnical Institute, Toronto. J. North. il Lib J 102:2132-4 O 15 '77
See also
British Columbia. University, Vancouver
Guelph. University, Ontario

China

Science education in China. BioScience 27:303 Ap '77

Colorado

See also
Colorado. University, Boulder
Denver. University

Connecticut

See also
Yale University

England

See also
Oxford. University

Florida

See also
Florida Institute of Technology
Miami-Dade Community College, Miami

Georgia

See also
Georgia. University, Athens
Toccoa Falls Institute, Toccoa Falls

Germany

Junior faculty in revolt: reform plan for Berlin University in 1848. E. J. C. Hahn. bibl f il Am Hist R 82:875-95 O '77

Great Britain

Science in Europe: attack on Marxists stirs controversy. N. Hawkes. Science 198:1230-1 D 23 '77
Writing across the Curriculum: the London projects; ERIC/RCS report; University of London. A. N. Applebee. bibl Engl J 66:81-5 D '77

Illinois

See also
Chicago. University
Illinois Institute of Technology, Chicago
Moraine Valley Community College, Palos Hills
Northwestern University, Evanston
Rush Medical College, Chicago
Wheaton College, Wheaton

Indiana

See also
DePauw University, Greencastle
Indiana State University, Terre Haute
Notre Dame. University, Notre Dame

Iowa

See also
Iowa. University, Iowa City

Israel

See also
College libraries—Israel

Italy

Italian dilemma: far too many students, poor universities, too few jobs. G. Ackley. por Duns R 109:9 My '77
Removing the Italian welcome mat; suspension of foreign enrollment. il Time 110:43 Jl 18 '77

Japan

Growing of grids; the Central Building of Tsukuba University; with introd by W. Marlin. il Archit Rec 161:107-12 Ap '77
See also
United Nations University, Tokyo

Louisiana

See also
Grambling College, Grambling
Louisiana. State University, Baton Rouge
New Orleans. University

Maine

See also
Maine. University, Orono

Maryland

See also
Johns Hopkins University, Baltimore
United States—Uniformed Services University of the Health Sciences, Bethesda

Massachusetts

See also
Boston University
Brandeis University, Waltham
Emerson College, Boston
Hampshire College, Amherst
Harvard University
Holy Cross College, Worcester
Massachusetts Institute of Technology, Cambridge
Radcliffe College, Cambridge
Simmons College, Boston
Smith College, Northampton
Wellesley College, Wellesley

Michigan

See also
Detroit. University
Hillsdale College, Hillsdale
Michigan State University, East Lansing

Minnesota

See also
Minnesota. University, Minneapolis

Missouri

See also
Missouri. University, Columbia

Nebraska

See also
Nebraska. University, Omaha

New Hampshire

See also
Dartmouth College, Hanover
New Hampshire. University, Durham

New Jersey

See also
New Jersey. Stockton State College, Pomona
Princeton University
Stevens Institute of Technology, Hoboken

New York (state)

Closing colleges; Briarcliff & Bennett. Time 110:82 Ag 15 '77
College for convicts; program at Attica. E. Cuddy. Progressive 41:53-5 F '77
See also
Briarcliff College, Briarcliff Manor
Columbia University
Fordham University
New York (state). State University
New York University
Rockefeller University
Sarah Lawrence College, Bronxville
Syracuse University, Syracuse
Vassar College, Poughkeepsie
Yeshiva University, New York

North Carolina

See also
Black Mountain College
Davidson College, Davidson
North Carolina. Appalachian State University, Boone
Wake Forest University, Winston Salem

Ohio

See also
Case Western Reserve University, Cleveland
Ohio. Kent State University, Kent
Wilmington College, Wilmington

Oklahoma

See also
Oklahoma City. South Oklahoma City Junior College

Oregon

See also
Oregon. University, Eugene

Pennsylvania

Entrance examination; U.S. probe into admissions practices of Philadelphia's medical and graduate schools. il por Time 109:14 Je 6 '77
See also
Bryn Mawr College, Bryn Mawr
Bucknell University, Lewisburg
Haverford College, Harverford
Pittsburgh. University

Rhode Island

See also
Providence College, Providence

Saudi Arabia

New college in Riyadh will train teachers and scientists. il Archit Rec 162:37 N '77

Texas

See also
Southern Methodist University, Dallas
Texas. University

COLLEGES and universities—*Continued*

United States

Make America smarter: the independent college; address, January 6, 1977. J. C. Sawhill. Vital Speeches 43:309-11 Mr 1 '77
What's going on in schools & colleges. Changing T 31:29-30 S '77
See also
Colleges and universities, State
Theological seminaries

Utah

See also
Utah. University, Salt Lake City

Washington, D.C.

See also
Catholic University of America

Washington (state)

See also
Washington (state). University, Seattle

COLLEGES and universities, Choice of. See Colleges, Choice of

COLLEGES and universities, Experimental
See also
Black Mountain College,
Hampshire College, Amherst, Mass.

COLLEGES and universities, Municipal
See also
New York (city). City University

COLLEGES and universities, State
Durability of reasonable autonomy for state universities. M. M. Chambers. Educ Digest 42:24-7 Ap '77
More blacks in colleges; integration order issued by HEW. il U.S. News 83:69 Jl 18 '77

COLLEGES for women
Academic profile; women's Catholic colleges. E. B. Wymard. Commonweal 104:652-7 O 14 '77
Closing colleges; Briarcliff & Bennett. Time 110:82 Ag 15 '77
See also
Bryn Mawr College, Bryn Mawr, Pa.
Smith College, Northampton, Mass.
Wellesley College, Wellesley, Mass.

COLLERD, Ray
Urban trapper. L. Pinck. por Outdoor Life 160:38 D '77 *

COLLET, Marjen H.
Making it on its own. por Forbes 119:78 Mr 1 '77 *

COLLI, Jean Claude
Selling sunshine to Saudis. por Forbes 120:110 D 1 '77 *

COLLIER, James Lincoln
Asimov, the human writing machine. por Read Digest 111:123-6 Ag '77
Mad, mad world of rock 'n records. Read Digest 111:13+ O '77

COLLIER, Richard
Bridge across the sky; condensation. il Read Digest 111:258-62+ N '77

COLLIER, Zena
John Newbery: publisher with a radical idea. il por Pub W 212:81-2 Jl 18 '77

COLLIER revolvers. See Revolvers

COLLIGAN, Douglas
What's happening to our weather? il Mech Illus 73:132+ My '77

COLLINS, Arthur Worth, Jr. See Collins, Bud

COLLINS, Bob
Two on the fifty. il Sat Eve Post 249:40-1 O '77

COLLINS, Bud
Farewell to Forest Hills. il N Y Times Mag p48-50+ S 11 '77
She can beat Evert—but does she really want to? il pors N Y Times Mag p35-6+ Je 19 '77
Tennis. Sports Illus 47:99-100 D 5 '77

COLLINS, Chase
Random voodoo; story. Ms 6:59-63 Ag '77

COLLINS, Clint
Dynamic symmetry of Ruth Egri. il Am Artist 41:46-51+ D '77

COLLINS, Frederick A. 1915-
Whatever happened to S&H? por Duns R 109:18-19 Ja '77 *

COLLINS, Gary R.
Burn-out: the hazard of professional people-helpers. Chr Today 21:12-14 Ap 1 '77

COLLINS, Janet, and Nickel, K. N.
Collegiate grading system: traditional or non-traditional. bibl il Clearing H 50:243-7 F '77

COLLINS, Judy
Judy Collins & the art of transition; interview, ed by S. Elliott. pors Hi Fi 27:123-6 Ap '77

COLLINS, Leighton
Learning to fly. Flying 101:301 S '77

COLLINS, Marva
Westside story. il por Time 110:39 D 26 '77 *

COLLINS, Mary
Meditating on the word's meaning. il New Cath World 220:36-7 Ja '77

COLLINS, Michael, 1930-
Orbiter is first spacecraft designed for shuttle runs. il Smithsonian 8:38-47 bibl(p 134) My '77
Showing Lindbergh the air and space museum. il Sat R 4:30-1+ Ap 16 '77

COLLINS, Morris William Hollowell, 1917-
How Carter will differ from Ford—an expert's view; interview. il por U.S. News 82:17-18 Ja 31 '77

COLLINS, Norm
Mayday now from any ocean. Yachting 141:184-3 My '77

COLLINS, Reid
Fisherman; story. Field & S 82:136-8 O '77

COLLINS, Richard L.
Aftermath. Flying 101:37+ Ag; 88+ O '77
Flying techniques. See issues of Flying
On top. See issues of Flying
Pilot error. See issues of Flying

about

Change of command. E. D. Muhlfeld. Flying 100:4 Mr '77
Passing the flag. E. D. Muhlfeld. il pors Flying 101:1+ O '77 *

COLLINS, Ruth Harvey
One-fourth of the world's children. Educ Digest 43:57-9 S '77

COLLINS, Thomas
Q&A about retiring. See issues of Retirement living

COLLINS, Verla
1977—the year of the nurse; address, June 11, 1977. Vital Speeches 43:590-3 Jl 15 '77

COLLISION avoidance systems. See Airplanes—Safety devices and measures; Automobiles—Safety devices and measures

COLLISIONS, Airplane. See Aviation—Accidents

COLLISIONS at sea
Soviet submarine, U.S. frigate collide; photographs. Aviation W 106:18-19 Mr 14 '77
Wreck of the two sisters; crash of the tank ships Venoil and Venpet. il map Time 110:31 D 26 '77

COLMAN, Libby. See Bing, E. jt auth

COLOGNE. See Perfumes

COLOGNE for men. See Perfumes for men

COLOMBIA
See also
Bogotá
Forests and forestry—Colombia
Medical care—Colombia

Economic conditions

Inequality in Colombia. D. K. Zschock. bibl f il Cur Hist 72:68-72+ F '77

Photographs

Photographer's eye: Colombia; work of Egar. A. L. Lowe. il Américas 29:8-9 Ja '77

Religious institutions and affairs

See also
Colombian Confederation of Evangelicals

COLOMBIAN Confederation of Evangelicals
In Bogotá, a banquet of hope. J. C. Hefley. il Chr Today 22:44-6 N 18 '77

COLOMBIAN cookery. See Cookery, Colombian

COLOMBIANS in the United States
See also
Queens, N.Y.—Foreign population

COLON (anatomy)
Thyrotropin-releasing hormone: stimulation of colonic activity following intracerebroventricular administration. J. R. Smith and others. bibl il Science 196:660-2 My 6 '77

COLONIAL history (United States) See United States—History—Colonial period, ca. 1600-1775

COLONIAL life and customs. See United States—Social life and customs—Colonial period, ca. 1600-1775

COLONIAL Village Church, Flint. See Michigan—Religious institutions and affairs

COLONIES
See also
United Nations—Special Committee on the Situation with Regard to the Implementation of the Declaration on the Granting of Independence to Colonial Countries and Peoples
United Nations—Trusteeship Council

COLONIES, Artists and authors. See Artists and authors colonies

COLONIES, Space. See Space colonies

COLONIZATION
See also
Africa—Colonization
Latin America—Colonization
Space colonies

COLONY, Joyce
Argument for Milton's Dalila. Yale R 66:562-75 Je '77

COLONY Square. See Atlanta—Buildings

COLOPHON, pseud
Notes on trade. Pub W 211:8 Je 13; 212:10 Jl 11; 6 Ag 15; 8 S 12; 10 O 31; 6 N 28; 16 D 26 '77

COLOR
Appearance of materials. T. B. Brill. bibl il por Chemistry 50:6-9 D '77
Color, format and abstract art: an interview with Kenneth Noland; ed by D. Waldman. K. Noland. il por Art in Am 65:99-105 My '77
Eugene Delacroix: color magician. A. Werner. il por Am Artist 41:38-43+ Ap '77

COLOR—*Continued*
Kenneth Noland: independence in the face of conformity. S. Polcari. il por Art N 76:153-5 Summ '77
Teaching color relationships: a conversation with Henry Hensche; interview, ed by C. Movalli. H. Hensche. il por Am Artist 41:34-9+ Mr '77
See also
Dyes and dyeing

Psychology

Gloria Vanderbilt on color; interview, ed by M. Gough. G. Vanderbilt. il por House B 119:76-7+ F '77
How does color hit you? P. R. Jackson. il House & Gard 149:136-7+ Mr '77
Personal palette; color personality quiz; ed by V. E. Towns. D. Vance. House B 119:98-9+ F '77
Yves Saint Laurent on color; interview, ed by P. O'Higgins. Y. M. St Laurent. il por House B 119:74-5+ F '77

Standards

New color standards for biologists. J. H. Frank. BioScience 27:762 N '77

COLOR after images. See After images
COLOR analyzers. See Photography—Processing—Apparatus and supplies
COLOR films. See Photography—Films
COLOR filters. See Light filters
COLOR in house decoration
America—show your colors! S. Van Zante and R. E. Dittmer. il Bet Hom & Gard 54:56-65 Ag '76
Color decorating energy. il House & Gard 149:101-29 S '77
Comfort gets a glow on; apartment of Mrs S. Joseph Tankoos, Jr. il House & Gard 149:90-3 F '77
Decorating: color makes it personal. il House B 119:62-83 F '77
Environmental eloquence; designed by Chvotzkin. R. Weil. il House B 119:94-103 N '77
Forecast! designers; views on color, comp by S. Schraub. il House B 119:84-9 F '77
How to decorate with color! J. Brothers. il Good H 184:128-33 My '77
I wanted a traditional air with the ripe, rich colors of today; work of designer John Leigh Spath. R. Weil. il House B 119:124-32 S '77
Late bloomer. J. Dektar. il House B 119:86-91 Je '77
Passion for color—in your house. il House & Gard 149:132-5 Mr '77
Peach power. P. Sadowsky. il Am Home 80:48-9+ My '77
Rainbow retreat; renovated log cottage. S. G Lewin. il House B 119:150-5 S '77
Spicy tones add zest to a spirited mix; work of designer Robert Metzger at Sea Pines Plantation, S.C. J. B. Reiter and S. Grossman. il House B 119:114-23 S '77
COLOR of animals
White lions. C. Panati and others. il Newsweek 89:96+ My 9 '77
See also
Albinos and albinism
COLOR of fishes
Color control: multihued fishes; excerpt from Underwater wilderness. C. Roessler. il Oceans 10:6-13 S '77
COLOR of food
See also
Coloring matter in cosmetics, food, etc.
COLOR of insects
See also
Mimicry (biology)
COLOR of leaves
Bright passage. B. Vogt. il Nat Wildlife 15:30-2 O '77
Fall's colorful country roads. P. Czura. il Travel 148:58-61+ S '77
COLOR of man
See also
Black race
COLOR photography
Can color shine on cloudy days? A. Grundberg. il Mod Phot 41:88-93 S '77
Ed Scully on color. E. Scully. See issues of Modern photography
Four photographers: four color viewpoints. J. Scully. il Mod Phot 41:84-93 Jl '77
New simple way to test color accuracy of slides or prints. H. Kimata and H. Keppler. il Mod Phot 41:98-9+ Ap '77
COLOR photography printing. See Photography—Printing processes
COLOR print processors. See Photography—Processing—Apparatus and supplies
COLOR processing. See Photography—Processing
COLOR sense
Lens that makes people see red; X-Chrom lens. F. Schumacher. McCalls 105:41 Ja '78
Line, not a space, represents visual distinctness of borders formed by different colors. B. W. Tansley and R. M. Boynton; reply with rejoinder. R. W. Rodieck. bibl Science 197:1195-6 S 16 '77
Retinex theory of color vision. E. H. Land. il Sci Am 237:108-20+ bibl(p 190) D '77
Trichromatic vision in the cat. J. Ringo and others. bibl il Science 198:753-5 N 18 '77
COLOR standards. See Color—Standards
COLOR television receivers. See Television receivers
COLOR vision. See Color sense
COLORADO
Making it happen in Colorado. F. Ruffin. il Redbook 149:82+ S '77
Science in Colorado: the second century begins. H. Lansford. il Science 195:477-9 F 4 '77
See also
Agriculture—Colorado
Architecture—Colorado
Art—Colorado
Banks and banking—Colorado
Coal mines and mining—Colorado
Colorado Plateau
Education—Colorado
Hunting—Colorado
Mesa Verde National Park
Music festivals—Colorado
Paleontology—Colorado
Recreation—Colorado
Regional planning—Colorado
Rocky Mountain National Park
Wilderness areas—Colorado
Wildlife sanctuaries—Colorado

Description and travel

Summer in Colorado ski country; eight resorts. D. Schlossberg. il Travel 147:38-43 Ap '77

Religious institutions and affairs

Religion and an ERA battle in the Rockies; Broomfield, Colo. M. H. Rush. Chr Cent 94:164-5 F 23 '77

COLORADO Chamber Orchestra. See Chamber orchestras
COLORADO floods. See Floods—United States
COLORADO Opera Festival. See Music festivals—Colorado
COLORADO Plateau
Canyon lands of the Colorado Plateau. L. A. Mohar. il Holiday 58:34-5+ Ap '77
COLORADO River
Battle over the mighty Colorado. G. Lichtenstein. il map N Y Times Mag p 10-13+ Jl 31 '77; Same abr. Read Digest 111:49-50+ N '77
Desert empire. G. Sibley. map Harpers 255:49-56+ O '77
Just keep your head above water; photographs; with report by M. Ludtke. J. Blaustein. Sports Illus 47:24-9 Ag 1 '77
Man's impact on the Colorado River in the Grand Canyon. R. R. Johnson and others. il Nat Parks & Con Mag 51:13-16 Mr '77
Remember when rivers were free? P. Singerman. Esquire 87:22+ F '77
See also
Powell, Lake
COLORADO Springs Symphony Orchestra. See Orchestras
COLORADO Trail. See Trails
COLORADO. University, Boulder

Graduate School of Public Affairs

Molding the new breed public officials; Graduate School of Public Affairs at the University of Colorado. R. C. Bobowski. il Am Educ 13:22-7 D '77

COLORED people (South Africa)
Apartheid's other victims. il Time 110:40+ O 3 '77
COLORING matter in cosmetics, food, etc.
Color it confusing. Changing T 31:40 Je '77
COLORING of metals. See Metals—Coloring
COLORS. See Color
COLOURED people (South Africa) See Colored people (South Africa)
COLQUIT, Jesse L.
Eliminating black cultural oppression in the school curriculum. Educ Digest 42:21-3 Mr '77
—and Hendrix, Elmira
So you are the new principal? il Clearing H 51:22-3+ S '77
COLQUITT, Betsy
Terrible peaceable kingdom; poem. Chr Cent 94:476 My 18 '77
COLT, Edward
Running—the new high. C. Seebohm. il House & Gard 149:89+ Jl '77 *
COLT revolvers. See Revolvers
COLTRANE, John
John Coltrane & Eric Dolphy: the Vanguard years. D. Heckman. pors Hi Fi 27:116-17 Ag '77 *
COLUMBIA (Goodyear blimp) See Airships
COLUMBIA, Md.

Religious institutions and affairs

See Maryland—Religious institutions and affairs

COLUMBIA Broadcasting System, Inc. See CBS, Inc

COLUMBIA Pictures Industries
Fallen star; D. Begelman of Columbia Pictures Industries. D. Pauly and M. Kasindorf. Newsweek 90:89-90 O 17 '77

COLUMBIA-Presbyterian Medical Center. See New York (city)—Hospitals

COLUMBIA State Historic Park. See California —Parks and reserves

COLUMBIA University
Student strike at Columbia; interview, ed by L. R. Obst. J. S. Kunen. il N Y Times Mag p43+ N 13 '77

Libraries

From Winchell's 8th to Sheehy's 9th; interview, ed by A. Plotnik. E. P. Sheehy. il Am Lib 8:129-32 Mr '77

On the ground floor of a new trend; Columbia University's new Augustus Long Health Sciences Library. A. G. Bushman. il Am Lib 8:80 F '77

School of International Affairs

Corruption at Columbia University: proposed appointment of H. Kissinger. Nat R 29:655-6 Je 10 '77

Kissinger: victim of liberal witch hunt at Columbia? F. W. Friendly. por U.S. News 82:33 Je 13 '77

Professor Kissinger. F. Getlein. Commonweal 104:388-90 Je 24 '77

Should Dr Kissinger be seated? Columbia's ethical red herring; address, April 26, 1977. M. Teitelman. Nation 224:658-60 My 28 '77

COLUMBUS, Christopher
Untitled duke's cryptic signature. A. Davies. Sci Digest 82:88 O '77 *

COLUMBUS, Ind.

Art

See Art—Indiana

City planning

See City planning—Indiana

Education

See Education—Indiana

COLUMBUS, Ohio
Why Columbus? F. M. Hechinger. Sat R 4:14 Ap 30 '77

Education

School without schools; creative solutions to closing of schools during fuel shortage. F. M. Hechinger. il Sat R 4:12+ Ap 30 '77; Same abr. Educ Digest 43:10-13 O '77

School without schools; televising lessons during gas shortage closings. P. Bonventre and J. Lowell. il Newsweek 89:39 F 21 '77

COLUMBUS and Franklin County, Ohio, Public Library of. See Libraries—Ohio

COLUMNS (newspapers) See Newspapers—Sections, columns, etc.

COLWELL, R. R. and others
Vibrio cholerae, vibrio parahaemolyticus, and other vibrios: occurrence and distribution in Chesapeake Bay. bibl il map Science 198:394-6 O 28 '77

COLWIN, Laurie
Boyish lover; story. McCalls 105:102-3 Ja '78
Girl skating; story. New Yorker 53:33-5 My 30 '77
Old-fashioned story; story. McCalls 104:122-3 Mr '77

COMAR, Cyril
Environmental assessment: a pragmatic view. Science 198:567 N 11 '77

COMBINATION squares. See Carpenters squares

COMBINATORIAL analysis
Structure in large sets: two proofs where there were none. G. B. Kolata. Science 195:767-8 F 25 '77
See also
Tessellations (mathematics)

COMBINED Communications Corporation
Rapid rise of a media giant. Bus W p30-1 Ap 4 '77

COMBINED immune deficiency diseases. See Immunologic diseases

COMBINES. See Harvesting machinery

COMBS, G. F. Jr. and Scott, M. L.
Nutritional interrelationships of vitamin E and selenium. bibl il BioScience 27:467-73 Jl '77

COMBS, Harry B.
Time out; excerpt from address, May 9, 1977. Flying 101:369+ S '77

COMBUSTION
Combustion of several 2,4,5-trichlorophenoxy compounds: formation of 2,3,7,8-tetrachlorodibenzo-p-dioxin. R. H. Stehl and L. L. Lamparski. bibl il Science 197:1008-9 S 2 '77
Fluid-bed combustion: a sleeper awakes; use by Ohio's coal mining industry. il Sci N 112:134 Ag 27 '77

COMEDIANS
How to beat Johnny Carson to the punch. A. Ripp. Horizon 20:91-5 N '77
See also
Chase, C.
Martin, S.
Marx, G.
Monty Python (comedy team)
Women comedians
Youngman, H.

COMEDIANS; drama. See Griffiths, T.

COMEDY
See also
Humor
Motion pictures—Comedy

COMEDY with music; revue. See Musical comedy, revue, etc.—Reviews—Single works

COMEN, Priscilla
Say it better with pictures. Writers Digest 57:27 My '77

COMER, James P.
How to control your anger; interview. il por U.S. News 83:53-4 O 10 '77

COMER, Larry
Small business award winner: a Georgian whose firm grew and grew. il por Nations Bus 65:34 Jl '77 *

COMER, Nancy Axelrad
How to make your doctor work for you. bibl Mademoiselle 83:106-9+ Jl '77
—See Gross, A. jt auth

COMETS
Comet digest. J. E. Bortle. See issues of Sky and telescope, July 1977-
1976 apparition of periodic Comet d'Arrest. J. E. Bortle. il Sky & Tel 53:152-6 F '77
Thomas Clap and the terrestrial comets. H. A. Smith. il Sky & Tel 53:420-2 Je '77
Tycho Brahe and the great comet of 1577. O. Gingerich. il Sky & Tel 54:452-8 D '77
W. A. Bradfield and his comet seeker. il por Sky & Tel 53:306-11 Ap '77
See also
Halley's comet

COMFORT, Alexander
Old age: facts and fancies; excerpt from A good age. Sat Eve Post 249:45 Mr '77

about

Staying young longer. C. Seebohm. il House & Gard 149:131+ Mr '77 *

COMFORT stations, Public. See Public comfort stations

COMFREY
See also
Cookery—Herbs

COMIC book heroes. See Comics (books, strips, etc)

COMICS (books, strips, etc)
Clean up the comic book badlands, now. R. Carnell. Parents Mag 52:8+ D '77
Dogpatch is ready for Freddie; retirement of A. Capp, Li'l Abner cartoonist. il Time 110:78 O 17 '77
Fantom, yu pren tru bilong mi; popularity of Phantom comics in Papua New Guinea. il Time 110:38 S 26 '77
Religion in the comics . . . the new thing. il Pub W 212:71-2 S 26 '77
Soap operas take to print; newspaper serials. il Time 110:42-3 Ag 8 '77
Super freaks; comic book heroes. Nat R 29:566-7 My 13 '77
Underestimated Duck; Howard the Duck. New Yorker 52:29-30 F 7 '77
Vive les Celtes! Astérix. il Nat Geog 151:632-3 My '77

COMISSIONA, Sergiu
Musician of the month: Sergiu Comissiona. C. Suttoni. por Hi Fi 27:MA8-9 My '77 *

COMMANDMENTS, Ten
Ten Commandments. K. Bockmuhl. Chr Today 21:43 Ag 26 '77

COMMEMORATIVE coins. See Coins

COMMEMORATIVE postage stamps. See Postage stamps

COMMEMORATIVE services. See Memorial services

COMMERCE
Commission on Trade Law approves draft convention on sale of goods. UN Chron 14:44 Jl '77
International trade without money. R. E. Weigand. Harvard Bus R 55:28-30+ N '77
See also
Balance of trade
Barter
Embargo
Foreign trade regulation
Shipping
Smuggling
also subhead Commerce under names of countries, e.g. France—Commerce

COMMERCE, Committee on. See United States—Congress—Senate—Commerce, Committee on

COMMERCE Department (United States) See United States—Commerce, Department of

COMMERCE Union Bank. See Nashville, Tenn.—Banks

COMMERCIAL Aeronautics. See Aeronautics, Commercial
COMMERCIAL blacklisting. See Blacklisting
COMMERCIAL catalogs. See Catalogs, Commercial
COMMERCIAL crimes
For business: advice from FBI on curbing crime. il U.S. News 83:69-70 N 14 '77
$40-billion crime wave swamps American business. il U.S. News 82:47-8 F 21 '77
SEC focuses on executive perks. Bus W p52+ Ap 18 '77
They blew it. il Forbes 120:P69-76+ S 15 '77
War on white-collar crime. Bus W p66+ Je 13 '77
White collar crime; address, May 9, 1977. H. E. Groves. Vital Speeches 43:525-7 Je 15 '77
See also
Computers and crime
COMMERCIAL journalism. See Journalism, Commercial
COMMERCIAL law
See also
Arbitration and award
Contracts
Maritime law
Trusts, Industrial—Law
COMMERCIAL paper. See Negotiable instruments
COMMERCIAL photography. See Photography, Commercial
COMMERCIAL policy
Droopy dollar. New Repub 177:5-6+ D 24 '77
Free-falling U.S. dollar. il Time 110:40-1 D 26 '77
Propping the dollar at last. il Time 111:38-40 Ja 16 '78
Saving the sick dollar. M. Ruby and others. il Newsweek 91:62+ Ja 16 '78
Turnabout to boost the dollar. il Bus W p30-1 D 26 '77
See also
Commodity control
Dumping (commercial policy)
Foreign trade regulation
United States—Commercial policy
COMMERCIAL products
Commodities. S. W. Angrist. See issues of Forbes
See also
Branded merchandise
Manufactures
Products, New
Quality of products
Unbranded merchandise

Endorsements

See Advertising—Testimonials

Safety devices and measures

Ban the ban; safety of products as judged by Consumer reports. Nat R 29:818-19 Jl 22 '77
What price safety? D. Pauly and J. Whitmore. il Newsweek 89:97 My 16 '77

Standards

Cooperation; standards program for miniature electric Christmas tree lights and decorations. D. Chaucer. Consumers Res Mag 60:37-8 Jl '77
Product technology and the consumer. G. F. Montgomery. il Sci Am 237:47-53 D '77

Testing

See also
Consumers' Research, Inc
Consumers Union of the United States
COMMERCIAL treaties and agreements
See also
General Agreement on Tariffs and Trade
COMMERCIALS. See Television advertising
COMMISSION of the European Communities
It's even worse in Brussels; civil servants of the Commission of the European Communities. J. T. Easley. New Repub 177:22-3 Jl 9 '77
Licensing furor in the EC. il Bus W p54-5 Jl 25 '77
COMMISSION on Personnel Interchange. See United States—President's Commission on Personnel Interchange
COMMISSIONS, Independent regulatory. See Independent regulatory commissions
COMMISSIONS, Public service. See Public service commissions
COMMISSIONS of the United Nations. See name of the commission as subhead under United Nations, e.g. United Nations—Commission on Narcotic Drugs
COMMISSIONS of the United States government. See name of commission as subhead under United States, e.g. United States—Commission on Civil Rights
COMMITMENT to the church
Returning to the fold: disbelief within the community of faith. D. E. Miller. Chr Cent 94:810-13 S 21 '77
COMMITTEE for the Scientific Investigation of Claims of the Paranormal. See Scientific societies
COMMITTEE of Twenty-four. See United Nations—Special Committee on the Situation with Regard to the Implementation of the Declaration on the Granting of Independence to Colonial Countries and Peoples
COMMITTEE on Human Values. See National Conference of Catholic Bishops
COMMITTEE on Non-governmental Organizations of the United Nations. See United Nations—Council Committee on Non-governmental Organizations
COMMITTEE on Periodic Reports on Human Rights. See United Nations—Commission on Human Rights
COMMITTEE on Science and Public Policy. See National Academy of Sciences—Committee on Science and Public Policy
COMMITTEE on Shipping. See United Nations Conference on Trade and Development
COMMITTEE on the Present Danger
Fresh warning to Americans about U.S.-Soviet Arms talks; report of the Committee on the Present Danger. il U.S. News 83:59-60 Jl 18 '77
COMMITTEES, Congressional. See United States—Congress—Committees
COMMITTEES of the United Nations. See name of the committee as subhead under United Nations, e.g. United Nations—Committee on Human Rights
COMMODITIES Exchange Center. See Commodity exchanges
COMMODITY control
At the summit talks: creeping cartelization; special section. il Bus W p64-7+ My 9 '77
Commodities: a better idea? commodity-stabilization agreements. A. J. Mayer and R. Thomas. il Newsweek 89:57 Ap 4 '77
Department testifies on international commodity agreements; statement, June 8, 1977. J. L. Katz. Dept State Bull 77:19-25 Jl 4 '77
More OPECs. Nat R 29:1408+ D 9 '77
Problem of exhaustible resources. S. F. Williams. il Nat R 29:1352-3+ N 25 '77
Trying to stabilize commodities; Conference on International Economic Cooperation. il Bus W p31-2 My 30 '77
U.S. commodity policy; address, October 3, 1977. C. F. Bergsten. Vital Speeches 44:57-61 N 1 '77
When nations try to rig commodity prices—. W. S. Wingo. il U.S. News 82:67 My 30 '77
See also
Rationing, Consumer
United Nations Negotiating Conference on a Common Fund
COMMODITY Credit Corporation. See United States—Agriculture, Department of—Commodity Credit Corporation
COMMODITY exchanges
Anatomy of a sweet investment; sugar futures. A. Tobias. Esquire 88:12+ S '77
Breaking the Hunts' grip on soybeans. pors Bus W p40-1 My 16 '77
Chicago's booming commodity markets: hotter than Wall Street. il U.S. News 82:81-2 Je 13 '77
Commodities. S. W. Angrist. See issues of Forbes
Commodities thrive on uncertainty. il Bus W p 143-4 D 26 '77
Commodity options: avoid setup for investment upset. Suc Farm 75:37 Je '77
Commodity traders find an electronic home; Commodities Exchange Center. R. Levy. il Duns R 110:88-91 O '77
Day Stanley Kroll quit; excerpt from The Midas touch. J. Train. il por Forbes 120:66+ O 1 '77
Fever of speculation afflicts Ginnie Mae. Bus W p28+ Jl 18 '77
Forward trading that vexes Treasury; Treasury bill futures. il Bus W p60-1 Ag 22 '77
Futures for you? corn hedge. D. Seim. il Farm J 101:24-6+ Ap '77
How to cash in on cash-futures price relationships. J. Sperbeck. il Suc Farm 75:no4 K12 Mr '77
How to gamble in bonds; Government National Mortgage Association futures. B. Weberman. Forbes 119:154 Ap 15 '77
How to speculate on the world's safest investment; treasury bill futures. L. Snyder. il Fortune 96:49-51 Jl '77
Hunts and the soybeans. M. Ruby and others. il pors Newsweek 89:77-8 My 9 '77
Las Vegas in Chicago; Government National Mortgage Association and Treasury bill futures. il Forbes 120:31-2 Jl 1 '77
New futures market reduces some risks; commercial paper and T-bill markets. Bus W p 105 O 10 '77
New way to cut the risk of running a business. W. D. Haggerty. Nations Bus 65:74+ D '77
Orange freeze heats futures prices. il Bus W p72 F 21 '77
Orange juice bucks the trend in futures. il Bus W p28 Je 27 '77
Say, boy, any cocoa in there? S. W. Angrist. Forbes 119:87 Ja 15 '77
Soybean speculators: did they help farmers this time? il Farm J 101:22 S '77

COMMODITY exchanges—*Continued*
Stability in swinging market. il Bus W p70-1 Ag 8 '77
Uncertain future of zinc trading. il Bus W p72 Jl 18 '77
Weather and the futures markets. L. Snyder. il Fortune 95:59-60+ Ap '77
Why commodity prices dropped so sharply. il Bus W p90-1 Je 27 '77
Why metals markets have started rising. il Bus W p29-30 F 7 '77
Why soybean prices blew the fuse. R. C. Black. Farm J 101:18B+ Je '77
See also
Government investigations—Commodity exchanges
Hedging (finance)
Stock exchanges—American Exchange
United States—Commodity Futures Trading Commission

Great Britain

U.S. rule stifles a London market; Commodity Futures Trading Commission regulation. Bus W p80-1 Je 6 '77

COMMODITY Futures Trading Commission. See United States—Commodity Futures Trading Commission

COMMODITY options. See Commodity exchanges

COMMODITY price stabilization policy. See Commodity control

COMMON Cause (organization)
Common Cause and campaign financing: reform liberals open up the system. H. Tolley, Jr. il Intellect 106:122-5 O '77
Money for campaigns. K. Bode. New Repub 176:8+ F 19 '77

COMMON Market in Western Europe. See European Economic Community

COMMON sense
Common sense; reason and intellectuals. G. Niemeyer. Nat R 29:557 My 13 '77

COMMONER, Barry
For a new energy policy. Current 191:17-22 Mr '77
Promise and perils of petrochemicals. N Y Times Mag p38-40+ S 25 '77
Risks, benefits, and carcinogens; adaptation of address, March 22, 1977. Chemistry 50:19-20 Je '77
Social cures, not palliatives; adaptation of address. il Nat Parks & Con Mag 51:14-15 My '77
We have enough oil for the next 50 to 60 years; interview. por U.S. News 82:45 Ap 18 '77

COMMONWEALTH Edison Company
CommEd: tomorrow's utility today. il por Bus W p58+ O 24 '77
Nuclear energy expert; C. Reed. il pors Ebony 32:64-6+ Je '77

COMMONWEALTH Forestry Association. See Forestry societies

COMMONWEALTH Oil Refining Company
Tesoro's $130 million burden. por Bus W p93-4 My 9 '77

COMMONWEALTH Oil Refining Company-Ashland Oil, Inc merger. See Petroleum industry—Acquisitions and mergers

COMMUNAL living. See Collective settlements

COMMUNES. See Collective settlements

COMMUNICABLE diseases
Drugs, coffee, alcohol, infections and your unborn baby; excerpt from Caring for your unborn child. R. E. Gots and B. A. Gots. Good H 186:68+ Ja '78
See also
Epidemiology
Insects as carriers of infection
Quarantine
United States—Public Health Service—Center for Disease Control
Vaccination
Waterborne infection
also names of communicable diseases, e.g Measles

COMMUNICATION
Openness: a formula for communication. P. H. Zonca. Clearing H 50:201-3 Ja '77
See also
Communications satellites
Computers—Communication use
Intercultural communication
Interstellar communication
Language arts
Light communication systems
Mass media
Oral communication
Persuasion (psychology)

International aspects

Now, a new international information order? H. I. Schiller. Intellect 106:42-3 Ag '77
World debate on information: flood-tide or balanced flow? symposium. il UNESCO Courier 30:4-33 Ap '77

Social aspects

Art of healthy communication; interview. E. L. Vogelsong. il Fam Health 9:26-8 Jl '77
Communications. il Forbes 120:P139-46 S 15 '77
In the heads of the listeners; address, September 9, 1977. W. W. Braden. Vital Speeches 44:42-4 N 1 '77
New communications. G. O. Robinson. Current 195:37-52 S '77
Pathology of gap-ology. K. Kolenda. Intellect 105:437-8 Je '77

Underdeveloped areas

See Underdeveloped areas—Communication

COMMUNICATION (theology)
Church teaching: content without context. L. Richards. il Chr Today 21:16-18 Ap 15 '77
Effective evangelism: a matter of marketing? interviews, ed by D. Kucharsky. J. F. Engel; H. W. Norton. il Chr Today 21:12-15 Ap 15 '77
Word and the words. L. Morris. Chr Today 21:40+ Je 3 '77
See also
Radio programs—Religious programs

COMMUNICATION, Animal. See Animal communication

COMMUNICATION, Chemical. See Pheromones

COMMUNICATION, Intercultural. See Intercultural communication

COMMUNICATION, Nonverbal
How well do you read body language? D. Archer and R. M. Akert. bibl il Psychol Today 11:68-9+ O '77
Making valid nonverbal judgments. B. Eckman. Engl J 66:72-4 N '77
Man who refuses to talk; J. Francis. il pors Ebony 33:114-16+ D '77
People watching; excerpt from Man-watching—a field guide to human behavior. D. Morris. il Good H 186:100-1+ Ja '78
See also
Gesture

COMMUNICATION and traffic
See also
Telecommunication

COMMUNICATION in education
Don't just sit there—say something! T. Hightower. Clearing H 51:148 D '77
Non-responsive students? Check the classroom communication channels. D. W. Olson. Clearing H 51:160-2 D '77

COMMUNICATION in government
High cost of whistling. T. Nicholson and others. pors Newsweek 89:75+ F 14 '77
When trouble strikes—how U.S. crisis management works. il U.S. News 82:28-9 F 21 '77

COMMUNICATION in management
Double loop learning in organizations. C. Argyris. il Harvard Bus R 55:115-25 S '77
Effective way to get employees on your side; program at Marlin Firearms Co. V. Louviere. il Nations Bus 65:38-9 Jl '77
High cost of whistling. T. Nicholson and others. pors Newsweek 89:75+ F 14 '77
In the grip of hands-on management; Eltra Corporation. A. M. Louis. il por Fortune 95:170-8 Mr '77
Losing something in the translation. F. F. Mauser. Harvard Bus R 55:14+ Jl '77
TV that competes with the office grapevine. il Bus W p49+ Mr 14 '77
See also
Report writing

COMMUNICATION in marketing
Managing your marketing communications program; excerpt from Creative communications for a successful design practice. S. A. Kliment. il Archit Rec 161:77-9 My '77
News release as marketing tool. S. A. Kliment. Archit Rec 162:55 Jl '77
Writing for marketing impact: letters, brochures, proposals. S. A. Kliment. Archit Rec 161:71+ Je '77

COMMUNICATION in science
Failure of scientists to communicate; address, October 25, 1977. T. C. Root, Jr. Vital Speeches 44:133-6 D 15 '77
Science court. N. Ponnamperuma. il por Sci Digest 82:21-3 S '77
Solutions to national problems through scientific consensus. H. Greber. il Intellect 106:72-3 Ag '77

COMMUNICATIONS, Military
See also
Communications satellites—Military use
Radio, Military

COMMUNICATIONS Satellite Corporation
Court of Appeals upholds FCC on Comsat, hits procedures. Aviation W 107:25 O 24 '77

COMMUNICATIONS satellites
Communications satellites. il Space World N-11-167:30-1 N '77
Comsat revolution. J. K. Beatty. il Sky & Tel 54:4-8 Jl '77; Same abr. with title Communications satellites: how your voice (or TV show) is routed geosynchronously. Sci Digest 82:53-5+ N '77
Domestic satellite service authorized. Aviation W 106:27 Ja 24 '77
Domsat war gets tougher and costlier. L. Smith. il Duns R 109:72-5 My '77

COMMUNICATIONS satellites—*Continued*
Dual mission complicates data relay satellite work. Aviation W 107:155+ O 17 '77
Global satellite communications. il map Sci Am 236:58-68+ bibl(p 138) F '77
Higher power broadens Satcom uses. K. Johnsen. il Aviation W 106:75-7 Mr 21 '77
Intelsat 5 design uses flight-proved hardware. il Aviation W 107:161-2+ O 17 '77
Intelsat-6 technical options studied. P. J. Klass. il Aviation W 107:77+ N 28 '77
Lincoln Experimental Satellites LES-8 and-9. il Space World N-10-166:30 O '77
NASA urged to resume talksat R&D. il Sci N 111:231 Ap 9 '77
NASA urged to study Satcom program. C. Covault. Aviation W 106:41-2 Mr 14 '77
Public satellite effort keyed to services, not hardware. Aviation W 107:54-5 O 24 '77
Radio interferometer with satellite link. Sci N 112:278 O 29 '77
Real-time, very-long-baseline interferometry based on the use of a communications satellite. J. L. Yen and others. bibl il Science 198:289-91 O 21 '77
Relay satellite to employ interim upper stage. Aviation W 106:36 Ap 25 '77
Satellite communications. B. I. Edelson and L. Pollack. bibl il map Science 195:1125-33 Mr 18 '77
TDRS to perform dual space missions. il Aviation W 107:97+ O 17 '77
TDRSS won by Western Union. C. Covault. il Aviation W 106:14-16 Ja 3 '77
Third intelset IV-A satellite launched. Sci N 111:359 Je 4 '77
Three new satellite systems planned; domestic services for China and the USSR and a regional system to be operated by the Arab Satellite Communications Organization. Aviation W 107:93 O 17 '77
Unesco's first teleconference by satellite: Symphonie experiment. E. L. Sommerlad. il UNESCO Courier 30:32-3 Ap '77

Accidents

See Space flight—Accidents

Data transmission use

Business users eye 1981 start date. Aviation W 107:94-5 O 17 '77
CIA satellite data link study revealed. J. M. Lenorovitz. Aviation W 106:25-6 My 2 '77
FCC lofts a new satellite network; Satellite Business Systems. Bus W p37 Ja 31 '77
I.B.M. reaches for a golden future in the heavens; Satellite Business Systems. B. Uttal. il Fortune 95:172-6+ Je '77

Educational use

Visitor to the village; Satellite Instructional Television Experiment. Y. Pal. il Bull Atom Sci 33:55-6 Ja '77

Government use

Videoconferences via satellite: opening Congress to the people? L. J. Carter. il Science 197:31-3 Jl 1 '77

Ground stations

SBS network to use unattended terminals. Aviation W 107:95 O 17 '77

International aspects

U.S. to oppose broadcast satellite plan. K. Johnsen. Aviation W 106:85-6 Ja 10 '77
See also
International Telecommunications Satellite Organization

Leasing and renting

Defense satcoms cut in effort to force commercial leasing. Aviation W 106:60 Je 6 '77

Maritime use

ESA presses Marots satcom proposals. R. R. Ropelewski. Aviation W 107:18-19 N 21 '77
Marisat. J. Powell. il Sci Digest 82:56-8+ Jl '77
Marisat owners eye European follow-on; ESA reconfiguring Marots for operational mission. Aviation W 107:138-9 O 17 '77
Shipping firms shifting to Marisat system. il Aviation W 107:46-7 O 3 '77

Medical use

House calls by long distance. R. Karen. il Fam Health 9:48-50+ O '77

Military use

Defense satcoms stress jam-resistance, flexibility. il Aviation W 107:116-17+ O 17 '77
NATO IIIB military communications satellite launched. il Space World N-8-164:26-7 Ag '77
Satcom tests stress jam-resistance. P. J. Klass. il Aviation W 107:68-9+ N 21 '77
Strategic satellite options weighed; USAF Satellite Communications System. Aviation W 107:123-4 O 17 '77
Upper stage shift studied for Satcom. B. Miller. il Aviation W 106:57-9 F 28 '77

Television broadcasting use

Broadcast satellite keyed to Ariane. il Aviation W 107:135+ O 17 '77

COMMUNICATIONS satellites, Arab
Communications satellite leader sought by Arabs. Aviation W 107:23 S 19 '77

COMMUNICATIONS satellites, Canadian
Canadian Satcom in qualification tests. K. J. Stein. il Aviation W 107:74-5+ D 12 '77
Telesat Canada perceives larger role. il Aviation W 107:101+ O 17 '77
Telesat Canada votes to appeal Commission decision to Cabinet. Aviation W 107:22 S 5 '77

COMMUNICATIONS satellites, European
Broadcast satellite keyed to Ariane. il Aviation W 107:135+ O 17 '77
ESA orbital test satellite nears launch. il map Aviation W 107:44-5 S 5 '77
Europe readies backup for lost OTS. Aviation W 107:24-5 S 19 '77
European satcoms near operational goal. il Aviation W 107:113+ O 17 '77
NATO studying new series of satellites. Aviation W 107:127-8 O 17 '77
OTS satellite: 5,4,3,2, 1—poof. Sci N 112:181 S 17 '77
Talks start on satellite development. Aviation W 107:61-2 Ag 8 '77

COMMUNION. See Catholic Church—Eucharist

COMMUNISM
Failure of Marxist scholarship. T. Molnar. Nat R 29:1430-2 D 9 '77
1517 and all that. F. Getlein. Commonweal 104:613-14 S 30 '77
Politics of envy. E. M. von Kuehnelt-Leddihn. Nat R 29:721 Je 24 '77
Spider's web: deceptive beauty. E. Schaeffer. Chr Today 21:25-6 Jl 29 '77
When is a nation Marxist? W. F. Buckley, Jr. Nat R 29:351 Mr 18 '77
See also
Communist parties
Motion picture industry—Communist activities
Socialism
Trade unions and communism

Anti-Communist measures

See United States—Foreign relations—Anti-Communist measures

Africa

I am not anti-Communist; excerpt from Battle for Africa. Andrew. Chr Today 22:28-30 D 9 '77
Triple play. Nat R 29:425 Ap 15 '77

China

Maoism is dead. F. B. Randall. il Nat R 29:258-63 Mr 4 '77
Marxism as a political religion; Maoist Marxism. W. H. Heard. il Nat R 29:1427+ D 9 '77

Cuba

Eyewitness account of life in Castro's Cuba. C. J. Migdail. il U.S. News 82:29-30+ Mr 28 '77
U.S. Christians and Cuba. D. Kirkpatrick. Chr Cent 94:685-7 Ag 3 '77

Europe

Europeanization of communism? C. Gati. bibl f For Affairs 55:539-53 Ap '77
See also
Communist parties—Europe

Europe, Western

Europe breaks apart. M. Ledeen. Commentary 63:53-7 My '77
Europe's future. M. Ledeen. New Repub 177:8-9 Jl 2 '77
See also
Communist parties—Europe, Western

France

See also
Communist Party (France)

Great Britain

Anglocommunism? R. Moss. Commentary 63:27-33 F '77; Discussion. Nation 224:298-300 Mr 12 '77; Commentary 63:6+ My; 64:18-19 Jl '77

Indochina

See also
Cambodian-Vietnamese conflict, 1977-

Italy

Italian communism at home and abroad: the new class. M. Lucentini; discussion. Commentary 63:20-2+ Mr '77
Trouble in Red City; tr by D. Betz. B. H. Levy. New Repub 177:23 O 8 '77
La Un-dolce vita. J. Ahern. Commonweal 104:521-8 Ag 19 '77
See also
Communist Party (Italy)

Laos

Inside the new Laos. J. Everingham. il Newsweek 90:37 Jl 18 '77

COMMUNISM—*Continued*

Russia

Russia's 60 years of communism: success or failure? special section. il map U.S. News 83: 42-54+ O 24 '77
See also
Communist Party (Russia)

Spain

See also
Communist Party (Spain)

United States

See also
Communist Party (United States)
Rosenberg, Julius and Ethel, case

Anti-Communist measures

See Anti-Communist movements

Vietnam

New Vietnam. L. T. Anh. Nat R 29:487-8 Ap 29 '77

COMMUNISM and literature
In my own time: Neruda's Memoirs: the making of a Stalinist. C. L. Mee, Jr. por Horizon 19:94-5 Ja '77

COMMUNISM and religion
Christianity in Communist Czechoslovakia. K. Winter. Chr Cent 94:919-20 O 12 '77
Enrico's encyclical; Communist-Catholic dialogue in Italy. il por Time 110:51 N 7 '77
French Catholicism faces the left. P. McCarthy. America 137:350-3 N 19 '77
Marxism as a political religion; Maoist Marxism. W. H. Heard. il Nat R 29:1427+ D 9 '77
U.S. Christians and Cuba. D. Kirkpatrick. Chr Cent 94:685-7 Ag 3 '77

COMMUNISPOND (firm) See Public speaking—Study and teaching

COMMUNIST countries
See also
Cambodia
China
Civil rights—Communist countries
Russia

Commerce

New directions in East-West trade. J. M. Hertzfeld. Harvard Bus R 55:93-9 My '77

United States

See United States—Commerce—Communist countries

Foreign relations

Five worlds of detente. N. B. Hannah. maps Nat R 29:541-5 My 13 '77; Reply. J. Burnham. 29:600 My 27 '77

United States

See United States—Foreign relations—Communist countries

Travel regulations

See Travel regulations

COMMUNIST defectors. See Defectors, Political

COMMUNIST dissenters. See Dissenters

COMMUNIST education
See also
Education—China

COMMUNIST parties

Europe

Soviet policy in Europe. A. Z. Rubinstein. bibl f Cur Hist 73:105-8+ O '77

Europe, Western

America's *ostpolitik*. R. N. Tannahill. Commonweal 104:142-3 Mr 4 '77
Apostle Carrillo. il por Time 110:47 N 21 '77
Brezhnev's nightmare: breakaway in Europe. il U.S. News 83:28-30 Ag 1 '77
Canopy of tyranny; address, October 29, 1977. G. R. Ford. Vital Speeches 44:130-3 D 15 '77
Carrillo in sheep's clothing; Madrid summit. E. M. von Kuehnelt-Leddihn. Nat R 29:556 My 13
Communism with little face; Eurocommunism. R. C. Christopher. il Horizon 20:60-5 D '77
Communist schism. M. R. Benjamin and others. Newsweek 90:37-8+ Jl 11 '77
Danger: Eurocommunism; views of H. Kissinger. il por Time 109:49 Je 20 '77
Euro-communism. il map Sr Schol 109:6-9+ Mr 10 '77
Eurocommunism after Madrid. J. O. Goldsborough. For Affairs 55:800-14 Jl '77
Eurocommunism and detente. A. Schlesinger, Jr. Current 196:42-5 O '77
Eurocommunism: Moscow's problem too. il Time 110:32-3 Jl 11 '77
Eurocommunism quandary. V. S. Kearney. America 137:347-50 N 19 '77
Eurocommunism—two views. Nat R 29:816 Jl 22 '77
Eurocommunists exposed; Madrid summit. M. Ledeen. New Repub 176:13-14 Mr 26 '77
Kremlin cracks the whip. M. Ledeen. New Repub 177:22-3 Ag 6 '77
Myths of Eurocommunism. J. F. Revel. bibl f For Affairs 56:295-305 Ja '78
New kind of communism? Commonweal 104:483-4 Ag 5 '77
News about Eurocommunism. M. Ledeen. Commentary 64:53-7 O '77
Not being too beastly to Moscow; meeting in Spain. il por Time 109:23 Mr 14 '77
Not remarkably entertaining; views of H. Kissinger. F. Getlein. Commonweal 104:452-4 Jl 22 '77
Notes on Eurocommunism. J. Burnham. Nat R 29:769 Jl 8 '77
Red scare in Moscow. R. H. Heindel. Intellect 106:116-17 O '77
Soviet policy in Europe. A. Z. Rubinstein. bibl f Cur Hist 73:108+ O '77

COMMUNIST Party (France)
France: Communists spurn power? J. Fromm. il U.S. News 83:38-9 O 17 '77
French have no word for it; possibility of a Union of Left election victory. J. Burnham. Nat R 29:711 Je 24 '77
Picking the lock; French Eurocommunism. J. Burnham. Nat R 29:821 Jl 22 '77
Some Euroquestions. J. Burnham. Nat R 29:873 Ag 5 '77

COMMUNIST Party (Italy)
Big brawl in Bologna; students against Italian Communist Party. il Time 110:47-8 O 3 '77
Cultural terrorism: the Italian press as public-relations organ for the Communist Party. M. A. Ledeen. Harpers 255:99-100 S '77
Enrico's encyclical; Communist-Catholic dialogue. il por Time 110:51 N 7 '77
First-hand appraisal of Communist threat in Italy; interview, ed by D. B. Richardson. G. Andreotti. por U.S. News 83:30-1 Ag 1 '77
Idea whose time is passing? H. Arkes. Nat R 29: 1108-10+ S 30 '77
Italian communism at home and abroad: the Soviet connection. M. Ledeen; discussion. Commentary 63:20-2+ Mr '77
Italy's Communist paradox. B. Sennett and M. Gordon. Progressive 41:37-9 My '77
Nearer the historic compromise. Time 110:33 Jl 11 '77
Red blues. F. Willey and L. Jenkins. Newsweek 89:39 My 23 '77
Reporter in Europe. J. Kramer. il New Yorker 53:107-13 My 2 '77
Reports & comment: Turin: nostalgic communism. G. Hodgson. il Atlantic 240:20+ Ag '77
Seeing red in Italy; interviews. il Sr Schol 109: 10-11 Mr 10 '77

COMMUNIST Party (Russia)
Brezhnev's year: politics in the U.S.S.R. R. G. Wesson. Cur Hist 73:109-11+ O '77
Communist schism. M. R. Benjamin and others. Newsweek 90:37-8+ Jl 11 '77
Eurocommunism: Moscow's problem too. il Time 110:32-3 Jl 11 '77
Europeanization of communism? C. Gati. bibl f For Affairs 55:539-53 Ap '77
New kind of communism? Commonweal 104:483-4 Ag 5 '77
Red scare in Moscow. R. H. Heindel. Intellect 106:116-17 O '77
Savaging a comrade; Russian attack on Spanish Communist Party. Time 110:19 Jl 4 '77
Soviet policy in Europe. A. Z. Rubinstein. Cur Hist 73:105-8+ O '77
Talk with Trotsky. P. Berlinrut. Harpers 254: 62-3+ F '77
Where the real power lies and the way it's exercised. il U.S. News 83:51 O 24 '77

Political Bureau

Brezhnev's purge; firing N. Podgorny. F. Willie and F. Coleman. por Newsweek 89:43-4 Je 6 '77
Unhitching Podgorny from the Troika. por Time 109:35 Je 6 '77

COMMUNIST Party (Spain)
Carrillo 'neath the elms; speeches at Yale. R. Brookhiser. Nat R 29:1420 D 9 '77
Communists out in the open. il Time 109:47 Ap 25 '77
Kremlin cracks the whip. M. Ledeen. New Repub 177:22-3 Ag 6 '77
Parfit gentil knyght. Nat R 29:137 F 4 '77
La Pasionaria: an exile ends. il pors Time 109: 50 My 23 '77
Quotations from Chairman Carrillo; excerpts from Eurocommunism and the state. S. Carrillo. por Time 110:32 Jl 11 '77
Rocky road to democracy; Communist Party and June 15 Spanish elections. R. Moss and M. Arostgui. Nat R 29:663-7 Je 10 '77
Savaging a comrade; Russian attack on Spanish Communist Party. Time 110:19 Jl 4 '77
Spain's red Luther. M. R. Benjamin and M. Acoca. por Newsweek 90:38 Jl 11 '77

COMMUNIST Party (United States)

Anecdotes, facetiae, satire, etc.

Comrade Yuri. D. K. Mano. Nat R 29:1313+ N 11 '77
Our hearts were young and red. M. E. Kinsley New Repub 177:43 O 8 '77

COMMUNIST strategy
Beyond Brezhnev? Nat R 29:137-8 F 4 '77

COMMUNISTS
See also
Communist parties

COMMUNITIES (ecology) See Ecosystems

COMMUNITIES Organized for Public Service. See Citizens associations

COMMUNITY and junior college libraries. See College libraries

COMMUNITY and junior college teachers. See College teachers

COMMUNITY and junior colleges
Future of the community college. E. J. Gleazer, Jr. il Intellect 106:152-4 O '77
See also
Miami-Dade Community College, Miami, Fla.
Moraine Valley Community College, Palos Hills, Ill.
Oklahoma City. South Oklahoma City Junior College

Administration

Recruiting and hiring practices of community college deans of instruction. J. L. Brown. il Clearing H 51:29-31 S '77

COMMUNITY and the individual. See Individual and society

COMMUNITY and the school. See School and the community

COMMUNITY art centers. See Art centers

COMMUNITY centers
See also
Mental health centers
Recreation centers
Senior centers

COMMUNITY chests. See United Way of America (organization)

COMMUNITY control of schools. See School management and organization

COMMUNITY development
Community problem-solver; Center for Community Organization and Area Development in rural area of South Dakota, Minnesota and Iowa. R. C. Bobowski. il Am Educ 13:16-19 Je '77
Washington architect Arthur Cotton Moore; design strategies for community development. W. Marlin. il Archit Rec 162:84-95 D '77
See also
Location in business and industry
Urban renewal

Federal aid

Block grant rules land HUD in court. il Am City & County 92:16 S '77
HUD tightens block grant rules. Am City & County 92:13-14 D '77
Housing and community development: an act to bleed the cities. J. M. Baer. Nation 224: 274-6 Mr 5 '77
1977 Housing and Community Development Act: some new tools for central-city revitalization. N. J. Parish and C. Teglas. Archit Rec 162: 61 D '77
Washington scene. B. Kravetz. Parks & Rec 12:16+ Je '77

COMMUNITY Development Block Grant program. See Community development—Federal aid

COMMUNITY development corporations
Hoosuck: a community story. M. Flad and H. Flad. il Craft Horiz 37:20-1+ Ap '77
New urban pioneers: homesteading in the slums; People's Development Corporation. R. M. Williams. il Sat R 4:8-14 Jl 23 '77

COMMUNITY education
Community education and its major components. P. A. Clark. Educ Digest 43:58-61 N '77
Community education and public libraries: cooperation or conquest? L. D. Fleming. bibl por Wilson Lib Bull 52:319-23 D '77
Update on the status of community education. D. Buchanan. Parks & Rec 12:70+ My '77

COMMUNITY fallout shelters. See Atomic bomb shelters

COMMUNITY gardens
Do it yourself: Texas gardeners grow bumper crop; Amarillo Senior Citizens Assn. il Aging 274:15 Ag '77
Unexpected harvest: California gardens that raise community consciousness. R. L. Tracy. il Horticulture 55:46-9 Jl '77

COMMUNITY leadership
Can do crusaders; women activists. R. Nader. Ladies Home J 94:146 Jl '77

COMMUNITY life
See also
Neighborhoods

COMMUNITY of Peace People. See Peace movements—Northern Ireland

COMMUNITY of the Living Spirit, Waukesha. See Wisconsin—Religious institutions and affairs

COMMUNITY organization
Community action:
Cross with a flag for safety; Laguna Beach Calif. il Sunset 159:32 N '77
Controlling medical expansion; protesting against Affiliated Hospitals Center's planned destruction of neighborhood housing in Boston. H. Waitzkin and J. A. Sharratt. il Society 14: 30-5 Ja '77
Popular power in Cuba. J. Miller. Progressive 41:33-4 Jl '77
See also
Citizens associations

History

Unwanted helping hand; Cincinnati Social Unit. N. Betten and M. Austin. bibl il Environment 19:13-20+ Ja '77

COMMUNITY-police relations. See Police—Public relations

COMMUNITY power
See also
Community leadership

COMMUNITY property
New light on property rights of farm wives. L. Lane. Farm J 101:K8 mid-Mr '77

COMMUNITY recreation. See Recreation

COMMUNITY schools
Community school movement; instruction in music and the arts. il Hi Fi 27:MA12-13 Jl '77

COMMUNITY service. See Citizens associations; Volunteer service

COMMUNITY Services Administration. See United States—Community Services Administration

COMMUNITY Services to International Visitors, National Council for. See National Council for Community Services to International Visitors

COMMUTER airlines. See Airlines—Local service

COMMUTERS
Commuter marriages—latest product of women's changing status. il U.S. News 83:109-10 O 24 '77

COMO, William
Editor's log. Dance Mag 52:23 Ja '78

COMPACT cameras. See Cameras

COMPACTION of soil. See Soil stabilization

COMPANIA Vale do Rio Doce (firm) See Iron industry—Brazil

COMPANIES. See Corporations

COMPANION crops
Beans, the perfect interplant companion. J. Ruttle. il Org Gard & Farm 24:66-8 F '77
Interplanting helps increase Central American food supply. T. Black and S. Black. il Org Gard & Farm 24:132-4+ Jl '77
Practical companion planting. il Org Gard & Farm 24:62-5 F '77

COMPANY stores
Return of the company store. J. C. Perham. il Duns R 110:50-2 Jl '77

COMPANY towns
See also
Midland, Mich.

COMPARATIVE advertising. See Advertising, Comparison

COMPARATIVE psychology. See Psychology, Comparative

COMPARATORS
Build a solar controller; electronic temperature comparator. J. M. Cogswell. il Pop Electr 12:69-70 Jl '77
Projection blinking: a way toward discovery. B. Mayer. il por Sky & Tel 54:246-9 S '77

COMPARISON advertising. See Advertising, Comparison

COMPASSION. See Sympathy

COMPATIBILITY (marriage) See Marriage

COMPENSATION (law)
Money problems that mercury wrought; compensation paid by Chisso Corp. for Minamata disease. il Bus W p38 Je 27 '77
See also
Damages
Insurance, Workmens compensation

COMPENSATION for victims of crime. See Reparation

COMPETITION
Competing with the giants. N. Howard. il Duns R 110:46-52 O '77
Meeting the greater competition of tomorrow; Monsanto Co. J. W. Hanley. pors Nations Bus 65:37-40 Mr '77
See also
Business intelligence

COMPETITION (biology) See Struggle for existence

COMPETITION, International
See also
Free trade and protection

COMPETITION, Unfair
See also
Dumping (commercial policy)

COMPETITIONS
It's shake, rumble and roll; tractor pulling. B. Gilbert. il Sports Illus 47:28-34+ Jl 11 '77
See also
Aviation—Competitions
Beauty contests
Music—Competitions
Navigation—Competitions
Truck driving—Competitions

COMPLAINTS
Complaining about government may not be in vain; Governor's Action Center in Pennsylvania. D. W. Hyman. Intellect 105:377 My '77
Consumer in the marketplace. Consumers Res Mag 60:215-18 O '77
Consumers complaint—does business respond? A. R. Andreasen and R. Best. il Harvard Bus R 55:93-101 Jl '77; Discussion. 55:68+ S '77
Could a complaint agency help you? Changing T 31:41-3 D '77
Cries of angry consumers: what they're telling officials now. U.S. News 82:61-2 Ap 18 '77
How to complain—and get results; excerpt from The Good housekeeping woman's almanac. Good H 185:208 N '77
How to send revolution through the mail. M. Rockwood. il Ms 6:85 Ja '78
Record number of complaints on auto insurance filed by drivers in New York. Ret Liv 17:13-14 My '77
When computers goof—consumers air their frustrations. U.S. News 82:61-2 My 2 '77
When your charter flight lets you down; where to complain. H. Hyans. McCalls 104:54 S '77

COMPLEAT Strategist bookstore, New York City. See Booksellers and bookselling—New York (state)

COMPLEMENTS (immunity)
Babesia rodhaini: requirement of complement for penetration of human erythrocytes. W. E. Chapman and P. A. Ward. bibl il Science 196:67-70 Ap 1 '77
Lysis of human cultured lymphoblastoid cells by cell-induced activation of the properdin pathway. A. N. Theofilopoulos and L. H. Perrin. bibl il Science 195:878-80 Mr 4 '77
Serum complement-like opsonic activities in human, animal, vegetable, and proprietary milks. M. E. Miller and R. G. Ganges. bibl il Science 196:1115-17 Je 3 '77

COMPLEXION. See Skin

COMPLIMENTS. See Praise

COMPOSERS
Recordings and the composer. C. Wuorinen. il Sat R 4:24-5 Jl 23 '77
See also
Black composers
Women composers

COMPOSERS, American
Group for Contemporary Music; Charles Wuorinen, Harvey Sollberger, and Nicolas Roussakis. M. Blechner. il Hi Fi 27:MA24-5 N '77
Milieu of the American composer. E. Carter. por Hi Fi 27:MA16+ S '77
Music West; festivals of American music in the San Francisco Bay area. R. Commanday. il Hi Fi 27:MA32-4 Mr '77
New music; Robert Ashley's videotapes of seven contemporary composers entitled Music with roots in the aether. J. La Barbara. il Hi Fi 27:MA14-15 Je '77
See also
Beach, A. M. C.
Bernstein, L.
Blitzstein, M.
Cage, J.
Carter, E.
Chadwick, G. W.
Copland, A.
Cowell, H.
Crumb, G.
Del Tredici, D.
Erb, D.
Farberman, H.
Floyd, C.
Foote, A.
Foster, S. C.
Franks, M.
Gershwin, G.
Glass, P.
Hannay, R.
Hanson, H.
Hellermann, B.
Hovhaness, A.
Imbrie, A. W.
Ives, C. E.
Kay, U.
Kirchner, L.
Laderman, E.
Lazarof, H.
Lees, B.
Marshall, I.
Mason, D. G.
Menotti, G. C.
Ornstein, L.
Persichetti, V.
Piston, W.
Read, G.
Sessions, R.
Shapey, R.
Siegmeister, E.
Sondheim, S.
Starer, R.
Thomson, V.
Trimble, L.
Tudor, D.
Varèse, E.
Weill, K.
Williams, P.

COMPOSERS, Argentine
See also
Ginastera, A.

COMPOSERS, Armenian
See also
Khachaturian, A. I.

COMPOSERS, Australian
Review of records. E. Schwartz. Mus Q 63:572-8 O '77

COMPOSERS, Austrian
See also
Berg, A.
Bruckner, A.
Haydn, F. J.
Mahler, G.
Mozart, J. C. W. A.
Schubert, F. P.
Strauss, J. Jr
Wolf, H.

COMPOSERS, Black. See Black composers

COMPOSERS, Brazilian
See also
Villa-Lobos, H.

COMPOSERS, British
Review of records. E. Schwartz. Mus Q 63:572-8 O '77

COMPOSERS, Czech
See also
Berg, J.
Dvořák, A.
Fibich, Z.
Janáček, L.
Smetana, B.
Suk, J.
Válek, J.

COMPOSERS, Danish
See also
Nielsen, C.

COMPOSERS, Dutch
See also
Obrecht, J.

COMPOSERS, English
Some Englishmen of note. I. Kolodin. Sat R 4:21 Je 11 '77
See also
Alwyn, W.
Brian, H.
Britten, B.
Elgar, E. W.
Gibbons, O.
Holst, G.
Purcell, H.
Sullivan, A.
Tippett, M.
Walton, W. T.

COMPOSERS, Filipino
Amer. Sym: Filipino composers; concert at Carnegie Hall on April 6. Hi Fi 27:MA24-5 Ag '77

COMPOSERS, Finnish
See also
Segerstam, L.
Sibelius, J. J. C.

COMPOSERS, French
See also
Berlioz, H.
Bizet, G.
Chabrier, E.
Charpentier, G.
Couperin, F.
David, F. C.
Debussy, C.
Fauré, G. U.
Franck, C. A.
Indy, V. d'
L'Affilard, M.
Lully, J. B.
Massenet, J.
Milhaud, D.
Offenbach, J.
Planquette, R.
Poulenc, F.
Rameau, J. P.
Ravel, M.
Saint-Saëns, C.

COMPOSERS, German
See also
Bach, J. S.
Beethoven, L. van
Brahms, J.
Handel, G. F.
Hindemith, P.
Humperdinck, E.
Kreutzer, K.
Lortzing, A.
Meyerbeer, G.
Neuhaus, M.
Nicolai, O.
Orff, C.
Strauss, R.
Ullmann, V.
Wagner, R.

COMPOSERS, German—See also—*Continued*
Weber, K. M. von
Weill, K.
Zimmermann, B. A.

COMPOSERS, Hungarian
See also
Bakfark, B.
Bartok, B.
Lehár, F.
Liszt, F.

COMPOSERS, Israeli
See also
Ran, S.

COMPOSERS, Italian
See also
Albinoni, T.
Bellini, V.
Berio, L.
Cilea, F.
Cimarosa, D.
Donaggio, P.
Donizetti, G.
Gagliano, M. da
Geminiani, F.
Giordano, U.
Grandi, A.
Leoni, F.
Montemezzi, I.
Monteverdi, C.
Peri, J.
Puccini, G.
Rossini, G.
Rota, N.
Scarlatti, A.
Verdi, G.
Vivaldi, A.
Wolf-Ferrari, E.

COMPOSERS, Japanese
See also
Takemitsu, T.

COMPOSERS, Jewish
Jewish contribution; influence on American music. G. Lees. Hi Fi 27:27-8+ Jl '77
See also
Pergament, M.

COMPOSERS, Mexican
See also
Revueltas, S.

COMPOSERS, Polish
See also
Chopin, F. F.
Penderecki, K.

COMPOSERS, Russian
See also
Glinka, M. I.
Kabalevsky, D.
Musorgskii, M. P.
Prokof'ev, S. S.
Rachmaninoff, S.
Rimskii-Korsakov, N. A.
Shostakovich, D. D.
Stravinsky, I. F.
Tchaikovsky, P. I.

COMPOSITION (art)
See also
Proportion (art)

COMPOSITION (music)
L'Affilard's published Sketchbooks; with views on early 18th century musical style. E. Schwandt. bibl f il Mus Q 63:99-113 Ja '77
Music of Edgard Varèse. R. P. Morgan. il por Hi Fi 27:78-82 F '77
Reappraisal of Schubert's methods of composition. L. M. Griffel. bibl f il Mus Q 63:186-210 Ap '77
Varèse in New York: from Ecuatorial to Intégrales; excerpt from Varèse: a looking glass diary, v2. L. Varèse. il pors Hi Fi 27:73-7 F '77

COMPOSITION (printing) See Typesetting

COMPOSITION, English. See English language—Composition

COMPOST
Amazing grape-seed greenhouse. R. Rodale. il pors Org Gard & Farm 24:48-52 D '77
Compost piles that work. J. Cox. il Org Gard & Farm 24:60-4 Ag '77
Compost recipe—little water. il Sunset 159:266 O '77
Composting in the solar greenhouse for CO_2 and heat; excerpt from The solar greenhouse book. D. Knapp. il Org Gard & Farm 24:60-2 D '77
Easy plan for making hot compost. H. Olkowski and W. Olkowski. il Horticulture 55:46-8 Mr '77
Inexorable march to composting. J. Goldstein. il Org Gard & Farm 24:145-8 My '77
Power in the blood meal. W. Wieclaw. il Org Gard & Farm 24:74-5 O '77

Preservation and storage

How Jenny Tam hides her compost. il Sunset 158:230 Je '77

COMPOST sifters. See Garden tools, equipment, and supplies

COMPOSTING and Waste Recycling Conference. See Refuse, Utilization of—Conferences

COMPOSTING toilets. See Sewage purification—Biological treatment

COMPREHENSION
See also
Reading comprehension

COMPREHENSIVE Employment and Training Act programs. See Unemployment—Relief measures

COMPRESSORS
Rotary compressor for auto air conditioners. il Pop Sci 210:180 Ap '77

COMPTON, Gail
Manta rays and stingrays. il Oceans 10:4-9 Ja '77

COMPTON, Joseph E.
Regulatory codes: one firm's check list for industrial projects. Archit Rec 161:65+ Je '77

COMPUGRAPHIC Corporation. See Phototypesetting

COMPULSIVE-obsessive behavior. See Behavior (psychology)

COMPULSORY education. See Education, Compulsory

COMPULSORY military service. See Military service, Compulsory

COMPULSORY retirement. See Retirement

COMPUTER art. See Computers—Art use

COMPUTER Automation, Inc. See Computer industry

COMPUTER chess. See Chess

COMPUTER circuits. See Computers—Circuits

COMPUTER clubs. See Clubs

COMPUTER crimes. See Computers and crime

COMPUTER equipment industry. See Computer industry

COMPUTER graphics
Build the Pixie graphic display. J. A. Weisbecker. il Pop Electr 12:41-6 Jl '77
Computer graphics for architecture: techniques in search of problems. il Archit Rec 162:98-105 mid-Ag '77

COMPUTER industry
After the coup at CalComp. por Bus W p35 Ap 25 '77
Amdahl's coup stuns the computer industry. por Duns R 109:23-4+ Ap '77
Cooling off a hot concept; Itel Corp. J. Grigsby. il Forbes 120:57-9 D 15 '77
Corny but true story; Storage Technology. Forbes 120:130 O 15 '77
Dataproducts: it expects to match IBM. por Duns R 109:18-19 F '77
Gene Amdahl takes aim at I.B.M. B. Uttal. il por Fortune 96:106-10+ S '77
Hassle over hardware; electronic banking equipment. il Bus W p95 Ap 18 '77
How Boothe Courier came bouncing back. il Bus W p44-5 Ag 22 '77
More tumult for the computer industry. il Bus W p58-61+ My 30 '77
Quotron's fast climb up from the depths; stock market data terminals. il por Bus W p 100 Je 27 '77
Surprising success; Computer Automation. por Forbes 119:120 Mr 15 '77
Vanishing species, venture-capital division; Tesdata Systems Corp. il Forbes 120:120+ N 15 '77
See also
Bunker-Ramo Corporation
Burroughs Corporation
Control Data Corporation
Data General Corporation
Electronic Data Systems Corporation
International Business Machines Corporation
NCR Corporation
Texas Instruments Inc

Acquisitions and mergers

Acquisition binge in computer services. il Bus W p82+ S 5 '77

Antitrust cases

How courts will treat IBM, AT&T. A. Hershman. por Duns R 110:76-7+ D '77
IBM's antitrust win could be a big one; decision against California Computer Products Inc. J. Madrick. il Bus W p62 Mr 7 '77
IBM's high-flying legal eagle. por Forbes 119:74 Ap 1 '77
Those cases that go on and on; U.S. v IBM. il Time 109:40+ Je 27 '77

Export-import trade

China pushes a trade decision. il Bus W p75 N 21 '77
Computer games; denial of license to export Cyber 76 to Russia. il Time 110:42+ Ag 1 '77
Secretary Kreps won't talk; sale of American computers to foreign governments. M. T. Klare. Nation 224:678-9 Je 4 '77

Finance

Beauty shows signs of aging. il Bus W p 113 O 17 '77
Information processing. il Forbes 121:110+ Ja 9 '78
More competition in a hot market. il Bus W p44+ Ja 9 '78

Securities

IBM's price war takes to the Street. il Bus W p 123+ Ap 18 '77

COMPUTER industry—*Continued*

France

France: at war with IBM over small computers. Bus W p48 Mr 21 '77

Japan

Coming Japanese computer push. il Forbes 119: 59-60 My 15 '77

Russia

Computer games. il Time 110:42+ Ag 1 '77

COMPUTER languages
High-level languages. H. Chamberlin. Pop Electr 12:88-9 N '77

COMPUTER leasing. See Computers—Leasing and renting

COMPUTER manuals. See Computers—Handbooks, manuals, etc.

COMPUTER Output Microfilm. See Computers—Input-output equipment

COMPUTER phototypesetting. See Phototypesetting

COMPUTER printers. See Computers—Print-out equipment

COMPUTER program language. See Computer languages

COMPUTER programming
Algorithms. D. E. Knuth. il Sci Am 236:63-6+ bibl(p 148) Ap '77
Debugging aids. H. Chamberlin. il Pop Electr 11:96-7 My '77
Komputer korner (cont) P. R. Rony and others. il Radio-Electr 48:24+ My '77
Komputer korner. J. Titus and others. Radio-Electr 48:22+ F '77
Monitors, or control programs. S. B. Gray. Pop Electr 11:95-6 Ap '77
Pixie animation program. E. C. Deveaux. Pop Electr 12:42-5 Jl '77
Software engineering. H. D. Mills. bibl il Science 195:1199-205 Mr 18 '77
See also
System Development Corporation

COMPUTER programming manuals. See Computers—Handbooks, manuals, etc.

COMPUTER renting. See Computers—Leasing and renting

COMPUTER science. See Computers

COMPUTER security. See Computers—Security measures

COMPUTER software. See Computer programming

COMPUTER stores. See Computers—Marketing

COMPUTERESE. See Jargon

COMPUTERIZED axial tomography. See Radiography, Medical

COMPUTERIZED typesetting. See Computers—Printing use

COMPUTERS
Computer bits:
More good news for the computer group. L. Solomon. il Pop Electr 12:97-100 O '77
Potpourri from here and there. L. Solomon. il Pop Electr 12:118-21+ D '77
Some new hardware and software. L. Solomon. il Pop Electr 11:109-11 Je '77
Evolution of computers and computing. R. M. Davis. bibl il Science 195:1096-102 Mr 18 '77
Human performance considerations in complex systems. H. O. Holt and F. L. Stevenson. bibl il Science 195:1205-10 Mr 18 '77
Microelectronics and computer science. I. E. Sutherland and C. A. Mead. il Sci Am 237:210-12+ bibl(p262) S '77
Microelectronics and the personal computer. A. C. Kay. il Sci Am 237:230-2+ S '77
New hobby computers you can build from a kit. il Radio-Electr 48:42-4 Ag '77
Post-human intelligence; excerpt from Until the sun dies. R. Jastrow. Natur Hist 86:12-13+ Je '77
Role of microelectronics in data processing. L. M. Terman. il Sci Am 237:162-4+ bibl(p260) S '77
See also
Calculators
Information storage and retrieval systems
Word processing equipment

Aeronautic use

Fuel-saving computer system studied. B. M. Elson. il Aviation W 106:40-1+ Mr 7 '77
Lufthansa computerizing maintenance. Aviation W 107:35 S 19 '77

Agricultural use

Computer terminals as near as your implement dealer; International Harvester's Pro-Ag package. B. Coffman. il Farm J 101:C4 Mr '77
Corn growing costs too high? Here's how to tell. Suc Farm 75:9 D '77
This feeding program predicts everything but the market prices; Fox-Black system. N. Reeder. il Farm J 101:Beef 10+ S '77
What? An electronic herdsman? C. S. Machan. il Farm J 101:Dairy 1-2 My '77
Your own computer. L. Lane. Farm J 101:J1 Ag '77

Airline use

Computers' role grows in fuel planning. K. J. Stein. Aviation W 107:28-9 N 21 '77

Architectural use

Automated project control system aims for improved profitability; Computer-Based Financial Management System. G. N. Harper. il Archit Rec 161:61 Mr '77

Art use

Can computers be programmed to appreciate art? M. J. Apter. Art N 76:18 Summ '77
Computerized cameras, knives sculpt quickly; work of Dynell Electronics Corp. R. Field. il Sci Digest 81:77-8 Ap '77

Astronomical use

Computer-enhanced photographs of galaxies. il Sky & Tel 53:170-2 Mr '77

Audio engineering use

Computer technology transforms speaker design. H. A. Rodgers. il Hi Fi 27:74-5 O '77

Automotive use

Leave the driving to the computer. il U.S. News 83:86 D 26 '77
See also
Automobiles—Electronic equipment

Banking use

Banking without cash a reality; electronic fund transfer on Long Island's North Shore. il U.S. News 83:81-2 D 26 '77
Checkless banking is bound to come. S. Rose. il Fortune 95:118-21+ Je '77
Computers in banking and marketing. F. E. Balderston and others. bibl Science 195:1115-19 Mr 18 '77
Electronic funds transfer: pitfalls and payoffs. J. B. Benton. il Harvard Bus R 55:16-17+ Jl '77
More bang for the buck: the magic of electronic banking; electronic funds transfer. S. Rose. Fortune 95:202-5+ My '77
Retreat from the cashless society. il map Bus W p80-3+ Ap 18 '77
See also
United States—Commission on Electronic Fund Transfers

Biological use

Computer readout translates body language into skills. P. Garfinkel. il Sci Digest 81:12-14 Mr '77

Bookselling use

See also
Book Industry Systems Advisory Committee

Business use

Card-key helps set flexible work hours. J. Free. il Pop Sci 210:176 F '77
Cash like a flash. B. Weberman. il Forbes 119:42+ Ap 1 '77
Controlling the costs of data services. R. L. Nolan. il Harvard Bus R 55:114-24 Jl '77
Electronic banking aims at businesses. Bus W p77 Ja 24 '77
Management and the computer; special report. il Duns R 110:65+ Jl '77

Cartographic use

Digitized mapping pays off for California city; Placentia. il Am City & County 92:111 S '77

Cataloging use

See Libraries—Automation

Chemical use

Computer-based chemical information system. S. R. Heller and others. bibl il Science 195: 253-9 Ja 21 '77
Empirical explorations of SYNCHEM. H. L. Gelernter and others. bibl il Science 197:1041-9 S 9 '77

Circuits

Plug-in circuits make home computers talk, listen, play music, and more. W. J. Hawkins. il Pop Sci 211:89-91+ N '77

College library use

See College libraries—Automation

Communication use

Computer communications; address, May 3, 1977. A. M. McMahon. Vital Speeches 43:529-32 Je 15 '77
Convergence of computing and telecommunications systems. D. Farber and P. Baran. Science 195:1166-70 Mr 18 '77

Control

Using existing house wiring for computer remote control. D. Sokol and others. il Pop Electr 12:60-5 D '77; 13:60-2 Ja '78

COMPUTERS—*Continued*

Control use

Impact of the electronics revolution on industrial process control. L. B. Evans. bibl il Science 195:1146-51 Mr 18 '77
Remote control. L. Solomon. il Pop Electr 12:88-9 Ag '77

Cryptographic use

Computer encryption and the National Security Agency connection. G. B. Kolata. il Science 197:438-40 Jl 29 '77
Cryptography: on the brink of a revolution? G. B. Kolata. Science 197:747-8 Ag 19 '77
Cryptology: scientists puzzle over threat to open research, publication. D. Shapley and G. B. Kolata. Science 197:1345-9 S 30 '77
How to decipher secret messages. F. W. Chesson. il Radio-Electr 48:48-50 D '77

Editing use

How Hendrix snatched the lead in text editing. Bus W p58-9 Jl 4 '77

Educational use

Decade of usage of the computers for instructional purposes. S. Charp and H. H. Altschuler. Educ Digest 42:41-3 F '77
When computers invade a city' school system—Flint, Mich. il U.S. News 83:80-1 D 26 '77

Engineering use

Building automation: energy optimization by computer. D. E. Ross. il Archit Rec 161:143-4 My '77
See also
Computer graphics

Equipment

Bus systems. H. Chamberlin. Pop Electr 13:77-9 Ja '78

Errors

How computers detect and correct transmission errors. J. May. il Pop Electr 11:70-2 Je '77
When computers goof—consumers air their frustrations. U.S. News 82:61-2 My 2 '77

Exhibitions

Digitizing; Personal Computing Expo. New Yorker 53:40-2 N 14 '77
First West Coast Computer Faire. T. Munnecke. il Pop Electr 12:74-5 S '77

Government use

Business is wary about Carter's volunteer plan; OMB computer task force. Bus W p36-7 D 26 '77
See also
Computers—Municipal use

Handbooks, manuals, etc.

Scelbi computer 8008/8080 programming manuals. il Radio-Electr 48:26-8 Ap '77

Home use

And now a computer for your home. il Changing T 31:39-40 D '77
Brain for a house; microprocessor. por House B 119:14+ S '77
Bytes and chips. New Yorker 53:30-1 Ap 4 '77
Computers move into the kitchen. F. K. Coffee. il Mech Illus 74:38+ Ja '78
Everyman's home computer is here. A. R. Curtis. il Pop Mech 148:92-3+ O '77
Future of home computers. A. P. Salsberg. Pop Electr 12:4 O '77
Home computer kits: the hottest new angle in America's newest hobby. I. Berger. il Pop Mech 147:98-100+ F '77
Home computers are on the way. L. Buckwalter. il Mech Illus 73:48-9+ O '77
I build my own home computer from a kit. A. Curtis. il Pop Mech 147:100+ F '77
I built my own home computer system. C. W. Prestia, Jr. il Pop Mech 148:79 Jl '77
Just set 35 dials—computer will budget your home energy use. il Sci Digest 82:47-8 O '77
New home computers can change your lifestyle. W. J. Hawkins. il Pop Sci 211:30+ O '77
Plug-in circuits make home computers talk, listen, play music, and more. W. J. Hawkins. il Pop Sci 211:89-91+ N '77
Plugging in everyman. il Time 110:39 S 5 '77
Remote control. L. Solomon. il Pop Electr 12:88-9 Ag '77
Soon: a computer in every home? il U.S. News 83:77-8 N 21 '77
Special focus on home computers; symposium. il Pop Electr 12:57-72 D '77
What it's like to build and use your own home computer. W. J. Hawkins. il Pop Sci 210:102-5+ My '77

Indexing use

Computerized word; indexing the Responsa for Jewish scholars. M. Montagno and M. J. Kubic. il Newsweek 89:61 Ap 11 '77

Industrial use

Computerized manufacturing pressed. Aviation W 107:57-8 Jl 11 '77
See also
Computers—Control use

Input-output equipment

Assemblers. H. Chamberlain. il Pop Electr 12:89-90 Jl '77
Computer corner; interrupt operation. D. G. Larsen and others. bibl Radio-Electr 48:16+ Je '77
Computer corner; interrupts. il Radio-Electr 48:22+ Jl '77
Hex-to-ASCII converter for your TVT-6. D. Lancaster. il Pop Electr 12:49-52 O '77
Interfacing a D/A converter. T. A. Titus and others. il Radio-Electr 48:76-7 O '77
More libraries switch to COM catalogs. Lib J 102:672 Mr 15 '77
See also
Information display systems
Speech processing systems

Investment use

Big Board's own national marketplace. il Bus W p34-5 D 5 '77
Quotron's fast climb up from the depths; stock market data terminals. il por Bus W p 110 Je 27 '77
Reviving the concept of a national market. Bus W p33-4 Ag 15 '77

Leasing and renting

Should it be lease or buy? Duns R 110:82-3+ Jl '77

Legal use

Lawyers—computers—and power; address, April 20, 1977. J. E. Murray. Vital Speeches 43:487-90 Je 1 '77

Library use

See Libraries—Automation

Marketing

Computer bits:
Computer stores. S. B. Gray. il Pop Electr 11:89-90 F '77
Computer stores: a new retailing phenomenon. S. Wantz. il Pop Electr 12:70-2 D '77

Medical use

New medical techniques from space technology; vascular image processing. D. H. Blankenhorn. Intellect 106:189 N '77

Memory systems

Bubble memory finally arrives. il Bus W p72+ Mr 28 '77
Core memories—how they work. M. A. Sala. il Radio-Electr 48:54-5 S '77
Memory testing. H. Chamberlin. Pop Electr 11:107-10 Mr '77
Microelectronic memories. il Sci Am 237:130-1+ bibl(p258) S '77
New memory technologies. J. A. Rajchman. bibl il Science 195:1223-9 Mr 18 '77
Product test reports:
North Star model MDS-A micro disk system. il Pop Electr 12:86-7 N '77
Stacks—what they are and how they're used. T. Barry. il Radio-Electr 48:22+ Mr '77

Meteorological use

History of the earth's atmosphere. il Sky & Tel 53:266+ Ap '77

Miniaturization

Build the COSMAC Elf: a low-cost experimenter's microcomputer (cont) J. Weisbecker. il Pop Electr 11:63-7 Mr; 12:41-6 Jl '77
Build 2650-based microcomputer system. J. Roloff. il Radio-Electr 48:31-5+ Ap; 45-8 My; 47-9+ Je '77
Computers: the move to micro. J. W. Moore and E. A. Moore. Sci Digest 82:69-70+ Jl '77
Desktop computers; use by local government. il Am City & County 92:61-4 F '77
Equipment reports:
Infinite UC1800 microcomputer. il Radio-Electr 48:27+ Ag '77
I build my own home computer from a kit. A. Curtis. il Pop Mech 147:100+ F '77
Impudent, magical silicon chip. K. Lamott. il Horizon 19:72-7 Jl '77
Komputer korner. See issues of Radio-electronics
Large-scale integration of microelectronic circuits. il Sci Am 237:82-94 bibl(p258) S '77
Radio-shack's new computer system. A. Kleiman. il Radio-Electr 48:101-2 O '77
You can take your pulse; micro-computer. Sci Digest 81:85 Je '77
See also
Microprocessors

Municipal use

Bright future seen for public works computer programs. S. S. Baxter. Am City & County 92:98 My '77
Desktop computers; use by local government. il Am City & County 92:61-4 F '77

COMPUTERS—Municipal use—*Continued*
Digitized mapping pays off for California city; Placentia. il Am City & County 92:111 S '77
Don't be a slave to your city's computer; minicomputer system in Wethersfield, Conn. il Am City & County 92:69-71 O '77
Make gasoline losses evaporate; computerized control over fuel records for municipal vehicles; Bloomington, Minn. H. G. Wurdelman. il Am City & County 92:39-40 Ja '77
Make money by computer; Melbourne, Fla. E. Watkins and J. Burger. il Am City & County 92:57-8 Ap '77
See also
Computers—Traffic control use

Musical use

Musecom II: musical notation computer. D. Heckman. il Hi Fi 27:106 Ag '77

Newspaper publishing use

Newspapers take a big step in automation; New York Daily news and Westchester Rockland Newspaper, Inc. il Bus W p58-60 Jl 4 '77

Optical equipment

See also
Optical scanners

Photographic use

Computer-painted enlargement. E. H. Ortner. il Pop Sci 210:92-3 Je '77

Police use

Central crime computer project draws mixed reviews. D. Shapley. Science 197:138-41 Jl 8 '77

Prices

IBM's price war takes to the Street. il Bus W p 123+ Ap 18 '77

Print-out equipment

Amazing daisies; industry competition for daisy wheel printing system. il Forbes 120:27-8 Ag 1 '77

Printing use

Book designer compiles specifications booklets for computer composition firms. P. Doebler. Pub W 211:64 Je 6 '77
Designer's perspective on technology and typography; report on Vision '77 symposium. J. Stoliar. il Pub W 212:63-4 Jl 4 '77
Printing by computer: a USN&WR gamble pays off; electronic composition system. il U.S. News 83:56-8 S 5 '77
United Methodists pioneer electronic printing facility. Pub W 212:72 S 26 '77

Programs

See Computer programming

Publishing use

APS tests computer system for publishing operations. il Phys Today 30:75 D '77
Market-wise; Compugraphic Corp. il Forbes 119:59-60 Mr 1 '77
See also
Book Industry Systems Advisory Committee
Computers—Newspaper publishing use
Computers—Printing use

Radio broadcasting use

Automated radio: the future is upon us. T. Everett. il Hi Fi 27:124-7 S '77

Real estate use

Computer appraises your home. N. Smith. il Pop Sci 210:168 My '77

Retail trade use

Computers in banking and marketing. F. E. Balderston and others. bibl Science 195:1115-19 Mr 18 '77
Tiny computer made to order. V. E. Smay. il Pop Sci 210:75 F '77

Scientific use

Computers and research. W. O. Baker and others. bibl il Science 195:1134-9 Mr 18 '77
Whole moon catalog; computer data intercomparative system. J. Eberhart. il Sci N 111:300-2 My 7 '77

Security measures

Computer privacy. Sci Am 236:50 F '77
Computer privacy. M. Davidson. Sci Digest 82:42-4 S '77
Computers: a seeing-eye watching you; identity verification. P. Meissner. il Sci Digest 81:64-7 Je '77
Growing threat to computer security. il Bus W p44-5 Ag 1 '77
See also
Computers—Cryptographic use

Space flight use

Self-healing computer in development. il Aviation W 107:57-60 Ag 15 '77

Sports use

Gideon Ariel and his magic machine; biomechanical analysis. K. Moore. il por Sports Illus 47:52-60 Ag 22 '77

Stock exchange use

See Computers—Investment use

Telephone use

Freak-proof computer arms Ma Bell against toll cheats. R. Field. Sci Digest 82:86-7 S '77

Traffic control use

Computerizing Tokyo's traffic. J. H. Douglas. il map Sci N 112:412-14 D 17 '77
Leave the driving to the computer. il U.S. News 83:86 D 26 '77

COMPUTERS, Used
Would you buy a used computer from this man? por Forbes 119:104 Mr 15 '77

COMPUTERS and civilization
What computers mean for man and society. H. A. Simon. bibl Science 195:1186-91 Mr 18 '77; Same with title Computers: changing man's view of himself. Current 193:39-51 My '77

COMPUTERS and crime
Annals of crime. T. Whiteside. New Yorker 53:35-8+ Ag 22; 34-6+ Ag 29 '77
Computer capers. il Time 110:53 Ag 8 '77
Computer criminals; excerpt from address. D. B. Parker. Intellect 106:187 N '77
Nagging feeling of undetected fraud. U.S. News 83:42 D 19 '77

COMSATS. See Communications satellites

CON Edison. See Consolidated Edison Company of New York

CON men. See Fraud

CONANT, Howard S.
Eccentric genius of Frank Lloyd Wright. bibl il por Intellect 106:164-7 O '77
Reassessment of Renaissance artist Carlo Crivelli. il Intellect 106:79-81 Ag '77

CONBOY, Joseph L.
Foam-cored fiberglass boats. il Yachting 141:98-101 Ap '77

CONCENTRATED study
Intensive education: the impact of time on learning. B. S. Powell. Educ Digest 42:6-9 Mr '77

CONCENTRATION. See Attention

CONCENTRATION camps

Germany

Miracle of barracks 28; Ravensbrück; excerpt from The hiding place. C. Ten Boom and others. il por Sat Eve Post 249:42-3+ Ap '77
Vanadium; memoir of Auschwitz; excerpt from Il sistema periodico; tr by G. Jochnowitz. P. Levi. Commentary 63:65-9 Mr '77

Poland

Who is in the dock? Maidanek trial in Dusseldorf. R. Carroll and T. Nater. il Newsweek 90:43 Jl 11 '77

Russia

Statement by prisoner H. I. Butman to the chief of the Perm administration of corrective labor establishments (ITK-35) H. Butman. il Nat R 29:822-5 Jl 22 '77

CONCERNED Farm Wives of South Central Kansas (organization) See Agricultural societies

CONCERT Dance Company of Boston. See Dance companies

CONCERT halls
Musical events; Orpheum. A. Porter. New Yorker 53:66-7 Jl 4 '77
Robin Hood Dell West: a new summer capital for Philadelphia's music lovers. il Archit Rec 161:129-32 Ja '77
See also
Opera houses

Acoustics

See Acoustics, Architectural

CONCERT stage (radio program) See Radio broadcasting—Music

CONCERTO and concertos
Aria structure and ritornello form in the music of Albinoni. J. E. Solie. bibl f il Mus Q 63:31-47 Ja '77
See also
Phonograph records—Concertos

CONCERTS
Avery Fisher Awards. I. Kolodin. Sat R 5:52-3 O 29 '77
See also
Phonograph records—Concert performances
Television broadcasting—Music

CONCERTS in prisons. See Prison recreation

CONCESSIONS (food, etc)
NPCA exposes concessioner's misrepresentation of profits. Nat Parks & Con Mag 51:23-4 S '77
Park Service discloses ripoff operations in land of Old Faithful. Nat Parks & Con Mag 51:26-7 Ag '77

CONCORD, Battle of, 1775

Personal narratives

Eyewitness to Concord. S. Cooper. il Am Hist Illus 12:20-1 Ap '77

CONCORDAT of 1929 (Italy) See Catholic Church in Italy

CONCORDE airliner. See Airplanes, Supersonic

CONCOURS d'Elegance. See Automobiles—Exhibitions

CONCRETE, Reinforced

PS guide to concrete reinforcing. R. Day. il Pop Sci 211:126-8+ Ag '77

CONCRETE blocks

Making your own concrete block wall. il Mech Illus 73:118+ My '77

Self-locking blocks go up without mortar. F. Albert. il Pop Sci 211:74 Ag '77

CONCRETE construction

Arresting view to the south; the Mexican embassy in Brasilia and the Colegio de Mexico in Mexico City. il Archit Rec 162:81-8 O '77

Maintenance and repair

Dry-pack repair for sagging concrete. J. Emmett. il Pop Sci 210:192 Ap '77

CONCRETE floors (swine houses) See Swine houses—Floors

CONCRETE mixers

Mobile concrete batchers save time, manpower and money; Baltimore. S. Cortese. il Am City & County 92:51-2 F '77

CONCRETE pavements. See Pavements

CONCRETE sewer pipes. See Sewer pipes

CONCRETE sidewalks. See Sidewalks

CONCRETE work

See also

Concrete blocks

CONDENSATION

Nucleation on photoexcited molecules. J. L. Katz and others. bibl il Science 196:1203-5 Je 10 '77

CONDIMENTS

See also

Pickles and relishes

CONDITIONED responses

Classical conditioning with auditory discrimination of the eye blink in decerebrate cats. R. J. Norman and others. bibl il Science 196:551-3 Ap 29 '77

Classical nictitating membrane conditioning in the awake normal, restrained cat. M. M. Patterson and others. bibl il Science 196:1124-6 Je 3 '77

Conditioned narcotic withdrawal in humans. C. P. O'Brien and others. bibl il Science 195: 1000-2 Mr 11 '77

Limbic system interrelations: functional division among hippocampal-septal connections. T. W. Berger and R. F. Thompson. bibl il Science 197:587-9 Ag 5 '77

See also

Biofeedback training

Reinforcement (psychology)

CONDOMINIUM (housing)

Apogee 1 Townhouses, Miami, Florida. il Archit Rec 161:112-13 mid-My '77

Butternut Hill Condominiums, Waitsfield, Vermont; vacation condominiums. il Archit Rec 161:110-11 mid-My '77

Custom tailored apartments in Nashville fit together like a high-rise jigsaw puzzle; Rokeby Condominium Apartments. il Archit Rec 162: 120-1 S '77

Directory of timeshare resorts. C. Burlingame. Holiday 58:16+ S '77

Embarcadero Condominiums, Newport, Oregon. il Archit Rec 161:114-15 mid-My '77

New England condo rondo; resorts for all seasons. S. M. Joynes. il Holiday 57:16+ N '76

New twists on vacation rentals. S. Birnbaum. Esquire 88:38+ S '77

Price-chopping eases the condominium glut. il Bus W p 151-2 Ap 18 '77

Sun living on the rise. il House & Gard 150:76-83+ Ja '78

Time-sharing: new way to buy a vacation home. il Changing T 32:40-2 Ja '78

Time sharing of resort homes. U.S. News 82:49 Mr 14 '77

Tower of power; New York's Olympic Tower. D. K. Shah and B. Carter. il Newsweek 91:63 Ja 9 '78

CONDOMINIUM auctions. See Auctions

CONDON, Jane

Backpacking gourmet. Harp Baz 110:88-9+ Ap '77

Hiking, backpacking & rafting. Harp Baz 110: 88+ Ap '77

CONDON, Richard

That's entertainment! Harpers 255:80+ S '77

about

Caroline, Como, and Condon. W. Cole. Sat R 4:43 Jl 23 '77 •

CONDUCT of life

Connecting the dots in organic living. J. Goldstein. Org Gard & Farm 24:114-17 Ap '77

How to come to terms with yourself; combatting instant gratification. N. Lande and A. Slade. Harp Baz 110:46-7+ Je '77

How to take charge of your life; excerpt. M. Newman and B. Berkowitz. il por Ladies Home J 94:56 Ap '77

If I should die before I wake. A. Whitman. Read Digest 111:217-20+ D '77

I'm not going; living a balanced life. J. Dake. Read Digest 110:205-6 Ap '77

New American dream. R. Rodale. il Org Gard & Farm 24:52-5 Ap '77

Poor Richard's way to wealth and happiness. B. Franklin. por Sat Eve Post 249:6-7 Jl '77

Special people; voluntary simplicity. R. Rodale. il pors Org Gard & Farm 24:54-8 Jl '77

Taking the scare out of scarcity. E. F. Schumacher. Psychol Today 11:16 S '77; Same abr. Read Digest 111:168-9 D '77

Thoughts for the new year; excerpt from The heritage book 1978. E. McCann. Good H 186: 127-8 Ja '78

You can't quit. H. H. Humphrey. por Read Digest 111:57-61 Ag '77

See also

Altruism
Anger
Avarice
Charm
Christian ethics
Christian life
Conscience
Contentment
Courtesy
Early rising
Efficiency
Etiquette
Faith
Forgiveness
Friendship
Happiness
Honesty
Human relations
Humanity
Hurry
Leisure
Love
Neatness
Pride and vanity
Resolutions
Responsibility
Self control
Self reliance
Simplicity
Spiritual life
Success
Temptation
Thrift
Time, Use of
Virtue
Work
Youth—Conduct of life

Anecdotes, facetiae, satire, etc.

Future doesn't work. B. Sloan. por Newsweek 90: 15 S 19 '77

CONDUCTING (music)

Karajan at Juilliard; classes in conducting. D. J. Soria. il pors Hi Fi 27:MA5+ Ap '77

See also

Conductors (music)

CONDUCTORS (music)

Orchestra conductors would make good porpoise trainers. K. Pryor. il por Psychol Today 10:61+ F '77

Outmoded music director. I. Kolodin. il Sat R 4:36-7 Je 25 '77

See also

Badea, C.
Berglund, P. A. E.
Bernstein, L.
Bloch, H.
Boulez, P.
Caldwell, S.
Comissiona, S.
Davis, A.
Davis, C.
Furtwängler, W.
Gavazzeni, G.
Haitink, B.
Karajan, H. von
Kleiber, E.
Krips, J.
Kubelik, R.
Ledger, P.
Levine, J.
Mata, E.
Mehta, Z.
Mengelberg, W.
Nazareth, D.
Ozawa, S.
Plasson, M.
Previn, A.
Rahn, E.
Rostropovich, M.

CONDUCTORS (music)—See also—*Continued*
Sabata, V. de
Schuller, G
Solti, G
Tennstedt, K.
Toscanini, A.
Weingartner, F.

Anecdotes, facetiae, satire, etc.

Pitfalls. L. Dreyer. il Opera N 42:26+ O '77

CONDUCTORS, Electric. See Electric conductors

CONE, Ceasar
Ceasarism at Cone Mills. Forbes 119:70 Mr 15 '77 *

CONE, Edward T.
One hundred metronomes. Am Scholar 46:443-57 Aut '77

CONE, Joan
Chuck full of flavor. il Outdoor Life 159:124 My '77

CONE, Kady
Paralytics: strangers in a strange land. il Chr Cent 94:589-92 Je 22 '77

CONE cells. See Rods and cones

CONE Mills Corporation
Ceasarism at Cone Mills. Forbes 119:70 Mr 15 '77

CONERLY, Richard Pugh
Bittersweet deal; Pott Industries sold to Houston Natural Gas Corp. por Forbes 119:76 Ap 1 '77 *

CONEY Island
Brighton Beach; ballroom dancing. New Yorker 53:22-4 Ag 22 '77

CONFECTIONERY
Christmas idea from Vienna—glacéed fruits on a stick. il Sunset 159:166 D '77
For Easter baskets—nougat. il Sunset 158:228 Ap '77
See also
Candy
Candy industry

CONFEDERATE States of America

Secret service

See United States—History—Civil War, 1861-1865—Secret service—Confederate States

CONFERENCE Board, Inc
Solid rise for business in '78—size-up by a panel of experts. il U.S. News 83:56-7 D 5 '77

CONFERENCE committees, Congressional. See United States—Congress—Committees

CONFERENCE of the Committee on Disarmament. See United Nations—Committee on Disarmament

CONFERENCE on Alternative State and Local Public Policies. See National Conference on Alternative State and Local Public Policies

CONFERENCE on Carriage of Goods by the Sea. 1978 (proposed) See United Nations Conference on Carriage of Goods by the Sea, 1978 (proposed)

CONFERENCE on College Composition and Communication
Playing tennis without a net; resolution accepting all dialects. J. Simon. Esquire 88:66+ O '77

CONFERENCE on Human Settlements, 1976. See United Nations Conference on Human Settlements, 1976

CONFERENCE on International Economic Cooperation. See Economic conferences

CONFERENCE on Laser Engineering and Applications. See Lasers—Conferences

CONFERENCE on National Energy Policy. See Energy policy—Conferences

CONFERENCE on Science and Technology for Development, 1979 (proposed) See United Nations Conference on Science and Technology for Development, 1979 (proposed)

CONFERENCE on Security and Cooperation in Europe
Carter backs off; Belgrade conference. C. Whipple and others. Newsweek 90:48+ O 10 '77
Caviar ending; Belgrade talks. Time 110:29-30 Ag 15 '77
Co-existence, détente and cooperation between nations and systems; report of Pugwash Conference. Bull Atom Sci 33:35-6 D '77
Conference on Security and Cooperation in Europe. Dept State Bull 77:404-10 S 26 '77
Department discusses implementation of economic provisions of the final act of the Helsinki Conference; statement, January 14, 1977. C. W. Robinson. Dept State Bull 76:108-13 F 7 '77
Détente with a human face; Belgrade conference. il Time 110:36 O 17 '77
Final acts and final solutions; effect of Helsinki agreement on Soviet Jews. W. Korey. bibl il Society 15:81-6 N '77
Human rights: confrontation in Belgrade. il Time 109:6-7 Je 27 '77
Human rights—roots of conflict; from Helsinki accords. U.S. News 82:18 Je 20 '77
Louder, please; Belgrade's post-Helsinki talks. Nat R 29:1283-4 N 11 '77
Reports & comment: Belgrade: spinning a European web. D. Cook. Atlantic 240:6+ N '77
Review meeting of the CSCE opens at Belgrade; statement, with outline, October 6, 1977. A. J. Goldberg. Dept State Bull 77:674-80 N 14 '77
Secretary discusses administration's objectives for Belgrade review conference on CSCE; statement, June 6, 1977. C. R. Vance. Dept State Bull 76:669-70 Je 27 '77
To Helsinki, with love. Nat R 29:253 Mr 4 '77
Understating the Communist threat; excerpt from address, July 1977. A. B. Bozeman. bibl Society 15:92-6 N '77
Writer, swine; complying with the Helsinki accord. F. Willey and others. il Newsweek 89:48+ Ja 24 '77
See also
United States—Commission on Security and Cooperation in Europe

CONFERENCE on the Law of the Sea. See United Nations Conference on the Law of the Sea

CONFERENCE on the Limitation of Armaments, Washington, D.C, 1921. See Disarmament—Conferences

CONFERENCE on Trade and Development. See United Nations Conference on Trade and Development

CONFERENCES
Conventions. See issues of American city & county to May 1977
See also
Authors conferences
Economic conferences
International conferences
Library conferences
Religious conferences
Technical conferences
also names of conferences, e.g., Pugwash Conference on Science and World Affairs; *also* subhead Conferences under various subjects, e.g. Music—Conferences

CONFESSION
See also
Confidential communications
Penance

CONFESSION in literature
To see life steady and to see it whole. V. S. Owens. il Chr Today 21:18-21 Mr 4 '77

CONFESSION story. See Short story

CONFESSIONS of faith. See Creeds

CONFIDENCE
Developing a climate of trust. D. Gerig. Chr Today 21:30 Ap 15 '77

CONFIDENCE men. See Fraud

CONFIDENCES, Personal. See Confidential communications

CONFIDENTIAL communications
Talk-it-over technique; ideas of B. Green. B. Russell. il House & Gard 149:30+ Je '77
Telling all; revealing personal secrets. H. LaBarre. Ladies Home J 94:77+ Jl '77
See also
Official secrets

Press

Prying out sources; jailing of reporter J. E. Shelledy. Time 110:114 N 14 '77

Psychotherapists

Therapist as double agent. F. Powledge. il Psychol Today 11:44-7 Jl '77

CONFINEMENT barns, Livestock. See Barns and stables

CONFINEMENT feeding of cattle. See Cattle—Confinement methods

CONFINEMENT feeding of swine. See Swine—Confinement methods

CONFIRMATION (sacrament)
Confirmation: pastoral letdown. J. L. Cunningham. America 136:164-6 F 26 '77

CONFLICT of generations. See Generation gap

CONFLICT of interests (business)
PR man helps select author of book on pollution case. L. J. Carter. Science 195:468 F 4 '77

CONFLICT of interests (public office)
Academics in New York and California fight disclosure policies. B. J. Culliton. Science 196:37-8 Ap 1 '77
Conflicts of interest. L. Komisar. Progressive 41:8-9 Mr '77
Persecution and character assassination of Howard (Bo) Callaway as performed by inmates of the U.S. Senate under the auspices of the Democratic Party. J. Hougan. Harpers 255:35-42+ Jl '77
Putting a lid on lawyers in Congress. J. A. Kidney. il U.S. News 83:39-41 S 12 '77
Seeking the litmus. M. Ruby and others. il Newsweek 90:62-3 Jl 25 '77
Too-high price of public service. il Fortune 96:158-62+ D '77
Unholy trinities that undermine America. J. N. Miller. Read Digest 110:61-7 Mr '77

CONFORD, Ellen
Children's records. Am Rec G 40:50-1 N '76; 48-50 Mr '77

CONFORMITY
See also
Eccentrics and eccentricities

CONGDON-MARTIN, Beth
Three young clergywomen: how they're changing their churches. J. T. Freeman. il Redbook 149:24+ Je '77 *

CONGENITAL heart defects. See Heart—Abnormalities and deformities

CONGER, Ben
Whitetail tactics. il Field & S 82:46-7+ O '77

CONGER, Dean
Five times to Yakutsk. il pors Nat Geog 152:256-69 Ag '77

CONGER, Lesley
Off the cuff. See issues of Writer

CONGLOMERATE corporations
Conglomerate with hidden values; Utilities & Industries Corp. D. G. Santry. Bus W p 104 N 28 '77
Hanging tough; Kay Corp. il Forbes 120:154 O 15 '77
Martin Processing: heating up for solar energy. por Duns R 109:18-19+ My '77
S.O.S: no help, thank you. por Duns R 109:19-20 Ja '77
Tyler: unsung, prosaic and very profitable. Duns R 109:21-2+ Mr '77
See also
American Financial Corporation
Arlen Realty and Development Corporation
Brunswick Corporation
Eltra Corporation
FMC Corporation
Foremost-McKesson, Inc
General Dynamics Corporation
Gulf & Western Industries, Inc
International Telephone and Telegraph Corporation
Johnson, S. C, and Son, Inc
LTV Corporation
Litton Industries, Inc
Meyer, Fred, Inc
Minnesota Mining and Manufacturing Company
Norris Industries, Inc
Rapid-American Corporation
Sperry Rand Corporation
TRW, Inc
Tenneco, Inc

Finance
Multicompanies. il Forbes 121:94-7 Ja 9 '78

Reorganization
Streamlining the management at SCM; reorganizing Glidden-Durkee Div. il Bus W p96+ F 21 '77

British Columbia
Government selloff in British Columbia; British Columbia Resources Development Corp. por Bus W p69-70 S 26 '77

Canada
How Genstar won its own identity in Canada. il Bus W p 144+ Ap 18 '77
Succeeding against government competition; Canadian Pacific; interview. I. D. Sinclair. il por Nations Bus 65:84-90 D '77

France
Threadbare; Rhône-Poulenc. por Forbes 120:190 N 15 '77

Great Britain
See also
Heron Group Ltd
Reed International Ltd
Trafalgar House, Ltd

Ireland
Heinz's O'Reilly winds down in Dublin; Fitzwilton Ltd. il Bus W p30-1 Jl 4 '77

Malaysia
Socking it to Swine Bobby; government takeover of Sime Darby. il Time 109:50 Ja 24 '77

Netherlands
Revived Miller-Wohl lures a Dutch bidder; Brenninkmeyers. il Bus W p34+ S 5 '77

CONGOLEUM Corporation
Analysts disagree about Congoleum. D. G. Santry. por Bus W p93 O 31 '77

CONGRAT-BUTLAR, Stefan
Brazilian writers meet with foreign editors, publishers, translators. il Pub W 212:24+ N 28 '77
Translators, at Montreal Congress, press for their professional rights. il Pub W 212:36-9 Jl 11 '77

CONGREGATION for Catholic Education
Catholic universities and the Vatican. R. J. Henle. America 136:315-22 Ap 9 '77

CONGREGATION for the Doctrine of the Faith
Open letter to the apostolic delegate; response to declaration on the ordination of women. Commonweal 104:204-6 Ap 1 '77
Vatican declaration: another view. D. Burrell. America 136:289-92 Ap 2 '77; Reply with rejoinder. D. L. Gelpi. 137:75-8 Ag 13 '77
Women, priesthood and the Vatican. J. R. Donahue. America 136:285-9 Ap 2 '77

CONGRESS (United States) See United States—Congress

CONGRESS for Recreation and Parks. See National Recreation and Park Association—Meetings

CONGRESS of Panama, 1826. See Panama Congress, 1826

CONGRESS on World Evangelization. See International Congress on World Evangelization

CONGRESS Party (India) See Political parties—India

CONGRESSIONAL aides. See Congressmen—Staff

CONGRESSIONAL Budget Office. See United States—Congress—Budget Office

CONGRESSIONAL campaigns. See Political campaigns

CONGRESSIONAL caucuses. See Caucuses

CONGRESSIONAL committees. See United States—Congress—Committees

CONGRESSIONAL Cup (race) See Yacht racing

CONGRESSIONAL internship programs for the aged. See Aged—Political activities

CONGRESSIONAL investigations. See Government investigations

CONGRESSIONAL science fellows. See Scientists in government

CONGRESSMEN
Congressmen debate own role as advisers in SALT treaty. Aviation W 107:14 N 21 '77
Freshman class in Congress—young but not rebellious. il U.S. News 82:21-2 F 21 '77
95th Congress: doing or dozing? il Sr Schol 109:6-8 F 24 '77
President Carter and the honeymooners; nonenacted legislation supported by Democratic congressmen. J. Drake and S. Petersen. il Nat R 29:433-6+ Ap 15 '77
Putting a lid on lawyers in Congress. J. A. Kidney. il U.S. News 83:39-41 S 12 '77
Rebels on the Hill; Democrats. R. Steele H. W. Hubbard. il Newsweek 90:19+ Ag 8 '77
See what your congressman can do for you. il Changing T 32:31-2 Ja '78
Who's who in Congress? il Sr Schol 109:20-1 F 24 '77
See also
Conflict of interests (public office)
Government investigations—Congressmen

Ethics
See Political ethics

Public relations
Tending to the home folks. D. M. Alpern and H. W. Hubbard. il Newsweek 89:26+ Ap 25 '77
There's no shortage of gripes when lawmakers talk to voters. H. Kennedy; R. Shoup; J. Hogue. il U.S. News 83:17-19 Ag 29 '77
What worries the voters? il Time 110:14-15+ S 5 '77
When congressmen talk to voters back home. il U.S. News 82:22 Ja 24 '77

Salaries, allowances, etc.
Ain't misbehaving; House code of ethics. Newsweek 89:16 Mr 14 '77
Congress adopts ethics code, but skepticism still runs strong. U.S. News 82:79 Ap 11 '77
Congress joins the billion-dollar club. Fortune 95:90 Ja '77
Congress's pay raise: House stands up to be counted. U.S. News 83:32 Jl 11 '77
Eccentricities of ethics. F. Getlein. Commonweal 104:228-9 Ap 15 '77
Ethics on Capitol Hill. Progressive 41:8-10 Ag '77
For the record: congressional perquisites; excerpt from CBS Evening News; December 24, 1976. Read Digest 110:203-4 Ap '77
For top officials: big pay raises in the works. il U.S. News 82:19 F 7 '77
In defense of Congress. . R. C. Byrd. il por U.S. News 82:74 Ap 18 '77
Mounting discontent with first billion-dollar Congress. il U.S. News 82:23-6+ Mr 7 '77
Power, fame and fortune too. New Repub 176:7-8 Mr 5 '77; Reply. M. Peretz. 176:6 Mr 12 '77
Same old gang? M. Stone. U.S. News 82:88 Mr 14 '77
They are paying the price of virtue; code of ethics. il Time 109:12-13 Mr 14 '77

Anecdotes, facetiae, satire, etc.
Perks. R. Lipez. Progressive 41:50 Je '77

Staff
Big pay hikes for Congress aides, too. il U.S. News 82:50 Je 20 '77
Capitol Hill staffs: hidden government in Washington. il U.S. News 82:37-40 Ap 4 '77
Human rights on Capitol Hill. M. Kondracke. New Repub 176:11+ Ap 9 '77
Knowing when to leave. J. B. Smith por Newsweek 90:13 O 3 '77
Why the Justice Department doesn't want you to know what happened between Otto Passman and Shirley Davis; charge of sex descrimination after dismissal of congressional aide. A. Northrop. il pors Ms 6:57-9 Ja '78

CONGRESSMEN—*Continued*

Term

Let's limit the length of congressional service. W. A. Barnstead. il por Duns R 110:101+ D '77

Limit a lawmaker's term in Congress? interviews. J. C. Danforth; A. Cranston. pors U.S. News 83:71-2 N 14 '77

Travel

Our junket-happy Congress: what secret records disclose. il U.S. News 82:19-22 Je 27 '77

CONGRESSMEN, Letters to. See Lobbyists and lobbying

CONGRESSWOMEN

Slim past, but a strong future. il Ebony 32:89-92+ Ag '77

Women of Congress speak out. il Good H 185: 26+ N '77

See also

Fenwick, M.
Jordan, B. C.

CONIC sections

See also

Hyperbola

CONIFERS

Cornbelt conifers. S. Reardon and D. Dickmann. il por Am For 83:8-10 Ag '77

CONIGLIARO, Tony

Hard-luck heroes. E. Keerdoja. il pors Newsweek 90:5+ Ag 1 '77 *

CONIGLIO, Adolph

Annals of medicine. B. Roueché. New Yorker 53:97-8+ S 12 '77 *

CONJUGATION (biology)

Conjugal transfer of the gonococcal penicillinase plasmid. B. I. Eisenstein and others. il Science 195:998-1000 Mr 11 '77

Increase in conjugational transmission frequency of nonconjugative plasmids; escherichia coli. N. J. Crisona and A. J. Clark. bibl il Science 196:186-7 Ap 8 '77

CONJUNCTIVITIS. See Eye—Diseases and defects

CONJURING

Classroom behavior problems solved with magic. L. Palmatier. Intellect 106:105 S '77

Goldfinger and Dove. il pors Ebony 32:88-90+ Ap '77

Anecdotes, facetiae, satire, etc.

Harried Houdini. J. Allen. Seventeen 36:60+ My '77

CONLON, James A.

Two; interview. New Yorker 53:23-5 Jl 18 '77

CONLON-HOFFMAN, Mrs

String training on the Cape. il Hi Fi 28:MA14-15 Ja '78

CONN, Bernard

State government on the road. il Parks & Rec 12:59-60+ Je '77

CONN, Richard

Labor Department mural: a complicated voyage; J. Beal's murals. B. Carter. il por Art N 76: 40-1 My '77 *

CONNALLY, John Bowden, 1917-

Dying party? interview. pors U.S. News 83:22 Ag 29 '77

about

Off to the races. T. Mathews and others. il por Newsweek 90:49 O 24 '77 *

CONNAUGHTON, Howard W.

Craftsmen in business: taxes; excerpt from Craftsmen in business: a guide to financial management and taxes. Ceram Mo 25:40-4 Mr '77

CONNECTICUT

See also

Air pollution—Connecticut
Architecture, Domestic—Connecticut
Booksellers and bookselling—Connecticut
Criminal justice, Administration of—Connecticut
Education—Connecticut
Fairfield County
Forests and forestry—Connecticut
Historic houses, sites, etc.—Connecticut
Housing—Connecticut
Lakes—Connecticut
Mianus River
Opera—Connecticut
Public health—Connecticut

Description and travel

Cruising the Nutmeg Valley. H. Sutton. il Sat R 5:48-9 O 1 '77

Politics and government

Surprises from Nation's two women governors. pors U.S. News 83:45 O 10 '77

Religious institutions and affairs

Born again in Darien; E. L. Fullam of St Paul's Episcopal Church. S. Heath. Sat R 4:14-15 S 17 '77

CONNECTICUT Ballet Company. See Ballet companies

CONNECTICUT General Mortgage & Realty Investments. See Real estate investment trusts

CONNECTICUT Opera Association. See Opera—Connecticut

CONNECTICUT River Raft Race. See Raft racing

CONNECTION, Press (newspaper) See Madison, Wis.—Newspapers

CONNECTIVE tissues

Diseases

See also

Lupus erythematosus

CONNECTORS

See also

Electric connectors

CONNELL, Dan

Fifteen-year war. il map Nation 224:337-40 Mr 19 '77

CONNELL, Evan

Aztec treasure house; excerpt from El Dorado and other pursuits. il Harpers 255:80-4 O '77

CONNELLY, Dolly

Strait of Magellan: the ultimate passage; with biographical sketch. il Sea Front 23:2-8, 62 Ja '77

CONNELLY, John L.

History (cont) America 136:84-5 Ja 29 '77

CONNER, Alice Anne

Elvis: the mystique. Read Digest 112:75-7 Ja '78

CONNER, Bruce

Bruce Conner is not Bruce Conner. J. Tarshis. il por Art N 76:80-2+ Ja '77 *

CONNER, Dennis

Dennis Conner on match racing; excerpt from No excuse to lose; winning sailboat races with Dennis Conner. il Yachting 142:74+ S '77

CONNER, J. D. and MacLeod, D. I. A.

Rod photoreceptors detect rapid flicker. bibl il Science 195:698-9 F 18 '77

CONNETT, Stephen M. H.

Go chase a shark. il Yachting 141:74-6 Mr '77

CONNIFF, Richard

Malevolent mosquito. il Read Digest 111:153-7 Ag '77

CONNOLLY, Harold X.

Assessing affirmative action. il Intellect 106: 134-6 O '77

CONNOLLY, Paul H.

Courts v. self-government. Nat R 29:1225-8 O 28 '77

CONNOLLY, Sybil Dee

How to make something from nothing. il por Am Lib 8:572-3 N '77

CONNOR, John Thomas

Our over-developed society; address, April 20, 1977. Vital Speeches 43:555-7 Jl 1 '77

about

Risk rewarded. il por Forbes 119:101-2 Mr 15 '77 *

CONNOR, Lawrence S.

Six million dollar murder. il por Sat Eve Post 249:54-5+ N '77

CONNORS, Jimmy

Borg's hot hand took all the tricks. C. Kirkpatrick. il pors Sports Illus 46:16-17 Ja 31 '77 *

He's a first-class tourist. J. Underwood. il por Sports Illus 46:78+ My 23 '77 *

Star you love to hate. T. Kornheiser. il pors N Y Times Mag p20-1+ Ap 10 '77 *

Wimbledon was never better. C. Kirkpatrick. il pors Sports Illus 47:12-15 Jl 11 '77 *

CONRAD, Barnaby, 3d

(ed) See Cunningham, I. Interview with Imogen Cunningham

CONRAD, Charles, 1930-

See also

Space stations—Skylab 2 (1st manned) mission

CONRAD, Douglas

Medical malpractice suits. bibl f il Cur Hist 73:22-6+ Jl '77

CONRAD, Joseph

Conrad's Lord Jim and the enigma of sublimation. J. Berman. bibl f Am Imago 33:380-402 Wint '76 *

CONRAD, Max

Living legends. D. Mosteller. Flying 101:50-1+ N '77 *

CONRAD, Paul

Drawing his own conclusions. H. Lebo. il pors Writers Digest 57:32-3 D '77 *

CONRAD, Peter

Situational hyperactivity: a social system approach. Educ Digest 43:39-41 O '77

CONRAD, Thomas

Winning hearts and minds for the all-volunteer military force. Progressive 41:28-31 S '77

CONRAIL. See Consolidated Rail Corporation

CONRAN, Terence Orby

Conrans in the country. E. Brown. il por N Y Times Mag p74-5 O 30 '77 *

CONRAN'S (store) See Furniture stores

CONRAT, Maisie, and Conrat, Richard

Farmers' frontier; excerpt from The American farm: a photographic history. il Am West 14: 22-33 Mr '77

How U.S. farmers became specialists in cash and debts; excerpt from The American farm. il Smithsonian 7:48-55 Mr '77

CONRAT, Richard
Hillside gardening without terraces. il Org Gard & Farm 24:61-2 Ap '77
—See Conrat, M. jt auth

CONROY, Barbara
CLENE: a success story. il por Lib J 102:1453-5 Jl '77

CONROY, Sarah Booth
House that Joan Mondale decorated. il pors Art N 76:56-7+ Summ '77

CONROY, William J.
Dust starts to settle at Farah. il por Bus W p52 Ap 18 '77 *

CONSANGUINITY
See also
Incest

CONSCIENCE
Educated persons should serve as society's conscience. R. Howell, Jr. por Intellect 106:185 N '77
See also
Guilt

CONSCIENTIOUS objectors
COs or cheap labor; West Germany. T. Heneghan. Commonweal 105:5-7 Ja 6 '78

CONSCIOUSNESS
How hypnosis aids in passing over the threshold of consciousness. T. Bay. il por Sci Digest 81:45-8 Je '77
Lost voices of the gods: reflections on the dawn of consciousness; interview, ed by S. Keen. J. Jaynes. il Psychol Today 11:58-60+ N '77
Lost voices of the gods; views of J. Jaynes. il por Time 109:51-2+ Mr 14 '77
Tuning in on the twilight zone. T. Budzynski. bibl il pors Psychol Today 11:38-9+ Ag '77
See also
Belief and doubt
Self

Anecdotes, facetiae, satire, etc.

Newest consciousness. F. P. Tullius. New Yorker 53:34-6 Mr 28 '77

CONSCIOUSNESS-raising groups. See Discussion groups

CONSERVATION associations
Dirge for the harp; work of B. Davies, director of the International Fund for Animal Welfare. D. Levin. il por Sports Illus 46:80+ Ap 18 '77
Pioneer conservationist A. P. Hill: he saved the redwoods; early work of the Sempervirens Club in Big Basin Redwoods State Park. V. T. Olson. il pors Am West 14:32-40 S '77
See also
Ducks Unlimited, Inc
National Audubon Society
National Parks and Conservation Association
National Wildlife Federation
Nature Conservancy (organization)
Wilderness Society
World Wildlife Fund

CONSERVATION education. See Conservation of resources—Study and teaching

CONSERVATION law. See Conservation of resources—Laws and legislation

CONSERVATION laws (physics)
Nucleon stability: a geochemical test independent of decay mode. J. C. Evans, Jr, and R. I. Steinberg. bibl il Science 197:989-91 S 2 '77
Ripples in physics: apparent failure of muon conservation. Sci N 111:116 F 19 '77

CONSERVATION movement. See Environmental movement

CONSERVATION of library materials. See College libraries—Technical processes; Libraries—Technical processes

CONSERVATION of resources
Conservation. G. Reiger. See issues of Field & stream
Conservation trails. il Outdoor Life 159:34+ F; 106+ Mr; 50+ Ap; 160:34+ N '77
Graying of responsibility. Parks & Rec 12:19 O '77
Immigration policy: the new environmental battlefield. G. Bikales. il Nat Parks & Con Mag 51:13-16 D '77
See also
Environmental movement
Environmental policy
Forest conservation
Landscape protection
Power resources—Conservation
Reclamation of land
Shore protection
Soil conservation
Stream conservation
United Nations—Committee on Natural Resources
United States—Interior, Department of the
Water conservation
Watersheds
Wilderness areas
Wildlife conservation

Awards, prizes, etc.

To honor an engineer; Joan Hodges Queneau Award. il Audubon 79:160 Ja '77

Bibliography

Books. il Liv Wildn 40:36-42 O '76; 44-9 Ja; 41:34-6 Ap '77

History

Eden ravished: the land, pioneer attitudes, and conservation. H. Hague. bibl il Am West 14:30-3+ My '77

Laws and legislation

Congress hooks snail darter; Endangered Species Act. E. J. Christy. BioScience 27:320 My '77
Conservation docket. See issues of National parks & conservation magazine
Deflowering of the Endangered Species Act. G. Moore. il Horticulture 55:36-9 My '77
Endangered Species Act. K. Shea. bibl il Environment 19:6-15 O '77
Endangered Species Act under fire. M. J. Bean. il Nat Parks & Con Mag 51:16-20 Je '77
Endangered Species: review of law triggered by Tellico impasse. C. Holden. Science 196:1426-8 Je 24 '77
Furbish lousewort is no joke; Endangered Species Act and public works projects. J. Wheelwright. New Repub 176:9-12 My 14 '77
Little fish inspires big ideas; snail darter and the Tellico Dam project. E. M. Leeper. map BioScience 27:697-9 O '77
Mighty, like a Furbish lousewort; Endangered Species Act. P. Steinhart. Audubon 79:121-5 My '77
Open season on wildlife laws; Endangered Species Act. il Nat Parks & Con Mag 51:21-2 My '77
Updating wildlife law; Endangered Species Act. U.S. News 82:66 Ap 25 '77
Washington lookout. R. Pardo. See issues of American forests
What they didn't tell you about the snail darter & the dam; question of Tennessee Valley Authority avoiding compliance with Endangered Species Act in Tellico Dam project. S. G. Cook and others. il map Nat Parks & Con Mag 51:10-13 My '77

Periodicals

See also
Conservationist (periodical)

Study and teaching

Energy and the schools. E. L. Boyer; K. C. Kryger; J. Silver and K. Johnson. bibl il Todays Educ 66:54-5+ S '77
Washington scene; Park Project on Energy Interpretation. B. Kravetz. Parks & Rec 12:48+ S '77
See also
Environmental education
United States—Youth Conservation Corps

Alaska

Fragile giant. R. F. Jones. Sports Illus 47:94-5 D 12 '77
Observations on Alaska. L. S. Clapper and others. il Am For 83:22-3+ F '77

CONSERVATION of works of art. See Art—Conservation and restoration

CONSERVATION officers
Environmental conservation officer. J. T. Lynch. il por Conservationist 32:28-31 N '77

CONSERVATION tillage. See Tillage

CONSERVATIONIST (periodical)
About this issue: change of editors. R. F. Hall. por Conservationist 31:43 Ja '77
All the smale foweles. J. J. DuPont. il Conservationist 31:1 My '77

CONSERVATISM
Balancing act; conservative publications by the Center for Constructive Alternatives, Hillsdale, Mich. M. J. Sobran, Jr. Nat R 29:1005-6 S 2 '77
Conservatives' drive for a stronger voice. P. L. Martin. il U.S. News 83:47 Jl 11 '77
Conservatives in the academy; educational organizations. R. Kirk. Nat R 29:889 Ag 5 '77
Glimpse of the American right; views of Newsweek. Nat R 29:1346 N 25 '77
Is America turning right? D. Gelman and others. il Newsweek 90:34-6+ N 7 '77
Memo to: Bill Brock, nat'l chairman, GOP. Nat R 29:1474+ D 23 '77
New activists. R. Boeth and others. il Newsweek 90:41 N 7 '77
Operation Trojan donkey. D. Lindquist. Nat R 29:1234-6 O 28 '77
Plunder on the right; movement to impeach A. Young. K. Bode. New Repub 177:11-12 N 12 '77
Second spring of American conservatism; adaptation of address. S. J. Tonsor. Nat R 29:1103-7 S 30 '77
Self-image of a natural aristocracy: what flows from neo-conservatism. I. Silver. Nation 225:44-51 Jl 9 '77
See also
Young Americans for Freedom (organization)

Bibliography

Right of center. J. M. Hillard. Wilson Lib Bull 52:74-5 S '77

CONSERVATIVE Judaism. See Judaism

CONSERVATORSHIPS. See Guardian and ward

CONSIDINE, Bob
Unforgettable Bob Considine. S. Pett. il Read Digest 111:87-90 Jl '77 *

CONSOLES (sound) See Sound—Apparatus

CONSOLIDATED Edison Company of New York
Bolt of lightning, then—; New York City blackout. il U.S. News 83:22-3 Jl 25 '77
Catharsis time again at Con Ed. il por Time 110:46-7 Jl 25 '77
Electrocuting Con Edison. il Time 110:51 Ag 15 '77
Environmentalism and the leisure class; public fight against building of Storm King plant. W. Tucker. il map Harpers 225:49-56+ D '77
Is the improvement real at Con Edison? il Bus W p44+ My 30 '77
Must we try for blackout III? J. Wicklein. il Progressive 41:16-20 N '77
New York blackout: weak links tie Con Ed to neighboring utilities. W. D. Metz. Science 197:441-2 Jl 29 '77
New York's Con Ed counts its casualties. il Bus W p 19-20 Ag 1 '77
Why it happened; New York City blackout. A. J. Mayer and others. il map Newsweek 90:27-9 Jl 25 '77
Why the lights went out. map Time 110:24-5 Jl 25 '77

Anecdotes, facetiae, satire, etc.

Good explanation. I. Frazier. New Yorker 53:27 Ag 1 '77

CONSOLIDATED Foods Corporation
John H. Bryan Jr. of Consolidated Foods: right place. por Forbes 119:95 F 15 '77

CONSOLIDATED Rail Corporation
After years of decay, the railroads are coming to life. il map U.S. News 82:70-2 F 21 '77
Conrail's first year: a good track record. il Bus W p96-7+ Ap 11 '77
How Buffalo dented the Conrail budget. Bus W p32 F 21 '77

CONSOLIDATION Coal Company. See Coal industry—United States

CONSOLIDATIONS and mergers. See Corporations—Acquisitions and mergers

CONSOLINO, Joseph
PW interviews; ed by I. Kropotkin. il por Pub W 212:8-10 Jl 25 '77

CONSOMMÉ. See Soups

CONSORTS (music) See Instrumental ensembles

CONSPIRACY of Pontiac. See Pontiac's Conspiracy, 1763-1765

CONSROE, Paul. See Martin, P. jt auth

CONSTANS, J. and Viau, M.
Group-specific components: evidence for two subtypes of the Gc[1] gene. bibl il Science 198:1070-1 D 9 '77

CONSTANTINE, Robert J.
Testing CB transceivers. il Radio-Electr 48:51-3+ S '77

CONSTELLATIONS
Canopus: only no. 2, but stars as a pilot. K. L. Franklin. il Sci Digest 82:20-2 Jl '77
Far-ultraviolet rocket survey of Orion. G. R. Carruthers and C. B. Opal. il Sky & Tel 53:270-5 Ap '77
Rambling through [the month] skies. G. Lovi. See issues of Sky and telescope

CONSTIPATION
Constipation. A. Frank and S. Frank. Mademoiselle 83:267 Ap '77

CONSTITUTIONAL amendments. See United States—Constitution—Amendments

CONSTITUTIONAL conventions
Why a constitutional convention is needed; human life amendment. E. J. McMahon. America 137:12-14 Jl 2 '77

CONSTITUTIONAL law
See also
Civil rights
Due process of law
United States—Constitutional law

CONSTITUTIONS
See also
Russia—Constitution
United States—Constitution

CONSTRUCCIONES Aeronauticas, S.A. See Airplane industry—Spain

CONSTRUCTION. See Building

CONSTRUCTION, Concrete. See Concrete construction

CONSTRUCTION, Modular. See Modular construction

CONSTRUCTION contracts. See Building—Contracts and specifications

CONSTRUCTION equipment
Alyeska Pipeline's hugh surplus sale: machines, materials, and construction camp facilities. il Bus W p35-6 Ja 31 '77

CONSTRUCTION industry
Boom in housing? Or a coming bust? il Forbes 119:293 My 15 '77
Builders see steady sales; farm builders. J. Russell. il Farm J 101:Hog 16 D '77
Construction's solid 1978. il Bus W p38-9 N 14 '77
Dodge/Sweet's construction outlook, 1977: first update; it's looking bigger by the minute. G. A. Christie. il Archit Rec 161:63+ Mr '77
Dodge/Sweet's construction outlook: 1978 the fuller development of nonresidential markets is expected. il Archit Rec 162:55+ N '77
Five-year forecast: is there growth after recovery? G. A. Christie. il Archit Rec 161:65-6 My '77
Fresh drive to put union label on more construction jobs. il U.S. News 82:79-80 F 28 '77
Homebuilders will keep on hammering hard. il Fortune 96:22+ O '77
Housing boom has strong coattails. Bus W p38+ Je 13 '77
Housing industry gets a new lease on life. il U.S. News 82:37-8 F 7 '77
Housing industry watches sales soften. il Bus W p34 O 24 '77
Housing's hot pace will cool. il Bus W p31-2 D 5 '77
If you can't move, improve; home improvement industry. H. Rudnitsky. il Forbes 120:46-8+ Ag 15 '77
Ira Koger's friendly rathole; suburban office builder Koger Properties, Inc. il Forbes 119:141-2 My 15 '77
Labor tests Carter with a picketing bill. Bus W p27 F 28 '77
Life after the post office; Blount, Inc. por Forbes 119:142 Ap 15 '77
New Levitt Corp. rises from the dust. il Bus W p27 Jl 11 '77
New start for housing: what we need most are new approaches. W. F. Wagner, Jr. Archit Rec 161:13 Ap '77
New year, new administration, new hope, new concerns. W. F. Wagner, Jr. Archit Rec 161:13 Ja '77
1977 Dodge/Sweet's construction outlook: second update: more gains in architectural work are expected. G. A. Christie. il Archit Rec 162:55+ Ag '77
Parsons: from family business to industry leader. por Duns R 109:18-19 My '77
Profile: W. J. Levitt. J. H. Ingersoll. il por House B 119:12+ Jl '77
Real estate without tears. por Forbes 119:57-8 Je 1 '77
Regional activity in 1976 showed the shifts have stabilized. G. A. Christie. il Archit Rec 161:67 F '77
Those happy homebuilders should be even happier. il Fortune 95:10+ Ap '77
See also
Associated General Contractors of America
Bechtel Corporation
Building materials industry
Collective bargaining—Construction industry
Contractors
Engineering construction companies
National Construction Industry Council
National Institute of Building Sciences

Acquisitions and mergers

Contractor buys some brains; Raymond International takeover of Kaiser Engineers. Forbes 120:32 O 15 '77

Employees

See also
Construction workers

Finance

Building financing. G. A. Christie. il Archit Rec 161:73 Ap; 162:51 Jl; 61 O '77
Construction. il Forbes 121:88+ Ja 9 '78

Information services

Inexpensive, fast estimating services provide second source costs; Wood and Tower, Inc. il Archit Rec 161:64-5 F '77
Southern newsletter delivers 12 new project leads per week; Consulting Opportunities newsletter. il Archit Rec 162:59 S '77

International aspects

Squeeze tightens on building overseas. il U.S. News 83:65 D 12 '77

Management

Construction management, in a Miami test, saves $1.5 million. il Archit Rec 161:75-8 Ja '77

Arab countries

Snag in Arab contracts. il Bus W p85 Ap 25 '77

Germany, West

Algerian venture sinks a developer; Bremer Treuhand. il Bus W p30-1 Jl 18 '77

Great Britain

Britain's economic travails leave a quarter of its architects unemployed and put a third of its private firms out of business. M. Burns and T. Marshall. Archit Rec 161:36 Ja '77

CONSTRUCTION industry—*Continued*

Italy

Salvage job to stave off a banking crisis. il Bus W p40 My 2 '77

Korea, South

Korea's crucial link to the Middle East. il Bus W p41 Ag 1 '77

CONSTRUCTION materials. See Building materials

CONSTRUCTION Safety Standards regulations. See Building laws and regulations

CONSTRUCTION sets, Toy. See Toys

CONSTRUCTION Specifications Institute. See Building—Contracts and specifications

CONSTRUCTION workers

Open-shop construction picks up momentum. il Bus W p 108-9 D 12 '77

See also

Trade unions—Construction workers

CONSULAR Service. See United States—Diplomatic and Consular Service

CONSULTANT writing. See Authorship

CONSULTANTS

How much insulation do you need? thermography consultants. House & Gard 149:96 S '77

See also

Agricultural consultants
Business consultants
Consulting engineers
Educational consultants
Government consultants
Public relations consultants
Tax consultants

CONSULTING engineers

All stick and no carrot; Ford, Bacon & Davis. il Forbes 119:73-4 Je 1 '77

Consulting for fun and profit. C. Goodman. bibl il Phys Today 30:44-6+ S '77

See also

American Consulting Engineers Council

CONSULTING Opportunities (firm) See Construction industry—Information services

CONSUMER bankruptcy. See Bankruptcy

CONSUMER complaints. See Complaints

CONSUMER credit. See Credit

CONSUMER education

Handbook of buying issue. il Consumers Res Mag 60:1-224 O '77

1978 buying guide issue. il Consumer Rep 42:1-431 D '77

See also

Consumer protection

CONSUMER Electronics Show. See Home electronics—Exhibitions

CONSUMER fraud. See Fraud

CONSUMER goods. See Commercial products

CONSUMER price index. See Price indexes

CONSUMER Product Safety Commission. See United States—Consumer Product Safety Commission

CONSUMER protection

Ban the ban; safety of products as judged by Consumer reports. Nat R 29:818-19 Jl 22 '77

Behind the fronts: phony consumer groups; industry-backed groups. D. H. Rothman. Nation 225:239-42 S 17 '77

Consumer information; Federal agencies and information centers. Consumer Rep 42:355-60 D '77

Consumerism and the economic dope habit; address, August 17, 1977. R. J. Buckley. Vital Speeches 44:145-50 D 15 '77

Consumers challenge legal monopoly. D. Maron. Intellect 105:333-5 Ap '77

Could a complaint agency help you? Changing T 31:41-3 D '77

Four women who can improve your life; government's new consumer advocates. J. Carper. il Am Home 80:42-3 Ag '77

Got a lemon? how to get the drop on Detroit. R. Lund. il Pop Mech 149:84-5+ Ja '78

Is Nader losing his clout? por U.S. News 83:18 D 19 '77

Local muscle for consumers; government agencies. il Bus W p 143-4+ S 26 '77

Nader group finds wide variations in medicare fees for common surgery; the Health Research Group. Ret Liv 17:15 Ap '77

Nader: success or excess? il por Time 110:76+ N 14 '77

Pain clinics. J. Greenwald. McCalls 104:46-7 Mr '77

Palooka principle. P. Fasolino. por Newsweek 89:11 Je 13 '77

Q&A about consumer concerns. C. Henry. See issues of Retirement living

Ralph Nader reports. R. Nader. See issues of Ladies' home journal

Things are getting better faster for consumers. il Changing T 31:17-18 F '77

What the Government can—and cannot—do to protect the public; interview. S. J. Byington. il por U.S. News 83:33-5 O 24 '77

When consumers tackle the phone companies—. il U.S. News 83:71 Jl 11 '77

See also

Better business bureaus
Consumers' Research, Inc
Consumers Union of United States
Quality of products
Unit pricing
United States—Agency for Consumer Advocacy (proposed)
United States—Consumer Product Safety Commission
Warranty

Laws and legislation

Coming: a rush of new consumer-safety rules. U.S. News 83:61 Jl 18 '77

Do-it-yourself consumerism. J. Carper. Am Home 80:18 Ag '77

Docket. See issues of Consumer reports

From Washington. See alternate issues of Changing times

Has emotion tipped the scales on consumer safety? address, October 17, 1977. J. W. Hanley. Vital Speeches 44:92-5 N 15 '77

We've been asked: about crackdown on bill collectors; Fair Debt Collection Practices Act. il U.S. News 83:48 O 10 '77

When the government's regulations boomerang—. C. E. Mayer. il U.S. News 83:89-91 S 19 '77

See also

House buying—Laws and legislation
United States—Federal Trade Commission

CONSUMER relations. See Customer relations

CONSUMER reports (periodical)

Ban the ban; safety of products as judged by Consumer reports. Nat R 29:818-19 Jl 22 '77

Whisperings in the press gallery; periodical correspondents banned from Congress. P. H. Schuck. Harpers 254:113-17 Mr '77; Reply. N. MacNeil. 254:113+ Mr '77

CONSUMERS

How U.S. consumers view energy crisis; University of Texas study. S. C. Lopreato and W. Cunningham. Intellect 106:95+ S '77

Metamorphosis in the marketplace? R. Levy. il Duns R 109:65-7 F '77

Power of women consumers. N. McKeon. Harp Baz 111:153+ N '77

Public trust in business: it's increasing, but—. il U.S. News 82:26-8 Je 27 '77

Speaker for the house. C. Montgomery. See issues of Good housekeeping

Tips for the consumer. See issues of Consumers' research magazine

See also

Consumer education
Consumer protection
Youth market

CONSUMERS Power Company

Nuclear partners: adversity breeds trouble between Dow and utility. L. J. Carter. Science 195:162-3 Ja 14 '77

Outrageous Mr Cherry and the underachieving nukes; controversy surrounding construction of nuclear power plant in Midland, Mich. F. Graham, Jr. il por Audubon 79:50-67 S '77; Discussion. 79:128-30 N '77

Who's in charge here? Forbes 119:60 Mr 1 '77

CONSUMERS' Research, Inc

50 years of faithful service to the consumer. il Consumers Res Mag 60:1-2 O '77

CONSUMERS Union of United States

Seven directors elected to seats on CU's board. Consumer Rep 43:6 Ja '78

U.S. court lowers barriers to CU legal directory. Consumer Rep 42:70 F '77

See also

Consumer reports (periodical)

CONSUMPTION (economics)

Americans: splurging in big ways, cutting back in small ones. il U.S. News 82:26-7 Ap 25 '77

Big shifts in how Americans spend their dollars. il U.S. News 83:76-7 O 31 '77

Coming slowdown in retail spending. S. H. Wildstrom. Bus W p32 Je 13 '77

Consumer: ready to spend. A. Hershman. il Duns R 110:55-7 N '77

Consumer spending extends its run. N. Jonas. Bus W p32 D 5 '77

Consumers in a buying mood—big lift for business. il U.S. News 82:27-8 Je 6 '77

Family spending habits; Bureau of Labor Statistics survey. Society 14:5-6 S '77

New breed of consumer: growing challenge to business. il U.S. News 83:45-6 Jl 25 '77

New two-tier market for consumer goods. il Bus W p80+ Ap 11 '77

On consuming the surplus; excerpt from Toward socialism in America. H. Freeman. Progressive 41:20-1 F '77

Surge ahead for business—. il U.S. News 82:20-1 Ap 4 '77

Tax that is killing investment: capital gains; views of W. F. Ballhaus. J. Cobbs. il Bus W p 14+ Ja 16 '78

Trade shows leave retailers wondering; Dallas home furnishings mart and the Chicago housewares exposition. il Bus W p55 Jl 25 '77

CONSUMPTION (economics)—*Continued*
Waiting for some Christmas cheer. Fortune 96: 19+ N '77
What lies beyond retailing's mini-recession. il Fortune 96:14 Ag '77
See also
Consumers

Poland

Wheeling and dealing; used-car capitalism in Warsaw. Time 109:40 Je 6 '77

CONTACT cement adhesives. See Adhesives

CONTACT improvisation. See Improvisation (dance)

CONTACT lenses
Contact lenses; soft lenses; interview. J. P. Dodd. Harp Baz 110:117+ Ag '77
Contacts. G. C. Larson. Flying 101:85 O '77
Cut-rate contacts. J. Carper. il Am Home 80:16 Jl '77
Development in contacts provide a wider choice. R. Field. il pors Sci Digest 82:86-7+ Jl '77
Future sight. J. Carper. Am Home 80:23+ S '77
Making contact. D. R. Zimmerman. il N Y Times Mag p66-7+ F 20 '77

CONTACT printing. See Photography—Printing processes

CONTAINER gardening
Containers give you more garden. M. C. Goldman. il Org Gard & Farm 24:80-3 O '77
Herbs in a small place. J. Meeker. il por Org Gard & Farm 24:53-6 N '77
Places rock gardeners get into. il Sunset 159: 224-5 N '77
Stand-up gardening at Shady Lane. E. Pearson. il Org Gard & Farm 24:106-8 My '77
Unlikely story—container melons. il Sunset 158: 260-1 My '77
What can you do about those thirsty pots? il Sunset 158:96-7 Je '77
See also
Balcony gardens, roof gardens, etc.
Flower boxes, planters, etc.
Hanging plants
Indoor gardening

CONTAINER industry
See also
American Can Company
Collective bargaining—Container industry
Continental Group, Inc

CONTAINERIZATION (freight)
Contagious tie-up on the docks. il Bus W p33-4 O 24 '77
Container woes in dockland. il Time 110:53-4 O 17 '77
General cargo: on the twenty-fifth anniversary of containerization. G. Knight. il Oceans 10: 38-45 Mr '77
Off the waterfront. T. Nicholson and D. Witherspoon. il Newsweek 90:93 O 24 '77
Ship containerization: an exploding industry. il Forbes 120:47-8 S 1 '77

CONTAINERS
Locking and sealing storage containers; ceramic containers for food storage. D. Hendley. il Ceram Mo 25:60-3 F '77
Profit in bottle laws; standardized reusable container system. L. D. Orr; reply with rejoinder. J. V. Waggoner. Environment 19:42-3 Ap '77
Wooden canisters you can build. il Org Gard & Farm 24:91-2 D '77
See also
Bags
Boxes, cases, etc.
Bottles
Cans
Incense burners and containers
Vases

CONTAINERS, Pressurized. See Pressure packaging

CONTAMINATED feeds. See Feeds—Contamination by drugs, pesticides, etc.

CONTAMINATED fish. See Fish contamination

CONTEMPLATION. See Meditation

CONTEMPORARY Chamber Players. See Chamber orchestras

CONTEMPORARY Dancers, Winnipeg. See Dance companies

CONTEMPORARY furniture. See Furniture

CONTENTMENT
Cancelling contentment. E. Schaeffer. Chr Today 21:27 Ag 26 '77
See also
Happiness

Les CONTES d'Hoffmann; opera. See Offenbach, J.

CONTESTS. See Competitions

CONTINENTAL Air lines
CAB proposes Continental for South Pacific. Aviation W 106:31 My 16 '77
Continental readies South Pacific push. J. M. Lenorovitz. Aviation W 107:31-3+ D 19 '77
Continental readying Pacific service. J. M. Lenorovitz. map Aviation W 107:36-7 S 5 '77
Landing rights clouding Continental Pacific route. Aviation W 107:30 Ag 1 '77
Saipan authority clouds Japanese bilateral talks. L. Doty. Aviation W 106:27-8 My 30 '77

CONTINENTAL Baking Company. See ITT Continental Baking Company

CONTINENTAL Congress. See United States—Continental Congress

CONTINENTAL Copper & Steel Industries, Inc
Copper and irony. il Forbes 119:56+ Je 15 '77

CONTINENTAL drift
Collision between India and Eurasia. P. Molnar and P. Tapponnier. il maps Sci Am 236:30-41 bibl(p 148) Ap '77
Continental drift affair. S. J. Gould. Natur Hist 86:12 F '77
Extra continent may have existed; Pacifica. il Sci N 111:389 Je 18 '77
New arrangement of southern continents. il Sci N 111:372 Je 11 '77

CONTINENTAL Group, Inc
How Bob Hatfield keeps Continental growing and prospering; interview. R. S. Hatfield. il pors Nations Bus 65:68-70+ S '77

CONTINENTAL Illinois Corporation
Chicago's unique unbranched banking. il Bus W p66-8 Jl 18 '77

CONTINENTAL Oil Company
Do coal and oil mix? ownership of Consolidation Coal. J. Cook. il Forbes 120:138+ O 15 '77

CONTINENTAL shelf
Danger to artifacts on the continental shelf. Intellect 105:304 Mr '77
Resources of continental margins: perspectives on a program for their management. C. N. K. Mooers and J. M. Hall. il Oceans 10:61-3 Mr '77

CONTINENTS
Oldest rocks and the growth of continents. S. Moorbath. il maps Sci Am 236:92-104 bibl (p 150) Mr '77
See also
Continental drift

CONTINUING education. See Adult education

CONTINUING Library Education Network and Exchange. See Library schools and education

CONTINUOUS sessions. See School year

CONTOUR farming
Terracing and contour farming to stop hillside erosion. G. Logsdon. il Org Gard & Farm 24:64-7 Ap '77

CONTRABAND trade. See Smuggling

CONTRACEPTION. See Birth control

CONTRACEPTIVES
Another alternative to the pill; Encare Oval. J. Chan. McCalls 105:40 Ja '78
Back to foam? excerpt from Women and the crisis in sex hormones. B. Seaman. Ms 6:16-18 Ag '77
Birth control: if not the pill, what? M. L. Schildkraut. il Good H 185:201-3 Ag '77
Birth control preview. E. Kaplan; K. Larson; J. Rodgers. Ladies Home J 94:60+ Ag '77
Birth control: what's new, safe and fool-proof. L. Pembrook. il Parents Mag 52:74+ N '77
Contraceptive use has changed dramatically since 1965. J. Gaylin. Psychol Today 11:43-4 O '77
Controls on male fertility now seem within our reach. A. Rosenfeld. il Smithsonian 8:36-43 Jl '77
Dalkon shield: collusion? Society 14:4 My '77
Facts about a controversial contraceptive; Depo-Provera. L. Prinz. McCalls 105:39-40 Ja '78
Final victory; connection between the pill and breast cancer. N. S. Greenfield. Good H 184: 103+ Ap '77
Long look at contraception. Fam Health 9:60 Ap '77
On the way: fail-safe birth control. A. A. Belson. Vogue 167:234-5+ Mr '77
Rating the contraceptives. J. H. Wear. Harp Baz 110:88-9+ Je '77
Safest diet for every woman on the pill; nutritional side effects. F. J. Stare and E. M. Whelan. Harp Baz 110:120+ Ag '77
Smoking and the pill. il Newsweek 89:65 Ap 11 '77
Steroid contraceptive use and cervical dysplasia: increased risk of progession. E. Stern and others. bibl il Science 196:1460-2 Je 24 '77
What we know now about the pill. il Changing T 31:21-3 Jl '77
Who shouldn't take the pill. J. Chan. McCalls 104:65-6 Jl '77

CONTRA COSTA County, Calif.
Sludge, garbage may fuel California sewage plant. R. B. Sieger and B. D. Bracken. il Am City & County 92:37-8 Ja '77

CONTRACTION, Muscular. See Muscle contraction

CONTRACTORS
Finding and working with a contractor. M. D. Hinds. House & Gard 149:110+ My '77
Texas-Saudi affair; Saudi investments in Sam P. Wallace Co. il Forbes 120:88 O 1 '77
Which contractors and why. S. Auerbach. Am Home 80:21 S '77
See also
Associated General Contractors of America

CONTRACTS
Gobbledygook; readability of legal agreements. R. Nader. Ladies Home J 94:68 S '77
Uranium thing; utilities suing Westinghouse over uranium contracts. A. J. Mayer and P. L. Abraham. il Newsweek 89:73 F 14 '77
See also
Artists contracts
Building—Contracts and specifications
Collective labor agreements
Gold clauses

Arbitration
See Arbitration and award

CONTRACTS, Agricultural
How and why farmers use forward contracts. L. Palmer. Farm J 101:L8 Ap '77
How to make a tax-tight deferred sales contract; grain contracts. A. Brennecke. Suc Farm 75: K2 S '77
Legal side of forward contracts. il Suc Farm 75: no4 L8 Mr '77
Sharing agreements. S. Cain. il Suc Farm 75: 30-1 O '77
What you should know about price later agreements; grain contracts. Suc Farm 75:8 S '77

CONTRACTS, Authors. See Authors and publishers

CONTRACTS, Government
Black capitalism runs into tough sledding. il U.S. News 83:26 D 5 '77
Boeing, Vought win rocket contracts. Aviation W 107:26 S 26 '77
Business, too, tests reverse discrimination; Associated General Contractors' suits. il Bus W p40-1 N 14 '77
Case for private industry—2. R. V. Paolucci. Aviation W 107:7 Ag 1 '77
Information Act invoked in contracting. E. Kozicharow. Aviation W 106:19+ F 7 '77
One way to shrink government employment; service contracts. W. Kroger. il Nations Bus 65: 39-42 D '77
Rockwell's bombshell; loss of the B-1 bomber program. D. Pauly and D. Gram. il Newsweek 90:61-2 Jl 11 '77
SBA scandals: whites bilk black fronts. A. Poinsett. il Ebony 32:75-6+ O '77
Solar awards mark multi-mission start. Aviation W 106:19 Ja 3 '77
Status of major U.S. European defense, aerospace programs. Aviation W 106:10-15 Mr 21 '77
Sweet crude, sweet profits. Forbes 120:40 N 15 '77
Swords and plowshares; project in Calif. area to sway companies from military contracts. S. H. Day, Jr. Bull Atom Sci 33:4-5 N '77
TDRSS won by Western Union. C. Covault. il Aviation W 106:14-16 Ja 3 '77
Thinking about tomorrow; address, October 17, 1977. R. E. Hilchey. Vital Speeches 44:88-92 N 15 '77
UTC prepares for shuttle booster role. Aviation W 106:15 Ja 3 '77
Uncle Sam as customer; service contracts. Forbes 119:22 F 1 '77
See also
Military-industrial complex
Municipal contracts
Munitions
Purchasing, Government
United States—Army—Procurement
United States—Defense, Department of—Procurement
United States—Labor, Department of—Federal Contract Compliance, Office of
United States—Navy—Procurement

International aspects
General Dynamics struggles to build a plane for all nations; F-16. L. Kraar. il Fortune 95: 180-4+ Mr '77

Renegotiation
Renegotiation hearing cites Lockheed. Aviation W 106:24-5 Je 20 '77
See also
United States—Renegotiation Board

Arab Countries
Petrogrants. M. Sheils. il Newsweek 90:75 Jl 4 '77

Australia
ITT's strategy may benefit a competitor. Bus W p57+ S 12 '77

Canada
Fighter contract tied to jobs. Bus W p42 S 12 '77

Iran
U.S. firms getting approval for Iranian avionics supply; Ibex system. Aviation W 106:15 Ja 10 '77

Iraq
New scramble for $8 billion in contracts. il Bus W p41 Je 6 '77

Poland
Dos and don'ts of landing a Polish contract. A. Hertzberg. Forbes 120:46 Jl 1 '77

Saudi Arabia
Saudis say wrong numbers to the U.S. Bus W p20-1 Ja 9 '78
Wrong number; Americans lose telecommunications contract. D. Pauly and E. Shannon. Newsweek 90:78 D 26 '77

Underdeveloped areas
Great world telephone war. W. Guzzardi, Jr. il Fortune 96:142-7+ Ag '77

CONTRACTS, Marriage. See Marriage contracts

CONTRERAS, Joseph
Practical inducements for studying foreign languages. bibl Clearing H 50:407-9 My '77

CONTROL Data Corporation
Reaction at computer firm: more pluses than minuses; alternative work schedule program. M. A. Hopp and C. R. Sommerstad. il M Labor R 100:69-71 F '77

CONTROL of insects. See Insect control

CONTROL of temperature. See Temperature—Control

CONTROL systems, Biological. See Biological control systems

CONTROLLED Ecosystem Pollution Experiment. See United States—National Science Foundation

CONTROLLERS. See Executives

CONVALESCENT homes. See Nursing homes

CONVENIENCE foods
Eating well—with convenience foods. il Redbook 149:120-1+ Jl '77
Fast food at home; with recipes. il Ladies Home J 94:138-9+ O; 106 N '77
Fast food shops. Mech Illus 73:20 My '77
Instant breakfasts nutritious junk food? il Consumer Rep 42:324-7 Je '77
Junk food diet; College survival tipsheet. J. S. Stern. Mademoiselle 83:178-9 Ag '77
No time to cook; menus with recipes. See issues of McCall's
Supermarket: camp cook outfitter. S. Bashline. il Field & S 82:70+ My '77

CONVENIENCE stores. See Food stores

CONVENTION delegates, Democratic. See National conventions, Democratic

CONVENTION expense deductions. See Income tax—Deductions

CONVENTION on International Trade in Endangered Species of Wild Fauna and Flora
International treaty boosted. il Nat Parks & Con Mag 51:26 F '77

CONVENTION on the Prevention and Punishment of the Crime of Genocide. See Genocide

CONVENTIONS
Conventions. See issues of American city & county to May 1977

CONVENTIONS, Constitutional. See Constitutional conventions

CONVENTS and nunneries
See also
Abbeys

CONVERSATION
Chop the chitchat—save time and money. C. H. Ford. il Nations Bus 65:35-6+ S '77
Conversation and literature; address, September 14, 1977. G. P. Rice, Jr. Vital Speeches 43:749-53 O 1 '77
Fine art of conversation. S. Schraub. House B 119:74+ N '77

CONVERSATION radio programs. See Radio programs—Conversation programs

CONVERSION
See also
Converts

CONVERSION tables
Quick hex-decimal conversions. R. J. Bell. il Pop Electr 12:72 D '77

CONVERTERS, Digital to analog. See Computers—Input-output equipment; Digital electronics

CONVERTERS, Frequency. See Frequency changers

CONVERTIBLE airplanes. See Airplanes, Convertible

CONVERTIBLE bonds. See Bonds, Convertible

CONVERTIBLE furniture. See Furniture, Convertible

CONVERTIBLES (automobiles) See Automobiles

CONVERTS
Flynt's odyssey. Chr Today 22:50-2 D 9 '77
Hustling for the Lord; question of L. Flynt's motivation. T. Schwartz and others. il pors Newsweek 90:61 D 5 '77
I'll be a hustler for the Lord; L. Flynt. il por Time 110:112 D 5 '77
Who will be next? L. Flynt. Chr Today 22:26-7 D 30 '77

CONVICT labor
Jobs behind bars: boon to prisoners and taxpayers. il U.S. News 82:60 Je 20 '77
Where prison shops run like businesses. il Bus W p56+ Jl 18 '77

CONVICTS. See Prisoners
CONVULSIONS
Cannabinoid induced behavioral convulsions in rabbits. P. Martin and P. Consroe; reply with rejoinder. D. M. Feeney. bibl Science 197:1301-2 S 23 '77
See also
Epilepsy
CONWAY, John Horton
Mathematical games: are they bona fide research? G. B. Kolata. Science 197:546 Ag 5 '77 *
CONWAY, William, Cardinal
Death comes for a cardinal. J. Cooney. Commonweal 104:326-7 My 27 '77 *
Requiem for a Cardinal. T. P. O'Mahony. America 136:445-6 My 14 '77 *
CONWAY, William G.
Case against urban dinosaurs. il Sat R 4:12+ My 14; 10 S 17 '77
People fire in the ghetto ashes. il Sat R 4:15-16 Jl 23 '77
COOK, Adrian
Ashes and blood. il Am Hist Illus 12:30-40 Ag '77
COOK, Arnold
Christian witness in Rhodesia. Chr Cent 94:444-5 My 11 '77
COOK, Barbara
Barbara Cook: fat can set you free; interview, ed by L. C. Pogrebin. il pors Ms 6:50-2 S '77
COOK, Betty
Betty Cook is one hard-driving lady. T. West. il por Motor B & S 140:64-5+ S '77 *
Out on the verge, but far from foolish. D. S. Looney. il por Sports Illus 46:16-17 Mr 14 '77 *
COOK, Chauncey William Wallace
Stricter code of ethics; excerpt from address. Intellect 106:186 N '77
COOK, Don
Reports & comment: Belgrade: spinning a European web. Atlantic 240:6+ N '77
Reports & comment: Common Market. por Atlantic 239:14-16+ Ap '77
Reports & comment: France: the making of the elite. il Atlantic 240:16-18+ Jl '77
COOK, Edward R. and Jacoby, G. C. Jr
Tree-ring—drought relationships in the Hudson Valley, New York. bibl il Science 198:399-401 O 28 '77
COOK, Edward Willingham
Ned Cook in the agonies of corporate confession. L. Beman. il por Fortune 95:340-3+ My '77 *
COOK, J. Marvin
Measurement of affective art objectives. il Sch Arts 77:14-17 O '77
COOK, Jimmie E.
Teacher survival kit: the dictionary. Educ Digest 42:36-7 Ja '77
COOK, Richard Okey
Reporter at large. J. McPhee. New Yorker 53:43-4+ Je 20; 55-72 Jl 11 '77 *
COOK, Robert Edward
Raymond Lindeman and the trophic-dynamic concept in ecology. bibl Science 198:22-6 O 7 '77
COOK, Rodger
25 Vette tips. il Hot Rod 30:52-5+ S '77
COOK, Sara Grigsby, and others
What they didn't tell you about the snail darter & the dam. il map Nat Parks & Con Mag 51:10-13 My '77
COOK, Terry
Wonderfulness of it all. il Car & Dr 23:81-2 S '77
COOK, Thomas, and Son, Ltd
Corporate travel revives Cook's. il Bus W p 116+ O 3 '77
COOK books. See Cookbooks
COOK County Jail. See Chicago—Prisons and reformatories
COOK Industries, Inc. See Grain trade
COOK Islands
See also
Rarotonga
COOKBOOKS
Community cookbook (cont) J. R. Stevens. il Ladies Home J 94:104+ F; 98+ Ap; 68+ Je; 98+ Jl; 144+ O '77
Culinary excursion; excerpts from Holiday magazine award cookbook; ed by R. L. Balzer and C. Turgeon. Holiday 57:6 N '76
Finding old cookbooks and new friends. J. Buie. House B 119:93+ Jl '77
Peter Rabbit's natural foods cookbook; excerpt. A. Dobrin. il McCalls 104:158-60+ My '77
Your own family's best-seller cookbook. M. Cavaiani. Ret Liv 16:39 D '76

Bibliography

Cookbooks: a gastronome's picks. il Time 110:63 D 19 '77
Cookbooks '77: a guide to the best of the year. H. McCully. House B 119:137+ O '77
Machine cookbooks; operating food processors. il House & Gard 149:131+ Je '77
Timesaving cookbooks. M. Hodgson. Am Home 80:72 Ag '77
COOKBOOKS for children
Basic ingredients: cookbooks for children. C. Jenks. bibl SLJ 23:120-1 Mr '77
Cookbooks for kids. K. Kushkin. il House & Gard 149:122+ My '77

Bibliography

Kids in the kitchen; with recipes. B. Foster. il N Y Times Mag p30-1 D 25 '77
COOKE, Alistair
Did Rose live happily ever after? il N Y Times Mag p60-4 My 8 '77
Mid-Atlantic man; interview, ed by R. Gelatt. por Sat R 5:46-7 O 1 '77
COOKE, Eileen D. and Henderson, C. C.
ALA Washington notes. See issues of Wilson library bulletin to June 1977
—and Sprouse, H. W.
ALA Washington notes. See issues of Wilson library bulletin, September 1977-
COOKE, Michael G.
No image for soccer. New Repub 177:28-9 Jl 23 '77
COOKE, Steve
Drives with one hound. il por Outdoor Life 160:90 S '77
COOKE, Tom
More winter sun in the Yucatán. House & Gard 149:114+ N '77
COOKERS, Fireless. See Fireless cookers
COOKERY
Bountiful kettle meals—the old ways and the new. R. Molter. il Parents Mag 52:70-2+ O '77
Classics from a slow cooker. il Bet Hom & Gard 55:58 S '77
Cook-off extravaganza. D. Eby and N. Byal. il Bet Hom & Gard 55:92-3 N '77
Cooking for busy families: how other families do it. S. P. Torpey. il Bet Hom & Gard 55:140-7+ My '77
Cooking for one or two. il Bet Hom & Gard 55:151-2 My '77
Cook's guide to food processors: new whiz in the kitchen; with recipes. il House & Gard 149:131+ Je '77
Crimson desserts—flaming. il Sunset 159:164 D '77
Date with a dish. See issues of Ebony
Delicious dollar-saving meatless meals. il Good H 185:144+ Ag '77
Eat. M. Cantwell. See issues of Mademoiselle
Fireplaces are for cooking, too. B. R. Rogers il Org Gard & Farm 24:132+ N '77
Flaming Christmas feasts. il Harp Baz 111:96-7+ D '77
Food. C. Claiborne and P. Franey. See issues of New York times magazine
Food. A. Gold and R. Fizdale. See issues of Vogue
Food for thought; questions and answers. C. Turgeon. Holiday 58:53+ Je '77
41 surefire ways to feed your family for less. H. P. Schoenberg. il Good H 184:208+ Ap '77
Fresh-from-the-garden cooking. R. Carrier. il pors House & Gard 149:151+ Mr '77
Good eating country style. M. Stewart. il pors House & Gard 149:134-5+ Je '77
Good Plains cooking from Rosalynn Carter; interview, ed by M. Burros. R. S. Carter. il por House & Gard 149:118-19+ F '77
Healthware; new cookware with recipes. il House & Gard 149:104-5+ Jl '77
Hot or cold cookbook. il Good H 185:130-9 Jl '77
House beautiful chef. J. Pepin. See issues of House beautiful
How I feed my husband, four children—and our dog—for $50 a week. il Good H 186:148+ Ja '78
Journal about home. See issues of Ladies' home journal
Joys of cooking with wood; excerpt from Wood heat. J. Vivian. il Org Gard & Farm 24:126+ N '77
Live-in bedrooms, moveable feasts. il Mademoiselle 83:192-9+ O '77
Lots for little: tempting high-protein dishes. il Parents Mag 52:64 Mr '77
Low-sodium recipes. il Bet Hom & Gard 55:182 Ap '77
McCall's cooking school. See issues of McCall's
Make now, serve later. il McCalls 105:224-5+ N '77
Matter of taste. R. Sokolov. See issues of Natural history
[Month] menus; with recipes. See issues of Sunset
Nobody ever tells you these things; questions and answers. H. McCully. See issue of House beautiful
101 marvelous main dishes. il Good H 185:148-61+ O '77
Opening moves: easy recipes from a hostess who knows the game; excerpt from Feast without fuss. P. Harlech. il Vogue 167:258+ S '77
Our compliments to the chefs. il McCalls 104:102-5+ Ap '77

COOKERY—*Continued*
Quick, delicious dinners for two. il McCalls 104:140-2+ Mr '77
Recipes from chefs at sea. Holiday 58:50-1 Je '77
Redbook's competent cook. See issues of Redbook
Skillet specials: terrific meals-in-one. S. B. Huffman. il Ladies Home J 94:128-30+ Ap '77
Some like it hot! il Seventeen 36:156-7 N '77
Streamlined homestyle. P. Sadowsky and G. Steves. il Am Home 80:31-5+ My '77
Summer-style eating; you never had it so fresh. S. P. Torpey. il Bet Hom & Gard 55:132-3+ Jl '77
Sunset's kitchen cabinet. See issues of Sunset
Super entrées with work-saving appliances. S. P. Torpey. il Bet Hom & Gard 55:134+ Jl '77
Susan, our beginning cook. See issues of Good housekeeping
Tasty dishes from low-sodium soups. il Bet Hom & Gard 55:36 Ag '77
There's so much more in Detroit! recipes from restaurants. W. Rossmann and I. Rossmann. il Sat Eve Post 249:18+ N '77
Try tabletop cookery. il Seventeen 36:136-8 F '77

See also
Appetizers
Aspic
Barbecue cookery
Bread
Breakfasts
Brunches
Buffet meals
Cake
Candy
Canning and preserving
Casserole cookery
Caterers and catering
Chowder
Christmas cookery
Confectionery
Cookbooks
Cookies
Crumbs (bread, cake, etc)
Curry
Custards
Desserts
Dinners and dining
Doughnuts
Dumplings
Entertaining
Fireless cookers
Food—Smoking
Food as gifts
Frying
Gastronomy
Ice cream, ices, etc.
Jelly, jam, etc.
Kitchen utensils and appliances
Lunches
Meals
Meringue
Microwave cookery
Pancakes, waffles, etc.
Pastry
Pickles and relishes
Pie
Puddings
Salads
Sandwiches
Sauces
Snacks
Soufflés
Soups
Steaming (cookery)
Stew
Tarts
Thanksgiving dinners
Toast
Wedding meals

Competitions

Announcing the winners of the great Bicentennial bake-out. il Sat Eve Post 249:102-4 S '77
Shakes; milkshake-making contest. New Yorker 53:32-3 Mr 28 '77

Anecdotes, facetiae, satire, etc.

Chicanery topples international chili king in Houston invitational! G. Lish. il Esquire 88:92+ N '77

Measurements

Do you know your cooking arithmetic? il Parents Mag 52:74 S '77
Take me to your liter; recipes with metric measurements. il Seventeen 36:258-9+ Ag '77

Study and teaching

LaVarenne: what's cooking in Paris. C. Turgeon. Holiday 58:50 Ap '77

Beer

Better batter. C. Claiborne and P. Franey. il N Y Times Mag p76 Je 5 '77

Cereals

See Cookery—Grain

Cheese

Cottage cheese delights. il Ladies Home J 94:96-8+ Je '77
Good to the last crumb. E. Jones. il N Y Times Mag p49 Ag 28 '77
No-meat loaf and cheese pie. Sunset 159:206 O '77
Say (gruyère) cheese. C. Claiborne and P. Franey. il N Y Times Mag p 106 Ap 24 '77
Three cheers for sour cottage sauce. il Sunset 159:68-9 Jl '77

See also
Cheesecake

Chocolate

Chocolate, the irresistable temptation; with recipes. H. McCully. House B 119:98-9+ Ap '77
Glorious chocolate. il Ladies Home J 94:132-3+ N '77

Dairy products

Delicious dairy dishes. il Ebony 32:138+ Je '77
Making a meal of eggs and cheese. il McCalls 105:178-9+ O '77

Eggs

Cheesy egg puff. E. W. Manning. il Farm J 101:58 Ja '77
Egg and us. C. Claiborne and P. Franey. il N Y Times Mag p64+ Je 26 '77
Eggs for two. il Sunset 158:218 My '77
Inviting new ideas for breakfast eggs. Parents Mag 52:46 Je '77
Original fast food. G. Steves. il Am Home 80:64-5+ Ap '77

See also
Omelets
Soufflés

Fish

Baking salmon the Indian way. B. C. Anderson. Field & S 82:99 Jl '77
Bass for the shore lunch. B. Cary. il Outdoor Life 159:122 Je '77
Chuck Marcusson has a way with fish; ed by M. Wiley. por Yachting 141:98 Je '77
Elegant fish dish; fillets of sole Florentine. M. J. Norton. il McCalls 104:109-10 Je '77
Fish for breakfast? il Sunset 158:130-1 Ap '77
Fish from sea to sea. N. Byal and G. Preator. il Bet Hom & Gard 55:136-42+ Ap '77
Fishing for compliments. . .the frozen way. H. Alpert. il Ret Liv 17:46-8 Ap '77
Five hard-to-find trout recipes. il Outdoor Life 159:152 Ap '77
From lake or stream to the table. il Ebony 32:144+ S '77
Go fish. G. Steves. il Am Home 80:60-1 Ap '77
Golden seafood platter. il McCalls 104:121-2 Ap '77
Great flavor catch! Fish dinners. il Good H 184:140-1 Mr '77
How to oven-fry a fish; excerpt from Seafood cook book. il Sunset 158:236 My '77
Inside the paper, fish smothered with shrimp, crab, shallot sauce. il Sunset 158:124 F '77
Master trout chef; recipes of Dick Haas. J. Cassell. il Outdoor Life 159:164 Mr '77
Pickled salmon as a starter. il Sunset 159:134 Jl '77
Quick, easy ways to fabulous fish. H. McCully. il House B 119:99+ Mr '77
Round, flat, and delicious; flounder. S. Bashline. il Field & S 82:76-7 Jl '77
Shad season. C. Claiborne and P. Franey. il N Y Times Mag p67 F 27 '77
Simple secrets of cooking fish. P. S. Soller. Redbook 149:116 Ag '77
Somewhere over the rainbow trout. il Fam Health 9:34-6+ My '77
Southern fish fries. J. Gould. il Outdoor Life 160:116 Ag '77
Succulent shad. S. Bashline. il Field & S 81:121-2 Ap '77
Whole fish spicily baked; red snapper Veracruz style. Sunset 159:204 O '77

See also
Chowder

Fruit

Alluring avocado. H. McCully. il House B 119:85-6+ Jl '77
Apple pizza for lunch or for dessert. il Sunset 158:232 Ap '77
Bananas: cook them for great new mealtime flavor! il Good H 185:169 Jl '77
Breakfast or dessert or wholesome snack—just fruit on toast. il Sunset 159:140 Ag '77
Cheese and figs into tulips. il Sunset 158:186 Je '77
Cherry plums in a tart—the pitting is easy. il Sunset 159:124 Jl '77
Citrus family in full 1977 dress. H. McCully. House B 119:109+ F '77
Cool and colorful ways with breakfast fruits. il Parents Mag 52:76 S '77
Fresh fruit & vegetable ideas from experts on the farm. S. P. Torpey. il Bet Hom & Gard 55:64-5+ Je '77
Grapes of plenty. il Ladies Home J 94:136-7+ O '77
Hot and cold bananas. il Ebony 32:132+ Jl '77
In praise of the versatile, beautiful banana. H. McCully. il House B 119:121+ O '77

COOKERY—Fruit—*Continued*
Let's go berrying! H. McCully. House B 119: 98-9+ Je '77
Melon. il Ladies Home J 94:66+ Ag '77
Melon treats. il Bet Hom & Gard 54:80-1 Ag '76
Mint and citrus consommé. il Sunset 159:246 O '77
Oranges. il Ladies Home J 94:126-7+ Ap '77
Palm readings; dates. R. Sokolov. il Natur Hist 86:114-17 O '77
Red, white, and blueberry. P. Schiller. Am Home 80:98 Je '77
Scandinavian soup uses dried fruits. il Sunset 158:208 Ap '77
Strawberry peak comes two weeks early this year; with recipes. il Sunset 158:198-9 Ap '77
Vitamin C-ooking. il Fam Health 9:42-3 F '77
We love apples. il House & Gard 149:171+ O '77
See also
Desserts

Game

Bushytail bonanza; squirrel dishes. S. Bashline. il Field & S 82:134+ N '77
Chuck full of flavor; woodchuck recipes. J. Cone. il Outdoor Life 159:124 My '77
Claiborne on deer and birds; recipes. C. Claiborne. Outdoor Life 160:172 O '77
Cooking venison: six traditional recipes from skilled game cooks. Outdoor Life 160:100 N '77
Creative ways to fix venison. S. Bashline. il Field & S 82:60+ D '77
Gardens & game: do-it-yourself meals; with recipes. S. Bashline. il Field & S 81:36+ F '77
My turn for the wurst; making sausages from pork and game meats. K. Green. Field & S 82:177-9+ N '77
Outdoor tips hasenpfeffer; traditional rabbit recipe. P. Kelsey. il Conservationist 31:44 N '76
Quail are quality. S. Bashline. il Field & S 82: 126+ O '77
See also
Stew

Garnishes

Elegant garnishes. il Good H 185:20 D '77
Give a pretty buildup to holiday foods. Parents Mag 52:94+ N '77

Grain

Converting to whole grains. M. Bremer. il Org Gard & Farm 25:128+ Ja '78
Cook's discovery; triticale; with recipes. il Sunset 158:222+ Ap '77
It's what makes whole grainers enthusiasts; triticale breads. il Sunset 159:210 N '77
Redbook's competent cook learns about grains. il Redbook 149:138-9+ O '77
Time for a bran new diet; South African research; with bran recipes. C. SerVaas. il Sat Eve Post 249:72-4 Mr '77
Whole grain cooking. Bet Hom & Gard 55:62 My '77

Herbs

Basics of cooking with herbs. B. Fisher. il Org Gard & Farm 24:96+ N '77
Bravo basil. D. Tobias. il Am Home 80:98-100 Ag '77
Green drink with comfrey. il Sunset 158:242 My '77
Herb-farm Christmas buffet for twelve. il Redbook 150:137-8 D '77
Quality of coriander; with recipe. R. Sokolov. Natur Hist 86:86-9 N '77

Honey

Just-for-fun recipes cooked up by food hobbyists. N. Byal. il Bet Hom & Gard 55:146-7+ O '77

Leftovers

Virtues of leftovers. C. Claiborne and P. Franey. il N Y Times Mag p88 Mr 13 '77

Liquors

ABC of fruit liqueurs. A. D. Blue. il House & Gard 149:160+ Mr '77
Cooking with wines/liqueurs. il Bet Hom & Gard 55:151-2 My '77
Sparkling Christmas spirits. E. Fried. il Harp Baz 111:98-9+ D '77
Sugar and spice liqueurs. A. D. Blue. il House & Gard 149:136+ D '77

Macaroni products

Buon appetito! pasta recipes. N. Hazelton. Nat R 29:156 F 4 '77
Chewy health noodles. il Sunset 158:118-19 My '77
Crusty noodle pancake—beef on top. il Sunset 158:192 My '77
Macaroni, cheese, two ways to go. Sunset 159: 244 O '77
Noodling around. il Seventeen 36:170-2+ O '77
Pasta perfect; using a pasta machine; with recipes. il McCalls 104:112+ F '77
Pastas. il Ebony 32:126+ Mr '77
Sauces, soup, cheese—with noodles. il Sunset 158:190 My '77
Spaghetti with a French accent. C. Claiborne and P. Franey. il N Y Times Mag p78+ O 2 '77

Maple syrup

Just-for-fun recipes cooked up by food hobbyists. N. Byal. il Bet Hom & Gard 55:142-3+ O '77

Meat

Appeal of veal. C. Claiborne and P. Franey. il N Y Times Mag p64 Je 19 '77
Barbecue innovations with less-expensive beef. il Sunset 159:80-2 Jl '77
Chinese-American beef ribs. il Bet Hom & Gard 55:188 N '77
Chinese jerky is moister and less brittle than cowboy jerky; beef jerky. Sunset 159:126 Jl '77
Chopped liver for gentiles. G. Lish. il Esquire 87:80-2 Mr '77
Close to the bone; braised shanks. C. Claiborne and P. Franey. il N Y Times Mag p 104 O 23 '77
Cold cut entrées. il Bet Hom & Gard 54:54 Ag '76
Cold meatballs for a warm night. il Sunset 159: 130 Ag '77
Cooking for two with a whole leg of lamb. il Sunset 158:122-3 F '77
Culinary champs solve hamburger problems. il Redbook 148:112-13+ F '77
Easter ham precarved and stuffed. E. W. Manning. il Farm J 101:41 Ap '77
Easy ground beef recipes. il Bet Hom & Gard 55:141-2 Jl '77
Favorites from the GH dining room; prune-stuffed roast pork. il Good H 185:310 N '77
15 all-time best meat buys and 20 stylish ways to serve them. il Bet Hom & Gard 55:106-14+ Mr '77
First you pound and brown two pounds of boneless round steak; Swiss steak. Sunset 158:194 Mr '77
Freeze-ahead main dishes for take-it-easy meals. R. Molter. il Parents Mag 52:48-50+ Jl '77
From Redbook readers: my favorite hamburger recipe. il Redbook 149:136-7+ S '77
Great ground beef casseroles. E. W. Manning. il Farm J 101:62-3 O '77
Ham bonuses. C. Claiborne and P. Franey. il N Y Times Mag p76 Ap 3 '77
Hamburger & hot dog cookbook. il Good H 184: 146-54 My '77
Hamburger high style. S. B. Huffman. il Ladies Home J 94:106-11+ S '77
Hearty meat pies of Quebec. il Sunset 159:158 D '77
International chef; Egyptian veal. L. Szathmary. Travel 148:16+ Jl '77
Italian beef rolls. il Good H 186:136 Ja '78
It's a Spanish-American hot dog bash. il Sunset 159:68-9 Ag '77
Lamb. il House & Gard 149:165-7 Ap '77
Make the most of meat. R. Molter. il Parents Mag 53:52-4+ Ja '78
Meat loaves. R. Molter. il Parents Mag 52:44-5+ Je '77
Meat loaves men like. E. W. Manning. il Farm J 101:42-3 F '77
Meat pies. il Bet Hom & Gard 55:117-18 Mr '77
Minute steak meals. il Bet Hom & Gard 55:184 N '77
Picnic salami. il Sunset 158:98-9 Je '77
Pork roast with caraway biscuits, sauerkraut, and black gravy. il Sunset 158:178 Mr '77
Roast dinner for two; pork tenderloin. il Bet Hom & Gard 55:188 S '77
Roast pork with winter vegetables. E. W. Manning. il Farm J 101:56-7 Ja '77
Round steak entrées. il Bet Hom & Gard 55: 131-2 F '77
Special savor of ham. il McCalls 104:156-7+ My '77
Spring comes in like a lamb. il McCalls 104:136-7+ Mr '77
Spring for lamb for spring. il Fam Health 9: 40-2+ Ap '77
Sublime meat loaf. C. Claiborne and P. Franey. il N Y Times Mag p40 Ja 30 '77
Succulent pork chops. il Good H 184:22 Mr '77
Summer suppers. il Bet Hom & Gard 55:119-20 Ag '77
Supercolossal stuffed burgers. il Bet Hom & Gard 55:78 Je '77
Sweet & sour meatballs. il Bet Hom & Gard 55:36 Je '77
This sauerbraten is braised deliciously in the oven. il Sunset 158:230 Ap '77
Tips from the butchers in an old family meat market. il Bet Hom & Gard 55:84-5+ O '77
Wake up to the aroma of sizzling meats. il Parents Mag 52:78+ O '77
See also
Barbecue cookery
Cookery—Game
Stew

Mushrooms

Delectable champignons. C. Claiborne and P. Franey. il N Y Times Mag p66 Ap 10 '77

Nuts

Christmastide treat; chestnuts. R. Sokolov. Natur Hist 86:94-6 D '77

COOKERY—*Continued*

Organic food

Holiday treats from Fitness House. il Org Gard & Farm 24:100-4 D '77
Instead of chocolate, what about carob? il Sunset 159:232+ O '77
Peter Rabbit's natural foods cookbook; excerpt. A. Dobrin. il McCalls 104:158-60+ My '77
Vegetables; excerpt from Cooking creatively with natural foods. E. Brown and S. Brown. House B 119:158+ My '77

Poultry

Chestnut chicken—teriyaki. il Sunset 159:194 N '77
Chicken, turkey, goose and duckling cookbook. il Good H 185:152-61+ N '77
Classic roast chicken. il McCalls 104:109-10 Ap '77
Company's coming for a ranch feast; roast turkey dinner Texas style; excerpt from Flavors. il Redbook 150:114-15 D '77
Complete guide to a traditional turkey holiday dinner. il Redbook 150:146+ D '77
Dozen delicious stuffings. il Good H 185:162-3+ N '77
English pie par excellence; chicken pot pie. C. Claiborne and P. Franey. il N Y Times Mag p 108 O 9 '77
Favorites from our dining room; chicken à la suisse. il Good H 185:208 D '77
Few uses for that leftover turkey. il Ebony 33:158+ N '77
For an elegant Thanksgiving, star small birds. R. Molter. il Parents Mag 52:86-8+ N '77
Fowl play: 6 new ways to make a chicken go farther. M. Moore-Betty. il pors House & Gard 149:122-3+ F '77
From Julia Child's kitchen; turkey roasting. J. Child. il por McCalls 105:155-6+ N '77
Juicy inside and crispy outside is how duck on the barbecue turns out. il Sunset 159:118-19 Ag '77
One to a hungry customer; rock cornish game hens. il Sunset 158:170-1 Mr '77
Other birds to be thankful for. il Redbook 150:134-5+ N '77
Party pâté; duck aspic and pâté. C. Claiborne and P. Franey. il N Y Times Mag p 141+ D 11 '77
Rice stuffing in your smoky bird. il Sunset 159:174 N '77
Roasting the holiday bird. il Bet Hom & Gard 55:52 N '77
Rock cornish hen. il Good H 185:50 S '77
Savory ground turkey—hot in a lettuce leaf. il Sunset 159:150-1 D '77
Special stuffings for the traditional turkey. il McCalls 105:226-7+ N '77
Thinking man's guide to Peking duck. A. Zich. Holiday 58:20 Mr '77
Two great meals using spare parts of the turkey. Sunset 159:116 Jl '77
Variations on a theme; chicken. C. Claiborne and P. Franey. il N Y Times Mag p80 Mr 20 '77
See also
Cookery—Game
Thanksgiving dinners

Rhubarb

Rhubarb bread, rhubarb muffins. Sunset 158:174 Je '77

Rice

Persians have a way with rice. il Sunset 158:184-6 My '77
Play it cool; rice salads. G. Steves. il Am Home 80:66-8 Ag '77
Rice. il Fam Health 9:30-2+ Ag '77
Rice is nice. il Ladies Home J 94:130-2+ My '77

Sea food

Great seafoods: favorite recipes from 6 chefs. il Redbook 149:112-13+ Ag '77
See also
Cookery—Fish
Cookery—Shellfish

Shellfish

Crab gets together with marrow. il Sunset 158:232 My '77
Light touch with crab. il Sunset 158:130 F '77
Lobster quadrille. C. Claiborne and P. Franey. il N Y Times Mag p26-7 Jl 3 '77
Mussel power. C. Claiborne and P. Franey. il N Y Times Mag p82 My 22 '77
Quick, make a mussel! E. Lax. il Esquire 88:98-100 Ag '77
Shellfish moist and tender from a microwave. Sunset 158:198 Je '77
See also
Chowder

Snails

Flavorful snail. C. Claiborne and P. Franey. il N Y Times Mag p 116 Mr 27 '77

Sugar

Boiling sugar. E. Alston. Redbook 150:166 D '77

Vegetables

Adaptable asparagus. il Bet Hom & Gard 55:174 Ap '77
Applying jalapeño's fire to ribs, beans, spoonbread; chile peppers. il Sunset 159:218+ O '77
Asparagus: a taste of spring. il McCalls 104:154-5+ My '77
Beans are making news. il Sunset 158:90-3 Je '77
Best way to cook vegetables; use of steamers. il McCalls 104:84+ Ag '77
Bright peppers are what make these preserves festive. il Sunset 159:248 O '77
Cool cucumbers. il Bet Hom & Gard 55:76 Ag '77
Corn: it's with us all year round. il Ebony 32:136+ Ap '77
Crazy baked beans. il Bet Hom & Gard 55:106 Jl '77
Creams of the crop. M. Moore-Betty. il por House & Gard 149:96-7+ Ag '77
Creamy dips, all are low calorie; tofu or soybean curd. il Sunset 159:146 D '77
Culture & notes; tomatoes. Horticulture 55:94 F '77
Devil's food! M. Kaytor. il Esquire 87:72-3+ F '77
Eggplant, Italian style. il McCalls 105:81-2 Ja '78
Favorite tempeh recipes. W. Shurtleff and A. Aoyagi. il Org Gard & Farm 24:112+ Je '77
Fresh fruit & vegetable ideas from experts on the farm. S. P. Torpey. il Bet Hom & Gard 55:64-5+ Je '77
Fresh garden vegetables. il Bet Hom & Gard 54:83-4 Ag '76
Garden-fresh green beans. il Bet Hom & Gard 55:34 Ag '77
Gardening with exotic vegetables from Europe; with recipes. K. Kraft and P. Kraft. il Horticulture 55:52-6 Mr '77
Glorious endive. A. Gold and R. Fizdale. il Vogue 167:166+, 320-1 O '77
Gourmet gardener; with recipes. il House & Gard 149:98-100 Ag '77
Gourmet grass; sorrel. C. Claiborne and P. Franey. il N Y Times Mag p44 My 29 '77
Growing, cooking, shopping for Chinese greens. il Sunset 158:102-3 Mr '77
How to treat the common cole; with recipe for Szechwan style broccoli. R. Sokolov. Natur Hist 86:22+ F '77
In good taste; molded vegetables. C. Claiborne and P. Franey. il N Y Times Mag p48 Ag 14 '77
Into these deep-dish pizzas go fresh vegetable fillings. il Sunset 159:214 O '77
Julienne vegetables. il Bet Hom & Gard 55:106 Ap '77
Keep summer in your freezer all year long! il Fam Health 9:46-50 Ja '77
Kohlrabi gives you options. il Sunset 158:194+ Je '77
Live green fast food: sprouts. A. Gold and R. Fizdale. il Vogue 167:166+, 366 S '77
Mild eggplant goes spicy. il Sunset 159:204+ N '77
One-inch new potatoes. Sunset 158:160 Je '77
Onions. S. B. Huffman. il Ladies Home J 94:100-2+ F '77
Perfect french fry; using mini-fryers. il Ladies Home J 94:70+ S '77
Pilaf, zesty stew—all with lentils. Sunset 159:202 N '77
Playing delicious games with tomatoes—slicing, stuffing, stacking. il Sunset 159:128 Ag '77
Potato pancakes almost any time. il Sunset 158:236 Ap '77
Puff-puff potatoes. C. Claiborne and P. Franey. il N Y Times Mag p82 My 15 '77
Roast pork with winter vegetables. E. W. Manning. il Farm J 101:56-7 Ja '77
Roots. Seventeen 36:120 My '77
Same vegetables day after day a bore? il Sunset 159:72-3 S '77
Stuffed quartet. C. Claiborne and P. Franey. il N Y Times Mag p92 My 1 '77
Sweet corn of summer. S. B. Huffman. il Ladies Home J 94:92-4+ Jl '77
Tantalizing tomatoes. C. Claiborne and P. Franey. il N Y Times Mag p56 Ag 21 '77
Tofu cooking. il Org Gard & Farm 24:106+ Ap '77
Too many tomatillos? Here's what to do; recipes. il Sunset 159:125 Ag '77
Unusual dishes from your garden. J. Goldstein. il Org Gard & Farm 24:142+ F '77
Vegetable garden into creamy soup; recipes. il Sunset 159:138 Ag '77
Vegetables; excerpt from Cooking creatively with natural foods. E. Brown and S. Brown. House B 119:158+ My '77
Vegetarian who came to dinner. L. DeMauro. Am Home 80:36 S '77
Viva la vegetable! J. Ellis. House & Gard 150:103-4+ Ja '78
You start with an eggplant or potato; buffet. il Sunset 159:236-7 O '77
Zucchini milk—a new discovery. M. Marvin. il Org Gard & Farm 24:100+ Jl '77
See also
Stew
Vegetables—Preservation

COOKERY—*Continued*

Vinegar

Vive vinaigre! C. Claiborne and P. Franey. il N Y Times Mag p 160+ N 6 '77

Yogurt

Food. C. Rossant. Vogue 167:88+ Ap '77
For yogurt-lovers, handy seagoing recipes. B. Leach. Yachting 142:86 Jl '77
Frozen yogurt made at home with fresh August fruit. il Sunset 159:76-7 Ag '77
Frozen yogurt—the anytime reviver; recipes. il Vogue 167:162 O '77
Yogurt lover's feast. il McCalls 104:152-4+ Ag '77

COOKERY, American
America's favorite foods. S. B. Huffman. il Ladies Home J 94:91-9 Mr '77
Best-of-the-best recipes; excerpt from Farm Journal's best-ever recipes. E. W. Manning. il Farm J 101:50-2 Mr '77
California hospitality . . . dinner and all the trimmings. il Am Home 80:66-7 D '77
Community cookbook; Starving artists cookbook; excerpt. il Ladies Home J 94:68+ Je '77
Company's coming for a ranch feast; roast turkey dinner Texas style; excerpt from Flavors. il Redbook 150:114-15 D '77
Down-on-the-farm cooking. D. Eby. il Bet Hom & Gard 54:70-8+ Ag '76
Heritage of hospitality; North Carolina; excerpt. il Ladies Home J 94:98+ Ap '77
Heritage of treasured recipes; excerpt from Heritage cookbook. J. Stevens. il Ladies Home J 94:144+ O '77
Redbook's special it's almost Christmas cookbook; Texas style. il Redbook 150:57-64 N '77
Redbook's Texas holiday cookbook. Redbook 150:131 D '77
Sensuous cook; J. Beard. M. Rourke. il por Newsweek 89:93 Ap 11 '77
Simple splendor of Pennsylvania Dutch cooking. il McCalls 105:108-14+ Ja '78
Six easy pieces. N. Hazelton. Nat R 29:1186-7 O 14 '77
Southern fish fries. J. Gould. il Outdoor Life 160:116 Ag '77
Southern hospitality . . . a Creole brunch. G. Steves. Am Home 80:68-70+ D '77
Texas digest. G. Hill. Field & S 82:22+ Ag '77
Treasury of southern cooking. M. Eckley. il McCalls 104:154-60+ F '77

COOKERY, British
Eating out: British picnic. il Am Home 80:52-5+ Jl '77

COOKERY, Chinese
China's red cooking. il Sunset 158:238 Ap '77
Chinese-American beef ribs. il Bet Hom & Gard 55:188 N '77
Chinese home cooking. il House & Gard 149:168-9+ Ap '77
Chinese jerky is moister and less brittle than cowboy jerky; beef jerky. Sunset 159:126 Jl '77
Chinese New Year: a sumptuous feast. il Ladies Home J 94:98-9+ F '77
Crusty noodle pancake—beef on top. il Sunset 158:192 My '77
Hospitality on a budget. V. J. Bergeron. il por House & Gard 149:152-3 S '77
How to make Chinese chicken and egg buns (guy bow) il Sunset 158:204 My '77
How to treat the common cole; with recipe for Szechwan style broccoli. R. Sokolov. Natur Hist 86:22+ F '77
Memoir of Christmas in China. H. McNulty. il House & Gard 149:74+ D '77
Orient express; ed by G. Steves. K. Lee. il por Am Home 80:60-1+ N '77
Savory ground turkey—hot in a lettuce leaf. il Sunset 159:150-1 D '77
Taste of China. G. Lang. il por N Y Times Mag p 108+ My 1 '77
These Szechwan fish rolls are simply delicious. il Sunset 158:164 Mr '77
Thinking man's guide to Peking duck. A. Zich. Holiday 58:20 Mr '77
World's greatest Chinese restaurant. A. Zich. Holiday 58:40-1+ Mr '77

COOKERY, Colombian
Two bread ideas we brought back from Colombia. il Sunset 158:195-6 My '77

COOKERY, Creole. See Cookery, American

COOKERY, Cuban
Floatable feast. J. Hemingway. il por Esquire 87:156-7 Ap '77
Our meal in Havana. G. Lang. il N Y Times Mag p 122+ O 16 '77

COOKERY, Czech
Pork roast with caraway biscuits, sauerkraut, and black gravy. il Sunset 158:178 Mr '77

COOKERY, Danish
Eating out: Danish smørrebrød. il Am Home 80:48-9+ Jl '77
Ebleskivers: a Danish delight. il McCalls 105:143-4+ O '77
Soup for dessert? the Danes don't bat an eye; buttermilk soup. il Sunset 159:104 Jl '77

COOKERY, Dutch
Before dinner the Dutch enjoy hot bites of bitterballen. il Sunset 158:231 My '77
Dutch treat—sausages baked in a pastry shell. il Sunset 158:180 Mr '77

COOKERY, English
But can you eat the food? M. H. Tenison. il Sat R 4:29-31+ Je 11 '77
Humble pie. R. Sokolov. il Natur Hist 86:80-3 Ap '77
Meat pie, nut cakes, pub style. il Sunset 158:182 Mr '77
Pub party; with menu and recipes. il Sunset 158:88-9 Mr '77

COOKERY, European
Three European delicacies. il McCalls 105:182-4+ O '77

COOKERY, Foreign. See Cookery, International

COOKERY, French
Cook on the light side; Le Coup de fusil. il por House & Gard 149:172-3 O '77
Cuisine surprise; recipes of F. Girardet. A. Gold and R. Fizdale. Vogue 167:108+, 176-9 F '77
Food: France's best; ed by A. Gold and R. Fizdale. P. Bocuse. il Vogue 167:214+ N '77
French cooking from farm to fame. A. Gold and R. Fizdale. il map Vogue 167:58+, 242-7+ My '77
French food without the calories; excerpt from Michel Guerard's cuisine mineur. M. Guérard. McCalls 104:179-86 F '77
French touch . . . in the galley. C. Daume. Yachting 142:134 S '77
From Julia Child's kitchen. J. Child. See issues of McCall's
Jet-set chefs; the new French chefs. R. Daley. il pors N Y Times Mag p76+ F 6 '77
One way the French make apple pie. il Sunset 159:214 N '77
Spaghetti with a French accent. C. Claiborne and P. Franey. il N Y Times Mag p78+ O 2 '77
Vive vinaigre! C. Claiborne and P. Franey. il N Y Times Mag p 160+ N 6 '77
With love to La Belle France. H. McCully. il House B 119:164-8+ S '77
Your own French country picnic. il Sunset 159:102-3 Jl '77

COOKERY, German
German feast: Sauerbraten. il McCalls 105:175-6 N '77
Oktoberfest. il Sunset 159:192-3 O '77

COOKERY, Greek
Grill it Greek-style: BBQ for a bunch. S. P. Torpey. il Bet Hom & Gard 55:128-31+ Jl '77
Moussaka for the masses. C. Claiborne and P. Franey. il N Y Times Mag p 126+ S 11 '77

COOKERY, Guatemalan
Guatamalan *boquitas*. il Sunset 159:170-1 N '77

COOKERY, Hawaiian
Eating out: Hawaiian luau. il Am Home 80:60-1+ Jl '77

COOKERY, Indian (American)
Baking salmon the Indian way. B. C. Anderson. Field & S 82:99 Jl '77

COOKERY, Indian (East Indian)
Eating out: Indian cookout. il Am Home 80:34-5+ Jl '77
Spice of life. S. D. Holkar. il por Holiday 58:44-5 Je '77
Tandoori mixed grill. il Sunset 159:122-3 S '77

COOKERY, Indonesian
Mild eggplant goes spicy. il Sunset 159:204+ N '77

COOKERY, International
Body and soul: why ethnic eating is here to stay. Parents Mag 52:42-3+ Mr '77
Christmas sweets from many lands. H. McCully and M. Siple. il House B 119:111-17 D '77
Deli directory from the experts behind the counter. S. P. Torpey. il Bet Hom & Gard 55:82-3+ My '77
How to diet in six languages. il Ladies Home J 94:78+ My '77
International chef. See issues of Travel
Many tastes of Christmas. G. Lang. il N Y Times Mag p81+ D 18 '77
Portfolio of culinary art; excerpt. J. R. Stevens. il Ladies Home J 94:104+ F '77
Round the world picnics: eating out; with recipes. P. Sadowsky and G. Steves. il Am Home 80:33-5+ Jl '77
26 super salads from around the world. il Good H 185:130-9+ Ag '77

COOKERY, Italian
Buon appetito! a festa Verdi for opera luminaries. F. Tobey. il Opera N 42:8-11 D 24 '77
Culinary ramblings in Italy. C. Claiborne and P. Franey. il N Y Times Mag p 124+ N 13 '77
La dolce vita; desserts. C. Claiborne and P. Franey. il N Y Times Mag p56 Ja 8 '78
Eggplant, Italian style. il McCalls 105:81-2 Ja '78
Food: best eating of Italy. A. Gold and R. Fizdale. Vogue 167:86+ Ag '77
Glories of Italian cooking. il McCalls 104:174-80+ S '77
Great cooking the Italian way. il Good H 184:118-27+ F '77
Into these deep-dish pizzas go fresh vegetable fillings. il Sunset 159:214 O '77

COOKERY, Italian—*Continued*
Mangia, mangia: celebrating the new Met production of La Bohème. R. Jacobson. il Opera N 41:8-13 Mr 19 '77
Pizza: at home on the range. il McCalls 104:112+ Mr '77
Sicilian variations. N. Hazelton. il N Y Times Mag p67 F 13 '77
See also
Cookery—Macaroni products

COOKERY, Japanese
Chestnut chicken—teriyaki. il Sunset 159:194 N '77
Heavenly food of Japan. C. Lucas. il Read Digest 110:38-40+ My '77
Kan-pei! Junidan-ya restaurant. R. L. Balzer. il Holiday 58:26-8 Mr '77
Tempura: what starts out lumpy ends up light and lacy. il Sunset 158:240 Ap '77
Wake up little Su-u-shi, wake up! M. A. Crenshaw. il Esquire 87:86-9 Ap '77

COOKERY, Jewish
Jewish sweet and sour. il Sunset 159:198-9 O '77
This Hanukkah feast mixes Europe, Middle East. il Sunset 159:138-9 D '77

COOKERY, Latin American
It's a Spanish-American hot dog bash. il Sunset 159:68-9 Ag '77
Latin American picnic pies; empanadas. il Sunset 158:102-3, 220 My '77
Milk candies of Latin America. Sunset 158:219 Ap '77

COOKERY, Marine
For yogurt-lovers, handy seagoing recipes. B. Leach. Yachting 142:86 Jl '77
French touch in the galley. C. Daume. Yachting 142:134 S '77
Lazy gourmet afloat. S. Stoddard. Yachting 141:96-7+ My '77

COOKERY, Mexican
Applying jalapeño's fire to ribs, beans, spoonbread; chile peppers. il Sunset 159:218+ O '77
Canned chili; with recipe for chili con carne. Consumer Rep 42:76-7 D '77
15 Mexican classics from scratch. R. Hutchinson. il Bet Hom & Gard 55:146-56+ S '77
Great chili cult conspiracy; with recipe. R. Starnes. Outdoor Life 160:10+ Jl '77
Mexican buffet for ten. J. Schwartz and M. Melby. il Redbook 150:132-3 D '77
Mexican candies from San Antonio. il Redbook 150:122+ D '77
Mexican main dishes. il Bet Hom & Gard 55:145-6 Ap '77
Plump tamale. il Sunset 159:118-19 N '77
Prom fiesta; Mexican party food. il Ladies Home J 94:94-5 Je '77
Tacos: a tasty Mexican treat; taco cooker and serving rack. il McCalls 104:142+ S '77
Tom's tacos. il Bet Hom & Gard 55:76 Ap '77
Traditional los posadas buffet for sixteen. M. A. Cisneros. il Redbook 150:135-7 D '77
Whole fish spicily baked; red snapper Veracruz style. Sunset 159:204 O '77

Anecdotes, facetiae, satire, etc.

Chicanery topples international chili king in Houston invitational! G. Lish. il Esquire 88:92+ N '77

COOKERY, Middle Eastern
Two delicious fila pastries. il Sunset 158:208 My '77

COOKERY, Moroccan
Moorish delight. C. Claiborne and P. Franey. il N Y Times Mag p48+ Jl 10 '77

COOKERY, Oriental
Crispy Oriental shrimp salad. il Sunset 159:150 S '77
See also
Cookery, Chinese
Cookery, Indonesian
Cookery, Japanese

COOKERY, Ornamental
Art of cake decorating. il McCalls 104:162+ Ap '77
Butter lamb for the Easter Sunday breakfast table. il Sunset 158:200 Ap '77
Finishing touches that make a meal a feast; excerpts from La technique. J. Pépin. il McCalls 104:133-40 Ap '77
Holiday centerpieces . . . good enough to eat! il Good H 185:126-35+ D '77
Holiday tree magic; molasses cookie Christmas trees. il Ladies Home J 94:102-5+ D '77
How to make our fairyland gingerbread house. il Good H 185:12+ D '77
It's an art! with recipes. il Redbook 148:130-2+ Ap '77
Look! A gingerbread dollhouse. il Good H 185:86+ D '77
Make Santa's gingerbread sleigh. il Good H 185:56+ D '77
Sweet hearts; Valentine's Day cookery. il Ladies Home J 94:96-7+ F '77
See also
Cookery—Garnishes
Cookies

COOKERY, Outdoor
Bass for the shore lunch. B. Cary. il Outdoor Life 159:122 Je '77
Cooking on the move; backpacking and picnicking. il Bet Hom & Gard 55:118-23+ Je '77
Field cooking without utensils. M. Marshall. il Outdoor Life 160:111-12 Jl '77
Fired up for springtime. il Sat Eve Post 249:100+ Ap '77
It's a Spanish-American hot dog bash. il Sunset 159:68-9 Ag '77
Southern fish fries. J. Gould. il Outdoor Life 160:116 Ag '77
See also
Camp cookery
Food—Smoking

Equipment and supplies

See also
Camp stoves

COOKERY, Persian
Persians have a way with rice. il Sunset 158:184-6 My '77

COOKERY, Scandinavian
Viking picnic. il Fam Health 9:34-7 Jl '77
See also
Cookery, Danish
Cookery, Swedish

COOKERY, South American
Spicy corn pie has an unusual vegetable-beef crust. il Sunset 159:148 S '77

COOKERY, Southern. See Cookery, American

COOKERY, Spanish
Inside Catalonia's kitchen. L. S. Harper. il Sat R 5:26-7 O 29 '77

COOKERY, Swedish
Swedish pudding cake. il Sunset 159:160 D '77

COOKERY, Swiss
Make it delicious; Swiss Christmas cookies of Marina Schinz Rubin. il House & Gard 149:98-9+ D '77

COOKERY, Turkish
Delights of Turkey. W. P. Rayner. il map N Y Times Mag p80+ S 18 '77
Mica Ertegün's Turkish ease. L. Davis. Vogue 167:66+ D '77

COOKERY, Vietnamese
Chicken salad from Vietnam. il Sunset 158:206 Mr '77
Stuffed leaves—Vietnamese; grape leaves. il Sunset 159:218 N '77
Vietnamese pork and shrimp omelet. Sunset 158:190 Je '77

COOKERY by children
Wonderful cookies for children to bake. il Redbook 150:128+ D '77
See also
Cookbooks for children

COOKERY by college students
Cooking in the dorm; recipes; excerpt from The international students' guide to cooking without getting caught. T. Fisher. Seventeen 36:160 F '77

COOKERY by men
Chefs of the West. See issues of Sunset
He cooks:
Chinese-American beef ribs. il Bet Hom & Gard 55:188 N '77
Cinnamon popovers. il Bet Hom & Gard 55:194 My '77
Crazy baked beans. il Bet Hom & Gard 55:106 Jl '77
Daniel W. coffee cake. il Bet Hom & Gard 55:78 D '77
Prune nut bread. il Bet Hom & Gard 55:20 Mr '77
Pumpkin gelatin pie. D. Tait. il por Bet Hom & Gard 55:74 Ag '77
Skip jack chowder. il Bet Hom & Gard 55:150 O '77
Sweet & sour meatballs. il Bet Hom & Gard 55:36 Je '77
Tom's tacos. il Bet Hom & Gard 55:76 Ap '77
Venison stew. J. Moran. il por Bet Hom & Gard 55:184 S '77
Whole wheat pancakes. il Bet Hom & Gard 55:144 F '77
Men at home: one man's muffins. L. Radwell. Am Home 80:59 Mr '77
Separate kitchen pleases us both. R. Wendorff. il por Ret Liv 17:49-50 Mr '77
Whole-earth gourmet. E. O'Bryan. il por Am Home 80:64-5 Jl '77

COOKERY contests. See Cookery—Competitions

COOKERY for diabetics. See Diabetes—Nutritional aspects

COOKERY on boats. See Cookery, Marine

COOKIE makers. See Kitchen utensils and appliances

COOKIES
Christmas cookies. il Bet Hom & Gard 55:121-2 D '77
Christmas therapy. N. Hazelton. Nat R 29:1444-5 D 9 '77
Coconut crisps and sandwich cookies. il Sunset 159:212 N '77

COOKIES—*Continued*
Cookie book '77. S. B. Huffman. il Ladies Home J 94:100-7+ D '77
Cookie-jar treats. il Parents Mag 53:58+ Ja '78
Cookie wise and pound foolish; excerpt from Maida Heatter's book of great cookies. M. Heatter. il N Y Times Mag p 134+ S 25 '77
Cookies check out. il Am Home 80:92-4 D '77
Cookies quick and wholesome. il Sunset 158:206 My '77
Cooky that's almost bigger than she is. il Sunset 158:176 Mr '77
How to bake a monster cookie. il Seventeen 36:266-7+ Ag '77
How to make *bizcochitos*, a treat from New Mexico. il Sunset 158:220 Ap '77
Make it delicious; Swiss Christmas cookies of Marina Schinz Rubin. il House & Gard 149:98-9+ D '77
No-bake cookies. il Bet Hom & Gard 55:186 N '77
Shimmering cookies to hang on the Christmas tree. il Sunset 159:168 D '77
Sugarless cookies—naturally sweet; date cookies. Sunset 159:242 O '77
These little cookies are sandwiches. il Sunset 158:166 Mr '77
24 cookie-jar favorites from just 4 doughs. R. C. Hutchinson. il Bet Hom & Gard 55:144-5 S '77
Wonderful cookies for children to bake. il Redbook 150:128+ D '77

COOKING. See Cookery

COOKING schools. See Cookery—Study and teaching

COOKING utensils and appliances. See Kitchen utensils and appliances

COOKS
Cooking up a living; catering, cooking schools and food shops. C. Calvert. il Mademoiselle 83:152+ D '77
Jet-set chefs; the new French chefs. R. Daley. il pors N Y Times Mag p76+ F 6 '77
Love in the kitchen. il Time 110:54-8+ D 19 '77
Six women chefs and their favorite recipes. A. C. Scotton. Redbook 149:116 Ag '77
What's cooking? teen-age cooks. il Seventeen 36:64 Ap '77
See also
Beard, J.
Cookery by men
Girardet, F.

COOKSEY, Donald
Obituary
Phys Today por 30:69-70 D '77. E. M. McMillan

COOKTOPS. See Stoves

COOKWARE. See Kitchen utensils and appliances

COOLEY, Robert O.
Sound teeth for life. il Parents Mag 52:28+ N '77

COOLIDGE, Calvin
Silent Cal. New Repub 177:2+ Ag 6 '77 *

COOLIDGE, Dane
Riding the Cherrycow chuck line. il Am West 14:36-47 N '77
about
Dane Coolidge western writer and photographer. O. Ulph. bibl il por Am West 14:32-5 N '77 *

COOLIDGE, Rita
Grooving with Kris and Rita. pors Time 110:71 Ag 15 '77 *

COOLING
Keep cool, save energy; household improvements. il Redbook 149:56+ Jl '77
See also
Automobile engines—Cooling
Heat pumps
Marine engines—Cooling
Water—Cooling

COOLING racks. See Kitchen utensils and appliances

COOLING systems, Automobile. See Automobile engines—Cooling

COOMBS, Orde
Black woman finds her roots. Redbook 149:56+ O '77
Ghetto criminals: do they have a choice il Psychol Today 11:102-3 O '77
Lena Horne is 60. por Esquire 88:66-8+ Ag '77

COON hunting. See Raccoon hunting

COONEN, Lester P.
Aristotle's biology. bibl BioScience 27:733-8 N '77

—and Porter, C. M.
Jefferson: quiet patron of nature and science; excerpt from BioScience, December 1976. por Sci Digest 81:40-1 Ap '77

COONEY, Caroline B.
Brain game; story. Seventeen 36:236-7 Ag '77

COONEY, John
Death comes for a cardinal. Commonweal 104:326-7 My 27 '77

COONEY, Judd
About hunting elk. il Field & S 82:50-1+ S '77

COONS. See Raccoons

COOPER, Ed
California; photographs. Am For 83:46-50 O '77

COOPER, Edward E.
Edward E Cooper & 10 greatest Negroes of 1890. W. B. Gatewood, Jr. bibl por Negro Hist Bull 40:708-10 My '77 *

COOPER, Gary
Stagecoach Mary; ed by M. Crawford. il pors Ebony 32:96-8+ O '77

COOPER, Gloria (Vanderbilt) See Vanderbilt, G.

COOPER, Jane
Flashboat; poem. New Yorker 53:34 Ja 9 '78

COOPER, Jim
Vest-pocket turtle; with biographical sketch. il map Natur Hist 86:2, 52-7 bibl(p 100) Ap '77

COOPER, Kenneth Hardy
How aerobics can help your heart—and the way you feel; excerpt from The aerobics way. Read Digest 112:117-21 Ja '78
about
Cooper's cohorts run down heart disease. P. Rosenfield. il Sat Eve Post 249:18-20 S '77 *
Get fit, trim, slim—and grin. J. Alexander. il Sat Eve Post 249:70-1 O '77 *

COOPER, Matt
Spinoffs. Am Rec G 40:48-9 D '76; 50-1 Mr '77

COOPER, Peggy
Statement to Congress. il por Hi Fi 27:MA16-18+ O '77

COOPER, Ray, and others
Cortical potentials associated with the detection of visual events. bibl il Science 196:74-7 Ap 1 '77

COOPER, Richard N.
Administration urges U.S. participation in the IMF supplementary financing facility; statement, September 20, 1977. il Dept State Bull 77:645-50 N 7 '77
Department discusses results of CIEC meeting; statement, June 21, 1977. Dept State Bull 77:92-8 Jl 18 '77
International debt: current issues and implications; statement, August 29, 1977. il Dept State Bull 77:469-75 O 10 '77
International economic situation; statement, April 6, 1977. Dept State Bull 76:378-84 Ap 18 '77
Role of investment in expanding an open international economic system; address, June 27, 1977. Dept State Bull 77:127-31 Jl 25 '77
Secretary Vance and other administration officials urge ratification of Panama Canal treaties; statement, September 30, 1977. Dept State Bull 77:626-9 N 7 '77
Secretary Vance attends ministerial meeting of the Conference on International Economic Cooperation; news conference, June 3, 1977. Dept State Bull 76:648-50 Je 20 '77
United States and ASEAN hold economic consultations in Manila; statement, transcript of joint press conference, and text of press release, September 8, 10, 1977. Dept State Bull 77:595-605 O 31 '77
U.S. position on international economic relations; statement, October 14, 1977. Dept State Bull 77:696-704 N 14 '77
about
Man with a message. por Time 109:49 Ja 24 '77 *

COOPER, Richard V. L.
Rating the volunteer Army. il Time 110:34+ O 10 '77

COOPER, Samuel
Eyewitness to Concord. il Am Hist Illus 12:20-1 Ap '77

COOPER, Theodore
Carter says no to Cooper; Fredrickson's future unsure. B. J. Culliton. Science 195:376 Ja 28 '76 *

COOPER, Tom
Best laid garden plans go oft awry. Horticulture 55:64 D '77

COOPER-DRIVER, Gillian
Chemical evidence for separating the psilotaceae from the filicales. bibl il Science 198:1260-2 D 23 '77

COOPERATION
See also
Collective settlements
College library cooperation
Intercommunity cooperation
International cooperation
Library cooperation

COOPERATION, Inter-American. See Inter-American relations

COOPERATIVE agriculture. See Agriculture, Cooperative

COOPERATIVE apartment houses. See Apartment houses—Cooperative ownership

COOPERATIVE associations
California co-op cuts bills in half; food cooperative for the elderly. il por Aging 274:3-5 Ag '77
Co-ops:
Financial co-ops; loans to small depositors, credit unions. il Am Home 80:20 F '77

COOPERATIVE associations—*Continued*
Maryland seniors find their roots; they're saving money, keeping active; food co-op. Aging 274:14 Ag '77
Retail sales cooperative; Yellow Springs Pottery, near Dayton, Ohio. L. Eder. il por Ceram Mo 25:51-4 N '77

Northern Ireland

Buying back Belfast? IRA business activities. M. Dammerman. il Forbes 119:25-7 Mr 15 '77

COOPERATIVE associations, Agricultural. See Agriculture, Cooperative
COOPERATIVE education. See Education, Cooperative
COOPERATIVE housing projects. See Housing projects, Cooperative
COOPERATIVE library systems. See Library networks
COOPERATIVE nursery schools. See Nursery schools
COOPERATIVE purchasing. See Purchasing, Cooperative
COOPERATIVE stores. See Cooperative associations
COOPERSTOWN, N.Y.
See also
National Baseball Hall of Fame and Museum
COORS, Adolph, Company
Bitter beercott; dispute over polygraph exams. il Time 110:15 D 26 '77
COOTE, Graeme
Seven in the sea; shipwreck off the coast of Fiji. M. Shadbolt. il Read Digest 110:95-100 Ap '77 *
CO-OWNERSHIP of property. See Joint tenancy
COP television shows. See Television programs—Crime programs
COPE, Myron
Better than working for a living. il Sports Illus 47:36-8+ S 12 '77
COPELAND, D. Eugene. See Brown, D. S. jt auth
COPELAND, Mary Shawn
Modern black movement and Marxism. bibl il New Cath World 220:134-9 My '77
COPELAND, Peter
Buried but still a treasure. B. Pearsall. il Sports Illus 46:56+ Mr 14 '77 *
COPENHAGEN

Music

See also
Opera—Denmark
COPERSUCAR (firm) See Brazil—Industries
COPLAND, Aaron
Second hurricane. Reviews
Hi Fi il 27:MA17-19 S '77 *
COPLANS, John
Weegee the famous. il por Art in Am 65:37-41 S '77
COPPAGE, Edwin J. Jr
Schwalberg at large. B. Schwalberg. il por Pop Phot 81:48+ S '77 *
COPPÉLIA; ballet. See Ballet reviews—Single works
COPPER
See also
Water supply—Copper content

Prices

Bullish copper takes another price jump. il Bus W p26-7 Ap 4 '77
Copper prices ride a speculative seesaw. il Bus W p39-40 My 16 '77
Plunge in prices hits copper output. il Bus W p25-6 S 5 '77

Stockpiling

See Stockpiling

COPPER coins. See Coins
COPPER industry
See also
Collective labor agreements—Copper industry

Federal aid

Copper producers gain Washington's ear. il Bus W p35-6 N 28 '77

International aspects

Why CIPEC's no OPEC. il Forbes 119:59-61 Je 1 '77

United States

See also
Collective labor agreements—Copper industry
Kennecott Copper Corporation
Revere Copper and Brass, Inc
COPPER mines and mining
See also
Kennecott Copper Corporation

Chile

Copper and irony; Continental Copper & Steel Industries. il Forbes 119:56+ Je 15 '77
COPPERWELD Corporation-Imetal merger. See Corporations—Acquisitions and mergers—International aspects
COPPOLA, Francis Ford
Case histories of business management: Hollywood artistic division. il Esquire 88:190+ N '77

about

Watching the Apocalypse. M. Orth. il pors Newsweek 89:57-8+ Je 13 '77 *
COPTIC Church
Religious freedom for Egypt's Copts. America 137:160 S 24 '77
COPTIC manuscripts. See Manuscripts, Coptic (papyri)
COPY writing. See Advertising copy
COPYING machines and processes
See also
Apeco Corporation
Photocopying machines and processes
Signature writing machines
Slides (photography)—Copying
COPYPERSONS. See Newspapers—Employees
COPYRIGHT
Introducing IRIS, the International Rights Information Service. D. F. Reaney. Pub W 212:99-114 S 19 '77
Mexico balks at revised copyright procedures; international copyright; ed by S. Wagner. S. Bistline. Pub W 212:26+ D 12 '77
See also
Royalties

Art

Copyright conundrums. B. Chamberlain. Am Artist 41:28 Je '77
New copyright law: help in half-measures. T. Crawford. Art in Am 65:11-12+ S '77

Book design

Copyrights for book designs. P. Doebler. il Pub W 212:59-60+ Jl 4 '77

Broadcasting rights

Right to replay? suit against Sony Corp.'s Betamax. il Time 109:64 Ap 11 '77
Technology versus tariffs; home video recorder. il Forbes 119:27-8 Ap 15 '77

Music

Of copyrights, creators, and phonorecords; questions raised by new federal copyright law. L. Feist. por Hi Fi 27:63-6 Je '77

Television rights

See Copyright—Broadcasting rights

Transfer

AIP will ask authors to transfer copyright under new law; with editorial comment. B. C. Carr. Phys Today 30:85-7, 104 S '77

Unauthorized reprints

See Copyright infringement

Great Britain

U.K.'s Whitford Report; faith, hope, clarity. G. Graham. Pub W 211:49 Ap 25 '77

United States

AAP & authors clash over copy fee scheme. Lib J 102:1083 My 15 '77
AAP and authors differ on copyright termination. S. Wagner. Pub W 211:29-30 Ja 10 '77
AAP seeks bids to run copy payments center. S. Wagner. Pub W 212:28 Jl 11 '77
AAP spells out clearinghouse plan for photocopying at CONTU meeting. S. Wagner. Pub W 211:28 Ap 11 '77
AAP to present plan for photocopying fees. S. Wagner. Pub W 211:27-8 Mr 28 '77
Authors, publishers divide on divisibility doctrine. S. Wagner. Pub W 212:20+ O 17 '77
Clearance Center forms amid photocopying uncertainty. S. Wagner. Pub W 212:19+ Ag 8 '77
Copyright dilemma; report of conference at the Graduate Library School of Indiana University. L. X. Besant. Lib J 102:1337-9 Je 15 '77
Copyright law dictates new procedures for authors. W. G. Peter. il BioScience 27:829-30 D '77
Copyright matters. Pub W 212:40 O 3 '77
Copyright, resource sharing, and hard times: a view from the field. R. De Gennaro. bibl Am Lib 8:430-5 S '77
Copyright: the clauses of '78. Writers Digest 57:22 Ag '77
Copyright workshop sees new forms, is cautioned on problems ahead. S. Wagner. Pub W 212:23-4 N 14 '77
Electronic journal is on the way; Copyright Clearance Center. H. L. Davis. Phys Today 30:104 O '77
Lawyers warn publishers: copyright countdown has begun; report of AAP seminar. S. Wagner. Pub W 211:56-8 Mr 7 '77
Librarian looks at the new copyright law. E. G. Holley. bibl il Am Lib 8:247-51 My '77
Library groups balk at new photocopying guidelines. S. Wagner. Pub W 212:20+ O 31 '77
Living in the gap of ambiguity; an attorney's advice to libraries on the copyright law. L. I. Flacks. il Am Lib 8:252-7 My '77

COPYRIGHT—United States—*Continued*
Majority of publishers oppose clearinghouses. W. D. Nelson. il Wilson Lib Bull 52:118-19 O '77
More copyright information. Am Lib 8:624-5 D '77
NCLIS to propose center for periodical copying. S. Wagner. Pub W 211:21-2 My 2 '77
New copyright law primer. S. Wagner. Pub W 212:37-42 D 26 '77
New copyright law—what it means for photographers. L. Kirschbrown. Pop Phot 80:73+ Mr '77
New copyright law's complex, long-lasting. Mod Phot 41:181+ D '77
Of copyrights, creators, and phonorecords; questions raised by new federal copyright law. L. Feist. il por Hi Fi 27:63-6 Je '77
Publishers v. libraries, a real possibility. W. D. Nelson. Wilson Lib Bull 52:285-6 D '77
Rights and permissions. P. S. Nathan. See issues of Publishers weekly
Sweeping revision of the copyright law. K. J. Wrinkler. Educ Digest 42:17-19 Ja '77
We've been asked: what stricter copyright law will mean. il U.S. News 83:58 D 19 '77
What writers should know about the new copyright law. Writer 91:25-7 Ja '78
Will Xerox kill Gutenberg? G. Hardin. Science 198:883 D 2 '77
Writers blast copyright registration concept. S. Wagner. Pub W 212:35 O 24 '77
See also
United States—Copyright Office
United States—National Commission on New Technological Uses of Copyrighted Works

COPYRIGHT infringement
Film producers charge N.Y. BOCES with infringement of copyrights. SLJ 24:9 D '77
New York times sues over Index. Pub W 211:28 Je 20 '77
Two writers question the originality of Roots. M. Reuter. Pub W 211:20 My 2 '77

COPYRIGHT Office. See United States—Copyright Office

CORAL Pink Sand Dunes States Reserve. See Utah—Parks and reserves

CORAL Reef State Park. See Florida—Parks and reserves

CORAL reefs and islands
Reef corals: mutualistic symbioses adapted to nutrient-poor environments. L. Muscatine and J. W. Porter. bibl il BioScience 27:454-60 Jl '77
Symbionts of sea fans & sea whips. L. P. Zann. il Oceans 10:10-15 Ja '77
Unlikely Flower Gardens. T. Caffrey. il Sea Front 23:242-6 Jl '77
Where Puerto Rico meets the sea; reefs surrounding La Parguera, Puerto Rico. P. L. Colin. il Sea Front 23:350-60 N '77
World under the reef. R. E. Thresher. il Sea Front 23:66-75 Mr '77
See also
Eniwetok
Florida Keys
Palau (islands)

CORAL snakes. See Snakes

CORAL Springs, Fla.
Coral Springs sues over bond advice. Am City & County 92:33 Ag '77

CORALS
Deep-water corals. S. D. Cairns. il Sea Front 23:84-9 Mr '77

CORBETT, John
More on hair dyes. Ms 5:21 F '77

CORBETT, Sarah Anne
Reversals; poem. Chr Cent 94:1033 N 9 '77

CORBIN, David
Accurate milliammeters on a budget. il Pop Electr 11:67-8 Je '77

CORBINO, Marcia
Ben Stahl: teaching art through television. il por Am Artist 41:24-7+ Mr '77

CORBUSIER, Le. See Le Corbusier

CORCO. See Commonwealth Oil Refining Company

CORCORAN, Thomas Gardiner
Fork in the road. E. Yoffe. New Repub 177:21-3 S 17 '77 *
New Deal: born again. T. Mathews and J. Doyle. il pors Newsweek 89:16-17 Mr 14 '77 *

CORCORAN Biennial. See Painting, American—Exhibitions

CORCORAN Gallery of Art, Washington, D.C.
First Family at the Corcoran. P. M. Kadis. il Art N 76:52-3 My '77

CORDASCO, Francesco
Bilingual education in American schools. Intellect 106:4 Jl '77

CORDELE, Ga.
Container collection cuts refuse service costs; Cordele, Ga. il Am City & County 92:40 Jl '77

CORDER, Foster
His business has gone to the dogs. il pors Ebony 32:50-1+ My '77 *

CORDIALS. See Liqueurs

CORDYCEPIN. See Antibiotics

CORE drilling. See Drilling and boring (ice); Underwater drilling

COREN, Stanley, and Porac, Clare
Fifty centuries of right-handedness: the historical record. bibl il Science 198:631-2 N 11 '77

CORI, Naja
Your trouble-free individual exercise program. il Harp Baz 110:122-3 F '77

CORIANDER
See also
Cookery—Herbs

CORK, Betty
I'm ready for full-time motherhood. Am Home 80:27 N '77

CORK, Linda Collins, and others
GM_2 ganglioside lysosomal storage disease in cats with β-hexosaminidase deficiency. bibl il Science 196:1014-17 My 27 '77

CORKSCREWS
How's this for openers? il Esquire 88:170-1 N '77

CORLISS, John B. and Ballard, R. D.
Oases of life in the cold abyss. il por map Nat Geog 152:440-53 O '77

CORMAN, Avery
Kramer & son; story; excerpt from Kramer versus Kramer. Esquire 89:82-4 Ja '78
PW interviews; ed by A. K. Turner. por Pub W 212:6-7 O 10 '77

CORMAN, James Charles
Excerpt from remarks on proposed Health Security Act, January 6, 1977. Cong Digest 56:206+ Ag '77
about
Carter's welfare fight. G. R. Rosen. por Duns R 110:53 N '77 *

CORMIER, John
Of dogbiters and other mythical beasts; address, April 19, 1977. Vital Speeches 43:472-5 My 15 '77

CORMIER, Robert
Interview with R. Cormier; ed by P. Janeczko. Engl J 66:10-11 S '77

CORN, Alfred
Declaration, July 4; poem. Yale R 66:576-9 Je '77
Fire: the people; Sunday mornings in Harlem; Summer vertigo; Orlando Furioso: Sicilian puppet theater; Fifty-seventh Street and Fifth; Photographs of old New York; Afternoon; Short story: a covenant; poems. Poetry 130:187-200 Jl '77
January; Nine to five; Spring and summer; Impression; Some new ruins; poems. Poetry 129:187-94 Ja '77
To a muse; poem. New Repub 177:25 S 3 '77
about
Comment. R. Howard. Poetry 129:226-8 Ja '77 *

CORN
Growing guide for extra-early sweet corn. J. Jankowiak. il por Org Gard & Farm 25:97-9 Ja '78
See also
Cookery—Vegetables
Feeds—Corn
Popcorn

Breeding

Corn breeding in a test tube. N. Reeder. il Farm J 101:26+ Mr '77

Cultivation

Corn craftsmanship:
Be your own weatherman. C. E. Sommers. il Suc Farm 75:19-24 My '77
Buckle down on pests—field by field. B. Brantley and C. E. Sommers. il Suc Farm 75:30-1+ Ja '77
Picking your tillage. B. Brantley and C. E. Sommers. il Suc Farm 75:no5 28-30 Mr '77
Schedule your planting. B. Brantley and C. E. Sommers. il Suc Farm 75:26-7+ Ap '77
These farmers put it to the test. C. Sommers. il Suc Farm 75:28-9 S '77
Turning on the nitrogen. B. Brantley and C. E. Sommers. Suc Farm 75:no3 24-5+ F '77
Corn growing costs too high? Here's how to tell. Suc Farm 75:9 D '77
Corn production costs projected to rise 4.5%. il map Farm J 101:B1 Ap '77
Double-crop corn: for livestock producers. il Suc Farm 75:no4 40 Mr '77
Farmers get paid to try no-till corn. B. Coffman. il Farm J 101:M1 Ja '77
Fast, nervous start for '77 crops. D. Seim; B. Coffman. il Farm J 101:17+ Je '77
I could grow corn all year. D. Seim. il Farm J 101:P2 N '77
In-row subsoiling. K. Copeland. il Farm J 101:24-6 O '77
Knock out problem weeds in corn. D. Seim. il Farm J 101:21-2+ mid-F '77
Plow deep, fertilize heavily and plant early. D. Seim. Farm J 101:C1 S '77
Researchers seek ways to grow corn after coal. Farm J 101:D1 Ag '77

CORPORATE lobby. See Lobbyists and lobbying
CORPORATE photography. See Photography in industry
CORPORATE pilots. See Air pilots
CORPORATE planning. See Business planning
CORPORATE profit. See Corporations—Finance
CORPORATE psychology. See Psychology, Industrial
CORPORATE reorganization. See Corporations—Reorganization
CORPORATE responsibility. See Business—Social aspects
CORPORATE secrets. See Trade secrets
CORPORATION for Public Broadcasting
Public TV focuses on older Americans. il Aging 275:8-10 S '77
Public TV: stop the waste. M. Stone. U.S. News 83:84 O 3 '77
See also
Public Broadcasting Service
CORPORATION law
Backfire from state takeover laws. A. L. Priest. Bus W p25 Ag 29 '77
Boss of General Motors' legal staff; O. M. Smith. il pors Ebony 33:33-5+ D '77
Chilling impact of litigation. il Bus W p58-62+ Je 6 '77
Emerging solution to corporate governance. R. M. Estes. bibl f Harvard Bus R 55:20-3+ N '77
Merger notification business can live with. Bus W p40 O 17 '77
New fire in the drive to reform corporation law. J. K. Lieberman. Bus W p98-100 N 21 '77
Treasury Secretary Blumenthal testifies on legislation on illicit payments abroad; statement, March 16, 1977. W. M. Blumenthal. Dept State Bull 76:351-5 Ap 11 '77

Netherlands

Turn to the right worries business. Bus W p47 D 26 '77
CORPORATION lawyers. See Lawyers
CORPORATION management. See Business management
CORPORATION meetings. See Corporations—Meetings
CORPORATION reports
Annual report for the young tells the business story; Wheelebrator-Frye report. il Nations Bus 65:52-3 Jl '77
Some painful candor in annual reports. il Bus W p96+ My 9 '77
See also
Financial statements

Anecdotes, facetiae, satire, etc.

Annual report. J. Munves. New Yorker 53:32-3 Mr 7 '77
CORPORATIONS
Federal chartering: nightmare for business. il Nations Bus 65:10 Ja '77
Five best-managed companies. il Duns R 110:47-52+ D '77
New companies that beat the odds. G. Bylinsky. il Fortune 96:76-80+ D '77
See also
Black business enterprises
Conglomerate corporations
Family corporations
Farm corporations
Government investigations—Corporations
Minority business enterprises
Public service commissions
Stockholders
Trusts, Industrial

Accounting

Accounting rules may discourage investment. il Bus W p68+ O 17 '77
Balance-sheet battle; replacement-cost accounting. Time 109:48-9 Ja 24 '77
Corporate scheme for currency swapping. Bus W p70 S 5 '77
Global snares for corporate accountants; International Accounting Standards Committee. Bus W p 162+ Jl 25 '77
Have the accountants really hurt the multinationals? new currency conversion rules. L. Snyder. il Fortune 95:85-6+ F '77
How current-value date affect the balance sheet. il Bus W p48 Je 27 '77
Industry's wasted billions; asset mismanagement. T. J. Murray. il Duns R 110:86-8 D '77
Inflation? Account for it; use of current cost accounting in Great Britain. Forbes 119:64-5 Mr 1 '77
Inflation accounting is here to stay. il Bus W p 109-10 D 26 '77
Making the audit committee work. M. L. Lovdal. il Harvard Bus R 55:108-14 Mr '77; Reply J. F. McNiff. 55:163 My '77
New management headache; foreign-exchange operation. L. Adkins. il Duns R 110:72-4+ O '77
Newest numbers game; replacement-cost accounting. il Bus W p85+ Je 20 '77
Numbers game. See occasional issues of Forbes
Sharper definition of the auditor's job; Cohen Commission report. il por Bus W p55-6 Mr 28 '77
Steel: biting the bullet. il Forbes 120:35-6 D 1 '77
Strengthening the functions of internal auditors; CBS Inc. M. L. Mace. Harvard Bus R 55:46-7 Jl '77
Treasurers sweat out the currency turmoil; effect of floating exchange rates on multinational corporations. Bus W p68 Ag 29 '77
Trying to outrun currency swings; effect of foreign exchange accounting rule on earnings. Bus W p 108+ F 14 '77
Why Britain still lacks inflation accounting. il Bus W p 102+ O 31 '77
Why we should account for inflation. T. D. Flynn. bibl f il Harvard Bus R 55:145-57 S '77
See also
Disclosure in accounting

Acquisitions and mergers

APL's bid for Pabst: a hasty try at growth by acquisition. por Bus W p85-6 Ja 9 '78
Acquisition-hungry Envirodyne leaps into steel. il por Bus W p96+ S 12 '77
Allegheny Ludlum's coup at Chemetron. por Bus W p54-5 S 26 '77
Amtel's former chief encourages a suitor; AMCA International Corp. Bus W p39-40 N 28 '77
Another publisher expands into broadcasting; Ziff Corporation's acquisition of Rust Craft Greeting Cards Inc. il Bus W p87 N 21 '77
Authors Guild asks U.S. to block BOMC purchase by Time. M. Reuter; S. Wagner. Pub W 212:16 Ag 15 '77
Bad day in court for takeover laws; ruling on tender offer laws in case prompted by Great Western United Corp.'s bid to acquire Sunshine Mining Co. Bus W p44-5 S 19 '77
Baldwin's intricate merger play; United Corp. il Bus W p81+ My 30 '77
Bittersweet deal; Pott Industries, sold to Houston Natural Gas Corp. por Forbes 119:76 Ap 1 '77
Blend of tobacco and life insurance; American Brands acquisition of Franklin Life Insurance. il Bus W p26-7 Ag 22 '77
Blood in the water at Babcock & Wilcox. Bus W p25-6 Je 6 '77
Bluhdorn is at it . . . again; proposed sale of Madison Square Garden Corporation to Gulf and Western Industries Inc. por Forbes 119:30-1 Ap 15 77
Carrier Corp. adds ink to its air conditioning; acquisition of Inmont Corp. Bus W p25-6 Ag 29 '77
Evans pounces again, this time with cash; Crane's offer to buy Chemetron Corp. Bus W p35 Ag 15 '77
Fighting for the wheel; Fuqua Industries purchase offer of Avis stock. por Time 109:57 Je 6 '77
Finance company hungers for food; Norin Corp. acquires companies in the food business. Bus W p28-9 Ap 4 '77
Flxibility? Grumman acquires Flxible. il Forbes 120:152 O 15 '77
Foremost-McKesson beats a takeover; Sharon Steel Corp. bid. Bus W p48 Ap 18 '77
GE-Utah International: more than just another merger. il Forbes 119:32-3 Ja 15 '77
General Electric's very personal merger; Utah International, Inc. L. Kraar. il pors Fortune 96:186-92+ Ag '77
Great takeover binge. il Bus W p 176-9+ N 14 '77
How McDermott won its Babcock victory. Bus W p40-1 S 12 '77
How Norton Simon latched on to Avis. il Bus W p50+ Jl 11 '77
In spite of the obstacles, the takeover feast goes on; with editorial comment. J. A. Briggs. il Forbes 119:6, 25-7 My 1 '77
Jaws tries to swallow Coke? MCA's bid for Coca-Cola Bottling Co. of Los Angeles. Time 110:76 O 24 '77
Kennecott and the white knights; takeover of Carborundum Co. Time 110:91-2 N 28 '77
Kennecott prospects for an acquisition. Bus W p22-3 Jl 18 '77
Kennecott's internal debate on diversifying; acquiring Carborundum. il Bus W p33-4 D 5 '77
Killing in Babcock & Wilcox; action of arbitrageurs regarding takeover of Babcock & Wilcox by J. Ray McDermott & Co. E. J. Tracy. il pors Fortune 96:266-9 O '77
LTV's play to cut its losses through a merger with Lykes. il Bus W p86+ Ja 9 '78
Low-keyed contest for Philadelphia Life; offers from Tenneco Inc and American Express Company. Bus W p55 S 26 '77
Lykes and LTV count on an antitrust break. il Bus W p64 N 21 '77
Mergers on the rebound. J. Perham. il Duns R 109:61-3 My '77

CORPORATIONS—Acquisitions and mergers—*Continued*

New champ of takeover; acquisition of Babcock & Wilcox by J. Ray McDermott & Co. il Time 110:34 S 5 '77

New route around capital gains taxes. D. G. Santry. Bus W p 104 S 19 '77

Not-so-tender offer United Technologies at attempted acquisition of Babcock & Wilcox. Time 109:64-5 Ap 11 '77

Oil makes Kewanee alluring to suitors. il Bus W p30-1 Mr 14 '77

Profit potential in spotting takeovers. il Bus W p 100-2 O 24 '77

Raytheon's plunge into word processing; takeover of Lexitron Corp. Bus W p56 D 12 '77

Return of the big deal. il Time 110:50+ Ag 29 '77

Riklis stock deal that may save Kenton; Rapid-American deal. D. Santry. por Bus W p 190 N 14 '77

Search for a leveraged buyout. J. M. Stancill. Harvard Bus R 55:8+ Jl '77

Takeover target's defender; M. A. Siegel. por Bus W p 160 My 16 '77

Takeover tussle at Sunshine Mining; bid by Great Western United Corp. Bus W p40 O 3 '77

Tender trap; Kennecott Copper and Carborundum. Newsweek 90:94 N 28 '77

Time and Book-of-the-Month agree to $63-million merger. M. Reuter. Pub W 212:74 Jl 18 '77

Try-harder war for Avis. T. Nicholson. il Newsweek 89:79 Je 20 '77

United Technologies fights on for Babcock. Bus W p56 Jl 25 '77

Unwelcome suitor keeps plugging away; United Technologies Corp.'s pursuit of Babcock & Wilcox Co. Bus W p48-9 Ap 18 '77

Wall Street's highest rollers; arbitrage action. il Time 110:54+ O 17 '77

Wall Street's tender trap. D. Pauly. il Newsweek 89:88 Ap 11 '77

Which client secrets must a lawyer reveal? SEC suits against law firms involved in National Student Marketing Corporation's fraudulent takeover attempt of Interstate National Corp. il Bus W p 124+ Ag 15 '77

Why Alleghany wants to up its stake in IDS. il Bus W p90+ O 3 '77

Why Bic dropped its U.S. razor deal; possible merger with American Safety Razor Co. il Bus W p23-4 Mr 7 '77

Why Eaton likes Carborundum. il Bus W p 116-17 N 21 '77

Why Fruehauf got a crush on Koehring. Bus W p27 Ja 24 '77

Why Houston Gas wants to haul coal; merging with Pott Industries Inc. Bus W p24-5 Mr 28 '77

Why it's cheaper to buy than to build. J. Costello. Nations Bus 65:70 N '77

Will Olive Ann marry? proposed Beech Aircraft-General Dynamics merger. il por Time 110:72 Jl 18 '77

You can bank on it; Entex's purchase of University Savings Association. il Forbes 120:52 S 1 '77

See also

Automobile industry—Acquisitions and mergers
Bank holding companies—Acquisitions and mergers
Banks and banking—Acquisitions and mergers
Brokers—Acquisitions and mergers
Chain stores—Acquisitions and mergers
Computer industry—Acquisitions and mergers
Construction industry—Acquisitions and mergers
Discount houses (retail trade)—Acquisitions and mergers
Electronic industries—Acquisitions and mergers
Food industry—Acquisitions and mergers
Investment banking—Acquisitions and mergers
Petroleum industry—Acquisitions and mergers
Publishers and publishing—Acquisitions and mergers
Railroads—Acquisitions and mergers
Real estate business—Acquisitions and mergers
Soft drink industry—Acquisitions and mergers
Supermarkets—Acquisitions and mergers

International aspects

Allegheny Ludlum diversifies again; Wilkinson Match Ltd. Bus W p 19-20 Ja 9 '78

Bank looks to Case to rescue a borrower; Poclain's proposed merger helping Credit du Nord's profit picture. il Bus W p42 Ap 11 '77

Bayer as buyer; proposed acquisition of Miles Laboratories, Inc. Time 110:71 O 10 '77

Bayer's cash offer gives Miles a jolt. Bus W p41 O 17 '77

Canadian Pacific's U.S. hunting trip; acquiring Bangor Punta Corp. Bus W p23 Jl 18 '77

Continuing wave of British takeovers. il Bus W p27-8 D 19 '77

French solution to foreign takeovers; offers for Rousselot and Gardinier. Bus W p56 O 3 '77

Imasco buys a slice of Hardee's food. Bus W p42+ F 14 '77

Marts of trade; Imetal-Copperweld Corporation merger. J. Brooks. New Yorker 52:80-90 F 7 '77

Northern Telecom keeps pushing south. Bus W p29 D 19 '77

Takeovers; Unilever Group-National Starch and Chemical Corp. merger. il Time 110:49 D 26 '77

Laws and regulations

See Corporation law

Charitable contributions

Better management urged for company contributions. por Nations Bus 65:58 Ag '77

New toughness in corporate giving; program at Exxon Corporation. J. Perham. il Duns R 109:68-70 Mr '77

Directories

Dimensions of American business: a roster of the U.S.'s biggest corporations. Forbes 119:202-9+ My 15 '77

Fifty largest industrial companies in the world. il Fortune 96:240-2 Ag '77

Forbes 500s; with directories. il Forbes 119:156-60 My 15 '77

Fortune directory; largest U.S. non-industrial corporations; with introd by M. Dann. il Fortune 96:160-75 Jl '77

Fortune directory of the 500 largest industrial corporations outside the U.S; with introd by R. Leggett. il Fortune 96:225-39 Ag '77

Fortune directory of the second 500 largest U.S. industrial corporations; with introd by A. M. Morrison. il Fortune 95:204-32 Je '77

Fortune directory; with introd by S. Wittebort. il Fortune 95:364-91 My '77

Where to find the company. il Forbes 121:39-42+ Ja 9 '78

Directors

Bittersweet victory for Gerber's directors; stockholders' suit over Anderson, Clayton bid. il Bus W p37 O 10 '77

Changing fashion in company directors. Bus W p32 Mr 14 '77

Consultants move to the executive suite. il Bus W p76+ N 7 '77

Corporate governance—new heat on outside directors? por Forbes 120:33 O 1 '77

Directors' squabble at Becton Dickinson. il por Bus W p40-1 O 3 '77

From the boardroom; ed by M. L. Mace. See issues of Harvard business review

Innovative boards. J. C. Perham. Duns R 110:92-4+ O '77

Rich legal links to the boardroom. il Bus W p24-5 Ja 24 '77

Working directors: putting muscle into the board. J. A. Patton. Duns R 109:71-2 Ja '77

See also

Corporations—Meetings

Anecdotes, facetiae, satire, etc.

Preserving the impotence of the board. M. C. Lauenstein. Harvard Bus R 55:36-8+ Jl '77

Salaries, pensions, etc.

See Executives—Salaries, pensions, etc.

Divestiture

Breaking up large American energy firms; excerpts from address. P. Davidson. por Intellect 105:295-6 Mr '77

Crimping the air power of the press; FCC ruling against newspaper-broadcasting stations crossownerships. Bus W p33 Mr 14 '77

Divestiture debate; newspaper-television-radio combinations. Newsweek 89:43 Mr 14 '77

Divestiture-competition or nationalization? address, March 22, 1977. M. T. Halbouty. Vital Speeches 43:379-82 Ap 1 '77

Down the chute with Peabody coal. C. J. Loomis. il Fortune 95:228-33+ My '77

Fighting for the wheel; Fuqua Industries purchase offer of Avis stock. por Time 109:57 Je 6 '77

Should we break up the oil companies? controversy surrounding horizontal and vertical divestiture. I. Ross. Read Digest 110:153-4+ Je '77

Teddy bared; Kennedy bill to prevent horizontal divestiture by oil companies. Nat R 29:1097-8 S 30 '77

U.S. energy crisis; horizontal divestiture; address, November 30, 1976. R. Warner, Jr. Vital Speeches 43:246-51 F 1 '77

Employees

See Employees

Finance

Controller: inflation gives him more clout with management. il Bus W p84-7+ Ag 15 '77

Debenture swaps that trim debt. Bus W p54 Jl 4 '77

Discouraging lag in first-quarter profits. Bus W p27 My 2 '77

European money tap for the second string. il Bus W p62 Ag 1 '77

CORPORATIONS—Finance—*Continued*
High yields pull U.S. corporate cash abroad. il Bus W p79-80 Ja 16 '78
How the bellwether industries face 1978; special section. il Bus W p36-40+ Ja 9 '78
Medium-sized companies: outflank the hungry bankers. P. S. Nadler. Harvard Bus R 55:8+ My '77
Mixed springtime. il Time 109:62 My 2 '77
More bang for the buck: the magic of electronic banking; electronic funds transfer. S. Rose. Fortune 95:202-5+ My '77
Profit seesaw in basic industries. il Bus W p36-7 F 14 '77
Profits at a record and heading higher. il U.S. News 83:57 Ag 8 '77
Profits in collecting preferred dividends. il Bus W p 118+ O 17 '77
Profits picture for '77: its meaning for investors. il U.S. News 82:69-70 F 14 '77
Profits start leveling off—. il U.S. News 83:87 N 7 '77
Profits: up again, and still climbing. il U.S. News 82:104 My 9 '77
Quality vs. quantity. il Forbes 119:71 F 1 '77
Reports of the death of common stocks are greatly exaggerated. B. Malkiel. il Fortune 96:156-60+ N '77
Responding to divisional profit crises. R. G. Hamermesh. Harvard Bus R 55:124-30 Mr '77
Roller-coaster to nowhere. il Time 110:44-6+ Ag 29 '77
Search for a leveraged buyout. J. M. Stancill. Harvard Bus R 55:8+ Jl '77
Second-quarter profits indicate solid growth. il Bus W p 17-18 Ag 1 '77
Third-quarter hint of a profit slowdown. il Bus W p30 O 31 '77
Thriving in a recession; medium-sized industrials. D. K. Clifford, Jr. il Harvard Bus R 55:57-65 Jl '77
U.S. companies flee the mark. il Bus W p78 My 23 '77
See also
Acceptances
Budget, Business
Capital
Corporations—Accounting
Corporations—Valuation
Corporations, International—Finance
Dividends
Employees as stockholders
Small business—Finance

Statistics

Forbes assets 500. il Forbes 119:165-6+ My 15 '77
Forbes market 500. il Forbes 119:177-8+ My 15 '77
Forbes profits 500. il Forbes 119:189-90+ My 15 '77
Forbes sales 500. il Forbes 119:157-60+ My 15 '77
Forbes yardsticks: 1977. il Forbes 121:38-42+ Ja 9 '78
Fortune directory; largest U.S. non-industrial corporations; with introd by M. Dann. il Fortune 96:160-75 Jl '77
Fortune directory of the second 500 largest U.S. industrial corporations; with introd by A. M. Morrison. il Fortune 95:204-32 Je '77
Fortune directory; with introd by S. Wittebort. il Fortune 95:364-91 My '77
Little less push from profits. il Bus W p91-8+ D 26 '77
Survey of corporate performance (title varies) (cont) il Bus W p77-84+ Mr 21; 88+ My 16; 61-8+ Ag 15; 105-9+ N 14 '77
Top 100 industrials: 1917, 1929, 1945, 1966, 1977. il Forbes 120:128-9+ S 15 '77
Who employs the most people; a roster of 500 largest private employers. il Forbes 119:285-7+ My 15 '77
Who's where in profitability. il Forbes 121:177-8+ Ja 9 '78

Foreign business

American business bribery shakes the world—can Americans remake it? R. H. Heindel. Intellect 105:312-13 Ap '77
Antitrusters aim overseas. il Bus W p 100+ Mr 14 '77
Canada's weak dollar yields little profit. il Bus W p58 N 21 '77
Case of the tangled transfer price. M. E. Barrett. il Harvard Bus R 55:20-2+ My '77
Coping with the new rules of conduct. Bus W p76-7 O 10 '77
Employment practices in South Africa; remarks, October 5, 1977. C. R. Vance. Dept State Bull 77:685-6 N 14 '77
Kissinger's complaint. Time 110:52 Jl 11 '77
Losing something in the translation. F. F. Mauser. Harvard Bus R 55:14+ Jl '77
National and multilateral action on corrupt practices; address, April 21, 1977. M. B. Feldman. Dept State Bull 76:554-6 My 30 '77
Profit in breaking Japanese traditions; management techniques of U.S. subsidiaries. il Bus W p51-2 F 14 '77
Rentier economy would threaten manufacturing jobs. G. Tyler. M Labor R 100:45-6 Mr '77
Report warns on danger of Iran sales corruption. E. Kozicharow. Aviation W 107:22-3 D 12 '77
Shadowy underside of international trade. T. N. Gladwin and I. Walter. Sat R 4:16+ Jl 9 '77
This Communist internationale has a capitalist accent; establishment of Soviet corporations in foreign countries to improve trade relations. H. E. Meyer. il Fortune 95:134-7+ F '77
Treasury Secretary Blumenthal testifies on legislation on illicit payments abroad; statement, March 16, 1977. W. M. Blumenthal. Dept State Bull 76:351-5 Ap 11 '77
See also
Export-import trade
Insurance companies—Foreign business

Foreign subsidiaries

See Corporations—Foreign business

Laws and legislation

See Corporation law

Location

See Location in business and industry

Meetings

Hidden agenda; board of directors' meetings. R. K. Mueller. bibl f Harvard Bus R 55:40-1+ S '77

Price policies

See Price policies

Psychological aspects

See Psychology, Industrial

Public relations

See Business—Public relations

Reorganization

Arden-Mayfair's fifth turnaround try. il Bus W p30 Mr 14 '77
See also
Conglomerate corporations—Reorganization

Size

Media goliath; sample of conglomerates in the communications industry. Harpers 255:28-9 Jl '77

Social aspects

See Business—Social aspects

Statistics

See also
Corporations—Finance—Statistics

Taxation

Another weapon against inflation: tax policy. il pors Bus W p94+ O 3 '77
Arab boycott of Israel. N. Turck. bibl f For Affairs 55:472-93 Ap '77
Business stakes are high. il Bus W p53+ Ag 29 '77
Carter's new option play; tax-based incomes policy. M. Ruby and others. il Newsweek 90: 91-2 N 28 '77
Coming tax reform: read the fine print. il Forbes 120:21-3 Ag 1 '77
How new state taxes will bite business. il Bus W p30 Jl 18 '77
Integration of income taxes: issues for debate. C. E. McLure, Jr and S. S. Surrey. il Harvard Bus R 55:169-81 S '77
Manifesto for a tax revolution. A. F. Ehrbar. il Fortune 95:90-5+ Ap '77
New bill in Congress, if enacted, spells tax relief for firms subjected to liability exposures; Product Liability Insurance Tax Equity Act of 1977. A. T. Kornblut. Archit Rec 162:53 D '77
Reforming the tax laws; views of four tax authorities. U.S. News 83:34-8 Jl 25 '77
Relief from double taxation of dividend income. D. T. Smith; discussion. Harvard Bus R 55: 168+ Mr; 164+ My '77
Shifting priorities for corporate taxation. por Bus W p24+ Jl 4 '77
Something for no one; A. Ullman's jobs tax credit bill. il por Time 109:44+ Mr 7 '77
Strange case of the IRS questionnaire; address, May 3, 1977. R. E. Hanson. Vital Speeches 43:498-501 Je 1 '77
Tax gimmickry at its finest; tax credit proposals in jobs bill. M. Friedman. Newsweek 89:90 Ap 11 '77
Tax outlook: hidden traps for business. R. R. Statham. il Nations Bus 65:22-4 N '77
Taxing the multistate company. il Bus W p36+ Ap 11 '77
See also
Corporations—Taxation
Mining industry and finance—Taxation
Petroleum industry—Taxation

Valuation

Who's where in the stock market. il Forbes 121: 201-3+ Ja 9 '78

CORPORATIONS, Foreign
See also
Corporations—Foreign business
CORPORATIONS, Government

Great Britain

BNOC: new power in international oil. J. Ross-Skinner. por Duns R 109:84 My '77
See also
British Steel Corporation

Guyana

Comrate capitalist; head of Guystac. por Forbes 119:148 Ap 15 '77
CORPORATIONS, International
Challenges facing the multinational corporation; address, September 21, 1977. N. B. Sommer. Vital Speeches 44:85-8 N 15 '77
Controlling the cost of international compensation. M. R. Foote. il Harvard Bus R 55:123-32 N '77
Developing codes of conduct for multinational enterprises; statement, September 7, 1977. P. H. Boeker. Dept State Bull 77:475-9 O 10 '77
Fortune directory of the 500 largest industrial corporations outside the U.S; with introd by R. Leggett. il Fortune 96:225-39 Ag '77
Multinational corporations. Dept State Bull 77:707-8 N 14 '77
Multinational investment and global purpose; address, June 17, 1977. L. A. Iacocca. Vital Speeches 43:720-4 S 15 '77
Multinationals as agents of social development. R. L. Meier. il Bull Atom Sci 33:30-2+ N '77
Myopia and multinationals; address, February 7, 1977. R. H. Malott. Vital Speeches 43:363-6 Ap 1 '77
Myth of the big, bad multinational. L. A. Iacocca. por Newsweek 90:21 S 12 '77
Role of investment in expanding an open international economic system; address, June 27, 1977. R. N. Cooper. Dept State Bull 77:127-31 Jl 25 '77
Why the multinational tide is ebbing. S. Rose. il Fortune 96:110-14+ Ag '77
See also
Bechtel Corporation
Collective bargaining—Multinational bargaining
Corporations—Foreign business
Eaton Corporation
Gillette Company
Philips of Eindhoven companies
United Nations—Ad Hoc Intergovernmental Working Group on the Problem of Corrupt Practices

Accounting

See Corporations—Accounting

Anecdotes, facetiae, satire, etc.

Uge: the inside story; excerpt from The age of uncertainty. J. K. Galbraith. il Horizon 19:4-13 Mr '77

Finance

Annual survey of international corporate performance: 1976. il Bus W p80-3+ Jl 25 '77
Guessing game for corporate treasurers. Bus W p70 O 3 '77
Trying to outrun currency swings; effect of foreign exchange accounting rule on earnings. Bus W p 108+ F 14 '77

Management

See Business management

Taxation

Multinationals rush to beat new taxes; West Germany. il Bus W p52 O 10 '77
CORPORATIONS and education. See Business and education
CORPS of Engineers. See United States—Army—Corps of Engineers
CORPULENCE. See Obesity
CORPUS allatum. See Insects—Anatomy
CORPUS CHRISTI, Tex.
Control sewer corrosion with H_2O_2. D. G. Matthews. Am City & County 92:65 F '77
CORPUSCLES (blood) See Blood cells
CORRECTIONAL institutions. See Reformatories
CORRELATION (education)
Interdisciplinary approach to curriculum and instruction: from purpose to method. B. I. Troutman, Jr. Clearing H 50:200-1 Ja '77
Interdisciplinary education: a continuing experiment. M. G. Wolman. bibl Science 198:800-4 N 25 '77
Reading improvement through art; success story from the Big Apple. S. K. Corwin; reply. I. Seidenberg. Sch Arts 77:66 S '77
CORRESPONDENCE. See International correspondence; Letter writing
CORRESPONDENCE schools and courses
Home study courses. Mech Illus 73:20 Ag '77
CORRESPONDENT banks. See Banks and banking—Correspondent banks
CORRESPONDENTS, Foreign. See Foreign correspondents
CORRESPONDENTS, War. See War correspondents
CORRIDA (sports car) See Sports cars
CORRIDORS. See Halls
Il CORRIERE della sera (newspaper) See Milan, Italy—Newspapers
CORRIGAN, Mairead
Good news from Norway. pors Chr Cent 94:973 O 26 '77 *
Is peace in Northern Ireland becoming possible at last? pors U.S. News 83:84+ O 24 '77 *
Two Peace Prizes from Oslo. il pors Time 110:54 O 24 '77 *
Two women of Ulster. K. Willenson and A. Collings. il pors Newsweek 90:61 O 24 '77 *
CORROSION and anticorrosives
Cathodic protection guards Cleveland water system. R. Klimko. il Am City & County 92:54-5 Mr '77
Control sewer corrosion with H_2O_2; Corpus Christi, Tex. D. G. Matthews. Am City & County 92:65 F '77
Detroit's war on car corrosion. G. Stone. il Pop Sci 212:84-7 Ja '78
Fighting rust, the perennial foe. T. Tappett il Mech Illus 73:112+ N '77
Sir Humphry Davy's battle with the sea. P. M. Lauren. bibl il pors Chemistry 50:14-17 S '77
Investigating the corrosion of iron. P. M. Lauren. bibl il Chemistry 50:25-7 S '77
Rust removal & prevention. il McCalls 104:44 Ag '77
Understanding corrosion; boats. il Motor B & S 139:80-2 Mr '77
CORRUPTION in politics. See Politics, Corruption in
CORRY, John
Golden clan; excerpt. il N Y Times Mag p 16-19+ Mr 13 '77
Koch story. il pors N Y Times Mag p 15-17+ O 30 '77
CORSARO, Frank
Don Giovanni as the ideal sensualist; excerpt from Maverick: a director's personal experience in theater and opera. por Hi Fi 27:MA6-7+ D '77

about

Boring the audience is unforgivable. P. Andrews. il pors Horizon 20:58-65 O '77 *
Music. D. Hamilton. Nation 224:601-2 My 14 '77 *
CORSICANS in literature. See French in literature
CORSO, Lee
Don't let 'em wear you down! J. Underwood. il pors Sports Illus 47:46-8+ N 14 '77 *
CORT, John C.
Growing strength of anti-capitalism. America 137:478-80 D 31 '77
Time for stock-taking. Commonweal 104:198-9 Ap 1 '77
CORTÉS, Margaret
Variations on poems by Ezra Pound. Poetry 131:63-6 N '77
CORTESE, Saverio
Mobile concrete batchers save time, manpower and money. il Am City & County 92:51-2 F '77
CORTÉZ, Sea of. See California, Gulf of
CORTICOSTEROIDS
Glucocorticoid in inflammatory proliferative skin disease reduces arachidonic and hydroxyeicosatetraenoic acids. S. Hammarström and others. bibl il Science 197:994-6 S 2 '77
CORTICOTROPIN. See ACTH
CORTISOL. See Hydrocortisone
CORTRIGHT, Barbara
Metalsmith. il Craft Horiz 37:32-9 Ap '77
(ed) See Wilson, M. Jr. Mortimer Wilson: romantic baroque in the Southwest
CORTRIGHT, David
Minimal coercion: the plan to revive the draft. Progressive 41:25-8 Je '77
—and Borosage, R. L.
It's budget time again. Nation 224:205-8 F 19 '77
CORUÑA, Spain
Black tide of la Coruña: oil spill off Spain. E. R. Gundlach and others. il map Oceans 10:56-60 Mr '77
CORVETTE (sports car) See Sports cars
CORWIN, Sylvia K.
Contemplation of form. il Sch Arts 77:18-19 O '77
COSBY, Bill
Dr Bill Cosby. L. Robinson. il pors Ebony 32:130-2+ Je '77 *
COSCINA, Donald V. and Stancer, H. C.
Selective blockade of hypothalamic hyperphagia and obesity in rats by serotonin-depleting midbrain lesions. bibl il Science 195:416-19 Ja 28 '77
COSELL, Hilary
Is it true what they say about private schools? Seventeen 36:138-9+ O '77
COSELL, Howard
Celebrity. B. DeMott. il Atlantic 240:81-2 Jl '77 *
COSERV. See National Council for Community Services to International Visitors

COSGRAVE, Liam
Gentleman Jack gets back. por Time 109:27 Je 27 '77 *
COSGRAVE, Mary Silva
Outlook tower. See issues of Horn book magazine
COSGROVE, John
Risk management: new ways for business to insure against loss. il Nations Bus 65:75-8+ N '77
COSMETIC allergy. See Allergy
COSMETIC surgery. See Surgery, Plastic
COSMETICS
About face: do-it-yourself facials; skin-care products. Seventeen 36:104-5 Ag '77
Beauty bazaar. See issues of Harper's bazaar
Beauty now: everything to know about mascara. il Vogue 167:130 O '77
De-mystifying beauty; using cosmetics safely. Mademoiselle 83:28 F '77
18 summer surprises. il Redbook 149:54+ Ag '77
For safer sunning. Fam Health 9:38-9 Je '77
Hand lotions and creams. il Consumer Rep 42: 448-51 Ag '77
Health & beauty update. R. Graham. See issues of House beautiful
Is your skin dying of thirst? moisturizers. M. Hill. il Am Home 80:46-7+ Jl '77
Moisturizers. . .how they work—and why. Vogue 167:83 Ap '77
Safe glow; sunscreens. A. Taylor. N Y Times Mag p74 F 6 '77
You & the sun & those tanning lotions. il Changing T 31:19-20 Je '77
See also
Beauty, Personal
Beauty shops
Make-up
Nail polish removers
Toilet preparations

Labeling

See Labels
COSMETICS for men
See also
Perfumes for men
COSMETICS industry
Beauty: color '77; new products. B. Morris. il Vogue 167:282-91 O '77
His-and-hers cosmetics team; Redken Laboratories Inc. il pors Bus W p 140 S 12 '77
Making an impression; women in the cosmetics industry. A. Penney. il N Y Times Mag p38-9 Jl 17 '77
Redken Labs: business is beautiful. il por Duns R 110:30-1 Jl '77
Scientific skin care; Scientific hair care. il Harp Baz 110:190-3 S '77
Second thoughts on going public; Charles of the Ritz Company. R. Salomon. il Harvard Bus R 55:126-31 S '77
See also
Avon Products, Inc

Finance

Personal products & health care. il Forbes 121: 126-8 Ja 9 '78
COSMIC physics
See also
Solar wind
COSMIC rays
Bolts from the heavens; theories of J. W. Follin. il Time 110:105 D 19 '77
Cosmic snooping; U-2 flights. P. Gwynne and S. Begley. il Newsweek 90:88 N 28 '77
Giving cosmic rays their bounce. Sci N 111:309 My 14 '77
COSMOCHEMISTRY. See Astrochemistry
COSMOGONY
See also
Universe
COSMOLOGY
Clustering of galaxies. E. J. Groth and others. il Sci Am 237:76-8+ bibl (p 163) N '77
Cosmic calendar; excerpt from The dragons of Eden. C. Sagan. il Read Digest 111:148-9 O '77
Cosmic snooping; U-2 flights. P. Gwynne and S. Begley. il Newsweek 90:88 N 28 '77
Cosmological constant and cosmological change; adaptation of address, December 1976. B. M. Tinsley. bibl il Phys Today 30:32-8 Je '77
Cosmology today. L. C. Green. il Sky & Tel 54:180-4 S '77
Creation according to cosmology. J. Marsh. Commentary 64:65-6 O '77
Deuterium quantity and cosmology. Sci N 111:55 Ja 22 '77
Einstein's world and the big numbers game. D. E. Thomsen. Sci N 112:157-8 S 3 '77
Flying through the cosmos. D. E. Thomsen. il Sci N 112:44-5 Jl 16 '77
How much deuterium? il Sky & Tell 53:253 Ap '77
Intergalactic gas: toward a closed universe. il Sci N 112:36 Jl 16 '77
It moves. Sci Am 237:70+ N '77
Out of chaos; excerpt. L. J. Halle. Sci Digest 82:16-20+ S '77
Physics and the cosmos. J. Bernstein. Natur Hist 86:106-7+ O '77
Protoscientific revolution; 12th-century cosmologists; with views of Tina Stiefel. Sci Am 238:68-9 Ja '78
Smoothing out the universe. D. E. Thomsen. il Sci N 111:41 Ja 15 '77
See also
Universe
COSMONAUTS. See Astronauts
COSMOS
How comely the cosmos. H. V. Wilson. il Horticulture 55:28-31 Je '77
COSMOS satellites. See Artificial satellites—Cosmos missions
COSS, Clare, and others
Daughters. Reviews
Ms 6:29-30 N '77 *
COST
See also
Labor cost
also subhead Cost under various subjects, e.g. Nucear reactors—Cost
COST (law)
Rich get rich, and the poor get lawyers. S. Chapman. New Repub 117:9-10+ S 24 '77
See also
Lawyers—Salaries, fees, etc.
COST benefit analysis. See Cost effectiveness
COST effectiveness
Controlling the cost of international compensation. M. R. Foote. il Harvard Bus R 55:123-32 N '77
Disasters as a necessary part of benefit-cost analyses. R. K. Mark and D. E. Stuart-Alexander. bibl Science 197:1160-2 S 16 '77
High costs of intervention; government regulation. il Bus W p65-6+ Ap 4 '77
Regulation's phantom benefits—ICC style. S. Zucker. il Bus W p83+ My 16 '77
COST of automobile operation. See Automobiles—Cost of operation
COST of food. See Food—Prices
COST of living
Cost-of-living indexes for Americans living abroad (cont) M Labor R 100:64 Ja; 78 Ap; 69 O '77
See also
Budget, Household
Income

United States

Inflation is only 6%. il Forbes 120:86 N 1 '77
Living with high prices: how people are changing their ways. il U.S. News 83:16-17 Jl 18 '77
Price data. See issues of Monthly labor review
Retiring? a guide to cheapest cities. il U.S. News 83:36 Ag 22 '77
Way living costs vary in 40 areas. il U.S. News 82:93 My 9 '77
Where are the greener pastures? il Changing T 31:4 Je '77
Your Mafia cost of living. il Esquire 87:80-1+ F '77
See also
Food—Prices
Price indexes
Prices—United States
COST of living wage adjustments. See Wages—Cost of living adjustments
COST of medical care. See Medical care, Cost of
COSTA, Horacio de la
Obituary
America 136: inside cover Ap 2 '77. J. O'Hare
COSTA RICA
See also
Botany—Costa Rica
Fishing—Costa Rica
Investments, American—Costa Rica

Politics and government

Don Pepe; interview, ed by K. Bode. J. Figueres. New Repub 176:13-15 Ap 23 '77; Reply. D. Oduber. 176:15 My 28 '77
See also
Elections—Costa Rica
Politics, Corruption in—Costa Rica
COSTAKIS, George
Momentous happening in Moscow. il por Time 109:75-6 Ap 11 '77 *
COSTAKIS, George, collection. See Art—Private collections
COSTANZA, Margaret
Jimmy and the folks. J. Osborne. New Repub 176:8+ Ap 30 '77 *
Midge Costanza: one door from the Oval Office. V. Cadden. il pors Ms 6:48-51+ Ja '78 *
Pantsuit powerhouse. E. Clift. por Newsweek 89: 32 F 14 '77 *
That other White House woman. por Time 110:14 S 12 '77 *
Trouble with Midge. T. Mathews and others. por Newsweek 90:49 N 7 '77 *

COSTELLO, Elvis
Elvis Costello: new wave rock classicist; My aim is true. S. Sutherland. por Hi Fi 27:138 D '77 *
England's Elvis: gut emotions. il por Time 110:60 D 26 '77 *

COSTELLO, Harry
Bishops play monopoly. D. Morrissey. Commonweal 104:528-30 Ag 19 '77 *

COSTELLO, John
Executive trends. See issues of Nation's business to December 1977

COSTEN, Bill
Up, up and away. il pors Ebony 32:88-90+ Jl '77 *

COSTERTON, J. W. and others
How bacteria stick; with biographical sketch. il Sci Am 238:12, 86-95 Ja '78

COSTIGAN, James
Eleanor and Franklin: the White House years; excerpt from screenplay. il Sr Schol 109:14-17 Mr 10 '77

COSTIGAN, Madeleine
House on twist road; story. McCalls 104:130-1 Je '77
Living room; story. McCalls 105:174-5 O '77
Some cold winter night; story. McCalls 104:130-1 Mr '77
Tuesday's heroine; story. McCalls 104:122-3 Jl '77
What do you learn at a writers conference? Writer 90:16-18+ D '77

COSTLE, Douglas Michael
EPA's new man. L. Langway and J. Bishop, Jr. por Newsweek 89:80-1+ F 21 '77 *
New day at the EPA? interview, ed by J. Doherty. por Nat Wildlife 15:18-19 Ag '77
New U.S. pollution challenge: a deluge of dangerous chemicals; interview. por U.S News 83:31-2 D 19 '77

COSTUME
Dressed to thrill: simple Halloween costumes. E. Gross. il Seventeen 36:58 O '77
See also
Fashion

Exhibitions

Style: the craft of being you. il Craft Horiz 37:12-13 D '77
See also
Metropolitan Museum of Art, New York—Costume Institute

Peru

Liberation à limeña; tapadas worn by women. V. C. Holmgren. il Américas 29:12-13 Je '77

Russia

From Russia, with opulence. E. R. Lipson. il N Y Times Mag p48-9+ Ja 16 '77
Russian costume; exhibition at the Metropolitan Museum of Art. S. B. Sherrill. il Antiques 111:266+ F '77

COSTUME, Theatrical
The cloak; symbol of love, violence, revenge, and despair in literature and opera. J. Kestner. il Opera N 41:24-6 F 26 '77
Madame Barbara Karinska: costumes to delight; ballet costumes. V. Huckenpahler. il pors Dance Mag 52:44-7 Ja '78
Name it, she'll make it; R. West. il pors Ebony 32:66+ My '77
What a wild idea: Lewitzky and Gernreich design a dance; Inscape. V. H. Swisher. il pors Dance Mag 51:75-7 Mr '77

Japan

Masterpieces of No. il Art N 76:116 S '77
Nō robe as perfection. J. Brzostoski. il Craft Horiz 37:22-7 Ag '77
Sumptuous robes from Japan; exhibition of Nō theater items at New York's Japan Society. R. Hughes. il Time 109:71 Je 13 '77
Tokugawa collection; exhibition of Nō drama objects. D. Leder. America 137:82 Ag 13 '77

COSTUME design
Craftsman's approach to apparel design. R. Hillestad. il Design (US) 78:22-5 Spr '77
Inaugural togs: less is more. il Time 109:69 Ja 24 '77
Renaissance of haute couture. B. Morris. il N Y Times Mag p76-8+ F 27 '77
See also
Fashion shows

History

Haute couture of decades past recollected by Penn and Vreeland in Viking book; interview, ed by R. Dahlin. I. Penn. il Pub W 211:44+ Ja 31 '77

COSTUME designers
California comers. M. McEvoy. il N Y Times Mag p60-3 Ja 8 '78
Great new looks from top designers. il Harp Baz 110:146-53 O '77
Here's how they spent the summer; photographs. B. Walz. N Y Times Mag p34-7 S 4 '77
Milan signals—where the action is; tr by G. Alhadeff. M. Pezzi. il Vogue 167:108-9+ Jl '77
Paris signals—new designers. M. Russell. il Vogue 167:106-7+ Jl '77
Unbuckled Sunbelt look; West Coast designers. il Time 109:46-7 F 21 '77
See also
Burrows, S.
Chanel, G.
Klein, C. R.
McFadden, M.
St Laurent, Y. M.
West, R.

COSTUME Institute. See Metropolitan Museum of Art, New York—Costume Institute

COTLER, Irwin. See Wisse, R. R. jt auth

COTTAGE cheese
See also
Cookery—Cheese

COTTAGE industries
Business begins at home. C. Jessup and G. Chipps. Am Home 80:63+ S '77
How to make money without taking a job. McCalls 104:76 Jl '77
How to set up a business in your home. J. Alter. bibl Bet Hom & Gard 55:26+ O '77

COTTAGES
What it's like to live in a rose-covered cottage. il House & Gard 149:122-5 Mr '77

COTTER, James Finn
Along King's highway; poem. Commonweal 104:818 D 23 '77
Forgiving Robert Frost. America 137:463-5 D 24 '77
Poetry is dead, long live poetry. bibl America 137:80-2 Ag 13 '77
Poetry of apocalypse. America 136:295-7 Ap 2 '77
Trailways to Jersey shore; poem. Commonweal 104:555 S 2 '77

COTTER, William R. See Ferguson, C. jt auth

COTTESLOE Theatre. See National Theatre (Great Britain)

COTTLE, Thomas J.
Cost of hope. America 136:125-7 F 12 '77
Jamie Horace Pinkerton. il America 136:370-3 Ap 23 '77
Nobody's special when they're poor. Yale R 66:388-98 Mr '77
Question of fault. Progressive 41:34-6 O '77
Thomas J. Cottle on behavior. New Repub 177:29-30 D 3 '77

COTTON

Marketing

Cottons natural comeback; Cotton Inc. por Forbes 119:80 Ap 1 '77

Prices

Government experts to deal with cotton trade problems. UN Chron 14:36 Jl '77

COTTON fabrics
More cotton in men's durable press shirts. il Consumers Res Mag 60:24-8 Mr '77

COTTON Inc. See Cotton—Marketing

COTTON industry

Export-import trade

Government experts to deal with cotton trade problems. UN Chron 14:36 Jl '77

COTTON workers. See Textile workers

COTTONTAILS. See Rabbits

COTTRELL, Joseph J.
Resurrecting a ruined company. P. Schwab. por Nations Bus 65:102 N '77 *

COTTRELL, Kim
Superstrain of oil-eating microbes. il Sea Front 23:28-31 Ja '77

COTURNIX. See Quails

COTZIAS, George Constantin, and Tang, L. C.
Adenylate cyclase of brain reflects propensity for breast cancer in mice. bibl Science 197:1094-6 S 9 '77

—and others
Levodopa, fertility, and longevity. bibl il Science 196:549-51 Ap 29 '77

COUCH, John A. and others
Kepone-induced scoliosis and its histological consequences in fish. bibl il Science 197:585-7 Ag 5 '77

COUCHES, Convertible. See Furniture, Convertible

COUGARS. See Pumas

COUGH medicines. See Medicines, Patent, proprietary, etc.

COUGHLIN, William P.
Deadly trade in under-built boats. il Motor B & S 139:61-5+ Ap '77

COULAN, Robert F.
Inter-service weapons rivalry. bibl il Bull Atom Sci 33:25-36 Je '77

COULTER, Steven Earl
Tracing your family tree. il Bet Hom & Gard 55:10+ Je '77

COUNCIL for American Private Education
Private schools: in support of diversity. R. L. Lamborn. Educ Digest 43:53-5 O '77

COUNCIL-manager government. See City manager plan

COUNCIL of Better Business Bureaus. See Better Business Bureaus
COUNCIL of Economic Advisers. See United States—Council of Economic Advisers
COUNCIL of Economic Priorities
More burning of coal offsets gains in air pollution control. L. J. Carter. Science 198:1233 D 23 '77
COUNCIL of Europe
Trends of the Twenties; exhibition of European art. W. S. Lieberman. il Art N 76:39-44 O '77
COUNCIL on Environmental Quality. See United States—Council on Environmental Quality
COUNCIL on Foreign Relations
Member of the CFR talks back. Z. Nagorski. Nat R 29:1416-19 D 9 '77
COUNCIL on Interracial Books for Children
Any writer who follows anyone else's guidelines ought to be in advertising. N. Hentoff. por SLJ 24:27-9 N '77
Humans vs. anti-humans in children's book world. Am Lib 8:176 Ap '77
Would-be censors of the left. L. N. Gerhardt; discussion. SLJ 23:3 Ap '77
COUNCIL on Library Resources, Inc
Council on Library Resources: a 20-year report. N. E. Gwinn. bibl il Lib J 102:330-4 F 1 '77
17 midcareer librarians get CLR fellowships. Lib J 102:1232 Je 1 '77
COUNCIL on Wage and Price Stability. See United States—Council on Wage and Price Stability
COUNCILMEN
Confessions of a town councilman; Bedford, N.Y. R. Lemon. Read Digest 110:122-5 My '77
COUNCILS and synods
See also
Synod of Bishops, 1977
Vatican Council, 2d
COUNSELING
Crisis counseling; program for students and parents at Yerba Buena High School in San Jose, Calif. S. B. Neill. il Am Educ 13:17-22 Ja '77
Guidance centers: where women can find themselves. J. Wilkins. Good H 184:152+ Je '77
Help! How to cope with it all. J. L. Barkas. Redbook 149:81-8 O '77
Help at the halfway point; counseling programs for women. L. Davis. Vogue 167:88 Je '77
How to make love not war; counseling for unmarried couples. M. Fabe. Mademoiselle 83: 119+ D '77
Relating; questions and answers. A. Wood. See issues of Seventeen
See also
Families Anonymous (organization)
Genetic counseling
Marriage counseling
Pastoral counseling
Personnel service in education
Telephone in counseling
Vocational guidance
COUNSELING, Financial. See Financial services
COUNSELORS
Burn-out: the hazard of professional people-helpers. G. R. Collins. Chr Today 21:12-14 Ap 1 '77
See also
Camp counselors
Student counselors
COUNTER, Allen
Bush Negroes carry on tradition of rebel ancestors. C. M. Turnbull. il Smithsonian 7:78-85 Mr '77 *
COUNTERCULTURE
Avant-garde parents: traditional infants. Sci N 111:262 Ap 23 '77
COUNTERCULTURE literature
See also
Mother earth news
COUNTERFEIT money. See Counterfeits and counterfeiting
COUNTERFEITING. See Counterfeits and counterfeiting
COUNTERFEITS and counterfeiting
How Levi's cracked a ring of counterfeiters. il Bus W p27 S 5 '77
Paper money—portraits and counterfeits. G. Rayner. Hobbies 82:131 My '77
See also
Forgery of works of art
COUNTERS, Frequency. See Frequency meters
COUNTERS, Kitchen. See Kitchen furniture
COUNTING machines and devices
Flip-flops and decade counters. F. M. Mims. il Pop Electr 11:75-6 F; 96-8 Mr '77
Timers and counters. L. Garner. il Pop Electr 11: 66-9+ F '77
COUNTING the ways; drama. See Albee, E.
COUNTRIES. See Nations
COUNTRY and city. See City and country
COUNTRY churches
Rural church and rural religion: analysis of data from children and youth. H. M. Nelsen and R. H. Potvin. bibl f il Ann Am Acad 429:103-14 Ja '77
COUNTRY clubs
Hampden Country Club designed by Paolo Riani Associates; golf club. il Archit Rec 161:122-3 F '77
We'll see you at the club; Country Club of Indianapolis. L. K. Howe. il McCalls 104:30+ F '77
COUNTRY Dance and Song Society of America. See Dance companies
COUNTRY doctors. See Medical care, Rural
COUNTRY houses
Country house, California style: Marin County. J. Friedman-Weiss and H. H. Wise. McCalls 104:104-6 S '77
See also
Farmhouses
COUNTRY houses, Remodeled. See Houses, Remodeled
COUNTRY inns. See Hotels, motels, etc.
COUNTRY life
Country living. G. Logsdon. See issues of Organic gardening and farming
For many fleeing the cities, rural life is no paradise. il U.S. News 83:44-6 Jl 18 '77
Joy in hard times. B. Gilbert. il Sports Illus 47: 100-4+ D 19 '77
Lion in the rain-rinsed morning. J. Curtis. il Atlantic 240:67-73 S '77
Quality of life in rural America. D. A. Dillman and K. R. Tremblay, Jr. bibl f Ann Am Acad 429:115-29 Ja '77
To know where we have been; excerpts from The Bob Timberlake collection; reproductions of paintings; with text by C. Kuralt and editorial comment. B. Timberlake. il Audubon **79:inside cover, 48-61 My '77. Same abr. Read Digest 111:136-42 S '77**
Today's country style; special section. il Am Home 80:45-51 S '77
You can't talk to the trees! remote country living in California's Sierras. G. Bergman. il Ret Liv 17:32-3 Je '77
See also
City and country
Farm life
Sociology, Rural

Anecdotes, facetiae, satire, etc.

Behind the roses 'round the door; life in an English country cottage. A. Menen. il Horticulture 55:61-5 Ap '77
COUNTRY life in art
She brings back the good old days; with interview with T. Kitchen. J. Strohm. il por Nat Wildlife 16:28-35 D '77
Winter in the country; Currier & Ives lithographs. il Am Hist Illus 12:38-41 D '77
COUNTRY music
Country goes pop. il Horizon 20:52-7 N '77
Country's angels. R. Blount, Jr. il pors Esquire 87:62-7+ Mr '77
George Jones: I'm never gonna sell pop. N. Tosches. il pors Hi Fi 27:103-5 My '77
In the heart of honky-tonk rock; Austin, Tex. il Time 110:86+ S 19 '77
Rose-colored map. B. Marsh. il Harpers 255:80-2 Jl '77
Singer Loretta Lynn tells why country music thrives. L. Lynn. pors U.S. News 83:71 O 24 '77
You've come a long way, Dolly; D. Parton. J. Hurst. il por Hi Fi 27:122-4 D '77
See also
Gospel music
Phonograph records—Country music
COUNTRYMAN, Vern
Out, damned spot. New Repub 177:15-17 O 8 '77
COUNTS, Charles
Interior monologue: a potter's thoughts amidst work. Ceram Mo 25:19+ D '77
COUNTY buildings
Impressive new government center around a grand atrium space; Hennepin County Government Center, Minneapolis. il Archit Rec 161:101-6 Mr '77
See also
Courthouses
COUNTY centers. See County buildings
COUNTY fairs. See Fairs
Le **COUP de Fusil (restaurant)** See New York (city)—Hotels, restaurants, etc.
COUPERIN, François
Concerts royaux; Nouveaux concerts; recording. W. L. Purcell. il Am Rec G 40:31-4 F '77 *
COUPLES, Unmarried. See Unmarried couples
COUPONS
Coupon clippers of '77; food discount coupons. L. Langway and J. Huck. il Newsweek 89: 75 Je 20 '77
COURAGE
Courage continued. E. Schaeffer. Chr Today 12: 23 Ag 12 '77
COURAGE North (camp) See Camps—Minnesota
COURBET, Gustave
Always controversial Monsieur Courbet. A. Werner. il por Am Artist 41:58-63+ S '77 *
Courbet: painting as politics; retrospective at the Grand Palais in Paris. R. Hughes. il Time 110:110-1 D 5 '77 *

COURCHESNE, Eric
Event-related brain potentials: comparison between children and adults. bibl il Science 197:589-92 Ag 5 '77

COURNAND, André Frederic
Code of the scientist and its relationship to ethics; address, May 27, 1977. bibl Science 198:699-705 N 18 '77

COURSES of study
Mini-course as an experiment in alternative education. S. C. Diamond. Clearing H 51:11 S '77
See also
Black studies
Colleges and universities—Curriculum
Curriculum planning
High schools—Curriculum
Peace studies
School schedules
Vocational education

Anecdotes, facetiae, satire, etc.

Charting new courses. D. Getz. Seventeen 36:28+ My '77

COURT houses. See Courthouses

COURT of King Arithmetic; drama. See Chaloner, G.

COURT stenographers. See Stenographers

COURTESY
Sexual courtesy. K. Durbin. Mademoiselle 83:147+ Mr '77
Who says manners are out of style? L. Baldridge. Seventeen 36:142-3 My '77
See also
Etiquette

COURTHOUSES
Nigeria's Court of Appeals will have six regional centers. il Archit Rec 161:41 Mr '77
Temples of democracy. C. Trillin. il Am Heritage 28:50-61 O '77

COURTLY love
See also
Troubadours

COURTRIGHT, Bill
Flowers in the rough. N. K. Koran. il por Ret Liv 17:42 Ap '77 *

COURTS
See also
Criminal procedure
Grand jury
Judges
Judicial review
Jury
Juvenile courts
Small claims courts
Trials
Video recorders and recording—Court use

California

Another first for California; R. E. Bird appointed Chief Justice of Supreme Court. por Time 109:69 F 28 '77
Case of the senile judge; M. McComb. por Newsweek 89:36 Ja 24 '77
Ms chief justice; R. E. Bird. P. Bonventre and W. J. Cook. il por Newsweek 89:70 F 28 '77

Great Britain

See also
Justice, Administration of—Great Britain

Massachusetts

See also
Boston—Courts

New York (state)

See also
New York (city)—Courts

Russia

In Soviet courts, acquittals are rare. R. Knight. il U.S. News 82:34 My 2 '77

Texas

Sins of Justice Yarbrough. por Time 110:44 Jl 18 '77

United States

Class actions shift to the state courts. Bus W p53-4 Ja 24 '77
Crisis in courts—new moves to speed up justice. il U.S. News 83:66-7 Jl 18 '77
Cuba. . .courts. . .coolies. M. Stone. U.S. News 82:84 Mr 28 '77
How liberals are making an end run around the Supreme Court; using state supreme courts. P. Oster. il U.S. News 82:50-1 Ja 31 '77
How to break logjam in courts; interview. W. E. Burger. il pors U.S. News 83:21-4+ D 19 '77
In the name of justice: unending rush to the courts; address, May 18, 1977. S. M. Hufstedler. Vital Speeches 43:572-6 Jl 1 '77
Inside the federal court system. il U.S. News 82:52+ My 9 '77
Just leave it to the states; decisions encouraging state court involvement in protecting civil liberties. Time 109:46 Ap 4 '77
We've got too much law! J. K. Footlick. Read Digest 110:96-100 My '77
See also
Judicial Conference of the United States
United States—Supreme Court

Utah

Feet-First Ritter under siege; controversial Federal judge. il por Time 110:63 N 7 '77

COURTS (for games)
See also
Basketball courts
Tennis courts

COURTS, International
See also
International Court of Justice, The Hague

COURTS, Municipal
See also
Boston—Courts
New York (city)—Courts

COURTS of small claims. See Small claims courts

COURTSHIP
See also
Dating
Love letters

COURTSHIP of birds
Chilean flamingo court and dance. J. Muñoz. il Natur Hist 86:72-8 D '77
Rites of spring. il Audubon 79:56-67 Mr '77
Trial balloon; frigate birds; excerpt from Galapagos: islands of birds. B. Nelson. il Audubon 79:42-3 My '77

COURTYARDS
See also
Atriums

COUSE, Eanger Irving
Eanger Irving Couse: the Indian as noble innocent. M. C. Nelson. il por Am Artist 42:48-53 Ja '78 *

COUSIN, Ronnellee
Black women/white men: the other mixed marriage. il Ebony 33:37-9+ Ja '78

COUSINS, Norman
Mysterious placebo: how mind helps medicine work. il Sat R 5:8-12+ O 1 '77
One chance in 500 to live. por Sat Eve Post 249:52-4+ My '77; Same with title Anatomy of an illness (as perceived by the patient) Sat R 4:4-6+ My 28 '77; Same abr Read Digest 110:130-4 Je '77
Where is the news leading us? il Todays Educ 66:26-7 Mr '77
World I have seen; photographs. Sat Eve Post 249:55-9 My '77

about

Norman Cousins. S. Schiefelbein. il por Sat Eve Post 249:32 My '77 *
Positive power of laughing. Sci Digest 82:19 N '77 *
Saturday's child. T. Schwartz. pors Newsweek 89:89-90 Mr 21 '77 *

COVELL, Mara
Facial pain. Vogue 167:34+ Je '77

COVENANT on Civil and Political Rights. See International Covenant on Civil and Political Rights

COVENANT on Economic, Social and Cultural Rights. See International Covenant on Economic, Social and Cultural Rights

COVENANTS (theology)
Covenant of Israel: old, new and one. J. M. Oesterreicher. il America 137:282-3 O 29 '77

COVENEY, John
Lotte Lehmann remembered. por Hi Fi 27:MA16-17+ Je '77

COVENT Garden Opera Company. See Opera—Great Britain

COVER crops
Hollow-stemmed cover crops for soil aeration. W. Pierce. il Org Gard & Farm 24:174-5 Je '77
See also
Clover
Legumes

COVER design. See Periodical covers

COVER plants
See also
Chamomile
Ivy

COVER-up conspiracy trial. See Watergate trials—Cover-up conspiracy trial

COVERLETS
New Jersey handwoven coverlets; exhibit at the Newark Museum. S. B. Sherrill. il Antiques 111:870+ My '77
See also
Afghans (coverlets)

COVERS, Book. See Book covers

COVERS, Periodical. See Periodical covers

COVERS, Phonograph record. See Phonograph record covers

COVETOUSNESS. See Avarice

COVINA, Calif.

Education

See Education—California

COVINO, Michael
Wim Wenders: a worldwide homesickness. il Film Q 31:9-19 Wint '77

COWAN, Edward
(ed) Dear Dr Schlesinger: here's what I would do about energy. il N Y Times Mag p58-60+ Ap 17 '77

COWAN, Frederick W.
Nazi of New Rochelle. T. Mathews and S. Agrest. il por Newsweek 89:30 F 28 '77 *
Season of savagery and rage. il Time 109:23-4 F 28 '77 *

COWAN, Paul
World of our children. il N Y Times Mag p64-70 Ap 3 '77

COWARD, E. Walter, Jr. See Saint, W. S. jt auth

COWART, Marolyn
Before the baby comes (cont) il Parents Mag 52:24 F '77

COWBIRDS
Species identification in the North American cowbird: appropriate responses to abnormal song. A. P. King and M. J. West. bibl il Science 195:1002-4 Mr 11 '77

COWBOY stories. See Western stories

COWBOYS
Cowboy's West: a special issue; symposium. bibl il Am West 14:4-5+ N '77
Marlboro man; D. Winfield. M. Smith. il pors Sports Illus 46:58-62+ Ja 17 '77
Profiles; H. Blanton. J. Kramer. New Yorker 53:44-6+ My 30; 40-4+ Je 6 '77
Real American cowboy; excerpt from Cowboys. W. H. Forbis. il Read Digest 110:27-30+ Je '77
See also
Rodeos

Bibliography

Best books on the cowboy; comp by W. H. Hutchinson. il Am West 14:49 N '77
Cowboy in myth and reality. O. Ulph. il Am West 14:55 Ja '77

Photographs

Riding the Cherrycow chuck line: a Dane Coolidge portfolio. D. Coolidge. il Am West 14:36-47 N '77

COWBOYS in art
Remington & Russell: delineators of the American cowboy; excerpt from Way west. P. H. Hassrick. il Am West 14:16-29 N '77

COWDEN, Peter. See Jacobs, F. jt auth

COWELL, Henry
Committee for 20th century music: Henry Cowell retrospective. por Hi Fi 27:MA25 Ag '77

COWEN, Robert C.
Climatic change. Current 195:53-6 S '77

COWENS, Dave
Back in business in Boston. J. Papanek. il por Sports Illus 46:22-4+ Ja 24 '77 *
This half, go out there and make statements! R. Blount, Jr. Esquire 87:44+ Ap '77 *

COWLE, Jerry
Something to strive for. il Read Digest 111:171-2+ O '77

COWLES, Chips
He turns kids' dreams into toys. J. Kraus. il pors Ret Liv 17:33+ D '77 *

COWLES, Timothy J. and others
Biological consequences of the 1975 El Niño. bibl il maps Science 195:285-7 Ja 21 '77

COWLEY, John M. and Lijima, Sumio
Electron microscopy of atoms in crystals. bibl il pors Phys Today 30:32-6+ Mr '77

COWLEY, Malcolm
Bruce Bliven. New Repub 176:8-9 Je 11 '77
Can a complete s.o.b. be a good writer? il Esquire 88:120-1+ N '77
Reconsiderations: the '60s. New Repub 177:37-40 Ag 20 '77

COWLEY, Susan (Cheever)
(ed) See Cheever, J. Duet of Cheevers

COWS
Culling cows by choice upgrades a herd faster. Suc Farm 75:no4 D8 Mr '77
See also
Calving
Dairying

Breeding

See Cattle breeding

Breeds

See Cattle—Breeds

Care

Down on the farm. M. Thomas. il Seventeen 36:74+ My '77
Watch out for health problems when you feed only corn silage. C. Bickers. Farm J 101:Dairy 10 O; LK4 N '77

Diseases and pests

Adequate response of plasma 1,25-dihydroxyvitamin D to parturition in paretic (milk fever) dairy cows. R. L. Horst and others. bibl il Science 196:662-3 My 6 '77
Fluorosis: new disease problem on Michigan farms. J. R. Borcherding. il Suc Farm 75: K6 S '77
Old diseases are still a threat to your industry; views of Dr F. Mulhern. Farm J 101:Dairy 14+ F '77
See also
Mastitis

Feeding

Feeding tips to use in drought stressed areas. J. R. Borcherding. il Suc Farm 75:A4 Ja '77
Give her the fuel for top production. il Farm J 101:Dairy 10-11 F '77
How to fit NH_3 treated corn silage to dairy rations. J. R. Borcherding and L. Reichenberger. il Suc Farm 75:C4 Ag '77
Whip disease with nutrition? R. E. Wanner. il Farm J 101:Dairy 10+ Ja '77

Leasing and renting

Cow-leasing generates cash to help you grow. E. Ainsworth. il Farm J 101:Dairy 1-2+ Ja '77

Milk production

See Milk—Production

COWS, Effect of temperature on
Heat stress: 100-1,000 lbs. production loss per cow. J. R. Borcherding. map Suc Farm 75: A2 Ag '77

COX, Archibald
Courts v. self-government. P. H. Connolly. Nat R 29:1225-8 O 28 '77 *
Saturday night live! excerpt from Not above the law. J. Doyle. il pors N Y Times Mag p40+ My 15 '77 *

COX, Elenor R. See Rizzo, P. J. jt auth

COX, Harvey
Eastern cults and western culture: why young Americans are buying Oriental religions; excerpt from Turning East. bibl il por Psychol Today 11:36-40+ Jl; 12+ O '77
More on a Dual-sex Eucharist. Commonweal 104:112-14 F 18 '77

about

Down the Marxist road with Harvey Cox; excerpt from On synthesizing Marxism and Christianity. D. Vree. Chr Today 21:12-14 Ag 26 '77 *

COX, Jeff
(ed) About books. See issues of Organic gardening and farming to December 1977

COX, Juanita
Comprehension revisited. Engl J 66:66-7 O '77

COX, Marilyn
Home-ground, homemade whole wheat. Org Gard & Farm 25:110+ Ja '78

COX, Maxine L.
Bicentennial mural. il Sch Arts 76:32 Ap '77

COX, Robert E. and Sinnott, R. W.
(eds) Gleanings for ATM's. See issues of Sky and telescope

COX, Vic
Murder of the porpoise: closing in on a solution. Sci Digest 82:46-7+ Jl '77
TDI: the unacknowledged poison. Nation 224: 530-2 Ap 30 '77

COX, William M.
Highways: which way to the future? il por Am City & County 92:91-2 O '77

COXEY, Jacob Sechler
Coxey's march on Washington, 1894. G. G. Eggert. il pors Am Hist Illus 12:20-31 O '77 *

COXEY'S Army, 1894
Coxey's march on Washington, 1894. G. G. Eggert. il pors Am Hist Illus 12:20-31 O '77

COYLE, Joseph T. and Molliver, M. E.
Major innervation of newborn rat cortex by monoaminergic neurons. bibl il Science 196: 444-7 Ap 22 '77
—See Herndon, R. M. jt auth

COYNE, John
(ed) See Farrell, J. Business of crafts

COYNE, John R. Jr
(ed) See Bukovsky, V. Word is freedom

COYOTE brush
They get by with little water; dudleya caespitosa and baccharis pilularis. il Sunset 158: 264 Ap '77

COZZENS, James Gould
James Gould Cozzens. N. Perrin. New Repub 177:43-5 S 17 '77 *

CRAB cactus. See Cactus

CRAB fisheries. See Shellfish fisheries

CRAB nebula. See Nebulae

CRABBE, Chris Wallace-. See Wallace-Crabbe, C.

CRABBE, George
Out of The borough; G. Crabbe's poem as the inspiration for B. Britten's opera Peter Grimes. G. Schmidgall. il por Opera N 42:8+ D 10 '77 *

CRABS
Aftermath of an oil spill: a black seven years; effects of Buzzards Bay oil slick on fiddler crab population. il Sci N 112:84 Ag 6 '77
Catching the Dungeness crab. O. W. Larson and H. J. Smith. il Field & S 82:108 Je '77
Long-term effects of an oil spill on populations of the salt-marsh crab uca pugnax. C. T. Krebs and K. A. Burns. bibl il Science 197: 484-7 Jl 29 '77
Nature's odd couples; dependency of hermit crabs on whelk shells and Calvaria major on dodos. S. J. Gould. il Natur Hist 87:38-41 Ja '78

CRABS—*Continued*
What's that coming out of your shirt? Oh, it's just Jo-Jo; G. Spence and hermit crabs. D. Levin. il por Sports Illus 46:44+ F 14 '77
Winter comes to the Bay; blue crabs; excerpt from Beautiful swimmers: watermen, crabs and the Chesapeake Bay. W. Warner. Yachting 141:75-7 F '77
See also
Cookery—Shellfish
CRABS as food. See Shellfish as food
CRABS eye. See Eye (crustaceans)
CRABTREE, Bruce
Bergs, bears and bald eagles. il Yachting 141: 72-4 F '77
By the mark. **See issues of Yachting to June 1977**
CRACKERS
See also
Nabisco, Inc
CRAFT centers. See Art centers
CRAFT fairs. See Arts and crafts—Exhibitions
CRAFT Film Festival, International. See Motion picture festivals
CRAFT horizons (periodical)
New craft era. R. Slivka. Craft Horiz 37:9 Je '77
CRAFT shops. See Art trade
CRAFTS. See Arts and crafts; Handicraft
CRAFTS schools. See Art schools
CRAFTSMEN. See Artisans
CRAIG, Carla. See Buntzen, L. jt auth
CRAIG, Edward Gordon. See Craig, G.
CRAIG, Gordon
Isadora reexamined. N. Macdonald. il pors Dance Mag 51:60-3 S '77 *
CRAIG, James B.
Man with roots. W. E. Towell. por Am For 83:inside back cover O '77 *
Redwoods: as the worm turns. il Am For 83:28-31+ Jl '77
CRAIG, James C.
Vibrotactile pattern perception: extraordinary observers. bibl il Science 196:450-2 Ap 22 '77
CRAIG, Marjorie
Miss Craig's summer shape-up plan. il McCalls 104:152-3+ My '77 *
CRAIG, Colo
Craig, Colorado: population unknown, elevation 6,185 feet; energy boom town. P. L. Fradkin. il Audubon 79:118-27 Jl '77
CRAIN, Marjorie Piga
Washington report (cont) Yachting 141:108 F '77
CRAMER, James
Becoming a pro. New Repub 177:14-16 N 12 '77
—See Rice, B. jt auth
CRAMER, Jerome
Alcoholics on the school staff. Educ Digest 43: 38-40 N '77
CRANBERRIES
Cranberry connection. H. Sutton. il Sat R 5:24-30 N 26 '77
CRANBERRY desserts. See Desserts
CRANBERRY industry. See Fruit industry
CRANBERRY sauce. See Sauces
CRANCH, Gene S.
Breast feeding is beautiful. il Parents Mag 52:50+ O '77
CRANDALL, Richard S. and Williams, Richard
Gravitational compression of crystallized suspensions of polystyrene spheres. bibl il Science 198:293-5 O 21 '77
CRANE, Philip Miller
Excerpt from remarks on national health care insurance, January 31, 1977. Cong Digest 56: 205+ Ag '77
Excerpts from address on U.S. African policy, September 22, 1976. Cong Digest 56:27+ Ja '77
CRANE, Sylvia E.
Reading Chinese tea leaves. Commonweal 104: 393-7 Je 24 '77
CRANE Company-Chemetron Corporation merger. See Corporations—Acquisitions and mergers
CRANE helicopters. See Helicopters
CRANES (birds)
Something to whoop about. il BioScience 27:760 N '77
Too sacred to survive? Japan's red crested cranes, tancho. F. H. Marks. il por Int Wildlife 8:20-5 Ja '78
Whooper rally. R. Barker. il map Natur Hist 86:22-4+ bibl(p96) Mr '77
CRANKS. See Eccentrics and eccentricities
CRANSTON, Alan
Limit a lawmaker's term in Congress? interview. por U.S. News 83:71-2 N 14 '77
CRAPPIE fishing
6 experts tell why their crappie techniques work. il Outdoor Life 159:76-9 Mr '77
CRARY, Calvert Horton
How courts will treat IBM, AT&T. A. Hershman. por Duns R 110:76-7+ D '77 *
CRASE, Douglas
Color-peak weekend; poem. New Yorker 53:50 O 24 '77
Lake effect; Experience and what to make of it; poems. Poetry 129:202-6 Ja '77
CRASKE, Brian
Perception of impossible limb positions induced by tendon vibration. bibl il Science 196:71-3 Ap 1 '77
CRATERS
Alaskan meteorite crater. Sky & Tel 54:107 Ag '77
Cratering in the solar system. W. K. Hartmann. il Sci Am 236:84-6+ bibl(p 132) Ja '77
Invisible crater. Sci Am 237:75 N '77
Meteorite crater identified in Alaska; Sithylemenkat Lake. il Sci N 111:405-6 Je 25 '77
Meteorite impact crater discovered in central Alaska with Landsat imagery; Sithylemenkat Lake. P. J. Cannon. il Science 196:1322-4 Je 17 '77
CRATTY, Bill
Spotlight on: Bill Cratty; interview, ed by L. Small. il pors Dance Mag 51:64-7 Ag '77
CRAVENS, Gwyneth
How Ma Bell is training women for management. il N Y Times Mag p 12-13+ My 29 '77
CRAVENS, Hamilton
Impact of evolutionary thought on American culture in the 20th century. bibl Intellect 106: 83-6 Ag '77
CRAWFORD, Alan
Fission on the right. Nation 224:104-8 Ja 29 '77
CRAWFORD, George, and others
Asymptomatic gonorrhea in men: caused by gonococci with unique nutritional requirements. bibl Science 196:1352-3 Je 17 '77
CRAWFORD, Joan
Joan Crawford's revealing last interviews; ed by R. Newsquist. il pors McCalls 104:90+ Ag '77
about
Hollywood's once and only star. il por Time 109:97 My 23 '77 *
Iron woman. J. Maslin. por Newsweek 89:73 My 23 '77 *
CRAWFORD, John S.
Wolfpack! il Outdoor Life 159:64-5 Ap '77
CRAWFORD, Marc
(ed) See Cooper, G. Stagecoach Mary
CRAWFORD, Patricia
Wonderful world of the two-year-old. il Parents Mag 52:39-41 F '77
CRAWFORD, Robert W.
Tribute to Joseph Lee. il por Parks & Rec 12:43-5 Ja '77
CRAWFORD, Tad
Is the Internal Revenue Service unfair to artists? Am Artist 41:8 Mr '77
New copyright law: help in half-measures. Art in Am 65:11-12+ S '77
Sky sports. il Harp Baz 110:85+ My '77
Taking care of the government's public art. Art in Am 65:19+ My '77
CRAWFORD, William Donham
Electricity: a necessity for the people; address, February 2, 1977. Vital Speeches 43:294-6 Mr 1 '77
CRAZY locomotive; drama. Witkiewicz, S. I.
CREAM puffs. See Pastry
CREATION
Scientists answer the creationists. Sci N 111:85 F 5 '77
See also
Chaos (theology)
Man—Origin and antiquity
Study and teaching
Creation at Michigan State. Sci Am 237:87 D '77
Creationism controversy in Dallas; biology texts. J. C. Evans. Chr Cent 94:188-9 Mr 2 '77
Unequal time; Indiana biology text case. Sci Am 236:61 Je '77
What Christian colleges teach about creation; interview, ed by D. Singer. J. Haas. R. Wright. il Chr Today 21:8-11 Je 17 '77
CREATION (literary, artistic, etc)
Freud and his literary doubles. M. Kanzer. bibl Am Imago 33:231-43 Fall '76
Mörike's Mozart on the way to Prague: stages and outcomes of the creative experience. U. Mahlendorf. bibl f Am Imago 33:304-27 Fall '76
See also
Creative ability
Creative writing
CREATIVE ability
Genius of everyman. J. H. Douglas. il Sci N 111:268-70, 284-7 Ap 23-30 '77
How to encourage your natural creativity. J. Bronowski. House & Gard 149:173+ N '77
Turning your creativity into future success; adaptation of address. G. Bylinsky. il por Sci Digest 81:50-4 Mr '77
CREATIVE Artists Public Service Program competition. See Art—Competitions

CREATIVE education
Save the eco system: support creative expression. C. R. Duke. bibl Clearing H 51:101-3 N '77
CREATIVE imagination. See Imagination
CREATIVE photography
Five unusual slide techniques. A. Grundberg. il Mod Phot 41:72-7 Mr '77
Hattersley class for beginners: expand your vision. R. M. Hattersley. il Pop Phot 81:106-7+ S '77
Mole's other masterpieces. il por Am Heritage 28:92-3 Je '77
CREATIVE writing

Study and teaching

Invisible stories become visible; program in Richmond, Va. R. L. Norris. Engl J 66:76-8 N '77
Little magazine: grow or die. G. Lyons. Nation 225:85-6 Jl 23 '77
Night campus; adult class. M. Schreiber. il Todays Educ 66:65-6 S '77
CREATIVITY. See Creative ability
CREDIT
Consumer credit. Consumer Rep 42:362-4 D '77
Credit: how to use it wisely. Hugh C. Sherwood. Harp Baz 110:50+ Je '77
Dollars and sense. G. Mahon. Mademoiselle 83:22+ N '77
How much credit can you afford? S. Auerbach. Am Home 80:9+ O '77
Merchants of debt. il Time 109:36-40 F 28 '77; Same abr. with title America's credit-card craze. Read Digest 110:137-40 Je '77
See also
Agricultural credit
Credit cards
Debt
Export credit
Finance companies
Instalment plan
Interest (economics)
Loans, Bank
Loans, Personal
Monetary policy
Negotiable instruments
Sex discrimination in consumer credit

Information services

See Credit bureaus

Rating

How lenders size you up; credit scoring. il Changing T 32:37-9 Ja '78
If you want a bank loan—new tests you have to pass. il U.S. News 83:65-6 Ag 22 '77
Who's a good credit risk? credit-scoring systems. J. Main. Read Digest 110:197+ My '77
See also
Credit bureaus

Regulation

Attack on Truth-in-lending. Consumer Rep 42:608-10 O '77
Credit rules that give women a fair shake; Equal Credit Opportunity Act. il Changing T 31:13-15 My '77
ECOA—in a nutshell. R. A. Lazarus. Ms 5:98 Mr '77
Equal Credit Opportunity Act: some good news, some not so good. L. C. Wohl. Ms 5:95-7 Mr '77
Married women get a credit rating; new provisions of Equal Credit Opportunity Act. il Bus W p28-9+ Je 6 '77
Things they must tell you when you lease something; amendment to the truth-in-lending law to cover leases. Changing T 31:41-2 Mr '77
You become creditable; Equal Credit Opportunity Act and sex discrimination. W. Flanagan. Vogue 167:184+ Je '77
CREDIT bureaus
Check out your credit rating. M. Daly. Bet Hom & Gard 55:240+ My '77
Credit bureau reports. Consumer Rep 42:364-5 D '77
Little company that could; Chilton Corp. Forbes 120:170 N 15 '77
CREDIT cards
As the race to sell credit cards heats up—. il U.S. News 83:62-4 S 5 '77
Credit cards today. Mech Illus 73:13 Mr '77
Hooked on credit and out of control. Changing T 31:34 F '77
Thumbs down for the credit card—eventually; use of thumbprints for credit. E. K. Sperling. il Intellect 106:44-5 Ag '77
Visa-card offensive angers the opposition; massive mailing effort by Citicorp. il Bus W p31 S 5 '77
West Germany: banks band together in a new credit card; Eurocard. il Bus W p44+ Ap 25 '77
See also
American Express Company
Government investigations—Credit cards
CRÉDIT du Nord. See Banks and banking—France
CREDIT rating. See Credit—Rating
CREDIT reporting agencies. See Credit bureaus
CREDIT unions
Co-ops: financial co-ops; loans to small depositors, credit unions. il Am Home 80:20 F '77
Credit unions move deeper into banking. Bus W p52 Ap 11 '77
More trouble for the banks. Forbes 120:98+ N 1 '77
Once-meek credit unions take on the banking industry. il U.S. News 82:85-6 F 21 '77
What can a credit union offer you? M. Daly. Bet Hom & Gard 55:8+ N '77
CREDITORS; drama. See Strindberg, A.
CREE Indians
On the wings of the wind; James Bay goose hunting. J. Knap. il Outdoor Life 159:72-5+ Mr '77
CREECH, Frances Gillum
Jokichi Takamine (1854-1922) il por Chemistry 50:5-6 My '77
CREEDS
Doctrinal hodgepodge in the churches. Chr Today 21:30-1 My 6 '77
Returning to the fold: disbelief within the community of faith. D. E. Miller. Chr Cent 94:810-13 S 21 '77
Southern Presbyterian dilemma; Proposed book of confessions. L. W. Posey. Chr Cent 94:142-5 F 16 '77; Discussion. 94:541-3, 765-6 Je 1, Ag 31 '77
CREEKS. See Brooks, creeks, etc.
CREESE, Ian, and others
Dopamine receptor binding enhancement accompanies lesion-induced behavioral supersensitivity. bibl il Science 197:596-8 Ag 5 '77
CRÈME brûlée. See Custards
CRENSHAW, Mary Ann
Wake up little Su-u-shi, wake up! il Esquire 87:86-9 Ap '77
CREOLE cookery. See Cookery, American
CREOLE music. See Music, Popular (songs, etc)
CREOLE poetry, West Indian. See West Indian poetry
CRÊPES. See Pancakes, waffles, etc.
CRESCITELLI, Frederick
Ionochromic behavior of gecko visual pigments. bibl il Science 195:187-8 Ja 14 '77
CRESPIN, Régine
Régine Crespin; interview, ed by G. S. Bourdain. il pors Hi Fi 27:86-9 S '77
CRESPO TORAL, Hernán
Quito. il map Américas 29:S4-12 Ap '77
CRESSMAN, George P.
Another frigid winter ahead? What a top authority says; interview. por map U.S. News 83:43-4 N 7 '77
CRESTED BUTTE, Colo.

Newspapers

See Newspapers—Colorado
CRESTS. See Heraldry
CRETACEOUS period. See Geology, Stratigraphic—Cretaceous; Paleontology—Cretaceous
CREUSOT-Loire (firm) See Steel industry—France
CREVICE gardens. See Gardens, Rock
CREW racing. See Rowing
CREWS, Harry
Grits. See issues of Esquire to August 1977
Trucker militant. il por Esquire 88:82-4+ Ag '77
CREWS, Airplane. See Airplane crews
CREWS, Boat. See Seamen
CRIB deaths. See Infant mortality
CRIBBEN, Carol
Buckaroo; poem. Mademoiselle 83:108 Mr '77
CRICHTON, J. Michael
Art. L. Alloway. Nation 225:571-2 N 26 '77 *
CRICHTON, Michael. See Crichton, J. M.
CRICHTON, Robert
Justice at the bar. il por Esquire 87:103-4+ Je '77
CRICKET (game)
Fending off vulgarity; International Cricket Conference vs K. Packer. il Time 110:45 Ag 8 '77
Sticky wicket; K. Packer's signing of players. P. Webb. il Newsweek 90:36 Ag 8 '77
CRICKETS
Ecdysis: neural orchestration of a complex behavioral performance. J. R. Carlson and D. Bentley. bibl il Science 195:1006-8 Mr 11 '77
Of cricket song and sex. W. Cade. il Natur Hist 87:64-73 bibl(p 108-9) Ja '78
CRIME and criminals
See also
Airplane hijacking
Assassins
Automobiles, Theft of
Blacks—Crime
Boats, Theft of

CRIME and criminals—See also—*Continued*
Bribery
Burglary and burglers
Capital punishment
Commercial crimes
Computers and crime
Convict labor
Crime and the press
Crime prevention
Criminal investigation
Criminal psychology
Embezzlement
Fraud
Gangs
Horse stealing
Juvenile delinquency
Kidnapping
Murder
Outlaws
Parole
Prisoners
Prisoners, Discharged
Prisons
Punishment
Rape
Robberies and assaults
Self defense for women
Shoplifting
Smuggling
Social work with delinquents and criminals
Stealing
Stolen goods, Receiving of
Terrorism
Terrorists
Trials
Victims of crimes
Wife beating
Women—Crime
Youth—Crime

Economic aspects

See also
Reparation

History

Contemporary crime in historical perspective: a comparative study of London, Stockholm, and Sydney. T. Gurr. bibl f il Ann Am Acad 434:114-36 N '77

Identification

Caught in the lineup; case of W. Walls, Jr. Time 110:44 Jl 18 '77
Line-up: a critical look. R. Buckhout and K. W. Ellison. bibl il Psychol Today 11:82-4+ Je '77
See also
Computers—Police use

Periodicals

True crime markets. Writers Digest 57:31 S '77

Research

See Criminal research

Africa

Crime and development in Africa. L. Sesay. Ann Am Acad 432:42-51 Jl '77

Alabama

Seventh son; shooting of Rev W. Maxwell in Alexander City, Ala. D. M. Alpern and V. E. Smith. il por Newsweek 90:21 Jl 4 '77
See also
Birmingham, Ala.—Crime

Arab countries

Crime or punishment? Islamic law. il Time 110:38 Jl 25 '77

Arizona

Investigative reporters' Arizona project. R. L. Friedly. Chr Cent 94:243-4 Mr 16 '77
Pack tackles the Mob. D. Gelman and others. il Newsweek 89:85-6 Mr 28 '77
Putting heat on the Sunbelt Mafia; work of the Investigative Reporters and Editors Association. il Time 109:21-2 Mr 28 '77
See also
Phoenix, Ariz.—Crime

Asia, Southeastern

Following the jade trail. il Time 111:24-5 Ja 9 '78

Australia

See also
Sydney, Australia—Crime

California

America's newest crime syndicate—the Mexican Mafia. N. M. Adams. Read Digest 111:97-102 N '77
Kidnapped bus; Chowchilla aftermath. P. S. Greenberg. il Newsweek 89:15 My 9 '77
Kidnapped! The ordeal that shook Chowchilla. J. P. Blank. il Read Digest 111:51-5+ S '77
Trash-bag murders; case of D. D. Hill and P. W. Kearney. D. A. Williams and J. Huck. il pors Newsweek 90:22 Jl 18 '77
Twenty-eight, and counting. . . ; arrest of mass murderers P. Kearney and D. Hill. il pors Time 110:49 Jl 18 '77
See also
Los Angeles—Crime
San Francisco—Crime

Caribbean Region

Cops & robbers offshore. T. Plate. il map Motor B & S 140:51-3 O '77

Colorado

See also
Denver—Crime

Egypt

Repentance, retreat and murder; case of Sheik Zahaby. il Time 110:32 Jl 18 '77

Europe, Western

Heroin plague. K. Labich. il Newsweek 89:47 Ap 25 '77

Florida

See also
Miami, Fla.—Crime

France

Bank heist of the century; robbery of the Societé Générale bank in Nice. R. Daley. il Read Digest 110:84-90 Ap '77
Francs a lot; hijacking of Bank of France coin shipment delivery truck. Time 110:41 Ag 8 '77
To lose a thief; escape of A. Spaggiari, Nice bank robber. F. Willey and E. Peer. il por Newsweek 89:44 Mr 21 '77
World's first—and greatest—detective; cases of F.-E. Vidocq. J. Stewart-Gordon. Read Digest 111:129-33 O '77

Great Britain

Candid camera; case of Y. McShane. il por Time 110:29 S 5 '77
No privacy? controversy surrounding the televising of a police film in Y. McShane case. Newsweek 90:47 S 5 '77
See also
London—Crime

Greece

On an unsolved mystery; 1948 murder of G. Polk. H. E. Salisbury. Progressive 41:24-5 My '77

Illinois

How one suburb deals with juvenile crime. J. Greenwald. McCalls 104:84 Je '77
See also
Chicago—Crime

Indiana

Six million dollar murder; murder of M. V. Jackson. L. S. Connor. il por Sat Eve Post 249:54-5+ N '77
Terror in Spring Mill; murder of M. Jackson. il por Time 109:42 My 23 '77
See also
Indianapolis—Crime

Italy

Love thief; case of R. Vallanzasca. K. Willenson. il por Newsweek 89:46+ Mr 7 '77
See also
Milan, Italy—Crime

Japan

Inalienable right to be robbed; comparison of Japanese and American crime prevention techniques. J. Gaylin. Psychol Today 11:34+ O '77
Putting the Mafia to shame; *yakuza*. il Time 110:40+ O 17 '77
Shaming gangsters from a life of crime—it's the Japanese way. D. Cohen. Psychol Today 11:97 Je '77

Kentucky

Million-dollar horse heist; theft of Fanfreluche from Claiborne Farm. M. Delnagro. il Sports Illus 47:30-2+ Ag 1 '77
Toast of Tompkinsville; recovery of thoroughbred Fanfreluche. W. F. Reed. il pors Sports Illus 47:95-6+ D 19 '77

Lebanon

See also
Jumblatt, K.—Assassination

Louisiana

From mob to supermob; C. Marcello. L. Velie. por Read Digest 112:49-54 Ja '78
Murder at Jupiter; political corruption and construction workers' union in Lake Charles, La. K. Y. Tomlinson. il Read Digest 111:115-19 Jl '77

Mexico

Dark and violent world of the Mexican connection; behind America's marijuana high. D. Harris. il map N Y Times Mag p 15-18+ D 18 '77

Michigan

They all trusted their killer; child killings in Oakland County, Mich. il Time 109:20 Ap 4 '77
Town that lives in terror; child murders in Birmingham, in Oakland County. B. Davidson. il Good H 185:136-7+ S '77

Missouri

See also
St Louis—Crime

Nevada

See also
Las Vegas, Nev.—Crime

CRIME and criminals—*Continued*

New England

New connection; drug traffic. D. A. Williams and R. Manning. il map Newsweek 90:38 O 3 '77
New England connection; drugs smuggling. il Time 110:26 O 3 '77

New Jersey

See also
Mafia

New York (state)

Guy with the edge; D. Sorkin's guilty plea in sports betting larceny case. P. Axthelm. il pors Newsweek 90:57 O 3 '77
Nazi of New Rochelle; case of F. Cowan. T. Mathews and S. Agrest. il por Newsweek 89:30 F 28 '77
Season of savagery and rage; F. W. Cowan's shooting spree in New Rochelle. il Time 109: 23-4 F 28 '77
See also
New York (city)—Crime

Pennsylvania

See also
Pittsburgh—Crime

Russia

Now it's Russia that fights a crime wave. il U.S. News 82:33-4 My 2 '77

Sweden

See also
Stockholm—Crime

Texas

Clmbing the tower; Austin, Texas site of 1966 murders by C. Whitman. H. Crews. Esquire 88:38-9 Ag '77
Night of terror; Wilson family kidnapping in Texas. W. Evans and D. R. Williams. il Good H 185:126-7+ O '77
Outlaw county: marijuana smuggling in Starr County, Tex. J. Lelyveld. il N Y Times Mag p 110 My 15 '77
Taming a tough county; marijuana smuggling. Time 109:58-9 My 2 '77

United States

Crime on the farm; rural property theft. J. K. Footlick and others. il Newsweek 90:101 O 3 '77
From an expert—some ideas on what's needed to fight crime; interview. N. Morris. il por U.S. News 82:61-3 Je 20 '77
How much crime? Sci Am 237:56+ Jl '77
Mobilizing eyewitnesses to crime: the use of radios and rewards. J. P. Levine. bibl il Intellect 105:254-7 F '77
New urban riots. M. Pousner. por Newsweek 89:11 Je 27 '77
Police blotter; crime in church circles. Chr Today 22:64+ O 7 '77
Thinking about crime. W. F. Buckley, Jr. Nat R 29:1012 S 2 '77
White collar crime; address, May 9, 1977. H. E. Groves. Vital Speeches 43:525-7 Je 15 '77
Why violent crime is now in fashion; interview. F. J. Hacker. il por U.S. News 82:57-8 F 28 '77
See also
Mafia
Police—United States
Prisons—United States
Vigilance committees
also subhead Crime under names of cities, e.g. Chicago—Crime

Statistics

As crime in the U.S. starts to level off—. il U.S. News 83:89-90 O 10 '77

Washington, D.C.

See Washington, D.C.—Crime

Western States

Deadly messenger of God; E. LeBaron. il por Time 110:31 Ag 29 '77
Only law; excerpts from 1926 articles, ed by A. B. Macdonald. F. Sutton. il por Sat Eve Post 249:62-3 Jl '77

Wisconsin

Caught in the lineup; case of W. Walls, Jr. Time 110:44 Jl 18 '77

CRIME and the press
How they covered Sam; press coverage. D. M. Alpern and others. il Newsweek 90:77+ Ag 22 '77
Investigative reporters' Arizona project. R. L. Friedly. Chr Cent 94:243-4 Mr 16 '77
Notes and comment; press treatment of Son of Sam story. New Yorker 53:21-2 Ag 15; 19-22 S 5 '77
Pack tackles the Mob. D. Gelman and others. il Newsweek 89:85-6 Mr 28 '77
Putting heat on the Sunbelt Mafia; work of the Investigative Reporters and Editors Association. il Time 109:21-2 Mr 28 '77
Tale of midnight; Son of Sam case. T. Powers. il Commonweal 104:594-6 S 16 '77
Terrorism and censorship. il Time 109:57 Mr 28 '77

CRIME code. See Criminal law

CRIME detection. See Criminal investigation

CRIME in literature
Conspiracy of silence. J. Epstein. il Harpers 255:77-80+ N '77
See also
Detective and mystery stories

CRIME novels. See Detective and mystery stories

CRIME prevention
AoA supports $4 million joint study on crime; reduce crimes against the elderly. Aging 275:7 S '77
For business: advice from FBI on curbing crime. il U.S. News 83:69-70 N 14 '77
From an expert—some ideas on what's needed to fight crime; interview. N. Morris. il por U.S. News 82:61-3 Je 20 '77
Inalienable right to be robbed; comparison of Japanese and American crime prevention techniques. J. Gaylin. Psychol Today 11:34+ O '77
Lighten up downtown alleys; Fort Madison, Iowa. il Am City & County 92:44 O '77
Step-up in fight on crimes against elderly. il U.S. News 82:62 Je 13 '77
Why government alone can't end the crime wave. G. M. Caplan. por U.S. News 82:82 Ap 11 '77
See also
Juvenile delinquency—Prevention
Police
Television in crime prevention
United States—Law Enforcement Assistance Administration

Citizen participation

Anti-crime citizen patrols on the rise. il Am City & County 92:50 My '77
How women can fight back against violent crime. Ladies Home J 94:65-73 Mr '77
We've been asked about making a citizen's arrest. U.S. News 84:56 D 12 '77
See also
Vigilance committees

CRIMES, Business. See Commercial crimes

CRIMES Against Women, International Tribunal on. See Feminism—Conferences

CRIMINAL investigation
City under seige; Son of Sam case. P. Axthelm. il Newsweek 90:18+ Ag 15 '77
Hunting the Son of Sam. T. Mathews and others. il map Newsweek 90:18-21 Jl 11 '77
Hunting the son of Sam; New York City killer. P. Axthelm and A. Lallande. il Newsweek 89:86 Je 20 '77
Man hunt for Son of Sam goes on. il Time 110: 13-15 Ag 15 '77
Sam told me to do it. . .Sam is the devil. il pors Time 110:22-3+ Ag 22 '77
Sick world of Son of Sam. P. Axthelm and others. il pors Newsweek 90:16-20+ Ag 22 '77
Son of Sam is not sleeping. il Time 110:61 Jl 11 '77
Son of Sam—the killer who terrorized New York. il por Read Digest 111:155-60 N '77
Strangler's grip; Los Angeles. D. A. Williams and others. il Newsweek 91:24-6 Ja 9 '78
Tracing of Beretta A47469; condensation. N. M. Adams. il Read Digest 112:203-6+ Ja '78
World's first—and greatest—detective; cases of F.-E. Vidocq. J. Stewart-Gordon. Read Digest 111:129-33 O '77
See also
Crime and criminals—Identification
Detectives
Electronics in criminal investigation, espionage, etc.
Informers
Lie detectors and detection
Public prosecutors
United States—Federal Bureau of Investigation

CRIMINAL justice, Administration of
United States, the most punitive nation; report of comparison study. J. Gaylin. Psychol Today 11:38 O '77
See also
Bail
Criminal law
Criminal procedure
Jury
Juvenile courts
Pleas (criminal procedure)
Probation
Public prosecutors
Punishment

Alabama

Arrest in Birmingham; charging R. E. Chambliss with 1963 church bombing. R. Boeth and V. E. Smith. il pors Newsweek 90:32+ O 10 '77

CRIMINAL justice, Administration of—*Cont.*

California

Dennis Banks's extradition fight; South Dakota vs California Uniform Criminal Extradition Act. H. Rubin. il Chr Cent 94:691-2 Ag 3 '77

Skyhorse and Mohawk: more than a murder trial. D. Blackburn. Nation 225:682-6 D 24 '77

When a state changes its sentencing laws; Uniform Determinate Sentencing Act. U.S. News 83:48 S 5 '77

Connecticut

New life of Reilly. E. Keerdoja. il por Newsweek 90:6+ Jl 25 '77

Cuba

Two years in Cuban jails; T. O'Hare and B. Mack. J. Huck. il por Newsweek 89:29 Je 27 '77

Georgia

Dawson boys; work of the Team Defense Project. M. Pinsky. Progressive 41:40-1 My '77

Illinois

Silent one; case of D. Lang. J. K. Footlick and E. Sciolino. Newsweek 90:89+ N 7 '77

Massachusetts

Killing time on death row; J. J. Kerrigan. P. Carlson. Nation 224:774-5 Je 25 '77

See also

Sacco-Vanzetti case

Mexico

Argument over Mexican justice. D. Harris. N Y Times Mag p68+ My 1 '77

New York (state)

See also

New York (city)—Criminal justice, Administration of

North Carolina

American Gulag; case of the Wilmington Ten. M. Pinsky. Progressive 41:9 N '77

Capital punishment—or suicide? L. Spear. Commonweal 104:742 N 25 '77

He didn't know half . . .; conviction of W. J. Spence for murder; Durham. B. Jacobs. Progressive 41:42 N '77

Sad footnote; Daniel R. Webster case. J. Deedy. Commonweal 104:772 D 9 '77

Rhode Island

Bill Bailey's Rhode Island blues. il por Time 109:70 Mr 21 '77

South Dakota

Dennis Banks's extradition fight; South Dakota vs California Uniform Criminal Extradition Act. H. Rubin. il Chr Cent 94:691-2 Ag 3 '77

Legal history of an Indian: South Dakota vs. Dennis Banks. H. Rubin. por Nation 225:113-15 Ag 6 '77

United States

Changing criminal sentences. J. Q. Wilson. Harpers 255:16-20 N '77

Crime and American society. B. Eckhardt. Current 196:33-41 O '77

Fixed sentences gain favor. il Time 110:98-9 D 12 '77

From an expert—some ideas on what's needed to fight crime; interview. N. Morris. il por U.S. News 82:61-3 Je 20 '77

I catch a burglar; Career Criminal Program. J. Berendt. il Read Digest 110:109-13 F '77

Stepped-up drive to make punishment fit the crime. U.S. News 83:47-8 S 5 '77

Three years to life; mandatory sentencing for gun crimes. E. B. Mann. Field & S 82:22+ N '77

War on white-collar crime Bus W p66+ Je 13 '77

White collar crime; address, May 9, 1977. H. E. Groves. Vital Speeches 43:525-7 Je 15 '77

See also

United States—National Advisory Commission on Criminal Justice Standards and Goals

Wisconsin

Rape and culture; controversial views of A Simonson. il por Time 110:41 S 12 '77

CRIMINAL Justice Standards and Goals, National Advisory Commission on. See United States—National Advisory Commission on Criminal Justice Standards and Goals

CRIMINAL law

Compromise on the code. J. K. Footlick and L. Howard. il Newsweek 89:78 My 16 '77

Needed: new crime code; proposed Criminal Code Reform Act of 1977. M. Stone. U.S. News 83:68 Ag 15 '77

Remaking of S-1. Time 109:46-7 Ap 4 '77

S. 1 again; criminal code revision. Progressive 41:7-8 O '77

See also

Capital punishment
Criminal justice, Administration of
Criminal procedure
Entrapment (law)
Obscenity (law)
Probation
Rape

CRIMINAL Laws and Procedures Subcommittee. See United States—Congress—Senate—Judiciary, Committee on the—Criminal Laws and Procedures Subcommittee

CRIMINAL procedure

Miranda still stands; case of R. Williams. C. Panati and L. Howard. por Newsweek 89:80+ Ap 4 '77

Undercutting Miranda: the Burger way with suspects. A. Berlow. Nation 224:498-500 Ap 23 '77

See also

Arrest
Bail
Criminal law
Executions and executioners
Extradition
Grand jury
Jury
Pleas (criminal procedure)
Probation
Searches and seizures
Trials

CRIMINAL psychology

Justice for whom? plea bargaining. S. Phillips. il por Psychol Today 10:70-2+ Mr '77

New ways to spot serious criminals early; study by Joan Petersilia and others. D. Cohen. Psychol Today 11:33+ D '77

Shy murderers. M. Lee and others. bibl il Psychol Today 11:68-70+ N '77

What happened to me is my fault. W. C. Spann. il Good H 185:44+ O '77

See also

Forensic psychiatry
Prison psychology

CRIMINAL research

Why government alone can't end the crime wave. G. M. Caplan. por U.S. News 82:82 Ap 11 '77

CRIMINALS. See Crime and criminals

CRIPPS, Edward J.

Food crisis? It's still there. il America 136:46-9 Ja 22 '77

CRISAN, George

Believers in Romania: divided they stand. E. E. Plowman. il pors Chr Today 21:18-21 My 20 '77 *

CRISCUOLO, Nicholas P.

PR and the classroom teacher. Educ Digest 42:46-7 Mr '77

—and Rossman, J. F.

Fresh look at secondary reading. bibl Clearing H 50:366-8 Ap '77

CRISIS centers. See Mental health centers

CRISONA, Nancy J. and Clarke, A. J.

Increase in conjugational transmission frequency of nonconjugative plasmids. bibl il Science 196:186-7 Ap 8 '77

CRISPNESS of foods. See Food texture

CRISPUS Attucks Memorial Monument. See Boston—Monuments, statues, etc.

CRISS, Charlie

Very short and sweet in Atlanta. J. Kirshenbaum. il por Sports Illus 47:89-91 N 14 '77 *

CRIST, Judith

Chairborne aviator at the flicks. il Sat R 4:24+ Ap 16 '77

Movies. See issues of Saturday review to August 6, 1977

CRISTOFER, Michael

I stress the emotions. il Horizon 19:78 Jl '77 *

Shadow box. Reviews

America 136:397 Ap 30 '77 *
Nation 224:507 Ap 23 '77 *
New Yorker 53:85 Ap 11 '77 *
Newsweek 89:89-90 Ap 25 '77 *
Sat R 4:42-3 My 14 '77 *
Time il 109:60 F 7 '77 *

CRITICAL phenomena (physics)

Critical phenomena: experiments show theory on right track. A. L. Robinson. il Science 196:861-3 My 20 '77

CRITICAL point

Critical-point universality and fluids. A. L. Sengers and others. bibl il Phys Today 30:42-8+ D '77

CRITICISM. See Critics and criticism

CRITICISM, Personal. See Self evaluation

CRITICS and criticism

Against the grain: why the arts have jumped the tracks. B. Levin. il Horizon 19:90-2 Ja '77

See also

Art critics and criticism
Book reviewers and reviewing
Drama critics and criticism
Education critics and criticism

CRITICS and criticism—See also—*Continued*
Food critics and criticism
Literary critics and criticism
Motion picture critics and criticism
Music critics and criticism
Press critics and criticism
Television critics and criticism
CRIVELLI, Carlo
Reassessment of Renaissance artist Carlo Crivelli. H. S. Conant. il Intellect 106:79-81 Ag '77 *
CROCE, Arlene
Dancing. See occasional issues of New Yorker
CROCHETING
Eight special sweaters. il McCalls 104:185-92 My '77
50 dazzling sweaters for you to knit or crochet. il Good H 184:104-11+ F '77
GH's needlework festival. il Good H 184:115+ Je '77
Soft, mohairy knits that are big-needle easy. il Mademoiselle 83:160 D '77
Super shawls! il Good H 186:96-8+ Ja '78
28 enchanting children's sweaters to knit and crochet. il Good H 185:140-7+ S '77
Warm hands, warm head, warm feet: lovely presents to knit and crochet for Christmas. il McCalls 105:249-55 N '77
CROCKER, Jack J.
Independents' best friend. il por Forbes 119:47-8 F 1 '77 *
CROCKERY cookery. See Cookery
CROCKETT, Edith S. and Mount, Ellis
(comps) Sci-tech books of 1976. il Lib J 102: 543-53 Mr 1 '77
CROCKETT, James Underwood
Mulching on. T. Schwartz and C. Foreman. il por Newsweek 90:103 S 12 '77 *
Rock garden that earns its keep. il por House & Gard 150:94-5+ Ja '78 *
CROCKETT, Lawrence J.
Those wildly successful, hateful plants; excerpt. il Sci Digest 82:38-40+ Ag '77
CROCODILES
Bad time to be a crocodile. R. Gore. il map Nat Geog 153:90-115 Ja '78
See also
Alligators
CROCODILES, Fossil
Crocodile with laterally compressed snout: first find in Australia. R. E. Molnar. bibl il Science 197:62-4 Jl 1 '77
CROFT, John. See Stapleton, J. C. jt auth
CROFUT, Bill
One-of-a-kind country look. B. Niles. il pors Am Home 80:46-9 S '77 *
CROISSANTS. See Bread
CROLAND, Carol
Thomas; poem. Redbook 150:66 D '77
CROMELIN, Richard
Down at the clubhouse with Dr Buzzard's Original Savannah Band. il Hi Fi 27:131-3 Jl '77
CROMER, Jim
Crisis in language. bibl Engl J 66:96-101 N '77
CROMPTON, John L.
Public-commercial joint venture. bibl Parks & Rec 12:20-3+ Jl '77
CRONIN, Sean
Death in Ireland. Commonweal 103:743-5; 104: 29+ N 19 '76, Ja 7 '77
CRONKITE, Kathy
My father Walter Cronkite. il pors McCalls 105: 222-3+ N '77
CRONKITE, Walter, 1916-
Behind Cronkite's coup. il por Time 110:47 N 28 '77 *
Cronkite summit? D. M. Alpern and B. Carter. il por Newsweek 90:129 N 28 '77 *
My father, Walter Cronkite. K. Cronkite. il pors McCalls 105:222-3+ N '77 *
CRONLEY, Jay
Drinking man's guide to Las Vegas. il Esquire 88:110+ D '77
Peeved at pets. il Esquire 87:134-5 F '77
CRONYN, Hume
Cards; interview. New Yorker 53:36-7 O 24 '77
CROOK, Mel
Racing scene. See issues of Yachting
You and your engine. See issues of Yachting
CROP experiments. See Field experiments (agriculture)
CROP reporting services
Editorial; question of Department of Agriculture's world crop yield forecasts and abnormal weather patterns. C. Whipple. Horticulture 55:6 Ap '77
Eye-in-the-sky: satellites add confidence to world crop estimates; Large Area Crop Inventory Experiment. Suc Farm 75:no2 50 F '77
How we see crop prospects. B. Coffman. il Farm J 101:20-1 Ag '77
Now—infrared can spot your crop problems. J. G. White. il Farm J 100:18-19+ D '76
Remote-sensing of crop yields. S. B. Idso and others. bibl il Science 196:19-25 Ap 1 '77
Soviet grain harvests: CIA study pessimistic on effects of weather. D. Shapley. Science 195: 377-8 Ja 28 '77
CROP reports. See Crop reporting services
CROP residues
Estimate your crop residue cover. C. E. Sommers. il Suc Farm 75:no4 L54-5 Mr '77
CROP rotation. See Rotation of crops
CROP share leases. See Leases
CROP yields
Blessings and problems of 1977's bumper crops. il U.S. News 83:32-4 S 19 '77
Bountiful crops—so why are farmers and bankers worried? ed by K. Sheets, P. Recer and others. il U.S. News 82:23-5 Je 27 '77
Electronic seed treatment: will it boost yields? G. W. Wormley. il Farm J 101:C1 Ag '77
Increasing crop production through more controlled photosynthesis. J. A. Bassham. bibl il Science 197:630-8 Ag 12 '77
Plant genetics: increasing crop yield. P. R. Day. bibl Science 197:1334-9 S 30 '77
Swollen silos, edgy farmers. il map Time 110:16-18 S 12 '77
This alcohol makes crops grow through night; triacontanol as a growth regulator. Farm J 101:10 Je '77
See also
Corn—Yield
Soybeans—Yield

Information services

See Crop reporting services
CROPS
Crop production costs in 1977. il Suc Farm 75:no4 9 Mr '77
World's crop plant germplasm—an endangered resource. H. G. Wilkes. bibl il map Bull Atom Sci 33:8-16 F '77
See also
Crop reporting services
Double cropping
Rotation of crops
also names of crops, e.g. Wheat
CROPS, Surplus. See Surplus products, Agricultural
CROPS and climate. See Plants, Effect of climate on
CROPS and cold weather. See Plants, Effect of temperature on
CROPS and soils
Crop management. C. E. Sommers. See issues of Successful farming
CROQUET
On the move; national championship tournament. il New Yorker 53:29-30 Je 6 '77
CROSBY, Bing
He could carry a tune. H. Saal. il pors Newsweek 90:101-2 O 24 '77 *
Indigenous music. N. Hentoff. Nation 224:542 Ap 30 '77 *
My 20 years with Bing; interview, ed by A. Ross. K. Crosby. il pors Ladies Home J 94: 110 O '77 *
Obituary
Nat R 29:1286 N 11 '77
Sweet singer for all seasons. F. Trippett. il pors Time 110:106+ O 24 '77 *
CROSBY, Donald G. and Wong, A. S.
Environmental degradation of 2,3,7,8-tetrachlorodibenzo-*p*-dioxin (TCDD) bibl il Science 195: 1337-8 Mr 25 '77
CROSBY, Joseph
Certification in the basics one hundred years ago. J. W. Velz. il Engl J 66:32-8 O '77 *
CROSBY, Kathryn
My 20 years with Bing; interview, ed by A. Ross. il pors Ladies Home J 94:110+ O '77
CROSLAND, Anthony
European communities' present stage of development; address, January 12, 1977. Vital Speeches 43:233-8 F 1 '77
Secretary Kissinger attends NATO ministerial meeting at Brussels and meets with British officials at London; text of joint news conference, December 10, 1976. Dept State Bull 76:6-9 Ja 3 '77
CROSS, Diana Harding
Battle of the Kegs. il Am Hist Illus 12:40-1 Ap '77
CROSS, Farrell
Try a campus vacation. il Read Digest 110:92-5 My '77
—and Cross, Wilbur
Cheers! A belly laugh can help you stay well; excerpt from The world of humor. il Sci Digest 82:15-18+ N '77
CROSS, Gertrude
New leisure class: gray but not blue. il Parks & Rec 12:32-5+ Je '77
CROSS, Wilbur. See Cross, F. jt auth
CROSS country running. See Running
CROSS country ski racing. See Ski racing
CROSS country skiing. See Skis and skiing
CROSS cultural studies. See Intercultural studies
CROSS Florida Barge Canal
Boondoggle busted? Nat Parks & Con Mag 51: 21-2 Mr '77
Coup de grâce for barge canal. G. Laycock. Audubon 79:147 Mr '77
CROSS ownership of mass media. See Mass media —Multiple ownership

CROSSBREEDING of cattle. See Cattle breeding

CROSSLAND, Fred E.
Faculty collective bargaining: impact on planning. por Intellect 106:67-70 Ag '77

CROSSLAND, Janice
Wastes endure. bibl il Environment 19:6-13 Je '77

CROSSWORD puzzles
Right sort of puzzle; a guide to the London Times crossword. J. A. Maxtone-Graham. il Horizon 19:94-5 Mr '77
Will Weng's farewell puzzle. W. Weng. pors N Y Times Mag p73 F 27 '77
Working the Double-Crostic. N. Ephron. Esquire 87:10+ My '77

CROTEAU, Suzanne
You call us, they'll call you. Educ Digest 42:16-18 Ap '77

CROUCH, Andrae
Hosanna in a spot of hell. J. Wilde. il por Time 111:14 Ja 9 '78 *

CROUCH, Dorothy Ruth
Going up! New rules for women on the job. il Redbook 149:102-3+ Ag '77

CROUCH, Stanley
Jazz lofts: a walk through the wild sounds. il N Y Times Mag p40-2+ Ap 17 '77

CROW, Porter J.
We the people; address, February 27, 1977. Vital Speeches 43:456-7 My 15 '77

CROW shooting
Great crow confusion. R. Starnes. por Outdoor Life 159:12+ Mr '77

CROWDER, John
Honorable discharge for the biggest pollutant. il Parks & Rec 12:28a-30a F '77

CROWDING stress
Crowding, death rates linked in humans. Sci N 112:341 N 19 '77
It's more pleasant being crowded with a woman. D. Cohen. Psychol Today 11:36 O '77
Too close for comfort: why one person's company is another's crowd; excerpt from Too close for comfort. P. M. Insel and H. C. Lindgren. bibl il pors Psychol Today 11:100-1+ D '77

CROWELL, Marnie Reed
St Lawrence. il Conservationist 31:2-9 Mr '77

CROWELL, Thomas Y, Company-Harper and Row, Publishers, Inc merger. See Publishers and publishing—Acquisitions and mergers

CROWLEY, Jill
Jill Crowley. il Ceram Mo 25:36-7 S '77 *

CROWLEY, Melvin
In God we trust; poem. Negro Hist Bull 40:704 My '77

CROWLEY, Robert
Team. New Yorker 53:16-18 Ja 2 '78 *

CROWN Central Petroleum Corporation. See Petroleum industry—United States

CROWNS
Ancient symbol stirs a storm for Carter; St Stephen's crown. il U.S. News 83:44 N 21 '77
Hungary's Crown. T. Beeson. Chr Cent 94:1158-9 D 14 '77
Kadar's crown; return of St Stephen's crown to Hungary. C. Fenyvesi. il New Repub 177: 15-17 N 19 '77
Meaning of a crown; return of St Stephen's crown to Hungary. Nation 225:516 N 19 '77
Return of an ancient symbol; Crown of St Stephen. il Time 111:25 Ja 9 '78

CROWS
Why scare the crows? R. Rodale. il Org Gard & Farm 24:50-4 My '77

CROZER-Chester Burn Center. See Burn care units

CRUCIBLE furnaces. See Furnaces

CRUELTY
See also
Police cruelty

CRUELTY to animals. See Animals—Treatment

CRUELTY to children. See Child abuse

CRUET stands, Silver. See Silverware

CRUICKSHANK, Alexander M.
Gordon Research Conferences. Science 195:1009-34 Mr 11 '77
Gordon Research Conferences: winter program, 1978. Science 198:323-6 O 21 '77

CRUIKSHANK, Nelson
Nelson Cruikshank new Federal Council head. il por Aging 274:20 Ag '77 *

CRUISE missiles. See Guided missiles

CRUISERS (pleasure boats)
Boats for cruising:
Amphora 37. T. Gibbs. il Yachting 142:26 Ag '77
Cornish Crabber. T. Gibbs. il Yachting 142: 54+ S '77
Down East 38. T. Gibbs. il Yachting 141:38+ Mr '77
Moody 33. T. Gibbs. Yachting 141:42+ My '77
Valiant 40. T. Gibbs. il Yachting 142:24 Jl '77
Choosing the right long distance cruising boat. J. Guzzwell. il Yachting 141:88-91 Ap '77
Clues to quality. il Motor B & S 141:125-7+ Ja '78
Comfortable compromise; cruising sailboats 32-40 feet. T. Meisel. il Motor B & S 140:72-7+ N '77
Condition report:
Dufour 2800. il Motor B & S 140:32+ Jl '77
Ericson 27. B. O'Donovan and O. Moore. il Motor B & S 140:41-4 S '77
Fales Explorer 42. W. E. Tobin. il Motor B & S 140:22+ D '77
Fuji 45. J. Hammond. il Motor B & S 139:66-7+ Ap '77
Morgan 37. E. B. Oldak. il Motor B & S 139:6819+ Mr '77
O'Day 32. W. E. Tobin. il Motor B & S 140:42+ Ag '77
Seafarer 26 cruising sloop. T. Meisel. il Motor B & S 141:56+ Ja '78
Seawind II. O. Moore. il Motor B & S 140:54-6 N '77
Valiant 32. W. E. Tobin. il Motor B & S 140: 40+ O '77
Everything for cruising; Hinckley Sou'wester 50. B. Robinson. il Yachting 142:60-3 D '77
Guide to:
Inboard cabin cruisers. il Motor B & S 140: 92-6 S '77
Stern-drive cruisers. J. Martenhoff. il Motor B & S 140:82-5 S '77
30-foot cruising sailboats. R. H. Perry. il Motor B & S 140:86-91 S '77
Man & his boat: built to take it. J. West. il Motor B & S 139:56-9+ F '77
Maximum bareboat; CSY-44. B. Robinson. il Yachting 141:66-9 Je '77
Measure for measure: 30 cruising sailboats compared. il Motor B & S 139:69-80 F '77
New boats in Yachting. See occasional issues of Yachting
New breed—classic setting; C&C Landfall 42. T. Gibbs. il Yachting 141:76-9 My '77
New power cruisers. il Motor B & S 141:132-41 Ja '78
Other way to cruise; the yacht, Pole Star. W. Fisher. il Yachting 142:88-90 N '77
Winter voyage through the Everglades; Skipjack 28. T. Gibbs. il Yachting 141:59-61 Je '77

Design

Client to designer; views of J. Mullen. T. Gibbs. il Yachting 142:100+ Ag '77
Yachting eyes:
Atlantic 44 long-range cruiser. J. Smith. il Yachting 141:70-3 Je '77
Bayliner 40. J. Smith. il Yachting 141:73-5 My '77
Egg Harbor 40 sedan cruiser. J. Smith. il Yachting 142:80-3 N '77
Hatteras 42 long range cruiser. J. Smith. il Yachting 141:78-9+ F '77
Silverton 34 Sedan. T. Gibbs. il Yachting 142:68-71 D '77
West Indian 36. il Yachting 141:94-5+ Mr '77

Testing

Performance test:
Atlantic 44. D. Hart. il Motor B & S 140:38-40 S '77
Bayliner 3350. D. Hart. il Motor B & S 139: 66-7+ Mr '77
Trojan F-30. D. Hart. il Motor B & S 139: 58-60+ Ap '77

CRUISES. See Cruising

CRUISES around the world. See Voyages around the world

CRUISING
Air/sea circuit; packaged fly/cruise vacation trips. T. B. Lesure. il Travel 148:28-31+ S '77
Armchair cruising; symposium. il map Yachting 141:66-81+ Mr '77
Cruise news. S. Birnbaum. Esquire 88:10+ D '77
Cruising blues and their cure. R. Pirsig. por Esquire 87:65-8 My '77
Cruising yachtsman; ed by T. Gibbs. See issues of Yachting
Float your cares away—use a cruise ship. D. Messineri. Vogue 167:164-8 Mr '77
Good tide-ings: the joys of taking a cruise vacation. Sat Eve Post 249:89+ Mr '77
Halfway south; North Carolina. B. Robinson. il map Yachting 142:58-61 Ag '77
Harbor-hopping the Pacific coast. B. Baker. il Motor B & S 140:68-9+ S '77
New York YC cruise. B. Robinson. il Yachting 142:216 O '77
Organizing a club cruise. D. White and H. White. Yachting 141:85 F '77
Return to the islands; southern New England. B. Robinson. il map Yachting 142:46-9 D '77
Special pleasures of a cruise and how to choose the right one for you. J. O'Reilly; D. Butwin. bibl il House & Gard 149:110+ O '77
Stern-driving Lake Superior. O. Moore. il Motor B & S 141:68-9+ Ja '78
Symphony in sea major. N. T. Clarke. il Sat Eve Post 249:74-5 N '77
Two-day circumnavigation; Huntington Bay, Long Island. J. Rousmaniere. il Yachting 142: 72-3 N '77

CRUISING—*Continued*
Wine tasters aweigh! H. Sutton. il Sat R 4:29 Ag 6 '77
Winter cruises—the bookings are at flood tide. il U.S. News 83:65-6 O 10 '77
See also
Voyages
Voyages around the world

Alaska

Bergs, bears and bald eagles. B. Crabtree. il Yachting 141:72-4 F '77
Cruising the microcosm of Alaska; from Juneau to Seattle. C. West. il map Yachting 142:65-7 N '77
Lessons of a long-distance cruiser; the inside passage through British Columbia and Alaska. B. Baker. il Motor B & S 141:122-4+ Ja '78
North to Alaska. B. Baker. il Motor B & S 140:40-3+ D '77
Passage north; Vancouver to Glacier Bay, Alaska. J. Hammond. il Motor B & S 141:118-21+ Ja '78

Arctic Regions

Farthest North; voyage of the Reindeer. E. N. Smith. il Yachting 141:68-72 My; 62-5 Je '77

Azores

Refreshing way station. R. M. Greenlee. il Yachting 141:77-9 Mr '77

Bahamas

Great train chase. J. Powell. il map Motor B & S 139:44-5+ Mr '77

Baltic Region

Spy who sailed in from the cold; excerpt from The saga of a wayward sailor. T. Jones. il Motor B & S 139:94-5+ My '77

British Columbia

See Cruising—Canada

California, Lower

Whale-watchers; natural history study cruise off Baja California. G. Reiger. il Audubon 79:74-6+ My '77

Canada

Cruising the microcosm of Alaska; from Juneau to Seattle. C. West. il map Yachting 142:65-7 N '77
Lessons of a long-distance cruiser; the inside passage through British Columbia and Alaska. B. Baker. il Motor B & S 141:122-4+ Ja '78
Passage north; Vancouver to Glacier Bay, Alaska. J. Hammond. il Motor B & S 141:118-21+ Ja '78
Warm water to the north; Gulf of St Lawrence. J. E. McKelvy, Jr. il map Yachting 141:67-9 Mr '77

Caribbean Region

Boom in sunshine cruises. il Time 111:47 Ja 16 '78
Cruising the Caribbean. T. B. Lesure. il Trav/Holiday 148:44-51 N '77
Discovering the Western Caribbean. W. T. Stone. il maps Yachting 142:52-5 Jl; 54-7 Ag '77
I'll see you in C-U-B-A; cruise on the Daphne. H. Sutton. il Sat R 4:42-5 Je 25 '77
Never waste a calm, but. . . C. Mitchell. il por map Yachting 142:61-4 N; 56-9+ D '77

England

Most relaxed way to cruise; the Thames: Oxford to Hampton Court; barge cruise. il Yachting 142:67-9 O '77

France

Most relaxed way to cruise. Canals of Burgundy. B. Robinson. il Yachting 142:63-6 O '77

Greece

Chartering in Greece. S. Hart. Yachting 141: 156-7 Je '77

Indonesia

Islands of Indonesia; cruise on the luxury ship Prinsendam. D. Bruce. il map Travel 148: 56-61 Ag '77

Mediterranean Region

Lessons learned: a practical lifestyle in the Med. R. Sutton. il Yachting 142:72-6 Ag '77
New area to bareboat: opening up the Sardinia-Corsica section of the Med. B. Robinson. il map Yachting 142:68-71 N '77
Sea full of islands. R. P. Sutton. il Yachting 141:70-3+ Mr '77

Mexico

Keeping cool in Cozumel. W. F. Buckley, Jr. il Motor B & S 139:37-9+ Mr '77

Norway

Glaciers, fjords, and the North Cape rock. P. R. Jackson. il House & Gard 150:49-50+ Ja '78

South America

South America by ship; cruises by Prudential Lines. T. B. LeSure. il Travel 147:34-9 Je '77

Turkey

Chartering in Greece. S. Hart. Yachting 141: 156-7 Je '77

United States

See Cruising

CRUMB, George
Lost souls; Star-child. F. J. Spieler. Harpers 255:102+ S '77 *
Musical events. A. Porter. New Yorker 53:126+ My 23 '77 *
N.Y. Phil: Crumb's Star-child. Hi Fi 27:MA26-7 Ag '77 *
Star-child: innocence and evil. W. Bender. il por Time 109:89-90 My 16 '77 *

CRUMBS (bread, cake, etc)
Sprinkle-on streusel. il Bet Hom & Gard 55: 196 N '77

CRUMMERE, Maria Elise
Horoscope. See issues of Vogue

CRUSHES (emotions) See Love

CRUSINBERRY, Jim
Black Sox scandal. D. Smith. il por Am Hist Illus 11:16-24 Ja '77 *

CRUSTACEANS
See also
Crabs
Eye (crustaceans)
Krill
Lobsters
Shrimps

CRUTCHFIELD, William
Transcending the machine. il Harpers 255:56-7 Ag '77

CRUZIC, Kathleen
Ten ways to build article sales. Writer 90:30-1 D '77

CRYER, Gretchen
Cryer & Ford: hang on to the good times. S. Dworkin. pors Ms 6:64-5 D '77 *

CRYING
See also
Infants—Crying

CRYOBIOLOGY
See also
Hypothermia

CRYOTHERAPY. See Cold—Therapeutic use

CRYPTOGRAPHY
See also
Ciphers
Computers—Cryptographic use

Conferences

Cryptography meeting goes smoothly. D. S. Shapley. Science 198:476 N 4 '77

CRYSTAL CITY, Tex.
Price of gas in Texas: Crystal City is cold. T. Brick. Nation 225:559-61 N 26 '77
When the gas stops. il Time 110:18 O 17 '77

CRYSTAL receivers. See Radio receivers

CRYSTAL testers. See Testing instruments

CRYSTALLINE lens
Method for detecting 8-methoxypsoralen in the ocular lens. S. Lerman and R. F. Borkman. bibl il Science 197:1287-8 S 23 '77
Vertebrate eye lens. H. Bloemendal. bibl il Science 197:127-38 Jl 8 '77
See also
Cataracts (eye defect)

CRYSTALLINE lens implants. See Eye—Surgery

CRYSTALLIZATION
Poor chemist's rotary crystallizer. L. Kershnar and M. P. Goodstein. bibl il pors Chemistry 50: 25-6 Mr '77

CRYSTALLOGRAPHY
Biocrystals. S. Inoué and K. Okazaki. il Sci Am 236:82-4+ bibl(p 148) Ap '77
Cholera toxin crystals suitable for X-ray diffraction. P. B. Sigler and others. bibl il Science 197:1277-9 S 23 '77
Electron microscopy of atoms in crystals. J. M. Cowley and S. Lijima. bibl il pors Phys Today 30:32-6+ Mr '77
Molecules in 3-D. il Time 109:81 F 14 '77
Monomeric forms of the acid ionophore lasalocid A (X-537A) from polar solvents. C. C. Chiang and I. C. Paul. bibl il Science 196: 1441-3 Je 24 '77
Ribulose bisphosphate carboxylase: a two-layered, square-shaped molecule of symmetry 422. T. S. Baker and others. bibl il Science 196:293-5 Ap 15 '77
Three-dimensional structure of transfer RNA. A. Rich and S. H. Kim. il Sci Am 238:52-62 Ja '78
Veatchine: coexistence of epimers in a crystal structure. W. H. De Camp and S. W. Pelletier. bibl il Science 198:726-7 N 18 '77
Will holography revolutionize crystallography? letter. C. K. Johnson. bibl Science 196:478+ Ap 29 '77
X-ray crystallography: 3-D structures by optical computing. T. H. Maugh, 2d. il Science 195:384 Ja 28 '77

CRYSTALS
Bell Labs reports manmade single-crystal monolayer alloys. G. B. Lubkin. il Phys Today 30:17-18 F '77

Dislocations

Disclinations. W. F. Harris. il Sci Am 237:130-6+ bibl(p 190) D '77

CSIKSZENTMIHALYI, Mihaly
Why fun is fun. W. B. Furlong. Read Digest 110:140-2 My '77 *

CSOÓRI, Sándor
I stole your face; Dreamers of my dream; poems; tr by D. Hoffman. New Repub 176:29 Mr 26 '77

CUBA
Cuba: a sense of purpose. J. Armstrong. Chr Cent 94:675-6 Ag 3 '77
Cuba: update on a revolution. L. S. Stavrianos. Nation 224:270-4 Mr 5 '77
Cuba's developing policies. G. W. Grayson. bibl f Cur Hist 72:49-52+ F '77
Inside Cuba today. F. Ward; reply. M. J. Sobran, Jr. Nat R 29:564-5 My 13 '77
See also
Baseball—Cuba
Communism—Cuba
Fishing—Cuba
Folklore—Cuba
Havana
Investments, American—Cuba
Prisons—Cuba
Secret service—Cuba
Tourist trade—Cuba
Visitors, Foreign—Cuba

Commerce
United States
See United States—Commerce—Cuba

Description and travel
Cruise to the new Cuba. N. Proffitt. il Newsweek 89:49-50 My 30 '77; Same with title Time for a Cuban connection? Sr Schol 110:16-17 S 8 '77
I'll see you in C-U-B-A; cruise on the Daphne. H. Sutton. il Sat R 4:42-5 Je 25 '77
Jazzing into Cuba. K. Tynan. il por Vogue 167:328-9+ S '77
Waiting for that Yankee dollar. il Time 109:39-40 My 9 '77

Economic conditions
Reports & comment: Cuba. S. Kinzer. il Atlantic 239:6+ My '77
See also
Communism—Cuba

Expropriation policy
Claimsmen and the traders: U.S. business squabbles over Cuba; reimbursement for expropriated properties. A. L. Padula, Jr. Nation 225:390-3 O 22 '77
Little matter of $1.8 billion. il Forbes 119:24 My 1 '77
Will U.S. companies recoup losses in Cuba? U.S. News 82:61 Je 13 '77

Foreign relations
Jamaica
Cuba's role in Jamaica. A. De Borchgrave. il por Newsweek 89:37-8 F 28 '77
United States
See United States—Foreign relations—Cuba

History
Invasion, 1961
Brigade 2506; survivors of the Bay of Pigs. E. Keerdoja. il Newsweek 90:20 D 12 '77
Schlesinger and Kennedy: historian in the service of power. R. Radosh. Nation 225:104-9 Ag 6 '77; Reply with rejoinder. A. Schlesinger, Jr. 225:147-8 Ag 20 '77
Missile Crisis, 1962
See Cuban Missile Crisis, 1962

History, Naval
Maritime history of Cuba; tr by R. Fagin. R. Montañés. il Oceans 10:16-21 S '77

Invasion
See Cuba—History—Invasion, 1961

Politics and government
Popular power in Cuba. J. Miller. Progressive 41:33-4 Jl '77
Reports & comment: Cuba. S. Kinzer. il Atlantic 239:6+ My '77
See also
Communism—Cuba
Socialism—Cuba

Social conditions
Secrets of the new Cuba. A. Walker. il por Ms 6:71-4+ S '77

Treaties
United States
See United States—Treaties—Cuba

CUBA and the United States
See also
United States—Foreign opinion—Cuban
CUBAN cookery. See Cookery, Cuban
CUBAN military assistance. See Military assistance, Cuban
CUBAN Missile Crisis, 1962
Cuban Missile Crisis: an anniversary. N. Cousins. Sat R 5:4 O 15 '77
Time of the angel: the U-2, Cuba, and the CIA. D. Moser. il Am Heritage 28:4-15 O '77
CUBAN poetry
Afro-Cuban poetry. J. Antonio León. il Américas 29:28-32 S '77
CUBAN terrorists. See Terrorists, Cuban
CUBANITE. See Sulfides
CUBANS in the United States
See also
Miami, Fla.—Foreign population
CUBISINO, Marjorie
Chop, peel, dice, slice, brew, bake: shopper's guide to new small kitchen appliances. McCalls 105:132+ N '77
No-nonsense guide to cookware. McCalls 104:186+ Ap '77
CUCKOOS
Relative fecundity and parental effort in communally nesting anis, crotophaga sulcirostris. S. L. Vehrencamp. bibl il Science 197:403-5 Jl 22 '77
CUCUMBER mosaic virus. See Viruses, Plant
CUCUMBERS
Having cucumber troubles? Try hand pollination. D. J. Young. il Org Gard & Farm 24:83-5 F '77
See also
Cookery—Vegetables
CUCUMIS. See Melons
CUCURBITS
See also
Chayotes
CUD-chewing animals. See Ruminants
CUDDY, Edward
College for convicts. Progressive 41:53-5 F '77
CUDLIPP, Edythe
New job discrimination: a matter of health. Harp Baz 110:87+ Ag '77
CUDMORE, L. L. Larison
Center of life; excerpt. il Sci Digest 82:41-6 N '77
about
To relieve the laboratory's fierce tensions: add ♀. por Sci Digest 82:47-8 N '77 *
CUELLAR, Hector S. and Cuellar, Orlando
Refractoriness in female lizard reproduction: a probable circannual clock. bibl il Science 197:495-7 Jl 29 '77
CUELLAR, Orlando
Animal parthenogenesis. bibl il maps Science 197:837-43 Ag 26 '77
—See Cuellar, H. S. jt auth
CUELLO excavations. See Belize—Antiquities
CUFFE, Edwin D.
Case of the with-it encyclopedia. America 137:182-4 O 1 '77
Christmas game. America 137:465 D 24 '77
Somewhat inconsequential ode. America 137:45 Jl 30 '77
CUFFE, Mary I.
Forgotten harvest. il Conservationist 31:16-18 Ja '77
CULHANE, John
Fantastical world of Maurice Sendak. il por Read Digest 110:104-8 F '77
Magical, madcap Muppets. il por Read Digest 111:23-5+ S '77
CULLEN, Millicent
Plastic surgery—true story. Vogue 167:195+ F '77
CULLINAN, Elizabeth
Good loser; story. New Yorker 53:32-8 Ag 15 '77
Idioms; story. New Yorker 52:31-5 Ja 31 '77
CULLINAN, Helen
Cleveland. il Art N 76:119-20 D '77
CULOT, Pierre
Farmhouse for art. N. Skurka. il por N Y Times Mag p42-3 Ag 14 '77 *
CULSHAW, John
Culshaw at large. See issues of High fidelity and Musical America
CULTIVATION. See Tillage
CULTIVATORS
Get multiple use from these tillage tools. L. Reichenberger. il Suc Farm 75:no2 40-1 F '77
His big disk does it all. R. Brunoehler. il Suc Farm 75:no3 F8 F '77
Mini-tillers—a lot of muscle for compact gardens. E. F. Lindsley. il Pop Sci 210:58+ My '77
New gear that makes yard work easier. M. Schultz. il Pop Mech 147:116-19 My '77
Power garden tillers; rototillers. il Changing T 31:45-7 S '77
Test shows the best way to incorporate soybean herbicides. B. Coffman. Farm J 101:C4 Ap '77
Woman's best friend could be her tiller. K. L. Carlsen. il Org Gard & Farm 24:81-3 Ag '77

CUPBOARDS
See also
Armoires
Kitchen cabinets
CUPIVAC; drama. See Boiko, C.
CURARE
Curare cure; treating pancreatitis. il Newsweek 89:74 My 2 '77
CURATORS. See Museum directors
CURCIO, Renato
Terrorism on trial in Italy. il por Time 110:58 Jl 4 '77 *
CURE, Karen
Great Austrian true-blue, down-on-the-farm Epiphany celebrations. il Holiday 57:22-3 N '76
Healthy hair. il Am Home 80:10+ F '77
Island on the edge of the world. il Holiday 58:41-3+ Je '77
CURING of meat. See Meat—Preservation
CURLING (sports)
Shuffleboard on ice—it's curling. il Sunset 159:82+ N '77
CURRAN, Donald R. and others
Dynamic failure in solids. il Phys Today 30:46-8+ Ja '77
CURRAN, M. and Seeman, P.
Alcohol tolerance in a cholinergic nerve terminal: relation to the membrane expansion-fluidization theory of ethanol action. bibl il Science 197:910-11 Ag 26 '77
CURRANTS
High voltage currant. A. De Mangelaere. il Org Gard & Farm 25:152+ Ja '78
CURRENCY. See Money
CURRENCY question
See also
Gold clauses
Monetary policy
CURRENT events
Events and people. See issues of Christian century
Images 1977; photographs. Time 111:37-45 Ja 2 '78
Month in review. See issues of Current history
News & views. J. Deedy. See issues of Commonweal
Pictures of '77; special issue. Newsweek 90:10, 16-24+ D 26 '77
Sr's top ten of '77. il Sr Schol 110:4-6 D 15 '77
Very special autumn; special issue, ed by H. Sutton. il Sat R 4:11-14+ Ag 6 '77
Washington diarist. See issues of New republic. January 22, 1977-

Poetry

See also titles of poems listed under Von Dreele, W. H.
CURRENT events in motion pictures. See Motion pictures—Plots, themes, etc.
CURRENTS, Ocean. See Ocean currents
CURREY, Stella Martin
You are so lovely; story. Good H 185:128-9 S '77
CURRICULUM. See Church colleges and universities—Curriculum; Colleges and universities—Curriculum; Courses of study; High schools—Curriculum; Junior high schools—Curriculum; Public schools—Curriculum
CURRICULUM planning
Curriculum: content and utility. B. O. Smith. Educ Digest 42:15-18 F '77
Developmental curriculum: an articulation model for grades K-12. S. Lehane. bibl il Clearing H 51:86-9 O '77
Developmental staging: in pursuit of comprehensive curriculum planning. J. W. Wiles. Clearing H 50:274-7 F '77
Planning for successful teaching. G. F. Horn. il Sch Arts 77:4-5 O '77
Politics of curriculum development. P. W. Doerrer and J. L. Pulley. bibl il Clearing H 50:260-1 F '77
Two new emphases in curriculum development. R. W. Tyler. Educ Digest 42:11-14 F '77
CURRIE, Elliott
Carter's welfare reform. Nation 225:230-3 S 17 '77
CURRIE, Malcolm Roderick
Technological superiority required. Aviation W 106:7 F 7 '77
CURRIER, Richard L.
Genes and human behavior: what Wilson has not proved. por Horizon 19:45 Mr '77
CURRIER, William W. and Strobel, G. A.
Chemotaxis of Rhizobium spp. to a glycoprotein produced by birdsfoot trefoil roots. bibl il Science 196:434-6 Ap 22 '77
CURRIER & Ives prints. See Lithographs
CURRY, Bill
I'm number 50! interview, ed by G. Plimpton; excerpt from One more July. il Read Digest 112:129-32 Ja '78
CURRY
Curry mystery. il Sunset 158:78-81 F '77
More curries—lamb, cheese with peas, fish, shrimp with pork. Sunset 158:126-7 F '77
CURSES! Foiled again; drama. See Cheatham, V. R.
CURSING sickness. See Nervous system—Diseases
CURTAIN and drapery fixtures
All about windows. il Redbook 149:205 S '77
Hanging curtain and traverse rods. McCalls 104:110 My '77
How to lengthen and shorten traverse rods. W. Gore. il Pop Mech 148:78 N '77
CURTAINS and draperies
Inner views. il Seventeen 36:206-7 Ap '77
Right way to measure your windows for curtains and draperies. il Good H 185:24 O '77
CURTIS, Charles B.
Bad news for oilmen? por Forbes 120:70 S 1 '77 *
CURTIS, Charlotte
New nightlife: dinner-partying. il Vogue 167:255+ N '77
CURTIS, Cyrus Hermann Kotzschman
Man from Maine. il por Sat Eve Post 249:4+ Jl '77 *
CURTIS, David. See Swanson, J. jt auth
CURTIS, David (poet)
Rainbow; poem. Chr Cent 94:425 My 4 '77
Thoughts while grading a student's sonnet; poem. Clearing H 51:156 D '77
CURTIS, Freda E.
Pregnant onion. il Org Gard & Farm 24:76-7 My '77
CURTIS, Jack
Lion in the rain-rinsed morning. il Atlantic 240:67-73 S '77
CURTIS, Jean
Children vs. your success drive; When should you go back to work? Child-care alternatives: good news. Harp Baz 110:176-7+ O '77
CURTIS, Joseph E.
Clustering services mustering cooperation. il Parks & Rec 12:68-9+ S '77
Cooperative department streamlines city services. il Am City & County 92:67 Ap '77
CURTIS, Kenneth Merwin
Democrats rediscover democracy. New Repub 176:8 Ap 16 '77 *
It's my party. New Repub 177:8-9 D 24 '77 *
CURTIS, William
Fox that climbs trees. il Nat Wildlife 15:20-7 Je '77
Sure, it looks cute. il Nat Wildlife 16:36-9 D '77
CURTIS Institute of Music, Philadelphia
Curtis Inst: Intermezzo. il Hi Fi 27:MA32 Jl '77
Viewpoint. R. Jacobson. Opera N 41:6 My '77
CURTIS Publishing Company
See also
Saturday evening post
CURTISS, Roy, 1934-
—See Maturin, L. jt auth

about

Making a safer microbe. por Time 109:45 Ap 18 '77 *
CURVATURE of the spine. See Spine—Abnormalities and deformities
CURVE tracers. See Testing instruments
CURVES
Fractals: a world of nonintegral dimensions. L. A. Steen. il Sci N 112:122-3 Ag 20 '77
CUSACK, Cyril
Confiteor; poem. Commonweal 104:39 Ja 21 '77
CUSACK, Isabel Langis
Lonely dollhouse; story. McCalls 105:208-9 N '77
CUSHMAN, William P.
Letter to parents. il Engl J 66:45-8 O '77
CUSTARDS
Custard. il Bet Hom & Gard 54:48 Ag '76
Luscious crème brûlée. il Good H 185:40 Ag '77
CUSTER, George Armstrong
Campaigning with Custer; excerpt from Life in Custer's cavalry: diaries and letters of Albert and Jennie Barnitz, 1867-68, ed by R. M. Utley. A. Barnitz and J. P. Barnitz. il pors Am West 14:4-9+ Jl '77 *
CUSTODIANSHIP accounts
Saving for college the tax-free way; establishing a custodial savings account for a child. E. G. Pascoe. McCalls 105:112 O '77
CUSTODY of children. See Parent and child (law)
CUSTOM feedlots. See Cattle feedlots
CUSTOMER relations
Consumers complain—does business respond? A. R. Andreasen and R. Best. il Harvard Bus R 55:93-101 Jl '77; Discussion. 55:68+ S '77
Corporate clout for consumers. il Bus W p 144+ S 12 '77
See also
Customer service
CUSTOMER service
Service with a scowl: what business is doing about it. il U.S. News 83:50-1 D 5 '77
CUSTOMS. See Manners and customs
CUSTOMS Service (United States) See United States Customs Service
CUSTOMS service and tourists
See also
Duty free importation

CUT flowers. See Flowers—Cut flowers
CUTLER, B. J.
Velvety wines for dessert. por maps House & Gard 150:110+ D '77
CUTLER, Bruce
Big sky, Switzerland; poem. Yale R 66:399-400 Mr '77
CUTLER, Carol
New healthier foodstyle. bibl il Am Home 80: 66-70 Je '77
CUTLER, Rupert
Rupert Cutler: the environmentalist in the farmer's back yard. N. Wade. Science 196:505-7 Ap 29 '77 *
USDA's profound change: to help farmers naturally. J. Cox. por Org Gard & Farm 24:48-52 S '77 *
CUTLERY
See also
Knives
CUTOUT work. See Paper work
CUTTER, Robert A.
Indy has a new boy in town. il Mech Illus 73: 126+ My '77
CUTTERS (boats) See Sailboats
CUTTHROAT trout fishing. See Trout fishing
CUTTILL, William J.
Audiovisual materials; 16mm sound films. See issues of Today's education
CUTTING fluids. See Lubrication and lubricants
CUTTING tools
See also
Knives
Saws
CUTTINGS, Plant. See Plant propagation
CVIJANOVICH, George
Low-cost solar collector. C. A. Miller. il pors Mech Illus 73:58+ D '77 *
CYANOTRIACETYLENE. See Acetylene
CYCADS. See Cycas
CYCAS
Easy to grow house plants:
Cycas. E. McDonald. il House B 119:36 Mr '77
CYCLADES (islands)
See also
Siphnos (island)
Thera (island)
CYCLES
If you look hard cycles are all over; work of E. R. Dewey. R. R. Ward. il por Smithsonian 7:104-10 Mr '77
Just how do cycles affect all of life? R. R. Ward. il Sci Digest 82:14-16+ Jl '77
See also
Biogeochemical cycles
Hydrologic cycle
CYCLES, Biological. See Biology—Periodicity
CYCLIC nucleotides. See Nucleotides
CYCLING
Big wheels; excerpt from Biking for grownups. J. Biermann and B. Toohey. il Fam Health 9:50-2 Ag '77
Bike hiking. K. Reading. Seventeen 36:68 S '77
Build bike paths to last; concrete pavement. E. G. Robbins. il Am City & County 92:70 Ap '77
Confessions of a bike bug. J. Stocker. il Ret Liv 17:24-5+ O '77
Energy plan may boost bikeways. il Am City & County 92:23 S '77
4-mile bike loop unlocks Boise River; Idaho. il Sunset 158:72 Je '77
Notes and comment. New Yorker 53:19-20 Jl 11 '77
Oakland bike loop; California. il map Sunset 159:40-1 Ag '77
This sport is not on the level; cycling up Fargo Street hill in Los Angeles. S. Pileggi. il Sports Illus 46:22-4 F 7 '77
See also
Bicycle racing
CYCLOHEXIMIDE
Incompatibility on Brassica stigmas is overcome by treating pollen with cycloheximide. T. E. Ferrari and D. H. Wallace. bibl il Science 196:436-8 Ap 22 '77
CYCLONES
India
Sudden death on the Bay of Bengal. il Time 110:52 D 5 '77
Varuna's sacrifice. H. Jensen. il map Newsweek 90:48 D 5 '77
CYCLOPS, pseud. See Leonard, John
CYCLOTRONS. See Accelerators (electrons, etc)
CYLINDER heads, Automobile. See Automobile engines—Cylinders
CYLINDERS (engines, etc)
See also
Automobile engines—Cylinders
Manufacture
Court orders OSHA to consider economics; noise controls at Turner Division plant. Bus W p46+ O 3 '77

CYNARA cardunculus. See Cardoons
CYPRESS
Cashmere cypress—watch for it. il Sunset 158: 232 Je '77
CYPRINIDS. See Minnows
CYPRUS
It's negotiable. A. Deming and others. Newsweek 89:48+ F 14 '77
President Carter's second report on Cyprus submitted to Congress; April 15, 1977. J. Carter. Dept State Bull 76:491-2 My 16 '77
President Carter's third report on Cyprus submitted to Congress; June 22, 1977. J. Carter. Dept State Bull 77:138-9 Jl 25 '77
President Carter's fourth report on Cyprus submitted to Congress; message, August 25, 1977. J. Carter. Dept State Bull 77:445 O 3 '77
President Carter's fifth report on Cyprus submitted to Congress; message, October 28, 1977. J. Carter. Dept State Bull 77:787-8 N 28 '77
President discusses Cyprus issue in periodic report to Congress; February 11, 1977. J. Carter. Dept State Bull 76:243 Mr 14 '77
Ready for a new beginning. il Time 108:29-30 F 28 '77
Seventh progress report on Cyprus submitted to the Congress; message, January 10, 1977. G. R. Ford. Dept State Bull 76:93-4 Ja 31 '77
See also
United Nations—Armed Forces—Forces in Cyprus
United Nations—Cyprus
Description and travel
Quartet from far corners. H. Sutton. il por Sat R 4:48-9 F 5 '77
CYPRUS cedar. See Cedar
CYPRUS Mines Corporation
Using copper to diversify. il Bus W p77-8 My 23 '77
CYR, Arthur
British politics in 1977. Cur Hist 73:153-5+ N '77
CYR, Don
Kids and kameras (cont) il por Pop Phot 80:58+ Mr; 38+ Je; 81:51+ Ag; 56+ O '77
CYSTIC fibrosis
Cystic fibrosis: an immune disease? Sci N 111: 232 Ap 9 '77
Lonely courage of Lisa Boyle. F. Deford. il Seventeen 36:188-9+ Ap '77
CYSTINURIA
Transport interaction of cystine and dibasic amino acids in renal brush border vesicles. S. Segal and others. bibl il Science 197:169-71 Jl 8 '77
CYTIDINE phosphates
Cytidine 3′,5′-monophosphate (cyclic CMP) formation in mammalian tissues. S. Y. Cech and L. J. Ignarro. bibl il Science 198:1063-5 D 9 '77
CYTOCHROMES
Cytochrome c: immunofluorescent localization of the testis-specific form. E. Goldberg and others. bibl il Science 196:1010-12 My 27 '77
CYTOLOGY
See also
American Society for Cell Biology
Cells
Methodology
Animal viruses: probes of cell function. G. B. Kolata. Science 196:417-18 Ap 22 '77
Quantitative single cell analysis and sorting. P. K. Horan and L. L. Wheeless, Jr. bibl il Science 198:149-57 O 14 '77
See also
Freeze fracturing
CYTOMEGALOVIRUSES. See Herpesviruses
CYTOSINE arabinoside
Phospholipid derivative of cytosine arabinoside and its conversion to phosphatidylinositol by animal tissue. C. R. H. Raetz and others. bibl il Science 196:303-5 Ap 15 '77
CYTOSOL
Specific high-affinity binding macromolecule for 1,25-dihydroxyvitamin D_3 in fetal bone. B. E. Kream and others. bibl il Science 197:1086-8 S 9 '77
CZAKY, David
After 18 years of searching: we're a family again! E. P. Frank. il pors Good H 185:111+ O '77 *
CZECH authors. See Authors, Czech
CZECH cookery. See Cookery, Czech
CZECHOSLOVAKIA
See also
Archives—Czechoslovakia
Civil rights—Czechoslovakia
Opera—Czechoslovakia
Visitors, Foreign—Czechoslovakia
Description and travel
Travel. M. Gough. House B 119:62+ O '77

CZECHOSLOVAKIA—*Continued*

Intellectual life

Intellectuals without influence: the window cleaners of Prague. P. Brennan. Nation 224:229-31 F 26 '77

Religious institutions and affairs

See also

Church and state in Czechoslovakia

CZURA, Pete

Fall's colorful country roads. il Travel 148:58-61+ S '77

D

DB. See Decibels

DBCP (dibromochloropropane) See Pesticides

DEHA (diethyl hydroxylamine) See Hydroxylamine

DES (diethylstilbestrol) See Stilbestrols

DGI (Dirección General de Intelligencia) See Secret service—Cuba

DINA (Dirección de Inteligencia Nacional) See Secret service—Chile

DNA

Bacterial genetics: action at a distance on DNA. G. B. Kolata. il Science 198:41-2 O 7 '77

DNA: laws, patents and a proselyte. N. Wade. Science 195:762 F 25 '77

DNA strand scission by benzo[*a*]pyrene diol epoxides. H. B. Gamper and others. bibl il Science 197:671-4 Ag 12 '77

Era of the jumping genes. il Sci N 111:164 Mr 12 '77

Full gene sequence of DNA virus solved. il Sci N 111:148-9 Mr 5 '77

Gene control: frog DNA in newt eggs. il Sci N 112:54-5 Jl 23 '77

Isolation of eukaryotic DNA fragments containing structural genes and the adjacent sequences. G. P. Georgiev and others. bibl il Science 195:394-7 Ja 28 '77

Newly evolved repeated DNA sequences in primates. D. Gillespie. bibl il Science 196:889-91 My 20 '77

Nucleotide sequence of a viral DNA. J. C. Fiddes. il Sci Am 237:54-67 D '77

Packaged DNA. Sci Am 237:72+ N '77

Packaging the message; viruses. il Chemistry 50:22-3 Mr '77

Psoralen-DNA photoreaction: controlled production of mono- and diadducts with nanosecond ultraviolet laser pulses. B. H. Johnston and others. bibl il Science 197:906-8 Ag 26 '77

Satellite DNA's. D. M. Skinner. bibl il BioScience 27:790-6 D '77

Secondary structure of histones and DNA in chromatin. G. J. Thomas, Jr and others. bibl il Science 197:385-8 Jl 22 '77

Superhelix densities of circular DNA's: a generalized equation for their determination by the buoyant method. W. B. Upholt. bibl Science 195:891 Mr 4 '77

Viral integration and excision: structure of the lambda *att* sites. A. Landy and W. Ross. bibl il Science 197:1147-60 S 16 '77

See also

Plasmids

Research

See Genetic research

DOT. See United States—Transportation, Department of

DSOC. See Democratic Socialist Organizing Committee

DX'ing (radio) See Radio audiences

DAANE, James

Creating a respect for theology. Chr Cent 94:89-90 F 2 '77

DABERTIN, Rita

Unsung heroine of the year. L. Hershey. il por Ladies Home J 94:4 Jl '77 *

DACEY, Philip

From the clearing; poem. Poetry 129:252-3 F '77

DACQUOISE. See Meringue

DADA, Idi Amin. See Amin Dada, I.

DADAISM

Nothing is here; Dada is its name; excerpt from The art world; ed by B. Diamonstein. il Art N 76:144+ N '77

DADDARIO, Emilio Quincy

Science digest interviews new AAAS president; ed by W. K. Stuckey. por Sci Digest 81:back cover, 80 Mr '77

about

Daddario resigns abruptly from OTA. P. M. Moffey. Science 196:1066 Je 3 '77 *

Impartial OTA future dubious; a launching pad for Kennedy? D. Gergen. Sci Digest 82:24-5+ S '77 *

OTA: Daddario's exit heightens strife over Kennedy role. C. Holden. Science 197:27-8 Jl 1 '77 *

DADDY; drama. See Bullins, E.

DADE County, Fla.

Aluminum poles help light saltwater highways. F. P. Seeley. il por Am City & County 92:35-6 Ja '77

Anita Bryant is mad about gays. M. Kondracke. New Repub 176:13-15 My 7 '77

Anita Bryant on the march: the lessons of Dade County. L. Van Gelder. il por Ms 6:75-8+ S '77

Anita Bryant's crusade. G. Steinem. Progressive 41:37 Je '77

Anita Bryant's crusade; ordinance banning discrimination against homosexuals. D. A. Williams. por Newsweek 89:39 Ap 11 '77

Anita Bryant's hollow victory. Progressive 41:8 S '77

Anita's circle; A. Bryant's drive to repeal ordinance barring discrimination against homosexuals. il por Time 109:76 My 2 '77

Battle over gay rights. T. Mathews and others. il por Newsweek 89:16-17+ Je 6 '77

Confronting the homosexual issue. Chr Today 21:36 Jl 8 '77

Enough! Enough! Enough! repeal of ordinance outlawing discrimination against homosexuals. il por Time 109:59-60 Je 20 '77

Gay rights showdown in Miami. il por Time 109:20 Je 13 '77

Homosexuality and civil rights. America 136:558 Je 25 '77; Discussion. 137:41 Jl 30 '77

How far out of the closet? G. F. Will. Newsweek 89:92 My 30 '77

Miami vote: tide turning against homosexuals? il por U.S. News 82:46 Je 20 '77

Myth of self-evident truths. W. Muehl. Chr Cent 94:1000-2 N 2 '77

No to the gays. R. Steele and H. Camp. il Newsweek 89:27+ Je 20 '77

Why the conservatives won in Miami. R. H. Ard. Chr Cent 94:677-9 Ag 3 '77

Education

See Education—Florida

DAFFODILS. See Narcissus

DAFORA, Asadata

Charles Moore dances and drums of Africa at the CUNY mall. M. Robertson. Dance Mag 51:32-3 O '77 *

DAGUERREOTYPES

Faces of slavery. E. Reichlin. il Am Heritage 28:4-11 Je '77

Time exposure. E. S. Lothrop, Jr. il Pop Phot 80:32+ Ap '77

DAGUIN, André

Jet-set chefs. R. Daley. il por N Y Times Mag p76+ F 6 '77 *

DAHL, Alan R. and Hodgson, Ernest

Complexes of stannous fluoride and other group IVB dihalides with mammalian hemoproteins. bibl il Science 197:1376-8 S 30 '77

DAHL, Dawn

So this is Little Rock. il Ret Liv 17:44-5 My '77

DAHL, Roald

Hitchhiker; story; excerpt from The wonderful story of Henry Sugar and six more. Atlantic 240:45-8 Ag '77

DAHLBERG, Charles Clay

Stroke; excerpt. il por Psychol Today 11:121-2+ Je '77

DAHLBERG, Edward

Obituary

Pub W 211:31 Mr 21 '77

DAHLIN, Robert

(ed) Trade news. See issues of Publishers weekly

(ed) See Kreuger, M. PW interviews

DAHMS, Alan M. and others

Adult education for the mildly retarded; College for Living program. Educ Digest 43:53-5 N '77

DAHOOD, Thomas S.

Bowl your students over with coiled clay. il Design (US) 79:6+ Fall '77

Stained glass design. il Design (US) 78:20-2 mid-Wint '77

DAHRENDORF, Ralf

International power: a European perspective. For Affairs 56:72-88 O '77

about

Science in Europe: a Brookings-style think tank is proposed. N. Hawkes. Science 195:659-60 F 18 '77 *

DAIGH, Chuck

Blueprint for power. J. Thomas. il Motor B & S 139:84-5+ Ap '77 *

DAIGH, Ralph

Maybe you should write a book; excerpt. Writer 90:19-22 S; 19-21 O '77

DAILEY, Bob

Philly gladly takes The Count. P. Gammons. il por Sports Illus 48:76-7 Ja 9 '78 *

DAILY mail (newspaper) See London—Newspapers

DAILY news, Chicago. See Chicago daily news

DAILY news, New York
How they covered Sam; press coverage. D. M. Alpern and others. il Newsweek 90:77+ Ag 22 '77
Notes and comment; experiences of a copy-person in 1941. New Yorker 53:25-6 Je 13 '77
Notes and comment; press treatment of Son of Sam story. New Yorker 53:21-2 Ag 15; 19-22 S 5 '77
Tale of midnight; Son of Sam case. T. Powers. il Commonweal 104:594-6 S 16 '77
DAILY racing form (periodical)
Pssst! Wanna tip on a hot horse? P. Axthelm. il Esquire 87:92-3 Ap '77
DAIMLER-Benz, AG. See Automobile industry—Germany, West
DAIRY farming. See Dairying
DAIRY lobby. See Lobbyists and lobbying
DAIRY price supports. See Agricultural administration—United States
DAIRY products
See also
Cheese
Cookery—Dairy products
Ice cream, ices, etc.
Yogurt

Advertising
See Dairying—Advertising

Marketing
See also
Milk—Marketing

Prices
See also
Milk—Prices
DAIRY substitutes. See Food substitutes
DAIRYING
Dairy extra (cont) Farm J 101:Dairy 1-2+ Ja; Dairy 1-2+ F; Dairy 1-2+ My; Dairy 1-2+ Je; Dairy 1-2+ Ag; Dairy 1-2 S; Dairy 1-2+ O; Dairy 1-2+ D '77
Dairy management. J. R. Borcherding. See issues of Successful farming
Determination got Randy Week into dairying. R. Brunoehler. il Suc Farm 75:no4 D10 Mr '77
Good near-term outlook, danger in rising stocks. C. S. Machan. il Farm J 101:Dairy 1-2 D '77
Making milk; Massachusetts farm of L. Totman. M. Kramer. il por Atlantic 240:80-4+ N '77
Seabolds cut herd size to improve their operation. il Suc Farm 75:no4 L14 Mr '77
Successful dairy management; ed by J. R. Borcherding. il Suc Farm 75:no4 D1-8+ Mr '77
You can start from scratch. C. S. Machan. il Farm J 101:Dairy 4-5 My '77
See also
Borden, Inc
Cheese industry
Computers—Agricultural use
Goats
Hood, H. P, and Sons, Inc
Milk industry

Advertising
Yogurt & the fountain of youth; filming of Dannon commercial in Soviet Georgia. C. Turgeon. il Sat Eve Post 249:18+ O '77

Export-import trade
How much do imports really hurt you? C. S. Machan. il Farm J 101:Dairy 6-7 D '77
DAITZ, Hortense Meyers
Snow doesn't give a soft white damn where it falls; poem. Am For 83:44 O '77
DAKE, June
I'm not going. Read Digest 110:205-6 Ap '77
DAKIN, R, & Company. See Toy industry
DAKIN family
Dakin coat-of-arms. H. K. Eilers. il Hobbies 82:140 Je '77
DALE, Clamma
Musician of the month: Clamma Dale; interview, ed by J. Hiemenz. por Hi Fi 27:MA4-5 D '77
DALE, Francis L.
U.N. myth; address, September 8, 1977. Vital Speeches 43:760-4 O 1 '77
DALE, Richard
South Africa and Namibia. bibl f Cur Hist 73: 209-13+ D '77
DALE, Robin
I couldn't cope alone. Seventeen 36:150-1+ N '77
DALE Books (firm) See Publishers and publishing—Paperback books
DALES, George F.
Strange relics of the crumbling, still-puzzling Indus culture. bibl (p 101) il map Smithsonian 8:56-65 Jl '77
D'ALESSIO, Pasquale, family
Twin miracles; open-heart surgery for D'Alessio twins. E. Keiffer. il Good H 186:75+ Ja '7?
DALEY, Kevin
$900 lesson in podium power. H. E. Meyer. il pors Fortune 96:196-8+ Ag '77 *
DALEY, Maxine
How to buy a house at a shameful savings. Am Home 80:23+ Je '77
DALEY, Richard J.
Chicago: A.D (After Daley) S. J. Ungar. il pors Atlantic 239:4+ Mr '77 *
Chicago library loses its no. 1 friend in Daley. L. R. Pearson. il pors Am Lib 8:60-1 F '77 *
Kindly omit flowers. K. Bode. New Repub 176: 12-14 Ja 15 '77 *
Organization man. R. Whitehead, Jr. Am Scholar 46:351-7 Summ '77 *
Salmon for Hizzoner. R. Telander. il Sports Illus 46:60+ Mr 28 '77 *
DALEY, Robert
Bank heist of the century; robbery of the Societé Générale bank in Nice. il Read Digest 110: 84-90 Ap '77
Great bargains of Bordeaux. il N Y Times Mag p98-112+ Mr 27 '77
Jet-set chefs. il por N Y Times Mag p76+ F 6 '77
DALIBOR; opera. See Smetana, B.
DALILA (literary character) See Women in literature
DALKON shield. See Contraceptives
DALLAS

Architecture
Texas Supreme Court ruling jeopardizes historic buildings. L. Smith. il Archit Rec 162:37 O '77

Art
Dallas (cont) (title varies) J. Kutner. il Art N 76:95-8 Mr; 96+ O; 102+ D '77

Education
Creationism controversy in Dallas; biology texts. J. C. Evans. Chr Cent 94:188-9 Mr 2 '77

Fire Department
Fast treatment keeps patients alive; Dallas Fire Department paramedics. il Am City & County 92:64 Ja '77

Galleries and museums
See also
Southern Methodist University, Dallas—Meadows Museum and Sculpture Court

Music
See also
Dallas Symphony Orchestra
Opera—Texas
DALLAS Civic Opera Company. See Opera—Texas
DALLAS County, Ala.

Police
See Police—Alabama
DALLAS Symphony Orchestra
Symphony appointment raises questions; conductor E. Mata. J. Ardoin. por Hi Fi 27:MA32-3 My '77
D'ALLEYRAND, Marc R.
Holograms: putting the third D into the catalog. bibl il Wilson Lib Bull 51:746-50 My '77
DALMAYRAC, B. and others
Two-billion-year granulites in the late Precambrian metamorphic basement along the southern Peruvian coast. bibl il map Science 198: 49-51 O 7 '77
DALOZE, Désiré. See Pasteels, J. M. jt auth
DALRYMPLE, Byron W.
Amazing mayfly. il Outdoor Life 159:65-7+ My '77
Bassing with bait. il Outdoor Life 159:78-81 Je '77
Channel cats; two ways. il Outdoor Life 159: 84-5+ Ap '77
Come summertime, the squirreling is easy. il Outdoor Life 159:80-1+ Mr '77
Deer hunter's handbook to field dressing, skinning, & butchering. il Outdoor Life 160:93-9 N '77
Nature is my calendar. il Outdoor Life 159:90-2+ Ap '77
New kind of chain for saws. il Mech Illus 73: 78 Mr '77
Stripers for everybody. il Outdoor Life 160:59-61+ Jl '77
Successful mule deer hunting. il Field & S 82: 44-5+ S '77
Successful whitetail hunting. il Field & S 82: 43-5+ D '77
Word to the compleat angler. il Holiday 58:48-9 Ap '77
DALTERIO, S. and others
Cannabinoids inhibit testosterone secretion by mouse testes in vitro. bibl il Science 196:1472-3 Je 24 '77
DALTON, John Nichols
Two tight gubernatorial races. il pors Time 110:25-6 N 7 '77 *
DALTON, Phyllis Irene
Upping the states' ante for libraries. Am Lib 8:621-2 D '77
DALTON Bookseller (firm) See Booksellers and bookselling—United States
DALTON Bookseller (firm), New York City. See Booksellers and bookselling—New York (state)
DALVEN, Rae
(tr) See Cavafy, C. P. Ithaca

DALY, Joseph M.
Construction management brings water plant in on time, under budget. il Am City & County 92:101-2 O '77

DALY, Margaret
Family money management. See issues of Better homes & gardens

DALY, Robert M.
Social and political forces affecting the mental health system; address, October 17, 1977. Vital Speeches 44:139-41 D 15 '77

DALY, William F.
Navajo woman; poem. Nation 225:697 D 24 '77

DAMADIAN, Raymond
Damadian's supermagnet. S. Renner-Smith. il pors Pop Sci 211:76-9+ D '77 *

DAMAGES
Brucellosis buyers win damages. Farm J 101: Dairy 11, Beef 13 Ag '77
First big test of a new antitrust law; price fixing lawsuits against oil companies. por Bus W p48+ S 12 '77
Putting a price on death; compensation awarded by legal systems of various countries. S. Phillips and M. Moller. il pors Psychol Today 10:70-2+ My '77
See also
Liability (law)

DAMARALAND, Colin O'Brien Winter, Bp of.
See Winter, C. O.

DAMICO, James
Let us now praise Cleveland. por Newsweek 90: 18-19 O 17 '77

DAMITZ, Ernst
Naïve artist rediscovered. S. B. Sherrill. il Antiques 111:234 F '77 *

DAMMERMAN, Marilyn
Buying back Belfast? il Forbes 119:25-7 Mr 15 '77
about
Doing business in Belfast. por Forbes 119:6 Mr 15 '77 *

DAMPERS
Automatic damper to cut heat losses. il Mech Illus 73:86 Ap '77

DAMPNESS in buildings
Cures for wet basements. il Bet Hom & Gard 55:42+ Ag '77
Leak-sealing applications are the key to a dry basement. il Pop Sci 210:148 Mr '77

DAMS
Auburn Dam: a faulty business H. Rubin. il Nation 224:563-4 My 7 '77
Auburn Dam: earthquake hazards imperil $1-billion project. L. J. Carter. map Science 197: 643-4+ Ag 12 '77
Bitter battle of the waterways. J. N. Miller. Read Digest 111:83-7 S '77
California dams revisited. Sci Am 236:46-7 Ja '77
Endangered species: review of law triggered by Tellico impasse. C. Holden. Science 196:1426-8 Je 24 '77
From symbolism to substance; views of C. D. Andrus and C. Warren. J. B. Craig. Am For 83:23 My '77
Furbish lousewort is no joke; Endangered Species Act and public works projects. J. Wheelwright. New Repub 176:9-12 My 14 '77
Georgia dam collapse renews concern for safety. R. J. Smith. Science 198:811 N 25 '77
Little fish inspires big ideas; snail darter and the Tellico Dam project. E. M. Leeper. map BioScience 27:697-9 O '77
Maine: damned if you do. . .Dickey-Lincoln project. D. Holt and others. il map Newsweek 91: 21 Ja 2 '78
Of dams and Kate Furbish; threat to Maine's rare plants by proposed Dickey-Lincoln Dams project. R. Saltonstall, Jr. il por Liv Wildn 40:42-3 Ja '77
On dumping Dickey and saving the St John; with editorial comment. R. Saltonstall, Jr. Liv Wildn 40:3, 20-1 O '76
What they didn't tell you about the snail darter & the dam; question of Tennessee Valley Authority avoiding compliance with Endangered Species Act in Tellico Dam project. S. G. Cook and others. il map Nat Parks & Con Mag 51:10-13 My '77

Failure

Awful truth about our federal dams; collapse of the Teton Dam. J. N. Miller. il Read Digest 110:92-6 Je '77
Boom after the burst; Teton Dam aftermath. E. Keerdoja and P. S. Greenberg. il Newsweek 89:9 Je 6 '77
Dam breaks in Georgia; Toccoa. il Time 110:34 N 21 '77
Disasters as a necessary part of benefit-cost analyses. R. K. Mark and D. E. Stuart-Alexander. bibl Science 197:1160-2 S 16 '77
Teton Dam verdict: a foul-up by the engineers. P. M. Boffey. Science 195:270-2 Ja 21 '77
Those uninspected dams: like a loaded shotgun; Toccoa, Ga. il U.S. News 83:69 N 21 '77
Toccoa and the flood. D. A. Williams and V. E. Smith. il Newsweek 90:53 N 21 '77
Torrent of litigation over Teton Dam; possible suit against U.S. Bureau of Reclamation. il Bus W p21-2 Ja 24 '77
Tragedy at Toccoa. E. E. Plowman. il Chr Today 22:48-50 D 9 '77

Panama

Deliverance! rescue of wildlife trapped by rising waters behind the Bayano Dam. J. Fisher. il Int Wildlife 7:40-7 Jl '77

DAMSELFISHES
Female fish produce mates when needed; anemone fish. Sci N 111:311 My 14 '77

DANA, Richard Henry
Return of Pilgrim. G. Jones. il Sea Front 23: 331-3 N '77 *

DANA, Robert
Astronomies; poem. New Yorker 53:60 Ag 1 '77
Mnemosyne; poem. New Yorker 53:34 S 26 '77

DANBURY, Conn.

Education

See Education—Connecticut

DANCE, Jim
Culture in Detroit takes no back seat. il Lib J 102:1116-20+ My 15 '77

DANCE, Kay
How to make a million before you're 34; interview, ed by D. Kaye and F. Ruffin. pors Redbook 149:60+ My '77

DANCE companies
Asakawalker: Graham-influenced; Japan House concert. J. Maskey. Hi Fi 28:MA10 Ja '78
Dance: coming of age in Boston. I. M. Fanger. il Dance Mag 51:16-17 Ag '77
Dance in Washington—it's happening; Washington, D.C. dance companies. F. C. Pannella. Dance Mag 51:92-3 Je '77
Dancers before dance. H. Saal. il por Newsweek 90:112 D 12 '77
Dancing:
Dancers company at the Roundabout Theatre. A. Croce. New Yorker 53:135-6 D 19 '77
Pilobolus Dance Theatre. A. Croce. New Yorker 53:133-5 D 19 '77
Twyla Tharp's Mud. A. Croce. New Yorker 53:106-7 Je 13 '77
Twyla Tharp's season at the Brooklyn Academy. A. Croce. New Yorker 53:106+ My 30 '77
Dancing in a January world: Winnipeg's Contemporary Dancers. J. Anderson. il por Dance Mag 51:44-9 Mr '77
Denishawn redivivus. R. Berenson. Nat R 29: 155 F 4 '77
Denishawn; Spirit of Denishawn program presented by the Danscompany. Hi Fi 27:MA11 Ap '77
Eleven seconds; rehearsal of Twyla Tharp's Half the one hundreds. New Yorker 53:28-9 My 23 '77
Eye witness; Brooklyn Academy of Music performances May 12-22 by Twyla Tharp dancers. T. Tobias. il Dance Mag 51:45-50 S '77
Fearful symmetry; Rockettes. J. Lahr. Harpers 255:83-4 Jl '77
Hirabayashi's seventh season; Marymount Manhattan Theatre. J. Maskey. Hi Fi 28:MA10-11 Ja '78
In contact with Mangrove; contact improvisation. J. Armstrong. il Dance Mag 51:42-5 D '77
Minnesota commotion: Loyce Houlton and the Minnesota Dance Theatre. J. Anderson. il Dance Mag 51:75-9 Ap '77
Monk's Quarry; performance at the Brooklyn Academy of Music by The House. J. La Barbara. il Hi Fi 27:MA12-13 Ap '77
On the road with dance and dancers; Georgia Dance Theatre Company. W. Terry. il Sat R 4:40-1 My 14 '77
Pilobolus: six mavericks in search of their own style. C. McLaughlin. il Horizon 20:23-7 N '77
Portland, Oregon: braving the new world; Portland Dance Theatre and the Portland Ballet Company. M. Aloff. il Dance Mag 51:124-5 My '77
Reviews:
Alonso Castro Dance Theatre. A. Smith. Dance Mag 52:80+ Ja '78
Asakawalker Dance Company at Japan House. L. Small. Dance Mag 51:101+ D '77
Chuck Davis Dance Company. L. Small. Dance Mag 51:98 My '77
Communitas/ego; performed by the Country Dance and Song Society of America. Dance Mag 51:33-4 My '77
Concert Dance Company of Boston performances at ATL October 6-9. M. Robertson. Dance Mag 51:33-4 D '77
Earth; Thunderbird American Indian Dancers at the McBurney YMCA. L. Small. Dance Mag 51:47-8 Ap '77
Isadora Duncan Centenary Dance Company at the theatre of the Riverside Church. Dance Mag 51:32 Ag '77
Louis Falco Dance Company's April 12-16 run at the Roundabout Theatre. A. Smith. Dance Mag 51:74+ Ag '77

DANCE companies—*Continued*
Reviews:—Cont
March olio; Trisha Brown Dance Company. J. Pikula. Dance Mag 51:74 Jl '77
Mariko Sanjo Dance Company. A. Smith. Dance Mag 51:108-9 My '77
Marion Rice's Denishawn Dancers. R. A. Thom. Dance Mag 51:114+ My '77
Norman Walker's The medicine wheel presented by the Adelphi Dance Theatre. L. Small. Dance Mag 51:83 Je '77
North Carolina Dance Theatre's February 26 performance in Winston-Salem. J. Dunning. Dance Mag 51:66 S '77
People/Dorothy Vislocky Dance Theatre. A. Smith. Dance Mag 52:82 Ja '78
Raymond Johnson Dance Company at Pace University's Schimmel Center. Dance Mag 51:84+ Je '77
Sanasardo Dance Company's June 14-19 season at the Roundabout Theatre. L. Small. il Dance Mag 51:22-4+ S '77
Steven Peck Jazz Dance Company; interview, ed by V. H. Swisher. S. Peck. il Dance Mag 51:78-9 Mr '77
Three spaces in three days; premiere of Abandoned prayer by the Sanasardo Dance Company. J. Silverman. Dance Mag 51:87-8 Mr '77
Viola Farber Dance Company series at the Diplomat Hotel. A. Smith. Dance Mag 51: 76+ Ag '77
St Mark's, Capitol Hill: patron of the arts. J. Warren. Chr Cent 94:632-3 Jl 6 '77
Sleight of limb; Pilobolus. H. Saal. il Newsweek 90:89 D 5 '77
See also
Alwin Nikolais Dance Theatre
Ballet companies
José Limón Dance Company
Martha Graham Dance Company
Merce Cunningham Dance Company
Murray Louis Dance Company
Paul Taylor Dance Company
Pearl Lang Dance Company

Finance

Dance funding. B. V. Bordelon. See issues of Dance magazine
Oumansky in queryland; attempts to fund the Valentina Oumansky Dramatic Dance Ensemble. V. H. Swisher. il por Dance Mag 52: 75 Ja '78

DANCE concerts
Dance; a special Saturday matinee by Dance Umbrella. J. Maskey. il Hi Fi 27:MA13 Je '77
Dance in Central Park; Delacorte Theatre September 2-12. J. Maskey. il Hi Fi 27:MA12-13 D '77
Isadora's dances; November and January programs performed by A. Gamson. J. Maskey. por Hi Fi 27:MA10 Ap '77
Remy's imaginative play; performance at American Theatre Laboratory. J. Maskey. Hi Fi 28: MA10 Ja '78
Reviews:
Bruce Becker and Jane Kosminsky's June 2 performance at the Marymount Manhattan Theatre. D. Hering. Dance Mag 51:86+ S '77
Choreographer's Showcase. A. Smith. Dance Mag 51:107 My '77
Contact improvisation; two concerts at The Kitchen. E. R. Luger. Dance Mag 51: 41-3 Ap '77
Critic-at-large: Joan Lombardi, Vic Stornant and Dancers at New York's Theatre of the Riverside Church. D. Hering. Dance Mag 51:40 Ap '77
Dance Theater Workshop's Choreographers Showcase; performances at American Theatre Laboratory. A. Smith. Dance Mag 51:88+ O '77
Dancing from inside; Mel Wong's Glass. J. Pikula. Dance Mag 51:35+ Mr '77
Daniel Nagrin Gala at Marymount Manhattan Theatre. L. Small. Dance Mag 51: 96+ D '77
First Decade Dance Showcase. L. Small. Dance Mag 51:99-100 My '77
Madeleine Denko and Susan Matthews' presentation of Dances. J. Silverman. Dance Mag 51:94+ D '77
R. Charlip's concert at the American Theatre Laboratory. J. Dunning. Dance Mag 51:26+ D '77
Rachel Lampert at the NYU School of the Arts. D. Vaughan. Dance Mag 51:40-1 O '77
Spokes of the Umbrella; Dance Umbrella fall series. A. Smith. Dance Mag 51:102-6 Mr '77
Technique is only half the game; Rebecca: a DanceMime Concert. J. Pikula. Dance Mag 51:43+ Ap '77
Vanaver and Drapkin Ensemble's June 19 performance. D. Hering. Dance Mag 51:84+ S '77
What's in a name? Dance Uptown programs at Barnard's Minor Latham Playhouse. D. Vaughan. Dance Mag 51:26+ Je '77

DANCE conferences
Canadian Conference: classical and contemporary ballet—the next twenty-five years; text of first session. il Dance Mag 51:50-8 Mr '77
Canadian Conference: funding, criticism and music; excerpts from text of second session. il Dance Mag 51:84-7 Ap '77
Conventions 1977. il Dance Mag 51:90 D '77

DANCE costume. See Costume, Theatrical

DANCE dramas, Korean. See Folk drama, Korean

DANCE exercises. See Exercise

DANCE festivals
Calendar of summer dance events 1977. il Dance Mag 51:52-7 My '77
Chicago; First North American International Ballet Festival. A. Barzel. Dance Mag 51:26+ N '77
Dance; First North American International Dance Festival. N. Goldner. Nation 225:28-30 Jl 2 '77
Delacorte; New York Dance Festival. T. Tobias. il Dance Mag 51:20-2+ D '77
Island festival: Cuba takes off: Havana's Fifth International Festival of Ballet. B. Fitzgerald. il Dance Mag 51:80-5 Mr '77
Musical theatre; Alvin Ailey's Duke Ellington Festival. D. Diether. il Am Rec G 40:52-3 N '76
National Association for Regional Ballet festivals—1977. S. Shelton. il Dance Mag 51:46-9 D '77
Reviews:
Los Angeles Dance Festival events. H. V. Swisher. Dance Mag 52:73 Ja '78
See also
Jacob's Pillow (festival and school of dance)

DANCE films. See Motion pictures—Dance films

DANCE institutes and workshops
See also
Jacob's Pillow (festival and school of dance)
School of American Ballet

DANCE magazine
Dance Magazine Awards 1977: Murray Louis, Peter Martins, Natalia Makarova; presentation ceremony. il pors Dance Mag 51:30-5 Jl '77

DANCE of death; drama. See Strindberg, A.

DANCE production
Eleven seconds; rehearsal of Twyla Tharp's Half the one hundreds. New Yorker 53:28-9 My 23 '77

DANCE studios

Floors

Dance floors: their selection and preparation. R. Gelabert. il Dance Mag 51:94-5 Mr '77
Rosin: its use and abuse; treatment of dance floors. R. Gelabert. Dance Mag 51:88 Ap '77

DANCE teachers
Dancers and teachers; ballet instruction. R. Gelabert. il Dance Mag 51:72-3 S '77
Terpsichore and Artemis: dance as therapy after mastectomy; programs of four dance teachers. W. A. Winkler. il Dance Mag 51:77-8 N '77

DANCE Theatre of Harlem
Dance Theatre of Harlem; Wollman Auditorium performances. D. Maskey. Hi Fi 27:MA27 N '77

DANCE therapy
Dance therapy. E. Feder and B. Feder. bibl il Psychol Today 10:76-8+ F '77
Psychomotor approach in the nursing home; dancing programs for the aged. L. R. Schoenfeld. il Dance Mag 51:82-4 O '77
Terpsichore and Artemis: dance as therapy after mastectomy; programs of four dance teachers. W. A. Winkler. il Dance Mag 51: 77-8 N '77

DANCERS
Dance is climbing the walls; Annabelle Gamson, Phoebe Neville, Dianne McIntyre, and Trisha Brown. J. Dunning. il Ms 6:46-8+ D '77
Dancers and choreographers. R. Gelabert. il Dance Mag 51:84-5 Je '77
Dancers and teachers; ballet instruction. R. Gelabert. il Dance Mag 51:72-3 S '77
Dancer's Christmas; gifts. il Dance Mag 51:92 D '77
Editor's log. W. Como. Dance Mag 52:23 Ja '78
Presstime news. See issues of Dance magazine
What she did for love. . . T. Hilfman. il por Dance Mag 51:54 D '77
See also
Clothing and dress—Dancers
also names of dancers, e.g. C. Gregory

Accidents and injuries

Dancers and medical science. R. Gelabert. il Dance Mag 51:74-5 D '77

Health and hygiene

Dancer's physique. R. Gelabert. il Dance Mag 51:78-80 N '77
Stage injuries; dancers' diet and health. R. Gelabert. il Dance Mag 51:30-1 Ag '77
See also
Posture

DANCERS—*Continued*

Nutrition

On eating. M. Louis. Dance Mag 51:96 S '77
Stage injuries; dancers' diet and health. R. Gelabert. il Dance Mag 51:30-1 Ag '77

Psychology

From the inside: on identity: the me-factor. M. Louis. Dance Mag 52:48-50 Ja '78

DANCERS (ballet company) See Ballet companies

DANCES, High school. See Student activities

DANCING
Brighton Beach; ballroom dancing. New Yorker 53:22-4 Ag 22 '77
Calendar of summer dance events 1977. il Dance Mag 51:52-7 My '77
Dance. J. Maskey. See issues of High fidelity and Musical America
Dancing. A. Croce. See occasional issues of New Yorker
Dancing in the seventies. J. Highwater. il Horizon 19:30-3 My '77
From the inside. M. Louis. See occasional issues of Dance magazine
Geometries: the song and dance of Laura Dean. R. Baker. il por Dance Mag 51:40-4 N '77
Man himself; J. Phillips. New Yorker 53:32-4 S 12 '77
New exercise. E. Schoen. il House & Gard 149:158-9+ My '77
Performance can have a dangerous connotation. K. Litz. por Dance Mag 51:131 My '77
Perspectives. See issues of Dance magazine
Presstime news. See issues of Dance magazine
Reviews. See issues of Dance magazine
Steven Peck Jazz Dance Company; interview, ed by V. H. Swisher. S. Peck. il Dance Mag 51:78-9 Mr '77
Why dance best expresses life in an electronic age. E. Feld. il U.S. News 83:68 O 10 '77
See also
Ballet
Choreography
Dance therapy
Discotheques
Folk dancing
Improvisation (dance)
Motion pictures—Dance films
Square dancing
Tango (dance)

Benefit performances

Ballet from the bleachers; benefit for the National Association for Regional Ballet. W. Terry. il Sat R 4:46-7 Je 11 '77

Bibliography

Book briefs (title varies) Dance Mag 51:98 Jl: 26-9 Ag; 100 S; 41 O; 74-6 N '77; 52:96 Ja '78
For very young dancers: a quickstep through recent books. A. Kellman. il SLJ 24:34-5 D '77

Photographs

Liveliest art. Horizon 19:14-25 Jl '77

Production and direction

See Dance production

Study and teaching

Education briefs. H. Von Obenauer. See issues of Dance magazine
On teachers. M. Louis. Dance Mag 51:84 F '77

DANCING, African
Charles Moore dances and drums of Africa at the CUNY mall. M. Robertson. Dance Mag 51:32-3 O '77

DANCING, Balinese
Bali Hoo; Barong dances and music. J. Culshaw. il Hi Fi 27:19+ Jl '77

DANCING, Indian (American) See Indians of North America—Dances

DANCING, Indian (East Indian)
Perspectives: Kathakali and other styles of Indian dance. S. Shelton. Dance Mag 51:71 S '77
Reviews; performances by Janak Khendry and Ritha Devi. S. Banes. Dance Mag 51:34+ F '77
Reviews; Y. Krishnamurti. S. Banes. Dance Mag 51:34-5 My '77

DANCING, Indonesian
See also
Dancing, Balinese

DANCING, Middle Eastern
From Medina to midtown; performances by Middle Eastern dancers in New York. L. Small. Dance Mag 51:100-2 Mr '77

DANCING, Oriental
Everybody is belly-dancing. J. Stewart-Gordon. il Read Digest 111:129-32 Ag '77

DANCING for the aged. See Aged—Recreation

DANCING in art
Degas' dancers; Degas in the Metropolitan exhibition. S. Banes. Dance Mag 51:72-4 Je '77

DANCING in religion, folklore, etc.
See also
Indians of North America—Dances

DANE, Jean
Why I cared for and fed my garden's caterpillars. il Org Gard & Farm 24:124-5 Je '77

DANFORTH, Douglas Dewitt
Energy and the economy; address, May 18, 1977. Vital Speeches 43:539-41 Je 15 '77

DANFORTH, Helen
Mussel's secret formula; with biographical sketch. il Sea Front 23:210-14, 254 Jl '77

DANFORTH, John Clagget
Limit a lawmaker's term in Congress? interview. por U.S. News 83:71-2 N 14 '77

about

5 freshman Senators who are moving into the spotlight. pors U.S. News 82:24-5 F 7 '77 *

DANGEROUS goods. See Hazardous substances

DANIEL, James
Garbage: a fuel for the future. il Read Digest 111:66+ D '77
Johnny Appleseed for our time. il por Read Digest 111:142-6 Ag '77

DANIEL, John B.
U.S. Appeals Court rules employee pension funds are subject to federal antifraud laws. Ret Liv 17:47 O '77 *

DANIEL Boone National Forest, Ky. See National forests

DANIELL, Martha L.
She shuns retirement; joins Peace Corps instead. por Aging 274:22 Ag '77 *

DANIELS, David
Winter into summer. New Yorker 53:19-22 Ja 9 '78 *

DANIELS, Derick January
Another Playboy hutch cleaning. por Time 110:95 S 26 '77 *
Skinning the rabbit. D. Pauly and C. J. Harper. il por Newsweek 90:66+ S 26 '77 *
Thinning the staff fattens Playboy. Bus W p59+ S 26 '77 *

DANIELS, Guy
(tr) See Chalidze, V. How important is Soviet dissent?

DANILOVA, Aleksandra
Belle of the Ballets Russes: Alexandra Danilova. A. Fay. il pors Dance Mag 51:55-70 O '77 *

DANISH cookery. See Cookery, Danish

DANISH pottery. See Pottery, Danish

DANKY, James P. and Fox, Michael
Alternative periodicals. il Wilson Lib Bull 51: 481-5, 662-6, 763-8 F, Ap-My '77

DANN, Blanche L.
More about the Dann Trio and Rudy Wiedoeft. J. Walsh. il pors Hobbies 82:35-6+ Jl; 35-6+ Ag '77 *

DANN, M. Felice
More about the Dann Trio and Rudy Wiedoeft. J. Walsh. il pors Hobbies 82:35-6+ Jl; 35-6+ Ag '77 *

DANNENBAUM, Julie
Tea for two. . .with homemade strudel. il Am Home 80:62-3+ F '77

DANSCOMPANY. See Dance companies

DANTE Alighieri
Love makes the world go round: Divine comedy. N. Tischler. Chr Today 21:22-3 Ag 26 '77 *

DANTLEY, Adrian
Finding a home with the Braves. il por Sports Illus 46:60+ Mr 14 '77

DANTZIG, Maurits van
Programmed connoisseurship. G. Schwartz. Art N 76:99-102 My '77 *

DANUBE River
Danube: river of many nations, many names. M. Edwards. il map Nat Geog 152:454-85 O '77

DANVILLE Hotel Territory Historical Site. See Historic houses, sites, etc.—California

DANZIGER, Sheldon, and Plotnick, Robert
Demographic change, government transfers, and income distribution. bibl il M Labor R 100: 7-11 Ap '77

D'AOUST, Brian G. and others
Venous gas bubbles: production by transient, deep isobaric counterdiffusion of helium against nitrogen. bibl il Science 197:889-91 Ag 26 '77

DARCY, Clare
Love's own promise; story; excerpt from Cecily; or, A young lady of quality. Good H 185:181-4 Ag '77

DARCY, Cornelius P.
Edmonia Lewis arrives in Rome. bibl f por Negro Hist Bull 40:688-9 Mr '77

DARDEN, Ellington
Vitamin update. Parents Mag 52:43+ Mr '77

DARDÓN, Hugo Cerezo. See Cerezo Dardón, H.

DAREHSHORI, Charlotte
Way it is. Todays Educ 66:46-8 Mr '77

DARIEN, Conn.

Religious institutions and affairs

See Connecticut—Religious institutions and affairs

DARK, S. K.
Gardening with the weather. il Org Gard & Farm 24:144-6 Jl '77
Making paprika from homegrown peppers. Org Gard & Farm 24:116 Ag '77

DARK glasses. See Sun glasses

DARKNESS in the Bible. See Light and darkness in the Bible

DARKROOM equipment. See Photography—Processing—Apparatus and supplies

DARKROOM technique in photography. See Photography—Processing

DARKROOM thermometers. See Thermometers and thermometry

DARKROOMS. See Photography—Studios and darkrooms

DARLING, Pamela W.
Preservation: a national plan at last? report of National Preservation Program Planning Conference. il Lib J 102:447-9 F 15 '77
—See Patton, F. jt auth

DARLING, Richard L. See Learmont, C. L. jt auth

DARMAN, Richard G.
Law of the sea: rethinking U.S. interests. bibl f For Affairs 56:373-95 Ja '78

DARNTON, John
Nigeria's dissident superstar. il pors N Y Times Mag p 10-12+ Jl 24 '77

DARR, Jack
Service clinic. See issues of Radio-electronics

DARR, Russell E.
Fiberglass, stainless steel stop deep well corrosion. il Am City & County 92:57 Jl '77

DARRELL, Robert Donaldson
Electrical recording: the convert revolution. il Hi Fi 27:79-85 Jl '77
Tape deck. See issues of High fidelity and Musical America

DART, John
Woody Allen, theologian. bibl Chr Cent 94:585-9 Je 22 '77

DARTMOUTH College, Hanover, N.H.
Lesson of the master; L. Edel, Vernon Visiting Professorship of Biography. por Time 110:47 Ag 22 '77
When business executives go back to school—. il U.S. News 83:61 Ag 22 '77

DARTMOUTH Conferences
Dartmouth at Jurmala. N. Cousins. Sat R 4:6-7+ S 3 '77
When writers meet; Soviet-American authors conference. N. Cousins. il Sat R 4:8-9+ S 17 '77

DARWIN, Charles Robert
Charlie Darwin was an underachiever. A. Franza. Engl J 66:12-14 Ap '77 *
Darwin and Melville: why a tortoise? J. Franzosa. bibl f Am Imago 33:361-79 Wint '76 *
Darwin's mistake. T. Bethell. bibl Chr Today 21:12-15 Je 17 '77 *
Overlooked link: Darwin and his flowers; excerpt from Darwin and his flowers. M. Allan. il por Horticulture 55:12-21 O '77 *

DARWINISM. See Natural selection

DASE, Johann
Johann Dase and some other mental calculators. J. Ashbrook. Sky & Tel 54:365 N '77

DAS GUPTA, Jyotirindra
Nation, region, and welfare: ethnicity, regionalism, and development politics in south Asia. bibl f il Ann Am Acad 433:125-36 S '77

DASH, Glen
Build this video modulator. il Radio-Electr 48:33-5+ Ag '77

DASH, Leon
Behind the lines. K. Willenson and L. H. Norman. il por Newsweek 90:38+ Ag 22 '77 *

DASHEFF, William. See Dearborn, L. jt auth

DASS, Ram. See Ram Dass

DASSAULT-Breguet (firm) See Airplane industry—France

DATA base systems. See Information storage and retrieval systems

DATA General Corporation
Advantage, Adler! il por Forbes 119:66-7 Ja 15 '77

DATA processing. See Electronic data processing

DATA Resources, Inc. See Economic forecasting

DATA storage and retrieval systems. See Information storage and retrieval systems

DATA transmission systems
Computer communications; address, May 3, 1977. A. M. McMahon. Vital Speeches 43:529-32 Je 15 '77
Speculative play in Graphic Scanning. D. G. Santry. il Bus W p92 Ja 16 '78
See also
Library networks

Europe, Western

IIA sees price war threat in European info tariffs; charges for use of Tymnet. Lib J 102:1982 O 1 '77

DATAPRODUCTS Corporation. See Computer industry

DATE palms. See Palms

DATES (fruit)
See also
Cookery—Fruit

DATING
How young America dates. W. B. Furlong. Seventeen 36:226-9+ Ag '77
I canceled the wedding of my dreams. il Good H 184:24+ My '77
Interfaith dating dilemma. Seventeen 36:57 S '77

Anecdotes, facetiae, satire, etc.

Looking for Mr Rightbar. A. Strickland. Mademoiselle 83:170+ Je '77

DATING, Radioactive. See Radiocarbon dating

DATSUN (automobile) See Automobiles, Foreign

DATTA, Rabinder S. See Howard, P. H. jt auth

DATTNER, Richard
Parks for the year 2000. il Am City & County 92:39-44 N '77

DAUGHERTY, Richard D.
Indian Pompeii. P. Gwynne and S. Gayle. il Newsweek 90:81-2 S 5 '77 *

DAUGHTERS; drama. See Coss, C. and others

DAUGHTERS and fathers. See Parent-child relationship

DAUGHTERS and mothers. See Parent-child relationship

DAUKSZA, Tony
Arctic almost killed me twice! il map Outdoor Life 159:88-91+ Je '77

D'AULAIRE, Emily and D'Aulaire, P. O.
Equal Rights Amendment: what's it all about? Read Digest 110:98-102 F '77
New hope for the childless. Read Digest 111:197-200+ D '77
Piranha: minijaws of the Amazon. il Read Digest 111:11-14+ S '77
16-day ordeal of John Vihtelic. il Read Digest 110:142-6+ Mr '77

D'AULAIRE, Per Ola. See D'Aulaire, E. jt auth

DAUME, Charlotte
French touch . . . in the galley. Yachting 142:134 S '77

DAUMIER, Honoré
Daumier goes a-sporting. il Am Artist 41:50-1 Jl '77 *

DAVAO, Philippines
Davao. I. M. Santiago. il Travel 148:36-41 Ag '77

DAVENPORT, Hazel Streeter
Not ready for the rocking chair. il por Ret Liv 17:32-4 D '77

DAVENPORT, J. C. and others
Program at Fermilab for minority students. il Phys Today 30:9+ Je '77

DAVERN, Jeanne M.
New kind of development. il Archit Rec 162:96-107 D '77

DAVID, Edward Emil, 1925-
Edward E. David, Jr, president-elect. J. R. Pierce. il por Science 196:336-7 Ap 15 '77 *

DAVID, Félicien César
Félicien David 1810-1876 and French romantic orientalism. P. Gradenwitz. bibl f il por Mus Q 62:471-506 O '76 *

DAVID, Gerard
Looking at paintings. B. Dunstan. il Am Artist 41:62-3 D '77 *

DAVID, Leonard
Students in space? maybe! il Sci Digest 81:15-17 Mr '77

DAVID, Lester
Best places to borrow money. il Mech Illus 73:56+ My '77
Control your temper. Seventeen 36:116-17+ F '77
I refused to give up my baby. il Seventeen 36:162-3+ Je '77
Jinx Melia: crusader for homemakers. il por Good H 184:154+ Je '77
Many faces of guilt. il Fam Health 9:22-5 Jl '77
Second sight. il por Ladies Home J 94:154+ Jl '77
Violence in our schools. il Good H 185:129+ N '77

DAVID, Michael John
Reporter at large. J. McPhee. New Yorker 53:40+ Jl 11 '77 *

DAVID-WEILL, Michel
Passing the baton at Lazard Frères. W. Robertson. il pors Fortune 96:116-20+ N '77 *

DAVID J. Greene and Company. See Investment advisers

DAVIDOFF, Zino
Man who saved Havanas. W. Galling. il pors Fortune 95:174-6 F '77 *

DAVIDON, Ann Morrissett
Macho obstacles to peace. Bull Atom Sci 33:22-4 Je '77
On rage remembered. Progressive 41:18-19 Je '77

DAVIDSON, Bill
Town that lives in terror. il Good H 185:136-7+ S '77

DAVIDSON, Diane W. See Brown, J. H. jt auth

DAVIDSON, Donald
Competition. Motor T 29:120-3 My; 118-19 Ag '77

DAVIDSON, Dorothy J. Buchanan-. See Buchanan-Davidson, D. J.

DAVIDSON, Erika
Dynamite U.S.S.R. il pors Opera N 42:26-8+ S '77
(ed) See Sass, S. Sylvia Sass: remember the name
DAVIDSON, Harvey Justin
Top of the world is flat. bibl f il Harvard Bus R 55:89-99 Mr '77
DAVIDSON, Mark
Computer privacy. Sci Digest 82:42-4 S '77
Stormy weather forecast for those who tinker. Sci Digest 81:74-5 Je '77
—and Ponnamperuma, Nirmali
Continued: the mystery of black holes that warp space /halt time. il Sci Digest 81:57-8 My '77
Old enigma: scientists and therapists gain in understanding your phobias. Sci Digest 82:60-4 Ag '77
Tossing & turning all night? Read this . . . and fall asleep; questions and answers. Sci Digest 81:13-17 Ap '77
DAVIDSON, Paul
Breaking up large American energy firms; excerpts from address. por Intellect 105:295-6 Mr '77
DAVIDSON, Ralph P.
Letter from the publisher. See issues of Time
DAVIDSON, Sara
Flirting with mysticism; excerpt from Loose change: three women of the sixties. il Ms 5:57-9+ Ap '77
Way we weren't; excerpt from Loose change: three women of the sixties. il Esquire 87:83-7+ Mr '77
about
Intelligent woman's guide to sex. J. Coburn. Mademoiselle 83:76 O '77 *
DAVIDSON, Trudi
Chances are one in a million. por Ret Liv 17:26-7 Je '77
DAVIDSON, Wendell
What makes Robert Redford run? il pors Sat Eve Post 249:42-3 My '77
DAVIDSON College, Davidson, N.C.
Ass. prof. GS-7; case of R. Linden and Davidson College. Nat R 29:818 Jl 22 '77
DAVIE, Donald
Tunstall forest; Seeing her leave; Wide France; Via Portello; To Helen Keller; Agave in the West; Morning; Hardness of light; Time passing, beloved; Among artisans' house; Fountain of Arethusa; excerpts from In the stopping train and Collected poems, 1950-1970. New Repub 177:21-4 O 22 '77
about
Poetry of Donald Davie. W. H. Pritchard. New Repub 177:24-8 O 22 '77 *
DAVIE, Earl W. See Vehar, G. A. jt auth
DAVIES, Brian
My sons are drowning! il Read Digest 111:78-81 Jl '77
about
Dirge for the harp. D. Levin. il por Sports Illus 46:80+ Ap 18 '77 *
DAVIES, Jane B.
Gothic revival furniture designs of Alexander J. Davis. bibl il Antiques 111:1014-27 My '77
DAVIES, Merton E.
Prime meridian of Mars and the longitudes of the Viking landers. bibl Science 197:1277 S 23 '77
DAVIES, Owen
Colds: 200 strains ache to get you. Sci Digest 81:21-5 Ap '77
Seven sources to help power your future. Sci Digest 82:77-82 O '77
DAVIES, Scrope Berdmore
Scrope's last throw. R. Holmes. Harpers 254:77-9+ Ap '77 *
DAVIES, Thomas A. and others
Estimates of Cenozoic oceanic sedimentation rates. bibl il Science 197:53-5 Jl 1 '77
DAVIGNON, Etienne, Viscount
Take your (ugh!) pills, boys. por Forbes 120:120 N 1 '77
DAVIS, Alexander Jackson
Gothic revival furniture designs of Alexander J. Davis. J. B. Davies. bibl il Antiques 111:1014-27 My '77 *
DAVIS, Andrew
Music: guest conductor. B. H. Haggin. New Repub 177:23 N 26 '77 *
DAVIS, Bernard D.
Debate by a spirited pair. Sci Digest 81:27-8 Je '77
DAVIS, Chester C.
Battle for the shrinking millions. il por Time 110:64+ Jl 4 '77 *
DAVIS, Clive J.
Clive's comeback. G. Stokes. il pors N Y Times Mag p70+ Ap 24 '77 *
DAVIS, Colin
Dvořak: Symphony no. 7 in D minor, op. 70. J. R. Oestreich. por Am Rec G 40:18-20 My '77 *
Sibelius: Symphony no. 2 in D, Boston Symphony Orchestra, conducted by C. Davis. J. W. Barker. por Am Rec G 40:41-2 O '77 *

DAVIS, Daniel J. and others
Birth order and intellectual development: the confluence model in the light of cross-cultural evidence. bibl il Science 196:1470-2 Je 24 '77
DAVIS, Daphne
Movies. See issues of American home
DAVIS, David E. Jr
Driver's seat. See issues of Car and driver
DAVIS, Dick
Little Tree in Forrest. por Writers Digest 57:24 My '77
DAVIS, Douglas F.
California—summer under fire. il Am For 83:8-12 O '77
DAVIS, Douglas M.
Due West: the Costakis collection comes out. il Art in Am 65:122-3+ N '77
Let's hear it for the cable. por Newsweek 90:29 N 21 '77
about
Art on the line. M. A. Tighe. il New Repub 176:24-6 Ap 16 '77 *
DAVIS, Eddie
Indigenous music. N. Hentoff. Nation 225:637 D 10 '77 *
DAVIS, Edward Michael
L.A.'s controversial cop. J. K. Footlick and M. Kasindorf. il por Newsweek 90:55 Ag 29 '77 *
DAVIS, Esther
World on your Christmas tree. il Ret Liv 17:37+ D '77
DAVIS, Flora
Sad but necessary facts about divorce. Redbook 149:223+ My '77
(ed) See Farson, R. Are you trying to be too good a parent?
DAVIS, Gary
Reviews. J. Anderson. Dance Mag 51:23-4 Ap '77 *
DAVIS, Glenn C. and others
Intravenous naloxone administration in schizophrenia and affective illness. bibl il Science 197:74-6 Jl 1 '77
DAVIS, Gwen
(ed) See Dunaway, F. Why I waited so long to marry
DAVIS, Howard
This was the start of something big. P. Putnam. il pors Sports Illus 46:18-19 Ja 24 '77 *
DAVIS, Howard W.
Profits on textbooks: a call for group action by college store managers. Pub W 212:37-8 N 28 '77
DAVIS, Hugh J.
Dalkon shield: collusion? Society 14:4 My '77 *
DAVIS, Jack
Jack Davis cover story. N. Meglin. il Am Artist 41:34-7+ Ap '77 *
DAVIS, Jeff C. Jr
Introduction to spectroscopy (cont) Chemistry 50:17-20 N '77
DAVIS, Jerry B.
Improving reading and the teaching of science. bibl Clearing H 50:390-2 My '77
DAVIS, Joe E.
Nursing the nursing homes back to health. il por Bus W p66+ D 5 '77 *
DAVIS, John D. See Wirtshafter, D. jt auth
DAVIS, Julia
Victorians thought her a downright scandal—as she was. il por Smithsonian 8:131-6+ O '77
DAVIS, Katherine T. and Shearn, Allen
In vitro growth of imaginal disks from drosophila melanogaster. bibl il Science 196:438-40 Ap 22 '77
DAVIS, Kingsley
Next 30 years—not very happy. Intellect 106:182 N '77
DAVIS, Laurie Lee
Just look at her now! GH's 1959 cover-baby winner. il pors Good H 185:56 O '77 *
DAVIS, Lorraine
Between us. See issues of Vogue
Sex switchers. Vogue 167:151+ Ag '77
DAVIS, Mendel Jackson
Excerpts from testimony on proposals relative to the President's powers of reorganization, March 1, 1977. Cong Digest 56:113+ Ap '77
DAVIS, Paul
Paul Davis: a personal vision; interview, ed by S. Bonhomme. il Am Artist 41:34-41+ My '77
DAVIS, Paxton
Small is beautiful. il Am Home 80:44-5+ Jl '77
DAVIS, Priscilla
Texas gothic. R. Steele and M. Kasindorf. il por Newsweek 89:30 Ap 4 '77 *
DAVIS, Rennie
Inner-space trip. pors Newsweek 90:24-5 S 5 '77 *
DAVIS, Robert Gorham
Need to know. Commonweal 104:236-9 Ap 15 '77
DAVIS, Ronald Wayne. See Benton, W. D; Cameron, J. R. jt auths
DAVIS, Rosalynd
More about the Dann Trio and Rudy Wiedoeft. J. Walsh. il pors Hobbies 82:35-6+ Jl; 35-6+ Ag '77 *

DAVIS, Ruth M.
Evolution of computers and computing. bibl il Science 195:1096-102 Mr 18 '77

DAVIS, Sam
History in houses. E. D. Garrett. il Antiques 111:560-7 Mr '77 *

DAVIS, Sam, Home, Smyrna. See Historic houses, sites, etc.—Tennessee

DAVIS, Shelby Cullom
Annals of higher education. E. J. Kahn, Jr. New Yorker 53:88+ My 23 '77 *

DAVIS, Shirley
Why the Justice Department doesn't want you to know what happened between Otto Passman and Shirley Davis. A. Northrop. il pors Ms 6:57-9 Ja '78 *

DAVIS, Stephen R.
How external speakers can improve mobile CB performance. il Pop Electr 11:54-7 Mr '77

DAVIS, T. Cullen, murder trial. See Trials (murder)

DAVIS, Vicky
Jet-set tycoon; interview, ed by M. Kunz. il pors Am Home 80:24+ Je '77

DAVIS, Virginia H.
My useful friend, the cinnabar moth. Org Gard & Farm 24:89-90 My '77

DAVIS, W. Doug
Some regional considerations concerning glazing materials; excerpt from The solar greenhouse book. Org Gard & Farm 24:67-8 D '77

DAVIS, William J. See Kovac, M. P. jt auth

DAVIS, William Virgil
Snow; poem. Chr Cent 94:1215 D 28 '77

DAVIS, William W. and Manar, H. E.
Ecoscene. il Parks & Rec 12:26-8+ Ja '77

DAVIS, Calif.
Thriftiest town of all. D. Pauly and W. J. Cook. il Newsweek 89:74 Ap 18 '77

DAVISON, Jane
Design (cont) N Y Times Mag p88-9 Ap 24; 73 My 15 '77

DAVISON, Peter
La bocca della verità; poem. Atlantic 240:42 S '77
Cross cut; poem. Atlantic 240:75 Jl '77
Day of wrath; poem. New Repub 177:27 S 3 '77
Zenith: Walker Creek; poem. New Yorker 53:38 Je 20 '77

DAVISON, Susan E.
But you can't do that! That's not fair! Todays Educ 66:68-9 Ja '77; Same abr. Educ Digest 42:36-7 My '77

DAVY, Sir Humphry
Sir Humphry Davy's battle with the sea. P. M. Lauren. bibl il pors Chemistry 50:14-17 S '77 *

DAW Books (firm) See Publishers and publishing—Paperback books

DAWKINS, Richard
Remarkable replicators; excerpt from The selfish gene. Natur Hist 86:34+ F '77
You—the gene machine. il Vogue 167:234-5+ My '77

about

Caring groups and selfish genes. S. J. Gould. Natur Hist 86:20+ D '77 *

DAWSON, Paul Dow
Science and socialization out-of-doors. Educ Digest 42:57-9 F '77

DAWSON, Paula
Closet crisis. Seventeen 36:32+ Ag '77

DAWSON, T. J.
Kangaroos; with biographical sketch. il map Sci Am 237:20, 78-85+ Ag '77

DAWSON, Ga.
Dawson boys; work of the Team Defense Project. M. Pinsky. Progressive 41:40-1 My '77

DAWSON Five murder trial. See Trials (murder)

DAY, Dorothy
Confronting Dorothy Day. A. McCarthy. Commonweal 104:297+ My 13 '77 *
Dollar for Dorothy. M. Mayer. por Progressive 41:40-1 N '77 *

DAY, Doug
You can repair winter's damage to your asphalt driveway. il Pop Sci 210:112-13 Je '77

DAY, Mark
Manzo raid. Nation 224:146-8 F 5 '77

DAY, Peter R.
Plant genetics: increasing crop yield. bibl Science 197:1334-9 S 30 '77

—and others
Somatic cell genetic manipulation in plants. bibl BioScience 27:116-18 F '77

DAY, R. C.
Coming of age in Sonoma; story. Redbook 148:94 F '77

DAY, Samuel H. Jr
Converting the weapons labs. Bull Atom Sci 33:27 Ja '77
Farewell. Bull Atom Sci 33:4-5 D '77
Nuclear weapons labs. il Bull Atom Sci 33:21-6 Ap '77
On the uses of science. Progressive 41:32-3 O '77
Swords and plowshares. Bull Atom Sci 33:4-5 N '77
Toward a more fragrant world. Bull Atom Sci 33:6-7 My '77

DAY care. See Children—Day care

DAY care centers
All about day care. S. Auerbach. il Parents Mag 52:40-1+ Ap '77
Dozen ways to solve your day-care problem. H. Hyans. McCalls 105:112-13 O '77
Drive-in day care; Kinder Cares. J. Lelyveld. il N Y Times Mag p 110 Je 5 '77

See also

Nursery schools

DAY dreams. See Fantasy

DAY lilies
Day lily is a delicious ornamental. R. Wallace. il Org Gard & Farm 24:95-6 My '77
Daylilies: the perfect perennials. R. O'Harra. il Bet Hom & Gard 55:102-3 Ag '77
Taking action with daylilies. il Sunset 159:150-1 Ag '77

DAY nurseries. See Day care centers

DAYAN, Moshe
Time for peace; excerpts from interview, ed by S. Sullivan and N. Proffitt. il por Newsweek 90:33 O 17 '77

about

Bazaar bargaining in Washington. il pors Time 110:31-2+ O 3 '77 *
Begin's strategy and Dayan's tactics: the conduct of Israeli foreign policy. A. Perlmutter. For Affairs 56:357-72 Ja '78 *
Begin's surprise maneuver. il por Time 109:36 Je 6 '77 *
Dayan's secret. A. De Borchgrave. il por Newsweek 90:43 O 3 '77 *
Minister and his mystery trip. il por Time 110:34+ O 3 '77 *
On the hustings with Moshe Dayan. il pors Time 110:34 O 17 '77 *
Strained alliance. R. Steele and others. il pors Newsweek 90:26-7+ O 17 '77 *
Trying to sell Geneva. A. Deming and others. il por Newsweek 90:56 O 24 '77 *
Two men who hold keys to Mideast peace talks. pors U.S. News 83:36 O 24 '77 *
Warrior-diplomat. A. Deming and M. J. Kubic. il pors Newsweek 90:28-9 O 17 '77 *

DAYAN, Yael
Israeli women—more feminine than feminist. il por N Y Times Mag p78-80 F 13 '77

DAYER, Jean-Michel, and others
Collagenase production by rheumatoid synovial cells: stimulation by a human lymphocyte factor. bibl il Science 195:181-3 Ja 14 '77

DAYLIGHT
Daylighting design aids emerge as interest grows in technique. il Archit Rec 161:152 Ja '77

DAYLILIES. See Day lilies

DAYSPRING Graphics, Inc. See Publishers and publishing—Art

DAYTON, Edward R.
Lifting ministers from the mud. Chr Today 21:10-12 Jl 29 '77

DAYTON, Paul K, and Oliver, J. S.
Antarctic soft-bottom benthos in oligotrophic and eutrophic environments. bibl il map Science 197:55-8 Jl 1 '77
—See Tegner, M. J. jt auth

DAYTON, Ohio
How one hard-hit city is buttoning up. il U.S. News 83:72 O 3 '77

Buildings

NCR corporate headquarters. il Archit Rec 162:97-102 N '77

Education

Conflicting signals; Supreme Court decision in case of the National Association for the Advancement of Colored People against the Dayton Board of Education. J. Miller. New Repub 177:10-11 Jl 23 '77
Tale of two cities; Supreme Court decisions on the proper role of Federal judges in school-desegregation cases. M. Sheils and others. il Newsweek 90:54 Jl 11 '77

Sanitary affairs

Peripheral mixing turns sludge into fuel gas. il Am City & County 92:58-9 Jl '77

DAYTON Hudson Corporation
Dayton Hudson's bid to climb from no. 8. Bus W p28-9 D 19 '77

DAYTONA 200. See Motorcycle racing

DAYTONA 500. See Automobile racing

DEACONS
No temporary deacons, please. A. C. Kammer. America 136:503-4 Je 4 '77

DEAD

See also

Undertakers and undertaking

DEAD Sea
Dead Sea. H. C. Howes. il Sea Front 23:90-5 Mr '77

DEAD Sea Scrolls
Newest of the Dead Sea Scrolls; Temple Scroll. il por Time 109:57-8 Ja 24 '77

DEADLY sins. See Sin

DEAF

Fastest woman on earth; K. O'Neil. P. Bowie. il pors Sat Eve Post 249:42-3+ Mr '77

Now, hearing-ear dogs. il Newsweek 89:39 Je 6 '77

Silent lives; children's relationship with deaf parents. L. Konner. il Seventeen 36:38+ Ap '77

Subtitles for TV and films; captions for the hearing-impaired. il Am Educ 13:18-22 Mr '77

Education

Breaking the silence; discrimination complaint by R. Nomeland against the Minnesota School for the Deaf. E. M. Gobble. Progressive 41:35 F '77

Can schools speak the language of the deaf? J. Greenberg and G. Doolittle. il N Y Times Mag p50+ D 11 '77

Employment

Breaking the silence; discrimination complaint by R. Nomeland against the Minnesota School for the Deaf. E. M. Gobble. Progressive 41:35 F '77

Means of communication

Can your eyes replace your ears? D. C. Guilbert. il Ret Liv 17:34-5+ Ag '77

Deaf children develop sign language on their own; study by Susan Goldin-Meadow and Heidi Feldman. J. Gaylin. Psychol Today 11:22+ D '77

Development of language-like communication without a language model. S. Goldin-Meadow and H. Feldman. bibl il Science 197:401-3 Jl 22 '77

Language in deaf children: an instinct. Sci N 112:70 Jl 30 '77

Recreation

See also

Camps for the handicapped

DEAF, Apparatus for the

See also

Hearing aids

DEAF-mutes

Silent one; case of D. Lang. J. K. Footlick and E. Sciolino. Newsweek 90:89+ N 7 '77

DEAFNESS

See also

Deaf

Hearing aids

Noise—Physiological effects

DEALERS, Automobile. See Automobile dealers

DEALY, J. Edward

Mountain-mahogany makes music. il por Am For 83:24-7 Je '77

DEAN, David, and Dean, Martha

Moma went to Congress and then to jail. il pors Am Hist Illus 12:37-43 N '77

DEAN, Jim

Old snaggletooth! il Field & S 82:38+ Je '77

DEAN, John Wesley, 3d

Doing time. por Newsweek 90:9 Jl 4 '77

DEAN, Laura

Dancing. A. Croce. New Yorker 53:222+ D 5 '77 *

Geometries: the song and dance of Laura Dean. R. Baker. il por Dance Mag 51:40-4 N '77 *

DEAN, Martha. See Dean, D. jt auth

DEAN, Phil

Know your rigging (cont) Motor B & S 139:48-9+ F '77

DEAN Witter Organization Inc-Reynolds Securities, Inc merger. See Brokers—Acquisitions and mergers

DEANE, Hamilton. See Balderston, J. L. jt auth

DEAR, Ian

Those glorious J-boats; excerpt from Enterprise to Endeavour: the J-class yachts. il Yachting 142:99-102+ S '77

DEARBORN, Laura, and Dasheff, William

Mopeds: somewhere between a Rolls and a tricycle. il Ms 6:27-30 S '77

DEARDORFF, Howard

Recall for greenways; excerpt from The public benefits of cleaned water; emerging greenway opportunities. il Parks & Rec 12:39a-40a F '77

DEATH

Do we have the right to die? J. W. Montgomery. Chr Today 21:49-50 Ja 21 '77

Dying in Oklahoma. R. Morris. New Repub 177:8-9 Jl 23 '77

Intending death: moral perspectives. K. Vaux. il Chr Cent 94:56-60 Ja 26 '77

Karen Ann a year later. E. Keerdoja. Newsweek 89:10 Mr 21 '77

Legislation and the living will. R. A. McCormick and A. E. Hellegers. America 136:210-13 Mr 12 '77

Mary's assumption, God's promise fulfilled. R. Kress. America 137:71-4 Ag 13 '77

O death, where is thy sting-a-ling-a-ling? L. H. Farber. Commentary 63:35-43 Je '77

Quiet death, with dignity. C. Holbert. il America 136:214-16 Mr 12 '77

Sudden happenings. E. Schaeffer. Chr Today 21:39 My 6 '77

Toward an anthropology of death. J. J. Preston. bibl f il Intellect 105:343-4 Ap '77

See also

Funeral rites and ceremonies

Future life

Heaven

Suicide

Terminal care

Anecdotes, facetiae, satire, etc.

Oh death where is thy story line? W. Saroyan. New Repub 178:29-30 Ja 7 '78

Bibliography

Death and therapy. J. Garvey. Commonweal 104:471-3 Jl 22 '77

Causes

See also

Mortality

Psychology

Dealing with death. M. L. Meyer. il America 137:109-11 Ag 27 '77

Dealing with death in the family. M. Fischer. bibl il N Y Times Mag p82+ Mr 13 '77

Emotional stress and sudden death. G. Engel. bibl il Psychol Today 11:114-15+ N '77

Hope of dying. G. Schurr. Chr Cent 94:935-6 O 19 '77

What the dying see. J. White. Sci Digest 81:71-2 F '77

See also

Children and death

Youth and death

DEATH, Apparent

See also

Resuscitation

DEATH and children. See Children and death

DEATH benefits (trade unions) See Trade unions—Benefit funds

DEATH in art

Fiesta of death. il UNESCO Courier 30:28-9 Ag '77

DEATH in literature

Death: the last taboo. A. I. Webb. Engl J 66:55-6 S '77

DEATH notices. See Obituaries

DEATH of God theology

Death of God: a belated personal postscript. J. W. Woelfel; discussion. Chr Cent 94:431-3 Mr 4 '77

Where have all the flower children gone? C. M. Spring. Chr Cent 94:952-4 O 19 '77

DEATH penalty. See Capital punishment

DEATH rate. See Mortality

DEATH VALLEY JUNCTION, Calif.

Why stop over in Death Valley Junction? Look; work of M. Becket. il pors Sunset 159:66 N '77

DEATHBED words. See Last words

DEAVER, Dick

Downwind control—not disaster! (cont) il Yachting 141:82-4+ F '77

Eccentric Admiral's Cup. il Yachting 142:50-2 D '77

DEBAKEY, Michael Ellis

Should US scientists trade data with USSR? por Sci Digest 81:32-7+ Je '77

DEBATES, Television. See Television in politics

DEBAYLE, Anastasio Somoza. See Somoza Debayle, A.

DE BEERS Consolidated Mines, Ltd

Extra glitter in diamond prices. Bus W p57-8 N 21 '77

DEBENTURES. See Bonds

DE BEVOISE, Arlene

Meditations of an errant pilgrim; poem. Chr Cent 94:1116 N 30 '77

DE BLIJ, Harm J.

Mozambique: fragile independence. bibl il map Focus 27:9-16 N '76

DE BOLT, William Walter

Exegesis for a New Year; poem. Chr Cent 94:1218 D 28 '77

Out of his youth; poem. Chr Cent 94:812 S 21 '77

Primal wedding; poem. Chr Cent 94:684 Ag 3 '77

DEBT

Brace your back for bigger debt in year 2000. Suc Farm 75:no5Cl Mr '77

How to adjust an out-of-balance debt load. il Suc Farm 75:8-9 Ag '77

See also

Bankruptcy

Collecting of accounts

Credit

DEBTS, External

Debts of the poor: preventing the crash. R. V. Roosa. New Repub 176:42-5 Ja 22 '77

International debt: current issues and implications; statement, August 29, 1977. R. N. Cooper. il Dept State Bull 77:469-75 O 10 '77

DEBTS, Public

See also

Debts, External

Europe, Eastern

East Europe's debt to the West: interdependence is a two-way street. R. Portes. bibl f il For Affairs 55:751-82 Jl '77

DEBTS, Public—*Continued*

Underdeveloped areas

Are the LDCs in over their heads? H. van B. Cleveland and W. H. B. Brittain. il For Affairs 55:732-50 Jl '77

United States

U.S. goes deeper and deeper in the hole. il U.S. News 83:46-7 O 10 '77
Up, up and away! The U.S. debt. A. Gallatin. Read Digest 111:107-9 S '77

DEBUSK, Robert F.
Stress and the heart. Intellect 106:190 N '77

DEBUSSY, Claude
Fall of the House of Usher (La Chute de la maison Usher) Reviews
Hi Fi 27:MA26-8 Je '77 *
Mus Q 62:536-53 O '76 *
New Yorker 53:130+ Mr 14 '77 *
Sat R 4:52-3 Ap 16 '77 *
Pelléas et Mélisande. Reviews
Nation 225:541-2 N 19 '77 *

DEBUTTS, John Dulany
Sponsor as star. por Forbes 119:66 F 1 '77 *

DECADE counters. See Counting machines and devices

DECADE for Women. See United Nations Decade for Women

DECADENCE in literature. See Literature—Themes

DE CAMP, Wilson H. and Pelletier, S. W.
Veatchine: coexistence of epimers in a crystal structure. bibl il Science 198:726-7 N 18 '77

DECARBOXYLASE
Ornithine decarboxylase may function as an initiation factor for RNA polymerase I. C.-A. Manen and D. H. Russell. bibl il Science 195:505-6 F 4 '77

DECATUR, Stephen
(ed) See Eastwood, C. Maggie & Clint
(ed) See Eastwood, M. Maggie & Clint
(ed) See Powers, S. Stefanie & Bill

DECAY, Dental. See Dental caries

DECENTRALIZATION in government
See also
Public administration

Belgium

Managing ethnic conflict in Belgium. M. O. Heisler. bibl f Ann Am Acad 433:32-46 S '77

DE CESARE, Lee
U.S. journal: Tampa, Florida; discrimination against women at the University Club. C. Trillin. New Yorker 53:105-7 Ap 11 '77 *

DECIBELS
Solving the dB mystery. L. Feldman. il Radio-Electr 48:65-7 Je '77

DECISION making
Decision making with uncertain inputs; excerpt from The genesis strategy. S. H. Schneider. BioScience 27:511 Ag '77
See also
Risk taking (psychology)

Anecdotes, facetiae, satire, etc.

Of two minds. J. Delton. Seventeen 36:32 N '77

DECK chairs. See Chairs

DECKER, Gerald L.
Getting to know each other. pors Forbes 120:62 Ag 1 '77 *

DECKER, John L.
Should US scientists trade data with USSR? por Sci Digest 81:35-7+ Je '77

DECKS, patios, terraces, etc.
Avid indoor gardeners transform a useless second-floor porch. il House B 119:98 S '77
Build your own patio in sand. D. Raffel. il House & Gard 149:42+ Jl '77
Clean sweep of space; rooms built of terraces. il House & Gard 149:140-3 Ap '77
Craftsman-era deck and trellis. il Sunset 158:158 My '77
Deck garden in water-scarce Marin makes it with gray water. il Sunset 158:256 Ap '77
Fence wraps around streetside deck. il Sunset 158:97 F '77
Festive canopy turns a big deck into an outdoor living room. il Sunset 158:171 Ap '77
Garage roof is a sunny beach. il Sunset 158:254 Je '77
Gazebo, deck, a staggered carport. il Sunset 158:162 My '77
Green patio jungle in 18 months. il Sunset 158:221 Mr '77
How did this garden grow? by adding decks, changing levels. il Sunset 159:234 N '77
How to deck a sloping yard. il Bet Hom & Gard 55:96 Jl '77
Live out and love it! N. Seney and S. Coulter. il Bet Hom & Gard 55:103-13 Je '77
Narrow side yard deserves a chance. il Sunset 158:146 Mr '77
Now they have a subtropical patio. il Sunset 158:70-1 F '77
Now this space works better and looks bigger. il Sunset 158:191 Ap '77
Outdoor exercise in privacy. il Sunset 158:184-5 Ap '77
Outdoor space at living-room level? Add a veranda. il Sunset 158:144 Ap '77
Porch pick-me-ups. V. Perlo. il Am Home 80:40-1+ Jl '77
Raise a deck. V. D. Chase. il Am Home 80:90+ Ap '77
Rebuild your deck for longer life. R. M. Engelbrecht. il Pop Sci 210:136+ Je '77
Summerize patios and porches. J. Cornell. Am Home 80:96 Ap '77
Two verandas and a new turnaround bring new life to a boxy bungalow. il Sunset 158:168 Ap '77
Up-and-up garden; two-level deck. il Sunset 158:302-3 My '77
Well-angled redwood deck you can build. il Bet Hom & Gard 55:118+ Ap '77
See also
Balcony gardens, roof gardens, etc.

Maintenance and repair

Porch-and-deck paints. il Consumer Rep 42:176-9 D '77

DECLARATION of Human Rights. See Universal Declaration of Human Rights

DECLARATION of Independence. See United States—Declaration of Independence

DECLARATION on the Strengthening of International Security. See United Nations Declaration on the Strengthening of International Security

DÉCO Art. See Art Déco

DECODERS, Stereophonic. See Audio systems—Equipment

DECODING of ciphers. See Ciphers

DE COMBRAY, Richard
One outsider's view of Arabian culture pictured in spring Doubleday book; interview, ed by R. Dahlin. il Pub W 212:33 N 28 '77

DECOMPOSITION (chemistry)
See also
Pesticides—Decomposition

DECOMPRESSION sickness
Venous gas bubbles: production by transient, deep isobaric counterdiffusion of helium against nitrogen. B. G. D'Aoust and others. bibl il Science 197:889-91 Ag 26 '77

DECONDE, Alexander
Quasi-War. il Am Hist Illus 12:4-9+ Ap '77

DECONTAMINATION from radioactive substances. See Radioactive decontamination

DECORATED eggs. See Eggs, Decorated

DECORATION and ornament
Arts in Mobile. S. A. Smith. il Antiques 112:482-91 S '77
French interiors; Wrightsman rooms at the Metropolitan Museum of Art. S. B. Sherrill. Antiques 112:818+ N '77
New look at decorating Brighton style; Royal Pavilion at Brighton exhibition. il House & Gard 149:136-9 Ap '77
Prince and the puritan; Royal Pavilion at Brighton exhibition. D. Davis. il Newsweek 89:77-77A Mr 28 '77
Royal Pavilion; exhibition at the Cooper-Hewitt Museum. New Yorker 53:30-1 Mr 21 '77
Seventeenth-and early eighteenth-century decorative motifs in New England; permanent display at the Boston Museum of Fine Arts. S. B. Sherrill. il Antiques 112:180 Ag '77
Seventeenth-century New England decorative and fine arts; exhibit at the Wadsworth Atheneum. il Antiques 111:1086+ Je '77
See also
Antiques
Art Déco
Candles
Christmas decorations
Church decoration and ornament
Cookery, Ornamental
Design
Design, Decorative
Eggs, Decorated
Firearms—Decoration
Flowers, Arrangement of
Furniture, Decorated
House decoration
Ironwork
Moldings (architecture)
Needlework
Paneling
Paper work
Pottery—Decoration
Shellwork
Stencil work
Table decoration
Textile design
Wood carving

DECORATION and ornament, Architectural
Address book; stores selling authentic period fixtures and reproductions. S. Sunderlin. House B 119:32+ Ap '77
Born New Yorker sight-revels in places most people miss; architectural ornaments. G. Emerson. Vogue 167:144 Mr '77
Doodles on the landscape: barn decorations in central New York. N. C. Hage. il Conservationist 31:42-3 N '76

DECORATION and ornament, Architectural—*Cont.*
Quito; church architecture and decoration of the colonial period. J. R. Chiriboga; H. Crespo Toral. il map Americas 29:S1-12 Ap '77
See also
Mural painting and decoration
Mural painting and decoration, Exterior

DECORATION and ornament, Personal
Henna for happiness: India's mehndi art of symbols for all seasons. J. Saksena. il UNESCO Courier 30:18-22 F '77

DECORATION Day. See Memorial Day

DECORATION of food. See Cookery—Garnishes

DECORATIVE arts. See Decoration and ornament

DECORATIVE design. See Design, Decorative

DECORATIVE plants. See Plants, Ornamental

DECOYS (hunting)
Art and craft of making decoys. il por Bet Hom & Gard 55:140-1 N '77
Duck decoys: to carve and collect. il Bet Hom & Gard 55:224 N '77
Really basic decoys; make silhouette-type goose decoys. il Mech Illus 73:133 Ap '77

DECRISTOFORO, David
Cabinet of real oak. il Mech Illus 74:76+ Ja '78

DECTER, Midge
Looting and liberal racism. Commentary 64:48-54 S; 34-5 D '77

DEDERICH, Charles
Life at Synanon is swinging. il por Time 110:18 D 26 '77 *

DEDICATIONS, Book. See Book dedications

DEDUCTIONS, Income tax. See Income tax—Deductions

DEEDY, John
News & views. See issues of Commonweal

DEEP sea drilling. See Underwater drilling

DEEP sea fauna. See Benthos

DEEP sea mining. See Ocean mining

DEEP sea research. See Oceanographic research

DEER
When dogs run wild; threat to deer. D. M. Duffey. il Outdoor Life 159:84-6+ Mr '77
Wolf-pack buffer zones as prey reservoirs. L. D. Mech. bibl Science 198:320-1 O 21 '77
See also
Caribou
Elk
Reindeer

DEER, Dressing of. See Game, Dressing of

DEER baits and repellents
Scent for a buck. J. Weiss. il Outdoor Life 160:70-1+ O '77

DEER hounds. See Hounds

DEER hunting
Behold the hunter. N. Bryant. il Atlantic 240:66-70 D '77
Complete tree-stand hunter—gun and bow. G. Helgeland. il Outdoor Life 160:74-7+ Ag '77
5 deer masters—how they hunt; symposium. il Outdoor Life 160:88-91+ S '77
For whitetails, the sneak play is in. C. Walton. il Outdoor Life 160:65-9 O '77
Girl learns to hunt; deer hunting by C. McRae in Montana. B. McRae. il por Field & S 82:40-1+ O '77
High-up, way-out ways of a rimrock guide; mule deer hunting guide, K. Clark. E. A. Bauer. il Outdoor Life 160:90-2 N '77
Hunting the quiet way. F. Bear. il Conservationist 31:17-19+ N '76
Hunting, the safe way. N. Geoffrey. Esquire 88:24+ N '77
Long-distance whitetails; experience in central Texas. D. Flores. il Field & S 82:28+ Ag '77
Missing impossible? gun sights. B. Brister. il Field & S 82:110-12+ O '77
Mule deer are where you find them. V. L. Oertle. il map Outdoor Life 160:76-9+ Jl '77
New bowhunting school. V. T. Sparano. il Outdoor Life 159:48+ F '77
Results of 1976 deer and bear seasons. il Conservationist 32:22 Jl '77
Scent for a buck. J. Weiss. il Outdoor Life 160:70-1+ O '77
Secret life of the cottontail deer. J. Madson. il Outdoor Life 159:92-4+ Je '77
Shotgunning for deer. J. Carmichel. il Outdoor Life 160:106-8+ O '77
Successful mule deer hunting; Western States. B. Dalrymple. il Field & S 82:44-5+ S '77
Successful whitetail hunting. B. W. Dalrymple. il Field & S 82:43-5 D '77
Update: deer/big game; ed by T. Paugh. il Outdoor Life 160:32 O; 54 N; 50 D '77; 161:50 Ja '78
We must harvest does or lose our herds. J. O. Cartier. il Outdoor Life 160:61-3+ D '77
What is a deer management permit? special hunting permits. P. Kelsey. il map Conservationist 32:35-7 N '77
Whitetail tactics. B. Conger. il Field & S 82:46-7+ O '77
Whitetails & wild tales. N. Strung. il Field & S 82:42-3+ N '77

DEER Island, Me.
Deer Island, Maine. G. Loehr and V. Loehr. il map Travel 147:24-9+ My '77

DEER meat cookery. See Cookery—Game

DEER poaching. See Poaching

DEERE and Company
Waterloo, Iowa: coming to terms with prosperity. M. King. il Forbes 120:48-52 N 15 '77

DEERFIELD, Ill.

Crime

See Crime and criminals—Illinois

DEES, Morris
Friends of the poor. J. K. Footlick and V. E. Smith. il por Newsweek 90:95 Jl 18 '77 *
Horror of death at Eastertime. J. M. Wall. Chr Cent 94:315-16 Ap 6 '77 *

DEFEAT (psychology) See Failure (psychology)

DEFECTORS, Political
Inside the Air Force; Chinese Commander Fan Yuan-yen's defection to Taiwan. M. Liu. il por Newsweek 90:50 Jl 25 '77
Timely defection; Chinese Communist pilot Fan Yuan-yeh's defection to Taiwan. il por Time 110:37 Jl 18 '77
See also
Asylum, Right of

DEFENSE appropriations. See United States—Defense, Department of—Appropriations and expenditures

DEFENSE contracts. See Contracts, Government

DEFENSE industries. See Munitions

DEFENSE information, Classified
Pyramider spy case; A. Lee and C. Boyce. R. Steele and N. Horrock. il por Newsweek 89:29 Ap 18 '77
Stealing the company store; case of C. Boyce and A. D. Lee. il por Time 109:19 My 9 '77
To be young, rich—and a spy; A. D. Lee and C. J. Boyce. R. Lindsey. il pors N Y Times Mag p 18+ My 22 '77

DEFENSE mechanisms (biology)
Cardiac glycosides in the defensive secretion of chrysomelid beetles: evidence for their production by the insects. J. M. Pasteels and D. Daloze. bibl il Science 197:70-2 Jl 1 '77
Escape! N. Smith. il Nat Wildlife 15:34-5 Je '77

DEFENSE spending, International. See Armed forces—Appropriations and expenditures

DEFEO murders. See Murder

DEFOLIATION
Mugging of a garden; question of defoliation along Long Island Railroad rights of way. R. Uldis. il Horticulture 55:18-23 Jl '77

DEFORD, Frank
After the last hurrah, a final murmur. il Sports Illus 46:30-2+ Mr 21 '77
Christmas gift for Fort Zack; story. Sports Illus 47:62-4 D 19 '77
Horse racing. Sports Illus 46:84+ My 23 '77
I don't date any women under 48. il pors Sports Illus 47:36-8+ D 5 '77
Lonely courage of Lisa Boyle. il Seventeen 36:188-9+ Ap '77
Mouth that soars. il pors Sports Illus 46:64-9+ My 30 '77
Move over for Oh-san. il pors Sports Illus 47:58-64+ Ag 15 '77
Movies. il Sports Illus 46:42 Mr 7; 66 Ap 11; 45 My 30; 47:48 Jl 11; 39 Ag 15; 55 S 12 '77
Promo wiz in kidvid bid. il por Sports Illus 46:30-3 F 7 '77
Site for tired eyes. il por Sports Illus 46:84-8+ Ap 18 '77
Sportsman of the year. il por Sports Illus 47:38-41+ D 19 '77
Tennis. Sports Illus 46:69-70+ Ap 11 '77
Three little syllables. il Sports Illus 46:30-5 Ja 24 '77
—See Kramer, J. jt auth
about
Letter from the publisher. J. Meyers. Sports Illus 47:6 D 19 '77 *

DEFORESTATION. See Forest ecology

DEFORMATION (mechanics)
Gravitational compression of crystallized suspensions of polystyrene spheres. R. S. Crandall and R. Williams. bibl il Science 198:293-5 O 21 '77
See also
Crystals—Dislocations
Fracture of solids

DEFORMITIES
Birth defects: how to prevent them. N. H. Clark. Harp Baz 110:86-7+ Jl '77
Fascination of freaks: excerpt from Freaks. L. Fiedler. il Psychol Today 11:56-9+ Ag '77
Female hormones and birth defects. Sci N 111:54 Ja 22 '77
Rebirth of Beth Thorne. J. L. Block. Good H 185:99+ Jl '77
Test to prevent birth defects. M. R. Skrocki. McCalls 104:67 Jl '77
Winning the war against birth defects: advances in genetic counseling and screening. R. Halcomb. il Parents Mag 52:37+ My '77

DEFORT, Wolfgang
East Germany: a vexing issue. R. D. Linder. Chr Today 22:54-5 N 18 '77 *
DEGAETANI, Jan
Queen of new music. H. Saal. por Newsweek 89:92-3 F 14 '77 *
DEGAS, Edgar
Art. J. E. Canaday. il New Repub 177:25-6+ N 12 '77 *
Degas' dancers. S. Banes. Dance Mag 51:72-4 Je '77 *
Painting and photography: the two-way street. B. Rose. il Vogue 167:236-7+ My '77 *
DE GAULLE, Charles. See Gaulle, C. de
DE GEER, Lars Erik
Airborne short-lived radionuclides of unknown origin in Sweden in 1976. il map Science 198: 925-7 D 2 '77
DE GENNARO, Richard
Copyright, resource sharing, and hard times: a view from the field. bibl Am Lib 8:430-5 S '77
Escalating journal prices: time to fight back. bibl il Am Lib 8:69-74 F '77
Wanted: a minicomputer serials control system. bibl Lib J 102:878-9 Ap 15 '77
DEGNAN, James P.
Can Tahoe be saved? Commonweal 105:13-14 Ja 6 '78
DEGRADATION (biology) See Biodegradation
DEGREES, Academic
Ph.D. population. Sci Am 237:96 S '77

Language requirements

See Colleges and universities—Graduation requirements
DEGREES, Honorary
Kudos. Time 109:44-5 My 30; 64+ Je 6; 46 Je 13 '77
DE GROOT, Roy Andries
Scotch would like to take you to bed. il Esquire 87:88-90+ F '77
DE GROOTE, Steven
Damn good shot. il por Horizon 20:33 D '77 *
Fifth Van Cliburn Piano Competition. A. Satz. il pors Hi Fi 28:MA16-18 Ja '78 *
DE HAVILLAND, Sir Geoffrey
DH and his marvelous Moths. J. Gilbert. il Flying 100:82-90+ My '77 *
De Havilland. J. Scott. il Flying 101:272-3 S '77 *
DE-HIRING consultant services. See Business consultants
DEHMELT, Hans G.
Elegant inquiry into the electron. Sci N 111:101 F 12 '77 *
DEHN, Virginia
Virginia Dehn paints inscapes. M. C. Nelson. il por Am Artist 41:50-3+ Mr '77 *
DEHUMIDIFIERS
Dehumidifiers: the low-cost way to take the sweat out of summer. M. Schultz. il Pop Mech 147:114-15+ Je '77
DEHYDRATION (physiology)
Thirst—dehydration alert. S. L. Halpern. Vogue 167:137 Ap '77
DEHYDRATORS. See Drying apparatus
DEHYDROGENASES
Hepatitis B "e" antigen: an apparent association with lactate dehydrogenase isozyme-5. G. N. Vyas and others. bibl il Science 198:1068-70 D 9 '77
DEIMOS (satellite) See Satellites
DEINZER, M. L. and others
Pyrrolizidine alkaloids: their occurrence in honey from tansy ragwort (senecio jacobaea L.) bibl il Science 195:497-9 F 4 '77
DEITIES. See Gods and goddesses
DE JOIE, Patricia K.
Wastes around the world. il Environment 19: 32-7 O '77
DE JONG, Gordon F. and Sell, R. R.
Population redistribution, migration, and residential preferences. bibl f il Ann Am Acad 429:130-44 Ja '77
DEKORNE, James
Constructing the attached greenhouse; excerpt from The solar greenhouse book. il Org Gard & Farm 24:63-7 D '77
DEL E. Webb Corporation. See Webb, Del E, Corporation
DELACORTE Festival. See Dance festivals
DELACROIX, Eugène
Eugene Delacroix: color magician. A. Werner. il por Am Artist 41:38-43+ Ap '77 *
DELAMOTTE, Yves
Reform of the enterprise in France. Ann Am Acad 431:54-62 My '77
DELANEY, Paul
Bakke case. Nation 225:498-9 N 12 '77
Carter and black Americans. Nation 225:132-3 Ag 20 '77
Chicago without Daley. Nation 224:646-9 My 28 '77
DELANEY clause. See Food laws and legislation
DE LANY, Richard N.
Will U.S. prosecute American volunteers? interview. por U.S. News 82:32 My 23 '77 *
DELAPORTE, Chris T.
NRPA interview: C. T. Delaporte tells what to expect from BOR; ed by B. Kravetz. il pors Parks & Rec 12:38-43 Ag '77

about

SPRE responds to BOR director on leisure curricula, research. Parks & Rec 12:46 D '77 *
DE LA RUE Company, Ltd
Why a money-maker is making more money. Bus W p58 Ag 8 '77
DELATINER, Barbara
Housewife's disease. Good H 184:84+ Je '77
DELAUNAY, Charles
Profiles. W. Balliett. pors New Yorker 52:43-6+ F 14 '77 *
DE LAURETIS, Teresa
Cavani's Night porter: a woman's film? Film Q 30:35-8 Wint '76
DELAWARE
See also
Blacks—Delaware
Chesapeake Bay
Education—Delaware
Historic houses, sites, etc.—Delaware
DELAWARE Historical Society. See Historical Society of Delaware
DELAWARE River Valley
Delaware River: evidence for its former extension to Wilmington Submarine Canyon. D. C. Twichell and others. bibl il map Science 195:483-5 F 4 '77
DELAY devices
IC application of the month: Reticon SAD-1024. il Radio-Electr 48:58-61+ Ap '77
See also
Charge transfer devices (electronics)
DELEGATES, Democratic convention. See National conventions, Democratic
DELEGATES to the United Nations. See United Nations—Delegates
DELEGATION of authority in business. See Personnel management
DE LEON, George
Baldness experiment. il por Psychol Today 11: 62-3+ O '77
DELEON, Marino, family
Keeping the old: a celebration at Norma and Marino De Leon's. L. W. Eckhardt. il pors Redbook 150:94+ D '77
DELILLO, Don
Players; story Esquire 87:102-4 Ap '77
DELINQUENT girls. See Girls, Delinquent
DELINQUENTS. See Juvenile delinquency
DELIUS, Jean
Bruno LaVerdiere. il Craft Horiz 37:46-8 O '77
DELIVERY of goods
Delivery dilemma: why is your furniture late? Am Home 80:8 S '77
DELL, Joseph
Cottontail rabbit. il por Conservationist 32:13-15 S '77
Varying hare. il Conservationist 31:3+ N '76
DELLS of the Wisconsin (valley)
Canoeing. G. Helgeland. il Travel 148:32-5+ Ag '77
Heigh-O the Dairy-O, the traveler in the Dells. L. McPherson. il Holiday 58:27+ Ap '77
DELNAGRO, Michael
Betting. Sports Illus 47:70+ D 5 '77
Football's week. il Sports Illus 47:55-6 N 7 '77
Million-dollar horse heist. il Sports Illus 47:30-2+ Ag 1 '77
Pool (cont) Sports Illus 46:52+ Je 27 '77
So it has come to pass. il Sports Illus 47:72-6 S 5 '77
DELOREAN, John Zachary
DeLorean's phantom book. A. J. Mayer and J. C. Jones. por Newsweek 90:65+ Ag 15 '77 *
Introducing the 1979 DeLorean—the car and the company. K. Ludvigsen. il por Motor T 29: 44-9+ S '77 *
John DeLorean builds a sports car: the DMC-12. P. Bedard. il Car & Dr 23:37-9+ Jl '77 *
DELOREAN Motor Company. See Automobile industry—United States
DEL REY Books (imprint) See Publishers and publishing—Science fiction
DELTA Air Lines
Delta offers New York-Miami low fare. L. Dunkelberg. il Aviation W 107:31 S 26 '77
Delta readies for Atlanta-London route. D. M. North. il Aviation W 107:30-2 D 5 '77
Delta's flying money machine. il Bus W p84-5+ My 9 '77
Flying high at Delta Air Lines. por Duns R 110:60-1 D '77
DELTA democrat-times (newspaper) See Newspapers—Mississippi
DELTON, Julie Ann
Fantasy impromptu; poem. Seventeen 36:30 Ap '77
Of two minds. Seventeen 36:32 N '77
Writer's daughter. Seventeen 36:86 Ag '77
DEL TREDICI, David
Musical events. A. Porter. New Yorker 53:114-8 Ap 11 '77 *
DELUCA, Tom. See Buell, J. jt auth

DELUGE
Noah, the flood, the facts. F. Warshofsky. map Read Digest 111:129-34 S '77
DELUSIONS, Paranoid. See Paranoia
DE MANGELAERE, Al
High voltage currant. il Org Gard & Farm 25: 152+ Ja '78
DE MARCELLUS, Robert
Failure in the West: a demographic insight. America 137:278-80 O 29 '77
DEMARCO, Michael
Fifth dimension of library service. S. Seward. bibl il por Wilson Lib Bull 51:741-5 My '77 *
DEMAREST, Christopher. See Lipez, R. jt auth
DE MENIL, Lois Pattison
Paris in June. New Repub 176:21 Je 18 '77
DEMENT, Sandy
Let lawyers advertise? interview. pors U.S. News 82:39-40 F 28 '77
DEMENTIA, Presenile. See Brain—Diseases
DE MEYER, Adolf, Baron
Viewpoint. R. Jacobson. il Opera N 41:4 Mr 5 '77 *
DEMIHA, Clara Oreskes
On the front line: Clara Demiha. L. Sharpe. il Ms 6:22 D '77 *
DEMING, Caren J. and Wahlstrom, B. J.
Hero, the harlot, and the glorified horse as mythic Americans. bibl Intellect 105:439-41 Je '77
DEMIREL, Suleyman
Pas de deux. por Time 111:30-1 Ja 16 '78 *
DEMOCRACY
Between freedom and despotism; self government; excerpt from address. B. F. Skinner. il por Psychol Today 11: 80-2+ S '77
Can our democratic government survive? address, September 9, 1977. D. F. Linowes. Vital Speeches 44:15-19 O 15 '77
Debating in the groves of Aspen. il pors Time 110:57 Jl 25 '77
Democracy: what? G. Niemeyer. Nat R 29:154 F 4 '77; Reply. H. V. Jaffa. 29:553 My 13 '77
Dulling the democratic mind. C. Wolfe. Clearing H 51:4 S '77
Is the Republican Party dead? C. B. Luce. Nat R 29:326-7 Mr 18 '77
Reasons for democracy; excerpt from The reason for democracy. K. H. Silvert. il Society 14:25-31 My '77
Retreat from democracy. L. H. Lapham. Harpers 225:11+ D '77
Trilateral Commission: have capitalism and democracy come to a parting of the ways? S. Bowles. il Progressive 41:20-3 Je '77
See also
Equality
Liberalism
Liberty
Town meetings
DEMOCRATIC Agenda Coalition. See Democratic Socialist Organizing Committee
DEMOCRATIC congressmen. See Congressmen
DEMOCRATIC convention delegates. See National conventions, Democratic
DEMOCRATIC conventions. See National conventions, Democratic
DEMOCRATIC Movement for Change. See Political parties—Israel
DEMOCRATIC National Committee
Democrats' new money man; J. Hay. por Bus W p 128 Mr 21 '77
Democrats rediscover democracy. New Repub 176:8 Ap 16 '77
It's my party. New Repub 177:8-9 D 24 '77
DEMOCRATIC Party
According to Hoyle; reform of delegate system for Presidential nominating conventions. New Repub 177:5-6 S 3 '77
Democrats have their own two-party system. E. C. Ladd, Jr. il Fortune 96:212-18+ O '77
Democrats in distress. H. Bruno. Newsweek 90: 25+ D 19 '77
Operation Trojan donkey. D. Lindquist. Nat R 29:1234-6 O 28 '77
Party of one; $1,000-a-plate assembly at the Waldorf-Astoria. P. Goldman and others. il por Newsweek 90:13-14 Jl 4 '77
Pluralist structures or interest groups? G. McGovern. Society 14:13-15+ Ja '77
Two feminists tell how they work; interview. ed by G. Steinem. K. Horbal. pors Ms 6:52+ Jl '77
See also
Democratic National Committee
Democratic Socialist Organizing Committee
National conventions, Democratic
DEMOCRATIC Socialist Organizing Committee
Growing strength of anti-capitalism; conference on full employment of the Democratic Agenda Coalition. J. C. Cort. America 137:478-80 D 31 '77
Passionate socialist. H. Fairlie. New Repub 176: 17-19 Mr 26 '77
Return to good nature; third annual convention. H. Fairlie. New Repub 176:12-15 Mr 5 '77
Time for stock-taking. J. C. Cort. Commonweal 104:198-9 Ap 1 '77
DE MOHRENSCHILDT, George
Are there new leads? D. M. Alpern and others. il por Newsweek 89:32+ Ap 11 '77 *
Assassination: now a suicide talks. il por Time 109:20 Ap 11 '77 *
DE MOLL, Louis
Housing, urban decay challenge Carter; excerpt from address. Am City & County 92:110+ My '77
DEMONIAC possession in literature. See Literature—Themes
DEMONOLOGY
See also
Devil
Evil eye
Exorcism
Witchcraft
DEMONSTRATION flying. See Aviation—Stunt flying
DEMOREST, Stephen
Pop gets juiced. il Sat R 4:26-7 Jl 23 '77
DEMOSS, Virginia
Houses that live in glass bottles. il Design (US) 78:8-11 Summ '77
DEMOTT, Benjamin
Culture watch. See occasional issues of Atlantic
Onward and downward from the ivory tower. il por Psychol Today 11:60-2+ S '77
Pick of the list. Sat R 4:62-3 Ag 6 '77
Two reporters: at peace and war. Atlantic 241: 91-3 Ja '78
DE MOTT, Helen
New landscape art. L. R. Lippard. il Ms 5:68-73 Ap '77 *
DEMPEWOLFF, Richard F.
Flight to remember. il por map Pop Mech 147: 81-3+ My '77
Your next house could have a grass roof. il Pop Mech 147:78-81+ Mr '77
DEMPSEY, Barbara Piattelli. See Dempsey, J. jt auth
DEMPSEY, Frank J.
Cavities and conscience pangs: candy can cause both. il Am Lib 8:231 My '77
DEMPSEY, Frederick R.
Wisdom in New York. Nat R 29:1052+ S 16 '77
DEMPSEY, Jack, and Dempsey, B. P.
Destruction of a giant; excerpt from Dempsey. il pors Am Heritage 28:72-83 Ap '77
DEMPSEY, Michael
Ken Russell, again. il Film Q 31:19-24 Wint '77
DEMPSTER, Nigel
Life & loves of Princess Margaret. por Ladies Home J 94:30+ D '77
DEMUTH, Jerry
Insurance redlining: a new urban setback. America 137:438-40 D 17 '77
Setback in Arlington Heights. America 136:167-8 F 26 '77
DEMYELINATIVE disorders. See Nervous system—Diseases
DENBY, David
Germans are coming! The Germans are coming! il pors Horizon 20:88-90+ S '77
DENDROCHRONOLOGY. See Tree rings
DENENBERG, Tia Schneider
Handling prison grievances: the labor model in practice. M Labor R 100:53-6 Mr '77
DENERVATION of muscle. See Muscle—Innervation
DENES, Magda
Performing abortions; excerpt from In necessity and sorrow: life and death in an abortion hospital. Commentary 62:33-7 O; 6 D '76; 63: 20+ Ja; 24-5 F '77
DENEUVE, Catherine
Why Catherine Deneuve gets depressed; interview, ed by A. E. Hotchner. por McCalls 105:176-7+ O '77
DENHARDT, Robert
How to set up a safe tent stove. il Outdoor Life 159:176 Mr '77
DENHOLTZ, Melvin
Dental flaws. Time 110:44 S 5 '77 *
DENIRO, Michael J. and Epstein, Samuel
Mechanism of carbon isotope fractionation associated with lipid synthesis. bibl il Science 197:261-3 Jl 15 '77
DENIRO, Robert
Close-up. E. Miller. por Seventeen 36:92 S '77 *
De Niro: a star for the '70s. J. Kroll. il pors Newsweek 89:80-4+ My 16 '77 *
De Niro: the phantom of the cinema. il pors Time 110:59-60 Jl 25 '77 *
What's Robert De Niro hiding? M. Brenner. il pors Redbook 149:116+ My '77 *
DENISHAWN Company. See Dance companies
DENMARK
See also
Art galleries and museums—Denmark
Greenland
Opera—Denmark
Publishers and publishing—Denmark
United Nations—Denmark
Antiquities
Who killed the bog men of Denmark? And why? theory of Tollund Man as victim of human sacrifice advanced by P. V. Blob. M. Shadbolt. il Read Digest 110:197-200+ Je '77

DENMARK—*Continued*

Colonies

See also
Faeroe Islands

Description and travel

Behind the scenes in Denmark. il Sunset 158:56 Ap '77

Foreign relations

Russia

See Russia—Foreign relations—Denmark

DENNETT, Joann Temple
Noisy silence: natural infrasound can warn of impending disaster. Sci Digest 81:27-8 My '77

DENNIS, Carl
Signs; poem. New Yorker 53:181 N 28 '77

about

Comment. D. Allen. Poetry 130:347-8 S '77 *

DENNIS, Hope
House exchanging; a way to go and stay awhile. il Ret Liv 17:27-9 Jl '77

DENNIS, J. Stacy
Q&A about money (cont) por Ret Liv 16:57 D '76; 17:58 F; 80+ Ap; 50 Jl; 14-15 O '77
7 mistakes retirees make about money. il Ret Liv 17:22-5 S '77

DENNIS, John V.
Deadly harvests and wildlife. il por Conservationist 31:26-7 My '77

DENNIS, Landt, and Dennis, Lisl
Fine art of collecting photographs; excerpt from Collecting photographs: a guide to the new art boom. il Horizon 19:80-5 My '77
Guatemala. il Travel 148:32-7 S '77
Gypsy carting in France. il Travel 147:58-63 Ap '77
Oasis playground. il Trav/Holiday 148:26-31 N '77
So you want to begin collecting photographs? excerpt from Collecting photographs: a guide to the new art boom. il Pop Phot 81:87-9+ S '77

DENNIS, Lisl
Tired of taking ho-hum travel pictures? il por Pop Phot 80:96-103+ Ap '77
—See Dennis, Landt, jt auth

DENNISTON, Lyle
After Gilmore. New Repub 176:10-12 Ja 29 '77

DENNISTON-THOMPSON, Katherine, and others
Physical structure of the replication origin of bacteriophage lambda. bibl il Science 198:1051-6 D 9 '77

DENNY, John
This Card is certainly no joker. B. Newman. il por Sports Illus 46:44+ Je 20 '77 *

DENNY'S Inc. See Restaurants—Chain and franchise operations

DENOMINATIONAL budgets. See Church finance

DENOMINATIONAL colleges. See Church colleges and universities

DENOMINATIONS, Religious. See Sects

DENSEN-GERBER, Judianne
What pornographers are doing to children: a shocking report. Redbook 149:86+ Ag '77

DENSITY of housing. See Housing—Density

DENT, John H.
Excerpt from remarks on proposed amendments to the Fair Labor Standards Act, February 22, 1977. Cong Digest 56:146+ My '77

DENTAL caries

Prevention

Coming: a vaccine against tooth decay. L. Edson. il N Y Times Mag p56-60 F 27 '77; Same abr. Read Digest 111:59-62 Jl '77
Cut your family's dental cavities by 85%. M. L. Schildkraut. Good H 185:205 Ag '77
Diet control can prevent decay. W. H. Bowen. il por Parents Mag 52:40-1+ Mr '77
Drop of prevention. . .; fluoridated water. Fam Health 9:33 Ap '77
How to have sound teeth for life. A. E. Nizel. por Parents Mag 52:41+ Mr '77

DENTAL decay. See Dental caries

DENTAL hygiene. See Teeth—Care and hygiene

DENTAL insurance. See Insurance, Dental

DENTISTRY
See also
Orthodontics
Periodontia
Teeth

DENTISTS
Dental flaws; views of M. Denholtz on competency of dentists. Time 110:44 S 5 '77
Dentists for kids only. I. Fiddler. il Fam Health 9:31-4 O '77
Supply of Federal physicians and dentists found adequate. M Labor R 100:50 My '77

Anecdotes, facetiae, satire, etc.

Imperial dentistry. R. Baker. N Y Times Mag p 10 My 22 '77

DENVER

Crime

Ron Lyle's last fight? R. Boeth and D. Gram. il pors Newsweek 91:29-30 Ja 16 '78

Galleries and museums

World's first Turner museum; Turner Museum of Colorado. Vasari. il Art N 76:30+ N '77

Hospitals

Breathe easy! program for asthmatic children at National Jewish Hospital and Research Center. S. H. Young. il Parents Mag 52:23+ Jl '77

Industries

Denver: the new Houston? T. J. Murray. il map Duns R 110:54-8 O '77

Libraries

See also
Denver Public Library

Music

Jazz-classical fusion: it's working. G. Lees. il por Hi Fi 27:MA26-7 N '77
See also
Opera—Colorado

Street traffic

Parking ticket gives Denver new headache. il Am City & County 92:30 My '77

Water supply

Eagles Nest—classic lesson in wilderness politics; defeat of two proposed water projects. F. Small. Audubon 79:128-31 Jl '77

DENVER Public Library
How Denver brings history to life; TimeAlive! program. il Sunset 159:58 Ag '77

DENVER. University
Ability plus science equal world's best; Human Performance Laboratory. L. Bortstein. il Sci Digest 81:10-11 Mr '77

DEODARS. See Cedar

DEOXYGLUCOSE
Suprachiasmatic nucleus; use of ^{14}C-labeled deoxyglucose uptake as a functional marker. W. J. Schwartz and H. Gainer. bibl il Science 197:1089-91 S 9 '77

DEOXYRIBONUCLEIC acid. See DNA

DE PALMA, Brian
Corruption and catastrophe: DePalma's Carrie. P. Matusa. il Film Q 31:32-8 Fall '77 *

DEPARTMENT of Housing and Urban Development. See United States—Housing and Urban Development, Department of

DEPARTMENT stores
Company in the gray flannel suit; Garfinckel, Brooks Bros, Miller & Rhoads. il Forbes 120:70+ N 15 '77
In-store decorating courses: worth your while? Bet Hom & Gard 55:45 Jl '77
Why the pressure is still on City Stores. il Bus W p94+ Ap 25 '77
See also
Abercrombie & Fitch Company
Carter Hawley Hale Stores, Inc
Dayton Hudson Corporation
Federated Department Stores, Inc.
Grant, W. T, Company
Kresge, S. S, Company
Macy, R. H, and Company
Marshall Field & Company
Penney, J. C, Company
Sears, Roebuck and Company
also subhead Stores under names of cities, e.g. New York (city)—Stores

Acquisitions and mergers

Shooting over Marshall Field; bid by Carter Hawley Hale Stores, Inc. il Bus W p35 D 26 '77
Takeovers; Carter Hawley Hale-Marshall Field & Co. merger. il Time 110:49 D 26 '77

Advertising

Notes and comment; Bloomingdale's promotion of India. New Yorker 53:43-4 N 7 '77

Employees

One-stop decorating; department store designers. C. Kriebel. il Am Home 80:24 F '77

Great Britain

Carter Hawley Hale backs out of Britain; House of Fraser Ltd. Bus W p42+ O 17 '77
See also
Marks & Spencer, Ltd

DE PAUW, Gommar A.
Tradition vs. traditionalists. Chr Today 21:62 S 9 '77 *

DEPAUW University, Greencastle, Ind.
Jungle mission; DePauw University student-volunteer program. Newsweek 91:66 Ja 9 '78

DEPILATION. See Hair, Removal of

DEPORTATION
England revives the star chamber; deportation of P. Agee. R. Clark. Nation 224:261-3 Mr 5 '77
See also
Asylum, Right of
Extradition
DEPRECIATION
Old depreciation game; automobiles. T. Cook. il Car & Dr 23:66+ N '77
Steel: biting the bullet. il Forbes 120:35-6 D 1 '77
See also
Investment tax credits

Taxation

Depreciation arithmetic; teach your pencil some new tricks. il Suc Farm 75:no2 9 F '77
Tax quiz: when is a repair not an improvement? Suc Farm 75:36 Ap '77
DEPREIST, James
Musician of the month: James DePreist; interview. ed by J. Hiemenz. por Hi Fi 27:MA8-9+ Mr '77
DEPRESSION, Business. See Business depression
DEPRESSION, Mental
Christmas depression syndrome. J. E. Rodgers. Mademoiselle 83:50 D '77
Cruising blues and their cure. R. Pirsig. por Esquire 87:65-8 My '77
Depression! il Good H 184:28+ Mr '77
How to cope with holiday hangups and hangovers; views of experts. R. Goldman. Harp Baz 111:134-5+ D '77
How to feel better when you're feeling rotten; cures for blues. J. Viorst. por Redbook 149:68+ My '77
Link between self-esteem and depression. D. Cohen. Psychol Today 11:96+ Jl '77
Psychiatrist's notebook; vacation blues. T. I. Rubin. Ladies Home J 94:70 Jl '77
Senility? It's more likely depression, says psychiatrist. Ret Liv 17:15 Mr '77
Spending money on yourself can up your bank account; depression alleviated by psychotherapy. M. Page. Vogue 167:236+ S '77
Treating depression. E. J. Stainbrook. por Intellect 105:299 Mr '77
What to do when you're really depressed. A. Kosner. il McCalls 105:220-1+ N '77
See also
Manic-depressive psychoses
DEPRIVATION, Maternal. See Maternal deprivation
DEPRIVATION, Sensory. See Sensory deprivation
DEPROGRAMMING
Brainwashing Moonies; conservatorship strategy. Time 109:73 Ap 4 '77
Deprogramming the brainwashed: even a Moonie has civil rights; use of conservatorship laws. T. Robbins. Nation 224:238-42 F 26 '77
Deprogramming: the cults fight back. Chr Today 21:36-7 Je 17 '77
Fighting cults: the Tucson tactic; deprogramming by the Freedom of Thought Foundation. R. Chandler. il Chr Today 21:57-61 F 4 '77
Letting go: everybody has the right to be wrong. J. C. Lyles. Chr Cent 94:451-3 My 11 '77
Parents v. Moonies: conservatorship orders. J. K. Footlick and P. S. Greenberg. il Newsweek 89:83 Ap 25 '77
Rescue from a fanatic cult. C. H. Edwards. il Read Digest 110:129-33 Ap '77
Setback for what? Commonweal 104:232+ Ap 15 '77
DEPTH indicators
Choosing a depth sounder. G. West. il Yachting 142:80-1+ O '77
Fish finders: chart your catch; Fish finders buyer's guide. il Motor B & S 139:62-4+, 68 F '77
Follow your depth finder. M. Meisels. il map Motor B & S 140:62-4+ D '77
Sounding out depthfinders. F. M. Paulson. il Field & S 81:98-100+ Mr '77
Sounding the depths. il Motor B & S 140:94-6 O '77
DEPTH of field. See Photography—Focusing
DEPTH perception. See Space perception
DERBER, Milton
Collective bargaining: the American approach to industrial democracy. bibl f Ann Am Acad 431:83-94 My '77
DERBY, Conn.

Air pollution

See Air pollution—Connecticut
DER HOVANESSIAN, Diana
Fisherman's mother; poem. Nation 224:566 My 7 '77
DERIAN, Patricia
Carter's point woman. A. Deming and S. Sullivan. por Newsweek 89:70 My 16 '77 *
DERING, William
Charles Bridges and William Dering; two Virginia painters, 1735-1750; excerpt. G. Hood. bibl il Antiques 112:934-8 N '77 *
DERINGERS. See Pistols
DERMATOLOGY. See Skin
DE ROSIS, Helen A.
Working mother's guilt complex. Harp Baz 110:178+ O '77
—and Pellegrino, V. Y.
Your declaration of independence. Harp Baz 110:98+ F '77
DERRINGERS. See Pistols
DERWINSKI, Edward Joseph
Excerpt from debate on bill to amend the Hatch Act, June 7, 1977. Cong Digest 56:297+ D '77
DESAI, Morarji
I have no ill will; excerpts from interview, ed by H. Jensen. Newsweek 89:36 Ap 4 '77
Morarji Desai: the ascetic activist; excerpts from interview, ed by L. Malkin and W. Stewart. il por Time 109:34 Ap 4 '77

about

Desai: a man of the cloth. F. Willey and others. il por Newsweek 89:35 Ap 4 '77 *
Fall of the Gandhis—mixed blessing for India? il por U.S. News 82:31-2 Ap 4 '77 *
India after Indira. A. Demig and others. il pors Newsweek 89:32-3+ Ap 4 '77 *
Letter from New Delhi. V. Mehta. New Yorker 53:119-22+ O 17 '77 *
Morarji in charge. M. Kondracke. New Repub 177:10-12 O 22 '77 *
Powerful vote for freedom. il por Time 109:30-1+ Ap 4 '77 *
DESAUTELS, Paul E.
Jade is a mystery 4,000 years old that transcends science. il Smithsonian 8:80-7 Ap '77
DESCARTES, René
Thinking man's philosopher. P. W. Schmidtchen. Hobbies 82:134-7 O '77 *
DESCENT. See Genealogy
DESCHIN, Jacob
Viewpoint. See issues of Popular photography
DESEGREGATION. See Catholic schools—Desegregation; Colleges and universities—Desegregation; Public schools—Desegregation
DESEGREGATION decision, 1954. See United States—Supreme Court—Decisions
DESERT. See Deserts
DESERT architecture. See Architecture and climate
DESERT ecology
Competition between seed-eating rodents and ants in desert ecosystems. J. H. Brown and D. W. Davidson. bibl il Science 196:880-2 My 20 '77
Desert greenhouse. il maps Environment 19:14-20 N '77
Desert made by man. S. Galal. il map Nat Parks & Con Mag 51:11-16 N '77
Earth's creeping deserts. il map Time 110:58-9 S 12 '77
Halt to desert advance; symposium. il UNESCO Courier 30:4-33 Jl '77
Spreading deserts. E. Eckholm and L. R. Brown. bibl il map Focus 28:1-11 S '77
See also
United Nations Conference on Desertification, 1977

Conferences

See Deserts—Conferences
DESERT fauna
Case study in survival: animal life in the Sahara. C. Grenot and R. Vernet. il UNESCO Courier 30:25-8 Jl '77
See also
Kangaroo rats
DESERT gardens. See Gardens, Desert
DESERT islands. See Islands
DESERT survival. See Wilderness survival
DESERT varnish
Desert varnish: the importance of clay minerals. R. M. Potter and G. R. Rossman. bibl il Science 196:1446-8 Je 24 '77
DESERT vegetation
Annual plants: adaptations to desert environments. T. W. Mulroy and P. W. Rundel. bibl BioScience 27:109-14 F '77
See also
Cactus
DESERT willow. See Willow
DESERTIFICATION. See Desert ecology; United Nations Conference on Desertification, 1977
DESERTION, Military. See United States—Armed Forces—Desertion
DESERTION and non-support
Getting child support from runaway fathers; Child Support Enforcement Program. B. Stephen. McCalls 104:84-5 Je 77
Rights of parents and children; conflicts of civil rights. T. R. Hayden. Current 190:24-7 F '77

DESERTS
Desert love affair; American deserts; excerpt from The journey home. E. Abbey. il Read Digest 111:39+ O '77
Great green walls of China; planting of forest barriers to check desert. il UNESCO Courier 30:32-3 Jl '77
See also
Libyan Desert
Sahara Desert
Sonoran Desert

Conferences

Nairobi conferees identify desertification indicators. Science 198:43 O 7 '77
See also
United Nations Conference on Desertification, 1977

DESIGN
Conversation with Charles Eames; ed by O. Gingerich. C. Eames. Am Scholar 46:326-37 Summ '77
Pushing future directions in modern design; New York Museum of Modern Art's Department of Architecture and Design. B. Diamonstein. il por Art N 76:43-5 S '77
Tut-o-mania. S. C. Cowley and others. il Newsweek 89:94-5 My 9 '77
See also
Architectural design
Book design
Costume design
Line (art)
Postage stamp design
Textile design

Exhibitions

Cooper-Hewitt and its concern for American taste; More Than Meets the Eye exhibit. R. Lynes. il Smithsonian 8:69-77 bibl(p 160-1) N '77
To celebrate the moment; exhibition at Cooper-Hewitt Museum. il Hobbies 82:119+ Ja '78

Study and teaching

Build a balloon—a 3-D project that flies. R. F. Salzberg. il Design (US) 78:10-12 Spr '77
Study of design. R. Moore. il Design (US) 78:27 Spr '77

DESIGN, Decorative
Repeat; pattern repetition. M. Sonday. il Craft Horiz 37:52-4 Ag '72
See also
Pottery—Decoration
Textile design
Textile fabrics

Plant forms

Rose is a rose. . .& so much more! il House B 119:57-71+ Je '77
Wildflowers—adapting floral designs for different types of needlework. N. Lindemeyer and G. Vaughan. il Bet Hom & Gard 55:64-76+ F '77

DESIGN, Industrial
Tribute to Russel Wright: pioneering industrial designer, 1903-1976. M. Greif. Craft Horiz 37:45 Ag '77
25 best-designed products. W. McQuade. il Fortune 95:270-7 My '77
See also
Human engineering
Mechanical drawing
Systems engineering
also subhead Design under various subjects e.g. Loudspeakers—Design

History

Mind's eye: nonverbal thought in technology. E. S. Ferguson. bibl il Science 197:827-36 Ag 26 '77

DESIGN firms
Consultant profile: the medical equipment planner; ISD Inc. il Archit Rec 162:59+ Ag '77
Graphic design companies grow from hired hands to publishing partners:
A Good Thing: the multimedia packaging of Slim Goodbody. P. Doebler. il Pub W 211:52+ My 2 '77
Tree Communications: outperforming the industry averages. P. Doebler. il Pub W 211:50-2 My 2 '77

DESIGNERS
Careers in art; industrial designers. P. Savino. il Sch Arts 76:8 Mr '77
First of all, I design for people; interview, ed by M. Gough and J. B. Reiter. A. Donghia. il por House B 119:48-56 Ag '77
Forecast! designers; views on color, comp by S. Schraub. il House B 119:84-9 F '77
See also
Costume designers
Design firms

DESIRE
Seven deadly sins today; excerpt. H. Fairlie. New Repub 177:18-21 O 8 '77

DESK furnishings
Build the ultimate desktop. M. McClintock. il Pop Mech 147:116-18 Ap '77
Study in naturals . . . a study in brights; decorating desks and desk furnishings. il Seventeen 36:252-3+ Ag '77

DESKS
Box on the wall is their desk by the phone. il Sunset 158:120 Je '77
Desk you can build in one evening. J. A. Birk. il Pop Sci 210:152 Mr '77
Easy as child's play: a table-desk you can build in a day; excerpt from Things to do in a day. il Redbook 150:136+ N '77
Study in naturals . . . a study in brights; decorating desks and desk furnishings. il Seventeen 36:252-3+ Ag '77

DESLAURIERS, Lorraine C.
Do you really need a yearly medical checkup? il Fam Health 9:32-4 F '77

DES MOINES

Music

See also
Opera—Iowa

DES MOINES Metro (opera company) See Opera—Iowa

DES MOINES Metro Summer Festival. See Music festivals—Iowa

DESOWITZ, Robert S.
Airs, waters, and places. Natur Hist 86:34+ O '77
Fly that would be king; with biographical sketch. il Natur Hist 86:8, 76-83 bibl(p 101) F '77
—and Miller, L. H.
Airs, waters, and places. il Natur Hist 86:10+ bibl(p 110) D '77

DESPARD, Lucy Edwards
(comp) Recent books on international relations. For Affairs 55:644-63 Ap '77

DESPOTOPOULOS, Constantine
Aristotle. por UNESCO Courier 30:31-3 O '77

DES PRES, Terrence
On the verge of a new morality: Wilson's message for humanists. por Horizon 19:46-7 Mr '77

DESSAINT, Alain Yvon
Chinese way of eating. il Natur Hist 86:94-5+ Ag '77

DESSAU, Germany

Architecture

See also
Bauhaus

DESSAUER, John P.
Too many books (?) revisited. Pub W 211:41-3 My 16 '77
U.S. consumer expenditures on books in 1976. il Pub W 211:39-40 Ap 25 '77

DESSERT toppings. See Icings

DESSERT wines. See Wine

DESSERTS
Apple desserts. il Bet Hom & Gard 55:159-60 N '77
Cheese and figs into tulips. il Sunset 158:186 Je '77
Chef Chapel's trio of desserts. C. Claiborne and P. Franey. il N Y Times Mag p77 My 8 '77
Christmas sweets from many lands. H. McCully and M. Siple. il House B 119:111-17 D '77
Classy canned-fruit desserts. il Bet Hom & Gard 55:210+ N '77
Coffee desserts. il Bet Hom & Gard 55:131-2 F '77
Company in the kitchen; Christmas desserts; ideas of Martha Stewart. il Mademoiselle 83:124-7+ D '77
Cool and sweet: fresh fruit desserts. R. Molter. il Parents Mag 52:50-2 Ag '77
Dairy desserts. il Bet Hom & Gard 55:117-18 Mr '77
Delectable holiday desserts for family baking. il House & Gard 149:131+ D '77
Desserts in a hurry. il Bet Hom & Gard 55:98 Jl '77
La dolce vita. C. Claiborne and P. Franey. il N Y Times Mag p56 Ja 8 '78
Festive cranberry desserts. il Bet Hom & Gard 55:50 D '77
Freeze-ahead holiday treats. il Bet Hom & Gard 55:112 N '77
Fresh fruit desserts. il Bet Hom & Gard 55:84 Ag '77
Fresh fruit desserts: cool and colorful. il McCalls 104:138-40+ Je '77
Getting your just desserts. il Fam Health 9:44-5 Mr '77
Gluten-free desserts. il Bet Hom & Gard 55:70 S '77
Golden floating island. il McCalls 104:93-4 S '77
Halloween treats. il Bet Hom & Gard 55:153-4 O '77
Heavenly dessert; four Christmas desserts. il Redbook 150:120+ D '77
How to make the layered fruit dessert. il Bet Hom & Gard 55:2 My '77
Jicama for dessert? Yes indeed. il Sunset 158:216 My '77
Lavish sauces and simple desserts—so right together. il Parents Mag 52:77 O '77
Menus for people who can't wait for dessert. il Redbook 149:120-1+ Je '77
Mighty mousses. C. Claiborne and P. Franey. il N Y Times Mag p 118 N 27 '77
Mud pies; good and easy desserts children can help make. il House & Gard 149:154-5 Mr '77

DESSERTS—*Continued*
Ne plus ultra mousse. C. Claiborne and P. Franey. il N Y Times Mag p60 F 20 '77
Our best apple desserts. il McCalls 105:180-1+ O '77
Peach melba? here are two ways. il Sunset 159:128 Jl '77
Pots de crème. il Good H 184:24 F '77
Pretty party desserts in a bowl. E. W. Manning. il Farm J 101:27-8 Je '77
Refrigerator desserts. il Bet Hom & Gard 54: 83-4 Ag '76
Small pleasures. il Redbook 148:110-11+ F '77
Soup for dessert? the Danes don't bat an eye; buttermilk soup. il Sunset 159:104 Jl '77
Summer's greatest desserts. il Good H 184:140-9 Je '77
Sweet cherry desserts. il Bet Hom & Gard 55: 44 Je '77
Sweet hearts. il Ladies Home J 94:96-7+ F '77
Tempting high-calorie come-on; toppings and desserts. il Sunset 159:238+ O '77
30-minute dessert; orange cream trifle. il Good H 185:290 N '77
Twist of lemon desserts. il Bet Hom & Gard 55:182 N '77
See also
Cake
Cheesecake
Cookies
Custards
Ice cream, ices, etc.
Meringue
Pastry
Pie
Puddings
Soufflés
Tarts

DE STAEBLER, Stephen
Painterly allegories and ceramic parables. T. Albright. il Art N 76:88-9 Ap '77 *

DESULFURIZATION of coal. See Coal—Sulfur content

DETECTION of crime. See Criminal investigation

DETECTIVE and mystery stories
Dorothy L. Sayers—for good work, for God's work. C. Forbes. Chr Today 21:16-18 Mr 4 '77
Issue is murder; symposium. il New Repub 177: 25-46 Jl 30 '77
Studies, both frivolous and serious, unravel clues to mysteries in Workman's Murder ink; interview, ed by R. Dahlin. D. Winn. Pub W 212:49 Jl 4 '77
See also
Publishers and publishing—Detective and mystery stories
Television programs—Crime programs

Authorship

Birth of a sleuth. N. Marsh. Writer 90:23-5 Ap '77
Making crime pay. C. W. Sasser. Writers Digest 57:29-32 S '77
Masters of white-collar homicide; coauthors of Emma Lathen and R. B. Dominic mysteries. pors Forbes 120:89 D 1 '77
Poirot's first case; excerpt from An autobiography. A. Christie. il por N Y Times Mag p41-2+ S 18 '77
Travels with le Carré; writing spy thriller, The honourable schoolboy. pors Newsweek 90:102 O 10 '77
Writing the library whodunit; Dewey decimated. C. A. Goodrum. il Am Lib 8:194-6 Ap '77

Bibliography

Mysteries (cont) R. Winks. New Repub 176:35-7 Mr 19; 35-7 Je 11; 177:37-9 S 24; 34-7 N 26 '77
World of mysteries—plus. J. L. Breen. See alternate issues of Wilson library bulletin

Periodicals

True crime markets. Writers Digest 57:31 S '77

Single works

Death in the air. A. Christie. Sat Eve Post 249:42-4 O; 33-5 N; 42-6 D '77
Johore murders. P. Theroux. Atlantic 239:93-4 Mr '77
Whodunits; excerpts from stories. il Sat Eve Post 249:54-6 Jl '77

Study and teaching

Anecdotes, facetiae, satire, etc.

Statistically significant genre teaching. A. Peetoom. Engl J 66:9-11 F '77

Technique

Elements of the police procedural novel. R. Burns. Writer 90:14-17 Jl '77
Keeping the reader breathless. A. Chamberlain. Writer 90:20-2+ Ag '77
Tricks and traps in writing suspense fiction. J. L. Backus. Writer 90:11-14 Mr '77
Writing the mystery short-short. B. Pronzini. Writer 90:19-23 D '77

DETECTIVE and mystery stories for children. See Childrens literature

DETECTIVE Bureau Hostage Negotiating Team. See New York (city)—Police

DETECTIVES
Long way from Philip Marlowe. J. G. Dunne. Esquire 88:76+ N '77
See also
Beltrante, N.
Vidocq, E. F.

DETECTORS
Detectors for lightwave communication. H. Melchior. bibl il Phys Today 30:32-9 N '77
Equipment reports:
Electrolert Fuzzbuster and Fuzzbuster II radar detectors. il Radio-Electr 48:17+ D '77
Germanium gamma-ray detectors. R. H. Pehl. bibl il Phys Today 30:50-4+ N '77
Getting on top of old smokey; radar detectors. R. Taylor. il Car & Dr 23:41-2+ S '77
Heat sensors cut the risk of. . .corn in big bins. D. Seim. il Farm J 101:20-1 D '77
If all else fails . . .; ECM; radar detector. P. Bedard. Car & Dr 23:62 S '77
Microchannel plates. B. Leskovar. bibl il Phys Today 30:42-9 N '77
Sniffing out Smokeys. A. Salsberg. Pop Electr 12:4 N '77
Using LED's as light detectors. F. M. Mims. il Pop Electr 11:86-8 My '77
Your right to bear radar detectors; radio transmissions under Communications Act of 1934. R. Taylor. Car & Dr 23:59-60 S '77
See also
Fire detectors

DETECTORS, Infrared
Aircraft detection system advances. B. Miller. Aviation W 106:22-3 Je 20 '77
Heat-leak locator. H. Shuldiner. il Pop Sci 212: 83 Ja '78
Infrared detectors. H. Levinstein. bibl il Phys Today 30:23-8 N '77
Infrared sensor sized for helicopters; forward-looking infrared (FLIR) sensor. P. H. Klass. il Aviation W 108:71-3 Ja 9 '78

DETENTE policy. See United States—Foreign relations—Russia

DETERGENTS
Detergent economizer kit. il Consumers Res Mag 60:25 My '77
Detergents, bleaches, softeners—when to use what. il Changing T 31:29-30 My '77
Dishwasher detergents and two rinsing aids. il Consumers Res Mag 60:14-17 Ag '77
Dishwashing detergents. il Consumers Res Mag 60:24-7 Ap '77
Dishwashing liquids. Consumer Rep 42:41-2 D '77
Water pollution: the Indiana experiment; phosphate-detergent ban. T. Wyman. Environment 19:2-4 Je '77

DETERMINISM. See Free will and determinism

DETHLEFSEN, Edwin S. and Jensen, Kenneth
Social commentary from the cemetery; with biographical sketches. il Natur Hist 86:2, 32-9 bibl(p 92) Je '77

DE TOLEDANO, Ralph
Karl Hess and the doppelgänger. Nat R 29:718-20 Je 24 '77
On re-reading W. H. Auden's Collected longer poems & Collected shorter poems; poem. Nat R 29:341 Mr 18 '77
Tip-off; poem. Nat R 29:1052 S 16 '77

DETOMBE, Robert E.
How to sidestep jogging hazards. il Parks & Rec 12:58-60+ S '77

DETONATORS
Dr Maynard and his primer. C. Worman. il Hobbies 81:142-3 F '77

DETRITUS
Detritus-based food webs: exploitation by juvenile chum salmon (oncorhynchus keta) J. Sibert and others. bibl il Science 196:649-50 My 6 '77

DETROIT
Culture in Detroit takes no back seat. J. Dance. il Lib J 102:1116-20+ My 15 '77
Focus on Detroit. il Lib J 102:1152-3 My 15 '77

Art

African clay; exhibition of art from Detroit collections. F. J. Cummings. il Ceram Mo 25:28-31 D '77

Banks

Commonwealth's continuing troubles. il Bus W p90-1 Ag 29 '77

Buildings

Detroit's new towers of hope; Renaissance Center. T. Nicholson and J. C. Jones. il Newsweek 89:60 Mr 28 '77
Detroit's palazzo; Renaissance Center. il Horizon 19:48 Jl '77
Facelift for Detroit; Renaissance Center. R. M. Williams. il Sat R 4:6-8+ My 14 '77
Henry Ford on Renaissance Center; interview. H. Ford. Sat R 4:11 My 14 '77
Motown meets the Renaissance. il Time 109:61+ Ap 18 '77
Parking deck saves money with tube columns and weathering steel. il Archit Rec 161:143-4 Je '77

DETROIT—Buildings—*Continued*
Renaissance. N. Von Hoffman. Progressive 41:32 Je '77
Renaissance Center—enough to revive Detroit? il U.S. News 82:83 Mr 28 '77
Renaissance in Detroit. R. E. McCabe. il Lib J 102:1128-31 My 15 '77

City planning

Renaissance in Detroit. R. E. McCabe. il Lib J 102:1128-31 My 15 '77

Crime

Juvenile justice; children on the witness stand at the Al Junior Lewis murder trial. D. A. Williams and J. C. Jones. il Newsweek 89:22 Je 27 '77
Leadership row at a Teamsters local. Bus W p38-9 N 28 '77

Description

Detroit: a bite at a time. W. Miller and others. il Am Lib 8:315+ Je '77
Editor walks those mean streets; a scouting report for ALA conferees. A. Plotnik. il pors Am Lib 8:311+ Je '77

Education

Motown blues; music education program. I. Kolodin. Sat R 4:14 S 3 '77
Tale of two cities; Supreme Court decisions on the proper role of Federal judges in school-desegregation cases. M. Sheils and others. il Newsweek 90:54 Jl 11 '77

History

Surrender of Detroit. L. H. Scott. il por map Am Hist Illus 12:28-36 Je '77
See also
Pontiac's Conspiracy, 1763-1765

Hotels, restaurants, etc.

Dining out in Detroit. M. Abraham. il Lib J 102:1148-51 My 15 '77
There's so much more in Detroit! W. Rossmann and I. Rossmann. il Sat Eve Post 249:18+ N '77

Housing

Born-again housing. D. A. Williams and others. il Newsweek 90:37-8 O 31 '77

Libraries

Detroit library network. N. Seabrooks. il Lib J 102:1123-7 My 15 '77
See also
Detroit Public Library

Music

Debuts & reappearances. il Hi Fi 27:MA30 F '77
See also
Detroit Symphony Orchestra
Opera—Michigan

Newspapers

See also
Detroit news

Sanitary affairs

Detroit goes to court over cleanup deadline. il Am City & County 92:13 Jl '77

Stores

Serving the fashion-conscious male; R. Jackson of J. L. Hudson's menswear department. il pors Ebony 32:99-100+ My '77

Transit systems

Heavy-rail transit looks best for Detroit. il Am City & County 92:42 My '77

DETROIT International Bridge Company
Seeking the shelter of a Detroit bridge; Ambassador Bridge, between Detroit and Windsor, Ont. il Bus W p24-5 N 7 '77

DETROIT news
Washing dirty laundry in Detroit; D. Riegle story. N. Ephron. Esquire 87:42-4 F '77

DETROIT Public Library
Library and Detroit's future. C. S. Jones. por Lib J 102:1113-15 My 15 '77

DETROIT Symphony Orchestra
Detroit Sym: Lees premiere; Concerto for string quartet and orchestra. por Hi Fi 27:MA30 F '77

DETROIT. University
Meanwhile, back in Detroit; crisis in Jesuit education. G. Pickering. Commonweal 104:49-51 Ja 21 '77

DETTRE, John R.
On creating the Stepford instructorship. Clearing H 51:120-2 N '77

DEUTCH, John Mark
Deutch and Thorne to fill two key DOE research posts. F. C. Bennett. pors Phys Today 30:93+ N '77 *
MIT chemist, Schlesinger ally assumes energy research post. W. D. Metz. por Science 198:1125-6 D 16 '77 *

DEUTERIUM
Deuterium quantity and cosmology. Sci N 111:55 Ja 22 '77
How much deuterium? il Sky & Tel 53:253 Ap '77

DEUTSCH, Babette
Nursery rhyme recalled; poem. Nation 224:730 Je 11 '77
Pot of crocuses; poem. Nation 225:664 D 17 '77
Remembering the animals; poem. New Repub 177:34 Ag 6 '77

DEUTSCH, Davida Tenenbaum
Washington memorial prints. bibl il por Antiques 111:324-31 F '77

DEUTSCH, Dennis J.
Electronic bell for a TVT-II. il Pop Electr 12:46 Jl '77

DEUTSCH, Herbert
Purchase AV equipment with care. SLJ 23:48 Ap '77

DEUTSCH, J. Anthony, and Walton, N. Y.
Diazepam maintenance of alcohol preference during alcohol withdrawal. bibl il Science 198:307-9 O 21 '77

DEUTSCHE Oper Berlin (opera company) See Opera—Germany, West

DEVEAUX, Edward C.
Pixie animation program. Pop Electr 12:42-5 Jl '77

DEVELOPING (photography) See Photography—Developing and developers

DEVELOPING nations. See Underdeveloped areas

DEVELOPMENT, Biological. See Morphogenesis

DEVELOPMENT banks
U.S. emphasizes role of international lending institutions in African development; statement, May 3, 1977. D. B. Bolen. Dept State Bull 76:576-9 My 30 '77
See also
African Development Bank

DEVELOPMENT of children. See Children—Growth and development

DEVELOPMENT Program of the United Nations. See United Nations—Development Program

DEVELOPMENTAL biology
Pattern regulation in epimorphic fields. V. French and others; reply. L. Glass. Science 198:321-2 O 21 '77

DEVI, Ritha
Reviews. S. Banes. Dance Mag 51:34+ F '77 *

DEVIL
Devil, demons & dogmatism. R. Modras. il Commonweal 104:71-5 F 4 '77
Jaws. E. Schaeffer. Chr Today 22:28 D 30 '77
See also
Exorcism

Anecdotes, facetiae, satire, etc.

Conversation with a patriot. R. Rosenblatt. New Repub 176:37-8 Mr 12 '77

DEVILFISH. See Rays (fishes)

DEVITO, Bobby
Neighborhood story. New Yorker 53:30-2 F 21 '77 *

DEVOE, Robert
How to dress up your projects. il Pop Electr 12:53-5 N '77

DEVORE, Irven
New science of genetic self-interest; interview, ed by S. Morris. il Psychol Today 10:42-6+ F '77

about

Man in the middle. S. Morris. por Psychol Today 10:44-5 F '77 *

DEVORE, Ophelia
Charm. New Yorker 53:30 Je 6 '77 *

DEVOTI, William
Where they lived; poem. Nation 224:668 My 28 '77

DEVOTIONAL literature

Bibliography

New genre of devotional writing. M. Boyd. Chr Cent 94:1066-8 N 16 '77
Some gold, much dross: devotional books. M. Boyd. Chr Cent 94:511-14 My 25 '77

DEVOTIONS. See Prayer

DE VRIES, Peter
Way down upon the Swami River; story, excerpt from Madder music. Horizon 20:96 O '77

DEW
To meet the morning dew. H. Pfletschinger. il Int Wildlife 8:44-7 Ja '78

DEWEY, Edward Russell
If you look hard cycles are all over. R. R. Ward. il por Smithsonian 7:104-10 Mr '77 *

DEWS, William
Side show. Reviews
Nation 224:410-11 Ap 2 '77 *
Sat R 4:42-3 My 14 '77 *

DEXTER, John
Classical music. B. H. Haggin. New Repub 176:27-8 My 28 '77 *
False prophet, true martyrs. R. Jacobson. il Opera N 41:30-1 Mr 19 '77 *

DEXTER, John—*Continued*
Music. B. H. Haggin. New Repub 178:28-9 Ja 7 '78 *
Playing Rigoletto up front. W. Bender. il Time 110:116 N 14 '77 *
DEY, Richard Morris
Cruising man goes racing. il Yachting 141:172+ My '77
DHARMA-WARDANA, M. W. C.
Self-help for third world scientists. il Bull Atom Sci 33:22-3 F '77
DHOPLE, A. M. and Hanks, J. H.
In vitro growth of mycobacterium lepraemurium, an obligate intracellular microbe. bibl il Science 197:379-81 Jl 22 '77
DIABETES
Diabetes: the prognosis is brighter. M. P. Scott. Bet Hom & Gard 55:46+ Je '77
On living with diabetes. M. Ginott. Mademoiselle 83:38+ My '77
Somatostatin: widespread abnormality in tissues of spontaneously diabetic mice. Y. C. Patel and others. bibl il Science 198:930-1 D 2 '77
3 musts that keep diabetics on the go. J. Mayer. il Fam Health 9:30-2 My '77

Nutritional aspects

Cooking for the diabetic. il Bet Hom & Gard 55:166 F '77
Revised food exchange lists for diabetics. il Bet Hom & Gard 55:160+ F '77
Special diets. il Bet Hom & Gard 55:54 Je '77
DIABETES research
Healy sisters—clues to diabetes. W. Stockton. il N Y Times Mag p88+ Je 12 '77
Major stride in the fight against diabetes. Sci Digest 82:82-5 Ag '77
New look at diabetes. P. Lehmann. Harp Baz 110:186 S '77
DIABLO Canyon plant. See Atomic power plants
DIACONATE. See Deacons
DIACONIS, Persi
Mathematics and magic: illumination and illusion. G. B. Kolata. Science 198:282-3 O 21 '77 *
DIACRIDINES. See Acridines
DIAGNOSIS
Casebook of the medical detective; work of H. Friedman of Philadelphia's Children's Hospital in attempting to diagnose Legionnaires' disease (cont) D. Russell. il Fam Health 9:40-1+ Ja '77
Diagnosis by the book; Symptoms: the complete home medical encyclopedia. Time 109:84 Mr 7 '77
Do-it-yourself medical tests. M. P. Scott. il Bet Hom & Gard 55:70+ D '77
Early warning signals of common diseases; excerpt from Symptoms; the complete home medical encyclopedia. S. Miller. Good H 184:223-5 Mr '77
Epidemic that was; Legionnaires' disease. E. Keerdoja and others. il Newsweek 90:6 Jl 18 '77
Found: the Philly killer, perhaps; Legionnaires' disease. Time 109:47 Ja 31 '77
Legion fever: failed investigation may be successful after all. B. J. Culliton. Science 195:469-70 F 4 '77
Tracking the killer fever; Legionnaires' disease. M. Clark. il Newsweek 89:78-9 Ja 31 '77
What your eyes tell you about your health. J. Maxwell. il Esquire 89:54-7 Ja '78
See also
Hospitals—Diagnostic services
Medicine—Practice
Radiography, Medical
also subhead Diagnosis under names of diseases, e.g. Cancer—Diagnosis
DIALECTS
See also
English language—Dialects
DIALECTS, Black. See Black-English dialects
DIALOGUE
He said she said. L. Block. Writers Digest 57:13+ F '77
Writing dialogue. J. Sayles. Writer 91:13-15 Ja '78
DIALOGUES of the Carmelites; opera. See Poulenc, F.
DIALYSIS
See also
Hemodialysis
DIAMANTOPOULOS, Alexis
Citadel in praise of peace. il UNESCO Courier 30:24-7 O '77
DIAMINOANISOLE sulfate. See Sulfates
DIAMOND, Edwin
How Carter is changing us. por Newsweek 89:21 Ap 11 '77
DIAMOND, Jared Mason, and May, R. M.
Species turnover rates on islands: dependence on census interval. bibl il Science 197:266-70 Jl 15 '77
DIAMOND, Matthew
Reviews. A. Smith. Dance Mag 51:104 My '77 *
DIAMOND, Rhea. See Carey, S. jt auth
DIAMOND, Stanley C.
Mini-course as an experiment in alternative education. Clearing H 51:11 S '77
DIAMOND industry
Diamonds and death; murder of P. Jaroslawicz. R. Steele and S. Agrest. il pors Newsweek 90:35-6 O 10 '77
Harry Winston: ace of diamonds. J. Stewart-Gordon. il Read Digest 112:183-4+ Ja '78
See also
De Beers Consolidated Mines, Ltd
DIAMOND mines and mining

South Africa

Glitter from the Dark Continent. il Holiday 58:13 Mr '77
See also
De Beers Consolidated Mines, Ltd
DIAMOND Shamrock Corporation
Diamond Shamrock in clover. por Forbes 120:37 D 15 '77
DIAMONDS
Diamond. H. D. Brown. il Hobbies 82:158 Ag '77
Magic word. S. T. Atlas and others. il Newsweek 90:95-6+ O 17 '77

Prices

Extra glitter in diamond prices; De Beers Consolidated Mines Ltd. Bus W p57-8 N 21 '77
DIAMONDS as an investment. See Gems as an investment
DIAMONSTEIN, Barbaralee
(ed) Art world: a seventy-five year treasury of ARTnews; excerpts. il Art N 76:141-4+ N '77
New York. Art N 76:109-12 D '77
Pushing future directions in modern design. il por Art N 76:43-5 S '77
DIANETICS
See also
Scientology
DIANNA, John
Editorially speaking. See issues of Hot rod
Triple threat; Hot rod's 3-in-1 Chevy II. il por Hot Rod 30:56-7+ Ag; 26-8+ S; 36-7+ O '77
DIAPERS
Disposable diapers. Consumer Rep 42:353-4 D '77
DIARIES
Dialogue weekend; Intensive Journal Workshop. R. A. Blake. America 136:105-6 F 5 '77
Write your own history. J. A. McCracken. Read Digest 111:7-9+ Ag '77

Anecdotes, facetiae, satire, etc.

Diary of me: Manhattan, 1976. R. M. Strozier. il Atlantic 239:83-5 Ap '77
DIARRHEA
See also
Acrodermatitis enteropathica
DIAZEPAM. See Tranquilizing drugs
DIBENZODIOXIN
Cleaning up Seveso: science, politics and chaos. il Chemistry 50:21-2 N '77
Combustion of several 2,4,5-trichlorophenoxy compounds: formation of 2,3,7,8-tetrachlorodibenzo-p-dioxin. R. H. Stehl and L. L. Lamparski. bibl il Science 197:1008-9 S 2 '77
Environmental degradation of 2,3,7,8-tetrachlorodibenzo-*p*-dioxin (TCDD); action of sunlight. D. G. Crosby and A. S. Wong. bibl il Science 195:1337-8 Mr 25 '77
Persistent poison; spread of dioxin pollution over Seveso, Italy. E. Keerdoja. map Newsweek 89:10 Je 13 '77
Poison that fell from the sky; dioxin poisoning following factory explosion in Seveso, Italy; condensation. J. G. Fuller. il map Read Digest 111:191-6+ Ag '77
Reporter at large. T. Whiteside. New Yorker 53:30-8+ Jl 25 '77
Seveso—one year later: aftermath of TCDD explosion at Icmesa chemical plant in Seveso, Italy. D. B. Richardson. il U.S. News 83:44-5 Ag 1 '77
Seveso: the questions persist where dioxin created a wasteland. J. Walsh. map Science 197:1064-7 S 9 '77
Small, prolonged exposure to dioxin harmful to monkeys. BioScience 27:370 My '77
DIBROMOCHLOROPROPANE. See Pesticides
DIBROMOPROPYL phosphate
Banning Tris; chemically treated nightwear. il Newsweek 89:67 Ap 18 '77
Fire retardant may pose cancer hazard. Sci N 111:23 Ja 8 '77
Flame-retardant ban dishevels an industry; childrens sleepwear chemical Tris-BP. il Bus W p45-6 Ap 18 '77
Tris—a sleepwear flame retardant banned. il Consumers Res Mag 60:4 Je '77
Tris: confusion over another cancer hazard. Consumer Rep 42:415-16 Jl '77
Tris controversy. P. H. Abelson. Science 197:113 Jl 8 '77; Reply. R. H. Harris. bibl 197:1132-3 S 16 '77
DIBUTYRYL cyclic adenosine monophosphate. See Adenosine monophosphate

DICARO, Paul
Busted in Mexico. D. Harris. il pors N Y Times Mag p26-30+ My 1 '77 *
DI CICCO, Dennis. See McDermott, A. T. jt auth
DICK, Philip Kindred
Philip K. Dick: exile in paradox. F. E. Warren. Chr Today 21:22-4 My 20 '77 *
DICK, Rebecca Ann
Build your own preposition box. il Engl J 66: 75-6 Ap '77
DICKELMAN, Robert A.
Cars. See issues of Better homes and gardens
Good news. See issues of Better homes and gardens
DICKENS, Charles
Christmas carol; dramatization. See Hackett, W.
Tale of two cities; dramatization. See Hackett, W.
DICKERMAN, Alexandra, and Dickerman, John
Quick-growing hydroponic gardens. il Bet Hom & Gard 55:100-1+ N '77
DICKERMAN, John. See Dickerman, A. jt auth
DICKEY, Beth
(ed) See Fox, W. P. Eccentric like a fox
DICKEY, Charley H.
Make pheasants fly! il Field & S 82:39+ N '77
Percentage quail hunting; excerpt from Charley Dickey's bobwhite quail hunting. il Outdoor Life 160:61-3+ N '77
DICKEY, James
Poet James Dickey on Carter and the born-again South. il por U.S. News 82:67 Ap 18 '77

about

Voice of the South. P. Axthelm. pors Newsweek 89:25 Ja 31 '77 *
DICKEY-Lincoln dams project. See Dams
DICKINSON, Edwin
Bordering on the surreal. N. T. Willig. il Art N 76:195-6 N '77 *
DICKINSON, Emily
Enigma of Emily. M. Klein. il por Am Hist Illus 12:4-11 D '77 *
DICKINSON, Fairleigh Stanton, 1919-
Directors' squabble at Becton Dickinson. il por Bus W p40-1 O 3 '77 *
DICKINSON, William Louis
Excerpts from remarks on U.S. African policy, April 29, 1976. Cong Digest 56:21+ Ja '77
DICKMAN, Robert L.
Bok globules; with biographical sketch. il Sci Am 236:18, 66-70+ bibl(p 142) Je '77
DICKMANN, Don. See Reardon, S. jt auth
DICKMANN, Zeev, and others
Does blastocyst estrogen initiate implantation? bibl Science 195:687-8 F 18 '77
DICKSON, Frank A.
Getting started. Writers Digest 57:46+ O '77
Thinking ahead. Writers Digest 57:28+ Je '77
DICKSON, John W.
Four snapshots of Aunt Claire; poem. Am Scholar 46:348-9 Summ '77
DICKSTEIN, Morris
Reconsideration. New Repub 176:36-7 Ja 29 '77
Winding down the '60s. Nation 224:632-3 My 21 '77
DICTAPHONE corporation
Conversations. New Yorker 53:27-9 D 19 '77
DICTATING machines
Dictating machines. il Consumers Res Mag 60: 21-5 Jl '77
DICTATION (educational method) See English language—Study and teaching
DICTATORS
Are South American dictators serious about stepping down? il map U.S. News 83:47-8 N 28 '77
Washington diarist. M. M. Kondracke. New Repub 177:52 O 15 '77
DICTION
See also
Singing—Diction
DICTIONARIES
See also
English language—Dictionaries
DIDATO, Salvatore V.
Are you ready for marriage? Harp Baz 110:51+ Je '77
DIDION, Joan
A book of common prayer; excerpt from novel. Mademoiselle 83:148-9+ F '77
The Coast. See alternate issues of Esquire to December 1977
Day in the life of Joan Didion; interview, ed by S. Brady. Ms 5:65-8+ F '77
Myth of fragility concealing a tough core; interview, ed by D. Diehl. Sat R 4:24 Mr 5 '77

about

Imagination of disaster. por Time 109:87-8 Mr 28 '77 *
Joan Didion & her characters. J. Romano. Commentary 64:61-3 Jl '77 *
DIEBENKORN, Richard
Amazing grace; retrospective at the Whitney Museum of American Art. M. Stevens. il Newsweek 89:83+ Je 20 '77 *
California in eupeptic color; retrospective at Whitney Museum. R. Hughes. il por Time 109:58-9 Je 27 '77 *
Problem solving in solitude. G. J. Hazlitt. il por Art N 76:76-9 Ja '77 *
DIEBOLD, Gerald J. and Zare, R. N.
Laser fluorimetry: subpicogram detection of aflatoxins using high-pressure liquid chromatography. bibl il Science 196:1439-41 Je 24 '77
DIEBOLD, John
Why things don't work any more. por Newsweek 90:8-9 Jl 18 '77
DIEGO Garcia Naval Base. See Navy yards and naval stations
DIEHL, Digby
(ed) See Didion, J. Myth of fragility concealing a tough core
DIENHART, Joe S.
Two on the fifty. B. Collins. il Sat Eve Post 249:40-1 O '77 *
DIENSTAG, Eleanor
Myth of creative divorce. il Psychol Today 10: 49-50+ Ap '77
DIESEL engines
Swing-beam crank system quiets opposed-piston diesel. D. Scott. il Pop Sci 211:74-5 D '77

Fuel

See Diesel fuels
DIESEL engines, Automotive
Are diesel autos finally going to make it big? il U.S. News 82:55-6 Je 13 '77
Coming of the diesels: emissions and the laws. Consumer Rep 42:520 S '77
Detroit's diesel; Oldsmobile 88. il Time 110:74 S 19 '77
Diesel power. A. J. Mayer. il Newsweek 89:63-4 Mr 7 '77
Diesel's advantages; letter. F. J. Hooven. Science 197:940 S 2 '77
Durable diesel. R. Taylor and J. Taylor. pors House & Gard 149:56+ N '77
New Chevy, Dodge, GMC fuel-stretching diesel pickups. J. Dunne. il Pop Sci 211:77+ O '77
New diesel pickups and bigger 4WD's. H. Shuldiner. il Outdoor Life 160:54+ O '77
Oldsmobile Diesel—the engineering story. E. F. Lindsley. il Pop Sci 212:78-9+ Ja '78
Oldsmobile Diesel V-8. K. Ludvigsen. il Motor T 29:84-7+ O '77
Special diesel section; Rabbit and Oldsmobile. il Pop Mech 148:82-7+ Jl '77
Special section: the diesel file. il Car & Dr 22: 67+ Je '77
Update on diesel. B. Behme. il Field & S 82: 72+ Jl '77
VW's 60-mpg turbo-diesel safety car. J. Dunne. il Pop Sci 211:104-5 O '77
Why the old diesel is the new hot engine. il Bus W p 108-9 Ja 31 '77

Maintenance and repair

You can do it yourself if you buy a diesel! Rabbit engine. P. Weissler. il Pop Mech 148: 86-7+ Jl '77

Manufacture

See also
Cummins Engine Company

Testing

Do diesel cars really make sense? R. G. Beason. il Mech Illus 73:50-1+ S '77
Double take: Peugeot 504D and Mercedes 240/300D. il Car & Dr 22:103-5 Je '77
Driving impression:
GMC's diesel pickup. G. Witzenburg. il Motor T 29:57-8 S '77
Driving the Terra diesel pickup. M. Lamm. il Pop Mech 147:36 Je '77
Oldsmobile Diesel: PS 10,000-mile test. R. Ceppos. il Pop Sci 212:80-2+ Ja '78
PS car test & driving report:
Diesel Rabbit. J. Dunne and R. Ceppos. il Pop Sci 211:34+ S '77
Road test:
International Diesel Scout Traveler. il Car & Dr 22:94+ Je '77
Oldsmobile Diesel. D. Sherman. il Car & Dr 23:55-8 D '77
Volkswagen Rabbit Diesel. il Car & Dr 22: 87-8+ Je '77
Volkswagen Rabbit Diesel. B. Hall. il Motor T 29:39-40+ Jl '77
We test:
Olds Diesel. B. Tripolsky. il Mech Illus 73: 43-5 O '77
VW's new diesel Rabbit. G. Wilkins. il Mech Illus 73:46-7 Ap '77

DIESEL engines, Marine
Blueprint for power; work of C. Daigh. J. Thomas. il Motor B & S 139:84-5+ Ap '77
Converting the iron jib to diesel. W. D. Teague. il Motor B & S 140:49-53 D '77
Fire; hazards with diesel engines. J. West. il Motor B & S 139:68-9+ Ap '77
Living with a diesel. C. Miller. il Yachting 142: 82-5 O '77

DIESEL fuels
Diesel fuel—feed your engine a proper diet. D. R. Hart. il Motor B & S 139:15-16+ Mr '77

DIESKAU, Dietrich Fischer-. See Fischer-Dieskau, D.

DIET
Anti-tension diet and exercise plan. M. Mercer. McCalls 104:54+ F '77
Bazaar's 1,200 calorie fresh fruit diet. Harp Baz 110:88+ My '77
Bite by bite, count yourself thin; method of R. D. Black. S. Mines. il Read Digest 112:176-8+ Ja '78
Busy woman's diet plan. L. L. Lindauer. il Ladies Home J 94:77 Ap '77
California diet; with recipes. J. S. Stern. il Mademoiselle 83:214-15+ Ap '77
Calorie cutting on the QT. Bet Hom & Gard 55:184 Ap '77
Daydream those pounds away; tips for youth on maintaining diets. A. A. Belson. Seventeen 36:234-5+ Ag '77
Diet crazes. M. Clark and others. il Newsweek 90:66-7+ D 19 '77
Diet menu. J. Goldberg. See issues of Family health incorporating Today's health
Diets work better in a crowd. D. Cohen. il Psychol Today 10:96 Ap '77
Dr Fredrick Stare rates the 10 top diets. F. J. Stare and E. M. Whelan. Harp Baz 110:40-3 Jl '77
Dr Neil Solomon's calorie-free diet; with recipes. N. Solomon. Harp Baz 110:130-1+ F '77
Dr Neil Solomon's youth diet: be beautiful forever. P. Lehmann. Harp Baz 110:137+ O '77
Dr Solomon's healthy dollar-a-day diet. N. Solomon and M. Dolinsky. Harp Baz 110:131+ Mr '77
Eat and grow beautiful. M. Weber. il Ladies Home J 94:74+ My '77
Feast yourself slim; food served at The Greenhouse health resort, Texas. il House & Gard 149:102 Jl '77
Feasting on fat; liquid protein. L. Langway and others. il Newsweek 90:83 D 5 '77
Feel good food; diet menu at Rancho la Puerta health resort; with recipes. il House & Gard 149:173-5+ My '77
Food factor: diet; McGovern report. Vogue 167:168 Ag '77
Forget calories: think yourself thin; with menus and recipes; interview. J. S. Nevid. Harp Baz 110:233+ S '77
French food without the calories; excerpt from Michel Guerard's cuisine mineur. M. Guérard. McCalls 104:179-86 F '77
Gourmet blowouts that don't blow your diet. il Mademoiselle 83:170-3+ N '77
How safe are the liquid protein diets? J. Cook. il McCalls 104:51-2 S '77
How to create a family food plan that's right for you. R. Mirenda. il por Parents Mag 52:38-9+ Mr '77
How to diet in six languages. il Ladies Home J 94:78+ My '77
Hungry and wise woman's diet. il Redbook 149:104+ Je '77
Junk food diet; College survival tipsheet. J. S. Stern. Mademoiselle 83:178-9 Ag '77
Losing; dieting for outdoorsmen. E. Rogers. Field & S 82:145 Je '77
Losing weight made me a new person—a novelist. E. Babitz. Vogue 167:200+ S '77
Mine is the simplest diet in the world; how Mrs Dick Gregory lost 140 pounds. il pors Ebony 32:64-5+ F '77
Miracle diet for hair, skin, and body; with recipes. Harp Baz 110:78-9+ Ap '77
My no-diet diet. W. A. Nolen. McCalls 105:30+ Ja '78
My 1,200-calorie-a-day diet; with recipes. J. Child. il McCalls 104:144+ Ap '77
NRG diet; with recipes. N. Solomon. il Good H 184:80+ My '77
New action food for campers. J. Galub. Pop Mech 147:229-30+ My '77
New healthier foodstyle; low fat dishes. C. Cutler. bibl il Am Home 80:66-70 Je '77
No-food diet; liquid-protein regimen. S. C. Cowley and P. J. Seth. il por Newsweek 90:74 Jl 11 '77
Office diet. K. W. McNutt. il Harp Baz 110:90-1+ Je '77
Pickle diet. L. S. Bernstein. House B 119:161+ O '77
Please pass the fiber; bread as diet food. A. Entelis and J. Johnston. Am Home 80:58-9 F '77
Protein fad. P. Bonventre and S. Agrest. il por Newsweek 90:71 D 19 '77
Redbook's wise woman's diet. il Redbook 149:140-2+ O '77
Safest diet for every woman on the pill. F. J. Stare and E. M. Whelan. Harp Baz 110:120-1+ Ag '77
Special diet:
Delicious diabetic crepes. il Bet Hom & Gard 55:54 Je '77
Gluten-free desserts. il Bet Hom & Gard 55:70 S '77
Guilt-free holiday feasting. Bet Hom & Gard 55:214 N '77
Low-sodium ideas; recipes. il Bet Hom & Gard 55:96 O '77
Low-sodium recipes. il Bet Hom & Gard 55:182 Ap '77
Recipes for a fat-controlled diet. il Bet Hom & Gard 55:184 My '77
Spice is right: James Beard gives new life to diet food. J. Beard. il por House & Gard 149:117+ F '77
Stay-warm diet. N. Solomon. il Ladies Home J 94:100+ O '77
Summer shape-up: 5 sure ways to lose weight. Bet Hom & Gard 55:114+ My '77
Think thin and get thin. J. Adams. Read Digest 110:113-16 Ap '77
Thinner with Skinner: a food critic's strategy for belly modification. R. Sokolov. il Psychol Today 11:98+ Je '77
Tips from dieters. Seventeen 36:122 Ag '77
Tips from top cooks; recipes for fat, salt and sugar modified diets. House & Gard 149:101+ Jl '77
Two cheers for the unfit. M. Greenfield Newsweek 91:68 Ja 2 '78
Two-week crash diet; with recipes. J. S. Stern. Mademoiselle 83:137 D '77
Why losing weight is easier for men. B. H. Hoffman. McCalls 104:67 Jl '77
Winning looks; winners of Seventeen's losers take all diet contest. il Seventeen 36:110 Mr '77
Woman doctor's diet; excerpt from A woman doctor's diet for women. B. Edelstein. il Ladies Home J 94:169-76 N '77
You and your diet. See issues of Good housekeeping
See also
Athletes—Nutrition
Blacks—Nutrition
Children—Nutrition
College students—Nutrition
Dancers—Nutrition
Fasting
Food habits
Infants—Nutrition
Iron in diet
Jews—Dietary laws
Obesity
Proteins
Vegetarianism
Vitamins
Weight Watchers, Inc
Youth—Nutrition
also headings beginning Nutrition

DIET in disease
Anti-migraine diet. J. B. Brainard. Harp Baz 111:159+ N '77
Common food allergies; with recipes. il Good H 184:172+ F '77
From soup and salad to suppleness; C. H. Dong. S. I. Hayakawa. por Sat Eve Post 249:39 Mr '77
Pauling: just try to find the answer; interview. L. Pauling. il por Sci Digest 82:54-7 Ag '77
Season food the smart way—it could lengthen your life; effect of salt on health. S. L. Halpern. Vogue 167:80 O '77
See also
Cancer—Nutritional aspects
Diabetes—Nutritional aspects
Heart—Diseases—Nutritional aspects
Mental illness—Nutritional aspects

DIET pills. See Weight reducing preparations

DIETARY laws, Jewish. See Jews—Dietary laws

DIETHER, Doris
Dance. il Am Rec G 40:52-3 N; 59-62 D '76; 55 Je; 49-51 O '77

DIETHYL hydroxylamine. See Hydroxylamine

DIETHYLSTILBESTROL. See Stilbestrols

DIETS. See Diet

DIETZ, George
Gee, I didn't know you did that well. il por Forbes 119:49 F 1 '77 *

DIETZ, J. Jeffrey. See Clay, K. jt auth

DIETZ, Lew. See Goodridge, H. jt auth

DIETZ, Robert S.
San Andreas: an oceanic fault that came ashore; with biographical sketch. il Sea Front 23:258-66, 318 S '77

DIFFERENTIALS, Wage. See Wage differentials

DIFFERENTIATION (biology)
Differentiating limb tissue affects neurite growth in spinal cord cultures. E. D. Pollack and V. Liebig. bibl il Science 197:899-900 Ag 26 '77
Glia maturation factor: effect on chemical differentiation of glioblasts in culture. R. Lim and others. bibl il Science 195:195-6 Ja 14 '77

DIFFERENTIATION (biology)—*Continued*
Goblet cells in embryonic intestine: accelerated differentiation in culture. B. L. Black and F. Moog. bibl il Science 197:368-70 Jl 22 '77
Stability of the individual globin genes during erythroid differentiation. E. Benz, Jr and others. bibl il Science 196:1213-14 Je 10 '77
See also
Morphogenesis
DIFFICULT children. See Problem children
DIFFILY, John
Field guide to Roger Tory Peterson. il por Am Artist 41:28-33+ Ap '77
DIFFUSION
Comparison of radioactive and stable Tl^{+} diffusion in potassium chloride: demonstration of a transmutation effect. G. C. T. Wei and B. J. Wuensch. bibl il Science 197:159-61 Jl 8 '77
Lateral diffusion in planar lipid bilayers. P. F. Fahey and others. bibl il Science 195:305-6 Ja 21 '77
Lateral transport of a lipid probe and labeled proteins on a cell membrane. J. Schlessinger and others. bibl il Science 195:307-9 Ja 21 '77
Transmutation products may influence radiotracer diffusion rates in an ionic solid. G. C. T. Wei and B. J. Wuensch. bibl il Science 197:157-9 Jl 8 '77
DIFLUBENZURON. See Insecticides
DIGBY, Lady Jane. See Ellenborough, J. E. D. L. Countess of
DIGENIC acid. See Kainic acid
DIGESTIVE system
Burp! food critics' gastrointestinal tracts. il Esquire 87:70-3+ Je '77
See also
Colon (anatomy)
Stomach
DIGIACOMO, James J.
Why Johnny can't pray. il America 137:414-18 D 10 '77
DI GIOVANNI, Norman Thomas
(tr) See Borges, J. L. Avelino Arredondo
(tr) See Borges, J. L. Mirror and the mask
(tr) See Borges, J. L. Night of the gifts
(tr) See Borges, J. L. Ulrike
(tr) See Borges, J. L. Undr
DIGITAL clocks, Electronic. See Clocks, Electronic
DIGITAL electronics
Flip-flops and decade counters. F. M. Mims. il Pop Electr 11:75-6 F; 96-8 Mr '77
From bits into pieces. I. Berger. il Sat R 4:32-3 Jl 23 '77
How to design TTL digital systems. J. Huffman. il Pop Electr 12:56-8 O '77
How's & why's of D/A and A/D converters. R. D. Pascoe. il Pop Electr 11:53-6 Ap '77
Logical look at digital circuits. J. Darr. il Radio-Electr 48:74+ O '77
DIGITAL readout displays. See Information display systems
DIGITAL to analog converters. See Computers—Input-output equipment
DIGITAL watches, Electronic. See Watches, Electric
DIHYDROCHALCONES. See Chalcones
DIHYDROFOLATE reductase. See Reductases
DIHYDROXYCHOLECALCIFEROL. See Vitamins—Vitamin D
DIHYDROXYVITAMIN D. See Vitamins—Vitamin D
DIISOCYANATES. See Isocyanates
DILIBERTO, Danny
Easy times the hard way. B. McDermott. il Sports Illus 47:54-62+ Ag 8 '77 *
DILL, Barbara
Picturely books for children. See issues of Wilson library bulletin to June 1977
DILL
All dilled up. R. Langer. il House & Gard 149:10 O '77
Thrill of dill. R. B. Lee. il Org Gard & Farm 24:90-1 N '77
DILLARD, Annie
Mirages; story. Harpers 225:84-5 D '77
DILLINGHAM, Leslie
Reviews. S. Banes. Dance Mag 51:34 Ap '77 *
DILLMAN, Bradford
To save a child. il McCalls 105:104+ N '77
DILLMAN, Don A. and Tremblay, K. R. Jr
Quality of life in rural America. bibl f Ann Am Acad 429:115-29 Ja '77
DILLON, Diane
Leo Dillon. Horn Bk 53:423-5 Ag '77
—See Dillon, L. jt auth
about
Diane Dillon. L. Dillon. Horn Bk 53:422-3 Ag '77 *
Leo and Diane Dillon. L. Dillon. il pors Horn Bk 53:425-6 Ag '77 *
DILLON, Elizabeth A.
Staff development: bright hope or empty promise? Educ Digest 42:12-15 Ap '77
DILLON, Jack
(ed) Shark. il Oceans 10:8-47 N '77
DILLON, Lee
Leo and Diane Dillon. il pors Horn Bk 53:425-6 Ag '77
DILLON, Leo
Diane Dillon. Horn Bk 53:422-3 Ag '77
—and Dillon, Diane
Caldecott Award acceptance; address, June 18, 1977. Horn Bk 53:415-21 Ag '77
about
Leo and Diane Dillon. L. Dillon. il pors Horn Bk 53:425-6 Ag '77 *
Leo Dillon. D. Dillon. Horn Bk 53:423-5 Ag '77 *
DILLON, Melinda
Wedding for Dillon. il por Horizon 21:93 Ja '78 *
DILS, Maynard
Mechanical collection puts lid on refuse inflation. il Am City & County 92:31-2 Ja '77
DILWORTH, Collett B. Jr
Reader as poet: a strategy for creative reading. bibl f il Engl J 66:43-7 F '77
To the external consultant from his/her audience: what we want to hear and see. Clearing H 51:180-2 D '77
DI MARE, Dominic
Paper, wood, and string of Dominic Di Mare; interview, ed by M. Fuller. il Craft Horiz 37:52-5 Je '77
DIMATTIA, Susan
(comp) Business books of 1976. il Lib J 102:554-9 Mr 1 '77
DIMENSIONAL analysis
Fractals: a world of nonintegral dimensions. L. A. Steen. il Sci N 112:122-3 Ag 20 '77
DIMETHYL sulfide. See Methyl sulfide
DIMICK, Horace E.
Guns by Dimick. C. Worman. il Hobbies 82:154-5 N '77 *
DIMMA, William A.
Toronto Star goes on a multimedia binge. por Bus W p68-9 F 7 '77 *
DIMORPHISM (biology)
Sexual dimorphism and mating systems: how did they evolve? G. B. Kolata. Science 195:382-3 Ja 28 '77
DINE, Jim
Jim Dine and the life of objects; interview, ed by J. Gruen. il pors Art N 76:38-42 S '77
about
Beaux arts; exhibition. R. Berenson. Nat R 29:342 Mr 18 '77 *
Color them masters; Pace Gallery show, New York city. M. Stevens. il Newsweek 89:80-1 F 14 '77 *
Self-portraits in empty robes; show at Manhattan's Pace Gallery. R. Hughes. il Time 109:65 F 14 '77 *
DINERS (restaurants) See Restaurants
DINESEN, Isak, pseud. See Blixen, K. D.
DINGHIES. See Boats and boating
DINH, Tran-van-. See Tran-van-Dinh
DINING. See Dinners and dining
DINING clubs. See Clubs
DINING rooms
Charming kitchen-dining room. il House & Gard 149:64-5+ Jl '77
Kitchen switched with dining room, now opens to the garden. il Sunset 159:126 O '77
New look at an old tradition. il McCalls 104:206-9 Ap '77
Shared traditions. il Ladies Home J 94:122-5 My '77
DINNEEN, G. P. and Frick, F. C.
Electronics and national defense: a case study. bibl il Science 195:1151-5 Mr 18 '77
DINNERS and dining
Adjustable dinner for 2 or 4. il Bet Hom & Gard 55:34 My '77
Art of eating out all alone. J. Villas. il por Esquire 88:101-2+ Jl '77
Be our guest: favorite dishes from McCall's dining room; with menu and recipes. il McCalls 104:106-7+ Ap '77
Dinner plans from Mary McFadden. M. McFadden. Vogue 167:146-7 D '77
Fast food at home; with recipes. il Ladies Home J 94:138-9+ O; 106 N '77
5 creative dinners, all ready to serve in just 30 minutes. H. McCully. il House B 119:136+ N '77
For working mothers: ready-on-time dinners; with recipes. R. Molter. il Parents Mag 52:48-50+ Ap '77
Gourmet blowouts that don't blow your diet. il Mademoiselle 83:170-3+ N '77
Great meals-in-minutes cookbook. M. Happel. il Good H 184:130-9+ Ap '77
How to be an instant gourmet; with recipes. M. Stevens. Harp Baz 110:129+ Ag '77
In the spirit of joy and some joy of the spirit; sports award banquet circuit. R. Reid. il Sports Illus 46:32-7 F 28 '77
It happened in New Orleans; grand banquet for the winners of the Holiday Fine Dining Awards. C. Turgeon. Holiday 58:14-15 Ja '77

DINNERS and dining—*Continued*
Long live Sunday dinner. G. Steves. il Am Home 80:66-7+ Mr '77
Menus for people who can't wait for dessert. il Redbook 149:120-1+ Je '77
New nightlife:
Dinner-partying. C. Curtis. il Vogue 167: 255+ N '77
Eating and drinking. J. Robinson. Vogue 167:251 N '77
No time to cook. See issues of McCall's
Redbook's competent cook serves a luxurious company dinner. il Redbook 149:142-3+ My '77
Sunday dinner—it's only the beginning! great two-for-one meals; with recipes. il Redbook 148:128-9+ Ap '77
Two-course sit-down dinner. il Bet Hom & Gard 55:148-9 N '77
See also
Buffet meals
Christmas dinners
Gastronomy
Thanksgiving dinners
DINNERWARE. See Pottery
D'INNOCENZO, Michael
Family under fire; address, March 23, 1977. Vital Speeches 43:431-5 My 1 '77
DINOFLAGELLATES
Histone occurrence in chromatin from peridinium balticum, a binucleate dinoflagellate. P. J. Rizzo and E. R. Cox. bibl il Science 198:1258-60 D 23 '77
DINOSAURS
Dinosaurs. J. Bosveld. il Sci Digest 82:31-2+ S '77
Rickety dinosaurs. il Chemistry 50:3 Jl '77
Telltale wishbone; Archaeopteryx and the question of direct descent of birds from dinosaurs. S. J. Gould. il Natur Hist 86:26+ N '77
See also
Plesiosaurs
DINOSEB. See Growth promoting substances (plants)
DINSMORE, Lee
Forgotten Kurds. Progressive 41:38-9 Ap '77
DIOCLEA
Degradation and detoxification of canavanine by a specialized seed predator. G. A. Rosenthal and others. bibl il Science 196:658-60 My 6 '77
DIODES
Detectors for lightwave communication. H. Melchior. bibl il Phys Today 30:32-9 N '77
Four-layer diode. F. M. Mims. il Pop Electr 12: 82-3 Ag '77
Laser diodes. F. M. Mims. il Pop Electr 12:94-5 S '77
Semiconductor diode. S. D. Prensky. il Pop Electr 11:101-4 Ap '77
Using LED's as light detectors. F. M. Mims. il Pop Electr 11:86-8 My '77
DIODES testers. See Testing instruments
DIOL epoxides. See Epoxy compounds
DIOMEDE Islands
Life on a cold rock. F. Bruemmer. il map Natur Hist 86:54-65 bibl(p97) Mr '77
DIOXIN. See Dibenzodioxin
DIOXIRANE
Dioxirane: nonradical route to smog. il Sci N 112:340 N 19 '77
DIPHENYL compounds
Bulrushes thrive on PCB's. BioScience 27:370 My '77
Chemical catastrophes; PCBs. D. Zwerdling. Progressive 41:15-19 F '77
Michigan episode; PBB contamination of feed. N. Cousins. Sat R 4:4 Mr 19 '77
PBBs: more effects and more exposure. Sci N 112:100-1 Ag 13 '77
Polychlorinated biphenyls: penetration into the deep ocean by zooplankton fecal pellet transport. D. L. Elder and S. W. Fowler. bibl il Science 197:459-61 Jl 29 '77
Reports & comment: Michigan; PBB feed contamination. E. Chen. il Atlantic 240:12+ Ag '77
Ron Thomas' horror story; my family was poisoned! E. Keiffer. il Good H 185:64+ Ag '77
Somebody simply goofed; PBB contamination of feed in Michigan. W. Chapman. Progressive 41:30-2 My '77
Town dilemma; PCB contamination of Bloomington, Ind. sewage. D. Jordan. il map Environment 19:6-15 Mr '77
Widespread PBB contamination can affect immune system. B. J. Culliton. Science 197:849 Ag 26 '77
DIPHENYLHYDANTOIN
Avian muscular dystrophy: functional and biochemical improvement with diphenylhydantoin. R. K. Entrikin and others. bibl il Science 195:873-5 Mr 4 '77
DIPLOMACY
See also
Diplomatic etiquette
International relations
DIPLOMATIC and consular service
See also
Diplomatic privileges and immunities
United States—Diplomatic and Consular Service
DIPLOMATIC etiquette
Marx and manners; Russia's standards of diplomatic deportment. Time 110:37 Jl 11 '77
Reflections on the Presidential style. W. F. Buckley, Jr. Nat R 29:512 Ap 29 '77
DIPLOMATIC immunities. See Diplomatic privileges and immunities
DIPLOMATIC privileges and immunities
Beyond the law. J. K. Footlick and J. Whitmore. il Newsweek 90:42 Ag 8 '77
DIPLOMATIC receptions. See Government entertaining
DIPLOMATIC recognition. See Recognition (international law)
DIPLOMATS
See also
Black diplomats
DI PRIMA, Diane
Loba recovers the memory of a mare; poem. Ms 5:66 My '77
DIPRIONID sawflies. See Sawflies
DIPS. See Appetizers
DIRECT energy conversion
Energy recovery from saline water by means of electrochemical cells. B. H. Clampitt and F. E. Kiviat; reply. A. F. Hadermann. il Science 197:598-9 Ag 5 '77
Pulsed power from explosions. D. E. Thomsen. il Sci N 112:281+ O 29 '77
See also
Fuel cells
Solar batteries
DIRECT mail advertising. See Advertising, Direct mail
DIRECTION, Theatrical. See Theater—Production and direction
DIRECTION finding
Survival in Boston; direction finding project for Arlington, Mass. school children. P. Orton and J Stevens. Educ Digest 42:19-21 Ap '77
DIRECTION finding apparatus
See also
Radio beacons
Radio direction finders
DIRECTORIES
Born again businessmen; Christian business directories. America 137:140 S 17 '77
Buying Christian; Christian business directories. A. B. Haines. Chr Cent 94:804-5 S 21 '77
Christian yellow pages. Chr Today 22:46-8 O 21 '77
God & mammon; Christian yellow pages. Time 110:114 N 28 '77
Tribulations for Christian ads; lawsuits against business directories for born-again Christians. il Bus W p 148 S 19 '77
See also
Camp sites, facilities, etc.—Directories
Resorts—Directories
Telephone directories
DIRECTORS, Bank. See Banks and banking—Directors
DIRECTORS, Camp. See Camp directors
DIRECTORS, Corporation. See Corporations—Directors
DIRECTORS, Motion picture. See Motion picture directors
DIRIGIBLES. See Airships
DIRKS, Raymond
High cost of whistling. T. Nicholson and others. pors Newsweek 89:75+ F 14 '77 •
DIRR, Michael
Fothergillas: a garden aristocrat. il Horticulture 55:38-9 D '77
DIRTY linen & New-found-land; drama. See Stoppard, T.
DIRTY words. See Words, Obscene
DISABILITY insurance. See Insurance, Disability
DISABILITY Insurance Trust Fund. See Social security—United States
DISABLED. See Handicapped
DISABLED veterans. See Veterans, Disabled
DISADVANTAGED children. See Socially handicapped children
DISARMAMENT
Amendments to Arms Control and Disarmament Act; statement, August 18, 1977. J. Carter. Dept State Bull 77:413 S 26 '77
Arms control impact statements again have little impact. P. M. Boffey. Science 196:1181 Je 10 '77
Arms control statement criticized. K. Johnsen. Aviation W 106:14-15 My 16 '77
Assembly to hold special session on disarmament questions next year; with text of resolutions. UN Chron 14:21, 102-4; 115-16 Ja '77
Date recommended for special session on disarmament. il UN Chron 14:28 O '77
Disarmament: new challenges and new opportunities; statement, October 18, 1977. A. S. Fisher. Dept State Bull 77:778-87 N 28 '77
Military and political challenges of the 80's; East-West relations; address, May 10, 1977. J. Carter. Vital Speeches 43:482-4 Je 1 '77; Same with title President Carter attends economic, Berlin, and NATO meetings at London with text of communique. J. Carter. Dept State Bull 76:597-602 Je 6 '77

DISARMAMENT—*Continued*
Non-nuclear arms control and disarmament; report of Pugwash Conference. Bull Atom Sci 33:34-5 D '77
Stonewalling on the arms control impact statements. B. R. Schneider. Bull Atom Sci 33:5 Ja '77
United States discusses disarmament issues in U.N. General Assembly debate; statements, with text of resolution, November 1, 18 and December 10, 1976. F. C. Iklé; J. Martin, Jr. Dept State Bull 76:17-29 Ja 10 '77
U.S. policy toward our NATO partners: traditional commitments and new directions; statement, May 23, 1977. A. A. Hartman. Dept State Bull 76:635-9 Je 13 '77
United States signs convention banning environmental warfare; statement, with text of joint US-USSR communique, May 17, 1977. C. R. Vance. Dept State Bull 76:633-4 Je 13 '77
What lies ahead in arms control? address, November 12, 1976. F. C. Ikle. Vital Speeches 43:166-8 Ja 1 '77
Why disarmament? J. Burnham. Nat R 29:486 Ap 29 '77
See also
Atomic weapons and disarmament
International security
United Nations—Committee on Disarmament
United States—Defenses

Conferences

Mr Waldheim states need for careful preparation for disarmament session. K. Waldheim. UN Chron 14:20 My '77
1921 SALT talks—and you are there. R. K. Massie. il pors N Y Times Mag p38-40+ O 2 '77
Western summation of 11th round of MBFR talks; statement, April 15, 1977. W. J. de Vos van Steenwyk. Dept State Bull 76:482-4 My 16 '77
Western summation of 12th round of MBFR talks; statement, July 21, 1977. W. J. de Vos Van Steenwyk. Dept State Bull 77:374-5 S 19 '77
See also
Strategic Arms Limitation Talks

DISARMAMENT Agency. See United States—Arms Control and Disarmament Agency
DISASTER insurance. See Insurance, Disaster
DISASTER relief
Climatic change: coping with nature's forces. R. C. Cowen. Current 195:53-6 S '77
National network on aging provides disaster assistance to the nation's elderly. il Aging 270:17-21 Ap '77
We've been asked: about the big surge in disaster aid. il U.S. News 83:55 S 19 '77
Where relief became disaster; south Florida. U.S. News 82:57 Mr 7 '77
See also
Emergency housing
United Nations Disaster Relief Office
DISASTER relief deductions. See Income tax—Deductions
DISASTER warning systems
Noisy silence: natural infrasound can warn of impending disaster. J. T. Dennett. Sci Digest 81:27-8 My '77
DISASTERS
See also
Avalanches
Cyclones
Disaster relief
Fires
Floods
Forest fires
Hurricanes
Tornadoes

Psychological aspects

Good news about disaster. V. Taylor. bibl il por Psychol Today 11:93-4 O '77
DISCH, Tom
Descriptions of the wilderness; poem. Poetry 129:249 F '77
DISCHARGED prisoners. See Prisoners, Discharged
DISCHARGES, Military. See Military discharges
DISCHE, Irene
Germany's terrorist lexicon. Nation 225:524-6 N 19 '77
DISCHI Ricordi (firm) See Phonograph record industry—Italy
DISCIPLES of Christ. See Christian Church, Disciples of Christ
DISCIPLINE
See also
Corporal punishment
Labor discipline
School discipline
Trade unions—Discipline
DISCIPLINE of children. See Children—Management and training
DISCLINATIONS in crystals. See Crystals—Dislocations
DISCLOSURE in accounting
Disclosure rules survive. il Bus W p86 N 14 '77
Inflation accounting is here to stay. il Bus W p 109-10 D 26 '77
Is forced disclosure inefficient? il Forbes 119:78 Je 1 '77
Sauce for the goose? accountants objecting to mandatory disclosure by small firms. Forbes 120:70 D 15 '77
DISCLOSURE (securities) laws and regulations. See Securities—Laws and regulations
DISCO dancing. See Dancing
DISCO music
Dancing in the seventies. J. Highwater. il Horizon 19:30-3 My '77
Down at the clubhouse with Dr Buzzard's Original Savannah Band. R. Cromelin. il Hi Fi 27:131-3 Jl '77
See also
Phonograph records—Disco music
DISCOTHEQUES
Dancing in the seventies. J. Highwater. il Horizon 19:30-3 My '77
Disco. S. Helgesen. Harpers 255:20-4 O '77
Disco beat. il Horizon 19:34-7 My '77
Disco survival system. il Mademoiselle 83:178-9 N '77
Discotheque scene. H. Johnson. il Ebony 32:54-6+ F '77
Hotpots of the urban night. il Time 109:56-7 Je 27 '77
Notes and comment; disco called New York New York. New Yorker 53:33 O 3 '77
DISCOUNT airline fares. See Airlines—Fares
DISCOUNT brokers. See Brokers
DISCOUNT houses (retail trade)
Day in the life of Sam Walton; Wal-Mart Stores, Inc. H. Seneker. il pors Forbes 120:45-6+ D 1 '77
See also
Arlen Realty and Development Corporation
Kresge, S. S, Company
Zayre Corporation

Acquisitions and mergers

A German expands in U.S. retailing; merger agreement between Vornado, Inc and Fed-Mart Corp. il Bus W p34-5 Ag 15 '77
DISCOVERY (law) See Civil procedure
DISCRIMINATION
Aspects of institutional discrimination. J. J. Harris, 3d and W. R. Bentzen. bibl il Clearing H 51:7-10 S '77
Bogus order of merit. New Repub 176:6+ Ap 2 '77
Conspiracy of merit. M. Kinsley. New Repub 177:22-4 O 15 '77
Emerging national consensus; public opinion on issue of reverse discrimination. S. M. Lipset and W. Schneider. New Repub 177:8-9 O 15 '77
Essay on the unfairness of life. L. Morrow. Horizon 20:34-7 D '77
Is reverse discrimination justified? interviews. F. Askin; E. V. Rostow. pors U.S. News 83:39-40 O 3 '77
Making up for past injustices: how Bakke could backfire; reverse discrimination. A. Etzioni. Psychol Today 11:18 Ag '77
Mr Califano on quotas. Commonweal 104:291-2 My 13 '77
Quota conflict; reverse discrimination vs affirmative action. Time 110:25 S 26 '77
Reverse discrimination: a brief against it. E. Van Den Haag. Nat R 29:492-5 Ap 29 '77
Sensible limits of non-discrimination; Time essay. F. Trippett. Time 110:52-3 Jl 25 '77
Should clubs have the right to be exclusive? M. Mead. Redbook 149:31+ Jl '77
Some are more equal; Supreme Court decisions affecting discrimination in education and political representation. B. Odom. Nat R 29:1114-15 S 30 '77
Trivializing discrimination. N. Lewin. New Repub 176:19-21 Ap 2 '77; Discussion. 176:9 Ap 30 '77
See also
Anti-Semitism
Race discrimination
Sex discrimination
United Nations—Sub-Commission on Prevention of Discrimination and Protection of Minorities

Anecdotes, facetiae, satire, etc.

Have-nots. R. Baker. il N Y Times Mag p4 Jl 24 '77
DISCRIMINATION (psychology)
See also
Visual discrimination
DISCRIMINATION in education
Follies of affirmative action. E. Loftus. Society 14:21-4 Ja '77
Question of fault; race problems in London schools. T. J. Cottle. Progressive 41:34-6 O '77
Science High; Bronx High School of Science. J. Lelyveld. il N Y Times Mag p 178 D 4 '77
See also
Bakke, Allan, case
Minorities—Education
Sex discrimination in education

DISCRIMINATION in employment
After cancer, the tough return to the job; study by the American Cancer Society's California Division. J. Gaylin. Psychol Today 10:30-2 F '77
Assessing affirmative action. H. X. Connolly. il Intellect 106:134-6 O '77
Blow to minorities; seniority systems decision by Supreme Court. H. Hill. il Commonweal 104: 552-5 S 2 '77
Bona fide seniority and racial bias; Supreme Court decision. bibl M Labor R 100:48-9 Ag '77
Calif. selection center eyes entry level skills. Lib J 102:1706-7 S 1 '77
Case of the 15 gardeners; racial discrimination suit against the National Institutes of Health. Nation 225:614 D 10 '77
Court strikes a blow for seniority. il Time 109:60 Je 13 '77
Day they didn't march. L. Bennett, Jr. il Ebony 32:128-30+ F '77
Eager new team tackles job discrimination. por Bus W p 116+ Jl 25 '77
Equal opportunity; address, November 21, 1976. J. L. Belser. Vital Speeches 43:251-3 F 1 '77
Fair play for drunks; Labor Department's proposal of affirmative action for alcoholics and drug addicts. E. Marshall. New Repub 177:7 Jl 23 '77
Fat people's fight against job bias. il U.S. News 83:78-80 D 5 '77
Furor over reverse discrimination. J. K. Footlick and others. il Newsweek 90:52-5+ S 26 '77
How to avoid charges of job discrimination; program at Motorola, Inc. V. Louviere. il Nations Bus 65:69 Mr '77
Immigrants, employers, and exclusion. B. W. Parlin. Society 14:23-6 S '77
Legal cloud over affirmative action. Bus W p40+ D 26 '77
New job discrimination: a matter of health. E. Cudlipp. Harp Baz 110:87+ Ag '77
Short people—are they being discriminated against? il U.S. News 82:68-9 Mr 28 '77
Statistical significance; case of alleged discrimination by Hazelwood School District, Mo. M Labor R 100:51 N '77
Supreme Court opens new term; cases involving public employees. G. J. Mounts. M Labor R 100:66 D '77
Taking a second look at equal employment opportunity. A. R. Weber. Duns R 110:9 O '77
See also
Age and employment
Deaf—Employment
Minorities—Employment
United States—Equal Employment Opportunity Commission
Women—Employment

Anecdotes, facetiae, satire, etc.
Life is unfair. W. Goodman. N Y Times Mag p6 Ag 28 '77

DISCRIMINATION in housing
Arlington Heights case. America 136:90-1 F 5 '77
Attempt to control thought; Justice Dept. complaint against American Institue of Real Esate Appraisers. J. J. Kilpatrick. Nations Bus 65:11-12 O '77
Common sense on race; Arlington Heights, Ill. zoning refusal case. G. F. Will. Newsweek 89: 80 Ja 24 '77
Intent, not impact; Supreme Court decision on Arlington Heights, Ill. zoning law. Time 109:52 Ja 24 '77
No singles allowed. T. Laver. Am Home 80:26-7 Ap '77
Right to refuse; rezoning refusal upheld by Supreme Court in Arlington Heights, Ill, case. J. K. Footlick and others. il Newsweek 89:77 Ja 24 '77
Setback in Arlington Heights; Supreme Court ruling on zoning. J. De Muth. America 136: 167-8 F 26 '77
Suburban iron curtain; Supreme Court decision on Arlington Heights, Ill. zoning law. Commonweal 104:99-100 F 18 '77
Zoning out low-income families in suburbia; Arlington Heights, Ill. J. S. Fuerst. Chr Cent 94:77-8 F 2 '77
See also
Blacks—Housing
Housing—Desegregation

DISCRIMINATION in sports. See Segregation in sports

DISCS, Video. See Video records

DISCUSSION groups
Consciousness-raising; truth and consequences. S. Arnold. il Ms 6:101-4+ Jl '77; Reply with rejoinder. H. M. Perl. 6:8+ N '77
How we grew a mothers' group. L. B. Hansen. il por Redbook 149:72+ S '77

DISEASE Control, Center for. See United States —Public Health Service—Center for Disease Control

DISEASE models, Animal. See Diseases—Animal models

DISEASE prevention. See Medicine, Preventive

DISEASES
Blood-type clues. M. Clark and D. Shapiro. Newsweek 91:70-1 Ja 9 '78
Casebook of the medical detective; work of H. Friedman of Philadelphia's Children Hospital in attempting to diagnose Legionnaires' disease (cont) D. Russell. il Fam Health 9:40-1+ Ja '77
Epidemic that was; Legionnaires' disease. E. Keerdoja and others. il Newsweek 90:6 Jl 18 '77
Found: the Philly killer, perhaps; Legionnaires' disease. Time 109:47 Ja 31 '77
Latest in health and medicine; more on Legionnaires' disease. il U.S. News 83:63 O 31 '77
Leads on the causes of Legionnaires' disease. il Sci N 112:180 S 17 '77
Legion disease: culprit caged. il Sci N 111:69-70 Ja 29 '77
Legion fever: failed investigation may be successful after all. B. J. Culliton. Science 195: 469-70 F 4 '77
Legionnaires' disease: nickel levels. J. R. Chen and others. bibl il Science 196:906-8 My 20 '77
Medical mailbox; questions and answers. C. Servaas. See issues of Saturday evening post
Need for a new medical model: a challenge for biomedicine. G. L. Engel. bibl Science 196: 129-36 Ap 8 '77
New clue to Legionnaires' disease. Sci N 111:39 Ja 15 '77
Philadelphia disease story; Legionnaires' disease. Chemistry 50:22 Mr '77
Profiles; views of L. Thomas. J. Bernstein. por New Yorker 53:27-32+ Ja 2 '78
Return of the Philly killer; Legionnaires' disease in a Vermont hospital. Time 110:68 O 17 '77
Tracking the killer fever; Legionnaires' disease. M. Clark. il Newsweek 89:78-9 Ja 31 '77
War on germs. M. Clark. il Newsweek 90:98 S 19 '77
See also
Communicable diseases
Diagnosis
Medicine—Practice
Parasitic diseases
also names of diseases, e.g. Lupus erythematosus; *also* subhead Diseases under organs and parts of the body, e.g. Heart—Diseases

Animal models
Antigen-antibody reactions in rat brain sites induce transient changes in drinking behavior. C. A. Williams, Jr, and N. Schupf. bibl il Science 196:328-30 Ap 15 '77
Basal ganglia cooling disables learned arm movements of monkeys in the absence of visual guidance. J. Hore and others. bibl il Science 195:584-6 F 11 '77
Bovine protoporphyria: the first nonhuman model of this hereditary photosensitizing disease. G. R. Ruth and others. bibl il Science 198: 199-201 O 14 '77
Cyclic GMP accumulation causes degeneration of photoreceptor cells: simulation of an inherited disease; retinitis pigmentosa. R. N. Lolly and others. bibl il Science 196:664-6 My 6 '77
Experimental diabetes reduces circulating 1,25-dihydroxyvitamin D in the rat. L. E. Schneider and others. bibl il Science 196:1452-4 Je 24 '77
Hypertension: increase of collagen biosynthesis in arteries but not in veins. K. Iwatsuki and others. bibl il Science 198:403-5 O 28 '77
Mucopolysaccharidosis in a cat with arylsulfatase B deficiency: a model of Maroteaux-Lamy syndrome. P. F. Jezyk and others. bibl il Science 198:834-6 N 25 '77
Niemann-Pick disease experimental model: sphingomyelinase reduction induced by AL-9944. N. Sakuragawa and others. bibl il Science 196:317-19 Ap 15 '77
Nude mouse: a new experimental model for pneumocystis carinii infection. P. D. Walzer and others. bibl il Science 197:177-9 Jl 8 '77
Paradoxical effects of amphetamine on preweanling and postweanling rats; possible animal model of minimal brain dysfunction hyperkinesis. B. A. Campbell and P. J. Randall. bibl il Science 195:888-91 Mr 4 '77
Prevention of autoimmunity in experimental lupus erythematosus by soluble immune response suppressor. R. S. Krakauer and others. bibl il Science 196:56-9 Ap 1 '77
Theta-sensitive cell and erythropoiesis: identification of a defect in W/Wv anemic mice. W. Wiktor-Jedrzejczak. bibl il Science 196: 313-15 Ap 15 '77

Causes and theories of causation
See also
Medicine, Psychosomatic

Nutritional aspects
See Diet in disease

Prevention
See Medicine, Preventive

Transmission by water
See Waterborne infection

DISEASES, Diet in. See Diet in disease

DISEASES, Hereditary. See Heredity of disease

DISEASES, Industrial

Health issues; ed by J. Waller and L. Whitehead; excerpts from De morbis artificum. B. Ramazzini. Craft Horiz 37:8+ O '77

Unhealthy jobs; excerpt from The picture of health: environmental sources of disease. E. Eckholm. bibl il Environment 19:29-38 Ag '77

See also

Anthrax

Industrial hygiene

Lungs—Dust diseases

DISEASES, Mental. See Mental illness

DISHES. See Pottery

DISHES, Soap. See Soap dishes, trays, etc.

DISHWASHING and drying machines

Built-in dishwashers. Consumer Rep 42:34-7 D '77

Portable and convertible automatic dishwashers. il Consumers Res Mag 60:7-13 S '77

You can make space to install a dishwasher. R. Stepler. il Pop Sci 210:116-17 F '77

DISHWASHING detergents. See Detergents

DISK tillers. See Cultivators

DISMISSAL of teachers. See Teachers—Dismissal

DISNEY, Dorothy Cameron

Can this marriage be saved? See issues of Ladies' home journal

DISNEY, Michael J. and Véron, Philippe

BL Lacertae objects; with biographical sketches. il Sci Am 237:20, 32-9 Ag '77

DISNEY, Walt

Gene slips us a Mickey. G. Shalit. il Ladies Home J 94:8+ D '77 *

Mouse that roared. D. D. Miller. il por Sat Eve Post 249:50 Jl '77 *

DISNEY, Walt, Productions

Disney way with the dollar. il Forbes 119:79-81 Mr 15 '77

Land exchange; case study involving Disney's resort plans and government land. R. F. Masse and C. Broussard. il map Parks & Rec 12:26-9+ D '77

Wonderful world of Disney—its psychological appeal; address, May 1975. M. Brody. bibl Am Imago 33:350-60 Wint '76

DISPLACEMENT (ships)

Bruce Farr talks about light displacement and the IOR; interview, ed by M. Pope. B. Farr. il por Yachting 142:72-5 O '77

How to calculate displacement. il Motor B & S 139:45-6 Ap '77

DISPLAY booths. See Exhibition booths

DISPLAY of antiques, art objects, etc.

How to make a room special with accessories. S. Van Zante and others. il Bet Hom & Gard 55:74-7 Mr '77

Living with things you love. il Good H 185: 122-5 Jl '77

They use hollow-core doors to make an art display. il Sunset 158:153 Mr '77

DISPLAY systems, Airborne. See Aeronautic instruments—Display systems

DISPLAY systems, Information. See Information display systems

DISPLAYS, Library. See Library exhibits

DISPOSAL of radioactive waste. See Radioactive waste disposal

DISPOSAL of refuse. See Refuse and refuse disposal

DISSENTERS

Censuring the Soviets; vote by the World Psychiatric Association. il Time 110:36 S 12 '77

Charge of treason; case of A. Shcharansky. F. Willey and F. Coleman. Newsweek 89:42+ Je 13 '77

Death in Cracow; dissenter S. Pyjas. F. Willey and P. Martin. Newsweek 89:50 My 30 '77

Dirty tricks—and worse. F. Willey and others. il Newsweek 89:37+ F 14 '77

Dissent and repression in the Soviet Union. R. Sharlet. bibl f Cur Hist 73:112-17+ O '77

Dissent in Czechoslovakia. M. Bergman. New Repub 176:12-13 F 26 '77

Dissidents v. Moscow. il Time 109:20-4+ F 21 '77

Dual messages to Washington. il por Time 109: 30+ F 14 '77

Eastern bloc voices that won't be silenced. A. H. Matthews. Chr Today 21:44-6 Mr 4 '77

Exile for heretics; East Germany. il Time 110:48 O 3 '77

From Russia, with dissent. il Read Digest 110: 102-6 Je '77

Fuse is laid for a new revolution; Russian dissident movement. B. Levin. il por U.S. News 83:66 O 24 '77

How important is Soviet dissent? tr by G. Daniels. V. Chalidze. bibl f Commentary 63: 57-62 Je '77

Inside Russia's psychiatric jails. L. Thorne. il N Y Times Mag p26-7+ Je 12 '77

Kremlin cracks down. F. Coleman. il Newsweek 89:69-70 My 16 '77

Mixed results on rights. Newsweek 89:63-4 My 2 '77

Nigeria's dissident superstar; Fela Anikulapo-Kuti. J. Darnton. il pors N Y Times Mag p 10-12+ Jl 24 '77

No to Maoism; Chinese. il Time 110:54 S 19 '77

Prisoner of conscience: the Bukovsky file. L. Elliott. por Read Digest 111:93-7 Ag '77

Rights—and wrongs. il Newsweek 89:54-5 Je 20 '77

Silent fall; Communist dissenters. M. W. Browne. il N Y Times Mag p63+ O 23 '77

Soviet psychiatric practices criticized; World Psychiatric Association. Sci N 112:164-5 S 10 '77

Statement by prisoner H. I. Butman to the chief of the Perm administration of corrective labor establishments (ITK-35) H. Butman. il Nat R 29:822-5 Jl 22 '77

Ten days that shook me up in Russia. B. Gelb N Y Times Mag p21+ S 18 '77

Wave of dissent in Russia's empire. U.S. News 82:35 Mr 7 '77

Writing on the party's terms; establishing the boundaries of Czech intellectual life. C. Sawyer. il Harpers 256:25+ Ja '78

DISTILLING industries. See Liquor industry

DISTORTION, Anamorphic. See Anamorphosis

DISTRESS signals. See Signals and signaling

DISTRIBUTION of goods

Improve distribution with your promotional mix. B. P. Shapiro. bibl f il Harvard Bus R 55:115-23 Mr '77

Logistics—essential to strategy. J. L. Heskett. il Harvard Bus R 55:85-96 N '77

DISTRIBUTION of motion pictures. See Motion pictures—Distribution

DISTRIBUTORS, Automobile. See Automobile engines—Ignition

DISTRICT heating. See Heating

DISTRICT of Columbia. See Washington, D.C.

DISTRICT schools. See Rural schools

DI SUVERO, Mark

Di Suvero in Grand Rapids: the public prevails. M. A. Tighe. il Art in Am 65:12-13+ Mr '77 *

DITCHES

Blasted ditches—new way to drain land. C. E. Sommers. il Suc Farm 75:no5 58 Mr '77

DITLEA, Steve

Music. il Am Home 80:19 F; 14 My; 14 Jl; 12 D '77

Platter patter: the top 40 music moguls. il Ms 6:66-7+ D '77

DITTA, Joseph M.

Winter poem; In another city; poems. Poetry 130:88-9 My '77

DITTMAR, David. See Benke, P. J. jt auth

DIURNAL rhythm. See Biology—Periodicity

DIVERSIFICATION in industry

Oil industry under siege: how it plans to meet the challenge. il U.S. News 83:73-4+ O 31 '77

Responding to divisional profit crises. R. G. Hamermesh. Harvard Bus R 55:124-30 Mr '77

See also

Corporations—Acquisitions and mergers

DIVESTITURE by corporations. See Corporations—Divestiture

DIVIDENDS

Dividends that grow and grow. il Forbes 119:72 Mr 1 '77

From one pocket into the other; dividend-reinvestment plans. Forbes 120:38 N 15 '77

Growth companies try a dividend tonic. il Bus W p89 My 23 '77

If you're looking for big dividends—. U.S. News 82:73 Je 27 '77

Multiplying dividends through stock swaps; W. Peters of Unicorn Group. J. Madrick. il Bus W p 126 Ap 18 '77

Profits in collecting preferred dividends. il Bus W p 118+ O 17 '77

Taxation

Coming tax reform: read the fine print. il Forbes 120:21-3 Ag 1 '77

Relief from double taxation of dividend income. D. T. Smith; discussion. Harvard Bus R 55: 168+ Mr; 164+ My '77

DIVIDERS, Room. See Partitions

DIVINE comedy; poem. See Dante Alighieri

DIVINE creation. See Creation

DIVINE healing. See Faith cure

DIVINE love. See Love (theology)

DIVINE providence. See God—Providence

DIVING

Diving champ at sixty; D. Brand. R. Bauman. por Ret Liv 17:49+ My '77

DIVING, Submarine

See also

Skin diving

Study and teaching

Diving into the future; program at the Florida Institute of Technology. G. Simmons. il Sea Front 23:38-42 Ja '77

DIVING by animals. See Animal locomotion
DIVING reflex. See Reflexes
DIVING stunts. See Stunts
DIVINITY schools. See Theological seminaries
DIVISION of powers. See Separation of powers
DIVONE, Eileen
Puppets, an educational experience. il Sch Arts 77:50-1 S '77
DIVORCE
Teaching about divorce. E. Bledsoe. Todays Educ 66:31 Ja '77
See also
Alimony
Children of divorced parents

Biblical teaching

Theology of divorce. R. F. Sinks. Chr Cent 94:376-9 Ap 20 '77; Discussion. 94:659-61 Jl 20 '77

Bibliography

Myth of creative divorce. E. Dienstag. il Psychol Today 10:49-50+ Ap '77

United States

Divorce kits. R. Barkin. McCalls 104:45 Mr '77
For women who wonder about divorce: a major report; excerpt from Divorce experience. M. Hunt and B. Hunt. Redbook 149:92+ S '77
Is divorce contagious? S. W. Olds. Ladies Home J 94:81+ F '77
Men's lib movement trains its guns on divorce courts. il U.S. News 83:42 S 12 '77
Pensions land in divorce court. Bus W p 104+ N 7 '77
Sad but necessary facts about divorce. F. Davis. Redbook 149:223+ My '77
Surge in no fault divorce and its spreading impact. il U.S. News 83:76 Jl 25 '77
What the Carters are doing to wipe out divorce in Washington. J. L. Block. il Good H 184:109+ Je '77
Why we can't stay married. T. D. Allman. il Am Home 80:66+ F '77
DIVORCE (canon law)
See also
Marriage—Annulment (canon law)
DIVORCED fathers
Divorced fathers. E. M. Hetherington and others. bibl il Psychol Today 10:42-3+ Ap '77
Fathers in name only. C. J. Lehr. il Parents Mag 52:44+ My '77
What divorced fathers miss most. M. R. Skrocki. McCalls 105:85 N '77
See also
Single parent families
DIVORCED persons. See Divorcees
DIVORCEES
Labor force patterns of divorced and separated women. A. S. Grossman. bibl f il M Labor R 100:48-53 Ja '77
Scenes from a divorce. C. K. Watts. por Redbook 148:82+ Ap '77
DIX, Eugene F.
Early graduation here to stay? Clearing H 50:219-20 Ja '77; Correction 50:319 Mr '77
DIXON, Jim
With diligence, you may find a treasure amid the junk. House B 119:54-5+ Ap '77
DIXON, Leon
Hang on to that balloon-tire bike! il Pop Mech 149:52-3+ Ja '78
DJANIKIAN, Gregory
After planting; poem. Nation 224:663 My 28 '77
DJIBOUTI
Ceremonies at the gate of sorrows. L. Griggs. il Time 110:27-8 Jl 4 '77
Lowering the Tricolor. E. Peer. il Newsweek 90:31+ Jl 11 '77
See also
United Nations—Djibouti
DO-it-yourself house building. See House construction
DO-it-yourself work
Doing it yourself is not always best. J. S. Russotto. il Ret Liv 17:39+ F '77
58 do-it-yourself decorating ideas all under $100. il Good H 185:118-27+ Ag '77
See also
Kit building

Bibliography

DIY—a Yankee tradition. A. Lees. il Pop Sci 210:158-60 Ap '77
Here's how to remodel by the book. House B 119:99 S '77
DO you turn somersaults? drama. See Arbuzov, A. N.
DOBBS, Jeannine
There's a little Helen Hokinson in all of us. il Ms 5:16-17 F '77
DOBEL, J. Patrick
Bearing witness and human rights. Chr Cent 94:751-3 Ag 31 '77
Stewards of the earth's resources: a Christian response to ecology. Chr Cent 94:906-9 O 12 '77
DOBELL, Elizabeth R.
Self-defense. Seventeen 36:194-5+ Ap '77
DOBLER, Conrad
I'll do anything I can get away with. D. Hurford. il pors Sports Illus 47:30-2+ Jl 25 '77 •
DOBRIANSKY, Lev E.
Whose shoes are you wearing? address, May 12, 1977. Vital Speeches 43:563-5 Jl 1 '77
DOBRIN, Arnold
Peter Rabbit's natural foods cookbook; excerpt. il McCalls 104:158-60+ My '77
DOBRYNIN, Anatolii Fedorovich
In the mirror: a Soviet reflects on the Soviets; interview. por Sr Schol 110:13 N 3 '77
about
Washington's favorite Russian. M. Kondracke. New Repub 177:19-21 N 19 '77 •
DOBSON, Rona
Rubens year: carnival in Flanders. il por Art N 76:176+ Summ '77
DOBYNS, Stephen
Rain song. New Yorker 53:36 My 2 '77
DOCKENS, William Silverington, 3d
Scholar who moonlights at T'ai chi ch'uan. il pors Ebony 32:44-6+ Jl '77 •
DOCKING in space. See Orbital rendezvous (space flight)
DOCKS, wharves, etc.
Easy-to-build boat dock. J. Seville. il Mech Illus 73:118-19 F '77
See also
Chicago—Docks, wharves, etc.
Marinas
DOCTER, Stephen
Businessman turns a dream into a reality. por Nations Bus 65:58 Ag '77 •
DR Buzzard's Original Savannah Band. See Rock groups
DR Seuss, pseud. See Geisel, T. S.
DOCTOROW, E. L.
New poetry; excerpt from introduction to The crowned cannibals. Harpers 254:92+ My '77
DOCTORS. See Physicians
DOCTRINAL theology. See Theology
DOCTRINE, Religious. See Theology
DOCTRINE of the Faith, Congregation for the. See Congregation for the Doctrine of the Faith
DOCUMENT ownership controversies. See Possession (law)
DOCUMENTA art festival, Kassel, Germany. See Art, Modern—Exhibitions
DOCUMENTARY motion pictures. See Motion pictures, Documentary
DOCUMENTARY photography. See Photography, Documentary
DOCUMENTARY television programs. See Television programs, Documentary
DOCUMENTATION
See also
Bibliographical control
DOCUMENTS
See also
Archives
Government publications
DODD, James P.
Contact lenses; interview. Harp Baz 110:117+ Ag '77
DODD, Robert T.
Kinky grass caper; story. Sat Eve Post 249:20-1 Mr '77
DODDS, Margaret Lacy
Christmas is coming. Chr Today 22:17-18 N 18 '77
DODGE, Marshall J. 3d
U.S. journal: Maine. C. Trillin. New Yorker 53:112+ O 10 '77 •
DODGE, Norton. See Hilton, A. jt auth
DODGSON, Charles Lutwidge. See Carroll, L. pseud
DODONAEA
Dense screen—only 4 years old. il Sunset 159:270 O '77
DODOS
Dodo ecology. Sci Am 237:81-2 O '77
Nature's odd couples; dependency of hermit crabs on whelk shells and Calvaria major on dodos. S. J. Gould. il Natur Hist 87:38-41 Ja '78
Plant-animal mutualism: coevolution with dodo leads to near extinction of plant. S. A. Temple. bibl Science 197:885-6 Ag 26 '77
DODSON, Fitzhugh
Weaving together two families into one; excerpt from How to discipline—with love. Fam Health 9:44-7+ S '77
DOEBLER, Paul D.
(ed) Book design and manufacturing. See first issue of every month of Publishers weekly
DOEFFINGER, Derek
Neither plant nor animal. il Conservationist 31:38-9 Mr '77
DOERDER, F. Paul, and others
Macronuclear subunits of tetrahymena thermophila are functionally haploid. bibl il Science 198:946-8 D 2 '77
DOERRER, Paul W. and Pulley, J. L.
Politics of curriculum development. bibl il Clearing H 50:260-1 F '77

DOG bites
How to prevent dog bites. J. E. Rodgers. il Ladies Home J 94:199-200 N '77

DOG collars. See Dogs—Equipment and supplies

DOG food. See Dogs—Food and feeding

DOG food industry. See Pet industries

DOG houses. See Kennels

DOG racing
Classic win for a precocious pup; Downing's victory in the World Greyhound Classic. P. Putnam. il Sports Illus 46:18-19 Mr 14 '77

DOG sleds and sledding
Aspen wilderness by dog sled. il Sunset 159:60 D '77

DOG stories. See Dogs—Stories

DOG training. See Dogs—Training

DOGFIGHTING maneuvers. See Military maneuvers

DOGS
How to find your lost dog. B. Tarrant. il Field & S 82:186-8 N '77
MS mystery; relationship between multiple sclerosis and pet dogs. Time 110:44 S 5 '77
Rapid brain cooling in exercising dogs; function of the carotid rete. M. A. Baker and L. W. Chapman. bibl il Science 195:781-3 F 25 '77
Tracking down a lost animal. M. W. Fox. McCalls 104:63-4+ Ag '77
Unusual dogs your family will love. B. Humeston. il Bet Hom & Gard 55:148+ Mr '77
When dogs run wild. D. M. Duffey. il Outdoor Life 159:84-6+ Mr '77
See also
Bloodhounds
Dog racing
Hunting dogs
Police dogs
Toy dogs
Watchdogs

Care

Basic yard rules for your outdoor dog. D. M. Lidster. Bet Hom & Gard 54:107 Ag '76
Dog bathing: easy if you know how. K. Larson. il Ladies Home J 94:198 My '77
How to be your dog's best friend; puppies. D. L. Hunter. Parents Mag 52:50 D '77
How to help your pet weather winter. B. Humeston. Bet Hom & Gard 55:266+ N '77

Diseases and pests

Does your dog have heartworms? Bet Hom & Gard 55:264 My '77
Guarding a new puppy's health. D. L. Hunter. il Parents Mag 52:40 S '77
How to pick a healthy pup; interview, ed by B. Tarrant. D. Royse. il Field & S 81:154+ Mr '77
Pet set: when your dog needs a doctor. D. L. Hunter. il Parents Mag 52:77 N '77
When your dog has worms. D. M. Duffey. il Outdoor Life 159:184-7 Ap '77

Equipment and supplies

Shock collars: training shortcuts or dog wreckers? D. M. Duffey. il Outdoor Life 159:152+ Je '77
Yabba-yabba, doodle-doodle; interview with inventors of the Doggie Washer. A. Blafford; C. Blafford. New Yorker 53:55-6 N 21 '77

Food and feeding

Pets; overweight dogs; excerpt from The good dog book. M. Siegal. House B 119:36 S '77
Strange truth about dog foods. M. O'Connell. il Mech Illus 73:110-12 Ag '77

Grooming

See Dogs—Care

Habits and behavior

See Animals—Habits and behavior

History

Man-made dogs. J. Clutton-Brock. bibl il Science 197:1340-2 S 30 '77

Kennels

See Kennels

Purchasing

Choose a dog you can live with. il Changing T 31:33-4 Je '77
How to pick a healthy pup; interview, ed by B. Tarrant. D. Royse. il Field & S 81:154+ Mr '77

Shedding

See Molting

Stories

Dog story. M. A. Robinson. Redbook 150:84 N '77
Dogs in our life; excerpt from The animals come first. M. Bowring. il Good H 184:68+ Ap '77
Lassie come home. E. Knight. il Sat Eve Post 249:60-1 Jl '77
Shaggy dog story. J. Yglesias and others. il por N Y Times Mag p87 F 20 '77

Training

Housebreaking your pup. B. Tarrant. il Field & S 81:162-4+ Ap '77
Now, hearing-ear dogs. il Newsweek 89:39 Je 6 '77
Preserving ancient skills; training Newfoundland dogs for sea rescues. il Time 110:72 S 5 '77
Your child can train his dog. M. S. Pierce. il Parents Mag 52:56-7 Jl '77
See also
Hunting dogs—Training

Caricatures and cartoons

Obedience school. S. Berenstein and J. Berenstain. il Good H 184:118-19 Mr '77

DOGS, Feral. See Feral animals

DOGS, Fossil
Chinese wolf, ancestor of new world dogs. S. J. Olsen and J. W. Olsen. bibl il Science 197:533-5 Ag 5 '77

DOGS, Wild. See Wild dogs

DOGS and children. See Children and animals

DOGS as actors. See Animals as actors

DOGS as drug detectors. See Narcotics, Control of

DOGS as gifts. See Pets as gifts

DOGS in police work. See Police dogs

DOGS in psychotherapy. See Psychotherapy

DOGWOOD
Dogwood and catbird. W. Trimm. il Conservationist 31:28 My '77
Native dogwoods. D. W. Stokes. il Horticulture 55:27-31 F '77

DOHAN, Mary Helen
In a word, history. il Am Educ 13:10-12 N '77

DOHERTY, Gail, and Doherty, P. C.
Literature (cont) America 136:81-2 Ja 29 '77

DOHERTY, James E.
At long last, we're planning for the future. il Int Wildlife 7:24-8 N '77
Hail, lobsterman. . .and farewell. il Nat Wildlife 15:42-9 Ap '77
(ed) See Costle, D. New day at the EPA?

DOHERTY, Paul C. See Doherty, G. jt auth

DOHERTY, Steve
Design on a small scale. il Sch Arts 76:80 F '77
Setting sail for Tahiti. il Mech Illus 73:104+ D '77

DOLAN, Robert, and others
Shoreline forms and shoreline dynamics. bibl il maps Science 197:49-51 Jl 1 '77

DOLE, Robert J.
Dole: a goat turns tiger. T. Mathews and J. J. Lindsay. il por Newsweek 90:39-40 D 5 '77 *
Path to 1980. J. Lelyveld. il pors N Y Times Mag p 110 O 2 '77 *

DOLINSKY, Marsha. See Solomon, N. jt auth

DOLL furniture
Smallest small packages. J. Goldman. Vogue 167:40 D '77

DOLL hospitals. See Dolls—Repairing

DOLL houses
Bottle houses for tiny dolls. il Sunset 159:107 D '77
It's the spare parts you buy that make your doll house convincing. il Sunset 159:126-7 D '77
See also
Doll furniture
Rooms, Miniature

DOLLAR. See Money—United States

DOLLAR sign
Birth of the great American $. J. Gustaitis. il Am Hist Illus 12:17-19 Jl '77

DOLLARD, John
Choice. C. Stephens. Chr Today 21:38 Jl 8 '77 *

DOLLARD, Peter
Lock the loonies in a stereotype! Lib J 102:1725-6 S 1 '77

DOLLIES. See Trucks (dollies)

DOLLS
Celebrity dolls; black dolls. il Ebony 33:153-4+ N '77
Dream of dolls; antique dolls. il Good H 185:156-9 D '77
Glossary of bisque doll terms. J. Chiara. il Hobbies 82:38-9 S '77
Mother Goose stitch 'n stuffs: nursery rhyme dolls and quilt. N. Lindemeyer. il Bet Hom & Gard 55:130-1 N '77
Mystery story: St Nicholas magazine doll. Hobbies 82:52 My '77
Papoose doll in one hour. il Sunset 158:136 My '77

Collectors and collecting

Dollology:
Baby dolls past and present. J. Chiara. il Hobbies 82:39 Ap '77
Celluloid dolls. J. Chiara. il Hobbies 82:38-54 Ja '78
China dolls. J. Chiara. il Hobbies 82:39 My; 38 Je '7
Dolls at the sea front. D. Hartlap. il Hobbies 82:39-40+ Mr '77
Forgotten facts about dolls of the past. J. Chiara. il Hobbies 81:39 F '77

DOLLS—Collectors and collecting—*Continued*
Dollology:—*Continued*
Kachina dolls. J. Chiara. il Hobbies 82:38 Jl '77
Parson and Jackson baby doll. J. Chiara. il Hobbies 82:38 D '77
Peddler dolls. J. Chiara. il Hobbies 82:38 O '77
Pennywooden doll. J. Chiara. il Hobbies 82:38 Ag '77

History

Dolls. il Sch Arts 76:33-40 Ap '77

Repairing

Moody business; New York Doll Hospital. New Yorker 53:17-19 D 26 '77

DOLPHINS (mammals)
Dolphins and/or tuna: an update on the problems of purse seining for yellowfin. S. M. Minasian. il Oceans 10:60-3 N '77
Hawaiian spinner; thermoregulatory behavior of the spinner dolphin. G. C. Whittow. il Sea Front 23:304-7 S '77
Lonely are the hunted; leopard seals, penguins and killer whales. F. Erize. il Int Wildlife 7:14-16 S '77
Memory for lists of sounds by the bottle-nosed dolphin: convergence of memory processes with humans? R. K. R. Thompson and L. M. Herman. bibl il Science 195:501-3 F 4 '77
Murder of the porpoise: closing in on a solution. V. Cox. Sci Digest 82:46-7+ Jl '77
Open season on wildlife laws; Marine Mammal Protection Act's regulation of porpoise kill by tuna industry. il Nat Parks & Con Mag 51:20-1 My '77
Orchestra conductors would make good porpoise trainers. K. Pryor. il Psychol Today 10:61+ F '77
Orcinus orca: separating facts from fantasies; killer whales. E. Hoyt. il Oceans 10:22-6 Jl '77
Photographic determination of group size, composition, and stability of coastal porpoises (tursiops truncatus) B. Würsig and M. Würsig. bibl il Science 198:755-6 N 18 '77
Troubled waters; effect of laws protecting porpoises in tuna fishing areas. il Forbes 119:56 Ap 1 '77
Tuna catch high, porpoise kill low. E. M. Leeper. BioScience 27:221-2 Mr '77
Tuna sandwiches cost at least 78,000 porpoise lives a year, but there is hope. K. S. Norris. il Smithsonian 7:44-53 bibl(p 152) F '77
U.S. tuna fleet fishes for foreigners; registry transfer due to new U.S. regulations that limit the kill of porpoises that swim with tuna. il Bus W p25 Ja 24 '77
View from the castle; pilot whale strandings on beaches. S. D. Ripley. Smithsonian 8:6 My '77
What price porpoises? Marine Mammal Protection Act and tuna fishermen. A. J. Mayer and J. Huck. il Newsweek 89:58 F 7 '77

Anecdotes, facetiae, satire, etc.

Summer of the porpoise. K. L. Fleming. il Nat Parks & Con Mag 51:17-20 N '77

DOLPHY, Eric
John Coltrane & Eric Dolphy: the Vanguard years. D. Heckman. pors Hi Fi 27:116-17 Ag '77 *

DOLPO. See Nepal

DOMALAIN, Jean-Yves
Confessions of an animal trafficker; excerpt from The animal connection. il Natur Hist 86:54-67 bibl(p94+) My '77

DOMANSKY, Yaroslav Vital'evich
Antiquity's great reporter-historian among the Scythians. il UNESCO Courier 29:9-14+ D '76

DOME Petroleum Ltd. See Petroleum industry—Canada

DOMES
See also
Geodesic domes

DOMESTIC animals
See also
Cats
Dogs
Goats
Pets

DOMESTIC appliances. See Household appliances

DOMESTIC architecture. See Architecture, Domestic

DOMESTIC Council. See United States—Domestic Council

DOMESTIC education. See Home education

DOMESTIC finance. See Finance, Personal

DOMESTIC quarrels. See Quarrels

DOMESTIC relations
See also
Divorce
Family
Family life
Home
Marriage
Marriage counseling
Unmarried couples

DOMINANCE, Ocular
Which is your better shooting eye? eye dominance. J. R. Gregg. il Field & S 81:90+ Mr '77

DOMINGO, Placido
Bel sogno; interview. ed by S. Von Buchau. pors Opera N 41:24-8 Mr 26 '77

DOMINI, John
Lessons from a lower level. il Sports Illus 47:72-6+ O 3 '77

DOMINICAN REPUBLIC
Dominican Republic: Caribbean comeback. J. Cerruti. il map Nat Geog 152:538-65 O '77
See also
Investments, American—Dominican Republic
Medical care—Dominican Republic
Santo Domingo

Description and travel

Dominican Republic: capital sights and sea sights. D. Hardie. il House & Gard 149:108+ N '77

Religious institutions and affairs

See also
Catholic Church in the Dominican Republic
Evangelistic work—Dominican Republic

DOMINION Bridge Company, Ltd. See Steel industry—Canada

DOMON, Ken
Ken Domon: a documentary pilgrimage; tr by M. Tsuji. T. Kishi. il Mod Phot 41:84-93 Mr '77 *

DOMSAT (domestic communications satellites)
See Communications satellites

DON Carlo; opera. See Verdi, G.

DON Giovanni; opera. See Mozart, J. C. W. A.

DON Giovanni (operatic character) See Characters in opera

DON Quixote; ballet. See Ballet reviews—Single works

DONADY, Bonnie, and Tobias, Sheila
Math anxiety. Educ Digest 43:49-52 D '77

DONAGGIO, Pino
Poignant backdrop for cinematic horrors; Carrie. R. S. Brown. il Hi Fi 27:80 My '77 *

DONAHUE, John R.
Women, priesthood and the Vatican. America 136:285-9 Ap 2 '77

DONAHUE, Phil
TV's Phil Donahue: bachelor father; interview, ed by E. Keiffer. il pors Good H 185:88+ O '77

about

Marlo Thomas: men, marriage & me; interview, ed by J. Ardmore. M. Thomas. por Ladies Home J 94:40+ D '77 *

DONALDSON, George
Carlson lecture: leisure time new challenge for the future. Camp Mag 49:4+ Ja '77

DONALDSON, Kenneth
Kenneth Donaldson's fight for freedom. R. Steinzor. Progressive 41:48-50 Ap '77 *

DONALDSON, William V.
Municipal departments must work together. por Am City & County 92:52 Ja '77 *

DONALDSON, Lufkin and Jenrette (firm) See Investment advisers

DONATION of organs, tissues, etc.
Give someone the gift of life: donor card. M. L. Schildkraut. Good H 185:250 O '77
Give yourself. Sci Digest 81:65+ Mr '77
Your cornea and kidney can outlive you. C. Hutchison. Ms 5:95-8 Ap '77
See also
Blood donors
Kidney donors

DONELSON, Kenneth L.
Forward to five basics in composition. Clearing H 51:60-3 O '77
Some responsibilities for English teachers who already face an impossible job. Engl J 66:27-32 S '77
YA literature comes of age. bibl il por Wilson Lib Bull 52:241-7 N '77

DONER, Landis W. and White, J. W. Jr
Carbon-13/carbon-12 ratio is relatively uniform among honeys. bibl il Science 197:891-2 Ag 26 '77

DONG, Collin H.
From soup and salad to suppleness. S. I. Hayakawa. por Sat Eve Post 249:39 Mr '77 *

DONGHIA, Angelo
First of all, I design for people; interview, ed by M. Gough and J. B. Reiter. il por House B 119:48-56 Ag '77 *
Now you can have top design for top value. il por House & Gard 149:80-3 Ag '77 *

DONIZETTI, Gaetano
Gemma di Vergy. A. Porter. il Hi Fi 27:86-8 Je '77 *
Like singing three Normas; M. Caballé records Donizetti's Gemma di Vergy. R. V. Lucano. il por Am Rec G 40:16-18 My '77 *
Lucia di Lammermoor. Reviews
Hi Fi 27:MA16 Ap '77 *

DONLAN, Dan
Drama and the three stages in the teaching of literature. il Engl J 66:74-6 F '77

DONN, William L.
Of rogue waves and little ripples. il Motor B & S 139:50-1+ Mr '77

DONNE, John
John Donne's The good-morrow. D. Grunes. Am Imago 33:261-5 Fall '76 *

DONNELLY, Doris
Child shall lead them. il New Cath World 220: 4-5 Ja '77

DONNELLY, Dorothy H.
This lover is faithful. New Cath World 220: 14-15 Ja '77

DONOHOE, Tony
Weekend with the Moonies. Intellect 105:338-9 Ap '77

DONOHUE, John W.
College-related church. America 137:122-5 S 10 '77
Cracks in the keystone. America 137:242 O 15 '77
Family ecology. America 137:456-9 D 24 '77
High school years. il America 136:107-9 F 5 '77
Island in the city. America 136:322-4 Ap 9 '77
Mr Hutchins' convictions. America 136:504-5 Je 4 '77
New Jersey mantra. America 137:360 N 19 '77
Patience. America 137:311-12 N 5 '77
Positive experience. America 136:236-8 Mr 19 '77
Vatican statement on education. America 137: 67-70 Ag 13 '77

about

We have a holy Bishop. America 136:539-42 Je 18 '77 *

DONORS, Organ. See Donation of organs, tissues, etc.

DONOVAN, Carrie
Clothes designed to celebrate the body. il N Y Times Mag p 123-8 N 27 '77
Milan designers come of age. il N Y Times Mag p 129-33 N 13 '77
What they're wearing at night. il N Y Times Mag p83-5 D 18 '77

DONOVAN, John, 1928-
Conference notes from all over. il SLJ 24:22-6 N '77

DONOVAN, John B. See Dyal, W. M. jt auth

DONOVAN, Mark
Platform tennis. il Sports Illus 46:74+ Ap 11 '77

DONUTS. See Doughnuts

DOOB, Penelope
National Ballet of Canada: two views from the present. il Dance Mag 51:63-7 Mr '77
Spotlight on: James Kudelka. il por Dance Mag 51:70-3 Mr '77

DOODLEBUGS. See Ant lions

DOOLITTLE, Glenn. See Greenberg, J. jt auth

DOOLITTLE, James Harold
Doolittle. P. Trenner. Flying 101:194 S '77 *

DOOR locks. See Locks and keys

DOORBELLS, Electric
Ready, world? A doorbell that changes its tune. il Consumer Rep 42:127 Mr '77

DOORKNOBS, pulls, etc.
American historical glass. M. Wollett and B. Wollett. il Hobbies 81:99 F '77

DOORS
Heat-wasting doors: you can plug the leaks. T. H. Jones. il Pop Sci 211:128+ D '77
Install a sliding door. V. D. Chase. Am Home 80: 87-8+ Ap '77
Lamu door carving. M. M. Michie. il Design (US) 78:26 mid-Wint '77
Metaphysical dimensions of a door. T. H. Troeger. Chr Cent 94:557-9 Je 8 '77
Patio doors that install in a day. R. Capotosto. il Mech Illus 73:114+ Ag '77
Product reports 78. il Archit Rec 162:61-6 mid-O '77
Windows and doors. M. Cubisino. McCalls 104: 123-4 S '77
See also
Garage doors

DOOYEWEERD, Herman
Obituary
Chr Today 21:30 Mr 18 '77

DOPA
L-dopa: selective toxicity for melanoma cells in vitro. M. M. Wick and others. bibl il Science 197:468-9 Jl 29 '77
L-dopa's second generation. Sci N 112:217 O 1 '77
Levodopa, fertility, and longevity. G. C. Cotzias and others. bibl il Science 196:549-51 Ap 29 '77

DOPAMINE
Brain self-stimulation: direct evidence for the involvement of dopamine in the prefrontal cortex. F. Mora and R. D. Myers. bibl il Science 197:1387-9 S 30 '77
Haloperidol: effect of long-term treatment on rat striatal dopamine synthesis and turnover. P. Lerner and others. bibl il Science 197:181-3 Jl 8 '77
Striatal efferent fibers play a role in maintaining rotational behavior in the rat. J. F. Marshall and U. Ungerstedt. bibl il Science 198:62-4 O 7 '77

DOPAMINE receptors. See Receptors, Neural

DOPE smuggling. See Smuggling

DOPING of semiconductors. See Semiconductors—Doping

DOPPLER microwave landing systems. See Airplanes—Landing

DOPPLER navigation system. See Air navigation—Aids and devices

DORAN, Bernadette
Feminist surge hits school boards. Educ Digest 43:28-30 O '77

DORDIGAN, Dennis, family
Giving thanks with Nancy and Dennis Dordigan. L. Henderson. il pors Redbook 150:93+ D '77

DORIAN, Frank
Along the memory trail; reprint from February 1934 issue of The music lover's guide. Am Rec G 40:58-60 F '77

DORMAN, J. Anderson
Illicit artifacts: a booming business. il Sci Digest 81:inside cover, 68 Je '77

DORMANCY (plants)
Greenhouse. J. Kilborn. Horticulture 55:48-9 D '77

DORMANN, Henry O.
Putting on the Ritz. il Holiday 58:8 Ja '77

DORMICE
Hibernation and body weight in dormice: a new type of endogenous cycle. N. Mrosovsky. bibl il Science 196:902-3 My 20 '77

DORMITORIES
Closet crisis; storing clothes in college dormitories. P. Dawson. Seventeen 36:32+ Ag '77
Coed dorms are a nuisance! J. Cohen. por Seventeen 36:67 Ag '77
Coed dorms are the greatest! K. Cady. por Seventeen 36:66 Ag '77

Fires and fire prevention

Holiday eve disaster; fire in Providence College dormitory. il Time 110:16-17 D 26 '77

DORMITORIES, Remodeled
Yale University is preserving its great late-19th-century architecture by remodeling the Old Campus. M. F. Schmertz. il Archit Rec 161:93-100 Mr '77

DORN, Edward
Comment. B. Howard. Poetry 130:287-8 Ag '77 *

DOROS, Paul E.
Tiffany glass at the Chrysler Museum, Norfolk, Virginia. bibl il Antiques 111:746-50 Ap '77

DORSAL column stimulators. See Medical electronics

DORSETT, Tony Drew
Tony D comes to big D. J. Marshall. il pors Sports Illus 47:38-43+ S 19 '77 *

DORSON, Richard M.
Squash memories. New Repub 177:29-31 Jl 23 '77

DOSTAL, Guel
Bottle fantasy. il Sch Arts 76:47 F '77
Missy goes Surrealistic. il por Sch Arts 77:22-3 N '77
Our own tax museum. il Sch Arts 77:64-5 O '77

DOSTOEVSKII, Fedor Mikhailovich
Crime and punishment; matricide and the woman question. D. Kiremidjian. bibl f Am Imago 33: 403-33 Wint '76 *
Dostoyevsky and the Grand Inquisitor; a study in atheism. S. R. Sutherland. Yale R 66:364-73 Mr '77 *

DOT (music) See Musical notation

DOTREMONT, Christian
Darling when you read this I shall be alive. M. Gibson. il Art N 76:104 O '77 *

DOTTED notes. See Musical notation

DOTY, Roy
Wordless workshop. See issues of Popular science

DOUBLE, D. D. and Hellawell, A.
Solidification of cement; with biographical sketches. il Sci Am 237:18, 82-6+ bibl(p 154) Jl '77

DOUBLE bass
Bass part in Haydn's early string quartets. J. Webster. bibl il Mus Q 63:390-424 Jl '77

DOUBLE cropping
Corn after wheat—a triple crop for Tom Justison. il Suc Farm 75:no4 K6 Mr '77
Double-crop corn: for livestock producers. il Suc Farm 75:no4 40+ Mr '77
Double cropping; symposium. il Suc Farm 75:no4 21-31+ Mr '77
How to get wheat off to plant soybeans earlier. G. Reynolds. il Farm J 101:M4-5 Ja '77
Interseeding and double cropping in a dry year. C. F. Marley. il Farm J 100:16-17 D '76
1,800 acres of crops on 1,200 acres of land. B. Coffman. Farm J 101:M8 Ap '77
Planter on combine speeds up double-cropping. C. F. Marley. il Farm J 101:H2 N '77
Two-story cropping; Hammons Products Company, world's largest processor of black walnuts. J. D. Ritchie. il Org Gard & Farm 24: 80+ S '77

DOUBLE-Crostic. See Crossword puzzles

DOUBLE stars. See Stars, Double

DOUBLEDAY, Abner
Way I see it. B. Catton. por Am Heritage 28:107 Ap '77 *

DOUBLEDAY & Company, Inc
Blood and money is target of $20-million libel suit. M. Reuter. Pub W 212:35 O 3 '77
Doubleday answers Haley; denies all charges. M. Reuter. Pub W 211:34-5 Ap 25 '77
Doubleday-Hotchner decision. M. Reuter. Pub W 211:22 Ap 11 '77

DOUBLEDAY & Company, Inc—*Continued*
Is Doubleday about to become an open book? il Forbes 119:28-9 Mr 15 '77
Two writers question the originality of Roots. M. Reuter. Pub W 211:20 My 2 '77
Why Alex Haley is suing Doubleday: an outline of the complaint. M. Reuter. Pub W 211:25 Ap 4 '77
DOUBLESPEAK. See Jargon
DOUGH
Sourdough explained. N. Albright. Org Gard & Farm 25:122-7 Ja '78
DOUGH modeling. See Modeling
DOUGHERTY, John J. Bp
Since we live by the Spirit, let us follow the Spirit's lead. New Cath World 220:32 Ja '77
DOUGHERTY, Mary Ellen
Christmas in Appalachia; poem. America 137:455 D 24 '77
DOUGHERTY, Richard M.
Innocents abroad. Am Lib 8:614 D '77
DOUGHERTY, Russell Elliott
U.S. strategic forces; address, March 16, 1977. Vital Speeches 43:584-90 Jl 15 '77
DOUGHNUT makers. See Kitchen utensils and appliances
DOUGHNUTS
Sugar and spice twists. il Sunset 159:196 O '77
Ummm. . .fresh warm doughnuts! with recipes. il McCalls 105:228-30+ N '77
DOUGLAS, Donald Wills
Douglas. G. C. Larson. il Flying 101:252 S '77 *
DOUGLAS, Jennie
Expand your garden with oriental vegetables. il Org Gard & Farm 24:78-81 D '77
DOUGLAS, John H.
[Articles on science and society] See issues of Science news
—and Miller, J. A.
Record breaking women. il Sci N 112:172-4 S 10 '77
DOUGLAS, Rose B.
Be careful where you aim those binoculars! il Ret Liv 17:28-9 Je '77
DOUGLAS, William Orville
C & O Canal dedicated to Justice Douglas. il por Nat Parks & Con Mag 51:20 Ag '77

about

Last word. il por Time 109:80+ Ap 11 '77 *
DOUGLAS-HAMILTON, Iain
Unforgettable elephants. J. C. Horn. il Psychol Today 10:88+ Ap '77 *
DOUGLASS, Frederick
Frederick Douglass on ethnology: a commencement address at Western Reserve College, 1854. A. McCluskey and J. McCluskey. bibl il por Negro Hist Bull 40:746-9 S '77 *
DOUKHOBORS. See Dukhobors
DOUTY, Harry Mortimer
Slowdown in real wages: a postwar perspective. bibl il M Labor R 100:7-12 Ag '77
DOVE shooting. See Pigeon shooting
DOVER, Del.

Education

See Education—Delaware
DOVETAIL joints. See Joints (carpentry)
DOW, Arthur Wesley
Arthur Wesley Dow. S. B. Sherrill. il Antiques 112:832 N '77 *
DOW, Ruth McNabb
How well do seniors eat? Title VII can help. Aging 274:12-14 Ag '77
DOW Chemical Company
Dow chemical's catalog of regulatory horrors. il Bus W p50 Ap 4 '77
Dow's pullout haunts California. Bus W p38 F 7 '77
Dow's strategy for an unfriendly new era. A. L. Morner. il por Fortune 95:312-15+ My '77
Nuclear partners: adversity breeds trouble between Dow and utility. L. J. Carter. Science 195:162-3 Ja 14 '77
Outrageous Mr Cherry and the underachieving nukes; controversy surrounding construction of nuclear power plant in Midland, Mich. F. Graham, Jr. il por Audubon 79:50-67 S '77; Discussion. 79:128-30 N '77
Reporter at large; effects of 2,4,5-T. T. Whiteside. New Yorker 53:30-8+ Jl 25 '77
See also
Dow Corning Corporation
DOW Corning Corporation
A shot—or two or three—in the breast; silicone breast injection. D. Larned. Ms 6:55+ S '77; Discussion. 6:4+ Ja '78
DOW Jones & Company, Inc. See Newspaper publishers and publishing
DOW-Jones averages. See Stocks—Price indexes and averages
DOWD, Nancy
Four-letter screenwriter. J. Maslin. il por Newsweek 89:68-9 Mr 7 '77 *
Slap shot controversy: did Nancy Dowd commit a personal foul? S. Braudy and H. Lyons. il Ms 6:31+ Jl '77 *
DOWD, Richard F.
Adjusting for risk in business investments. Intellect 105:355-6 Ap '77
DOWD, Timothy
Hunting the Son of Sam. T. Mathews and others. il map Newsweek 90:18-21 Jl 11 '77 *
DOWELL, David R.
Certification: more study needed. bibl Lib J 102:1720-1 S 1 '77
DOWELS
How to turn dowels on your drill press. C. Baker. il Pop Mech 147:174 Je '77
DOWLING, Colette
Confessions of an American guru. il pors N Y Times Mag p41-3+ D 4 '77
Going home. il N Y Times Mag p68-9+ D 11 '77
Outrage called Kiss. il N Y Times Mag p 18+ Je 19 '77
DOWLING, Elizabeth
(ed) See Ashe, A. Arthur Ashe: on politics & sports
DOWLING, John, Jr
Nuclear debate in film. il Bull Atom Sci 33:52-4 F '77
DOWN, A. Graham
Why basic education? Educ Digest 43:2-5 N '77
DOWN, Lesley Anne
Shall we compare thee to Lesley-Anne Down? R. Brown. il pors Esquire 88:104-5 Jl '77 *
DOWNES, Mollie Panter-. See Panter-Downes, M.
DOWNEY, Gregg W.
Is it time we started teaching children how to take tests? Educ Digest 42:6-8 Ap '77
DOWNING, George
How to massage your spouse. il Sat Eve Post 249:66-9 O '77
DOWNRIGGERS. See Fishing boats—Equipment
DOWNS, Hugh
Resources of space. il por Space World N-3-159: 8-17 Mr '77
DOWNS, Linda B.
Case for rosé. House B 119:97+ Je '77
Red, light & true. House B 119:159+ My '77
DOWN'S syndrome. See Mongolism
DOWNTOWN areas. See Business districts
DOWTY, Alan
Don't bank on it: the phantom of a West Bank PLO state. New Repub 177:15-18 Ag 20 '77
DOWTY, Leonhard
Miranda's star; story. Good H 185:112-13 Jl '77
DOWTY Aviation Division. See Airplane industry —Great Britain
DOXEY, W. S.
At the nudist camp; poem. Esquire 87:30 My '77
Snowbound; poem. Esquire 88:54 S '77
DOYLE, David
Angel named David Doyle. P. Herz. por Sr Schol 110:28 N 3 '77 *
DOYLE, James
Saturday night live! excerpt from Not above the law. il pors N Y Times Mag p40+ My 15 '77
DOYLE, Robert E.
Rivers wild and pure: a priceless legacy. il Nat Geog 152:2-11 Jl '77
DOYLE, Wayne
What is the problem? What is the solution? Educ Digest 43:14-16 O '77
D'OYLY Carte Opera Company
Gilbert and Sullivan: The grand duke or The Statutory duel. W. Botsford. Am Rec G 41:15 N '77
DOZIER, Carroll Thomas, Bp
Reconciliation in Memphis. R. R. Holton. Commonweal 104:38-9 Ja 21 '77 *
Rome vs. Memphis. Commonweal 104:355-6 Je 10 '77 *
DRABBLE, Margaret
Ice age; excerpt; story. Ms 6:68-70 N '77
Jane Fonda: her own woman at last? il pors Ms 6:51-3+ O '77
DRACAENAS
Houseplant how-to. il Bet Hom & Gard 55:270-1 My '77
DRACE, Terry
Bionic bassing. **il Motor B & S 139:84-6+ Je '77**
DRACHMAN, Daniel B. See Kao, I. jt auth
DRACULA, Prince of Wallachia. See Vlad II, Dracul, Prince of Wallachia
DRACULA; dramatization. See Balderston, J. L. and Deane, H.
DRACULA returns; drama. See Majesti, B.
DRAEGIN, Lois
After Isadora: her art as inspiration. il por Dance Mag 51:67-71 Jl '77
DRAFT, Military. See Military service, Compulsory
DRAFT resisters. See Military service, Compulsory —Draft resisters
DRAFT riot, 1863
Ashes and blood: the New York City draft riots. A. Cook. il Am Hist Illus 12:30-40 Ag '77
DRAFTING, Automatic. See Computer graphics
DRAFTING, Mechanical. See Mechanical drawing

DRAFTING of baseball players. See Baseball players—Recruiting
DRAFTING tables. See Tables
DRAG boat racing. See Motor boat racing
DRAG racing
Bracket nationals. il Hot Rod 30:84-5 D '77
Bracket racing America: [state] G. Baskerville and D. Wallace. il Hot Rod 30:35-8 S '77
Bracket racing America: [state] D. Wallace. il Hot Rod 30:28-32 Ag; 29-32 O; 35-8 N; 32-6 D '77
Cha Cha waltzed home; Summernationals. B. Newman. il por Sports Illus 47:26-7 Jl 18 '77
Drag wars; Winston championship. il Hot Rod 30:82-7 N '77
Heat wave; 1977 Winternationals, with editorial comment. il Hot Rod 30:7, 34-6+ Ap '77
Instant replay; Street Rod and Street Machine Nationals, with editorial comment. il Hot Rod 30:7+, 53-4+ N '77
Roddin' at random. See issues of Hot rod
Ruth & Shirley show; NHRA'S Summernationals. D. Wallace. il Hot Rod 30:42-4+ O '77
Too close for comfort. D. Wallace. il pors Hot Rod 30:22-3 D '77
DRAG racing cars. See Automobiles, Racing
DRAG racing drivers. See Automobile racing drivers
DRAGONETTE, Jessica
Historical tape recordings. L. Dumont. por Hobbies 82:58-9 Ag; 58-9+ S; 58-9+ O '77 *
DRAGONWAGON, Crescent, pseud. See Parsons, E.
DRAIN cleaners. See Cleaning compositions
DRAIN cleaning. See Plumbing—Maintenance and repair
DRAINAGE
How to keep your tile drains working. B. Gergen il Suc Farm 75:no4 L6 Mr '77
New tiling boosts corn yield up to 20 bu. il Farm J 101:26-7 N '77
Tiling still pays: drainage boosts efficiency, yields. G. Vincent. il Suc Farm 75:41 S '77
See also
Ditches
Storm sewers
DRAKE, Elisabeth, and Reid, R. C.
Importation of liquefied natural gas; with biographical sketches. il map Sci Am 236:20, 22-9 bibl(p 148) Ap '77
DRAKE, Frank Donald
NASA bans sex from outer space. N. Wade. Science 197:1163-5 S 16 '77 *
DRAKE, George R.
New tools for spatter-free pad painting. il Pop Sci 210:48+ Ap '77
DRAKE, Gilbert, Jr
Hunters of the flats. il Field & S 82:56-8+ Je '77
DRAKE, James A.
(ed) See Ponselle, R. Rosa Ponselle reminisces
DRAKE, John, and Peterson, Svend
President Carter and the honeymooners. il Nat R 29:433-6+ Ap 15 '77
DRAKE, Michael L.
Opening the locks to the past. il map Parks & Rec 12:22-7+ Mr '77
DRAKE, Robert
Forty-two game. Chr Cent 94:1224-6 D 28 '77
DRAKE, Ruth
Leadership: the teacher's option. bibl Clearing H 50:291-3 Mr '77
DRAKE, Samantha
Electrolysis: in praise of a new method. Am Home 80:24-5 N '77
DRAKE, Sylvie
Rothschild, tapestry, Mouton, and Picasso. il Holiday 58:48-9+ Ja '77
DRAKE Hotel. See Chicago—Hotels, restaurants, etc.
DRAKE Relays. See Running
DRAMA
Album of a play doctor. S. Kauffmann. Am Scholar 47:87-94 Wint '77
See also
Browning, E. B.—Drama
Christmas plays
Hale, N.—Drama
Halloween—Drama
Japanese drama
Lincoln, A.—Drama
Melodrama
Opera
Television broadcasting—Drama
Thanksgiving Day—Drama
Valentines Day—Drama
Washington, G.—Drama
Women in drama

Study and teaching

Case of the divorced reader. C. R. Duke. bibl f il Engl J 66:33-6 F '77
Spotlight on books. See issues of Plays
Student drama in the classroom: a solution to the end-of-the-year blahs. H. G. Larsen. il Engl J 66:54-6 F '77

Technique

How to write and sell that play. T. Kelly. Writers Digest 57:19-23 My '77
Playwriting: hints from a first reader; with list of theaters. J. Calender. Writer 91:16-20 Ja '78
DRAMA critics and criticism
Count Dracula of Shubert Alley; J. Simon. por Time 110:34 D 26 '77
Critic and the reviewer: responsibilities and expectations. D. B. Wilmeth. Intellect 105:423 Je '77
See also
Drama reviews
DRAMA festivals
Cervantes at Chamizal; Siglo de Oro Drama Festival, El Paso, Tex. W. M. Reid. il Américas 29:19-24 S '77
Forsaking the barn; Williamstown Theatre Festival. S. R. Lawson. Am Scholar 46:377-83 Summ '77
See also
Shakespeare festivals

Scotland

See also
International Festival of Music and Drama, Edinburgh
DRAMA in education. See Dramatization in education
DRAMA production and direction. See Theater—Production and direction
DRAMA reviews
Goings on about town. See issues of New Yorker
Off Broadway. E. Oliver. See occasional issues of New Yorker
Theater. Nat R 29:394-5, 504-5 Ap 1, 29 '77
Theatre. H. Clurman. See issues of Nation
Theatre. B. Gill. See occasional issues of New Yorker
Theatre. C. Hughes. See occasional issues of America
Theater. S. Kauffmann. See occasional issues of New republic
Theater (cont) J. Richardson. Commentary 63:74-5 Ap '77
Theater. G. Rogoff. il Sat R 4:46-7 Mr 5; 46-7 Mr 19; 36-7 Ap 2; 36-7 Ap 30; 42-3 My 14; 38-9 My 28; 48-9 Je 11; 50-1 Jl 9; 57-8 Ag 6 '77
Theater (cont) il Ms 5:34+ Mr; 6:29-30 N '77
Year's best. Time 111:59 Ja 2 '78

Single works

See name of author for full entry
Absent friends. A. Ayckbourn
Agamemnon. Aeschylus
All for love. J. Dryden
Almost perfect person. J. Ross
American buffalo. D. Mamet
Anna Christie. E. G. O'Neill
Archbishops ceiling. G. Weales
As to the meaning of words. M. Eichman
Ashes. D. Rudkin
Basic training of Pavlo Hummel. D. Rabe
Boseman and Lena. A. Fugard
Brontosaurus. L. Wilson
Caesar and Cleopatra. G. B. Shaw
Caucasian chalk circle. B. Brecht
Chapter two. N. Simon
Cherry orchard. A. P. Chekhov
Chez nous. P. Nichols
Cockfight. E. Jackson
Cold storage. R. Ribman
Comedians. T. Griffiths
Counting the ways. E. Albee
Crazy locomotive. S. I. Witkiewicz
Creditors. A. Strindberg
Daddy. E. Bullins
Dance of death. A. Strindberg
Daughters. C. Coss and others
Dirty linen & New-found-land. T. Stoppard
Do you turn somersaults? A. N. Arbuzov
Dracula. J. L. Balderston and H. Deane
Dusa, Fish, Stas & Vi. P. Gems
Dybbuk. S. Ansky
Equus. P. Shaffer
Eulogy for a small-time thief. M. Piñero
Exiles. J. Joyce
G.R. point. D. Berry
Gathering. E. O'Brien
Gemini. A. Innaurato
Ghost sonata. A. Strindberg
Ghosts. H. Ibsen
Gin game. D. L. Coburn
Golda. W. Gibson
Guardsman. F. Molnár
Hagar's children. E. Joselovitz
History of the American film. C. Durang
I was sitting on my patio this guy appeared I thought I was hallucinating. R. Wilson
Importance of being Earnest. O. Wilde
In the summer house. J. Bowles
Isadora Duncan sleeps with the Russian Navy. J. Wanshel
Jules Feiffer's hold me! J. Feiffer
Ladies at the Alamo. P. Zindel
Landscape of the body. J. Guare
Last street play. R. Wesley
Life in the theatre. D. Mamet

DRAMA reviews—Single works—*Continued*
Listening. E. Albee
Man and superman. G. B. Shaw
Man with bags. E. Ionesco
Mandrake. N. Machiavelli
Marco Polo sings a solo. J. Guare
Memphis is gone. R. Hobson
Merchant. A. Wesker
Miss Margarida's way. R. Athayde
Mr Puntila and his chauffeur Matti. B. Brecht
Molly. S. Gray
My life. C. L. Jacker
Naked. L. Pirandello
New York idea. L. E. Mitchell
Night of the tribades. P. O. Enquist
Night shift. M. Goldsmith
No man's land. H. Pinter
Oedipus. L. A. Seneca
Offering. G. Edwards
Old country. A. Bennett
Otherwise engaged. S. Gray
Pages from Parra. N. Parra
Passing game. S. Tesich
Passion of Dracula. B. Hall and D. Richmond
Past tense. J. Zeman
Peg o' my heart. J. H. Manners
Photograph. N. Shange
Play and other plays. S. Beckett
Rum an Coca-Cola. M. Matura
Saint Joan. G. B. Shaw
Savages. C. Hampton
Shadow box. M. Cristofer
Side show. W. Dews
Sly fox. L. Gelbart
Sorrow beyond dreams. P. Handke
Survival. F. D. Kekana and others
Tales from the Vienna woods. O. von Horváth
Tartuffe. J. B. P. Molière
Terra nova. T. Tally
Three sisters. A. P. Chekhov
Touch of the poet. E. G. O'Neill
Transfiguration of Benno Blimpie. A. Innaurato
Treats. C. Hampton
Trip back down. J. Bishop
Ulysses in traction. A. Innaurato
Uncommon women and others. W. Wasserstein
Vieux Carré. T. Williams
Volpone. B. Jonson
Waiting for Godot. S. Beckett
Water engine. D. Mamet
Wayside Motor Inn. A. R. Gurney
White marriage. T. Różewicz
You never can tell. G. B. Shaw

DRAMATIC criticism. See Drama critics and criticism

DRAMATIC festivals. See Drama festivals

DRAMATIC readings
Off Broadway; Negro Ensemble Company's Square root of soul. New Yorker 53:54 Je 27 '77

DRAMATISTS, American
New blood. J. Kroll. il Newsweek 90:86-8 D 19 '77
See also
Hellman, L.
Mamet, D.
O'Neill, E. G.
Simon, N.

DRAMATISTS, English
The play's still the thing. R. Morley. il Sat R 4:12-13 Je 11 '77
See also
Stoppard, T.

DRAMATISTS, French
See also
Beaumarchais, P. A. C. de
Beckett, S.
Ionesco, E.

DRAMATISTS, German
See also
Brecht, B.
Wedekind, F.

DRAMATISTS, Irish
See also
Shaw, G. B.

DRAMATISTS, Latin American
Dramatists in revolt. F. P. Hebblethwaite. il Américas 29:6-9 Mr '77

DRAMATIZATION in education
Close-up: drama in the classroom; special section. Engl J 66:68-78 My '77
Creative drama in the junior high. G. B. Siegel. Engl J 66:110-12 Ja '77
Drama and the three stages in the teaching of literature. D. Donlan. il Engl J 66:74-6 F '77
Facilitating class discussion: another way. A. V. Beale and A. M. McLeod. Clearing H 51:67-70 O '77
See also
Role playing

DRAPERIES. See Curtains and draperies

DRAWBRIDGES
San Francisco's drawbridges will perform two days in April. il Sunset 158:70 Ap '77

DRAWERS
Drawers match odd angles and corners. il Sunset 158:148 Ap '77
Three cheers for drawer glides. il Sunset 158:98 F '77

DRAWING
See also
Architectural drawing
Mechanical drawing
Pastel drawing
Portrait drawing
Scratchboard drawing

Study and teaching

Surrealistic anatomy studies. A. N. Sponzilli. il por Sch Arts 77:24-5 N '77
Take off your shoes. W. Bitautas. il Sch Arts 76:40-1 Je '77

DRAWING and photography. See Art and photography

DRAWINGS, Childrens. See Childrens art

DRAZEK, Stanley J.
Adult continuing education growth: no time for complacency. bibl il Intellect 106:49-51 Ag '77

DREAMS
Art of dreaming; excerpt from The second ring of power. C. Castaneda. il Psychol Today 11:34-6+ D '77
Dream machine: end of a fantasy? il Sci N 112:405 D 17 '77
Dreams and your health. T. Beckwith. il House & Gard 149:28+ S '77
New vision of dreams. L. Cherry. il N Y Times Mag p9-13+ Jl 3 '77; Same abr. with title Why you need to dream. Read Digest 111:139-42 O '77
What's in a dream; studies by J. Allan Hobson and Robert McCarley. J. Seligmann and S. Begley. Newsweek 91:50 Ja 16 '78
Women's dreams; ideas of R. Van deCastle. E. Howard. il Ladies Home J 94:50+ Je '77

DREAMS in motion pictures. See Motion pictures—Plots, themes, etc.

DREDGING
Honorable discharge for the biggest pollutant; dredged and fill materials. J. Crowder. il Parks & Rec 12:28a-30a F '77

DREGNE, Harold Ernest
Sands of wrath: America's Dust Bowl in retrospect. il UNESCO Courier 30:14-17 Jl '77

DREIFUS, Claudia
(comp) Do I want a baby? discussion. il McCalls 105:203+ N '77
22 myths & realities about your body. il Seventeen 36:125-9+ Je '77

DRELL, Sidney D.
Beyond SALT II—a missile test quota. bibl il Bull Atom Sci 33:34-42 My '77

DRESANG, Eliza T.
There are no other children; special children in library media centers. il SLJ 24:19-23 S '77

DRESDEN

Music

See also
Opera—Germany, East

DRESDNER Bank. See Banks and banking—Germany, West

DRESS. See Clothing and dress

DRESS accessories
Good looks. See issues of McCall's

Manufacture

But will it last? Swank's fashion accessories. por Forbes 120:33 Ag 15 '77

DRESS designers. See Costume designers

DRESSING of game. See Game, Dressing of

DRESSING tables
Bathroom niche is just 4 feet wide; bathroom vanity. il Sunset 158:104 Mr '77
Old sideboard in the bathroom. il Sunset 158:108 Mr '77
Squeeze in a vanity area. il Bet Hom & Gard 55:282 O '77

DREW, Elizabeth Brenner
Our far-flung correspondents. New Yorker 53:82-8 F 28 '77
Reporter at large. New Yorker 53:99-117 Ap 4; 112-14+ My 23; 36-8+ Jl 18; 70-4+ Ag 22; 156-62+ O 10 '77; 32-6+ Ja 9 '78
Reporter in Washington, D.C. (cont) New Yorker 52:48+ Ja 17 '77

DREWIEN, Rod
Whooper rally. R. Barker. il map Natur Hist 86:22-4+ bibl(p96) Mr '77 *

DREXLER, Arthur
Pushing future directions in modern design. B. Diamonstein. il por Art N 76:43-5 S '77 *

DREXLER, Rosalyn
Is womanhood worth it? Vogue 167:94 F '77

DREYER, June Teufel
Ethnic relations in China. bibl f Ann Am Acad 433:100-11 S '77

DREYER, Leslie
Pitfalls. il Opera N 42:26+ O '77

DREYFUS, Rene
Woman we would have loved to love. B. Yates. Car & Dr 22:18-19 Mr '77 *

DREYFUS Tax-exempt Bond Fund. See Investment trusts

DREYFUSS, Joel
Black progress myth and ghetto reality. Progressive 41:21-5 N '77

DREYFUSS, Richard
Hollywood's flying object. pors Time 110:87+ D 5 '77 *
DRIED flowers. See Flowers, Dried
DRIED food. See Food, Dried
DRIED meat. See Meat, Dried
DRIED milk. See Milk, Dried
DRIESSCHE, W. van. See Lindemann, B. jt auth
DRIFTING of continents. See Continental drift
DRILLING and boring
Plastic cube with memory. il Mech Illus 73:153 O '77
DRILLING and boring (earth and rocks)
See also
Underwater drilling
DRILLING and boring (ice)
Devon Island ice cap: core stratigraphy and paleoclimate. R. M. Koerner. bibl il map Science 196:15-18 Ap 1 '77
DRILLING and boring machinery
Craftsman hammer drill. M. McClintock. il Pop Mech 147:44 Mr '77
Drill presses that go with you. R. Capotosto. il Mech Illus 73:108+ N '77
How to outwit a drill press; precision drilling guide. W. G. Waggoner. il Pop Sci 210:188+ Ap '77
How to turn dowels on your drill press. C. Baker. il Pop Mech 147:174 Je '77
Impact drills: the hot new tool. T. H. Jones. il Mech Illus 73:128-9 Je '77
Looking for a new drill? J. Roy. il Am Home 80:14 D '77
Versatile guide for precision drilling. D. Day. il Pop Sci 210:142 Je '77
See also
Bits (drilling and boring)
Jigs
DRILLING rigs, Gas well. See Gas well drilling rigs
DRILLING rigs, Oil well. See Oil well drilling rigs
DRILLS (machinery) See Drilling and boring machinery
DRILLS, Seed. See Planters (farm machines)—Equipment
DRINAN, Robert Frederick
Repression in Argentina. Commonweal 104:103-4 F 18 '77
DRINKING (physiology)
Antigen-antibody reactions in rat brain sites induce transient changes in drinking behavior. C. A. Williams, Jr and N. Schupf. bibl il Science 196:328-30 Ap 15 '77
Overdosing on water; case of T. Christopherson. Newsweek 89:46 Mr 14 '77
DRINKING and the clergy. See Alcohol and the clergy
DRINKING and traffic accidents
Drinking & driving: how many drinks are too many. A. Rosenblum. Good H 184:226 My '77
Drinking & the holidays. R. A. Dickelman. Bet Hom & Gard 55:10+ D '77
Smash-up! T. Morando. il por Good H 184:102+ Je '77
DRINKING and women. See Alcohol and women
DRINKING and youth. See Alcohol and youth
DRINKING customs
Revolution in drinking reshapes the liquor industry. il U.S. News 82:71-3 Mr 21 '77
Surprising changes in American drinking habits. C. G. Burck. Read Digest 110:163-4+ F '77

Anecdotes, facetiae, satire, etc.

Drinking man's guide to Las Vegas. J. Cronley. il Esquire 88:110+ D '77
DRINKING vessels
American historical glass. M. Wollett and B. Wollett. il Hobbies 82:99 Mr '77
Art you can hold in your hand. M. Siple. il House B 119:10+ N '77
Garfield memorial goblet. M. Wollett and B. Wollett. il Hobbies 82:99 S '77
McKinley milk glass tumbler. M. Wollett and B. Wollett. il Hobbies 82:99 Ja '78
DRINKING water
Drinking water safe? Needs research. Sci N 111:374 Je 11 '77
See also
Water, Bottled

Microbiology

See Water—Microbiology

Pollution

See Water pollution

Purification

See Water purification

Standards

Chlorine still best water purifier. BioScience 27:704 O '77
Drinkable, but. . F. S. Sterrett. bibl il Environment 19:28-36 D '77
If our drinking water gets tainted, you'll now be told; EPA standards. M. Zeldin. Audubon 79:127 My '77

DRINKS. See Alcoholic beverages; Beverages
DRIP irrigation. See Irrigation; Watering of gardens, lawns, etc.
DRISCOLL, Everly
Alfalfa yields a mystery chemical that spurs plant growth, even in the dark. il por Horticulture 55:8+ Ag '77
DRISKELL, Tony
Bromeliad boys at Nature's Way. C. Seagraves. il pors Horticulture 55:36-7 D '77 *
DRIVE-away system. See Automobiles—Transportation
DRIVER, Gillian Cooper-. See Cooper-Driver, G.
DRIVER training schools. See Automobile driving —Study and teaching
DRIVEWAYS
In the paving cracks, alyssum and much else. il Sunset 159:256 O '77
Lawn and concrete blocks get together in Hawaii. il Sunset 158:228 Je '77

Maintenance and repair

Fixup for driveways. il Mech Illus 73:122+ N '77
Patching and sealing a driveway. il McCalls 104:94 Ap '77
You can repair winter's damage to your asphalt driveway. D. Day. il Pop Sci 210:112-13 Je '77
DRIVING, Automobile. See Automobile driving
DROOZ, A. T. and others
North American egg parasite successfully controls a different host genus in South America. bibl il Science 197:390-1 Jl 22 '77
DROPS
Amateur scientist; persistence of water drops on hot surfaces. J. Walker. il Sci Am 237: 126-31 Ag '77
DROSOPHILA
Aldehyde oxidase compartmentalization in drosophila melanogaster wing imaginal disks. D. T. Kuhn and G. N. Cunningham. bibl il Science 196:875-7 My 20 '77
Courtship of patchwork flies. J. A. Miller. il Sci N 111:107+ F 12 '77
Genetic rescue of a lethal null activity allele of 6-phosphogluconate dehydrogenase in drosophila melanogaster. M. B. Hughes and J. C. Lucchesi. bibl il Science 196:1114-15 Je 3 '77
In vitro growth of imaginal disks from drosophila melanogaster. K. T. Davis and A. Shearn. bibl il Science 196:438-40 Ap 22 '77
Induction of acetylcholinesterase activity by β-ecdysone in a drosophila cell line. P. Cherbas and others. bibl il Science 197:275-7 Jl 15 '77
Isolation of eukaryotic DNA fragments containing structural genes and the adjacent sequences. G. P. Georgiev and others. bibl il Science 195:394-7 Ja 28 '77
Mechanism of suppression in drosophila: control of sepiapterin synthase at the purple locus. J. J. Yim and others. bibl il Science 198: 1168-70 D 16 '77
Temporal control of urate oxidase activity in drosophila: evidence of an autonomous timer in Malpighian tubules. T. B. Friedman and D. H. Johnson. bibl il Science 197:477-9 Jl 29 '77
DROUGHT resistance of plants. See Plants—Drought resistance
DROUGHTS
Aluminum smelters pray for more rain; Northwestern states. il Bus W p30 Mr 28 '77
As drought worsens: fears for the immediate future. map U.S. News 83:35 Jl 18 '77
Blue skies may mean brown links; effect on northern California golf courses. S. Pileggi. il Sports Illus 46:54+ Ap 4 '77
California fire report. J. McGuire Am For 83:6 O '77
California orchardists face the drought. M. C. Goldman. il Org Gard & Farm 24:60-3 My '77
Climate as accomplice; droughts, rainfall and desertification. F. K. Hare. il UNESCO Courier 30:6-10 Jl '77
Deep freeze, drought hit local budgets. il Am City & County 92:13 Mr '77
Drought fails to wilt California's harvest. Bus W p40 O 24 '77
Drought; Great Britain. Audubon 79:150-1 Ja '77
Drought watch: gloomy to grim. il Time 109:9-10 My 30 '77
Drought; Western and Great Plains States. il U.S. News 82:46-8+ Ap 4 '77
Droughts linked to sunspot cycle. il Chemistry 50:23-4 My '77
Dry threat to the West. L. Langway and W. J. Cook. il Newsweek 89:72 F 14 '77
Dust concentration in the atmosphere of the equatorial North Atlantic: possible relationship to the Sahelian drought. J. M. Prospero and R. T. Nees. bibl il Science 196:1196-8 Je 10 '77
Europe's sizzling summer. R. Ferguson. il Read Digest 110:131-4 My '77
Forest Service is ready; fire hazards resulting from drought in the Pacific Northwest. J. B. Craig. Am For 83:6 Ag '77

DROUGHTS—*Continued*
Going dry; San Francisco. S. Fraker and W. J. Cook. il Newsweek 89:32 Ap 18 '77
Great California drought; adaptation of address, June 3, 1977. J. H. Lauten. il Am For 83:16-19 O '77
Great western drought of 1977. il map Time 109:76-81 Mr 7 '77
In California, new perils from unbroken drought. U.S. News 82:24 Je 27 '77
In the West, drought is the worry. U.S. News 82:41 Ja 31 '77
Just trying to survive; Southeast. il map Time 110:30+ Jl 11 '77
Long dry winter; western U.S. S. Fraker and others. il Newsweek 89:22+ Mr 7 '77
1976 and 1977 drought in California: extent and severity. M. L. Shelton. il map Weatherwise 30:139-46+ Ag '77
Our changing weather. G. Alexander. il maps Pop Sci 211:90-4 S '77
Science, the public and the American drought. il Sci N 111:132 F 26 '77
Scorched earth; San Joaquin Valley. P. Brinkley-Rogers. il Newsweek 89:40 Ap 11 '77
Spreading impact of worst drought in decades. il map U.S. News 82:55-7 Mr 7 '77
Tree-ring—drought relationships in the Hudson Valley, New York. E. R. Cook and G. C. Jacoby, Jr. bibl il Science 198:399-401 O 28 '77
Tree rings warn us; droughts in Western States. il Sunset 159:296 O '77
Tuolumne River: the drought in a microcosm. P. L. Fradkin. map Audubon 79:132-5 Jl '77
Water: the next resource crisis? il Nations Bus 65:50-2+ S '77
Waterless West. Time 110:23-4 Ag 15 '77
Western states adapt to dry-weather siege. Am City & County 92:68 My '77
Western U.S. drought area depicted by Landsat imagery. il Aviation W 106:16-17 My 9 '77
Will drouth ease in 1977? D. Seim. il Farm J 101:17+ F '77
See also
Dust storms

DROWNING
Kondiba's daring dive; rescue of Indian boy by blind beggar. A. Sadhu. il Read Digest 111:11-12+ D '77
My sons are drowning! B. Davies. il Read Digest 111:78-81 Jl '77
See also
Respiration, Artificial

DROWNPROOFING. See Swimming—Safety devices and measures

DRUG abuse
Cocaine, alcohol & amphetamines: thrillers or killers? J. C. Wang. Harp Baz 110:86-7+ Je '77
See also
Marijuana

DRUG addicts. See Narcotic addicts

DRUG Enforcement Administration. See United States—Drug Enforcement Administration

DRUG implants. See Implantation, Subcutaneous

DRUG industry
Drive to limit the antibiotics in animal feed. il Bus W p55-6 Ja 16 '78
Feasting on fat; liquid protein. L. Langway and others. il Newsweek 90:83 D 5 '77
One small step beyond mankind; recombinant DNA research by drug companies. J. Rifkin. Progressive 41:21 Mr '77
Prescription drugs: problems for public policy. M. C. Hornbrook. bibl f il Cur Hist 72:215-22+ My '77
See also
Baxter Travenol Laboratories, Inc
Searle, G. D, and Company
Smithkline Corporation
United States—Congress—Joint Commission on Prescription Drug Use

Advertising

Pained Bayer cries foul; ad refuting Tylenol's claims. il Bus W p 142 Jl 25 '77
Painkiller war. L. Langway and J. Whitmore. il Newsweek 90:79-80 Jl 18 '77

Employees

How a stillborn child started a NIOSH study; case of employee at Wyeth Laboratories. il por Bus W p76-7 Ag 29 '77

Finance

Personal products & health care. il Forbes 121:126-8 Ja 9 '78

Laws and legislation

See Drug laws and legislation

Public relations

Hawking the estrogen fix; campaign by Ayerst Laboratories. M. Mintz and V. Cohn. Progressive 41:24-5 S '77

DRUG laws and legislation
Damn the doctors—and Washington. il map Time 109:50+ Je 20 '77
Laetrile: should it be banned? M. Clark and others. il Newsweek 89:48-53+ Je 27 '77
Laetrile: the political success of a scientific failure. Consumer Rep 42:444-7 Ag '77
Prescription drugs: problems for public policy. M. C. Hornbrook. bibl f il Cur Hist 72:215-22+ My '77
See also
United States—Food and Drug Administration

DRUG metabolism. See Drugs—Metabolism

DRUG plants. See Botany, Medical

DRUG pushers. See Narcotics, Control of

DRUG receptors
Benzodiazepine receptor: demonstration in the central nervous system. H. Mohler and T. Okada. bibl il Science 198:849-51 N 25 '77
Brain makes its own narcotics! R. Restak. il Sat R 4:6-11 Mr 5 '77
Brain's own tranquilizer? il Chemistry 50:26 Jl '77
Endogenous opiate receptor ligand: electrically induced release in the guinea pig ileum. M. Puig and others. bibl il Science 195:419-20 Ja 28 '77
Membrane adenosinetriphosphatase: a digitalis receptor? T. Akera. bibl il Science 198:569-74 N 11 '77
Opiate receptors and internal opiates. S. H. Snyder. il Sci Am 236:44-56 bibl(p 150) Mr '77
Stereospecific and nonstereospecific effects of (+)-and(-)-morphine: evidence for a new class of receptors? Y. F. Jacquet and others. bibl il Science 198:842-5 N 25 '77

DRUG research. See Pharmaceutical research

DRUG stores. See Drugstores

DRUG testing. See Drugs—Testing

DRUG trade. See Drug industry

DRUGGISTS. See Pharmacists

DRUGS
How safe are the drugs you take? interview. D. Kennedy. il pors U.S. News 83:65-6 N 21 '77
Toxified society. N. Cousins. Sat R 4:4 Mr 5 '77
When and why medicine goes bad. J. L. Lippert. Good H 186:168-9 Ja '78
Your doctor's prescription: is it Greek to you? L. Lamberg. Bet Hom & Gard 55:47-8+ F '77
See also
Antidepressants
Botany, Medical
Hypnotics
Medicines, Patent, proprietary, etc.
Narcotics
Placebos
Swine—Contamination by drugs, pesticides, etc.
United States—Congress—Joint Commission on Prescription Drug Use
United States—Food and Drug Administration
also names of drugs, e.g. Stilbestrols

Advertising

See Drug industry—Advertising

Anecdotes, facetiae, satire, etc.

Say aaaahrrrrgh. D. K. Mano. Nat R 29:1445-6 D 9 '77

Laws and legislation

See Drug laws and legislation

Metabolism

Reduced warfarin binding of albumin variants. G. Wilding and others. bibl il Science 195:991-4 Mr 11 '77
World safe from smallpox. Sci Digest 81:88 F '77

Physiological effects

Aspirin. il Sci Digest 82:54-7 S '77
Cocaine, alcohol & amphetamines: thrillers or killers? J. C. Wang. Harp Baz 110:86-7+ Je '77
Cures that can kill. T. A. Vonder Haar. Progressive 41:40-3 Ap '77
New treatments vs. unknown risks. A. A. Belson. Vogue 167:132-3+ Jl '77
What women don't know about the medicines they take. A. Lake. McCalls 104:117+ Je '77
See also
Drugs—Metabolism
Fetus, Effect of drugs on the

Prices

Comparison shop for drugs. Mademoiselle 83:146 My '77
Prescription drugs: problems for public policy. M. C. Hornbrook. bibl f il Cur Hist 72:215-22+ My '77

Psychological effects

See Psychopharmacology

Research

See Pharmaceutical research

Side effects

See Drugs—Physiological effects

DRUGS—*Continued*

Testing

Mind-bending disclosures; CIA testing. il Time 110:9 Ag 15 '77
Mind bending—latest CIA scandal. U.S. News 83:22 Ag 15 '77
Mind controllers; CIA testing. F. Getlein. Commonweal 104:548-9 S 2 '77

DRUGS and youth. See Narcotics and youth

DRUGSTORES
Bigelow II; Roosevelt Island, New York City. New Yorker 52:29-31 F 14 '77
Home-baked bread, anyone? TV sets? Blue jeans? Skaggs-Albertson's combination stores. il Forbes 119:144+ My 15 '77
Pride goeth before a fall; Rite Aid Corp. il Forbes 120:40+ S 1 '77
Skaggs-Albertson's amicable separation; dissolution of joint venture. Bus W p39+ F 14 '77
Skaggs charts a recession-proof combo. il Bus W p50+ Je 6 '77
See also
Supermarkets—Drug and cosmetic departments

Great Britain

How's the water there? Boots Co, Ltd. Forbes 119:51-2 Je 15 '77

DRUKKER, Leendert
Focus on film (title varies) il por Pop Phot 80:74+ My; 81:22+ Jl; 56+ Ag; 50+ S; 58+ D '77

DRUM, Bob
Step right up and take a whirl. Sports Illus 47:38-41 N 7 '77

DRUM
Drums of Calanda. T. Eigeland. il Natur Hist 86:58-63 Ap '77

DRUM synthesizers. See Musical instruments, Electronic

DRUMMOND, A. H, Jr
Hypothermia: the chill that kills. il Motor B & S 139:52-3+ F '77
Winter warmers. il Motor B & S 140:58-61+ D '77

DRUMMOND, Lord David
Legacy of a Scottish lord; Innerpeffray. G. Thomson. il Wilson Lib Bull 51:844-7 Je '77 *

DRUMS. See Drum

DRUNKENNESS. See Alcoholism; Liquor problem

DRURY, Michael
Dilemma; poem. Good H 185:177 Ag '77

DRUSKA, John
Aspects of Robert Lowell. Commonweal 104:783-8 D 9 '77

DRUYAN, Anne, and Ferris, Timothy
Earth's greatest hits. N Y Times Mag p 12-13 S 4 '77

DRY cell batteries. See Electric batteries

DRY farming
Dry farming: energy saver. A. L. Huebner. Sci Digest 82:59-61 Jl '77

DRY rot
Cuckolded boat owner. D. Bradley. il Motor B & S 139:10+ F '77

DRY TORTUGAS (islands)
See also
Fort Jefferson National Monument

DRYDEN, G. L. and Anderson, J. N.
Ovarian hormone: lack of effect on reproductive structures of female Asian musk shrews. bibl il Science 197:782-4 Ag 19 '77

DRYDEN, John
All for love. Reviews
New Repub 177:22-3 S 24 '77 *

DRYDEN Flight Research Center. See United States—National Aeronautics and Space Administration—Flight Research Center

DRYERS, Clothes. See Clothes dryers

DRYING
See also
Food—Drying
Lumber—Drying
Photography—Drying (films and prints)

DRYING (crops)
See also
Corn—Drying
Soybeans—Drying

DRYING apparatus
Solar drying: it's energy free. Org Gard & Farm 24:100-2 Ag '77
Step-by-step to a food dehydrator. il Bet Hom & Gard 55:23 Jl '77
Super-dehydrator does much more. J. Stephens. il Org Gard & Farm 24:108-9 Ag '77
See also
Clothes dryers
Grain dryers

DRYING of flowers. See Flowers, Dried

DUALISM
See also
Mind and body

DUBAS, Susan Mennear-. See Mennear-Dubas, S.

DUBBERLY, Ron
Options to improve delivery. il Lib J 102:170-1 Ja 15 '77

DUBIE, Norman
Ambassador diaries of Jean de Bosschère and Edgar Poe; poem. Poetry 129:324-30 Mr '77
Elizabeth's war with the Christmas bear: 1601; poem. New Yorker 53:30 D 26 '77
Hours; poem. New Yorker 52:38 F 7 '77
Norway; poem. New Yorker 53:42 My 16 '77

DUBINSKY, Rostislav
Last days in Russia; Borodin Quartet; tr by A. Vergun. il Hi Fi 27:MA10-11+ N '77

DUBIVSKY, Barbara
How to feast and fast in flight. N Y Times Mag p28 S 4 '77
Nail file. il N Y Times Mag p72+ F 27 '77

DUBLIN

Art

Dublin. K. Moffett. il Art N 76:215-16+ N '77

DUBOIS, Grant E. and others
Nonnutritive sweeteners: taste-structure relationships for some new simple dihydrochalcones. bibl il Science 195:397-9 Ja 28 '77

DUBOIS, William Edward Burghardt
W.E.B. DuBois: his journalistic career. D. S. Green. bibl f il pors Negro Hist Bull 40:672-7 Mr '77 *

DUBOS, Rene Jules
Despairing optimist. See issues of American scholar

DUBROW, Marsha
Competition vs. femininity. Harp Baz 110:85+ My '77

DUBS, Adolph
Department discusses south Asia and U.S. assistance programs; statement, March 22, 1977. Dept State Bull 76:344-6 Ap 11 '77

DUBUFFET, Jean
Warring complexities of Jean Dubuffet; interview, ed by M. Peppiatt. il por Art N 76:68-70 My '77

about

Right to raze. Vasari. il por Art N 76:19 S '77 *

DUBUQUE, Ia.
Rocky comes to Dubuque; location shooting of F.I.S.T. F. Maier. il pors Newsweek 89:28 Je 27 '77

DUBUS, Andre
Eavesdropping on the quotidian. G. Lyons. Nation 224:248-50 F 26 '77 *

DUCHAMP, Gaston. See Villon, J. pseud

DUCHAMP, Marcel
Duchamp & Leonardo: L.H.O.O.Q.-alikes; adaptation of address, February 17, 1974. T. Reff. bibl il Art in Am 65:82-93 Ja '77; Discussion. 65:5 My; 5 Jl '77 *
Duchamp's acephalic symbolism; analysis of bookstore window display called Lazy Hardware. C. F. Stuckey. bibl il Art in Am 65:94-9 Ja '77 *
Merce Cunningham's Walkaround time; hommage to Duchamp. J. Mueller. Dance Mag 51:94-5 Je '77 *
Private joke between myself and myself. J. Hobhouse. il por Art N 76:41-3 Ap '77 *

DUCHAMP-VILLON, Raymond
Paris celebrates: a new art center and the brothers Duchamp. F. Steegmuller. Atlantic 239:88-90 Je '77 *

DUCHENNE dystrophy. See Dystrophy, Muscular

DUCHIN, Cheray (Zauderer) See Duchin, P. O. jt auth

DUCHIN, Peter Oelrichs, and Duchin, C. Z.
Joyful place of light and color; interview, ed by R. Weil. il House B 119:28-35 Ag '77

DUCK as food. See Cookery—Poultry

DUCK aspic. See Aspic

DUCK blinds. See Blinds (camouflage)

DUCK boats. See Boats and boating

DUCK decoys. See Decoys (hunting)

DUCK shooting
How they cracked duck hunting's isle of shame: Pruitt's Paradise Inc on Tangier Island. J. Phillips. il Outdoor Life 161:64-5+ Ja '78
It's ok to ignore steel shot (if you don't mind losing your duck hunting) B. Brister. Field & S 82:112-14+ S '77
Move with 'em or lose 'em. W. L. Bourne. il Outdoor Life 160:92-3+ S '77
Retrievers good and bad; hunting in Montana. N. MacLean. Esquire 88:22+ O '77
Woodies on the wing again. J. H. Phillips. il Outdoor Life 159:94-5+ My '77

DUCKENS, Silvia
Casey Jones would be proud. il pors Ebony 32:53-4+ Mr '77 *

DUCKS
Call of the duck. G. Gottlieb. Natur Hist 86:40+ O '77
Raising Muscovy ducks for the table. M. Bonta. il Org Gard & Farm 24:134-6 Je '77

DUCKS, Wild
Build a wood duck nest box. il Outdoor Life 159:164 My '77
Mr Wood Duck; F. Leopold. H. Bradshaw and V. Bradshaw. por Outdoor Life 160:100 Ag '77

DUCKS, Wild—*Continued*
Refuge ducks are swamped by powerboats, politicians; Ruby Lake National Wildlife Refuge. G. Laycock. Audubon 79:152-3 N '77
Simple wood duck box. K. Schultz. il Field & S 82:200 N '77
Sociobiology of rape in mallards anas platyrhynchos: responses of the mated male. D. P. Barash. bibl Science 197:788-9 Ag 19 '77
Wood duck. P. Schnell. il Conservationist 32:43 Jl '77
See also
Duck shooting
DUCKS Unlimited, Inc
Art of shooting and the shooting arts; Ducks Unlimited Midwest Wildlife Art Show. B. Tarrant. il Field & S 81:144-8 F '77
DUCKWORTH, Garrett
Country doctor. C. Remsberg. il por Fam Health 9:36-9+ Ap '77 *
DUCKWORTH, Ruth
Ceramics of Ruth Duckworth. A. Westphal. il por Craft Horiz 37:48-51 Ag '77 *
DUCTS, Bile. See Bile ducts
DUDAR, Helen
America discovers child pornography. Ms 6:45-7+ Ag '77
Price of blowing the whistle. il pors N Y Times Mag p41-2+ O 30 '77
DUDDERAR, Glenn R.
Bird study aids camp enrichment. il Camp Mag 49:6-7 Je '77
DUDE ranches. See Ranches
DUDEK, F. Edward. See Pinsker, H. M. jt auth
DUDLEY, Jean Hogan
The beginning; poem. Chr Today 21:18 Ja 21 '77
DUDLEY, Mary Neary
My husband and I are equal partners. McCalls 104:46+ F '77
DUDLEYA caespitosa. See Echeveria
DUE process of law
Due process in discipline. C. E. Alberti. bibl Clearing H 51:12-14 S '77
Insuring procedural due process in expulsion cases. C. Hestor. Clearing H 50:256-7 F '77
See also
Right to counsel
DUFAULT, Peter Kane
Equinoctial; poem. Atlantic 241:85 Ja '78
DUFAY, Guillaume
Fifteen songs; Transformations. W. Purcell. Am Rec G 40:28-30 S '77 *
Missa Se la face ay pale. W. L. Purcell. Am Rec G 40:27-8 D '76 *
DUFF, Katharyn
At Liz and Billy Green's: a Christmas on the prairie. il pors Redbook 150:89+ D '77
DUFF, Marilyn
Helping readers to visualize. Todays Educ 66:56-7 Mr '77
DUFFETT, John L.
Understanding paint chemistry. il Motor B & S 139:43-5 Ap '77
DUFFEY, David Michael
Hunting dogs. See issues of Outdoor life
DUFFEY, Joseph Daniel
Humanist at the Humanities. New Repub 177:8+ Ag 20 '77 *
Joe Duffey's new job. Chr Cent 94:742 Ag 31 '77 *
Populism vs. elitism. R. Steele and others. il Newsweek 90:39 O 31 '77 *
Rights and wrongs of scholarship. por Horizon 20:57 O '77 *
DUFFY family
American family. J. P. Blank. il Read Digest 111:107-12 Jl '77
DUGDALE, John
Grand Prix racing in the thirties. il pors Car & Dr 23:105-6+ N '77
DUGGAN, Moira
International scene. por Pub W 211:43-4 Ja 17 '77
DUHE, Camille
Health and beauty (cont) Am Home 80:10+ Mr '77
DUKAKIS, Michael Stanley
Hard times liberal. W. A. Henry, 3d. New Repub 176:20-3 Ja 15 '77 *
Workfare and welfare. H. Lipman. Nation 225:141-4 Ag 20 '77 *
Working on welfare. Time 109:12 Je 27 '77 *
DUKE, Charles R.
Case of the divorced reader. bibl f il Engl J 66:33-6 F '77
Save the eco system: support creative expression. bibl Clearing H 51:101-3 N '77
Vocational oversell. Clearing H 50:284 Mr '77
DUKE, David
Great white hope. D. A. Williams and others. il por Newsweek 90:45 N 14 '77 *
DUKE, Debbie
Jobscope. Mademoiselle 83:197 F; 12+ Ap '77
—and others
How to transplant & survive. il Mademoiselle 83:205+ Ap '77
DUKE Ellington Festival. See Dance festivals
DUKES, Anne K.
Drive. See issues of Mademoiselle

DUKHOBORS
British Columbia's Doukhobors. il map Sunset 158:62 Je '77
DULLES, Avery
Anathemas and orthodoxy. L. Gilkey. Chr Cent 94:1026-9 N 9 '77; Reply. A. Dulles. 94:1053-4 N 16 '77 *
DU MAURIER, Dame Daphne
Place has taken hold of me; Menabilly; excerpt from Myself when young. il pors Sat Eve Post 249:48-50 D '77
DUMMLING and the golden goose; dramatization. See Thane, A.
DUMOND, Jesse William Monroe
Obituary
Phys Today por 30:74-5 Mr '77. E. R. Cohen
DUMONT, Alberto Santos-. See Santos-Dumont, A.
DUMONT, Lou
Historical tape recordings. See issues of Hobbies
DUMPING (commercial policy)
Antitrust question about Japanese steel. Bus W p32+ D 19 '77
Carter plan to aid steel—will it work? il U.S. News 83:67 D 19 '77
Cautious approval for U.S. reference prices. il Bus W p30 Ja 16 '78
First step in rescuing steel. il Bus W p34-5 N 28 '77
Protecting steel. New Repub 177:8-9 D 17 '77
Steel builds its dumping case. il Bus W p 128+ O 17 '77
Trigger to curb dumping; steel. Time 111:45-6 Ja 16 '78
Why steel's dumping cases may backfire. il Bus W p48 N 14 '77
Zeroing in on dumping. Time 110:107-8 N 7 '77
DUMPLINGS
Great dumpling cookbook. M. Polushkin. il por Redbook 148:126-7+ Mr '77
DUN, Nae J. and others
Dopamine and adenosine 3',5'-monophosphate responses of single mammalian sympathetic neurons. bibl il Science 197:778-80 Ag 19 '77
DUNAWAY, Faye
Why I waited so long to marry; interview. ed by G. Davis. il por McCalls 104:22+ Mr '77
DUNAWAY, Vic
Snook: getting down to basics. il Field & S 81:28+ F '77
DUNBAR, Bonnie S. See Shivers, C. A. jt auth
DUNBAR, Gary, and Lang, Martin
Public utilities can serve more than one use. il pors Am City & County 92:49-50 N '77
DUNCAN, Charles William, 1926-
Collective security and confidence; excerpt from address. Aviation W 107:7 S 12 '77
DUNCAN, David
Environmental game plan for successful indoor gardening. il Horticulture 55:40-3 D '77
DUNCAN, Gurl
Froggy green decision; story. Redbook 148:108+ Ap '77
Unnamed but not unloved; story. McCalls 104:140-1+ My '77
DUNCAN, Isadora
After Isadora: her art as inspiration. L. Draegin. il por Dance Mag 51:67-71 Jl '77 *
Annabelle Gamson: Gamson dances Isadora; interview, ed by J. Dunning. A. Gamson. il pors Dance Mag 51:47-50 F '77 *
Isadora reexamined; excerpt from Isadora Duncan. N. Macdonald. il pors Dance Mag 51:51-66 Jl; 42-6 Ag; 60-3 S; 79-81 O; 45-7 N; 71-3 D '77 *
Isadora: the last year. M. B. Geddes. il pors Dance Mag 52:67-70 Ja '78 *
Isadora's childhood: clearing away the clouds. P. Hertelendy. il por Dance Mag 51:48-50 Jl '77 *
Year of Isadora. il por Horizon 20:26 S '77 *
DUNCAN, Isadora, Centenary Dance Company. See Dance companies
DUNCAN, Joe
Build a fluorescent utility lamp. il Pop Electr 12:53-5 O '77
DUNCAN, John James
Excerpt from address on Comprehensive Health Care Insurance Act, January 17, 1977. Cong Digest 56:201+ Ag '77
DUNCAN, Lois
Graduate in the family. il por Good H 185:102+ O '77
DUNCAN, Mary R.
Child's play in Northern Ireland. il Parks & Rec 12:27-30 Ag '77
DUNCAN, Patricia
Zephyr; story. Harpers 254:58-60 Je '77
DUNCAN, Rodger Dean
Medical quacks: today's merchants of menace. Ret Liv 17:25-6+ F '77
DUNES, Sand. See Sand dunes
DUNES National Lakeshore. See Indiana Dunes National Lakeshore
DUNGENESS crab. See Crabs
DUNICZ, Boleslaw L.
Device for detecting carbonates. il Chemistry 50:27 Ap '77

DUNIFER, Stephen
Display quad signals on your scope. il Radio-Electr 48:42-3 Je '77
DUNKELL, Samuel
What our sleep position reveals; excerpt from Sleep positions: the night language of the body. il Read Digest 111:137-9 Jl '77
What your sleeping position reveals about you; interview, ed by N. A. Comer. il Mademoiselle 83:176-7+ Mr '77
DUNKIN' Donuts of America, Inc. See Restaurants—Chain and franchise operations
DUNLAP-PIANKA, Helen, and others
Ovarian dynamics in heliconiine butterflies: programmed senescence versus eternal youth. bibl il Science 197:487-90 Jl 29 '77
DUNLEAVY, Steve
Mr Blood-and-guts. T. Schwartz. il por Newsweek 90:67 O 17 '77 *
DUNLINS. See Sandpipers
DUNLOP, John Thomas
Unofficial adviser on labor-management. por Bus W p33-4 Je 13 '77 *
DUNLOP, Peter
Herbs for health. il House & Gard 149:102+ F '77
DUNN, Bob
Baseball (cont) Sports Illus 47:42-4+ Ag 8 '77
DUNN, Diana R.
Women in recreation. bibl il Parks & Rec 12:24-30 Jl '77
DUNN, Douglas
Dance. N. Goldner. Nation 224:638 My 21 '77 *
DUNN, Lewis A.
Nuclear proliferation and world politics. Ann Am Acad 430:96-109 Mr '77
DUNN, Lucia, and Ullman, Jackie
These proud Americans. il Sat Eve Post 249:42-4+ S '77
DUNN, Robert
Memory; poem. New Yorker 53:174 N 21 '77
DUNN, Stephen
Beached whales off Margate; poem. Nation 224:119 Ja 29 '77
DUNN-RANKIN, Peter
Visual characteristics of words; with biographical sketch. il Sci Am 238:12, 122-30 Ja '78
DUNNAN, Nancy
British are coming! Lib J 102:2311-16 N 15 '77
DUNNE, Bill
Broker profile; interview. por Motor B & S 140:117 N '77
DUNNE, Bronwyn
Tunisia. il Trav/Holiday 149:26-33+ Ja '78
DUNNE, Jim
Detroit report. See issues of Popular science
—and Ceppos, Rich
PS car test & driving report. See issues of Popular science
DUNNE, John Gregory
The Coast. See alternate issues of Esquire to November 1977
Day in the life of Joan Didion; interview, ed by S. Braudy. Ms 5:65-8+ F '77
DUNNING, Jennifer
Dance is climbing the walls. il Ms 6:46-8+ D '77
DUN'S review
Dun's extends Midwest coverage with new bureau. por Duns R 110:3 Ag '77
New feature makes its debut in this issue; Footnotes. il Duns R 109:3 Mr '77
Reviewing Dun's. il Duns R 109:3 Ja '77
DUNSMORE, Barrie
(ed) See Vance, C. R. Secretary Vance interviewed on Issues and answers
DUNSTAN, Bernard
Looking at paintings. See issues of American artist
DUNSTAN, John C. Jr
Ethnic circular painting. il Design (US) 78:20-1 Summ '77
DUNTON, William Herbert
William Herbert Dunton: from yankee to cowboy. M. C. Nelson. il por Am Artist 42:60-3+ Ja '78 *
DUPLEX apartments. See Apartments
DUPLICATING films. See Photography—Films
DUPLICATING processes. See Photocopying machines and processes
DUPONT, Alfred I, trust. See Trusts and trustees
DU PONT, Diane, pseud
Story behind a record-breaking sale. Writer 90:15-17 N '77

about

Garage sale. J. Briskin. por Writers Digest 57:48+ D '77 *
DU PONT, Henry Francis, Winterthur Museum. See Henry Francis du Pont Winterthur Museum
DU PONT, John J.
About this issue. R. F. Hall. por Conservationist 31:43 Ja '77 *
DU PONT, Pierre Samuel, 1935-
Delaware: toils of champagne Pete. H. Bruno. il por Newsweek 89:45 Ap 11 '77 *

DU PONT DE NEMOURS, E. I, and Company
American economy; address, August 28, 1977. I. S. Shapiro. Vital Speeches 43:738-41 O 1 '77
Health records face a privacy challenge; Du Pont challenges NIOSH on claim to undisputed access. il Bus W p38 O 31 '77
Sign of the times. Forbes 119:39 Je 15 '77
DUPUY, Frank C.
No support from Washington; what a border agent tells Carter. il por U.S. News 82:36-7 Ap 25 '77
DURANG, Christopher
History of the American film. Reviews
Time il 109:108 My 23 '77 *
DURANT, Ariel
Birthday party. N. Cousins. Sat R 5:4-5 Ja 7 '78 *
DURANT, Thomas Clark
Great race; excerpt from Hear that lonesome whistle blow. D. Brown. il Am West 14:4-15+ My '77 *
DURANT, William James
What I have learned; excerpt from address. Sat R 5:5 Ja 7 '78

about

Birthday party. N. Cousins. Sat R 5:4-5 Ja 7 '78 *
DURATION of life. See Longevity
DURAZZO, Michelangelo
Borobudur—Nirvana in central Java. il Holiday 58:36-9 Mr '77
DURBIN, Karen
Intelligent woman's guide to sex. See issues of Mademoiselle to July 1977
Men & women: towards a new eroticism. Mademoiselle 83:156-7+ N '77
New sexual pyramid. il Mademoiselle 83:142+ F '77
Sexual courtesy. Mademoiselle 83:147+ Mr '77
DURFEE, Jay
Passing the flag. E. D. Muhlfeld. il pors Flying 101:1+ O '77*
DURIE, Brian G. M.
Scintillator distribution in high-speed autoradiography. Science 195:208 Ja 14 '77
DURKA, Gloria
Revelation, faith and catechesis. il por New Cath World 220:69-73 Mr '77
DURRELL, Lawrence
Sicilian carousel; excerpt. il Sat Eve Post 249:72-3+ N '77
DURROW, Book of. See Book of Durrow
DURSO, Joseph
Secret lives of the super jocks. il Sat Eve Post 249:40-1+ Mr '77
(ed) See Ford, W. Confessions of a gunkball artist
DUSA, Fish, Stas & Vi; drama. See Gems, P.
DU SABLE, Jean Baptiste. See Pointe du Sable, J. B.
DÜSSELDORF, Germany

Music

See also
Opera—Germany, West
DUST, Interstellar. See Matter, Interstellar
DUST Bowl. See Great Plains
DUST diseases. See Lungs—Dust diseases
DUST glazing. See Glazes and glazing (ceramics)
DUST jackets, Phonograph record. See Phonograph record covers
DUST pans
King-sized cleanup pan. W. Asa. il Org Gard & Farm 24:95 Ap '77
DUST storms
Coping with today's drought—scenes from a parched land. il U.S. News 82:48-50 Ap 4 '77
Dust storm tracked across U.S. il Space World N-11-167:32 N '77
Earth, Mars dust storms photographed. il Aviation W 106:43 Mr 14 '77
DUSTAN, Harriet P.
Latest in fight against heart disease; interview. il por U.S. News 83:83-4+ N 14 '77
DUSTAN, Phillip
Besieged reefs of Florida's Keys; with biographical sketch. il Natur Hist 86:4, 72-6 bibl(p 101) Ap '77
DUSTPANS. See Dust pans
DUTCH, Von
Von Dutch: machine age gypsy; interview, ed by T. Kramer. il por Hot Rod 30:44-8+ Mr '77
DUTCH, Pennsylvania. See Pennsylvania Germans
DUTCH cookery. See Cookery, Dutch
DUTCH elm disease. See Elm—Diseases and pests
DUTCH National Ballet. See Ballet—Netherlands
DUTCH ovens, Outdoor. See Camp stoves
DUTCH propaganda. See Propaganda, Dutch
DUTCHESS County, N.Y.

Historic houses, sites, etc.

See Historic houses, sites, etc.—New York (state)

DUTTON, E. P, and Company. See Publishers and publishing—United States

DUTTON, Geoffrey
(tr) See Akhmadulina, B. Tale about rain in several episodes

DUTTON, Joan Parry
English arrangement. il Horticulture 55:64-9 F '77

DUTY
See also
Conscience

DUTY free importation
Bringing back the goods. S. Birnbaum. Esquire 87:42+ Ap '77

DUVAL, Denise
Voice of Poulenc; interview, ed by L. Rasponi. por Opera N 41:17-19 F 5 '77

DUVAL, Isaac Harding
Overland to California; memoirs, ed by G. C. Stein. il por Am Hist Illus 12:26-36 My '77

DUVAL, Julian
New hope for endangered species. il Américas 29:19-23 Ja '77

DU VAL, Miles P. 1896-
Panama Canal question; address, July 29, 1977. Vital Speeches 43:685-9 S 1 '77

DUVALL, Shelley
Afternoon of a star: a day in the park with Shelly Duvall; interview, ed by A. Lovell. il pors Mademoiselle 83:190-1+ S '77
What's happening; interview, ed by G. Shalit. il por Ladies Home J 94:8+ Ag '77

DUVOISIN, Roger
PW interviews; ed by M. Freeman. il pors Pub W 211:54-5 F 28 '77

DVOŘÁK, Antonín
Dvořák plain vs. Dvořák fancified; recordings of G minor piano concerts by S. Richter. H. Goldsmith. por Hi Fi 27:73-4 D '77 *
Rusalka. B. Hastings. Am Rec G 40:30-2 S '77 *
String quartet no. 6 in F major (American) op. 96; String quintet no. 3 in E flat major, op. 97. J. Diether. Am Rec G 40:20-1 N '76 *
Symphony no. 7 in D minor, op. 70. J. R. Oestreich. por Am Rec G 40:18-20 My '77 *
Water-sprite, The noonday witch and Symphonic variations; Deutsche Grammophon recording. L. M. Smoley. il Am Rec G 41:28-32 D '77 *

DWARF fruit trees. See Fruit trees, Dwarf

DWARF mistletoe. See Mistletoe

DWARF palms. See Palms

DWARF trees. See Trees, Dwarf

DWELL meters
Auto maintenance basics: how to use a dwell tach. R. Hill. il Pop Sci 211:160+ S '77
Auto tune-up equipment; dwell tachometers and ignition-timing lights. Consumer Rep 42:419-22 D '77

DWIGHT, Edward H.
Along the Oriskany. il Conservationist 31:20-2 N '76

DWIGHT Twilley Band. See Rock groups

DWORKIN, Andrea
Phalic imperialism: why economic recovery will not work for us. Ms 5:101-2+ D '76; Correction 5:14 F '77

DWORKIN, James B.
How final-offer arbitration affects baseball bargaining. bibl il M Labor R 100:52-3 Mr '77

DWORKIN, Martin S.
Jaws in retrospect. il Society 14:78-81 My '77

DWORKIN, Ronald Myles
Treating people as equals. D. Beckwith. il por Time 110:54 S 5 '77 *

DWORKIN, Susan
Cryer & Ford: hang on to the good times. pors Ms 6:64-5 D '77
Great man syndrome: Saul Bellow & me. por Ms 5:72-3 Mr '77

DWYER, James, and Albert, John
Dwarf fruit trees: big producers in tiny plots. il Pop Mech 147:94-6+ Ap '77

DYAL, William M. Jr, and Donovan, J. B.
Identity and change: does development imply dependency? il Américas 29:13-18 Ap '77

DYBBUK; drama. See Ansky, S.

DYBEK, Stuart
Undertow; story. Atlantic 240:74-8 S '77

DYCK, Arthur J.
Alternative views of moral priorities in population policy. bibl BioScience 27:272-6 Ap '77

DYE, James L.
Anions of the alkali metals; with biographical sketch. il Sci Am 237:18+, 92-6+ bibl(p 154) Jl '77

DYER, Richard
Gilbert and Sullivan discography. il Hi Fi 27:52-8 My '77

DYER, Wayne W.
Happiness—it's only natural. Read Digest 111: 84-6 Jl '77
How to stop those same old family fights. Read Digest 111:25-8 O '77
How you can worry less; excerpt from Your erroneous zones. Read Digest 110:81-4 F '77

about
Australia: Dyer's new best selling zone. il por Pub W 212:40 D 12 '77 *

DYER-BENNET, Richard
Musical events; performances of Die schöne Mullerin. A. Porter. New Yorker 53:93-4 F 28 '77 *

DYES and dyeing
Do-it-yourself dye jobs. Bet Hom & Gard 55: 252+ My '77
Grow your own colors; natural dyes for yarn. il House & Gard 149:168-9+ My '77
Tie dye--designing with color; excerpt from Designing in batik and tie dye. N. Belfer. il Sch Arts 76:12-17 Ap '77
Wild colors, natural dyes. L. Borgeson. il Nat Wildlife 15:50-5 Ap '77
See also
Batik
Coloring matter in cosmetics, food, etc
Fluorescein
Hair—Dyeing and bleaching
Henna
Textile painting

DYES as indicators
Internal calcium changes in a bursting pacemaker neuron measured with arsenazo III. M. V. Thomas and A. L. F. Gorman. bibl il Science 196:531-3 Ap 29 '77

DYING. See Death

DYING patients, Care of. See Terminal care

DYMOCK, James
Blue bloods. il Sat Eve Post 249:84 Jl '77

DYNAMIC range enhancers. See Sound—Apparatus

DYNAMIC symmetry. See Proportion (art)

DYNAMICS
See also
Transients (dynamics)

DYRNESS, William A.
Redeeming Indian culture. il Chr Today 21:26-7 Mr 18 '77

DYSART, W. D.
Functions and makeup of lubricants. il Motor B & S 139:79-80 Mr '77

DYSLEXIA, Developmental. See Reading disability

DYSMENORRHEA. See Menstruation—Disorders

DYSPLASIA of the cervix. See Cervix—Diseases

DYSTEL, Oscar
Paperback revolution: where has it gone? adaptation of address, October 1977. por Pub W 212:31-3 N 14 '77

DYSTROPHY, Muscular
Avian muscular dystrophy: functional and biochemical improvement with diphenylhydantoin. R. K. Entrikin and others. bibl il Science 195: 873-5 Mr 4 '77
Duchenne dystrophy: alteration in muscle plasma membrane structure. D. L. Schotland and others. bibl il Science 196:1005-7 My 27 '77
Erythrocyte lipids in heterozygous carriers of duchenne muscular dystrophy. J. L. Howland and S. L. Iyer. bibl il Science 198:309-10 O 21 '77

E

ECE. See United Nations—Economic Commission for Europe

ECLA. See United Nations--Economic Commission for Latin America

EDS. See Electronic Data Systems Corporation

EEC. See European Economic Community

EEG. See Electroencephalography

EEI. See Edison Electric Institute

EEOC. See United States—Equal Employment Opportunity Commission

EFLA. See Educational Film Library Association

E. I. Du Pont de Nemours and Company. See Du Pont de Nemours, E. I. and Company

E. P. Dutton and Company. See Publishers and publishing—United States

EPA. See United States—Environmental Protection Agency

EPIRB (Emergency position indicating radio beacon) See Radio beacons

ERA (Equal Rights Amendment [proposed]) See United States—Constitution—Amendments

ERDA. See United States—Energy Research and Development Administration

ERIC. See Eric

ERISA (Employee Retirement Income Security Act) See Pensions—Laws and regulations

ESA. See European Space Agency

ESCAP. See United Nations—Economic and Social Commission for Asia and the Pacific

ESP. See Extrasensory perception

EST. See Erhard Seminars Training

ESV (experimental safety vehicles) See Automobiles, Experimental

ETS. See Educational Testing Service
ETS (Evangelical Theological Society) See Religious societies
EADS, Valerie
(ed) See Kinzler, K. West Point woman
EAGLE, Joanna Shaw-. See Shaw-Eagle, J.
EAGLE, Alaska
Reporter at large. J. McPhee. New Yorker 53: 43-4+ Je 20; 58-80 Je 27; 33-6+ Jl 4; 30-40+ Jl 11 '77
EAGLE Lake
Water aplenty in mile-high Eagle Lake. il Sunset 159:52-3+ Ag '77
EAGLE-Picher Industries Inc
Eagle-what? il Forbes 120:53+ Ag 15 '77
EAGLES
Birds in the hand; reestablishment of bald eagles in New York state. A. Wolff. Sat R 4: 55 F 5 '77
In quest of the snatcher; harpy eagles. N. Rettig. il map Audubon 79:26-49 N '77
Tomorrow's dinosaurs? bald eagles. il Sr Schol 109:11 Ap 21 '77
EAGLES Nest Wilderness. See Wilderness areas—Colorado
EAGLESON, Alan
Hockey 1977-78; interview. il pors Sports Illus 47:36-41 O 17 '77
EAGLESON, Robert Alan. See Eagleson, A.
EAGLETON, Thomas Francis
1977: year of opportunity in the Middle East? address, December 8, 1976. Vital Speeches 43: 201-4 Ja 15 '77
Why rent controls don't work. Read Digest 111: 108-11 Ag '77
EAKER, Ira Clarence
War to war. il Flying 101:180-3 S '77
EAKINS, Susan (Macdowell)
Mr and Mrs Eakins. il pors Harpers 255:69-71 O '77 *
EAKINS, Thomas
Hipped on nudes. il Horizon 21:35 Ja '78 *
Mr and Mrs Eakins. il pors Harpers 255:69-71 O '77 *
EAMES, Charles
Conversation with Charles Eames; ed by O. Gingerich. Am Scholar 46:326-37 Summ '77
EAMES, David
Watching Wiseman watch. il N Y Times Mag p96-102+ O 2 '77
EAMES chairs. See Chairs
EAR
See also
Hearing

Protection

Hearing protectors. Consumer Rep 42:155-6 D '77
EAR (animals)
Critical period for acoustic trauma in the hamster and its relation to cochlear development. G. R. Bock and J. C. Saunders. bibl il Science 197:396-8 Jl 22 '77
EARECKSON, Joni
Joni's story. P. Yancey. il pors Sat Eve Post 249:75+ S '77 *
EARHART, Amelia
Earhart. D. Mosteller. por Flying 101:160 S '77 *
EARL, Ralph
Paintings of Ralph Earl at the Litchfield Historical Society. L. F. Ballard, Jr. il Antiques 112:959-63 N '77 *
EARLE, Jane
Se habla español. Todays Educ 66:76-7 N '77
EARLY, Daniel
Amaranth secrets of the Aztecs. il Org Gard & Farm 24:69-73 D '77
EARLY California Industries. See Food industry
EARLY rising
Notes and comment. New Yorker 53:37-9 O 17 '77
EARLY warning airplanes. See Airplanes, Military
EARNINGS, Corporate. See Corporations—Finance
EARTH
What the exploration of Mars tell us about earth. S. I. Rasool and others. il Phys Today 30:23-30+ Jl '77
See also
Atmosphere
Biosphere
Cosmology
Creation
Geography
Ocean

Internal structure

Flow of heat from the earth's interior. H. N. Pollack and D. S. Chapman. il maps. Sci Am 237: 60-8+ bibl(p 140) Ag '77
Hot spots. P. R. Vogt. il maps Natur Hist 86:36-45 bibl(p 100) Ap '77
Mysterious inner earth. J. Goldsmith. Intellect 106:14-15 Jl '77

Mantle

See Earth—Internal structure

Observations from space

See also
Artificial satellites—Earth sciences use

Orbit

Head south with all deliberate speed: ice may return in a few thousand years. N. Calder. il Smithsonian 8:32-41 bibl(p 114) Ja '78
Mean winters. il Chemistry 50:21 Mr '77
Sea-floor data link glaciation to earth's orbital motion. G. B. Lubkin. il Phys Today 30:17+ My '77
Variations in the earth's orbit: pacemaker of the ice ages. J. D. Hays and others; reply with rejoinder. D. L. Evans and H. J. Freeland. bibl il Science 198:528-30 N 4 '77

Photographs from space

America shines; lights as seen from space. H. W. Brandli and E. I. Johnson. il Environment 19:6-9 D '77
Brazilian coffee crop frost damage shown. il Aviation W 106:46 Ap 4 '77
Earth shown in infrared, visible regions. Aviation W 108:50-1 Ja 9 '78
Expanding desert creates grim beauty but also threatens crucial cropland; Western Desert of Egypt. F. El-Baz. il Smithsonian 8:34-41 Je '77
Massive dust cloud tracked in GOES-1 satellite image. il Aviation W 107:58-60 Jl 25 '77
Metsat imagery depicts East, West coasts. il Aviation W 106:40-1 Ap 18 '77
NASA improves Skylab scanner imagery. Aviation W 106:40-1 F 21 '77
NASA, NOAA satellites photograph giant iceberg. il Aviation W 106:42-3 Ap 25 '77
NOAA satellites track winter storms. Aviation W 106:50-1 F 21 '77
Satellite image depicts severe winter weather in U.S, Canada. Aviation W 106:26-7 F 7 '77
Techniques tomorrow; Landsat. B. Sherman. il Mod Phot 41:49+ S '77
Want a photo of your house taken from space? M. L. Schildkraut. il Good H 184:229 My '77
Western U.S. drought area depicted by Landsat imagery. il Aviation W 106:16-17 My 9 '77

Radiation

Planetary radiation balance as a function of atmospheric dust: climatological consequences. S. B. Idso and A. J. Brazel. bibl il Science 198:731-3 N 18 '77

Size

Twin-engined spaceship earth. S. J. Gould. il Natur Hist 86:72-6 Mr '77

Surface

Ancient lithosphere: its role in young continental volcanism. C. Brooks and others; reply with rejoinder. F. Chayes. bibl Science 196:1234-5 Je 10 '77
Mars on earth. il Sci Digest 81:80-1 F '77
Slow leak of earth's surface water. W. S. Fyfe and J. S. Levine. Intellect 105:386-7 My '77
See also
Continents
Deserts
Faults (geology)
EARTH, Destruction of. See End of the world
EARTH, Effect of man on. See Man—Influence on nature
EARTH, Wind, and Fire (rock group) See Rock groups
EARTH art. See Environment (art)
EARTH Camp One. See Camps—California
EARTH movements
High rates of vertical crustal movement near Ventura, California. R. S. Yeats. bibl il map Science 196:295-8 Ap 15 '77
EARTH sciences
Earth sciences (cont) Sci N 111:139, 202, 393; 112:120, 264, 297, 408 F 26, Mr 26, Je 18, Ag 20, O 22, N 5, D 17 '77
See also
Artificial satellites—Earth sciences use
Geography
Meteorology
Oceanography
Radar in earth sciences
EARTH temperature
Flow of heat from the earth's interior. H. N. Pollack and D. S. Chapman. il maps Sci Am 237:60-8+ bibl(p 140) Ag '77
See also
Geothermal resources
Global temperature changes
EARTHENWARE, English. See Pottery, English
EARTHQUAKE prediction
California's shifting crust: slip sliding away. Sci N 112:404 D 17 '77
Can animals anticipate earthquakes? E. Shaw. Natur Hist 86:14+ N '77
China's quake forecasting: 50-50. Sci N 112:133-4 Ag 27 '77
Forecast: future shock; study by J. E. Haas and D. S. Mileti. il Time 109:83 Ja 24 '77
If pandas scream, an earthquake is coming! P. Magida. il Int Wildlife 7:36-9 S '77
Next big earthquake is on its way; United States. il Changing T 31:36-8 F '77

EARTHQUAKE prediction—*Continued*
Relation between earthquakes, weather, and soil tilt. M. D. Wood and N. E. King. bibl il Science 197:154-6 Jl 8 '77
Social hazards of earthquake prediction. Sci N 111:20-1 Ja 8 '77
Swelling earth; Palmdale bulge. E. Keerdoja and M. Kasindorf. il Newsweek 89:10 Mr 21 '77

Anecdotes, facetiae, satire, etc.

Dr Matrix goes to California to apply punk to rock study. M. Gardner. il Sci Am 237:17-18+ D '77

EARTHQUAKES
Motion of the ground in earthquakes. D. M. Boore. il map Sci Am 237:68-78 bibl(p 190) D '77
Volcanic activity and great earthquakes at convergent plate margins. M. J. Carr. bibl il map Science 197:655-7 Ag 12 '77
Year of the earthquake. Sci N 111:85 F 5 '77
See also
Tidal waves

Prediction

See Earthquake prediction

China

Did a moving ripple cause China quake? map Sci N 111:342 My 28 '77
Tangshan quake: protrait of a catastrophe. Sci N 111:388 Je 18 '77

Guatemala

Earthquake injuries related to housing in a Guatemalan village. R. I. Glass and others. bibl il map Science 197:638-43 Ag 12 '77
Guatemala remembers; work of CEPA, Permanent Evangelical Committee for Aid. S. Sywulka. Chr Today 21:55-6 Ap 1 '77

Rumania

Bad dream comes true. il Time 109:38 Mr 21 '77
Earth's madness. il Time 109:29 Mr 14 '77
Springtime after Romania's quake. E. E. Plowman. Chr Today 21:54-5 Ap 1 '77
Tanks take Bucharest. R. Carroll. il map Newsweek 89:28 Mr 14 '77

United States

Earthquake hazard in New England. A. F. Shakal and M. N. Toksöz. bibl il map Science 195:171-3 Ja 14 '77
Huntington Beach: disaster waits impatiently in wings; excerpt from Acts of God, acts of man. W. Marx. Audubon 79:126-8 Mr '77

History

Two hundred years of California earthquakes; excerpt from California quake. L. L. Meyer. il Am West 14:4-9+ Ja '77
See also
San Francisco—Earthquake and fire, 1906

EARTHQUAKES and building
Earthquake injuries related to housing in a Guatemalan village. R. I. Glass and others. bibl il map Science 197:638-43 Ag 12 '77
Visualizing the effect of earthquakes on the behavior of building structures. P. Weidlinger. il Archit Rec 161:139-42 My '77

EARTHS, Rare
Magnetism of rare-earth metals. A. R. Mackintosh. bibl il Phys Today 30:23-30 Je '77
See also
Promethium

EARTHWATCH (organization) See Scientific expeditions

EARTHWORK
See also
Filling (earthwork)

EARTHWORKS (archeology)
Intaglios-ancient earth paintings; Arizona. il Sunset 158:61-2 Ap '77

EARTHWORKS (art) See Environment (art)

EARTHWORM culture
Hercules of the soil—the earthworm. J. F. Farmer. Read Digest 111:83-6 N '77
Profitable way to get rid of solid waste; North American Bait Farms experiment. V. Louviere. por Nations Bus 65:65 Ja '77

EARTHWORMS
King of worms; interview, ed by J. Skow. G. Sroda. il Outdoor Life 159:84-6+ F '77
See also
Earthworm culture

EASEMENTS
Bold bid to preserve scenery; easement proposal in Jackson Hole. il Bus W p94 N 21 '77

EASLEY, Joe Tom
It's even worse in Brussels. New Repub 177:22-3 Jl 9 '77

EASMAN, William S. Jr
Why the market acts the way it does. por Forbes 119:68+ Mr 1 '77 *

EASON, Al
Bass boom south of the border. il map Outdoor Life 161:82-4+ Ja '78
War and peace in a bass boat: slob guides, kooky clients. Outdoor Life 160:95-6+ O '77

EAST, Ben
Make the river do the work. il por Outdoor Life 160:78-81+ O '77
(ed) See Stamm, F. W. I will survive
—See Mol, C. jt auth

EAST (United States) See Atlantic States

EAST AFRICAN Airways (firm) See Airlines—Africa, East

EAST and West in music
Félicien David 1810-1876 and French romantic orientalism. P. Gradenwitz. bibl f il por Mus Q 62:471-506 O '76
Turkish affect in the land of the Sun King; French music from about 1625 to 1700. M. R. Obelkevich. bibl il Mus Q 63:367-89 Jl '77

EAST BERLIN. See Berlin (East Berlin)

EAST GERMAN exiles. See Exiles

EAST GERMANY. See Germany, East

EAST River, N.Y.

Bridges

See New York (city)—Bridges

EAST Side House Settlement Winter Antiques Show, New York. See Antiques— Exhibitions

EAST TIMOR. See Timor (island)

EAST-West relations. See International relations

EAST-West trade. See Communist countries—Commerce

EASTBURN, David P.
Modification in minimum wage is one approach; interview. por U.S. News 82:59-60 F 21 '77

EASTCOTT, John. See Momatiuk, Y. jt auth

EASTER
Message of Easter. R. C. Stapleton. por Ladies Home J 94:107+ Ap '77
See also
Jesus Christ—Resurrection and Ascension

EASTER breads. See Bread

EASTER candy. See Candy

EASTER cookery, Ornamental. See Cookery, Ornamental

EASTER eggs. See Eggs, Decorated

EASTER Island
Bound for glory; excerpt from Aku-Aku: the secret of Easter Island. T. Heyerdahl. il Sat Eve Post 249:18 Jl '77
Eye which sees heaven. W. Barnstone. il Holiday 58:44-5+ Mr '77

EASTER table decoration. See Table decoration

EASTERN Airlines
Airbus faces weight limitations. W. H. Gregory. Aviation W 107:25-6 O 31 '77
Eastern A-300B crew training started. L. Dunkelberg. il Aviation W 107:27+ S 5 '77
Eastern Airlines foresees need for 50 airbus-type aircraft. Aviation W 106:30 My 16 '77
Eastern leases four A-300Bs. Aviation W 106:22-3 My 9 '77
Eastern to get new terminal for air shuttle. il Aviation W 107:29 D 5 '77
Eastern to pay no lease fee for Airbus A-300s. J. M. Lenorovitz. Aviation W 106:28-9 My 30 '77
Eastern weighing reequipment needs. W. H. Gregory. Aviation W 107:27+ Ag 1 '77
Eastern weighs buy of 28 A-300Bs. Aviation W 107:25 D 19 '77
Eastern's engineering size, functions pared. W. C. Wetmore. Aviation W 107:27-8 N 28 '77
Long-term Eastern shuttle growth seen. D. M. North. Aviation W 107:34 O 10 '77
McDonnell Douglas, Eastern oppose Boeing on carrier talks. Aviation W 107:35 O 10 '77
Moon Man turns Eastern around; work of F. Borman. il pors Time 109:53 F 7 '77
Now, the poor man's jumbo jet; A300 Airbus. il Time 110:56+ O 17 '77
Shuttle serves as economic barometer. L. Doty. il Aviation W 106:26-8 F 14 '77

EASTERN Orthodox Church in the United States. See Orthodox Eastern Church in the United States

EASTERN religions. See Religions

EASTERN Test Range. See Proving grounds

EASTHAM, William K.
Inspiring public confidence in private enterprise; interview. il pors Nations Bus 65:50-4+ My '77

EASTLAKE, William
Mrs Gage in her bed of pain with a nice cup of gin; story; excerpt from The long naked descent into Boston. Ms 5:78-80 Mr '77

EASTMAN, Charles Alexander
Indian boyhood. A. L. Stensland. Engl J 66:59 Mr '77 *

EASTMAN, John
Walking the railroads. Natur Hist 86:90-3 N '77

EASTMAN, Max
Claude McKay as an artist. S. Warren. bibl f por Negro Hist Bull 40:685-7 Mr '77 *

EASTMAN Kodak Company
At the company that never rests. por Fortune 95:19 Ja '77
Case for Kodak. R. J. Flaherty. il Forbes 120:122 D 1 '77

EASTMAN Kodak Company—*Continued*
Kodak's blitz. A. J. Mayer and P. E. Simons. il Newsweek 89:58+ Ap 4 '77
Market manhandles a blue chip. il Bus W p70-3+ Je 20 '77
No joy for Kodak in GAF's departure. Bus W p23-4 Ag 8 '77
EASTMAN School of Music. See Rochester. University, Rochester, N.Y.—Eastman School of Music
EASTON, Carol
Sex and violence in the library: scream a little louder, please. il Am Lib 8:484-8 O '77
EASTWOOD, Clint
Maggie & Clint; interview; ed by S. Decatur. pors Ladies Home J 94:76+ N '77
about
Good ole Burt; cool-eyed Clint. R. Schickel. il pors Time 111:48-54 Ja 9 '78 *
EASTWOOD, Maggie
Maggie & Clint; interview; ed by S. Decatur. pors Ladies Home J 94:76+ N '77
EATING. See Diet; Gastronomy; Nutrition
EATING habits. See Food habits
EATON, Cyrus Stephen, 1883-
Profiles. E. J. Kahn, Jr. New Yorker 53:50-2+ O 10; 54-6+ O 17 '77 *
EATON, Quaintance
Wagner's Rienzi. il Hi Fi 27:MA30+ Ag '77
(ed) See Gish, L. Silent mimi talks
EATON Corporation
High gear. il Forbes 119:52-3 Je 1 '77
Where white-collar status boosts productivity. il Bus W p80+ My 23 '77
EATON Corporation-Carborundum Company merger. See Corporations—Acquisitions and mergers
EAUCLAIRE, Sally
Fashion, from barons to guys. il Mod Phot 41: 104-5 D '77
EAVESDROPPING, Electronic. See Electronics in criminal investigation, espionage, etc.
EBALITE inscriptions. See Cuneiform inscriptions
EBEL, Robert L.
Declining scores: two explanations. Educ Digest 42:2-5 F '77
EBER, Dorothy Harley
Eskimo tales. il Natur Hist 86:126-9 O '77
How it really was; excerpt from People from our side; with biographical sketch. il por Natur Hist 86:8, 70-5 bibl(p 101) F '77
EBERHARD, William G.
Aggressive chemical mimicry by a bolas spider. bibl il Science 198:1173-5 D 16 '77
EBERHART, Jonathan
[Articles on the natural sciences] See issues of Science news
Sense of Mars. il Chemistry 50:7-16 N '77
about
[Jonathan Eberhart] K. Frazier. por Sci N 111: 83 F 5 '77 *
EBERLE, Nancy Hartley
Hurry, hurry, hurry. McCalls 105:91+ Ja '78
100,000 pounds of lobster tail. il Oceans 10:30-2 S '77
EBERLY, Donald J.
National youth service. Current 192:3-12 Ap '77
EBERSTADT, Nicholas
Underappreciated India. New Repub 176:14-16 Ja 15 '77
EBERT, Alan
Exercise secrets of a Hollywood body doctor. il por Ladies Home J 94:50+ F '77
EBLAN excavations. See Syria—Antiquities
EBLESKIVERS. See Cookery, Danish
EBONY Fashion Fair. See Fashion shows
ECCENTRICS and eccentricities
Grass roots art. C. Carlson. il Ms 6:64-8 O '77
Scientific cranks: how to recognize one and what to do until the doctor arrives. Am Scholar 47:8+ Wint '77
Caricatures and cartoons
Eccentrics of the world. P. Le-Tan. il Horizon 19:88-9 Ja '77
ECCLESIASTICAL architecture. See Church architecture
ECCLESIASTICAL art. See Christian art and symbolism
ECCLESIASTICAL law
See also
Canon law
ECDYSIS. See Molting
ECDYSONE
2-Deoxy-α-ecdysone from ovaries and eggs of the silkworm, bombyx mori. E. Ohnishi and others. bibl il Science 197:66-7 Jl 1 '77
3β-Hydroxy-5α-cholestan-6-one: a possible precursor of α-ecdysone biosynthesis. S. Sakurai and others. bibl il Science 198:627-9 N 11 '77
Induction of acetylcholinesterase activity by β-ecdysone in a drosophila cell line. P. Cherbas and others. bibl il Science 197:275-7 Jl 15 '77
ECEVIT, Bülent
Harmony time for a poet-warrior. il por Time 109:44 Je 20 '77 *
Pas de deux. por Time 111:30-1 Ja 16 '78 *
ECHEVARRI, Javier. See Olano, M. jt auth
ECHEVARRÍA, Evelio A.
Poem of the pampas. il Américas 29:2-5 Ap '77
ECHEVERIA
They get by with little water; dudleya caespitosa and baccharis pilularis. il Sunset 158:264 Ap '77
ECHEVERRÍA ALVAREZ, Luis
Echeverria's economic policy. C. P. Blair. bibl f Cur Hist 72:124-7+ Mr '77 *
Mexican education: Echeverria's mixed legacy. G. Perissinotto. bibl f il Cur Hist 72:115-19+ Mr '77 *
Mexican foreign policy. G. W. Grayson. bibl f Cur Hist 72:97-101+ Mr '77 *
Mexico's government in crisis. S. Bizzarro. bibl f Cur Hist 72:102-5+ Mr '77 *
ECHINODERMS
See also
Sea urchins
ECHINOPS. See Thistles
ECHOLOCATION (physiology)
Amplitude spectrum representation in the Doppler-shifted-CF processing area of the auditory cortex of the mustache bat. N. Suga. bibl il Science 196:64-7 Ap 1 '77
Echo-detecting characteristics of neurons in inferior colliculus of unanesthetized bats. G. Pollak and others. bibl il Science 196:675-8 My 6 '77
Echolocation: cetaceans' sixth sense. R. McNally. il Oceans 10:27-33 Jl '77
ECHOLS, Evelyn
Ask Holiday; questions and answers. See issues of Holiday
ECKERD, Jack M.
Get involved with government—you can make it better. pors Nations Bus 65:61-3 Je '77
ECKERT, Roger, and Lux, H. D.
Calcium-dependent depression of a late outward current in snail neurons. bibl il Science 197: 472-5 Jl 29 '77
ECKERT, Thor, Jr
Karajan Orchestra Competition. il por Hi Fi 27: MA34-5+ Ap '77
ECKHARDT, Edris
New Deal ceramics: the Cleveland workshop. K. A. Marling. il por Ceram Mo 25:25-31 Je '77 *
ECKHARDT, Linda West
Keeping the old: a celebration at Norma and Marino DeLeon's. il pors Redbook 150:94+ D '77
ECKHARDT, Robert Christian
Crime and American society. Current 196:33-41 O '77
ECKHERT, Curtis D. and others
Zinc binding: a difference between human and bovine milk. bibl il Science 195:789-90 F 25 '77
ECKHOLM, Erik P.
Other energy crisis: firewood; excerpt from Losing ground: environmental stress and world food prospects. bibl il Focus 27:9-16 Mr '77; Same abr. with title Poor man's energy crisis. il UNESCO Courier 30:29-31 Jl '77; Same abr. with title Poor man's crisis: firewood. Sci Digest 82:59 O '77
Shrinking forests; excerpt from Losing ground: environmental stress and world food prospects. bibl il Focus 28:12-16 S '77
Unhealthy jobs; excerpt from The picture of health: environmental sources of disease. bibl il Environment 19:29-38 Ag '77
Unnatural history of tobacco; with biographical sketch. il Natur Hist 86:2, 22-4+ Ap; 76-7 Je '77
—and Brown, L. R.
Spreading deserts. bibl il map Focus 28:1-11 S '77
ECKMAN, Bruce
Making valid nonverbal judgments. Engl J 66:72-4 N '77
ECKSTEIN, Otto
To the prophet for the profits. il por Time 110: 90+ S 26 '77 *
ECLIPSES
Eclipses of Jupiter's satellites. il Sky & Tel 53:230-3 Mr '77
Eclipses of Iapetus by Saturn's rings. il Sky & Tel 54:190-1 S '77
Observations of eclipses of Jupiter's moons. J. Ashbrook. Sky & Tel 54:153 Ag '77
See also
Occultations
ECLIPSES, Lunar
April's partial lunar eclipse. il Sky & Tel 53: 423-6 Je '77
Julius Schmidt and his book about lunar eclipses. J. Ashbrook. il por Sky & Tel 153: 173-4 Mr '77
Notes on the lunar eclipse. il Sky & Tel 54:533-5 D '77
Partial lunar eclipse next month. il Sky & Tel 53:191 Mr '77
Reports on November's penumbral lunar eclipse. il Sky & Tel 53:149-51 F '77
ECLIPSES, Photography of. See Astronomical photography

ECLIPSES, Solar
Eclipse at sea. D. Di Cicco. il Sky & Tel 54:470-4 D '77
1977 solar eclipse in Colombia. A. A. Tinker. il maps Sky & Tel 53:267-9 Ap '77
Partial phases of this month's solar eclipse. il Sky & Tel 54:276-7 O '77
Two solar eclipses in 1977. maps Sky & Tel 53:184-5 Mr '77

History

Solar eclipses and ancient artistic motifs; letter. R. M. Sinclair. bibl Science 196:715-17 My 13 '77

ECLIPSING binaries. See Stars, Eclipsing binary

ECO, Umberto
De interpretatione, or the difficulty of being Marco Polo (on the occasion of Antonioni's China film); tr by C. Leefeldt. Film Q 30:8-12 Summ '77

L'ECOLE Nationale d'Administration. See National School of Administration, France

ECOLOGICAL communities. See Ecosystems

ECOLOGICAL models
Economic models in ecology. D. J. Rapport and J. E. Turner. bibl il Science 195:367-73 Ja 28 '77

ECOLOGICAL movement. See Environmental movement

ECOLOGICAL research
See also
Institute of Ecology
International biological program

ECOLOGISTS
Earthly pleasures; careers for women in ecology. A. M. Cunningham. Seventeen 36:72 O '77
Ecologists, ethics, and the environment. P. R. Ehrlich. BioScience 27:239 Ap '77
Yesterday's flower children were called conservationists. A. Hershman. Duns R 109:31-2+ Ap '77

Caricatures and cartoons

Ecologist. G. Watt. Am For 83:36-7 O '77

ECOLOGISTS in government. See Scientists in government

ECOLOGY
Boundary conditions in energy and ecology. H. G. Cassidy. bibl Bull Atom Sci 33:31-2 Mr '77
Emergence of ecology as a new integrative discipline. E. P. Odum. bibl Science 195:1289-93 Mr 25 '77
Gaia: the harmony of our sphere; theories of J. Lovelock and L. Margulis. F. Hapgood. Atlantic 240:100-4 D '77
See also
Botany—Ecology
Desert ecology
Ecosystems
Environment
Fishes—Ecology
Forest ecology
Fresh water ecology
Human ecology
Island ecology
Marine ecology
Marsh ecology
Population biology
Religion and ecology
Zoology—Ecology

Awards, prizes, etc.

Odum: ecology's highest award; Tyler Ecology Award. por Sci N 111:263 Ap 23 '77

History

Ecology: some historical perspective. Sci N 112:151 S 3 '77

Africa

Fly that would be king. R. S. Desowitz. il Natur Hist 86:76-83 bibl(p 101) F '77

Florida

35 percent of south Florida down the drain? Geological Survey report. Nat Parks & Con Mag 51:25 Mr '77

Idaho

Phosphate fate will determine Idaho high country's fate. E. Chaney. Audubon 79:123-6 Mr '77

Massachusetts

Dangerous nymphs of Nantucket. R. S. Desowitz and L. H. Miller. il Natur Hist 86:10+ bibl(p 110) D '77

Papua New Guinea

Wau Institute studies unique Papuan biota. J. L. Gressitt. map BioScience 27:149-50 F '77

Underdeveloped areas

See Underdeveloped areas—Ecology

ECOLOGY (periodical)
Raymond Lindeman and the trophic-dynamic concept in ecology. R. E. Cook. bibl Science 198:22-6 O 7 '77

ECOLOGY, Human. See Human ecology

ECOLOGY art. See Assemblage (art)

ECONOMETRIC models. See Economic models

ECONOMIC Adjustment, Office of. See United States—Defense, Department of—Economic Adjustment, Office of

ECONOMIC advisers. See Economists

ECONOMIC and Social Commission for Asia and the Pacific. See United Nations—Economic and Social Commission for Asia and the Pacific

ECONOMIC assistance
Economic aid urged for Angola, Comoros, Mozambique, Sao Tome and Principe. UN Chron 14:41-2 Ja '77
See also
International Bank for Reconstruction and Development
Underdeveloped areas

ECONOMIC assistance, American
Foreign aid authorizing bills transmitted to the Congress; text of letters, March 28, 1977. J. Carter. Dept State Bull 76:490-1 My 16 '77
President Carter outlines goals of foreign assistance program; message to Congress, March 17, 1977. J. Carter. Dept State Bull 76:340-2 Ap 11 '77
Secretary testifies on Administration's approach to foreign assistance; statement, February 24, 1977. C. R. Vance. Dept State Bull 76:236-41 Mr 14 '77
Secretary Vance emphasizes importance of foreign assistance programs; statement, March 23, 1977. C. R. Vance. Dept State Bull 76:336-9 Ap 11 '77
Secretary Vance gives overview of foreign assistance programs; statement, March 2, 1977. C. R. Vance. Dept State Bull 76:284-9 Mr 28 '77
See also
Food relief
Overseas Private Investment Corporation
United States—Agency for International Development

Africa

Administration supports increased U.S. contributions to the African Development Fund; statement, April 18, 1977. Dept State Bull 76:471-4 My 9 '77
Is the U.S. short-changing Africa? il A. Poinsett. il Ebony 33:84-5+ D '77
U.S. emphasizes role of international lending institutions in African development; statement, May 3, 1977. D. B. Bolen. Dept State Bull 76:576-9 My 30 '77

Asia, Southeastern

U.S. assistance programs in southeast Asia; statement, March 17, 1977. R. B. Oakley. Dept State Bull 76:342-4 Ap 11 '77

Asia, Southern

Department discusses south Asia and U.S. assistance programs; statement, March 22, 1977. A. Dubs. Dept State Bull 76:344-6 Ap 11 '77

Egypt

Sadat's sorry state. M. Kondracke. New Repub 176:14-16 Mr 19 '77

Europe, Western

History

Marshall plan: a memory, a beacon; Time essay. F. Trippett. il Time 109:43-4 Je 6 '77
Partners in a common enterprise: building for the future; Marshall plan address, June 2, 1977. W. M. Christopher. Dept State Bull 76:681-4 Je 27 '77

Far East

U.S. economic and security assistance programs in East Asia; statement, March 10, 1977. R. C. Holbrooke. Dept State Bull 76:322-6 Ap 4 '77

Korea, South

Korea, Inc. T. Szulc. New Repub 176:20-2 Ja 29 '77

Latin America

New unity and a new hope in the Western hemisphere: economic growth with social justice; statement, May 3, 1977. A. J. Young, Jr. Dept State Bull 76:567-76 My 30 '77

Lebanon

Lebanese delegation discusses rehabilitation needs; Department statement. Dept State Bull 76:91-2 Ja 31 '77
U.S. increases relief aid to Lebanon. Dept State Bull 76:234 Mr 14 '77

Portugal

Balance-of-payments assistance for Portugal; statement, June 9, 1977. P. H. Boeker. Dept State Bull 77:136-8 Jl 25 '77

Underdeveloped areas

Aid to developing countries: a third world trade unionist view. K. W. Nyoike. M Labor R 100:38-9 Mr '77
America's stake in the developing world; address, September 27, 1977. J. J. Gilligan. Dept State Bull 77:687-91 N 14 '77
Let's create wealth, not allocate shortages; address, May 24, 1977. W. B. Wriston. Vital Speeches 43:653-6 Ag 15 '77

ECONOMIC assistance, American—*Continued*

Vietnam, North

Dirty linen sale; secret Kissinger agreement. Nation 224:611-12 My 21 '77
Former President Nixon's message to Prime Minister Pham Van Dong; February 1, 1973. R. M. Nixon. Dept State Bull 76:674-5 Je 27 '77
Kissinger's double-cross for peace: The broken promise to Hanoi. G. Porter. Nation 224:519-21 Ap 30 '77

ECONOMIC assistance, Domestic
How to clean up the mess in Washington. Duns R 109:40-1 F '77
Memo to the White House. G. McGovern. il Harpers 255:33-5 O '77
New urban riots. M. Pousner. por Newsweek 89:11 Je 27 '77
Recounting the poor. T. M. Smeeding. bibl il Intellect 106:222-5 D '77
See also
Community development
Food relief—United States
Grants-in-aid
Negative income tax
Old age assistance
Project Head Start
United States—Commerce, Department of—Economic Development Administration
United States—Community Services Administration

Scandinavia

Welfare state at the crossroads. J. Logue. Progressive 41:34-7 S '77

ECONOMIC assistance, German

United States

Berlin remembers; donations to the American Red Cross by West Berliners. il Time 109:63 Mr 7 '77

ECONOMIC assistance, Kuwaiti

Underdeveloped areas

View from the upper deck; Kuwait Fund for Arab Economic Development. por Forbes 119:120 Je 15 '77

ECONOMIC assistance in Egypt
Egypt: if belt-tightening fails, what next? il Bus W p42 F 7 '77

ECONOMIC assistance in Rhodesia
Department discusses proposal for Zimbabwe Development Fund; statement, April 28, 1977. W. E. Schaufele, Jr. Dept State Bull 76:528-30 My 23 '77

ECONOMIC assistance in South Africa
States condemned for supporting foreign economic interests which exploit territories; with text of resolution. UN Chron 13:45-6, 81-2 D '76

ECONOMIC assistance in underdeveloped areas. See Underdeveloped areas

ECONOMIC botany. See Botany, Economic

ECONOMIC boycott. See Boycott

ECONOMIC Commission for Africa. See United Nations—Economic Commission for Africa

ECONOMIC Commission for Europe. See United Nations—Economic Commission for Europe

ECONOMIC Commission for Latin America. See United Nations—Economic Commission for Latin America

ECONOMIC Commission for Western Asia. See United Nations—Economic Commission for Western Asia

ECONOMIC conditions
Business around the world. See issues of U.S. news and world report
Department discusses international economic importance of enactment of the President's energy program; statement, May 17, 1977. J. L. Katz. Dept State Bull 76:640-2 Je 13 '77
Energy and the world economy; statement, January 5, 1977. J. L. Katz. Dept State Bull 76:61-7 Ja 24 '77
Fighting a global lull. M. Ruby and others. il Newsweek 90:89-90 O 10 '77
Harder times abroad—a threat to U.S? il U.S. News 83:48-9 O 3 '77
International buddy system. Forbes 119:77 Ja 15 '77
International business. See issues of Business week
International economic situation; statement, April 6, 1977. R. N. Cooper. Dept State Bull 76:378-84 Ap 18 '77
On a disappointing year, an enduring crisis, and an opportunity. S. Lens. Progressive 41:12-13 D '77
Quality vs. quantity. B. Strumpel. Intellect 105:378 My '77
Spreading gloom in foreign economies. il Bus W p63-4 D 26 '77
Strong U.S. leads the recovery. il Time 109:63-4 My 16 '77
World economy. J. McCaull. il Environment 19:34-44 N '77
World on the mend. il Fortune 96:122-7 Ag '77
Year of opportunity. P. A. Samuelson. Newsweek 89:67 Ja 31 '77
See also
Business depression
Cost of living
Poverty
also subhead Economic conditions under names of countries, states, cities, etc, e.g. Russia—Economic conditions

ECONOMIC conferences
Assembly concerned at Paris Conference failure to achieve concrete results; Conference on International Economic Co-operation; with text of resolution. UN Chron 13:50-1, 82 D '76
Conflict between North and South; Conference on International Economic Cooperation, Paris. il Time 109:30 Je 13 '77
Department discusses CIEC and developing country debt; statement, June 29, 1977. R. J. Ryan, Jr. Dept State Bull 77:179-82 Ag 8 '77
Department discusses results of CIEC meeting; statement, June 21, 1977. R. N. Cooper. Dept State Bull 77:92-8 Jl 18 '77
Limited progress made at Paris talks—Mr Waldheim; report on Conference on International Economic Co-operation. UN Chron 14:36 Jl '77
London economic summit. J. Novak. America 136:518-20 Je 11 '77
No meeting of minds in Paris; Conference on International Economic Cooperation, Paris. America 136:535 Je 18 '77
Package for the have-nots; Conference on International Cooperation and Development. Nation 224:739-40 Je 18 '77
Paris Economic Co-operation Conference seen as contributing to broader understanding. il UN Chron 14:46-7 Jl '77
Progress in Paris. il Newsweek 89:78 Je 13 '77
Requiem for the North-South conference; Conference on International Economic Cooperation. J. Amuzegar. bibl f For Affairs 56:136-59 O '77
Resumed Assembly session fails to agree on Paris conference achievements. il UN Chron 14:32-5 O '77
Secretary Vance attends ministerial meeting of the Conference on International Economic Co-operation; address, news conference, with text of communique, May 30, June 3, 1977. C. R. Vance; R. N. Cooper. Dept State Bull 76:645-52 Je 20 '77
Third try at the summit; London conference. Time 109:76+ Mr 21 '77
Trying to stabilize commodities; Conference on International Economic Cooperation. il Bus W p31-2 My 30 '77
What it will take to restore global prosperity; Washington D.C. meeting of finance ministers. il U.S. News 83:62-3 O 10 '77
What the third world wants; Conference on International Economic Cooperation. il Bus W p80-1 My 9 '77
See also
Employment—Conferences
Foreign trade regulation—Conferences
United Nations Conference on Science and Technology for Development, 1979 (proposed)

ECONOMIC cooperation. See Economic relations

ECONOMIC development
Closet conservatives; works of E. F. Schumacher and F. Hirsch. M. Mayer. Am Scholar 46:230+ Spr '77
Dilemma in reflation for the IMF. E. Mervosh. Bus W p40 O 10 '77
Human scene: growth: how big? How far? How risky? il Sr Schol 109:6-8+ Ja 27 '77
Idea whose time has come? appropriate technology; application of E. F. Schumacher's concepts. J. Ross-Skinner. il por Duns R 110:118-20+ O '77
Mr Small; theories of E. F. Schumacher. S. Fraker and G. C. Lubenow. il por Newsweek 89:18 Mr 28 '77
St George for growth; views of W. Beckerman. por Time 109:63 Je 6 '77
Slow economic growth intensifies political conflict. G. Almond. Intellect 105:209 Ja '77
Socioeconomic fix: the easy way out? A. J. Fedanzo, Jr. bibl Intellect 106:55-7 Ag '77
Third-world poverty: don't blame us. M. Singer and P. Bracken. Read Digest 110:114-17 F '77
U.S. position on international economic relations; statement, October 14, 1977. R. N. Cooper. Dept State Bull 77:696-704 N 14 '77
What ails the world economy. Fortune 96:103 N '77
Why the industrial nations aren't growing; GATT economists' report. il Bus W p 138+ N 21 '77
See also
Development banks
Independent Commission on International Development Issues
Institute for International Development, Inc
Organization for Economic Cooperation and Development
Underdeveloped areas
United Nations Industrial Development Organization

Conferences

See Economic conferences

ECONOMIC Development Administration. See United States—Commerce, Department of—Economic Development Administration

ECONOMIC education. See Economics—Study and teaching

ECONOMIC forecasting
Ahead: at least 3 years of prosperity; interview. W. M. Blumenthal. il por U.S. News 82:31-4 Ap 11 '77
Bad case of frostbite. il Bus W p32-3 F 14 '77
Bears are prowling again. Bus W p24-5 S 5 '77
Declining interest rates forecast; study by the Academy for Contemporary Problems. il Am City & County 92:34 S '77
Economic impact; energy policy. M. Ruby and others. il Newsweek 89:21-2+ My 2 '77
Economics. il Sr Schol 110:30-1 S 22; 22-5 O 6; 13-16 N 17 '77
Forecasts for Carter years. J. Carlson. por Nations Bus 65:28+ Ja '77
Hearing the inflation beat. M. Ruby and others. il Newsweek 89:75-6 F 21 '77
How little stimulus will be enough? il Time 109:65 My 9 '77
Inflation breeds a few bears. il Bus W p23 Mr 28 '77
International economic outlook; address, April 20, 1977. L. G. McGinnis. Vital Speeches 43:478-80 My 15 '77
Investment outlook 1978; special section. il Bus W p52-3+ D 26 '77
Next recession? 1978? il Forbes 119:81 Mr 1 '77
Outlook for borrowers: plenty of money but it'll cost more. il U.S. News 83:82-4 O 31 '77
Parliament of owls. M. S. Forbes, Jr. por Forbes 119:6 Ja 15 '77
Passing of the age of affluence. T. Bender. Current 197:23-33 N '77
Recovery gets its second wind. il Fortune 95:7-8+ Ja '77
Recovery on a tightrope. il Time 110:75-7 O 3 '77
'78 outlook: one more good year; Time Board of Economists report. il Time 110:79-82 D 19 '77
Slower, but no pause. il Time 110:35-6 Ag 1 '77
Solid rise for business in '78—size-up by a panel of experts; Conference Board economic forum. il U.S. News 83:56-7 D 5 '77
Still a good year. P. A. Samuelson. Newsweek 91:53 Ja 9 '78
Storm warnings. Nat R 29:1039-40 S 16 '77
Sunny midyear outlook. il U.S. News 83:16-18 Jl 4 '77
Tests for Carter's balanced-budget plans. Bus W p31-2 Je 13 '77
That awful weather won't slow us down. Fortune 95:9-10 Mr '77
There's no slowdown in sight. il Bus W p 16-17 Ag 1 '77
To the prophet go the profits; Data Resources, Inc. il por Time 110:90+ S 26 '77
Tough times ahead. W. W. Rostow. por Intellect 105:377 My '77
Turn of the tide. P. A. Samuelson. il Newsweek 89:88 Mr 14 '77
Uneasy balance for the U.S. economy. il Bus W p52-3+ D 26 '77
Warm autumn for the west; OECD report. P. A. Samuelson. Newsweek 90:80 Jl 18 '77
Weather economics. P. A. Samuelson. Newsweek 89:84 F 21 '77
What to expect if prices keep going up. il U.S. News 82:22-3 My 30 '77
When company chiefs look ahead—. U.S. News 83:25 O 24 '77
Will energy conservation throttle economic growth? with interview with J. R. Schlesinger. il Bus W p66-72+ Ap 25 '77
See also
Business forecasting
Economic indicators
Economic models

ECONOMIC growth. See Economic development

ECONOMIC history
It started with Adam (Smith) J. K. Galbraith. il por N Y Times Mag p23-4+ My 15 '77
John Kenneth Galbraith's marathon television series. G. Stigler. il Nat R 29:601-4 My 27 '77
See also
Great Britain—Economic history
United States—Economic history

ECONOMIC indicators
Economy '78: a graphic look. il Duns R 110:46-9 S '77
New role for economic indicators. J. Shiskin. M Labor R 100:3-5 N '77
See also
Price indexes
Seasonal variations (economics)

ECONOMIC models
Econometrics and politics. P. C. Roberts. Nat R 29:549-51 My 13 '77
Economic models in ecology. D. J. Rapport and J. E. Turner. bibl il Science 195:367-73 Ja 28 '77

ECONOMIC policy
After the summit: a widening gap between weak and strong. E. Mervosh and J. Pearson. il Bus W p92 My 23 '77
Backlash from U.S. growth. il Bus W p 16-17 Jl 4 '77
Stoking the West's economic locomotive. E. Mervosh. Bus W p29 Jl 11 '77
Trilateral reform and world justice. J. Novak. America 137:106-9 Ag 27 '77
Widening split over growth policies; OECD meeting. Bus W p37+ D 5 '77
World roundup. See issues of Business week
See also
Commercial policy
Economic development
Inflation (finance)
also subhead Economic policy under names of countries, e.g. Israel—Economic policy

ECONOMIC relations
Against the New Economic Order. P. T. Bauer and B. S. Yamey. bibl f Commentary 63:25-31 Ap '77; Reply with rejoinder. J. Novak. 64:4+ Jl '77
Assembly acts on economic co-operation; with text of resolution. UN Chron 14:55, 106-7 Ja '77
Department discusses implementation of economic provisions of the final act of the Helsinki Conference; statement, January 14, 1977. C. W. Robinson. Dept State Bull 76:108-13 F 7 '77
Economic relations between developed and developing countries. S. S. Ramphal. M Labor R 100:37-8 Mr '77
Equality of opportunities among nations. R. H. Heindel. Intellect 105:292 Mr '77
International economic report transmitted to the Congress; message, January 18, 1977. G. R. Ford. Dept State Bull 76:129-32 F 14 '77
News conference of Secretary Vance and Secretary Blumenthal, May 8. C. R. Vance and W. M. Blumenthal. Dept State Bull 76:586-93 Je 6 '77
On power; symposium. bibl f For Affairs 56:1-110 O '77
President Carter attends economic, Berlin, and NATO meeting at London; remarks, with text of declarations, NATO communique, and question and answer session, May 5, 8-11, 1977. J. Carter. Dept State Bull 76:581-6+ Je 6 '77
Stewardship and the NIEO. P. Land. il New Cath World 220:244-9 S '77
Trilateral world approach; report of Trilateral Commission task force. Current 192:54-61 Ap '77
U.S. position on international economic relations; statement, October 14, 1977. R. N. Cooper. Dept State Bull 77:696-704 N 14 '77
World economy. J. McCaull. il Environment 19:34-44 N '77
See also
Balance of payments
European Economic Community
General Agreement on Tariffs and Trade
Independent Commission on International Development Issues
Organization for Economic Cooperation and Development
Trilateral Commission, Inc
United States—Economic relations

ECONOMIC, Social and Cultural Rights, International Covenant on. See International Covenant on Economic, Social and Cultural Rights

ECONOMIC research
See also
American Enterprise Institute for Public Policy Research
Brookings Institution
Trilateral Commission, Inc

ECONOMIC statistics
Economics. il Sr Schol 110:30-1 S 22; 22-5 O 6; 13-16 N 17 '77
See also
Gross national product
Seasonal variations (economics)
Unemployment—Statistics

ECONOMIC status of women. See Women—Economic conditions

ECONOMIC theory. See Economics

ECONOMIC zoology. See Zoology, Economic

ECONOMICS
Decadence of economic theory; J. M. Keynes and Keyesianism. E. Meadows. Nat R 30:23-5+ Ja 6 '78
Great hamburger paradox. D. Warsh. il Forbes 120:166-7 S 15 '77
Haggis & the Wealth of nations; Bicentennial celebration of the publication of Adam Smith's great work. E. Van Den Haag. Nat R 29:268 Mr 4 '77
Inflation is now too serious a matter to leave to the economists. D. Warsh and L. Minard; discussion. il Forbes 119:44-6 Ja 15 '77
Is Keynes dead? M. Ruby and others. il Newsweek 89:74-5 Je 20 '77
1977 Nobel Prize in economics. C. P. Kindleberger. pors Science 198:813-14+ N 25 '77

ECONOMICS—*Continued*
Taking the scare out of scarcity. E. F. Schumacher. Psychol Today 11:16 S '77; Same abr. Read Digest 111:168-9 D '77
See also
Bible—Economic aspects
Capital
Capitalism
Debt
Efficiency, Industrial
Employment
Free enterprise
Income
Inflation (finance)
Leisure class
Property
Socialism
Stock exchanges
Urban economics
Wealth

Bibliography

Robert Lekachman on economics. R. Lekachman. New Repub 177:32-4 N 26 '77

History

See Economic history

Study and teaching

Economics gap. H. Flieger. U.S. News 82:76 Ja 31 '77
Getting economic basics across to children. V. Louviere. il Nations Bus 65:57 Ag '77
Keynes goes to kindergarten. L. Smith. il Duns R 109:42-3 Ja '77
Why business finds it tough to polish its own image. U.S. News 83:64 S 19 '77

ECONOMICS and politics
Let us now praise (faintly) famous economists. J. K. Galbraith. Esquire 87:70-1+ My '77
Redistribution of wealth means bloody politics; Project: Knowledge 2000 conference; excerpts from address. G. A. Almond. por Intellect 105:205-6 Ja '77
Slow economic growth intensifies political conflict. G. Almond. Intellect 105:209 Ja '77

ECONOMISTS
Big business in credibility. il Bus W p84+ Mr 7 '77
Let us now praise (faintly) famous economists. J. K. Galbraith. Esquire 87:70-1+ My '77
New clout for corporate economists. P. Smith. Duns R 109:62-4 Ja '77
Who's who in no 2. il Newsweek 89:62-3 Ja 31 '77
Why few government economists resign in protest; excerpt from Professional Standards for the Performance of the Government Economist. J. B. Henderson. M Labor R 100:74 F '77
See also names of economists, e.g. R. N. Cooper

ECONOMY. See Thrift

ECOSYSTEMS
Ecosystems analysis and population biology: lessons for the development of community ecology. T. C. Foin and S. K. Jain. bibl il BioScience 27:532-8 Ag '77
Frenetic life forms that flourish in suburban lawns. J. H. Falk. il Smithsonian 8:90-6 bibl(p 147) Ap '77
How much are nature's services worth? W. E. Westman. bibl Science 197:960-4 S 2 '77
Pygmies on the fourth terrace, rain forest on the second; ecosystem of new state park north of Mendocino, Calif. il Sunset 159:38-9 Jl '77
Raymond Lindeman and the trophic-dynamic concept in ecology. R. E. Cook. bibl Science 198:22-6 O 7 '77
This fragile earth. See issues of International wildlife to May 1977
Tree nobody liked; red mangrove in Florida Gulf Coast area. R. Gore. il map Nat Geog 151:668-89 My '77

ECUADOR
See also
Churches—Ecuador
Galápagos Islands
Otavalo
Quito
Railroads—Ecuador

Antiquities

San Pablo corn kernel and its friends. C. Zevallos and others. bibl il map Science 196:385-9 Ap 22 '77

Commerce

Israel

See Israel—Commerce—Ecuador

Native races

See Indians of South America—Ecuador

Religious institutions and affairs

See also
Catholic Church in Ecuador

ECUMENICAL conferences. See Religious conferences

ECUMENICAL Council, 2d. See Vatican Council, 2d

ECUMENICAL movement
Eastern view of ecumenism. P. M. Gregorios. il America 137:400-1 D 3 '77
Ecumenism in Latin America. America 136:228 Mr 19 '77
Ecumenism; symposium; with editorial comment. bibl New Cath World 220:158+ Jl '77
Fourteen years after Unity in mid-career. A. J. Van der Bent. Chr Cent 94:565-7 Je 8 '77
Of many things. J. O'Hare. America 136:inside cover Mr 5 '77
Severed roots of American Christianity; results of ecumenism. P. Williams; rejoinder. Nat R 29:270-1 Mr 4 '77
Ultimum verbum—promitto! J. J. Lynch. Nat R 29:887+ Ag 5 '77

EDDIES, Ocean. See Ocean currents

EDDY, Edward Danforth, 1921-
Quality of life; address, May 21, 1977. Vital Speeches 43:593-5 Jl 15 '77

EDDY, John A.
Case of the missing sunspots; with biographical sketch. il Sci Am 236:15, 80-8 My '77
—and others
Anomalous solar rotation in the early 17th century. bibl il Science 198:824-9 N 25 '77

EDDY, Otis
Schoharie Aqueduct. A. S. Fick. il por Conservationist 32:16-17 N '77 *

EDEL, Leon
Portrait of the artist as an old man. Am Scholar 47:52-68 Wint '77
about
Lesson of the master. por Time 110:47 Ag 22 '77 *

EDEL, Matthew
Continuing Keynesian economics. Society 14:17-19 My '77

EDELMAN, Gerald Maurice
Theory of the brain: Edelman's quest for unity. por Sci N 112:112-13 Jl 9 '77 *

EDELMAN, Susanne Popper
Virtue, weep if I die. il por Opera N 41:10-13 Mr 26 '77

EDELSON, Burton I.
Global satellite communications; with biographical sketch. il map Sci Am 236:16, 58-68+ bibl(p 138) F '77
—and Pollack, Louis
Satellite communications. bibl il map Science 195:1125-33 Mr 18 '77

EDELSON, Edward
Aura phenomenon puzzles experts. il Smithsonian 8:109-14 bibl(p 148) Ap '77
Great ozone debate. il Pop Sci 210:82-6 Je '77

EDELSON, Mark
Bastille Day '77. Nat R 29:870 Ag 5 '77

EDELSTEIN, Barbara
Woman doctor's diet; excerpt from A woman doctor's diet for women. il Ladies Home J 94:169-76 N '77

EDELSTEIN, Leon M.
Can blackness prolong life? il pors Ebony 32:124-7 Je '77 *

EDEMA
See also
Reye's syndrome

EDEN, Anthony, 1st Earl of Avon. See Avon, A. E.

EDEN, Dorothy
PW interviews; ed by J. F. Baker. por Pub W 211:8-9 Mr 28 '77

EDEN, John
Eye myths. Harp Baz 110:115 Ag 77

EDER, Lynn
Retail sales cooperative. il por Ceram Mo 25:51-4 N '77

EDER, Richard
Andrei Serban's theater of terror and beauty. il pors N Y Times Mag p42-3+ F 13 '77
Conversations west of Seville. Sat R 5:12-13 O 29 '77
New visionary in German films. il pors N Y Times Mag p24-6+ Jl 10 '77
Theater USA. il Horizon 20:20-9 O '77
Those mean and dirty streets. il Horizon 19:4-10 My '77

EDER, Sid, and Williamson, Jed
From the mountains to the classrooms. il Am Educ 13:17-22 N '77

EDEY, Marion
CEQ nominee learns judge not, lest ye be judged. L. J. Carter. Science 198:473 N 4 '77 *

EDGAR; opera. See Puccini, G.

EDGERTON, Susan Ketchin
Teachers in role conflict: the hidden dilemma. Educ Digest 43:17-19 D '77

EDGINTON, Christopher R. See Williams, J. G. jt auth

EDGLEY, Charles. See Turner, R. E. jt auth

EDIBLE greens. See Greens, Edible

EDIBLE plants. See Plants, Edible

EDIGER, Donald, and Parisi, A. J.
Commentary/energy. il Bus W p 142-3 Ap 18 '77

EDIGER, Marlow
Open space education: success or failure. Clearing H 50:262-3 F '77

EDINBURGH Festival. See International Festival of Music and Drama, Edinburgh

EDISON, Thomas Alva
At the creation. R. R. Wile. bibl il por Am Rec G 40:6-10 F '77 *
Centennial of the phonograph. G. A. Stahl. bibl il por Chemistry 50:10-12 D '77 *
Edison concept; drawings of early phonographs; comp by R. R. Wile. Am Rec G 41:10-13 D '77 *
Edison's baby: from tinfoil to tape. I. Kolodin. il por Sat R 4:20-2 Jl 23 '77 *
First 100 years of the phonograph. H. Fantel. il por Pop Mech 148:87+ Ag '77 *
Genius to genius: comp by R. R. Wile. J Hofmann. Am Rec G 40:6-8+ S '77 *
In nature's laboratory. P. W. Metzler. il pors Conservationist 32:30-3+ Jl '77 *

EDISON Electric Institute
Electricity: a necessity for the people; address, February 2, 1977. W. D. Crawford. Vital Speeches 43:294-6 Mr 1 '77
Mind control, the Edison Electric way. M. Zeldin. Audubon 79:115-17 Jl '77
Nuclear game; Energy-Environment game. il Progressive 41:10 N '77
Selling the nuclear faith. Progressive 41:22 S '77

EDISON National Historic Site. See Historic houses, sites, etc.—New Jersey

EDITH Bunker (television character) See Women in television

EDITING. See Editors and editing

EDITIONS of works of art. See Multiple art

EDITORIAL cartoons. See Caricatures and cartoons

EDITORIALS
Good grey bananas. M. J. Sobran, Jr. Nat R 29:1251-2 O 28 '77
Looking back at Christmas; newspaper editorials and poems. Sat Eve Post 249:18-19+ D '77
Where to sell op-ed articles. Writer 90:23-4 My '77

Anecdotes, facetiae, satire, etc.

Point and counterpoint. M. E. Marty. Chr Cent 94:495 My 18 '77

EDITORS and editing
Cave of the winds. L. H. Lapham. Nat R 29: 1055-8+ S 16 '77
Of editors and imprints. W. Cole. Sat R 4:37 My 14 '77
See also
Authors and editors
Proofreading

Awards, prizes, etc.

Robert D. Loomis of Random House wins fourth Roger Klein Award for creative editing; interview, ed by M. Reuter. R. D. Loomis. il por Pub W 211:25+ My 9 '77

EDMISTON, Susan
Celebrity shrinks. il pors Esquire 88:53-6+ Ag '77
Mrs Greene's steps to successful family life. por Good H 185:70+ S '77

EDMONDSON, Madeleine
Confessions of a soap addict. por Newsweek 90: 3 Ag 22 '77

EDMONDSON, William B.
Department testifies on U.S policy toward Rhodesia; statement, June 8, 1977. Dept State Bull 77:98-9 Jl 18 '77

EDMUNDSON, Allen B. See Capra, J. D. jt auth

EDSON, Lee
Coming: a vaccine against tooth decay. il N Y Times Mag p56-60 F 27 '77; Same abr. Read Digest 111:59-62 Jl '77
Why laetrile won't go away. il N Y Times Mag p41+ N 27 '77

EDUCATION
See also
Accountability (education)
Business and education
Business education
Carnegie Foundation for the Advancement of Teaching
Coeducation
College education
Communication in education
Community education
Computers—Educational use
Correlation (education)
Creative education
Dramatization in education
Education, Compulsory
Education of women
Educators
Engineering education
Foreign study
Group work in education
Illiteracy
International education
Learning, Psychology of
Medical education
Minorities
Moral education
Motion pictures in education
Motivation (education)
Museum education
Newspapers in education
Outdoor education
Physical education and training
Professional education
Religious education
Role playing
Segregation in education
Self culture
Teachers
Teaching
Technical education
Telephone in education
Theological education
Travel study courses
Video recorders and recording—Educational use
Vocational education
Volunteer workers in education
also headings beginning School; *also* subhead Education under various subjects, e.g. Handicapped—Education

Aims and objectives

I like behavioral objectives because... J. F. Newport. Clearing H 51:182-3 D '77
See also
College education—Aims and objectives
Educational sociology

Bibliography

Books. See issues of Today's education
New educational materials. See issues of Education digest

Conferences

Clearing the air in career education; Houston conference. S. B. Neill. il Am Educ 13:6-9+ Mr '77
Dates of the month. See issues of Education digest
National Conference on Issues That Impact on the Black Community. J. R. Picott. Negro Hist Bull 40:693 My '77
Sexism: curing the disease vs. masking the symptoms; National Conference on Non-Sexist Early Childhood Education. P. D. Pollack; discussion. SLJ 23:52 Mr; 4 Ap '77
See also
Conference on College Composition and Communication

Curricula

See Courses of study

Economic aspects

School budgets cheat children. S. D. Frank. por Intellect 106:9-10 Jl '77
See also
College education—Cost

Evaluation

Evaluation and politics in Education. G. E. Sroufe. Educ Digest 43:20-3 D '77
See also
Accountability (education)

Experimental methods

Mini-course as an experiment in alternative education. S. C. Diamond. Clearing H 51:11 S '77
New school plan from toddlers to pre-teens; Kramer Project in Little Rock, Ark. B. M. Caldwell. il Parents Mag 52:56-7+ S '77
School without schools; creative solutions to closing of Columbus, Ohio schools during fuel shortage. F. M. Hechinger. il Sat R 4:12+ Ap 30 '77; Same abr. Educ Digest 43:10-13 O '77
See also
Concentrated study
Educational innovations
Open plan schools
Schools, Experimental

Federal aid

Carter budget: at last, better news for book, library and reading programs. S. Wagner. Pub W 211:32-4 Mr 7 '77
Education funding: a look at bills before Congress. S. Wagner. Pub W 211:36-7 Je 27 '77
Failure richly rewarded; New York City. M. Kempton. Progressive 41:45 O '77
Federal funds. See issues of American education
House-Senate conferees agree on education funds. S. Wagner. Pub W 212:46 Ag 1 '77
How to ask for Federal funding. C. L. Battaglia. il Am Educ 13:6-9 Jl '77; Same abr. Educ Digest 43:24-7 D '77
Let's reward for success—not failure. R. B. Love. Educ Digest 42:20-1 Ja '77
One-third federal funding. J. Ryor. Todays Educ 66:6 Mr '77
PL 94-142—getting the money to make it work. E. Brooke. Todays Educ 66:50-2 N '77
Theoretical and policy implications of case study findings about federal efforts to improve public schools. N. Gross. bibl f Ann Am Acad 434:71-87 N '77
Unfinished work of the 95th Congress. Todays Educ 66:80 S '77

EDUCATION—Federal aid—*Continued*
U.S. expected to propose new Education Department. S. Wagner. Pub W 212:27 D 26 '77
See also
Catholic schools—Federal aid
Colleges and universities—Federal aid
Project Head Start
School libraries—Federal aid
Student aid
Voucher plan in education

Finance

Coming battles over school-finance reform. S. Leggett. Read Digest 110:21-4+ F '77
New battles over school budgets; question of property tax financing in Serrano case in California. R. Lindsey. il N Y Times Mag p 17-19+ S 18 '77
Ohio squeeze. M. Sheils. il Newsweek 90:111 O 31 '77
Paying for schools in Washington. C. Polsgrove. Progressive 41:44 N '77
School finance: the case for equalization of opportunity. J. Gwynne. bibl Intellect 105:420-2 Je '77
School tax credits? D. Holt and others. il Newsweek 90:76 D 26 '77
Schools that ran out of money. M. R. Skrocki. McCalls 104:66 My '77
Time to cut strings; Moynihan-Packwood bill. America 137:470 D 31 '77
See also
Colleges and universities—Finance
Education—Economic aspects
Private schools—Finance

International aspects

What they teach abroad; secondary education. Time 110:71 N 14 '77

Laws

See Educational laws and legislation

Objectives

See Education—Aims and objectives

Periodicals

See also
English journal

Philosophy

Alternative schooling: language and meaning. J. I. Goodlad. il Todays Educ 66:84-6 Ja '77
Back to basics: its meaning for school media programs. M. Weber. bibl por SLJ 24:83-5 O '77
Back to basics: the movement and its meaning. B. Brodinsky. Educ Digest 42:2-5 My '77
Back to basics: what does it really mean? E. H. Schuster. Clearing H 50:237-9 F '77
Battle for the little red schoolhouse. M. S. Miller. il Ladies Home J 94:60+ N '77
Cult of anti-rationalism in education. R. Hoffman. Educ Digest 42:57-60 Ja '77
Look at the fundamental school concept; address, November 20, 1976. J. K. Wellington. Vital Speeches 43:215-20 Ja 15 '77
Mr Hutchins' convictions. J. W. Donohue. America 136:504-5 Je 4 '77
The more we spend, the less children learn; excerpt from Our children's crippled future: how American education has failed. F. E. Armbruster. il N Y Times Mag p9-11+ Ag 28 '77; Same abr. with title Why American education is failing. Read Digest 112:106-9 Ja '78
1976 declaration of education; address, November 4, 1976. B. O. Wireman. Vital Speeches 43:220-3 Ja 15 '77
Pedestrian-idealist's approach to education; College Life Project at the University of New Orleans. W. Barnwell. Chr Cent 94:944-8 O 19 '77
What's basic about the curriculum? A. W. Foshay. Educ Digest 43:5-9 D '77
Which basics? A. Lemke. Clearing H 51:14-16 S '77; Same abr. Educ Digest 43:6-8 N '77
Why basic education? A. G. Down. Educ Digest 43:2-5 N '77

Research

See Educational research

Societies

See Educational associations

Standards

Are forty percent of our children really unsatisfactory? W. D. Hedges. bibl il Clearing H 50:417-22 My '77; Same abr. Educ Digest 43:31-3 O '77
Basic training; Chicago's minimum competence standards for elementary school students. M. Sheils and S. Monroe. Newsweek 90:44 Ag 15 '77
Chains of functional illiteracy. G. H. Cole. Educ Digest 43:10-13 D '77
Competency-based education. W. G. Spady. Educ Digest 42:21-4 My '77
Education now; judging a school system. S. Wilson. Sat R 5:68-9 D 10 '77
Need for elite education. J. R. Silber. Harpers 254:22-4 Je '77

State aid

See also
Catholic schools—State aid
Church schools—State aid

Statistics

Statistics of the month. See issues of American education
See also
United States—Education, Office of—National Center for Education Statistics

Study and teaching

See also
Student teaching
Teachers—Education

Africa

Professor James Emman Kwegyir Aggrey's personality. D. C. Yancey. bibl Negro Hist Bull 40:722-4 Jl '77
See also
Education—Rhodesia

Africa, East

Educational change in Africa. S. Kay. bibl il Intellect 106:217-20 D '77

Appalachian Region

Appalachian reading instruction: the pragmatic social factor. G. Giordano. Engl J 66:31-2 My '77

Arizona

Classroom in the cactus; Arizona-Sonora Desert Museum. J. Stocker. il Am Educ 13:6-11 D '77

Arkansas

Little Rock revisited. E. Keerdoja. il Newsweek 90:8 S 5 '77
New school plan from toddlers to pre-teens; Kramer Project in Little Rock. B. M. Caldwell. il Parents Mag 52:56-7+ S '77

Asia

Exploring the exotic East; teacher study tour of Asian schools. V. N. Kobayashi. Todays Educ 66:74-6 S '77

California

As we see it; desegregation resolution drafted by Stockton, Calif, students; excerpt from television script. il Sr Schol 110:17-18+ S 22 '77
Career education—the California R.O.P.—revisited. V. A. Gallo. bibl Clearing H 51:26-9 S '77
Croquet, anyone? athletic-injury awards. L. Langway and D. Gram. il Newsweek 90:72-3 S 5 '77
Early childhood education, California-style; Barranca Elementary School, Covina, Calif. M. McVey. Educ Digest 43:14-16 D '77
Early childhood: the crucial years for learning; Early Childhood Education (ECE) program. C. Luetje. Parents Mag 52:18 Ag '77
Family that fought back; use of Ritalin in Taft schools. J. N. Bell. il McCalls 104:26+ My '77
Los Alamitos: the School Library Media Program of 1977; views of school system representatives. il SLJ 24:74-9 O '77
New battles over school budgets; question of property tax financing in Serrano case. R. Lindsey. il N Y Times Mag p 17-19+ S 18 '77
Potter's pentathlon; Marin County high schools. R. Jolliffe and R. Richards. il por Ceram Mo 25:43-6 N '77
School before school can be the answer; work of the Delayed Development Center at Redondo Beach, Calif. C. Luetje. il Parents Mag 53:37+ Ja '78
Today's weather: courtesy of 12-year-olds; Meyers school, Lake Tahoe. P. Zauner. il Sci Digest 81:81-2 Ap '77
See also
Idyllwild School of Music and the Arts
Los Angeles—Education
Los Angeles County, Calif.—Education
Oakland, Calif.—Education
Pasadena, Calif.—Education

Canada

See also
Colleges and universities—Canada

China

One-fourth of the world's children. R. H. Collins. Educ Digest 43:57-9 S '77
Politics in Chinese higher education. C. T. Hu. Cur Hist 73:79-83+ S '77
See also
Colleges and universities—China

Colombia

Inequality in Colombia. D. K. Zschock. bibl f il Cur Hist 72:68-72+ F '77

Colorado

Se habla espanol; the story of the Chicano Education Projet. J. Earle. Todays Educ 66:76-7 N '77

EDUCATION—*Continued*

Connecticut

Sign that took three years to build; Stadley Rough School, Danbury. R. Farrell. il Sch Arts 76:46-7 Ap '77

See also

Hartford, Conn.—Education

New Haven, Conn.—Education

Delaware

Of youth and time; teaching in Dover. G. Henry. Engl J 66:9+ My '77

England

From the mouths of babes; music education in Birmingham. J. Culshaw. Hi Fi 28:64 Ja '78

See also

London—Education

Florida

Citizen advisory committees. G. E. Greenwood and others. Educ Digest 43:6-9 S '77

Construction management, in a Miami test, saves $1.5 million; Dade County School District. il Archit Rec 161:75-8 Ja '77

Osceola teacher education center. L. Olson and others. Todays Educ 66:75-6+ Mr '77

See also

Miami Beach, Fla.—Education

St Petersburg, Fla.—Education

Georgia

Earth log: the Foxfire wildfire. P. Hendrickson. il por Audubon 79:108-12 Mr '77

Preparing teenagers for the world of work; Georgia's Career Awareness Program. A. Bledsoe. il Parents Mag 52:23-4 My '77

Germany

See also

Colleges and universities—Germany

Germany, West

Downhill race. E. M. von Kuehnelt-Leddihn. Nat R 29:386 Ap 1 '77

Great Britain

Letter from England. T. Newkirk. Engl J 66:10-12 Mr; 15-16 Ap '77

Planning and education. B. Wicker. Commonweal 104:134-5 Mr 4 '77

See also

Colleges and universities—Great Britain

Open plan schools

Schools—Great Britain

Idaho

Training model for junior high school communication aides; reading center at West Junior High School, Nampa. L. McMillin. Engl J 66:52-3 Ap '77

Illinois

Hurrah for HEW; experiences of Kenilworth school. Time 110:39 D 26 '77

Peotone fights school failure; special classes for kindergartners with learning disabilities. J. Bone. il Am Educ 13:32-5 Ja '77

See also

Chicago—Education

Indiana

Supergraphics: student art that keeps on giving; project at Columbus East High School, Columbus. M. Lewman and P. Miller. il Sch Arts 77:38-40 D '77

Unequal time; Indiana biology text case. Sci Am 236:61 Je '77

Italy

See also

Colleges and universities—Italy

Japan

See also

Colleges and universities—Japan

Kentucky

Censorship and the schools: a different perspective; studying community standards of obscenity. S. I. Mour. bibl f il Engl J 66:18-20 F '77

Counterattack; controversy over church schools. R. Kirk. Nat R 29:1434 D 9 '77

See also

Louisville—Education

Maryland

Our school-made solar project; Central Senior High School, Seat Pleasant. J. Silver and K. Johnson. il pors Todays Educ 66:62-4 S '77

Project ARTS; public school program in Montgomery County, Md. C. B. Fowler. il Hi Fi 27:MA12-13+ My '77

RIF for teenagers. N. L. Marqua. SLJ 23:45 My '77

Using parents as teaching partners; reading program in Montgomery County public schools. A. Breiling. Educ Digest 42:50-2 F '77

See also

Baltimore—Education

Massachusetts

One way it can be; evaluation system at the Cambridge Alternative Public School, Mass. B. S. Engel. il Todays Educ 66:50-2 Mr '77

School board bans poem; defense committee sues; Chelsea High School library. SLJ 24:10 N '77

String training on the Cape; music education program of the Barnstable, Mass, public school system. Mrs Conlon-Hoffman. il Hi Fi 28:MA14-15 Ja '78

Survival in Boston; direction finding project for Arlington school children. P. Orton and J. Stevens. Educ Digest 42:19-21 Ap '77

Why the GLUB went mobile; Groton-Lowell Upward Bound Program. J. Helyar. il Am Educ 13:22-6 Ag '77

See also

Boston—Education

Mexico

Mexican education: Echeverria's mixed legacy. G. Perissinotto. bibl f il Cur Hist 72:115-19+ Mr '77

Michigan

Prep makes parents more intelligenter; early-intervention program for pre-schoolers and parents; Redford Union School District. J. Wagner. il Am Educ 13:9-12 O '77

When computers invade a city's school system —Flint, Mich. il U.S. News 83:80-1 D 26 '77

See also

Detroit—Education

Minnesota

Busiest outdoor school; Environmental Learning Center, Isabella, Minn. S. J. Marcovich. il Am Educ 13:28-30 My '77

Mississippi

Segregation by sex; black boycott of policy prohibiting mingling of sexes in classrooms in Amite County, Miss. M. Sheils. il Newsweek 90:97 S 19 '77

Missouri

Saturday School; Parent-Child Early Education program, Ferguson-Florissant, Mo, School District. P. L. Williamson. il Am Educ 13:14-17 Mr '77; Same abr. Educ Digest 43:25-7 S '77

See also

St Louis—Education

Montana

Building a human resources file: a model; Missoula Area Resource Center. K. Clay and J. J. Dietz. Clearing H 50:337-40 Ap '77

Namibia

Namibians train for tomorrow. H. G. Geingob. il UNESCO Courier 30:20-1 N '77

New Jersey

Art appreciation: a practical approach; a volunteer program in Monmouth County schools. C. K. Sills. il Sch Arts 76:44+ Mr '77

New Jersey mantra; Federal court ruling on transcendental meditation in public schools. J. W. Donohue. America 137:360 N 19 '77

New York (state)

Beyond the handicap; preparations for White House Conference on Handicapped Individuals by New York educators. J. H. Hoyt. Am Educ 13:25-6 Ap '77

Class of '77: all's quiet at Scarsdale High. J. Feron. il N Y Times Mag p20+ Je 26 '77

Constitutionality of book ban challenged by NYCLU; suit filed by the New York Civil Liberties Union against Island Trees School District. Lib J 102:530+ Mr 1 '77

Film producers charge N.Y. BOCES with infringement of copyrights. SLJ 24:9 D '77

Four Island Trees students sue book-banning school board. M. Reuter. Pub W 211:29 Ja 10 '77

Organizing clusters in a traditional building; Denonville Middle School, Penfield. R. W. Barber. Clearing H 50:314-15 Mr '77

Smoking in school; Suffern High School. W. V. Woodward. Educ Digest 43:56-7 N '77

Students & NYCLU file lawsuit against the Island Trees Board. SLJ 23:17 F '77

Substitute for substitutes; Enrichment Program at Syosset High School. N. Schwartz. Educ Digest 43:36-7 N '77

See also

Buffalo, N.Y.—Education

Colleges and universities—New York (state)

New York (city)—Education

New York State United Teachers

Rochester, N.Y.—Education

North Carolina

CETA funds—a boon to North Carolina; employment programs for artists and musicians. C. B. Fowler. il Hi Fi 27:MA16-18 D '77

Detecting learning problems before children start school; North Carolina's Statewide Preschool Screening Program. F. Peterson and J. R. Kesselman. il McCalls 104:69-70 Ag '77

EDUCATION—North Carolina—*Continued*
Ecoscene; introduction to eighteenth century customs in environmental education program, Greensboro. W. W. Davis and H. E. Manar. il Parks & Rec 12:26-8+ Ja '77
In North Carolina, its working; teacher education centers sponsored by Appalachian State University and local schools. K. D. Jenkins. il Clearing H 50:268-71 F '77

Ohio

Learning to cope with the future; futurology course at Milford, Ohio Junior High School. J. E. Smith. Educ Digest 42:38-40 Ja '77
New model me; program in Lakewood high schools. F. Beatty. il Am Educ 13:23-6 Ja '77
See also
Cincinnati—Education
Cleveland—Education
Columbus, Ohio—Education
Dayton, Ohio—Education

Pennsylvania

Middle school student council; Fred S. Engle Middle School, West Grove. J. P. Oakley. Clearing H 50:296-7 Mr '77
Special treatment for the gifted; program for gifted and talented children of the Riverside Center for the Arts, Harrisburg, Pa. C. B. Fowler. il Hi Fi 27:MA14-15 Ap '77
See also
Colleges and universities—Pennsylvania
Philadelphia—Education

Poland

Glimpses of education in Poland and Romania. G. E. Mitchell. il Am Educ 13:16-24 Ap '77

Rhodesia

Teaching African literature: the case of Zimbabwe. K. Phaswana. bibl f il Engl J 66:46-8 Mr '77

Rumania

Glimpses of education in Poland and Romania. G. E. Mitchell. il Am Educ 13:16-24 Ap '77

Russia

Art educators' odyssey, USSR. A. Hurwitz. il Sch Arts 76:56-8+ Ap '77
Education: unequal opportunity; U.S.-Soviet comparison. M. Sheils and others. il Newsweek 90:62+ O 10 '77
See also
Moscow—Education

Sweden

How PRYO worked for one student; Sweden. R. E. Belding. il Am Educ 13:12-13 Ag '77
Sweden's vocational strategy. R. Carlson. il Am Educ 13:9-11+ Ag '77

Switzerland

See also
Schools—Switzerland

Texas

Gifted, talented child; programs in Texas to help the top 5 percent. M. Wightman. Educ Digest 43:51-3 S '77
See also
Dallas—Education
Houston, Tex.—Education

Underdeveloped areas

See Underdeveloped areas—Education

United States

And they lived unhappily ever after. W. Mahood. Clearing H 50:373-4 Ap '77
Cracks in the keystone; documentaries on contemporary education. J. W. Donohue. America 137:242 O 15 '77
Drive for better schools—what the government plans; interview. E. L. Boyer. il por U.S. News 83:63-4 Jl 11 '77
Education. M. Daly. See occasional issues of Better homes and gardens
Education briefs. See issues of Education digest
Latest in schools and colleges. il U.S. News 83:75 Jl 25; 55 S 5; 66 O 17; 94 N 14 '77
On opening day America's schools ponder some sobering lessons; How to get quality back into schools. G. E. Jones. il U.S. News 83:28-34 S 12 '77
U.S. Department of Education: the case for it; the case against it. J. Ryor; G. E. Sroufe. Current 193:16-30 My '77
With education in Washington. J. Mathews. See issues of Education digest
See also
Adult education
Blacks—Education
Community and junior colleges
Community schools
Educational equalization
Educational innovations
Educational laws and legislation—United States
Indians of North America—Education
National Education Association
Private schools
Public schools—Desegregation
Public schools—United States
United States—Education, Department of (proposed)
United States—Education, Office of
United States—Navy—Education
Vocational education
Voucher plan in education

Vermont

It's all downhill from here; Burke Mountain Academy. D. S. Looney. il Sports Illus 48:22-5 Ja 2 '78

Virginia

Babel reversed; ESL program, Glen Forest Elementary School, Fairfax County. I. Carpenter. il Am Educ 13:27-30 Ag '77
Goodbye to the rubber diploma; minimal competency program in Greensville County, Va. schools. il por Time 110:46 S 26 '77
School where students have to measure up; work of S. Owen of Greensville County. J. Greenwald. McCalls 104:58 Ap '77
See also
Richmond, Va.—Education

Washington, D.C.

See Washington, D.C.—Education

Washington (state)

Paying for schools in Washington. C. Polsgrove. Progressive 41:44 N '77
Winning play at home base; home visitation program for parents of preschoolers in Yakima, Wash. V. Hedrich. il Am Educ 13:27-30 Jl '77
See also
Seattle—Education

West Virginia

Historical goodies crammed in old camelback trunks; West Virginia Heritage Trunk project. D. Sherwood. il Smithsonian 8:106+ Je '77

Wisconsin

Law-and-order principal; M. McKee of LaCrosse. P. Haslanger. Progressive 41:45 N '77
See also
Madison, Wis.—Education

Zaïre

Reversal in Zaire; returning administration of public primary and secondary schools to the churches. R. L. Niklaus. Chr Today 21:43 Ja 7 '77

EDUCATION, Adult. See Adult education
EDUCATION, Architectural. See Architectural education
EDUCATION, Art. See Art education
EDUCATION, Bilingual
Bilingual education in American schools. F. Cordasco. Intellect 106:4 Jl '77
Bilingual teaching for newly arrived immigrant children; use of adult and peer tutors. J. J. Hassett. Clearing H 50:409-12 My '77
Bring back the melting pot. M. Stone. U.S. News 83:92 D 5 '77
Preparing for bilingual education. L. J. Glickman. il Am Educ 13:31-2 Ag '77
Se habla espanol; the story of the Chicano Education Project; Colorado. J. Earle. Todays Educ 66:76-7 N '77
Some aspects of bilingualism for the English teacher. F. Pialorsi. bibl Engl J 66:94-7 Ja '77
Teaching in English—plus. M. Sheils and others. il Newsweek 89:64-5 F 7 '77
EDUCATION, Boards of. See School boards
EDUCATION, College. See College education
EDUCATION, Compulsory
Is compulsory attendance necessary? S. O. Wilde. Educ Digest 42:2-5 Mr '77
EDUCATION, Consumer. See Consumer education
EDUCATION, Cooperative
Career education: success for the potential dropout; cooperative work program, Egbert Junior High School, Staten Island. A. J. Keller. Clearing H 51:70-2 O '77
Hartford's workplaces become the classroom. il Bus W p 117-18 D 5 '77
EDUCATION, Department of (proposed) See United States—Education, Department of (proposed)
EDUCATION, Elementary
Early childhood education, California-style; Barranca Elementary School, Covina, Calif. M. McVey. Educ Digest 43:14-16 D '77
Early childhood: the crucial years for learning; California's Early Childhood Education (ECE) program. C. Luetje. Parents Mag 52:18 Ag '77
Individualization: subversion of elementary schooling. K. Kepler and J. W. Randall. Educ Digest 43:17-20 O '77
See also
Nursery schools
Open plan schools
Private schools

EDUCATION, Experimental. See Education—Experimental methods
EDUCATION, Higher. See College education
EDUCATION, Humanistic
Behind the push to revive the liberal arts in U.S. colleges. il U.S. News 82:49 My 2 '77
Beyond education's watershed. C. R. Rogers. Educ Digest 43:2-5 O '77
Bring back elitist universities. J. Epstein. il N Y Times Mag p86-8+ F 6 '77
Faculty of liberal learning; address, August 22, 1977. F. A. Johnson. Vital Speeches 43:724-31 S 15 '77
Rediscovering the liberal arts. il Time 109:98 Ap 11 '77
Scholar and the pedagogue: different breeds of humanists. D. T. Wolfe, Jr. Clearing H 50:206-8 Ja '77
EDUCATION, Individual. See Individual instruction
EDUCATION, Intercultural. See Intercultural education
EDUCATION, Moral. See Moral education
EDUCATION, Museum. See Museum education
EDUCATION, Office of. See United States—Education, Office of
EDUCATION, Parent. See Parent education
EDUCATION, Physical. See Physical education and training
EDUCATION, Preschool
Prep makes parents more intelligenter; early-intervention program for pre-schoolers and parents; Redford Union School District, Mich. J. Wagner. il Am Educ 13:9-12 O '77
Preschool and the politics of sexism; excerpt from address, October 11, 1976. S. Greenberg. SLJ 23:126 Mr '77
Printing and evaluation. J. W. Burgner. il Sch Arts 76:36-8+ Je '77
Saturday School; Parent-Child Early Education program, Ferguson-Florissant, Mo. School District. P. L. Williamson. il Am Educ 13:14-17 Mr '77; Same abr. Educ Digest 43:25-7 S '77
School before school can be the answer; work of the Delayed Development Center at Redondo Beach Calif. C. Luetje. il Parents Mag 53:37+ Ja '78
Vindication of early childhood programs. Sci N 111:151 Mr 5 '77
Winning play at home base; home visitation program for parents of preschoolers in Yakima, Wash. V. Hedrich. il Am Educ 13:27-30 Jl '77
See also
Kindergarten
Nursery schools
Project Head Start
EDUCATION, Professional. See Professional education
EDUCATION, Rural
See also
Rural schools
EDUCATION, Secondary
Educate teenagers to become people. R. P. Mathur. Clearing H 51:170-2 D '77
Recommendations on the education of adolescents. Educ Digest 42:2-5 Ja '77
See also
High schools
EDUCATION, Technical. See Technical education
EDUCATION, Urban
City schools in crisis. M. Sheils and others. il Newsweek 90:62-4+ S 12 '77
Developing self-concepts of urban children; Success program for parents of young children. K. R. Washington. Educ Digest 43:44-6 N '77
Wasted decade. D. Ravitch. New Repub 177:11-13 N 5 '77
EDUCATION, Value of
Why? Because it's relevant. J. Rensch. bibl il Clearing H 50:203-5 Ja '77
The why of teaching. M. Rothstein. il Todays Educ 66:50-2 Ja '77
See also
College education, Value of
EDUCATION, Vocational. See Vocational education
EDUCATION and business. See Business and education
EDUCATION and Labor, Committee on. See United States—Congress—House—Education and Labor, Committee on
EDUCATION and manpower
How business management improves government. V. Louviere. il Nations Bus 65:37-8 Ap '77
EDUCATION and politics. See Politics and education
EDUCATION and public opinion. See School and the community
EDUCATION and social problems. See School and social and economic problems
EDUCATION and society. See Educational sociology
EDUCATION and state
Ass. prof, GS-7; case of R. Linden and Davidson College. Nat R 29:818 Jl 22 '77
Campus handicap? colleges complying with HEW's rules. M. Sheils and others. il Newsweek 90:58 Ag 8 '77
Defensive education; University of Texas conference. Intellect 105:297 Mr '77
Discouraging word? address, October 13, 1977. A. Brown. Vital Speeches 44:78-81 N 15 '77
Follies of affirmative action. E. Loftus. Society 14:21-4 Ja '77
Higher education and government; address, January 18, 1977. E. Bartell. Vital Speeches 43:389-94 Ap 15 '77
Impact of Federal regulations at a university. D. C. Spriestersbach and W. J. Farrell. bibl Science 198:27-30 O 7 '77
My personal commitment to education. J. Carter. por Todays Educ 66:26-7 Ja '77
Reschooling society. J. Featherstone. New Repub 176:40+ Ja 22 '77
School race problems: the states move in. il U.S. News 83:50 N 28 '77
Teachers' feature. J. Carter. por Sr Schol 109: TE15 Ja 13 '77
Trumpeting a certain note; address, February 23, 1977. J. A. Howard. Vital Speeches 43:428-31 My 1 '77
Vast changes ahead for U.S. schools? il U.S. News 82:62 F 14 '77
See also
Education—Federal aid
Educational laws and legislation
Voucher plan in education
EDUCATION associations. See Educational associations
EDUCATION critics and criticism
American scholar, 1977. A. Kazin. Esquire 88:34+ S '77
Crash and creativeness in education. H. H. Punke. Clearing H 50:306-8 Mr '77
Drastic change in roles of schools. W. C. Morse. por Intellect 105:382-3 My '77
How to get quality back into schools; symposium. il U.S. News 83:31-4 S 12 '77
I wants to go to the prose. S. B. Jordan. por Newsweek 90:23 N 14 '77
The more we spend, the less children learn; excerpt from Our children's crippled future: how American education has failed. F. E. Armbruster. il N Y Times Mag p9-11+ Ag 28 '77; Same abr. with title Why American education is failing. Read Digest 112:106-9 Ja '78
Need for elite education. J. R. Silber. Harpers 254:22-4 Je '77
New voice for the schools. H. S. Broudy. Todays Educ 66:28-31 Mr '77
Preaching pride; J. L. Jackson. M. Sheils and S. Monroe. il por Newsweek 89:64 Je 27 '77
PUSH for excellence; J. Jackson's program. A. Poinsett. il pors Ebony 32:104-6+ F '77
EDUCATION for family life. See Family life, Education for
EDUCATION for Publishing Committee. See Association of American Publishers—Education for Publishing Committee
EDUCATION of children
Education now; parents role in childrens' learning. F. M. Hechinger. Sat R 5:50 O 15 '77
Equality now! For girls and boys; non-sexist schooling project of Women's Action Alliance. B. Sprung. il Parents Mag 52:44+ S '77
Letter to parents. W. P. Cushman. il Engl J 66:45-8 O '77
Sea and shores as classrooms; sailing on the Aquarius. M. Herron. il pors Smithsonian 8:99-104 S '77
See also
Camping—Educational aspects
Childrens reading
Education, Elementary
Education, Preschool
Home education
Moral education
Museum education
Nature study
Nursery schools
Outdoor education
Play
Sex education
EDUCATION of Indian children (American) See Indians of North America—Education
EDUCATION of librarians. See Library schools and education
EDUCATION of the aged. See Aged—Education
EDUCATION of women
Courses that women can count on; colleges offering math-anxiety classes. E. Pascoe. il McCalls 104:68 Jl '77
Daughters of the middle class; excerpt from We must march my darlings. D. Trilling. Harpers 254:31-6+ Ap '77
Graduate in the family; college commencement for mother of five. L. Duncan. il por Good H 185:102+ O '77
Little courses that grew. C. Grosgebauer. il Am Educ 13:10-13 Je '77; Same abr. Educ Digest 43:21-4 O '77
Math mystique: fear of figuring. Time 109:36 Mr 14 '77
Mom goes to law school. M. Smith. il Ms 6:16-18 S '77
Mother goes to school. R. Gross. Parents Mag 52:18+ Ap '77

EDUCATION of women—*Continued*
On juggling a family, a home and a college education. J. L. Smith Mademoiselle 83:32+ Ag '77
Your future is now; college education. L. Davis. Vogue 167:94 Ag '77
See also
Colleges for women
Vocational education of women

EDUCATION of workers. See Labor and laboring classes—Education

EDUCATIONAL achievements. See Student achievements

EDUCATIONAL administration. See School management and organization

EDUCATIONAL associations
Conservatives in the academy. R. Kirk. Nat R 29:889 Ag 5 '77
See also
National Council of Teachers of English
National Education Association
New York State United Teachers
Parents and teachers associations

EDUCATIONAL change. See Educational innovations

EDUCATIONAL conferences. See Education—Conferences

EDUCATIONAL consultants
To the external consultant from his/her audience: what we want to hear and see. C. B. Dilworth, Jr. Clearing H 51:180-2 D '77

EDUCATIONAL correlation. See Correlation (education)

EDUCATIONAL criticism. See Education critics and criticism

EDUCATIONAL discrimination. See Discrimination in education

EDUCATIONAL equalization
I wants to go to the prose. S. B. Jordan. por Newsweek 90:23 N 14 '77
Law, politics, and equal educational opportunity. D. L. Kirp. Educ Digest 43:32-5 S '77
New battles over school budgets; question of property tax financing in Serrano case in California. R. Lindsey. il N Y Times Mag p 17-19+ S 18 '77
Normative assumptions in educational policy research: the case of Jencks's Inequality. L. B. Joseph. bibl f Ann Am Acad 434:101-13 N '77

EDUCATIONAL evaluation. See Education—Evaluation

EDUCATIONAL expense deductions. See Income tax—Deductions

EDUCATIONAL extension. See University extension

EDUCATIONAL Film Library Association
Film. D. Hare. Craft Horiz 37:6+ O '77
Year's top educational films. D. Boyle. il Am Lib 8:451-2 S '77

EDUCATIONAL forecasting
Most realistic future. A. A. Schmieder. Educ Digest 42:31-3 Ap '77

Anecdotes, facetiae, satire, etc.

Lion's roar. A. Burgess. il por Lib J 102:327-9 F 1 '77

EDUCATIONAL games
Mind control, the Edison Electric way; Energy-Environment Game. M. Zeldin. Audubon 79: 115-17 Jl '77
Nuclear game; Energy-Environment Game distributed by Edison Electric Institute. il Progressive 41:10 N '77
Serious play—using games to teach and learn; work of B. Lawson. J. Gaylin. Psychol Today 11:28+ Jl '77

EDUCATIONAL guidance. See Personnel service in education

EDUCATIONAL innovations
Creating learning environments. A. A. Glatthorn. Educ Digest 43:9-12 N '77
Initiating structure for educational change. J. W. Licata and others. Educ Digest 43:21-4 S '77
Innovative education: little effect. Sci N 111:39 Ja 15 '77
A little magic. R. Wheeler. bibl Clearing H 50: 345-8 Ap '77
Politics of changing schools. D. Mann. Educ Digest 43:6-9 O '77
Special section on revamping the schools; symposium. il Parents Mag 52:55-66+ S '77
Theoretical and policy implications of case study findings about federal efforts to improve public schools. N. Gross. bibl f Ann Am Acad 434:71-87 N '77
Trends, titles, taxonomies—alas! D. T. Wolfe, Jr. Clearing H 50:236 F '77
Wasted decade. D. Ravitch. New Repub 177:11-13 N 5 '77
What is the problem? What is the solution? W. Doyle. Educ Digest 43:14-16 O '77

EDUCATIONAL laws and legislation
See also
Colleges and universities—Laws and legislation
Education, Compulsory

United States

Controversial English lessons and the law. A. K. Hoy. bibl il Engl J 66:21-5 F '77
Education amendments of 1976. A. L. Alford. Am Educ 13:6-11 Ja '77
Fighting fraud in education. G. E. Arnstein. il Am Educ 13:27-30 Ap '77
NEA's legislative program; 95th Congress. Todays Educ 66:81-3 Ja '77
Road is paved with good intentions; Title IX and sex discrimination; address, January 25, 1977. E. Green. Vital Speeches 43:300-3 Mr 1 '77
Title IX: antisexism's big legal stick. B. Sandler. il Am Educ 13:6-9 My '77
With education in Washington. J. Mathews. See issues of Education digest
Women's Educational Equity Act. C. Hoffman. Am Educ 13:28-9 D '77
See also
Education—Federal aid

EDUCATIONAL leadership. See Leadership

EDUCATIONAL literature
See also
Publishers and publishing—Educational literature
Sex education literature

EDUCATIONAL malpractice. See Malpractice

EDUCATIONAL materials. See Teaching—Aids and devices

EDUCATIONAL Materials Review Center. See United States—Education, Office of—Educational Materials Review Center

EDUCATIONAL measurements. See Educational tests and measurements

EDUCATIONAL news
Latest in schools and colleges. il U.S. News 83:75 Jl 25; 55 S 5; 66 O 17; 94 N 14 '77

EDUCATIONAL Paperback Association
Educational Paperback Association seeks larger share of the education market; report of symposium. J. Marshall. il Pub W 211:82+ Mr 7 '77

EDUCATIONAL philosophy. See Education—Philosophy

EDUCATIONAL planning
Planning and education; Great Britain. B. Wicker. Commonweal 104:134-5 Mr 4 '77
Utopianism and education. E. Wynne. Educ Digest 42:50-3 My '77
See also
Curriculum planning
Educational innovations

EDUCATIONAL policy. See Education and state

EDUCATIONAL Priorities Panel. See School management and organization—Parent participation

EDUCATIONAL records. See School reports and records

EDUCATIONAL reform. See Educational innovations

EDUCATIONAL research
Conceptions of research and development for education in the United States. B. Holzner and L. Salmon-Cox. bibl f Ann Am Acad 434:88-100 N '77
Research clues. J. H. Hollifield. See issues of Today's education
See also
Colleges and universities—Research

EDUCATIONAL resource centers. See Instructional materials centers

EDUCATIONAL Resources Information Center. See Eric

EDUCATIONAL segregation. See Segregation in education

EDUCATIONAL sociology
Education, history, and the press; address, February 8, 1977. H. E. Foster. Vital Speeches 43: 349-52 Mr 15 '77
Interpersonal relations and education. C. M. Galloway. Educ Digest 42:42-4 My '77
Race and desegregation; symposium. il Society 14:32-48 My '77
Society and the failure of the schools. M. Lee. Todays Educ 66:64-5 N '77
See also
College education—Aims and objectives
Education—Aims and objectives
School and social and economic problems
Socially handicapped children—Education

EDUCATIONAL standards. See Education—Standards

EDUCATIONAL statistics. See Education—Statistics

EDUCATIONAL study tours. See Travel study courses

EDUCATIONAL surveys
Assessing instructional needs in your district. P. J. Berrie. bibl Clearing H 50:221-3 Ja '77
Yin and Yang: Baptist and Methodist college surveys. Chr Cent 94:933-5 O 19 '77

EDUCATIONAL technology
Keeping ed tech in the picture. L. N. Gerhardt. SLJ 23:7 Ap '77
See also
Teaching—Aids and devices

EDUCATIONAL television stations. See Television stations, Educational

EDUCATIONAL Testing Service
ETS's star chamber; Law School Admissions Test and the exemption of the Educational Testing Service from the Family Education Rights and the Privacy Act of 1974. K. Masters. New Repub 176:13-14 F 5 '77
Nadir is to Nader as lowest is to. . . ; investigation of ETS. G. V. Glass. Nat R 29:776-7 Jl 8 '77

EDUCATIONAL tests and measurements
All those tests your children take and what they really mean. M. Daly and J. Daubenmier. il Bet Hom & Gard 55:178+ O '77
Basic training; Chicago's minimum competence standards for elementary school students. M. Sheils and S. Monroe. Newsweek 90:44 Ag 15 '77
Declining scores: two explanations. R. L. Ebel; V. R. Rogers and J. Baron. Educ Digest 42:2-7 F '77
Detecting learning problems before children start school; North Carolina's Statewide Preschool Screening Program. F. Peterson and J. R. Kesselman. il McCalls 104:69-70 Ag '77
How much must a student master? minimal competency testing. il Time 109:74 F 28 '77
Improve your classroom testing skills. J. S. Taylor. Clearing H 50:381-5 My '77
Is it time we started teaching children how to take tests? G. W. Downey. Educ Digest 42:6-8 Ap '77
Power to the person. W. W. Turnbull. Educ Digest 43:28-31 N '77
What do diplomas mean? proficiency testing. M. Sheils. il Newsweek 91:65 Ja 9 '78
What the kids' test scores mean. il Changing T 32:13-15 Ja '78
What's wrong with standardized testing? symposium; ed by Bernard McKenna. il Todays Educ 66:35-42+ Mr '77
See also
Achievement tests
American College Testing program
College Entrance Examination Board—Scholastic Aptitude Test
Intelligence tests
Students—Rating

Anecdotes, facetiae, satire, etc.

Pencils down. A. Ward. Atlantic 239:77-81 My '77

EDUCATIONAL tests and measurements, Publishing of. See Publishers and publishing—Educational literature

EDUCATIONAL theory. See Education—Philosophy

EDUCATIONAL workshops
How to improve student writing; Bay Area Writing Project and teachers workshops. S. B. Neill. Educ Digest 42:44-7 Ja '77

EDUCATOR Records (firm) See Phonograph record industry

EDUCATORS
Political role of educators. T. M. Black. Educ Digest 42:30-2 Mr '77
See also
College presidents
College teachers
Teachers

EDWARD VI, King of England
Boy kings. P. W. Schmidtchen. il Hobbies 82:134-6 S '77 *

EDWARD, C.
Marats, Dantons, and Robespierres. il Am Hist Illus 12:10-16 Jl '77

EDWARDES, Michael Owen
Last chance for Leyland. il por Time 110:82 N 14 '77 *
New whiz kid at British Leyland. por Bus W p58+ N 14 '77 *

EDWARDS, A. G, & Sons, Inc. See Brokers

EDWARDS, Audrey
Hey, lady, who's in charge here? por Redbook 148:64+ F '77

EDWARDS, Bruce
Minister's farewell to Plains, Georgia. V. Cadden. il por McCalls 104:115+ Jl '77 *
Pressure in Plains. Chr Today 21:51-2 Mr 18 '77 *
Schism in Plains. M. Montagno and others. il por Newsweek 89:76 Mr 7 '77 *
To the lions. Time 109:14 Mr 7 '77 *

EDWARDS, Carl M.
Trailer hitching. il Consumers Res Mag 60:18-20 Jl '77

EDWARDS, Charles H.
Rescue from a fanatic cult. il Read Digest 110:129-33 Ap '77

EDWARDS, Danny
Down the Bobby Jones Expressway. W. Bingham. il Sports Illus 46:28 Ap 18 '77 *

EDWARDS, David V.
Politics and the aged. il Intellect 106:181 N '77
Will a Carter foreign policy make a difference? Intellect 105:319-21 Ap '77

EDWARDS, Don
(ed) See Gardner, J. Conversation with John Gardner

EDWARDS, Donald
Wiley withholds book with possible CIA link; interview. ed by S. Wagner. Pub W 211:37-8 F 7 '77

EDWARDS, Duane
Reaction to student evaluation. Educ Digest 42:54-6 My '77

EDWARDS, Ellen
Lipchitz legacy. Art N 76:166-8 Summ '77

EDWARDS, Gus
Offering. Reviews
New Yorker 53:92 D 12 '77 *

EDWARDS, Mike W.
Danube: river of many nations, many names. il map Nat Geog 152:454-85 O '77

EDWARDS, Owen
From rags to photographic riches. il N Y Times Mag p 151-4 N 6 '77
Journalist of the plague years. il Sat R 5:43-5 Ja 7 '78
Small world in a room. il Sat R 5:34-6 O 1 '77
(ed) See Penn, I. Perspectives of Penn

EDWARDS, Richard
Self-watering sprout grower. il Org Gard & Farm 24:124+ D '77

EDWARDS, Ross B. and Szamier, R. B.
Defective phagocytosis of isolated rod outer segments by RCS rat retinal pigment epithelium in culture. bibl il Science 197:1001-3 S 2 '77

EDWARDS, Steven
Establishing a student-built pottery. il Ceram Mo 25:37-9 F '77

EDWARDS, Thomas C.
Who says concept stocks are dead. P. Berman. il por Forbes 120:30-1 Ag 15 '77 *

EDWARDS, V. C. Wynne-. See Wynne-Edwards, V. C.

EELLS, Eleanor P.
FAC marks 15th year in camping. Camp Mag 50:6-7+ S '77

EELS
Misunderstood morays. W. MacElwain. il Sea Front 23:96-100 Mr '77

EFF, Elaine, and Fennimore, D. L.
Folk art from the Henry Francis du Pont Winterthur Museum. il Antiques 112:506-13 S '77

EFF, Johannes
Lass's lib; poem. Nat R 29:555 My 13 '77
Vladimir Nabokov meets Madame Butterfly; poem. Nat R 29:830 Jl 22 '77

EFFICIENCY
Get smart. J. S. King. Am Home 80:38+ My '77

EFFICIENCY, Administrative
Can our democratic government survive? address, September 9, 1977. D. F. Linowes. Vital Speeches 44:15-19 O 15 '77
Need to act. T. Bethell. il Harpers 255:34-6+ N '77

EFFICIENCY, Industrial
Human dimension in productivity; address, January 19, 1977. T. C. McDermott. Vital Speeches 43:306-9 Mr 1 '77
Thinking about tomorrow; address, October 17, 1977. R. E. Hilchey. Vital Speeches 44:88-92 N 15 '77
Your service shop, how does it rate? J. Darr. il Radio-Electr 48:81-2+ My '77
See also
Labor productivity
Office management

EFIRD, Susan
Nebuchadnezzar's robes; poem. Poetry 130:94-5 My '77

EFRON, Bradley, and Morris, Carl
Stein's paradox in statistics; with biographical sketches. il map Sci Am 236:18, 119-27 bibl (p 148) My '77

EFTINK, Bill
Beef management. See issues of Successful farming
(ed) Successful beef management (cont) Suc Farm 75:no3 B1-3+ F '77

EGAN, Carol
Viola Farber moving on. il por Dance Mag 51:80-3 Ap '77

EGAN, James
Tour of the LBJ ranch. il por Good H 185:112-17+ O '77

EGAR (photographer)
Photographer's eye: Colombia. A. L. Lowe. il Américas 29:8-9 Ja '77

EGELSTON, P.
In winter; poem. Sat Eve Post 249:88 Mr '77

EGELSTON, Roberta J.
Stalking the wild job; or, A career library from the ground up. bibl il Wilson Lib Bull 52:330-5 D '77

EGERTON, John
As Jamaican as apple pie. Progressive 41:37-40 D '77
Fannie Lou Hamer. Progressive 41:7 My '77
On utopianism; excerpt from Visions of Utopia. Progressive 41:20-1 Jl '77

EGG beaters. See Kitchen utensils and appliances

EGG decoration. See Eggs, Decorated

EGG laying. See Oviposition

EGG shell mosaics. See Mosaics

EGG tempera painting. See Tempera painting

EGG timers. See Timing devices

EGGERT, Gerald G.
Coxey's march on Washington, 1894. il pors Am Hist Illus 12:20-31 O '77
EGGLESTON, William
Color. J. Malcolm. il New Yorker 53:107-11 O 10 '77 *
EGGPLANT
See also
Cookery—Vegetables
EGGS
Egg & you. il Am Home 80:66 Ap '77
See also
Birds—Eggs
Cookery—Eggs
Eggs, Decorated
EGGS (ova) See Ova
EGGS, Decorated
Create a classic Easter egg. P. Angell. il Pop Mech 147:102 Ap '77
Easter eggs dyed and decorated the natural way. J. Browne. il Org Gard & Farm 24:108+ Mr '77
Eggs à la art. il Seventeen 36:204-5 Ap '77
Glorious Easter eggs. S. Purdy. il Ladies Home J 94:80+ Ap '77
EGLEVSKY Ballet Company
Guests at home; performances by the Eglevsky Ballet Company at Nassau Coliseum. A. J. Shaw. Dance Mag 51:41+ Mr '77
Reviews; April program at Hofstra University. R. A. Thom. Dance Mag 51:82+ Ag '77
Reviews; new staging of Coppélia at Hofstra University. M. Robertson. Dance Mag 52:32-3 Ja '78
EGO. See Self
EGOISM
See also
Self love
EGRI, Kit. See Egri, T. jt auth
EGRI, Ruth
Dynamic symmetry of Ruth Egri. C. Collins. il Am Artist 41:46-51+ D '77 *
EGRI, Ted
Ted Egri: the survival of a sculptor; interview, ed by M. C. Nelson. il por Am Artist 41:56-61+ Je '77
—and Egri, Kit
Walter Ufer: passion and talent. il por Am Artist 42:64-7+ Ja '78
EGYPT
See also
Airplanes, Military—Egypt
Crime and criminals—Egypt
Economic assistance, American—Egypt
Economic assistance in Egypt
Investments, American—Egypt
Investments, Foreign—Egypt
Libyan Desert
Petroleum pipelines—Egypt
Red Sea
Suez Canal
Visitors, Foreign—Egypt

Antiquities

Dazzling legacy of an ancient quest. A. J. Hall. il Nat Geog 151:292-311 Mr '77
Egyptian souvenir spoons. L. M. Plogger. il Hobbies 82:153 S '77
Treasures of King Tut; discovery of tomb by H. Carter. S. Flythe, Jr. il Sat Eve Post 249: 68-71+ My '77
See also
Mummies
Temples—Egypt
Tutenkhamûn, King of Egypt

Commerce

France

See France—Commerce—Egypt

Israel

See Israel—Commerce—Egypt

United States

See United States—Commerce—Egypt

Description and travel

Astronomer's impressions of ancient Egypt. D. A. Allen. il map Sky & Tel 54:15-19 Jl '77
Egypt. T. J. Abercrombie. il map Nat Geog 151: 312-43 Mr '77
Fantastic Egypt. A. T. Fleming. il Vogue 167: 66+ Jl '77
Gift of the River Nile. il map Time 111:18-21 Ja 2 '78
Well traveled camera. H. Keppler. il Mod Phot 41:46 Ag; 112+ N; 99-100 D '77

Economic conditions

Egypt: if belt-tightening fails, what next? il Bus W p42 F 7 '77
Promises, promises. W. E. Schmidt. il Newsweek 90:51-2 N 28 '77
Sadat in trouble. Nat R 29:372 Ap 1 '77
What Sadat will seek from Carter; interview, ed by L. H. Young and R. Taggiasco. A. Sadat. pors Bus W p96-9 Ap 4 '77

Economic policy

Sadat's sorry state. M. Kondracke. New Repub 176:14-16 Mr 19 '77
Will Sadat survive Egypt's mounting woes? il U.S. News 82:21-2 F 28 '77

Foreign relations

See also
Cairo conference, 1977

Israel

Middle East: driller discord in the Gulf of Suez. map Bus W p47 Mr 21 '77
Peace crusader; work of A. Nathan. E. Keerdoja and M. J. Kubic. il pors Newsweek 91:5 Ja 2 '78
See also
Begin, M.—Visit to Egypt, 1977
Sadat, A.—Visit to Israel, 1977

Libya

Arab vs. Arab. M. R. Benjamin and W. Schmidt. il map Newsweek 90:29 Ag 1 '77
Libya-Egypt clash—latest threat to Mideast peace; with interview with M. al-Qaddafi. il map U.S. News 83:36-8 Ag 8 '77
Maxi-plots behind a strange mini-war. il Time 110:33-4 Ag 8 '77
Revenge in the desert. pors map Time 110:20 Ag 1 '77

Middle East

Anwar Sadat: architect of a new Mideast. il pors Time 111:10-17 Ja 2 '78

Saudi Arabia

Why the Saudis are silent. W. Wynn. il Time 110:40 D 12 '77

United States

See United States—Foreign relations—Egypt

Kings and rulers

See also
Tutenkhamûn, King of Egypt

Politics and government

Cairo: Sadat's bold gamble. B. Came. il por Newsweek 89:28-9 F 21 '77
Why Egypt needs peace. D. B. Richardson. il map U.S. News 83:18 D 5 '77
Will Sadat survive Egypt's mounting woes? il U.S. News 82:21-2 F 28 '77

Religious institutions and affairs

See also
Coptic Church
Muslims in Egypt

Riots

Sadat's darkest hour. R. Carroll and others. il por Newsweek 89:51-2 Ja 31 '77
Sound and the fury of the poor. il Time 109: 29-30 Ja 31 '77
EGYPT and the United States
Message to America. A. Sadat. por Time 109:35 F 28 '77
EGYPT-United States Joint Working Group on Technology, Research and Development. See Technology—International aspects
EGYPTIAN art. See Art, Egyptian
EGYPTIAN design. See Design
EGYPTIAN jewelry. See Jewelry, Egyptian
EHEMANN, Jane
Highway map as a social studies resource. Clearing H 51:165-6 D '77
EHRBAR, A. F.
IMF lays down the law; with report by A. Stuart. il Fortune 96:98-102+ Jl '77
Manifesto for a tax revolution. il Fortune 95: 90-5+ Ap '77
Radical prescription for medical care. il Fortune 95:164-70+ F '77
Those pension plans are even weaker than you think. il Fortune 96:104-8+ N '77
EHRENKRANTZ, Louis
Reviewing the reviewers. Intellect 106:246-8 D '77
EHRENSTEIN, Gerald
Ion channels in nerve membranes. bibl il Phys Today 29:33-6+ O '76; 30:15+ Je '77
EHRLICH, Arnold W.
Algonquin at 75. il N Y Times Mag p 126-7+ O 16 '77
(ed) See Nash, N. R. PW interviews
(ed) See Reid, A. PW interviews
(ed) See Schwed, P. PW interviews
(ed) See Wendell, B. PW interviews
EHRLICH, Paul R.
Ecologists, ethics, and the environment. BioScience 27:239 Ap '77
EHRLICHMAN, John D.
Ehrlichman's novel comes to TV. K. E. Meyer. il Sat R 4:38-9 S 3 '77 *
EICHBAUM, William M.
Hotspur story. il Yachting 141:151-4 Je '77
EICHMAN, Mark
As to the meaning of words. Reviews Time 109:31 Ap 18 '77 *
EICHMANN, Adolf
Murderous mind. M. Selzer. il pors N Y Times Mag p35-7+ N 27 '77 *

EIDT, Robert C.
Detection and examination of anthrosols by phosphate analysis. bibl il Science 197:1327-33 S 30 '77

EIFFEL Tower
Ailing grande dame. il Time 110:37-8 Jl 18 '77

EIGELAND, Tor
Drums of Calanda; with biographical sketch. il Natur Hist 86:4, 58-63 Ap '77

EIGHTEEN hundred and seventy-seven
Meanwhile, back in the 1877. il Sr Schol 110:7-8 D 15 '77

EILBERG, Joshua
New curbs on illegal aliens. G. R. Rosen. il por Duns R 110:49 Jl '77 *

EILENBERGER, Robert F.
Topsy-turvy or the fright pot. il Sch Arts 76:54-7 Mr '77

EILERS, Hazel Kraft
At the sign of the crest. See issues of Hobbies

EINSTEIN, Albert
Einstein and his closest friend. G. M. Spruch. pors Phys Today 30:9+ Mr '77 *

EINSTEIN theory. See Relativity (physics)

EISELEY, Loren Corey
Buzzards; Mars; Dreamed in a dark millennium; Shore haunters; poems. Harpers 254:56-7 Je '77
How brief upon the wind; poem; excerpt from Another kind of autumn. Sci Digest 82:82 S '77
Snowstorm; poem; excerpt from The innocent assassins. por Audubon 79:inside cover S '77
Sparrow hawk resting; poem; excerpt from Another kind of autumn. il Audubon 79:48-9 Mr '77
Star thrower; excerpt from The unexpected universe. il Oceans 10:54-7 S '77
There came a cry of joy; excerpt from The immense journey. il Read Digest 110:97-9 Mr '77
Two hours from now; poem. Poetry 130:33 Ap '77
Wind child; poem. il Audubon 79:20-1 My '77

about

Eiseley: into the ultimate night. Sci N 112:63 Jl 23 '77 *

EISEN, Jonathan
Greening of Vermont. Commonweal 104:7 Ja 7 '77

EISENBERG, Howard B.
Long arm of the library: prison law collections. bibl il Wilson Lib Bull 51:514-18 F '77

EISENBERG, Leon
Social imperatives of medical research. bibl Science 198:1105-10 D 16 '77

EISENBERG, Norman
High fidelity pathfinders. See issues of High fidelity and Musical America

EISENBERGER, Katherine E.
Declining enrolments: implications for the school curriculum. Educ Digest 42:6-9 My '77

EISENHOWER, David
Grandpa Ike; excerpt from The sixties, ed by L. Obst. il por Ladies Home J 94:18+ N '77
Sins of Washington. il por Newsweek 90:104 S 19 '77

EISENHOWER, Dwight David
Ike's wartime letters to Mamie; excerpt from Letters to Mamie, ed by J. S. D. Eisenhower. il McCalls 105:92-3+ Ja '78

about

Eisenhower's other warning; excerpts from address, April 26, 1976. H. F. York. por Phys Today 30:9+ Ja '77 *
Grandpa Ike; excerpt from The sixties, ed by L. Obst. D. Eisenhower. il por Ladies Home J 94:18+ N '77 *
Mamie; excerpt from Special people. J. N. Eisenhower. il pors Ladies Home J 94:105-7+ Je '77 *
Perspectives on the past. M. Blumenson. Am Hist Illus 12:48 O '77 *

Staff

See also
Adams, S.

EISENHOWER, Dwight David, 2d. See Eisenhower, D.

EISENHOWER, John Sheldon Doud
(ed) See Eisenhower, D. D. Ike's wartime letters to Mamie

EISENHOWER, Julie (Nixon)
Mamie; excerpt from Special people. il pors Ladies Home J 94:105-7+ Je '77
My college diary; interview, ed by L. R. Obst. il por N Y Times Mag p97-9 N 13 '77
(ed) See Meir, G. Golda Meir

EISENHOWER, Mamie Geneva (Doud)
Ike's wartime letters to Mamie; excerpt from Letters to Mamie, ed by J. S. D. Eisenhower. D. D. Eisenhower. il McCalls 105:92-3+ Ja '78 *
Mamie; excerpt from Special people. J. N. Eisenhower. il pors Ladies Home J 94:105-7+ Je '77 *

EISENMAN, Peter
House as sculptural object. P. Goldberger. il N Y Times Mag p74-6+ Mr 20 '77 *

EISENSTADT, Marvin
Short 'n sweet. por Forbes 120:80 Jl 15 '77 *

EISENSTAEDT, Alfred
Splendor of autumn; photographs. Horticulture 55:36-43 S '77

about

1937 available light revisited. B. Schwalberg. il por Pop Phot 80:120-1+ My '77 *

EISENSTEIN, B. I. and others
Conjugal transfer of the gonococcal penicillinase plasmid. bibl il Science 195:998-1000 Mr 11 '77

EISNER, Thomas, and others
Stink of stinkpot turtle identified: ω-phenylalkanoic acids. bibl il Science 196:1347-9 Je 17 '77

EISNER, Will
Remedial tennis. il Esquire 88:78-9 Jl '77

EIZENSTAT, Stuart Elliot
Stuart Eizenstat: an inside look at how the White House operates; interview, ed by R. L. Lesher. il pors Nations Bus 65:36-41 Ag '77

about

Clear it with Stu. P. Goldman and E. Clift. il por Newsweek 89:18+ Je 13 '77 *
Growing power of Stuart Eizenstat. por Bus W p42+ O 10 '77 *
Quiet Georgian makes it to the top. por U.S. News 83:35 D 5 '77 *

EJECTION devices (airplanes) See Airplanes—Escape devices

EKLUND, Coy Glenwood
Corporate social responsibility; address, November 30, 1976. Vital Speeches 43:168-70 Ja 1 '77

EKLUND, Sigvard
We must move forward with all deliberate speed. il Bull Atom Sci 33:42-7 O '77

EL-BAZ, Farouk
Expanding desert creates grim beauty but also threatens crucial cropland. il Smithsonian 8:34-41 Je '77
Onslaught on the Nile. il UNESCO Courier 30:23-4+ Jl '77

EL-KASSAS, Mohammed
Are deserts man-made? il UNESCO Courier 30:4-6 Jl '77

EL MEZRAB, Jane Elizabeth (Digby) See Ellenborough, J. E. D. L. Countess of

EL NIMIERI, Gaafar Mohamed. See Nimieri, G. M.

ELACHI, C. and others
Ocean wave patterns under Hurricane Gloria: observation with an airborne synthetic-aperture radar. bibl il Science 198:609-10 N 11 '77

ELASTASE
Elastase release from human alveolar macrophages: comparison between smokers and nonsmokers. R. J. Rodriguez and others. bibl il Science 198:313-14 O 21 '77

ELATTAR, A. and others
Intermetallic compounds of the type MNi_5 as methanation catalysts. bibl il Science 196:1093-4 Je 3 '77

ELBERT, Joan
Universal and unconditional. Chr Cent 94:134-5 F 16 '77

EL CARISO Park and Golf Course, Los Angeles. See Golf courses

EL CHAPOTE Ranch, Texas. See Ranches

ELDER, D. L. and Fowler, S. W.
Polychlorinated biphenyls: penetration into the deep ocean by zooplankton fecal pellet transport. bibl il Science 197:459-61 Jl 29 '77

ELDER, Jim
Black art of Black Bart. il por Motor B & S 140:61-3+ Jl '77
Muskie man. il por Motor B & S 139:60-1+ Je '77

ELDER, William Voss, 2d
Maryland furniture, 1760-1840. bibl il Antiques 111:354-61 F '77

ELDERLY. See Aged

ELDREDGE, Niles
Evolution's erratic pace. S. J. Gould. Natur Hist 86:12+ My '77 *

ELDRIDGE, Ronnie
Political update: New York's finest—Bella, Ronnie, & Carol. L. Sherr. il pors Ms 6:60-1 S '77 *

ELE, Robert S.
More vegetables in less space. il Org Gard & Farm 24:78-9 F '77

ELECTION Day
Election Day weather—2 November 1976. F. C. Parmenter. map Weatherwise 29:301 D '76

ELECTION districts
See also
Apportionment (election law)
Gerrymander

ELECTION expenses. See Campaign funds

ELECTION fraud. See Elections—Corrupt practices

ELECTION laws
See also
Voters, Registration of

United States

Common sense at work. M. Stone. U.S. News 83:72 Ag 29 '77
Everybody vote; proposed postcard registration law. W. F. Buckley, Jr. Nat R 29:456 Ap 15 '77
How should we vote. D. M. Alpern and others. il Newsweek 89:22-4 Ap 4 '77
Pitfalls in election reform proposals. J. J. Kilpatrick. Nations Bus 65:9-10 My '77
Reforming our election laws. T. Wicker; A. S. Miller; S. Fuzesi, Jr. Current 189:3-10 Ja '77
See also
Campaign funds—Laws and legislation

ELECTIONS
See also
Political campaigns
Referendum

Corrupt practices

Bell ringers; fraud investigation of R. Tonry in Louisiana. S. Fraker and others. por Newsweek 89:30+ Ap 18 '77
LBJ accused; 1948 Texas Democratic Senatorial primary. D. A. Williams and L. Donosky. il pors Newsweek 90:27 Ag 8 '77
L.B.J: the softer they fall; 1948 Texas primary. H. Sidey. il por Time 110:10 Ag 15 '77
Vote forever; 1948 Texas primary. W. F. Buckley, Jr. Nat R 29:1013 S 2 '77

Australia

Second term for Fraser. il por Time 110:38 D 19 '77

Costa Rica

Costa Rica, democratic anomaly. K. Bode. New Repub 176:8-11 Ap 16 '77

France

Catholic vote in France; municipal elections. A. Woodrow. Commonweal 104:261-3 Ap 29 '77
France: a leftist surge. A. Deming and E. Peer. il Newsweek 89:46 Ap 4 '77
White knight in a graveyard; municipal elections. il pors Time 109:37-8 Mr 28 '77

Great Britain

Britain: right wing landslide; municipal elections. Nat R 29:596 My 27 '77

Greece

Victory without triumph. il pors Time 110:51 D 5 '77

India

Department of amplification. V. Mehta. New Yorker 53:67-8+ My 9 '77
Fall of the Gandhis—mixed blessing for India? il por U.S. News 82:31-2 Ap 4 '77
Good news from India. New Repub 176:5-6 Ap 2 '77
India after Indira. A. Demig and others. il pors Newsweek 89:32-3+ Ap 4 '77
India and Indira Gandhi. N. Cousins. Sat R 4:4 Ap 30 '77
India without Indira. Chr Cent 94:347-8 Ap 13 '77
India's election: backing into the future. L. I. Rudolph and S. H. Rudolph. For Affairs 55: 836-53 Jl '77
Indira Gandhi's day of reckoning. America 136: 282 Ap 2 '77
Indira's defeat. R. Watson and H. Jensen. por Newsweek 89:40 Mr 28 '77
It's wait and see after India's election. il Bus W p32 Ap 4 '77
Notes and comment. New Yorker 53:27-8 Ap 4 '77
On the phone to Bombay. P. Gupte. Nation 224: 421-2 Ap 9 '77
Powerful vote for freedom. il por Time 109:30-1+ Ap 4 '77
Reflections on the Indian experience. W. F. Buckley, Jr. Nat R 29:456-7 Ap 15 '77
Voting with their brains. Nation 224: 386-7 Ap 2 '77
See also
Political campaigns—India

Ireland

Gentleman Jack gets back. por Time 109:27 Je 27 '77
How the cruiser was grounded and Finn MacCool returned. H. Kenner. Nat R 29:874-7 Ag 5 '77
Upset at the polls. D. Fisher. Commonweal 104: 518-19 Ag 19 '77

Israel

Begin the Begin. New Repub 176:5-6+ My 28 '77
Israel: day of the hawks. R. Carroll and others. il pors Newsweek 89:32-3+ My 30 '77
Israel thumps the Bible. Nation 224:674 Je 4 '77
Israel turns to the right. Progressive 41:10 Jl '77
Israel under Begin: changing horses in the old stream. I. L. Gendzier. Nation 224:742-4 Je 18 '77
Israeli election and the Begin victory. H. L. Chandler. il por Chr Cent 94:650-4 Jl 20 '77
Israeli election shakes up the Street. il Bus W p80 Je 6 '77
Israel's election shocker: setback for U.S. peace hopes? il por U.S. News 82:27-8 My 30 '77
Likud's victory. B. J. Wattenberg. Harpers 255: 14-17 Ag '77
Middle Eastern prospects. Commonweal 104:387-8 Je 24 '77
Mideast: what's next; views of five Mideast observers. il Newsweek 89:38+ My 30 '77
Triumph of a superhawk. il por map Time 109: 22-3+ My 30 '77

Jamaica

Cuba's role in Jamaica. A. De Borchgrave. il por Newsweek 89:37-8 F 28 '77

Pakistan

Bitter victory. por Time 109:42+ Ap 11 '77
Rioting for a recount. M. Sheils and T. Clifton. il por Newsweek 89:39+ Ap 25 '77

Rhodesia

Boost for Ian Smith. M. R. Benjamin and others. il por Newsweek 90:38-40 S 12 '77
End of a chapter; victory of I. Smith. il por Time 110:24+ S 12 '77

South Africa

Avalanche for Vorster. il por Time 110:46 D 12 '77
Color line. B. Pogrund. New Repub 177:15-17 D 17 '77

Spain

Leftist ground swell in Spain. J. Stewart. Progressive 41:46-7 O '77
Personal reflection. T. Szulc. New Repub 177:24-5 Jl 2 '77
Reign in Spain. K. E. Moore. Commonweal 104: 460-3 Jl 22 '77
Rocky road to democracy; Communist Party and June 15 Spanish elections. R. Moss and M. Arostegui. Nat R 29:663-7 Je 10 '77
Spain at the polls. A. Joseph. New Repub 177: 22-5 Jl 2 '77
Spain returns to the ballot box. B. Koeppel. Nation 224:135-8 F 5 '77
Spain strides toward democracy. T. S. Goslin. Chr Cent 114:615 Jl 6 '77
Spain: the Socialist initiative. Nation 225:2-3 Jl 2 '77
Spain: up the middle. R. Carroll and others. il por Newsweek 89:38-40 Je 27 '77
Spain's free election: now a move to join Europe? D. B. Richardson. il por U.S. News 82:30 Je 27 '77
Spain's future. E. M. von Kuehnelt-Leddihn. Nat R 29:945 Ag 19 '77
Voters say *si* to democracy. il pors Time 109: 18-23 Je 27 '77
See also
Political campaigns—Spain

Sri Lanka

End of a dynasty. K. Willenson and B. Came. il por Newsweek 90:33-4 Ag 1 '77

Turkey

Harmony time for a poet-warrior; election of B. Ecevit. il por Time 109:44 Je 20 '77

United States

New faces of election '77. il Newsweek 90:42-3+ N 21 '77
November 8: wot happened? Nat R 29:1343-4 N 25 '77
Referenda lessons. Progressive 41:11 Mr '77
Victory for the middle. il Time 110:16-18 N 21 '77
What '77 elections show. il U.S. News 83:19-20 N 21 '77
See also
Presidents—United States—Election
United States—Federal Election Commission
also subhead Politics and government under names of states and cities, e.g. Georgia—Politics and government

History

Close election of 1876. il Hobbies 81:53-4 F '77

ELECTORAL college
Abolishing the electoral college. T. Wicker. Current 189:3-4 Ja '77
Bad idea whose time has come. New Repub 176:5-6+ My 7 '77; Reply. M. E. Kinsley. 176: 6+ Je 25 '77
Direct election of the president. Nat R 29:135-6 F 4 '77
Don't fool with the electoral college. G. F. Will. Newsweek 89:96 Ap 4 '77
Unworthy idea; direct-election amendment proposed by B. Bayh. M. Stone. U.S. News 82: 100 My 16 '77
Vote to close down the college. il Time 109:12 Ap 4 '77

ELECTRIC analgesia. See Analgesia
ELECTRIC apparatus and appliances
Product reports 78. il Archit Rec 162:165-77 mid-O '77
ELECTRIC automobiles. See Automobiles, Electric
ELECTRIC barbecue grills. See Barbecue grills
ELECTRIC batteries
Battery selection becomes bewildering. R. Field. Sci Digest 81:67-8 Mr '77
Flashlight batteries (D-cell) il Consumers Res Mag 60:29-31 Ag '77
Photo-electronics; high-voltage dry batteries. E. Farber. il Pop Phot 80:66+ My '77
Photo-electronics; testing dry batteries. E. Farber. il por Pop Phot 81:58+ Jl; 58+ O '77
Photo-electronics; use in cameras and photographic equipment. E. Farber. il por Pop Phot 80:60+ Je '77
Protechniques; battery dating. E. Meyers. il Pop Phot 81:62+ Jl '77
Short, bright life of flashlight batteries. Changing T 31:47 My '77
What's ahead in batteries? J. Bailey. il Mod Phot 41:73-4+ S '77
See also
Fuel cells
Storage batteries
Storage battery industry

Charging

Photoelectronics; recharging dry batteries. E. Farber. il por Pop Phot 81:32+ S '77

Manufacture

See Electric battery industry
ELECTRIC battery industry

Germany, West

Spunky newcomer in the battery market; Ucar Batterien. Bus W p42-3 Ja 16 '78
ELECTRIC Boat Division. See General Dynamics Corporation
ELECTRIC boats. See Boats and boating
ELECTRIC cables
See also
Electric lines
ELECTRIC charges
Evidence for fractional electric charge. il Sci N 111:276 Ap 30 '77
ELECTRIC conductivity
See also
Superconductivity
ELECTRIC conductors
High-conductivity graphite compounds. B. G. Levi. bibl il Phys Today 30:18-19 Jl '77
Lithium-sodium beta alumina: first of a family of co-ionic conductors? W. L. Roth and G. C. Farrington. bibl il Science 196:1332-4 Je 17 '77
ELECTRIC connectors
New solderless coax connector. F. Shunaman. il Radio-Electr 48:54 F '77
ELECTRIC current converters
See also
Frequency changers
ELECTRIC current rectifiers
SCR, triac, diac and quadrac. E. Savage. il Radio-Electr 48:70-1 D '77
ELECTRIC discharges
See also
Electric sparks
ELECTRIC doorbells. See Doorbells, Electric
ELECTRIC drills. See Drilling and boring machinery
ELECTRIC engineering
Most subtle layering of architecture and light. il Archit Rec 161:131-6 F '77
ELECTRIC fans. See Fans, Electric
ELECTRIC fences. See Fences, Electric
ELECTRIC fields

Physiological effects

See Electricity—Physiological effects
ELECTRIC filters
Active filters. F. M. Mims. il Pop Electr 11:75-6 Ap '77
Noise filtering for hi-fi. J. Hirsch. il Pop Electr 12:32-3 Jl '77
See also
Radio filters
ELECTRIC fuses
Compact plug-in car fuse. W. J. Hawkins. il Pop Sci 210:52 F '77
ELECTRIC generators
See also
Fuel cells
ELECTRIC generators, Alternating current
Alternator charging circuit; excerpt from Your boat's electrical system. C. Miller. il Motor B & S 139:99-101 F '77
ELECTRIC hair dryers and stylers. See Hair dryers
ELECTRIC heaters. See Heaters
ELECTRIC household appliances. See Household appliances
ELECTRIC industries
See also
Electric utilities

Finance

Electronics & electrical equipment. il Forbes 121:98-9+ Ja 9 '78

Germany, West

Payoff in Braun's Americanized style. il Bus W p60+ Ap 18 '77

Great Britain

Action learning comes to industry; Great Britain's General Electric Company. N. Foy. bibl f Harvard Bus R 55:158-68 S '77

Japan

See also
Matsushita Electric Industrial Company, Ltd

United States

Harvey Hubbell, Harvey Hubbell. Forbes 120:28 Ag 1 '77
See also
Emerson Electric Company
General Electric Company
Reliance Electric Company
Western Electric Company
Westinghouse Electric Corporation
ELECTRIC kitchen utensils and appliances. See Kitchen utensils and appliances
ELECTRIC lamps
Akari lamps by Noguchi. il Craft Horiz 37:36-7 D '77
Home improvement ideas for the house fixer: 5 easy steps to rewire a lamp. D. Raffel. il House & Gard 150:44+ Ja '78
Incandescent to fluorescent lamp conversion. P. Eisenhut. il Pop Sci 210:142 F '77
Making a lamp from wood scraps. il Mech Illus 73:168-70 My '77
New lamps: there's a design that's right for any room. S. Grossman. il House B 119:54+ O '77
See also
Lighting fixtures
ELECTRIC lamps, Fluorescent
Build a fluorescent utility lamp. J. Duncan. il Pop Electr 12:53-5 O '77
Compact, throwaway fluorescent light stick. W. J. Hawkins. il Pop Sci 211:126 Jl '77
Fluorescent lights and hyperactivity in children: an experiment. M. Painter. Educ Digest 42:36-7 Ap '77
Tough emergency light—handiest and safest yet. E. F. Lindsley. il Pop Sci 210:179 Je '77
ELECTRIC lamps, Incandescent
Bulb to brighten lighting costs. Sci N 112:135 Ag 27 '77
Lights up, energy down; light bulbs. E. A. Meehan. il House & Gard 149:82+ S '77
ELECTRIC lamps, Photoflash
Instant photography; uneven flash intensity. D. Leavitt. il por Pop Phot 80:62+ My '77
ELECTRIC lawn mowers. See Lawn mowers
ELECTRIC light fixtures. See Lighting fixtures
ELECTRIC lighting
Modern designs for farmstead lighting. L. Reichenberger. il Suc Farm 75:44-5 S '77
10 ways to lower the cost of lighting your home. Good H 184:214 F '77
See also
Electric lamps
Lighting, Architectural and decorative
Street lighting
Theater—Stage lighting

Control

See also
Electric switches
ELECTRIC lines
Confrontation on the prairie; farmers' opposition to power lines; Minnesota. P. D. Wellstone and L. Tarbox. Progressive 41:41-3 D '77
Great energy standoff; opposition to high-voltage transmission lines crossing Minnesota farms. L. P. Gerlach. Natur Hist 87:22+ Ja '78
New opposition to high-voltage lines. il Bus W p27 N 7 '77
Watts up must come down? E. Meves. bibl il Parks & Rec 12:29-31 O '77
ELECTRIC meters
Build 3 low cost CB test meters. W. E. Osborne. il Radio-Electr 48:40-1+ O '77
Digital capacitance meter. T. R. Fox. il Pop Electr 11:50-2 Ap '77
Digital multimeters. il Radio-Electr 48:55-7 N '77
Don't electrocute your car battery. J. Sandler. il Pop Mech 148:68+ O '77
Equipment reports:
Data Precision model 175 digital multimeter. il Radio-Electr 48:34+ Mr '77
Fluke model 8020A digital multimeter. il Radio-Electr 48:22+ O '77
Simpson model 461 digital multimeter. il Radio-Electr 49:20+ Ja '78
VIZ WV-534A Voltohmyst V. il Radio-Electr 48:104 S '77

ELECTRIC meters—*Continued*
High sensitivity SWR meter for low-power communications equipment. W. Vancura. il Pop Electr 12:59-61 O '77
Measure capacitance on a digital readout. J. Vernon. il Radio-Electr 48:37-9 D '77
Multimeters for electronics (cont) C. J. Hallmark. il Pop Electr 11:31-2+ F '77
New energy monitor lets you keep track of electrical costs. S. Walton. il Pop Mech 148: 42 O '77
Product test reports:
Fluke model 8020A digital multimeter. il Pop Electr 12:85-6 Ag '77
Heathkit model IM-2202 digital multimeter kit. il Pop Electr 11:78-9 F '77
Sabtronics model 2000 digital multimeter kit. il Pop Electr 12:99-100+ D '77
Sencore model DVM37 digital multimeter. il Pop Electr 13:75-6 Ja '78
Servicing with multimeters. A. N. M. Kluijtmans. il Radio-Electr 48:67-9+ Ap '77
What you should know about DMM's. C. M. Gilmore. il Radio-Electr 48:53-5+ Jl '77
See also
Ammeters
Frequency meters
Voltohmmeters
Wattmeters

ELECTRIC motors
Little motor that saves; C. Wanlass' design. M. Ruby and M. Kasindorf. il por Newsweek 89:78 My 9 '77
See also
Automobiles, Electric

ELECTRIC organs in fishes
Flashlight fishes. J. E. McCosker. il Sci Am 236:106-12+ bibl(p 150) Mr '77

ELECTRIC outlet testers. See Testing instruments

ELECTRIC plants
Good things in small packages; fuel cell power plants. il Forbes 119:66 Mr 1 '77
See also
Atomic power plants
Electric utilities
Hydroelectric plants

Environmental aspects

Cheyennes drive for clean-air rights; redesignating air quality status to prevent industrial development. il Bus W p29 Ap 4 '77
Montana and Canada clash over pollution; power plant site 8 mi. across U.S. border. map Bus W p27-8 Je 27 '77
More burning of coal offsets gains in air pollution control. L. J. Carter. Science 198:1233 D 23 '77
New end run around EPA air standards. il Bus W p64 O 31 '77
No boomtown on the Kaiparowits Plateau: who made the decision and why? J. M. Rock. bibl il Intellect 105:248-50 F '77
Public health hazards from electricity-producing plants. J. Neyman. bibl il Science 195:754-8 F 25 '77
Quetico-Superior: international negotiators must head off pollution of borderland wilderness; proposed Atikokan Generating Station, Ontario. Nat Parks & Con Mag 51:20-1+ O '77
REA expansion plans bump into landowners. il Bus W p36+ O 31 '77
Western coal darkens Ohio's mining future; electric plants threaten switch from high sulfur variety. il Bus W p28 My 2 '77

Interconnection

Must we try for blackout III? proposal for regional grid system. J. Wicklein. il Progressive 41:16-20 N '77

Load

Leveling the load. Sci Am 237:58-9 Jl '77

Canada

Montana and Canada clash over pollution; power plant site 8 mi. across U.S. border. map Bus W p27-8 Je 27 '77
Quetico-Superior: international negotiators must head off pollution of borderland wilderness; proposed Atikokan Generating Station, Ontario. Nat Parks & Con Mag 51:20-1+ O '77

Great Britain

Coal to the rescue. W. C. Patterson. il Environment 19:4+ Ap '77

ELECTRIC power
See also
Electric plants
Electric utilities
Hydroelectric plants
Hydroelectric power
New York (city)—Electric power
St Louis—Electric power
Tennessee Valley Authority
United States—Agriculture, Department of—Rural Electrification Administration

Rates

See Electric utilities—Rates

ELECTRIC power, Solar. See Solar energy

ELECTRIC power distribution
See also
Electric plants—Interconnection

ELECTRIC power failures
Around City Hall; question of federal aid after blackout looting in New York City. A. Logan. New Yorker 53:64-72 Ag 15 '77
Bastille Day '77; blackout looting in New York City. M. Edelson. Nat R 29:870 Ag 5 '77
Blackout justice; New York City. M. Sheils and others. il Newsweek 90:67-8 Ag 1 '77
Blackout; New York City. J. A. Schnepper. Intellect 106:121 O '77
Bolt of lightning, then—; New York City blackout. il U.S. News 83:22-3 Jl 25 '77
Counting losses in the rubble; effects of blackout looting in New York City. il Time 110:14+ Ag 1 '77
Heart of darkness; New York City blackout; symposium. il Newsweek 90:16-31 Jl 25 '77
Light on the blackout. Nat R 29:930-1 Ag 19 '77
Looting and liberal racism: blackout looting in New York City. M. Decter. Commentary 64: 48-54 S '77; Discussion. 64:4+ N; 30+ D '77
Mugging of New York. New Repub 177:5-6+ Jl 30 '77
Must we try for blackout III? J. Wicklein. il Progressive 41:16-20 N '77
New York blackout. A. McGowan. Environment 19:48-9 Ag '77
New York blackout: weak links tie Con Ed to neighboring utilities. W. D. Metz. Science 197: 441-2 Jl 29 '77
New York's Con Ed counts its casualties. il Bus W p 19-20 Ag 1 '77
Night of terror; New York City blackout and looting. il Time 110:12-22 Jl 25 '77
Night of the transistor; New York. D. M. Alpern. il Newsweek 90:58 Jl 25 '77
Notes and comment; blackout in New York City. New Yorker 53:19-27 Jl 25 '77
Notes and comment; looting during New York City blackout. New Yorker 53:15-17 Ag 8 '77
People in the dark; New York City power failure. Nation 225:100 Ag 6 '77
Picking up the pieces; economic impact of New York's blackout. T. Nicholson and M. Reese. il Newsweek 90:60-1 Ag 1 '77
Rip-off time; blackout looting in New York City. Nat R 29:869 Ag 5 '77
Shock of recognition; New York City blackout. G. F. Will. Newsweek 90:80 Jl 25 '77
Steep price tag on the blackout; New York City. il Bus W p20-1 Ag 1 '77
What to do when a blackout hits. G. Williams, 3d. il Pop Mech 148:96-9+ N '77
When the news tickers fell silent; blackout in New York City. il Time 110:43 Jl 25 '77
Why the lights went out; can it happen elsewhere? il Time 110:24-6 Jl 25 '77

Anecdotes, facetiae, satire, etc.

Good explanation. I. Frazier. New Yorker 53: 27 Ag 1 '77

ELECTRIC power lines. See Electric lines

ELECTRIC power plants. See Electric plants

ELECTRIC power production
Saving energy the cogeneration way; using waste heat from industrial plants. il Bus W p99-100 Je 6 '77
See also
Direct energy conversion

ELECTRIC power production from chemical action
See also
Fuel cells

ELECTRIC power supply. See Electricity supply

ELECTRIC precipitators
How to select electrostatic precipitators. R. L. Bump. il Am City & County 92:76-7 My '77

ELECTRIC rates. See Electric utilities—Rates

ELECTRIC saws. See Saws

ELECTRIC shock
Electroshock experiment at Albany violates ethics guidelines. R. J. Smith. Science 198:383-6 O 28 '77; Discussion. 198:1099-100 D 16 '77
Guarding against shock. Consumer Rep 42:152-5 D '77

ELECTRIC sparks
Spark discharge: application to multielement spectrochemical analysis. J. P. Walters. bibl il Science 198:787-97 N 25 '77

ELECTRIC stoves. See Stoves

ELECTRIC switches
Don't fight, switch. J. Roy. il Am Home 80:16 S '77
How to connect a second wall switch to your ceiling light. il Bet Hom & Gard 55:200 My '77
Replacing an electrical switch. D. Raffel. House & Gard 149:68 Ap '77
Tachometer-speed switches. L. Garner. il Pop Electr 11:86-9 Mr '77

ELECTRIC tools
Power tool workout. il Hot Rod 30:84+ Ag '77

Manufacture

Managing a comeback with Skil. il Duns R 110:28+ N '77

ELECTRIC tools, Portable

Manufacture

See Electric tools—Manufacture

ELECTRIC transmission
See also
Electric lines

ELECTRIC typewriters. See Typewriters, Electric

ELECTRIC utilities
Confrontation on the prairie; farmers' opposition to power lines; Minnesota. P. D. Wellstone and L. Tarbox. Progressive 41:41-3 D '77
Electric power: who pays for expansion? D. J. Newburger. Environment 19:50-2 Je '77
Great energy standoff; opposition to high-voltage transmission lines crossing Minnesota farms. L. P. Gerlach. Natur Hist 87:22+ Ja '78
Issues on trial in the Westinghouse lawsuits; suits charging failure to deliver on uranium supply contracts. Bus W p 125-6+ S 26 '77
Night the lights almost went out. P. Lancaster. Fortune 95:57 My '77
No boomtown on the Kaiparowits Plateau: who made the decision and why? J. M. Rock. bibl il Intellect 105:248-50 F '77
Public power: its time has come. R. Munson. Progressive 41:26-9 My '77
Solar energy and electric utilities: should they be interfaced? J. G. Asbury and R. O. Mueller. bibl il Science 195:445-50 F 4 '77
Uranium pattern Westinghouse buys. Bus W p33 D 26 '77
Uranium thing; utilities suing Westinghouse over uranium contracts. A. J. Mayer and P. L. Abraham. il Newsweek 89:73 F 14 '77
See also
Commonwealth Edison Company
Consolidated Edison Company of New York
Consumers Power Company
Edison Electric Institute
Houston Lighting and Power Company
Pennsylvania Power and Light Company
Public Service Electric and Gas Company
Union Electric Company

Federal aid

REA expansion plans bump into landowners. il Bus W p36+ O 31 '77

Finance

Nuclear denting plagues the utilities. Bus W p20-1 Jl 4 '77

Fuel requirements

Texas power companies converting from natural gas to coal, lignite. J. Walsh. il map Science 198:471-4 N 4 '77
Why utilities are fired up over lignite; Texas plants. il Bus W p78-9 N 28 '77

Public relations

Selling the nuclear faith; campaign by Edison Electric Institute. Progressive 41:22 S '77

Rates

Energy: eastern power companies to warn before pulling plug. Aging 274:16 Ag '77
Knock the peaks off your power bills. L. Schotsch. il Farm J 101:A4-5 S '77
Leveling the load. Sci Am 237:58-9 Jl '77
New federal hand on electricity rates. il Bus W p29-30 F 28 '77
$16 to start your truck? J. Gillies. il Farm J 101:43-5 Ag '77
Utility's experiment in rate-setting; Public Service Company of New Mexico. il Bus W p84 S 26 '77
Why it's tougher to justify rate boosts. il Bus W p56+ N 7 '77
Why utility rates will keep going up. il Changing T 31:41-4 F '77

Regulation

Electricity: a necessity for the people; address, February 2, 1977. W. D. Crawford. Vital Speeches 43:294-6 Mr 1 '77
New end run around EPA air standards. il Bus W p64 O 31 '77
See also
Electric utilities—Rates

Reports to government

Full disclosure that may be too full; Justice Department intervention in fuel price information case. Bus W p28+ Ag 8 '77

Securities

Electric utility stocks are shining again; interview, ed by A. Hershman. C. Benore. por Duns R 110:73-5 Ag '77
Good time to buy utilities? J. Fraser. U.S. News 83:89 N 7 '77
How can the utilities raise the money? il Forbes 120:96 O 1 '77
Why Northern utilities may prove a good buy. J. Madrick. il Bus W p73 F 21 '77

Canada

Angling for the cash at Hydro-Quebec. Bus W p39-40 Je 27 '77
Arabs with a French accent; James Bay project of Hydro-Quebec. P. Sturm. il map Forbes 120:63-5 D 15 '77

ELECTRIC vehicles
Michael Hackleman: electric truck is wind-powered, too. E. Moran. il Pop Sci 210:78-9 Ap '77
Running out of steam. A. W. Reitze, Jr. bibl il Environment 19:34-40 Je '77
See also
Automobiles, Electric
Buses, Electric

ELECTRIC voltage. See Voltage

ELECTRIC water heaters. See Water heaters

ELECTRIC wire and wiring
Coping with wire and cable. F. Belt. il Radio-Electr 49:34-6 Ja '78
Flexible wiring systems: a catalog of current technology. il Archit Rec 162:114-20 mid-Ag '77
No-fuss wire splicing. D. Richmond. il Mech Illus 73:74 Mr '77
Wire-wrapping techniques for computer hobbyists. A. Mangieri. il Pop Electr 12:74-6+ D '77
See also
Automobiles—Electric wiring
Boats—Electric equipment
Electric switches

ELECTRICAL phonograph recording. See Phonograph records—Recording

ELECTRICAL stimulation of the brain. See Electronic behavior control

ELECTRICITY
See also
Atmospheric electricity
Fuel cells

Physiological effects

Watts up must come down? E. Meves. bibl il Parks & Rec 12:29-31 O '77

ELECTRICITY, Animal. See Electrophysiology

ELECTRICITY, Injuries from
See also
Electric shock

ELECTRICITY on boats. See Boats—Electric equipment

ELECTRICITY on the farm
Knock the peaks off your power bills. L. Schotsch. il Farm J 101:A4-5 S '77
$16 to start your truck? J. Gillies. il Farm J 101:43-5 Ag '77

ELECTRICITY supply
Electricity: a necessity for the people; address, February 2, 1977. W. D. Crawford. Vital Speeches 43:294-6 Mr 1 '77
Night the lights almost went out. P. Lancaster. Fortune 95:57 My '77
No boomtown on the Kaiparowits Plateau: who made the decision and why? J. M. Rock. bibl il Intellect 105:248-50 F '77
Why it's tougher to justify rate boosts. il Bus W p56+ N 7 '77

ELECTROACOUSTICS
See also
Acoustic surface wave devices

ELECTROBIOLOGY. See Electrophysiology

ELECTROCHEMISTRY
Electrochemical growth of organic charge-transfer complexes. D. F. Williams. Science 197:1194 S 16 '77
Energy recovery from saline water by means of electrochemical cells. B. H. Clampitt and F. E. Kiviat; reply. A. F. Hadermann. il Science 197:598-9 Ag 5 '77
See also
Electrolysis
Fuel cells

ELECTROCONVULSIVE therapy. See Shock therapy

ELECTRODES
Antibody binding measurements with hapten-selective membrane electrodes. M. Meyerhoff and G. A. Rechnitz. bibl il Science 195:494-5 F 4 '77

ELECTRODYNAMICS
See also
Quantum electrodynamics

ELECTROENCEPHALOGRAPHY
Alpha blocking: absence in visuobehavioral deprivation. J. D. Glass. bibl il Science 198:58-60 O 7 '77
Appetitive and replacement naps; EEG and behavior. F. J. Evans and others. bibl il Science 197:687-9 Ag 12 '77
Cortical potentials associated with the detection of visual events. R. Cooper and others. bibl il Science 196:74-7 Ap 1 '77
Event-related brain potentials: comparison between children and adults. E. Courchesne. bibl il Science 197:589-92 Ag 5 '77

ELECTROENCEPHALOGRAPHY—*Continued*
Neurometrics. E. R. John and others. bibl il Science 196:1393-410 Je 24 '77
Visual association cortex and vision in man: pattern-evoked occipital potentials in a blind boy. I. Bodis-Wollner and others. bibl il Science 198:629-31 N 11 '77
See also
Brain waves

ELECTROETCHING of metals. See Metal etching

ELECTROFORMING
Forming and etching as a plating process. J. R. Gianatasio and A. M. Grutter. il Sch Arts 77:30-3 D '77

ELECTROIMMUNODIFFUSION. See Immunodiffusion

ELECTROLYSIS
Electrolysis: how and why it can affect your boat and what to do about it; metal parts on boats. J. Pazereskis. il Yachting 142:53-5 D '77
Photoassisted electrolysis of water by visible irradiation of a *p*-type gallium phosphide electrode. M. Tomkiewicz and J. M. Woodall. bibl il Science 196:990-1 My 27 '77

ELECTROLYSIS (hair removal) See Hair, Removal of

ELECTROLYTES
Polyelectrolytes: potential chloroform precursors. K. L. E. Kaiser and J. Lawrence. bibl il Science 196:1205-6 Je 10 '77

ELECTROMAGNETIC theory
See also
Blackbody radiation

ELECTROMYOGRAPHY
Permeation of manganese, cadmium, zinc, and beryllium through calcium channels of an insect muscle membrane. J. Fukuda and K. Kawa. bibl il Science 196:309-11 Ap 15 '77

ELECTRON beam fusion. See Nuclear fusion

ELECTRON beams. See Electrons—Beams

ELECTRON microscopes and microscopy
Electron microscopy of atoms in crystals. J. M. Cowley and S. Lijima. bibl il pors Phys Today 30:32-6+ Mr '77
Electronic voyage through an invisible world; scanning electron microscope. K. F. Weaver. il Nat Geog 151:274-90 F '77
Hominoid enamel prism patterns. D. G. Gantt and others. bibl il Science 198:1155-7 D 16 '77
Human factor VIII: morphometric analysis of purified material in solution. H. K. Tan and J. C. Andersen. bibl il Science 198:932-4 D 2 '77
Magnifications; scanning electron microscope; excerpt. D. Scharf. il Harpers 255:55-9 Jl '77
Micro macabre; photography of insects using the scanning electron microscope. D. Scharf. il Int Wildlife 7:18-23 S '77
Mouse chromosome translocations: visualization and analysis by electron microscopy of the synaptonemal complex. M. J. Moses and others. bibl il Science 196:892-4 My 20 '77
Neurogenesis in the adult rat: electron microscopic analysis of light radioautographs. M. S. Kaplan and J. W. Hinds. bibl il Science 197:1092-4 S 9 '77
See also
Freeze fracturing

ELECTRON multipliers. See Photoelectric multipliers

ELECTRON probe microanalysis
Electron probe microanalysis: new uses in physiology. T. H. Maugh, 2d. Science 197:356-8 Jl 22 '77

ELECTRON spectroscopy. See Spectrum analysis

ELECTRON storage rings. See Accelerators (electrons, etc)

ELECTRONIC air cleaners. See Air filters

ELECTRONIC alarm systems
Build a field disturbance sensor for security. K. Powell. il Pop Electr 12:60-2 N '77
Build this electronic security system. C. D. Wadsworth. il Radio-Electr 48:36-9 S '77
Two-way cable TV protects America's safest town; The Woodlands, Tex. D. Lynch. il Pop Sci 211:70-1 Jl '77

ELECTRONIC apparatus and appliances
How to custom design plastic cases for projects. J. Huff. il Pop Electr 12:81-4 S '77
New products. See issues of Popular electronics including Electronics world
New products. See issues of Radio-electronics
See also
Airplanes—Electronic equipment
Automobiles—Electronic equipment
Blind, Apparatus for the
Boats—Electronic equipment
Computers
Electronics in surveying
Handicapped, Apparatus for the

Exhibitions

Big June trial balloon; Consumer Electronics Show. R. Hodges. il Pop Electr 12:22+ O '77

Instrument panels

See Instrument panels

Maintenance and repair

Service clinic. J. Darr. See issues of Radio-electronics

Power supply

Bring your car stereo or mobile CB home with this 12-v. power supply. W. D. Goldberg. il Pop Mech 147:175-6 F '77
Current foldback protects power supply and load. J. May. il Pop Electr 11:59-60 F '77
Equipment reports:
Heath IP2718 Tri-Power supply. il Radio-Electr 48:87+ Mr '77
Switching regulators reduce power supply cost. D. Raudenbush. il Pop Electr 11:60+ Ap '77

Safety devices and measures

How to handle MOS devices without destroying them. L. Solomon. il Pop Electr 12:67-70 Ag '77

Testing

Equipment reports. See issues of Radio-electronics
Product test reports. See issues of Popular electronics including Electronics world

ELECTRONIC behavior control
Schedule control of behavior reinforced by electrical stimulation of the brain. R. J. Beninger and others. bibl il Science 196:547-9 Ap 29 '77

ELECTRONIC circuits
Experimenter's corner. F. M. Mims. See issues of Popular electronics including Electronics world
RC circuit quiz. R. P. Balin. il Pop Electr 12:26 Jl '77
See also
Computers—circuits
Printed circuits
Radio circuits
Television circuits

Design

Homebrew breadboard. E. R. Savage. il Radio-Electr 48:70-1 Ag; 72-3+ S '77; Correction. 48:69+ N '77

Manufacture

Fabrication of microelectronic circuits. W. G. Oldham. il Sci Am 237:110-14+ bibl(p258) S '77

ELECTRONIC circuits, Integrated
Custom-design microcircuit cost cut; Interdesign, Inc. P. J. Klass. il Aviation W 106:52-3 F 14 '77
IC application of the month:
Reticon SAD-1024. il Radio-Electr 48:58-61+ Ap '77
IC bricklaying for miniature projects. W. T. Cardwell, Jr. il Radio-Electr 48:58-60 D '77
IC's for test instruments. L. Garner. il Pop Electr 12:77-81 Jl '77
Impudent, magical silicon chip. K. Lamott. il Horizon 19:72-7 Jl '77
Large-scale integration of microelectronic circuits. il Sci Am 237:82-94 bibl(p258) S '77
Large-scale integration: what is yet to come? R. N. Noyce. il Science 195:1102-6 Mr 18 '77
Programmable read-only memories. F. M. Mims. il Pop Electr 12:77-9 N '77
Read/write memories (RAM's) F. M. Mims. il Pop Electr 12:90-1+ D '77; 13:67-8 Ja '78
Six CMOS circuits for experimenters. D. Lancaster. il Pop Electr 11:46-7 Ap '77
State of solid state; National LM1812 ultrasonic transceiver. K. Savon. il Radio-Electr 48:100-4 F '77
State of solid state; two rhythm generators designed for electronic organs. K. Savon. il Radio-Electr 48:78-80 Mr '77
Tachometer-speed switches. L. Garner. il Pop Electr 11:86-9 Mr '77
What's new in IC's. Radio-Electr 48:61 D '77
Z-80. W. Barden, Jr. il Radio-Electr 48:72-3 D '77; 49:68-9 Ja '78
See also
Charge coupled devices (electronics)
Microprocessors

ELECTRONIC clocks. See Clocks, Electronic

ELECTRONIC communication. See Telecommunication

ELECTRONIC control
Role of microelectronics in instrumentation and control. B. M. Oliver. il Sci Am 237:180-1+ bibl(p260) S '77
See also
Camera shutters—Control
Photoelectric cells—Control use

ELECTRONIC cookery. See Microwave cookery

ELECTRONIC countermeasures on military airplanes. See Airplanes, Military—Electronic equipment

ELECTRONIC data processing
New trends in data processing. Duns R 110:93+ Jl '77
See also
Computers
Data transmission systems

ELECTRONIC data processing—*Continued*

Security measures

See Computers—Security measures

ELECTRONIC Data Systems Corporation
H. Ross Perot's new game plan at EDS. il por Bus W p92+ Ap 11 '77

ELECTRONIC funds transfer systems. See Computers—Banking use

ELECTRONIC gadgets. See Gadgets

ELECTRONIC games
Action football game. R. F. Graf and G. J. Whalen. il Radio-Electr 48:60-1+ Mr '77
Another new video game; RCA's Studio II. R. D. Freed. il Mech Illus 73:20 N '77
Build the LED target game. A. Russell. il Pop Electr 11:50-2 Je '77
Build this electronic slot machine. G. W. Hart. il Radio-Electr 48:39-43 Jl '77
How to prevent TV damage from video game-playing. Consumer Rep 42:252 My '77
Multiplayer LED racing game. W. J. Prudhomme. il Pop Electr 11:77-9+ Mr '77
New 1978 electronic games. K. Jensen. il Pop Electr 13:33-5+ Ja '78
New TV games: livelier, smarter. D. Sagrin. il Pop Mech 148:92-3 D '77
Programmable TV games. il Radio-Electr 49: 46-7 Ja '78
Quiz-game electronics. M. S. Robbins. il Pop Electr 11:64-5 F '77
Sociable Pong; television game. C. Tucker. Sat R 5:56 N 26 '77
Solid-state fun. T. Ferris. il Esquire 87:100-1+ Mr '77
TV electronic games grow up. A. Salsberg. Pop Electr 12:4 S '77
Those amazing new TV games. R. D. Freed. il Mech Illus 73:110+ My '77
To the electronic races! J. Barbarello. il Pop Electr 12:52-5 D '77
Video games. il Consumer Rep 42:630-4 N '77
See also
Pinball machines

ELECTRONIC industries
See also
Audio equipment industry
Avionics industry
Computer industry

Acquisitions and mergers

Hot bidding war to capture Milgo; controversy between Applied Digital Data Systems Co. and Racal Electronics Ltd. Bus W p33-4 F 7 '77
Racal's mistakes in the Milgo bidding. J. Madrick. il Bus W p75 F 28 '77
Siemens buys its way into U.S. expertise; Advanced Micro Devices Inc. il Bus W p42 O 17 '77
What made Motorola spend $89 million; attempt to acquire Codex Corp. Bus W p27-8 F 21 '77

Export-import trade

Brazil: even components must be Brazilianized. il Bus W p34 Ja 24 '77
Crackdown on electronics smugglers. il Bus W p39 Mr 21 '77
International trade in electronics: U.S.-Japan competition. J. Walsh. bibl il Science 195:1175-9 Mr 18 '77

Finance

Electronics & electrical equipment. il Forbes 121:98-9+ Ja 9 '78
Sure bet for first-half growth; semi-conductors. il Bus W p55-6+ Ja 9 '78

Marketing

Mess in consumer electronics. T. J. Murray. il Duns R 109:72-3+ Je '77

Brazil

Brazil: even components must be Brazilianized. il Bus W p34 Ja 24 '77

France

Setback in trying to Frenchify phones; Thomson-CSF. Bus W p68 N 21 '77

Germany, West

Here comes Siemens! il Forbes 119:31-2 Ja 15 '77

Japan

International trade in electronics: U.S.-Japan competition. J. Walsh. bibl il Science 195: 1175-9 Mr 18 '77
Japanese challenge in semiconductors. il Bus W p72-4 Jl 11 '77
Reluctant invader; Sharp Corp. il Forbes 120:59+ N 1 '77
See also
Matsushita Electrical Industrial Company, Ltd
Sony Corporation

Netherlands

See also
Philips of Eindhoven companies

Norway

Trying once again to bail out Tandberg. il Bus W p55-6 S 19 '77

United States

Advantage, Adler! il por Forbes 119:66-7 Ja 15 '77
Custom-design microcircuit costs cut; Interdesign, Inc. P. J. Klass. il Aviation W 106:52-3 F 14 '77
Good life beckons; Intel Corporation. il por Forbes 119:53 Ap 15 '77
How Hendrix snatched the lead in text editing. Bus W p58-9 Jl 4 '77
Intellectual and economic fuel for the electronics revolution. J. G. Linvill and C. L. Hogan. bibl il Science 195:1107-14 Mr 18 '77
Litronix cuts out of consumer products. Bus W p32-3 F 28 '77
Surplus labor; Loral Corp. por Forbes 120: 98 Jl 1 '77
Take the cash and let the credit go; CTS Corp. P. Berman. por Forbes 120:26-7 S 1 '77
See also
Bunker-Ramo Corporation
Fairchild Camera and Instrument Corporation
Harris Corporation
Leeds and Northrup Company
Motorola, Inc
National Semiconductor Corporation
RCA Corporation
Tandy Corporation
Texas Instruments, Inc

ELECTRONIC locks. See Locks and keys

ELECTRONIC mail. See Electronics in postal service

ELECTRONIC music. See Music, Electronic

ELECTRONIC music boxes. See Music boxes

ELECTRONIC music synthesizers. See Musical instruments, Electronic

ELECTRONIC musical instruments. See Musical instruments, Electronic

ELECTRONIC noise
See also
Audio systems—Noise

ELECTRONIC ovens. See Microwave ovens

ELECTRONIC photoflash units. See Photography —Electronic equipment

ELECTRONIC repair shops
Mac's service shop (cont) J. T. Frye. il Pop Electr 11:106-8 Je '77
Your service shop, how does it rate? J. Darr. il Radio-Electr 48:81-2+ My '77

ELECTRONIC scoreboards. See Scoreboards

ELECTRONIC technicians
Careers in audio: choosing a course. S. Traiman. il Hi Fi 27:134-7 Jl '77
See also
Television repairmen

ELECTRONIC thermometers. See Thermometers and thermometry

ELECTRONICS
Electronics revolution; special issue with editorial comment. bibl il Science 195:1085, 1087-240 Mr 18 '77
Electronics: snapshot of a developing revolution; Science's special issue of March 18, 1977. Sci N 111:184 Mr 19 '77
Hanging fire. A. Salsberg. il Pop Electr 11:4 F '77
Hobby scene; questions and answers. J. McVeigh. See issues of Popular electronics including Electronics world
Inside basic electronics. S. D. Prensky. See issues of Popular electronics including Electronics world
See also
Avionics
Delay devices
Digital electronics
Home electronics
Microelectronics
Pulse techniques (electronics)
Semiconductors
Transistors

Bibliography

Electronics library. See issues of Popular electronics including Electronics world

Caricatures and cartoons

World of electronics. F. Bolle. il Pop Electr 12:67 Jl '77

Gadgets

See Gadgets

History

Roots of solid-state research at Bell Labs. L. H. Hoddeson. bibl il Phys Today 30:23-6+ Mr '77

Military use

Electronic warfare gains given emphasis by Navy. il Aviation W 106:245-6 Ja 31 '77
Electronics and national defense: a case study. G. P. Dinneen and F. C. Frick. bibl il Science 195:1151-5 Mr 18 '77
Navy tactical situation display readied; liquid-crystal projector. P. J. Klass. il Aviation W 108:42-4 Ja 2 '78

ELECTRONICS—Military use—*Continued*
United States firms getting approval for Iranian avionics supply; Ibex system. Aviation W 106:15 Ja 10 '77
See also
Airplanes, Military—Electronic equipment
United States—Army Electronics Command

Study and teaching

Careers in audio: choosing a course. S. Traiman. il Hi Fi 27:134-7 Jl '77

Tools

See Tools

ELECTRONICS, Automotive. See Automobiles—Electronic equipment

ELECTRONICS as a profession
See also
Electronic technicians

ELECTRONICS in agriculture
Electronic seed treatment: will it boost yields? G. W. Wormley. il Farm J 101:C1 Ag '77
It's time for electronic ID. J. Russell. por Farm J 101:Hog 24 Ag '77

ELECTRONICS in astronomy
CCD: new eye on the sky. J. Eberhart. il Sci N 111:169+ Mr 12 '77

ELECTRONICS in aviation. See Avionics

ELECTRONICS in criminal investigation, espionage, etc.
Antitrust suit against Bell winds onward. D. Shapley. Science 198:278 O 21 '77
Case of the bugged physicist; Verfassungsschutz' bugging of K. R. Traube's home. il por Time 109:28 Mr 14 '77
Death of a wireman; murder of F. Chin. il por Time 109:19 F 21 '77
Was Wilson bugged? Former Prime Minister, H. Wilson. Newsweek 90:31 Ag 15 '77
See also
Wiretapping

ELECTRONICS in fishing
Bionic bassing. T. Drace. il Motor B & S 139:84-6+ Je '77
Fish finder. J. Fullum. il Conservationist 31:43 Ja '77
See also
Depth indicators

ELECTRONICS in medicine. See Medical electronics

ELECTRONICS in photography
Photo-electronics. E. Farber. il por Pop Phot 80:8+ Mr; 60+ Je; 81:58+ Jl; 32+ S; 58+ O; 80+ D '77
See also
Photography—Electronic equipment

ELECTRONICS in postal service
Electronic mail. R. J. Potter. bibl il Science 195:1160-4 Mr 18 '77

ELECTRONICS in sports
See also
Electronics in fishing

ELECTRONICS in surveying
Surveying instruments. il Am City & County 92:63-6 Ap '77

ELECTRONS
Exoelectrons. E. Rabinowicz. il Sci Am 236:74-82 bibl(p 132) Ja '77
See also
Neutrons
Positronium
Quantum electrodynamics

Beams

Fusions by electron beam produced at Sandia. Sci N 112:4 Jl 2 '77
U.S. electron beam tests trigger fusion. W. C. Wetmore. il Aviation W 107:22-4 Jl 4 '77

ELECTROPHOTOGRAPHY
Aura phenomenon puzzles experts; Kirlian photography. E. Edelson. il Smithsonian 8:109-14 bibl(p 148) Ap '77

ELECTROPHYSIOLOGY
Cortical mechanisms that augment or reduce evoked potentials in cats. J. H. Lukas and J. Siegel. bibl il Science 198:73-5 O 7 '77
Dopamine and adenosine 3',5'-monophosphate responses of single mammalian sympathetic neurons. N. J. Dun and others. bibl il Science 197:778-80 Ag 19 '77
Electricity and natural healing. il Sci N 112:343 N 19 '77
Gating of neuronal transmission in the hippocampus: efficacy of transmission varies with behavioral state. J. Winson and C. Abzug. bibl il Science 196:1223-5 Je 10 '77
Ion channels in nerve membranes. G. Ehrenstein; reply with rejoinder. M. W. P. Strandberg. bibl Phys Today 30:13+ Je '77
Licking behavior: evidence of hypoglossal oscillator. Z. Wiesenfeld and others. bibl il Science 196:1122-4 Je 3 '77
Membrane currents examined under voltage clamp in cultured neuroblastoma cells. W. H. Moolenaar and I. Spector. bibl il Science 196:331-3 Ap 15 '77
Membrane potential of mitochondria measured with microelectrodes. B. L. Maloff and others. bibl il Science 195:898-900 Mr 4 '77
Pontine reticular formation neurons: relationship of discharge to motor activity. J. M. Siegel and D. J. McGinty. bibl il Science 196:678-80 My 6 '77
Skin batteries and limb regeneration. R. B. Borgens. il Natur Hist 86:84-9 bibl(p 123) O '77
Sodium-specific membrane channels of frog skin are pores: current fluctuations reveal high turnover. B. Lindemann and W. van Driessche. bibl il Science 195:292-4 Ja 21 '77
Transmitter release during repetitive stimulation: selective changes produced by Sr^{2+} and Ba^{2+}. J. E. Zengel and K. L. Magleby. bibl il Science 197:67-9 Jl 1 '77
Visual input to the visuomotor mechanisms of the monkey's parietal lobe. T. C. T. Yin and V. B. Mountcastle. bibl il Science 197:1381-3 S 30 '77
See also
Electric organs in fishes
Electricity—Physiological effects
Electroencephalography
Electromyography

Apparatus

Laser interferometer measurement of changes in crayfish axon diameter concurrent with action potential. B. C. Hill and others. bibl il Science 196:426-8 Ap 22 '77
Long-term unit recording from somatosensory neurons in the spinal ganglia of the freely walking cat. G. E. Loeb and others. bibl il Science 197:1192-4 S 16 '77

ELECTROPHYSIOLOGY of plants
Osmotically induced changes in electrical properties of plant protoplast membranes. R. H. Racusen and others. bibl il Science 198:405-7 O 28 '77
Pyroelectricity and induced pyroelectric polarization in leaves of the palmlike plant encephalartos villosus. S. B. Lang and H. Athenstaedt. bibl il Science 196:985-6 My 27 '77

ELECTROPLATING
See also
Electroforming

ELECTROSHOCK. See Electric shock

ELECTROSTATIC accelerators. See Accelerators (electrons, etc.)

ELECTROSTATIC precipitators. See Electric precipitators

ELECTROSTATIC sprayers. See Spraying apparatus

ELECTROTHERAPY
See also
Shock therapy

ELEGANT, Robert S.
Eternal China, eternal conspiracies. il map Nat R 29:1167+ O 14 '77
Robert S. Elegant: journalist into novelist; interview, ed by R. Dahlin. por Pub W 212:48 O 10 '77

ELEMENTARY education. See Education, Elementary

ELEMENTARY particles. See Particles (nuclear physics)

ELEPHANT poaching. See Poaching

ELEPHANTS
Perilous future of the elephant. il Sci N 111:327 My 21 '77
Under the gun. M. Myers; discussion. il Int Wildlife 7:18-19 Mr '77
Unforgettable elephants; work of I. Douglas-Hamilton. J. C. Horn. il Psychol Today 10:88+ Ap '77
See also
Ivory

Training

School for elephants. D. D. Gray. il Int Wildlife 8:36-43 Ja '78
Trunkful of talent. K. Jones. il Seventeen 36:112 Ap '77

ELEPHANTS, Fossil
See also
Mammoths
Mastodons

ELEPHANTS, Photography of. See Photography of animals

ELEVATED railroads. See Railroads, Elevated

ELEVATORS
Elevator space requirements in high-rise buildings. J. K. Ochsner and others. il Archit Rec 162:117-18 Jl '77

ELEVATORS, Grain. See Grain elevators

ELFENBEIN, Julien, Jr
Broker profile; interview. por Motor B & S 140:108 Ag '77

ELFIN, Margery
Vice Presidential home on Naval Observatory hill. il pors Smithsonian 8:62-9 S '77

ELGAR, Sir Edward William, 1st Bart
Dream of Gerontius. J. Diether. Am Rec G 40:32-3 S '77 *
Symphony no. 2 in E flat, London Philharmonic Orchestra conducted by Sir Adrian Boult. J. Diether. Am Rec G 40:27 O '77 *

ELGIN, Suzette Haden
From the author. Engl J 66:17-19 My '77
ELIAS IV, Patriarch
Visitor from the Middle East. Chr Today 21:39-40 Ag 26 '77 *
ELIAS, Morris
Stars in their eyes. E. R. Walsh. por Ret Liv 17:31+ Ag '77 *
ELIAV, Arie
Tough talk from a dove; excerpt from interview, ed by M. Bruzonsky. Nation 225:688-9 D 24 '77
ELICKER, Paul H.
Long turnaround at SCM Corp. por Duns R 109:22-3 Ap '77 *
ELIOT, Alexander
J. Paul Getty's legacy; what is in store for the garden of the billionaire's whim? il Horticulture 55:10-13 N '77
Rubens' garden. il Horticulture 55:52+ My '77
Sackville-West's Sissinghurst. bibl il Horticulture 55:12-15 Jl '77
ELIOT, Jane
Get with child a mandrake root. Horticulture 55:12-13+ Je '77
ELIOT, John
Japan's warriors of the wind. il Nat Geog 151:550-61 Ap '77
ELIOT Feld Ballet
Dance. N. Goldner. Nation 224:412-14 Ap 2 '77
Eliot Feld Ballet; engagement at the City Center. J. Maskey. il Hi Fi 27:MA11 Jl '77
Eliot Feld's animated cartoons; Eliot Feld Ballet season at City Center. A. Smith. il por Dance Mag 51:63-5 Je '77
Feld magic. H. Saal. il por Newsweek 89:60-1 Mr 21 '77
Misha meets Yankee Doodle. J. Downs. il Time 109:88 Mr 21 '77
ELITE (social sciences)
How the establishment got established; excerpt from The emergence of society. J. Pfeiffer. il Horizon 19:62-7 Mr '77
Italian communism at home and abroad: the new class. M. Lucentini; discussion. Commentary 63:20-2+ Mr '77
Reasons for democracy; excerpt from The reason for democracy. K. H. Silvert. il Society 14:25-31 My '77
ELIZABETH II, Queen of Great Britain
All about the Queen; excerpt from Majesty. R. Lacey. il pors N Y Times Mag p28-31+ Ja 30 '77 *
Days of Jubilee. R. Carroll and A. Collings. il pors Newsweek 89:35-8 Je 20 '77 *
God save the Queen. G. F. Will. Newsweek 89:104 Je 13 '77 *
Inner Queen. R. West. il Vogue 167:232-3+ My '77 *
Jubilee bash for the Liz they love. il pors Time 109:36-8+ Je 20 '77 *
Letter from London. M. Panter-Downes. New Yorker 53:52-3 Je 27 '77 *
Profiles. A. Bailey. New Yorker 53:42-4+ Ap 11; 51-2+ Ap 18 '77 *
The Queen. J. Bradshaw. il Esquire 88:74-6 Ag '77 *
Queen Elizabeth at 51; excerpt from Queens of England. N. Lofts. por Ladies Home J 94:67-8+ Jl '77 *
Queen for our day. A. Deming and others. il pors Newsweek 89:29-31+ Je 13 '77 *
Vivat Regina. H. Fairlie. New Repub 176:12 Je 18 '77 *

Visit to Northern Ireland, 1977
Letter from Belfast: post-Elizabethan blues. T. P. O'Mahony. America 137:147-8 S 17 '77
Royal blitz in a troubled realm. il por Time 110:39 Ag 22 '77
ELIZABETH; drama. See Garver, J.
ELK
Elk in the shrub-steppe region of Washington: an authentic record. W. H. Rickard and others. il Science 196:1009 My 27 '77
ELK hunting
About hunting elk; Colorado. J. Cooney. il Field & S 82:50-1+ S '77
Bugle your elk; Rocky Mountains. C. J. Farmer. il Field & S 82:40-1+ N '77
Day of the elk; New Mexico. J. Samson. il Field & S 82:48-9 O '77
Elk hunting today—a comparison of 11 states. V. L. Oertle. Outdoor Life 160:85+ Ag '77
Elk that was king; new Pope & Young world record; ed by D. Schuh. D. Kittredge. il por Outdoor Life 160:98-100+ S '77
Three-for-three elk hunt; in Uncompahgre National Forest, Colo. R. Tinsley. il map Outdoor Life 159:70-1+ Je '77
To the elk kingdom. E. A. Bauer. il Outdoor Life 160:80-4 Ag '77
We go on an elk hunt; Vermejo Park ranch in New Mexico. P. Barrett. il Mech Illus 73:24+ S '77
ELKIND, David
What young children need most in changing society; interview. il Parents Mag 52:40-1+ Jl '77
ELKINS, Valmai How
Great beginnings. K. McLean. il pors Am Home 80:30-2 Mr '77 *
ELLAISSI, M. I.
Working. Engl J 66:65-6 S '77
ELLAM, Patrick
To the Great Lakes. Yachting 141:146+ Je '77
ELLENA, Gina. See Ellena, N. jt auth
ELLENA, Nick, and Ellena, Gina
Ladakh: a journey. il map Travel 147:24-31+ F '77
ELLENBOROUGH, Jane Elizabeth (Digby) Law, Countess of
Passions of Lady Jane Digby. M. F. Schmidt. il por Ms 5:78-80+ My '77 *
ELLETT, William H.
Litchfield's golden age. il Américas 29:14-20 Je '77
ELLINGSON, Marnie
Happiest day; story. Good H 185:134-5 O '77
Little magic in the spring; story. McCalls 104:202-3 Ap '77
Thank you, Allen French; story. McCalls 104:124-5 Ag '77
Under the family tree; story. Good H 184:98-9 F '77
ELLINGTON, Duke
Indigenous music. N. Hentoff. Nation 224:314-15 Mr 12 '77 *
ELLINGTON Festival. See Dance festivals
ELLIOT, Arthur H.
Turning it around in education with student tutoring. bibl il Clearing H 50:285-90 Mr '77
ELLIOT, James L.
Discoverers provide details of Uranus rings. Space World N-8-164:25 Ag '77 *
—and others
Discovering the rings of Uranus. il Sky & Tel 53:412-16+ Je '77
Occultation of ε Geminorum by Mars: evidence for atmospheric tides? bibl il Science 195:485-6 F 4 '77
ELLIOT, Jeffrey M.
(ed) See Angelou, M. Maya Angelou: in search of self
(ed) See Burke, Y. B. Congressional Black Caucus
(ed) See Lindsay, G. Dynamics of black local politics: an interview with G. Lindsay
—See Rein, M. jt auth
ELLIOTT, Charles
Channel cats; two ways. il Outdoor Life 159:86-7+ Ap '77
Enemies of gamebirds. il Outdoor Life 160:74-7+ S '77
Fall gobblers are different. il Outdoor Life 160:72-3+ O '77
Fox in the treetops. il map Outdoor Life 160:70-1+ Jl '77
Snakebite! What to know—what to do. il Outdoor Life 160:84-7+ S '77
Ugh! Fish. Outdoor Life 160:67+ D '77
ELLIOTT, Gordon
19th century Staffordshire; with excerpts from 1827 pamphlet. Ceram Mo 25:29-36 Mr '77
ELLIOTT, Lawrence
Challenging Hidden Peak. il Read Digest 111:102-7 D '77
French correction. il Read Digest 111:117-20 Ag '77
Monte Albán, city of the gods. il Read Digest 110:202-4+ My '77
Prisoner of conscience: the Bukovsky file. por Read Digest 111:93-7 Ag '77
ELLIOTT, Marion L.
My name is not Kevin . . . it's Michelangelo! il Sch Arts 77:21 N '77
ELLIOTT, Osborn
From city desk to City Hall: the odyssey of an erstwhile journalist. il pors N Y Times Mag p30-1+ Ag 28 '77
ELLIOTT, Paul. See Williams, M. jt auth
ELLIOTT, Robert M.
Levitz redecorates its image. il por Bus W p59 Ag 8 '77 *
ELLIOTT, Susan
Billy Joel: up from Piano man. pors Hi Fi 28:110-13+ Ja '78
(ed) See Collins, J. Judy Collins & the art of transition
ELLIOTT, Ted
One of a kind. O. Moore. il pors Motor B & S 140:58-60+ Jl '77 *
ELLIS, H. F.
Ancestral voices. New Yorker 53:33-5 Mr 14 '77
Autobiographer manqué. New Yorker 53:25-6 S 5 '77
ELLIS, Harry
Woods are alive with salamanders. il Nat Wildlife 15:42-5 O '77
ELLIS, Jib
Arp & Friend, Inc. il pors Hi Fi 28:114-16 Ja '78
ELLIS, Joan
Joan Ellis: Fireball class commodore. E. Horan. il Yachting 142:48+ O '77 *

ELLIS, Richard
Of men, whales, and Captain Scammon. il map Nat Parks & Con Mag 51:8-13 O '77
Predators: the swordfish and the mako shark; excerpt from The book of sharks. il Oceans 10:18-20 N '77
ELLIS, Richard Williamson
Richard Ellis honored for his book designs by Franklin Club. F. Harrington. il por Pub W 212:95-6 Ag 1 '77 *
ELLIS, William Donohue
Hardware U.—the great American learning center. il Read Digest 111:120-3 S '77
Put that small idea to work. Read Digest 111: 123-5 N '77
ELLIS, William N.
A.T: the quiet revolution. il Bull Atom Sci 33: 24-9 N '77
ELLIS, William S.
Japan's amazing Inland Sea. il map Nat Geog 152:830-63 D '77
Loch Ness: the lake and the legend. il map Nat Geog 151:758-79 Je '77
Malaysia: youthful nation with growing pains. il map Nat Geog 151:634-67 My '77
South Africa's lonely ordeal. il map Nat Geog 151:780-819 Je '77
ELLIS family
Ellis coat-of-arms. H. K. Eilers. il Hobbies 82: 150-1 D '77
ELLIS Island
Ellis Island. New Yorker 53:20 Jl 11 '77
ELLISON, Katherine White. See Buckhout, R. jt auth
ELLISON, Ralph
Little man at Chehaw Station. Am Scholar 47: 25-48 Wint '77
about
Flying home. M. W. Mintz. Engl J 66:67-8 Mr '77 *
ELLMANN, Richard
Richard Ellmann on biography. il New Repub 177:26+ N 26 '77
ELLSBERG, Daniel
Ellsberg: a punk talks back. il por Newsweek 89:19 My 30 '77
ELLSWORTH, Henry
How the Department got its start. S. B. Sutton. il Horticulture 55:33-7 Ap '77 *
ELLSWORTH, Randolph A. and Willson, D. D.
Another visit to the world of grading. il Clearing H 51:188-9 D '77
ELM
Diseases and pests
Death of an aged monarch; Dutch elm disease on White House grounds. H. Sidey. il Time 111:13 Ja 16 '78
Their elm forest is doomed, but Twin Cities are ready; Dutch elm disease control program. F. Graham, Jr. Audubon 79:136-9 Jl '77
ELMBLAD, Mary
Something to celebrate; story. Ladies Home J 94:130-1 N '77
Squared-up petunia; story. Ladies Home J 94: 52 Ag '77
ELMEN, Paul
Death of an elfking. por Chr Cent 94:1057-60 N 16 '77
EL MORRO National Monument
History on the rocks; Inscription Rock. B. A. Branson. il Américas 29:10-14 Ja '77
ELMS, Alan C.
Alias Johnny Hooker. Psychol Today 10:17 F '77
ELOCUTION
Power to the eloquent. J. Hitchcock. Yale R 66:374-87 Mr '77
See also
Public speaking
ELON, Florence
Pain killer; poem. Atlantic 240:62 Jl '77
Transformation of father; poem. New Yorker 53:66 N 21 '77
EL PASO, Tex.
Foreign population
Benign neglect; Mexicans. J. Lelyveld. il N Y Times Mag p 178 N 20 '77
EL PASO Company
El Paso's big deal excites investors. J. Madrick. il Bus W p72 My 30 '77
EL SEGUNDO blue butterfly. See Butterflies
ELSEN, Albert
Arts bills: pluses and minuses. il por Art N 76:52-4 O '77
California's art resale law: the failure of innocence. Art in Am 76:15-16 Mr '77
Mind bending with George Segal. il por Art N 76:34-7 F '77
ELTRA Corporation
In the grip of hands-on management. A. M. Louis. il por Fortune 95:170-8 Mr '77
ELWELL, Richard
Inevitable metric advance. Educ Digest 42:17-20 Mr '77
ELWYN family
Elwyn coat-of-arms. H. K. Eilers. il Hobbies 82:146 Mr '77

ELY, Alice
Chef's chatter (cont) Holiday 57:54 N '76
ELY, David
Partisan; story. Atlantic 239:35-40 F '77
EMBALMING
See also
Mummies
EMBARGO
Case of the missing thistleseed; question of embargo by India. G. Reiger. Audubon 79:161 N '77
If the world tries to block South Africa's trade—. il U.S. News 83:38 N 7 '77
Limited action against apartheid; UN imposition of mandatory arms embargo on South Africa. il Time 110:35-6 N 14 '77
Loneliness is an enemy; proposed arms embargo of South Africa. il Time 110:36-7 N 7 '77
Message to Pretoria. R. Steele and others. il Newsweek 90:30-1 N 7 '77
Mood in South Africa: defiance, bitterness, anger; with interview with B. J. Vorster. K. M. Chrysler. il U.S. News 83:38-40 N 21 '77
South Africa: post-diplomatic options. A. Silk. Nation 225:677 D 24 '77
U.N. Security Council condemns South Africa's apartheid policy and imposes a mandatory arms embargo; statements, with text of resolutions, October 31 and November 4, 1977. A. J. Young. Dept State Bull 77:859-66 D 12 '77
Voting the embargo; UN vote on South Africa. K. Willenson and others. il Newsweek 90:62 N 14 '77
EMBASSIES (buildings)
USA embassy office building, Tokyo. il Archit Rec 161:101-6 Ap '77
EMBELLISHMENT (music)
Second thoughts on the performance of Beethoven's trills. R. Winter. bibl f il Mus Q 63: 483-504 O '77
EMBEZZLEMENT
Embezzler; B. L. Campbell of the Calhoun First National Bank. S. Fraker and others. por Newsweek 90:27 S 19 '77
Swinging sergeant; embezzlement case of German Air Force Sergeant S. Schmidt. il por Time 109:46 Ap 11 '77
Wayward bookman; question of embezzlement by Milwaukee public librarian and ALA president K. A. Linderfelt. W. A. Wiegand. bibl il Am Lib 8:134-7, 197-200 Mr-Ap '77
EMBLEMS
See also
Fleur-de-lis
EMBLEMS, National
Russia
Caricatures and cartoons
Hammer and the sickle. D. Suter. il Harpers 255:70-1 N '77
EMBOLISM
Just be ready! first aid given to pulmonary embolism victim. A. H. Bridges. Read Digest 111:83-7 O '77
EMBRACING
Commentary; hugging of children. P. Knauth. MH 61:2 Spr '77
Did you hug your child today? A. Silberman. Read Digest 110:143-6 F '77
EMBRAER (firm) See Airplane industry—Brazil
EMBROIDERY
Crafts; chairs covered with original needlepoint at the governor's mansion in Indiana. A. Kline. il House B 119:26+ O '77
Easy-to-master stitchery painting. N. Lindemeyer and others. il Bet Hom & Gard 55:84-7+ My '77
Heraldic embroidery from Miss Balch's in Providence; ed by K. M. Jones. il Antiques 112:754+ O '77
Revolutionary needlepoint; new stitches by Paul Himmel and Shirlee Lantz. il House & Gard 149:166-7+ My '77
What makes the sweater interesting is what you do to it. il Sunset 159:136 O '77
See also
Samplers
Patterns
In praise of butterflies. N. Lindemeyer and C. Vaughan. il Bet Hom & Gard 54:66-9+ Ag '76
EMBRY-Riddle Aeronautical University, Daytona Beach, Fla. See Aviation schools
EMBRYO transplantation. See Ova—Transplantation
EMBRYOLOGY
See also
Blastocysts
Fertilization (biology)
Fetus
Morphogenesis
Neoteny
Parthenogenesis
Amphibia
Evidence for abnormal heart induction in cardiac-mutant salamanders (ambystoma mexicanum) L. F. Lemanski and others. bibl il Science 196:894-6 My 20 '77

EMBRYOLOGY—*Continued*

Birds

Axial bending in the early chick embryc by a cyclic adenosine monophosphate source. A. Robertson and A. R. Gingle. bibl il Science 197:1078-9 S 9 '77

Morphologies of cells from 1-day chick embryos. A. R. Gingle and A. Robertson. bibl il Science 196:59-60 Ap 1 '77

EMBRYOLOGY, Experimental

See also

Ova—Transplantation

EMERGENCIES. See Accidents

EMERGENCIES, Assistance in. See Assistance in emergencies

EMERGENCY briefing of airline passengers. See Aviation—Safety devices and measures

EMERGENCY communication systems

See also

Disaster warning systems

Telephone—Emergency use

EMERGENCY Decontamination Facility. See United States—Energy Research and Development Administration—Emergency Decontamination Facility

EMERGENCY first aid. See First aid in illness and injury

EMERGENCY housing

After the strip floods: relief is the real disaster; emergency housing for Mingo County, W.Va. R. E. Wise, Jr. il Nation 225:18-20 Jl 2 '77

EMERGENCY medical care. See Medical care

EMERGENCY position indicating radio beacon. See Radio beacons

EMERGENCY powers. See War and emergency powers

EMERGENCY signals. See Signals and signaling

EMERGENCY telephone operators. See Telephone operators

EMERGENCY trucks. See Trucks in rescue work

EMERSON, Gloria

Born New Yorker sight-revels in places most people miss. Vogue 167:144 Mr '77

PW interviews; ed by J. F. Baker. por Pub W 211:8-9 Ja 10 '77

Voodoo vendetta. il Esquire 87:102-3 Je '77

Your father's daughter. Vogue 167:303+ O '77

about

Critical amnesia. M. Young. Nation 224:406-8 Ap 2 '77 *

Virgins of Times Square. C. Williamson, Jr. Nat R 29:616-19 My 27 '77 *

EMERSON, Ken

Chocolate city and beyond. il por Sat R 5:48-9 N 12 '77

EMERSON, Ralph Waldo

Transcendentalism and the expectation of dawn: Emerson and Thoreau. E. Ardura. il pors Américas 29:36-41 Ag '77 *

EMERSON College, Boston

Tuning in and turning on; address, September 15, 1977. G. Turbeville. Vital Speeches 43:747-9 O 1 '77

EMERSON Electric Company

Charles F. Knight of Emerson Electric: direct approach. por Forbes 119:94 F 15 '77

Emerson Electric: the unique manager. il por Duns R 110:52+ D '77

EMERSON Lake & Palmer (rock group) See Rock groups

EMERSONS, Ltd. See Restaurants—Chain and franchise operations

EMERY, Lin

Special tax problem: no profits. P. Schwab. il por Nations Bus 65:100 N '77 *

EMERY, Noemie

Home away from home for writers. il Pub W 211:39-40 Ja 17 '77

EMIGH, Virginia D. and Farrar, D. R.

Gemmae: a role in sexual reproduction in the fern genus vittaria. bibl il Science 198:297-8 O 21 '77

EMIGRATION. See Immigration and emigration

EMIGRATION and immigration law. See Immigration and emigration law

EMILIANI, Cesare

Oxygen isotopic analysis of the size fraction between 62 and 250 micrometers in Caribbean cores P6304-8 and P6304-9. bibl il Science 198: 1255-6 D 23 '77

EMINENT domain (international law)

Managing against expropriation. D. G. Bradley. il map Harvard Bus R 55:75-83 Jl '77

See also

Cuba—Expropriation policy

EMLEN, Stephen Thompson, and Oring, L. W.

Ecology, sexual selection, and the evolution of mating systems. bibl il Science 197:215-23 Jl 15 '77

EMMANUEL, Sister Marie. See Marie Emmanuel, Sister

EMMER, Harry

Fireplace man; interview. il New Yorker 53:31-2 My 2 '77

EMMERICH, André

Is New York City vital to an artist's success? pors Am Artist 41:17 Ag '77

EMMETT, Edward A. and others

Phototoxic keratoconjunctivitis from coal-tar pitch volatiles. bibl il Science 198:841-2 N 25 '77

EMMINGER, Otmar

Can Germany avoid catching the U. S. disease? E. Mervosh and W. Wolman. por Bus W p 122 O 17 '77 *

Hard-liner takes over at the Bundesbank. il por Bus W p94+ Je 20 '77 *

EMMONS, Chansonette (Stanley)

Timeless summers in old-time Maine. D. Seiberling. il pors N Y Times Mag p 18-19+ Jl 24 '77 *

EMMONS, Howard W.

More research on flammability, ignition, other factors needed. Sci Digest 82:12-13 Ag '77

EMOTIONAL illness. See Mental illness

EMOTIONAL problems of children

Why worry helps; pre-operation anxiety. E. Lauter. il Parents Mag 53:40+ Ja '78

EMOTIONALLY disturbed. See Mentally ill

EMOTIONALLY disturbed children. See Problem children

EMOTIONS

Borderline behavior; diagnosing emotional or behavioral problems. E. B. Wilson. Harp Baz 110:228-9+ S '77

Brain and emotions. J. Greenberg. il por Sci N 112:74-5 Jl 30 '77

Breakup: how he feels when it's over. V. Billings. Seventeen 36:94-5 Jl '77

Putting it back where it belongs. W. Gaylin. il Psychol Today 11:25 Je '77

Seven basic emotional problems & what you can do about them. N. Lande and A. Slade. Harp Baz 110:98-9+ Ap '77

When feelings clash; parents and children. J. Neary. il Parents Mag 53:44+ Ja '78

See also

Anger
Anxiety
Bashfulness
Desire
Emotional problems of children
Empathy
Facial expression
Hate
Intimacy
Jealousy
Love
Mind and body
Moods
Sensitiveness
Worry

EMPATHY

On the nature of empathy. F. W. Kaslow. bibl Intellect 105:273-7 F '77

EMPEREUR, James L.

Catechesis for a worshiping community. il por New Cath World 220:84-8 Mr '77

EMPEROR of Atlantis; opera. See Ullmann, V.

EMPEROR penguins. See Penguins

EMPEROR Seamounts. See Seamounts

EMPHYSEMA

Elastase release from human alveolar macrophages: comparison between smokers and nonsmokers. R. J. Rodriguez and others. bibl il Science 198:313-14 O 21 '77

EMPIRE Brass Quintet. See Wind quintets

EMPIRICAL argument. See God—Proof, Empirical

EMPLOYEE absenteeism. See Absenteeism

EMPLOYEE benefits. See Non-wage payments

EMPLOYEE incentives. See Incentives in industry

EMPLOYEE morale

See also

Incentives in industry
Job satisfaction

EMPLOYEE motivation. See Motivation (psychology)

EMPLOYEE ownership

How to buy out your own company. L. Adkins. il Duns R 110:74-6+ N '77

EMPLOYEE participation in management. See Employees representation in management

EMPLOYEE Retirement Income Security Act. See Pensions—Laws and regulations

EMPLOYEE rights. See Employees—Civil rights

EMPLOYEE rules. See Work rules

EMPLOYEE seniority. See Seniority, Employee

EMPLOYEE stock ownership. See Employees as stockholders

EMPLOYEE stores. See Company stores

EMPLOYEE suggestions. See Suggestion systems

EMPLOYEE thefts. See Stealing

EMPLOYEES
Who employs the most people; a roster of 500 largest private employers. il Forbes 119:285-7+ My 15 '77
See also
Industrial relations
Job satisfaction
Labor turnover
Personnel management
Suggestion systems
also subhead Employees under various subjects, e.g. Newspapers—Employees; *also* classes of employees, e.g. School employees

Attitudes

Service with a scowl: what business is doing about it. il U.S. News 83:50-1 D 5 '77

Civil rights

Employees' rights; excerpt from Freedom inside the organization. D. W. Ewing. il Society 15: 104-11 N '77
High cost of whistling. T. Nicholson and others. pors Newsweek 89:75+ F 14 '77
Law and your job; legal rights of women. M. P. Rowe. Parents Mag 53:10 Ja '78
Myth of the oppressive corporation. M. Ways. Fortune 96:149+ O '77
What business thinks about employee rights. D. W. Ewing. bibl f il Harvard Bus R 55: 81-94 S '77

Discipline

See Labor discipline

Dismissal

See also
Executives—Dismissal
Layoff systems

Personnel records

See Personnel records

Psychology

See Psychology, Industrial

Reinstatement

Credit the vet; rehiring a returning veteran. M Labor R 100:71 O '77

Relocation

Corporate travel revives Cook's. il Bus W p 116+ O 3 '77
For lots of reasons, more workers are saying no to job transfers. il U.S. News 82:73-4 F 14 '77

Seniority

See Seniority, Employee

Training

See also
Apprentices
Education and manpower

Transfer

See also
Executives—Transfer

EMPLOYEES, International. See International officials and employees

EMPLOYEES, Recruiting of. See Recruiting of employees

EMPLOYEES as stockholders
ESOP: how it fits in estate planning; farm corporations. Suc Farm 75:9 My '77
When the workers are bosses. L. Smith. il Duns R 109:84-6+ Je '77

EMPLOYEES health insurance. See Insurance, Health

EMPLOYEES representation in management
Democracy in the workplace. V. P. Mainelli; reply. J. C. Meisner. America 136:117 F 12 '77
How Volvo adapts work to people; excerpt from People at work. P. G. Gyllenhammar. il Harvard Bus R 55:102-13 Jl '77
Industrial democracy in international perspective; symposium, ed by J. P. Windmuller. bibl f Ann Am Acad 431:1-140 My '77
Participative management urged as best option; views of M. Beckman. Lib J 102:321-2 F 1 '77
Process of work restructuring, and its impact on collective bargaining. L. A. Schlesinger and R. E. Walton. M Labor R 100:52-5 Ap '77
Stonewalling plant democracy; General Foods Topeka plant. il Bus W p78+ Mr 28 '77
Triumph of Marx. J. A. Schnepper. Intellect 105:395 Je '77
Volvo way: efficiency without pain; views of Pehr Gyllenhammar. J. Gaylin. Psychol Today 11:45 O '77
Workers can set their own wages—responsibly. E. E. Lawler. il por Psychol Today 10:109-10+ F '77
See also
Employee ownership
Industrial democracy

EMPLOYER-employee relations. See Industrial relations; Personnel management

EMPLOYMENT
Best job bets for 1985. Sr Schol 109:5 F 10 '77
Employment and unemployment in 1976. R. W. Bednarzik and S. M. St Marie. bibl il M Labor R 100:3-13 F '77
Employment: how full is full? il Progressive 41: 6-7 N '77
Full and part time: a review of definitions. J. N. Hedges and S. L. Gallogly. bibl il M Labor R 100:21-8 Mr '77
Full employment and fiscal integrity. T. D. Kane. bibl Intellect 105:246-7 F '77
Impact of electronics on employment: productivity and displacement effects. A. L. Robinson. bibl il Science 195:1179-84 Mr 18 '77
Job problem. E. Ginzberg. il Sci Am 237:43-51 bibl(p 163) N '77
More jobs at any cost: organized labor's goal for 1977. il Nations Bus 65:23-6 F '77
Overlooked boom. H. Flieger. U.S. News 82: 68 F 7 '77
Where the jobs go begging. il Bus W p34-5 O 10 '77
Why higher oil prices mean fewer jobs; theories of D. W. Jorgenson. S. Zucker. il por Bus W p 134+ S 12 '77
See also
Age and employment
Applications for positions
Discrimination in employment
Handicapped
Part time employment
Self employed
Student employment
Unemployment
Women—Employment
Youth—Employment

Conferences

Growing strength of anti-capitalism; conference on full employment of the Democratic Agenda Coalition. J. C. Cort. America 137:478-80 D 31 '77

Statistics

Employment and unemployment during the first half of 1977. S. M. St Marie. il M Labor R 100:3-6 Ag '77
Employment data from household survey. See issues of Monthly labor review
Employment ratio as an indicator of aggregate demand pressure. C. Green. bibl il M Labor R 100:25-32 Ap '77
Impact of the winter of 1977 on payroll employment. E. Dmytrow. il M Labor R 100:43-5 Ag '77
Occupational data program yielding big dividends. H. N. Goodson. M Labor R 100:44-5 O '77
See also
Unemployment—Statistics
United States—National Commission on Employment and Unemployment Statistics

EMPLOYMENT, Seniority in. See Seniority, Employee

EMPLOYMENT, Supplementary. See Supplementary employment

EMPLOYMENT, Temporary
One way to get good workers; older people as temporary employees. R. Ross. Nations Bus 65:39-40 S '77

EMPLOYMENT agencies
See also
Theatrical agencies

EMPLOYMENT counseling. See Vocational guidance

EMPLOYMENT interviewing
Bitter beercott; dispute over polygraph exams at Adolph Coors Co. il Time 110:15 D 26 '77
Facing the interview. J. Berendt. Esquire 88:57-9 Jl '77
Why they hired the ones they did; views of interviewers. bibl Sr Schol 110:26 S 22 '77

EMPLOYMENT security. See Job security

EMPRESS Hotel. See Victoria, British Columbia —Hotels, restaurants, etc.

EMPRESS tree. See Paulownia

EMSLEY, Michael G.
Creature from outer space? il Int Wildlife 7: 44-7 Mr '77

ENAMELS and enameling
See also
Cloisonné

ENCARE Oval. See Contraceptives

ENCEPHALARTOS
Pyroelectricity and induced pyroelectric polarization in leaves of the palmlike plant encephalartos villosus. S. B. Lang and H. Athenstaedt. bibl il Science 196:985-6 My 27 '77

ENCEPHALITIS
Fatal disease; primary amebic meningoencephalitis. S. A. Carter. bibl il Environment 19:16-20 Ap '77

ENCEPHALITIS, Experimental allergic. See Immunologic diseases

ENCEPHALOGRAPHY
See also
Electroencephalography

ENCEPHALOMYELITIS, Experimental allergic. See Immunologic diseases

ENCOUNTER groups. See Group relations training

ENCYCLOPEDIAS
Case of the with-it encyclopedia; Random House encyclopedia. E. D. Cuffe. America 137:182-4 O 1 '77
Colorpedia Americana; Random House encyclopedia. il Time 110:106 O 10 '77
Encyclopedists; Random House encyclopedia; interview. J. Mitchell. New Yorker 53:36-7 O 3 '77
How to buy an encyclopedia. A. Rosenblum. Good H 185:267 N '77
Images at Random; Random House Encyclopedia. H. Kenner. il Harpers 225:102+ D '77
New Columbia Encyclopedia. W. T. Johnston. Consumers Res Mag 60:13 F '77
Outer limits; Encyclopaedia of ignorance. il Time 111:60 Ja 9 '78
Sausage and Lucille Ball; Random House encyclopedia. W. Clemons. il Newsweek 90:105 O 10 '77
Story behind the project: Random House encyclopedia; symposium. il Pub W 211:33+ My 9 '77
See also
Photography—Dictionaries and encyclopedias
Publishers and publishing—Encyclopedias

Advertising
See Books—Advertising

END of the world
20 ways the world could end. I. Asimov. il Pop Mech 147:86-9+ Mr '77

ENDANGERED species. See Rare animals; Rare plants

ENDANGERED Species, Office of. See United States—Fish and Wildlife Service

ENDANGERED Species Act. See Conservation of resources—Laws and legislation

ENDIVE
See also
Cookery—Vegetables

ENDOMETRIOSIS
Cause and treatment of a common female disorder. M. L. Schildkraut. il Good H 184:223 F '77

ENDOPLASMIC reticulum
Age-related changes in the hepatic endoplasmic reticulum: a quantitative analysis. D. L. Schmucker and others. bibl il Science 197:1005-8 S 2 '77

ENDORPHINS
Blood bath; isolation of leu-endorphin by Frank Ervin and Roberta Palmour. Time 110:119 N 21 '77
Brain makes its own narcotics! R. Restak. il Sat R 4:6-11 Mr 5 '77
Brain peptides as psychiatric drugs. Sci N 112:182 S 17 '77
Curing the mind; beta-endorphin. S. Drake. il Newsweek 90:68-9 Ag 29 '77
Endogenous opiate receptor ligand: electrically induced release in the guinea pig ileum. M. Puig and others. bibl il Science 195:419-20 Ja 28 '77
β-Endorphin and adrenocorticotropin are secreted concomitantly by the pituitary gland. R. Guillemin and others. bibl il Science 197:1367-9 S 30 '77
β-Endorphin; endogenous opiate or neuroleptic? D. S. Segal and others. bibl il Science 198:411-14 O 28 '77
Hyperalgesia induced by naloxone follows diurnal rhythm in responsivity to painful stimuli. R. C. A. Frederickson and others. bibl il Science 198:756-8 N 18 '77
Internal opiates. Sci Am 236:50+ F '77
See also
Enkephalins

ENDORSEMENTS in advertising. See Advertising—Testimonials

ENDOTHELIUM. See Epithelium

ENDOTOXINS. See Toxins and antitoxins

ENDT, Friso
In praise of Darwin, Rembrandt, Mendel and other famous tulips. il Horticulture 55:26-8+ Ag '77

ENEA, Horace, and Reykjalin, John
Introducing Speechlab: the first hobbyist vocal interface for a computer! il Pop Electr 11:43-50 My '77

ENEMAS
Ritual enemas. P. T. Furst and M. D. Coe. il Natur Hist 86:88-91 bibl(p97) Mr '77

ENERGETICS, Biological. See Bioenergetics

ENERGY, Department of. See United States—Energy, Department of

ENERGY, Vital. See Vitality

ENERGY budget (geophysics)
See also
Hydrologic cycle

ENERGY conservation. See Power resources—Conservation

ENERGY Conversion Devices, Inc. See Solar energy industry

ENERGY crisis. See Fuel supply; Petroleum supply; Power resources

ENERGY industry. See Fuel industry

ENERGY lobby. See Lobbyists and lobbying

ENERGY metabolism
Minimum size of mammalian homeotherms: role of the thermal environment. C. R. Tracy. bibl il Science 198:1034-5 D 9 '77

ENERGY policy
Aid for energy development pledged; proposals of J. Carter. Am City & County 92:17-18 Je '77
Answering OPEC. D. Yergin. New Repub 176:45-7 Ja 22 '77
Appeals for a different energy approach. il Nations Bus 65:18-19 S '77
Bard of oil; Rep. R. Krueger's efforts on behalf of the petroleum industry lobby. T. Mathews and H. W. Hubbard. il por Newsweek 89:75-6 Je 20 '77
Battle begins. A. J. Mayer and others. il Newsweek 89:22-4 My 9 '77
Beware of Russians bearing gas. il Forbes 119:91+ Mr 15 '77
Blinding glare of profit; national energy plan. Nation 224:452 Ap 16 '77
Breaking up large American energy firms; excerpts from address. P. Davidson. por Intellect 105:295-6 Mr '77
Building an energy plan. M. Ruby and J. Bishop, Jr. il por Newsweek 89:59-60 Mr 7 '77
Burst of energy. A. J. Mayer and others. il Newsweek 89:14-15 Je 13 '77
Business cites flaws in energy plan. Nations Bus 65:21 Jl '77
CO_2 pollution may change the fuel mix. il Bus W p25 Ag 8 '77
Call to all Americans. M. Stone. U.S. News 82:96 Ap 25 '77
Can do. A. J. Mayer and H. W. Hubbard. Newsweek 89:68+ My 30 '77
Can we save ourselves? M. Stone. U.S. News 83:80 Jl 4 '77
Carter energy message; how stiff a prescription? L. J. Carter. Science 196:630-2 My 6 '77
Carter energy proposal holds far-reaching aviation impact. Aviation W 106:48 Ap 25 '77
Carter on energy: the R&D impact. il Sci N 111:277 Ap 30 '77
Carter plan. W. F. Buckley, Jr. Nat R 29:572-3 My 13 '77
Carter's first big test; Jimmy's carrot-and-stick plan. il pors Time 109:8-14 Ap 25 '77
Carter's melodrama. G. F. Will. il Newsweek 89:84 My 2 '77
Carter's modest energy proposals. J. M. Wall. Chr Cent 94:419-20 My 4 '77
Carter's program: will it work? il Time 109:17-18+ My 2 '77
Clean sweep for Jimmy. Time 110:46+ Ag 15 '77
Coal option; General Accounting Office report. Sci Am 238:64 Ja '78
Combating the energy lobbyists. J. M. Wall. Chr Cent 94:395 Ap 27 '77
Congress and the cozy triangles: the case of energy. B. M. Casper. Bull Atom Sci 33:5 My '77
Dear Dr Schlesinger: here's what I would do about energy; ed by E. Cowan. il N Y Times Mag p58-60+ Ap 17 '77
Dr Schlesinger's threshing machine. L. Schaller. Chr Cent 94:902-4 O 12 '77
Economic appraisal of President Carter's energy program. W. J. Mead. bibl Science 197:340-5 Jl 22 '77
Electrical equipment industry; energy needs; address, November 9, 1976. R. E. Kirby. Vital Speeches 43:186-9 Ja 1 '77
Emerging national consensus on energy policy: options before the Carter administration; address, November 29, 1976. F. X. Gannon. Vital Speeches 43:181-6 Ja 1 '77
Energy: America at the crossroads. il Nations Bus 65:18-21 Ap '77
Energy and defense; excerpt from testimony before the Senate Armed Services Subcommittee on Military Construction and Stockpiles. G. Marienthal. Aviation W 107:7 D 5 '77
Energy and national will. Nation 224:514 Ap 30 '77
Energy and the environment: putting the brakes on RV's? H. Shuldiner. il Outdoor Life 160:122+ S '77
Energy and the future of America. M. McCormack. Intellect 105:314-17 Ap '77
Energy basics. P. A. Samuelson. Newsweek 89:70 Ap 25 '77
Energy: beyond the Carter program. Fortune 95:183 My '77
Energy brownout. Nation 224:706-8 Je 11 '77
Energy conservation is not enough. P. H. Abelson. Science 196:1159 Je 10 '77
Energy crisis: made in U.S.A. M. R. Laird. Read Digest 111:56-60 S '77
Energy crisis on the Hill. New Repub 176:5-6 Je 25 '77
Energy crisis solution: shining a new light on the problem. J. A. Schnepper. Intellect 106:221 D '77

ENERGY policy—*Continued*
Energy debacle; Energy Policy Project of the Ford Foundation. L. H. Lapham. Harpers 255:58-61+ Ag '77; Discussion. 255:6+ O '77
Energy: estimates and issues. R. B. Morrissey. America 136:523-4 Je 11 '77
Energy: fallacy of controlled scarcity; address, May 2, 1977. R. G. Lugar. Vital Speeches 43: 520-2 Je 15 '77
Energy gets top priority. il Am City & County 92:56-8 Je '77
Energy plan: what's at stake. R. L. Collins. Flying 100:44 Je '77
Energy policy for leaner times. Bus W p40+ Mr 21 '77
Energy program. Progressive 41:5-6 Je '77
Energy rhetoric. M. Friedman. Newsweek 89: 82 Je 13 '77
Energy squeeze coming for all Americans. por U.S. News 82:26 Ap 11 '77
Energy strategy: the road not taken? A. B. Lovins; discussion. For Affairs 55:636-40; 891-900 Ap, Jl '77
Energy war. il por Time 109:10-14 My 2 '77
Energy, water, environment—a top official looks ahead; interview. C. D. Andrus. il por U.S. News 82:62-4 Je 27 '77
Energy: where intervention is inevitable. il Bus W p80-1 Ap 4 '77
Energy: who wins and loses. Bus W p24-5 My 2 '77
Energy: will Americans pay the price? Carter's 7 energy goals for 1985. il por U.S. News 82:13-17 My 2 '77
Equivalence and equivocation; President Carter's call for a "moral equivalent of war." F. Getlein. Commonweal 104:292-3 My 13 '77
Everyone a conservationist. J. B. Craig. Am For 83:6 Je '77
Failure seen for big-scale, high-technology energy plans. L. J. Carter. Science 195:764 F 25 '77
Far-sighted energy program. B. T. Feld. Bull Atom Sci 33:9 Je '77
For a new energy policy; toward using solar energy. B. Commoner. Current 191:17-22 Mr '77
From pariah to messiah: recent history of coal; address, February 28, 1977. E. R. Phelps. Vital Speeches 43:366-9 Ap 1 '77
Future: energy and wisdom; address, July 14, 1977. W. E. Callahan. Vital Speeches 43:656-9 Ag 15 '77
Give-and-take spirit. D. M. Alpern and others. Newsweek 89:17-18 Je 27 '77
Helping shape legislative policy; American Physics Society Congressional Fellows. A. Hoffman and others. il Phys Today 30:42-8 Ag '77
Hit us hard, please, Mr Carter. G. F. Will. il Newsweek 89:112 Ap 18 '77
How businessmen view energy policy. Nations Bus 65:22-3 Ap '77
How the energy shortage will change life in America; with interview with J. Schlesinger. il U.S. News 82:22-5 F 14 '77
How to save energy. A. J. Mayer and others. il Newsweek 89:70-1+ Ap 18 '77
Icy grip tightens. il Time 109:6-11 F 14 '77
Last resorts. W. D. Carey. Science 197:327 Jl 22 '77
Less delay, more supply. il Time 110:30-1 S 5 '77
Letter from Washington. R. H. Rovere. New Yorker 53:136-8+ My 9 '77; 54-8 Ja 2 '78
Lobbying the Carter UFO. il Time 109:74-5 Je 20 '77
Lubrication of the American economy. J. A. Schnepper. Intellect 106:33 Ag '77
Memo to JC. W. F. Buckley, Jr. Nat R 29:1452 D 9 '77
Millions for taxes; proposals of J. Carter. Nat R 29:534 My 13 '77
Moral equivalent of war; address, April 20, 1977. J. Carter. Vital Speeches 43:420-3 My 1 '77
More heat than light. J. Midgley. Harpers 254: 30+ My '77
My case for national planning; with editorial comment. T. Bradshaw. il por Fortune 95:97, 100-4 F '77
National energy plan. K. H. Hohenemser. il Environment 19:4-5 O '77
National energy policy: hard choices can't be avoided. E. R. Zausner. por Duns R 109:97-8+ Je '77
Net energy analysis: an economic assessment. D. A. Huettner; discussion. Science 196:259+ Ap 15 '77
No rush. E. Marshall. New Repub 177:13-14 Ag 20 '77
No simple solutions to the energy crisis. T. Orme. il Motor T 29:9-10+ Jl '77
Not serious; J. Carter's energy proposal. J. Burnham. Nat R 29:540 My 13 '77
Notes and comment. New Yorker 53:29 My 2 '77
Of, by, and for the regulators. Nat R 29:929-30 Ag 19 '77
On the altar of oil. B. W. Tuchman. New Repub 176:37-8 Ja 22 '77
On tiptoe toward the big battle ahead. Time 109: 75-6 My 9 '77
Our energy goals: how clean are they? Sci N 112:231 O 8 '77
Our energy problem; address, May 23, 1977. J. E. Swearingen. Vital Speeches 43:569-72 Jl 1 '77
People are still wondering—is energy shortage for real? il U.S. News 82:28-30 My 9 '77
Prescriptions for a drastic program; Jim's overnight task force. il Time 109:58-60 F 21 '77
President Carter offers his comprehensive energy program to Congress. W. Hickman. Archit Rec 161:34 Je '77
President's proposed energy policy; address, April 18, 1977. J. Carter. Vital Speeches 43: 418-20 My 1 '77
Prometheus rebound. New Repub 176:5-6+ My 21 '77
Republican version; Senate Republican Energy Initiative. Time 109:63 My 23 '77
Resistance wanes to the energy bill. Bus W p31 Je 27 '77
Scientists urge President: stop reliance on coal and nuclear fuel; Go for development of uniform solar power. J. E. Persico. Sci Digest 82:8-9+ O '77
Secretary Vance testifies on energy program; statement, May 4, 1977. C. R. Vance. Dept State Bull 76:564-6 My 30 '77
Seen through the mists. W. F. Buckley, Jr. Nat R 29:1256 O 28 '77
Setback on energy; coalition of environmental and consumer groups. A. J. Mayer and J. B. Copeland. il Newsweek 89:93 My 16 '77
Should we break up the oil companies? controversy surrounding horizontal and vertical divestiture. I. Ross. Read Digest 110:153-4+ Je '77
Sizing up the winners and losers; effects of Carter program on industry. il Time 109:78-9 My 9 '77
Soft technology energy debate: Limits to growth revisited? A. L. Hammond. Science 196:959-61 My 27 '77; Reply. A. B. Lovins. 196:1384 Je 24 '77
Special report—energy roundup. S. Novick. il Environment 19:29-33 Je '77
Strong medicine. New Repub 176:5-6+ Ap 30 '77
Superbrain's superproblem. il pors Time 109:58-61+ Ap 4 '77
TRB from Washington. New Repub 176:2 Ap 30 '77
Tax impact of new energy plan—who's helped, who's hurt. il U.S. News 82:73-4 My 2 '77
Team approach to energy planning. P. M. Morse. por Bull Atom Sci 33:68-9 Mr '77
That man is energy Czar James R. Schlesinger and he has plans for all of us; interview. J. R. Schlesinger. il pors Sr Schol 110:4-7+ S 8 '77
Thinking soft; views of A. Lovins. A. J. Mayer. il por Newsweek 90:108+ N 14 '77
Tough oil tax in the energy plan. il Bus W p32 Ap 11 '77
Tough talk on energy. D. M. Alpern and others. il Newsweek 89:21-2 Ap 25 '77
Uphill road. Nation 224:546-7 My 7 '77
What America makes; question of energy policy taxes and rebates on automobiles. New Repub 176:5-6 Je 4 '77
What Carter could do if his energy bills fail. Bus W p34-6 Ja 16 '78
What price energy? symposium. il por Newsweek 89:12-16+ My 2 '77
What to do about energy crisis—advice from five experts; symposium. il U.S. News 82:41-5 Ap 18 '77
Where Carter's program goes from here. il U.S. News 83:36-8 Jl 18 '77
Where the Carter energy plan goes astray. Nations Bus 65:72 Je '77
Which way the energy plan? W. F. Buckley, Jr. Nat R 29:512-13 Ap 29 '77
Why Carter may not meet his coal deadline. il Bus W p31 Jl 11 '77
Will energy conservation throttle economic growth? with interview with J. R. Schlesinger. il Bus W p66-72+ Ap 25 '77
See also
Power resources—Laws and legislation
United States—Congress—House—Energy, Ad Hoc Select Committee on
United States—Energy, Department of

Conferences

Carter's energy plan: a first step; report of Conference on National Energy Policy. N. C. Joyce. Science 197:39-40 Jl 1 '77

Environmental aspects

Carter's bid: both energy and clean air. J. McWethy. il U.S. News 82:18 My 2 '77

International aspects

Department discusses international economic importance of enactment of the President's energy program; statement, May 17, 1977. J. L. Katz. Dept State Bull 76:640-2 Je 13 '77
Energy and the world economy; statement, January 5, 1977. J. L. Katz. Dept State Bull 76: 61-7 Ja 24 '77

ENERGY policy—*Continued*

Brazil

Energy: Brazil seeks a strategy among many options. A. L. Hammond. Science 195:566-7 F 11 '77

California

California's answer to an energy riddle; Canadian and Mexican gas. Bus W p24-5 Ag 22 '77
California's fight for the sun; attempt by gas industry to control solar energy. F. Branfman. Nation 224:749-51 Je 18 '77
Oil will soon flow, but where will it go? P. L. Fradkin. il Audubon 79:86-8+ Ja '77

Canada

Why Canadians want an Alcan gas route. map Bus W p20 Jl 18 '77

China

Intermediate energy technology in China. V. Smil. bibl il map Bull Atom Sci 33:25-31 F '77

Great Britain

Britain's new jackpot. il pors Forbes 119:118 Mr 15 '77
Science in Europe: Benn and British rethink energy policy. N. Hawkes. Science 196:146-7 Ap 8 '77

Latin America

Energy; adaptation of address, May 23, 1977. A. Orfila. il Américas 29:6-12 O '77

Minnesota

Conservation: the Minnesota plan; excerpts from address, September 28, 1977. J. P. Millhone. Science 198:1207 D 23 '77

Sweden

Efficient energy use and well-being: the Swedish example. L. Schipper and A. J. Lichtenberg; reply with rejoinder. C. Starr and S. Field. bibl Science 196:121-2+ Ap 8 '77
How the Swedes live well while consuming less energy. P. M. Boffey. Science 196:856 My 20 '77

Texas

Texas is testing ground for impact of coal use on economic growth. J. Walsh. Science 198:586+ N 11 '77

United States

See Energy policy

Utah

Son of a gun, it's son of Kaiparowits! P. L. Fradkin. Audubon 79:146-8 My '77

ENERGY Policy Project. See Ford Foundation

ENERGY research. See Power resources—Research

ENERGY Research and Development Administration. See United States—Energy Research and Development Administration

ENERGY resources. See Power resources

ENERGY supply. See Power resources

ENERGY Transportation Security Act of 1977. See Maritime law

ENERGY Week. See Special days, weeks, and months

ENEWETAK. See Eniwetok

ENGEL, Brenda S.
One way it can be. il Todays Educ 66:50-2 Mr '77

ENGEL, George L.
Emotional stress and sudden death. bibl il Psychol Today 11:114-15+ N '77
Need for a new medical model: a challenge for biomedicine. bibl Science 196:129-36 Ap 8 '77

ENGEL, James F.
Effective evangelism: a matter of marketing? interview, ed by D. Kucharsky. il Chr Today 21:12-15 Ap 15 '77

ENGEL, Lyle Kenyon
Engel's millions. A. Myers. il por Writers Digest 57:35-6 O '77 •

ENGELBRECHT, Robert Martin
Rebuild your deck for longer life. il Pop Sci 210:136+ Je '77

ENGINEERING
See also
Audio engineering
Bioengineering
Computers—Engineering use
Electric engineering
Environmental engineering
Highway engineering
Structural engineering
Systems engineering
Water supply engineering

Study and teaching

Changing the specifications for engineers; program for prospective minority students at the Illinois Institute of Technology. D. Milesko-Pytel. il Am Educ 13:27-31 Ja '77

ENGINEERING, Ethics of. See Engineers, Professional ethics for

ENGINEERING, Genetic. See Genetic engineering

ENGINEERING construction companies
Loner relaxes his grip; Jacobs Engineering. il Bus W p 132+ N 21 '77
Mirage made real; VTN. por Forbes 120:82 D 15 '77
See also
Morrison-Knudsen Company, Inc

Belgium

Belgium hits Badger for shutting an office. Bus W p30+ Mr 28 '77

ENGINEERING consultants. See Consulting engineers

ENGINEERING education
Engineering and society programs in engineering education. W. R. Lynn. bibl Science 195:150-5 Ja 14 '77
See also
Engineering—Study and teaching

ENGINEERING societies
See also
American Society of Civil Engineers
Institute of Electrical and Electronic Engineers
National Academy of Engineering

ENGINEERS
COFPAES meeting indicates support to retain Brooks Law; COFPAES renews its costs and audits argument; Committee on Federal Procurement of Architect-Engineer Services. W. Hickman. Archit Rec 161:34, 75 Ap '77
To honor an engineer; Joan Hodges Queneau Award. il Audubon 79:160 Ja '77
See also
Black engineers
Consulting engineers
Locomotive engineers
Mechanical engineers
Petroleum engineers

Legal status, laws, etc.

Legal perspectives. A. T. Kornblut. Archit Rec 161:57 F; 55+ Mr; 67+ Ap; 162:63 Ag; 53 D '77
See also
Liability (law)

Selection and appointment

Don't wait! Seek out those graduate engineers. S. S. Baxter. Am City & County 92:22 F '77

Supply and demand

Measuring the supply of scientific personnel. R. R. Trumble. M Labor R 100:47-8 O '77

ENGINEERS, Professional ethics for
On trial, profession assesses charges. Sci Digest 81:79-80 Ap '77

ENGINES
See also
Air engines
Airplane engines
Automobile engines
Automobiles, Racing—Engines
Diesel engines
Locomotives
Motorcycle engines
Tractor engines
Turbines

Collectors and collecting

Fix'em up and show 'em off. D. Fales. il Pop Mech 147:108-9 My '77

ENGLAND, David W.
Hearing from the teacher when nothing is wrong. Engl J 66:42-4 S '77

ENGLAND
See also
Agriculture—England
Architecture, Domestic—England
Blacks in England
Churches—England
Cruising—England
Education—England
English
Festivals—England
Gardens—England
Great Britain
Guernsey (island)
Historic houses, sites, etc.—England
Hunting—England
Music—England
Music festivals—England
Salisbury
Thames River
Water supply—England
Weston

Antiquities, Roman

See Great Britain—Antiquities, Roman

Description and travel

Best bits of Britain. S. Birnbaum. Esquire 88:20+ N '77
Going places, finding things in Britain. N. Richardson. il House & Gard 149:58+ F '77
Midsummer feast: English gardens with Kenneth for your guide; Hidcote and Sissinghurst. Kenneth. bibl il por House & Gard 149:48+ Jl '77

ENGLAND—*Continued*

Economic history

See Great Britain—Economic history

Industries

See also
Potteries

Religious institutions and affairs

See also
Church of England

Social conditions

In England now. D. J. M. Cornwell. pors N Y Times Mag p34-5+ O 23 '77

Social life and customs

Austen-ized village; Weston. M. Green. Atlantic 240:77-81 Jl '77

Domestic manners of the English. L. Lewis. Atlantic 240:92+ N '77

ENGLEWOOD, Ohio
Match utility rates to system costs. R. T. Holland and J. Niccolls. il Am City & County 92:53-5 Ap '77

ENGLISH, Diane
Are you a secret TV addict? Vogue 167:184-5 F '77
TV. See issues of Vogue

ENGLISH, Isobel
Cousin Dot; story. Chr Cent 94:1034 N 9 '77

ENGLISH, Maurice
Temple University: starting a press in the 70s. por Pub W 212:37-40 Jl 4 '77

ENGLISH
John Benton-Harris: Yankee eye on the English. P. Turner. il Mod Phot 41:128-37 O '77

Anecdotes, facetiae, satire, etc.

Behind the roses 'round the door; life in an English country cottage. A. Menen. il Horticulture 55:61-5 Ap '77

ENGLISH architecture. See Architecture, English

ENGLISH art. See Art, British

ENGLISH as a second language. See English language—Study and teaching—Foreigners

ENGLISH CHANNEL
See also
Channel Islands (English Channel)

ENGLISH Channel swims. See Swimming

ENGLISH cheese. See Cheese

ENGLISH composition. See English language—Composition

ENGLISH cookery. See Cookery, English

ENGLISH dictionaries. See English language—Dictionaries

ENGLISH dramatists. See Dramatists, English

ENGLISH flower arrangements. See Flowers, Arrangement of

ENGLISH furniture. See Furniture, English

ENGLISH grammar. See English language—Grammar

ENGLISH journal
Editor's page (cont) S. N. Judy. Engl J 66:5 S; 5-6 O '77

ENGLISH language
Blind idiot: the problems of translation; adaptation of address, May 4, 1976. E. Fenton. Horn Bk 53:505-13 O '77

Brotherly love in today's Church. J. Chittister. il America 136:233-6 Mr 19 '77

Definition of Partridge. I. Shenker. pors N Y Times Mag p41-2 O 2 '77

The language. J. Simon. See issues of Esquire

Light refractions. T. H. Middleton. See issues of Saturday review

Profession in perspective. Engl J 66:6-7 F; 6-9 Mr; 6-9 Ap; 8-9+ My; 6-9 S '77
See also
Sex discrimination in language
Vocabulary

Accents and accentuation

Anecdotes, facetiae, satire, etc.

Eyes on the White House lawn. S. L. Varnado. Nat R 29:496 Ap 29 '77

Business English

Mystery of the business graduate who can't write; teaching specialized writing courses at business schools. il Nations Bus 65:60-2 F '77

Composition

Close-up: what do college students write? special section. Eng J 66:58-69 N '77

Ethnic and regional literature: making connections with composition. S. Burns and L. Burns. il Engl J 66:34-6 Mr '77

Focus: teaching writing; symposium. bibl f Engl J 66:26-61 D '77

Forward to five basics in composition. K. Donelson. Clearing H 51:60-3 O '77

From Newsweek; From the author. M. Sheils; S. H. Elgin. il Engl J 66:16-19 My '77

Great American writing crisis. P. Zagano. Educ Digest 43:56-9 O '77

How to improve student writing; Bay Area Writing Project and teachers workshops. S. B. Neill. Educ Digest 42:44-7 Ja '77

No help for teachers of English; panel discussion at the Graduate Center of the City University of New York. J. Simon. il Esquire 87:12+ Je '77

Perils of paper grading. G. G. Sloan. Engl J 66:33-6 My '77

Steps to correct functional writing. J. W. Cunningham and P. M. Cunningham. Educ Digest 43:60-1 D '77

Teaching thinking on paper; work of A. D. Van Nostrand. il por Time 109:74 Ap 18 '77

That special something that you know better: six inventions for individualizing the writing process. J. W. Halpern Engl J 66:74-8 Mr '77

Writing across the Curriculum: the London projects; ERIC/RCS report; University of London. A. N. Applebee. bibl Engl J 66:81-5 D '77
See also
Conference on College Composition and Communication
Creative writing
Student themes and reports

Aids and devices

Designing writing assignments. E. M. Hoffman and J. P. Schifsky. il Engl J 66:41-5 D '77

Exploring quality as definition. W. Palmer. Engl J 66:46-8 D '77

Getting it out, getting it down: adapting Zoellner's talk-write. V. Wixon and P. Stone. bibl f il Engl J 66:70-3 S '77

It's in the cards: a new deal for student writers. M. F. Vargas. Engl J 66:48-51 S '77

Bibliography

Annotated bibliography of resources for teachers of composition; ERIC/RCS report. R. Barth. Engl J 66:68-72 Ja '77

Dialects

Playing tennis without a net; resolution accepting all dialects passed by the Conference on College Composition and Communication. J. Simon. Esquire 88:66+ O '77
See also
Black-English dialects

Dictionaries

Arbiter of words; Oxford English Dictionary. il por Horizon 20:30-1 O '77

Haarlem to Nzima; Oxford English dictionary. Time 109:66 Ja 24 '77

Many shades of Webster. L. A. Spinks. Writers Digest 57:38+ My '77

Wit and wisdom of catch phrases. J. Simon. Esquire 88:46+ N '77

Word king; E. Partridge's A dictionary of catch phrases. por Time 110:75-6 O 17 '77

Gender

See also
Sex discrimination in language

Grammar

American grammatical revolution. P. A. Moody. Educ Digest 42:58-61 Ap '77

Grammar barrier; Southern usage. R. S. Barnett. Nat R 29:210 F 18 '77

Grammar instruction: what we know; ed by A. R. Petrosky. bibl Engl J 66:86-8 D '77
See also
English language—Usage
Sentences (grammar)

Jargon

See Jargon

Periodicals

See also
Quarrel (periodical)

Prefixes and suffixes

On-ess's, essential and non-. T. H. Middleton. Sat R 4:59 F 19 '77

Prepositions

Build your own preposition box. R. A. Dick. il Engl J 66:75-6 Ap '77

Pronouns

Maybe he isn't so bad after all. T. H. Middleton. Sat R 4:50 My 14 '77

Pondering the personal pronoun problem. T. H. Middleton. Sat R 4:59 Mr 5 '77

Remedial teaching

Focus: English for the non-college bound; symposium. il Engl J 66:28-52 N '77

Resources for the non-college bound; ed by C. Kuykendall. il Engl J 66:84-7 N '77

Success without college; ERIC/RCS report. K. Steiner. bibl Engl J 66:90-3 N '77

ENGLISH language—*Continued*

Study and teaching

Censorship, the law, and the teacher of English; symposium. A. A. Glatthorn. bibl il Engl J 66:12-25 F '77
Creating learning environments. A. A. Glatthorn. Educ Digest 43:9-12 N '77
EJ curriculum catalog; comp by S. Koch. Engl J 66:53-67 S '77
English classroom 1977; EJ readership survey. C. Gillis and others. il Engl J 66:55-8 Ja; 20-6 S '77
Focus: middle and junior high schools; symposium, ed by A. R. Gere. il Engl J 66:25-51 Ap '77
Getting to some basics that the back-to-basic movement doesn't get to. C. Weingartner. bibl f il Engl J 66:39-44 O '77
Hearing from the teacher when nothing is wrong. D. W. England. Engl J 66:42-4 S '77
JHS/MS idea factory; ed by J. Golub and B. Horst. Engl J 66:76-8 N; 64-5 D '77
Learning democratically. T. Wagner. il Engl J 66:33-7 S '77
Letter from England. T. Newkirk. Engl J 66:10-12 Mr; 15-16 Ap '77
Letter to parents. W. P. Cushman. il Engl J 66:45-8 O '77
Of youth and time; teaching in Dover, Del. G. Henry. Engl J 66:9+ My '77
Profession in perspective. See issues of English journal
Reading skills in the English class. R. H. White. il Clearing H 51:32-5 S '77
Teacher survival kit: the dictionary. J. E. Cook. Educ Digest 42:36-7 Ja '77
Teacher who gets results; L. Lovelace's class at Wendell Phillips High in Chicago. J. Seligmann and S. Monroe. il por Newsweek 90:67 S 12 '77
Teachers should be dictators. G. Schofer. Educ Digest 43:42-3 O '77
Teaching LD adolescents; ed by J. Singleton. M. Brown. Todays Educ 66:43-6 N '77
To confess a fault freely; address. C. F. Greiner. Engl J 66:5-6 My '77
U.S. literacy level not bad; excerpts from address. F. Hechinger. il Intellect 106:104-5 S '77
W. Wilbur Hatfield—some reflections of his mind and spirit. W. W. Hatfield. Engl J 66:6-7 F '77
Whatever happened to the new English? A. Tibbetts and C. Tibbetts. Clearing H 51:183-8 D '77

See also

Dramatization in education
English language—Composition
English language—Grammar
English language—Remedial teaching
English literature—Study and teaching
English teachers
National Council of Teachers of English

Aids and devices

Case for filmstrips: producing filmstrips in the classroom. D. P. Miller. il Engl J 66:70-2 O '77
EJ workshop, ed by B. B. Kaufman. See issues of English journal
Film and television research. R. Beach. bibl Engl J 66:90-3 Mr '77
Going beyond motivation to involvement at the junior high/middle school level. J. Golub. Engl J 66:80-3 F '77
Multi-media; ed by N. C. Thompson. il Engl J 66:100-4 F; 92-5 Ap '77
New products and publications for 1977; ed by A. Crouch. il Engl J 66:27-50 Ja '77
Resource directory: ideas and materials for the teaching of English. il Engl J 66:61-72+ Ja '77
Selecting instructional materials. J. W. Sabol. il Engl J 66:9-14 Ja '77
Short film; ed by R. Fulginiti (cont) Engl J 66:90-3 S '77
Teaching ideas: educating the in-betweener; symposium. Engl J 66:55-72 Ap '77
Teaching materials; ed by C. Kuykendall (cont) Engl J 66:86-90 F; 82-5 Ap; 78-82 S; 84-7 N '77

Anecdotes, facetiae, satire, etc.

Alice in schoolroom land. P. Smith. Engl J 66:22-6 My '77
Likely story. S. N. Judy. Engl J 66:7-8 D '77

Bibliography

More sources of free and inexpensive material. T. Ball, Jr. Engl J 66:100-6 Ja '77
New products and publications for 1977; ed by A. Crouch. il Engl J 66:27-50 Ja '77
Once over; ed by S. Koch and L. Rosen. Engl J 66:80-2 Mr; 80-1 Ap; 79-80 My; 76-7 S; 76-7 O; 80-2 N; 74-5 D '77
Professional publications; ed by D. Kirby. il Engl J 66:82-6 O; 76-80 D '77
Professional publications; ed by C. Suhor (cont) Engl J 66:84-8 Mr; 81-2 My '77
Research roundup; ed by A. R. Petrosky (cont) bibl Engl J 66:90-3 Mr; 96-8 O; 86-8 D '77

Foreigners

Babel reversed; ESL program, Glen Forest Elementary School, Fairfax County, Va. I. Carpenter. il Am Educ 13:27-30 Ag '77
Letter; request for pen pals to aid English language study. B. Lee. por Sch Arts 76:52 Ap '77
Some aspects of bilingualism for the English teacher. F. Pialorsi. bibl Engl J 66:94-7 Ja '77
Tutoring Vietnamese refugees. J. Koster. Todays Educ 66:32-4 N '77

Russia

See English language in Russia

Terms and phrases

See also

Jargon
Slang

Usage

Attack and counterattack. J. Simon. Esquire 88:20+ D '77
Civil tongue; excerpt. E. Newman. Read Digest 110:189-90+ My '77
Conciseness in F major. F. Rathbun. Writers Digest 57:45-7 Ag '77
I passed my A*C*T test. J. W. Ney. Engl J 66:10-12 D '77
In your head. H. B. Maloney. Engl J 66:10-11 O '77
Machining of America. R. L. King. Commonweal 104:340-2 My 27 '77
NCTE and English usage. R. C. Pooley. Engl J 66:18-19 D '77
State of the language, 1977; Time essay. S. Kanfer. Time 111:36 Ja 2 '78
Usage. New Yorker 53:20 Jl 4 '77

ENGLISH language in Europe, Western

English spoken here; the common language of European business and multinationals. J. Ross-Skinner. il Duns R 109:56-7 Mr '77

ENGLISH language in Russia

English studies in the Soviet Union: a specialized language school in Moscow. P. E. Zevin. bibl f il Eng J 66:14-16 N '77

ENGLISH literature

See also

English poetry

Catalogs

Brute indeed! working on the second edition of A short-title catalogue of books printed in England, Scotland, & Ireland and of English books printed abroad 1475-1640. New Yorker 53:30-2 Mr 28 '77

History

Literary legacy. C. P. Snow. il Sat R 4:14-15 Je 11 '77

Study and teaching

Censorship and the classroom teacher. A. A. Glatthorn. Engl J 66:12-15 F '77; Same abr. Educ Digest 43:54-6 S '77
Helping readers to visualize. M. Duff. Todays Educ 66:56-7 Mr '77
Where will our future English teachers come from? D. Badaczewski. Educ Digest 42:54-5 Mr '77

See also

Shakespeare, W.—Study and teaching

ENGLISH manuscripts. See Manuscripts, English

ENGLISH National Opera. See Opera—Great Britain

ENGLISH poetry

Poetic responses to the Copernican revolution. M. M. Byard. il Sci Am 236:120-9 bibl(p 142) Je '77

ENGLISH portraits. See Portraits, British

ENGLISH pottery. See Pottery, English

ENGLISH prints. See Prints

ENGLISH professors. See English teachers

ENGLISH silverware. See Silverware

ENGLISH teachers

Changing times for teachers of English. Educ Digest 42:41-3 Ja '77
How are English teachers reacting to declining college entrance scores? C. Tibbetts and A. M. Tibbetts. Engl J 66:13-16 D '77
JHS/MS teacher: penal, pastural, or preparatory. W. J. Bosher, Jr. Engl J 66:64-5 D '77
Newspeak generation. R. Whittemore. Harpers 254:16+ F '77
Scholar and the pedagogue: different breeds of humanists. D. T. Wolfe, Jr. Clearing H 50:206-8 Ja '77
Some responsibilities for English teachers who already face an impossible job. K. Donelson. Engl J 66:27-32 S '77
Those doctoral dilemmas; lack of professorial job openings. A. Swan and E. McGrath. il Time 111:57 Ja 9 '78
U.S. journal: Manhattan; status of college teachers. C. Trillin. New Yorker 53:84+ Mr 7 '77

See also

National Council of Teachers of English

Anecdotes, facetiae, satire, etc.

Teacher 1999. S. Judy. Engl J 66:5-6 O '77

ENGRAVING
Challenges of engraving. J. Opalak. il Design (US) 78:14-16 Summ '77
Tomoe Yokoi's mezzotints. E. Zeifer. il por Am Artist 41:40-5+ O '77
See also
Etching
Glass engraving
ENGRAVING on firearms. See Firearms—Decoration
ENGRAVINGS
See also
Etchings
Collectors and collecting
Engravings of George Washington in the Stanley DeForest Scott collection. S. W. Grote. il Antiques 112:128-33 Jl '77
ENHANCED radiation warheads. See Neutron bombs
ENIWETOK
Calcium carbonate production of the mare incognitum, the upper windward reef slope, at Enewetak Atoll. S. V. Smith and J. T. Harrison. bibl il Science 197:556-9 Ag 5 '77
ENKEPHALINS
Analog of enkephalin having prolonged opiate-like effects in vivo. J. M. Walker and others. bibl il Science 196:85-7 Ap 1 '77
Enkephalins: more than just pain killers; effect on learning ability. J. Arehart-Treichel. il Sci N 112:59+ Jl 23 '77
Internal opiates. Sci Am 236:50+ F '77
Morphine and enkephalin: analgesic and epileptic properties. G. Urca and others. bibl il Science 197:83-6 Jl 1 '77
Opiate receptors and internal opiates. S. H. Snyder. il Sci Am 236:44-56 bibl(p 150) Mr '77
ENLARGERS, Photographic. See Photography—Enlargers and enlarging
ENLOE, Cynthia H.
Police and military in the resolution of ethnic conflict. bibl f Ann Am Acad 433:137-49 S '77
ENQUIRER (newspaper). See National enquirer (newspaper)
ENQUIST, Per Olov
Night of the tribades. Reviews
New Yorker 53:143 O 24 '77 *
Newsweek 90:85 O 24 '77 *
Time il 110:123 O 24 '77 *
ENROLLMENT, School. See School attendance
ENSEMBLES (music) See Instrumental ensembles
ENSIGN, Tod, and Uhl, Michael
Unorganizing GIs. Progressive 41:8-9 D '77
—See Uhl, M. jt auth
ENSOR, James, Baron
Energy of rot. M. Stevens. il por Newsweek 89:57 Ja 31 '77 *
Ensor: much possessed by death; retrospective at the Guggenheim Museum. R. Hughes. il por Time 109:51 Mr 7 '77 *
Outrageously unique; retrospective at the Guggenheim Museum. H. Rosenberg. New Yorker 53:108+ Ap 11 '77 *
ENSRUD, Barbara
Seven great wines. il Horizon 20:38-46 D '77
ENSTROM, James E. and Austin, D. F.
Interpreting cancer survival rates. bibl il Science 195:847-51 Mr 4 '77
ENTEBBE raid. See Guerrillas—Israel
ENTENMANN, Martha
Mother knows best. il por Forbes 119:52 Mr 15 '77 *
ENTENMANN'S Inc. See Bakers and bakeries
ENTERPRISE, Free. See Free enterprise
ENTERTAINERS
Entertainers of the year. R. Rosenblatt. New Repub 176:28-30 F 12 '77
November action in San Francisco; street entertainers. il Sunset 159:51-2 N '77
See also
Actors and actresses
Black entertainers
ENTERTAINING
Angela Cummings; an independent hostess; interview, ed by N. H. Clark. A. Cummings. il por Harp Baz 110:136-7+ F '77
Charlotte Ford entertains. C. Porcelli. il por House B 119:100-1 Je '77
Donna Karan gives a party. il por Harp Baz 110:126-7+ Ag '77
Easy-does-it party ideas. P. Pollock. il Bet Hom & Gard 55:152+ N '77
Eleanor Lambert entertains. C. Porcelli. il por House B 119:122-3 O '77
Entertain beautifully on a budget. C. Porcelli. il Harp Baz 110:130-1+ Mr '77
For bridge, backgammon or rap sessions. il Ebony 32:150+ Ag '77
Fresh-from-the-garden party food; with menus and recipes. House & Gard 149:174+ Ap '77
Gloria & Emlen Etting entertain. C. Porcelli. il House B 119:110-11 F '77
Great meal you hardly have to cook. D. Fredericks. il pors House & Gard 149:120-1+ F '77
Have a wine & cheese tasting party. il Good H 184:214 My '77
Have your company in the kitchen. il House & Gard 149:72-5 Ag '77
Hosting without hassle. S. P. Torpey. il Bet Hom & Gard 55:146-7 N '77
How to feed houseguests and still have fun. Bet Hom & Gard 55:94 O '77
How to give a great party; with recipes. il House & Gard 149:197-9 N '77
How to set up a party. A. Fraser. Mademoiselle 83:112 Ag '77
How we entertain in New York; ed by P. Pierce. B. Sills. il por McCalls 104:132-3+ Je '77
How we entertain in the South. R. Carter. il por McCalls 104:152-3+ F '77
John Anthony gives a party; with recipes. J. Anthony. il por Harp Baz 110:210-11+ S '77
Keep-in-touch party; Kitchen-sink party. il Seventeen 36:168-72+ My '77
Kenneth Jay Lane entertains. C. Porcelli. il por House B 119:102-3 Mr '77
Marina & Guy de Brantes entertain. C. Porcelli. il por House B 119:158-9 S '77
Mica Ertegün's Turkish ease; with recipes. L. Davis. Vogue 167:66+ D '77
Mystery ride; cocktail party in motor home given by Harrison and Sonja Eiteljorg. F. A. Birmingham. il Holiday 58:52-4 S '77
Natchez entertains. il Am Home 80:42-3 Mr '77
Our dinner-party secrets. A. Gold and R. Fizdale. il Vogue 167:248-50+ Mr '77
Parties in flower; with recipes. il Seventeen 36:166-7+ Je '77
Party food—fast, fabulous; with recipes; excerpt from Feasts without fuss. P. Harlech. il pors House & Gard 149:150-1+ S '77
Partygoing; New York City. New Yorker 53: 43-5 N 28 '77
Ready, set, party! Kitchen buffet. il House & Gard 149:174-5+ O '77
Social Sundays; party drink recipes. A. Fraser. Mademoiselle 83:116 O '77
Summer favorites; no-fuss entertaining; with recipes. il Redbook 149:122-3+ Jl '77
Taste of perfection; entertaining by Countess Ulla Wachtmeister; with recipes. il por House & Gard 149:176-80+ My '77
Tom Tryon entertains. C. Porcelli. il por House B 119:102-3 Ap '77
Vegetables plus; party food. il House & Gard 150:106-7+ Ja '78
Wine tasting party. il Ladies Home J 94:124-5 Ap '77
See also
Buffet meals
Business entertaining
Caterers and catering
Childrens parties
Christmas entertaining
Games
Guests
Teas
Anecdotes, facetiae, satire, etc.
Mrs Armand Reef likes to entertain. G. W. S. Trow. New Yorker 53:25-6 Jl 4 '77
Showdown at generation gap. W. Stanton. Read Digest 111:134-6 O '77
ENTEX, Inc-University Savings Association merger. See Corporations—Acquisitions and mergers
ENTRANCE halls. See Halls
ENTRANCE requirements, College. See Colleges and universities—Entrance requirements
ENTRAPMENT (law)
How prosecutors are nabbed. J. Lardner. New Repub 176:22-5 Ja 29 '77
ENTREPRENEURS
Hall of Fame for Business Leadership. M. Ways. Fortune 95:117-23 Ja '77
Put that small idea to work. W. D. Ellis. Read Digest 111:123-5 N '77
See also
Business enterprises
Kaiser, E. F. Jr
Ronson, G. M.
Thomas, K. R.
ENTRIKIN, Richard K. and others
Avian muscular dystrophy: functional and biochemical improvement with diphenylhydantoin. bibl il Science 195:873-5 Mr 4 '77
ENTROPY
Entropy estimates for some silicates at 298°K from molar volumes. S. K. Saxena; reply with rejoinder. S. Cantor. bibl il Science 198:206-7 O 14 '77
ENVIRODYNE, Inc-Wisconsin Steel merger. See Corporations—Acquisitions and mergers
ENVIRONMENT
Environment (cont) Sci N 111:44; 112:185, 392, 425 Ja 15, S 17, D 10, 24 '77
National wildlife's readers rank the top ten environmental issues. il Nat Wildlife 15:35 Ap '77
Prescription for world survival; a report of U.N.'s Environment Program. il Time 109:59 Je 13 '77

ENVIRONMENT—*Continued*
Unfinished agenda—a special report. J. L. Fox. il Chemistry 50:22-4 Ap '77
Unfinished agenda; report of the Rockefeller Brothers Fund. A. W. Smith. Nat Parks & Con Mag 51:2+ Mr '77
See also
Airplanes, Supersonic—Environmental aspects
Coke plants—Environmental aspects
Ecology
Express highways—Environmental aspects
Human ecology
Industry and the environment
Man—Influence of environment
Man—Influence on nature

Bibliography

Environment update: a review of environmental literature and developments in 1976. G. H. Siehl. il por Lib J 102:981-7 My 1 '77
Overview: books. See issues of Environment

Conferences

See also
United Nations Conference on Desertification, 1977

Economic aspects

Behind the growing backlash against environmentalists. il U.S. News 83:29-30 D 19 '77
Environment and the economy: finding common ground. F. Smith. il por Duns R 110:83-4+ S '77

Laws and legislation

See Environmental law

Periodicals

Big as all outdoors; environmental writing. C. Schoenfeld. Writers Digest 57:21-3 S '77
Canada's environmental magazines. R. C. Paehlke. Environment 19:5+ Je '77
Environmental markets. D. Sandhage and W. Brohaugh. Writers Digest 57:22-3 S '77
See also
Conservationist (periodical)
Environment (periodical)

Statistics

1977 Environmental Quality Index: the year of the invisible crisis; with editorial comment. il Nat Wildlife 15:3, 17-32 F '77

Study and teaching

See also
Environmental education

ENVIRONMENT (art)
Art out of nature which is about nothing but nature; work of M. Singer. B. Forgey. il por Smithsonian 8:62-4+ Ja '78
Fence to remember; Christo's project. E. Keerdoja and L. Burgess. il Newsweek 89:8 F 21 '77
Michael Heizer: you might say I'm in the construction business; interview, ed by J. Gruen. M. Heizer. il por Art N 76:96-9 D '77
New landscape art: four contemporary artists go back to nature. L. R. Lippard. il Ms 5:68-73 Ap '77
Onward and upward with the arts: Running fence. C. Tomkins. il New Yorker 53:43-6+ Mr 28 '77
Quarrymaster of Saugerties; H. Fite's Opus 40. Vasari. il por Art N 76:23-4+ O '77

Anecdotes, facetiae, satire, etc.

Strutting pasta. S. Chawkins. il Atlantic 239: 90-2 F '77

ENVIRONMENT (periodical)
SIPI sells (out?) Environment magazine. D. Shapley. Science 198:1128-9 D 16 '77
ENVIRONMENT and cancer. See Cancer—Causes
ENVIRONMENT and state. See Environmental policy
ENVIRONMENT Program of the United Nations. See United Nations—Environment Program
ENVIRONMENT records. See Phonograph records —Sounds
ENVIRONMENTAL bioethics. See Bioethics
ENVIRONMENTAL Conservation, Department of. See New York (state)—Environmental Conservation, Department of
ENVIRONMENTAL design
Ian McHarg: champion for design with nature. C. Holden. por Science 195:379-82 Ja 28 '77
Some news in the right direction from Washington. W. Wagner. Archit Rec 162:13 O '77

Study and teaching

Three-dimensional design: the environment. L. F. Lisitrano. bibl il Sch Arts 76:26-8 Ap '77

ENVIRONMENTAL diseases
Chemical assault on our natural defenses. J. Cox. Org Gard & Farm 24:174-81 O '77
See also
Diseases, Industrial

ENVIRONMENTAL education
Busiest outdoor school; Environmental Learning Center, Isabella, Minn. S. J. Marcovich. il Am Educ 13:28-30 My '77
Earth log: the Audubon road show; Audubon Mobile Environmental Education Project. G. H. Harrison. il pors Audubon 79:102-3+ My '77
Ecoscene; introduction to eighteenth century customs in environmental education program, Greensboro, N.C. W. W. Davis and H. E. Manar. il Parks & Rec 12:26-8+ Ja '77
Many faces of an organic education. J. Goldstein. il Org Gard & Farm 24:112-14+ D '77
New classroom for environmental education; wastewater treatment facilities. D. L. Hall. il Parks & Rec 12:36a-38a F '77
Seacamp: a unique environment for a unique education; Big Pine Key, Fla. R. E. Bachert, Jr. il Camp Mag 49:8-10 F '77
YCC: a recipe for youth development; Outdoor Environmental Education Center, Camp Owahta, New York. B. E. Matthews and C. H. Yaple. il pors Conservationist 32:11-12 S '77
See also
Conservation of resources—Study and teaching

ENVIRONMENTAL engineering
Colonizing Mars: the age of planetary engineering begins. A. L. Robinson. il Science 195: 668 F 18 '77

ENVIRONMENTAL engineering (buildings)
Building an energy-saving house; excerpt from How to plan, buy or build your leisure home. H. Wicks. il Pop Mech 148:124-5+ N '77
Buried bookstore saves energy, saves space, saves the view; Williamson Hall, University of Minnesota. S. J. Marcovich. il Pop Sci 211:96-7 S '77
Energy-saving wall. V. E. Smay. il Pop Sci 210: 73 Je '77
Notes from the field: how architects, and their consultants, approach solar design. M. F. Gaskie. il Archit Rec 162:108-13 mid-Ag '77
Owner-built homes—low-cost, energy-efficient. E. Tozer. il por Pop Sci 211:114-17 S '77
President Carter offers his comprehensive energy program to Congress. W. Hickman. Archit Rec 161:34 Je '77
Round table on cost-effective strategies for saving energy in buildings; with editorial comment. il Archit Rec 162:7, 92-7 mid-Ag '77
Solar energy: some hopes and some concerns. W. F. Wagner, Jr. Archit Rec 161:13 Je '77
Tech House: an experiment in future living; developed by NASA. il Consumers Res Mag 50:41 Ag '77
See also
Computers—Engineering use
Johnson Controls Inc

Laws and regulations

See Building laws and regulations

ENVIRONMENTAL health
Convention urges control of hazards in work environment. UN Chron 14:45 Jl '77
Environmental balance sheet: cost benefits of the cleanup; excerpt from Building 6: the tragedy of Bridesburg. S. D. Solomon and W. S. Randall. Nation 225:431-4 O 29 '77
Hazards of toxic substances; excerpt from The unfinished agenda: the citizen's policy guide to environmental issues. Nat Parks & Con Mag 51:10-13 Jl '77
New breed of pollutants: the dangers they carry. il U.S. News 82:42-6 F 7 '77
Public health hazards from electricity-producing plants. J. Neyman. bibl il Science 195: 754-8 F 25 '77
See also
Industrial hygiene

ENVIRONMENTAL impact statements. See Environmental policy
ENVIRONMENTAL indexes. See Environment—Statistics
ENVIRONMENTAL law
Out of court. por Forbes 119:142 Ap 15 '77
Overview: law. See issues of Environment
Payoff for business initiative on the environment. N. Orloff. Harvard Bus R 55:8+ N '77
Role for biologists in climate program; National Climate Program Act. K. Weaver. BioScience 27:518 Ag '77
See also
Air pollution—Laws and legislation
Land utilization—Laws and regulations
Pollution—Laws and legislation
Refuse and refuse disposal—Laws and regulations
Shore protection—Laws and legislation
Strip mining—Laws and legislation

ENVIRONMENTAL literature
See also
Environment—Bibliography

ENVIRONMENTAL movement
Behind the growing backlash against environmentalists. il U.S. News 83:29-30 D 19 '77
Despairing optimist... R. Dubos. Am Scholar 46:280-1+ Summ '77
Environmentalists try to win labor over. Bus W p 104 O 3 '77
Organic living almanac. See issues of Organic gardening and farming
Whatever happened to the cranberry crisis? J. F. Henahan. Atlantic 239:29-36 Mr '77; Discussion. 239:26-7 Je '77
See also
Cleaning of lakes, rivers, etc.
Industry and the environment

History

Yesterday's flower children were called conservationists. A. Hershman. Duns R 109:31-2+ Ap '77

Alaska

From my corner. C. Hunter. Liv Wildn 41:61-3 Jl '77

California

Its fate is up in the air; protecting the habitat of the El Segundo blue butterfly. R. H. Boyle. il Sports Illus 46:54+ F 28 '77

Canada

Nuclear waste. R. Paehlke. Environment 19:2-3 Ag '77

Cape Cod

Siege of the Province Lands; question of proposed CeeJay Marina in Provincetown Harbor. W. O. Johnson. il map Audubon 79:22-35 My '77

Massachusetts

See also
Environmental movement—Cape Cod

Montana

New grassroots reform movement checks the great raid on Montana's resources. T. Judge. Horticulture 55:12+ Ag '77

New Jersey

Coordinated advertising campaign to combat environmental pollution. B. A. Jones. il Sch Arts 76:30-1 Ap '77

New York (state)

Environmentalism and the leisure class; public fight against building of Storm King plant by Con Ed. W. Tucker. il map Harpers 225:49-56+ D '77
Hudson: that river's alive. A. J. Hall. il map Nat Geog 153:62-89 Ja '78

Pennsylvania

Battle of Whiskey Run; community battle to save Woodland Park. D. Linton. il Parks & Rec 12:64-7+ S '77

Texas

Can they head off the tankers at the pass? proposed Harbor Island superport off Texas coast. D. G. Schueler. Audubon 79:146-8 N '77

Vermont

Vermont's magnificent amateur; special issue; with editorial comment. Am For 83:4, 6+ S '77

ENVIRONMENTAL news
Econotes. D. Hanson. See issues of Audubon
News notes. Nat Parks & Con Mag 51:26 F; 25-6 Mr; 27 Jl; 26-9 Ag; 27-9 N; 23-4 D '77
Spectrum. See issues of Environment

ENVIRONMENTAL policy
American springtime. A. W. Smith. Nat Parks & Con Mag 51:2+ Je '77
Audubon talks with Andrus; interview, ed by G. Reiger. C. D. Andrus. Audubon 79:148-50 My '77
Carter and the environment: better, but still not good enough. L. S. Clapper. il Nat Wildlife 15:18-19 Je '77
Carter environmental message: landmark action plan would shift conservation program into high gear; May 23 message to Congress. Nat Parks & Con Mag 51:26-9 Ag '77
Carter places environment high on agenda. L. J. Carter. Science 196:1065 Je 3 '77
Carter's hard line on the environment. il U.S. News 82:88 Je 6 '77
DNA debate prompts review of environmental impacts. E. M. Leeper. il BioScience 27:515-17 Ag '77
EIS: the program that grew and grew. M. Hornblower. Am For 83:20-1 My '77
Energy and the environment: putting the brakes on RV's? H. Shuldiner. il Outdoor Life 160:122+ S '77
Energy, water environment—a top official looks ahead; interview. C. D. Andrus. il por U.S. News 82:62-4 Je 27 '77
Environment update: a review of environmental literature and developments in 1976. G. H. Siehl. il por Lib J 102:981-7 My 1 '77
Environmental assessment: a pragmatic view. C. Comar. Science 198:567 N 11 '77
Environmental impact statements; adaptation of address, December 1976. J. Gruenfeld. pors Am For 83:18-19 My '77
Forging ahead. A. W. Smith. Nat Parks & Con Mag 51:2+ D '77
From my corner; President Carter's May 23 message to Congress. C. Hunter. por Liv Wildn 41:39 Ap '77
Letter to the new President. A. W. Smith. Nat Parks & Con Mag 51:2+ Ja '77; Reply. C. D. Andrus. 51:21 Je '77
Man from Putney; G. D. Aiken. H. N. Muller, 3d. il por Am For 83:18-21+ S '77
More than half a loaf. il Conservationist 32:1 N '77
National outlook. C. H. Callison. See issues of Audubon to May 1977
New environment at Interior; C. Andrus. J. Shepherd. il por N Y Times Mag p36+ My 8 '77
New for scientists: RFP's from USDA, EIS's from NIH. E. M. Leeper. il BioScience 27:297-8 Ap '77
Odum urges: speed up worldwide data gathering now; interview, ed by E. M. Leeper. E. P. Odum. por BioScience 27:755-8 N '77
Price of environmentalism—the blacklash begins. J. A. Briggs. il Forbes 119:36-40 Je 15 '77
Social cures, not palliatives; adaptation of address. B. Commoner. il Nat Parks & Con Mag 51:14-15 My '77
Throwaways. Audubon 79:150 Ja '77
Washington scene; analysis of President Carter's environmental message. B. Kravetz. Parks & Rec 12:10+ Jl '77
What needs to be done to save the environment; interview. D. P. Rall. il por U.S. News 82:51-3 F 7 '77
See also
Conservation of resources
Environmental law
Industry and the environment
Man—Influence on nature
Pollution—Control
United States—Council on Environmental Quality
United States—Environmental Protection Agency

Anecdotes, facetiae, satire, etc.

Jaundiced eye. S. Novick. See issues of Environment to June 1977

International aspects

Department discusses approach to environmental issues; requiring international environmental impact statements; statement March 31, 1977. P. T. Mink. Dept State Bull 76:385-7 Ap 18 '77
Double standard? requiring environmental impact statements for U.S. agencies operating outside the country. Int Wildlife 7:41 Mr '77
ECE to consider convening high-level meeting on protecting environment. il UN Chron 14:30-1 My '77
Environmental hazards of global concern; report of Pugwash Conference. Bull Atom Sci 33:38-9 D '77
One earth. P. W. Quigg. See issues of Audubon
Polecats, beavers, and détente; U.S.-U.S.S.R. Agreement on Cooperation in the Field of Environmental Protection. G. Reiger. Field & S 81:20+ Ap '77
See also
United Nations—Environment Program

California

California: the state takes on the public interest. T. J. Murray. il Duns R 109:48-9 Ap '77

Canada

Asbestos, maple trees, and Mounties. R. Paehlke. Environment 19:3-4 Ja '77
Overview: Canada. R. C. Paehlke. See issues of Environment

Greece

Ill-provisioned voyage: Greece sails into this century. J. W. Brown. il Nation 225:38-41 Jl 9 '77

Idaho

New man at Interior; with interview with C. D. Andrus. E. A. Bauer. il por Outdoor Life 159:106+ Mr '77

Italy

See also
Industry and the environment—Italy

Maine

Boys from Buffalo Creek; proposed Pittston Company refinery in Eastport, Me. J. E. Chappell, Jr. Progressive 41:11 N '77
Maine; damned if you do... Dickey-Lincoln project. D. Holt and others. il map Newsweek 91:21 Ja 2 '78

Michigan

Navy project goes aground in Michigan; Seafarer. por Bus W p28 Ap 11 '77
Project Seafarer: Michigan's war against the Navy. J. Magney. Progressive 41:22-4 Jl '77
Seafarer: project still homeless as Milliken says no to Navy. L. J. Carter. Science 197:964-8 S 2 '77

ENVIRONMENTAL policy—*Continued*

Montana

Montana and Canada clash over pollution; power plant site 8 mi. across U.S. border. map Bus W p27-8 Je 27 '77

New York (state)

See also
New York (state)—Environmental Conservation, Department of

Ohio

In search of a final SO_2 plan. il Bus W p78+ S 26 '77

Panama

Panama Canal treaties: conservationists fear squatters will cut forests. E. M. Leeper. il map BioScience 27:717-20 N '77

Washington (state)

Dixy rocks the Northwest. il pors map Time 110: 26-9+ D 12 '77

ENVIRONMENTAL pollution. See Pollution

ENVIRONMENTAL Protection Agency. See United States—Environmental Protection Agency

ENVIRONMENTAL psychology
Buildings may be hazardous to your health. C. W. Taylor. Intellect 106:101-2 S '77

ENVIRONMENTAL satellites. See Artificial satellites—Earth sciences use

ENVIRONMENTAL warfare

International control

United States signs convention banning environmental warfare; statement, with text of joint US-USSR communique, May 17, 1977. C. R. Vance. Dept State Bull 76:633-4 Je 13 '77

ENVIRONMENTALISTS. See Ecologists

ENVY
Seven deadly sins today; excerpt. H. Fairlie. New Repub 177:29-31 S 17 '77
See also
Jealousy

ENZYME deficiency diseases. See Metabolism, Disorders of

ENZYME polymorphism. See Polymorphism (biology)

ENZYMES
Adenylate cyclase of brain reflects propensity for breast cancer in mice. G. C. Cotzias and L. C. Tang. bibl il Science 197:1094-6 S 9 '77
Arginyl residues: anion recognition sites in enzymes. J. F. Riordan and others. bibl il Science 195:884-6 Mr 4 '77
Can we live forever? E. K. Pye. por Sat Eve Post 249:35+ Mr '77; Same abr. Sci Digest 82:14-15 S '77
Cigarette smoke activates guanylate cyclase and increases guanosine 3′,5′-monophosphate in tissues. W. P. Arnold and others. bibl il Science 198:934-6 D 2 '77
Dopamine-sensitive adenylate cyclase; location in substantia nigra. K. Gale and others. bibl il Science 195:503-5 F 4 '77
Folate conjugase: two separate activities in human jejunum. A. M. Reisenauer and others. bibl il Science 198:196-7 O 14 '77
Formation of a serine enzyme in the presence of bovine factor VIII (anti-hemophilic factor) and thrombin. G. A. Vehar and E. W. Davie. bibl il Science 197:374-6 Jl 22 '77
Localization of nigral dopamine-sensitive adenylate cyclase on neurons originating from the corpus striatum. P. F. Spano and others. bibl il Science 196:1343-5 Je 17 '77
See also
Acetylcholinesterase
Adenosine triphosphatase
Carbonic anhydrase
Carboxylases
Cellulases
Collagenase
Decarboxylase
Dehydrogenases
Elastase
Oxidases
Papain
Peptidases
Reductases
Synthetases
Transferases

Inactivation

Inhibition of a lymphocyte membrane enzyme by Δ^9-tetrahydrocannabinol in vitro. J. H. Greenberg and others. bibl il Science 197:475-7 Jl 29 '77

ENZYMES, Plant
Leucine 2,3-aminomutase: a cobalamin-dependent enzyme present in bean seedlings. J. M. Poston. bibl il Science 195:301-2 Ja 21 '77

EPEL, David
Program of fertilization; with biographical sketch. il Sci Am 237:16, 128-34+ N '77

EPHRON, Delia
How to eat like a child. N. Y. Times Mag p95 F 27 '77; Same abr. Read Digest 110:71 Je '77
State of the union. il Esquire 87:63-7 F '77

EPHRON, Nora
Academic gore. il por Esquire 88:76-8+ S '77
Media. See issues of Esquire to July 1977

EPIDEMICS
Red death on the Missouri; American Indian epidemic of smallpox. K. C. Tessendorf. il Am West 14:48-53 Ja '77
See also
Influenza
Quarantine

EPIDEMIOLOGY
Using cancer's rates to track its cause. map Bus W p69-70+ N 14 '77
See also
United States—Public Health Service—Center for Disease Control

EPIDERMAL growth factor
Control of a cell surface major glycoprotein by epidermal growth factor. L. B. Chen and others. bibl il Science 197:776-8 Ag 19 '77

EPIGRAMS
See also
Proverbs

EPIGRAPHY. See Inscriptions

EPILEPSY
Congratulations, you're an epileptic! L. Wolf. Psychol Today 11:94+ D '77
Epilepsy. M. P. Scott. il Bet Hom & Gard 55: 65-6+ My '77
Morphine and enkephalin: analgesic and epileptic properties. G. Urca and others. bibl il Science 197:83-6 Jl 1 '77
New hope for epileptics—but we still have a long way to go; interview. R. Masland. il por U.S. News 83:53-4 S 5 '77
New method of controlling seizures; work of Robert Feldman and Norman Paul. G. Gregg. Psychol Today 10:30 Mr '77

EPINEPHRINE. See Adrenalin

EPIPHANY
Great Austrian true-blue, down-on-the-farm Epiphany celebrations. K. Cure. il Holiday 57:22-3 N '76

EPISCIAS
Flame violets. M. Kartuz. il Horticulture 55: 60-2 F '77

EPISCOPAL Church. See Protestant Episcopal Church

EPITHELIUM
Endothelial damage and thrombocyte adhesion in pigeon atherosclerosis. J. C. Lewis and B. A. Kottke. bibl il Science 196:1007-9 My 27 '77
Sodium-specific membrane channels of frog skin are pores: current fluctuations reveal high turnover. B. Lindemann and W. van Driessche. bibl il Science 195:292-4 Ja 21 '77
See also
Goblet cells

EPOXIDES. See Epoxy compounds

EPOXY adhesives
You never know; J. Birdsall, developer of Aquatapoxy. New Yorker 53:30-1 Ap 11 '77

EPOXY compounds
Benzo [α] pyrene diol epoxides: mechanism of enzymatic formation and optically active intermediates. S. K. Yang and others. bibl il Science 196:1199-201 Je 10 '77

EPPE bookstore, Paris. See Booksellers and bookselling—France

EPPLER, Heinz
Copycat. por Forbes 120:68 S 1 '77 •

EPSTEIN, Emanuel
Role of roots in the chemical economy of life on earth. bibl il BioScience 27:783-7 D '77

—and Norlyn, J. D.
Seawater-based crop production: a feasibility study. bibl il Science 197:249-51 Jl 15 '77

EPSTEIN, Helen
Heirs of the holocaust. il por N Y Times Mag p 12-15+ Je 19 '77
Notes from the orchestra pit. Ms 5:106+ Ap '77
(ed) See Horowitz, V. Grand eccentric of the concert hall

EPSTEIN, Joseph
Bring back elitist universities. il N Y Times Mag p86-8+ F 6 '77
Conspiracy of silence. il Harpers 255:77-80+ N '77
Rediscovering Mencken. Commentary 63:47-52 Ap '77
What makes Vidal run. Commentary 63:72-5 Je '77

EPSTEIN, Leslie
Skaters on wood; story. Esquire 88:109-11 S '77

EPSTEIN, Louis
Pickwick's founder reminisces about his early bookselling days. Pub W 211:55-6 Ja 10 '77

EPSTEIN, Mel H. and others
Cerebrospinal fluid production: stimulation by cholera toxin. bibl il Science 196:1012-13 My 27 '77

EPSTEIN, Noel
On the use and abuse of data. Society 14:36-8 My '77

EPSTEIN, Renee
Theater. Ms 5:34+ Mr '77

EPSTEIN, Robert L.
Criminalist—the forensic scientist. il Intellect 105:258-60 F '77

EPSTEIN, Samuel, and others
Oxygen and hydrogen isotopic ratios in plant cellulose. bibl il Science 198:1209-15 D 23 '77
—See DeNiro, M. J. jt auth

EPSTEIN, Samuel S.
Cancer and the environment. bibl il Bull Atom Sci 33:22-30 Mr '77
Case for a consumer protection agency. Bull Atom Sci 33:6-7 S '77

EPSTEIN, William
Time to bury deterrence. Bull Atom Sci 33:6-7 Je '77
Why states go—and don't go—nuclear. Ann Am Acad 430:16-28 Mr '77

EPSTEIN-Barr viruses. See Herpesviruses

EQUAL Credit Opportunity Act. See Credit—Regulation

EQUAL Employment Opportunity Commission. See United States—Equal Employment Opportunity Commission

EQUAL Rights Amendment (proposed) See United States—Constitution—Amendments

EQUALITY
Dominance syndrome. J. M. Luecke. Chr Cent 94:405-7 Ap 27 '77
Equality's uneven hand. T. Griffith. Atlantic 241:28-9 Ja '78
Note on the new equality. E. M. McCarthy. Commentary 64:53-5 N '77
See also
Democracy
Educational equalization
Race relations

EQUALIZATION, Educational. See Educational equalization

EQUALIZERS (sound) See Sound—Apparatus

EQUATORIAL Guinea
See also
Pigalu (island)

EQUESTRIANISM. See Horsemanship

EQUIPMENT industry. See Industrial equipment industry

EQUIPMENT leasing. See Lease and rental services

EQUITABLE Life Assurance Society of the United States
Equitable alchemy; Teamsters' pension fund management. il Time 110:52+ Jl 11 '77
Equitable courts small business. Bus W p 114 Je 20 '77
Equitable Life goes on a realty investment spree. il Bus W p 114+ N 7 '77

EQUUS; drama. See Shaffer, P.

ERB, Donald
Rochester Philharmonic: Erb prem. por Hi Fi 27:MA36 F '77 *

ERBE, Pamela
Imperfect chords; story. Ms 6:68-71 Ja '78
Mementos of our trip; story. Redbook 149:102-3 Jl '77

ERDDIG Park, Wrexham. See Historic houses, sites, etc.—Wales

ERDMAN, Paul
Doom for fun and profit. il por Time 109:64+ Je 13 '77 *

ERDÖS, Paul
Mathematician Paul Erdös: total devotion to the subject. G. B. Kolata. por Science 196:144-5 Ap 8 '77 *

ERGENBRIGHT, Ric
Shutter tripper. il Travel 148:20-1+ O '77 (cont as) Trav/Holiday 148:8+ N; 16+ D '77; 149:10+ Ja '78

ERGOTISM
Ergot reconsidered; Salem Witch trials. Chemistry 50:20 Mr '77

ERHARD, Ludwig
Obituary
Nat R 29:657 Je 10 '77

ERHARD Seminars Training
Est-erical behavior? Newsweek 89:95 My 9 '77
Serpentine serenity of EST. K. Garvey. Chr Today 21:13-15 Ja 21 '77

ERIC
Eric clearinghouse goes to Syracuse, N.Y. Lib J 102:529 Mr 1 '77

ERICKSENN, Lief
First look. il Pop Phot 81:96 D '77

ERICKSON, Kenneth A.
Disruptive youth and the rights of others. Todays Educ 66:40-1 Ja '77

ERICKSON, Milton Hyland
Secrets of a modern Mesmer. D. Goleman. bibl il por Psychol Today 11:62+ Jl '77 *

ERICKSON, Ralph O. See Maksmowych, R. jt auth

ERIE, Pa.
Winter wasteland. T. Fuller. il Newsweek 89:40 Ja 31 '77

ERIE, Lake
See also
Kelley's Island

ERIE Canal. See Canals—New York (state)

ERIKSON, Erik Homburger
Psychobiography of everyday life. R. W. Noland. Nation 224:570-2 My 7 '77*

ERITREA. See Ethiopia

ERIZE, Francisco
Lonely are the hunted. il Int Wildlife 7:14-16 S '77

ERLANGER, Ellen
Most valuable in-put. il por Sr Schol 109:14 Mr 24 '77

ERON, Carol
Anatomy of a cold. Read Digest 111:110-13 S '77

EROSION
Soil deterioration and the growing world demand for food. R. A. Brink and others. bibl il Science 197:625-30 Ag 12 '77
Where are our children's farms? loss of topsoil. R. Rodale. il Org Gard & Farm 24:62-7 S '77
See also
Coast changes
Dust storms

Photographs

Erosion. M. Keller. il Oceans 10:48-55 N '77

EROSION prevention and control
Concrete waffle for erosion control. il Parks & Rec 12:47-8+ My '77
New stitches sew up erosion control. il Am City & County 92:73-4 My '77
Soil erosion: the problem persists despite the billions spent on it. L. J. Carter. il Science 196:409-11 Ap 22 '77
See also
Contour farming
Crop residues
Terraces (agriculture)

EROTICA
Where have you gone, Boccaccio? M. Greenfield. Newsweek 90:96 S 26 '77

ERRORS, Logical. See Fallacies (logic)

ERRORS, Popular
Happiness—it's only natural; five popular errors refuted. W. W. Dyer. Read Digest 111:84-6 Jl '77
Sorry, wrong number. M. E. Marty. Chr Cent 94:519 My 25 '77
See also
Medical delusions

ERRORS, Scientific
Science myths, or, It ain't necessarily so. B. Brown. il Sci Digest 81:72-5 My '77

Anecdotes, facetiae, satire, etc.

Scientific cranks: how to recognize one and what to do until the doctor arrives. J. Bernstein. Am Scholar 47:8+ Wint '77

ERTEGÜN, Mica
Mica Ertegün: for her, the impossible works. W. P. Rayner. il por Vogue 167:209+ D '77 *

ERVIN, Samuel James, 1896-
Excerpt from statement on the ERA, January 24, 1977. Cong Digest 56:171+ Je '77

ERVING, Julius Winfield, Jr
Doctor J's toughest case. G. Hoenig. il pors N Y Times Mag p56-61 F 13 '77 *

ERWIN, Tanya Lee
Indiana Dunes: another border to defend. il map Nat Parks & Con Mag 51:4-7 O '77

ERWITT, Elliott
Festival of F-stops in France; photographs. N Y Times Mag p 10-11 Ag 14 '77

ERXLEBEN, Russell
They're kicking up a real storm. J. Jares. il pors Sports Illus 47:26-9 N 7 '77 *

ERYTHROCYTES
Fluidity in the membranes of adult and neonatal human erythrocytes. M. Kehry and others. bibl il Science 195:486-7 F 4 '77
Prelytic damage of red cells in filtrates from peroxidizing microsomes. M. K. Roders and others. bibl il Science 196:1221-2 Je 10 '77

ERYTHROPOIESIS
Growth hormone: species-specific stimulation of erythropoiesis in vitro. D. W. Golde and others. bibl il Science 196:1112-13 Je 3 '77
Theta-sensitive cell and erythropoiesis: identification of a defect in W/Wv anemic mice. W. Wiktor-Jedrzejczak. bibl il Science 196:313-15 Ap 15 '77

ERYTHROPOIETIN. See Hormones

ESALEN Institute, Big Sur, California
Weekend at the heart of the Human Potential Movement. A. Gross. il Mademoiselle 83:202+ Ap '77

ESCALANTE Canyon, Utah. See Canyons

ESCAPES
Capture in the Cumberlands; case of J. E. Ray. il por map Time 109:10-12 Je 27 '77
Critic in exile; D. Woods' escape from South Africa. il por Time 111:31 Ja 16 '78
Great escape; H. Kappler. K. Willenson and others. il por Newsweek 90:43 Ag 29 '77
Great escape; D. Woods' flight from South Africa. S. Strasser and P. Younghusband. il por Newsweek 91:48 Ja 16 '78
Great escape? two Philippine political prisoners. C. Whipple and others. il pors Newsweek 90:62 O 17 '77
Missing cancer patient; H. Kappler. il por Time 110:42-3 Ag 29 '77
Ray's breakout. il pors Time 109:12-16 Je 20 '77
Ray's capture. P. Goldman and others. il por Newsweek 89:25+ Je 27 '77

ESCAPES—*Continued*
Ray's escape; breakout at Brushy Mountain State Prison, Tenn. P. Goldman and others. il pors map Newsweek 89:22-4+ Je 20 '77
Return of the native; escape of Nazi H. Kappler. F. Getlein. Commonweal 104:580-2 S 16 '77; Discussion. 104:642 O 14 '77
To lose a thief; escape of A. Spaggiari, Nice bank robber. F. Willey and E. Peer. il por Newsweek 89:44 Mr 21 '77

ESCHATOLOGY
See also
Second Advent

ESCHENMOSER, Albert, and Wintner, C. E.
Natural product synthesis and vitamin B_{12}. bibl il Science 196:1410-20 Je 24 '77

ESCHERICHIA coli
Cloning of cauliflower mosaic virus (CLMV) DNA in escherichia coli. W. W. Szeto and others. bibl il Science 196:210-12 Ap 8 '77
Cloning of yeast transfer RNA genes in escherichia coli. J. S. Beckmann and others. bibl il Science 196:205-8 Ap 8 '77
DNA and insulin; recombinant DNA research. Newsweek 89:74 Je 6 '77
E. coli at work. Time 110:56 N 14 '77
E. coli: elusive enemy of the gut. J. Arehart-Treichel. il Sci N 112:189-90 S 17 '77
Effects of escherichia coli and yeast DNA insertions on the growth of lambda bacteriophage. J. R. Cameron and R. W. Davis. bibl il Science 196:212-15 Ap 8 '77
Excision and recombination of adenovirus DNA fragments in escherichia coli. M. Perricaudet and others. bibl il Science 196:208-10 Ap 8 '77
Expression in escherichia coli of a chemically synthesized gene for the hormone somatostatin. K. Itakura and others. bibl il Science 198:1056-63 D 9 '77
Genetic disarmament. Sci Am 236-53-5 My '77
Increase in conjugational transmission frequency of nonconjugative plasmids. N. J. Crisona and A. J. Clark. bibl il Science 196: 186-7 Ap 8 '77
Naturally occurring plasmid carrying genes for enterotoxin production and drug resistance. C. L. Gyles and others. bibl il Science 198:198-9 O 14 '77
One for the gene engineers; inserting human insulin gene into DNA of escherichia coli. il Time 109:68 Je 6 '77
One strand equivalent of the escherichia coli genome is transcribed: complexity and abundance classes of mRNA. W. E. Hahn and others. bibl il Science 197:582-5 Ag 5 '77

ESCLARMONDE; opera. See Massenet, J.

ESCOBEDO, Reuben John
Night of terror. W. Evans and D. R. Williams. il Good H 185:126-7+ O '77 *

ESKIMO villages
See also
Barrow, Alaska

ESKIMOS
Eskimo tales. D. H. Eber. il Natur Hist 86: 126-9 O '77
How it really was; excerpt from People from our side. D. H. Eber. il por Natur Hist 86:70-5 bibl(p 101) F '77
Life on a cold rock; Siberian and Alaskan Eskimos of the Diomede Islands. F. Bruemmer. il map Natur Hist 86:54-65 bibl(p97) Mr '77
Still Eskimo, still free; Inuit of Umingmaktok. Y. Momatiuk and J. Eastcott. il map Nat Geog 152:624-47 N '77
See also
Aleuts

Economic conditions

Alaskan tragedy. B. Lopez. map Harpers 255: 30-3 S '77

Hunting

Bowhead whales; ban on Eskimo hunting. Dept State Bull 77:740-1 N 21 '77
Hunt for the narwhal: unicorn of the Arctic seas; Inuits of the Canadian Arctic. R. R. Reeves. il Oceans 10:50-7 Jl '77
Issue of survival: bowhead vs. tradition; Eskimo whaling. J. R. Bockstoce. Audubon 79:142-5 S '77
Managing bowhead, sperm whale hunts. Sci N 112:406 D 17 '77
Moratorium for the bowhead: Eskimo whaling on ice? J. Walsh. il Science 197:847-50 Ag 26 '77
Saving the bowheads. P. Gwynne and W. J. Cook. il map Newsweek 90:113 N 7 '77
Whale of a problem for the administration; Eskimo hunting of the bowhead whale. J. Walsh. Science 198:384-5 O 28 '77

ESKIMOS in literature
Eskimo and his literature. C. Klose. Engl J 66: 60-1 S '77

ESKRIDGE, Rob. See Kaplan, N. jt auth

ESMARK, Inc.
Tough numbers man sets up the Esmark derby. D. P. Kelly. il por Fortune 95:17+ Ap '77

ESPING, Mardel
Students write about their artwork. il Sch Arts 76:36-8 F '77

ESPIONAGE
Sam Jaffe and the new blacklist. T. Branch Esquire 87:36+ Mr '77
See also
Electronics in criminal investigation, espionage, etc.
Secret service
Trials (espionage)

ESPIONAGE, American
Behind the purge at CIA. il U.S. News 83:37 N 21 '77
Firm guilty in technology export case. Aviation W 106:55 F 21 '77
Honorable schoolboy; FBI's domestic counterespionage; attempted recruiting of Russian exchange student A. R. Lusis. Time 110:26 N 14 '77

ESPIONAGE, German
Mischa meets his match; East German spies in West Germany. il por Time 110:37-8 Jl 25 '77
NATO modifies defense plans in spying case. Aviation W 108:22-3 Ja 2 '78
Spies with many secrets; East German spying in West Germany; Lutze case. il pors Time 110:25 D 26 '77

ESPIONAGE, Industrial. See Business intelligence

ESPIONAGE, Russian
Despite détente, Soviet spying is on the increase around the world. il U.S. News 83:89-91 O 17 '77

Norway

From Russia with lovers; arrest of G. G. Haavik, Soviet spy. il por Time 109:32 F 28 '77

United States

Bugs in the system; Soviet interception of US phone calls. K. Keegan. New Repub 177:14-15 Ag 6 '77
Business stake in Soviet snooping; phone message interceptions. Bus W p57-8 D 12 '77
Espionage: the dark side of détente; KGB agents. J. Barron. Read Digest 112:78-82 Ja '78
Pyramider spy case; A. Lee and C. Boyce. R. Steele and N. Horrock. il por Newsweek 89:29 Ap 18 '77
Stealing the company store; case of C. Boyce and A. D. Lee. il por Time 109:19 My 9 '77
To be young, rich—and a spy; A. D. Lee and C. J. Boyce. R. Lindsey. il pors N Y Times Mag p 18+ My 22 '77

ESPOSITO, Ralph, and Kornetsky, Conan
Morphine lowering of self-stimulation thresholds: lack of tolerance with long-term administration. bibl il Science 195:189-91 Ja 14 '77

ESPY, Willard R.
PW interviews; ed by J. F. Baker. por Pub W 211:6+ Ap 11 '77

ESQUIRE (periodical)
Best of Dubious. D. Newman. il Esquire 88: 99-104 O '77
Clay Felker, Esq. T. Schwartz. il por Newsweek 90:47 S 5 '77
Esquire's dubious achievement awards for 1977. il Esquire 89:45-9 Ja '78
Familiar voice for Esquire; sale to C. Felker. Time 110:41 S 5 '77

ESQUIRE, Inc
Esquire sans Esquire. Forbes 120:36 O 1 '77

ESSEX (warship) See Warships—United States

ESSEX Institute, Salem, Mass.
Furniture at the Essex Institute, Salem, Massachusetts. A. Farnam. il Antiques 111:958-73 My '77
Historic houses owned by the Essex Institute in Salem, Massachusetts. G. W. R. Ward and B. M. Ward. bibl il Antiques 112:1130-47 D '77

ESSILOR (firm) See Optical industry—France

ESTAING, Valéry Giscard d'. See Giscard d'Estaing, V.

ESTATE planning
ESOP: how it fits in estate planning; employee stock ownership of farm corporations. Suc Farm 75:9 My '77
Estate planning for business owners. W. L. McPeters. il por Nations Bus 65:67-8+ Je '77
Estate planning; symposium. L. Kruse. il Suc Farm 75:31-41+ N '77
Farm corporation. C.-L. Davis. il Suc Farm 75:26-7+ My '77
For your family's future: latest on planning an estate; with interview with W. C. Clay. il por U.S. News 82:47-50 My 30 '77
How a trust could save your life's work. M. Kilgore. il Farm J 101:D2 Ap '77
How to settle an estate—peacefully. L. Lane. il Farm J 101:31-3 My '77
State of your estate. P. Gross. House & Gard 149:30+ My '77
Word tools of estate planning. Suc Farm 75:9 N '77
See also
Inheritance tax

ESTATE tax. See Inheritance tax

ESTERASES
See also
Acetylcholinesterase

ESTES, Billie Sol
Return of Pecos Billie. M. Ruby and L. Donosky. pors Newsweek 90:71-2 S 5 '77 *
ESTES, Elliott M.
Auto safety dialogue: tough gap to narrow; interview, ed by J. Norris. pors Motor T 29:13-14 O '77
about
Motor Trend Man of the Year Awards to Thomas A. Murphy and E. M. "Pete" Estes. pors Motor T 29:34+ F '77 *
Nepotism question at General Motors. por Bus W p41 S 19 '77 *
ESTES, Robert Manson
Emerging solution to corporate governance. bibl f Harvard Bus R 55:20-3+ N '77
ESTHETICS. See Aesthetics
ESTIMATES, Tax. See Income tax—Estimates
ESTRADIOL
Estradiol shortens the period of hamster circadian rhythms. L. P. Morin and others. bibl il Science 196:305-7 Ap 15 '77
Heart: a target organ for estradiol. W. E. Stumpf and others. bibl il Science 196:319-21 Ap 15 '77
ESTREMADURA, Spain
Extremadura: cradle of conquistadors. C. L. Soper and M. Blanch de Alcolea. il Américas 29:34-40 O '77
ESTROGEN receptors. See Hormone receptors
ESTROGENS
Catechol estrogens: presence in brain and endocrine tissues. S. M. Paul and J. Axelrod. bibl il Science 197:657-9 Ag 12 '77
Clomid or nafoxidine administered to neonatal rats causes reproductive tract abnormalities. J. H. Clark and S. McCormack. bibl il Science 197:164-5 Jl 8 '77
Competition of Δ^9-tetrahydrocannabinol with estrogen in rat uterine estrogen receptor binding. A. B. Rawitch and others. bibl il Science 197:1189-91 S 16 '77
Does blastocyst estrogen initiate implantation? Z. Dickmann and others. bibl Science 195:687-8 F 18 '77
Effect of delta-9-tetrahydrocannabinol on uterine and vaginal cytology of ovariectomized rats. J. Solomon and others. bibl il Science 195:875-7 Mr 4 '77
Estrogen-cancer link faces challenge. Sci N 111:294 My 7 '77
Estrogen: doctors' complete update on dangers, needs. Vogue 167:86+ Ap '77
Estrogen: the rewards and the risks. P. Weideger. McCalls 104:70+ Mr '77
Estrogens: can they hold back the clock? M. Steinmann. il Fam Health 9:24-7 My '77
Final victory; connection between the pill and breast cancer. N. S. Greenfield. Good H 184:103+ Ap '77
Hawking the estrogen fix; campaign by Ayerst Laboratories. M. Mintz and V. Cohn. Progressive 41:24-5 S '77
Ovarian hormone: lack of effect on reproductive structures of female Asian musk shrews. G. L. Dryden and J. N. Anderson. bibl il Science 197:782-4 Ag 19 '77
Uterotrophic effect of delta-9-tetrohydrocannabinol in ovariectomized rats. J. Solomon and others; reply with rejoinder. A. B. Okey and G. P. Bondy. bibl Science 195:904-6 Mr 4 '77
See also
Estradiol
ESTRUS
Catch cycling cows every time; estrus probes. E. Ainsworth. il Farm J 101:Dairy 1-2, Beef 26 O '77
ESTY, Janet
How to make a million before you're 34; interview. ed by D. Kaye and F. Ruffin. pors Redbook 149:60+ My '77
ESTY, William, Company. See Advertising agencies
ETA Carinae nebula. See Nebulae
ETCHING
Michael Jacques: a double career in art; interview, ed by P. T. Nagano. M. Jacques. il Am Artist 41:86-9+ F '77
Shell game. J. M. Wood. il Design (US) 78:6-7 Summ '77
See also
Etchings
Metal etching
ETCHINGS
Picasso's cries of children. . .cries of stones; series of etchings entitled The Dream and Lie of Franco. P. Failing. bibl il Art N 76:55-8+ S '77
When god was a woman. Z. Blum. il por Horizon 20:82-5 O '77
ETHANOL. See Alcohol
ETHEL & Albert (radio program) See Radio programs—Humorous programs
ETHICAL education. See Moral education
ETHICS
See also
Advertising ethics
Altruism
Bioethics
Business ethics
Conscience
Courage
Guilt
Honesty
Hunting—Ethical aspects
Journalistic ethics
Justice
Legal ethics
Lying
Medical ethics
Natural law
Political ethics
Professional ethics
Religious ethics
Responsibility
Simplicity
Sin
Television broadcasting—Moral and religious aspects
Values
Women—Social and moral questions
ETHICS, Religious. See Religious ethics
ETHICS and law. See Law and ethics
ETHICS and science. See Science and ethics
ETHICS Commission. See United States—National Commission for the Protection of Human Subjects of Biomedical and Behavioral Research
ETHICS Committee. See United States—Congress—House—Standards of Official Conduct, Committee on; United States—Congress—Senate—Standards and Conduct, Select Committee on
ETHIOPIA
See also
Churches—Ethiopia
Military assistance, Cuban—Ethiopia
Military assistance, Russian—Ethiopia
Radio broadcasting—Ethiopia

Foreign relations

Somalia

Blood and bullets. E. Peer. il Newsweek 90:40+ S 5 '77
Conflict in the African Horn. F. Shams. bibl f map Cur Hist 73:199-204+ D '77
Crossed wires. A. De Borchgrave. il por Newsweek 90:42-3 S 26 '77
Horning in. C. Legum. New Repub 177:18-21 O 1 '77
Shifting sands on the Horn. map Time 110:34+ Ag 22 '77
Somalia: sending Moscow a message. E. Peer. il Newsweek 90:37-8 Ag 29 '77
State of siege. J. Pringle. il Newsweek 90:43 S 26 '77
Sticks, stones and rockets. il map Time 110:48-9 O 24 '77
Under fire in the Ogaden. J. Pringle. il map Newsweek 90:54+ O 17 '77
U.S.-Soviet struggle to control the Horn of Africa. D. Mullin. il map U.S. News 83:43-5 Ag 29 '77

United States

See United States—Foreign relations—Ethiopia

Politics and government

And then there were sixty; execution of Teferi Benti. il Time 109:37 F 14 '77
Chaos and fear in Ethiopia. M. A. Swanson. Chr Cent 94:580-1 Je 22 '77
Conflict in the African Horn. F. Shams. bibl f map Cur Hist 73:199-204+ D '77
Cubans in Ethiopia. C. Legum. New Repub 176:15-16 Je 11 '77
Despot at war on all fronts. map Time 109:45-6 My 23 '77
Ethiopia: how big a loss for U.S? il map U.S. News 82:38 My 9 '77
Fifteen-year war: Ethiopia, Eritrea & U.S. policy. D. Connell. il map Nation 224:337-40 Mr 19 '77
Raging war on the Horn of Africa; Eritrea: with report by D. Brelis. il map Time 110:34-6 Jl 25 '77
Reign of war in the land of Sheba. M. T. Kaufman. il N Y Times Mag p 16-19+ Ja 8 '78
Shoot-out in the Dirgue. il Newsweek 89:48 F 14 '77

Religious institutions and affairs

See also
Missions—Ethiopia
ETHIOPIAN painting. See Painting, Ethiopian
ETHNIC barriers
Cultural movements and ethnic change. D. L. Horowitz. bibl f Ann Am Acad 433:6-18 S '77
ETHNIC boundaries. See Ethnic barriers
ETHNIC conflict. See Culture conflict
ETHNIC cookery. See Cookery, International
ETHNIC differences. See Ethnopsychology
ETHNIC diseases. See Heredity of disease

ETHNIC minorities. See Minorities

ETHNIC neighborhoods. See Neighborhoods

ETHNICITY
Ethnic conflict in the world today; symposium, ed by M. O. Heisler. bibl f Ann Am Acad 433: 1-160 S '77
Limits of ethnicity. I. Howe. New Repub 176:17-19 Je 25 '77
Limits of ethnicity. H. F. Stein and R. F. Hill. Am Scholar 46:181-9 Spr '77
Troubling future of ethnicity. P. Perlmutter. Chr Cent 94:718-21 Ag 17 '77

ETHNOLOGY
Frederick Douglass on ethnology: a commencement address at Western Reserve College, 1854. A. McCluskey and J. McCluskey. bibl il por Negro Hist Bull 40:746-9 S '77
See also
Anthropometry
Ethnic barriers
Ethnicity
Ethnopsychology

ETHNOPSYCHOLOGY
Ethnic conflict in the world today: an introduction. M. O. Heisler. bibl f Ann Am Acad 433:1-5 S '77
Majorities and minorities: a comparative survey of ethnic violence. C. Hewitt. bibl f il Ann Am Acad 433:150-60 S '77
Police and military in the resolution of ethnic conflict. C. H. Enloe. bibl f Ann Am Acad 433: 137-49 S '77
Psychiatry labeling in cross-cultural perspective. J. M. Murphy; discussion. bibl Science 196: 480+ Ap 29 '77
See also
Culture conflict

ETHRIDGE, John
Brief test. il Motor T 29:67-9 F; 70-2+ Mr '77
Road test. il Motor T 29:63-4+ Ap; 32-4, 105-9 My; 44-6 Je; 61-2+ Jl; 81+ Ag; 42-4+ N '77

ETHYL alcohol. See Alcohol

ETHYL alcohol as fuel. See Alcohol as fuel

ETHYLENE
Why chemical companies are nervous; expansion of ethylene production by oil companies. Forbes 120:68 D 15 '77

ETIQUETTE
Emily Post. E. Oettinger. por Am Heritage 28: 38-9 Ap '77
Evangelical tongues at 10:50; church etiquette. C. F. H. Henry. Chr Today 21:20-1 Je 3 '77
New Emily Post. E. L. Post. See issues of Good housekeeping
New etiquette; for single couples. R. L. Green. Harp Baz 110:119+ My '77
New etiquette; symposium. il Esquire 88:129-36+ D '77
Remarriage: survival manual; excerpt from Rewedded bliss: love, alimony, incest, ex-spouses, and other domestic blessings. D. Mayleas. Vogue 167:64+ N '77
Test your P's and Q's; table manners. A. Storipan. Seventeen 36:32 F '77
See also
Charm
Courtesy
Diplomatic etiquette
Guests
Hand shaking
Salutations

ETNA, Mount
Case of earthly indigestion. il Time 110:61 Ag 29 '77

ETTMAN, Jay
Their yen for bluefin. D. Levin. il Sports Illus 47:103-4+ O 10 '77 *

ETZIONI, Amitai
Can schools teach kids values? Todays Educ 66:28-30+ S '77
Creative response to our crisis. Bull Atom Sci 33:24 F '77
Family: is it obsolete? Current 195:3-12 S '77
Making up for past injustices: how Bakke could backfire. Psychol Today 11:18 Ag '77
Old people and public policy. Current 192:21-34 Ap '77
One and a half cheers for social science. Psychol Today 11:168 D '77
Opting out: the waning of the work ethic. Psychol Today 11:18 Jl '77
Politics of promises. Read Digest 110:121-2 My '77
Science and the future of the family. Science 196:487 Ap 29 '77
Toward a Swedenized America? Current 190: 11-15 F '77
When rights collide. Psychol Today 11:158 O '77
When to see a therapist. Psychol Today 10:16 Ap '77
Will power and your health. Intellect 105:429 Je '77

EUCALYPTUS
Eucalyptus bark. E. S. Ayensu. il Natur Hist 86: 36-9 D '77

EUGENE Onegin; opera. See Tchaikovsky, P. I.

EUGENICS
Science and values: the eugenics movement in Germany and Russia in the 1920s. L. R. Graham. bibl f Am Hist R 82:1133-64 D '77
See also
Genetic engineering

EUGLENA
Cloned ribosomal RNA genes from chloroplasts of euglena gracilis. M. I. Lomax and others. bibl il Science 196:202-5 Ap 8 '77

EULER, Leonhard
Efficiency of algorithms. H. R. Lewis and C. H. Papadimitriou. il maps Sci Am 238:96-109 bibl(p 138+) Ja '78 *

EULOGY for a small-time thief; drama. See Piñero, M.

EUPHORBIACEAE
Easy to grow house plants. E. McDonald. il House B 119:42 Ap '77

EURASIA
See also
Geology—Eurasia

EUREKA, Calif.
Redwood protest; loggers demonstration against major expansion of Redwood National Park. S. Fraker and G. C. Lubenow. il map Newsweek 89:30 Ap 25 '77

EUROBOND market
Action in bonds moves to Europe. il Bus W p53 My 9 '77
Continental swing in Eurobond financing. il Bus W p58 Ja 24 '77
Eurobond hedge against a rising yen. Bus W p86 Ap 11 '77
European money tap for the second string. il Bus W p62 Ag 1 '77

EUROCARD. See Credit cards

EUROCOMMUNISM. See Communist parties—Europe, Western

EURODOLLAR market
Bank of England's fall from grace: it can take London's bankers with it. il Bus W p60-4+ Mr 14 '77
Foreign investors thrash the dollar. il Bus W p92-4 O 31 '77

EUROPE
See also
Industry and state—Europe
Music festivals—Europe
Railroads—Europe
United States—Air Force—Forces in Europe

Antiquities

Ancient Europe is older than we thought. C. Renfrew. il map Nat Geog 152:614-23 N '77
Celts. M. Severy. il Nat Geog 151:582-630, supp (folded map) My '77

Defenses

See also
Conference on Security and Cooperation in Europe
United States—Air Force—Forces in Europe

Description and travel

Europe! package tours. il Seventeen 36:126+ Ap '77

Anecdotes, facetiae, satire, etc.

Hop on a bus, Gus: American package tours through Europe. D. Shaw. il Holiday 58:28-31 Ja '77

Economic conditions

See also
United Nations—Economic Commission for Europe

Foreign relations

Russia

See Russia—Foreign relations—Europe

United States

See United States—Foreign relations—Europe

History

Bibliography

Reviews of books: modern Europe. See issues of American historical review

1517-1648

Rubens: emissary of peace in strifetorn Europe. F. Baudouin. il UNESCO Courier 30:23-6 Je '77

1789-1815

Imprisonment of Lafayette. J. W. Baker. il Am Heritage 28:86-91 Je '77

20th century

See also
World War, 1914-1918

1945-

Who started the cold war? with introduction and discussion. C. L. Lee, Jr; W. A. Harriman; E. Abel. il pors Am Heritage 28:8-23 Ag '77

Kings and rulers

See also
Hapsburg, House of

EUROPE—*Continued*

Maps

Map section. Sr Schol 110:25 O 20 '77

Nationalism

How unhappy minorities upset Europe's calm. il U.S. News 82:37-9 Ja 31 '77

Politics and government

See also
Communism—Europe
Communist parties—Europe

EUROPE, Eastern

See also
Catholic Church—Relations (diplomatic)—Europe, Eastern
Civil rights—Europe, Eastern
Debts, Public—Europe, Eastern
Industrial relations—Europe, Eastern
Loans, Bank—Europe, Eastern
Rumania

Commerce

France

See France—Commerce—Europe, Eastern

Defenses

Military spending rises in East Europe. Aviation W 107:18-19 S 19 '77
Nightmare for NATO. A. De Borchgrave. il map Newsweek 89:36-8 F 7 '77

Description and travel

Danube: river of many nations, many names. M. Edwards. il map Nat Geog 152:454-85 O '77

Economic conditions

Private enterprise vs. Eastern Europe. il Nations Bus 65:51-4+ Ag '77
Recession, Communist style. J. Dornberg. il Duns R 109:82-6 Ap '77
Trouble in Eastern Europe, too. il U.S. News 82:24-5 My 9 '77

Economic relations

Russia

See Russia—Economic relations—Europe, Eastern

Foreign relations

Russia

See Russia—Foreign relations—Europe, Eastern

Industries

See also
Shipping—Europe, Eastern

Religious institutions and affairs

See also
Evangelistic work—Europe, Eastern

Social conditions

Wire—and other vignettes of life in eastern Europe; excerpts from The wonderful years. R. Kunze. il Fortune 95:89 Je '77

Travel regulations

See Travel regulations

EUROPE, Western

Fresh worry for U.S.—a Europe beset by stagnation, self-doubt and violence. J. Fromm. il U.S. News 83:38-40+ O 17 '77
See also
Agricultural administration—Europe, Western
Airlines—Europe, Western
Airplanes, Military—Europe, Western
Atomic power—Europe, Western
Canals—Europe, Western
Capital investments—Europe, Western
Christmas—Europe, Western
City planning—Europe, Western
Collective labor agreements—Europe, Western
Commission of the European Communities
Council of Europe
Crime and criminals—Europe, Western
Data transmission systems—Europe, Western
English language in Europe, Western
Gypsies—Europe, Western
Hours of labor—Europe, Western
Housing—Europe, Western
Investments, American—Europe, Western
Investments, European
Migrant labor—Europe, Western
Photography—Europe, Western
Public health—Europe, Western
Railroads—Europe, Western
Restaurants—Europe, Western
Science—Europe, Western
Technology—Europe, Western
Telephone—Europe, Western
Tourist trade—Europe, Western
Visitors, Foreign—Europe, Western
Youth—Europe, Western

Armed Forces

See also
Trade unions—Servicemen

Commerce

Europe's booming arms trade. il Fortune 96:170-3 N '77

Hong Kong

EC threat to textile exports. il Bus W p46 D 5 '77

Israel

Cost of losing a tariff shelter. il Bus W p42-3 Jl 11 '77

Japan

Europe fights Japanese imports. J. Ross-Skinner. il Duns R 109:68-70+ F '77

Russia

See Russia—Commerce—Europe, Western

United States

See United States—Commerce—Europe, Western

Commercial policy

Growing worry over world trade war. U.S. News 83:24 Ag 8 '77

Defenses

See also
Nato
United States—Armed Forces—Forces in Europe

Description and travel

Autumn excursions. R. S. Kane. il Harp Baz 110:12+ S '77
Children's continent. P. Krasilovsky. il Sat Eve Post 249:90-1+ My '77
Europe's scenic train rides. J. Andrews. il Travel 147:53-9 Mr '77
Guide to European package tours. N. Kuehnl. il Bet Hom & Gard 55:153-4+ Mr '77
Into Europe; symposium. bibl il Mademoiselle 83:90-4+ F '77
Untrapped tourist. T. Griffith. Atlantic 240:20+ S '77

Anecdotes, facetiae, satire, etc.

Six glorious weeks in Europe—on a buying spree; shopping for writing equipment. P. O'Toole. Vogue 167:254+ Mr '77

Droughts

See Droughts

Economic conditions

But Europe is in a stall. il Time 110:48-9 S 12 '77
Europe's economies: the magic is gone. il U.S. News 82:95 Ap 11 '77
Harder times abroad—a threat to U.S? il U.S. News 83:48-9 O 3 '77
Slow, slow, slow; OECD report. Time 111:39+ Ja 9 '78
Trade war: the first skirmishes? T. Szulc. il Forbes 120:29-30 O 15 '77
Trouble in Western Europe . . . il U.S. News 82:24-5 My 9 '77
Why Europe fears sag in business. K. S. Smith. il U.S. News 84:47-8 Ja 9 '78
Winter of discontent. S. P. Kramer. Commonweal 104:167-8 Mr 18 '77
See also
Unemployment—Europe, Western

Economic policy

Europe toys with reflation. il Bus W p22-3 Ag 29 '77
Failure of indexation. J. Ross-Skinner. Duns R 110:76-7+ S '77
Forced reflation from London to Tokyo. Bus W p 18-19 Ag 1 '77
New European unity: a conservative war on inflation. il Bus W p86-7 Je 27 '77

Economic relations

United States

See United States—Economic relations—Europe, Western

Economic union

See European Economic Community

Foreign opinion

Giant from afar: visions of Europe from Algiers to Tokyo. F. Stern. bibl f For Affairs 56:111-35 O '77

Foreign relations

Giscard speaks out; excerpts from interview, ed by A. De Borchgrave. V. Giscard d'Estaing. il por Newsweek 90:45-8 Jl 25 '77
International power: a European perspective. R. Dahrendorf. For Affairs 56:72-88 O '77

Russia

See Russia — Foreign relations — Europe, Western

United States

See United States—Foreign relations—Europe, Western

EUROPE, Western—*Continued*

Industries

See also
Aerospace industries—Europe, Western
Airplane industry—Europe, Western
Automobile industry—Europe, Western
Chemical industries—Europe, Western
Petroleum industry—Europe, Western
Radio apparatus industry—Europe, Western
Shipbuilding—Europe, Western
Shipping—Europe, Western
Steel industry—Europe, Western
Textile industry—Europe, Western

Nationalism

Europe breaks apart. M. Ledeen. Commentary 63:53-7 My '77

Politics and government

Cooperation among European nations; excerpts from address. O. R. Borch. por Intellect 106: 97-8 S '77
How to spoil a birthday party. il Time 109:24+ Ap 4 '77
Reflections (cont) W. Pfaff. New Yorker 53:87-92 My 16 '77
West Europe, 1977; symposium. bibl Cur Hist 73:145-73+ map(inside back cover) N '77
See also
Communist Parties—Europe, Western
Europe, Western—Nationalism
Socialism—Europe, Western

Social conditions

Crisis of modernity. E. M. von Kuehnelt-Leddihn. Nat R 29:1117 S 30 '77

EUROPE and Latin America
Latin America and Europe—today. F. X. Gannon. Américas 29:29 O '77

EUROPE and the United States
See also
United States—Foreign opinion—European

EUROPE-United States Cooperative Science Program. See Science—International aspects

EUROPEAN art. See Art, European

EUROPEAN artificial satellites. See Artificial satellites, European

EUROPEAN Common Market. See European Economic Community

EUROPEAN communications satellites. See Communications satellites, European

EUROPEAN Communities, Commission of the. See Commission of the European Communities

EUROPEAN Community Biologists Association
Toward a common biology curriculum. BioScience 27:636 S '77

EUROPEAN cookery. See Cookery, European

EUROPEAN Economic Community
Compromise speeds the Tokyo Round; agricultural concession between the U.S. and the European Community. il Bus W p53-4 Jl 25 '77
Cooperation among European nations; excerpts from address. O. R. Borch. por Intellect 106: 97-8 S '77
EC nations fight Communist tactics. il Bus W p69-70 D 12 '77
EC threat to textile exports; Hong Kong quota reduction. il Bus W p46 D 5 '77
Europe seen weighing F-16 import duty snag. R. R. Ropelewski. Aviation W 107:22-3 O 3 '77
European communities' present stage of development; address, January 12, 1977. A. Crosland. Vital Speeches 43:233-8 F 1 '77
European Economic Community; address, May 25, 1977. A. Jacomet. Vital Speeches 43:581-4 Jl 15 '77
European steelmen try U.S.-style protection. il Bus W p29-30 Ja 16 '78
Europe's farmers—tougher competitors than you think. R. C. Black. il Farm J 101:K1+ Ja '77
Growing worry over world trade war. U.S. News 83:24 Ag 8 '77
Reports & comment: Common Market. D. Cook. por Atlantic 239:14-16+ Ap '77
South Africa: multinationals are caught in the middle again; race discrimination in employment guidelines. il Bus W p49-50 O 24 '77
Take your (ugh!) pills, boys. por Forbes 120:120 N 1 '77
Tricky transition to EC membership; Greece. Bus W p69-70 N 21 '77
See also
Commission of the European Communities

EUROPEAN fiction
Human dialogues are born; Eastern Europe. I. Sanders. Nation 224:504-7 Ap 23 '77

EUROPEAN Organization for Nuclear Research
Conditions of success in international enterprises in science and technology. L. Kowarski. Bull Atom Sci 33:44-8 S '77

EUROPEAN painting. See Painting, European

EUROPEAN pottery. See Pottery, European

EUROPEAN Science Foundation. See Science—Europe, Western

EUROPEAN Security Conference. See Conference on Security and Cooperation in Europe

EUROPEAN Southern Observatory. See Astronomical observatories—Chile

EUROPEAN Space Agency
ESA presses Marots satcom proposals. R. R. Ropelewski. Aviation W 107:18-19 N 21 '77
ESA, to have responsibility for resource satellite effort. Aviation W 106:20 Ja 3 '77
Europe space activity at record pace. il Aviation W 106:71-3 Mr 21 '77
European Space Agency defining responsibilities. R. R. Ropelewski. Aviation W 106:52-3 F 28 '77
European space officials ponder budget, program. R. R. Ropelewski. Aviation W 106:16-17 F 14 '77
Would you buy a rocket from this agency? J. Walsh. Science 198:385 O 28 '77

EUROPEAN technical assistance. See Technical assistance, European

EUROPEAN War, 1914-1918. See World War, 1914-1918

EUSTIS, Warren
Legal advice helps lessen directors' worries. Camp Mag 49:10-12+ Ja '77

EUTROPHICATION
Evolution of phosphorus limitation in lakes. D. W. Schindler. bibl il Science 195:260-2 Ja 21 '77
Great Lakes eutrophication: the effect of point source control of total phosphorus. S. C. Chapra and A. Robertson. bibl il Science 196:1448-50 Je 24 '77
See also
Water bloom

EUTYCHUS VIII, pseud
Things they didn't tell you at your seminary graduation. Chr Today 21:6 My 20 '77

EVACUATION of civilians
See also
Vietnamese War, 1957-1975—Evacuation of civilians

EVALUATION (education) See Education—Evaluation

EVALUATION of students. See Students—Rating

EVALUATION of works of art. See Art—Valuation

EVANGELICAL advertising. See Religious advertising

EVANGELICAL churches
See also
Assemblies of God
National Association of Evangelicals

EVANGELICAL churches in Canada
Circulating saints. V. M. Parachin. Chr Cent 94: 396 Ap 27 '77

EVANGELICAL churches in Rumania
Josif Ton's fight for rights. E. E. Plowman. il por Chr Today 21:40-1 My 20 '77

EVANGELICAL Lutheran Church, Association of. See Lutheran Church in the United States

EVANGELICAL Lutheran Church of Tanzania. See Lutheran Church in Africa

EVANGELICAL Press Association
Evangelical press: issues and awards. il Chr Today 21:36-7 Je 3 '77

EVANGELICAL Theological Society. See Religious societies

EVANGELICAL theology. See Theology

EVANGELICALISM
Anglican evangelicals: a view from the north. J. D. Douglas. Chr Today 21:41 Jl 8 '77
Anglican evangelicals speak out; Nottingham statement. J. R. W. Stott. Chr Today 21:30-1 Jl 8 '77
Back to that oldtime religion. il Time 110:52-8 D 26 '77
Chicago Call. D. Tinder. Chr Today 21:32-3 Je 3 '77
Chicago Call: an appeal to evangelicals; with editorial comment. Chr Today 21:27-9 Je 17 '77
Evangelical summertime? C. F. H. Henry. Chr Today 21:38+ Ap 1 '77
Evangelicals and activists. M. Novak. Chr Cent 94:469-70 My 18 '77
Love, power and justice. P. B. Henry. il Chr Cent 94:1088-92 N 23 '77
Progeny of programmers: evangelical religion and the television age. J. A. Taylor. il Chr Cent 94:379-82 Ap 20 '77; Discussion. 94:788+ S 14 '77
Public schools: equal time for evangelicals. J. R. McQuilkin. il Chr Today 22:8-11 D 30 '77
Roots for evangelicals; Chicago Call. K. L. Woodward and F. Maier. il Newsweek 89:76 My 23 '77
Rules of decency. Time 109:52 My 30 '77
When piety prevails; Chicago Call. Chr Today 21:22 Jl 29 '77
Why the evangelical upswing? D. Tinder. Chr Today 22:10-12 O 21 '77
Yes, there are semi-evangelicals. J. Bayly. Chr Today 21:23 Jl 29 '77

Anecdotes, facetiae, satire, etc.

Some semi-tough questions. M. E. Marty. Chr Cent 94:415 Ap 27 '77; Reply. J. Bayly. Chr Today 21:23 Jl 29 '77

Bibliography

Choice evangelical books; key books of '76. D. Tinder. Chr Today 21:24-5 Mr 18 '77

Theology

See Theology

EVANGELICALISM and politics. See Religion and politics
EVANGELICALS, National Association of. See National Association of Evangelicals
EVANGELICALS for Social Action (organization) See Church and social problems
EVANGELISTIC work
Effective evangelism: a matter of marketing? interviews, ed by D. Kucharsky. J. F. Engel; H. W. Norton. il Chr Today 21:12-15 Ap 15 '77
Graham scores at Notre Dame. A. H. Matthews. il por Chr Today 21:30-1 Je 3 '77
Honoring a homegrown prophet; B. Graham. crusade in Ashville, N.C. A. H. Matthews. Chr Today 21:55-6 Ap 15 '77
Is America over-evangelized? D. W. Hillis. Chr Today 21:16-17 My 20 '77
Kindling fires along the Ohio; B. Graham crusade at Cincinnati's Riverfront Coliseum. A. Toalston. Chr Today 22:47-9 N 18 '77
Rex Humbard's 25-25 vision. P. Geiger and N. Kennedy. il pors Chr Today 21:53-6 My 6 '77
See also
Campus Crusade for Christ (organization)
Church growth
International Congress on World Evangelization
Inter-Varsity Christian Fellowship
Missions
National Association of Evangelicals
Youth for Christ International (organization)

Finance

Billy Graham on financing evangelism. B. Graham. pors Chr Today 21:18-20 Ag 26 '77

Asia

Missions momentum in Asia. C. F. H. Henry. Chr Today 21:34+ Mr 4 '77

Colombia

See also
Colombian Confederation of Evangelicals

Dominican Republic

Caribbean crusade. J. C. Hefley. Chr Today 22:46-7 N 18 '77

Europe, Eastern

Graham: back to the bloc. Chr Today 21:40 Ag 12 '77

Hungary

Billy in Budapest: Hungary opens its heart. E. E. Plowman. il pors Chr Today 22:52-4 O 7 '77
Graham and the Gospel: welcome in Hungary. E. E. Plowman. Chr Today 21:44-5 S 23 '77
Graham goes East. K. L. Woodward. il por Newsweek 90:70 Ag 29 '77
Gulyas and the Gospel; B. Graham. il pors Time 110:83 S 19 '77

Latin America

Evangelical's duty to the Latin American poor. H. B. Kuhn. Chr Today 21:67-8 F 4 '77; Reply. 21:23-4 Je 3 '77
Palau power in Latin America. il por Time 110:123 N 7 '77

Nigeria

Black culture—the Bible is the judge; Second World Black and African Festival of Arts and Culture, FESTAC. W. H. Fuller. Chr Today 21:51-2 Ap 1 '77

Philippines

Billy Graham's mission to Manila. H. Lindsell. il Chr Today 22:36-7 D 30 '77

Sweden

Graham: warm-up in Sweden. B. Graham. Chr Today 21:51-2 F 18 '77

EVANGELISTS
If Christ were alive today . . . : views of five TV evangelists. il Ladies Home J 94:58+ D '77
See also
Graham, B.
Humbard, R.
EVANIER, David
Man who refused to watch the Academy Awards; story. Commentary 63:53-9 Ap '77
EVANOFF, Vlad
Fishing on a budget. il Ret Liv 17:24-5 Ag '77
EVANS, Bill
Bill Evans: a modern day dance frontiersman; interview, ed by A. Smith il pors Dance Mag 51:67-70 F '77
EVANS, Cicely Louise
Your life in fiction. Writer 90:21-2+ F '77
EVANS, David L.
Bush Negroes carry on tradition of rebel ancestors. C. M. Turnbull. il Smithsonian 7:78-85 Mr '77 *
EVANS, David S.
Photoelectric observing of occultations. il Sky & Tel 54:164-6 S; 289-92 O '77
EVANS, Donald
Obituary
Art in Am por 65:14-15 Jl '77. S. Gablik
EVANS, Elisabeth Murawski
For Alun Lewis (1915-44); poem. New Repub 176:25 F 5 '77
Tinder; poem. Chr Cent 94:902 O 12 '77

EVANS, Frederick J.
—and others
Appetitive and replacement naps: EEG and behavior. bibl il Science 197:687-9 Ag 12 '77
about
Taking a nap: what it can do for you. C. Seebohm. il House & Gard 149:26+ F '77 *
EVANS, Harold J. and Barber, L. E.
Biological nitrogen fixation for food and fiber production. bibl il Science 197:332-9 Jl 22 '77
EVANS, Howard Ensign
Extrinsic versus intrinsic factors in the evolution of insect sociality. bibl BioScience 27:613-17 S '77
EVANS, James Hurlburt
1977: taxation at the crossroads; address, June 7, 1977. Vital Speeches 43:615-18 Ag 1 '77
about
Highball from a Harriman. il por Fortune 96:17 Ag '77 *
EVANS, John C. Jr, and Steinberg, R. I.
Nucleon stability: a geochemical test independent of decay mode. bibl il Science 197:989-91 S 2 '77
EVANS, Lawrence B.
Impact of the electronics revolution on industrial process control. bibl il Science 195:1146-51 Mr 18 '77
EVANS, M. Stanton
Dark horses. See issues of National review
Kemp & Co. Nat R 29:670 Je 10 '77
EVANS, Marion B.
Systematic approach to contrary opinions. J. Madrick and D. G. Santry. por Bus W p61 Ag 1 '77 *
EVANS, Michael
Confessions of a camp counselor. Seventeen 36:140 Jl '77
Hangin' on. il Seventeen 36:174 Mr '77
Walkin' on water. Seventeen 36:186+ Ag '77
EVANS, Robert
Phyllis & Bob. K. Gilman. pors Ladies Home J 94:78+ N '77 *
EVANS, Therman E.
Is your doctor ripping you off? Ebony 32:45-6+ S '77
On the health of black Americans. por Ebony 32:112 Mr '77
EVANS, Thomas Mellon
Is history repeating? interview, ed by R. Flaherty. Forbes 119:104+ Je 15 '77
about
Evans pounces again, this time with cash. Bus W p35 Ag 15 '77 *
EVANS, Wanda, and Williams, D. R.
Night of terror. il Good H 185:126-7+ O '77
EVAPORATION
Estimating evaporation: difficulties of applicability in different environments. J. D. Kalma and others. bibl Science 196:1354 Je 17 '77
EVAPORATORS
Inexpensive evaporator for backyard syrup making. L. E. Weeks, Jr. il Org Gard & Farm 24:138-41 F '77
EVEARITT, Daniel J.
Key to Stevie Wonder. Chr Today 21:30 F 18 '77
Paul Simon: the only living boy in New York. Chr Today 22:22-3 O 21 '77
Phil Keaggy's new song. Chr Today 21:18 Ag 12 '77
EVENING and continuation schools
See also
Adult education
University extension
EVENING clothes. See Clothing and dress
EVENING flowers. See Plants, Night blooming
EVEREST, Mount
Trekking on Everest: making a living from wanderlust; interview, ed by G. Lichtenstein. S. B. Larrabee. bibl il Ms 5:26+ Mr '77
EVERETT, Barbara
John Barry, fighting Irishman. il pors map Am Hist Illus 12:18-25 D '77
EVERETT, Todd
Automated radio: the future is upon us. il Hi Fi 27:124-7 S '77
Independent that could: A&M Records. il pors Hi Fi 27:132-4 Ap '77
EVERGLADES National Park
Open tap for Taylor Slough. L. L. Purkerson and D. Morrow. il Parks & Rec 12:31a-34a F '77
EVERGREEN, Colo.
Tennis on a tank; Evergreen, Colo. J. S. Blair. il Parks & Rec 12:35a F '77
EVERGREENS
See also
Arborvitae
Christmas greens
Christmas trees
Holly
EVERIST, Burton
Church and the coming electronic revolution; interview, ed by P. Rossman. Chr Cent 94:1167-8 D 14 '77

EVERLASTING flowers
Everlastings. K. Kraft and P. Kraft. il Horticulture 55:66-9, 86-7 Ap '77
EVERS, Carl G.
Carl Evers. N. Meglin. il por Am Artist 41:62-5 Jl '77 *
EVERT, Chris
Ambush on the comeback trail. W. Bingham. il pors Sports Illus 47:34-5 N 14 '77 *
Chrissie Evert. il pors Vogue 167:160-3 Ag '77 *
Extra! Chrissie loses first set! J. Jares. il por Sports Illus 46:24-5 Ap 4 '77 *
EVES, Edward
Retrospect. il Motor T 30:66-8 Ja '78
EVETT, Kenneth
Earthbound and sublime. New Repub 176:29-31 Mr 5 '77
EVETTS, Deborah
Book art. il pors House & Gard 149:160-1+ O '77
EVICTION
U.S. journal: San Francisco: some thoughts on the International Hotel controversy. C. Trillin. New Yorker 53:116-20 D 19 '77
EVIDENCE (law)
Legal house of cards. A. M. Rosenblatt and J. C. Rosenblatt. Harpers 255:18-21 Jl '77
Use of illegally obtained evidence; excerpts from address. Intellect 105:378-9 My '77
See also
Witnesses
EVIDENCES of the Bible. See Bible—Evidence, authority, etc.
EVIL eye
Evil eye—a stare of envy. S. Bush. Psychol Today 11:154+ D '77
EVOKED potentials (electrophysiology) See Electrophysiology
EVOLUTION
Deuterolysis of amino acid precursors: evidence for hydrogen cyanide polymers as protein ancestors. C. Matthews and others. bibl il Science 198:622-5 N 11 '77
Dodo ecology. Sci Am 237:81-2 O '77
Early chemical evolution of nucleic acids: a theoretical model. D. A. Usher. bibl il Science 196:311-13 Ap 15 '77
Ecology, sexual selection, and the evolution of mating systems. S. T. Emlen and L. W. Oring. bibl il Science 197:215-23 Jl 15 '77
Evolution and tinkering; address, March 1977. F. Jacob bibl Science 196:1161-6 Je 10 '77
Evolution in a time-varying environment. R. A. Armstrong and M. E. Gilpin. bibl il Science 195:591-2 F 11 '77
Evolution of primate chromosomes. D. A. Miller. bibl il Science 198:1116-24 D 16 '77
Extrinsic versus intrinsic factors in the evolution of insect sociality. H. E. Evans. bibl BioScience 27:613-17 S '77
Human evolution: hominoids of the miocene. G. B. Kolata. Science 197:244-5+ Jl 15 '77
Impact of evolutionary thought on American culture in the 20th century. H. Cravens. bibl Intellect 106:83-6 Ag '77
Modeling early evolution with clay. Sci N 112:277 O 29 '77
New theory of protein evolution. il Sci N 111:228 Ap 9 '77
New view of evolution; protein structure analysis. il Time 109:47 Ap 4 '77
Plant-animal mutualism: coevolution with dodo leads to near extinction of plant. S. A. Temple. bibl Science 197:885-6 Ag 26 '77
Remarkable replicators; molecular evolution and the law of survival of the stable; excerpt from The selfish gene. R. Dawkins. Natur Hist 86:34+ F '77
Scientists answer the creationists. Sci N 111:85 F 5 '77
Sexual dimorphism and mating systems: how did they evolve? G. B. Kolata. Science 195:382-3 Ja 28 '77
This view of life. S. J. Gould. See issues of Natural history
You—the gene machine. R. Dawkins. il Vogue 167:234-5+ My '77
See also
Biology
Creation
Homology (biology)
Man—Origin and antiquity
Natural selection
Ontogeny
Plants—Evolution
Species
Stars—Evolution
EWING, David W.
Discovering your problem-solving style. il por Psychol Today 11:68-70+ D '77
Employees' rights; excerpt from Freedom inside the organization. il Society 15:104-11 N '77
What business thinks about employee rights. bibl f il Harvard Bus R 55:81-94 S '77
EWING, James Eugene
Church of Compassion: going for broke. R. Chandler. Chr Today 21:42 Je 17 '77 *
EWING, Maria
Maria Ewing: sharing; interview, ed by S. Wadsworth. por Opera N 41:24-5 Mr 5 '77

EXAMINATIONS
See also
Civil service—Examinations
College Entrance Examination Board
Educational tests and measurements
Law schools—Entrance examinations
Physical examinations
EXCAVATING machinery
See also
Bulldozers (machines)
Graders (excavating machinery)
EXCAVATIONS (archeology)
Amateur archaeology: the joy of the dig. E McCoy. il House & Gard 149:50+ Mr '77
Want to go on a dig? il Changing T 31:24 My '77
See also
Carthage, Africa
Earthworks (archeology)
also subhead Antiquities under names of continents, countries, states, etc. e.g. Russia—Antiquities
EXCESS government property. See Surplus government property
EXCHANGE (barter) See Barter
EXCHANGE, Foreign. See Foreign exchange
EXCHANGE National Bank of Chicago. See Chicago—Banks
EXCHANGE rates. See Foreign exchange
EXCHANGES, Commodity. See Commodity exchanges
EXCHANGES, Literary and scientific
Should US scientists trade data with USSR? symposium. il Sci Digest 81:30-7+ Je '77
U.S.-Soviet exchange results; conference at Stanford University. Intellect 105:301 Mr '77
Web of relations: where détente is doing well; assorted joint projects. R. Knight. il U.S. News 82:26 Mr 28 '77
EXCOMMUNICATION (Jewish law)
Why Spinoza was excommunicated. Y. Yovel. Commentary 64:46-52 N '77
EXCURSIONS
Up by seaplane from Lake Union. il Sunset 158:56 F '77
EXCURSIONS, School. See School excursions
EXECUTION Rocks Lighthouse. See Lighthouses
EXECUTIONS and executioners
After Gilmore. L. Denniston. New Repub 176:10-12 Ja 29 '77
After Gilmore, who's next to die? Idyll of Gary and Amber Jim. il pors Time 109:48-9 Ja 31 '77
Death penalty—issue that won't go away. il U.S. News 82:47 Ja 31 '77
Death watch in Salt Lake City; case of G. Gilmore. il por Time 109:51 Ja 24 '77
Gilmore gets his wish. D. A. Williams and others. il pors Newsweek 89:31-2 Ja 31 '77
Gilmore saga. il Newsweek 90:12 S 19 '77
Gilmore's countdown. T. Mathews and P. S. Greenberg. por Newsweek 89:35 Ja 24 '77
Gilmore's victory. E. Shorris. il Harpers 254:16+ Ap '77
Hell's agent; L. Schiller's merchandising of the G. Gilmore execution. R. Friedman. il Esquire 88:75-8+ O '77
Ringmaster at the circus; L. Schiller's selling of the media rights to the G. M. Gilmore execution. D. Gelman and others. il por Newsweek 89:77-8 Ja 31 '77
Speculative spectaculars; question of publicly televised executions. F. Getlein. Commonweal 104:4-5 Ja 7 '77
See also
Capital punishment
EXECUTIVE ability
See also
Leadership
EXECUTIVE advisory bodies
Carter reducing plan adds pounds. R. J. Smith. il Science 198:900 D 2 '77
If they held a meeting there'd be no one to come. B. J. Culliton. Science 198:592 N 11 '77
EXECUTIVE departments (United States) See United States—Executive departments
EXECUTIVE Interchange Program. See United States—President's Commission on Personnel Interchange
EXECUTIVE liability. See Liability (law)
EXECUTIVE Office of the President. See United States—Executive Office of the President
EXECUTIVE power
See also
Judicial review
Presidents—United States—Powers and duties
War and emergency powers
EXECUTIVE public speaking. See Public speaking
EXECUTIVE stock options. See Stock purchase options
EXECUTIVES
Businessmen and terrorism. A. J. Mayer and others. il Newsweek 90:82-4+ N 14 '77
Choosing a second career. il Bus W p 119-21 S 19 '77
Chop the chitchat—save time and money. C. H. Ford. il Nations Bus 65:35-6+ S '77
Controller: inflation gives him more clout with management. il Bus W p84-7+ Ag 15 '77

EXECUTIVES—*Continued*

Executive trends. J. Costello. See issues of Nation's business to December 1977
Faces behind the figures. See issues of Forbes
Forum. See issues of Dun's review
Here come the young turks! chief executive officers. il Forbes 119:93-5 F 15 '77
How much room at the top? J. C. Perham. il Duns R 109:82-5 Mr '77
Lessons of leadership. See issues of Nation's business
Managers with impact: versatile and inconsistent; operating managers; excerpt from Manufacturing in the corporate strategy. W. Skinner and W. E. Sasser. il Harvard Bus R 55:140-8 N '77
Managing your time by managing yourself. C. L. Hamman. il Nations Bus 65:54-6 Ap '77
Money men. See issues of Forbes
Spotlight. See issues of Dun's review
Staying out of trouble. A. J. Mayer. il Newsweek 90:84 N 14 '77
Too smart to be in business? L. Smith. il Duns R 110:100-2+ O '77
Understanding today's young executive; survey of deans at business schools. il Nations Bus 65:90-1+ S '77
U.S. business throws billions into a fight against terrorists. il U.S. News 83:24-6 N 21 '77
What it takes to run a big company. il U.S. News 83:69 D 12 '77

See also

Banks and banking—Directors
Corporations—Directors
Entrepreneurs
Leadership
United States—President's Commission on Personnel Interchange
Women executives

Anecdotes, facetiae, satire, etc.

Lunch of champions. R. Baker. il N Y Times Mag p 14 My 1 '77

Attitudes

Is the ethics of business changing? readers' survey. S. N. Brenner and E. A. Molander; discussion. il Harvard Bus R 55:47-+ Mr '77
Profits before ethics: Harvard business review survey. S. Bush. Psychol Today 11:30 Jl '77
What business thinks about employee rights. D. W. Ewing. bibl f il Harvard Bus R 55:81-94 S '77

Compensation

See Executives—Salaries, pensions, etc.

Dismissal

Bosses on the beach. D. Pauly and E. Sciolino. il Newsweek 90:84-5 D 5 '77
Flourishing new business of recycling executives; out-placement or dehiring firms. H. E. Meyer. il Fortune 95:328-30+ My '77

Education

When business executives go back to school—; Dartmouth's summer institute. il U.S. News 83:61 Ag 22 '77

Health and hygiene

Fighting stress; biofeedback training. L. Smith. il Duns R 109:59-61 Ja '77
Heart disease: new ways to reduce the risk. il Bus W p 135-7+ O 17 '77

Language

English spoken here; the common language of European business and multinationals. J. Ross-Skinner. il Duns R 109:56-7 Mr '77

Promotion

Are R&D organizations obsolete? P. H. Thompson and G. W. Dalton; discussion. Harvard Bus R 55:173+ Ja; 174-5 Mr '77

Psychology

Age of the gamesman; views of M. Maccoby. il Time 109:57-8 F 14 '77
Gamesman; behavioral theories of M. Maccoby. L. Langway. il por Newsweek 89:70 Ja 24 '77
Living well is more than the best revenge; study by G. E. Vaillant. por Forbes 120:62-3 D 1 '77
Managers and leaders: are they different? A. Zaleznik. bibl f Harvard Bus R 55:67-78 My '77; Discussion. 55:148-9 Jl '77
Mobile managers—well paid and discontent. T. J. Johnston. il Harvard Bus R 55:6-7 S '77
Power, dependence, and effective management. J. P. Kotter. bibl f Harvard Bus R 55:125-36 Jl '77; Discussion. 55:74 S '77

Public relations

See Business—Public relations

Recreation

Executive gardener. il Bus W p85-7+ My 2 '77
On your own time. See issues of Fortune

Recruiting

Bright prospects in the executive job market. il Nations Bus 65:30-2+ F '77
Executive placement; work of Paul R. Ray & Co; address, November 16, 1976. P. R. Ray. Vital Speeches 43:204-6 Ja 15 '77

Relocation

Alarming exodus of business talent. Bus W p46 My 23 '77
Job transfers: help for wives. V. E. Towns. House B 119:14+ S '77
Mobile managers—well paid and discontent. T. J. Johnston. il Harvard Bus R 55:6-7 S '77

Retirement

Over 65—and still in charge. il Bus W p 18-19 Ja 9 '78

Salaries, pensions, etc.

Annual survey of executive compensation. il Bus W p48-9+ My 23 '77
Are corporate executives overpaid? J. C. Baker. bibl f Harvard Bus R 55:51-6 Jl '77; Discussion. 55:60+ S '77
Changing compensation package. J. Perham. il Duns R 110:50-2 S '77
Comeback for restricted stock plans. L. J. Brindisi, Jr. il Harvard Bus R 55:14+ S '77
Compensation of directors. M. L. Mace. Harvard Bus R 55:52+ S '77
Controlling the cost of international compensation. M. R. Foote. il Harvard Bus R 55:123-32 N '77
Double standard for women managers' pay. il Bus W p61+ N 28 '77
Men who set your salary; board of directors' compensation committee. J. Perham. il Duns R 109:75-6+ F '77
SEC focuses on executive perks. Bus W p52+ Ap 18 '77
Stock options for outside directors. Harvard Bus R 55:47 Jl '77
Superstars, supermoney. P. Berman and S. Hardesty. il Forbes 119:30-2 Ap 1 '77
This bonus is a real incentive; R. Puga's bonus pay at Suave Shoe Corp. il por Bus W p54+ Mr 14 '77
Tightening squeeze on white-collar pay. il Bus W p82-5+ S 12 '77
Top-echelon pay follows profits up. Bus W p28-9 Ap 11 '77
When the boss gets a raise. J. Lelyveld. N Y Times Mag p47 Jl 24 '77
Who are industry's highest-paid executives? il U.S. News 82:75-7 Je 6 '77
Who gets the most pay; a roster of 767 chief executives. il Forbes 119:244-8+ My 15 '77
Why executives are not overpaid. R. E. Sibson. il Nations Bus 65:51-4 N '77

See also

Executives—Taxation
Expense accounts (business)

Selection and appointment

Board and the new CEO. M. L. Mace. Harvard Bus R 55:16-17+ Mr '77

Supply and demand

Boom in executive jobs; with editorial comment. J. C. Perham. il Duns R 110:3, 80-7+ N '77
Coming glut in executives. T. J. Murray. il Duns R 109:64-5+ My '77

Taxation

Curbing the three-martini lunch: does Carter plan have a chance? il U.S. News 83:87-8 D 5 '77
Halving the expense account. Time 110:69 O 10 '77
Hunting of the perk. D. Pauly and others. Newsweek 90:97 O 10 '77
In defense of the martini; expense account dining. H. Sidey. il Time 110:38 O 24 '77
Morality and the martini lunch. G. F. Will. Newsweek 90:120 O 17 '77
Tax reform remodels the pay package; effect on executive's qualified stock option. il Bus W p48+ F 28 '77
Three-martini tax bill. T. Nicholson and others. il Newsweek 91:48-9 Ja 2 '78

Training

Action learning comes to industry; Great Britain's General Electric Company. N. Foy. bibl f Harvard Bus R 55:158-68 S '77
Big business of teaching managers. il Bus W p 106+ Jl 25 '77
How Ma Bell is training women for management. G. Cravens. il N Y Times Mag p 12-13+ My 29 '77

Transfer

Unshackle your comers; moving middle managers across divisional lines. R. A. Pitts. bibl f Harvard Bus R 55:127-36 My '77

Travel

See Business travel

EXECUTIVES (American) in foreign countries. See Americans in foreign countries

EXECUTIVES as college teachers. See College teachers

EXECUTIVES as jazz musicians. See Jazz musicians

EXECUTIVES as photographers. See Photographers

EXECUTIVES wives
Job transfers: help for wives. V. E. Towns. House B 119:14+ S '77
My wife, the homemaker: still a status symbol. M. Marcus. Psychol Today 11:32 O '77

EXECUTORS and administrators
See also
Probate law and practice

EXEMPTION from taxation. See Taxation, Exemption from

EXERCISE
Aerobics program—try it; with heart rated exercises. Vogue 167:132-3 Ap '77
Alex on exercise. A. Jaskewicz. il Harp Baz 110:129 Mr '77
. . .And four to go. L. T. V. Whedbee. il Redbook 148:102-3 F '77
Anti-tension diet and exercise plan. M. Mercer. McCalls 104:54+ F '77
Are you getting the right kind of exercise? Changing T 32:33-6 Ja '78
Back talk; back exercises. il Mademoiselle 83:68+ My '77
Conditioners. il Seventeen 36:148-9 N '77
Cooper's cohorts run down heart disease; Tyler Cup Invitational and aerobic exercise. P. Rosenfield. il Sat Eve Post 249:18-20 S '77
Coronary curb; study by R. Paffenbarger. Time 110:80 D 12 '77
Dance! the exercises you don't know you're doing. il Mademoiselle 83:174-7 N '77
Dance your way to beauty. M. Lynch. il Ladies Home J 94:100-3 Mr '77
Easy isometrics; excerpt from Exercise in the office. R. R. Spackman, Jr. il Fam Health 9:48-51 My '77
Energize with exercise. L. Beech. Sr Schol 110:40 S 22 '77
Energy blitz; health and exercise programs at the Institute for Environmental Stress and California spas. M. R. C. Berg. il Mademoiselle 83:180-7 Ap '77
Exercise and exercise devices—which ones are really useful? M. B. Howorth. il Consumers Res Mag 60:31-2+ N '77
Exercise and your heart. il Consumer Rep 42:254-8 My '77
Exercise: it ain't watcha do, it's the way that ya do it. B. Maness. il Fam Health 9:34-5 Ap '77
Exercise secrets of a Hollywood body doctor; R. Fletcher. A. Ebert. il por Ladies Home J 94:50+ F '77
Exercises to help you bowl them over. il Fam Health 9:58-9 Mr '77
Exer-sex. B. Prudden. il Ladies Home J 94:42+ Ag '77
Feel fit; excerpt from Manya Kahn body rhythms. M. Kahn. il Ladies Home J 94:82-5 Jl '77
Find your best self by using more sense; excerpt from Secrets of The Golden Door. D. S. Mazzanti. il Fam Health 9:36-9 D '77
Fitness in flight; Lufthansa's program. Time 110:53 Ag 1 '77
5 exercises to keep your back in shape. R. Kuhn. il Ret Liv 17:22 Ja '77
Five-minute cure. M. Mannes. por Am Home 80:26-7 My '77
Formulas for fitness:
  Choosing the right exercise. J. E. Brody. Read Digest 112:121-3 Ja '78
  How aerobics can help your heart—and the way you feel; excerpt from The aerobics way. K. H. Cooper. Read Digest 112:117-21 Ja '78
Get fit, trim, slim—and grin; ideas of K. H. Cooper. J. Alexander. il Sat Eve Post 249:70-1 O '77
Give your back a break. M. Mercer. il McCalls 105:106-7+ Ja '78
Give your legs a lift. C. Seebohm. il House & Gard 149:30+ Mr '77
Handling your anxieties; with exercises. J. Segal and Z. Segal. il Seventeen 36:146-7 Mr '77
How I stay in shape. J. La Lanne. il Sat Eve Post 249:34 Mr '77
How it helps—and hurts. M. Clark and M. Gosnell. il Newsweek 89:82-3 My 23 '77
How to start your personal exercise plan. L. Rothman. il Bet Hom & Gard 55:46+ Ap '77
Inside story; easy stomach exercises. C. Seebohm. il House & Gard 149:38+ My '77
It takes two: the exercises you do together. il Seventeen 36:232-3 Ag '77
Marvelous new route to total body awareness; excerpt from The body has its reasons. T. Berthèrat and C. Bernstein. Mademoiselle 83:165+ My '77
Miss Craig's summer shape-up plan. il McCalls 104:152-3+ My '77
New exercise; dancing. E. Schoen. il House & Gard 149:158-9+ My '77
New exercise splash; bath exercises. P. Markham. il House & Gard 149:28+ Jl '77
Over 60? Exercise! il Sci Digest 81:87 F '77
Ready, set. . .sweat! il Time 109:82-3+ Je 6 '77; Same abr. Read Digest 111:51-2+ O '77
Shaping up. N. Gittelson. bibl il McCalls 105:63-70 O '77
Spring shape-up guide; exercise class. D. Kaye. il N Y Times Mag p44+ Mr 27 '77
Summer shape-up: 5 sure ways to lose weight. Bet Hom & Gard 55:114+ My '77
Taking exercise to heart. C. P. Gilmore. il pors N Y Times Mag p38-42+ Mr 27 '77; Same abr. with title Does exercise really prolong life? Read Digest 111:140-3 Jl '77
Taking the bore out of chores: exercising around the house; 12 ways to shape up doing housework. P. Markham. il House & Gard 149:51 N '77
Three simple stretches that will change your life; excerpt from The power of positive stretching. E. Loewendahl. il Good H 185:16 N '77
What to do about low-back pain. A. Rosenblum. il Good H 185:208 Jl '77
Your trouble-free individual exercise program. N. Cori. il Harp Baz 110:122-3 F '77
See also
Body building
Gymnastics
Health clubs
Jogging
Physical education for the aged
Sports
T'ai chi ch'üan
Walking

Anecdotes, facetiae, satire, etc.
Firmer Erma. E. Bombeck. il Ladies Home J 94:32 Ag '77

EXERCISE clubs. See Health clubs

EXERCISES, Military. See Military maneuvers

EXERCISING equipment
Do those bust developers really work? Good H 185:152+ Ag '77
Exercise devices. il Consumer Rep 42:259-63 My '77
To soften your calisthenics, a pad of towels and foam. il Sunset 159:156 N '77

Anecdotes, facetiae, satire, etc.
They do it all for me. D. Wolters. Progressive 41:32 Mr '77

EXHAUST systems
See also
Automobile engines—Exhaust

EXHAUSTION, Heat. See Heatstroke

EXHIBITION booths
Booth design at Northeast Craft Fair. il Ceram Mo 25:62-3 My '77
Booth design; design of Winter Market booth. J. Yesberger and M. Saffer. il Craft Horiz 37:57 Je '77

EXHIBITIONS
Conversation with Charles Eames; ed by O. Gingerich. C. Eames. Am Scholar 46:326-37 Summ '77
Doin' the home shows. A. Lees. il Pop Sci 210:152+ Je '77
March look at the new hardware; First New Earth Exposition. il Sunset 158:33 Mr '77
Orchid diplomacy; trip to Canton Fair in attempt to import orchids to U.S. W. K. Glikbarg. Horticulture 55:8-13 My '77
Trade shows leave retailers wondering; Dallas home furnishings mart and the Chicago housewares exposition. il Bus W p55 Jl 25 '77
See also
Book exhibits
Library exhibits
School exhibitions
also subhead Exhibitions under various subjects, e.g. Art—Exhibitions

Anecdotes, facetiae, satire, etc.
Mementos and memories of the 1936 Cairo World's fair. B. McCall. il Esquire 88:95-100 Jl '77

EXHIBITIONS, Traveling
See also
School exhibitions, Traveling

EXHIBITIONS Committee, International. See American Federation of Arts—International Exhibitions Committee

EXILES
Exile for heretics; East Germany. il Time 110:48 O 3 '77
Exiles' silent world, Russian writers. C. D. May. pors Newsweek 89:51 Ap 4 '77
On political exile. C. Belfrage. Progressive 41:20-1 Ag '77

EXILES; drama. See Joyce, J.

EX-IM Bank. See Export-Import Bank of the United States of America

EX-NUNS, priests, etc.
Wayward bus; J. E. Groppi. E. Keerdoja and S. Monroe. il por Newsweek 90:16+ O 31 '77

EXOBIOLOGY. See Life on other planets
EXOCYTOSIS. See Cells—Physiology
EXORCISM
Satan: alive and well? practice of exorcism. J. Benjamin. il Sat Eve Post 249:56-7 Ap '77
Tovil: exorcism by white magic; ceremony of Sri Lanka's Buddhists. M. M. Ames. il Natur Hist 87:42-9 bibl(p 108) Ja '78
EXPANDERS, Audio. See Sound—Apparatus
EXPANDING universe. See Cosmology
EXPANSION, House. See Houses, Remodeled
EXPECTATION of life. See Longevity
EXPEDITIONS, Scientific. See Scientific expeditions
EXPENSE accounts (business)
Curbing the three-martini lunch: does Carter plan have a chance? il U.S. News 83:87-8 D 5 '77
Halving the expense account. Time 110:69 O 10 '77
Hunting of the perk. D. Pauly and others. Newsweek 90:97 O 10 '77
In defense of the martini. H. Sidey. il Time 110:38 O 24 '77
Morality and the martini lunch. G. F. Will. Newsweek 90:120 O 17 '77
Three-martini tax bill. T. Nicholson and others. il Newsweek 91:48-9 Ja 2 '78
EXPERIENCE (religion)
Of tidy doctrine and truncated experience; relationalist and charismatic views of evangelical experimental theology. R. K. Johnston. il Chr Today 21:10-14 F 18 '77
EXPERIMENTAL Aircraft Association
Big fly-in at Oshkosh. il Time 110:60-1 Ag 15 '77
Homebuilder heaven. P. Garrison. il Flying 101:72-4+ N '77
That thing flies? Oshkosh convention. S. C. Cowley and P. E. Simons. il Newsweek 90:23-4 Ag 15 '77
EXPERIMENTAL airplanes. See Airplanes, Experimental
EXPERIMENTAL automobiles. See Automobiles, Experimental
EXPERIMENTAL education. See Education—Experimental methods
EXPERIMENTAL farms, Organic. See Farms, Organic
EXPERIMENTAL motion pictures. See Motion pictures, Experimental
EXPERIMENTAL music. See Music, Experimental
EXPERIMENTAL Negotiating Agreement. See Collective bargaining—Steel industry
EXPERIMENTAL safety vehicles. See Automobiles, Experimental
EXPERIMENTAL schools. See Schools, Experimental
EXPERIMENTAL theater. See Theater, Experimental
EXPERIMENTATION on animals. See Animal experimentation
EXPERIMENTATION on man. See Medical research—Experimentation on man
EXPERTISING in art. See Art—Expertising
EXPERTS. See Specialists
EXPLORATION
See also
Antarctic exploration
Honduras—Exploring expeditions
EXPLORERS
Bound for glory; T. Heyerdahl, R. E. Byrd and R. C. Andrews. il Sat Eve Post 249:18-19 Jl '77
EXPLORERS, Polynesian
Voyaging canoes and the settlement of Polynesia. B. R. Finney. bibl il maps Science 196:1277-85 Je 17 '77
EXPLOSIONS
Blast no one can explain; 1908 explosion over Siberia. D. Valentry. Mech Illus 73:94 Mr '77
Pulsed power from explosions. D. E. Thomsen. il Sci N 112:281+ O 29 '77
See also
Coal mines and mining—Accidents and explosions
EXPLOSIVES
Tagged explosives—reading the code after the blast. il Chemistry 50:23-4 S '77
See also
Torpedoes
EXPORT controls, American. See United States—Commercial policy
EXPORT credit
Exim aircraft credits to remain at 30%. il Aviation W 106:115-16 Je 6 '77
EXPORT-Import Bank of the United States of America
Exim aircraft credits to remain at 30%. il Aviation W 106:115-16 Je 6 '77
EXPORT-import trade
Abroad, new name-calling in the trade battle. U.S. News 82:67 F 14 '77
America's improving competitiveness promotes export growth. W. N. Walker. M Labor R 100:47-8 Mr '77
How smaller firms are profiting from sales abroad. il Nations Bus 65:67-70+ D '77
See also
Aerospace industries—Export-import trade
Air freight service—Export-import trade
Airplane industry—Export-import trade
Atomic power industry—Export-import trade
Automobile equipment industry—Export-import trade
Automobiles—Export-import trade
Avionics industry—Export-import trade
Birds—Export-import trade
Books—Export-import trade
Cattle industry—Export-import trade
Chromium—Export-import trade
Coffee industry—Export-import trade
Computer industry—Export-import trade
Corn—Export-import trade
Dairying—Export-import trade
Dumping (commercial policy)
Electronic industries—Export-import trade
Gas industry—Export-import trade
Grain trade
Livestock industry—Export-import trade
Meat industry—Export-import trade
Munitions—Export-import trade
Petroleum equipment industry—Export-import trade
Petroleum industry—Export-import trade
Plants—Export-import trade
Produce trade
Reptiles—Export-import trade
Shoe industry—Export-import trade
Soybeans—Export-import trade
Steel industry—Export-import trade
Sugar industry—Export-import trade
Television apparatus industry—Export-import trade
Textile industry—Export-import trade
Tropical fishes—Export-import trade
Wildlife—Export-import trade
also subhead Commerce under names of countries, e.g. Israel—Commerce

Laws and regulations

See Foreign trade regulation
EXPOSURE (photography) See Photography—Exposure
EXPOSURE meters
David Vestal's photo workbook: light meters & metering. D. Vestal. Pop Phot 81:69-70 Ag '77
Exposure meters. E. Farber. il Pop Phot 81:125+ Jl '77
Hand-held meters hold on. D. L. Miller. il Mod Phot 41:94-5 Ap '77
View from Kramer; Spectra Combi II. A. Kramer. il Mod Phot 41:64-5+ S '77
EX-PRESIDENTS of the United States. See Presidents—United States
EXPRESS highways
Highways: which way to the future? W. M. Cox. il por Am City & County 92:91-2 O '77
Interstate numbers game. il Mech Illus 73:21 Ap '77
Sorry, can't make it; interstate highway system. J. Burnham. Nat R 29:377+ Ap 1 '77

Environmental aspects

Up a Notch; routing Interstate Highway 93 through Franconia Notch State Park. il Time 110:51 D 26 '77

Federal aid

Diverting the Highway Fund. M. Gerrard. Environment 19:4-5 Je '77
Road funds under transit attack. Am City & County 92:29 Jl '77
Road groups oppose trust fund bill. Am City & County 92:24 O '77

Finance

Goodbye yellow brick road; interstate system. F. M. H. Gregory. il Car & Dr 23:83-4+ Jl '77

Safety devices and measures

See Roads—Safety devices and measures

Canada

North to adventure—following the Yellowhead Highway through British Columbia. il map Sunset 159:40+ Jl '77

Maryland

Asbestos hazard on U.S. roads? use of asbestos-carrying crushed stone in Montgomery County. il Am City & County 92:36 Ag '77

New Hampshire

Up a Notch; routing Interstate Highway 93 through Franconia Notch State Park. il Time 110:51 D 26 '77

EXPRESS highways—*Continued*

New York (state)

New York's debate over building Westway. il Bus W p28+ Ja 24 '77

Notes and comment; New York City public hearings on Westway. il New Yorker 53:27-8 Je 6 '77

Southern States

Along the Natchez Trace. E. Cheatham and P. Cheatham. il Travel 148:52-9+ O '77

Texas

Cold recycling of asphalt pavement meets conservation ethic. W. S. Foster. Am City & County 92:36 N '77

Virginia

Relieve summertime pavement blowups; pressure relief joints for concrete highways. K. H. McGhee. il Am City & County 92:38-9 Jl '77

Western States

Away from Interstate 5; attractions in California, Oregon and Washington. il maps Sunset 158:80-9 Je '77

Wisconsin

Is pavement reinforcing worth its cost? concrete pavements. R. C. Blum and C. E. Solberg. il Am City & County 92:59-61 D '77

EXPRESSION

See also

Communication, Nonverbal

Elocution

EXPRESSION, Facial. See Facial expression

EXPRESSION, Genetic. See Genetic regulation

EXPROPRIATION. See Eminent domain (international law)

EXPULSION and suspension, Student. See Student suspension and expulsion

EXTENSION education

See also

Telephone in education

University extension

EXTERIOR mural painting and decoration. See Mural painting and decoration, Exterior

EXTERMINATION of termites. See Termite control

EXTERMINATORS, Pest. See Pest control operators

EXTRACTORS. See Tools

EXTRADITION

L'affaire Daoud: too hot to handle. il por Time 109:29-31 Ja 24 '77

Arch-terrorist who went scot-free; Abu Daoud. D. Reed. Read Digest 111:114-18 S '77

Dennis Banks's extradition fight; South Dakota vs California Uniform Criminal Extradition Act. H. Rubin. il Chr Cent 94:691-2 Ag 3 '77

Legal history of an Indian: South Dakota vs. Dennis Banks. H. Rubin. por Nation 225:113-15 Ag 6 '77

Terrorist cross fire; releasing Abu Daoud. A. Deming and others. il por Newsweek 89:43+ Ja 24 '77

EXTRA-MARITAL relationships. See Adultery

EXTRAS (opera) See Opera—Production and direction

EXTRASENSORY perception

Test your ESP. P. Lutus. il Pop Electr 11:46 Je '77

What do we really know about psychic phenomena? L. E. Bartlett. Read Digest 111:82-7 Ag '77

When children have psychic powers; excerpt from Psychic children. S. H. Young. il McCalls 104:204-5+ Ap '77

Win, place and glow; L. Harribance's use of ESP in betting. R. Cantwell. il Sports Illus 47:32-4+ Ag 29 '77

EXTRATERRESTRIAL life. See Life on other planets

EXTREMADURA, Spain. See Estremadura, Spain

EXXON Corporation

Does Exxon have a future? J. Flanigan. il por Forbes 120:37-41 Ag 15 '77

Excerpt from testimony on retirement age policy, March 16, 1977. H. J. Lartigue, Jr. Cong Digest 56:275+ N '77

First and forgotten pipeline; the War Department's Canol project and Imperial Oil Ltd. P. L. Fradkin. il pors map Audubon 79:58-79 N '77

New toughness in corporate giving. J. Perham. il Duns R 109:68-70 Mr '77

What makes Exxon give? R. Gelatt. il Sat R 4:34 Je 25 '77

EXXON Enterprises, Inc.

Exxon has its eye on more than oil. B. Uttal. Fortune 95:166-8 Ap '77

EYE

See also

Crystalline lens

Flicker phenomena

Iris (eye)

Retina

Vision

Visual purple

Accommodation and refraction

How to beat the odds when you drive at night. B. Hampton. il Pop Mech 147:75-7+ Mr '77

Lead-sabotaged vision: low-level link. Sci N 111:292 My 7 '77

Night glasses for safer highway driving. Sci N 112:85 Ag 6 '77

Nightime driving accidents and selective visual degradation; letter. H. W. Leibowitz and D. A. Owens. bibl Science 197:422-3 Jl 29 '77

Scotopic vision deficits in young monkeys exposed to lead. P. M. Bushnell and others. bibl il Science 196:333-5 Ap 15 '77

Care and hygiene

All the news in sight; symposium. Harp Baz 110:112-17+ Ag '77

Protecting your eyesight: an expert's advice; interview. B. R. Straatsma. il por U.S. News 82:79-81 Ap 25 '77; Same abr. with title What you should know about eye care. Read Digest 111:147-50 Ag '77

Diseases and defects

Cyclic GMP accumulation causes degeneration of photoreceptor cells: simulation of an inherited disease; retinitis pigmentosa. R. N. Lolley and others. bibl il Science 196:664-6 My 6 '77

Eye and its troubles. il Consumer Rep 42:642-6 N '77

Eye diseases: what can be done about them? P. Lehmann. Harp Baz 110:116+ Ag '77

How eyes change with age. Consumers Res Mag 60:31 S '77

Lesson of retrolental fibroplasia. W. A. Silverman. il Sci Am 236:100-7 bibl(p 142) Je '77

Little known diseases; retinitis pigmentosa. A. Belson. Fam Health 9:42-4+ My '77

Phototoxic keratoconjunctivitis from coal-tar pitch volatiles. E. A. Emmett and others. bibl il Science 198:841-2 N 25 '77

Protecting your eyesight: an expert's advice; interview. B. R. Straatsma. il por U.S. News 82:79-81 Ap 25 '77

See also

Blindness

Cataracts (eye defect)

Glaucoma

Myopia

Strabismus

Examination

When should you have your eyes examined? M. P. Scott and T. Walsh. il Bet Hom & Gard 55:57-8 Jl '77

Movements

Eye contact and face scanning in early infancy. M. M. Haith and others. bibl il Science 198:853-5 N 25 '77

Eyes have it; eye roll and susceptibility to hypnotism. Time 110:53 D 19 '77

Look into my eyes: an infant's view. il Sci N 112:373 D 3 '77

Visual input to the visuomotor mechanisms of the monkey's parietal lobe. T. C. T. Yin and V. B. Mountcastle. bibl il Science 197:1381-3 S 30 '77

Protection

Essential workshop insurance, eye/face protectors. M. Philips. il Pop Sci 210:136 My '77

See also

Goggles

Surgery

Corneal endothelium damage with intraocular lenses: contact adhesion between surgical materials and tissue. H. E. Kaufman and others. bibl il Science 198:525-7 N 4 '77

Eye surgery: new facts everyone should know. M. P. Scott. il Bet Hom & Gard 55:52+ Mr '77

Facing surgery for new sight, new life. B. B. Carter. il por Ret Liv 16:27-8+ D '76

Spectacle within the eye; lens implants. il Time 110:68+ O 17 '77

Wounds and injuries

Eye-safety guide. L. Wingerson. Harp Baz 110:113+ Ag '77

EYE (amphibia)

Amacrine cells in necturus retina: evidence for independent γ-aminobutyric acid- and glycine-releasing neurons. R. F. Miller and others. bibl il Science 198:748-50 N 18 '77

EYE (animals)

Eyes of the wild. A. Odum. il Int Wildlife 7:22-3 N '77

See also

Vision (animals)

EYE (crustaceans)

Efferent optic nerve fibers mediate circadian rhythms in the limulus eye. R. B. Barlow, Jr and others. bibl il Science 197:86-9 Jl 1 '77

EYE (fishes)
Interactions between rod and cone systems in the goldfish retina. J. M. Shefner and M. W. Levine. bibl il Science 198:750-3 N 18 '77
Neuronal architecture of on and off pathways to ganglion cells in carp retina. E. V. Famiglietti, Jr and others. bibl il Science 198:1267-9 D 23 '77
Structural basis for on- and off-center responses in retinal bipolar cells. W. K. Stell and others. bibl il Science 198:1269-71 D 23 '77
EYE (insects)
Compound eye of insects. G. A. Horridge. il Sci Am 237:108-20 bibl(p 154) Jl '77
See also
Vision (insects)
EYE (reptiles)
Ionochromic behavior of Gecko visual pigments. F. Crescitelli. bibl il Science 195:187-8 Ja 14 '77
EYE, Evil. See Evil eye
EYE, Instruments and apparatus for
Eye opener; oculometers. P. Gwynne and C. Panati. il Newsweek 89:74 Je 6 '77
EYE dominance. See Dominance, Ocular
EYE make-up. See Make-up
EYE movements. See Eye—Movements
EYE roll. See Eye—Movements
EYEGLASS industry. See Optical industry
EYEGLASSES
Glamorous new looks in glasses. il Good H 184:92+ Je '77
Good look at good looks and glasses. il Redbook 148:116-17+ Mr '77
Growing up bespectacled. A. Bayer. Seventeen 36:138-9 S '77
Professionals and their product. il Consumer Rep 42:646-9 N '77
Your frame and lens shapes; Your frame and make-up colors. il Harp Baz 110:114 Ag '77
See also
Contact lenses
Sun glasses

Purchasing

Guide to buying eyeglasses. il Bet Hom & Gard 55:236+ S '77
EYES. See Eye
EYEWITNESSES. See Witnesses
EYTAN, Walter
Television. P. Sourian. Nation 224:603-4 My 14 '77 *
EZRA, Derek
Britain's new jackpot. il pors Forbes 119:118 Mr 15 '77 *

F

F-14 (airplane) See Airplanes, Military
F-16 (airplane) See Airplanes, Military
F-18 (airplane) See Airplanes, Military—United States
FAA. See United States—Federal Aviation Administration
FAMOUS (French-American Mid-ocean Undersea Survey) See Oceanographic research
FAO. See Food and Agriculture Organization of the United Nations
FBI. See United States—Federal Bureau of Investigation
FBI agents. See United States—Federal Bureau of Investigation
FBI informers. See Informers
FCC. See United States—Federal Communications Commission
FCCSET. See United States—Federal Coordinating Council of Science, Engineering and Technology
FDA. See United States—Food and Drug Administration
FDIC. See Federal Deposit Insurance Corporation
FHA. See United States—Agriculture, Department of—Farmers Home Administration; United States—Federal Housing Administration
FHLBB. See United States—Federal Home Loan Bank Board
FIAC (Foire Internationale d'Art Contemporain) See Art, Modern—Exhibitions
FIC. See United States—Federal Information Center
FLIR (foreward-looking infrared) sensors. See Detectors, Infrared
FM antennas. See Radio antennas
FM receivers. See Radio receivers
FM tuners. See Radio receivers—Tuning
FMC Corporation
Drinking water: getting rid of the carbon tetrachloride. J. L. Marx. Science 196:632-6 My 6 '77
Myopia and multinationals; address, February 7, 1977. R. H. Malott. Vital Speeches 43:363-6 Ap 1 '77
FPC. See United States—Federal Power Commission
FTC. See United States—Federal Trade Commission
FTF. See Freedom of Thought Foundation
F. W. Woolworth Company. See Woolworth, F. W., Company
FWS. See United States—Fish and Wildlife Service
FABE, Maxene
How to make love not war. Mademoiselle 83:119+ D '77
FABLES
See also
Parables

Anecdotes, facetiae, satire, etc.

Fabulas rasas; tr by A. Reid. il New Repub 177:28-9 D 24 '77
FABRIC collage. See Collage
FABRIC crafts. See Textile crafts
FABRIC softeners. See Softening agents
FABRIC wall coverings. See Wall coverings
FABRICS. See Textile fabrics
FABRIQUE Nationale Herstal SA-Browning (firm) merger. See Firearms industry—Acquisitions and mergers
FACE
On creating a new face through plastic surgery. M. G. Haddad. il Mademoiselle 83:53+ O '77
See also
Beauty, Personal
Facial expression
FACE in art. See Head in art
FACES, Recognition of. See Recognition (psychology)
FACIAL expression
Reflections on the face in film. L. Shaffer. il Film Q 31:2-8 Wint '77
FACIAL hair, Removal of. See Hair, Removal of
FACIAL pain
Facial pain; therapy for women practiced by Marbach. M. Covell. Vogue 67:34+ Je '77
FACIALS. See Skin—Care and hygiene
FACSIMILES of rare books. See Book rarities—Facsimiles
FACTOR VIII. See Blood—Coagulation
FACTORIES
See also
Asphalt plants
Breweries
Chemical plants
Factory management
Paper mills
Potteries

Environmental aspects

See also
Petroleum refineries—Environmental aspects
Steel works—Environmental aspects
FACTORY management
Big man at Ford; Chicago plant manager L. M. Callaway, Jr. il pors Ebony 32:62-4+ Mr '77
Gone-fishing syndrome; earned time concept of Harman International industries. J. Lelyveld. N Y Times Mag p62 My 29 '77
How Volvo adapts work to people; excerpt from People at work. P. G. Gyllenhammar. il Harvard Bus R 55:102-13 Jl '77
Volvo way: efficiency without pain; views of Pehr Gyllenhammar. J. Gaylin. Psychol Today 11:45 O '77
FACTORY produced houses. See Houses, Prefabricated
FACTORY stores. See Stores
FACTORY workers. See Labor and laboring classes
FACULTY, College. See College teachers
FACULTY unions. See Teachers unions
FADIMAN, Anne, and Sedgwick, John
Writing on the walls of ivy. il Esquire 88:113-14 S '77
FAEROE Islands
Edge of Europe. J. F. West. il Natur Hist 86:40-7 bibl(p 110) D '77
FAGEN, Richard Rees
Realities of U.S.-Mexican relations. For Affairs 55:685-700 Jl '77
FAGER, Charles E.
Dan Berrigan in Santa Cruz. Chr Cent 94:654-7 Jl 20 '77
Small is beautiful, and so is Rome. Chr Cent 94:325-8 Ap 6 '77
FAGIN, Richard
(tr) See Montañés, R. Maritime history of Cuba
FAHD, Prince of Saudi Arabia
Crown Prince Fahd of Saudi Arabia visits Washington; exchange of toasts, May 24, 1977. Dept State Bull 76:671-2 Je 27 '77
Fahd: it's up to Israel; excerpts from interview, ed by A. De Borchgrave. pors Newsweek 89:54 Je 6 '77
about
Arab brings a warning for Carter. por U.S. News 82:28 My 30 '77 *

FAHD, Prince of Saudi Arabia—*Continued*

Visit to the United States, 1977

Crown Prince Fahd of Saudi Arabia visits Washington; exchange of toasts, with remarks, May 24-25, 1977. Fahd; J. Carter. Dept State Bull 76:670-4 Je 27 '77
Keeping up the pressure. A. Deming and others. il pors Newsweek 89:14-15 Je 6 '77

FAHEY, John L.
Cancer and the immune response. bibl il por Chemistry 50:6-10 Je '77

FAHEY, P. F. and others
Lateral diffusion in planar lipid bilayers. bibl il Science 195:305-6 Ja 21 '77

FAHLSTROM, Oyvind
Obituary
Art in Am por 65:19+ Mr '77. S. Gablik

FAHMY, Ismail
Bazaar bargaining in Washington. il pors Time 110:31-2+ O 3 '77 *
Two men who hold keys to Mideast peace talks. pors U.S. News 83:36 O 24 '77 *

FAILEY, Dean F.
Seventeenth- and eighteenth-century Long Island furniture. il Antiques 112:732-41 O '77

FAILING, Patricia
How the seed money in Portland has grown. il Art N 76:58-61 My '77
Maryhill investigation. Art N 76:128-30+ S '77
Maryhill Museum: a case history of cultural abuse. il Art N 76:83-90 Mr '77
Picasso's cries of children . . . cries of stones. bibl il Art N 76:55-8+ S '77
Portland's starving grande dame. il Art N 76:85-8 O '77

FAILURE (psychology)
Turning failure into success. F. Maynard. Read Digest 111:123-6 D '77

FAILURE Analysis Associates. See Mechanical engineers

FAILURE of solids. See Fracture of solids

FAILURES in business. See Business failures

FAIN, Elaine
Selection and soapboxes: an ideological primer. Wilson Lib Bull 52:136-9 O '77

FAIR Debt Collection Practices Act. See Collecting of accounts

FAIR labor standards. See Labor standards

FAIR Labor Standards Act. See Labor laws and legislation—United States

FAIRCHILD Camera and Instrument Corporation
Fairchild's problems: more than watches. il Bus W p 116+ Ag 15 '77

FAIRFAX County, Va.

Education

See Education—Virginia

Water supply

See Water supply—Virginia

FAIRFAX County, Va, Public Library. See Libraries—Virginia

FAIRFIELD County, Conn.
New York's loss is Fairfield County's gain. il Bus W p 121-2 Ap 25 '77

FAIRGROUND organ. See Musical instruments, Mechanical

FAIRLIE, Henry
Politician's art. Harpers 225:33-6+ D '77
Seven deadly sins today; excerpt. New Repub 177:17-20 S 10; 29-31 S 17; 18-21 S 24; 23-5 O 1; 18-21 O 8; 16-19 O 22; 20-3 O 29; 19-23 N 12 '77

about

Kennan, elites and consensus. Nation 226:4-5 Ja 7 '78 *

FAIRNESS. See Justice

FAIRS
Lets go to the fair; summer calendar of state and county fairs. il Travel 147:10 Je '77
Special report: a children's learning fair; project of Jackson County, Ore, Public Library. V. C. Munn. il Wilson Lib Bull 52:122-3 O '77
State fairs: bigger and brassier than ever. W. L. MacDougall. il U.S. News 83:43-5 S 5 '77
See also
Bazaars, Charitable
Book fairs
Exhibitions
Science fairs

FAIRY tales
Fairy tales for a liberated age. A. Lurie. il Horizon 19:80-5 Jl '77
Modern magic. C. Forbes. Chr Today 21:30 F 4 '77
Vladimir Propp in Hollywood; analysis of plots according to fairy tale models. J. L. Fell. bibl il Film Q 30:19-28 Spr '77

al-FAISAL, Saud, Prince of Saudi Arabia. See Saud al Faisal

FAITH
God is great—pass it on. G. McCauley. America 136:452-3 My 14 '77
Journey to faith. J. Bishop. Read Digest 111:163-4+ Ag '77
Keeping track. G. McCauley. America 136:89 Ja 29 '77
No cowardly spirit. G. McCauley. America 137: inside backcover S 24 '77
See also
Creeds
Trust in God

FAITH and Order, World Conference on. See World Conference on Faith and Order

FAITH cure
Jimmy Carter's sister: how faith can heal; interview, ed by J. West. R. C. Stapleton. por McCalls 104:32+ Ap '77
Miraculous truth can stand a test. Chr Today 21:30 Mr 4 '77
Walking people out of their past; interview. R. C. Stapleton. pors Chr Today 22:10-14 N 4 '77
See also
Mental healing

FAITH healing. See Faith cure

FAKERS. See Quacks and quackery

FALCO, K. Mathea
Narcotics control program in Bolivia; statement, October 14, 1977. Dept State Bull 77:826-7 D 5 '77

FALCO, Louis, Dance Company. See Dance companies

FALCON Jet Corporation
Facilities expansion under way. Aviation W 107:58 Ag 29 '77

FALCON Seaboard Inc. See Holding companies

FALCONS
Stereopsis in the falcon. R. Fox and others. bibl il Science 197:79-81 Jl 1 '77
Super summer for falcons; peregrine falcons. R. Sayre. Audubon 79:141-2 N '77
There came a cry of joy; capture of a sparrow hawk; excerpt from The immense journey. L. Eiseley. il Read Digest 110:97-9 Mr '77

FALICOV, L. M. See Cohen, M. L. jt auth

FALK, Carol H.
Supreme Court and civil rights. Current 191:13-16 Mr '77

FALK, John H.
Frenetic life forms that flourish in suburban lawns. il Smithsonian 8:90-6 bibl(p 147) Ap '77
Roots: the saga of the American house plant. il Horticulture 55:14-17 N '77

FALK, Richard A.
Mobilizing social science. bibl Society 14:23-4 My '77

FALKENSTEIN, Lynda C.
Action learning: a model for in-service teacher education. Clearing H 50:188-91 Ja '77

FALKLAND Islands
Scotia Sea: waterway of the future. J. F. Lohr and M. Castleman. il Oceans 10:36-41 My '77

FALL. See Autumn

FALL of man
The fall: two perspectives. C. S. Lewis and H. Thielicke. il Chr Today 21:10-15 Mr 4 '77

FALL of the House of Usher; opera. See Debussy, C.

FALLACIES (logic)
Valid and fallacious reasoning: some shades of gray. H. C. Jent. Intellect 106:62-6 Ag '77

FALLOUT, Radioactive. See Radioactive fallout

FALLOUT shelters. See Atomic bomb shelters

FALSE imprisonment
Sawyer brothers—their only crime was being poor; erroneous sentence for kidnapping. S. Pearlman. pors Good H 185:82+ Ag '77

FALSE personation
Phony photographer; impersonation of R. Avedon. R. Boeth and others. il por Newsweek 90:43 S 19 '77
You ought to be in pictures; rapist-con man O. E. Kendall's use of psychology in impersonation of R. Avedon. R. Rosenblatt. New Repub 177:45-6 O 1 '77

FALSEY, John
Bachelors; story. New Yorker 53:24-6 Ja 9 '78

FALSTAFF; opera. See Verdi, G.

FALTER, Mary Elizabeth
Auto suggestions. House & Gard 149:54+ My '77

FALTERMAYER, Edmund K.
How to stop worrying about natural gas. il map Fortune 96:156-9+ Ag '77
Man who keeps those Maytag repairmen lonely. il pors Fortune 96:192-5+ N '77

FAME
Notes on fame. J. Lahr. Harpers 256:77-80 Ja '78
See also
Celebrities

FAMIGLIETTI, Edward V. Jr, and others
Neuronal architecture of on and off pathways to ganglion cells in carp retina. bibl il Science 198:1267-9 D 23 '77

FAMILIES Anonymous (organization)
Families anonymous: help for distressed parents. M. Brenton. Good H 184:94+ My '77
Tough love: new way to help teens in trouble. N. C. Baker. il Parents Mag 52:43+ Jl '77

FAMILY
All our children; report of the Carnegie Council on Children. Time 110:118 S 19 '77
American family. J. A. Michener. il Ladies Home J 94:87+ D '77
American family in decline. U. Bronfenbrenner. Current 189:39-47 Ja '77
American family in trouble; symposium. il Psychol Today 10:39-43+ My '77
American family; it ain't what it used to be. R. T. Williams. il MH 60:24-7 Wint '77
Baby talk; E. Whelan's counseling service. B. Carter. il por Newsweek 90:73 Ag 8 '77
Can Carter revitalize the American family? G. E. Jones. il U.S. News 82:35 F 28 '77
Can the American family survive? M. Mead. il Redbook 148:91+ F '77
Disturbing changes in the American family. U. Bronfenbrenner. Educ Digest 42:22-5 F '77
Do I want a baby? discussion; comp by C. Dreifus. il McCalls 105:203+ N '77
Family ecology; studies by J. F. Kett and the Carnegie Council on Children. J. W. Donohue. America 137:456-9 D 24 '77
Family impact on a changing America; interviews, ed by E. Stone and others. Parents Mag 52:54-7+ O '77
Family: is it obsolete? A. Etzioni. Current 195:3-12 S '77
Family: it is changing, not breaking up; study by the Carnegie Council on Children. J. Gaylin. Psychol Today 11:36+ O '77
Family: new breed v. the old; a study based on Yankelovich poll. Time 109:76 My 2 '77
Family under fire; address, March 23, 1977. M. D'Innocenzo. Vital Speeches 43:431-5 My 1 '77
How the government affects family life. J. Chan. McCalls 104:63-4 My '77
Let's get rid of families! C. S. Bell. por Newsweek 89:19 My 9 '77
New approaches to statistics on the family. J. L. Norwood. bibl il M Labor R 100:31-4 Jl '77
Nobody's special when they're poor. T. J. Cottle. Yale R 66:388-98 Mr '77
Problems of raising children in a changing society; Yankelovich study. il Intellect 106:177-9 N '77
Remarriage: survival manual; excerpt from Rewedded bliss: love, alimony, incest, ex-spouses, and other domestic blessings. D. S. Mayleas. Vogue 167:64+ N '77
Science and the future of the family. A. Etzioni. Science 196:487 Ap 29 '77
Tomorrow's family. R. S. Pickett. bibl f Intellect 105:330-2 Ap '77
U.S. children give families high marks. Sci N 111:214 Ap 2 '77
Viewing the family from the Oval Office. W. G. Pippert. Chr Today 21:60-1 S 9 '77
What's happening to the American family? questionnaire. il Bet Hom & Gard 55:125-8 S; 119-22 O '77
See also
Birth order
Childlessness
Children
Divorce
Eugenics
Family life
Fathers
Foster home care
Grandparents
Home
Home education
Husbands
Jewish families
Marriage
Mothers
National Organization for Non-parents
Parents
Single parent families
FAMILY, Size of
Why have more than one? A. Roiphe. N Y Times Mag p49-50+ Je 5 '77
See also
Childlessness
FAMILY agencies. See Social agencies
FAMILY budget. See Budget, Household
FAMILY businesses. See Family corporations
FAMILY care for the mentally ill. See Mentally ill—Home care
FAMILY cookbooks. See Cookbooks
FAMILY corporations
Chips off the executive block; being the boss's son. R. Levy. il Duns R 110:38-40 Ag '77
FAMILY counseling. See Counseling
FAMILY Court, New York City. See New York (city)—Courts
FAMILY doctors. See Physicians
FAMILY finance. See Finance, Personal
FAMILY health (periodical)
As we see it. H. Steirman. See issues of Family health incorporating Today's health
FAMILY history. See Genealogy
FAMILY income. See Income

FAMILY life
American family; Duffy family of Arkansas. J. P. Blank. il Read Digest 111:107-12 Jl '77
Bitterness tinged with hope; the stories of four families. il U.S. News 82:52-5 My 2 '77
Equinox. M. E. Marty. Chr Cent 94:967 O 19 '77
Focus on the family. G. Baisinger. por Parents Mag 52:12 S '77
How today's couples are making it as parents. C. Safran. il Redbook 148:108-9+ Mr '77
I am the mother of eight, a housewife, a feminist—and happy: Jane Broderick's story; interview, ed by J. Lazarre. J. Broderick. il por Ms 5:51-5+ My '77
Meet superstar O. J. Simpson: home is always where the heart is. P. Baum. il por Parents Mag 52:42-3+ F '77
New-breed parents have doubts; Yankelovich study. J. Gaylin. Psychol Today 11:21-2 Jl '77
New goals for young families; special section. il Parents Mag 52:29-33+ D '77
Parents and children speak out on family life. il Good H 185:213 S '77
Plug-in drug; influence on family life; excerpt. M. Winn. Sat Eve Post 249:40-1+ N '77
You and your family; questions and answers. L. Salk. See issues of McCall's
See also
Aged—Family relationships
Marriage counseling
Parent-child relationship

Anecdotes, facetiae, satire, etc.

Man next door. B. Hillis. See issues of Better homes & Gardens

Caricatures and cartoons

It's all in the family (cont) S. Berenstain and J. Berenstain. il Good H 184:118-19 Mr; 124-5 Je; 185:114-15 Ag; 168+ S; 160-1 D '77
FAMILY life, Education for
Marry-go-round; California YWCA's Responsibility, Experience and Alternatives for Life program for high school students. L. Katz. Seventeen 36:55 Je '77
School as a resource for families. M. Hover. Clearing H 50:415-16 My '77
Teaching about divorce. E. Bledsoe. Todays Educ 66:31 Ja '77
FAMILY medicine
Family medicine program and Duke aging center cooperate in venture. Aging 268:20 F '77
FAMILY names. See Names, Personal
FAMILY planning. See Birth control
FAMILY psychotherapy
You are cordially invited to help save a life; network intervention. J. Gaylin. il Psychol Today 10:108+ Mr '77
FAMILY quarrels. See Quarrels
FAMILY reunions
How to plan an old-fashioned family reunion. il Bet Hom & Gard 55:56+ N '77
Why not plan a vacation reunion? M. L. Ludeman. il Farm J 101:24A-24C Je '77
FAMILY rooms. See Recreation rooms
FAMILY size. See Family, Size of
FAMILY therapy. See Family psychotherapy
FAMILY Union (agency) See Social agencies
FAMILY vacations. See Vacations
FAMINES

France

Siege of Paris. G. Carson. il Natur Hist 86:68-77 O '77
FAMOUS men and women. See Celebrities
FAN, Tsai Y. and others
N-nitrosodiethanolamine in synthetic cutting fluids: a part-per-hundred impurity. bibl il Science 196:70-1 Ap 1 '77
FAN, Yuan-yen
Inside the Air Force. M. Liu. il por Newsweek 90:50 Jl 25 '77 *
Timely defection. il por Times 110:37 Jl 18 '77 *
FAN letters. See Letters
La FANCIULLA del west; opera. See Puccini, G.
FANDEL, John
Weight of a few words. Commonweal 104:791-4 D 9 '77
FANEUIL Hall Marketplace. See Boston—Markets
FANGER, Donald
(tr) See Markish, S. Example of Isaac Babel
FANGIO, Juan Manuel
Foyt, Fangio and the sponsor's ego. D. E. Davis, Jr. Car & Dr 23:7 O '77 *
FANNIE Mae. See Federal National Mortgage Association
FANNING, James
Gardener's notes. See issues of House & garden incorporating Living for young homemakers
FANNING, John Harold
Man who heads NLRB now. il por Nations Bus 65:26+ S '77 *
FANNING, Katherine (Woodruff)
Feud in Anchorage. il por Time 109:86-7 Mr 21 '77 *
She keeps Anchorage a two-paper town. E. Munro. Ms 6:19 N '77 *

FANS, Electric
Consumer's guide to: electric fans. il Mech Illus 73:22 Je '77
Fans can help you make energy savings. V. McNiff. il House & Gard 149:88+ S '77

FANS, Ventilating. See Ventilators

FANTASIES, Literary
Quest: the search for meaning through fantasy. L. Rochelle. Engl J 66:54-5 O '77
See also
Publishers and publishing—Fantasies, Literary

Bibliography

Fantasy; ed by M. Parish. il Engl J 66:90-3 O '77

FANTASTIC art. See Art, Fantastic

FANTASY
Daydream those pounds away; tips for youth on maintaining diets. A. A. Belson. Seventeen 36:234-5+ Ag '77
Liberation of sexual fantasy. D. Goleman and S. Bush. bibl il Psychol Today 11:48-9+ O '77
Pleasure and pain of that first crush. A. Bayer. il Seventeen 36:144-5+ My '77
We daydream about our problems; study by Leonard Giambra. M. Marcus. Psychol Today 11:44+ O '77
What do our masochistic fantasies really mean? sexual fantasy; excerpt from Going too far: the personal chronicle of a feminist. R Morgan. Ms 5:66-8+ Je '77
See also
Childrens fantasies
Fairy tales

FANTEL, Hans H.
Hi-fi: at the frontier. Opera N 42:32-3 D 17 '77
Hi-fi: fair values. Opera N 42:66-7 S '77
Hi fi: sound dollar '77. il Opera N 42:64-5 N '77
Hi-fi: the once and future phonograph. il Opera N 41:28-9 Je '77
Keep in touch from anywhere. il Pop Mech 147:98-100+ My '77
Keeping it clean: solutions for record care. Opera N 41:38-9 Ap 2 '77
Loudspeaker guidelines. Esquire 88:147-8+ O '77
Murder of the Orient express. il map Pop Mech 147:71-5+ Ap '77
Silent partners. il Opera N 41:34-5 F 12 '77
Taping off the air. il Esquire 88:119-20+ Ag '77
They're still inventing hi-fi loudspeakers. il Pop Sci 211:58+ S '77

FAR East
See also
Economic assistance, American—Far East
Investments, American—Far East

Description and travel

Far East. S. Fockler. il Trav/Holiday 148:28-32+ D '77
First pass at the Pacific. S. Birnbaum. il Esquire 88:42+ Ag '77
Pacific overture. S. Birnbaum. il Esquire 88:85-93 Ag '77

FARAH Manufacturing Company
Dust starts to settle at Farah. il por Bus W p52 Ap 18 '77

FARB, Nathan
Portraits at an exhibition; ed by D. Seiberling. N Y Times Mag p57-9 N 20 '77

FARBER, David, and Baran, Paul
Convergence of computing and telecommunications systems. Science 195:1166-70 Mr 18 '77

FARBER, Ed
Photo-electronics. il por Pop Phot 80:8+ Mr; 60+ Je; 81:58+ Jl; 32+ S; 58+ O; 80+ D '77

FARBER, Leslie H.
O death, where is thy sting-a-ling-a-ling? Commentary 63:35-43 Je '77

FARBER, Viola
Viola Farber: moving on. C. Egan. il por Dance Mag 51:80-3 Ap '77 *

FARBER, Viola, Dance Company. See Dance companies

FARBERMAN, Harold
Colorado Springs Symphony: Farberman's War cry. por Hi Fi 27:MA19-20 Mr '77 *

FARER, Tom J.
Exaggerating the Communist menace; excerpt from Human rights and American foreign policy. il Society 15:87-91 N '77

FARES. See subhead Fares under various subjects, e.g. Airlines—Fares

FAREWELLS. See Salutations

FARIA, Carlo
Bel canto duet. il pors Opera N 41:16-19 Je '77
(ed) See Barbieri, F. Old pros: Tajo & Barbieri
(ed) See Scotto, R. Revelation
(ed) See Tajo, I. Old pros: Tajo & Barbieri

FARIS, William
William Faris Sr, his sons, and journeymen—Annapolis silversmiths. J. S. Brown. bibl il Antiques 111:378-85 F '77 *

FARJEON, Eleanor
Second look: glass slipper. S. B. Andrews. Horn Bk 53:193-4 Ap '77 *

FARLEY, Carole Ann
Real Lulu: Carole Farley; interview, ed by S. Wadsworth. por Opera N 41:14 Ap 2 '77

about

Lulu and the Cinderella from Idaho. W. Bender. il por Time 109:96 Mr 28 '77 *

FARLEY, John H.
Building costs. il Archit Rec 162:53 Jl '77

FARLEY, Reynolds
Integrating residential neighborhoods. il Society 14:38-41 My '77

The FARM (collective settlement) See Collective settlements

FARM animals. See Livestock

FARM auctions. See Auctions

FARM building industry. See Construction industry

FARM buildings
Nifty British ideas. il Farm J 101:Dairy 20 Ja '77
See also
Calf pens
Swine houses

Heating and ventilation

Plan your buildings to collect solar heat. il Farm J 101:14-16 Je '77
Solar drying makes better hay. C. F. Marley. il Farm J 101:36 N '77

Leasing and renting

See also
Swine houses—Leasing and renting

FARM Bureau Federation, American. See American Farm Bureau Federation

FARM cooperatives. See Agriculture, Cooperative

FARM corporations
Farm corporation:
Estate planning. C.-L. Davis. il Suc Farm 75:26-7+ My '77
Fringe benefits and taxes: not dodges, just good planning. C. L. Davis. il Suc Farm 75:29-31 Ap '77
Setting it up. il Suc Farm 75:no5 20-1 Mr '77
Take stock of your future. il Suc Farm 75:no5 19 Mr '77
Let's stop the big grab for farmland. R. C. Black. il Farm J 101:14-15+ S; 20-1+ O '77; Discussion. 101:C4 D '77
What you should know before you incorporate. P. Brustowicz. Suc Farm 75:35 N '77

Taxation

ESOP: how it fits in estate planning; employee stock ownership. Suc Farm 75:9 My '77
Estate planning. C.-L. Davis. il Suc Farm 75:26-7+ My '77
Fringe benefits and taxes: not dodges, just good planning. C. L. Davis. il Suc Farm 75:29-31 Ap '77
How Congress landed on tax-loss farming. R. C. Black. il Farm J 101:18-19 F '77
How the new law cracks down on corporate farming. Farm J 101:5 Ja '77
In the shade of the FDIC: the tax-shelter farmers. R. B. Taylor. Nation 224:590-4 My 14 '77
Your family corporation can pay your life insurance. Farm J 101:B2 O '77

FARM electricity. See Electricity on the farm

FARM equipment
Farm & shop. il Farm J 101:J4 S; N2+ N '77
Home-made and handy; photographs. See issues of Farm journal
Pick up your shop, and go. il Suc Farm 75:C8 Ag '77
Sharing agreements. S. Cain. il Suc Farm 75:30-1 O '77
See also
Bins
Grain dryers
Swine farms—Equipment

FARM equipment industry. See Agricultural machinery industry

FARM finance
Estate planning; symposium. L. Kruse. il Suc Farm 75:31-41+ N '77
Getting started farming: the Minnesota family farm plan. Suc Farm 75:no4 9 Mr '77
Getting started in farming: it's still a hard row to hoe. R. Blobaum. il Org Gard & Farm 24:69-71 Ag '77
How to adjust an out-of-balance debt load. il Suc Farm 75:8-9 Ag '77
How to handle taxes on money you get from Uncle Sam. L. Lane. Farm J 101:30-1+ N '77
Money management. L. Kruse and S. Cain. See issues of Successful farming
These kids learn farming means business. il Suc Farm 75:no4 8 Mr '77

FARM houses. See Farmhouses

FARM income. See Income

FARM labor
Add an employee—get tax credit. il Suc Farm 75:C32 D '77
Apple picker blues; question of importing Jamaican pickers. D. McGhee. New Repub 177:15-16 O 29 '77

FARM labor—*Continued*
As Jamaican as apple pie; apple harvest workers in Virginia. J. Egerton. Progressive 41:37-40 D '77
Doubly difficult apple to pluck; foreign pickers. il Time 110:28 N 7 '77
Farm labor. V. Fuller and B. Mason. bibl f il Ann Am Acad 429:63-80 Ja '77
Good help in getting started. . .; working for older people. C. Bickers. il Farm J 101:L4+ O '77
Good way to hire help; campus interviews. Farm J 101:D4 Je '77
Gypsies of harvest. N. Proffitt. il Newsweek 90: 65-6 Jl 4 '77
How much extra income to add an employee? il Suc Farm 75:11 Je '77
People management: these employees grow with the farm. S. Cain. il Suc Farm 75:26-7 S '77
Why labor leaves the farm. C. S. Machan. Farm J 101:Dairy 8 F '77
Why labor really leaves the farm. C. S. Machan. Farm J 101:Beef 4 F; LK8 Mr '77
See also
Migrant labor
United Farm Workers

FARM labor laws. See Labor laws and legislation

FARM land. See Land

FARM land values. See Land values

FARM leases. See Leases

FARM life
Back to the farm; F. and J. Riley. il pors House & Gard 149:88-9+ F '77
Farm family living. See issues of Farm journal
Farm people. See issues of Farm journal
Rarity of June; excerpt from Ox bells and fireflies. E. Buckler. il Read Digest 110:114-16 Je '77
Some difficulties to think about before buying a farm. W. Berry. il Org Gard & Farm 24:59-61 Jl '77
Why we leave the hall light on all night. D. Predmore. il Farm J 101:L15-16 Ap '77
See also
Sociology, Rural

History

Self-reliance and hard work; three centuries of farming in New England. M. Franz. Org Gard & Farm 24:138-41 My '77

FARM lighting. See Electric lighting

FARM magazines. See Agriculture—Periodicals

FARM management
Can you ride it out? il Farm J 101:19-21 N '77
Don't let the spring rush overpower you. G. Lepper. il Suc Farm 75:no3 22-3 F '77
Expansion: taller? Or wider? Suc Farm 75:K9 Ap '77
Farm better on scattered fields. D. K. O'Brien. il Farm J 101:M2-3 Ap '77
How Russell Newlin prescription farms. R. Brunoehler. il Suc Farm 75:no4 44 Mr '77
How the family farm can harvest millions. il Bus W p68-70 Jl 4 '77
Much ado about weather. Farm J 101:60 Ag '77
Multiple management: a plan, not an accident. S. Cain. il Suc Farm 75:C6-7 Ag '77; Same. 75:C28 D '77
Multiple management: the mom and pop approach. R. Brunoehler. Suc Farm 75:L4 Je '77
New farmers for a new era. N. Reeder. il Farm J 101:22-5 Mr '77
Page one. Suc Farm 75:23-34 Ag; 21-32 S; 27-30 O; 31-41+ N; 23-34 D '77
Quit producing at a loss. K. Carter. Farm J 101:B4 S '77
See also
Cattle farm management
Computers—Agricultural use
Farm corporations
Farm records
Farms, Size of
Farms, Small
Father-son farm operating agreements
Swine farm management

FARM management consultants. See Agricultural consultants

FARM manure. See Fertilizers and manures

FARM operating agreements, Father and son. See Father-son farm operating agreements

FARM ownership
Changing American farm. H. F. Breimyer. bibl f il map Ann Am Acad 429:12-22 Ja '77
How to get started in farming. C. Bickers. il Farm J 101:D1-2 D '77
Joint venture: an alternative to partnership. il Suc Farm 75:45 O '77
Keep your business intact. Farm J 101:Hog 27 Ja '77
Let's stop the big grab for farmland. R. C. Black. il Farm J 101:14-15+ S; 20-1+ O '77; Discussion. 101:C4 D '77
See also
Farm partnership

Laws and legislation

See Agricultural laws and legislation

FARM partnership
Four-family operation that works. J. D. Ritchie. il Farm J 101:Hog 10-11 Ag '77
How to retire a small farm gracefully. G. Vincent. il Suc Farm 75:40-1+ N '77
How to save a partnership: buy-sell plans ease land transfer. G. Vincent. il Suc Farm 75:no4 L32 Mr '77
Partnerships: three ways to share income. il Suc Farm 75:8 My '77
Risk capital. G. L. Vincent. il Suc Farm 75: 32-3+ Ja '77
Why we stick with a parnership. D. Seim. Farm J 101:F1-2 mid-Mr '77

FARM policy. See Agricultural administration

FARM ponds. See Ponds

FARM population. See Rural population

FARM produce
Buying to supplement your harvest. il Org Gard & Farm 24:145-6 Ag '77
See also
Surplus products, Agricultural
also names of farm produce, e.g. Corn

Marketing

Marketing. L. Kruse and S. Cain. See issues of Successful farming
Marketing skills separate superior from good farmers. Suc Farm 75:C8 D '77
Successful farming's marketing section. G. Lepper and others. il Suc Farm 75:11-13 D '77
See also
Cotton—Marketing
Markets, Farmers

Prices

Farm outlook for 1978. R. D. Wennblom. Farm J 101:17+ D '77
Global props for U.S. farm prices. il Bus W p74+ My 9 '77
NFO sets price goals. R. D. Wennblom. Farm J 101:37 Ja '77
New farm bill. il Farm J 101:13+ S '77
New farm bill—a mixed bag. Farm J 101:44 S '77
Price impact of Florida's freeze. il Bus W p30-1 F 7 '77
What's in the administration's new farm bill. R. Wennblom. il Farm J 101:15-17 My '77
Why Farm Bureau endorsed target prices. R. D. Wennblom. Farm J 101:33 Mr '77
Your '77 outlook: steady to strong. R. D. Wennblom. Farm J 101:13 D '76
See also
Agricultural administration—United States

FARM records
Every field a profit center. J. D. Boyd. il Farm J 101:18-18A+ Je '77
How to use records to improve profits. J. Russell. il Farm J 101:Hog 10-11 D '77
Livestock charts: take the guesswork out of selling. G. Johnston. il Suc Farm 75:H18 D '77
Simple way to schedule sows; tablet sheet. H. Pike. il Farm J 101:Hog 6 S '77

FARM shops. See Workshops

FARM size. See Farms, Size of

FARM subsidies. See Agricultural administration—United States

FARM tenancy
See also
Leases

FARM vacations. See Vacations

FARM wagons. See Wagons

FARM workers. See Farm labor

FARMER, Charles J.
Bugle your elk. il Field & S 82:40-1+ N '77
Go the drop camp way. il Outdoor Life 159: 68-71+ F '77
Hunt your own sheep. il Field & S 82:60-1+ S '77
Waterhole pronghorns. il Field & S 82:52-4+ Ag '77

FARMER, James
Scapegoats of '77. por Newsweek 90:13 Ag 8 '77

FARMER, Jean
Hercules of the soil—the earthworm. Read Digest 111:83-6 N '77
Little league lunacy. il Org Gard & Farm 24: 120+ My '77
Slicer-shredder. il Org Gard & Farm 24:118-19 O '77

FARMER, Richard N.
Business prospects in the inner city. Intellect 105:263-4 F '77

FARMERS
Farm people. See issues of Farm journal
New era for agriculture. R. C. Black. Farm J 101:21 Mr '77
Polish farmers learn about free enterprise. V. Louviere. il Nations Bus 65:44 F '77
See also
Farm management
Strikes—United States—Farmers

Attitudes

Ag-pulse. L. Palmer. Farm J 101:C1-3 Ja; 16+ mid-F; L8 Ap; B2 Ag '77
Hear me. Farm J 101:9 Mr; B4 S '77

FARMERS—*Continued*

Political activities

Get ready to battle for your property rights. L. Lane. il Farm J 101:K3-4+ mid-Mr '77
Plowshares into swords. il Time 110:28+ O 24 '77
Uneven squeeze on the U.S. farmer. il Bus W p70-1 D 19 '77

Public relations

See Agriculture—Public relations

FARMERS Home Administration. See United States—Agriculture, Department of—Farmers Home Administration
FARMERS markets. See Markets, Farmers
FARMERS wives
It's a mighty good life; Charlena Lewis of Hinds County, Miss. il Ebony 32:73 Ag '77
New light on property rights of farm wives. L. Lane. Farm J 101:K8 mid-Mr '77

Agricultural societies

See Agricultural societies

FARMHOUSES
Antique farmhouse with indoor-outdoor charm; house of Ivan Chermayeff. il House & Gard 149:60-3 Ag '77
Tighten up your house. il Farm J 101:A4-5 D '77

Leasing and renting

Little house that spreads happiness; vacation retreat in Clayton County, Ia. J. Gillies. il Farm J 100:33A-33C D '76

FARMHOUSES, Remodeled. See Houses, Remodeled
FARMING. See Agriculture
FARMING, Organic. See Organic farming
FARMING, Truck. See Truck farming
FARMS
Crime on the farm; rural property theft. J. K. Footlick and others. il Newsweek 90:101 O 3 '77
See also
Farm management
Farm ownership
Plantations

Sanitation

Sanitation laws squeeze out small producers. W. Berry and G. Logsdon. il Org Gard & Farm 24:43-6+ O '77

FARMS, Incorporated. See Farm corporations
FARMS, Organic
Urban farm; Integral Urban House, Berkeley, Calif. K. Brower. il Atlantic 241:58-63 Ja '78
FARMS, Size of
Changing American farm. H. F. Breimyer. bib f il map Ann Am Acad 429:12-22 Ja '77
Reversing agricultural priorities; Southern Regional Council report. Society 14:5 S '77
Size isn't everything. B. M. Wilkinson. il Farm J 101:D2 Mr '77
See also
Farms, Small
FARMS, Small
How to retire a small farm gracefully. G. Vincent. il Suc Farm 75:40-1+ N '77
Organizing knowledge for small farmers. J. Goldstein. il Org Gard & Farm 25:146+ Ja '78
FARNAM, Anne
Furniture at the Essex Institute, Salem, Massachusetts. il Antiques 111:958-73 My '77
FAROE Islands. See Faeroe Islands
FARR, Bruce
Bruce Farr talks about light displacement and the IOR; interview, ed by M. Pope. il por Yachting 142:72-5 O '77
FARR, Louise
(ed) See Nolan, K. Kathleen Nolan: from sit-com star to SAG prexy
FARRAR, Donald R. See Emigh, V. D. jt auth
FARRAR, Estelle Sinclaire
Master engravers of Corning, New York. bibl il Antiques 112:726-31 O '77
FARRAR, Straus and Giroux, Inc. See Publishers and publishing—United States
FARRELL, James H, Jr
Market comment. por Forbes 121:230-1 Ja 9 '78
FARRELL, Joan
Business of crafts; opening a craft store; ed by J. Coyne. Ceram Mo 25:19+ My '77
FARRELL, Ray M.
Sign that took three years to build. il Sch Arts 76:46-7 Ap '77
FARRELL, Robert J.
Market trends. por Forbes 119:102-3 Ja 15 '77
FARRELL, Suzanne
Three independent views; interview, ed by D. Lurie. il por Harp Baz 110:97 F '77
FARRELL, William E.
Hawk on a mission of peace. il pors N Y Times Mag p9-11+ Jl 17 '77
FARRELL, William J. See Spriestersbach, D. C. jt auth
FARREN, David, pseud. See McFerran, D. D.
FARRINGTON, Gregory C. See Roth, W. L. jt auth
FARRIS, Nancy Pierson
For a pleasant surprise, try okra. Org Gard & Farm 24:170+ F '77
Something growing, something green. il Org Gard & Farm 24:70-1 O '77
FARROWING houses, Swine. See Swine houses
FARSON, Richard
Are you trying to be too good a parent? interview, ed by F. Davis. il Redbook 148:88+ Ap '77
FARTASH, Manoutchehr
Disarmament club at work. il por Bull Atom Sci 33:57-62 Ja '77
FASCELL, Dante Bruno
Excerpts from testimony on proposals to renew the reorganization powers of the President, March 1, 1977. Cong Digest 56:108+ Ap '77
FASCIOLIASIS. See Liver—Diseases
FASCISM

Great Britain

British anti-Semitism; then and now; controversy surrounding David Pryce-Jones's Unity Mitford: a quest. D. R. Katz. New Repub 176:21 F 5 '77
Not their finest hour; British aristocrats sympathetic to Hitler. D. Pryce-Jones. il New Repub 176:12-16 My 14 '77

United States

See also
Nazis in the United States

FASHION
Cream of the cream. Vogue 167:259 O '77
Fashion. A. Hollander. il New Repub 177:27 D 17 '77
How you look; symposium, ed by E. L. Gross. Vogue 167:116-18+ Je '77
On and off the avenue; British fashion. K. Fraser. New Yorker 53:107-10+ N 7; 149-50+ N 14 '77
On and off the avenue; New York City boutiques. K. Fraser. New Yorker 53:91-8 Ap 11 '77
People are talking about. . .fashion. Vogue 167:48 O; 48 N; 28 D '77
What's up in Paris. il Mademoiselle 83:88-9 Jl '77
See also
Clothing and dress
Costume
Costume design
Dress accessories
Hairdressing

Study and teaching

Fashion lecture. New Yorker 53:35 O 10 '77

FASHION designers. See Costume designers
FASHION photography. See Photography, Fashion
FASHION shows
Clothes designed to celebrate the body; Paris shows. C. Donovan. il N Y Times Mag p 123-8 N 27 '77
Fashion: oxygen for an aging lady; Paris shows. il Time 109:76 F 7 '77
Fashions and business set her lifestyle; E. W. Johnson; director of Ebony Fashion Fair. il pors Ebony 32:74 Ag '77
Knees news; Paris spring collections. M. A. Kellogg and C. Mitchelmore. il Newsweek 89:78 F 7 '77
Long-ago and far-away romance; showings of the French couture collections for autumn. il Time 110:47-8 Ag 8 '77
Milan designers come of age. C. Donovan. il N Y Times Mag p 129-33 N 13 '77
On and off the avenue; New York fall shows. K. Fraser. New Yorker 53:76-81 Jl 11; 63-9 Jl 18 '77
Paris ragtime; spring collections. S. C. Cowley and J. Friedman. il Newsweek 90:70-1 N 7 '77
Put-ons, take-offs and dress-ups; Paris showings of spring clothes. il Time 110:54-5 N 7 '77
FASI, Frank
Rotten system. T. Mathews and G. C. Lubenow. il pors Newsweek 90:47 N 14 '77 •
FASOLINO, Peter
Palooka principle. por Newsweek 89:11 Je 13 '77
FASSBINDER, Rainer Werner
Current cinema. P. Gilliatt. New Yorker 53:104-5 My 30 '77 •
Fassbinder: the poetry of the inarticulate. P. Thomas. il Film Q 30:2-17 Wint '76 •
Germans are coming! The Germans are coming! D. Denby. il pors Horizon 20:88-90+ S '77 •
FAST, Betty
Mediacentric (cont) Wilson Lib Bull 51:572-3, 732-3; 52:133-5 Mr, My, O '77

about

Obituary
Am Lib il por 8:369 Jl '77
SLJ por 24:15 S '77. T. J. Galvin
FAST, Jonathan
Problems and pleasures of living together; interview, ed by I. Silden. pors Harp Baz 110:116-17 My '77

FAST food restaurants. See Restaurants—Chain and franchise operations
FAST foods. See Convenience foods
FASTENINGS
How to hang anything on a wall. A. Rosenblum. il Good H 185:207 Jl '77
Hung up on a hollow wall. J. Roy. Am Home 80:16 My '77
See also
Bolts and nuts
FASTING
Benefits of fasting. P. Martin. il Chr Cent 94:298-301 Mr 30 '77
Fastest diet—is it for you? M. Goodwin. Read Digest 110:108-11 Je '77
Fasting: asceticism in a new key. J. Kopas. America 136:190-1 Mr 5 '77
Fasting: is it a safe way to lose weight? E. Schoen. House & Gard 149:130+ Mr '77
High protein fasting: is it for you? M. L. Schildkraut. il Good H 184:227 My '77
Should you starve yourself thin? J. Mayer. il Fam Health 9:24-6 F '77
Suppression of sympathetic nervous system during fasting. J. B. Young and L. Landsberg. bibl il Science 196:1473-5 Je 24 '77
Your family's health: protein-sparing modified fast. D. R. Zimmerman. Ladies Home J 94:96+ O '77
FASTS and feasts
See also
Advent
Carnival
Epiphany
Hanukkah (Feast of Lights)
Lent
Passover

Catholic Church

Going to glory; Feast of Christ the King. G. McCauley. America 137:inside back cover N 12 '77

Hinduism

Holiest day in history; Kumbh Mela or Jar Festival in India. il Time 109:43-4 Ja 31 '77
FAT
See also
Obesity
FAT bodies. See Adipose tissues
FAT content of foods. See Food—Fat content
FAT tissues. See Adipose tissues
FATAH (organization) See Palestine Liberation Organization
FATHAUER, Theodore F.
1976-77 winter in Alaska: unsettled and exceptionally mild. il maps Weatherwise 30:76-9+ Ap '77
—and Wilson, W. J.
Alaska tornadoes. il maps Weatherwise 30:106-10 Je '77
FATHER-son corporations. See Family corporations
FATHER-son farm operating agreements
Starting a new family deal? Save grief with a trial run. D. Seim. Farm J 101:F3 Ag '77
FATHERLESS families. See Single parent families
FATHERS
Day I found my father. S. Albert. Good H 184:158+ Je '77
Do fathers make good mothers? views of J. A. Levine. J. Greenwald. McCalls 104:65 F '77
Fathering: it's a major role. R. D. Parke and D. B. Sawin. bibl il pors Psychol Today 11:108-9+ N '77
Fathers can make good mothers, too. E. Stukane. Harp Baz 110:179+ O '77
Helping husbands to be better fathers. T. B. Brazelton. Redbook 149:93+ My '77
I was a mother for six months. E. Susman. il Good H 185:74+ Jl '77
See also
Desertion and non-support
Divorced fathers
Single parent families
Stepparents

Anecdotes, facetiae, satire, etc.

Harried Houdini. J. Allen. Seventeen 36:60+ My '77
FATHERS and daughters. See Parent-child relationship
FATHERS and sons. See Parent-child relationship
FATHERS Day

Poetry

Poems for Father's Day. Ms 5:64-5 Je '77
FATHERS Day gifts. See Gifts
FATIGUE
See also
Relaxation
FATIGUE of metals. See Metals—Fatigue
FATIO, Louise
PW interviews; ed by M. Freeman. il pors Pub W 211:54-5 F 28 '77
FATTY acids. See Acids, Fatty
FAUCETS. See Plumbing
FAUDE, Wilson H.
Candace Wheeler, textile designer. bibl il por Antiques 112:258-61 Ag '77
FAULKNER, Douglas
Still living fossil, the nautilus, glides through the ages. il Smithsonian 8:76-81 Je '77

about

Images from the deep. D. Steigman. il Pop Phot 81:92-7+ S '77 *
FAULKNER, William
Tomorrow; story; excerpt from Knight's gambit. il Sat Eve Post 249:68-9 Jl '77

about

Faulkner filmography. B. F. Kawin. bibl il Film Q 30:12-21 Summ '77 *
FAULKNER Hospital, Boston. See Boston—Hospitals
FAULTS (geology)
Deep drilling in the Galapagos Rift. il Sci N 112:85 Ag 6 '77
Research dives probe the Galapagos Rift. Sci N 111:182 Mr 19 '77
San Andreas: an oceanic fault that came ashore. R. S. Dietz. il Sea Front 23:258-66 S '77
FAUNA, Desert. See Desert fauna
FAURÉ, Gabriel Urbain
Formidable achievement; G. Fauré's songs. P. L. Miller. Am Rec G 40:5-9 Je '77 *
Songs; two recordings by Connoisseur Society and Musical Heritage. D. Hamilton. Hi Fi 27:80+ Ag '77 *
FAUST, Irving M. and others
Adipose tissue regeneration following lipectomy. bibl il Science 197:391-3 Jl 22 '77
Surgical removal of adipose tissue alters feeding behavior and the development of obesity in rats. bibl il Science 197:393-6 Jl 22 '77
FAUVISM. See Painting, French
FAUX, Jeff. See Alperovitz, G. jt auth
FAVA beans. See Beans
FAVIA-ARTSAY, Aida
Historical records. See issues of Hobbies to April 1977
FAVICCHIO, John
Going motorhome part-time. il Ret Liv 17:31-2 F '77
FAWCETT-MAJORS, Farrah
Face looks vaguely familiar; interview, ed by M. A. Sharpe. il pors Sat Eve Post 249:54-5+ S '77
Farrah talks about looking and feeling beautiful; interview, ed by M. Mercer. por McCalls 105:94+ O '77
Farrah's way; interview, ed by B. Sabol. il por Vogue 167:128-9 Ap '77

about

Barbie doll as sex symbol. K. E. Meyer. Sat R 5:45 O 1 '77 *
Don't change a hair for me. R. Rosenblatt. por New Repub 176:29-30 F 26 '77
Farrah factor. M. S. Miller. por Ladies Home J 94:34+ Je '77 *
Farrah Fawcett-Majors: an unlikely sex symbol. C. Champlin. il por McCalls 104:28+ Ap '77 *
Little girl who became Farrah Fawcett-Majors. K. Maugham. il pors Good H 185:128-9+ Ag '77 *
May I see you after class . . . Miss Fawcett? il pors Esquire 88:97-8 S '77 *
FAY, Anthony
Alicia Markova: her appearances in America. il pors Dance Mag 51:47-55 Je '77
Belle of the Ballets Russes: Alexandra Danilova. il pors Dance Mag 51:55-70 O '77
FAY, James S.
Missing billions. Nation 224:294-5 Mr 12 '77
FAY, Maxine
Saving the old homestead; drama. Plays 36:25-32 Mr '77
FAYETTE County, Pa.
Fayette County, Pa.—the coal heap. S. Agrest. il Newsweek 89:26 F 14 '77
FAYETTE County, W.Va.
Nutrition site becomes emergency kitchen. Aging 274:9 Ag '77
FEAR
See also
Anxiety
Bashfulness
Nervousness
Phobias
School phobia
FEARS, J. Wayne
Cold-weather survival. il Outdoor Life 161:119-20 Ja '78
Day pack and survival kit. il Outdoor Life 160:163-4 O '77
Finding and preparing edible wild roots. il Outdoor Life 159:129-30 Ap '77
FEAST of Lights. See Hanukkah (Feast of Lights)
FEASTS. See Fasts and feasts

FEATHERSTONE, Richard L. and Romano, Louis
Evaluation of administrative performance. Clearing H 50:412-15 My '77

FEAVER, William
London. See issues of Art news

FEAZEL, Charles T.
Oil under the Gulf. il Oceans 10:33-7 S '77

FEBRUARY
And it all happened in February! excerpt from The almanac of dates. L. Millgate. il Good H 184:219 F '77

FECHTER, Laurence D. and Annau, Zoltan
Toxicity of mild prenatal carbon monoxide exposure. bibl il Science 197:680-2 Ag 12 '77

FED Mart Corporation-Vornado, Inc merger. See Discount houses (retail trade)—Acquisitions and mergers

FEDANZO, Anthony J. Jr
Socioeconomic fix: the easy way out? bibl Intellect 106:55-7 Ag '77

FEDAYEEN
See also
Palestine Liberation Organization

FEDER, Bernard. See Feder, E. jt auth

FEDER, Elaine, and Feder, Bernard
Dance therapy. bibl il pors Psychol Today 10:76-8+ F '77

FEDER, R. and others
High-resolution soft X-ray microscopy. bibl il Science 197:259-60 Jl 15 '77

FEDERAL agencies. See United States—Executive departments

FEDERAL aid
See also
Grants-in-aid
also subhead Federal aid under various subjects, e.g. Atomic power industry—Federal aid

FEDERAL and municipal relations
See also
Intergovernmental fiscal relations
Intergovernmental tax relations

FEDERAL and state relations
How absurd federal rules victimize the state. P. J. Lucey. por Nations Bus 65:43-6 My '77
New trial for states' rights; upcoming Supreme Court decisions. Bus W p38 O 10 '77
What the Supreme Court is really telling business. W. Guzzardi, Jr. il Fortune 95:147-54 Ja '77
See also
Decentralization in government

History

Marats, Dantons, and Robespierres; Hartford Convention of 1814. C. Edward. il Am Hist Illus 12:10-16 Jl '77

FEDERAL Art Project
Boston; WPA art projects in New England. J. H. Kay. Art N 76:116-18 D '77
Extensions downtown. New Yorker 53:24-5 F 28 '77
New Deal ceramics: the Cleveland workshop. K. A. Marling. il por Ceram Mo 25:25-31 Je '77

FEDERAL Aviation Administration. See United States—Federal Aviation Administration

FEDERAL boards, bureaus, commissions, etc. of the United States government. See names of boards, bureaus, commissions, etc. as subheads under United States, e.g. United States—Federal Communications Commission

FEDERAL buildings. See Public buildings

FEDERAL Coal Mine Health and Safety Act. See Coal mines and mining—Laws and legislation

FEDERAL Company
Let 'em eat bread. Forbes 119:76 Ap 1 '77

FEDERAL Contract Compliance, Office of. See United States—Labor, Department of—Federal Contract Compliance, Office of

FEDERAL Coordinating Council of Science, Engineering and Technology. See United States—Federal Coordinating Council of Science, Engineering and Technology

FEDERAL Council on the Aging. See United States—Aging, Administration on

FEDERAL courts. See Courts—United States

FEDERAL crop insurance. See Insurance, Government

FEDERAL debt (United States) See Debts, Public—United States

FEDERAL Deposit Insurance Corporation
Biggest liquidator of them all. il Forbes 119:55+ F 15 '77
Billion-dollar banks go on the watch list; FDIC list. Bus W p23-4 Mr 28 '77
In the shade of the FDIC: the tax-shelter farmers; failure of the U.S. National Bank in San Diego. R. B. Taylor. Nation 224:590-4 My 14 '77
Liabilities of sitting on a bank board. il Bus W p86-7 S 26 '77

FEDERAL Election Commission. See United States—Federal Election Commission

FEDERAL employees. See Government employees

FEDERAL Express Corporation. See Air freight service

FEDERAL flood insurance. See Insurance, Government

FEDERAL funds rate. See Interest (economics)

FEDERAL government
See also
Democracy
United States—Politics and government

FEDERAL Grain Inspection Service. See United States—Federal Grain Inspection Service

FEDERAL Home Loan Bank Board. See United States—Federal Home Loan Bank Board

FEDERAL Home Loan Mortgage Corporation
Ginnie Mae's kid brothers grows up; Freddie Mac. Forbes 119:100+ Je 15 '77

FEDERAL Housing Administration. See United States—Federal Housing Administration

FEDERAL Information Centers. See United States—Federal Information Centers

FEDERAL judges. See Judges

FEDERAL lands. See Public lands—United States

FEDERAL libraries. See Libraries, Government

FEDERAL Mediation and Conciliation Service
See United States—Federal Mediation and Conciliation Service

FEDERAL-municipal fiscal relations. See Intergovernmental fiscal relations

FEDERAL National Mortgage Association
Carterizing Fannie Mae. Bus W p38 Je 20 '77
Feuding over who runs Fannie Mae. il por Bus W p74+ S 12 '77

FEDERAL prosecutors. See Public prosecutors

FEDERAL register
Turning federalese into plain English. Bus W p58 My 9 '77

FEDERAL Reserve banks
Sticking with Burns. Nat R 29:817 Jl 22 '77

FEDERAL Reserve Board. See United States—Federal Reserve System

FEDERAL-state tax relations. See Intergovernmental tax relations

FEDERAL Trade Commission. See United States—Federal Trade Commission

FEDERATED Department Stores, Inc
Burdines Department Store holds up a mirror to passers-by; with introd by G. Allen. il Archit Rec 161:115-23 Mr '77

FEDERICI, Tommaso
Church and Israel. M. B. Martin. Nat R 29:1435 D 9 '77 *

FEDO, Michael W.
With the help of a friend. America 136:463-4 My 21 '77

FEDOROV, Konstantin N.
Hidden dynamos of Neptune's powerhouse. il UNESCO Courier 30:24-7 Ja '77

FEDOROVA, Viktoria
Only in America. B. Carter. il pors Newsweek 89:9 Mr 7 '77 *

FEE, Rodney J.
(ed) Successful hog management (cont) il Suc Farm 75:no3 H1 F '77

—and Johnston, Gene
Hog management. See issues of Successful farming

FEED additives. See Feed supplements

FEED mixers and mixing
Farm feed mixing saves money, but takes good plan. Suc Farm 75:no2 52 F '77

FEED supplements
Are we losing our animal feed additives? G. Johnston. il Suc Farm 75:no3 19+ F '77
Whip disease with nutrition? R. E. Wanner. il Farm J 101:Dairy 10+ Ja '77

FEED supplements, Antibiotic. See Antibiotic feed supplements

FEEDBACK (psychology)
See also
Biofeedback training

FEEDERS (birds) See Bird feeders

FEEDING behavior, Animal. See Animals—Food and feeding

FEEDLOTS
See also
Cattle feedlots
Swine feedlots

FEEDS
See also
Feed mixers and mixing
Milo
Silage
also subhead Feeding under names of animals, e.g. Cows—Feeding

Contamination by drugs, pesticides, etc.

Michigan episode; PBB contamination of feed. N. Cousins. Sat R 4:4 Mr 19 '77
PBBs: more effects and more exposure. Sci N 112:100-1 Ag 13 '77
Reports & comment: Michigan; PBB feed contamination. E. Chen. il Atlantic 240:12+ Ag '77

FEEDS—Contamination by drugs, pesticides, etc. —*Continued*
Ron Thomas' horror story: my family was poisoned! E. Keiffer. il Good H 185:64+ Ag '77
Somebody simply goofed; PBB contamination of feed in Michigan. W. Chapman. Progressive 41:30-2 My '77

Corn

Cut costs with grain processing? K. Parker. il Suc Farm 75:no3 B6 F '77
Get more for corn by feeding? R. C. Black. il Farm J 101:18-19 D '77

Cornstalks

Can stalks replace corn silage? B. Eftink. il Suc Farm 75:14 O '77
Extra feed from stalks and stubble. il Farm J 101:24-5 N '77

Grain

Wet brewers grains can help you stretch feed dollars. C. S. Machan. il Farm J 101:Dairy 9 O '77

Grasses

They're bred to make it on grass. il Farm J 101:G4 D '77

Hay

Baled hay feeding losses. il Farm J 101:Beef 10+ F '77
Our livestock love soybean-millet hay. D. Langsner and L. Langsner. il Org Gard & Farm 24:214+ F '77

Medicated feed

See also
Antibiotic feed supplements

Pelleted feed

Pelleting pays pork profits. il Suc Farm 75:no2 A1 F '77

Protein content

Top return from your protein bill. N. Reeder. il Farm J 101:Beef 20+ O '77

Sawdust

Sawdust steaks in your future? M. Lobrovich. Sci Digest 82:79-80 N '77

Urea

How to put urea into dairy rations this winter. Suc Farm 75:D7 D '77

Waste products

Waste products into beef. C. S. Machan. il Farm J 101:Beef 20+ Ag '77

Weeds

Weeds as feed for healthier stock. L. Langsner. il Org Gard & Farm 24:84-7 My '77

FEELINGS. See Emotions

FEENEY, Joseph J.
Nature's round makes jubilee: Hopkins's priestly centenary. il America 137:394-7 D 3 '77

FEENEY, Leonard
Update on Leonard Feeney. J. Deedy. Commonweal 104:5-7 Ja 7 '77 *

FEES, Bank. See Banks and banking—Service charges

FEES, Legal. See Cost (law); Lawyers—Salaries, fees, etc.

FEES, Trade union. See Trade unions—Dues, fees, etc.

FEET. See Foot

FEICK, Stuart
Certain style. il por Forbes 119:68 My 1 '77 *

FEIFER, George
Rostropovich in midpassage. pors Sat R 4:35-9 Mr 5 '77

FEIFFER, Jules
Jules Feiffer's hold me! Reviews
Nation 224:189 F 12 '77
New Yorker 53:65 Mr 14 '77 *
Newsweek 89:93 Mr 7 '77 *

FEIGENBAUM, Rita
Faneuil family silver cruet stand rediscovered. il Antiques 112:120-1 Jl '77

FEIL, V. J. and others
Carbon-14—labeled diethylstilbestrol synthesis by the McMurry method: concurrent formation of hexestrol. bibl Science 198:510-11 N 4 '77

FEIN, Leonard J.
War inside the Jews. New Repub 177:16-18 O 15 '77

FEINBERG, Irwin, and others
Flurazepam effects on slow-wave sleep: stage 4 suppressed but number of delta waves constant. bibl il Science 198:847-8 N 25 '77

FEINBERG, Susan
Classroom's no longer prime time. Todays Educ 66:78-9 S '77; Same abr. Educ Digest 43:38-40 D '77

FEINER, Muriel
(ed) See Trujillo, B. Lady in the bullring

FEINGOLD, Ben F.
No-additives diet; interview. il por Good H 185:292+ N '77

about

Diet not cause of hyperactivity. Sci N 111:406-7 Je 25 '77 *

FEINGOLD, Michael
Apple for Miss Parsons. Sat R 5:51 O 29 '77

FEININGER, Andreas
Feininger's guide to identifying trees. il Horticulture 55:32-49 Je '77

about

Feininger's fantasia. M. R. Weiss. il Sat R 5:40 O 15 '77 *

FEININGER, Laurence
Laurence Feininger 1909-1976: life, work, legacy. E. E. Lowinsky. bibl il por Mus Q 63:327-66 Jl '77 *

FEINSTEIN, Sherman
Psychoquiz: how neurotic are you? Harp Baz 110:229+ S '77

FEINWELL, Dick
Pushbutton dialer with memory. il Radio-Electr 48:38-41+ Je '77

FEIST, Leonard
Of copyrights, creators, and phonorecords; por Hi Fi 27:63-6 Je '77

FEITELSON, Rose, and Salomon, George
New oil prices: impact and response. Intellect 105:327-9 Ap '77

FEIVESON, Harold A. and Taylor T. B.
Security implications of alternative fission futures. il Bull Atom Sci 32:14-18+ D '76; 33:59 My '77

FELD, Bernard Taub
Far-sighted energy program. Bull Atom Sci 33:9 Je '77
Hard-nosed but soft-headed. Bull Atom Sci 33:9 Ap '77
Let's not panic prematurely. Bull Atom Sci 33:8-9 My '77
1976-1977: time for a shock. Bull Atom Sci 33:8-9 Ja '77
Nuclear dilemma revisited. Bull Atom Sci 33:7 F '77
Ode to diversity. Bull Atom Sci 33:10-11 O '77
Way to begin is to stop. Bull Atom Sci 33:9 Mr '77

FELD, Eliot
Why dance best expresses life in an electronic age. il U.S. News 83:68 O 10 '77

about

Eliot Feld's animated cartoons. A. Smith. il por Dance Mag 51:63-5 Je '77 *
Feld magic. H. Saal. il por Newsweek 89:60-1 Mr 21 '77 *

FELD, Eliot, Ballet. See Eliot Feld Ballet

FELD, Lipman Goldman
Before you make your will. il Ret Liv 17:26-9 Mr '77
Training against ship disaster; with biographical sketch. il Sea Front 23:280-6, 318 S '77

FELDBERG, Stanley
Education of Sumner and Stanley Feldberg. il pors Forbes 119:61-2 My 1 '77 *

FELDBERG, Sumner
Education of Sumner and Stanley Feldberg. il pors Forbes 119:61-2 My 1 '77 *

FELDHUSEN, John F. and others
Curriculum materials for vocational youth organizations. bibl Clearing H 50:224-6 Ja '77

FELDMAN, Elane
Sheet savvy. il Am Home 80:23-4 Mr '77

FELDMAN, Heidi. See Goldin-Meadow, S. jt auth

FELDMAN, Irving
Comment. J. D. McClatchy. Poetry 130:52-3 Ap '77 *

FELDMAN, Joan
Winged woman. il Sat R 4:36+ Ap 16 '77

FELDMAN, Leonard
Amplifier/speaker interface—a new concept. il Radio-Electr 48:64-6 F '77
Binaural/biphonic sound. il Radio-Electr 48:37-9+ Mr '77
Broadcast systems for AM stereo. il Radio-Electr 48:51-3 D '77
Classes of audio amplifiers. il Pop Electr 11:74-6 Mr '77
Creative recording with 4-channel tape recorders. il Pop Electr 11:73-6 Je '77
Getting rid of RFI. il Radio-Electr 48:43-6+ Mr '77
Hi-fi components that think. il Esquire 88:122-4+ N '77
IHF sensitivity—what it really means. il Radio-Electr 48:62-4 N '77
Increase dynamic range for better hi-fi. il Radio-Electr 48:46-8 Ap '77
New way to room equalization. il Radio-Electr 48:42-4 My '77
Pulse-width modulation for hi-fi. il Radio-Electr 48:59-61 S '77
Radio-electronics tests. See issues of Radio-electronics
Tomorrow's hi-fi gear. il Radio-Electr 48:40-2+ Mr '77

FELDMAN, Linda
Kosher meals a specialty at New York Luncheon Club. il Aging 274:6-8 Ag '77

FELDMAN, M. A.
Place to grow. il por Opera N 41:20-2 Je '77

FELDMAN, Mark B.
National and multilateral action on corrupt practices; address, April 21, 1977. Dept State Bull 76:554-6 My 30 '77

FELDMAN, Silvia
Psychology and the arts (cont) Psychol Today 10:18+ F; 22 Mr; 24 Ap; 11:26 Je '77

FELDMAN, Trude B.
Rosalynn Carter: my extraordinary mother. il por McCalls 104:116+ My '77
Young Carters' crisis. il pors McCalls 105:18+ Ja '78
(ed) See Carter R. S. Rosalynn Carter at 50

FELGER, Richard Stephen. See Nabhan, G. P. jt auth

FELIX, David
Income inequality in Mexico. bibl f Cur Hist 72:111-14+ Mr '77

FELIX, Regina
Racing shape. il pors Seventeen 36:184-5 Ap '77 *

FELIX, W. Robert, Jr
Questions for the doctor. por Consumers Res Mag 60:41 S; 41 N; 38 D '77

FELKER, Clay S.
Clay Felker, Esq. T. Schwartz. il por Newsweek 90:47 S 5 '77 *
Familiar voice for Esquire. Time 110:41 S 5 '77 *

Anecdotes, facetiae, satire, etc.

Revitalization of Clay Filter: yet another passage. N. Ephron. Esquire 87:28+ Ap '77

FELL, Barry
Who really discovered America? T. Fleming. il Read Digest 110:69-73 F '77 *

FELL, Derek
Everything you always wanted to know about the tomato. il Horticulture 55:16-18+ F '77
Horticulture's 1978 garden catalog preview. Horticulture 55:14+ D '77
[Month] in the garden. See issues of Horticulture

FELL, John L.
Vladimir Propp in Hollywood. bibl il Film Q 30:19-28 Spr '77

FELLATIO. See Sexual behavior

FELLIG, Arthur
Bad and the beautiful. M. Stevens. il por Newsweek 90:72-3 S 26 '77 *
He was there. A. Quindlen. il pors N Y Times Mag p40-3 S 11 '77 *
Seeing pictures. J. Scully. il Mod Phot 41:8+ D '77 *
Weegee the famous. J. Coplans. il por Art in Am 65:37-41 S '77 *
Weegee's brilliant flash of light. N. Ffrench-Frazier. il Art N 76:230+ N '77 *

FELLINI, Federico
Fellini's unlovable Casanova. P. Schwartzman. il N Y Times Mag p22-4+ F 6 '77 *
Screen. C. L. Westerbeck, Jr. Commonweal 104:240-1, 277-8, Ap 15, 29 '77 *
Two views on Fellini's Casanova. D. Willis; A. Johnson. il Film Q 30:24-31 Summ '77 *

FELLNER, William John
What's needed is to adjust for the impact of inflation; interview. por U.S. News 83:38 Jl 25 '77

FELLOWS, Martha
Student classification and legal implications for administrators. bibl Clearing H 51:80-5 O '77

FELLOWSHIP of Catholic Scholars
Conservative response. W. J. Parente. America 137:313 N 5 '77

FELSTINER, John
Through a Spanish looking glass: Williams' poetry in translation. Américas 29:5-8 N '77

FEM bass contests. See Fishing—Competitions

FEMININITY (psychology)
Competition vs. femininity. M. Dubrow. Harp Baz 110:85+ My '77
Is womanhood worth it? Vogue 167:94 F '77
New sexual pyramid; The club. K. Durbin. il Mademoiselle 83:142+ F '77
Who's afraid of bulging biceps? A call to arms for women athletes. C. McCall. il Ms 5:26+ My '77

FEMINISM
Brotherly love in today's Church. J. Chittister. il America 136:233-6 Mr 19 '77
Can women's lib sell its program? National Women's Conference in Houston. il U.S. News 83:31 D 5 '77
Clunks! J. O'Reilly. Ms 6:66-7 Jl '77
Have you ever supported equal pay, child care, or women's groups? The FBI was watching you; with excerpts from FBI files. L. C. Pogrebin. Ms 5:37-44+ Je; 6:7-8+ O '77
I am the mother of eight, a housewife, a feminist—and happy: Jane Broderick's story; interview, ed by J. Lazarre. J. Broderick. il por Ms 5:51-5+ My '77; Discussion. 6:7-8+ S '77
Intelligent woman's guide to sex; anti-feminist bias. K. Durbin. Mademoiselle 83:173+ F '77
Liberated woman: identity crisis. G. Serban. Harp Baz 110:232+ S '77
Loneliness of a teenage feminist. D. Shaw. il por Ms 6:112-13 N '77
Now that men can cry . . . W. Sheed. N Y Times Mag p38-40+ O 30 '77
Sexual courtesy. K. Durbin. Mademoiselle 83:147+ Mr '77
Special 5th anniversary issue. G. Steinem. il Ms 6:47 Jl '77
State of the movement. M. Sheils and others. il Newsweek 90:59-60+ N 28 '77
Talking to a friend—an interview with Simone de Beauvoir; ed by A. Schwarzer. S. de Beauvoir. por Ms 6:12-13+ Jl '77
Two feminists tell how they work; interviews, ed by G. Steinem. C. Bunch; K. Horbal. pors Ms 6:52-3+ Jl '77
Why women's lib is in trouble. il U.S. News 83:29-32 N 28 '77
Woman's art: it's the only goddam energy around; interview, ed by H. Lyons. M. Schapiro. il por Ms 6:40-3+ D '77
See also
Sex discrimination
Women's Action Alliance

Conferences

Crimes against women; International Tribunal on Crimes Against Women. D. E. H. Russell. Ms 5:81-3+ F '77
See also
National Women's Political Caucus
Women—Conferences

History

Framing our foremother; A. K. Foster. M. Bacon. por Ms 6:22 O '77
Pantsuited pioneer of Women's lib, Dr Mary Walker. A. Lockwood. il pors Smithsonian 7:113-14+ Mr '77
Victorians thought her a downright scandal—as she was; V. Woodhull. J. Davis. il por Smithsonian 8:131-6+ O '77

Language question

See Sex discrimination in language

Periodicals

Bibliography

Hot off the feminist presses: new journals. L. Van Gelder. il Ms 6:95-8 N '77

FEMINIST Press (firm) See Publishers and publishing—United States

FEMMES fatals in opera. See Women in opera

FENCES
Fence it in! Bet Hom & Gard 55:102+ My '77
Six great fence designs. il Mech Illus 73:72-3+ Ap '77
Storing the trailer behind a removable fence. il Sunset 159:107 S '77

FENCES (receivers of stolen goods) See Stolen goods, Receiving of

FENCES, Electric
Electric fences. il Farm J 101:Beef 14-15 Ja '77
Electric fencing: tips to keep yours tops. Suc Farm 75:no2 62 F '77

FENDERS, Automobile. See Automobiles—Fenders

FENDERSON, G. K.
This article will lead you down the primrose path. il Horticulture 55:50-5 Je '77

FENFLURAMINE. See Weight reducing preparations

FÉNIX Institute. See Spanish language—Study and teaching

FENNIMORE, Donald L. See Eff, E. jt auth

FENSELAU, Catherine, and others
Mandelonitrile β-glucuronide: synthesis and characterization. bibl il Science 198:625-7 N 11 '77

FENSTERHEIM, Herbert, and Baer, Jean
Stop running scared; excerpts. Good H 185:116+ N '77; 186:40+ Ja '78

FENSTERMACHER, Ted
Our retirement plans are working. il Org Gard & Farm 24:108-10 My '77

FENTON, Edward
Blind idiot: the problems of translation; adaptation of address, May 4, 1976. Horn Bk 53:505-13, 633-41 O-D '77

FENTON Pottery (firm) See Potteries—History

FENWICK, Millicent (Hammond)
Congresswoman who cares. S. Burnham. por McCalls 104:36+ Je '77 *
Grandmother is a sophomore. S. J. Ungar. por Atlantic 240:35 Jl '77 *

FENYVESI, Charles
Aging gracefully. New Repub 176:11-12 F 19 '77
(ed) Conversations with Italians; interviews. New Repub 178:18-19 Ja 7 '78
From the concrete floor. New Repub 176:16-17 Mr 26 '77
Kadar's crown. il New Repub 177:15-17 N 19 '77
Lace and velvet. New Repub 177:13-15 N 5 '77
Living with a fearful memory. por Psychol Today 11:61+ O '77
Red raspberries. New Repub 177:15 Ag 20 '77

FERACA, Jean
South paradise hotel; poem. Nation 224:184 F 12 '77

FERAL animals
Feral dogs: threat to man, too? C. Elliott. il Outdoor Life 159:88+ Mr '77
Summary of NPCA survey of feral animals in the national park system. il Nat Parks & Con Mag 51:16-20 Jl '77

FERCH, John A.
Strengthening the Public Law 480 food aid program; statement, April 5, 1977. Dept State Bull 76:447-51 My 2 '77

FERDMAN, Saul, and Kline, R. L.
Space solar power—an available energy source. il Space World M-12-156:4-17 D '76

FERGUSON, Clyde, and Cotter, W. R.
South Africa: what is to be done. bibl f For Affairs 56:253-74 Ja '78

FERGUSON, Eugene S.
Mind's eye: nonverbal thought in technology. bibl il Science 197:827-36 Ag 26 '77

FERGUSON, Francis E.
Uncommon risk-taker. por Forbes 119:85-6 F 15 '77 *

FERGUSON, Roy
Europe's sizzling summer. il Read Digest 110: 131-4 My '77

FERGUSON, Mo.
Education
See Education—Missouri

FERLEGER, David
Battle over children's rights. bibl il por Psychol Today 11:88-91 Jl '77

FERLINGHETTI, Lawrence
Sea and ourselves at Cape Ann; poem. N Y Times Mag p 142 S 11 '77
about
Poetry is dead, long live poetry. J. F. Cotter. bibl America 137:80-2 Ag 13 '77 *

FERM, Virgil H. See Kilham, L. jt auth

FERMI National Accelerator Laboratory. See National Accelerator Laboratory

FERMIONS. See Particles (nuclear physics)

FERNANDEZ, Steve
Boy wonder of fly tying. L. Green. il por Field & S 81:50-2 Ap '77 *

FERNANDEZ-MORENO, Cesar
Tango tangle. il UNESCO Courier 30:60-2 Ag '77

FERNANDEZ RETAMAR, Roberto
Debunking the black legend. il UNESCO Courier 30:54-5+ Ag '77

FERNS
Chemical evidence for separating the psilotaceae from the filicales. G. Cooper-Driver. bibl il Science 198:1260-2 D 23 '77
Easy to grow house plants:
Bear's-paw fern. E. McDonald. il House B 119:50 F '77
Staghorn ferns. E. McDonald. il House B 119:96 My '77
Gemmae: a role in sexual reproduction in the fern genus vittaria. V. D. Emigh and D. R. Farrar. bibl il Science 198:297-8 O 21 '77
Gift plant to treasure; maidenhair fern. il Sunset 159:178-9 D '77
Growing ferns from spores. il Sunset 159:154-5 Jl '77
Plants around the house: the fern craze. R. Langer. il House & Gard 149:84+ N '77

FERNS, Fossil
Evidence for a pollination-drop mechanism in Paleozoic pteridosperms. G. W. Rothwell. bibl il Science 198:1251-2 D 23 '77

FERNSTROM, John D. See Markovitz, D. C. jt auth

FERON, James
Class of '77: all's quiet at Scarsdale High. il N Y Times Mag p20+ Je 26 '77
Israelis of New York. il N Y Times Mag p 14-15+ Ja 16 '77

FERORELLI, Enrico
Letter from the publisher. J. Meyers. il por Sports Illus 47:6 D 5 '77 *

FERRARA, Armand B.
Blue concords are his favorites. il Org Gard & Farm 24:84-5 D '77
Rose care tips worth remembering. il Org Gard & Farm 24:95-7 Mr '77

FERRARI, Ermanno Wolf-. See Wolf-Ferrari, E.

FERRARI, Thomas E. and Wallace, D. H.
Incompatibility on Brassica stigmas is overcome by treating pollen with cycloheximide. bibl il Science 196:436-8 Ap 22 '77

FERRARI (sports car) See Sports cars

FERRENIEA, Viki
Wild flowers that will grow in your garden. il Horticulture 55:40-1 My '77

FERRER, José Figueres. See Figueres Ferrer, J.

FERRER, Rafael
Ferrer: a voyage with *salsa*: show at Manhattan's Nancy Hoffman Gallery. R. Hughes. il Time 109:67 F 28 '77 *

FERRETTI, Carlo
Historical records. A. F. Artsay. il por Hobbies 82:37+ Mr '77 *

FERRETTI, Fred
Mister Untouchable. il pors N Y Times Mag p 15-17+ Je 5 '77
Sending the best of America abroad. il Art N 76:62-5 Summ '77

FERREZ, Gilberto, and Naef, W. J.
Pioneer photographers of Brazil; excerpt from Pioneer photographers of Brazil, 1840-1920. il Society 14:74-6 My '77

FERRI, Jim
Black Hills & the Badlands. il Travel 147:30-3 Je '77
Manila today. il Trav/Holiday 149:40-3+ Ja '78
Oregon's magnificent Southwest. il Travel 47: 38-41+ Mr '77
Touch of the Dutch. il Holiday 58:44-7+ Ja '77
Vancouver and Victoria. il Travel 147:30-5 My '77

FERRIES
San Francisco launches world's first water-jet ferry. J. Zmuda. il Pop Sci 210:102 Ap '77
To get from here to there a pleasant way, take a ferry. il Smithsonian 8:76-81 Jl '77

FERRIS, Charles Daniel
FCC nomination causes some static. il por Bus W p41-2 O 3 '77 *

FERRIS, Susan
Making of Julia. il por Horizon 20:86-90+ O '77
Secrets of anamorphic art. il Horizon 19:16-23 Ja '77

FERRIS, Timothy
Seeking an end to cosmic loneliness. il N Y Times Mag p30-2+ O 23 '77
Solid-state fun. il Esquire 87:100-1+ Mr '77
—See Druyan A. jt auth

FERTILITY
Levodopa, fertility, and longevity. G. C. Cotzias and others. bibl il Science 196:549-51 Ap 29 '77
Monosodium glutamate administration to the newborn reduces reproductive ability in female and male mice. W. J. Pizzi and others. bibl il Science 196:452-4 Ap 22 '77

FERTILITY, Human
Controls on male fertility now seem within our reach. A. Rosenfeld. il Smithsonian 8:36-43 Jl '77

FERTILITY awareness method. See Birth control

FERTILITY of soils. See Soil fertility

FERTILITY symbols. See Symbols

FERTILIZATION (biology)
Hooks and eyes of sperm and eggs. il Sci N 112:356 N 26 '77
Program of fertilization. D. Epel. il Sci Am 237: 128-34+ bibl(p 161) N '77
See also
Conjugation (biology)
Spawning

FERTILIZATION, Artificial. See Artificial insemination, Human

FERTILIZATION of plants
Coevolution of foraging in bombus and nectar dispensing in chilopsis: a last dreg theory. T. G. Whitham. bibl il Science 197:593-6 Ag 5 '77
Evidence for a pollination-drop mechanism in Paleozoic pteriodosperms. G. W. Rothwell. bibl il Science 198:1251-2 D 23 '77
Game of the bees. B. Heinrich. il Horticulture 55:38-9+ Jl '77
Having cucumber troubles? Try hand pollination. D. J. Young. il Org Gard & Farm 24: 83-5 F '77
Pesticides and pollution. H. M. Caine. bibl il Environment 19:28-33 N '77
See also
Pollen

FERTILIZER industry
Enough fertilizer for 1977. D. Seim. Farm J 101:9+ mid-Mr '77
Fertilizer slump weakens a strong man; Beker Industries Corp. por Bus W p38 F 14 '77
Fertilizer's gloomy outlook. il Bus W p 180+ Mr 21 '77
See also
Williams Companies

FERTILIZERS and manures
Apply manure on phosphate basis. Suc Farm 75:36 Ag '77
Cut fertilizer costs without skimping on rates. B. Coffman. il Farm J 101:J2 O '77
Do's and don'ts of fall fertilizing; trees. R. Foster. Am City & County 92:114 S '77
Feed your vegetables chicken. E. Ruggeri. il Org Gard & Farm 24:76-7 Je '77
Fishing for good vegetables. J. Meeker. il Org Gard & Farm 24:86-7 D '77
Garden honey pot. J. J. Meeker. il Org Gard & Farm 25:142-5 Ja '78
Get the most from wood ashes. R. Young. il Org Gard & Farm 24:160-3 F '77
He's brewing up some manure tea. il Sunset 159:166 Jl '77
Putting the right things into the ground. M. Franz. Org Gard & Farm 24:136+ Ap '77
Seaweed: manure, mulch and fertilizer free from the sea. J. Plotkin. Org Gard & Farm 24:148-9 S '77
Starter fertilizer pays on cold soil. Suc Farm 75:no4 L44 Mr '77

FERTILIZERS and manures—*Continued*
Tips on mixing organic fertilizer. J. Jaisun. il Org Gard & Farm 24:78-9 My '77
Will fertilizers harm ozone as much as SST's? D. Shapley. Science 195:658 F 18 '77
See also
Compost
Lime
Liquid fertilizers and manures
Nitrapyrin
Refuse as fertilizer
Sewage as fertilizer
Sewage irrigation

Handling

Airpower moves manure for less. C. S. Machan. il Farm J 101:Dairy 1-2 Je '77
But officer, it's just fertilizer! C. Bickers. Farm J 101:Dairy 15 S '77
Can your cattle pay for confinement? W. Kester. il Farm J 101:Beef 10-11 O '77
How to match manure to crop needs. il Farm J 101:Hog 8 F '77
It's kept me in hogs; manure digester. E. Ainsworth. il Farm J 101:Hog 22-3 Ja '77
Pump selection for waste handling. G. L. Vincent. il Suc Farm 75:no4 LS1+ Mr '77
TRU recycles manure into odorless bedding. il Suc Farm 75:no4 D12 Mr '77
Tailor your manure system to fit your farm. Farm J 101:Hog 5+ F '77
What's ahead in pollution control rules? D. Seim. Farm J 101:Beef 9 My '77
Zero run-off system for $20 a cow. W. Kester. il Farm J 101:Dairy 6-8 O '77

Spray applications

Foliar fertilizers flunk big test on soybeans. B. Coffman. Farm J 100:29 D '76

FERTL, Inc. See Garden tools, equipment, and supplies—Manufacture

FESCE, Joseph P.
Just out. See issues of Popular photography

FESCUE
New fescue varieties on the way. C. Bickers. Farm J 101:E4 N '77

FESHBACH, Herman
For science policy—an opportunity. Phys Today 30:128 My '77

—and Sheldon, Eric
Recent advances in neutron physics. bibl il Phys Today 30:40-3+ F '77

FESTAC. See Festivals—Nigeria

FESTIVAL Canada. See Music festivals—Canada

FESTIVAL of American Folklife. See Festivals—Washington, D.C.

FESTIVAL of Contemporary Music. See Music festivals—Massachusetts

FESTIVAL of Two Worlds, Spoleto. See Festivals—Italy

FESTIVAL of Youth Orchestras. See Music festivals—Washington, D.C.

FESTIVALS
Fables, fantasies and folklore; spring festivals. Seventeen 36:60 Mr '77
See also
Drama festivals
Fasts and feasts
Motion picture festivals
Music festivals
Shakespeare festivals

California

California's Renaissance Faire. A. Sirdofsky. il Travel 147:40-1 My '77

Chile

Pilgrimage to La Tirana; celebration of religious festival. S. Valderrama. il Américas 29:17-20 Ag '77

England

Islam goes to England; World of Islam Festival in London. A. Goldin. bibl il Art in Am 65:106-13 Ja '77

Italy

Artist life; Spoleto Festival events and conductors. D. J. Soria. pors Hi Fi 27:MA8-10+ D '77
Menotti's two worlds; Spoleto Festival comes to Charleston, S.C. J. Gruen. il Opera N 41:12-17 My '77
Spoleto:
Operas at the Festival of Two Worlds. W. Weaver. Opera N 42:50-1 S '77

Japan

Japan's warriors of the wind; city's annual tribute to its first-born sons. J. Eliot. il Nat Geog 151:550-61 Ap '77

New Mexico

Santa Fe Festival: electicism and a high-noon showdown. W. Peterson. il Art N 76:78-9 D '77

Nigeria

Black culture—the Bible is the judge; Second World Black and African Festival of Arts and Culture, FESTAC. W. H. Fuller. Chr Today 21:51-2 Ap 1 '77
Festac '77; with editorial comment. il Ebony 32:33-6+, 48-9 My '77
International exchange: the 2nd World Festival of Black Art and Culture; Lagos. C. Morgan. il Dance Mag 51:90 Jl '77
Searching for black roots; World Black and African Festival of Arts and Culture. J. Pringle. il Newsweek 89:40+ F 14 '77

Scotland

See also
International Festival of Music and Drama, Edinburgh

South Carolina

Artist life; Spoleto U.S.A. Festival. D. J. Soria. il Hi Fi 27:MA6-8 O '77
Charleston, S.C; operatic productions at the Spoleto festival. R. Jacobson. il Opera N 42:38+ Ag '77
Loaf of bread, a glass of wine, and hushpuppies; Spoleto Festival U.S.A. Horizon 19:86-7 My '77
Menotti's two worlds; Spoleto Festival comes to Charleston. J. Gruen. il Opera N 41:12-17 My '77
Musical events; Spoleto Festival U.S.A. A. Porter. New Yorker 53:96+ Je 13 '77
Neglected sculptor at Spoleto U.S.A. J. Gruen. il Art N 76:122+ S '77
Newest U.S. immigrant: Spoleto. il por Time 109:72+ Je 6 '77
Spoleto comes to Charleston. J. Kroll. il por Newsweek 89:56-7+ Je 6 '77
Spoleto Festival U.S.A. S. Fleming. il Hi Fi 27:MA32-4 O '77
Spoleto U.S.A. G. Glueck. il por N Y Times Mag p20-2+ My 22 '77
Spoleto U.S.A: a world celebration. W. Terry. il Sat R 4:42-3 Jl 9 '77

Spain

Song of sack; sherry festival in Jerez. N. Hazelton. Nat R 29:1312-13 N 11 '77

Switzerland

Seasons of vineyards; Fête des Vignerons. E. Schaeffer. Chr Today 22:36+ O 7 '77

United States

American Indian pow-wow. L. M. Rhodes. il Travel 147:48-53 F '77
Merry Kwanza! S. C. Cowley and M. Lord. il Newsweek 90:103 D 19 '77

Uruguay

Night of nights in Montevideo; Llamadas festival. C. Páez Vilaró. il Américas 29:58-9 N '77

Washington, D.C.

Cajun fiddles, Hindustani veenas and dulcimers; Smithsonian's Folklife Festival. R. Rinzler and P. Seitel. il Smithsonian 8:142+ O '77
View from the castle; Smithsonian's Festival of American Folklife. S. D. Ripley. Smithsonian 8:6 Ap '77

FETAL research. See Fetus

FÊTE des Vignerons wine festival. See Festivals—Switzerland

FETOLOGY. See Fetus

FETUS
Still forbidden fruit; fetal research report of the National Commission for the Protection of Human Subjects of Biomedical and Behavioral Research. G. Meilaender, Jr. il Chr Today 21:16-19 Ja 21 '77

Diseases

Therapy

Healing babies before they're born. E. Kiester, Jr. il Fam Health 9:26-8+ O '77

FETUS, Effect of drugs on the
Drugs, coffee, alcohol, infections and your unborn baby; excerpt from Caring for your unborn child. R. E. Gots and B. A. Gots. Good H 186:68+ Ja '78
Dubious drugs for pregnant women. M. Cimons. McCalls 104:63 F '77
Methadone and motherhood. J. Schinto. Progressive 41:40-2 Mr '77
On popping pills and potions during pregnancy. M. Newton. Fam Health 9:20+ My '77
Pregnancy no-no's; substances that may be risky to unborn. G. Carro. il Ladies Home J 94:24 S '77

FETUS, Effect of smoking on the
Toxicity of mild prenatal carbon monoxide exposure. L. D. Fechter and Z. Annau. bibl il Science 197:680-2 Ag 12 '77

FEUDALISM
Organized peace in southern France and Catalonia, ca. 1140-ca. 1233. T. N. Bisson. bibl f map Am Hist R 82:290-311 Ap '77

FEUER, Lewis S.
Arthur O. Lovejoy. Am Scholar 46:358-66 Summ '77
Herberg as political philosopher. por Nat R 29:882-3 Ag 5 '77

FEVER ticks. See Ticks

FIAT (automobile) See Automobiles, Foreign

FIAT Company. See Automobile industry—Italy

FIBER crafts. See Textile crafts

FIBER in food. See Food—Fiber content

FIBER optics
Fiber lightguide. A. G. Chynoweth; reply. A. G. Revesz. bibl Phys Today 30:84+ Mr '77
Fiber optics for controls being studied. il Aviation W 108:45 Ja 2 '78
Photons in fibers for telecommunication. S. E. Miller. bibl il Science 195:1211-16 Mr 18 '77

FIBERGLASS boats. See Boats—Materials

FIBICH, Zdenek
Quintet in D major, op. 42; Trio in F minor. J. Ringo. Am Rec G 40:29-30 D '76 *

FIBKINS, Robert J.
Publisher's letter. Horticulture 55:96 F '77

FIBONACCI numbers
Cornering a queen leads unexpectedly into corners of the theory of numbers. M. Gardner. il Sci Am 236:134+ Mr '77
Phyllotaxis and the Fibonacci series. G. J. Mitchison. bibl il Science 196:270-5 Ap 15 '77

FIBREBOARD Corporation
When a good try was not enough. Bus W p36-7 O 10 '77

FIBROBLASTS
Testing the commitment theory of cellular aging. R. Holliday and others. bibl il Science 198:366-72 O 28 '77

FIBROSIS, Cystic. See Cystic fibrosis

FICHTER, George S.
Bizarre world of undersea lights. il Int Wildlife 8:12-15 Ja '78

FICHTER, Joseph H.
Alcohol addiction: priests and prelates. America 137:258-60 O 22 '77
Spirituality, religiosity and alcoholism. America 136:458-61 My 21 '77

FICK, Alvin S.
Schoharie aqueduct. il por Conservationist 32:16-17 N '77

FICO, Rosario M. and others
Bifunctional intercalators: relationship of antitumor activity of diacridines to the cell membrane. bibl il Science 198:53-6 O 7 '77

FICTION
Playing with the facts. T. Griffith. il Time 110:92-3 S 19 '77
That's entertainment! on the role of the novel. R. Condon. Harpers 255:80+ S '77
See also
Blacks in literature
Characters in literature
Christmas stories
Detective and mystery stories
Novelists
Politics in literature
Publishers and publishing—Fiction
Realism in literature
Science fiction
Women in literature
World War, 1914-1918—Fiction
also European fiction; Russian fiction; etc.

Authorship

Cheever's triumph. W. Clemons. il pors Newsweek 89:61-2+ Mr 14 '77
Conversation with John Gardner; interview, ed by D. Edwards and C. Polsgrove. J. Gardner. pors Atlantic 239:43-4+ My '77
Does genius have a gender? J. Burroway and C. Ozick. pors Ms 6:56-7+ D '77
Duet of Cheevers; interview, ed by S. Cheever Cowley. J. Cheever. il pors Newsweek 89:68-70+ Mr 14 '77
Eccentric like a Fox; interview, ed by B. Dickey. W. P. Fox. il por Writers Digest 57:41 F '77
Fiction. L. Block. See alternate issues of Writer's digest
Gold mine of experience. C. Brink. Writer 90:11-14 Ag '77
How to write a novel. M. L. West. Writer 90:9-11 My '77
Joseph Heller: some things happen. L. Grobel. por Writers Digest 57:24-5 O '77
Literary life anything but romantic; excerpts from address. W. Stegner. por Intellect 106:107 S '77
Little Tree in Forrest; work of F. Carter. D. Davis. por Writers Digest 57:24 My '77
Ludlum conspiracy; R. Ludlum. L. Block. por Writers Digest 57:25-6 S '77
Novelist's identity crisis. H. Van Slyke. Writer 90:11-14 N '77
Plots brew in Kansas; L. V. Roper. B. Townsend. il por Writers Digest 57:30-1 Mr '77
Questions they never asked me. W. Percy. il pors Esquire 88:170-2+ D '77
Risks and rewards in writing the saga novel. S. Howatch. Writer 90:11-13+ Je '77
Studs Lonigan in the Bronx; interview, ed by A. Auster and L. Quart. R. Price. Nation 224:725-7 Je 11 '77
Thomas Gifford: the bestsell factor. S. L. Muellner. por Writers Digest 57:50-1 Jl '77
What makes a fiction writer? B. J. Chute. Writer 90:9-11 O '77
What you do know can hurt you. J. McKimmey. Writer 90:18-20 Je '77
Witches and aspirin; interview, ed by M. Allen. S. King. il por Writers Digest 57:26-7 Je '77
Workshop trio. P. D. Boles. Writer 90:15-17 My '77
Your life in fiction. C. L. Evans. Writer 90:21-2+ F '77

Anecdotes, facetiae, satire, etc.

New big one. R. Lipez. Atlantic 241:88-9 Ja '78

Collaboration

See Authorship—Collaboration

Bibliography

Fiction (cont) G. C. Reedy. America 136:421-3 My 7; 137:336+ N 12 '77
John Gardner on fiction. J. Gardner. New Repub 177:33-4 D 3 '77

Competitions

Between the lines; winners of Redbook's Young Writers' Contest; short stories. A. M. Smith. il Redbook 149:20 Ag '77

Study and teaching

Aids and devices

How to encourage the unwilling reader of fiction. N. A. Rabianski. il Engl J 66:64-9 F '77
Of bags and boxes: how to banish the book report form without getting fired. B. L. Warren. il Engl J 66:70-3 F '77

Technique

Absorbing reality into fiction. M. C. Banning. Writer 90:12-14+ O '77
Angle of vision. R. Brown. Writer 90:15-18+ S '77
Beyond the obvious. A. S. Turnbull. Writer 90:23-4 S '77
Experimenting with perspective. B. Rohde. Writer 91:9-12+ Ja '78
Five W's and how! L. Floren. Writers Digest 57:39-40+ Jl '77
Four tests for a paragraph. J. Ball. Writer 90:15-16+ Ja '77
Great man syndrome: Saul Bellow & me. S. Dworkin. por Ms 5:72-3 Mr '77
How to be an expert on anything. F. G. Slaughter. Writer 90:11-13 Jl '77
Leaving the reader satisfied. P. A. Whitney. Writer 90:13-16+ Ap '77
One way through the woods. R. M. Stern. Writer 90:11-13 F '77
Ordinary thoughts on the writing of a novel. J. Guest. Writer 90:11-14+ Ja '77
See also
Characterization
Dialogue
Plots (drama, novel, etc)
Short story

Themes

See Literature—Themes

FICTION and society. See Literature and society

FICTION collections in libraries. See Libraries—Fiction collections

FICTION collective (firm) See Publishers and publishing—Fiction

FICTION contests. See Fiction—Competitions

FICTION in periodicals and newspapers
Good fiction, plain and fancy; fiction in Redbook and in little magazines. G. Lyons. Nation 225:405-6 O 22 '77
Redbook fiction, from the inside. J. Johnson. Writer 90:18-21 N '77
Theory of the silver bullet. L. S. Bernstein. Writer 90:28-9 Ag '77
What do you learn at a writers conference? M. Costigan. Writer 90:16-18+ D '77

FICTION writing. See Fiction—Authorship

FICUS. See Fig trees

FIDDES, John C.
Nucleotide sequence of a viral DNA; with biographical sketch. il Sci Am 237:10, 54-67 D '77

FIDDLE. See Violin

FIDDLER, Ileen
Dentists for kids only. il Fam Health 9:31-4 O '77

FIDDLER crabs. See Crabs

FIDDLER on the roof; musical comedy. See Musical comedy, revue, etc.—Reviews—Single works

FIDELIO; opera. See Beethoven, L. van

FIDELITY Bank of Philadelphia. See Philadelphia—Banks

FIDLER, Isaiah J. and Kripke, M. L.
Metastasis results from preexisting variant cells within a malignant tumor. bibl il Science 197:893-5 Ag 26 '77
Tumor growth and spread. bibl il pors Chemistry 50:18-24 Ja '77

FIDRYCH, Mark
Bird flaps again and doesn't flop. P. Gammons. il por Sports Illus 46:20-1 Je 6 '77 *
He's not a bird, he's a human. R. Fimrite. il Sports Illus 46:44-6+ Ap 11 '77 *
FIEDLER, Arthur
Arthur Fiedler discusses the future of American music. pors U.S. News 82:44 Mr 7 '77
What's happening; interview, ed by G. Shalit. il por Ladies Home J 94:14+ N '77
FIEDLER, Leslie A.
Fascination of freaks; excerpt from Freaks. il Psychol Today 11:56-9+ Ag '77
FIEL, Maxine Lucille
Starcast. See issues of Mademoiselle
FIELD, James A. Jr
Comments: America: experiment or destiny? Am Hist R 82:523-7 Je '77
FIELD, Jane Tylor
Classroom tips. See issues of Today's education
FIELD, Michael
Eat; excerpt from Michael Field's cooking school. M. Cantwell. Mademoiselle 83:102 S '77 *
FIELD, Roger
Consumer notebook (cont of) Science and the consumer. See issues of Science digest
Here's how to use your own TV to locate twisters. Sci Digest 81:14-16 My '77
FIELD and stream (periodical)
Editor; policy affecting manuscripts. D. E. Petzal. Field & S 82:6 D '77
Editorial; staff awards. M. J. O'Neill. Field & S 82:4 O '77
FIELD crops. See Crops
FIELD experiments (agriculture)
Test plots help this farmer compare crop varieties. Suc Farm 75:no2 59 F '77
Testing; 1, 2, 3, testing... C. E. Sommers. Suc Farm 75:no3 F13 F '77
FIELD glasses
Better look at binoculars. J. Samberg. Field & S 82:20+ Ag '77
Binoculars. il Consumers Res Mag 60:7-11 Mr '77
See how they run! il Esquire 87:94-5 Ap '77
FIELD goal kickers. See Football players
FIELD mice. See Mice
FIELD theory (physics)
Future of unified gauge theories; adaptation of address, February 8, 1977. S. Weinberg. bibl il Phys Today 30:42-3+ Ap '77
Physics and the cosmos; gauge theories. J. Bernstein. Natur Hist 86:106-7+ O '77
Unified gauge theories: an atomic fly in the ointment. A. L. Robinson. Science 198:908-9 D 2 '77
FIELD trips, Educational. See School excursions
FIELDCREST Mills, Inc
How basic management principles pay off; interview. W. C. Battle. pors Nations Bus 65:46-8+ Mr '77
Kingpin of upstairs linen. il Forbes 120:98 O 1 '77
FIELDS, Cheryl M.
Anti-bias safeguards don't apply to teachers. Educ Digest 43:46-7 S '77
FIELDS, Mary
Stagecoach Mary; ed by M. Crawford. G. Cooper. il pors Ebony 32:96-8+ O '77 *
FIELDS, Totie
Happy courage of Totie Fields; interview, ed by S. D. Scott. por Ladies Home J 94:68+ My '77
FIELDSTON School. See Bronx, N.Y.—Education
FIESTA (automobile) See Automobiles, Foreign
FIFTY Books of the Year exhibit. See Book exhibits
FIG trees
Fig trees from cuttings. Sunset 159:190 D '77
Houseplant how-to; ficuses. il Bet Hom & Gard 55:262 O '77
Versatile fig named celeste. V. F. Shockley. il Org Gard & Farm 24:82-3 D '77
FIGARO (operatic character) See Characters in opera
FIGHTING. See Boxing
FIGHTING (psychology)
See also
Aggressiveness (psychology)
FIGHTING, Hand-to-hand. See Hand-to-hand fighting
FIGS
See also
Cookery—Fruit
FIGUERES FERRER, José
Don Pepe; interview, ed by K. Bode. New Repub 176:13-15 Ap 23 '77
about
Costa Rica imbroglio. K. Bode. New Repub 176:12-16 My 28 '77 *
FIGUEROA, Alfonso
Alfonso Figueroa and the Birmingham Ballet; interview, ed by L. Small. Dance Mag 52:73-4 Ja '78
FIGURE drawing
See also
Portrait drawing
FIGURE painting
See also
Portrait painting
FIGURE skating. See Skating
FIGURINES
Santons of Provence. R. D. Sullivan. il Hobbies 82:116-17+ D '77
FIGURINES, Wooden. See Wood carving
FIJI
See also
Lauthala (island)

Description and travel

Fiji. T. Talamini. Trav/Holiday 148:32+ D '77
FILAR micrometers. See Micrometers
FILARTIGA, Joel
Political murder in Paraguay. A. Cabral. il America 136:376-8 Ap 23 '77 *
FILARTIGA, Joelito
Political murder in Paraguay. A. Cabral. il America 136:376-8 Ap 23 '77 *
FILES and filing (documents, etc)
Desk top file or rack for books. il Sunset 158:106 Mr '77
FILES and rasps
Workshop mini-course: files and rasps. H. Wicks. il Pop Mech 148:132 O '77
FILIBUSTERING in legislation. See United States—Congress—Senate—Rules and practice
FILICALES. See Ferns
FILIPINO composers. See Composers, Filipino
FILIPINOS in the United States
Brain drain Philippinos. A. J. A. Pido. bibl Society 14:50-3 S '77
La **FILLE** mal gardée; ballet. See Ballet reviews—Single works
FILLERS (in periodicals) See Periodical fillers
FILLETS, Fish. See Fish as food
FILLING (earthwork)
Golf at the town dump. G. Cornish. il Parks & Rec 12:28-9+ My '77
Honorable discharge for the biggest pollutant; dredged and fill materials. J. Crowder. il Parks & Rec 12:28a-30a F '77
How much leachate can we afford? question of groundwater pollution at landfill sites. J. J. Reinhardt. il Am City & County 92:48-9 Jl '77
Los Angeles County loses landfill fight. il Am City & County 92:30 Je '77
Solid waste recovers land for industry use; New Orleans. il Am City & County 92:46-8 Ap '77
What's new in landfill liners. il Am City & County 92:54-6 F '77
FILM adaptations. See Motion picture adaptations
FILM containers. See Photography—Apparatus and supplies
FILM festivals. See Motion picture festivals
FILM Library Association, Educational. See Educational Film Library Association
FILM propaganda. See Motion pictures—Propaganda films
FILM speeds. See Photography—Exposure
FILM strips. See Filmstrips
FILMS
See also
Photography—Films
FILMS, Motion picture. See Motion Pictures
FILMS from books. See Motion picture adaptations
FILMSTRIPS
Case for filmstrips; producing filmstrips in the classroom. D. P. Miller. il Engl J 66:70-2 O '77
FILMSTRIPS in religious education
Filmstrips. D. Sanders. Chr Today 22:36 N 4; 42 D 9 '77
Return of the filmstrip. D. Sanders. Chr Today 21:38+ F 18; 38-9 Mr 18 '77
FILMWRITING. See Motion picture authorship
FILTERS, Light. See Light filters
FILTERS, Radio. See Radio filters
FILTERS and filtration
Don't drink the water; home charcoal filters. J. Carper. il Am Home 80:16 N '77
End taste and odor complaints with granular activated carbon; water. C. A. Blanck. il por Am City & County 92:89-90 O '77
How cost effective is direct filtration? water filtration. G. P. Fulton. il Am City & County 92:43-4 Ja '77
New guide to water filters. F. K. Coffee. il Mech Illus 73:122+ Mr '77
See also
Air filters
Automobile engines—Filters
Marine engines—Filters
FIMRITE, Ron
Baseball (cont) Sports Illus 46:69-70+ My 2 '77
Baseball 1977. Sports Illus 46:36-7 Ap 11 '77
Giving Joe a big hello. il por Sports Illus 47:8-11 Ag 15 '77
Good guys against the bad guys. il Sports Illus 47:18-25 O 24 '77
He's not a bird, he's a human. il Sports Illus 46:44-6+ Ap 11 '77
In Cuba, it's viva el grand old game. il Sports Illus 46:68-72+ Je 6 '77

FIMRITE, Ron—*Continued*
Lot of person. il pors Sports Illus 46:76-80+ Ap 4 '77
Make way for the Sultan of Swipes. il pors Sports Illus 47:24-30 Ag 22 '77
Melding of men all suited to a T. il Sports Illus 47:90-100 S 5 '77
Pro basketball. Sports Illus 46:63-5 My 9 '77
Reds are singing the blues. il Sports Illus 47: 16-19 Ag 22 '77
Reg-gie! Reg-gie!! Reg-gie!!! il pors Sports Illus 47:28-30+ O 31 '77
Script written by God. il Sports Illus 47:21-3 O 17 '77
This guy Tanana's no second banana. il pors Sports Illus 47:38-43 Jl 11 '77
Tip of the hat, cut of the bat. Sports Illus 46: 24-5 Ap 25 '77
Yankee Clipper. il pors Sports Illus 47:122-6+ O 10 '77

FINANCE
See also
Banks and banking
Bonds
Bonds, Government
Budget
Capital
Church finance
Commerce
Credit
Farm finance
Inflation (finance)
Interest (economics)
Investment trusts
Investments
Money
Money markets
Municipal finance
Negotiable instruments
Securities
Stock exchanges
Stocks
also subhead Finance under various subjects, e.g. Small business—Finance

Alaska

Way up there. Forbes 119:23-4 F 15 '77

Arab countries

Arabs breed a new capital market. il Bus W p76 Ap 18 '77

Canada

Why Canadian dollars are migrating south. il Bus W p42+ N 28 '77
See also
Banks and banking—Canada
Canada—Monetary policy

Chile

Trying to cash in on a stronger economy. Bus W p42+ Ap 11 '77

Europe, Eastern

See also
Debts, Public—Europe, Eastern

France

See also
France—Monetary policy
Securities—France

Great Britain

See also
Bank of England
Bonds, Government—Great Britain
Budget—Great Britain

Italy

Credit shadow over foreign trade. Bus W p56+ N 14 '77
Credit stretched to the breaking point. Bus W p68 D 12 '77
Swiss shuffle. D. Pauly. il Newsweek 89:81 My 9 '77
See also
Securities—Italy

Japan

See also
Securities—Japan
Stock exchanges—Tokyo Exchange

Michigan

Pension plan crisis looming; public employee pension plans. Am City & County 92:27 D '77

New York (state)

War between the states; D. P. Moynihan speech of July 27. W. F. Buckley, Jr. Nat R 29:905 Ag 5 '77

Russia

Olympics send Russians off on a profit-making spree. il U.S. News 83:55 D 5 '77

Singapore

Asiadollar market starts to sprout. Bus W p44 Jl 11 '77

South Africa

See also
Budget—South Africa

Texas

Bonds of Texas. Forbes 119:136 My 15 '77

United States

Finance trends. See issues of U.S. news and world report
See also
Banks and banking—United States
Budget—United States
Debts, Public—United States
Local finance
United States—Appropriations and expenditures
United States—Economic conditions
United States—Federal Reserve System
United States—Monetary policy
also subhead Finance under names of cities, e.g New York (city)—Finance

FINANCE, International
Cure for depression; excerpts from interview, ed by A. de Borchgrave. J. Javits. por Newsweek 90:71 S 26 '77
High-yielding currency hedge; use of floating rate by multinationals. il Bus W p67 F 21 '77
Petro-dollar pinch tightens. il U.S. News 82:22 My 9 '77
Why so much worry about a world financial crisis. il U.S. News 82:84-5 F 14 '77
See also
Asiadollar market
Balance of payments
Banks and banking, International
Bonds
Debts, External
Eurobond market
Eurodollar market
Financial institutions, International
Foreign exchange
International Bank for Reconstruction and Development
International Monetary Fund

FINANCE, Local. See Local finance

FINANCE, Personal
American families optimistic; findings of Yankelovich study. Intellect 106:183 N '77
Bitterness tinged with hope; the stories of four families. il U.S. News 82:52-5 My 2 '77
Changing times saving & investment yardstick. il Changing T 31:41 Je; 25-8 O '77
Dollars and sense; money management for married and unmarried couples. G. Mahon. Mademoiselle 83:42+ S '77
Family money management. M. Daly. See issues of Better homes & gardens
Family spending habits; Bureau of Labor Statistics survey. Society 14:5-6 S '77
Financial mistakes even smart people make. il Changing T 31:7-9 D '77
Focus: on finances. Seventeen 36:60-1 S '77
How 8 young women punch up their lives; symposium. il Mademoiselle 83:129-31+ Je '77
How much do I love thee? Let me count the change . . . ; family money quarrels. V. Grey. il Am Home 80:82-3 F '77
How to handle your money: latest from an expert; interview. J. S. Rosenbloom. il pors U.S. News 83:67-8+ S 19 '77
Is his money your money too? S. W. Olds. il Redbook 149:120+ S '77
It's not only men with extra cash; with interview with V. VanCaspel. il U.S. News 83:32-4 D 5 '77
Living with high prices: how people are changing their ways. il U.S. News 83:16-17 Jl 18 '77
Managing your money. J. Train. por Forbes 120:134-5 N 1; 206 N 15; 130-1 D 1; 94-5 D 15 '77; 121:232-3 Ja 9 '78
Managing your money in '78. il Changing T 32: 6-10 Ja '78
Money. W. Flanagan. See occasional issues of Vogue
Money. A. Tobias. See issues of Esquire
Money matters. P. Gross. por House & Gard 149:30+ My; 44+ S; 58+ O; 22-3+ N '77
Money problems of the stars. R. Kisner. il Ebony 32:142-6+ My '77
Money questions and answers (cont of) Answers to your questions on money. N. G. Rollins. See issues of Good housekeeping
Money talks. P. Nelson. por McCalls 104:74+ F; 96+ Ap; 68+ Je; 76+ Jl; 105:46+ N '77
Money: the subject harder to talk about than sex. C. Tarvis. Ms 6:63-7 N '77
Planning your personal financial strategy. M. Pollard. Archit Rec 161:59 Mr; 77 Ap '77
Q&A about investments. S. Shulsky. See issues of Retirement living
Q&A about money (cont) J. S. Dennis. por Ret Liv 16:57 D '76; 17:58 F; 80+ Ap; 50 Jl; 14-15 O '77
7 mistakes retirees make about money. J. S. Dennis. il Ret Liv 17:22-5 S '77
Spending money on yourself can up your bank account; depression alleviated by psychotherapy. M. Page. Vogue 167:236+ S '77
Spending your money; questions and answers. S. Porter. See issues of Ladies' home journal
What's that about the poor little woman? O. Sanderlin. il Ret Liv 17:25+ S '77

FINANCE, Personal—*Continued*
Why women can't save money. P. Nelson. Harp Baz 110:98+ Mr '77
See also
Bankruptcy
Budget, Household
Credit
Debt
Estate planning
Investments
Wealth

FINANCE, Public
See also
Local finance
Paper money
State finance

FINANCE Committee, Senate. See United States—Congress—Senate—Finance, Committee on

FINANCE companies
New credit packages for the smaller borrower; competition for business loan customers. il Bus W p74-5 S 5 '77

Australia

Citicorp's Australian salvage operation; Industrial Acceptance Corp. Bus W p36 My 2 '77

FINANCIAL Accounting Standards Board. See Accounting—Standards

FINANCIAL analysts. See Investment advisers

FINANCIAL consultants. See Financial services

FINANCIAL counseling. See Financial services

FINANCIAL institutions
Finance. il Forbes 121:119-22 Ja 9 '78
See also
American Financial Corporation
Banks and banking
Finance companies
Investment trusts
Savings and loan associations

Investments

See Institutional investments

Statistics

Fifty largest diversified-financial companies. il Fortune 96:166-7 Jl '77

FINANCIAL institutions, International
Department urges appropriation of funds for international financial institutions; statement, February 16, 1977. P. H. Boeker. Dept State Bull 76:198-201 Mr 7 '77
See also
Banks and banking, International

FINANCIAL Institutions Supervision, Regulation and Insurance Subcommittee. See United States—Congress—House—Banking, Currency and Housing, Committee on—Financial Institutions Supervision, Regulation and Insurance Subcommittee

FINANCIAL journalism. See Journalism, Commercial

FINANCIAL planning. See Business planning

FINANCIAL ratios
Ratios of manufacturing. il Duns R 110:92-3+ D '77
Ratios of retailing. il Duns R 110:80-1 S '77
Ratios of the wholesalers. il Duns R 110:124-6 O '77

FINANCIAL services
How to get help with your money problems. P. Nelson. por McCalls 104:68+ Je '77
See also
Accountants
Goldman, Sachs & Company
Investment advisers
Tax consultants

FINANCIAL statements
Annual survey of corporate balance sheets. il Bus W p72-6+ O 17 '77
Obfuscation, Inc. por Forbes 119:78-9 F 15 '77
See also
Corporation reports
Disclosure in accounting

FINCASTLE, Va.
Small is beautiful. P. Davis. il Am Home 80:44-5+ Jl '77

FINCH, Joyce H.
Design your own historical quilt. il Design (US) 78:2-6 mid-Wint '77

FINCHER, Jack
And now, atomic clocks. Read Digest 111:34+ N '77

FINCHES
See also
Goldfinches

FINDLEY, Myrtle
Why my dried apricots don't shrivel up. Org Gard & Farm 24:112-13 Ag '77

FINE, Daniel I.
Rhodesia: a gingerly diplomacy. Nation 225:199-201 S 10 '77

FINE, Jacob
Rx: a peer review system for physicians. il Bull Atom Sci 33:38-43 S '77

FINE, John C.
NESS: National Environmental Satellite Service; with biographical sketch. il Sea Front 23:198-203, 254 Jl '77

FINE, Max W.
Case for national health insurance. bibl f Cur Hist 73:13-16+ Jl '77; Same. Current 196:26-32 O '77

FINE, William M.
Fad, fashion, or style? il Sat R 4:52-3 F 5 '77

FINE Arts Quartet. See String quartets

FINEBERG, Richard A.
Promises and betrayals. Nation 225:293-7 O 1 '77

FINEMAN, Herbert
Entrance examination. il por Time 109:14 Je 6 '77 *

FINEMAN, Morton
Draw a very big circle; story. Ladies Home J 94:78-9+ Je '77
From two to three; story. Ladies Home J 94:60 S '77
Laura, herself; story. Ladies Home J 94:106-7 My '77

FINES, Library. See Libraries—Fines

FINGER Lakes Region
New York's land of dreamers and doers. E. A. Starbird. il map Nat Geog 151:702-24 My '77

FINGER prints. See Fingerprints

FINGERHOOD, Shirley
New child-care tax credit: what will it do for you? Ms 5:101-4 Ap '77

FINGERNAILS. See Nails (anatomy)

FINGERNAILS, Manicuring of. See Manicuring

FINGERPRINTS
Inkless fingerprints help fight bad checks. il Bus W p33+ F 28 '77
Thumb down for the credit card—eventually; use of thumbprints for credit. E. K. Sperling. il Intellect 106:44-5 Ag '77

FINISHING, Wood. See Wood finishing

FINKELSTEIN, Edward
New Macy's greets Christmas. il por Time 110:60 D 5 '77 *

FINKELSTEIN, Stan N.
Blood pressure measurement devices. il Consumers Res Mag 60:7-10 F '77

FINLAND
See also
Booksellers and bookselling—Finland
Music festivals—Finland
Publishers and publishing—Finland

Description and travel

Finland. A. Henkels. il Sat Eve Post 249:91+ My '77

Foreign relations

Russia

See Russia—Foreign relations—Finland

FINLAY, Ian Hamilton
Submarines in the evergreens. W. Feaver. Art N 76:220+ N '77 *

FINLAYSON, Alice Bell
Unique Southwest educational program. il Negro Hist Bull 40:658 Ja '77

FINN, James
Second Call to Action. Commonweal 104:269-72 Ap 29 '77

FINNAN, T. L.
Sailor's Bimini top. il Motor B & S 139:132 Je '77

FINNEY, Ben R.
Voyaging canoes and the settlement of Polynesia. bibl il maps Science 196:1277-85 Je 17 '77

FINNISH Americans
Maid from Finland; B. Hiltunen family. T. Schwartz and others. il Newsweek 90:32 Jl 4 '77

FINNS in the United States
See also
Finnish Americans

FIR

Diseases and pests

See also
Spruce budworms

FIRE
Anatomy of fire! Newer technologies fighting the unknown. M. Grosswirth. il Sci Digest 82:7-11 Ag '77

Anecdotes, facetiae, satire, etc.

Fire safety controversy. V. L. Highland. Bull Atom Sci 33:54-5 O '77

FIRE and casualty insurance companies. See Insurance companies

FIRE ants. See Ants

FIRE arms. See Firearms

FIRE codes. See Fire prevention—Laws and regulations

FIRE companies. See Fire departments

FIRE departments
Yes, we now have firewomen; volunteers in Rollingwood, Tex. D. Lampe. il House B 119:21+ Mr '77
See also
Dallas—Fire Department
New York (city)—Fire Department

FIRE detectors
About smoke detectors for the home. il U.S. News 82:63 My 16 '77
Blazing market for smoke alarms. il Bus W p32 Mr 7 '77
Buy your smoke detector with care. R. Field. il Sci Digest 82:87-90 N '77
Caution: smoke detectors may be dangerous to your health; use of americium. M. C. Olson. Progressive 41:22-5 Ag '77
Consumer watch; smoke detectors. J. Carper. Am Home 80:20 Mr '77
Electronics aids security; fire and smoke detectors. A. Salsberg. Pop Electr 11:4 Ap '77
Home smoke-detectors win praise from safety experts, but controversy erupts over some types of units. Ret Liv 17:14 F '77
Inexpensive solution to fatal home fires. G. M. Chamberlain. Am City & County 92:106 Ap '77
Residential fire detectors. W. F. Jenaway. il Consumers Res Mag 60:16-20 My '77
Smoke detectors. Consumer Rep 42:303-4 D '77
Smoke detectors win Chicago council vote. il Am City & County 92:26 My '77
Update: smoke detectors. Consumer Rep 42:283 My '77

Manufacture
See also
Gillette Company

Testing
Fiery debate over smoke-alarm efficiency; controversy surrounding claims made by Gillette and ADT concerning their photoelectric detectors. il Bus W p95-6+ S 26 '77

FIRE engine industry. See Truck industry

FIRE engines
Foaming out air-crash fires; airport fire trucks. C. Haas. il Mech Illus 73:120 O '77

FIRE extinction
See also
Fire sprinklers
Women firefighters

History
Hinckley fire; 1894 fire fighting in Pine County, Minn. R. F. Snow. il Am Heritage 28:90-6 Ag '77

FIRE extinguishers
Fire extinguishers. Consumer Rep 42:305-6 D '77
Fire extinguishers; equipment for motor vehicles and boats. B. Behme. il Field & S 82:130+ Je '77
PS guide to fire extinguishers. C. Salit. il Pop Sci 211:58+ D '77

FIRE fighting. See Fire extinction

FIRE houses, Converted. See Buildings, Remodeled

FIRE Island
See also
Architecture, Domestic—Fire Island

FIRE making
If you get lost in the wilderness. J. Lord il Conservationist 31:35 My '77
My flaming affair with firewood. R. Starnes. Outdoor Life 161:12+ Ja '78

FIRE prevention
See also
Boats—Fires and fire prevention
Fireproof construction
Fireproofing of textiles
Forest fires—Prevention and control
Houses—Fires and fire prevention
Skyscrapers—Fires and fire prevention
United States—Commerce, Department of—National Fire Prevention and Control Administration

Laws and regulations
Concerned homemaker expresses her views on furniture flammability legislation; proposed flammable upholstered furniture law. M. Nervig. Consumers Res Mag 60:27+ Je '77
Local law 5; New York fire code for high-rise office buildings. D. Oliver. Nat R 29:387+ Ap 1 '77; Reply. J. T. O'Hagan. 29:717 Je 24 '77
Smoke detectors win Chicago council vote. il Am City & County 92:26 My '77

Research
More research on flammability, ignition, other factors needed; summary of paper. H. W. Emmons. Sci Digest 82:12-13 Ag '77

FIRE research. See Fire prevention—Research

FIRE sprinklers
Sprinkler system installer invents a bar joist that is part sprinkler pipe. il Archit Rec 162:119 Jl '77

FIRE trucks. See Fire engines

FIREARMS
Don't sell the short gun short; handguns. T. Trueblood. il Field & S 82:10+ Ag '77
Firearms. C. Worman. See issues of Hobbies
Getting the range (cont) J. Carmichel. il Outdoor Life 159:144+ F; 146+ Mr '77
Guns that shoot two ways. A. Maher. il Mech Illus 73:80-1 Jl '77
New guns for 1977. J. Carmichel. il Outdoor Life 159:129+ Mr '77
On target. P. Wahl. See issues of Popular science
Special hats, high ribs, and other news; firearms at the National Sporting Goods Show. B. Brister. il Field & S 82:114-16+ My '77
See also
Air guns
Gunstocks
Machine guns
Pistols
Revolvers
Rifles
Shotguns

Collectors and collecting
How much is that old gun worth? E. B. Mann. il Field & S 81:112-14 F '77

Decoration
Art of the engraver. J. Carmichel. il Outdoor Life 159:118-20+ My '77

Laws and regulations
Carter/Knox team wins a big one; handgun debates at the sixth conference of Game Conservation International in San Antonio. J. Samson. pors Field & S 82:41+ S '77
Cruising gun. V. Russell. il Motor B & S 140:54-5 O '77
Editorial; FAA proposed ban on carrying weapons in airports. J. Samson. Field & S 82:4 S '77
Great American gun war. W. F. Buckley, Jr. Nat R 29:223 F 18 '77
Gun control. I. Block. Society 14:10 Ja '77
Our endangered tradition. E. B. Mann. See issues of Field & stream

Anecdotes, facetiae, satire, etc.
Right to bear arms. D. Weil. il Atlantic 239:64-7 F '77

Protection against theft
Safeguarding your guns. C. Worman. il Hobbies 82:142-3 My '77

Safety devices and measures
How to fireproof your firearms. B. McKeown. il Pop Mech 147:103 Je '77
Pressure: the dangerous friend. J. Carmichel. il Outdoor Life 160:92-5 Jl '77

Sights
Missing impossible? B. Brister. il Field & S 82:110-12+ O '77
Of peeps and posts; iron sights. J. Wootters. il Field & S 81:142-5 Ap '77
Right scope. B. Bell. il Outdoor Life 160:83 N '77

FIREARMS industry
Effective way to get employees on your side; program at Marlin Firearms Co. V. Louviere. il Nations Bus 65:38-9 Jl '77
Traffic (legal and illegal) in guns. S. Brill. il Harpers 255:37-44 S '77

Acquisitions and mergers
Belgian arms maker bids for Browning; Fabrique Nationale acquiring Browning. il Bus W p27-8 Ag 22 '77

FIREARMS museums. See Museums

FIREBALL racing. See Sailboat racing

FIREBALLS. See Meteors

FIREBIRD; ballet. See Ballet reviews—Single works

FIRELESS cookers
Bring back the fireless cooker. H. Hunt. il Conservationist 31:32-3 Ja '77

FIREMEN
True soot; South Bronx firemen; excerpts from Firehouse. D. Smith and J. Freedman. il Esquire 87:97-9 My '77
See also
Trade unions—Firemen

Psychological examinations
Fire drill; Jersey City, N.J. Nation 224:708 Je 11 '77

FIREMENS strike (Great Britain) See Strikes—Great Britain

FIREPLACE cookery. See Cookery

FIREPLACES
Cluster of fireplaces. il Sunset 159:166-7 N '77
Energy-saving fireplace accessories. E. Moran. il Pop Sci 211:48+ N '77
Fabled fireplaces. G. B. Jackson. bibl il Antiques 112:1148-55 D '77

FIREPLACES—*Continued*
Fireplace addition that fits the spot. il Bet Hom & Gard 55:75 My '77
Fireplaces. B. Niles. il Am Home 80:91-3+ S '77
Freestanding fireplace. E. Moran. il Pop Sci 211:10+ S '77
Gene Feeney, fireplace grate for total heating. E. Moran. il Pop Sci 210:34-5 Je '77
Handbuilt fireplace facade. F. Simons. il Ceram Mo 25:59-61 N '77
Measure your fireplace for top performance. G. A. Repas. il Pop Sci 211:118-19 D '77
Turn your fireplace into a furnace. N. Smith. il Pop Sci 211:170 O '77
Useful heat from a cone fireplace. G. D. Jones. il Mech Illus 73:32+ O '77

Anecdotes, facetiae, satire, etc.

Keeping the home fires burning. W. Stanton. il Good H 185:78+ N '77

Fuel

Make your own gas log. P. Troke. il Mech Illus 73:84+ F '77

Marketing

Fireplace man; interview with senior partner in the William H. Jackson Company. H. Emmer. il New Yorker 53:31-2 My 2 '77

FIREPROOF construction
Fireproof retreat. A. Lees. il Pop Sci 211:106-7 S '77

FIREPROOFING
See also
Fireproof construction

FIREPROOFING of textiles
Banning Tris; chemically treated nightwear. il Newsweek 89:67 Ap 18 '77
Fire retardant may pose cancer hazard. Sci N 111:23 Ja 8 '77
Flame-retardant ban dishevels an industry; childrens sleepwear chemical Tris-BP. il Bus W p45-6 Ap 18 '77
Tris—a sleepwear flame retardant banned. il Consumers Res Mag 60:4 Je '77
Tris: confusion over another cancer hazard. Consumer Rep 42:415-16 Jl '77
Tris controversy. P. H. Abelson. Science 197:113 Jl 8 '77; Reply. R. H. Harris. bibl 197:1132-3 S 16 '77

FIRES
Hinckley fire. R. F. Snow. il Am Heritage 28:90-6 Ag '77
Ma Bell, firebug. F. Warner. Nation 224:684-8 Je 4 '77
St Francis YC destroyed in fire. J. Carrick. il Yachting 141:166 F '77
Your house is on fire! excerpt from Fire and you. H. R. Owen. Sat Eve Post 249:26 S '77
See also
Airplanes—Fires and fire prevention
Airports—Fires and fire prevention
Arson
Boats—Fires and fire prevention
Brush fires
Dormitories—Fires and fire prevention
Fire prevention
Forest fires
Harvesting machinery—Fires and fire prevention
Houses—Fires and fire prevention
Night clubs—Fires and fire prevention
Prisons—Fires and fire prevention
Skyscrapers—Fires and fire prevention

FIRESTONE, Harvey Samuel, 1898-
In nature's laboratory. P. W. Metzler. il pors Conservationist 32:30-3+ Jl '77 *

FIREWOMEN. See Women firefighters

FIREWOOD. See Wood as fuel

FIREWOOD bins. See Woodbins, racks, etc.

FIREWOOD racks. See Woodbins, racks, etc.

FIRING
See also
Kilns—Firing

FIRING of pottery. See Pottery—Firing

FIRMS, Architectural. See Architectural firms

FIRST aid for animals
First aid for pets. R. Caras. il Ladies Home J 94:156 Je '77
First aid for pets. A. Rosenblum. il Good H 185:206 Ag '77
What to do in an emergency. D. L. Hunter. il Parents Mag 53:64+ Ja '78

FIRST aid in illness and injury
Emergency techniques that save lives. M. Gosnell. il Ms 6:83-6 Ag '77
First aid for kids; views of M. Green. S. C. Cowley. il Newsweek 90:48 S 5 '77
In a medical emergency, can you get help fast? Changing T 31:21-4 O '77
New, fast help for the injured; paramedic teams in L.A. County. M. Spiegel. il Mech Illus 73:56+ O '77
Rx for campers. D. Larned. Harp Baz 110:89+ Ap '77
Simulated wounds for use in first-aid training. D. Lampe. il Sci Digest 82:76-8 N '77
Snakebite! What to know—what to do. C. Elliott. il Outdoor Life 160:84-7+ S '77
What's your first-aid I.Q? J. L. Lippert. Good H 185:266 N '77
See also
Ambulance service
Ambulances
Burns and scalds
Medical supplies
Poisons
Rescue work
Respiration, Artificial
Resuscitation

Bibliography

First-aid book in your backpack. Sunset 158:50 Mr '77

FIRST amendment to the Constitution. See United States—Constitution—Bill of Rights

FIRST American Bank, Canton, S.D. See Banks and banking—South Dakota

FIRST Banc Group of Ohio. See Bank holding companies

FIRST Chicago Corporation
Chicago's unique unbranched banking. il Bus W p66-8 Jl 18 '77

FIRST Kentucky National Corporation. See Bank holding companies

FIRST ladies. See Presidents—United States—Wives

FIRST National Bank of Atlanta. See Atlanta—Banks

FIRST National Bank of Chicago. See Chicago—Banks

FIRST National Bank of Commerce. See New Orleans—Banks

FIRST National City Corporation. See Citicorp

FIRST National Stores Inc-Pick-N-Pay Super Markets Inc merger. See Supermarkets—Acquisitions and mergers

FIRST State Bank and Trust Company. See Banks and banking—Texas

FIRST Union Real Estate Investments. See Real estate investment trusts

FIRTH, John
(ed) See Cheever, J. Talking with John Cheever
(ed) See Trilling, D. Talking with Diana Trilling

FISCH, Arline
Crafts in industry; ed by A. Gold. il por Craft Horiz 37:10-15 Ag '77
Problems, prospects of production craft; adaptation of address, September 1976. Craft Horiz 37:10+ F '77
SNAG: meet shines with studies. Craft Horiz 37:43 Ag '77

FISCH, Harold
Sanctification of literature. Commentary 63:63-9 Je '77

FISCHER, David Hackett
David Hackett Fischer on history. New Repub 177:21+ D 3 '77
Dealing with old age. Current 194:45-8 Jl '77

FISCHER, Hal
Outsider's view of the 30's. il Mod Phot 41:62 F '77

FISCHER, Lawrence
American ethnic studies. Engl J 66:58-9 S '77

FISCHER, Lucy
Enthusiasm: from kino-eye to radio-eye. bibl il por Film Q 31:25-34 Wint '77
(ed) See Kubelka, P. Restoring Enthusiasm

FISCHER, Muriel
Dealing with death in the family. bibl il N Y Times Mag p82+ Mr 13 '77

FISCHER, Virlis L.
Does the BLM belong in Nevada? il Am For 83:18-21 D '77

FISCHER-DIESKAU, Dietrich
Schubert: the melody and the misery. I. Kolodin. por Sat R 5:42-3 O 1 '77 *
Wolf: Lieder, vol. 2. D. Arthur. il Am Rec G 40:44-5 My '77 *

FISCHER-WILLIAMS, Barbara
Beyond Figaro. il Opera N 41:26-8 Mr 5 '77
Harry Theyard: full of surprises. por Opera N 41:26 Je '77

FISCHLER, Stan, and Friedman, R. A.
Stars in their eyes. il por Ret Liv 17:31-3 Ag '77
—and Rubenstein, Dave
Not ready for the rocking chair. il por Ret Liv 17:33-4+ F '77

FISCO, Benjamin P. Jr
Are high-pressure sewer cleaners safe? il Am City & County 92:45 Jl '77

FISH, Peter
I voted for a man who . . . Mademoiselle 83:174+ F '77

FISH. See Fishes

FISH, Canned
Canned sardines. il Consumer Rep 42:78-80 D '77

FISH, Freezing of. See Freezing of food

FISH, Frozen
Fishing for compliments. . .the frozen way. H. Alpert. il Ret Liv 17:46-8 Ap '77

FISH and Wildlife Service. See United States—Fish and Wildlife Service

FISH as fertilizer. See Fertilizers and manures

FISH as food
Delicious fish in Australia; local fish served in restaurants. il Sunset 158:60+ My '77
Fish & seafood basics. il Bet Hom & Gard 55: 142 Ap '77
How to bone a fish. il Am Home 80:68+ Mr '77
Marketing the shark. S. Lissau. il Oceans 10: 34-6 N '77
That's good fish! Bite-size shark. D. Holtkamp. Sci Digest 81:35-6 Ap '77
Those other fish; preparing fish fillets; with recipes. B. D. Shupp and J. Goerg. il pors Conservationist 31:32-4 My '77
See also
Cookery—Fish
Sea food

FISH carving. See Carving (meat, etc)

FISH contamination
Eight hot issues that affect you now. S. French. il Outdoor Life 159:50+ Ap '77
Fish and food poisoning. B. L. Gordon. il Sea Front 23:218-27 Jl '77
Ralph Nader reports. R. Nader. Ladies Home J 94:198 Ap '77

FISH culture
Fish culture: problems and prospects. A. H. Weatherley and B. M. G. Cogger. bibl il Science 197:427-30 Jl 29 '77
Fish gardening is coming of age. R. Rodale. il Org Gard & Farm 24:52-5 Mr '77
Great put-and-take controversy; attitudes of trout fishermen toward stocking. P. Miller. il Outdoor Life 159:61-3+ Ap '77
New opportunities in fish culture. S. Smyser and T. Gettings. il Org Gard & Farm 24:62-8 Mr '77
Polyculture increases protein supply. Sci Digest 82:81 Jl '77
Progress of marine fish farming in Britain. T. Holloway. il Sea Front 23:48-54 Ja '77
Ranching Atlantic bluefin; work of Janel Fisheries Limited in St Margarets Bay, Nova Scotia. L. Buchanan. il Sea Front 23:172-80 My '77
Salmon for Hizzoner; stocking the Chicago River. R. Telander. il Sports Illus 46:60+ Mr 28 '77
Stripers for everybody! B. W. Dalrymple. il Outdoor Life 160:59-61 Jl '77
Their yen for bluefin; J. Ettman's Janel Fisheries tuna farm in Nova Scotia. D. Levin. il Sports Illus 47:103-4+ O 10 '77
See also
Shellfish culture

Anecdotes, facetiae, satire etc.

Cast your car in the pond and reap fish. M. Hamman. Smithsonian 8:104 Ag '77

FISH farming. See Fish culture

FISH fertilizer. See Fertilizers and manures

FISH finders, Electronic. See Electronics in fishing

FISH genetics
Heteromorphic sex chromosomes in male rainbow trout. G. H. Thorgaard. bibl il Science 196: 900-2 My 20 '77
Socially induced inhibition of genetically determined maturation in the platyfish, xiphophorus maculatus. J. J. Sohn. bibl il Science 195:199-201 Ja 14 '77

FISH hooks. See Fishhooks

FISH introduction
Changing bowls. B. A. Branson. bibl il Environment 19:25-30 Ap '77

FISH markets, New York City. See New York (city)—Markets

FISH nets. See Fishing nets

FISH populations
Understanding our bass population. B. D. Shupp. il Conservationist 32:26-9 Jl '77

FISH records. See Fishing records

FISH salads. See Salads

FISH sounds
Voices in the deep. W. B. Hendrickson, Jr. il Sea Front 23:234-41 Jl '77

FISH soups. See Chowder

FISH tagging
Tagging: a stitch in time. J. Hearst, Jr. il Motor B & S 140:30+ Ag '77

FISHBEIN, Morris
Ask the doctor; questions and answers. por Fam Health 9:8 Ja; 8 F; 8 Mr; 10 Ap; 8 My '77

FISHER, Adrian Sanford
Disarmament: new challenges and new opportunities; statement, October 18, 1977. Dept State Bull 77:778-87 N 28 '77

FISHER, Arthur
Living sea. il Int Wildlife 7:4-11 My '77
Science newsfront. See issues of Popular science

FISHER, Bonnie
Basics of cooking with herbs. il Org Gard & Farm 24:96+ N '77
Herb garden for the bees. il Org Gard & Farm 24:85-7 F '77
Instant fruit—it's hard to ask more. il Org Gard & Farm 24:74-5 Je '77
Protecting the home with herbs. il Org Gard & Farm 24:148-51 Ap '77
—See Fisher, D. jt auth

FISHER, Carrie
Hollywood girl; interview, ed by E. Miller. il pors Seventeen 36:146-7+ My '77

FISHER, Dave, and Fisher, Bonnie
Gift from the woods. il Org Gard & Farm 24:95-6 S '77

FISHER, Desmond
Exporting death to Ireland. Commonweal 104: 356-8, 501-2 Je 10, Ag 5 '77
Police brutality in Ireland. Commonweal 104: 230-1 Ap 15 '77
Upset at the polls. Commonweal 104:518-19 Ag 19 '77
Welcome initiative. Commonweal 104:612-13 S 30 '77

FISHER, Donald W.
James Hall. il pors Conservationist 31:12-16 N '76

FISHER, Elsie
Youth camp safety—yes. Camp Mag 50:18+ S '77

FISHER, Jonathan
Deliverance! il Int Wildlife 7:40-7 Jl '77
John O'Neill doesn't just paint birds. il por Int Wildlife 7:30-7 N '77

FISHER, Knute A. and Stoeckenius, Walther
Freeze-fractured purple membrane particles: protein content. bibl il Science 197:72-4 Jl 1 '77

FISHER, Melvin A.
Fortune to find a fortune. F. Casey. il Mech Illus 73:24 F '77 *
Guns of Atocha. R. F. Burgess. il Oceans 10:26-9 S '77 *

FISHER, Nancy Alice
My favorite winter vegetables are herbs. il Org Gard & Farm 24:71-3 Jl '77
Raised beds for year-around gardening. il Org Gard & Farm 24:140-1 Je '77
When to harvest and when to propagate your herbs. Org Gard & Farm 24:77-8 N '77

FISHER, Terry
Cooking in the dorm: recipes; excerpt from The international students' guide to cooking without getting caught. Seventeen 36:160 F '77

FISHER, Vernon
Capricious places. J. Kutner. il Art N 76:102+ D '77 *

FISHER, Warren
Other way to cruise. il Yachting 142:88-90 N '77

FISHERIES
Murder of the porpoise: closing in on a solution. V. Cox. Sci Digest 82:46-7+ Jl '77
Tuna sandwiches cost at least 78,000 porpoise lives a year, but there is hope. K. S. Norris. il Smithsonian 7:44-53 bibl(p 152) F '77
Vanishing tuna. J. N. Cole. il Read Digest 110: 132-5 Mr '77; Discussion. Atlantic 239:28+ Ap '77
See also
Shellfish fisheries

Fuel requirements

Nutritional outputs and energy inputs in seafoods. M. Rawitscher and J. Mayer. bibl il Science 198:261-4 O 21 '77

International aspects

Department comments on fishery agreements with EEC and Japan; statement, February 22, 1977. R. L. Ridgway. Dept State Bull 76:272-3 Mr 21 '77
Department reviews developments in international fisheries policy; statement, February 3, 1977. R. L. Ridgway. Dept State Bull 76: 175-8 F 28 '77
Politics of fish; experiences aboard factory trawler. W. W. Warner. il Atlantic 240:35-44 Ag '77; Same abr. with title Aboard a fish trawler in the North Atlantic. Read Digest 111:142-7 N '77
Reciprocal fisheries agreement with the United Kingdom; message to Senate, October 7, 1977. J. Carter. Dept State Bull 77:708-9 N 14 '77
U.S-Canada maritime boundary and resource negotiations. Dept State Bull 77:896-7 D 19 '77
U.S, Canada to negotiate maritime issues; announcement, July 27, 1977. Dept State Bull 77:282 Ag 29 '77
U.S, Cuba agree on maritime boundaries and fishery matters. map Dept State Bull 76:686-7 Je 27 '77
U.S, Mexico sign fishery agreement; set provisional maritime boundaries. Dept State Bull 75:758-9 D 27 '76
See also
Fishery laws and legislation

Law

See Fishery laws and legislation

FISHERIES—*Continued*

Research

Cape Vincent; Great Lakes Fisheries Research Station. W. A. Pearce. il Conservationist 31:19-20 Mr '77
When scientists and oystermen cooperate; oyster culture and research in Brittany. C. Jones. il Sea Front 23:106-12 Mr '77

Belize

100,000 pounds of lobster tail; Caribeña Producers Cooperative Society Limited of San Pedro, Belize. N. Eberle. il Oceans 10:30-2 S '77

Canada

Ranching Atlantic bluefin; work of Janel Fisheries Limited in St Margarets Bay, Nova Scotia. L. Buchanan. il Sea Front 23:172-80 My '77
Their yen for bluefin; J. Ettman's Janel Fisheries tuna farm in Nova Scotia. D. Levin. il Sports Illus 47:103-4+ O 10 '77
200-mile limit; showdown at sea. S. Kimber. il pors Int Wildlife 7:41-5 S '77

Germany, West

Politics of fish; experiences aboard factory trawler. W. W. Warner. il Atlantic 240:35-44 Ag '77; Same abr. with title Aboard a fish trawler in the North Atlantic. Read Digest 111:142-7 N '77

Grenadines (islands)

Spiny lobster fishing in the Grenadines. J. E. Adams. il map Sea Front 23:322-30 N '77

Japan

Fishing to get around the 200-mi. limit. map Bus W p36+ My 9 '77
Japan: pinched between 200-mile limits. il U.S. News 82:70 F 28 '77
Sharp boost for your exports. R. C. Black. Farm J 101:H2 O '77

Korea, South

Fishing to get around the 200-mi. limit. map Bus W p36+ My 9 '77

Mexico

Shark fishermen of Mexico. M. Bendix. il Oceans 10:12-17 N '77

United States

All-porpoise war limiting kill of porpoises caught by tuna fishermen. G. M. Prather. Nat R 29:439+ Ap 15 '77
Dolphins and/or tuna: an update on the problems of purse seining for yellowfin. S. Minasian. il Oceans 10:60-3 N '77
Down to the sea with money. M. King. il map Forbes 120:41-3+ O 15 '77
Open season on wildlife laws; Marine Mammal Protection Act's regulation of porpoise kill by tuna industry. il Nat Parks & Con Mag 51:20-1 My '77
Talking tuna; commercial fisherman, J. Alioto. R. Vaughan. il Motor B & S 139:66-9+ Je '77
Troubled waters; effect of laws protecting porpoises in tuna fishing areas. il Forbes 119:56 Ap 1 '77
Tuna catch high, porpoise kill low. E. M. Leeper. BioScience 27:221-2 Mr '77
What price porpoises? Marine Mammal Protection Act and tuna fishermen. A. J. Mayer and J. Huck. il Newsweek 89:58 F 7 '77

FISHERS (animals)
What is a fisher? J. Wood. il Nat Wildlife 15:18-21 Ap '77

FISHERY Conservation and Management Act of 1976. See Fishery laws and legislation

FISHERY laws and legislation
Case of red herring; Coast Guard seizure of two Russian trawlers. T. Mathews and R. Manning. il Newsweek 89:23+ Ap 25 '77
Crackdown on Russian poachers—a taste of more to come. il map U.S. News 82:43-4 Ap 25 '77
Department reviews developments in international fisheries policy; effects of the Fishery Conservation and Management Act of 1976; statement, February 3, 1977. R. L. Ridgway. Dept State Bull 76:175-8 F 28 '77
Equity in global fisheries management. G. Kent. il Oceans 10:60-4 S '77
Fishing laws: United States & Canada. Field & S 81:168-70 Ap '77
Fishing seasons (cont) Outdoor Life 159:56+ Ap '77
Fishing to get around the 200-mi. limit; Japanese and Koreans. map Bus W p36+ My 9 '77
Indians and the courts: allies against wildlife; question of applying fish and game laws to Indians. R. Starnes. il Outdoor Life 159:8+ Je '77
Little stink about a lot of fish; violation of U.S. 200 mile fishing zone by Russian ships. il Time 109:42+ Ap 25 '77
Net gain along the shores; 200-mile U.S. limit. il map Time 109:17 Mr 14 '77
New frontier: planned or plundered? Fishery Conservation and Management Act of 1976; excerpt from address, December 8, 1976. G. Reiger. Field & S 81:22+ Mr '77
Our man in Havana; T. Todman fishing rights mission. F. Willey and L. E. Nelson. il Newsweek 89:44 My 9 '77
Provisional limits established for fishery conservation zone; statement, March 1, 1977. F. Z. Brown. Dept State Bull 76:273-4 Mr 21 '77
Racism and fishing rights; Michigan Indians. J. H. Moore. Nation 225:236-8 S 17 '77
Sport fishermen; Fisheries Conservation and Management Act. F. T. Moss. Yachting 141:52+ Ap '77
Tough new Coast Guard mission; policing today's vast 200-mile limit. R. Petrow. il map Pop Mech 148:72-5+ Ag '77
200-mile limit and you. J. Hearst, Jr. il Motor B & S 139:27-8 My '77
200-mile limit; showdown at sea. S. Kimber. il pors Int Wildlife 7:41-5 S '77
200-mile zone: a shot in the arm for U.S. fishermen. il U.S. News 82:69-70 F 28 '77
U.S. tuna fleet fishes for foreigners; registry transfer due to new U.S. regulations that limit the kill of porpoises that swim with tuna. il Bus W p25 Ja 24 '77

FISHES
Fright posture of the plesiopid fish calloplesiops altivelis: an example of Batesian mimicry. J. E. McCosker. bibl il Science 197:400-1 Jl 22 '77
How to mimic an eel: look mean; calloplesiops altivelis. il Sci N 112:71 Jl 30 '77
Ugh! Fish; fishes unpopular with fishermen. C. Elliott. Outdoor Life 160:67+ D '77
See also
Aquariums
Color of fishes
Electric organs in fishes
Fisheries
Poisonous fishes
Rare fishes
Teeth (fishes)
Tropical fishes
also headings beginning Fish; *also* names of fishes, e.g. Eels

Anatomy

Overlapping platelets: a diffusion barrier in a teleost swimbladder. D. S. Brown and D. E. Copeland. bibl il Science 197:383-4 Jl 22 '77

Diseases and pests

Kepone-induced scoliosis and its histological consequences in fish. J. A. Couch and others. bibl il Science 197:585-7 Ag 5 '77

Ecology

Native fish in troubled waters; fresh water fishes: with reproductions of paintings by G. L. Schelling. G. Reiger. il Audubon 79:18-41 Ja '77
See also
Fish introduction

Eye

See Eye (fishes)

Food and feeding

Amazing mayfly; fishing during mayfly hatches. B. Dalrymple. il Outdoor Life 159:65-7+ My '77
Detritus-based food webs: exploitation by juvenile chum salmon (oncorhynchus keta) J. Sibert and others. bibl il Science 196:649-50 My 6 '77

Geographical distribution

See also
Fish populations

Habits and behavior

Developmental neuroethology: changes in escape and defensive behavior during growth of the lobster. F. Lang and others. bibl il Science 197:682-5 Ag 12 '77
Meanmouth; research on hybrid bass behavior by W. Childers. K. Schultz. il Field & S 82:84-5+ Je '77
pHish pfinder, using acidity of alkalinity of water to determine fish populations. J. Scott. il Field & S 82:58+ Jl '77
Socially induced inhibition of genetically determined maturation in the platyfish, xiphophorus maculatus. J. J. Sohn. bibl il Science 195:199-201 Ja 14 '77

Locomotion

See Animal locomotion

Reproduction

Ovoviviparous volutes. T. Bratcher. il Sea Front 23:374-6 N '77

Tagging

See Fish tagging

FISHES, Color of. See Color of fishes

FISHES, Deep sea
See also
Swordfish
Tuna fish

FISHES, Effect of temperature on
Fish survival in subfreezing temperatures. E. Golanty. il Oceans 10:52-3 My '77
Visual pigment changes in rainbow trout in response to temperature. A. T. C. Tsin and D. D. Beatty. bibl il Science 195:1358-60 Mr 25 '77

FISHHOOKS
Unusual hooks and how to fish them. B. Stearns. il Outdoor Life 159:82-3 Mr '77

FISHING
Amazing mayfly; fishing during mayfly hatches. B. Dalrymple. il Outdoor Life 159:65-7+ My '77
Fishing. J. Gibbs. See issues of Outdoor life to August 1977
Fishing. K. Schultz. See issues of Field & stream
Fishing. E. Zern. See issues of Field & stream
Fishing facts. J. Fullum. See issues of Conservationist
Fishing for the fun of it; advice to young fishermen. J. Bashline. il Field & S 81:130-5 Mr '77
Fishing moves to metrics. R. D. Stearns. Outdoor Life 159:82-3 Ap '77
Fishing on a budget. V. Evanoff. il Ret Liv 17:24-5 Ag '77
Fly and fish; Pacific, Gulf of Mexico and the Caribbean. il Ebony 33:110-12+ Ja '78
Have boat, will travel; fishing vacations. F. M. Paulson. il Field & S 82:88-90 Jl '77
How to plan your big fishing fling. J. Bashline. il Field & S 82:102+ Jl '77
Leap. J. Gibbs. il Outdoor Life 160:67-71+ N '77
Look who's fishing now. H. Circle. il Am Home 80:68-9+ Jl '77
Lucky losses. T. Trueblood. il Field & S 82:8+ Je '77
Nature is my calendar; determining hunting and fishing seasons by natural signs. B. W. Dalrymple. il Outdoor Life 159:90-2+ Ap '77
Solunar tables for [month] See issues of Field & stream
Ugh! Fish; fishes unpopular with fishermen. C. Elliott. Outdoor Life 160:67+ D '77
Update: fishing; ed by J. Gibbs. il Outdoor Life 160:28 O; 106 N '77; 161:52 Ja '78
Update: fishing; ed by T. Paugh. il Outdoor Life 160:56 D '77
Watch the birds catch more fish. J. Weiss. il Outdoor Life 159:76-81+ F '77
Where to go. M. Worby. See issues of Outdoor life

See also
Bait
Casting (fishing)
Fisheries
Indians of North America—Fishing
Salt water fishing
Trawls and trawling
also Bass fishing; Pike fishing; and similar headings

Accidents and injuries
Death stalked the ice; ed by D. Richey. S. Lupo. il Outdoor Life 160:74-5+ O '77
See also
Fishing—Safety devices and measures

Anecdotes, facetiae, satire, etc.
Fishing lesson. P. F. McManus. Field & S 82:146-9 My '77
Miracle of the fish plate. P. F. McManus. il Field & S 81:136-9 F '77

Competitions
Bass tournaments—one man's view. E. Zern. il Field & S 82:146-7 Je '77
Behold the new fisherperson; FEM, America's oldest women's bass tournament. P. Miller. il Outdoor Life 159:56-9+ F '77
Bimini blues; Bimini Big Game Club's Members Tournament for billfish. O. Moore. il Motor B & S 140:76-7+ Ag '77
Many ways to catch bass; sixth annual Bass Masters Classic. K. Schultz. il Field & S 81:116-19 F '77
1976 Field & Stream Fishing Contest winners. Field & S 81:152+ Ap; 82:140+ My; 164+ Je '77
Pool party: catfish for 600; Pohick Bay Regional Park, Va. R. G. Bowers. il Parks & Rec 12:38-40+ Mr '77
Pursuing Papa's marlin; Hemingway Billfish Tournament. R. F. Jones. il Sports Illus 47:54-8+ Ag 1 '77
Tournaments and tomorrow; funding for fishing tournaments. G. Reiger. Field & S 82:24+ Ag '77

Implements and appliances
Fishing accessories; boat equipment. F. M. Paulson. il Field & S 81:146-50 Ap '77
See also
Depth indicators
Electronics in fishing
Fishing nets
Fishing tackle

History
Capturing fishes. B. L. Gordon. il Sea Front 23:43-7 Ja '77

Law
See Fishery laws and legislation

Safety devices and measures
Ice safety and rescue. D. Richey. il Outdoor Life 160:123-4 D '77

Study and teaching
New boom in fishing schools. J. Gibbs. il Outdoor Life 159:68-71+ Mr '77

Alaska
About fishing and bears; encounter with brown bears while salmon fishing. B. Brister. il Field & S 82:46-8+ Je '77
Land of geese and plenty. R. F. Jones. il Sports Illus 47:84-8+ D 12 '77

Argentina
Boca brookies. P. Miller. il Outdoor Life 160:88-93+ O '77

Arizona
Landlocked striper tops previous record. il Outdoor Life 160:52 Ag '77

Atlantic States
Stripers and bait. N. Bryant. il Field & S 82:42-6 Ag '77

Australia
Bitten from the records; marlin caught by N. Green off Australia. M. Sloan. il Motor B & S 139:52-5+ Mr '77
Great Barrier marlin! J. Troy. il Field & S 81:130-5 F '77

Bahamas
Hunters of the flats; shark fishing. G. Drake, Jr. il Field & S 82:56-8+ Je '77

Belize
Turneffe Islands cornucopia; bonefish. J. Bashline. il Field & S 82:160-4 N '77

Bermuda
Bermuda grab bag. B. Roberts. Field & S 82:91 Jl '77

California
Best fishing for surfperch is now or soon in California, later up north. il Sunset 158:48+ F '77
Custom-caught big brown; trout fishing in California; ideas of B. Bringhurst. C. Garrison. il por Field & S 82:76+ Je '77
Midnight stripers; San Francisco Bay. R. Chatham. il Field & S 81:136-8+ Mr '77
More fish this year in East Bay lakes. il Sunset 158:66 My '77
On these two official wild trout streams you put your catch back; Hat Creek and Fall River. il map Sunset 158:68+ Je '77
Smith River steelheads. M. Fong. il Field & S 81:68-72 F '77
To kill a monster; sturgeon in San Francisco Bay. L. Green. il Field & S 81:64+ Mr '77

California, Lower
Bank of the giant sea bass; Uncle Sam Bank, Baja California. C. Garrison. il Field & S 82:94-5+ My '77
Escape to Pescadero; fishing on the lower Baja Peninsula. C. Garrison. il Field & S 81:56-8+ Mr '77
Frankenheimer; marlin fishing off Baja California. O. Moore. il pors Motor B & S 141:100-3+ Ja '78

Canada
Canadian fishing roundup. J. Knap. il Field & S 82:99-102+ Je '77
How to catch trophy brook trout. D. Richey. il por Field & S 81:78-80+ Ap '77
King of the North; pike fishing. E. A. Bauer. il map Outdoor Life 159:82-5+ My '77
Lady of Great Bear Lake; fishing guide, Susan Stechly. J. Fowler. Outdoor Life 160:44 Jl '77
Portland hitch on the Pinware; salmon fishing in Labrador. A. Cameron. il Field & S 81:62-4+ Ap '77
River that calls to the bold; Back River in the Northwest Territories. P. Smith. il map Outdoor Life 160:69-73+ Ag '77
Tale of two rivers; salmon fishing in Canada and Norway. E. Zern. il Field & S 82:62-3 Jl '77
Word to the compleat angler; how to plan a fishing trip. B. W. Dalrymple. il Holiday 58:48-9 Ap '77

Caribbean Region
Fishing world of Johnny Harms. J. Borgzinner. il por Motor B & S 139:58-9+ Je '77
Like a neon shadow in the sea; blue marlin; with reproductions of paintings. S. Meltzoff. il Sports Illus 47:22-9 Jl 25 '77

Chesapeake Bay
Shad in the surf. N. Karas. il Field & S 81:96+ Ap '77

FISHING—*Continued*

Costa Rica

Grand fish at night: the ultimate action; tarpon fishing at the mouth of the Parismina River. S. Apte. il Outdoor Life 160:66-7+ Jl '77

Cuba

First anglers into Cuba. E. A. Bauer. il map Outdoor Life 160:69-73+ S '77
Pursuing Papa's marlin; Hemingway Billfish Tournament. R. R. Jones. il Sports Illus 47:55-8+ Ag 1 '77
Treasure lives; bass fishing in Treasure Lake. K. Schultz. il Field & S 82:114-22+ Ag '77

Florida

Bass methods for big bream; bluegill fishing. F. Sargeant. il Field & S 82:66-71 Jl '77
Denizens of the dark; Florida swordfish fishing. D. Levin. il Sports Illus 47:44-5+ Ag 15 '77
Magnificent tarpon; fishing off Punta Gorda Isles. C. R. Meyer. il Field & S 81:26-7+ Ap '77
Out for blood; shark fishing. J. Rudloe. il Sports Illus 46:76-80+ Ap 25 '77
Snook: getting down to basics. V. Dunaway. il Field & S 81:28+ F '77
To a different beat; bonefish fishing in Biscayne Bay. J. Bashline. il Field & S 81:184+ Ap '77

Honduras

Bass boom south of the border. A. Eason. il map Outdoor Life 161:82-4+ Ja '78

Idaho

40-minute forward 40-year backward walk; trout fishing. T. Trueblood. il Field & S 81:8+ Ap '77

Ireland

Fishing in Ireland: it's close. J. Gibbs. il Outdoor Life 159:66-7+ F '77

Labrador

See Fishing—Canada

Massachusetts

See also
Fishing—Nantucket Island

Mexico

Bass boom south of the border. A. Eason. il map Outdoor Life 161:82-4+ Ja '78
South of the border on a shoestring. N. Strung. il Field & S 81:158-9+ F '77
See also
Fishing—California, Lower

Michigan

Day the pike put the move on Herman; use of suckerfish when pike ice fishing. R. Rau. il Sports Illus 46:38-40+ F 28 '77
For big steelhead only. D. Bowring. il Field & S 82:46-7+ S '77
Hemingway fished here. J. Harrison. il Esquire 88:38+ Jl '77
Racism and fishing rights; Michigan Indians. J. H. Moore. Nation 225:236-8 S 17 '77

Missouri

Incredible paddlefish; spoonbills. G. Reiger. il Field & S 82:62+ N '77

Nantucket Island

Tumult on a wild shore; bluefish fishing. W. Humphrey. il Sports Illus 47:42-4+ N 7 '77

New Mexico

Great grandfather brown; brown trout of New Mexico's Rio Grande River. D. Kline. il Field & S 81:48-50+ Mr '77

New York (state)

Bad show at the mud hole; Sheepshead Bay. C. Gammon. Sports Illus 46:36-8+ Je 6 '77
Magic of musky fishing. H. E. Herrick, Jr. il Conservationist 31:26-7 Mr '77
Midnight Medusa; fishing for bullheads in Chataugua Lake. D. Walrod. il Field & S 81:34+ Mr '77
Miramichi it ain't, so all right, it's 116th St. J. Bryan. Sports Illus 47:81-2+ O 17 '77
Musky fishing. J. Brabant. il por Conservationist 31:21-3 Mr '77
New York State Record Fish Program. R. C. Brewer. il Conservationist 31:29 My '77
Steelhead of the East. D. Mermon. il por Field & S 81:42-4+ Mr '77

New Zealand

Catch and don't release; trout fishing in Lake Taupo. E. Zern. il Field & S 82:96+ Ag '77

Northwest Territories

See Fishing—Canada

Norway

Tale of two rivers; salmon fishing in Canada and Norway. E. Zern. il Field & S 82:62-3 Jl '77

Oregon

Seattle salmon fishing. il Sunset 158:92+ Ap '77

Panama

Fish story that was all too true. C. Gammon. il Sports Illus 46:56-9+ F 14 '77

Pennsylvania

Care and feeding of a trout stream; Letort stream. A. Lee. il Sports Illus 46:30-2 Ja 31 '77
How now brown trout? excerpt from Masters of the dry fly, ed by M. Migel. E. Zern. Field & S 82:90-3 My '77
Trout and the summer angler. R. L. Henry. il Field & S 82:20-1+ Jl '77

United States

Word to the compleat angler; how to plan a fishing trip. B. W. Dalrymple. il Holiday 58:48-9 Ap '77

Utah

Monster brown: new record—but will it last? J. Zumbo. il Outdoor Life 159:68-9+ Je '77

Vermont

Brute; trout fishing. T. Vargish. il Nat R 29:507 Ap 29 '77

Washington (state)

Hang on for my life; boating accident while steelhead trout fishing. B. Knoll. il Outdoor Life 159:76-7+ My '77

Western States

Neglected nomad of the saltwater; fishing for cutthroat trout from Alaska to California. C. H. Williams. il Field & S 82:54-6 Jl '77

Wyoming

Rocky Mountain high time of your life. V. Landi. il Outdoor Life 159:70-5+ My '77

FISHING, Winter

Catch 'em cold; advice from four experts; ed by J. Zumbo. il Outdoor Life 161:70-3 Ja '78
Day the pike put the move on Herman; use of suckerfish when pike ice fishing in Michigan. R. Rau. il Sports Illus 46:38-40+ F 28 '77
Winter bass: the cold hard facts. D. Morris. il Outdoor Life 160:78-81+ N '77

Accidents and injuries

See Fishing—Accidents and injuries

Safety devices and measures

See Fishing—Safety devices and measures

FISHING boats

Best new boats for bass. B. McKeown. il Pop Mech 147:84-5+ My '77
Blow-up boat; inflatables for fishermen. F. M. Paulson. il Field & S 82:124-6+ S '77
Center consoles for fun and fish. J. Martenhoff. il Motor B & S 139:95+ Je '77
Doughnuts are dandy. E. Bauer. il Outdoor Life 159:78-9+ Ap '77
Fish craft for '77. F. M. Paulson. il Field & S 81:104-6+ F '77
Whatever happened to those bass boats? A. J. McMasters. il Mech Illus 73:20+ D '77

Anecdotes, facetiae, satire, etc.

Wynken, Blynken, and Cod. P. Stegner. Atlantic 240:39-45 Jl '77

Chartering

See Fishing boats—Leasing and renting

Design

Warship; the ultimate sportfishing boat. J. Hearst, Jr and T. West. il Motor B & S 139:70-2+ Je '77
Yachting eyes:
Harris 36 sport fisherman. J. Smith. il Yachting 142:120-3 S '77
Pacemaker 40 sport fisherman. J. Smith. il Yachting 142:64-6 Jl '77

Electronic equipment

See also
Electronics in fishing

Equipment

Personal touch; customizing a center console boat. J. Martenhoff. il Motor B & S 141:71-2 Ja '78
Who? Me use a downrigger? H. L. Lawrence. il Outdoor Life 160:88-90 Jl '77

Leasing and renting

Cost-efficient sportfishing. J. Hearst, Jr. il Motor B & S 140:78-81+ N '77
Fly and fish; Pacific, Gulf of Mexico and the Caribbean. il Ebony 33:110-12+ Ja '78

Purchasing

Right boat for you. J. Hearst, Jr. il Motor B & S 140:31 S '77

FISHING boats—*Continued*

Testing

Performance test:
Penn Yan 30 sportfisherman. D. Hart. il Motor B & S 140:48-50 N '77
Stamas 32 sport cruiser. D. Hart. il Motor B & S 140:30+ O '77

FISHING by animals. See Animals—Food and feeding

FISHING flies. See Fishing lures, flies, etc.

FISHING for the blind. See Sports for the blind

FISHING guides. See Guides

FISHING in art
Outdoor prints: a sporting chance for pleasure and profit. P. Miller. il Outdoor Life 159:72-7+ Je '77
Tom Allen. N. Meglin. il por Am Artist 41:52-5 Jl '77

FISHING industry. See Fisheries

FISHING lines. See Fishing tackle

FISHING literature
Lord of the flies; R. Haig-Brown. R. Chatham. Esquire 87:16+ Mr '77

FISHING lures, flies, etc.
AC/DC trout flies. F. McKinley. il Field & S 81:52-4+ F '77
Bait walker. K. Schultz. il Field & S 82:152 S '77
Bass and the worm. K. Schultz. il por Field & S 82:84-9 My '77
Blue dun bonanza; raising roosters to supply feathers for fishing flies. S. Paulakavich. por Outdoor Life 159:31 Je '77
Bye bye, wet fly? excerpt from The masters on the nymph. E. Zern. il Field & S 82:108-10 D '77
Catching the Dungeness crab. O. W. Larson and H. J. Smith. il Field & S 82:108 Je '77
Fancy worms for hungry bass. P. Barrett. il Mech Illus 73:10+ Ag '77
Fly of the month:
Caddis larva. E. Peper. il Field & S 82:133 Ag '77
Comparadun. E. Peper. il Field & S 81:84 F '77
Cooper bug. E. Peper. il Field & S 81:88 Mr '77
Floating nymph. E. Peper. il Field & S 82:55 O '77
Muddler minnow. E. Peper. il Field & S 81:167 Ap '77
Poly-wing spinner. E. Peper. il Field & S 82:102 S '77
Sparkle caddis pupa. E. Peper. il Field & S 82:133 N '77
Spring wiggler. E. Peper. il Field & S 82:107 D '77
Thunder Creek Series. E. Peper. il Field & S 82:71 Jl '77
Tying your own. E. Peper. Field & S 82:72 Je '77
Wooly worm. E. Peper. il Field & S 82:160 My '77
Get more strikes and hookups with these hot new worming systems. J. Gibbs. il Outdoor Life 159:18+ My '77
Getting deep with flies. J. Gibbs. il Outdoor Life 159:30+ Ap '77
Gripper; Grip Lip by Cordell Tackle. K. Schultz. il Field & S 82:120 Ag '77
It bubbles and vigrates; ringworms. K. Schultz. il Field & S 82:89 My '77
Malarkey flies; trout lures. P. Barrett. il Field & S 82:50+ O '77
Old African thread trick; rigged baits. J. Bashline. il Field & S 81:188 Ap '77
Old stalwart goes weedless; Jitterbug. K. Schultz. il Field & S 82:133 Je '77
100-year-old wet fly technique; trout fishing. J. Bashline. il Field & S 82:172+ My '77
Spring's the thing; spinnerbait. K. Schultz. il Field & S 81:92 Ap '77
Teasers today. J. Hearst. il Motor B & S 140:22 Jl '77
Top to bottom; floating-diving plugs. Conservationist 32:39 Jl '77
Triple-threat trolling rig. O. W. Larson. il Field & S 81:150 Ap '77
Up with the jig! J. Gibbs. il Outdoor Life 160:108+ Ag '77
See also
Fly casting

Anecdotes, facetiae, satire, etc.

Cast your car in the pond and reap fish. M. Hamman. Smithsonian 8:104 Ag '77

Collectors and collecting

Boy wonder of fly tying; S. Fernandez. L. Green. il por Field & S 81:50-2 Ap '77

Manufacture

Bass' Mann; Tom Mann Bait Company; interview, ed by P. Miller. T. Mann. il pors Outdoor Life 159:55-7+ Mr '77

FISHING maps. See Topographic maps

FISHING nets
Tuna sandwiches cost at least 78,000 porpoise lives a year, but there is hope. K. S. Norris. il Smithsonian 7:44-53 bibl(p 152) F '77

FISHING records
Landlocked striper tops previous record. il Outdoor Life 160:52 Ag '77
Monster brown: new record—but will it last? J. Zumbo. il Outdoor Life 159:68-9+ Je '77
New world-record fish. Field & S 81:74+ F '77
New York State Record Fish Program. R. C. Brewer. il Conservationist 31:29 My '77
Record bass: the quest is getting frantic. P. Miller. il Outdoor Life 160:94-7+ S '77
Sports fishermen; 1976. F. T. Moss. Yachting 141:54+ My '77
3 records about to fall:
Coho salmon. D. Rickey. il Outdoor Life 159:66-7 Je '77
Largemouth bass. C. Farmer. il Outdoor Life 159:66-7 Je '77
Smallmouth bass. H. L. Lawrence. il Outdoor Life 159:68-9 Je '77

Anecdotes, facetiae, satire, etc.

Tuesday night with Cody, Jimbo and a fish of some proportion. H. Crews. Esquire 87:26+ F '77

FISHING reels. See Fishing tackle

FISHING rods. See Fishing tackle

FISHING schools. See Fishing—Study and teaching

FISHING tackle
All about fishing lines. C. B. Pfeiffer. il Outdoor Life 161:91-8 Ja '78
Big-game fly reel; Billy Pate Reel. J. Samson. il Field & S 82:141-2+ O '77
Finger on accuracy; push-button reels. L. Mueller. il Outdoor Life 159:170 Mr '77
Fish-hook float. E. Robbins. il Pop Sci 211:26 Ag '77
Fishing lines: separating the turkeys from the trophies. K. Schultz. il Field & S 81:110-12+ Mr '77
Fly-fishing reels. Consumer Rep 42:131-4 D '77
Head with many faces; shooting head. T. Trueblood. il Field & S 81:12+ Mr '77
Long rod back; fly casting rods. L. Kreh. il Outdoor Life 159:72-3+ F '77
New fishing gear engineered to hook more big ones. A. J. Hand. il Pop Sci 210:112-13 F '77
New fishing tackle report. K. Schultz. il Field & S 82:66+ N '77
New tackle that lands the lunkers. M. Sosin. il Pop Mech 147:100-1+ Ap '77
Revolutionary new rod. J. Gibbs. il Outdoor Life 159:26+ Mr '77
Spinning for trout. A. J. Acerrano. il Field & S 82:50-1+ D '77
Tackle selection for the beginner. J. Bashline. il Field & S 82:112+ Je 77
Take me to your leader. J. Bashline. il Field & S 82:52-3+ D '77
What's new in angling equipment for '77. J. Gibbs. il Outdoor Life 159:113-16+ F '77
See also
Fishhooks
Fishing lures, flies, etc.

Maintenance and repair

Tackle repairs in the field. M. Marshall. il Outdoor Life 159:155-6 Mr '77

Storage

Rod carrier for quick-draw fishing. S. Stall. il Pop Mech 148:103 Jl '77

FISHING thermometers. See Themometers and thermometry

FISHING tournaments. See Fishing—Competitions

FISHING trips. See Fishing

FISHLOCK, Trevor
Cleanly flows the Thames. il Int Wildlife 8:33-5 Ja '78

FISHMAN, Melvin
Bookstore improves net profit via Book Distributors' new ordering service. P. D. Doebler. il Pub W 211:47-8 My 16 '77 *

FISHWORMS. See Earthworms

FISKE, Edward B.
Issue that won't go away. il N Y Times Mag p58 Mr 27 '77

FISSION, Atomic. See Nuclear fission

FIT to be tied; drama. See Martens, A. C.

FITE, Harvey
Quarrymaster of Saugerties. Vasari. il por Art N 76:23-4+ O '77 *

FITTINGS, Boat. See Boats—Equipment

FITZELLE, Edward H.
Peking & Wavertree. il Oceans 10:4-10 My '77

FITZGERALD, Brendan
Island festival: Cuba takes off. il Dance Mag 51:80-5 Mr '77

FITZGERALD, Ed
Off the force. M. J. Albrecht. Progressive 41:42 My '77 *

FITZGERALD, Ernest
Price of blowing the whistle. H. Dudar. il pors N Y Times Mag p41-2+ O 30 '77 *
FITZGERALD, Frances
Jamaican limbo. Harpers 255:10+ Jl '77
FITZGERALD, Francis Scott Key
Harmony in Great Neck: the friendship of Ring Lardner and F. Scott Fitzgerald; excerpt from Ring: a biography of Ring Lardner. J. Yardley. il pors Sat R 4:23-5+ Jl 9 '77 *
Humiliation in Hollywood. S. Koch. il Harpers 254:102-4 Mr '77 *
This side of Hollywood. J. Rascoe. il Atlantic 239:92-4 F '77 *
FITZGERALD, Marianne
Country music; poem. America 137:161 S 24 '77
FITZGERALD, Paul A.
Panama Canal: use and ownership. America 137:473-6 D 31 '77
FITZGERALD, Robert
Robert Lowell, 1917-1977. il New Repub 177:10-12 O 1 '77
FITZGERALD, Scott. See Fitzgerald, F. S. K.
FITZGIBBONS, Virginia
Sizzling designs with a soldering iron. il Design (US) 79:23 Fall '77
FITZJOHN, Tony
Locked in the lion's jaws. A. Shapiro. il Read Digest 110:82-6 My '77 *
FITZPATRICK, Elysia
This happy home; story. Good H 186:94-5 Ja '78
FITZPATRICK, Franklin E.
Church and the Cherry orchard. America 136: 266-7 Mr 26 '77
FITZPATRICK, Joseph P.
Self and society. America 136:86-7 Ja 29 '77
FITZPATRICK, Tom, 3d
25 & married; story. Redbook 149:116 O '77
FITZWILTON, Ltd. See Conglomerate corporations—Ireland
FIVE College Radio Astronomy Observatory. See Astronomical observatories
FIXATION of nitrogen. See Nitrogen—Fixation
FIZDALE, Robert. See Gold, A. jt auth
FJARE, Paul S.
Planning & development. Camp Mag 49:16-17 F; 17-18 My '77
FLACH, Frederic F.
How to cope with change at 30. Harp Baz 110:133+ O '77
FLACKS, Lewis I.
Living in the gap of ambiguity; an attorney's advice to libraries on the copyright law. il Am Lib 8:252-7 My '77
FLACKS. See Press agents
FLAD, Harvey. See Flad, M. jt auth
FLAD, Mary, and Flad, Harvey
Hoosuck: a community story. il Craft Horiz 37:20-1+ Ap '77
FLAGELLARIA
Apical dichotomy demonstrated in the angiosperm flagellaria. P. B. Tomlinson and others. bibl il Science 196:1111-12 Je 3 '77
FLAGELLATES
See also
Euglena
Trypanosomes
FLAGS
Make your own private signal; boat flag. K. Kirkpatrick and D. Kirpatrick. il Motor B & S 140:104-5 Ag '77

United States

Birth of the flag. il U.S. News 82:47-8 Je 13 '77
FLAGS of convenience. See Ships—Registration and transfer
FLAGSTAD, Kirsten
Kirsten Flagstad sings from Norway; recording. P. L. Miller. Am Rec G 40:47 F '77 *
FLAHERTY, Peter F.
Flaherty's promise. P. Peckarsky. New Repub 177:9-10 D 10 '77 *
FLAHERTY, Robert J.
Streetwalker. Forbes 120:122 D 1 '77
FLAHERTY, Robert Joseph
Helen Van Dongen: an interview; ed by B. Achtenberg. H. Van Dongen. bibl il pors Film Q 30:46-57 Wint '76 *
FLAHERTY seminars. See Motion pictures—Study and teaching
FLAME violets. See Episcias
FLAMING (cookery) See Cookery
FLAMINGO Stakes. See Horse racing
FLAMINGOS
Chilean flamingo court and dance. J. Muñoz. il Natur Hist 86:72-8 D '77
FLAMMABLE Fabrics Act (proposed) See Fire prevention—Laws and regulations
FLAMMARION, Camille
About an astronomical woodcut. J. Ashbrook. il Sky & Tel 53:356-7+ My '77 *
Mars centennial. K. L. Franklin. il Sci Digest 82:66-9 S '77 *
FLANAGAN, Brian P.
Airwar 1914-1918. il Flying 101:75-8 S '77
FLANAGAN, William
Employers are insisting on women managers and supervisors. Vogue 167:222 Mr '77
Money. See occasional issues of Vogue
Pick a tax pro now for a happier '78. Vogue 167:238 D '77
FLANDERMEYER, Robert R. See Nelson-Rees, W. A. jt auth
FLANDERS, Jane
Cloisonne; poem. Nation 225:281 S 24 '77
FLANIGAN, James
Side lines. il por Forbes 119:6 Mr 1 '77 *
FLANNELLY, Kevin. See Lore, R. jt auth
FLARE stars. See Stars, Variable
FLARES, Solar. See Solar flares
FLASH cords. See Photography—Electronic equipment
FLASH units. See Electric lamps, Photoflash; Photography—Electronic equipment
FLASHLIGHT batteries. See Electric batteries
FLASHLIGHT fish. See Electric organs in fishes
FLASHLIGHT photography. See Photography, Flashlight
FLASTE, Richard
How to pick a camp. il N Y Times Mag p86+ Mr 20 '77
FLATHEAD River
Our wild and scenic rivers. D. H. Chadwick. il Nat Geog 152:12-19 Jl '77
FLATLEY, Guy
Sound that shook Hollywood. il N Y Times Mag p34-7+ S 25 '77
FLATS, Tidal. See Tidal flats
FLAVIN, Joseph B.
Back to basics. por Forbes 119:72 Ja 15 '77 *
FLAVONES and flavonoids
Chemical evidence for separating the psilotaceae from the filicales. G. Cooper-Driver. bibl il Science 198:1260-2 D 23 '77
Chemistry of still-green fossil leaves. Sci N 111:391 Je 18 '77
Flavonoid and other chemical constituents of fossil miocene celtis and ulmus (succor creek flora) D. E. Giannasi and K. J. Niklas. bibl il Science 197:765-7 Ag 19 '77
Flavonoids and other chemical constituents of fossil miocene zelkova (ulmaceae) K. J. Niklas and D. E. Giannasi. bibl il Science 196:877-8 My 20 '77
Geochemistry and thermolysis of flavonoids. K. J. Niklas and D. E. Giannasi. bibl il Science 197:767-9 Ag 19 '77
See also
Quercetin
Quercitrin
Rutin
FLEA markets. See Markets
FLEAS
I've got you under my skin. B. Gilbert. il Sports Illus 47:30-4 Ag 15 '77; Same abr. with title There's no fleeing the flea. Read Digest 112: 11-12+ Ja '78
FLECK, K. M.
Elegant comfort: alternatives for after dark. il N Y Times Mag p72-3 O 30 '77
FLEETWOOD Mac (rock group) See Rock groups
FLEISCHHAUER, F. William
And some plumbing projects. il Motor B & S 140:98-9 N '77
Maintaining your ice supply. Motor B & S 140: 100-2 Jl '77
FLEMING, Anne Taylor
Bad love. por Newsweek 90:9 Ag 1 '77
Does total woman add up? Vogue 167:76 Ag '77
Fantastic Egypt. il Vogue 167:66+ Jl '77
Flirting. il Redbook 148:22+ F '77
That week in Houston. il N Y Times Mag p 10-13+ D 25 '77
What do you still want—that you're not getting —from your father? il Redbook 149:42+ Jl '77
When you give up dolls. . .you can begin to love men. Vogue 167:350+ O '77
FLEMING, Erin
At the circus go west; E. Fleming vs. Arthur Marx. R. Rosenblatt. il por New Repub 176: 60-2 My 21 '77 *
FLEMING, Karol L.
Summer of the porpoise. il Nat Parks & Con Mag 51:17-20 N '77
FLEMING, Lois D.
Community education and public libraries: cooperation or conquest? bibl por Wilson Lib Bull 52:319-23 D '77
FLEMING, Robert L. Jr
Nepal's downhill flyers. il Int Wildlife 7:46-7 S '77
FLEMING, Shirley
Spoleto Festival U.S.A. il Hi Fi 27:MA32-4 O '77
Sydney International Piano Competition. il Hi Fi 27:MA36-8 D '77
FLEMING, Thomas James, 1927-
Divided shepherds of a restive flock. il N Y Times Mag p9+ Ja 16 '77
How proudly we hailed! il Read Digest 111:63-72 Jl '77

FLEMING, Thomas James, 1927-—*Continued*
Meaning of Mihajlov. America 137:145-7 S 17 '77
PW interviews; ed by B. A. Bannon. por Pub W 212:12-13 Jl 4 '77; Discussion. 212:34 Jl 25 '77
Who really discovered America? il Read Digest 110:69-73 F '77

FLEMING County, Ky.
Some say it will kill you; Maxey Flats nuclear waste disposal site; reprint from Audubon, November 1976 issue. G. Laycock. il Redbook 148:102+ Ap '77

FLEMING H. Revell Company. See Publishers and publishing—Religious literature

FLEMISH painting. See Painting, Flemish

FLEMMING, Ray
Pines of Rome; poem. New Repub 177:27 S 3 '77

FLETCHER, Edward A. and Moen, R. L.
Hydrogen and oxygen from water. bibl il Science 197:1050-6 S 9 '77

FLETCHER, Louise
Louise Fletcher in search of herself; interview, ed by E. Kaye. por Ladies Home J 94:54+ Jl '77

FLETCHER, Ron
Exercise secrets of a Hollywood body doctor. A. Ebert. il por Ladies Home J 94:50+ F '77 *

FLETEMEYER, John R.
Rare albino turtle. il Sea Front 23:233 Jl '77

FLEUR-de-lis
Button collecting: Fleur-de-lis. D. F. Brown. il Hobbies 82:138-9 S '77

FLEURAGE. See Pictures

FLEXITIME. See Hours of labor

FLICK, Bill
Glory be to man for dappled things. M. Smith. il Sports Illus 46:40-2+ My 23 '77 *

FLICK, Earl
Oregon trails. il por Am For 83:36-7 My '77

FLICKER phenomena
Rod photoreceptors detect rapid flicker. J. D. Conner and D. I. A. MacLeod. bibl il Science 195:698-9 F 18 '77

Der **FLIEGENDE** Holländer; opera. See Wagner, R.

FLIEGER, Howard
Editorial. See issues of U.S. news and world report to March 7, 1977

FLIES
See also
Drosophila
Lacewings
Sawflies
Tsetse flies
White flies

Control

Whitefly whammy? il Sunset 159:78-9 Ag '77

FLIES, Artificial. See Fishing lures, flies, etc.

FLIES as carriers of infection
See also
Tsetse flies

FLIESS, Elenore Stratton, and Fliess, Robert
Shakespeare's Juliet and her nurse. bibl f Am Imago 33:244-60 Fall '76

FLIESS, Robert. See Fliess, E. S. jt auth

FLIGHT
See also
Aeronautics
Gliding and soaring

Physiological aspects

See Aviation—Physiological aspects

FLIGHT attendants. See Airlines—Flight attendants

FLIGHT controllers (instruments) See Aeronautic instruments

FLIGHT crews. See Airplane crews

FLIGHT Research Center. See United States—National Aeronautics and Space Administration—Flight Research Center

FLIGHT Safety International Inc. See Air pilots—Training

FLIGHT Service Stations. See United States— Federal Aviation Administration—Flight Service Stations

FLIGHT simulators
Competition spurs enhanced simulation. il Aviation W 106:316-17+ Je 6 '77
Simulators key to flying time cuts. il Aviation W 106:239-40 Ja 31 '77
Single-pilot effectiveness of F-18 tested in simulator. D. M. North. il Aviation W 106:64-5+ Ja 31 '77
See also
Space flight simulators

FLIGHT training. See Air pilots—Training

FLINT, Jerry
Cars had faces then. il Esquire 88:111-15 N '77

FLINT, Mich.

Education

See Education—Michigan

FLINTLOCK rifles. See Rifles

FLIP-flops. See Multivibrators

FLIRTING. See Women and men

FLITTNER, Glenn
What your weatherman doesn't tell you; interview, ed by J. Cameron. il map Motor B & S 139:76-8+ My '77

FLOAT (banking) See Banks and banking—Float

FLOAT hunting. See Hunting

FLOAT trips. See River trips

FLOATING element lenses. See Lenses, Photographic

FLOATING exchange rates. See Foreign exchange

FLOATING hospitals. See Hospital ships

FLOATING island (dessert) See Desserts

FLOATING nuclear power plants. See Atomic power plants

FLOATING rate notes. See Securities

FLOATPLANES. See Seaplanes

FLOATS (fishing) See Fishing tackle

FLOCKS of birds. See Birds—Habits and behavior

FLOOD, The. See Deluge

FLOOD insurance, Government. See Insurance, Government

FLOOD prevention and control
How Baltimore County keeps its residents high and dry. J. D. Seyffert. il por Am City & County 92:78-80 S '77
See also
Rivers—Regulation

FLOODS

United States

After the flood; relief measures for Pineville, Ky, flood. J. S. Golden. il Sat Eve Post 249:52-3+ D '77
After the floods; Tug Valley, West Virginia. C. McCarthy. Progressive 41:44-7 D '77
After the strip floods: relief is the real disaster. R. E. Wise, Jr. il Nation 225:18-20 Jl 2 '77
Bethlehem's bind in Johnstown. il Bus W p40+ Ag 15 '77
Big Thompson flood of 1976 in Colorado. J. F. Henz and others. il maps Weatherwise 29:278-85 D '76
Cloudburst; Big Thompson flood of 1976. Sci Am 236:60 Ap '77
Double disaster in Appalachia; Tug Fork River flood, West Virginia. C. McCarthy. America 136:536-9 Je 18 '77
Flood relief; Kansas City. Chr Today 22:39 O 21 '77
Floodtrap city: Johnstown, Pa. B. Gilbert. il map Audubon 79:2-9 N '77
Great strip mine flood. P. Primack. Nation 224 691-2 Je 4 '77
Huntington Beach: disaster waits impatiently in wings; excerpt from Acts of God, acts of man. W. Marx. Audubon 79:126-8 Mr '77
Kansas City's deluge. T. Mathews and S. Monroe. il Newsweek 90:37 S 26 '77
Rain of fear in Kansas City. il Time 110:28 S 26 '77
We'll dig out again; Johnstown, Pa. T. Mathews. il Newsweek 90:16 Ag 1 '77
Will cruel weather ever let up? il U.S. News 82:59-60 Ap 18 '77
See also
Dams—Failure

FLOOR cleaning appliances
See also
Vacuum cleaners

FLOOR coverings
Floor treatments. Redbook 148:186+ Ap '77; Same with title Floors. Ladies Home J 94:180+ Ap '77
Floors. Ladies Home J 94:150+ S '77; Same with title Floors: the fifth wall. Redbook 149:192+ S '77
See also
Rugs and carpets

Manufacture

See also
Congoleum Corporation

FLOOR tile laying. See Tile laying

FLOORING
Cut-up lumber scraps make handsome parquet. il Sunset 158:124-5 My '77
Masonry floors for easy-care beauty that doesn't wear out. V. E. Smay. il Pop Sci 210:114-17+ My '77
Parquet floors you can install yourself. S. Renner-Smith. il Pop Sci 210:114-17 Mr '77

FLOORING, Plastic
Flooring by the roll: a quick put-down. il Pop Mech 148:126-7+ D '77
Sheet-vinyl floor coverings. Consumer Rep 42:306-7 D '77
Shoot down this new floor covering with a staple gun; Premier Sundial. il Pop Mech 148:18 Ag '77

FLOORS
Floor shows. S. Van Zante and others. il Bet Hom & Gard 55:90-7 Ag '77
How to stencil a floor. M. Stewart. il por House & Gard 149:54+ Je '77
Modified light-gage steel units frame hospital's interstitial floors. il Archit Rec 161:151 Ja '77
See also
Dance studios—Floors
Floor coverings
Swine houses—Floors

Maintenance and repair
Hardwood floor refinishing—a $750 job for $95. il Sunset 159:86-7 Ag '77

FLORA. See Botany
FLORAL decoration. See Flowers, Arrangement of
FLORAL design. See Design, Decorative—Plant forms
FLORAL pictures. See Pictures
FLOREN, Lee
Five W's and how! Writers Digest 57:39-40+ Jl '77
FLORENCE

Music
New light on the Accademia degli Elevati of Florence. E. Strainchamps. bibl f il Mus Q 62:507-35 O '76
See also
Opera—Italy

Theater
We open in Florence; production of The abdication. R. Wolff. il por N Y Times Mag p50-2+ D 4 '77

FLORENCE, Ky.
Submersible pumps speed sewage flow. J. E. Ransom. il Am City & County 92:70 Je '77
FLORENCIA shipwreck. See Shipwrecks
FLORENSKY, C. P. and others
Geomorphic degradations on the surface of Venus: an analysis of Venera 9 and Venera 10 data. bibl il Science 196:869-71 My 20 '77
FLORENTINE Opera Company. See Opera—Wisconsin
FLORES, Dan L.
Long-distance whitetails. il Field & S 82:28+ Ag '77
Long-range whitetails. il por Outdoor Life 160:88-90 S '77
FLORICULTURE
Cutting garden: what to plant for fresh flowers all summer. C. Stone. il Horticulture 55:42-9 My '77
Gardener's notes. J. Fanning. See issues of House & garden incorporating Living for young homemakers
Greenhouse. J. Kilborn. See issues of Horticulture
Practical plan for a cutting garden. R. Keller. il Org Gard & Farm 24:88-90 F '77
Wild flowers that will grow in your garden. V. Ferreniea. il Horticulture 55:40-1 My '77
See also
Bulbs

Bibliography
Green-thumb reading. J. Fanning. House & Gard 149:72+ Ap '77

FLORIDA
Making it happen in Florida. J. Carter and F. Ruffin. il Redbook 149:70+ O '77
Sunny Florida: foreshadowing our future? impact of the aged. J. R. Wooten. map U.S. News 84:34-5 Ja 9 '78
See also
Agriculture—Florida
Architecture, Domestic—Florida
Big Cypress National Preserve
Biscayne Bay
Broward County
Camps—Florida
Dade County
Ecology—Florida
Education—Florida
Everglades National Park
Fishing—Florida
Fort Jefferson National Monument
Hunting—Florida
Libraries—Florida
Opera—Florida
Police—Florida
Strip mining—Florida
Suwannee River

Economic conditions
Miami: saved again. P. Berman. il Forbes 120:37-41 N 1 '77

Industries
See also
Cirtus fruit industry

Parks and reserves
Besieged reefs of Florida's Keys; John Pennekamp Coral Reef State Park. P. Dustan. il Natur Hist 86:72-6 bibl(p 101) Ap '77

Restaurants
See Restaurants—United States

FLORIDA East Coast Railway
Little railroad that did. M. Frazier. Read Digest 110:111-15 My '77
No cabooses, no brakeman, but on-time trains and profits. U.S. News 82:98 My 16 '77
Railroad fights it's way into the 20th century. O. K. Armstrong. il Nations Bus 65:58-61+ Jl '77
FLORIDA Institute of Technology

Jensen Beach campus
Diving into the future. G. Simmons. il Sea Front 23:38-42 Ja '77

FLORIDA Keys
Besieged reefs of Florida's Keys. P. Dustan. il Natur Hist 86:72-6 bibl(p 101) Ap '77
Vacation discoveries in the Florida Keys. G. Bush. il Bet Hom & Gard 55:173-4+ D '77
See also
Key West, Fla.
FLORIDA National Banks of Florida, Inc. See Bank holding companies
FLORISSANT, Mo.

Education
See Education—Missouri

FLORMAN, Samuel C.
Hired scapegoats. Harpers 254:26-9 My '77
Small is dubious. Harpers 255:10-12 Ag '77
Thoughts from the dais. Harpers 254:29-30 F '77
FLOTATION equipment. See Boats and boating—Safety devices and measures
FLOUNDER
See also
Cookery—Fish
FLOUR
Converting to whole grains. M. Bremer. il Org Gard & Farm 25:128+ Ja '78
See also
Dough
FLOUR mills
1765 mill grinds into action; restoration of Rest Place Mill, High Falls, N.Y. by Tang and Jane Hansen. B. Russell. il House & Gard 149:36+ Je '77
FLOUR mills, Converted. See Houses, Remodeled
FLOW microfluorometry. See Fluorimetry
FLOWER arrangements. See Flowers, Arrangement of
FLOWER auctions. See Auctions
FLOWER boxes, planters, etc.
Fixing up your window box. D. Raffel. il House & Gard 149:62+ Je '77
Plant stand for a corner. il Sunset 159:146+ O '77
Plantable box: a new way to start roses. E. Bonanno and S. Mechlin. il Horticulture 55:50-1 My '77
Planter-rail is decorative and it's very safe. il Sunset 159:86 Jl '77
Summer start for windows; making a window box. il House & Gard 149:12 Je '77
Throwing a double-walled planter. P. Wood. il Ceram Mo 25:59-61 My '77
2 planters you can use indoors or out. il Pop Mech 148:200+ O '77
Winners! Redbook's plant contest; decorative ways to display indoor plants. il Redbook 149:160 S '77
FLOWER exhibits
Garden events in [month] (title varies) See issues of Sunset
Summer garden sampler; excerpt from A joy of gardening. V. M. Sackville-West. il Horticulture 55:16-17 Jl '77
FLOWER formation. See Fruit-bud development
FLOWER gardening. See Floriculture
FLOWER photography. See Photography of flowers, plants, trees, etc.
FLOWER pictures. See Pictures
FLOWER shows. See Flower exhibits
FLOWER stands
Indoor garden 5 feet tall. il Sunset 158:188 Ap '77
Put some air under your house plant pots. il Sunset 158:162+ F '77
FLOWERING of plants. See Plants, Flowering of
FLOWERING onions. See Alliums
FLOWERING trees
See also
Dogwood
FLOWERREE, Robert Edmund
Best of everything. por Forbes 119:59-60 Mr 15 '77 *
FLOWERS
Favorite flowers for a cutting garden. M. Brandies. il Org Gard & Farm 24:90-1 F '77
See also
Annuals (plants)
Bulbs
Everlasting flowers
Fertilization of plants
Floriculture
Forcing (plants)
Perennials (plants)
Wild flowers
also names of flowers, e.g. Orchids

FLOWERS—*Continued*

All-America Selections

See Plants—All-America Selections

Collection and preservation

See also

Flowers, Dried

Cut flowers

Plant workshop: making cut flowers last. Seventeen 36:14 F '77

Drying

See Flowers, Dried

Odors

See Odors

FLOWERS, Arrangement of

Ceramics and flowers; Ikebana, the art of Japanese flower arranging. D. Rudoff. il Sch Arts 77:26-7 S '77

English arrangement. J. P. Dutton. il Horticulture 55:64-9 F '77

Let the flowers speak; views of C. Masson. il pors House & Gard 149:74-7 Jl '77

Romantic bouquets. C. Masson, Jr. il House & Gard 149:40 Jl '77

Three ways to arrange flowers: how to do it with your own plants. C. Warren. il Horticulture 55:70-1 F '77

See also

Bouquets

Flowers, Dried

Fruits, vegetables, etc. in decoration

Vases

FLOWERS, Artificial

Boom in blooms. il Newsweek 89:92 Ap 18 '77

Deck the halls with roses. il Ladies Home J 94:96-7+ D '77

Spice up your Christmas; artificial bouquets and herb and spice gifts. il Sat Eve Post 249:78-9 D '77

FLOWERS, Dried

Everlastings. K. Kraft and P. Kraft. il Horticulture 55:66-9, 86-7 Ap '77

Fine art of fleurage; pressed flower pictures. H. White. il por Horticulture 55:26-8 O '77

Flowers that last forever. il McCalls 104:146-9+ Ag '77

Preserving summer flowers. E. Simmons. il por Conservationist 32:19-22 S '77

Second life for your flowers: how to preserve plants for winter arrangements. B. Kent. il Horticulture 55:58-9 S '77

See also

Potpourri

FLOWERS, Forcing of. See Forcing (plants)

FLOWERS, Pressed. See Flowers, Dried

FLOWERS, Wild. See Wild flowers

FLOWERS as food

Day lily is a delicious ornamental. R. Wallace. il Org Gard & Farm 24:95-6 My '77

FLOYD, Carlisle

Susannah. Reviews

Hi Fi 27:MA28 S '77 •

FLU. See Influenza

FLUDAS, John

Fatal women. il Opera N 41:14-16+ F 12 '77

FLUE dampers. See Dampers

FLUG, James F.

Carter on oil & gas. Nation 224:652-8 My 28 '77

FLUID-bed combustion. See Combustion

FLUID dynamics

Salt fountain and other curiosities based on the different density of fluids. J. Walker. il Sci Am 237:142+ O '77

FLUIDS

Critical-point universality and fluids. A. L. Sengers and others. bibl il Phys Today 30:42-8+ D '77

FLUORESCEIN

Liposome-cell interaction: transfer and intracellular release of a trapped fluorescent marker. J. N. Weinstein and others. bibl il Science 195:489-92 F 4 '77

FLUORESCENCE

Defined dimensional changes in enzyme cofactors: fluorescent "stretched-out" analogs of adenine nucleotides. D. I. C. Scopes and others. bibl il Science 195:296-8 Ja 21 '77

See also

Immunofluorescence

FLUORESCENT indicators in biological research

Lateral transport of a lipid probe and labeled proteins in a cell membrane. J. Schlessinger and others. bibl il Science 195:307-9 Ja 21 '77

Pesticide uptake into membranes measured by fluorescence quenching. G. Omann and J. R. Lakovicz. bibl il Science 197:465-7 Jl 29 '77

Regions of cerebral ischemia located by pyridine nucleotide fluorescence. F. A. Welsh and others. bibl il Science 198:951-3 D 2 '77

Reverse banding on chromosomes produced by a guanosine-cytosine specific DNA binding antibiotic olivomycin. J. H. Van De Sande. bibl il Science 195:400-2 Ja 28 '77

See also

Fluorescein

FLUORESCENT lamps and lighting. See Electric lamps, Fluorescent

FLUORIDATION. See Water supply—Fluoridation

FLUORIDES

Complexes of stannous fluoride and other group IVB dihalides with mammalian hemoproteins. A. R. Dahl and E. Hodgson. bibl il Science 197:1376-8 S 30 '77

FLUORIMETRY

Characterization of bacterial growth by means of flow microfluorometry. J. E. Bailey and others. bibl il Science 198:1175-6 D 16 '77

FLUOROCARBONS

Aerosol ban has lost its sting. il Bus W p30-1 My 30 '77

Fluorocarbons out, new systems in. Sci N 111:324-5 My 21 '77

Great ozone debate. E. Edelson. il Pop Sci 210:82-6 Je '77

Psst! aerosol alternatives. P. Gwynne and others. il Newsweek 89:99 My 9 '77

Son of aerosol; Aquasol. il Time 109:72 My 23 '77

Why ban fluorocarbons in aerosol sprays? interview. F. S. Rowland. Read Digest 110:35-6+ F '77

FLUOROMETRY. See Fluorimetry

FLUOROSIS in cows. See Cows—Diseases and pests

FLUOXETINE

Fenfluramine and fluoxetine spare protein consumption while suppressing caloric intake by rats. J. J. Wurtman and R. J. Wurtman. bibl il Science 198:1178-80 D 16 '77

FLURAZEPAM

Flurazepam effects on slow-wave sleep: stage 4 suppressed but number of delta waves constant. I. Feinberg and others. bibl il Science 198:847-8 N 25 '77

FLUSHING Airport. See New York (city)—Airports

FLUTE

Mountain-mahogany makes music. J. E. Dealy. il por Am For 83:24-7 Je '77

FLUTE music

See also

Phonograph records—Flute music

FLXIBLE Company-Grumman Corporation merger. See Corporations—Acquisitions and mergers

FLY casting

Bye, bye, wet fly? excerpt from The masters on the nymph. E. Zern. il Field & S 82:108-10 D '77

Flyrod bream: don't settle for runts; fishing for bluegills. L. Kreh. il por Outdoor Life 159:86-7+ Je '77

Rain is catching time. N. Strung. il por Outdoor Life 159:96+ My '77

Spin a fly. G. Paust. il Field & S 82:92+ Je '77

Terrestrial tricks for low-water trout. S. R. Slaymaker, 2d. il por Outdoor Life 160:78-9+ S '77

Versatile flyfisherman; D. Whitlock. N. Lyons. il pors Outdoor Life 160:74-7+ D '77

FLY control. See Flies—Control

FLY fishing. See Fly casting

FLY rods. See Fishing tackle

FLY tying. See Fishing lures, flies, etc.

FLYGARE, Thomas J.

Teachers' private lives and legal rights. Educ Digest 42:26-8 F '77

FLYING (periodical)

Change of command; new editor. E. D. Muhlfeld. Flying 100:4 Mr '77

Passing the flag. E. D. Muhlfeld. il pors Flying 101:1+ O '77

24-carat gold: Flying's fiftieth birthday issue. E. D. Muhlfeld. Flying 101:3 S '77

FLYING, Fear of. See Phobias

FLYING boats. See Airplanes, Amphibious; Seaplanes

FLYING clubs. See Aviation clubs

FLYING Dutchman; opera. See Wagner, R.

FLYING machines

See also

Aeronautics—History

FLYING saucers. See UFOs

FLYING schools. See Aviation schools

FLYING Tiger Corporation

Flying Tiger adding cargo capacity. J. M. Lenorovitz. il Aviation W 106:55+ Ap 25 '77

Freight carriers track trade restraints. J. M. Lenorovitz. il Aviation W 106:331-4 Je 6 '77

Underachiever. Forbes 120:48 S 1 '77

FLYNN, Thomas D.

Why we should account for inflation. bibl f il Harvard Bus R 55:145-57 S '77

FLYNT, Candace

Their day off; story. Redbook 149:66-7 Ag '77

FLYNT, John James, 1914-

John Flynt. E. Roeder and A. Berlow. Nation 225:201-5 S 10 '77 •

FLYNT, Larry
Bad case makes worse law. il por Time 109:51-2 F 21 '77 *
Confusion worse confounded. L. H. Lapham. Harpers 254:12+ Ap '77 *
Dirty book goes to jail. P. Bonventre and others. il por Newsweek 89:34 F 21 '77 *
Flynt's odyssey. Chr Today 22:50-2 D 9 '77 *
Has the first amendment met its match? R. Neville. il N Y Times Mag p 18 Mr 6 '77 *
Hustler and freedom. Nat R 29:252 Mr 4 '77 *
Hustling for the Lord. T. Schwartz and others. il pors Newsweek 90:61 D 5 '77 *
I'll be a hustler for the Lord. il por Time 110:112 D 5 '77 *
Intelligent woman's guide to sex; L. Flynt's obscenity trial. K. Durbin. Mademoiselle 83:94 My '77 *
Justice for Hustler. A. Kretchmer. Newsweek 89:13 F 28 '77 *
Man of the year at Wake Forest. Chr Today 21:36 Ap 1 '77 *
When freedom is difficult to live with. J. J. Kilpatrick. Nations Bus 65:9-10 Ap '77 *
Who will be next? Chr Today 22:26-7 D 30 '77 *

FLYTHE, Starkey, Jr
Good morning, David Hartman. il pors Sat Eve Post 249:45-7+ S '77
Not going all the way. il Holiday 57:24-5+ N '76
Treasures of King Tut. il Sat Eve Post 249:68-71+ My '77

FOAM contraceptives. See Contraceptives

FOAM plastics. See Plastic foams

FOCHEK, Frank
Tennis tips and products. il Consumers Res Mag 60:13-15 Ap '77

FOCKLER, Shirley
Far East. il Trav/Holiday 148:28-32+ D '77

FOCUS Gallery, San Francisco. See Photography—Galleries and museums

FOCUSING. See Photography—Focusing

FOEGEN, J. H.
How figures can fool you. Ret Liv 17:35-6 Jl '77

FOERSTNER, George C.
Figuring out what consumers want; interview. il pors Nations Bus 65:46-8+ F '77

FOG
See also
Aviation—Fog hazards

FOGELMAN, Phyllis J.
Mildred D. Taylor. por Horn Bk 53:410-14 Ag '77

FOGHAT (rock group) See Rock groups

FOIN, T. C. and Jain, S. K.
Ecosystems analysis and population biology: lessons for the development of community ecology. bibl il BioScience 27:532-8 Ag '77

FOKKER, Anthony Herman Gerard
Fokker. J. Gilbert. Flying 101:273 S '77 *

FOKKER-VFW (firm) See Aerospace industries—Europe, Western

FOLATE conjugase. See Enzymes

FOLDING bathtubs. See Bathtubs

FOLDING boats. See Boats and boating

FOLDING screens. See Screens (furniture)

FOLEY, Dennis
Foley's return. New Yorker 53:33-4 My 9 '77 *

FOLEY, Michael W.
Turning thirty with The graduate. America 137:78-80 Ag 13 '77

FOLGER Company. See Coffee industry

FOLIAGE plants. See Plants, Ornamental

FOLIAR feeding of plants. See Plants—Nutrition

FOLIAR fertilizers. See Fertilizers and manures—Spray applications

FOLK architecture. See Architecture, Amateur

FOLK art
Henna for happiness: India's mehndi art of symbols for all seasons. J. Saksena. il UNESCO Courier 30:18-22 F '77
Pennsylvania German folkart. il Sch Arts 76:33-40 Mr '77
Shaker crafts. il Sch Arts 77:39-46 S '77
She brings back the good old days; with interview with T. Kitchen. J. Strohm. il por Nat Wildlife 16:28-35 D '77

Exhibitions

American folk art highlights; exhibition at Museum of American Folk Art. il Hobbies 82:148-9 Ag '77
American folk painting; exhibition. S. B. Sherrill. il Antiques 112:1026+ D '77
Folk art from the Henry Francis du Pont Winterthur Museum. E. Eff and D. L. Fennimore. il Antiques 112:506-13 S '77
Pippin's folk heroes. M. Stevens. il Newsweek 90:59-60 Ag 22 '77
Spanish America in today's New Mexico; Santa Fe's Museum of International Folk Art. il map Sunset 158:94-9 My '77

FOLK dancing
Communitas/ego; performance by the Country Dance and Song Society of America. S. Banes. Dance Mag 51:33-4 My '77
See also
Square dancing

FOLK drama, Korean
Masked messages; masked dance dramas. A. M. Cunningham. il Natur Hist 86:42-7 bibl(p96) Mr '77

FOLK literature, Tanzanian
After literacy, what next? Tanzanian folk tales in readers. S. Malya. il UNESCO Courier 30:23-7 F '77

FOLK lore. See Folklore

FOLK music
See also
Phonograph records—Folk music
Radio broadcasting—Music

FOLK music, African
Song for every season. S. Mbabi-Katana. il UNESCO Courier 30:26-8 My '77

FOLK music, American
See also
Country music

FOLK songs
See also
Sailors songs

FOLK songs, American
Centuries of song in her garage; E. H. Linscott's collection of New England folk songs. J. W. Steinbergh. il Ms 6:22 S '77
Just what in the hell has gone wrong here anyhow? F. Turner. il pors Am Heritage 28:34-43 O '77

FOLK tales. See Folklore

FOLKLORE
See also
Animal lore
Evil eye
Geographical myths

Bibliography

Student as folklorist. L. Trout. Engl J 66:83-7 My '77
What tall tales teach. C. Forbes. Chr Today 21:22 Ja 21 '77

Cuba

Afro-Cuban poetry. J. Antonio León. il Américas 29:28-32 S '77

United States

Children, humor, and folklore. A. Schwartz. il Horn Bk 53:280-7, 471-6 Je, Ag '77
Film; work of the Center for Southern Folklore in Memphis, Tenn. D. Hare. Craft Horiz 37:7+ Je '77

FOLKLORE of plants. See Plant lore

FOLKMAN, Moses Judah
Harvard and Monsanto: the $23-million alliance. B. J. Culliton. pors Science 195:759-63 F 25 '77 *

FOLLIN, James W. 1919-
Bolts from the heavens. il Time 110:105 D 19 '77 *

FOLSOM, Clyde H. Jr
Interview with an alcoholic. il MH 61:6-9 Summ '77

FONDA, Jane
Four successful women talk about what they want—and can't have. pors Redbook 148:92-3+ F '77
Growing Fonda of Jane; interview, ed by W. Rademaekers. il pors Time 110:90-1 O 3 '77
Jane Fonda, the woman; interview, ed by F. Robbins. il por Vogue 167:286-7+ N '77
Will the real Jane Fonda please stand up; interview, ed by J. Atlas. il pors Parents Mag 52:34-5+ D '77

about

Fonda at forty. A. Harmetz. il por McCalls 105:104-5+ Ja '78 *
Hollywood's new heroines. J. Kroll and others. il pors Newsweek 90:78-82+ O 10 '77 *
Jane Fonda: her own woman at last? M. Drabble. il pors Ms 6:51-3+ O '77 *
Politics under the palms. B. Burlingham. il pors Esquire 87:47-52+ F '77 *

FONER, Eric
Men and the symbols. il Nation 225:135-41 Ag 20 '77

FONER, Simon. See Schwartz, B. B. jt auth

FONG, Michael W.
Smith River steelheads. il Field & S 81:68-72 F '77

FONTANA, Vincent J.
Summer colds—allergies in disguise? il Mademoiselle 83:60 Je '77

FOOD
Food and nutrition. B. T. Hunter. Consumers Res Mag 60:104-12 O '77
Q&A. il Good H 185:222 N '77
See also
Boats and boating—Food problems
Carbohydrates
Convenience foods
Cookery
Diet
Dinners and dining
Fasting
Fish as food
Gastronomy
Insects as food

FOOD—See also—*Continued*
Proteins
School lunches
Shellfish as food
Vitamins
also names of foods, e.g. Cake

Canning and preserving

See Canning and preserving

Contamination

See Food contamination

Drying

Do-it-yourself food drying. il Bet Hom & Gard 55:18+ Jl '77
Dry your own foods the easy way. il Good H 185:242 S '77
See also
Fruit—Drying
Vegetables—Drying

Fat content

Facts on fat: it's not all bad; excerpt from NutriScore. R. Fremes and Z. Sabry. il Good H 185:210 S '77
4 keys to live-longer diets. P. Shriever. il Ret Liv 17:44-6 N '77

Fiber content

Confusion over fiber. il Chemistry 50:23-4 O '77
Diet with fiber. il Time 110:64+ S 12 '77
Dietary fiber: a panacea? B. T. Hunter. Consumers Res Mag 60:32-3 Jl '77
Facts about fiber. Parents Mag 52:42+ Mr '77
High-fiber diet's value questioned. W. O'Reilly, Jr. Sci Digest 81:26-8 Ap '77
New study casts doubts on high-fiber diets effectiveness in preventing heart disease. il Ret Liv 17:13 Ja '77
Please pass the fiber; bread as diet food. A. Entelis and J. Johnston. Am Home 80:58-9 F '77
Time for a bran new diet; South African research. C. SerVaas. il Sat Eve Post 249:72-4 Mr '77
Why the feud over high-fiber foods? J. Mayer. il Fam Health 9:32-4 Mr '77

Grading

See also
Meat—Grading

Irradiation

See Food, Effect of radiation on

Labeling

FDA to take a solid look at solid-weight labeling. Consumer Rep 42:313 Je '77
Peachy idea is finally ripening; weight labels on canned food. il Consumer Rep 42:65 F '77

Marketing

Strong trends in marketing organic foods. M. C. Goldman. il Org Gard & Farm 24:147-8+ Ag '77

Preservation

See Food preservation and preservatives

Prices

Bad news at the supermarket. il U.S. News 82:71 My 16 '77
Economics of a Thanksgiving dinner. il Sr Schol 110:12 N 17 '77
Food prices: what the winter wrought. il Fortune 95:14 Ap '77
Good news about food. L. Langway and others. il Newsweek 90:50-1 Ag 22 '77
Much higher food prices coming? il U.S. News 82:20 F 14 '77
National cheap food policy #1; plan of the Exploratory Project for Economic Alternatives. Farm J 101:52 Ap '77
What it costs to eat around the world; chart. U.S. News 82:25 Je 27 '77

Ready-to-cook food

See Convenience foods

Smoking

Meat smoking. il Sunset 159:172-3 N '77
Smoke an outdoor dinner. il Ebony 32:150+ My '77
Smoked turkey cold or piping. il Sunset 159:110-11 N '77

Storage

Canned food storage. Bet Hom & Gard 55:151 Je '77
See also
Freezing of food
Fruit—Storage
Vegetables—Storage

Texture

See Food texture

FOOD, Canned. See Canned food
FOOD, Choking on. See Choking
FOOD, Contaminated. See Food contamination
FOOD Convenience. See Convenience foods
FOOD, Cost of. See Food—Prices
FOOD, Dried
How to used dried foods. R. Beasley. il Org Gard & Farm 24:104+ Ag '77
See also
Food—Drying
Meat, Dried
Milk, Dried
FOOD, Effect of radiation on
Whatever happened to: Army plan to irradiate food: total failure. U.S. News 83:77 S 26 '77
FOOD, Fermented
See also
Tempeh
FOOD, Frozen
Frozen entrées. il Consumer Rep 42:277-81 My '77
How to handle frozen foods to keep them safe from spoilage. Good H 184:214 Je '77
Keep summer in your freezer all year long! il Fam Health 9:46-50 Ja '77
See also
Fish, Frozen
Freezing of food
Ice cream, ices, etc.
FOOD, Irradiated. See Food, Effect of radiation on
FOOD, Organic
Love and the food you eat. J. Goldstein. Org Gard & Farm 24:132+ Mr '77
Organic living almanac. See issues of Organic gardening and farming
See also
Cookery—Organic food

Marketing

See Food—Marketing

FOOD, Sensitivity to. See Food allergy
FOOD, Synthetic. See Food substitutes
FOOD, Wild
See also
Plants, Edible
FOOD additives
Diet not cause of hyperactivity. Sci N 111:406-7 Je 25 '77
Eat with caution! FDA's second look at additives will take five more years. Sci Digest 82:70-3 Ag '77
Eating food additives and having them too. il Sci N 111:198 Mr 26 '77
Growing worry over the chemicals in our food. il Changing T 31:37-40 Je '77
Is law on food additives too strict? views on Delaney clause; interviews. J. W. Hanley; S. M. Wolfe. pors U.S. News 82:25-6 My 30 '77
Let's subtract additives. J. Mayer. Fam Health 9:42-3 D '77
Pizen squad; USDA Board of Food and Drug Inspection. il pors Chemistry 50:18-21 S '77
Polymeric food additives. il Chemistry 50:23 Je '77
Research disputes link between hyperactivity and food additives. J. Gaylin. Psychol Today 11:46+ O '77
Screening for cancer; FDA use of the Ames test. M. Weinstock. Environment 19:2-4 D '77
Why ban reason from the consumer safety debate? address, June 14, 1977. J. W. Hanley. Vital Speeches 43:626-9 Ag 1 '77
See also
Butylated hydroxytoluene
Monosodium glutamate
Sodium nitrite
FOOD adulteration and inspection
Pizen squad; USDA Board of Food and Drug Inspection. il pors Chemistry 50:18-21 S '77
See also
Food laws and legislation
FOOD allergy
Common food allergies. il Good H 184:172+ F '77
Food allergies may be causing more headaches than you know. C. A. Frazier. House B 119:42+ Je '77
How biocriminology's clues show diet's relationship to violence! T. O. Marsh. por Sci Digest 82:17-19 Jl '77
Hyperactivity or chocolate milk? T. G. Banville. Educ Digest 42:48-9 My '77
FOOD and Agriculture Organization of the United Nations
FAO Council adopts $206 million budget proposal. UN Chron 14:37+ Jl '77
Hunger in the midst of plenty. J. J. DuPont. Conservationist 32:1 S '77
International cooperation to protect the whales; UNEP and FAO. S. J. Holt. il Oceans 10:62-4 Jl '77
FOOD and Drug Administration. See United States—Food and Drug Administration
FOOD and Drug Inspection, Board of. See United States—Agriculture, Department of
FOOD and Nutrition Service. See United States—Agriculture, Department of—Food and Nutrition Service

FOOD as gifts
Apt wraps for food gifts. Bet Hom & Gard 55:60-2 N '77
Bake-ahead presents in giveaway containers. il House & Gard 149:200+ N '77
Food gifts by mail. il Sunset 159:120+ N; 130 D '77
For a marvelous make-ahead Christmas. il House & Gard 149:146-9 N '77
44 super gifts to make now for next Christmas; with recipes. il Good H 185:126-9+ Jl '77
Gifts from the earth. S. Tait. il Org Gard & Farm 24:119-20 D '77
Gourmet gifts from your kitchen. il Good H 185:162-3+ D '77
Homemade food gifts. E. W. Manning. il Farm J 101:50-1+ N '77
Spice up your Christmas; artificial bouqets and herb and spice gifts. il Sat Eve Post 249:78-9 D '77
Sweets and treats you make. il Mademoiselle 83:108-9+ D '77
Treats that travel. il Good H 185:274 N '77
Try the supermarket. G. Franck. il Ret Liv 16:38 D '76

FOOD buying. See Purchasing, Household

FOOD chains (ecology)
See also
Detritus

FOOD chemistry
See also
Food additives

FOOD containers. See Containers

FOOD contamination
Case for food chemicals. J. Carper. por Newsweek 89:11 Mr 7 '77
Pesticides, insects in foods, and cosmetic standards. D. Pimentel and others. bibl il BioScience 27:178-85 Mr '77
See also
Fish contamination
Swine—Contamination by drugs, pesticides, etc.

FOOD cooperatives. See Cooperative associations

FOOD crispness. See Food texture

FOOD critics and criticism
Burp! il Esquire 87:70-3 Je '77

FOOD customs. See Food habits

FOOD decoration. See Cookery—Garnishes; Cookery, Ornamental

FOOD discount coupons. See Coupons

FOOD drying apparatus. See Drying apparatus

FOOD for infants. See Infants—Nutrition

FOOD for Peace program. See Food relief

FOOD freezers. See Freezers

FOOD habits
Are you eating right? S. N. Wellborn. il U.S. News 83:39-43 N 28 '77
Chinese way of eating. A. Y. Dessaint. il Natur Hist 86:94-5+ Ag '77
Communion as a culinary art. W. H. Willimon. Chr Cent 94:829-30 S 21 '77
Did your mother make you fat? Ebony 32:50-60+ My '77
Food we eat: enough is not enough. B. Myerson. por Redbook 148:96+ Ap '77
4 keys to live-longer diets. P. Shriever. il Ret Liv 17:44-6 N '77
How to control your sweet tooth. M. Mercer. il McCalls 104:112+ Jl '77
How to gear your mind to think yourself slim; interview, ed by C. Seebohm. F. M. Stern. House & Gard 149:22+ Ag '77
Learning to be thin; views of S. Simon. McCalls 105:81-2 O '77
Love in the kitchen. il Time 110:54-8+ D 19 '77
Those food-related cues magnify your weight problem. A. R. Weiss. Sci Digest 81:33-4 Ap '77
Want food fast? Here's fast food. P. Gray. il Time 110:42-3 Jl 4 '77
What you eat today can decide your health tomorrow. H. Alpert. il Ret Liv 17:26-30 S '77
See also
Gluttony

Anecdotes, facetiae, satire, etc.

How to eat like a child. D. Ephron. N Y Times Mag p95 F 27 '77; Same abr. Read Digest 110:71 Je '77

FOOD in the Bible. See Bible—Food

FOOD industry
Baby's business; Baker/Beech-Nut Corporations' reformulated natural products. L. Langway and M. Reese. il Newsweek 89:72 Mr 21 '77
Early California gears up for the olive war. por Duns R 110:22-3 S '77
Gargling with peanut butter; snack foods by Lance. il Forbes 120:114 O 15 '77
Mushrooming business. Forbes 120:48-9 Jl 15 '77
Panacea, placebo, nostrum, amen; Shaklee Corp. il Forbes 120:83-4+ O 15 '77
Pizza to go, heavy on the soybeans; Universal Foods. por Forbes 119:76 Mr 1 '77
Sprouts; Sun-Mee Company producer for bean sprouts. New Yorker 53:16-17 Ag 1 '77
See also
Beatrice Foods Company
Borden, Inc
Candy industry
Consolidated Foods Corporation
Federal Company
Food additives
Food service
Fruit industry
General Foods Corporation
General Mills, Inc
Heinz, H. J, Company
Herb industry
Hershey Foods Corporation
Mueller, C. F, Company
Pet, Inc
Pillsbury Company
Standard Brands, Inc
Vlasic Foods, Inc
Ward Foods Inc

Acquisitions and mergers

Bittersweet victory for Gerber's directors; stockholders' suit over Anderson, Clayton bid. il Bus W p37 O 10 '77
Nothing-is-too-good-for-our-stockholders department; proposed Anderson, Clayton and Gerber Products merger. Forbes 119:55 My 15 '77
Why Gerber makes such an inviting target; Anderson, Clayton & Co. takeover plan. il Bus W p26 Je 27 '77

Advertising

See also
Dairying—Advertising

Finance

Food & drink. il Forbes 121:156+ Ja 9 '78

Management

When a family company outgrows the family; Shaklee Corporation. por Bus W p68-9 Ag 1 '77

Switzerland

Bottle-baby disease; boycott of Nestle products in attempt to stop promotion of infant formula in underdeveloped countries. B. L. Benderly. Ms 6:20 D '77

FOOD inspection. See Food adulteration and inspection

FOOD laws and legislation
Has emotion tipped the scales on consumer safety? address, October 17, 1977. J. W. Hanley. Vital Speeches 44:92-5 N 15 '77
Is law on food additives too strict? views on Delaney clause; interviews. J. W. Hanley; S. M. Wolfe. pors U.S. News 82:25-6 My 30 '77
Opting for cancer; Delaney amendment. J. Cox. il Org Gard & Farm 24:115+ Je '77
Why ban reason from the consumer safety debate? address, June 14, 1977. J. W. Hanley. Vital Speeches 43:626-9 Ag 1 '77
See also
United States—Food and Drug Administration

FOOD mail order business. See Mail order business

FOOD mixers. See Kitchen utensils and appliances

FOOD plants. See Plants, Edible

FOOD poisoning
Watch out for food poisoning. Changing T 31:4 Jl '77
See also
Botulism
Ergotism

FOOD policy. See Agricultural administration

FOOD preservation and preservatives
Salting and brining. M. Stoner. il Org Gard & Farm 24:117-18+ Ag '77
See also
Canning and preserving
Food—Drying
Food, Effect of radiation on
Freezing of food
Meat—Preservation

FOOD processing industry. See Food industry

FOOD processors. See Kitchen utensils and appliances

FOOD relief
Challenging the world food crisis. G. Borgstrom. Intellect 105:322-4 Ap '77
Food for Peace or food for power? M. Marchino and R. K. Musil. il Chr Cent 94:714-18 Ag 17 '77
Is it time to end Food for Peace? E. Rothschild. N Y Times Mag p 15+ Mr 13 '77
Strengthening the Public Law 480 food aid program; statement, April 5, 1977. J. A. Ferch. Dept State Bull 76:447-51 My 2 '77
U.S. agripower and a hungry world. D. Morgan. Current 191:30-7 Mr '77
See also
Food and Agriculture Organization of the United Nations

FOOD relief—*Continued*

Underdeveloped areas

See Underdeveloped areas—Food relief

United States

How to reach out to hungry America. A. Northrop. il Ms 6:91-4 O '77
Hungry women in America. L. Schwartz. il Ms 6:60-3+ O '77
Stamp act; proposed reforms. M. S. Evans. Nat R 29:1116 S 30 '77

FOOD research
See also
Nutrition research

FOOD sensitiveness. See Food allergy

FOOD service
Best of everything; trains, airplanes and ocean liners. R. E. M. Whitaker. New Yorker 53: 29-32 D 19 '77
Cooking up a living: catering, cooking schools and food shops. C. Calvert. il Mademoiselle 83:152+ D '77
New food giants? H. Seneker. il Forbes 119: 53-4 Ap 1 '77
See also
Airlines—Beverage and food service
Camps—Food service
Ocean liners—Food service

FOOD service employees
See also
Waiters and waitresses

FOOD stamp plan. See Food relief—United States

FOOD storage. See Food—Storage

FOOD storage containers. See Containers

FOOD stores
Convenience stores: a $7.4 billion mushroom. il Bus W p61-2+ Mr 21 '77
Special sharing of favorite holiday recipes; with recipes. il Bet Hom & Gard 55:104-11+ D '77
See also
Supermarkets

FOOD substitutes
Case for food chemicals. J. Carper. por Newsweek 89:11 Mr 7 '77
How ersatz foods shortchange you. J. L. Kent. Sci Digest 82:20-1 Jl '77
It isn't cheese. N. Von Hoffman. Progressive 41:52 My '77
Top banana. Chemistry 50:3 Jl '77
See also
Coffee substitutes

Anecdotes, facetiae, satire, etc.

Soy of cooking. J. Lardner. New Repub 176:11 F 26 '77

FOOD supply
Challenging the world food crisis. G. Borgstrom. Intellect 105:322-4 Ap '77
Food and agriculture: symposium; discussion. Sci Am 236:8+ Ja '77
Food crisis? It's still there. E. J. Cripps. America 136:46-9 Ja 22 '77
Panel calls for global food and nutrition research drive. C. Holden. Science 197:140 Jl 8 '77
Place of U.S. food in eliminating world hunger. G. E. Brandow. bibl f il Ann Am Acad 429:1-11 Ja '77
Roots of hunger. D. Morgan. Natur Hist 86:118-21 O '77
Soil deterioration and the growing world demand for food. R. A. Brink and others. bibl il Science 197:625-30 Ag 12 '77
See also
Crop yields
Famines
Food and Agriculture Organization of the United Nations
Grain supply
Production, Agricultural
United Nations International Fund for Agricultural Development (proposed)
United Nations World Food Council

Poland

Poland: meat and potatoes. P. Martin. Newsweek 91:26 Ja 2 '78

FOOD texture
Is a chip crisp if you can't hear it crunch? il Chemistry 50:28 Jl '77

FOOD values
See also
Nutrition

FOOD wrapping materials. See Wrapping materials

FOOT

Care and hygiene

Common-sense foot care. il Good H 186:154 Ja '78
Great-looking summer feet. A. Taylor. il N Y Times Mag p92-6 Ap 17 '77
Handle with care. C. B. Abbott. Am Home 80: 32+ D '77
If your feet hurt. W. A. Nolen. McCalls 104:46+ Ap '77
What to do for your aching feet. L. Lamberg. Bet Hom & Gard 55:231-2 S '77

Diseases

See also
Athlete's foot (disease)

FOOT bridges. See Bridges, Foot

FOOT racing. See Running

FOOTBALL
Moral equivalent to football. W. E. Washburn. New Repub 177:33-6 Jl 23 '77
See also
Rugby football
Soccer

FOOTBALL, Childrens
Parents egos take the fun out of Little League; research by Keith Henschen and Leon Griffin. J. Horn. Psychol Today 11:18+ S '77

FOOTBALL, College
Alabama stole the show; USC game. J. Jares. il Sports Illus 47:65-6 O 17 '77
Bedeviled, not beaten; Penn State vs Arizona State in the Fiesta Bowl. B. McDermott. il Sports Illus 48:48 Ja 2 '78
College football 1977. il Sports Illus 47:28-40+ S 5 '77
Don't let 'em wear you down! L. Corso, coach of Indiana. J. Underwood. il pors Sports Illus 47:46-8+ N 14 '77
Down and out can be upsetting; Texas vs Oklahoma. D. S. Looney. il Sports Illus 47:24-5 O 17 '77
End to the bickering; Iowa vs Iowa State. W. Bingham. il Sports Illus 47:50+ S 26 '77
Explosive Woody Hayes; Ohio State. J. Brondfield. il Read Digest 111:98-102 S '77
Football. See issues of New Yorker published during the football season
He really pounds it out; Texas A&M vs Texas Tech. J. Jares. il Sports Illus 47:44+ O 3 '77
Hello, big time, so long, streak; Penn State vs Rutgers. P. Putnam. il Sports Illus 47:62+ S 12 '77
In the second half it was pure Aggie-ny; Michigan vs Texas A&M. J. Jares. il Sports Illus 47:28-30 O 10 '77
Is Colgate going to be squeezed out again? M. DelNagro. il Sports Illus 47:55-6 N 7 '77
Longhorns of plenty; University of Texas. il Time 110:118 N 28 '77
Maybe it's the luck of the Irish; Notre Dame vs University of Pittsburgh. J. Underwood. il Sports Illus 47:20-2+ S 19 '77
Minnesota's miracle; victory over Michigan. W. O. Johnson. Sports Illus 47:23 O 31 '77
Mowed down by a Thompson; Washington State vs Nebraska. K. Hannon. por Sports Illus 47: 70+ S 19 '77
Nary a bomb in the rockets' red glare; Arizona State vs Brigham Young. W. Bingham. il Sports Illus 47:20-1 N 21 '77
Never too late for the Sooners; Oklahoma vs Ohio State. J. Underwood. il Sports Illus 47:14-17 O 3 '77
Pags packs his bags; Yale vs Harvard. J. Papanek. il Sports Illus 47:56+ N 21 '77
Setting up a showdown in Dallas; selections for bowl games. J. Underwood. il Sports Illus 47: 26-30+ D 19 '77
Shake down the thunder; bowl games; symposium. il Sports Illus 48:6-11 Ja 9 '78
So it's two in a row for Bo; Michigan vs Ohio State. J. Underwood. il Sports Illus 47:20-3 N 28 '77
They sure didn't come up short; Western Carolina University. J. Kirshenbaum. il Sports Illus 47:90+ N 28 '77
They were dressed to kill; Notre Dame vs USC. D. S. Looney. il Sports Illus 47:20-3 O 31 '77
Tips from a fearsome foursome; handicapping the college bowl games. P. Axthelm. il Newsweek 91:44-5 Ja 2 '78
Togetherness pays off at Kentucky. W. F. Reed. il Sports Illus 47:72+ N 14 '77
Two on the fifty; letters to Purdue ticket seller J. S. Dienhart. B. Collins. il Sat Eve Post 249: 40-1 O '77
Week; college football. See issues of Sports Illustrated published during the football season
What a way to wind it up; symposium. il Sports Illus 47:20-5 D 5 '77
Who's number one? B. Wilkinson. il Sat Eve Post 249:64-5+ O '77
See also
Football players

Awards, prizes, etc.

Hail to the chief; college football trophies. B. Weber. il Sr Schol 110:48-9 O 20 '77
Idea that deserves no trophy; televising the Heisman Awards. D. S. Looney. il Sports Illus 47:68 D 5 '77

Conferences

Words spoke louder than action; NCAA convention. J. Underwood. Sports Illus 46:48-9 Ja 31 '77

FOOTBALL, College—*Continued*

Ethical aspects

Fewer is finer except for some flaws; football scholarships. J. Underwood. il Sports Illus 47:28-31+ S 5 '77

History

Legend vs. legend; annual Notre Dame-Southern Cal games. N. B. Read, Jr. il Sat Eve Post 249:58-9+ N '77
Melding of men all suited to a T; 1940 Stanford team. R. Fimrite. il Sports Illus 47:90-100 S 5 '77

FOOTBALL, High school
At tackle, Ms Tammy Lee Mercer. J. E. Maslow. por Sat R 5:49-51 N 26 '77
Mightiest of the highs; Moeller vs Farrell. W. Bingham. il Sports Illus 47:60+ O 10 '77
That senior season: Vicksburg, Mich. B. Gilbert. il Sports Illus 47:104-8+ N 14; 38-40+ N 21 '77

Anecdotes, facetiae, satire, etc.

What are we doing at a football game? high school football. V. J. Richards. Seventeen 36:198+ Ag '77

FOOTBALL, Professional
Fly now, swoop later plan; Atlanta Falcons. J. Marshall. Sports Illus 47:78+ O 24 '77
Football. See issues of New Yorker published during the football season
Giving Joe a big hello; Los Angeles Rams. R. Fimrite. il por Sports Illus 47:8-11 Ag 15 '77
Interest centers on the Central; Cincinnati Bengals vs Cleveland Browns. R. Reid. il Sports Illus 47:32-3 N 14 '77
It's Denver and Dallas; Super Bowl. il Time 111:64-6+ Ja 16 '78
It's hard to buck the Broncos; Super Bowl pick. P. Axthelm. il Newsweek 91:72-3 Ja 16 '78
Kickoff time! P. Axthelm. il Newsweek 90:60-1 S 26 '77
Matter of higher math; potential playoff matchups. D. Jenkins. il Sports Illus 47:20-3 D 19 '77
Miles high in the Mile High City; Denver Broncos. Time 110:70-1 D 26 '77
New charge for the Chargers. J. Marshall. il Sports Illus 47:20-2 Ag 22 '77
Once more, with no hard feelings; Oakland-Pittsburgh game. D. Jenkins. il Sports Illus 47:22-4+ O 3 '77
One giant step for L.A. while Oakland limps. J. Marshall. il Sports Illus 47:67-8 D 12 '77
Pro football '77. Sports Illus 47:30-4+ S 19 '77
Raiders were all suped up; Super Bowl. D. Jenkins. il Sports Illus 46:10-15 Ja 17 '77
Raiding party; Raiders vs Vikings in Super Bowl. P. Axthelm. il Newsweek 89:54-5 Ja 24 '77
Really Joe, is all this necessary? J. Thomas, general manager of the San Francisco 49ers. J. Marshall. il por Sports Illus 47:90+ O 31 '77
Roger, over and in; Dallas vs Minnesota. D. Jenkins. il Sports Illus 47:18-21 S 26 '77
Say hello to the fearsome threesome; the 3-4 defense. J. Marshall. il Sports Illus 47:26-8+ O 17 '77
Taking to the Super highway; playoffs; symposium. il Sports Illus 48:10-17 Ja 2 '78
Too tall, too mean, too much; Dallas vs Minnesota for NFC title. J. Marshall. il Sports Illus 48:14-16 Ja 9 '78
Trying the patient of the Saints. R. F. Jones. il Sports Illus 47:20-1 Ag 29 '77
Upending the upstarts; Oakland Raiders vs Denver Broncos. J. Marshall. il Sports Illus 47:22-5 N 7 '77
Whole town's sacking the Jones boy; New England Patriots vs Baltimore Colts. D. Jenkins. il Sports Illus 47:26-7 O 31 '77
Wholly Moses for Denver; Denver vs Oakland for AFC title. D. Jenkins. il Sports Illus 48:14-16+ Ja 9 '78
Why women like football. K. Gilman. Vogue 167:60 N '77
See also
Collective bargaining—Football, Professional
Football players

Accidents and injuries

I'm number 50! interview, ed by G. Plimpton; excerpt from One more July. B. Curry. il Read Digest 112:129-32 Ja '78

Ethical aspects

Walk on the sordid side; G. Atkinson's slander suit against C. Noll. W. O. Johnson. il por Sports Illus 47:10-15 Ag 1 '77

History

Super Bowl. H. Rosenthal. il Sports Illus 48:31-2+ Ja 9 '78

Organization and administration

Party became a lynching; firing of San Francisco 49er coach M. Clark by general manager J. Thomas. J. Marshall. por Sports Illus 46:68+ Ap 18 '77
Pro football's mismatch. P. Axthelm. il Newsweek 90:121 D 12 '77
Vince, you wouldn't believe it; American Football Conference vs National Football Conference. J. Marshall. il Sports Illus 47:24-6+ N 21 '77

Radio broadcasting

See Radio broadcasting—Sports

Refereeing

Now for the zebras. . . il Time 111:70 Ja 16 '78

Television broadcasting

See Television broadcasting—Sports

Canada

Snow stopped for Sonny; Edmonton Eskimos vs Montreal Alouettes in Grey Cup game. R. F. Jones. il Sports Illus 47:87-8 D 5 '77

FOOTBALL coaches
Better than working for a living; Pittsburgh Steeler assistant coaches. M. Cope. il Sports Illus 47:36-8+ S 12 '77
See also
Bryant, B.
Clark, M.
Corso, L.
Halas, G. S.
Hayes, W. W.
Johnson, W. O.
Majors, J.
Shaughnessy, C.

FOOTBALL fields
Gridiron of the future? conversion of football fields to metric system. il Sr Schol 110:9 D 1 '77

FOOTBALL gambling. See Gambling

FOOTBALL in art. See Sports in art

FOOTBALL players
All American notes. B. Weber. il Sr Schol 109:26 Mr 10 '77
Annual football roundup. il Ebony 33:163-6+ N '77
Becoming a pro; Philadelphia Eagles. J. Cramer. New Repub 177:14-16 N 12 '77
Getting inside their 'Skins; Washington Redskins in broadcasting. B. Newman. Sports Illus 47:49 D 12 '77
Leaders of a new air force; college quarterbacks. Sports Illus 47:76 S 5 '77
My vacation was nifty. R. F. Jones. il Sports Illus 47:62-6+ Jl 11 '77
1976 High School All-American Football Team. B. Weber. Sr Schol 109:35 Mr 24 '77
Runts in the big league. il Time 110:75-6 D 5 '77
They're kicking up a real storm; Southwest Conference field goal kickers. J. Jares. il pors Sports Illus 47:26-9 N 7 '77
See also
Albert, F.
Alzado, L.
Atkinson, G.
Bell, R.
Blount, M.
Dobler, C.
Dorsett, T. D.
Griese, B.
Haden, P.
Hipp, I. M.
King, H.
Mansfield, R.
Namath, J. W.
Pagliaro, J.
Papale, V.
Payton, W.
Simpson, O. J.
Stabler, K.
Thompson, J.
Williams, D.
Woodard, G.

Anecdotes, facetiae, satire, etc.

Sandy Frazier dream team. I. Frazier. il New Yorker 53:46-7 N 28 '77

Recruiting

Draft evasion. P. Bonventre. il Newsweek 89:79 F 7 '77
That orange shirt means something; J. Major's recruiting for Tennessee. J. Underwood. il Sports Illus 46:68-72+ Mr 28 '77

Salaries, pensions, etc.

This agent's no secret; work of M. Trope. J. Marshall. il por Sports Illus 46:60+ My 16 '77
See also
Collective bargaining—Football, Professional

FOOTBALL scouting
Scout: sports' indefatigable spy. B. Surface. Read Digest 111:53-4+ D '77

FOOTE, Arthur
Foote: Sonata in G minor for violin & piano; Beach: Sonata in A minor for violin & piano. W. Simmons. Am Rec G 40:27-8 O '77 *

FOOTE, Barbara
Three machines for your kitchen. il Org Gard & Farm 24:110+ O '77

FOOTE, Jim
Getting started in organic farming. il Org Gard & Farm 24:86-9 Mr '77

FOOTE, Marion R.
Controlling the cost of international compensation. il Harvard Bus R 55:123-32 N '77

FOOTE, Robert Thaddeus
Pizza to go, heavy on the soybeans. por Forbes 119:76 Mr 1 '77 *

FOOTE, Theodore P.
(comp) News: people, places, events. See issues of School arts

FOOTE, Timothy
Inventing the centerboard. il por Motor B & S 140:139-42 S '77

FOOTLICK, Jerrold K.
We've got too much law! Read Digest 110:96-100 My '77

FOOTWEAR. See Shoes, boots, rubbers, etc.

FOR Eyes Optical Company. See Optical industry

FORAGE harvesters. See Harvesting machinery

FORAGE plants
Poison! foraging. R. E. Arnold. Field & S 81: 134-5 F '77
See also
Alfalfa
Grasses
Silage
Sorghum

FORAKER, J. D.
Pick windowsill peppers all year long. il Org Gard & Farm 24:88-90 Ag '77

FORAMINIFERA
Sand-covered, tree-shaped sea creatures. il Sci N 112:292-3 N 5 '77

FORAMINIFERA, Fossil
Glacial-Holocene transition in deep-sea carbonates: selective dissolution and the stable isotope signal. W. H. Berger and J. S. Killingley. bibl il Science 197:563-6 Ag 5 '77
Isoleucine epimerization of dating marine sediments: importance of analyzing monospecific foraminiferal samples. K. King and C. Neville. bibl il Science 195:1333-5 Mr 25 '77
Oxygen isotopic analysis of the size fraction between 62 and 250 micrometers in Caribbean cores P6304-8 and P6304-9. C. Emiliani. bibl il Science 198:1255-6 D 23 '77

FORBES, Cheryl A.
Dorothy L. Sayers—for good work, for God's work. Chr Today 21:16-18 Mr 4 '77

FORBES, Christopher Charles
Those were the good old days? il por Forbes 119:8 F 15 '77 *

FORBES, Malcolm Stevenson, Jr
Parliament of owls. por Forbes 119:6 Ja 15 '77

FORBES, Reginald D.
Obituary
Am For 83:4 Mr '77

FORBES (periodical)
Forbes readers have their say—1917-1977: selection of letters to the editors. Forbes 120:244+ S 15 '77
Greater expectations. il Forbes 120:121-2 S 15 '77
Why we're so fat; magazine's 60th birthday. Forbes 120:12 S 15 '77

FORBES House, Milton. See Historic houses, sites, etc.—Massachusetts

FORBIS, William H.
Real American cowboy; excerpt from Cowboys. il Read Digest 110:27-30+ Je '77

FORCE and energy
See also
Mass (physics)

FORCE of destiny; opera. See Verdi, G.

FORCED labor camps. See Concentration camps

FORCINELLI, Joseph
I taught ethics in high school. Todays Educ 66: 70-1 Ja '77

FORCING (plants)
Greenhouse: pot-et-fleur, or mixed pan. J. Kilborn. il Horticulture 55:50+ O '77
How to force winter branches to blossom for an early spring indoors. M. M. Herweg. il Horticulture 55:32-3 F '77

FORD, Barbara
Books. See issues of Science digest

FORD, Bob, Jr
InSights. Hi Fi 27:131-3 Mr '77

FORD, Charles H.
Chop the chitchat—save time and money. il Nations Bus 65:35-6+ S '77

FORD, Charlotte
Charlotte Ford entertains. C. Porcelli. il por House B 119:100-1 Je '77 *

FORD, Corey
Letter to a grandson; story. Field & S 82:56-7 D '77

FORD, Cristina. See Ford, M. C. V. A.

FORD, Edsel Bryant
Frustrations and strains of being the boss's son. C. Mueller. pors Duns R 110:21-2 Ag '77 *

FORD, Elizabeth (Bloomer)
Harper, Reader's Digest to copublish Fords' memoirs. M. Reuter. il pors Pub W 211:25-6 Mr 21 '77 *
Keeping up with Betty Ford. M. MacPherson. il por McCalls 105:206-7+ N '77 *

Photographs

My White House scrapbook. S. E. Ford. il por Good H 184:126-9 Je '77

FORD, Freeman A.
What to expect of solar pool heaters. Parks & Rec 12:44-5 My '77

FORD, Gerald Rudolph
Bill of Rights Day, Human Rights Day and Week, 1976. Dept State Bull 76:29 Ja 10 '77
Canopy of tyranny; address, October 29, 1977. Vital Speeches 44:130-3 D 15 '77
International economic report transmitted to the Congress; message, January 18, 1977. Dept State Bull 76:129-32 F 14 '77
Lessons from the Presidency; address, May 28, 1977. por Chr Today 21:18-19 Jl 29 '77
President Ford responds to action by OPEC increasing oil prices; statement, December 17, 1976. Dept State Bull 76:67 Ja 24 '77
Prime Minister Andreotti of Italy visits Washington; exchange of remarks, December 6, 1976. Dept State Bull 76:12-13 Ja 3 '77
Second Sinai Support Mission report transmitted to the Congress; message, January 11, 1977. Dept State Bull 76:134 F 14 '77
Seventh progress report on Cyprus submitted to the Congress; message, January 10, 1977. Dept State Bull 76:93-4 Ja 31 '77
Sixteenth annual report of ACDA transmitted to the Congress; text of letter, January 19, 1977. Dept State Bull 76:132-3 F 14 '77
State of the Union 1977; address, January 12, 1977. Vital Speeches 43:226-30 F 1 '77; Same abr. Dept State Bull 76:97-101 F 1 '77; Excerpts. il por U.S. News 82:28 Ja 24 '77
U.S. signs articles of agreement of Agricultural Development Fund; statement, December 22, 1976. Dept State Bull 76:70-1 Ja 24 '77
What Ford thinks of Carter's style; interview. il pors U.S. News 83:20-2 Jl 4 '77

about

Advice from the former tenants. Nation 224:482-4 Ap 23 '77 *
Cheaper Ford. Nation 224:773 Je 25 '77 *
Ford era—highlights of a pivotal 2½ years. il pors U.S. News 82:26-7 Ja 24 '77 *
Ford in retirement: busy, rich and happy. il pors U.S. News 82:26 Mr 21 '77 *
Ford overturns Atlantic decision. R. K. Ellingsworth. Aviation W 106:25 Ja 3 '77 *
Good riddance. New Repub 176:3-4+ Ja 15 '77 *
Graceful exit. Chr Today 21:51 F 4 '77 *
Harper, Reader's Digest to copublish Fords' memoirs. M. Reuter. il pors Pub W 211:25-6 Mr 21 '77 *
How Carter will differ from Ford—an expert's view; interview. M. W. H. Collins, Jr. il por U.S. News 82:17-18 Ja 31 '77 *
Ironic farewell. R. Hotz. Aviation W 106:9 Ja 17 '77 *
It's just citizen Ford now. B. Angelo. il por Time 109:19-20 Ja 31 '77 *
Reporter in Washington D.C. (cont) E. B. Drew. New Yorker 52:48+ Ja 17 '77 *
Rocky Mountain high. T. Mathews and T. M. DeFrank. il pors Newsweek 90:40-1 Ag 1 '77 *
Suited to a tee. T. M. DeFrank. il por Newsweek 89:29-30 Ja 31 '77 *
Sunny world of Palm Springs. T. Schwartz and M. Kasindorf. il Newsweek 89:68-70 Mr 28 '77 *
TRB from Washington (cont) New Repub 176: 2 Ja 15; 2+ Ap 9 '77 *
Watson, but not so elementary; participation in the Bing Crosby National Pro-Am. D. Jenkins. il Sports Illus 46:12-15 Ja 31 '77 *

Addresses, messages, etc.

See also
Ford, G. R.—State of the Union Message, January 12, 1977

Photographs

My White House scrapbook. S. E. Ford. il por Good H 184:126-9 Je '77

Press relations

Poor Jody Powell. R. H. Nessen. por Newsweek 89:9 Ja 31 '77

State of the Union Message, January 12, 1977

Making it easier for the new man. il por Time 109:14 Ja 24 '77

FORD, Henry, 1863-1947
Frustrations and strains of being the boss's son. C. Mueller. pors Duns R 110:21-2 Ag '77 *
Henry the first. R. L. Strout. il New Repub 176:16-18 My 21 '77 *
In nature's laboratory. P. W. Metzler. il Conservationist 32:30-3+ Jl '77 *

FORD, Henry, 1917-

Henry Ford on Renaissance Center; interview. Sat R 4:11 My 14 '77

Rap with Hank the deuce; excerpts from interview, ed by J. C. Jones. il pors Newsweek 89:66+ Ap 25 '77

about

Another Ford farewell. por Time 109:24 Ja 24 '77 *

Facelift for Detroit. R. M. Williams. il Sat R 4:6-8+ My 14 '77 *

Ford's new trimotor. T. Nicholson and J. C. Jones. il pors Newsweek 89:65 Ap 25 '77 *

Ford's parting shot. il por Newsweek 89:69 Ja 24 '77 *

Separate ways. E. Keerdoja and J. C. Jones. Newsweek 90:10 Ag 22 '77 *

'77 Ford trimotor. il pors Time 109:76-7 Ap 25 '77 *

Why Ford quit Ford Foundation. por U.S. News 82:62 Ja 24 '77 *

FORD, Henry, Museum. See Greenfield Village and Henry Ford Museum, Dearborn, Mich.

FORD, Leighton

Update Lausanne; interview. por Chr Today 22:16-18+ D 9 '77

FORD, Maria Cristina Vettore Austin

Separate ways. E. Keerdoja and J. C. Jones. Newsweek 90:10 Ag 22 '77 *

FORD, Nancy

Cryer & Ford; hang on to the good times. S. Dworkin. pors Ms 6:64-5 D '77 *

FORD, Nancy (Torbett)

U.S. journal: Tampa, Florida; discrimination against women at the University Club. C. Trillin. New Yorker 53:102-3 Ap 11 '77 *

FORD, Richard

Walker Percy: not just whistling Dixie. Nat R 29:558+ My 13 '77

FORD, Susan Elizabeth

My White House scrapbook. il por Good H 184:126-9 Je '77

FORD, Whitey

Confessions of a gunkball artist; excerpt from Whitey and Mickey, ed by J. Durso. il pors N Y Times Mag p38-41 Ap 3 '77

—and Mantle, M.

Life with Casey Stengel; excerpt from Whitey and Mickey; ed by J. Durso. il pors Sat Eve Post 249:44-5+ My '77

FORD, Bacon & Davis, Inc (firm) See Consulting engineers

FORD Foundation

Another Ford farewell. por Time 109:24 Ja 24 '77

Bundy touch. L. Minard. Forbes 120:105 N 1 '77

Energy debacle; Energy Policy Project. L. H. Lapham. Harpers 255:58-61+ Ag '77; Discussion. 255:6+ O '77

Ford Foundation activities related to college and university faculty. Intellect 106:71 Ag '77

Ford-MITRE study: nuclear power yes, plutonium no. W. D. Metz. Science 196:41 Ap 1 '77

Ford's parting shot. il por Newsweek 89:69 Ja 24 '77

Nuclear power policy issues; recommendations of the Nuclear Energy Policy Study Group. K. H. Hohenemser. Environment 19:3-5 Ag '77

Why Ford quit Ford Foundation. por U.S. News 82:62 Ja 24 '77

See also

Council on Library Resources, Inc

FORD Motor Company

Ford streaks. D. E. Davis, Jr. Car & Dr 23:7 S '77

Ford's Fiesta: $800 million bet. J. Ross-Skinner. il Duns R 110:62-4 Ag '77

Ford's new management. pors Motor T 29:17 Jl '77

Ford's new trimotor. T. Nicholson and J. C. Jones. il pors Newsweek 89:65 Ap 25 '77

Multinational investment and global purpose; address, June 17, 1977. L. A. Iacocca. Vital Speeches 43:720-4 S 15 '77

Rap with Hank the deuce; excerpts from interview, ed by J. C. Jones. H. Ford. il pors Newsweek 89:66+ Ap 25 '77

'77 Ford trimotor. il pors Time 109:76-7 Ap 25 '77

Slaying Ford's dragon. J. Norris. il Motor T 29:102-3+ Ap '77

FORD Motor Company, Ltd

Funny you should ask; British Ford. por Forbes 120:64 Ag 1 '77

FORDE, Alfred Nathaniel

Danse macabre in Barbados. il Américas 29:29-31 My '77

FORDHAM, Christopher Columbus, 1926-

Califano loses Fordham as assistant secretary. B. J. Culliton. Science 196:635 My 6 '77 *

Christopher Fordham named assistant secretary for health. B. J. Culliton. Science 196:148 Ap 8 '77 *

FORDHAM University

Colleges challenge value-free education; program developed by Fordham College. R. J. Roth. America 136:324-6 Ap 9 '77

FORE, William F.

Mass media's mythic world: at odds with Christian values. bibl Chr Cent 94:32-8 Ja 19 '77

FORE (native race) See Papua New Guinea—Native races

FORECASTING

Catastrophe model: can it see crises? P. P. Luedtke. il por Sci Digest 81:68-70 F '77

Future flight; symposium. il Flying 101:350-60+ S '77

History and happenstance. N. Cousins. Sat R 4:6 Ag 6 '77

Learning to cope with the future; futurology course at Milford, Ohio Junior High School. J. E. Smith. Educ Digest 42:38-40 Ja '77

Nightmare life without fuel; Time essay. I. Asimov. Time 109:33 Ap 25 '77; Same abr. with title Life without fuel. Read Digest 111:126-8 Ag '77

Outlook '78: a pivotal year. il U.S. News 83:16-17 D 26 '77

Tomorrow: newsgram. See issues of U.S. news and world report

Visions of futures past; Lindisfarne Association. S. Helgesen. il Harpers 254:80-6 Mr '77

Which future for tomorrow? address, July 20, 1977. W. W. Harman. Vital Speeches 43:696-700 S 1 '77

See also

Agricultural forecasting
Business forecasting
Economic forecasting
Educational forecasting
Nineteen hundred and eighty-five
Political forecasting
Population forecasting
Prophecies
Social forecasting
Technological forecasting
Two thousand two (year)
Weather forecasting

FOREIGN affairs (periodical)

Soft technology energy debate: Limits to growth revisited? A. L. Hammond. Science 196:959-61 My 27 '77; Reply. A. B. Lovins 196:1384 Je 24 '77

FOREIGN aid. See Economic assistance, American

FOREIGN automobiles. See Automobiles, Foreign

FOREIGN cookery. See Cookery, International

FOREIGN correspondents

Beating the press; incarceration of reporters M. Goldsmith and J. C. Randal. D. M. Alpern and others. il pors map Newsweek 90:54 Ag 29 '77

China without gee whiz; Canadian R. H. Munro's coverage. il por Time 110:99 N 7 '77

Dodging the spooks: an American journalist in Prague. C. Sawyer. Nation 225:325-8 O 8 '77

Getting tough with the press; Philippines. B. Wideman. Progressive 41:47-8 O '77

Hava nagila in Egypt; Israeli correspondents in Cairo. W. Stewart. il Time 110:24 D 26 '77

Journalists as spooks; CIA use of newsmen for intelligence operations. H. Bray. Progressive 41:9-10 F '77

Reporting from the third world. M. Rosenblum. For Affairs 55:815-35 Jl '77

Revolution that wasn't; press coverage of Argentinian violence. T. Powers. Commonweal 104:19-20 Ja 7 '77

Spooking the press; CIA ties. Newsweek 91:30 Ja 16 '78

Who can be a paid spook? journalists and the CIA. il Time 111:12 Ja 9 '78

FOREIGN debts. See Debts, External

FOREIGN enlistment

Smith's Yankee recruits. A. De Borchgrave. il Newsweek 90:40 S 12 '77

Why Americans are fighting on Rhodesia's front lines. S. Hempstone. il map U.S. News 82:31-2 My 23 '77

FOREIGN exchange

Anticipate your long-term foreign exchange risks. H. Hagemann. il Harvard Bus R 55:81-8 Mr '77

Corporate scheme for currency swapping. Bus W p70 S 5 '77

Exchange-rate jitters. M. Friedman. il Newsweek 90:74 S 5 '77

Floating exchange rates: the calm before an economic storm. il Bus W p68-72+ O 3 '77

Hard currency problems spur Soviet export push. E. Kozicharow. Aviation W 106:17-18 Ap 11 '77

Have the accountants really hurt the multinationals? new currency conversion rules. L. Snyder. il Fortune 95:85-6+ F '77

New management headache. L. Adkins. il Duns R 110:72-4+ O '77

Rip-offs in faraway places. R. Gates. Changing T 31:37-8 D '77

Stabilized yen drives up the mark. Bus W p32 D 19 '77

Treasurers sweat out the currency turmoil; effect of floating exchange rates on multinational corporations. Bus W p68 Ag 29 '77

Trying to outrun currency swings; effect of foreign exchange accounting rule on earnings. Bus W p 108+ F 14 '77

FOREIGN exchange—*Continued*
World currencies turn skittish. il Bus W p94 My 30 '77
See also
Asiadollar market
Balance of payments
Eurobond market
Eurodollar market
International Monetary Fund

FOREIGN exchange brokers

Antitrust cases

Closed currency club; Sarabex Ltd. charges against London banks, and brokers. il Bus W p 114+ O 24 '77

FOREIGN investments. See Investments, Foreign

FOREIGN languages. See Languages, Modern

FOREIGN missions. See Missions

FOREIGN opinion of Europe, Western. See Europe, Western—Foreign opinion

FOREIGN opinion of the United States. See United States—Foreign opinion

FOREIGN population. See Immigration and emigration; *also* Foreign population under names of countries, cities, etc, e.g. Tucson, Ariz.—Foreign population

FOREIGN relations. See International relations; *also* subhead Foreign relations under names of countries, e.g. France—Foreign relations

FOREIGN sports cars. See Sports cars

FOREIGN station wagons. See Station wagons, Foreign

FOREIGN students in France
Seventeen in Paris; thoughts of an American student. C. Guigui. il Seventeen 36:150 F '77

FOREIGN students in Great Britain
Sherry and skepticism: Oxford days; an American student at Balliol College. L. Wieseltier. Am Scholar 46:483-95 Aut '77

FOREIGN students in Italy
Removing the Italian welcome mat; suspension of foreign enrollment. il Time 110:43 Jl 18 '77

FOREIGN students in Rumania
Rumanian solution; American medical students. il Time 109:80+ Je 20 '77

FOREIGN students in the Netherlands
Summer search; American language student in Friesland. R. Goldberg. map Seventeen 36:68-9 Ag '77

FOREIGN students in the United States
Making of a man; South African Nieman fellow at Harvard, P. Qoboza. L. Sloane. il por Newsweek 90:58 O 31 '77
Oil dollars, too, are flooding U.S. campuses. il U.S. News 82:58 Ja 24 '77

FOREIGN study
Bogota connection; recreology students from University of Ottawa, studying in Colombia, South America. T. L. Goodale. il Parks & Rec 12:54-7+ S '77
Students immerse selves in foreign living and fun, too; Intercultural Action Learning Program. D. Brelis and J. Reader. il Smithsonian 8:48-55 bibl(p 146) Ap '77
Studying abroad. il U.S. News 82:57-8 Ja 24 '77

FOREIGN subsidiaries. See Corporations—Foreign business

FOREIGN trade. See Commerce

FOREIGN trade regulation
News conference of Secretary Vance and Secretary Blumenthal, May 8. C. R. Vance and W. M. Blumenthal. Dept State Bull 76:586-93 Je 6 '77
See also
General Agreement on Tariffs and Trade

Conferences

At the summit talks: creeping cartelization; special section. il Bus W p64-7+ My 9 '77

FOREIGN trade regulation, American. See United States—Commercial policy

FOREIGN trucks. See Trucks, Foreign

FOREIGN visitors. See Visitors, Foreign

FOREIGN visitors in the United States. See Visitors, Foreign—United States

FOREIGN workers. See Alien labor

FOREIGNER (rock group) See Rock groups

FOREMAN, Carl
Foreman sets course; interview, ed by P. S. Nathan. Pub W 211:43 Ap 25 '77

FOREMAN, Clark
Clark Foreman. C. McWilliams. Nation 225:5-6 Jl 2 '77 •

FOREMAN, Dale I. See Allen, S. J. jt auth

FOREMAN, George
Jeemy Young! Jeemy Young! Jeemy Young! P. Putnam. il pors Sports Illus 46:22-3 Mr 28 '77 •

FOREMAN, John. See Zizmor, J. jt auth

FOREMAN, Laura
Reviews. J. Dunning. Dance Mag 51:19+ Jl '77 •

FOREMAN, Laura (journalist)
Philadelphia story. T. Schwartz and L. Howard. il por Newsweek 90:48 N 14 '77 •

FOREMOST-McKesson, Inc
Curing the lethargy syndrome at Foremost. il Bus W p98-9 Je 27 '77
See also
Mueller, C. F, Company

FOREMOST-McKesson, Inc-Sharon Steel Corporation merger. See Corporations—Acquisitions and mergers

FORENSIC hematology
Human bloodstains: individualization by crossed electroimmunodiffusion. G. H. Sweet and J. W. Elvins; discussion. bibl il Science 198:427 O 28 '77

FORENSIC psychiatry
Should psychiatrists get out of the courtroom? J. Robitscher and R. Williams. bibl il Psychol Today 11:84-6+ D '77

FOREST Acres Camp for Girls. See Camps—Maine

FOREST clearcutting. See Clearcutting

FOREST conservation
Redwoods: as the worm turns; with letter by N. B. Livermore, Jr. J. B. Craig. il Am For 83:28-31+ Jl '77; Discussion. 83:4+ O '77
See also
Forest fires—Prevention and control

Laws and regulations

See Forestry laws and regulations

FOREST ecology
Awakening. J. P. Jackson. il Am For 83:8-11 Ap '77
Carbon dioxide question. G. M. Woodwell. il map Sci Am 238:34-43 Ja '78
Different view of the forest. R. M. Brett. Am For 83:10+ D '77
How does a forest grow? J. P. Jackson. il Am For 83:32-3+ Jl '77
Nitrogen budget for an aggrading northern hardwood forest ecosystem. F. H. Bormann and others. bibl il Science 196:981-3 My 27 '77
Pygmies on the fourth terrace, rain forest on the second; ecosystem of new state park north of Mendocino, Calif. il Sunset 159:38-9 Jl '77
Shrinking forests; deforestation; excerpt from Losing ground; environmental stress and world food prospects. E. Eckholm. il Focus 28:12-16 S '77
See also
Forest influences
Rain forests

FOREST fire fighting. See Forest fires—Prevention and control

FOREST Fire Medal, North American. See North American Forest Fire Medal

FOREST fires
California fire report. J. McGuire. Am For 83:6 O '77
California—summer under fire. D. F. Davis. il Am For 83:8-12 O '77
Enormous cost of fires in the West. il Bus W p27 Ag 29 '77
Summer of the forest fire. map Newsweek 90:22 Ag 15 '77
Tillamook: a modern success story. B. Keil. il Am For 83:20-3+ Mr '77

Prevention and control

Battle of Marble Cone; Los Padres National Forest. P. S. Greenberg. il Newsweek 90:26-7 Ag 22 '77
Forest inferno in the West. il Time 110:21 Ag 22 '77
Forest Service is ready; fire hazards resulting from drought in the Pacific Northwest. J. B. Craig. Am For 83:6 Ag '77
Member deplores NPS fire policy; NPS resource specialist responds; letters to the editor. G. M. Schoepfle; D. B. Butts. il Nat Parks & Con Mag 51:27-8 Mr '77
See also
North American Forest Fire Medal

FOREST HILLS Tennis Club. See Sports clubs

FOREST influences
Fresh air-clean water exchange. F. H. Bormann and G. E. Likens. il Natur Hist 86:62-71 bibl(p 118) N '77

FOREST insects
See also
Spruce budworms

FOREST management
American forest policy in development. W. Koehler. por Am For 83:12-13+ Ag '77
American people are being robbed! K. Wiegner. il Forbes 120:102+ O 15 '77
Bankers aren't always right; Can you afford to operate a tree farm? adaptation of address, March 1977. N. Ormonde. il Am For 83:12-14 Je '77
Conscience of a forester. L. S. Minckler. Am For 83:10-11 Mr '77
Managing your woods. W. K. Newbury. il Horticulture 55:74-7 Mr '77
Thirty years in a woodlot; tree farming in New York State. H. S. Kernan. il por map Conservationist 32:32-4 N '77
Tree farmers. J. B. Craig. il pors Am For 83:8-11+ My '77

FORESTS and forestry—*Continued*

Vermont

Vermont's state foresters. il Am For 83:28-29 S '77

Virginia

Jefferson's country. D. A. Tice. il por Am For 83:24-7 My '77

FORESTS in cities. See Trees in cities

FORESTS Subcommittee. See United States—Congress—House—Agriculture, Committee on—Forests Subcommittee

FORGERIES, Art. See Forgery of works of art

FORGERY

Inkless fingerprints help fight bad checks. il Bus W p33+ F 28 '77

See also

Counterfeits and counterfeiting

FORGERY of antiques

Beware! Antiques fakery is thriving again; American furniture. N. Pratt. il House B 119: 12+ Jl '77

See also

Antiques—Expertising

FORGERY of works of art

Ars gratia artis? B. Wicker. Commonweal 104: 622-4 S 30 '77

Collector beware! Which of these ambrotypes are fake? R. Busch. il Pop Phot 80:110-11+ My '77

Secondhand saint; St Catherine altarpiece at the Cleveland Museum of Art found to be a forgery. Vasari. il Art N 76:24+ D '77

See also

Art—Expertising

FORGEY, Benjamin F.

American art 1910-1940: a neglected vision. il Art N 76:66-8 O '77

Art out of nature which is about nothing but nature. il por Smithsonian 8:62-4+ Ja '78

Artist for all decades. il por Art N 76:34-6 Ja '77

Canada—a new national vision. il Art N 76: 70-2+ Ap '77

Horace Pippin's personal spiritual journey. il Art N 76:74-5 Summ '77

Jack Beal's history of American labor. il Art N 76:38 Ap '77

Matisse cutouts. il por Art N 76:66-9 D '77

Restless experiments of Hans Hofmann. il por Art N 76:62-3 F '77

Washington (title varies) (cont) il Art N 76: 86-7 F; 106+ My; 168+ Summ '77

Whitney Biennial. il Art N 76:120-1 Ap '77

FORGING and forgings

See also

Blacksmithing

FORGIVENESS

Fine point. G. McCauley. America 136:260-1 Mr 19 '77

FORMAN, David C. and Richardson, Penny

Open learning and guidelines for the design of instructional materials. Educ Digest 42:41-4 Ap '77

FORMAN, Harrison

Canal a million farmers built. il Horticulture 55:30-5 My '77

FORMISANO, Ronald P.

Comments: ideology and political culture. Am Hist R 82:568-77 Je '77

FORMOSA. See Taiwan

FORMS, blanks, etc.

See also

Tax forms

FORNAY, Alfred R. Jr

Beautiful black woman. il Ebony 32:138-42 F '77

FORREST, G. H.

Shorthanded sail shortening. il Motor B & S 139:81-3 F '77

FORRESTER, Maureen

Maureen Forrester, contralto; New York recital in Town Hall. por Hi Fi 27:MA24 Mr '77 *

FORSCHER, Martin B.

Such good friends. R. Wolters. Writers Digest 57:16+ D '77 *

FORSHEY, Gerald

Film (cont) Chr Cent 94:178-9 F 23 '77

Harry, Joe and Al: the authenticity of death. Chr Cent 94:1022-4 N 9 '77

FORSYTH, Frederick

Shepherd; condensation of novel. il Read Digest 111:244-8+ D '77

FORT, Larry

Build tone probe for testing digital IC's. il Radio-Electr 48:76-7 Mr '77

FORT, Robert A.

Booksellers flock to 4th annual regional. il Pub W 212:49-50 N 14 '77

FORT JEFFERSON National Monument

Fort Jefferson: confessions of a tour guide. N. O'Shea. il Nat Parks & Con Mag 51:20-2 S '77

FORT LEE Historic Park. See New Jersey—Parks and reserves

FORT MADISON, Iowa

Lighten up downtown alleys. il Am City & County 92:44 O '77

FORT NIOBRARA National Wildlife Refuge. See Wildlife sanctuaries—Nebraska

FORT TICONDEROGA

Ethan Allen and the Green Mountain Boys; capture of Fort Ticonderoga. D. B. Sabine. il pors Am Hist Illus 11:8-15 Ja '77

FORT UNION National Monument

Fort Union, New Mexico. il Nat Parks & Con Mag 51:28 Mr '77

FORT VANCOUVER National Historic Site. See Historic houses, sites, etc.—Washington (state)

FORT WAYNE, Ind.

500% more light with 47% less energy. il Am City & County 92:56 Mr '77

FORT WORTH, Tex.

We motivate mechanics for high-production maintenance. R. S. Menefee. il por Am City & County 92:51-2 Mr '77

Galleries and museums

How to build a museum with diplomacy, guile and charm; views of R. F. Brown of the Kimbell Art Museum. J. Kutner. il por Art N 76: 87-90 D '77

FORTAS, Abe

Case against capital punishment. il N Y Times Mag p8-9+ Ja 23 '77

FORTESCUE, Peter

Comparative breeding characteristics of fusion and fast reactors. il Science 196:1326-9 Je 17 '77

FORTIES, The. See Nineteen hundred and forties

FORTIN, Ernest L.

Christian mission and spirituality: Roman Catholics and Methodists in dialogue. il New Cath World 220:191-5 Jl '77

FORTUNA, J.

Foil car thieves with Digistart, the electronic security lock. il Pop Electr 11:48-9 Ap '77

FORTUNE telling

See also

I ching (Book of changes)

42d Street. See New York (city)—Streets

FORWARDING companies

See also

Air freight service

La FORZA del destino; opera. See Verdi, G.

FORZANO, Giovacchino

Forzano remembered; a Trittico librettist. Opera N 41:14 F 26 '77 *

FOSBURGH, Lacey

Carol Burnett & Dick Van Dyke: what alcoholism did to their lives. pors Ladies Home J 94:34+ S '77

Make-believe world of teen-age maternity. il N Y Times Mag p29-30+ Ag 7 '77

Patty today. il por N Y Times Mag p 19-22+ Ap 3 '77

FOS-Marseilles port complex. See Ports—France

FOSHAY, Arthur Wellesley

What's basic about the curriculum? Educ Digest 43:5-9 D '77

FOSSIL algae. See Algae, Fossil

FOSSIL angiosperms. See Angiosperms, Fossil

FOSSIL arthropods. See Arthropods, Fossil

FOSSIL birds. See Birds, Fossil

FOSSIL cats. See Cats, Fossil

FOSSIL crocodiles. See Crocodiles, Fossil

FOSSIL ferns. See Ferns, Fossil

FOSSIL foraminifera. See Foraminifera, Fossil

FOSSIL fuels. See Fuel

FOSSIL hoaxes. See Hoaxes

FOSSIL leaves. See Leaves, Fossil

FOSSIL mammals. See Mammals, Fossil

FOSSIL man. See Man, Prehistoric

FOSSIL microorganisms. See Micropaleontology

FOSSIL pollen. See Pollen, Fossil

FOSSIL sharks. See Sharks, Fossil

FOSSIL swine. See Swine, Fossil

FOSSIL teeth. See Teeth, Fossil

FOSSILS. See Paleontology

FOSSILS, Living. See Living fossils

FOSSO, D. R.

Opposing; Salute; Volume; poems. Poetry 130: 21-2 Ap '77

FOSTER, Abigail (Kelley)

Framing our foremother. M. Bacon. por Ms 6:22 O '77 *

FOSTER, Barbara

Kids in the kitchen. il N Y Times Mag p30-1 D 25 '77

FOSTER, Bristol

Africa's gentle giants. il map Nat Geog 152: 402-17 S '77

FOSTER, Catharine Osgood

Making your plants live forever. il Org Gard & Farm 24:65-7 O '77

FOSTER, Edward J.
How to interpret loudspeaker tests. il Hi Fi 27:46-9 Je '77
How to judge record-playing equipment. il Hi Fi 27:60-3 Ap '77
Interpreting FM tuner specs. il Hi Fi 27:72-3+ N '77
Sorting out amp and preamp specs. il Hi Fi 27:60-3 D '77
Step by step through our tape recorder tests. il Hi Fi 27:48-51 Ag '77
FOSTER, G. Allen
Woman who saved the Union Navy. il Ebony 33:131-2+ D '77
FOSTER, George
Hypnotic hitter. P. Bonventre and D. Gram. il por Newsweek 90:52 O 3 '77 *
No, it's the year of the lively bat. L. Keith. il por Sports Illus 47:18-19 S 19 '77 *
FOSTER, Harry E.
Education, history, and the press; address, February 8, 1977. Vital Speeches 43:349-52 Mr 15 '77
FOSTER, Larry
Leviathan model brings us the whale we could never see. M. Herron. il pors Smithsonian 8:52-9 bibl(p 114) Ja '78 *
FOSTER, Laura Louise
Anyplace rock gardens. il Am Home 80:54-5+ S '77
FOSTER, M. E.
Electronics: buying the basics. il Motor B & S 139:76-9+ Ap '77
FOSTER, Michael
Printed mural. il Sch Arts 77:48-50 D '77
FOSTER, Ruth S.
Urban forestry (cont) Am City & County 92:69 Mr; 100 My; 73 Jl; 114 S '77
FOSTER, Stephen Collins
Foster: Songs—vol. 2; recordings. P. L. Miller. Am Rec G 40:50 F '77 *
FOSTER, William S.
Worth trying. See alternate issues of American city & county
FOSTER children, Care of. See Foster home care
FOSTER day care
See also
Day care centers
FOSTER Grandparent Program. See United States—ACTION
FOSTER home care
Homes for the unwanted. R. J. Stout. Chr Cent 94:849-51 S 28 '77
FOSTER parents
Greatest gift; a true story about Lorene and Julian Vela. N. Rodgers and E. Lynch. il Good H 185:79-82+ D '77
FOTHERGILLAS
Fothergillas: a garden aristocrat. M. Dirr. il Horticulture 55:38-9 D '77
FOUCAULT test for mirrors. See Telescopes—Mirrors
FOULKES, Fred K. and Morgan, H. M.
Organizing and staffing the personnel function. Harvard Bus R 55:142-54 My '77
FOUND objects
See also
Assemblage (art)
FOUNDATION garments
See also
Brassieres
FOUNDATIONS
Drought-caused house settling; making foundation repairs. il Sunset 159:189 O '77
FOUNDATIONS, Charitable and educational
Confrontation: Greenpeace Foundation puts itself on the line. E. Perlman. il Oceans 10:58-61 Jl '77
Soap bubble of the Enlightenment; Teyler's Foundation in Haarlem, Netherlands. G. Schwartz. il Art N 76:96-7 F '77
See also
Albert and Mary Lasker Foundation
Carnegie Corporation of New York
FOUNDRIES
Wages and hours
Recasting pay factors in nonferrous foundries. E. D. Schilling. il M Labor R 100:49-51 Je '77
FOUNDRY workers
See also
Foundries—Wages and hours
FOUNTAIN, David W. and others
Lectin release by soybean seeds. bibl il Science 197:1185-7 S 16 '77
FOUNTAIN, Eric A. Jr
Canada lynx. il Conservationist 31:2 N '76
FOUNTAIN, John W. and Larson, S. M.
New satellite of Saturn? bibl il Science 197:915-17 Ag 26 '77
FOUNTAINS
Shaping water into art. A. T. Baker. il Time 110:32-3 S 12 '77
FOUR channel tape recorders. See Tape recorders and recording
FOUR-color problem. See Graph theory
FOUR-day week. See Hours of labor
4-H clubs
Arts-In! What is it? J. Schultz. il Sch Arts 76:18-21 Ap '77
Reading poles. G. D. Walker. il Am For 83:31 Je '77
FOUR poster beds. See Beds
FOUR wheel drive jeeps. See Jeep automobiles—Four wheel drive
FOUR wheel drive motor vehicles. See Motor vehicles—Four wheel drive
FOUR wheel drive vans. See Vans—Four wheel drive
FOURIER analysis. See Mathematical analysis
FOURNIER, Marc
Honk, tweet, blare: sounds of the fair. R. Chelminski. il por Smithsonian 8:78-83 Ja '78 *
FOURNIER, René
French way. P. Garrison. Flying 100:43 F '77 *
FOURTEENTH Amendment to the Constitution. See United States—Constitution—Amendments
FOURTH of July
First Fourth. il Am Heritage 28:28-9 Je '77
201. il Newsweek 90:14-16 Jl 18 '77
Anecdotes, facetiae, satire, etc.
Colonel Pierce and the peach tree; excerpt from In a year of Our Lord. J. Mullen. il Read Digest 111:187-9+ Jl '77
FOWL shooting. See Fowling; Game bird shooting; Water bird shooting
FOWLER, Charles B.
On education. See issues of High fidelity and Musical America
FOWLER, Charles W.
Making the most of the school day. Educ Digest 43:28-9 D '77
When superintendents fail. Educ Digest 42:18-20 My '77
FOWLER, Neal
Art of short course tactics. il Yachting 141:46+ Je '77
FOWLER, Scott W. See Elder, D. L. jt auth
FOWLER, William A.
Physics in 1976—a personal account. il Phys Today 30:33-8+ Ap '77
FOWLES, John
Distant summer; story; excerpt from Daniel Martin. McCalls 105:166-7 O '77
FOWLING
Bird hunting without a dog. P. Barrett. il Mech Illus 73:8+ D '77
Bird lovers. E. R. Ricciuti. il Audubon 79:68-72+ S '77
See also
Game bird shooting
FOX, Bette-Lee, and others
(ed) Annual buyers' guide 1977. Lib J 102:1590-4+ Ag '77; Same. SLJ 24:48-52+ S '77
FOX, Charles
Keeping the faith. il pors Car & Dr 23:97-8+ Ag; 89-91 S '77
FOX, Charles K.
Care and feeding of a trout stream. A. Lee. il Sports Illus 46:30-2 Ja 31 '77 *
FOX, Donna M.
Puddle jumpers. il Parks & Rec 12:33 My '77
FOX, Edward Whiting, and Safford, J. O. 3d
Political uncertainty in France. Cur Hist 73:149-52+ N '77
FOX, H. B.
Laughingstock of Oat Hill; story; excerpt from The 2000-mile turtle. Read Digest 110:102-5 Mr '77
FOX, Irving H. and others
Purine nucleoside phosphorylase deficiency: altered kinetic properties of a mutant enzyme. bibl Science 197:1084-6 S 9 '77
FOX, James A.
Letter from Paris (cont) Pop Phot 80:62+ F '77
FOX, Lorraine
Lorraine Fox: illustrator, painter, teacher, alchemist. M. Tinkelman. il pors Am Artist 41:38-45+ D '77 *
FOX, Michael. See Danky, J. P. jt auth
FOX, Michael W.
Understanding your pet. See issues of McCall's
FOX, Patricia Ann
Rates of spring. Writers Digest 57:20-1 Mr '77
FOX, Paula
Cracking open the geode. A. Bach. il Horn Bk 53:514-21 O '77 *
FOX, Robert, and others
Stereopsis in the falcon. bibl il Science 197:79-81 Jl 1 '77
FOX, Siv Cedering
Lyre; poem. New Repub 177:36 Ag 6 '77
FOX, Thomas R.
Digital capacitance meter. il Pop Electr 11:50-2 Ap '77
FOX, Virgil
Virgil Fox, organ; concert at Kennedy Center. Hi Fi 27:MA26 S '77 *
FOX, William Price
Eccentric like a fox; interview, ed by B. Dickey. il por Writers Digest 57:41 F '77

FOXES
Fox that climbs trees; gray fox. W. Curtis. il Nat Wildlife 15:20-7 Je '77
Smell signals in fox scavenging. J. Arehart-Treichel. il Sci N 112:348-9 N 19 '77
FOXFIRE (periodical)
Earth log: the Foxfire wildfire. P. Hendrickson. il por Audubon 79:108-12 Mr '77
FOY, Lewis Wilson
If the steel industry is to survive . . . ; interview. il por U.S. News 83:90+ N 21 '77
No fooling! address, April 1, 1977. Vital Speeches 43:435-7 My 1 '77
about
Bethlehem's bind in Johnstown. il Bus W p40+ Ag 15 '77 *
FOY, Nancy
Action learning comes to industry. bibl f Harvard Bus R 55:158-68 S '77
FOYER, Jim
PHRF: what it is; how it works. il Yachting 141:54+ F '77
FOYERS. See Halls
FOYT, A. J.
A. J, you're amazing. S. Moses. il por Sports Illus 46:16-19 Je 6 '77 *
Fingers in the sky. L. A. Taylor. por Motor T 29:117-18 O '77 *
Foyt, Fangio and the sponsor's ego. D. E. Davis, Jr. Car & Dr 23:7 O '77 *
Foyt stands alone in Indy history. il por Motor T 29:118-19 Ag '77 *
Old man still plays rough. M. Jordan. il pors Car & Dr 23:120 O '77 *
Running fast and furious. S. Moses. il por Sports Illus 47:52-3 Jl 4 '77 *
FRACCI, Carla
Bel canto duet. C. Faria. il pors Opera N 41: 16-19 Je '77 *
FRACTALS. See Curves
FRACTIONATION. See Isotope separation
FRACTIONS
Study and teaching
See Mathematics—Study and teaching
FRACTURE of solids
Dynamic failure in solids. D. R. Curran and others. il Phys Today 30:46-8+ Ja '77
FRADKIN, Philip L.
Craig, Colorado: population unknown, elevation 6,185 feet. il Audubon 79:118-27 Jl '77
First and forgotten pipeline. il pors map Audubon 79:58-79 N '77
Oil will soon flow, but where will it go? il Audubon 79:86-8+ Ja '77
Summer with Alex. il por Audubon 79:36-41 My '77
Tuolumne River: the drought in a microcosm. map Audubon 79:132-5 Jl '77
FRAGIPAN soils. See Soils, Hardpan
FRALEY, Elizabeth
Nursing an ambulance and a county. D. Lampe. il pors Fam Health 9:28-30 Je '77 *
FRAME, George W. and Frame, L. H.
Dog days on the Plains. il Int Wildlife 7:48-55 S '77
FRAME, Lory Herbison. See Frame, G. W. jt auth
FRAME looms. See Looms
FRAMES for mirrors. See Mirror frames
FRAMES for pictures. See Picture frames
FRAMING (building)
Plastic-composite design cuts steel tonnage in Johns-Manville's new headquarters building. W. J. LeMessurier. il Archit Rec 162:127-8 S '77
FRANCE, Bill
Day at the races—Southern style. pors Forbes 119:106+ Mr 15 '77 *
FRANCE
See also
Airlines—France
Airplanes, Military—France
Alps
Americans in France
Architecture, Domestic—France
Art and state—France
Atomic power—France
Atomic power plants—France
Automobile driving—France
Automobile racing—France
Aviation and state—France
Banks and banking—France
Blacks in France
Booksellers and bookselling—France
Bordeaux
Burgundy
Cathedrals—France
Christmas—France
Cities and towns—France
Conglomerate corporations—France
Crime and criminals—France
Cruising—France
Famines—France
Foreign students in France
French
Government ownership—France
Hotels, motels, etc.—France
Hunting—France
Industrial relations—France
Industry and state—France
Investments, French
Loans, Bank—France
Loire Valley
Marseilles
Money—France
Mont Saint Michel
Morale, National—France
Motion pictures—France
Music—France
National cemeteries—France
National School of Administration, France
Newspapers—France
Opera—France
Paris
Periodicals—France
Ports—France
Provence
Restaurants—France
Rheims
St Emilion
Strikes—France
Telephone—France
Versailles, Palaces of
Zoology—France

Civilization
Le mal français: is there a reason for being Cartesian? A. Burgess. il N Y Times Mag p46-8+ My 29 '77

Commerce
Banks find ways to boost lending. Bus W p44+ O 31 '77
Algeria
Once-sure market becomes competitive. Bus W p62+ Ap 18 '77
Egypt
French, Egyptians draw closer on deal for Mirage fighters. Aviation W 106:16 Ja 17 '77
Europe, Eastern
French exports seed future competition. il Bus W p34 My 23 '77
Russia
See Russia—Commerce—France

Commercial policy
Achetez Français. D. Pauly and J. Friedman. il Newsweek 89:62+ Mr 7 '77

Description and travel
Day of variety in the French countryside; La Dombes. il map Sunset 159:92 O '77
Gypsy carting in France. L. Dennis and L. Dennis. il Travel 147:58-63 Ap '77
With love to La Belle France. H. McCully. il House B 119:164-8+ S '77

Economic policy
Adding stimulation to the austerity plan. il Bus W p30 Ag 1 '77
Businessmen begin to breathe easier again. Bus W p38 N 7 '77
French take to a new conservatism; with interview with R. Barre. il Bus W p64-6 Mr 7 '77
Professor's gamble; policies of R. Barre. il por Time 110:72+ O 24 '77
Trying to placate a hostile labor force. il Bus W p44 Ap 25 '77

Foreign relations
Abu Daoud and the law. S. E. Rapoport. Commentary 63:70-2 Mr '77; Reply. S. Liskofsky. 63:10-11+ My '77
L'affaire Daoud: too hot to handle. il por Time 109:29-31 Ja 24 '77
Arch-terrorist who went scot-free; A. Daoud. D. Reed. Read Digest 111:114-18 S '77
End of an ordeal; France's efforts to secure release of F. Claustre from rebels in Chad. il por Time 109:38 F 14 '77
French recipe for cowardice; release of Abu Daoud. Nation 224:98-9 Ja 29 '77
Giscard speaks out; excerpt from interview, ed by A. De Borchgrave. V. Giscard d'Estaing. il por Newsweek 90:45-8 Jl 25 '77
Terrorist cross fire; releasing Abu Daoud. A. Deming and others. il por Newsweek 89:43+ Ja 24 '77
Madagascar
No, man, it's my island; dispute over Tromelin. il map Time 110:32 D 26 '77
Mauritius
No, man, it's my island; dispute over Tromelin. il map Time 110:32 D 26 '77

History
Medieval period, 987-1515
Organized peace in southern France and Catalonia, ca. 1140-ca. 1233. T. N. Bisson. bibl f map Am Hist R 82:290-311 Ap '77

FRANCE—History—*Continued*

Revolution, 1789-1799

Robespierre and the French Revolution; seven studies. J. I. Shulim. bibl Am Hist R 82:20-38 F '77

Virtue, weep if I die: the real André Chénier. S. P. Edelman. il por Opera N 41:10-13 Mr 26 '77

Third Republic, 1870-1940

See also
Paris—Siege, 1870-1871

Industries

See also
Airplane industry—France
Automobile industry—France
Computer industry—France
Electronic industries—France
Gas industry—France
Helicopter industry—France
Household appliances industry—France
Optical industry—France
Solar energy industry—France
Steel industry—France
Trading companies—France
Wine industry—France

Intellectual life

Bête noire of France's Left; J. F. Revel. D. Pryce-Jones. il pors N Y Times Mag p54-5+ D 11 '77
See also
Philosophy, French

Monetary policy

Trying to outwit the French. il Bus W p 108 S 12 '77

Moral conditions

Pots of wine; bribery. R. Chelminski. Sat R 4: 14-15 Jl 9 '77

Politics and government

Dangerous left turn ahead in France. R. Ball. il Fortune 96:130-3+ Ag '77
France: ready for the left. E. Peer. il Newsweek 89:48+ Je 13 '77
French have no word for it; possibility of a Union of Left election victory. J. Burnham. Nat R 29:711 Je 24 '77
French socialism and Europe. M. Rocard. For Affairs 55:554-60 Ap '77
Giscard gets the message. il Time 109:41 Ap 11 '77
Giscard reshuffles for political survival. por Bus W p33+ Ap 11 '77
Giscard's blues. K. Willenson and E. Peer. por Newsweek 89:53 F 14 '77
If the left wins; French novel, The 180 days of Mitterrand. il Time 110:28 S 5 '77
M. le Maire de Paris; Mayor J. Chirac's challenge to V. Giscard d'Estaing. G. Ross. New Repub 176:17-19 Ap 9 '77
Mortal illness hits France's left. il Bus W p32+ My 30 '77
Plight of Giscard d'Estaing. J. O. Goldsborough. il pors N Y Times Mag p37-9+ S 11 '77
Reporter in Europe. J. Kramer. New Yorker 53:72-81 Jl 4 '77
See also
Communist Party (France)
Elections—France
Political campaigns—France
Political parties—France
Socialism—France

Religious institutions and affairs

See also
Catholic Church in France
Catholics in France

Social history

On Lamennais, Chaadaev, and the romantic revolt in France and Russia. N. V. Riasanovsky. bibl f pors Am Hist R 82:1165-86 D '77
Rules of inheritance and strategies of mobility in prerevolutionary France. R. E. Giesey. bibl f Am Hist R 82:271-89 Ap '77

Territories and possessions

See also
Afars and the Issas, French Territory of
Tromelin (island)

FRANCE and Quebec (province)
See also
Lévesque, R.—Visit to France, 1977

FRANCE and the United States
Reflections. W. Pfaff. New Yorker 52:66-70+ Ja 24 '77
See also
United States—History—Revolution—French participation

FRANCE-United States Cooperative Program in Oceanography. See Oceanography—International aspects

FRANCE-United States Cooperative Science Program. See Science—International aspects

FRANCHISE system
Franchising comes of age. T. J. Murray. il Duns R 110:58-60 Ag '77
Going into business the franchise way. Changing T 31:7-10 Ap '77
See also
Automobile service stations—Chain and franchise operations
Restaurants—Chain and franchise operations

Antitrust cases

Court switches franchising signals; Schwinn Bicycle Company ruling. Bus W p30 Jl 11 '77

FRANCIS, John
Man who refuses to talk. il pors Ebony 33: 114-16+ D '77 *

FRANCIS, Robert
Comment. R. B. Shaw. Poetry 131:106-10 N '77 *

FRANCIS, Terry Tucker
Microclimatology. il Org Gard & Farm 24:107-10 F '77

FRANCIS Lewis High School. See Queens, N.Y.—Education

FRANCIS Marion National Forest, S. C. See National forests

FRANCISCO, Leon
Stalk for a cannibal brown. il Outdoor Life 160: 68-9+ Jl '77

FRANCK, César Auguste
D'Indy: Symphony on a French mountain air. Franck: Symphonic variations and Les djinns. J. Waxman. Am Rec G 40:21-2 Je '77 *
Psyché. J. Ringo. Am Rec G 40:21 N '76 *
Symphony in D minor; Symphonic variations for piano and orchestra. J. Waxman. Am Rec G 40:24 Je '77 *

FRANCK, Georgann
Try the supermarket. il Ret Liv 16:38 D '76

FRANCKE, Linda Bird
Abortion and men; excerpt from The ambivalence of abortion. il Esquire 89:58-60 Ja '78
I hate sports. Harp Baz 110:91+ My '77
Myth of the liberated housewife. Harp Baz 110: 101+ F '77

FRANCKE, Sue, and Horacek, Bruce
Festival of education for older people. il Aging 275:24-5 S '77

FRANCO, John M.
Rochester school supt. wins AASL service award. por SLJ 23:14+ My '77 *

FRANCO, Marjorie
Genevieve's birthday money; story. Redbook 149:94 Ag '77

FRANCO-German War, 1870-1871
See also
Paris—Siege, 1870-1871

FRANCOEUR, Robert Thomas
Sex films. bibl il Society 14:33-7 Jl '77

FRANCONIA NOTCH State Park. See New Hampshire—Parks and reserves

FRANEY, Pierre. See Claiborne, C. jt auth

FRANGIAMORE, Catherine Lynn
Landscape wallpaper in the Jeremiah Lee Mansion. bibl il Antiques 112:1174-9 D '77

FRANK, Anthony Melchior
An interview with Anthony Frank—new thoughts on old mortgages. por Forbes 119:62 Ja 15 '77

FRANK, Arthur, and Frank, Stuart
Health. See issues of Mademoiselle

FRANK, Dick
House as sculptural object. P. Goldberger. il N Y Times Mag p74-6+ Mr 20 '77 *

FRANK, Elizabeth Pope
After 18 years of searching: we're a family again! il pors Good H 185:111+ O '77
What are they doing to our children? il Good H 185:99+ Ag '77

FRANK, Reuven
Spiritual energy crisis. Atlantic 240:76-7 Jl '77

FRANK, Stanley D.
School budgets cheat children. por Intellect 106: 9-10 Jl '77

FRANK, Stuart. See Frank, A. jt auth

FRANK, Suzanne
House as sculptural object. P. Goldberger. il N Y Times Mag p74-6+ Mr 20 '77 *

FRANKEL, Marvin E.
Immodest proposal. il N Y Times Mag p92-4+ D 4 '77

FRANKENBERGER, Elizabeth
Garden primer for pre-schoolers. Horticulture 55:48-9 N '77

FRANKENFELD, Miguel
Workers' banks in Latin America. il Américas 29:2-6 Ag '77

FRANKENHEIMER, John Michael
Frankenheimer. O. Moore. il pors Motor B & S 141:100-3+ Ja '78 *

FRANKENHUIS, Jean Pierre
How to get a good consultant. il Harvard Bus R 55:133-9 N '77

FRANKENSTEIN, Alfred
Evaluating the Bicentennial exhibitions. bibl Art in Am 65:10-11+ My '77
IRCAM—underground and underway. il Hi Fi 28:MA28-9+ Ja '78

FRANKENSTEIN, Alfred—*Continued*
Lords, ladies and common folk at Yale. il Art N 76:40-3 Summ '77
San Francisco. Art N 76:94+ O '77
Spring Opera: a death-dealing triple bill. il Hi Fi 27:MA30-1 O '77
Toward a complete history of art: Women Artists, 1550-1950. il Art in Am 65:66-9 Mr '77

FRANKENTHALER, Helen
Sophisticated lady; exhibition at the André Emmerich Gallery in New York. M. Stevens. il Newsweek 90:94 D 5 '77 *

FRANKFURT Book Fair. See Book fairs

FRANKFURTER, Alfred M.
Picasso in retrospect 1939-1900; excerpt from The art world; ed by B. Diamonstein. il Art N 76:156+ N '77

FRANKFURTER, Felix
F. F; exhibit at Harvard Law School; with interview. P. A. Freund. New Yorker 53:42-3 N 28 '77 *

FRANKFURTERS
See also
Cookery—Meat

FRANKLIN, Benjamin
Poor Richard's way to wealth and happiness. por Sat Eve Post 249:6-7 Jl '77

about

Benjamin Franklin's residence in France: the Hôtel de Valentinois in Passy. M. Martindale. bibl il Antiques 112:262-73 Ag '77 *

FRANKLIN, Bruce
Oxford University Press unlocks prison writing to show its integration in American culture. R. Dahlin. Pub W 212:41+ Ag 22 '77 *

FRANKLIN, Jerry F.
Biosphere reserve program in the United States. bibl il map Science 195:262-7 Ja 21 '77

FRANKLIN, Kenneth Linn
Canopus: only no. 2, but stars as a pilot. il Sci Digest 82:40-2 Jl '77
Mars centennial. il Sci Digest 82:66-9 S '77

FRANKLIN, Marte
Phantom Ranch: yesterday and a mile deep. il Nat Parks & Con Mag 51:4-9 D '77

FRANKLIN, Tony
They're kicking up a real storm. J. Jares. il pors Sports Illus 47:26-9 N 7 '77 *

FRANKLIN, William B.
(ed) Business outlook. See issues of Business week

FRANKLIN, State of. See Tennessee—History

FRANKLIN Book Programs, Inc
Franklin Book Programs expands worldwide activities. C. B. Grannis. Pub W 211:34+ Mr 7 '77

FRANKLIN Delano Roosevelt Island
Bigelow II; pharmacy. New Yorker 52:29-31 F 14 '77
Just 5 minutes from downtown. il U.S. News 83:76-9 D 26 '77
New way to go to work; Roosevelt Island's aerial tramway. C. A. Miller. il Mech Illus 73:52 Je '77

FRANKLIN Delano Roosevelt memorial (proposed)
See Washington, D.C.—Monuments, statues, etc.

FRANKLIN Life Insurance Company-American Brands Inc merger. See Corporations—Acquisitions and mergers

FRANKLIN Mint Corporation
Costly troubles at Franklin Mint. il Bus W p28-9 My 30 '77
How Franklin Mint keeps new products flowing. il Bus W p60+ Ap 25 '77
Krugerrand vs. Franklin Mint. J. O'Hanlon. il Forbes 120:64+ Jl 15 '77

FRANKS, Lucinda
In search of a novel at MacDowell. il por N Y Times Mag p72+ My 1 '77

FRANKS, Michael
Michael Franks is no three-chord composer. il Hi Fi 27:142+ Mr '77 *

FRANKS
See also
Charlemagne, King of the Franks

FRANXMAN, James J.
Technical writing: career opportunities. bibl il por Chemistry 50:19-21 Ap '77

FRANZ, Frederick
End is near (contd.) Time 110:64+ Jl 11 '77 *

FRANZ, Maurice
Garden calendar. See issues of Organic gardening and farming

FRANZA, August
Broadsides & ballads (cont) Engl J 66:12-14 Ap '77

FRANZONI, Giovanni Battista
Giovanni Battista Franzoni, one year after laicization. E. Carrillo. il por Chr Cent 94:1093-5 N 23 '77 *

FRANZOSA, John
Darwin and Melville: why a tortoise? bibl f Am Imago 33:361-79 Wint '76

FRASER, Alan
Drink. See issues of Mademoiselle

FRASER, Andrew
Making digital electronic clocks immune to AC flicker. il Pop Electr 12:58 N '77

FRASER, Lady Antonia (Pakenham)
(comp) For Valentine's Day: immortal love letters. il por N Y Times Mag p 16-18 F 13 '77
Trifles and treasures. il Sat Eve Post 249:64-7+ D '77

FRASER, Douglas A.
New leader for Auto Workers: you'll see a different style; interview. por U.S. News 82:69 My 30 '77
UAW's Doug Fraser looks ahead; interview. Nation 225:171-6 S 3 '77

about

Piping in a new chief. il por Time 109:67 My 30 '77 *
UAW elects its last Reuther-generation president. L. H. LeGrande. M Labor R 100:35-7 Ag '77 *
UAW's new chief: an ear to the young. il por Bus W p 135+ My 16 '77 *

FRASER, James
Taking stock. U.S. News 82:81 Mr 28; 93 Ap 25; 94 My 23; 77 Je 20; 72 Jl 18; 83:65 Ag 15; 64 Ag 29; 84 S 12; 92 S 26; 90 O 10; 102 O 24; 89 N 7; 105 N 21; 89 D 5; 78 D 19; 91 D 26 '77

FRASER, John Malcolm. See Fraser, M.

FRASER, Kennedy
On and off the avenue. New Yorker 53:91-8 Ap 11; 76-81 Jl 11; 63-9 Jl 18; 107-10+ N 7; 149-50+ N 14 '77

FRASER, LeRoy B, 3d. See Barrett, M. E. jt auth

FRASER, Malcolm
Prime Minister Fraser of Australia visits Washington; exchange of remarks, June 22, 1977. Dept State Bull 77:132-3 Jl 25 '77

about

From Whitlam to Fraser. T. B. Millar. For Affairs 55:854-72 Jl '77 *
Second term for Fraser. il por Time 110:38 D 19 '77 *

Visit to the United States, 1977

Prime Minister Fraser of Australia visits Washington; exchange of remarks, June 22, 1977. M. Fraser; J. Carter. Dept State Bull 77:132-3 Jl 25 '77

FRASER, Ron
He's a one-man Hurricane. J. Underwood. il pors Sports Illus 46:46+ My 30 '77 *

FRASER, Russell
Reconsideration. New Repub 176:36-8 F 5 '77

FRAUD
After high school, what? fraudulent practices of trade schools. W. D. Green. Am Educ 13:19-22 O '77
Alias Johnny Hooker; con games and social psychologists. A. C. Elms. Psychol Today 10:17 F '77
Be sure the yuletide laugh isn't on you. U.S. News 83:47 N 21 '77
Beware! You can be robbed by mail—or phone. J. L. Lippert. Good H 184:201 Ap '77
Burt report: fraud? Society 14:4+ My '77
Catching double-dealers; welfare fraud. Time 110:12-13 Jl 4 '77
Classic experiment—mistake or deliberate fraud? C. Burt's heredity research. J. Gaylin. Psychol Today 10:33+ F '77
Crime and no punishment; Home-Stake oil swindle. J. K. Galbraith. il Esquire 88:102+ D '77
Did Sir Cyril Burt fake his research on heritability of intelligence? O. Gillie; A. R. Jensen. Educ Digest 42:43-5 Mr '77
Fake sheiks; phony Arabs in Europe. Newsweek 90:64-5 Ag 1 '77
Fighting fraud in education. G. E. Arnstein. il Am Educ 13:27-30 Ap '77
Fraud in the insulation business. Changing T 32:4 Ja '78
Golden fleecing of union funds; Teamster pension funds. L. Velie. Read Digest 111:88-92 O '77
Great fakes of science. M. Gardner. il Esquire 88:88-91 O '77
Guarding the border; sham marriages with illegal aliens. New Repub 176:2+ Mr 12 '77
Here's an offer you can resist: door-to-door con artists. J. Froelich. il Ret Liv 17:21-2 Ag '77
How I became a saint; Big Con conference. P. S. Prescott. il Newsweek 89:97 My 23 '77
How people cheat Uncle Sam out of billions. D. C. Bacon. il U.S. News 83:16-19 Jl 11 '77
IQ and heredity: suspicion of fraud beclouds classic experiment. N. Wade; discussion. il Science 195:246-8 Ja 21 '77
Local campaign against consumer fraud; San Francisco. il Bus W p66 Je 13 '77
Medicaid fraud: a bitter pill for the Nation's poor. F. J. Butler. America 136:414-15 My 7 '77
Model for fraud: Michigan's Medicaid rip-off. E. E. Chen. Nation 224:242-4 F 26 '77

FRAUD—*Continued*
New York ticket fraud plot foiled. Aviation W 107:24 N 21 '77
Not so-simple case of larceny; automobile auctions fraud. R. J. Gottlieb. Motor T 29:64-5 Mr '77
Offside in Pittsburgh? investigation of football players for possible involvement in fraud against a job-training program. S. Fraker and S. Lesher. pors Newsweek 89:40 My 9 '77
One more plan to end fraud in welfare; interview. J. A. Califano, Jr. il pors U.S. News 84:41-4 Ja 9 '78
Our multibillion-dollar medicaid scandal. D. Thomasson and C. West. Read Digest 110: 87-91 My '77
Researcher admits he faked journal data. Sci N 111:150-1 Mr 5 '77
Rx for medifraud; medicaid. P. Bonventre and others. il Newsweek 89:92 My 9 '77
SEC gets slapped for double-dealing; stock fraud investigation of TDA Industries, Inc. Bus W p36 Je 20 '77
Scandal in heavens: renowned astronomer accused of fraud. N. Wade. por Science 198:707-9 N 18 '77
Story of Adela H; A. Holzer's investment fraud. por Time 109:60 Ap 18 '77
U.S. Appeals Court rules employee pension funds are subject to Federal antifraud laws. Ret Liv 17:47 O '77
Unscientific phenomenon: fraud grows in laboratories. Sci Digest 81:38-40 Je '77
Ways con men cash in on the energy crisis. il U.S. News 83:58-9 Ag 8 '77
Which client secrets must a lawyer reveal? SEC suits against law firms involved in National Student Marketing Corporation's fraudulent takeover attempt of Interstate National Corp. il Bus W p 124+ Ag 15 '77
Winging a Broadway angel; A. Holzer's investment fraud. il por Time 110:51 Jl 25 '77
See also
Computers and crime
False personation
Forgery
Forgery of works of art
Quacks and quackery

Anecdotes, facetiae, satire, etc.

Getting streetwise. D. K. Mano. Nat R 30:43-4 Ja 6 '78

FRAZETTA, Frank
Incredible paintings of Frank Frazetta. D. Newlove. il por Esquire 87:86-94+ Je '77 *

FRAZIER, Claude A.
Child abuse: society's symptom of stress. il Chr Today 21:6-8 Je 3 '77
Food allergies may be causing more headaches than you know. House B 119:42+ Je '77

FRAZIER, Ian
End of Bob's Bob House. New Yorker 53:35 S 12 '77
Good explanation. New Yorker 53:27 Ag 1 '77
Sandy Frazier dream team. il New Yorker 53: 46-7 N 28 '77

FRAZIER, Mark
Little railroad that did. Read Digest 110:111-15 My '77
More on space freeport. Space World N-12-168: 27 D '77

FRAZIER, Walt
Clyde, laughing Cavalier. J. Papanek. il por Sports Illus 47:74+ N 7 '77 *

FREAKS. See Deformities

FRED, Mark Simon
Two Argonne scientists win Optical Society's Meggers Award. pors Phys Today 30:75 S '77 *

FRED Meyer, Inc. See Meyer, Fred, Inc

FREDDIE Mac. See Federal Home Loan Mortgage Corporation

FREDERICK, Jane
Plainly, Jane has a penchant for the pentathlon. J. Marshall. il pors Sports Illus 47:32-7 N 21 '77 *

FREDERICKS, Carlton
High-fiber diet; interview. il por Good H 185: 294+ N '77

FREDERICKS, Devon
Great meal you hardly have to cook. il pors House & Gard 149:120-1+ F '77

FREDERICKSON, Christopher J. and Gerken, G. M.
Masking of electrical by acoustic stimuli: behavioral evidence for tonotopic organization. bibl il Science 198:1276-8 D 23 '77

FREDRICKSON, Donald S.
Cancer—the outlaw cell. il por Chemistry 50: 9-10 Ja '77

about

Califano praises NIH, retains Fredrickson as director. B. J. Culliton. il por Science 195:663 F 18 '77 *

FREDERICKSON, Robert C. A. and others
Hyperalgesia induced by naloxone follows diurnal rhythm in responsivity to painful stimuli. bibl il Science 198:756-8 N 18 '77

FREE, John R.
Look and listen. See issues of Popular science

FREE Church of Scotland
Scotland: a path still overgrown. J. D. Douglas. Chr Today 22:70+ O 7 '77

FREE enterprise
Future of capitalism: the intellectual and the businessman; address, February 9, 1977. M. Friedman. Vital Speeches 43:333-7 Mr 15 '77
Get involved with government—you can make it better. J. Eckerd. pors Nations Bus 65: 61-3 Je '77
Going down the drain; excerpts from address. F. Byrom. Intellect 105:210 Ja '77
Halting government intervention in economic affairs; excerpts from address. M. Friedman. Intellect 105:295 Mr '77
Leading businesswoman's perspective on management; interview. J. Spain. il pors Nations Bus 65:70-2+ Mr '77
Our fragile freedom; address, April 29, 1977. R. M. Brown, Jr. Vital Speeches 43:553-5 Jl 1 '77
Polish farmers learn about free enterprise. V. Louviere. il Nations Bus 65:44 F '77
Public use of private interest: excerpt from Godkin lectures. C. L. Schultze. Harpers 254: 43-50+ My '77
Sixty years of American business: the pursuit of happiness through the pursuit of profit. J. Brooks. Forbes 120:69-76+ S 15 '77
We are losing the freedom to decide; address, August 6, 1977. T. A. Murphy. Vital Speeches 43:714-17 S 15 '77
Winter's chill—and the cold hand of government; address, February 7, 1977. E. B. Speer. Vital Speeches 43:303-6 Mr 1 '77
See also
Competition

FREE-lance writers. See Authors

FREE-lance writing. See Authorship

FREE Library of Philadelphia. See Philadelphia Free Library

FREE periodicals. See Periodicals

FREE press. See Freedom of the press

FREE radicals. See Radicals (chemistry)

FREE speech
ALA ExecBoard delays distribution of film; The speaker. W. R. Eshelman. Wilson Lib Bull 51:794-5 Je '77
Attempt to control thought; Justice Dept. complaint against American Institute of Real Estate Appraisers. J. J. Kilpatrick. Nations Bus 65:11-12 O '77
Black Caucus vetoes patching: The speaker stand as is. Am Lib 8:405-6 S '77
Controversy continues over ALA's The speaker. SLJ 24:10 N '77
Day the first amendment died; address, September 16, 1977. J. R. Bittner. Vital Speeches 44: 24-8 O 15 '77
Debate nobody won; The speaker; criticism of the film; with editorial comment. J. Berry. il Lib J 102:1543, 1573-80 Ag '77; Discussion. 102:2289-90 N 15 '77
Even for Nazis; Skokie, Ill. right-to-march controversy. Progressive 41:6-7 D '77
First amendment blues. il Time 110:40 Ag 15 '77
For all or for none; right-to-march case of the American Nazi Party in Skokie, Ill. Nation 225: 354-5 O 15 '77
Freedom of expression: too much of a good thing? excerpt from Too much of a good thing. J. Sparrow. Am Scholar 46:165-80 Spr '77
Freedom of speech for The speaker. A. Plotnik. il Am Lib 8:337 Je '77
Jones asks for panel to review The speaker. SLJ 24:9 D '77
Reflections on The speaker. C. S. Jones. il Wilson Lib Bull 52:51-5 S '77
Right not to speak; Wooley v. Maynard. C. McWilliams. Nation 225:69-70 Jl 23 '77
Son of Speaker; with comments by readers. D. Broderick. Am Lib 8:502-5 O '77
Speaker: step or misstep into filmmaking? symposium. il Am Lib 8:371-6 Jl '77
Whimper for freedom; controversy surrounding the film, The speaker. J. Berry. Lib J 102: 1227 Je 1 '77
See also
Academic freedom
Freedom of the press
Libel and slander

FREE trade and protection
Fighting a global lull. M. Ruby and others. il Newsweek 90:89-90 O 10 '77
Free trade in jeopardy. il Time 110:48+ O 17 '77
Keep trade free. S. Luxenberg. New Repub 177: 13-15 S 3 '77
What ails the world economy. Fortune 96:103 N '77
See also
Balance of trade
Foreign trade regulation
General Agreement on Tariffs and Trade
Tariff
United States—Commercial policy
United States—International Trade Commission

FREE verse
Rhythm revived. J. Jerome. Writers Digest 57:16+ Jl '77

FREE will and determinism
Listening to B. F. Skinner. J. W. Woelfel. Chr Cent 94:1112-16 N 30 '77
Science's now cloudy crystal ball; effects of S. W. Hawking's findings on black holes. F. R. Haig. America 136:192-3 Mr 5 '77

FREED, Robert D.
Those amazing new TV games. il Mech Illus 73:110+ My '77

FREEDMAN, Dan
New tactics in the textile war. il Nation 225:618-21 D 10 '77

—and Krauss, Clifford
Peru runs out of credit. il Nation 225:466-8 N 5 '77

FREEDMAN, Dan. See Goldsmith, F. jt auth

FREEDMAN, Daniel X.
Governmental interference with medical care; excerpts from address. por Intellect 106:100-1 S '77

FREEDMAN, Jill. See Smith, D. jt auth

FREEDMAN, Jonathan, and Norton, Gay
GH's happiness survey—the surprising results. il Good H 185:82+ S '77

FREEDMAN, Martha H.
Candlelight and vintage years. Aging 274:11 Ag '77

FREEDMAN, Maurice Julius, 1939-
Public libraries, the Library of Congress, and the national bibliographic network; adaptation of address, February 1977. il Lib J 102:2211-15 N 1 '77

FREEDMAN, Michael B.
Centrifuge ends drying bed chores for Pennsylvania water plant. il Am City & County 92:63-4 N '77

FREEDOM. See Liberty

FREEDOM (theology)
See also
Free will and determinism

FREEDOM, Intellectual. See Intellectual liberty

FREEDOM of information. See Information, Freedom of

FREEDOM of Information Act. See Information, Freedom of

FREEDOM of religion. See Religious liberty

FREEDOM of speech. See Free speech

FREEDOM of teaching. See Academic freedom

FREEDOM of the air. See Airspace (international law)

FREEDOM of the press
Censorship and man's right to know; radio news; address; December 17, 1976. K. R. Giddens. Vital Speeches 43:280-3 F 15 '77
Danger: pendulum swinging: using the courts to muzzle the press. A. U. Schwartz. Atlantic 239:29-34 F '77
Fairness doctrine for the press? N. Cousins. Sat R 5:4 N 12 '77
First amendment pixillation; A. Goldstein. Nat R 29:1349-50 N 25 '77
Free press for a free people; excerpt from address, March 28, 1977. E. Sevareid. por Society 15:11+ N '77
Mass media and society:
American viewpoint. W. G. Harley. il UNESCO Courier 30:28-31 Ap '77
Soviet viewpoint. Y. N. Zasursky and Y. I. Kashlev. il UNESCO Courier 30:24-7 Ap '77
Press, privacy and the Constitution. F. Abrams. il N Y Times Mag p 11-13+ Ag 21 '77; Same with title What of the privacy explosion? Current 196:7-17 O '77; Discussion. N Y Times Mag p26+ S 18 '77
See also
Government and the press
Press law

FREEDOM of Thought Foundation
Fighting cults: the Tuscon tactic. R. Chandler. il Chr Today 21:57-61 F 4 '77
Is deprograming legal? using conservatorship laws to obtain custody of young cultists. M. Montagno. por Newsweek 89:44 F 21 '77

FREEDOM to Read Foundation
FRF looks over its legal repertoire. P. Harper. Wilson Lib Bull 51:564-5 Mr '77
Uphill struggles for the FRF; board of trustees meeting. P. Harper. Wilson Lib Bull 52:121 O '77

FREEDOM to travel. See Travel regulations

FREEMAN, Don
Dr Seuss at 72—going like 60. il por Sat Eve Post 249:8+ Mr '77

FREEMAN, Harold
On consuming the surplus; excerpt from Toward socialism in America. Progressive 41:20-1 F '77

FREEMAN, Harry B. Jr
Can America finance future prosperity? por Nations Bus 65:58 Je '77

FREEMAN, Jean Todd
Three young clergywomen: how they're changing their churches. il Redbook 149:24+ Je '77

FREEMAN, John W.
Pride of Bergamo. por Opera N 41:30 Ap 9 '77
Records. See issues of Opera news

FREEMAN, Larry
Prang Christmas cards. il Hobbies 82:118-19 D '77

FREEMAN, M.
(ed) See Duvoisin, R. and Fatio, L. PW interviews

FREEMAN, Neal B.
Down among the bureaucrats. Nat R 29:1229 O 28 '77

FREEMAN, Richard B.
Does it pay to go to college? pors U.S. News 82:59-60 Ja 24 '77
Economic gains of black workers; excerpts from address. Intellect 106:102-3 S '77

FREEMAN, S. David
Carter's mandate to transform TVA. por Bus W p29-30 S 5 '77 *
Energy debacle. L. H. Lapham. Harpers 255:58-61+ Ag '77; Discussion. 255:6+ O '77 *

FREEMAN'S Farm, Battle of, 1777. See Saratoga Campaign, 1777

FREEMARK Abbey. See Wine industry

FREESTYLE skiing. See Skis and skiing

FREEWAY Park. See Seattle—Parks and playgrounds

FREEZE fracturing
Freeze-fractured purple membrane particles: protein content. K. A. Fisher and W. Stoeckenius. bibl il Science 197:72-4 Jl 1 '77

FREEZER thermometers. See Thermometers and thermometry

FREEZERS
Consumer's guide to: home freezers. il Mech Illus 73:22 Ag '77
Freezers. il Consumer Rep 42:56-61 D '77
Managing my home freezer. E. Trull. il por Org Gard & Farm 24:104-5 Jl '77

FREEZING
Hot water freezes faster than cold water. Why does it do so? J. Walker. il Sci Am 237:246+ bibl(p262) S '77
See also
Frostbite

FREEZING and opening of lakes, rivers, etc.
See Ice on rivers, lakes, etc.

FREEZING of food
Freeze-ahead main dishes for take-it-easy meals. R. Molter. il Parents Mag 52:48-50+ Jl '77
Home freezing: fruits and vegetables, poultry, meat and fish; main dishes, breads, desserts. il Good H 184:194+ Je '77
Wrapping meat for your freezer. il Bet Hom & Gard 55:98 O '77

FREEZING of fruits. See Freezing of food

FREEZING of vegetables. See Freezing of food

FREIDBERG, Sidney
Just wear a camera and a smile. il Mod Phot 41:96-9+ F '77

FREIGHT and freightage
See also
Air freight service
Shipping
Trucking

FREIGHT handling
See also
Containerization (freight)
Loading and unloading

FREIGHT rates. See Railroads—Rates

FREIGHTERS
See also
Tank ships

Inspection

See Ships—Inspection

FREIGHTLINER Corporation. See Truck industry

FREIS, Richard
Life story; Beach motel; poems. Poetry 130:256-7 Ag '77

FRELIER, P. and others
Sarcocystosis: a clinical outbreak in dairy calves. bibl il Science 195:1341-2 Mr 25 '77

FREMES, Ruth, and Sabry, Zak
Facts on fat: it's not all bad; excerpt from NutriScore. il Good H 185-210 S '77

FRENCH, Bevan M.
Planetary comparisons. il Space World N-1-157:30-1 Ja '77
What's new on the moon? il Sky & Tel 53:164-9 Mr; 257-61 Ap '77

FRENCH, Beverlee. See Maina, W. jt auth

FRENCH, Daniel Chester
Daniel Chester French. S. B. Sherrill. Antiques 112:188+ Ag '77 *
Irving memorial created by Daniel Chester French. Hobbies 82:145 D '77 *
Long labor of making nation's favorite statue. M. Richman. il Smithsonian 7:54-61 bibl(p 152) F '77 *

FRENCH, Hector
Average, peak, and rms values. il Pop Electr 12:68 Jl '77

FRENCH, Marilyn
Fearful and the innocent. il Horizon 21:30-3 Ja '78

FRENCH, Sally
Eight hot issues that affect you now. il Outdoor Life 159:50+ Ap '77
FRENCH
Gadfly in France. il por Horizon 20:56-7 O '77
FRENCH art. See Art, French
FRENCH artificial satellites. See Artificial satellites, French
FRENCH CANADA. See Quebec (province)
FRENCH chefs. See Cooks
FRENCH cookery. See Cookery, French
FRENCH costume designers. See Costume designers
FRENCH decorative arts. See Decoration and ornament
FRENCH fry cookers. See Kitchen utensils and appliances
FRENCH glass. See Glassware
FRENCH horn. See Horn (musical instrument)
FRENCH in literature
Mateo Falcone; P. Merimee's Corsican short story. B. J. Khalil. Engl J 66:66-7 Mr '77
FRENCH intensive gardening. See Organic gardening
FRENCH language
Anecdotes, facetiae, satire, etc.
French correction. L. Elliott. Read Digest 111: 117-20 Ag '77
FRENCH literature
See also
French poetry
FRENCH philosophy. See Philosophy, French
FRENCH poetry
Virtue, weep if I die: the real André Chénier. S. P. Edelman. il por Opera N 41:10-13 Mr 26 '77
FRENCH pottery. See Pottery, French
FRENCH Revolution. See France—History—Revolution, 1789-1799
FRENCH Somaliland. See Afars and the Isaas, French Territory of
FRENCH songs. See Songs, French
FRENCH tarragon. See Tarragon
FRENCH toast. See Toast
FRENCH wines. See Wine
FRENI, Mirella
Mirella ritornata; interview, ed by R. Jacobson. il pors Opera N 42:18-23 O '77
FRENZEL, Bill
End tax breaks for capital gains? interview. pors U.S. News 83:71-2 D 19 '77
Excerpts from address on Federal Elections Campaign Act Amendments, April 1, 1976. Cong Digest 56:91+ Mr '77
FREQUENCY changers
Build programmable frequency divider. G. Baumgras. il Radio-Electr 48:37-41 My '77
Equipment reports:
Sencore model CB44 27-MHz scope frequency converter. il Radio-Electr 49:31 Ja '78
FREQUENCY counters. See Frequency meters
FREQUENCY dividers. See Frequency changers
FREQUENCY equalizers. See Sound—Apparatus
FREQUENCY generators. See Signal generators
FREQUENCY measurement
Spectrum analyzer in hi-fi measurements. J. Hirsch. il Pop Electr 13:49-53 Ja '78
FREQUENCY meters
Build a 10-Hz to 1-MHz EPUT meter. J. F. Hollabaugh. il Pop Electr 11:68-9 Mr '77
Build 30-MHz CB frequency counter. G. Santi. il Radio-Electr 48:43-5+ S '77
Equipment reports:
Lunar electronics DX-555 signal generator /frequency counter. il Radio-Electr 48:32 O '77
40-MHz frequency counter. B. Green. il Pop Electr 11:64-6 Je '77
Frequency counters. il Radio-Electr 48:53-5 N '77
Product test reports:
Continental Specialties Model Max-100 frequency counter. il Pop Electr 12:93 O '77
FREQUENCY synthesizers. See Signal generators
FRÈREBEAU, Mariel
What is Montmartre? Nothing! What should it be? Everything! tr by G. Needham. il Art N 76:60-2 Mr '77
FRERS, German
New boats for the SORC. Yachting 141:100 F '77
FRESH water biology
Familiar ponds harbor mysteries, exotic animals. C. W. Hart, Jr. il Smithsonian 8:84-8+ bibl(p 115) Ja '78
See also
Plankton
FRESH water ecology
Vernal pools. D. M. Small. il Am For 83:30-3 My '77
FRESH water fauna
Unseen life of a mountain stream. W. H. Amos. il Nat Geog 151:562-80 Ap '77
See also
Fishes
FRESH water mussels. See Mussels, Fresh water
FRESNO, Calif. State University. See California. State University, Fresno
FREUD, Lucian
Relentlessly personal vision of Lucian Freud; interview, ed by J. Gruen. il por Art N 76: 60-3 Ap '77
FREUD, Sigmund
Freud and his literary doubles. M. Kanzer. bibl Am Imago 33:231-43 Fall '76 *
FREUDENHEIM, Tom Lippmann
It's like love, a one-to-one relationship between a human being and a work of art. R. Bongartz. il por Art N 76:78-80+ My '77 *
FREUDENTHAL, Juan R.
Special report: SALALM in Gainesville. Wilson Lib Bull 52:24 S '77
FREUND, Paul A.
F. F; interview. New Yorker 53:42-3 N 28 '77
FREUND, Ron
Carter and the B-1 bomber. Chr Cent 94:53-4 Ja 26 '77
FREY, Donald Nelson
Don Frey's dilemma. il pors Forbes 120:74-5 D 1 '77 *
FREY, Peter
Driving impression. il Motor T 29:91-2 S '77
FREYRE, Gilberto
Afro-Brazilian experiment. il UNESCO Courier 30:13-18 Ag '77
FRIBOURG, Michael
World of extremes; address, April 27, 1977. Vital Speeches 43:527-9 Je 15 '77
FRICK, F. C. See Dinneen, G. P. jt auth
FRICK Collection, New York
Echoes at the Frick; display of orchids. New Yorker 53:27-8 Ap 11 '77
Shaping of a garden; design for garden of the Frick Collection. R. Page. il por House & Gard 149:34+ Jl '77
Versailles in Indiana limestone; addition to the Frick Collection. G. Henry. il Art N 76:117 S '77
FRICKER, John, and Sims, E. H.
Airwar 1939-1945. il Flying 101:185-99 S '77
FRIDOVICH, Irwin
Oxygen is toxic! bibl il BioScience 27:462-6 Jl '77
FRIED, Eunice
Sherry flip. il Sat R 5:28-9 O 29 '77
Sparkling Christmas spirits. il Harp Baz 111:98-9+ D '77
FRIED, John J.
Pneumonia is still a killer. Read Digest 110: 178-81 My '77
FRIED, Miriam
Musician of the month: Miriam Fried; interview, ed by S. Fleming. por Hi Fi 27:MA8-9 Jl '77
FRIED, Sherman, and others
Retention of plutonium and americium by rock. bibl il Science 196:1087-9 Je 3 '77
FRIEDAN, Betty
Women at Houston. New Repub 177:15-19 D 10 '77
FRIEDBERG, Milton R.
What you should know about CB antennas. il Radio-Electr 48:64-6+ O '77
FRIEDLAND, Joan, and others
Angiotensin converting enzyme: induction by steroids in rabbit alveolar macrophages in culture. bibl il Science 197:64-5 Jl 1 '77
FRIEDLY, Robert L.
Investigative reporters' Arizona project. Chr Cent 94:243-4 Mr 16 '77
FRIEDMAN, Arthur
Letting the employees set their own salaries. Nations Bus 65:44 F '77 *
FRIEDMAN, Bruce Jay
Lonely guy's grooming guide. Esquire 88:116-18+ N '77
Sex and the lonely guy. il Esquire 88:114-17+ O '77
FRIEDMAN, Deborah
Busted in Mexico. D. Harris. il pors N Y Times Mag p26-30+ My 1 '77 *
FRIEDMAN, Edward
How to save your child's good sight. il Parents Mag 52:46-7+ F '77
FRIEDMAN, Herbert
40-channel CB's—lots of new choices. il Pop Sci 210:84-6 My '77
FRIEDMAN, John S.
(ed) See Roth, H. On being blocked & other literary matters
FRIEDMAN, Leon
How to get your file. Ms 5:42 Je '77
FRIEDMAN, Mel
Judicial thicket. Nation 225:110-13 Ag 6 '77

FRIEDMAN, Milton
Courage to take it. Nat R 29:1478 D 23 '77
Future of capitalism; address, February 9, 1977. Vital Speeches 43:333-7 Mr 15 '77
Halting government intervention in economic affairs; excerpts from address. Intellect 105: 295 Mr '77
Leaning against next year's wind; interview, ed by F. Kutchins. il por Sat Eve Post 249:16+ My '77
Path we dare not take. Read Digest 110:110-14 Mr '77
Sincerely yours, next. . .Sincerely yours, next. . . il Sr Schol 109:8-9+ My 5 '77
Where Carter is going wrong; interview. il pors U.S. News 82:20-2 Mr 7 '77

about

En-Nobeling Milton Friedman. R. Skole. Nation 224:68-70 Ja 22 '77 *

FRIEDMAN, Myra
Is this any way to make a living? Esquire 88: 66-7+ Jl '77

FRIEDMAN, Richard, and Iwai, Junichi
Genetic predisposition and stress-induced hypertension. bibl il Science 193:161-2, 198:80 Jl 9 '76, O 7 '77

FRIEDMAN, Richard Allen. See Fischler, S. jt auth

FRIEDMAN, Robert
Hell's agent. il Esquire 88:75-8+ O '77

FRIEDMAN, Shirley
Long wait: a study in determination. Chr Cent 94:348-9 Ap 13 '77 *

FRIEDMAN, Stephen
Expert strategists in the acquisition game. pors Bus W p 182-3 N 14 '77 *

FRIEDMAN, Sylvia M. and O'Shaughnessy, Helaine
Reading made easy for beginners. il Parents Mag 52:62-3+ S '77

FRIEDMAN, Thomas B. and Johnson, D. H.
Temporal control of urate oxidase activity in drosophila: evidence of an autonomous timer in Malpighian tubules. bibl il Science 197:477-9 Jl 29 '77

FRIEDMAN-WEISS, Jeffrey, and Wise, H. H.
Americans at home; excerpt from Good lives. il McCalls 104:98-100+ S '77

FRIEDMANN, Lynda
Saving old Orleans. P. Brooks. il por Ms 6:21 Ag '77 *

FRIEDRICH, Otto
Clover and Henry Adams—a most unusual love story. il pors Smithsonian 8:58-64+ bibl(p 146-7) Ap '77

FRIEND, David
Arp & Friend, Inc. J. Ellis. il pors Hi Fi 28:114-16 Ja '78 *

FRIENDLY, Alfred
Admiral Beaufort charted coasts for ships of the world. il por map Smithsonian 8:68-70+ bibl(p 101) Ag '77
Great Book of Kells in shining exhibit of ancient Irish art. il Smithsonian 8:66-75 bibl(p 160) O '77

FRIENDLY, Fred W.
Kissinger: victim of liberal witch hunt at Columbia? por U.S. News 82:33 Je 13 '77

FRIENDS, Society of
Getting the Quakers together. H. H. Ward. Chr Cent 94:724-6 Ag 17 '77

FRIENDSHIP
Alternative life-styles; sexually intimate friendships. J. W. Ramey. bibl il Society 14:43-7 Jl '77
Can men and women be friends? Answers from famous women and men; ed by L. Werner. il Redbook 149:31-2 O '77
Focus on friendship. Seventeen 36:52-3 N '77
Friends, good friends—and such good friends. J. Viorst. Redbook 149:31-2+ O '77
Friends: when does caring become interference? J. Shapiro. Mademoiselle 83:174-5 O '77
Friendship Force. P. Davis. Bet Hom & Gard 55:204+ N '77
How to keep sex from screwing up a friendship; platonic relationships. S. Haller. Mademoiselle 83:118+ D '77
It's 1977. Do you know who your friends are? special section. il Esquire 87:81-93+ My '77
Making friends abroad, down-home style; Friendship Force. il U.S. News 83:58 S 19 '77
Somebody else should be your own best friend. R. Brain. bibl il por Psychol Today 11:83-4+ O '77
Your friends, my friends, our friends. A. Gross. Redbook 149:76+ My '77

FRIENDSHIP Force program. See Friendship

FRIESIAN language
Summer search; American language student in Friesland. R. Goldberg. map Seventeen 36: 68-9 Ag '77

FRIESLAND
Summer search; American language student in Friesland. R. Goldberg. map Seventeen 36: 68-9 Ag '77

FRIGATE birds
Trial balloon; excerpt from Galapagos: islands of birds. B. Nelson. il Audubon 79:42-3 My '77

FRIGATES. See Warships

FRIMBO, Ernest M. pseud. See Whitaker, R. E. M.

FRINGE benefits. See Non-wage payments

FRISBEE (game)
And now, frisbee golf. il Newsweek 90:48 S 5 '77
Around the Mall and beyond. E. Park. il Smithsonian 8:14-16 Ja '78
Play it where it lays; Frisbee golf in Central Park. P. J. O'Rourke. il N Y Times Mag p24-5 Je 12 '77

FRISCH, Ann, and Partie, Dianne
How to recognize a good relationship. . .and a bad one; quiz. Mademoiselle 83:165-6 S '77
Power strategies: how to play the game—and win. Mademoiselle 83:166-7 My '77

FRISIAN language. See Friesian language

FRITZ, Robert S.
Spruce grouse in the Adirondacks. il Conservationist 31:19-22 Ja '77

FROELICH, Jeffrey
Here's an offer you can resist. il Ret Liv 17:21-2 Ag '77

FROGS
Albumin phylogeny for clawed frogs (xenopus) C. A. Bisbee and others. bibl il Science 195: 785-7 F 25 '77
Infrared reflectance in leaf-sitting neotropical frogs. P. A. Schwalm and P. H. Starrett. bibl il Science 196:1225-7 Je 10 '77
Leopard frog supply; letter. J. T. Bagnara and J. S. Frost. bibl Science 197:106-7 Jl 8 '77
Thyrotropin-releasing hormone: abundance in the skin of the frog, rana pipiens. I. M. D. Jackson and S. Reichlin. bibl il Science 198: 414-15 O 28 '77

See also

Tree frogs and tree toads

FROMKIN, David
Drawing the line. New Repub 176:12-14 Je 4 '77

FROMM, Erich
How to be happy with who you are; interview, ed by C. Seebohm. il House & Gard 149:152-3+ Ap '77

FROMM, Gary
Shifting priorities for corporate taxation. por Bus W p24+ Jl 4 '77 *

FROMME, Robert A.
Clay whistle. il Ceram Mo 25:60-3 Mr; 58-62 Ap '77

FRONT wheel drive automobiles. See Automobiles—Front wheel drive

FRONTIER and pioneer life

Canada

Roughing it in the Yukon. J. Hope. il Int Wildlife 7:20-7 Jl '77

United States

Campaigning with Custer; excerpt from Life in Custer's cavalry; diaries and letters of Albert and Jennie Barnitz, 1867-68, ed by R. M. Utley. A. Barnitz and J. P. Barnitz. il pors Am West 14:4-9+ Jl '77
Eden ravished: the land, pioneer attitudes, and conservation. H. Hague. bibl il Am West 14:30-3+ My '77
Farmers' frontier; excerpt from The American farm: a photographic history. M. Conrat and R. Conrat. il Am West 14:22-33 Mr '77
Meadowlark song; memories of an Oklahoma childhood. L. W. Bartley and S. J. Wolfe. il Am West 14:34-7 Mr '77
Shelters on the plains. R. Welsch. il Natur Hist 86:48-53 bibl(p94) My '77
Trailing the alias; nicknames in the old West. W. Koop. Am West 14:32-5 Ja '77

See also

Cowboys
Homesteads
Overland journeys to the Pacific

FRONTIER Days Rodeo, Cheyenne, Wyo. See Rodeos

FROSCH, Robert A.
Frosch sees period of evolutionary exploration for NASA. F. C. Bennett. por Phys Today 30: 85+ S '77 *
NASA chief designate selection keyed to issues facing agency. Aviation W 106:61 My 9 '77 *
NASA nominee to stress applications. Aviation W 106:79-80 Je 20 '77 *
Space chief nominee stresses need for good science. D. Sharpley. por Science 196:1301-3 Je 17 '77 *
Woods Hole's Frosch to be NASA nominee. Sci N 111:279 Ap 30 '77 *

FROST, Dan
1,000-yard chucks. il Outdoor Life 160:82-3+ Jl '77

FROST, David
David can be a Goliath. il por Time 109:33 My 9 '77 *
Nixon speaks. D. M. Alpern and others. il pors Newsweek 89:25+ My 9 '77 *
Nixon talks. il pors Time 109:22-4+ My 9 '77 *

FROST, David—*Continued*
Notes and comment. New Yorker 53:31-2 My 16 '77 *
Struggle to find sponsors for Nixon. pors Bus W p33-4 My 9 '77 *
Watching Nixon; symposium. il pors Newsweek 89:28-9+ My 16 '77 *
When the President does it. I. L. Horowitz. Nation 224:751-4 Je 18 '77 *
Why Nixon went on the witness stand. pors U.S. News 82:27-9 My 16 '77 *

Anecdotes, facetiae, satire, etc.

David and Pariah. H. Fairlie. il New Repub 176:43-5 My 21 '77 *

FROST, Richard
Animal graves; poem. Esquire 88:54 N '77
I stroke my sleeping son; poem. Am Scholar 46:513 Aut '77

FROST, Robert
For girls: from Birches to Wild grapes. H. Bacon. Yale R 67:13-29 O '77 *
Forgiving Robert Frost. J. F. Cotter. America 137:463-5 D 24 '77 *
Poetry and power. S. Maloff. il por Commonweal 104:215-18 Ap 1 '77 *
Robert Frost: two anecdotes. J. Ciardi. Sat R 4:48 S 3 '77 *
Vanity, fame, love, and Robert Frost; excerpt from Remembering poets. D. Hall. Commentary 64:51-61 D '77 *

FROST, William
Chaucerian crux. Yale R 66:551-61 Je '77

FROST protection of plants. See Plants, Protection of

FROSTBITE
Frostbitten winter. J. A. Seligmann. il Newsweek 89:77 F 14 '77
Have fun in the snow—but be careful! V. T. Sparano. il Nat Wildlife 16:26-7 D '77

FROUD, Brian
Lovely monsters of Brian Froud. il Esquire 88:179-83 D '77 *

FROWICK, Roy Halston. See Halston (fashion designer)

FROZEN desserts. See Ice cream, ices, etc.

FROZEN dinners. See Food, Frozen

FROZEN fish. See Fish, Frozen

FROZEN food. See Food, Frozen

FROZEN meat. See Meat, Frozen

FRUEHAUF Corporation-Koehring Company merger. See Corporations—Acquisitions and mergers

FRUIT
Adventures in eating. il Ladies Home J 94:114+ Mr '77
Spinning rotation of ash and tulip tree samaras. C. W. McCutchen. bibl il Science 197:691-2 Ag 12 '77
See also
Citrus fruits
Cookery—Fruit
also names of fruits, e.g. Grapes

Diseases and pests

See also
Codling moths

Drying

Dry up! S. Bashline. il Field & S 82:140+ Je '77
Why my dried apricots don't shrivel up. M. Findley. Org Gard & Farm 24:112-13 Ag '77

Storage

Keeping fruits & vegetables fresh. il Changing T 31:34-6 Jl '77
Stocking the cold cellar. R. B. Yepsen, Jr. il Org Gard & Farm 24:109-10+ S '77

Varieties

How to choose new varieties for your 1978 garden. M. C. Goldman. il Org Gard & Farm 25:74-9 Ja '78

FRUIT, Freezing of. See Freezing of food

FRUIT, Pickled. See Pickles and relishes

FRUIT-bud development
Switching flowers on and off. il Sci N 112:39 Jl 16 '77

FRUIT cake. See Cake

FRUIT culture
California orchardists face the drought. M. C. Goldman. il Org Gard & Farm 24:60-3 My '77
Reviving an old orchard; excerpt from Fruits and berries for the home garden. L. Hill. il Org Gard & Farm 24:64-8 My '77
Soil fertility in the orchard. H. Lisle. il Org Gard & Farm 24:93-5 Je '77
See also names of fruits, e.g. Bananas

FRUIT desserts. See Desserts

FRUIT dryers. See Drying apparatus

FRUIT flies
See also
Drosophila

FRUIT industry
Apple picker blues; question of importing Jamaican pickers. D. McGhee. New Repub 177:15-16 O 29 '77
As Jamaican as apple pie; apple harvest workers in Virginia. J. Egerton. Progressive 41:37-40 D '77
Baiter Award; National Peach Council's recommendation to use DBCP as form of birth control. J. G. Mitchell. Audubon 79:168 N '77
Cranberry bogs of Long Island. T. Huss. il por Conservationist 32:5-8 N '77
Doubly difficult apple to pluck; foreign pickers. il Time 110:28 N 7 '77
See also
Citrus fruit industry
United Brands Company

FRUIT juices
New and better way to preserve juice; use of steam juicer. il Org Gard & Farm 24:96-7 Jl '77
See also
Orange juice

FRUIT salads. See Salads

FRUIT tarts. See Tarts

FRUIT trees
Fruit crosses you can grow. Sunset 158:168 F '77
Whip-and-tongue graft: easy way to more fruit in half the time. R. Kurle. il Org Gard & Farm 25:84-7 Ja '78
See also
Apple trees
Fig trees
Persimmons

FRUIT trees, Dwarf
Dwarf fruit trees: big producers in tiny plots. J. Dwyer and J. Albert. il Pop Mech 147:94-6+ Ap '77
Grow your own rootstock; dwarf apple trees. M. Averre. Org Gard & Farm 25:82-3 Ja '78
Guide to dwarf fruits. V. McElwain. Horticulture 55:28-30+ S '77

FRUITCAKE. See Cake

FRUITS, vegetables, etc. in decoration
Nuts, pods, weeds and seeds. B. Kent. il Org Gard & Farm 24:138+ N '77

FRUTKIN, Ren
Will a solar home save you money? Sci Digest 82:70-1 N '77

FRYE, Christopher
Dairy that delivers organic farm foods. il Org Gard & Farm 24:150+ S '77
How one farmer controls weeds naturally. il Org Gard & Farm 24:87-9 My '77

FRYE, John
Supertankers—coming or going? with biographical sketch. il Sea Front 23:76-83, 126 Mr '77

FRYE, John T.
Mac's service shop (cont) il Pop Electr 11:106-8 Je '77

FRYE, Mariella
National catechetical directory: Origins and vision. il por New Cath World 220:56-9 Mr '77

FRYER, Jerome M.
Gabriel plays a new game and wins hands down. por Duns R 109:20-1 Mr '77 *

FRYERS. See Kitchen utensils and appliances

FRYING
Better batter; use of beer. C. Claiborne and P. Franey. il N Y Times Mag p76 Je 5 '77
It's quick! Easy! Terrific! Stir-fry. il Redbook 149:138-40+ S '77

FRYING pans. See Kitchen utensils and appliances

FUCHS, Bernard
Watering holes; reproductions of paintings. Sports Illus 47:32-6 S 5 '77

about

Letter from the publisher. J. Meyers. por Sports Illus 47:4 S 5 '77 *

FUCHS, Fritz
Coping with the threat of premature birth. il Parents Mag 52:20 Mr '77

FUCHSIAS
Giving fuchsias a fresh start. il Sunset 158:160-1 F '77

FUEL
Energy solution in China; biogas generation. V. Smil. bibl il Environment 19:27-31 O '77
Growing oil; fossil fuel. por Forbes 120:64 Ag 1 '77
Is energy use overheating world? fossil fuels. il U.S. News 83:71 Jl 25 '77
See also
Airplane engines, Jet—Fuel consumption
Alcohol as fuel
Automobile engines—Fuel consumption
Coal
Diesel fuels
Gas, Natural—Reserves
Lignite
Liquefied petroleum gas
Motor vehicle engines—Fuel consumption
Peat
Recreational vehicles—Fuel consumption
Refuse as fuel
Synthetic fuels
Wood as fuel
also subhead Fuel under various subjects, e.g. Automobile engines—Fuel

FUEL—*Continued*

Conservation

Energy savers. Mech Illus 73:20 S '77
Energy-saver's quiz. S. Porter. Ladies Home J 94:16+ O '77
How to get in on those energy benefits. F. Casey. il Mech Illus 73:50+ O '77
Infrared energy spies. il Chemistry 50:23-4 N '77
Look around the house to save $'s. Consumers Res Mag 60:219 O '77
Saving fuel abroad—lots of talk, less action. il U.S. News 82:30 Je 6 '77
Tighten up your house. il Farm J 101:A4-5 D '77
Trees can cool and heat your house. Farm J 101: H2 S '77
Upgrade thermal efficiency:
Heat-wasting doors: you can plug the leaks. T. H. Jones. il Pop Sci 211:128+ D '77
Window heat loss. A. J. Hand. bibl il Pop Sci 212:97-8+ Ja '78
Useful gadgets that help save fuel. R. Wolkomir. il Mech Illus 73:46-7 N '77
Watch that convective heat loss! Nine tips to cut your energy cost. R. Field. il Sci Digest 82:83-5 O '77
Watt you can do to save energy. G. Reiger. Field & S 82:24+ O '77
See also
Energy policy
Gasoline—Conservation
Heating
Temperature—Control

Prices

After the chill comes the bitter bill. il Time 109:46-7 F 28 '77
Setting energy prices. H. Willens and L. S. Wyler. Progressive 41:7 S '77

FUEL cells
Good things in small packages; fuel cell power plants. il Forbes 119:66 Mr 1 '77
On the way: power for electric grids from fuel cells. R. Gorman. il Pop Sci 210:84-5+ Mr '77
Potential chemical fuel cell. il Chemistry 50:24 Je '77

FUEL conservation. See Fuel—Conservation

FUEL filters
See also
Marine engines—Filters

FUEL industry
Houston Oil's freehand approach to growth. Bus W p97+ Je 13 '77
How Tom Brown is fooling the shorts. D. G. Santry. il Bus W p 108 D 5 '77
See also
Coal industry
Gas industry
Mapco Inc
Petroleum industry

Accounting

Earnings cut from oil exploration. D. G. Santry. il Bus W p67 D 19 '77
FASB ruling hurts oil exploration; successful-efforts accounting for oil and gas companies. Bus W p41-2 O 10 '77

Finance

Energy. il Forbes 121:152-4 Ja 9 '78
Pity the suppliers. Time 109:63 Mr 7 '77

Laws and regulations

Divestiture—competition or nationalization? address, March 22, 1977. M. T. Halbouty. Vital Speeches 43:379-82 Ap 1 '77

Securities

Why energy stocks are still vigorous. il Bus W p60 Ag 1 '77

FUEL injection systems. See Automobile engines—Fuel feeding

FUEL lines, Boat. See Marine engines—Fuel feeding

FUEL oil. See Petroleum as fuel

FUEL pumps
Electric pump meters fuel in the field. D. K. O'Brien. il Farm J 101:7 Ja '77

FUEL sheds. See Sheds

FUEL supply
Cheerier outlook for winter fuel. il Bus W p36 O 24 '77
Direst fears disappear. il Time 109:75 Je 20 '77
Fueling up for winter. Time 110:30 D 5 '77
Go get it, fellows! il Forbes 119:25-7 Je 1 '77
How the energy shortage will change life in America; with interview with J. Schlesinger. il U.S. News 82:22-5 F 14 '77
Recovery in a deep-freeze. il Time 109:32 F 7 '77
Winter to remember; 1976-77. il U.S. News 82: 40-1 Ja 31 '77
Winter's legacy: step-up in search for fuel supplies. il U.S. News 82:19-20 F 21 '77
See also
Agriculture—Fuel requirements
Airlines—Fuel requirements
Aluminum industry—Fuel requirements
Aviation—Fuel requirements
Boats and boating—Fuel requirements
Cattle industry—Fuel requirements
Electric utilities—Fuel requirements
Fisheries—Fuel requirements
Gas supply
Industry—Fuel requirements
Petroleum supply
Public buildings—Fuel requirements
Schools—Fuel requirements

FUEL systems, Boat. See Marine engines—Fuel feeding

FUEL tanks
See also
Space vehicles—Fuel tanks

FUELS, Nuclear. See Nuclear fuels

FUERBRINGER, Otto
Time Inc.'s internal war over Vietnam; excerpt from The powers that be. D. Halberstam. il pors Esquire 89:94-100+ Ja '78 *

FUERST, J. S.
Achievable miracles in subsidized housing. Chr Cent 94:147-9 F 16 '77
Zoning out low-income families in suburbia. Chr Cent 94:77-8 F 2 '77

——and Petty, Roy
Case history in Providence. Nation 224:428-31 Ap 9 '77
Supreme Court and quotas. il Chr Cent 94:948-52 O 19 '77

FUERTES, Louis Agassiz
Fuertes portfolio. il por Conservationist 31:8-15 Ja '77

FUGARD, Athol
Boseman and Lena. Reviews
New Yorker 52:68 F 7 '77 *

FUGITIVES from justice
Aging radical comes home; M. Rudd. pors Time 110:25 S 26 '77
Return of Mark Rudd. R. Boeth and others. il pors Newsweek 90:34 S 26 '77
Rich man, poor man; capture of thief R. C. Rees. il por Time 109:22+ Ja 24 '77
See also
Escapes

FUJITA, T. Theodore
Anticyclonic tornadoes. bibl il Weatherwise 30: 51-64 Ap '77

FUKUDA, Jun, and Kawa, Kazuyoshi
Permeation of manganese, cadmium, zinc, and beryllium through calcium channels of an insect muscle membrane. bibl il Science 196:309-11 Ap 15 '77

FUKUDA, Takeo
What Asian nations want most from Carter; interview, ed by J. N. Wallace and H. Tanakadate. por U.S. News 82:76-7 Mr 28 '77

about

Japan gets the message. il por Time 110:71-2 D 12 '77 *
Ready to deal. F. Willey and others. il Newsweek 90:69-70 D 12 '77 *

Visit to the United States, 1977

How to avoid future *shokkus*. il Time 109:34+ Mr 28 '77
Japan's Prime Minister comes calling—. il U.S. News 82:76-7 Mr 28 '77
Prime Minister Fukuda of Japan visits Washington; text of joint communique, March 22, 1977. Dept State Bull 76:375-7 Ap 18 '77

FULBRIGHT, James William
International education: focus for corporate support. Harvard Bus R 55:137-41 My '77

FULFILLMENT (ethics) See Self realization

FULFORD, Robert
Canada's restive nationalism. il Art N 76:76-8 Ap '77
Canadian couple look to American market. pors Pub W 212:48 O 24 '77

FULGINITI, Rebecca
(ed) Short film (cont) Engl J 66:90-3 S '77

FULL employment. See Employment

FULL Employment and Balanced Growth Act of 1976. See Labor laws and legislation—United States

FULLAM, Everett L.
Born again in Darien. S. Heath. Sat R 4:14-15 S 17 '77 *

FULLER, Buckminster. See Fuller, R. B.

FULLER, John
In a railway compartment; Cook's lesson; All the members of my tribe are liars; Annotations of giant's town; Evening signs at Gallt-y-Ceiliog; Cairn; Boundaries; Sleeping out at Gallt-y-Ceiliog; poems. New Repub 176:29-32 My 28 '77

about

Comment. J. Matthias. Poetry 129:340-7 Mr '77 *
Poetry of John Fuller. E. Mendelson. New Repub 176:32-5 My 28 '77 *

FULLER, John G.
Poison that fell from the sky. il map Read Digest 111:191-6+ Ag '77

FULLER, Loie
La Loie. G. Morris. il pors Dance Mag 51:36-41 Ag '77 *

FULLER, Mary
(ed) See Di Mare, D. Paper, wood, and string of Dominic Di Mare

FULLER, Meta Vaux Warrick
Meta Vaux Warrick Fuller: her life and art. V. J. Hoover. il por Negro Hist Bull 40:678-81 Mr '77 *

FULLER, Peter Davenport
Inner life of a wealthy warrior. M. Maddocks. il pors Sports Illus 46:54-6+ My 23 '77 *

FULLER, Richard Buckminster
Buckminster Fuller on minds instead of muscle. il pors U.S. News 83:49 D 5 '77
Fifty years ahead of my time. por Sat Eve Post 249:44+ Mr '77

about

Book of the century: Fuller's Tetrascroll; with introd by P. Lada-Mocarski. R. Minsky and P. Seidler. il pors Craft Horiz 37:18-21+ O '77 *
Goldilocks' cosmic teach-in. M. Hoelterhoff. il pors Art N 76:19-21 Mr '77 *
Not ready for the rocking chair. E. Berger. il pors Ret Liv 17:30-2 O '77 *

FULLER, Robert G. and others
Can physics develop reasoning? bibl il Phys Today 30:23-8 F '77

FULLER, Varden, and Mason, Bert
Farm labor. bibl f il Ann Am Acad 429:63-80 Ja '77

FULLER, W. Harold
Black culture—the Bible is the judge. Chr Today 51:21-2 Ap 1 '77
Evangelicals in Africa. il Chr Today 21:38 Ag 26 '77

FULLUM, Jay
Fishing facts. See issues of Conservationist

FULTON, George P.
How cost effective is direct filtration? il Am City & County 92:43-4 Ja '77

FULTON Fish Market. See New York (city)—Markets

FULTZ, Karla
One woman's war against rape. M. Gross. por Good H 184:84+ Ap '77 *

FUNCTION generators. See Signal generators

FUND for Advancement of Camping
FAC marks 15th year in camping. E. P. Eells. Camp Mag 50:6-7+ S '77

FUND raising
Beggar's opera; fund raising by cultural institutions. L. H. Lapham. Harpers 255:16+ O '77
Catered crepe. il Seventeen 36:104-5+ Jl '77
Contributor as a consumer; public disclosure of church financial affairs. Chr Today 21:61-3 My 6 '77
Disclosure by charities. U.S. News 83:65 Jl 4 '77
Disclosure is closer; financial disclosure by charitable organizations. Chr Today 21:35-6 Ag 26 '77
Get equipment for your school—free! M. L. Schildkraut. Good H 184:228 Mr '77
Giving and getting taken; cases of Boys Town, Pallottine Fathers, and others. Chr Today 22:59-61 D 9 '77
H.R. 41: the state demands church disclosures. W. Proctor. Chr Today 22:15-17 N 4 '77
Way to increase charitable contributions; selling-up technique. J. Horn. Psychol Today 10:32-3 F '77
Writing for the hidden markets; fundraising groups. A. R. Blackburn. Writers Digest 57:41-3 Jl '77
See also
Bazaars, Charitable
Campaign funds
Dancing—Benefit performances
United Way of America (organization)

Anecdotes, facetiae, satire, etc.

Nine steps to fiscal solvency. G. Weales. N Y Times Mag p 123 Mr 27 '77

FUNDAMENTAL particles. See Particles (nuclear physics)

FUNDIDORA de Monterrey (firm) See Steel industry—Mexico

FUNDS, Pension. See Pensions—Finance

FUNERAL directors. See Undertakers and undertaking

FUNERAL parlors. See Undertakers and undertaking

FUNERAL rites and ceremonies
Funeral of Henry Clay. J. S. Brown. il Antiques 112:110-11 Jl '77
Horses for the hereafter; excavations at Arzhan. M. P. Gryaznov. il UNESCO Courier 29:38-41 D '76
What you should know about funerals. Good H 185:268 N '77

FUNERALS, Cost of
See also
Undertakers and undertaking

FUNGAL genetics
Genetic engineering: the origin of the long-distance rumor. J. L. Marx. Science 198:388 O 28 '77

FUNGI
Elemental sulfur: accumulation in different species of fungi. R. Pezet and V. Pont. bibl il Science 196:428-9 Ap 22 '77
See also
Aspergillus
Mushrooms
Wood decaying fungi

FUNGICIDES
See also
Spraying and dusting

FUNK, Ben
Swept away. il N Y Times Mag p38-40+ S 18 '77

FUNK, Fanchon F. and others
Assessing your student teaching program. il Clearing H 51:108-12 N '77

FUNK, Karen. See Kruschke, D. jt auth

FUNK, Peter
It pays to enrich your word power. See issues of Reader's digest

FUNK, Robert
Robert Funk. D. Steigman. il Pop Phot 81:108-11 Jl '77 *

FUNNY cars. See Automobiles, Racing

FUQUA Industries, Inc.-Avis, Inc merger. See Corporations—Acquisitions and mergers

FUR bearing animals
See also
Beavers
Fishers (animals)
Foxes
Otters
Seals (animals)
Trapping

FUR farming
Kinky minks; mink rancher. L. W. Bennett. por Forbes 119:106 My 15 '77

FUR industry
Take back your mink. il Forbes 119:105-6+ My 15 '77

FUR trade
See also
Fur farming
Hudson's Bay Company

FURBISH, Kate
Of dams and Kate Furbish. R. Saltonstall, Jr. il por Liv Wildn 40:42-3 Ja '77 *
Woman behind the wildflower that stopped a dam. J. Cole. il por Horticulture 55:30-5 D '77 *

FURIE, Kenneth
Diagnosis: slipped discography. il Wilson Lib Bull 51:755-9 My '77
In the opera house: how much does neatness count? il por Hi Fi 27:71-3 Ag '77

FURLING (sails) See Sails

FURLONG, William Barry
Ferment in Georgetown. il Horizon 19:4-13 Jl '77
How young America dates. Seventeen 36:226-9+ Ag '77
Mondale's Minnesota. il pors Horizon 20:66-74 O '77
Take me out to the scoreboard. il Horizon 20:66-71 D '77
Why fun is fun. Read Digest 110:140-2 My '77

FURLOUGHS, Prison. See Prison furloughs

FURMAN, Laura
Free and clear; story. New Yorker 53:28-32 Mr 7 '77
Kindness of strangers; story. New Yorker 53:34-9 Ap 11 '77
Real estate; story. New Yorker 53:28-32 S 5 '77
Seesaw; story. Redbook 149:134-5 O '77

FURNACES
Feed logs to your oil burner? Multi-fuel furnaces. V. D. Chase. il Pop Sci 211:106-9 O '77
Free home heating from a car-engine furnace. D. Scott. il Pop Sci 211:10 Ag '77
Now it may pay to switch furnaces. il Mech Illus 73:92-3 S '77
Superhot homebuilt furnace for metalworking; crucible furnace. P. L. Conant. il Pop Mech 148:126-7 N '77
Thermal-storage furnace—can it make electric heat practical? E. Powell. il Pop Sci 211:70+ N '77
See also
Gas furnaces
Oil burners

Dampers

See Dampers

Maintenance and repair

Furnace fix-ups that save fuel and money. M. Schultz and M. McClintock. il Pop Mech 147:104-7+ F '77
Furnace fix-ups you can do. G. Way. il Mech Illus 73:100+ D '77

Ventilation

See Ventilation

FURNESS, Betty
ABA's Smith censures Furness and Today show. J. Giusto. Pub W 212:36+ O 24 '77 *

FURNESS, Pauline Tymon
Try role playing. bibl Todays Educ 66:94-5 Ja '77

FURNISHINGS, Household. See Household furnishings

FURNITURE

Almost instant furniture; do-it-yourself furniture construction; ideas of S. Zakas. il Time 111:62 Ja 9 '78
Antiques: a family bet that worked. B. Brennan. House B 119:48 N '77
Furnishing the museum rooms of the William Paca House. G. R. Weidman. bibl il Antiques 111:165-71 Ja '77
Furniture now. il House & Gard 149:146-55 O '77
Great finds! antiques; with excerpts from Living places and Made with oak. il Good H 184:134-9+ Je '77
New contemporary. K. Mahoney. il House B 119:133-9 S '77
Tube/clamp system—furniture your kids will never outgrow. R. Stepler. il Pop Sci 210:100-1 Je '77

See also

Beds
Bookcases
Cabinets (furniture)
Chairs
Chests
Desks
Drawers
Kitchen cabinets
Kitchen furniture
Office furniture
Screens (furniture)
Sofas
Tables
Upholstery
Veneers and veneering
Wood carving
Woodworking

Care

Art of staying old; conservation of antique furniture. C. Stapleton. il Am Home 80:6+ Mr '77
Use and care of rattan furniture. il Redbook 149:49+ Jl '77

Decorating and painting

See Furniture, Decorated; Furniture Painted

Design

Comfort con brio: Italian design '77; work of Mario Bellini and Giuseppe Raimondi. il House & Gard 149:144-5 Ap '77
Enduring splendor of Mies van der Rohe. A. L. Huxtable. il por N Y Times Mag p70-1+ F 27 '77
Wood. W. Weed. il Craft Horiz 37:18-19 Je '77

Finishing

After the room is remodeled, what of the furniture? S. Schraub. House B 119:100 S '77
Art of antiquing. il McCalls 105:60 N '77
Complete guide to furniture finishing. P. Angell. il Pop Mech 147:115-17+ F '77
Creative furniture finishing. P. Corbin. House & Gard 149:60+ Je '77
Finishing new furniture and refinishing old. il Sunset 159:140 O '77
Gentle art of refinishing old furniture. il Chang-ing T 31:31-2 F '77
How to refurbish furniture. M. Principe. il House & Gard 149:14 O '77
How to strip furniture and refinish with hot wax. M. Principe. il House & Gard 149:12 F '77
New looks for old furniture. Redbook 149:208 S '77

See also

Stains and staining

Leasing and renting

Rented furniture: a new design for living. il Bus W p 107+ Mr 14 '77

Marketing

See Furniture industry—Marketing

Painting

See Furniture, Painted

Purchasing

Furniture facts. Redbook 148:194+ Ap '77

Refinishing

See Furniture—Finishing

FURNITURE, American

Address book; dealers in Shaker furniture. House B 119:32+ My '77
American furniture; special issue. il Antiques 111:958-1040 My '77
Best of early American. il Good H 184:122-7 Ap '77
Beware! Antiques fakery is thriving again. N. Pratt. il House B 119:12+ Jl '77
Furniture of the River Road plantations in Louisiana. J. J. Poesch. bibl il Antiques 111:1184-8 Je '77
John Shaw, cabinetmaker of Annapolis. L. Bartlett. bibl il Antiques 111:362-77 F '77
Maryland furniture, 1760-1840. W. V. Elder, 3d. bibl il Antiques 111:354-61 F '77
North Carolina furniture; exhibition. S. B. Sherrill. il Antiques 112:588 O '77
Seventeenth- and eighteenth-century Long Island furniture. D. F. Failey . il Antiques 112:732-41 O '77

See also

House decoration, American

FURNITURE, Arrangement of

How to shape up the space at your place. S. Van Zante and R. E. Dittmer. il Bet Hom & Gard 55:126-31 Ap '77

FURNITURE, Built in

Space savers; excerpt from Spacemaker book. E. Liman. il Am Home 80:17 Ag '77

FURNITURE, Childrens

Build-it-yourself furniture that grows with your kids. D. Ashe and D. Haupert. il Bet Hom & Gard 55:116-17 F '77
Handsome, versatile sleep/play platform. il Pop Sci 210:118-19 My '77
Step-by-step project scrapbook: kid's furniture. il Bet Hom & Gard 55:54 Jl '77

See also

Desks
Nurseries

FURNITURE, Convertible

Build PM's couch and get a double bed, too. il Pop Mech 148:105-7 Ag '77

Purchasing

Sleep sofas. il Seventeen 36:76 F '77

FURNITURE, Decorated

Stenciling a new face for old furniture. il Redbook 148:66+ Ap '77

FURNITURE, Doll. See Doll furniture

FURNITURE, English

Britain's bric-a-brac boom. J. Ross-Skinner. il Duns R 109:76-9 Je '77

FURNITURE, Gothic

Gothic revival furniture designs of Alexander J. Davis. J. B. Davies. bibl il Antiques 111:1014-27 My '77

FURNITURE, Miniature

Patent model by John Henry Belter. R. Roth. bibl il Antiques 111:1038-40 My '77
Techniques in building miniatures; interview, ed by S. A. Parvin. J. Shellhaas. Hobbies 82:120-1 My '77

See also

Doll furniture

FURNITURE, Modern. See Furniture

FURNITURE, Outdoor

At home anywhere. C. Jones. il Am Home 80:76-7+ Ap '77
Casual furniture for indoors and out. il Bet Hom & Gard 55:94+ My '77
Garden furniture made to last. R. Weinsteiger. il Org Gard & Farm 24:176-7+ S '77
Outdoor furniture with up-front style. P. Angell. il Pop Mech 147:128-9+ Ap '77
Sun finds. il House & Gard 150:92-3 Ja '78
Update outdoor furniture. J. Cornell. il Am Home 80:98-100+ Ap '77

See also

Benches
Parks—Equipment

FURNITURE, Painted

Painted furniture; exhibition at the Renwick Gallery. S. B. Sherrill. il Antiques 111:844+ My '77
Painted wood furniture. il Craft Horiz 37:55-7+ Ag '77

FURNITURE, Prefabricated

Easy way to a room in a day; knockdown furniture. E. Brown. il N Y Times Mag p74-6 O 2 '77
Furniture in a box! knocked-down furniture. K. Mahoney. il House B 119:57-65 Ag '77

FURNITURE, School. See School furniture, equipment, etc.

FURNITURE, Victorian

Beastly chic. R. Reif. il N Y Times Mag p74-5 My 15 '77

FURNITURE deliveries. See Delivery of goods

FURNITURE finishing. See Furniture—Finishing

FURNITURE industry

From a humble beginning to triumph in business; Broyhill Industries; interview. J. E. Broyhill. il pors Nations Bus 65:44-6+ Ja '77

See also

Levitz Furniture Corporation
Office furniture industry

Marketing

U.S. journal: High Point, N.C. C. Trillin. il New Yorker 53:94-9 Je 6 '77

FURNITURE stores

Chic on the cheap; Conran's. il Newsweek 90:83-4 N 7 '77

FURNITURE stripping. See Furniture—Finishing

FURRER, Fredrick James

Shopping for shocks (cont) Motor T 29:82-4+ F; 76-8+ Mr '77

FURRIERS. See Fur industry

FURST, Peter T. and Coe, M. D.

Ritual enemas; with biographical sketches. il Natur Hist 86:8, 88-91 bibl(p97) Mr '77

FÜRSTENBERG, Diane, Prinzessin von und zu
Diane von Furstenberg's total-spa bathroom. F. De La Renta. il Vogue 167:370-1 S '77 *
FURSTENBERG, Friedrich
West German experience with industrial democracy. bibl f Ann Am Acad 431:44-53 My '77
FURTH, M. E. and others
Genetic structure of the replication origin of bacteriophage lambda. bibl il Science 198:1046-51 D 9 '77
FURTWÄNGLER, Wilhelm
Furtwangler on Brahms; Symphony no. 1 in C minor, op. 68. G. S. Fox. Am Rec G 40:16-17 N '76 *
FUSES, Electric. See Electric fuses
FUSION, Nuclear. See Nuclear fusion
FUSION reactors. See Nuclear reactors
FUSSELL, Edwin
Comment. R. Siegel. Poetry 130:110-11 My '77 *
FUTEHALLY, Zafar
Prospects for India's wildlife. il Nat Parks & Con Mag 51:17-19 Mr '77
FUTRELLE, Jacques
Murder without air. E. L. Gilbert. New Repub 177:33-4 Jl 30 '77 *
FUTURE
I have to spend the rest of my life in the future. H. Wittcoff. bibl il Chemistry 50:8-12 Mr '77
Intergenerational distributive justice and environmental responsibility. R. M. Green. bibl BioScience 27:260-5 Ap '77
See also
Forecasting
Nineteen hundred and eighty-five
Prophecies
Two thousand two (year)
FUTURE life
Back from the brink. D. Goleman. bibl il Psychol Today 10:56-9 Ap '77
City of light, realm of shadow; excerpt from Reflections on life after life. R. A. Moody, Jr. Read Digest 111:151-4 Jl '77
Cosmic consciousness; excerpt from Life after death. A. Koestler. il por Psychol Today 10: 52-4+ Ap '77
Is there life after death? R. A. Moody, Jr. il Sat Eve Post 249:66-7+ My '77
People who return from death; studies by Dr Michael Sabom and Sarah Kreutziger. L. Norment. Ebony 33:135-6+ N '77
Under the perspective of eternity. K. Bockmuhl. Chr Today 21:64-5 F 18 '77
See also
Heaven
FUTURES. See Commodity exchanges
FUTUROLOGY. See Forecasting
FUXE, Kjell and others
Prolactin-like immunoreactivity: localization in nerve terminals of rat hypothalamus. bibl il Science 196:899-900 My 20 '77
FUZESI, Stephens, Jr
Reforming the succession laws. Current 189:7-10 Ja '77
FYODOROVA, Viktoria. See Fedorova, V.

G

G. Fox & Company book department. See Booksellers and bookselling—Connecticut
G. Heileman Brewing Company. See Brewing industry
GAC. See United States—Government Advisory Committee on International Book and Library Programs
GAF Corporation
No joy for Kodak in GAF's departure. il Bus W p23-4 Ag 8 '77
GAO. See United States—General Accounting Office
GATT. See General Agreement on Tariffs and Trade
GATX Corporation
They shudda stayed on dry land. il Forbes 120: 46-7 Jl 15 '77
G. D. Searle and Company. See Searle, G. D. and Company
GE. See General Electric Company
GEICO. See Government Employees Insurance Company
G. K. Hall (firm) See Publishers and publishing—United States
GM. See General Motors Corporation
GMP. See Guanosine monophosphate
GNP. See Gross national product
GOP (Grand Old Party) See Republican Party
G.R. point; drama. See Barry, D.
GRC. See United States—National Institutes of Health—Gerontology Research Center
GSA. See Genetics Society of America; United States—General Services Administration

GABELLI, Mario
Mario Gabelli's orphan asylum. il por Forbes 120:69-70+ Jl 15 '77 *
GABELLI & Company. See Investment advisers
GABO, Naum
Obituary
Art N il por 76:62 O '77. A. Elsen
GABON
Glories of Gabon; OAU summit meeting. J. Pringle. por map Newsweek 90:33 Jl 18 '77
See also
Investments, Foreign—Gabon
Uranium mines and mining—Gabon
GABRIEL, Ann
I won $25,000 on a TV game show; $25,000 pyramid; ed by M. Siegel. il por Good H 184:154+ Mr '77
GABRIEL Industries Inc. See Games—Manufacture
GABRIELL, Terri
Believe-it-or-not herbal. il Org Gard & Farm 24: 82-4 N '77
GABRIELSON, Ira Noel
Obituary
Am For por 83:4+ N '77. L. W. Swift
Nat Parks & Con Mag por 51:18-21 D '77
GADDAFI, Muammar. See Qaddafi, M.
GADDIE, Ronald E.
Profitable way to get rid of solid waste. V. Louviere. por Nations Bus 65:65 Ja '77 *
GADDIS, John Lewis
Containment: a reassessment. bibl f For Affairs 55:873-87; 56:440-1 Jl '77, Ja '78
GADGETS
What you need to know about tools and handy gadgets. F. Belt. il Radio-Electr 49:33-42 Ja '78
GADSKI, Johanna Emilia Agnes
Exciting voice; Club 99 recordings. P. L. Miller. por Am Rec G 40:19-21 Jl '77 *
GAEBELEIN, Frank E.
Paradoxes of prayer. Chr Today 21:33-4 S 9 '77
GAELS. See Celts
GAFFNEY, James
Catechesis for a worshiping community. il por New Cath World 220:89-91 Mr '77
Catechesis for social ministry. il por New Cath World 220:92-5 Mr '77
Diverging paths in Catholic sexual ethics. il New Cath World 220:276-9 N '77
Religion (cont) America 136:417+ My 7; 137: 338-40 N 12 '77
GAG rules. See Press law
GAGE, Joan. See Gage, N. jt auth
GAGE, Nicholas
Has the Mafia penetrated the F.B.I? il N Y Times Mag p 14-16+ O 2 '77
—and Gage, Joan
Treasures from a golden tomb. il por map N Y Times Mag p 14-19+ D 25 '77
GAGLIANO, Marco da
La Dafne. R. V. Lucano. Am Rec G 41:32 D '77 *
New light on the Accademia degli Elevati of Florence. E. Strainchamps. bibl f il Mus Q 62:507-35 O '76 *
GAGNÉ, Sarah
Views on science books. il Horn Bk 53:77-9, 336-9, 557-9 F, Je, O '77
GAIL, Max
TV's Polish detective. P. Herz. il por Sr Schol 110:31 N 17 '77 *
GAILLARD, Frye
Labor victory. Progressive 41:8 N '77
Organizing J. P. Stevens. Progressive 41:37 F '77
GAINER, Harold, and Sarne, Yosef
Neurophysin biosynthesis: conversion of a putative precursor during axonal transport. bibl il Science 195:1354-6 Mr 25 '77
—See Schwartz, W. J. jt auth
GAINES, Diana
Historical novel: a trip. Writer 90:18-20 F '77
GAINES, James R.
More than wit flourished at the Round Table: there were creative blocks too, says HBJ book; interview, ed by R. Dahlin. il Pub W 211:89+ Je 13 '77
GAINES, Joan B.
Arts are for learning. il Todays Educ 66:72-4 N '77
GAITHER, W. S.
Policy for ocean resource development. Science 196:383 Ap 22 '77
GAITHER Trio. See Singers
GAJDUSEK, Daniel Carleton
Unconventional viruses and the origin and disappearance of Kuru. bibl il maps Science 197: 943-60 S 2 '77
GALACTOCEREBROSIDES. See Cerebrosides
GALAL, Salah
Desert made by man. il map Nat Parks & Con Mag 51:11-16 N '77
GALANTE, Carmine
Cigar for the Mafia. il por Time 109:15 Mr 7 '77 *
Mafia's new godfather. P. S. Meskil. por Read Digest 110:141-4 Je '77 *

GALAPAGOS ISLANDS
Three, two, one tortoise; Pinta Island. P. C. H. Pritchard. il map Natur Hist 86:90-100 bibl (p 123) O '77
View from the castle. S. D. Ripley. Smithsonian 8:8 D '77
GALAPAGOS Rift. See Faults (geology)
GALAPAGOS Rift Expedition. See Oceanographic research
GALAXIES
Clustering of galaxies. E. J. Groth and others. il Sci Am 237:76-8+ bibl(p 163) N '77
Deep-sky wonders. W. S. Houston. See issues of Sky and telescope
Dwarf galaxy in Carina. il Sky & Tel 54:105-6 Ag '77
Evolving questions about galaxies. D. E. Thomsen. il Sci N 112:324-5 N 12 '77
How ring galaxies are formed. il Sci Digest 81:78 F '77
Ring galaxies. S. P. Maran. il Natur Hist 86: 106+ N '77
Survey of galaxies sheds light on shape. il Sci N 111:86 F 5 '77
Whither thou goest..; recession velocities of remote spiral galaxies. Sky & Tel 53:111-12 F '77
X-rays from superclusters of galaxies. il Sky & Tel 54:105 Ag '77
See also
Radio sources (astronomy)
GALAXIES, Photography of. See Astronomical photography
GALAXY (Milky Way) See Milky Way
GALAZEN, Thomas
At our expense; government funding of recombinant DNA research. Progressive 41:22 D '77
Harnessing the wind: a way of life. il pors Org Gard & Farm 24:36+ O '77
GALBRAITH, Evan
Self-liquidating junta. Nat R 29:1494 D 23 '77
GALBRAITH, John Kenneth
Crime and no punishment. il Esquire 88:102+ D '77
Galbraithian guide to the economic folkways of Americans. por Fortune 96:97-8+ Ag '77
It started with Adam (Smith) il por N Y Times Mag p23-4+ My 15 '77
Let us now praise (faintly) famous economists. Esquire 87:70-1+ My '77
My forty years with the F.B.I. il por Esquire 88:122-6+ O '77
Uge: the inside story; excerpt from The age of uncertainty. il Horizon 19:4-13 Mr '77
about
John Kenneth Galbraith's marathon television series. G. Stigler. il Nat R 29:601-4 My 27 '77 *
Watch this man. S. Hampshire. il por Vogue 167:240-1+ My '77 *
GALDSTON, Richard
Coping with behavior problems (cont) Parents Mag 52:46 Jl; 97 O '77
GALE, Gloria
Doctor, lawyer, merchant, chief. il Design (US) 78:23 mid-Summ '77
GALE, K. and others
Dopamine-sensitive adenylate cyclase: location in substantia nigra. bibl il Science 195:503-5 F 4 '77
GALE, Roger W.
New U.S. lake in the Pacific. map Progressive 41:50-2 My '77
GALESBURG, Ill.
Midwest gets Main Street Projects. il Am City & County 92:22-3 N '77
GALILEI, Galileo
Science and humanism in the Italian renaissance; Galileo and his followers. E. Cochrane. bibl f Am Hist R 81:1039-57 D '76 *
GALLAGHER, Dorothy
Four waitresses: their secret world. il Redbook 150:104+ N '77
Murder in Morningside Park. il pors N Y Times Mag p26-9+ Ag 28 '77
Tracing their roots. il N Y Times Mag p48+ F 20 '77
GALLAGHER, Joel P. and Shinnick-Gallagher, Patricia
Cyclic nucleotides injected intracellularly into rat superior cervical ganglion cells. bibl il Science 198:851-2 N 25 '77
GALLAGHER, John
Lipstick cases, typewriter parts melded into motorcycle art. S. Parker. il por Design (US) 79: 14-16 Fall '77 *
GALLAGHER, Michela, and others
Memory formation: evidence for a specific neurochemical system in the amygdala. bibl il Science 198:423-5 O 28 '77
GALLAGHER, Patricia Shinnick-. See Shinnick-Gallagher, P.
GALLAGHER, Thomas
View from the 44th precinct; interview. Sat R 4:16-17 Mr 19 '77

GALLANT, Mavis
Doctor; story. New Yorker 53:33-42 Je 20 '77
Potter; story. New Yorker 53:36-44 Mr 21 '77
GALLATIN, A. pseud
Up, up and away! The U.S. debt. Read Digest 111:107-9 S '77
GALLÉ, Émile
Gallé: transcendence in glass or wood. H. Littleton. il Craft Horiz 37:32-6+ Ag '77 *
GALLEONS. See Sailing vessels
GALLERIES and museums, Art. See Art galleries and museums
GALLEY equipment. See Boats—Equipment
GALLEYS (boats) See Boats—Galleys
GALLIGAN, Edward L.
Impolite speculations on higher education. Educ Digest 43:50-2 O '77
GALLINA, Gino
Victim no. 21. Time 110:39 N 21 '77 *
GALLING, Walter
Hotel in Rome with a name people remember. il Fortune 96:219-20 Ag '77
Man who saved Havanas. il pors Fortune 95: 174-6 F '77
GALLIUM sulfide
Anomalous temperature dependence for a partial vapor pressure. J. A. Roberts, Jr and A. W. Searcy. bibl il Science 196:525-7 Ap 29 '77
GALLMAN, Alice
Triumph of Alice Gallman. il por Good H 185:148-9+ N '77
GALLO, Vincent
Miracle of the reborn bells. C. W. Moodie. il por Read Digest 111:9-12+ N '77 *
GALLO, Vincent A.
Career education—the California R.O.P.—revisited. bibl Clearing H 51:26-9 S '77
GALLOGLY, Stephen J.
Workers on long hours and premium pay, May 1976. il M Labor R 100:42-5 My '77
GALLOWAY, Charles M.
Interpersonal relations and education. Educ Digest 42:42-4 My '77
GALLOWAY, L. Thomas. See McAteer, J. D. jt auth
GALLUP, Gordon G. Jr
Self-awareness: humans are not alone. il Sci N 111:340 My 28 '77 *
GALLUZZO, Tony
Movie making. See issues of Modern photography
GALLWEY, W. Timothy
How to overcome self-doubt and think your way to total confidence; ed by C. Seebohm. il House & Gard 149:22+ D '77
Playing the inner game of working, living; interview. por Mademoiselle 83:203+ Ap '77
—and Kriegel, Robert
Fear of skiing; excerpt from Inner skiing. il pors Psychol Today 11:78-9+ N '77
about
Inner gamesman. G. Lichtenstein. por Psychol Today 11:86+ N '77 *
GALSTON, Arthur William
Bios (cont) Natur Hist 86:94-7 N '77
GALTON, Lawrence
Nervous stomach and what to do about it. Harp Baz 110:127+ Mr '77
GALTON, Peter M. See Olsen, P. E. jt auth
GALUB, Jack
MAST to the rescue. il Pop Mech 148:88-91+ O '77
GALVESTON
Banks
See Banks and banking—Texas
GALVIN, Brendan
Glass; poem. New Yorker 53:30 Ag 29 '77
North-northeast; poem. New Yorker 53:130 My 16 '77
Photo of miners; poem. New Yorker 53:100 My 2 '77
about
Comment. E. Butscher. Poetry 130:167-8 Je '77 *
GALVIN, Hoyt R. and Ashbury, B. N.
Public library building in 1977. il Lib J 102: 2402-9 D 1 '77
GALVIN, James
Lemon ode for Neruda. Nation 225:342 O 8 '77
Notes for the first line of a Spanish poem. Nation 224:629 My 21 '77
Rosary of conspiracies; poem. Nation 225:502 N 12 '77
Something to save us; poem. Nation 224:758 Je 18 '77
Stone's throw; poem. Nation 225:246 S 17 '77
That falling we fall; poem. Nation 224:534 Ap 30 '77
GALVIN, Thomas J.
Elizabeth T. Fast: a tribute. SLJ 24:15 S '77
—and Kent, Allen
Use of a university library collection: a progress report on a Pittsburgh study. Lib J 102:2317-20 N 15 '77
GALWAY Blazer II (boat) See Sailboats

GAMBIA
See also
Villages—Gambia

Genealogy

Limits of faction. K. L. Woodward and A. Collings. il por Newsweek 89:87 Ap 25 '77
My search for roots; excerpt. A. Haley. il por Read Digest 110:148-52 Ap '77
Roots; condensation; reprint of 1974 article. A. Haley. il Read Digest 110:153-79 Ap; 145-68 My '77

GAMBLE, Bertin Clyde
Fierce palace politics at Gamble-Skogmo. il por Bus W p80+ Jl 11 '77 *

GAMBLE-Skogmo, Inc
Fierce palace politics at Gamble-Skogmo. il por Bus W p80+ Jl 11 '77

GAMBLER; opera. See Prokof'ev, S. S.

GAMBLING
Atlantic City gambles on casinos. D. Schlossberg. il Travel 148:50-1+ O '77
Atlantic City: soon to be Las Vegas of the East. D. L. Battle. il U.S. News 83:40-1 Ag 22 '77
Big gamble; Atlantic City. D. Pauly and M. Reese. il Newsweek 90:66-7 Ag 8 '77
Care to join our little old game? Professional Gamblers Invitational golf tournament. E. Shrake. il Sports Illus 47:16-18+ Ag 15 '77
Cashing in a sure thing; football tipster D. Sheridan. M. DelNagro. il Sports Illus 47:70+ D 5 '77
Gambling fever! il Changing T 31:36-8 S '77
Gambling goes legit. il Read Digest 110:180-2+ Mr '77
Guy with the edge; D. Sorkin's guilty plea in sports betting larceny case. P. Axthelm. il por Newsweek 90:57 O 3 '77
Las Vegas: city built by losers; excerpt from Inside Las Vegas. M. Puzo. il Holiday 58:32-3+ Ap '77
More cities going on gambling spree? il U.S. News 84:53 Ja 9 '78
Picking winners; football predictions of D. Sheridan. L. Linderman. por Esquire 88:177-8+ D '77
States muscle in on the numbers game. il Bus W p 113-14 My 9 '77
Taking the risk out of gambling; Harrah's casinos. J. Quirt. il Time 110:78 N 21 '77
Tips from a fearsome foursome; handicapping the college bowl games. P. Axthelm. il Newsweek 91:44-5 Ja 2 '78
Trouble in Las Vegas East; casino gambling in Atlantic City, N.J. il Time 111:14-15 Ja 16 '78
See also
Blackjack (game)
Horse race betting
Lotteries

International aspects

Why gambling is world's no. 1 growth industry. il U.S. News 82:86-90 Ap 11 '77

Taxation

Taxman cometh. S. T. Atlas and G. C. Lubenow. Newsweek 90:64+ Jl 11 '77

Great Britain

Her majesty's bookies; Ladbroke Group. G. Smith. il Forbes 119:67-8 Mr 15 '77

Russia

Where gambling helps good causes. U.S. News 82:89 Ap 11 '77

United States

See Gambling

GAMBLING machines

Manufacture

Big spender hits Atlantic City; Bally Mfg. Corp. il Bus W p47 Ap 18 '77
Jackpot for Bally? T. O'Hanlon. il Forbes 119: 57-61 Ja 15 '77
Pinball wisdom; investing in Bally Manufacturing. A. Tobias. Esquire 88:24+ O '77

GAMBOA, George J. See Breed, M. D. jt auth

GAMBUSIAS
Big Bend gambusia: . . . then there were three. J. M. Schlatter. il Nat Parks & Con 51:8-10 N '77

GAME
See also
Cookery—Game
Hunting

Food and feeding

Tall oaks and fat squirrels. L. Line. Field & S 82:110 N '77

GAME, Dressing of
Deer hunter's handbook to field dressing, skinning, & butchering. B. Dalrymple. il Outdoor Life 160:93-9 N '77

GAME, Photography of. See Photography of animals

GAME bird shooting
He did not go gentle; Oregon game bird shooting. M. Baughman. il Sports Illus 47:66+ O 3 '77
Settling down in Texas; bird hunting at McFaddin Ranch. V. Kraft. il Sports Illus 47:74+ N 21 '77
Tough shots. B. Brister. Field & S 82:32+ D '77
See also
Duck shooting
Goose shooting
Grouse shooting
Mourning dove shooting
Pheasant shooting
Quail shooting
Rail shooting
Water bird shooting
Woodcock shooting

Anecdotes, facetiae, satire, etc.

Catching flies and the art of wingshooting. R. Starnes. il Outdoor Life 160:8+ N '77

GAME birds
Enemies of gamebirds. C. Elliott. il Outdoor Life 160:74-7+ S '77
See also
Cookery—Game
Grouse
Water birds

Breeding

Hobby becomes thriving enterprise; Marsh Manufacturing, Inc. V. Louviere. Nations Bus 65:60 Je '77

GAME birds in art. See Birds in art

GAME calls. See Animal calling

GAME laws
Baiting laws are a mess; waterfowl baiting. J. Phillips. il Outdoor Life 159:63-5+ Je '77
Boy who fired too soon; game law violated by goose shooter; excerpt from Halt! I'm a federal game warden. W. J. Parker and C. Robinson. il Read Digest 111:170-4 S '77
Great crow confusion. R. Starnes. por Outdoor Life 159:12+ Mr '77
Hunt Alaska now; state laws and wildlife populations. J. Rearden. il Field & S 82:60-1+ Ag '77
Hunting seasons 1977-1978. Outdoor Life 160:44+ S '77
Indians and the courts: allies against wildlife; question of applying fish and game laws to Indians. R. Starnes. il Outdoor Life 159:8+ Je '77
Twilight for lead shot? regulations designed to reduce number of waterfowl dying of lead poisoning. J. Phillips. il Outdoor Life 160:90-1+ Ag '77
See also
Poaching
Trapping—Laws and regulations

GAME preserves
See also
Shooting preserves

GAME protection
See also
Conservation officers
Game laws
Game wardens
Wildlife conservation

GAME ranches. See Ranches

GAME shows. See Television programs—Game shows

GAME wardens
See also
Roberts, C.

Anecdotes, facetiae, satire, etc.

Sneed. P. F. McManus. il Field & S 82:98+ N '77

GAMELAN music. See Music, Balinese

GAMES, Lew
Case of the murderess cat; ed by J. Carmichel. il Outdoor Life 159:58-9+ Mr '77

GAMES
41 games for the family—some new, some old. il Changing T 31:10-12 D '77
Fun machines; sports games. R. Cantwell. il Sports Illus 47:24-9 Jl 4 '77
Games people play. E. Bilgore. il House & Gard 149:128+ N '77
Games people play: 1977. il Time 110:62-3+ D 26 '77
Selection of games, puzzles and toys: sidelines that educate and entertain. D. Maryles. il Pub W 211:41-52 Mr 7 '77
Water relays. D. Pick. Camp Mag 49:11+ F '77
What kids can do on a rainy day . . . on a sunny day. M. R. Skrocki. il McCalls 104:72-3 Ag '77
See also
Backgammon
Billiards
Chess
Croquet
Educational games
Electronic games

GAMES—See also—*Continued*
Frisbee (game)
Pinball machines
Puzzles
Table tennis
War games

Manufacture

Gabriel plays a new game and wins hands down. por Duns R 109:20-1 Mr '77

GAMES, Mathematical. See Mathematical recreations

GAMMA ray detectors. See Detectors

GAMMA rays
First gamma-ray sky catalog. D. E. Thomsen. il Sci N 112:14 Jl 2 '77
Gamma-ray stars. il Sky & Tel 54:192-3 S '77

GAMMON, Clive
Bad show at the mud hole. Sports Illus 46:36-8+ Je 6 '77
Boxing. Sports Illus 47:52+ Ag 15 '77
Cosmos reach their goal. il Sports Illus 47:14-17 S 5 '77
Fish story that was all too true. il Sports Illus 46:56-9+ F 14 '77
Nothing but blue skies does Woosnam see. il por Sports Illus 46:38-40+ My 30 '77
Recovery from *kulturschock.* il pors Sports Illus 46:28-9 Je 13 '77
Slim pickings at the cabbage patch. il Sports Illus 47:26-8+ O 24 '77
Soccer. il Sports Illus 47:59-60 Jl 11 '77

GAMMON, Max
Gammon's black holes. M. Friedman. por Newsweek 90:84 N 7 '77 *

GAMMON, Tim
Black freedmen of the Cherokee Nation. bibl il Negro Hist Bull 40:732-5 Jl '77

GAMMONS, Peter
Baseball (cont) Sports Illus 46:53+ My 16; 47 Je 27; 47:38-9 Ag 1; 40-1 Ag 15; 37-9 Ag 22; 62+ S 26; 83+ N 14 '77
Bird flaps again and doesn't flop. il por Sports Illus 46:20-1 Je 6 '77
Bumper crop of boys from the farm. il Sports Illus 46:24-6 Mr 28 '77
Chi, oh my! il Sports Illus 47:8-13 Jl 25 '77
College hockey. il Sports Illus 46:65-6 Ap 4 '77
Hockey (cont) Sports Illus 46:49-50 F 14; 54-5 F 21; 50+ Mr 7; 52+ Mr 14; 72+ Ap 25; 78+ My 2; 47:86+ O 31; 102+ D 5 '77; 48:76-7 Ja 9 '78
Hockey 1977-78: scouting reports. il Sports Illus 47:42-4+ O 17 '77
Just what the doctor ordered. il Sports Illus 47:22-3 N 21 '77
Stating their case. il Sports Illus 46:16-19 My 9 '77
They ruined the Bruins. il Sports Illus 46:24-7 My 23 '77
They saved the best for the very last. il Sports Illus 46:26-7 Ap 11 '77
Wherever you find Orr, he glitters. il pors Sports Illus 46:20-1 Ja 24 '77
Wild Willie gets a new lease on life. il pors Sports Illus 47:28-30+ N 28 '77

about

Letter from the publisher. J. Meyers. por Sports Illus 46:6 My 9 '77 *

GAMPER, Howard B. and others
DNA strand scission by benzo[*a*]pyrene diol epoxides. bibl il Science 197:671-4 Ag 12 '77

GAMSON, Annabelle
Annabelle Gamson: Gamson dances Isadora; interview, ed by J. Dunning. il pors Dance Mag 51:47-50 F '77

about

Isadora's dances. J. Maskey. por Hi Fi 27: MA10 Ap '77 *

GANDHI, Indira (Nehru)
Mrs Gandhi: relief but few regrets; interview, ed by L. Malkin and K. K. Sharma. por Time 110:30 S 12 '77
They are afraid of me; excerpts from interview, ed by H. Jensen. por Newsweek 90:49 S 12 '77

about

Closing in on Mrs Gandhi. R. K. Manoff. Nation 225:355-6 O 15 '77 *
Coup that failed. R. Manoff. Nation 224:550-1 My 7 '77 *
Deft re-entry. il por Time 110:39 Ag 15 '77 *
Department of amplification (cont) V. Mehta. New Yorker 53:67-8+ My 9 '77 *
Election—at last. il por Time 109:32-3 Ja 31 '77 *
Empress in distress. il por Time 110:37 O 17 '77 *
Fall of the Gandhis—mixed blessing for India? il por U.S. News 82:31-2 Ap 4 '77 *
Good news from India. New Repub 176:5-6 Ap 2 '77 *
Ill winds batter Indira Gandhi. il por Time 109: 34-5 Mr 21 '77 *
India: a bungled arrest. R. Carroll and others. il por Newsweek 90:53-4 O 17 '77 *
India after Indira. A. Demig and others. il pors Newsweek 89:32-3+ Ap 4 '77 *
India and Indira Gandhi. N. Cousins. Sat R 4:4 Ap 30 '77 *
India: back in touch. il por Sr Schol 109:20-1 My 5 '77 *
India without Indira. Chr Cent 94:347-8 Ap 13 '77 *
India's election: backing into the future. L. I. Rudolph and S. H. Rudolph. For Affairs 55: 836-53 Jl '77 *
India's game of surprises. H. Jensen. il por Newsweek 89:41+ Mr 21 '77 *
India's net closes. H. Jensen. il pors Newsweek 90:46 S 12 '77 *
Indira Gandhi's day of reckoning. America 136: 282 Ap 2 '77 *
Indira's defeat. R. Watson and H. Jensen. por Newsweek 89:40 Mr 28 '77 *
Indira's sure thing. F. Willey. il por Newsweek 89:52-3 Ja 31 '77 *
Letter from New Delhi. V. Mehta. New Yorker 53:119-22+ O 17 '77 *
Mrs Gandhi changes trains. Nation 224:132 F 5 '77 *
Mrs Gandhi's defectors. A. Deming. il Newsweek 89:45+ F 14 '77 *
Morarji in charge. M. Kondracke. New Repub 177:10-12 O 22 '77 *
New Delhi notebook. P. Gupte. Nation 224:649-52 My 28 '77 *
Notes and comment. New Yorker 53:27-8 Ap 4 '77 *
One cheer for Indira Gandhi. Chr Cent 94: 163-4 F 23 '77 *
Opposition strikes back. il por Time 109:37-8 F 14 '77 *
Powerful vote for freedom. il por Time 109:30-1 Ap 4 '77 *
Price India pays for Indira Gandhi's reforms. J. N. Wallace. il por U.S. News 82:37-40 Ja 24 '77 *
Rebels' rally. il por Time 111:30 Ja 16 '78 *
Reporter at large. V. Mehta. New Yorker 52:56-60+ F 14 '77 *
Son also rises. F. Willey. il pors Newsweek 89:36 F 28 '77 *
Travels with Indira. R. Ramanuiam. Newsweek 90:67+ N 14 '77 *
Uniting against Indira. il por Time 109:37-8 Mr 7 '77 *

GANDHI, Mohandas Karamchand
Special people. R. Rodale. il pors Org Gard & Farm 24:54-8 Jl '77 *

GANDHI, Sanjay
Closer to Indira. il por Time 110:29 S 5 '77 *
Closing in on Sanjay. F. Willey and others. il por Newsweek 89:64 My 2 '77 *
Family affairs. por Newsweek 89:56 Ap 11 '77 *
India's crown prince. W. Borders. il por N Y Times Mag p 13-15+ F 13 '77 *
India's net closes. H. Jensen. il pors Newsweek 90:46 S 12 '77 *
Sanjay in the dock. K. Willenson and R. Ramanujam. il por Newsweek 90:45 S 5 '77 *
Son also rises. F. Willey. il pors Newsweek 89:36 F 28 '77 *

GANDOLF, Ray
This program is a real eye-opener. M. Ludtke. il por Sports Illus 46:42 F 14 '77 *

GANGES, Roland G. See Miller, M. E. jt auth

GANGES River
Consensus adopted on Ganges Waters dispute between Bangladesh, India. UN Chron 13:35-6 D '76

GANGLIOSIDOSIS
GM_2 ganglioside lysosomal storage disease in cats with β-hexosaminidase deficiency. L. C. Cork and others. bibl il Science 196:1014-17 My 27 '77

GANGS
Civil war in Chinatown; San Francisco. D. A. Williams and others. il Newsweek 90:39 S 26 '77
Cripplers in the war zone. il Time 110:20 Jl 11 '77
New gangs of Chinatown; New York City. B. Rice. il Psychol Today 10:60-1+ My '77
Rumble this time. W. Miller. il por Psychol Today 10:52-4+ My '77
Savage skulls. J. Bradshaw. il Esquire 87: 74-83+ Je '77
Violence starts at home; study by Jack Friedman. N. Napp. Psychol Today 10:131 Ap '77

GANN, Ernest K.
Around Cape Horn the easy way. il por map Flying 101:69-72+ Jl; 56-9+ Ag '77
Thirty-three hours that changed the world. il por Sat R 4:7-10 Ap 16 '77

about

Time machine. S. Wilkinson. il Flying 101:210-15 S '77 *

GANNETT, Deborah (Sampson)
More on Deborah Sampson. C. C. Ritter. il Am Hist Illus 12:28-9 N '77 *

GANNON, Francis X.
Emerging national consensus on energy policy; address, November 29, 1976. Vital Speeches 43:181-6 Ja 1 '77
Latin America and Europe—today. Américas 29:29 O '77
Stalemate or catalyst? il Américas 29:2-6 S '77

GANNON, Robert
Alaska pipeline. il Pop Sci 210:90-3 Ap '77
GANS, Carl, and Baic, Dusan
Regional specialization of reptilian scale surfaces: relation of texture and biologic role. bibl il Science 195:1348-50 Mr 25 '77
GANSLER, Jacques S.
Let's change the way the Pentagon does business. il Harvard Bus R 55:109-18 My '77
GANTT, David G. and others
Hominoid enamel prism patterns. bibl il Science 198:1155-7 D 16 '77
GAP junctions. See Junctions (physiology)
GARAGE doors
Bifolding doors were the answer. il Sunset 158:92 F '77
Control
Radio opener for garage doors. R. G. Beason. il Mech Illus 73:148+ N '77
GARAGE storage platforms. See Platforms
GARAGES
Between trips, storing the RV. il Sunset 158:116 My '77
Carport on the shop. il Farm J 101:F1 Ja '77
Detached carport with storage, too. A. S. Jetter. il Mech Illus 73:69-70 Mr '77
Parking the garage. N. Harris. New Repub 176:21-4 F 19 '77
Step by step to building your own garage with a little help from your friends. D. Haupert. il Bet Hom & Gard 55:58-61 Ag '77
This convertible carport sometimes is a pass-through. il Sunset 158:84 F '77
See also
Automobile parking
GARAGES, Converted. See Houses, Remodeled
GARAGES, Municipal
Avoiding parking garage design errors. il Am City & County 92:65 Ag '77
Parking deck saves money with tube columns and weathering steel. il Archit Rec 161:143-4 Je '77
GARAI, Gábor
Vigil at dawn; poem, tr by D. Hoffman. New Repub 176:30 Mr 26 '77
GARBAGE. See Refuse and refuse disposal
GARBAGE as fuel. See Refuse as fuel
GARBAGE dumps. See Municipal dumps
GARBAGE trucks. See Refuse collection trucks
GARBER, Marjorie
Coming of age in Shakespeare. Yale R 66:517-33 Je '77
GARDEN, Alexander
Dr Garden's wonderfully scented and almost imaginary namesake; excerpt from Species of eternity. J. Kastner. il Horticulture 55:64 N '77 *
GARDEN benches. See Benches
GARDEN carts. See Carts
GARDEN catalogs. See Catalogs, Seed and plant
GARDEN contests. See Gardening—Competitions
GARDEN design
See also
Landscape gardening
GARDEN equipment. See Garden tools, equipment, and supplies
GARDEN exhibits
Garden events in [month] (title varies) See issues of Sunset
GARDEN furniture. See Furniture, Outdoor
GARDEN hose
Garden hoses and nozzles. il Consumers Res Mag 60:32-6 Ag '77
GARDEN houses, shelters, etc.
Build PM's everything shed. M. McClintock. il Pop Mech 147:121-4+ Ap '77
How to build your own summerhouse. J. Fanning. il House & Gard 149:185 F '77
Pitch a room outdoors; screen houses. il Pop Mech 148:94-5 Jl '77
Romantic fantasy; gazebo. J. B. Reiter. il House B 119:26-7 Ag '77
Shelf-screen makes a work center. il Sunset 158:249 Mr '77
Storage sheds. Consumer Rep 42:203-6 D '77
Their garden work center is a bunker of railroad ties. il Sunset 158:260 Ap '77
GARDEN huckleberries
Instant fruit—it's hard to ask more. B. Fisher. il Org Gard & Farm 24:74-5 Je '77
GARDEN literature
See also
Publishers and publishing—Garden literature
GARDEN of Allah (hotel) See Hollywood, Calif.—Hotels, restaurants, etc.
GARDEN ornaments
Sculpture cut to your taste; commissioning art work for a garden ornament. A. Ogden. House B 119:10+ Ap '77
See also
Trellises
GARDEN paths. See Garden walks
GARDEN pests. See Insects, Injurious and beneficial
GARDEN pools
Backyard fountains; septic-tank fountain, bathtub waterfall. C. Stem and W. Gerler. il Pop Sci 210:126 My '77
Dig it: lily pools. L. Riotte and C. Riotte. il Am Home 80:20-1 Jl '77
Home for fish, snails, aquatic plants. il Sunset 159:140 Jl '77
GARDEN power equipment. See Garden tools, equipment, and supplies
GARDEN rooms
Garden room for a beach house. il Sunset 158:125 Je '77
Live-in plants. il House & Gard 149:162-7 O '77
This used to be their old bare backyard; greenhouse room. il Sunset 159:176-7 O '77
Vestibule garden room. il Bet Hom & Gard 55:270-1 N '77
GARDEN sculpture. See Garden ornaments
GARDEN theater. See Theater, Open-air
GARDEN tillers. See Cultivators
GARDEN tools, equipment, and supplies
4 PM projects for successful summer gardening. M. McClintock. il Pop Mech 147:96-9 Mr '77
Greenhouse frame, water wand; using polyvinyl chloride pipe. il Sunset 158:256+ My '77
Turn your gardening into a power trip. E. McDonald. House B 119:54-5+ Je '77
20 new work-saving garden tools. il Pop Mech 147:121-3 Mr '77
What the serious compost maker needs is a good sifter. il Sunset 158:232 Mr '77
See also
Cultivators
Garden hose
Hoes
Indoor gardening—Equipment and supplies
Lawn tools, equipment, and supplies
Lime spreaders
Pruning apparatus and equipment
Spraying apparatus
Maintenance and repair
Garden tool shape-up. Bet Hom & Gard 55:64 Ap '77
Now's the time to recondition garden tools for an active spring. J. Robinson. il Pop Sci 210:118-19 Mr '77
Manufacture
Old folks at work; Fertl, Inc. S. T. Atlas and M. Reese. il por Newsweek 90:64 S 26 '77
GARDEN tractors. See Tractors
GARDEN walks
Garden walk is wood blocks. il Sunset 159:119 S '77
Instant patio or path. V. D. Chase. il Am Home 80:95 Ap '77
Landscape idea collection—pathways in Mexico. il Sunset 159:178-9 O '77
GARDENIAS
Dr Garden's wonderfully scented and almost imaginary namesake; excerpt from Species of eternity. J. Kastner. il Horticulture 55:64 N '77
GARDENING
Carefree gardener. R. W. Langer. il N Y Times Mag p24-7+ Mr 13 '77
Culture & notes. See issues of Horticulture
8-hour garden. il House & Gard 149:164-5 My '77
Garden calendar. M. Franz. See issues of Organic gardening and farming
Gardener's notes. J. Fanning. See issues of House & garden incorporating Living for young homemakers
Gardening in [month] See issues of Better homes and gardens
Gardening tips you can use this fall. Farm J 101:B1 O '77
Good start for bedding plants. il Sunset 158:270 My '77
It's back to the soil for millions of home gardeners. il U.S. News 82:66-7 Mr 28 '77
[Month] in the garden. D. Fell. See issues of Horticulture
[Month] in your garden. See issues of Sunset
New leaf. L. Nathanson. il Am Home 80:38 Jl '77
Old wisdom for new gardens; excerpt from Old wives' lore for gardeners. B. Boland and M. Boland. il House & Gard 149:80+ My '77
Retirement gardening; symposium. il Org Gard & Farm 24:104-12 My '77
Summer garden sampler; excerpt from A joy of gardening. V. M. Sackville-West. il Horticulture 55:16-17 Jl '77
See also
Artificial light gardening
Bulbs
Catalogs, Seed and plant
Cold frames
Container gardening
Cover crops
Fertilizers and manures
Floriculture
Fruit culture
Grafting
Greenhouses
Herbs
Horticulture

GARDENING—See also—*Continued*
Indoor gardening
Irrigation
Landscape gardening
Lawns
Nurseries (horticulture)
Organic gardening
Plant propagation
Plants, Protection of
Pruning
Seeds
Spraying and dusting
Tillage
Vegetable gardening
Watering of gardens, lawns, etc.
Weeds

Anecdotes, facetiae, satire, etc.

Questions & answers. A. Buchwald. Horticulture 55:2-3 My '77
When in knead. . . R. Baker. il N Y Times Mag p4 My 29 '77

Bibliography

Green-thumb reading. J. Fanning. House & Gard 149:72+ Ap '77

Competitions

Everything's coming up sunflowers! il Org Gard & Farm 24:174 Ap '77
Garden contest winners for 1976. il Sunset 158: 112-13 Ap '77

Equipment and supplies

See Garden tools, equipment and supplies

Planting plans and tables

See also
Vegetable gardening—Planting plans and tables

Safety devices and measures

Your garden: lovely to look at, but is it safe? W. H. Weiss. il Ret Liv 17:19-20 Ag '77

Study and teaching

Gardening school, Swiss style; Gärtnerinnen-Schule Hünibach. R. Wolf. il Org Gard & Farm 25:160+ Ja '78

Therapeutic use

Green-thumb cure for hospital fears; plant therapy. J. Horn. Psychol Today 11:99 Jl '77

California

Water-short gardening; northern California. il Sunset 158:126-9 Ap '77
See also
Organic gardening—California

United States

See Gardening

GARDENING by children. See Childrens gardens

GARDENING literature. See Garden literature

GARDENS
Garden is a song of praise; interview, ed by C. Seebohm. R. Page. il por House & Gard 149:92-7+ Jl '77
My secret garden. M. R. Carter. Mademoiselle 83:142-3 Jl '77
Romance of a walled garden. il House & Gard 149:158-9 Ap '77
See also
Balcony gardens, roof gardens, etc.
Botanical gardens
Childrens gardens
Community gardens
Terrariums

Color

Something's always in bloom. B. Garrett and others. il Bet Hom & Gard 55:120-5 Ap '77

Belgium

Rubens' garden. A. Eliot. il Horticulture 55:52+ My '77

California

J. Paul Getty's legacy: what is in store for the garden of the billionaire's whim? A. Eliot. il Horticulture 55:10-13 N '77
Turning steep land into gardens. T. Gettings. il Org Gard & Farm 24:57-60 Ap '77
Water-frugal garden in Pasadena; R. Ross' garden. il Sunset 159:76-7 Jl '77
See also
Los Angeles—Gardens
Sacramento, Calif.—Gardens
San Diego, Calif.—Gardens

England

Lunatic asylum; excerpt from My garden in spring. E. A. Bowles. Horticulture 55:72-5 F '77
Midsummer feast: English gardens with Kenneth for your guide; Hidcote and Sissinghurst. Kenneth. bibl il por House & Gard 149:48+ Jl '77
Sackville-West's Sissinghurst: a garden of surprising privacies. A. Eliot. bibl il Horticulture 55:12-15 Jl '77

Long Island

Stand up and garden; Jack Lenor Larsen's garden. il House & Gard 149:120-1 D '77

Maryland

Paca House garden restored. S. Wright. bibl il Antiques 111:172-3 Ja '77

Massachusetts

Five great gardens. K. Bast. il Horticulture 55:28+ Mr '77

New Jersey

Look what's happened to the backyard; Princeton garden of Paul and Mary Ritts. il House & Gard 149:106-7+ F '77

New York (state)

See also
Gardens—Long Island
New York (city)—Gardens

Pennsylvania

For next year's garden: plant ahead; perennial garden of John B. Leake family. il House & Gard 149:142-5 S '77
Glory to the flowers; Longwood Gardens. il House & Gard 149:106-9 D '77

GARDENS, Childrens. See Childrens gardens

GARDENS, Community. See Community gardens

GARDENS, Desert
Ancient crops for desert gardens. G. P. Nabhan and R. S. Felger. il Org Gard & Farm 24:34+ F '77

GARDENS, Herb. See Herbs

GARDENS, Hillside
It just won't work in Los Angeles. il Sunset 158:90-3 Mr '77
New life for neglected land; symposium. il Org Gard & Farm 24:56-71 Ap '77

GARDENS, Indoor
Rise and fall of the Roman house plant; world's first indoor gardens unearthed in Pompeii. A. Menen. il Horticulture 55:26-9 D '77

GARDENS, Rock
Anyplace rock gardens. L. L. Foster. il Am Home 80:54-5+ S '77
Flowers for a rock wall garden; crevice gardens. P. Harper. il Horticulture 55:20-3 Je '77
Gardening on the rocks. il House & Gard 149: 90-1 Ag '77
How to turn a slope into a rock garden. B. Garrett and R. O'Harra. il Bet Hom & Gard 54:40-1 Ag '76
It just won't work in Los Angeles. il Sunset 158:90-3 Mr '77
Rock garden that earns its keep; J. U. Crockett's garden. il por House & Gard 150:94-5+ Ja '78
Taming the steepest slopes. S. Chappell. il Org Gard & Farm 24:60-1 Ap '77
See also
Rock plants

GARDENS, Roof. See Balcony gardens, roof gardens, etc.

GARDENS, Vegetable. See Vegetable gardening

GARDENS, Watering of. See Watering of gardens, lawns, etc.

GARDEY, Jon
Fire near the sun. il Sci Digest 82:8-10 N '77

GARDINER, John Rolfe
Going on like this; story. New Yorker 53:24-7 Ag 29 '77
Prior claim; story. New Yorker 53:33-5 D 19 '77

GARDNER, Betty
Hang a garden in your house. il Am Home 80:82+ Mr '77
Plants (cont) Am Home 80:22+ F '77

GARDNER, Hugh
McGovern vs. the farmers. il Nation 224:456-61 Ap 16 '77

GARDNER, Isabella
Telephone; poem. Poetry 130:208 Jl '77

GARDNER, Joann Evans. See Bonk, K. jt auth

GARDNER, John
Gang of Four and Chinese science. bibl il Bull Atom Sci 33:24-30 S '77

GARDNER, John Champlin, 1933-
Conversation with John Gardner; interview, ed by D. Edwards and C. Polsgrove. pors Atlantic 239:43-4+ My '77
John Gardner on fiction. New Repub 177:33-4 D 3 '77
Redemption; story. Atlantic 239:48-50 My '77
Southern Illinois. Vogue 167:156-7 Mr '77

GARDNER, John W.
Excerpt from statement on financing of campaigns, December 1976. Cong Digest 56:92+ Mr '77

about

Money for campaigns. K. Bode. New Repub 176:8+ F 19 '77 *

GARDNER, Martin
Great fakes of science. il Esquire 88:88-91 O '77
How logical are you? excerpt from Mathematical magic show. Read Digest 112:139-40 Ja '78
Mathematical games. See issues of Scientific American

GARDNER, Paul (soccer columnist)
Making soccer an American sport. il Horizon 20:76-81 N '77

GARDNER, Peter
(ed) See Wetering, J. van de. PW interviews

GARDNER, Sherwin
How much is enough? address, March 24, 1977. Vital Speeches 43:457-9 My 15 '77

GARDOZO, Yvette
St Augustine: old Spain in the New World. il Trav/Holiday 148:52-7 N '77

GAREY, L. J. and Blakemore, Colin
Monocular deprivation: morphological effects on different classes of neurons in the lateral geniculate nucleus. bibl il Science 195:414-16 Ja 28 '77

GARFIELD, R. E. and others
Gap junctions: their presence and necessity in myometrium during parturition. bibl il Science 198:958-60 D 2 '77

GARFINCKEL, Brooks Brothers, Miller & Rhoads Inc. See Department stores

GARFINKEL, Perry
Computer readout translates body language into skills. il Sci Digest 81:12-14 Mr '77

GARIBALDI, Giuseppe
Anita and Giuseppe Garibaldi: a love story on two continents. G. Arciniegas. il pors Américas 29:2-7 My '77 *

GARIS, Robert
Dance. New Repub 177:29-31 Ag 20 '77

GARLIC
Garlic studied as a remedy; work of Alan Tsai. M. Clark. Sci Digest 81:31-2 Ap '77

GARLINGTON, Aubrey S. Jr
German romantic opera and the problem of origins. il Mus Q 63:247-63 Ap '77

GARLOCK, Ruthanne
Feminist power: the battle of Houston. il Chr Today 22:38-40 D 30 '77

GARMENT factories. See Clothing factories

GARMENT workers
New sweatshop; Bronx, N.Y. shop. M. Ruby and J. Concannon. il Newsweek 90:87 D 12 '77
See also
Amalgamated Clothing and Textile Workers Union

GARN, Edwin Jacob
Debating abortion. Nat R 29:1299+ N 11 '77
Should U.S recognize Peking? interview. pors U.S. News 83:27-8 Ag 29 '77
Welfare reform; address, April 1, 1977. Vital Speeches 43:484-7 Je 1 '77

GARN, Jake. See Garn, E. J.

GARNER, Alan
Letter from England: a matter of balance; Stone book. A. Chambers. Horn Bk 53:479-82 Ag '77 *

GARNER, Arthur E. See Haynes, A. F. Jr, jt auth

GARNER, Erroll
Jazz. W. Balliett. New Yorker 53:98 F 21 '77 *

GARNER, Fradley
Lost Norse mystery. il Oceans 10:4-9 Mr '77

GARNER, Louis E. Jr
Solid state. See issues of Popular electronics including Electronics world

GARNETS
First occurrence of the garnet-ilmenite transition in silicates. L. G. Liu. bibl il Science 195:990-1 Mr 11 '77

GARNETT, William Ashford
Eye of Bill Garnett looks down on the commonplace and sees art. E. Park. il por Smithsonian 8:74-81 My '77 *

GARNISHES in cookery. See Cookery—Garnishes

GARRETT, Beverly
Down-to-earth guide to growing vegetables. il Bet Hom & Gard 55:91-7 Mr '77

GARRETT, Donald Everett
Budgeting for basics. por Forbes 119:118 Je 15 '77 *

GARRETT, Elisabeth Donaghy
History in houses. il Antiques 111:560-7 Mr '77
Living with antiques. il Antiques 111:990-1001 My; 112:514-21 S '77

GARRETT, Patrick Floyd
New Mexico incident. W. H. Hutchinson. bibl il pors Am West 14:4-7+ N '77 *

GARRETT, Stephen A.
Détente and the military balance. bibl il Bull Atom Sci 33:10-20 Ap '77
Morality at the water's edge. Commonweal 104:170-5 Mr 18 '77

GARRICK, Leslie D. and Lang, J. W.
Alligator revealed; with biographical sketches. il Natur Hist 86:6, 54-61 bibl(p92-3) Je '77

GARRISON, Bruce
Real estate without tears. por Forbes 119:57-8 Je 1 '77 *

GARRISON, Chuck
Bank of the giant sea bass. il Field & S 82:94-5+ My '77
Custom-caught big brown. il por Field & S 82:76+ Je '77

GARRISON, Peter
Your own worst enemy. il Flying 101:82+ N '77

GARRISON Diversion Unit. See Irrigation canals and ditches

GARRY, Fred W.
Crucial year for Rohr's survival. por Bus W p86-7 F 28 '77 *

GARTER snakes. See Snakes

GARTH, David
Prince maker strikes again. il por Time 110:19-20 N 21 '77 *
Rafshoon vs. Garth. J. Lelyveld. il pors N Y Times Mag p78 Ag 21 '77 *

GARTON, Leland
(ed) See Landon, M. Eugene Orowitz makes good

GARVER, Fred A. and others
Radioimmunoassay for abnormal hemoglobins. bibl il Science 196:1334-6 Je 17 '77

GARVER, Juliet
Elizabeth; drama. Plays 37:71-7 O '77

GARVEY, Edward R.
Finding square one. J. Marshall. por Sports Illus 46:63-4 Mr 7 '77 *

GARVEY, John
Death and therapy. Commonweal 104:471-3 Jl 22 '77
Man becomes God. il Commonweal 104:815-16+ D 23 '77

GARVEY, Kevin
Serpentine serenity of EST. Chr Today 21:13-15 Ja 21 '77

GARVIN, Clifton Canter, 1921-
Does Exxon have a future? J. Flanigan. il por Forbes 120:37-41 Ag 15 '77 *

GARWIN, Richard L.
Scientists and public policy, help or hindrance? excerpt from address, April 27, 1976. Phys Today 30:9+ F '77

GARWOOD, S. Gray
Name game: handle or handicap? il por Sci N 111:23 Ja 8 '77 *

GAS, Natural
See also
Gas industry
Gas supply
Liquefied natural gas

Laws and regulations

See Gas laws and regulations

Leases

See Oil and gas leases

Pipelines

Alaska natural gas transportation system; text of letter, September 1, 1977. J. Carter. Dept State Bull 77:479 O 10 '77
Alaskan gas: impact of pipeline on Canadian North stirs a debate. M. Panitch. map Science 195:1308-11 Mr 25 '77
Alaskan gas: NEPA brings out a strong new pipeline applicant. L. J. Carter. map Science 196:1068-70 Je 3 '77
Berger report: northern frontier, northern homeland; excerpt from Northern frontier, northern homeland; with editorial comments. T. R. Berger. il por maps Liv Wildn 41:3, 4-33 Ap '77
California's answer to an energy riddle; Canadian and Mexican gas. Bus W p24-5 Ag 22 '77
Canada: a major victory. R. C. Paehlke. map Environment 19:2-4 O '77
Canada: a northern pipeline. R. Paehlke. Environment 19:5+ Mr '77
Canada's pipeline battle. R. L. Moellering. il Chr Cent 94:982-5 O 26 '77
Cinderella's pipeline; Alcan Pipeline's winning route. A. J. Mayer and W. J. Cook. il por map Newsweek 90:87+ S 12 '77
Department testifies on Alcan project; statement, October 12, 1977. S. W. Bosworth. Dept State Bull 77:822-6 D 5 '77
Gas bonanza; Pemex' Mexican pipeline plan. S. T. Atlas and W. J. Cook. il map Newsweek 90:61-2 Ag 1 '77
Getting Alaska's gas to the lower 48; Alcan pipeline. map U.S. News 83:47 Ag 22 '77
Pemex wants dollars for a new gas line. il Bus W p42 My 23 '77
Piping Alaska's gas. D. Pauly and J. Bishop, Jr. map Newsweek 89:71 F 14 '77
Pressuring the U.S. over the price of gas; Pemex' Mexican pipeline. map Bus W p32 Ja 9 '78
Some relief on the distant horizon; proposed Alaskan pipelines. map Time 109:10-11 F 14 '77
U.S.-Canada agreement on natural gas pipeline; joint statement, message to Congress, with fact sheet, September 8, 22, 1977. P. E. Trudeau; J. Carter. map Dept State Bull 77:609-14 O 31 '77
Why Canadians want an Alcan gas route. map Bus W p20 Jl 18 '77
See also
Pipeline companies

Prices

See Gas, Natural—Rates

Prospecting

Lower 48. Time 110:50+ Ag 1 '77
See also
Pennzoil Company

GAS, Natural—*Continued*

Rates

Bard of oil; Rep R. Krueger's efforts on behalf of the petroleum industry lobby. T. Mathews and H. W. Hubbard. il por Newsweek 89:75-6 Je 20 '77
Blitz by Fritz; ending the gas deregulation filibuster. P. Goldman and others. por Newsweek 90:34+ O 17 '77
Carter on oil & gas: fudging away from a hard line. J. F. Flug. Nation 224:652-8 My 28 '77
Filibuster ends, but not the gas war. il por Time 110:10-11+ O 17 '77
Gas crisis: weather or Washington? M. Friedman. il Newsweek 89:69 F 28 '77
Gas: the Texas test. D. A. Williams and L. Donosky. il Newsweek 90:39 O 17 '77
Home for Christmas. R. Boeth and others. il por Newsweek 90:75-6 D 26 '77
How the winter of '77 started in the summer of '54. il Duns R 109:29-30 Mr '77
How to stop worrying about natural gas; with editorial comment. E. Faltermayer. il map Fortune 96:109, 156-9+ Ag '77
Just like the good old days. A. J. Mayer and others. il Newsweek 89:62+ Ja 24 '77
Needed more than ever: realistic gas pricing. A. J. Parisi. Bus W p 101 F 14 '77
Night of the long winds; Senate filibuster. il por Time 110:12-14 O 10 '77
Pressuring the U.S. over the price of gas; Pemex' Mexican pipeline. map Bus W p32 Ja 9 '78
Price of gas in Texas: Crystal City is cold. T. Brick. Nation 225:559-61 N 26 '77
Push to control OPEC gas. il Bus W p72-4 Ja 9 '78
Senator Byrd: more than just a manager. por Bus W p38 O 17 '77
Sky full of Learjets; gas industry and gas consumer lobbies. il Time 110:14 O 17 '77
They're giving us gas, all right; gas industry efforts to force deregulation through inaccurate reports of reserves. J. N. Miller. New Repub 176:15-17 F 12 '77
Wasted energy; passage of amendment to deregulate price of natural gas. Nat R 29:1220-1 O 28 '77
What natural gas shortage? B. Weidner. Progressive 41:19-23 Ap '77
When the gas stops; gas cut off in Crystal City, Tex. il Time 110:18 O 17 '77
Why Congress hasn't deregulated natural gas. B. Krueger. il por Nations Bus 65:24+ Ap '77
Why natural gas probably won't be deregulated. il Forbes 120:26 Ag 1 '77
Why utility rates will keep going up. il Changing T 31:41-4 F '77

Reserves

Giant gas gusher in Louisiana; Tuscaloosa Sand reserves. il map Time 110:71-2 D 5 '77
Reserves: the new math. A. J. Mayer and others. il Newsweek 89:71-3 Je 27 '77

Well drilling rigs

See Gas well drilling rigs

Alaska

Alaska natural gas transportation system; text of letter, September 1, 1977. J. Carter. Dept State Bull 77:479 O 10 '77
Alaskan gas: impact of pipeline on Canadian North stirs a debate. M. Panitch. map Science 195:1308-11 Mr 25 '77
Alaskan gas: NEPA brings out a strong new pipeline applicant. L. J. Carter. map Science 196:1068-70 Je 3 '77
Getting Alaska's gas to the lower 48; Alcan pipeline. map U.S. News 83:47 Ag 22 '77
Piping Alaska's gas. D. Pauly and J. Bishop, Jr. map Newsweek 89:71 F 14 '77
Some relief on the distant horizon. map Time 109:10-11 F 14 '77
Submarine seepage of natural gas in Norton Sound, Alaska. J. D. Cline and M. L. Holmes. bibl il map Science 198:1149-53 D 16 '77

Alberta

See Gas, Natural—Canada

Canada

Alberta finds itself a surplus of gas. Bus W p26 My 30 '77

Mexico

Gas bonanza; Pemex' Mexican pipeline plan. S. T. Atlas and W. J. Cook. il map Newsweek 90:61-2 Ag 1 '77
Pemex wants dollars for a new gas line. il Bus W p42 My 23 '77

Russia

Beware of Russians bearing gas. il Forbes 119:91+ Mr 15 '77

GAS and oil engines
See also
Automobile engines
Briggs and Stratton Corporation
Motor boat engines
Motorcycle engines
Outboard motors
Tractor engines

GAS appliances

Ignition

See Gas burners—Ignition

GAS Association, American. See American Gas Association

GAS burners
Make your own gas log. P. Troke. il Mech Illus 73:84+ F '77

Ignition

Whatchamacallit for lighting the burner or oven of a gas range. il Consumers Res Mag 60:33-4 S '77

GAS centrifugation. See Centrifugation

GAS companies
California's fight for the sun; attempt by gas industry to control solar energy. F. Branfman. Nation 224:749-51 Je 18 '77
How a business fights housing blight; Brooklyn Union Gas Co. V. Louviere. il Nations Bus 65:59 Je '77
Liquefied natural gas: bombs floating in our harbors; California. H. Rubin. Nation 225:557-9 N 26 '77
Telling students the truth about business; program at Southern California Gas Co. V. Louviere. il Nations Bus 65:67+ Mr '77

GAS detectors
Gas detector that really works. il Mech Illus 73:94 Ap '77

GAS distribution
NICOR: from gas distribution to total energy. por Duns R 110:22-3+ S '77

GAS-fired barbecues. See Barbecue grills

GAS furnaces
Good news for next heating season! R. A. Cutter. il Mech Illus 73:43-4+ Ap '77

GAS industry
Gas: the Texas test. D. A. Williams and L. Donosky. il Newsweek 90:39 O 17 '77
Go get it, fellows! il Forbes 119:25-7 Je 1 '77
Hidden gas: fresh doubts. M. Ruby and others. il Newsweek 89:66-7 F 28 '77
Price of gas in Texas: Crystal City is cold; Lo-Vaca Gathering Company. T. Brick. Nation 225:559-61 N 26 '77
Roy Huffington: life begins at 50: Huffington Inc's Indonesian gas project. J. Flanigan. por Forbes 120:28+ S 1 '77
Surplus of suspicion; natural gas production. il Time 109:60+ F 21 '77
Why the big shortage? D. Pauly and J. Bishop, Jr. il Newsweek 89:19-20 F 7 '77
See also
American Gas Association
El Paso Company
Gas companies

Export-import trade

High hurdles for imports. il Time 109:46 Mr 14 '77
Importation of liquefied natural gas. E. Drake and R. C. Reid. il map Sci Am 236:22-9 bibl(p 148) Ap '77

Finance

Out of foresight . . . opportunity; investment in oil and gas drilling ventures. il Forbes 119:23 F 15 '77

Regulation

See Gas laws and regulations

Australia

Australia: set to spend billions on liquefied gas. map Bus W p43-4 Mr 14 '77

France

Air Liquide protects its 80%. il Bus W p 170+ My 16 '77
Gazocéan's expensive flying in a new field. il Bus W p43-4 Jl 11 '77

GAS industry lobby. See Lobbyists and lobbying

GAS laws and regulations
Big energy buyers go straight to the source; law allowing industries to purchase gas directly from producers. il Bus W p27 Mr 7 '77
Energy policy starts to emerge. Bus W p30 F 28 '77
Gas crisis: weather or Washington? M. Friedman. Newsweek 89:69 F 28 '77
Icy grip tightens. il Time 109:6-11 F 14 '77
Infectious gas shortage. il Bus W p 100-1+ F 14 '77
Now, the gas crisis. R. Steele and others. il maps Newsweek 89:14-19 F 7 '77
Weather crisis. il U.S. News 82:11-13 F 7 '77
White House point man; J. Schlesinger. S. Fraker and J. Bishop. il por Newsweek 89:16 F 7 '77

GAS leases. See Oil and gas leases

GAS manufacture and works
See also
Coal gasification

GAS mileage, Automobile. See Automobile engines—Fuel consumption

GAS mileage, Motor vehicle. See Motor vehicle engines—Fuel consumption

GAS pipeline companies. See Pipeline companies
GAS pipelines. See Gas, Natural—Pipelines
GAS prices. See Gas, Natural—Rates
GAS reserves. See Gas, Natural—Reserves
GAS stations. See Automobile service stations
GAS supply
Big scramble to keep plants running. U.S. News 82:65 Mr 14 '77
Days dwindle down for a precious fuel. F. Kendig. il Sci Digest 82:44-6 O '77
Furnace? Yes! Boiler? no! il Forbes 120:31-2 O 1 '77
Gas: the Texas test. D. A. Williams and L. Donosky. il Newsweek 90:39 O 17 '77
Hidden gas: fresh doubts. M. Ruby and others. il Newsweek 89:66-7 F 28 '77
How the winter of '77 started in the summer of '54; natural-gas shortage. il Duns R 109:29-30 Mr '77
How to stop worrying about natural gas; with editorial comment. E. Faltermayer. il map Fortune 96:109, 156-9+ Ag '77
Icy grip tightens. il Time 109:6-11 F 14 '77
Irony of holding too much natural gas. Bus W p56+ Jl 25 '77
Just like the good old days. A. J. Mayer and others. il Newsweek 89:62+ Ja 24 '77
Long and short of gas supplies. Sci N 111:135+ F 26 '77
Luck runs out on natural gas. il Time 109:35-6 Ja 31 '77
Now, the gas crisis. R. Steele and others. il maps Newsweek 89:14-19 F 7 '77
Old-style winter disrupts the economy. il Bus W p44 Ja 31 '77
Primer on a fuel shortage that's growing worse. il U.S. News 82:14 F 7 '77
They're giving us gas, all right; gas industry efforts to force deregulation through inaccurate reports of reserves. J. N. Miller. New Repub 176:15-17 F 12 '77
What natural gas shortage? B. Weidner. Progressive 41:19-23 Ap '77
Wheedling extra gas out of the Southwest. Bus W p26-7 Mr 7 '77
Why propane fuel is harder to get. il Bus W p34 F 21 '77
Why the big shortage? D. Pauly and J. Bishop, Jr. il Newsweek 89:19-20 F 7 '77
Winter's tale. R. Steele. il map Newsweek 89:25 F 14 '77
Winter's toll: worse to come. il U.S. News 82:19-20 F 14 '77
Withholding gas? Nat R 29:315 Mr 18 '77
GAS turbines, Aircraft. See Airplane engines, Jet
GAS utilities. See Gas companies
GAS well drilling
See also
Gas, Natural—Prospecting
GAS well drilling rigs
One of our rigs is missing; Geological Survey report on sinking of Pennzoil's Platform A. J. G. Mitchell. Audubon 79:149-51 N '77
Pumping fuel under water. G. Taber. il Time 109:47 Mr 14 '77
GAS Works Park. See Seattle—Parks and playgrounds
GASCOIGNE, Bamber
Without religiosity, a September Morrow title examines Christianity's birth and growth. R. Dahlin. il Pub W 211:28 My 30 '77 *
GASCOIGNE, Christina
Without religiosity, a September Morrow title examines Christianity's birth and growth. R. Dahlin. il Pub W 211:28 My 30 '77 *
GASES
See also
Atmosphere
See also names of gases, e.g. Carbon dioxide

Industrial applications

Air Liquide protects its 80%. il Bus W p 170+ My 16 '77

Liquefaction

See also
Liquefied natural gas

Physiological effects

See also
Decompression sickness
GASES, Intergalactic. See Matter, Interstellar
GASES, Liquefied
See also
Liquefied natural gas
GASES, Rare
Primordial noble gases in chondrites: the abundance pattern was established in the solar nebula. L. Alaerts and others. bibl il Science 198:927-30 D 2 '77
GASIFICATION of coal. See Coal gasification
GASKIE, Margaret F.
Notes from the field: how architects, and their consultants approach solar design. il Archit Rec 162:108-13 mid-Ag '77

GASOLINE
All about gasoline. Changing T 31:45-7 O '77
Gasoline—facts, figures and forewarnings. D. R. Hart. il Motor B & S 139:16+ F '77
See also
Society of Independent Gasoline Marketers of America

Additives

Latest gasoline additive backfires. Consumer Rep 42:191 Ap '77
MMT: a gasoline additive that should be subtracted. Consumer Rep 42:441-3 Ag '77
MMT backfires as an octane booster; manganese additives. il Bus W p34 Ap 4 '77
Why getting the lead out may not be enough; MMT additives. R. Taylor. Car & Dr 23:28 Jl '77

Anti-knock and anti-knock mixtures

New octane race quietly revs up. il Bus W p38-9 Ja 31 '77
Return of red gas. R. L. Collins. Flying 100:15 My '77

Conservation

Recreation planning for energy conservation. S. M. Gold. il Parks & Rec 12:61-3+ S '77

Prices

Collusion at the gas pump: independents they are not. D. Zielenziger. Nation 224:551-4 My 7 '77
If people cut back on driving. . .how business will deal with it. il U.S. News 82:29-30 Je 6 '77
Wages of hoodwinking: little oil's slippery slope. D. Zielenziger. Nation 225:434-6 O 29 '77

Rationing

On energy: a modest proposal. R. Lekachman. Nation 225:659-60 D 17 '77

Taxation

Alternative to the taxation of gasoline consumption. M. Cetingok. Intellect 106:46-8 Ag '77
GASOLINE cans. See Cans
GASOLINE industry. See Petroleum industry—United States
GASOLINE-powered saws. See Saws
GASOLINE substitutes
See also
Alcohol as fuel
Automobile engines—Fuel
Methanol
GASQUE, W. Ward
Is man's purpose an enigma? Chr Today 21:15-17 Jl 29 '77
GASS, William H.
Statues; poem. New Yorker 53:48 D 5 '77
GASTON, Lyle K. and others
Controlling the pink bollworm by disrupting sex pheromone communication between adult moths. bibl il Science 196:904-5 My 20 '77
GASTROINTESTINAL tract. See Digestive system
GASTRONOMY
Dinner with the big boys; Lucullus Circle. C. Stinnett. il Atlantic 239:26-7 Ap '77
Love in the kitchen. il Time 110:54-8+ D 19 '77
Specialties of the house at the great clubs. il Fortune 95:150-5 F '77
See also
Food critics and criticism
Gluttony
GASTROPODS
Behavioral choice: neural mechanisms in pleurobranchaea. M. P. Kovac and W. J. Davis. bibl il Science 198:632-4 N 11 '77
Function of shell sculpture in marine gastropods: hydrodynamic destabilization in ceratostoma foliatum. A. R. Palmer. bibl il Science 197:1293-5 S 23 '77
See also
Abalones
Sea hares
Slugs
Snails
GATES, A. P.
Fertilizer slump weakens a strong man; Beker Industries Corp. por Bus W p38 F 14 '77 *
GATES, Elgin
If you call him old folks, be prepared to duck. V. Kraft. il por Sports Illus 47:34-6+ Ag 8 '77 *
GATES, Ralph
Rip-offs in faraway places. Changing T 31:37-8 D '77
GATES
Cable control for a driveway gate. J. Pond. il Pop Sci 210:160 My '77
GATES OF THE ARCTIC NATIONAL PARK (proposed) See National parks and reserves—Alaska
GATEWAY National Recreation Area. See Recreation areas
GATEWOOD, Willard B. Jr
Edward E. Cooper & 10 greatest Negroes of 1890. bibl por Negro Hist Bull 40:708-10 My '77
GATHERERS and hunters. See Hunters and gatherers

GATHERING; drama. See O'Brien, E.
GATI, Charles
Europeanization of communism? bibl f For Affairs 55:539-53 Ap '77
GAUCHOS
See also
Baretta, A.
GAUCHOS in literature. See Literature—Themes
GAUDIER-BRZESKA, Henri
Gaudier-Brzeska: a great unknown. E. Schwartz. il Art N 76:178+ N '77 *
GAUGE theories (physics) See Field theory (physics)
GAUGHAN, Norbert F.
God becomes man. il Commonweal 104:811-14 D 23 '77
GAULLE, Charles de
De Gaulle: the man behind the legend. por Read Digest 110:47-8+ Mr '77 *
GAUNT, Arthur
Ararat's mystery ship; with biographical sketch. il Sea Front 23:167-71, 190 My '77
GAUSS, Karl Friedrich
Gauss. I. Stewart. il por map Sci Am 237:122-31 bibl(p 154) Jl '77 *
GAUTHIER, Clarence Joseph
NICOR; from gas distribution to total energy. por Duns R 110:22-3+ S '77 *
GAUVIN, Aimé
As Baxter Park burns, so burns Maine. il maps Audubon 79:146-53 S '77
GAVAZZENI, Gianandrea
Pride of Bergamo. J. W. Freeman. por Opera N 41:30 Ap 9 '77 *
GAY, Ruth
Outwitting the final solution. il Horizon 19:42-7 Ja '77
GAY news. See London—Newspapers
GAYLIN, Jody
You are cordially invited to help save a life. il Psychol Today 10:108+ Mr '77
GAYLIN, Willard
Putting it back where it belongs. il Psychol Today 11:25 Je '77
GAYLORD, Alan T.
Master storyteller in search of a voice. Hi Fi 27:74-6 Je '77
GAYNOR, Lee
Paperback publishers approach a critical point in their use of broadcast advertising. il Pub W 212:36-8 D 5 '77
GAZEBOS. See Garden houses, shelters, etc.
GAZOCÉAN (firm) See Gas industry—France
GEAR bags. See Bags
GEARY, John D.
Irrigation, flood control, navigation and user taxes; address, May 6, 1977. Vital Speeches 43:536-9 Je 15 '77
GEBEL-WILLIAMS, Gunther
Greatest showman on earth. C. Kirkpatrick. il pors Sports Illus 47:82-6+ S 26 '77 *
GEBHARDT, Richard
Imagination and discipline in the writing class. bibl f il Engl J 66:26-32 D '77
GECKOS. See Lizards
GEDDES, Minna Hyman (Besser)
Isadora: the last year. il pors Dance Mag 52:67-70 Ja '78 *
GEDDES, Robert
Possibilities in architecture. il Archit Rec 162:103-8 N '77
GEDDY, Pam McLellan
Cosmo Alexander's travels and patrons in America. bibl il Antiques 112:972-7 N '77
GEDIN, Per
Novel in a changing society; excerpt from Literature in the marketplace; tr by G. Bisset. por Pub W 212-20-2 N 28 '77
GEDZELMAN, Stanley David
Mountain wave weather in New York City. il maps Weatherwise 30:202-6 O '77
GEE, Thomas C.
Integrated, student-centered language-arts assignment. Clearing H 50:294-5 Mr '77
GEESE
What I've learned about raising geese. C. Steffan. Org Gard & Farm 24:156-60 S '77
GEESE, Wild
Encore for the snow goose? G. Gruenefeld. il Int Wildlife 7:17-20 N '77
Snow geese are coming! The snow geese are coming! J. H. Phillips. il por Int Wildlife 7:21 N '77
Uncle Sam says scram! efforts to reduce Canada geese population in Horicon Marsh refuges. B. Gilbert. il maps Audubon 79:42-55 Ja '77
View from the castle: Ross's geese. S. D. Ripley. Smithsonian 8:8 N '77
See also
Goose shooting
GEIBERGER, Al
It was a day unlike any other day. C. Gillespie. il pors Sports Illus 46:50+ Je 20 '77 *
GEICO. See Government Employees Insurance Company
GEIGER, Peter, and Kennedy, N. L.
Rex Humbard's 25-25 vision. il pors Chr Today 21:53-6 My 6 '77
GEIGER-TOREL, Herman Berthold
Obituary
Opera N por 41:32 F 19 '77
GEINGOB, Hage G.
Namibians train for tomorrow. il UNESCO Courier 30:20-1 N '77
GEISEL, Ernesto
Why angry Brazil shaped up as Rosalynn's toughest challenge. J. Benham. il pors map U.S. News 82:44-5 Je 13 '77 *
GEISEL, Theodor Seuss
Dr Seuss at 72—going like 60. D. Freeman. il por Sat Eve Post 249:8+ Mr '77 *
GEISLER, Norman L.
Philosophy: the roots of vain deceit. Chr Today 21:8-12 My 20 '77
GEISLER, Richard M.
Era ends in big-league baseball. il por Nations Bus 65:38 Ap '77 *
GEISSINGER, Dorothy
922 Oak Street: a personal remembrance of the San Francisco earthquake. il por Am West 14:26-31 Ja '77
GELABERT, Raoul
Dance floors: their selection and preparation. il Dance Mag 51:94-5 Mr '77
Dancers and choreographers. il Dance Mag 51:84-5 Je '77
Dancers and medical science. il Dance Mag 51:74-5 D '77
Dancers and teachers. il Dance Mag 51:72-3 S '77
Dancer's physique. il Dance Mag 51:78-80 N '77
Myth of dance-induced pain. il Dance Mag 51:96-7 My '77
Posture. il Dance Mag 51:85-7 O '77
Rosin: its use and abuse. Dance Mag 51:88 Ap '77
Stage injuries. il Dance Mag 51:86-7 Jl; 30-1 Ag '77
Turning out. il Dance Mag 51:86-7 F '77
GELATIN desserts. See Desserts
GELATT, Dorothy S.
How to get your photo book into print. il Pop Phot 80:74-7+ Mr '77
GELATT, Roland
Artsletter. See issues of Saturday review
Cool conscience of a hot industry. il pors Sat R 4:28-9 Jl 23 '77
Echoing from the past. il Opera N 42:14-18+ Ag '77
Picasso's legacy. il pors Sat R 5:8-10 N 12 '77
GELB, Barbara
Cool-headed cop who saves hostages. il por N Y Times Mag p30-3+ Ap 17 '77
Great Scott! il pors N Y Times Mag p 10-12+ Ja 23 '77
Ten days that shook me up in Russia. il N Y Times Mag p21+ S 18 '77
Touch of the tragic. il pors N Y Times Mag p43-5+ D 11 '77
GELB, Betsy D.
When compulsory retirement at 65 is ended. . . Harvard Bus R 55:6-8 Jl '77
GELBAND, Myra
Letter from the publisher. D. Jenkins. il por Sports Illus 46:6 Ap 4 '77
GELBART, Larry
Sly fox; adaption of Volpone by B. Jonson. Reviews
America 136:60 Ja 22 '77 *
New Repub 176:24 Ja 15 '77
GELD, Ellen Bromfield
Reports & comment: Brazil. il Atlantic 240:6+ Ag '77
GELERNTER, H. L. and others
Empirical explorations of SYNCHEM. bibl il Science 197:1041-9 S '77
GELFAND, Quinn and Associates. See Investment advisers
GELL-MANN, Murray
Quark; interview. New Yorker 53:22-3 Jl 18 '77
GELLER, Harvey
Nathan Stubblefield: the radio prophet of the Kentucky fields. il pors Hi Fi 27:79-83 N '77
GELLER, Uri
Psychic power of Uri Geller. K. Toffler. il pors Sat Eve Post 249:58-9+ O '77 *
GELLES, Walter
Harper & Row, District 65 agree on new contract. il Pub W 211:154 My 23 '77
William Jovanovich delivers keynote address at graduation of publishing workshop. il Pub W 211:42 Je 27 '77
GELLONA, Olga Kliwadenko
Flavor of Santiago. il Américas 29:19-25 Mr '77
GELPI, Donald L.
Lent, repentance: a parable. America 136:223-4 Mr 12 '77
GELSTHORPE, Edward
Buy frogurt, or else. il por Forbes 119:56 My 15 '77 *
Marketer who put H. P. Hood on the map. il por Duns R 110:30-1 Jl '77 *
GELVIN, Ed, family
Reporter at large. J. McPhee. New Yorker 53:33-6+ Jl 4 '77

GEMINI; drama. See Innaurato, A.
GEMINI Ltd. See Publishers and publishing—Art
GEMINIANI, Francesco
Six cello sonatas. E. Belov. Am Rec G 40: 16-17 Mr '77 *
GEMMAE
Gemmae: a role in sexual reproduction in the fern genus vittaria. V. D. Emigh and D. R. Farrar. bibl il Science 198:297-8 O 21 '77
GEMS, Pam
Dusa, Fish, Stas & Vi. Reviews
New Yorker 53:97-8 Mr 7 '77 *
GEMS
Diamonds and other prized gems. il Changing T 31:19-20 D '77
See also
Diamonds
Jewelry
Precious stones
Exhibitions
Around the Mall and beyond; Victoria-Transvaal diamond and emerald brooch at Washington's Museum of Natural History. E. Park. il Smithsonian 8:28+ D '77
GEMS as an investment
Gems: a good hedge against inflation? il U.S. News 82:64 F 7 '77
Money. W. Flanagan. Vogue 167:54+ Ap '77
Now the diamond bugs? il Forbes 119:130+ Ap 15 '77
GENAUER, Emily
Leonardo and the stain. por Newsweek 90:27 D 12 '77
GENDEL, Milton
Giovanni Urbani and restoration Italian-style. il por Art N 76:146-8 Summ '77
GENDZIER, Irene L.
Assassination of Jumblatt. Nation 224:388-9 Ap 2 '77
Begin in Middle East perspective. Nation 225: 102-4 Ag 6 '77
Israel under Begin. Nation 224:742-4 Je 18 '77
GENE expression. See Genetic regulation
GENE mapping. See Chromosome mapping
GENE-splicing research. See Genetic research
GENEALOGY
Alex Haley on kids in search of their roots; interview, ed by G. M. Landau. A. Haley. pors Parents Mag 52:60-1+ S '77
Back where they came from. B. DeMott. Atlantic 239:88-91 My '77
Climbing all over the family trees; Time essay. S. Kanfer. il Time 109:54 Mr 28 '77
Everybody's search for roots. D. Gelman and others. il Newsweek 90:26-7+ Jl 4 '77
Game of the name. H. Sutton. Sat R 4:45-7 Ap 2 '77
Granite is forever; Granite Mountain Genealogical Vault. il Am Heritage 28:81 Je '77
How to trace your family tree. M. Burgen. il Ebony 32:52-4+ Je '77
How to trace your own roots. L. M. Skalka. il Ret Liv 17:34-5+ Je '77
Maid from Finland; B. Hiltunen family. T. Schwartz and others. il Newsweek 90:32 Jl 4 '77
Negro boy Alfred. T. Schwartz and H. Camp. por Newsweek 90:29 Jl 4 '77
Roots and the biologist. G. B. Moment. BioScience 27:589 S '77
Roots spin-off; school project. P. Tapogna. Todays Educ 66:48 S '77
Tracing their roots. D. Gallagher. il N Y Times Mag p48+ F 20 '77
Tracing your family tree. S. E. Coulter. il Bet Hom & Gard 55:10+ Je '77
Tracing your own roots—advice from an expert; interview. J. D. Walker. por U.S. News 82:57 Mr 14 '77
Tracking down your kinfolk; using Mormon Church libraries. il Sunset 158:36 Je '77
Up from the DAR. M. Barton. Nat R 29:1252-3 O 28 '77
What Roots means to me. A. Haley. Read Digest 110:73-6 My '77
White roots: looking for great-grandpa. il Time 109:43-4 Mr 28 '77
Who am I? D. Carlinsky. Seventeen 36:202 My '77
See also
Gambia—Genealogy
New England Historical Genealogical Society
Anecdotes, facetiae, satire, etc.
Now, Jewish roots. I. Shenker. N Y Times Mag p42-5 Mr 20 '77
Bibliography
How to find your roots. S. C. Cowley and B. Carter. il Newsweek 90:35 Jl 4 '77
GENEEN, Harold Sydney
Geneen's legacy. D. Pauly. pors Newsweek 89: 80 F 21 '77 *
Harold Geneen rests his case. R. J. Flaherty. il pors Forbes 119:42+ Je 15 '77 *
GENENTECH Inc
Commercial debut for DNA technology. il Bus W p 128+ D 12 '77
GENERAL Accounting Office. See United States—General Accounting Office
GENERAL Agreement on Tariffs and Trade
Compromise speeds the Tokyo Round; agricultural concession between the U.S. and the European Community. Bus W p53-4 Jl 25 '77
Freedom to trade; question of American markets for agricultural products and the GATT trading rules; address, December 6, 1976. D. L. Hume. Vital Speeches 43:244-6 F 1 '77
Growing worry over world trade war. U.S. News 83:24 Ag 8 '77
Stakes go higher in new trade talks. Bus W p22-3 Mr 7 '77
Talking to defuse a trade war. il Bus W p36-8 O 3 '77
Why the industrial nations aren't growing; GATT economists' report. il Bus W p 138+ N 21 '77
GENERAL American Transportation Corporation. See GATX Corporation
GENERAL Assembly of the United Nations. See United Nations—General Assembly
GENERAL aviation. See Aviation
GENERAL Aviation Manufacturers Association
General Aviation group expects additional sales gains in 1977. Aviation W 106:22 Ja 17 '77
GENERAL Dynamics Corporation
Cost-cutter climbs all over Electric Boat; P. T. Veliotis. por Bus W p42+ N 14 '77
General Dynamics struggles to build a plane for all nations; F-16. L. Kraar. il Fortune 95: 180-4+ Mr '77
Rescue mission at Electric Boat; Navy contracts. il Bus W p34 O 31 '77
Settling for less on Navy contracts; General Dynamics Corp.'s Electric Boat Div. and Tenneco Inc.'s Newport News Shipbuilding & Dry Dock Co. il Bus W p27-8 Ap 11 '77
GENERAL Dynamics Corporation-Beech Aircraft Corporation merger. See Corporations—Acquisitions and mergers
GENERAL Electric Company
GE's new billion-dollar small businesses. il Bus W p78-9 D 19 '77
Opposites: GE grows while Westinghouse shrinks. il Bus W p60-4+ Ja 31 '77
GENERAL Electric Company, Ltd. See Electric industries—Great Britain
GENERAL Electric Company-Utah International Inc merger. See Corporations—Acquisitions and mergers
GENERAL Foods Corporation
How to get coffee prices for sugar and vegetable oil. Consumer Rep 42:184-5 Ap '77
Stonewalling plant democracy; Topeka plant. Bus W p78+ Mr 28 '77
GENERAL information tests. See Information tests
GENERAL Mills, Inc
Bruce's bowl; truth-in-advertising suit. il pors Time 110:36 D 5 '77
GENERAL Motors Corporation
Big payoff at General Motors. Duns R 110:48-50 D '77
Bob Jones speaks, General Motors listens; canceling sponsorship of television program, Jesus of Nazareth. J. M. Wall. Chr Cent 94:291 Mr 30 '77
Boss of General Motors' legal staff; O. M. Smith. il pors Ebony 33:33-5+ D '77
Christianity's Hanafis; General Motors withdrawal of sponsorship of F. Zeffirelli's Jesus of Nazareth. M. E. Marty. Chr Cent 94:367 Ap 13 '77
DeLorean's phantom book. A. J. Mayer and J. C. Jones. por Newsweek 90:65+ Ag 15 '77
End of the great engine flap; settlement of suit against GM for use of Chevrolet engines in other cars. Time 111:66 Ja 2 '78
Engine trouble; use of Chevrolet engines in Oldsmobiles. Time 109:66 My 9 '77
Excerpt from testimony on retirement age policy, March 16, 1977. G. B. Morris, Jr. Cong Digest 56:285+ N '77
GM takes its lumps. T. Nicholson. Newsweek 89:89-90 Ap 11 '77
Hell on wheels. F. Getlein. Commonweal 104:420-2 Jl 8 '77
How's your new Chevrolet? engine switch in GM cars. Nation 224:549 My 7 '77
Nepotism question at General Motors; lawsuits charging E. M. Estes with furthering his sons' careers. por Bus W p41 S 19 '77
We are losing the freedom to decide; address, August 6, 1977. T. A. Murphy. Vital Speeches 43:714-17 S 15 '77
You're damned if you do. . . il Forbes 121:33-6 Ja 9 '78
Cadillac Motor Division
Mark of dominance. il Forbes 119:62+ Ap 1 '77
Chevrolet Division
Men behind the Car of the Year. il pors Motor T 29:36-8 F '77
Truck and Coach Division
GMC puts new bus on the road. Am City & County 92:19 N '77

GENERAL Services Administration. See United States—General Services Administration

GENERAL Signal Corporation
General Signal cashes in on federal dollars. por Bus W p 166 Mr 21 '77

GENERALS, Israeli. See Israel—Armed Forces—Officers

GENERATION gap
Bringing your grandchildren into your life. A. P. Boyle. il Ret Liv 17:16-18 Ag '77
Generation gap is wider than it needs to be. S. Taylor. por Seventeen 36:78 My '77

GENERATIVE organs
Ovarian hormone: lack of effect on reproductive structures of female Asian musk shrews. G. L. Dryden and J. N. Anderson. bibl il Science 197:782-4 Ag 19 '77
See also
Genito-urinary organs
Orgasm

Abnormalities and deformities
Clomid or nafoxidine administered to neonatal rats causes reproductive tract abnormalities. J. H. Clark and S. McCormack. bibl il Science 197:164-5 Jl 8 '77
Effect of delta-9-tetrahydrocannabinol on uterine and vaginal cytology of ovariectomized rats. J. Solomon and others. bibl il Science 195:875-7 Mr 4 '77

Surgery
Functioning artificial penis. Sci N 111:246-7 Ap 16 '77

GENERATORS, Neutron. See Neutron sources

GENES
Animal genes do it differently. il Sci N 112:70-1 Jl 30 '77
Era of the jumping genes. il Sci N 111:164 Mr 12 '77
Gene parts sandwich surprise segments. Sci N 112:214 O 1 '77
Gene transfer in mammalian cells: mediated by chromosomes. J. L. Marx. il Science 197:146-8 Jl 8 '77
Group-specific component: evidence for two subtypes of the Gc[1] gene. J. Constans and M. Viau. bibl il Science 198:1070-1 D 9 '77
Overlapping genes: more than anomalies? G. B. Kolata. Science 196:1187-8 Je 10 '77
Remarkable replicators; excerpt from The selfish gene. R. Dawkins. Natur Hist 86:34+ F '77
Stability of the individual globin genes during erythroid differentiation. E. Benz, Jr and others. bibl il Science 196:1213-14 Je 10 '77
Success in deciphering human genes. Sci N 111:294-5 My 7 '77
To clone a gene. Sci Am 236:47-9 Ja '77
Two genes control seasonal isolation in sibling species. C. A. Tauber and others. bibl il Science 197:592-3 Ag 5 '77
Yeast and mold genes work in bacteria. Sci N 111:165-6 Mr 12 '77
See also
Heredity of disease

GENESCO, Inc
Choices narrow for troubled Genesco. Bus W p41-2 S 19 '77
Does Genesco face a takeover bid? Bus W p29 Ap 11 '77
What undid Jarman: paperwork paralysis. il por Bus W p67-8 Ja 24 '77

GENETIC code
Amended dogma; onegene, one-protein hypothesis. Sci Am 236:50 My '77
How many anticodons? T. H. Jukes. bibl il Science 198:319-20 O 21 '77
New view of evolution; protein structure analysis. il Time 109:47 Ap 4 '77
Nucleotide sequence of a viral DNA. J. C. Fiddes. il Sci Am 237:54-67 D '77

GENETIC control. See Genetic engineering

GENETIC counseling
Winning the war against birth defects. R. Halcomb. il Parents Mag 52:37+ My '77

GENETIC diseases. See Heredity of disease

GENETIC engineering
Genetic engineering: the origin of the long-distance rumor. J. L. Marx. Science 198:388 O 28 '77
Nitrogen fixation: prospects for genetic manipulation. J. L. Marx. il Science 196:638-41 My 6 '77
People shapers; excerpt. V. Packard. Sat R 4:33-48 Ag 6 '77
Recombinant DNA: clashing views aired. Sci N 111:181 Mr 19 '77
Who should play God? excerpt. T. Rifkin and T. Howard. il Progressive 41:16-22 D '77

GENETIC polymorphism. See Polymorphism (biology)

GENETIC psychology
See also
Intelligence levels

GENETIC regulation
Recombinational switch for gene expression. J. Zieg and others. bibl il Science 196:170-2 Ap 8 '77

GENETIC research
Application of genetic and cellular manipulations to agricultural and industrial problems. B. B. Hoskins and others. bibl BioScience 27:188-91 Mr '77
At our expense; government funding of recombinant DNA research. T. Galazen. Progressive 41:22 D '77
Biologists oppose DNA research bills. Sci N 112:36 Jl 16 '77
Cambridge may O.K. gene research. Sci N 111:70 Ja 29 '77
Cambridge resumes genetic research. Sci N 111:103 F 12 '77
Caution: gene transplants. P. Gwynne. il Newsweek 89:57-8 Mr 21 '77
Confusion breaks out over gene splice law. Science 198:176 O 14 '77
Construction of chimeric phages and plasmids containing the origin of replication of bacteriophage lambda. D. D. Moore and others. bibl il Science 198:1041-6 D 9 '77
Continuing saga of recombinant DNA: Senate hears proposals for regulation without legislation. E. M. Leeper. BioScience 27:775-6 D '77
Creating new forms of life—blessing or curse? il U.S. News 82:80-1 Ap 11 '77
DNA and insulin; recombinant DNA research. Newsweek 89:74 Je 6 '77
DNA debate. J. Randal. Progressive 41:11-12 My '77
DNA: laws, patents, and a proselyte. N. Wade. Science 195:762 F 25 '77
DNA legislation: status report. A. J. Grimes. BioScience 27:573 Ag '77
DNA lobby. J. Randal. Progressive 41:12 O '77
DNA research. il Time 110:56 Ag 15 '77
DNA rules backed by administration. Sci N 111:245-6 Ap 16 '77
DNA: will the future curse science's decisions today? M. Reisner. il Sci Digest 82:62-5+ Jl '77
Dialogue via satellite: NIH director meets students. E. M. Leeper. il BioScience 27:428-9 Je '77
Dicing with nature: three narrow escapes. N. Wade. Science 195:378 Ja 28 '77
E. coli at work. Time 110:56 N 14 '77
Gene legislation NAS urges caution. Sci N 111:293 My 7 '77
Gene rules: violation and revisions. Sci N 112:420 D 24 '77
Gene scene. I. Asimov. il Sat Eve Post 249:12+ S '77
Gene-splicing: at grass-roots level a hundred flowers bloom. N. Wade. Science 195:558-60 F 11 '77
Gene-splicing bills suffer setback. Sci N 112:229 O 8 '77
Gene-splicing: Cambridge citizens OK research but want more safety. N. Wade. il por Science 195:268-9 Ja 21 '77
Gene splicing: Congress starts framing law for research. N. Wade. Science 196:39-40 Ap 1 '77
Gene-splicing: critics of research get more brickbats than bouquets. N. Wade. Science 195:466-7+ F 4 '77
Gene splicing preemption rejected. N. Wade. Science 196:406 Ap 22 '77
Gene-splicing research: some safety advice from virus scientists. J. A. Miller. Sci N 111:141 F 26 '77
Gene splicing: Senate bill draws charges of Lysenkoism. N. Wade. por Science 197:348+ Jl 22 '77; Reply. W. P. Rowe. 198:563+ N 11 '77
Gene-splicing: the eighth day of creation. D. J. Sullivan. il America 137:441-3 D 17 '77
Genetic disarmament. il Sci Am 236:53-5 My '77
Genetic roulette: the hazards of altering nature. J. Milton. Nation 225:361-5 O 15 '77
Genetic structure of the replication origin of bacteriophage lambda. M. E. Furth and others. bibl il Science 198:1046-51 D 9 '77
In defense of DNA. J. D. Watson. New Repub 176:11-14 Je 25 '77
Insulin gene researchers admit breach of rules. Sci N 112:212 O 1 '77
Kennedy bill unchanged by scientists' visit. P. R. Day. BioScience 27:594 S '77
Life from the labs: who will control the new technology? J. Randal. Progressive 41:16-20 Mr '77; Same with title Who will control new living organisms? Current 193:52-60 My '77
NIH seeks law on gene-splice research. N. Wade. Science 195:859 Mr 4 '77
New P4 laboratories: containing recombinant DNA. J. L. Marx. il Science 197:1350-2 S 30 '77
Novel screening procedure for recombinant plasmids. J. Telford and others. bibl il Science 195:391-3 Ja 28 '77
One for the gene engineers; inserting human insulin gene into DNA of escherichia coli. il Time 109:68 Je 6 '77
One small step beyond mankind; recombinant DNA research by drug companies. J. Rifkin. Progressive 41:21 Mr '77

GENETIC research—*Continued*
Physical structure of the replication origin of bacteriophage lambda. K. Denniston-Thompson and others. bibl il Science 198:1051-6 D 9 '77
Politics of deoxyribonucleic acid. A. Budrys New Repub 176:18-21 Ap 16 '77
Rat insulin gene spliced into bacteria. Sci N 111:340 My 28 '77
Recombinant DNA. P. H. Abelson. Science 197: 721 Ag 19 '77
Recombinant DNA: a critic questions the right to free inquiry. N. Wade; discussion. Science 195:131-3 Ja 14 '77
Recombinant DNA: clashing views aired. Sci N 111:181 Mr 19 '77
Recombinant-DNA debate. C. Grobstein. il Sci Am 237:22-33 bibl(p 154) Jl '77
Recombinant DNA debate. M. F. Singer. Science 196:127 Ap 8 '77
Recombinant DNA debate shakes science community; symposium. Sci Digest 81:21-9 Je '77
Recombinant DNA: examples of present-day research; symposium. bibl il Science 196:159-221 Ap 8 '77
Recombinant DNA: fact and fiction. S. N. Cohen. bibl Science 195:654-7 F 18 '77; Same abr. with title Gene splicing: fact and fantasy. Parents Mag 52:72-3+ N '77
Recombinant DNA forum-stellar cast; gripping plot; but no new message. E. M. Leeper. il BioScience 27:317-19 My '77
Recombinant DNA legislation—what next? H. O. Halvorson. Science 198:357 O 28 '77
Recombinant DNA: NIH rules broken in insulin gene project. N. Wade. Science 197:1342-5 S 30 '77
Recombinant DNA research. J. A. Miller. il Sci N 111:216-17 Ap 2 '77
Recombinant DNA research; symposium. il Bull Atom Sci 33:10-16+ My '77
Recombinant DNA technology: who shall regulate? S. Wright. Bull Atom Sci 33:4-5 O '77
Recombinant DNA-the containment debate. L. B. Riesenberg. bibl il Chemistry 50:13-17 D '77
Recombinant lab for DNA and my 95 days in it; H. Boyer's Lab at the University of California's School of Medicine in San Francisco. J. L. Hopson. il pors Smithsonian 8:54-63 Je '77
Research in a box; recombinant DNA research. J. McCaull. il Environment 19:31-7 Ap '77
Rogers lists advantages of his DNA bill; interview, ed by E. M. Leeper. P. G. Rogers. por BioScience 27:591-3 S '77
Science that frightens scientists: the great debate over DNA. B. William and J. Gurin. il Atlantic 239:43-50+ F '77
Scientists ask Congress to control DNA research. E. M. Leeper. BioScience 27:141-3 F '77
Somatic cell genetic manipulation in plants. P. R. Day and others. bibl BioScience 27: 116-18 F '77
Song, signs and spite spice DNA talks. Sci N 111:165 Mr 12 '77
Tinkering with life. il Time 109:32-4+ Ap 18 '77
UK biologists claim DNA controls too broad. E. M. Leeper. BioScience 27:12 Ja '77
Update on DNA research regulation. A. J. Grimes. BioScience 27:720 N '77
Yeast and mold genes work in bacteria. Sci N 111:165-6 Mr 12 '77
See also
Genentech Inc
Genetic engineering

Bibliography

Splice of life. J. Milton. Sat R 5:26+ O 15 '77

GENETIC screening. See Heredity of disease

GENETIC transformation
Feline oncornavirus-associated cell membrane antigen: expression in transformed non-producer mink cells. A. H. Sliski and others. bibl il Science 196:1336-9 Je 17 '77

GENETICS
See also
Allelomorphism
Animal genetics
Behavior genetics
Chromosomes
Fish genetics
Fungal genetics
Heredity
Human genetics
Immunogenetics
Insect genetics
Microbial genetics
Mosaics (biology)
Mutation (biology)
Ontogeny
Plant genetics
Population genetics

Conferences

Developmental genetics of the early embryo. G. M. Malacinski and A. J. Brothers. BioScience 27:279-80 Ap '77

Research

See Genetic research

GENETICS Society of America
Genetic differences in intelligence. Intellect 105: 214-15 Ja '77

GENEVA, Switzerland

Music

See also
Opera—Switzerland

Stores

Man who saved Havanas: Z. Davidoff's cigar store. W. Galling. il pors Fortune 95:174-6 F '77

GENG, Veronica
My Mao. New Yorker 53:32-4 Mr 21 '77

GENICULATE body. See Thalamus

GENIESSE, Jane
Adolescent in the house. McCalls 104:31+ Jl '77

GENITAL herpesviruses. See Herpesviruses

GENITO-urinary organs
Vasoactive intestinal polypeptide occurs in nerves of the female genitourinary tract. L. I. Larsson and others. bibl il Science 197: 1374-5 S 30 '77

GENIUS
See also
Children. Gifted
College students, Mentally superior

GENOCIDE
Administration recommends Senate approval of Genocide Convention; message, with text of statements, May 23-24, 1977. J. Carter and others. Dept State Bull 76:676-80 Je 27 '77

GENOISE. See Cake

GENOVESI, Vincent J.
Birth into poverty. America 137:459-60 D 24 '77

GENSTAR Ltd. See Conglomerate corporations—Canada

GEOCHEMICAL Ocean Sections program. See Oceanographic research

GEODESIC domes
Fifty years ahead of my time. R. B. Fuller. por Sat Eve Post 249:44+ Mr '77
Home sweet dome. il Time 109:34-5 Mr 14 '77

GEODYNAMICS
See also
Continental drift

GEOGRAPHICAL distribution of animals and plants
Ectoparasitic mites on rodents: application of the island biogeography theory? with reply by B. O'Connor and others. A. M. Kuris and A. R. Blaustein. bibl Science 195:596-8 F 11 '77

GEOGRAPHICAL medicine. See Medical geography

GEOGRAPHICAL myths
Quest in the jungle; search for the lost city of Ciudad Blanca, Honduras. J. Underwood. il Sports Illus 48:86-90+ Ja 9 '78
Shamans and shamanism: epic journeys to a legendary land. G. M. Bongard-Levin and E. A. Grantovsky. il UNESCO Courier 29:42-7 D '76

GEOGRAPHICAL names. See Names, Geographical

GEOGRAPHICAL societies
See also
National Geographic Society

GEOGRAPHY
See also
Boundaries
Maps
Medical geography

Study and teaching

Highway map as a social studies resource. J. Ehemann. Clearing H 51:165-6 D '77

GEOGRAPHY, Historical
See also
Maps, Early

GEOGRAPHY, Political. See Geopolitics

GEOLOGICAL research
See also
Antarctic research

GEOLOGICAL Society of America
Earth sciences; summaries of papers. K. Frazier. Sci N 112:345, 360 N 19-26 '77

GEOLOGICAL Survey (United States) See United States—Geological Survey

GEOLOGICAL time
Oldest rocks and the growth of continents. S. Moorbath. il maps Sci Am 236:92-104 bibl(p 150) Mr '77
See also
Amino acid dating
Radiocarbon dating

GEOLOGY
See also
Caves
Deluge
Faults (geology)
Forests, Submerged
Geological Society of America
Geysers
Hydrogeology
Mountains
Paleogeography
Rocks
Slopes (physical geography)
Submarine geology

GEOLOGY—*Continued*

Algeria

Capsian escargotières. D. Lubell and others. bibl il Science 191:910-20 Mr 5 '76; Correction. 196:335 Ap 15 '77

Australia

Fluid inclusion assemblages of the stratiform Broken Hill ore deposit, New South Wales, Australia. R. W. T. Wilkins. bibl il Science 198:185-7 O 14 '77

California

California's shifting crust: slip sliding away. Sci N 112:404 D 17 '77
Exploring an ominous bulge; Palmdale bulge. map Time 111:54 Ja 16 '78
High rates of vertical crustal movement near Ventura, California. R. S. Yeats. bibl il map Science 196:295-8 Ap 15 '77
Palmdale bulge: puzzling changes in shape. Sci N 111:167 Mr 12 '77
Swelling earth; Palmdale bulge. E. Keerdoja and M. Kasindorf. il Newsweek 89:10 Mr 21 '77

Canada

Oldest macroborers: lower Cambrian of Labrador. N. P. James and others. bibl il map Science 197:980-3 S 2 '77

Eurasia

Collision between India and Eurasia. P. Molnar and P. Tapponnier. il maps Sci Am 236:30-41 bibl(p 148) Ap '77

Great Britain

Getting the axe; stone axes from Neolithic sites. Sci Am 238:69 Ja '78

Hawaii

Hot spots. P. R. Vogt. il maps Natur Hist 86:36-45 bibl(p 100) Ap '77

Iceland

Hot spots. P. R. Vogt. il maps Natur Hist 86:36-45 bibl(p 100) Ap '77

Labrador

See Geology—Canada

Michigan

Geology, vegetation, and vertebrate fauna of Michigan. F. W. Cambray. bibl map BioScience 27:349-50 My '77

Peru

Two-billion-year granulites in the late Precambrian metamorphic basement along the southern Peruvian coast. B. Dalmayrac. bibl il map Science 198:49-51 O 7 '77

South Dakota

Evidence for late tertiary volcanic activity in the northern Black Hills, South Dakota. J. G. Kirchner. bibl Science 196:977 My 27 '77

United States

See also
United States—Geological survey

GEOLOGY, Stratigraphic
See also
Paleontology

Cambrian

Oldest macroborers: lower Cambrian of Labrador. N. P. James and others. bibl il map Science 197:980-3 S 2 '77

Cenozoic

Explosive cenozoic volcanism and climatic implications. D. Ninkovich and W. L. Donn; reply. J. P. Kennett and R. C. Thunell. bibl il Science 196:1231-4 Je 10 '77

Cretaceous

Grand Banks and J-anomaly ridge: a geological comparison. F. M. Gradstein and others. bibl il map Science 197:1074-6 S 9 '77

Paleozoic

See also
Geology, Stratigraphic—Cambrian

Pleistocene

Delaware River: evidence for its former extension to Wilmington Submarine Canyon. D. C. Twichell and others. bibl il map Science 195:483-5 F 4 '77

Pre-Cambrian

Two-billion-year granulites in the late Precambrian metamorphic basement along the southern Peruvian coast. B. Dalmayrac and others. bibl il map Science 198:49-51 O 7 '77

Tertiary

Evidence for late tertiary volcanic activity in the northern Black Hills, South Dakota. J. G. Kirchner. bibl Science 196:977 My 27 '77

GEOLOGY, Structural
Awesome force that shaped our planet; plate tectonics. R. Schiller. maps Read Digest 112:112-16 Ja '78
Collision between India and Eurasia. P. Molnar and P. Tapponnier. il maps Sci Am 236:30-41 bibl(p 148) Ap '77
Continental drift affair; question of plate tectonics theory. S. J. Gould. Natur Hist 86:12 F '77
Did asteroid impacts help shape earth? Sci N 112:341 N 19 '77
Emperor Seamounts: hotspot candidates. il Sci N 112:215 O 1 '77
Exploring an ominous bulge; Palmdale bulge. map Time 111:54 Ja 16 '78
Flow of heat from the earth's interior. H. N. Pollack and D. S. Chapman. il maps Sci Am 237:60-8+ bibl(p 140) Ag '77
Hot spots. P. R. Vogt. il maps Natur Hist 86:36-45 bibl(p 100) Ap '77
Oldest rocks and the growth of continents. S. Moorbath. il maps Sci Am 236:92-104 bibl(p 150) Mr '77
Swelling earth; Palmdale bulge. E. Keerdoja and M. Kasindorf. il Newsweek 89:10 Mr 21 '77
Volcanic activity and great earthquakes at convergent plate margins. M. J. Carr. bibl il map Science 197:655-7 Ag 12 '77
See also
Continental drift
Faults (geology)

GEOMAGNETISM. See Magnetism, Terrestrial

GEOMETRY
Thermodynamics and geometry. F. Weinhold; discussion. bibl il Phys Today 30:11+ Ja '77
See also
Curves

GEOPHYSICS
See also
American Geophysical Union
Earth—Internal structure
Earth movements
Seismology

GEOPOLITICS
Five worlds of detente. N. B. Hannah. maps Nat R 29:541-5 My 13 '77; Reply. J. Burnham. 29:600 My 27 '77

GEORGE, David Lloyd, 1st Earl Lloyd George of Dwyfor. See Lloyd George of Dwyfor, D. L. G.

GEORGE, Donald W.
Climbing Kilimanjaro. il Mademoiselle 83:188+ N '77

GEORGE, Emery
Solstice; poem. Poetry 130:249-50 Ag '77

GEORGE, Jean (Craighead)
White-water high. il Read Digest 111:74-7 S '77

GEORGE, Phyllis
Phyllis & Bob. K. Gilman. pors Ladies Home J 94:78+ N '77 *

GEORGE, Sally
How to be your own exterminator. il Ms 5:27-8+ F '77
Louise Atkins: pest-control operator; story. Redbook 149:131 S '77

GEORGE, William Henry Krome
Doing it by the numbers. por Forbes 119:71 F 15 '77 *

GEORGE, William W.
Task teams for rapid growth. il Harvard Bus R 55:71-80 Mr '77

GEORGE C. Page Museum of La Brea Discoveries, Los Angeles
Opening soon in Los Angeles: a new home for the skeletons of ice age animals. il Sunset 158:64 Ap '77

GEORGE Washington University, Washington, D.C.

National Law Center

Washington memo; Paralegal Training for Seniors program at Institute of Law and Aging. R. D. Westgate. Ret Liv 17:16 F '77

GEORGES Pompidou Center. See Paris—Georges Pompidou Center

GEORGESCU-ROEGEN, Nicholas
Steady state and ecological salvation: a thermodynamic analysis. bibl il BioScience 27:266-70, 646-7 Ap; O '77

GEORGETOWN. See Washington, D. C.

GEORGIA
Georgia seeks its disabled citizens; The Search. Aging 274:24 Ag '77
See also
Banks and banking—Georgia
Blacks—Georgia
Cumberland Island
Cumberland Island National Seashore
Education—Georgia
Libraries—Georgia
Opera—Georgia
Recreation areas—Georgia
Sea Islands

Description and travel

Blue Ridge of Georgia. R. Magruder and M. Magruder. il Travel 147:36-41+ F '77
Georgia on my mind. R. Schiller. il map Read Digest 110:152-6+ Mr '77

GEORGIA—*Continued*

Politics and government

Realpolitik in Georgia; question of special elections in the 5th Congressional district. K. Bode. New Repub 176:19-21 Mr 5; 10 Ap 9 '77

Realpolitik in Georgia: the fight for Young's seat; House of Representatives. P. Kovler. Nation 224:400-1 Ap 2 '77

Religious institutions and affairs

Carter and the church. N.King. il Nat R 29: 384-5+ Ap 1 '77

Easing the pains in Plains; J. Carter's visit to Plains Baptist and Maranatha Baptist. Chr Today 21:37 Ag 26 '77

Minister's farewell to Plains, Georgia; B. Edwards ousted as head of Plains Baptist Church. V. Cadden. il por McCalls 104:115+ Jl '77

Pilgrimage to Plains. L. Sandon, Jr. Chr Cent 94:145-6 F 16 '77

Plains Baptists. E. Keerdoja and H. Camp. il Newsweek 90:12 O 17 '77

Pressure in Plains; Plains Baptist Church. Chr Today 21:51-2 Mr 18 '77

Schism in Plains; ousting B. Edwards from pastorship of Plains Baptist Church. M. Montagno and others. il por Newsweek 89:76 Mr 7 '77

Strain in Plains. il Time 109:51 Je 27 '77

To the lions; B. Edwards' resignation as pastor of Plains Baptist Church. Time 109:14 Mr 7 '77

GEORGIA, Russia

Princesses for ransom: abduction in the grand style. F. MacLean. il pors Horizon 19:82-7 Mr '77

GEORGIA Dance Theatre Company. See Dance companies

GEORGIA Museum of Art. See Georgia. University, Athens—Georgia Museum of Art

GEORGIA-Pacific Corporation

Best of everything. por Forbes 119:59-60 Mr 15 '77

GEORGIA. University, Athens

Georgia Museum of Art

American artist from loner to lobbyist; Open to new Ideas: a Collection of New Art for Jimmy Carter. C. Ratcliff. il Art in Am 65:10-12 Mr '77

Carter's conceptualists and Uncle Alton. Vasari. Art N 76:23-6 Ap '77

Libraries

High cost of hiring. R. Christofferson. il por Lib J 102:677-81 Mr 15 '77

GEORGIANS

Bound for fun—and glory; attending J. Carter's inauguration. G. Taber. il Time 109:18 Ja 31 '77

GEORGIEV, G. P. and others

Isolation of eukaryotic DNA fragments containing structural genes and the adjacent sequences. bibl il Science 195:394-7 Ja 28 '77

GEOSECS program. See Oceanographic research

GEOTHERMAL energy. See Geothermal resources

GEOTHERMAL power plants. See Steam power plants

GEOTHERMAL resources

Energy from hot dry rock. E. Keller. Chemistry 50:21-2 S '77

Geothermal energies. J. Bosveld. il Sci Digest 82:73-6 O '77

Geothermal energy development. J. C. Rowley. bibl il Phys Today 30:36-8 Ja '77

Geothermal energy: ERDA leaves it lay. S. Bierman and G. T. Hunt. Nation 225:487-9 N 12 '77

How to harness earth's heat. il U.S. News 82:71 F 28 '77

Power of letting off steam; geothermal energy. K. F. Weaver. il map Nat Geog 152:566-79 O '77

See also

Geysers

GERANIUMS

For nonstop color—geraniums. R. Langer. il House & Gard 149:76 Mr '77

Greenhouse; show or regal geraniums. J. Kilborn. Horticulture 55:60-1 My '77

This geranium is a special treat; peppermint geranium. il Sunset 158:288 Ap '77

GERARD, Mark

Great Belmont Park sting. il Time 110:122 N 21 '77 *

Is this horse that horse? W. Leggett. il por Sports Illus 47:28-31 N 14 '77 *

Winner by any name. P. Axthelm. il por Newsweek 90:73 N 7 '77 *

GERBER, Judianne Densen-. See Densen-Gerber, J.

GERBER, Merrill Joan

Key word; story. Redbook 148:98 F '77

Lover's knot; story. Good H 185:138-9 S '77

GERBER Products Company-Anderson, Clayton & Company merger. See Food industry—Acquisitions and mergers

GERBILS

Jirds are ideal models for schistosomiasis research. BioScience 27:68 Ja '77

Small pets, little trouble. M. W. Fox. McCalls 104:122+ My '77

GERBNER, George

Proliferating violence. Society 14:8+ S '77

about

Networks hold the line. J. A. Schneider. Society 14:9+ S '77 *

GERE, Anne Ruggles

(ed) Eleven going on sixteen...in their own words. il Engl J 66:25-7 Ap '77

Writing and writing. bibl f Engl J 66:60-4 N '77

GERGEN, David

Impartial OTA future dubious; a launching pad for Kennedy? Sci Digest 82:24-5+ S '77

GERHARDT, Lillian N. and others

ALA Midwinter Meeting '77. il SLJ 23:110-19 Mr '77

(ed) Book review. See issues of School library journal

Issues, arguments, actions: ALA in Detroit. il SLJ 24:26-37 S '77

GERIATRICS. See Aged—Care and hygiene

GERIATRICS as a profession

Dr Robert M. Butler issues urgent call for more doctors trained in geriatrics. por Ret Liv 16: 14-15 D '76

GERICKE, Dick

Three relics; Gericke's Organic Farm, Staten Island. New Yorker 53:28-9 Je 20 '77 *

GERIG, Donald

Minister's workshop. Chr Today 21:30 Ap 15 '77

GERKEN, George M. See Frederickson, C. J. jt auth

GERLACH, Luther P.

Great energy standoff. Natur Hist 87:22+ Ja '78

GERM-free isolators

David's debut into the world; isolation suit for child with combined immunodeficiency disease. il Sci N 112:314-15 N 12 '77

GERMACRENE

Aphids foiled by false alarm. W. S. Bowers. il Chemistry 50:23 Jl '77

Sesquiterpene progenitor, germacrene A: an alarm pheromone in aphids. W. S. Bowers and others. bibl il Science 196:680-1 My 6 '77

GERMAN AMERICANS

Profiles; Hermann, Mo. B. Roueché. New Yorker 53:37-40 F 28 '77

GERMAN art. See Art, German

GERMAN cookery. See Cookery, German

GERMAN legends. See Legends, German

GERMAN measles. See Rubella

GERMAN pottery. See Pottery, German

GERMAN prisoners of war in the United States. See Prisoners of war in the United States

GERMAN songs. See Songs, German

GERMAN terrorists. See Terrorists, German

GERMAN war criminals. See World War, 1939-1945—War criminals

GERMAN wines. See Wine

GERMANS

See also

Berliners

GERMANS in Pennsylvania. See Pennsylvania Germans

GERMANS in the United States

See also

German Americans
Pennsylvania Germans

GERMANY

See also

Berlin
Colleges and universities—Germany
Concentration camps—Germany
Jews in Germany
Motion pictures—Germany
Radio broadcasting—Germany
Technology—Germany
World War, 1939-1945—Campaigns and battles—Germany

Boundaries

G.I. watch on a deadly border. B. W. Mader. il Time 110:38 Jl 18 '77

Foreign relations

Great Britain

See Great Britain—Foreign relations—Germany

History

1933-1945

See also

World War, 1939-1945—Germany

Intellectual life

See also

Colleges and universities—Germany

GERMANY—*Continued*

National socialist movement

See National socialism

Politics and government

See also
National socialism

Social history

Science and values: the eugenics movement in Germany and Russia in the 1920s. L. R. Graham. bibl f Am Hist R 82:1133-64 D '77

GERMANY, East

Behind the Berlin wall: socialism with a German face. J. Steele. Nation 225:397-400 O 22 '77

See also
Berlin (East Berlin)
Espionage, German
Historic houses, sites, etc.—Germany, East
Opera—Germany, East
Political prisoners—Germany, East

Foreign relations

See also
Berlin question, 1945-

Russia

See Russia—Foreign relations—Germany, East

Politics and government

See also
Berlin question, 1945-

Religious institutions and affairs

See also
Catholic Church in Germany, East
Church and state in Germany, East

GERMANY, West

West Germany: a pessimistic giant. J. Fromm. il U.S. News 83:39-40 O 17 '77

West Germany: continuing miracle. J. J. Putman. il map Nat Geog 152:148-81 Ag '77

See also
Accounting—Germany, West
Airlines—Germany, West
Alien labor—Germany, West
Ballet—Germany, West
Banks and banking—Germany, West
Berlin (West Berlin)
Cities and towns—Germany, West
Economic assistance, German
Education—Germany, West
Espionage, German
Historic houses, sites, etc.—Germany, West
Hours of labor—Germany, West
Hunting—Germany, West
Industrial relations—Germany, West
Intelligence service—Germany, West
Investments, American—Germany, West
Investments, German
Journalism—Germany, West
Money—Germany, West
Motion pictures—Germany, West
Munich
Music festivals—Germany, West
Opera—Germany, West
Police—Germany, West
Publishers and publishing—Germany, West
Regensburg
Rösrath
Ruhr Valley
Taxation—Germany, West
Terrorism—Germany, West
Trade unions—Germany, West
Trials—Germany, West

Air Force

Swinging sergeant; embezzlement case of Sergeant S. Schmidt. il por Time 109:46 Ap 11 '77

Armed Forces

COs or cheap labor. T. Heneghan. Commonweal 105:5-7 Ja 6 '78

Commerce

Strong D-mark, pressure on exports. Bus W p68-9 D 12 '77

United States

See United States—Commerce—Germany, West

Cultural relations

Fifth U.S.-German cultural talks held at Washington; text of communique, April 27, 1977. Dept State Bull 76:556-7 My 30 '77

Defenses

See also
United States—Army—Forces in Germany, West

Description and travel

German wineland tour. N. Karas. il Travel 147:42-7 My '77

Economic conditions

West Germany: can moderate stimulation do the job? Bus W p48 Ja 31 '77

Economic policy

Behind Germany's refusal to reflate its economy. G. T. Gibson. il Bus W p65 Jl 18 '77

Can Germany avoid catching the U.S. disease? E. Mervosh and W. Wolman. por Bus W p 122 O 17 '77

West Germany: can moderate stimulation do the job? Bus W p48 Ja 31 '77

See also
Price regulation by government—Germany, West

Economic relations

United States

See United States—Economic relations—Germany, West

Foreign opinion

European

Visions of hobnails; European criticism of West Germany's anti-terrorist measures. M. Ledeen. New Repub 177:17-19 N 19 '77

Foreign relations

Germany, East

See also
Berlin question, 1945-
Espionage, German

United States

See United States—Foreign relations—Germany, West

Industries

See also
Aerospace industries—Germany, West
Atomic power industry—Germany, West
Audio equipment industry—Germany, West
Automobile equipment industry—Germany, West
Automobile industry—Germany, West
Book industries—Germany, West
Chemical industries—Germany, West
Clothing industry—Germany, West
Construction industry—Germany, West
Electric battery industry—Germany, West
Electric industries—Germany, West
Electronic industries—Germany, West
Fisheries—Germany, West
Motion picture industry—Germany, West

Politics and government

Facing a Helmut problem. por Time 110:16 Jl 4 '77

Schmidt rides a new crest of confidence. por Bus W p46-7 D 5 '77

Under the lid of West Germany: a cauldron of paradoxes. N. Birnbaum. Nation 225:520-4 N 19 '77

West Germany: a balance sheet. G. Braunthal. Cur Hist 73:156-9+ N '77

Social conditions

Forgetting the holocaust. C. McConkey. Chr Cent 94:669-70 Jl 20 '77

Once again, the Führer's ghost is haunting Germany. il U.S. News 83:59 N 7 '77

GERMINATION

Easiest seed germinator yet. S. A. McDonald. il Org Gard & Farm 25:67-8 Ja '78

Simple seed sprouting. T. L. Gettings. il Org Gard & Farm 25:65-6 Ja '78

GERMOND, Jack W.

Congress and Carter: who's in charge? il por N Y Times Mag p22+ Ja 30 '77

GERNREICH, Rudi

What a wild idea: Lewitzky and Gernreich design a dance. V. H. Swisher. il pors Dance Mag 51:75-7 Mr '77 *

GERONTOLOGICAL Society

Annual meeting of Gerontological Society draws 2000 professionals. il Aging 268:9-12 F '77

GERONTOLOGY

Conferences

Conference calendar. See issues of Aging

First Lady hosts discussion on the Nation's elderly; NCOA conference provides forum for national leaders; Washington D.C. il por Aging 272:3-5 Je '77

Mrs Carter chairs special White House conference on aging. Ret Liv 17:15 Jl '77

National organizations form Ad Hoc Coalition on Aging. Aging 270:5 Ap '77

Puerto Rico holds first Governor's Conference on Aging. il Aging 266:14-15 D '76

See also
Gerontological Society
National Association of Area Agencies on Aging
National Council on the Aging

Study and teaching

Course calendar. Aging 268:25-6 F; 270:28-31 Ap; 272:26-8 Je '77

First Gerontology Training Institute under Jewish auspices created. Aging 266:22 D '76

GERONTOLOGY Research Center. See United States—National Institutes of Health—Gerontology Research Center

GEROVITAL. See Antidepressants

GERRARD, Michael
Overview: law. Environment 19:4-5 Je '77
This man was made possible by a grant from Mobil Oil. il Esquire 89:62-4+ Ja '78
GERROLD, David
Trouble with tribbles; drama; excerpt from television script of Star trek. Plays 37:1-16, 38 O '77
GERRYMANDER
Court docket; gerrymander challenge by Hasidic Jews of Brooklyn; Supreme Court decision. J. K. Footlick. Newsweek 89:97-8 Mr 14 '77
GERSBACH, Jo
Start of something; drama. Plays 37:53-6 O '77
GERSHMAN, Carl. See Rustin, B. jt auth
GERSHWIN, George
Catfish Row revisited; Porgy and Bess recording performed by the Houston Grand Opera. E. Jablonski. il por Am Rec G 40:10-15 S '77 *
Catfish Row springs to life; RCA recording. D. Hamilton. il Hi Fi 27:92-4 S '77
Gershwin. W. Youngren. New Repub 176:21-4 Ap 23; 27-30 Ap 30; 23-6 My 7 '77 *
Porgy and Bess. Reviews
New Repub 176:23-7 My 14 '77 *
GERSTEN, Leon
Encounter in Moscow. America 137:30-1 Jl 16 '77
GERSTMAN, Maria K.
Spontaneous mosaics. il Design (US) 78:10-11 mid-Summ '77
Three basic methods to approach art, creatively. il Design (US) 78:14-17 mid-Wint '77
GERSTON, Jill
Acne: all the facts. Seventeen 36:36+ Jl '77
How to avoid freshman weight gain. Seventeen 36:70 Mr '77
GERTZ, Kathryn Rose
Do you have a compulsive personality? Harp Baz 110:86+ Ag '77
15 ways to land a job. Harp Baz 110:47+ Je '77
GERULAITIS, Vitas
It's *veni, vidi, vici* for Vitas. B. McDermott. il pors Sports Illus 47:24-7 Ag 15 '77 *
GERVASI, Tom
Arsenal of democracy; excerpt from Arsenal for democracy: a catalogue of American weapons. il Harpers 254:68-9 Je '77
GESNERIACEAE
Gesneriads: beyond the African violet. R. Langer. il House & Gard 149:52 F '77
GESNERIADS. See Gesneriaceae
GESTURE
Hand signals; excerpt from Manwatching—a field guide to human behavior. D. Morris. il Good H 186:100-1 Ja '78
Secrets of man's unspoken language; excerpt from Manwatching: a field guide to human behavior. D. Morris. Read Digest 112:55-8 Ja '78
GETCHELL, Robert
Bound for glory; excerpt from screenplay. il pors Sr Schol 109:2-4+ F 10 '77
GETLEIN, Frank
Washington report. See issues of Commonweal
Word from Washington. Progressive 41:12-13 S; 14-15 O; 14-15 N; 14-15 D '77
GETOFF, Mary M.
Old-fashioned sun-cooked preserves. il Org Gard & Farm 24:110-11 Ag '77
GETTINGS, Tom L. See Smyser, S. jt auth
GETTY, Ann
House with a heart. il pors Vogue 167:322-7 O '77 *
GETTY, Eugene Paul, 1957?-
Golden hippie. E. Keerdoja. il pors Newsweek 90:24+ N 28 '77 *
GETTY, Gordon Peter
House with a heart. il pors Vogue 167:322-7 O '77 *
GETTY Museum. See Malibu, Calif.—Galleries and museums
GETZ, David
Art of being cool. Seventeen 36:70-1+ Ag '77
Charting new courses. Seventeen 36:28+ My '77
GEWIRTZ, Geraldine, and Martin, R. J.
Retiring alone to the country. pors Ret Liv 17:30-1 Je '77
GEYER, Georgie Anne
Cubans in Africa. New Repub 176:11-13 Ap 2 '77
GEYSERS
USGS earth science series. il Sci Digest 81:83 F '77
GEZARI, Temima
Carnival of two centuries. il Sch Arts 76:52-3 Mr '77
GHANA
See also
Americans in Ghana
Arts and crafts—Ghana

Politics and government

Decline of Ghana's military government. J. Kraus. il Cur Hist 73:214-17+ D '77
GHANGAS, Gurdev S. and Milman, Gregory
Hypoxanthine phosphoribosyltransferase: two-dimensional gels from normal and Lesch-Nyhan hemoyzates. bibl il Science 196:1119-20 Je 3 '77
GHETTOS (slums) See Slums
GHOST sonata; drama. See Strindberg, A.
GHOST writing. See Authorship—Collaboration
GHOSTS
Our dream house was haunted; scene of the De Feo murders and home of the G. L. Lutzes. P. Hoffman. il Good H 184:119+ Ap '77
Our haunted house on the Hudson. H. H. Ackley. il Read Digest 110:217-19+ My '77
GHOSTS; drama. See Ibsen, H.
GHOZALA, Hani Abu
Money is no object. por Forbes 120:97 Jl 1 '77 *
GIAMATTI, Angelo Bartlett
Hyperbole's child. Harpers 225:117-18+ D '77
Tom Seaver's farewell. il Harpers 255:93-4+ S '77

about

Humanist. por Time 111:68 Ja 2 '78 *
Renaissance man. M. Sheils and P. Malamud. por Newsweek 91:45 Ja 2 '78 *
GIANATASIO, Joan R. and Grutter, A. M.
Forming and etching as a plating process. il Sch Arts 77:30-3 D '77
GIANNASI, David E. and Niklas, K. J.
Flavonoid and other chemical constituents of fossil miocene celtis and ulmus (succor creek flora) bibl il Science 197:765-7 Ag 19 '77
—See Niklas, K. J. jt auth
GIAP, Vo-nguyen-. See Vo-nguyen-Giap
GIASONE; opera. See Cavalli, F.
GIBB, John
Expert-ski: heli-skiing in the Canadian Rockies. il House & Gard 149:76+ D '77
GIBBERELLINS
Phyllotaxis in xanthium shoots altered by gibberellic acid. R. Maksymowych and R. O. Erickson. bibl il Science 196:1201-3 Je 10 '77
GIBBONS, Edward F.
Woolworth: the last stand of the variety store. il por Bus W p84-5 Ja 9 '78 *
GIBBONS, J. F. and others
Tutored videotape instruction: a new use of electronics media in education. bibl il Science 195:1139-46 Mr 18 '77
GIBBONS, Orlando
Reviews of records: madrigals and motets. H. L. Clarke. Mus Q 63:146-8 Ja '77 *
GIBBONS, Russell W.
Fear Valley, U.S.A. Commonweal 104:720-2 N 11 '77
GIBBS, Andy
Music people; interview, ed by E. Miller. por Seventeen 36:90 N '77
GIBBS, Jerry
Fishing. See issues of Outdoor life to August 1977
Leap. il Outdoor Life 160:67-71+ N '77
Secrets of the strike. il Outdoor Life 160:61-5+ Ag '77
(ed) Update. il Outdoor Life 160:28, 34, 100 O; 52, 102, 106 N; 52, 110 D '77; 161:44, 52, 106 Ja '78
GIBBS, Tony
(ed) Cruising yachtsman. See issues of Yachting
Rough log. See issues of Yachting
GIBNEY, Frank
Report & comment: Japan. il por Atlantic 239:6-9+ Je '77
Ripple effect in Korea. For Affairs 56:160-74 O '77
GIBSON, Campbell
Elusive rise in the American birthrate. bibl il Science 196:500-3; 197:110 Ap 29, Jl 8 '77
GIBSON, Michael
Paris. il Art N 76:101-2 Ap; 104 O; 123 D '77
Paris' contemporary art fair. il Art N 76:92 S '77
GIBSON, Ralph
Masters of the darkroom; excerpt from Darkroom. il por Pop Phot 80:110-15+ Mr '77
GIBSON, Raymond E.
Total spiritual fitness—in 30 minutes a week. Chr Cent 94:197-8 Mr 2 '77
GIBSON, William
Golda. Reviews
America 137:423 D 10 '77 *
Nation 225:605 D 3 '77 *
New Repub 177:18-19 D 3 '77 *
New Yorker 53:81 N 28 '77 *
Newsweek 90:80 N 28 '77 *
Time il 110:103 N 28 '77 *
GIDDENS, Kenneth Rabb
Censorship and man's right to know; address; December 17, 1976. Vital Speeches 43:280-3 F 15 '77
GIEREK, Edward
Poland: meat and potatoes. P. Martin. Newsweek 91:26 Ja 2 '78 *
Polish road to communism. P. Osnos. For Affairs 56:209-20 O '77 *
Trying to prop up Poland's shaky government. S. W. Sanders. il por Bus W p44 D 19 '77 *
GIESEY, Ralph E.
Rules of inheritance and strategies of mobility in prerevolutionary France. bibl f Am Hist R 82:271-89 Ap '77

GIFFORD, J. Nebraska
(ed) See Tucker, M. Marcia's not there to take artistic chances

GIFFORD, Thomas
Thomas Gifford: the bestsell factor. S. L. Muellner. por Writers Digest 57:50-1 Jl '77 *

GIFT boxes. See Boxes, cases, etc.

GIFT shops
See also
Museum stores

GIFT wrappings. See Wrapping of packages

GIFTED and Talented, Office for the. See United States—Education, Office of—Gifted and Talented, Office for the.

GIFTED children. See Children, Gifted

GIFTS
Cleopatra's choice; gifts from museum stores. L. Nooger. il Am Home 80:13 N '77
Ghastly gifts, or, the art of graceful giving. J. Viorst. il Redbook 150:29+ D '77
Gifts for the old man; Fathers Day. il Esquire 87:106-7 Je '77
10 cheers for mom. il Am Home 80:13 My '77
12 gifts fathers want most. il Mech Illus 73:50-1 Je '77
See also
Books as gifts
Christmas gifts
Food as gifts
Giving
Liquors as gifts
Money as gifts
Pets as gifts
Phonograph records as gifts
Plants as gifts

GIFTS for children
See also
Christmas gifts for children

GIGANTE, Cathy M.
Airborne; poem. Seventeen 36:96 Ag '77

GIGOT, Paul
Tokyo Rose in New York. Nat R 29:1488 D 23 '77

GILBERT, Arthur
Great collection of tiny artistry—how it was made. M. Zucker. il Smithsonian 8:84-91 My '77 *

GILBERT, Arthur, mosaic collection. See Art—Private collections

GILBERT, Barrie
My God, I've gotten too close. D. Richey. il Outdoor Life 161:58-9+ Ja '78 *

GILBERT, Bentley Brinkerhoff
David Lloyd George: land, the budget, and social reform. bibl f Am Hist R 81:1058-66 D '76

GILBERT, Bil
College basketball. il Sports Illus 46:59+ Ap 4 '77
Facing old king cold. il Sports Illus 46:74-8+ Mr 14 '77
Floodtrap city: Johnstown, Pa. il map Audubon 79:2-9 N '77
Hellish spot in heavenly surroundings. il maps Audubon 79:30-47 Mr '77
It's shake, rumble and roll. il Sports Illus 47:28-34+ Jl 11 '77
I've got you under my skin. il Sports Illus 47:30-4 Ag 15 '77; Same abr. with title There's no fleeing the flea. Read Digest 112:11-12+ Ja '78
Joy in hard times. il Sports Illus 47:100-4+ D 19 '77
Nature. il Sports Illus 46:75-7 My 2 '77
That senior season (title varies) il Sports Illus 47:104-8+ N 14; 38-40+ N 21 '77
Uncle Sam says scram! il maps Audubon 79:42-55 Ja '77
about
Letter from the publisher. J. Meyers. Sports Illus 47:6 D 19 '77 *

GILBERT, Cass
World's tallest building. S. Klaw. il pors Am Heritage 28:86-98 F '77 *

GILBERT, Craig
Men at home. Am Home 80:12 O '77
Television. Am Home 80:14 S '77

GILBERT, Elliot Lewis
Murder without air. New Repub 177:33-4 Jl 30 '77

GILBERT, Fred. See Balaban-Malenbaum, G. jt auth

GILBERT, Jack
My graveyard in Tokyo; Breakfast; Mistrust of bronze; Sects; Rainy forests of Northern California; Love poem; Ostinato rigore; Alba; poems. Esquire 88:124-5 Ag '77

GILBERT, John P. and others
Statistics and ethics in surgery and anesthesia. bibl il Science 198:684-9 N 18 '77

GILBERT, Neil
Burgeoning social service payload. il Society 14:63-5 My '77

GILBERT, Perry Webster
Two decades of shark research: a review. bibl il por BioScience 27:670-3 O '77

GILBERT, Sandra M.
On the edge of the estate. Poetry 129:296-301 F '77
Sculpture: naiad/fountain; Elegy; poems. Poetry 131:67-8 N '77

GILBERT, Steven W.
Crunch. Educ Digest 42:46-9 F '77

GILBERT, Thomas L.
Success stories in multiple-use. il Parks & Rec 12:22a-24a F '77

GILBERT, William S.
Gilbert and Sullivan discography. R. Dyer. il Hi Fi 27:52-8 My '77 *

GILBERT and Sullivan opera
Gilbert and Sullivan this spring in Davis, S.F., San Jose, Stanford. il Sunset 158:34+ Mr '77
Secret diaries of Sir Arthur Sullivan. A. Jacobs. il pors Hi Fi 27:46-50 My '77
See also
D'Oyly Carte Opera Company
Phonograph records—Gilbert and Sullivan opera

GILCHRIST, Alan L.
Perceived lightness depends on perceived spatial arrangement. bibl il Science 195:185-7 Ja 14 '77

GILCHRIST, Jane
Shopwalk. Sports Illus 47:9 N 21 '77

GILCHRIST, Sandra. See Abele, L. G. jt auth

GILDER, Jules
Build amplifier for hands-off telephone. il Radio-Electr 48:60-1 My '77

GILELS, Elena
Elena Gilels, piano; debut program at the YMHA. por Hi Fi 27:MA22 My '77 *

GILES, Kenneth L.
Genetic engineering: the origin of the long-distance rumor. J. L. Marx. Science 198:388 O 28 '77 *

GILES, Louise Jones
Obituary
Am Lib por 8:59 F '77
Wilson Lib Bull por 51:633 Ap '77. E. J. Josey

GILHOOLEY, James J.
On the road to Drogheda. il Commonweal 104:178-80 Mr 18 '77

GILILLAND, James B.
New Mexico incident. W. H. Hutchinson. bibl il pors Am West 14:4-7+ N '77 *

GILKEY, Langdon
Anathemas and orthodoxy. Chr Cent 94:1026-9 N 9 '77

GILL, Bernard
Second coming. B. Brenner. Chr Today 21:43-4 Ja 21 '77 *

GILL, Brendan
Lindbergh alone; condensation. il pors Read Digest 110:225-8+ My '77
Theatre. See occasional issues of New Yorker

GILL, June M.
Films of Gunvor Nelson. bibl il Film Q 30:28-36 Spr '77

GILL, Michael
Heritage of Royal heritage. R. Gelatt. il por Sat R 4:33-4 Ap 30 '77 *

GILL, Robert Lee
Living with antiques. E. D. Garrett. il Antiques 111:990-1001 My '77 *

GILLAM, Isaac Thomas, 4th
Space shuttle research chief. il pors Ebony 32:124-6+ Ap '77 *

GILLAM, Richard
Richard Hofstadter, C. Wright Mills, and the critical ideal. Am Scholar 47:69-85 Wint '77

GILLERS, Stephen
Maze of school desegregation. Nation 224:688-91 Je 4 '77
Nitpicking justice. Nation 224:110-13 Ja 29 '77

GILLES de la Tourette syndrome. See Nervous system—Diseases

GILLESPIE, Charles
Golf. Sports Illus 46:50+ Je 20 '77

GILLESPIE, David
Newly evolved repeated DNA sequences in primates. bibl il Science 196:889-91 My 20 '77

GILLESPIE, Dizzy
Indigenous music. N. Hentoff. Nation 224:350 Mr 19 '77 *

GILLESPIE, Gregory J.
Gregory Gillespie's dense reality; interview, ed by J. Gruen. il por Art N 76:78-81 Mr '77

GILLESPIE, Jonathan
Survivor; poem. Poetry 130:80 My '77

GILLET, Renaud
Threadbare. por Forbes 120:190 N 15 '77 *

GILLETTE, Wyo.
Coal on the range. A. J. Mayer and J. B. Copeland. il Newsweek 89:67-8 Je 6 '77

GILLETTE Company
Fiery debate over smoke-alarm efficiency; controversy surrounding claims made by Gillette and ADT concerning their photoelectric detectors. il Bus W p95-6+ S 26 '77
Gillette after the diversification that failed. il Bus W p58-62 F 28 '77
Payoffs in Braun's Americanized style. il Bus W p60+ Ap 18 '77
Why Gillette stopped its digital watches. Bus W p37-8 Ja 31 '77

GILLIATT, Michael T.
Big brother I.Q? bibl Clearing H 51:166-9 D '77

GILLIATT, Penelope
Current cinema. See issues of New Yorker, March 28, 1977 to September 19, 1977
Fleeced; story. New Yorker 53:40-6 My 2 '77
Profiles: L. Buñuel. New Yorker 53:53-4+ D 5 '77

GILLIE, Oliver
Did Sir Cyril Burt fake his research on heritability of intelligence? Educ Digest 42:43-5 Mr '77

GILLIES, Thomas D.
Missouri science library nixes online service. Lib J 102:1547 Ag '77 *

GILLIGAN, John Joyce
America's stake in the developing world; address, September 27, 1977. Dept State Bull 77:687-91 N 14 '77
United States seeks improved U.N. programs to meet basic needs of world's poor; address, June 16, 1977. Dept State Bull 77:204-7 Ag 15 '77

about

Appropriate technology. A. Von Lazar and K. Bode. New Repub 176:11-13 Je 11 '77 *

GILLILAND, J. Richard. See Little, P. L. jt auth

GILLIS, Candida, and others
English classroom 1977; EJ readership survey. il Engl J 66:55-8 Ja; 20-6 S '77

GILLISON, Gillian
Fertility rites and sorcery in a New Guinea village. il map Nat Geog 152:124-46 Jl '77

GILMAN, Kay
Phyllis & Bob. pors Ladies Home J 94:78+ N '77
Sports. See issues of Vogue

GILMORE, C. P.
Taking exercise to heart. il pors N Y Times Mag p38-42+ Mr 27 '77; Same abr. with title Does exercise really prolong life? Read Digest 111:140-3 Jl '77
When, not if, is now key to solar power. Sci Digest 81:42-5 Mr '77

GILMORE, Charles M.
All about RF signal generators. il Radio-Electr 48:49-51+ Ag; 56-8+ S; 67-9+ O '77
Analog voltmeters (cont) il Radio-Electr 48:75-7 F; 69-71+ Mr '77
What you should know about DMM's. il Radio-Electr 48:53-5+ Jl '77

GILMORE, Gary Mark
After Gilmore. L. Denniston. New Repub 176:10-12 Ja 29 '77 *
After Gilmore, who's next to die? il pors Time 109:48-9 Ja 31 '77 *
Death watch in Salt Lake City. il por Time 109:51 Ja 24 '77 *
Deterrent to the deterrent argument. Chr Cent 94:132-3 F 16 '77 *
Gilmore gets his wish. D. A. Williams and others. il pors Newsweek 89:31-2 Ja 31 '77 *
Gilmore saga. il Newsweek 90:12 S 19 '77 *
Gilmore's countdown. T. Mathews and P. S. Greenberg. por Newsweek 89:35 Ja 24 '77 *
Gilmore's victory. E. Shorris. il Harpers 254:16+ Ap '77 *
Heard round the world. Nat R 29:133-4 F 4 '77 *
Hell's agent. R. Friedman. il Esquire 88:75-8+ O '77 *
Ringmaster at the circus. D. Gelman and others. il por Newsweek 89:77-8 Ja 31 '77 *

GILPIN, Frank I.
Check hypo, stop print curl and water waste. il Mod Phot 41:138-9 O '77

GILPIN, Laura
Laura Gilpin: photographer of the Southwest; interview, ed by D. Vestal. il por Pop Phot 80:100-5 F '77

GILPIN, Laura Crafton
Hub of the Universe; poem, excerpt from the Hocus pocus of the universe. McCalls 104:114 F '77

GILPIN, Michael E. See Armstrong, R. A. jt auth

GIMI (native race) See Papua New Guinea—Native races

GIN game; drama. See Coburn, D. L.

GINASTERA, Alberto
Piano concerto no. 2, op. 37; Quintet for piano and strings. G. S. Fox. Am Rec G 40:25-6 Je '77 *

GINGERBREAD houses, ornaments, etc. See Cookery, Ornamental

GINGERICH, Owen
Laboratory exercises in astronomy: the Crab Nebula. il Sky & Tel 54:378-82 N '77
PhD language requirement. il Phys Today 30:9+ N '77
Tycho Brahe and the great comet of 1577. il Sky & Tel 54:452-8 D '77
(ed) See Eames, C. Conversation with Charles Eames

GINGLE, Alan R. and Robertson, Anthony
Morphologies of cells from 1-day chick embryos. bibl il Science 196:59-60 Ap 1 '77
—See Robertson, A. jt auth

GINOTT, Alice
Christmas and the Jewish child. Ladies Home J 94:26 D '77
How to drive your child sane. il Ladies Home J 94:48+ Ag '77

GINOTT, Mimi
On living with diabetes. Mademoiselle 83:38+ My '77

GINSBERG, Allen
PW interviews; ed by G. Stuttaford. por Pub W 212:6-7 N 14 '77

GINSBERG, Robert
British tried to discredit Declaration of Independence. por Intellect 105:387 My '77

GINSBURG, Harvey J.
Child altruism: saving Johnny not mommy. Sci N 112:358-9 N 26 '77 *

GINSBURG, Helen
Jobs for all. Nation 224:138-43 F 5 '77

GINSBURG, Ruth Bader
Discriminating protection. New Repub 176:9 Ap 30 '77

GINSENG
Crackdown on a fabled root. il Time 110:34 S 5 '77

GINZBERG, Eli
Job problem; with biographical sketch. il Sci Am 237:15, 43-51 bibl(p 163) N '77
Real college pay-off. Parents Mag 52:59+ S '77
When mothers work. Parents Mag 52:34+ Ap '77

about

How you going to get 'em back in the kitchen? You aren't. J. A. Briggs. il por Forbes 120:177-80+ N 15 '77 *

GINZBURG, Alexander Ilich
Dual messages to Washington. il por Time 109:30+ F 14 '77 *

GIOBBI, Edward
Is your child gifted? interview, ed by C. Leon. House & Gard 149:40 Ap '77
Whole-earth gourmet. E. O'Bryan. il por Am Home 80:64-5 Jl '77 *

GIORDANO, Gerard
Appalachian reading instruction: the pragmatic social factor. Engl J 66:31-2 My '77

GIORDANO, Umberto
Andrea Chénier. Review
Opera N il 41:16+ Mr 26 '77 *
In the opera house: how much does neatness count? recordings of Andrea Chénier and La forza del destino, conducted by J. Levine. K. Furie. il por Hi Fi 27:71-4 Ag '77 *
Love and revolution; Andrea Chénier. W. Ashbrook. Opera N 41:14-15 Mr 26 '77 *
Outstanding effort; Andrea Chénier; RCA recording. D. Arthur. il Am Rec G 40:29-31 O '77 *

GIORDMAINE, J. A.
Solid-state electronics: scientific basis for future advance. bibl il Science 195:1235-40 Mr 18 '77

GIRAFFES
Africa's gentle giants. B. Foster. il map Nat Geog 152:402-17 S '77
Lo, the poor giraffe; death of Victor at the Marwell Zoo in England. il Newsweek 90:51 O 3 '77
Rescuing the Rothschild. C. B. Patterson. il Nat Geog 152:402-17 S '77

GIRARD, Joe
Selling Joe Girard. por Forbes 120:120 N 1 '77 *

GIRARD, Tanner. See Kolb, L. jt auth

GIRARDET, Freddy
Cuisine surprise. A. Gold and R. Fizdale. Vogue 167:108+, 176-9 F '77 *

GIRARDI, Joseph Samuel. See Girard, J.

GIRDERS
Sprinkler system installer invents a bar joist that is part sprinkler pipe. il Archit Rec 162:119 Jl '77
Wood I-beams. B. Lopez. il Pop Sci 211:92 D '77

GIRL Scouts
Scouts survive island and vice versa. C. Lewis. il Camp Mag 49:6-9 Ja '77

GIRLS
Relating; questions and answers. A. Wood. See issues of Seventeen
See also
Adolescence
Sex differences

GIRLS, Delinquent
Unequal justice unter the juvenile law. D. Cohen. Psychol Today 11:26 O '77

GIRLS, Tall. See Stature

GIRLS as actresses. See Children as actors and actresses

GIRLS clubs
See also
Girl Scouts

GISCARD D'ESTAING, Valéry
Giscard speaks out; excerpts from interview, ed by A. De Borchgrave. il por Newsweek 90:45-8 Jl 25 '77

about

Center holds. il por Time 110:51-2 N 7 '77 *
France: a leftist surge. A. Deming and E. Peer. il Newsweek 89:46 Ap 4 '77 *
Fun and games in Paris; L. Brezhnev's visit to France. Nat R 29:765 Jl 8 '77 *

GISCARD D'ESTAING, Valéry—about—*Continued*
Giscard gets the message. il por Time 109:41 Ap 11 '77 *
Giscard reshuffles for political survival. por Bus W p33+ Ap 11 '77 *
Giscard's blues. K. Willenson and E. Peer. por Newsweek 89:53 F 14 '77 *
M. le Maire de Paris. G. Ross. New Repub 176:17-19 Ap 9 '77 *
Paris is worth a race. K. Willenson and others. pors Newsweek 89:53-4 Ja 31 '77 *
Plight of Giscard d'Estaing. J. O. Goldsborough. il pors N Y Times Mag p37-9+ S 11 '77 *
Political uncertainty in France. E. W. Fox and J. O. Safford, 3d. Cur Hist 73:149-52+ N '77 *
Reporter in Europe. J. Kramer. New Yorker 53: 72-81 Jl 4 '77 *
Shot from Paris. D. Martin and others. il pors Newsweek 90:44 Jl 25 '77 *
White knight in a graveyard. il pors Time 109: 37-8 Mr 28 '77 *

GISELLE; ballet. See Ballet reviews—Single works

GISH, Lillian
Silent mimi talks; interview, ed by Q. Eaton. por Opera N 42:18-19+ D 24 '77

GITLIN, Todd
Reunion and intimation. Nation 225:400-4 O 22 '77

GITTELSON, Natalie
Shaping up. bibl il McCalls 105:63-70 O '77

GITTLER, Allan
Old sound, new model. por Horizon 20:51 S '77 *

GIUSTO, Joann
ABA regional in Washington, D.C: low turnout, high spirits. il Pub W 212:66-8 O 17 '77
—See Maryles, D; Smith, R. H. jt auths

GIVING
Peanuts, emeralds and the art of giving. W. J. Byron. America 137:461-3 D 24 '77
See also
Charities
Christmas gifts
Church finance
Gifts

GLACÉED fruit. See Confectionery

GLACIAL epochs
Head south with all deliberate speed: ice may return in a few thousand years. N. Calder. il Smithsonian 8:32-41 bibl(p 114) Ja '78
On the trail of Wisconsin's Ice Age. A. LaBastille. il pors map Nat Geog 152:182-205 Ag '77
Pleistocene volcanism and glacial initiation. J. R. Bray. bibl il Science 197:251-4 Jl 15 '77
Sea-floor data link glaciation to earth's orbital motion. G. B. Lubkin. il Phys Today 30:17+ My '77
Variations in the earth's orbit: pacemaker of the ice ages. J. D. Hays and others; reply with rejoinder. D. L. Evans and H. J. Freeland. bibl il Science 198:528-30 N 4 '77

GLADE, Luba B.
New Orleans. Art N 76:163-6 Summ '77

GLADE, William
Camelot revisited. Society 14:20-1 My '77

GLADIOLUS
Rainbow of glad colors. Bet Hom & Gard 55:191 Je '77

GLADSTONE, Bernard
(ed) Boatkeeper. il Motor B & S 140:93-100 N; 97-104 D '77

GLADSTONE, Mo.
Contract services stretch sewer maintenance budget. D. C. Anderson. il Am City & County 92:53 F '77

GLADWIN, Thomas N. and Walter, Ingo
Shadowy underside of international trade. Sat R 4:16+ Jl 9 '77

GLAESSNER, Verina
(ed) See Brownlow, K. Winstanley

GLANDER, Kenneth E.
Poison in a monkey's Garden of Eden; with biographical sketch. Natur Hist 86:4, 34-41 bibl(p96) Mr '77

GLANDS
Gland dictates death to aging octopus. il Sci N 112:375 D 3 '77
Hormonal inhibition of feeding and death in octopus: control by optic gland secretion. J. Wodinsky. bibl il Science 198:948-51 D 2 '77
Octopus's life; aging process impeded by optic gland removal. il Newsweek 90:81 D 12 '77
See also
Prostate gland

Diseases

See also
Cystic fibrosis

GLASCOCK, H. R. Jr
Why not an American forestry policy—now? adaptation of address. Am For 83:22+ Ap '77

GLASER, Paul Michael
Starsky & Hutch; interview, ed by M. Cohen. pors Ladies Home J 94:50+ Mr '77
Sticking with Starsky; interview, ed by E. Miller. il pors Seventeen 36:156-7+ S '77

GLASER, Peter Edward
Solar power from satellites; adaptation of address, October 1976. bibl il Phys Today 30: 30-2+ F; 9+ Jl '77

GLASGOW, Vaughn L.
G.P.A. Healy and his Louisiana portraits. bibl il Antiques 111:1204-9 Je '77

GLASGOW

Music

See also
Opera—Great Britain

GLASS, Bentley
Scientist: trustee for humanity. bibl BioScience 27:277-8 Ap '77

GLASS, Gene V.
Nadir is to Nader as lowest is to. . . Nat R 29: 776-7 Jl 8 '77

GLASS, Humphrey, and Shirk, Martha
Transkei's empty independence. Progressive 41: 28-31 Mr '77

GLASS, Jay D.
Alpha blocking: absence in visuobehavioral deprivation. bibl il Science 198:58-60 O 7 '77

GLASS, Jeanne A.
Paperback historical romance. Writer 90:33-5 Ap '77

GLASS, Leon. See Mackey, M. C. jt auth

GLASS, Philip
New music; Another look at harmony, part 4. J. La Barbara. Hi Fi 27:MA14-15 N '77 *

GLASS, Roger I. and others
Earthquake injuries related to housing in a Guatemalan village. bibl il map Science 197: 638-43 Ag 12 '77

GLASS
Shock-produced olivine glass: first observation. R. Jeanloz and others. bibl il Science 197:457-9 Jl 29 '77
See also
Glassware
Glazes and glazing (glass)
Windows

GLASS, Optical
Techniques tomorrow. B. Sherman. Mod Phot 41: 84+ O '77

GLASS, Ornamental
See also
Glass engraving

GLASS, Stained. See Glass painting and staining

GLASS boxes. See Boxes, cases, etc.

GLASS cleaners. See Cleaning compositions

GLASS construction
Corporate slick; mirror glass architectural design. R. Jensen. il Horizon 20:70-3 N '77

GLASS containers
Sculpture lids for gift jars; baker's clay. il Sunset 159:80-1 D '77

GLASS doors. See Doors

GLASS engraving
Master engravers of Corning, New York. E. S. Farrar. bibl il Antiques 112:726-31 O '77

GLASS fibers, Optical. See Fiber optics

GLASS gardens
See also
Terrariums

GLASS hydration dating. See Hydration rind dating

GLASS industry
Midland: how to specialize. N. Howard. il Duns R 110:49-50 O '77
See also
Corning Glass Works

History

Greentown glass: Indiana Tumbler and Goblet Company. C. B. Lippert and J. S. Measell. bibl il Antiques 111:774-81 Ap '77

Sweden

Swedish treat: beautiful glass in a rustic landscape; touring southeastern Sweden. D. Otis. il House & Gard 149:48+ Jl '77

GLASS manufacture. See Glass industry

GLASS painting and staining
Chartres: through a glass darkly. il Time 109: 54-5 Ja 31 '77
Devotion to stained glass; window created by A. Rattner for the Chicago Loop Synagogue. Vasari. il Art N 76:20+ My '77
Stained glass design. T. S. Dahood. il Design (US) 78:20-2 mid-Wint '77
Tiffany window displayed at Corning, N.Y. Museum of Glass. il(p 1) Hobbies 82:118 Mr '77
Treasures from Laurelton Hall; collection of Tiffany glass of the Hugh F. McKeans. M. R. Grant. il Antiques 111:752-9 Ap '77

GLASSER, Selma
Writing selected shorts; excerpt from How to write and sell fillers, light verse and short humor. Writer 90:26-9 N '77

GLASSER, William
Needed for America: the kind of recreation that frees the mind; interview. il por U.S. News 82:74-6 My 23 '77
10 steps to good discipline. il Todays Educ 66: 60-3 N '77

GLASSES (spectacles) See Eyeglasses

GLASSES, Drinking. See Drinking vessels

GLASSWARE
American historical glass:
Bryan-Kern paperweight. M. Wollett and B. Wollett. il Hobbies 82:99 O '77
Cleveland tumbler and shot glass. M. Wollett and B. Wollett. il Hobbies 82:99 Mr '77
Dewey canteen. M. Wollett and B. Wollett. il Hobbies 82:99 N '77
Fitzhugh Lee plate. M. Wollett and B. Wollett. il Hobbies 82:99 Ap '77
Fort Meigs cup plate. M. Wollett and B. Wollett. Hobbies 82:99 D '77
Garfield memorial goblet. M. Wollett and B. Wollett. il Hobbies 82:99 S '77
Lafayette-Franklin sulphide doorknobs. M. Wollett and B. Wollett. il Hobbies 81:99 F '77
Liberty Bell water pitcher. M. Wollett and B. Wollett. il Hobbies 82:99 Je '77
Liberty's hand with torch lamp. M. Wollett and B. Wollett. il Hobbies 82:99 Jl '77
McKinley milk glass tumbler. M. Wollett and B. Wollett. il Hobbies 82:99 Ja '78
Salt Lake City Temple bread tray. M. Wollett and B. Wollett. il Hobbies 82:99 Ag '77
Teddy Roosevelt figural bottle. M. Wollett and B. Wollett. il Hobbies 82:99 My '77
Glass relating to William III. P. Warren. bibl il Antiques 112:742-9 O '77
Master engravers of Corning, New York. E. S. Farrar. bibl il Antiques 112:726-31 O '77
Renee Lalique. il Hobbies 82:95-7 Ja '78
Tiffany glass at the Chrysler Museum, Norfolk, Virginia. P. E. Doros. bibl il Antiques 111:746-50 Ap '77
Wine finery. P. Pollock. il Bet Hom & Gard 55:126+ Je '77
See also
Corning Glass Center, Corning, N.Y.
Drinking vessels
Paperweights
Salt and pepper grinders, shakers, etc.

Collectors and collecting

Treasures from Laurelton Hall; collection of Tiffany glass of the Hugh F. McKeans. M. R. Grant. il Antiques 111:752-9 Ap '77

Exhibitions

American glass; Corning Museum exhibition. S. B. Sherrill. il Antiques 111:1088+ Je '77
Coburger Glaspreis 1977. T. Buechner. il Craft Horiz 37:16-27 D '77
First exhibition of cut and engraved glass from one American city at the Corning Museum of Glass. il Hobbies 82:68-9 My '77

GLASTONBURY Abbey. See Abbeys

GLATTHORN, Allan A.
Censorship and the classroom teacher. Engl J 66:12-15 F '77; Same abr. Educ Digest 43:54-6 S '77
Creating learning environments. Educ Digest 43:9-12 N '77
On finding some real alternatives. il Todays Educ 66:68-71 N '77

GLAUCOMA
Can marijuana cure glaucoma? il pors Ebony 32:108+ S '77

GLAZE, Andrew
Dr Freud; poem. Atlantic 239:81 Je '77
Eyes of the heart; poem. New Yorker 53:40 Mr 14 '77
Fantasy Street; poem. New Yorker 53:40-1 Ap 11 '77
September; poem. New Yorker 53:32 S 5 '77

GLAZE, Eleanor
Spider stories; story. Redbook 148:111-13+ Ap '77

GLAZER, Nathan
Herberg as sociologist. Nat R 29:881-2 Ag 5 '77

GLAZES and glazing (ceramics)
Arabian luster glazes. R. Behrens. Ceram Mo 25:46 Je '77
Barium glazes. R. Behrens. il por Ceram Mo 25:64-5 My '77
Cone 5 to 8 oxidation glazes. R. Behrens. il Ceram Mo 25:56-7 D '77
Dust glazing. D. Parks. il Ceram Mo 25:23-7 O '77
Japanese ash glazes. H. Sasaki. il por Ceram Mo 25:53-9 F '77
Lead and cadmium release; WHO conference on ceramic foodware safety. il Ceram Mo 25:69+ D '77
Manganese glazes. R. Behrens. Ceram Mo 25:64 Mr '77
Oxidation glazes, slips, stains, and bodies for cone 6. R. Zakin. il Ceram Mo 25:33-43 Ap '77

GLAZES and glazing (glass)
New glazing materials for your home, greenhouse, or solar collector. G. Stone. il Pop Sci 211:128+ S '77
Some regional considerations concerning glazing materials; excerpt from The solar greenhouse book. W. D. Davis. Org Gard & Farm 24:67-8 D '77

GLAZIER, Kenneth M.
Separatism and Quebec. bibl f Cur Hist 72:154-7+ Ap '77

GLAZUNOV, Ilya
Ars brevis for a Soviet painter. il Time 110:35+ Jl 11 '77 *
Defiant Russian painter. F. Willey and F. Coleman. il Newsweek 89:44 Je 6 '77 *
Reliable Soviet citizen. J. E. Bowlt. Art N 76:109-11 O '77 *
Soviet painter poses a question. S. F. Starr. il por Smithsonian 8:101-4+ bibl(p 135) D '77 *

GLEASNER, Bill. See Gleasner, D. C. jt auth

GLEASNER, Diana C. and Gleasner, Bill
Bay of Islands. il map Trav/Holiday 148:42-5 D '77
Ohio's Erie Islands. il Travel 148:36-9 Jl '77

GLEASON, Joseph
Excerpt from testimony on proposed revisions of the Hatch Act, February 23, 1977. Cong Digest 56:306+ D '77

GLEASON, Thomas William
Automation again threatens peace on the docks. il Bus W p64+ S 5 '77 *

GLEAZER, Edmund John, 1916-
Future of the community college. il Intellect 106:152-4 O '77

GLEN Echo Park. See Maryland—Parks and reserves

GLENDALE Federal Savings and Loan Association. See Savings and loan associations—California

GLENN, Constance W.
Roy Lichtenstein: ceramic sculpture. il Ceram Mo 25:40-5 My '77

GLENN, John Herschel, 1921-
Critical mass. New Repub 176:2+ My 28 '77 *

GLENN, Mike
Glenn plus ball makes two. B. McDermott. il por Sports Illus 46:38+ Ja 31 '77 *

GLENN, Norval D. and Hill, Lester, Jr
Rural-urban differences in attitudes and behavior in the United States. bibl f il Ann Am Acad 429:36-50 Ja '77

GLIAL cells. See Nerve cells

GLICKMAN, Jane
Preparing for bilingual education. il Am Educ 13:31-2 Ag '77

GLICKMAN, L. Jane. See Glickman, J.

GLICKSTEIN, Ira
Van bench/bed clears away for cargo. il Pop Sci 211:110-11 Jl '77

GLIDDEN-Durkee Division. See SCM Corporation

GLIDERS (aeronautics)
From Japan—nimble new motor glider. B. Kocivar. il Pop Sci 211:75 Jl '77
Hang glider with an engine. W. Thoms. il Mech Illus 73:52+ Ap '77
It's a plane, it's a glider . . . it's both! S. M. Gallager. il Pop Mech 147:170+ F '77
Now they're hanging engines on hang gliders. B. Allen. il Pop Mech 148:62-4+ Ag '77
Powered sailplane takes to the air without a tow. B. Kocivar. il Pop Sci 210:44 Ap '77
Wright glider gets re-invented. R. Q. Riley. il Mech Illus 73:36 Je '77

Testing

Pilot report:
Sperber RF5B, sailplane of independent means. G. Baxter. il Flying 100:40-3 F '77

GLIDING and soaring
He soars through the air. M. Jailer. il por Ret Liv 17:16-17 Ap '77
Sky sports: the thrill of flight. T. Crawford. Harp Baz 110:85+ My '77

GLIKBARG, W. K.
Orchid diplomacy. Horticulture 55:8-13 My '77

GLIMM, Adele
Come back, my love; story. Good H 184:110 Je '77

GLINKA, Mikhail Ivanovich
Russlan and Ludmilla. Reviews
Hi Fi 27:MA32-3 Ag '77 *
New Yorker 53:105-6 Mr 28 '77 *
Newsweek il 89:62 Mr 21 '77 *
Time il 109:66 Mr 21 '77 *

GLINN, Burt
Burt Glinn: the right lens for the right look. M. O'Grady. il Mod Phot 41:78-83 Ag '77 *

GLOB, Peter V.
Who killed the bog men of Denmark? And why? M. Shadbolt. il Read Digest 110:197-200+ Je '77 *

GLOBAL studies. See International education

GLOBAL temperature changes
CO_2 pollution may change the fuel mix. il Bus W p25 Ag 8 '77
Carbon dioxide and climate: carbon budget still unbalanced. R. A. Kerr. Science 197:1352-3 S 30 '77
Carbon dioxide question. G. M. Woodwell. il map Sci Am 238:34-43 Ja '78
Caution: the greenhouse effect. W. Sullivan. Sci Digest 82:58 O '77
Climate and the planets. R. Goody. il Natur Hist 87:84-93 Ja '78
Coal and climate: a yellow light on CO_2. il Sci N 112:68 Jl 30 '77

GLOBAL temperture changes—*Continued*
Coal and the coming (?) superinterglacial. Sci N 111:356 Je 4 '77
Cold shower for climatologists N. Wade. Science 197:647 Ag 12 '77
Desert greenhouse; fossil fuels and climate. il maps Environment 19:14-20 N '77
Devon Island ice cap: core stratigraphy and paleoclimate. R. M. Koerner. bibl il map Science 196:15-18 Ap 1 '77
Has the weather gone mad? B. J. Mason. New Repub 177:21-3 Jl 30 '77
Hazards of coal dependence. W. S. Broecker. il Natur Hist 86:8+ O '77
Head south with all deliberate speed: ice may return in a few thousand years. N. Calder. il Smithsonian 8:32-41 bibl(p 114) Ja '78
Is energy use overheating world? fossil fuels. il U.S. News 83:71 Jl 25 '77
Our changing weather. G. Alexander. il maps Pop Sci 211:100-3+ O '77
Question of climate. J. Norwine. bibl il maps Environment 19:6-13+ N '77
Threats of climate change. il Weatherwise 30: 138 Ag '77
Upsetting the climatic balance. il Chemistry 50: 26-7 O '77
Variations in the earth's orbit: pacemaker of the ice ages. J. D. Hays and others; reply with rejoinder. D. L. Evans and H. J. Freeland. bibl il Science 198:528-30 N 4 '77
What's happening to our climate? S. W. Matthews. il Read Digest 110:88-92 Mr '77
What's happening to our weather? D. Colligan. il Mech Illus 73:132+ My '77

GLOBE thistles. See Thistles

GLOBULAR clusters. See Stars—Clusters

GLOMAR Challenger (ship) See Ships, Research

GLOVE industry
Surprise attack on trade with China; Work Glove Manufacturers Assn. Bus W p32 D 26 '77

GLOVES
Fit the glove to the job. P. Angell. il Pop Mech 148:108-9 Ag '77

GLOXYLATES
Increasing photosynthesis by inhibiting photorespiration with glyoxylate. D. J. Oliver and I. Zelitch. bibl il Science 196:1450-1 Je 24 '77

GLUCAN
Cellulases can enhance β glucan synthesis. Y. S. Wong and others. bibl Science 195:679-81 F 18 '77

GLUCK, Christoph Willibald
Gluck: opera arias. P. L. Miller. Am Rec G 40:17-18 Mr '77 *
Orfeo ed Euridice. Reviews
New Yorker 53:91-4 Je 27 '77 *

GLUCK, Harold
Target: the checks in your mailbox. il Ret Liv 16:25-6+ D '76

GLÜCK, Louise
Blind girl; poem. New Yorker 53:111 Mr 28 '77
Scraps; poem; excerpt from Firstborn, a collection of poems. Redbook 150:76 D '77

GLUCK, Peter
Shinjuku. il Archit Rec 162:101-4 S '77

GLUCKIN, Neil
Electric vehicles (EV's) in your future. il Sci Digest 82:7-13+ S '77
Wind. il Sci Digest 82:26-32 O '77

GLUCKSBERG, Sam. See Krauss, R. M. jt auth

GLUCOCORTICOIDS. See Corticosteroids

GLUCOSE
Hunger in humans induced by 2-deoxy-D-glucose: glucoprivic control of taste preference and food intake. D. A. Thompson and R. G. Campbell. bibl il Science 198:1065-8 D 9 '77
See also
Deoxyglucose

GLUE
Glue you can sand. il Mech Illus 73:114 D '77
See also
Adhesives

GLUECK, Grace
Annenberg controversy. por Art N 76:63-4 My '77
Dissidence as a way of art. il pors N Y Times Mag p33-5 My 8 '77
Moving in on the Met. il por N Y Times Mag p20-2+ F 27 '77
Spoleto U.S.A. il por N Y Times Mag p20-2+ My 22 '77
(ed) 20th-century artists most admired by other artists. il Art N 76:78-103 N '77
Woman as artist. il N Y Times Mag p48-50+ S 25 '77

GLUNT, Ruth Reynolds
Tidal flats in the Hudson. il por Conservationist 31:30-1 My '77

GLUTAMINE synthetase. See Synthetases

GLUTAMYL hydrolase. See Enzymes

GLUTTONY
Seven deadly sins today; excerpt. H. Fairlie. New Repub 177:16-19 O 22 '77

GLYCANS
Peptidoglycan in the cell wall of the primary intracellular symbiote of the pea aphid. E. J. Houk and others. bibl il Science 198:401-3 O 28 '77

GLYCERIN
Body weight: reduction by long-term glycerol treatment. D. Wirtshafter and J. D. Davis. bibl il Science 198:1271-4 D 23 '77

GLYCEROL. See Glycerin

GLYCOCALYX
How bacteria stick. J. W. Costerton and others. il Sci Am 238:86-95 Ja '78

GLYCOPROTEINS
Chemotaxis of rhizobium spp. to a glycoprotein produced by birdsfoot trefoil roots. W. W. Currier and G. A. Strobel. bibl il Science 196:434-6 Ap 22 '77
Control of a cell surface major glycoprotein by epidermal growth factor. L. B. Chen and others. bibl il Science 197:776-8 Ag 19 '77

GLYCOSIDES
See also
Cardiac glycosides
Rutin

GLYNDEBOURNE Festival. See Music festivals—England

GOALIES. See Hockey players

GOATS
Full-time goat dairy: how one family does it. L. Tilton. il Org Gard & Farm 24:162+ O '77
See also
Ibex

Anecdotes, facetiae, satire, etc.

Why does a falling down goat not fall down? D. Snell. il Horticulture 55:36-9 O '77

GOBBI, Tito
Artist life. D. J. Soria. il por Hi Fi 27:MA6-7+ Ag '77 *

GOBBLE, Edward M.
Breaking the silence. Progressive 41:35 F '77

GOBLET cells
Goblet cells in embryonic intestine: accelerated differentiation in culture. B. L. Black and F. Moog. bibl il Science 197:368-70 Jl 22 '77
Stimulation by immune complexes of mucus release from goblet cells of the rat small intestine. W. A. Walker and others. bibl il Science 197:370-2 Jl 22 '77

GOBLETS. See Drinking vessels

GOD
Divine inhabitant. R. Goetz. Chr Cent 94:1085 N 23 '77
Fire, ashes, beauty: fire, power, purpose. E. Schaeffer. Chr Today 21:30-1 My 20 '77
Martin Buber: I and Thou. L. S. Cunningham. Chr Cent 94:246-7 Mr 16 '77
Myth of the self-sufficient man; excerpt from address. M. N. Beck. Chr Today 21:12-16 S 23 '77
Questions God asks. E. Schaeffer. Chr Today 21:36-7 Mr 18 '77
Truth by any other name; propositional revelation. R. H. Nash. Chr Today 22:17-19+ O 7 '77
What witness will God give? E. Schaeffer. Chr Today 22:28-9 O 21 '77
See also
Atheism
Christianity
Creation
Death of God theology
Jesus Christ
Logos (theology)
Religion
Theology
Trinity
Trust in God

Love

See Love (theology)

Proof, Empirical

God and Norman Bloom. C. Sagan. il Am Scholar 46:460-6 Aut '77

Providence

Attraction of life on Mars. L. Morris Chr Today 21:56-7 Mr 4 '77

Will

Is man's purpose an enigma? W. W. Gasque. Chr Today 21:15-17 Jl 29 '77

GOD in literature. See Religion in literature

GOD in poetry. See Religion in poetry

GOD is dead theology. See Death of God theology

GODARD, Jean Luc
Review; Numéro deux. S. Schwartz. Film Q 30: 61-3 Wint '76 *

GODDARD, Robert Hutchings
Goddard. R. P. Hallion. Flying 101:319 S '77 *

GODDEN, Rumer
Writing for children; excerpts from address. Writer 90:18-19 Jl '77

GODFREY, Michael A.
Inevitable forest; excerpt from A closer look. il Nat Wildlife 15:14-16+ Ag '77

GODILLO, Svetlana
Washington's star stargazer. M. A. Kellogg. il por N Y Times Mag p 12-13+ Ja 16 '77 *

GODS and goddesses
Young girl called Kumari: Nepal's current living goddess. D. O'Connor and P. O'Connor. il Ms 5:30 Mr '77

GODTSENHOVEN, Patrick van
Shipwreck! interview. ed. by E. Keiffer, W. F. van Godtsenhoven. il Good H 184:51+ Ap '77 *
GODTSENHOVEN, Wendy Farr van
Shipwreck! interview, ed. by E. Keiffer. il Good H 184:51+ Ap '77
GODWIN, Gail
Southern men, Southern lies. il Esquire 87:126-9 F '77
GOEBBELS, Joseph
Inside the götterdämmerung. il por Time 111:32 Ja 16 '78 *
Springtime with Hitler. il por Newsweek 91:49 Ja 16 '78 *
GOEDICKE, Patricia
For the path she must follow; poem. Harpers 255:72 Jl '77
GOEPPERT, Klaus
Frontier: three big publishing houses; tr by T. Weyr. il Pub W 212:43-4 S 12 '77
GOERG, John. See Shupp, B. D. jt auth
GOERGEN, Robert B.
Development banking à la DLJ. il por Forbes 119:56-7 Ap 15 '77 *
GÖERSCHNER, Ted
Conversation with Ted Göerschner; interview, ed by C. Movalli. il por Am Artist 41:52-7+ S '77
GOETZ, Ronald
Advent meditation. Chr Cent 94:1085 N 23 '77
GOFF, Dorothy L.
Retiring to the Ozarks. il Ret Liv 17:44+ My '77
GOFFMAN, Erving
Genderisms. il Psychol Today 11:60-3 Ag '77
GOGGLES
Heated goggles don't fog up. R. L. Stepler. il Pop Sci 210:73 Mr '77
GOITER
Increasing frequency of thyroid goiters in coho salmon (oncorhynchus kisutch) in the Great Lakes. R. D. Moccia and others. bibl il Science 198:425-6 O 28 '77
GOLANTY, Eric
Fish survival in subfreezing temperatures. il Oceans 10:52-3 My '77
Scripps Institution of Oceanography. il Oceans 10:2-7 N '77
GOLD, Aaron
Rush Street, that lush street. il Holiday 58:50-1+ S '77
GOLD, Andrew
Andrew Gold gets into the picture. por Hi Fi 27:146-7 F '77 *
GOLD, Annalee
(ed) See Fisch, A. Crafts in industry
GOLD, Arthur, and Fizdale, Robert
Food. See issues of Vogue
Insiders' drink. il Vogue 167:192-4 Ap '77
Our dinner-party secrets. il Vogue 167:248-50+ Mr '77
GOLD, Herbert
Television's little dramas. il Harpers 254:88-93 Mr '77
A walk on San Francisco's gay side. il N Y Times Mag p67-9+ N 6 '77
GOLD, Seymour M.
Recreation planning for energy conservation. il Parks & Rec 12:61-3+ S '77
GOLD
See also
Goldsmithing

Prices

Gold stages a comeback—what's sparking it. il U.S. News 82:85-6 Mr 14 '77
GOLD as an investment
Fever chart. il Newsweek 90:76+ N 7 '77
For the gold bugs. S. W. Angrist. il por Forbes 119:92-3 Ap 1 '77
Foreign investors buy a golden hedge. il Bus W p 148 Mr 21 '77
Gold and the dollar. P. A. Samuelson. Newsweek 90:70 O 31 '77
Investing in gold: mining shares, coin or bullion? interview, ed by A. Hershman. J. Kuhn. por Duns R 110:107+ D '77
GOLD as money
Role of gold in the international monetary system; address, December 3, 1976. F. L. Widman. Vital Speeches 43:199-201 Ja 15 '77
See also
Gold clauses
GOLD clauses
U.S. legalizes multicurrency deals. il Bus W p23-4 N 7 '77
GOLD mines and mining

Canada

Scaling Chilkoot even today is a fearful ordeal; retracing the 1897-98 Gold rush ascent. J. Hope. il Smithsonian 7:106-13 bibl(p 154+) F '77

Nicaragua

Let the record show; question of the ownership of Bonanza gold mine in Nicaragua by Asarco, Inc. Nation 225:291-2 O 1 '77

United States

Gold rush '77; California. Time 110:46-7 S 12 '77
GOLD prospecting. See Prospecting
GOLD rush days; drama. See Reay, N.
GOLD rush of 1897-1898. See Gold mines and mining—Canada
GOLD work. See Goldsmithing
GOLDA; drama. See Gibson, W.
GOLDBERG, Alan L.
Rediscovering the joy of good eating for good health. il Parents Mag 52:37+ Mr '77
GOLDBERG, Arthur Joseph
Review meeting of the CSCE opens at Belgrade; statement, October 6, 1977. Dept State Bull 77:674-9 N 14 '77
GOLDBERG, Bernard
Growing feud at American Distilling. D. G. Santry. por Bus W 106 D 12 '77 *
GOLDBERG, Dan
Retailing: eyes right. D. Pauly and B. Keough. il por Newsweek 91:50+ Ja 2 '78 *
GOLDBERG, Edward D.
What can we do about marine pollution? D. Behrman. il UNESCO Courier 30:27-8 Ja '77 *
GOLDBERG, Erwin, and others
Cytochrome c: immunofluorescent localization of the testis-specific form. bibl il Science 196:1010-12 My 27 '77
GOLDBERG, Jeanne
Diet menu. See issues of Family health incorporating Today's health
GOLDBERG, Leo
Donald Howard Menzel. il pors Sky & Tel 53:244-51 Ap '77
GOLDBERG, Norman
Shop talk. See issues of Popular photography
GOLDBERG, Reuben Lucius. See Goldberg, Rube
GOLDBERG, Richard
Summer search. map Seventeen 36:68-9 Ag '77
GOLDBERG, Robert
Creating a showcase is not an easy task. House B 119:74 O '77
Power of the pen. House B 119:80 N '77
GOLDBERG, Rube
Solving the energy crisis. il Am Heritage 28:30-1 O '77 *
GOLDBERG, Vicki
Do body rhythms really make you tick? Read Digest 110:181-2+ Je '77
Psychology and the arts. bibl il Psychol Today 11:24+ N '77
What can we do about jet lag. bibl il Psychol Today 11:68-9+ Ag '77
GOLDBERGER, Paul
Architecture. il N Y Times Mag p 74-5+ Je 5; p34-7 Jl 24; p42-4 Ag 7; p 106-8 O 23; p 146-8+ D 11 '77
Brash, young and post-modern. il N Y Times Mag p 18-20+ F 20 '77
Design (cont) il N Y Times Mag p46-7+ Ja 16; 66-9 Mr 13; 74-6+ Mr 20 '77
Lower Manhattan takes on a new character. il Horizon 20:28-37 N '77
Space age comes to the Empire state. il Horizon 19:60-71 Jl '77
Triumph of style: one man's home and his collections. il Smithsonian 8:100-4+ bibl(p 147-8) Ap '77
GOLDBLUM, Jacob
FM gabbai. M. Singer. Atlantic 240:98-100 O '77 *
GOLDE, David W. and others
Growth hormone: species-specific stimulation of erythropoiesis in vitro. bibl il Science 196:1112-13 Je 3 '77
GOLDEN, Bruce
Swimsuit optional zone. Progressive 41:41-2 My '77
GOLDEN, Francis
North again; reproductions of paintings. il Audubon 79:18-22+ Mr '77
GOLDEN, James S.
After the flood. il Sat Eve Post 249:52-3+ D '77
GOLDEN Gate Park. See San Francisco—Parks and playgrounds
GOLDEN trout. See Trout
GOLDEN Trout Wilderness Study Area. See Wilderness areas—California
GOLDENBERG, Ronald, and McNair, Bruce
Child no one knows. Educ Digest 43:36-8 O '77
GOLDENDALE Observatory, Vancouver, Wash. See Astronomical observatories
GOLDFINCHES
Wild canaries; American goldfinch. L. Line. Field & S 82:100 S '77
GOLDFISH eye. See Eye (fishes)
GOLDIN, Amy
Alexander Calder, 1898-1976. il por Art in Am 65:70-3 Mr '77
Islam goes to England. bibl il Art in Am 65:106-13 Ja '77
Report from Toronto & Montreal. il Art in Am 65:35-45+ Mr '77
—and Smith, Roberta
Present tense: new art and the New York museum. il Art in Am 65:92-104 S '77
GOLDIN-MEADOW, Susan, and Feldman, Heidi
Development of language-like communication without a language model. bibl il Science 197:401-3 Jl 22 '77

GOLDMAN, Albert
Charleston! Charleston! il Esquire 87:110-13+ Je '77
Farewell to flesh: Rio goes Hollywood; excerpt from Carnival in Rio. il Esquire 89:66-72+ Ja '78
Recordings. Esquire 88:44+ O '77
GOLDMAN, James A.
Baconian imperative. bibl il Intellect 105:430-2 Je '77
GOLDMAN, Judith
Collecting. See issues of Vogue
Master printer of Bedford, N.Y. il pors Art N 76:50-4 S '77
GOLDMAN, Rita
How to cope with holiday hangups and hangovers. Harp Baz 111:134-5+ D '77
GOLDMAN, William
Bridge too far; excerpt from screenplay. il map Sr Schol 109:21-4 Ap 21 '77
GOLDMAN, Sachs & Company
Coral Springs sues over bond advice. Am City & County 92:33 Ag '77
GOLDMARK, Susan. See Bird, K. jt auth
GOLDNER, Nancy
Dance (cont) Nation 224:186-8, 250-2, 412-14, 637-8, 666-8, 697-8, 794+; 225:28-30, 88+, 568-9 F 12, 26, Ap 2, My 21-Je 4, 25-Jl 2, 23, N 26 '77
GOLDSBOROUGH, James O.
Eurocommunism after Madrid. For Affairs 55:800-14 Jl '77
Plight of Giscard d'Estaing. il pors N Y Times Mag p37-9+ S 11 '77
GOLDSCHLAG, Harry
Reading by listening. Ret Liv 17:44-5 D '77
GOLDSCHMIDT, Neil
Urban mayor offers some sensible strategies in searching for a new urban policy; ed by W. F. Wagner, Jr. Archit Rec 161:13 Mr '77
GOLDSCHMIDT, Richard Benedict
Return of hopeful monsters; theories of R. Goldschmidt. Natur Hist 86:22+ Je '77 *
GOLDSMITH, Arthur
Editorial. por Pop Phot 80:10 Ap; 8 My; 81:12 D '77
GOLDSMITH, Frank, and Freedman, Dan
Coke and cancer. il Nation 224:113-16 Ja 29 '77
GOLDSMITH, Harris
Weingartner, Kleiber, De Sabata: a matter of record. pors Hi Fi 27:94-6 S '77
GOLDSMITH, Sir James Michael
Sir Jimmy's cross-Channel fiefdom. il por Time 109:51-2 Ap 18 '77 *
GOLDSMITH, Julian
Mysterious inner earth. Intellect 106:14-15 Jl '77
GOLDSMITH, Martin
Night shift. Reviews
Nation 225:541 N 19 '77 *
GOLDSMITH, Michael
Beating the press. D. M. Alpern and others. il pors map Newsweek 90:54 Ag 29 '77 *
GOLDSMITHING
Great golden art of the ancient Peruvian artisans; at New York's Museum of Natural History. T. Belcher and E. Belcher. il Smithsonian 8:84-91 bibl(p 135) D '77
Scythians: nomad goldsmiths of the open steppes; symposium. il UNESCO Courier 29:4-49 D '76
GOLDSMITHS
SNAG: a solid gold hit; Society of North American Goldsmiths. Craft Horiz 37:47 Je '77
SNAG: meet shines with studies. A. Fisch. Craft Horiz 37:43 Ag '77
GOLDSTEIN, Al
First amendment pixillation. Nat R 29:1349-50 N 25 '77 *
Obscenity: who's to say? R. Boeth and E. Sciolino. il por Newsweek 90:53 N 7 '77 *
United States versus the princes of porn. T. Morgan. il pors N Y Times Mag p 16-17+ Mr 6 '77 *
GOLDSTEIN, Dora B. See Chin, J. H. jt auth
GOLDSTEIN, Doris S.
J. B. Bury's philosophy of history: a reappraisal. bibl f por Am Hist R 82:896-919 O '77
GOLDSTEIN, Eric A.
Containing waste. bibl il Environment 19:42-4 O '77
GOLDSTEIN, Jerome
Organizing knowledge for small farmers. il Org Gard & Farm 25:146+ Ja '78
GOLDSTEIN, Joan. See Baxter, P. J. jt auth
GOLDSTEIN, Michael J. See Woodward, J. A. jt auth
GOLDSTEIN, Milton
Grand Canyon: color portfolio; excerpt from The magnificent West. il Am West 14:39-47 Jl '77
GOLDSTEIN, Tom
Corporate law firms respond to Nader. N Y Times Mag p84+ N 20 '77
GOLDTHWAITE, John
Notes on the children's book trade. Harpers 254:76+ Ja; 6 Mr '77
GOLDWASSER, Anita
No job for mom; story. Ms 6:75-8 Ag '77
GOLDWASSER, Eugene. See Van Zant, G. jt auth
GOLDWATER, Barry Morris, 1909-
Senate reform too modest—Moss, Goldwater protest. por BioScience 27:10-11 Ja '77
GOLEMAN, Daniel
Back from the brink. bibl il Psychol Today 10:56-9 Ap '77
Hypnosis comes of age. il Psychol Today 11:54-6+ Jl '77
Meditation without mystery; excerpt from The varieties of the meditative experience. il Psychol Today 10:54-6+ Mr '77
Secrets of a modern Mesmer. bibl il por Psychol Today 11:62+ Jl '77
Split-brain psychology; fad of the year. il Psychol Today 11:88-90+ O '77
(ed) See Montagu, A. Don't be adultish!
—and Bush, Sherida
Liberation of sexual fantasy. bibl il Psychol Today 11:48-9+ O '77
GOLEMBIEWSKI, Robert T. and Hilles, R. J.
Drug company workers like new schedules. M Labor R 100:65+ F '77
GOLF
Defensive golf. T. Gunn. New Repub 177:31-3 Jl 23 '77
To hell with golf! C. Price. Esquire 87:150-2 My '77
Weekend with Arnold Palmer; winners of the Ladies home journal golf contest. il Ladies Home J 94:78-9 O '77
See also
United States Golf Association

Lightning hazards

On lightning damage to a golf course green. E. P. Krider. bibl il Weatherwise 30:111 Je '77

Television broadcasting

See Television broadcasting—Sports

Tournaments

Accepting with pleasure his kind invitation; Jack Nicklaus' Memorial tournament. D. Jenkins. il por Sports Illus 46:24-6+ My 30 '77
And away we go; celebrities on the pro-am circuit; with photographs by T. Triolo. Sports Illus 48:20-5 Ja 9 '78
Another rabbit is in the lettuce patch; Los Angeles Open. S. Pileggi. il Sports Illus 46:22-3 F 28 '77
Augusta's Mr Cool; T. Watson's Masters win. P. Axthelm. por Newsweek 89:75 Ap 25 '77
Battle of the ages; PGA Championship. D. Jenkins. il Sports Illus 47:12-15 Ag 22 '77
Braw brawl for Tom and Jack; British Open. D. Jenkins. il pors Sports Illus 47:28-30+ Jl 18 '77
Bringing in the new year with a bang; World Series. D. Jenkins. il Sports Illus 47:82+ S 19 '77
Care to join our little old game? Professional Gamblers Invitational. E. Shrake. il Sports Illus 47:16-18+ Ag 15 '77
Down the Bobby Jones Expressway; D. Edwards in the Masters. W. Bingham. il Sports Illus 46:28 Ap 18 '77
From Is Molas to Memorial to Augusta National; the Masters. H. W. Wind. New Yorker 53:108+ My 16 '77
His putter has the sputters; J. Miller in the Tucson Open. D. Jenkins. il por Sports Illus 46:55-6+ Ja 24 '77
In a class all by itself—for now; Tournament Players Championship. D. Jenkins. il Sports Illus 46:64+ Mr 28 '77
Isn't it warm, isn't it cozy, side by side; Pepsi Mixed Team Championship. W. Bingham. il Sports Illus 47:22-3 D 12 '77
It was a day unlike any other day; A. Geiberger's tour record at the Danny Thomas Memphis Classic. C. Gillespie. il pors Sports Illus 46:50+ Je 20 '77
Let's hear it for Croatia; Amateur Public Links Championship. J. Papanek. il por Sports Ilus 47:44+ Jl 25 '77
None of them will win the Masters. D. Jenkins. il Sports Illus 46:40-2+ Ap 4 '77
Pair of kings for openers; Phoenix Open. B. McDermott. il Sports Illus 46:50+ Ja 17 '77
Roar of pro golf's young lions; Professional Golfers Association tour. J. Radosta. il N Y Times Mag p 17-18+ Ag 21 '77
Stacy's not spacey anymore; Women's Open. J. Papanek. il por Sports Illus 47:45-7 Ag 1 '77
Step right up and take a whirl; satellite tournaments. B. Drum. Sports Illus 47:38-41 N 7 '77
Talk about total pressure; H. Green's victory in the U.S. Open. D. Jenkins. il por Sports Illus 46:14-19 Je 27 '77
They didn't make a dent; Walker Cup. S. Pileggi. il Sports Illus 47:88-9 S 5 '77
To the right, to the left, hold it! USGA's preparation of Southern Hills course for U.S. Open. S. Pileggi. il Sports Illus 46:36-9 Je 13 '77
Tulsa and Turnberry: two exceptional Opens. H. W. Wind. New Yorker 53:47-65 Ag 8 '77

GOLF—Tournaments—*Continued*
Watson, but not so elementary; Bing Crosby National Pro-Am. D. Jenkins. il Sports Illus 46:12-15 Ja 31 '77
What a beauty of a Masters. D. Jenkins. il pors Sports Illus 46:24-7+ Ap 18 '77
Wood can be a putter; National Junior Championship. B. McDermott. por Sports Illus 47:50-1 Ag 8 '77

History

Bobby Jones: paragon of the links. F. Hannigan. il Read Digest 111:146-50 Jl '77

GOLF, Childrens
Have a whale of a time. J. Nicklaus. il Sports Illus 47:44-6+ O 10 '77

GOLF clubs (sticks)

Manufacture

See Sporting goods industry

GOLF clubs. See Country clubs

GOLF courses
Blue skies may mean brown links; effect of drought on northern California courses. S. Pileggi. il Sports Illus 46:54+ Ap 4 '77
Coping with a water shortage; care of grass in recreation facilities. J. R. Watson. il Parks & Rec 12:54-5+ Jl '77
Designers go to the poles; El Cariso Park and Golf Course. il Parks & Rec 12:36 My '77
Golf at the town dump. G. Cornish. il Parks & Rec 12:28-9+ My '77
Link to Scotland; Shinnecock Hills course, Southampton, N.Y. F. Hannigan. il Sports Illus 47:32-5 Ag 22 '77
None of them will win the Masters; Augusta National course. D. Jenkins. il Sports Illus 46:40-2+ Ap 4 '77
To the right, to the left, hold it! USGA's preparation of Southern Hills course for U.S. Open. S. Pileggi. il Sports Illus 46:36-9 Je 13 '77

Anecdotes, facetiae, satire, etc.

Golf's impossible holes; imaginary courses painted by B. Chapman. il Read Digest 112:146-50 Ja '78

Design

From Is Molas to Memorial to Augusta National. H. W. Wind. New Yorker 53:108+ My 16 '77

GOLF gambling. See Gambling

GOLF records. See Sports records

GOLFERS
Big-money swingers; women golfers. K. Gilman. il Vogue 167:34 Jl '77
New reign in Spain. B. Wright. il Sports Illus 47:30-3 Ag 8 '77
Roar of pro golf's young lions. J. Radosta. il N Y Times Mag p 17-18+ Ag 21 '77
78 victories and she's still counting; young women professionals. S. Pileggi. il Sports Illus 46:30-2+ Ap 11 '77
See also
Austin, D.
Bolt, T.
Geiberger, A.
Green, H.
Nicklaus, J.
Palmer, A.
Rankin, J.
Stacy, H.
Vidovic, J.
Watson, T.
Wood, W.

GOLFFING, Francis
Question; poem. New Yorker 53:58 N 7 '77

GOLOVIN, Anne Castrodale
William King Jr, Georgetown furniture maker. bibl il por Antiques 111:1032-7 My '77

GOLSAN, Lucy B.
Liem's story. il Chr Cent 94:976-82 O 26 '77

GOLUB, Jeff
Going beyond motivation to involvement at the junior high/middle school level. Engl J 66:80-3 F '77
—and Horst, Bill
(eds) JHS/MS idea factory. Engl J 66:76-8 N; 64-5 D '77

GOLUB, Leon
Art. L. Alloway. Nation 224:221-2 F 19 '77 •

GOLUEKE, Clarence G.
Three options to turn waste into resources. il Org Gard & Farm 24:142+ S '77

GOMEZ, Joseph A.
Peter Watkins's Edvard Munch. bibl f il pors Film Q 30:38-46 Wint '76

GONADOTROPIN-releasing hormone. See Pituitary hormone releasing factors

GONADOTROPINS
Human chorionic gonadotropin-like substance in nonendocrine tissues of normal subjects. Y. Yoshimoto and others. bibl il Science 197:575-7 Ag 5 '77
Tumor antigen and human chorionic gonadotropin in CaSki cells: a new epidermoid cervical cancer cell line. R. A. Pattillo and others. bibl il Science 196:1456-8 Je 24 '77

GONADS
See also
Testicles

GONÇALVES, Maria Eduarda
Who owns the oceans? il UNESCO Courier 30:4-8 Ja '77

GONICK, C. W.
Is Canada falling apart? Current 191:38-47 Mr '77

GONOCOCCI. See Neisseria

GONORRHEA
Asymptomatic gonorrhea in men: caused by gonococci with unique nutritional requirements. G. Crawford and others. bibl Science 196:1352-3 Je 17 '77

Vaccines

New hope for a gonorrhea vaccine. Sci N 112:22 Jl 9 '77

GONZÁLEZ, Adolfo Suárez. See Suárez González, A.

GONZALEZ, Fernando A. and Byrd, L. D.
Mathematics underlying the rate-dependency hypothesis. bibl il Science 195:546-50; 198:1182-3 F 11, D 16 '77

GONZALEZ, Henry B.
Self-inflicted wounds. D. M. Alpern and others. pors Newsweek 89:18+ F 21 '77 •

GOOCH, Bob
Trapping: new angles on an old controversy. il Ret Liv 17:41-2 F '77

GOOD, Patricia K. and others
Should we teach about work in the social studies? Educ Digest 42:57-9 My '77

GOOD, Raymond Francis
New face jolts Pillsbury. il por Bus W p92+ My 2 '77 •

GOOD, Robert Alan. See Miké, V. jt auth

GOOD, Robert C.
Twenty-first century is now. Current 194:8-17 Jl '77

GOOD and evil
See also
Sin
Temptation

GOOD deeds of Pacca; dramatization. See Winther, B.

GOOD Friday
Drums of Calanda. T. Eigeland. il Natur Hist 86:58-63 Ap '77

GOOD HOPE, Cape of
Behind the Cape route theory: NATO flirts with South Africa. P. L. Smith. Nation 225:262-4 S 24 '77

GOOD housekeeping (periodical)
Child's garden of memories; Good housekeeping covers; excerpt from Jessie Willcox Smith. S. M. Schnessel. il Good H 184:142-5 My '77
Editor's notebook. J. M. Carter. See issues of Good housekeeping
GH poll results: the ten most admired women. il Good H 186:28+ Ja '78
Just look at her now! GH's 1959 cover-baby winner. il pors Good H 185:56 O '77
Look who won our cover-baby contest! il Good H 185:136-7 O '77
Portfolio of Christmases past; Good housekeeping covers. il Good H 185:103-9 D '77
Women in Passage II. il Good H 185:94+ Ag '77

GOOD News Bible. See Bible—Versions

A **GOOD Thing (firm)** See Design firms

GOOD times gazette. See Ithaca, N.Y.—Newspapers

GOODALE, Thomas L.
Bogota connection. il Parks & Rec 12:54-7+ S '77

GOODBAN, Mary Jane
St John: a trip through time. il Nat Parks & Con Mag 51:16-18 F '77

GOODBYE to litter; drama. See Marra, D. B.

GOODFIELD, June
Humanity in science: a perspective and a plea; address, February 24, 1977. bibl Science 198:580-5 N 11 '77

GOODLAD, John I.
Alternative schooling: language and meaning. il Todays Educ 66:84-6 Ja '77

GOODMAN, Benny
Our local correspondents. W. Balliett. il por New Yorker 53:33-4+ D 26 '77 •

GOODMAN, Clark
Consulting for fun and profit. bibl il Phys Today 30:44-6+ S '77

GOODMAN, Corey S.
Neuron duplications and deletions in locust clones and clutches. bibl il Science 197:1384-6 S 30 '77

GOODMAN, Elizabeth B.
Touch, listen, and smell. il Nat Parks & Con Mag 51:14-15 Jl '77

GOODMAN, Ellen
Here's to the crazy ladies. por Ms 5:22 My '77

GOODMAN, Jack
Different slopes for different folks. il Holiday 57:42-3+ N '76

GOODMAN, Mark, and Wilson, Tim
Million dollar dream. il por Motor B & S 139:51-3+ Ap '77

GOODMAN, Mort, and Solomon, Bennie
Supporting the life style of retired men through community service; a two-way street. il Aging 266:7 D '76

GOODMAN, Paul
Attitude of anarchism. T. Stoehr. Nation 224: 437-40 Ap 9 '77 *
Cunning, fraud or flight. T. Stoehr. Nation 224:373-6 Mr 26 '77 *

GOODMAN, Roy Matz
Odd man out. R. Steinberg. il por N Y Times Mag p 18-19+ O 30 '77 *

GOODMAN, Ryah Tumarkin
Business of living; poem. New Repub 177:36 Ag 6 '77

GOODMAN, Walter, 1927-
Life is unfair. N Y Times Mag p6 Ag 28 '77
Presidential call-in. N Y Times Mag p 10 F 27 '77
(ed) See Talese, G. Coming of bold pornography
(ed) See Van den Haag, E. Coming of bold pornography

GOODNER, Charles J. and others
Insulin, glucagon, and glucose exhibit synchronous, sustained oscillations in fasting monkeys. bibl il Science 195:177-9 Ja 14 '77

GOODNOUGH, Robert
Pollock paints a picture; excerpt from The art world; ed by B. Diamonstein. il pors Art N 76:162+ N '77

GOODPASTER, Andrew Jackson
West Point faces life. S. Kinzer. New Repub 177:14-17 D 3 '77 *

GOODRICH, B. F, Company
Goodrich proposes binding arbitration plan. L. Bornstein and others. M Labor R 100:59 My '77
Goodrich's cash cow starts to deliver. il Bus W p78+ N 14 '77

GOODRIDGE, Harry, and Dietz, Lew
Andre the sociable seal; excerpt from A seal called Andre. il Read Digest 110:134-8 Ap '77

GOODRUM, Charles A.
Writing the library whodunit. il Am Lib 8:194-6 Ap '77

GOODSTEIN, Madeline P. See Kershnar, L. jt auth

GOODWIN, Archie
Murder Ink honors maitre d'tective Rex Stout. Pub W 212:50+ N 14 '77

GOODWIN, Doris Kearns
Back at the LBJ ranch; interview, ed by L. R. Obst. il pors N Y Times Mag p42-3 N 13 '77
Becoming great. New Repub 176:29+ Ja 22 '77
Second lady. il por Ladies Home J 94:56+ Je '77

GOODWIN, Hugh Wesley
Should this judge be benched? V. Vogelzang and E. E. Plowman. por Chr Today 22:56-7 N 4 '77 *

GOODWIN, Michael
Children: sometimes poker chips. N Y Times Mag p 15 My 22 '77
Famous long ago. il N Y Times Mag p 18 My 8 '77
Fastest diet—is it for you? Read Digest 110:108-11 Je '77

GOODWIN, Shirley B.
Pains and pleasures of being thrown out at 65. pors Time 110:33 O 10 '77 *

GOODY, Richard
Climate and the planets; with biographical sketch. il por Natur Hist 87:6, 84-93 Ja '78

GOODYEAR blimp (Columbia) See Airships

GOODYEAR Tire and Rubber Company
Charles Pilliod was the odd man in at Goodyear. A. M. Louis. il pors Fortune 95:280-3+ My '77
Goodyear rolls out a gas-saving tire. Bus W p28 Ag 8 '77

GOOLAGONG, Evonne
Hand that rocks the cradle. B. McDermott. por Sports Illus 47:74+ O 17 '77 *

GOOSE as food. See Cookery—Poultry

GOOSE decoys. See Decoys (hunting)

GOOSE shooting
Blessing of the snows. C. Michaels. il Field & S 82:54-5+ D '77
Boy who fired too soon; game law violated by goose shooter; excerpt from Halt! I'm a federal game warden. W. J. Parker and C. Robinson. il Read Digest 111:170-4 S '77
Joys of hunting geese; Montezuma National Wildlife Refuge. N. Bryant. il Field & S 82: 28-9+ Je '77
On the wings of the wind. J. Knap. il Outdoor Life 159:72-5+ Mr '77
Snow fever; goose shooting in Kansas. B. Tarrant. il Field & S 82:39+ O '77
So you want to buy a goose hunt; commercial goose hunting. J. O. Cartier. il Outdoor Life 160:76-7+ O '77
Weep no more for the widowed goose; Canada goose. R. Starnes. Outdoor Life 160:8+ O '77

GOOSEBERRIES
See also
Currants

GORAK, Diane
What the books don't tell working mothers. il por Redbook 148:77+ Mr '77

GORDON, Alfred M.
Kodak vs. Fuji: which fast color film does it all best? il Mod Phot 41:88-93+ Ag '77
—and Schneider, Jason
35mm slide films: which look best. . .and when? il Mod Phot 41:94-101+ S '77

GORDON, Bernard Ludwig
Capturing fishes; with biographical sketch. il Sea Front 23:43-7, 62 Ja '77
Fish and food poisoning; with biographical sketch. il Sea Front 23:218-27, 254 Jl '77

GORDON, David
Reviews. J. Dunning. Dance Mag 51:88-9 Jl '77 *

GORDON, Dexter
Back in the U.S.A. T. Outhwaite. Nat R 29: 1125-6 S 30 '77 *
Jazzman comes home. T. Schwartz. il pors Newsweek 90:100 N 21 '77 *
Pepper and Gordon. M. A. Ullman. il pors New Repub 177:35-7 O 1 '77 *

GORDON, Don
Fourth world; poem. Harpers 255:82 Jl '77

GORDON, Harris
Stars in their eyes. S. Fischler and R. Friedman. il por Ret Liv 17:31-3 Ag '77 *

GORDON, James Stewart-. See Stewart-Gordon, J.

GORDON, Kurtiss J.
Laboratory exercises in astronomy—pulsars. il Sky & Tel 53:178-80 Mr '77

GORDON, Leah Shanks
Help wanted at the Met. il N Y Times Mag p 13-15+ Je 26 '77

GORDON, Mary
Kindness; story. Mademoiselle 83:224 O '77
Serious person; story. Redbook 149:61-2 Ag '77
Sisters; story. Ladies Home J 94:78-9 Jl '77

GORDON, Max. See Sennett, B. jt auth

GORDON, Richard, pseud. See Ostlere, G.

GORDON, Russell T.
Art on the rebound. Vasari. Art N 76:26 O '77 *

GORDON, Sol
Let's put sex education back where it belongs—in the home. il Good H 185:66+ O '77

GORDON, Theodore J.
Lifestyle of the future; address, May 19, 1977. Vital Speeches 43:557-63 Jl 1 '77

GORDON, William S.
Dynamic noise reduction systems and expanders. il Pop Electr 12:60-2 S '77

GORDON Research Conferences
Gordon Research Conferences. A. M. Cruickshank. Science 195:1009-34 Mr 11 '77
Gordon Research Conferences: winter program, 1978. A. M. Cruickshank. Science 198:323-6 O 21 '77

GORE, Daniel
Things your boss never told you about library management; excerpt from To know a library. Lib J 102:765-70 Ap 1 '77

GORE, George J.
Ethics: another kind of oil shortage; address, January 29, 1977. Vital Speeches 43:292-4 Mr 1 '77

GORE, Rick
Bad time to be a crocodile. il map Nat Geog 153:90-115 Ja '78
Striking it rich in the North Sea. il map Nat Geog 151:518-49 Ap '77
Tree nobody liked. il map Nat Geog 151:668-89 My '77

GORELL, Frank
Sweet sound of. . . il por Forbes 119:72 Je 1 '77 *

GOREY, Edward St John
Edward Gorey onstage. P. Andrews. il pors Horizon 20:12-15 N '77 *
Gorey goes batty. M. Gussow. il por N Y Times Mag p40-2+ O 16 '77 *
Gothics by Gorey. D. Ansen and P. Malamud. il por Newsweek 90:81 O 31 '77 *

GOREY, Hays
Joe Kennedy comes of age. il pors N Y Times Mag p6-11+ My 29 '77

GORILLAS
Pursuit of reason. H. T. P. Hayes. il pors N Y Times Mag p21-3+ Je 12 '77; Reply. B. DeMott. Atlantic 240:86+ S '77

GORIN, Henry Jerome
Landing ship medium (LSM) il Oceans 10:46-9 Mr '77

GORKY, Arshile
Cheating the philistines. Vasari. il Art N 76:20-2 S '77 *

GORMAN, A. L. F. See Thomas, M. V. jt auth

GORMAN, Robert
Coal-based power cycle. il Pop Sci 211:102-5 Ag '77
No-fill, no fuss batteries. il Pop Sci 210:114-17+ Je '77
On the way: power for electric grids from fuel cells. il Pop Sci 210:84-5+ Mr '77
Wall systems. il Pop Sci 210:104-7 Ap '77

GORSE, R. A. Jr, and others
Hydroxyl radical reactivity with diethylhydroxylamine. bibl il Science 197:1365-7 S 30 '77

GORSKY, Sulima
Finding my niche—at 61. McCalls 104:56+ Mr '77

GORTON, Richard A.
Parent apathy: problem or symptom. bibl Clearing H 51:93-4 O '77
Responding to student misbehavior. Educ Digest 42:2-5 Ap '77

GORTON, Slade
First big test of a new antitrust law. por Bus W p48+ S 12 '77 *

GOSAIBI, Gazi
Candles were a luxury; interview. por Forbes 119:32 Je 1 '77

GOSHGARIAN, Gary
Earthwatch expeditions are the real thing. Todays Educ 66:67-9 Mr '77

GOSLING, J. T. and Hundhausen, A. J.
Waves in the solar wind; with biographical sketches. il Sci Am 236:22, 36-43 bibl(p 150) Mr '77

GOSLING, Jean O. See Orne, J. jt auth

GOSLING, Nigel
Things exactly as they are. il pors Horizon 20:46-51 N '77

GOSNELL, John W.
Relationship between work experience and occupational aspiration and attrition from teaching. bibl il Clearing H 51:176-9 D '77

GOSNELL, Mariana
Carlsbad's famous bats are dying off. il Nat Wildlife 15:28-33 Je '77
Emergency techniques that save lives. il Ms 6:83-6 Ag '77
On patrol with Africa's new park rangers. il pors Int Wildlife 7:4-13 S '77

GOSPEL music
First lady of gospel; S. Caesar. il por Ebony 32:98-100+ S '77
Gonna shout, gonna shine. B. Overton. il Sat Eve Post 249:22-4+ N '77
People like honest sounds; Gaither Trio. S. B. Walton. il Sat Eve Post 249:46-7+ Ap '77

GOSPEL singers. See Singers

GOSSETT, Philip
Happy ending for a tragic finale. il por Opera N 42:34-5+ O '77

GOSSIP columns. See Newspapers—Sections, columns, etc.

GOSSIP in mass media
People perplex. H. F. Waters. il Newsweek 89:89-90 Je 6 '77
Where has all the privacy gone? M. Mead. por Redbook 148:44+ Ap '77

Anecdotes, facetiae, satire, etc.

Schlemiel. R. Baker. N Y Times Mag p4 Ag 7 '77

GOSSMAN, Francis Joseph, Bp
Praying because I needed to pray. . . il New Cath World 220:24+ Ja '77

GOTHIC revival in furniture. See Furniture, Gothic

GOTHIC sculpture. See Sculpture, Gothic

GOTS, Barbara A. See Gots, R. E. jt auth

GOTS, Ronald E. and Gots, B. A.
Drugs, coffee, alcohol, infections and your unborn baby; excerpt from Caring for your unborn child. Good H 186:68+ Ja '78

GOTTFRIED, Brian
New stars of the court. P. Axthelm and J. B. Cumming, Jr. pors Newsweek 89:95 Ap 11 '77 *
What's with who's that? F. Deford. por Sports Illus 46:69-70+ Ap 11 '77 *

GOTTFURCHT, Adolph
Chinese words of science. il por Chemistry 50:17-19 Mr '77

GOTTLIEB, Gilbert
Call of the duck. Natur Hist 86:40+ O '77

GOTTLIEB, Robert J.
Classic comments. See issues of Motor trend
Retrospect (cont) il Motor T 29:109-12+ Ap '77

GOTTSTEIN, Klaus
Nuclear energy for the third world; tr by S. Libich. Bull Atom Sci 33:44-8 Je '77

GOUDSMIT, Samuel Abraham
Irrelevant debate. por Bull Atom Sci 33:67 Mr '77

GOUGES. See Chisels

GOUGH, Marion
Balearics. Sat R 5:31+ O 29 '77

GOULD, Elizabeth B.
Transition and adaptation in Mobile architecture. il Antiques 112:466-75 S '77

GOULD, Jane
Southern fish fries. il Outdoor Life 160:116 Ag '77

GOULD, Jay
Man of mystery. M. Klein. il pors Am Hist Illus 12:10-18 O '77 *

GOULD, Lois
My college essay. il pors N Y Times Mag p29 Ja 16 '77

GOULD, R. Gordon
Forgotten inventor emerges from epic patent battle with claim to laser. N. Wade. il por Science 198:379-81 O 28 '77 *
Laser man. T. Nicholson and E. Clark. il por Newsweek 91:66+ Ja 16 '78 *
Laser patent that upsets the industry. il por Bus W p 122+ O 24 '77 *

GOULD, Robert E.
Psychiatrist answers teen questions about homosexuality. Seventeen 36:152-3+ S '77

GOULD, Stephen Jay
This view of life. See issues of Natural history

GOULD, William B.
Unions and Carter. Nation 224:466-8 Ap 16 '77

GOURMET clubs. See Clubs

GOURMETS. See Gastronomy

GOUSSELAND, Pierre
Moly's baby-sitter takes on the whole family. por Fortune 95:33+ Je '77 *

GOVE, Clayton. See Blatchley, D. jt auth

GOVERNMENT. See Nationalism; Political science

GOVERNMENT, Resistance to
Case of civil disobedience; protest against gymnasium construction at Kent State University. E. G. McGehee. Chr Cent 94:1217-23 D 28 '77; Same abr. Progressive 41:24-5 D '77

Poland

Unrest in Poland. Progressive 41:10 Mr '77

GOVERNMENT administrative efficiency. See Efficiency, Administrative

GOVERNMENT advisory boards. See United States—Executive advisory bodies

GOVERNMENT Advisory Committee on International Book and Library Programs. See United States—Government Advisory Committee on International Book and Library Programs

GOVERNMENT agencies (United States) See United States—Executive departments

GOVERNMENT airplanes. See Airplanes, Government

GOVERNMENT and agriculture. See Agricultural administration

GOVERNMENT and art. See Art and state

GOVERNMENT and aviation. See Aviation and state

GOVERNMENT and business. See Industry and state

GOVERNMENT and medicine. See Medical policy

GOVERNMENT and science. See Science and state

GOVERNMENT and technology. See Technology and state

GOVERNMENT and the arts. See The Arts and state

GOVERMENT and the individual. See Individual and state

GOVERNMENT and the press
Editors telling secrets. T. Griffith. il Time 109:80 Mr 14 '77
Inspired leak; leakage of information by the government and the press. B. Catton. il Am Heritage 28:44-9 F '77
Mass media and society: American viewpoint. W. G. Harley. il UNESCO Courier 30:28-31 Ap '77
Our national flacks. R. Reeves. Esquire 88:68+ D '77
Pulling the big switch; journalists as government employees. D. Gelman and L. Howard. il Newsweek 89:55 F 21 '77
Secrecy lives. New Repub 177:9-10 N 26 '77
Social relationships between journalists and government officials; excerpts from address. D. Halberstam. por Intellect 106:100 S '77
Supreme embarrassment; news leak describing Supreme Court action on appeals in the Watergate cover-up trial. J. K. Footlick and L. Howard. por Newsweek 89:66 My 9 '77
Terrorism and censorship. il Time 109:57 Mr 28 '77
Unplugged leaks; H. M. Jackson and the progress of the Strategic Arms Limitation Talks. New Repub 177:2+ N 26 '77
What secrets are sacred? decision to print the King Hussein-CIA story by the Washington post. D. Gelman and others. il por Newsweek 89:40+ Mr 14 '77
Whisperings in the press gallery; periodical correspondents banned from Congress. P. H. Schuck. Harpers 254:113-17 Mr '77; Discussion. 254:113+ Mr; 6+ Ap '77
Working for the Company? journalists and the CIA. il Time 110:60 S 26 '77
See also
Newspapers and politics
Presidents—United States—Press relations
Press law
United States—Congress—Reporters and reporting

Central African Empire

Beating the press; incarceration of reporters M. Goldsmith and J. C. Randal. D. M. Alpern and others. il pors map Newsweek 90:54 Ag 29 '77

Great Britain

England revives the star chamber; deportation of P. Agee. R. Clark. Nation 224:261-3 Mr 5 '77
Roadblocks on Fleet Street. il Time 109:79 Mr 14 '77

GOVERNMENT and the press—*Continued*

Philippines

Getting tough with the press; foreign journalists. B. Wideman. Progressive 41:47-8 O '77

Russia

Mass media and society: Soviet viewpoint. Y. N. Zasursky and Y. I. Kashlev. il UNESCO Courier 30:24-7 Ap '77

South Africa

Black journalists in Johannesburg; shutdown of The world in Johannesburg. A. Silk. Nation 225:454-6 N 5 '77
Critic in exile; D. Woods' escape. il por Time 111:31 Ja 16 '78
Great escape; D. Woods' flight. S. Strasser and P. Younghusband. il por Newsweek 91:48 Ja 16 '78
In a South African prison; P. Qoboza. R. Javers. Commonweal 104:808-9 D 23 '77
Notes and comment; arrest of P. Qoboza, editor of World. New Yorker 53:41-2 N 28 '77
Rewards of moderation; government suppression of Johannesburg's The world newspaper. New Repub 177:5-6 O 29 '77
Silent bystander; banning of D. Woods, East London daily dispatch editor. W. McWhirter. il por Time 110:38 N 7 '77
South African muzzle: Vorster bullies the press. A. Silk. il Nation 224:618-21 My 21 '77

Underdeveloped areas

Reporting from the third world. M. Rosenblum. For Affairs 55:815-35 Jl '77

Vietnam

Vietnam: a new numbers game; post-war coverage. R. K. Musil. Progressive 41:32-3 S '77

GOVERNMENT bonds. See Bonds, Government

GOVERNMENT buildings. See Public buildings

GOVERNMENT consultants
Business is wary about Carter's volunteer plan; OMB computer task force. Bus W p36-7 D 26 '77
Government consultants: a booming industry comes under fire. U.S. News 83:41-2 Ag 15 '77

GOVERNMENT contracts. See Contracts, Government

GOVERNMENT decentralization. See Decentralization in government

GOVERNMENT dentists. See Dentists

GOVERNMENT documents. See Government publications

GOVERNMENT economists. See Economists

GOVERNMENT employees
Bureaucrats: the real power? map U.S. News 82:59-60 My 9 '77
Can your budget afford unemployment compensation? local government employees. Am City & County 92:103-4+ S '77
Carter plans commission to review excessive military pension costs. Ret Liv 17:14 Ap '77
Crystal gazing about the labor front. A. Leggat. Am City & County 92:32 N '77
Cutting the cost of local government; overstaffing. R. A. Smardon. Harvard Bus R 55; 8+ Mr '77
Double dippers. New Repub 176:6+ F 12 '77
Double dippers; retirement of veterans. Sat Eve Post 249:36+ N '77
Federal agencies—which are worst? U.S. News 83:42 N 14 '77
Federal employees see increase in productivity; excerpt from Flexitime for increased productivity. T. F. Cowley and B. L. Fiss. M Labor R 100:66 F '77
Inside look at our runaway bureaucracy; with interview with A. Campbell. J. S. Lang. il U.S. News 83:22-4+ O 3 '77
Price of blowing the whistle. H. Dudar. il pors N Y Times Mag p41-2+ O 30 '77
Scapegoats of '77. J. Farmer. por Newsweek 90:13 Ag 8 '77
Supreme Court opens new term; discrimination cases involving public employees. G. J. Mounts. M Labor R 100:66 D '77
When workers blow whistle on federal waste, fraud. il U.S. News 83:55 D 19 '77
Why the fuss over retired officers in federal jobs; double dipping. il U.S. News 82:39 F 7 '77
Witnesses of the new order. T. Bethell. Harpers 254:34-5+ Je '77
See also
American Federation of State, County, and Municipal Employees
Bureaucracy
Civil service
Collective agreements—Government employees
Collective bargaining—Government employees
Conflict of interests (public office)
Congressmen—Staff
Municipal employees
Public officers
State employees
Strikes—United States—Government employees
Trade unions—Government employees

Appointment, qualifications, tenure, etc.

If you want to go to work for the government—. U.S. News 82:60 My 9 '77

Pensions

See Civil service pensions

Political activities

Batten down that Hatch; proposed revision of the Hatch Act. Nat R 29:597 My 27 '77
Hands off the Hatch Act. M. Stone. il U.S. News 82:80 Je 27 '77
This month's feature: controversy over proposed revision of the Hatch Act. Cong Digest 56: 289-91+ D '77

Retirement

In government, many step down before 65. U.S. News 83:72 N 7 '77

Salaries, allowances, etc.

Are government workers overpaid? il U.S. News 83:35-6 S 12 '77
Down among the bureaucrats. N. B. Freeman. Nat R 29:1229 O 28 '77
Federal pay increase. L. Bornstein and others. M Labor R 100:71-2 D '77
Washington high on the hog. Nation 224:642-3 My 28 '77

GOVERNMENT Employees Insurance Company
Geico's plans to stay in the black. il Bus W p98+ Je 20 '77

GOVERNMENT entertaining
Making of a state dinner; White House dinner for J. Callaghan. S. Fraker and J. Whitmore. il por Newsweek 89:30-1 Mr 21 '77
No frills at the White House. il Horizon 21:62 Ja '78
Now that Carters have put their stamp on White House social life. il U.S. News 82:55-6 Ap 4 '77
147 good reasons for bypassing the caviar; entertaining at the UN. S. A. Korle. il por Sat Eve Post 249:37+ S '77
Rosalynn Carter gets a big hand from 37 craftsmakers at White House luncheon. por Craft Horiz 37:41 Je '77
Sans caviare; diplomatic receptions. J. Lukacs. il Nat R 29:450-2 Ap 15 '77
White House crafts & craftsmen; luncheon for Senator's wives, May 16, 1977. E. K. Canavier. il Ceram Mo 25:47-55 D '77
White House menu. J. Child. il N Y Times Mag p55+ Ja 16 '77
White House showcase for crafts; luncheon in honor of the Senate wives. J. B. Reiter and J. Macurdy. il pors House B 119:116-19 O '77

GOVERNMENT ethics. See Political ethics

GOVERNMENT guaranty of loans. See Loans, Bank—Guaranty

GOVERNMENT immunity. See Government liability

GOVERNMENT information
Bureaucrats above the law: double-entry intelligence files. A. Theoharis. Nation 225:393-7 O 22 '77
Coalition seeks access to Kissinger records. S. Wagner. Pub W 211:28+ Ja 31 '77
Have you ever supported equal pay, child care or women's groups? The FBI was watching you; with excerpts from FBI files. L. C. Pogrebin. Ms 5:37-44+ Je; 6:7-8+ O '77
Man who called Walter Cronkite a spy; S. Jaffe. T. Branch. il Esquire 87:34-6+ Ap '77
Mining the dossiers; SEC files on corporate payments. il Newsweek 89:71+ My 30 '77
My forty years with the F.B.I. J. K. Galbraith. il por Esquire 88:122-6+ O '77
One man's files. G. C. Zahn. America 135:438-42 D 18 '76; Correction. 136:62 Ja 29 '77
Sam Jaffe and the new blacklist. T. Branch. Esquire 87:36+ Mr '77
Secretary Kreps won't talk; sale of American computers to foreign governments. M. T. Klare. Nation 224:678-9 Je 4 '77
See also
Government and the press
Information, Freedom of
Official secrets
United States—Federal Information Centers

GOVERNMENT information services. See Information services, Government

GOVERNMENT investigations

Accountants

CPAs get another lashing; Senate Subcommittee report. Bus W p76 Ja 31 '77
More CPAs chime in on self-regulation; testimony before the Senate Subcommittee on Reports, Accounting, and Management. il Bus W p84+ Je 6 '77
Should CPAs be management consultants? staff study of the Senate Subcommittee on Reports, Accounting and Management. il Bus W p70+ Ap 18 '77

Airlines

FAA hit on regulatory reform safety role, collision avoidance. Aviation W 107:31-2 D 12 '77

GOVERNMENT investigations—*Continued*

Amateurism (sports)

Cracking down on the payoffs; payments to track stars. il Time 109:55-6 Je 13 '77

Central Intelligence Agency

Brotherhood of liars. Nation 224:226-7 F 26 '77
Carter and Helms. J. Osborne. New Repub 177:10-13 N 19 '77
Guarding the secrets; testimony of R. Helms. Nation 225:482-3 N 12 '77
Helms cops a plea. R. Steele and others. por Newsweek 90:31 N 14 '77
Helms file. por Newsweek 90:31-2 O 10 '77
Helms makes a deal. il por Time 110:18+ N 14 '77
Helmsmen, what quarry? F. Getlein. Commonweal 104:740-1 N 25 '77
Importance of Richard Helms. Nat R 29:1348 N 25 '77
Mind-bending disclosures; drug testing. il Time 110:9 Ag 15 '77
Mind bending—latest CIA scandal. U.S. News 83:22 Ag 15 '77
Mind controllers. F. Getlein. Commonweal 104:548-9 S 2 '77
Spare that spook! case of R. M. Helms. New Repub 177:5+ N 19 '77
Spooking the press. Newsweek 91:30 Ja 16 '78
They never laid a hand on him; R. Helms. Nation 225:514-15 N 19 '77
Up against Citizen Helms. J. K. Larson. Chr Cent 94:1108-10 N 30 '77
What national security? Nation 225:546 N 26 '77
Who can be a paid spook? journalists. il Time 111:12 Ja 9 '78

Commodity exchanges

Bucketing beans; investigation of Chicago Board of Trade. il Time 109:65 Je 27 '77

Commodity Futures Trading Commission

Futures regulator comes under fire. il Bus W p97-8 Ag 15 '77

Congressmen

All about Koreagate. D. M. Alpern and others. il pors Newsweek 90:17+ Ag 1 '77
As the Korean bribery scandal unfolds—. il U.S. News 83:27 O 31 '77
Civil rights for Tongsun Park. Nation 225:261 S 24 '77
Fresh stirrings on Koreagate. il Time 110:19-20 S 5 '77
Investigative asymmetry; proposed reestablishment of House Internal Security Committee. M. S. Evans. Nat R 29:997 S 2 '77
Jaworski comes back. Time 110:8 Ag 1 '77
KCIA game plan. D. Holt and E. Shannon. il Newsweek 90:34 D 12 '77
Korea stonewalls. New Repub 177:7-8 N 5 '77
Lid finally blows off Korean bribery scandal. il por U.S. News 83:28+ S 19 '77
Memories of Ice Mountain; House Ethics Committee investigation of South Korea's attempts to bribe Congressmen. Time 110:16 O 31 '77
New scandal in Congress. J. S. Lang. il por U.S. News 83:9-12 Ag 1 '77
Paper chase; piecing together the business records of T. Park. D. A. Williams and N. Horrock. Newsweek 89:33-4 Je 6 '77
Park stays put. Newsweek 90:44 S 19 '77
Park's lobby hobby. K. Willenson and others. il por Newsweek 90:37 S 5 '77
Patriarch's blessing. R. Steele and E. Shannon. il Newsweek 90:38 O 31 '77
Sordid example. M. Stone. U.S. News 83:68 Ag 1 '77
Still waiting for harvest time; indictment of T. Park. il por Time 110:21-2 S 19 '77
Swindler from Seoul. Time 110:8+ Jl 4 '77
System fixer; L. Jaworski heading investigation. Nation 225:98 Ag 6 '77
Talking with Tongsun Park; interview. ed by B. Krisher. T. Park. pors Newsweek 90:36-8 O 3 '77

Anecdotes, facetiae, satire, etc.

How it might have gone. W. F. Buckley, Jr. Nat R 29:1194-5 O 14 '77

Corporations

Corporate governance—new heat on outside directors? por Forbes 120:33 O 1 '77

Credit cards

Hard congressional look at credit cards. Bus W p96-7 F 7 '77

Federal Bureau of Investigation

Griffin Bell's dilemma. Newsweek 90:35 D 19 '77
Prosecution of FBI, CIA agents: an idea coming under fire. il por U.S. News 83:56 S 12 '77
Putting the FBI in the dock. il Time 109:46 Ap 18 '77
What national security? case of J. J. Kearney. Nation 225:546-7 N 26 '77
When G-men break the law. P. Goldman and N. Horrock. il Newsweek 89:28+ My 30 '77

Intelligence service

Public or private papers? The arrogance of the intelligence community. A. G. Theoharis. Intellect 106:118-20 O '77
See also
United States—Congress—Senate—Select Committee to Study Governmental Operations with Respect to Intelligence Activities

International Telephone and Telegraph Corporation

ITT under the gun. T. Szulc and E. Yoffe. New Repub 177:18-22 Ag 6 '77

Medical care

Medical cheats who fleece taxpayers; Congressional report. U.S. News 82:38 Mr 28 '77

Public officers

Lance affair fallout: are security checks really tough? U.S. News 83:63 Ag 29 '77
Persecution and character assassination of Howard (Bo) Callaway as performed by inmates of the U.S. Senate under the auspices of the Democratic Party. J. Hougan. Harpers 255:35-42+ Jl '77

Small Business Administration

SBA scandals: whites bilk black fronts. A. Poinsett. il Ebony 32:75-6+ O '77

Smithsonian Institution

Cold-shower time at the Smithsonian. I. Ross. il pors Fortune 96:132-4+ S '77
Now, the venerable Smithsonian is a target of Congress. il por U.S. News 82:58+ Je 27 '77
Smithsonian: the nation's attic undergoing new federal scrutiny. C. Holden. por il Science 196:857-60 My 20 '77

Trade unions

Momentum builds against the top Teamsters. il Bus W p 108+ O 10 '77

United States marshals

Your cover is showing. R. Boeth and others. il Newsweek 90:66+ N 28 '77

Watergate case

Teamsters' Watergate connection. il Time 110:28 Ag 8 '77

India

Closer to Indira. il por Time 110:29 S 5 '77
Closing in on Sanjay. F. Willey and others. il por Newsweek 89:64 My 2 '77
Empress in distress; case of I. Gandhi. il por Time 110:37 O 17 '77
Family affairs; S. Gandhi. por Newsweek 89:56 Ap 11 '77
India: a bungled arrest. R. Carroll and others. il por Newsweek 90:53-4 O 17 '77
India's net closes. H. Jensen. il pors Newsweek 90:46 S 12 '77
Letter from New Delhi. V. Mehta. New Yorker 53:119-22+ O 17 '77
Sanjay in the dock. K. Willenson and R. Ramanujam. il por Newsweek 90:45 S 5 '77
They are afraid of me; excerpts from interview. ed by H. Jensen. I. Gandhi. por Newsweek 90:49 S 12 '77

GOVERMENT laboratories. See Laboratories, Government

GOVERNMENT liability
Epidemic of swine flu suits. il Bus W p32-3 My 23 '77
Policy accountability. P. G. Brown. Society 14:8 Jl '77
Suing City Hall; sovereign immunity. Time 110:42 S 12 '77
Surprising trend: you can beat city hall; citizens taking their governments to court. U.S. News 83:67-8 Ag 8 '77
Swine flu claims pile up in Washington. Bus W p23-4 Ja 24 '77
Weapon against abuse of government power. J. J. Kilpatrick. il Nations Bus 65:13-14 N '77
Whatever happened to. . .swine-flu suits: running into the billions of dollars. il U.S. News 84:58 Ja 9 '78
Who is responsible for workplace safety? J. S. Shaw. Bus W p42 D 26 '77

GOVERNMENT libraries. See Libraries, Government

GOVERNMENT National Mortgage Association futures. See Commodity exchanges

GOVERNMENT officials. See Public officers

GOVERNMENT ownership
California may become a banker. Bus W p46 O 3 '77

Argentina

Government loosens its hold on business. il Bus W p68-9 N 21 '77

British Columbia

Government selloff in British Columbia. por Bus W p69-70 S 26 '77

GOVERNMENT ownership—*Continued*

Canada

Workplace democracy: a Canadian experiment; nationalization of Kootney Forest Products. J. Lembcke. Progressive 41:29-32 Jl '77

France

Leftists eye Dassault nationalization. Aviation W 108:18 Ja 9 '78
Moving in on Dassault. il Time 109:78-9 Je 20 '77
Profit picture colors French takeover. R. R. Ropelewski. Aviation W 107:22-3 Ag 1 '77

Great Britain

British industry braced for nationalization move. D. A. Brown. il Aviation W 106:42-3+ Mr 21 '77
Is there any hope for Britain? interview, ed by G. Smith. A. Robens of Woldingham. il por Forbes 119:65-6 My 15 '77

Malaysia

Socking it to Swine Bobby; government takeover of Sime Darby. il Time 109:50 Ja 24 '77

United States

More regulation or deregulation of the airlines? nationalization may be the answer for the future; address, December 8, 1976. C. C. Tillinghast. Vital Speeches 43:206-9 Ja 15 '77
Public control of public money; state-owned banks. J. Rowen. Progressive 41:47-52 F '77
Public power: its time has come. R. Munson. Progressive 41:26-9 My '77

GOVERNMENT physicians. See Physicians
GOVERNMENT procurement. See Purchasing, Government
GOVERNMENT property
See also
Surplus government property
GOVERNMENT publications
Fishbowl approach to agency lobbying; recent U.S. Court of Appeals decision. Bus W p31-2 My 23 '77
Government, business try plain English for a change. U.S. News 83:46+ N 7 '77
Look at all the ways the government will help you. Changing T 31:31-4 Ag '77
Trying to regulate the regulators. H. Sidey. Time 110:33 D 5 '77
Turning federalese into plain English. Bus W p58 My 9 '77
Waging war on legalese. il Time 111:60 Ja 16 '78
See also
Security classification (government documents)

Bibliography

Congressional documents relating to foreign policy. See occasional issues of Department of State bulletin
Publications. See issues of Department of State bulletin
Source material; comp by J. Rigney. For Affairs 55:664-70 Ap '77
Ten most wanted government booklets. Good H 185:203 Jl '77

GOVERNMENT publicity
See also
Government and the press

Taiwan

Getting to know you; Pacific Cultural Foundation's sponsoring of Taiwan junkets. A. Deming and others. il Newsweek 89:54-5 Ja 31 '77

GOVERNMENT records. See Public records
GOVERNMENT regulation of industry. See Industry and state
GOVERNMENT secrecy. See Official secrets
GOVERNMENT service. See Public officers
GOVERNMENT service contracts. See Contracts, Government
GOVERNMENT spending policy. See United States—Appropriations and expenditures
GOVERNMENTAL Affairs, Committee on. See United States—Congress—Senate—Governmental Affairs, Committee on
GOVERNMENTS. See Nations
GOVERNORS
Governors: new faces of '77. T. Mathews and others. pors Newsweek 89:45-6 Ap 11 '77
GOWANS, James Learmonth
Medical research in England: new director seeks to boost morale. N. Wade. por Science 198:1021-2 D 9 '77 •
GOWER, Ronald
Drop camp by rail. il map Outdoor Life 159:70-1 F '77
GOYEN, William
Right here at Christmas; story. Redbook 150:77-8 D '77
GRABILL, Paul
God's lights; poem. Chr Cent 94:623 Jl 6 '77
GRACE Patricia, Consort of Rainier III, Prince of Monaco
Other Princess Grace; interview, ed by B. Schulberg. por Ladies Home J 94:82+ My '77
Princess Grace's Monaco. . .; interview, ed by J. Winslow. il por Holiday 58:36-9+ Ja '77

about

Grace Kelly broke my heart; excerpt from Sun and shadow. J. P. Aumont. Vogue 167:166+ My '77 •
Smashing; christening of the Cunard Princess by Princess Grace of Monaco. New Yorker 53:28-9 Ap 11 '77 •

GRACE, Nancy C.
Unlisted number. Atlantic 239:88-9 Ap '77
GRACE, W. R. & Company
Grace's latest stab at consumer markets. il Bus W p33 Je 13 '77
See also
Baker and Taylor Companies
GRACE H. Flandrau Planetarium, Tucson, Ariz. See Planetariums
GRACIE at the bat; drama. See Boiko, N.
GRACKLES
Sex-ratio adjustment in the common grackle. H. F. Howe. bibl il Science 198:744-6 N 18 '77
GRADE, Chaim
In praise of Chaim Grade. R. R. Wisse. Commentary 63:70-3 Ap '77 •
GRADE, Sir Lew
Lew Grade, superstar. il por Forbes 119:42+ My 1 '77 •
Making of a modern-day movie mogul. il por Bus W p 117 My 16 '77 •
GRADEN, Maynard
Build the Light Genie. il Pop Electr 11:57-9 Ap '77
GRADENWITZ, Peter
Félicien David 1810-1876 and French romantic orientalism. bibl f il por Mus Q 62:471-506 O '76
GRADERS (excavating machinery)
Articulated graders tackle county roads; San Bernardino County, Calif. il Am City & County 92:30 Ja '77
Move more snow with motorgraders. D. Hurlugson. il Am City & County 92:73 Ap '77
GRADIE, J. and Zellner, B.
Asteroid families: observational evidence for common origins. bibl il Science 197:254-5 Jl 15 '77
GRADING and marking (students)
Another visit to the world of grading. R. A. Ellsworth and D. D. Willson. Clearing H 51:188-9 D '77
Collegiate grading system: traditional or nontraditional. J. Collins and K. N. Nickel. bibl il Clearing H 50:243-7 F '77
Goodbye to the rubber diploma; minimal competency program in Greensville County, Va. schools. il por Time 110:46 S 26 '77
Grading: new alternatives to an old question. C. Spratling. Bet Hom & Gard 55:42+ O '77
Perils of paper grading. G. G. Sloan. Engl J 66:33-5 My '77
Social promotion: problem or solution? W. G. Cunningham and R. C. Owens. Educ Digest 42:10-12 Ja '77
See also
Ability grouping in education
Students—Rating
GRADING of meat. See Meat—Grading
GRADSTEIN, F. M. and others
Grand Banks and J-anomaly ridge: a geological comparison. bibl il map Science 197:1074-6 S 9 '77
GRADUATE school admission. See Colleges and universities—Admission
GRADUATE work. See Colleges and universities—Graduate work
GRADUATES, College. See College graduates
GRADUATION requirements. See High schools—Graduation requirements
GRADY, Ruth Ellen
Library work without an M.L.S. Lib J 102:1726 S 1 '77
GRAEFE, Gernot
Amazing grape-seed greenhouse. R. Rodale. il por Org Gard & Farm 24:48-52 D '77 •
GRAF, Rudolph F. and Whalen, G. J.
Action football game. il Radio-Electr 48:60-1+ Mr '77
GRAFF, Gerald
Fear and trembling at Yale. Am Scholar 46:467-78 Aut '77
GRAFF, Marv
Craftsman's approach to apparel design. R. Hillestad. il Design (US) 78:22-5 Spr '77 •
GRAFFITI
Writing on the walls of ivy. A. Fadiman and J. Sedgwick. il Esquire 88:113-14 S '77
GRAFT in politics. See Politics, Corruption in
GRAFTING
Tree grafting methods; symposium. Org Gard & Farm 25:82-96 Ja '78
GRAFTON, Sue
Creative cycle. Writer 90:11-15 D '77

GRAGG, Larry
Ragged Mat, the Democrat. il Am Hist Illus 12:20-5 My '77

GRAHAM, Alma
Words that make women disappear. Redbook 148:72+ Mr '77

GRAHAM, Benjamin
Ben Graham's last will and testament. P. Blustein. il por Forbes 120:43-5 Ag 1 '77 *

GRAHAM, Bill
Counter counterculture shock. E. Melton. por Forbes 120:103 N 15 '77 *

GRAHAM, Billy
Billy Graham on financing evangelism. pors Chr Today 21:18-20 Ag 26 '77
I can't play God any more; interview, ed by J. M. Beam. il pors McCalls 105:100-1+ Ja '78
PW interviews; ed by G. Stuttaford. por Pub W 211:10-11 Je 20 '77
Taking the world's temperature; interview. pors Chr Today 21:16-19 S 23 '77
Who was this man called Jesus? excerpt from How to be born again. il Sat Eve Post 249:22-3+ D '77

about

Billy Graham: issues and answers; with editorial comment. Chr Today 22:27, 44-5 O 21 '77 *
Billy Graham's mission to Manila. H. Lindsell. il Chr Today 22:36-7 D 30 '77 *
Billy in Budapest: Hungary opens its heart. E. E. Plowman. il pors Chr Today 22:52-4 O 7 '77 *
Graham and the Gospel: welcome in Hungary. E. E. Plowman. Chr Today 21:44-5 S 23 '77 *
Graham and the press: new look at ledgers. Chr Today 21:36-7 Jl 29 '77 *
Graham: back to the bloc. Chr Today 21:40 Ag 12 '77 *
Graham: feted by Jews; American Jewish Committee's first national interreligious award. A. H. Matthews. Chr Today 22:49-50 N 18 '77 *
Graham goes East. K. L. Woodward. il por Newsweek 90:70 Ag 29 '77 *
Graham scores at Notre Dame. A. H. Matthews. il por Chr Today 21:30-1 Je 3 '77 *
Graham: warm-up in Sweden. Chr Today 21:51-2 F 18 '77 *
Graham's new sermon. por Time 110:67-8 Jl 25 '77 *
Gulyas and the Gospel. il pors Time 110:83 S 19 '77 *
Honoring a homegrown prophet. A. H. Matthews. Chr Today 21:55-6 Ap 15 '77 *
Kindling fires along the Ohio. A. Toalston. Chr Today 22:47-9 N 18 '77 *
Pray, pay and sin no more. Nation 225:389-90 O 22 '77 *

GRAHAM, Charles
Shape of sounds to come. il Am Rec G 40:48 N '76; 56-7 Mr '77
Soundwise. See issues of American record guide

GRAHAM, Douglas
World's first Turner museum. Vasari. il Art N 76:30+ N '77 *

GRAHAM, Frank, 1925-
Endangered birds: tinkering for time. Audubon 79:137-41 N '77
Outrageous Mr Cherry and the underachieving nukes. il por Audubon 79:50-67 S '77

GRAHAM, Gordon
After the consent decree: a new era in the marketing of English-language books. Pub W 211:38-40 Ja 31 '77
Letter from London. Pub W 211:49 Ap 25 '77

GRAHAM, James A. Maxtone. See Maxtone Graham, J. A.

GRAHAM, Jorie
How morning glories could bloom at dust; poem. Nation 225:214 S 10 '77

GRAHAM, Jory
Time to write. il por Time 110:94+ N 14 '77 *

GRAHAM, Katharine (Meyer)
Krusty Kay tightens her grip. por Time 109:70 F 7 '77 *

GRAHAM, Loren R.
Science and values: the eugenics movement in Germany and Russia in the 1920s. bibl f Am Hist R 82:1133-64 D '77

GRAHAM, Martha
Martha Graham then and now; filmed version of Appalachian spring. J. Mueller. Dance Mag 51:107 D '77 *

GRAHAM, Martha. Dance Company. See Martha Graham Dance Company

GRAHAM, Nicholas E.
Weather surrounding the Santa Barbara fire: 26 July 1977. il Weatherwise 30:158-9 Ag '77

GRAHAM, Rubye
Health & beauty update. See issues of House beautiful

GRAHAM, Sharon K.
How to grow pots of tomatoes in your windowsill garden. il House & Gard 149:82+ N '77

GRAIN
See also
Barley
Corn
Feeds—Grain
Milo
Rice
Rye
Sorghum

Drying

See also
Grain dryers

Grading

See also
Corn—Grading

Handling

See Grain handling

Harvesting

High costs boost do-it-yourself harvest, storage. Farm J 101:B2 N '77

Inspection

See also
United States—Federal Grain Inspection Service

Marketing

Farmers who market together make it together. L. Kruse. il Suc Farm 75:30-1 D '77
40 grain sales a year spread the risk. D. K. O'Brien. Farm J 101:K1 My '77
Grain marketing for the next decade; address, September 12, 1977. W. B. Saunders. Vital Speeches 44:37-9 N 1 '77
How government programs may fit your grain marketing strategy. il Suc Farm 75:8 O '77
Marketing of the crop 1976. L. Kruse. il Suc Farm 75:C3-7 D '77
New set of rules for your marketing game. G. Lepper. il Suc Farm 75:32-3 D '77
Should you sell it before you grow it? R. Brunoehler. Farm J 101:K2 N '77
Survey: delayed pricing becoming top marketing tool. Suc Farm 75:34 D '77
Will it pay you to take a shortcut to market? B. Coffman. il Farm J 101:12-13 Mid-F '77
Will new marketing pools get more for your grain? G. Lorang and G. Reynolds. il Farm J 101:24-5+ F '77

Milling

Grain grinder from a kit. il Mech Illus 73:64 N '77
Productivity in grain mill products: output up, employment stable. J. A. Urisko. bibl M Labor R 100:38-43 Ap '77
See also
Flour
Flour mills

Prices

How to make a tax-tight deferred sales contract. A. Brennecke. Suc Farm 75:K2 S '77
Price of farm products in the future. W. W. Cochrane. bibl f Ann Am Acad 429:23-35 Ja '77
What you should know about price later agreements. Suc Farm 75:8 S '77

Storage

Grain storage. L. Kruse and G. Lepper. il Suc Farm 75:21-5 S '77
High costs boost do-it-yourself harvest, storage. Farm J 101:B2 N '77
Hold for higher price? Watch the hidden costs. Suc Farm 75:C24 D '77
What about storage when the bins are full? L. Reichenberger. il Suc Farm 75:L2 Je '77
See also
Grain elevators

Transportation

Can you go 10 extra miles for a 2¢ higher bid? C. P. Baumel and C. O'Riley. il Suc Farm 75:42 S '77
Predicts few transportation bottlenecks. Suc Farm 75:12 Ap '77

GRAIN banks. See Grain elevators

GRAIN contracts. See Contracts, Agricultural

GRAIN dryers
Dryeration: cut fuel costs 25% and double your capacity. L. Reichenberger. il Suc Farm 75:30-3 Ag '77
Four farmers: one drying facility. D. Allen. il Suc Farm 75:45 Je '77
How to get more corn through your dryer. D. Seim. il Farm J 101:20-1 S '77

GRAIN elevators
Are grain banking services a good buy? il Suc Farm 75:41 Je '77

GRAIN handling
Dries and harvests 4,000 bu. a day; corn handling. il Farm J 101:A1 O '77
Dump pits and wet holding—easiest way to gear up for a fast harvest. G. Lepper. il Suc Farm 75:32-3 O '77
Easy ways to clean corn. il Farm J 101:A8 N '77
Improve the value of your harvest: reduce grain handling damage; corn. G. Lepper. il Suc Farm 75:26-7 Je '77

GRAIN handling—*Continued*
Simplicity ensures success for this grain system. il Suc Farm 75:L3 Je '77
What it will take to get. . .top prices for your corn. G. W. Wormley. il Farm J 101:22-3 D '77
See also
Grain elevators

GRAIN mills. See Grain—Milling

GRAIN supply
Carter's gamble on crop cutbacks. il Bus W p44-5 S 12 '77
Paying farmers not to work. J. Solkoff. New Repub 177:19-21 S 17 '77
They're asking you to pay for the grain reserve. Farm J 101:64 N '77
Wheat farmers lose out at the White House. Farm J 101:72 O '77
World grain reserve. B. Jones. il New Cath World 220:250-3 S '77

GRAIN surplus. See Surplus products, Agricultural

GRAIN trade
Another Soviet grain sting. il Time 110:88+ N 28 '77
Behind the cash bind at Cook Industries. Bus W p30 Je 20 '77
Exports record high, but not high enough. Farm J 101:F2 Ag '77
Good news: farmers are exporting grain. Farm J 101:56 F '77
Grain marketing for the next decade; address, September 12, 1977. W. B. Saunders. Vital Speeches 44:37-9 N 1 '77
It looks like another grain robbery for Russia. il U.S. News 83:29 N 21 '77
Ned Cook in the agonies of corporate confession. L. Beman. il por Fortune 95:340-3+ My '77
Productivity in grain mill products: output up, employment stable. J. A. Urisko. bibl M Labor R 100:38-43 Ap '77
Russia shops for grain again. il Bus W p52-3 N 21 '77
Russian poker. Nation 225:579 D 3 '77
Soviet agriculture and United States-Soviet relations. D. G. Johnson. Cur Hist 73:118-22+ O '77
U.S. exports of grain; statement, July 13, 1977. J. L. Katz. Dept State Bull 77:265-7 Ag 22 '77
U.S. grain exports may drop as world supply soars. Farm J 101:44 Ja '77
U.S. leads world in exporting grain—but not by enough. Farm J 101:K4 N '77
Why Russia will continue to buy our farm products. R. Krumme. map Suc Farm 75:27 O '77
See also
United States Feed Grains Council
Wheat trade

GRAINGER, Stuart E.
Useful knots; excerpt from Creative ropecraft. il Yachting 142:125 S '77

GRAINS
Introduction to grains. F. Greenberg. il Redbook 149:166+ O '77

GRAMBLING College, Grambling, La.
Prez' talks up a breeze. A. Swan. il por Time 109:96 Mr 21 '77

GRAMBS, Jean Dresden
Women and administration: confrontation or accommodation? Educ Digest 42:39-42 Mr '77
Working mothers. . .the wonder women. Parents Mag 52:33+ Ap '77

GRAMICK, Jeannine
Set the captives free. il New Cath World 220:292-5 N '77

GRAMLICH, Edward M.
This way to the morass: a guide to New York City's fiscal crisis. il Intellect 106:226-30 D '77

GRAMMAR, English. See English language—Grammar

GRAMS, Ralph R.
Double-drum roller furling. il Motor B & S 140:106 Ag '77
Slick finish for teak. Motor B & S 140:99 Jl '77

GRAND, Jürg
Behind the scenes. Hi Fi 27:72+ My '77 *

GRAND BANKS (submarine plateau)
Grand Banks and J-anomaly ridge: a geological comparison. F. M. Grandstein and others. bibl il map Science 197:1074-6 S 9 '77

GRAND Canyon
Canyon fever. M. Hamilton. il Am Home 80:40-1 Ap '77
First photographers of the Grand Canyon. G. Simmons and V. Simmons. il Am West 14:34-8+ Jl '77
Grand Canyon high; hiking the Bright Angel Trail on the South Rim. M. Kasindorf. il Newsweek 90:59-60 Jl 18 '77

Photographs

Grand Canyon; color portfolio; excerpt from The magnificent West. M. Goldstein. il Am West 14:39-47 Jl '77

GRAND Canyon National Park
Man's impact on the Colorado River in the Grand Canyon. R. R. Johnson and others. il Nat Parks & Con Mag 51:13-16 Mr '77
Phantom Ranch: yesterday and a mile deep. M. Franklin. il Nat Parks & Con Mag 51:4-9 D '77

GRAND jury
Grand juries & human rights. Nation 225:197 S 10 '77
Grand jury abuse; investigations of Seattle radicals. R. C. Kelley. Progressive 41:34-5 F '77
Reforming grand juries. Time 110:58+ Jl 4 '77
Reforming the grand jury. J. K. Footlick and D. Camper. il Newsweek 90:46 Ag 22 '77

GRAND MONADNOCK. See Monadnock, Mount

GRAND piano. See Piano

GRAND Prix racing. See Automobile racing

GRAND RAPIDS, Mich.
Di Suvero in Grand Rapids: the public prevails. M. A. Tighe. il Art in Am 65:12-13+ Mr '77

GRAND STRAND, S.C. (resort) See Seaside resorts

GRAND TETON climb. See Mountaineering

GRAND TETON National Park
Don't expect a peaceful winter retreat; snowmobiling. il Nat Parks & Con Mag 51:19+ My '77
Rocky Mountain high time of your life. V. Landi. il Outdoor Life 159:70-5+ My '77

GRANDE, Rutilio
Blood poured out. J. R. Brockman. America 136:328-9 Ap 9 '77 *
Witness to justice. E. Moran. il America 136:410-14 My 7 '77 *

GRANDFATHER clocks. See Clocks

GRANDFATHERS. See Grandparents

GRANDI, Alessandro
Music for San Marco, Venezia, San Giorgio, Ferrara, & Santa Maria Maggiore, Bergamo. J. W. Barker. Am Rec G 40:30 D '76 *

GRANDMOTHERS. See Grandparents

GRANDPARENTS
Bringing your grandchildren into your life. A. P. Boyle. il Ret Liv 17:16-18 Ag '77
Grandparents as educators. M. Mead. il Sat Eve Post 249:54-9 Mr '77
Heard what your grandchildren are saying about you? comp by R. Turner. il Ret Liv 16:29+ D '76
Letter to my grandmother. S. Jacoby. il McCalls 105:118+ O '77
When you give up dolls. . .you can begin to love men. A. T. Fleming. Vogue 167:350+ O '77

GRANDPARENTS in childrens literature. See Childrens literature—Themes

GRANETZ, Marc
Coming and going; story. Mademoiselle 83:48 Ag '77

GRANITE Mountain Genealogical Vault. See Libraries, Church

GRANNIS, Chandler Brinkerhoff
American imports and exports; international title output. il Pub W 212:93-6 S 19 '77

GRANT, Cary
Other Cary Grant. W. Hoge. il pors N Y Times Mag p 14-15+ Jl 3 '77 *

GRANT, Doug
Smoking the bee. il Org Gard & Farm 24:146-7 Ap '77

GRANT, Jim
End-of-season sail maintenance. il Motor B & S 140:116-17 O '77

GRANT, M. Colin
Who's catering the theological smorgasbord? Chr Cent 94:428-31 My 4 '77

GRANT, Marena R.
Treasures from Laurelton Hall. il Antiques 111:752-9 Ap '77

GRANT, W. T, Company
It's expensive to go broke; legal costs surrounding W. T. Grant bankruptcy case. H. Seneker. Forbes 119:21-2 F 1 '77

GRANTOVSKY, Edvin A. See Bongard-Levin, G. M. jt auth

GRANTS-in-aid
Grantsmanship reforms look promising for cities. H. V. Semling. Am City & County 92:16 My '77
Secrets of success in getting U.S. funds. il U.S. News 83:60 Ag 15 '77
See also
Housing—Federal aid

GRANVILLE-BARKER, Frank
New dimensions: Rigoletto. Opera N 42:36-7 D 3 '77

GRANZIG, William A. See Peck, E. jt auth

GRAPE ivy. See Ivy

GRAPE seed compost. See Compost

GRAPES
Grape products: virus killers. Sci N 111:138 F 26 '77
See also
Cookery—Fruit
Viticulture

GRAPH theory
Mathematical games; in which joining sets of points by lines leads into diverse (and diverting) paths; Ramsey theory. M. Gardner. il Sci Am 237:18-19+ N '77
Solution of the four-color-map problem. K. Appel and W. Haken. il map Sci Am 237:108-9+ bibl(p 152) O '77

GRAPHIC arts
Creative pendulum of Mike Vogel: graphic artist and entrepreneur; founder of the Dayspring Graphics. M. C. Nelson. il por Am Artist 41:70-5+ O '77
Technologists trace graphic arts trends for AIGA Clinic. P. Doebler. Pub W 211:55-6 My 2 '77
See also
Drawing
Engraving
Etching
Lithography
Prints
Push Pin Studios, Inc

Study and teaching

Supergraphics: student art that keeps on giving; project at Columbus East High School, Columbus, Ind. M. Lewman and P. Miller. il Sch Arts 77:38-40 D '77
What's in this building, anyway? supergraphic project. M. Scherer. il Design (US) 78:13-17 Spr '77

GRAPHIC design firms. See Design firms
GRAPHIC equalizers. See Sound—Apparatus
GRAPHIC methods
See also
Nomography (mathematics)
GRAPHIC Scanning Corporation. See Data transmission systems
GRAPHICS, Computer. See Computer graphics
GRAPHITE
High-conductivity graphite compounds. B. G. Levi. bibl il Phys Today 30:18-19 Jl '77
GRAPHOLOGY
Handwriting of history's celebrities. W. Rodger. Hobbies 82:138-9 Ja '78
Handwriting's on the wall. il Seventeen 36:102-3 Jl '77
GRASS, Günter
Floundering with Grass. M. Moorcroft. il por Commonweal 104:435-8 Jl 8 '77 *
GRASS. See Grasses
GRASS seed. See Grasses—Seed
GRASS ski racing. See Ski racing
GRASS trimmers. See Lawn tools, equipment and supplies
GRASSES
Culture & notes; lawngrasses. Horticulture 55:84-5 Mr '77
Irrigated grass pays as well as crops; orchardgrass in Wyoming. il Farm J 101:J2 N '77
Nitrogen fixation in grasses inoculated with spirillum lipoferum. R. L. Smith and others; reply with rejoinder. A. C. Rogerson. Science 195:1362 Mr 25 '77
Reed canarygrass: an answer for your wet fields. E. D. Thomas. Suc Farm 75:41 Ap '77
Texas natives. D. Snell. il pors Horticulture 55:38-51 Ap '77
What are your choices in less thirsty grass? il Sunset 159:258-9 O '77
What is the grass? choosing the best grass for your lawn. R. W. Schery. il Horticulture 55:20-1+ Mr '77
See also
Alfalfa
Bamboo
Clover
Feeds—Grasses
Fescue
Lawns

Seed

Grass seed. il Consumers Res Mag 60:28-30 S '77

Seeding

See Pastures—Seeding
GRASSKIING. See Skis and skiing
GRASSO, Ella (Tambussi)
Surprises from Nation's two women governors. pors U.S. News 83:45 O 10 '77 *
GRASSO, John T.
High school curriculum from a policy point of view. Educ Digest 43:13-16 N '77
GRATITUDE
One leper thanks you. G. McCauley. America 137:inside back cover O 1 '77
See also
Thanksgiving
GRATUITIES. See Tipping
GRATZ, Roberta Brandes
Never again! Never again? Can we lose our right to abortion? il Ms 6:54-5 Jl '77
GRAU, C. R. and others
Altered yolk structure and reduced hatchability of eggs from birds fed single doses of petroleum oils. bibl il Science 195:779-81 F 25 '77
GRAUBARD, Paul S.
How I stopped nagging and started teaching my children to behave; excerpt from Positive parenthood. McCalls 104:90+ My '77
GRAUL, Donald, Jr
Seasickness. Yachting 141:130+ Ap '77
GRAUSTEIN, William C. and others
Calcium oxalate: occurrence in soils and effect on nutrient and geochemical cycles. bibl il Science 198:1252-4 D 23 '77
GRAVEL, Mike
Excerpts from testimony on nuclear energy production, February 26, 1976. Cong Digest 56:45+ F '77
GRAVEL
Ground cover? It's rock. il Sunset 159:70-3 Ag '77
Rock ground cover can work as a cover-up. il Sunset 159:156-7 Ag '77
GRAVELY, Samuel L. Jr
Guardian of the Pacific. il pors Ebony 32:66-8+ S '77 *
GRAVES, Ben E.
Modernization: everybody's doing it. Educ Digest 43:17-19 N '77
GRAVES, Elizabeth Minot
Children's books for the trail; Selected list of children's books. il Commonweal 104:726-35 N 11 '77
GRAVES, James, and Graves, Joan
What makes an interracial marriage work: interviews, ed by E. Stone. il pors Parents Mag 52:54+ O '77
GRAVES, Joan. See Graves, J. jt auth
GRAVES, Michael
Pillar of cloud; poem. Chr Today 22:17 N 4 '77
GRAVES, Nancy
New landscape art. L. R. Lippard. il Ms 5:68-73 Ap '77 *
Out in front. B. Rose. pors Vogue 167:152-3+ Je '77 *
GRAVES, Steven
Early invitations; poem. Yale R 66:401-3 Mr '77
Small anthem; Cancellation; poems. Poetry 131:19-20 O '77
GRAVES. See Cemeteries; Tombs
GRAVESTONES. See Sepulchral monuments
GRAVITATION
Supergravity. Sci Am 237:59-60 Jl '77
Will supergravity unify quantum theory with general relativity? G. B. Lubkin. Phys Today 30:17-19 Je '77
See also
Relativity (physics)
GRAVITT, T. O.
Phone calls and philandering. il pors Time 110:32-3 S 5 '77 *
GRAY, Allan
Aubade; Family argument; poems. Poetry 129:335-6 Mr '77
Two theories for the Muses' mother; poem. Poetry 130:140-2 Je '77
GRAY, Betty
Episcopal Church: an endangered species. Chr Cent 94:1052-3 N 16 '77
GRAY, Colin S.
Arms control in a nuclear armed world? Ann Am Acad 430:110-21 Mr '77
GRAY, Denis D.
School for elephants. il Int Wildlife 8:36-43 Ja '78
GRAY, Francine (du Plessix)
Manners of deceit and the case for lying. Esquire 88:134-5+ D '77
GRAY, Gale
I'm gonna miss you. J. P. Blank. Read Digest 111:233-4+ N '77 *
GRAY, Garry
H.C. Haynes: barber & inventor. bibl il Negro Hist Bull 40:751-2 S '77
GRAY, H. Peter
Rethinking free trade. New Repub 176:12-13 Mr 19 '77
GRAY, Hanna (Holborn)
Chicago's woman. M. Sheils and F. Maier. por Newsweek 90:88 D 19 '77 *
Mme President. por Time 110:90 D 19 '77 *
GRAY, Harry Jack
Not-so-tender offer. Time 109:64-5 Ap 11 '77 *
GRAY, Ira
Adirondack guide. R. F. Hall. por Conservationist 31:48 Ja '77 *
GRAY, Jim
Watercolor page. il por Am Artist 41:50-3+ Ap '77
GRAY, John
Water. . .; poem. Sci Digest 81:84-5 Ap '77
GRAY, Lois S.
Academic degrees for labor studies—a new goal for unions. bibl il M Labor R 100:15-20 Je '77
GRAY, Patricia
That awful age! Engl J 66:28-30 Ap '77
GRAY, Patrick Worth
I do not know the city; poem. Chr Cent 94:225 Mr 9 '77
Wild geese; poem. Chr Cent 94:1033 N 9 '77
GRAY, Robert C. and Bresler, R. J.
Why weapons make poor bargaining chips. Bull Atom Sci 33:8-9 S '77

GRAY, Simon
Molly. Review
Time il 109:75 Je 6 '77 *
Otherwise engaged. Reviews
America 136:148 F 19 '77 *
Commentary 63:75 Ap '77 *
Nation 224:219-21 F 19 '77 *
New Repub 176:20-1 F 26 '77 *
New Yorker 52:53 F 14 '77 *
Newsweek 89:66 F 14 '77 *
Psychol Today 11:28 Je '77 *
Sat R 4:46-7 Mr 19 '77 *
Time il 109:85 F 14 '77 *

GRAY, Stephen B.
Computer bits. il Pop Electr 11:89-90 F; 95-6 Ap '77

GRAY foxes. See Foxes

GRAY Panthers (pressure group)
Whatever happened to: Gray Panthers: aiming at new targets. U.S. News 82:79 Ja 24 '77

GRAY whales. See Whales

GRAYSON, Charles Jackson, 1923-
Productivity center wins broad backing. por Bus W p39 F 14 '77

GRAYSON, Donald K.
Pleistocene avifaunas and the overkill hypothesis. bibl Science 195:691-3 F 18 '77

GRAYSON, George W. Jr
Cuba's developing policies. bibl f Cur Hist 72: 49-52+ F '77
Mexican foreign policy. bibl f Cur Hist 72:97-101+ Mr '77
Portugal's crisis. bibl f Cur Hist 73:169-73+ N '77

GRAZING
Corn belt cow herd goes south for the summer. il Suc Farm 75:no3 F48 F '77

GREAT Atlantic & Pacific Tea Company
Jonathan Scott of A&P: hunted head. por Forbes 119:94 F 15 '77
Price and pride on the skids. il Time 110:79 D 12 '77
Travels of Ann Page. Forbes 119:85 Je 15 '77

GREAT BRITAIN
I'm not all right, Jack. C. Brogan. Nat R 29: 151-2 F 4 '77
What makes Britain great. . .no matter what; symposium. il Sat R 4:6-10+ Je 11 '77
See also
Accounting—Great Britain
Aged—Great Britain
Airlines—Great Britain
Airplanes, Military—Great Britain
Art galleries and museums—Great Britain
Atomic power—Great Britain
Automobile rallies—Great Britain
Aviation—Great Britain
Ballet—Great Britain
Blacks in Great Britain
Bonds, Government—Great Britain
Book wholesalers—Great Britain
Booksellers and bookselling—Great Britain
Children—Great Britain
Civil rights—Great Britain
Coal mines and mining—Great Britain
Colleges and universities—Great Britain
Commodity exchanges—Great Britain
Communism—Great Britain
Copyright—Great Britain
Corporations, Government—Great Britain
Crime and criminals—Great Britain
Drugstores—Great Britain
Education—Great Britain
Elections—Great Britain
Electric plants—Great Britain
Energy policy—Great Britain
England
Foreign students in Great Britain
Forests and forestry—Great Britain
Gambling—Great Britain
Government and the press—Great Britain
Government ownership—Great Britain
Historic houses, sites, etc.—Great Britain
Immigration and emigration—Great Britain
Income tax—Great Britain
Industrial relations—Great Britain
Intelligence service—Great Britain
Investments, American—Great Britain
Investments, British
Justice, Administration of—Great Britain
Law—Great Britain
Loans, British
Morale, National—Great Britain
Motion pictures—Great Britain
Museums—Great Britain
Newspaper publishers and publishing—Great Britain
Newspapers—Great Britain
Northern Ireland
Opera—Great Britain
Periodicals—Great Britain
Power resources—Great Britain
Publishers and publishing—Great Britain
Research institutions—Great Britain
Rockall (island)
Schools—Great Britain
Science—Great Britain
Securities—Great Britain
Stone Age—Great Britain
Strikes—Great Britain
Theater—Great Britain
Trade unions—Great Britain
Trials—Great Britain
United States—Diplomatic and consular service—Great Britain
Wages—Great Britain
Youth—Great Britain

Antiquities

Celtic farmstead in southern Britain. G. Wainwright. il Sci Am 237:156-64+ bibl(p 190) D '77

Antiquities, Roman

Frontier post in Roman Britain; Vindolanda excavations. R. Birley. il maps Sci Am 236:38-46 bibl(p 138) F '77

Armed Forces

Appropriations and expenditures

British defense programs tailored to pared budget. Aviation W 106:22 Mr 7 '77

Colonies

See also
Bermuda
United States—History—Colonial period, ca. 1600-1775

Commerce

See also
European Economic Community

Poland

Big ship order stranded in the yards. il Bus W p46 D 26 '77

Russia

See Russia—Commerce—Great Britain

United States

See United States—Commerce—Great Britain

Culture, Popular

See Great Britain—Popular culture

Description and travel

Fabulous fortnight in the British Isles. il Mademoiselle 83:92-3+ Je '77

Diplomatic and Consular Service

See also
Ambassadors

Drought

See Droughts

Economic conditions

Britain—a visitor's prognosis. M. S. Forbes, Jr. Forbes 120:27 D 15 '77
Britain: back from the brink. J. Fromm. il U.S. News 83:40+ O 17 '77
Britain: sink or swim. Nat R 29:1412-13 D 9 '77
Britain starts back up. Time 110:82 O 3 '77
Britain's inexhaustible complacence. T. D. Allman. Harpers 254:18+ My '77
Gloomy spring. B. Wicker. Commonweal 104: 263-4 Ap 29 '77
Is Britain an awful warning to America? R. Marris. New Repub 177:23-5 S 17 '77
North Sea oil: a mixed blessing for Britain. J. Ross-Skinner. il Duns R 110:82-3+ D '77
Prince Philip: the new battle of Britain . . . and how to win it; interview, ed by G. Bull. Philip. pors Sat R 4:8-10+ Je 11 '77
Problems beyond today's oil wealth. il Bus W p52-3 O 17 '77
Queen's silver jubilee: a hard day's night. il map Sr Schol 109:4-7 My 5 '77
Roots of Britain's troubles. S. G. Slappey. il Nations Bus 65:77-80+ D '77
This sickled isle. . . .Nat R 29:316 Mr 18 '77
What a little oil can do. A. Collings. il Newsweek 90:59+ O 17 '77

Economic history

Early energy crisis and its consequences; J. U. Nef. il map Sci Am 237:140-2+ bibl(p 164) N '77

Economic policy

After the fireworks. A. Lejeune. Nat R 29:1111 S 30 '77
Can the British economy recover? T. Beeson. Chr Cent 94:177-8 F 23 '77
How the conservatives would deal with Britain's troubles; interview. M. Thatcher. il por U.S. News 83:69-71 S 12 '77
Letter from London. M. Panter-Downes. New Yorker 53:194-6 N 14 '77
Now Britain is pushing reflation. Bus W p28 N 7 '77
Time to be bullish on Britain? il Time 111:64-5 Ja 2 '78
What North Sea oil won't do for Britain. R. Ball. il Fortune 95:138-42+ Ap '77
See also
Budget—Great Britain

Economic relations

See also
European Economic Community

GREAT BRITAIN—*Continued*

Foreign relations

Detente, Helsinki and human rights: the British view; address, March 3, 1977. D. Owen. Vital Speeches 43:369-72 Ap 1 '77

Doctor's new practice; D. Owen chosen as Foreign Secretary. il por Newsweek 89:46 Mr 7 '77

How the conservatives would deal with Britain's troubles; interview. M. Thatcher. il por U.S. News 83:69-71 S 12 '77

Germany

Churchill and us; question of policies toward military preparedness in pre-World War II Great Britain and in the United States today. E. N. Luttwak. Commentary 63:44-9 Je '77

United States

See United States—Foreign relations—Great Britain

History

Roman period 55 B.C.—449 A.D.

See also
Great Britain—Antiquities, Roman

Revolution of 1688

Propaganda in the Revolution of 1688-89. L. G. Schwoerer. bibl f il Am Hist R 82:843-74 O '77

1760-1789

See also
United States—History—Revolution, 1775-1783

1800-1837

See also
United States—History—War of 1812

20th century

David Lloyd George: land, the budget, and social reform. B. B. Gilbert. bibl f Am Hist R 81:1058-66 D '76

Industries

Britain: a new upbeat mood for investment. il Bus W p41-2 F 21 '77

Inflation? Account for it; use of current cost accounting. Forbes 119:64-5 Mr 1 '77

See also
Aerospace industries—Great Britain
Airplane industry—Great Britain
Atomic power industry—Great Britain
Automobile equipment industry—Great Britain
Automobile industry—Great Britain
Biscuit and cracker industry—Great Britain
Cigarette industry—Great Britain
Coal industry—Great Britain
Construction industry—Great Britain
Electric industries—Great Britain
Fish culture
Pearson, S, & Son, Ltd
Petroleum industry—Great Britain
Phonograph record industry—Great Britain
Real estate business—Great Britain
Retail trade—Great Britain
Shipbuilding—Great Britain

Kings and rulers

Happy and glorious. H. Sutton. il Sat R 4:6-7 Je 11 '77

Inner Queen; Elizabeth II and her predecessors. R. West. il Vogue 167:232-3+ My '77

See also
Elizabeth II, Queen of Great Britain
William III, King of Great Britain

Medical Research Council

See Medical Research Council (Great Britain)

Military policy

Churchill and us; question of policies toward military preparedness in pre-World War II Great Britain and in the United States today. E. N. Luttwak. Commentary 63:44-9 Je '77

National Health Service

British National Health Service in international perspective. J. G. Simanis. bibl f Cur Hist 73:27-9+ Jl '77

Navy

See also
United States—History—War of 1812—Naval operations

Nobility

Gathering; first American edition of Debrett's peerage and baronetage. New Yorker 53:37-8 D 12 '77

Peerage

See Great Britain—Nobility

Politics and government

Britain: an October election? J. E. Pluenneke. il Bus W p44 Ap 11 '77

British politics in 1977. A. Cyr. Cur Hist 73:153-5+ N '77

Callaghan's moment of truth. il por Time 109:38 Mr 28 '77

Heating up. W. F. Buckley, Jr. Nat R 29:958 Ag 19 '77

Letter from London (cont) M. Panter-Downes. New Yorker 53:96-7 Mr 7; 122 Ap 11 '77

Margaret Thatcher: Britain's next prime minister? C. Sterling. il por Read Digest 110:172-6 My '77

Poor old Harold the henpecked; J. Haines' book depicting Prime Minister H. Wilson and secretary M. Williams. pors Time 109:43 F 21 '77

Queen's silver jubilee: a hard day's night. il map Sr Schol 109:4-7 My 5 '77

Sick man of Europe. F. Mount. Nat R 29:727-30 Je 24 '77

Thatcher: we shall win; interview. ed by H. Nickel. M. Thatcher. por Time 110:44 S 19 '77

This sickled isle... Nat R 29:316 Mr 18 '77

Why Labor loses ground in Britain; with interview with M. Thatcher. R. A. Haeger. il U.S. News 83:68-71 S 12 '77

See also
Elections—Great Britain
Fascism—Great Britain
Legislation—Great Britain
Political parties—Great Britain

Popular culture

Plastic punks. A. Burgess; J. Lombardi. il Psychol Today 11:120-2+ N '77

Prime Ministers

See also
Avon, Anthony Eden, 1st Earl of

Race question

Belt up, you big bore; views of E. Powell. por Time 109:44-5 F 7 '77

Bit of hell in Notting Hill. il Time 110:28 S 12 '77

Britain's new ultra-right; the National Front. P. Webb and M. MacPherson. il Newsweek 90:44 Ag 29 '77

Coloreds must go! National Front party; with report by E. Amfitheatrof. il Time 110:50+ D 12 '77

Violence in Lewisham. T. Beeson. Chr Cent 94:803-4 S 21 '77

Violence in the streets. B. Wicker. Commonweal 104:582-4 S 16 '77

Religious institutions and affairs

Was Jesus merely man? theological controversy. il Time 110:45 Ag 15 '77

See also
Baptists in Great Britain
Catholic Church in Great Britain
Religious conferences—Great Britain

Riots

Violence in the streets. B. Wicker. Commonweal 104:582-4 S 16 '77

See also
London—Riots

Royal family

See also
Great Britain—Kings and rulers

Social history

David Lloyd George: land, the budget, and social reform. B. B. Gilbert. bibl f Am Hist R 81:1058-66 D '76

Social life and customs

History

Book of gentlemanly conduct. P. W. Schmidtchen. il Hobbies 82:134-6+ Mr '77

Treaties

United States

See United States—Treaties—Great Britain

GREAT BRITAIN in miniature. See Models of cities, towns, etc.

GREAT BRITAIN-United States air agreement. See Aviation—International aspects

GREAT Connecticut River Raft Race. See Raft racing

GREAT Depression. See Business depression, 1929-1939

GREAT FISH River. See Back River

GREAT Lakes

Great Lakes eutrophication: the effect of point source control of total phosphorus. S. C. Chapra and A. Robertson. bibl il Science 196:1448-50 Je 24 '77

See also
Superior, Lake
Water pollution—Great Lakes

GREAT Lakes Fisheries Research Station, Cape Vincent. See New York (state)—Environmental Conservation, Department of

GREAT Lakes shipping. See Inland water transportation

GREAT men and women

America's 10 most powerful women. il Harp Baz 111:150-1 N '77

Gentle conquerors: P. Cushman, H. Keller and M. Curie. il Sat Eve Post 249:80 Jl '77

Saturday review honor roll 1977. il Sat R 5:10-11 D 10 '77

GREAT men and women—*Continued*

Anecdotes, facetiae, satire, etc.

Things the history books don't tell us. T. H. Middleton. Sat R 4:59 Ja 22 '77

Photographs

Many faces of Yousuf Karsh; excerpt from Karsh portraits. Y. Karsh. il Read Digest 110:153-9 F '77

GREAT PLAINS

History

Dust! R. D. Hurt. il Am Heritage 28:34-5 Ag '77
Dust Bowl. R. D. Hurt. bibl il Am West 14: 22-7+ Jl '77
Route 66: ghost road of the Okies. T. W. Pew, Jr. il Am Heritage 28:24-33 Ag '77
Sands of wrath: America's Dust Bowl in retrospect. H. E. Dregne. il UNESCO Courier 30:14-17 Jl '77

GREAT PLAINS National Park (proposed) See National parks and reserves—United States

GREAT SALT Lake
Salt Lake spills over. il Bus W p 116 Ap 25 '77
Splendor at the shore; photographs. C. G. Summers, Jr. Nat Wildlife 15:42-7 Je '77

GREAT SMOKY Mountains
Pocket of the past: the Great Smokies. B. A. Branson. il Américas 29:9-15 F '77
See also
Great Smoky Mountains National Park

GREAT SMOKY Mountains National Park
Could the Smokies be shrinking? Nat Parks & Con Mag 51:22-3 Je '77
NPS reveals decisions on future of Smokies. Nat Parks & Con Mag 51:29 O '77
Problems in the Smokies. G. S. Kephart. il por Am For 83:28-31 Ag '77; Discussion. 83:2-4 D '77

GREAT Southwest Corporation
Great Southwest's ride toward solvency. il Bus W p54+ Ap 25 '77

GREAT Western United Corporation-Sunshine Mining Company merger. See Corporations—Acquisitions and mergers

GREAT women. See Great men and women

GREATER Miami Opera Association. See Opera—Florida

GREB, G. Allen. See York, H. F. jt auth

GREBEN, Seymour
Reaching everyman: Shakespeare in the streets. il Parks & Rec 12:39-40+ Ap '77

GREBER, Henry
Solutions to national problems through scientific consensus. il Intellect 106:72-3 Ag '77

GREBMEIER, Ralph
Police for hire. il por Time 109:52 Ja 24 '77 *

GREECE
See also
Botany—Greece
Crime and criminals—Greece
Cruising—Greece
Publishers and publishing—Greece
Shipping—Greece
Siphnos (island)
Tourist trade—Greece

Antiquities

Art. L. Alloway. Nation 225:60-1 Jl 9 '77
Ill-provisioned voyage: Greece sails into this century. J. W. Brown. il Nation 225:38-41 Jl 9 '77
Paleogeographic reconstructions of coastal Aegean archaeological sites. J. C. Kraft and others. bibl il maps Science 195:941-7 Mr 11 '77
See also
Athens, Greece—Acropolis
Parthenon
Tombs—Greece

Anecdotes, facetiae, satire, etc.

Clumsy fool—careful with that vase! R. Vicker. il Read Digest 110:133-5 F '77

Commerce

See also
European Economic Community

Description and travel

New voyager: Greece for travelers, not tourists. C. Ingham. bibl Ms 5:56-9+ F '77

Economic relations

See also
European Economic Community

Foreign relations

Cyprus

See Cyprus

Turkey

Turks, Greeks, Congress and Carter. il Time 109:50 My 16 '77

United States

See United States—Foreign relations—Greece

Industries

See also
Potteries

Politics and government

See also
Elections—Greece

Religious institutions and affairs

See also
Orthodox Eastern Church in Greece

GREECE, Ancient

History

Citadel in praise of peace. A. Diamantopoulos. il UNESCO Courier 30:24-7 O '77

GREED. See Avarice

GREEK AMERICANS
Great American melting pot. H. M. Petrakis. Holiday 58:24-5 Ap '77
Growing up Greek American. C. C. Moskos, Jr. il por Society 14:64-71 Ja '77

GREEK cookery. See Cookery, Greek

GREEK poetry

Translations into English

Ithaca; excerpt from The complete poems of Cavafy, tr by R. Dalven. C. P. Cavafy. Ms 5: 57 F '77

GREEK pottery. See Pottery, Greek

GREEK revival architecture. See Architecture, Greek revival

GREEK sculpture. See Sculpture, Greek

GREEK vases. See Vases, Greek

GREEKS in the United States
See also
Greek Americans

GREEN, Adele
Consider the lilies of the terrace. il Horticulture 55:44-5 N '77

GREEN, Alice M.
Her son, the teen-aged ascetic; story. Commentary 64:68-79 D '77

GREEN, Bernard
Talk-it-over technique. B. Russell. il House & Gard 149:30+ Je '77 *

GREEN, Bill
40-MHz frequency counter. il Pop Electr 11:64-6 Je '77
Power your projects with solar energy! il Pop Electr 12:41-7 D '77

GREEN, Christopher
Employment ratio as an indicator of aggregate demand pressure. bibl il M Labor R 100: 25-32 Ap '77

GREEN, Constance
I'm a friend of your son's. il Ret Liv 17:32-3 S '77

GREEN, Cynthia P. and Lowe, S. J.
Teenage pregnancy. Current 192:35-40 Ap '77

GREEN, Dan S.
W.E.B. DuBois: his journalistic career. bibl f il pors Negro Hist Bull 40:672-7 Mr '77

GREEN, Edith
Road is paved with good intentions; address, January 25, 1977. Vital Speeches 43:300-3 Mr 1 '77

GREEN, Elmer
Biofeedback: what it is and how it can help you; interview. il pors U.S. News 82:63-4 Ap 4 '77

GREEN, G. Kenneth
Obituary
Phys Today por 30:78-80 O '77. J. Blewett

GREEN, Gerald
PW interviews; ed by J. F. Baker. il por Pub W 211:10-11 Mr 7 '77
Spell; story. Seventeen 36:82-5 Jl '77

GREEN, Hannah
Mister Nabokov. New Yorker 52:32-5 F 14 '77

GREEN, Harold P.
Oppenheimer case: a study in the abuse of law. il pors Bull Atom Sci 33:12-16+ S '77

GREEN, Hubert
Talk about total pressure. D. Jenkins. il por Sports Illus 46:14-19 Je 27 '77 *

GREEN, James Frederick
NGOs. bibl il Society 15:65-70 N '77

GREEN, Karen
Hearty small-game stews. il Outdoor Life 159: 158 F '77
My turn for the wurst. Field & S 82:177-9+ N '77

GREEN, Louis C.
Cosmology today. il Sky & Tel 54:180-4 S '77
Radio galaxies and quasars. il Sky & Tel 54: 384-9 N '77
Some new developments in X-ray astronomy. il Sky & Tel 53:340-3 My '77
Supernovae today. il Sky & Tel 54:11-14 Jl '77

GREEN, Marc A. and others
Comparison of Fourier analysis and feature analysis in pattern-specific color aftereffects. bibl il Science 192:147-8; 198:209 Ap 9 '76, O 14 '77

GREEN, Mark J.
Consumer agency; pro. New Repub 176:14-16 Je 18 '77
Too much conscience is unprofessional. Nation 224:485-8 Ap 23 '77
—See Nader, R. jt auth

GREEN, Martin
Austen-ized village. Atlantic 240:77-81 Jl '77
Visible college in British science. Am Scholar 47:105-17 Wint '77

GREEN, Martin I.
First aid for kids. S. C. Cowley. il Newsweek 90:48 S 5 '77 *

GREEN, Maureen
Always something to do at Britain's National Theatre. il Smithsonian 8:66-73 Je '77
In praise of beasts: round-the-world museum observance. il Smithsonian 8:108-14 bibl(p 162) N '77
Pevsner choices among the fine English buildings. il pors Smithsonian 7:96-103 bibl(p 154) F '77

GREEN, Neville
Bitten from the records. M. Sloan. il Motor B & S 139:52-5+ Mr '77 *

GREEN, Olivia Harris
Unsung melody; poem. Negro Hist Bull 40:750 S '77

GREEN, Philip
Australia's feathered playboy. il Nat Geog 152: 864-72 D '77

GREEN, Philip, 1932-
Heredity and ideology. Nation 224:341-3 Mr 19 '77

GREEN, Robert L.
Fast feast. il por N Y Times Mag p 158+ N 20 '77
Mostly for men. il N Y Times Mag p 162+ D 4 '77
New etiquette. Harp Baz 110:119+ My '77

GREEN, Ronald M.
Intergenerational distributive justice and environmental responsibility. bibl BioScience 27: 260-5 Ap '77

GREEN, Timothy
Man's obsession reveals the riches of a hidden world. il por Smithsonian 8:80-7 bibl(p 161) N '77

GREEN, William D.
After high school, what? Am Educ 13:19-22 O '77

GREEN, William Henry, family
At Liz and Billy Green's: a Christmas on the prairie. K. Duff. il pors Redbook 150:89+ D '77

GREEN-ARMYTAGE, Stephen
Breathtaking ride through the autumn countryside. il Sports Illus 47:28-32 O 3 '77

GREEN BAY (city), Wis.
Gazetteer. il Ret Liv 17:39+ S '77

GREEN beans. See Beans

GREEN Haven prison. See Prisons—New York (state)

GREEN lacewings. See Lacewings

GREEN Mountain Boys. See United States—History—Revolution, 1775-1783—American forces

GREENAMYER, Darryl
Speed dash in a homemade jet. R. L. Emerson. il Pop Mech 147:102+ Je '77 *

GREENBAUM, Elias
Photosynthetic unit of hydrogen evolution. bibl il Science 196:879-80 My 20 '77

GREENBAUM, Everett
Fine piece of machinery. il Sat Eve Post 249: 56-7+ N '77

GREENBERG, Daniel S.
Danger for our research/technology. il Sci Digest 81:20-3+ F '77
Official circles. See issues of Science digest

GREENBERG, Donald P.
Computer graphics for architecture: techniques in search of problems. il Archit Rec 162:98-105 mid-Ag '77 *

GREENBERG, Emanuel, and Greenberg, Madeline
Adventures with wines. House B 119:128-9 D '77
Independent woman's wine cellar. Harp Baz 110:137+ F '77

GREENBERG, J. H. and others
Inhibition of a lymphocyte membrane enzyme by Δ^9-tetrahydrocannabinol in vitro. bibl il Science 197:475-7 Jl 29 '77

GREENBERG, Joanne, and Doolittle, Glenn
Can schools speak the language of the deaf? il N Y Times Mag p50+ D 11 '77

GREENBERG, Joel
[Articles on the behavioral sciences] See issues of Science news
Stress-illness link: not if but how. il Sci N 112: 394-5+ D 10 '77

GREENBERG, Madeline. See Greenberg, E. jt auth

GREENBERG, Michael J. See Price, D. A. jt auth

GREENBERG, Selma
Preschool and the politics of sexism; excerpt from address, October 11, 1976. SLJ 23:126 Mr '77

GREENBURG, Dan
Sweet grapes of wrath. il por Esquire 87:100-2 Je '77

GREENBURGH Public Library, Elmsford. See Libraries—New York (state)

GREENE, Bob, 1948-
Are books an endangered species? por Newsweek 89:9 My 2 '77

GREENE, Caty
Cause célèbre of Caty Greene; excerpt from Caty. J. F. Stegeman and J. A. Stegeman. il por Am Hist Illus 12:8-16 Je '77 *

GREENE, David J.
Elderly kid in a candy store. H. Rudnitsky. por Forbes 119:110+ My 1 '77 *

GREENE, Graham
Staying power and the glory. M. Mewshaw. Nation 224:469-72 Ap 16 '77 *

GREENE, Jeannette (Lofas)
Mrs Greene's steps to successful family life. S. Edmiston. por Good H 185:70+ S '77 *

GREENE, Jeffrey
Block Island; poem. Nation 224:534 Ap 30 '77
Charleston R.I; poem. Nation 225:508 N 12 '77
Winter in Plainfield N.H; poem. Nation 225:156 Ag 20 '77

GREENE, Johnny
Selling off the Old South. il map Harpers 254: 39-42+ Ap '77

GREENE, Joyce G.
Managing your house plant's hormones. il Horticulture 55:18-20 N '77

GREENE, Nathanael
Cause célèbre of Caty Greene; excerpt from Caty. J. F. Stegeman and J. A. Stegeman. il por Am Hist Illus 12:8-16 Je '77 *

GREENE, Richard Lawrence
Fertility symbols on the Hadley chests. bibl il Antiques 112:250-7 Ag '77

GREENFIELD, Edward
Glyndebourne's Giovanni & Covent Garden's Fanciulla. il Hi Fi 27:MA38-9 O '77

GREENFIELD, Jeff
Absent left. Harpers 255:19-21+ S '77
Growing up cynical with TV; excerpt from Television: the first fifty years. Horizon 20:96 S '77
Perfect tennis partner. il Esquire 87:110-11+ My '77
Showdown at ABC News. il pors N Y Times Mag p32-4+ F 13 '77

GREENFIELD, Lois
Senegal. il Trav/Holiday 148:38-43+ N '77

GREENFIELD, Natalee S. pseud
Final victory. Good H 184:103+ Ap '77

GREENFIELD, Stanley R.
National directory of addresses and telephone numbers; interview, ed by R. Dahlin. Pub W 212:34 D 5 '77

GREENFIELD Village and Henry Ford Museum, Dearborn, Mich.
What's happening at: Greenfield Village and Henry Ford Museum. Hobbies 82:155 Ja '78

GREENGARD, Paul. See Nathanson, J. A. jt auth

GREENHILL, Robert F.
Expert strategists in the acquisition game. pors Bus W p 182-3 N 14 '77 *

GREENHOUSE, Tex (resort) See Health resorts, watering places, spas, etc.

GREENHOUSE effect. See Atmosphere

GREENHOUSES
For people who want to live in glass houses. S. Oddo. il House & Gard 150:36+ Ja '78
Fossil plants you can still grow. M. M. Whitson. il Horticulture 55:22-5 O '77
Front yard greenhouse is both courteous and efficient. il Sunset 158:274-5 Ap '77
Greenhouse. J. Kilborn. See issues of Horticulture
Greenhouse gardening. J. Fanning. bibl il House & Gard 150:156-7 Ja '78
Make room for plants. il Bet Hom & Gard 55:69 O '77
New upstairs is conservatory. New downstairs is work center. il Sunset 158:166-7 F '77
Revolution in greenhouses. il Sunset 158:96-9 Mr '77
Solar greenhouses; symposium. il Org Gard & Farm 24:53-68 D '77
Stretch your greenhouse space. K. L. Carlsen. il Org Gard & Farm 24:121-5 S '77
Sun power makes window greenhouse self-ventilating. G. Stone. il Pop Sci 211:108-10 D '77
Sunpit for propagation. F. Lape. il Org Gard & Farm 24:100-3 F '77
Their old courtyard now has a greenhouse on top. il Sunset 159:98 Ag '77
Two-story greenhouse is three-way heater for this Santa Fe adobe. il Sunset 158:146+ My '77
See also
Cold frames
Garden rooms

Anecdotes, facetiae, satire, etc.

Aluminum wedding. G. Ostlere. il Horticulture 55:17 Je '77

Heating and ventilation

Amazing grape-seed greenhouse. R. Rodale. il por Org Gard & Farm 24:48-52 D '77
Composting in the solar greenhouse for CO_2 and heat; excerpt from The solar greenhouse book. D. Knapp. il Org Gard & Farm 24:60-2 D '77

Lighting

Winter light for greenhouse gardening; excerpt from The solar greenhouse book. J. White. il Org Gard & Farm 24:58-9 D '77

GREENING, W. E.
Separation threat fuels Quebec crisis. Chr Cent 94:754 Ag 31 '77

GREENLAND

Antiquities

Lost Norse mystery; disappearance of Greenland settlements in Middle Ages. F. Garner. il Oceans 10:4-9 Mr '77

GREENLEE, Ralph M.
Refreshing way station. il Yachting 141:77-9 Mr '77

GREENLER, Robert G. and others
Form and origin of the Parry arcs. bibl il Science 195:360-7 Ja 28 '77

GREENOUGH, James W.
Arctic splendor along the Noatak. il maps Nat Parks & Con Mag 51:4-9 Je '77

GREENPEACE Foundation. See Foundations, Charitable and educational

GREENS, Edible
Chinese greens—freezing or pickling. il Sunset 158:169 Mr '77
Growing, cooking, shopping for Chinese greens. il Sunset 158:102-3 Mr '77
New use for an old device: growing greens in a coldframe for fresh winter salads. K. Kraft and P. Kraft. il Horticulture 55:56-7 S '77
Taking action on Oriental greens. Sunset 158: 236 Mr '77
See also
Herbs
Kale

GREENSBORO, N.C.

Education

See Education—North Carolina

GREENSPAN, Alan
Debate: how to stop inflation. pors Fortune 95:116-20 Ap '77

GREENSPAN, Donald
Physics without limits. D. E. Thomsen. il Sci N 112:186-7 S 17 '77 *

GREENSPAN, Martin
Greenspan and Jeffress win ASA silver medals. pors Phys Today 30:67 D '77 *

GREENSVILLE County, Va.

Education

See Education—Virginia

GREENVILLE, Miss.

Newspapers

See Newspapers—Mississippi

GREENWALD, Judith
Souvenirs you shouldn't bring back. McCalls 104:66-7 My '77

GREENWALD, Michael
Good stove is priceless. il Motor B & S 141: 104-7+ Ja '78

GREENWALT, Lynn A.
In Washington, the policy-makers fret and sweat. J. H. Phillips. il Nat Wildlife 15:12-13 Ag '77 *

GREENWELL, George Robert
Pricking up their ears. J. Kirshenbaum. il por Sports Illus 47:94+ O 31 '77 *

GREENWICH Village, New York. See New York (city)—Greenwich Village

GREENWOOD, Gordon E. and others
Citizen advisory committees. Educ Digest 43:6-9 S '77

GREENWOOD, John
Big John's comeback. B. Yates. il pors Car & Dr 23:104-6+ O '77 *

GREENWOOD, L. C.
Offside in Pittsburgh? S. Fraker and S. Lesher. pors Newsweek 89:40 My 9 '77 *

GREEP, Roy O.
Population explosion; excerpt from address, August 1977. Society 15:9 N '77 *

GREER, Georgeanna H.
Alkaline glazes and groundhog kilns: Southern pottery traditions. il Antiques 111:768-73 Ap '77

GREER, Gordon G.
Of concern now. il Bet Hom & Gard 55:10+ Mr '77

GREETING cards
Departed. . .deceased. . .but never dead; sympathy card language. J. Horn. Psychol Today 11:152 O '77
Salute to autumn leaves. J. Bear and F. Bear. il por Conservationist 32:38-9 N '77
This month's special market list; poetry. Writer 90:31-42+ Mr '77
See also
Christmas cards
Valentines

GREETINGS. See Salutations

GREGER, Debora
After Iceland, William Morris dreams of Panama; poem. New Yorker 53:129 D 5 '77
Armorer's daughter; poem. New Yorker 53:107 Mr 7 '77
Closing; poem. Nation 224:534 Ap 30 '77
Inventing the third person; poem. New Yorker 53:128 Ap 11 '77
Seduction of solitude; Body of work; Not you; poems. Nation 225:629 D 10 '77
Woman of my description; poem. Nation 225:573 N 26 '77

GREGG, Fred M.
New teacher, pupil at Sunday school. C. Nannes. por Chr Today 21:52-3 Ap 1 '77 *

GREGG, James R.
Which is your better shooting eye? il Field & S 81:90+ Mr '77

GREGG, Linda
As when the blowfish perishing; poem. Nation 225:217 S 10 '77

GREGOR, Arthur
Cul-de-sac; poem. New Yorker 53:38 Ap 25 '77
Markings; poem. Nation 224:509 Ap 23 '77
Two-sided; poem. Nation 224:700 Je 4 '77

about

Comment. J. D. McClatchy. Poetry 130:47-9 Ap '77 *

GREGORIOS, Paulos Mar
Eastern view of Ecumenism. il America 137: 400-1 D 3 '77

GREGORY, Cynthia
Dancing. A. Croce. New Yorker 53:68-70 Jl 4 '77 *
Flying high. por Time 109:77 Ja 24 '77 *
No swan song for Cynthia. J. Kaplan. il por Seventeen 36:18+ Jl '77 *

GREGORY, Donnelly. See Russo, T. jt auth

GREGORY, Fred M. H.
Goodbye yellow brick road. il Car & Dr 23:83-4+ Jl '77
Retrospect (cont) il Motor T 28:101-4 D '76

GREGORY, Lillian
Mine is the simplest diet in the world. il pors Ebony 32:64-5+ F '77 *

GREGORY, Mary
Kostes Palamas: Patrides; poems. Poetry 130: 211-17 Jl '77

GREIF, Martin
Tribute to Russel Wright: pioneering industrial designer, 1903-1976. Craft Horiz 37:44 Ag '77

GREINER, Charles F.
Humanizing education: the possible dream. il Engl J 66:28-31 N '77
To confess a fault freely; address. Engl J 66:5-6 My '77

GRENADA

Photographs

Grenada portfolio; with introduction by A. J. Lowe. Américas 29:33-40 S '77

GRENADINES (islands)
See also
Bequia (island)
Fisheries—Grenadines (islands)

GRENOT, Claude, and Vernet, Roland
Case study in survival. il UNESCO Courier 30:25-8 Jl '77

GRESSITT, J. Linsley
Symbiosis runs wild on the backs of high-living weevils. il Smithsonian 7:135-6+ bibl(p 156) F '77

GRESSON, Aaron D. and Carter, D. G.
In search of the potentially gifted: suggestions for the school administrator. bibl Clearing H 50:369-71 Ap '77

GREULICH, Constance
Patron saints. Sat Eve Post 249:41+ Ap '77

GREY, Jo, and Grey, Joel
Jo and Joel Grey's brunch. Vogue 167:62+ Je '77

GREY, Joel
—See Grey, Jo, jt auth

about

Barefoot in New York. L Davis. il pors Vogue 167:158-61+ Je '77 *

GREY, M. Cameron
Heuriger; story. Mademoiselle 83:22 F '77

GREY, Tony
Bird in the bush; Pancontinental Mining. M. Dammerman. por Forbes 119:31-2 Je 15 '77 *

GREY, Vivian
How much do I love thee? Let me count the change. . . il Am Home 80:82-3 F '77

GREY, Zane
Earth log: the trammeling of Rainbow Bridge. G. Reiger. il Audubon 79:114-15+ N '77 *

GREY Cup. See Football, Professional—Canada

GREYHOUND racing. See Dog racing

GREYWATER. See Water reuse

GRIBBIN, John R.
Black holes. Sci Digest 81:45-7 Ap '77
Concept opening way to a scientific world of fantasy. il Smithsonian 8:100-7 bibl(p 161-2) N '77

GRIBBINS, Joseph
(ed) Boatkeeper. See issues of Motor boating & sailing

GRIDDLE cakes. See Pancakes, waffles, etc.

GRIDIRONS, Football. See Football fields

GRIEF
Death in the family. J. Seligmann and S. Agrest. il Newsweek 89:89 Je 20 '77
Help for bereaved parents; ideas of H. S. Schiff. J. Chan. McCalls 105:114 O '77
How to cope with tragedy. A. F. Poussaint. il Ebony 32:94-6+ F '77

GRIES, George Alexander
Open new doors through biology education. BioScience 27:7 Ja '77
about
New officers stress building membership. por BioScience 27:41 Ja '77 *

GRIESE, Bob
Spectacles make him spectacular. D. Jenkins. por Sports Illus 47:111-12+ O 10 '77 *

GRIEVANCE procedures
Handling prison grievances: the labor model in practice. T. S. Denenberg. M Labor R 100:53-6 Mr '77

GRIEVES, Robert T. and Strack, David
Press lord comes to Buffalo. Nation 225:590-2 D 3 '77

GRIFFEL, L. Michael
Reappraisal of Schubert's methods of composition. bibl f il Mus Q 63:186-210 Ap '77

GRIFFIN, Donald R.
Anthropomorphism. bibl BioScience 27:445-6 Jl '77

GRIFFIN, Mike
Five pounds of firefighting. il Motor B & S 140:99-101 Ag '77

GRIFFIN, R. M.
Leveling; story. Redbook 149:112-13 Je '77

GRIFFIN, Rachael
New peak at Timberline. il Craft Horiz 37:14-17 O '77

GRIFFIN, Robert
Personal meaning and personal learning as educational concepts. Clearing H 50:227-30 Ja '77

GRIFFIN, Robert P.
Message to the professions; address, August 27, 1977. Vital Speeches 44:82-5 N 15 '77

GRIFFIN, Sunny
Calling on Avon. M. R. Carter. Mademoiselle 83:72 Je '77 *

GRIFFITH, F. H.
Old mechanical banks. See issues of Hobbies

GRIFFITH, Jack W.
There is an alternative to fines. SLJ 23:50 Ap '77

GRIFFITH, Mary
Month in yachting. Yachting 142:206-8 O '77

GRIFFITH, Thomas
Newswatch. See occasional issues of Time
Party of one. See every other issue of Atlantic
Weyerhaeuser gets set for the 21st century. il Fortune 95:74-9+ Ap '77

GRIFFITH, William E.
Let's resolve the Middle East crisis—now! Read Digest 110:73-7 Ap '77

GRIFFITHS, Edgar H.
RCA off the roller coaster, onto the escalator? J. Grigsby. por Forbes 119:25-8 F 15 '77 *

GRIFFITHS, Trevor
Comedians. Review
Commentary 63:74 Ap '77 *

GRIGSON, Geoffrey
Death for the undying; poem. Poetry 131:147 D '77

GRILL cookery. See Barbecue cookery

GRILLS, Barbecue. See Barbecue grills

GRIMALDI, Alberto
Messy fight for the final cut. il Time 109:70-1 My 2 '77 *

GRIMM, Clayford T.
Designing brick masonry walls to avoid structural problems. il Archit Rec 162:124-8 O '77

GRIMM, Jack
Amateur is burned at high stakes; World Series of Poker. E. Shrake. il por Sports Illus 46:56+ My 30 '77 *

GRIMM Brothers
Dummling and the golden goose; dramatization. See Thane, A.
One eye, two eyes and three eyes; dramatization. See Lavin, R. C.

GRINDAL, Gracia
Stopping by the pit stop. bibl il Chr Cent 94:453-7 My 11 '77

GRINDING machines
Hand grinders—versatile tools for your shop. T. H. Jones. il Pop Sci 210:128+ My '77

GRINGO (term)
Notes on the gringo. W. E. Hoy. Américas 29:15-16 Ag '77

GRININS, Tekla A.
Will the real Abraham Lincoln please stand up? drama. Plays 36:71-4 F '77

GRINKER, Roy R., Jr
Poor rich. bibl il Psychol Today 11:74-6+ O '77

GRINNELL, Richard M. and Kyte, N. S.
Crisis. il MH 60:11-13 Wint '77

GRINSPOON, Lester, and Bakalar, J. B.
Cocaine—a social history; excerpt from Cocaine: a drug and its social evolution. bibl il pors Psychol Today 10:36-9+ Mr '77
Kick from cocaine. il Psychol Today 10:41-2+ Mr '77

GRIS, Charles Édouard Jeanneret-. See Le Corbusier

GRISHKOT, Walter
Adirondack Hot-Air Balloon Festival 1977. il Conservationist 32:30-1 S '77

GRIST mills. See Flour mills

GRIZZLY bears. See Bears

GROBEL, Larry
Joseph Heller: some things happen. por Writers Digest 57:24-5 O '77

GROBSTEIN, Clifford
Recombinant-DNA debate; with biographical sketch. il Sci Am 237:18, 22-33 bibl(p 154) Jl '77

GROCERY trade
Independents' best friend; Super Valu Stores, Inc. il por Forbes 119:47-8 F 1 '77
New greengrocers; Koreans in New York City. New Yorker 53:20-3 Jl 4 '77
No-brand groceries. il Time 110:80 N 21 '77
Output per unit of labor input in the retail food store industry. J. L. Carey and P. F. Otto. bibl f il M Labor R 100:42-6 Ja '77
Wetterau: a maverick grocery wholesaler. il Bus W p 121-2 F 14 '77
See also
Arden-Mayfair, Inc
Food stores
Great Atlantic & Pacific Tea Company

Finance

Supermarkets & wholesalers. il Forbes 121:146+ Ja 9 '78

GRODZINS, Lee
Changing career opportunities for physicists. G. B. Lubkin. por Phys Today 30:85-6 O '77 *

GROENE, Gordon
Plate-glass varnish. il Motor B & S 139:101-4 Ap '77

GROENE, Janet
Choosing the galley stove; excerpt from The galley book. Yachting 141:90-1 My '77
Privacy (and comfort) afloat starts with a basic bed. Yachting 142:78-9 N '77

GROLIER, Inc
How Grolier lost $13 a share. il Bus W p31 Ap 4 '77

GROMYKO, Andreĭ Andreevich
Secretary Vance and Soviet Foreign Minister Gromyko hold talks at Geneva; transcript of news conference, with joint communique, May 21, 1977. Dept State Bull 76:628-33 Je 13 '77
about
Breaking the ice; SALT talks in Geneva. S. Fraker and others. pors Newsweek 89:16-17 My 30 '77 *

GROOMING of pets. See Pets—Care

GROPPI, James Edward
Wayward bus. E. Keerdoja and S. Monroe. il por Newsweek 90:16+ O 31 '77 *

GROSBEAKS
Art print of the year: rose-breasted grosbeak. B. Vogt. il Nat Wildlife 15:24 O '77

GROSGEBAUER, Clare
Little courses that grew. il Am Educ 13:10-13 Je '77; Same abr. Educ Digest 43:21-4 O '77

GROSMAN, Tatyana
Goldilocks' cosmic teach-in. M. Hoelterhoff. il pors Art N 76:19-21 Mr '77 *

GROSS, Amy
Marriage counseling for unwed couples. N Y Times Mag p52+ Ap 24 '77
Verbal sex—the world's greatest noncontact sport. Mademoiselle 83:149+ Je '77
Weekend at the heart of the Human Potential Movement. il Mademoiselle 83:202+ Ap '77
Your friends, my friends, our friends. Redbook 149:76+ My '77
—and Comer, N. A.
Power dressing. Mademoiselle 83:188-9+ S '77

GROSS, Leonard H.
How to do more by taking it easy; excerpt from Maximum performance. il Good H 184:202-3 Ap '77

GROSS, Marthe
One woman's war against rape. por Good H 184:84+ Ap '77

GROSS, Neal
Theoretical and policy implications of case study findings about federal efforts to improve public schools. bibl f Ann Am Acad 434:71-87 N '77

GROSS, Norman
Teaching about the law: perceptions and implications. Educ Digest 43:34-5 O '77

GROSS, Paul
Health insurance: are you covered? House & Gard 149:46+ Ap '77
How to buy your place in the sun. il House & Gard 150:77+ Ja '78
Money matters. por House & Gard 149:30+ My; 44+ S; 58+ O; 22-3+ N '77

GROSS, Philip J.
How to make that trip abroad more exciting. Harvard Bus R 55:14 Mr '77

GROSS, Richard
Faculty growth contracts. Educ Digest 43:28-31 S '77

GROSS, Robert Alfred
Nuclear fusion's promise grows. P. Raeburn. il Sci Digest 82:8-10 Jl '77 *

GROSS, Ronald
Mother goes to school. Parents Mag 52:18+ Ap '77

GROSS national product
Carter's only choice may be a tax cut. N. Jonas and S. H. Wildstrom. Bus W p24 N 7 '77

GROSSBARDT, Andrew
No good reason; poem. Am Scholar 47:103 Wint '77
Winter in mid-country; poem. Nation 224:344 Mr 19 '77

GROSSBERGER, Lewis
Sorry, wrong number. Sports Illus 47:42-4+ Jl 18 '77

GROSSET and Dunlap, Inc
G&D buys hardcover rights to Nixon memoirs. M. Reuter. Pub W 211:40 Mr 14 '77

GROSSMAN, Allen
O great O north cloud; Runner; Nightmare; poems. Poetry 129:321-3 Mr '77

about

Comment. J. D. McClatchy. Poetry 130:50-2 Ap '77 *

GROSSMAN, Allyson Sherman
Almost half of all children have mothers in the labor force. bibl il M Labor R 100:41-4 Je '77

GROSSMAN, Lee
Shuffling too much paper? Here's how to reduce it; interview. por U.S. News 82:53 Ap 18 '77

GROSSMAN, Robert
There's a surprise in every package; caricatures. il Sports Illus 46:38-43 Ap 11 '77

GROSSMAN, Robert G. and Seregin, Aleksandr
Glial-neural interaction demonstrated by the injection of Na^+ and Li^+ into cortical glia. bibl il Science 195:196-8 Ja 14 '77

GROSSWIRTH, Marvin
Anatomy of a fire! Newer technologies fighting the unknown. il Sci Digest 82:7-11 Ag '77
Can inventions make you rich? il Mech Illus 73:30+ My '77
Impaired MDs now recognized as a peril to patients. il Sci Digest 81:8-11+ Je '77
Research crunch. Sci Digest 82:27-9+ N '77

GROSVENOR, Gilbert M.
Geographic faces life. T. Schwartz and J. Whitmore. il por Newsweek 90:111 S 12 '77 *

GROSVENOR, Verta Mae
Is a woman over the hill at 40? il por Ebony 32:144-6+ Ag '77
Why where you from has replaced what's your sign. Mademoiselle 83:96-7+ Jl '77

GROSZ, George
Bright side of Weimar. R. Berenson. Nat R 29:1124-5 S 30 '77 *

GROTE, Margaret D.
Public schools can study religion. por Intellect 106:105-6 S '77

GROTE, Suzy Wetzel
Engravings of George Washington in the Stanley DeForest Scott collection. il Antiques 112:128-33 Jl '77

GROTH, Edward J. and others
Clustering of galaxies; with biographical sketches. il Sci Am 237:15, 76-8+ bibl(p 163) N '77

GROTON, Mass.

Education

See Education—Massachusetts

GROUEFF, Stéphane
Nation as concentration camp. Nat R 29:988-90 S 2 '77

GROUND cherries. See Husk tomatoes

GROUND effect machines. See Air cushion vehicles

GROUND meat cookery. See Cookery—Meat

GROUND sloths, Fossil. See Sloths, Fossil

GROUND squirrels
Nepotism and the evolution of alarm calls. P. W. Sherman. bibl il Science 197:1246-53 S 23 '77

GROUNDHOGS. See Woodchucks

GROUNDS, Vernon C.
Faith to face failure, or what's so great about success? por Chr Today 22:12-13 D 9 '77

GROUNDSEL
See also
Tansy ragwort

GROUNDWATER pollution. See Water pollution

GROUNI, H. N. See Billing, J. R. jt auth

GROUP for Contemporary Music. See Instrumental ensembles

GROUP leadership. See Leadership

GROUP legal-service plan. See Insurance, Litigation

GROUP psychotherapy
See also
Family psychotherapy

GROUP relations training
I couldn't cope alone. R. Dale. Seventeen 36:150-1+ N '77
Personal power at work; excerpt from Carl Rogers on personal power. C. Rogers. il por Psychol Today 10:60-2+ Ap '77
Weekend at the heart of the Human Potential Movement; Esalen. A. Gross. il Mademoiselle 83:202+ Ap '77

GROUP work in education
Students who work together like each other more. J. Horn. Psychol Today 10:95-6 Ap '77

Bibliography

Literature of the interactive education movement. F. Carlson and D. Shroyer. Engl J 66:84-8 Mr '77

GROUPING by ability. See Ability grouping in education

GROUPS (sociology)
Influence of peer groups on secondary school students. R. C. Maxon and B. Malone. bibl Clearing H 50:191-3 Ja '77
Why a woman can't be a good boss—because no one will let you; group leadership studies by C. Beauvais and Z. Schachtel. Mademoiselle 83:120+ Jl '77

GROUPS, Discussion. See Discussion groups

GROUSE
Rites of spring. il Audubon 79:56-67 Mr '77
Spruce grouse in the Adirondacks. R. S. Fritz. il Conservationist 31:19-22 Ja '77
Track on the beach; efforts to identify birds as either sharp-tailed grouse or heath hens. P. Matthiessen. il Audubon 79:68-9+ Mr '77

GROUSE shooting
Art of grouse finding. T. Trueblood. il Field & S 82:28+ N '77
Fateful chop, chop, chop, pop, hisssss; auerhahn shooting in Austria. V. Kraft. il Sports Illus 46:49+ F 21 '77
5-for-5 grouse hunters; interviews with five ruffed grouse hunters. ed by J. O. Cartier. il Outdoor Life 160:84-7 O '77
Glorious grouse; shooting in England's County of Yorkshire. A. Oglesby. il Field & S 82:28-30+ Jl '77
How to pick the best grouse dog. D. M. Duffey. il Outdoor Life 161:150+ Ja '78

GROVE, Noel
Vestmannaeyjar: up from the ashes. il map Nat Geog 151:690-701 My '77

GROVE Press, Inc. See Publishers and publishing—United States

GROVES, Harry E.
White collar crime; address, May 9, 1977. Vital Speeches 43:525-7 Je 15 '77

GROW Chemical Corporation. See Chemical industries

GROWTH
See also
Chemotaxis
Maturation (biology)
Maturity
Regeneration (biology)

GROWTH (bacteria)
Characterization of bacterial growth by means of flow microfluorometry. J. E. Bailey and others. bibl il Science 198:1175-6 D 16 '77

GROWTH (mollusks)
Anaerobiosis and a theory of growth line formation. R. A. Lutz and D. C. Rhoads. bibl il Science 198:1222-7 D 23 '77

GROWTH (plants)
How does a forest grow? J. P. Jackson. il Am For 83:32-3+ Jl '77
Managing your house plant's hormones. J. G. Greene. il Horticulture 55:18-20 N '77
NASA launches a new experiment to explore how plants react to stress. C. Mitchell. il pors Horticulture 55:10-13 S '77
See also
Tree rings

GROWTH, Economic. See Economic development

GROWTH hormone. See Pituitary hormones

GROWTH inhibiting substances (plants)
Growth regulator controls Johnson grass in soybeans; mefluidide. Farm J 101:M4 N '77
See also
Gloxylates

GROWTH of children. See Children—Growth and development

GROWTH of cities and towns. See Cities and towns—Growth

GROWTH promoting substances
See also
Epidermal growth factor
Nerve growth promoting factor

GROWTH promoting substances (plants)
Alfalfa yields a mystery chemical that spurs plant growth, even in the dark; triacontanol. E. Driscoll. il por Horticulture 55:8+ Ag '77
More corn from dinoseb? N. Reeder. il Farm J 101:20-1 Ap '77
Plant growth regulators—where they are now. Suc Farm 75:38 Je '77
Triacontanol: a new naturally occurring plant growth regulator. S. K. Ries and others. bibl il Science 195:1339-41 Mr 25 '77

GRUBBS, Clinton J.
13-*cis*-Retinoic acid: inhibition of bladder carcinogenesis induced in rats by *N*-butyl-*N*-(4-hydroxybutyl)nitrosamine. bibl il Science 198:743-4 N 18 '77

GRUEN, John
Charleston. il Art N 76:122+ S '77
Copenhagen. il Art N 76:105-6 O '77
(ed) Far-from-last judgments; or, Who's overrated now? And underrated. il Art N 76:106-20 N '77
Menotti's two worlds. il Opera N 41:12-17 My '77
Nureyev's Valentino tango. il por Vogue 167:148-9+ Ag '77
Paris. il Art N 76:109-11 S '77
(ed) See Dine, J. Jim Dine and the life of objects
(ed) See Freud, L. Relentlessly personal vision of Lucian Freud
(ed) See Gillespie, G. Gregory Gillespie's dense reality
(ed) See Heizer, M. You might say I'm in the construction business
(ed) See LaFosse, E. Spotlight on Edmund La Fosse
(ed) See Rauschenberg, R. Robert Rauschenberg: an audience of one
(ed) See Strong, R. Privilege and passion of directing museums

GRUENEFELD, George
Encore for the snow goose? il Int Wildlife 7:17-20 N '77

GRUENFELD, Jay
Environmental impact statements; adaptation of address, December 1976. pors Am For 83:18-19 My '77

GRUENING, Ernest
Gruening we knew. C. McWilliams. Nation 225:454 N 5 '77 *

GRUENINGER, Walter F.
Recorded music in review. See issues of Consumers' research magazine

GRUENSFELDER, Robert C.
Law enforcers lend a hand. il por Wilson Lib Bull 51:510-13 F '77

GRUENSTEIN, Peter
Alaska's natives, inc. Progressive 41:33-8 Mr '77

GRUMBACH, Doris
Fine print. Sat R 5:30-1 O 1; 33 O 15; 44 O 29; 30 N 12; 43 N 26; 54-5 D 10 '77; 41 Ja 7 '78
Multifarious horses of instruction. Commonweal 104:87-9 F 4 '77
Washingtonian's Book Fair—first edition. il Pub W 211:56-8 Je 6 '77

GRUMMAN, Leroy Randle
Grumman. D. Scheuer. il Flying 101:250-1 S '77 *

GRUMMAN Corporation
Grumman's chance to bag a NATO plane; E-2C Hawkeye. il Bus W p49+ Ap 18 '77

GRUMMAN Corporation-Flxible Company merger. See Corporations—Acquisitions and mergers

GRUNDKE, Russell, and Vederman, Ron
Successful pre-camp training program instills confidence, helps motivate working team. Camp Mag 49:14-15 Ap '77

GRUNES, Dennis
John Donne's The good-morrow. Am Imago 33:261-5 Fall '76

GRÜNEWALD, Matthias
Secondhand saint. Vasari. il Art N 76:24+ D '77 *

GRUNFELD, Frederic V.
Life and loves of Lady Hamilton: a melodrama in several acts. il pors Horizon 19:72-81 Ja '77
Skating on the canals. il Horizon 19:20-3 Mr '77

GRUNWALD, Henry Anatole
Letter from the publisher. R. P. Davidson. por Time 110:7 O 10 '77 *

GRUSKY, Oscar
Psychology and the arts. il Psychol Today 11:21-2 O '77

GRUSSING, Don
Castles in the air. il Nat Wildlife 15:12-16 F '77

GRUTKA, Andrew G. Bp
Freedom and parochial schools. R. Kirk. Nat R 29:441-2+ Ap 15 '77 *

GRUTTER, Anna Marie. See Gianatasio, J. R. jt auth

GRYAZNOV, Mikhail Petrovich
Horses for the hereafter. il UNESCO Courier 29:38-41 D '76

GUADELOUPE
Going places, finding things. N. Richardson. il House & Gard 149:74+ Ap '77

GUANAJUATO, Mexico
Guanajuato. R. Magruder and M. Magruder. il Travel 148:38-43 O '77

GUANOSINE monophosphate
Cigarette smoke activates guanylate cyclase and increases guanosine 3',5'-monophosphate in tissues. W. P. Arnold and others. bibl il Science 198:934-6 D 2 '77
Cyclic GMP accumulation causes degeneration of photoreceptor cells: simulation of an inherited disease; retinitis pigmentosa. R. N. Lolly and others. bibl il Science 196:664-6 My 6 '77
Efflux of cyclic nucleotides from rat pineal: release of guanosine 3',5'-monophosphate from sympathetic nerve endings. M. Zatz and R. F. O'Dea. bibl il Science 197:174-6 Jl 8 '77
Hormone-induced cyclic guanosine monophosphate secretion from guinea pig pancreatic lobules. C. L. Kapoor and G. Krishna. bibl il Science 196:1003-5 My 27 '77
Localization of cyclic GMP and cyclic AMP in cardiac and skeletal muscle: immunocytochemical demonstration. S. H. Ong and A. L. Steiner. bibl il Science 195:183-5 Ja 14 '77

GUANYLATE cyclase. See Enzymes

GUARANI Indians. See Indians of South America

GUARANI language. See Paraguay—Languages

GUARANTEED income. See Public welfare—United States

GUARANTY. See Warranty

GUARANTY of loans. See Loans, Bank—Guaranty

GUARD cells. See Stomata

GUARD dogs. See Watchdogs

GUARDIAN and ward
Brainwashing & religious freedom. T. Robbins. Nation 224:518 Ap 30 '77
Brainwashing Moonies; conservatorship strategy. Time 109:73 Ap 4 '77
Deprogramming the brainwashed: even a Moonie has civil rights; use of conservatorship laws. T. Robbins. Nation 224:238-42 F 26 '77
Deprogramming: the cults fight back. Chr Today 21:36-7 Je 17 '77
Fighting cults: the Tucson tactic; deprogramming by the Freedom of Thought Foundation. R. Chandler. il Chr Today 21:57-61 F 4 '77
Is deprograming legal? using conservatorship laws to obtain custody of young cultists. M. Montagno. il por Newsweek 89:44 F 21 '77
Letting go: everybody has the right to be wrong; deprogramming issue. J. C. Lyles. Chr Cent 94:451-3 My 11 '77
Parents v. Moonies; conservatorship orders. J. K. Footlick and P. S. Greenberg. il Newsweek 89:83 Ap 25 '77
Setback for what? deprogramming issue. Commonweal 104:232+ Ap 15 '77
See also
Parent and child (law)

GUARDSMAN; drama. See Molnar, F.

GUARE, John
Landscape of the body. Reviews
Nation 225:505 N 12 '77 *
New Yorker 53:144 O 24 '77 *
Newsweek il 90:86 O 24 '77 *
Marco Polo sings a solo. Reviews
New Yorker 52:53-4 F 14 '77 *
Newsweek 89:66+ F 14 '77 *
Time il 109:57 F 21 '77 *

GUATEMALA
Guatemala beyond bananas. S. Kinzer. il New Repub 176:21-3+ Mr 5 '77
See also
Earthquakes—Guatemala

Description and travel

Guatemala. L. Dennis and L. Dennis. il Travel 148:32-7 S '77

History

José Cecilio del Valle. il pors Américas 29:7-14 Ag '77

Industries

See also
Coffee industry—Guatemala

Relief work

Guatemala remembers; work of CEPA, Permanent Evangelical Committee for Aid. S. Sywulka. Chr Today 21:55-6 Ap 1 '77

GUATEMALAN cookery. See Cookery, Guatemalan

GUAYULE
Chemical bioinduction of rubber in guayule plant. H. Yokoyama and others. bibl il Science 197:1076-8 S 9 '77
Domestic rubber—an old idea recapped. il Chemistry 50:4 Jl '77
Guayule: a native natural rubber. il Sci N 111:232 Ap 9 '77
Guayule and jojoba: agriculture in semiarid regions. T. H. Maugh, 2d. Science 196:1189-90 Je 10 '77
Guayule bounces back. A. W. Galston. Natur Hist 86:94-7 N '77
Real tire plant. C. E. Downey. il Mech Illus 73:128 Mr '77
Rubber plant. il Newsweek 89:66 Ap 11 '77

GUCCIONE, Robert
Sex in the seventies; interview, ed by L. Sanford. pors Am Home 80:46-8+ F '77
about
Merchants of raunchiness. T. Griffith. il por Time 110:69+ Jl 4 '77 *

GUELPH. University, Guelph, Ontario

Library

Participative management urged as best option; views of M. Beckman. Lib J 102:321-2 F 1 '77

GUÉRARD, Michel
French food without the calories; excerpt from Michel Guerard's cuisine minceur. McCalls 104:179-86 F '77
about
Quartet from far corners. H. Sutton. il por Sat R 4:49-50 F 5 '77 *

GUERNICA, Bombing of, 1938. See Spain—History —Civil War, 1936-1939—Atrocities

GUERNSEY, Bruce
Certain providence; poem. Atlantic 239:60 My '77

GUERNSEY, Duane L. and Stevens, E. D.
Cell membrane sodium pump as a mechanism for increasing thermogenesis during cold acclimation in rats. bibl il Science 196:908-10 My 20 '77

GUERNSEY (island)
Why writers need islands. C. Northcote Parkinson. il Sat R 5:33-4 Ja 7 '78

GUERRARD, Philip
Silence; poem. New Yorker 53:130 D 19 '77

GUERRILLAS
See also
Terrorists

Angola

Behind the lines; UNITA forces. K. Willenson and L. H. Norman. il por Newsweek 90:38+ Ag 22 '77

Arab countries

See also
Palestine Liberation Organization

Israel

Year after Entebbe. E. Keerdoja and M. J. Kubic. il Newsweek 90:7 Jl 4 '77

Mozambique

Dealing or double-dealing. il por map Time 110:49 D 12 '77
Mozambique's porous front. J. Pringle. il map Newsweek 89:36+ Ap 25 '77
Talk-talk, fight-fight. K. Willenson and others. il Newsweek 90:62+ D 12 '77

Nicaragua

Return of the rebels; Sandinistas. R. Moreau. il map Newsweek 90:61-2 N 7 '77

Rhodesia

Caught in the middle. X. Smiley. Time 110:25 S 12 '77
Devil himself. C. Legum. il New Repub 177:17-19 D 17 '77
Rhodesia and her neighbors. R. W. Hull. Cur Hist 73:218-22+ D '77

Somalia

Blood and bullets. E. Peers. il Newsweek 90:40+ S 5 '77

Thailand

War against the night; insurgency by Communist guerrillas. il map Time 109:33-4 Ja 31 '77

Western Sahara

Shadowy war in the Sahara; Polisario. A. de Borchgrave. il map Newsweek 89:34 My 23 '77

GUEST, Judith
Ordinary thoughts on the writing of a novel. Writer 90:11-14 Ja '77

GUEST houses. See Hotels, motels, etc.

GUEST Keen and Nettlefolds, Ltd. See Automobile equipment industry

GUEST ranches. See Ranches

GUEST rooms
Invisible guest room. B. Niles. Am Home 80:56 My '77

GUESTS
Guestmanship; houseguests. C. Stinnett. Atlantic 240:28+ D '77
See also
Entertaining

GUGGENHEIM, Solomon R, Museum, New York. See Solomon R. Guggenheim Museum, New York

GUIDANCE. See Counseling; Personnel service in education; Vocational guidance

GUIDE books. See Guidebooks

GUIDEBOOKS
Quick guide to travel guidebooks. bibl il Chang T 31:35-7 My '77
Short guide to guidebooks. S. Birnbaum. il Esquire 87:130+ F '77

GUIDED missile bases
Conversation; visit to Davis-Monthan Air Force Base. K. Alfven. il Bull Atom Sci 33:43-4 My '77
MX basing mode concepts analyzed. J. M. Lenorovitz. il Aviation W 107:62-3+ N 21 '77

GUIDED missile industries
Missile X becomes a hostage to SALT. Bus W p32+ Je 27 '77

GUIDED missile submarines. See Submarine boats, Atomic powered

GUIDED missiles
After the B-1; cruise missile. Nation 225:66-8 Jl 23 '77
Air intercept missile options evaluated. Aviation W 107:16-17 Ag 29 '77
Arms control: the Russians are cheating! M. R. Laird. Read Digest 111:97-101 D '77
B-1 no, cruise yes. S. Fraker and others. il por Newsweek 90:14-17 Jl 11 '77
Battle over the N-bomb; lance Enhanced Radiation Warhead. M. R. Benjamin and L. H. Norman. il Newsweek 90:44-5 Jl 4 '77
Beyond SALT II—a missile test quota. S. D. Drell. bibl il Bull Atom Sci 33:34-42 My '77
Carter and the new weapons. Nat R 29:868 Ag 5 '77
Carter's big decision: down goes the B-1, here comes the cruise. il por Time 110:8-12 Jl 11 '77
Congress report warns Soviets boosting first-strike capability. Aviation W 108:59+ Ja 9 '78
Cruise missile halt considered. C. A. Robinson, Jr. il Aviation W 106:16-20 My 23 '77
Cruise missiles. K. Tsipis. il Sci Am 236:20-9 F '77; Reply with rejoinder. J. Deutch and others. 237:8+ Ag '77
DOD pressing for joint missile efforts. C. A. Robinson, Jr. il Aviation W 106:22-5 Mr 21 '77
First-strike capability: from MARV to holocaust. R. C. Aldridge. Nation 224:360-4 Mr 26 '77
$49.50 cruise missile and another moratorium. Nat R 29:1097 S 30 '77
Germans weighing alternative Patriot acquisition techniques. Aviation W 107:47-8 Ag 29 '77
Good news and bad; decision to exchange cruise missiles for B-1. B. T. Feld. Bull Atom Sci 33:10-11 S '77
ICBM, guidance curbs alarm planners. C. A. Robinson, Jr. il Aviation W 107:14-18 Jl 11 '77
Innovation advances Tomahawk effort. P. J. Klass. Aviation W 107:58-9 O 31 '77
Jimmy's weapons choice; B-1 decision. R. Hotz. Aviation W 107:7 Jl 11 '77
Laser-powered rockets and dark satellites. E. Ulsamer. Space World N-5-161:30-2 My '77
Legacy of James Schlesinger. R. J. Bresler and R. C. Gray. Intellect 105:228-9 F '77
Look at the cruise missile. il U.S. News 83:14 Jl 11 '77
MX deployment urged for parity. C. A. Robinson, Jr. il Aviation W 107:12-15 D 5 '77
MX strategic missile. K. H. Hohenemser. il Environment 19:4-5 My '77
Missile accuracies: overlooked program could undermine SALT. D. Shapley. il Science 196:1185-6 Je 10 '77
Missile engineering: modernization marks Soviet missiles. il Aviation W 107:82-3 D 12 '77
Missile the Russians fear most; cruise missile. R. K. Bennett. il Read Digest 110:129-32 F '77
Missile X becomes a hostage to SALT. Bus W p32+ Je 27 '77
Now, a push for another supermissile; MX. il U.S. News 83:58 Jl 18 '77
Roland 2 nearing U.S. production. D. E. Fink. il Aviation W 106:57-61 Ja 17 '77
SALT: outgunned? Russian ICBMs. Newsweek 90:46 S 26 '77
Shell game; missile X. Sci Am 236:58+ Mr '77
Soviet strategic capabilities: the superpower balance. C. G. Jacobsen. Cur Hist 73:97-9+ O '77
Strategic force structure to face stiff debate. C. A. Robinson, Jr. il Aviation W 106:16-19 Ap 18 '77
Technology rampant: the case of the cruise missile. R. J. Bresler. Intellect 106:96 S '77
Technology revolution in weaponry. J. H. Douglas. il Sci N 112:60-2 Jl 23 '77
USAF plans test of MX trench concept. il Aviation W 107:17-19 O 17 '77
USSR submarines pose heavy threat. C. A. Robinson, Jr. il Aviation W 106:35-7+ Ja 24 '77
USSR unveils new anti-tank missiles; photographs. Aviation W 107:19 D 5 '77
U.S.-built missiles to arm U.K. aircraft, submarines. Aviation W 107:21-2 Ag 22 '77
U.S. prepares for production of Roland 2 missile. D. E. Fink. il Aviation W 106:92-3+ Je 6 '77
Zeroing in on the silo busters; U.S.—Soviet arms race. il Time 109:18 My 9 '77

Control

Missile guidance proposals sought. Aviation W 106:26 My 2 '77
New radar-guided weapon under study. B. Miller. il Aviation W 106:42-3 F 14 '77
See also
Inertial guidance systems

Cost

Minuteman production funds released. K. Johnsen. il Aviation W 107:23-4 O 24 '77
Senate stalls quick expansion in funding for cruise missiles. Aviation W 107:17 Jl 18 '77

GUIDED missiles—*Continued*

Defenses

Challenges in the 1980s; Triad missile concept and Soviet defenses; address, January 17, 1977. T. C. Reed. Vital Speeches 43:268-71 F 15 '77
Charged debate erupts over Russian beam weapon. N. Wade. Science 196:957-9 My 27 '77
Great Russian death-beam flap. J. H. Douglas and D. E. Thomsen. il Sci N 111:329+ My 21 '77
Particle beams as ABM weapons: general and physicists differ. N. Wade. por Science 196: 407-8 Ap 22 '77
Soviets push for beam weapon; with editorial comment. C. A. Robinson, Jr. il Aviation W 106:11, 16-23 My 2 '77
U.S-U.S.S.R. communique on antiballistic missile systems; treaty review, November 21, 1977. Dept State Bull 77:856 D 12 '77
Whole new ball game? announcement of Russian particle beam weapon by Aviation week & space technology. Nat R 29:596-7 My 27 '77

Launching from airplanes

B-1 cost-effectiveness claimed; study by Rockwell on B-1 cruise missile launchers. D. E. Fink. il Aviation W 107:14-16 D 12 '77
B-1 for cruise missiles urged. E. Kozicharow. Aviation W 107:14-15 S 19 '77
Boeing proposes 747 as missile launcher. R. G. O'Lone. il Aviation W 107:17-18 S 5 '77
Boeing restarting SRAM production. B. M. Elson. il Aviation W 106:53-5 Ap 11 '77
Boeing set for cruise missile speedup. R. G. O'Lone. Aviation W 107:19 Jl 11 '77
Boeing USAF missile effort set; $6.7 million obligated. Aviation W 106:23 Mr 14 '77
C-5 cruise missle launcher tested. S. W. Harlamor. il Aviation W 108:40-2+ Ja 9 '78
Congress initiates studies on cruise missile stress. K. Johnsen. Aviation W 107:18-19 Jl 25 '77
Cruise missile flyoff planned; with editorial comment. C. A. Robinson, Jr. il map Aviation W 107:7, 12-17 Jl 18 '77
Improved reliability of missiles primary aim of Navy. B. Miller. il Aviation W 106:164-7+ Ja 31 '77
Munitions for air-to-surface exhibited; photographs. Aviation W 107:44-7 Jl 11 '77
New radar-guided weapon under study. B. Miller. il Aviation W 106:42-3 F 14 '77
Quantity cruise missile production set. C. Brownlow. Aviation W 106:20 F 21 '77
USAF, Marines eye Hellfire adoption. C. A. Robinson, Jr. il Aviation W 106:14-16 My 30 '77
USAF pushes long-range cruise missile version. Aviation W 106:19-20 Ap 18 '77

Launching from submarine boats

Inside subs: abroad the Thomas Jefferson. T. Buckley. il Esquire 87:81-4+ Ap '77

Launching sites

See Guided missile bases

Nozzles

MX missile movable nozzle fails in test. Aviation W 107:23 O 3 '77
Rocket nozzle exit cone system tested. Aviation W 108:23 Ja 2 '78

Propulsion systems

MX upper stage technology demonstrated. Aviation W 106:22-3 F 14 '77
Ramjet facility tested; photographs. Aviation W 106:87 Ja 10 '77

Specifications

Leading international missiles; tables. Aviation W 106:102-3 Mr 21 '77
USSR missiles; tables. Aviation W 106:91 Mr 21 '77
U.S. missiles; tables. Aviation W 106:83-4 Mr 21 '77

Testing

Aerial combat test to advance. C. A. Robinson. il Aviation W 106:28-31 Ap 25 '77
Fighter, missile gains pressed; Navy, USAF joint test. C. A. Robinson, Jr. Aviation W 106: 12-14 Ap 4 '77
Tomahawk development tests begin. D. E. Fink. il Aviation W 106:16-19 Ap 4 '77
Weather chief problem in Trident tests. il Aviation W 107:46-7 O 31 '77
See also
Proving grounds

GUIDES

Adirondack guide. R. F. Hall. por Conservationist 31:48 Ja '77
Bear of a man; adventures of C. Atwood. B. Brady. il por Outdoor Life 159:88-9+ My '77
Fisherman's guide to guides. J. F. Daubel. Field & S 82:124 Je '77
Go the drop camp way. C. J. Farmer. il Outdoor Life 159:68-71+ F '77
High-up, way-out ways of a rimrock guide; mule deer hunting guide, K. Clark. E. A. Lauer. il Outdoor Life 160:90-2 N '77
Lady of Great Bear Lake; fishing guide, Susan Stechly. J. Fowler. Outdoor Life 160:44 Jl '77
Trekking on Everest: making a living from wanderlust: interview, ed by G. Lichtenstein. S. B. Larrabee. bibl il Ms 5:26+ Mr '77
War and peace in a bass boat: slob guides, kooky clients. J. Weiss; A. Eason. il Outdoor Life 160:94-6+ O '77

GUIDRY, Ron

Getting fat with the thin man. H. Weiskopf. por Sports Illus 47:76 S 19 '77 *

GUIGUI, Catherine

Seventeen in Paris. il Seventeen 36:150 F '77

GUILBERT, David C.

Can your eyes replace your ears? il Ret Liv 17:34-5+ Ag '77

GUILD, Tricia

Lively romantic. il por House & Gard 149:156-61 N '77 *

GUILDER, James

Turn-on appliances via long distance. il Radio-Electr 48:39-42+ Ap '77

GUILLAIN-Barré syndrome. See Neuritis, Multiple

GUILLEMIN, Roger

—and others

β-Endorphin and adrenocorticotropin are secreted concomitantly by the pituitary gland. bibl il Science 197:1367-9 S 30 '77

about

1977 Nobel Prize in physiology or medicine. J. Meites. il pors Science 198:594-6 N 11 '77 *
Nobel Prizes: seven in '77. pors Sci N 112:260-1 O 22 '77 *

GUILLÉN, Jorge

Appreciation. E. L. King. il New Repub 176:27-9 Ap 9 '77 *

GUILLEN, Michael

Quarks: merely Joycean or the ultimate McCoy? Sci Digest 81:38-41+ Mr '77

GUILLORY, Richard J. and others

Covalent labeling of the tetrodotoxin receptor in excitable membranes. bibl il Science 196:883-5 My 20 '77

GUILT

Many faces of guilt. L. David. il Fam Health 9:22-5 Jl '77
Working mother's guilt complex. H. De Rosis. Harp Baz 110:178+ O '77

GUINEA pigs

Human drama in a small cage. A. Roiphe. N Y Times Mag p52-3 Je 26 '77
Understanding your pet. M. W. Fox. McCalls 104:60+ Mr '77

GUINNESS, Sir Alec

Second strike. por Time 111:72 Ja 2 '78 *

GUION, Polly

Diary of a 19th-century lass; excerpts, ed by A. Barry. il Seventeen 36:118+ Ap '77

GÜIRALDES, Ricardo

Poem of the pampas. E. A. Echevarría. il Américas 29:2-5 Ap '77 *

GUITAR

Design

Old sound, new model; Gittler guitar. por Horizon 20:51 S '77

GUITARISTS

See also
Benson, G.

GULATI, Jagdish. See Palmer, L. G. jt auth

GULF & Western Industries, Inc

Blues for Mr Charlie. il pors Time 110:71-2 Jl 18 '77
Church investments: challenging G&W. J. E. Mulligan. Chr Cent 94:64-7 Ja 26 '77
Taking on big business; S. Hersh's series in the New York times. D. M. Alpern and others. il por Newsweek 90:81-2 Ag 8 '77

GULF & Western Industries, Inc-Madison Square Garden Corporation merger. See Corporations—Acquisitions and mergers

GULF of California. See California, Gulf of

GULF of Mexico. See Mexico, Gulf of

GULF of St Lawrence. See St Lawrence, Gulf of

GULF of Suez-Mediterranean pipeline. See Petroleum pipelines—Egypt

GULF Oil Corporation

Corporate Patty Hearst; investigating Gulf's role in uranium cartel price fixing. D. Pauly. Newsweek 89:69 Je 27 '77
Darkening storm over Gulf; membership in uranium price-fixing cartel. il Time 109:62-3 Je 27 '77
Gulf Oil goes back to what it knows best. il por Bus W p78+ Ja 31 '77
Gulf Oil: yesterday's villain. L. Minard. il Forbes 120:95-7+ O 15 '77
Leading businesswoman's perspective on management; interview. J. Spain. il pors Nations Bus 65:70-2+ Mr '77
Uranium cartel's fallout. il Time 110:96+ N 21 '77

GULF States
Retiring along the 5-state Gulf coast. J. B. Truscott. il Ret Liv 17:30-1+ Ja '77

Description and travel

Great springtime vacations along the Gulf of Mexico. G. Bush. il Bet Hom & Gard 55:173-4+ F '77

GULF Stream
Gulf Stream analyses. R. Mairs. map Yachting 142:36+ D '77
Gulf Stream flow shown by NOAA-5; photograph. Aviation W 106:68 Je 20 '77
Oceanography: a closer look at Gulf Stream rings. R. A. Kerr. map Science 198:387-9+ O 28 '77

GULHATI, Kaval
Compulsory sterilization: the change in India's population policy. bibl il Science 195:1300-5 Mr 25 '77

GULINO, Samuel J.
What's wrong with junior high—everything! il Parents Mag 52:58+ S '77

GULL, G. E. See Houck, J. R. jt auth

GULLBERG, Hjalmar Robert
Balloons; poem; tr by J. Moffett. New Yorker 53:188 D 12 '77

GULLIS, Robert J.
Researcher admits he faked journal data. Sci N 111:150-1 Mr 5 '77 *

GULLS

Sexual behavior

See Sexual behavior—Birds

GUM chewing
See also
Chewing gum

GUMMERE, Walter Cooper
Never volunteer! por Forbes 120:106 D 1 '77 *

GUMS

Diseases

Expensive way to keep your teeth; periodontal disease or pyorrhea. G. Subak-Sharpe. il N Y Times Mag p56-9 Ap 10 '77
How to save your teeth. J. Calem. McCalls 104:74 Ag '77
Periodontal disease: zeroing in on the greatest threat to your teeth. M. P. Scott and L. Rothman. il Bet Hom & Gard 55:26+ Jl '77
Tooth or consequences; preventing periodontitis. R. Hendley. Seventeen 36:59 S '77
See also
Periodontia

GUMS and resins
Rosin: its use and abuse; treatment of dance floors. R. Gelabert. Dance Mag 51:88 Ap '77
See also
Terpenes

GUN, Milton J.
Sportscasters score the cities. il Holiday 58:22-5 Je '77

GUN control legislation. See Firearms—Laws and regulations

GUN dogs. See Hunting dogs

GUN engraving. See Firearms—Decoration

GUN museums. See Museums

GUN sights. See Firearms—Sights

GUN stocks. See Gunstocks

GUN tackers. See Staple guns

GUNDERMAN, Karen
Karen Gunderman. il Ceram Mo 25:44 S '77 *

GUNDERSON, Mary
Coffee breaks. Am Home 80:75 S '77

GUNDLACH, Erich R.
Oil tanker disasters. il map Environment 19:16-20 D '77
—and others
Black tide of la Coruña: oil spill off Spain. il map Oceans 10:56-60 Mr '77

GUNDRY, Robert H.
Salvation according to Scripture: no middle ground. Chr Today 22:14-16 D 9 '77

GUNN, Peggy
At home with my cactus family. il Org Gard & Farm 24:160+ D '77
Earth rich on retirement income. il Org Gard & Farm 24:110-11 My '77

GUNN, Scout Lee, and Peterson, C. A.
Therapy and leisure education. il Parks & Rec 12:22-5+ N '77

GUNN, Timothy
Defensive golf. New Repub 177:31-3 Jl 23 '77

GUNS (small arms) See Firearms; Pistols; Revolvers

GUNSKY, Frederic R.
Legacy of Ishi. il Liv Wildn 40:4-11 Ja '77

GUNSTOCKS
Open letter to rifle makers. J. Carmichel. il Outdoor Life 160:112-14+ Ag '77

GUNSTON Hall, Lorton. See Historic houses, sites, etc.—Virginia

GUNTER, Pete A. Y.
Big Thicket, born again. il map Nat Wildlife 15:4-11 Je '77

GUNTERSVILLE, Ala.
Guntersville, Ala.—life below zero. V. E. Smith. il Newsweek 89:26 F 14 '77

GUNTHER, Max
Five ways to improve your luck; excerpt from The luck factor. Read Digest 110:77-80 My '77
What are your rights with the IRS? Bet Hom & Gard 55:78+ F '77
(comp) Your rights with the police. il Bet Hom & Gard 55:13+ Ap '77

GUPTE, Pranay
Lion in winter. Nation 224:677 Je 4 '77
Nepal: despotism in tranquillity. il Nation 224:781-4 Je 25 '77
New Delhi notebook. Nation 224:649-52 My 28 '77
On the phone to Bombay. Nation 224:421-2 Ap 9 '77
Passage to a new India. il Atlantic 240:59-66 Ag '77

GUPTILL, Arthur
Editor remembers; reprint from June 1962 issue; excerpts. E. W. Watson. por Am Artist 41:35-6 F '77 *

GURGANUS, Allan
Comfort; story. Mademoiselle 83:70 Je '77

GURIN, Joel. See Bennett, W. jt auth

GURNEY, A. R. Jr
Wayside Motor Inn. Reviews
Nation 225:604-5 D 3 '77 *
New Yorker 53:143-4 N 21 '77 *

GURR, Ted Robert
Contemporary crime in historical perspective: a comparative study of London, Stockholm, and Sydney. bibl f il Ann Am Acad 434:114-36 N '77

GURUS
See also
Muktananda, B.
Rajneesh, B. S.
Ram Dass

GUSH Emunim (organization) See Political clubs and associations—Israel

GUSSOW, Mel
Basic training of Al Pacino. il pors N Y Times Mag p21-2+ Je 5 '77
European pleasures. il Horizon 19:34-7 Jl '77
Gorey goes batty. il por N Y Times Mag p40-2+ O 16 '77

GUSTAFSON, Eleanor H.
(ed) Clues and footnotes. See issues of Antiques
Museum accessions. See issues of Antiques

GUSTAFSSON, T. See Plummer, E. W. jt auth

GUSTAITIS, Joseph
Birth of the great American $. il Am Hist Illus 12:17-19 Jl '77
J.-K. Huysmans and France's Catholic revival. map America 136:394-6 Ap 30 '77

GUSTY goat to the rescue; drama. See Albert, R.

GUTHEIL-SCHODER, Marie
Theaterblut. G. Breuer. pors Opera N 42:14-16 Ja 7 '78 *

GUTHRIE, Woody
Bound for glory; excerpt from screenplay. R. Getchell. il pors Sr Schol 109:2-4+ F 10 '77 *
Just what in the hell has gone wrong here anyhow? F. Turner. il pors Am Heritage 28:34-43 O '77 *

GUTIERREZ, Peter L. See Swartz, H. M. jt auth

GUTMAN, Herbert G.
Black conjugations. J. D. Anderson. Am Scholar 46:384+ Summ '77 *

GUTMANN, John
Outsider's view of the 30's. H. Fischer. il Mod Phot 41:62 F '77 *

GUTTENTAG, Jack M.
How to sell your house and keep it too. il Ret Liv 17:36-9+ Ja '77

GUYANA
See also
Birds—Guyana
Corporations, Government—Guyana
Investments, Foreign—Guyana

Politics and government

Guyana: old scars break open. T. J. Spinner, Jr. Nation 225:723-4 D 31 '77

GUYER, Donna Dickey
Writing poems to sell. Writers Digest 57:52-3 S '77

GUYSTAC Corporation. See Corporations, Government—Guyana

GUZZARDI, Walter, Jr
C.P. Wong makes Bulova tick again. il por Fortune 95:154-7+ Ap '77
Great world telephone war. il Fortune 96:142-7+ Ag '77
Way to escape the Washington stockade. il Fortune 95:175-6 Ja '77
What the Supreme Court is really telling business. il Fortune 95:147-54 Ja '77

GUZZWELL, John
Choosing the right long distance cruising boat. il Yachting 141:88-91 Ap '77

GWATHMEY & Siegal Architects. See Architectural firms

GWINN, Nancy E.
Council on Library Resources: a 20-year report. bibl il Lib J 102:330-4 F 1 '77

GWIRTZMAN, Milton S.
Knocking sense into form 1040. New Repub 176:15-18 Ap 16 '77

GWITT, Carolyn D.
Special report: a winning role for the school library. bibl il Wilson Lib Bull 52:295-8 D '77

GWYNNE, James
School finance: the case for equalization of opportunity. bibl Intellect 105:420-2 Je '77

GWYNNE, Peter
Get ready Antarctica . . . here comes the boom! il Int Wildlife 7:4-11 N '77

GWYNNE-JONES, Arthur, Chalfont, Baron. See Chalfont, A. G.-J.

GYLES, Carlton L. and others
Naturally occurring plasmid carrying genes for enterotoxin production and drug resistance. bibl il Science 198:198-9 O 14 '77

GYLLENHAMMAR, Pehr Gustaf
How Volvo adapts work to people; excerpt from People at work. il Harvard Bus R 55:102-13 Jl '77
Humanizing mass production jobs. il Intellect 105:380-1 My '77

GYMNASTICS
Gymnastics fever. A. Verschoth. il Horizon 19:62-9 My '77
It all began with Olga. K. Gilman. Vogue 167:42+ D '77

Equipment

Backyard gymnastics; making equipment. il Sunset 158:110-11 My '77

GYMNASTICS for the mentally handicapped. See Sports for the handicapped

GYNECOLOGIC examinations
See a specialist: when and why you need a gynecologist. A. Machiaverna. Seventeen 36:56 Mr '77

GYNECOLOGISTS and patients
When to visit the gynecologist. M. Newton. Fam Health 9:12+ D '77

GYORGY, Anna
France kills its first protester. Nation 225:330-3 O 8 '77

GYPSIES

Europe, Western

Last of the Romanovs. R. Carroll and T. Nater. il Newsweek 89:55 Ja 31 '77

GYPSY moths
Rapid response to selection for a nondiapausing gypsy moth. M. A. Hoy. bibl il Science 196:1462-3 Je 24 '77

GYPSY wagons. See Wagons

GYRATORS
Introduction to gyrator theory. B. T. Morrison. il Pop Electr 12:58-9 Jl '77

GYROSCOPES
Laser gyros find increased applications. P. J. Klass. il Aviation W 107:44-7 Jl 25 '77

GYROSCOPIC instruments
See also
Automatic pilot (boats)

H

H-2 locus. See Immunogenetics

H-Y antigen. See Antigens and antibodies

HEAO (high energy astronomy observatory) See Artificial satellites—Astronomical use

HEW. See United States—Health, Education and Welfare, Department of

H. J. Heinz Company. See Heinz, H. J, Company

HLA (histocompatability complex) See Immunological tolerance

HMO (health maintenance organizations) See Insurance, Health—United States

HNH (firm) See Phonograph record industry

H. P. Hood and Sons, Inc. See Hood, H. P, and Sons, Inc

HUD. See United States—Housing and Urban Development, Department of

HAACK, Robert William
Anderson to succeed Haack as Lockheed's chief executive. Aviation W 107:24 Ag 8 '77 *
How Lockheed got back its wings. L. Kraar. il por Fortune 96:198-202+ O '77 *
Lockheed: up from the ashes. T. J. Murray. il por Duns R 109:53-5+ Mr '77 *

HAAKON, Paul
Paul Haakon; interview, ed by J. Gruen. il pors Dance Mag 51:51-66 N '77

HAARLEM, Netherlands

Art

See Art—Netherlands

HAARMAN, Dorothy
Lunch with the principal. Educ Digest 43:60 O '77

HAARSTICK, Steve
Problems in sail design. il Yachting 141:50+ Je '77

HAAS, Ernst
Offbeat. N. Rothschild. il Pop Phot 81:9+ Jl '77 *

HAAS, George H.
German hunting: it's the tradition that counts. il Int Wildlife 7:38-43 N '77

HAAS, Jack
What Christian colleges teach about creation; interview, ed by D. Singer. il Chr Today 21:8-11 Je 17 '77

HAAS, John Eugene
Forecast: future shock. il Time 109:83 Ja 24 '77 *

HAASE, Ashley T. and others
Slow persistent infection caused by visna virus: role of host restriction. bibl il Science 195:175-7 Ja 14 '77

HAAVIK, Gunvor Galtung
From Russia with lovers. il por Time 109:32 F 28 '77 *

HABASH, George
Habash: Israel will fall; excerpts from interview, ed by D. Brelis. por Time 110:33 D 19 '77

HABIB, Philip Charles
Cuban Interest Section opens in Washington; statement, September 1, 1977. Dept State Bull 77:572-3 O 24 '77
Ratification recommended for treaties with U.S.S.R. restricting nuclear testing; statements, July 28, 1977. Dept State Bull 77:312-14 S 5 '77
Relations with the Soviet Union; address, November 14, 1977. Dept State Bull 77:854-6 D 12 '77
Southern Africa in the global context; statement, March 3, 1977. Dept State Bull 76:318-21 Ap 4 '77
Under Secretary Habib interviewed on Face the Nation; transcript of program, November 20, 1977; ed by G. Herman and others. Dept State Bull 77:886-91 D 19 '77
Withdrawal of U.S. ground forces from South Korea; statement, June 10, 1977. Dept State Bull 77:48-50 Jl 11 '77

HABITAT, Animal. See Zoology—Ecology

HABITAT '76. See United Nations Conference on Human Settlements, 1976

HABITS
See also
Idiosyncrasies

HABSBURG, Otto von. See Otto, Archduke of Austria

HACHARD, Marie Madeleine
Little adventures of Madeleine Hachard. P. Robbins. il Am Hist Illus 12:36-42 Jl '77 *

HACHETTE (firm) See Publishers and publishing —France

HACKER, Frederick J.
Why violent crime is now in fashion; interview. il por U.S. News 82:57-8 F 28 '77

HACKER, Marilyn
Comment. R. Holland. Poetry 129:292-3 F '77 *

HACKER, William. See Selverstone, R. jt auth

HACKETT, Regina
(ed) See Washington, J. Jr. James Washington: secrets in stone

HACKETT, Walter
Christmas carol; dramatization of story by C. Dickens. Plays 37:85-95 D '77
Tale of two cities; dramatization of novel by C. Dickens. Plays 37:84-96 N '77

HACKLE, Sparse Grey, pseud
Still going strong. J. Cassell. por Outdoor Life 160:35 S '77 *

HADAS, Rachel
September song; poem. New Repub 177:25 S 3 '77

HADDAD, M. George
On creating a new face through plastic surgery. il Mademoiselle 83:53+ O '77
20 hot tips for tabs. Writers Digest 57:23 Jl '77

HADDOX, John H.
Dependence or interdependence? Américas 29:2-5 Mr '77

HADEN, Sir Francis Seymour
Commitment to the past. G. Weisberg. il Art N 76:150-2 Summ '77 *

HADEN, Pat
Giving Joe a big hello. R. Fimrite. il por Sports Illus 47:8-11 Ag 15 '77 *

HADEN, Sir Seymour. See Haden, F. S.

HAENKE, David
Trenches and sawdust: huge potatoes from hard clay. il Org Gard & Farm 24:80-1 Mr '77

HAGANS, Orville R.
On time. See issues of Hobbies

HAGAR'S children; drama. See Joselovitz, E.

HAGARTY, Hazel
Help for people society often ignores. il pors U.S. News 83:46-7 Ag 1 '77 *

HAGE, Jerald, and Hollingsworth, J. R.
First steps toward the integration of social theory and social policy. bibl f il Ann Am Acad 434:1-23 N '77

HAGE, Nancy C.
Doodles on the landscape. il Conservationist 31: 42-3 N '76

HAGEMAN, George
George Hageman. il Ceram Mo 25:44-5 Je '77 *

HAGEMANN, Helmut
Anticipate your long-term foreign exchange risks. il Harvard Bus R 55:81-8 Mr '77

HAGER, Barry M. See Reeves, R. jt auth

HAGGADAH. See Jews—Prayer books and devotions

HAGGARD, William, pseud. See Clayton, R.

HAGGERTY, William D.
New way to cut the risk of running a business. Nations Bus 65:74+ D '77

HAGGIN, Bernard H.
Ballet (cont) New Repub 177:28-31 Ag 6 '77
Music (title varies) (cont) New Repub 176: 25-7 Ja 15; 25-7 Mr 12; 27-8 My 28; 177:23-4 S 3; 30-2 O 1; 21-3 N 26; 23-5 D 17 '77; 27-9 Ja 7 '78
New records in review. See issues of Yale review
Opera. New Repub 176:21-3 Je 3; 177:28-30 N 5 '77

HAGOPIAN, Louis Thomas
Giving impact to ideas; address, October 11, 1977. Vital Speeches 44:154-7 D 15 '77

HAGUE, Harlan
Eden ravished: the land, pioneer attitudes, and conservation. bibl il Am West 14:30-3+ My '77

HAGUE, The

International Court of Justice

See International Court of Justice, The Hague

HAHAMOVITCH, Bernard Moses
Deadly trade in under-built boats. W. P. Coughlin. il Motor B & S 139:61-5+ Ap '77 *

HAHN, Erich J. C.
Junior faculty in revolt: reform plans for Berlin University in 1848. bibl f il Am Hist R 82:875-95 O '77

HAHN, William E. and others
One strand equivalent of the escherichia coli genome is transcribed: complexity and abundance classes of mRNA. bibl il Science 197: 582-5 Ag 5 '77

HAIDENTHALLER, Ingo
Low-cost root cellar solves winter storage problems. il Org Gard & Farm 24:114-16 S '77

HAIG, Alexander Meigs, 1924-
NATO: Haig speaks out; excerpts from interview, ed by A. de Borchgrave. por Newsweek 91:39 Ja 9 '78

about

Kissinger, Haig and the Koreans. Nation 225: 227-8 S 17 '77 *
Western alliance seeks to update nuclear capability. D. A. Brown. il maps Aviation W 107: 12-15 Ag 1 '77 *

HAIG, Frank R.
Science's now cloudy crystal ball. America 136: 192-3 Mr 5 '77

HAIG-BROWN, Roderick
Lord of the flies. R. Chatham. Esquire 87:16+ Mr '77 *

HAIL
Paradox of hail suppression. D. Atlas. bibl il Science 195:139-45 Ja 14 '77

HAIL insurance. See Insurance, Hail

HAILMAN, Jack P.
Ethos. BioScience 27:715 N '77

HAILSHAM of Saint Marylebone, Quintin McGarel Hogg, Baron
How Britain lays down the law. il Sat R 4:26+ Je 11 '77

HAINES, Aubrey B.
Buying Christian. Chr Cent 94:804-5 S 21 '77

HAINES, Gerald L.
Ethics, medical malpractice and the church. Chr Cent 94:1003-5 N 2 '77

HAINES, Joe
Poor old Harold the henpecked. pors Time 109: 43 F 21 '77 *

HAINES, John Meade
If the owl calls again; Snowy night; Sound of animals in the night; poems; excerpt from Winter news. Liv Wildn 41:63 Jl '77

HAIR
Hair element content in learning disabled children. R. O. Pihl and M. Parkes. bibl il Science 198:204-6 O 14 '77
Proton-induced X-ray emission analysis of single human hair roots. E. C. Henley and others. bibl il Science 197:277-8 Jl 15 '77
See also
Baldness
Haircutting
Hairdressing
Wigs

Care

Advice for the groom; excerpt from Looking good. C. Hix. il Sat Eve Post 249:44-7+ N '77
Bazaar's complete guide for black skin & hair; questions and answers. il Harp Baz 110:156-9 O '77
Beauty today. il Vogue 167:186-93 F '77
By the roots of your hair. L. Beech. Sr Schol 109:14 Ap 7 '77
Common-sense beauty guide: hair. il Harp Baz 110:80-1 Je '77
Fall shape-up for your hair; questions and answers. Harp Baz 110:134 S '77
Hair now. See issues of Vogue
Hair; the inside story from 10 mile staffers; interviews. il Mademoiselle 83:158-63 Mr '77
Heads up. L. Beech. Sr Schol 110:18 O 6 '77
Healthy hair. K. Cure. il Am Home 80:10+ F '77
How to individualize your hair care. Harp Baz 110:125 F '77
How to make your hair your best accessory. il Mademoiselle 83:132-47 Je '77
Jump into summer & hang loose! skin and hair care. il Mademoiselle 83:124-37 My '77
Miracle workers for your hair. il Harp Baz 110:82-3 Ap '77
Recharge! Make the most of your looks, your time. il Mademoiselle 83:108-13 F '77
Scientific hair care. il Harp Baz 110:192-3 S '77

Dyeing and bleaching

At-home perm & color guide. il Seventeen 36: 120-1 O '77
Bazaar's complete hair-coloring handbook. il Harp Baz 110:100-5 Ag '77
Beauty of shadow shading. M. Lynch. il Ladies Home J 94:112-15 N '77
Busy woman's guide to hair coloring. il McCalls 105:50-3+ O '77
Household worries; sodium nitrite as meat preservative and diaminoanisole sulfate as hair dye component. P. Gwynne and J. B. Copeland. il Newsweek 90:109 O 31 '77
How to individualize your hair color. il Harp Baz 110:120-1 F '77
Making black hair more beautiful. il McCalls 105:92+ N '77
More on hair dyes. J. Corbett. Ms 5:21 F '77
Naturals for summer hair. il Seventeen 36:70 Je '77
Sunny highlights for your hair: paint it—frost it—streak it. S. Beck. il Parents Mag 52:18-19 F '77
Take care of yourself. il Vogue 167:164-5 Je '77

HAIR; musical comedy. See Musical comedy, revue, etc.—Reviews—Single works

HAIR, Removal of
Electrolysis: in praise of a new method; Laurier IB Probe. S. Drake. Am Home 80:24-5 N '77
Facial hair. A. Frank and S. Frank. Mademoiselle 83:72 Mr '77
Hair removers. Seventeen 36:34 S '77

HAIR cutting. See Haircutting

HAIR dressing. See Hairdressing

HAIR dryers
Blow dryers. il Consumer Rep 42:626-9 N '77
Hand-held hair dryers. il Consumers Res Mag 60:11-15 D '77
Hand-held hair dryers and stylers. il Good H 184:210+ My '77

HAIR dyes. See Hair—Dyeing and bleaching

HAIR pieces. See Wigs

HAIR preparations
At-home perm & color guide. il Seventeen 36: 120-1 O '77
See also
Shampoos

Manufacture

See Cosmetics industry

HAIR streaking. See Hair—Dyeing and bleaching

HAIR styles. See Hairdressing

HAIR styling equipment. See Hair dryers

HAIRCUTTING
Above all, the cut. M. Lynch. il Ladies Home J 94:108-13 Ap '77
Beauty is a family affair; the Jerry McDevitts. M. Lynch. il Ladies Home J 94:80-3 Ag '77
Homemade haircuts—here's how. il Mademoiselle 83:108 Ag '77
It takes two: the haircuts you give each other. il Seventeen 36:230-1 Ag '77
Next-to-no-time haircut. il Mademoiselle 83:124-5 F '77
Our new no-work cuts for your kind of hair. il Harp Baz 110:124 F '77
Short cuts for problem hairlines. il McCalls 104:150-1+ My '77

HAIRDOS. See Hairdressing

HAIRDRESSERS. See Beauty operators

HAIRDRESSING
Advice for the groom; men's hair styles; excerpt from Looking good. C. Hix. il Sat Eve Post 249:44-7+ N '77
Beauty/New focus . . . hair; ideas of Christiaan. il Vogue 167:212-15 Mr '77
15 fast, no-fuss, pretty hairdos. il Mademoiselle 83:128-33 D '77
Flowering of longer hair. il McCalls 104:132-5 Mr '77
Hair: dressing it up. il Seventeen 36:129 Jl '77
Hair now. See issues of Vogue

HAIRDRESSING—*Continued*
Hair update '77. il Mademoiselle 83:192-7 S '77
Happy haircuts; children's hairstyles. S. Beck. il Parents Mag 52:34-5 O '77
How to make short work of long hair. il Mademoiselle 83:180-1 Ag '77
How to make your hair your best accessory. il Mademoiselle 83:132-47 Je '77
New for fall! 24 terrific hairdos. il Good H 185:118-27+ S '77
New wave in hair; au naturel. A. Penny. il N Y Times Mag p94-5 Ap 24 '77
New wave of permanents. A. Penney. il N Y Times Mag p 123-4 S 11 '77
Ready-to-wear hair collections. il Harp Baz 110:102-3 Ap '77
Romantic dos that work with the soft new clothes. il Mademoiselle 83:90-3 Jl '77
Subtle changes that look sensational. il Redbook 149:132-3 S '77
Summer headliners. il Seventeen 36:130 Jl '77
20 beautiful new hairstyles for fall. il McCalls 104:140-5 Ag '77
24 spring hairdos. il Good H 184:108-17+ Mr '77
Who's the Farrahest? T. Schwartz. il Newsweek 89:58 Je 27 '77

HAIRPIECES. See Wigs

HAITH, Marshall M. and others
Eye contact and face scanning in early infancy. bibl il Science 198:853-5 N 25 '77

HAITI

Description and travel

By donkey up the hill to Haiti's Citadelle. il map Sunset 159:53-4 O '77
This is Haiti. il Mademoiselle 83:108-9+ My '77

History

Work and discipline. J. Cook. por Forbes 119:40 My 1 '77

HAITIAN refugees. See Refugees, Haitian

HAITINK, Bernard
Haitink's Mahler: much to commend; Des Knaben Wunderhorn. J. Diether. il Am Rec G 41:21-2+ N '77 *

HAKEN, Wolfgang. See Appel, K. jt auth

HALACY, Daniel Stephen, 1919-
Energy crossroads: despite a time bind picture is hopeful. . .but it's our move! excerpt from Earth, water, wind & sun, our energy alternatives. Sci Digest 82:6-7 O '77

HALAKHA. See Jewish law

HALAS, George Stanley
I don't date any woman under 48. F. Deford. il pors Sports Illus 47:36-8+ D 5 '77 *

HALASZ, Piri
Upward reappraisal. Art N 76:100-1 Ja '77

HALBERSTAM, David
Social relationships between journalists and government officials; excerpts from address. por Intellect 106:100 S '77
Time Inc.'s internal war over Vietnam; excerpt from The powers that be. il pors Esquire 89:94-100+ Ja '78

HALBERT, Rick
Reports & comment. E. Chen. il Atlantic 240:12+ Ag '77

HALBOUTY, Michel Thomas
Divestiture—competition or nationalization? address, March 22, 1977. Vital Speeches 43:379-82 Ap 1 '77

HALCOMB, Ruth
Winning the war against birth defects. il Parents Mag 52:37+ My '77

HALDANE, W. R.
Radio hams use amateur bands for global TV. Sci Digest 81:90-1 My '77

HALDEMAN, Harry Robbins
Nos 24171-157 and 01489-163(B) il pors Time 110:11 Jl 4 '77 *

HALDEMAN, Michael
Small press movement. bibl por Lib J 102:2477-81 D 15 '77

HALE, Bob
Michael Manley: Jamaica's born-again socialist. por Chr Cent 94:1117-19 N 30 '77

HALE, J. Russell
Looking from the inside out. por Time 110:85 O 3 '77 *

HALE, Nathan

Drama

Hiding Mr Hale. C. Boiko. Plays 37:47-52 O '77

HALE, Robert
When you care enough to sing the very best; interview, ed by C. Forbes. por Chr Today 21:8-11 Ag 26 '77

HALE, Robert Beverly
Profiles. P. Hamburger. il New Yorker 53:41-2+ Je 13 '77 *

HALE, Robert D.
Hathaway House Bookshop. il Horn Bk 53:121-7 Ap '77
Robert D. Hale—on ABA and its new projects; interview, ed by D. Maryles. por Pub W 211:94-5 Je 27 '77

HALEY, Albert
Juvenile dice; story. Atlantic 240:88-90 O '77

HALEY, Alex
Alex Haley on kids in search of their roots; interview, ed by G. M. Landau. pors Parents Mag 52:60-1+ S '77
Haley's Rx: talk, write, reunite; interview, ed by W. Marmon. il Time 109:72+ F 14 '77
Interview with Alex Haley; ed by W. McGuire and M. S. Clayton. Todays Educ 66:46-7 S '77
My search for roots; excerpts. il por Read Digest 110:148-52 Ap '77
Roots; condensation; reprint of 1974 article. il Read Digest 110:153-79 Ap '77
What Roots means to me. Read Digest 110:73-6 My '77

about

After Haley's comet. H. F. Waters. il por Newsweek 89:97-8 F 14 '77 *
Alex Haley in Juffure. H. J. Massaquoi. il pors Ebony 32:31-3+ Jl '77 *
Alex Haley: the man behind Roots. H. J. Massaquoi. il pors Ebony 32:33-6+ Ap '77 *
Black man's burden. L. H. Lapham. Harpers 254:15-16+ Je '77 *
Doubleday answers Haley; denies all charges. M. Reuter. Pub W 211:34-5 Ap 25 '77 *
From these Roots; the real significance of Haley's phenomenon. C. Forbes. Chr Today 21:19-22 My 6 '77 *
Haley's quest for Roots. por Forbes 119:24 F 15 '77 *
Limits of faction. K. L. Woodward and A. Collings. il por Newsweek 89:87 Ap 25 '77 *
Roots. M. Rein and J. M. Elliot. il por Negro Hist Bull 40:664-7 Ja '77 *
Roots of victory, roots of defeat. P. H. Wood. New Repub 176:27-8 Mr 12 '77 *
Two writers question the originality of Roots. M. Reuter. Pub W 211:20 My 2 '77 *
Uncle Tom's Roots. M. Greenfield. il Newsweek 89:100 F 14 '77 *
Why Alex Haley is suing Doubleday: an outline of the complaint. M. Reuter. Pub W 211:25 Ap 4 '77 *

HALEY, Delphine
Let's help the Atlantic loggerhead. il map Nat Parks & Con Mag 51:12-15 F '77

HALEY, William
Rest in prose: the art of the obituary. Am Scholar 46:206-11 Spr '77

HALL, Alice J.
Dazzling legacy of an ancient quest. il Nat Geog 151:292-311 Mr '77
Hudson: that river's alive. il map Nat Geog 153:62-89 Ja '78

HALL, Asaph
Asaph Hall finds the moons of Mars. J. Ashbrook. il por Sky & Tel 54:20-1 Jl '77 *

HALL, Beverly
Wild bunch. il Nat Wildlife 15:4-11 Ap '77

HALL, Bob
Driving impression. il Motor T 29:68-9 Ag; 80-1 O; 54-5 N '77
Road test. il Motor T 29:96-8+ Ap; 55-6+ My; 111-12+ Je; 39-40+ Jl; 35-6+, 107-9, 113-15 Ag; 77+ S; 71-2+ D '77

HALL, Bob (dramatist) and Richmond, David
Passion of Dracula; dramatization of Dracula by B. Stoker. Reviews
New Yorker 53:91-2 O 10 '77 *
Newsweek il 90:74-5+ O 31 '77 *
Time il 110:93 O 31 '77 *

HALL, Carlyle W. Jr
Role of public interest law firms. Current 192:41-6 Ap '77

HALL, Craig
Me and Time Inc. il por Forbes 120:81 D 15 '77 *

HALL, Danelle
Library training program for native Americans. Wilson Lib Bull 51:751-4 My '77

HALL, Debra L.
New classroom for environmental education. il Parks & Rec 12:36a-38a F '77

HALL, Donald
E. B. White on the exercycle. Nat R 29:671-2 Je 10 '77
Names of horses; poem. New Yorker 53:207 N 14 '77
Other voices, other tones. Atlantic 240:100+ O '77
Ox cart man; poem. New Yorker 53:44 O 3 '77
Vanity, fame, love, and Robert Frost; excerpt from Remembering poets. Commentary 64:51-61 D '77

HALL, Donald N. B.
Shu and Hall win Astronomical Society prizes. pors Phys Today 30:95 My '77

HALL, Douglas Kent
Van art. il Esquire 88:115-17 S '77

HALL, G. K. (firm) See Publishers and publishing—United States

HALL, Graham M.
College racing. See issues of Yachting

HALL, J. Michael. See Mooers, C. N. K. jt auth

HALL, James
James Hall. D. W. Fisher. il pors Conservationist 31:12-16 N '76 *

HALL, James Baker
In the meadow; poem. Am Scholar 46:503-4 Aut '77

HALL, Jim (guitarist)
Jazz. M. Ullman. il New Repub 177:23-5 N 19 '77 *

HALL, Joyce Clyde
Hall of Fame for Business Leadership. M. Ways. por Fortune 95:123 Ja '77 *

HALL, Richard, kidnapping
I'll have vengeance. il por Time 109:19 F 21 '77
Three days of rage. D. M. Alpern and S. Monroe. il por Newsweek 89:22 F 21 '77

HALL, Robert
$4 billion barrel of pork? G. R. Rosen. por Duns R 109:71 My '77 *

HALL, Robert F.
About this issue. por Conservationist 31:43 Ja '77
61 days. il Conservationist 31:48 Mr '77

HALL, Walter
Taming the holy terror: a homily on living at peace with one's chain saw; excerpt from Barnacle Parp's chain saw guide. il Org Gard & Farm 24:138-42 O '77

HALL of Fame for Business Leadership. See Halls of fame

HALL of Fame for Great Americans. See Halls of fame

HALL of Reptiles and Amphibians. See American Museum of Natural History, New York

HALLAHMI, Benjamin Beit-. See Beit-Hallahmi, B.

HALLBERG, Clarice L.
Visual order in the art room. il Sch Arts 77:28-9 N '77

HALLE, Louis J.
Out of chaos; excerpt. Sci Digest 82:16-20+ S '77

HALLENBECK, Lulu
First-time cruising with the very young. Yachting 142:20 D '77

HALLER, Henry
Holiday dinner at the White House. il Ladies Home J 94:110-11+ N '77

HALLER, Scot
Finish line; story. Mademoiselle 83:50 Ag '77
How to keep sex from screwing up a friendship. Mademoiselle 83:118+ D '77
Very ready for laughs. il Horizon 20:81-3 D '77

HALLEY, Laurence, pseud
Easter on Atlantis. il Sat R 5:24+ Ja 7 '78
Hometown in Britain. Sat R 5:22 N 26 '77

HALLEY'S comet
Halley's comet. Sky & Tel 54:363-4 N '77

HALLEY'S comet mission (proposed) See Space flight

HALLIDAY, E. M.
Carving the American colossus. il por Am Heritage 28:18-27 Je '77

HALLIDAY, Robert William
Big catch. il pors Forbes 120:76 D 15 '77 *

HALLINAN, Kevin M.
Are line-ups fair? A cop's eye view. Psychol Today 11:84 Je '77

HALLMARK, Clayton L.
Guide to oscilloscopes. il Pop Electr 11:59-63 Je '77
Multimeters for electronics (cont) il Pop Electr 11:31-2+ F '77

HALLORAN, Judith
(ed) See Merrill, R. Yes I can!

HALLOWEEN
Cheerful pumpkins to greet your Halloween visitors. il Sunset 159:160 O '77
Mad Halloween hatter comes up with a bear, an elephant, a crocodile. il Sunset 159:118-19 O '77
What is happy about Halloween? J. W. Howe. il Chr Today 22:16-17 O 21 '77
Why not paint the pumpkin? il Sunset 159:181 O '77

Drama

Test for a witch. E. MacLellan and C. V. Schroll. Plays 37:65-70 O '77

Photographs

Halloween in the good old days. il Am Hist Illus 12:46-7 O '77

HALLOWEEN costumes. See Costume

HALLS
How to Brighton up a hall. il House & Gard 149:52+ Ap '77
Light and heat, sight and messages go up and down. il Sunset 159:100 S '77

HALLS of fame
Another honor for the peanut man; G. W. Carver named to the Hall of Fame of Great Americans. il pors Ebony 32:102-4+ Jl '77
Hall of Fame for Business Leadership. M. Ways. Fortune 95:117-23 Ja '77
Pop; Songwriters' Hall of Fame. New Yorker 52:25-6 Ja 31 '77

HALLUCINATION and illusion producing plants
Ritual enemas. P. T. Furst and M. D. Coe. il Natur Hist 86:88-91 bibl(p97) Mr '77

HALLUCINATIONS and illusions
Hallucinations. R. K. Siegel. il Sci Am 237:132-40+ O '77

HALLUCINOGENIC drugs
See also
LSD

HALMAN, Talât Sait
(tr) See Jalāl al-Dēn, R. Ghazal

HALOGENS in the body
Complexes of stannous fluoride and other group IVB dihalides with mammalian hemoproteins. A. R. Dahl and E. Hodgson. bibl il Science 197:1376-8 S 30 '77

HALOPERIDOL
Haloperidol: effect of long-term treatment on rat striatal dopamine synthesis and turnover. P. Lerner and others. bibl il Science 197:181-3 Jl 8'77

HALOS (meteorology)
Form and origin of the Parry arcs. R. G. Greenler and others. bibl il Science 195:360-7 Ja 28 '77
Solar halo complexes. il Sky & Tel 54:185-7 S '77

HALOS (mineralogy)
Evidence for superheavies in mica looks weaker. G. B. Lubkin. il Phys Today 30:17+ Ja '77

HALPERIN, Morton H.
Notes and comment. New Yorker 53:19-21 Ag 22 '77 *

HALPERN, Bobby
Making a comeback from nowhere. P. Zimmerman. il pors Sports Illus 47:106-9+ D 5 '77 *

HALPERN, Daniel
Aubade; I hear nothing; poems. Atlantic 240:75 Ag '77
Let me tell you; poem. Nation 225:189 S 3 '77
Still; poem. New Yorker 53:28 Jl 11 '77
Take for example; Blue suspension; poems. Harpers 254:12 Je '77

HALPERN, Howard
How to come to terms with your parents; interview. Harp Baz 110:47+ Je '77

HALPERN, Jeanne W.
That special something that you know better: six inventions for individualizing the writing process. Engl J 66:74-8 Mr '77

HALPERN, Seymour L.
Season food the smart way—it could lengthen your life. Vogue 167:80 O '77
Thirst—dehydration alert. Vogue 167:137 Ap '77

HALPRIN, Lawrence
FDR and the cherry blossoms. il por Horizon 19:56-61 My '77 *

HALSBAND, Frances
Mapping and remapping; with introd by G. Allen. il Archit Rec 161:103-10 F '77 *

HALSTED, Thomas A.
Sandwiches and beer for the press at ACDA? L. J. Carter. Science 197:1063 S 9 '77 *

HALSTON (fashion designer)
Halston gives a party. il por Harp Baz 110:154-5+ O '77

about

Essence of understatement. M. Gough and others. il por House B 119:94-7+ O '77 *
Halston's hideaway. P. Goldberger. il N Y Times Mag p34-7 Jl 24 '77 *

HALVERSON, Robert E.
Fighting the white death. Outdoor Life 161:69+ Ja '78

HALVORSON, Harlyn O.
Recombinant DNA legislation—what next? Science 198:357 O 28 '77

HAM
See also
Cookery—Meat

HAM radio. See Radio, Amateur

al-HAMAD, Abdlatif
View from the upper deck; Kuwait Fund for Arab Economic Development. por Forbes 119:120 Je 15 '77 *

HAMAMATSU, Japan
Japan's warriors of the wind; city's annual tribute to its first-born sons. J. Eliot. il Nat Geog 151:550-61 Ap '77

HAMBERLIN, Emiel
Chicago teacher makes his classes come alive. B. Rhoden. il pors Ebony 32:43-6+ Mr '77 *

HAMBLETONIAN race. See Harness racing

HAMBLIN, Dora Jane
Maladies of Venice: decay, delay and that old sinking feeling. il map Smithsonian 8:40-53 bibl(p 160) N '77

HAMBURG, David A.
Coping with stress effectively. por Intellect 106:13-14 Jl '77

HAMBURG, Germany

Music

See also
Opera—Germany, West

HAMBURG State Opera Ballet. See Ballet—Germany, West

HAMBURG State Opera Company. See Opera—Germany, West

HAMBURGER, Anne W. and Salmon, S. E.
Primary bioassay of human tumor stem cells. bibl il Science 197:461-3 Jl 29 '77

HAMBURGER, Philip
Profiles; R. B. Hale. il New Yorker 53:41-2+ Je 13 '77

HAMBURGER Hamlets Inc. See Restaurants—Chain and franchise operations

HAMBURGERS. See Cookery—Meat

HAMELIN pays the piper; drama. See Thornton, J. F.

HAMER, Dean H.
Interbacterial transfer of escherichia coli-drosophila melanogaster recombinant plasmids. bibl il Science 196:220-1 Ap 8 '77

HAMER, Fannie Lou
Fannie Lou Hamer. J. Egerton. Progressive 41:7 My '77 *
Woman who changed the South. E. H. Norton. por Ms 6:51+ Jl '77 *

HAMERMESH, Richard G.
Responses to divisional profit crises. Harvard Bus R 55:124-30 Mr '77

HAMERSTROM, Frances
This raptor keeps a low profile. il Nat Wildlife 15:20-5 Ag '77

HAMES, Jerry
Canadian Anglicans debate life-and-death issues. Chr Cent 94:772-3 S 14 '77

HAMILL, Pete
Libraries' decay speaks volumes. il Wilson Lib Bull 52:48-50 S '77
New nightlife; jazz. il Vogue 167:250+ N '77

HAMILTON, Buzz
Ancram's Victorian Christmas. il Ret Liv 16:32-4 D '76

HAMILTON, David
Catfish Row springs to life. il Hi Fi 27:92-4 S '77
Crux of the Ring. il Opera N 41:8-12 F 19 '77
Music (cont) Nation 224:318, 444-6, 600-2, 731-2, 797-8; 225:221, 411-12, 541-2 Mr 12, Ap 9, My 14, Je 11, 25, S 10, O 22, N 19 '77
Records (cont) Nation 224:92-4, 253-4, 381-2, 509-10, 797-8; 225:318, 477-8, 602-4, 734 Ja 22, F 26, Mr 26, Ap 23, Je 25, O 1, N 5, D 3, 31 '77
Records 1977. Nation 225:666-7 D 17 '77

HAMILTON, Emma Hart, Lady
Life and loves of Lady Hamilton: a melodrama in several acts. F. V. Grunfeld. il pors Horizon 19:72-81 Ja '77 *

HAMILTON, G. D. and Pilipowskyj, S.
Passage of Typhoon Pamela over Guam. il map Weatherwise 30:147-53 Ag '77

HAMILTON, Iain Douglas-. See Douglas-Hamilton, I.

HAMILTON, Lyman Critchfield, 1926-
Fastest antelope of them all. il por Fortune 95:17 Mr '77 *
Geneen's legacy. D. Pauly. pors Newsweek 89:80 F 21 '77 *

HAMILTON, Margo
Canyon fever. il Am Home 80:40-1 Ap '77

HAMILTON, Patricia
Backing into sculpture; interview, ed by Vasari. Art N 76:21-2+ Mr '77

HAMILTON, Sir William, 1730-1803
Greek art from the Atlantic depths. A. Birchall. il Horizon 19:66-71 Ja '77 *
Life and loves of Lady Hamilton: a melodrama in several acts. F. V. Grunfeld. il pors Horizon 19:72-81 Ja '77 *

HAMILTON, William B.
American characters. il por Am Heritage 28:62-3 O '77

HAMILTON Gallery of Contemporary Art. See New York (city)—Galleries and museums

HAMLET; drama. See Shakespeare, W.—Plays

HAMMACHER Schlemmer (store) See New York (city)—Stores

HAMMAN, Charles L.
Managing your time by managing yourself. il Nations Bus 65:54-6 Ap '77

HAMMAN, Mary
Cast your car in the pond and reap fish. Smithsonian 8:104 Ag '77
Nessie no, but Yeti yes: an abominable abdomen. Smithsonian 7:132 Mr '77
Purple martins, the ingrates, don't read their own paper. Smithsonian 8:144 My '77

HAMMARSKJOLD, Knut
World airline industry; interview. por U.S. News 82:56+ Mr 21 '77

HAMMARSTROM, David, Jr
Coming to grips. il Atlantic 240:84-5 Ag '77

HAMMARSTROM, Sven, and others
Glucocorticoid in inflammatory proliferative skin disease reduces arachidonic and hydroxyeicosatetraenoic acids. bibl il Science 197:994-6 S 2 '77

HAMMER and sickle emblem. See Emblems, National—Russia

HAMMER drills. See Drilling and boring machinery

HAMMERS
Hammers. il Consumers Res Mag 60:16-18 Ap '77
Striking and struck tools. A. Lees. il Pop Sci 211:112+ Jl '77
Using a claw hammer. H. Wicks. il Pop Mech 147:119 Je '77

HAMMETT, Dashiell
Murder in the dark. F. Occhiogrosso. New Repub 177:28-30 Jl 30 '77 *

HAMMITT, Andrew G.
Power play. il Motor B & S 139:50-1+ F '77

HAMMOND, Frank, and Hammond, Ora
Over, under, and through arches. il Ret Liv 17:24-6 Ja '77

HAMMOND, Geoffrey F.
At the helm. See issues of Motor boating & sailing

HAMMOND, Jeff. See Hammond, G. F.

HAMMOND, John
Jazz. New Yorker 53:60-2 Ja 9 '78 *

HAMMOND, Margo
Archbishop Lefebvre's religion. Commonweal 104:422-3 Jl 8 '77
Display of unity. Commonweal 104:774-6 D 9 '77
End of the Concordat? Commonweal 104:584-5 S 16 '77
Two Christs in Italy. Commonweal 104:358-9 Je 10 '77

HAMMOND, Norman
Earliest Maya; with biographical sketch. il maps Sci Am 236:24, 116-23+ bibl(p 150) Mr '77

HAMMOND, Ora. See Hammond, F. jt auth

HAMMOND-Harwood House, Annapolis. See Historic houses, sites, etc.—Maryland

HAMMONS Products Company. See Nut industry

HAMNER, Peggy, and Hamner, W. M.
Chemosensory tracking of scent trails by the planktonic shrimp acetes sibogae australis. bibl il Science 195:886-8 Mr 4 '77

HAMNER, William M. See Hamner, P. jt auth

HAMPDEN Country Club, Hampden, Mass. See Country clubs

HAMPSHIRE, Stuart
Watch this man. il por Vogue 167:240-1+ My '77

HAMPSHIRE College, Amherst, Mass.
Comes the counterrevolution. B. Rice and J. Cramer. il Psychol Today 11:56-7+ S '77

HAMPTON, Christopher
Savages. Review
New Yorker 53:66+ Mr 14 '77 *
Treats. Review
New Yorker 53:144-5 O 24 '77 *

HAMPTON, Mark
Warmth of country traditions rekindled in a city apartment. J. B. Reiter. il por House B 119:96-101 D '77 *

HAMPTON, Ruth E.
My solution to the feathered berry thieves. Org Gard & Farm 24:156 Je '77

HAMS (radio) See Radio operators, Amateur

HAMSTERS
Critical period for acoustic trauma in the hamster and its relation to cochlear development. G. R. Bock and J. C. Saunders. bibl il Science 197:396-8 Jl 22 '77
Estradiol shortens the period of hamster circadian rhythms. L. P. Morin and others. bibl il Science 196:305-7 Ap 15 '77
Melatonin induction of gonadal quiescence in pinealectomized Syrian hamsters. L. Tamarkin and others. bibl il Science 198:953-5 D 2 '77
Small pets, little trouble. M. W. Fox. McCalls 104:122+ My '77

HANAFI Muslims. See Muslims in the United States

HANCOCK, Herbie
Herbie Hancock's fifth incarnation; interview, ed by L. Lyons. il pors Hi Fi 27:121-3 S '77

HANCOCK Tower, Boston. See Boston—Buildings

HAND, A. J.
Wood stains . . . keys to a fine finish. il Pop Sci 211:131-4+ O '77

HAND
See also
Gesture
Manicuring

HAND creams. See Cosmetics

HAND puppets. See Puppets and puppet plays

HAND railings
Planter-rail is decorative and it's very safe. il Sunset 159:86 Jl '77

HAND shaking
Coming to grips. D. Hammarstrom, Jr. il Atlantic 240:84-5 Ag '77
Handshake; excerpt from Manwatching—a field guide to human behavior. D. Morris. il Good H 186:101+ Ja '78

HAND stamps
Bold wrapping paper stamped with fruits and vegetables. il Sunset 159:104 D '77

HAND-to-hand fighting
Fighting street dance; capoeira. il Horizon 19:70 My '77

HAND-to-hand fighting, Oriental
Call this one a game of feet; matches in Las Vegas. J. Jares. il Sports Illus 46:88-4 My 2 '77
Khalilah Ali: karate disciplines her new life. R. Kisner. il pors Ebony 32:78-80+ S '77
Writing for the martial arts market. J. Murray. il Writers Digest 57:29-30 Je '77

HAND tools. See Tools

HANDBAGS
Macrame: a sampler becomes a handbag. S. La Pierre. il Design (US) 78:28-9 mid-Wint '77
Make a keyboard clutch. E. Gross. il Seventeen 36:54 My '77
106 sensational handbags to make. C. K. Toth. il Good H 184:112-19 My '77

HANDBALL
Served up, imperially, under glass; work of R. Kendler. M. Sharnik. il pors Sports Illus 46:44-6+ My 2 '77
See also
Racquetball

HANDBOOKS
See also
Camps—Handbooks, manuals, etc.

HANDEDNESS. See Left- and right-handedness

HANDEL, Georg Friedrich
Another Messiah. R. V. Lucano. Am Rec G 40:19-21 Mr '77 *
Belshazzar; Telefunken recording. J. Noble. Hi Fi 28:94-7 Ja '78 *
Complete concerti for keyboard and orchestra. J. W. Barker. Am Rec G 40:13-14 Ag '77 *
Complete sonatas for wind instrument and basso continuo; recording. J. W. Barker. Am Rec G 40:35 F '77 *
Concerti for organ and orchestra complete. J. W. Barker. Am Rec G 40:21-2 My '77 *
Ears of an untoward make: Pope and Handel. M. R. Brownell. bibl f il Mus Q 62:554-70 O '76 *
Israel in Egypt. R. V. Lucano. Am Rec G 40:24-5 N '76 *
Judas Maccabeus; recording. R. V. Lucano. Am Rec G 40:34 F '77 *
Messiah sing-alongs—bring your own score, join in. il Sunset 159:72 D '77 *
Semele. R. V. Lucano. Am Rec G 40:21-2 Mr '77 *
16 organ concertos. P. Pfunke. por Am Rec G 40:23 Mr '77 *
Twenty years of Messiah recordings. R. V. Lucano. il Am Rec G 40:6-9 D '76 *

HANDGUNS. See Firearms

HANDICAPPED
Georgia seeks its disabled citizens; The Search. Aging 274:24 Ag '77
Handicapped: hidden no longer. S. Kleinfield. Atlantic 240:86-90+ D '77
Handicapped resource group members work for barrier elimination. il Science 195:475-6 F 4 '77
Latest on helping the handicapped; interview. H. B. Betts. il por U.S. News 82:61-3 Ja 31 '77
What's being done for 35 million handicapped. il U.S. News 83:58 Ag 29 '77
Wheelchair route to open San Diego for handicapped. Aging 274:26 Ag '77
See also
Architecture and the handicapped
Blind
Children, Handicapped
Deaf
Deformities
International Year for Disabled Persons, 1981 (proposed)
Libraries—Services to the handicapped
Mentally handicapped
Mentally handicapped children
Paralytics
Physical education for the handicapped
Veterans, Disabled
White House Conference on Handicapped Individuals, 1977

Civil rights
Campus handicap? colleges complying with HEW's rules. M. Shiels and others. il Newsweek 90:58 Ag 8 '77
Hire the handicapped. S. Fraker and H. McGee. il Newsweek 89:39 My 9 '77
It's a new day for disabled people. il Am Educ 13:17-18+ D '77
Overlooked minority. C. A. Robbins. McCalls 104:82 Je '77
Rights for the handicapped—new rules stir turmoil. il U.S. News 82:84 My 9 '77
Sweeping rules on employing the handicapped. J. J. Kilpatrick. Nations Bus 65:11-12 Jl '77
See also
Mentally handicapped children—Civil rights

Education
Campus handicap? colleges complying with HEW's rules. M. Sheils and others. il Newsweek 90:58 Ag 8 '77
Handicapped and science: moving into the mainstream. E. Walsh. Science 196:1424-6 Je 24 '77

Employment
Disabled employee: separating myth from fact. R. B. Nathanson. Harvard Bus R 55:6-8 My '77
Employment problems of disabled persons; excerpt from Jobs for the disabled. S. A. Levitan and R. Taggart. bibl il M Labor R 100:3-13 Mr '77
Hire the handicapped librarian! W. A. Zerface. bibl il por Wilson Lib Bull 51:656-60 Ap '77
Rehabilitating the employer. J. A. Nesbitt and P. Hippolitus. il Parks & Rec 12:36-7+ N '77
See also
Deaf—Employment

Recreation
Leisure and handicapped persons; symposium. il Parks & Rec 12:21-44+ N '77
Mobilizing for a barrier-free zoo; Knoxville Zoological Park. il Parks & Rec 12:30+ My '77
Planning for the handicapped. Am City & County 92:42 N '77
See also
Camps for the handicapped
Sports for the handicapped

Transportation
What price transit accessibility? il Am City & County 92:18 O '77

HANDICAPPED, Apparatus for the
Electronics and the handicapped. A. Salsberg. il Pop Electr 13:4 Ja '78
Help for the handicapped. bibl il Changing T 31:41-2 N '77
Product news. il Parks & Rec 12:65-6 N '77

HANDICAPPED, Libraries for the
Barrier free; Alabama Regional Library for the Blind and Physically Handicapped. A. G. Bushman. il Am Lib 8:303-4 Je '77
See also
Illinois Regional Library for the Blind and Physically Handicapped, Chicago

HANDICRAFT
Pazyryk; Altaian tombs excavated. M. P. Zavitukhina. il UNESCO Courier 29:30-3+ D '76
Things to make by the batch for bazaars. C. Vaughan and C. Deery. il Bet Hom & Gard 55:136-9+ S '77
Weaving affairs; innovative handicraft program. M. Zipadelli and V. Satalino. il pors Sch Arts 76:66-7 Mr '77
See also
Arts and crafts
Arts and crafts movement
Basket making
Christmas projects
Eggs, Decorated
Folk art
Jewelry making
Patchwork
Shellwork
Stencil work
Textile crafts
Weaving

Equipment and supplies
Address book; handicraft kits. House B 119:20+ N '77
Address book; supply dealers. S. Sunderlin. House B 119:28 S '77

HANDICRAFT kits. See Handicraft—Equipment and supplies

HANDICRAFT shops. See Art trade

HANDKE, Peter
Left-handed woman; story, tr by R. Manheim. New Yorker 53:50-60 N 7 '77
Two authors, two points of view; interview, ed by H. R. Lottman. por Pub W 212:54-5 S 12 '77
about
Sorrow beyond dreams. Reviews
Nation 224:189 F 12 '77 *
New Yorker 52:69 F 7 '77 *

HANDLER, Bruce
Politics of water. il Sat R 4:16-19 My 14 '77

HANDLER, Philip
Academy shifts emphases to keep up with the times; interview. por BioScience 27:241-4+ Ap '77

HANDLIN, Oscar
Living in a valley. Am Scholar 46:301-12 Summ '77

HANDLING of materials. See Materials handling

HANDMADE paper. See Paper making

HANDMAN, Edward
Department of amplification. New Yorker 53:136-8 O 3 '77

HANDSHAKING. See Hand shaking

HANDVILLE, Robert T.
Robert Handville. M. Tinkelman. il por Am Artist 41:56-61 Jl '77 *

HANDWRITING. See Writing

HANDWRITING analysis. See Graphology

HANDY men. See Repairmen

HANES Corporation
Hosiery giant jumps from L'eggs to faces. il Bus W p87 Ag 22 '77

HANEY, Marilyn Plowman
James and John revisited; poem. Chr Cent 94:274 Mr 23 '77
To a young Christian friend in Rhodesia; poem. Chr Cent 94:563 Je 8 '77

HANG gliders. See Gliders (aeronautics)
HANGING plants
Hang a garden in your house. B. Gardner. il Am Home 80:82 Mr '77
Ivy balls in the window. il Sunset 159:226-7 N '77
HANGINGS, Wall. See Wall hangings
HANIFF, Ghulam M.
Education for a global society. Current 194:17-22 Jl '77
HANIGAN, John Leonard
Choices narrow for troubled Genesco. Bus W p41-2 S 19 '77 *
HANKER, Jacob S. and Romanovicz, D. K.
Phi bodies: perovidatic particles that produce crystalloidal cellular inclusions. bibl il Science 197:895-8 Ag 26 '77
HANKIN, Robert A.
Why America must have national health insurance. Intellect 105:340-1 Ap '77
HANKS, J. H. See Dhople, A. M. jt auth
HANKS, Nancy
Nancy Hanks on craft grants; excerpt from address. Craft Horiz 37:6 F '77

about

NEA; will success spoil our biggest patron? M. N. Carter. il por Art N 76:32-40+ My '77 *
Nancy Hanks resigns NEA post. B. V. Bordelon. Dance Mag 51:4 N '77 *
HANLEY, James R.
Not ready for the rocking chair. il por Ret Liv 17:40-1 Jl '77
HANLEY, John W.
Voluntarism in America; address, May 23, 1977. Vital Speeches 43:634-7 Ag 1 '77
HANLEY, John Weller
Has emotion tipped the scales on consumer safety? address, October 17, 1977. Vital Speeches 44:92-5 N 15 '77
Is law on food additives too strict? interview. por U.S. News 82:25-6 My 30 '77
Meeting the greater competition of tomorrow. pors Nations Bus 65:37-40 Mr '77
Why ban reason from the consumer safety debate? address, June 14, 1977. Vital Speeches 43:626-9 Ag 1 '77
HANNAH, Barry
Coming close to Donna; story. Esquire 87:146 Ap '77
Pete resists the man of his old room; story. Esquire 87:147-8 Ap '77
HANNAH, Norman Britton
Five worlds of detente. maps Nat R 29:541-5 My 13 '77
HANNAY, Roger
Bucknell Univ: New Music. por Hi Fi 27:MA20-1 Mr '77 *
HANNIGAN, Frank
Bobby Jones: paragon of the links. il Read Digest 111:146-50 Jl '77
Link to Scotland. il Sports Illus 47:32-5 Ag 22 '77
HANNON, Bruce M.
Negative energy impact of modern rail transit systems. bibl Science 195:596 F 11 '77
HANNON, Kent
Baseball (cont) Sports Illus 46:67-8 My 23; 44+ Je 6 '77
Blue-collar coach in a button-down league. il pors Sports Illus 48:26-30 Ja 2 '78
Boom! il Sports Illus 47:10-15 Jl 4 '77
College basketball (cont) Sports Illus 46:38+ F 14; 44+ Mr 14 '77; 48:35-6 Ja 2; 72-3 Ja 9 '78
College football. por Sports Illus 47:70+ S 19 '77
Everybody is courting the King. il por Sports Illus 46:18-19 F 7 '77
Idea that's gotten way off the ground. Sports Illus 47:43-4+ N 28 '77
Pro basketball. il Sports Illus 46:56+ Mr 7 '77
Road to success passes four corners. Sports Illus 46:19-20 Mr 28 '77
Softball. il Sports Illus 46:66+ Je 13 '77
Tennis. Sports Illus 46:52-3 My 30 '77
Week; baseball. Sports Illus 47:56+ Jl 18 '77
Week; college basketball (cont) Sports Illus 47:82+ D 5 '77

about

Letter from the publisher. J. Meyers. por Sports Illus 48:4 Ja 2 '78 *
HANOI, Vietnam
Hanoi: souvenirs and spontaneity. S. Talbott. il Time 109:45 Ap 4 '77
HANRAHAN, John D.
Foreign agents in our midst. il Progressive 41:31-5 N '77
HÄNSCH, Theodor W.
High-resolution spectroscopy of atoms and molecules. bibl il Phys Today 30:34-6+ My '77
HANSELL, Herbert J.
Administration officials testify on the Panama Canal treaties; statement, August 17, 1977. Dept State Bull 77:533-5 O 17 '77
Administration recommends Senate approval of Genocide Convention; statement, May 24, 1977. Dept State Bull 76:678-80 Je 27 '77
Department discusses War Powers Resolution; statement, July 15, 1977. Dept State Bull 77:291-3 Ag 29 '77
HANSEN, Arlen J.
Imagination gap. por Newsweek 90:9 Jl 25 '77
HANSEN, Harvey
Nature photography is easy? il Mod Phot 41:106-11+ My '77
HANSEN, Laura Barnett
How we grew a mothers' group. il por Redbook 149:72+ S '77
HANSEN, Susan K.
Valley of 10,000 wonders. il por Am For 83:26-9 F '77
HANSEN'S disease. See Leprosy and lepers
HANSON, Angus Alexander
Beltsville scientists await new congressional priorities. E. M. Leeper. il por BioScience 27:85-8 F '77 *
HANSON, Christopher
American political asylum. Nation 224:527-30 Ap 30 '77
HANSON, Dennis
Econotes. See issues of Audubon
HANSON, Dick
Across the editor's desk. See issues of Successful farming
HANSON, Duane
It's the real thing. R. Bongartz. il pors Horizon 20:72-81 S '77 *
HANSON, Howard
Howard Hanson: eightieth birthday tributes. il por Hi Fi 27:MA36-7 F '77 *
HANSON, Jeannie Kitchen
Energy from the biomass. Current 190:39-42 F '77
HANSON, Robert E.
Strange case of the IRS questionnaire; address, May 3, 1977. Vital Speeches 43:498-501 Je 1 '77
HANUKKAH (Feast of Lights)
Star of David (Mogen David) mobiles. il Design (US) 79:18 N '77
HANUKKAH cookery. See Cookery, Jewish
HAPGOOD, Fred
Gaia: the harmony of our sphere. Atlantic 240:100-4 D '77
Naked coward. Atlantic 240:88-91 Ag '77
Reformation in science. Atlantic 239:107-10 Mr '77
HAPKE, Bruce W. See Wells, E. jt auth
HAPLOIDY. See Chromosomes
HAPPILY ever after; ballet. See Ballet reviews—Single works
HAPPINESS
Despairing optimist . . .: pursuit of happiness and the quality of life, defining joie de vivre. R. Dubos. Am Scholar 46:424+ Aut '77
GH's happiness survey—the surprising results. J. Freedman and G. Norton. il Good H 185:82+ S '77
Happiness—it's only natural; five popular errors refuted. W. W. Dyer. Read Digest 111:84-6 Jl '77
Happiness: who's got it? How you can get it! S. Walton. il Sat Eve Post 249:48-51+ S '77
How happy are you? questionnaire. il Good H 184:49-50 Mr '77
How to be happy with who you are: interview, ed by C. Seebohm. E. Fromm. il House & Gard 149:152-3+ Ap '77
Search for poor, happy people; Gallup/Kettering Global Survey on Human Needs and Satisfactions. S. Bush. Psychol Today 10:34+ Ap '77
75 easy ways to punch up your life. J. O'Reilly. Mademoiselle 83:128-31+ Je '77
You can be happier; Option Process method. Seventeen 36:51 Je '77
See also
Contentment

Anecdotes, facetiae, satire, etc.

Pursuit of unhappiness. R. Baker. il N Y Times Mag p 12 My 15 '77
HAPPY end; musical comedy. See Musical comedy, revue, etc.—Reviews—Single works
HAPSBURG, Otto von. See Otto, Archduke of Austria
HAPSBURG, House of
Raiser Max: first among the Hapsburgs. H. R. Trevor-Roper. il pors Horizon 19:68-81 Mr '77
See also
Maria Theresa, Empress of Austria
HAPTICS. See Touch
HARAM, Michael Sue
Learning to live in the real world. il por Redbook 149:40+ O '77
HARBORS
See also
Marinas
Petroleum shipping terminals
HARCOURT Brace Jovanovich, Inc
HBJ's new Jove paperback line will share functions with hardcover trade side. Pub W 211:68 Ap 4 '77
Money-saving coupons is the come-on in HBJ's fall trade paperback campaign. Pub W 212:55 Jl 11 '77

HARCOURT Brace Jovanovich Publishing Laboratory. See Publishers and publishing—Study and teaching
HARD of hearing. See Deaf
HARDEE'S Food Systems Inc-Imasco Ltd. merger. See Corporations—Acquisitions and mergers—International aspects
HARDEN, Jack
Get in line! il Yachting 141:82-5 Je '77
HARDENBURGH, N.Y.
Small-town tax rebellion; ordination of residents. D. Jacobs. McCalls 104:69 F '77
HARDENING of the arteries. See Arteriosclerosis
HARDESTY, Robert L.
Squandered national resource. por Newsweek 89:11 Mr 14 '77
HARDIE, Dee
Nantucket offers the perfect autumn vacation. il House & Gard 149:43+ Ag '77
Upholstery in 6 easy lessons. il House & Gard 149:66+ My '77
HARDIN, Garrett
Will Xerox kill Gutenberg? Science 198:883 D 2 '77
HARDIN, Paul, 1931-
College-related church. J. W. Donohue. America 137:122-5 S 10 '77 *
HARDIN, Robert
(ed) See Massine, L. Conversation with Leonid Massine
HARDING, Bertrand Morrison
Excerpt from testimony on proposed revisions of the Hatch Act, February 24, 1977. Cong Digest 56:303+ D '77
HARDISKY, Michael, and Reimold, R. J.
Salt-marsh plant geratology. bibl il Science 198:612-14 N 11 '77
HARDISON, O. B. Jr
In the palazzo of Pellucid; poem. New Repub 177:35-6 Ag 6 '77
HARDPAN soils. See Soils, Hardpan
HARDWARE
See also
Bolts and nuts
Curtain and drapery fixtures
Fastenings
HARDWARE stores
Hardware U.—the great American learning center; Vanderhoof's hardware store, Concord, Mass. W. D. Ellis. Read Digest 111:120-3 S '77
See also
Home improvement centers
HARDWOODS
6 scientists working hard on the hardwoods. J. Marks. il Am For 83:16-19+ N '77
HARDY, Hugh Gelston
Recycling architectural masterpieces—and other buildings not so great; ed by M. Holzman and N. Pfeiffer. il Archit Rec 162:81-92 Ag '77
HARDY Holzman Pfeiffer Associates. See Architectural firms
HARE, Cyril, pseud. See Clark, A. A. G.
HARE, David
American Surrealist; Cronus series on display at the Guggenheim Museum. H. Rosenberg. New Yorker 53:155-8 O 24 '77 *
David Hare: American surrealist. K. Kuh. il Sat R 5:38-40 O 1 '77 *
HARE, Denise
Film (cont) Craft Horiz 37:16+ F; 12+ Ap; 7+ Je; 6+ O; 6+ D '77
HARE, F. Kenneth
Climate as accomplice. il UNESCO Courier 30:7-10 Jl '77
HARE, Jimmy
Images of war: Jimmy Hare's photojournalism. E. M. Halliday. il por Am Heritage 28:74-81 Ag '77 *
HARE, Nathan
Many ways men pimp their women. il Ebony 33:145-6+ N '77
HARE hunting
Think small for hares; snowshoes. R. P. Smith. il Outdoor Life 160:72-3+ N '77
HARE Krishna consciousness. See Mysticism—Hinduism
HARES
Varying hare. J. Dell. il Conservationist 31:3+ N '76
HARGROVE, Erwin Charles, 1930-
Leading authority sizes up Carter's performance so far; interview. il pors U.S. News 82:23-4 My 2 '77
HÄRING, Bernard
Sex and the celibate. il New Cath World 220:272-5 N '77
HARKNESS, Ned
No heels in the Achilles. P. Putnam. il por Sports Illus 46:46+ F 7 '77 *
Union all but sundered? il por Time 111:63 Ja 9 '78 *
HARLECH, Pamela
Opening moves: easy recipes from a hostess who knows the game; excerpt from Feast without fuss. il Vogue 167:258+ S '77
Party food—fast, fabulous; excerpt from Feast without fuss. il pors House & Gard 149:150-1+ S '77
HARLEM. See New York (city)—Harlem
HARLEM Dance Theatre. See Dance Theatre of Harlem
HARLEY, J. Preston
Diet not cause of hyperactivity. Sci N 111:406-7 Je 25 '77 *
HARLEY, William G.
Mass media and society: American viewpoint. il UNESCO Courier 30:28-31 Ap '77
HARLOW, LeRoy F.
Local government; address, October 3, 1977. Vital Speeches 44:70-3 N 15 '77
HARLOW, Michael
Devotion to the small; poem. Nation 224:282 Mr 5 '77
HARMAN, Willis Walter
Which future for tomorrow? address, July 20, 1977. Vital Speeches 43:696-700 S 1 '77
HARMAN International Industries, Inc
Gone-fishing syndrome: earned time concept. J. Lelyveld. N. Y. Times Mag p62 My 29 '77
HARMETZ, Aljean
Fonda at forty. il por McCalls 105:104-5+ Ja '78
How they filmed a classic; excerpt from Making of the Wizard of Oz. il Read Digest 111:73-4+ N '77
HARMON, Clifford B.
Harmon trophy. T. West. il Flying 101:98 S '77 *
HARMON, Ronald Lynd
American rustic: the Ozarks. il Travel 148:42-5 Ag '77
HARMONY (aesthetics)
Tyranny of harmony. J. P. Sisk. Am Scholar 46:193-205 Spr '77
HARMS, Johnny
Fishing world of Johnny Harms. J. Borgzinner. il por Motor B & S 139:58-9+ Je '77 *
HARMSTONE, Teresa Rakowska-. See Rakowska-Harmstone, T.
HARNER, Michael
Enigma of Aztec sacrifice; with biographical sketch. il map Natur Hist 86:2, 46-51 bibl(p 100) Ap; 22 My '77
HARNESS racing
Generation gap: half a length. D. S. Looney. il Sports Illus 46:20-1 Je 27 '77
Governor had a ball; Little Brown Jug. D. S. Looney. il Sports Illus 47:58+ O 3 '77
Green Speed was red hot to trot; Hambletonian. D. S. Looney. il Sports Illus 47:22-3 S 12 '77
Red, white and true; Gold Cup. D. S. Looney. Sports Illus 47:52 Ag 8 '77
Sure way to get his goat; Governor Skipper's victory in the Adios. D. S. Looney. il Sports Illus 47:48-50 Ag 22 '77
View from the end of a horse. P. Axthelm. il Newsweek 89:56-7 Mr 14 '77
See also
Horses, Race
HARNETT, William Michael
My candidate for mayor. D. K. Mano. Nat R 29:787-8 Jl 8 '77 *
Still-life paintings of William Michael Harnett their reflections upon nineteenth-century American musical culture. C. J. Oja. bibl f il Mus Q 63:505-23 O '77 *
HAROLD, Franklin M. and Van Brunt, Jennifer
Circulation of H^+ and K^+ across the plasma membrane is not obligatory for bacterial growth. bibl il Science 197:372-3 Jl 22 '77
HARP seals. See Seals
HARPER, Buzz, family
Sharing the good life in Natchez. il pors Am Home 80:44-5 Mr '77
HARPER, G. Neil
Automated project control system aims for improved profitability. il Archit Rec 161:61 Mr '77
HARPER, Heather
Irish Heather. S. Wadsworth. il pors Opera N 42:25-7 D 10 '77 *
HARPER, Leon
New president elected for National Assn. of AAA's in Washington. por Aging 275:32 S '77 *
HARPER, Lisl Stedronski
Inside Catalonia's kitchen. il Sat R 5:26-7 O 29 '77
HARPER, Pamela
Clematis, the queen of garden climbers. il Horticulture 55:76-81 F '77
Flowers for a rock wall garden. il Horticulture 55:20-3 Je '77
Virtuoso viburnums. il Horticulture 55:52-5 S '77
HARPER, Valerie
Valerie Harper: what Rhoda taught me about marriage & divorce; ed by M. F. Cohen. por Ladies Home J 94:36+ S '77
HARPER, William
Magic of cloisonné: William Harper. il Craft Horiz 37:54-7 D '77
HARPER & Row, Publishers, Inc
Harper & Row, District 65 agree on new contract. W. Geles. il Pub W 211:154 My 23 '77
Harper & Row, District 65 brace for strike. M. Reuter. Pub W 211:21 My 9 '77

HARPER & Row, Publishers, Inc—*Continued*
Harper, Reader's Digest to copublish Fords' memoirs. M. Reuter. il pors Pub W 211:25-6 Mr 21 '77
Robert E. Baensch: the global man at Harper & Row; interview, ed by H. R. Lottman. R. E. Baensch. il por Pubs W 212:87+ S 19 '77
220 union members walk out at Harper & Row. M. Reuter. il Pub W 211:28-9 My 16 '77
HARPER & Row, Publishers, Inc mergers. See Publishers and publishing—Acquisitions and mergers
HARPER'S (periodical)
Harping at Harper's. L. N. Gerhardt. SLJ 23:7 F '77
Posters; E. Penfield's advertising posters. E. Penfield. il por Harpers 225:57-70 D '77
HARPER'S young people (periodical) See Childrens periodicals
HARPY eagles. See Eagles
HARRAGAN, Betty L.
Why corporations are teaching men to think like women. . .and other secret game plans that you may not have been briefed on; excerpt from Games mother never taught you: corporate gamesmanship for women. il Ms 5:62-3+ Je '77
HARRAH'S Automobile Collection, Reno, Nev.
Harrah's Automobile Collection. C. Scully. il Trav/Holiday 148:36-7+ N '77
HARRAH'S casinos. See Gambling
HARRIBANCE, Lalsingh
Win, place and glow. R. Cantwell. il Sports Illus 47:32-4+ Ag 29 '77 *
HARRIER (airplane) See Airplanes, Military
HARRIMAN, Leslie O.
Nordic initiatives on southern Africa very significant—Chairman. UN Chron 14:24-5 My '77 *
HARRIMAN, William Averell
Who started the cold war? il pors Am Heritage 28:8-23 Ag '77
about
Ancient mariner. New Repub 177:18-20 Ag 20 '77 *
HARRIMAN State Park. See New York (state)—Parks and reserves
HARRING, Ruth
Missing link. Educ Digest 42:48-9 Ja '77
HARRINGTON, Bob
Bob and Madalyn's fight to the finish. J. C. Hefley and E. E. Plowman. il por Chr Today 21:34-5 Ag 26 '77 *
Combat zone. Chr Today 22:50-1 N 18 '77 *
On tour. Chr Today 22:58-9 O 7 '77 *
Soul mates. M. Montagno and F. Maier. pors Newsweek 90:72 S 19 '77 *
HARRINGTON, Frank
Richard Ellis honored for his book designs by Franklin Club. il por Pub W 212:95-6 Ag 1 '77
HARRINGTON, Michael
Hiding the other America. New Repub 176:15-17 F 26 '77
July in January? New Repub 176:60+ Ja 22 '77
Marxism in America. il New Cath World 220:118-21 My '77
Old comrades meet. Harpers 254:26-8 F '77
Status quo economy. Harpers 255:34-5 S '77
Sweden's swing to the right overstated. Current 190:18-20 F '77
HARRIS, Arthur S. Jr
Timing the submission. Writer 90:19-21+ Mr '77
HARRIS, Bruce
Best friends of bestsellers. Writers Digest 57:26 O '77
HARRIS, David
Busted in Mexico. il pors N Y Times Mag p26-30+ My 1 '77
Dark and violent world of the Mexican connection. il map N Y Times Mag p 15-18+ D 18 '77
HARRIS, Franco
Offside in Pittsburgh? S. Fraker and S. Lesher. pors Newsweek 89:40 My 9 '77 *
HARRIS, George S.
Ethnic conflict and the Kurds. bibl f Ann Am Acad 433:112-24 S '77
HARRIS, Herbert E. 2d
Excerpt from debate on proposed Federal Employees' Political Activities Act, May 18, 1977. Cong Digest 56:300+ D '77
HARRIS, J. John, 3d, and Bentzen, W. R.
Aspects of institutional discrimination. bibl il Clearing H 51:7-10 S '77
Theoretical framework for analyzing poverty as a subculture. bibl Clearing H 50:209-11 Ja '77
HARRIS, J. M. See White, T. D. jt auth
HARRIS, Jana
Clackamas; poem. Nation 225:504 N 12 '77
HARRIS, Joan R.
Stopping white flight. bibl il Society 14:44-6 My '77
HARRIS, Joel Chandler
Why the frog has no tail; poem. Sat Eve Post 249:50 Jl '77
HARRIS, John
Death by incompetence. Nation 226:18-20 Ja 7 '78
HARRIS, John Benton-. See Benton-Harris, J.
HARRIS, Kenneth
Watercolor page. il por Am Artist 41:48-51+ S '77
HARRIS, Leon
Satan's lexicographer. il pors Am Heritage 28:56-63 Ap '77
HARRIS, Lusia
Delta State's irresistible force. L. Norment. il pors Ebony 32:86-8+ F '77 *
HARRIS, Maria
Organization for catechesis. il por New Cath World 220:101-3 Mr '77
HARRIS, Marvin
Why men dominate women. il N Y Times Mag p46+ N 13 '77
HARRIS, Neil
Parking the garage. New Repub 176:21-4 F 19 '77
HARRIS, Patricia (Roberts)
How much more federal aid can cities expect? interview. por U.S. News 83:63-4 D 12 '77
about
Erosion of aid to the cities. por Bus W p36 Ag 15 '77 *
HUD Secretary Harris puts priority on good design. D. Loomis. Archit Rec 161:34 F '77 *
Patronizing Proxmire. Nation 224:66-7 Ja 22 '77 *
Secretary Harris picks top aides, seeks more housing funds. D. Loomis. Archit Rec 161:34 Ap '77 *
Secretary Harris seeks more subsidized housing. D. Loomis. Archit Rec 161:34 My '77 *
HARRIS, Philip
Advice for the new trustee negotiator. por Wilson Lib Bull 52:237-40 N '77
HARRIS, Richard E.
Reflections: crime in the F.B.I. New Yorker 53:30-2+ Ag 8 '77
Reporter at large (cont) New Yorker 53:48-50+ Ap 25; 56+ S 26 '77
HARRIS, Richard W.
Management approach to park maintenance. il Parks & Rec 12:32-4 D '77
HARRIS, William F.
Disclinations; with biographical sketch. il Sci Am 237:10+, 130-6+ bibl(p 190) D '77
HARRIS Bankcorp Inc. See Bank holding companies
HARRIS Corporation
Technology transfer's master. il Bus W p 120+ O 10 '77
HARRISBURG, Pa.
Education
See Education—Pennsylvania
HARRISON, Anne Blaine
Obituary
New Repub 176:9 Je 18 '77. A. McCarthy
HARRISON, Barbara F.
Second look. Gilgamesh: man's first story. il Horn Bk 53:74-6 F '77
HARRISON, Barbara Grizzuti
How TV can be good for children. il McCalls 105:165+ O '77
Papa mia. il por Ms 5:30+ Je '77
Profound hypochondriac. il Ms 5:71-3+ My '77
Riddle of Robert Redford. il por McCalls 104:42+ My '77
Why some women feel secure—and so many don't. Redbook 148:48+ Mr '77
Write the truth, my son said. Write about me. il Ms 6:14-18 Ja '78
HARRISON, Charles H.
Proper study of government. il Am Educ 13:10-14 Jl '77
HARRISON, Edward
Chesapeake spring. J. Lelyveld. il N Y Times Mag p 110 Ap 3 '77 *
HARRISON, George H.
Attract more birds this winter. il Nat Wildlife 16:40-5 D '77
Behold, a multitude of penguins. il Int Wildlife 7:36-9 Jl '77
Earth log; the Audubon road show. il pors Audubon 79:102-3+ My '77
Is the bluegill America's favorite fish? il Nat Wildlife 15:36-41 Je '77
Making of the world's number one bird watcher. il pors Am For 83:18-21+ F '77
Maynard Reece paints—memories on canvas. il pors Am For 83:24-7 Jl '77
Rare look at wildlife in Russia. il por map Int Wildlife 8:4-11 Ja '78
(ed) See Peterson, R. T. Dean of bird watchers
HARRISON, J. T. See Smith, S. V. jt auth
HARRISON, James
Changing male roles. il Am Educ 13:20-6 Jl '77
HARRISON, Jim
Outdoors. il Esquire 88:38+ Jl '77
HARRISON, John H.
Whale and the wild jojoba; with biographical sketch. il Sea Front 23:267-72, 319 S '77

HARRISON, K. C.
Proudly, British Library Association joins centenarian club. Am Lib 8:473-4 O '77

HARRISON, Lowell H.
George Rogers Clark and the conquest of Illinois. il pors map Am Hist Illus 11:4-7+ F '77

HARRISON, Newton
Should the art school curriculum include professional job training? il Am Artist 41:17 O '77

HARRISON, Rex
Last gentleman-actor? G. Rogoff. por Sat R 4:46-7 Mr 5 '77 *

HARRISON, Richard V.
Berried anemone; with biographical sketch. il Sea Front 23:194-7, 255 Jl '77

HARSHBARGER, John C. and others
Chlamydiae (with phages), mycoplasmas, and rickettsiae in Chesapeake Bay bivalves. bibl il Science 196:666-8 My 6 '77
—See Rose, F. L. jt auth

HART, C. W. Jr
Familiar ponds harbor mysteries, exotic animals. il Smithsonian 8:84-8+ bibl(p 115) Ja '78

HART, Dexter R.
Below decks with Dex. See issues of Motor boating & sailing
Performance test. See occasional issues of Motor boating & sailing

HART, Donna
Enlarging the American dream. il Am Educ 13:10-16 My '77

HART, Ernest H.
Which pet is right for you? excerpt from Living with pets. Am Home 80:28 N '77

HART, Gregory W.
Build this electronic slot machine. il Radio-Electr 48:39-43 Jl '77

HART, Jeffrey
Is the Republican Party dead? Nat R 29:327-8 Mr 18 '77
NBC as a Soviet megaphone. il Sat Eve Post 249:31 O '77
Truth and culture. Nat R 29:992-5 S 2 '77
White flannels, grass courts. New Repub 177:21-4 Jl 23 '77

HART, Michael H.
History of the earth's atmosphere. il Sky & Tel 53:266+ Ap '77 *

HART, Moss
Christmases with my father; excerpt from Act one. Redbook 150:63-4 D '77

HART, Philip A.
Philip Hart. E. J. McCarthy. New Repub 176:6+ Ja 15 '77 *

HART, Sandra
Antigua: sailing, tennis, relaxing. il Harp Baz 110:12+ My '77
Chartering in Greece. Yachting 141:156-7 Je '77

HARTACK, Willie
Hero who has gone on to Happy Valley. F. Deford. por Sports Illus 46:84+ My 23 '77 *

HARTER, Walter
Dressing better—yet saving money. il Ret Liv 17:32-3 My '77

HARTFORD, Bill
Imports & motorsports. See issues of Popular mechanics

HARTFORD, Conn.
Detour to Hartford. H. Koenig and G. Koenig. il Travel 147:64-9 Mr '77

Bookstores

See Booksellers and bookselling—Connecticut

Education

Hartford's workplaces become the classroom. il Bus W p 117-18 D 5 '77

Housing

Core city fight for housing not over; with editorial comment. il Am City & County 92:33-4, 138 O '77
Homesteading in Hartford. E. V. Warren. il House B 119:10+ F '77

Monuments, statues, etc.

Andre's square one; Stone Field. Vasari. il Art N 76:29 N '77
Connecticut rocks; Stone Field Sculpture. il por Horizon 20:59 N '77
Indentations in space; Stone Field Sculpture; interview. C. Andre. New Yorker 53:51-2 N 21 '77

Music

See also
Opera—Connecticut

HARTFORD Appeal. See Religious conferences

HARTFORD Ballet Company. See Ballet companies

HARTFORD Convention of 1814. See New England—History

HARTFORD Fire Insurance Company
ITT's Hartford deal still worries the SEC; Lazard Frères stock sale arrangement. Bus W p26-7 Je 6 '77

HARTLAP, Diane
Dollology. il Hobbies 82:39-40+ Mr '77

HARTLE, Terry W. See Baratz, J. C. jt auth

HARTLEY, Gregg L. and Tucker, Larry
Mobile I and R unit serves elderly in southwest Missouri. il Aging 266:16-18 D '76

HARTMAN, Arthur A.
U.S. policy toward our NATO partners: traditional commitments and new directions; statement, May 23, 1977. Dept State Bull 76:635-9 Je 13 '77

HARTMAN, Charles O.
Essayist; Stars: flat. blue, large stars. Nothing; poems. Poetry 131:99-100 N '77

HARTMAN, Curtis
Sunday afternoon in Mexico City. il Holiday 57:32-3 N '76

HARTMAN, David
David Hartman's impossible dream. A. Rankin. il por Read Digest 110:78-82 Ap '77 *

HARTMAN, David Downs
Nice man to wake up to; interview, ed by C. Anderson. il por Good H 184:66+ My '77

about

Good morning, David Hartman. S. Flythe, Jr. il por Sat Eve Post 249:45-7+ S '77 *
Television. P. H. Herz. por Sr Schol 109:37-8 F 24 '77 *

HARTMAN, Geoffrey
Genius loci; poem. Poetry 131:138-40 D '77
Malraux mystery. New Repub 176:27-30 Ja 29 '77

HARTMAN, Guy L.
Pediatrician's advice to parents on poisonous garden plants. il Horticulture 55:18-25 Ag '77

HARTMAN, John J. and others
Stones of madness. bibl f il Am Imago 33:266-95 Fall '76

HARTMAN, Suzanne Forse
It's your move; story. Ladies Home J 94:22 N '77

HARTMANN, William K.
Cratering in the solar system; with biographical sketch. il Sci Am 236:16, 84-6+ bibl(p 132) Ja '77

HARTNETT, Edith
J. K. Huysmans: a study in decadence. Am Scholar 46:367-76 Summ '77

HARTSEN, Kay
Roadblocks to beauty. il Conservationist 32:36 S '77

HARTT, Frederick
Philadelphia. Art N 76:100+ O '77

HARVARD advocate. See College and school journalism

HARVARD University
Comes the counterrevolution. B. Rice and J. Cramer. il Psychol Today 11:56-7+ S '77
Incomplete candor; policy toward ex-Communist faculty members in the 1950s. K. L. Woodward. pors Newsweek 90:77 Jl 25 '77
Writing on the walls of ivy. A. Fadiman and J. Sedgwick. il Esquire 88:113-14 S '77

Graduate School of Public Health

Harvard under fire for mishandling grant money. B. J. Culliton. Science 197:1262 S 23 '77

John F. Kennedy School of Government

Institute of Politics

Learning to lead. M. Sheils and P. Malamud. il Newsweek 89:121 My 16 '77

Law School

Mom goes to law school. M. Smith. il Ms 6:16-18 S '77
Tears and terror; S. Turow's views. J. K. Footlick. il por Newsweek 90:76 O 17 '77

Libraries

Harvard's underground understatement: Nathan Marsh Pusey Library. E. P. Mitchell. il Am Lib 8:114-16 Mr '77
Preservation at Harvard: guidelines and goals set. Lib J 102:1230 Je 1 '77

Medical School

Harvard and Monsanto: the $23-million alliance. B. J. Culliton. pors Science 195:759-63 F 25 '77
Tosteson new Harvard dean: Chicago bitter about his leaving. B. J. Culliton. Science 195:160-2 Ja 14 '77

HARVARD University Press. See University presses

HARVEST labor. See Farm labor

HARVESTING
Russia's harvest: a battle against the elements. il U.S. News 83:60 O 31 '77
What harvesting losses cost. il Suc Farm 75:10 Je '77
See also
Vegetables—Harvesting

HARVESTING machinery
Dairy study: low-cost forage system not the best. il Suc Farm 75:no4 L20 Mr '77
Keep the combine moving. il Farm J 101:16-17 S '77
Rotary threshing engineering design of the future? L. Reichenberger. il Suc Farm 75:22-5 Je '77
Tough tomatoes; mechanical harvesting in California. P. Barnett. Progressive 41:32-6 D '77

Equipment

Planter on combine speeds up double-cropping. C. F. Marley. il Farm J 101:H2 N '77

Fires and fire prevention

Combine makes a great fire. . .unless it's yours. T. Vaughan. il Farm J 101:A4 O '77

HARVEY, Frank L.
Time of eagles. il Flying 101:276-80 S '77
HARVEY, George
Terrestrial tricks for low-water trout. S. R. Slaymaker, 2d. il por Outdoor Life 160:78-9+ S '77 *
HARVEY Hubbell Inc. See Electric industries—United States
HARVEY'S Chelsea Restaurant. See New York (city)—Hotels, restaurants, etc.
HARVEY'S Wine Museum, Bristol. See Museums—Great Britain
HARWOOD, Edwin
Pluralist press. bibl Society 15:10+ N '77
HASCHICK, A. D. and others
Water vapor maser turn-on in the HII region W3 (OH) bibl il Science 198:1153-5 D 16 '77
HASELER, Stephen
Europe: the collapse of the social democrats. Commentary 64:42-6 D '77
HASELTINE, Robert W.
Welfare costs vs. the negative income tax. Intellect 106:141-2 O '77
HASENPFEFFER. See Cookery—Game
HASHIM, G. A.
Experimental allergic encephalomyelitis in Lewis rats: chemical synthesis of disease-inducing determinant. bibl il Science 196:1219-21 Je 10 '77
HASKELL, Harry
Setting an example. il por Opera N 42:48-9 S '77
HASKELL, Molly
As the lens turns: women photograph men; excerpt from Women photograph men. il Ms 6:31-2+ S '77
Focus: reel women; excerpt from From reverence to rape: the treatment of women in the movies. il Seventeen 36:52-3 My '77
Tatum O'Neal and Jodie Foster: their combined age is 27—what is Hollywood trying to tell us? il pors Ms 5:49-51 Ap '77
(ed) See Peck, G. Gregory Peck remembers
HASKETT, James A. See Wegener, J. E. jt auth
HASKINS, Caryl P. See Hölldobler, B. jt auth
HASLAM, Gerald
What about the Okies? il Am Hist Illus 12:28-39 Ap '77
HASLANGER, Phil
Law-and-order principal. Progressive 41:45 N '77
HASLER, August B.
Was Vatican I rigged? il pors Time 110:92-3 N 14 '77 *
HASS, Hans
Quartet from far corners. H. Sutton. il por Sat R 4:47-8 F 5 '77 *
HASSAN II, King of Morocco
Africa's policeman; excerpts from interview, ed by A. De Borchgrave. por Newsweek 89:58+ My 16 '77
HASSELL, Mea
Mounting a molehill. Seventeen 36:66-7 Jl '77
HASSETT, James
New look at living together. il Psychol Today 11:82-3 D '77
—and Schwartz, G. E.
Why can't people take humor seriously? il N Y Times Mag p 103 F 6 '77
HASSETT, John J.
Bilingual teaching for newly arrived immigrant children. Clearing H 50:409-12 My '77
HASSLER, Jon
Passion of Agatha McGee; story. McCalls 104:132-3 Jl '77
HASSLER, Warren W. Jr
Perspectives on the past. Am Hist Illus 11:50 F; 12:50 Ag; 44-6 N; 37 D '77
HASSNER, Pierre
View from Europe. por U.S. News 82:48-9 Je 27 '77
HASSRICK, Peter H.
Buffalo Bill Historical Center. il Am West 14:16-29 My '77
Remington & Russell; excerpt from Way west. il Am West 14:16-29 N '77
HASTE. See Hurry
HASTIE, William Henry
Judge William H. Hastie civilian aide to the Secretary of War, 1940-1943. P. McGuire. por Negro Hist Bull 40:712-13 My '77 *
HASTINGS, Lana
One company's waste, another's wealth. il Environment 19:38-40 O '77
HASTINGS, William M.
In praise of regurgitation. Intellect 105:349-50 Ap '77
HATCH, Orrin G.
More appropriations—more unemployment. il Nat R 29:942-3 Ag 19 '77

about

5 freshman Senators who are moving into the spotlight. pors U.S. News 82:24-5 F 7 '77 *
HATCH, Robert
Films. See occassional issues of Nation
HATCH Act. See Government employees—Political activities
HATE
Sometimes I hate my husband. J. Viorst. Read Digest 110:19+ Mr '77
See also
Misogyny
HATFIELD, Henry
Achieving the impossible: Thomas Mann. Yale R 66:501-16 Je '77
HATFIELD, Mark Odom
Go ahead with neutron bomb? interview. il por U.S. News 83:25-6 Jl 25 '77
HATFIELD, Robert Sherman
How Bob Hatfield keeps Continental growing and prospering; interview. il pors Nations Bus 65:68-70+ S '77
HATFIELD, Thomas A.
Art program and the metric system. il Sch Arts 76:60-1 Mr '77
HATFIELD, W. Wilbur
W. Wilbur Hatfield—some reflections of his mind and spirit. Engl J 66:6-7 F '77
HATHAWAY, Lodene Brown
For my mother; poem. Chr Cent 94:170 F 23 '77
HATHAWAY, William Dodd
Maine: damned if you do. . . D. Holt and others. il map Newsweek 91:21 Ja 2 '78 *
HATHAWAY House Bookshop, Wellesley, Mass. See Booksellers and bookselling—Massachusetts
HATHORN, Reginald H.
Frontloader in the treetops. il por Outdoor Life 160:91+ S '77
HATS
Mad Halloween hatter comes up with a bear, an elephant, a crocodile. il Sunset 159:118-19 O '77
HATTERAS National Seashore, Cape. See Cape Hatteras National Seashore
HATTERSLEY, Ralph
Hattersley class for beginners. See issues of Popular photography
HAUCK, Eugene M.
Conservation of mass and mole relationships. il por Chemistry 50:25-6 Je '77
HAUEISEN, Kathryn
Rationale for collecting. House B 119:46+ Mr '77
HAUGE, Gabriel
Choosing strategies for business success; interview. pors Nations Bus 65:32-5 Je '77
HAUNTED houses. See Ghosts
HAUPERT, David
Making big rooms out of little ones. il Bet Hom & Gard 55:68-73 Mr '77
HAUPT, Christopher Lehmann-. See Lehmann-Haupt, C.
HAUPTMANN, Bruno Richard
We cannot be sure. Nation 224:420 Ap 9 '77 *
HAURAKI Gulf Maritime Park. See National parks and reserves—New Zealand
HAUSER, Ernest O.
Dream called Kashmir. il map Read Digest 112:164-6+ Ja '78
Tidings of comfort and joy. il Read Digest 111:27-8+ D '77
HAUSER, Glenn
DX listening (cont) Pop Electr 11:102-3 Mr; 100-1 My; 12:112-14 S; 93+ N '77
How to DX earth radio from outer space. il Pop Electr 11:37-40 Ap '77
HAUSER, Joseph
Golden fleecing of union funds. L. Velie. Read Digest 111:88-92 O '77 *
HAUSER, Philip M.
Including population problems in the curriculum. Educ Digest 42:14-16 Mr '77
HAUSMAN, Louis
Older Americans: a national resource; address; November 18, 1976. Vital Speeches 43:189-92 Ja 1 '77
HAUST, M. Daria, and others
Fat-containing uterine smooth muscle cells in toxemia: possible relevance to atherosclerosis? bibl il Science 195:1353-4 Mr 25 '77
HAVANA

Description

Cuba opens up—is it for you? il Sunset 159:30+ D '77

HAVENS, Elizabeth Maret-. See Maret-Havens, E.

HAVERFORD College, Haverford, Pa.
Bryn Mawr v. coeducation. Time 109:64 Ja 31 '77

HAVLICEK, John
Complete basketball player. H. W. Wind. New Yorker 53:86-104 Mr 28 '77 *

HAWAII
See also
Architecture, Domestic—Hawaii
Botany—Hawaii
Geology—Hawaii
Hawaii Volcanoes National Park
Hilo
Honolulu
Kahoolawe (island)
Kauai (island)
Kilauea (crater)
Kona
Maui (island)
Molokai (island)
Money—Hawaii
Oahu (island)
Opera—Hawaii
School libraries
Tourist trade—Hawaii

Description and travel

Aloha 'oe. J. Lord. il por Holiday 58:42-5+ Ap '77
Blind teens touch Hawaii via travel camp. N. Kaplan and R. Eskridge. il Camp Mag 49:14-16 Mr '77
8 paradise islands called Hawaii. R. L. Balzer. il Trav/Holiday 149:48-9+ Ja '78
Hawaii on a budget. R. S. Kane. il Ret Liv 17:36-7+ Je '77
Hawaii: the sun and fun islands. S. C. Cowley and G. C. Lubenow. il map Newsweek 91:30-3+ Ja 2 '78
Three little syllables. F. Deford. il Sports Illus 46:30-5 Ja 24 '77

Economic conditions

Paradise closed? il Forbes 120:98-9 N 15 '77

History

Bibliography

Historic Hawaii; comp by H. B. Melendy. il Am West 14:55 S '77

Industries

See also
Amfac, Inc

Politics and government

See also
Politics, Corruption in—Hawaii

Social life and customs

Viewpoint; delayed sports telecasts in Hawaii. T. Horton. Sports Illus 47:6-7 O 17 '77

HAWAII (island)
Mini-holiday. B. Jeffer. map Holiday 58:17-18+ Mr '77

HAWAII Opera Theatre. See Opera—Hawaii

HAWAII Volcanoes National Park
Volcanoes of Hawaii. D. Bush. il Nat Parks & Con Mag 51:10-12 Mr '77

HAWAIIAN cookery. See Cookery, Hawaiian

HAWAIIAN seals. See Seals (animals)

HAWES, Diana
Oil dollars go into music. por Hi Fi 27:MA33+ N '77

HAWK, Richard L.
Onions tie the gardening year together. Org Gard & Farm 24:72-3 O '77

HAWKEN, William R.
Making big ones out of little ones: current trends in micrographics. il Lib J 102:2127-31 O 15 '77

HAWKES, Nigel
Science in Europe (cont) Science 195:659-60, 962-3; 196:146-7, 636-7, 1067-8; 197:141-3, 1167-9; 198:709-12, 1230-1 F 18, Mr 11, Ap 8, My 6, Je 3, Jl 8, S 16, N 18, D 23 '77

HAWKING, Stephen W.
Quantum mechanics of black holes; with biographical sketch. il Sci Am 236:16, 34-40 bibl(p 132) Ja '77

about

Out from under the cosmic censor: Stephen Hawking's black holes. O. Overbye. il por Sky & Tel 54:84-9+ Ag '77 *
Peering into black holes. P. Gwynne. por Newsweek 89:78-9 Ja 24 '77 *
Science's now cloudy crystal ball. F. R. Haig. America 136:192-3 Mr 5 '77 *

HAWKINS, Robert
Nets sink, Bubbles rises. K. Hannon. il Sports Illus 46:56+ Mr 7 '77 *

HAWKS
Hawk is flying. H. Crews. il Esquire 87:24+ Je '77
Keeping track of hawks. D. R. Zimmerman. il Audubon 79:2-12 Jl '77
This raptor keeps a low profile; red-shouldered hawk. F. Hamerstrom. il Nat Wildlife 15:20-5 Ag '77
Winter hawk; rough-legged hawks. J. F. Traynor. il por Conservationist 32:2-4 N '77
See also
Falcons

HAWN, Shirley
Shaggy mane—the safe fall mushroom. il Field & S 81:150 Mr '77

HAWRYLSHYN, George
Perspective on development: Brazil and the United States, 1776. il Américas 29:12-13 My '77

HAWTHORN Books, Inc-Allen, W. H, Publishers Inc merger. See Publishers and publishing—Acquisitions and mergers

HAWTHORNE, Calif.

Police

See Police—California

HAWTHORNE Studies in personnel management. See Personnel management

HAY, Jess Thomas
Democrats' new money man. por Bus W p 128 Mr 21 '77 *

HAY, John
Menhaden in Maine. il Liv Wildn 40:48-9 O '76

HAY
See also
Feeds—Hay

Drying

Solar drying makes better hay. C. F. Marley. il Farm J 101:36 N '77

Marketing

Hay growers get serious about marketing. Farm J 101:44 N '77
Top dollar for your hay. D. Braun. il Farm J 101:M1 Mr '77
With this California co-op. . .12 salesmen sell your hay; San Joaquin Valley Hay Growers Association. D. Braun. Farm J 101:J4 Ag '77

HAY boxes. See Fireless cookers

HAY cooperatives. See Agriculture, Cooperative

HAY fever
Summer colds—allergies in disguise? V. J. Fontana. il Mademoiselle 83:60 Je '77
What's good for hay fever? il Consumer Rep 42:342-5 Je '77

HAY handling
Baled hay feeding losses. il Farm J 101:Beef 10+ F '77

HAYAKAWA, Samuel Ichiyé
From soup and salad to suppleness. por Sat Eve Post 249:39 Mr '77
Mr Hayakawa goes to Washington. il Harpers 256:39-43 Ja '78

HAYDÉE, Marcia
Keeper of the flame. H. Saal. il pors Newsweek 89:81 Je 27 '77 *

HAYDEN, Robert Earl
Comment. W. Logan. Poetry 130:226-8 Jl '77 *
Robert Hayden poet laureate. H. J. Scarupa. il pors Ebony 33:78-80+ Ja '78 *

HAYDEN, Sterling
PW interviews; ed by J. F. Baker. por Pub W 211:242-3 Ja 24 '77

HAYDEN, Thomas Emmett
Fonda at forty. A. Harmetz. il por McCalls 105:104-5+ Ja '78 *
Port Huron to Santa Barbara. K. Lynch. Nat R 29:1112 S 30 '77 *

HAYDEN, Trudy R.
Rights of parents and children. Current 190:24-31 F '77

HAYDEN, William
Funny you should ask. por Forbes 120:64 Ag 1 '77 *

HAYDN, Franz Joseph
Bass part in Haydn's early string quartets. J. Webster. bibl il Mus Q 63:390-424 Jl '77 *
Cello concertos in C major and D major conducted by P. Makanowitzky. P. L. Althouse. Am Rec G 41:34 D '77 *
Haydn's mad knight; Orlando Paladino. R. V. Lucano. il Am Rec G 41:16-17 N '77 *
Haydn's Orlando Paladino: a heroic-comic delight; Philips recording. P. H. Lang. il Hi Fi 27:107 D '77 *
L'infedeltà delusa; Hungaroton recording. R. V. Lucano. Am Rec G 40:31-2 O '77 *
L'infedeltà delusa; La vera costanza; recordings by Hungarton and Philips. A. Porter. il Hi Fi 27:83-4+ Ag '77 *
Piano trios H xv no. 13 in C minor, no. 16 in D, no. 17 in F. E. Belov. il Am Rec G 40:22-3 My '77 *
Piano works, v 1, R. Buchbinder soloist. R. Kammerer. Am Rec G 40:36 S '77 *
Symphonies; Barenboim and Previn discs. J. W. Barker. Am Rec G 40:22-3 Jl '77 *
La vera costanza. R. V. Lucano. il Am Rec G 40:14-16 Ag '77 *

HAYES, Denis
Biological sources of commercial energy; excerpt from Rays of hope. bibl BioScience 27:540-6 Ag '77
about
Academics urged to join Sun Day observance. L. J. Carter. Science 198:472 N 4 '77 *
HAYES, Harold Thomas Pace
PW interviews: ed by J. F. Baker. por Pub W 211:10-11 F 7 '77
Pursuit of reason. il pors N Y Times Mag p21-3+ Je 12 '77
Push Pin conspiracy. il N Y Times Mag p 19-22 Mr 6 '77
HAYES, James L.
Want to be a better boss? interview. il por U.S. News 82:68-70 Mr 21 '77
HAYES, John P.
Curious case of an IRS agent. Nation 225:17-18 Jl 2 '77
Man who played Santa Claus. il Good H 185: 118-19+ D '77
New York newsletter. See issues of Writer's digest
HAYES, Samuel L. 3d
Capital commitments and the high cost of money. bibl f Harvard Bus R 55:155-61 My '77
HAYES, Wayne Woodrow
Explosive Woody Hayes. J. Brondfield. il Read Digest 111:98-102 S '77 *
HAYES, Will
Totally at the whim of the elements; excerpt from The complete ballooning book. il Sci Digest 82:11-14 N '77
HAYES, Woody. See Hayes, W. W.
HAYFLICK, Leonard
Biology of aging; with biographical sketch. Natur Hist 86:4, 22+ bibl(p 116) Ag '77
HAYHURST, Elizabeth
Art room mural. il Sch Arts 76:13 Je '77
HAYLAGE. See Silage
HAYMAN, Jane
Kate, 10 days old; poem. Nation 224:90 Ja 22 '77
HAYNES, A. Ford, Jr, and Garner, A. E.
Sharing administrative decision making. bibl Clearing H 51:53-7 O '77
HAYNES, H. C.
H. C. Haynes: barber & inventor. G. Gray. bibl il Negro Hist Bull 40:751-2 S '77 *
HAYNES, John R. See Vanderweil, G. it auth
HAYS, Anne M.
Boats in blue: sailing at the U.S. Naval Academy. Yachting 141:158+ Je '77
Louise Burke. il pors Yachting 142:74-5 Jl '77
Tank-testing Enterprise. il Yachting 141:66-8 F '77
HAYS, James D. and others
Variations in the earth's orbit: pacemaker of the ice ages. bibl il Science 194:1121-32; 198: 529-30 D 10 '76, N 4 '77
HAYS, Timothy, and others
Patron is not the public. bibl il Lib J 102:1813-18 S 15 '77
HAYS-Kiser House, Antioch. See Historic houses, sites, etc.—Tennessee
HAYSTACK Mountain School of Crafts, Deer Isle, Me. See Art schools
HAYUM, Walter
Protechniques. E. Meyers. il por Pop Phot 80:68+ Ap '77 *
HAYWARD, Brooke
Brooke Hayward talks about her children; interview, ed by C. M. Dobrish. il pors Parents Mag 52:52-3 O '77
Haywire; excerpt. il por Ladies Home J 94:110-11 Jl '77
Hollywood hay days—every parent a star; excerpt from Haywire. il pors Vogue 167:224-7+ Mr '77
about
Children of paradise. P. Prescott. il pors Newsweek 89:76-7 Mr 14 '77 *
Spoiled children. A. Sarris. il por Harpers 254: 77-80 Je '77 *
HAYWARD, John
Carolingian fairy tale. Vasari. Art N 76:33 N '77 *
HAYWARD, Leland
Children of paradise. P. S. Prescott. il pors Newsweek 89:76-7 Mr 14 '77 *
Hollywood hay days—every parent a star; excerpt from Haywire. B. Hayward. il pors Vogue 167:224-7+ Mr '77 *
HAYWARD Annual. See Art, British—Exhibitions
HAYWOOD, L. Julian
How to survive a heart attack. Intellect 105: 427-8 Je '77
HAZARDOUS substances
See also
Chemicals
Disposal
Oregon desert graveyard for leaking herbicide wastes. P. L. Fradkin. Audubon 79:127 Ja '77
Wastes endure. J. Crossland. bibl il Environment 19:6-13 Je '77
See also
Radioactive waste disposal

HAZELTON, Nika Standen
Delectations. See occasional issues of National review
Sicilian variations. il N Y Times Mag p67 F 13 '77
Surprise of Sicily. il Harp Baz 110:20+ Mr '77
HAZLITT, Gordon J.
Los Angeles (cont) Art N 76:89-90 Ja; 104 My; 117+ S; 91-2 O '77
Problem solving in solitude. il por Art N 76:76-9 Ja '77
HAZO, Samuel
Statutes from a January river; poem. Nation 224:695 Je 4 '77
about
Comment. R. Holland. Poetry 129:290-2 F '77 *
Literary licentiousness. G. Lyons. Nation 224: 378-9 Mr 26 '77 *
HAZZARD, Shirley
Crush on Doctor Dance; story. New Yorker 53: 36-44 S 26 '77
HEACOCK, Anne M. and Agranoff, B. W.
Clockwise growth of neurites from retinal explants. bibl il Science 198:64-6 O 7 '77
HEAD, Bessie
Collector of treasures; story. Ms 5:58-61 Je '77
HEAD, Gwen
Not sleeping; poem. Poetry 129:263 F '77
HEAD, Howard
Howard Head strikes again. por Forbes 119:76 Je 1 '77 *
HEAD, K. Maynard
Why not write a newspaper column? Chr Today 21:29 Ag 26 '77
HEAD
See also
Face
Transplantation
See Brain—Transplantation
HEAD in art
About faces: the new work of Peter Campus. R. Smith. il Art in Am 65:85-7 Mr '77
Throw a head. M. Sapiro. il Sch Arts 77:20-7 O '77
See also
Portrait drawing
HEAD Start, Project. See Project Head Start
HEADACHE
Anti-migraine diet. J. B. Brainard. Harp Baz 111:159+ N '77
Battle against migraine. il Time 110:84-5 N 7 '77
Headaches: the causes & the cures; interview, ed by P. Lehmann. J. W. Lance. Harp Baz 111:158-9+ N '77
Help for your headaches. il Changing T 31:45-7 Mr '77
How to handle a persistent headache. M. P. Scott. Bet Hom & Gard 55:52+ O '77
Managing headache. A. Anderson, Jr. il N Y Times Mag p48+ My 8 '77
Migraine headaches. A. Frank and S. Frank Mademoiselle 83:22 Jl '77
Nerves are a real headache. D. Rice. Harp Baz 110:124+ Mr '77
Preventing-and curing-headaches. W. A. Nolen. McCalls 104:60+ S '77
HEADBOARDS. See Beds
HEADPHONES
How headphones are tested. J. Hirsch. il Pop Electr 11:26+ My '77
Julian Hirsch audio reports:
Koss model K/145 stereo headphones. il Pop Electr 12:36 Jl '77
Sennheiser model HDI 434 infrared headphones. il Pop Electr 11:32+ My '77
New equipment reports:
B&O's smartly styled headset; model U-70. il Hi Fi 28:55 Ja '78
Koss ESP/10 submerges the ears in music. il Hi Fi 27:41 Ag '77
Stax SR-44 sounds like a dream. il Hi Fi 27:54-5 Mr '77
Superex TRL-77—a comfortable way to listen. il Hi Fi 27:39 D '77
Stereo headphones. il Consumer Rep 42:224-6 D '77
HEADS (automobile engines) See Automobile engines—Cylinders
HEALEY, Denis Winston
Bittersweets for Britain. L. Langway and A. Collings. il por Newsweek 89:87 Ap 11 '77 *
Britain's turnaround? R. Carroll and A. Collins. il por Newsweek 90:56+ N 7 '77 *
Early Christmas. il por Time 110:114 N 7 '77 *
HEALING, Divine. See Faith cure
HEALING, Mental. See Mental healing
HEALTH
Alert. See issues of Family health incorporating Today's health
Ask the doctor; questions and answers. M. Fishbein. por Fam Health 9:8 Ja; 8 F; 8 Mr; 10 Ap; 8 My '77
Ask the doctor; questions and answers. R. L. Landau and C. Landau. See issues of Family health incorporating Today's health, June 1977-

HEALTH—*Continued*
Autumn ought-to's. S. Mennear-Dubas. il Fam Health 9:28-9 S '77
Beauty nightlife. il Vogue 167:268-73+ N '77
Doctoring isn't just for doctors; self-care. R. C. Yeager. Read Digest 111:237-8+ D '77
Doctor's 20-day pleasure program for health; interview, ed by C. Seebohm. A. Ulene. il por House & Gard 150:24+ Ja '78
Find your best self by using more sense; excerpt from Secrets of The Golden Door. D. S. Mazzanti. il Fam Health 9:36-9 D '77
Good health is a family affair. il Ebony 32:107-8+ My '77
Guide to good family health; symposium, ed by W. W. McCrory. il Parents Mag 52:65-73+ N '77
Health. See issues of Better homes and gardens
Health (cont) M. P. Scott. Bet Hom & Gard 55:84+ F '77
Health. J. B. Smith. Nat R 29:786-7 Jl 8 '77
Health. M. Weber. See issues of Vogue
Health & medicine. P. Lehmann. Harp Baz 110:186-9+ S '77
Health, psychology, sex; questions and answers. R. Tyson and M. C. Tyson. pors House & Gard 149:36+ F; 50 Ap; 50+ Je '77
Health/sex/psychology; questions and answers. M. C. Tyson. por House & Gard 149:72+ O; 66+ N '77
How to beat the elements. il Seventeen 36:144-7 N '77
How to stop risking your life; with health quiz. K. L. Woodward. McCalls 105:154+ O '77
Latest in health and medicine (cont) U.S. News 82:84 F 21; 59 Mr 21; 82 Ap 25; 78 Je 6; 83:60 Jl 11; 39 Ag 22; 86 S 26; 63 O 31; 82 D 5 '77
Medical mailbox; questions and answers. C. SerVaas. See issues of Saturday evening post
Nation's health today. R. M. Scheffler and L. Paringer. Cur Hist 72:193-5+ My '77
Questions for the doctor. W. R. Felix, Jr. por Consumers Res Mag 60:41 S; 41 N; 38 D '77
Responsibility for health. J. H. Knowles. Science 198:1103 D 16 '77
Should US scientists trade data with USSR? symposium. il Sci Digest 81:30-7+ Je '77
Surefire ways to ruin your summer vacation. J. Mayer. il Fam Health 9:22-4 Ag '77
22 myths & realities about your body. C. Dreifus. il Seventeen 36:125-9+ Je '77
Your family's health. Consumers Res Mag 60:97-103 O '77
See also
Aged—Care and hygiene
Blacks—Health and hygiene
Dancers—Health and hygiene
Diet
Environmental health
Executives—Health and hygiene
Exercise
Hygiene
Longevity
Nutrition
Public health
Sleep
Women—Health and hygiene

Information services
Health info for all; San Diego meet. W. Maina and B. French. Lib J 102:1552-3 Ag '77

HEALTH, Mental. See Mental hygiene
HEALTH and weather. See Weather—Mental and physiological effects
HEALTH care. See Medical care
HEALTH care costs. See Medical care, Cost of
HEALTH care policy. See Medical policy
HEALTH centers. See Health facilities
HEALTH clinics. See Health facilities
HEALTH clubs
Don't join a health spa! Until you read this. A. Rosenblum. il Good H 185:211 S '77
Tough is good for you; strenuous-exercise clubs; New York. A. Penney. il N Y Times Mag p50+ Ag 14 '77
HEALTH discrimination in employment. See Discrimination in employment
HEALTH education
See also
Health workers—Training
Mental hygiene—Study and teaching
Physical education and training
HEALTH, Education and Welfare, Department of. See United States—Health, Education and Welfare, Department of
HEALTH examinations. See Physical examinations
HEALTH facilities
Chronic pain; clinics. E. H. McCleary. il Fam Health 9:26-9+ Ag '77
Come-and-go surgery. il Time 110:96 O 10 '77
Health facilities in the United States. D. P. Rice. bibl f il Cur Hist 72:211-14+ My '77
Now, surgery at discount rates; surgical centers. il U.S. News 83:73 Jl 18 '77
See also
Birth control clinics
Burn care units
Hospitals
Mental health centers

Finance
Unhealthy state of coalfield health care; 50 clinics. Bus W p38-9 Ag 15 '77

HEALTH fads. See Medical delusions
HEALTH insurance. See Insurance, Health
HEALTH maintenance organizations. See Insurance, Health—United States
HEALTH news. See Medical news
HEALTH planning
Local rein on health costs; Central Ohio River Valley Association for Health Planning & Resource Development. il Bus W p 114+ O 31 '77
HEALTH quizzes. See Information tests
HEALTH records. See Medical records
HEALTH Research Group. See Consumer protection
HEALTH resorts, watering places, etc.
Beauty now; spas. il Vogue 167:68 Ag '77
But it's always hot-spring time in the Rockies. C. Brown. il Smithsonian 8:90-7 bibl(p 161) N '77
Energy blitz; health and exercise programs at the Institute for Environmental Stress and California spas. M. R. C. Berg. il Mademoiselle 83:180-7 Ap '77
Feast yourself slim; food served at The Greenhouse health resort, Texas. il House & Gard 149:102 Jl '77
Feel good food; diet menu at Rancho la Puerta health resort. il House & Gard 149:173-5+ My '77
Shape-up at a spa retreat. il Harp Baz 110:134-6 O '77
Toughest spa in America: The Ashram in Calabasas, Calif. il Vogue 167:126-31 Jl '77
See also
Abano Terme, Italy
HEALTH Services Administration. See United States—Health, Education and Welfare, Department of—Health Services Administration
HEALTH Systems Agencies. See Health planning
HEALTH workers
Fast treatment keeps patients alive; Dallas Fire Department paramedics. il Am City & County 92:64 Ja '77
Health employment and the Nation's health. C. E. Bishop. bibl f Cur Hist 72:207-10+ My '77
New, fast help for the injured; paramedic teams in L.A. County. M. Spiegel. il Mech Illus 73:56+ O '77
Occupational mobility of health workers. P. Wash. bibl il M Labor R 100:25-9 My '77
Paraprofessionals in a multiservice community mental health center. M. B. Ahmed and A. Birenbaum. il Intellect 106:149-51 O '77

Training
Programming mental health care for the world of work. S. H. Akabas and S. Bellinger. il MH 61:4-8 Spr '77
To the rescue; sex discrimination in education of paramedic L. Knop. G. D. Miklowitz. il pors Seventeen 36:102 Je '77

HEALY, David
Make your own astrophotographs. il Pop Phot 81:110-11+ O '77
HEALY, George Peter Alexander
G.P.A. Healy and his Louisiana portraits. V. L. Glasgow. bibl il Antiques 111:1204-9 Je '77 •
HEALY, John, family
Healy sisters—clues to diabetes. W. Stockton. il N Y Times Mag p88+ Je 12 '77
HEALY, Paul F.
(ed) See Wall, L. A. S. My sister, Rosalynn
HEALY, Timothy S.
Ignatian heritage for today's college. America 137:304-6 N 5 '77
HEANEY, Seamus
Pigeon shoot; poem. New Yorker 52:34 Ja 31 '77

about
Comment R. B. Shaw. Poetry 129:236-9 Ja '77 •
HEANY, Donald F. See Hobbs, J. M. jt auth
HEARD, William H.
Marxism as a political religion. il Nat R 29:1427+ D 9 '77
HEARD Museum, Phoenix, Ariz. See Indians of North America—Museums
HEARING
How to keep your sense of hearing. L. David. il Mech Illus 73:102+ Ap '77
See also
Audiometry
Ear
Echolocation (physiology)

HEARING (animals)
Amplitude spectrum representation in the Doppler-shifted-CF processing area of the auditory cortex of the mustache bat. N. Suga. bibl il Science 196:64-7 Ap 1 '77
See also
Ear (animals)

HEARING (birds)
Receptive fields of auditory neurons in the owl. E. I. Knudsen and others. bibl il Science 198: 1278-80 D 23 '77

HEARING aids
Hearing aids. Consumer Rep 42:320-1 D '77
How helpful are hearing aids? Bet Hom & Gard 55:84+ N '77
New protection for hearing-aid buyers. N. G. Rollins. Good H 185:206 Ag '77

HEARINGS, Legislative. See Government investigations

HEARN, Michael Patrick
Second look. il Horn Bk 53:563-6 O '77

HEARNE, Betsy. See Sutherland, Z. B. jt auth

HEARON, Shelby
Treasured offerings from Becky and Dow Patterson. il pors Redbook 150:91+ D '77

HEARST, James
Calendar's mischief; poem. America 137:161 S 24 '77

HEARST, John Jr
Fighting chair. See issues of Motor boating & sailing

HEARST, Patricia Campbell
Patty Hearst: my prisoner, my friend; excerpt from My prisoner; ed by T. Berkman. J. Jimenez. pors Ladies Home J 94:51-8 S '77 *
Patty Hearst: the way it really was—and is; ed by P. Battelle. J. A. Johnson. il por Good H 184:104-5+ Mr '77 *
Patty today. L. Fosburgh. il por N Y Times Mag p 19-22+ Ap 3 '77 *
Real story of Patty Hearst; ed by P. Battelle. J. A. Johnson. il pors Good H 184:94-7+ F '77 *

HEART
See also
Cardiopulmonary system
Pulse

Abnormalities and deformities
Conquering childhood heart disease; views of experts on surgery for congenital heart defects. M. A. Poust. Parents Mag 52:16+ O '77

Analysis and chemistry
Adrenergic stimulation of taurine transport by the heart. R. Huxtable and J. Chubb. bibl il Science 198:409-11 O 28 '77

Arteries
See Arteries

Diseases
Aging heart: changes in function and response to drugs. G. B. Kolata. Science 195:166-7 Ja 14 '77
Cholesterol ... is just one heart threat. N. Lyon. il Sci Digest 81:28-31 Ap '77
Experimental infarct sizing using computer processing and a three-dimensional model. M. Lewis and others. bibl il Science 197:167-9 Jl 8 '77
Heart attack emergency... D. Seim. il Farm J 101:P6-7 N '77
Heart disease: new ways to reduce the risk. il Bus W p 135-7+ O 17 '77
How to survive a heart attack. L. J. Haywood. Intellect 105:427-8 Je '77
Latest in fight against heart disease; interview. H. P. Dustan. il por U.S. News 83:83-4+ N 14 '77
Progress in coping with heart disease. il U.S. News 82:64 Ja 31 '77
Stress and the heart. R. F. DeBusk. Intellect 106:190 N '77
Tobacco protein may lead to heart disease. Sci N 112:214 O 1 '77
See also
Cardiacs

Nutritional aspects
Failed hypothesis; low-fat, low-cholesterol diet to reduce incidence of coronary heart disease. Sci Am 237:86-7 D '77
Low cholesterol diet: it won't prevent heart attacks. H. J. Johnson. il Duns R 109:93-4+ Mr '77
New study casts doubts on high-fiber diets effectiveness in preventing heart disease. il Ret Liv 17:13 Ja '77

Personal narratives
How to survive a heart attack; personal narratives of celebrities. S. W. Olds. il Fam Health 9:34-7 Ja '77

Prevention
AMIS trial: can aspirin prevent heart attacks? J. L. Marx. Science 196:1075 Je 3 '77
Alcohol: a heart disease preventive? Sci N 112:102-3 Ag 13 '77
Clinical trials: methods and ethics are debated. G. B. Kolata. Science 198:1127-31 D 16 '77
Coronary curb; effects of exercise; study by R. Paffenbarger. Time 110:80 D 12 '77
Exercise and your heart. il Consumer Rep 42: 254-8 My '77
Hard work and healthy hearts; Heart attacks go down as you go up. J. Gaylin. Psychol Today 11:25-6 Jl '77
How you can make your heart healthier. M. P. Scott and D. Sonnenburg. il Bet Hom & Gard 55:10+ O '77
Young at heart. J. Powell. il Sci Digest 82:66-9 N '77

Psychological aspects
Heart disease and life stress; identical twin studies by Einar Kringlen. Sci N 112:166 S 10 '77

Therapy
Liposome accumulation in regions of experimental myocardial infarction. V. J. Caride and B. L. Zaret. bibl il Science 198:735-8 N 18 '77

Muscle
Aging heart: changes in function and response to drugs. G. B. Kolata. Science 195:166-7 Ja 14 '77
Heart: a target organ for estradiol. W. E. Stumpf and others. bibl il Science 196:319-21 Ap 15 '77
Possible cyclic nucleotide regulation of calcium mediating myocardial contraction. A. Schwartz and others. bibl il Science 195:982+ Mr 11 '77

Rhythm
See Heart beat

Surgery
Bloodless surgery saves heart victim. Sci N 112:5 Jl 2 '77
Christiaan Barnard: South Africa's premier surgeon; interview, ed by W. Bradley. C. N. Barnard. il por Sat Eve Post 249:62-4 Mr '77
Conquering childhood heart disease; views of experts on surgery for congenital heart defects. M. A. Proust. Parents Mag 52:16+ O '77
Is this cut necessary? coronary-bypass operations. Newsweek 90:102 O 3 '77
New freeways for the heart; coronary bypass performed by R. Mamiya. G. Cant. il por Time 109:55-6 My 9 '77
Twin miracles; open-heart surgery for D'Alessio twins. E. Keiffer. il Good H 186:75+ Ja '78

Transplantation
Baboon heart. J. Seligmann and P. Young-Husband. il por Newsweek 90:60 Jl 4 '77

HEART beat
Cardiac pacemaking: an obligatory role of catecholamines? G. R. Pollack. bibl il Science 196. 731-8 My 13 '77
See also
Pacemaker, Artificial (heart)
Pulse

HEART defects. See Heart—Abnormalities and deformities

HEART diseases. See Heart—Diseases

HEART muscle. See Heart—Muscle

HEART patients. See Cardiacs

HEART rated exercises. See Exercise

HEARTWORM disease. See Dogs—Diseases and pests

HEAT
See also
Hot weather
Temperature—Control
Waste heat

Physiological effects
How to handle hot weather emergencies. M. P. Scott. il Bet Hom & Gard 55:78+ Ag '77
See also
Heatstroke

Therapeutic use
See Thermotherapy

Transmission
How to choose a heat sink. T. Zwaska. il Pop Electr 11:89 Je '77

HEAT collectors, Solar. See Solar collectors

HEAT detectors. See Detectors

HEAT detectors, Infrared. See Detectors, Infrared

HEAT exhaustion. See Heatstroke

HEAT in animals. See Estrus

HEAT production (biology) See Temperature, Animal and human

HEAT pumps
David and Cynthia Edney: solar-assisted heat pump. E. Moran. il Pop Sci 211:84+ O '77
Heat pump appears to do the impossible. il Sunset 159:126-8 N '77
Heat pump makes a comeback. il Mech Illus 73: 56+ Je '77
Pumping heat; Carrier Corp's new product. il Forbes 119:75-6 Mr 15 '77

HEAT resistant alloys. Seee Alloys

HEAT sensors. See Detectors

HEAT sinks. See Heat—Transmission

HEAT stroke. See Heatstroke
HEAT therapy. See Thermotherapy
HEAT transmission. See Heat—Transmission
HEATERS
Camping equipment: stoves and catalytic heaters. il Consumers Res Mag 60:26-31 Jl '77
Get more heat by burning wood. il Pop Mech 148:138+ S '77
Portable electric heaters. Consumer Rep 42:291-4 D '77
See also
Water heaters
HEATH, Aloise Buckley
It says here. . . Nat R 30:30-1 Ja 6 '78
HEATH, Barrie
There's a lot of G.K.N. in Europe's cars. R. Ball. il por Fortune 95:156-61+ Ja '77 *
HEATH, Donald F. and others
Solar proton event: influence on stratospheric ozone. bibl il Science 197:886-9 Ag 26 '77
HEATH, Jennifer
Art on the range. il Ms 5:43+ My '77
HEATH, Susan
Born again in Darien. Sat R 4:14-15 S 17 '77
HEATH hens
Track on the beach; efforts to identify birds as either sharp-tailed grouse or heath hens. P. Matthiessen. il Audubon 79:68-9+ Mr '77
HEATHROW International Airport. See London—Airports
HEATING
A-frame energy saver; Taos, N.M. il Mech Illus 73:70 O '77
Fall warm-up: home improvement & decorating guide. B. Niles. il Am Home 80:77+ S '77
Get set for winter. il Changing T 31:6-8 N '77
Heating the home. il Consumers Res Mag 60:130-5 O '77
How five families save money on home heating. il Good H 185:270+ N '77
How to keep warm for pennies. . .Japanese style. W. Shurtleff. il Org Gard & Farm 24:120-2+ Mr '77
1977 homeowner's guide to saying energy and money. M. Cubisino. il McCalls 104:121-8 S '77
Prospects for district heating in the United States. J. Karkheck and others. bibl il Science 195:948-55 Mr 11 '77
Remodeling notebook; windows and heat loss. J. H. Ingersoll. House B 119:22 Ag '77
10 ways to conserve heat. M. Mandell. il Mech Illus 73:68-9+ O '77
Wind power for home heating. E. F. Lindsley. il Pop Sci 211:62+ N '77
See also
Fireplaces
Hospitals—Heating and ventilation
Insulation (heat)
School buildings—Heating and ventilation
Solar heating
Thermostats
Ventilation

Costs

How to cut those costly home heating bills. J. H. Ingersoll. House B 119:82-3 S '77
HEATING equipment
Air deflectors improve register efficiency. M. Philips. il Pop Sci 210:138 My '77
Home fuel-saving devices. Consumer Rep 42:270-2 D '77
See also
Furnaces
Gas burners
Heat pumps
Oil burners
Radiators
Stoves
HEATON, Herbert
Inflation protection for retired employees. il Harvard Bus R 55:8+ S '77
HEATSTROKE
Heat exhaustion and sunstroke. A. Frank and S. Frank. Mademoiselle 83:87 Ag '77
HEATTER, Maida
Cookie wise and pound foolish; excerpt from Maida Heatter's book of great cookies. il N Y Times Mag p 134+ S 25 '77
HEAVEN
Destination heaven. S. E. Wirt. il Chr Today 21:10-12 Ag 12 '77
HEBBLETHWAITE, Frank P.
Dramatists in revolt. il Américas 29:6-9 Mr '77
HEBBLETHWAITE, Peter
Anglican/R. C. agreement? Commonweal 104:106-8 F 18 '77
Christian-Marxist dialogue. il New Cath World 220:140-4 My '77
HEBERLING, R. L. and others
Oncornavirus: isolation from a squirrel monkey (saimiri sciureus) lung culture. bibl il Science 195:289-92 Ja 21 '77
HEBREW literature
See also
Talmud

HECHINGER, Fred Michael
Education now. Sat R 5:50 O 15 '77
Full speed backward. Sat R 4:14 My 28 '77
Reappraising the open classroom. Sat R 4:6+ Mr 19 '77
School without schools. il Sat R 4:12+ Ap 30 '77; Same abr. Educ Digest 43:10-13 O '77
U.S. literacy level not bad; excerpts from address. il Intellect 106:104-5 S '77
HECHT, Anthony
Sestina d'inverno; poem. Mademoiselle 85:51 F '77

about

Comment. R. Howard. Poetry 131:103-6 N '77 *
HECHT, Ben
Caballero of the law; story. Sat Eve Post 249:34-6 S '77
HECHT, Ernest
Ernest Hecht, of London's Souvenir Press, a pocket publisher with best selling ideas. H. R. Lottman. il por Pub W 211:48-9 Mr 28 '77 *
HECHT, George Joseph
More help needed for children. por Parents Mag 52:32+ F '77
HECHT, Julie
Love is blind; story. Harpers 255:73-8 O '77
HECKLER Jonellen
Argument between siblings; poem. Ladies Home J 94:64 Jl '77
Confession to a daughter; poem. Ladies Home J 94:59 Ag '77
HECKMAN, Don
A-team west: L.A.'s most valuable players. il Hi Fi 27:142-7 Jl '77
Studio circuit. il Hi Fi 27:134-6 F '77
Tom Oberheim's magical music machines. il Hi Fi 27:127-30 Ap '77
—and Wilson, J. S.
Jazz. Hi Fi 27:144 Mr; 120 My; 142 S '77
HEDGES, William D.
Are 40 percent of our children really unsatisfactory? bibl il Clearing H 50:417-22 My '77; Same abr. Educ Digest 43:31-3 O '77
HEDGES
Dense screen—only 4 years old; Dodonaea viscosa. il Sunset 159:270 O '77

Pruning

See Pruning
HEDGING (finance)
Cash in early on hedge sales? corn. Suc Farm 75:22 O '77
Futures for you? Corn hedge. D. Seim. Farm J 101:24-6+ Ap '77
His bank meets margin calls; swine contract hedging at First American Bank, Canton, S. D. D. Seim. il Farm J 101:Hog 7+ Je '77
Margin call headaches; broker-lender-farmer hedging account. Suc Farm 75:9 O '77
Protect feeding profits with hedges? W. Kester. Farm J 101:Beef 16 S '77
Steer clear of trading troubles; views of B. Kovacs. J. McNabney. por Farm J 101:Beef 16 Ag '77
This banker talks farmer to city brokers. il Suc Farm 75:37 My '77
HEDIN, Mary
Lovelier than roses on the vine. McCalls 104:137+ My '77
HEDIN, R. S.
Build a digital camera shutter timer. il Pop Electr 12:59+ Ag '77
HEDLUND, Laurence, and others
Melatonin: daily cycle in plasma and cerebrospinal fluid of calves. bibl il Science 195:686-7 F 18 '77
HEDRICH, Vivian
Rainbow in industrial arts. Educ Digest 42:53-6 F '77
Winning play at home base. il Am Educ 13:27-30 Jl '77
HEENAN, David A.
Global cities of tomorrow. bibl f Harvard Bus R 55:79-92 My '77
HEENAN, John Carmel
Fight on! And on and on; excerpt from The great prize fight. A. Lloyd. il pors Sports Illus 47:54-60+ Jl 25 '77 *
HEEZEN, Bruce C. and Rawson, Michael
Visual observations of the sea floor subduction line in the middle-America trench. bibl il Science 196:423-6 Ap 22 '77
HEFNER, Hugh Marston
Middle-aged rabbit. il por Forbes 119:29-32 Je 1 '77 *
HEIDEGGER, Martin
Martin Heidegger: in memoriam. W. J. Richardson. Commonweal 104:16-18 Ja 7 '77 *
HEIDELBERGER, Cecil
Time to retire. il por Time 109:42 My 23 '77 *
HEIDEN, Eric
Call him Kid Cool. K. Moore. por Sports Illus 47:56-8+ D 19 '77 *
HEIFERS
Forget about weight gains on heifers? il Farm J 101:Beef 8 My '77
New ways to get heifers bred earlier. W. Kester. il Farm J 100:LK3 D '76

HEIFERS—*Continued*

Feeding

Heifers feed as good as steers? il Farm J 101: Beef 5 F; LK4 Mr '77

HEIFETZ, Daniel
Daniel Heifetz, violin; New York bow at Tully Hall. por Hi Fi 27:MA24 S '77 *

HEIFETZ, Jascha
Heifetz chamber music collections. E. Belov. Am Rec G 41:40-1 D '77 *
Heifetz Piatigorsky concerts; recording. E. Belov. Am Rec G 40:48-9 F '77 *

HEIGHT of man. See Stature

HEILBRON, John L.
J. J. Thomson and the Bohr atom. il pors Phys Today 30:23-4+ Ap '77

HEILEMAN, G, Brewing Company. See Brewing industry

HEILES, Carl
Structure of the interstellar medium; with biographical sketch. il Sci Am 238:12, 74-84 Ja '78

HEILMANN, Caroline
Creative ways of book reporting. SLJ 23:49 F '77

HEIM, S. Mark
Divine principle and the Second Advent. por Chr Cent 94:448-51 My 11 '77

HEIMAEY (island)
Vestmannaeyjar: up from the ashes. N. Grove. il map Nat Geog 151:690-701 My '77

HEIMAN, Grover
Business: a look ahead. See issues of Nation's business

HEIMANN, John Gaines
Big showdown over banker Bert. il por Time 110:19-20 Ag 22 '77 *
Closer watch on bank takeovers. por Bus W p29 Ag 22 '77 *
Lance affair: an official report gives an inside look at banking. il por U.S. News 83:62-4 Ag 29 '77 *
What the report says. M. Ruby and others. il Newsweek 90:18-19 Ag 29 '77 *

HEIMLICH, Henry J.
Four minutes to live. . .this maneuver can save you. il por Sci Digest 82:66-7 Jl '77 *
Hug of life. E. Keerdoja. il por Newsweek 89: 12 My 30 '77 *

HEIMLICH maneuver. See Choking

HEINDEL, Richard H.
International affairs. Intellect 105:292 Mr '77
State of the world. See alternate issues of Intellect

HEINECKEN, Robert
Multi-moded Heinecken proves multi-media has come of age. il Mod Phot 41:77 My '77 *

HEINEMAN, Ben Walter
Railroads: rags to riches. D. Pauly and F. Maier. il Newsweek 91:50 Ja 2 '78 *

HEINEMANN, Robert E.
Writing for business: the bucks start here. Writers Digest 57:19-23 O '77

HEINO, Otto
Otto and Vivika Heino. E. Levin. il pors Ceram Mo 25:38-45 O '77 *

HEINO, Vivika
Otto and Vivika Heino. E. Levin. il pors Ceram Mo 25:38-45 O '77 *

HEINRICH, Bernd
Game of the bees. il Horticulture 55:38-9+ Jl '77

HEINS, Ethel L. and others
Booklist (title varies) See issues of Horn book magazine

HEINSELMAN, Miron L.
Crisis in the canoe country. il maps Liv Wildn 40:12-24 Ja '77

HEINSHEIMER, Hans W.
Alban Berg; as I knew him. il por Opera N 41: 10-13 Ap 2 '77
Born in exile. il por Opera N 42:16-17 D 10 '77
Mistress Musgrave. por Opera N 42:44-6 S '77
Scribe factory. por Opera N 41:16-19 Ja 29 '77
Zeroing in. il por Opera N 41:12-15 Ap 16 '77

HEINTZ, Carl M.
Powering round the globe. il Motor B & S 139: 46-9 Mr '77

HEINTZE, Walter
Styling. J. Gribbins. il por Motor B & S 139: 54-7+ Ap '77 *

HEINZ, Donald
Consuming self. America 136:498-501 Je 4 '77

HEINZ, H. J, Company
Heinz comes home and discovers advertising. il Bus W p224+ N 14 '77

HEIRLOOMS
Gems among your junk? Sotheby Parke Bernet's Heirloom Discovery Days. B. H. Schneider. McCalls 105:110 O '77
Treasure of trash? Sotheby Parke Bernet's Heirloom Discovery Day. M. Kasindorf. il Newsweek 89:10 Mr 14 '77

HEIRS. See Inheritance

HEISLER, Martin O.
(ed) Ethnic conflict in the world today. bibl f Ann Am Acad 433:1-160 S '77
Managing ethnic conflict in Belgium. bibl f Ann Am Acad 433:32-46 S '77
—and Peters, B. G.
Toward a multidimensional framework for the analysis of social policy. bibl f Ann Am Acad 434:58-70 N '77

HEISMAN Trophy. See Football, College—Awards, prizes, etc.

HEIZER, Michael
You might say I'm in the construction business; interview, ed by J. Gruen. il por Art N 76:96-9 D '77

HELCK, Peter
Life and art of Peter Helck. W. S. Jackson. il Motor T 29:72-5 F '77 *
Peter Helck. M. Tinkelman. il por Am Artist 41:40-5 Jl '77 *

HELDMAN, Julie
Tennis tips (cont) il por Seventeen 36:34+ F; 40+ Je '77
Tracy Austin tops Seventeen netters second annual Tennis Tournament of Champions. il Seventeen 36:140-1+ S '77

HELENA, Mont.
Montana community honors young children. il SLJ 24:13 S '77

HELENA (warship) See World War, 1939-1945—Naval operations

HELGELAND, Glenn B.
Canoeing. il Travel 148:32-5+ Ag '77
Complete tree-stand hunter—gun and bow. il Outdoor Life 160:74-7+ Ag '77
Get out on a limb! il Nat Wildlife 15:34-5 Ag '77

HELGESEN, Sally
Disco. Harpers 255:20-4 O '77
Official avant-garde. il Harpers 225:28-31 D '77
Students of the subjective. Harpers 254:26-7+ Je '77
Visions of futures past. il Harpers 254:80-6 Mr '77

HELICOPTER airlines
Highs and lows; Rocky Mountain Helicopters. por Forbes 120:104 O 1 '77

HELICOPTER campers. See Helicopters, Remodeled

HELICOPTER industry
Technology sparks helicopter sales. il Aviation W 107:61+ S 26 '77

France

Aerospatiale, Dassault vie for helicopter role. Aviation W 108:21 Ja 2 '78
New helicopter lifts Aerospatiale's hopes. il Bus W p42 Ja 16 '78

United States

Resurgence of helicopter market seen. H. J. Coleman. il Aviation W 106:31+ Mr 21 '77
See also
United Technologies Corporation—Sikorsky Aircraft Division

HELICOPTERS
Bell taking orders on new helicopter. Aviation W 106:63 F 7 '77
Chopper they call when the chips are down; Sikorsky Skycrane. J. F. Pearson. il Pop Mech 147:84-6+ F '77
Coast Guard helicopter buy awaited. D. M. North. Aviation W 106:18-19 My 16 '77
Helicopters: who needs 'em? J. W. Olcott. il Flying 100:62-6+ Mr '77
New helicopters expand world market. il Aviation W 106:258-9+ Je 6 '77
RotorWay revolution. G. C. Larson. il Flying 100:56-61+ F '77
U.S. helicopters get Paris exposure. il Aviation W 106:53-5 Je 27 '77
Up collective. E. D. Muhlfeld. il Flying 100:6 F '77
See also
Helicopter airlines

Accidents

Chopper turns deadly; New York City. il Newsweek 89:27 My 30 '77
Flights of folly; crash of Sikorsky S-61 helicopter on roof of the PanAm building in Manhattan. Nation 224:644 My 28 '77
Strut attachment cited in helicopter accident. E. H. Kolcum. il Aviation W 106:30-1 My 23 '77
Whirling death on a rooftop; New York City. il Time 109:19 My 30 '77

Chartering

See also
Okanagan Helicopters Ltd

Design

Long-term potential seen for S-76. W. H. Gregory. il Aviation W 106:19-22 Ja 17 '77
Reliability emphasized in UH-60 design. W. C. Wetmore. il Aviation W 106:44-7 Ap 11 '77

HELICOPTERS—*Continued*

Electronic equipment

Infrared sensor sized for helicopters. P. J. Klass. il Aviation W 108:71-3 Ja 9 '78

See also

Air navigation—Aids and devices

Military use

Few YAH-64 design changes expected. D. E. Fink. il Aviation W 106:82-3 Ja 10 '77
Helicopters play new role in Europe. D. A. Brown. Aviation W 107:62-3+ N 28 '77
Hind D carries added weapons; photographs. Aviation W 106:21 F 21 '77
Hughes starts phase 2 on YAH-64. D. E. Fink. Aviation W 106:17-19 Ja 3 '77
Lamps' avionics validation completed. il Aviation W 106:146-7+ Ja 31 '77
Mi-24 attack version can fly troops; photographs. Aviation W 106:16-17 Ja 31 '77
Marines acquiring attack helicopters. W. C. Wetmore. il Aviation W 106:193-5 Ja 31 '77
NATO AH-64 coproduction weighted. D. E. Fink. il Aviation W 107:43-5 N 21 '77
Navy supports continuation of CH-53E. H. J. Coleman. Aviation W 106:23-4 Mr 7 '77
New commonality policy clouds helicopter growth. C. Brownlow. Aviation W 106:26 Je 20 '77
Tale of two cities; UTTAS contract awarded to Sikorsky. E. Shields. il Time 109:51+ F 14 '77
UH-60 termed low technical risk. W. C. Wetmore. il Aviation W 106:59-63 Ap 4 '77
U.S. evaluates helicopter air threat. D. E. Fink. Aviation W 107:20-1 N 28 '77
Vertol assured full lamps evaluation. W. C. Wetmore. il Aviation W 107:47+ Ag 1 '77
Vertol extending Chinook service life. W. C. Wetmore. il Aviation W 107:48-9+ O 3 '77

Rotors

Vertol to exploit new rotor technology. D. M. North. il Aviation W 106:46-7 Ja 24 '77

Specifications

Leading international rotary-wing aircraft; tables. Aviation W 106:113 Mr 21 '77
U.S. rotary-wing aircraft; tables. Aviation W 106:111 Mr 21 '77

Testing

Aviation week pilot report:
- Ease of handling stressed for AS 350. R. R. Ropelewski. il Aviation W 106:49+ Ja 17 '77
- Hughes 500D demonstrates versatility. D. E. Fink. il Aviation W 106:56-9 F 14 '77

Early flight tests indicate S-76 exceeds wind tunnel forecasts. il Aviation W 106:19-20 My 9 '77
Pilot report:
- Five-blade Hughes 500D. J. W. Olcott. il Flying 101:75-9 Ag '77

HELICOPTERS, Military. See Helicopters—Military use

HELICOPTERS, Remodeled
And now, the ultimate Arvee; Heli-Homes. M. Demarest. il Time 109:90 Ap 18 '77
Flying RV—the ultimate camper; Heli-Home. il Pop Mech 148:102-3 S '77

HELICOPTERS in rescue work
MAST to the rescue. J. Galub. il Pop Mech 148:88-91+ O '77

HELICOPTERS in skiing
Adventure in the high Bugaboos. P. A. Langan. il Fortune 96:25+ D '77
Expert-ski: heli-skiing in the Canadian Rockies. J. Gibb. il House & Gard 149:76+ D '77

HELICOPTERS in the petroleum industry
Oil exploration spurs increased helicopter use; photographs. Aviation W 106:257 Je 6 '77

HELI-HOMES. See Helicopters, Remodeled; Recreational vehicles

HELIOS solar research spacecraft. See Artificial satellites—Astronomical use

HELIOSTATS
Power with heliostats. A. F. Hildebrandt and L. L. Vant-Hull. bibl il Science 197:1139-46 S 16 '77
Super sun power from mirrors; ERDA project in New Mexico. C. A. Miller. il Mech Illus 73:86+ S '77

HELIUM, Liquid
Quantum statistics and liquid helium-3—helium-4 mixtures. E. G. D. Cohen. bibl il Science 197:11-16 Jl 1 '77

HELLAWELL, A. See Double, D. D. jt auth

HELLBRUNN Palace Festival. See Music festivals—Austria

HELLBUSCH, Ronald A.
For results, get citizens involved early. Am City & County 92:50 Ja '77

HELLEGERS, André E. See McCormick, R. A. jt auth

HELLER, Joseph
Heller moves back to S&S for third novel. M. Reuter. Pub W 211:37 F 7 '77 *
Joseph Heller: some things happen. L. Grobel. por Writers Digest 57:24-5 O '77 *

HELLER, S. R. and others
Computer-based chemical information system. bibl il Science 195:253-9 Ja 21 '77

HELLERMANN, Bill
New music; What? J. La Barbara. il Hi Fi 27: MA14-15 N '77 *

HELLMAN, Geoffrey T.
Obituary
- New Yorker 53:192 O 10 '77

HELLMAN, Lillian
Legend of Lillian Hellman. A. Kazin. il Esquire 88:28+ Ag '77 *
Making of Julia. S. Ferris. il por Horizon 20: 86-90+ O '77 *
Night of the cuckoo. W. F. Buckley, Jr. Nat R 29:513 Ap 29 '77 *
Starring . . . the writer. M. Knelman. Atlantic 240:96-8 N '77 *

HELLMAN, Peter
Lure of surf fishing. il N Y Times Mag p20-1+ O 2 '77

HELLS Canyon
Hells Canyon. W. Ashworth. il map Am Heritage 28:12-23 Ap '77

HELLYER, David
Lost da Vinci may yield its secret to ultrasonic science. il Sci Digest 82:16-19 Ag '77

HELM, Levon
Good ole rock. M. Orth. Newsweek 90:101-2 O 31 '77 *

HELMS, Harry L. Jr
Chasing foreign DX on the broadcast band. il Pop Electr 11:78-83 Je '77
End that utility futility. il Pop Electr 12:53-5 Jl '77
Piracy on the airwaves. il Pop Electr 12:56-8 N '77

HELMS, Jesse
Should Senate OK Panama treaties? interview. pors U.S. News 83:33-4 D 12 '77

HELMS, Richard McGarrah
Ambassador for sale. Nation 225:580 D 3 '77 *
Brotherhood of liars. Nation 224:226-7 F 26 '77 *
Carter and Helms. J. Osborne. New Repub 177: 10-13 N 19 '77 *
Guarding the secrets. Nation 225:482-3 N 12 '77 *
Helms cops a plea. R. Steele and others. por Newsweek 90:31 N 14 '77 *
Helms file. por Newsweek 90:31-2 O 10 '77 *
Helms makes a deal. il por Time 110:18+ N 14 '77 *
Helmsmen, what quarry? F. Getlein. Commonweal 104:740-1 N 25 '77 *
Importance of Richard Helms. Nat R 29:1348 N 25 '77 *
Making punishment fit the crime. M. Greenfield. il Newsweek 90:144 N 21 '77 *
Spare that spook! New Repub 177:5+ N 19 '77 *
Staying a step ahead of them. H. Sidey. il Time 110:23 N 14 '77 *
They never laid a hand on him. Nation 225: 514-15 N 19 '77 *
Up against Citizen Helms. J. K. Larson. Chr Cent 94:1108-10 N 30 '77 *

HELPING behavior
People help a woman more if she's embarrassed; study by Jack Levin and Judith Feingold. J. Horn. il Psychol Today 11:151 D '77
Who wouldn't help a lost child? You, maybe. H. Takooshian and others. bibl il pors Psychol Today 10:67-8+ F '77
Why we leave the hall light on all night. D. Predmore. il Farm J 101:L15-16 Ap '77

See also

Assistance in emergencies

HELSINKI

Bookstores

See Booksellers and bookselling—Finland

HELSINKI Summit. See Conference on Security and Cooperation in Europe

HELSTEIN, Toni J. See Piers, M. W. jt auth

HELTON, George B. and others
Grouping for instruction: 1965, 1975, 1985. Educ Digest 43:53-6 D '77

HELYAR, John
Why the GLUB went mobile. il Am Educ 13:22-6 Ag '77

HEMATOLOGY, Forensic. See Forensic hematology

HEMATOPOIESIS. See Blood—Formation

HEMENWAY, Pat
At last—help for innocent victims of crime. A. Rule. il Good H 185:84+ Jl '77 *

HEMEROCALLIS. See Day lilies

HEMES
Metals as regulators of heme metabolism. M. D. Maines and A. Kappas. bibl il Science 198: 1215-21 D 23 '77

HEMINGWAY, Ernest
Farewell to machismo. A. Latham. il pors N Y Times Mag p52-5+ O 16 '77 *
Hemingway fished here. J. Harrison. il Esquire 88:38+ Jl '77 *
Hemingway the painter. A. Kazin. por New Repub 176:21-8 Mr 19 '77 *
Papa's letters. por Horizon 19:27 Jl '77 *

HEMINGWAY, Joan
Floatable feast. il por Esquire 87:156-7 Ap '77

HEMINGWAY, Margaux
Margaux Hemingway; interview, ed by M. Cantwell. il por Mademoiselle 83:188-9 Ap '77

HEMINGWAY, Mariel
New faces on the big screen; interview, ed by E. Miller. pors Seventeen 36:123 Mr '77

about

Look at Mariel run. il pors Seventeen 36:124-31 Mr '77 *

HEMINGWAY Billfish Tournament. See Fishing—Competitions

HEMISPHERIC dominance. See Laterality

HEMMING, Roy
Back page. **See issues of Retirement living**

—and Alpert, Helen
25 things to do this summer. il Ret Liv 17:22-5 Je '77

HEMODIALYSIS
Rendezvous with a machine; Medicare's kidney program. E. Marshall. New Repub 176:16-19 Mr 19 '77

HEMOGLOBIN
Blood corpuscles and blood hemoglobins: a possible example of coevolution. G. K. Snyder. bibl il Science 195:412-13 Ja 28 '77
New way to detect variant hemoglobins. Sci N 111:407 Je 25 '77
Radioimmunoassay for abnormal hemoglobins. F. A. Garver and others. bibl il Science 196: 1334-6 Je 17 '77

HEMOLYTIC anemia. See Anemia

HEMOPOIESIS. See Blood—Formation

HEMOPROTEINS
Complexes of stannous fluoride and other group IVB dihalides with mammalian hemoproteins. A. R. Dahl and E. Hodgson. bibl il Science 197: 1376-8 S 30 '77

HEMORRHOIDS
Hemorrhoids. A. Frank and S. Frank. Mademoiselle 83:86+ Je '77

HEMPSTONE, Smith
Why Americans are fighting on Rhodesia's front lines. il map U.S. News 82:31-2 My 23 '77

HENAHAN, Donal
Perils of a first-time farmer. il Read Digest 110:107-10 My '77

HENAHAN, John F.
Whatever happened to the cranberry crisis? Atlantic 239:29-36 Mr; 27 Je '77

HENDERSON, Brian
Segmentation. Film Q 31:57-65 Fall '77

HENDERSON, Carol C. See Cooke, E. D. jt auth

HENDERSON, Charles P. Jr
Charles P. Henderson, Jr: a new element of contrition. Chr Cent 94:6 Ja 5 '77

HENDERSON, Henry F. Jr
Quiet success of a talented engineer. H. Johnson. il pors Ebony 32:72-4+ F '77 *

HENDERSON, John B.
Why few government economists resign in protest. M Labor R 100:74 F '77

HENDERSON, Joseph
Jackson Pollock's drawings under analysis; B. Carter. il Art N 76:58-60 F '77 *
Laying the Pollock case to rest. A. Frankenstein. Art N 76:94+ O '77 *

HENDERSON, Lana
Giving thanks with Nancy and Dennis Dordigan. il pors Redbook 150:93+ D '77

HENDERSON, Steve
This Stevie is also a wonder. P. Gammons. il por Sports Illus 47:40-1 Ag 15 '77 *

HENDERSON Industries. See Process control equipment industry

HENDLEY, David E.
Locking and sealing storage containers. il Ceram Mo 25:60-3 F '77

HENDRICKSON, Paul
Earth log: the Foxfire wildfire. il por Audubon 79:108-12 Mr '77

HENDRICKSON, Walter B. Jr
Robots are here! il Sci Digest 82:21-6 N '77
Voices in the deep; with biographical sketch. il Sea Front 23:234-41, 255 Jl '77

HENDRIX, Elmira. See Colquit, J. L. jt auth

HENDRIX Electronics, Inc. See Electronic industries—United States

HENEGHAN, Tom
COs or cheap labor. Commonweal 105:5-7 Ja 6 '78
More government pressure. Commonweal 104: 454-5 Jl 22 '77
Vatican's *ostpolitik*. Commonweal 104:137-42 Mr 4 '77

HENINGTON, David M.
Keeping options open. por Lib J 102:169-70 Ja 15 '77

HENKEL, Stephen C.
Proper pushpit for Pipit. il Yachting 141:92-4 Ap '77

HENKIN, Alan B. See Henkin, C. S. jt auth

HENKIN, Carole S. Henkin, A. B.
Culture, poverty and educational problems of Mexican Americans. bibl Clearing H 5:316-19 Mr '77

HENKIN, Robert I.
Power of perfume; interview. Harp Baz 111: 123 N '77

HENLE, Peter
Social security and pressure politics. il Society 14:57-9 My '77

HENLE, Robert J.
Catholic universities and the Vatican. America 136:315-22 Ap 9 '77
Demystification of life. Commonweal 104:457-60 Jl 22 '77

HENLEY, E. C. and others
Proton-induced X-ray emission analysis of single human hair roots. bibl il Science 197:277-8 Jl 15 '77

HENLEY Regatta. See Rowing

HENN, Mary Ann
Ashes; poem. Chr Cent 94:978 O 26 '77

HENNA
Henna for happiness: India's mehndi art of symbols for all seasons. J. Saksena. il UNESCO Courier 30:18-22 F '77

HENNE, Frances Elizabeth
Teeth for the professionally nameless. L. N. Gerhardt. SLJ 24:7 D '77 *

HENNEPIN County Medical Center. See Minneapolis—Hospitals

HENNIG, Margaret
Let's huddle, women. Time 109:63 My 2 '77 *

HENNIN, Pat
Owner-built homes—low-cost, energy-efficient. E. Tozer. il por Pop Sci 211:114-17 S '77 *

HENNING, Laura
Little league composer. il Opera N 42:49 N '77

HENNINGER, Alice
Who do you think will fight for your raises? Am Lib 8:579 N '77

HENNINGER, Joseph
Joseph Henninger: the artist as teacher. D. C. Hines. il por Am Artist 41:52-7+ My '77 *

HENRIE, J. O.
Ocean thermal gradients—a practical source of energy? bibl Science 195:206-7 Ja 14 '77

HENRIOT, Peter J. See Holland, J. jt auth

HENRY, Carl F. H.
On saying good-bye. Chr Today 21:47-8 S 9 '77
Repressive powers. Chr Today 21:30-1 Ja 21 '77

about

Theology for the tent meeting. por Time 109:82 F 14 '77 *

HENRY, Catherine
Q&A about consumer concerns. See issues of Retirement living

HENRY, Constance. See Knoke, D. jt auth

HENRY, George H.
Of youth and time. Engl J 66:9+ My '77

HENRY, Gerrit
Act of alteration. Art N 76:115-16 My '77
Backward look at American printmaking. il Art N 76:64-6 Mr '77
New York. il Art N 76:117 S '77
Paris-New York: a continuing romance. il Art N 76:60-2 D '77

HENRY, Jean
Sequoia star stomp. il por Sky & Tel 53:262-5 Ap '77

HENRY, Mary Roblee
New Paris focus. Vogue 167:106-8+ Ap '77

HENRY, Paul B.
Love, power and justice. il Chr Cent 94:1088-92 N 23 '77

HENRY, R. C. and Sloan, A. B.
Space shuttle and Vandenberg Air Force Base. bibl il pors map Space World N-2-158:29-36 F '77

HENRY, Richard L.
He's a woods bird now. il Outdoor Life 160: 82-3+ O '77
Trout and the summer angler. il Field & S 82: 20-1+ Jl '77

HENRY, William A. 3d
Hard times liberal. New Repub 176:20-3 Ja 15 '77

HENRY Ford Museum. See Greenfield Village and Henry Ford Museum, Dearborn, Mich.

HENRY Francis du Pont Winterthur Museum
Folk art from the Henry Francis du Pont Winterthur Museum. E. Eff and D. L. Fennimore. il Antiques 112:506-13 S '77

HENRY Regnery Company. See Publishers and publishing—United States

HENSCHE, Henry
Teaching color relationships: a conversation with Henry Hensche; interview, ed by C. Movalli. il por Am Artist 41:34-9+ Mr '77

HENSCHEN, Robert
New sound in review. Consumers Res Mag 60: 32 D '77

HENSEL, Carl
Anniversary present. New Yorker 53:40-1 O 17 '77 *

HENSON, Carolyn
'77 NASA summer study: no show stoppers! il Space World N-12-168:26 D '77

HENSON, Jim
Magical, madcap Muppets. J. Culhane. il por Read Digest 111:23-5+ S '77 *

HENSON, Kenneth T.
New concept of discipline. Clearing H 51:89-91 O '77
Questions teachers ask. Clearing H 50:193-5 Ja '77
HENTOFF, Nat
Any writer who follows anyone else's guidelines ought to be in advertising. por SLJ 24:27-9 N '77
Indigenous music. See occasional issues of Nation
HENZ, John F. and others
Big Thompson flood of 1976 in Colorado. il maps Weatherwise 29:278-85 D '76
HEPATIC encephalopathy. See Reye's syndrome
HEPATITIS
Australia antigen and the biology of hepatitis B; Nobel prize lecture, December 13, 1976. B. S. Blumberg. bibl il Science 197:17-25 Jl 1 '77
Viral hepatitis. J. L. Melnick and others. il Sci Am 237:44-52 bibl(p 154) Jl '77
HEPATITIS B antigen. See Antigens and antibodies
HEPBURN, James
Theater in London. New Repub 176:21-3 Je 25 '77
HEPBURN, Katharine
Hepburn; interview, ed by R. Homer. por Ladies Home J 94:50+ Mr '77
HEPLER, P. K. See Zeiger, E. jt auth
HEPPNER, Frank
Birds of a feather indeed flock together. il Audubon 79:16-19 S '77
HERALD-examiner, Los Angeles. See Los Angeles—Newspapers
HERALDRY
At the sign of the crest. H. K. Eilers. See issues of Hobbies
China trade armorial porcelain in America. C. Le Corbeiller. bibl il Antiques 112:1124-9 D '77
See also
Emblems, National
Fleur-de-lis
HERALDS-trumpets
Tropical jungle at your house; (beaumontia grandiflora) il Sunset 158:250 Ap '77
HERB gardens. See Herbs
HERB industry
How we got started in the herb business. T. Attmore. il por Org Gard & Farm 24:85-7 N '77
HERB lore. See Plant lore
HERB tea. See Tea (beverage)
HERBARIUMS
Exploring the herbarium. S. von R. Altschul. il Sci Am 236:96-104 My '77
HERBERG, Will
Obituary
Nat R 29:429 Ap 15 '77
Will Herberg: a tribute; symposium. pors Nat R 29:880-6 Ag 5 '77 •
HERBERT, Anthony Bernard
Herbert's war. Time 110:103 N 21 '77 •
HERBERT, Victor
Acquiring new information while retaining old ethics. bibl il Science 198:690-3 N 18 '77
HERBICIDES
Buckle down on pests—field by field. B. Brantley and C. E. Sommers. il Suc Farm 75:30-1+ Ja '77
Combustion of several 2,4,5-trichlorophenoxy compounds: formation of 2,3,7,8-tetrachlorodibenzo-p-dioxin. R. H. Stehl and L. L. Lamparski. bibl il Science 197:1008-9 S 2 '77
How to commit herbicide. P. L. Carpenter. il Horticulture 55:16-21 My '77
How to diagnose a sick pond. il Farm J 101: H4-5+ D '77
Knock out problem weeds in corn. D. Seim. il Farm J 101:21-2+ mid-F '77
1977 weed and insect control guide. il Suc Farm 75:35-7+ Ja '77
Stop tough weeds in soybeans. D. Seim. il Farm J 101:32+ Mr '77
Surfactants may injure crops. Suc Farm 75:no4 L52 Mr '77
Test shows the best way to incorporate soybean herbicides. B. Coffman. Farm J 101:C4 Ap '77
Word to the wise: 2, 4-D backfires. BioScience 27:224 Mr '77

Disposal

Odyssey of Agent Orange ends in the Pacific. Science 197:966 S 2 '77

Injurious effects

In defense of my organic homestead. H. Seaver. il por Org Gard & Farm 24:184+ O '77
Mugging of a garden; question of defoliation along Long Island Railroad rights of way. U. Roze. il Horticulture 55:18-23 Jl '77
Reporter at large; effects of 2,4,5-T. T. Whiteside. New Yorker 53:30-8+ Jl 25 '77

Residues

Herbicide residues: how serious in 1977? C. E. Sommers. il Suc Farm 75:W1 Ja '77
Oregon desert graveyard for leaking herbicide wastes. P. L. Fradkin. Audubon 79:127 Ja '77

HERBICIDES as defoliants. See Defoliation
HERBS
Eight extra-special herbs: how to grow them, how to use them. J. L. Lippert. il Good H 184:206 Ap '77
Exciting world of herbs; symposium. il Org Gard & Farm 24:46-68+ bibl(p32-5) N '77
Growing things. Seventeen 36:108 S '77
Herb garden for the bees. B. Fisher. il Org Gard & Farm 24:85-7 F '77
Herb tea gardening. il Sunset 158:262 Ap '77
Herbs. New Yorker 53:22-3 Ag 15 '77
Herbs for health; bathroom plants. P. Dunlop. il House & Gard 149:102+ F '77
Lore of herbs revived for kitchen and for cures; with views of John Williamson. E. V. Warren. il House B 119:14+ O '77
My favorite winter vegetables are herbs. N. A. Fisher. il Org Gard & Farm 24:71-3 Jl '77
Protecting the home with herbs. B. Fisher. il Org Gard & Farm 24:148-51 Ap '77
See also
Borage
Chamomile
Cookery—Herbs
Dill
Garlic
Ginseng
Potpourri
Sages (plants)
Tarragon

Bibliography

Herbals: great and small. J. Cox. Org Gard & Farm 24:32-5 N '77
HERBS, Medicinal. See Botany, Medical
HERBST, Robert L.
Sportsman in the Cabinet. B. East. por Outdoor Life 160:38 D '77 •
HERCULES, Frank
To live in Harlem. . . il Nat Geog 151:178-207 F '77; Same abr. Read Digest 110:175-6+ Je '77
HERCULES X-1. See Neutron stars
HEREAFTER. See Future life
HEREDITY
Roots and the biologist. G. B. Moment. BioScience 27:589 S '77
See also
Albinos and albinism
Blood groups
Eugenics
Evolution
Genes
HEREDITY and intelligence. See Intelligence levels
HEREDITY of disease
Alzheimer's disease, trisomy 21, and myeloproliferative disorders: associations suggesting a genetic diathesis. L. L. Heston. bibl il Science 196:322-3 Ap 15 '77
Birth defects: not for babies only. A. Rosenfeld. Sat R 5:47-8 N 26 '77
HLA and disease. Sci Am 238:64+ Ja '78
Hereditary hemolytic anemia with increased red cell adenosine deaminase (45- to 70-fold) and decreased adenosine triphosphate. W. N. Valentine and others. bibl il Science 195:783-5 F 25 '77
New way to predict genetic disease; research by Steven Rosenberg and others. J. Horn. Psychol Today 11:28-9+ D '77
Tale of 3 diseases: a common cause? pathological microtubules. Sci N 111:263 Ap 23 '77
Winning the war against birth defects; advances in genetic counseling and screening. R. Halcomb. il Parents Mag 52:37+ My '77
See also
Acrodermatitis enteropathica
Huntington's chorea
Metabolism, Disorders of
Phenylketonuria
Porphyria

Genetic counseling

See Genetic counseling
HEREN, Louis
Fleet Street and the free press. il Sat R 4:24-5 Je 11 '77
HERE'S Life, America campaign. See Campus Crusade for Christ (organization)
HERHOLD, Robert M.
Letting go of Richard Nixon. Chr Cent 94:582-3 Je 22 '77
HERMAN, Edward S. See Chomsky, N. jt auth
HERMAN, George, and others
(ed) See Habib, P. C. Under Secretary Habib interviewed on Face the Nation
HERMAN, Ken
Small-town moxie. Nation 224:580 My 14 '77 •
HERMAN, Louis Marvin. See Thompson, R. K. R. jt auth
HERMAN, Mary W.
Health care and the patient's needs. bibl f Cur Hist 73:1-4+ Jl '77
HERMAN, Woody
Indigenous music. N. Hentoff. Nation 224:636 My 21 '77 •

HERMANN, Mo.
Profiles. B. Roueché. New Yorker 53:37-40+ F 28 '77
HERMAPHRODITISM
H-Y antigen: expression in human subjects with the testicular feminization syndrome. G. C. Koo and others. bibl il Science 196:655-6 My 6 '77
See also
Sex reversal
HERMES, Julius
Martin Processing: heating up for solar energy. por Duns R 109:18-19+ My '77 *
HERMIT crabs. See Crabs
HERNANDEZ, Antonio Martinez-. See Martinez-Hernandez, A.
HERNDON, Gordon
Stop a week in Sri Lanka. il map House & Gard 149:74+ Je '77
HERNDON, James H.
Summer sun—how to guard against dangers; interview. il U.S. News 82:55 My 30 '77
HERNDON, Robert M. and Coyle, J. T.
Selective destruction of neurons by a transmitter agonist. bibl il Science 198:71-2 O 7 '77
—and others
Regeneration of oligodendroglia during recovery from demyelinating disease. bibl il Science 195:693-4 F 18 '77
HERNMARCK, Helena Barynina
Photorealism in a medieval medium. A. Knight. il por Horizon 20:58-9 D '77 *
HERODOTUS
Egyptian way of death; excerpt from Book II of The history. il Sr Schol 109:17 Ap 7 '77
about
Antiquity's great reporter-historian among the Scythians. Y. V. Domansky. il UNESCO Courier 29:9-14+ D '76 *
Father of history. P. W. Schmidtchen. il por Hobbies 82:134-6 My '77 *
HEROES
Do you agree? results of NISO poll on heroes. J. Brothers. il por Sr Schol 109:14-15 F 10 '77
Let's bring back heroes. W. J. Bennett. por Newsweek 90:3 Ag 15 '77; Same abr. il Read Digest 111:91-2+ D '77
Will young people ever have heroes again? ed by J. N. Bell. S. T. Black. il pors Seventeen 36:136-7+ S '77
See also
Mythology
HEROES, Legendary American. See Legends, American
HEROIN
Drugs to help addicts kick the heroin habit. H. J. Sanders. il Chemistry 50:22-3 S '77
Fix for pain? use of heroin and marijuana for terminal cancer patients. M. Clark and others. il Newsweek 91:41 Ja 2 '78
Heroin plague; Western Europe. K. Labich. il Newsweek 89:47 Ap 25 '77
Mexican heroin flow continues unabated. C. Holden. Science 196:509 Ap 29 '77
Mister Untouchable; N. Barnes. F. Ferretti. il pors N Y Times Mag p 15-17+ Je 5 '77
New kings of heroin. N. M. Adams. Read Digest 110:117-21 Ap '77
New look at heroin could spur better medical use of narcotics. C. Holden. Science 198:807-9 N 25 '77
New strategy against drug rings—dramatic story of a successful bust; central tactical units—CENTAC 1. O. Kelly. il U.S. News 83:64-6 O 31 '77
HERON Group Ltd
Last British tycoon? por Forbes 120:52+ O 1 '77
HERPES simplex viruses. See Herpesviruses
HERPESVIRUS diseases
Antiviral drugs: possibilities against herpes. il Sci N 112:116 Ag 20 '77
Drug for treatment of herpes encephalitis. T. H. Metz. Science 197:973 S 2 '77
Drug for viruses; use of ara-A in treatment of herpes viruses. J. Seligmann and E. Clark. il Newsweek 90:80 Ag 22 '77
New drug effective against virus. il Chemistry 50:27 O '77
Viral antidote; adenine arabinoside. il Time 110:75 Ag 22 '77
Vaccines
Malaria, herpes vaccines: progress. Sci N 112:55 Jl 23 '77
HERPESVIRUSES
Cytomegalovirus: the newborn's enemy. Sci N 111:373 Je 11 '77
Establishment of a cell line with associated Epstein-Barr-like virus from a leukemic orangutan. S. Rasheed and others. bibl il Science 198:407-9 O 28 '77
Herpes: it can be treated—but not cured; genital herpes. J. Kagan. Ms 6:38-40 Ja '78
Herpesviruses—a link in the cancer chain? A. C. Hollinshead and W. A. Knaus. bibl il Chemistry 50:17-21 My '77
HERRERA, Hayden
Manhattan seven. bibl il Art in Am 65:50-63 Jl '77
HERRERA, Omar Torrijos. See Torrijos Herrera, O.
HERRESHOFF, Louise
Upward reappraisal. P. Halasz. Art N 76:100-1 Ja '77 *
HERRICK, Harold E. Jr
Magic of musky fishing. il Conservationist 31:26-7 Mr '77
HERRIOT, James
All things wise and wonderful; story; excerpt from novel. il Read Digest 111:233-42+ O '77
All things wise and wonderful; story; excerpt from novel. McCalls 104:130-9 Ag '77
Mrs Ainsworth's Christmas cat; story, excerpt from All things wise and wonderful. Read Digest 111:118-22 D '77
HERRMANN, Kathleen
Fine arts festival. il Sch Arts 76:47 Je '77
HERRMANN, Nina L.
Go out in joy; condensation. il Read Digest 110:249-60+ Ap '77
HERRON, Matthew
Leviathan model brings us the whale we could never see. il pors Smithsonian 8:52-9 bibl(p 114) Ja '78
Sea and shores as classrooms. il pors Smithsonian 8:99-104 S '77
HERSCHEL, Sir William
Herschel's large 20-foot telescope. J. Ashbrook. il Sky & Tel 54:174-5 S '77 *
HERSEY, John
In their hour of triumph. il Yachting 142:86-91+ S '77
Walnut door; condensation of novel. Redbook 149:219-41 O '77
HERSH, Evan M. See Schafer, L. A. jt auth
HERSH, Richard H. and Paolitto, D. P.
Moral development: implications for pedagogy. Educ Digest 42:13-16 Ja '77
HERSH, Seymour M.
Taking on big business. D. M. Alpern and others. il por Newsweek 90:81-2 Ag 8 '77 *
HERSHENSON, Martin
Color in your darkroom. il por Mod Phot 41:50+ O; 10+ N; 40+ D '77
Kodacolor? Vericolor? What's the difference? il Mod Phot 41:118-19+ N '77
HERSHEY, Lenore
Editor's diary. See issues of Ladies home journal
HERSHEY Foods Corporation
Chocolate bars by the battalion; Hershey plant in Oakdale, Calif. il Sunset 159:37 Jl '77
HERSHFIELD, Michael S. and others
Adenine and adenosine are toxic to human lymphoblast mutants defective in purine salvage enzymes. bibl il Science 197:1284-7 S 23 '77
HERSKOWITZ, Mickey. See Rather, D. jt auth
HERST, Herman, Jr
Stamps. See issues of Hobbies
HERTELENDY, Paul
Isadora's childhood. il por Dance Mag 51:48-50 Jl '77
HERTZ Corporation
Getting tough at Hertz. Forbes 120:116 N 1 '77
HERTZBERG, Alex
Dos and don'ts of landing a Polish contract. Forbes 120:46 Jl 1 '77
HERTZFELD, Jeffrey M.
New directions in East-West trade. Harvard Bus R 55:93-9 My '77
HERWEG, Mabel Mariá
How to force winter branches to blossom for an early spring indoors. il Horticulture 55:32-3 F '77
HERZ, Peggy Hudson
Television. See occasional issues of Senior scholastic including World week
HERZLINGER, Regina
Why data systems in nonprofit organizations fail. Harvard Bus R 55:81-6 Ja; 54+ Mr '77
HERZOG, Chaim
Peace in the Middle East; address, December 6, 1976. Vital Speeches 43:170-3 Ja 1 '77
HERZOG, Werner
Germans are coming! The Germans are coming! D. Denby. il pors Horizon 20:88-90+ S '77 *
Man on the volcano: a portrait of Werner Herzog. G. Bachmann. il por Film Q 31:2-10 Fall '77 *
New visionary in German films. R. Eder. il pors N Y Times Mag p24-6+ Jl 10 '77 *
Screen. C. L. Westerbeck, Jr. Commonweal 104:596-7, 624-5 S 16-30 '77 *
Traveling man. C. L. Westerbeck, Jr. Commonweal 104:596-7 S 16 '77 *
HESBURGH, Theodore Martin
Prince of priests, without a nickel. R. Ajemian. il pors Time 109:74-5 My 2 '77 *
HESKETT, James Lee
Logistics—essential to strategy. il Harvard Bus R 55:85-96 N '77
HESS, Karl
Karl Hess and the doppelgänger. R. De Toledano. Nat R 29:718-20 Je 24 '77 *

HESS, Leon
Playing for high stakes in the Virgin Islands. T. Szulc. Forbes 120:53-5 Ag 1 '77 *

HESS, M. Whitcomb
Edmund Spenser and the angels; poem. Chr Today 21:21 Mr 4 '77

HESS, Stephen
Irrelevant forum. New Repub 176:34+ Ja 22 '77
U.S. reaffirms commitment to self-determination and independence for Namibia; statement, December 10, 1976. Dept State Bull 76:44-6 Ja 17 '77
United States urges peaceful change in South Africa; statement, November 3, 1976. Dept State Bull 76:48-9 Ja 17 '77

HESS, Thomas B.
Photo—luxe; Irving Penn: time is luxury. il Vogue 167:332-3+ S '77

HESSEN, Tatiana Moritz von, Princess. See Tatiana, M. von H.

HESTON, Leonard L.
Alzheimer's disease, trisomy 21, and myeloproliferative disorders: associations suggesting a genetic diathesis. bibl il Science 196:322-3 Ap 15 '77

about

Tale of 3 diseases: a common cause? Sci N 111:263 Ap 23 '77 *

HESTOR, Charles
Insuring procedural due process in expulsion cases. Clearing H 50:256-7 F '77

HETHERINGTON, Eileen Mavis, and others
Divorced fathers. bibl il Psychol Today 10:42-3+ Ap '77

HEUBLEIN, Inc
Behind the profit plunge at Heublein. il Bus W p64-6 Jl 4 '77

HEVER, Thomas
Culture & notes. Horticulture 55:78-9 Je '77

HEWITT, Christopher
Majorities and minorities: a comparative survey of ethnic violence. bibl f il Ann Am Acad 433:150-60 S '77

HEWITT, Geof
Raising your own small business; excerpt from Working for yourself. Org Gard & Farm 24:68-77 S '77

HEWITT, Peter F.
(ed) Fall religious issue. il pors Pub W 212:63-102 S 26 '77
Record attendance at 28th annual Christian Booksellers Convention. il Pub W 212:50-2 Ag 15 '77

HEXADECIMAL conversion tables. See Conversion tables

HEYEN, William
Mushrooms; poem. New Yorker 53:48 O 3 '77

HEYERDAHL, Thor
Bound for glory; excerpt from Aku-Aku: the secret of Easter Island. il Sat Eve Post 249:18 Jl '77

about

Eye which sees heaven; Easter Island. W. Barnstone. il Holiday 58:44-5+ Mr '77 *
From Eden to India. il Time 110:116 N 28 '77 *

HEYMANN, Philip
(ed) See Allen, J. Education of John Allen

HEYNEN, Jim
Iowa poem: winter, Oregon. Redbook 150:74 D '77

HEYWARD family
Heyward coat-of-arms. H. K. Eilers. Hobbies 82:140 Jl '77

HEYWOOD, Lloyd A.
Day care with a difference. il Parks & Rec 12:16-19 Jl '77
—and Warnick, R. B.
Campus recreation. Educ Digest 42:33-5 Ja '77

HIATT, Travis
One man's afghan, another man's purl. E. A. Yeager. il pors Ret Liv 17:43 Ap '77 *

HIBBERD, Fred
Other ways to furl and reef. Yachting 141:32+ F '77

HIBBS, John B. Jr, and others
Macrophage tumor killing: influence of the local environment. bibl il Science 197:279-82 Jl 15 '77
—See Chapman, H. A. Jr, jt auth

HIBERNATION
Can humans be "taught" to hibernate? work of H. Swan. A. Rosenfeld. Sat R 4:34-5 Je 11 '77
Hibernation and body weight in dormice: a new type of endogenous cycle. N. Mrosovsky. bibl il Science 196:902-3 My 20 '77

HICKEY, T. L.
Postnatal development of the human lateral geniculate nucleus: relationship to a critical period for the visual system. bibl il Science 198:836-8 N 25 '77

HICKMAN, Charles W.
Labor organizations' fees and dues. bibl il M Labor R 100:19-24 My '77

HICKMAN, Frederic W.
Urged: an end to double tax on corporate dividends; interview. por U.S. News 83:36-7 Jl 25 '77

HICKMAN, William
New ANSI standards on barrier-free design expected in 1978. Archit Rec 162:63 D '77

HICKOK, James Butler
Only law; excerpts from 1926 articles, ed by A. B. Macdonald. F. Sutton. il por Sat Eve Post 249:62-3 Jl '77 *

HICKS, Louise (Day)
Boston after Louise Day Hicks. H. Husock. il por Nation 225:710-12 D 31 '77 *

HICKS, Mark
24 facts that'll help you bag more squirrels. il Outdoor Life 160:80-1+ S '77

HICKS, Warren B. and Tillin, A. M.
Libraries and technology—some future concerns; excerpt from Managing multi-media libraries. pors SLJ 23:27-32 Ap '77

HIDALGO, Marty Adair
Wicked stepmother doesn't live here any more. il por Redbook 149:22+ Ag '77

HIDATSA Indians
Winter at Fort Clark: Maximilian and Bodmer among the tribes of the Upper Missouri, 1833-1834; with reproductions of paintings; excerpt from People of the first man, ed by D. Thomas and K. Ronnefeldt. A. P. Maximilian. Am West 14:36-47 Ja '77

HIDING Mr Hale; drama. See Boiko, C.

HI-FI industry. See Audio equipment industry

HI-FI sound systems. See Audio systems

HIGGINS, Edward
Green frogs; poem. Org Gard & Farm 24:159 Ap '77

HIGGINS, Victor
Victor Higgins: creative explorer; with editorial comment. M. C. Nelson. il por Am Artist 42:6+, 54-9+ Ja '78 *

HIGH altitude, Influence of. See Altitude, Influence of

HIGH altitude flying. See Aviation—Altitude flying

HIGH-altitude sickness. See Altitude, Influence of

HIGH blood pressure. See Hypertension

HIGH Commissioner for Refugees. See United Nations—High Commissioner for Refugees

HIGH density housing. See Housing—Density

HIGH Energy Astronomy Observatory (satellite) See Artificial satellites—Astronomical use

HIGH FALLS, N.Y.

Historic houses, sites, etc.

See Historic houses, sites, etc.—New York (state)

HIGH fidelity and Musical America (periodical)
Best records of 1977; annual High Fidelity/International Record Critics Awards; with remarks by L. Marcus. il Hi Fi 27:48-55 D '77
High fidelity weds Schwann. L. Marcus. Hi Fi 27:4 Mr '77

HIGH fidelity sound systems. See Audio systems

HIGH interest-low vocabulary books. See Readability and readable books

HIGH jumping. See Jumping

HIGH lysine corn. See Corn—Hybrids

HIGH POINT, Mich.

Recreation

See Recreation—Michigan

HIGH pressure (science)
High pressures on small areas. A. L. Ruoff and J. Wanagel. bibl il Science 198:1037-8 D 9 '77
Strange world of superpressure. J. S. Wilentz. il Pop Sci 210:78-81+ F '77

HIGH pressure phase transitions. See Phase transitions

HIGH school athletics. See School athletics

HIGH school coaches. See Coaches (athletics)

HIGH school libraries. See School libraries

HIGH school student opinion. See Student opinion

HIGH school students
Senior serial: the halls of Haywood High. K. Lance. See issues of Senior scholastic including World week
See also
Scholastic Research Center
School management and organization—Student participation
Student activities
Teen-age pregnancy

Adjustment

Think you're ready for high school? D. Simon. Seventeen 36:52+ S '77

HIGH school students—*Continued*

Attitudes

Class of '77: all's quiet at Scarsdale High. J. Feron. il N Y Times Mag p20+ Je 26 '77
Does the use of newspapers in the classroom affect attitudes of students? study made in a Houston high school. Z. Verner and L. Murphy. il Clearing H 50:350-1 Ap '77
What young Americans know about Hitler. D. Kaiser. Nation 225:613 D 10 '77

Social and economic status

See Students—Social and economic status

HIGH school students, Black. See Black students

HIGH school students and smoking. See Smoking and youth

HIGH schools

High schools under fire. il Time 110:62-5+ N 14 '77
House plan in secondary schools. C. R. Kraegel. Clearing H 50:392-4 My '77
See also
Education, Secondary

Curriculum

Career investigation and planning in the high school English curriculum. R. E. Roberts. bibl Engl J 66:49-52 N '77
Declining enrollments: implications for the school curriculum. K. E. Eisenberger. Educ Digest 42:6-9 My '77
EJ curriculum catalog; comp by S. Koch. Engl J 66:53-67 S '77
Economics gap. H. Flieger. U.S. News 82:76 Ja 31 '77
High school curriculum from a policy point of view. J. T. Grasso. Educ Digest 43:13-16 N '77
I taught ethics in high school. J. Forcinelli. Todays Educ 66:70-1 Ja '77
Reshaping secondary education; International Baccalaureate program at Francis Lewis High School, Queens, N.Y. J. R. Adams. Educ Digest 43:2-4 D '77
Substitute for substitutes; Enrichment Program at Syosset High School, New York. N. Schwartz. Educ Digest 43:36-7 N '77
Vanished past of the American school; curricular change. A. Tibbetts and C. Tibbetts. Clearing H 50:380 My '77

Graduation requirements

Early graduation here to stay? E. F. Dix. Clearing H 50:219-20 Ja '77; Correction. 50:319 Mr '77
What do diplomas mean? proficiency testing. M. Sheils. il Newsweek 91:65 Ja 9 '78

HIGH speed films. See Photography—Films

HIGH-voltage batteries. See Electric batteries

HIGHER education. See College education

HIGHER education and state. See Education and state

HIGHLAND, Virgil L.

Fire safety controversy. Bull Atom Sci 33:54-5 O '77

HIGHRISE buildings. See Skyscrapers

HIGHTOWER, Toby E.

Don't just sit there—say something! Clearing H 51:148 D '77
More power to young administrators. Educ Digest 42:36-7 F '77

HIGHWATER, Jamake

Dancing in the seventies. il Horizon 19:30-3 My '77

HIGHWAY engineering

Road building cost shows sharp rise. il Am City & County 92:46 O '77

HIGHWAY patrols. See Traffic police

HIGHWAY rest rooms. See Public comfort stations

HIGHWAY safety. See Roads—Safety devices and measures; Traffic safety

HIGHWAY safety laws. See Traffic regulations

HIGHWAY sculpture. See Roadside improvement

HIGHWAY Trust Fund. See Express highways—Federal aid

HIGHWAYS. See Express highways

HIJACKING. See Robberies and assaults

HIJACKING of airplanes. See Airplane hijacking

HIJACKING of boats. See Boat hijacking

HIKING

Have fun in the snow—but be careful! V. T. Sparano. il Nat Wildlife 16:26-7 D '77
In Switzerland—ride up, hike down. il Sunset 158:74+ Je '77
Mountain; day hikes and climbing Mount Rainier. il map Sunset 159:60-7 bibl(p58) Jl '77
Reporter at large: memories of a day's walk from Massachusetts to Maine. A. Bailey. New Yorker 53:158+ N 21 '77
Three to six-day Holland walks. il Sunset 158:78 Ap '77
Trekking on Everest: making a living from wanderlust; interview, ed by G. Lichtenstein. S. B. Larrabee. bibl il Ms 5:26+ Mr '77
Walk across America. P. G. Jenkins. il map Nat Geog 151:466-99 Ap '77
Walking beach in wild Washington; Olympic National Park. il map Sunset 158:76+ My '77
Walking the railroads. J. Eastman. Natur Hist 86:90-3 N '77
See also
Backpacks and backpacking
Trails

HILCHEY, Robert E.

Thinking about tomorrow; address, October 17, 1977. Vital Speeches 44:88-92 N 15 '77

HILDEBRANDT, Alvin F. and Vant-Hull, L. L.

Power with heliostats. bibl il Science 197:1139-46 S 16 '77

HILFMAN, T.

What she did for love.... Dance Mag 51:54 D '77

HILL, Andrew Putnam

Pioneer conservationist A. P. Hill; he saved the redwoods. V. T. Olson. il pors Am West 14:32-40 S '77 *

HILL, Archie

Patience. J. W. Donohue. America 137:311-12 N 5 '77 *

HILL, Bruce C. and others

Laser interferometer measurement of changes in crayfish axon diameter concurrent with action potential. bibl il Science 196:426-8 Ap 22 '77

HILL, David D.

Trash-bag murders. D. A. Williams and J. Huck. il pors Newsweek 90:22 Jl 18 '77 *
Twenty-eight, and counting. il pors Time 110:49 Jl 18 '77 *

HILL, Gene

Hill country. See issues of Field & stream
Woodcock days past, but lovingly remembered. il Field & S 82:48-9+ S '77

HILL, Gladwin

Power play. Nat Wildlife 14:38-9 O '76; 15:38-9 F '77

HILL, Herbert

Blow to minorities. il Commonweal 104:552-5 S 2 '77

HILL, Jim

If only luck will be a lady. D. S. Looney. il pors Sports Illus 46:40-1+ Je 13 '77 *

HILL, Lester, Jr. See Glenn, N. D. jt auth

HILL, Lewis

Do plants shiver in the north wind? il Org Gard & Farm 24:92-4 O '77
Make it butternuts for the North. il Org Gard & Farm 24:92-4 S '77
Natural steps to beat apple scab. il Org Gard & Farm 24:84-7 Ag '77
Reviving an old orchard; excerpt from Fruits and berries for the home garden. il Org Gard & Farm 24:64-8 My '77

HILL, Loren Gilbert

pHish pfinder? J. Scott. il Field & S 82:58+ Jl '77 *

HILL, Lowell D.

How good (or bad) is our export corn? excerpt from address. por Farm J 101:Jl S '77

HILL, Mary Shadow

More than a blender. il Org Gard & Farm 24:119-20 O '77
Preserving in the garden. il Org Gard & Farm 24:104+ S '77

HILL, Murie

Get up and glow. il Am Home 80:54-5 Ap '77
Is your skin dying of thirst? il Am Home 80:46-7+ Jl '77

HILL, Nellie

Fisherman; poem. Commonweal 104:336 My 27 '77

HILL, Ray

Auto-maintenance basics. il Pop Sci 211:160+ S; 138+ N; 104-7 D '77
Motorcycling. See issues of Popular science

HILL, Richard A.

Canon law after Vatican II: renewal or retreat? America 137:298-300 N 5 '77

HILL, Robert Charles

Argentina today; address, June 28, 1977. Vital Speeches 43:612-15 Ag 1 '77

HILL, Robert F. See Stein, H. F. jt auth

HILL, Rochelle

Alice in Wonderland; dramatization of story by L. Carroll. Plays 36:75, 83-92 My '77

HILL, Ronald W.

One middle-school approach. Todays Educ 66:41 Ja '77

HILL, Sandy

Jane Pauley & Sandy Hill. A. L. Ball. pors Redbook 150:94+ N '77 *

HILL agriculture. See Hill farming

HILL farming

Farming the edge of the Andes. S. B. Brush. il Natur Hist 86:32-41 bibl(p94) My '77
High-altitude growing in California. F. Blanchard. il Org Gard & Farm 25:80-1 Ja '78

HILL slopes. See Slopes (physical geography)
HILLARD, James M.
Right of center (cont) Wilson Lib Bull 51:668-9 Ap; 52:74-5 S '77
HILLENBRAND, Robert, and Ryan, M. F.
Project Parsec goes to Mars. il Sky & Tel 54: 464-5 D '77
HILLES, Richard J. See Golembiewski, R. T. jt auth
HILLESTAD, Robert
Craftsman's approach to apparel design. il Design (US) 78:22-5 Spr '77
HILLIARD, Mary Ellen Verheyden-. See Verheyden-Hilliard, M. E.
HILLIS, Burton
Man next door. See issues of Better homes and gardens
HILLIS, Don W.
Is America over-evangelized? Chr Today 21:16-17 My 20 '77
HILLMAN, Brenda
Walking the dunes; On the pier; Effort to enter into morning; poems. Poetry 130:83-4 My '77
HILLMAN, Bruce Joel
Farm markets. Writers Digest 57:28-30 Ag '77
—See Alpert, H. jt auth
HILLMAN, William S.
Ecofreaks, technofreaks, and one-armed biologists; excerpt from address. BioScience 27:315 My '77
HILLS, Carla Anderson
America—passing out of adolescence; excerpts from address. por Intellect 105:207-8 Ja '77
HILLS, Patricia
Art. L. Alloway. Nation 225:124-5 Ag 6 '77 *
HILLS, Roderick M.
What awaits Hills at Peabody. por Bus W p 18-19 Jl 4 '77 *
HILLSDALE College, Hillsdale, Mich.

Center for Constructive Alternatives

Balancing act; conservative publications. M. J. Sobran, Jr. Nat R 29:1005-6 S 2 '77
HILLSIDE architecture
Chiu residence, Vancouver, British Columbia. il Archit Rec 161:72-3 mid-My '77
Country house, California style; Marin County. J. Friedman-Weiss and H. H. Wise. il McCalls 104:104-6 S '77
House in the hill; Alexander house near Santa Barbara. P. Goldberger. il N Y Times Mag p42-4 Ag 7 '77
Lieto residence, Westchester, New York. il Archit Rec 161:78-81 mid-My '77
HILLSIDE gardens. See Gardens, Hillside
HILO, Hawaii
In Hilo, tropical plant discovery; nurseries. il Sunset 159:44 Ag '77
HILTON, Alison, and Dodge, Norton
Soviet unofficial art in the U.S. bibl il Art in Am 65:113-19 N '77
HILTUNEN, Bob, family
Maid from Finland. T. Schwartz and others. il Newsweek 90:32 Jl 4 '77
HIMALAYAN climbs. See Mountaineering
HIMALAYAS
See also
Everest, Mount
Ladakh
HINCKLEY, Henry R.
Aristocrat of boat builders. A. F. Ehrbar. il por Fortune 95:122-9 Ap '77 *
HINCKLEY, Henry R, and Company. See Boatbuilding
HINCKLEY fire. See Fires
HINDEMITH, Paul
Konzertmusik fur Blasorchester, op. 41; Symphonia serena; Geschwindmarsch; Symphony in B flat. J. Ringo. Am Rec G 40:27 Je '77 *
Reviews of records: The complete sonatas for brass and piano. W. Hilse. Mus Q 63:144-6 Ja '77 *
HINDS, James W. See Kaplan, M. S. jt auth
HINDS, Michael DeCourcy
Finding and working with a contractor. House & Gard 149:110+ My '77
New Harmony. il House & Gard 149:84-5+ Ag '77
Restoring a historic house. il House & Gard 149:58+ Ap '77
HINDU painting. See Painting, Indian (East Indian)
HINDUISM
See also
Fasts and feasts—Hinduism
Krishna
Mysticism—Hinduism
HINE, Darlene Clark
NAACP and the Supreme Court: Walter F. White and the defeat of Judge John J Parker, 1930. bibl il por Negro Hist Bull 40: 753-7 S '77
HINE, Lewis Wickes
Hine's Ellis Island pilgrims. A. S. Wooster. il Art N 76:126 My '77 *
Recording angel of labor; retrospective at the Brooklyn Museum. R. Hughes. il Time 109: 63-4 Mr 28 '77 *
HINEGARDNER, Ralph T. See Coffaro, K. A. jt auth
HINES, Benjamin Franklin
Westerlies. G. C. Larson. il Flying 100:21-2+ F '77 *
HINES, Diane Casella
Jessie James: painting from the heart. il por Am Artist 41:54-9+ N '77
Joseph Henninger: the artist as teacher. il por Am Artist 41:52-7+ My '77
HINES, Earl
National Public Radio. W. Youngren. il por New Repub 177:23+ S 24 '77 *
HINES, Henry, 3d
He teaches the pros. il pors Ebony 32:134-6+ O '77 *
HINES, William
Anti-nuclear ferment in Europe. Progressive 41: 19-21 S '77
—and Randal, Judith
Behind the saccharin uproar. Progressive 41:13-17 Je '77
HINGES
Not-so-crazy hinge. J. O'Boyle. il Pop Mech 148: 208 O '77
HINNERS, Noel W.
Science as exploration; excerpts from address, February 1977. Aviation W 106:7 F 14 '77
HINRICHS, Marie A.
Q&A about health. See issues of Retirement living
HINSDALE, Ill.
Tale of two suburbs: near Chicago . . . P. Delaney. il Time 109:23 My 2 '77
HINSON, E. Glenn
Southern Baptist context. Chr Cent 94:93-5 F 2 '77
HIPKINS, Clifton A.
Man and his boat. E. Horan. il por Yachting 141:92-3 Mr '77 *
HIPP, I. M.
I.M. the wonder walk-on. D. S. Looney. il Sports Illus 47:57-8+ O 24 '77 *
HIPPIES
Generation that was never going to have to work. M. Jacobson. il Esquire 88:52-4+ Jl '77
HIPPOCAMPUS (brain) See Brain
HIPPOLITUS, Paul. See Nesbitt, J. A. jt auth
HIRABAYASHI, Kazuko, Dance Theatre. See Dance companies
HIROHITO, Emperor of Japan
Recording that ended World War II. F. Bowers. il Hi Fi 27:87-90 O '77 *
HIROSHIMA
Continuing body count at Hiroshima and Nagasaki. F. Barnaby. il Bull Atom Sci 33:48-51+ D '77
Physical and medical effects of the Hiroshima and Nagasaki bombs; report of Natural Science Group. Bull Atom Sci 33:54-6 D '77
Survivor's story: friends, please forgive us. K. Osamu. Bull Atom Sci 33:52 D '77
HIRSCH, Julian D.
How FM tuners work. il Pop Electr 12:48-51 D '77; 13:58-9 Ja '78
Julian Hirsch audio reports. See issues of Popular electronics including Electronics world
HIRSCH, Richard
Richard Hirsch. il Ceram Mo 25:32-3 Je '77 *
HIRSCHL & Adler Galleries, Inc. See New York (city)—Galleries and museums
HIRT, Joseph
Extending guidance functions into the classroom. bibl Clearing H 51:113-17 N '77
HIRUMI, H. and others
African trypanosomes: cultivation of animal-infective trypanosoma brucei in vitro. bibl il Science 196:992-4 My 27 '77
HISPANIC AMERICAN art. See Art, Latin American
HISPANIC AMERICAN history. See Latin America—History
HISPANIC literature. See Latin American literature
HISPANICS in the United States. See Latin Americans in the United States
HISPANIOLA (island)
See also
Dominican Republic
HISS, Alger
Weinstein's controversial Hiss-Chambers probe now scheduled for April release by Knopf; ed by R. Dahlin. A. Weinstein. Pub W 212:43 D 12 '77 *
HISS, Anthony
Profiles; H. Youngman. New Yorker 53:46-8+ S 12 '77
—and Lewis, Jeff
The Mad generation. il N Y Times Mag p 14-16+ Jl 31 '77
Moped revolution. il N Y Times Mag p96-7 My 15 '77

HISTAMINE receptors. See Hormone receptors
HISTIDINEMIA. See Metabolism, Disorders of
HISTOCOMPATIBILITY. See Immunological tolerance
HISTOCOMPATIBILITY Y antigen. See Antigens and antibodies
HISTONES
Histone occurrence in chromatin from peridinium balticum, a binucleate dinoflagellate. P. J. Rizzo and E. R. Cox. bibl il Science 198: 1258-60 D 23 '77
Secondary structure of histones and DNA in chromatin. G. J. Thomas, Jr and others. bibl il Science 197:385-8 Jl 22 '77
HISTORIANS, American
See also
Hofstadter, R.
Nevins, A.
Parkman, F.
Rhodes, J. F.
Webb, W. P.
HISTORIANS, English
See also
Bury, J. B.
HISTORIANS, French
See also
Braudel, F.
HISTORIANS, Greek
See also
Herodctus
HISTORIANS and publishers. See Authors and publishers
HISTORIC house museums. See Historic houses, sites, etc.
HISTORIC houses, sites, etc.
See also
Houses, Restored

Alabama
Historic preservation in Mobile. D. L. Young. il Antiques 112:460-5 S '77
Living with antiques: the Marshall-Hixon house in Mobile. M. R. Ingate. il Antiques 112:492-5 S '77

Belgium
See also
Antwerp, Belgium—Historic houses, sites, etc.

California
Early California in Danville; Danville Hotel Territory Historical Site. il Sunset 159:41 N '77
Reminder of San Jose's past, Roberto Adobe. il Sunset 159:54 Jl '77

Connecticut
Litchfield's golden age. W. H. Ellett. il Américas 29:12-20 Je '77

Delaware
Historic homes: authentic charm, modern comfort; renovated interiors of historic houses in New Castle, Del. il McCalls 104:116-21 Jl '77

England
In King Arthur country, the Glastonbury ruins. il Sunset 158:66 Ap '77
Letter from London; Mentmore Towers. M. Panter-Downes. New Yorker 53:123-4 Ap 11 '77
Pevsner choices among the fine English buildings. M. Green. il pors Smithsonian 7:96-103 bibl(p 154) F '77
Place has taken hold of me; Menabilly; excerpt from Myself when young. D. Du Maurier. il pors Sat Eve Post 249:48-50 D '77

France
See also
Paris—Historic houses, sites, etc.
Versailles, Palaces of

Georgia
See also
Savannah, Ga—Historic houses, sites, etc.

Germany, East
East Germany restores Gropius's Bauhaus workshop for its 50th anniversary. il Archit Rec 161:35 Je '77

Germany, West
Wahnfried restored; cite of Bayreuth Festival. G. Loney. il Opera N 41:14-15 F 19 '77

Great Britain
Collections of kings; treasures of the British crown. J. H. Plumb. il por Horizon 20:86-93 D '77

Indiana
New Harmony: a heritage restored. M. D. Hinds. il House & Gard 149:84-5+ Ag '77

Maryland
Furnishing the museum rooms of the William Paca House. G. R. Weidman. bibl il Antiques 111:165-71 Ja '77
Great houses from the golden age of Annapolis. G. B. Tatum. bibl il Antiques 111:174-85 Ja '77
Hammond-Harwood House: a colonial masterpiece; Annapolis. W. H. Pierson, Jr. bibl il Antiques 111:186-93 Ja '77
Paca House garden restored. S. Wright. bibl il Antiques 111:172-3 Ja '77
Restoration of the interior of the William Paca House. R. J. Wright. il Antiques 111:162-4 Ja '77
Saving the William Paca House; Annapolis. S. Wright. il Antiques 111:160-1 Ja '77

Massachusetts
History in houses; the Jeremiah Lee Mansion in Marblehead, Massachusetts. N. G. Chamberlain. bibl il Antiques 112:1164-73 D '77
Landscape wallpaper in the Jeremiah Lee Mansion. C. L. Frangiamore. bibl il Antiques 112: 1174-9 D '77
Rediscovering Chinese export in America; Museum of the American China Trade (Forbes House) Milton, Mass. C. Seebohm. il House & Gard 149:48+ My '77
Riches from the China trade; Museum of the American China Trade (Forbes House) Milton. il House & Gard 149:160-3 My '77
See also
Salem, Mass.—Historic houses, sites, etc.

Mississippi
Auburn in Natchez. M. McGehee. bibl il Antiques 111:546-53 Mr '77
Historic preservation in Natchez, Mississippi. R. W. Miller. il Antiques 111:538-45 Mr '77
Tour of antebellum Natchez. A. Scharffenberger and B. Niles. il Am Home 80:36-7 Mr '77

Missouri
See also
Kansas City, Mo.—Historic houses, sites, etc.

New Jersey
Enchanted evening at the Thomas A. Edison's laboratory; Edison National Historic Site (cont) J. Walsh. il Hobbies 81:35-6+ F; 82: 35-6+ Mr '77

New York (state)
Ancram's Victorian Christmas. B. Hamilton. il Ret Liv 16:32-4 D '76
Caramoor; festival and house of Walter and Lucie Rosen. N. Hazelton. Nat R 29:1062+ S 16 '77
1765 mill grinds into action; restoration of Rest Place Mill, High Falls, N.Y. by Tang and Jane Hansen. B. Russell. il House & Gard 149:36+ Je '77
Sleepy Hollow Restorations; Sunnyside. il Hobbies 82:141+ D '77
Styles; Dutchess County. New Yorker 53:17-19 Ag 8 '77
Sunnyside. C. Morgan. il por Am For 83:26-9 Ap '77
See also
Bronx, N.Y.—Historic houses, sites, etc.
New York (city)—Historic houses, sites, etc.

Northeastern States
Fairs, fleas and historic houses. M. D. Schwartz. Art N 76:144 Summ '77

Pennsylvania
Allegheny Portage Railroad. il Nat Parks & Con Mag 51:25 Jl '77
See also
Philadlephia—Historic houses, sites, etc.
Valley Forge, Pa.

South Carolina
Charleston way. il House & Gard 149:146-9 O '77

Southern States
House touring in the South. N. Richardson. il House & Gard 149:84+ Mr '77
See also
Plantations

Tennessee
History in houses: the Sam Davis home, Smyrna, Tennessee. E. D. Garrett il Antiques 111:560-7 Mr '77
Living with antiques: the Hays-Kiser house, Antioch, Tennessee. J. Kiser. il Antiques 111: 526-9 Mr '77

Texas
See also
Houston, Tex.—Historic houses, sites, etc.

United States
Hard times for others, too. U.S. News 83:93 O 24 '77
Historic houses, landmarks, and museums. See issues of Antiques
Many-sided splendors; American polygonal architecture. R. Taylor. il House & Gard 149:58+ My '77
See also
National Trust for Historic Preservation

Anecdotes, facetiae, satire, etc.
Tour. R. Lipez. Progressive 41:66 F '77

HISTORIC houses, sites, etc.—*Continued*

Virginia

Living with antiques:
In Alexandria, Virginia. S. B. Sherrill. il Antiques 111:1002-5 My '77
New generation for High Street; Petersburg. J. Canup and T. Canup. il Ret Liv 17:35-7+ F '77
Restoring a historic house; Boush-Tazewell house, Norfolk. M. DeCourcy Hinds. il House & Gard 149:58+ Ap '77
Visitors' center for an historic house; at Gunston Hall in Lorton. il Archit Rec 162:105-8 O '77
See also
Monticello (historic house)
Mount Vernon

Wales

Although a rascal, Eli Yale used his means effectively; Erddig Park. M. Waterson. il por Smithsonian 8:91-7 O '77

Washington (state)

Fort Vancouver: fur trade capital of the Pacific Northwest. J. A. Hussey. bibl il por Am West 14:12-19+ S '77

Western States

Western history today. Am West 14:54 Ja; 54 Mr; 56+ My; 48+ Jl; 54 S '77

HISTORIC sites. See Historic houses, sites, etc.
HISTORIC trails. See Trails
HISTORICAL farms. See Agricultural museums
HISTORICAL fiction

Authorship

Historical novel: a trip. D. Gaines. Writer 90:18-20 F '77

HISTORICAL literature
Historical story: is it relevant today? children's books. G. Trease. il Horn Bk 53:20-8 F '77
See also
History—Bibliography
HISTORICAL museums
Buffalo Bill Historical Center. P. H. Hassrick. il Am West 14:16-29 My '77
Buffalo Bill story; dedication of Winchester Gun Museum at Buffalo Bill Historical Center, Cody, Wyo. D. E. Petzal. il Field & S 82:150-1+ My '77
See also
Greenfield Village and Henry Ford Museum, Dearborn, Mich.
Louisiana. State University, Baton Rouge—Rural Life Museum
HISTORICAL societies
See also
American Antiquarian Society, Worcester, Mass.
Litchfield Historical Society
New England Historical Genealogical Society
Western History Association
HISTORICAL Society of Delaware
Decorative arts in Delaware; exhibit of the collection of the Historical society of Delaware. S. B. Sherrill. il Antiques 111:1108+ Je '77
HISTORIOGRAPHY
Why I see it (cont) B. Catton. por Am Heritage 28:79 F; 107 Ap; 63 Je; 97 Ag; 44-5 O '77
See also
United States—History—Historiography
HISTORY
History and happenstance. N. Cousins. Sat R 4:6 Ag 6 '77
See also
Archives
Chronology
Current events
Historical literature
Oral history
Records, Ancient
also names of years, decades and centuries, e.g. Nineteen hundred and twenties; *also* subhead History under various subjects, e.g. Astronomy—History, and under names of countries, cities, states, etc, e.g. France—History

Bibliography

David Hackett Fischer on history. D. H. Fischer. New Repub 177:21+ D 3 '77
History (cont) J. L. Connelly. America 136:84 Ja 29 '77
History (cont) T. H. O'Connor. America 136:425-6 My 7 '77
Other books received. See issues of American historical review
Reviews of books: general. See issues of American historical review

Philosophy

J. B. Bury's philosophy of history: a reappraisal. D. S. Goldstein. bibl f por Am Hist R 82:896-919 O '77
Living in a valley; historical perspective. O. Handlin. Am Scholar 46:301-12 Summ '77
On challenging the inevitable. L. Morrow. il Time 111:74 Ja 9 '78

Psychological aspects

History's 50-minute hour. K. L. Woodward and others. il Newsweek 89:96+ Ap 18 '77

Sources

See also
Oral history

Study and teaching

Repeating history. R. Kirk. Nat R 29:1054 S 16 '77
Some thinking skills defined in historiographical terms. C. E. Traugh. bibl Clearing H 51:76-7 O '77
See also
United States—History—Study and teaching
HISTORY, Ancient
See also
Greece, Ancient—History

Bibliography

Reviews of books: ancient. See issues of American historical review
HISTORY of the American film; drama. See Durang, C.
HITCH, Charles J.
Unfreezing the future. Science 195:825 Mr 4 '77
HITCH hiking. See Hitchhiking
HITCHCOCK, James
Power to the eloquent. Yale R 66:374-87 Mr '77
HITCHENS, Christopher
Faded laurel crown. Harpers 255:114-17 N '77
HITCHES (automobile) See Automobiles—Equipment
HITCHES (tractors) See Tractors—Equipment
HITCHHIKING
Writer on the road. J. D. Vickery. il por Writers Digest 57:20 Ap '77
HITE, Shere
Discover your own sexuality; interview. Harp Baz 110:100+ F '77
Hite report and female sexuality; interview, ed by S. Moore. Read Digest 110:121-3 Je '77
Women can reach orgasm as easily as men. Vogue 167:220 Mr '77
HITES, Ronald A. and others
Sedimentary polycyclic aromatic hydrocarbons: the historical record. bibl il Science 198:829-31 N 25 '77
HITLER, Adolf
Hitler and the Holocaust. K. L. Woodward and A. Collings. il por Newsweek 90:77 Jl 11 '77 *
Hitler and the revisionists; J. Lukacs and controversy surrounding D. Irving's Hitler's war. W. F. Buckley, Jr. Nat R 29:1072-3 S 16 '77 *
Hitler without cheers or tears; documentary movie. por Time 110:43 Ag 29 '77 *
Not their finest hour. D. Pryce-Jones. il New Repub 176:12-16 My 14 '77 *
Once again, the Führer's ghost is haunting Germany. il U.S. News 83:59 N 7 '77 *
Son of Hitler? por Time 110:45 N 14 '77 *
Speer: Hitler knew; excerpts from interview, ed by A. Zarca. A. Speer. il pors Newsweek 90:56 S 19 '77 *
What young Americans know about Hitler. D. Kaiser. Nation 225:613 D 10 '77 *
HIX, Charles
Advice for the groom; excerpt from Looking good. il Sat Eve Post 249:44-7+ N '77
HJORTSBERG, William
Outdoors (cont) Esquire 88:142-4 Ag '77
HOADLEY, Walter E.
Economy (cont) Duns R 109:9 Mr; 9 Je; 110:11 S; 9 D '77
HOAGLAND, Hudson
Brain evolution and the biology of belief. Bull Atom Sci 33:41-4 Mr '77
HOAN, Nguyen-cong-. See Nguyen-cong-Hoan
HOAXES
Nature fakers and science. E. M. Reilly, Jr. il Conservationist 31:28-31 Ja '77
Paleontological hoaxes; Calaveras skull, Piltdown man, and Beringer fossil hoaxes. A. M. Keen. Natur Hist 86:24+ My '77
War of Longitude Lane; cannon hoax. W. Ripley. il Am Hist Illus 11:20-3 F '77
HOBBIES
He wouldn't do that—would he? B. Norman. Ret Liv 17:46 Jl '77
Hobbies and activities; symposium. il Ret Liv 17:40-4 Ap '77
Self-renewal takes new directions in hobbies, culture, back-to-school. il U.S. News 82:64-9 My 23 '77
See also
Collectors and collecting

Bibliography

Books reviewed. See issues of Hobbies

HOBBS, Fritz
What do you do when you grow up? J. Kaplan. il pors Sports Illus 47:37-8 Jl 4 '77 *

HOBBS, Harry Jason
Flexible veneer—easy, inexpensive route to elegant furniture. il Pop Sci 210:124+ F '77

HOBBS, John M. and Heany, D. F.
Coupling strategy to operating plans. Harvard Bus R 55:119-26 My '77

HOBBS, Peter V. and others
Eruptions of the St Augustine volcano: airborne measurements and observations. bibl il Science 195:871-3 Mr 4 '77

HOBHOUSE, Janet
Jasper Johns: the passionless subject passionately painted. il Art N 76:46-9 D '77
Private joke between myself and myself. il por Art N 76:41-3 Ap '77
Some unresolved questions. Art N 76:58-9 F '77

HOBOES. See Tramps

HOBSON, Richard
Memphis is gone. Reviews
New Yorker 52:67 F 7 '77 *

HOCHACHKA, P. W. and others
Pulmonary metabolism during diving: conditioning blood for the brain. bibl il Science 198: 831-4 N 25 '77

HOCHFIELD, Sylvia
Wonderful things. il Art N 76:54-7 Ja '77

HOCKER
Game any number can play. V. Kraft. il por Sports Illus 47:40-1 Ag 22 '77

HOCKEY

Study and teaching

Joy of deprogramming sport; Can/Am Hockey School in Guelph. R. Kahn. il Time 110:50 Ag 22 '77

HOCKEY, College
No heels in the Achilles; Union College. P. Putnam. il por Sports Illus 46:46+ F 7 '77
Union all but sundered? coach N. Harkness of Union College. il por Time 111:63 Ja 9 '78

Tournaments

Revelry in the morgue; NCAA championship. P. Gammons. il Sports Illus 46:65-6 Ap 4 '77

HOCKEY, Professional
Away advantage; Philadelphia Flyers vs Toronto Maple Leafs in Stanley Cup quarterfinals. P. Gammons. il Sports Illus 46:72 Ap 25 '77
Les Canadiens: the politics of pucks. R. Kahn. il Time 109:63-4 F 14 '77
Cash was laundered; Boston Bruins vs Los Angeles Kings in Stanley Cup quarterfinals. P. Gammons. il Sports Illus 46:78+ My 2 '77
He was a two-time loser; Boston Bruins vs Montreal Canadiens in Stanley Cup finals. J. Kirshenbaum. il pors Sports Illus 46:73-6 My 16 '77
Hockey 1977-78: scouting reports. P. Gammons. il Sports Illus 47:42-4+ O 17 '77
Hockey on thin ice. J. E. Maslow. il Sat R 5: 70-1 D 10 '77
Hockey's super team; Montreal Canadiens. P. Axthelm. il Newsweek 89:71+ My 2 '77
Just what the doctor ordered; Canadiens, Flyers and Islanders. P. Gammons. il Sports Illus 47:22-3 N 21 '77
On the whole, it's the donut line; Montreal Canadiens. J. Kirshenbaum. il pors Sports Illus 46:26-9 F 7 '77
Shoveling out from under; Buffalo Sabres. P. Gammons. il Sports Illus 46:54-5 F 21 '77
Stating their case; Stanley Cup semi-finals. P. Gammons. il Sports Illus 46:16-19 My 9 '77
They ruined the Bruins; Canadiens' Stanley Cup victory. P. Gammons. il Sports Illus 46:24-7 My 23 '77
They saved the best for the very last. P. Gammons. il Sports Illus 46:26-7 Ap 11 '77
Welcome back, Scarface; T. Lindsay, general manager of the Detroit Red Wings. P. Gammons. il pors Sports Illus 47:86+ O 31 '77
Wherever you find Orr, he glitters; Chicago Black Hawks. P. Gammons. il pors Sports Illus 46:20-1 Ja 24 '77
See also
Hockey players

Acquisitions and mergers

Will the world end? proposed World Hockey Association-National Hockey League merger. J. Kirshenbaum. Sports Illus 46:52 Je 6 '77

Economic aspects

Cleveland's not barren; plan to save the Barons from bankruptcy. P. Gammons. il Sports Illus 46:50+ Mr 7 '77
Socializing of slap shots. R. Kahn. il Time 109:62 Mr 21 '77

Ethical aspects

Wild Willie gets a new lease on life; case of W. Trognitz. P. Gammons. il por Sports Illus 47:28-30+ N 28 '77

Organization and administration

Hockey 1977-78; interview. A. Eagleson; J. A. Ziegler, Jr. il pors Sports Illus 47:36-41 O 17 '77
Would you buy a used hockey player from this man? S. Pollock, general manager of the Montreal Canadiens. J. Kirshenbaum. por Sports Illus 46:46-8+ Ap 18 '77

HOCKEY coaches
See also
Harkness, N.

HOCKEY players
How Montreal's dynasty was built. Sports Illus 46:51 Ap 18 '77
Reincarnation and 13 pairs of socks; goalies' superstitions. J. Kirshenbaum. il Sports Illus 46:30-3 Mr 28 '77
Three Islanders unto themselves; Bryan Trottier, Mike Bossy and Clark Gillies. J. Kirshenbaum. il Sports Illus 47:20-1 D 12 '77
Young and restless; WHA's young stars. P. Gammons. il por Sports Illus 46:52+ Mr 14 '77
See also
Cashman, W.
Cheevers, G.
Dailey, B.
Howe, G.
Schultz, D.
Trognitz, W.

HOCKNEY, David
Stylish realist; show at the André Emmerich Gallery in New York city. M. Stevens. il Newsweek 90:73+ N 14 '77 *
Things exactly as they are. N. Gosling. il pors Horizon 20:46-51 N '77 *

HODDES, Eric
Does sleep help you study? Psychol Today 11:69 Je '77

HODDESON, Lillian Hartmann
Roots of solid-state research at Bell Labs. bibl il Phys Today 30:23-6+ Mr '77

HODGE, Norman E.
Share buildings for better operations. Am City & County 92:92 S '77

HODGES, David A.
Microelectronic memories; with biographical sketch. il Sci Am 237:14, 130-1+ bibl(p258) S '77

HODGES, Ralph
Stereo scene. See issues of Popular electronics including Electronics world

HODGES, Tom
This orchard drips with success. il Org Gard & Farm 24:90-2 Jl '77

HODGIN, Ellis
Orphans without a home. Lib J 102:1722 S 1 '77

HODGINS, Maibelle Dickey
Woodpecker at my window. il Am For 83:26-7 D '77

HODGKIN'S disease
Cancer in clusters; cases in Breckenridge, Mich. M. Clark and others. il Newsweek 90:119 O 17 '77

HODGSON, Alice Doan
History in towns: Orford, New Hampshire. il Antiques 112:712-25 O '77

HODGSON, Bryan
Montenegro: Yugoslavia's black mountain il map Nat Geog 152:662-83 N '77

HODGSON, Ernest. See Dahl, A. R. jt auth

HODGSON, Godfrey
Reports & comment: Turin. il Atlantic 240:20+ Ag '77

HODGSON, Moira
Timesaving cookbooks. Am Home 80:72 Ag '77

HOEKEMA, Anthony A.
Thinking positively about self. Chr Today 21:32-3 My 20 '77

HOEKSTRA, Harry D.
Off with your pants. Ret Liv 17:34 My '77

HOELTERHOFF, Manuela
Goldilocks' cosmic teach-in. il pors Art N 76:19-21 Mr '77

HOENIG, Gary
Doctor J's toughest case. il pors N Y Times Mag p56-61 F 13 '77

HOERR, John
Commentary (cont) Bus W p28 F 28 '77

HOES
Warren hoe. P. Koepke. il Org Gard & Farm 24:166-7 Je '77

HOEY, Richard B.
Market trends (cont) por Forbes 121:234-5 Ja 9 '78
Stock trends (cont) por Forbes 119:80 F 1; 90-1 Mr 1; 94 Ap 1; 304-5 My 15; 136-7 Je 15; 120:95 Jl 15; 177 O 1; 208-9 N 15 '77

HOFF, M. Edward, Jr
Brain for a house. por House B 119:14+ S '77 *

HOFFA, Harlan
Encouraging children's interest in art. il Intellect 105:304 Mr '77

HOFFER, William
Blood: it's safe to give, but sometimes dangerous to receive. il Fam Health 9:36-9 Mr '77

HOFFERT, Sylvia
This one great evil. bibl il Am Hist Illus 12:37-41 My '77

HOFFMAN, Alice
Property of; story; excerpt from novel. Ms 5:69-71 F '77
HOFFMAN, Allan Richard, and others
Helping shape legislative policy. il Phys Today 30:42-8 Ag '77
HOFFMAN, Arlene
Yogurt & the fountain of youth. C. Turgeon. il Sat Eve Post 249:18+ O '77 *
HOFFMAN, Mrs Conlon-. See Conlon-Hoffman, Mrs
HOFFMAN, Charlotte K.
Women's Educational Equity Act. Am Educ 13: 28-9 D '77
HOFFMAN, Daniel
Voyeurs; poem. Am Scholar 46:190-1 Spr '77
(tr) See Csoóri, S. I stole your face; Dreamers of my dream
(tr) See Gerai, G. Vigil at dawn
(tr) See Somlyó, G. Tale of the double helix; Fairy tale of the cosmos
(tr) See Zelk, Z. Moment; Alone
HOFFMAN, David J. and Niyogi, S. K.
Metal mutagens and carcinogens affect RNA synthesis rates in a distinct manner. bibl il Science 198:513-14 N 4 '77
HOFFMAN, Eleanor M. and Schifsky, J. P.
Designing writing assignments. il Engl J 66: 41-5 D '77
HOFFMAN, George
International development of energy; excerpts from address. Intellect 105:207 Ja '77
HOFFMAN, Kenneth A.
Polarity transition records and the geomagnetic dynamo. bibl il Science 196:1329-32 Je 17 '77
HOFFMAN, Nancy Yanes
Violet Weingarten. por Commonweal 104:533-5 Ag 19 '77
HOFFMAN, Paul
Our dream house was haunted. il Good H 184: 119+ Ap '77
HOFFMAN, Robert
Cult of anti-rationalism in education. Educ Digest 42:57-60 Ja '77
HOFFMANN, Stanley
Not a single issue in which we can impose our will. por U.S. News 82:45 Je 27 '77
Toward world order. New Repub 176:10-12 Mr 19 '77
Uses of American power; excerpt from The lure of primacy and the logic of world order. bibl f For Affairs 56:27-48 O '77
HOFMANN, Adele D.
Adolescents, sex, and education. Educ Digest 43:24-7 N '77
HOFMANN, Hans
Restless experiments of Hans Hofmann. B. Forgey. il por Art N 76:62-3 F '77 *
HOFMANN, Josef
Genius to genius; correspondence with the Edison Laboratories; comp by R. R. Wile. Am Rec G 40:6-8+ S '77
HOFSTADTER, Richard
Richard Hofstadter, C. Wright Mills, and the critical ideal. R. Gillam. Am Scholar 47:69-85 Wint '77 *
HOGAN, Clarence Lester. See Linvill, J. G. jt auth
HOGAN, Douglas
Sex therapy. bibl il Society 14:38-42 Jl '77
HOGAN, Paul
Reaching high point with a playground. il Parks & Rec 12:26-9 N '77
HOGE, James Fulton, 1935-
Press and President. New Repub 176:25-6 Ja 22 '77

about

Hoge gives them Hecht. D. Gelman and others. il por Newsweek 89:52 F 7 '77 *
HOGE, Warren
Other Cary Grant. il pors N Y Times Mag p 14-15+ Jl 3 '77
HOGG, Quintin McGarel, Baron Hailsham of Saint Marylebone. See Hailsham of Saint Marylebone, Q. M. H.
HOGS. See Swine
HOHEISEL, Peter
Limestone and iron; poem. Nation 224:124 Ja 29 '77
HOHENEMSER, Christoph, and others
Distrust of nuclear power. bibl il Science 196: 25-34 Ap 1 '77
HOHENEMSER, Kurt H.
Overview: energy. See issues of Environment
HOHENSTEIN, C. Louis
State-of-the-art electronics. il Yachting 142:40+ Ag '77
HOHLER, Robert
My father played for me. il Read Digest 111:156-9 D '77
HOISTING machinery
See also
Winches
HOISTS, Truck. See Trucks—Equipment
HOKANSON, Garth
Anthrax: the deadly fruit of the loom. Craft Horiz 37:9+ F '77
HOKINSON, Helen Elna
There's a little Helen Hokinson in all of us. J. Dobbs. il Ms 5:16-17 F '77 *
HOLADAY, John W. and others
Synchronized ultradian cortisol rhythms in monkeys: persistence during corticotropin infusion. bibl il Science 198:56-8 O 7 '77
HOLBERT, Cornelia
Quiet death, with dignity. il America 136:214-16 Mr 12 '77
HOLBROOK, Hal
Mark Twain tonight! Nat R 29:504-5 Ap 29 '77 *
HOLBROOKE, Richard C.
Department discusses MIA's in Vietnam and Laos; statement, July 27, 1977. Dept State Bull 77:359-61 S 12 '77
Human rights situation in Cambodia; statement, July 26, 1977. Dept State Bull 77:323-4 S 5 '77
Recommendation to parole Indochinese refugees; statement. August 4, 1977. Dept State Bull 77: 411-13 S 26 '77
U.S. economic and security assistance programs in East Asia; statement, March 10, 1977. Dept State Bull 76:322-6 Ap 4 '77
HOLBY, Grethe
Reviews. J. Pikula. Dance Mag 51:42+ My '77 *
HOLD-ups. See Robberies and assaults
HOLDEN, Larry
Incredibly rich tabloid market. Writers Digest 57:19-22 Jl '77
HOLDEN, Michael
From Wall Street to auto sales—a success story. V. Louviere. il pors Nations Bus 65:76 S '77 *
HOLDEN, Robert H.
We're gonna get our asses kicked. Nation 225: 461-3 N 5 '77
HOLDEN, William
Problems and pleasures of living together; interview, ed by I. Silden. S. Powers. pors Harp Baz 110:114-15+ My '77 *
Stefanie & Bill; interview, ed by S. Decatur. S. Powers. il pors Ladies Home J 94:78+ N '77 *
HOLDER, Ken
Poems on various subjects, religious and moral; P. Wheatley's poetry. Engl J 66:68 Mr '77
HOLDING, Robert Earl
Earl has bought a pearl. W. O. Johnson. il por Sports Illus 47:93-4+ N 14 '77 *
HOLDING companies
NICOR: from gas distribution to total energy. por Duns R 110:22-3+ S '77
Raising the ante; Falcon Seaboard. J. Flanigan. Forbes 120:150 O 15 '77
Why Maremont is going after Pemcor; success of Pemcor's Jensen sound Laboratories. Bus W p95 Ag 29 '77
See also
Amfac, Inc
Bank holding companies
Esmark, Inc.
Insurance holding companies
Kaiser Industries Corporation
Merrill Lynch & Company, Inc
Summa Corporation
Triad Holding Corporation
Union Pacific Corporation

Belgium

Lambert's widening beachhead in the U.S; Lambert Brussels Corp. il por Bus W p 102-3 F 21 '77

Great Britain

See also
Pearson, S. & Son, Ltd
HOLDING Corporation of America. See Insurance holding companies
HOLDING devices (machine work)
Hold-down for the Workmate. H. Wicks. il Pop Mech 149:24 Ja '78
Toolpost holder for hand grinder. C. A. Traub. il Pop Mech 148:117 Ag '77
See also
Clamps
Jigs
Vises
HOLDREGE, Neb.
New confidence. il U.S. News 82:30-1 Je 13 '77
HOLIDAY (periodical)
Speaking of Holiday. See issues of Holiday to April 1977
See also
Travel/Holiday (periodical)
HOLIDAY Inns, Inc
Place to worship; chaplains at Holiday Inns. K. Wilson. il por Sat Eve Post 249:37 Ap '77
Profits are back, but the thrill is gone. por Forbes 120:56 D 15 '77
What? Me nonessential? il Forbes 119:79 Je 1 '77
HOLIDAY parties. See Christmas entertaining
HOLIDAY travel. See Travel
HOLIDAYS
See also
Vacations
also names of holidays, e.g. Fourth of July

HOLKAR, Shalini Devi
Spice of life. il por Holiday 58:44-5 Je '77
HOLLABAUGH, John F.
Build a 10-Hz to 1-MHz EPUT meter. il Pop Electr 11:68-9 Mr '77
HOLLAND, Barbara
Children are scared of the dark; story. Ladies Home J 94:60 F '77
Day's work; story. Ms 6:54-8 Ag '77
HOLLAND, Isabelle
Interview with Isabelle Holland; ed by P. Janeczko. Engl J 66:14-16 Mr '77
HOLLAND, Joe, and Henriot, P. J.
New challenge for world labor. America 137:209-12 O 8 '77
HOLLAND, Max, and Bird, Kai
State department clientism. Nation 224:334-7 Mr 19 '77
—See Bird, K. jt auth
HOLLAND, Raymond T. and Niccolls, John
Match utility rates to system costs. il Am City & County 92:53-5 Ap '77
HOLLAND, Robert
Six or seven fools. Poetry 129:285-95 F '77
HOLLAND. See Netherlands
HOLLAND Festival. See Music festivals—Netherlands
HOLLANDER, Anne
Fashion. il New Repub 177:27 D 7 '77
When fat was in fashion. il N Y Times Mag p36-7+ O 23 '77
HOLLANDER, John
From spectral emanations; poems. Poetry 129: 214-25 Ja '77
Indian summer, 1975; poem. New Yorker 53: 46 N 14 '77

about

Comment. J. D. McClatchy. Poetry 130:41-4 Ap '77 *
HOLLANDER, Lorin
AMSA competition—something different. J. Wierzbicki. il por Hi Fi 27:MA28-9 O '77 *
Lorin Hollander, piano; concert at the 92nd Street YMHA. por Hi Fi 27:MA25-6 Mr '77 *
HÖLLDOBLER, Berthold K. and Haskins, C. P.
Sexual calling behavior in primitive ants. bibl il Science 195:793-4 F 25 '77
—and Wilson, E. O.
Weaver ants: social establishment and maintenance of territory. bibl il Science 195:900-2 Mr 4 '77
Weaver ants; with biographical sketches. il Sci Am 237:15, 146-8+ D '77
HOLLELEY, Douglas
Nude redefined. M. R. Cipnic. il Pop Phot 81: 112-15 Jl '77 *
HOLLEY, Edward G.
Librarian looks at the new copyright law. bibl il Am Lib 8:247-51 My '77
HOLLEY, Terry L. See Beagley, W. K. jt auth
HOLLIDAY, R. and others
Testing the commitment theory of cellular aging. bibl il Science 198:366-72 O 28 '77
HOLLIFIELD, John H.
Research clues. See issues of Today's education
HOLLIGER, Heinz
Heinz Holliger: now that's charisma. R. D. Darrell. il por Hi Fi 27:97 O '77 *
HOLLINGSWORTH, J. Rogers
(ed) Social theory and public policy. bibl f il Ann Am Acad 434:1-198 N '77
—See Hage, J. jt auth
HOLLINGSWORTH, Leslie
Silent night; drama. Plays 37:45-50, 72 D '77
HOLLINSHEAD, Ariel C. and Knaus, W. A.
Herpesviruses—a link in the cancer chain? bibl il Chemistry 50:17-21 My '77
HOLLIS, J. P. See Joshi, M. M. jt auth
HOLLIS, James
On Margate sands: literature and ideas. Intellect 105:362-5 Ap '77
HOLLMAN, Doug
Piano aboard: the sound of music on the water. il Yachting 141:195-7 Ap '77
HOLLOWAY, James Lemuel, 1922-
Secretary Vance and other administration officials urge ratification of Panama Canal treaties; statement, September 27, 1977. Dept State Bull 77:621-2 N 7 '77
HOLLOWAY, Trevor
Britain in miniature. il Travel 147:50-3 Je '77
Progress of marine fish farming in Britain. il Sea Front 23:48-54 Ja '77
HOLLY
Holly for Christmas. il Sunset 159:198 D '77
HOLLY SPRINGS, Miss.
Cemetery at Holly Springs. W. D. Miller. America 137:194-5 O 1 '77
HOLLYHOCK begonias. See Begonias
HOLLYWOOD, Calif.

Hotels, restaurants, etc.

Hollywood's Garden of Allah. G. Oppenheimer. il Am Heritage 28:82-7 Ag '77

Industries

See also
Motion picture industry—United States

Moral conditions

Cleaning up the act in Hollywood. il Time 110: 16+ Ag 15 '77
HOLMES, Barbara Ware
Touching bottom; story. Redbook 149:109 Jl '77
HOLMES, Charlotte Amalie
Impossible man; poem. Mademoiselle 83:139 Ag '77
HOLMES, Currier J.
Iowa beef becomes a test for management. Bus W p28-9 Mr 14 '77 *
HOLMES, Ernie
Offside in Pittsburgh? S. Fraker and S. Lesher. pors Newsweek 89:40 My 9 '77 *
Pittsburgh Fats dodges a silver bullet. R. Kennedy. il por Sports Illus 46:24-6+ Mr 7 '77 *
HOLMES, Linda G.
Teenage drinking. il Good H 184:58+ F '77
HOLMES, Mark L. See Cline J. D. jt auth
HOLMES, Richard
Scrope's last throw. Harpers 254:77-9+ Ap '77
HOLMES, Ruth Vickery
King John and the Abbot of Canterbury; dramatization of English legend. Plays 36:49-56 Ap '77
HOLMGREN, Virginia C.
Liberation à la limeña. il Américas 29:12-13 Je '77
HOLOCAUST, Jewish (1939-1945) See World War, 1939-1945—Jews
HOLOCENE period. See Paleontology—Quaternary
HOLOGRAMS. See Holography
HOLOGRAPHY
Holograms: putting the third D into the catalog. M. R. D'Alleyrand. bibl il Wilson Lib Bull 51: 746-50 My '77
Holography gets closer to your neighborhood theater. S. Walton. il Pop Mech 148:94 D '77
Holography—gimmick or new visual art? P. Sealfon and others. il Pop Phot 81:100-3+ S '77
Interview with two practitioners. S. Cohen; A. Rezny. il pors Pop Phot 81:104-5+ S '77
Molecules in 3-D. il Time 109:81 F 14 '77
Will holography revolutionize crystallography? letter. C. K. Johnson. bibl Science 196:478 Ap 29 '77
X-ray crystallography: 3-D structures by optical computing. T. H. Maugh, 2d. il Science 195: 384 Ja 28 '77
HOLOGRAPHY, Museum of, New York. See Photography—Galleries and museums
HOLST, Gustav
The planets—suite for large orchestra, op. 32. J. Diether. Am Rec G 40:27 N '76 *
HOLSTON River
Chemical plants leave unexpected legacy for two Virginia Rivers; mercury pollution. L. J. Carter. map Science 198:1015-20 D 9 '77
HOLT, H. O. and Stevenson, F. L.
Human performance considerations in complex systems. bibl il Science 195:1205-10 Mr 18 '77
HOLT, Patricia
ABA fever grips publishers in the West. il Pub W 211:40-1 Ap 18 '77
ABA in Denver presents a new kind of regionalism. il Pub W 212:47-8+ N 21 '77
Cody's Books of Berkeley: after 21 years, the Cody's move on. il pors Pub W 212:48-9+ N 7 '77
Letter from the Bay Area. il Pub W 212:49-51 O 17 '77
New approaches to old ideas made two western success stories. il Pub W 211:44-5 My 16 '77
Steel bookstore fixtures—a winning concept. il por Pub W 212:115-17 S 12 '77
Western religious publishers see phenomenal growth period. Pub W 212:73-4 S 26 '77
(ed) See Lorentz, A. PW interviews
(ed) See Surguine, R. Ray and Mary Jane Surguine retire
HOLT, Sidney J.
International cooperation to protect the whales. il Oceans 10:62-4 Jl '77
HOLT, Victoria
Devil on horseback; story; excerpt from novel. Good H 185:115-17 S '77
HOLTKAMP, Dorothy
That's good fish! Bite-size shark. Sci Digest 81: 35-6 Ap '77
HOLTMANN, Carrie
Braced for the best. por Seventeen 36:36 My '77
HOLTON, George
Antarctic coast: a land where man cannot live; photographs. il Oceans 10:14-19 My '77
HOLTON, Robert R.
Reconciliation in Memphis. Commonweal 104:38-9 Ja 21 '77
HOLTON, William C.
Large-scale integration of microelectronic circuits; with biographical sketch. il Sci Am 237: 14, 82-94 bibl(p258) S '77

HOLTZMAN, Elizabeth
Excerpt from remarks on proposal to amend the Hatch Act, June 16, 1977. Cong Digest 56:299+ D '77

HOLVEY, Dora
Day my husband lost his job. il McCalls 104:54+ My '77

HOLY Cross College, Worcester, Mass.
Holy Cross case; crisis in Jesuit education. D. O'Brien; discussion. Commonweal 104:45-8 Ja 21 '77

HOLY days. See Fasts and feasts

HOLY Ghost. See Holy Spirit

HOLY Scriptures. See Bible

HOLY Shroud
News on the Shroud. Nat R 29:656 Je 10 '77
That man in question. K. Lindskoog. Chr Cent 94:934 O 19 '77
Truth and culture; analysis of Holy Shroud. J. Hart. Nat R 29:992-5 S 2 '77

HOLY Spirit
Of tidy doctrine and truncated experience; relationalist and charismatic views of evangelical experiential theology. R. K. Johnston. il Chr Today 21:10-14 F 18 '77
Spiritual lift no one is talking about; analysis of Paul's letter to the Corinthians. L. Samuel. il Chr Today 21:10-12 Ja 21 '77
See also
Pentecost
Trinity

HOLY Week
See also
Good Friday

HOLY Week in art. See Jesus Christ—Art

HOLZER, Adela
Story of Adela H. por Time 109:60 Ap 18 '77 *
Winging a Broadway angel. il por Time 110:51 Jl 25 '77 *

HOLZER, Edith
Home is where the hearth is to the kitchen kollector. il Hobbies 82:116-18 Ja '78

HOLZER, Harold
Lincoln in death: bigger than life. il pors Hobbies 82:115-16 My '77

HOLZMAN, Malcolm
(ed) See Hardy, H. Recycling architectural masterpieces—and other buildings not so great

HOLZNER, Burkart, and Salmon-Cox, Leslie
Conceptions of research and development for education in the United States. bibl f Ann Am Acad 434:88-100 N '77

HOLZWARTH, G. and Prestridge, E. B.
Multistranded helix in xanthan polysaccharide. bibl il Science 197:757-9 Ag 19 '77

HOME
Going home. C. Dowling. il N Y Times Mag p68-9+ D 11 '77
Home: an American obsession. R. Price. Sat R 5:9-14+ N 26 '77
Home—how to take it along when you move. A. J. Waterhouse. House B 119:72+ O '77
Notes and comment; *querencia*. New Yorker 53:27-8 S 26 '77
Segregating the home into male and female territories. G. Melson. Intellect 106:186-7 N '77
See also
Christmas gifts for the home
Family
Family life
Foster home care

HOME and the school. See School and the home

HOME aquariums. See Aquariums

HOME bars. See Bars for the home

HOME building. See House construction

HOME building industry. See Construction industry

HOME business deductions. See Income tax—Deductions

HOME buying. See House buying

HOME care services
House calls are back again. Forbes 120:27 S 1 '77

HOME computers. See Computers—Home use

HOME cooling. See Cooling

HOME decoration. See House decoration

HOME economics
Around the house. J. Keely. See issues of Good housekeeping
Ask Rufus; questions and answers. See issues of Mechanix illustrated
Danger in the combat zones; devices that solve household problems. D. Davis. il Am Home 80:40-1 F '77
Future for working women; ed by R. J. Leaper; excerpt from Women and the American economy: a look to the 1980's. J. Kreps. por Ms 5:56-7 Mr '77
Help. See issues of Mademoiselle
Home economics for guys. il Esquire 87:68-71 Mr '77
Home works. See issues of Redbook
Househusbands. L. C. Pogrebin. Ladies Home J 94:30+ N '77
How women really feel about housework; responses to questionnaire. N. Gittelson. il McCalls 104:129+ F '77
I hereby resign as keeper of this house . . . love mom; family housekeeping. S. Roberts. il por Ms 5:56-7 My '77
Journal about home. See issues of Ladies home journal
Keeping up with keeping house. M. Davidson. il Parents Mag 53:75-9 Ja '78
No-care apartment; Francesca Paolozzi's apartment. il Harp Baz 110:128+ Ag '77
Streamlined, carefree, timesaving house. il N. Williams. Am Home 80:77-8 O '77
300 ingenious ways to make your life easier. il House & Gard 149:114-21 Je '77
Taking the bore out of chores: exercising around the house; 12 ways to shape up doing housework. P. Markham. il House & Gard 149:51 N '77
When you both work; labor-saving appliances. M. Davidson. il Parents Mag 52:66-8 Ap '77
See also
Budget, Household
Computers—Home use
Finance, Personal
Housewives
Mechanics, Household
Storage in the home

Study and teaching
See also
Cookery—Study and teaching

HOME education
Do-it-yourself nursery school. K. A. Wright. il por Redbook 149:38+ Jl '77
Get with child a mandrake root. J. Eliot. Horticulture 55:12-13+ Je '77
How to make your kids smarter. R. Bahr. il Am Home 80:44-5 Je '77
Should you teach your child to read? preparing the preschooler. S. A. Jackson. bibl Am Educ 13:27-9 O '77
We banished the unhappy hour. K. R. Olenzak. il por Redbook 148:49+ Ap '77

HOME electronics
Look and listen. J. Free. See issues of Popular science
New electronics for the home. H. Fantel. il Redbook 150:53+ N '77
See also
Audio systems
Phonograph
Radio receivers
Tape recorders and recording
Television receivers

Exhibitions
See Electronic apparatus and appliances—Exhibitions

Purchasing
Sound advice. il Seventeen 36:154-5 Mr '77

HOME energy conservation. See Power resources—Conservation

HOME equipment. See Household appliances

HOME fire prevention. See Houses—Fires and fire prevention

HOME fires. See Fires

HOME freezers. See Freezers

HOME furnishings. See Household furnishings

HOME grounds
How to dress up your yard with brick. P. Angell. il Pop Mech 147:104-6+ My '77
Live out and love it! N. Seney and S. Coulter. il Bet Hom & Gard 55:103-13 Je '77
Natural look: alternatives to the lawn. M. Wexler. il Nat Wildlife 15:10-11 F '77
This used to be their old bare backyard; greenhouse room. il Sunset 159:176-7 O '77
Winterize the yard, too. il Changing T 31:8-9 N '77
See also
Lawns
Playgrounds, Home

HOME improvement centers
Home centers: 1-stop shopping for Mrs Fixit. S. Schraub. House B 119:48 Ap '77
See also
Hardware stores

HOME improvement deductions. See Income tax—Deductions

HOME improvements. See Houses—Maintenance and repair

HOME industries. See Cottage industries

HOME inspection. See Building inspection

HOME insurance. See Insurance, Homeowners

HOME labor
See also
Cottage industries

HOME life. See Family life

HOME life, Education for. See Family life, Education for

HOME made toys. See Toys

HOME mechanics. See Mechanics, Household

HOME movies. See Motion pictures, Amateur
HOME offices. See Offices
HOME ownership
8 ways to protect your investment in your home. R. Rosefsky. Bet Hom & Gard 55:37+ Ap '77
Good investment, but a bad business. J. Train. por Forbes 120:206 N 15 '77
How to sell your house and keep it too; split equity. J. M. Guttentag. il Ret Liv 17:36-9+ Ja '77
Is owning a home still a sound investment? G. G. Greer. il Bet Hom & Gard 55:10+ Mr '77
Moral dimension of housing. J. M. Wall. Chr Cent 94:243 Mr 16 '77
Tax-saving tips for home-owners. il U.S. News 82:74 Mr 21 '77
See also
House buying
Urban homesteading
HOME playgrounds. See Playgrounds, Home
HOME remedies. See Medicines, Patent, proprietary, etc.
HOME remodeling industry. See Construction industry
HOME run records. See Sports records
HOME safety devices and measures. See Accidents—Prevention
HOME selling. See House selling
HOME shows. See Exhibitions
HOME-Stake Production Company. See Petroleum industry—United States
HOME storage. See Storage in the home
HOME study courses. See Correspondence schools and courses
HOME-swapping vacations. See Vacations
HOME swimming pools. See Swimming pools, Home
HOME towns. See Birthplaces
HOME visitations. See School and the home
HOME waste disposal appliances. See Refuse and refuse disposal—Apparatus
HOME water purifiers. See Water purifiers, Domestic
HOME water supply. See Water heaters
HOMEMAKERS. Housewives
HOMEMAKING. See Home economics
HOMEOWNER insurance. See Insurance, Homeowners
HOMER
Southern gentleman and Pope's Homer. R. S. Sugg, Jr. il por Smithsonian 7:125-30+ F '77 *
HOMER, Frank X. J.
Biography (cont) America 136:428-30 My 7 '77
HOMER, Larena
Alone in a retirement community. il pors Ret Liv 17:29-30 Ag '77
HOMER, Ron
(ed) See Hepburn, K. Hepburn
HOMER, Winslow
Winslow Homer in Texas. K. M. Jones. il Antiques 112:892 N '77 *
HOMES, Institutional
See also
Nursing homes
HOMESTEADING, Urban. See Urban homesteading
HOMESTEADS
Closing the frontier. H. Flieger. U.S. News 82:88 F 28 '77
Farmers' frontier; excerpt from The American farm: a photographic history. M. Conrat and R. Conrat. il Am West 14:22-33 Mr '77
Homestead venture that works. G. Logsdon. il Org Gard & Farm 24:147-53+ Jl '77
Last Idaho land rush: growth at any cost? E. Chaney. Audubon 79:154-7 N '77
Two homesteading newcomers to the Ozarks. T. Gettings. il Org Gard & Farm 24:111-15 F '77
HOMETOWNS. See Birthplaces
HOMICIDE. See Murder
HOMILETICS. See Preaching
HOMINIDS. See Man, Prehistoric
HOMOLOGY (biology)
Orthogenesis of the hominids: an exploration using biorthogonal grids. F. L. Bookstein. bibl il Science 197:901-4 Ag 26 '77
HOMOSEXUALITY
Anita Bryant is mad about gays. M. Kondracke. New Repub 176:13-15 My 7 '77
Anita Bryant on the march: the lessons of Dade County. L. Van Gelder. il por Ms 6:75-8+ S '77
Anita Bryant's crusade. G. Steinem. Progressive 41:37 Je '77
Anita Bryant's crusade; ordinance banning discrimination against homosexuals in Dade County, Fla. D. A. Williams. por Newsweek 89:39 Ap 11 '77
Anita Bryant's hollow victory. Progressive 41:8 S '77
Anita's circle; A. Bryant's drive to repeal Dade County's ordinance barring discrimination against homosexuals. il por Time 109:76 My 2 '77
Band gets bigger. il Time 110:30 Jl 11 '77
Battle over gay rights. T. Mathews and others. il por Newsweek 89:16-17+ Je 6 '77
Confronting the homosexual issue. Chr Today 21:36 Jl 8 '77
Cooler crusader; A. Bryant. S. Drake and B. Brubaker. il por Newsweek 90:11-12 O 3 '77
Education now. P. Schrag. Sat R 5:53-4 N 12 '77
Enough! Enough! Enough! repeal of ordinance outlawing discrimination against homosexuals, Dade County, Fla. il por Time 109:59-60 Je 20 '77
Freedom to sin; letter. M. R. Sills. Chr Cent 94:963-5 O 19 '77
Gay genius and the gay mob. A. Kazin. Esquire 88:33-4+ D '77
Gay power in San Francisco. S. Fraker and G. C. Lubenow. il Newsweek 89:25 Je 6 '77
Gay rights showdown in Miami. il por Time 109:20 Je 13 '77
Gay sex in the schools. J. Merrow. Parents Mag 52:66+ S '77
Gaycott turns ugly. il por Time 110:33 N 21 '77
Homosexuality. A. Frank and S. Frank. Mademoiselle 83:108 O '77
Homosexuality and civil rights; repeal of Dade County, Fla. ordinance. America 136:558 Je 25 '77; Discussion. 137:41 Jl 30 '77
How far out of the closet? G. F. Will. Newsweek 89:92 My 30 '77
Legitimizing homosexuality. M. Spector. bibl il Society 14:52-6 Jl '77
Miami vote: tide turning against homosexuals? il por U.S. News 82:46 Je 20 '77
Mystical poetry in a court of law; conviction of D. Lemon, editor of Gay news, in London. T. Beeson. Chr Cent 94:838-9 S 28 '77
No to the gays. R. Steele and H. Camp. il Newsweek 89:27+ Je 20 '77
Not so gay; vote to repeal the homosexual rights bill. Nat R 29:763 Jl 8 '77
Not yet equal under the law. il Time 109:60 Je 20 '77
On trial for blasphemy; Gay news trial in Great Britain. Time 110:54 Jl 25 '77
Out in the open: gay rights: the coming struggle. K. Ross. Nation 225:526-30 N 19 '77
Out of the closet. Nation 225:34-5 Jl 9 '77
Psychiatrist answers teen questions about homosexuality. R. Gould. Seventeen 36:152-3+ S '77
Returning sex to the bedroom. C. Tucker. Sat R 4:60 Jl 23 '77
Toujours gai; N. Podhoretz's article in Harper's magazine. Nat R 29:1160 O 14 '77
Trash-bag murders; case of D. D. Hill and P. W. Kearney in California. D. A. Williams and J. Huck. il pors Newsweek 90:22 Jl 18 '77
Twenty-eight, and counting. . .; arrest of mass murderers P. Kearney and D. Hill. il pors Time 110:49 Jl 18 '77
United fruit. D. K. Mano. Nat R 29:898-9 Ag 5 '77
A walk on San Francisco's gay side. H. Gold. il N Y Times Mag p67-9+ N 6 '77
When your teenager needs you the most: learning to talk openly about homosexuality; excerpt from What every parent should know about sex and the American teenager. M. M. Kappelman. il Fam Health 9:44-6 Ag '77
Why the conservatives won in Miami. R. H. Ard. Chr Cent 94:677-9 Ag 3 '77
Yes, Virginia, there is a PIE; Paedophile Information Exchange. Nat R 29:1221-2 O 28 '77
See also
Church work with homosexuals
Lesbianism

Bibliography

Books on homosexuality: a current checklist. D. Maryles and R. Dahlin. Pub W 212:50-1 Ag 8; 58+ O 17 '77
HOMOSEXUALITY and Christianity
Disciples decide; homosexuality issue and the Christian Church, Disciples of Christ. Chr Today 22:56-7 N 18 '77
Gay get-together. R. Christopher. Chr Today 21:33-5 Je 3 '77
Homosexual ordination: bishops feel the flak. Chr Today 21:51 Mr 4 '77
Homosexuality and Christian faith: a theological reflection. T. W. Jennings. Chr Cent 94:137-42 F 16 '77
Leveling of John McNeill. D. Berrigan. Commonweal 104:778-83 D 9 '77
Sexual differences: a cultural convention? J. M. Batteau. Chr Today 21:8-10 Jl 8 '77; Reply. J. E. Runions. 22:11 O 7 '77
See also
Ordination of homosexuals
HOMOSEXUALITY in literature
Even little gulls do it. W. F. Buckley, Jr. Nat R 30:49 Ja 6 '78
See also
Homosexuality—Bibliography

HOMOSEXUALITY in the Bible
Sexual differences: a cultural convention? J. M. Batteau. Chr Today 21:8-10 Jl 8 '77; Reply. J. E. Runions. 22:11 O 7 '77
Speaking literally. M. E. Marty. Chr Cent 94: 639 Jl 6 '77

HONDA (automobile) See Automobiles, Foreign

HONDA Motor Company. See Automobile industry—Japan

HONDERICH, Beland H.
Toronto star goes on a multimedia binge. por Bus W p68-9 F 7 '77 *

HONDURAS
See also
Fishing—Honduras
Women—Honduras

Exploring expeditions

Quest in the jungle; search for the lost city of Ciudad Blanca. J. Underwood. il Sports Illus 48:86-90+ Ja 9 '78

Religious institutions and affairs

See also
Church and social problems—Honduras

HONESTY
See also
Cheating in school work

Anecdotes, facetiae, satire, etc.

I embrace the new candor. G. W. S. Trow. New Yorker 53:36-7 My 9 '77

HONEY
Carbon-13/carbon-12 ratio is relatively uniform among honeys. L. W. Doner and J. W. White, Jr. bibl il Science 197:891-2 Ag 26 '77
Pyrrolizidine alkaloids: their occurrence in honey from tansy ragwort (senecio jacobaea L.) M. L. Deinzer and others. bibl il Science 195:497-9 F 4 '77
See also
Bee culture
Bees
Cookery—Honey

HONEYBEES. See Bees

HONG KONG
See also
Americans in Hong Kong
Hotels, motels, etc.—Hong Kong

Commerce

Europe, Western

See Europe, Western—Commerce—Hong Kong

Description and travel

Hong Kong. T. Randall. il pors Holiday 58:30-3+ Mr '77

Industries

See also
Watch industry—Hong Kong

HONG KONG influenza virus. See Influenza viruses

HONGISTO, Richard
Sheriff behind bars. il por Time 109:85 My 16 '77

HONIGBERG, B. M. See Cunningham, I. jt auth

HONOLULU

Description

Tour of Honolulu's old and new Chinatown. il Sunset 159:50 Ag '77

Hotels, restaurants, etc.

Beyond fish and poi and little grass shacks. R. L. Balzer. il Holiday 58:46-7+ Ap '77
Kings, queens, and a full house. H. Sutton. il Sat R 4:51-3 F 19 '77

Music

See also
Opera—Hawaii

Parks and playgrounds

Century in the life of Kapiolani Park. E. L. Bryden and T. Robinson. bibl il Parks & Rec 12:49-53 Jl '77

HONOLULU Marathon. See Running

HONOR students
Don't call me egghead! B. Lumpkins. Seventeen 36:74 S '77

HONOR system in education. See Self government in education

HONORARY degrees. See Degrees, Honorary

HOOD, Graham
Charles Bridges and William Dering; two Virginia painters, 1735-1750; excerpt. bibl il Antiques 112:934-8 N '77

HOOD, H. P, and Sons, Inc
Buy frogurt, or else. il por Forbes 119:56 My 15 '77
Marketer who put H. P. Hood on the map; E. Gelsthorpe. il por Duns R 110:30-1 Jl '77

HOOD, Joyce E.
Sight words are not going out of style. Educ Digest 42:53-5 Ap '77

HOOD, Ted
In their hour of triumph. J. Hersey. il Yachting 142:86-91+ S '77 *
One on one. R. Vaughan. il pors Motor B & S 140:78-80+ Ag '77 *
Tuning with Ted. J. Rousmaniere. il Yachting 141:63-5 F '77 *

HOOK, J. N.
My love song. Engl J 66:14-17 O '77

HOOK, Sidney
Fanaticism and absolutism. il por Intellect 105: 387-8 My '77

HOOKED rugs. See Rugs and carpets

HOOKS, Benjamin Lawson
Washington notebook. S. Booker. Ebony 33:22 Ja '78 *

HOOPER, Glenda Todd
Special report: rejoycing at the library. il Wilson Lib Bull 51:718-19 My '77

HOOPER, Lucien O.
Market comment. See issues of Forbes

HOOPES, David T.
Alaska's interior forests: in the eye of the storm. il Am For 83:16-19+ Je '77

HOOPES, Roy
Taped talk: storing tomorrow's source materials. il Hi Fi 27:61-5 Ag '77

HOOPMAN, Harold Dewaine
Marathon man sprints. por Forbes 119:70+ Ap 15 '77 *

HOOSUCK Community Resources Corporation. See Community development corporations

HOOVER, David
Digital tuners. il Pop Sci 211:92-3+ N '77

HOOVER, John Edgar
JFK killing: FBI files raise questions, give no answers. il U.S. News 83:15 D 19 '77 *
JFK: what the FBI found. R. Boeth and others. il pors Newsweek 90:28+ D 19 '77 *

HOOVER, Suzanne R.
Teaching: Nadia Boulanger. Am Scholar 46:496-502 Aut '77

HOOVER, Velma J.
Meta Vaux Warrick Fuller: her life and art. il por Negro Hist Bull 40:678-81 Mr '77

HOPE, Jack
Roughing it in the Yukon. il pors Int Wildlife 7:20-7 Jl '77
Scaling Chilkoot even today is a fearful ordeal. il Smithsonian 7:106-13 bibl(p 154+) F '77

HOPE, Marjorie
What have they done to the rain? Chr Cent 94: 693-5 Ag 3 '77

HOPE (project) See Underdeveloped areas—Medical care

HOPE (ship) See Hospital ships

HOPE Seminar. See Religious conferences—Israel

HOPEFUL Stakes (race) See Horse racing

HOPI Indians
Kachina dolls. J. Chiara. il Hobbies 82:38 Jl '77
Nampeyo: Hopi potter. K. A. Way. il por Ceram Mo 25:51-3 Mr '77

HOPKINS, Bernie
Art and craft of making decoys. il por Bet Hom & Gard 55:140-1 N '77 *

HOPKINS, Edwin E.
Using hand calculators in schools. Educ Digest 42:44-5 F '77

HOPKINS, Ellen Moore
Nurse Hopkins, 30 years later. il pors Ebony 32:80+ Ap '77 *

HOPKINS, Gerard Manley
Gerard Manley Hopkins: exploding for Christ. M. R. Brown. Chr Today 21:20+ Ja 7 '77 *
Nature's round makes jubilee: Hopkins's priestly centenary. J. J. Feeney. il America 137:394-7 D 3 '77 *

HOPKINS, John C.
Why not stop testing? por Bull Atom Sci 33:30-1 Ap '77

HOPKINS, Joseph Martin
Armstrong's Worldwide Church of God: musical chairs of change. Chr Today 21:20-3 Ap 1; 22-4 Ap 15 '77
(ed) See Jacks, D. Children of God: disciples of deception
(ed) See Wasson, J. Children of God: disciples of deception

HOPKINS, Robert A.
Metrics ahead: how you can cope; excerpt from Metric. . .in a nutshell. il Sci Digest 81:44-8+ F '77

HOPKINSON, Francis
Battle of the Kegs; poem. Am Hist Illus 12:42 Ap '77

HOPP, Michael A. and Sommerstad, C. R.
Reaction at computer firm: more pluses than minuses. il M Labor R 100:69-71 F '77

HOPP, R. J. and Vittum, M. T.
Nature's own weather bureau. il Org Gard & Farm 24:127-9 Ap '77

HOPP, Ralph H.
Minnesota library profile. il por Lib J 102:1238-9+ Je 1 '77 *

HOPPER'S jazz club, New York City. See Night clubs

HOPSON, Janet L.
Recombinant lab for DNA and my 95 days in it. il pors Smithsonian 8:54-63 Je '77

HORACE Mann School. See Washington, D.C.—Education

HORACEK, Bruce. See Francke, S. jt auth

HORAN, Ellen
(ed) Notes from the classes (cont of) With the racing classes. See issues of Yachting

HORAN, Paul K. and Wheeless, L. L. Jr
Quantitative single cell analysis and sorting. bibl il Science 198:149-57 O 14 '77

HORBAL, Koryne
Two feminists tell how they work; interview ed by G. Steinem. pors Ms 6:52+ Jl '77

HORE, J. and others
Basal ganglia cooling disables learned arm movements of monkeys in the absence of visual guidance. bibl il Science 195:584-6 F 11 '77

HORICON Marsh wildlife refuges. See Wildlife sanctuaries—Wisconsin

HORIZON (periodical)
Monthly Horizon. Horizon 20:2 S '77

HORMAN, Charles E.
Charles Horman. J. Deedy. Commonweal 104:738 N 25 '77 *
What happened to Horman? Nation 225:453 N 5 '77 *

HORMONE fattening of cattle. See Cattle—Hormone fattening

HORMONE receptors
Competition of Δ^9-tetrahydrocannabinol with estrogen in rat uterine estrogen receptor binding. A. B. Rawitch and others. bibl il Science 197:1189-91 S 16 '77
Drug design: developing new criteria. G. B. Kolata. Science 197:36-7 Jl 1 '77
Hormone receptors: how are they regulated? G. B. Kolata. Science 196:747-8+ My 13 '77
Human breast cancer: biologically active estrogen receptor in the absence of estrogen? D. T. Zava and others. bibl il Science 196:663-4 My 6 '77
Selective display of histamine receptors on lymphocytes. W. Roszkowski and others. bibl Science 195:683-5 F 18 '77
Thyroid hormone action: the mitochondrial pathway. K. Sterling and others. bibl il Science 197:996-9 S 2 '77

HORMONES
Hepatic regeneration and erythropoietin production in the rat. B. A. Naughton and others. bibl il Science 196:301-2 Ap 15 '77
Primary structure of cholera toxin β-chain: a glycoprotein hormone analog? A. Kurosky and others. bibl il Science 195:299-301 Ja 21 '77
Simultaneous effects of erythropoietin and colony-stimulating factor on bone marrow cells. G. Van Zant and E. Goldwasser. bibl il Science 198:733-5 N 18 '77
See also
Adrenalin
Chalones
Ecdysone
Epidermal growth factor
Hydrocortisone
Hypothalamic hormones
Juvenile hormones
Malatonin
Oxytocin
Parathyroid hormone
Pituitary hormone releasing factors
Prostaglandins
Stilbestrols
Thyroid hormones
Thyrotropin releasing factor

HORMONES, Plant
Switching flowers on and off. il Sci N 112:39 Jl 16 '77
See also
Auxins

HORMONES, Sex
Female hormones and birth defects. Sci N 111:54 Ja 22 '77
Hormones taken during pregnancy affect the child's personality; study by June Reinisch. J. Gaylin. Psychol Today 11:31-2 O '77
New cure: the impotence and frigidity pill. Harp Baz 111:153 N '77
Primate sex preference at ovulation. il Sci N 111:118-19 F 19 '77
Relaxin: a disulfide homolog of insulin. C. Schwabe and J. K. McDonald. bibl il Science 197:914-15 Ag 26 '77
See also
Androgens
Estrogens
Gonadotropins
Testosterone

HORN, George
Not ready for the rocking chair. S. Fischler and D. Rubenstein. il por Ret Liv 17:33-4+ F '77 *

HORN, Jack C.
(ed) Newsline. See issues of Psychology today
Unforgettable elephants. il Psychol Today 10:88+ Ap '77

HORN, Stephen
Ethics, due process, diversity, and balance; address, March 25, 1977. Vital Speeches 43:463-8 My 15 '77

HORN, Zoia
Library Bill of Rights vs. the Racism and Sexism Awareness Resolution. Lib J 102:1254-5 Je 1 '77

HORN, Cape
Inside Cape Horn; excerpts. H. Roth. il por map Motor B & S 139:40-3 Mr; 70-3+ Ap; 68-71+ My; 78-80+ Je; 140:56-7+ Jl; 50-3+ S; 64-7+ O; 86-7+ N; 44-8+ D '77; 141:86-9+ Ja '78

HORN (musical instrument)
Profiles; Barry Tuckwell. W. Sargeant. por New Yorker 53:45-6+ Mr 14 '77

HORNBLOWER, Margot
Alaska: develop or conserve? Issue is moving toward a showdown. il map Smithsonian 8:38-49 bibl(p 134) D '77
EIS: the program that grew and grew. Am For 83:20-1 My '77

HORNBROOK, Mark C.
Prescription drugs: problems for public policy. bibl f il Cur Hist 72:215-22+ My '77

HORNE, Lena
Lena Horne is 60. O. Coombs. por Esquire 88:66-8+ Ag '77 *

HORNER, Joyce
Words for music; poem. Commonweal 104:272 Ap 29 '77

HORNER, Karla
Out of tune; poem. Seventeen 36:96 Ag '77

HORNER, Matina Souretis
Did fear of success fail? L. Shapiro. Ms 6:19 Jl '77 *

HOROSCOPE. See Astrology

HOROWITZ, Donald L.
Cultural movements and ethnic change. bibl f Ann Am Acad 433:6-18 S '77

HOROWITZ, Irving Louis
Science, sin, and sponsorship. por Atlantic 239:98-102 Mr; 26 Je '77
Social science and Presidential choices. bibl Society 14:21-3 My '77
When the President does it. Nation 224:751-4 Je 18 '77

HOROWITZ, Norman H.
Search for life on Mars; with biographical sketch. il Sci Am 237:15, 52-61 bibl(p163) N '77

HOROWITZ, Sheldon, and others
Induction of suppressor T cells in systemic lupus erythematosus by thymosin and cultured thymic epithelium. bibl il Science 197:999-1001 S 2 '77

HOROWITZ, Ted
Ted Horowitz. R. Busch. il por Pop Phot 81:98-105+ Ag '77 *

HOROWITZ, Vladimir
Grand eccentric of the concert hall; interview, ed by H. Epstein. il pors N Y Times Mag p 12-15+ Ja 8 '78
Musician of the month: Vladimir Horowitz; interview ed by H. Kupferberg. il por Hi Fi 28:MA8-9 Ja '78
about
King of pianists. S. Lipman. Commentary 63:62-6 My '77 *
Unknown recordings of Vladimir Horowitz. C. Alder. pors Hi Fi 28:69-74 Ja '78 *

HORRIDGE, G. Adrian
Compound eye of insects; with biographical sketch. il Sci Am 237:108-20, bibl(p 154) Jl '77
Mechanistic teleology and explanation in neuroethology; excerpt from Identified neurons and behavior of arthropods, ed by G. Hoyle. bibl BioScience 27:725-32 N '77

HORROCKS, Norman
A few new projects. . . Lib J 102:688-9 Mr 15 '77
Increasing CLA effectiveness. il por Lib J 102:1732-5 S 1 '77

HORROR films. See Motion pictures—Horror films

HORROR in art
Horror in art: the good, the mad, and the ugly. V. Goldberg. bibl il Psychol Today 11:24+ N '77

HORS d'oeuvres. See Appetizers

HORSE auctions. See Auctions

HORSE breeding
Morgan Horse Farm—you are invited. il Sunset 158:13 Je '77
New York's gentle industry. A. Carl. il por Conservationist 31:10-15 My '77

HORSE diving stunts. See Stunts

HORSE farms. See Horse breeding

HORSE race betting
Days of wine and races. A. Beyer. Esquire 87:92-3+ Ap '77
Pssst! Wanna tip on a hot horse? P. Axthelm. il Esquire 87:92-3 Ap '77
Running their own race; betting messenger services in Illinois. J. Schulian. Sports Illus 47:63-4 D 12 '77
Win, place and glow; L. Harribance's use of ESP in betting. R. Cantwell. il Sports Illus 47:32-4+ Ag 29 '77

HORSE racing
Bound for glory and a wreath of roses; Seattle Slew in the Flamingo. W. Leggett. il Sports Illus 46:36-9 Ap 4 '77
California, here we are! foreign horses racing at Santa Anita. W. Leggett. Sports Illus 46:42+ Ja 31 '77
Eeny meeny miney mo; Alydar's victory in the Champagne Stakes. W. Leggett. il Sports Illus 47:76-7 O 24 '77
Fine way to affirm his worth; Affirmed's victory in the Hopeful Stakes. W. Leggett. il Sports Illus 47:85-7 S 5 '77
For the moment, on the scent of roses; Kentucky Derby; with photographs and report by D. S. Looney. W. Leggett. il Sports Illus 46:34-9 My 9 '77
Good but not great; Seattle Slew's win in the Kentucky Derby. P. Axthelm. il Newsweek 89:77 My 16 '77
He brought down the house; Seattle Slew's Belmont victory and Triple Crown title. W. Leggett. il Sports Illus 46:16-19 Je 20 '77
He flew for the crew; Seattle Slew's Kentucky Derby victory. W. Leggett. il Sports Illus 46:18-23 My 16 '77
Here's mud in your eye! Forego's victory in the Woodward Stakes. W. Leggett. il Sports Illus 47:78+ S 26 '77
Horse nouveau; special section. il Esquire 87:90-7 Ap '77
How to beat Seattle Slew; Kentucky Derby. P. Axthelm. il Newsweek 89:100 My 9 '77
If only luck will be a lady; owners of Seattle Slew. D. S. Looney. il pors Sports Illus 46:40-1+ Je 13 '77
Near the head of the class; Cum Laude Laurie's victory in the Ruffian Handicap. W. Leggett. il Sports Illus 47:70-1 O 3 '77
New York's gentle industry. A. Carl. il por Conservationist 31:10-15 My '77
No plater, but is he sterling? Silver Series' victory in the Hutcheson Stakes. W. Leggett. il Sports Illus 46:20-1 F 21 '77
No sweat for Slew in the Wood. W. Leggett. il Sports Illus 46:89-90 My 2 '77
Now there's just one more dance to go; Seattle Slew's Preakness victory. W. Leggett. il Sports Illus 46:20-1 My 30 '77
Race he should've forgone; Forego's Whitney loss. W. Leggett. il Sports Illus 47:56-7 Ag 15 '77
Race track. A Minor. See issues of New Yorker
Seattle Slew gallops to a coronation. il Time 109:61 Je 20 '77
Seattle Slew strides home by two; Kentucky Derby. il Time 109:60 My 16 '77
Slew blew west test; Swaps Stakes at Hollywood Park. W. Leggett. il Sports Illus 47:54+ Jl 11 '77
Three's a Crown; Seattle Slew at Belmont. P. Axthelm. il Newsweek 89:71 Je 20 '77
Tomato Patch George at the spa; the Travers. W. Leggett. il Sports Illus 47:18-19 Ag 29 '77
Triple Crown trainer; W. H. Turner. J. L. Phillips. il pors N Y Times Mag p47-8+ N 13 '77
See also
Harness racing
Horses, Race
Race tracks

Ethical aspects
Great Belmont Park sting. il Time 110:122 N 21 '77
Is this horse that horse? Cinzano/Lebón question at Belmont Park. W. Leggett. il por Sports Illus 47:28-31 N 14 '77
Winner by any name; switching horses in Belmont race. P. Axthelm. il por Newsweek 90:73 N 7 '77

Periodicals
See also
Daily racing form (periodical)

HORSE racing, Photography of. See Photography of sports
HORSE stables. See Barns and stables
HORSE stealing
Million-dollar horse heist; theft of Fanfreluche from Kentucky's Claiborne Farm. M. Delnagro. il Sports Illus 47:30-2+ Ag 1 '77
Toast of Tompkinsville; recovery of thoroughbred Fanfreluche. W. F. Reed. il por Sports Illus 47:95-6+ D 19 '77
HORSE trails. See Trails
HORSE training
Triple Crown trainer; W. H. Turner. J. P. Phillips. il pors N Y Times Mag p47-8+ N 13 '77
HORSEBACK riding. See Horsemanship
HORSEMANSHIP
How to ride a mountain horse. S. Netherby. il Field & S 82:150-1 S '77
Taking a quantum jump; American Jumping Derby. J. Papanek. il Sports Illus 47:118+ O 10 '77
When developing horse sense, use common sense. B. J. Rankin. Consumers Res Mag 60:41 My '77
See also
Polo

HORSES
Mustang roundup. D. A. Williams and P. S. Greenberg. il Newsweek 90:22 S 5 '77
New York's gentle industry. A. Carl. il por Conservationist 31:10-15 My '77
Once-again Prince. I. Townsend. il Read Digest 110:126-8 My '77
Wild bunch; mustangs. B. Hall. il Nat Wildlife 15:4-11 Ap '77
Wild horse dilemma; Bureau of Land Management's Adopt-a-Horse program. il Sunset 158:304 My '77

Breeding
See Horse breeding

Diseases and pests
They're paying through the nose; race horse sickness at Meadowlands. D. S. Looney. il Sports Illus 48:18-21 Ja 2 '78

Equipment and supplies
See also
Saddlery

Periodicals
Horse markets. W. Brohaugh. il Writers Digest 57:31-3 Ag '77

Purchasing
Get a horse? excerpt from The Roger Caras pet book. R. Caras. il Ladies Home J 94:142 S '77

Training
See Horse training

HORSES, Photography of. See Photography of animals
HORSES, Race
And the nightingales sing; owning a racehorse. N. Perlmutter. il Nat R 29:996+ S 2 '77
Champ named Slew. P. Axthelm. il Newsweek 89:76-7+ Je 6 '77
Every other colt met his match. W. Leggett. Sports Illus 46:44 Je 13 '77
Freight pulled in late; trotter ABC Freight. il Sports Illus 46:62+ Je 13 '77
Horse right here; Seattle Slew. J. Morgan. New Repub 177:26-8 Jl 23 '77
No million-dollar baby; Sexetary. W. F. Reed. il Sports Illus 46:68+ Ap 25 '77
Race track. A. Minor. See issues of New Yorker
Racehorse. . .a fast profit? W. Flanagan. Vogue 167:378 S '77
Reverie between the acts; Seattle Slew's Belmont race day routine. D. S. Looney. il Sports Illus 46:20-1 Je 20 '77
See also
Horse racing

Auctions
See Auctions

Diseases and pests
See Horses—Diseases and pests

Thefts
See Horse stealing

Training
See Horse training

HORSES in art
Missy goes Surrealistic; work of M. Stang. G. Dostal. il por Sch Arts 77:22-3 N '77
HORSMANDEN family
Horsmanden. H. K. Eilers. il Hobbies 82:150 S '77
HORST, Bill. See Golub, J. jt ed
HORST, R. L. and others
Adequate response of plasma 1,25-dihydroxyvitamin D to parturition in paretic (milk fever) dairy cows. bibl il Science 196:662-3 My 6 '77
HORSTMAN, James R.
Choosing portable & mobile tape recorders. il Pop Electr 12:43-5 Ag '77
HORTICULTURAL research
See also
Saratoga Horticultural Foundation
HORTICULTURAL societies
See also
Massachusetts Horticultural Society
HORTICULTURE
See also
Bulb industry
Floriculture
Forcing (plants)
Gardening
Greenhouses
Nurseries (horticulture)
Vegetable gardening

Bibliography
Books. See issues of Horticulture
HORTICULTURE (periodical)
1977 garden club yearbook contest award winners. Horticulture 55:52-3 D '77
Publisher's letter; question of advertising ethics in nursery mailorder business. R. J. Fibkins. Horticulture 55:96 F '77

HORTICULTURE magazine photography contest. See Photography—Competitions
HORTICULTURE therapy. See Gardening—Therapeutic use
HORTON, Frank
Excerpts from testimony on reorganization plans for the Executive Branch, March 1, 1977. Cong Digest 56:112+ Ap '77
HORTON, Paul B.
Sexless vocabulary for a sexist society. Educ Digest 42:36-8 Mr '77
HORTON, Tom
Viewpoint. Sports Illus 47:6-7 O 17 '77
HORVAT, Paul
Help for people society often ignores. il por U.S. News 84:48 Ag 1 '77 *
HORVATH, Joseph
Joe Horvath is adding up your dollars of happiness. J. Skow. il por Outdoor Life 159:66-7+ Mr '77 *
HORVATH, Odön von
Tales from the Vienna woods. Reviews Nation 225:92-4 Jl 23 '77 *
HORVITZ, Wayne Louis
Experienced hand for labor mediator. Bus W p27 Mr 28 '77 *
Labor: trouble ahead? G. R. Rosen. por Duns R 110:57 S '77 *
HORWITZ, Simi
Are you a secret bigot? il Seventeen 36:110-11+ F '77
Is business school for you? Seventeen 36:36 Ap '77
HOSE
See also
Garden hose
HOSIERY
Layered look for legs. il Time 110:46 S 12 '77
Now they've put the panties in panty hose! il Good H 185:182+ S '77
Year of the leg. il Newsweek 90:81 S 12 '77
HOSIERY industry
See also
Hanes Corporation
HOSKINS, B. B. and others
Application of genetic and cellular manipulations to agricultural and industrial problems. bibl BioScience 27:188-91 Mr '77
HOSOBUCHI, Yoshio, and others
Pain relief by electrical stimulation of the central gray matter in humans and its reversal by naloxone. bibl il Science 197:183-6 Jl 8 '77
HOSOE, Eikoh
Masters of the darkroom; excerpt from Darkroom. il por Pop Phot 81:102-7+ Jl '77
HOSPICES (terminal care) See Terminal care facilities
HOSPITAL care
Are hospitals really no place for sick people? letters from readers; comp by R. Guss. Good H 185:270+ O '77
Carter's stab at health care. il Forbes 119:53-4 My 15 '77
Hospitals are no place for sick people. A. Kern and E. Keiffer. Good H 184:111+ My '77
10,000 nurses speak out: a startling report on hospitals and doctors. il Fam Health 9:36-8 Ag '77
See also
Children—Hospital care

Cost

Bitter pill for U.S. hospitals. il Time 109:32 My 2 '77
Blue Cross bearing down. il Time 110:67 Ag 29 '77
Carter proposes setting strict controls on what hospitals can charge patients. Ret Liv 17:11-12 Je '77
Carter's first shot in war on medical costs. il U.S. News 82:79 My 9 '77
HEW's half-measure. E. Marshall. New Repub 176:8-10 My 7 '77
9% flaw in Carter's hospital plan. I. Pave. Bus W p 36 My 9 '77
Race to cut medical costs. A. Hershman. il Duns R 109:48-53+ My '77
Ready to clamp down on hospital rates. Bus W p30+ Mr 7 '77
Uncle Sam's dangerous prescriptions. M. S. Evans. Nat R 29:1368 N 25 '77
HOSPITAL chaplains. See Chaplains, Hospital
HOSPITAL employees. See Hospitals—Staff
HOSPITAL nursing. See Nurses and nursing
HOSPITAL records. See Medical records
HOSPITAL service, Cost of. See Hospital care—Cost
HOSPITAL ships
New HOPE; history of the S.S. Hope and plans for new Project HOPE. J. Cergol. il Américas 29:17-22 O '77
HOSPITAL supply industry

Securities

Growth power in hospital-supply stocks; interview, ed by A. Hershman. F. Prunier. por Duns R 110:105-6+ N '77

HOSPITALITY
American hospitality (cont) McCalls 104:152-3+ F; 132-3+ Je '77
See also
Entertaining
Guests
HOSPITALIZATION insurance. See Insurance, Health
HOSPITALS
See also
Burn care units
Hospital care
Hospital ships
Nurses and nursing
Nursing homes
Terminal care facilities

Administration

Chain: a survival formula for hospitals. il Bus W p 113-14 Ja 16 '78
HEW's half-measure. E. Marshall. New Repub 176:8-10 My 7 '77
Hospitals begin crack-down on smokers. Sci Digest 81:84-5 Je '77
Humana's hopes; Humana Inc. il por Forbes 120:24-5 S 1 '77
Major move against the tide. Forbes 121:127 Ja 9 '78
Revived interest in hospital stocks; management companies. Bus W p73 Jl 18 '77

Architecture

Building types study: hospitals: how are they? with introd by W. Marlin. il Archit Rec 162:113-28 Ag '77

Chaplains

See Chaplains, Hospital

Diagnostic services

Small company manages to take itself public; Omnimedical Services Inc. il por Bus W p88-9 Ja 31 '77

Employees

See Hospitals—Staff

Equipment and supplies

Consultant profile: the medical equipment planner; ISD Inc. il Archit Rec 162:59+ Ag '77
See also
Hospital supply industry

Finance

Great hospital war. E. Marshall. New Repub 176:22-5 My 28 '77

Heating and ventilation

All of hospital's heat is from off-peak power. il Archit Rec 161:153 Ja '77

Management and regulation

See Hospitals—Administration

Outpatient services

Hospital without walls; New Zealand. il Time 109:57 Ap 25 '77

Public relations

Controlling medical expansion; protesting against Affiliated Hospitals Center's planned destruction of neighborhood housing in Boston. H. Waitzkin and J. A. Sharratt. il Society 14:30-5 Ja '77

Regulation

See Hospitals—Administration

Securities

Great expectations at the proprietary hospitals. L. Schiff. il Fortune 96:57-8+ D '77

Staff

Hospitals trim off their staffing fat. il Bus W p 127+ My 16 '77
Private hospitals nearing wage levels in state, local government hospitals. M. Sieling. il M Labor R 100:46-7 My '77

Volunteer workers

Prize is life. L. Pope, Jr. Chr Cent 94:916-18 O 12 '77
Shalom. . .a gut yontiff. . .and a Merry Christmas; Holy Redeemer Hospital in Meadowbrook, Pa. M. Lichtig. il por Ret Liv 16:35 D '76

California

All in the family; permitting children to witness birth of siblings at Mendocino Coast Hospital, Fort Bragg. Newsweek 89:90 My 30 '77
Dr Myers and Dr Myers; internship at Stanford Medical Center. il pors Ebony 33:107-8+ N '77
To save a child; rattlesnake venom victim at UCLA Medical Center. B. Dillman. il McCalls 105:104+ N '77
See also
Los Angeles—Hospitals

HOSPITALS—*Continued*

Maine

Penobscot Bay Medical Center, Rockport, Maine; with introd by W. Marlin. il Archit Rec 162:113, 122-5 Ag '77

Maryland

See also
Baltimore—Hospitals

Massachusetts

See also
Boston—Hospitals

Minnesota

See also
Minneapolis—Hospitals

New York (state)

Amateur hour; alleged surgery performed by medical supply salesman W. MacKay at Smithtown General Hospital. il Time 110:94 N 14 '77
Amateur surgeons; alleged surgery performed by medical supply salesman W. MacKay at Smithtown General Hospital. M. Clark and D. Shapiro. il por Newsweek 90:125 N 14 '77
See also
New York (city)—Hospitals

New Zealand

Hospital without walls. il Time 109:57 Ap 25 '77

Oklahoma

Oral Roberts' gift adds to a hospital glut; proposed teaching hospital and diagnostic clinic in Tulsa. il Bus W p35 O 31 '77

Pennsylvania

Breath of death; use of laughing gas for oxygen at Suburban General Hospital in Norristown. Time 110:56 Ag 15 '77

Russia

See also
Hospitals, Psychiatric—Russia

Texas

Hospitals trim off their staffing fat. il Bus W p 127+ My 16 '77

United States

See also
United States—Veterans Administration hospitals

Washington (state)

See also
United States—Energy Research and Development Administration—Emergency Decontamination Facility

HOSPITALS, Military
Medical mailbox; C. Chung and the Acupuncture Research Clinic of Taipei. C. SerVaas. il Sat Eve Post 249:138-9 D '77
See also
United States—Veterans Administration hospitals

HOSPITALS, Psychiatric
Making it as a mental patient. M. Katz and P. Zimbardo. bibl il pors Psychol Today 10:122-4+ Ap '77
Trust treatment; Ward 56 of Utah State Hospital. J. Seligmann and P. S. Greenberg. il Newsweek 89:78 F 14 '77
See also
Mentally handicapped—Institutional care

Russia

Censuring the Soviets; vote by the World Psychiatric Association. il Time 110:36 S 12 '77
Inside Russia's psychiatric jails. L. Thorne. il N Y Times Mag p26-7+ Je 12 '77
Serbsky treatment; interview, ed by E. F. Torrey. V. Bukovsky. il por Psychol Today 11:38-9+ Je '77
Soviet cure for religion. J. A. Broun. America 137:26-9 Jl 16 '77
Soviet psychiatric practices criticized; World Psychiatric Association. Sci N 112:164-5 S 10 '77

HOSTAGES
America's menacing misfits; taking of hostages by terrorists. Time 109:20 Mr 21 '77
Cool-headed cop who saves hostages; F. Bolz of the New York Detective Bureau Hostage Negotiating Team. B. Gelb. il pors N Y Times Mag p30-3+ Ap 17 '77
Delicate art of handling terrorists. P. Goldman and others. il Newsweek 89:25-7 Mr 21 '77
From the concrete floor: thoughts while being held hostage; Washington, D.C. siege by Hanafi Muslims. C. Fenyvesi. New Repub 176:16-17 Mr 26 '77
Hostage mentality. D. Rabinowitz. Commentary 63:70-2 Je '77; Discussion. 64:7-9 Ag '77
How to play the waiting game. Time 109:18-19 Mr 21 '77
Is there a treatment for terror? effects of Washington, D.C. seige by Hanafi Muslims. M. Belz and others. il Psychol Today 11:54-6+ O '77
Living with a fearful memory; effects of the Washington, D.C. seige by Hanafi Muslims. C. Fenyvesi. por Psychol Today 11:61+ O '77
Year after Entebbe. E. Keerdoja and M. J. Kubic. il Newsweek 90:7 Jl 4 '77
See also
United Nations—Ad Hoc Committee on the Drafting of an International Convention Against the Taking of Hostages

HOSTAL Nicolás de Ovando. See Santo Domingo, Dominican Republic—Hotels, restaurants, etc.

HOSTESSES, Air. See Airlines—Flight attendants

HOSTICK, King V.
Autographs. See issues of Hobbies

HOSTILITY (psychology)
See also
Anger

HOT air balloons. See Balloons

HOT dog skiing. See Skis and skiing

HOT rods. See Automobiles, Remodeled

HOT SPRINGS, S.D.
Midwest gets Main Street Projects. il Am City & County 92:22-3 N '77

HOT springs resorts. See Health resorts, watering places, etc.

HOT tubs. See Bathtubs

HOT water supply
See also
Water heaters

HOT weather
Simmer of '77. R. Boeth. il map Newsweek 90:14-16 Ag 1 '77
Weather with a vengeance: heat, storm and flood. il Time 110:10-11 Ag 1 '77
Where all that sticky weather came from. il U.S. News 83:32 Ag 1 '77
See also
Summer

HOTCAPS for plants. See Plants, Protection of

HOTCHIN, John, and Buckley, Ruth
Latent form of scrapie virus: a new factor in slow-virus disease. bibl il Science 196:668-71 My 6 '77

—and Seegal, Richard
Virus-induced behavioral alteration of mice. bibl il Science 196:671-4 My 6 '77

HOTCHKIN, John F.
Ecumenical view from a Catholic perspective—1977. il New Cath World 220:160-3 Jl '77

HOTCHNER, Aaron Edward
Doubleday-Hotchner decision. M. Reuter. Pub W 211:22 Ap 11 '77 *
(ed) See Bergen, C. Candy Bergen has a question
(ed) See Deneuve, C. Why Catherine Deneuve gets depressed

HÔTEL de Valentinois, Passy. See Paris—Historic houses, sites, etc.

HOTEL management
City hotels: alive and well. L. Smith. il Duns R 110:44-7 Jl '77
Making life more bearable for the traveler. J. J. Kilpatrick. Nations Bus 65:11-12 D '77
See also
Webb, Del E. Corporation

HOTELS, motels, etc.
Bed & board. See issues of Fortune
New look in grand hotels. N. Richardson. il House & Gard 149:70+ My '77
Why not the best? S. Birnbaum. il Esquire 88:149-53 N '77
See also
Holiday Inns, Inc
also subhead Hotels, restaurants, etc. under names of cities, e.g. Chicago—Hotels, restaurants, etc.

Architecture

Building types study: design for leisure: two urban hotels, a riverboat and recreational village; with introd by M. F. Schmertz. il Archit Rec 162:109-24 O '77
Rooms with a view. H. Sutton. il Sat R 4:52-4 S 17 '77

Conservation and restoration

See Architecture—Conservation and restoration

Finance

Recovering from too much growth. il Bus W p 114+ O 17 '77

History

Room at the Ritz. H. Sutton. il por Sat R 4:45-7 My 14 '77

Securities

Gambling stocks are riding a winning streak; hotels and casinos. L. Snyder. il Fortune 96:65-6+ S '77

Asia, Southeastern

Grand old hotels of the Orient. G. Plimpton. il Holiday 58:42-3+ Mr; 36-7+ Ap '77

Canada

Walker's guide to the mountains of Québec; trails and country inns. R. Rudner. Mademoiselle 83:44-6 Jl '77
See also
Toronto—Hotels, restaurants. etc.

HOTELS, motels, etc.—*Continued*

France

Richard the Lion-Hearted slept here; the Relais et Châteaux hotel group. T. Thompson. il N Y Times Mag p 16-19+ Je 26 '77

Hawaii

See also
Honolulu—Hotels, restaurants, etc.

Hong Kong

Grand old hotels of the Orient; Peninsula. G. Plimpton. il Holiday 58:36-7+ Ap '77

Ireland

Live the Irish country life; country house hotels. C. Spicer. il House & Gard 149:74+ Je '77

Israel

See also
Jerusalem—Hotels, restaurants, etc.

Italy

See also
Rome (city)—Hotels, restaurants, etc.

Macao

Grand old hotels of the Orient; Bela Vista. G. Plimpton. Holiday 58:71-2 Ap '77

Saudi Arabia

Toughest hotel in the world to get into; Riyadh Inter-Continental. W. McQuade. il por Fortune 95:229-30 Mr '77

Singapore

Grand old hotels of the Orient; Raffles. G. Plimpton. Holiday 58:66-7+ Mr '77

Spain

Paradores: Spain's castle hotels. E. Berman. il Harp Baz 110:12+ Je '77

United States

Castle in Peoria; Jumer's Castle Lodge. A. Morner. il Fortune 95:171-2 Ap '77
City hotels: alive and well. L. Smith. il Duns R 110:44-7 Jl '77
New shape for an urban hotel; Hyatt Regency Cambridge, Cambridge, Mass. il Archit Rec 162:110-13 O '77
Retiring alone to the country; running Brook Farm guest house in Lenox, Mass. G. Gewirtz and R. J. Martin. pors Ret Liv 17:30-1 Je '77
Sleeping space in and near Big Sur. Sunset 159: 26 S '77
Whatever happened to...: the grand hotels of America. il U.S. News 83:74-7 D 5 '77
Which hotels and motels offer discounts to retirees? il Ret Liv 16:15 D '76
See also subhead Hotels, restaurants, etc under names of cities, e.g. San Francisco—Hotels restaurants, etc.

History

American hotels on early Staffordshire. F. Stefano, Jr. bibl il Antiques 112:274-7 Ag '77

HOTHOUSES. See Greenhouses

HOTLINES, Information service. See Telephone information service

HOTSPUR (cutter) See Sailboats

HOUCK, J. C. and others
Lymphocyte and fibroblast chalones: some chemical properties. bibl il Science 196:896-7 My 20 '77

HOUCK, James R. and Gull, G. E.
Cornell's 25-inch training telescope. il Sky & Tel 54:264-6 O '77

HOUCK, Oliver Austin
Best present of all; dramatization. See Sollid, L.

HOUGAN, Jim
Persecution and character assassination of Howard (Bo) Callaway as performed by inmates of the U.S. Senate under the auspices of the Democratic Party. Harpers 255:35-42+ Jl '77

HOUGH, Gordon Letts
Planning and policy; address, February 4, 1977. Vital Speeches 43:344-7 Mr 15 '77

HOUGHTON, Amory, 1926-
Trials of Amory Houghton Jr. il por Forbes 120: 33-7 Ag 1 '77 *

HOUK, Edward J. and others
Peptidoglycan in the cell wall of the primary intracellular symbiote of the pea aphid. bibl il Science 198:401-3 O 28 '77

HOULIHAN, John F.
Energy: roots of the problem, seeds of the solution. il Intellect 106:237-40 D '77

HOULIHAN, Patrick
Indian art—living with the political realities; excerpt from The art museum as educator: a collection of studies as guides to practice and policy; ed by B. Y. Newsom and A. Z. Silver. il Art N 76:92-5 D '77 *

HOULTON, Jennifer
Soap opera teen. il pors Seventeen 36:77-8 N '77

HOULTON, Loyce
Minnesota commotion: Loyce Houlton and the Minnesota Dance Theatre. J. Anderson. il Dance Mag 51:75-8 Ap '77 *

HOUNDS
Bluetick hounds: bawling and treeing. G. Norman. il Esquire 89:16+ Ja '78
Drives with one hound; using deer hounds to hunt in southern Ontario. S. Cooke. il por Outdoor Life 160:90 S '77
See also
Bloodhounds

HOURS of labor
Changes in the number of days in the workweek, 1973-76. J. N. Hedges. il M Labor R 100:72-3 Ap '77
Easing the constraints of time-oriented work. I. Bernstein. bibl M Labor R 100:58-60 F '77
Education, work, and leisure: must they come in that order? F. Best and B. Stern. bibl il M Labor R 100:3-10 Jl '77
Employment, hours, and earnings data from establishment surveys. See issues of Monthly labor review
Flexitime: a new work style catches on. L. Smith. il Duns R 109:61+ Mr '77
For more and more workers, an end to the 9-to-5 day. U.S. News 82:80-1 Ap 4 '77
Gone-fishing syndrome; earned time concept. J. Lelyveld. il N Y Times Mag p62 My 29 '77
How blue-collar workers on 4-day workweeks use their time; excerpt from The four-day workweek. D. M. Maklan. bibl il M Labor R 100:18-26 Ag '77
Macho of time; question of length of public officials' work day. New Repub 177:2+ Ag 20 '77
New way to work: pick your own shift. L. David. il Mech Illus 73:44-5+ N '77
Special flexitime reports; symposium. M Labor R 100:62-74 F '77
Swelling ranks of workers who set their own hours; flextime. il U.S. News 83:62-3 Ag 1 '77
Thank God it's Thursday? four-day work week? Time 109:58+ Je 6 '77
Workers on long hours and premium pay, May 1976. S. J. Gallogly. il M Labor R 100:42-5 My '77
Working on the Sabbath; Supreme Court decision. Time 109:50-1 Je 27 '77
See also subhead Wages and hours under names of industries, e.g. Textile industry—Wages and hours

Europe, Western

Flexiyear schedules—only a matter of time? B. Teriet. bibl f M Labor R 100:62-5 D '77

Germany, West

It started in Germany—and keeps growing. J. Dornberg. il Duns R 109:62+ Mr '77

HOUSE, Connie
Bibliotherapy project in Texas. il por Wilso[n] Lib Bull 51:530-3 F '77

HOUSE building. See House construction

HOUSE buying
Better to buy now than wait till later. il Time 109:61-2 My 2 '77
Buy or rent a home? il U.S. News 82:86 Ap 25 '77
How to buy a house at a shameful savings. M. Daley. Am Home 80:23+ Je '77
How to keep down the cost of buying a home. il U.S. News 82:39-42 Mr 21 '77
It's easy to write and self-publish a consumer manual: the hard part is getting it to consumers. J. D. Bowers. Writers Digest 57:23-4 Ap '77
Private building inspection before you buy? Sunset 159:108+ S '77
Right nest for you. S. Auerback. Am Home 80:32+ Ap '77
Spending your money; questions and answers S. Porter. Ladies Home J 94:20+ Ag '77
Steps to follow when house shopping. Bet Hom & Gard 55:272 My '77
See also
Housing finance
Mortgages

Laws and legislation

Home closing costs: do you know your rights? Real Estate Settlement Procedures Act. M. Daly. Bet Hom & Gard 55:10+ Jl '77

HOUSE cleaning
Vacuuming, dusting and tidying up. il Redbook 149:88+ Je '77

Anecdotes, facetiae, satire, etc.

Lift your feet. A. Ward. Atlantic 239:86-8+ F '77

HOUSE committees. See United States—Congress—House—Committees

HOUSE construction
Sweat equity: finish a house yourself and save. K. Petersen. il Bet Hom & Gard 55:54-7 Ag '77
Unfinished house; building a weekend retreat. P. H. Matson. Am Home 80:24 D '77

HOUSE construction—*Continued*

Study and teaching

Homemade houses; Shelter Institute in Bath, Me. J. Edwards. McCalls 104:73 Ag '77
Owner-built homes—low-cost, energy-efficient; Shelter Institute. E. Tozer. il por Pop Sci 211:114-17 S '77
You can too build your own house; Shelter Institute in Maine. E. McPherson. il Ms 5:49-51+ Je '77

HOUSE decoration

At home with Helen Reddy. il por Good H 186:102-5 Ja '78
Booklets. House B 119:84+ My; 42+ O '77
California revival. il Mademoiselle 83:216-17 Ap '77
Confessions of a home clutterer. L. Schoenhoff. Read Digest 111:20+ Ag '77
Dear House & garden; 5 redecorating schemes. il House & Gard 149:136-41 My '77
Dear House & garden. . . ; questions and answers. House & Gard 149:24 O; 38-9 N; 54+ D '77; 150:30 Ja '78
Decorating special: how to create the romantic look at home. il House & Gard 149:101-9+ Mr '77
Decorating to taste; house of Clotilde Alvarez. il House & Gard 149:78-83 Jl '77
Decorator showhouses around the country. House & Gard 149:38 Ap '77
Designer's guide to instant decorating. C. Varney. House B 119:46-7 Ag '77
Do-it-yourself decorating. il House & Gard 149:102+ Ap '77
Early American. il Bet Hom & Gard 55:123-31 O '77
Echoing old world manors; home of Welter Budd Holden and Steven Browne. R. Weil. il House B 119:84-93 O '77
Essence of understatement; Halston's Manhattan town house. M. Gough and others. il por House B 119:94-7+ O '77
Family plan excitement. J. Macurdy and J. H. Ingersoll. il House B 119:100-7 F '77
Farmhouse for moderns; home of Brian and Marrisa Stone. il House & Gard 149:166-71 N '77
Few silk purses from sows' ears. M. A. Sharp. il Sat Eve Post 249:64-7 N '77
First of all, I design for people; interview, ed by M. Gough and J. B. Reiter. A. Donghia. il por House B 119:48-56 Ag '77
For country living that's blithely graceful; house of Arthur Hannett. J. Macurdy. il House B 119:92-5 Ap '77
For ever & today; interior of Williamsburg house designed by Chuck Winslow in Aurora, Ill. J. Macurdy. il House B 119:62-73 Ap '77
Good living. See issues of McCall's
Help! We're trapped in a basic box house. il Bet Hom & Gard 55:105-13 F '77
Here's how to plan your decorating right now, and create your rooms in stages. il House & Gard 149:134-9 O '77
Home improvement and decorating guide. il Am Home 80:85+ Ap '77
Home offices that work. il Am Home 80:60-2 S '77
House where Lucille Ball lives! il pors Good H 185:132-5 S '77
House with a heart; house of G. and A. Getty in San Francisco. il pors Vogue 167:322-7 O '77
How to create your own personal space; 8 case histories. il House & Gard 149:126-35 My '77
Imagination, country style; house of S. Parish in Maine. il House & Gard 149:110-15 D '77
Improving your home for winter; special section. il Ladies Home J 94:145+ S '77
In the California manner; an air of casual chic; house of Mr and Mrs Marty Pasetta. R. Weil. il House B 119:74-9 Ap '77
It all fits together; home of Sandy Gallin, Beverly Hills. R. Weil. il House B 119:72-9 Je '77
It's home improvement time! J. H. Ingersoll. House B 119:43-4+ My '77
It's time to turn if into now. il House B 119:117-55 My '77
Joyful place of light and color; interview, ed by R. Weil. P. Duchin and C. Duchin. il House B 119:28-35 Ag '77
Ladies' home journal home improvement and decorating guide. il Ladies Home J 94:165+ Ap '77
Lively romantic; home of T. Guild. il por House & Gard 149:156-61 N '77
Most creative house in America; home of the Wolfman family. P. Sadowsky. il Am Home 80:34-9 Ag '77
New directions in decorating. N. Mandelbaum. il Ladies Home J 94:84-7 Je '77
One-step decorating; department store designers. C. Kriebel. il Am Home 80:24 F '77
Painless guide to redecorating. A. F. Rush and M. Cubisino. il McCalls 104:91-8 Mr '77
Perfect backdrop. S. G. Lewin. il House B 119:92-5 Je '77
Perfectionists; houses of celebrities. P. O'Higgins. House B 119:90-1+ Ap '77
Quick and easy decorating for a holiday haven; Fire Island home. J. Macurdy and K. Mahoney. il House B 119:66-71 Ag '77
Redbook's guide to home improvement and decorating. il Redbook 148:173+ Ap; 149:189+ S '77
Renaissance of a villa. N. Skurka. il N Y Times Mag p46-7 Ag 28 '77
Renew! C. Seebohm. il House & Gard 149:116-31+ Ap '77
Renewal: a total break from the routine. S. G. Lewin. il House B 119:114-19 N '77
Rethinking closets, kitchens, and other forgotten spaces. S. Torre and others. il Ms 6:54-5 D '77
Romantic rooms. P. Sadowsky. il Am Home 80:39-43 O '77
Rustic with class; house designed for Arthur Williams. il House & Gard 149:72-7 F '77
Sensational barn of your own; prefabricated house. il House & Gard 149:122-7 Je '77
Serenity was their goal. S. G. Lewin. il House B 119:80-5 Je '77
Special home decorating guide. il Am Home 80:39-41+ My '77
Stay in touch with the land; adobe house. il House & Gard 149:66-9 Ag '77
Summer rental re-do. N. Skurka. il N Y Times Mag p78+ My 22 '77
To Turkey with joy: Mica and Ahmet Ertegün's house. il Vogue 167:202-9 D '77
Tour of the LBJ ranch. J. Egan. il por Good H 185:112-17+ O '77
Trends in decorating; interviews, ed by J. Lynch. il Harp Baz 110:112+ S '77
What's new? What's coming? il House & Gard 150:58-65 Ja '78

See also

Antiques
Apartments
Art in the home
Bathrooms
Beams, Artificial
Bedrooms
Ceilings
Christmas decorations
Color in house decoration
Curtains and draperies
Decoration and ornament, Architectural
Dining rooms
Display of antiques, art objects, etc.
Do-it-yourself work
Electric lamps
Fireplaces
Floor coverings
Floors
Fruits, vegetables, etc. in decoration
Furniture, Arrangement of
Guest rooms
Halls
Household furnishings
Interior decorators
Kitchens
Laundries
Lighting, Architectural and decorative
Living rooms
Mirrors
Painting, Industrial and practical
Paneling
Recreation rooms
Rooms
Screens (furniture)
Shelves
Shutters
Slip covers
Table decoration
Textile fabrics
Upholstery
Wall coverings
Wallpaper and wallpapering
Walls
Window shades
Windows

Study and teaching

In-store decorating courses: worth your while? Bet Hom & Gard 55:45 Jl '77

HOUSE decoration, American

It fit together like a jigsaw puzzle; home of C. Barnes in Winston-Salem, N.C. M. Gough and J. Macurdy. il por House B 119:104-13 N '77

See also

Furniture, American

HOUSE decoration, Colonial and early American. See House decoration, American

HOUSE decoration, Exterior

See also

Christmas decorations, Outdoor
House painting

HOUSE exchanging vacations. See Vacations

HOUSE expansion. See Houses, Remodeled

HOUSE fires. See Fires

HOUSE fittings. See Building fittings

HOUSE guests. See Guests

HOUSE heating. See Heating

HOUSE insulation. See Insulation (heat)
HOUSE lighting. See Electric lighting
HOUSE models
American houses in miniature: Sturbridge Village Richardson saltbox. S. A. Parvin. il Hobbies 82:123+ S '77
He bottles houses. il Pop Mech 148:128+ D '77
Houses that live in glass bottles. V. DeMoss. il Design (US) 78:8-11 Summ '77
Metcalf house, townhouse cabinet. S. A. Parvin. il Hobbies 82:120 Je '77
Miniature architectural environments. S. A. Parvin. il Hobbies 82:120 Mr '77
Techniques in building miniatures; interview, ed by S. A. Parvin. J. Shellhaas. Hobbies 82:120 My '77
HOUSE moving. See Moving of structures, etc.
HOUSE museums. See Historic houses, sites, etc.
HOUSE of Fraser, Ltd. See Department stores—Great Britain
HOUSE of Representatives. See United States—Congress—House
HOUSE paint. See Paint
HOUSE painting
Housepainting with a regional flavor. H. Wicks. il Pop Mech 148:92-5 S '77
Preparing your house for paint. D. Raffel. House & Gard 149:76 S '77
HOUSE painting, Interior. See Painting, Industrial and practical
HOUSE plans. See Architecture, Domestic—Designs and plans
HOUSE plants
Best plant gifts. B. Mulligan. il Am Home 80:21 D '77
Cold-weather survival guide for houseplants. G. Abraham and K. Abraham. il Org Gard & Farm 25:166-71 Ja '78
Easy to grow house plants:
Bear's-paw fern. E. McDonald. il House B 119:50 F '77
Beaucarnea recurvata or ponytail plant. E. McDonald. il House B 119:32 Jl '77
Bird-of-paradise. E. McDonald. il House B 119:38 S '77
Bromeliads. E. McDonald. il House B 119:40 O '77
Cactuses. E. McDonald. il House B 119:38 N '77
Cycas. E. McDonald. il House B 119:36 Mr '77
Dwarf palm. E. McDonald. il House B 119:80 D '77
Euphorbia trigona. E. McDonald. il House B il 119:42 Ap '77
Rickrack cactus. E. McDonald. il House B 119:30 Je '77
Staghorn ferns. E. McDonald. il House B 119:96 My '77
Enjoy the outdoors indoors. C. L. Busch. il Harp Baz 110:138-9+ Ap '77
For indoor jungle lovers. il Sunset 159:240 N '77
Green gifts. il Seventeen 36:66 Je '77
Growing things; minimum-care, easy-to-grow greens. il Seventeen 36:46 Ag '77
Houseplant how-to. See occasional issues of Better homes and gardens
Houseplant pronunciation guide. Bet Hom & Gard 55:76+ My '77
Houseplants in bloom! S. Coulter. il Bet Hom & Gard 55:142-5 N '77
How to stop killing your house plants. V. E. Towns. House B 119:90-1+ Mr '77
Indoor plants. See issues of Horticulture
Instant care for indoor plants. B. Mulligan. il Am Home 80:8 O '77
Kick your plants outside for the summer. A. Rosenblum. Good H 184:224 Je '77
Living room jungle at the Suva's place. il Sunset 159:248-9 N '77
Plant collections. il Seventeen 36:78 O '77
Plant savers, pot pointers. il Redbook 149:22+ My '77
Plants around the house:
Captivating cacti. R. Langer. il House & Gard 149:32+ Ag '77
Dramatic accents—bromeliads. R. Langer. il House & Gard 149:68 Je '77
Fern craze. R. Langer. il House & Gard 149:84+ N '77
For nonstop color—geraniums. R. Langer. il House & Gard 149:76+ Mr '77
Gardening by lights. R. Langer. il House & Gard 150:32+ Ja '78
Gesneriads: beyond the African violet. R. Langer. il House & Gard 149:52 F '77
How to brighten up your house with an indoor bulb garden. R. Langer. il House & Gard 149:92 O '77
How to keep your holiday plants blooming. R. Langer. il House & Gard 149:30+ D '77
Jungle gems: bamboo and palm. R. Langer. il House & Gard 149:82+ Ap '77
Miniature roses. R. Langer. il House & Gard 149:78 My '77
Orchids—exotics indoors. R. Langer. House & Gard 149:32 Jl '77
Plants for night people; odoriferous flowering plants. R. Langer. il House & Gard 149:42+ S '77
Roots: the saga of the American house plant. J. H. Falk. il Horticulture 55:14-17 N '77
What can a plant do for you? J. U. Crockett. il Horticulture 55:4-5 Mr '77
Your guide to indoor trees. V. E. Towns. il House B 119:106-7+ O '77
See also
Amaryllis
Artificial light gardening
Aspidistra
Begonias
Bromeliads
Cactus
Coleus
Dracaenas
Episcias
Ferns
Garden rooms
Geraniums
Gesneriaceae
Hanging plants
Ivy
Kafir lilies
Orchids
Poinsettias
Soils, Potting

Anecdotes, facetiae, satire, etc.

Plants: the roots of all evil. F. Lebowitz. Mademoiselle 83:52 F '77
Urban fauna. R. Baker. N Y Times Mag p 10 N 27 '77

Purchasing

How to buy a plant. il Seventeen 36:96 Mr '77
HOUSE prices. See Housing—Costs
HOUSE protection
See also
Burglary protection
Locks and keys
HOUSE purchasing. See House buying
HOUSE selling
How to help a realtor sell your home. P. L. Stewart. il Ret Liv 17:40-1+ My '77
Selling your house yourself. Sunset 158:130+ Je '77
Which home improvements pay off best when you sell? M. Daly. Bet Hom & Gard 55:46+ My '77
Yes, you can sell your house yourself. il Changing T 31:19-22 Mr '77
HOUSE sparrows. See Sparrows
HOUSE-swapping vacations. See Vacations
HOUSECLEANING. See House cleaning
HOUSEHOLD, Geoffrey Edward West
PW interviews; ed by B. A. Bannon. por Pub W 211:6-7 Ap 4 '77
HOUSEHOLD accounts. See Budget, Household
HOUSEHOLD appliance repairmen. See Repairmen
HOUSEHOLD appliances
How to save $300 a year on utility bills. il Good H 185:266+ O '77
Report from the housewares show. Redbook 149:200 My '77
What it costs to use your appliances. N. G. Rollins. il Good H 185:264 N '77
When you both work; labor-saving appliances. M. Davidson. il Parents Mag 52:66-8 Ap '77
See also
Cleaning machinery and appliances
Clothes dryers
Coffee pots, percolators, etc.
Dishwashing and drying machines
Freezers
Home electronics
Household appliances industry
Kitchen utensils and appliances
Washing machines

Labeling

EPA's next target: noisy appliances. Bus W p 100+ O 10 '77

Maintenance and repair

Appliance clinic; questions and answers. See issues of Popular mechanics
Housepower clinic; questions and answers (cont) E. Powell. il Pop Sci 210:136+ F; 166 My; 211:152-4 S '77

Noise labeling

See Household appliances—Labeling

Purchasing

Housewares. Consumers Res Mag 60:4-12 O '77
HOUSEHOLD appliances industry
Figuring out what consumers want; Amana Refrigeration, Inc; interview. G. C. Foerstner. il pors Nations Bus 65:46-8+ F '77
Overcooked? Rival Manufacturing Co. Forbes 120:68 S 1 '77
Rival toughs it out in a tough market. N. Howard. il Duns R 110:50-1 O '77
Tom Swift and his electric hamburger cooker; National Presto. Forbes 120:112 O 15 '77
See also
Maytag Company

HOUSEHOLD appliances industry—*Continued*

Finance

Household products & apparel. il Forbes 121: 162+ Ja 9 '78

Marketing

Distributors bring back the Crosley appliance. il Bus W p92-3 Ja 31 '77

France

Appliance maker scouts for a U.S. site; Moulinex. Bus W p38-40 My 30 '77

HOUSEHOLD budget. See Budget, Household

HOUSEHOLD cleaning preparations. See Cleaning compositions

HOUSEHOLD employees insurance. See Insurance, Workmens compensation

HOUSEHOLD energy conservation. See Power resources—Conservation

HOUSEHOLD furnishings

Can-do canvas furnishings. P. W. Cullison and others. il Bet Hom & Gard 55:66-9 Je '77

Essence of understatement; Halston's Manhattan town house. M. Gough and others. il por House B 119:94-7+ O '77

58 do-it-yourself decorating ideas all under $100. il Good H 185:118-27+ Ag '77

House furnishings. il Consumers Res Mag 60: 136-43 O '77

How to make a room special with accessories. S. Van Zante and others. il Bet Hom & Gard 55:74-7 Mr '77

New for you. See issues of House beautiful

New York: where to shop for your house within walking distance of the hotel. N. Richardson. il House & Gard 149:62+ S '77

Now you can have top design for top value; furnishings by A. Donghia. il por House & Gard 149:80-3 Ag '77

100 ideas under $100. il Bet Hom & Gard 55:75-91+ Jl '77

Rustic with class; house designed for Arthur Williams. il House & Gard 149:72-7 F '77

Trends. Am Home 80:58 My '77

See also

Christmas gifts for the home

Color in house decoration

Electric lamps

HOUSEHOLD furnishings, Moving of. See Moving

HOUSEHOLD furnishings industry

See also

Congoleum Corporation

HOUSEHOLD management. See Home economics

HOUSEHOLD mechanics. See Mechanics, Household

HOUSEHOLD pest control

See also

Termite control

HOUSEHOLD pests

See also

Fleas

HOUSEHOLD purchasing. See Purchasing, Household

HOUSEHOLD scales. See Scales (weighing instruments)

HOUSEHOLD water purifiers. See Water purifiers, Domestic

HOUSEKEEPING. See Home economics

HOUSEL, Thomas J.

Finding allies in the fight against shoplifting. il Nations Bus 65:64-6 S '77

HOUSEMAN, Gerald L.

Rights of movement. bibl Society 14:16-19 Jl '77

HOUSER, David, and Stepler, R.

Dual-use solar wall: pool heat plus handball backboard. il Pop Sci 210:110-13+ Ap '77

HOUSER, George M.

Needed: a change in U.S. policy in Southern Africa. Chr Cent 94:244-6 Mr 16 '77

HOUSES

Houses that endure. E. Schaeffer. Chr Today 21:24 Jl 8 '77

Other people's houses. L. Lewis. Atlantic 241: 86-8 Ja '78

See also

Architecture, Domestic

Architecture and climate

City houses

Condominium (housing)

Cottages

Farmhouses

Sod houses

Storage in the home

Vacation houses

Automation

See Computers—Home use

Cooling

See Cooling

Finance

See Housing finance

Fires and fire prevention

Burglar and fire protection. il Consumers Res Mag 60:156-8 O '77

Leasing and renting

Buy or rent a home? il U.S. News 82:86 Ap 25 '77

Special pleasures of renting a house of your own in St Martin. W. P. Rayner. il House & Gard 149:62+ S '77

See also

Farmhouses—Leasing and renting

Maintenance and repair

8 ways to protect your investment in your home. R. Rosefsky. Bet Hom & Gard 55:37+ Ap '77

Fall cleanup. Mech Illus 73:38 O '77

Fall home value ideas; symposium. il Pop Sci 211:138+ O '77

Fall warm-up: home improvement & decorating guide. B. Niles. il Am Home 80:77+ S '77

Get set for winter. Changing T 31:6-8 N '77

Give your house an energy update; how a systems engineer can help you. V. McNiff. il House & Gard 149:38 Jl '77

Home centers: 1-stop shopping for Mrs Fixit; women making household repairs. S. Schraub. House B 119:48+ Ap '77

Home energy guide. H. Wicks and others. il Pop Mech 148:115+ S '77

Home improvement and decorating guide. il Am Home 80:85+ Ap '77

Home-improvement ideas; symposium. il Pop Sci 211:113-26+ S '77

Home improvement section. il Mech Illus 73:58+ Ap '77

Home maintenance. bibl il Consumers Res Mag 60:113-19 O '77

House for sale. P. Gross. House & Gard 149:36+ My '77

Improving your home for winter; special section. il Ladies Home J 94:145+ S '77

It's home improvement time. J. H. Ingersoll. House B 119:43-4+ My '77

Ladies' home journal home improvement and decorating guide. il Ladies Home J 94:165+ Ap '77

9 new products for home improvement. il Pop Mech 148:90-1 S '77

1977 homeowner's guide to saving energy and money. M. Cubisino. il McCalls 104:121-8 S '77

Redbook's guide to home improvement and decorating. il Redbook 148:173+ Ap; 149:189+ S '77

Shop talk. A. Lees. See issues of Popular science

Weather stripping; winter proofing. il Consumer Rep 42:110-12 F '77

See also

Mechanics, Household

Bibliography

Remodeling notebook. J. H. Ingersoll. House B 119:98 My '77

Prices

See Housing—Costs

Ventilation

See Ventilation

HOUSES, Historic. See Historic houses, sites, etc.

HOUSES, Miniature. See House models

HOUSES, Octagonal

PS leisure home of the month: octagon on piers. A. Lees. il Pop Sci 210:132 F '77

HOUSES, Prefabricated

How you can afford a home of your own; factory houses. A. M. Watkins. Redbook 150:199+ N '77

Is the precut house a bargain? il Sunset 158:104-9 My '77

Sensational barn of your own. il House & Gard 149:122-7 Je '77

See also

Mobile homes

HOUSES, Remodeled

Add an energy-efficient room at the top. A. M. Watkins. il Pop Sci 210:140+ Mr '77

Adding to older houses: many approaches, many choices. il Archit Rec 162:81-92 N '77

Architect's choice; home of B. Thompson. J. Davison. il N Y Times Mag p88-9 Ap 24 '77

At home in half a barn; weekend home of the Winthrop Faulkners. N. Skurka. il N Y Times Mag p56-8 F 20 '77

Conrans in the country; English home. E. Brown. il por N Y Times Mag p74-5 O 30 '77

Don't move—improve. B. Niles. il Am Home 80:51-3 Ap '77

Family living—open house; California. il House & Gard 150:84-7 Ja '78

Farmhouse for moderns; home of Brian and Marrisa Stone. il House & Gard 149:166-71 N '77

Few silk purses from sows' ears. M. A. Sharp. il Sat Eve Post 249:64-7 N '77

Finding and working with a contractor. M. D. Hinds. House & Gard 149:110+ My '77

For more living space in your home, enclose a porch. R. Stepler. il Pop Sci 211:115 Jl '77

Garage into bedroom for $3,500. il Sunset 159:144 O '77

HOUSES, Remodeled—*Continued*
Halston's hideaway; remodeled New York carriage house. P. Goldberger. il N Y Times Mag p34-7 Jl 24 '77
Home is where you find it; converted schoolhouse, tugboat and ice house. il Good H 184:96+ Mr '77
House splicing. M. Philips. il Pop Sci 210:121-3 Ap '77
How not to do it yourself. C. Scarborough. il por Am Home 80:24+ S '77
How to afford home improvements. F. Casey. il Mech Illus 73:110-1 Jl '77
How to make an old tract house live like new. D. Haupert and C. Scott. il Bet Hom & Gard 55:96-103 S '77
In just two years, transformation; Portland, Ore. il Sunset 158:100-3 Je '77
It's time to turn if into now. il House B 119: 117-55 My '77
Let there be light: remodelings that bring the outdoors in. il House & Gard 149:108-13 Je '77
Making big rooms out of little ones. D. Haupert. il Bet Hom & Gard 55:68-73 Mr '77
More openness, an end to traffic confusion. il Sunset 158:144 Je '77
New upstairs is conservatory, new downstairs is work center. il Sunset 158:166-7 F '77
Old house spreads its wing; R. Stern. il House & Gard 149:122-7 D '77
Once a bar, this house proves again urban life's resiliency. il House B 119:50+ My '77
One-of-a-kind country look; farmhouse of the Bill Crofut family. B. Niles. il pors Am Home 80:46-9 S '77
Open up for more light; remodeling easily with windows and sliding glass doors. M. McClintock. il Pop Mech 147:142+ Ap '77
Opening up an outdated old house. il Bet Hom & Gard 55:42 My '77
Over the living room is a new loft. il Sunset 158:82 F '77
Private residence, New York State. il Archit Rec 161:94-7 mid-My '77
Rainbow retreat; renovated log cottage. S. G. Lewin. il House B 119:150-5 S '77
Remodeling? Don't hire just anybody. Changing T 31:4 F '77
Remodeling: garage conversions that add low-cost living space. D. Haupert. il Bet Hom & Gard 55:132-5 My '77
Remodeling: how to make an ordinary house something special. D. Haupert. il Bet Hom & Gard 55:124-7 My '77
Remodeling notebook. J. H. Ingersoll. See occasional issues of House beautiful
Remodeling report. J. H. Ingersoll. bibl il House B 119:69-70+ bibl(p99) S '77
Remodeling: stretch space to make your house more livable. R. A. Dickelman. il Bet Hom & Gard 54:34-9 Ag '76
Residential remodeling and addition, Chevy Chase, Maryland. il Archit Rec 161:82-3 mid-My '77
Starting from scratch; idle garage space becomes an apartment. il House B 119:43-4+ My '77
They built an indoor-outdoor hideaway. il Sunset 159:98 S '77
They raised the roof. il Sunset 158:152 Ap '77
We put the wood place to work. W. Willis. il Ret Liv 17:42-3+ My '77
We wanted the new house to have the same flavor as the old; remodeled Victorian house, Washington, D.C. il House & Gard 149:142-5 My '77
Weekend wonderplace: the Antenor-Patiños French country house; remodeled seventeenth-century mill near Fontainebleau. il Vogue 167:166-9 Ap '77
With true pioneer spirit; house of Richard and Rita Burns. N. Craig. il House B 119:84-9 Mr '77

HOUSES, Restored
Back Bay update. J. Davison. il N Y Times Mag p73 My 15 '77
Historic homes: authentic charm, modern comfort; renovated interiors of historic houses in New Castle, Del. il McCalls 104:116-21 Jl '77
It fit together like a jigsaw puzzle; home of C. Barnes in Winston-Salem, N.C. M. Gough and J. Macurdy. il por House B 119:104-13 N '77
New generation for High Street; Petersburg, Va. J. Canup and T. Canup. il Ret Liv 17:35-7+ F '77
Restoration of San Francisco (St Frusquin) Reserve, Louisiana. H. W. Krotzer, Jr. il Antiques 111:1194-1203 Je '77
Restoring a historic house. M. DeCourcy Hinds. il House & Gard 149:58+ Ap '77
See also
Historic houses, sites, etc.

HOUSES, Seashore. See Beach architecture

HOUSES, Solar. See Solar houses

HOUSES, Tree. See Tree houses

HOUSES, Underground
Underground houses. V. E. Smay. bibl il Pop Sci 210:84-9+ Ap '77
Your next house could have a grass roof. R. F. Dempewolff. il Pop Mech 147:78-81+ Mr '77

HOUSES in bottles. See House models

HOUSEWARES. See Household appliances

HOUSEWIVES
Help for women suddenly on their own; Alliance for Displaced Homemakers. il Changing T 32: 45-7 Ja '78
Housewife's disease; agoraphobia. B. Delatiner. Good H 184:84+ Je '77
I am the mother of eight, a housewife, a feminist—and happy: Jane Broderick's story; interview, ed by J. Lazarre. J. Broderick. il por Ms 5:51-5+ My '77; Discussion. 6:7-8+ S '77
I'm ready for full-time motherhood. B. Cork. Am Home 80:27 N '77
Myth of the liberated housewife. L. B. Francke. Harp Baz 110:101+ F '77
Occupation: homemaker—a professional guide; symposium. Ms 5:91-4 My '77
When women on their own are thrown onto the job market; work of the Alliance for Displaced Homemakers. il U.S. News 83:55-6 S 26 '77
See also
Marriage

HOUSEWORK. See Home economics

HOUSING
See also
Aged—Housing
Condominium (housing)
Discrimination in housing
Emergency housing

Costs

District of Columbia/open today; prices of houses in Georgetown. R. Rosenblatt. il New Repub 177:39-40 Jl 9 '77
Housing: it's outasight. il Time 110:50-4+ S 12 '77; Same abr. with title House prices: they're outasight. Read Digest 112:135-8 Ja '78
Housing: raising the roof. T. Nicholson and others. il Newsweek 89:77-8 Je 13 '77
How to keep down the cost of buying a home. il U.S. News 82:39-42 Mr 21 '77
Soaring housing prices: will galloping costs of ownership kill the boom? W. E. Hoadley. por Duns R 109:9 Je '77
Why Fannie, Ginnie, and Freddy can't do it. S. Rose. il Fortune 95:111+ Mr '77
Why home prices are soaring. il Nations Bus 65:82-4+ S '77

Density

Building types study: high density housing; with introd by J. Nairn. il Archit Rec 162:111-26 S '77

Desegregation

Luring blacks, keeping whites; integration in the San Fernando Valley, Calif. and Oak Park, Ill. il Time 110:16+ O 31 '77
Success in Oak Park. D. A. Williams and others. Newsweek 90:47 O 17 '77

Federal aid

Big boost for housing. il U.S. News 82:42 Mr 14 '77
Born-again housing; Detroit. D. A. Williams and others. il Newsweek 90:37-8 O 31 '77
HEW vs. HUD; controversy over housing allowances. S. Kaplan. New Repub 177:15-16 Ag 6 '77
Housing and community development: an act to bleed the cities. J. M. Baer. Nation 224: 274-6 Mr 5 '77
1977 Housing and Community Development Act: some new tools for central-city revitalization. N. J. Parish and C. Teglas. Archit Rec 162:61 D '77
Secretary Harris seeks more subsidized housing. D. Loomis. Archit Rec 161:34 My '77

Finance

See Housing finance

Algeria

Algerian venture sinks a developer; Bremer Treuhand. il Bus W p30-1 Jl 18 '77

California

Banks help the cities rebuild. il Bus W p 124+ N 21 '77
Luring blacks, keeping whites; integration in the San Fernando Valley. il Time 110:16+ O 31 '77
Wild speculation in California homes. il Bus W p31+ My 2 '77
See also
Los Angeles—Housing
San Francisco—Housing

Colombia

See also
Bogotá, Colombia—Housing

Connecticut

Award winning community; Lakeridge in Connecticut. il Bet Hom & Gard 55:89 Ag '77
See also
Hartford, Conn.—Housing

HOUSING—*Continued*

Europe, Western

European experience with rent controls. E. J. Howenstine. bibl il M Labor R 100:21-8 Je '77

Illinois

Achievable miracles in subsidized housing; Crestview Village and Edgewood Commons, Kankakee, Ill. J. S. Fuerst. Chr Cent 94:147-9 F 16 '77
Arlington Heights case. America 136:90-1 F 5 '77
Common sense on race; Arlington Heights zoning refusal case. G. F. Will. Newsweek 89:80 Ja 24 '77
Deviating into sense; Arlington Heights, Ill. zoning law. Nat R 29:136 F 4 '77
Intent, not impact; Supreme Court decision on Arlington Heights, Ill. zoning law. Time 109: 52 Ja 24 '77
Luring blacks and keeping whites; integration in Oak Park. il Time 110:16+ O 31 '77
Right to refuse; rezoning refusal upheld by Supreme Court in Arlington Heights case. J. K. Footlick and others. il Newsweek 89:77 Ja 24 '77
Setback in Arlington Heights; Supreme Court ruling on zoning. J. De Muth. America 136: 167-8 F 26 '77
Suburban iron curtain; Supreme Court decision on Arlington Heights zoning law. Commonweal 104:99-100 F 18 '77
Success in Oak Park. D. A. Williams and others. Newsweek 90:47 O 17 '77
Zoning out low-income families in suburbia; Arlington Heights. J. S. Fuerst. Chr Cent 94: 77-8 F 2 '77

Iran

See also
Housing projects—Iran

Maryland

Maryland pioneers new concept in housing; sheltered housing for elderly. D. F. Thomas. il Aging 268:21-4 F '77

Mexico

Urban housing policy for developing countries; report from the Colloquium on Urban Development Problems in Mexico City. M. Kilbridge. Archit Rec 161:37+ Ap '77

Michigan

Youngest landlord in Michigan; F. Simmons of Pontiac. il pors Ebony 32:140+ S '77
See also
Detroit—Housing

Middle East

Texas-Saudi affiar. il Forbes 120:88 O 1 '77

New York (state)

See also
New York (city)—Housing

Rhode Island

See also
Providence, R.I.—Housing

Saudi Arabia

See also
Housing projects—Saudi Arabia

South Africa

Destruction of an African community. M. Nash. Chr Cent 94:985 O 26 '77

Tennessee

See also
Nashville, Tenn.—Housing

Underdeveloped areas

See Underdeveloped areas—Housing

United States

Housing, urban decay challenge Carter; excerpt from address. L. De Moll. Am City & County 92:110+ My '77
Moral dimension of housing. J. M. Wall. Chr Cent 94:243 Mr 16 '77
Urban mayor offers some sensible strategies in searching for a new urban policy; ed by W. F. Wagner, Jr. Archit Rec 161:13 Mr '77
Urban pioneers gamble on the inner city. il Bus W p 144+ Jl 25 '77
See also
Blacks—Housing
Construction industry
Housing finance
Housing projects
Housing projects, Cooperative
United States—Federal Housing Administration
United States—Housing and Urban Development, Department of

West Virginia

After the strip floods: relief is the real disaster; emergency housing for Mingo County, W.Va. R. E. Wise, Jr. il Nation 225:18-20 Jl 2 '77

HOUSING, Cooperative
See also
Apartment houses—Cooperative ownership
Housing projects, Cooperative

HOUSING, Discrimination in. See Discrimination in housing

HOUSING allowances. See Housing—Federal aid

HOUSING and Urban Development, Department of. See United States—Housing and Urban Development, Department of

HOUSING authority bonds. See Bonds, Housing authority

HOUSING construction industry. See Construction industry

HOUSING density. See Housing—Density

HOUSING finance
Banks help the cities rebuild; California banks. il Bus W p 124+ N 21 '77
Hope at last for families who want their own first home; individual housing accounts; proposed Young Families Housing Acts. M. Daly. Bet Hom & Gard 55:10 Ap '77
House buying: how to dig up that down payment. Bet Hom & Gard 55:32+ Je '77
Is owning a home still a sound investment? G. G. Greer. il Bet Hom & Gard 55:10+ Mr '77
More about money: how much you need, where to get. it. Redbook 148:178+ Ap '77
S&Ls find many reasons to be happy. il Bus W p41-2 N 28 '77
S&Ls will write a program for city neighborhood lending. D. Loomis. Archit Rec 161:34 Je '77
See also
Federal Home Loan Mortgage Corporation
Federal National Mortgage Association
Housing—Federal aid
Mortgages
United States—Federal Home Loan Bank Board

HOUSING laws and legislation
Hope at last for families who want their own first home; individual housing accounts; proposed Young Families Housing Act. M. Daly. Bet Hom & Gard 55:10 Ap '77
See also
Building laws and regulations
Housing—Federal aid
Rent laws

HOUSING projects
Achievable miracles in subsidized housing; Crestview Village and Edgewood Commons, Kankakee, Ill. J. S. Fuerst. Chr Cent 94: 147-9 F 16 '77
Landings near Buffalo, New York. il Archit Rec 161:118-19 mid-My '77
Whalers' Cove Apartments, Foster City, California. il Archit Rec 161:124-6 mid-My '77
See also
Apartment houses
New York (city)—Housing
Providence, R.I.—Housing

Iran

Levittshahr will bring development housing to Tehran. D. Higgins. il Archit Rec 162:37 Ag '77

Saudi Arabia

Town-in-town will house 8,000 in suburban Riyadh. il Archit Rec 162:37 D '77

HOUSING projects, Cooperative
U.S. journal: the Bronx; the coops. C. Trillin. il New Yorker 53:49-54 Ag 1 '77

HOUSING projects, Government
See also
New York (city)—Housing
Providence, R.I.—Housing

HOUSING subsidies. See Housing—Federal aid

HOUSTON, Charles
Murder in Morningside Park. D. Gallagher. il pors N Y Times Mag p26-9+ Ag 28 '77 *

HOUSTON, Jean
Margaret Mead at seventy-five. por Sat R 4:6+ F 5 '77

HOUSTON, John
Do we have rights to everything? U. S. News 83:34 O 31 '77

HOUSTON, Rob
Biggest littlest shows on earth. il pors Ebony 32:90-2+ Mr '77 *

HOUSTON, Walter Scott
Deep-sky wonders. See issues of Sky and telescope

HOUSTON, Tex.

Art

Deep in the art of Texas. C. Moser. il Ms 5:33-5 F '77
Houston (cont) C. Moser. il Art N 76:92-4 F; 94+ Ap; 92-4 O; 101-2 D '77
Houston's new cultural decision makers. C. Moser. il Art N 76:74-6 F '77

Banks

Why foreign banks like Houston so much. il Bus W p39+ D 5 '77

Buildings

Nobody here but us Texans. . ; foreign investments in Houston. il Forbes 119:52-4 F 1 '77

HOUSTON, Tex.—*Continued*

City planning

Waiting for the future; Texas Eastern's Houston Center. E. Bailey. il Forbes 120:50+ S 1 '77

See also
Houston, Tex.—Metropolitan area

Description

Houston. R. Magruder and M. Magruder. il Travel 147:36-9 My '77
Houston: supercity. D. A. Williams and N. Proffitt. il Newsweek 90:41 D 12 '77
Rodeo in the Astrodome. N. Richardson. il House & Gard 150:49+ Ja '78

Economic conditions

Houston: then and now; with editorial comment. il Forbes 119:6, 48 Mr 1 '77
Houston's Arab connection. N. Proffitt. il Newsweek 89:88+ Je 13 '77

Education

Does the use of newspapers in the classroom affect attitudes of students? study made in a Houston high school. Z. Verner and L. Murphy. il Clearing H 50:350-1 Ap '77

Historic houses, sites, etc.

Living with antiques: Old Richmond, the Houston guest cottage of Mr and Mrs Fred T. Couper Jr. E. D. Garrett. il Antiques 112:514-21 S '77

Metropolitan area

Octopus. il Newsweek 89:27 Je 13 '77

Music

See also
Opera—Texas

Police

Blue Monday; sentences of two Houston policemen. Nation 225:421 O 29 '77
Police story: two hard towns. il Time 110:29-30 S 19 '77
Wild bunch. J. K. Footlick. il Newsweek 89:80-1 Je 6 '77

Politics and government

Women's advocacy: showdown in Houston. L. Gillan. il Ms 6:19 S '77

Public health

Deadly mosquitoes dealt knockout blow. il Am City & County 92:53 Mr '77

HOUSTON Ballet Company. See Ballet companies

HOUSTON Lighting and Power Company
Don't say we're lucky. il Forbes 119:74 Ja 15 '77
Wrong kind of foresight. Forbes 120:66 N 1 '77

HOUSTON Natural Gas Corporation-Pott Industries Inc. merger. See Corporations—Acquisitions and mergers

HOUSTON Oil and Minerals Corporation. See Fuel industry

HOUSTON Opera. See Opera—Texas

HOUSTON Public Library

Branches

Keeping options open. D. M. Henington. il Lib J 102:169-70 Ja 15 '77

HOUSTON Ship Channel
Pollution can be licked. il U.S. News 82:49 F 7 '77

HOUSTOUN, Diana
Murder in Argentina. E. Magalis. Chr Cent 94:1030-3 N 9 '77 *

HOUTZ, Elsa
Path to the evangelicals is straight and narrow—but easy to follow. Writers Digest 57:24-5 D '77

HOVEN, Vern
Where should you live in retirement? il Ret Liv 16:20-2 D '76

HOVER, Margot
School as a resource for families. Clearing H 50:415-16 My '77

HOVERCRAFT. See Air cushion vehicles

HOVHANESS, Alan
Minn. orch: Hovhaness premiere; Symphony no. 29. Hi Fi 27:MA24 Ag '77

HOVING, Thomas Pearsall Field
Hoving years; interview, ed by M. N. Carter. pors Art N 76:37-40 Ja '77

about

Who should manage museums? P. M. Kadis. il por Art N 76:46-51 O '77 *

HOWARD, Alan
Lofty rhetoric and business interests. Nation 225:365-70 O 15 '77

HOWARD, Ben
Four voices. Poetry 130:285-92 Ag '77
Two deer; poem. Poetry 130:258-9 Ag '77

HOWARD, David M.
Nixon's Watergate—man's depravity. Chr Today 21:12-14 Je 3 '77

HOWARD, Edward Neal
Library bond campaign to bank on. Am Lib 8:622 D '77

HOWARD, Elizabeth
Women's dreams. il Ladies Home J 94:50+ Je '77

HOWARD, Jane
Books. See issues of Mademoiselle

HOWARD, John Addison
Trumpeting a certain note; address, February 23, 1977. Vital Speeches 43:428-31 My 1 '77

HOWARD, Philip H. and Datta, R. S.
Desulfurization of coal by use of chemical comminution. bibl il Science 197:668-9 Ag 12 '77

HOWARD, Richard
Art or knack? Poetry 129:226-32 Ja '77
Charles Garnier; poem. Poetry 131:101-2 N '77
Shadows. Poetry 131:103-6 N '77

about

Comment. R. K. Martin. Poetry 130:36-40 Ap '77 *

HOWARD, Richard Alden
Legacy of Sri Lanka's Royal Botanic Gardens. il Horticulture 55:66 Mr '77

HOWARD, Ross H.
20 years a landlord & how it paid. Changing T 31:40-2 O '77

HOWARD, Ted. See Rifkin, T. jt auth

HOWARD, Thomas
Who am I? Who am I? Chr Today 21:10-13 Jl 8 '77

HOWARD the Duck comic books. See Comics (books, strips, etc)

HOWARD University Hospital. See Washington, D.C.—Hospitals

HOWARDS, Stuart S. See Johnson, A. L. jt auth

HOWATCH, Susan
Rich are different; story; excerpt from novel. Ladies Home J 94:111-13 Jl '77
Risks and rewards in writing the saga novel. Writer 90:11-13+ Je '77

HOWE, Don
65% loan rate can help. Farm J 101:9 Mr '77

HOWE, Elias, 1819-1867
Singer: making a business of Howe's invention. A. Hershman. il Duns R 109:28+ Je '77 *

HOWE, Gordon
Rub-a-dub-dub, that's my daddy in the tub. P. Gammons. il por Sports Illus 47:102+ D 5 '77 *

HOWE, Harold, 2d
Does it pay to go to college? pors U.S. News 82:59-60 Ja 24 '77

HOWE, Henry F.
Sex-ratio adjustment in the common grackle. bibl il Science 198:744-6 N 18 '77

HOWE, Irving
Cities' secret. New Repub 176:55-7 Ja 22 '77
Limits of ethnicity; address, June 25, 1977. New Repub 176:17-19 Je 25 '77; Same with title What role for ethnicity? Current 195:13-17 S '77
Strangers. Yale R 66:481-500 Je '77
What Henry heard; excerpts from address, February 1977. New Repub 176:20-1 Mr 26 '77

HOWE, John W.
What is happy about Halloween? il Chr Today 22:16-17 O 21 '77

HOWE, Louise Kapp
Summer in the life of a beauty parlor: the stories of 5 women who work there; excerpt from Pink collar workers. Ms 5:52-5+ Mr '77
We'll see you at the club. il McCalls 104:30+ F '77
What American women want. McCalls 105:198+ N '77
Women who sell houses. McCalls 104:123+ Ag '77

HOWELL, Barbara
Make your office look successful. il Harp Baz 110:98-9+ Mr '77
Manipulation: shortcut to the top. Harp Baz 110:84+ Ag '77

HOWELL, Henry Evans, 1920-
Carter strikes out in Virginia. R. Mackenzie. Nat R 29:1425-6 D 9 '77 *
Howell for Virginia. New Repub 177:6 O 29 '77 *
Howlin' Henry's surprise win. R. Mackenzie. Nat R 29:778 Jl 8 '77 *
Statehouse derby. R. Boeth and others. il pors Newsweek 90:42+ O 17 '77 *
Two tight gubernatorial races. il pors Time 110:25-6 N 7 '77 *

HOWELL, John A.
Treatment of effluents: modern methods of sewage disposal. il Oceans 10:63-7 My '77

HOWELL, Roger, 1936-
Educated persons should serve as society's conscience. por Intellect 106:185 N '77

HOWELL, Suzanne
Research paper redux. Engl J 66:52-5 D '77
Unlocking the box: an experiment in literary response. il Engl J 66:37-42 F '77

HOWES, Helen Claire
Dead sea; with biographical sketch. il Sea Front 23:90-5, 126 Mr '77

HOWLAND, John L. and Iyer, S. L.
Erythrocyte lipids in heterozygous carriers of duchenne muscular dystrophy. bibl il Science 198:309-10 O 21 '77

HOWLER, Walter
Case for fiscal irresponsibility. Nat R 29:605 My 27 '77
HOWLER monkeys. See Monkeys
HOWLETT, Duncan
New forests of Scotland (cont) il Am For 83: 32-5+ F '77
HOWORTH, M. Beckett
Exercise and exercise devices—which ones are really useful? il Consumers Res Mag 60:31-2+ N '77
HOWZE, Joseph Lawson, Bp
Black bishop for Mississippi. G. V. Murry. America 137:32 Jl 16 '77 *
HOY, Alice Kathleen
Controversial English lessons and the law. bibl il Engl J 66:21-5 F '77
HOY, Marjorie A.
Rapid response to selection for a nondiapausing gypsy moth. bibl il Science 196:1462-3 Je 24 '77
HOY, Wilton E.
Notes on the gringo. Américas 29:15-16 Ag '77
HOYT, Erich
Orcinus orca: separating facts from fantasies. il Oceans 10:22-6 Jl '77
HOYT, Jane Hauser
Beyond the handicap. Am Educ 13:25-6 Ap '77
HOYT, Kenneth B.
According to Hoyt; interview. ed by S. B. Neill. il por Am Educ 13:10-13 Mr '77
Career education defined; excerpt from Career education for special populations. Am Educ 13:inside cover Mr '77
HRDY, Sarah Blaffer
Animals that kill their young. il Time 111:64 Ja 9 '78 *
HRUBECKY, Henry
Worldwide view of technology. por Intellect 106: 14 Jl '77
HRUBY, Sarka, and others
Synthetic galactocerebrosides evoke myelination-inhibiting antibodies. bibl il Science 195: 173-5 Ja 14 '77
HU, C. T.
Politics in Chinese higher education. Cur Hist 73:79-83+ S '77
HU, Hsiang-yun Yang, and others
Inducibility of transferrin receptors on Friend erythroleukemic cells. bibl il Science 197:559-61 Ag 5 '77
HU, Mary Lee
Mary Lee Hu: high on the wire. E. Breckenridge. il por Craft Horiz 37:40-3+ Ap '77 *
HUANG, Hua
Secretary Vance visits China and Japan August 20-27; exchanges of toasts. Dept State Bull 77:365-8 S 19 '77
HUANG-ti, Emperor of China. See Ch'in Shih-huang-ti
HUBBELL, Harvey, Inc. See Electric industries—United States
HUBBELL, John G.
Here comes the 100-mile-an-hour Navy! Read Digest 111:112-16 Ag '77
Medical wonders of Dr Robert White. por Read Digest 110:138-42 F '77
HUBER, D. M. and others
Nitrification inhibitors—new tools for food production. bibl il BioScience 27:523-9 Ag '77
HUBERT, Saint
St Hubertus: a conservation legacy. F. Knapp. il Int Wildlife 7:42-3 N '77 *
HUBERT, Henry
View from here: a publisher's rep attends ABA/NACS booksellers school. Pub W 211:47-8 My 2 '77
HUCK, Winnifred Spraghe (Mason)
Moma went to Congress and then to jail. D. Dean and M. Dean. il pors Am Hist Illus 12: 37-43 N '77 *
HUCKENPAHLER, Victoria
Madame Barbara Karinska: costumes to delight. il pors Dance Mag 52:44-7 Ja '78
HUCKLEBERRIES, Garden. See Garden huckleberries
HUCKLEBERRY Finn (literary character) See Characters in literature
HUDNALL, James
In the company of great whales. il Audubon 79:62-73 My '77
HUDSON, Gossie Harold
Not for entertainment only. bibl f por Negro Hist Bull 40:682-3 Mr '77
HUDSON, Grace (Carpenter)
Pomo Indian portraits of Grace Carpenter Hudson; excerpt from The painter lady. S. R. Boynton. il por Am West 14:20-9 S '77 *
HUDSON, J. L, Company. See Detroit—Stores
HUDSON, James R.
Municipal bureaucracies and municipal power. Intellect 105:396-8 Je '77
HUDSON, James W.
Raising the rooftop consciousness. il Parks & Rec 12:32-5+ Ap '77
HUDSON, Richard
Changing the United Nations. Current 189:48-55 Ja '77
For a law of the seas. Current 198:44-51 D '77
International struggle for a law of the sea. il Bull Atom Sci 33:14-20 D '77
HUDSON, Rock
Rock Hudson talks about Rock Hudson—finally! interview, ed by J. Wilkie. por Good H 184: 152+ Mr '77
HUDSON (television character) See Characters in television
HUDSON River
Hudson: that river's alive. A. H. Hall. il map Nat Geog 153:62-89 Ja '78
Tidal flats in the Hudson. R. R. Glunt. il por Conservationist 31:30-1 My '77
HUDSON'S Bay Company
American characters: John McLoughlin. D. Lavender. por Am Heritage 28:64-5 Je '77
Fort Vancouver: fur trade capital of the Pacific Northwest. J. A. Hussey. bibl il por Am West 14:12-19+ S '77
HUEBNER, Albert L.
Dry farming: energy-saver. Sci Digest 82:59-61 Jl '77
No-win war against cancer. Progressive 41:26-8 O '77
HUEY, Raymond B. and Pianka, E. R.
Natural selection for juvenile lizards mimicking noxious beetles. bibl il Science 195:201-3 Ja 14 '77
HUFF, Betty Tracy
Case of the missing masterpiece; drama. Plays 36:23-32 Ap '77
HUFF, Darrell
Calcu-letter. il Pop Sci 211:23-4 N '77; 212:8 Ja '78
Incredible tale of the 37-year puzzle. il por Pop Sci 211:26+ O '77
HUFF, John
How to custom design plastic cases for projects. il Pop Electr 12:81-4 S '77
HUFFINGTON, Roy Michael
Roy Huffington: life begins at 50. J. Flanigan. por Forbes 120:28+ S 1 '77 *
HUFFINGTON, Roy M, Inc. See Gas industry
HUFFMAN, James R.
How to design TTL digital systems. il Pop Electr 12:56-8 O '77
HUFFMAN, John L. and Trauth, D. M.
Cable television: diversity or duplication? Intellect 106:157-8 O '77
HUFFMAN Manufacturing Company. See Bicycle industry
HUFSTEDLER, Shirley (Mount)
In the name of justice: unending rush to the courts; address, May 18, 1977. Vital Speeches 43:572-6 Jl 1 '77
HUGER, Francis Kinloch
Imprisonment of Lafayette. J. W. Baker. il Am Heritage 28:86-91 Je '77 *
HUGER family
Huger coat-of-arms. H. K. Eilers. Hobbies 82: 150-1 O '77
HUGGING. See Embracing
HUGHES, Art
Auto-maintenance basics (cont) il Pop Sci 210: 164-6 F '77
HUGHES, Catharine R.
Antic arts. il Holiday 57:12 N '76; 58:26 Ja '77
Theatre. See occasional issues of America
HUGHES, Charles Evans, 1862-1948
1921 SALT talks—and you are there. R. K. Massie. il pors N Y Times Mag p38-40+ O 2 '77 *
HUGHES, Dee
My family, his family and my job. McCalls 104:58+ Ag '77
HUGHES, Helen MacGill
Wasp/woman/sociologist. il pors Society 14:69-80 Jl '77
HUGHES, Howard Robard
Battle for the shrinking millions. il por Time 110:64+ Jl 4 '77 *
Howard Hughes: man of wings. R. B. Parke. il por Flying 101:184 S '77 *
Howard Hughes' messy legacy. il Time 110:78+ O 3 '77 *
Those cases go on and on. Time 109:42+ Je 27 '77 *
HUGHES, Ina
How I found the real Santa Claus. il Good H 185:60+ D '77
HUGHES, Joseph V. and Johnson, T. C.
Hyperphenylalanemia: effect on brain polyribosomes can be partially reversed by other amino acids. bibl il Science 195:402-4 Ja 28 '77
HUGHES, Langston
Not without laughter. M. J. Moran. Engl J 66:58 Mr '77 *
HUGHES, M. Beatrice, and Lucchesi, J. C.
Genetic rescue of a lethal null activity allele of 6-phosphogluconate dehydrogenase in drosophila melanogaster. bibl il Science 196:1114-15 Je 3 '77
HUGHES, Paul
Remember Paul Hughes. W. F. Buckley, Jr. Nat R 29:403 Ap 1 '77 *
HUGHES, Robert
Art of the Japanese sword. il Horizon 19:50-61 Mr '77
Casanova myth. il Vogue 167:228-9 Mr '77

HUGHES, Spike
Beaumarchais: Figaro's playwright. Opera N 41:13-15 Mr 5 '77
Drawn from life. il Opera N 42:12-14+ D 24 '77
Notes on the Flute. il Opera N 41:12-14 Ja 22 '77
HUGO, Adèle
Victor Hugo's wayward daughter. T. Morgan. il pors Horizon 19:34-41 Ja '77 •
HUGO, Richard F.
Poet's statements of faith. il Atlantic 239:79-82 Ap '77
HUGO, Victor Marie, Comte
Tale of turmoil; adaptation of V. Hugo's play Le roi s'amuse into Verdi's opera Rigoletto. G. R. Marek. il por Opera N 42:10-14 D 3 '77 •
Victor Hugo: the painter. C. Barth. il Design (US) 78:6-9 mid-Summ '77 •
HUICHOLS Indians. See Indians of Mexico
HULL, Richard W.
Rhodesia and her neighbors. Cur Hist 73:218-22+ D '77
HULL, William
Surrender of Detroit. L. H. Scott. il por map Am Hist Illus 12:28-36 Je '77 •
HULLETT, Arthur
Singapore Handicraft Centre. il Trav/Holiday 148:32-5 N '77
HULLS (naval architecture)
Aluminum hull construction. il Motor B & S 140:47 Ag '77
Resistance to motion. E. Clement. il Motor B & S 141:46+ Ja '78
Rough-water powerboat design; excerpt from Power yachts. R. Mudie and C. Mudie. il Yachting 142:162+ O '77
Semisubmersible ships. il Sea Front 23:215-17 Jl '77
Ski hull takes the bounce out of boating. D. D. Vigren. il Pop Sci 210:104-5 F '77
What to know about trihulls. A. J. McMasters. il Mech Illus 73:32+ Mr '77

Decoration

See Boat decoration
HULTÉN, Pontus
Beaubourg preview; interview, ed by E. Baker. por Art in Am 65:100-2 Ja '77
HUMAN behavior. See Behavior (psychology)
HUMAN beings. See Man
HUMAN chorionic gonadotropin. See Gonadotropins
HUMAN Development Services, Office of. See United States—Human Development Services, Office of
HUMAN ecology
Ecofreaks, technofreaks, and one-armed biologists; excerpt from address. W. S. Hillman. BioScience 27:315 My '77
Human ecology; address, March 25, 1977. C. E. Bishop. Vital Speeches 43:470-2 My 15 '77
See also
Man—Influence on nature

Moral and religious aspects

Scientist and environmental bioethics; symposium. bibl BioScience 27:251-8+ Ap '77
HUMAN embryo. See Fetus
HUMAN engineering
Human performance considerations in complex systems. H. O. Holt and F. L. Stevenson. bibl il Science 195:1205-10 Mr 18 '77
HUMAN experimentation. See Medical research—Experimentation on man
HUMAN factors in engineering design. See Human engineering
HUMAN fertility. See Fertility, Human
HUMAN figure in art
It's the real thing; D. Hanson's lifelike figures. R. Bongartz. il pors Horizon 20:72-81 S '77
Mind bending with George Segal. A. Elsen. il por Art N 76:34-7 F '77
See also
Anatomy, Artistic
Portrait drawing
Portrait painting
Women in art
HUMAN genetics
Group-specific component: evidence for two subtypes of the Gc[1] gene. J. Constans and M. Viau. bibl il Science 198:1070-1 D 9 '77
Hemoglobin ontogenesis: test of the gene excision hypothesis. T. Papayannopoulou and others. bibl il Science 196:1215-16 Je 10 '77
Human globin messenger RNA: importance of cloning for structural analysis. J. T. Wilson and others. bibl il Science 196:200-2 Ap 8 '77
Mapping the locus of the H-Y gene on the human Y chromosome. G. C. Koo and others. bibl il Science 198:940-2 D 2 '77
New genetic marker in human parotid saliva (pm) S. Ikemoto and others. bibl il Science 197:378-9 Jl 22 '77
Status of the gene map of the human chromosomes. V. A. McKusick and F. H. Ruddle. bibl il Science 196:390-405 Ap 22 '77
See also
Behavior genetics
Genetic engineering
Heredity of disease

Social aspects

Are we born to be good? theories of E. O. Wilson; with editorial comment. N. Calder. il por Horizon 19:42-9 Mr '77
New science of genetic self-interest; interview, ed by S. Morris. I. DeVore. il Psychol Today 10:42-6+ F '77
HUMAN information processing
Auditory evoked potentials as probes of hemispheric differences in cognitive processing. D. W. Shucard and others. bibl il Science 197:1295-8 S 23 '77
Reading disability: an information-processing analysis. F. J. Morrison and others. bibl Science 196:77-9 Ap 1 '77
HUMAN interest columns. See Newspapers—Sections, columns, etc.
HUMAN Life Amendment (proposed) See United States—Constitution—Amendments
HUMAN mechanics
Computer readout translates body language into skills. P. Garfinkel. il Sci Digest 81:12-14 Mr '77
Gideon Ariel and his magic machine; computerized biomechanical analysis. K. Moore. il por Sports Illus 47:52-60 Ag 22 '77
HUMAN milk. See Milk, Human
HUMAN nature (periodical)
Bipedal party. New Yorker 53:33-5 O 24 '77
HUMAN Performance Laboratory, University of Denver. See Denver. University
HUMAN Potential Movement. See Group relations training; Self realization
HUMAN race. See Man
HUMAN relations
Enormous party; human beings and altruism. L. Thomas. il House & Gard 149:86-9+ D '77
Gift of you; emotional gifts. D. A. Sugarman. Good H 185:98+ D '77
Halo effect—it only affects the other guy; research by Richard Nisbett and Timothy DeCamp Wilson. J. Horn. Psychol Today 11:116 S '77
How to recognize a good relationship...and a bad one; quiz. A. Frisch and D. Partie. Mademoiselle 83:165-6 S '77
How will you know unless I tell you? expressing appreciation. J. Lindstrom. Read Digest 110:43-4 Ap '77
Interpersonal relations and education. C. M. Galloway. Educ Digest 42:42-4 My '77
Power strategies: how to play the game—and win. A. Frisch and D. Partie. Mademoiselle 83:166-7 My '77
See also
Communication—Social aspects
Conversation
Courtesy
Friendship
Group relations training
Helping behavior
Intimacy
Jealousy
Loneliness
Love
Marriage
Parent-child relationship
Popularity
Praise
Prejudice
Race relations
Rejection (psychology)
Sensitiveness
Sympathy
Youth-adult relationship

Study and teaching

Human relations training; camp counselors. R. Selverstone and W. Hacker. Camp Mag 49:9+ Ap '77
See also
Esalen Institute, Big Sur, California
HUMAN Relations Work-Study Center. See New School for Social Research, New York
HUMAN rights. See Civil rights
HUMAN Rights, American Convention on. See American Convention on Human Rights
HUMAN Rights, Committee on. See United Nations—Committee on Human Rights
HUMAN Rights, Universal Declaration of. See Universal Declaration of Human Rights
HUMAN Rights Commission of the United Nations. See United Nations—Commission on Human Rights
HUMAN Rights Day and Week
Bill of Rights Day, Human Rights Day and Week, 1976; proclamation, G. R. Ford. Dept State Bull 76:29 Ja 10 '77
Human Rights Day observed. UN Chron 14:63-4 Ja '77
HUMAN sacrifice. See Sacrifice, Human
HUMANA Inc. See Hospitals—Administration
HUMANISM
See also
Philosophical anthropology
Renaissance

HUMANISTIC education. See Education, Humanistic

HUMANITIES
See also
American Association for the Advancement of the Humanities
Education, Humanistic
National Humanities Center (proposed)
Science and the humanities

Study and teaching

Career guides for the arts and humanities; guidebooks produced by the Technical Education Research Center. E. B. Roth. il Am Educ 13:14-15 Je '77

HUMANITIES and science. See Science and the humanities

HUMANITY
Artist's plea for harmony; address. R. Bearden. il Sch Arts 77:72-3 S '77

HUMBARD, Rex
If Christ were alive today. por Ladies Home J 94:60+ D '77

about

Rex Humbard's 25-25 vision. P. Geiger and N. Kennedy. il pors Chr Today 21:53-6 My 6 '77 *

HUMBOLDT County, Calif.
Letters and comment; spaced out West. S. Poss. Yale R 66:472-80 Mr '77

HUME, David L.
Freedom to trade; address, December 6, 1976. Vital Speeches 43:244-6 F 1 '77

HUME, John
Stopping violence in Northern Ireland; excerpts from address. por Intellect 105:374-5 My '77

HUME, Ruth
Selling the Swedish Nightingale. il pors Am Heritage 28:98-107 O '77

HUMES, Charles W. 2d
Some operational problems in an on-going gifted program. Clearing H 51:163-5 D '77

HUMESTON, Barbara
Learn-to-do-something-new vacations. il Bet Hom & Gard 55:199-200+ Ap '77
Pets. Bet Hom & Gard 55:199 F; 148+ Mr; 264+ My; 240+ S; 272+ O; 266+ N '77

HUMIDIFIERS
Humidifiers. il Consumers Rep 42:294-7 D '77

HUMIDITY
See also
Hot weather

HUMOR
Children, humor, and folklore. A. Schwartz. il Horn Bk 53:280-7, 471-6 Je, Ag '77
Kutting kapers with komical ks. T. H. Middleton. Sat R 4:57 F 5 '77
No laughing matter; humor in executives' speeches; views of R. Orben. P. Steinfels. Commonweal 104:434 Jl 8 '77
Time for laughter; anecdotes of W. C. Fields, Will Rogers, and Jack Benny. il Sat Eve Post 249:22 Jl '77
Why can't people take humor seriously? J Hassett and G. E. Schwartz. il N Y Times Mag p 103 F 6 '77
See also
Laughter
Puns and punning
Radio programs—Humorous programs
Television programs—Humorous programs

Authorship

Martin Levin: the good humor man; interview. ed by L. Taylor. M. Levin. por Writers Digest 57:29 O '77
Now that's a laugh; with list of markets. R. S. Aldrich. Writers Digest 57:27-34 O '77
Sharpening the one-liners; ideas of Robert Orben. D. Link. Writers Digest 57:30 O '77

Psychological aspects

Understanding Lily Tomlin; or, we're all in this alone. E. Stone. il Psychol Today 11: 14+ Jl '77

HUMOR, English
Humorists: in jest or in jail? P. Campbell. il Sat R 4:16+ Je 11 '77

HUMOR, Pictorial
See also
Caricatures and cartoons

HUMPBACK whales. See Whales

HUMPERDINCK, Engelbert
Joining of words and music in late romantic melodrama. E. F. Kravitt. bibl f il Mus Q 62:571-90 O '76 *

HUMPHREY, Hubert Horatio, 1911-1978
Excerpt from remarks on U.S. African policy, April 27, 1976. Cong Digest 56:12+ Ja '77
Look at the fun we've had; interview, ed by N. Thimmesch. il pors McCalls 104:138-9+ My '77
You can't quit. por Read Digest 111:57-61 Ag '77

about

Humphrey's cancer. por Newsweek 90:27 Ag 29 '77 *
Humphrey's newest life. T. Mathews and others. il pors Newsweek 90:38+ Jl 25 '77 *
Immortality of H.H.H. A. Latham. il Esquire 88:84-6+ O '77 *
Indomitable Senator returns. B. Angelo. il pors Time 110:23+ N 7 '77 *
Tribute to Hubert Horatio Humphrey from the opposition. W. F. Buckley, Jr. il Nat R 29: 1489-92+ D 23 '77 *
Welcome home, Hubert! J. J. Lindsay. il por Newsweek 90:33 N 7 '77 *

HUMPHREY, J. H.
Challenge of parasitic diseases. il Bull Atom Sci 33:46-53 Mr '77

HUMPHREY, John H. and Pedley, J. G.
Roman Carthage; with biographical sketches. il maps Sci Am 238:12, 110-17+ Ja '78

HUMPHREY, Muriel
Look at the fun we've had; interview, ed by N. Thimmesch. il pors McCalls 104:138-9+ My '77

HUMPHREY, William
Tumult on a wild shore. il Sports Illus 47:42-4+ N 7 '77
Ugly, pestiferous and prepotent. il Sports Illus 46:58-62+ F 7 '77

HUMPHREY-Hawkins Full Employment and Balanced Growth Act of 1976. See Labor laws and legislation—United States

HUMPHREYS, Rob
European news (title varies) See occasional issues of Yachting

HUNDERTWASSER, Friedensreich
Hundertwasser art book features cover done specially by the artist. P. Doebler. il Pub W 212:96 Ag 1 '77 *

HUNDHAUSEN, A. J. See Gosling, J. T. jt auth

HUNG, Akey C. F. and Vinson, S. B.
Interspecific hybridization and caste specificity of protein in fire ant. bibl il Science 196:1458-60 Je 24 '77

HUNGARIAN poetry

Translations into English

Chairs above the Danube; tr by W. J. Smith. S. Várady. New Yorker 53:34 F 28 '77
Contemporary Hungarian poets; tr by D. Hoffman. New Repub 176:29-30 Mr 26 '77
Mr T. S. Eliot cooking pasta; tr by R. Wilbur. J. Tornai. New Yorker 53:35 F 28 '77

HUNGARIAN refugees. See Refugees, Hungarian

HUNGARY
See also
Ballet—Hungary
Budapest
Opera—Hungary

Description and travel

How free is the freest? M. L. Kahn. America 136:53-4 Ja 22 '77

Foreign relations

United States

See United States—Foreign relations—Hungary

Industries

See also
Book industries—Hungary

Religious institutions and affairs

Hungary: an open door and a time for healing. E. E. Plowman. Chr Today 21:48-52 Ap 15 '77
See also
Catholic Church in Hungary
Evangelistic work—Hungary

HUNGER
End hunger by 2000—a possible dream. E. M. Leeper. BioScience 27:571-3 Ag '77
Hunger in humans induced by 2-deoxy-D-glucose: glucoprivic control of taste preference and food intake. D. A. Thompson and R. G. Campbell. bibl il Science 198:1065-8 D 9 '77
Stewardship and property; symposium; with editorial comment. bibl il New Cath World 220: 210-32+ S '77
See also
Famines

HUNGER in the Bible
Biblical perspective on the problem of hunger. W. Brueggemann. il Chr Cent 94:1136-41 D 7 '77

HUNT, Amber Edwina
Idyll of Gary and Amber Jim. il por Time 109: 49 Ja 31 '77 *

HUNT, Bernice. See Hunt, M. jt auth

HUNT, Chester L.
Carter's moral foreign policy and Philippine martial law. bibl por Intellect 106:130-3 O '77

HUNT, Earl W.
Encounters in a winter wilderness; excerpt from The living wilderness. il Read Digest 112:124-8 Ja '78

HUNT, Everette Howard, 1918-
How America looks to me now. por Newsweek 89:15 Ap 4 '77
about
Hunt's tales of Watergate. D. A. Williams and R. Manning. por Newsweek 89:22 Mr 7 '77 *
Who doubts he did it? por Newsweek 89:39 My 16 '77 *

HUNT, Gaillard T. See Bierman, S. jt auth

HUNT, Geoffrey
It was hard, but easy. J. Kaplan. il por Sports Illus 46:44-5 F 7 '77 *

HUNT, George L. Jr, and Hunt, M. W.
Female-female pairing in western gulls (larus occidentalis) in southern California. bibl il Science 196:1466-7 Je 24 '77

HUNT, Gerard J.
Process to close the gap. MH 61:9-11 Spr '77

HUNT, Hamlen
Bring back the fireless cooker. il Conservationist 31:32-3 Ja '77

HUNT, Jack R.
Learning to fly. Flying 101:301 S '77

HUNT, James
Hunt scores a homespun win at Silverstone. J. Norris. il por Motor T 29:126 N '77 *

HUNT, James F.
Commercial vessel safety: Cost Guard inspection of United States Merchant Marine. il Oceans 10:28-31 Mr '77

HUNT, Molly Warner. See Hunt, G. L. Jr, jt auth

HUNT, Morton, and Hunt, Bernice
After divorce: who gets married again—and when? excerpt from The divorce experience: a new look at the world of the formerly married. il Redbook 149:106+ O '77
For women who wonder about divorce: a major report; excerpt from The divorce experience. Redbook 149:92+ S '77

HUNT, Nelson Bunker
Breaking the Hunts' grip on soybeans. pors Bus W p40-1 My 16 '77 *
Hunts and the soybeans. M. Ruby and others. il pors Newsweek 89:77-8 My 9 '77 *

HUNT, Percival
On writing well. R. S. Wolper. Nation 224:345-6 Mr 19 '77 *

HUNT, Ray L.
Nice Hunt. por Time 110:45-6 Ag 22 '77 *

HUNT, W. Herbert
Breaking the Hunts' grip on soybeans. pors Bus W p40-1 My 16 '77 *
Hunts and the soybeans. M. Ruby and others. il pors Newsweek 89:77-8 My 9 '77 *

HUNT-JONES, Conover
Remember the ladies: women in America, 1750-1815. il Antiques 111:762-7 Ap '77

HUNTER, Alberta
Our local correspondents. W. Balliett. por New Yorker 53:100-1+ O 31 '77 *
Rebirth of the blues. H. Saal. il pors Newsweek 90:101 O 31 '77 *

HUNTER, Allan Oakley
Feuding over who runs Fannie Mae. il por Bus W p74+ S 12 '77 *

HUNTER, Beatrice Trum
Dietary fiber: a panacea? Consumers Res Mag 60:32-3 Jl '77
Food and nutrition. Consumers Res Mag 60:104-12 O '77
Papain meat tenderizers: objectionable for all and hazardous for some. Consumers Res Mag 60:36 S '77

HUNTER, Celia
From my corner (cont of) President's page. See issues of Living wilderness

HUNTER, David L.
Guarding a new puppy's health. il Parents Mag 52:40 S '77
Pet set. il Parents Mag 52:77 N; 50 D '77; 53:64+ Ja '78

HUNTER, George Charles
Should Methodists buy the church growth package? J. C. Lyles. Chr Cent 94:1214-15 D 28 '77 *

HUNTER, Jim (skier)
Jungle Jim and the rocky run. S. Moses. il por Sports Illus 48:43-4 Ja 2 '78 *

HUNTER, Kristin
Soul brothers and sister Lou. N. Stimpfle. Engl J 66:61 Mr '77 *

HUNTER, Lynn S.
Piscataway's puppet program. il pors SLJ 23:32-4 My '77

HUNTER, Madeline
Right-brained kids in left-brained schools. Educ Digest 42:8-10 F '77
Tri-dimensional approach to individualization. Educ Digest 43:17-20 S '77

HUNTER, Mel
Revolution in hand-drawn lithography. il Am Artist 41:52-9+ O '77

HUNTER, Sylvia
(tr) See Levi, P. Iron: a memoir

HUNTERS
Are you in shape for hunting season? exercise for hunters. S. Netherby. il Field & S 82:148-9+ Ag '77
See also
Women hunters

HUNTERS and gatherers
Life before horticulture; the !Kung San. M. Shostak. il Horticulture 55:38-57 F '77

HUNTING
Amphibious hunter; float hunting. F. M. Paulson. il Field & S 82:182-3+ O '77
Bear of a man; adventures of C. Atwood. B. Brady. il por Outdoor Life 159:88-9+ My '77
Nature is my calendar; determining hunting and fishing seasons by natural signs. B. W. Dalrymple. il Outdoor Life 159:90-2+ Ap '77
Solunar tables for [month] See issues of Field & stream
Update: deer/big game; ed by T. Paugh. il Outdoor Life 160:32 O; 54 N; 50 D '77; 161:50 Ja '78
Update: upland game; ed by T. Paugh. il Outdoor Life 160:98 O; 108 N; 54 D '77; 161:100 Ja '78
Walk 'em up; small game. R. Beck. il Outdoor Life 160:86-9 Ag '77
Where to go. M. Worby. See issues of Outdoor life
See also
Duck shooting
Eskimos—Hunting
Fowling
Game, Dressing of
Game laws
Hunting with bow and arrow
Poaching
Sealing
Trapping
Whaling
also Elk hunting; Squirrel hunting and similar headings

Accidents and injuries

Mistake. J. Poling. il Outdoor Life 159:74-5+ F '77; Same abr. Read Digest 110:117-20 Je '77

Caricatures and cartoons

Daumier goes a-sporting. il Am Artist 41:50-1 Jl '77

Equipment and supplies

Complete tree-stand hunter—gun and bow. G. Helgeland. il Outdoor Life 160:74-7+ Ag '77
Frontloader in the treetops. R. H. Hathorn. il por Outdoor Life 160:91+ S '77
Go the drop camp way. C. J. Farmer. il Outdoor Life 159:68-71+ F '77
Hunting camp & you; equipment checklist. S. Netherby. il Field & S 81:160-2 Mr '77
Ladies only; gift ideas for sportsmen. B. Tarrant. il Field & S 82:118-19+ D '77
See also
Blinds (camouflage)
Decoys (hunting)

Ethical aspects

Anti-hunting sentiment: can we fight it? D. L. Shaw. il Field & S 82:56+ N '77
Behold the hunter. N. Bryant. il Atlantic 240:66-70 D '77
Let's wipe out slobbery. E. B. Mann. Field & S 82:16+ S '77
Weep no more for the widowed goose; Canada goose. R. Starnes. Outdoor Life 160:8+ O '77
What about this anti-hunting thing? J. Madson; discussion. il Conservationist 31:38-9 Ja; 40-1 Mr '77
Whose world is it? hunters and endangered species. E. B. Mann. Field & S 81:16 Ap '77

History

First hunters; cave paintings. D. Mazonowicz. il Field & S 82:130+ My '77

Study and teaching

Basics for bowhunters. R. Methot. por Outdoor Life 161:22 Ja '78
New bowhunting school. V. T. Sparano. il Outdoor Life 159:48+ F '77
Training New York's bowhunters. P. Kelsey. il Conservationist 32:32-3 S '77

Africa

Possible dream: going on safari! P. Barrett. il Mech Illus 73:22+ My '77

Alabama

Lonely stillhunter. W. Atchison. il Outdoor Life 160:118+ S '77

Alaska

Hunt Alaska now; state laws and wildlife populations. J. Rearden. il Field & S 82:60-1+ Ag '77
Land of geese and plenty. R. F. Jones. il Sports Illus 47:84-8+ D 12 '77
Stalk for a cannibal brown. L. Francisco. il Outdoor Life 160:68-9+ Jl '77

HUNTING—*Continued*

Arizona

Elk that was king; new Pope & Young world record; ed by D. Schuh. D. Kittredge. il por Outdoor Life 160:98-100+ S '77

Swing. . .swing. . .swing and you'll hit those doves. J. Carmichel. il Outdoor Life 160:62-3+ Jl '77

Austria

Fateful chop, chop, chop, pop, hissss; auerhahn shooting. V. Kraft. il Sports Illus 46:49+ F 21 '77

British Columbia

See Hunting—Canada

Canada

Drives with one hound; using deer hounds to hunt in southern Ontario. S. Cooke. il por Outdoor Life 160:90 S '77

High-country moose; Besa River, British Columbia. S. Netherby. il Field & S 81:150+ F '77

On the wings of the wind; James Bay goose shooting. V. Knap. il Outdoor Life 159:72-5+ Mr '77

Colorado

About elk hunting. J. Cooney. il Field & S 82:50-1+ S '77

Three-for-three elk hunt; in Uncompahgre National Forest. R. Tinsley. il map Outdoor Life 159:70-1+ Je '77

England

Glorious grouse; shooting in England's County of Yorkshire. A. Oglesby. il Field & S 82:28-30+ Jl '77

Florida

At Payson's place he's just plain Charlie; Florida hunting ranch. V. Kraft. il por Sports Illus 46:54+ Ap 18 '77

Poaching gators for fun and profit. H. Crews. il Esquire 87:54+ Ap '77

France

Ugly, pestiferous and prepotent; boar hunting. W. Humphrey. il Sports Illus 46:58-62+ F 7 '77

Germany, West

German hunting: it's the tradition that counts. G. H. Haas. il Int Wildlife 7:38-43 N '77

Kansas

Snow fever; goose shooting. B. Tarrant. il Field & S 82:39+ O '77

Kentucky

Move with 'em or lose 'em; duck hunting. W. L. Bourne. il Outdoor Life 160:92-3+ S '77

Kenya

End of the game. P. Webb. il Newsweek 89:78 My 30 '77

Great Kenya wildlife ripoff. J. Samson. il Field & S 82:48-9 D '77

Mexico

South of the border on a shoestring. N. Strung. il Field & S 81:158-9+ F '77

Winged treasure below the border; waterfowl of northcentral Mexico. J. Samson. il Field & S 82:46-7+ N '77

Mississippi

Clever footwork fools a clever bird. J. Carmichel. il Outdoor Life 159:86-7+ My '77

Montana

Girl learns to hunt; deer hunting by C. McRae. B. McRae. il por Field & S 82:40-1+ O '77

Retrievers good and bad; duck hunting. N. MacLean. Esquire 88:22+ O '77

Mozambique

Terrible-tempered ox; Cape buffalo. P. Barrett. il Field & S 82:48-50+ N '77

New Mexico

Day of the elk. J. Samson. il Field & S 82:48-9+ O '77

We go on an elk hunt; Vermejo Park ranch. P. Barrett. il Mech Illus 73:24+ S '77

New York (state)

Results of 1976 deer and bear seasons. il Conservationist 32:22 Jl '77

Spring is turkey time. D. Knight. il Field & S 81:84-6+ Mr '77

Training New York's bowhunters. P. Kelsey. il Conservationist 32:32-3 S '77

Ontario

See Hunting—Canada

Oregon

He did not go gentle; Oregon game bird shooting. M. Baughman. il Sports Illus 47:66+ O 3 '77

Pennsylvania

He's a woods bird now; ringnecks. R. L. Henry. il Outdoor Life 160:82-3+ O '77

1,000-yard chucks. D. Frost. il Outdoor Life 160:82-3+ Jl '77

Russia

Hunting the Soviet Union. B. Tarrant. il por Field & S 81:42-4+ Ap '77

Texas

Long-distance whitetails; experience in central Texas. D. Flores. il Field & S 82:28+ Ag '77

Settling down in Texas; bird hunting at McFaddin Ranch. V. Kraft. il Sports Illus 47:74+ N 21 '77

United States

History

Hunting with Teddy Roosevelt; ed by B. Vint. T. Roosevelt. il Field & S 82:166+ My '77

Virginia

How they cracked duck hunting's isle of shame; Pruitt's-Paradise Inc on Tangier Island. J. Phillips. il Outdoor Life 161:64-5+ Ja '78

I will survive; duck boat adrift in Chesapeake Bay; ed by B. East. F. W. Stamm. il Outdoor Life 160:80-1+ D '77

Western States

Bugle your elk; Rocky Mountains. C. J. Farmer. il Field & S 82:40-1+ N '77

Elk hunting today—a comparison of 11 states. V. L. Oertle. Outdoor Life 160:85+ Ag '77

Hunt your own sheep. C. J. Farmer. il Field & S 82:60-1+ S '77

Successful mule deer hunting. B. Dalrymple. il Field & S 82:44-5+ S '77

Wyoming

Double on antelope. E. A Bauer. il Outdoor Life 159:60-3+ F '77

No bull moose hunt. E. A. Bauer. il Outdoor Life 160:64-6 N '77

Quality hunting you can afford. B. Taylor. il Outdoor Life 159:68-9+ My '77

HUNTING clothes. See Clothing and dress—Sports clothes

HUNTING dogs

Gun dogs. B. Tarrant. See issues of Field & stream

Hunting dogs. D. M. Duffey. See issues of Outdoor life

Which is the best all-round dog? D. M. Duffey. il Outdoor Life 159:78-81+ My '77

See also

Hounds

Retrievers

Anecdotes, facetiae, satire, etc.

Dog day afternoon. R. Starnes. por Outdoor Life 159:10+ F '77

Care

How to winterize your dog. D. M. Duffey. il Outdoor Life 160:140+ D '77

Diseases and pests

See Dogs—Diseases and pests

Training

Avoiding dog gyps. D. M. Duffey. il Outdoor Life 159:202+ Mr '77

Chain gang; teaching dogs with check cords. B. Tarrant. il Field & S 82:156-8 Je; 94-8 Jl; 136-9 Ag '77

Happiness is . . . beagles and rabbits. D. M. Duffey. il Outdoor Life 160:196+ N '77

Shock collars: training shortcuts or dog wreckers? D. M. Duffey. il Outdoor Life 159:152+ Je '77

Six ways to make a better gun dog. D. M. Duffey. il Outdoor Life 160:40+ Jl '77

Training scents: do they really work? D. M. Duffey. il Outdoor Life 159:182+ My '77

Transportation

Traveling with gun dogs. D. M. Duffey. il Outdoor Life 160:175-6+ S '77

HUNTING dogs in art. See Animals in art

HUNTING films. See Motion pictures—Sports films

HUNTING guides. See Guides

HUNTING in art

First hunters; cave paintings. D. Mazonowicz. il Field & S 82:130+ My '77

Outdoor prints: a sporting chance for pleasure and profit. P. Miller. il Outdoor Life 159:72-7+ Je '77

HUNTING laws. See Game laws

HUNTING licenses. See Licenses

HUNTING outfits. See Hunting—Equipment and supplies

HUNTING ranches. See Ranches

HUNTING records
Elk that was king; new Pope & Young world record; ed by D. Schuh. D. Kittredge. il por Outdoor Life 160:98-100+ S '77

HUNTING stands. See Hunting—Equipment and supplies

HUNTING with bow and arrow
Blunt hunt for cottontails. R. Tinsly. il Outdoor Life 159:82-3+ F '77
Bowhunter's camp northwest Canada. F. Bear. il por Field & S 82:64-6+ My '77
Bowhunting; questions and answers. See issues of Outdoor life
Elk that was king; new Pope & Young world record; ed by D. Schuh. D. Kittredge. il por Outdoor Life 160:98-100+ S '77
Hunting the quiet way. F. Bear. il Conservationist 31:17-19+ N '76
Hunting, the safe way. N. Geoffrey. Esquire 88:24+ N '77
Endless fall. N. Strung. il Field & S 82:76-8+ S '77

Study and teaching
See Hunting—Study and teaching

HUNTINGTON, Roger
1978 Detroit model review. il Consumers Res Mag 60:12-16 N '77
So you want a motorcycle. il Consumers Res Mag 60:12-15 Mr '77

HUNTINGTON, Trumbull
Russians came to browse in Hartford bookstore. Pub W 211:62-3 Mr 28 '77

HUNTINGTON, Vt.
New England: rites of March; town meeting. J. Bell. il Time 109:18-19 Mr 14 '77

HUNTINGTON Beach, Calif.
Huntington Beach: disaster waits impatiently in wings; excerpt from Acts of God, acts of man. W. Marx. Audubon 79:126-8 Mr '77

HUNTINGTON'S chorea
Huntington's disease: delayed hypersensitivity in vitro to human central nervous system antigens. D. S. Barkley and others. bibl il Science 195:314-16 Ja 21 '77
In Woody Guthrie's memory; work of the committee to combat Huntington's disease. S. Weiss. McCalls 104:67 My '77
Little-known diseases. A. Belson. Fam Health 9:42-4+ My '77
New way to predict genetic disease; research by Steven Rosenberg and others. J. Horn. Psychol Today 11:28-9+ D '77

HUNTLEY, Charlotte
Special report: book return lag? Try promos. Wilson Lib Bull 52:294-5 D '77

HUNTLEY, Chet
Clouded Sky. E. Keerdoja. il Newsweek 90:13 S 12 '77 •

HUNTS POINT. See Bronx, N.Y.

HUPP, Robert P.
United States urges peaceful change in South Africa; statement, November 9, 1976. Dept State Bull 76:49-51 Ja 17 '77

HURFORD, Daphne
Driven by mo-ped madness. il Sports Illus 47:24-7 Ag 8 '77
I'll do anything I can get away with. il pors Sports Illus 47:30-2+ Jl 25 '77

HURLEY, Michael C.
Annapolis. il Travel 147:40-5 Je '77

HURLEY, Neil P.
Drop-ins: mass media and the poor. America 137:377-8 N 26 '77

HURLUGSON, Dan
Move more snow with motorgraders. il Am City & County 92:73 Ap '77

HURRICANES
Atlantic hurricane season of 1976. M. B. Lawrence. il map Weatherwise 30:10-17 F '77
Foul weather forecast? S. Mennear-Dubas. il Fam Health 9:30 S '77
Ocean wave patterns under Hurricane Gloria: observation with an airborne synthetic-aperture radar. C. Elachi and others. bibl il Science 198:609-10 N 11 '77
Swept away; danger to coastal communities from hurricanes. B. Funk. il N Y Times Mag p38-40+ S 18 '77
See also
Boats and boating—Storm hazards

HURRY
Hurry, hurry, hurry. N. H. Eberle. McCalls 105:91+ Ja '78

HURST, Jack
You've come a long way, Dolly. il pors Hi Fi 27:122-4 D '77

HURT, R. Douglas
Dust! il Am Heritage 28:34-5 Ag '77
Dust bowl. bibl il Am West 14:22-7+ Jl '77

HURVITZ, Alan
Turmoil in Texas. il Car & Dr 23:75-8 Ja '78

HURWITZ, Al
Art educators' odyssey, USSR. il Sch Arts 76:56-8+ Ap '77

HURWITZ, Sidney
Breakthrough! Doctors find improved acne treatments; interview, ed by N. Simon. Vogue 167:389+ S '77

HUSAYN, Saddam
Why Iraq won't deal with Israel; interview, ed by D. Mullin. il por U.S. News 82:96 My 16 '77

HUSBAND and wife. See Marriage

HUSBAND and wife quarrels. See Quarrels

HUSBANDS
Househusbands. L. C. Pogrebin. Ladies Home J 94:30+ N '77
How to live with a difficult man. S. W. Olds. il Ladies Home J 94:58+ Ap '77
My husband was unfaithful. il Good H 184:28+ F '77
My job vs. my husband's pride. C. Bocardo. McCalls 105:57+ N '77
Sometimes I hate my husband. J. Viorst. Read Digest 110:19+ Mr '77
See also
Adultery
Divorce
Marriage
Marriage counseling
Widowers

Anecdotes, facetiae, satire, etc.
Stow it till the commercial! E. Bombeck. il Read Digest 111:120-2 Jl '77

HUSK tomatoes
Instant fruit—it's hard to ask more. B. Fisher. il Org Gard & Farm 24:74-5 Je '77

HUSOCK, Howard
Boston after Louise Day Hicks. il por Nation 225:710-12 D 31 '77

HUSS, Tim
Cranberry bogs of Long Island. il por Conservationist 32:5-8 N '77

HUSSEIN, King of Jordan
Hussein: close ranks; excerpts from interview, ed by A. de Borchgrave. por Newsweek 90:59-60+ D 12 '77
Hussein on his CIA money; excerpts from interview, ed by A. de Borchgrave. il por Newsweek 89:16-18 Mr 7 '77
King Hussein of Jordan visits Washington; exchange of toasts, and remarks, April 25-26, 1977. Dept State Bull 76:521-2 My 23 '77
Time to take a gamble; interview, ed by W. Wynn. il por Time 109:34 F 14 '77
Two Arab leaders reply to Begin; excerpts from interview, ed by A. de Borchgrave. pors Newsweek 90:30-2 Ag 1 '77

about

Carter and the CIA. A. S. Miller. Progressive 41:9-10 My '77 •
Carter's oversight. J. Osborne. New Repub 176:8-10 Mr 19 '77 •
Cutting off the King's dole. il por Time 109:13 F 28 '77 •
Dayan's secret. A. De Borchgrave. il por Newsweek 90:43 O 3 '77 •
Easier lies the Hashemite head. il Time 109:33-4 F 14 '77 •
Genius for survival. pors Time 109:28 F 28 '77 •
Hussein flap: cui bono? Nat R 29:313 Mr 18 '77 •
King's pay packet. D. M. Alpern and others. il por Newsweek 89:18-19 F 28 '77 •
Letter from Washington. R. H. Rovere. New Yorker 53:111-14 Mr 7 '77 •
Other jubilee. D. Pryce-Jones. New Repub 176:14-17 Je 25 '77 •
What secrets are sacred? D. Gelman and others. il por Newsweek 89:40+ Mr 14 '77 •

Visit to the United States, 1977
King Hussein of Jordan visits Washington; exchange of toasts, and remarks, April 25-26, 1977. J. Carter; Hussein. Dept State Bull 76:520-3 My 23 '77

HUSSEY, John A.
Fort Vancouver. bibl il por Am West 14:12-19+ S '77

HUSTAD, Donald P.
Music speaks . . . but what language? Chr Today 21:16-18 My 6 '77

HUSTLER (periodical)
Bad case makes worse law; trial of publisher. L. Flynt. il por Time 109:51-2 F 21 '77
Dirty book goes to jail; Hustler publisher L. Flynt. P. Bonventre and others. il por Newsweek 89:34 F 21 '77
First amendment hustle; trial of Hustler magazine publishers. Nation 224:99-100 Ja 29 '77
Has the first amendment met its match? R. Neville. il N Y Times Mag p 18 Mr 6 '77
Hustler and freedom. Nat R 29:252 Mr 4 '77
Intelligent woman's guide to sex; L. Flynt's obscenity trial. K. Durbin. Mademoiselle 83:94 My '77
Justice for Hustler. A. Kretchmer. Newsweek 89:13 F 28 '77

HUSTON, John
Careers of two major Hollywood directors unreel in a pair of spring titles. R. Dahlin. il por Pub W 212:40 N 21 '77 •

HUTCHESON, Richard G. Jr
Pluralism and consensus: why mainline church mission budgets are in trouble. Chr Cent 94: 618-24 Jl 6 '77
HUTCHESON Stakes. See Horse racing
HUTCHINS, Robert Maynard
Intellectual community. Educ Digest 42:38-41 My '77
about
Mr Hutchins' convictions. J. W. Donohue. America 136:504-5 Je 4 '77 *
Obituary
Nat R 29:656-7 Je 10 '77
Progressive 41:7-8 Jl '77. M. Mayer
Sat R 4:4 Je 11 '77. N. Cousins
HUTCHINSON, Joe
From a tour boat on Crater Lake; poem. Nation 224:477 Ap 16 '77
HUTCHINSON, Nan S.
Goal, a program and a community. il por Aging 272:13-17 Je '77 *
HUTCHINSON, W. H.
(comp) Best books on the cowboy. il Am West 14:49 N '77
New Mexico incident. bibl il pors Am West 14: 4-7+ N '77
HUTCHINSON, Warner Alton, 1929-
Story behind the book: Good News Bible; interview, ed by R. Dahlin. Pub W 211:78 Mr 14 '77
HUTCHISON, Bruce
Canada's time of troubles. For Affairs 56:175-89 O '77
HUTCHISON, Charlotte
Your cornea and kidney can outlive you. Ms 5:95-8 Ap '77
HUTTNER, J. J. and others
Fatty acids and their prostaglandin derivatives: inhibitors of proliferation in aortic smooth muscle cells. bibl il Science 197:289-91 Jl 15 '77
HUTTNER, Marian A.
Branches to rebuild cities. por Lib J 102:168-9 Ja 15 '77
HUXTABLE, Ada Louise
Enduring splendor of Mies van der Rohe. il por N Y Times Mag p70-1+ F 27 '77
Most influential architect in history. il N Y Times Mag p22-5 Jl 17 '77
Unbuilt buildings. il N Y Times Mag p44-5+ Ja 30 '77
You can have your city's past and use it too. Vogue 167:222 Mr '77
HUXTABLE, Ryan, and Chubb, James
Adrenergic stimulation of taurine transport by the heart. bibl il Science 198:409-11 O 28 '77
HUYSMANS, Joris Karl
J. K. Huysmans: a study in decadence. E. Hartnett. Am Scholar 46:367-76 Summ '77 *
J.-K. Huysmans and France's Catholic revival. J. Gustaitis. map America 136:394-6 Ap 30 '77 *
HYACINTHS, Water. See Water hyacinths
HYATT, I. Ralph
Assessing one's sanity. bibl Intellect 106:147-8 O '77
Mental labels and tattoos. il Intellect 106:74-5 Ag '77
HYATT Regency Cambridge, Cambridge, Mass. See Hotels, motels, etc.—United States
HYBRID cells. See Cells
HYBRIDIZATION
Cull of the wild. Sci Am 237:81 O '77
In praise of Darwin, Rembrandt, Mendel and other famous tulips; with photographs by D. Kessel. F. Endt. Horticulture 55:26-39 Ag '77
Interspecific hybridization and caste specificity of protein in fire ant. A. C. F. Hung and S. B. Vinson. bibl il Science 196:1458-60 Je 24 '77
See also
Plant breeding
HYDANTOINS
See also
Diphenylhydantoin
HYDE, Charlotte. See Welsh, A. L. jt auth
HYDE, Tom
That fabulous mix of metal and miracle—the car. il Sat Eve Post 249:48-51 N '77
HYDE, Vic
Two's a motorcycle, three's a . . . very strange car. M. Lamm. il pors Pop Mech 148:102-4+ N '77 *
HYDRA (zoology)
Polarity reversal in nerve-free hydra. B. A. Marcum and others. bibl il Science 197:771-3 Ag 19 '77
HYDRATION rind dating
Glass hydration: a method of dating glass objects. W. A. Lanford. bibl il Science 196:975-6 My 27 '77
HYDRAULIC engineering
See also
Canals
Channels (hydraulic engineering)
HYDRAULIC turbines. See Turbines
HYDRIDES
See also
Boron hydrides

HYDROCARBONS
Sedimentary polycyclic aromatic hydrocarbons: the historical record. R. A. Hites and others. bibl il Science 198:829-31 N 25 '77
See also
Germacrene
HYDROCORTISONE
Synchronized ultradian cortisol rhythms in monkeys: persistence during corticotropin infusion. J. W. Holaday and others. bibl il Science 198:56-8 O 7 '77
HYDRODYNAMICS
See also
Drops
Magnetohydrodynamics
HYDROELECTRIC plants
Environmentalism and the leisure class; public fight against building of Storm King plant by Con Ed. W. Tucker. il map Harpers 225: 49-56+ D '77
Lost megawatts flow over nation's myriad spillways. D. E. Lilienthal. il Smithsonian 8:82-9 S '77; Same abr. with title Let's put our rivers back to work! Read Digest 112:25-8+ Ja '78
Canada
Arabs with a French accent; James Bay project of Hydro-Quebec. P. Sturm. il map Forbes 120: 63-5 D 15 '77
Latin America
50-cycle politics; dispute over Itapú project. J. R. Brockman. map America 137:484 D 31 '77
HYDROELECTRIC power
Water power for your home. E. F. Lindsley. bibl il Pop Sci 210:87-93 My '77
See also
Tide power
United States—Bonneville Power Administration
HYDROFOILS
Jetfoil with wings beneath the waves. L. Wood. il Oceans 10:35-7 Mr '77
Skimming the waves between Belgium and Britain; jetfoil Flying Princess. C. S. Foltz, Jr. il U.S. News 83:41 N 7 '77
HYDROGEN
Analyzing hydrogen with nuclear reactions. S. T. Picraux. bibl il Phys Today 30:42-3+ O '77
Hydrogen. P. Luedtke. por Sci Digest 82:68-72 O '77
Quarks with unit charge: a search for anomalous hydrogen. R. A. Muller and others. bibl il Science 196:521-3 Ap 20 '77
Isotopes
Oxygen and hydrogen isotopic ratios in plant cellulose. S. Epstein and others. bibl il Science 198:1209-15 D 23 '77
See also
Deuterium
HYDROGEN as fuel
See also
Automobile engines—Fuel
HYDROGEN bombs. See Atomic bombs
HYDROGEN ion concentration
pHish pfinder? using acidity or alkalinity of water to determine fish populations. J. Scott. il Field & S 82:58+ Jl '77
See also
Soil acidity
HYDROGEN peroxide
Hydrogen peroxide induces spawning in mollusks, with activation of prostaglandin endoperoxide synthetase. D. E. Morse and others. bibl il Science 196:298-300 Ap 15 '77
HYDROGEN sulfide
Innocent packages; fumes from drain cleaners. R. E. Arnold. Field & S 81:104+ Mr '77
Interaction of Beggiatoa and rice plant: detoxification of hydrogen sulfide in the rice rhizosphere. M. M. Joshi and J. P. Hollis. bibl il Science 195:179-80 Ja 14 '77
HYDROGEOLOGY
Slow leak of earth's surface water. W. S. Fyfe and J. S. Levine. Intellect 105:386-7 My '77
HYDROGRAPHIC surveying
Admiral Beaufort charted coasts for ships of the world. A. Friendly. il por map Smithsonian 8:68-70+ bibl(p 101) Ag '77
HYDROGRAPHY
See also
Hydrographic surveying
HYDROLASES. See Enzymes
HYDROLOGIC cycle
Underground reservoirs to control the water cycle. R. P. Ambroggi. il map Sci Am 236: 21-7 My '77
HYDROLOGY
See also
Hydrogeology
HYDROPLANE racing
Racing scene. M. Crook. il Yachting 142:64+ S '77

HYDROPONICS
Quick-growing hydroponic gardens. A. Dickerman and J. Dickerman. il Bet Hom & Gard 55:100-1+ N '77

HYDRO-QUEBEC (firm) See Electric utilities—Canada

HYDROTHERAPY
See also
Baths, Whirlpool

HYDROXYCHOLECALCIFEROL. See Vitamins—Vitamin D

HYDROXYL
Anthropogenic CO emissions: implications for the atmospheric CO-OH-CH_4 cycle. N. D. Sze. bibl Science 195:673-5 F 18 '77
Hydroxyl radical reactivity with diethylhydroxylamine. R. A. Gorse, Jr and others. bibl il Science 197:1365-7 S 30 '77

HYDROXYLAMINE
Enhancement of photochemical smog by N,N' diethylhydroxylamine in polluted ambient air. J. N. Pitts, Jr and others. bibl il Science 197:255-7 Jl 15 '77
Hydroxyl radical reactivity with diethylhydroxylamine. R. A. Gorse, Jr and others. bibl il Science 197:1365-7 S 30 '77

HYENAS
Critter nobody loves; excerpt from Cult of the wild. B. Rensberger. il Int Wildlife 7:12-16 N '77

HYGIENE
Cleaning up. Seventeen 36:76+ Ag '77
See also
Charm
Health
Medicine, Preventive
Posture
Women—Health and hygiene

HYGIENE, Mental. See Mental hygiene

HYLAND, William G.
Dealing with the Russian leaders. il por Time 110:28 N 21 '77 •

HYLTON, Delmer P.
Obfuscation, Inc. por Forbes 119:78-9 F 15 '77 •

HYMAN, Morton P.
Old Glory sails again. il por Forbes 119:34-5 F 1 '77 •

HYMAN, Sylvia
Elly and Willy Kuch. il por Ceram Mo 25:50-7 My '77
Workshop in Belgium. il Ceram Mo 25:31-4 O '77

HYMENOPTERA
Genetics of generation gap in insects. Sci N 111:278 Ap 30 '77
Local mate competition and parental investment in social insects. R. D. Alexander and P. W. Sherman. bibl Science 196:494-500 Ap 29 '77
See also
Wasps

HYMN Society of America
Hymnologists in an age of prose; convention. J. C. Lyles. Chr Cent 94:614-15 Jl 6 '77

HYMNS
See also
Gospel music
Hymn Society of America

HYMOVITZ, Leon
Multicultural education in America: melting pot atonement or at-one-ment? il Engl J 66:25-8 Mr '77

HYNEK, Josef Allen
Great UFO debate. Current 196:21-4 O '77
about
Galileo of UFOlogy. P. Gwynne and K. Ames. il por Newsweek 90:97 N 21 '77 •

HYPERACTIVE children
Diet not cause of hyperactivity. Sci N 111:406-7 Je 25 '77
Family that fought back; use of Ritalin in Taft. Calif. schools. J. N. Bell. il McCalls 104:26+ My '77
Fluorescent lights and hyperactivity in children: an experiment. M. Painter. Educ Digest 42:36-7 Ap '77
Hyperactive children—problems of coping. H. K. Panjwani. Consumers Res Mag 60:21-2 S '77
Hyperactives as teens: problems linger. Sci N 112:389 D 10 '77
Hyperactivity or chocolate milk? T. G. Banville. Educ Digest 42:48-9 My '77
Methylphenidate in hyperkinetic children: differences in dose effects on learning and social behavior. R. L. Sprague and E. K. Sleator. bibl il Science 198:1274-6 D 23 '77
Research disputes link between hyperactivity and food additives. J. Gaylin. Psychol Today 11:46+ O '77

HYPERACTIVITY. See Hyperkinesis

HYPERBOLA
Mathematical games. M. Gardner. il Sci Am 237:24+ S '77

HYPERKINESIS
Paradoxical effects of amphetamine on preweanling and postweanling rats; possible animal model of minimal brain dysfunction hyperkinesis. B. A. Campbell and P. J. Randall. bibl il Science 195:888-91 Mr 4 '77
Situational hyperactivity: a social system approach. P. Conrad. Educ Digest 43:39-41 O '77
See also
Hyperactive children

HYPEROSMOLALITY. See Solution (chemistry)

HYPERPHAGIA
Gorging-purging syndrome; bulimarexia. M. Boskind-Lodahl and J. Sirlin. il Psychol Today 10:50-2+ Mr '77

HYPERPHENYLALANEMIA. See Metabolism, Disorders of

HYPERSENSITIVITY. See Allergy

HYPERSONIC airplane engines. See Airplane engines, Jet

HYPERSONIC airplanes. See Airplanes, Supersonic

HYPERTENSION
Blood pressure measurement devices. S. N. Finkelstein. il Consumers Res Mag 60:7-10 F '77
Checking children for high blood pressure. M. Norman. McCalls 104:44 Mr '77
Design of specific inhibitors of angiotensin-converting enzyme: new class of orally active antihypertensive agents. M. A. Ondetti and others. bibl il Science 196:441-4 Ap 22 '77
Fix high blood pressure before it fixes you. M. Weber. Vogue 167:147 Mr '77
Genetic predisposition and stress-induced hypertension. R. Friedman and J. Iwai; reply with rejoinder. M. Peters. bibl Science 198:80 O 7 '77
High blood pressure: a heart disease you can control. L. Palmer. il Farm J 101:37-9 Ap '77
Hypertension: increase of collagen biosynthesis in arteries but not in veins. K. Iwatsuki and others. bibl il Science 198:403-5 O 28 '77
Lowering blood pressure. J. Arehart-Treichel. il Sci N 111:347 My 28 '77
Silent killer; National High Blood Pressure Education Program. M. Clark and D. Shapiro. il Newsweek 90:123 N 14 '77
Stress: role in hypertension debated. J. L. Marx. Science 198:905-7 D 2 '77

HYPNOSIS
Tolerance for incongruity. New Yorker 53:29-30 Mr 28 '77

HYPNOTICS
Insomnia remedies: which ones work best? Sleep medications. il Consumer Rep 42:568-70 O '77
See also
Flurazepam

HYPNOTISM
Blister formation—another test of hypnotic suggestion; research by Theodore Barber and R. F. Q. Johnson. Psychol Today 11:28+ S '77
Eyes have it; eye roll and susceptibility to hypnotism. Time 110:53 D 19 '77
Facts about hypnosis; questions and answers. R. C. Mastrovito. il Seventeen 36:159 My '77
How hypnosis aids in passing over the threshold of consciousness. T. Bay. il por Sci Digest 81:45-8 Je '77
How self-hypnosis worked for me. B. Bloy. Seventeen 36:158+ My '77

Therapeutic use

Hypnosis comes of age. D. Goleman. il Psychol Today 11:54-6+ Jl '77
Hypnosis technique. M. Clark and D. Shapiro. il Newsweek 89:54 Mr 7 '77
Hypnosis: will medicine recognize its use in therapy? T. Bay. il Sci Digest 81:53-6+ My '77
Pain control with hypnosis. C. Holden. Science 198:808 N 25 '77
Secrets of a modern Mesmer; work of M. Erickson. D. Goleman. bibl il por Psychol Today 11:62+ Jl '77

HYPOCHONDRIA
Profound hypochondriac. B. G. Harrison. Ms 5:71-3+ My '77

HYPODERMIC injections. See Injections, Hypodermic

HYPOGEUSIA. See Taste

HYPOGLOSSAL nerve. See Nerves

HYPOGLYCEMIA. See Blood sugar

HYPOLIPIDEMIC drugs. See Antilipemic agents

HYPOTHALAMIC hormones
Bacteria synthesize brain hormone; somatastatin. Sci N 112:310 N 12 '77
Expression in escherichia coli of a chemically synthesized gene for the hormone somatostatin. K. Itakura and others. bibl il Science 198:1056-63 D 9 '77
GnRH—What it is, how it works. il Suc Farm 75:no4 D4 Mr '77
Medicine: spotlight on hormones. Sci N 112:260 O 22 '77
1977 Nobel Prize in physiology or medicine. J. Meites. il pors Science 198:594-6 N 11 '77

HYPOTHALAMIC hormones—*Continued*
Somatostatin: analogs with selected biological activities. M. Brown and others. bibl il Science 196:1467-9 Je 24 '77
Somatostatin: electron microscope immunohistochemical localization in secretory neurons of rat hypothalamus. G. Pelletier and others. bibl il Science 196:1469-70 Je 24 '77
Somatostatin: widespread abnormality in tissues of spontaneously diabetic mice. Y. C. Patel and others. bibl il Science 198:930-1 D 2 '77
See also
Pituitary hormone releasing factors
Thyrotropin releasing factor

HYPOTHALAMUS
Axon-sparing brain lesioning technique: the use of monosodium-L-glutamate and other amino acids. E. L. Simson and others. bibl il Science 198:515-17 N 4 '77
Hypothalamic stimulation facilitates contralateral visual control of a learned response. W. K. Beagley and T. L. Holley. bibl il Science 196:321-2 Ap 15 '77
Prolactin-like immunoreactivity: localization in nerve terminals of rat hypothalamus. M. Fuxe and others. bibl il Science 196:899-900 My 20 '77
Selective blockade of hypothalamic hyperphagia and obesity in rats by serotonin-depleting midbrain lesions. D. V. Coscina and H. C. Stancer. bibl il Science 195:416-19 Ja 28 '77

HYPOTHERMIA
Cold water survival. S. A. Schwartz. il Conservationist 31:6-7 Ja '77
Have fun in the snow—but be careful! V. T. Sparano. il Nat Wildlife 16:26-7 D '77
Hypothermia: the chill that kills. A. H. Drummond, Jr. il Motor B & S 139:52-3+ F '77

HYPOXIA. See Anoxemia

I

IAEA. See International Atomic Energy Agency
IAM. See International Association of Machinists and Aerospace Workers
IATA. See International Air Transport Association
IB (International Baccalaureate) See International education
IBEX system. See Electronics—Military use
IBM. See International Business Machines Corporation
IBP. See International Biological Program
IC Industries, Inc
See also
Midas-International Corporation
ICAO. See International Civil Aviation Organization
ICBA. See International Community of Booksellers Associations
ICBM (intercontinental ballistic missiles) See Guided missiles
ICC. See International Controls Corporation; United States—Interstate Commerce Commission
ICMA. See International City Management Association
IEEE. See Institute of Electrical and Electronic Engineers
IFC. See American Library Association—Intellectual Freedom Committee
IFLA. See International Federation of Library Associations
IFR flying. See Aviation—Instrument flying
IFS Industries. See Undertakers and undertaking
IGE (individually guided education) See Individual instruction
IHS (Indian Health Service) See Indians of North America—Health and hygiene
IIA. See Information Industry Association
ILA. See International Longshoremen's Association
ILHR. See International League for Human Rights
ILO. See International Labor Organization
ILS (instrument landing system) See Airplanes—Landing
ILWU. See International Longshoremen's and Warehousemen's Union
IMF. See International Monetary Fund
IMS. See International Musicological Society
INA (Insurance Company of North America) See Insurance companies
INFCE (International Nuclear Fuel Cycle Evaluation) See Nuclear fuels
IOB. See United States—Intelligence Oversight Board
IOC. See International Olympic Committee
IOI. See International Ocean Institute
IOS. See Investors Overseas Services, Ltd
IPM (Integrated Pest Management) services. See Pest control operators
IQ. See Intelligence quotient
IQ tests. See Intelligence tests
IRA. See Irish Republican Army
IRCAM (Institut de Recherche et Coordination Acoustique/Musique) See Paris—Georges Pompidou Center
IRIS (International Rights Information Service) See Copyright
IRS. See United States—Internal Revenue Service
ISAD. See American Library Association—Information Science and Automation Division
ISCM. See International Society for Contemporary Music
ISD Inc. See Design firms
ISEE (International Sun-Earth Explorer) satellites. See Artificial satellites—Meteorological use
ISOMATA. See Idyllwild School of Music and the Arts
ITT. See International Telephone and Telegraph Corporation
ITT Continental Baking Company
ITT branches out. E. Marshall. New Repub 176:9-11 Ap 2 '77; Reply with rejoinder. R. B. Keane. 176:7+ My 21 '77
IVCF. See Inter-Varsity Christian Fellowship
I-beams. See Girders
I ching (Book of changes)
I ching on libraries. J. Berry. Lib J 102:2101 O 15 '77
I love my wife; musical comedy. See Musical comedy, revue, etc.—Reviews—Single works
I was sitting on my patio this guy appeared I thought I was hallucinating; drama. See Wilson, R.
IACOCCA, Lee Anthony. See Iacocca, Lido Anthony
IACOCCA, Lido Anthony
Multinational investment and global purpose; address, June 17, 1977. Vital Speeches 43:720-4 S 15 '77
Myth of the big, bad multinational. por Newsweek 90:21 S 12 '77
IACONIO, Frankie
Too close for comfort. D. Wallace. il pors Hot Rod 30:22-3 D '77 •
IAMS, Denise Z.
Success in math. Clearing H 50:362-3 Ap '77
IAPETUS (satellite). See Satellites
IBARRURI, Dolores
La Pasionaria: an exile ends. il pors Time 109:50 My 23 '77 •
IBBOTSON, Eva
Perfect potions; story. Seventeen 36:120-1+ F '77
IBEX
Ibex in Israel; Nubian ibex. L. Aronson. il Natur Hist 87:50-5 bibl(p 108) Ja '78
IBSEN, Henrik
Ghosts. Reviews
Time il 109:66 Je 20 '77 •
ICE
See also
Icebergs

Harvesting
See Ice harvesting

Polar Regions
Devon Island ice cap: core stratigraphy and paleoclimate. R. M. Koerner. bibl il map Science 196:15-18 Ap 1 '77
ICE accidents
Ice safety and rescue. D. Richey. il Outdoor Life 160:123-4 D '77
Prisoners of the ice; rescue of Italian couple swallowed by crevasse. F. Schell. il Read Digest 112:66-71 Ja '78
ICE Age Trail. See Trails
ICE ages. See Glacial epochs
ICE boats and ice boating
Hard water sailing. J. Beals. il Conservationist 31:2-5 Ja '77
Mark rounding lessons. G. Bowers. il por Yachting 141:60+ Mr '77
ICE break; opera. See Tippett, M.
ICE caps. See Ice—Polar Regions
ICE cream, ices, etc.
Adult ice creams; adding alcoholic beverages to ice cream. il Am Home 80:8 Je '77
Crimson desserts—flaming. il Sunset 159:164 D '77
Freezer pleasers. C. Claiborne and P. Franey. il N Y Times Mag p32-3 Jl 31 '77
Homemade ice cream without all the fuss; ice-cream maker and recipes. il McCalls 104:91-2 Jl '77
Ice cream: dairymen imperiled by FDA's recipe. N. Wade. Science 197:844-5+ Ag 26 '77
It's refreshment in mid-dinner; wine sherbet. il Sunset 158:174 Mr '77
Just-for-fun recipes cooked up by food hobbyists. N. Byal. il Bet Hom & Gard 55:140-1+ O '77

ICE cream, ices, etc.—*Continued*
Month of sundaes. S. B. Huffman. il Ladies Home J 94:84-5 Ag '77
Thirty-one favors; dairy lobby's campaign against new ice cream standards. N. Wade. New Repub 177:15-17 N 5 '77
Two dips of milk-derived products on a sugar cone. Chemistry 50:26 N '77
See also
Milkshakes
ICE cream makers. See Kitchen utensils and appliances
ICE cream parlors
Old-fashioned ice cream parlors in the gold country; California. il Sunset 159:28+ Ag '77
ICE drilling. See Drilling and boring (ice)
ICE fishing. See Fishing, Winter
ICE harvesting
Forgotten harvests. M. I. Cuffe. il Conservationist 31:16-18 Ja '77
ICE hazards in aviation. See Airplanes—Ice protection
ICE industry
Forgotten harvests; industry in New York. M. I. Cuffe. il Conservationist 31:16-18 Ja '77
ICE on rivers, lakes, etc.
Ice inevitably wins; Lake Champlain; with photographs. C. H. Smith. il Audubon 79:56-65 Ja '77
ICE skating. See Skating
ICE skating rinks. See Skating rinks
ICE yachts. See Ice boats and ice boating
ICEBERGS
Experts ponder icebergs as relief for world water dilemma. C. Holden. il Science 198: 274-6 O 21 '77
Huge iceberg in Antarctic spotted by RCA-built environmental satellite. il Space World N-10-166:34 O '77
Iceberg cometh; a possibility of towing icebergs from Antarctica to Saudi Arabia. P. Gwynne and others. il Newsweek 90:72 Jl 4 '77
Iceberg express; towing icebergs from Antarctica to Saudi Arabia. il map Sr Schol 110:10-12 D 1 '77
Icebergs for Arabia: the talk heats up. Bus W p21 Jl 4 '77
Icebergs for the desert: cool calculations. il Sci N 112:244 O 15 '77
Indian Ocean on the rocks. Chemistry 50:3 S '77
Is there an iceberg in your future? K. Frazier. il Sci N 112:298-300 N 5 '77
NASA, NOAA satellites photograph giant iceberg. il Aviation W 106:42-3 Ap 25 '77
Rise and fall of Antarctic ice: the rest of the iceberg. I. Ashkenazy. il Oceans 10:26-30 My '77
Towing icebergs. il Time 110:65 O 17 '77
World's biggest moving job—icebergs! E. D. Fales, Jr. il Pop Mech 149:47-51 Ja '78
ICEBOATS. See Ice boats and ice boating
ICELAND
See also
Geology—Iceland
Heimaey (island)

Description and travel

Island on the edge of the world. K. Cure. il Holiday 58:41-3+ Je '77
ICHNIOWSKI, Thomas
Father Bill and the voices of the night. il America 136:50-2 Ja 22 '77
ICHTHYORNIS. See Birds, Fossil
ICINGS
Tempting high-calorie come-on; toppings and desserts. il Sunset 159:238+ O '77
IDA, Queen. See Queen Ida
IDAHO
See also
Bird sanctuaries—Idaho
Education—Idaho
Environmental policy—Idaho
Fishing—Idaho
Hells Canyon
Land—Idaho
Police—Idaho
Salmon River (Idaho)
Strip mining—Idaho
IDEAL states. See Utopias
IDEALISM
See also
Romanticism
IDEAS in business
Put that small idea to work. W. D. Ellis. Read Digest 111:123-5 N '77
See also
Suggestion systems
IDENTICAL twins. See Twins
IDENTIFICATION
See also
Birds—Identification
Crime and criminals—Identification
Fingerprints
Swine—Identification
IDENTIFICATION (religion)
One personality, one life, one death. E. Schaeffer. Chr Today 22:36-7 D 9 '77
IDENTIFICATION cards, certificates, etc.
Coping with the credit crunch; cashing checks without backup identification. H. Alpert. il Ret Liv 17:22-4+ F '77
National identification card? W. F. Buckley, Jr. Nat R 29:1385 N 25 '77
IDENTIFICATION tags, bracelets, etc.
In case of emergency . . .; medic alert tags. H. Steirman. Fam Health 9:4 Jl '77
Medic Alert program celebrates 20th anniversary throughout U.S. il Ret Liv 17:11+ Ja '77
IDENTITY (psychology)
Individual and mass identity in urban art: the New York case. D. B. Kuspit. bibl il Art in Am 65:66-77 S '77
Liberated woman: identity crisis. G. Serban. Harp Baz 110:232+ S '77
One personality, one life, one death. E. Schaeffer. Chr Today 22:36-7 D 9 '77
IDEOLOGY
Ideology and political culture from Jefferson to Nixon; with discussion. R. Kelley. bibl f Am Hist R 82:531-82 Je '77
IDIOPATHIC hypogeusia. See Taste
IDIOSYNCRASIES
Does your quirk irk you. . .and others, too? N. Ashby. Fam Health 9:40-3 Mr '77
IDLEMAN, Peter
Cross-country skiing. il Consumers Res Mag 60:27-30 N '77
IDOMENEO; opera. See Mozart, J. C. W. A.
IDSO, Sherwood B. and Brazel, A. J.
Planetary radiation balance as a function of atmospheric dust: climatological consequences. bibl il Science 198:731-3 N 18 '77
—and others
Remote-sensing of crop yields. bibl il Science 196:19-25 Ap 1 '77
IDYLLWILD School of Music and the Arts
Idyllwild School of Music and the Arts; Idyllwild, Calif. il Bet Hom & Gard 55:204+ Ap '77
IFE Book Fair. See Book fairs
IGNARRO, Louis J. See Cech, S. Y. jt auth
IGNATIUS of Loyola, Saint. See Loyola, Ignatius of
IGNATOW, David
Question; poem. Atlantic 241:74 Ja '78
IGNEOUS rocks. See Rocks, Igneous
IGNITION devices. See Gas burners—Ignition; Magnetos
IGNITION timing lights. See Testing instruments
IGNORANCE, Encyclopedia of. See Encyclopedias
IGUANAS
Social behavior in hatchling green iguanas: life at a reptile rookery. G. M. Burghardt and others. bibl il Science 195:689-91 F 18 '77
IHARA, Toni. See Warner, R. jt auth
IJAPA, the tortoise; dramatization. See Winther, B.
IKARD, Frank Neville
International development of energy; excerpts from address. Intellect 105:207 Ja '77
Solving the energy problem; address, October 19, 1977. Vital Speeches 44:117-20 D 1 '77
IKEBANA. See Flowers, Arrangement of
IKEDA, Toshiya, and others
Chemical basis for feeding adaptation of pine sawflies neodiprion rugifrons and neodiprion swainei. bibl il Science 197:497-9 Jl 29 '77
IKEMOTO, Shigenori, and others
New genetic marker in human parotid saliva (pm) bibl il Science 197:378-9 Jl 22 '77
IKER, Gladys McKee
Of bread. . .and love; poem. Ladies Home J 94: 200 Ap '77
IKLÉ, Fred Charles
United States discusses disarmament issues in U.N. General Assembly debate; statement, November 18, 1976. Dept State Bull 76:22-6 Ja 10 '77
What lies ahead in arms control? address, November 12, 1976. Vital Speeches 43:166-8 Ja 1 '77
What to hope for, and worry about, in SALT. il por Fortune 96:176-9+ O '77
ILLEGAL aliens. See Aliens
ILLEGAL literature. See Underground literature
ILLEGAL radio stations. See Radio stations, Illegal
ILLINOIS
See also
Architecture, Domestic—Illinois
Booksellers and bookselling—Illinois
Champaign County, Ill.
Chicago River
Crime and criminals—Illinois
Criminal justice, administration of—Illinois
Education—Illinois
Libraries—Illinois
Music festivals—Illinois
Natural areas—Illinois
Prisons—Illinois
Protests, demonstrations, etc.—Illinois
School libraries—Illinois

ILLINOIS—*Continued*

Description and travel

Southern Illinois. J. Gardner. Vogue 167:156-7 Mr '77

Politics and government

Big Jim; J. Thompson. K. Bode. New Repub 177:16-19 D 24 '77

ILLINOIS Institute of Technology, Chicago
Changing the specifications for engineers program for prospective minority students. D. Milesko-Pytel. il Am Educ 13:27-31 Ja '77

ILLINOIS mud turtles. See Turtles

ILLINOIS Regional Library for the Blind and Physically Handicapped, Chicago
Library for everyone. il Horizon 21:93 Ja '78

ILLINOIS State Library, Springfield
More local library input sought for Ill. 5-year plan. Lib J 102:536 Mr 1 '77

ILLITERACY
Chains of functional illiteracy. G. H. Cole. Educ Digest 43:10-13 D '77
Equal chance for everyone; illiteracy and the problems of youth; excerpt from Unesco's Medium-Term Plan (1977-1982) il UNESCO Courier 30:26-7 Mr '77
Newspeak generation. R. Whittemore. Harpers 254:16+ F '77
U.S. literacy level not bad; excerpts from address. F. Hechinger. il Intellect 106:104-5 S '77

Anecdotes, facetiae, satire, etc.

Likely story. S. N. Judy. Engl J 66:7-8 D '77

Tanzania

After literacy, what next? Tanzanian folk tales in readers. S. Malya. il UNESCO Courier 30:23-7 F '77

ILLUMINATION of books and manuscripts
Manuscript initials a fine art form. W. Rodger. il Hobbies 82:150-2 Jl '77
See also
Book of Durrow
Book of Kells

ILLUSION and hallucination producing plants. See Hallucination and illusion producing plants

ILLUSTRATED books
See also
Picture books

ILLUSTRATION
Child's garden of memories; Good housekeeping covers; excerpt from Jessie Willcox Smith. S. M. Schnessel. il Good H 184:142-5 My '77
Contemporary look at Kafka: illustrations for four stories of alienation. A. Cober. il Horizon 20:74-7 D '77
Mortimer Wilson: romantic baroque in the Southwest; interview, ed by B. Cortright. M. Wilson, Jr. il por Am Artist 41:52-5+ Je '77
My life as an illustrator; with portfolio of magazine covers. N. Rockwell. il Sat Eve Post 249:73-9 Jl '77
Paul Calle; interview, ed by N. Meglin. P. Calle. il por Am Artist 41:66-9 Jl '77
See also
Illumination of books and manuscripts
Picture books for children
Scientific illustration

History

Empathy with the humanity of the streets; illustrations of turn of the century Paris by T. A. Steinlen. P. D. Cate. il Art N 76:56-9 Mr '77
Frank Schoonover's frontier; excerpt from Frank Schoonover. C. Schoonover. il por Am West 14:38-47 Mr '77

Study and teaching

Illustrators Workshop: an original approach to teaching tomorrow's artists. N. Meglin. il Am Artist 41:42-7+ My '77
Jim Spanfeller: the illustrator as instructor. N. Meglin. il Am Artist 41:46-9+ Mr '77

ILLUSTRATORS
Careers in art: illustration. P. Savino. Sch Arts 76:4 F '77
New generation of writers and artists brings fresh vision to children's books. J. F. Mercier. Pub W 211:99-100 F 28 '77
Paul Davis: a personal vision; interview, ed by S. Bonhomme; with editorial comment. P. Davis. il Am Artist 41:7-9, 34-41+ My '77
See also
Allen, D.
Allen, T.
Anderson, W. I.
Davis, J.
Dillon, D.
Dillon, L.
Fox, L.
Frazetta, F.
Froud, B.
Geisel, T. S.
Gorey, E. S.
Handville, R. T.
Henninger, J.
Hokinson, H. E.
Jonson, J.
Lansdowne, J. F.
Neiman, L.
Pitz, H. C.
Santore, C.
Schoonover, F.
Sendak, M.
Smith, J. W.
Spanfeller, J.
Steinlen, T. A.
Whitmore, C.

ILLUSTRATORS Workshop. See Illustration—Study and teaching

ILMENITE
First occurrence of the garnet-ilmenite transition in silicates. L. G. Liu. bibl il Science 195:990-1 Mr 11 '77

IMAGE of God. See Man (theology)

IMAGINAL disks. See Insects—Development

IMAGINARY conversations
Deadly conversation. R. L. Woods. il Esquire 87:108-9 Ap '77

IMAGINATION
Centering as a process for children's imaging. R. B. Kent. bibl il Sch Arts 77:18-20 N '77
Imagination gap. A. J. Hansen. por Newsweek 90:9 Jl 25 '77
See also
Creative ability
Fantasy

IMAGINETICS International, Inc. See Toy industry

IMAI, Ryukichi
Safeguards against diversion of nuclear material: an overview. Ann Am Acad 430:58-69 Mr '77

IMASCO Ltd-Hardee's Food Systems Inc merger. See Corporations—Acquisitions and mergers—International aspects

IMBER, Peg
Identity crisis no. 14; poem. Seventeen 36:70 Mr '77

IMBRIE, Andrew Welsh
Angle of repose. Reviews
Am Rec G 40:58-9 D '76 *
Hi Fi il 27:MA30-1 Mr '77 *

IMETAL-Copperweld Corporation merger. See Corporations—Acquisitions and mergers—International aspects

IMIDES
See also
Cycloheximide

IMITATION
Don't stick out your tongue at a newborn; study by Andrew Meltzoff and M. Keith Moore. J. Gaylin. Psychol Today 11:24+ D '77
Imitation of facial and manual gestures by human neonates. A. N. Meltzoff and M. K. Moore. bibl il Science 198:75-8 O 7 '77

IMLAY, Marc J.
Mollusc expert resists transfer. C. Holden. Science 196:1427 Je 24 '77 *

IMMATURITY, Emotional. See Maturity

IMMIGRANTS in the United States
New immigrant wave; symposium. bibl il Society 14:18-42+ S '77
New peril. A. McCarthy. Commonweal 104:40+ Ja 21 '77
See also
Aliens
Chinese in the United States
Ellis Island
Filipinos in the United States
Indians (East Indian) in the United States
Italians in the United States
Jews in the United States
Latin Americans in the United States
Mexicans in the United States
Vietnamese in the United States

History

What Roots means to me. A. Haley. Read Digest 110:73-6 My '77

IMMIGRATION and emigration
See also
Alien labor
Aliens
Assimilation (sociology)
Refugees

Law

See Immigration and emigration law

Canada

Canada has second thoughts about its open door to immigrants. K. M. Chrysler. il U.S. News 83:60+ O 3 '77

Great Britain

Alarming exodus of business talent. Bus W p46 My 23 '77
See also
Deportation

Israel

Israelis of New York. J. Feron. il N Y Times Mag p 14-15+ Ja 16 '77

IMMIGRATION and emigration—*Continued*

Latin America

History

Enduring heritage; influence of early Spanish settlers in Latin America. I. Vásquez de Acuña. il map Américas 29:30-3 O '77

Puerto Rico

Why Puerto Ricans migrated to the United States in 1947-73. R. M. Maldonado; reply with rejoinder. S. P. Zell. bibl il M Labor R 100: 29-35 Ag '77

Rhodesia

Land of opportunity—maybe. il Time 110:56 O 24 '77

Taking the chicken run; emigrating. il Time 110:27 Ag 1 '77

Russia

Refuseniks of Kiev. W. Steif. il Sat R 4:20-1+ S 17 '77

Soviets turn deaf ear to pleas for Levich. C. Holden. por Science 197:349 Jl 22 '77

History

Passage to the New World; Jewish family's escape from Czarist Russia; with introd by C. Ozick. S. R. Ozick. il por Ms 6:70-4+ Ag '77

Sweden

Racial time bomb. Time 110:41 Ag 8 '77

United States

Back where they came from; Haitians. Nation 225:260-1 S 24 '77

Indochinese refugees. K. Keegan. New Repub 177:11-12 Jl 23 '77

Recent immigration and current data collection. R. Warren. bibl il M Labor R 100:36-41 O '77

Why Puerto Ricans migrated to the United States in 1947-73. R. M. Maldonado; reply with rejoinder. S. P. Zell. bibl il M Labor R 100:29-35 Ag '77

Yanks go west; American Jews in the West Bank. M. J. Kubic. il Newsweek 90:46 S 26 '77

See also

Aliens
Ellis Island
United States—Immigration and Naturalization Service

IMMIGRATION and emigration law

Evolution of U.S. immigration policy. A. E. Kellogg. Cong Digest 56:227-9+ O '77

Highlights of the present basic law; Immigration and Nationality Act. Cong Digest 56:230 O '77

Immigration policy: the new environmental battlefield. G. Bikales. il Nat Parks & Con Mag 51:13-16 D '77

Political refugees; question of liberalization of US immigration law. New Repub 177:6+ D 3 '77

Soviet side; McCarran-Walter Act. F. Willey and others. il Newsweek 89:30 F 21 '77

U.S. opens its doors to the floating refugees; parole section of the Immigration and Nationality Act. U.S. News 83:21 Ag 15 '77

See also

Asylum, Right of

IMMIGRATION and Nationality Act. See Immigration and emigration law

IMMIGRATION service. See United States—Immigration and Naturalization Service

IMMORAL literature and pictures

See also

Obscenity (law)

IMMORTALITY

See also

Future life
Reincarnation

IMMUNE deficiency diseases. See Immunologic diseases

IMMUNE response. See Immunity

IMMUNITIES of foreign states

See also

Diplomatic privileges and immunities

IMMUNITY

Immune response in the sea urchin lytechinus pictus. K. A. Coffaro and R. T. Hinegardner. bibl il Science 197:1389-90 S 30 '77

Spotting invaders: which cells decide? Sci N 111:358 Je 4 '77

Stress-induced modulation of the immune response. A. A. Monjan and M. I. Collector. bibl il Science 196:307-8 Ap 15 '77

See also

Antigens and antibodies
Complements (immunity)
Immunochemistry
Immunosuppressive agents
Vaccination
Vaccines

IMMUNITY (exemption) See Diplomatic privileges and immunities

IMMUNIZATION

See also

Vaccination

IMMUNOCHEMISTRY

Prolactin-like immunoreactivity: localization in nerve terminals of rat hypothalamus. K. Fuxe and others. bibl il Science 196:899-900 My 20 '77

Somatostatin: electron microscope immunohistochemical localization in secretory neurons of rat hypothalamus. G. Pelletier and others. bibl il Science 196:1469-70 Je 24 '77

IMMUNODIFFUSION

Human bloodstains: individualization by crossed electroimmunodiffusion. G. H. Sweet and J. W. Elvins; discussion. bibl il Science 198:427 O 28 '77

IMMUNOFLUORESCENCE

Cytochrome c: immunofluorescent localization of the testis-specific form. E. Goldberg and others. bibl il Science 196:1010-12 My 27 '77

Immunofluorescence localization of proteins of high molecular weight along intracellular microtubules. P. Sherline and K. Schiavone. bibl il Science 198:1038-40 D 9 '77

IMMUNOGENETICS

Glyoxalase I polymorphism in the mouse: a new genetic marker linked to H-2. T. Meo and others. bibl il Science 198:309-10 O 21 '77

Immunological resolution of a diploid-tetraploid species complex of tree frogs. L. Maxson and others. bibl il Science 197:1012-13 S 2 '77

Lymphocyte-defined loci in cattle. W. R. Usinger and others. bibl il Science 196:1017-18 My 27 '77

IMMUNOGLOBULINS

Myasthenic immunoglobulin accelerates acetylcholine receptor degradation. I. Kao and D. B. Drachman. bibl il Science 196:527-9 Ap 29 '77

See also

Lectins

IMMUNOHISTOCHEMISTRY. See Immunochemistry

IMMUNOLOGIC diseases

David's debut into the world; isolation suit for child with combined immunodeficiency disease. il Sci N 112:314-15 N 12 '77

EAE model: a tentative connection to multiple sclerosis. T. H. Maugh. Science 195:969-71 Mr 11 '77

Experimental allergic encephalomyelitis in Lewis rats: chemical synthesis of disease-inducing determinant. G. A. Hashim. bibl il Science 196:1219-21 Je 10 '77

See also

Lupus erythematosus
Myasthenia gravis

IMMUNOLOGICAL tolerance

HLA and disease. Sci Am 238:64+ Ja '78

Marek's disease: effects of B histocompatibility alloalleles in resistant and susceptible chicken lines. W. E. Briles and others. bibl il Science 195:193-5 Ja 14 '77

IMMUNOLOGY

See also

Cancer—Immunological aspects
Tumors—Immunological aspects

IMMUNOPATHOLOGY. See Immunologic diseases

IMMUNOSUPPRESSIVE agents

Prevention of autoimmunity in experimental lupus erythematosus by soluble immune response suppressor. R. S. Krakauer and others. bibl il Science 196:56-9 Ap 1 '77

IMMUNOTHERAPY

See also

Cancer—Therapy

IMPEACHMENTS

See also

Johnson, A.—Impeachment

IMPERIAL ivory-billed woodpeckers. See Woodpeckers

IMPERIAL Oil Ltd. See Exxon Corporation

IMPERIAL Valley, Calif.

Fairness for farmers. New Repub 177:2+ N 12 '77

Populist Doc; attempts to cut off federal irrigation water to large farms. por Forbes 120:190 N 15 '77

IMPERIALISM

Passing of the old imperialisms. C. Northcott. Chr Cent 94:268-9 Mr 23 '77

IMPERSONATION (law) See False personation

IMPEYAN pheasants. See Pheasants

IMPLANTATION, Subcutaneous

How you implant makes a difference. T. Grandin. il Suc Farm 75:no3 B18-19 F '77

IMPLANTATION of blastocysts. See Blastocysts

IMPLEMENTS, utensils, etc.

See also

Indians of North America—Implements
Kitchen utensils and appliances
Stone implements and weapons
Tools

IMPORT tax. See Tariff

IMPORT trade. See Export-import trade

IMPORTANCE of being Earnest; drama. See Wilde, O.

IMPOSTERS and imposture

See also

Quacks and quackery

IMPREGNATION, Artificial. See Artificial insemination, Human

IMPRESARIOS
Counter counterculture shock; B. Graham. E. Melton. por Forbes 120:103 N 15 '77
Lew Grade, superstar. il por Forbes 119:42+ My 1 '77
See also
Theatrical agencies

IMPRESSIONISM (art)
Berthe Morisot: paintings from a private place. W. P. Scott. il Am Artist 41:66-71 N '77
Impressionists arrive; excerpt from The art world; ed by B. Diamonstein. il Art N 76:150+ N '77
Looking at paintings; C. Monet's Old St. Lazare Station, Paris. B. Dunstan. il Am Artist 41:54-5 Ap '77
Looking at paintings; A. Renoir's The Luncheon of the Boating Party. B. Dunstan. il Am Artist 41:28-9 Mr '77
See also
Post-impressionism (art)

IMPRISONMENT. See Prisons

IMPRISONMENT, False. See False imprisonment

IMPROVISATION (dance)
In contact with Mangrove; contact improvisation. J. Armstrong. il Dance Mag 51:42-5 D '77

IN-service teacher education. See Teachers—Education in service

IN the summer house; drama. See Bowles, J.

INAUGURATIONS
See also
Carter, J.—Inauguration

INCANDESCENT electric lamps. See Electric lamps, Incandescent

INCARNATION
Debating the incarnation. T. Beeson. Chr Cent 94:740-2 Ag 31 '77
From myth to myth. E. Schaeffer. Chr Today 21:45-6 S 9 '77
Is the incarnation a myth? J. R. W. Stott. Chr Today 22:34-5 N 4 '77
Man becomes God. J. Garvey. il Commonweal 104:815-16+ D 23 '77
Mystery at Bethlehem. H. Lindsell. il Chr Today 22:22-5 D 9 '77
Was Jesus merely man? theological controversy in Great Britain. il Time 110:45 Ag 15 '77

INCENSE burners and containers
Japanese incense boxes. il Ceram Mo 25:22-7 N '77

INCENTIVES in industry
Even a millionaire couldn't buy something like that. J. O'Hanlon. il Forbes 120:88+ N 1 '77
How to keep workers happy on the job. il U.S. News 83:85-6 D 26 '77
See also
Profit sharing

INCEST
Incest: sexual abuse begins at home. E. Weber. Ms 5:64-7 Ap '77; Discussion. 6:89-92 S '77
Story of Mary C. J. Stucker. Ms 5:66-7+ Ap '77

INCINERATORS. See Refuse incinerators

INCLAN, Hilda
Incident. T. Branch and J. Rothchild. il pors Esquire 87:57 Mr '77 *

INCO. See International Nickel Company of Canada

INCOME
Demographic change, government transfers, and income distribution. S. Danziger and R. Plotnick. bibl il M Labor R 100:7-11 Ap '77
Family income: where your state stands. il U.S. News 83:80 D 12 '77
Gap in wealth and income. Progressive 41:11 Jl '77
How much extra income to add an employee? il Suc Farm 75:11 Je '77
Income inequality in Mexico. D. Felix. bibl f Cur Hist 72:111-14+ Mr '77
Measuring income inequality with extended earnings periods. E. Steinberg. bibl il M Labor R 100:29-31 Je '77
Middle class poor. S. Fraker and others. il Newsweek 90:30-1+ S 12 '77
New two-tier market for consumer goods. il Bus W p80+ Ap 11 '77
Official look at rising family income. il U.S. News 83:77 O 17 '77
Partnerships: three ways to share income. il Suc Farm 75:8 My '77
Personal income. See occasional issues of Business week
Surge in incomes—which states do best. il U.S. News 82:79 My 23 '77
249 billions to prop incomes—where government money goes. il U.S. News 83:98-9 N 28 '77
Where people's incomes run highest; top 100 counties in the U.S. il U.S. News 82:66 Je 20 '77
Why inflation hits some people less than others. A. Brimmer. il por Nations Bus 65:38-40+ F '77
See also
Negative income tax
Retirement income
Salaries
Wages
Wealth

INCOME insurance. See Insurance, Life—Income policy

INCOME investments. See Investments

INCOME tax
See also
Corporations—Taxation
Non-wage payments—Taxation
Pensions—Taxation

Auditing

See Tax auditing

Capital gains tax

Business stakes are high. il Bus W p53+ Ag 29 '77
End tax breaks for capital gains? interviews. L. C. Thurow and B. Frenzel. pors U.S. News 83:71-2 D 19 '77
New route around capital gains taxes; corporate acquisitions. D. G. Santry. Bus W p104 S 19 '77
Tax that is killing investment; views of W. F. Ballhaus. J. Cobbs. il Bus W p 14+ Ja 16 '78
Time to plan tax selling. J. Fraser. U.S. News 83:105 N 21 '77
See also
Real property and taxation

Deductions

Artists' tax bills. B. Chamberlain. Am Artist 42:18+ Ja '78
Beggar thy neighbor; overseas conventions. il Forbes 120:48 O 15 '77
Buffer casualty losses with tax deduction. Suc Farm 75:54 N '77
Claim another tax exemption when you support a parent. Suc Farm 75:44 Je '77
Curbing the three-martini lunch: does Carter plan have a chance? il U.S. News 83:87-8 D 5 '77
Deducting at-home entertainment expenses. Bus W p90 My 30 '77
Early advice for taxpayers. il Mech Illus 74:26+ Ja '78
Educational expenses. Consumers Res Mag 60:41 Ap '77
Get full value from charitable contributions. Suc Farm 75:A4 O; C33 D '77
Get set to save on your income tax. il Changing T 32:17-19 Ja '78
Give a car but not the title. Farm J 101:K4 Ap '77
Halving the expense account. Time 110:69 O 10 '77
Hirshhorn waltz. Vasari. Art N 76:27-8 Ja '77
Household list that could save you money; disaster relief. J. Block. McCalls 105:40 Ja '78
How the new laws can save you tax money. il Mech Illus 73:50 Mr '77
How to profit from the new tax laws. B. Surface. N Y Times Mag p70-5 Mr 13 '77
How you can deduct legal fees. Farm J 101:39 Ja '77
Hunting of the perk. D. Pauly and others. Newsweek 90:97 O 10 '77
International conferences and tax reform. L. M. Branscomb. Science 196:719 My 13 '77
It may pay to keep a diary on your vacation; business expenses. Farm J 101:B1 Ag '77
Long-range tax planning softens blow of net operating loss. il Suc Farm 75:8 N '77
Middle class loophole; mortgage interest deduction. S. Chapman. New Repub 177:12-14 D 3 '77
Money matters: business at home; artists. G. Krefetz. Craft Horiz 37:49+ D '77
Morality and the martini lunch. G. F. Will. Newsweek 90:120 O 17 '77
Plan ahead to save in 1977. S. Auerbach. Am Home 80:92 Mr '77
Q&A about taxes (cont) L. A. Miller. il Ret Liv 17:48 Ja; 66+ F; 13 Ag; 14-15 S; 12-13 D '77
Remodeling notebook; deducting home improvements. J. Block. House B 119:44 Mr '77
Saving international conferences. H. L. Davis. Phys Today 30:88 Je '77
Should the purchase of art be tax deductible? pro and con discussion. T. M. Rees; T. Crawford; reply. R. Blumberg. Am Artist 41:5+ Mr '77
Some thoughts on a librarian's income tax. Am Lib 8:62-3 F '77
States expand tax incentives for solar energy users. il Ret Liv 17:49 D '77
Tax break for working parents. M. R. Skrocki. McCalls 104:48 Mr '77
Tax break you don't want; theft loss. J. Block. il Mech Illus 73:26 Jl '77
Tax loopholes for everyone—roadblock to reform. il U.S. News 83:64-5 Ag 1 '77
Tax quiz: when is a repair not an improvement? Suc Farm 75:36 Ap '77
Tax-saving tips for home-owners. il U.S. News 82:74 Mr 21 '77
Tax tips to save you money; boat deductions. J. Cameron. Motor B & S 139:82+ Ap '77
Taxes: are you making the most of medical deductions? questions and answers. Bet Hom & Gard 55:32+ D '77

INCOME tax—Deductions—*Continued*
Taxes for the craftsman (title varies) (cont) E. Marcum. Craft Horiz 37:12+ F '77
Three-martini tax bill. T. Nicholson and others. il Newsweek 91:48-9 Ja 2 '78
Time to think about next year's tax return. Changing T 31:19-20 Ap '77
Use tax planning when you support both parents. Suc Farm 75:K4 S '77
Volunteer helpers of youth groups: take a tax break. Suc Farm 75:K5 Je '77
See also
Tax planning

Estimates

Should you file a tax estimate? Suc Farm 75:48 N '77

Forms

See Tax forms

Records

See Tax records

Returns

See Tax returns

Great Britain

Bittersweets for Britain. L. Langway and A. Collings. il por Newsweek 89:87 Ap 11 '77
Reluctant exiles. A. Lejeune. Nat R 29:551-2 My 13 '77

Ireland

Little bit of haven. il Time 110:115-16 O 10 '77

United States

Answers to your tax questions. il Changing T 31:33-4 Mr '77
Anti-inflation gospel; turnabout on tax rebate plan. A. J. Mayer and others. il Newsweek 89:63-4 Ap 25 '77
Artists and taxes. J. A. Mondale. il Ceram Mo 25:73-5 O '77
Carter's only choice may be a tax cut. N. Jonas and S. H. Wildstrom. Bus W p24 N 7 '77
Carter's tax reforms—who'll be helped, who'll be hurt. il U.S. News 83:79-80+ O 3 '77
Corporate expatriates fight a U.S. tax law. Bus W p44+ Ap 11 '77
Craftsmen in business: taxes; excerpt from Craftsmen in business: a guide to financial management and taxes. H. W. Connaughton. Ceram Mo 25:40-4 Mr '77
Crucial issue of capital to pay for tomorrow. il Nations Bus 65:41-2+ S '77
Dance funding: the Richmond Arts and Education Bill. B. V. Bordelon. Dance Mag 51:14-15 Ag '77
Econometrics and politics. P. C. Roberts. Nat R 29:549-51 My 13 '77
Effect of tax policies on initiative. il Nations Bus 65:20-1 D '77
Energy pushes back tax reform. il Time 110:71-2 O 24 '77
Fiscal fix; tax cuts. Nat R 29:1476 D 23 '77
Get set to save on your income tax. il Changing T 32:17-19 Ja '78
Hanging bookshelves on tax brackets. A. Tobias. Esquire 88:42+ Jl '77
Here comes the tax cut. il por Time 110:13-14 D 12 '77
How the new tax law will affect you. J. L. Lippert. Good H 184:230 Mr '77
How to avoid the pitfalls in this year's tax return. U.S. News 82:80 Mr 7 '77
How to handle taxes on money you get from Uncle Sam. L. Lane. il Farm J 101:30-1+ N '77
How to save on '77 taxes. U.S. News 83:99-102 O 24 '77
If Carter really wants a simple tax plan... il U.S. News 82:72-3 Ja 31 '77
Jumping the gun on Carter's tax reform. N. Jonas. Bus W p39 O 17 '77
Knocking sense into form 1040. M. Gwirtzman. New Repub 176:15-18 Ap 16 '77
Last-minute tax tips. F. Casey. il Mech Illus 73: 88+ Ap '77
Long batting for Carter. il Time 109:75-6 Mr 28 '77
Manifesto for a tax revolution. A. F. Ehrbar. il Fortune 95:90-5+ Ap '77
Minimum tax: you may owe it and not know it. il Farm J 101:B3 O '77
Nation's taxpayers are getting angry—and getting organized. il U.S. News 82:69-70 Ap 25 '77
Never too late to get it straight. R. C. Black. Farm J 101:38 Mr '77
New tax cut—what you have coming. il U.S. 83:26-8 Jl 18 '77
Next: you'll pay taxes on your fringe benefits; interview. J. Kurtz. il por U.S. News News 82:62-3 F 7 '77
1977: taxation at the crossroads; address, June 7, 1977. J. H. Evans. Vital Speeches 43:615-18 Ag 1 '77
On the mark, get set, calculate. Time 109:74-5 Mr 21 '77
Our tax system; address, July 20, 1977. W. M. Blumenthal. Vital Speeches 43:674-7 S 1 '77
Pick a tax pro now for a happier '78. W. Flanagan. Vogue 167:238 D '77
Rebates may drown in a spat over water. Bus W p43-4 Ap 18 '77
Redoing Carter's package. il Time 109:66 F 21 '77
Reforming the tax laws; views of four tax authorities. U.S. News 83:34-8 Jl 25 '77
Requiem for a rebate. R. M. Solow. New Repub 176:11-13 My 7 '77
Retreat on the rebate. Progressive 41:7 Je '77
Rising rumble over taxes. H. Sidey. Time 110: 18 N 28 '77
So you married a crook. . . ; innocent-spouse status. J. Block. Vogue 167:58+ N '77
Stop these secret tax hikes! index linking. J. T. Lynn. Read Digest 111:197-8+ N '77
Sudden spring thaw. D. Pauly and others. il Newsweek 89:52+ Mr 28 '77
TRB from Washington; proposed tax rebates. New Repub 176:2+ F 5 '77
Tax burden—heading for a new record? il U.S. News 82:30 My 23 '77
Tax changes worth knowing about. Changing T 31:31-2 S '77
Tax cut in '78—a sure thing. il U.S. News 83:23-4 N 14 '77
Tax cut in the making. M. Ruby and R. Thomas. il Newsweek 90:50+ D 19 '77
Tax laws must be made simpler as part of any reform package. C. Morgello. por Duns R 110: 84 Ag '77
Tax package made for stimulus. E. Lewis. Bus W p91 Ja 9 '78
Tax plans. Time 111:51 Ja 2 '78
Tax reform: is the battle lost before it begins? J. M. Berry. il Forbes 120:31-2 O 15 '77
Tax reform: not so fast. D. Pauly and others. il Newsweek 90:94 O 10 '77
Tax reform takes shape. il Time 110:85-6 S 26 '77
Tax support for visual arts. B. Chamberlain. Am Artist 41:14-15 Ap '77
Taxing situation; filling out short form 1040A. il Sr Schol 109:32-3 Ap 7 '77
Taxpayers on a seesaw; tax laws for single and married people. Fortune 96:53 Jl '77
10 questions retirees ask most about the new tax laws. L. A. Miller. il por Ret Liv 17:22-5 Mr '77
Tips on how to cut your income tax. U.S. News 82:47-50 F 28 '77
Understanding the new tax laws. P. Nelson. McCalls 104:96+ Ap '77
Wanted: a broader base and a simpler system. il Bus W p48-9 Ag 29 '77
We still need better income tax laws. il Changing T 31:25-8 My '77
When is a form too simple. Chr Today 22:29 N 4 '77
When more is not enough; proposed $50 rebate. il Time 109:51 F 7 '77
Year-end tips to cut your tax bill. M. Daly. Bet Hom & Gard 55:40+ D '77
You need a pro to figure your taxes. L. Lane. Farm J 101:17 mid-F '77
Your stake in coming cuts. il U.S. News 84: 62-3 Ja 9 '78
See also
Tax returns
United States—Internal Revenue Service

Anecdotes, facetiae, satire, etc.

Taxpayer's prayer. R. Baker. N Y Times Mag p 12 Ap 10 '77

History

Short history of form 1040. P. Meyer. il Harpers 254:22-4 Ap '77

INCOME tax, Negative. See Negative income tax
INCOME tax, State
State income taxes—who pays most, least. il U.S. News 82:72 Ap 4 '77
INCOME tax consultants. See Tax consultants
INCOME tax credit. See Tax credits
INCOMES policy. See Wage-price policy
INCREASE of population. See Population, Increase of
INCURABLES
See also
Terminal care
INDECENT assault
See also
Child molesters
Rape
INDEPENDENCE, Personal. See Self reliance
INDEPENDENCE, Political. See Autonomy
INDEPENDENCE Day. See Fourth of July
INDEPENDENT Commission on International Development Issues
Brandt's plan. S. Strasser and T. Nater. por Newsweek 90:70 D 12 '77
In search of an LDC solution. S. W. Sanders. por Bus W p75 D 12 '77

INDEPENDENT regulatory commissions
Business-regulatory agency interlocking: big brother keeps it all in the family. J. A. Schnepper. Intellect 105:325 Ap '77
Controversial world of the regulatory agencies. T. K. McCraw. Am Heritage 28:40-7 Ap '77
Federal agencies move out of the shadows; Sunshine Act. il Bus W p74-5 Mr 14 '77
Federal regulators: impact on every American. il U.S. News 82:61-2 My 9 '77
Fishbowl approach to agency lobbying; recent U.S. Court of Appeals decision. Bus W p31-2 My 23 '77
Grand scale of federal intervention. Bus W p52-3+ Ap 4 '77
Jimmy Carter's not-so-new faces; 25 regulatory appointees. P. Sturm. il Forbes 120:35-6 O 15 '77
Let the sunshine in? Government in the Sunshine Act. il Sr Schol 109:12-13 Mr 10 '77
Program you will be FOR; Comprehensive Program for Reasonable Regulation. Farm J 101: 52 D '77
Rage over rising regulation. Time 111:48-50 Ja 2 '78
Regulating the regulators. W. F. Buckley, Jr. Nat R 29:402-3 Ap 1 '77
Regulating the regulators. A. Hershman. il Duns R 109:34-6 Ja '77
Reorganizing U.S. executive agencies. H. C. Relyea. Current 189:17-21 Ja '77
Social watchdogs act in unison. il Bus W p36 Je 13 '77
Sunshine Act gets clouded results. il U.S. News 83:58 Jl 4 '77
Taking public hearings public; proposed bill to finance public participation in hearings at all federal agencies. Bus W p43-4 Mr 7 '77
Weapon against abuse of government power. J. J. Kilpatrick. il Nations Bus 65:13-14 N '77
What happened to Carter's pledge to slash red tape? il U.S. News 82:47-9 Je 20 '77
When the government's regulations boomerang —. C. E. Mayer. il U.S. News 83:89-91 S 19 '77
Why not the second best? Carter appointments. Nation 225:483-4 N 12 '77

INDEPENDENT schools. See Private schools

INDEPENDENT Schools Orchestra. See School orchestras

INDEX investment trusts. See Investment trusts

INDEX linking (economics)
Failure of indexation; western Europe. J. Ross-Skinner. Duns R 110:76-7+ S '77
Inflation protection for retired employees. H. Heaton. il Harvard Bus R 55:8+ S '77
Netherlands: close to a showdown over indexation. Bus W p50 F 7 '77
Stop these secret tax hikes! J. T. Lynn. Read Digest 111:197-8+ N '77
U.S. legalizes multicurrency deals. Bus W p23-4 N 7 '77
Utility's experiment in rate-setting; Public Service Company of New Mexico. il Bus W p84 S 26 '77

INDEX numbers (economics)
Business week index. See issues of Business week
Forbes index. See alternate issues of Forbes
See also
Index linking (economics)
Price indexes

INDEXATION. See Index linking (economics)

INDEXES
See also
Newspapers—Indexes
Periodicals—Indexes

INDEXES, Environmental. See Environment—Statistics

INDEXING
See also
Computers—Indexing use

INDIA
See also
Airlines—India
Birth control—India
Calcutta
Cities and towns—India
Cyclones—India
Government investigations—India
Industrial relations—India
Kashmir
Ladakh
Political prisoners—India
Poor—India
Protests, demonstrations, etc.—India
Rajasthan
Regionalism—India
Visitors, Foreign—India
Wildlife management—India
Women—India
Zoology—India

Antiquities

See also
Indus Valley—Antiquities

Commerce

United States

See United States—Commerce—India

Description and travel

India. S. Fockler. Trav/Holiday 148:72 D '77

Economic conditions

Elephant turns frisky. il Time 109:55 F 7 '77
Nation, region, and welfare: ethnicity regionalism, and development politics in South Asia. J. Das Gupta. bibl f il Ann Am Acad 433:125-36 S '77

Economic policy

It's wait and see after India's election. il Bus W p32 Ap 4 '77

Expropriation policy

IBM withdraws from India. il Time 110:92 N 28 '77
India may swallow Coke. il Time 110:44 Ag 22 '77
Sweet stuff; action of the Indian government toward Coca-Cola. Nation 225:228-9 S 17 '77

Foreign relations

Honeymoon is about over between India and Russia; interview. W. B. Saxbe. por U.S. News 82:41-2 Ja 24 '77

Bangladesh

Consensus adopted on Ganges waters dispute between Bangladesh, India. UN Chron 13:35-6 D '76

Russia

See Russia—Foreign relations—India

United States

See United States—Foreign relations—India

Industries

See also
Airplane industry—India

Politics and government

Coup that failed: Indira was willing. R. Manoff. Nation 224:550-1 My 7 '77
Deft re-entry. il por Time 110:39 Ag 15 '77
Democracy scoring a break through in India? L. J. Hansen. il map U.S. News 82:35-7 Je 27 '77
Election—at last. il por Time 109:32-3 Ja 31 '77
I have no ill will; excerpts from interview, ed by H. Jensen. M. Desai. Newsweek 89:36 Ap 4 '77
India: back in touch. il por Sr Schol 109:20-1 My 5 '77
India diarist. M. M. Kondracke. New Repub 177: 46 N 12 '77
India, my India! excerpt; with introd by C. A. Martin. J. P. Narayan. il pors N Y Times Mag p35-7+ Mr 27 '77
India's crown prince; S. Gandhi. W. Bordes. il por N Y Times Mag p 13-15+ F 13 '77
India's permanent emergency. K. Bird and S. Goldmark. Progressive 41:43-6 Mr '77
Indira's sure thing. F. Willey. il por Newsweek 89:52-3 Ja 31 '77
Lion in winter; J. P. Narayan. P. Gupte. Nation 224:677 Je 4 '77
Mrs Gandhi changes trains. Nation 224:132 F 5 '77
Mrs Gandhi: relief but few regrets; interview, ed by L. Malkin and K. K. Sharma. I. Gandhi. por Time 110:30 S 12 '77
Mrs Gandhi's defectors. A. Deming. il Newsweek 89:45+ F 14 '77
Morarji Desai: the ascetic activist; excerpts from interview, ed by L. Malkin and W. Stewart. M. Desai. il por Time 109:34 Ap 4 '77
Morarji in charge. M. Kondracke. New Repub 177:10-12 O 22 '77
New Delhi notebook: euphoria in a hot season. P. Gupte. Nation 224:649-52 My 28 '77
One cheer for Indira Gandhi. Chr Cent 94:163-4 F 23 '77
Opposition strikes back. il por Time 109:37-8 F 14 '77
Passage to a new India. P. Gupte. il Atlantic 240:59-66 Ag '77
Price India pays for Indira Gandhi's reforms. J. N. Wallace. il por U.S. News 82:37-40 Ja 24 '77
Reporter at large. V. Mehta. New Yorker 52: 56-60+ F 14 '77
Underappreciated India. N. Eberstadt. New Repub 176:14-16 Ja 15 '77
See also
Elections—India
Political campaigns—India
Political parties—India
Politics, Corruption in—India

Religious institutions and affairs

Master of Ganeshpupri; Swami Muktananda. P. Zweig. il Harpers 254:85-8+ My '77
See also
Religious conferences—India
Sikhism

INDIA—*Continued*

Social conditions

See also
Women—India

Social life and customs

Henna for happiness: India's mehndi art of symbols for all seasons. J. Saksena. il UNESCO Courier 30:18-22 F '77
Purdah in India: life behind the veil. D. W. Jacobson. il por map Nat Geog 152:270-86 Ag '77

INDIAN Airlines. See Airlines—India
INDIAN art (East Indian) See Art, Indian (East Indian)
INDIAN blankets, rugs, etc (American)
Navajo rug auction in New Mexico. il Sunset 159:48 N '77
INDIAN cookery (American) See Cookery, Indian (American)
INDIAN cookery (East Indian) See Cookery, Indian (East Indian)
INDIAN Creek School, Crownsville, Md. See Private schools
INDIAN dancing (East Indian) See Dancing, Indian (East Indian)
INDIAN folk art (East Indian) See Folk art
INDIAN Health Service. See United States—Health, Education and Welfare, Department of—Health Services Administration
INDIAN languages (American) See Indians of North America—Languages
INDIAN moccasins. See Moccasins
INDIAN Ocean
Deep western boundary current in the eastern Indian Ocean. B. A. Warren. bibl map Science 196:53-4 Ap 1 '77
Indian Ocean on the rocks. Chemistry 50:3 S '77
Somali Current: recent measurements during the southwest monsoon. J. G. Bruce. bibl maps Science 197:51-3 Jl 1 '77
See also
Seychelles (islands)
United Nations—Ad Hoc Committee on the Indian Ocean
INDIAN painting (East Indian) See Painting, Indian (East Indian)
INDIAN Peaks. See Rocky Mountains
INDIAN pipes (American) See Tobacco pipes
INDIAN rock carvings (American) See Petroglyphs
INDIAN rugs (American) See Indian blankets, rugs, etc (American)
INDIAN tobacco pipes (American) See Tobacco pipes
INDIAN warfare (American)
See also
Scalping
INDIAN weaving (American) See Weaving
INDIANA, Robert
We had this nice big rectangle. So why not put a painting on it? Vasari. il por Art N 76:24 D '77 *
INDIANA
See also
Architecture—Indiana
Art—Indiana
Crime and criminals—Indiana
Education—Indiana
Historic houses, sites, etc.—Indiana
Libraries—Indiana
Water pollution—Indiana
INDIANA Dunes National Lakeshore
Indiana Dunes: another border to defend; proposed location of the Bailly nuclear power plant. T. L. Erwin. il map Nat Parks & Con Mag 51:4-7 O '77
Indiana Dunes: tying up loose ends. J. P. Laue. Audubon 79:125-6 Ja '77
INDIANA State University, Terre Haute
Indiana State University. R. Bonham. il Ceram Mo 25:28-33 N '77
INDIANA Tumbler and Goblet Company. See Glass industry—History
INDIANAPOLIS

Crime

I'll have vengeance; A. Kiritsis' kidnapping of R. Hall. il por Time 109:19 F 21 '77
Three days of rage; R. Hall kidnapping. D. M. Alpern and S. Monroe. il por Newsweek 89:22 F 21 '77

INDIANAPOLIS, Country Club of. See Country clubs
INDIANAPOLIS 500. See Automobile racing
INDIANS
See also
Indians of Mexico
Indians of North America
Indians of South America
Paleo-Indians

INDIANS (American) in art
George Catlin's life amongst the Indians. J. R. Millichap. il pors Am Hist Illus 12:4-9+ Ag '77
How did an Indian chief really look? lithographic copies of Charles Bird King portraits. H. J. Viola. il Smithsonian 8:100-2+ Je '77
Pomo Indian portraits of Grace Carpenter Hudson; excerpt from The painter lady. S. R. Boynton. il por Am West 14:20-9 S '77
Taos art colony; special issue; with editorial comments. M. C. Nelson. Am Artist 42:6+, 27-63+ Ja '78
When you wish upon a star . . . ; work of A. Battles. M. Battles. il Design (US) 79:2-5 Fall '77
Winter at Fort Clark: Maximilian and Bodmer among the tribes of the Upper Missouri, 1833-1834; with reproductions of paintings; excerpt from People of the first man, ed by D. Thomas and K. Ronnefeldt. A. P. Maximilian. Am West 14:36-47 Ja '77
INDIANS (American) in literature
Forget the masked man. Who was his Indian companion? Tonto. M. Kendall. il Smithsonian 8:113-20 S '77
Indian boyhood; C. A. Eastman's autobiography. A. L. Stensland. Engl J 66:59 Mr '77
Indian presence in American literature. A. L. Stensland. bibl f il Engl J 66:37-41 Mr '77
Man who killed the deer; F. Waters' novel. H. Welch. Engl J 66:60 Mr '77
Second decade of Little big man. F. Turner. Nation 225:149-51 Ag 20 '77
INDIANS (American) in songs. See Songs, American
INDIANS (East Indian) in literature
Nectar in a sieve; K. Markandaya's novel. M. R. Oran. Engl J 66:62-3 Mr '77
INDIANS (East Indian) in the United States
Our local correspondents: naturalized citizen no. 9845165. V. Mehta. New Yorker 53:68-78 Ag 29 '77
See also
New York (city)—Foreign population
INDIANS, Treatment of
But was it history? P. W. Schmidtchen. il Hobbies 82:134-7+ N '77
Memory of ancient wrongs. C. Miles. Hobbies 82:146 Jl '77
INDIANS, Wooden
Wooden Indians. R. Moore. il Sch Arts 76:68 Mr '77
INDIANS of Alaska. See Indians of North America—Alaska
INDIANS of Canada. See Indians of North America—Canada
INDIANS of Central America
See also
Mayas
INDIANS of Mexico
See also
Aztecs
Yaqui Indians

Antiquities

See Mexico—Antiquities

Architecture

Monte Albán, city of the gods; Zapotec and Mixtec antiquities discovered by A. Caso. L. Elliott. il Read Digest 110:202-4+ My '77

Art

Pot shows in New Mexico, Colorado; Maxwell and Taylor Museums. il Sunset 158:49 My '77

Industries

Indian arts and crafts from Phoenix; Heard Museum exhibit of Mexican Indian crafts. il Sunset 158:68-9 My '77

Religion and mythology

Art of dreaming; excerpt from The second ring of power. C. Castaneda. il Psychol Today 11:34-6+ D '77
Don Juan's power trip. S. Keen. il por Psychol Today 11:40-2+ D '77
Matter of life and death; Aztec myths and Christian beliefs; excerpt from The labyrinth of solitude. O. Paz. il UNESCO Courier 30:20-1+ Ag '77

Social life and customs

Huichols: Mexico's people of myth and magic. J. Norman. il map Nat Geog 151:832-53 Je '77

INDIANS of North America
Pomo Indian portraits of Grace Carpenter Hudson; excerpt from The painter lady. S. R. Boynton. il por Am West 14:20-9 S '77
See also
Abnaki Indians
Aleuts
American Indian Movement
Apache Indians
Cherokee Indians

INDIANS of North America—See also—*Continued*
Cheyenne Indians
Eskimos
Hopi Indians
Mandan Indians
Navaho Indians
Nez Percé Indians
Pueblo Indians
Yahi Indians

Antiquities

Earlier Americans. Sci Am 236:61-2 Je '77
Indian relics. C. Miles. See issues of Hobbies
See also
Arizona—Antiquities
Maine—Antiquities
Washington (state)—Antiquities

Architecture

See also
Pueblo architecture

Art

See also
Petroglyphs

Exhibitions

Embraces of nature; Sacred Circles exhibition and Art Institute of Chicago show. M. Stevens. il Newsweek 90:82-3 S 12 '77
Living magic of Indian art: exhibition at the Nelson Gallery, Atkins Museum of Fine Arts, Kansas City. il Read Digest 111:170-5 D '77

Astronomy

See Astronomy, Indian (American)

Bibliography

Some books. C. Miles. Hobbies 82:140 Mr '77

Civil rights

Native Americans' new clout. W. Chapman. Progressive 41:30-2 Ag '77

Civilization

See Indians of North America—Culture

Claims

Cheyennes drive for clean-air rights; redesignating air quality status to prevent industrial development. il Bus W p 29 Ap 4 '77
Native Americans' new clout. W. Chapman. Progressive 41:30-2 Ag '77
U.S. Indians demand a better energy deal; Council of Energy Resource Tribes. por Bus W p53 D 19 '77

Cookery

See Cookery, Indian (American)

Costume and adornment

See also
Moccasins

Culture

Culture areas. C. S. Miles. il Hobbies 82:146-8 D '77
Indian summer for wayfarers; teaching Indian culture to children in natural areas. K. Kaltenbronn. il Parks & Rec 12:49-50 Je '77

Dances

Earth; Thunderbird American Indian Dancers at the McBurney YMCA. L. Small. Dance Mag 51:47-8 Ap '77

Diseases

Red death on the Missouri; American Indian epidemic of smallpox. K. C. Tessendorf. il Am West 14:48-53 Ja '77

Dwellings

See also
Cliff dwellers and cliff dwellings

Education

Students write about their artwork. M. Esping. il Sch Arts 76:36-8 F '77

Fishing

Racism and fishing rights; Michigan. J. H. Moore. Nation 225:236-8 S 17 '77

Government relations

Congress is the problem. P. Kovler. Nation 225:233-6 S 17 '77
Indians and the courts: allies against wildlife; question of applying fish and game laws to Indians. R. Starnes. il Outdoor Life 159:8+ Je '77
Leonard Peltier and the posse: still fighting the Indian wars. B. Johansen. por Nation 225:304-7 O 1 '77
See also
Indians of North America—Claims
Indians of North America—Land tenure
Indians of North America—Wars

History

Terror of the wilderness; spread of Western civilization; excerpt from The cost of living. F. Turner. il Am Heritage 28:58-65 F '77

Implements

Knives. C. S. Miles. il Hobbies 82:146-9 N '77
Some Indian tools. C. Miles. il Hobbies 82:146-7 S '77
Wooden utensils. C. Miles. il Hobbies 82:140-1 Ap '77

Industries

Alaska's natives, inc; corporate organizations. P. Gruenstein. Progressive 41:33-8 Mr '77
Alaska's natives—rich but troubled. U.S. News 83:51 Jl 11 '77
Rocky road to capitalism for Alaskan natives. il map Bus W p 114-15+ N 28 '77
See also
Indian blankets, rugs, etc (American)

Land tenure

As Maine goes. . . ? claims of the Passamaquoddy and Penobscot Indians. map Time 109:21 Mr 14 '77
Carter's first Indian test; Penobscot and Passamaquoddy of Maine. Chr Cent 94:680 Ag 3 '77
Century of Pyrrhic victories: Indian lawsuits and white power; Passamaquoddy and Penobscot tribes. P. T. Shattuck and J. Norgren. il Nation 225:12-16 Jl 2 '77
Giving it back to the Indians; claims of Passamaquoddy and Penobscot Indians to land in Maine. R. McLaughlin. il map Atlantic 239:70-4+ F '77
If Indian tribes win legal war to regain half of Maine—Penobscot and Passamaquoddy tribes. il map U.S. News 82:53-4 Ap 4 '77
Indians on the lawpath; Penobscot and Passamaquoddy tribes. S. Taylor. il New Repub 176:16-21 Ap 30 '77
Redeeming the time and the land; epilogue to 1776; claims of Penobscot and Passamaquoddy Indians. J. K. Larson. il Chr Cent 94:356-61 Ap 13 '77
Should we give the U.S. back to the Indians? Time essay. F. Trippett. il Time 109:51-2 Ap 11 '77
This land is my land; Maine's Passamaquoddy and Penobscot Indians. D. M. Alpern and others. il map Newsweek 89:18+ Mr 14 '77

Languages

Forget the masked man. Who was his Indian companion? Tonto. M. Kendall. il Smithsonian 8:113-20 S '77

Legal status, laws, etc.

See Indians of North America—Government relations

Libraries

Library training program for native Americans; Paraprofessional Training of Aides for American Indian Information Centers. D. Hall. Wilson Lib Bull 51:751-4 My '77

Medical care

Health care via TV in a rural area; STARPAHC unit used on Papago Indian reservation in Ariz. il U.S. News 83:79-80 D 26 '77

Medicine

See also
Medicine men

Missions

Church between cultures: missions on Indian reservations. C. F. Starkloff; reply. E. L. Schusky. il Chr Cent 94:303-6 Mr 30 '77

Museums

Indian art—living with the political realities; the Heard Museum in Phoenix; excerpt from The art museum as educator: a collection of studies as guides to practice and policy; ed by B. Y. Newsom and A. Z. Silver. il Art N 76:92-5 D '77
Indian arts and crafts from Phoenix; Heard Museum. il Sunset 158:68-9 My '77
See also
British Columbia. University, Vancouver— Museum of Anthropology

Periodicals

Native Americans. J. P. Danky and M. Fox. il Wilson Lib Bull 51:481-5, 662-6 F, Ap '77

Pottery

Nampeyo: Hopi potter. K. A. Way. il por Ceram Mo 25:51-3 Mr '77

Rites and ceremonies

American Indian pow-wow. L. M. Rhodes. il Travel 147:48-53 F '77
See also
Scalping

Schools

See Indians of North America—Education

Treatment

See Indians, Treatment of

INDIANS of North America—*Continued*

Wars

Campaigning with Custer; excerpt from Life in Custer's cavalry: diaries and letters of Albert and Jennie Barnitz, 1867-68, ed by R. M. Utley. A. Barnitz and J. P. Barnitz. il pors Am West 14:4-9+ Jl '77

Chief Joseph; Nez Perce War of 1877. W. A. Allard. il por map Nat Geog 151:408-34 Mr '77

See also

Pontiac's Conspiracy, 1763-1765

Weaving

See Weaving

Women

And then there were none; Indian Health Service's sterilization practices. J. K. Larson. Chr Cent 94:61-3 Ja 26 '77

Alaska

Alaska's interior forests: in the eye of the storm. D. T. Hoopes. il Am For 83:16-19+ Je '77

Alaska's natives, inc; corporate organizations. P. Gruenstein. Progressive 41:33-8 Mr '77

Alaska's natives—rich but troubled. U.S. News 83:51 Jl 11 '77

Rocky road to capitalism for Alaskan natives. il map Bus W p 114-15+ N 28 '77

Where have all the *tuttu* gone? with editorial comment. J. G. Mitchell. il Audubon 79:inside cover; 2-15 Mr '77

Canada

Berger report; northern frontier, northern homeland; excerpt from Northern frontier, northern homeland; with editorial comments. T. R. Berger. il por maps Liv Wildn 41:3, 4-33 Ap '77

Canada's pipeline battle. R. L. Moellering. il Chr Cent 94:982-5 O 26 '77

See also

Cree Indians

INDIANS of North America and blacks

Black freedmen of the Cherokee Nation. T. Gammon. bibl il Negro Hist Bull 40:732-5 Jl '77

INDIANS of North America in art. See Indians (American) in art

INDIANS of South America

Antiquities

See also

Ecuador—Antiquities

Civilization

See Indians of South America—Culture

Culture

Communities in crisis, Indians of South America. J. E. Adoum. il UNESCO Courier 30:46-50 Ag '77

Human species: the tribe that talks peace and makes war; the Yanomamo. J. Pfeiffer. il Horizon 19:92-3 Ja '77

Living legacy of the Andes. P. Macera. il UNESCO Courier 30:38-45 Ag '77

Medicine

Medical secrets of the Amazon. N. Maxwell. il por Américas 29:2-8 Je '77

Weaving

See Weaving

Amazon Valley

Medical secrets of the Amazon. N. Maxwell. il por Américas 29:2-8 Je '77

Ecuador

Looms of Otavalo. J. B. Casagrande. il Natur Hist 86:48-59 O '77

Paraguay

Paraguay's lost paradise; Guarani Reductions. C. J. McNaspy. il America 136:72-4 Ja 29 '77

INDICATORS, Dye. See Dyes as indicators

INDICATORS, Economic. See Economic indicators

INDIG, George

But what can it do? por Forbes 120:104 O 1 '77 *

INDIVIDUAL and society

Individual and mass identity in urban art: the New York case. D. B. Kuspit. bibl il Art in Am 65:66-77 S '77

Place called community. P. J. Palmer. Chr Cent 94:252-6 Mr 16 '77

INDIVIDUAL and state

Let's get rid of families! C. S. Bell. por Newsweek 89:19 My 9 '77

Missing the people's message; address, October 24, 1977. P. Lesly. Vital Speeches 44:141-5 D 15 '77

People's sense of powerlessness; excerpts from address. J. L. Buckley. por Intellect 106:95 S '77

INDIVIDUAL differences

See also

Sex differences

INDIVIDUAL instruction

IGE as a focus for educational reform and renewal. F. S. Chase. Educ Digest 42:48-50 Mr '77

Individualization: subversion of elementary schooling. K. Kepler and J. W. Randall. Educ Digest 43:17-20 O '77

Practitioner's guide to machete-swinging in the paperwork jungle: record keeping and individualized instruction. D. G. Armstrong and R. E. Pinney. il Clearing H 50:196-9 Ja '77

Rainbow in industrial arts; Occupational Versatility program; Puget Sound Junior High, Seattle. V. Hedrich. Educ Digest 42:53-6 F '77

Tri-dimensional approach to individualization. M. Hunter. Educ Digest 43:17-20 S '77

See also

Children, Handicapped—Education

INDIVIDUALISM

Special people; voluntary simplicity. R. Rodale. il pors Org Gard & Farm 24:54-8 Jl '77

See also

Individual and state

INDIVIDUALITY

Class and style; poll of Ebony readers. il Ebony 33:33-6+ N '77

See also

Self

INDIVIDUALIZED instruction. See Individual instruction

INDOCHINA

See also

Cambodia
Communism—Indochina
Vietnam
Vietnam, South

Politics and government

Insurgents: a new-old battle. il map Time 110:20+ Jl 4 '77

INDOCHINESE conflict, 1977-. See Cambodian-Vietnamese conflict, 1977-

INDOCHINESE in the United States

See also

Vietnamese in the United States

INDOCHINESE refugees. See Refugees, Indochinese

INDOCTRINATION

Politics in Chinese higher education. C. T. Hu. Cur Hist 73:79-83+ S '77

Thought control in Mao's China; interview with Chinese intellectual, ed by W. Berkson. Nat R 29:1173-7+ O 14 '77

INDOLE

Vegetables thwart drug efficiency. Sci Digest 81:88 F '77

INDOMETHACIN

Fatty acids and their prostaglandin derivatives: inhibitors of proliferation in aortic smooth muscle cells. J. J. Huttner and others. bibl il Science 197:289-91 Jl 15 '77

INDONESIA

Land of promise: the wealth of a troubled paradise. il Time 109:46-7 My 16 '77

See also

Bali
Civil rights—Indonesia
Cruising—Indonesia
Investments, Foreign—Indonesia
Investments, Indonesian
Loans, Bank—Indonesia
Military assistance, American—Indonesia
Political prisoners—Indonesia
Timor (island)
United Nations—Indonesia

Description and travel

Indonesia. S. Fockler. il Trav/Holiday 148:71-2 D '77

Industries

See also

Petroleum industry—Indonesia

Politics and government

Letter from Indonesia. R. Shaplen. il New Yorker 53:153-6+ D 12 '77

Territorial expansion

Department testifies on East Timor; statement, July 19, 1977. G. H. Aldrich. Dept State Bull 77:324-6 S 5 '77

U.S. diplomacy and human rights: the cruel case of Indonesia. A. S. Kohen. map Nation 225:553-7 N 26 '77

INDONESIAN cookery. See Cookery, Indonesian

INDOOR gardening

Environmental game plan for successful indoor gardening. D. Duncan. il Horticulture 55:40-3 D '77

Herbs for health; bathroom plants. P. Dunlop. il House & Gard 149:102+ F '77

Home is where the herbs grow. M. C. Goldman. il Org Gard & Farm 24:74-6 N '77

INDOOR gardening—*Continued*
How to grow pots of tomatoes in your window-sill garden. S. K. Graham. il House & Gard 149:82+ N '77
See also
Artificial light gardening
Greenhouses
House plants

Equipment and supplies

Indoor gardening aids. Consumer Rep 42:530-2 S '77

INDOOR gardens. See Gardens, Indoor

INDOOR plants. See House plants

INDOOR trees. See House plants

INDRISES. See Lemurs

INDUCTANCE
Introduction to gyrator theory. B. T. Morrison. il Pop Electr 12:58-9 Jl '77

INDUCTION, Mathematical. See Logic, Symbolic and mathematical

INDUS Valley

Antiquities

Strange relics of the crumbling, still-puzzling Indus culture. G. F. Dales. bibl il map Smithsonian 8:56-65 Jl '77

INDUSTRIAL Acceptance Corporation. See Finance companies—Australia

INDUSTRIAL arts
See also
Engineering

INDUSTRIAL buildings
Building types study; achieving economy and efficiency in environmentally sound buildings for industry; with introd by C. E. Hamlin. il Archit Rec 161:127-42 Je '77
Regulatory codes: one firm's check list for industrial projects. J. E. Compton. Archit Rec 161:65+ Je '77

INDUSTRIAL capacity
Limits on capacity won't slow growth. il Bus W p92-4 Jl 11 '77
Prices rise in spite of spare capacity. il Bus W p 120-3+ Mr 21 '77
Specter of shortages—with unemployment. il Fortune 95:14 Mr '77

INDUSTRIAL democracy
Heresy of worker participation. A. H. Raskin. Psychol Today 10:111 F '77
Industrial democracy in international perspective; symposium, ed by J. P. Windmuller. bibl f Ann Am Acad 431:1-140 My '77
See also
Employees representation in management

INDUSTRIAL design. See Design, Industrial

INDUSTRIAL designers. See Designers

INDUSTRIAL Development Board of the United Nations. See United Nations Industrial Development Organization

INDUSTRIAL development bond. See Bonds, Industrial development

INDUSTRIAL Development Organization. See United Nations Industrial Development Organization

INDUSTRIAL discipline. See Labor discipline

INDUSTRIAL diseases. See Diseases, Industrial

INDUSTRIAL districts
Park that reversed a brain drain; Research Triangle Park. il Fortune 95:148-53 Je '77
Research: alive and well in N.C; Research Triangle Park. il Time 110:46 Ag 1 '77

INDUSTRIAL diversification. See Diversification in industry

INDUSTRIAL drawing. See Mechanical drawing

INDUSTRIAL efficiency. See Efficiency, Industrial

INDUSTRIAL equipment

Leasing and renting

See also
Banks and banking—Leasing business

INDUSTRIAL equipment industry
See also
Bucyrus-Erie Company
Machine tool industry

Finance

Industrial equipment. il Forbes 121:68-70 Ja 9 '78

INDUSTRIAL espionage. See Business intelligence

INDUSTRIAL expansion
See also
Capital investments

INDUSTRIAL feeding
See also
Canteen Corporation

INDUSTRIAL hygiene
Carcinogens in the workplace: where to start cleaning up. T. H. Maugh, 2d. Science 197:1268-9 S 23 '77
Dilemma of regulating reproductive risks; safeguarding women's rights and health. Bus W p76-7+ Ag 29 '77
TDI: the unacknowledged poison; toluene diisocyanate. V. Cox. Nation 224:530-2 Ap 30 '77
Workplace hazards: no women need apply. D. McGhee. Progressive 41:20-5 O '77
See also
Diseases, Industrial
United States—Occupational Safety and Health Administration

INDUSTRIAL laws and legislation
See also
Labor laws and legislation

INDUSTRIAL management. See Business management

INDUSTRIAL museums
See also
Greenfield Village and Henry Ford Museum, Dearborn, Mich.

INDUSTRIAL parks. See Industrial districts

INDUSTRIAL photography. See Photography in industry

INDUSTRIAL poisons. See Poisons, Industrial

INDUSTRIAL prices. See Prices

INDUSTRIAL production. See Production

INDUSTRIAL psychology. See Psychology, Industrial

INDUSTRIAL relations
Developments in industrial relations. L. Bornstein and others. See issues of Monthly labor review
Industrial democracy and industrial relations. J. P. Windmuller. bibl f Ann Am Acad 431:22-31 My '77
Myth of the oppressive corporation. M. Ways. Fortune 96:149+ O '77
New chill in labor relations. il Bus W p32-3 O 24 '77
Significant decisions in labor cases. C. Polhemus. See issues of Monthly labor review
Tough talk won't be about wages this time. il U.S. News 83:92-3 D 26 '77
What's coming in labor relations? G. S. McIsaac. bibl f Harvard Bus R 55:22-3+ S '77
See also
Collective bargaining
Collective labor agreements
Communication in management
Employees representation in management
Grievance procedures
Labor boards, councils, etc.
Layoff systems
Strikes
United States—Labor policy
United States—National Labor Relations Board

Europe, Eastern

Soviet model of industrial democracy. J. L. Porket. bibl f Ann Am Acad 431:123-32 My '77

France

Reform of the enterprise in France. Y. Delamotte. Ann Am Acad 431:54-62 My '77

Germany, West

West German experience with industrial democracy. F. Furstenberg. bibl f Ann Acad 431:44-53 My '77

Great Britain

British labor problems dim Chrysler's hopes. il Bus W p53-4 N 21 '77
New focus on industrial democracy in Britain. A. W. J. Thomson. bibl f Ann Am Acad 431:32-43 My '77

India

Participative management in India: utopia or snare? S. Kannappan and V. N. Krishnan. bibl f Ann Am Acad 431:95-102 My '77

Israel

Worker participation in Israel: experience and lessons. E. Rosenstein. bibl f Ann Am Acad 431:113-22 My '77

Netherlands

Between harmony and conflict: industrial democracy in the Netherlands. W. Albeda. Ann Am Acad 431:74-82 My '77
Dutch grope for a new social contract. il Bus W p46+ Ag 8 '77

Peru

Industrial community in Peru. W. F. Whyte and G. Alberti. Ann Am Acad 431:103-12 My '77

Russia

Soviet model of industrial democracy. J. L. Porket. bibl f Ann Am Acad 431:123-32 My '77

Scandinavia

Industrial democracy in Scandinavia. B. Schiller. bibl f Ann Am Acad 431:63-73 My '77

South Africa

South Africa: multinationals are caught in the middle again; European Community race discrimination in employment guidelines. il Bus W p49-50 O 24 '77

Yugoslavia

Self-management in Yugoslavia. M. J. Broekmeyer. Ann Am Acad 431:133-40 My '77

INDUSTRIAL Relations Research Association
Conference papers; excerpts (cont) M Labor R 100:52-61 F; 51-7 Mr; 44-5 Ap '77

INDUSTRIAL research
Are R&D organizations obsolete? P. H. Thompson and G. W. Dalton; discussion. Harvard Bus R 55:173+ Ja; 174-5 Mr '77
Baconian imperative. J. A. Goldman. bibl il Intellect 105:430-2 Je '77
Budgeting for basics. por Forbes 119:118 Je 15 '77
See also
Industrial districts

Federal aid

NSF: pressures mount to provide grants for industrial researchers. P. M. Boffey. Science 196:142-3 Ap 8 '77

Finance

What 600 companies spend for research. il Bus W p62-9+ Je 27 '77

INDUSTRIAL revenue bonds. See Bonds, Industrial development

INDUSTRIAL safety
Who is responsible for workplace safety? J. S. Shaw. Bus W p42 D 26 '77
See also
United States—Occupational Safety and Health Administration

Laws and legislation

Furor spreads over safety rules for workers; Occupational Safety and Health Act of 1970. il U.S. News 82:69-70 Ja 31 '77

INDUSTRIAL security measures. See Industry—Security measures

INDUSTRIAL shows
Star-studded polyester; Milliken & Co. industrial show. M. Orth. il Newsweek 89:75-6 Je 27 '77

INDUSTRIAL standards. See Labor standards

INDUSTRIAL stores. See Company stores

INDUSTRIAL waste. See Trade waste

INDUSTRIAL workers. See Labor and laboring classes

INDUSTRY
See also
Corporations
Location in business and industry
Manufactures
Production

Fuel requirements

Big energy buyers go straight to the source; law allowing industries to purchase gas directly from producers. il Bus W p27 Mr 7 '77
Big scramble to keep plants running. U.S. News 82:65 Mr 14 '77
Energy conservation's impact on R&D. il Bus W p52-5+ Je 27 '77
Energy management: a crisis in industry. H. L. Breckenridge. bibl f Intellect 105:352-4 Ap '77
How some companies are coping with the energy crunch. Nations Bus 65:28-9 Ap '77
Industry can save energy without stunting its growth. T. Alexander. il Fortune 95:186-9+ My '77
Saving energy the cogeneration way; using waste heat from industrial plants. il Bus W p99-100 Je 6 '77
See also
Aluminum industry—Fuel requirements

Security measures

Businessmen and terrorism. A. J. Mayer and others. il Newsweek 90:82-4+ N 14 '77
Staying out of trouble. A. J. Mayer. il Newsweek 90:84 N 14 '77
U.S. business throws billions into a fight against terrorists. il U.S. News 83:24-6 N 21 '77
See also
American District Telegraph Company

INDUSTRY, Nationalization of. See Government ownership

INDUSTRY and art. See Art and industry; Art patronage

INDUSTRY and education. See Business and education

INDUSTRY and state
Budget unit asks caution in shift to private sector. K. Johnsen. Aviation W 107:16-17 N 28 '77
Bureaucratic Babylon; address, September 23, 1977. W. L. Wearly. Vital Speeches 44:44-9 N 1 '77
Business policy and the public welfare: the excesses of government regulations; address, January 14, 1977. M. L. Weidenbaum. Vital Speeches 43:317-20 Mr 1 '77
Does future look bright for business? It does indeed; interview. J. M. Kreps. pors U.S. News 83:17-19 Ag 1 '77
Getting the economic impact into regulatory decision-making. Bus W p90-1 Je 6 '77
Government intervention; special issue. il pors Bus W p42-3+ Ap 4 '77
Government regulation: a smooth ride to the bank; New Jersey. J. McLaughlin. Nation 224:679-82 Je 4 '77
Has emotion tipped the scales on consumer safety? address, October 17, 1977. J. W. Hanley. Vital Speeches 44:92-5 N 15 '77
How government looks at business. U.S. News 82:28 Je 27 '77
Juanita Kreps: more active role for Commerce; interview. J. M. Kreps. il pors Nations Bus 65:30-4 S '77
My case for national planning; with editorial comment. T. Bradshaw. il por Fortune 95:97, 100-4 F '77
News-lines: what you can and cannot do if you run a business. See issues of U.S. news and world report
OMB director Bert Lance seeks business help; interview, ed by R. L. Lesher. T. B. Lance. il pors Nations Bus 65:18-22+ My '77
Plain talk from brother Billy. B. Carter. il por Newsweek 89:71 My 30 '77
Pluralism run amok. S. Chapman. New Repub 176:36-9 My 21 '77
Public use of private interest; excerpt from Godkin lectures. C. L. Schultze. Harpers 254:43-50+ My '77
Real costs of regulation. R. A. Leone. il Harvard Bus R 55:57-66 N '77
Regulating the regulators. A. Hershman. Duns R 109:34-6 Ja '77
Social cures, not palliatives; adaptation of address. B. Commoner. il Nat Parks & Con Mag 51:14-15 My '77
Spur to business spending: ideas White House has in mind. il U.S. News 82:82-3 F 14 '77
Talking back to the SEC. A. Hershman. il Duns R 109:78-80 Mr '77
Thoughts about government and business; address, June 23, 1977. J. M. Kreps. Vital Speeches 43:610-12 Ag 1 '77
Toughest business battles in 1978. R. T. Gray. il Nations Bus 65:22-6+ D '77
Unlocking the gilded cage of regulation. P. H. Weaver. il Fortune 95:178-82+ F '77
Washington. G. R. Rosen. See issues of Dun's review
What businessmen dislike most about government regulation. Nations Bus 65:28 Jl '77
What happened to Carter's pledge to slash red tape? il U.S. News 82:47-9 Je 20 '77
What the Supreme Court is really telling business. W. Guzzardi, Jr. il Fortune 95:147-54 Ja '77
When the government's regulations boomerang —. C. E. Mayer. il U.S. News 83:89-91 S 19 '77
Why not zero based regulation? address, May 23, 1977. I. S. Shapiro. Vital Speeches 43:605-7 Jl 15 '77
World roundup. See issues of Business week
See also
Contracts, Government
Electric utilities—Regulation
Free enterprise
Government ownership
Independent regulatory commissions
Labor laws and legislation
Land utilization—Laws and regulations
Military-industrial complex
Public service commissions
Publishers and publishing—Federal aid
Railroads and state
Shoe industry—Federal aid
Steel industry—Federal aid
Transportation—Laws and regulations
Trusts, Industrial
United States—Federal Trade Commission
United States—Labor policy
United States—President's Commission on Personnel Interchange
also subhead Reports to government under names of industries, e.g. Electric utilities—Reports to government

Anecdotes, facetiae, satire, etc.

26,911 little words; government regulations. New Repub 176:9-10 Ap 23 '77

History

Businessman and the government; corruption, yesterday and today. J. Brooks. il Am Heritage 28:66-73 Je '77

Africa, Southern

Five black nations; living with more activist government. Bus W p77-8+ F 14 '77

Argentina

See also
Government ownership—Argentina

Europe

London letter. J. Ross-Skinner. Duns R 109:127-8 Je; 110:8 Jl; 79-80 Ag; 103-4 S; 149-50 O; 111-12 N; 113-14 D '77

France

French solution to foreign takeovers; offers for Rousselot and Gardinier. Bus W p56 O 3 '77

INDUSTRY and state—*Continued*

Italy

Industrial giants need salvaging again. il Bus W p68 S 26 '77

Will politics drown a debt-ridden giant? Montedison. il Bus W p72-5+ Jl 25 '77

Japan

Reports & comment: Japan; collusion between industry and politicians. F. Gibney. il por Atlantic 239:6-9+ Je '77

INDUSTRY and the arts. See The Arts and industry

INDUSTRY and the church. See Church and industry

INDUSTRY and the environment

American economy; address, August 28, 1977. I. S. Shapiro. Vital Speeches 43:738-41 O 1 '77

Environment and the economy: finding common ground. F. Smith. il por Duns R 110:83-4+ S '77

Getting to know each other. pors Forbes 120:62 Ag 1 '77

Giant battle in redwood country; controversy surrounding expansion of Redwood National Park. il Bus W p30-1 Ap 25 '77

Industry cries overkill on clean-water rules. il Bus W p41 O 10 '77

Jobs and the environment; views of the United Automobile Workers. R. F. Hall. il Conservationist 31:1 N '76

Joe Horvath is adding up your dollars of happiness. J. Skow. il por Outdoor Life 159:66-7+ Mr '77

Lumbermen vs. environmentalists: growing fight over what to do with nation's forests. il U.S. News 83:62-4 Ag 22 '77

New U.S. pollution challenge: a deluge of dangerous chemicals; interview. D. M. Costle. por U.S. News 83:31-2 D 19 '77

Now small business can pay its pollution tab. il Bus W p90 N 21 '77

Opportunity—an obligation; recent actions of New York's Department of Environmental Conservation. J. J. DuPont. Conservationist 31:1 Mr '77

Partnership that pays off for the public; American Land Trust. il Nations Bus 65:46-8+ Jl '77

Payoff for business initiative on the environment. N. Orloff. Harvard Bus R 55:8+ N '77

Price of environmentalism—the blacklash begins. J. A. Briggs. il Forbes 119:36-40 Je 15 '77

Redwood protest; loggers demonstration against major expansion of Redwood National Park. S. Fraker and G. C. Lubenow. il map Newsweek 89:30 Ap 25 '77

Taking the profit out of pollution. Bus W p27 D 19 '77

To drill or not to drill; controversy surrounding proposed oil lease of Michigan Audubon Society's Bernard W. Baker Sanctuary. J G. Mitchell. il Audubon 79:78-85 Ja '77

We can work with you; donations to the Nature Conservancy. D. Morine. il Am For 83:10-12 N '77

Italy

Seveso—one year later: aftermath of TCDD explosion at Icmesa chemical plant in Seveso. D. B. Richardson. il U.S. News 83:44-5 Ag 1 '77

INDY, Vincent d'

D'Indy; Symphony on a French mountain air. Franck: Symphonic variations and Les djinns. J. Waxman. Am Rec G 40:21-2 Je '77 •

INEBRITY. See Alcoholism

INERTIAL guidance systems

MX inertial units built; photographs. Aviation W 106:79 Ap 4 '77

Standard inertial system effort enters key phase. Aviation W 106:64-5 My 23 '77

Standoff delivery capability advances. il Aviation W 107:65 Jl 18 '77

INFALLIBILITY of the Pope. See Popes—Infallibility

INFANT learning. See Infants—Growth and development

INFANT mortality

Impaired regulation of alveolar ventilation and the sudden infant death syndrome. D. C. Shannon and D. Kelly. bibl il Science 197:367-8 Jl 22 '77

Preventing sudden infant deaths; identifying risk factors. Sci N 112:167 S 10 '77

Reversal of cardiopulmonary failure during active sleep in hypoxic kittens: implications for sudden infant death. T. L. Baker and D. J. McGinty. bibl il Science 198:419-21 O 28 '77

What experts are learning about crib death. A. Rosenblum. il Good H 184:220 F '77

INFANT psychology

Avant-garde parents: traditional infants. Sci N 111:262 Ap 23 '77

Fathering: it's a major role. R. D. Parke and D. B. Sawin. bibl il pors Psychol Today 11:108-9+ N '77

First day of life. C. Spezzano and J. Waterman. bibl il pors Psychol Today 11:110+ D '77

How babies learn about love. T. B. Brazelton. il Redbook 149:101+ Jl '77

INFANTE, Guillermo Cabrera. See Cabrera Infante, G.

INFANTICIDE. See Murder

INFANTILE autism. See Autism

INFANTS

How babies smell. M. R. Carter. Mademoiselle 83:104-5 F '77

Look who won our cover-baby contest! il Good H 185:136-7 O '77

See also

Fetus

Maternal deprivation

Accidents

See Accidents

Care and hygiene

Are you risking your child's health? E. B. Wilson. il Harp Baz 110:87+ Jl '77

I was a mother for six months; father caring for infant. E. Susman. il Good H 185:74+ Jl '77

Infant care: a touching story. E. McCoy. por House & Gard 149:68+ Mr '77

New mothers want to know; questions and answers. M. A. Wessel. See issues of Parents' magazine & better homemaking

See also

Baby sitters

Infants—Nutrition

Clothing

See also

Diapers

Crying

How I learned to cope with my difficult baby. S. Weisser. il por Redbook 150:42+ N '77

Diseases

See also

Allergy

Food and feeding

See Infants—Nutrition

Growth and development

Baby's first year; development of motor coordination. il Good H 185:110-11 Ag '77

Busy, purposeful world of a baby. M. Lewis. bibl il por Psychol Today 10:53-4+ F '77

Infant's world: how babies learn about taste, touch and smell. T. B. Brazelton. il por Redbook 150:24+ N '77

Vestibular stimulation influence on motor development in infants. D. L. Clark and others. bibl il Science 196:1228-9 Je 10 '77

See also

Infant psychology

Names

See Names, Personal

Nutrition

Baby food. il Good H 185:238+ S '77

Baby food revisited. il Consumer Rep 42:165 Mr '77

Baby foods grow up. J. Mayer. il Fam Health 9:36-7+ O '77

Getting your baby off to a good start. J. Chan. McCalls 105:83 N '77

Two baby-food makers take first few faltering steps. Consumer Rep 42:620-1 N '77

When it's time for a bottle. S. F. Trien. il Parents Mag 52:51+ O '77

See also

Breast feeding

Milk, Dried

Psychology

See Infant psychology

Vision

See Vision

INFANTS, Adoption of. See Adoption

INFANTS, Deformed. See Deformities

INFANTS, Newborn

Don't stick out your tongue at a newborn; study by Andrew Meltzoff and M. Keith Moore. J. Gaylin. Psychol Today 11:24+ D '77

Imitation of facial and manual gestures by human neonates. A. N. Meltzoff and M. K. Moore. bibl il Science 198:75-8 O 7 '77

Infant's world: how babies learn about taste, touch and smell. T. B. Brazelton. il por Redbook 150:24+ N '77

Deformities

See Deformities

Diseases

Cytomegalovirus: the newborn's enemy. Sci N 111:373 Je 11 '77

Hospital care

Double miracle that's saving high risk newborns; unit at New York Hospital-Cornell Medical Center. C. M. Dobrish. il Parents Mag 52:35-7 Je '77

INFANTS, Newborn—*Continued*

Psychology

See Infant psychology

Vision

See Vision

INFANTS, Premature

Lesson of retrolental fibroplasia. W. A. Silverman. il Sci Am 236:100-7 bibl(p 142) Je '77

See also

Respiratory distress syndrome

INFANTS food. See Infants—Nutrition

INFANTS rooms. See Nurseries

INFARCTION, Myocardial. See Heart—Diseases

INFECTION

See also

Waterborne infection

INFECTIOUS diseases. See Communicable diseases

INFERTILITY. See Sterility

INFIDELITY, Marital. See Adultery

INFLAMMATION

Inflammatory effects of endotoxin-like contaminants in commonly used protein preparations. L. Z. Bito. bibl il Science 196:83-5 Ap 1 '77

INFLAMMATORY skin diseases. See Skin—Diseases

INFLATABLE boats. See Boats and boating

INFLATION (finance)

Anti-inflation gospel. A. J. Mayer and others. il Newsweek 89:63-4 Ap 25 '77

Behind the fears of another price explosion. il U.S. News 82:38-9 Mr 14 '77

Built-in drag on the stock market—secular inflation. J. Carson-Parker. Bus W p82-3 Mr 14 '77

Burns on the outside. M. Friedman. por Newsweek 91:52-3 Ja 9 '78

Capital commitments and the high cost of money. S. L. Hayes, 3d. bibl f Harvard Bus R 55:155-61 My '77; Discussion. 55:177-8 Jl '77

Carter tackles inflation. D. Pauly and R. Thomas. il Newsweek 89:80+ Ap 11 '77

Case for overthrowing the government; address, June 17, 1977. J. M. Snyder. Vital Speeches 43:717-20 S 15 '77

Debate: how to stop inflation. A. Greenspan; A. Okun. pors Fortune 95:116-20 Ap '77

Drive to keep prices from soaring higher. il U.S. News 82:23-5 Ap 25 '77

Galloping new inflation of fears. Time 109:38+ Mr 14 '77

Great hamburger paradox. D. Warsh. il Forbes 120:166-7 S 15 '77

Great stagflation swamp; address, October 6, 1977. A. M. Okun. Vital Speeches 44:120-5 D 1 '77

Hearing the inflation beat. M. Ruby and others. il Newsweek 89:75-6 F 21 '77

How 80 years of inflation have shrunk your dollar. il U.S. News 83:19 Jl 4 '77

How government itself keeps prices rising. il U.S. News 82:16-17 Ap 18 '77

How inflation swindles the equity investor. W. E. Buffett. il por Fortune 95:250-4+ My '77

Inflation & unemployment: the double whammy! il Sr Schol 110:13-16 N 17 '77

Inflation, interest rates and the Fed; address, July 26, 1977. J. J. Balles. Vital Speeches 43:741-4 O 1 '77

Inflation is now too serious a matter to leave to the economists. D. Warsh and L. Minard; discussion. il Forbes 119:44-6 Ja 15 '77

Inflation is only 6%. il Forbes 120:86 N 1 '77

Inflation: why can't this headache be cured? with interview with H. Stein. il U.S. News 83:15-16+ Ag 22 '77

Is inflation really coming under control? il U.S. News 83:80+ O 17 '77

Is the Federal Reserve building future inflation today? W. Wolman. il Bus W p 110+ S 26 '77

It takes long-range planning to lick inflation. A. Meltzer. il Fortune 96:96-100+ D '77

Jimmy in Wonderland; views of A. Okun and L. Thurow. New Repub 178:2+ Ja 7 '78

Money madness. Nat R 29:1347 N 25 '77

More appropriations—more unemployment. O. G. Hatch. il Nat R 29:942-3 Ag 19 '77

New case of inflationary jitters. il Bus W p26-30 Ap 25 '77

New European unity: a conservative war on inflation. il Bus W p86-7 Je 27 '77

Now it's government itself pushing prices higher and higher. il U.S. News 83:16-17 D 19 '77

Pay, inflation and unemployment; address, September 6, 1977. J. Callaghan. Vital Speeches 44:34-7 N 1 '77

Plan for fighting the double digits. il Time 109:59-60 Ap 18 '77

Prices rise in spite of spare capacity. il Bus W p 120-3+ Mr 21 '77

Real cause of inflation; address, March 16, 1977. H. S. Richey. Vital Speeches 43:386-9 Ap 15 '77

Reports of the death of common stocks are greatly exaggerated. B. Malkiel. il Fortune 96:156-60+ N '77

Scrambling for an inflation policy. E. Lewis. Bus W p 153 D 26 '77

Sinai curve. Nat R 29:983-4 S 2 '77

Stagflation. M. J. Ulmer. New Repub 177:11-13 O 29 '77

What inflation's doing to hunting, fishing. J. O. Cartier. Outdoor Life 160:66+ S '77

Why inflation hits some people less than others. A. Brimmer. il por Nations Bus 65:38-40+ F '77

Why inflation is so hard to stop. il Changing T 31:33-6 Ap '77

Why inflation persists. M. Friedman. il Newsweek 90:84 O 3 '77

Why we should account for inflation. T. D. Flynn. bibl f il Harvard Bus R 55:145-57 S '77

See also

Index linking (economics)

INFLUENCE (psychology)

See also

Persuasion (psychology)

INFLUENZA

Epidemiology of influenza. M. M. Kaplan and R. G. Webster. il map Sci Am 237:88-92+ D '77

New/old flu; A/USSR/77. Time 111:53 Ja 2 '78

1918: the plague year. J. E. Persico. il Sci Digest 81:76-9 Mr '77

Preventive inoculation

Epidemic of swine flu suits. il Bus W p32-3 My 23 '77

Flu shots: another try. J. Seligmann. Newsweek 89:73 F 21 '77

Guillain-Barré: rare disease paralyzes swine flu campaign. P. M. Boffey. Science 195:155-9 Ja 14 '77; Reply. H. M. Gelfand. 195:728-9 F 25 '77

Limited use of flu shots resumed. Sci N 111:117-18 F 19 '77

Mass vaccination: probability of three sudden deaths, letter. M. Gail. il Science 195:934+ Mr 11 '77; Reply. M. Kac and S. I. Rubinow. 196:480 Ap 29 '77

Off-again, on-again flu shots. Time 109:47 F 21 '77

Real victims of the swine-flu fiasco. A. T. Brett. il U.S. News 82:73 Ja 24 '77

Roll down your sleeves. Chemistry 50:5-6 Mr '77

Science is no gentleman's club: lessons of the swine flu debacle. G. A. Silver. Nation 224:166-9 F 12 '77

Swine flu claims pile up in Washington. Bus W p23-4 Ja 24 '77

Swine flu: lessons from a non-epidemic. il Sci N 111:324 My 21 '77

Swine flu vaccinations halted by federal officials. Ret Liv 17:12 F '77

Swine flu vs the people. Sci Digest 81:75-6 F '77

Whatever happened to. . .swine-flu suits: running into the billions of dollars. il U.S. News 84:58 Ja 9 '78

Vaccines

Control of influenza and poliomyelitis with killed virus vaccines. J. Salk and D. Salk. bibl il Science 195:834-47 Mr 4 '77

Swine influenza virus vaccine: potentiation of antibody responses in rhesus monkeys E. L. Stephen and others. bibl il Science 197:1289-90 S 23 '77

INFLUENZA viruses

Fine dissection of virus: no pandemic. il Sci N 111:117 F 19 '77

Persistence of Hong Kong influenza virus variants in pigs. K. F. Shortridge and others. bibl il Science 196:1454-5 Je 24 '77

INFORMANTS. See Informers

INFORMATION, Communication of. See Communication

INFORMATION, Freedom of

Bureaucracy's great paper chase; Freedom of Information Act. Time 110:23-4 D 19 '77

Federal agencies move out of the shadows; Sunshine Act. il Bus W p74-5 Mr 14 '77

Freedom of information: up against the stone wall; Freedom of Information Act. M. Michaelson. Nation 224:614-18 My 21 '77

Growing role of mass media noted by committee. UN Chron 14:33-4 Mr '77

Information Act invoked in contracting. E. Kozicharow. Aviation W 106:19+ F 7 '77

Moon selects target: U.S. information policy; address, June 21, 1977. E. Moon. por Am Lib 8:381 Jl '77

Moonshine; question of rights of the young to access to information. E. Moon; L. N. Gerhardt. SLJ 24:9 S; 5 N '77

Reorganizing U.S. executive agencies. H. C. Relyea. Current 189:17-21 Ja '77

Sunshine Act gets clouded results. il U.S. News 83:58 Jl 4 '77

See also

Freedom of the press

Government and the press

Government information

Intellectual liberty

Journalistic ethics

Security classification (government documents)

INFORMATION, Government. See Government information

INFORMATION display systems
Build the TVT-6: a low-cost direct video display. D. E. Lancaster. il Pop Electr 12:47-52 Jl; 49-55 Ag '77
Digital frequency readout for shortwave receivers. D. L. Mattis. il Pop Electr 11:49-51+ F '77
Everything's coming up digits. M. Meisels. il Motor B & S 139:20+ My '77
Morse code automatic readout on a TV screen. G. R. Steber. il Pop Electr 11:64-5 My '77
See also
Aeronautic instruments—Display systems

INFORMATION Industry Association
10 years old, Information Industry Association grapples with far-reaching issues; annual meeting. P. Doebler. Pub W 212:25-6 N 7 '77

INFORMATION processing, Human. See Human information processing

INFORMATION science
See also
Library science
United States—National Commission on Libraries and Information Science

INFORMATION Science and Automation Division. See American Library Association—Information Science and Automation Division

INFORMATION scientists
Alternative info careers eyed in Syracuse. D. R. Smith. por Lib J 102:1712 S 1 '77

INFORMATION services
AoA issues findings on I&R services. Aging 275: 12-13 S '77
Mobile I and R unit serves elderly in southwest Missouri. G. L. Hartley and L. Tucker. il Aging 266:16-18 D '76
See also
Construction industry—Information services
Health—Information services
Information Industry Association
Libraries—Reference services
Telephone information service
United States—Federal Information Centers
White House Conference on Library and Information Services (proposed)

Finance

SLA/ASIS Janus meet: costs of information scrutinized. N. Savage. Lib J 102:540-1 Mr 1 '77

INFORMATION services, Government
Help! How to cope with it all; national and governmental organizations. J. L. Barkas. Redbook 149:81-8 O '77
Look at all the ways the government will help you. Changing T 31:31-4 Ag '77
See also
Telephone—Government use

INFORMATION storage and retrieval systems
Trends in computers and computing: the information utility. S. E. Madnick. bibl il Science 195:1191-9 Mr 18 '77
See also
College libraries—Automation
Computers
Electronic data processing
Eric
Libraries—Automation

Rates

Database vendors in a price war? Lib J 102:665 Mr 15 '77
IIA sees price war threat in European info tariffs. Lib J 102:1982 O 1 '77

Science

Computer-based chemical information system. S. R. Heller and others. bibl il Science 195:253-9 Ja 21 '77
Three computer-based bibliographic retrieval systems for scientific literature; AGRICOLA, BIOSIS and CAB. M. L. Cittadino and others. il BioScience 27:739-42 N '77

INFORMATION systems, Management
Why data systems in nonprofit organizations fail. R. Herzlinger; discussion. Harvard Bus R 55:54+ Mr '77

INFORMATION tests
Bizquiz. il Duns R 110:33+ S; 37+ O; 39 N; 29+ D '77
Christmas quiz (cont) New Repub 176:32-3 Ja 15 '77
Do you have a space-age mind? G. M. Spruch and L. Spruch. Read Digest 110:127-9 Mr '77
Educators' quiz. M. Rosenberg. See issues of Education digest
Energy-saver's quiz. S. Porter. Ladies Home J 94:16+ O '77
Family quiz game (cont) Parents Mag 52:20+ F; 22 Mr; 34 My; 20 O; 46 N '77
Focus on sunglasses. Fam Health 9:61+ My '77
Food fun: games to teach kids the ABC's of good nutrition. Parents Mag 52:42-3+ Mr '77
Sex test; quiz, excerpt from WNBC television program. D. Luftig. Read Digest 111:78-80 S '77
Take this wintertime safe-driving quiz. J. L. Lippert. il Good H 184:221 F '77
Teenagers & alcohol; quiz. il Sr Schol 110:14-15 O 6 '77
Test your P's and Q's; table manners. A. Storipan. Seventeen 36:32 F '77
What's your nutrition I.Q? Consumer Rep 42: 78-80 F '77; Same abr. with title Test your nutrition I.Q. Read Digest 111:158-60 Ag '77
Will you live to be 100? D. S. Woodruff. il Sr Schol 110:10-11 N 17 '77
You auto take this test. J. Brewer. il Sat Eve Post 249:6+ N '77

INFORMERS
Has the Mafia penetrated the F.B.I? N. Gage. il N Y Times Mag p 14-16+ O 2 '77
Man who called Walter Cronkite a spy; S. Jaffe. T. Branch. il Esquire 87:34-6+ Ap '77
Your cover is showing. R. Boeth and others. il Newsweek 90:66+ N 28 '77

INFRARED agricultural photography. See Photography, Agricultural

INFRARED astronomy
Infrared studies of star formation. M. W. Werner and others. bibl il Science 197:723-32 Ag 19 '77

INFRARED communication systems. See Light communication systems

INFRARED detectors. See Detectors, Infrared

INFRARED films. See Photography—Films

INFRARED photography. See Photography, Infrared

INFRARED radiometers. See Radiometers

INFRARED rays
Infrared reflectance in leaf-sitting neotropical frogs. P. A. Schwalm and P. H. Starrett. bibl il Science 196:1225-7 Je 10 '77
Noninvasive, infrared monitoring of cerebral and myocardial oxygen sufficiency and circulatory parameters. F. F. Jöbsis. bibl il Science 198: 1264-7 D 23 '77

INFRASOUND. See Sound waves

INFRINGEMENT of copyright. See Copyright infringement

INGATE, Margaret Rose
Living with antiques. il Antiques 112:476-81, 492-5 S '77

INGELS, Marty
Problems and pleasures of living together; interview, ed by I. Silden. pors Harp Baz 110: 117+ My '77

INGERSOLL, John H.
Remodeling notebook. See occasional issues of House beautiful

INGERSOLL-Rand Company
Bureaucratic Babylon; address, September 23, 1977. W. L. Wearly. Vital Speeches 44:44-9 N 1 '77

INGERSON, Thomas E. See Walborn, N. R. jt auth

INGHAM, Curtis
New voyager: Greece for travelers, not tourists. bibl Ms 5:56-9+ F '77

INGRAM M-10 machine guns. See Machine guns

INGRES, Jean Auguste Dominique
Looking at paintings. B. Dunstan. il Am Artist 41:74-5 Ag '77 *

INHERITANCE
Rules of inheritance and strategies of mobility in prerevolutionary France. R. E. Giesey. bibl f Am Hist R 82:271-89 Ap '77
See also
Estate planning
Probate law and practice
Wills

INHERITANCE (biology) See Heredity

INHERITANCE of diseases. See Heredity of disease

INHERITANCE tax
Artists' tax bills. B. Chamberlain. Am Artist 42:18+ Ja '78
Burden of joint tenancy. Suc Farm 75:53 N '77
Death and taxes; Philip K. Wrigley family. L. Langway and F. Maier. il Newsweek 90:62 Ag 1 '77
How long to pay estate taxes? B. Harris. Suc Farm 75:56 N '77
Law and your will; interview. W. C. Clay, Jr. il por U.S. News 82:49-50 My 30 '77
Marital deduction: how big? Suc Farm 75:K8 N '77
Tax breaks that help you pass on more to your heirs. il Changing T 31:7-11 Je '77
Will the new estate tax law increase land prices? Suc Farm 75:K2 N '77
See also
Real property and taxation

INHIBITION of enzymes. See Enzymes—Inactivation

INHIBITORS, Metabolic. See Metabolism inhibiting substances

INJECTIONS, Hypodermic
A shot—or two or three—in the breast; silicone breast injection. D. Larned. Ms 6:55+ S '77; Discussion. 6:4+ Ja '78

INJUNCTIONS
U.S. injunction against Stevens? il Time 110:76 D 12 '77

INJURIES. See Burns and scalds; First aid in illness and injury
INLAND navigation
Cracking the tanker safety problem. J. Cameron. il Fortune 95:150-2 Ap '77
See also
Canals—United States
INLAND Sea
Japan's amazing Inland Sea. W. S. Ellis. il map Nat Geog 152:830-63 D '77
INLAND shipping. See Inland water transportation
INLAND Steel Company
Industry problems catch up with Inland. Bus W p72 S 19 '77
INLAND water transportation
Hundred years' war; controversy between barge and railroad transportation in Mississippi Valley. Forbes 119:54 Ja 15 '77
Irrigation, flood control, navigation and user taxes; address, May 6, 1977. J. D. Geary. Vital Speeches 43:536-9 Je 15 '77
New canals for Europe: Russia's invasion path? map U.S. News 82:81 Mr 21 '77
Shipping profits sink with the Great Lakes. il Bus W p29 My 23 '77

Taxation

Taxing waterway use. U.S. News 83:66 S 26 '77
INLAND Waterway. See Intracoastal Waterway
INMONT Corporation-Carrier Corporation merger. See Corporations—Acquisitions and mergers
INNAURATO, Albert
Gemini. Reviews
America 136:363 Ap 16 '77 *
Nation 224:410-11 Ap 2 '77 *
New Yorker 53:84 Mr 28 '77 *
Time 109:95 Mr 28 '77 *
Transfiguration of Benno Blimpie. Reviews
America 136:363-4 Ap 16 '77 *
Nation 224:410-11 Ap 2 '77 *
New Yorker 53:77 Mr 21 '77 *
Sat R 4:42-3 My 14 '77 *
Time 109:95 Mr 28 '77 *
Ulysess in traction. Reviews
Horizon 21:62 Ja '78 *
New Yorker 53:112 D 19 '77 *
INNERPEFFRAY library. See Libraries—Scotland
INNERVATION of brain. See Brain—Innervation
INNERVATION of muscle. See Muscle—Innervation
INNISFREE meteorite. See Meteorites
INNOVATIONS, Technological. See Technological innovations
INNOVATIONS in education. See Educational innovations
INNS. See Hotels, motels, etc.
INNS, Photography of. See Photography of buildings and structures
INOCULATION. See Vaccination
INOSITOL
See also
Phosphatidylinositol
INOUÉ, Shinya, and Okazaki, Kayo
Biocrystals; with biographical sketches. il Sci Am 236:20, 82-4 bibl(p 148) Ap '77
INQUIRER, Philadelphia. See Philadelphia inquirer
INSANE
See also
Mentally ill

Legal status, laws, etc.

See Insanity—Jurisprudence
INSANE, Criminal and dangerous
See also
Forensic psychiatry
Insanity—Jurisprudence
INSANITY
See also
Eccentrics and eccentricities

Jurisprudence

Will he stand trial? D. Berkowitz. D. M. Alpern and S. Agrest. il por Newsweek 90:27-8 Ag 29 '77
See also
Forensic psychiatry
Mentally ill children—Civil rights
INSANITY in art
Stones of madness; psychoanalytic study of Dutch paintings. J. J. Hartman and others. bibl f il Am Imago 33:266-95 Fall '76
INSANITY in motion pictures. See Motion pictures—Plots, themes, etc.
INSCRIPTION Rock. See El Morro National Monument
INSCRIPTIONS
Who really discovered America? ideas of B. Fell. T. Fleming. il Read Digest 110:69-73 F '77
See also
Graffiti
Tablets (paleography)
INSCRIPTIONS, Cuneiform. See Cuneiform inscriptions
INSCRIPTIONS, Sumerian. See Cuneiform inscriptions
INSECT baits and repellents
Insect repellents. il Consumer Rep 42:403-5 Jl '77
INSECT bites and stings
Allergic reaction to insect sting. A. Frank and S. Frank. Mademoiselle 83:134 S '77
Poison! black widow. R. E. Arnold. Field & S 82:37 O '77
Season for insect stings—ways to protect yourself; interview. J. I. Tennenbaum. il U.S. News 82:73 My 9 '77
Sting outdraws bite. il Sci Digest 81:84-5 F '77
INSECT calls. See Insect sounds
INSECT camouflage. See Mimicry (biology)
INSECT control
Applied ecology: showing the way to better insect control. J. L. Marx. il Science 195:860-2 Mr 4 '77
Best plants for chasing bugs. R. Tirrell. il Org Gard & Farm 24:57-61 N '77
Bug juice method: how safe? How effective? il Org Gard & Farm 24:164-9+ My '77
Getting garden pests to bug off. M. C. Goldman. il Org Gard & Farm 24:149-55 Je '77
Greenhouse. J. Kilborn. Horticulture 55:74-5 Ap '77
Operation tsetse fly; livestock vs wildlife in United Nations tsetse fly control project. N. Myers. il Int Wildlife 7:33-5 My '77
Plant traps: a way to outwit your insect foes. K. Kaule and A. Kaule. Org Gard & Farm 24:178-80 Je '77
Protecting the home with herbs. B. Fisher. il Org Gard & Farm 24:148-51 Ap '77
Syringing: a simple, workable insect control. W. Asa. il Org Gard & Farm 24:134+ My '77
What to do about those annoying household pests. bibl il Consumers Res Mag 60:20-3 Ap '77
See also
Cockroach control
Flies—Control
Insecticides
Mosquito control
Pest control operators
Spruce budworms—Control
Termite control

Biological control

Business of biological control. K. Shea. bibl il Environment 19:15-19 My '77
Controlling the pink bollworm by disrupting sex pheromone communication between adult moths. L. K. Gaston and others. bibl il Science 196:904-5 My 20 '77
Exotic forest saved by foreign sting. il Sci N 112:69 Jl 30 '77
Improving lady beetle efficiency. il Org Gard & Farm 25:46-9 Ja '78
North American egg parasite successfully controls a different host genus in South America. A. T. Drooz and others. bibl il Science 197:390-1 Jl 22 '77
Suppressing insects pays off. J. Goldstein. il Org Gard & Farm 24:148+ N '77
USDA's profound change: to help farmers naturally. J. Cox. por Org Gard & Farm 24:48-52 S '77
Viruses and the biological control of insect pests. T. W. Tinsley. bibl il BioScience 27:659-61 O '77
INSECT eating by animals. See Animals—Food and feeding
INSECT evolution. See Evolution
INSECT genetics
Extrinsic versus intrinsic factors in the evolution of insect sociality. H. E. Evans. bibl BioScience 27:613-17 S '77
Genetic rescue of a lethal null activity allele of 6-phosphogluconate dehydrogenase in drosophila melanogaster. M. B. Hughes and J. C. Lucchesi. bibl il Science 196:1114-15 Je 3 '77
Mechanism of suppression in drosophila: control of sepiapterin synthase at the purple locus. J. J. Yim and others. bibl il Science 198:1168-70 D 16 '77
Neuron duplication and deletions in locust clones and clutches. C. S. Goodman. bibl il Science 197:1384-6 S 30 '77
Sympatric speciation based on allelic changes at three loci: evidence from natural populations in two habitats. C. A. Tauber and M. J. Tauber. bibl Science 197:1298-9 S 23 '77
Two genes control seasonal isolation in sibling species. C. A. Tauber and others. bibl il Science 197:592-3 Ag 5 '77
INSECT repellents. See Insect baits and repellents
INSECT sex attractants
Are you what you eat? il Chemistry 50:22 My '77
Controlling the pink bollworm by disrupting sex pheromone communication between adult moths. L. K. Gaston and others. bibl il Science 196:904-5 My 20 '77
Identification of the female Japanese beetle sex pheromone: inhibition of male response by an enantiomer. J. H. Tumlinson and others. bibl il Science 197:789-92 Ag 19 '77

INSECT sex attractants—*Continued*
Moth mating: role of diet challenged. Sci N 111:37 Ja 15 '77
Sexual calling behavior in primitive ants. B. Hölldobler and C. P. Haskins. bibl il Science 195:793-4 F 25 '77

INSECT societies
Behavioral control of workers by queens in primitively eusocial bees. M. D. Breed and G. J. Gamboa. bibl il Science 195:694-6 F 18 '77
Genetics of generation gap in insects. Sci N 111:278 Ap 30 '77
Local mate competition and parental investment in social insects. R. D. Alexander and P. W. Sherman. bibl Science 196: 494-500 Ap 29 '77

INSECT song. See Insect sounds

INSECT sounds
Of cricket song and sex. W. Cade. il Natur Hist 87:64-73 bibl(p 108-9) Ja '78

INSECT traps
Easy-to-build insect traps. S. Smyser and R. Weinsteiger. il Org Gard & Farm 24:112-14+ Jl '77

INSECTICIDES
Chemical insect control—a troubled pest management strategy. R. F. Luck and others. bibl il BioScience 27:606-11 S '77
Chitin synthesis inhibitors: new class of insecticides; diflubenzuron. J. L. Marx. il Science 197: 1170+ S 16 '77
Consumer's guide to: insect fighters. il Mech Illus 73:18 Jl '77
Insecticide solvents: interference with insecticidal action. L. B. Brattsten and C. F. Wilkinson. bibl il Science 196:1211-13 Je 10 '77
Polychlorobornane components of toxaphene: structure-toxicity relations and metabolic reductive dechlorination. M. A. Saleh and others. bibl il Science 198:1256-8 D 23 '77
Rootworm buildup threatens 1977 corn. D. Seim. il Farm J 101:34-5+ Ja '77
Safe insecticides; chitin synthesis inhibitors. il Chemistry 50:23 N '77
See also
Insect baits and repellents

Injurious effects

Canada's moth war; efforts to halt spruce budworm spraying program due to increase in Reye's syndrome cases. E. E. May. bibl il map Environment 19:16-24 Ag '77
Careless Kepone; James River contamination. F. S. Sterrett and C. A. Boss. bibl il map Environment 19:30-6 Mr '77
Kepone-induced scoliosis and its histological consequences in fish. J. A. Couch and others. bibl il Science 197:585-7 Ag 5 '77
Pollution postscripts; Minamata disease and Kepone poisoning. E. Keerdoja. il Newsweek 89:12 Ap 4 '77
Profile of a deadly pesticide; Phosvel. K. Shea. bibl il Environment 19:6-12 Ja '77

INSECTIVOROUS plants
Leafy jaws: the plants that eat animals; excerpt from Carnivorous plants of the United States and Canada. D. E. Schnell. il Sci Digest 81:7-10+ My '77

INSECTS
See also
Fertilization of plants
Nervous system—Insects
Parasites—Insects
Photography of insects
also names of insects, e.g. May flies

Anatomy

Antiallatotropins: inhibition of corpus allatum development. W. S. Bowers and R. Martinez-Pardo. bibl il Science 197:1369-71 S 30 '77
See also
Malpighian vessels

Control

See Insect control

Development

Aldehyde oxidase compartmentalization in Drosophila melanogaster wing imaginal disks. D. T. Kuhn and G. N. Cunningham. bibl il Science 196:875-7 My 20 '77
In vitro growth of imaginal disks from drosophila melanogaster. K. T. Davis and A. Shearn. bibl il Science 196:438-40 Ap 22 '77
Temporal control of urate oxidase activity in drosophila: evidence of an autonomous timer in Malpighian tubules. T. B. Friedman and D. H. Johnson. bibl il Science 197:477-9 Jl 29 '77

Export-import problems

Keeping insects in the zoo. BioScience 27:72-3 Ja '77

Eyes

See Eye (insects)

Food and feeding

Are you what you eat? il Chemistry 50:22 My '77
Chemical basis for feeding adaptation of pine sawflies neodiprion rugifrons and neodiprion swainei. T. Ikeda and others. bibl il Science 197:497-9 Jl 29 '77
Degradation and detoxification of canavanine by a specialized seed predator. G. A. Rosenthal and others. bibl il Science 196:658-60 My 6 '77
Extraordinary images show how beetles have adapted to live off plants, and each other. J. Lawrence. il Horticulture 55:8-13 D '77
Game of the bees. B. Heinrich. il Horticulture 55:38-9+ Jl '77
Herbivore-plant interactions: mixed-function oxidases and secondary plant substances. L. B. Brattsten and others. bibl il Science 196: 1349-52 Je 17 '77
Moth mating: role of diet challenged. Sci N 111:37 Ja 15 '77

Habits and behavior

Extrinsic versus intrinsic factors in the evolution of insect sociality. H. E. Evans. bibl BioScience 27:613-17 S '77
Man's obsession reveals the riches of a hidden world; Dr S. Y. Lee. T. Green. il por Smithsonian 8:80-7 bibl(p 161) N '77
Pit and the antlion. H. Topoff. il Natur Hist 86: 64-71 bibl(p 100-1) Ap '77
Resource partitioning in bumble bees: the role of behavioral factors. D. H. Morse. bibl il Science 197:678-80 Ag 12 '77
Weaver ants: social establishment and maintenance of territory. B. Holldobler and E. O. Wilson. bibl il Science 195:900-2 Mr 4 '77
See also
Insect societies
Mimicry (biology)
Sexual behavior—Insects

Host plants

See Insects—Food and feeding

Molting

See Molting

Photographs

Magnifications; excerpt. D. Scharf. il Harpers 255:55-9 Jl '77

Reproduction

Ovarian dynamics in heliconiine butterflies: programmed senescence versus eternal youth. H. Dunlap-Pianka and others. bibl il Science 197: 487-90 Jl 29 '77

Periodicity

See Biology—Periodicity

Temperature

See Temperature, Animal and human

Vision

See Vision (insects)

INSECTS, Aquatic
Unseen life of a mountain stream. W. H. Amos. il Nat Geog 151:562-80 Ap '77

INSECTS, Effect of temperature on
Insects and spiders—how they spend the winter. J. Serrao. il Conservationist 31:26-8 N '76

INSECTS, Injurious and beneficial
Buggy cosmopolis in your garden; identifying and photographing common insects. il Sunset 158:112-17 bibl(p291) My '77
Garden critters worth cultivating. S. Coulter. il Bet Hom & Gard 55:202+ My '77
See also
United States—Agriculture, Department of—Animal and Plant Health Inspection Service
also names of insects, e.g. Ladybirds

Biological control

See Insect control—Biological control

Control

See Insect control

INSECTS, Predatory
See also
Ladybirds

INSECTS, Sound production by. See Insect sounds

INSECTS, Stinging
See also
Insect bites and stings

INSECTS and children. See Children and animals

INSECTS as carriers of infection
Mrs Murray's mystery disease; Lyme arthritis discovered. E. Keiffer. il por Good H 184:80+ Mr '77
See also
Mosquitoes as carriers of infection

INSECTS as food
Layman's guide to entomophagy. P. Magida; discussion. il Int Wildlife 7:34-5 Jl '77

INSEL, Paul M. and Lindgren, H. C.
Too close for comfort; excerpt. bibl il pors Psychol Today 11:100-1+ D '77

INSEMINATION, Artificial. See Artificial insemination; Artificial insemination, Human

INSOMNIA
Can't get a good night's sleep? Changing T 31:13-15 Ap '77
Do you dream (perchance) of sleeping? C. Kahn. Fam Health 9:36-9+ S '77
How to get a night's sleep; interview. E. D. Weitzman. il por U.S. News 83:62-4 Ag 8 '77
Tossing & turning all night? Read this . . . and fall asleep; questions and answers. M. Davidson and N. Ponnamperuma. Sci Digest 81:13-17 Ap '77
See also
Hypnotics
INSPECTION of buildings. See Building inspection
INSPECTION of food. See Food adulteration and inspection
INSPECTION of ships. See Ships—Inspection
INSTALMENT plan
Whose car is it? il Forbes 120:197 N 15 '77
INSTANT print cameras. See Cameras, Instant print
INSTANT print motion picture cameras. See Motion picture cameras, Instant print
INSTITUT de Recherche et Coordination Acoustique/Musique. See Paris—Georges Pompidou Center
INSTITUTE for International Development, Inc
Saying God loves you to a starving man; interview, ed by D. Kucharsky. A. A. Whittaker. pors Chr Today 21:17-21 Ap 1 '77
INSTITUTE for Policy Studies
IPS faces life. E. Yoffe. New Repub 177:16-18 Ag 6 '77
INSTITUTE for Political and Legal Education. See Political science—Study and teaching
INSTITUTE for the Future
Camelia report; teleconferencing systems. Sci Digest 82:48-53 S '77
INSTITUTE of Ecology
Ecology interns report—new perspectives gained from Washington experience. E. J. Christy and K. Weaver. il pors BioScience 27:631-3 S '77
TIE: a new beginning for a child of promise. E. M. Leeper. BioScience 27:495-8 Jl '77
INSTITUTE of Electrical and Electronic Engineers
Getting and Hogan win IEEE races. J. Walsh. Science 198:1018 D 9 '77
IEEE: a policy challenge for big engineering society. J. Walsh. Science 197:741-4 Ag 19 '77
INSTITUTE of Law and Aging. See George Washington University, Washington, D.C.—National Law Center
INSTITUTE of Politics, John F. Kennedy School of Government. See Harvard University—John F. Kennedy School of Government—Institute of Politics
INSTITUTE of Society, Ethics and Life Sciences
Ethics of miracles. K. L. Woodward. il Newsweek 90:115+ S 19 '77
INSTITUTE of Scrap Iron and Steel
Scrap dealers see red over salvage bill; Texas regulation of automobile salvage business. Am City & County 92:28 Ap '77
INSTITUTE of Student Opinion. See Scholastic Research Center
INSTITUTES, Library. See Library institutes and workshops
INSTITUTIONAL investments
Who owns American industry? the big shifts under way. il U.S. News 83:70-1 Jl 18 '77
INSTITUTIONS, Correctional. See Reformatories
INSTITUTIONS, Financial. See Financial institutions
INSTITUTIONS, Nonprofit
Getting management help to the nonprofit sector; Volunteer Urban Consulting Group of New York City. R. A. Mittenthal and B. W. Mahoney. il Harvard Bus R 55:95-103 S '77
Lobbying rules for nonprofits: new option sets specific limits. J. Walsh. Science 196:40+ Ap 1 '77
Why data systems in nonprofit organizations fail. R. Herzlinger; discussion. Harvard Bus R 55:54+ Mr '77

Taxation

IRS theology; definition of church. Chr Cent 94:213 Mr 9 '77
INSTITUTO Fénix. See Spanish language—Study and teaching
INSTRASTATE airlines. See Airlines—Local service
INSTRUCTION. See Education; Teaching
INSTRUCTIONAL materials. See Teaching—Aids and devices
INSTRUCTIONAL materials centers
Center for audio-visual development; the Clark Kerr Learning Resources Hall on the University of California campus in Santa Barbara; with introd by J. Nairn. il Archit Rec 162:85-8 Jl '77
Congress enacts NEA teacher center bill. Todays Educ 66:74-5 Mr '77
Mediacentric. D. P. Baker. Wilson Lib Bull 52:308-9 D '77
Mediacentric (cont) B. Fast. Wilson Lib Bull 51:572-3, 732-3; 52:133-5 Mr, My, O '77
Osceola teacher education center. L. Olson and others. Todays Educ 66:75-6+ Mr '77
Teacher utilization of instructional media centers in secondary schools. H. R. Johnson. bibl Clearing H 51:117-20 N '77
See also
School libraries
United States—Education, Office of—Educational Materials Review Center
INSTRUMENT flying. See Aviation—Instrument flying
INSTRUMENT landing. See Airplanes—Landing
INSTRUMENT panels
How to dress up your projects. R. Devoe. il Pop Electr 12:53-5 N '77

Lighting

See also
Boats—Instrument panels—Lighting
INSTRUMENTAL ensembles
Group for Contemporary Music; Charles Wuorinen, Harvey Sollberger, and Nicolas Roussakis. M. Blechner. il Hi Fi 27:MA24-5 N '77
New York (city); Waverly Consort performance of Le roman de Fauvel. F. J. Warnke. Opera N 41:29 Ja 22 '77
Strike up the shawm; Waverly Consort at the Cloisters. H. Saal. il Newsweek 91:55 Ja 2 '78
Waverly Consort: Fauvel; performance on October 20. il Hi Fi 27:MA34 F '77
See also
Quartets, Instrumental
Trios, Instrumental
INSTRUMENTAL music
See also
Keyboard instrument music

Instruction and study

See Music—Instruction and study
INSTRUMENTAL trios. See Trios, Instrumental
INSTRUMENTS
See also
Musical instruments
Nautical instruments
Scientific apparatus and instruments
INSULATING materials

Manufacture

See Building materials industry
INSULATING shutters. See Shutters
INSULATING window panels. See Panel construction
INSULATION (heat)
Energy outlook for windows. S. Oddo. il House & Gard 149:134-5+ S '77
For cozy, fuel-saving winter survival, build a warm room. E. Powell. il Pop Sci 211:110-12 N '77
Four ways to cut your home-heating costs. il Good H 185:240+ O '77
Give your house an energy update. V. McNiff. House & Gard 149:38 Jl '77
Happiness is a warm room. il Mech Illus 73:108+ D '77
Heat-leak locator. H. Shuldiner. il Pop Sci 212:83 Ja '78
Heat-wasting doors: you can plug the leaks. T. H. Jones. il Pop Sci 211:128+ D '77
Here comes winter; is your house ready? Ladies Home J 94:145+ S '77; Same. il Redbook 149:215 S '77
How much insulation do you need? thermography consultants. House & Gard 149:96 S '77
Insulation. B. Niles. il Am Home 80:82+ S '77; Same. McCalls 104:122-3 S '77
Insulation: making your house snug. J. Morgan. House & Gard 149:102 My '77
Insulation shortage. il Am Home 80:14 D '77
Insulation upgrade—plug those leaks your builder left. A. Lees. il Pop Sci 211:144+ S '77
Sales heat up for home insulation. il Bus W p31-2 F 28 '77
Super insulation for your attic. il Mech Illus 74:98-9 Ja '78
See also
Clothing, Cold weather
Weatherstripping

Tax credit

See Tax credits
INSULATORS, Acoustic. See Audio systems—Equipment
INSULIN
DNA and insulin; recombinant DNA research. Newsweek 89:74 Je 6 '77
One for the gene engineers; inserting human insulin gene into DNA of escherichia coli. il Time 109:68 Je 6 '77
Rat insulin gene spliced into bacteria. Sci N 111:340 My 28 '77
INSULTS, Verbal. See Invective
INSURANCE
How much insurance? J. Train. por Forbes 120:134-5 N 1 '77
How to cut your insurance costs and still be safe. M. Daly. Bet Hom & Gard 55:86+ Ap '77

INSURANCE—*Continued*
Q & A about insurance. A. F. Blum. por Ret Liv 17:48 Je; 16 N '77
Ye olde negative sell; underwriting by Americans at Lloyd's. il Forbes 120:127+ N 15 '77

Laws and legislation

See Insurance law

Marketing

Insurance sales; careers for women. D. Duke. Mademoiselle 83:197 F '77
See also
Insurance agents

Policies

Insurance. L. David. Mech Illus 73:22 N '77
Rig writer. por Forbes 119:78 Mr 1 '77
Why women need insurance, too. R. Provost. Parents Mag 52:20+ Ap '77
See also
Insurance, Life—Policies

Rates and tables

Why insurance premiums pay off for everybody. il Nations Bus 65:90+ N '77
See also
Insurance, Automobile—Rates and tables

Reinsurance

Insurance companies' insurance company; Swiss Reinsurance Company. R. Ball. il Fortune 95:154-9 Je '77

Risks

Big push in risk management. J. Perham. il Duns R 109:62-4 Je '77
Risk management: new ways for business to insure against loss. J. Cosgrove. il Nations Bus 65:75-8+ N '77

INSURANCE, Accident
See also
Insurance, Liability

INSURANCE, Agricultural
See also
Insurance, Government

Hail

See Insurance, Hail

INSURANCE, Atomic hazards
Testing the liability of nuclear operators; Price-Anderson Act. il Bus W p38-9 O 10 '77

INSURANCE, Automobile
Auto insurance. J. Scagnetti. il Motor T 29:93-8 D '77; 30:71-7 Ja '78
Automotive redlining draws consumer fire. map Bus W p24 Je 6 '77
Buying auto insurance. A. K. Dukes. Mademoiselle 83:113 O '77
Changes in auto insurance that may affect you. Changing T 31:37-8 Ap '77
Fresh boost for no-fault auto insurance. U.S. News 82:70 Je 27 '77
Insurance ratings: how to beat their system. T. Cook. Car & Dr 22:28 Je '77
Managing your auto insurance. il Consumer Rep 42:318-20, 375-84, 484-9 Je-Ag '77
No-fault insurance—how it's working. il map U.S. News 83:35-6 S 26 '77
Record number of complaints on auto insurance filed by drivers in New York. Ret Liv 17:13-14 My '77
Rising cost of auto insurance. R. Taylor. il Car & Dr 22:63+ Ap '77
Who will pay that auto insurance claim? Changing T 31:29-30 Ag '77
Yes or no for no-fault insurance. J. O'Connell. il America 137:261-5 O 22 '77
See also
Allstate Insurance Company

Rates and tables

Car insurance: how your rates are set. R. Clayton. il Pop Mech 147:177-8+ F '77

INSURANCE, Aviation
Tenerife case may alter liability rules. il Aviation W 106:32 Ap 4 '77

INSURANCE, Business
Equitable courts small business. Bus W p 114 Je 20 '77

INSURANCE, Casualty
See also
Insurance, Disaster
Insurance, Property

INSURANCE, Dental
Insurance that covers the dentist bills. il Changing T 31:43-4 My '77

INSURANCE, Disability
Rush for disability pay proves a mounting burden for taxpayers. il U.S. News 83:104-6 O 17 '77
Work injuries and earnings of partially disabled men in California. W. Vroman. il M Labor R 100:58-60 Ap '77
Workers' compensation compared with other disability programs. M. Berkowitz. il M Labor R 100:57-8 Ap '77

INSURANCE, Disaster
Congress mulls over disaster insurance. R. D. Wennblom. Farm J 101:27 Ap '77

INSURANCE, Fire
See also
Arson

INSURANCE, Flood
See also
Insurance, Government

INSURANCE, Government
Congress may gut Federal floodplains policy. B. J. Culliton. Science 197:848 Ag 26 '77
Crop insurance based on your yield records; Federal plans. Farm J 101:62 N '77
Insurance: a freshet of flood coverage; Federal flood insurance. Bus W p38 Ap 11 '77
Under water; flood insurance program. Forbes 120:58 O 1 '77
Wanted: an agent for HUD's flood insurance. Bus W p48+ S 19 '77

INSURANCE, Hail
Should you carry hail insurance? D. Allen. Suc Farm 75:no3 F20 F '77

INSURANCE, Health
Are national health service systems converging? Predictions for the United States. O. W. Anderson. bibl f Ann Am Acad 434:24-38 N '77
See also
Insurance, Dental
Insurance, Disability

Great Britain

See also
Great Britain—National Health Service

United States

AMA vs. HMOs. E. Marshall. New Repub 177:9-11 O 29 '77
AMA's health plan. R. E. Palmer. por Newsweek 89:11 Je 6 '77
Abortion double standard; medicaid vs health insurance coverage. New Repub 177:12 O 15 '77
Adding insult to injury; Blue Cross. il Forbes 119:33-4 Mr 1 '77
Blue Cross. E. Marshall. New Repub 177:9-12 Jl 2 '77
Blue Cross bearing down. il Time 110:67 Ag 29 '77
Carter going slow on national health insurance. B. J. Culliton. Science 195:467 F 4 '77
Carter's health plans; labor's push for national health insurance. E. Marshall. New Repub 177:10-12 D 10 '77
Case for national health insurance. M. W. Fine. bibl f Cur Hist 73:13-16+ Jl '77; Same. Current 196:26-32 O '77
Chances for health Insurance—bleak in '77. U.S. News 82:35 F 14 '77
Coming: an overhaul of health programs. il U.S. News 82:76 F 28 '77
Containing the cost of employee health plans; health maintenance organizations. il Bus W p74-6 My 30 '77
Cutting medical-insurance costs; new Blue Shield programs. J. Chan. il McCalls 104:57 S '77
Danse macabre; Hyde amendment. M. Kinsley. New Repub 177:13+ N 19 '77
Health costs containment; address, August 9, 1977. W. E. Ryan. Vital Speeches 43:753-6 O 1 '77
Health insurance: are you covered? P. Gross. House & Gard 149:46+ Ap '77
Health insurance: how much coverage do you need? T. Cohen and M. Miner. Harp Baz 110:87+ Ag '77
Health insurance stalled. D. S. Greenberg. Sci Digest 81:55-7 Mr '77
How business can help cut health-care costs. il Nations Bus 65:16-20 F '77
Kaiser and the desert doctors: a way to cut medical bills; prepaid health care. L. Smith. il Duns R 109:23+ My '77
Michigan's clamp on doctor bills; Blue Cross and Blue Shield plan. Bus W p34 D 19 '77
National health care planning; address, October 27, 1977. J. A. Califano. Vital Speeches 44:112-14 D 1 '77
National health insurance: a social placebo? K. Leffler. bibl f Cur Hist 73:17-21+ Jl '77
Proposed health insurance plans in the United States, 1977-1978. Cur Hist 73:inside back cover Jl '77
Radical cure for high medical costs. C. Peters. por Newsweek 89:11 Mr 18 '77
Radical prescription for medical care. A. F. Ehrbar. il Fortune 95:164-70+ F '77
This month's feature: controversy in Congress over national health insurance proposals. Cong Digest 56:193-224 Ag '77
Uproar over medical bills; with interview with W. J. McNerney. J. Mann. il U.S. News 82:35-40+ Mr 28 '77
Voluntary health insurance. W. J. McNerney. Cur Hist 73:9-12+ Jl '77
Why America must have national health insurance. R. A. Hankin. Intellect 105:340-1 Ap '77
Your health insurance: be sure you have what you need. il Changing T 31:45-7 Je '77
See also
Medicare

INSURANCE, Homeowners
Filing home-insurance claim? you may be in for a shock. il U.S. News 82:77-8 F 21 '77

INSURANCE, Hospitalization. See Insurance, Health

INSURANCE, Liability
Croquet, anyone? athletic-injury awards in California. L. Langway and D. Gram. il Newsweek 90:72-3 S 5 '77
Premiums on city life; municipal liability insurance. L. Minard. Forbes 119:96+ Mr 15 '77
Suppose someone sues you for a million. Changing T 31:34 N '77
See also
Insurance, Atomic hazards
Insurance, Aviation
Insurance, Malpractice liability
Insurance, Products Liability
Insurance, Space flight

INSURANCE, Life
See also
Annuities

Agents

See Insurance agents

Income policy

Menopause: it's a disease, says insurance company; exclusion from income protection policies. B. Canon. Ms 5:22 Mr '77

Marketing

See Insurance—Marketing

Policies

Adjustable life insurance. il Changing T 31:17-19 O '77
Answers to some life insurance questions. Changing T 31:29-30 D '77
Campus life insurance at best a delusion, at worst a snare. il Consumer Rep 42:168-71 Mr '77
Life insurance: what you'd better know before you buy. il Changing T 31:36-40 Mr '77
Your family corporation can pay your life insurance. Farm J 101:B2 O '77

INSURANCE, Litigation
Another option: the group legal-service plan. Consumer Rep 42:288-90 My '77
Consumers challenge legal monopoly. D. Maron. Intellect 105:333-5 Ap '77
Insurance to cover the lawyer's bill; Blue Cross plan. Bus W p46-7 Ap 18 '77
New fringe benefit: prepaid legal help. il U.S. News 83:70 Ag 29 '77

INSURANCE, Malpractice liability
Dip in malpractice rates; Aetna's and St Paul Fire's loss control programs. il Bus W p 109-10 O 3 '77
Functions of an insurance company: insurance aspects of legal malpractice; address, February 26, 1977. F. J. McCarthy. Vital Speeches 43:394-8 Ap 15 '77
Malpractice policies that earn profits. Bus W p37-8 Mr 21 '77
Medical malpractice. Consumer Rep 42:544-8, 598-601, 674-7 S-N '77

INSURANCE, Maternity
See also
Maternity benefits

INSURANCE, Motor vehicle
Insurance for mobile sportsmen. B. Behme. Field & S 82:52-3 Jl '77
Transportation projects face insurance coverage problems. Aging 275:11-12 S '77

INSURANCE, Municipal liability. See Insurance, Liability

INSURANCE, No-fault. See Insurance, Automobile; Insurance, Liability

INSURANCE, Physicians liability. See Insurance, Malpractice liability

INSURANCE, Products liability
Business and the products liability crisis; legal aspects of no-fault insurance; address, October 27, 1976. J. O'Connell. Vital Speeches 43:278-80 F 15 '77
Europe: a liability threat to U.S.-bound exports. il Bus W p42 Mr 14 '77
New bill in Congress, if enacted, spells tax relief for firms subjected to liability exposures; Product Liability Insurance Tax Equity Act of 1977. A. T. Kornblut. Archit Rec 162:53 D '77
Sue syndrome. D. Pauly and others. il Newsweek 89:61-2 Ap 4 '77

INSURANCE, Property
Insurance redlining: a new urban setback. J. De Muth. America 137:438-40 D 17 '77
See also
Insurance, Homeowners

INSURANCE, Social. See Social security

INSURANCE, Space flight
Interest in satellite insurance grows. Aviation W 107:53-4 O 24 '77

INSURANCE, Surgical. See Insurance, Health

INSURANCE, Survivors. See Social security

INSURANCE, Unemployment

United States

Behind the unemployment numbers. M. Friedman. il Newsweek 89:63 F 7 '77
Can your budget afford unemployment compensation? local government employees. Am City & County 92:103-4+ S '77
Hidden crisis in jobless pay. il Bus W p20-1 Ja 24 '77
Jobless pay funds go deeper in debt. il Bus W p30 F 21 '77
6 ways to cut the jobless taxes you pay. J. Carroll. Nations Bus 65:64+ Mr '77
State unemployment insurance: legislative changes in 1976. J. A. Hickey. il M Labor R 100:46-51 F '77
Tightening up unemployment pay rules. Nations Bus 65:58-60+ Mr '77
Unemployment comp is middle-class welfare. E. Marshall. New Repub 176:16-18 F 19 '77
Unemployment insurance data. See issues of Monthly labor review

INSURANCE, Workmens compensation
For a better workers' compensation system. D. M. Kasper. Harvard Bus R 55:6-8 Mr '77
From the people who brought you full employment; insurance coverage of boatyard and marina workers. B. O'Donovan. il Motor B & S 139:81-3+ Je '77
How job-injury benefits are rising. il Nations Bus 65:38-40 Je '77
Who pays when household help gets hurt? Changing T 31:16 S '77
Will workers' compensation standards be mandated by federal legislation? J. F. Burton. bibl M Labor R 100:55-7 Ap '77
Work injuries and earnings of partially disabled men in California. W. Vroman. il M Labor R 100:58-60 Ap '77
Workers' compensation compared with other disability programs. M. Berkowitz. il M Labor R 100:57-8 Ap '77
Workers' compensation laws: major amendments in 1976. A. S. Hribal and G. Minor. il M Labor R 100:39-45 F '77
Workers' compensation laws—significant enactments in 1977. A. S. Hribal. M Labor R 100:25-33 D '77

INSURANCE agents
New arms for an army of insurance agents; life insurance agents. E. Carruth. Fortune 95:132-4 Ap '77

INSURANCE companies
Bounce-back champ; SAFECO. il Forbes 119:80+ Je 15 '77
Country slicker's progress; Republic Financial Services. por Forbes 120:67+ D 1 '77
Dip in malpractice rates; Aetna's and St Paul Fire's loss control programs. il Bus W p 109-10 O 3 '77
Directors who get to the heart of a problem; United Services Life Insurance Co. il Nations Bus 65:36-7 Jl '77
Functions of an insurance company: insurance aspects of legal malpractice; address, February 26, 1977. F. J. McCarthy. Vital Speeches 43:394-8 Ap 15 '77
Heck of a sales force; American Family Life Assurance Co. B. McMennamin. por Forbes 119:53-5 Mr 1 '77
In prosperity, prepare for adversity; Insurance Company of North America. Forbes 120:132 N 15 '77
Labor's own Union Labor Life Insurance Co. Forbes 119:88 My 15 '77
Life and casualty insurers meet head-on. il Bus W p86-7 Ag 29 '77
Magic returns for mortgage insurers. il Bus W p 104+ D 5 '77
Malpractice policies that earn profits; bedpan mutuals. Bus W p37-8 Mr 21 '77
Profitable exclusivity; United Services Automobile Association. E. Bailey. il Forbes 120:111 N 15 '77
Ticor launches another round of diversification. por Bus W p 113-14 O 31 '77
Wanted: an agent for HUD's flood insurance. Bus W p48+ S 19 '77
What insurance companies do to women: a new look. B. Myerson. por Redbook 149:74+ Je '77
See also
Allstate Insurance Company
Bankers Life and Casualty Company
Equitable Life Assurance Society of the United States
Government Employees Insurance Company
Hartford Fire Insurance Company
Metropolitan Life Insurance Company
Northwestern Mutual Life Insurance Company
Prudential Insurance Company of America

Acquisitions and mergers

Sweeter offer for Richmond Corp; American General Insurance Company offer. il Bus W p30 Ap 11 '77

Employees

See also
Insurance agents

INSURANCE companies—*Continued*

Finance

Finance. il Forbes 121:119-22 Ja 9 '78
How to create value by moving assets around. Bus W p70 Je 6 '77
Insurance companies turn to public markets. Bus W p98 O 24 '77
Story behind casualty insurance companies' roller-coaster years. il Nations Bus 65:82+ N '77

Foreign business

Germans are coming! Germans are coming! foreign property and casualty insurance companies in United States. il Forbes 120:74-5 O 1 '77

Holding companies

See Insurance holding companies

Securities

Mergers may revive life insurance stocks. D. G. Santry. il Bus W p 107 S 12 '77

Social aspects

Impact of the insurance enterprise on socio-economic forces; address, August 10, 1977. J. S. Kemper Vital Speeches 43:708-10 S 15 '77

Statistics

Fifty largest life-insurance companies. il Fortune 96:164-5 Jl '77

Great Britain

See also
Lloyd's, London

Switzerland

Insurance companies' insurance company; Swiss Reinsurance Company. R. Ball. il Fortune 95: 154-9 Je '77

INSURANCE Company of North America. See Insurance companies

INSURANCE holding companies
Insurer's spectacular rise; Holding Corp of America. il por Bus W p69-70+ Je 6 '77

INSURANCE industry. See Insurance companies

INSURANCE law
Bringing sexual equality to insurance. il Bus W p 116 My 23 '77
Emerging scandal in medical coverage; Multiple Employer Benefit Trusts. Bus W p22-3 Jl 4 '77

INSURANCE policies. See Insurance—Policies

INSURANCE premiums. See Insurance—Rates and tables

INSURANCE salesmen. See Insurance agents

INSURANCE stocks. See Insurance companies—Securities

INTAKE manifolds. See Manifolds

INTEGRAL Urban House, Berkeley, Calif. See Farms, Organic

INTEGRATED circuit testers. See Testing instruments

INTEGRATED circuits. See Electronic circuits, Integrated

INTEGRATED optics
See also
Fiber optics
Light communication systems

INTEGRATED Pest Management services. See Pest control operators

INTEGRATION of public schools. See Public Schools—Desegregation

INTEL Corporation. See Electronic industries—United States

INTELLECT
See also
Intelligence

INTELLECTUAL development of children. See Children—Growth and development

INTELLECTUAL liberty
Treason of the clerisy. C. Williamson, Jr. Harpers 256:88-90+ Ja '78
See also
Academic freedom
American Civil Liberties Union
American Library Association—Intellectual Freedom Committee
Libraries and intellectual liberty
Science, Freedom of

INTELLECTUAL life
See also subhead Intellectual life under names of countries, e.g. Russia—Intellectual life

INTELLECTUALS
Common sense; reason and intellectuals. G. Niemeyer. Nat R 29:557 My 13 '77
Educated persons should serve as society's conscience. R. Howell, Jr. por Intellect 106:185 N '77
Political superstition and the intellectuals. A. Kazin. Esquire 88:42+ N '77
See also
Scholars

INTELLIGENCE
Post-human intelligence; excerpt from Until the sun dies. R. Jastrow. Natur Hist 86:12-13+ Je '77

INTELLIGENCE, Business. See Business intelligence

INTELLIGENCE, Military. See Military intelligence

INTELLIGENCE, Select Committee on. See United States—Congress—House—Intelligence, Select Committee on; United States—Congress—Senate—Intelligence, Committee on

INTELLIGENCE levels
Burt report: fraud? Society 14:4+ My '77
Classic experiment—mistake or deliberate fraud? C. Burt's heredity research. J. Gaylin. Psychol Today 10:33+ F '77
Did Sir Cyril Burt fake his research on heritability of intelligence? O. Gillie; A. R. Jensen. Educ Digest 42:43-5 Mr '77
Heredity and ideology. P. Green. Nation 224: 341-3 Mr 19 '77
IQ and heredity: suspicion of fraud beclouds classic experiment. N. Wade; discussion. il Science 195:246-8 Ja 21 '77
Jensen: environment is a factor in IQ. Sci N 111:390 Je 18 '77
Why men and women think differently. K. Lamott. il Horizon 19:40-5 My '77
See also
Intelligence tests

Blacks

New light on black I.Q. T. Sowell. il N Y Times Mag p56-8+ Mr 27 '77; Discussion. p7+ My 1 '77
Second opinion from Jensen. por Time 110:75 Ag 8 '77

INTELLIGENCE Operations, Select Committee on. See United States—Congress—Senate—Select Committee to Study Governmental Operations with Respect to Intelligence Activities

INTELLIGENCE Oversight Board. See United States—Intelligence Oversight Board

INTELLIGENCE quotient
Childhood IQ's as predictors of adult educational and occupational status. R. B. McCall. bibl il Science 197:482-3 Jl 29 '77
Genetic differences in intelligence; Genetics Society of America, statement. Intellect 105:214-15 Ja '77
IQ, culture and adopted children; findings of S. Scarr. Sci N 112:150 S 3 '77
Second opinion from Jensen. por Time 110:75 Ag 8 '77
Too smart to be in business? L. Smith. il Duns R 110:100-2+ O '77

INTELLIGENCE service
Foreign agents in our midst. J. D. Hanrahan. il Progressive 41:31-5 N '77
Foreign nationals and American law. D. E. La Voy. bibl Society 15:58-64 N '77
See also
Military intelligence
Secret service

Chile

After DINA; Central Nacional de Informaciónes (CNI) R. Moreau. il Newsweek 90:50 S 12 '77

Germany, West

Case of the bugged physicist; Verfassungsschutz' bugging of K. R. Traube's home. il por Time 109:28 Mr 14 '77

Great Britain

Was Wilson bugged? former Prime Minister, H. Wilson. Newsweek 90:31 Ag 15 '77

Israel

Uranium: the Israeli connection. il map Time 109:32-4 My 30 '77

Korea, South

Inside South Korea's C.I.A. T. Szulc. il N Y Times Mag p41-2+ Mr 6 '77
KCIA game plan. D. Holt and E. Shannon. il Newsweek 90:34 D 12 '77
Korean connection. Nation 224:772-3 Je 25 '77
What a former Korean agent told Congress. U.S. News 83:24 Jl 4 '77

United States

Carter and spyland. J. Osborne. New Repub 176:9-11 Je 11 '77
Happenings; government reorganization. J. Osborne. New Repub 177:9-12 D 17 '77
Inside story of battle to control spying. J. Fromm. pors U.S. News 83:27 Ag 8 '77
Intelligence superchief: Turner's new challenge. por U.S. News 83:22 Ag 15 '77
Major intelligence shifts set. Aviation W 107: 14-16 Ag 8 '77
Man who called Walter Cronkite a spy; S. Jaffe. T. Branch. il Esquire 87:34-6+ Ap '77
Organization and functions of intelligence community. Dept State Bull 77:306-7 S 5 '77
Sam Jaffe and the new blacklist. T. Branch. Esquire 87:36+ Mr '77
Turner disavows any intention to become intelligence czar. Aviation W 107:16 Ag 15 '77

INTELLIGENCE service—United States—*Cont.*
Watch list for intelligence reform. J. K. Larson. Chr Cent 94:688-91 Ag 3 '77
See also
Government investigations—Intelligence service
United States—Central Intelligence Agency
United States—Intelligence Oversight Board

INTELLIGENCE tests
Big brother I.Q? M. T. Gilliatt. bibl Clearing H 51:166-9 D '77
IQ tests and the culture issue. A. C. Ornstein. Educ Digest 42:9-11 Ap '77
Issue that won't go away. E. B. Fiske. il N Y Times Mag p58 Mr 27 '77; Discussion. p7+ My 1 '77
Tests that cheat our children. A. Silberman. Read Digest 111:127-30 Jl '77; Same. McCalls 104:191+ Ap '77
What ever became of geniuses? il Time 110:89 D 19 '77
See also
Intelligence quotient

INTELSAT. See International Telecommunications Satellite Organization

INTELSAT satellites. See Communications satellites

INTEMPERANCE. See Alcoholism; Temperance

INTENSIVE education. See Concentrated study

INTENSIVE gardening method. See Organic gardening

INTER-AMERICAN Conference of Major Religious Superiors
New missions at home. America 137:453 D 24 '77

INTER-AMERICAN conferences
See also
Panama Congress, 1826

INTER-AMERICAN cooperation. See Inter-American relations

INTER-AMERICAN Defense Board
See also
Inter-American Defense College, Washington, D.C.

INTER-AMERICAN Defense College, Washington, D.C.
Fort Lesley J. McNair: grad school for juntas. J. Stein. Nation 224:621-4 My 21 '77

INTER-AMERICAN relations
Can Latin America and the United States modernize their traditional special relationship? address, August 19, 1977. A. Orfila. Vital Speeches 44:21-4 O 15 '77
Dependence or interdependence? J. H. Haddox. Américas 29:2-5 Mr '77
New horizons for progress and freedom in the Americas; address, February 24, 1977. A. Orfila. Vital Speeches 43:411-13 Ap 15 '77
See also
Latin America and the United States
Organization of American States
Pan American Day and Week
United States—Commerce—Latin America
United States—Foreign relations—Latin America

INTERCELLULAR junctions. See Junctions (physiology)

INTERCOMMUNITY cooperation
Share buildings for better operations. N. E. Hodge. Am City & County 92:92 S '77
To Plains with love; sister city of Kaohsiung, Taiwan. il Newsweek 90:35 Ag 29 '77

INTERCONNECTION of power systems. See Electric plants—Interconnection

INTERCONTINENTAL ballistic missiles. See Guided missiles

INTERCOURSE, Sexual. See Sexual behavior

INTERCULTURAL Action Learning Program. See Foreign study

INTERCULTURAL communication
Cross-cultural communication; possibilty or pipe-dream? J. A. Willings. il UNESCO Courier 30:12-16 Ap '77
Now, a new international information order? H. I. Schiller. Intellect 106:42-3 Ag '77

INTERCULTURAL education
Focus: multicultural literature; symposium. il Engl J 66:24-52 Mr '77
Multicultural literature to teach; symposium, comp by S. Koch. Engl J 66:57-70 Mr '77
Students immerse selves in foreign living and fun, too; Intercultural Action Learning Program. D. Brelis and J. Reader. il Smithsonian 8:48-55 bibl(p 146) Ap '77

INTERCULTURAL studies
Birth order and intellectual development: the confluence model in the light of cross-cultural evidence. D. J. Davis and others. bibl il Science 196:1470-2 Je 24 '77
Brain and emotions. J. Greenberg. il por Sci N 112:74-5 Jl 30 '77

INTERDENOMINATIONAL Theological Center, Atlanta, Ga.
Living out the gospel in seminary life. G. S. Shockley. Chr Cent 94:90-1 F 2 '77

INTERDESIGN, Inc. See Electronic industries—United States

INTERDISCIPLINARY studies. See Correlation (education)

INTEREST (economics)
Adjusting for risk in business investments. R. F. Dowd. Intellect 105:355-6 Ap '77
Appealing rate trend. B. Weberman. Forbes 120:98 D 1 '77
Bargain rates on medium-term money. Bus W p 105 Mr 28 '77
Bond market falls into a Fed trap; raising the Federal funds rate. il Bus W p 187+ N 14 '77
Calmer outlook for the money markets. il Fortune 95:44+ My '77
Costlier credit: no threat to recovery—yet. il U.S. News 82:59 Je 20 '77
Costlier money casts a shadow. il Bus W p34-5 O 17 '77
Declining interest rates forecast; study by the Academy for Contemporary Problems. il Am City & County 92:34 S '77
Exodus begins from long-term bonds. il Bus W p90+ N 7 '77
Fed's sudden tightening: has Burns gone too far? S. H. Wildstrom. por Bus W p43 N 14 '77
I can get it for you wholesale; banks undercutting their own prime rate. B. Weberman. il Forbes 119:23-4 My 1 '77
Inflation, interest rates and the Fed; address, July 26, 1977. J. J. Balles. Vital Speeches 43:741-4 O 1 '77
New softness in the prime. il Bus W p34 Je 27 '77
Rising interest rates revive the dollar. il Bus W p35-6 O 17 '77
Shaky truce on money. il Bus W p22-3 N 7 '77
Sudden recovery in long-term rates. il Bus W p57 Ja 24 '77
Surprising powers of short-term rates; effects on capital spending. il Bus W p70-1 Ag 22 '77
What might hold interest rates down. il Bus W p90 My 23 '77
Why the prime may rise again. il Bus W p79-80 My 30 '77
Why the surprising jump in interest rates. il U.S. News 82:71 Ja 31 '77
See also
Instalment plan
Investments
Savings deposits—Interest

INTEREST deductions. See Income tax—Deductions

INTEREST groups, Political. See Pressure groups

INTERFACES (computers) See Computers—Equipment

INTERFAITH dating. See Dating

INTERFERENCE, Radio. See Radio interference

INTERFEROMETRY
Binary-star speckle interferometry. H. A. McAlister. il Sky & Tel 53:346-50 My '77
Exorcising the demon of the atmosphere; speckle interferometry. il Sci N 112:320-1 N 12 '77
Laser interferometer measurement of changes in crayfish axon diameter concurrent with action potential. B. C. Hill and others. bibl il Science 196:426-8 Ap 22 '77
Radio interferometer with satellite link. Sci N 112:278 O 29 '77
Real-time, very-long-baseline interferometry based on the use of a communications satellite. J. L. Yen and others. bibl il Science 198:289-91 O 21 '77

INTERFERON
Interferon: an inducer of macrophage activation by polyanions. R. M. Schultz and others. bibl il Science 197:674-6 Ag 12 '77
Protective chemistry: sensitive cell control. il Sci N 111:308 My 14 '77
Status of interferon. D. C. Burke. il Sci Am 236:42-50 bibl(p 148) Ap '77

INTERGOVERNMENTAL Council of Copper Exporting Countries. See Trusts, Industrial—International trusts

INTERGOVERNMENTAL fiscal relations
Carter policy: no quick fix for urban America. H. V. Semling. Am City & County 92:18 F '77
Everyone's in the act; Montgomery County, Ohio. H. Flieger. U.S. News 82:88 F 21 '77
Federal conservation push signals trouble ahead. W. L. Forestell. Am City & County 92:98 D '77
How much more federal aid can cities expect? interview. P. R. Harris. por U.S. News 83:63-4 D 12 '77
Jobs and money—Carter's plan to save the cities. il U.S. News 83:37-8 N 28 '77
Mayors call for help. il Time 110:12-13 D 12 '77
Northeast versus the Sunbelt. R. S. Morris. Current 189:22-5 Ja '77
Policy options for beleaguered cities. A. K. Campbell and J. V. Burkhead. Intellect 105:208 Ja '77
Pork-barrel war between the states. il U.S. News 83:39-41 D 5 '77
Still seeking an urban policy. E. Lewis. Bus W p 119-20 Ja 16 '78
See also
Grants-in-aid
Intergovernmental tax relations

INTERGOVERNMENTAL Oceanographic Commission
UNESCO and the oceans. il UNESCO Courier 30:14-15 Ja '77

INTERGOVERNMENTAL tax relations
How federal policies are hurting the cities. il map Bus W p86-8 D 19 '77
Social security $$ fuel N.C. library info center; Wake County Public Libraries System. Lib J 102:148 Ja 15 '77

INTERIOR, Department of the. See United States—Interior, Department of the

INTERIOR and Insular Affairs, Committee on. See United States—Congress—House—Interior and Insular Affairs, Committee on

INTERIOR decoration
Building types study: Record Interiors of 1977; with introd by B. Gordon. il Archit Rec 161: 101-28 Ja '77
See also
Boat decoration
House decoration
Office decoration
School decoration

INTERIOR decorators
California contribution. E. Brown. il N Y Times Mag p52-3 Ja 8 '78
Careers in art. P. Savino. il Sch Arts 76:9 Mr '77
One-stop decorating; department store designers. C. Kriebel. il Am Home 80:24 F '77
See also
Parish, Mrs H.

INTERIOR Design Award Program. See Architectural record (periodical)

INTERIOR designers. See Interior decorators

INTERLIBRARY loans
ILL policy directory: making sharing easier. R. L. Barclay. Lib J 102:2322-3 N 15 '77
Living in the gap of ambiguity; an attorney's advice to libraries on the copyright law. L. I. Flacks. il Am Lib 8:252-7 My '77
More copyright information. Am Lib 8:624-5 D '77
New interlibrary loan form unveiled. W. R. Eshelman. Wilson Lib Bull 52:115-16 O '77
Resource sharing in libraries; 1976 Pittsburgh conference. K. Nyren; discussion. Lib J 102: 299 F 1 '77

INTERLOCKING puzzles. See Puzzles

INTERMARRIAGE of races. See Interracial marriage

INTERMETALLIC compounds
Intermetallic compounds of the type MNi_5 as methanation catalysts. A. Elattar and others. bibl il Science 196:1093-4 Je 3 '77

INTERMEZZO; opera. See Strauss, R.

INTERNAL migration. See Migration, Internal

INTERNAL Revenue Service. See United States—Internal Revenue Service

INTERNAL security
Civil liberties and national security: the outlook in Congress. I. Shapiro. Intellect 105:230-3 F '77
Ecology and national security. C. Holden. Science 198:712 N 18 '77
Lips that sink ships; security investigation of HEW employees. J. McClellan and D. Anderson. Progressive 41:47-9 My '77
Police and military in the resolution of ethnic conflict. C. H. Enloe. bibl f Ann Am Acad 433:137-49 S '77
See also
Loyalty investigations

INTERNAL Security, Committee on. See United States—Congress—House—Internal Security, Committee on

INTERNAL Security Subcommittee. See United States—Congress—Senate—Judiciary, Committee on the—Internal Security Subcommittee

INTERNATIONAL Accounting Standards Committee. See Accounting—Standards

INTERNATIONAL agencies
Conditions of success in international enterprises in science and technology. L. Kowarski. Bull Atom Sci 33:44-8 S '77
Department discusses U.S. participation in international organizations; statement, June 15, 1977. C. W. Maynes. Dept State Bull 77:100-3 Jl 18 '77
Doing well by doing good. Nation 225:643-4 D 17 '77
See also
Organization of American States

INTERNATIONAL Air Transport Association
Deregulation mess. W. H. Gregory. Aviation W 107:7 N 21 '77
IATA turmoil in rates continues. Aviation W 107:21-2 N 21 '77
IATA unit studies plans to meet Laker challenge. Aviation W 107:29 Jl 18 '77
Skytrain spurs IATA fares reduction. Aviation W 107:32 Ag 22 '77
Super Apex negotiations seen dominating IATA conference. Aviation W 107:29 O 3 '77
World airline industry; interview. K. Hammarskjöld. por U.S. News 82:56+ Mr 21 '77

INTERNATIONAL Association of Machinists and Aerospace Workers
Aerospace labor disputes continue. J. M. Lenorovitz. Aviation W 107:22-3 O 31 '77
Aerospace labor woes continue. Aviation W 107: 15 D 19 '77
IAM locals at P&W work under new labor contract. W. C. Wetmore. Aviation W 107:24 D 12 '77
IAM strikes Lockheed's installations in California. Aviation W 107:24-5 O 17 '77
Labor, management adamant in Lockheed strike positions. J. M. Lenorovitz. Aviation W 107: 23-4 D 12 '77
Lockheed contract offer rejected by machinists. Aviation W 108:22 Ja 2 '78
Lockheed details offer to machinists. Aviation W 107:21-2 N 28 '77
Lockheed employes return to jobs. J. M. Lenorovitz. Aviation W 108:17 Ja 9 '78
Lockheed strike continued despite union member rift. J. M. Lenorovitz. Aviation W 107:21-2 D 5 '77
Seniority snags aerospace talks. il Bus W p45+ N 14 '77
Why Lockheed's strike is a holy war. il Bus W p31 D 19 '77
Wimpy takes command. por Time 110:51-2 Jl 11 '77
Winpisinger: forging a new left coalition. por Bus W p78-9 F 21 '77

INTERNATIONAL Atomic Energy Agency
IAEA asked to assess role of nuclear power as alternative energy source. UN Chron 13:34-5 D '76
Safeguards against diversion of nuclear material: an overview. R. Imai. Ann Am Acad 430: 58-69 Mr '77

INTERNATIONAL Automobile Show. See Automobiles—Exhibitions

INTERNATIONAL Baccalaureate. See International education

INTERNATIONAL Bank for Reconstruction and Development
Congressional threat to the World Bank; attaching conditions to U.S. contributions. Bus W p40-1 O 10 '77
House built on sand. J. Miller. New Repub 177: 19-21 S 3 '77
Push to tap new resources. il Bus W p 18-19 Jl 18 '77
Under fire: excessive salaries at the World Bank. U.S. News 83:63 O 10 '77
World Bank head calls for special efforts to relieve poverty; excerpt from address, September 1977. R. S. McNamara. UN Chron 14:40 O '77

INTERNATIONAL Bauxite Association. See Trusts, Industrial—International trusts

INTERNATIONAL Biennial of Tapestry. See Tapestry—Exhibitions

INTERNATIONAL Biological Program
Bits, Bytes, and IBP. D. B. Botkin. BioScience 27:385 Je '77
Evaluation of three biome programs. R. Mitchell and others; discussion. Science 195:822-3, 902-4 Mr 4 '77

INTERNATIONAL Boat Show. See Boats—Exhibitions

INTERNATIONAL Book and Library Programs, Government Advisory Committee on. See United States—Government Advisory Committee on International Book and Library Programs

INTERNATIONAL Brotherhood of Teamsters, Chauffeurs, Warehousemen and Helpers of America
Big union that's haunted by its own success. U.S. News 83:75-6 Ag 8 '77
Can anybody clean up the Teamsters? A. H. Raskin; reply with rejoinder. R. Billings. N Y Times Mag p62-3 Ja 16 '77
Cesar's triumph. T. Nicholson and W. J. Cook. il Newsweek 89:70+ Mr 21 '77
Equitable alchemy; pension fund management under Equitable Life Assurance Society. il Time 110:52+ Jl 11 '77
Fitzsimmons, three others quit pension fund; Central States Pension Fund. L. Bornstein and others. M Labor R 100:57 My '77
Golden fleecing of union funds. L. Velie. Read Digest 111:88-92 O '77
Hoffa's legacy. J. Lelyveld. il por N Y Times Mag p 142 N 27 '77
Leadership row at a Teamsters local; Detroit local. Bus W p38-9 N 28 '77
Momentum builds against the top Teamsters. il Bus W p 108+ O 10 '77
Render unto Cesar. il por Time 109:81 Mr 21 '77
Sticky fingers; trusteeship of the Teamsters' Central States Pension Fund. Nation 224:355-6 Mr 26 '77
Teamsters' Watergate connection. il Time 110: 28 Ag 8 '77
Truce ends 10-year jurisdictional dispute on farms. L. Bornstein and others. M Labor R 100:57-8 My '77
U.S. Appeals Court rules employee pension funds are subject to Federal anti-fraud laws. Ret Liv 17:47 O '77
We're gonna get our asses kicked: the teamster dissidents mobilize. R. H. Holden. Nation 225: 461-3 N 5 '77

INTERNATIONAL Business Machines Corporation
Amazing daisies; industry competition for daisy wheel printing system. il Forbes 120:27-8 Ag 1 '77
At IBM, privacy is a top priority. Bus W p 108 Ap 4 '77
France: at war with IBM over small computers. Bus W p48 Mr 21 '77
Gene Amdahl takes aim at I.B.M. B. Uttal. il por Fortune 96:106-10+ S '77
How courts will treat IBM, AT&T. A. Hershman. por Duns R 110:76-7+ D '77
IBM buys itself. Time 109:50 Mr 7 '77
I.B.M. reaches for a golden future in the heavens; satellite business systems. B. Uttal. il Fortune 95:172-6+ Je '77
IBM tries to break up a computer lottery. Bus W p32+ Je 6 '77
IBM withdraws from India. il Time 110:92 N 28 '77
IBM's antitrust win could be a big one; decision against California Computer Products Inc. J. Madrick. il Bus W p62 Mr 7 '77
IBM's cash problem: too much to handle. il Bus W p62+ D 5 '77
IBM's high-flying legal eagle. por Forbes 119: 74 Ap 1 '77
IBM's price war takes to the Street. il Bus W p 123+ Ap 18 '77
IBM's Santa Teresa Laboratory. J. Nairn. il Archit Rec 162:99-104 Ag '77
Jimmy Carter's computer connection; selection of IBM directors for Cabinet. il Forbes 119: 27-8 Ja 15 '77
Low profile for IBM; with introd by M. F. Schmertz. il Archit Rec 161:141-6 Ja '77
New IBM line likely in next year or so. il Duns R 110:100-1+ Jl '77
One firm's family. A. J. Mayer and M. Ruby. il Newsweek 90:82-4+ N 21 '77
Those cases that go on and on; U.S. v IBM. il Time 109:40+ Je 27 '77
Why IBM looks good. R. B. Hoey. por Forbes 119:80 F 1 '77

INTERNATIONAL cartels. See Trusts, Industrial—International trusts

INTERNATIONAL Center for Living Aquatic Resources Management. See Aquaculture

INTERNATIONAL Center of Photography, New York. See Photography—Galleries and museums

INTERNATIONAL City Management Association
ICMA: defend council-manager government, or lose it. W. S. Foster. Am City & County 92: 108 F '77
We can learn from Europe's cities; ICMA European Task Force; address, September 26, 1976. T. Tedesco. Vital Speeches 43:209-11 Ja 15 '77

INTERNATIONAL Civil Aviation Organization
Adoption of landing aid stymied. Aviation W 106:24-5 F 7 '77
Air transport can help strengthen Africa's economy, ICAO study finds. UN Chron 14:30-1 Mr '77
Expanded economic role for ICAO recommended. R. K. Ellingsworth. Aviation W 106:24-5 Ja 10 '77
Head of Governing Council speaks of ICAO role. UN Chron 14:30 Mr '77
ICAO moves toward landing system choice. Aviation W 107:21 Jl 4 '77
ICAO parley isolates problems. R. K. Ellingsworth. Aviation W 106:32-3 My 2 '77
ICAO unit sets landing system vote next April. Aviation W 106:70 Je 6 '77
Scanning-beam landing aid wins vote. P. J. Klass. Aviation W 106:26-7 Mr 28 '77
Swing votes key to landing aid choice. P. J. Klass. il Aviation W 106:46-8 F 21 '77

INTERNATIONAL civil service. See International officials and employees

INTERNATIONAL Civil Service Commission
Assembly authorizes salary changes recommended by civil service body. UN Chron 14:75 Ja '77
Mr Waldheim opens International Civil Service Commission session. K. Waldheim. UN Chron 14:40 Mr '77

INTERNATIONAL collective bargaining. See Collective bargaining—Multinational bargaining

INTERNATIONAL commercial policy. See Commercial policy

INTERNATIONAL commodity control. See Commodity control

INTERNATIONAL Community of Booksellers Associations
ICBA meeting focuses on bookseller problems. H. R. Lottmann and S. Wagner. il Pub W 212:55-6+ Jl 4 '77

INTERNATIONAL Conference in Support of the Peoples of Zimbabwe and Namibia, 1977
Conference to mobilize support for peoples of Namibia and Zimbabwe. UN Chron 14:31-3 Ja '77
Guidelines for Maputo conference approved. UN Chron 14:28 My '77
Joint committee endorses plan for Southern Africa conference. UN Chron 14:26-7 Ap '77
United States reiterates support for the independence of Namibia and Zimbabwe at Maputo conference; statements, with text of declaration, May 19 and 21, 1977. A. J. Young; C. W. Maynes. Dept State Bull 77:55-65 Jl 11 '77
Young at heart; A. Young's visit. J. Pringle. il por Newsweek 89:44 My 30 '77

INTERNATIONAL Conference of Trade Unions Against Apartheid. See Trade unions—Conferences

INTERNATIONAL Conference on the Unity of the Sciences. See Science—Conferences

INTERNATIONAL conferences
After summit cheers—real challenges lie ahead; hope for practical results of the London meetings. il U.S. News 82:25-6 My 23 '77
After the summit: a widening gap between weak and strong; London summit. E. Mervosh and J. Pearson. il Bus W p92 My 23 '77
Best foot forward; J. Carter's London summit trip. A. Deming and others. il Newsweek 89: 29-30 My 23 '77
Carter's crucial summit; London summit. il por U.S. News 82:21-4 My 9 '77
Carter's maiden flight; London summit. A. Deming and others. il por Newsweek 89:43-4 My 9 '77
Despairing optimist. R. Dubos. Am Scholar 46: 152-3+ Spr '77
Eurocommunists exposed; Madrid summit. M. Ledeen. New Repub 176:13-14 Mr 26 '77
Hey, look me over; London and Geneva conferences. S. Franker and others. il Newsweek 89: 26-8 My 16 '77
Innocent abroad; London economic summit. J. Osborne. New Repub 176:13-14+ My 21 '77
International conferences and tax reform. L. M. Branscomb. Science 196:719 My 13 '77
London economic summit. J. Novak. America 136:518-20 Je 11 '77
No meeting of minds in Paris; Conference on International Economic Cooperation, Paris. America 136:535 Je 18 '77
Not being too beastly to Moscow; Western European Communist meeting in Spain. il por Time 109:23 Mr 14 '77
Pledging a tithe that binds; summit meeting of Arab and black African leaders. il Time 109:32-3 Mr 21 '77
President Carter attends economic, Berlin, and NATO meetings at London; remarks, with text of declarations, NATO communique, and question and answer session, May 5, 8-11, 1977. J. Carter. Dept State Bull 76:581-6+ Je 6 '77
Saving international conferences. H. L. Davis. Phys Today 30:88 Je '77
Socko performance at the summit; J. Carter's role at London meetings. il pors Time 109:12-15 My 16 '77
Summit at Downing Street; seven-nation conference in London. il por Time 109:14-16 My 9 '77
Will Europe follow Carter? il U.S. News 82: 19-23 My 16 '77
See also
Cairo conference, 1977
Conference on Security and Cooperation in Europe
Economic conferences
Organization of Petroleum Exporting Countries—Conferences

INTERNATIONAL Congress of Organists
International Congress of Organists. S. Cantrell. Hi Fi 28:MA26-7 Ja '78

INTERNATIONAL Congress on World Evangelization
Update Lausanne; interview. L. Ford. por Chr Today 22:16-18+ D 9 '77

INTERNATIONAL Controls Corporation
International Controls: the lively corpse. por Forbes 120:63-4 O 15 '77

INTERNATIONAL cookery. See Cookery, International

INTERNATIONAL cooperation
Trilateral world approach; report of Trilateral Commission task force. Current 192:54-61 Ap '77
See also
Communications satellites—International aspects
Economic assistance
Inter-American relations
International agencies
Meteorology—International aspects
Nato
Oceanography—International aspects
Science—International aspects
Technology—International aspects
United Nations
Wildlife conservation—International aspects

INTERNATIONAL copyright. See Copyright

INTERNATIONAL corporations. See Corporations, International

INTERNATIONAL correspondence
Letter; request for pen pals to aid English language study. B. Lee. por Sch Arts 76:52 Ap '77

INTERNATIONAL Council on Biblical Inerrancy
Campaign for inerrancy. Chr Today 22:51-2 N 4 '77

INTERNATIONAL Court of Justice, The Hague
Judges salaries to be reviewed next four years. il UN Chron 14:80 Ja '77
Whatever happened to: World Court: on the ropes. il U.S. News 82:68 Ja 31 '77

INTERNATIONAL Covenant on Civil and Political Rights
Implementing United Nations covenants. A. G. Mower, Jr. bibl il Society 15:76-80 N '77
President Carter signs covenants on human rights; remarks, October 5, 1977. J. Carter. Dept State Bull 77:586-7 O 31 '77

INTERNATIONAL Covenant on Economic, Social and Cultural Rights
President Carter signs covenants on human rights; remarks, October 5, 1977. J. Carter. Dept State Bull 77:586-7 O 31 '77

INTERNATIONAL Craft Film Festival. See Motion picture festivals

INTERNATIONAL Day for the Elimination of Racial Descrimination
United Nations marks day for elimination of race discrimination. il UN Chron 14:30-3 Ap '77

INTERNATIONAL Day of Solidarity with the Struggling People of South Africa
Anniversary of Soweto incident observed. il UN Chron 14:27-8 Jl '77

INTERNATIONAL debts. See Debts, External

INTERNATIONAL economic policy. See Economic policy

INTERNATIONAL economic relations. See Economic relations

INTERNATIONAL education
Education for a global society. G. M. Haniff; R. C. Good. Current 194:8-22 Jl '77
Helping Americans understand world affairs; address, June 27, 1977. C. W. Bray, 3d. Dept State Bull 77:402-4 S 26 '77
International education: focus for corporate support. J. W. Fulbright. Harvard Bus R 55: 137-41 My '77
Reshaping secondary education; International Baccalaureate program at Francis Lewis High School, Queens, N.Y. J. R. Adams. Educ Digest 43:2-4 D '77
See also
United Nations—Study and teaching

INTERNATIONAL Exhibition of Modern Art. See Art, Modern—Exhibitions

INTERNATIONAL Exhibitions Committee. See American Federation of Arts—International Exhibitions Committee

INTERNATIONAL Fair of Contemporary Art, Paris. See Art, Modern—Exhibitions

INTERNATIONAL Federation of Library Associations
Another view from the Belgian front. S. M. Malinconico. Lib J 102:2484-5 D 15 '77
Even greater expectations; symposium. il Am Lib 8:606-14+ D '77
IFLA meets in Brussels; research round table set. SLJ 24:14 N '77
IFLA turns fifty. S. Havens. il Lib J 102:2482-4 D 15 '77
IFLA's 50th anniversary session in Brussels. W. R. Eshelman. il Wilson Lib Bull 52:218-22 N '77

INTERNATIONAL Federation of Translators. See Translators

INTERNATIONAL Festival of Music and Drama, Edinburgh
Edinburgh; Scottish Opera's performance of Carmen and Mary, Queen of Scots. N. Goodwin. Opera N 42:66-8 N '77
Musical events:
Scottish Opera's production of Carmen. A. Porter. New Yorker 53:102-5 S 26 '77
Report from Edinburgh. S. Kauffmann. New Repub 177:22-3 S 24 '77

INTERNATIONAL Film Seminars. See Motion pictures—Study and teaching

INTERNATIONAL Freedom to Publish Committee. See Association of American Publishers—International Freedom to Publish Committee

INTERNATIONAL Fund for Agricultural Development (proposed) See United Nations International Fund for Agricultural Development (proposed)

INTERNATIONAL Fund for Animal Welfare. See Conservation associations

INTERNATIONAL Harvester Company
Computer terminals as near as your implement dealer; Pro-Ag package. B. Coffman. il Farm J 101:C4 Mr '77
Five International Harvesters in one. H. Seneker. il por Forbes 119:60+ Ap 15 '77

INTERNATIONAL herald tribune
Trib may abandon Paris. il Bus W p29 Je 27 '77

INTERNATIONAL Hill Land Symposium. See Agriculture—Conferences

INTERNATIONAL Hotel, San Francisco. See San Francisco—Hotels, restaurants, etc.

INTERNATIONAL Human Powered Speed Championships. See Bicycle racing

INTERNATIONAL institutions. See International agencies

INTERNATIONAL Joint Commission (United States and Canada)
U.S., Canada to study river water quality; Poplar River Basin. Dept State Bull 77:282-3 Ag 29 '77

INTERNATIONAL Labor Organization
Convention urges control of hazards in work environment. UN Chron 14:45 Jl '77
Human-rights dilemma of leaving the ILO. il Bus W p 130+ S 19 '77
ILO tightens standards for maritime safety. J. P. Goldberg. bibl M Labor R 100:25-30 Jl '77
I.L.O. under fire. Time 110:113-14 N 7 '77
Impact of U.S. pullout from ILO. il U.S. News 83:102-3 N 14 '77
Leaving the ILO. Newsweek 90:69 N 14 '77
Meany and business vs. the ILO: will we pick up our marbles? B. Koeppel. Nation 225:429-31 O 29 '77
New challenge for world labor. J. Holland and P. J. Henriot. America 137:209-12 O 8 '77
Of many things; U.S. withdrawal. J. O'Hare. America 137:inside cover N 12 '77
Why the U.S. plans to quit the UN's labor arm. il Nations Bus 65:28-33 O '77

INTERNATIONAL law
Abu Daoud and the law. S. E. Rapoport. Commentary 63:70-2 Mr '77; Reply. S. Liskofsky. 63:10-11+ My '77
Court judgments go international; U.S.—British treaty providing for reciprocal recognition and enforcement of judgments in civil cases. Bus W p50+ F 21 '77
See also
Airspace (international law)
Asylum, Right of
Embargo
Eminent domain (international law)
Extradition
Fishery laws and legislation
International Court of Justice, The Hague
Maritime law
Recognition (international law)
Sanctions (international law)
Space law
Territorial waters
United Nations—Charter
United Nations—International Law Commission
United Nations Conference of Plenipotentiaries on Succession of States in Respect of Treaties

INTERNATIONAL Law Commission. See United Nations—International Law Commission

INTERNATIONAL Law of the Sea Conference. See United Nations Conference on the Law of the Sea

INTERNATIONAL League for Human Rights
Human rights as an International League. L. S. Wiseberg and H. M. Scoble. bibl il Society 15: 71-5 N '77

INTERNATIONAL Longshoremen's and Warehousemen's Union
Mellowed Bridges talks of reconciliation. por Bus W p40+ My 9 '77

INTERNATIONAL Longshoremen's Association
Automation again threatens peace on the docks. il Bus W p64+ S 5 '77
Contagious tie-up on the docks. il Bus W p33-4 O 24 '77
Container woes in dockland. il Time 110:53-4 O 17 '77
Industry split snarls the ILA talks. Bus W p56 S 26 '77
Method acting; FBI infiltration. Time 109:32+ F 7 '77
Off the waterfront. T. Nicholson and D. Witherspoon. il Newsweek 90:93 O 24 '77
Pinch on the docks. T. Nicholson and P. E. Simons. il Newsweek 90:77 N 21 '77
That tricky trike strike. il Time 110:77 N 21 '77

INTERNATIONAL Monetary Fund
Administration urges U.S. participation in the IMF supplementary financing facility; statement, September 20, 1977. R. N. Cooper. il Dept State Bull 77:645-50 N 7 '77
Austerity now—and hopes for IMF aid; Turkey's financial condition. Bus W p53+ O 17 '77
Credit stretched to the breaking point. Bus W p68 D 12 '77
Dilemma in reflation for the IMF. E. Mervosh. Bus W p40 O 10 '77
Europe's sickest man; question of loan to Italy. M. Ledeen. New Repub 176:8-10 F 12 '77
Fighting a global lull. M. Ruby and others. il Newsweek 90:89-90 O 10 '77
IMF lays down the law; with report by A. Stuart. A. F. Ehrbar. il Fortune 96:98-102+ Jl '77
IMF: no sign of that Saudi money. Bus W p36 My 2 '77
IMF wields sudden new power. il Bus W p86+ Mr 28 '77
Lender of last resort. il por Time 110:52-3 Ag 15 '77
Lot more clout for the superbank. il U.S. News 82:89-90 Je 6 '77
New funds—and strains—for the IMF. E. Mervosh. Bus W p73 Ag 22 '77
Portugal: a hard test for the IMF. S. W. Sanders. il Bus W p35 Ja 9 '78
Role of gold in the international monetary system; address, December 3, 1976. F. L. Widman. Vital Speeches 43:199-201 Ja 15 '77

INTERNATIONAL Monetary Fund—*Continued*
Toward international equilibrium: a strategy for the longer pull; address, May 25, 1977. W. M. Blumenthal. Dept State Bull 77:13-18 Jl 4 '77
Will the IMF let the Saudis buy in? B. Nussbaum. por Bus W p 154 My 16 '77

INTERNATIONAL Municipal Signal Association
School to replace IMSA conference. il Am City & County 92:26 O '77

INTERNATIONAL Musicological Society
Commentary: the IMS at Berkeley. J. Peyser. Mus Q 63:545-8 O '77
International Musicological Congress; IMS conference in Berkeley. B. Schwarz. il Hi Fi 27: MA27-9 D '77

INTERNATIONAL Nickel Company of Canada
Inco: nowhere to go but up? il Forbes 120:56+ O 1 '77

INTERNATIONAL Nuclear Fuel Cycle Evaluation. See Nuclear fuels

INTERNATIONAL Ocean Institute
International Ocean Institute. E. M. Borgese. il Oceans 10:52-7 Ja '77

INTERNATIONAL officials and employees
Doing well by doing good. Nation 225:643-4 D 17 '77
It's even worse in Brussels; civil servants of the Commission of the European Communities. J. T. Easley. New Repub 177:22-3 Jl 9 '77
See also
International Civil Service Commission

INTERNATIONAL Olympic Committee
Waiving the rules. Nat R 29:1040 S 16 '77

INTERNATIONAL organizations. See International agencies

INTERNATIONAL Publishers Association
Per A. Sjögren: the pressing need for IPA; interview, ed by A. Johnson. P. A. Sjögren. por Pub W 212:86+ S 19 '77

INTERNATIONAL Race of Champions. See Automobile racing

INTERNATIONAL relations
Alternatives to political paranoia. F. M. Wilhoit. il por Intellect 105:289-90 Mr '77
American stake in Israel; a lesson in international relations. E. V. Rostow. Commentary 63:32-46 Ap '77; Discussion. 64:16+ Jl '77
Cost of global stability. D. Simon. Intellect 106: 182-3 N '77
Détente, then and now; J. B. Alberdi and H. Kissinger. G. H. Watson. il pors Américas 29: 2-7 Ja '77
Foreign affairs: a guide for the political globe-watcher. B. Kalb. Sat R 4:12-13 Ag 6 '77
Islands of contention. S. Karnow. Sat R 5:30-2 Ja 7 '78
Military and political challenges of the 80's; East-West relations; address, May 10, 1977. J. Carter. Vital Speeches 43:482-4 Je 1 '77; Same with title President Carter attends economic, Berlin and NATO meetings at London and with text of communique. J. Carter. Dept State Bull 76:597-602 Je 6 '77
Nth powers of the future. A. Kapur. Ann Am Acad 430:84-95 Mr '77
Nuclear proliferation and world politics. L. A. Dunn. Ann Am Acad 430:96-109 Mr '77
On power; symposium. bibl f For Affairs 56:1-110 O '77
Party & international politics. D. P. Moynihan. Commentary 63:56-9 F '77
State of the world. R. H. Heindel. See alternate issues of Intellect
Toward world order. S. Hoffmann. New Repub 176:10-12 Mr 19 '77
U.S. gives views on U.S.S.R. proposal for world treaty on the non-use of force; statements, October 28, 29 and November 22, 1976. R. Rosenstock; A. W. Sherer, Jr. Dept State Bull 76: 30-5 Ja 10 '77
U.S. policy toward our NATO partners: traditional commitments and new directions; statement, May 23, 1977. A. A. Hartman. Dept State Bull 76:635-9 Je 13 '77
World affairs: a more cheerful perspective. B. Manning. Yale R 67:1-12 O '77
See also
Balance of power
Business Council for International Understanding
Columbia University—School of International Affairs
Committee on the Present Danger
Council on Foreign Relations
Disarmament
Economic policy
Geopolitics
International conferences
International cooperation
International Court of Justice, The Hague
International law
International security
Militarism
Peace
Radio broadcasting—International aspects
Recognition (international law)
Tariff
Travel regulations
Trilateral Commission, Inc
United Nations
War
World politics
also subhead Foreign relations under names of countries, e.g. Israel—Foreign relations

Bibliography

Recent books on international relations; comp by L. E. Despard. See issues of Foreign affairs
Source material; comp by J. Rigney. For Affairs 55:664-70 Ap '77

Study and teaching

See also
United Nations—Study and teaching

INTERNATIONAL Rights Information Service. See Copyright

INTERNATIONAL Rowing Association Championship. See Rowing

INTERNATIONAL security
Peace and security in a changing world; reports of working groups of Pugwash Conference. Bull Atom Sci 33:33-9 D '77
To strengthen the American alliance: better training and equipment in NATO forces; address, May 11, 1977. H. Brown. Vital Speeches 43:522-5 Je 15 '77
We citizens cannot sit back and relax: world security; address, April 20, 1977. R. W. Peterson. Vital Speeches 43:490-3 Je 1 '77
See also
Atomic power—International control
United Nations
United Nations—Security Council
United Nations—Special Committee on Peace-keeping Operations

INTERNATIONAL Ski Film Festival. See Motion picture festivals

INTERNATIONAL Society of Contemporary Music
ISCM World Days; Bonn festival. E. Schwartz. il Hi Fi 27:MA34-5+ S '77
ISCM World Music Days; October 1976 festival held in Boston. S. Carlin. il Hi Fi 27:MA30-1+ Ap '77

INTERNATIONAL style (architecture) See Architecture, Modern

INTERNATIONAL Sun-Earth Explorer satellites. See Artificial satellites—Meteorological use

INTERNATIONAL Tattoo Artists Association. See Tattooing

INTERNATIONAL Telecommunications Satellite Organization
Intelsat faces numerous challenges. il maps Aviation W 107:71+ O 17 '77
Intelsat moves toward permanent form. il Aviation W 106:90-1 Ja 10 '77

INTERNATIONAL Telephone and Telegraph Corporation
Fastest antelope of them all; L. C. Hamilton Jr. il por Fortune 95:17 Mr '77
Geneen's legacy. D. Pauly. pors Newsweek 89: 80 F 21 '77
Harold Geneen rests his case. R. J. Flaherty. il pors Forbes 119:42+ Je 15 '77
ITT's strategy may benefit a competitor. Bus W p57+ S 12 '77
See also
Government investigations—International Telephone and Telegraph Corporation
Hartford Fire Insurance Company

INTERNATIONAL television. See Television broadcasting—International aspects

INTERNATIONAL trade. See Commerce

INTERNATIONAL Trade Commission. See United States—International Trade Commission

INTERNATIONAL trade regulation. See Foreign trade regulation

INTERNATIONAL traffic in arms. See Munitions—Export-import problems

INTERNATIONAL Tribunal on Crimes Against Women. See Feminism—Conferences

INTERNATIONAL trusteeships
See also
United Nations—Trusteeship Council

INTERNATIONAL trusts. See Trusts, Industrial—International trusts

INTERNATIONAL Volleyball Association. See Volleyball

INTERNATIONAL Whaling Commission
Bowhead whales; ban on Eskimo hunting. Dept State Bull 77:740-1 N 21 '77
IWC slashes quotas, bans Eskimo hunt. C. Van Note. Audubon 79:141-2 S '77
Moratorium for the bowhead: Eskimo whaling on ice? J. Walsh. il Science 197:847-50 Ag 26 '77
To kill a whale. R. McNally. il Oceans 10:62-5 Ja '77

INTERNATIONAL Women's Year
See also
United States—National Commission on the Observance of International Women's Year

INTERNATIONAL Year for Disabled Persons, 1981 (proposed)
Assembly acts on disabled persons, narcotics, world social situation. UN Chron 14:67-9 Ja '77

INTERNATIONAL Year of the Child, 1979 (proposed)
1979 proclaimed International Year of the Child by Assembly; with text of resolution. UN Chron 14:55-7, 115 Ja '77
INTERNATIONALISM
Global challenges; excerpt from Bulletin of the atomic scientists, December, 1976. S. Chase. Sci Digest 81:70-2 Ap '77
Our world gets smaller and smaller. il U.S. News 83:24-5 Jl 18 '77
INTERNS (civil service)
Molding the new breed public officials; Graduate School of Public Affairs at the University of Colorado. R. C. Bobowski. il Am Educ 13:22-7 D '77
INTERPERSONAL relations. See Human relations
INTERPLANETARY flight. See Space flight
INTERPLANTING. See Companion crops
INTERRACIAL adoption. See Adoption
INTERRACIAL marriage
Negro: by definition; state laws prohibiting interracial marriage. R. Poe. bibl Negro Hist Bull 40:668-70 Ja '77
This one great evil; miscegenation prior to the Civil War. S. Hoffert. bibl il Am Hist Illus 12:37-41 My '77

Personal narratives

Black women/white men: the other mixed marriage. S. D. Lewis; R. Cousin. il Ebony 33:37-9+ Ja '78
What makes an interracial marriage work; interviews, ed by E. Stone. J. Graves and J. Graves. il pors Parents Mag 52:54-5+ O '77
INTERRACIAL relations. See Race relations
INTERRUPT devices, Computer. See Computers—Input-output equipment
INTERSEEDING. See Seeding
INTERSTATE commerce
See also
United States—Interstate Commerce Commission
INTERSTATE highway system. See Express highways
INTERSTATE National Corporation-National Student Marketing Corporation merger. See Corporations—Acquisitions and mergers
INTERSTELLAR communication
All ears. Sci Am 237:84+ D '77
Earth's greatest hits; audio-visual record on Voyager. A. Druyan and T. Ferris. N Y Times Mag p 12-13 S 4 '77
Eavesdropping on the galaxy. H. Mark and others. Intellect 106:190-2 N '77
Listening for intelligent aliens. il Sci N 112: 313 N 12 '77
NASA bans sex from outer space; information disc designed for Voyagers. N. Wade. Science 197:1163-5 S 16 '77
Seeking an end to cosmic loneliness. T. Ferris. il N Y Times Mag p30-2+ O 23 '77
Voyager: multiplanet mission has message. Sci N 112:86 Ag 6 '77
Voyager's message: record reviews. J. Eberhart. Sci N 112:211+ O 1 '77
What to say to the space probe when it arrives. R. Bracewell. il Horizon 19:48-53 Ja '77
When outer space speaks. . . L. Thomas. Read Digest 111:181-2 Jl '77
Who (if anyone) is living way out there? T. Bay. Sci Digest 82:64-9 Ag; 46-7 S '77
World on a record; audio-visual recording on Voyager flights. J. Eberhart. il Sci N 112:124-5 Ag 20 '77
INTERSTELLAR matter. See Matter, Interstellar
INTERSTITIAL alloys. See Alloys
INTERVALS (music) See Musical intervals and scales
INTER-VARSITY Christian Fellowship
Urbana '76: declaring God's glory and word. A. H. Matthews. il Chr Today 21:38-40 Ja 21 '77
INTERVIEWING
Tape your interviews for radio. M. S. Bucki. Writers Digest 57:23-5 F '77
Yes, but what was His Holines wearing? descriptions of interviewees in the New York times. G. Weales. Nation 225:533-5 N 19 '77
See also
Employment interviewing
INTERVIEWS, Taping of. See Tape recorders and recording
INTESTINES
Folate conjugase: two separate activities in human jejunum. A. M. Reisenauer and others. bibl il Science 198:196-7 O 14 '77
See also
Colon (anatomy)

Cancer

See Cancer

Diseases

See also
Appendicitis
Constipation

Surgery

Drastic methods to lose weight; intestinal bypass surgery. M. Burgen. il Ebony 32:124-6+ O '77
INTIMACY
Alternative life-styles; sexually intimate friendships. J. W. Ramey. bibl il Society 14:43-7 Jl '77
Intimacy; symposium. Mademoiselle 83:115-16+ D '77
Intimate terrorism. M. V. Miller. bibl il por Psychol Today 10:78-80+ Ap '77
Varieties of intimacy; excerpt from No-fault marriage. M. Lasswell and N. M. Lobsenz. Read Digest 111:115-18 N '77
See also
Embracing
Kissing
INTOLERANCE. See Prejudice
INTOXICATION. See Alcoholism; Liquor problem
INTRACOASTAL Waterway
Brief encounters on the Inland Waterway. K. Vonnegut, Jr. il Motor B & S 140:88-91+ N '77
INTRODUCTION of animals. See Animal introduction
INUITS. See Eskimos
INVASION ships. See Landing craft
INVECTIVE
Insult artistry; work of R. Aman. Time 111:64-5 Ja 9 '78
Mental labels and tattoos; effect of name calling on one's self image. I. R. Hyatt. il Intellect 106:74-5 Ag '77
INVENTIONS
How-to; excerpt from How to turn your idea into a million dollars. D. Kracke. Sci Digest 82:26-30 S '77
Inventors: here's where to go with bright ideas; innovation centers. Sci Digest 81:34-7 Mr '77
New ideas from the inventors. See issues of Popular science
Selling an idea to a big company. L. Combs. il Mech Illus 73:74 Jl '77
Solving the energy crisis. il Am Heritage 28: 30-3 O '77
Super-slurper soaks up awards; Association for the Advancement of Invention and Innovation. il Sci Digest 81:82-3 Ap '77
Thomas Jefferson and the growth of American technology. H. A. Meier. por Intellect 106:192 N '77
Yankee ingenuity plugs away at the energy problem. il U.S. News 83:78-9 O 10 '77
See also
Inventors
Patents
Technological innovations

Anecdotes, facetiae, satire, etc.

Jaundiced eye; suppressed inventions. S. Novick. Environment 19:inside cover Ap '77
INVENTORIES
Higher inventories, but fewer fears. il Bus W p22-3 Ag 8 '77
Industry's wasted billions; asset mismanagement. T. J. Murray. il Duns R 110:86-8 D '77
Inventories are tightening—and that's good. il Fortune 96:12 Ag '77
Inventories may be a drag again. il Bus W p30-1 D 5 '77
Will inventories buoy growth? il Bus W p22-3 Je 6 '77
INVENTORS
Young inventor sheds light on a tricky problem; device for reading and writing in the dark; interview, ed by A. Koral. B. Schroeder. por Seventeen 36:104 Ap '77
See also
Inventions
also names of inventors, e.g. T. A. Edison

Anecdotes, facetiae, satire, etc.

Inventors of the faith. M. E. Marty. Chr Cent 94:207 Mr 2 '77
INVENTORY control. See Inventories
INVERTEBRATES
See also
Marine invertebrates
Sexual behavior—Invertebrates
Skeleton (invertebrates)
Vision (invertebrates)
INVESTIGATIONS, Government. See Government investigations
INVESTIGATIVE Reporters and Editors Association. See Crime and the press
INVESTMENT advisers
Analysts who don't ignore bad news; T. L. O'Glove and R. A. Olstein. J. Madrick. pors Bus W p81 Je 6 '77
Development banking a la DLJ. il por Forbes 119:56-7 Ap 15 '77
Disclosure rules hit the advisers; New York State registration requirements. por Bus W p55-6 D 12 '77
Elderly kid in a candy store; David J. Greene and Co. H. Rudnitsky. por Forbes 119:110+ My 1 '77

INVESTMENT advisers—*Continued*
Exploding market in specialized research. Bus W p 128 D 26 '77
Finding good deals for corporate treasurers; Gelfand, Quinn & Associates. il Bus W p66-7 D 19 '77
Index funds: queering Wall Street's money game. C. Welles. Nation 224:300-4 Mr 12 '77
Mario Gabelli's orphan asylum; Gabelli & Co. il por Forbes 120:69-70+ Jl 15 '77
Multiplying dividends through stock swaps; W. Peters of Unicorn Group. J. Madrick. il Bus W p 126 Ap 18 '77
Profit potential in spotting takeovers. il Bus W p 100-2 O 24 '77
Rating a company by its market share; Mitchell, Hutchins Inc. D. Santry. Bus W p89 O 3 '77
Red faces and red ink; Winters & Co. il Forbes 119:27-8 Je 1 '77
Systematic approach to contrary opinions; M. B. Evans. J. Madrick and D. G. Santry. por Bus W p61 Ag 1 '77
Think tank that manages money; Unicorn Group. il Bus W p45-6 Jl 4 '77
Those investment advisory services—what you get for your money. Changing T 31:24-8 Ag '77
When star analysts look less lustrous; institutional analysts in retail brokerage. Bus W p 106-7 S 26 '77
See also
Brokers
Feick, S.
Patterson, S. P.

INVESTMENT advisory services. See Investment advisers

INVESTMENT analysis. See Security analysis

INVESTMENT annuities. See Annuities

INVESTMENT banking
Can Kuhn Loeb rebuild its muscle? il Bus W p 136+ F 14 '77
Commercial vs. investment bankers. H. H. Angermueller; M. A. Taylor. il Harvard Bus 55: 132-44 S '77
Expert strategists in the acquisition games; R. F. Greenhill and S. Friedman. pors Bus W p 182-3 N 14 '77
ITT's Hartford deal still worries the SEC; Lazard Frères stocks sale arrangement. Bus W p26-7 Je 6 '77
Jimmy Carter's Little Rock connection; Stephens Inc. il pors Bus W p88 Ap 11 '77
Passing the baton at Lazard Frères. W. Robertson. il pors Fortune 96:116-20+ N '77
See also
Goldman, Sachs & Company
Merrill Lynch & Company, Inc

Acquisitions and mergers

Our crowd, less one; Lehman Brothers and Kuhn Loeb merger. M. Ruby and P. L. Abraham. Newsweek 90:96+ D 12 '77
Shell shock on Wall Street; Lehman, Kuhn Loeb merging. Time 110:76+ D 12 '77

Advertising

Street is bullish on ad campaigns. il Bus W p 104 O 10 '77

INVESTMENT companies. See Investment trusts

INVESTMENT counselors. See Investment advisers

INVESTMENT fraud. See Fraud

INVESTMENT services, Bank. See Banks and banking—Services

INVESTMENT tax credit
Investment credit on confinement units: in pursuit of a decision. il Suc Farm 75:9 S '77
Utilities fight to escape a tax-credit trap. il Bus W p96+ D 5 '77

INVESTMENT trusts
Annual mutual fund survey: 1977. il Forbes 120:65+ Ag 15 '77
Bond funds designed as high-tax shelters. D. G. Santry. il Bus W p61 Ag 22 '77
Bond funds vs. unit trusts. Bus W p 132 Jl 25 '77
Dealing with your mutual fund. il Changing T 31:21-3 N '77
Fidelity's experiment with index funds. J. Madrick. il Bus W p 107 F 14 '77
Funds. See issues of Forbes
Funds hope to improve on 1977's gain. il Bus W p 118+ D 26 '77
Income without taxes? municipal-bond funds. W. Flanagan. il Vogue 167:320 N '77
Index funds: more than a passing fad. J. Madrick. il Bus W p78 Jl 11 '77
Index funds: queering Wall Street's money game. C. Welles. Nation 224:300-4 Mr 12 '77
Inside look at a new, hot municipal bond fund; Dreyfus Tax-exempt Bond Fund; interview, ed by A. Hershman. R. Moynihan. por Duns R 110:141-4+ O '77
John Marks Templeton: serving God and hunting bargains; Templeton Growth Fund. R. J. Flaherty. il por Forbes 119:72+ My 15 '77
Money fund extends the float; Capital Preservation Fund Inc. Bus W p 118 Mr 21 '77
Mutual funds for small investors. Mademoiselle 83:210 S '77
Mutual funds that pay tax-free income. il Changing T 31:6-9 Mr '77
On the rebound. Newsweek 89:80 Je 20 '77
Option funds: a popular cushion for investors. il Bus W p90-2 Ja 16 '78
Stock indexing wins more fans. il Bus W p75+ D 26 '77
Tortoise and the hare; W. J. Ruane's Sequoia fund. por Forbes 119:56-7 F 1 '77
What makes the funds look so much better. il Bus W p91-2 Je 20 '77
See also
Investors Overseas Services, Ltd
Real estate investment trusts

Finance

Forbes fund ratings—1977. il Forbes 120:68+ Ag 15 '77

INVESTMENTS
Best ways to beat inflation. il U.S. News 83:48-52 N 21 '77
Can America finance future prosperity? H. B. Freeman, Jr. por Nations Bus 65:58 Je '77
Changing times saving & investment yardstick. il Changing T 31:41 Je; 25-8 O '77
Exotica: the appeal of tangible objects. il Bus W p 146-8 D 26 '77
Farmland still best bet for rocking chair set. R. Krumme. il Suc Farm 75:23 Ag '77
How to invest for income. bibl il Changing T 31:6-10 Jl '77
Investment outlook 1978; special section. il Bus W p52-3+ D 26 '77
Investment trends. P. A. Samuelson. il Newsweek 89:74 Je 27 '77
Is owning a home still a sound investment? G. G. Greer. il Bet Hom & Gard 55:10+ Mr '77
Markets and investments. See issues of Business week
Money and investments. See issues of Forbes
Money plan for your retirement. S. Shulsky. il Ret Liv 17:30-7 N; 24-31 D '77
Money: where to put it now? interviews. U.S. News 83:50-4 D 26 '77
Personal investing. See issues of Fortune
Q&A about investments. S. Shulsky. See issues of Retirement living
Racehorse. . . a fast profit? W. Flanagan. Vogue 167:378 S '77
Strategy for young investors. J. Fraser. U.S. News 83:90 O 10 '77
Tax-saving investments your family can make. M. Daly. il Bet Hom & Gard 55:193-4+ O '77
Tax that is killing investment; capital gains; views of W. F. Ballhaus. J. Cobbs. il Bus W p 14+ Ja 16 '78
What investors are looking for. J. Fraser. U.S. News 83:64 Ag 29 '77
What would you do with $10,000? W. Flanagan. Vogue 167:190 Ag '77
What's ahead for farm investing? il Suc Farm 75:no5A4 Mr '77
Where should you invest your money now? interview. E. Shapiro. il Changing T 31:6-10 My '77
Where women should invest their money; interview. V. VanCaspel. il por U.S. News 83:33-4 D 5 '77
See also
Annuities
Banks and banking—Investments
Bonds, Government
Brokers
Capital
Capital investments
Coins as an investment
Dividends
Gold as an investment
Institutional investments
Interest (economics)
Investment trusts
Real estate investment
Saving and savings
Securities
Small business investment companies
Stockholders
Stocks

Advisers

See Investment advisers

Bibliography

Christmas shopping list. J. Train. por Forbes 120:130-1 D 1 '77

Statistics

Investment figures of the week. See issues of Business week

INVESTMENTS, American
Christmas cheer. R. H. Heindel. Intellect 106: 201 D '77
Developing codes of conduct for multinational enterprises; statement, September 7, 1977. P. H. Boeker. Dept State Bull 77:475-9 O 10 '77
High yields pull U.S. corporate cash abroad. il Bus W p79-80 Ja 16 '78
Why the multinational tide is ebbing. S. Rose. il Fortune 96:110-14+ Ag '77
See also
Overseas Private Investment Corporation

INVESTMENTS, American—*Continued*

Africa, Southern

Doing business with a blacker Africa. il Bus W p64-8+ F 14 '77

Belgium

Belgium hits Badger for shutting an office. Bus W p30+ Mr 28 '77

Brazil

J. I. Case's optimism about Brazil's future. Bus W p76 D 5 '77

Canada

Canada's weak dollar yields little profit. il Bus W p58 N 21 '77

Yankee dollars are welcome again. Bus W p59 My 16 '77

Caribbean Region

U.S. business community and the Caribbean: partners in growth and development; excerpt from address, June 23, 1977. T. A. Todman. Dept State Bull 77:214-18 Ag 15 '77

Chile

Four years after the fall. T. Szulc. New Repub 177:14-16 S 10 '77

ITT under the gun. T. Szulc and E. Yoffe. New Repub 177:18-22 Ag 6 '77

Costa Rica

Costa Rica's Vescogate. M. R. Benjamin and others. por Newsweek 89:47 Je 13 '77

Cuba

Claimsmen and the traders: U.S. business squabbles over Cuba; reimbursement for expropriated properties. A. L. Padula, Jr. Nation 225:390-3 O 22 '77

Will U.S. companies recoup losses in Cuba? il U.S. News 82:61 Je 13 '77

Dominican Republic

Church investments: challenging G&W. J. E. Mulligan. Chr Cent 94:64-7 Ja 26 '77

Egypt

Hell paved with good intentions. J. Berry. il Forbes 120:39-40 N 15 '77

Europe, Western

Radio Shack's rough trip. il Bus W p55 My 30 '77

Far East

Peaceful Asia beckons investors. R. Rowan. il Fortune 96:188-94+ O '77

France

Trying to outwit the French. il Bus W p 108 S 12 '77

Germany, West

Cookie crumbles for Xox-Nabisco. il Bus W p46+ Je 13 '77

Great Britain

American chance to buy more of BP. il Bus W p49+ Ap 25 '77

Japan

If you can't beat the Japanese, why not join them? il Forbes 120:96-7 D 1 '77

Latin America

Leadership role for private enterprise in Latin America; address, June 27, 1977. T. A. Todman. Dept State Bull 77:464-8 O 10 '77

Lofty rhetoric and business interests: the real Latin American policy. A. Howard. Nation 225:365-70 O 15 '77

Nigeria

Rhetoric and reality. por Forbes 120:122 N 1 '77

Poland

Dos and don'ts of landing a Polish contract. A. Hertzberg. Forbes 120:46 Jl 1 '77

Puerto Rico

Catch 936. il Forbes 120:96 N 1 '77

Russia

Innocents abroad; Kama River plant. W. F. Buckley, Jr. Nat R 29:168-9 F 4 '77

Profiting from Pepskis. il Time 109:39 Ja 31 '77

Soviet-American trade: trick or treat? J. Barron. Read Digest 111:67-8+ O '77

Soviet Union: Bendix breaks ground in trade with Russia. Bus W p49 Ja 31 '77

Saudi Arabia

Saudis say wrong numbers to the U.S. Bus W p20-1 Ja 9 '78

Wrong number; Americans lose telecommunications contract. D. Pauly and E. Shannon. Newsweek 90:78 D 26 '77

South Africa

Employment practices in South Africa; remarks, October 5, 1977. C. R. Vance. Dept State Bull 77:685-6 N 14 '77

Peddling apartheid in America. H. Glass and M. Shirk. Progressive 41:30 Mr '77

Reducing investments in South Africa. R. E. Lambert. map America 136:130-2 F 12 '77

U.S. companies feel pressure for change. Bus W p68 F 14 '77

Spain

Hedging on the peseta. il Bus W p71-2 My 2 '77

Underdeveloped areas

Let's create wealth, not allocate shortages; address, May 24, 1977. W. B. Wriston. Vital Speeches 43:653-6 Ag 15 '77

Multinational investment and global purpose; address, June 17, 1977. L. A. Iacocca. Vital Speeches 43:720-4 S 15 '77

Role of investment in expanding an open international economic system; address, June 27, 1977. R. N. Cooper. Dept State Bull 77:127-31 Jl 25 '77

United Arab Emirates

How taxes force Americans to leave a key Arab region. D. Mullin. il map U.S. News 83:75-6 S 19 '77

Virgin Islands

Playing for high stakes in the Virgin Islands; Amerada Hess. T. Szulc. il Forbes 120:53-5 Ag 1 '77

INVESTMENTS, Arab

Super-connector from Saudi Arabia; A. M. Khashoggi. L. Kraar. il pors Fortune 95:108-14+ Je '77

Very popular new issue. il por Forbes 120:188 N 15 '77

INVESTMENTS, Belgian

United States

Lambert's widening beachhead in the U.S; Lambert Brussels Corp. il por Bus W p 102-3 F 21 '77

INVESTMENTS, British

United States

Continuing wave of British takeovers. il Bus W p27-8 D 19 '77

Putting more pounds into U.S. property; British pension funds. il Bus W p57 O 10 '77

W. H. Smith subsidiary pondering U.S. distribution network. P. Kleinman. Pub W 212:23 Ag 8 '77

INVESTMENTS, Canadian

United States

Canadians like the look of U.S. real estate. il Bus W p55 Ag 1 '77

Northern Telecom keeps pushing south. Bus W p29 D 19 '77

Why Canadian dollars are migrating south. il Bus W p42+ N 28 '77

INVESTMENTS, European

United States

Europe's money on the run. M. Ruby and others. il Newsweek 90:58-60 Ag 1 '77

INVESTMENTS, Foreign

When a declining dollar helps the investor. il Bus W p 131-2+ D 26 '77

See also

Corporations—Foreign business

Debts, External

Algeria

Once-sure market becomes competitive. Bus W p62+ Ap 18 '77

Arab countries

Arabs diversify into the arms business. Bus W p31-2 O 31 '77

Australia

Sale of Rigby's shares heats up debate over foreign ownership; publishing industry. M. G. Zifcak. Pub W 212:74-6 S 19 '77

Brazil

Second thoughts on CVRD's partners; Companhia Vale do Rio Doce. il map Bus W p38 Ag 22 '77

Chile

Despotism is not enough: the big money shuns Chile. V. Bergesen. Nation 224:682-4 Je 4 '77

Egypt

Foreign investors start moving in. Bus W p52-3+ My 16 '77

Gabon

Africa's oil nations tempt investors. Bus W p77 F 14 '77

Germany, West

Multinationals rush to beat new taxes. il Bus W p52 O 10 '77

INVESTMENTS, Foreign—*Continued*

Guyana

Kissing the hand you just bit. il map Forbes 119:64-5 Je 15 '77

Indonesia

New courtship of foreign investors. il Bus W p56+ S 19 '77

Why foreign investors are scared. il Bus W p60 Ap 18 '77

Ireland

Books of Killeen. por Forbes 120:112 D 1 '77

Rake's progress. il Time 109:79 Je 20 '77

Malta

New gateway to Arab markets. il Bus W p52 Je 13 '77

Nigeria

Africa's oil nations tempt investors. Bus W p77 F 14 '77

But it still hurts. Forbes 120:26 Jl 15 '77

South Africa

South Africa tightens its grip on capital. Bus W p54 Ap 18 '77

South Africa: wary investing policy—until reform. il Bus W p67-8+ F 14 '77

Spain

Spain: smoothing the way for foreign investors. il Bus W p34-5 Ja 24 '77

Taiwan

Even brighter lure for foreign capital. il Bus W p42 Je 20 '77

Thailand

Junta sets out new bait for investors. il Bus W p52+ N 28 '77

Trinidad and Tobago

Using oil wealth to industrialize; luring foreign interest. Bus W p39-40 Ag 22 '77

Turkey

Stung by Turkey's foreign exchange crisis. il Bus W p55 Jl 4 '77

Underdeveloped areas

Assembly calls for sound investment in developing countries of resources of Pension Fund. UN Chron 14:76 Ja '77

United States

Foreign buyers snap up more U.S. farmland. D. Braun. Farm J 101:E2 D '77

Foreign investment in the U.S.—it grows. . .but slowly. il Forbes 120:158-60+ N 15 '77

Germans are coming! Germans are coming! foreign property and casualty insurance companies. il Forbes 120:74-5 O 1 '77

Invasion of the American heartland: a report on how and why foreign investors are gobbling up choice U.S. farms. C. H. Stern. il Sat R 5:18-20+ O 15 '77

Nobody here but us Texans. . ; foreign investments in Houston. il Forbes 119:52-4 F 1 '77

Role of foreign investment in the U.S. A. Brittain, 3d. por Nations Bus 65:54+ Mr '77

Safe haven for frightened funds. il Time 110: 49-50 Jl 25 '77

Scramble to buy U.S. land spreads all over the world. il U.S. News 83:78-9 S 12 '77

Skittish view from overseas. il Bus W p80 D 26 '77

Why foreign investors turn their eyes toward America. il U.S. News 82:92+ Ap 18 '77

Vietnam

Let's be practical. por Forbes 120:63 Ag 1 '77

INVESTMENTS, French

How the French do it. por Forbes 119:114+ Mr 15 '77

United States

Appliance maker scouts for a U.S. site; Moulinex. Bus W p38-40 My 30 '77

France dives deeply into commercial paper. Bus W p97 F 7 '77

Why so many French are tackling the U.S. il Bus W p30 Jl 4 '77

INVESTMENTS, German

Algeria

Algerian venture sinks a developer; Bremer Treuhand. il Bus W p30-1 Jl 18 '77

United States

A German expands in U.S. retailing; merger agreement between Vornado, Inc. and Fed-Mart Corp. il Bus W p34-5+ Ag 15 '77

How Bayer is building in the U.S. market. il Bus W p72-3 Ag 1 '77

Pollution may kill VW's Rabbit plant; EPA ruling. il Bus W p26 Mr 7 '77

INVESTMENTS, Indonesian

United States

Bitter *rijsttafel;* U.S. corporate contributors to the Ramayana restaurant. por Time 109:58 F 14 '77

INVESTMENTS, Iranian

United States

Super Bowl winner; investment in New Orleans land development. por Forbes 120:78 D 15 '77

INVESTMENTS, Japanese

Pressures to invest more money abroad. il Bus W p63 N 14 '77

Brazil

Japan's investment ardor cools off. il Bus W p54 O 3 '77

Singapore

Welcome injection of petrochemicals. Bus W p46 Je 13 '77

United States

Japan's ways thrive in the U.S. il Bus W p 156+ D 12 '77

Tactics to outwit U.S. protectionists. il Bus W p36 Mr 28 '77

INVESTMENTS, Korean

Arab countries

Korea's crucial link to the Middle East; South Korea. il Bus W p41 Ag 1 '77

INVESTMENTS, Latin American

United States

Miami: saved again. P. Berman. il Forbes 120: 37-41 N 1 '77

INVESTMENTS, Libyan

Italy

What Fiat will do with Libya's money. il Bus W p97+ Mr 14 '77

INVESTMENTS, Russian

This Communist international has a capitalist accent. H. E. Meyer. il Fortune 95:134-7+ F '77

INVESTMENTS, Saudi Arabian

United States

Lance's mysterious rescuer; G. Pharaon's offer to buy National Bank of Georgia stock. il por Time 111:45 Ja 9 '78

New targets for Saudi cash. il Bus W p88 N 7 '77

Still a good old boy; sale of National Bank of Georgia stock to the Saudi Research and Development Corporation. Nation 225:707-8 D 31 '77

Surprising turn in saga of Bert Lance; purchase of National Bank of Georgia stock by G. Pharaon. pors U.S. News 84:36 Ja 9 '78

Texas-Saudi affair. il Forbes 120:88 O 1 '77

INVESTMENTS, Scottish

United States

Scots who buy American. il Bus W p72 Ag 22 '77

INVESTORS. See Stockholders

INVESTORS Diversified Services, Inc-Alleghany Corporation Merger. See Corporations—Acquisitions and mergers

INVESTORS Overseas Services, Ltd

Cornfeld the crusader. M. Dammerman. il por Forbes 120:64+ O 15 '77

IO (satellite) See Satellites

IOANNISIANI, Bagrat K.

Soviet 6-meter altazimuth reflector. il map Sky & Tel 54:356-62 N '77

ION implantation

See also

Semiconductors—Doping

IONESCO, Eugéne

Antidotes from Ionesco. por Horizon 21:34 Ja '78 •

Man with bags. Review

Nation 225:349 O 8 '77 •

IONS

Anions of the alkali metals. J. L. Dye. il Sci Am 237:92-6+ bibl(p 154) Jl '77

See also

Electrolysis

Plasma (ionized gases)

IOWA

See also

Banks and banking—Iowa

Libraries—Iowa

Music festivals—Iowa

Opera—Iowa

Description and travel

Little house that spreads happiness; vacation retreat in Clayton County. J. Gillies. il Farm J 100:33A-33C D '76

IOWA Beef Processors, Inc

Iowa beef becomes a test for management. Bus W p28-9 Mr 14 '77

IOWA. University, Iowa City
Impact of Federal regulations at a university. D. C. Spriestersbach and W. J. Farrell. bibl Science 198:27-30 O 7 '77

IPI-Tombi; musical comedy. See Musical comedy, revue, etc.—Reviews—Single works

IRAN
See also
Airplanes, Military—Iran
Americans in Iran
Civil rights—Iran
Contracts, Government—Iran
Kurds
Teheran
Zoology—Iran

Commerce

United States

See United States—Commerce—Iran

Economic conditions

Iran rebuilds its confidence. il Bus W p54+ Ja 31 '77

Economic policy

Iran rebuilds its confidence. il Bus W p54+ Ja 31 '77
Our world must not be divided; address, May 7, 1977. A. Zahedi. Vital Speeches 43:517-20 Je 15 '77
Shah cools his overheated economy. Bus W p46-7 D 26 '77
Tough talk on oil, arms, investments; interview, ed by R. Taggiasco. Mohammed Reza Pahlevi. por Bus W p36+ Ja 24 '77

Foreign relations

Oil power in the Middle East. J. C. Campbell. bibl f For Affairs 56:89-110 O '77
Our world must not be divided; address, May 7, 1977. A. Zahedi. Vital Speeches 43:517-20 Je 15 '77

United States

See United States—Foreign relations—Iran

Kings and rulers

See also
Mohammed Reza Pahlevi

Politics and government

Shah on war and peace; excerpts from interview, ed by A. de Borchgrave. Mohammed Reza Pahlevi. por map Newsweek 90:69-71 N 14 '77

IRANIAN authors. See Authors, Iranian

IRAQ
Iraq: determined to upset U.S. plan for Mideast peace. D. Mullin. il map U.S. News 82:93-4+ My 16 '77
Iraq starts to thaw. T. Clifton. il Newsweek 90:52 Jl 4 '77
See also
Contracts, Government—Iraq
Kurds

Foreign relations

Why Iraq won't deal with Israel; interview, ed by D. Mullin. S. Husayn. il por U.S. News 82:96 My 16 '77

IRELAND, Jill
I love being Mrs Charles Bronson, but. . . ; interview, ed by J. Ardmore. il pors McCalls 105:28+ N '77

IRELAND
See also
Astronomical observatories—Ireland
Conglomerate corporations—Ireland
Dublin
Fishing—Ireland
Hotels, motels, etc.—Ireland
Income tax—Ireland
Investments, Foreign—Ireland
Music festivals—Ireland
Northern Ireland
Police—Ireland
Visitors, Foreign—Ireland

Industries

New exodus from Ireland. M. Dammerman. il Forbes 119:69-70 Ap 1 '77

Politics and government

See also
Elections—Ireland

Religious institutions and affairs

See also
Catholic Church in Ireland

IRELAND, Northern. See Northern Ireland

IRION, Mary Jean
House, woman, rock, sea; poem. Chr Cent 94:1060 N 16 '77

IRIS (eye)
What your eyes tell you about your health. J. Maxwell. il Esquire 89:54-7 Ja '78

IRISES
Iris with the golden writing. E. Pasahow. il Horticulture 55:14-15 My '77

IRISH, Paul
Death in detention in South Africa. Chr Cent 94:8 Ja 5 '77

IRISH AMERICANS
Exporting death to Ireland; arms purchased with American donations. D. Fisher. Commonweal 104:356-8 Je 10 '77; Discussion. 104:500-2 Ag 5 '77
Golden clan; excerpt. J. Corry. il N Y Times Mag p 16-19+ Mr 13 '77

IRISH art. See Art, Irish

IRISH in the United States
See also
Irish Americans

IRISH Republican Army
Buying back Belfast? IRA business activities. M. Dammerman. il Forbes 119:25-7 Mr 15 '77
Exporting death to Ireland; arms purchased with American donations. D. Fisher. Commonweal 104:356-8 Je 10 '77; Discussion. 104:500-2 Ag 5 '77
IRA's young Turks. M. MacPherson. Newsweek 89:30-1 F 21 '77
Irish paradox. D. O'Brien. il N Y Times Mag p96-8+ S 11 '77

IRISH unification question
See also
Ulster Defense Association

IRMSCHER, William F.
Teaching of writing in terms of growth. il Engl J 66:33-6 D '77

IRON
See also
Wrought iron

IRON, Sponge
Sponge iron in steel's future. S. Rose. il Fortune 95:106-10+ Ja '77

IRON Age
From bronze to steel. Sci Am 236:61 My '77
How the Iron Age began. R. Maddin and others. il Sci Am 237:122-31 O '77

Africa

Spread of the Bantu language. D. W. Phillipson. il maps Sci Am 236:106-14 bibl(p 148) Ap '77

IRON-clad vessels. See Armored vessels

IRON deficiency anemia. See Anemia

IRON in diet
Anemia epidemic; correcting iron deficiency in women by diet. J. C. Wang. Harp Baz 110:91+ Je '77

IRON industry

Brazil

Second thoughts of CVRD's partners; Compania Vale do Rio Doce. il map Bus W p38 Ag 22 '77

IRON metallurgy
See also
Iron, Sponge

IRON miners
See also
Strikes—United States—Iron miners

IRON mines and mining

United States

Shades of Adirondack iron; Salisbury Iron Mine. D. L. Tuttle. il Conservationist 31:33-5 Mr '77
See also
Reserve Mining Company

IRON rust. See Corrosion and anticorrosives

IRON silicates
See also
Olivine

IRONCLADS. See Armored vessels

IRONWORK
Iron candlestands: made where, when, and by whom? C. F. Montgomery and G. W. R. Ward. bibl il Antiques 112:282-4 Ag '77
See also
Blacksmithing

Collectors and collecting

Address book; dealers in iron objects. S. Sunderlin. House B 119:32+ Mr '77

IRRADIATED food. See Food, Effect of radiation on

IRRIGATION
Drip irrigation. K. Shoji. il Sci Am 237:62-8 N '77
Water management can offset higher irrigation costs. Suc Farm 75:no538 Mr '77
See also
Sewage irrigation
Watering of gardens, lawns, etc.

Arizona

Where the sun waters the desert; solar-power irrigation system near Gila Bend. D. Halacy. il Mech Illus 73:78+ D '77

California

Drip irrigation case history. il Sunset 158:292-3 Ap '77

Idaho

Last Idaho land rush: growth at any cost? E. Chaney. Audubon 79:154-7 N '77

IRRIGATION—*Continued*

Nebraska

They irrigate by phone. W. Waltner and E. Waltner. il Farm J 101:MM1+ Mr '77

Russia

Winning battle against destruction; reclamation of Russian steppes in Central Asia by irrigation. A. G. Babaev and N. S. Orlovsky. il UNESCO Courier 30:18-22 Jl '77

South Dakota

McGovern vs. the farmers: South Dakota's water showdown; Oahe Irrigation Project. H. Gardner. il Nation 224:456-61 Ap 16 '77

Texas

This orchard drips with success. T. Hodges. il Org Gard & Farm 24:90-2 Jl '77

United States

See also
United States—Reclamation, Bureau of

Wyoming

Irrigated grass pays as well as crops; orchardgrass. il Farm J 101:J2 N '77

IRRIGATION canals and ditches
Canal a million farmers built; Red Flag Canal in Linhsien, China. H. Forman. il Horticulture 55:30-5 My '77
Garrison Diversion. Audubon 79:163 N '77

IRRIGATION machinery
Financing irrigation: lender's point of view. Suc Farm 75:no2 8 F '77

IRRIGATION water
Take advantage of free water. D. Royal. il Org Gard & Farm 24:87-8 Jl '77

Salt content

Growing crops on sand dunes? L. Wood. il Sea Front 23:228-32 Jl '77
Salty irrigation: bringing in the sheaves. il Sci N 112:53 Jl 23 '77
Seawater-based crop production: a feasibility study. E. Epstein and J. D. Norlyn. bibl il Science 197:249-51 Jl 15 '77

IRVIN, Amanda
Steamed up; poem. Seventeen 36:96 Ag '77

IRVIN, Robert W.
Ed Cole was a friend. por Motor T 29:106 Ag '77

IRVINE Company mergers. See Real estate business—Acquisitions and mergers

IRVING, David John Cawdell
Caveat lector. J. Lukacs. Nat R 29:946-8+ Ag 19 '77 *
Hitler and the Holocaust. K. L. Woodward and A. Collings. il por Newsweek 90:77 Jl 11 '77 *
Hitler and the revisionists. W. F. Buckley, Jr. Nat R 29:1072-3 S 16 '77 *

IRVING, John
Dog in the alley, child in the sky; story. Esquire 87:108-9 Je '77

IRVING, Washington
Rip Van Winkle; dramatization. See Thane, A.

about

Historical group recreates Old Christmas. P. Doebler. il Pub W 212:51 S 5 '77 *
Sleepy Hollow Restorations. il Hobbies 82:141+ D '77 *
Sunnyside. C. Morgan. il por Am For 83:26-9 Ap '77 *

IRWIN, Howard S.
History of the Airflow car; with biographical sketch. il Sci Am 237:20, 98-104+ bibl(p 140) Ag '77

IRWIN, John B.
Case of the setting sun. il Sky & Tel 54:167-70 S '77

IRWIN, Manley R. and Johnson, S. C.
Information economy and public policy. bibl Science 195:1170-4 Mr 18 '77

IRWIN, Mark
Frog's advice to a young girl in love; poem. Commonweal 104:210 Ap 1 '77

IRWIN, Robert
Robert Irwin: everything I've done in the last five years doesn't exist; interview, ed by T. Albright. il Art N 76:49-54 Summ '77

about

Black plane; Whitney Museum retrospective. New Yorker 53:28-9 Je 6 '77 *
Floating a line in space. E. Schwartz. Art N 76:52-3 Summ '77 *

ISAAC (biblical character) See Bible—Biography

ISABELLA I, Queen of Spain
Autographs. K. V. Hostick. Hobbies 82:142 O '77 *

ISABELLA, Minn.

Education

See Education—Minnesota

ISADORA Duncan Centenary Dance Company. See Dance companies

ISADORA Duncan sleeps with the Russian Navy; drama. See Wanshel, J.

ISCHEMIA, Cerebral. See Cerebrovascular disease

ISEMAN, Frederick
Nothing happened. Esquire 88:74-5+ S '77

ISEMAN, Peter A.
Last of the Bedouin. il Horizon 19:32-9 Mr '77

ISHI (Indian)
Legacy of Ishi. F. R. Gunsky. il Liv Wildn 40:4-11 Ja '77 *
Wild man of Orville. C. W. Campbell. il por Am Hist Illus 12:18-26+ Je '77 *

ISHI Country Wilderness Area (proposed) See Wilderness areas—California

ISLA MUJERES
Isla Mujeres: Mexico's sleeping island. C. B. Barrington. il Travel 148:52-7 S '77

ISLAM
Islam. il Sr Schol 109:6-8 Mr 24 '77
Islam on the march. K. L. Woodward and W. E. Schmidt. il Newsweek 90:72+ D 5 '77

ISLAMIC art. See Art, Islamic

ISLAMIC civilization. See Civilization, Islamic

ISLAMIC law
Crime or punishment? il Time 110:38 Jl 25 '77

ISLAND ecology
Species turnover rates on islands: dependence on census interval. J. M. Diamond and R. M. May. bibl il Science 197:266-70 Jl 15 '77

ISLAND life. See Islands

ISLAND Trees, N.Y. School District. See Education—New York (state)

ISLANDS
Island fever. F. Powledge. il Esquire 87:88-93+ Mr '77
Islands! symposium; ed by H. Sutton. il Sat R 5:17-20+ Ja 7 '78
Need for a boat; islands in the National Park System. G. Soucie. il Nat Parks & Con Mag 51:4-7 F '77
See also
Barrier Islands
Coral reefs and islands

Caricatures and cartoons

Rolling in the isles. il Read Digest 112:94-5 Ja '78

ISLANDS, Artificial. See Artificial islands

ISLANDS, Bay of
Bay of Islands. D. Gleasner and B. Gleasner. il Trav/Holiday 148:42-5 D '77

ISLANDS of the Pacific
See also
Oceania

ISLE AU HAUT
Park service capitulates, plans Isle au Haut giveaway. Nat Parks & Con Mag 51:22-3 D '77

ISOCYANATES
TDI: the unacknowledged poison; toluene diisocyanate. V. Cox. Nation 224:530-2 Ap 30 '77

ISOLATION, Sensory. See Sensory deprivation

ISOLATION chambers
Use of isolators in recombinant DNA research. P. Kourilsky. bibl il Science 196:215-16 Ap 8 '77

ISOLATIONISM (United States) See United States—Foreign relations

ISOLATORS, Germ-free. See Germ-free isolators

ISOLEUCINE epimerization. See Amino acid dating

ISOMETRIC exercise. See Exercise

ISOTOPE separation
Laser separation of isotopes. R. N. Zare. il Sci Am 236:86-7+ F '77
Mechanism of carbon isotope fractionation associated with lipid synthesis. M. J. DeNiro and S. Epstein. bibl il Science 197:261-3 Jl 15 '77
Photophysics and photochemistry. V. S. Letokhov. bibl il Phys Today 30:23-32 My '77
See also
Uranium metallurgy

ISOTOPES
See also subhead Isotopes under names of various elements, e.g. Plutonium—Isotopes

ISRAEL, Gordon
Living legends. G. C. Larson. il por Flying 100:62-3+ Ap '77 *

ISRAEL
Epistle of a Gentile to Saul Bellow; importance of Israel to Jews and to the world. H. Fairlie. New Repub 176:18-20+ F 5 '77
Israel journal: 1972-1976: reflections on a troubled people; with photographs by M. Bar-Am. T. Smith. Sat R 4:8-16+ F 5 '77
Jerusalem diarist. M. Peretz. New Repub 177:42 N 5 '77
See also
Airplanes, Military—Israel
Atomic power—Israel
Ballet—Israel
Collective settlements—Israel
College libraries—Israel
Dead Sea
Guerrillas—Israel
Immigration and emigration—Israel
Intelligence service—Israel

ISRAEL—See also—*Continued*
Jerusalem
Mental hygiene—Israel
Music festivals—Israel
National parks and reserves—Israel
Political attitudes—Israel
Political prisoners—Israel
Power resources—Israel
Television broadcasting—Israel
Trade unions—Israel
United Nations—Israel
United Nations—Special Committee to Investigate Israeli Practices Affecting the Human Rights of the Population of the Occupied Territories
Visitors, Foreign—Israel
Women—Israel
Zionism
Zoology—Israel

Armed Forces

Officers

Israel's generals: polished brass. il Time 110:14-15 Jl 4 '77

Boundaries

Bible: a fallible guide. map Time 110:32 Jl 25 '77

Commerce

Ecuador

Rabin sees no change possible in block of Kfirs for Ecuador. Aviation W 106:24 Mr 14 '77

Egypt

Egypt is cool to trade with Israel. il Bus W p38-9 D 19 '77

Europe, Western

See Europe, Western—Commerce—Israel

United States

See United States—Commerce—Israel

Commercial policy

See also
Tariff—Israel

Defenses

Solutionist delusions. S. Rosen. New Repub 177:14-16 N 26 '77
See also
Radar defense networks

Description and travel

Stranger in Holy Land. S. Reiner. il Atlantic 239:85-7 Ap '77

Economic conditions

Between survival and solvency. E. Pawel. il Nation 224:584-7 My 14 '77

Economic policy

Entebbe again. M. Friedman. il Newsweek 90:90-1 N 14 '77
Nation braces for a round of austerity. Bus W p40-1 My 2 '77
Push toward capitalism. il Time 110:36 N 14 '77
Right turn for Israel. M. Ruby and others. il Newsweek 90:90-1 N 14 '77
Strong first step away from socialism. il Bus W p56 N 14 '77
See also
Socialism—Israel
Tariff—Israel

Foreign opinion

American

Begin's American bandwagon. il pors Time 110:22-3 S 5 '77
Is U.S. public opinion shifting? New look at Israel. D. Caploe. Nation 225:70-2 Jl 23 '77
Why Breira? criticism of Israeli policy. J. Shattan. Commentary 63:60-6 Ap '77; Discussion. 63:4+ Je '77

Foreign relations

Begin's strategy and Dayan's tactics: the conduct of Israeli foreign policy. A. Perlmutter. For Affairs 56:357-72 Ja '78

Egypt

See Egypt—Foreign relations—Israel

Lebanon

Border violence, hands of peace. il map Time 110:40-1 N 21 '77
An eye for a tooth. K. Willenson and others. il map Newsweek 90:61+ N 21 '77
Israel's secret war. il Time 110:29 Ag 22 '77
Major turn in a mini war. il maps Time 110:28+ O 3 '77

Panama

See also
Torrijos Herrera, O.—Visit to Israel, 1977

South Africa

Friend in need. K. Willenson and others. il Newsweek 90:44 S 12 '77

United States

See United States—Foreign relations—Israel

History

Begin without smears. E. Breindel. New Repub 176:16-18 Je 18 '77

Politics and government

Begin without smears. E. Breindel. New Repub 176:16-18 Je 18 '77
Begin's surprise maneuver. il por Time 109:36 Je 6 '77
Between survival and solvency. E. Pawel. Nation 224:584-7 My 14 '77
Israel: Begin takes charge. M. R. Benjamin and M. J. Kubic. il por Newsweek 90:50 Jl 4 '77
Israel's hardening line in the Middle East. D. Mullin. il por map U.S. News 83:59-61 Jl 4 '77
Journey through a land of doubts. M. Kalb. il N Y Times Mag p 12-13+ Jl 17 '77
Rabin sums it up; excerpts from interview, ed by M. J. Kubic. Y. Rabin. il por Newsweek 90:51 Jl 4 '77
Rabin's sudden exit. A. Deming and M. J. Kubic. il pors map Newsweek 89:37-8+ Ap 18 '77
Sad downfall of Yitzhak Rabin. il por Time 109:23-4 Ap 18 '77
Stormy start for a stylish hard-liner. il por Time 110:14-16 Jl 4 '77
Why Israel needs peace. il map U.S. News 83:19 D 5 '77
See also
Elections—Israel
Political campaigns—Israel
Political clubs and associations—Israel
Political parties—Israel
Socialism—Israel

Religious institutions and affairs

Zionism and Jewish identity; adaptation of address. J. Katz. Commentary 63:48-52 My '77
See also
Religious conferences—Israel

Social conditions

Feminist goes to Israel. L. C. Pogrebin. il Ms 6:69-72+ O '77

Territorial expansion

See also
Arab countries—Israeli occupation, 1967-
Israel-Arab Wars, 1967- —Territorial questions
Jordan—Israeli occupation, 1967-

ISRAEL-Arab relations. See Jewish-Arab relations

ISRAEL-Arab War, 1948-1949

Photographs and photography

Jerusalem of 1948 and its survivors today counterpoint in Dial Press/James Wade title; interview, ed by R. Dahlin. J. Phillips. il Pub W 211:47-8 Ja 10 '77

ISRAEL-Arab Wars, 1967-

Peace and mediation

Across the divide; interviews. M. Begin; H. Assad. il pors Newsweek 91:40-2+ Ja 16 '78
After the Vance mission: signs of hope. il pors Time 109:26-9 F 28 '77
After Vance trip: peace no closer in Mideast. D. Mullin. U.S. News 83:22 Ag 22 '77
Again, the Mid East. Commonweal 104:195-6 Ap 1 '77
Anatomy of a bold action; interview, ed by M. Gart and W. Wynn. A. Sadat. por Time 111:30+ Ja 2 '78
Anwar Sadat: architect of a new Mideast. il pors Time 111:10-17 Ja 2 '78
Assembly calls for resumption of Geneva peace talks not later than March this year with PLO participation; with texts of resolutions. UN Chron 14:17-19, 101-2 Ja '77
Bazaar bargaining in Washington; visit of M. Dayan. il pors Time 110:31-2+ O 3 '77
Begin brings his plans for peace. il pors Time 110:31-3 Jl 25 '77
Begin in Middle East perspective: new factor in an old equation. I. L. Gendzier. Nation 225:102-4 Ag 6 '77
Begin, the winner. M. Kondracke. New Repub 177:11-13 D 24 '77
Begin's strategy and Dayan's tactics: the conduct of Israeli foreign policy. A. Perlmutter. For Affairs 56:357-72 Ja '78
Behind Carter's gamble in the Middle East. il U.S. News 83:30-1 O 17 '77
Carter and Israel. S. L. Spiegel. Commentary 64:35-40 Jl '77; Discussion. 64:29-31 S '77
Carter plan. A. Deming and others. il por map Newsweek 89:32+ Mr 21 '77
Caution signs on the road to Geneva. il Time 109:35-6 My 9 '77
Charmer named Begin. S. Fraker and others. il pors Newsweek 90:27-8 Ag 1 '77
Christmas in Geneva? A. Deming and others. il map Newsweek 90:41+ O 3 '77
Christmas summit. K. Willenson and others. il pors Newsweek 91:12-14 Ja 2 '78
Council debates Secretary-General's report on Middle East question. il UN Chron 14:16-23+ Ap '77
Dayan's secret. A. De Borchgrave. il por Newsweek 90:43 O 3 '77

ISRAEL-Arab Wars, 1967- —Peace and mediation —*Continued*
Department discusses U.S. efforts in search for Middle East peace; statement, June 8, 1977. A. L. Atherton, Jr. Dept State Bull 77:25-7 Jl 4 '77
Does Washington have the means to impose a settlement on Israel? S. J. Rosen and M. Moustafine. Commentary 64:25-32 O '77
Don't call it treason: the need to talk with the PLO. A. I. Waskow. Nation 224:178-80 F 12 '77
Don't deliver Israel. New Repub 177:5+ Ag 6 '77
Editors and news directors interview President Carter; excerpts from transcript, September 16, 1977. J. Carter. Dept State Bull 77:570-2 O 24 '77
Egypt, Israel, and Isaiah. Chr Today 22:26 D 30 '77
Elusive Camelot; C. R. Vance's visit to the Middle East. il por Time 110:28-30 Ag 22 '77
Ends and beginnings. F. Getlein. Commonweal 105:4 Ja 6 '78
An eye for a tooth. K. Willenson and others. il map Newsweek 90:61+ N 21 '77
Face to face with Israel. R. Steele and others. il por Newsweek 90:32-3 Jl 25 '77
Fahd: it's up to Israel; excerpts from interview, ed by A. De Borchgrave. Fahd. pors Newsweek 89:54 Je 6 '77
Framework for Middle East peace: shaping a more stable world; address, June 17, 1977. W. F. Mondale. Dept State Bull 77:41-6 Jl 11 '77
Friendly talk, but outlook for Mideast peace still dim. D. Mullin. il por U.S. News 83:23 Ag 1 '77
From Geneva up to Geneva down. il Time 110:21-2 Ag 1 '77
Geneva, ho. T. Szulc. New Repub 177:12-14 N 12 '77
Geneva: push comes to shove. il Time 110:24-8+ O 17 '77
Geneva: the Palestinian problem. il Time 110:51-2 O 10 '77
Getting ready to face Carter. il Time 110:51 S 19 '77
Gloom in Israel, joy for the Arabs; American policy statement on Palestinian representation. il Time 110:33-4 S 26 '77
Goal of real peace; address, November 10, 1977. C. R. Vance. Dept State Bull 77:763-6 N 28 '77
Habash: Israel will fall; excerpts from interview, ed by D. Brelis. G. Habash. por Time 110:33 D 19 '77
High price to U.S. for peace in Mideast. D. Mullin. U.S. News 82:43 Je 13 '77
How to save Israel in spite of herself. G. W. Ball. For Affairs 55:453-71 Ap '77; Discussion. 55:888-90; 56:221-5 Jl-O '77
How to welcome President Sadat. il New Repub 176:5-6+ Ap 9 '77
Hussein on his CIA money; excerpts from interview, ed by A. de Borchgrave. Hussein. il por Newsweek 89:16-18 Mr 7 '77
Interview with Secretary Vance on February 8 by Egyptian and Syrian media representatives; transcript of interview, ed by A. Fawzi and G. Rifai. C. R. Vance. Dept State Bull 76:224-8 Mr 14 '77
Interview with Secretary Vance on February 10 by Israeli media representatives; transcript of interview, ed by E. Nissan and others. C. R. Vance. Dept State Bull 76:228-34 Mr 14 '77
Into the Mideast crunch. S. Fraker and others. Newsweek 90:17 Jl 18 '77
Is '77 the year? M. Kondracke. New Repub 176:13-15 F 12 '77
Israel and Munich. G. F. Will. il Newsweek 90:80 Jl 11 '77
Israel: day of the hawks. R. Carroll and others. il pors Newsweek 89:32-3+ My 30 '77
Israel hangs tough. S. Fraker and others. il por Newsweek 90:36-7 Ag 22 '77
Israel thumps the Bible. Nation 224:674 Je 4 '77
Israel turns to the right. Progressive 41:10 Jl '77
Israel's dilemma. S. Avineri. Commentary 64:47-50 D '77
Jimmy and Menachem. M. Kondracke. New Repub 177:13-15 Jl 30 '77
Latest U.S. peace effort—will it save Egypt's Sadat? D. Mullin. il por map U.S. News 83:23-4 Ag 15 '77
Let's resolve the Middle East Crisis—now! W. E. Griffith. Read Digest 110:73-7 Ap '77
Letter from Washington. R. Rovere. New Yorker 53:56-8 Ag 1 '77
Long road to Geneva; C. Vance's Mideast mission. A. Deming and others. pors Newsweek 90:27-9 Ag 15 '77
Making room for reason; interview, ed by W. Cowan and R. Hoyt. R. Lekachman. Current 197:34-49 N '77
Media shuttle. Nation 225:706 D 31 '77
Middle East: no quick fix. J. Miller. Progressive 41:7-8 F '77
Middle East realities. F. Getlein. Commonweal 104:260-1 Ap 29 '77; Reply. R. G. Hoyt. 104:419+ Jl 8 '77
Middle East; symposium. Dept State Bull 77:875-93 D 19 '77
Mideast: a time to hush up. M. Stone. U.S. News 83:84 D 12 '77
Mideast impasse. W. F. Buckley, Jr. Nat R 29:1194 O 14 '77
Mideast: what's next; views of five Mideast observers. il Newsweek 89:38+ My 30 '77
Minister and his mystery trip; meetings between M. Dayan and Arab leaders. il por Time 110:34+ O 3 '77
New friends upset a special relation. il Time 109:44-5 My 23 '77
No peace by proxy. N. Cousins. Sat R 4:4 Jl 23 '77
No slip of the tongue; Jimmy Carter's pronouncements. A. de Borchgrave. il Newsweek 89:35 Mr 21 '77
No to the P.L.O. il Time 110:26 S 12 '77
Nutcracker suite. il Time 110:28-9 Ag 15 '77
PLO still hangs tough; excerpts from interview, ed by W. E. Schmidt. F. al-Kaddoumi. il por Newsweek 89:37 Mr 14 '77
Peace, but not this year; excerpts from interview, ed by W. Wynn. H. Assad. por Time 109:32+ Ja 24 '77
Peace in the Middle East; address, December 6, 1976. C. Herzog. Vital Speeches 43:170-3 Ja 1 '77
Peace in the Middle East: Mr Carter grasps that nettle. M. A. Bruzonsky. il por Nation 224:489-92 Ap 23 '77
Personal touch; C. Vance's Mideast trip. A. Deming and others. il Newsweek 89:27-8 F 21 '77
President Carter comments on Middle East; exchange of remarks, August 8, 1977. J. Carter. Dept State Bull 77:379-80 S 19 '77
President Carter holds meetings with Middle East officials; September 19, 21 and 28, 1977. Dept State Bull 77:634-7 N 7 '77
President Carter interviewed by ABC news correspondents; excerpts from transcript of program, August 10, 1977; ed by H. Reasoner. J. Carter. Dept State Bull 77:395-6 S 26 '77
President Carter's news conference: November 10, 1977. J. Carter. Dept State Bull 77:839-40 D 12 '77
President Carter's remarks at Clinton, Mass, town meeting; excerpts from remarks and question and answer session, March 16, 1977. J. Carter. Dept State Bull 76:334-5 Ap 11 '77
Prospect with Peres; peace settlement. D. Caploe. il Nation 224:587-90 My 14 '77
Return to Geneva: will Carter boot it? D. R. Caploe. Nation 225:359-61 O 15 '77
Road to Tel Aviv. T. Powers. Commonweal 104:275-7 Ap 29 '77
Sadat: why Russia balks at peace; interview; ed by D. B. Richardson. A. Sadat. por U.S. News 83:13 D 19 '77
Sadat's confidence restored. il pors Time 111:24+ Ja 16 '78
Sadat's stormy wake. R. Steele and others. il Newsweek 90:51+ D 12 '77
Saud on war and oil; excerpts from interview, ed by A. de Borchgrave. Saud al Faisal. pors Newsweek 90:64 O 31 '77
Saudi Foreign Minister meets with President Carter; October 25, 1977. Dept State Bull 77:766-7 N 28 '77
Secretary Vance meets at London with Israeli foreign minister; remarks, May 11, 1977. C. R. Vance and Y. Allon. Dept State Bull 76:607-9 Je 6 '77
Secretary Vance reaffirms factors for Mideast conference; exchange of remarks, October 6, 1977. C. R. Vance; M. Riad. Dept State Bull 77:637-9 N 7 '77
Secretary Vance's visit to the Middle East and London July 31-August 13; text of press conferences and remarks, with statement. C. R. Vance. Dept State Bull 77:329-45+ S 12 '77
Secretary Vance's visit to the Middle East, February 14-21; remarks and texts of news conferences. C. R. Vance. Dept State Bull 76:209-23 Mr 14 '77
Security Council told main elements of Middle East issue remain difficult. UN Chron 14:14-15+ Mr '77
Sending Israel a message. R. Steele and others. il map Newsweek 90:28-9 Jl 11 '77
Setback to peace. K. Willenson and others. il Newsweek 90:33-4 Ag 8 '77
Settling the Arab-Israeli conflict. B. Lewis. Commentary 63:50-6 Je '77
Solutionist delusions. S. Rosen. New Repub 177:14-16 N 26 '77
Star in the East. F. Getlein. Commonweal 104:805-6 D 23 '77
Status of Palestinians in peace negotiations; statement, September 12, 1977. Dept State Bull 77:463 O 10 '77
Sticking point. Nat R 29:865-6+ Ag 5 '77
Strained alliance; M. Dayan's U.S. diplomacy. R. Steele and others. il pors Newsweek 90:26-7+ O 17 '77
They are fated to succeed. H. Kissinger. il por Time 111:34-5 Ja 2 '78
Thoughts on the Middle East. Nat R 29:1473-4 D 23 '77

ISRAEL-Arab Wars, 1967- —Peace and mediation —*Continued*
Time for decision. America 137:90-1 Ag 27 '77
Time for peace; excerpts from interview, ed by S. Sullivan and N. Proffitt. M. Dayan. il por Newsweek 90:33 O 17 '77
Time to forbear. Nation 225:610 D 10 '77
Time to meet the players, C. Vance's Middle East trip. il por Time 109:38 F 21 '77
Time to take a gamble; interview, ed by W. Wynn. Hussein. il por Time 109:34 F 14 '77
Too casual diplomacy. New Repub 177:10-11 O 15 '77
Tough talk from a dove; excerpt from interview, ed by M. Bruzonsky. A. Eliav. Nation 225:688-9 D 24 '77
Toward a just peace; Time magazine's plan. maps Time 110:49-50 D 5 '77
Triumph of a superhawk. il por map Time 109: 22-3+ My 30 '77
Trying to sell Geneva. A. Deming and others. il por Newsweek 90:56 O 24 '77
Two Arab leaders reply to Begin; excerpts from interviews, ed by A. de Borchgrave. Hussein; H. Assad. pors Newsweek 90:30-2 Ag 1 '77
Two men who hold keys to Mideast peace talks. pors U.S. News 83:36 O 24 '77
U.S. gives views in General Assembly debate on the Middle East; statement, with text of resolutions, December 9, 1976. W. W. Scranton. Dept State Bull 76:37-40 Ja 17 '77
U.S. Mideast plan? R. Carroll and others. il Newsweek 89:27+ My 23 '77
U.S. responsibility toward peace and human rights; address, November 2, 1977. J. Carter. Dept State Bull 77:759-62 N 28 '77
U.S, U.S.S.R. issue statement on the Middle East; text, October 1, 1977. Dept State Bull 77:639-40 N 7 '77
Warning shot across Begin's bow. por Time 110:34 Jl 11 '77
What role for U.S. in Mideast? il U.S. News 83:11-12 D 19 '77
What Sadat will seek from Carter; interview, ed by L. H. Young and R. Taggiasco. A. Sadat. pors Bus W p96-9 Ap 4 '77
What Vance will find: Mideast peace hopes on rise, but no quick breakthrough. D. Mullin. map U.S. News 82:34-5 F 21 '77
Which Mideast problem? J. Burnham. Nat R 29: 1480 D 23 '77
Why Breira? criticism of Israeli policy on question of negotiation with the PLO. J. Shattan. Commentary 63:60-6 Ap '77; Discussion. 63:4+ Je '77
Why U.S. takes tougher line on Mideast. D. Mullin. il U.S. News 83:35-6 O 3 '77
Will the working paper work? il Time 110:46-7 O 24 '77
See also
Begin, M.—Visit to Egypt, 1977
Cairo conference, 1977
Sadat, A.—Visit to Israel, 1977

Public opinion

Carter vs. Israel: what the polls reveal. S. M. Lipset and W. Schneider. Commentary 64:21-9 N '77
Is U.S. public opinion shifting? New look at Israel. D. Caploe. Nation 225:70-2 Jl 23 '77
Katz in the mountains; meeting with American rabbis. J. Lelyveld. il por N Y Times Mag p63 Jl 10 '77

Territorial questions

Begin the Begin. New Repub 176:5-6+ My 28 '77
Begin's trouble at home. E. M. Breindel. New Repub 178:10-11 Ja 7 '78
Bible: a fallible guide. map Time 110:32 Jl 25 '77
Committee urges implementation of recommendations. il UN Chron 14:31 O '77
Creating facts in the desert. il map Time 109: 26-7 F 28 '77
Don't bank on it: the phantom of a West Bank PLO state. A. Dowty. New Repub 177:15-18 Ag 20 '77
Elusive boundaries of peace in the Holy Land. B. K. Nijim. bibl f maps Intellect 106:202-5 D '77
Israel, West nations of Security Council asked for positions. il UN Chron 14:21 My '77
Israeli settlements in occupied territories; statement, October 19, 1977. A. L. Atherton. Dept State Bull 77:828-9 D 5 '77
Israel's soul. M. Kempton. Progressive 41:11 D '77
Proposal for a Palestinian state. E. R. F. Sheehan. il map N Y Times Mag p8-11 Ja 30 '77; Reply. C. Herzog. p 12 F 27 '77
U.S. position on Israeli settlements; statement, with text of resolution, October 28, 1977. A. J. Young. Dept State Bull 77:821-2 D 5 '77
See also
Arab countries—Israeli occupation, 1967-
Jordan—Israeli occupation, 1967-

ISRAEL Ballet (company) See Ballet—Israel
ISRAEL Broadcasting Authority. See Television broadcasting—Israel
ISRAEL Festival. See Music festivals—Israel
ISRAELI occupation of Arab countries, 1967-. See Arab Countries—Israeli occupation, 1967-
ISRAELI occupation of Jordan, 1967-. See Jordan—Israeli occupation, 1967-
ISRAELI visitors in Egypt. See Visitors, Foreign —Egypt
ISRAELIS
Israel journal: 1972-1976: reflections on a troubled people; photographs. M. Bar-Am. Sat R 4:8-16+ F 5 '77
ISRAELIS in the United States
See also
New York (city)—Foreign population
ISSEROFF, Hadar, and others
Fascioliasis: role of proline in bile duct hyperplasia. bibl il Science 198:1157-9 D 16 '77
ISTANBUL

Riots

May Day in Istanbul. il Newsweek 89:50 My 16 '77
ISTHMUS of Panama. See Panama, Isthmus of
ISTITUTO Centrale del Restauro. See Italy—Istituto Centrale del Restauro
ISTOMIN, Eugene
Conversation with Fingers. il pors N Y Times Mag p56-7+ O 9 '77

about

First Casals concerts; Primeras Jornadas Internacionales Casals. S. Fleming. pors Hi Fi 27: MA36-7 My '77 *
ISTOMIN, Marta Casals (Montañez)
First Casals concerts; Primeras Jornadas Internacionales Casals. S. Fleming. pors Hi Fi 27: MA36-7 My '77 *
ITAKURA, Keiichi, and others
Expression in escherichia coli of a chemically synthesized gene for the hormone somatostatin. bibl il Science 198:1056-63 D 9 '77
ITALIAN AMERICANS
Reporter at large; South Greenwich Village. R. E. Harris. New Yorker 53:48-50+ Ap 25 '77
ITALIAN architecture. See Architecture, Italian
ITALIAN bread. See Bread
ITALIAN cookery. See Cookery, Italian
ITALIAN costume designers. See Costume designers
ITALIAN girl in Algiers; opera. See Rossini, G.
ITALIAN International Bank Ltd. See Banks and banking—Italy
ITALIAN prisoners of war in the United States. See Prisoners of war in the United States
ITALIAN straw hat; opera. See Rota, N.
L'ITALIANA in Algeri; opera. See Rossini, G.
ITALIANS in literature
Bread and wine; I. Silone's novel. J. Martin. Engl J 66:65-6 Mr '77
ITALIANS in the United States
Certain complications; excerpt from O America. L. Barzini. Am Heritage 28:64-7 Ap '77
See also
Italian Americans
ITALY
See also
Abano Terme
Abortion—Laws and legislation—Italy
Architecture, Domestic—Italy
Art—Italy
Ballet—Italy
Banks and banking—Italy
Bologna
Christmas—Italy
Colleges and universities—Italy
Communism—Italy
Crime and criminals—Italy
Festivals—Italy
Finance—Italy
Florence
Foreign students in Italy
Industry and state
Industry and the environment—Italy
Investments, Libyan—Italy
Labor and laboring classes—Italy
Loans, Foreign—Italy
Milan
Music festivals—Italy
Opera—Italy
Political attitudes—Italy
Protests, demonstrations, etc.—Italy
Restaurants—Italy
Rome (city)
Shopping and shoppers—Italy
Sicily
Taormina
Television broadcasting—Italy
Terrorism—Italy
Trials—Italy
Turin
Umbria
Venice
Wages—Italy
World War, 1939-1945—Campaigns and battles—Italy

Antiquities

Rural life in ancient Italy; excavation team at Pizzica. J. C. Carter. il Intellect 106:106-7 S '77
See also
Pompeii

ITALY—*Continued*

Commerce

Credit shadow over foreign trade. Bus W p56+ N 14 '77

Description and travel

Head for the—Italian—hills. H. Calisher. Vogue 167:108 S '77

Economic conditions

Italian economy at a crossroad; address, March 3, 1977. L. Pirelli. Vital Speeches 43:382-4 Ap 1 '77

See also
Labor and laboring classes—Italy

Economic policy

Europe's sickest man. M. Ledeen. New Repub 176:8-10 F 12 '77
Italy: the new austerity starts to work. il Bus W p42-3 Mr 14 '77

Economic relations

United States

See United States—Economic relations—Italy

History

See also
Renaissance

19th century

Anita and Giuseppe Garibaldi: a love story on two continents. G. Arciniegas. il pors Americas 29:2-7 My '77

1922-1945

Iron: a memoir; excerpt from Il sistema periodico, tr by S. Hunter and M. Risk. L. Primo. Commentary 64:45-9 Ag '77

Industries

See also
Automobile industry—Italy
Chemical industries—Italy
Construction industry—Italy
Phonograph record industry—Italy

Istituto Centrale del Restauro

Giovanni Urbani and restoration Italian-style. M. Gendel. il por Art N 76:146-8 Summ '77

Politics and government

Disintegrating Italy. E. M. von Kuehnelt-Leddihn. Nat R 29:1498 D 23 '77
Italy: a new adventure. P. Nazzaro. bibl f Cur Hist 73:160-4+ N '77
Italy awaits Caesar. M. Ledeen. New Repub 178: 16-20 Ja 7 '78
Left and right in bed together: Italy's uncomfortable politics. N. Birbaum. Nation 225:177-81 S 3 '77
Nearer the historic compromise. Time 110:33 Jl 11 '77
Tottering once more at the edge. J. Bonfante. il Time 111:21 Ja 9 '78

See also
Communist Party (Italy)

Religious institutions and affairs

See also
Catholic Church in Italy

ITALY-United States air agreement. See Aviation—International aspects

ITAPÚ hydroelectric project. See Hydroelectric plants—Latin America

ITEL Corporation. See Computer industry

ITHACA, N.Y.

Newspapers

Try small newspapers; Good times gazette. P. Nussman. Writers Digest 57:35 Mr '77

ITO, Michio

Michio Ito: American pioneer. H. Caldwell. il por Dance Mag 51:88-91 My '77 *

ITOH, C. and Company. See Trading companies—Japan

IT'S your move; drama. See Nolan, P. T.

IVACIC, Pero

Non-aligned countries pool their news. il UNESCO Courier 30:18-20 Ap '77

IVAN the Terrible; ballet. See Ballet reviews—Single works

IVANOV, Boris, and Bogdanovsky, Georgy

Four months under space-simulated conditions. Space World N-8-164:24 Ag '77

IVES, Charles Edward

Complete works for solo piano. D. Garvelmann. il Am Rec G 40:16-19 Ag '77 *
Ives: 19 song recording. P. L. Miller. Am Rec G 40:36-7 F '77 *
Ives's position in social and musical history. S. Blum. bibl f il Mus Q 63:459-82 O '77 *
Symphony no. 4; Central Park in the dark, conducted by S. Ozawa. W. D. Curtis. Am Rec G 40:32-4 O '77 *

IVO, Tommy

Tommy Ivo's silver anniversary; ed by A. Scalzo. il pors Hot Rod 30:22-4 S '77

IVORIES

Carolingian fairy tale. Vasari. Art N 76:33 N '77

IVORY

Great Kenya wildlife ripoff; endangered elephants. J. Samson. il Field & S 82:48-9+ D '77

IVORY-billed woodpeckers. See Woodpeckers

IVORY carving

Enduring art of the ivory carver. W. Rodger. il Hobbies 82:152-3+ Ap '77

See also
Ivories
Scrimshaw

IVORY Coast

Ivory Coast: political stability and economic growth. A. Taylor and others. bibl il maps Focus 27:1-15 Ja; 1-14 My '77

IVY

Grape ivy has an oak-leaf relative. il Sunset 159:144 Jl '77
Greenhouse. J. Kilborn. Horticulture 55:52-3 Jl '77
Ivy balls in the window. il Sunset 159:226-7 N '77

IVY poisoning. See Poison ivy

IWAI, Junichi. See Friedman, R. jt auth

IWATSUKI, K. and others

Hypertension: increase of collagen biosynthesis in arteries but not in veins. bibl il Science 198:403-5 O 28 '77

IXTAPA (resort) See Seaside resorts—Mexico

IYER, Susheela L. See Howland, J. L. jt auth

IZU Peninsula

Japan's Izu Peninsula. J. Bowen. il Travel 147: 60-5 F '77

IZUMI, Walter Shearer-. See Shearer-Izumi, W.

J

J. Paul Getty Museum. See Malibu, Calif.—Galleries and museums

J. C. Penney Company. See Penney, J. C. Company

JCS. See United States—Joint Chiefs of Staff

JET (Joint European Torus) See Tokamaks

J. P. Stevens and Company. See Stevens, J. P. and Company

JPL. See Jet Propulsion Laboratory

JABBAR, Kareem Abdul-. See Abdul-Jabbar, K.

JABS, Carolyn

Ten uses for wood ashes. Org Gard & Farm 24:130-1 N '77

JACARANDA Wiley (firm) See Publishers and publishing—Australia

JACK, Homer A.

Disarmament scoreboard. Bull Atom Sci 33:54-8 Mr '77

JACK the Ripper (operatic character) See Characters in opera

JACKER, Corinne L.

My life. Reviews
Nation 224:190 F 12 '77 *
New Yorker 52:67-8 F 7 '77 *

JACKLET, Jon W.

Neuronal circadian rhythm: phase shifting by a protein synthesis inhibitor. bibl il Science 198:69-71 O 7 '77

JACKS, David

Children of God: disciples of deception; interview, ed by J. M. Hopkins. il por Chr Today 21:18-23 F 18 '77

JACK'S Peak Regional Park. See California—Parks and reserves

JACKSON, Andrew

Andrew & Rachel Jackson. P. Robbins. il pors Am Hist Illus 12:22-8 Ag '77 *

JACKSON, Arlyne A.

Small business development and management. Harvard Bus R 55:182+ S '77

JACKSON, Donald

George Washington's beautiful Nelly. il por Am Heritage 28:80-5 F '77

JACKSON, Donald Dale

Fighting beak and claw. il Sports Illus 46:78-82+ My 16 '77

JACKSON, Elaine

Cockfight. Reviews
New Yorker 53:116-17 O 31 '77 *

JACKSON, Elinor

It's never too late to grab a chunk of life. il Ebony 33:123-4+ N '77

JACKSON, Eugene D.

Equality in industry for U.S. blacks. por Nations Bus 65:91 D '77

JACKSON, George B.

Fabled fireplaces. bibl il Antiques 112:1148-55 D '77

JACKSON, Henry Martin
Reporter at large. E. Drew. New Yorker 53: 99-117 Ap 4 '77 *
Senatorial saboteur. Nation 225:515-16 N 19 '77 *
Unplugged leaks. New Repub 177:2+ N 26 '77 *

JACKSON, Ivor M. D. and Reichlin, Seymour
Thyrotropin-releasing hormone: abundance in the skin of the frog, rana pipiens. bibl il Science 198:414-15 O 28 '77

JACKSON, James P.
Awakening. il Am For 83:8-11 Ap '77
How does a forest grow? il Am For 83:32-3+ Jl '77

JACKSON, James Thomas
Ned Bobkoff and me. il pors Writers Digest 57:16-18+ F '77

about

James Thomas Jackson and me. N. Bobkoff. il pors Writers Digest 57:19 F '77 *

JACKSON, Jesse L.
Andy Young and the truth. por Newsweek 90:9 Jl 11 '77
Jesse Jackson speaks out; interview, ed by M. S. Clayton. il Todays Educ 66:42-6 Ja '77
You can pray if you want to; interview, ed by G. Arnold. por Chr Today 21:12-16 Ag 12 '77

about

PUSH for excellence. A. Poinsett. il pors Ebony 32:104-6+ F '77 *
Preaching pride. M. Sheils and S. Monroe. por Newsweek 89:64 Je 27 '77 *

JACKSON, Joseph H.
Jackson: keeping it cool. Chr Today 22:63 O 7 '77 *

JACKSON, Marguarite
Terror in Spring Mill. il por Time 109:42 My 23 '77 *

JACKSON, Marjorie V.
Six million dollar murder. L. S. Connor. il por Sat Eve Post 249:54-5+ N '77 *

JACKSON, Mary H.
Prospects for foreign language education. Educ Digest 43:48-9 O '77

JACKSON, Maynard Holbrook, 1938-
Crying Wurf. K. Bode. New Repub 177:14-17 Jl 2 '77 *
Strikebreaker. T. Mathews and V. E. Smith. il por Newsweek 89:29-30 Ap 25 '77 *

JACKSON, Paula Rice
How does color hit you? il House & Gard 149:136-7+ Mr '77

JACKSON, Philip W.
Lonely at the top. Educ Digest 43:10-13 S '77

JACKSON, Rachel (Donelson) Robards
Andrew & Rachel Jackson. P. Robbins. il pors Am Hist Illus 12:22-8 Ag '77 *

JACKSON, Reggie
Meet Reggie (Dr Jekyll) Jackson (Mr Hyde) H. Stein. il por Esquire 88:92-4+ Jl '77 *
Reg-gie. P. Axthelm. il por Newsweek 90:45+ O 31 '77 *
Reg-gie! Reg-gie! ! Reg-gie! ! ! R. Fimrite. il pors Sports Illus 47:28-30+ O 31 '77 *
Ups and downs of Reggie Jackson. B. Rhoden. il pors Ebony 32:60-2+ O '77 *

JACKSON, Robert
Serving the fashion-conscious male. il pors Ebony 32:99-100+ My '77 *

JACKSON, Rosemary H.
Critical focus. K. Poli. il por Pop Phot 80:6+ Mr '77 *

JACKSON, Shirley A.
Should you teach your child to read? bibl Am Educ 13:27-9 O '77

JACKSON, William H, Company. See Fireplaces—Marketing

JACKSON, William Henry
William Henry Jackson in Mexico. W. C. Jones. il por Am West 14:10-21 Jl '77 *

JACKSON, William S.
Life and art of Peter Helck. il Motor T 29:72-5 F '77
Retrospect (cont) il Motor T 29:103-6+ Mr; 113-19 My; 59-62+ Ag; 86+ N '77

JACKSON, Miss.

Music

See also
Opera—Mississippi

JACKSON and Mary Burke collection. See Art—Private collections

JACKSON County, Ore, Public Library. See Libraries—Oregon

JACKSON Heights, N.Y. See Queens, N.Y.

JACKSON HOLE Valley
Bold bid to preserve scenery; easement proposal in Jackson Hole. il Bus W p94 N 21 '77

JACKSONVILLE, Fla.
Jacksonville: bold new city of the South. il Nations Bus 65:93-4+ D '77

Galleries and museums

Cummer Gallery of Art. R. W. Schlageter. il Antiques 112:954-8 N '77

JACOB, François
Evolution and tinkering; address, March 1977. bibl Science 196:1161-6 Je 10 '77

JACOB, John
Kingsrider; Area; poems. Poetry 130:85-6 My '77

JACOB, Louis
(tr) See Leens, A. Manifesto for revolution in world library meetings

JACOBS, Arthur
Secret diaries of Sir Arthur Sullivan. il pors Hi Fi 27:46-50 My '77

JACOBS, Barry
He didn't know half. . . Progressive 41:42 N '77

JACOBS, Daniel
Ride; poem. New Yorker 53:50 O 17 '77

JACOBS, Donald
NLRB licenses lying. Nation 225:176-7 S 3 '77

JACOBS, Frederic, and Cowden, Peter
Relevance of recurrent education to worker satisfaction. bibl M Labor R 100:61-4 Ap '77

JACOBS, Gerald H.
Visual sensitivity: significant within-species variations in a nonhuman primate. bibl il Science 197:499-500 Jl 29 '77

JACOBS, Harvey C.
Schoolmaster to a nation. il por Sat Eve Post 249:62-3+ Ap '77

JACOBS, Irwin
Alchemist. E. Dyson. por Forbes 119:34 Ja 15 '77 *
What's up, Irwin? por Forbes 120:78 D 15 '77 *

JACOBS, Lou, Jr
My return to the view camera. il por Pop Phot 81:138-41+ D '77

JACOBS, Robert
And now a few words on writing for radio. Writers Digest 57:15-19 Ap '77

JACOBS, Walter C.
Design public works shops to increase productivity. por Am City & County 92:91-2 S '77

JACOBS Engineering Group Inc. See Engineering construction companies

JACOB'S Pillow (festival and school of dance)
Look at Jacob's Pillow. J. Warren. Chr Cent 94: 41-2 Ja 19 '77

JACOBSEN, Arne
Exhibitions in sight. B. Wasserman. il Sch Arts 76:48-51 Ap '77 *

JACOBSEN, C. G.
Soviet strategic capabilities: the superpower balance. Cur Hist 73:97-9+ O '77

JACOBSON, Bruce S. and Branton, D.
Plasma membrane: rapid isolation and exposure of the cytoplasmic surface by use of positively charged beads. bibl il Science 195:302-4 Ja 21 '77

JACOBSON, Doranne Wilson
Purdah in India: life behind the veil. il por map Nat Geog 152:270-86 Ag '77

JACOBSON, Mark
Generation that was never going to have to work il Esquire 88:52-4+ Jl '77

JACOBSON, Robert
Mangia, mangia; celebrating the new Met production of La Bohème. il pors Opera N 41:8-13 Mr 19 '77
News from Vienna. il Opera N 41:32-5 Mr 12 '77
Search for perfection. il pors Opera N 41:24-7 Ja 22 '77
Viewpoint. See issues of Opera news
(ed) See Freni, M. Mirella ritornata
(ed) See Milanov, Z. Most beautiful voice in the world
(ed) See Sayão, B. La demoiselle elue

JACOBY, Gordon C. Jr. See Cook, E. R. jt auth

JACOBY, Neil H. and others
Misty line between bribery and extortion; excerpt from Bribery and extortion in world business. Sat R 4:9 Jl 9 '77

JACOBY, Susan
Letter to my grandmother. il McCalls 105:118+ O '77
$73,000 abandoned babies. il N Y Times Mag p55-61 Mr 6 '77
We did overcome. il N Y Times Mag p62-4+ Ap 10 '77

JACOMET, André A.
European Economic Community; address, May 25, 1977. Vital Speeches 43:581-4 Jl 15 '77

JACQUES, Michael
Michael Jacques: a double career in art; interview, ed by P. T. Nagano. il Am Artist 41:86-9+ F '77

JACQUET, Yasuko F. and others
Stereospecific and nonstereospecific effects of (+)-and(-)- morphine: evidence for a new class of receptors? bibl il Science 198:842-5 N 25 '77

JACQUETTE, Yvonne
New landscape art. L. R. Lippard. il Ms 5:68-73 Ap '77 *

JADE
Jade is a mystery 4,000 years old that transcends science. P. E. Desautels. il Smithsonian 8:80-7 Ap '77

JADE smuggling. See Smuggling

JAFFA, Harry V.
Democracy, good and bad. Nat R 29:553 My 13 '77

JAFFE, Arnold
Murder with dignity. il New Repub 177:41-3 Jl 30 '77

JAFFE, M. J.
Experimental separation of sensory and motor functions in pea tendrils. bibl il Science 195: 191-2 Ja 14 '77
JAFFE, Rona
Joy of staying single. Harp Baz 110:92+ Mr '77
JAFFE, Sam
Man who called Walter Cronkite a spy; T. Branch. Esquire 87:34-6+ Ap '77 *
Sam Jaffe and new blacklist. T. Branch. Esquire 87:36+ Mr '77 *
JAGUAR (automobile) See Automobiles, Foreign
JAILS. See Prisons
JAIMES, Judit
Judit Jaimes, piano; concert at Tully Hall. Hi Fi 27:MA24 S '77 *
JAIN, S. K. See Foin, T. C. jt auth
JAISUN, Jef
Tips on mixing organic fertilizer. il Org Gard & Farm 24:78-9 My '77
JAKI, Stanley L.
Lambert: self-taught physicist. bibl il por Phys Today 30:25-30+ S '77
JAKOBSON, Roman
Jan Patočka. New Repub 176:26-8 My 7 '77
JALĀL AL-DĪN, Rūmī
Ghazal; poem; tr by W. S. Merwin and T. S. Halman. Nation 224:190 F 12 '77
JAM. See Jelly, jam, etc.
JAMAICA
Michael Manley: Jamaica's born-again socialist. B. Hale. por Chr Cent 94:1117-19 N 30 '77

Description and travel

Where the sun shines daily on the mountaintop. K. Klassen. il Holiday 57:28-31+ N '76

Economic conditions

Jamaican limbo. F. Fitzgerald. Harpers 255:10+ Jl '77

Foreign relations

Cuba

See Cuba—Foreign relations—Jamaica

Politics and government

Heavy manners in Jamaica: Michael Manley's race with time. A. Bonner. Nation 224:80-4 Ja 22 '77
Jamaican limbo. F. Fitzgerald. Harpers 255:10+ Jl '77
Talk with Manley; excerpt, ed by A. De Borchgrave. M. Manley. por Newsweek 89:38 F 28 '77
See also
Elections—Jamaica
JAMAICAN rock. See Rock music (songs, etc)
JAMAICANS in the United States
Apple picker blues; question of importing Jamaican pickers. D. McGhee. New Repub 177: 15-16 O 29 '77
As Jamaican as apple pie; apple harvest workers in Virginia. J. Egerton. Progressive 41: 37-40 D '77
JAMES, B. Thomas
Don't stand for it. Nat R 29:1113 S 30 '77
JAMES, Erin
In search of a real John Hancock. il Sat Eve Post 249:12-13+ My '77
(ed) See Newman, P. Paul Newman: at home with himself
JAMES, George William
Airlines' capital challenge; excerpts from address. Aviation W 107:9 N 28 '77
JAMES, Henry, 1843-1916
Portrait of the artist as an old man. L. Edel. Am Scholar 47:58-68 Wint '77 *
JAMES, Jessie
Jessie James: painting from the heart. D. C. Hines. il por Am Artist 41:54-9+ N '77 *
JAMES, N. P. and others
Oldest macroborers: lower Cambrian of Labrador. bibl il map Science 197:980-3 S 2 '77
JAMES, Nancy Esther
Cameo: an old man's face; poem. Chr Cent 94: 1029 N 9 '77
JAMES, Shirley M.
Evolution of a language arts program for pre- and early adolescent students. il Engl J 66:47-51 Ap '77
JAMES Bay Cree Indians. See Cree Indians
JAMES Bay hydroelectric project. See Hydroelectric plants—Canada
JAMESON, Vic
Presbyterian austerity. Chr Cent 94:28 Ja 19 '77
JAMIESON, John Kenneth
Top managers try venturing. il por Bus W p 101+ My 9 '77 *
JAMISON, Stephen
Star of his sleep; poem. New Yorker 52:34 F 14 '77
JAMMES, André
Digging up the past. D. Davis. il Newsweek 90: 116+ N 28 '77 *
JANÁČEK, Leoš
Choral works for female voices. W. D. Curtis. Am Rec G 40:37 S '77 *
Kátya Kabanova; London recording. D. Hamilton. Hi Fi 28:97-100 Ja '78 *
Their muses faced East and West. J. Ringo. Am Rec G 41:8-10+ N '77 *
JANDA, James
Christmastide; poem. America 137:471 D 31 '77
Iñigo de Loyola; poem. America 136:437 My 14 '77
Russian Easter; poem. America 136:329 Ap 9 '77
Veni sancte spiritus; poem. America 136:182 Mr 5 '77
JANE, Leslie
Reviews. J. Pikula. Dance Mag 51:42 My '77 *
JANECZKO, Paul B.
(ed) In their own words; interviews (cont) Engl J 66:14-16 Mr; 10-11 S; 20-1 O '77
JANEDIS, Jane
I challenged the Deliverance river—and loved it! il Redbook 148:55-6 Ap '77
JANEL Fisheries Ltd. See Fisheries—Canada
JANES, Kelly
To St Mary of Magdala; poem. Chr Cent 94: 326 Ap 6 '77
JANICK, Jules
Stalking the long purple. il Horticulture 55:28-31 N '77
JANKLOW, William
Dennis Banks's extradition fight. H. Rubin. il Chr Cent 94:691-2 Ag 3 '77 *
Legal history of an Indian. H. Rubin. por Nation 225:113-15 Ag 6 '77 *
JANKOVITZ, Frank R.
Senior citizen cultural revolution. il Aging 270. 12-16 Ap '77
JANKOWIAK, James
All the oysters don't grow in the ocean. il Org Gard & Farm 24:156+ Ap '77
Best way I know to grow big broccoli. il Org Gard & Farm 24:77-9 Mr '77
Borage goes like spinach. il Org Gard & Farm 24:74-5 My '77
Cultivating faster and bigger yields. il Org Gard & Farm 24:80-2 F '77
Growing guide for extra-early sweet corn. il por Org Gard & Farm 25:97-9 Ja '78
Ingredients for top-quality summer lettuce. il por Org Gard & Farm 24:122-3 Je '77
Manzanita: the ornamental with practical value. il Org Gard & Farm 24:128-30 D '77
Take the sting out of stinging nettles. il Org Gard & Farm 24:65-7 Ag '77
Turnips: the multipurpose vegetable. il Org Gard & Farm 24:134+ S '77
JANKOWSKI, Gene F.
Excerpt from testimony on retirement age policy, March 16, 1977. Cong Digest 56:269+ N '77
JANNASCH, Holger W. and Wirsen, C. O.
Microbial life in the deep sea; with biographical sketches. il Sci Am 236:18, 42-52 bibl(p 142) Je '77
JANOS, Barbara S.
Collecting. il House B 119:24+ Mr '77
JANOS, Leo
Travel: the South Pacific. il Sat Eve Post 249: 111-18+ D '77
JANOWITZ, Morris
Outlook for middle class: I am mildly optimistic; interview. por U.S. News 82:56-7 My 2 '77
JANOWITZ, Phyllis
Soon the final decree; poem. Esquire 87:10 Je '77
Years later; poem. Esquire 88:22 N '77
JANOWITZ, Tama
How to run away from college. bibl Mademoiselle 83:130+ Ag '77
JANTZ, Harold
Visit in Viet Nam. il Chr Today 21:49-51 F 18 '77
JANTZEN, Ellen E.
Succession planting chart. il Org Gard & Farm 24:72-3 F '77
JANTZEN, Steven L.
NCSS-1976. il Sr Schol 109:TE7-10 Ja 13 '77
JANZ, Robert
Female Prometheus, David and Bathsheba. M. Wortz. il Art N 76:162-3 Summ '77 *
JAPAN
Tokyo has risen. M. Kondracke. New Repub 177:11-14 S 10 '77
See also
Accounting—Japan
Airlines—Japan
Airplanes, Military—Japan
Americans in Japan
Architecture, Domestic—Japan
Atomic power—Japan
Banks and banking—Japan
Baseball, Professional—Japan
Birds—Japan
Business management—Japan
Cities and towns—Japan
Colleges and universities—Japan
Costume, Theatrical—Japan
Crime and criminals—Japan
Festivals—Japan
Forests and forestry—Japan
Hamamatsu
Hiroshima

JAPAN—See also—*Continued*
Industry and state—Japan
Inland Sea
Investments, Japanese
Izu Peninsula
Japanese
Kyoto
Military assistance, American—Japan
Money—Japan
Paleontology—Japan
Radio broadcasting—Japan
Securities—Japan
Space research—Japan
Technology—Japan
Tokyo

Antiquities

Paleoenvironment and human settlement in Japan and Korea. R. Pearson. bibl il maps Science 197:1239-46 S 23 '77

Commerce

At brink of trade war—Japan backs away. il U.S. News 83:38-9 D 12 '77
Japan gets the message. il por Time 110:71-2 D 12 '77
No sign of slowdown in the export flood. il Bus W p48 O 24 '77
See also
Japan—Industries

Europe, Western

See Europe, Western—Commerce—Japan

United States

See United States—Commerce—Japan

Commercial policy

Cracking down on Japan. D. Pauly and others. il Newsweek 90:75+ N 21 '77
Half a loaf. K. Willenson and others. Newsweek 90:41 D 19 '77
Is the stimulus too little and too late? il Bus W p36 Ag 8 '77
Japan: pressure to slow exports. G. B. Ringwald. Bus W p47 F 7 '77
Japan rebuffed in first round. il Time 110:41 D 26 '77
Japan relents on exchange rules. Bus W p94 My 30 '77
Protectionist scare sobers the Japanese. Bus W p53-5 D 12 '77
Ushiba: maneuvering room; excerpts from interview. ed by B. Krisher. N. Ushiba. il por Newsweek 91:32 Ja 9 '78
See also
Tariff—Japan

Defenses

Boots in Japan's military funding pressed by GAO. H. J. Coleman. Aviation W 106:24 Je 27 '77

Description and travel

Four fabled cities of Japan. il Mademoiselle 83: 134-6+ O '77
Japan. S. Fockler. il Trav/Holiday 148:28-31 D '77

Economic conditions

High cost of doing business with Japan. D. Kirk. il Sat R 4:20-6 Mr 19 '77
What Japan's prosperity looks like from the inside. il U.S. News 83:56-8 Ag 1 '77
See also
Japan—Industries

Economic policy

Forced reflation from London to Tokyo. Bus W p 18-19 Ag 1 '77
Is the stimulus too little and too late? il Bus W p36 Ag 8 '77
Push for Japan. Time 110:74+ S 19 '77
Ready to deal. F. Willey and others. il Newsweek 90:69-70 D 12 '77
See also
Budget—Japan

Economic relations

United States

See United States—Economic relations—Japan

Emperors and empresses

See also
Hirohito, Emperor of Japan

Foreign relations

United States

See United States—Foreign relations—Japan

History

See also
World War, 1939-1945—Japan

Industries

Japanese connection; address, October 10, 1977. W. F. Rockwell. Vital Speeches 44:61-4 N 1 '77
Worry for world business: how to compete with Japan; with interview with J. N. Wallace. il U.S. News 83:43-6 S 26 '77
See also
Aerospace industries—Japan
Automobile industry—Japan
Brewing industry—Japan
Chemical industries—Japan
Computer industry—Japan
Electronic industries—Japan
Fisheries—Japan
Office equipment industry—Japan
Photographic industry—Japan
Shipbuilding—Japan
Steel industry—Japan
Trading companies—Japan

Nationalism

Frontiersmen of Nippon. F. H. Tucker. il Intellect 251-3 D '77

Navy

See also
World War, 1939-1945—Naval operations

Politics and government

Future of democracy in Japan; address, June 10, 1977. T. Miki. Vital Speeches 43:659-61 Ag 15 '77
See also
Political campaigns—Japan
Politics, Corruption in—Japan

Treaties

United States

See United States—Treaties—Japan

JAPAN Camera Show. See Photography—Exhibitions

JAPAN Trench. See Submarine valleys

JAPAN-United States air agreement. See Aviation —International aspects

JAPANESE
Americanization of Japan. R. Payne. il Society 14:81-4 Jl '77
PW interviews; ed by J. F. Baker. E. O. Reischauer. por Pub W 211:6-8 Ap 18 '77

JAPANESE art. See Art, Japanese

JAPANESE artificial satellites. See Artificial satellites, Japanese

JAPANESE beetles. See Beetles

JAPANESE cookery. See Cookery, Japanese

JAPANESE drama
Nō robe as perfection. J. Brzostoski. il Craft Horiz 37:22-7 Ag '77
That's talent; Nō. il Horizon 19:26-7 Jl '77

JAPANESE flower arrangements. See Flowers, Arrangement of

JAPANESE kites. See Kites

JAPANESE literature
See also
Japanese drama

JAPANESE maple. See Maple

JAPANESE packaging. See Packaging

JAPANESE pottery. See Pottery, Japanese

JAPANESE prisoners of war in the United States. See Prisoners of war in the United States

JAPANESE quails. See Quails

JAPANESE screen painting. See Painting, Japanese

JAPANESE swords. See Swords

JAPONICAS. See Camellias

JAR Festival. See Fasts and feasts—Hinduism

JARDIM, Anne
Let's huddle, women. Time 109:63 My 2 '77 *

JAREMKO, Andrew
Add sound to your home movies. il Radio-Electr 48:45-8+ Ag '77

JARES, Joe
Baseball (cont) Sports Illus 47:40+ Jl 4 '77
College basketball (cont) Sports Illus 46:41-2 F 7; 47:81-2 D 5; 50+ D 12 '77
College football (cont) Sports Illus 47:44+ O 3 '77
Extra! Chrissie loses first set! il por Sports Illus 46:24-5 Ap 4 '77
Extra week of room service for Al McGuire. il Sports Illus 46:18-19 Mr 28 '77
Golf. Sports Illus 46:56-7 F 21 '77
In the second half it was pure Aggie-ny. il Sports Illus 47:28-30 O 10 '77
Karate. il Sports Illus 46:83-4 My 2 '77
TV radio. Sports Illus 47:70 Ag 29 '77
Tennis (cont) Sports Illus 46:48-9 Ja 17 '77
They're kicking up a real storm. il pors Sports Illus 47:26-9 N 7 '77
Volleyball (cont) Sports Illus 46:88+ My 23; 47:44-5 Ag 22 '77
Zing go the strings of our hearts. il Sports Illus 47:16-18+ Jl 25 '77

JARGON
Camus on doublespeak. D. Lazere. Engl J 66: 24-6 O '77
Doublespeaking. Time 110:33 D 5 '77
In your head. H. B. Maloney. Engl J 66:10-11 O '77

JARGON—*Continued*
Interface your output with computerese; excerpt from The phrase-dropper's handbook. J. T. Beaudoin and E. Mattlin. il Sci Digest 81:43-6 My '77
Semantic spinach; or, Mellowing out in sunny California. C. McFadden. N Y Times Mag p51+ N 20 '77
Speaking out. E. Newman. Clearing H 51:52 O '77
See also
Slang

Anecdotes, facetiae, satire, etc.

Minimizing intelligibility; bureaucratic English. R. Baker. N Y Times Mag p4 Jl 3 '77

JARMAN, Franklin Maxey
What undid Jarman: paperwork paralysis. il por Bus W p67-8 Ja 24 '77 *

JARMAN, Mark
Goodbye to a poltergeist; poem. Poetry 130:146 Je '77

JARMUSCH, Ann
Philadelphia (cont) Art N 76:92-4+ Ja; 89+ Ap; 170+ Summ; 194-5 N '77

JAROSLAWICZ, Pinchos
Diamonds and death. R. Steele and S. Agrest. il por Newsweek 90:35-6 O 10 '77 *

JARRETT, Keith
Jarrett: various works. W. Simmons. Am Rec G 40:34+ O '77 *
National Public Radio. W. Youngren. il por New Repub 177:23+ S 24 '77 *
Two free spirits. H. Saal. il pors Newsweek 90: 52-3 Ag 8 '77 *

JARS, Glass. See Glass containers

JASINSKI, Donald R. and others
Lithium: effects on subjective functioning and morphine-induced euphoria. bibl il Science 195: 582-4 F 11 '77

JASKEWICZ, Alex
Alex on exercise. il Harp Baz 110:129 Mr '77

JASON, Philip K.
Definition; poem. Commonweal 104:278 Ap 29 '77

JASTROW, Robert
Post-human intelligence; excerpt from Until the sun dies; with biographical sketch. Natur Hist 86:2, 12-13+ Je '77
Report from Mars; excerpt from Until the sun dies; with biographical sketch. il Natur Hist 86:8, 48-53 bibl(p96-7) Mr '77

JAVA

Antiquities

See also
Borobudur

JAVERS, Ron
In a South African prison. Commonweal 104:808-9 D 23 '77

JAVITS, Jacob Koppel
Cure for depression; excerpts from interview, ed by A. de Borchgrave. por Newsweek 90:71 S 26 '77

JAWORSKI, Diane, and Rodgers, M. A.
To lose weight, I had my jaws wired shut. Good H 185:76+ Ag '77

JAWORSKI, Leon
Active conspirator. por Newsweek 89:33 My 16 '77

about

Fresh stirrings on Koreagate. il Time 110:19-20 S 5 '77 *
Jaworski comes back. Time 110:8 Ag 1 '77 *
Jaworski rides again. D. M. Alpern and L. Donosky. il por Newsweek 90:17 Ag 1 '77 *
Second coming of Leon Jaworski. J. Lelyveld. il por N Y Times Mag p71 Ag 28 '77 *
System fixer. Nation 225:98 Ag 6 '77 *

JAWS (fishes)
Jaws of jaws; shark teeth and jaws. S. Lissau. il Oceans 10:31-3 N '77

JAY, Antony
Rate yourself as a client. il Harvard Bus R 55:84-92 Jl '77

JAY, Herman
Hollywood and American literature: the American novel on the screen. Engl J 66:82-6 Ja '77

JAY, Peter
Son-in-law also rises. K. Willenson and M. MacPherson. il por Newsweek 89:30 My 23 '77 *

JAYNES, Julian
Lost voices of the gods: reflections on the dawn of consciousness; interview, ed by S. Keen. il Psychol Today 11:58-60+ N '77

about

Julian Jaynes: portrait of the psychologist as a maverick theorizer. S. Keen. por Psychol Today 11:66-7 N '77 *
Lost voices of the gods. il por Time 109:51-2+ Mr 14 '77 *

JAYS
Bashful blue jay. H. Borland. il Audubon 79:2-5 My '77
Visual detection of cryptic prey by blue jays (cyanocitta cristata) A. T. Pietrewicz and A. C. Kamil. bibl il Science 195:580-2 F 11 '77

JAZZ Alive (radio program) See Radio broadcasting—Music

JAZZ bands. See Bands (music)

JAZZ clubs. See Night clubs

JAZZ dance. See Dancing

JAZZ festivals. See Music festivals

JAZZ music
. . . And all that jazz! J. Landman and P. Lippincott. il Sr Schol 109:2-5 Mr 24 '77
Big bands. G. Lees. Hi Fi 27:24-6 S '77
Indigenous music. N. Hentoff. See occasional issues of Nation
Jazz (cont) W. Balliett. New Yorker 53:98-104 F 21; 84-90 Ap 4; 94-8+ Ap 25; 120-2+ Je 6; 92-7 Je 20; 80-6+ Jl 18 '77; 60-9 Ja 9 '78
Jazz. A. Ripp. il Horizon 19:50-5 Jl '77
Jazz. M. A. Ullman. New Repub 177:35-7 O 1; 23-5 N 19; 19-21 D 3; 23-5 D 24 '77
Jazz-classical fusion: it's working; Denver. G. Lees. il por Hi Fi 27:MA26-7 N '77
Jazz comes back! H. Saal and A. Kuflik. il Newsweek 90:50-6 Ag 8 '77
Jazz in April in New Orleans; New Orleans Jazz & Heritage Festival. il Sunset 158:98+ Ap '77
Jazz: music of exile; contributions of blacks. G. Lees. Hi Fi 27:19-20 Je '77
Jazz: pop or classical? G. Lees. Hi Fi 27:22+ My '77
New nightlife; jazz. P. Hamill. il Vogue 167: 250+ N '77
Profiles; H. Panassié and C. Delaunay. W. Balliett. por New Yorker 52:43-6+ F 14 '77
Swing era; jazz music of the big bands. G. Lees. Hi Fi 27:19-20 Ag '77
See also
Blues (songs, etc)
Phonograph records—Jazz music
Radio broadcasting—Music

JAZZ musicians
At a nation's heart; ethnicity of sounds in jazz. G. Lees. Hi Fi 27:22+ Mr '77
Music: a reflection of jazz women. L. Kuehl. Commonweal 104:625-6 S 30 '77
New directions. M. A. Ullman. New Repub 176:45-7 My 21 '77
Tuning in on the jazz revival; executives. M. Wellmeyer. il Fortune 96:37-8+ Jl '77
See also
Carrington, T.
Coltrane, J.
Dolphy, E.
Garner, E.
Goodman, B.
Gordon, D.
Hines, E.
Jarrett, K.
Liston, M.
Venuti, J.
Wilber, B.

JAZZ societies. See Musical societies

JEALOUSY
How to handle sexual jealousy. M. Lasswell and N. Lobsenz. McCalls 104:86+ Jl '77
Self-inflicted pain of jealousy; excerpt from Jealousy. G. Clanton and L. G. Smith. il Psychol Today 10:44-7+ My '77
See also
Envy

JEANLOZ, Raymond, and others
Shock-produced olivine glass: first observation. bibl il Science 197:457-9 Jl 29 '77

JEANNERET-GRIS, Charles Edouard. See Le Corbusier

JEANS. See Pants

JEAVONS, John, and Leler, Robin
Intensive gardening—less water and higher yields. il Org Gard & Farm 24:78-80 Jl '77

JEBB, Robert
North Country Book Express: a mobile service for mountain booksellers (and publishers) il Pub W 211:63-5 Ap 11 '77

JEDRZEJCZAK, Wieslaw Wiktor-. See Wiktor-Jedrzejczak, W.

JEEP automobiles
Cheap (?) 4x4. B. Kilpatrick. il Field & S 82: 82+ S '77

Equipment

Gearing up for offroading. W. Childress. il Mech Illus 73:114-16 S '77

Four wheel drive

Torque for every tire: full-time four-wheel drive. Car & Dr 22:46 Mr '77
Wheels afield:
Toyota 4WD Jamboree. B. Kovacik. il Motor T 29:99-101 D '77

Testing

AMC Cherokee Chief. il Car & Dr 22:43-8 Mr '77

JEFFER, Bruce
Mini-holiday. See issues of Holiday

JEFFERS, Leroy
Let lawyers advertise? interview. pors U.S. News 82:39-40 F 28 '77

JEFFERSON, Thomas
Passage of the Potomac; excerpt from Notes on Virginia, with photographs by William A. Bake. il por Read Digest 110:194-9 Ap '77

about

Jefferson: quiet patron of nature and science; excerpt from BioScience, December 1976. L. P. Coonen and C. M. Porter. por Sci Digest 81: 40-1 Ap '77 *
Jefferson's country. D. A. Tice. il por Am For 83:24-7 My '77 *
Thomas Jefferson and the growth of American technology. H. A. Meier. por Intellect 106:192 N '77 *

JEFFERSON County, Ky.

Education

See Education—Kentucky

JEFFERY, David
Arizona's suburbs of the sun. il supp (folded map) Nat Geog 152:486-517 O '77
Audubon on the wing. il por Nat Geog 151:148-77 F '77

JEFFRESS, Lloyd Alexander
Greenspan and Jeffress win ASA silver medals. pors Phys Today 30:67 D '77 *

JEFFREYS, Garland
Garland Jeffreys; interview. New Yorker 53:22-3 Jl 11 '77

JEHOVAH'S Witnesses
End is near (contd.) Time 110:64+ Jl 11 '77

JEJEUNUM. See Intestines

JELLINEK, George
Fidès tradition. il Opera N 41:20-1 Ja 29 '77
Ponselle legacy. por Opera N 41:30-1 Mr 12 '77

JELLY, jam, etc.
Bright peppers are what make these preserves festive. il Sunset 159:248 O '77
Jams in a jiffy. G. Steves. il Am Home 80: 66-7+ S '77
Old-fashioned sun-cooked preserves. M. M. Getoff. il Org Gard & Farm 24:110-11 Ag '77
Summer jams and jellies. il Bet Hom & Gard 55:141-2 Jl '77

JELLYFISH
Electrically coupled, photosensitive neurons control swimming in a jellyfish. P. A. V. Anderson and G. O. Mackie. bibl il Science 197:186-8 Jl 8 '77
Poison! Jellyfish. R. E. Arnold. Field & S 82:150 Je '77

JENAWAY, William F.
Residential fire detectors. il Consumers Res Mag 60:16-20 My '77

JENCKS, Christopher
Normative assumptions in educational policy research: the case of Jencks's Inequality. L. B. Joseph. bibl f Ann Am Acad 434:101-13 N '77 *

JENDRZEJCZYK, L. Michael
Dismantling the cross: a case against capital punishment. Chr Cent 94:296-7 Mr 30 '77

JENKINS, Dan
Accepting with pleasure his kind invitation. il por Sports Illus 46:24-6+ My 30 '77
Battle of the ages. il Sports Illus 47:12-15 Ag 22 '77
Braw brawl for Tom and Jack. il por Sports Illus 47:28-30+ Jl 18 '77
Did old Tom throw that club? il por Sports Illus 46:36-8+ Je 20 '77
Golf. Sports Illus 46:55-6+ Ja 24; 64+ Mr 28; 47:82+ S 19 '77
In the main, waters. il Sports Illus 48:15-16 Ja 2 '78
Letter from the publisher. il por Sports Illus 46: 6 Ap 4 '77
List of naughty and nice. Sports Illus 47:30-4+ S 19 '77
Matter of higher math. il Sports Illus 47:20-3 D 19 '77
None of them will win the Masters. il Sports Illus 46:40-2+ Ap 4 '77
Once more, with no hard feelings. il Sports Illus 47:22-4+ O 3 '77
Pro football (cont) Sports Illus 47:111-12+ O 10 '77
Raiders were all suped up. il Sports Illus 46: 10-15 Ja 17 '77
Roger, over and in. il Sports Illus 47:18-21 S 26 '77
Semi-tough goes to the movies. il Sports Illus 47:78-82+ N 7 '77
Talk about total pressure. il por Sports Illus 46:14-19 Je 27 '77
Watson, but not so elementary; Bing Crosby National Pro-Am. il Sports Illus 46:12-15 Ja 31 '77
What a beauty of a Masters. il pors Sports Illus 46:24-7+ Ap 18 '77
Whole town's sacking the Jones boy. il Sports Illus 47:26-7 O 31 '77
Wholly Moses for Denver. il Sports Illus 48:14-16+ Ja 9 '78

JENKINS, Hayden
From Nigeria, guarded optimism; from Montreal, guarded pessimism. Pub W 211:30+ My 16 '77

JENKINS, Kenneth D.
In North Carolina, its working. il Clearing H 50:268-71 F '77

JENKINS, Lyll Becerra de. See Becerra de Jenkins, L.

JENKINS, Peter Gorton
Walk across America. il map Nat Geog 151: 466-99 Ap '77

JENKINS, Roy Harris
Reports & comment: Common Market. D. Cook. por Atlantic 239:14-16+ Ap '77 *

JENKINS, Russell. See Taylor, J. jt auth

JENKINS, Thomas M.
Mona Lisa, revised. il Design (US) 78:23 Summ '77

JENKINS, W. J.
Tritium-helium dating in the Sargasso Sea: a measurement of oxygen utilization rates. bibl il Science 196:291-2 Ap 15 '77

JENKS, Carolyn K.
Basic ingredients: cookbooks for children. bibl SLJ 23:120-1 Mr '77

JENNER, Bruce
Back to Bruce in a moment. First, this commercial. B. McDermott. il pors Sports Illus 47:42-4+ S 26 '77 *
Bruce's bowl. il pors Time 110:36 D 5 '77 *

JENNINGS, Elizabeth
Rhodes; poem. Poetry 130:87 My '77

about

Comment. J. Matthias. Poetry 129:347-50 Mr '77 *

JENNINGS, J. L. Sibley, Jr, and Sánchez, Néstor
Beyond beautification: cities with souls. il Américas 29:50-7 N '77

JENNINGS, Jan
Frederick Whitaker: Mister Watercolor. il Am Artist 41:68-73+ Ag '77

JENNINGS, Kate
Rural route; poem. Am Scholar 47:85 Wint '77
Stock pot; poem. Am Scholar 46:376 Summ '77

JENNINGS, Theodore W.
Homosexuality and Christian faith: a theological reflection. Chr Cent 94:137-42 F 16 '77
Steve Biko: liberator and martyr. Chr Cent 94: 997-9 N 2 '77

JENNINGS, Tom
Hustler meets an artist. M. DelNagro. il pors Sports Illus 46:52+ Je 27 '77 *

JENNISON, Peter S.
Keep on truckin': two days in the life of publisher as book peddler. il por Pub W 211:66-7 Ap 4 '77

JENSEN, Albert C.
Lobster aquaculture in New York. il por map Conservationist 31:16-19 My '77

JENSEN, Arthur Robert
Did Sir Cyril Burt fake his research on heritability of intelligence? Educ Digest 42:45 Mr '77

about

Dispute over Jensen election as fellow flares in council. P. M. Boffey. Science 195:965 Mr 11 '77 *
Jensen: environment is a factor in IQ. Sci N 111:390 Je 18 '77 *
Jensen's AAAS fellowship; letters. Science 196: 831-2+ My 20 '77 *
Second opinion from Jensen. por Time 110:75 Ag 8 '77 *

JENSEN, Eileen
Where the action is. Writers Digest 57:27-8 S '77

JENSEN, Homer, and others
Side-looking airborne radar; with biographical sketches. il Sci Am 237:15, 84-95 bibl(p 152) O '77

JENSEN, Kenneth. See Dethlefsen, E. S. jt auth

JENSEN, Kris
Auto-maintenance basics. il Pop Sci 211:124-5+ Ag '77
New 1978 electronic games. il Pop Electr 13:33-5+ Ja '78
Self-contained module lets you build your own digital clock. il Pop Sci 211:123-4 N '77

JENSEN, Laura
Heavy snowfall in a year gone past; poem. New Yorker 52:38 Ja 31 '77
Kite; poem. New Yorker 53:34 Ag 1 '77

JENSEN, Lloyd
Evaluating U.S. SALT bargaining strategies. Intellect 106:26-9 Ag '77

JENSEN, Robert
Corporate slick. il Horizon 20:70-3 N '77

JENSEN Sound Laboratories (firm) See Audio equipment industry—United States

JENT, H. Clay
Valid and fallacious reasoning: some shades of gray. Intellect 106:62-6 Ag '77

JERDEE, Thomas H. See Rosen, B. jt auth

JEREZ, Spain
Sherry flip. E. Fried. il Sat R 5:28-9 O 29 '77
Sherry sampling in Spain's Jerez. il map Sunset 159:30+ S '77
Song of sack; sherry festival. N. Hazelton. Nat R 29:1312-13 N 11 '77

JERNIGAN, Kenneth
To every thing there is a season; address, July 7, 1977. Vital Speeches 43:666-71 Ag 15 '77

JERKED meat. See Meat, Dried

JEROME, Judson
Poetry. See issues of Writers digest

JEROME, Lawrence E.
Mangroves: trees that help build the land. il Oceans 10:38-45 S '77

JERSEY CITY, N.J.

Water supply

See Water supply—New Jersey

JERUSALEM
Jerusalem. T. Kollek. For Affairs 55:701-16 Jl '77

Art

Jerusalem (cont) M. Ronnen. il Art N 76:97-101 F '77

City planning

New Mamillah will rise outside Jerusalem's walls. il Archit Rec 162:37 O '77

Description

Jerusalem diarist. New Repub 176:42 Ap 16 '77

Foreign population

From Berkeley to Jerusalem; Diaspora Yeshiva, Jerusalem. M. Brenner. il N Y Times Mag p71-3+ Ap 3 '77

Hotels, restaurants, etc.

Bold hotel tower for a Jerusalem hill; Jerusalem Hilton. il Archit Rec 162:122-3 O '77

JERUSALEM International Book Fair. See Book fairs

JESSUP, Claudia, and Chipps, Genie
Business begins at home. Am Home 80:63+ S '77
(eds) Everyone works. il Am Home 80:38-9 F '77
—See Chipps, G. jt auth; jt ed

JESUIT colleges and universities. See Catholic colleges and universities

JESUITS
Tennessee Williams and the Jesuits. G. D. Phillips. America 136:564-5 Je 25 '77

Missions

Paraguay's lost paradise; Guarani Reductions. C. J. McNaspy. il America 136:72-4 Ja 29 '77
Priests in peril; conditions in El Salvador. K. L. Woodward. il Newsweek 90:50 Ag 1 '77

JESUS CHRIST
If Christ were alive today. . .: views of five TV evangelists. il Ladies Home J 94:58+ D '77
Jesus and the tax collectors; defining church. M. E. Marty. Chr Cent 94:343 Ap 6 '77
Message of Easter. R. C. Stapleton. por Ladies Home J 94:107+ Ap '77
Myth of the self-sufficient man; excerpt from address. M. N. Beck. Chr Today 21:12-16 S 23 '77
Staff of life. Chr Today 22:33 O 7 '77
Who was this man called Jesus? excerpt from How to be born again. B. Graham. il Sat Eve Post 249:22-3+ D '77
Word and the words. L. Morris. Chr Today 21:40+ Je 3 '77
See also
Holy Shroud
Lord's Prayer
Salvation
Trinity

Apparitions and miracles (modern)

Strange visions in Shamokin; shadows resembling face of Jesus on tabernacle cloth at Holy Trinity Episcopal Church. il Time 109:52 My 30 '77

Art

Week that changed the world; Holy Week in art. S. Thomas. il Sat Eve Post 249:64-7 Ap '77

Atonement

See Atonement

Birth

See Jesus Christ—Nativity

Drama

See also
Passion plays

Incarnation

See Incarnation

Jewish interpretations

How Jews see Jesus. K. L. Woodward and others. il Newsweek 89:88 Ap 18 '77

Nativity

Angel Gabriel dissents. P. Steinfels. Commonweal 104:819 D 23 '77
Birth into poverty. V. J. Genovesi. America 137:459-60 D 24 '77
Christmas as it was; views of R. E. Brown. K. L. Woodward. il por Newsweek 90:89+ D 19 '77
Freeing the puppets. J. A. O'Hare. America 137:454 D 24 '77
God becomes man. N. F. Gaughan. il Commonweal 104:811-14 D 23 '77
Mystery at Bethlehem. H. Lindsell. il Chr Today 22:22-5 D 9 '77
See also
Christmas cribs
Incarnation

Passion

True to form. G. McCauley. America 136:280-inside back cover Mr 26 '77

Poetry

See also
Christmas poems

Resurrection and Ascension

After three days and three nights. . . H. Lindsell. Chr Today 21:14-16 Ap 1 '77
Icon tree; excerpt from Irrational season. M. L'Engle. Chr Cent 94:321-4 Ap 6 '77
In memoriam. G. McCauley. America 136:116-inside back cover F 5 '77
Red-haired saint: is Mary Magdalene the key to the Easter narratives? J. T. Baker. il Chr Cent 94:328-32 Ap 6 '77
Stumbling block: the paschal story. E. F. Shaw. America 136:330 Ap 9 '77
What difference does it make? Chr Today 21:32 Ap 15 '77
What seminaries don't believe. Chr Today 22:29-31 N 4 '77

Second Advent

See Second Advent

Teachings

Seasons of vineyards. E. Schaeffer. Chr Today 22:36+ O 7 '77

Temptation

When the spirit hits you. G. McCauley. America 136:156-7 F 19 '77

JESUS CHRIST in art. See Jesus Christ—Art

JESUS CHRIST in literature
Dostoyevsky and the Grand Inquisitor: a study in atheism. S. R. Sutherland. Yale R 66:364-73 Mr '77
Gerald Manley Hopkins: exploding for Christ. M. R. Brown. Chr Today 21:20+ Ja 7 '77

JESUS CHRIST in poetry. See Jesus Christ in literature

JESUS movement
Jesus mania: bigotry in the name of the Lord. D. Walls. il Sat R 4:12-15+ S 17 '77
See also
Jews for Jesus movement

JET airplane engines. See Airplane engines, Jet

JET airplanes. See Airplanes, Jet

JET boats. See Boats, Jet

JET Propulsion Laboratory
Added funding spurs planetary studies. D. E. Fink. Aviation W 106:17-18 Ja 17 '77
Sailing to Halley's comet. il Time 109:54 Mr 14 '77
Sailing with Halley's Comet—and other space spectaculars for the 1980s. J. F. Pearson. il Pop Mech 147:67-71 F '77
Space technology—a way to help solve biomedical problems. il Space World N-3-159:24-5 Mr '77
Specialized film lab plays key role as scientists probe secrets of Mars. il Space World N-10-166:20-3 O '77

JET trainers. See Airplanes, Training

JETFOILS. See Hydrofoils

JETTER, Albert S.
Detached carport with storage, too. il Mech Illus 73:69-70 Mr '77

JEWELRY
Art Deco jewelry: plastic and precious. M. D. Schwartz. il Art N 76:106-7 Ja '77
Buyers guide to jewelry. R. Rosefsky. Bet Hom & Gard 55:108+ Ap '77
Crafts in industry: five jewelers join skills with Reed & Barton; ed by A. Gold. A. Fisch. il por Craft Horiz 37:10-15 Ag '77
Fabulous one-of-a-kind jewels. il Harp Baz 111:112-17 D '77
Jewelry's new dazzle. S. C. Cowley and others. il pors Newsweek 89:64-5+ Ap 4 '77
See also
Diamonds
Gems
Necklaces

Cleaning

How to clean your jewelry. A. Rosenblum. Good H 184:229 Mr '77

JEWELRY, Egyptian
Craft of King Tut's jewels. J. A. Black. il Craft Horiz 37:20-3 F '77

JEWELRY boxes, cases, etc.
Jewelry display rack. il Bet Hom & Gard 55:264 O '77

JEWELRY making
Eye-catching jewelry. R. Wrenn. il Design (US) 78:31 mid-Wint '77
Forming and etching as a plating process. J. R. Gianatasio and A. M. Grutter. il Sch Arts 77:30-3 D '77

JEWELRY making—*Continued*
Getting into the real world. G. Saunders. il Craft Horiz 37:44-5 O '77
Magic of cloisonné: William Harper. W. Harper. il Craft Horiz 37:54-7 D '77
Make-ahead presents: cut-and-paste jewelry. il Seventeen 36:128-9 N '77
Mary Lee Hu: high on the wire. E. Breckenridge. il por Craft Horiz 37:40-3+ Ap '77
Seed jewelry: hobby. L. H. Snyder. il BioScience 27:502 Jl '77
Spare that hardwood! J. Ward. il Design (US) 78:16-18 mid-Summ '77
Workshop: titanium: metal of many colors. J. B. Ward. il Craft Horiz 37:20-1+ Ag '77

JEWELS. See Gems; Jewelry

JEWISH-Arab relations
Arafat: solutions, not theatrics; excerpts from interview, ed by M. Gart and W. Wynn. Y. Arafat. il por Time 109:33 Mr 21 '77
Chairman reports on contacts with West members of Security Council; question of Palestine. UN Chron 14:19-20 Jl '77
Israeli-Arab labor relations. Intellect 105:291+ Mr '77
Palestinians: a new unity. il Time 110:41-2 Ag 29 '77
Proposal for a Palestinian state. E. R. F. Sheehan. il map N Y Times Mag p8-11 Ja 30 '77; Reply. C. Herzog. p 12 F 27 '77
See also
Israel-Arab wars, 1967-

Conferences

Hope in Jerusalem. D. J. Moore. America 137:236-9 O 15 '77

History

American stake in Israel; a lesson in international relations. E. V. Rostow. Commentary 63:32-46 Ap '77; Discussion. 64:16+ Jl '77

JEWISH-Arab War, 1948-1949. See Israel-Arab War, 1948-1949

JEWISH art and symbolism
Devotion to stained glass; window created by A. Rattner for the Chicago Loop Synagogue. Vasari. il Art N 76:20+ My '77

JEWISH catacombs. See Catacombs

JEWISH Committee, American. See American Jewish Committee

JEWISH composers. See Composers, Jewish

JEWISH cookery. See Cookery, Jewish

JEWISH education. See Jews—Education

JEWISH families
Problems of American Jewish families. M. H. Riseman. il por Intellect 105:385-6 My '77
Strengths and weaknesses of the Jewish family; study by Gerald Zuk. D. Cohen. Psychol Today 11:146+ D '77

JEWISH Holocaust in childrens fiction. See Childrens literature—Themes

JEWISH identity. See Jews—Identity

JEWISH law
Computerized word; indexing the Responsa for Jewish scholars. M. Montagno and M. J. Kubic. il Newsweek 89:61 Ap 11 '77
Dilemma of Conservative Judaism; halakha. L. J. Kaplan; discussion. Commentary 63:6-8+ F '77
See also
Excommunication (Jewish law)

JEWISH literature
See also
Talmud
Yiddish literature

JEWISH literature (American) See American literature—Jewish authors

JEWISH musicians. See Musicians, Jewish

JEWISH theater. See Theater—Jews

JEWISH women
Woman's Passover Haggadah and other revisionist rituals. E. M. Broner and N. Nimrod. Ms 5:53-6 Ap '77

JEWS
Epistle of a Gentile to Saul Bellow; importance of Israel to Jews and to the world. H. Fairlie. New Repub 176:18-20+ F 5 '77
See also
Anti-Semitism
Catholic Church—Relations—Jews
Samaritans
Zionism

Dietary laws

Kosher meals a specialty at New York Luncheon Club. L. Feldman. il Aging 274:6-8 Ag '77

Education

From Berkeley to Jerusalem; Diaspora Yeshiva, Jerusalem. M. Brenner. il N Y Times Mag p71-3+ Ap 3 '77
World of our children; school founded by community of West Side Jews in New York. P. Cowan. il N Y Times Mag p64-70 Ap 3 '77

Emigration

See Immigration and emigration—Russia; Immigration and emigration—United States

History

See also
Bible—Old Testament
World War, 1939-1945—Jews

Identity

Zionism and Jewish identity; adaptation of address. J. Katz. Commentary 63:48-52 My '77

Liturgy and ritual

Grocery; afternoon prayers at L. Bistritzky's kosher grocery in New York City. New Yorker 53:29-30 My 23 '77
See also
Passover

Nationalism

See also
Jews—Identity
Zionism

Persecutions

See also
World War, 1939-1945—Jews

Political and social conditions

See also
Zionism

Prayer books and devotions

Woman's Passover Haggadah and other revisionist rituals. E. M. Broner and N. Nimrod. Ms 5:53-6 Ap '77

Psychology

Heirs of the Holocaust; children of survivors. H. Epstein. il por N Y Times Mag p 12-15+ Je 19 '77; Discussion. p 14+ Jl 24 '77

Radicalism

See Radicalism—Jews

Rites and ceremonies

See also
Hanukkah (Feast of Lights)
Passover

Social life and customs

See also
Excommunication (Jewish law)

Women

See Jewish women

JEWS and blacks
Historical impressions of black-Jewish relations prior to World War II. O. R. Williams, Jr. bibl Negro Hist Bull 40:728-31 Jl '77

JEWS and Catholics. See Catholic Church—Relations—Jews

JEWS and Christians. See Christianity and other religions

JEWS and Christmas
Christmas and the Jewish child. A. Ginott. Ladies Home J 94:26 D '77
Shalom. . .a gut yontiff. . .and a Merry Christmas; Holy Redeemer Hospital in Meadowbrook, Pa. M. Lichtig. il por Ret Liv 16:35 D '76

JEWS and World War II. See World War, 1939-1945—Jews

JEWS for Jesus movement
Jews for Jesus. D. K. Mano. Nat R 29:1126-7 S 30 '77; Discussion. 29:1433+ D 9 '77
Yeshua is the Messiah. il Time 110:76 Jl 4 '77

JEWS in Argentina
Get out, Jews. K. Bird and R. Moreau. il Newsweek 90:31 Ag 15 '77
Jews and leftists tremble: anti-Semitism in Argentina. H. Maurer. Nation 224:170-3 F 12 '77

JEWS in Canada
Quebec's Jews: caught in the middle. R. R. Wisse and I. Cotler. Commentary 64:55-9 S '77

JEWS in Germany
Outwitting the final solution; Jews in Berlin. R. Gay. il Horizon 19:42-7 Ja '77

JEWS in literature
The chosen, The promise, and My name is Asher Lev; C. Potok's novels. A. D. Sgan. Engl J 66:63-4 Mr '77
See also
American literature—Jewish authors

JEWS in motion pictures
Whatever happened to Bernie Schwartz? Jews in American films. L. Quart. Intellect 105:399 Je '77

JEWS in Palestine
Assimilationist dilemma: Ambassador Morgenthau's story; adaptation of address, December 1976. B. W. Tuchman. Commentary 63:58-62 My '77; Discussion. 64:12+ Ag '77

JEWS in Portugal
See also
Maranos

JEWS in Quebec (province) See Jews in Canada

JEWS in Russia
Encounter in Moscow. L. Gersten. America 137:30-1 Jl 16 '77
Final acts and final solutions. W. Korey. bibl il Society 15:81-6 N '77
Long wait: a study in determination. S. Friedman. Chr Cent 94:348-9 Ap 13 '77
Refuseniks of Kiev. W. Steif. il Sat R 4:20-1+ S 17 '77

JEWS in Russia—*Continued*
Statement by prisoner H. I. Butman to the chief of the Perm administration of corrective labor establishments (ITK-35) H. Butman. il Nat R 29:822-5 Jl 22 '77
Ten days that shook me up in Russia. B. Gelb. il N Y Times Mag p21+ S 18 '77

Emigration

See Immigration and emigration—Russia

JEWS in Syria
Syria: daylight in the Middle East? S. Cain. Chr Cent 94:592-3 Je 22 '77

JEWS in the Netherlands
Why Spinoza was excommunicated. Y. Yovel. Commentary 64:46-52 N '77

JEWS in the United States
American Jews: still a distinctive group. C. S. Liebman. Commentary 64:57-60 Ag '77
Assimilationist dilemma: Ambassador Morgenthau's story; adaptation of address, December 1976. B. W. Tuchman. Commentary 63:58-62 My '77; Discussion. 64:12+ Ag '77
Judaism: an ancient faith looks to a new kind of challenge. il U.S. News 82:68-9 Ap 11 '77
New York and/or Jerusalem. R. Alter. Commentary 64:50-6 Ag '77; Reply. H. Halkin. 64:10+ N '77
Problems of American Jewish families. M. H. Riseman. il por Intellect 105:385-6 My '77
Two aleins. C. Levine. Commonweal 105:6-7 Ja 6 '78
U.S. journal: the Bronx; the coops. C. Trillin. il New Yorker 53:49-54 Ag 1 '77
War inside the Jews; question of the Bakke case. L. Fein. New Repub 177:16-18 O 15 '77
Who is Israel? attitudes of American Jews. J. Neusner. il Nat R 29:714-16 Je 24 '77
See also
American Jewish Committee
Radicalism—Jews

Emigration

See Immigration and emigration—United States

Political activities

American Jews and Mr Carter. Commonweal 104:773-4 D 9 '77
Begin's American bandwagon. il pors Time 110:22-3 S 5 '77
Carter and the worried Jews. R. Steele and others. il por Newsweek 89:21-2 Je 27 '77
Carter, the world and the Jews. il por Time 109:8-10 Je 27 '77
Jimmy woos the Jewish leaders. il por Time 110:11-12 Jl 18 '77
Katz in the mountains; meeting with American rabbis. J. Lelyveld. il por N Y Times Mag p63 Jl 10 '77
On the hustings with Moshe Dayan. il por Time 110:34 O 17 '77

JEZYK, Peter F. and others
Mucopolysaccharidosis in a cat with arylsulfatase B deficiency: a model of Maroteaux-Lamy syndrome. bibl il Science 198:834-6 N 25 '77

JICAMAS
Jicama for dessert? Yes indeed. il Sunset 158:216 My '77

JICARILLA Apaches. See Apache Indians

JICINSKI, B.
That slanderous pamphlet. Nat R 29:383 Ap 1 '77

JIG saws. See Saws

JIGS
Doweling jig lines 'em up. D. Scott. il Pop Sci 210:58 Ap '77
Sharpening jigs—use them like a pro. M. Philips. il Pop Sci 210:72+ My '77
Twist-drill sharpening jig. H. Wicks. il Pop Mech 148:164 Ag '77

JIGS, Fishing. See Fishing lures, flies, etc.

JIMENEZ, Janey
Patty Hearst: my prisoner, my friend; excerpt from My prisoner; ed by T. Berkman. pors Ladies Home J 94:51-8 S '77

JIRDS. See Gerbils

JOAN Miró Foundation. See Barcelona—Galleries and museums

JOB, Book of. See Bible—Old Testament—Job

JOB descriptions
No longer entitled; Austrian civil service job titles. Time 110:56 D 12 '77

JOB discrimination. See Discrimination in employment

JOB hopping. See Labor turnover

JOB hunting. See Applications for positions

JOB interviews. See Employment interviewing

JOB mobility. See Occupational mobility

JOB placement guidance. See Vocational guidance

JOB satisfaction
Criteria for job satisfaction: is interesting work most important? B. J. White. bibl il M Labor R 100:30-5 My '77
Giving up on the problem: life on the job. B. Smoot. Nation 225:81-4 Jl 23 '77
Growing number of mismatched employees. C. C. Clogg. Intellect 106:103-4 S '77
Happy laborers and the sad professionals; study by Charles Weaver. J. Horn. il Psychol Today 11:30+ N '77
Heresy of worker participation. A. H. Raskin. Psychol Today 10:111 F '77
How do you like your job? questionnaire. il Psychol Today 11:72-9 S '77
How to keep workers happy on the job. il U.S. News 83:85-6 D 26 '77
Look at factors affecting the quality of working life; excerpt from Public economics and the quality of life, ed by L. Wingo and A. W. Evans. H. C. Morton. M Labor R 100:64-5 O '77
Quality of working life and productivity; address, April 28, 1977. J. M. Rosow. Vital Speeches 43:496-8 Je 1 '77
Relevance of recurrent education to worker satisfaction. F. Jacobs and P. Cowden. bibl M Labor R 100:61-4 Ap '77
White-collar unions and the work humanization movement. E. M. Kassalow. bibl il M Labor R 100:9-13 My '77

JOB security
From wage hikes to job security: the unions' new tune. P. Rosenstiel. Nation 225:720-3 D 31 '77
Hard line on lifetime security; can-manufacturing industry. il Bus W p33-4 O 31 '77
How lifetime security might work; USW bargaining program. Bus W p28 F 28 '77
Lifetime pay, come what may. Fortune 95:71 Ap '77
Lifetime security in steel? il Time 109:45 F 28 '77
Steel industry's expensive settlement. Bus W p28-9 Ap 25 '77
Tough talk won't be about wages this time. il U.S. News 83:92-3 D 26 '77

JOB sharing. See Part time employment

JOB stress. See Stress (psychology)

JOB success. See Success

JOB titles. See Job descriptions

JOB training. See Technical education; Vocational education

JOB transfers. See Employees—Relocation; Executives—Transfer

JOBBERS, Book. See Book wholesalers

JOBS. See Employment; Occupations

JÖBSIS, Frans F.
Noninvasive, infrared monitoring of cerebral and myocardial oxygen sufficiency and circulatory parameters. bibl il Science 198:1264-7 D 23 '77

JOBSON, Gary
How to improve your sailing skills. il por Yachting 141:58+ Ap '77

JOCHNOWITZ, George
(tr) See Levi, P. Vanadium

JOCKEYS
See also
Cauthen, S.
Hartack, W.

JOCKEYS; musical comedy. See Musical comedy, revue, etc.—Reviews—Single works

JOEL, Billy
Billy Joel: up from Piano man. S. Elliott. pors Hi Fi 28:110-13 Ja '78 *

JOFFE, Carol
(comp) Guide to OE-administered programs, fiscal year 1977. il Am Educ 13:36-43 Ja '77

JOFFREY Ballet. See City Center Joffrey Ballet

JOGGERS kidney. See Kidneys—Diseases

JOGGING
How to sidestep jogging hazards. R. F. DeTombe. il Parks & Rec 12:58-60+ S '77
Jogging. A. Frank and S. Frank. Mademoiselle 83:92+ My '77
Jogging. il Seventeen 36:80+ N '77
Put on those jogging shoes and run for your life! B. Ribakove. il Fam Health 9:48-9 F '77
Ready, set. . .sweat! il Time 109:82-3+ Je 6 '77; Same abr. Read Digest 111:51-2+ O '77
Taking exercise to heart. C. P. Gilmore. il pors N Y Times Mag p38-42+ Mr 27 '77

JOGGING clothes. See Clothing and dress—Sports clothes

JOHANNESBURG
Soweto: The Children take charge. W. McWhirter. il map Time 109:28-30 Je 27 '77

Newspapers

See Newspapers—South Africa

JOHANNSEN, Marilyn
Planning an absentee garden. il Org Gard & Farm 24:92-4 F '77

JOHANSEN, Bruce
Leonard Peltier and the posse. por Nation 225:304-7 O 1 '77

JOHN, E. Roy, and others
Neurometrics. bibl il Science 196:1393-410 Je 24 '77

JOHN, Olivia Newton-. See Newton-John, O.

JOHN F. Kennedy Center for the Performing Arts, Washington, D.C.
Big ticket item. S. Chapman. New Repub 177:13-14 Jl 9 '77
Kennedy Center: the first five years. I. Lowens. il Hi Fi 27:MA16-17 F '77

JOHN F. Kennedy Center for the Performing Arts, Washington, D.C.—*Continued*

Musical Theatre Lab

At Kennedy Center: a laboratory for musical theater; Musical Theatre Lab. C. B. Fowler. il Hi Fi 27:MA8-9 Ag '77

JOHN F. Kennedy International Airport. See New York (city)—Airports

JOHN F. Kennedy School of Government. See Harvard University—John F. Kennedy School of Government

JOHN Hancock Tower, Boston. See Boston—Buildings

JOHN Pennekamp Coral Reef State Park. See Florida—Parks and reserves

JOHN Wornall House. See Kansas City, Mo—Historic houses, sites, etc.

JOHNCOCK, Gordon

Man in the fiber glass mask. S. Moses. il por Sports Illus 46:36-8+ Je 27 '77 *

JOHNNY'S World Famous Beef Restaurant. See Bronx, N.Y.—Hotels, restaurants, etc.

JOHNS, Jasper

What is pop art? interview, ed by G. R. Swenson; excerpt from The art world; ed by B. Diamonstein. il Art N 76:170+ N '77

about

Art. L. Alloway. Nation 225:571-2 N 26 '77 *

Enigmas and double visions. E. White. il pors Horizon 20:48-55 O '77 *

Jasper Johns: the passionless subject passionately painted. J. Hobhouse. il Art N 76:46-9 D '77 *

Pictures at an inhibition; retrospective at New York's Whitney Museum. R. Hughes. il por Time 110:84-6 O 31 '77 *

Super artist; retrospective at the Whitney Museum. M. Stevens and C. McGuigan. il pors Newsweek 90:66-8+ O 24 '77 *

To know Jasper Johns. B. Rose. il pors Vogue 167:280-5 N '77 *

Twenty years of Jasper Johns; retrospective at the Whitney Museum. H. Rosenberg. New Yorker 53:42-5 D 26 '77 *

JOHNS Hopkins University, Baltimore

Smorgasbord for an IQ of 150; Study of Mathematically Precocious Youth program. il Time 109:64 Je 6 '77

Young prodigies take off under special program; Study of Mathematically Precocious Youth. D. Nevin. il por Smithsonian 8:76-81 bibl(p 160) O '77

Applied Physics Laboratory

Physicians + physicists=far-out medicine. D. Lampe. il Fam Health 9:48-50 S '77

JOHNS-Manville Corporation

At Johns-Manville, it's back to basics. il por Bus W p76+ O 31 '77

Johns-Manville world headquarters building—a winner for J-M and TAC. M. F. Schmertz. il Archit Rec 162:89-100 S '77

JOHNSON, Alvar

(ed) See Sjögren, P. A. Per A. Sjögren: the pressing need for IPA

JOHNSON, Andrew

Impeachment

I looked down into my open grave; excerpt from Profiles in courage. J. F. Kennedy. il Sr Schol 109:17-19 F 24 '77

JOHNSON, Anne L. and Howards, S. S.

Hyperosmolality in intraluminal fluids from hamster testis and epididymis: a micropuncture study. bibl il Science 195:492-3 F 4 '77

JOHNSON, Belton Kleberg

Rancher's revenge. pors Forbes 119:68 Ja 15 '77 *

JOHNSON, Carl J. and others

Plutonium hazard in respirable dust on the surface of soil. bibl il Science 193:488-90; 196:1126 Ag 6 '76, Je 3 '77

JOHNSON, Carl Tennis

Bear fever. B. East. por Outdoor Life 160:7 O '77 *

JOHNSON, Carolyn

After 18 years of searching: we're a family again! E. P. Frank. il pors Good H 185:111+ O '77 *

JOHNSON, Chalmers

Terror. bibl il Society 15:48-53 N '77

Wide of the mark. New Repub 177:12-14 N 26 '77

JOHNSON, Clarence Leonard

Johnson. J. W. Olcott. il Flying 101:388-9 S '77 *

No more frontiers. il por Forbes 120:118 N 1 '77 *

JOHNSON, Claudia Alta (Taylor)

Christmas in the Southwest. il Redbook 150:99+ D '77

about

Life with mother. L. B. J. Robb. pors Ladies Home J 94:117+ My '77 *

Tour of the LBJ ranch. J. Egan. il por Good H 185:112-17+ O '77 *

JOHNSON, D. Gale

Soviet agriculture and United States-Soviet relations. Cur Hist 73:118-22+ O '77

JOHNSON, Daniel H. See Friedman, T. B. jt auth

JOHNSON, Edith I. See Brandli, H. W. jt auth

JOHNSON, Eunice W.

Fashions and business set her lifestyle. il pors Ebony 32:74 Ag '77 *

JOHNSON, Evert

Get it hot and hit it is blacksmiths' cry. il Craft Horiz 37:9 F '77

JOHNSON, F. Ross

GE alumni revamp Standard Brands. il por Bus W p41-2 My 16 '77 *

JOHNSON, Frank M. Jr

Alabama judge is picked for FBI—the challenge he faces. il U.S. News 83:20-1 Ag 29 '77 *

Gilt-edged choice for the FBI. il pors Time 110:11-12 Ag 29 '77 *

Hope for the FBI. Nation 225:164 S 3 '77 *

Judge for the FBI. R. Boeth and D. Camper. por Newsweek 90:26-7 Ag 29 '77 *

Most wanted. E. Yoffe. New Repub 177:10-11 S 3 '77 *

JOHNSON, Franklyn Arthur

Faculty of liberal learning; address, August 22, 1977. Vital Speeches 43:724-31 S 15 '77

JOHNSON, Gen, and others

Do cellular slime molds form intercellular junctions? bibl Science 197:1300 S 23 '77

JOHNSON, George, Jr

Linda's haunting vision. C. Bakal. il por Read Digest 110:68-72 Mr '77 *

JOHNSON, Harlan R.

Teacher utilization of instructional media centers in secondary schools. bibl Clearing H 51: 117-20 N '77

JOHNSON, Harriett

Man of Toulouse. por Opera N 41:34-5 F 5 '77

JOHNSON, Harry G.

Economist's economist. E. Meadows. Nat R 29: 725 Je 24 '77 *

JOHNSON, Harry Julius

Low cholesterol diet: it won't prevent heart attacks. il Duns R 109:93-4+ Mr '77

JOHNSON, Herschel

Discotheque scene. il Ebony 32:54-6+ F '77

George Benson: still breezin'. il pors Ebony 33: 114-16+ N '77

Quiet success of a talented engineer. il pors Ebony 32:72-4+ F '77

$660,000 farewell. il pors Ebony 32:47-8+ F '77

JOHNSON, J. Albert

Patty Hearst: the way it really was—and is; ed by P. Battelle. il por Good H 184:104-5+ Mr '77

Real story of Patty Hearst: ed by P. Battelle. il pors Good H 184:94-7+ F '77

JOHNSON, Jacqueline

Redbook fiction, from the inside. Writer 90: 18-21 N '77

JOHNSON, James S.

Student teacher as self. Educ Digest 42:28-31 My '77

JOHNSON, Kurt. See Silver, J. jt auth

JOHNSON, Lady Bird. See Johnson, C. A. T.

JOHNSON, Laurie

Brainstorming and name forming. Parks & Rec 12:36+ Je '77

JOHNSON, Lawrence B.

Florentine Opera Company—ups & downs. il Hi Fi 27:MA34-6 Ag '77

JOHNSON, Lester

Lester Johnson and the kaleidoscopic crowd. B. Chernow. il Intellect 105:357-9 Ap '77 *

JOHNSON, Lucille

Christmas traditions—is it time to break a few? il Ret Liv 16:30-1 D '76

JOHNSON, Lyndon Baines

Back at the LBJ ranch; interview, ed by L. R. Obst. D. K. Goodwin. il pors N Y Times Mag p42-3 N 13 '77 *

LBJ accused. D. A. Williams and L. Donosky. il pors Newsweek 90:27 Ag 8 '77 *

L.B.J: the softer they fall. H. Sidey. il por Time 110:10 Ag 15 '77 *

Vote forever. W. F. Buckley, Jr. Nat R 29: 1013 S 2 '77 *

JOHNSON, Lyndon Baines, family

Christmas in the Southwest. C. A. T. Johnson. il Redbook 150:99+ D '77 *

JOHNSON, Nora

Second time around; story. McCalls 104:139-40 F '77

JOHNSON, Paul

Parting company. Nat R 29:1099 S 30 '77 *

JOHNSON, Philip Cortelyou

Profiles. C. Tomkins. por New Yorker 53:43-4+ My 23 '77 *

JOHNSON, Pyke, Jr

What publishers should know about the public library: a book editor's firsthand report. il pors Pub W 211:40-2 Mr 28 '77

JOHNSON, R. Roy, and others

Man's impact on the Colorado River in the Grand Canyon. il Nat Parks & Con Mag 51:13-16 Mr '77

JOHNSON, Richard D.

Organic chemistry in space. bibl il Chemistry 50:17-22 O '77

JOHNSON, Ross
Ross Johnson of Standard Brands: showdown. por Forbes 119:94 F 15 '77 *

JOHNSON, S. C. and Son, Inc
Inspiring public confidence in private enterprise; president of Johnson Wax; interview. W. K. Eastham. il pors Nations Bus 65:50-4+ My '77
S. C. Johnson tries again on personal care. il Bus W p54+ F 14 '77

JOHNSON, Samuel
Dr Johnson as apologist. J. W. Montgomery. Chr Today 21:62-3 Ap 15 '77 *

JOHNSON, Sharon Leijoy
Court rules against woman biochemist. C. Holden. Science 197:743 Ag 19 '77 *

JOHNSON, Stephen
Over the edge. il Read Digest 111:126-30 N '77
Philippines: a nation in transition. il por Read Digest 110:37-8+ Je '77

JOHNSON, Steven C. See Irwin, M. R. jt auth

JOHNSON, Terry C. See Hughes, J. V. jt auth

JOHNSON, Thomas
Ark; Reunion; poems. Yale R 67:68-9 O '77

JOHNSON, Thomas Edward, 1948-
Catechism; poem. Nation 224:443 Ap 9 '77

JOHNSON, Tom
Supper on the terrace; poem. New Repub 177:28 S 3 '77

JOHNSON, U. Alexis
From a veteran diplomat: how to deal with the Russians; interview. il pors U.S. News 82:25-6 Ap 4 '77

JOHNSON, Virginia E. See Masters, W. H. jt auth

JOHNSON, Warren A. and others
Energy conservation in Amish agriculture. bibl il Science 198:373-8 O 28 '77

JOHNSON, William A.
Kennedy, GAO criticize NSF; grant renewal is rejected. P. M. Boffey. Science 195:556-8 F 11 '77 *

JOHNSON, William Oscar
Contract with the Kremlin. il Sports Illus 46:14-19 F 21 '77
It all just sort of happened. Sports Illus 46:33 F 14 '77
Minnesota's miracle. Sports Illus 47:23 O 31 '77
Olympics (cont) Sports Illus 47:64+ N 7 '77
Passionate suitors for a wild paradise. il por Sports Illus 47:8, 50-2+ O 10 '77
Rising above it all. il Sports Illus 47:59-60+ D 5 '77
Siege of the Province Lands. il map Audubon 79:22-35 My '77
Skiing. il Sports Illus 47:93-4+ N 14 '77
They doubled the pleasure. il pors Sports Illus 46:12-15 Mr 14 '77
This strange and perilous joint. il Sports Illus 47:84-8+ O 24 '77
Walk on the sordid side. il por Sports Illus 47:10-15 Ag 1 '77

JOHNSON CITY, Tex.
LBJ's hometown. E. Keerdoja and L. Donosky. il Newsweek 90:10 Ag 22 '77

JOHNSON Controls Inc
Merger time? il Forbes 120:102-4 D 1 '77

JOHNSON grass. See Sorghum

JOHNSON Space Center. See United States—Lyndon B. Johnson Space Center

JOHNSON Wax. See Johnson, S. C. and Son. Inc

JOHNSTON, Arthur P.
Intensity of belief: a pragmatic concern for church growth; interview, ed by D. E. Kucharsky. pors Chr Today 21:10-14 Ja 7 '77

JOHNSTON, Brian H. and others
Psoralen-DNA photoreaction controlled production of mono- and diadducts with nanosecond ultraviolet laser pulses. bibl il Science 197:906-8 Ag 26 '77

JOHNSTON, Gene. See Fee, R. J. jt auth

JOHNSTON, Harold S.
Will fertilizers harm ozone as much as SST's? D. Shapley. Science 195:658 F 18 '77 *

JOHNSTON, J. Bruce
Steel negotiator looks at election issues; address, December 16, 1976. Vital Speeches 43:238-43 F 1 '77

JOHNSTON, Jeremiah
Class project: rewrite history. J. Kraus. Educ Digest 43:36-7 S '77 *

JOHNSTON, Joanne
On the other hand. Am Home 80:29 S '77

JOHNSTON, Richard W.
Maui is in the chips. il maps Sports Illus 46:44-7 Ja 24 '77

JOHNSTON, Robert K.
John Updike's theological world. por Chr Cent 94:1061-6 N 16 '77
Of tidy doctrine and truncated experience. il Chr Today 21:10-14 F 18 '77

JOHNSTON, Robert L.
Church in China. Commonweal 104:394-5 Je 24 '77

JOHNSTON, Thomas J.
Mobile managers—well paid and discontent. il Harvard Bus R 55:6-7 S '77

JOHNSTOWN, Pa. floods. See Floods—United States

JOIE de vivre (joy of life) See Happiness

JOINT adventures
Arabs diversify into the arms business. Bus W p31-2 O 31 '77
Home-baked bread, anyone? TV sets? Blue jeans? Skaggs-Albertson's combination stores. il Forbes 119:144+ My 15 '77
Joint venture: an alternative to partnership; farm arrangements. il Suc Farm 75:45 O '77
Public-commercial joint venture. J. L. Crompton. bibl Parks & Rec 12:20-3+ Jl '77
Skaggs-Albertson's amicable separation. Bus W p39+ F 14 '77
Soviet Union: Bendix breaks ground in trade with Russia. Bus W p49 Ja 31 '77

JOINT Chiefs of Staff. United States—Joint Chiefs of Staff

JOINT Commission on Prescription Drug Use. See United States—Congress—Joint Commission on Prescription Drug Use

JOINT European Torus. See Tokamaks

JOINT tenancy
Burden of joint tenancy. Suc Farm 75:53 N '77
His and hers ownership. S. Auerbach. il Am Home 80:68 F '77
Ins & outs of joint ownership. M. Daly. Bet Hom & Gard 55:50+ Jl '77
See also
Condominium (housing)

JOINT ventures. See Joint adventures

JOINTERS (woodworking machinery)
How to use a jointer. H. Wicks. il Pop Mech 148:116-19+ D '77
Swiss spliner. C. E. Maurer. il Pop Sci 210:66 Mr '77

JOINTS

Diseases

See also
Arthritis

JOINTS (carpentry)
How to make dovetail joints. R. Capotosto. il Pop Mech 148:102-4+ Ag '77
Mortising kit—strong joints made easy. A. J. Hand. il Pop Sci 210:147 Je '77

JOINTS, Artificial
Surgical replacement of the human knee joint; spherocentric prosthesis. D. A. Sonstegard and others. il Sci Am 238:44-51 bibl(p 138) Ja '78

JOISTS. See Girders

JOJOBA
Guayule and jojoba: agriculture in semiarid regions. T. H. Maugh, 2d. Science 196:1189-90 Je 10 '77
Real wax plant. il Mech Illus 73:116 O '77

JOJOBA oil. See Oils and fats

JOKES. See Humor

JOKL, Ernst
Kentuckian predicts new world records. J. Alsofrom. Sci Digest 81:14 Mr '77 *

JOLLIFFE, Ronald, and Richards, Robert
Potter's pentathlon. il por Ceram Mo 25:43-6 N '77

JOMO, K. S.
Kuala Juru's struggle for survival. il map Environment 19:41-2 O '77

JONAH, Kathleen
Traveling by bus. il Ret Liv 17:33-6 O '77

JONAH, Book of. See Bible—Old Testament—Jonah

JONAS, George
Canadian couple look to American market. R. Fulford. pors Pub W 212:48 O 24 '77 *

JONAS, Joan
Suspended in shadow. A. Jarmusch. il Art N 76:89+ Ap '77 *

JONAS, Paul
Home thoughts from abroad. Harpers 254:20-1 Ap '77

JONES, Andrew
Ray Bolger: leprechaun of the light fantastic. il Read Digest 110:124-8 Ap '77

JONES, Ann
Narciso-Perez case. Nation 225:584-8 D 3 '77

JONES, Antony Charles Robert Armstrong-, 1st Earl of Snowdon. See Snowdon, A. C. R. A.-J.

JONES, Arthur Gwynne-, Chalfont, Baron. See Chalfont, A. G.-J.

JONES, Barbara A.
Coordinated advertising campaign to combat environmental pollution. il Sch Arts 76:30-1 Ap '77

JONES, Bob, and Marsh, Richard
1/2-octave real time audio analyzer. il Pop Electr 12:47-54 S; 66-9 O '77

JONES, Bob, 1911-
Bob Jones speaks, General Motors listens. J. M. Wall. Chr Cent 94:291 Mr 30 '77 *

JONES, Bobby
Bobby Jones: paragon of the links. F. Hannigan. il Read Digest 111:146-50 Jl '77 *

JONES, Bonnie
Helping teachers teach the LD student. Todays Educ 66:46-8 N '77

JONES, Brennon
Rx for Carter: heed the poor nations. il Commonweal 104:9-12 Ja 7 '77
World grain reserve. il New Cath World 220:250-3 S '77

JONES, Clara Stanton
Liberating, not repressive: ALA President views the racism/sexism resolution. Am Lib 8:244-5 My '77
Library and Detroit's future. por Lib J 102:1113-15 My 15 '77
Reflections on The speaker. il Wilson Lib Bull 52:51-5 S '77
—and Morgan, J. H.
Branches—a visible presence. il pors Lib J 102:172-3 Ja 15 '77
about
Jones asks for panel to review The speaker. SLJ 24:9-10 D '77 *
JONES, Colin
When scientists and oystermen cooperate; with biographical sketch. il Sea Front 23:106-12, 126 Mr '77
JONES, Conover Hunt-. See Hunt-Jones, C.
JONES, David Allen
Humana's hopes. il por Forbes 120:24-5 S 1 '77 *
JONES, David Cadwalader
Three billy goats Gruff; dramatization of folktale. Plays 37:16, 77-80 N '77
JONES, David Pryce-. See Pryce-Jones, D.
JONES, Donald G.
Herberg as teacher. Nat R 29:886 Ag 5 '77
—and Richey, R. E.
Jones and Richey: a harmonizing of moral claims. Chr Cent 94:4-5 Ja 5 '77
JONES, Edgar
Blue chips at Reno. J. Jares. il por Sports Illus 47:50+ D 12 '77 *
JONES, Evan
Good to the last crumb. il N Y Times Mag p49 Ag 28 '77
JONES, Franklin R.
If we stay here, we'll die. il Read Digest 110:122-6 Mr '77
JONES, George
George Jones: I'm never gonna sell pop. N. Tosches. il pors Hi Fi 27:103-5 My '77 *
JONES, Gordon
Return of Pilgrim. il Sea Front 23:331-3 N '77
JONES, James
Million-dollar wound; story; excerpt from Whistle. Esquire 88:106-10 N '77
about
Good-bye, gentleman-ranker. J. Didion. Esquire 88:50+ O '77
Obituary
Nat R 29:598 My 27 '77
Pub W 211:160 My 23 '77
Taps for enlisted man Jones. por Time 109:107 My 23 '77 *
JONES, James Robert
Better than a Rolls any day. H. Sidey. il por Time 110:13 Jl 4 '77 *
JONES, Jim
Temple trouble. K. L. Woodward and others. il por Newsweek 90:79 Ag 15 '77 *
JONES, Judy, and Wilson, William
100 things every college graduate should know. il Esquire 88:91-6 S '77
JONES, Karen M.
American furniture in the Milwaukee Art Center. il Antiques 111:974-83 My '77
Collectors' notes. See issues of Antiques
JONES, Kari
Trunkful of talent. il Seventeen 36:112 Ap '77
JONES, Kirby
Cuban hustle. J. Miller. il por New Repub 177:11-14 O 8 '77 *
Middleman in Havana. por Newsweek 90:67 Jl 4 '77 *
JONES, Louise
Soups from vegetable scraps. il Org Gard & Farm 24:106-8 Jl '77
JONES, Marion Patrick. See O'Callaghan, M.
JONES, Mark
Sam Waller: eyewitness to history. il pors Ebony 32:79-80+ F '77
JONES, Marvin
Build the Phlanger for dramatic music effects. il Radio-Electr 48:42-5+ O '77
JONES, N. D.
Norman Jones, Vermont cabinetmaker. il por Antiques 111:1028-31 My '77
JONES, Norman
Norman Jones, Vermont cabinetmaker. N. D. Jones. il por Antiques 111:1028-31 My '77 *
JONES, Paul C.
Lively old fox. por Forbes 120:154 O 15 '77 *
JONES, Ralph Waldo Emerson
Prez' talks up a breeze. A. Swan. il por Time 109:96 Mr 21 '77 *
JONES, Reginald H.
GE-Utah International: more than just another merger. il Forbes 119:32-3 Ja 15 '77 *
General Electric's very personal merger. L. Kraar. il pors Fortune 96:186-92+ Ag '77 *
JONES, Richmond
Friends of mine: Richmond Jones. A. Goldsmith. il por Pop Phot 80:100-9+ Mr '77 *
JONES, Robert E. and Paxton, J. S.
296 million acre myth. Am For 83:6+ N '77
JONES, Robert F.
Gettin' nowhere fast. il pors Sports Illus 47:88-92+ S 19 '77
Land of geese and plenty. il Sports Illus 47:84-8+ D 12 '77
My vacation was nifty. il Sports Illus 47:62-6+ Jl 11 '77
Pro football (cont) Sports Illus 47:87-8 D 5 '77
Pursuing Papa's marlin. il Sports Illus 47:54-8+ Ag 1 '77
Recovering from a Rocky start. il pors Sports Illus 47:34-6+ O 3 '77
Trying the patient of the Saints. il Sports Illus 47:20-1 Ag 29 '77
Where the whales put on a whale of a show. il Sports Illus 46:34-6+ Mr 28 '77
about
Letter from the publisher. J. Meyers. il por Sports Illus 47:4 Ag 1 '77 *
JONES, Robert T.
You won't play the piano anymore. il por Read Digest 111:103-7 N '77
JONES, Rochelle and Woll, Peter
Carter vs the bureaucrats. Nation 224:402-4 Ap 2 '77
JONES, Ron
Acorn people. il Psychol Today 11:70-2+ Je '77
JONES, Shirley
Problems and pleasures of living together; interview, ed by I. Silden. M. Ingels. pors Harp Baz 110:117+ My '77 *
JONES, Susan
Light-hearted I take to the open road. il Holiday 58:54-6 Ap '77
JONES, Thad
National Public Radio. W. Youngren. il por New Repub 177:23+ S 24 '77 *
JONES, Thomas Harding
Annals of higher education. E. J. Kahn, Jr. New Yorker 53:88+ My 23 '77 *
JONES, Thomas Victor
Discipline urged in budgetary process; statement to the Congressional Joint Committee on Defense Production. por Aviation W 107:46-7+ O 24 '77
New arms export policy; excerpts from address. Aviation W 107:9 Ag 8 '77
Stabilizing defense budgets; excerpts from address. Aviation W 106:9 Ja 3 '77
about
Comeback of Tom Jones. D. Pauly and others. il por Newsweek 89:70 Ja 31 '77 *
JONES, Tom
Moloch's place; poem. New Repub 176:25 F 5 '77
Nearing Palenque; poem. Yale R 66:406 Mr '77
JONES, Tom H.
Heat-wasting doors: you can plug the leaks. il Pop Sci 211:128+ D '77
JONES, Trevor O.
Some recent and future automotive electronic developments. bibl il Science 195:1156-60 Mr 18 '77
JONES, Tristan
Shortening sail offshore. il Motor B & S 140:66-7+ S '77
Voyaging with Tristan Jones. il Motor B & S 139:54-5+ F; 62-3+ Mr; 10+ Ap; 94-5+ My '77
JONES, Turk. See Jones, W. G.
JONES, William C.
William Henry Jackson in Mexico. il por Am West 14:10-21 Jl '77
JONES, William Gwynne
Johnny Appleseed for our time. J. Daniel. il Read Digest 111:142-6 Ag '77 *
Modern Johnny Appleseed. J. Cassell. por Outdoor Life 159:31 Je '77 *
JONES & Laughlin Steel Corporation
LTV also is shaking up its steelmaker. Bus W p86 O 3 '77
JONES & Laughlin Steel Corporation-Youngstown Sheet & Tube Company merger. See Steel industry—Acquisitions and mergers
JONG, Erica Mann
Being a woman. Vogue 167:158+ Mr '77
East-west blues: a New Yorker goes west. Mademoiselle 83:201+ Ap '77
Fear of flying's Isadora Wing soars again—more outrageous than ever; story; excerpt from How to save your own life. Mademoiselle 83:146-7+ Mr '77
His tuning of the night; poem. New Yorker 53:47 N 28 '77
PW interviews; ed by B. A. Bannon. il por Pub W 211:8-9+ F 14 '77
Problems and pleasures of living together; interview, ed by I. Silden. pors Harp Baz 110:116-17 My '77
Speaking of love. por Newsweek 89:11 F 21 '77
Take a lover; story; excerpt from How to save your own life. Vogue 167:164-5 Ap '77
Two women: Liv Ullmann & Erica Jong—an intimate conversation. pors Redbook 149:104-5+ Ag '77
JONSON, Ben
Volpone. Review
Time il 110:89 O 3 '77 *
Volpone; adaptation. See Gelbart, L. Sly fox

JONSON, Jim
Acoustic era; with reproductions of paintings. R. Long. Hi Fi 27:69-72 Ap '77 *
Cylinder era; with reproductions of paintings. Hi Fi 27:67-70 F '77 *
Electrical era; with reproductions of paintings. R. Long. Hi Fi 27:73-6 Jl '77 *
Jim Jonson. M. Tinkelman. il por Am Artist 41: 74-7 Jl '77 *
Microgroove era; with reproductions of paintings. R. Long. il Hi Fi 27:81-5 O '77 *

JOPP, Martin
Harnessing the wind: a way of life. T. Galazen. il pors Org Gard & Farm 24:36+ O '77 *

JORDAN, Barbara C.
Barbara Jordan: brains + voice = power; interview, ed by E. Dowling. pors Sr Schol 110: 8-10 O 6 '77
about
Barbara Jordan—new voice in Washington. I. Ross. por Read Digest 110:148-52 F '77 *
Jordan reads her compass. por Newsweek 90:23 D 19 '77

JORDAN, Charles M.
Men behind the Car of the Year. il pors Motor T 29:37 F '77 *

JORDAN, David C.
Argentina's military government. bibl f Cur Hist 72:57-60+ F '77

JORDAN, Don
Looking in on us. il Environment 19:6-11 Ag '77; Same with title Surveilling the earth. Current 198:34-41 D '77
Town dilemma. il map Environment 19:6-15 Mr '77

JORDAN, Hamilton
How Carter operates; interview. il pors U.S. News 82:16-18 F 21 '77
about
Ham Jordan's new suit. T. M. DeFrank. por Newsweek 90:32 Ag 22 '77 *
Hannibal astride the Potomac. il por Time 109:14 Mr 14 '77 *
Making of a White House chief. E. Lewis. Bus W p 121 N 7 '77 *
President's boys. il pors Time 109:16-18+ Je 6 '77 *

JORDAN, June
Ah, momma; poem; excerpt from Things that I do in the dark. Redbook 150:74 D '77
Second thoughts of a black feminist; adaptation of address, February 1976. Ms 5:113-15 F '77

JORDAN, Peter A. See Shaw, J. H. jt auth

JORDAN, Robert Paul
Turkey. il map Nat Geog 152:88-123 Jl '77

JORDAN, Ruth
Growing up white in D.C. schools. Educ Digest 43:41-3 N '77

JORDAN, Suzanne Britt
I wants to go to the prose. por Newsweek 90:23 N 14 '77

JORDAN, Vernon Eulion, 1935-
Federal government and social rights. il Intellect 105:293-4 Mr '77
Voluntarism in America; address, April 25, 1977. Vital Speeches 43:493-5 Je 1 '77
about
Black monolith. W. F. Buckley, Jr. Nat R 29:1452-3 D 9 '77 *
Fallout between friends. por Time 110:27-8 Ag 8 '77 *
Family squabble. P. Goldman and others. il pors Newsweek 90:16-18 Ag 8 '77 *
Washington notebook. S. Booker. Ebony 33:22 Ja '78 *

JORDAN, William B.
Prado of the prairie. J. Kutner. il por Art N 76:74-7 My '77 *

JORDAN
See also
Bedouins in Jordan
Dead Sea

Israeli occupation, 1967-

Begin's challenge. M. Sheils and others. il por Newsweek 90:38+ Ag 29 '77
Bypassing the PLO? D. Holt and others. il por Newsweek 90:33 D 5 '77
Christmas summit; West Bank discussion. K. Willenson and others. il pors Newsweek 91:12-14 Ja 2 '78
Committee takes decisions on Cyprus, West Bank of Jordan River situations. UN Chron 14:40-1 Ag '77
Dayan's secret. A. De Borchgrave. il por Newsweek 90:43 O 3 '77
From the West Bank: Israel is in no mood to give up anything. D. Mullin. il map U.S. News 83:31-2 O 17 '77
Israel and its Bloc of Faithful; Gush Emunim. C. E. Brewster. Chr Cent 94:174-6 F 23 '77
Israeli-Arab labor relations. Intellect 105:291+ Mr '77
Israeli lawyer who defends Arabs; F. Langer. L. Rivlin. Ms 6:21 O '77
Israel's Patton; A. Sharon. M. R. Benjamin and M. J. Kubic. il por Newsweek 90:65 S 19 '77
Mr Waldheim regrets establishment of new Israeli settlements. UN Chron 14:20 Ag '77
Other jubilee. D. Pryce-Jones. New Repub 176: 14-17 Je 25 '77
Palestinian issue: anatomy of a slogan. B. Akzin. Intellect 106:198-200 D '77
Sending Israel a message. R. Steele and others. il map Newsweek 90:28-9 Jl 11 '77
Springing some more surprises. por Time 110: 36+ Ag 29 '77
Those disputed settlements. il map Time 110:12 Ag 8 '77
Time bomb on the West Bank. map U.S. News 83:59 Jl 25 '77
We are here to stay; Israeli legalization of three settlements. P. Martin. il Newsweek 90: 34-5 Ag 8 '77
We cannot give up Judea and Samaria; excerpts from interview, ed by M. J. Kubic. M. Begin. il por map Newsweek 89:36-7 My 30 '77
West Bank: decade of occupation. il map Time 109:31+ Je 13 '77
West Bank settlements. J. M. Wall. Chr Cent 94: 1155-7 D 14 '77
West Bank today. M. J. Kubic. il map Newsweek 89:55 Je 13 '77
Yanks go West; American Jews. M. J. Kubic. il Newsweek 90:46 S 26 '77

Kings and rulers

See also
Hussein

Politics and government

Easier lies the Hashemite head. il Time 109:33-4 F 14 '77
Other jubilee. D. Pryce-Jones. New Repub 176: 14-17 Je 25 '77

JORDEN, William John
Secretary Vance and other administration officials urge ratification of Panama Canal treaties; statement, September 29, 1977. Dept State Bull 77:622-6 N 7 '77

JORDON, Charles. See Jordon, J. jt auth

JORDON, Don
Reviews. J. Pikula. Dance Mag 51:45-6 Ap '77 *

JORDON, Joann, and Jordon, Charles
Daniel Boone's Kentucky. il Travel 148:46-51 Jl '77
Sod house frontier. il Travel 148:50-5 Ag '77

JORGENSON, Dale Weldeau
Why higher oil prices mean fewer jobs. S. Zucker. il por Bus W p 134+ S 12 '77 *

JOSÉ Limón Dance Company
Survivals: the José Limón Dance Company; season at the Roundabout, April 18-23. L. Small. il Dance Mag 51:63-4 Ag '77

JOSELOVITZ, Ernest
Hagar's children. Reviews
Nation 224:443-4 Ap 9 '77 *
New Yorker 53:82 Ap 4 '77 *

JOSEPH (Nez Perce Indian Chief)
Chief Joseph. W. A. Allard. il por map Nat Geog 151:408-34 Mr '77 *

JOSEPH, James
Re-engined: your car as good as new? questions and answers. il Motor T 29:105-9 Je '77
Used car buyer's guide. il Motor T 29:95-6+ Je '77

JOSEPH, James A.
U.N. Conference on Desertification; statement. map Dept State Bull 77:453-7 O 10 '77

JOSEPH, Lawrence B.
Normative assumptions in educational policy research: the case of Jencks's Inequality. bibl f Ann Am Acad 434:101-13 N '77

JOSEPH E. Seagram and Sons (firm) See Seagram, Joseph E. and Sons (firm)

JOSEPH Magnin Company. See Clothing industry —United States

JOSEPH Schlitz Brewing Company. See Schlitz, Joseph, Brewing Company

JOSEPHS, Allen
Spain at the polls. New Repub 177:22-5 Jl 2 '77
Spain is coming into her own: Aleixandre's Nobel Prize. il por New Repub 177:25-7 D 24 '77

JOSEPHSON, Marvin
Marvin Josephson: no business like 10% off the top. por Duns R 109:22-3 Ap '77 *

JOSEY, E. J.
Resolution on Racism & Sexism Awareness revisited. Wilson Lib Bull 51:727-8 My '77

JOSHI, M. M. and Hollis, J. P.
Interaction of Beggiatoa and rice plant: detoxification of hydrogen sulfide in the rice rhizosphere. bibl il Science 195:179-80 Ja 14 '77

JOSTEN, Monica L.
Unlikely censor. Engl J 66:15-17 F '77

JOURNAL, Philadelphia. See Philadelphia—Newspapers

JOURNALISM
See also
Crime and the press
Freedom of the press
Government and the press
Interviewing

JOURNALISM—See also—*Continued*
Journalistic ethics
News
Newsletters
Reporters and reporting
Sports journalism
Television broadcasting—News

Authorship

Once again, into the bank; selling reprint rights to Sunday newspaper magazine editors. F. J. O'Rourke. Writers Digest 57:54 S '77
Special tabloid issue; writing for the tabloid press; symposium. il Writers Digest 57:19-28 Jl '77
Try small newspapers. P. Nussman. Writers Digest 57:35 Mr '77
Where to sell op-ed articles. Writer 90:23-4 My '77

Awards, prizes, etc.

Editorial; staff awards. M. J. O'Neill. Field & S 82:4 O '77

International aspects

Reporting from the third world. M. Rosenblum. For Affairs 55:815-35 Jl '77
Word war of the worlds; third world nations protesting Western coverage of their affairs. il Time 109:89 Je 20 '77

Social aspects

Where is the news leading us? N. Cousins. il Todays Educ 66:26-7 Mr '77
See also
Muckraking

Study and teaching

Woodstein U: notes on the mass production and questionable education of journalists. B. H. Bagdikian. il Atlantic 239:80-92 Mr '77; Discussion. 239:30+ My; 22 Je '77

Canada

Of dogbiters and other mythical beasts; address, April 19, 1977. J. Cormier. Vital Speeches 43: 472-5 My 15 '77

Germany, West

Great impostor; work of G. Wallraff. il pors Time 110:103-4 O 24 '77

Underdeveloped areas

See Underdeveloped areas—Journalism

JOURNALISM, Agricultural
Farm markets. B. J. Hillman. Writers Digest 57:28-30 Ag '77
Writing for the farm magazines. C. A. Radimer. il Writers Digest 57:25-7 Ag '77

JOURNALISM, Commercial
Reporting the stock market. A. Hershman. il Duns R 110:36-9 Jl '77
Writing for business: the bucks start here. R. E. Heinemann. Writers Digest 57:19-23 O '77

JOURNALISM, Outdoor

Awards, prizes, etc.

See Journalism—Awards, prizes, etc.

JOURNALISM, Religious
Campus ministries: bread from heaven. C. G. Scully. Writers Digest 57:44 Ag '77
Free-lancing for the religious markets; list of markets. P. Wolff. Writer 90:27-9+ D '77
Gospel truths of religious writing. M. Emanuel. Writers Digest 57:20-1 D '77
I hate you! . . . love, Jeff; inspirational articles. J. Martin. Writers Digest 57:22 D '77
Path to the evangelicals is straight and narrow—but easy to follow. E. Houtz. Writers Digest 57:24-5 D '77

JOURNALISTIC ethics
Great impostor; work of G. Wallraff. il pors Time 110:103-4 O 24 '77
Greening of a guerrilla; R. Scheer. T. Griffith. por Time 109:56 Ap 4 '77
Is the press living by a double standard? A. P. Sanoff. il U.S. News 83:29 O 10 '77
Mr Blood-and-guts; sensational style of S. Dunleavy. T. Schwartz. il por Newsweek 90: 67 O 17 '77
Philadelphia story; conflict of interest charges against reporter L. Foreman. T. Schwartz and L. Howard. il por Newsweek 90:48 N 14 '77
Social relationships between journalists and government officials; excerpts from address. D. Halberstam. por Intellect 106:100 S '77
Washing dirty laundry in Detroit; D. Riegle story in the Detroit news. N. Ephron. Esquire 87:42-4 F '77
See also
Confidential communications—Press
Crime and the press

JOURNALISTIC photography. See Photography, Journalistic

JOURNALISTS
Other end of the telescope. por Time 109:49 My 9 '77
Our national flacks. R. Reeves. Esquire 88:68+ D '77
Overdose. N. Ephron. Esquire 88:35 Jl '77
Pulling the big switch; journalists as government employees. D. Gelman and L. Howard. il Newsweek 89:55 F 21 '77
Working for the Company? journalists and the CIA. il Time 110:60 S 26 '77
See also
Foreign correspondents
War correspondents
also names of journalists, e.g. S. Dunleavy

Anecdotes, facetiae, satire, etc.

Point and counterpoint. M. E. Marty. Chr Cent 94:495 My 18 '77

JOURNALS. See Periodicals

JOURNALS, Personal. See Diaries

JOURNEYS. See Travels

JOVANOVIC, Lois, and others
Screening for twin pregnancy. bibl il Science 198: 738 N 18 '77

JOVE imprint. See Harcourt Brace Jovanovich, Inc

JOWELL, Jeffrey
Our far-flung correspondents. C. Trillin. New Yorker 53:149-52+ N 21 '77 *

JOYCE, Charles
LSCA in Massachusetts: Bureau under fire anew. Lib J 102:1545 Ag '77 *
Massachusetts Bureau chief ousted by commissioners. Lib J 102:2302-3 N 15 '77 *
Massachusetts mess. J. Berry. Lib J 102:2195 N 1 '77 *

JOYCE, James
Exiles. Reviews
Nation 224:732-3 Je 11 '77 *
New Yorker 53:84+ My 30 '77 *
Reverberations of Ulysses still felt. J. Kent. por Intellect 106:189 N '77 *

JOYCE, Marshall
Conversation with Marshall Joyce; interview, ed by C. Movalli. il por Am Artist 41:90-5+ F '77

JOYCE, Rosemary
Coil springs at the Union Dime. New Yorker 53:32-4 My 16 '77 *

JOYCE, William
Eyes for the fish cutter; poem. Mademoiselle 83: 192 N '77

JUAN Carlos I, King of Spain
Political transformation of Spain. S. G. Payne. Cur Hist 73:165-8+ N '77 *
Reports & comment: Spain. S. Meisler. por Atlantic 239:14+ My '77 *

JUAN, Don, 1891-1973?
Don Juan's power trip. S. Keen. il por Psychol Today 11:40-2+ D '77 *

JUANTORENA, Alberto
El Caballo is off and running. J. Kirshenbaum. il pors Sports Illus 47:26-31 Ag 29 '77 *

JUBILEE; opera. See Kay, U.

JUD, G. Donald, and Walker, J. L.
How racial bias and social status affect the earnings of young men. bibl M Labor R 100:44-6 Ap '77

JUDAISM
Dilemma of Conservative Judaism. L. J. Kaplan; discussion. Commentary 63:6-8+ F '77
FM gabbai; J. Goldblum of Miami Beach. M. Singer. Atlantic 240:98-100 O '77
See also
Jesus Christ—Jewish interpretations
Jews—Liturgy and ritual
Messiah
Synagogues
Talmud
Zionism

JUDAISM and abortion. See Abortion—Moral and religious aspects

JUDAISM and Christianity. See Christianity and other religions

JUDD, Leda R.
Federal involvement in health care after 1945. bibl f il Cur Hist 72:201-6+ My '77

JUDGE, Thomas Lee
New grassroots reform movement checks the great raid on Montana's resources. Horticulture 55:12+ Ag '77

JUDGES
See also
Frankfurter, F.
Goodwin, H. W.
Judicial Conference of the United States
Marshall, J.
Parker, J. J.
United States—Supreme Court
Warren, E.

Appointment, qualifications, tenure, etc.

Case of the senile judge; M. McComb of California. por Newsweek 89:36 Ja 24 '77
Feet-First Ritter under siege; controversial Utah Federal judge. il por Time 110:63 N 7 '77
Judging Carter's judges. il Time 110:76 D 5 '77
Sins of Justice Yarbrough. por Time 110:44 Jl 18 '77

Attitudes

Report card on Supreme Court. il U.S. News 82:60-6+ Mr 7 '77

JUDGES—*Continued*

Salaries, allowances, etc.

Judges salaries to be reviewed next four years; International Court of Justice. il UN Chron 14:80 Ja '77

JUDGMENT
See also
Common sense

JUDICIAL Conference of the United States
Dark doings among the judges. J. P. MacKenzie. Sat R 4:18-19 My 28 '77

JUDICIAL review
Britain's Bill of Rights: judicial review is there to stay. D. J. Scheffer. Nation 224:364-7 Mr 26 '77

JUDICIARY. See Courts; Judges

JUDICIARY and the press. See Government and the press

JUDITH; opera. See Chadwick, G. W.

JUDSON, Arthur
Colorado's avalanche warning program. bibl il map Weatherwise 29:268-77 D '76

JUDY, Stephen N.
Editor's page (cont) Engl J 66:5 S; 5-6 O; 5-7 N; 7-8 D '77

JUFFURE, Gambia. See Villages—Gambia

JUICERS, Steam. See Canning and preserving—Equipment and supplies

JUICES, Fruit. See Fruit juices

JUICES, Vegetable. See Vegetable juices

JUILLIARD American Opera Center. See Lincoln Center for the Performing Arts, New York—Juilliard School

JUILLIARD School. See Lincoln Center for the Performing Arts, New York—Juilliard School

JUKES, Thomas H.
How many anticodons? bibl il Science 198:319-20 O 21 '77

JULES Feiffer's hold me! drama. See Feiffer, J.

JULIAN of Norwich. See Juliana, Anchoret

JULIANA, Anchoret
Julian of Norwich: revelations of divine love. L. S. Cunningham. Chr Cent 94:215 Mr 9 '77 *

JULIET (literary character) See Shakespeare, W. —Characters

JULY Fourth. See Fourth of July

JUMBLATT, Kamal

Assassination

Assassination of Jumblatt. I. L. Gendzier. Nation 224:388-9 Ap 2 '77
about
Revenge, revenge, revenge. il por Time 109:28 Mr 28 '77 *

JUMER'S Castle Lodge, Peoria, Ill. See Hotels, motels, etc.—United States

JUMP rope. See Rope jumping

JUMPING
Just an old-fashioned lad; high jumper V. Yashchenko. M. Clark. il por Sports Illus 47:48+ Jl 25 '77
Mouth that soars; high jumper D. Stones. F. DeFord. il pors Sports Illus 46:64-9+ My 30 '77

JUMPING (horsemanship) See Horsemanship

JUMPING by fish. See Animal locomotion

JUMPING rope. See Rope jumping

JUNCO DE MEYER, Victoria
Women in Mexican society. bibl f Cur Hist 72: 120-3+ Mr '77

JUNCTIONS (physiology)
Do cellular slime molds form intercellular junctions? G. Johnson and others. bibl Science 197: 1300 S 23 '77
Gap junctions: their presence and necessity in myometrium during parturition. R. E. Garfield and others. bibl il Science 198:958-60 D 2 '77

JUNGMAN, Royce
Funnel flash makes bare bulb light for only 39¢. il Mod Phot 41:102 F '77

JUNIDAN-ya (restaurant) See Kyoto, Japan—Hotels, restaurants, etc.

JUNIOR college libraries. See College libraries

JUNIOR high school teachers. See Teachers

JUNIOR high schools
What's wrong with junior high—everything! S. J. Gulino. il Parents Mag 52:58+ S '77

Curriculum

Focus: middle and junior high schools; symposium, ed by A. R. Gere. il Engl J 66:25-51 Ap '77
Teaching ideas: educating the in-betweener; symposium. Engl J 66:55-72 Ap '77

JUNK art. See Assemblage (art)

JUNK cars. See Automobiles—Wrecking

JUNK dealers
Junkyard jamboree; locating and using parts for rods and vans. il Hot Rod 30:70-4+ F '77

JUNK food snacks. See Snacks

JUNKER, Howard
Who erased the seventies? il Esquire 88:152-5+ D '77

JUNKINS, Donald
Approaches to Blue Hill Bay: chart no. 13313; poem. New Yorker 53:38 Je 27 '77

JUPITER, Claire
Black woman finds her roots. O. Coombs. Redbook 149:67 O '77 *

JUPITER (planet)
Mars, Jupiter, and Saturn for the coming year. R. C. Victor. il Sky & Tel 53:125-6 F '77
See also
Space flight—Voyager flights
Space flight to Jupiter

Atmosphere

Carbon monoxide on Jupiter and implications for atmospheric convection. R. G. Prinn and S. S. Barshay. bibl il Science 198:1031-4 D 9 '77

Satellites

See Satellites

JUPITER orbiter probe. See Space flight to Jupiter

JURANITCH, John A.
Sharpening secrets of a pro. il Pop Sci 210:118-21 F '77

JURISPRUDENCE
See also
Insanity—Jurisprudence
Sociological jurisprudence

JURY
Blind jurors. Newsweek 90:70 O 10 '77
Defending the jury system. J. Sanders and D. Colasanto. Intellect 105:296-7 Mr '77
See also
Grand jury

JUST, Ward S.
Reports & comment: Washington. il Atlantic 241: 6+ Ja '78

JUSTICE, Donald
Mild despair of Tremayne; Contentment of Tremayne; poems. New Yorker 53:30 Jl 4 '77

JUSTICE
Beyond masochism: a white male primal scream. R. C. Morgan. Chr Cent 94:1141-3 D 7 '77
Fair versus free. M. Friedman. Newsweek 90: 70 Jl 4 '77
Love, power and justice. P. B. Henry. il Chr Cent 94:1088-92 N 23 '77

Biblical teaching

Biblical vision of justice. J. Walsh. il New Cath World 220:145-7 My '77

JUSTICE, Administration of
See also
Actions and defenses
Courts
Criminal justice, Administration of
Due process of law
Judges
Public prosecutors
Searches and seizures

California

Ardent suitor; personal harassment of G. Morton. J. K. Footlick. il pors Newsweek 90:59 Jl 4 '77
Sheriff behind bars; R. Hongisto. il por Time 109:85 My 16 '77

Great Britain

Britain's Bill of Rights: judicial review is there to stay. D. J. Scheffer. Nation 224:364-7 Mr 26 '77

United States

Access to the courts: the justices slam the door. R. Nader and G. A. Spann. Nation 225: 495-8 N 12 '77
Nitpicking justice: unequal access to the courts. S. Gillers. il Nation 224:110-13 Ja 29 '77
See also
Courts—United States
United States—Justice, Department of
United States—National Advisory Commission on Criminal Justice Standards and Goals

Washington (state)

See also
Seattle—Justice, Administration of

JUSTICE, Department of. See United States—Justice, Department of

JUSTICES. See Judges

JUSTICES, Supreme Court. See United States—Supreme Court

JUSTIN G. Schiller, Ltd. See Booksellers and bookselling—Great Britain

JUVENILE courts
Games in kiddie court; Family Court. L. I. Barrett. il Time 110:27 Jl 11 '77

JUVENILE delinquency
Ethnic comparison of juvenile offenses and socioeconomic status. G. Calhoun, Jr. bibl il Clearing H 51:58-9 O '77
Sociological criminology and models of juvenile delinquency and maladjustment. D. Szabo. bibl f Ann Am Acad 434:137-50 N '77
Teenage criminals: time to get tougher on toughs? il Sr Schol 109:18-19 Ap 7 '77
See also
Gangs
Girls, Delinquent
Problem children
Reformatories

Prevention

Don't let them take me back! visits by juvenile offenders to Rahway State Prison. R. Tunley. il Read Digest 112:96-100 Ja '78
How one suburb deals with juvenile crime; Deerfield, Ill. J. Greenwald. McCalls 104:84 Je '77
Two answers—tough ordinances, tougher words. J. Gaylin. il Psychol Today 10:98+ My '77

JUVENILE hormones
Antiallatotropins: inhibition of corpus allatum development. W. S. Bowers and R. Martinez-Pardo. bibl il Science 197:1369-71 S 30 '77

JUVENILE sports. See Sports for children

K

K-MART Enterprises, Inc. See Kresge, S. S. Company

K-TEL International, Inc. See Phonograph record industry

KGB. See Secret service—Russia

KKK. See Ku Klux Klan

KYUS, Miles City, Mont. See Television stations

KABALEVSKY, Dmitri
Colas Breugnon, opp. 24/90. Hi Fi 27:104-5 Ap '77 *

KABUKI
Kabuki, a dance-drama art form of Japan. G. J. Michaelis. il Dance Mag 51:83-7 My '77
Reviews; September performances by the Grand Kabuki National Theatre of Japan in New York City. R. Philp. il Dance Mag 52:20-1+ Ja '78
Theatre. H. Clurman. Nation 225:285-6 S 24 '77

KACHEL, A. Theodore
Good baptism is not an end in itself. Chr Cent 94:500-1 My 25 '77

KACHINA dolls. See Dolls

KÁDÁR, János
Kadar's crown. C. Fenyvesi. il New Repub 177: 15-17 N 19 '77 *

KADDAFI, Muammar. See Qaddafi, M.

al-KADDOUMI, Farouk
PLO still hangs tough; excerpts from interview, ed by W. E. Schmidt. il por Newsweek 89:37 Mr 14 '77

KADIS, Phillip M.
Jimmy Carter: a big grin for culture. il por Art N 76:50-4 My '77
Who should manage museums? il por Art N 76: 46-51 O '77

KAEL, Pauline
Current cinema. See issues of New Yorker to March 21, 1977; September 26, 1977-

KAFIR lilies
Clivia: South African flower for a duchess. I. Zucker. il Horticulture 55:53-5 O '77

KAFKA, Franz
Contemporary looks at Kafka: illustrations for four stories of alienation. A. Cober. il Horizon 20:74-7 D '77 *

KAGAN, Jerome
All about day care. il Parents Mag 52:40-1+ Ap '77

KAGAN, Julia
Herpes: it can be treated—but not cured. Ms 6:38-40 Ja '78

KAHANER, Larry
Teletypewriter fundamentals for hams, SWL'ers & computer hobbyists. il Pop Electr 12:43-8 O '77

KAHN, Carol
Do you dream (perchance) of sleeping? Fam Health 9:36-9+ S '77

KAHN, Ely Jacques, 1916-
Annals of higher education. New Yorker 53:88+ My 23 '77
Profiles; C. S. Eaton. New Yorker 53:50-2+ O 10; 54-6+ O 17 '77
Quarter a point isn't twenty-five cents. Sports Illus 46:34-6 F 7 '77

KAHN, Frank
Sissy. por Forbes 120:100 Ag 15 '77 *

KAHN, Louis Isadore
New stately home. D. Davis. il Newsweek 89: 90-1 Ap 18 '77 *
Yale Center for British Art. V. Scully, Jr. il Archit Rec 161:95-104 Je '77 *

KAHN, Manya
Feel fit; excerpt from Manya Kahn body rhythms. il Ladies Home J 94:82-5 Jl '77

KAHN, Marcia L.
How free is the freest? America 136:53-4 Ja 22 '77

KAHN, Renee
Instant urban renewal. il Design (US) 78:2-4 mid-Summ '77

KAHN, Roger
Byplay (cont) Time 109:63-4 F 14; 62 Mr 21; 78 Ap 11; 90 Ap 25; 60 My 9; 79 Je 6; 69 Ag 1; 110:50 Ag 22; 63 S 12 '77

KAHOOLAWE (island)
Return of the natives to Kahoolawe; protesting Navy bombing. J. Wilde. il Time 110:32 Ag 8 '77

KAINEN, Jacob
Jacob Kainen: vision and technique. B. Forgey. il Art N 76:86 F '77 *

KAINIC acid
Selective destruction of neurons by a transmitter agonist. R. M. Herndon and J. T. Coyle. bibl il Science 198:71-2 O 7 '77

KAINJI Dam resettlement. See Rural planning—Nigeria

KAIPAROWITS electric power project. See Electric plants

KAISER, David
What young Americans know about Hitler. Nation 225:613 D 10 '77

KAISER, Edgar Fosburgh, Jr
Here comes another Kaiser. R. Loving, Jr. il pors Fortune 95:156-8+ F '77 *
Young Kaiser feels his oats. por Bus W p 131-2 D 5 '77 *

KAISER, Klaus L. E. and Lawrence, John
Polyelectrolytes: potential chloroform precursors. bibl il Science 196:1205-6 Je 10 '77

KAISER Aluminum and Chemical Corporation
Case for another aluminum price rise. il Bus W p25-6 Je 27 '77
Into the promised land. por Forbes 120:30-1 Jl 15 '77

KAISER Engineers Inc-Raymond International Inc merger. See Construction industry—Acquisitions and mergers

KAISER Industries Corporation
Kaisers and their empire. il Fortune 95:159 F '77

KAISER-Permanente Organization. See Insurance, Health—United States

KAISER Resources Ltd. See Coal industry—Canada

KAISER Steel Corporation
Behind the shake-up at Kaiser Steel. il Bus W p26 Jl 11 '77
EPA threatens to blacklist Kaiser; Fontana, Calif. plant. il Bus W p27 My 2 '77

KAKAR, R. K. and others
Mars: microwave detection of carbon monoxide. bibl il Science 196:1090-1 Je 3 '77

KALAUPAPA leper colony. See Leprosy and lepers

KALB, Bernard
Foreign affairs: a guide for the political globe-watcher. Sat R 4:12-13 Ag 6 '77

KALB, Marvin
Journey through a land of doubts. il N Y Times Mag p 12-13+ Jl 17 '77

KALDOR, Mary H.
Military technology and social structure. il Bull Atom Sci 33:49-53 Je '77

KALE
Something growing, something green; collards. N. P. Farris. il Org Gard & Farm 24:70-1 O '77
Yankee's love affair with collards. V. F. Shockley. il Org Gard & Farm 24:62-4 Jl '77

KALER, Theodor Schmidt-. See Schmidt-Kaler, T.

KALIMANTAN
See also
Zoology—Kalimantan

KALKE, David J.
El Salvador: a test of fire. Chr Cent 94:722-4 Ag 17 '77

KALMA, Jetse D. and others
Estimating evaporation: diffulties of applicability in different environments. bibl Science 196: 1354 Je 17 '77

KALTENBORN, H. V.
Rustic chivalry; home of H. V. Kaltenborn. Nat R 29:506 Ap 29 '77 *

KALTENBRONN, Kyra
Indian summer for wayfarers. il Parks & Rec 12:49-50 Je '77

KAMEN, Joseph M.
Controlling just noticeable differences in quality. Harvard Bus R 55:12+ N '77

KAMIL, Alan C. See Pietrewicz, A. T. jt auth

KAMMER, Alfred C.
No temporary deacons, please. America 136:503-4 Je 4 '77

KAMPUCHEA. See Cambodia

KANAGA, William S.
Business and accounting; address, January 21, 1977. Vital Speeches 43:274-8 F 15 '77

KANAPAUX, Martha Kelly
Creative teacher's approach. Todays Educ 66: 33-4 Ja '77

KANAWHA River
Drinking water: getting rid of the carbon tetrachloride. J. L. Marx. Science 196:632-6 My 6 '77
KANE, Art
Tank heaven for not so little girls; photographs. Sports Illus 46:36-43 Ja 24 '77
KANE, Eneas D.
Solving the energy crisis: we're not even taking the first step; interview, ed by J. Cook. por Forbes 120:91+ N 1 '77
KANE, Jean M.
Mongolia. il Travel 147:26-9+ Je '77
KANE, Robert S.
Autumn excursions to Europe. il Harp Baz 110: 12+ S '77
Canada's lively cities. il Redbook 149:120+ O '77
Hawaii on a budget. il Ret Liv 17:36-7+ Je '77
Travel: Canada. il Vogue 167:97-8+ Ag '77
Unexpected Pacific Northwest. il Harp Baz 110:16+ Ap '77
KANE, Tim D.
Full employment and fiscal integrity. bibl Intellect 105:246-7 F '77
KANEGIS, Arthur
Hair-raising brass propaganda. Nation 225:486-7 N 12 '77
KANFER, Stefan
Soft-shoe routine. il N Y Times Mag p 12 Mr 6 '77
KANGAROO rats
Morro Bay kangaroo rat: rodent in danger. S. Medders. il map Nat Parks & Con Mag 51:10-12 D '77
KANGAROOS
Kangaroos. T. J. Dawson. il map Sci Am 237: 78-85+ Ag '77
KANNAPPAN, Subbiah, and Krishnan, V. N.
Participative management in India: utopia or snare? bibl f Ann Am Acad 431:95-102 My '77
KANSAS
Codell, revisited; 3 years of tornadoes. M. Smith. bibl il Weatherwise 30:112-13 Je '77
See also
Hunting—Kansas
Opera—Kansas
Organic farming—Kansas
Paleontology—Kansas
School libraries—Kansas
KANSAS (rock group) See Rock groups
KANSAS CITY, Mo.

Historic houses, sites, etc.

John Wornall House, Kansas City, Missouri. K. N. Taggart. il Antiques 111:530-7 Mr '77

Libraries

See also
Linda Hall Library

Music

See also
Opera—Missouri
KANSAS CITY, Mo, flood. See Floods—United States
KANSAS CITY, Mo, Public Library
Kansas City story: capital recovery through continuing education. B. M. Nichols. por Lib J 102:1456-7 Jl '77
KANSAS CITY Lyric Opera. See Opera—Missouri
KANTAR, Edwin B.
Bowl of good cheer; quiz. il Sports Illus 47:92-3+ D 19 '77
KANTER, George
Boxing fits this old boy like a glove. D. Levin. il por Sports Illus 46:46-8+ Ap 4 '77 *
KANTER, Rosabeth Moss
Power games in the corporation; excerpt from Men and women of the corporation. il por Psychol Today 11:48-9+ Jl '77
KANTOR, Seth
Washing dirty laundry in Detroit. N. Ephron. Esquire 87:42-4 F '77 *
KANTROWITZ, Arthur
Science court experiment: criticisms and responses. bibl Bull Atom Sci 33:44-8+ Ap '77

about

Science court. N. Ponnamperuma. il por Sci Digest 82:21-3 S '77 *
KANTZER, Kenneth Sealer
Kenneth Kantzer: a biographical sketch. por Chr Today 21:36-7 S 9 '77 *
KANZER, Mark
Freud and his literary doubles. bibl Am Imago 33:231-43 Fall '76
KAO, Ing, and Drachman, D. B.
Myasthenic immunoglobulin accelerates acetylcholine receptor degradation. bibl il Science 196:527-9 Ap 29 '77
KAOHIUNG, Taiwan
To plains with love; sister city of Kaohsiung. il Newsweek 90:35 Ag 29 '77
KAOHSIUNG, Taiwan. See Kaohiung, Taiwan
KAPER, J. M.
—and Waterworth, H. E.
Cucumber mosaic virus associated RNA 5: causal agent for tomato necrosis. bibl il Science 196: 429-31 Ap 22 '77

about

Editorial. P. Trachtman. Horticulture 55:10-11 Jl '77 *
KAPER, Robert
Lethal seepage of nuclear waste. Nation 224: 266-70 Mr 5 '77
KAPIOLANI Park. See Honolulu—Parks and playgrounds
KAPLAN, Alice, collection. See Art—Private collections
KAPLAN, Barry Jay
Meyer and Kaplan: two into one will go; interview, ed by R. Dahlin. il pors Pub W 212:46 N 21 '77
KAPLAN, Gabe
From the Sweathogs to the National Gallery. P. Herz. por Sr Schol 110:22-3 D 15 '77 *
KAPLAN, James
In Miami, last winter; story. Esquire 88:144-6 D '77
Love and painting; story. New Yorker 53:40-8 My 16 '77
Vemler's Elm Street group. il New Yorker 53: 29-30 F 28 '77
KAPLAN, Janice E.
Sports. See occasional issues of Seventeen
Tracy Austin: is she tennis' next Chris Evert? il pors Seventeen 36:176-7+ Ap '77
What do you do when you grow up? il pors Sports Illus 47:30-2+ Jl 4 '77
KAPLAN, Jay L.
Locked up with fear. il Nation 225:530-2 N 19 '77
KAPLAN, Jim
Baseball (cont) Sports Illus 46:62+ Ap 25; 52+ Je 13; 47:56+ S 12; 52-4+ O 3 '77
Chess. Sports Illus 47:42 Ag 22 '77
College baseball. Sports Illus 46:55+ Mr 21 '77
College basketball. Sports Illus 46:48-9 F 28 '77
Squash (cont) Sports Illus 46:44-5 F 7 '77
Week; baseball (cont) Sports Illus 46:70+ My 2; 52+ My 9; 54+ My 16; 68+ My 23; 40+ Jl 25 '77
KAPLAN, Karel
Secrets from the Prague spring. il Time 109:38 My 9 '77 *
KAPLAN, Lawrence J.
Dilemma of Conservative Judaism. Commentary 62:44-7 N '76; 63:14+ F '77
KAPLAN, Martin Mark, and Webster, R. G.
Epidemiology of influenza; with biographical sketches. il map Sci Am 237:10, 88-92+ D '77
KAPLAN, Michael S. and Hinds, J. W.
Neurogenesis in the adult rat: electron microscopic analysis of light radioautographs. bibl il Science 197:1092-4 S 9 '77
KAPLAN, Norman, and Eskridge, Rob
Blind teens touch Hawaii via travel camp. il Camp Mag 49:14-16 Mr '77
KAPLAN, Peter B.
Focus on flowers. R. Busch. il por Pop Phot 80:116-25+ Je '77 *
KAPLAN, Seth
Clerking for the Supremes. New Repub 177:25-6 O 15 '77
KAPOOR, C. L. and Krishna, G.
Hormone-induced cyclic guanosine monophosphate secretion from guinea pig pancreatic lobules. bibl il Science 196:1003-5 My 27 '77
KAPPAS, Attallah. See Maines, M. D. jt auth
KAPPELMAN, Murray Martin
When your teenager needs you the most; excerpt from What every parent should know about sex and the American teenager. il Fam Health 9:44-6 Ag '77
KAPPLER, Herbert
Great escape. K. Willenson and others. il por Newsweek 90:43 Ag 29 '77 *
Missing cancer patient. il por Time 110:42-3 Ag 29 '77 *
Return of the native. F. Getlein. Commonweal 104:580-2 S 16 '77; Discussion. 104:642 O 14 '77 *
KAPUR, Ashok
Nth powers of the future. Ann Am Acad 430: 84-95 Mr '77
KARAJAN, Herbert von
Karajan at Juilliard. D. J. Soria. il pors Hi Fi 27:MA5+ Ap '77 *
Karajan Orchestra Competition. T. Eckert, Jr. il por Hi Fi 27:MA34-5+ Ap '77 *
Second time around; works by Brahms performed by the Berlin Philharmonic Orchestra conducted by H. von Karajan. P. L. Althouse. il por Am Rec G 40:24-6 O '77 *
KARAJAN Orchestra Competition. See Music—Competitions
KARAN, Donna
Donna Karan gives a party. il por Harp Baz 110:126-7+ Ag '77 *
KARAS, Nicholas
German wineland tour. il Travel 147:42-7 My '77
Shad in the surf. il Field & S 81:96+ Ap '77
KARATE. See Hand-to-hand fighting, Oriental
KAREN, Robert
House calls by long distance. il Fam Health 9: 48-50+ O '77

KARINSKA, Barbara
Madame Barbara Karinska: costumes to delight. V. Huckenpahler. il pors Dance Mag 52:44-7 Ja '78 *

KARKASHIAN, John Edward
Dealing with international terrorism; statement, September 14, 1977. Dept State Bull 77:605-9 O 31 '77

KARKHECK, J. and others
Prospects for district heating in the United States. bibl il Science 195:948-55 Mr 11 '77

KARL, Jean
PW interviews; ed by J. F. Mercier. por Pub W 212:66-7 Jl 18 '77

KARNAKY, Karl J. Jr, and others
Chloride transport across isolated opercular epithelium of killifish: a membrane rich in chloride cells. bibl il Science 195:203-5 Ja 14 '77

KARNIG, Jack J.
Forestry at West Point. il Am For 83:24-5+ F '77

KARNISH, Mariam
Found poetry. Engl J 66:73-5 Ap '77

KARNOW, Stanley
Carter and human rights. il Sat R 4:6-11 Ap 2 '77; Same. Current 193:3-11 My '77
Islands of contention. Sat R 5:30-2 Ja 7 '78
Our next move on China. il N Y Times Mag p7-9+ Ag 14 '77

KARP, Ivan
Is New York City vital to an artist's success? pors Am Artist 41:16-17 Ag '77

KARP, Walter
How to think about politicians. il por Horizon 19:14-15 Ja '77

KARSH, Yousuf
Many faces of Yousuf Karsh; excerpt from Karsh portraits. il Read Digest 110:153-9 F '77
Portrait of a Pope. por Sat Eve Post 249:28 Ap '77

KARSTEN Manufacturing Corporation. See Sporting goods industry

KARTUZ, Michael
Flame violets. il Horticulture 55:60-2 F '77

KÄSEBIER, Gertrude Stanton
Gertrude Käsebier lost and found. M. A. Tighe. bibl il Art in Am 65:94-8 Mr '77 *

KÄSEMANN, Elisabeth
Murder in Argentina. E. Magalis. Chr Cent 94:1030-3 N 9 '77 *

KASHLEV, Yuri I. See Zasursky, Y. N. jt auth

KASHMIR
Dream called Kashmir. E. O. Hauser. il map Read Digest 112:164-6+ Ja '78
See also
Ladakh

KASLOW, Florence W.
On the nature of empathy. bibl Intellect 105:273-7 F '77

KASPER, Daniel M.
For a better workers' compensation system. Harvard Bus R 55:6-8 Mr '77

KASS, Philip and Olmert, Michael
Violin-making as American art. il Smithsonian 8:106-10 bibl(p 131) S '77

KASSALOW, Everett M.
White-collar unions and the work humanization movement. bibl il M Labor R 100:9-13 My '77

KASSEL, Germany

Music

See also
Opera—Germany, West

KASTER, Howard B.
Weather course; ed by M. Pyzel. il map Motor B & S 140:54-6 Ag; 70-2+ S '77

KASTIN, Abba J.
Measuring melanin in the brain. Sci N 112:6-7 Jl 2 '77 *

KASTLER, Alfred
Challenge of the century. por Bull Atom Sci 33:20-2 S '77

KASTNER, Joseph
Colonial botanist, self-taught, filled European gardens; excerpt from A species of eternity. il Smithsonian 8:122-9 bibl(p 161) O '77
Dr Garden's wonderfully scented and almost imaginary namesake; excerpt from Species of eternity. il Horticulture 55:64 N '77
Innocent botanist who herbalized the West; excerpt from A species of eternity. il por Horticulture 55:44-51 S '77

KASUN, Jacqueline R.
Population bomb threat: a look at the facts. Intellect 105:412-14 Je '77

KATANA, Solomon Mbabi-. See Mbabi-Katana, S.

KATMAI, Mount
See also
Katmai National Monument

KATMAI National Monument
Valley of 10,000 wonders. S. K. Hansen. il Am For 83:26-9 F '77

KATONA, George
Recession-recovery fluctuations. Intellect 106:6-7 Jl '77

KATSENELINBOIGEN, Aron, and Levine, H. S.
Some observations on the plan-market relationship in centrally planned economies. bibl f il Ann Am Acad 434:186-98 N '77

KATSH, Ethan. See Arons, S. jt auth

KATYA Kabanová; opera. See Janáček, L.

KATZ, Alex
Broadway babies. Vasari. il Art N 76:19-20 S '77 *

KATZ, David H.
Britain's Labour Party at the crossroads. il Intellect 106:206-7 D '77

KATZ, Donald R.
British anti-Semitism, then and now. New Repub 176:21 F 5 '77
Slave trade. New Repub 176:19-21 Je 4 '77

KATZ, Jacob
Zionism and Jewish identity; adaptation of address. Commentary 63:48-52 My '77

KATZ, Joseph L. and others
Nucleation on photoexcited molecules. bibl il Science 196:1203-5 Je 10 '77

KATZ, Julius Louis
Department discusses coffee prices; statement, February 22, 1977. il Dept State Bull 76:292-301 Mr 28 '77
Department discusses international economic importance of enactment of the President's energy program; statement, May 17, 1977. Dept State Bull 76:640-2 Je 13 '77
Department discusses proposal to extend the authority of OPIC; statement, June 23, 1977. Dept State Bull 77:135-6 Jl 25 '77
Department testifies on International commodity agreements; statement, June 8, 1977. Dept State Bull 77:19-25 Jl 4 '77
Department urges passage of bill to halt importation of Rhodesian chrome; statement, February 10, 1977. Dept State Bull 76:172-4 F 28 '77
Energy and the world economy; statement, January 5, 1977. Dept State Bull 76:61-7 Ja 24 '77
U.S. exports of grain; statement, July 13, 1977. Dept State Bull 77:265-7 Ag 22 '77

KATZ, Michael, and Zimbardo, P. G.
Making it as a mental patient. bibl il pors Psychol Today 10:122-4+ Ap '77

KATZ, Richard
It wasn't all in the cards. W. Bingham. il pors Sports Illus 46:22-5 Ap 11 '77 *

KATZ, Shmuel
Katz in the mountains. J. Lelyveld. il por N Y Times Mag p63 Jl 10 '77 *

KATZ, William
Best titles of 1977: LJ's small press roundup. Lib J 102:2467-8 D 15 '77
(ed) Magazines. Lib J 102:893 Ap 15 '77

KATZENBERG, Dena S.
Copperplate-printed Irish textile. il Antiques 111:760-1 Ap '77

KATZNELSON, Ira
Redefining social science. Society 14:12-14 My '77

KAUAI (island)
Kauai: the island that's still Hawaii. E. A. Starbird. il map Nat Geog 152:584-613 N '77
Mini-holiday. B. Jeffer. map Holiday 58:17-18+ Mr '77

Churches

See Churches—Hawaii

KAUFFMAN, George B.
Calendar of science and technology. il bibl Chemistry 50:27-9 Mr '77
Left-handed and right-handed molecules. bibl il por Chemistry 50:14-18 Ap '77

KAUFFMAN, Janet
Off-loom weaving; poem. Nation 224:346 Mr 19 '77

KAUFFMAN, Robert B.
English gate. il Camp Mag 49:15+ F '77
Opinion; water sports. Camp Mag 49:5+ Je '77

KAUFFMANN, Angelica
Art isn't a man's world. W. Rodger. Hobbies 82:148-9 S '77 *

KAUFFMANN, John M.
Our wild and scenic rivers. il map Nat Geog 152:52-9 Jl '77

KAUFFMANN, Stanley
Album of a play doctor. Am Scholar 47:87-94 Wint '77
Films. See occasional issues of New republic
Money in focus. New Repub 176:42-3 My 21 '77
Theater. See occasional issues of New republic

KAUFMAN, Bel
Unlock the liberty. il Read Digest 110:47-8 My '77

KAUFMAN, Betsy B.
(ed) EJ workshop. See issues of English journal

KAUFMAN, Glen
Fiber. il Craft Horiz 37:15-16+ Je '77

KAUFMAN, Herbert E. and others
Corneal endothelium damage with intraocular lenses: contact adhesion between surgical materials and tissue. bibl il Science 198:525-7 N 4 '77

KAUFMAN, Irving Robert
Out, damned spot. V. Countryman. New Repub 177:15-17 O 8 '77 *

KAUFMAN, Michael T.
Reign of war in the land of Sheba. il N Y Times Mag p 16-19+ Ja 8 '78

about

Fellow-traveling in Mozambique. R. Moss. Nat R 29:1495-6 D 23 '77 *
Our man in Maputo. Nat R 29:1413 D 9 '77 *

KAUFMAN, Scott
Optimizing ratings. il Yachting 142:48+ N '77

KAUFMAN, Wallace
Attack on the queen; story. Mademoiselle 83:64 D '77
On a platform over the river; story. Redbook 149:122 S '77

KAUL, Mohan L.
Physical child abuse and its prevention. bibl il Intellect 105:270-2 F '77

KAULE, Al. See Kaule, K. jt auth

KAULE, Kathleen, and Kaule, Al
Plant traps: a way to outwit your insect foes. Org Gard & Farm 24:178-80 Je '77
Seed gardening for better nutrition. il Org Gard & Farm 25:63-4 Ja '78

KAUNDA, Kenneth David
Kaunda: I see no settlement; interview, ed by D. Wood. por Time 110:35-6 Ag 8 '77

KAUPER, Thomas E.
Public distrust and government service. por Intellect 106:2 Jl '77

KAURI pine
New Zealand's king kauri. E. R. Yarham. il Am For 83:16-19+ Ag '77

KAVANAGH, Aidan
Prayer is the choreography, the poetry, the symphony of existence. New Cath World 220: 11 Ja '77

KAVEN, Robert
Locating sleep; poem. New Yorker 53:135 Ap 25 '77

KAWA, Kazuyoshi. See Fukuda, J. jt auth

KAWAKAMI, Rokuo
Rokuo Kawakami: simplicity revived. H. O. Martin. il Mod Phot 41:100-5 My '77 *

KAWIN, Bruce F.
Faulkner filmography. bibl il Film Q 30:12-21 Summ '77

KAY, Alan C.
Microelectronics and the personal computer; with biographical sketch. il Sci Am 237:20, 230-2+ S '77

KAY, Jane Holtz
Architectural book marks (cont) Nation 224: 408-10 Ap 2 '77
Architecture (cont) Nation 224:474-6; 225:90-2, 245-7, 635-6 Ap 16, Jl 23, S 17, D 10 '77
Books on architecture. Nation 225:665 D 17 '77
Boston (cont) il Art N 76:96+ Ja; 98-101 Mr; 115-18 D '77
Designs and documents. Sat R 4:27 My 14 '77
Recycling of Boston. il Sat R 4:38-40 F 5 '77
Sixty million graves. Nation 224:209-12 F 19 '77

KAY, Stafford
Educational change in Africa. bibl il Intellect 106:217-20 D '77

KAY, Ulysses
Jubilee. Reviews
Hi Fi 27:MA19 Ap '77 *

KAY Corporation. See Conglomerate corporations

KAYAK racing
See also
Running rapids

KAYAKS and kayaking
Arctic splendor along the Noatak; combined kayaking and backpacking trip through the proposed Noatak National Preserve. il maps Nat Parks & Con Mag 51:4-9 Je '77
Kayaking; Snake River Kayak School. il Bet Hom & Gard 55:184+ Jl '77

KAYE, Danny
Lot of person. R. Fimrite. il pors Sports Illus 46:76-80+ Ap 4 '77 *

KAYE, Dena
(comp) Redbook traveler; where the stars take their romantic vacations. il Redbook 148:37-9 F '77
Spring shape-up guide. il N Y Times Mag p44+ Mr 27 '77

KAYE, Elizabeth
Is all this muscle all that healthy? il por Fam Health 9:20-4 D '77
(ed) See Fletcher, L. Louise Fletcher in search of herself
(ed) See Winkler, H. Fonzie

KAYE, Evelyn
What concerned parents can do about TV. il McCalls 104:53 Ap '77

KAYTOR, Marilyn
Devil's food! il Esquire 87:72-3+ F '77

KAZDIN, Andrew
Toward a super-refined music reproducer. il Hi Fi 28:76-8 Ja '78

KAZIN, Alfred
Books. See issues of Esquire
Hemingway the painter. por New Repub 176:21-8 Mr 19 '77
View from the sixties; excerpt from New York Jew. por New Repub 177:33-41 O 15 '77
Wisdom in exile. New Repub 177:12-14 Jl 23 '77

KAZUKO Hirabayashi Dance Theatre. See Dance companies

KEAGGY, Phil
Phil Keaggy's new song. D. J. Evearitt. Chr Today 21:18 Ag 12 '77 *

KEALY, Janet
Shooting on the run: how to make a vacation film. il por Pop Phot 81:126-7+ Ag '77

KEANE, John
Hercule Pawret. il por Time 110:53 Ag 1 '77 *

KEANE, John G.
Coming marketing internationale; address, May 18, 1977. Vital Speeches 43:532-6 Je 15 '77

KEANE, Philip
Theological anthropology of the man/woman relationship; excerpt from Sexual morality. il New Cath World 220:284+ N '77

KEARN, J. N.
1,436-acre legacy. D. Wooldridge. por Outdoor Life 161:22 Ja '78 *

KEARNEY, John J.
Defense fund. W. F. Buckley, Jr. Nat R 29:793 Jl 8 '77 *
Fortess breached. Nation 224:482 Ap 23 '77 *
Griffin Bell believes in law. Nation 224:547-8 My 7 '77 *
Prosecution of FBI, CIA agents: an idea coming under fire. il por U.S. News 83:56 S 12 '77 *
What national security? Nation 225:546 N 26 '77 *

KEARNEY, Patrick W.
Trash-bag murders. D. A. Williams and A. Huck. il pors Newsweek 90:22 Jl 18 '77 *
Twenty-eight, and counting. il pors Time 110: 49 Jl 18 '77 *

KEARNEY, Vincent S.
Eurocommunism quandary. America 137:347-50 N 19 '77
International affairs (cont) America 136:85-6 Ja 29 '77
Panama and Suez. America 137:477-8 D 31 '77
World scene (cont) America 136:426-8 My 7 '77

KEARNEY, Neb, Public Library. See Libraries—Nebraska

KEARNS, David T.
Distance man. il por Forbes 120:192 N 15 '77 *

KEARNS, Richard
Annapolis cityscape. il Antiques 111:194-200 Ja '77
Urban design. il Antiques 111:158-9 Ja '77

KEARTON, Christopher Frank Kearton, Baron
BNOC: new power in international oil. J. Ross-Skinner. por Duns R 109:84 My '77 *

KEATING, Justin
Rake's progress. il Time 109:79 Je 20 '77 *

KEATING, Kate
Education (cont) il Bet Hom & Gard 55:82+ Ap '77

KEATING, Kathleen Irwin
Allelopathic influence on blue-green bloom sequence in a eutrophic lake. bibl il Science 196:885-7 My 20 '77

KEATING, Tom
Ars gratia artis? B. Wicker. Commonweal 104: 622-4 S 30 '77 *

KEATON, Buster
More is less: comedy and sound. P. Warshow. il pors Film Q 31:38-45 Fall '77 *

KEATON, Diane
What's happening? interview, ed by G. Shalit. il por Ladies Home J 94:12+ Jl '77

about

Love, death and la-de-dah. il pors Time 110: 68-72+ S 26 '77 *
Woody Allen's breakthrough movie. il por Time 109:70-1 Ap 25 '77 *

KECK, James M.
Future air warfare; excerpts from address. Aviation W 106:7 F 21 '77

KEDOURIE, Elie
Real T. E. Lawrence. Commentary 64:49-56 Jl; 18 O '77

KEECH, Andy
Winging it on the way down. il Sports Illus 46:36-9 My 23 '77

KEEFAUVER, John
Man who couldn't find himself. Nat R 29:147 F 4 '77

KEEGAN, George J. Jr
New assessment put on Soviet threat; address, with biographical sketch. il por Aviation W 106:38-43+ Mr 28 '77

about

General goes zap. M. Kondracke. New Repub 177:19-22 Jl 2 '77 *
Particle beams as ABM weapons: general and physicists differ. N. Wade. por Science 196: 407-8 Ap 22 '77 *

KEELER, Harry Stephen
Murder like crazy. F. M. Nevins, Jr. il New Repub 177:25-8 Jl 30 '77 *

KEELEY, Lawrence H.
Functions of paleolithic flint tools; with biographical sketch. il Sci Am 237:15-16, 108-11+ N '77

KEELS
Are centerboards obsolete? splayed-out. H. A. Scheel. il Yachting 141:110+ Mr '77
Heel-keel. H. Kelly. il Motor B & S 139:102 F '77
Inventing the centerboard; J. Schank. T. Foote. il por Motor B & S 140:139-42 S '77

KEELY, Jane
Around the house. See issues of Good housekeeping

KEEN, A. Myra
Paleontological hoaxes. Natur Hist 86:24+ My '77

KEEN, Sam
Chasing the blahs away: boredom and how to beat it. il por Psychol Today 10:78-80+ My '77
Don Juan's power trip. il por Psychol Today 11:40-2+ D '77

KEEN, W. W.
President's operation. il Sat Eve Post 249:106+ Jl '77

KEENAN, James F.
Dead trees, dying communities. America 137:265-8 O 22 '77

KEENAN, Joseph H.
Obituary
Phys Today 30:74+ N '77. A. Shapiro

KEENELAND Race Track. See Race tracks

KEENS, William
Skull house, heart flower; How it feels to walk on the moon; poems. Poetry 129:276-77 F '77

KEENY, Spurgeon Milton, 1924-
Proposed modifications to nonproliferation legislation; statement, September 13, 1977. Dept State Bull 77:671-3 N 14 '77

KEEP America Beautiful, Inc
. . . helps beautify land; Clean Community System. R. W. Powers. Camp Mag 49:8-9 Je '77

KEES, Weldon
Comment. B. Howard. Poetry 130:285-7 Ag '77 *

KEFNER, John, pseud
Dragon and the bear: Asian perceptions of a Sino-Soviet war. map America 137:162-4 S 24 '77

KEHL, D. G.
Gimlet eye of D. Keith Mano. Chr Today 21:20-1 Je 17 '77

KEHRY, M. and others
Fluidity in the membranes of adult and neonatal human erythrocytes. bibl il Science 195:486-7 F 4 '77

KEIFFER, Elisabeth
Mrs Murray's mystery disease. il por Good H 184:80+ Mr '77
Ron Thomas' horror story: my family was poisoned! il Good H 185:64+ Ag '77
Twin miracles. il Good H 186:75+ Ja '78
(ed) See Donahue, P. TV's Phil Donahue: bachelor father
(ed) See Godtsenhoven, W. F. van. Shipwreck
—See Kern, A. jt auth

KEIL, Bill
Tillamook: a modern success story. il Am For 83:20-3+ Mr '77

KEILLOR, Garrison
Don: the true story of a young person. New Yorker 53:38-43 My 30 '77

KEITH, Larry
Baseball (cont) Sports Illus 46:50+ My 9; 47-38+ Jl 25 '77
Big change in the affairs of State. il por Sports Illus 47:24-6+ D 12 '77
College basketball (cont) Sports Illus 46:40-1 Ja 17; 48-9 Ja 24; 48:87 D 19 '77
Devil of a time for the Angels. il Sports Illus 47:16-17 Ag 1 '77
In L.A. it's up, up and away with Cey. il por Sports Illus 46:24-8+ My 16 '77
Infusion of fresh Dodger-blue blood. il pors Sports Illus 46:36-8+ Mr 14 '77
Is it daft—or deft—to raft? il Sports Illus 47:30-2+ N 7 '77
Macy had the goods in every department. il Sports Illus 48:12-13 Ja 9 '78
Minny gets the max from a minimum. il Sports Illus 46:22-3 Je 20 '77
No, it's the year of the lively bat. il por Sports Illus 47:18-19 S 19 '77
Off on a rampage. il Sports Illus 47:14-17 Ag 29 '77
On the trip to the pit the Bruins got bit. il Sports Illus 46:20-1 F 28 '77
Revival and survival. il Sports Illus 47:16-19 Ag 8 '77
Series full of flip-flops. il Sports Illus 47:18-21 O 17 '77
Somebody old and somebody new. il Sports Illus 46:30-1 Ap 18 '77
They kept cool during a cold streak. il Sports Illus 46:30-2+ My 2 '77
They're knocking the stuffing out of it. il Sports Illus 46:22-5+ Je 13 '77
Three applications for one vacancy. il Sports Illus 46:20-1 F 14 '77
Tom Terrific arms the Red arsenal. il por Sports Illus 46:22-4+ Je 27 '77
True tests of talent. il Sports Illus 47:18-21 O 3 '77
Week; baseball (cont) Sports Illus 46:49-50 My 30 '77
(ed) See McGuire, A. Conversation with chairman Al
about
Letter from the publisher. J. Meyers. il por Sports Illus 46:6 Je 13 '77 *

KEKANA, Fana D. and others
Survival. Reviews
New Yorker 53:145-6 O 24 '77 *

KELBER, Mim
UN's dirty little secret. Ms 6:51+ N '77

KELLEHER, Stephen J.
Catholic annulments: a dehumanizing process. il Commonweal 104:363-8 Je 10 '77

KELLER, Allan
Pontiac's conspiracy. il map Am Hist Illus 12:4-8+ My '77

KELLER, Arnold J. and Raffone, Arnold
Career education: success for the potential dropout. Clearing H 51:70-2 O '77

KELLER, Hans Ulrich
New West German planetarium. il Sky & Tel 54:375-7 N '77

KELLER, Mark
Erosion; photographs. il Oceans 10:48-55 N '77

KELLER, Marthe
Very modern Marthe Keller, interview, ed by K. Madden. il por Vogue 167:116-17+ Jl '77

KELLER, Rudy
Practical plan for a cutting garden. il Org Gard & Farm 24:88-90 F '77

KELLERMAN, Jonathan
Of drooling dogs and periwinkles. por Newsweek 89:11 My 23 '77

KELLEY, Ben
Make motorcyclists wear helmets? interview. il pors U.S. News 83:39-40 Jl 18 '77

KELLEY, Clarence Marion
Is the F.B.I. obsolete? address, May 18, 1977. Vital Speeches 43:578-81 Jl 15 '77
about
Still wanted. Time 110:16 D 12 '77 *

KELLEY, Jerome E.
Picture yourself tripling your income as a writer. Writers Digest 57:26-8 F '77

KELLEY, Kitty
Rosalynn and Jimmy Carter's Washington. il por Redbook 149:82+ Je '77

KELLEY, Richard C.
Grand jury abuse. Progressive 41:34-5 F '77

KELLEY, Robert
Ideology and political culture from Jefferson to Nixon. bibl f Am Hist R 82:531-62 Je '77

KELLEY'S Island
Ohio's Erie islands. D. Gleasner and B. Gleasner. il Travel 148:36-9 Jl '77

KELLMAN, Amy
For very young dancers. il SLJ 24:34-5 D '77

KELLOGG, Arthur E.
Evolution of U.S. immigration policy. Cong Digest 56:227-9+ O '77

KELLOGG, Mary Alice
Washington's star stargazer. il por N Y Times Mag p 12-13+ Ja 16 '77

KELLOGG, Rhoda
Is your child gifted? interview, ed by C. Leon. House & Gard 149:40 Ap '77

KELLS, Book of. See Book of Kells

KELLY, D. See Shannon, D. C. jt auth

KELLY, Dianne
(ed) See Allen, J. Education of John Allen

KELLY, Donald P.
Tough numbers man sets up the Esmark derby. il por Fortune 95:17+ Ap '77 *

KELLY, Ellsworth
Cover. M. Schiller. il Am Artist 41:6+ Ag '77 *

KELLY, Grace. See Grace Patricia, Consort of Rainier III, Prince of Monaco

KELLY, Hal
Super patching kit. il Mech Ilus 73:88 Mr '77

KELLY, Hartleigh
Heel-keel. il Motor B & S 139:102 F '77

KELLY, James
Cosmetic lib for men. il N Y Times Mag p 119-20+ S 25 '77

KELLY, Kathleen
Long-awaited well-respected community center. il Archit Rec 162:95-8 O '77

KELLY, Tim
How to write and sell that play. Writers Digest 57:19-23 My '77

KELMAN, Steven J.
No mad scientists. New Repub 176:8+ Mr 26 '77
OSHA under fire. New Repub 176:18-20+ My 21 '77

KELP culture. See Aquaculture

KELSEY, Paul M.
Training New York's bowhunters. il Conservationist 32:32-3 S '77
What is a deer management permit? il map Conservationist 32:35-7 N '77

KELSEY, William G.
Hiroshima echo. il Progressive 41:28-30 N '77

KELTS. See Celts

KEMP, Geoffrey
Scarcity and strategy. For Affairs 56:396-414 Ja '78

KEMP, Jack F.
Needed—tax reform that will create jobs. Read Digest 110:103-7 Ap '77

about

Kemp & Co. M. S. Evans. Nat R 29:670 Je 10 '77 *

KEMP, Lee
Suppression of his aggression. D. S. Looney. il pors Sports Illus 46:28-31 F 21 '77 *

KEMP, Walt
Bessie Baxter Pine; poem. Sat Eve Post 249: 54-5 Ap '77
MacNamara Vale; poem. Sat Eve Post 249:60-1 My '77
Sara Sims; poem. Sat Eve Post 249:45-7 O '77

KEMPER, James Scott, 1914-
Impact of the insurance enterprise on socio-economic forces; address, August 10, 1977. Vital Speeches 43:708-10 S 15 '77

KEMPIS, Thomas à. See Thomas à Kempis

KEMPNER, Harris L. Jr
Small Texas bank's high-powered portfolio. il Bus W p 102 S 19 '77 *

KEMPTON, Murray
Coca-colonialism. Progressive 41:35 Ag '77
Easy to fool. Progressive 41:17 Ap '77
Failure richly rewarded. Progressive 41:45 O '77
Giggling newscasters. Progressive 41:52 Mr '77
Israel's soul. Progressive 41:11 D '77
Musical chairs. Progressive 41:42 F '77
Numbers game. Progressive 41:49 My '77

KENAI Fjords National Monument (proposed)
See National monuments

KENDALL, Alan G. and Tashian, R. E.
Erythrocyte carbonic anhydrase I: inherited deficiency in humans. bibl il Science 197:471-2 Jl 29 '77

KENDALL, Dave
How to go near the water safely. il Ret Liv 17:20-3 Jl '77

KENDALL, Elaine
L.A: at home in the land of instant gratification. Vogue 167:196+ O '77

KENDALL, Elizabeth
Twyla Tharp, in motion. New Repub 176:19-20 F 12 '77

KENDALL, F. and others
Nuclear morphometry during the cell cycle. bibl il Science 196:1106-9 Je 3 '77

KENDALL, Martha
Forget the masked man. Who was his Indian companion? il Smithsonian 8:113-20 S '77

KENDALL, Oscar E.
You ought to be in pictures. R. Rosenblatt. New Repub 177:45-6 O 1 '77 *

KENDIG, Frank
Days dwindle down for a precious fuel. il Sci Digest 82:44-6 O '77

KENDLER, Robert
Served up, imperially, under glass. M. Sharnik. il pors Sports Illus 46:44-6+ My 2 '77 *

KENDRICK, Rebecca
Cooking organic quick breads. il Org Gard & Farm 25:134-5 Ja '78

KENIGSBERG, Jana Lyn
Gift of life; excerpt. por Sr Schol 109:24 My 5 '77

KENILWORTH, Ill.

Education

See Education—Illinois

KENISTON, Kenneth
More rights for children—what an expert says; interview. por U.S. News 83:33 O 31 '77 *

about

Citizens who need us most. C. Tucker. Sat R 5:56 O 15 '77 *

KENNAN, George Frost
Containment: a reassessment. J. L. Gaddis. bibl f For Affairs 55:873-87 Jl '77; Reply with rejoinder. E. Mark. 56:430-41 Ja '78 *
Mr X^2. H. Fairlie. New Repub 177:9-11 D 24 '77; Reply. Nation 226:4-5 Ja 7 '78 *
Strange case of George F. Kennan. E. N. Luttwak. Commentary 64:30-5 N '77 *

KENNECOTT Copper Corporation
Bothersome billion. il Time 110:42 Ag 1 '77
Costly copper pact stuns the industry. Bus W p24-5 Jl 18 '77
Could 1977 be the year for Kennecott? J. Madrick. il Bus W p59 Ja 24 '77
Down the chute with Peabody Coal. C. J. Loomis. il Fortune 95:228-33+ My '77
Kennecott prospects for an acquisition. Bus W p22-3 Jl 18 '77
Ocean mining: former negotiator now lobbies for Kennecott. D. Shapley. Science 196:964-5 My 27 '77

KENNECOTT Copper Corporation-Carborundum Company merger. See Corporations—Acquisitions and mergers

KENNEDY, Cora Wright
Tools & techniques. See issues of Popular photography

KENNEDY, Donald
How safe are the drugs you take? interview. il pors U.S. News 83:65-6 N 21 '77

about

Biologist Kennedy to head FDA. Sci N 111:168 Mr 12 '77 *
Donald Kennedy to head FDA. B. J. Culliton. por Science 195:1307 Mr 25 '77 *
FDA ready to turn corner. . .if it's still able. D. S. Greenberg. Sci Digest 81:71-2 Je '77 *

KENNEDY, Edward Moore
Excerpt from address on mandatory tax supported health insurance, January 11, 1977. Cong Digest 56:200+ Ag '77
Excerpts from remarks on U.S. African policy, March 23, 1976. Cong Digest 56:14+ Ja '77
Excerpts from statement on federal subsidies for congressional election campaigns, February 2, 1976. Cong Digest 56:76+ Mr '77

about

Gene splicing: Senate bill draws charges of Lysenkoism. N. Wade. por Science 197:348+ Jl 22 '77 *
Impartial OTA future dubious; a launching pad for Kennedy? D. Gergen. Sci Digest 82:24-5+ S '77 *
Kennedy bill unchanged by scientists' visit. P. R. Day. BioScience 27:594 S '77 *
Kennedy, GAO criticize NSF; grant renewal is rejected. P. M. Boffey. Science 195:556-8 F 11 '77 *
NSF: pressures mount to provide grants for industrial researchers. P. M. Boffey. Science 196:142-3 Ap 8 '77 *
OTA: Daddario's exit heightens strife over Kennedy role. C. Holden. Science 197:27-8 Jl 1 '77 *

KENNEDY, Jeffrey P.
Retrospect. Motor T 29:55-8 Jl '77

KENNEDY, John Clifford
United States discusses environmental problems; statement, October 20, 1977. Dept State Bull 77:868-71 D 12 '77

KENNEDY, John Fitzgerald, 1917-1963
Bringing JFK up to date. N. N. Minow. por Newsweek 89:13 My 30 '77 *
CIA and Cuba. W. F. Buckley, Jr. Nat R 29: 792-3 Jl 8 '77 *
I looked down into my open grave; excerpt from Profiles in courage. il Sr Schol 109:17-19 F 24 '77
JFK, Castro—and controversy. D. Gelman. il pors Newsweek 90:85 Jl 18 '77 *
Kennedy without end, amen. T. Wicker. il por Esquire 87:65-9 Je '77 *
Kennedy's cold war. T. Szulc. New Repub 177: 19-21 D 24 '77 *
Schlesinger and Kennedy. R. Radosh. Nation 225:104-9 Ag 6 '77; Reply with rejoinder. A. Schlesinger, Jr. 225:147-8 Ag 20 '77 *
Television; B. Moyers' The CIA's secret army. P. Sourian. Nation 225:155-7 Ag 20 '77 *

Assassination

FBI story on J.F.K.'s death; with report by H. Gorey. il Time 110:18+ D 19 '77
JFK killing: FBI files raise questions, give no answers. il U.S. News 83:15 D 19 '77
J.F.K.-R.I.P. T. Powers. Commonweal 104:337-9 My 27 '77; Reply with rejoinder. G. Mitchell. 104:451+ Jl 22 '77
JFK: what the FBI found. R. Boeth and others. il pors Newsweek 90:28+ D 19 '77
Marina & Lee; excerpt. P. J. McMillan. il pors Ladies Home J 94:175-82+ O; 122-3+ N '77
Opening the JFK file; FBI file. P. Bonventre and others. il Newsweek 90:34-5 D 12 '77

See also

United States—Congress—House—Assassinations, Select Committee on
United States—Congress—Senate—Select Committee to Study Governmental Operations with Respect to Intelligence Activities

KENNEDY, Joseph Patrick, 1952-
Joe Kennedy comes of age. H. Gorey. il pors N Y Times Mag p6-11+ My 29 '77 *

KENNEDY, Mopsy Strange
Lastborn speaks out—at last. por Newsweek 90: 22-3 N 7 '77

KENNEDY, Nell L. See Geiger, P. jt auth

KENNEDY, R. Scott
(ed) See McDonnell, N. Northern Ireland's guerrillas of peace
(ed) See Williams, B. Northern Ireland's guerrillas of peace

KENNEDY, Ray
Amateur night on the Americus plan. il Sports Illus 46:32-6+ F 21 '77
Little night music. il pors Sports Illus 47:82-6+ N 21 '77
Miracle in the Meadows. il por Sports Illus 47: 74-9+ S 12 '77
Pittsburgh Fats dodges a silver bullet. il por Sports Illus 46:24-6+ Mr 7 '77

KENNEDY, Ray—*Continued*
Revved up to ride on an ocean of trouble. il por Sports Illus 46:30-2+ Je 27 '77
Who are these guys? il Sports Illus 46:50-8+ Ja 31 '77
about
Letter from the publisher. J. Meyers. il por Sports Illus 47:4 N 21 '77 *

KENNEDY, Robert Francis, 1925-1968
Last day of the RFK campaign; interview, ed by L. R. Obst. J. Witcover. il por N Y Times Mag p85+ N 13 '77 *
Assassination
Murder of Robert Kennedy: suppressed evidence of more than one assassin? A. K. Lowenstein. il por Sat R 4:6-10+ F 19 '77

KENNEDY, Stephen J. and others
Synthetic peptides form ion channels in artificial lipid bilayer membranes. bibl il Science 196:1341-2 Je 17 '77

KENNEDY, Ted. See Kennedy, E. M.

KENNEDY, Terry
Catcher who's caught their fancy. J. Kaplan. por Sports Illus 46:55+ Mr 21 '77 *

KENNEDY Center for the Performing Arts. See John F. Kennedy Center for the Performing Arts, Washington, D.C.

KENNEDY International Airport. See New York (city)—Airports

KENNEDY School of Government. See Harvard University—John F. Kennedy School of Government

KENNEDY Space Center. See United States—John F. Kennedy Space Center

KENNELL, John D. See Linneman, R. E. jt auth

KENNELS
Definitive doghouse—and you can build it! D. M. Lidster. il Bet Hom & Gard 54:106 Ag '76
How to choose a boarding kennel. B. Humeston. Bet Hom & Gard 55:176+ Je '77

KENNER, Hugh
How the cruiser was grounded and Finn MacCool returned. Nat R 29:874-7 Ag 5 '77
Images at Random. il Harpers 225:102+ D '77

KENNETH
Midsummer feast: English gardens with Kenneth for your guide. bibl il por House & Gard 149:48+ Jl '77

KENNEY, Edward
Muskellunge. il Conservationist 31:24-5 Mr '77

KENNEY, Nathaniel T.
Our wild and scenic rivers. il map Nat Geog 152:46-51 Jl '77

KENNEY, Richard
Grotesques; Desperados; poems. Yale R 66:400-1 Mr '77
Night's La Brea; poem. Am Scholar 47:86 Wint '77
Notes from Greece; poem. New Yorker 53:41 O 24 '77

KENNY, John T. and Blass, E. M.
Suckling as incentive to instrumental learning in preweanling rats. bibl il Science 196:898-9 My 20 '77

KENT, Allen. See Galvin, T. J. jt auth

KENT, Betsy
Nuts, pods, weeds and seeds. il Org Gard & Farm 24:138+ N '77
Second life for your flowers: how to preserve plants for winter arrangements. il Horticulture 55:58-9 S '77

KENT, Francis B.
Teenagers around the world. il Sr Schol 109:16-17 Ja 13 '77

KENT, Fraser
Commonest phobia of all: shutting out the world; excerpt from Nothing to fear. il Fam Health 9:44-6+ O '77

KENT, George
Equity in global fisheries management. il Oceans 10:60-4 S '77

KENT, John
Reverberations of Ulysses still felt. por Intellect 106:189 N '77

KENT, John L.
How ersatz foods shortchange you. Sci Digest 82:20-1 Jl '77

KENT, Mary Day
Relinquishing the Canal. Chr Cent 94:755-6 Ag 31 '77

KENT, Robert B.
Centering as a process for children's imaging. bibl il Sch Arts 77:18-20 N '77

KENT, Rosemary
Cavorting in the cellar. il Horizon 20:78-80 D '77
Home in an adobe. il pors N Y Times Mag p46-7+ Ja 23 '77

KENT, Wallace
Portrait lenses at budget prices. il Mech Illus 73:48-9+ My '77

KENT Opera Company. See Opera—Great Britain

KENT State University. See Ohio. Kent State University, Kent

KENTON Corporation-Rapid-American Corporation merger. See Corporations—Acquisitions and merger

KENTUCKY
See also
Crime and criminals—Kentucky
Education—Kentucky
Fleming County
Hunting—Kentucky
Mammoth Cave National Park
Opera—Kentucky
Organic farming—Kentucky
Strip mining—Kentucky
Water pollution—Kentucky
Description and travel
Daniel Boone's Kentucky. J. Jordan and C. Jordan. il Travel 148:46-51 Jl '77
Parks and reserves
Socialism with a southern face; State Resort Parks. J. Burnham. Nat R 29:1102 S 30 '77
Restaurants
See Restaurants—United States

KENTUCKY caves. See Caves

KENTUCKY Derby. See Horse racing

KENTUCKY Fried Chicken Corporation
How to make a million after you're 65. H. Sanders. il por Sat Eve Post 249:46-7 Mr '77

KENTUCKY Opera Association. See Opera—Kentucky

KENYA
Other side of the coin; repression under Kenyatta. R. W. Thompson. Nat R 29:332 Mr 18 '77
Whither East Africa? W. A. E. Skurnik. Cur Hist 73:205-8+ D '77
See also
Hunting—Kenya
Lamu (island and town)
Marriage law—Kenya
Nairobi
National parks and reserves—Kenya
Wildlife conservation—Kenya
Description and travel
Kenya. N. Milford. il Holiday 57:36-9+ N '76

KENYATTA, Jomo
Other side of the coin. R. W. Thompson. Nat R 29:332 Mr 18 '77 *

KEPES, Gyorgy
Shows we've seen. J. Murray. il Pop Phot 80:87+ Ap '77 *

KEPHART, George S.
Problems in the Smokies. il por Am For 83:28-31 Ag '77

KEPHART, Horace
Problems in the Smokies. G. S Kephart. il por Am For 83:28-31 Ag '77 *

KEPLER, Karen, and Randall, J. W.
Individualization: subversion of elementary schooling. Educ Digest 43:17-20 O '77

KEPONE. See Insecticides

KEPPLER, Herbert
Keppler on the SLR. See issues of Modern photography
about
Such good friends. R. Wolters. Writers Digest 57:16+ D '77 *

KERATOCONJUNCTIVITIS. See Eye—Diseases and defects

KERER, Rudolf
Brahms: Piano concerto no. 1 in D minor. G. S. Pietri. il UNESCO Courier 30:30-8+ Ag '77

KERN, Arthur, and Keiffer, Elisabeth
Hospitals are no place for sick people. Good H 184:111+ My '77

KERN County, Calif.
Great Kern County mouse war. K. P. Maize. il Audubon 79:158-60 N '77

KERNAN, Alvin
Place and plot in Shakespeare. Yale R 67:48-56 O '77

KERNAN, Henry S.
Thirty years in a woodlot. il por map Conservationist 32:32-4 N '77

KERNAN, Michael
Breathing life into dry bones. il por Smithsonian 7:116-18+ F '77

KERNER, Estelle
(ed) See Milstein, N. Nathan Milstein: Brahmin with violin

KERR, Ed
Jim Mixon: the man they didn't eat for breakfast. por Am For 83:12-13+ My '77

KERR, James Robert
Avco gets its act together—for profit. por Bus W p 115-16 O 3 '77 *

KERR, Jean
Confessions of a soap-opera addict. il McCalls 104:36+ S '77

KERR, M. E.
Why of people: the novels of M. E. Kerr. M. Kingsbury. Horn Bk 53:288-95 Je '77 *

KERRIDGE, J. F. See MacDougall, J. D. jt auth

KERRIGAN, James Leo
Competitor asks: is this the way to run a railroad? por Duns R 109:99-100+ Ap '77

KERRIGAN, John J.
Killing time on death row. P. Carlson. Nation 224:774-5 Je 25 '77 *

KERSHNAR, Lawrence and Goodstein, M. P.
Poor chemist's rotary crystallizer. bibl il pors Chemistry 50:25-6 Mr '77

KERWIN, Joseph Peter
House calls in space: a doctor-astronaut's view. il por Space World N-3-159:26-9 Mr '77

KESSEL, Dmitri
In praise of Darwin, Rembrandt, Mendel and other famous tulips; photographs. Horticulture 55:29-37 Ag '77

KESSELMAN, Judi R. and Peterson, Franklynn
Miracle machine. il Fam Health 9:28-30+ Ja '77. Same Sci Digest 82:70-4 S '77

KESSINGER, Dale
I don't do this on purpose! ed by J. Singleton. Todays Educ 66:36-9 N '77

KESSLER, Francis P.
Kissinger's legacy: a Latin American policy. bibl f Cur Hist 72:76-8+ F '77

KESSLER, Irving Kenneth
Product is born. A. L. Morner. il Fortune 95: 124-9+ F '77 *

KESSLER, Milton
Standpoint; poem. Nation 225:380 O 15 '77

KESTER, Warren
Your beef business. il Farm J 101:Beef 28 Ja; Beef 32 O '77

KESTNER, Joseph
The cloak. il Opera N 41:24-6 F 26 '77
Woe to the vanquished. il Opera N 41:14-17 Mr 19 '77

KETCHES. See Sailboats

KETT, Joseph F.
Family ecology. J. W. Donohue. America 137: 456-9 D 24 '77 *

KEVLAR boats. See Boats—Materials

KEWANEE Industries Inc
Oil makes Kewanee alluring to suitors. il Bus W p30-1 Mr 14 '77

KEY WEST, Fla.
Key West, the living end. H. Sutton. il Sat R 5:26+ Ja 7 '78

KEY WEST offshore race. See Motor boat racing

KEYBOARD instrument music
Bach on the piano? Why not? comparison with other keyboard instruments. R. Tureck. il por Hi Fi 27:91-3 O '77

KEYBOARD instruments
See also
Phonograph records—Keyboard instruments
Piano

KEYES, Ralph
Bionic boom. por Newsweek 89:9 F 7 '77

KEYES, Robert W.
Microstructure fabrication. bibl il Science 196: 945-9 My 27 '77
Physical limits in semiconductor electronics. bibl il Science 195:1230-5 Mr 18 '77

KEYNES, John Maynard Keyes, 1st Baron
Decadence of economic theory. E. Meadows. Nat R 30:23-5+ Ja 6 '78 *

KEYNESIAN economics. See Economics

KEYS, Kerry Shawn
Arctic museum; poem. Nation 226:23 Ja 7 '78

KEYS, William E.
Switchel—the Yankee haymakers' drink. il Org Gard & Farm 24:100-1 Je '77

KEYS, Florida. See Florida Keys

KEYSER, Marty
When Wendy's brother died. Read Digest 111: 95-7 Jl '77

KEYSERLING, Leon H.
Tax cuts versus spending. G. R. Rosen. por Duns R 109:67 Mr '77 *

KHAALIS, Khalifa Hamaas Abdul. See Abdul Khaalis, K. H.

KHACHATURIAN, Aram Ilyich
Gayne ballet suites nos. 1, 2 and 3. M. Mark. il Am Rec G 40:19-20 Ag '77 *

KHALID, King of Saudi Arabia
Failing king. R. Carroll. por Newsweek 89:34 F 28 '77 *

KHALIFE, Raymond
Toughest hotel in the world to get into. W. McQuade. il por Fortune 95:229-30 Mr '77 *

KHALIL, Beverley J.
Mateo Falcone; P. Merimee's Corsican short story. Engl J 66:66-7 Mr '77

KHASHOGGI, Adnan M.
Super-connector from Saudi Arabia. L. Kraar. il pors Fortune 95:108-14+ Je '77 *

KHMER Rouge. See Revolutionists, Cambodian

KHRUSHCHEV, Nikita Sergeevich
Immodest proposal: Nikita to Adlai; excerpt from Adlai Stevenson and the world. J. B. Martin. il por Am Heritage 28:88-9 Ag '77 *
Why of Sputnik. bibl f il por map Space World N-12-168:4-15 D '77 *

KIAM, Victor Kermit, 1926-
Benrus gets out of the watch business—almost. por Duns R 109:20-1 Mr '77 *

KIANG, T.
Recent astronomical research in China. il map Sky & Tel 54:260-3 O '77

KIBBUTZIM. See Collective settlements—Israel

KICKBACKS. See Bribery

KIDDER, Margot
Margot Kidder; interview, ed by A. Gross. il por Mademoiselle 83:151+ N '77

KIDDER, Tracy
Tinkering with sunshine. il Atlantic 240:70-83 O '77

KIDDER Peabody Company, Inc. See Brokers

KIDNAPPING
Don't let her suffer; Italian kidnapping cases. il Time 110:46 O 17 '77
Kidnap epidemic; cases in Italy. il Newsweek 90:61 O 17 '77
Kidnapped bus; Chowchilla aftermath. P. S. Greenberg. il Newsweek 89:15 My 9 '77
Kidnapped! The ordeal that shook Chowchilla. J. P. Blank. il Read Digest 111:51-5+ S '77
See also
Caransa, Maurits, kidnapping
Hall, Richard, kidnapping
Lazzaroni, Paolo, kidnapping
Schleyer, Hanns-Martin, kidnapping
Wilson, A. L, family, kidnapping

History

Princesses for ransom: abduction in the grand style. F. MacLean. il pors Horizon 19:82-7 Mr '77

KIDNEY donors
Kidney donors—how they feel nine years later; study by John Marshall and Carl Fellner. J. Horn. Psychol Today 11:87 Ag '77

KIDNEY Transplant Center, Howard University Hospital. See Washington, D.C.—Hospitals

KIDNEYS

Diseases

Jogger's ills; pseudonephritis. il Time 111:56 Ja 16 '78
Ribavirin: efficacy in the treatment of murine autoimmune disease. L. W. Klassen and others. bibl il Science 195:787-9 F 25 '77

Surgery

Unilateral nephrectomy: effect on survival in NZB/NZW mice. M. M. Beyer and others. bibl il Science 198:511-13 N 4 '77

Transplantation

Kidney transplant center; Howard University Hospital in Washington, D.C. M. Burgen. il Ebony 32:59-62+ Ap '77
New kidney from Moscow. il Time 109:84 Mr 7 '77
See also
Kidney donors

KIDNEYS, Artificial
See also
Hemodialysis

KIEL, Germany

Music

See also
Opera—Germany, West

KIEL Week. See Sailboat racing

KIERS, Eric J.
Madame Mercedes-Benz: merchant of Togo. il Ms 5:112+ Ap '77

KIESTER, Edwin, Jr
Healing babies before they're born. il Fam Health 9:26-8+ O '77
Suicide: let's separate fact from fiction. Bet Hom & Gard 55:66+ Ap '77

KILAUEA (crater)
Angry goddess on a rampage. il Time 110:21 O 17 '77
Madame Pele's fiery face. il Newsweek 90:49 O 17 '77

KILBORN, Jean
Greenhouse. See issues of Horticulture
Growing vegetables in containers: our own trials. il Horticulture 55:49-51 Mr 77

KILBRIDGE, Maurice
Urban housing policy for developing countries. Archit Rec 161:37+ Ap; 37+ My '77

KILBY, Clyde Samuel
How to beat the beaten path; interview, ed by C. Forbes. por Chr Today 21:30-2 S 9 '77

KILHAM, Lawrence, and Ferm, V. H.
Congenital anomalies induced in hamster embryos with ribavirin. bibl il Science 195:413-14 Ja 28 '77

KILIMANJARO climbs. See Mountaineering

KILLEEN, Michael
Books of Killeen. por Forbes 120:112 D 1 '77 *

KILLEFER, Tom
Chasing the coupon clippers. il por Forbes 119: 56-7 My 1 '77 *

KILLER bees. See Bees

KILLER whales. See Dolphins (mammals)

KILLIFISHES
Chloride transport across isolated opercular epithelium of killifish: a membrane rich in chloride cells. K. J. Karnaky, Jr, and others. bibl il Science 195:203-5 Ja 14 '77

KILLINGLEY, J. S. See Berger, W. H. jt auth

KILMARTIN, Edward J.
Orthodox-Roman Catholic consultation in the U.S.A. il New Cath World 220:179-80+ Jl '77

KILN drying of wood. See Lumber—Drying

KILNS
O ye gods! kiln gods. C. Lakofsky. bibl f Ceram Mo 25:17+ Ap '77
Two wood-fired kilns:
A natural-draft, brick design. E. McEndarfer. il por Ceram Mo 25:36-8 D '77
Smug: a kiln of clay. J. Shurtliff. il Ceram Mo 25:39-41 D '77

Equipment and supplies

Making cranks for production firing. G. Wettlaufer and N. Wettlaufer. il Ceram Mo 25:64-6 S '77

Firing

Bendel burner. D. Bendel. il Ceram Mo 25:48-9 S '77

KILPATRICK, Bill
Giant miners for a new coal age. il map Pop Mech 148:77-81+ O '77
Vehicles. il Field & S 82:82+ S; 90+ O; 106+ N; 104+ D '77

KILPATRICK, James Jackson
Abortion, equal rights, and Robert's rules of order. Nat R 29:1481-5 D 23 '77
[Column] See issues of Nation's business
Our blessed land; excerpt from The foxes' union. Read Digest 111:193-4+ D '77
Waste no pity upon these foxes; excerpt from The foxes' union. il Smithsonian 8:85-7 Ag '77

KILSON, Marion
Black women in the professions, 1890-1970. bibl il M Labor R 100:38-41 My '77

KILVERT, Ian Scott-. See Scott-Kilvert, I.

KIM, Chi Ha
Prophetic minority. J. Baker. Commonweal 104:550-1 S 2 '77 *

KIM, Nelli
New look for Nelli. il pors Seventeen 36:178-9 Ap '77 *

KIM, Norman
Fearless and the humorless. Chr Cent 94:733-4 Ag 17 '77

KIM, Sung-hou. See Rich, A. jt auth

KIM, Untae. See Bernacki, R. J. jt auth

KIMATA, Hiroshi, and Schneider, Jason
Modern's inside your camera series (title varies) (cont) il Mod Phot 41:78-9+ Mr; 96-7+ Ap; 98-9+ Ag '77

KIMBALL, David T.
Perils of success. por Forbes 119:120 Je 15 '77 *

KIMBALL, Spencer Woolley
How Mormons cope with deterioration in morals; interview. il por U.S. News 83:60-1 D 19 '77

KIMBALL, Thomas L.
Why we need the biosphere program. il por Int Wildlife 7:29 N '77

KIMBELL Art Museum. See Fort Worth, Tex.—Galleries and museums

KIMBER, Stephen
200-mile limit: showdown at sea. il pors Int Wildlife 7:41-5 S '77

KIMMEL, Carol
Parents' PTA page (cont) por Parents Mag 52:29 Mr '77

KIMMEL, Eric A.
Confronting the ovens: the Holocaust and juvenile fiction. Horn Bk 53:84-91 F '77

KINDELBERGER, James Howard
Atwood-Kindelberger. J. A. Slocum. il Flying 101:251 S '77 *

KINDER, Marsha
Art of dreaming in Three women and Providence: structures of the self. il Film Q 31:10-18 Fall '77
Reflections on Jeanne Dielman. il Film Q 30:2-8 Summ '77

KINDER-Care centers. See Day care centers

KINDERGARTEN
Peotone fights school failure; special classes for kindergartners with learning disabilities. J. Bone. il Am Educ 13:32-5 Ja '77
See also
Nursery schools

KINESTHESIA. See Muscular sense

KINETIC art
Out of the tropics, an avant-garde art. A. Uslar-Pietri. il UNESCO Courier 30:30-8+ Ag '77

KINETIC sculpture
But will they like it in Chicago? the Los Angeles Triforium. Vasari. il Art N 76:20+ O '77
See also
Mobiles

KING, Albert
Everybody is courting the King. K. Hannon. il por Sports Illus 46:18-19 F 7 '77 *

KING, Andrew P. and West, M. J.
Species identification in the North American cowbird: appropriate responses to abnormal song. bibl il Science 195:1002-4 Mr 11 '77

KING, Angus S. Jr
Why Congress doesn't work. por Newsweek 91:9 Ja 9 '78

KING, Barbara
Single parenthood. Harp Baz 110:96+ Mr '77

KING, Billie Jean (Moffitt)
Ambush on the comeback trail. W. Bingham. il pors Sports Illus 47:34-5 N 14 '77 *

KING, Carole
Carole King: optimistic craftsmanship. D. Heckman. por Hi Fi 27:142+ O '77 *

KING, Clennon
Plains Baptists. E. Keerdoja and H. Camp. il Newsweek 90:12 O 17 '77 *

KING, Don
Black eye for TV boxing. P. Bonventre. il pors Newsweek 89:81-2 My 2 '77 *
King-size scandal in the ring. por Time 109:64 My 2 '77 *
Some very wrong numbers. R. H. Boyle. il por Sports Illus 46:22-7 My 2 '77 *
They've boxed themselves in. W. Leggett. por Sports Illus 47:68 S 19 '77 *

KING, Edmund L.
Appreciation. il New Repub 176:27-9 Ap 9 '77

KING, Francis
Villa Serbelloni; Down by the lake, up at the villa; Intruders; Lago di Como; Dawn; poems. Poetry 130:251-5 Ag '77

KING, George
Comrade capitalist. por Forbes 119:148 Ap 15 '77 *

KING, Glen I. See Blaurock, A. E. jt auth

KING, Horace
Detroit's new models. pors Sports Illus 47:91-2+ O 17 '77 *

KING, James C. and others
Some requirements for successful in-service education. Educ Digest 43:14-16 S '77

KING, James R.
Richard Wright: his life and writings. bibl il por Negro Hist Bull 40:738-43 S '77

KING, Janet Spencer
Cashing in on cooling. Am Home 80:80+ My '77
Get smart. Am Home 80:38+ My '77
Playing the numbers. Am Home 80:101 O '77

KING, Kenneth, Jr, and Neville, C.
Isoleucine epimerization for dating marine sediments: importance of analyzing monospecific foraminiferal samples. bibl il Science 195:1333-5 Mr 25 '77

KING, Martin Luther, 1929-1968
Day the black revolution began. L. Bennett, Jr. il pors Ebony 32:54-6+ S '77 *

Assassination

Question of conspiracy. il por Time 109:16-18 Je 20 '77
Saga of Jimmy Ray. T. Mathews and others. pors Newsweek 89:24-5 Je 20 '77
See also
United States—Congress—House—Assassinations, Select Committee on

KING, N. E. See Wood, M. D. jt auth

KING, Nicholas
Battle for the last frontier. il Nat R 29:722-4 Je 24 '77
Carter and the church. il Nat R 29:384-5+ Ap 1 '77
Yachting. Nat R 29:1187-8 O 14 '77
(tr) See Groueff, S. Nation as concentration camp

KING, Paul L.
Men behind the Car of the Year. il pors Motor T 29:38 F '77 *

KING, Robert L.
Machining of America. Commonweal 104:340-2 My 27 '77

KING, Stephen
PW interviews; ed by J. F. Baker. por Pub W 211:12-13 Ja 17 '77
Witches and aspirin; interview, ed by M. Allen. il por Writers Digest 57:26-7 Je '77

KING, W. B. Leslie
Galway Blazer II. il Yachting 141:139-41 Je '77

KING, William, Jr
William King Jr, Georgetown furniture maker. A. C. Golovin. bibl il por Antiques 111:1032-7 My '77 *

KING and I; musical comedy. See Musical comedy, revue, etc.—Reviews—Single works

KING John and the Abbot of Canterbury; dramatization. See Holmes, R. V.

KING Kong (motion picture character) See Characters in motion pictures

KINGERY, Alan
Getting bludgeoned by a telephone. Sat Eve Post 249:76 N '77

KINGFISHERS
Coarrangement of kingfishers; photographs; with introd by F. Hartmann. M. Olano and J. Echevarri. il Natur Hist 86:58-63 F '77

KINGMAN, Lee
Bookshop for Boys and Girls. il Horn Bk 53:209-14 Ap '77

KINGS and rulers
Royal flush. il Sat Eve Post 249:46 Jl '77
See also
Great Britain—Kings and rulers

KINGSBURY, Anne
Anne Kingsbury. il Ceram Mo 25:58 My '77 *

KINGSBURY, Mary
Why of people: the novels of M. E. Kerr. Horn Bk 53:288-95 Je '77

KINGSBURY, Pamela D.
Enoch Wood earthenware found in St Paul's Church, Burslem. bibl il Antiques 112:122-7 Jl '77

KINGSLEY, Bettina, pseud. See Kaplan, B. J.

KINGSLEY, Elizabeth (Seelman)
Working the Double-Crostic. N. Ephron. Esquire 87:10+ My '77 *

KINGSTON, Maxine Hong
Duck boy. il N Y Times Mag p54-5+ Je 12 '77
Susan Brownmiller talks with Maxine Hong Kingston; interview. il por Mademoiselle 83: 148-9+ Mr '77

KINKEAD, Eugene
Our local correspondents. New Yorker 52:56-60+ Ja 31 '77

KINKS (rock group) See Rock groups

KINSOLVING, Lester
Managing leaks. Nat R 29:706 Je 24 '77
about
Credentials controversy. Chr Today 21:57-8 Mr 18 '77 *
Gospel according to. . . Chr Today 21:58-9 Ap 15 '77 *

KINTE family
From these Roots; the real significance of Haley's phenomenon. C. Forbes. Chr Today 21:19-22 My 6 '77
Roots; condensation; reprint of 1974 article. A. Haley. il Read Digest 110:153-79 Ap; 145-68 My '77
What Roots means to me. A. Haley. Read Digest 110:73-6 My '77

KINZER, Stephen
El Salvador. New Repub 177:15-17 S 3 '77
Guatemala beyond bananas. il New Repub 176: 21-3+ Mr 5 '77
Nicaragua, a wholly owned subsidiary. New Repub 176:14-17 Ap 9 '77
Reports & comment: Cuba. il Atlantic 239:6+ My '77
West Point faces life. New Repub 177:14-17 D 3 '77

KINZIE, Mary
Human face; Bamberger reiter; poems. Poetry 129:331-4 Mr '77
Olympiad; Accidie, Chagall in his sickness; Nature morte; poems. Poetry 131:93-8 N '77

KINZLER, Karen
West Point woman; ed by V. Eads. il por Seventeen 36:74+ Ap '77

KIOKO, Joseph M.
On patrol with Africa's new park rangers. il pors Int Wildlife 7:4-13 S '77 *

KIPLING, Rudyard
Eyes of Asia. il Sat Eve Post 249:86-8+ Jl '77

KIPNIS, Igor
Bach: Partitas 1 and 2 performed by I. Kipnis. C. Greenleaf. Am Rec G 40:16-17 S '77 *

KIPP, Allan F.
Here's looking at you, kid! poem. Chr Cent 94: 587 Je 22 '77

KIPP, Laurence J.
(ed) Books for the thoughtful executive. Harvard Bus R 55:158-60 N '77

KIRBO, Charles Hughes
Carter's performance so far—insights from a personal adviser; interview. il pors U.S. News 83:19-20 D 12 '77
about
Carter's Georgia guru. J. T. Wooten. il pors N Y Times Mag p 14-18 Mr 20 '77 *
First friend. T. Mathews and J. Doyle. il por Newsweek 89:24 Ja 24 '77 *

KIRBY, Christine L.
Survey of inmates' reading habits. Wilson Lib Bull 51:503 F '77

KIRBY, Dan
(ed) Professional publications. il Engl J 66:82-6 O; 76-80 D '77

KIRBY, Robert Emory
Electrical equipment industry; address, November 9, 1976. Vital Speeches 43:186-9 Ja 1 '77
about
Why is this man smiling. por Forbes 119:66 My 1 '77 *

KIRCHNER, James G.
Evidence for late tertiary volcanic activity in the northern Black Hills, South Dakota. bibl Science 196:977 My 27 '77

KIRCHNER, Leon
Lily. Reviews
Hi Fi 27:MA17-18 Ag '77 *
Hi Fi por 27:MA6-7+ Ap '77 *
Nation 224:600-1 My 14 '77 *
New Yorker 53:124-6+ My 2 '77 *
Newsweek il 89:103 Ap 25 '77 *
Time il 109:78 Ap 25 '77 *
Musician of the month: Leon Kirchner. R. S. Brown. por Hi Fi 27:MA6-7+ Ap '77 *
Zeroing in; adaptation of Kirchner's opera Lily from S. Bellow's Henderson, the rain king. H. Heinsheimer. il por Opera N 41:12-15 Ap 16 '77 *

KIREMIDJIAN, David
Crime and punishment: matricide and the woman question. bibl f Am Imago 33:403-33 Wint '76

KIRGO, Julie
(ed) See Winkler, H. Chicken soup and fear

KIRIN Brewery Company, Ltd. See Brewing industry—Japan

KIRITSIS, Anthony George
I'll have vengeance. il por Time 109:19 F 21 '77 *
Three days of rage. D. M. Alpern and S. Monroe. il por Newsweek 89:22 F 21 '77 *

KIRK, Albert
Reconciliation in Memphis: a diocese prepared. America 136:146-8 F 19 '77

KIRK, Donald
High cost of doing business with Japan. il Sat R 4:20-6 Mr 19 '77
Made in Japan. Sat R 4:24 Ja 22 '77

KIRK, Kathleen
Curses, spoiled again! poem. Seventeen 36:68 O '77

KIRK, Russell
Freedom and parochial schools. Nat R 29:441-2+ Ap 15 '77
From the academy. See alternate issues of National review

KIRKLAND, Gelsey
Celebration; interview, ed by T. Tobias. il pors Dance Mag 51:52 D '77
about
Dancing. A. Croce. New Yorker 53:68-70 Jl 4 '77 *

KIRKLAND, Joseph Lane
Labor's interests vital in setting trade policies. M Labor R 100:34-5 Mr '77
Should U.S. curb imports? interview. pors U.S. News 83:25-6 Ag 8 '77

KIRKPATRICK, Curry
All for one sure beats one for all. il Sports Illus 46:30-2+ Je 13 '77
At full tilt into the playoffs. il Sports Illus 46:32-4+ Ap 18 '77
Bearing of the green. il Sports Illus 46:20-3 Ap 25 '77
Blasting off in Houston. il Sports Illus 46:16-17 Ja 17 '77
Borg's hot hand took all the tricks. il pors Sports Illus 46:16-17 Ja 31 '77
Calvin discovers Murphy's law. il por Sports Illus 47:14-15 Ag 15 '77
Couple of babes in the woods. il Sports Illus 46: 22-3 My 9 '77
Fantastico, Guillermo! il Sports Illus 47:12-17 S 19 '77
Fever called Blazermania. il Sports Illus 47:36-8 O 31 '77
Good, but why not the best? il Sports Illus 46:22-5 Mr 21 '77
Greatest showman on earth. il pors Sports Illus 47:82-6+ S 26 '77
It's a wild West show. il Sports Illus 46:14-17 F 14 '77
L.A. couldn't move the mountain. il Sports Illus 46:28-9 My 23 '77
Little bit better than Lagos. por Sports Illus 46: 20-1 F 7 '77
Pro basketball (cont) Sports Illus 48:46-7 Ja 2 '78
Storms over the Atlantic. il pors Sports Illus 47:20-1 D 12 '77
Tennis. il por Sports Illus 47:49-51 Jl 4 '77
There's no place like home court. il Sports Illus 46:22-3 Je 6 '77
Wimbledon was never better; Ginny fizz becomes Ginny tonic. il pors Sports Illus 47:12-17 Jl 11 '77
about
Letter from the publisher. J. Meyers. il Sports Illus 47:6 S 26 '77 *

KIRKPATRICK, Dorothy
Giving it back to their employer. il Ret Liv 17: 48-9 N '77
—See Kirkpatrick, K. jt auth

KIRKPATRICK, Dow
U.S. Christians and Cuba. Chr Cent 94:685-7 Ag 3 '77

KIRKPATRICK, Eileen M. See Stern, P. C. jt auth

KIRKPATRICK, Jeane
Behavior: habit-kicking; excerpt from Turnabout; help for a new life. Vogue 167:186+ N '77
Jeane Kirkpatrick on politics. New Repub 177: 36-8 D 3 '77
Why the new right lost. bibl f Commentary 63:34-9 F; 22+ My '77

KIRKPATRICK, Kirk, and Kirkpatrick, Dorothy
Make your own private signal. il Motor B & S 140:104-5 Ag '77

KIRKUP, James
Mystical poetry in a court of law. T. Beeson. Chr Cent 94:838-9 S 28 '77 *

KIRLIAN photography. See Electrophotography

KIROV Ballet
Children of Theatre Street; film of dancers at the Kirov School. N. M. Stoop. il Dance Mag 51:63-5 S '77

KIRP, David L.
Law, politics, and equal educational opportunity. Educ Digest 43:32-5 S '77

KIRSCH, Jonathan
(ed) See Kirsch, R. PW interviews
(ed) See Lindsey, H. PW interviews

KIRSCH, Robert R.
PW interviews; ed by J. Kirsch. por Pub W 212: 10-11 D 12 '77

KIRSHENBAUM, Jerry
Bottom was on top in very fast company. il Sports Illus 46:26-7 Ap 4 '77
Bottom was up to topping a Mark. Sports Illus 47:18-19 S 5 '77
College football. il Sports Illus 47:90+ N 28 '77
El Caballo is off and running. il pors Sports Illus 47:26-31 Ag 29 '77
Gimmicks, gadgets, goodby records. il Sports Illus 46:40-2+ Ap 25 '77
Hockey (cont) Sports Illus 46:73-6 My 16; 52 Je 6 '77
On the other hand. . .il Sports Illus 46:60-3+ Ja 24 '77
On the whole, it's the donut line. il pors Sports Illus 46:26-9 F 7 '77
Pro basketball. il Sports Illus 47:89-91 N 14 '77
Reincarnation and 13 pairs of socks. il Sports Illus 46:30-3 Mr 28 '77
Sports medicine. il Sports Illus 47:94+ O 31 '77
Swimming (cont) Sports Illus 46:59-60 F 28; 47:76+ Ag 29 '77
Three Islanders unto themselves. il Sports Illus 47:16-19 N 21 '77
Would you buy a used hockey player from this man? por Sports Illus 46:46-8+ Ap 18 '77

KIRST, Hans Hellmut
Two authors, two points of view; interview, ed by H. R. Lottman. por Pub W 212:55-6 S 12 '77

KISER, John
Living with antiques. il Antiques 111:526-9 Mr '77

KISHI, Tetsuo
Ken Domon: a documentary pilgrimage; tr by M. Tsuji. il Mod Phot 41:84-93 Mr '77

KISNER, Ronald E.
Khalilah Ali: karate disciplines her new life. il pors Ebony 32:78-80+ S '77
Money problems of the stars. il Ebony 32:142-6+ My '77

KISS (rock group) See Rock groups

KISSING
Great kissing epidemic; Time essay. L. Morrow. il Time 109:66-7 F 7 '77

KISSINGER, Henry Alfred
America's continuing concerns in the Middle East; remarks, January 11, 1977. Dept State Bull 76:90-1 Ja 31 '77
Continuity and change in American foreign policy; excerpt from address, September 19, 1977. bibl por Society 15:97-103 N '77
Laying the foundation of a long-term policy; remarks, with transcript of question and answer session, January 10, 1977. Dept State Bull 76: 81-7 Ja 31 '77
My valedictorian address; January 10, 1977. Vital Speeches 43:265-7 F 15 '77
Present U.S. policy: text of the Kissinger statement; April 27, 1976. Cong Digest 56:7-9+ Ja '77
Secretary Kissinger attends NATO ministerial meeting at Brussels and meets with British officials at London; statement, with texts of news conferences, December 7 and 10, 1976. Dept State Bull 76:1-9 Ja 3 '77
Secretary Kissinger emphasizes need for nonpartisan foreign policy; remarks, January 11, 1977. Dept State Bull 76:88-90 Ja 31 '77
Secretary Kissinger interviewed for the New York times; ed by J. Reston and others, January 20, 1977. Dept State Bull 76:102-7 F 7 '77
Secretary Kissinger pays tribute to the Foreign Service; remarks, January 19, 1977. Dept State Bull 76:127-9 F 14 '77
Secretary reaffirms continuity of U.S.-Mexican relations; remarks, November 30, 1976. Dept State Bull 75:749-50 D 27 '76
They are fated to succeed. il pors Time 111:34-5 Ja 2 '78
Thoughts from the lone cowboy; interview, ed by H. Sidey. por Time 109:20+ F 28 '77

about

Advice from the former tenants. Nation 224: 482-4+ Ap 23 '77 *
American foreign policy: the limits of power in the absence of purpose. J. A. Nathan. bibl il Intellect 106:208-12 D '77 *
Coalition seeks access to Kissinger records. S. Wagner. Pub W 211:28+ Ja 31 '77 *
Corruption at Columbia University. Nat R 29:655-6 Je 10 '77 *
Danger: Eurocommunism. il por Time 109:49 Je 20 '77 *
Détente, then and now. G. H. Watson. il pors Américas 29:2-7 Ja '77 *
Dirty linen sale. Nation 224:611-12 My 21 '77 *
Eurocommunism and detente. A. Schlesinger, Jr. Current 196:42-5 O '77 *
Good riddance. New Repub 176:3-4+ Ja 15 '77 *
Graves of academe. Commonweal 104:36-8 Ja 21 '77 *
Henry Kissinger going out. Nat R 29:169 F 4 '77 *
Henry Kissinger: so near & yet so far. S. H. Day, Jr. Bull Atom Sci 33:4-5 F '77 *
Henry: watching, waiting, worried. H. Sidey. il Time 110:26-7 Ag 8 '77 *
His legacy: realism and allure. J. Schecter. il Time 109:16+ Ja 24 '77 *
Kissinger emeritus. Nation 224:259-60 Mr 5 '77 *
Kissinger, Haig and the Koreans. Nation 225: 227-8 S 17 '77 *
Kissinger signs with Little, Brown for memoirs. il por Pub W 211:28 F 21 '77 *
Kissinger: victim of liberal witch hunt at Columbia? F. W. Friendly. por U.S. News 82:33 Je 13 '77 *
Kissinger years: morals and moralism. America 136:63 Ja 29 '77 *
Kissinger's complaint. Time 110:52 Jl 11 '77 *
Kissinger's double-cross for peace. G. Porter. Nation 224:519-21 Ap 30 '77 *
Kissinger's legacy: a Latin American policy. F. P. Kessler. bibl f Cur Hist 72:76-8+ F '77 *
Narrowing options for Rhodesia. T. Beeson. Chr Cent 94:133-4 F 16 '77 *
New glory without the old power. T. Mathews and others. il pors Newsweek 89:20-1+ My 23 '77 *
Nixon: pride in his diplomacy. pors U.S. News 82:35 My 23 '77 *
Not remarkably entertaining. F. Getlein. Commonweal 104:452-4 Jl 22 '77 *
Professor Kissinger. F. Getlein. Commonweal 104:388-90 Je 24 '77 *
Should Dr Kissinger be seated? address, April 26, 1977. M. Teitelman. Nation 224:658-60 My 28 '77 *
Tales of the K. P. Goldman and H. Bruno. il Newsweek 89:43 My 16 '77 *
Vance v. Kissinger: a matter of style. C. Ogden. Time 109:19 Ap 11 '77 *
What was Kissinger saying? Nat R 29:134 F 4 '77 *
Will a Carter foreign policy make a difference? D. V. Edwards. Intellect 105:319-21 Ap '77 *

KISTIAKOWSKY, George B.
Arms race: is paranoia necessary for security? il N Y Times Mag p52-4+ N 27 '77

KISWAHILI language. See Swahili language

KIT amplifiers. See Amplifiers

KIT building

Anecdotes, facetiae, satire, etc.

If you don't mind, I'll do it myself! P. F. McManus. Field & S 82:144-5+ S '77

KIT furniture. See Furniture, Prefabricated

KIT sports cars. See Sports cars

KITCHEN, Tella
She brings back the good old days. J. Strohm. il por Nat Wildlife 16:28-35 D '77 *

KITCHEN cabinets
Kitchen cabinets—great in any room. R. Gorman. il Pop Sci 211:108-11+ S '77
Making the most of kitchen storage. E. Liman. il Am Home 80:15 S '77
This unusual kitchen uses particle board for cabinets, shelves. il Sunset 158:136 Je '77

KITCHEN canisters. See Containers

KITCHEN dividers. See Partitions

KITCHEN furniture
Island octagon is a mini-kitchen in itself. il Sunset 159:129 O '77
Multipurpose center island. il Bet Hom & Gard 55:32 Jl '77
New ceramic-tile countertop. . .right over the old one. il Pop Mech 148:114-15 D '77
See also
Kitchen cabinets

KITCHEN ranges. See Stoves

KITCHEN scales. See Scales (weighing instruments)

KITCHEN storage. See Storage in the home

KITCHEN utensils and appliances
Are you ready for a food processor? R. Wolf. Org Gard & Farm 24:108-9 O '77
Blenders. il Consumer Rep 42:350-3 Je '77
Buying guide to food processors. il Good H 185: 230+ N '77
Chop, peel, dice, slice, brew, bake: shoppers guide to new small kitchen appliances. M. Cubisino. McCalls 104:132+ N '77
Computers move into the kitchen. F. K. Coffee il Mech Illus 74:38+ Ja '78
Cook's guide to food processors: new whiz in the kitchen; with recipes. il House & Gard 149: 131+ Je '77
Countertop broiler: three variations; broiler-ovens. il Consumer Rep 42:452-7 Ag '77
Cuisinart and three imitators. il Consumer Rep 42:321-3 Je '77
Donut makers. il Good H 186:116 Ja '78
Electric can openers. il Consumers Res Mag 60: 7-11 N '77
Electric frypans. il Consumers Res Mag 60:30-3 F '77
Electric mini-fryers. il Consumer Rep 42:623-5 N '77
Electric stirrer. il Consumers Res Mag 60:34 S '77

KITCHEN utensils and appliances—*Continued*
Flourishes with food:
Art of cake decorating. il McCalls 104:162+ Ap '77
Barbecue with charcoal all year round. il McCalls 105:138+ Ja '78
Best way to cook vegetables; with steamers. il McCalls 104:84+ Ag '77
Ebleskivers: a Danish delight; special pan. il McCalls 105:143-4+ O '77
Elegant single-serving cakes: bundt cake pans. il McCalls 105:179-80+ N '77
Homemade ice cream without all the fuss; ice-cream maker and recipes. il McCalls 104:91-2 Jl '77
Most versatile bake pan. il McCalls 104:112+ My '77
Pasta perfect; using a pasta machine. il McCalls 104:112+ F '77
Pizza: at home on the range. il McCalls 104:112+ Mr '77
Tacos: a tasty Mexican treat; taco cooker and serving rack. il McCalls 104:142+ S '77
Food processors. il Consumer Res Mag 60:16-20 D '77
GE's new Peeling Wand works no magic. Consumer Rep 43:4 Ja '78
Gift tools for the baker. il Sunset 159:137 D '77
Good-looking racks for cooling cakes. il Sunset 158:86 F '77
Gourmet breakthrough; food processors. L. Langway and M. Reese. il Newsweek 89:83 F 21 '77
Great American Frying Machine may be hazardous. il Consumer Rep 43:4 Ja '78
Harvest of helpers. N. Craig. il House B 119:101-2+ My '77
Healthware; new cookware with recipes. il House & Gard 149:104-5+ Jl '77
Major kitchen appliances. il Consumers Res Mag 60:194-205 O '77
Making yogurt the easy way; yogurt makers and recipes. il Good H 185:140+ Jl '77
Meat grinders. Consumer Rep 42:19-22 D '77
Mini-fryers. il Good H 185:238 D '77
Miniature deep fryers. il Consumers Res Mag 60:34-6 Je '77
Miracle machines: chefs' delights; electric processors and mixers. il Time 110:62 D 19 '77
More than a blender; Vita Mix. M. S. Hill. il Org Gard & Farm 24:119-20 O '77
New kitchen speed-ups and work savers. il House & Gard 149:156-8 Mr '77
No-nonsense guide to cookware. M. Cubisino. McCalls 104:186+ Ap '77
Notes and comment; KitchenAid food mixers and Cuisinart food processors. New Yorker 53:23-4 Mr 7 '77
Now it's easy to make your own pasta! il Good H 184:150 Je '77
Other labor-saving kitchen machines. il Sunset 158:140 Mr '77
Perfect french fry; using mini-fryers. il Ladies Home J 94:70+ S '77
Pick of the steamers. il Am Home 80:76 Mr '77
Pots & pans. Changing T 31:16-17 Ag '77
Ready world? Now you can beat an egg inside its shell. il Consumer Rep 42:373 Jl '77
Slicer-shredder; Cuisinart. J. Farmer. il Org Gard & Farm 24:118-19 O '77
Small electric appliances. Consumers Res Mag 60:65-77 O '77
Special cookie makers. il Ladies Home J 94:102+ N '77
Stamp out energy guzzlers. A. Scharffenberger. il Am Home 80:96+ S '77
Supersmall small appliances. il Redbook 149:76+ Ag '77
Task masters: the best of the new housewares. House B 119:148-9+ N '77
Those new do-almost-anything food machines. il Changing T 31:41-2 My '77
Three machines for your kitchen; food processing units. B. Foote. il Org Gard & Farm 24:110+ O '77
Tools for the competent cook. il Redbook 149:146+ My '77
Update on kitchen equipment. N. Craig. il House B 119:41+ Jl '77
See also
Dishwashing and drying machines
Stoves
Toaster ovens

Collectors and collecting

Home is where the hearth is to the kitchen kollector. E. Holzer. il Hobbies 82:116-18 Ja '78

Exhibitions

English domestic pottery. il Ceram Mo 25:20-3 D '77
Style: the craft of joyful eating. il Craft Horiz 37:14-15 D '77

KITCHENS
All the way with the open kitchen. il Sunset 158:174+ Ap '77
Big kitchen made better by design & a deft brush of color. il House B 119:90+ S '77
Blow ups. il Am Home 80:54-5 My '77
Can this kitchen be saved? Redbook 148:197+ Ap '77; Same. Ladies Home J 94:184+ Ap '77
Charming kitchen-dining room. il House & Gard 149:64-5+ Jl '77
Converting a city kitchen to country ways. J. McCloskey. il Bet Hom & Gard 55:104-6 S '77
Cook's tour; special issue. il House B 119:43-67+ Jl '77
Country-stable-inspired kitchen. il Sunset 158:182 Ap '77
Custom kitchen you can build yourself. J. McCloskey and D. Ashe. il Bet Hom & Gard 55:136-9+ My '77
Easing the task: a two-stage kitchen remodeling. il House B 119:76 My '77
Four-wall kitchen plans. il Bet Hom & Gard 55:190 Ap '77
Have your company in the kitchen. il House & Gard 149:72-5 Ag '77
Her island-idea kitchen. il Sunset 158:76-7 F '77
How to cheer up a dreary kitchen. J. McCloskey. il Bet Hom & Gard 55:70-3 Je '77
How to keep all your pleasures at hand. il House & Gard 149:144-5+ Mr '77
Idea packed kitchen portfolio. il Good H 184:128-34 F '77
James Beard's recipe for living; new kitchen in his Greenwich Village town house. il por House & Gard 149:108-13 F '77
Keep the eye moving with bold color, mirror, and flowing graphics. il House & Gard 149:140-1 O '77
Kitchen done over. il Sunset 158:146 Ap '77
Kitchen magic: you do it yourself! il Mech Illus 73:58+ Ap '77
Kitchen re-do—from dull to a dream. M. Davidson. il Parents Mag 52:108-11 S '77
Kitchen switched with dining room, now opens to the garden. il Sunset 159:126 O '77
Kitchens that bring the whole house together. J. McCloskey. il Bet Hom & Gard 55:132-5 Ap '77
Many kitchens are playrooms. il Sunset 158:164 Ap '77
Minus low ceiling and wall, kitchen is open and airy. il Sunset 158:154 My '77
Non-stop kitchen. N. Mandelbaum. il Ladies Home J 94:124-9+ N '77
Old farmhouse gets a new kitchen and a spacious picnic deck. il Sunset 159:104 Ag '77
One big room where we could cook and socialize; living room-kitchen. il House & Gard 149:146-9 My '77
Opening up one of the kitchen's blind corners. il Sunset 158:153 Je '77
Redo of a barn. N. Craig. il House B 119:102-3 Je '77
Reworking a tight space. il House B 119:76+ S '77
Shipshape as a galley. N. Craig. il House B 119:160-2 My '77
Small kitchens with big ideas. il McCalls 105:210-13 N '77
Snug kitchen is wide open to expansive living room. il Sunset 159:102 S '77
To get counter space and light, they pushed out the kitchen. il Sunset 159:84 Jl '77
Welcoming, workable kitchen. K. L. Petersen. il Bet Hom & Gard 55:138-9 O '77
Whiz of a kitchen. J. McCloskey. il Bet Hom & Gard 55:114-15 F '77
Who needs a kitchen really? communal kitchens in apartments. R. Sokolov. il Am Home 80:9 F '77
Wonder kitchen. il Good H 184:148-50 Mr '77
Your kitchen: the spice of homelife. Ladies Home J 94:148+ S '77; Same. il Redbook 149:192 S '77

Anecdotes, facetiae, satire, etc.

What's new in my kitchen? P. Shook. Am Home 80:31 Jl '77

KITCHENWARE. See Kitchen utensils and appliances

KITES
Japan's warriors of the wind. J. Eliot. il Nat Geog 151:550-61 Ap '77
This big reel for a kite holds a mile of string. il Sunset 158:116 Mr '77
To fly like a bird. D. H. Bryan. il Mech Illus 73:74-5 My '77
Two exciting kites you can build from scratch. M. Eden. il Pop Mech 148:96-8+ Ag '77
See also
Balloons, Kite

KITS, Handicraft. See Handicraft—Equipment and supplies

KITTEL, Dorothy A.
Library councils could spearhead co-op. Lib J 102:440+ F 15 '77

KITTREDGE, Doug
Elk that was king; new Pope & Young world record; ed by D. Schuh. il por Outdoor Life 160:98-100+ S '77

KITTREDGE, George
Exploring the briny deep in your own submarine. J. Kornfeld. il por Sci Digest 81:53-7 Je '77 *

KIVENGERE, Festo, Bp
How a Ugandan bishop views Africa's upheaval; excerpts from interview. por U.S. News 82:30 Ap 4 '77
Making headway painfully in Uganda. Chr Today 21:20-1 Ap 15 '77

about

Chaos in Uganda. America 136:349 Ap 16 '77 *

KIVES, Philip
K-Tel grows by selling other people's music. il por Bus W p62+ My 2 '77 *

KIWI fruit. See Yangtaos

KLAGSBRUN, Francine
Preventing teenage suicide; excerpt from Too young to die. il Fam Health 9:21-3 Ap '77

KLAPWIJK, Gerrit C.
Challenge from Europe; excerpts from address. Aviation W 107:9 O 31 '77 *

KLAR, Flavia
Sentinel in the sound. il Sea Front 23:361-4 N '77

KLARE, Michael T.
America's top arms merchants; table. Bull Atom Sci 33:20-1 Je '77
Arms sales unlimited. Progressive 41:9-11 D '77
How we practice arms restraint. Nation 225: 268-9+ S 24 '77
Proliferating arms industry. Nation 224:173-8 F 12 '77
Secretary Kreps won't talk. Nation 224:678-9 Je 4 '77

KLASS, Philip J.
Great UFO debate. Current 196:18-21+ O '77

KLASSEN, Kathryn
Speaking of Holiday (cont) Holiday 57:5 N '76; 58:6 Ja; 23 Ap '77
Where the sun shines daily on the mountaintop. il Holiday 57:28-31+ N '76

KLASSEN, Lynell W. and others
Ribavirin: efficacy in the treatment of murine autoimmune disease. bibl il Science 195:787-9 F 25 '77

KLAW, Barbara
(ed) See Anderson M. Voice one hears in a hundred years

KLAW, Spencer
Belly-my-grizzle. il por Am Heritage 28:96-105 Je '77
World's tallest building. il pors Am Heritage 28: 86-98 F '77

KLEEGE, Georgina
Picking up the tone; story. Redbook 148:88 Mr '77

KLEIBER, Erich
Weingartner, Kleiber, De Sabata: a matter of record. H. Goldsmith. pors Hi Fi 27:94-6 S '77 *

KLEIMAN, Art
Heathkit GR-2001: programmable color TV. il Radio-Electr 48:49-51+ My '77

KLEIMAN, Devra Gail
Monogamous mammals: variations on a scheme. M. G. Riegel. il Sci N 112:76-8 Jl 30 '77 *

KLEIN, Calvin Richard
Calvin Klein's romantic season. A. Chambers il pors N Y Times Mag p46-8 Ja 30 '77 *

KLEIN, Donald W.
Foreign policy of the People's Republic. Cur Hist 73:54-8+ S '77

KLEIN, Edmund
Skin cancer: the avoidable killer; interview, ed by D. Robinson. Read Digest 111:123-6 Jl '77

KLEIN, Jerry
All quiet on the Western Front. il Read Digest 111:227-8 N '77

KLEIN, Lawrence R. Awards. See Monthly labor review (periodical)

KLEIN, Maury
Enigma of Emily. il por Am Hist Illus 12:4-11 D '77
Life upon the wicked stage. il Am Hist Illus 11:36-43 F '77
Man of mystery. il pors Am Hist Illus 12:10-18 O '77

KLEIN, Norma
Sunshine Christmas; story; excerpt from novel. Ladies Home J 94:125-32 D '77

KLEIN, Oskar
Obituary
Phys Today por 30:67-8 Je '77. S. Deser

KLEIN, Peter
Judge Jenk; poem. Atlantic 239:60 My '77

KLEIN, Richard G.
Ecology of early man in Southern Africa. bibl il map Science 197:115-26 Jl 8 '77

KLEIN, Roger. Award. See Editors and editing—Awards, prizes, etc.

KLEINDIENST, Richard G.
Golden fleecing of union funds. L. Velie. Read Digest 111:88-92 O '77 *

KLEINER, Morris M.
Interstate occupational migration: an analysis of data from 1965-70. bibl il M Labor R 100:64-7 Ap '77

KLEINFIELD, Sonny
Handicapped: hidden no longer. il Atlantic 240: 86-90 D '77

KLEINMAN, Philip
BASH, and other bookselling ideas. Pub W 211: 57 Je 13 '77
British book clubs brace for Bertelsmann invasion. Pub W 211:30-1 F 14 '77
London Book Fair 1977: bigger, and still growing. il Pub W 212:97 S 19 '77

KLEINPOPPEN, Paul
Anniversary; Domination of yellow; poems. Poetry 130:147-8 Je '77

KLEIST, Heinrich von
Broken jug; adaptation. See Nolan, P. T.

KLERMAN, Gerald Lawrence
New ADAMHA head expected to lead, not just coordinate. C. Holden. por Science 197:846 Ag 26 '77 *

KLEZMORIM (musicians) See Musicians, Jewish

KLIBAN, B.
PW interviews; ed by B. Bannon. il por Pub W 212:40 Ag 1 '77

KLIM, Donald G.
How salty is the ocean? with biographical sketch. il Sea Front 23:152-8, 191 My '77

KLIMAN, M. L.
Controlling inflation in Canada. bibl f Cur Hist 72:166-9 Ap '77

KLIMENT, R. M.
Mapping and remapping; with introd by G. Allen. il Archit Rec 161:103-10 F '77 *

KLIMENT, Stephen A.
Getting published: an unraveled mystery. Archit Rec 161:59+ F '77
Managing your marketing communications program; excerpt from Creative communications for a successful design practice. il Archit Rec 161:77-9 My '77
News release as marketing tool. Archit Rec 162:55 Jl '77
Writing for marketing impact: letters, brochures, proposals. Archit Rec 161:71+ Je '77

KLIMKO, Ronald
Cathodic protection guards Cleveland water system. il Am City & County 92:54-5 Mr '77

KLINE, Carol
Planning problem-free book fairs. il SLJ 23:36-40 F '77

KLINE, Doyle
Killing of a wild river. il Field & S 82:104+ S '77

KLINE, Richard L. See Ferdman, S. jt auth

KLINGER, Georgette
Skin game. il McCalls 105:40-1+ O '77 *

KLINGER, Max
Max Klinger: a realm of privileged suspension; ed by E. Streicher; excerpt from The graphic works of Max Klinger. K. Varnedoe. il Art N 76:46-50 Mr '77 *

KLOSE, Charlotte
Eskimo and his literature. Engl J 66:60-1 S '77

KLOSS, Doris
Varoom! Goes the preacher. il Ret Liv 17:42+ Mr '77

KLOSSOWSKI, Balthus. See Balthus

KLOTZ-CHAMBERLIN, Peter
(ed) See McDonnell, N. Northern Ireland's guerrillas of peace
(ed) See Williams, B. Northern Ireland's guerrillas of peace

KLUIJTMANS, A. N. M.
Servicing with multimeters. il Radio-Electr 48: 67-9+ Ap '77

KMETZ, Gail Kessler
Olive Schreiner—woman of the Karroo. por Ms 6:90-4 Ag '77

KNAP, Jerome J.
Canadian fishing roundup. il Field & S 82:99-102+ Je '77
On the wings of the wind. il Outdoor Life 159: 72-5+ Mr '77
You can't sneak up on a marmot. il Int Wildlife 7:42-7 My '77

KNAPP, Dan
Composting in the solar greenhouse for CO_2 and heat; excerpt from The solar greenhouse book. il Org Gard & Farm 24:60-2 D '77

KNAPP, Ian M.
Sewage sludge and how to sell it. il Am City & County 92:63-5 O '77

KNAUS, William A. See Hollinshead, A. C. jt auth

KNAUTH, Percy
Commentary (cont) MH 60:2 Wint; 61:2 Spr '77

KNEE

Wounds and injuries

This strange and perilous joint; dealing with knee injuries. W. O. Johnson. il Sports Illus 47:84-8+ O 24 '77

KNEE, Artificial. See Joints, Artificial

KNELLER, George F.
In-depth courses in breadth. Intellect 105:351 Ap '77

KNELMAN, Martin
Starring. . .the writer. por Atlantic 240:96-8 N '77

KNEPPER, Jimmy
Jazz. W. Balliett. New Yorker 53:98-100 F 21 '77 *
KNEPPER, Mike
Driving impression (cont) il Motor T 28:81-2+ D '76
KNICKERBOCKER Toy Company. See Toy industry
KNIFE racks
Knife rack for Christmas. il Sunset 159:128-9 D '77
Knife rack for safekeeping. il Org Gard & Farm 24:92 D '77
KNIFE sharpening. See Sharpening
KNIGHT, Anne
Fashions in fashion photography. il Horizon 20:59-65 S '77
Jerzy Kosinski, self-searcher. por Horizon 20:96 N '77
Photorealism in a medieval medium. il por Horizon 20:58-9 D '77
There'll always be an England in New Haven. il Horizon 20:60-5 N '77
KNIGHT, Charles F.
Charles F. Knight of Emerson Electric: direct approach. por Forbes 119:94 F 15 '77 *
Emerson Electric: the unique manager. il por Duns R 110:52+ D '77 *
KNIGHT, Eric
Lassie come home; story. Sat Eve Post 249:60-1 Jl '77
KNIGHT, George
General cargo: on the twenty-fifth anniversary of containerization. il Oceans 10:38-45 Mr '77
KNIGHT, Lucy
Facts about Mr Buckley's amendment. Am Educ 13:6-9 Je '77
KNIGHT, Thomas J.
Passing of the Cold War generation. il Intellect 105:238-41 F '77
KNITTING
Eight special sweaters. il McCalls 104:185-92 My '77
50 dazzling sweaters for you to knit or crochet. il Good H 184:104-11+ F '77
Fireside sweatering. A. B. Bradley. il Ladies Home J 94:124-5+ O '77
New looks in new yarns; sweaters. N. Lindemeyer and C. Vaughan. il Bet Hom & Gard 55:132-7+ O '77
Soft, mohairy knits that are big-needle easy. il Mademoiselle 83:160 D '77
Super shawls! il Good H 186:96-8+ Ja '78
28 enchanting children's sweaters to knit and crochet. il Good H 185:140-7+ S '77
Warm hands, warm head, warm feet: lovely presents to knit and crochet for Christmas. il McCalls 105:249-55 N '77
KNIVES
About knives. Redbook 149:162+ My '77
Chef's knives you can make. M. McClintock. il Pop Mech 147:108-11 F '77

Exhibitions

Custom knives and knife makers; 1976 International Knife and Edged Weapon Exposition, Dallas. S. Latham. il Field & S 81:78-80+ Mr '77
KNIVES, Indian (American) See Indians of North America—Implements
KNOCKDOWN furniture. See Furniture, Prefabricated
KNODEL, John
Breast-feeding and population growth. bibl il Science 198:1111-15 D 16 '77
KNOEDLER & Company, Inc. See New York (city)—Galleries and museums
KNOKE, David, and Henry, Constance
Political structure of rural America. bibl f il Ann Am Acad 429:51-62 Ja '77
KNOLE Cottage. See Playhouses
KNOLL, Andrew H. and Barghoorn, E. S.
Archean microfossils showing cell division from the Swaziland System of South Africa. bibl il Science 198:396-8 O 28 '77
KNOLL, Bernie
Hang on for my life. il Outdoor Life 159:76-7+ My '77
KNOLL, Erwin
Do we want to trust the FBI? il Progressive 41:11 S '77
Obituary; the same old Nixon. Progressive 41:13 Jl '77
That agony is our triumph. Progressive 41:11 Ag '77
We simply sit. . .and wait. . . Progressive 41:13 O '77
KNOP, Laurie
To the rescue. G. D. Miklowitz. il pors Seventeen 36:102 Je '77 *
KNOPF, Alfred A.
Historian and publisher. pors Am Heritage 28:100-6 Ap '77

about

Bennett Cerf remembers; excerpt from At Random. B. Cerf. por Pub W 212:26-9 Ag 22 '77 *
KNOPF, Helen
Memories; poem. Atlantic 240:54 Ag '77
KNOTS and splices
Useful knots; excerpt from Creative ropecraft. S. E. Grainger. il Yachting 142:125 S '77
What knot to do. S. Netherby. il Field & S 81:178+ Ap '77
See also
Macramé
KNOTT, John L. Jr
Remodeling notebook (cont) House B 119:59 F '77
KNOTTING. See Macramé
KNOWLEDGE
100 things every college graduate should know. J. Jones and W. Wilson. il Esquire 88:91-6 S '77
See also
Information, Freedom of
KNOWLEDGE, Sociology of
Little knowledge. P. Steinfels. Commonweal 104:392+ Je 24 '77; Reply with rejoinder. M. Novak. 104:642-3+, 646+ O 14 '77
KNOWLEDGE, Theory of
Out of chaos; excerpt. L. J. Halle. Sci Digest 82:16-20+ S '77
See also
Belief and doubt
KNOWLEDGE 2000 Project. See United States—Centennial celebrations, etc.—Science
KNOWLES, Christopher
1970 solid gold: Everything is beautiful; A horse with no name; poems. New Yorker 53:30 Mr 7 '77
KNOWLES, John Hilton
Responsibility for health. Science 198:1103 D 16 '77
KNOX, Neal
Carter/Knox team wins a big one. J. Samson. pors Field & S 82:41+ S '77 *
KNOXVILLE Zoological Park. See Zoological gardens
KNUDSEN, Conrad Calvert
MacMillan Bloedel retreats to the woods. il por Bus W p28-9 Mr 7 '77 *
KNUDSEN, Eric I. and others
Receptive fields of auditory neurons in the owl. bibl il Science 198:1278-80 D 23 '77
KNUDTSON, Peter M.
Case of the missing monk seal; with biographical sketch. il Natur Hist 86:4, 78-83 bibl(p 122-3) O '77
KNUTH, Donald E.
Algorithms; with biographical sketch. il Sci Am 236:20, 63-6+ bibl(p 148) Ap '77
KO, P. K. and others
Denervated skeletal muscle fibers develop discrete patches of high acetylcholine receptor density. bibl il Science 196:540-2 Ap 29 '77
KOBAYASHI, Victor N.
Exploring the exotic East. Todays Educ 66:74-6 S '77
KOBYLARZ, Curt
Build the hi-fi/tv audio-minder. il Pop Electr 11:41-4 Ap '77
KOCH, Charles R.
Keeneland: coming out party for racing royalty. il Sat Eve Post 249:30-2+ Mr '77
KOCH, Edward I.
Around City Hall. A. Logan. New Yorker 53:142-8+ O 3; 134+ O 31; 203-11 N 21; 54-6 D 26 '77 *
Cool man for a hot seat. L. I. Barrett. il por Time 110:22-3 O 3 '77 *
Forked tongue in New York. Nation 225:229 S 17 '77 *
Koch for New York City. New Repub 177:8-9 S 24 '77 *
Koch story. J. Corry. il pors N Y Times Mag p 15-17+ O 30 '77 *
Money hangover for New York's mayor. por Bus W p56-7 N 21 '77 *
New face for New York. D. M. Alpern and others. il pors Newsweek 91:22-3 Ja 9 '78 *
Rafshoon vs. Garth. J. Lelyveld. il pors N Y Times Mag p78 Ag 21 '77 *
Raucous round 1 in New York. il pors Time 110:22+ S 19 '77 *
Two for the seesaw. T. Mathews and S. Agrest. il pors Newsweek 90:38 S 19 '77 *
KOCH, Jeanne Mason
Eccentric hard edge. J. Kutner. il Art N 76:96+ O '77 *
KOCH, Joanne
When children meet death. bibl il por Psychol Today 11:64-6+ Ag '77
KOCH, Kenneth
Pursuing a gray-haired muse. il por Time 109:52 Ap 4 '77 *
KOCH, Klaus-Friedrich
Fabulous Timbuktu; with biographical sketch. il Natur Hist 86:9, 68-72+ bibl(p96) My '77
KOCH, LaDonna Rae
Interpretations: an encounter with Rouault. il Sch Arts 76:23 F '77
KOCH, Stephen
Humiliation in Hollywood. il Harpers 254:102-4 Mr '77

KOCH, Susan
(comp) EJ curriculum catalog. Engl J 66:53-67 S '77
(comp) Multicultural literature to teach. Engl J 66:57-70 Mr '77
(ed) Once over. Engl J 66:80-2 Mr; 80-1 Ap; 79-80 My; 76-7 S; 76-7 O; 80-2 N; 74-5 D '77

KOCHAN, Thomas A. See Wheeler, H. N. jt auth

KODAK Company. See Eastman Kodak Company

KODNER, Karen
On smallness. Progressive 41:26-7 S '77

KOEGLER, Horst
Hamburg's stylish dream of A dream. il pors Dance Mag 51:48-50 N '77
Hanseatic tricentennial. il Opera N 42:8-13 Ja 7 '78
John Neumeier's new tour de force: Legend of Joseph. il Dance Mag 51:89 Je '77
Kenneth MacMillan's Requiem. il Dance Mag 51:56-8 Ap '77

KOEHLER, Walter O.
Auto-maintenance basics (cont) il Pop Sci 210: 128+ Mr '77
How to check vacuum systems. il Pop Sci 212: 106+ Ja '78
How to use a timing light. il Pop Sci 210:123-4+ My '77

KOEHLER, Wolfgang
American forest policy in development. por Am For 83:12-13+ Ag '77

KOEHN, Ilse
PW interviews; ed by S. Steinberg. por Pub W 212:6-7 N 21 '77

KOEHRING Company-Freuhauf Corporation merger. See Corporations—Acquisitions and mergers

KOENIG, Gea. See Koenig, H. jt auth

KOENIG, Helmut, and Koenig, Gea
Brussels. il Travel 148:26-31 Ag '77
Detour to Hartford. il Travel 147:64-9 Mr '77
Madrid: soul of the new Spain. il Travel 148: 26-33 O '77
Return to Lisbon. il Trav/Holiday 148:58-63+ N '77
Zagreb stop-over. il Travel 148:32-5+ Jl '77

KOENIG, M. E. D.
Toy theory of Western history. il Bull Atom Sci 33:16-18 O '77

KOENIG, Peter
Oil comes to the Shetlands. maps Audubon 79: 129-33 Mr '77

KOEPKE, Paul
Warren hoe. il Org Gard & Farm 24:166-7 Je '77

KOEPPEL, Barbara
Meany and business vs. the ILO. Nation 225: 429-31 O 29 '77
Spain returns to the ballot box. Nation 224:135-8 F 5 '77

KOERNER, R. M.
Devon Island ice cap: core stratigraphy and paleoclimate. bibl il map Science 196:15-18 Ap 1 '77

KOESTLER, Arthur
Cosmic consciousness; excerpt from Life after death. il por Psychol Today 10:52-4+ Ap '77

KOFFLER, David, and others
Radioimmunoassay for antibodies to cytoplasmic ribosomes in human serum. bibl il Science 198: 741-3 N 18 '77

KOGER Properties, Inc. See Construction industry

KOHÁK, Erazim Voclav
Road less traveled. il Harpers 225:21-2+ D '77
Taste of Quebec. il Commonweal 104:76-8 F 4 '77

KOHEN, Andrew I. See Andrisani, P. J. jt auth

KOHEN, Arnold S.
U.S. diplomacy and human rights. map Nation 225:553-7 N 26 '77

KOHL, Herbert
Not so loudmouthed and foolish. il por Time 109: 66 Ja 24 '77 *

KOHL, James V.
Bolivia: Andean power shift. map Progressive 41: 39-42 F '77
Secret war in Brazil. Progressive 41:33-5 Ag '77

KOHLBERG, Lawrence
Lawrence Kohlberg: why Johnny can be good without being religious. R. Beechick. il Chr Today 22:12-14 D 30 '77 *

KOHLHASE, C. E.
MJS '77: a space odyssey. il Space World N-3-159:30-1 Mr '77

KOHLRABI
Mechanically induced wall appositions of plant cells can prevent penetration by a parasitic fungus. J. R. Aist. bibl il Science 197:568-71 Ag 5 '77
See also
Cookery—Vegetables

KOJAK (television character) See Characters in television

KOK, Bessel. See Radmer, R. jt auth

KOLASA, Gary
Tips for summer photo fun. Camp Mag 49:12-13 My '77

KOLB, Larry and Girard, Tanner
Cumberland; the end of a fairytale. il Nat Parks & Con Mag 51:8-11 F '77

KOLBE, Harry
Make your own solar collector! il Mech Illus 73:43-5 Mr '77

KOLBE, Robert A.
Butterworths. il Pub W 213:23-5 Ja 2 '78

KOLE, K. C.
Creative ways to raise the cash. il Motor B & S 141:130-1+ Ja '78

KOLENDA, Konstantin
Pathology of gap-ology. Intellect 105:437-8 Je '77

KOLLEK, Teddy
Jerusalem. For Affairs 55:701-16 Jl '77

KOLLER, John
Cover. M. Schiller. il Am Artist 41:6+ Ag '77 *

KOLLER, Marvin R.
Retirement, no—back to college, yes! bibl il Intellect 106:52-4 Ag '77

KOLODIN, Irving
Edison's baby: from tinfoil to tape. il por Sat R 4:20-2 Jl 23 '77
Headphone hunting at 30,000 feet. Sat R 4:20+ Ap 16 '77
Music to my ears. See issues of Saturday review
Recordings (cont of) Fresh faces and first encounters (cont) Sat R 4:42 F 19; 42 My 28; 48-9 Jl 9 '77
Sounds for the silver screen. Sat R 5:44+ N 12 '77

KOMAR, Vitaly
Art on the line. M. A. Tighe. il New Repub 176:24-6 Ap 16 '77 *
Dissidence as a way of art. G. Glueck. il pors N Y Times Mag p33-5 My 8 '77 *

KOMISAR, Lucy
Conflicts of interest. Progressive 41:8-9 Mr '77
Getting a kick from cocaine. il Read Digest 111:103-6 Jl '77
With the women at Houston. Nation 225:624-7 D 10 '77

KOMISCHE Oper. See Opera—Germany, East

KOMOSKI, P. Kenneth
Materials and equipment. See issues of Todays education

KONA, Hawaii
Hawaiis Kona Coast. E. Cheatham and P. Cheatham. il Travel 147:42-7+ F '77

KONNER, Linda
Make New Year's resolutions in October. Seventeen 36:46-7 S '77
Should you try to change your parents? il Seventeen 36:154-5+ O '77
Silent lives. il Seventeen 36:38+ Ap '77

KONNER, Mel J.
Brain and emotions. J. Greenberg. il por Sci N 112:74-5 Jl 30 '77 *

KONOPA, Charles
Forests of stone. il Am For 83:8-11+ Je '77

KONRAD, Evelyn
Machine-tool stocks may soon be hot again. il Fortune 95:69-70+ Ja '77

KOO, Gloria C. and others
H-Y antigen: expression in human subjects with the testicular feminization syndrome. bibl il Science 196:655-6 My 6 '77
Mapping the locus of the H-Y gene on the human Y chromosome. bibl il Science 198:940-2 D 2 '77

KOO, Wellington
Oral history; interview. il New Yorker 53:32-5 Ap 18 '77

KOONTZ, Dan
Long-distance cruising with children: a second opinion. il Yachting 142:28+ N '77

KOOP, Waldo
Trailing the alias. Am West 14:32-5 Ja '77

KOOTNEY Forest Products (firm) See Forest products industry—Canada

KOPAS, Jane
Fasting: asceticism in a new key. America 136:190-1 Mr 5 '77

KOPECKY, Gini
(ed) What it's like for singles who adopt: four family stories. il Ms 5:45-8+ Je '77

KOPISCHKE, John L.
Library-based blind service fought by nat'l blind group. Lib J 102:148-9, 1222 Ja 15, Je 1 '77

KOPPEL, Ted
Turning the tables. T. Schwartz and S. Sullivan. il por Newsweek 91:56 Ja 16 '78 *

KOPPMAN, Lionel. See Postal, B. jt auth

KORAN, Nancy Klem
Flowers in the rough. il por Ret Liv 17:42 Ap '77

KORAN

Law

See Islamic law

KORCHNOI, Viktor
Taut duel for two old comrades. J. D. Reed. il Sports Illus 47:40-2+ D 12 '77 *

KORDA, Michael
Job power. Harp Baz 111:152+ N '77

KOREA

Antiquities

Paleoenvironment and human settlement in Japan and Korea. R. Pearson. bibl il maps Science 197:1239-46 S 23 '77

History

Admiral Yi and the turtle boats; ironclad warships in sixteenth century Asian war. B. I. Wiley. il por Am Hist Illus 12:44-8 Je '77

KOREA (Republic) See Korea, South

KOREA, North

Foreign relations

History

See also
Pueblo incident, 1968

United States

See United States—Foreign relations—Korea, North

KOREA, South

See also
Civil rights—Korea, South
Economic assistance, American—Korea, South
Intelligence service—Korea, South
Investments, Korean
Loans, Bank—Korea, South
Military assistance, American—Korea, South
Political prisoners—Korea, South

Commerce

South Korea's powerful economic offensive. il Bus W p36+ Ag 1 '77

United States

See United States—Commerce—Korea, South

Defenses

See also
United States—Armed Forces —Forces in Korea, South
United States—Army—Forces in Korea, South

Economic conditions

South Korea's powerful economic offensive. il Bus W p36+ Ag 1 '77
There's also some good news about South Korea. R. Rowan. il Fortune 96:170-6 S '77

Foreign relations

United States

See United States—Foreign relations—Korea, South

Industries

See also
Construction industry—Korea, South
Fisheries—Korea, South

Politics and government

Fearless and the humorless. N. Kim. Chr Cent 94:733-4 Ag 17 '77
Letter from Seoul. W. McGleish. map America 136:99-101 F 5 '77
Repressive powers. C. F. H. Henry. Chr Today 21:30-1 Ja 21 '77
South Korea with sympathy. M. Kondracke. New Repub 177:12+ S 17 '77
South Korean exposure: bad news for President Park. J. Stentzel. Nation 224:77-80 Ja 22 '77

Religious institutions and affairs

See also
Catholic Church in Korea, South
Christians in Korea, South

KOREAN drama
See also
Folk drama, Korean

KOREAN War, 1950-1953

Aerial operations

Time of eagles. F. L. Harvey. il Flying 101:276-80 S '77

KOREANS in the United States
See also
Los Angeles—Foreign population
New York (city)—Foreign population

KORETZ, Gene
(ed) Economic diary (cont) il Bus W p 13-14 F 14; 16+ F 28; 14+ Mr 28; 18 Je 20; 20+ Ag 15; 10 Ag 29; 21+ O 24; 18 O 31; 14+ N 7 '77

KOREY, William
Final acts and final solutions. bibl il Society 15:81-6 N '77

KORIAKIN, Igor Mezhakoff-. See Mezhakoff-Koriakin, I.

KORLE, Sinan A.
147 good reasons for bypassing the caviar. il pors Sat Eve Post 249:37+ S '77

KORNBLUT, Arthur T.
Legal perspectives. Archit Rec 161:57 F; 55+ Mr; 67+ Ap; 73 My; 162:63 Ag; 63 N; 53 D '77

KORNETCHUK, Elena
Politics of Soviet art. bibl il Bull Atom Sci 33:32-7 O '77

KORNETSKY, Conan. See Esposito, R. jt auth

KORNFELD, Joseph
Dirigibles: a comeback? il Sci Digest 81:38-42 My '77
Exploring the briny deep in your own submarine. il Sci Digest 81:53-7 Je '77

KORNHEISER, Tony
Gospel according to Willis. il por N Y Times Mag p43-4+ O 16 '77
Star you love to hate. il pors N Y Times Mag p20-1+ Ap 10 '77

KOROLEV, Sergei Pavlovich
Why of Sputnik. bibl f il por map Space World N-12-168:4-15 D '77 *

KORSAKOV, Nicholay Andreyevich Rimsky-. See Rimsky-Korsakov, N. A.

KORVETTE, E. J, Inc. See Arlen Realty and Development Corporation

KOSHER food. See Jews—Dietary laws

KOSHLAND, Daniel Edward, 1920-
Response regulator model in a simple sensory system; adaptation of address. bibl il Science 196:1055-63 Je 3 '77

KOSINSKI, Jerzy Nikodem
Psychological novelist as portable man; interview, ed by G. Sheehy. il por Psychol Today 11:52-3+ D '77

about

Horatio Algers of the nightmare. E. Stone. il por Psychol Today 11:59-60+ D '77 *
Jerzy Kosinski, self-searcher. A. Knight. por Horizon 20:96 N '77 *

KOSKELA, Roger
NBEA: when the Bible bumps blackness. Chr Today 21:58 My 6 '77

KOSLOW, Evan E.
Aposematic statement on nuclear war: ultraviolet radiation in the postattack environment. bibl BioScience 27:409-13 Je '77

KOSLOW, Sally Platkin
(ed) Politics of persuasion; interviews with women lobbyists. il Mademoiselle 83:58+ F '77

KOSLOW, Stephen H. and Butler, I. J.
Biogenic amine synthesis defect in dihydropteridine reductase deficiency. bibl il Science 198:522-3 N 4 '77

KOSNER, Alice
What to do when you're really depressed. il McCalls 105:220-1+ N '77

KOSTELANETZ, André
Unforgettable Leopold Stokowski. por Read Digest 112:101-5 Ja '78

KOSTELANETZ, Richard
New York Fair highlights growing interest in books by specialized publishers. il Pub W 212:28-30 N 14 '77

KOSTER, John
Creature feature: what was the New Zealand monster? il Oceans 10:56-9 N '77
Tutoring Vietnamese refugees. Todays Educ 66:32-4 N '77

KOTCHIAN, A. Carl
Lockheed's 70-day mission to Tokyo; excerpt from Lockheed sales mission: seventy days in Tokyo. il Sat R 4:7-12 Jl 9 '77

KOTKER, Zane
Words of life. C. Forbes. Chr Today 21:22 Ja 7 '77 *

KOTLER, Philip
From sales obsession to marketing effectiveness. il Harvard Bus R 55:67-75 N '77

KOTLOWITZ, Robert
Looking back. D. Merkin. Commentary 64:63-5 Jl '77 *
Television. P. Sourian. Nation 225:732-4 D 31 '77 *

KOTTAK, Conrad P.
Rituals at McDonald's; with biographical sketch. il Natur Hist 87:6, 74-83 bibl(p 109) Ja '78

KOTTER, John P.
Power, dependence, and effective management. bibl f Harvard Bus R 55:125-36 Jl '77

KOTTKE, Bruce A. See Lewis, J. C. jt auth

KOTZ, Mary Lynn
(ed) See O'Keeffe, G. Georgia O'Keeffe at 90
(ed) See Pryor, B. L. How her job saved their marriage

KOTZ, Nick
Can labor's tired leaders deal with a troubled movement? il por N Y Times Mag p8-11+ S 4 '77
Politics of welfare reform. New Repub 176:16-21 My 14 '77

KOUBEK, Richard F.
Father's instincts. Am Home 80:18+ Je '77

KOUNITZ, E. Jan
There is a Santa Claus. il Society 14:80-1 Ja '77

KOUNS, Betty
Thirteen steps to library orientation. SLJ 23:125 Mr '77

KOURILSKY, Philippe
Use of isolators in recombinant DNA research. bibl il Science 196:215-16 Ap 8 '77

KOVAC, Mark P. and Davis, W. J.
Behavioral choice: neural mechanisms in pleurobranchaea. bibl il Science 198:632-4 N 11 '77

KOVACIK, Bob
Wheels afield. See issues of Motor trend

KOVACS, William P.
Steer clear of trading troubles. J. McNabney. por Farm J 101:Beef 16 Ag '77 *

KOVALCIK, Alfred L.
Another look at reading readiness. Educ Digest 43:48-50 S '77

KOVDA, Victor Abramovitch
Precarious balance upset. il map UNESCO Courier 30:11-14 Jl '77

KOVIC, Ron
On the eve of the Tet offensive; interview, ed by L. R. Obst. il por N Y Times Mag p40-2 N 13 '77

KOVLER, Peter
Congress is the problem. Nation 225:233-6 S 17 '77
Realpolitik in Georgia. Nation 224:400-1 Ap 2 '77

KOWAL, Charles T.
Planetoid between Saturn and Uranus. il Sci N 112:311 N 12 '77 *
Puzzle in the sky. map Newsweek 90:141 N 21 '77 *
Return of Adonis: an asteroid refound. Sci N 111:183 Mr 19 '77 *
Tenth planet? Time 110:98 N 21 '77 *

KOWAL, Michael
Heinrich Mann and Der Untertan. Nation 225: 346-8 O 8 '77

KOWARSKI, Lew
Conditions of success in international enterprises in science and technology. Bull Atom Sci 33:44-8 S '77

KOZAK, Lola Jean. See Perlstadt, H. jt auth

KOZIARA, Karen S.
Agricultural labor relations laws in four states —a comparison. bibl M Labor R 100:14-18 My '77

KRAAR, Louis
General Dynamics struggles to build a plane for all nations. il Fortune 95:180-4+ Mr '77
General Electric's very personal merger. il pors Fortune 96:186-92+ Ag '77
Glory that was Troy, New York. il Fortune 95: 142-5 Ja '77
How Lockheed got back its wings. il por Fortune 96:198-202+ O '77
Super-connector from Saudi Arabia. il pors Fortune 95:108-14+ Je '77

KRACKE, Don
How-to; excerpt from How to turn your idea into a million dollars. Sci Digest 82:26-30 S '77

KRAEGEL, Charles R.
House plan in secondary schools. Clearing H 50: 392-4 My '77

KRAFT, Elizabeth
(tr) See Serebrennikov, N. Pas de deux

KRAFT, Frank J.
Line can be beautiful. il Sch Arts 76:51 F '77

KRAFT, John C. and others
Paleogeographic reconstructions of coastal Aegean archaeological sites. bibl il maps Science 195:941-7 Mr 11 '77

KRAFT, Joseph
Books. New Yorker 53:140-6+ D 19 '77

about

Kraft flunks Carter. Nation 225:4-5 Jl 2 '77 *
Spare that spook! New Repub 177:5+ N 19 '77 *

KRAFT, Ken, and Kraft, Pat
Everlastings. il Horticulture 55:66-9, 86-7 Ap '77
Exotic oriental vegetables. il Horticulture 55: 22-4+ My '77
Gardening with exotic vegetables from Europe. il Horticulture 55:52-6 Mr '77
New use for an old device: growing greens in a coldframe for fresh winter salads. il Horticulture 55:56-7 S '77
Perennial vegetables. il Horticulture 55:44-6 O '77

KRAFT, Pat. See Kraft, K. jt auth

KRAFT, Virginia
Archery (cont) Sports Illus 47:77+ O 31 '77
At Payson's place he's just plain Charlie. il por Sports Illus 46:54+ Ap 18 '77
Hocker. il por Sports Illus 47:40-1 Ag 22 '77
Hunting. Sports Illus 46:49+ F 21; 47:74+ N 21 '77
If you call him old folks, be prepared to duck. il por Sports Illus 47:34-6+ Ag 8 '77

KRAKAUER, R. S. and others
Prevention of autoimmunity in experimental lupus erythematosus by soluble immune response suppressor. bibl il Science 196:56-9 Ap 1 '77

KRAKER, Joseph H.
Cleveland vs. Mary Hartman. America 136:484-7 My 28 '77

KRAM, Mark
Why ain't I in the Hall? il por Sports Illus 46: 88-90+ Ap 11 '77

KRAMER, Arthur
View from Kramer. See issues of Modern photography

KRAMER, Hilton
American in Paris. il pors N Y Times Mag p 16-17+ Je 19 '77
France's new culture palace. il N Y Times Mag p 13 Ja 23 '77
Notes on Irving Penn. il New Repub 177:27-9 O 29 '77
Vollard: dealer for the demigods. il pors N Y Times Mag p28-30+ Je 5 '77

KRAMER, Jack, 1921-, and Deford, Frank
Little hanky-panky, but no fixes. il Sports Illus 48:26-30+ Ja 9 '78
So everything was Jake. il Sports Illus 48:50-8 Ja 2 '78

KRAMER, Jake. See Kramer, Jack

KRAMER, Jane
Profiles; H. Blanton. New Yorker 53:44-6+ My 30; 40-4+ Je 6 '77
Reporter in Europe. New Yorker 53:98+ Mr 21; 101-13 My 2; 72-81 Jl 4 '77

KRAMER, Leslie
Real looks: how four young women dress for job/home/night. il pors Mademoiselle 83:170-5 S '77 *

KRAMER, Mark
Making milk. il pors Atlantic 240:80-4+ N '77

KRAMER, Paul Jackson
Botanists capture distinguished service awards. pors BioScience 27:346 My '77 *

KRAMER, Reed
Bankers' stakes in Zaire. map Nation 224:521-4 Ap 30 '77

KRAMER, Steven Philip
Winter of discontent. Commonweal 104:167-8 Mr 18 '77

KRAMER, Thomas E.
Invitation to participate in the third and final consultation. il por New Cath World 220:60-4 Mr '77

KRAMMER, Arnold Paul
Nazi coal conversion methods reviewed. C. Holden. Science 196:508-9 Ap 29 '77 *

KRANTZLER, Mel
Learning to love again; excerpt. il Good H 185: 130-1+ S '77

KRANZLER, David
One and one-tenth lives of a librarian/scholar; interview, ed by A. Plotnik. por Am Lib 8:65 F '77

KRASEMANN, Stephen J.
We rafted down Canada's notorious Nahanni. il Int Wildlife 7:48-55 Mr '77

KRASILOVSKY, Phyllis
Children's continent. il Sat Eve Post 249:90+ My '77

KRASNE, Franklin B. and Lee, S. H.
Regenerating afferents establish synapses with a target neuron that lacks its cell body. bibl il Science 198:517-19 N 4 '77

KRASNER, Lee
Jackson Pollock's drawings under analysis; B. Carter. il Art N 76:58-60 F '77 *

KRASS, Allan S.
Laser enrichment of uranium: the proliferation connection. bibl il Science 196:721-31 My 13 '77

KRAUS, Jon
Decline of Ghana's military government. il Cur Hist 73:214-17+ D '77

KRAUS, Joseph
Class project: rewrite history. Educ Digest 43: 36-7 S '77
He turns kids' dreams into toys. il pors Ret Liv 17:33+ D '77

KRAUS, Richard
Urban alternative: making do with volunteers. il Parks & Rec 12:35-7+ Mr '77

KRAUSS, Clifford. See Freedman, D. jt auth

KRAUSS, Robert M. and Glucksberg, Sam
Social and nonsocial speech; with biographical sketches. il Sci Am 236:16, 100-5 bibl(p 138) F '77

KRAVETZ, Beth
Washington scene. See issues of Parks & recreation

KRAVITT, Edward F.
Joining of words and music in late romantic melodrama. bibl f il Mus Q 62:571-90 O '76

KREAM, B. E. and others
Specific high-affinity binding macromolecule for 1,25-dihydroxyvitamin D_3 in fetal bone. bibl il Science 197:1086-8 S 9 '77

KREBS, Charles T. and Burns, K. A.
Long-term effects of an oil spill on populations of the salt-marsh crab uca pugnax. bibl il Science 197:484-7 Jl 29 '77

KREFETZ, Gerald
Money matters: business at home. Craft Horiz 37:49+ D '77

KREH, Lefty
Flyrod bream: don't settle for runts. il por Outdoor Life 159:86-7+ Je '77
Long rod back. il Outdoor Life 159:72-3+ F '77

KREMENTZ, Jill
Woman behind the credit: photo by Jill Krementz. D. K. Mano. il Esquire 87:16+ F '77 *

KREMER, Gidon
Gidon Kremer: gaunt and gripping. por Time 109:77 Ja 24 '77 *
Gidon Kremer, violin; New York debut recital. Hi Fi 27:MA23 My '77 *

KREMER, M. D.
Santa lets his hair down; interview, ed by P. M. Jones. il pors Sr Schol 110:2-3 D 15 '77
KREN, Margo
Hand lift sling looms. il Sch Arts 76:18-19 F '77
KRENZELOK, Steven R.
Water quality: Oceanic Society monitors San Francisco Bay. Oceans 10:65 Mr '77
KREPS, Juanita (Morris)
Does future look bright for business? It does indeed; interview. pors U.S. News 83:17-19 Ag 1 '77
Future for working women; ed by R. J. Leaper; excerpt from Women and the American economy: a look to the 1980's. por Ms 5:56-7 Mr '77
Juanita Kreps: more active role for Commerce; interview. il pors Nations Bus 65:30-4 S '77
Thoughts about government and business; address, June 23, 1977. Vital Speeches 43:610-12 Ag 1 '77

about

First lady of Commerce. il por Newsweek 89:61 F 7 '77 *
Halo game. Nation 225:516-17 N 19 '77 *
Secretary Kreps won't talk. M. T. Klare. Nation 224:678-9 Je 4 '77 *
KRESGE, S. S, Company
Hot discounter: K-Mart stores. L. Langway and others. Newsweek 89:69-70 Ap 25 '77
K Mart has to open some new doors on the future. E. Carruth. il Fortune 96:144-7+ Jl '77
KRESS, Robert
Mary's assumption, God's promise fulfilled. America 137:71-4 Ag 13 '77
KRETCHMER, Arthur
Justice for Hustler. Newsweek 89:13 F 28 '77
KREUGER, Miles
PW interviews; ed by R. Dahlin. por Pub W 213:8-9 Ja 2 '78
KREUTZBERG, Harald
Films: Harald Kreutzberg's dances of death. J. Mueller. il por Dance Mag 51:28 Ap '77 *
KREUTZER, Konradin
Das Nachtlager in Granada. J. Ringo. Am Rec G 40:24-5 My '77 *
KRICH, Charles
Fastest growing American sport is camp's least understood program. il Camp Mag 49:14-15+ My '77
KRIDER, E. Philip
On lightning damage to a golf course green. bibl il Weatherwise 30:111 Je '77
KRIEBEL, Charles
One-stop decorating. il Am Home 80:24 F '77
KRIEGEL, Leonard
Mann letters. Nation 225:309-11, 343-6 O 1-8 '77
KRIEGEL, Robert. See Gallwey, W. T. jt auth
KRIEGER, David M.
What happens if...? Terrorist, revolutionaries, and nuclear weapons. Ann Am Acad 430:44-57 Mr '77
KRIEGER, Dolores
Her hands may heal. L. Davis. Vogue 167:105 My '77 *
KRIEGER, Dorothy T. and others
Suprachiasmatic nuclear lesions do not abolish food-shifted circadian adrenal and temperature rhythmicity. bibl il Science 197:398-9 Jl 22 '77
KRIEGER, Leonard
Idea of authority in the West. bibl f Am Hist R 82:249-70 Ap '77
KRILL, John
Treasure trove in the weeds. il Org Gard & Farm 24:137-8 Je '77
KRILL
Antarctic problems: tiny krill to usher in new resource era. D. Shapley. il map Science 196: 503-5 Ap 29 '77
Antarctica: rich around the edges. R. Burton. il Sea Front 23:287-95 S '77
Heating up: global race for Antarctic's riches. J. F. McWethy. il U.S. News 82:62-6 F 28 '77
Krill. J. F. Lohr. il Oceans 10:54-5 My '77
KRIPKE, Margaret L. See Fidler, I. J. jt auth
KRIPKE, Saul
New frontiers in American philosophy. T. Branch. il pors N Y Times Mag p 12-14+ Ag 14 '77 *
KRIPS, Josef
Mozart: Symphonies nos. 23, 28, 30, 31 and 38, performed by the Concertgebouw Orchestra under J. Krips. L. M. Smoley. Am Rec G 40: 41-2+ S '77 *
KRISHNA
Krishna: god as a troublesome youth. A. Menen. il Horizon 19:54-65 Ja '77 *
KRISHNA, G. See Kapoor, C. L. jt auth
KRISHNA, K. G. V.
Smallholder agriculture in Africa—constraints and potential. Ann Am Acad 432:12-25 Jl '77
KRISHNA consciousness movement. See Mysticism —Hinduism
KRISHNAMURTI, Yamini
Reviews. S. Banes. Dance Mag 51:34-5 My '77 *
KRISHNAN, V. N. See Kannappan, S. jt auth
KRISTEIN, Marvin M. and others
Health economics and preventive care. bibl il Science 195:457-62 F 4 '77
KRISTOFFERSON, Karl E.
Come ride the space shuttle. il Read Digest 110: 66-70 Je '77
KRISTOFFERSON, Kris
Grooving with Kris and Rita. pors Time 110:71 Ag 15 '77 *
Star is reborn. L. Minton. por McCalls 105:182+ N '77 *
KRISTOL, Irving
Memoirs of a Trotskyist. il por N Y Times Mag p42-3+ Ja 23 '77
Post-Watergate morality, a dubious legacy. Read Digest 110:169-171 My '77
KROC, Ray A.
Self-discipline called key to success; excerpt from address. por Intellect 106:185-6 N '77
KRÖCHER-TIEDEMANN, Gabriele
Link to Carlos? S. Strasser and P. Martin. il por Newsweek 91:25 Ja 2 '78 *
KROCH'S and Brentano's (bookstore) See Booksellers and book selling—Illinois
KROGER William
One way to shrink government employment. il Nations Bus 65:39-42 D '77
KROLL, Howard W. and Moren, D. K.
Effect of appearance on requests for help in libraries. il Am Lib 8:489 O '77
KROLL, Jack
Save the Music Hall! por Newsweek 91:15 Ja 16 '78
KROLL, Jules
Big rip-off in purchasing. R. Levey. il Duns R 109:76-7+ Mr '77 *
KROLL, Stanley
Day Stanley Kroll quit; excerpt from The Midas touch. J. Train. il por Forbes 120:66+ O 1 '77 *
KROPOTKIN, Igor
(ed) See Consolino, J. PW interviews
KROTZER, Henry W. Jr
Restoration of San Francisco (St Frusquin), Reserve, Louisiana. il Antiques 111:1194-1203 Je '77
KROWNAPPLE, Una
Baiting the hook. J. M. Hopkins. Chr Today 22:40-1 D 30 '77 *
KRUEGER, Robert Charles
Why Congress hasn't deregulated natural gas. il por Nations Bus 65:24+ Ap '77

about

Bard of oil. T. Mathews and H. W. Hubbard. il por Newsweek 89:75-6 Je 20 '77 *
KRUGER, James Thomas
I must keep this country safe; interview, ed by W. McWhirter. pors Time 110:38 O 17 '77
KRÜGER, Joachim
Great Mozart-Beethoven caper. P. Moor. il Hi Fi 27:72-7 Mr '77 *
KRUGMANN, Hartmut, and Von Hippel, Frank
Radioactive wastes: a comparison of U.S. military and civilian inventories. bibl il Science 197:883-5 Ag 26 '77
KRUSCHKE, David, and Funk, Karen
Our solar green-home; excerpt from The solar greenhouse book. il Org Gard & Farm 24:54-7 D '77
KRUSE, Loren, and Cain, Steve
Marketing. See issues of Successful farming
Money management. See issues of Successful farming
KRUUK, Hans
Critter nobody loves; excerpt from Cult of the wild. B. Rensberger. il Int Wildlife 7:12-16 N '77 *
KRYGER, King C.
Some guidelines for energy programs. bibl Todays Educ 66:60-2 S '77
KRYNSKI, Magnus
(tr) See Rózewicz, T. Méliès
KRYPTON

Isotopes

Meteorological consequences of atmospheric krypton-85. W. L. Boeck; reply with rejoinder. H. L. Gjorup. Science 196:380-1+ Ap 22 '77
KSZYSTYNIAK, Richard. See Stone, E. L. jt auth
KU KLUX Klan
Great white hope. D. A. Williams and others. il por Newsweek 90:45 N 14 '77
KUBELIK, Rafael
Kubelik and the mighty nine; Beethoven symphonies. G. S. Fox. Am Rec G 40:16-17 D '76 *
KUBELKA, Peter
Restoring Enthusiasm; interview, ed by L. Fisher. il Film Q 31:35-6 Wint '77
KUBIAK, T. J.
Rhodesia (Zimbabwe); white minority rule in a black state. bibl il map Focus 27:1-8 N '76
KUCH, Elly
Elly and Willy Kuch. S. Hyman. il pors Ceram Mo 25:50-7 My '77 *
KUCH, Wilhelm
Elly and Willy Kuch. S. Hyman. il pors Ceram Mo 25:50-7 My '77 *

KUCHARSKY, David Eugene
New post for David E. Kucharsky. por Chr Today 22:26 O 21 '77 *
(ed) See Van Til, C. At the beginning, God

KUCINICH, Dennis
Dennis the menace. D. M. Alpern and J. Lowell. il pors Newsweek 91:20 Ja 2 '78 *

KUDELKA, James
Spotlight on: James Kudelka. P. Doob. il por Dance Mag 51:70-3 Mr '77 *

KUECHENMEISTER, G. Arthur
Pains and pleasures of being thrown out at 65. pors Time 110:33 O 10 '77 *

KUEHL, Linda
Music: a reflection of jazz women. Commonweal 104:625-6 S 30 '77

KUEHNELT-LEDDIHN, Erik Maria, Ritter von
Letter from the Continent (title varies) (cont) Nat R 29:153, 386, 556, 721, 945, 1117, 1300, 1498 F 4, Ap 1, My 13, Je 24, Ag 19, S 30, N 11, D 23 '77

KUEHNL, Neil
Guide to European package tours. il Bet Hom & Gard 55:153-4+ Mr '77

KUERTI, Anton
Liszt: Sonata in B minor; Glazounov: Sonata no. 1 in B-flat minor; Aquitane recording. L. Radcliffe. por Am Rec G 41:35-6 D '77 *

KUETTNER, Klaus E. and others
Tumor cell collagenase and its inhibition by a cartilage-derived protease inhibitor. bibl il Science 196:653-4 My 6 '77

KUH, Katharine
Fine arts (cont) Sat R 4:44-6 Ja 22; 43-5 Mr 5; 55-6+ Ap 16; 34-6 My 28; 44+ Jl 9; 52-4+ Ag 6; 5:38-40 O 1 '77

KUHN, Annette
Post-war collecting: the emergence of phase III. Art in Am 65:110-11+ S '77

KUHN, Bob
Flap of vultures. il Audubon 79:56-7 N '77

KUHN, David T. and Cunningham, G. N.
Aldehyde oxidase compartmentalization in drosophila melanogaster wing imaginal disks. bibl il Science 196:875-7 My 20 '77

KUHN, Harold B.
World hunger and Christian conscience. Chr Today 21:68-9 My 6 '77

about

Evangelical's duty to the Latin American poor. Chr Today 21:23-4 Je 3 '77 *

KUHN, Irene Corbally
Munich. il Trav/Holiday 148:52-7 D '77
New Harmony. il Travel 148:48-51+ S '77

KUHN, John
Investing in gold: mining shares, coin or bullion; interview, ed by A. Hershman. por Duns R 110:107+ D '77

KUHN, P. M. and others
Clear air turbulence: detection by infrared observations of water vapor. bibl il Science 196:1099-100 Je 3 '77

KUHN, Reni
5 exercises to keep your back in shape. il Ret Liv 17:22 Ja '77

KUHN, Robert L.
Armstrong's Worldwide Church of God: musical chairs of change. J. M. Hopkins. Chr Today 21:20-3 Ap 1; 22-4 Ap 15 '77 *

KUHN, Thomas Samuel
Thomas S. Kuhn: revolutionary theorist of science. N. Wade. por Science 197:143-5 Jl 8 '77; Reply. R. J. Wurtman. 197:514 Ag 5 '77 *

KUHN, Loeb & Company. See Investment banking

KUHN, Loeb & Company-Lehman Brothers, Inc merger. See Investment banking—Acquisitions and mergers

KUHNE, Sharon Lea
All the evidence on pot isn't in! por Seventeen 36:32 Ap '77

KUIPER, T. B. H. and Morris, M.
Searching for extraterrestrial civilizations. bibl il Science 196:616-21 My 6 '77

KUJUNDZIC, Zeljko
Ceramic air cooler. il Ceram Mo 25:56-7 S '77

KULINICZ, Regina
Baby-sitting adventures. Seventeen 36:122+ My '77

KULTURA (periodical) See Periodicals—Poland

KUMBH Mela (festival) See Fasts and feasts—Hinduism

KUMIN, Maxine (Winokur)
July, against hunger; poem. New Yorker 53:34 Jl 11 '77
Remembering Pearl Harbor at the Tutankhamun exhibit; poem. New Repub 176:48 My 21 '77

KUMM, Bjorn
Utopia in trouble. Harpers 256:33-7 Ja '78

KUNEN, James Simon
Student strike at Columbia; interview, ed by L. R. Obst. il N Y Times Mag p43+ N 13 '77

KUNG, Hans
Finding sense when it makes no sense; excerpt from On being a Christian, tr by E. Quinn. il Sat Eve Post 249:50-1+ Ap '77

KUNG (native race) See Bushmen

KUNHARDT, Philip Bradish, 1928-
Hold still—don't move a muscle: you're on Brady's camera! excerpt from Mathew Brady and his world. il Smithsonian 8:58-67 bibl(p 101) Ag '77
Images of which history was made bore the Mathew Brady label; excerpts from Mathew Brady and his world. il pors Smithsonian 8:24-35 Jl '77

KUNTA Kinte family. See Kinte family

KUNZ, Marji
(ed) See Davis, V. Jet-set tycoon

KUNZE, Reiner
Wire—and other vignettes of life in eastern Europe; excerpts from The wonderful years. il Fortune 95:89 Je '77

KUNZLE, David
200 years of the great American freedom to complain. il Art in Am 65:99-105 Mr '77

KUPERSCHMID, Eileen
Whalers of Bequia. il map Motor B & S 139:40-5 F '77

KUPFERBERG, Herbert
(ed) See Horowitz, V. Musician of the month: Vladimir Horowitz

KUPFERBERG, Seth
Right-to-work fad. New Repub 178:20-3 Ja 7 '78

KURALT, Charles
To know where we have been; excerpt from The Bob Timberlake collection; with editorial comment. Audubon 79:inside cover, 48+ My '77. Same abr. Readers Digest 111:136-42 S '77

KURDS
Ethnic conflict and the Kurds. G. S. Harris. bibl f Ann Am Acad 433:112-24 S '77
Forgotten Kurds. L. Dinsmore. Progressive 41:38-9 Ap '77

KURIS, Armand M. and Blaustein, A. R.
Ectoparasitic mites on rodents: application of the island biogeography theory? bibl Science 195:596-8 F 11 '77

KURLE, Robert
Whip-and-tongue graft: easy way to more fruit in half the time. il Org Gard & Farm 25:84-7 Ja '78

KUROSKY, Alexander, and others
Primary structure of cholera toxin β-chain: a glycoprotein hormone analog? bibl il Science 195:299-301 Ja 21 '77

KURTZ, Bruce
Artists' video at the crossroads. il Art in Am 65:36-40 Ja '77

KURTZ, Jerome
Next: you'll pay taxes on your fringe benefits; interview. il por U.S. News 83:26-8 Jl 18 '77

KURU. See Nervous system—Diseases

KURZ, Gretchen
Sexual freedom: is it worth the hassle? Mademoiselle 83:207 Ag '77

KURZMAN, Cal
University libraries in Israel. il Wilson Lib Bull 51:824-31 Je '77

KUSACHI, Sachiko, and Loetterle, Fred
Puppets. il Design (US) 78:18-19 Summ '77

KUSKOKWIM Community College. See Alaska. University, Fairbanks—Kuskokwim Community College

KUSPIT, Donald B.
Charles Biederman's abstract analogues for nature. bibl il Art in Am 65:80-3 My '77
George Segal: on the verge of tragic vision. il Art in Am 65:84-5 My '77
Individual and mass identity in urban art: the New York case. bibl il Art in Am 65:66-77 S '77
Sol LeWitt: the look of thought. Art in Am 65:5+ Ja '77

KUSSMAUL, Dorothy S.
Urban urge. House B 119:66+ N '77

KUTAS, Marta, and others
Augmenting mental chronometry: the P300 as a measure of stimulus evaluation time. bibl il Science 197:792-5 Ag 19 '77

KUTCHINS, Fred
(ed) See Friedman, M. Leaning against next year's wind

KUTI, Fela Anikulapo-. See Anikulapo-Kuti, F.

KUTNER, David
Major shifts planned for Baker & Taylor Texas facility; interview, ed by J. Giusto. Pub W 212:55 O 10 '77

KUTNER, Janet
Dallas (cont) (title varies) il Art N 76:95-8 Mr; 96+ O; 102+ D '77
How to build a museum with diplomacy, guile and charm. il Art N 76:87-90 D '77
Prado of the prairie. il por Art N 76:74-7 My '77
Texas' small museums discovering each other. il Art N 76:77-80+ F '77

KUWAIT
See also
Economic assistance, Kuwaiti

KUWAIT Fund for Arab Economic Development. See Economic assistance, Kuwaiti

KUYKENDALL, Carol
(ed) Teaching materials (cont) Engl J 66:86-90 F; 82-5 Ap; 78-82 S; 84-7 N '77

KUYPERS, Henricus G. J. M. See Moll L. jt auth

KUZMA, Greg
Dead; poem. New Yorker 53:228 D 5 '77
KUZNETSOV, Vasilii Vasil'evich
Veep in Moscow. por Time 110:40 O 17 '77 *
KWANZA (festival) See Festivals—United States
KWAPONG, Alexander, Adum
U.N.U; interview. New Yorker 53:33-5 O 3 '77
KWITNY, Jonathan
Dirty little secret of lie detectors. il Esquire 89:73-6+ Ja '78
KWONG, Eva
Eva Kwong. il Ceram Mo 25:47 N '77 *
KY, Nguyen-cao-. See Nguyen-cao-Ky
KYEMBA, Henry
Henry Kyemba awaits the end of Idi Amin; interview, ed by G. Stuttaford. por Pub W 212:44 O 3 '77

about

Ace to issue its first instant title on Amin. M. Reuter. Pub W 212:74+ Jl 18 '77 *
Big Daddy in books. il pors Time 110:46 S 19 '77 *
Death and coffee in Uganda. J. M. Wall. Chr Cent 94:971-3 O 26 '77 *
KYLE, Chester
Bicycles built for speed. R. Bongartz. il Horizon 19:56-9 Jl '77 *
KYLE, George M.
BOR looks at water quality. il Parks & Rec 12:19a-21a F '77
KYOTO, Japan

Hotels, restaurants, etc.

Kan-pei! Junidan-ya restaurant. R. L. Balzer. il Holiday 58:26-8 Mr '77
KYTE, Nancy S. See Grinnell, R. M. jt auth

L

L-dopa. See Dopa
LAMPF (Los Alamos Meson Physics Facility) See Accelerators (electrons, etc)
LAMPS (light airborne multi-purpose systems) helicopters. See Helicopters—Military use
LC catalog cards. See Catalog cards
LC subject headings. See Subject headings
LDCs (less developed countries) See Underdeveloped areas
LEAA. See United States—Law Enforcement Assistance Administration
LED (light emitting diodes) See Diodes
LMSC. See Lockheed Missiles and Space Company
LNG. See Liquefied natural gas
LSCA (Library Services and Construction Act) See Library laws and legislation
LSCA (Library Services and Construction Act) funds. See Libraries—Federal aid
LSD
CIA's electric kool-aid acid test. T. Szulc. il Psychol Today 11:92-4+ N '77
LSD: yesterday, today, and tomorrow. J. Hassett. Psychol Today 11:101 N '77
LSD (life-span development) See Life
LSM (landing ship medium) See Landing craft
LSS. See Lutheran Social Service
LTV Corporation
LTV also is shaking up its steelmaker. Bus W p86 O 3 '77
LTV's campaign to save Vought; effect of defense budget cuts. il Bus W p24-5 Mr 7 '77
LTV Corporation-Lykes Corporation merger. See Corporations—Acquisitions and mergers
LA BARBARA, Joan
New music. See issues of High fidelity and Musical America
LA BARRE, Harriet
New Weight Watchers diet. Ladies Home J 94:119-26 F '77
Telling all. Ladies Home J 94:77+ Jl '77
LABASTILLE, Anne
How do they make it through the winter? il Nat Wildlife 16:20-5 D '77
On the trail of Wisconsin's Ice Age. il pors map Nat Geog 152:182-205 Ag '77
LABELS
Bumper crop of slogans. J. D. Reed. il Sports Illus 47:80+ D 12 '77
Crating up the California dream. J. L. Phillips. il Am Heritage 28:88-93 Ap '77
On the road with better bumper stickers. il Sky & Tel 54:32 Jl '77
What the new cosmetics labels tell you. M. P. Scott. Bet Hom & Gard 55:86+ Je '77
When the label reads medicated: what it really means. il Good H 185:220+ S '77
See also
Food—Labeling
Household appliances—Labeling
Unit pricing
Wine—Labeling

LABOR (obstetrics) See Childbirth
LABOR, Department of. See United States—Labor, Department of
LABOR, Migrant. See Migrant labor
LABOR absenteeism. See Absenteeism
LABOR agreements. See Collective labor agreements
LABOR and laboring classes
See also
Absenteeism
Age and employment
Apprentices
Children—Employment
Church and labor
Diseases, Industrial
Employment
Hours of labor
Job satisfaction
Middle classes
Open and closed shop
Right to labor
Socialism
Unemployment
Work
also classes of laborers, e.g. Migrant labor; *also* headings beginning Industrial; *also* subhead Employees under various subjects, e.g. Railroads—Employees

Bibliography

Book reviews. See issues of Monthly labor review
Labor force trends: a bibliography. R. M. Devens. M Labor R 100:12-15 O '77
Publications received. See issues of Monthly labor review

Discipline

See Labor discipline

Education

Educational attainment of workers, March 1976. K. Michelotti. bibl il M Labor R 100:62-5 Mr '77
Educational attainment of workers, March 1977. K. Michelotti. il M Labor R 100:53-7 D '77
Relevance of recurrent education to worker satisfaction. F. Jacobs and P. Cowden. bibl M Labor R 100:61-4 Ap '77

Newspapers

See Labor press

Non-wage payments

See Non-wage payments

Photographs

Working class; B. Owens' subjects. D. Davis. il Newsweek 90:75 O 10 '77

Political activities

See Trade unions—Political activities

Psychology

See Phychology, Industrial

Statistics

Current labor statistics. See issues of Monthly labor review
Federal-State approach to labor statistics. J. Hanna. M Labor R 100:43-4 O '77
New approaches to statistics on the family. J. L. Norwood. bibl il M Labor R 100:31-4 Jl '77
See also
Unemployment—Statistics
United States—Labor Statistics, Bureau of

Wages

See Wages

Germany, West

See also
Berlin (West Berlin)—Labor and laboring classes

Italy

Italy's secret economy: illegal cellar factories and moonlighting. il Time 110:46 Ag 22 '77

South Africa

South Africa's captive work-force. il UNESCO Courier 30:14-15 N '77

United States

Labor month in review. See issues of Monthly labor review
Lunch pails and safety shoes—newest badges of worker affluence; blue collar, industrial, and factory laborers. il U.S. News 82:83-4 Ap 25 '77
Rentier economy would threaten manufacturing jobs. G. Tyler. M Labor R 100:45-6 Mr '77
Research summaries. See issues of Monthly labor review
Rethinking free trade; displacement of unskilled workers. H. Peter Gray. New Repub 176:12-13 Mr 19 '77
State labor legislation enacted in 1977. R. R. Nelson and D. A. Levy. M Labor R 100:3-24 D '77

LABOR and laboring classes—United States —*Continued*
Trends in labor. See issues of U.S. news and world report
Work in the year 2001. W. Abbott. Current 193:31-9 My '77
See also
Labor laws and legislation—United States
Labor supply—United States
Strikes—United States
Wages—United States
LABOR and the church. See Church and labor
LABOR boards, councils, etc.
Carter says yes to a labor-business panel. Bus W p33 Mr 21 '77
Unofficial adviser on labor-management; J. T. Dunlop. por Bus W p33-4 Je 13 '77
See also
United States—National Labor Relations Board
LABOR contracts
See also
Collective labor agreements
LABOR cost
Productivity and costs in the first quarter, 1977. J. R. Norsworthy and L. J. Fulco. il M Labor R 100:38-40 Ag '77
Productivity and costs in the second quarter. J. R. Norsworthy and L. J. Fulco. il M Labor R 100:34-8 N '77
Productivity and costs in the third quarter, 1976. J. R. Norsworthy and L. J. Fulco. il M Labor R 100:75-9 F '77
Productivity and unit labor costs in 12 industrial countries. B. Boner and A. Neef. bibl il M Labor R 100:11-17 Jl '77
LABOR discipline
Discipline without tears: be positive, not punitive; views of Richard Grote. J. Horn. Psychol Today 11:34+ N '77
See also
Work rules
LABOR disputes
See also
Collective bargaining
Injunctions
Strikes
United States—Federal Mediation and Conciliation Service
LABOR ethics
Can anybody clean up the Teamsters? A. H. Raskin; reply with rejoinder. R. Billings. N Y Times Mag p62-3 Ja 16 '77
LABOR force. See Labor supply
LABOR in politics. See Trade unions—Political activities
LABOR incentives. See Incentives in industry
LABOR laws and legislation
See also
Hours of labor
Insurance, Workmens compensation

Canada

Pro-union bill scares Quebec business. il Bus W p 108 O 24 '77

Quebec (province)

See Labor laws and legislation—Canada

United States

AFL-CIO rebuffed on shoe imports, situs picketing. L. Bornstein and others. M Labor R 100:64 Je '77
AFL-CIO: set to bargain hard with Congress. il Bus W p68+ Mr 7 '77
Agricultural labor relations laws in four states—a comparison; approaches to bargaining rights and strikes. K. S. Koziara. bibl M Labor R 100:14-18 My '77
Battle that's brewing over changes in labor laws. il U.S. News 83:77-8 Jl 25 '77
Big labor's big defeat; common-situs picketing bill. T. Nicholson and others. il Newsweek 89:54+ Ap 4 '77
Business fights union power grab; proposed reforms of National Labor Relations Act. il Nations Bus 65:21-4+ S '77
Carter's detente; proposed reforms of the National Labor Relations Act. T. Nicholson and J. B. Copeland. Newsweek 90:64+ Jl 25 '77
Dealing for jobs; Humphrey-Hawkins Full Employment and Balanced Growth Act of 1976. J. Osborne. New Repub 177:6+ N 12 '77
Don't just stand there! Do something! J. A. Briggs. il Forbes 120:29-31 O 1 '77
Endorsed by Carter: nationwide job policy; Full Employment and Balanced Growth Act. U.S. News 83:38 N 28 '77
Get ready to battle for your property rights. L. Lane. il Farm J 101:K3-4+ mid-Mr '77
Guaranteed jobs for economists; Humphrey-Hawkins Full Employment and Balanced Growth Act. New Repub 177:5-6 D 17 '77
Hot battle over labor law reform. J. M. Berry. il Forbes 120:21-2 S 1 '77
Job on jobs; unemployment legislation. F. Getlein. Commonweal 104:776-7 D 9 '77
Jobs for youth; the Youth Employment and Demonstration Projects Act. F. H. Armstrong. il Am For 83:30-3+ N '77
Labor reform faces potent opposition. Bus W p34+ My 2 '77
Labor sets wage, overtime policy; Fair Labor Standards Act. Am City & County 92:44 S '77
Labor tests Carter with a picketing bill. Bus W p27 F 28 '77
Labor's call on Carter; AFL-CIO program. T. Nicholson and T. Joyce. il por Newsweek 89:60-1 Mr 7 '77
Labor's new Southern strategy; AFL-CIO support of Labor Reform Act of 1977. il map Bus W p28-9 F 7 '77
Man Carter counts on to bolster ties with labor. il por U.S. News 83:87-8 O 10 '77
Meany draws up his shopping list; with report on Bal Harbour, Fla. executive council meeting by P. Taubman. il por Time 109:43-4 Mr 7 '77
Mixed results of labor-law reform. il Bus W p86 N 7 '77
New chill in labor relations. il Bus W p32-3 O 24 '77
New union drive for one-sided labor law. il Nations Bus 65:18-21 Jl '77
Peace with Jimmy, war on the Hill. il Time 110:47-8 Jl 25 '77
Rapid decline in political clout; AFL-CIO. il Time 109:55+ Ap 11 '77
Sanitizing of Humphrey-Hawkins. N. Jonas. Bus W p41 N 28 '77
Significant decisions in labor cases. C. Polhemus. See issues of Monthly labor review
Significant labor decision—an analysis. C. E. Polhemus. bibl f M Labor R 100:36-41 Ja '77
State labor legislation enacted in 1976. D. T. Bond. M Labor R 100:25-38 F '77
Storm brews over union demands on Congress; AFL-CIO. il U.S. News 82:88-9 Mr 7 '77
Unemployed youth: now a global worry; youth employment bill. il Bus W p21-2 Ag 1 '77
Unemployment and taxes; Humphrey-Hawkins bill. A. B. Laffer. il Nat R 29:148-50 F 4 '77
Unemployment goal? Humphrey-Hawkins bill. il Time 110:89+ N 28 '77
Unions and Carter: prospects for labor-law reform. W. B. Gould. Nation 224:466-8 Ap 16 '77
Unions hit the comeback trail in Congress. U.S. News 83:112+ O 17 '77
Unions' sweet hopes turn sour. F. W. Frailey. U.S. News 82:93 Ap 11 '77
What job for you? age eligibility provisions of the Fair Labor Standards Act. il Sr Schol 110:29 S 22 '77
What situs taught the unions. il Bus W p 100 Ap 11 '77
Who speaks for labor? defeats of common situs picketing bill and large increase in the minimum wage. Nation 224:418 Ap 9 '77
See also
Arbitration, Industrial—United States
Minimum wage—United States

Taft-Hartley law

Is Congress becoming more practical? il Nations Bus 65:30-3 N '77
Should we repeal 14B? L. A. O'Donnell. America 136:354-5 Ap 16 '77
LABOR leaders. See Trade unions—Officials
LABOR lobby. See Lobbyists and lobbying
LABOR-management cooperation. See Employees representation in management
LABOR mobility
New layer of structural unemployment; older blue-collar workers. il map Bus W p 142+ N 14 '77
Revolving door. K. Bode. New Repub 177:11-12 Jl 9 '77
LABOR movement. See Trade unions—United States—History
LABOR newspapers. See Labor press
LABOR officials. See Trade unions—Officials
LABOR output. See Labor productivity
LABOR Party (Great Britain)
Anglocommunism? R. Moss. Commentary 63:27-33 F '77; Discussion. Nation 224:298-300 Mr 12 '77; Commentary 63:6+ My; 64:18-19 Jl '77
Britain: a real estate flop embarrasses Labor Bus W p42+ F 7 '77
Britain's Labour Party at the crossroads. D. H. Katz. il Intellect 106:206-7 D '77
Parting company; P. Johnson. Nat R 29:1099 S 30 '77
See also
Trades Union Congress
LABOR Party (Israel) See Political parties—Israel
LABOR Party Properties Ltd. See Real estate business—Great Britain
LABOR press
Sorry state of the labor press. R. Nader. Progressive 41:29-31 O '77
30 million readers. Nation 225:452-3 N 5 '77
LABOR productivity
Human dimension in productivity; address, January 19, 1977. T. C. McDermott. Vital Speeches 43:306-9 Mr 1 '77
More inflation talk—and why. il Newsweek 89:61 Mr 7 '77

LABOR productivity
New-car dealers experience long-term gains in productivity. J. Duke. bibl il M Labor R 100:29-33 Mr '77
Output per unit of labor input in the retail food store industry. J. L. Carey and P. F. Otto. bibl f il M Labor R 100:42-6 Ja '77
Productivity and costs in the first quarter, 1977. J. R. Norsworthy and L. J. Fulco. il M Labor R 100:38-40 Ag '77
Productivity and costs in the second quarter. J. R. Norsworthy and L. J. Fulco. il M Labor R 100:34-8 N '77
Productivity and costs in the third quarter, 1976. J. R. Norsworthy and L. J. Fulco. il M Labor R 100:75-9 F '77
Productivity and costs in the fourth quarter. J. R. Norsworthy and L. J. Fulco. bibl il M Labor R 100:68-71 Ap '77
Productivity and unit labor costs in 12 industrial countries. B. Boner and A. Neef. bibl il M Labor R 100:11-17 Jl '77
Productivity—at what price? Progressive 41:8 Ap '77
Productivity center wins broad backing. por Bus W p39 F 14 '77
Productivity data. See issues of Monthly labor review
Productivity in grain mill products: output up, employment stable. J. A. Urisko. bibl il M Labor R 100:38-43 Ap '77
Productivity in sawmills increases as labor input declines substantially. J. Duke and C. Huffstutler. bibl il M Labor R 100:33-7 Ap '77
Productivity is a worry again. il Bus W p22-3 Ag 22 '77
Productivity rates rose in 1976 for almost all industries surveyed. A. S. Herman. il M Labor R 100:57-60 O '77
Productivity slowdown and the outlook to 1985. R. E. Kutschter and others. bibl il M Labor R 100:3-8 My '77
Productivity: the road to improvement leads back to basics. A. R. Weber. por Duns R 110:11 Jl '77
Quality of working life and productivity; address, April 28, 1977. J. M. Rosow. Vital Speeches 43:496-8 Je 1 '77
Report on productivity gains in selected industries; manufacturing, mining, and other industries. A. S. Herman. bibl il M Labor R 100:80-3 F '77
Where white-collar status boosts productivity; Eaton Corp. il Bus W p80+ My 23 '77

LABOR Reform Act of 1977. See Labor laws and legislation—United States

LABOR Relations Board, National. See United States—National Labor Relations Board

LABOR standards
Establishing international fair labor standards. J. P. Windmuller. M Labor R 100:35-6 Mr '77

LABOR statistics. See Labor and laboring classes—Statistics

LABOR Statistics, Bureau of. See United States—Labor Statistics, Bureau of

LABOR studies. See Colleges and universities—Curriculum

LABOR supply
See also
College graduates—Employment
Education and manpower
Labor mobility
Unemployment
Women—Employment
Youth—Employment

Canada

Employment ratio as an indicator of aggregate demand pressure. C. Green. bibl il M Labor R 100:25-32 Ap '77

United States

Another look at working-age men who are not in the labor force. W. V. Deutermann, Jr. il M Labor R 100:9-14 Je '77
Education, work, and leisure: must they come in that order? F. Best and B. Stern. bibl il M Labor R 100:3-10 Jl '77
Employment ratio as an indicator of aggregate demand pressure. C. Green. bibl il M Labor R 100:25-32 Ap '77
Great male cop-out from the work ethic. il Bus W p 156+ N 14 '77
Growing number of mismatched employees. C. C. Clogg. Intellect 106:103-4 S '77
Labor force trends: a synthesis and analysis. R. W. Bednarzik and D. P. Klein. bibl il M Labor R 100:3-12 O '77
Specter of shortages—with unemployment. il Fortune 95:14 Mr '77
Where the jobs go begging. il Bus W p34-5 O 10 '77
Work experience of the population, 1976. A. M. Young. il M Labor R 100:43-7 N '77

LABOR turnover
Interstate occupational migration: an analysis of data from 1965-70. M. M. Kleiner. bibl il M Labor R 100:64-7 Ap '77
Job absence and turnover: a new source of data. M. G. Miner. il M Labor R 100:24-31 O '77
Why newly employed college graduates quit. F. S. Endicott. Intellect 106:103 S '77
Your job: the itch to switch. Changing T 31:25-8 D '77
See also
Labor mobility

LABOR unions. See Trade unions

LABORATORIES
See also
Atomic research laboratories
Biological laboratories
Johns Hopkins University, Baltimore—Applied Physics Laboratory
Medical laboratories
Sandia Laboratories
Testing laboratories

Architecture

IBM's Santa Teresa Laboratory. J. Nairn. il Archit Rec 162:99-104 Ag '77

LABORATORIES, Government
National laboratories: focused goals and field work hinted under DOE. W. D. Metz. il Science 198:901-4 D 2 '77
See also
Atomic research laboratories
United States—National Institutes of Health—Laboratories

LABORATORY animals
Are rats relevant? J. A. Miller. il Sci N 112:12-13 Jl 2 '77
Conserving nonhuman primates. il BioScience 27:228-9 Mr '77
See also
Animal experimentation
Diseases—Animal models
also names of laboratory animals, e.g. Mice

LABORATORY architecture. See Laboratories—Architecture

LABRANT, Lou
Profession in perspective. Engl J 66:6-9 Mr '77

LA BREA Discoveries Museum. See George C. Page Museum at La Brea Discoveries, Los Angeles

LABREQUE, Mort
Garbage—refuse or resource? il Pop Sci 210:95-8+ Je '77

LA BRIE, Henry G. 3d
Black press: 150 years old. bibl il Negro Hist Bull 40:705-7 My '77

LACARRIÈRE, Jacques
Village life among the ruins. il UNESCO Courier 30:29-30 O '77

LA CERRA, Patrick
(ed) See Scudo, P. Prophetic words

LACERTAE objects. See Radio sources (astronomy)

LACEWINGS
Meet the green lacewing. M. Sipe. il Org Gard & Farm 24:144+ Je '77
Sympatric speciation based on allelic changes at three loci: evidence from natural populations in two habitats. C. A. Tauber and M. J. Tauber. bibl Science 197:1298-9 S 23 '77
Two genes control seasonal isolation in sibling species. C. A. Tauber and others. bibl il Science 197:592-3 Ag 5 '77

LACEY, Robert
All about the Queen; excerpt from Majesty. il pors N Y Times Mag p28-31+ Ja 30 '77

LACHENALIAS. See Cape cowslips

LACHENBRUCH, David
Looking ahead. See issues of Radio-electronics
New boom in videocassette recorders. il House & Gard 149:62+ N '77

LACHKY, John
Process home movies at home? il Mod Phot 41:46+ Je '77

LACK, Larry
Land trusts: a practical route back to the land. il Org Gard & Farm 24:72-5 Ag '77

LA CORUÑA, Spain. See Coruña, Spain

LACOVARA, Philip A.
All about Koreagate. D. M. Alpern and others. il pors Newsweek 90:17+ Ag 1 '77 *

LACROSSE, Wis.
We built our service center on a landfill. il Am City & County 92:89-90 S '77

Education

See Education—Wisconsin

LACROSSE
Cornell's wild Irish rose; victory over Johns Hopkins for the NCAA crown. J. Marshall. il Sports Illus 46:63-4+ Je 6 '77
Lacrosse comes west; where to see major spring tournaments. il Sunset 158:60 Mr '77
You can't beat this game with a stick; photographs; with report by M. Donavan. D. Baliotti. Sports Illus 46:34-9 Ap 25 '77

LA CROSSE virus. See Viruses

LACTATE dehydrogenase. See Dehydrogenases

LACTOFERRIN
Bactericidal effect for human lactoferrin. R. R. Arnold and others. bibl il Science 197:263-5 Jl 15 '77

LADAKH
Adventureland: the Himalayas; visiting Tibetan Buddhist monasteries. G. Baeyens. il Vogue 167:180+ My '77
Ladakh: a journey. N. Ellena and G. Ellena. il map Travel 147:24-31+ F '77
LADBROKE Group. See Gambling—Great Britain
LADD, Everett Carll, Jr
Democrats have their own two-party system. il Fortune 96:212-18+ O '77
Reform is wrecking the U.S. party system. il Fortune 96:176-81+ N '77
Unmaking of the Republican Party. il maps Fortune 96:90-5+ S '77
LADDERS
McCall's handywoman. il McCalls 104:84 Mr '77
LADEN, Lenny
Help for people society often ignores. il pors U.S. News 83:47 Ag 1 '77 *
LADENSON, Alex
Is the library an educational institution? il por Wilson Lib Bull 51:576-81 Mr '77
LADERMAN, Ezra
Laderman works are commissioned and aired on CBS. Hi Fi 27:MA35 Jl '77 *
LADIES at the Alamo; drama. See Zindel, P.
LADIES' home journal
Weekend with Arnold Palmer; winners of the Ladies home journal golf contest. il Ladies Home J 94:78-9 O '77
Women of the year 1977. il Ladies Home J 94:75-7 Je '77
LADNER, Joyce A.
Black woman today. il por Ebony 32:33-6+ Ag '77
Mixed families: white parents and black children; excerpt from Mixed families: adopting across racial boundaries. bibl il Society 14:70-8 S '77
LADY beetles. See Ladybirds
LADYBIRDS
Improving lady beetle efficiency. il Org Gard & Farm 25:46-9 Ja '78
LADYBUGS. See Ladybirds
LAETRILE
Battle to legitimize laetrile continues unabated. C. Holden. Science 196:854 My 20 '77
Cancer researcher looks at laetrile. B. H. Morrison. il Chemistry 50:21-3 Jl '77
Challenging the apricot-pit gang; Senate investigation. il Time 110:58 Jl 25 '77
Cruel hope. Nation 224:645 My 28 '77
Damn the doctors—and Washington. il map Time 109:50+ Je 20 '77
Freedom of choice and apricot pits; Time essay. F. Golden. il Time 109:54 Je 20 '77
Hard look at laetrile. A. E. Nourse. Good H 185:44+ S '77
Laetrile apricot pits brew up cancer therapy storm. Sci Digest 82:20-2+ Ag '77
Laetrile at Sloan-Kettering: a question of ambiguity. N. Wade. Science 198:1231-4 D 23 '77
Laetrile: should it be banned? M. Clark and others. il Newsweek 89:48-53+ Je 27 '77
Laetrile: the political success of a scientific failure. Consumer Rep 42:444-7 Ag '77
Laetrile: the science behind the controversy. J. Arehart-Treichel. il Sci N 112:92-5 Ag 6 '77
Latest in health and medicine. il U.S. News 82:78 Je 6 '77
Legalize laetrile as a cancer drug? interviews. S. D. Symms; D. T. Carr. pors U.S. News 82:51-2 Je 13 '77
Legalizing laetrile. J. Seligman. il Newsweek 89:74 My 2 '77
Mandelonitrile β-glucuronide: synthesis and characterization. C. Fenselau and others. bibl il Science 198:625-7 N 11 '77
Testing laetrile—sort of. Newsweek 89:39 Je 6 '77
Three case histories. J. Seligmann. il Newsweek 89:52-3 Je 27 '77
U.S. government and laetrile. N. Cousins. Sat R 5:11 O 1 '77
Victories for laetrile's lobby. il Time 109:97-8 My 23 '77
Why laetrile won't go away. L. Edson. il N Y Times Mag p41+ N 27 '77
LAFAYETTE, Marie Joseph Paul Yves Roch Gilbert du Motier, Marquis de
Imprisonment of Lafayette. J. W. Baker. il Am Heritage 28:86-91 Je '77 *
LAFAYETTE, Calif.
New confidence. il U.S. News 82:26+ Je 13 '77
LAFFER, Arthur B.
Unemployment and taxes. il Nat R 29:148-50 F 4 '77
L'AFFILARD, Michel
L'Affilard's published Sketchbooks. E. Schwandt. bibl f il Mus Q 63:99-113 Ja '77 *
LAFLEUR, Guy
On the whole, it's the donut line. J. Kirshenbaum. il pors Sports Illus 46:26-9 F 7 '77 *
LAFOSSE, Edmund
Spotlight on: Edmund LaFosse; interview, ed by J. Gruen. il pors Dance Mag 51:66-9 Je '77
LAGERFELD, Karl
Chez Kenzo, chez Karl. M. Russell. il pors N Y Times Mag p 130-1 N 27 '77 *
LAGONDA (automobile) See Automobiles, Foreign
LAGOONS, Sewage. See Sewage lagoons
LAGOS, Nigeria
Political transition in urban Africa; Mushin sector. S. T. Barnes. bibl f Ann Am Acad 432:26-41 Jl '77
LAGUARDIA, Robert
Soap gets in your eyes. il Sat Eve Post 249:40-1+ S '77
LAHR, John
Fearful symmetry. Harpers 255:83-4 Jl '77
Notes on fame. Harpers 256:77-80 Ja '78
LAING, Hector
Touch of British realism. por Forbes 119:32 Ap 15 '77 *
LAIRD, Emil Matthew
Laird. T. West. il Flying 101:74 S '77 *
LAIRD, Melvin R.
Arms control: the Russians are cheating! Read Digest 111:97-101 D '77
Energy crisis: made in U.S.A. Read Digest 111:56-60 S '77
LAITY

Catholic Church

Assessment and anticipation; Chicago declaration of Christian concern. Commonweal 104:803-4 D 23 '77
New secretariat. A. McCarthy. Commonweal 104:586+ S 16 '77
LAJEUNESSE, William J.
Inherit the winds. il Sat Eve Post 249:52-3+ S '77
LAKAT, Michael F.
In pursuit of hunger: physiological considerations. bibl il Intellect 105:261-2 F '77
LAKE, Alice
Little boy who cheated death. il por Good H 185:96+ S '77
What women don't know about the medicines they take. McCalls 104:117+ Je '77
(ed) When your love affair turns into marriage. il Redbook 148:72+ F '77
LAKE, Anthony
Africa in a global perspective; October 27, 1977. Dept State Bull 77:842-8 D 12 '77
LAKE, C. Raymond, and Ziegler, M. G.
Lesch-Nyhan syndrome: low dopamine-β-hydroxylase activity and diminished sympathetic response to stress and posture. bibl il Science 196:905-6 My 20 '77
LAKE, Laura Marie
Out of court. por Forbes 119:142 Ap 15 '77 *
LAKE CHAMPLAIN. See Champlain, Lake
LAKE CHARLES, La.

Crime

See Crime and criminals—Louisiana
LAKE CLARK National Park (proposed) See National parks and reserves—Alaska
LAKE County, Oregon
Oregon desert graveyard for leaking herbicide wastes. P. L. Fradkin. Audubon 79:127 Ja '77
LAKE HAVASU City race. See Motor boat racing
LAKE pollution. See Water pollution
LAKE POWELL. See Powell, Lake
LAKE SUPERIOR. See Superior, Lake
LAKE TAHOE, Calif

Education

See Education—California
LAKE TAHOE Regional Planning Agency
Can Tahoe be saved? J. Degnan. Commonweal 105:13-14 Ja 6 '78
LAKE WINONA (Minnesota) See Winona, Lake (Minnesota)
LAKER, Frederick Alfred
Champ of the cheap flight. G. Sereny. il pors N Y Times Mag p 14+ S 4 '77 *
Sing a song of Skytrain. S. Birnbaum. Esquire 88:17-18 Jl '77 *
Skytrain: I'm Freddie. Fly me. il por Time 109:37 Ja 31 '77 *
Swashbuckler in the sky. H. Sutton. il por Sat R 4:50+ Mr 19 '77 *
LAKER, Rosalind
Promises to keep; story; excerpt from Ride the blue riband. Good H 184:187-90 My '77
LAKER Airways. See Airlines—Great Britain
LAKES
9 up-and-coming lakes; bass fishing; symposium. il Outdoor Life 159:66-73+ Ap '77
See also
Great Lakes
Water pollution

Temperature

See also
Ice on rivers, lakes, etc.

Alaska

Meteorite crater identified in Alaska; Sithylemenkat Lake. il Sci N 111:405-6 Je 25 '77
Meteorite impact crater discovered in central Alaska with Landsat imagery; Sithylemenkat Lake. P. J. Cannon. il Science 196:1322-4 Je 17 '77

LAKES—*Continued*

California

Highest reservoir-lakes in Marin welcome you. il map Sunset 158:48 Mr '77

Connecticut

Allelopathic influence on blue-green bloom sequence in a eutrophic lake. K. I. Keating. bibl il Science 196:885-7 My 20 '77

Michigan

Return to Sage Lake. R. Rau. il Nat Wildlife 15:36-9 Ap '77

Minnesota

See also
Winona, Lake

LAKES, Artificial
See also
Powell, Lake
Reservoirs

LAKESIDE Studio (firm)
Lakeside Studio: conserving the printmaking tradition. C. Shapiro and D. Shapiro. il por Art N 76:51-4 Mr '77

LAKEWOOD, N.J.
Gazetteer. il Ret Liv 17:39+ S '77

LAKEWOOD, Ohio

Education

See Education—Ohio

LAKOFSKY, Charles
Comment (cont) bibl f Ceram Mo 25:17+ Ap '77

LAKOWICZ, Joseph R. See Omann, G. jt auth
Closer to Indira. il por Time 110:29 S 5 '77 *

LAL, Bansi
Closer to Indira. il por Times 110:29 S 5 '77 *
Sanjay in the dock. K. Willenson and R. Ramanujam. il por Newsweek 90:45 S 5 '77 *

LAL, D.
Oceanic microcosm of particles. bibl il maps Science 198:997-1009 D 9 '77

LALANNE, Claude
Risible, visible—who cares as long as it's fun. R. Wernick. il pors Smithsonian 7:74-5+ F '77 *

LALANNE, François Xavier
Risible, visible—who cares as long at it's fun. R. Wernick. il pors Smithsonian 7:74-5+ F '77 *

LA LANNE, Jack
How I stay in shape. il Sat Eve Post 249:34 Mr '77

LALIQUE, René Jules
Renee Lalique. il Hobbies 82:95-7 Ja '78 *

LALIQUE glass. See Glassware

LALL, Betty Goetz
Mutual deterrence: the need for a new definition. Bull Atom Sci 33:10-11 D '77

LALLO (poet)
Harvester; poem. Nation 224:444 Ap 9 '77

LAMARCK, Jean Baptiste Pierre Antoine de Monet de
Piaget and Lamarck. F. J. Thomas. Educ Digest 43:47-9 N '77 *

LAMAZE method. See Childbirth

LAMB, Claudia
Heather Hartman, Heather Hartman . . . Claudia Lamb, Claudia Lamb . . . il pors Seventeen 36:140-3 Je '77 *

LAMB, James C.
Who controls rudderless regulatory ship-of-state? excerpt from address, August 1976. Am City & County 92:76+ Mr '77

LAMB, Julia
Boating. il Sports Illus 46:55-6+ Je 6 '77

LAMB, Lawrence E.
Energy and how to have more of it. Harp Baz 110:89+ My '77

LAMB, Robert
Mystery of steel prices. il Fortune 95:158-60 Mr '77
New crop of M.B.A.'s goes looking for that fast track. Fortune 95:160+ Je '77
Professional schools: cram courses in tension and trauma. il N Y Times Mag p49+ N 20 '77

LAMB, Russ
Mt Rainier inside and out; photographs. il Am For 83:39-40 Mr '77

LAMB (meat)
See also
Cookery—Meat

LAMBDIN, Bethany B. See Bacot, H. P. jt auth

LAMBERG, Lynne
Grooming. Bet Hom & Gard 55:59-60 F; 26+ Ap; 162+ Je; 34+ Jl; 74+ N '77
Health. Bet Hom & Gard 55:47-8+ F '77
What to do for your aching feet. Bet Hom & Gard 55:231-2 S '77

LAMBERG, Walter J.
Helping reluctant readers help themselves: interest inventories. bibl f il Engl J 66:40-4 N '77

LAMBERT, Eleanor
Eleanor Lambert entertains. C. Porcelli. il por House B 119:122-3 O '77 *

LAMBERT, Johann Heinrich
Lambert: self-taught physicist. S. L. Laki. bibl il por Phys Today 30:25-30+ S '77 *

LAMBERT, Léon Jean Gustave, Baron
Lambert's widening beachhead in the U. S. il por Bus W p 102-3 F 21 '77 *

LAMBERT, Rollins E.
Reducing investments in South Africa. map America 136:130-2 F 12 '77

LAMBERT, Saul
Letter from the publisher. J. Meyers. il Sports Illus 46:4 Mr 14 '77 *

LAMBERT Brussells Corporation. See Holding companies—Belgium

LAMBORGHINI (sports cars) See Sports cars

LAMBORN, Robert L.
Private schools: in support of diversity. Educ Digest 43:53-5 O '77

LAMBRAY, Maureen
Best friends. il Esquire 87:83-6 My '77

LAMENNAIS, Hugues Felicité Robert de
On Lamennais, Chaadaev, and the romantic revolt in France and Russia. N. V. Riasanovsky. bibl f pors Am Hist R 82:1165-86 D '77 *

LAMM, Michael
Retrospect. il Motor T 29:119-23 Je; 66+ O '77

LAMMEY, W. Clyde
Homeowners' clinic; questions and answers. See issues of Popular mechanics

LAMONT, Donal R. Bp
Bishop Lamont deported. America 136:312 Ap 9 '77 *

LAMOTT, Kenneth
Impudent magical silicon chip. il Horizon 19:72-7 Jl '77
Why men and women think differently. il Horizon 19:40-5 My '77

LAMPARSKI, L. L. See Stehl, R. H. jt auth

LAMPE, David
Ersatz gasoline. Sci Digest 82:65-7 O '77
Nursing an ambulance and a county. il pors Fam Health 92:28-30 Je '77
Physicians + physicists=far-out medicine. il Fam Health 9:48-50 S '77
Simulated wounds for use in first-aid training. il Sci Digest 82:76-8 N '77
Unloved and unloving, the armadillo blunders on. il Nat Wildlife 15:34-7 F '77
Vast balloons create confusion. Sci Digest 82:33-5 Jl '77
Yes, we now have firewomen. il House B 119:12+ Mr '77

LAMPERT, Rachel
Reviews; Rachel Lampert at the NYU School of the Arts. D. Vaughan. Dance Mag 51:40-1+ O '77 *

LAMPMAN, Ben Hur
Storm on the river; excerpt from Where would you go? il Read Digest 111:33-4 Ag '77

LAMPMAN, Robert J.
Who pays for social security? il Society 14:54-6 My '77

LAMPORT, Felicia
It takes a heap of compost to make a house a mess; poem. Atlantic 240:102 N '77
Middle-aged spread. il McCalls 105:216-17 N '77

LAMPS
American historical glass. M. Wollett and B. Wollett. il Hobbies 82:99 Jl '77
Lamps and candlesticks of the Meriden Britannia Company. R. L. Bowen, Jr. bibl il Antiques 111:332-7 F '77
See also
Electric lamps

LAMU (island and town)
Lamu door carving. M. M. Michie. il Design (US) 78:26 mid-Wint '77

LANCASTER, Donald E.
Build the TVT-6: a low-cost direct video display. il Pop Electr 12:47-52 Jl; 49-55 Ag '77
Hex-to-ASCII converter for your TVT-6. il Pop Electr 12:49-52 O '77
Six CMOS circuits for experimenters. il Pop Electr 11:46-7 Ap '77

LANCASTER, Paul
Night the lights almost went out. Fortune 95:57 My '77

LANCASTER, Pa.

Water supply

See Water supply—Pennsylvania

LANCE, James W.
Headaches: the causes & the cures; interview, ed by P. Lehmann. Harp Baz 111:158-9+ N '77

LANCE, Kathryn
Senior serial. See issues of Senior scholastic including World week

LANCE, Thomas Bertram
Carter's Mr Inside; excerpts from interview, ed by L. Martz and R. Thomas. por Newsweek 89:86 Ap 11 '77
OMB director Bert Lance seeks business help; interview, ed by R. L. Lesher. il pors Nations Bus 65:18-22+ My '77
Top official spells out Carter's plans for business; interview. il por U.S. News 82:16-18 F 7 '77

about

And at home, the Lance case puts Carter on the spot. por U.S. News 83:15 S 5 '77 *
Assistant president. M. Berss. il pors Forbes 119:27-9 Mr 1 '77 *

LANCE, Thomas Bertram—about—*Continued*
Atlanta banker at the cutting edge. por Fortune 95:87 Ja '77 *
Beat goes on. S. Fraker and others. il por Newsweek 90:17-18 S 5 '77 *
Bert, I'm proud of you. il pors Time 110:8-10 Ag 29 '77 *
Bert Lance's bind. M. Ruby and others. il por Newsweek 90:69-70+ Jl 18 '77 *
Bert Lance's OMB plays weaker role. il Bus W p23-4 Ag 29 '77 *
Big showdown over banker Bert. il por Time 110:19-20 Ag 22 '77 *
Budget chief's balance sheet. por Time 109:38 My 23 '77 *
Can Carter afford Lance? Why Jimmy stays loyal. il pors Time 110:8-10 S 12 '77 *
Case against Lance—and his reply. il pors U.S. News 83:21-2 S 26 '77 *
Close to the exit? S. Fraker and others. il por Newsweek 90:25-6 S 12 '77 *
Conservative sensationalism. Nat R 29:1038-9 S 16 '77 *
Dangling Justice. M. Stone. U.S. News 83:94 O 10 '77 *
Don't underestimate Bert. P. Taubman. por Time 109:16 F 28 '77 *
Double standard. F. Getlein. Commonweal 104:644-5 O 14 '77 *
Dumping Bert. J. Osborne. New Repub 177:8+ S 17 '77 *
For budget chief: a money problem all his own. por U.S. News 83:65 Jl 25 '77 *
Funny money banking. Nation 225:196-7 S 10 '77 *
Genial sharper. Nation 225:258-9 S 24 '77 *
Getting your man; B. Lance case. T. Griffith. Time 110:79 O 17 '77 *
Going to bat for beleaguered Bert. il por Time 110:26+ Jl 25 '77 *
Headaches pile up for Carter in Lance affair. il U.S. News 83:25-6 S 19 '77 *
Higher standard. J. M. Wall. Chr Cent 94:771-2 S 14 '77; Discussion. 94:1035-6 N 9 '77 *
His life and good times. R. Steele and others. il pors Newsweek 90:23+ Ag 29 '77 *
How bankers view Bert. Time 110:16+ S 19 '77 *
I'll never lie to you. Commonweal 104:611-12 S 30 '77 *
In-hock director. Nation 225:98-9 Ag 6 '77 *
Is Bert Lance losing his clout? il por U.S. News 83:21 Ag 8 '77*
Is he home free? P. Goldman and others. il pors Newsweek 90:16-17+ Ag 29 '77 *
Jimmy behind closed doors. H. Sidey. Time 110:10 S 19 '77 *
Jimmy Carter gets mixed marks in economics. I. J. Cameron. il pors Fortune 95:98-102+ Je '77 *
Lance: a gathering storm. M. Ruby and others. Newsweek 90:49-50 Ag 22 '77 *
Lance affair: an official report gives an inside look at banking. il por U.S. News 83:62-4 Ag 29 '77 *
Lance alone. D. M. Alpern and others. por Newsweek 90:14-15 Ag 15 '77 *
Lance and Carter. M. Stone. U.S. News 83:88 S 12 '77 *
Lance, bent but not broke. Nation 225:164-5 S 3 '77 *
Lance, Carter, Babbitt and Gantry. G. F. Will. Newsweek 90:122 S 19 '77 *
Lance comes out swinging. il pors Time 110:12-18+ S 26 '77 *
Lance: going, going...; Country slicker. il pors Time 110:6-10+ S 19 '77 *
Lance is rethinking the role of the SEC. Bus W p36+ F 28 '77 *
Lance on the carpet. M. Ruby and R. Thomas. il por Newsweek 90:57-8 Ag 1 '77 *
Lance on the offense. R. Steele and others. il pors Newsweek 90:20-3+ S 26 '77 *
Lance on the rise. T. Nicholson and J. Walcott. il por Newsweek 90:66+ O 31 '77 *
Lancegate: why Carter stuck it out. W. Safire. il pors N Y Times Mag p37-9+ O 16 '77 *
Lance's contribution to tough banking laws. Bus W p28-9 S 5 '77 *
Lance's loan. Time 110:10 Ag 15 '77 *
Letter from Washington. R. Rovere. New Yorker 53:131-4 S 12 '77 *
Ovation for Bert. il por Time 110:34 O 10 '77 *
Patting Bert on the back. por Time 110:31 Ag 8 '77 *
Perils of Bert Lance. A. J. Mayer and others. il por Newsweek 90:62 Ag 8 '77 *
Public morality after Bert Lance. J. Castelli. America 137:280-2 O 29 '77 *
Reporter at large. E. B. Drew. New Yorker 53:156-62+ O 10 '77 *
Send Lance back to banking. por New Repub 177:10-12 Ag 6 '77 *
Sharpening battle over Bert Lance. il por Time 110:6-8 Ag 1 '77 *
Spenders vs. savers: split in the Cabinet. W. C. Bryant. il pors U.S. News 82:18 Ap 18 '77 *
Sticking it to Bert. J. Osborne. New Repub 177:10-11 S 10 '77 *
Sticking up for Bert. J. Osborne. New Repub 177:8-10 S 3 '77 *
Still a good old boy. Nation 225:707-8 D 31 '77 *
Suddenly everybody is looking at the way banks do business. U. S. News 83:51-3 S 12 '77 *
Surprising turn in saga of Bert Lance. pors U.S. News 84:36 Ja 9 '78 *
Turning the bird dogs loose; press coverage. Time 110:117 S 19 '77 *
Was he hounded out? D. Gelman and L. Howard. Newsweek 90:35 O 3 '77 *
What damage to Carter? R. Steele and others. il pors Newsweek 90:24-6+ S 19 '77 *
What the report says. M. Ruby and others. il Newsweek 90:18-19 Ag 29 '77 *

Anecdotes, facetiae, satire, etc.

How it might have gone. W. F. Buckley, Jr. Nat R 29:1194-5 O 14 '77
Talk with a banker. New Repub 177:2+ O 1 '77

Resignation

Back to denim. R. Boeth and others. il Newsweek 90:24-5 O 3 '77
Bad day all around. Nation 225:290 O 1 '77
Behind the painful decision to quit. il Time 110:16-18+ O 3 '77
Lance, finis. New Repub 177:5+ O 1 '77
Lance heads home—Carter picks up the pieces. il por U.S. News 83:17-20 O 3 '77
Lance: wounding Carter. il pors Time 110:14-16 O 3 '77
Picking up the pieces. R. Steele and others. il pors map Newsweek 90:22-3+ O 3 '77
Whistling Dixie. Nation 225:322 O 8 '77

LANCE, Inc. See Food industry

LANCE missiles. See Guided missiles

LANCIA (automobile) See Automobiles, Foreign

LANCIA & Company. See Automobile industry—Italy

LAND, Edwin Herbert
Retinex theory of color vision; with biographical sketch. il Sci Am 237:10, 108-20+ bibl(p 190) D '77

about

Land's new wonder. L. Langway and others. il por Newsweek 89:75+ My 9 '77 *

LAND, Philip
Stewardship and the NIEO. il New Cath World 220:244-9 S '77

LAND, Thomas
Portugal's returnees. Progressive 41:50 D '77

LAND
What is marginal land? L. Reichenberger. il Suc Farm 75:23+ Ja '77
See also
Easements
Land utilization
Public lands
Real estate business
Real property
Reclamation of land
Wetlands

Prices

See Land values

Taxation

See Real property tax

California

Farmers vs. agribusiness: the new winning of the West; controversy over enforcement of the National Reclamation Law. M. E. Leary. Nation 225:646-50 D 17 '77

Idaho

Last Idaho land rush: growth at any cost? E. Chaney. Audubon 79:154-7 N '77

Missouri

1,436-acre legacy; donation of farm land to state. D. Wooldridge. por Outdoor Life 161:22 Ja '78

United States

Gaining momentum: a drive to stop suburban sprawl; farmland. il U.S. News 82:82-4 Mr 21 '77
Scramble to buy U.S. land spreads all over the world. il U.S. News 83:78-9 S 12 '77
Soaring farmland values: the way your state compares. il U.S. News 82:61 F 7 '77
See also
Public lands—United States

Wisconsin

Soil deterioration and the growing world demand for food. R. A. Brink and others. bibl il Science 197:625-30 Ag 12 '77

LAND and Water Conservation Fund. See United States—Interior, Department of the—Appropriations and expenditures

LAND buying. See Real Estate investment

LAND development business. See **Real estate business**

LAND fills. See **Filling (earthwork)**

LAND Management, Bureau of. See United States—Land Management, Bureau of

LAND planning. See Land utilization
LAND reclamation. See Reclamation of land
LAND reform
Down on the farm; regulations preventing ownership of more than 160 acres of federally watered land. A. J. Mayer and others. il Newsweek 90:67-8 S 5 '77
Fairness for farmers; question of enforcing limit on ownership of federally watered land. New Repub 177:2+ N 12 '77
Farmers vs. agribusiness: the new winning of the West; controversy over enforcement of the National Reclamation Law. M. E. Leary. Nation 225:646-50 D 17 '77
Homestead Act hits home. il Time 110:20 O 17 '77
U.S. Interior Department moves to enforce the law to break up big farms. Farm J 101:14 O '77

Great Britain

David Lloyd George: land, the budget, and social reform. B. B. Gilbert. Am Hist R 81:1058-66 D '76
LAND snails. See Snails
LAND speculation. See Real estate investment
LAND speed records. See Automobile speed records
LAND tenure
Concentrated ownership of land: a problem of stewardship and world hunger. M. M. Pignone. bibl il New Cath World 220:254-9 S '77
See also
Indians of North America—Land tenure
Land reform

Alaska

Observations on Alaska; question of Alaska Native Claims Settlement Act. L. S. Clapper and others. il Am For 83:22-3+ F '77

Canada

Canada's pipeline battle. R. L. Moellering. il Chr Cent 94:982-5 O 26 '77

Hawaii

Return of the natives to Kahoolawe; protesting Navy bombing. J. Wilde. il Time 110:32 Ag 8 '77

Maine

As Maine goes. . . ? claims of the Passamaquoddy and Penobscot Indians. map Time 109:21 Mr 14 '77
Carter's first Indian test; Penobscot and Passamaquoddy of Maine. Chr Cent 94:680 Ag 3 '77
Century of Pyrrhic victories: Indian lawsuits and white power; Passamaquoddy and Penobscott tribes. P. T. Shattuck and J. Norgren. il Nation 225:12-16 Jl 2 '77
Giving it back to the Indians; claims of Passamaquoddy and Penobscot Indians to land in Maine. R. McLaughlin. il map Atlantic 239: 70-4+ F '77
If Indian tribes win legal war to regain half of Maine—Penobscot and Passamaquoddy tribes. il map U.S. News 82:53-4 Ap 4 '77
Indians on the lawpath; Penobscot and Passamaquoddy tribes. S. Taylor. il New Repub 176:16-21 Ap 30 '77
Redeeming the time and the land: epilogue to 1776; claims of Penobscot and Passamaquoddy Indians. J. K. Larson. il Chr Cent 94:356-61 Ap 13 '77
This land is my land; Maine's Passamaquoddy and Penobscot Indians. D. M. Alpern and others. il map Newsweek 89:18+ Mr 14 '77

Oregon

From this valley they say we are going. J. E. Ross. bibl BioScience 27:254-8 Ap '77

United States

See also
Homesteads
LAND trusts
Partnership that pays off for the public; America Land Trust. il Nations Bus 65:46-8+ Jl '77
LAND use. See Land utilization
LAND utilization
Development vs. preservation. J. A. Behnke. BioScience 27:513 Ag '77
How is the land to be used? S. Smyser. Org Gard & Farm 24:68 Ag '77
Land exchange; case study involving Disney's resort plans and government land. R. F. Masse and C. Broussard. il map Parks & Rec 12:26-9+ D '77
Land use battles on the way out? study by Academy for Contemporary Problems. Am City & County 92:37 Ap '77
Meaning of multiple use. G. Reiger. Field & S 82:44+ Jl '77
Recreation review may stall PL 92-500 projects; coordination of wastewater treatment and open space and recreational planning. il Am City & County 92:13 O '77
Three axioms for land use. R. C. Austin. il Chr Cent 94:910-11+ O 12 '77
Vermont I know. C. Reidel. il Am For 83:30-3+ S '77
Washington scene; emerging options for preservation. B. S. Tindall. Parks & Rec 12:13+ D '77
See also
City planning
Regional planning
Shore protection
Suburbs

Conferences

Land-water symposium asks how to avert a crisis. E. M. Leeper. il BioScience 27:653-4 O '77

Laws and regulations

Administration discloses 92-million-acre Alaskan land proposal. il Nat Parks & Con Mag 51:28-30 N '77
Alaska: develop or conserve? Issue is moving toward a showdown; Alaska National Interest Lands Conservation Act. M. Hornblower. il map Smithsonian 8:38-49 bibl(p 134) D '77
Alaska national interest lands. Nat Parks & Con Mag 51:27-9 Je '77
Alaska's dilemma of untapped wealth. il map Bus W p 120+ Je 20 '77
Are conservationists asking for too much? national interest lands in Alaska. Nat Parks & Con Mag 51:26-9 S '77
Battle for the last frontier; Alaska National Interest Lands Conservation Act. N. King. il Nat R 29:722-4 Je 24 '77
Federal voice in private land-use: two views. M. K. Udall; S. D. Symms. pors Nations Bus 65: 18-20 Ag '77
Gaining momentum: a drive to stop suburban sprawl; farmland. il U.S. News 82:82-4 Mr 21 '77
Great Alaskan land battle. J. N. Miller. il Read Digest 111:128-34 D '77
Land use planning: coming in bits and pieces. G. L. Vincent. il Suc Farm 75:28-9+ Ja '77
NPCA urges approval of Alaska National Interest Lands Conservation Act. il Nat Parks & Con Mag 51:21-4+ Jl '77
Race to save wild Alaska; the Alaska National Interest Lands Conservation Act and related legislation. R. Cahn. il Liv Wildn 41:13-19 Jl '77
Viewpoint; managing Alaska's land. J. G. Deane. Liv Wildn 41:3 Jl '77
Washington control of land use feared. il Nations Bus 65:6 F '77
Who will win the battle of Alaska? J. N. Miller. map Read Digest 112:88-93 Ja '78
See also
Easements
LAND values
Land prices are running a fever! D. Paarlberg. por map Farm J 101:17-19 Ap '77
Midwest farmland values soaring. Farm J 101: J4 Mr '77
Soaring farmland values: the way your state compares. il U.S. News 82:61 F 7 '77
Why you can pay $2,000. . .$3,000. . .for farmland. L. Kruse. il Suc Farm 75:28+ Ap '77
Will the new estate tax law increase land prices? Suc Farm 75:K2 N '77
See also
Assessment
Real property—Valuation
LANDAU, Annette Henkin
Jewish sons; story. Commentary 63:40-2 F '77
LANDAU, Claire. See Landau, R. L. jt auth
LANDAU, Richard L. and Landau, Claire
Ask the doctor; questions and answers. See issues of Family health incorporating Today's health, June 1977-
LANDAU, Saul, and Stavins, Ralph
Letelier/Moffitt murder. por Nation 224:358-60 Mr 26 '77
LANDE, Nathaniel, and Slade, Afton
How to come to terms with yourself. Harp Baz 110:46-7+ Je '77
Nerves: mind and body therapies. Harp Baz 110:128-9+ Mr '77
Power of beauty. Harp Baz 111:122+ N '77
Psychotherapies: what's what; methods of noted therapists. Harp Baz 110:230+ S '77
Seven basic emotional problems & what you can do about them. Harp Baz 110:98-9+ Ap '77
Turning off: the great energizer. Harp Baz 110: 121+ Ag '77
LANDEGGER, Carl Clement
Where others fear to tread. il por Forbes 119: 96+ My 15 '77 *
LANDER, Kathleen
Printing calculators. il Pop Sci 212:59-61 Ja '78
LANDER, Toni
Bruce Marks and Toni Lander: breaking ground at Ballet West. J. Cumming. il pors Dance Mag 51:62-5 D '77 *
LANDERS, Ann, pseud
What my readers teach me. por Read Digest 111:175-8 N '77
LANDFILLS. See Filling (earthwork)

LANDI, Val
Historic trails to the wild country. il Outdoor Life 159:84-5+ Je '77
New maps & guides to adventure canoeing. Outdoor Life 160:72+ Ag '77
Rocky Mountain high time of your life. il Outdoor Life 159:70-5+ My '77

LANDING craft
Landing ship medium (LSM) H. J. Gorin. il Oceans 10:46-9 Mr '77

LANDING gear, Airplane. See Airplanes—Landing gear

LANDING ship medium. See Landing craft

LANDLORD and tenant
Money & your home. C. Carlson; J. M. Guttentag. il Ret Liv 17:34-9+ Ja '77
20 years a landlord & how it paid; investment in a single-family dwelling. R. H. Howard. il Changing T 31:40-2 O '77
Youngest landlord in Michigan; F. Simmons of Pontiac. il pors Ebony 32:140+ S '77
See also
Eviction

LANDMAN, Jonathan
Day in the life of Congressman David Obey. il pors Sr Schol 109:9-12 F 24 '77
(ed) See Alexander, C. Secretary of the Army Clifford Alexander . . . wants you
(ed) See Nader, R. Ralph Nader: You've got to make it work
(ed) See Porter, E. Photo and word views of pioneer photographer Eliot Porter

LANDMARKS, Historic. See Historic houses, sites, etc.

LANDON, Brooks
Radical Americanist. Nation 225:151-3 Ag 20 '77

LANDON, Butler
Transition diary. il por Newsweek 89:26+ Ja 24 '77

LANDON, Michael
Eugene Orowitz makes good; interview, ed by L. Garton. por Writers Digest 57:27 Ap '77

LANDOR, R. A.
Kittens; poem. New Repub 177:35 Ag 6 '77

LANDSBERG, Hans H.
Coal: the new swing fuel? Science 197:9 Jl 1 '77

LANDSBERG, Lewis. See Young, J. B. jt auth

LANDSCAPE architecture
Ground cover? It's rock. il Sunset 159:70-3 Ag '77
How to remodel your entry without remodeling. H. Wicks. il Pop Mech 148:128-31+ O '77
Landscape with timbers. V. D. Chase. Am Home 80:95-6 Ap '77
Landscaping with rock in the Tucson desert. il Sunset 159:268 O '77
Rock ground cover can work as a cover-up. il Sunset 159:156-7 Ag '77
Using a slide projector to help plan your garden. il Sunset 159:144-5 Ag '77
See also
Environmental design

LANDSCAPE gardening
How to shade and landscape your house to save energy; planting shade trees. J. Fanning. il House & Gard 149:35-6 Ag '77
It's all in 30 by 65 feet, all done on a budget: garden of Don and Juanita Walker. il Sunset 159:148-9 Jl '77
Landscaping with the not-too-thirsty succulents. il Sunset 159:238-9 N '77
Replant the lawn? What other attractive, unthirsty options? il Sunset 159:190-1 S '77
Sculptor's outdoor gallery; garden of William Snyder. il Sunset 159:150-1 Jl '77
Shaping of a garden; design for garden of the Frick Collection. R. Page. il por House & Gard 149:34+ Jl '77
Take-it-easy gardening. L. V. Power. il Am Home 80:22-3 Ap '77
Your own valuable space. W. R. Titus. il Horticulture 55:58-9 F '77
See also
Decks, patios, terraces, etc.
Driveways
Hedges
Home grounds
Lawns
also headings beginning Garden, Gardening, Gardens

LANDSCAPE of the body; drama. See Guare, J.

LANDSCAPE painting
Duane Wakeham: sharing a way of seeing; interview, ed by J. McCord. D. Wakeham. il por Am Artist 41:60-5 N '77
Forrest Moses: a man and his sanctuary; interview, ed by M. C. Nelson. F. Moses. il por Am Artist 41:44-9+ Ap '77
Looking for patterns: a conversation with Carl W. Peters; interview, ed by C. Movalli. C. W. Peters. il por Am Artist 41:56-61+ D '77
New landscape art: four contemporary artists go back to nature. L. R. Lippard. il Ms 5:68-73 Ap '77
Watercolor page: winter landscapes. W. B. Romeling. il Am Artist 41:52-5+ D '77
Winter landscapes; exhibition. S. B. Sherrill. il Antiques 112:1018 D '77

LANDSCAPE photography. See Photography—Landscapes

LANDSCAPE protection
Views. A. Brandt. il Atlantic 240:46-9 Jl '77
See also
Environmental movement
Nature Conservancy (organization)
Shore protection
Stream conservation
Wilderness areas

Maryland

Wye Island. D. J. Preston. il Am For 83:20-2+ N '77

Massachusetts

Yankee heritage is secured without government aid; Trustees of Reservations of Massachusetts. F. J. Pratson. il Smithsonian 8:92-9 Je '77

Vermont

Vermont I know. C. Reidel. il Am For 83:30-3+ S '77

Wyoming

Bold bid to preserve scenery; easement proposal in Jackson Hole. il Bus W p94 N 21 '77

LANDY, Arthur, and Ross, Wilma
Viral integration and excision: structure of the lambda *att* sites. bibl il Science 197:1147-60 S 16 '77

LANE, Frank E.
Extra hand at the tiller. il Motor B & S 139:88-9 F '77

LANE, Kenneth Jay
Kenneth Jay Lane entertains. C. Porcelli. il por House B 119:102-3 Mr '77 *

LANE, Marie Irene
Preschool craft activities. il SLJ 23:43 My '77

LANES, Selma G.
Case for The five Chinese brothers. il SLJ 24:90-1 O '77
Second look: Clever Bill. il Horn Bk 53:694-6 D '77

LANEY, James T.
Identity crisis in the seminaries. Chr Cent 94:95+ F 2 '77

LANFORD, William A.
Glass hydration: a method of dating glass objects. bibl il Science 196:975-6 My 27 '77

LANG, Daniel
Reporter in Germany. New Yorker 53:47-50+ O 3 '77

LANG, Donald
Silent one. J. K. Footlick and E. Sciolino. Newsweek 90:89+ N 7 '77 *

LANG, Frederick, and others
Developmental neuroethology: changes in escape and defensive behavior during growth of the lobster. bibl il Science 197:682-5 Ag 12 '77

LANG, George
Many tastes of Christmas. il N Y Times Mag p81+ D 18 '77
Our meal in Havana. il NY Times Mag p 122+ O 16 '77
Taste of China. il por N Y Times Mag p 108+ My 1 '77

about

Mangia, mangia; celebrating the new Met production of La Bohème. R. Jacobson. il pors Opera N 41:8-13 Mr 19 '77 *
Potpourri of George Lang. E. Brown. il por N Y Times Mag p 166-7 N 20 '77 *

LANG, Gertrude
Tips for over-55s traveling abroad. il Ret Liv 17:31-6 Ap '77
What's in your medicine cabinet? And what should be. il Ret Liv 17:35-7 My '77

LANG, Jeffrey W. See Garrick, L. D. jt auth

LANG, Jonathan
Winter night; Winter tree; Winter music; Winter landscape; poems. Poetry 130:23-4 Ap '77

LANG, Martin. See Dunbar, G. jt auth

LANG, Pearl, Dance Company. See Pearl Lang Dance Company

LANG, Sidney B. and Athenstaedt, Herbert
Pyroelectricity and induced pyroelectric polarization in leaves of the palmlike plant encephalartos villosus. bibl il Science 196:985-6 My 27 '77

LANGAN, Patricia A.
On your own time. il Fortune 96:25+ D '77

LANGER, Felicia
Israeli lawyer who defends Arabs. L. Rivlin. Ms 6:21 O '77 *

LANGER, Richard W. pseud
Carefree gardener. il N Y Times Mag p24-7+ Mr 13 '77
For nonstop color—geraniums. il House & Gard 149:76 Mr '77
Gesneriads: beyond the African violet. il House & Gard 149:52 F '77
Plants around the house. See issues of House & garden incorporating Living for young homemakers
Whale of a time. il House & Gard 149:62-4+ Ap '77

LANGERHANS, Fritz
Ship that hunted itself. C. Simpson. il pors map Read Digest 111:188-92+ S '77 *

LANGEWIESCHE, Wolfgang
Flying the F4U. il Flying 100:52-3+ Je '77

LANGLAND, Joseph
Intimations of the ordinary truth; poem. New Yorker 53:36 Mr 7 '77

LANGMUIR, Irving
Nobelist Langmuir's persistence proved cloud-seeding possible despite skeptics. V. Westervelt. Sci Digest 81:23-6 My '77 *

LANGS, David A. and others
Conformations of prostaglandin $F_{2\alpha}$ and recognition of prostaglandins by their receptors. bibl il Science 197:1003-5 S 2 '77

LANGSNER, Drew, and Langsner, Louise
Our livestock love soybean-millet hay. il Org Gard & Farm 24:214+ F '77

LANGSNER, Louise
Weeds as feed for healthier stock. il Org Gard & Farm 24:84-7 My '77
—See Langsner, D. jt auth

LANGUAGE, Obscene. See Words, Obscene

LANGUAGE, Psychology of. See Language and languages—Psychology

LANGUAGE and languages
See also
Communication
Conversation
English language
Executives—Language
French language
Languages, Modern
Religion and language
Rhetoric
Sex discrimination in language
Spanish language
Translations and translating

Psychology

Art of implying more than you say; work of Richard Harris. S. Bush. Psychol Today 10:36+ My '77
Art of the word: significance in stories for young people. P. Neumeyer. bibl Engl J 66:27-30 My '77

Rhythm

Words into music; rhythmic influence of language on music. G. Lees. Hi Fi 27:18+ Ap '77

Sociological aspects

See Sociolinguistics

Study and teaching

See also
Languages, Modern—Study and teaching
Latin language—Study and teaching

LANGUAGE and religion. See Religion and language

LANGUAGE and society. See Sociolinguistics

LANGUAGE arts

Study and teaching

Evolution of a language arts program for pre-and early adolescent students. S. M. James. il Engl J 66:47-51 Ap '77
In a word, history. M. H. Dohan. il Am Educ 13:10-12 N '77
Integrated, student-centered language-arts assignment. T. C. Gee. Clearing H 50:294-5 Mr '77
Working. M. I. Ellaissi. Engl J 66:65-6 S '77

Aids and devices

Crisis in language. J. Cromer. bibl Engl J 66:96-101 N '77
Language as art and art as language. L. Mueller. bibl il Engl J 66:49-53 O '77

LANGUAGE games. See Literary recreations

LANGUAGE of animals. See Animal communication

LANGUAGE requirement (graduate degrees) See Colleges and universities—Graduation requirements

LANGUAGES, Modern
See also
Modern Language Association of America
Spanish language
Thai language

Study and teaching

Foreign language and area research program. W. A. Bailey. Am Educ 13:26-7 N '77
Practical inducements for studying foreign languages. J. Contreras. bibl Clearing H 50:407-9 My '77
Prospects for foreign language education. M. Jackson. Educ Digest 43:48-9 O '77
Why Johnny can't parler. M. Sheils and others. il Newsweek 90:56 D 5 '77

LANGURS. See Monkeys

LANIER, Robin S.
New hope for TV sound. Hi Fi 27:76-8 N '77

LANIER, Thomas P.
Operaphiles' Baedeker 1977. il Opera N 41:20-2+ My '77
(ed) See Shicoff, N. Zealot: Neil Shicoff

LANKARD, Tom
View from the other side. Car & Dr 23:32 Ja '78

LANSDOWNE, James Fenwick
Wings. D. Grumbach. Sat R 5:43 N 26 '77 *

LANSFORD, Henry
Science in Colorado: the second century begins. il Science 195:477-9 F 4 '77

LANSING, Mich

Music

See also
Opera—Michigan

LANTERNS
Camp lanterns. il Consumer Rep 42:328-30 Je '77
Camping equipment: lanterns. il Consumers Res Mag 60:22-6 Je '77

LAOS
See also
Communism—Laos

LAPAGE, Wilbur F.
Plea for mediocrity. Parks & Rec 12:25-6+ Ag '77

LA PARGUERA, Puerto Rico. See Villages—Puerto Rico

LAPAROSCOPY. See Sterilization, Sexual

LAPAUTRE, Michelle
Michelle Lapautre. H. R. Lottman. por Pub W 211:25-6 My 30 '77 *

LAPE, Fred
Sunpit for propagation. il Org Gard & Farm 24:100-3 F '77

LAPHAM, Lewis H.
Capitalist paradox. il Harpers 254:31-4+ Mr '77
Cave of the winds. Nat R 29:1055-8+ S 16 '77
Easy chair. See issues of Harper's

LA PIERRE, Sharon
Macrame: a sampler becomes a handbag. il Design (US) 78:28-9 mid-Wint '77

LAPLAND
See also
Lapps

LAPORTE, Roy S. Bryce-. See Bryce-Laporte, R. S.

LAPPS
Norway's reindeer Lapps. S. Anderson. il map Nat Geog 152:364-79 S '77

LAQUEUR, Walter
Confronting the problems. Commentary 63:33-41 Mr '77
Europe: the specter of Finlandization. Commentary 64:37-41 D '77
Issue of human rights. Commentary 63:29-35 My '77
Perils of détente. N Y Times Mag p 16+ F 27 '77
Russia—beyond Brezhnev. Commentary 64:39-44 Ag '77
Third world fantasies. Commentary 63:43-8 F '77

LARCENY. See Stealing

LARDNER, George, Jr
Congress and the assassinations. il Sat R 4:14-17 F 19 '77

LARDNER, James
How prosecutors are nabbed. New Repub 176:22-5 Ja 29 '77
Soy of cooking. New Repub 176:11 F 26 '77
Television. il New Repub 177:32-5 O 1; 29-31 N 12; 24-6 D 10 '77

LARDNER, Ring, 1885-1933
There'll never be another. . . ; from March 4, 1914 article. il Sat Eve Post 249:36-8 Jl '77

about

Everybody knew me Al; excerpt from Ring, a biography of Ring Lardner. J. Yardley. il Sports Illus 47:82-6+ Ag 29 '77 *
Harmony in Great Neck: the friendship of Ring Lardner and F. Scott Fitzgerald; excerpt from Ring: a biography of Ring Lardner. J. Yardley. il pors Sat R 4:23-5+ Jl 9 '77 *

LARGE print books
See also
Publishers and publishing—Large print books

LARGE-scale integration. See Electronic circuits, Integrated

LARGEMOUTH bass fishing. See Bass fishing

LARGEY, Gale
Reversible sterilization. Society 14:57-9 Jl '77

LARGO, Fla.
Sewage sludge and how to sell it. I. M. Knapp. il Am City & County 92:63-5 O '77

LARKIN, Kathy
Kathy Larkin of Kroch's & Brentano's: total enthusiasm for the customer. I. Ballantine. il por Pub W 212:83-4 Jl 18 '77 *

LARKIN, Ronald P. and Sutherland, P. J.
Migrating birds respond to Project Seafarer's electromagnetic field. bibl il Science 195:777-9 F 25 '77

LARNED, Deborah
Rx for campers. Harp Baz 110:89+ Ap '77
A shot—or two or three—in the breast. Ms 6:55+ S '77

LAROUCHE, Janice
Game's played that way, lady! il pors Forbes 120:56+ Jl 15 '77 *

LARRABEE, Sarah B.
Trekking on Everest: making a living from wanderlust; interview, ed by G. Lichtenstein. bibl il Ms 5:26+ Mr '77

LARSEN, David G. and others
Computer corner. bibl Radio-Electr 48:16+ Je; 78-9+ S '77

LARSEN, Eric
Flirting with guilt and tyranny. il Harpers 225: 95-8+ D '77
Katie's eyes are normal now. il Parents Mag 52:37-9 Ag '77

about

Harper's bizarre. G. Lyons. Nation 226:24-6 Ja 7 '78 *

LARSEN, Helen G.
Student drama in the classroom: a solution to the end-of-the-year blahs. il Engl J 6:54-6 F '77

LARSEN, P. R. See Silva, J. E. jt auth

LARSEN, Robert L.
Place to grow. M. A. Feldman. il por Opera N 41:20-2 Je '77 *

LARSON, Alan H.
Energy: the sun and economics. il por Chemistry 50:12-13 Ap '77

LARSON, Charles R.
Invitation to a wedding; story. McCalls 104:128-9 Ag '77

LARSON, George C.
Outbound. See issues of Flying, May 1977-
Westerlies. See issues of Flying to April, 1977

LARSON, Janet Karsten
And then there were none. Chr Cent 94:61-3 Ja 26 '77
Redeeming the time and the land: epilogue to 1776. il Chr Cent 94:356-61 Ap 13 '77
Schemes from a marriage. il Chr Cent 94:535-40 Je 1 '77
Watch list for intelligence reform. Chr Cent 94: 688-91 Ag 3 '77

LARSON, Karen
Pet journal (cont) il Ladies Home J 94:156 Mr; 198 My; 72 Jl '77

LARSON, Kay
Rooms with a point of view. il Art N 76:32-8 O '77
Six art institutes: on the long lonesome road of the avant-garde. il Art N 76:50-4 D '77

LARSON, Stephen M. See Fountain, J. W. jt auth

LARSON, Timothy V. and others
Ammonia in the human airways: neutralization of inspired acid sulfate aerosols. bibl il Science 197:161-3 Jl 8 '77

LARSSON, L. I. and others
Vasoactive intestinal polypeptide occurs in nerves of the female genitourinary tract. bibl il Science 197:1374-5 S 30 '77

LARTIGUE, Henry J. Jr
Excerpt from testimony on retirement age policy, March 16, 1977. Cong Digest 56:275+ N '77

LARVAE
Extraordinary images show how beetles have adapted to live off plants, and each other. J. Lawrence. il Horticulture 55:8-13 D '77
See also
Caterpillars

LASALOCID. See Antibiotics

LA SCALA Opera, Milan. See Opera—Italy

LA SCALA Opera House, Milan. See Opera houses

LASER diodes. See Diodes

LASER fluorimetry. See Fluorimetry

LASER fusion. See Nuclear fusion

LASER gyroscopes. See Gyroscopes

LASER holography. See Holography

LASER isotope separation. See Isotope separation

LASER rifles. See Rifles

LASER uranium enrichment. See Uranium metallurgy

LASERS
Applications of lasers in research; symposium. bibl il Phys Today 30:23-32+ My '77
Carbon dioxide laser: fusion at last. Sci N 111: 166 Mr 12 '77
First operation of a free-electron laser. il Sci N 111:260 Ap 23 '77
Free-electron laser. Sci Am 236:62+ Je '77
Nuclear laser power up 100-fold. Sci N 112:69 Jl 30 '77
Short-wavelength laser: a new record. Sci N 111:309 My 14 '77

Art use

Have laser, will travel; cleaning industrial pollutants; work of J. Asmus. C. Panati and D. Gram. por Newsweek 89:87 Mr 28 '77

Astronomical use

Mobile lunar laser ranging station; University of Texas McDonald Observatory. il Intellect 105: 300-1 Mr '77

Chemical use

Chemistry by laser light. D. E. Thomsen. il Sci N 112:26-7 Jl 9 '77
Laser alchemy is just around the corner. G. Bylinski. Fortune 96:186-90 S '77
Lasers shed light on ozone reaction. Chemistry 50:21 S '77

Conferences

Washington is the site for the sixth CLEA. B. C. Carr. il Phys Today 30:60-2 My '77

Industrial use

Industry puts the laser to work. L. Smith. il Duns R 110:30-4 Ag '77

Military use

Progress made on high-energy laser. P. J. Klass. Aviation W 106:16-17 Mr 7 '77
Toward laser weapons in space. Sci N 111:158 Mr 5 '77

Patents

Forgotten inventor emerges from epic patent battle with claim to laser. N. Wade. il por Science 198:379-81 O 28 '77
Laser man; R. G. Gould. T. Nicholson and E. Clark. il por Newsweek 91:66+ Ja 16 '78
Laser patent that upsets the industry; R. G. Gould's patent. il pors Bus W p 122+ O 24 '77

Photographic use

See also
Holography

Space flight use

Space vehicles could be propelled by remote lasers. G. B. Lubkin. il Phys Today 30:17+ Ag '77

LASH, Joseph P.
American heritage announces the presentation of the 1977 Samuel Eliot Morison Award to Joseph P. Lash for Roosevelt and Churchill. il por Am Heritage 28:96-7 O '77 *

LASKER awards. See Albert and Mary Lasker Foundation

LASKEY, Harold H.
The pull of paperback displays. il por SLJ 23:31-5 F '77

LASKY, Melvin J.
Sweet dream. J. Burnham. Nat R 29:780-1 Jl 8 '77 *

LASKY, Victor
Old defense: they all did it. il por Time 110:20+ S 12 '77 *

LASORDA, Tom
Infusion of fresh Dodger-blue blood. L. Keith. il pors Sports Illus 46:36-8+ Mr 14 '77 *

LASSWELL, Marcia, and Lobsenz, N. M.
How children can hurt a marriage. McCalls 104: 161+ S '77
Varieties of intimacy; excerpt from No-fault marriage. Read Digest 111:115-18 N '77
Women and men; questions and answers. McCalls 104:86+ Jl; 46+ Ag; 127+ O; 105:50+ N '77; 24+ Ja '78

LASSWELL, Thomas E.
Six styles of loving. por Intellect 105:294-5 Mr '77 *

LAST stop; drama. See Cable, H.

LAST street play; drama. See Wesley, R.

LAST words
Famous last apothegms. P. Andrews. il Horizon 19:96 Ja '77

LAS VEGAS, Nev.

Anecdotes, facetiae, satire, etc.

Drinking man's guide to Las Vegas. J. Cronley. il Esquire 88:110+ D '77

Crime

Another Hoffa case? E. A. Bramlet. R. Steele and M. Kasindorf. il por Newsweek 89:23 Mr 14 '77
Vegas vanishing act; disappearance of E. A. Bramlet. por Time 109:21 Mr 14 '77

Description

Message from Las Vegas. J. R. Petitti. il por Parks & Rec 12:56-8 My '77

Hotels, restaurants, etc.

Getting the Vegas willies. J. Didion. Esquire 87:32+ My '77
See also
Casinos

LATCHES
Child protective latch for cabinets and drawers. il Consumers Res Mag 60:32 S '77

LATERALITY
Auditory evoked potentials as probes of hemispheric differences in cognitive processing. D. W. Shucard and others. bibl il Science 197: 1295-8 S 23 '77
Centering as a process for children's imaging. R. B. Kent. bibl il Sch Arts 77:18-20 N '77
Cerebral lateralization of haptic perception: interaction of responses to Braille and music reveals a functional basis. M. O. Smith and others. bibl il Science 197:689-90 Ag 12 '77

LATERALITY—*Continued*
Developmental dyslexia: two right hemispheres and none left. S. F. Witelson. bibl Science 195: 309-11 Ja 21 '77
Dyslexia: a hemispheric explanation. Sci N 111:55 Ja 22 '77
Interdependence of the nigrostriatal dopaminergic systems on the two sides of the brain in the cat. A. Nieoullon and others. bibl il Science 198: 416-18 O 28 '77
Lost voices of the gods; views of J. Jaynes. il por Time 109:51-2+ Mr 14 '77
Music education and the human brain. T. A. Regelski. Educ Digest 43:44-7 O '77
Right brain: surviving retardation. Sci N 112: 229-30 O 8 '77
Right-brained kids in left-brained schools. M. Hunter. Educ Digest 42:8-10 F '77
Split-brain psychology: fad of the year. D. Goleman. il Psychol Today 11:88-90+ O '77
Variations in writing posture and cerebral organization. J. Levy and M. Reid; discussion. il Science 195:441 F 4 '77
See also
Left- and right-handedness

LATERAN Pact, 1929. See Catholic Church in Italy

LATEX paint. See Paint

LATEX stains. See Stains and staining

LATHAM, Aaron. See Latham, J. A.

LATHAM, John Aaron
Adversaria. Esquire 88:78+ D '77
Farewell to machismo. il pors N Y Times Mag p52-5+ O 16 '77
Immortality of H.H.H. il Esquire 88:84-6+ O '77
National Velveeta. il pors Esquire 88:101-5+ N '77
PW interviews; ed by S. Steinberg. por Pub W 211:12+ Je 27 '77

LATHAM, Sid
Custom knives and knife makers. il Field & S 81:78-80+ Mr '77

LATHEN, Emma, pseud
Masters of white-collar homicide. pors Forbes 120:89 D 1 '77 *

LATHES
Little lathe for metal cutting. M. Philips. il Pop Sci 210:158 Mr '77
Optical template for easier wood-turning. J. Murphy. il Pop Sci 210:186 Ap '77
We try out a basic wood lathe. il Mech Illus 73:124-5+ S '77

LATIN AMERICA
Latin American development in an interdependent world; excerpt from address, May 29, 1977. T. A. Todman. Dept State Bull 77:440-5 O 3 '77
Myths about Latin America—setting the record straight. J. Benham and C. J. Migdail. il U.S. News 82:37-8 Je 6 '77
Our America; special section, ed by A. J. Lowe. il maps Américas 29:16-49 N '77
See also
Americans in Latin America
Banks and banking—Latin America
Blacks in Latin America
Cities and towns—Latin America
Civil rights—Latin America
Coffee industry—Latin America
Energy policy—Latin America
Hydroelectric plants—Latin America
Immigration and emigration—Latin America
Investments, American—Latin America
Investments, Latin American—United States
Power resources—Latin America
South America
Technical assistance, European—Latin America
Technology—Latin America

Civilization
Latin America: composite profile of a continent; symposium. UNESCO Courier 30:4-69 Ag '77

Colonization
City planning in the Spanish colonies. G. de Zéndegui. il map Américas 29:S1-12 F '77
Enduring heritage; influence of early Spanish settlers in Latin America. I. Vázquez de Acuña. il map Américas 29:30-3 O '77

Commerce
United States
See United States—Commerce—Latin America

Defenses
See also
Inter-American Defense College, Washington, D.C.

Economic conditions
Latin America and today's world economy; address, December 6, 1976. W. D. Rogers. Dept State Bull 75:751-4 D 27 '76
Never-to-be developed countries of Latin America. R. L. Clinton. bibl il Bull Atom Sci 33:19-26 O '77
See also
United Nations—Economic Commission for Latin America

Economic relations
Forging economic unity. A. Bono. Commonweal 104:618-20 S 30 '77
International business in Latin America; address, March 1, 1977. W. B. Wolf. Vital Speeches 43:443-7 My 1 '77
United States
See United States—Economic relations—Latin America

Foreign relations
United States
See United States—Foreign relations—Latin America

History
Key to the past; archival collections in Madrid relating to Latin American history. J. Luján Muñoz. il Américas 29:42-3 O '77
Bibliography
Reviews of books: Latin America. See issues of American historical review
Wars of independence, 1806-1830
Bolivar and the Congress of Panama. A. Uslar-Pietri. il por UNESCO Courier 30:28-32 F '77

Languages
See also
Spanish language in Latin America

Maps
Map section. Sr Schol 110:23 O 20 '77

Politics and government
Are South American dictators serious about stepping down? il map U.S. News 83:47-8 N 28 '77
Dependence or interdependence? J. H. Haddox. Américas 29:2-5 Mr '77
50-cycle politics; dispute over Itapú hydroelectric project. J. R. Brockman. map America 137: 484 D 31 '77
Latin America, 1977; symposium. bibl il map Cur Hist 72:49-78+ F '77

Religious institutions and affairs
Ecumenism in Latin America. America 136:228 Mr 19 '77
More on liberation theology. H. B. Kuhn. Chr Today 22:66-7 N 4 '77
See also
Catholic Church in Latin America
Christians in Latin America
Church and social problems—Latin America
Evangelistic work—Latin America

Treaties
United States
See United States—Treaties—Latin America

LATIN AMERICA and Europe. See Europe and Latin America

LATIN AMERICA and Spain. See Spain and Latin America

LATIN AMERICA and the United States
Hemisphere of misunderstanding; address, September 19, 1977. J. St John. Vital Speeches 44:5-9 O 15 '77
See also
Inter-American relations
Pan American Day and Week

LATIN AMERICAN art. See Art, Latin American

LATIN AMERICAN cookery. See Cookery, Latin American

LATIN AMERICAN drama
See also
Dramatists, Latin American

LATIN AMERICAN dramatists. See Dramatists, Latin American

LATIN AMERICAN literature
Spanish-American literature; address, December 4, 1976. O. Paz. New Repub 176:23-7 Ap 9 '77
Vargas Llosa, visionary realist; interview, ed by T. Bridges. M. Vargas Llosa. il pors Américas 29:2-5 O '77
See also
Latin American poetry

LATIN AMERICAN music. See Music, Latin American

LATIN AMERICAN poetry

Bibliography
Latin American poetry. J. Felstiner. New Repub 176:32-3 Ap 9 '77

LATIN AMERICANS in the United States
Female factor in resettlement. L. M. Cohen. bibl il Society 14:27-30 S '77
Marxism and the Hispanic movement of the United States. A. M. Stevens-Arroyo. il New Cath World 220:126-8+ My '77
Washington notebook. S. Booker. Ebony 32:30 O '77

Periodicals
See also
Nuestro (periodical)

LATIN language

Study and teaching

Back to the ablative absolute. M. Greenfield. Newsweek 90:112 S 12 '77

Pueri et puellae certantes; Latin Olympics. il Time 110:82 Ag 15 '77

LATIN Mass. See Mass

LATIN poetry

Translations into English

Epigrammatum liber primus; Epigrammatum liber secundus; tr by S. Ratcliffe. T. Campion. Poetry 130:90-3 My '77

LA TIRANA, Chile. See Villages—Chile

LATOUR, Martine

Bits (cont of) Show biz, arts, etc. See issues of Mademoiselle

LATTER-Day Saints. See Mormons and Mormonism

LATTIME, Edmund C. and Strausser, H. R.

Arteriosclerosis: is stress-induced immune suppression a risk factor? bibl il Science 198:302-3 O 21 '77

LATTIMORE, Richmond

Gehenna; poem. New Yorker 53:129 Je 6 '77

about

Poetry of Richmond Lattimore. S. Lea. New Repub 176:37-9 Ap 30 '77 *

LATVIA

Religious institutions and affairs

See also

Church and state in Latvia

LAU, Glenn

Smallmouth bass: facts that can change your fishing; interview, ed by J. Gibbs. il pors Outdoor Life 160:86-7+ Jl '77

Walleyes: find 'em-then it's easy; interview, ed by J. Gibbs. il por Outdoor Life 159:104+ Je '77

LAUCALA. See Lauthala (island)

LAUDA, Niki

Driving to the limit. P. Bonventre. il pors Newsweek 90:66+ Ag 29 '77 *

LAUE, John Paul

Indiana Dunes: tying up loose ends. Audubon 79:125-6 Ja '77

LAUENSTEIN, Milton C.

Preserving the impotence of the board. Harvard Bus R 55:36-8+ Jl '77

LAUGHING gas. See Nitrous oxide

LAUGHLIN, Clarence John

Clarence John Laughlin: phantoms and metaphors. M. L. Tucker. il Mod Phot 41:100-9+ Ap '77 *

LAUGHLIN, J.

In another country; poem. Harpers 256:44-5 Ja '78

LAUGHTER

See also

Humor

Psychological aspects

Cheers! A belly laugh can help you stay well; excerpt from The world of humor. F. Cross and W. Cross. il Sci Digest 82:15-18+ N '77

Sigmund, here's a joke on you; laughter as a release of tension. D. Cohen. il Psychol Today 10:30+ Ap '77

LAUMER, Frank

Talisman/Ford 1930 Model A. D. Sherman. il por Car & Dr 23:81-4 O '77 *

LAUNCHING of boats. See Boats—Launching

LAUNCHING of ocean liners. See Ocean liners—Launching

LAUNDRIES

Planning a laundry area. Bet Hom & Gard 55:54 N '77

6 super laundries. J. McCloskey. il Bet Hom & Gard 55:96-9 N '77

LAUNDRY

Laundry problems solved. Bet Hom & Gard 55:202 N '77

LAUNDRY equipment

Home laundry appliances. il Consumers Res Mag 60:30-7 O '77

See also

Clothes dryers

Washing machines

LAUNDRY products

Cleaning aids for the kitchen and laundry. il Consumers Res Mag 60:144-8 O '77

Guide to laundry aids. il Good H 184:216+ My '77

Three more prewash preparations. il Consumers Res Mag 60:20-1 F '77

See also

Bleaching materials

Detergents

LAUREN, Bruce

Re-rigging (cheaply) with Norseman fittings. il Motor B & S 139:129-31 Je '77

LAUREN, Paul M.

Investigating the corrosion of iron. bibl il Chemistry 50:25-7 S '77

Sir Humphry Davy's battle with the sea. bibl il pors Chemistry 50:14-17 S '77

LAURENTIAN Mountains

Walker's guide to the mountains of Québec; trails and country inns. R. Rudner. Mademoiselle 83:44-6 Jl '77

LAURIE, Andrew

What I learned stalking Indian rhinos. il Int Wildlife 7:6-16 Jl '77

LAURIE, Pete

Carolina haven for red wolf. Audubon 79:152 Ja '77

LAUSANNE Conference on Faith and Order. See World Conference on Faith and Order

LAUSANNE Congress on World Evangelization. See International Congress on World Evangelization

LAUSANNE Covenant. See International Congress on World Evangelization

LAUSTSEN, S.

First light for the ESO 3.6-meter telescope. il Sky & Tel 53:96-103 F '77

LAUTEN, John H.

Great California drought; adaptation of address, June 3, 1977. il Am For 83:16-19 O '77

LAUTER, Evelyn

Why worry helps. il Parents Mag 53:40+ Ja '78

LAUTERBACH, Ann

Window; poem. Nation 224:409 Ap 2 '77

LAUTHALA (island)

Company has gone to the movies. il Forbes 119:6 Ap 1 '77

LAVA

Lava flow causes 70 deaths; Nyiragongo volcano in Zaire. il Sci N 111:388 Je 18 '77

Oregon's astonishing lava lands. il map Sunset 159:64-7 Ag '77

See also

Basalt

LAVARENNE cooking school, Paris. See Cookery—Study and teaching

LAVARNWAY, Catherine

My heart doesn't care where the wild goose goes. il Read Digest 110:223-6 Ap '77

LAVE, Charles A.

Negative energy impact of modern rail transit systems. bibl Science 195:595-6; 197:938+ F 11, S 2 '77

LAVELLI, Jorge

Jorge Lavelli, stage director. D. J. Soria. por Hi Fi 27:MA7+ My '77 *

LAVENDER, David Sievert

American characters: John McLoughlin. por Am Heritage 28:64-5 Je '77

First crossing; excerpt from Winner take all. il por Am West 14:4-11+ S '77

LAVER, Tina

No singles allowed. Am Home 80:26-7 Ap '77

LAVERDIERE, Bruno

Bruno LaVerdiere. J. Delius. il Craft Horiz 37:46-8 O '77 *

Bruno LaVerdiere: clay sculptures. R. Zakin. il Ceram Mo 25:26-7 S '77 *

LAVIN, Richard C.

One eye, two eyes and three eyes; dramatization of fairy tale by the Brothers Grimm. Plays 36:58-64 Mr '77

LA VOY, Diane Edwards

Foreign nationals and American law. bibl Society 15:58-64 N '77

LAW

See also

Civil rights

Computers—Legal use

Contracts

Copyright

Corporation law

Courts

Criminal law

Inheritance

International law

Islamic law

Jury

Justice, Administration of

Lawyers

Legislation

Liability (law)

Libel and slander

Maritime law

Natural law

also subheads Law, Laws and legislation, Laws and regulations, Legal status, laws, etc. under various subjects, e.g. Atomic power—Laws and regulations

Practice

See Procedure (law)

Sociology

See Sociological jurisprudence

Study and teaching

How an elementary teacher does it. B. Miles. Todays Educ 66:76-7 Ja '77

Law Focused Education: a new thrust in education; seminars for teachers. W. L. Black. Clearing H 50:304-6 Mr '77

LAW—Study and teaching—*Continued*
Teaching about the law: perceptions and implications. N. Gross. Educ Digest 43:34-5 O '77
Teaching kids about law. C. J. White, 3d. Todays Educ 66:74-6 Ja '77
See also
Law teachers

Terminology

Gobbledygook; readability of legal agreements. R. Nader. Ladies Home J 94:68 S '77
Government, business try plain English for a change. U. S. News 83:46+ N 7 '77
Trying to regulate the regulators. H. Sidey. Time 110:33 D 5 '77
Turning federalese into plain English. Bus W p58 My 9 '77
Waging war on legalese. il Time 111:60 Ja 16 '78

California

California royalty bill: milestone or mistake? pro and con discussion. J. H. Merryman; H. Sandison. pors Am Artist 41:60-1 F '77
California's art resale law: the failure of innocence. A. Elsen. Art in Am 65:15-16 Mr '77
Do we have the right to die? J. W. Montgomery. Chr Today 21:49-50 Ja 21 '77
Legislating royalties for artists. S. Hochfield; reply. B. K. Brill. Art N 76:34 Ap '77
Noise and the home mechanic; effects of car noise law. Mech Illus 73:120 Ag '77

Great Britain

How Britain lays down the law. Q. M. H. Hailsham of Saint Marylebone. il Sat R 4:26+ Je 11 '77

Italy

See also
Abortion—Laws and legislation—Italy

New York (state)

Disclosure rules hit the advisers; registration requirements. por Bus W p55-6 D 12 '77
Publishers and librarians protest child porn provision in New York law. SLJ 24:64 O '77
St Martin's wins round against N.Y. obscenity law; case of Show me! M. Reuter. Pub W 212:23-4 D 12 '77

United States

Q&A about the law (cont) J. L. Alpert. por Ret Liv 17:56-7 F; 18 D '77
See also
Aged—Legal status, laws, etc.
American Bar Association
Courts—United States
Marriage law—United States
Teachers—Legal status, laws, etc.
United States—Constitution
United States—Constitutional law
United States—Supreme Court
Women—Legal status, laws, etc.

Anecdotes, facetiae, satire, etc.

Letter to the editor; recodification of state laws. R. Lipez. Progressive 41:66 Mr '77

LAW, Jewish. See Jewish law
LAW, Natural. See Natural law
LAW and ethics
Essay on the unfairness of life. L. Morrow. Horizon 20:34-7 D '77
LAW and religion. See Religion and law
LAW and science. See Science and law
LAW and society. See Sociological jurisprudence
LAW books. See Legal literature
LAW clerks, Supreme Court. See United States—Supreme Court—Employees
LAW enforcement
See also
Conservation officers
Police
United States—Law Enforcement Assistance Administration
LAW Enforcement Assistance Administration. See United States—Law Enforcement Assistance Administration
LAW firms. See Law partnership
LAW Focused Education, Inc. See Law—Study and teaching
LAW insurance. See Insurance, Litigation
LAW libraries
See also
Washington (state). University, Seattle—School of Law—Library
LAW libraries in prisons. See Prison libraries
LAW of nature. See Natural law
LAW of succession. See Inheritance
LAW of the Sea Conference. See United Nations Conference on the Law of the Sea
LAW partnership
Challenging media monopolies; public-interest law firm, Citizens Communications Center. D. Carmody. il N Y Times Mag p21-4 Jl 31 '77
Role of public interest law firms. C. W. Hall, Jr. Current 192:41-6 Ap '77
LAW professors. See Law teachers
LAW schools
See also
Harvard University—Law School
New York University—School of Law
Washington (state). University, Seattle—School of Law

Accreditation

See also
United States—Advisory Committee on Accreditation and Institutional Eligibility

Entrance examinations

ETS's star chamber; Law School Admissions Test. K. Masters. New Repub 176:13-14 F 5 '77
LAW societies
Washington notebook; W. S. Thompson of World Peace Through Law. S. Booker. Ebony 32:29 My '77
LAW teachers
Ten teachers who shape the future; law school professors. il Time 109:56-8 Mr 14 '77
LAWANI, S. M.
Citation analysis and the quality of scientific productivity. bibl BioScience 27:26, 443-4 Ja, Jl '77
LAWLER, Edward E.
Workers can set their own wages—responsibly. il por Psychol Today 10:109-10+ F '77
LAWN mowers
Lawn scene: cut, mulch, whip. F. K. Coffee. il Mech Illus 74:48-9+ Ap '77
Manual lawn mowers. Consumer Rep 42:194-5 D '77
Pedaled lawn mower. D. G. Wilson. il Org Gard & Farm 24:87 Je '77
Rotary power mowers are fancier and safer. Changing T 31:45-6 Ap '77
Safer lawn mower: the Roper Whip Stik. il Consumer Rep 42:391 Jl '77
Safer rotary power lawn mower? il Consumers Res Mag 60:28 Ag '77
Take your pick of the '77 mowers. M. Schultz. il Pop Mech 147:118-20+ Mr '77
Two new rider/bagger mowers. E. F. Lindsley. il Pop Sci 211:60 Jl '77

Equipment

Two riding-mower accessories you can make; mulcher and power rake. R. S. Wilkes. il Pop Mech 148:47 O '77
LAWN seed. See Grasses—Seed
LAWN sprinklers. See Sprinklers
LAWN tools, equipment, and supplies
Filament-type grass trimmers. il Consumer Rep 42:459-61 Ag '77
Get rid of fall litter with lawn vacs and blowers. M. Lindsley. il Pop Sci 211:70+ O '77
How to use those handy string trimmers. A. J. Hand. il Pop Sci 210:190 My '77
New bladeless electric weed and grass trimmers. il Consumers Res Mag 60:13-15 Jl '77
New gear that makes yard work easier. M. Schultz. il Pop Mech 147:116-19 My '77
String trimmers—fast, safe way to control weeds. A. J. Hand. il Pop Sci 210:50+ My 77

Storage

Yard-equipment storage—a little care now saves a lot of care next spring. G. R. Drake. il Pop Sci 211:152+ O '77
LAWN tractors. See Tractors
LAWNS
Frenetic life forms that flourish in suburban lawns. J. H. Falk. il Smithsonian 8:90-6 bibl(p 147) Ap '77
Grass-roots advice about lawns. J. Fanning. il House & Gard 149:85-8 Ap '77
Green-grass Q&A. House & Gard 149:90+ Ap '77
Greening of a ball field. R. Thomas. il Parks & Rec 12:26-7+ My '77
Now's the time to improve your lawn: yes, in the fall! N. G. Rollins. il Good H 185:214 S '77
Still time for a better lawn. Changing T 31:35 Mr '77
Summer, the drought and your lawn. M. Franz. Org Gard & Farm 24:126-8 Je '77
See also
Grasses

Anecdotes, facetiae, satire, etc.

Rub-out. A. Ward. il Horticulture 55:16-19 Mr '77
LAWNS, Watering of. See Watering of gardens, lawns, etc.
LAWRENCE, Charles, 3d
Bakke case: are racial quotas defensible? il Sat R 5:10-16 O 15 '77; Same. Current 198:3-11 D '77
LAWRENCE, David
Someday—a real Christmas. il U.S. News 83: 96+ D 26 '77
LAWRENCE, David Herbert
Whales weep not; poem; excerpt from The complete poems of D. H. Lawrence. il Oceans 10: 21 Jl '77
LAWRENCE, Deanna
U.S. journal: Tampa, Florida; discrimination against women at the University Club. C. Trillin. New Yorker 53:103-5 Ap 11 '77

LAWRENCE, G. M. and others
Excitation of the Venus night airglow. bibl il Science 195:573-4 F 11 '77

LAWRENCE, H. Lea
Who? Me use a downrigger? il Outdoor Life 160:88-90 Jl '77

LAWRENCE, Harding L.
Air transportation leadership; excerpts from address. Aviation W 106:11 My 23 '77

LAWRENCE, Harold
Gina Bachauer remembered. il por Hi Fi 27:MA18-19 F '77

LAWRENCE, John. See Kaiser, K. L. E. jt auth

LAWRENCE, John Francis
Extraordinary images show how beetles have adapted to live off plants, and each other. il Horticulture 55:8-13 D '77

LAWRENCE, Miles B.
Atlantic hurricane season of 1976. il map Weatherwise 30:10-17 F '77

LAWRENCE, R. D.
Paddy—orphan of the wild; condensation of Paddy; a naturalist's story of an orphan beaver. il Read Digest 110:206-16+ Je '77

LAWRENCE, Thomas Edward
Real T. E. Lawrence. E. Kedourie. Commentary 64:49-56 Jl '77; Discussion. 64:10-12+ O '77

LAWRENCE R. Klein Awards. See Monthly labor review (periodical)

LAWRENCE Radiation Laboratory, Livermore, Calif. See California. University—Lawrence Radiation Laboratories

LAWRENSON, Helen
How now, fellatio! Why dost thou tarry? excerpt from Whistling girl. Esquire 87:128+ My '77

LAWSON, Barry
Serious play—using games to teach and learn. J. Gaylin. Psychol Today 11:28+ Jl '77 *

LAWSON, Dale R.
Polymer cuts cost of Rochester water. il por Am City & County 92:97-8 S '77

LAWSON, Slick
Balloon is a moon. R. Blount, Jr. Esquire 88:46+ D '77 *

LAWSON, Stephen R.
Forsaking the barn. Am Scholar 46:377-83 Summ '77
José, Jason, and Gene. il pors Horizon 21:36-42 Ja '78
Language equals action. il pors Horizon 20:40-5 N '77

LAWSUITS. See Actions and defenses

LAWYERS
At 100, the bar confronts reform. Time 110:52 Ag 8 '77
Get yourself a good lawyer. il Changing T 31:39-40 My '77
How to choose a lawyer and what to do then. Consumer Rep 42:284-6+ My '77
Judging Carter's judges. il Time 110:76 D 5 '77
Law: executives criticize their counsel. Bus W p32 Ag 29 '77
Too much conscience is unprofessional: the big board-room lawyers; corporate lawyers. M. Green. Nation 224:485-8 Ap 23 '77
Watch out for trial lawyers. F. L. Bailey. por Newsweek 91:7 Ja 2 '78
See also
American Bar Association
Law partnership
Legal aid
Legal ethics
Malpractice
National Lawyers Guild
Patent lawyers

Advertising

ABA misses the mark on advertising. J. K. Lieberman. Bus W p74 Ag 29 '77
Advertisers-at-law; Supreme Court decision. J. K. Footlick and L. Howard. il Newsweek 90:47-8 Jl 11 '77
Bar's blushing maidens; Supreme Court decision. N. Lewin. New Repub 177:17-19 S 17 '77
Let lawyers advertise? interviews. S. DeMent; L. Jeffers. pors U.S. News 82:39-40 F 28 '77
Now that lawyers can advertise. . . U.S. News 83:21 Jl 11 '77
Supreme Court rules that attorneys may advertise, and speculation flourishes among the other professions. W. Hickman. Archit Rec 162:34 Ag '77

Anecdotes, facetiae, satire, etc.

Terminal jurisprudence. R. Baker. N Y Times Mag p 12 Mr 20 '77

Attitudes

Report card on Supreme Court. il U.S. News 82:60-6+ Mr 7 '77

Directories

U.S. court lowers barriers to CU legal directory. Consumer Rep 42:70 F '77

Salaries, fees, etc.

Corporate law firms respond to Nader. T. Goldstein. N Y Times Mag p84+ N 20 '77
Good news for the geese; fighting IRS. il por Forbes 119:30-1 Ap 15 '77
It's expensive to go broke; legal costs surrounding W. T. Grant bankruptcy case. H. Seneker. Forbes 119:21-2 F 1 '77
Nader's advice to big business: don't pay those high legal bills. R. Nader and M. Green. N Y Times Mag p53+ N 20 '77
Rich legal links to the boardroom il Bus W p24-5 Ja 24 '77
Top-dollar lawyers; Washington lawyers. J. K. Footlick and L. Howard. il Newsweek 89:97 Mr 14 '77
See also
Insurance, Litigation

LAWYERS and clients
In the heads of the listeners; address, September 9, 1977. W. W. Braden. Vital Speeches 44:42-4 N 1 '77
Masters of disruption; attorneys for West German terrorists. Time 110:38 S 19 '77
Which client secrets must a lawyer reveal? SEC suits against law firms involved in National Student Marketing Corporation's fraudulent takeover attempt of Interstate National Corp. il Bus W p 124+ Ag 15 '77

LAWYERS as Congressmen. See Congressmen

LAWYERS as public officers. See Public officers

LAWYERS in politics
Can Chuck Morgan keep Jimmy Carter honest? T. Branch. Esquire 87:14+ F '77

LAWYERS liability insurance. See Insurance, Malpractice liability

LAX, Eric
Nasty! il por Esquire 87:96-9+ Mr '77
Quick, make a mussel! il Esquire 88:98-100 Ag '77

LAXALT, Paul
On limiting the size of government. il Nat R 29:437-8 Ap 15 '77

LAYCOCK, George
Everybody's favorite bear. il Audubon 79:6-19 My '77
Refuge ducks are swamped by powerboats, politicians. Audubon 79:152-3 N '77
Some say it will kill you; reprint from Audubon, November 1976 issue. il Redbook 148:102+ Ap '77
Wildlife roulette. il Outdoor Life 159:34+ F '77

LAYMEN. See Laity

LAYOFF systems
End for Steel City? closing of Youngstown Sheet & Tube Co. works. il Time 110:78 O 3 '77
Fear Valley, U.S.A.; closing of Youngstown Sheet & Tube Company plant. R. W. Gibbons. Commonweal 104:720-2 N 11 '77
Hard times come to steeltown. L. Smith. il Fortune 96:86-93 D '77
Huge pink slip for an Ohio city; Youngstown Sheet & Tube Co. Bus W p39-40 O 3 '77
Steel blues; closing Youngstown Sheet & Tube Co. plant. D. Pauly and J. Lowell. il Newsweek 90:80+ O 3 '77
Steel companies announce layoffs. L. Bornstein and others. M Labor R 100:71 D '77

LAZARD, Naomi
Ordinance on arrival; In answer to your query; poems; excerpts from Ordinances. il Ms 6:74 Ja '78

LAZARD Frères and Company. See Investment banking

LAZAROF, Henri
Lazarof: Spectrum; Concerto for flute and orchestra. J. Ringo. Am Rec G 41:18-19 N '77 *

LAZAROW, Paul B.
Three hypolipidemic drugs increase hepatic palmitoyl-coenzyme A oxidation in the rat. bibl il Science 197:580-1 Ag 5 '77

LAZARRE, Jane
(ed) See Broderick, J. I am the mother of eight, a housewife, a feminist—and happy: Jane Broderick's story

LAZARUS, Andrew J.
Taormina. il Travel 148:46-9 Ag '77

LAZARUS, Emma
Liberty stands on her words; excerpt from American Jewish landmarks: a travel guide and history. B. Postal and L. Koppman. il por Ms 6:22 Ag '77 *

LAZARUS, Gerald S. and others
Polymorphonuclear leukocytes: possible mechanism of accumulation in psoriasis. bibl il Science 198:1162-3 D 16 '77

LAZARUS, Rosalind Avnet
ECOA—in a nutshell. Ms 5:98 Mr '77

LAZERE, Donald
Camus on doublespeak. Engl J 66:24-6 O '77

LAZINESS
Seven deadly sins today; excerpt. H. Fairlie. New Repub 177:20-3 O 29 '77

LAZZARA, Vince
Boatbuilder and his dream yacht. T. Gibbs. il por Yachting 142:74-7 N '77 *

LAZZARONI, Paolo, kidnapping
Kidnapped; P. Lazzaroni. C. B. Pepper. il pors N Y Times Mag p42-6+ N 20 '77

LEA, Barbara
Indigenous music. N. Hentoff. Nation 225:350 O 8 '77 *

LEA, Sydney
Poetry of Richmond Lattimore. New Repub 176: 37-9 Ap 30 '77

LEACH, Barbara
For yogurt-lovers, handy seagoing recipes. Yachting 142:86 Jl '77

LEACH, Bernard Howell
Bernard Leach. il pors Ceram Mo 25:47-58 Je '77 *
Pottery: the seventh Kenzan; retrospective at London's Victoria and Albert Museum. il por Time 109:76 Ap 4 '77 *

LEACH, Morgan
Convict and the boy. J. P. Blank and M. J. Mueller. il Read Digest 110:135-9 My '77 *

LEACH, Richard H.
Canada and the United States: a special relationship. bibl f Cur Hist 72:145-9+ Ap '77

LEACH, Robin
(ed) See Trudeau, M. S. Margaret Trudeau's own story

LEACHING, Soil. See Soil percolation

LEAD
Lead and cadmium release; WHO conference on ceramic foodware safety. il Ceram Mo 25: 69+ D '77

Prices

Big Russian buys jack up lead prices. Bus W p28 Mr 14 '77
Why lead prices are so buoyant. il Bus W p34-5 D 26 '77

LEAD industry

Environmental aspects

Making lead as costly as gold; new OSHA rule. il Bus W p26 Ja 24 '77

LEAD poisoning
Lead poisoning: still a threat to young children. M. A. Wessel. Parents Mag 53:14+ Ja '78
Lead-sabotaged vision: low-level link. Sci N 111: 292 My 7 '77
Lead shot; question of waterfowl mortality resulting from lead shot ingestion. Audubon 79:140 Jl '77
Scotopic vision deficits in young monkeys exposed to lead. P. J. Bushnell and others. bibl il Science 196:333-5 Ap 15 '77
Twilight for lead shot? regulations designed to reduce number of waterfowl dying of lead poisoning. J. Phillips. il Outdoor Life 160:90-1+ Ag '77

Prevention

Lead poisoning from paint: the end of the road? Consumer Rep 42:124-5 Mr '77

LEAD shot. See Shot

LEADERS, Fishing. See Fishing tackle

LEADERSHIP
Curriculum materials for vocational youth organizations; leadership instruction. J. F. Feldhusen and others. bibl Clearing H 50:224-6 Ja '77
Educational leadership. K. A. Berg. bibl Clearing H 50:212-14 Ja '77
Leadership: the teacher's option. R. Drake. bibl Clearing H 50:291-3 Mr '77
Managers and leaders: are they different? A. Zaleznik. bibl f Harvard Bus R 55:67-78 My '77; Discussion. 55:148-9 Jl '77
Top of the world is flat. H. J. Davidson. bibl f il Harvard Bus R 55:89-99 Mr '77
Two cheers for Jimmy! M. Stone. U.S. News 82:96 Ap 18 '77
Who runs America: annual survey. il U.S. News 82:28-36+ Ap 18 '77
Whom you like least. . .it's a clue to your style of leadership and LPC. Sci Digest 82:46-9 Ag '77
Why a woman can't be a good boss—because no one will let you; group leadership studies by C. Beauvais and Z. Schachtel. Mademoiselle 83:120+ Jl '77
See also
Black leadership
Christian leadership
Community leadership
Elite (social sciences)

LEAF blowers. See Lawn tools, equipment, and supplies

LEAF rollers
Moth mating: role of diet challenged. Sci N 111:37 Ja 15 '77

LEAFLETS. See Pamphlets

LEAGUE for Proletarian Socialism. See Socialism—United States

LEAGUE of Women Voters of the United States
Women behind the Presidential debates: League of Women Voters. M. McLaughlin. McCalls 104:65 F '77

LEAKEY, Richard E. F.
—and Lewin, Roger
Is it our culture, not our genes, that makes us killers? excerpt from Origins. il por Smithsonian 8:56-8+ bibl(p 160) N '77

about

Puzzling out man's ascent. il pors Time 110: 64-7+ N 7 '77; Reply. Chr Today 22:34 D 9 '77 *

LEAPER, R. John
(ed) See Kreps, J. Future for working women

LEAR, Frances
Work is not a four-letter word. por Newsweek 90:22-3 O 24 '77

LEAR, William Powell
King Lear. il por Forbes 119:74 Mr 1 '77 *
Lear. P. Garrison. por Flying 101:255 S '77 *

LEARMONT, Carol L. and Darling, R. L.
Placements & salaries 1976: a year of adjustment. il pors Lib J 102:1345-51 Je 15 '77

LEARNED, Michael
Michael Learned: a woman in passage; interview, ed by J. Stone. por Ladies Home J 94: 52+ Jl '77

LEARNING, Psychology of
Developmental curriculum: an articulation model for grades K-12. S. Lehane. bibl il Clearing H 51:86-9 O '77
Lawrence Kohlberg: why Johnny can be good without being religious. R. Beechick. il Chr Today 22:12-14 D 30 '77
Only one-third of children learning; advocation of mastery learning approach. B. S. Bloom. il Intellect 106:184-5 N '77
Piaget and Lamarck. F. J. Thomas. Educ Digest 43:47-9 N '77
Right-brained kids in left-brained schools. M. Hunter. Educ Digest 42:8-10 F '77
Structural learning and open education. J. M. Scandura. Clearing H 50:215-19 Ja '77; Same abr. Educ Digest 42:28-30 Ap '77
See also
Animal learning
Learning disabilities
Memorizing
Memory

Emotional aspects

Personal meaning and personal learning as educational concepts. R. Griffin. Clearing H 50:227-30 Ja '77

LEARNING ability. See Ability

LEARNING and scholarship
See also
Education
Scholars

LEARNING centers. See Instructional materials centers

LEARNING disabilities
Bright child, school failure. M. A. Wessel. bibl Parents Mag 53:36+ Ja '78
Detecting learning problems before children start school; North Carolina's Statewide Preschool Screening Program. F. Peterson and J. R. Kesselman. il McCalls 104:69-70 Ag '77
Grouping for instruction: 1965, 1975, 1985. G. B. Helton and others. Educ Digest 43:53-6 D '77
Hair element content in learning disabled children. R. O. Pihl and M. Parkes. bibl il Science 198:204-6 O 14 '77
Helping learning-disabled children; work of the New York Institute for Child Development. J. Gaylin. Psychol Today 10:96+ Ap '77
Lead, cadmium linked to learning problems. Sci N 112:262 O 22 '77
Learning disabilities linked to elements. il Chemistry 50:21-2 D '77
School before school can be the answer; work of the Delayed Development Center at Redondo Beach, Calif. C. Luetje. il Parents Mag 53:37+ Ja '78
Special feature on learning disabilities. Todays Educ 66:36-48+ N '77
Suspect your child has a learning disability? A. Rosenblum. il Good H 186:167 Ja '78

LEARNING materials. See Teaching—Aids and devices

LEARNING technology. See Educational technology

LEARNING theory. See Learning, Psychology of

LEARSON, T. Vincent
Department discusses international approaches to problem of oil spills from vessels: statement, January 11, 1977. Dept State Bull 76:113-16 F 7 '77

LEARY, Mary Ellen
Farmers vs. agribusiness. Nation 225:646-50 D 17 '77

LEARY, Timothy
Faces of Timothy Leary. D. K. Mano. Nat R 29:449-50 Ap 15 '77 *

LEASE and rental services
Things they must tell you when you lease something; amendment to the truth-in-lending law to cover leases. Changing T 31:41-2 Mr '77
See also
Agricultural machinery—Leasing and renting
Airplanes—Leasing and renting
Automobiles—Leasing and renting
Banks and banking—Leasing business

LEASE and rental services—See also—*Continued*
Computers—Leasing and renting
Farmhouses—Leasing and renting
Furniture—Leasing and renting
Swine houses—Leasing and renting
Tank ships—Leasing and renting
Yachts—Leasing and renting

LEASES
50-50 split isn't always so; crop share lease. Suc Farm 75:no2 54 F '77
See also
Eviction
Mining leases
Oil and gas leases

LEASEWAY Transportation Corporation
There are many ways to make money. il Forbes 119:61-2 F 1 '77

LEATHER braces, Orthopedic. See Orthopedic braces

LEATHER work
Address book; supply stores. S. Sunderlin. House B 119:26+ O '77
Workshop: wet forming in leather. M. Lloyd. il Craft Horiz 37:49-51 Je '77

LEATON, Anne
This domain, that dominion; story. Esquire 87: 118-19 My '77

LEAVES
Feininger's guide to identifying trees. A. Feininger. il Horticulture 55:32-49 Je '77
See also
Color of leaves
Phyllotaxis
Stomata

LEAVES, Fossil
Flavonoid and other chemical constituents of fossil miocene celtis and ulmus (succor creek flora) D. E. Giannasi and K. J. Niklas. bibl il Science 197:765-7 Ag 19 '77

LEAVES in art
Salute to autumn leaves. J. Bear and F. Bear. il por Conservationist 32:38-9 N '77

LEAVITT, Donald
Color prints at Tri-X speed. il Pop Phot 81:82-9+ Ag '77
Fujicolor F-11 400. il Pop Phot 80:83-7+ Mr '77
Ilford HP5: how it compares to Tri-X. il Pop Phot 80:98-103+ My '77
Instant photography. il por Pop Phot 80:62+ My; 66+, 128+ Je; 81:141+ S; 74+ O; 68+ D '77

LEAX, John
Grace soften my dreams—John Berryman. Chr Today 21:25-6 Ap 1 '77

LEBANON
See also
Beirut
Economic assistance, American—Lebanon
Villages—Lebanon

Civil War, 1975-

Lebanon flare-up: new threat to Mideast peace. map U.S. News 83:36 O 3 '77
War that won't go away. J. M. Markham. il N Y Times Mag p33+ O 9 '77

Peace and mediation

Edgy cease-fire; with report by D. Brelis and Abu Said Abu Rish. il Time 110:52+ O 10 '77
Leaky truce and lingering misery. il U.S. News 82:38 My 16 '77

Foreign relations

Israel

See Israel—Foreign relations—Lebanon

Politics and government

Beirut: better, but not yet well. il map Time 110:42-3 N 14 '77
Right and left in Lebanon. B. Lewis. New Repub 177:20-3 S 10 '77

Relief work

Lebanese delegation discusses rehabilitation needs; Department statement. Dept State Bull 76:91-2 Ja 31 '77
U.S. increases relief aid to Lebanon. Dept State Bull 76:234 Mr 14 '77

Religious institutions and affairs

Right and left in Lebanon. B. Lewis. New Repub 177:20-3 S 10 '77

LEBARON, Ervil
Deadly messenger of God. il por Time 110:31 Ag 29 '77 *

LEBLANC, Rena Dictor
Tatum O'Neal: a child once again. por Good H 184:56+ Je '77

LEBO, Harlan
Drawing his own conclusions. il pors Writers Digest 57:32-3 D '77

LE BOYER, Frederick
Leboyer's babies. R. J. Trotter. il Sci N 111:59 Ja 22 '77 *

LEBOYER method. See Childbirth

LE CARRÉ, John, pseud. See Cornwell, D. J. M.

LE CORBEILLER, Clare
China trade armorial porcelain in America. bibl il Antiques 112:1124-9 D '77

LE CORBUSIER
Death of the moderns. W. Von Eckardt. il New Repub 177:31-3 Ag 6 '77 *
House that modernism built; Corbusian revival. N. Silver. il Harpers 255:77+ Ag '77 *

LECTINS
Lectin release by soybean seeds. D. W. Fountain and others. bibl il Science 197:1185-7 S 16 '77
Lectins. N. Sharon. il Sci Am 236:18, 108-16+ bibl (p 142) Je '77
Looking at lectins: do they function in recognition processes? J. L. Marx. il Science 196: 1429-30+ Je 24 '77

LED Zeppelin (rock group) See Rock groups

LEDBETTER, Eve
Siblings; poem. Good H 185:160 Jl '77

LEDDIHN, Erik Maria, Ritter von Kuehnelt. See Kuehnelt-Leddihn, E. M. von

LEDEEN, Michael A.
Cultural terrorism. Harpers 255:99-100 S '77
Eurocommunists exposed. New Repub 176:13-14 Mr 26 '77
Europe breaks apart. Commentary 63:53-7 My '77
Europe's future. New Repub 177:8-9 Jl 2 '77
Europe's sickest man. New Repub 176:8-10 F 12 '77
Eurosocialism? New Repub 177:25 O 8 '77
Italian communism at home and abroad: the Soviet connection. Commentary 62:51-4 N '76; 63:26+ Mr '77
Italy awaits Caesar. New Repub 178:16-20 Ja 7 '78
Kremlin cracks the whip. New Repub 177:22-3 Ag 6 '77
News about Eurocommunism. Commentary 64: 53-7 O '77
Unknown catacombs. Commentary 64:64-6 S; 17-18 N '77
Visions of hobnails. New Repub 177:17-19 N 19 '77
(ed) See Mosse, G. L. On Nazism

LEDER, Dennis
Calder's universe. America 136:298-9 Ap 2 '77
European Master Paintings from Swiss Collections. America 136:149-50 F 19 '77
Fine arts. America 137:35-6, 244-5, 422 Jl 16, O 15, D 10 '77
Tokugawa collection. America 137:82 Ag 13 '77

LEDER, P. and others
EK2 derivatives of bacteriophage lambda useful in the cloning of DNA from higher organisms: the λgtWES system. bibl il Science 196:175-7 Ap 8 '77

LEDERER, Esther Pauline (Friedman) See Landers, A. pseud

LEDGER, Philip
Purcell: selected works conducted by P. Ledger. J. W. Barker. Am Rec G 41:27-9 N '77 *

LEE, Amy S. and others
Interspersion of short repetitive sequences studied in cloned sea urchin DNA fragments. bibl il Science 196:189-92 Ap 8 '77

LEE, Andrew Daulton
Pyramider spy case. R. Steele and N. Horrock. il por Newsweek 89:29 Ap 18 '77 *
Stealing the company store. il por Time 109:19 My 9 '77 *
To be young, rich—and a spy. R. Lindsey. il pors N Y Times Mag p 18+ My 22 '77 *

LEE, Art
Care and feeding of a trout stream. il Sports Illus 46:30-2 Ja 31 '77

LEE, Arthur M.
Facing up to the vo-ed information demand. Educ Digest 42:50-3 Ja '77

LEE, Benjamin W.
Obituary
Phys Today por 30:76-8 S '77. C. Quigg and S. Weinberg

LEE, Bong-ja
Letter. por Sch Arts 76:52 Ap '77

LEE, Dinah
On knowing when to come home. Mademoiselle 83:34+ Jl '77

LEE, Galen
Echoes at the Frick. New Yorker 53:27-8 Ap 11 '77 *

LEE, Jeremiah, Mansion, Marblehead. See Historic houses, sites, etc.—Massachusetts

LEE, Joseph
Tribute to Joseph Lee. il por Parks & Rec 12: 43-5 Ja '77 *

LEE, Karen
Orient express; ed by G. Steves. il por Am Home 80:60-1+ N '77

LEE, Kuan-yew
Singapore, where 1984 is now. H. Wasserman. map Progressive 41:34-8 Ap '77 *

LEE, Kuo-hsiung, and others
Sesquiterpene antitumor agents: inhibitors of cellular metabolism. bibl il Science 196:533-6 Ap 29 '77

LEE, Laurel
Patience. J. W. Donohue. America 137:311-12 N 5 '77 *

LEE, Lois
Herbs for beauty, health and sex. il Am Home 80:19+ My '77

LEE, M. Owen
Only a matter of time. il Opera N 42:20-2+ S '77

LEE, Melvin, and others
Shy murderers. bibl il Psychol Today 11:68-70+ N '77

LEE, Mildred
Nightmare of Mildred Lee. F. W. Wright, Jr. por Writers Digest 57:38-9 D '77 *

LEE, Myrra
Society and the failure of the schools. Todays Educ 66:64-5 N '77

about

America's teacher of the year. M. S. Miller. por Ladies Home J 94:40 Ap '77 *

LEE, Oliver Milton
New Mexico incident. W. H. Hutchinson. bibl il pors Am West 14:4-7+ N '77 *

LEE, Rand B.
Thrill of dill. il Org Gard & Farm 24:90-1 N '77

LEE, Sook Won, and others
25-Hydroxycholecalciferol to 1,25-dihydroxycholecalciferol: conversion impaired by systemic metabolic acirosis. bibl il Science 195:994-6 Mr 11 '77

LEE, Sun-hee. See Krasne, F. B. jt auth

LEE, Sung-yang
Man's obsession reveals the riches of a hidden world. T. Green. il por Smithsonian 8:80-7 bibl(p 161) N '77 *

LEE, Wayne C.
How much is enough? Writers Digest 57:34+ D '77

LEE, William G.
Helping patients to vote. il MH 61:14-16 Summ '77

LEEDS, M. C.
Vets' reunions. . .with a purpose. Ret Liv 17:48+ My '77

LEEDS and Northrup Company
Perils of success. por Forbes 119:120 Je 15 '77

LEEFELDT, Christine
(tr) See Eco, U. De interpretatione, or the difficulty of being Marco Polo (on the occasion of Antonioni's China film)

LEENS, Alain
Manifesto for revolution in world library meetings; tr by L. Jacob. il por Am Lib 8:609-10 D '77

LEES, Al
Shop talk. See issues of Popular science

LEES, Benjamin
Detroit Sym: Lees premiere. por Hi Fi 27:MA30 F '77 *

LEES, Gene
Lees side. See issues of High fidelity and Musical America

LEETMAA, Ants
Effects of the winter of 1976-1977 on the northwestern Sargasso Sea. bibl il Science 198:188-9 O 14 '77

LEEUWENHOEK, Anthony van
Van Leeuwenhoek: father of microbiology. J. W. M. La Rivière. il por UNESCO Courier 30:34-6 Je '77 *

LEFEBER, Dirk W.
In praise of Darwin, Rembrandt, Mendel and other famous tulips. F. Endt. il Horticulture 55:26-39 Ag '77 *

LEFEBVRE, Marcel, Abp
Archbishop Lefebvre's religion. M. Hammond. Commonweal 104:422-3 Jl 8 '77; Reply. R. G. Cipolla. 104:610 S 30 '77 *
Church is full of wolves. il por Time 110:64 Jl 11 '77 *
Lefebvre's defiance. il por Newsweek 90:78 Jl 11 '77 *
Threat of schism. America 137:23-4 Jl 16 '77 *
Tradition vs. traditionalists. Chr Today 21:62 S 9 '77 *
When an archbishop rebels against the Pope. il por U.S. News 83:62 Jl 25 '77 *

LEFF, Deborah Jackson
Whitney's welcome; story. Seventeen 36:148-9 Mr '77

LEFF, Joel
Pension-fund manager's cautious investment strategy; interview, ed by A. Hershman. por Duns R 109:125-6+ My '77

LEFFLAND, Ella
Gorm; story. Atlantic 240:43-8 S '77
House of angels; story. Harpers 254:77-8 F '77

LEFFLER, Keith
National health insurance: a social placebo? bibl f Cur Hist 73:17-21+ Jl '77

LEFKOWITZ, Louis J.
A legal officer's dilemma. por Bull Atom Sci 33:11 My '77

LEFKOWITZ, Rochelle
Help for the sexually harassed. Ms 6:49 N '77

LEFT and right (political science) See Right and left (political science)

LEFT- and right-handedness
Fifty centuries of right-handedness: the historical record. S. Coren and C. Porac. bibl il Science 198:631-2 N 11 '77
Leonardo was a southpaw; left-handed artists. Vasari. il Art N 76:22-3 Ap '77
New findings about left-handed people. il U.S. News 82:33-4 Je 20 '77
On the other hand. . ; left-handed athletes. J. Kirshenbaum. il Sports Illus 46:60-3+ Ja 24 '77
On the other hand; products designed for lefties. J. Johnston. Am Home 80:29 S '77
Sinister companions: the left handed. C. Pogash. Sci Digest 81:17-20 Je '77
Variations in writing posture and cerebral organization. J. Levy and M. Reid; discussion. il Science 195:441 F 4 '77

Anecdotes, facetiae, satire, etc.

Meeting the challenges of a left-handed world. H. Robboy. Psychol Today 11:34-5 Je '77

LEFT wing (politics) See Right and left (political science)

LEFTOVERS. See Cookery—Leftovers

LEG exercises. See Exercise

LEGAL aid
Dawson boys; work of the Team Defense Project. M. Pinsky. Progressive 41:40-1 My '77
Friends of the poor; Southern Poverty Law Center. J. K. Footlick and V. E. Smith. il por Newsweek 90:95 Jl 18 '77
Immodest proposal; National Legal Service. M. E. Frankel. il N Y Times Mag p92-4+ D 4 '77
Lawyers with little clients; Legal Services for Children, Inc. E. Coyle. McCalls 104:53 S '77
Legal clinics: lawyers in storefronts. Consumer Rep 42:287 My '77
New clinics for kids in trouble; San Francisco's Legal Services for Children. il Time 109:46+ Ap 18 '77
Not-so-new South: legal aid in the death belt; Team Defense Project. M. Pinsky. il Nation 224:367-8 Mr 26 '77

See also

Legal Services Corporation

LEGAL assistance to the aged
Corporation, AoA sign pact aimed at legal needs of aged; Legal Services Corporation. Aging 272:7 Je '77
Washington memo; Paralegal Training for Seniors program at George Washington University's Institute of Law and Aging. R. D. Westgate. Ret Liv 17:16 F '77

LEGAL assistants

See also

United States—Supreme Court—Employees

LEGAL clinics. See Legal aid

LEGAL costs insurance. See Insurance, Litigation

LEGAL education. See Law—Study and teaching

LEGAL ethics
FTC challenge to the legal profession. Bus W p23 Ja 9 '78
Lawyers—can they police themselves? J. Kidney. il U.S. News 82:33-5 Je 6 '77
Tangling with an IRS code for professionals; rules of conduct for lawyers and accountants arguing tax cases. Bus W p84 F 14 '77

See also

Lawyers and clients

LEGAL fees. See Cost (law); Lawyers—Salaries, fees, etc.

LEGAL literature
Jailhouse law book; manual by J. L. Potts. A. Wolff. Sat R 4:54 Mr 19 '77

See also

Publishers and publishing—Legal literature

LEGAL profession. See Lawyers

LEGAL Services Corporation
Rich get rich, and the poor get lawyers. S. Chapman. New Repub 177:9-10+ S 24 '77

LEGAL Services for Children, Inc. See Legal aid

LEGAL services for the aged. See Legal assistance to the aged

LEGAL tender

See also

Paper money

LEGAL terms. See Law—Terminology

LEGALESE. See Law—Terminology

LEGECKIS, Richard
Long waves in the eastern equatorial Pacific Ocean: a view from a geostationary satellite. bibl il Science 197:1179-81 S 16 '77

LEGEND of Joseph; ballet. See Ballet reviews—Single works

LEGENDS

See also

Folklore
Mythology

LEGENDS, American
West that wasn't. C. L. Sonnichsen. il Am West 14:8-15 N '77

LEGENDS, German
St Hubertus: a conservation legacy. il Int Wildlife 7:42-3 N '77

LEGGAT, Al
Labor relations. See occasional issues of American city & county

LEGGE, Walter
Callas remembered: La Divina. pors Opera N 42:8-11+ N '77
Rosa: an eightieth birthday homage. il pors Opera N 41:10-15 Mr 12 '77

about

Music to my ears. I. Kolodin. il por Sat R 4:47 Ja 22 '77 *
Schwarzkopf-Legge master classes; singing classes at Juilliard. D. J. Soria. pors Hi Fi 27:MA5-6+ Mr '77 *
Search for perfection. R. Jacobson. il pors Opera N 41:24-7 Ja 22 '77 *

LEGGETT, Paul
Of heroes and devils: the supernatural on film. il Chr Today 22:19-21 N 18 '77

LEGGETT, Stanton
Coming battles over school-finance reform. Read Digest 110:21-4+ F '77

LEGGETT, William
Bound for glory and a wreath of roses. il Sports Illus 46:36-9 Ap 4 '77
For the moment, on the scent of roses. il Sports Illus 46:34-8 My 9 '77
He brought down the house. il Sports Illus 46:16-19 Je 20 '77
He flew for the crew. il Sports Illus 46:18-23 My 16 '77
Horse racing (cont) Sports Illus 46:42+ Ja 31; 89-90 My 2; 47:54+ Jl 11; 56-7 Ag 15; 85-7 S 5; 78+ S 26; 70-1 O 3; 76-7 O 24 '77
Is this horse that horse? il por Sports Illus 47:28-31 N 14 '77
No plater, but is he sterling? il Sports Illus 46:20-1 F 21 '77
Now there's just one more dance to go. il Sports Illus 46:20-1 My 30 '77
TV/radio. See occasional issues of Sports illustrated
This could be the start. il pors Sports Illus 46:16-21 Mr 7 '77
Tomato Patch George at the spa. il Sports Illus 47:18-19 Ag 29 '77

LEGHOLD traps. See Traps

LEGIONNAIRES' disease. See Diseases

LEGISLATION
See also
Judicial review
Referendum

Great Britain

Kilt bill; defeat of home rule for Wales and Scotland. F. Willey and M. MacPherson. il Newsweek 89:43+ Mr 7 '77
Labor runs afoul of a muddy loch; home rule bill for Scotland and Wales. Time 109:31-2 Mr 7 '77
On hanging on to Scotland; devolution bill. A. Lejeune. Nat R 29:330-1 Mr 18 '77

United States

Capitol Hill issues. U.S. News 82:66 Ap 25; 83:65 Jl 4; 66 S 26 '77
Cleaning the in box. P. Goldman and others. Newsweek 90:16-18 Ag 15 '77
Flurry in the Capital. il U.S. News 83:15-16 Ag 15 '77
How a bill becomes law. U.S. News 82:50-1 My 9 '77
See also
Library laws and legislation
United States—Congress
also subheads Law; Laws and legislation; Laws and regulations; Legal status, laws, etc. under various subjects, e.g. Industrial safety—Laws and legislation

LEGISLATIVE advocates. See Lobbyists and lobbying

LEGISLATIVE bodies

United States

See also
United States—Congress

LEGISLATORS
Lawyers lose ground in the statehouses. il map U.S. News 84:64 Ja 9 '78
See also
Congressmen

LEGROS, Alphonse
Commitment to the past. G. Weisberg. il Art N 76:150-2 Summ '77 *

LE GUIN, Ursula Kroeber
Gwilan's harp; story. Redbook 149:229-30 My '77

about

Fantasy. M. Parish. il Engl J 66:90-3 O '77 *

LEGUM, Colin
Avoiding disaster in Southern Africa. New Repub 176:11-13 F 12 '77
Cubans in Ethiopia. New Repub 176:15-16 Je 11 '77
Devil himself. il New Repub 177:17-19 D 17 '77
Horning in. New Repub 177:18-21 O 1 '77

LEGUMES
No-till corn: adding a legume to cover crop boosts yields. Suc Farm 75:35 S '77
Six steps for sod seeding old pastures and hayfields. Suc Farm 75:no2 56 F '77
See also
Alfalfa
Beans
Birdsfoot trefoil
Dioclea
Leucaena
Peanuts
Soybeans

LEGVOLD, Robert
Nature of Soviet power. For Affairs 56:49-71 O '77

LEGWEAR. See Hosiery

LEHANE, Stephen
Developmental curriculum: an articulation model for grades K-12. bibl il Clearing H 51:86-9 O '77

LEHAR, Franz
Merry widow. Review
Hi Fi 28:MA21 Ja '78 *

LEHMAN, David
Comment. Poetry 131:159-64 D '77
Heroic couple; poem. Poetry 130:209-10 Jl '77

LEHMAN Brothers, Inc-Kuhn, Loeb & Company merger. See Investment banking—Acquisitions and mergers

LEHMANN, Lotte
Lotte Lehmann remembered. J. Coveney. por Hi Fi 27:MA16-17+ Je '77 *

LEHMANN, Phyllis
Cutting sex bias out of vocational education. Educ Digest 42:33-5 Mr '77
Eye diseases: what can be done about them? Harp Baz 110:116+ Ag '77
Health & medicine. Harp Baz 110:186-9+ S '77
(ed) See Lance, J. W. Headaches: the causes and the cures

LEHMANN-HAUPT, Christopher
Lehmann-Haupt, two three, four. D. K. Mano. Esquire 87:34+ Mr '77 *

LEHR, Claire Joyce
Fathers in name only. il Parents Mag 52:44+ My '77

LEHRER, Jim
Should US scientists trade data with USSR? il Sci Digest 81:30-7+ Je '77

LEIDAHL, Lois C. See Moltz, H. jt auth

LEIDENFROST, Johann Gottlieb
Amateur scientist. J. Walker. il Sci Am 237:126-31 Ag '77 *

LEIGH, Cindy
Playground blend. il Camp Mag 49:6-8 My '77

LEIGH, Monroe
U.S. calls for responsible measures against international terrorism; statement, December 6, 1976. Dept State Bull 76:75-7 Ja 24 '77

LEIGHNINGER, Robert D. Jr
Science and the arts; excerpt from Society, December 1976. il Sci Digest 81:61-4 Ap '77

LEIGHTON, Alexander H.
Fabulous zoo. il Américas 29:16-18 F '77

LEINWAND, Leslie, and Ruddle, F. H.
Stimulation of in vitro translation of messenger RNA by actinomycin D and cordycepin. bibl il Science 197:381-3 Jl 22 '77

LEINWOLL, Stanley
1979 world radio conference how it will affect you. il Radio-Electr 48:77-80+ My '77
Will sunspots affect CB communications? il Pop Electr 11:51-4 Mr '77

LEISER, Dorothy
Merciful; poem. Chr Cent 94:327 Ap 6 '77

LEISER, Wayne
In order to be born again; poem. Chr Cent 94:426 My 4 '77

LEISURE
Beating the weekend blues; Make the most of your weekend. Seventeen 36:25-7 F '77
Carlson lecture: leisure time new challenge for the future. Camp Mag 49:4+ Ja '77
Education, work, and leisure: must they come in that order? F. Best and B. Stern. bibl il M Labor R 100:3-10 Jl '77
How Americans pursue happiness: special section. il U.S. News 82:60-72+ My 23 '77
If people cut back on driving . . . how business will deal with it. il U.S. News 82:29-30 Je 6 '77
Leisure. il Forbes 121:77-8+ Ja 9 '78
Living. See issues of House & garden incorporating Living for young homemakers
People are shelling out more than ever for a good time. il U.S. News 82:40-2 F 21 '77
Recreation renaissance: excerpt from Play behavior. J. Levy. Parks & Rec 12:16-20 D '77
See also
Hobbies
Time, Use of

LEISURE class
Veblen revisited. L. H. Lapham. Harpers 255:8+ N '77

LEITER, Robert
Certain light; story. Redbook 150:82 N '77

LEITZ Canada (firm) See Photographic industry—Canada

LEJEUNE, Anthony
Letter from London. Nat R 29:330-1, 1111 Mr 18, S 30 '77

LEKACHMAN, Robert
Carter's welfare plan: Nixon warmed over? Sat R 5:9 D 10 '77
Gnomes of Manhattan. Nation 225:715-20 D 31 '77
Making room for reason; interview, ed by W. Cowan and R. Hoyt. Current 197:34-49 N '77
On energy: a modest proposal. Nation 225:659-60 D 17 '77
Robert Lekachman on economics. New Repub 177:32-4 N 26 '77
Specter of full employment. Harpers 254:35-40 F '77; Same. Current 192:13-20 Ap '77

LELER, Robin. See Jeavons, J. jt auth

LELYVELD, Joseph
In America. See issues of New York times magazine
Our new voice at the U.N. il pors N Y Times Mag p 17-19+ F 6 '77

LEMANN, Nicholas
Seats at the banquet. il New Repub 177:16-20 O 29 '77

LE MANS Endurance Race. See Automobile racing—France

LEMANSKI, Larry F. and others
Evidence for abnormal heart induction in cardiac-mutant salamanders (ambystoma mexicanum) bibl il Science 196:894-6 My 20 '77

LEMBCKE, Jerry
Workplace democracy: a Canadian experiment. Progressive 41:29-32 Jl '77

LEMELLE, Wilbert J.
Nairobi—a brother. por Newsweek 90:70 N 21 '77 *

LEMESSURIER, William J.
Plastic-composite design cuts steel tonnage in Johns-Manville's new headquarters building. il Archit Rec 162:127-8 S '77

LEMKE, Alan
Which basics? Clearing H 51:14-16 S '77; Same abr. Educ Digest 43:6-8 N '77

LEMMON, Jack
Desperation in Hollywood: actor Jack Lemmon's view. il pors U.S. News 83:44 Ag 22 '77

LEMON, Denis
Mystical poetry in a court of law. T. Beeson. Chr Cent 94:838-9 S 28 '77 *

LEMON, Mattie Florence
Washington notebook. S. Booker. por Ebony 32:50 Ag '77 *

LEMON, Richard
Confessions of a town councilman. Read Digest 110:122-5 My '77

LEMON, Robert E.
Bird song: an acoustic flag. bibl BioScience 27:402-8 Je '77

LEMON desserts. See Desserts

LEMON rolls. See Cake

LEMONS, Abe
Shot of Lemons to cure the blues. E. Shrake. por Sports Illus 46:32-4+ Ja 17 '77

LEMONS
Good news about lemons. P. Schiller. Am Home 80:47 Ap '77

LEMURS
Mystery no more: Madagascar's intriguing indris. J. Pollock. il por Int Wildlife 7:12-16 Mr '77

LENARD, John. See Rothman, J. E. jt auth

L'ENGLE, Madeleine
Icon Tree; excerpt from Irrational season. Chr Cent 94:321-4 Ap 6 '77

LENGTH of life. See Longevity

LENIN, Vladimir Il'ich
Lenin: the myth that lives on. U.S. News 83:51 O 24 '77 *

LENINGRAD

Description

Across the Neva; Vasilyevsky Island. N. Lo Bello. il Travel 147:50-1 Ap '77

Social conditions

Slice of life. F. Coleman. il Newsweek 90:59 N 14 '77

LENINGRAD Philharmonic Orchestra. See Orchestras

LENS, Sidney
Arms race: a primer. Progressive 41:37-42 O '77; Same. il Current 197:50-61 N '77
Capitalism's last gasp. Current 195:27-36 S '77
Coming revolt in labor. Progressive 41:26-30 Ap '77
Jimmy Carter and the new reality. il por Chr Cent 94:10-14 Ja 5 '77
Perspectives. See issues of Progressive
Puerto Rico: trouble in the showcase. Progressive 41:13-19 Ag '77

LENS industry. See Optical industry

LENS of the eye. See Crystalline lens

LENS of the eye implants. See Eye—Surgery

LENS tissue. See Photography—Apparatus and supplies

LENSES
Lens that makes people see red; X-Chrom lens. F. Schumacher. McCalls 105:41 Ja '78
What is a Fabry lens? J. Africano and R. Quigley. il Sky & Tel 54:60-2 Jl '77
See also
Contact lenses
Eyeglasses
Glass, Optical

LENSES, Photographic
Burt Glinn: the right lens for the right look. M. O'Grady. il Mod Phot 41:78-83 Ag '77
Editorial; the ideal SLR lens. A. Goldsmith. por Pop Phot 81:12 D '77
First look:
Sun macro to wide-angle zoom. N. Rothschild. il Pop Phot 80:140+ Ap '77
Floating elements: do they really help? B. Sherman. il Mod Phot 41:78-9+ Jl '77
Hattersley class for beginners; what lenses do. R. Hattersley. il Pop Phot 80:96-9+ Mr '77
How to get close, closer, closest with any zoom lens. N. Rothschild. il Pop Phot 80:96-9+ F '77
Lenses. N. Goldberg. il Pop Phot 80:98-9+ Je '77
Movie methods; zoom lens. L. Drukker. il por Pop Phot 81:58+ D '77
1978 interchangeable lens list. D. L. Miller. Mod Phot 41:142-53+ N '77
Off beat: lens quality. N. Rothschild. il por Pop Phot 80:10+ Mr '77
Portrait lenses at budget prices. W. Kent. il Mech Illus 73:48-9+ My '77
Protechniques; selecting the right lens by focal length. E. Meyers. il Pop Phot 81:140+ S '77
Schwalberg at large; SLR interchangeable lens smorgasbord. B. Schwalberg. Pop Phot 80:58+ Ap '77
Schwalberg at large; ultrawide-angle lenses. B. Schwalberg. Pop Phot 80:55+ My '77
Shutter tripper. R. Ergenbright. il Trav/Holiday 149:10+ Ja '78
Super 8 zoomsmanship. N. R. Seider. il Pop Phot 80:126-9+ Ap '77
Techniques tomorrow:
High performance lenses. B. Sherman. il Mod Phot 41:57-8+ Jl '77
View from Kramer; Jena view-camera lenses. A. Kramer. il Mod Phot 41:58+ Ag '77
Wide-angle-to-telephoto macro zoom lenses. N. Goldberg. il Pop Phot 81:105-25+ D '77
Zoom lenses—now they're wide-angle, too! D. Sagarin. il Pop Mech 147:106-7+ Ap '77

Design

Shop talk. N. Goldberg. il Pop Phot 80:64+ Mr; 14+ My; 81:14+ D '77
Techniques tomorrow. B. Sherman. Mod Phot 41:66+ F; 17-18+ Ap '77

Testing

Modern tests:
55mm f/2.2 Fujinon; 24mm EBC Fujinon SW; Soligor C/D macro zoom. il Mod Phot 41:168-9 N '77
Komuranon 715 II and Komuranon 821. il Mod Phot 41:121 Ap '77
Komuranon zoom and Tessar, Yashinon, and Asahi telephoto lenses. il Mod Phot 41:106-8 F '77
Pentax-M 28 and 135mm lenses and Nikkor 50mm lens. il Mod Phot 41:118-21+ My '77
60mm Distagon, 150mm Sonnar, Sun 24-40mm and Vivitar 90mm Macro lenses. il Mod Phot 41:127-30+ Je '77
29mm f/2.8 Pentacon Electric, 135 mm f/2.8 Pantacon Electric and 35mm f/1.4 Zeiss Distagon. il Mod Phot 41:125-6 S '77
Shop talk:
New lens-testing system. N. Goldberg. il Pop Phot 81:18+ S '77
Testing for flare. N. Goldberg. il Pop Phot 81:10+ O '77

LENT, Blair
There's much more to the picture than meets the eye. il Wilson Lib Bull 52:161-4 O '77

LENT
Faith in focus:
Dimensions of the wheel. S. M. Schneiders. America 136:203-4 Mr 5 '77
Lent, repentance: a parable. D. L. Gelpi. America 136:223-4 Mr 12 '77
Lenten lethargy and the invisible neighbor. T. L. Schubeck. America 136:274-5 Mr 26 '77
Suffering, responsibility and ethics: a Lenten reflection. J. A. Coleman. America 136:300-1 Ap 2 '77
Sufferings of Job. R. A. F. MacKenzie. America 136:242 Mr 19 '77
To fill up the sufferings of Christ. J. A. Tetlow. America 136:169 F 26 '77
See also
Good Friday

LENTILS
See also
Cookery—Vegetables

LEON, Darryl
Where to take your parents in London. il por House & Gard 149:58+ F '77

LEÓN, Julio Antonio
Afro-Cuban poetry. il Américas 29:28-32 S '77
LEON, Karen
Nutty about squirrels. il por Seventeen 36:94+ My '77
LEON County Public Library, Tallahassee. See Libraries—Florida
LEONARD, George B.
Running for your life. Read Digest 110:43-4+ F '77
LEONARD, Jacob
More on J. Leonard. il Antiques 112:84-5 Jl '77 •
LEONARD, James F.
U.N. Disengagement Observer Force in Israel-Syria sector extended; statement, May 26, 1977. Dept State Bull 77:90-1 Jl 18 '77
U.N. Emergency Force in the Sinai extended for one year; statement, October 21, 1977. Dept State Bull 77:866-7 D 12 '77
U.N. Force in Cyprus extended for six months; statement, June 16, 1977. Dept State Bull 77: 133-4 Jl 25 '77
U.S. supports expansion of sanctions against Rhodesia; statement, May 27, 1977. Dept State Bull 77:66 Jl 11 '77
LEONARD, John
Case for remarriage. . .among friends. Ms 6:26-7 Ag '77
My college essay. il pors N Y Times Mag p28 Ja 16 '77
TV news is good, even when the news is bad. Vogue 167:221+ Mr '77
What do men really want from women? Mademoiselle 83:94 Jl '77
What have American writers got against businessmen? Forbes 119:117-22+ My 15 '77
LEONARD, Ray Charles
Day the gold turned green. P. Putnam. il Sports Illus 46:18-19 F 14 '77 •
LEONARDO da Vinci
Duchamp & Leonardo: L.H.O.O.Q-alikes; adaptation of address, February 17, 1974. T. Reff. bibl il Art in Am 65:82-93 Ja '77; Discussion. 65:5 My; 5 Jl '77 •
Leonardo da Vinci: a man for all ages. K. MacLeish. il Nat Geog 152:296-329 S '77 •
Lost da Vinci may yield its secret to ultrasonic science. D. Hellyer. il Sci Digest 82:16-19 Ag '77 •
LEONE, Robert A.
Real costs of regulation. il Harvard Bus R 55: 57-66 N '77
LEONHARD, William Edward
Parsons: from family business to industry leader. por Duns R 109:18-19 My '77 •
LEONI, Franco
Star-baritone's opera; L'Oracolo. D. Arthur. Am Rec G 40:38-40 S '77 •
LEOPARD seals. See Seals (animals)
LEOPARDS
Prince of cats. A. Singh. il por Nat Parks & Con Mag 51:4-9 Ap '77
LEOPOLD, Frederic
Mr Wood Duck. H. Bradshaw and V. Bradshaw. por Outdoor Life 160:100 Ag '77 •
LEOVY, Conway B.
Atmosphere of Mars; with biographical sketch. il Sci Am 237:18, 34-43 bibl(p 154) Jl '77
LEPÈRE, Auguste Louis
Commitment to the past. G. Weisberg. il Art N 76:150-2 Summ '77 •
LEPERS. See Leprosy and lepers
LE PICHON, Xavier
Expedition FAMOUS. il UNESCO Courier 30:30-2 Ja '77
LEPIDOPTERA
See also
Butterflies
LEPPER, Greg, and Reichenberger, Larry
Machinery management. See issues of Successful farming
LEPROSY and lepers
After Damien; Kalaupapa leper colony. G. Cant. il Time 110:114-16+ S 19 '77
Hellish spot in heavenly surroundings; Kalaupapa leper colony on Molokai. B. Gilbert. il maps Audubon 79:30-47 Mr '77
Molokai's celebrated leper colony. Sunset 159:94 O '77
LEPROSY research
In vitro growth of mycobacterium lepraemurium, an obligate intracellular microbe. A. M. Dhople and J. H. Hanks. bibl il Science 197:379-81 Jl 22 '77
LEPTONS. See Particles (nuclear physics)
LEPTOPHOS. See Insecticides
LERMAN, Eleanor
Comment. D. Allen. Poetry 130:348-50 S '77 •
LERMAN, Leo
People are talking about. . . See issues of Vogue
LERMAN, Robert I.
Jobs and income for the poor. il Society 14:60-2 My '77
LERMAN, Sidney, and Borkman, R. F.
Method for detecting 8-methoxypsoralen in the ocular lens. bibl il Science 197:1287-8 S 23 '77
LERNER, Alfred
Country cousin. por Forbes 119:44 Mr 15 '77 •
LERNER, Pauline, and others
Haloperidol: effect of long-term treatment on rat striatal dopamine synthesis and turnover. bibl il Science 197:181-3 Jl 8 '77
LERNOUX, Penny
El Salvador suppresses the church. Nation 225: 100-2 Ag 6 '77
Our S.O.B.s. il map Nation 225:72-7 Jl 23 '77
Popular religiosity. Nation 224:199-205 F 19 '77
LEROY, Jean F.
Compound ovary with open carpels in winteraceae (magnoliales) evolutionary implications. bibl il Science 196:977-8 My 27 '77
LESBIANISM
I am a second-generation lesbian; excerpt from We are everywhere: a celebration of lavender culture. S. Malcolm. Ms 6:13-16 O '77
Lesbian priest; ordination of E. Barrett. por Time 109:58 Ja 24 '77
Two feminists tell how they work; interview, ed by G. Steinem. C. Bunch. pors Ms 6:53+ Jl '77
Who's afraid of lesbian sex? A. Roiphe. Vogue 167:150-1+ Ag '77
LESCH-Nyhan syndrome
Hypoxanthine phosphoribosyltransferase: two-dimensional gels from normal and Lesch-Nyhan hemolyzates. G. S. Ghangas and G. Milman. bibl il Science 196:1119-20 Je 3 '77
Lesch-Nyhan syndrome: low dopamine-β-hydroxylase activity and diminished sympathetic response to stress and posture. C. R. Lake and M. G. Ziegler. bibl il Science 196:905-6 My 20 '77
LESHAN, Eda
Case of the beautiful blonde. il Parents Mag 52: 42+ Jl '77
Discipline do's and dont's. Parents Mag 52:26+ O '77
What do the experts know about your child? il Parents Mag 52:40-1+ Je '77
LESHAN, Lawrence
Two faces of meditation. il Parents Mag 52:71+ N '77
LESHER, Richard L.
(ed) See Eizenstat, S. E. Stuart Eizenstat: an inside look at how the White House operates
(ed) See Lance, B. OMB director Bert Lance seeks business help
LESIONS, Brain. See Brain damage
LESKOVAR, Branko
Microchannel plates. bibl il Phys Today 30:42-9 N '77
LESLIE, Eleanor
Breakfast at Brennan's; story. Redbook 148:112-13 Mr '77
LESLY, Philip
Missing the people's message; address, October 24, 1977. Vital Speeches 44:141-5 D 15 '77
LESOTHO
See also
United Nations—Lesotho

Foreign relations

South Africa

See South Africa—Foreign relations—Lesotho
LESTER, Henry A.
Response to acetylcholine; with biographical sketch. il Sci Am 236:16; 106-16+ F '77
LESURE, Thomas B.
Air/sea circuit; packaged fly/cruise vacation trips. il Travel 148:28-31+ S '77
Cruising the Caribbean. il Trav/Holiday 148: 44-51 N '77
South America by ship. il Travel 147:34-9 Je '77
LE-TAN, Pierre
Eccentrics of the world. il Horizon 19:88-9 Ja '77
LETELIER, Orlando
Blow-up. K. Lynch. Nat R 29:320 Mr 18 '77 •
CIA's apprentices. Nation 224:772 Je 25 '77 •
Letelier/Moffitt murder. S. Landau and R. Stavins. por Nation 224:358-60 Mr 26 '77 •
Letelier-Moffitt mystery. J. Stein. Progressive 41:36-9 N '77 •
LETOKHOV, V. S.
Photophysics and photochemistry. bibl il Phys Today 30:23-32 My '77
LETTER stocks. See Stocks
LETTER writing
Sincerely yours, next. . .Sincerely yours next. . ; prefabricated letters and automatic signature machine answering letters to J. Carter. M. Friedman. il Sr Schol 109:8-9+ My 5 '77
See also
International correspondence
LETTER writing by children. See Letters by children
LETTERED olive snails. See Snails
LETTERING
See also
Calligraphy

LETTERS
Great soap opera fan letters; excerpt from Letters from soap opera fans; comp by B. Adler. Good H 184:76+ Mr '77
See also
Chain letters
Love letters
LETTERS by children
Kids' letters to President Carter; excerpt; comp by B. Adler. il McCalls 105:165+ N '77
LETTERS of complaint. See Complaints
LETTERS to Congressmen. See Lobbyists and lobbying
LETTERS to President Carter. See Carter. J.—Correspondence
LETTERS to the editor. See Periodicals—Letters to the editor
LETTUCE
Ingredients for top-quality summer lettuce. J. Jankowiak. il por Org Gard & Farm 24:122-3 Je '77
LEUCAENA
Today a weed—tomorrow a crop. il BioScience 27:825 D '77
LEUCINE
Ratio of plasma alpha amino-*n*-butyric acid to leucine as an empirical marker of alcoholism: diagnostic value. M. Y. Morgan and others. il Science 197:1183-5 S 16 '77
LEU-ENDORPHIN. See Endorphins
LEUKEMIA
Leukemia fighters in the bloodstream. Sci N 112:86-7 Ag 6 '77

Causes

See Cancer—Causes

Personal narratives

When Wendy's brother died. M. Keyser. Read Digest 111:95-7 Jl '77

Therapy

Leukemia breakthrough ... it can be cured! D. J. Buchanan-Davidson. il Parents Mag 52:22+ N '77
New signs of progress in battle against leukemia. il U.S. News 83:70-1 D 12 '77
Survival of Scott Helt; a case of acute myelocytic leukemia. D. Lund. Good H 184:91+ F '77
LEUKEMIA cells. See Cancer cells
LEUKEMIA inhibiting substances. See Cancer inhibiting substances
LEUKOCYTES
Direct resorption of bone by human monocytes. G. R. Mundy and others. bibl il Science 196:1109-11 Je 3 '77
Polymorphonuclear leukocytes: possible mechanism of accumulation in psoriasis. G. S. Lazarus and others. bibl il Science 198:1162-3 D 16 '77
LEUQUET, Paul
Challenges of engraving. J. Opalak. il Design (US) 78:14-16 Summ '77 *
LEVENSON, Marc D.
Coherent Raman spectroscopy. bibl il Phys Today 30:44-9 My; 52 D '77
LEVENSON, Mary Bess
Frankly speaking. por Seventeen 36:36 O '77
LEVENTHAL, Robert S.
Publicker: can the ailing distiller be turned around? por Duns R 110:26-7 N '77 *
LÉVÊQUE, Michel
French ceramist. C. Barth. il por Ceram Mo 25:48-50 N '77 *
LEVER, Janet
Child's play: what every parent needs to know. il Ms 5:22 F '77
LEVERTOV, Denise
Long way 'round; poem. il Ms 5:72-3 F '77
On the 32nd anniversary of the bombing of Hiroshima and Nagasaki: poem. Harpers 225:83 D '77
LÉVESQUE, René
Quebec; address, January 25, 1977. Vital Speeches 43:283-7 F 15 '77
We're a satellite; excerpts from interview, ed by A. de Borchgrave. il por Newsweek 90:54-5 D 5 '77
Why Quebec wants out—there are two nations here; interview, ed by K. M. Chrysler. il por U.S. News 83:70-2 S 26 '77

about

Canada: trouble above the border. R. H. Heindel. il por Intellect 105:226-7 F '77 *
Happy birthday, bonne chance. il Time 110:38 Jl 11 '77 *
Levesque checked. por Time 109:44 F 7 '77 *
Obsession with unity. A. Astrachan. New Repub 177:21-3 Ag 20 '77; Same. Current 196:46-52 O '77 *
Separatism and Quebec. K. M. Glazier. bibl f Cur Hist 72:154-7+ Ap '77 *
Trottier affair. K. Willenson and R. Manning. il por Newsweek 89:31 F 21 '77 *

Visit to France, 1977

France with love. il por Newsweek 90:67 N 14 '77
Gallic mischief. Nation 225:547 N 26 '77
LEVI, Herbert W.
Oh, what a tangled web. il Sci Digest 82:inside cover S '77
LEVI, Primo
Iron: a memoir; excerpt from Il sistema periodico, tr by S. Hunter and M. Risk. Commentary 64:45-9 Ag '77
Vanadium; memoir of Auschwitz; excerpt from Il sistema periodico. tr by G. Jochnowitz. Commentary 63:65-9 Mr '77
LEVI-MONTALCINI, Rita
NGF may hold the key—but to what? J. Arehart-Treichel. il por Sci N 111:330-1+ My 21 '77 *
LEVI Strauss and Company. See Strauss, Levi, and Company
LEVICH, Benjamin G.
Soviets turn deaf ear to pleas for Levich. C. Holden. por Science 197:349 Jl 22 '77 *
LEVIN, Bernard
Against the grain. il Horizon 19:90-2 Ja; 88-9 Mr '77
Fuse is laid for a new revolution. il por U.S. News 83:66 O 24 '77
LEVIN, Bruce R. and Stewart, F. M.
Probability of establishing chimeric plasmids in natural populations of bacteria. bibl il Science 196:218-20 Ap 8 '77
LEVIN, Burton
Human rights situation in the Republic of China; statement, June 14, 1977. Dept State Bull 77:50-4 Jl 11 '77
LEVIN, Dan
Boxing fits this old boy like a glove. il por Sports Illus 46:46-8+ Ap 4 '77
Fishing (cont) Sports Illus 47:44-5+ Ag 15 '77
Foreign affair ends a domestic dispute. il Sports Illus 47:18-19 Jl 11 '77
Nature. il Sports Illus 46:44+ F 14; 80+ Ap 18; 47:103-4+ O 10; 70+ N 7 '77
Rowing (cont) Sports Illus 46:54-5 My 30; 70+ Je 13 '77
LEVIN, Elaine
Children meet artists. il Sch Arts 76:20-2 Je '77
Definition Clay L.A. il Ceram Mo 25:40-2 N '77
Otto and Vivika Heino. il pors Ceram Mo 25:38-45 O '77
Ralph Bacerra. il pors Ceram Mo 25:21-7 Ap '77
LEVIN, Grigory M. Bongard-. See Bongard-Levin, G. M.
LEVIN, Martin
Martin Levin: the good humor man; interview, ed by L. Taylor. por Writers Digest 57:29 O '77
LEVINE, Anne
Publix, the Cleveland bookstore that could not go out of business, celebrates its 40 years. E. Batdorff. il pors Pub W 212:347-50 Ag 29 '77 *
LEVINE, Arnold J.
Cancer and viruses. bibl il por Chemistry 50:7-11 My '77
LEVINE, Carol
Two aliens. Commonweal 105:6-7 Ja 6 '78
LEVINE, Carole
3 not-so-easy pieces: a sexual journal; story. Ms 6:77-80 O '77
LEVINE, Elaine
American time line. il Sch Arts 76:30-2 Je '77
LEVINE, Elizabeth
Three construction projects with wood scraps. il Sch Arts 76:16-17 Je '77
LEVINE, Herbert Samuel. See Katsenelinboigen, A. jt auth
LEVINE, James
In the opera house: how much does neatness count? recordings of Andrea Chénier and La forza del destino. K. Furie. il por Hi Fi 27:71-4 Ag '77 *
Out of music, chaos? K. Monson. il por Hi Fi 27:MA28-30 N '77 *
LEVINE, James A.
Do fathers make good mothers? J. Greenwald. McCalls 104:65 F '77 *
LEVINE, James P.
Mobilizing eyewitnesses to crime: the use of radios and rewards. bibl il Intellect 105:254-7 F '77
LEVINE, Marc V.
Institution design and the separatist impulse: Quebec and the antebellum American South. bibl f Ann Am Acad 433:60-72 S '77
LEVINE, Marilyn
Ceramics of Marilyn Levine; interview, ed by S. Peterson. il Craft Horiz 37:40-3+ F '77
LEVINE, Michael W. See Shefner, J. M. jt auth
LEVINE, Milton Isra, and Seligmann, J. H.
Yes, there is a Santa Claus. Harp Baz 111:132+ D '77

LEVINE, Philip
Gift; poem. New Yorker 53:154 O 24 '77
Here and now; poem. Poetry 130:319-20 S '77
Last step; poem. New Yorker 53:123 S 19 '77
Life ahead; poem. New Yorker 53:188 N 28 '77
Miracle; poem. New Yorker 53:42 Mr 21 '77
We came back; poem. New Yorker 53:133 O 3 '77
You; Secret of their voices; New season; On the birth of good & evil during the long winter of '28; poems; excerpts from Names of the lost. Sat R 4:34-5 S 3 '77

about

Comment. J. Parini. Poetry 130:298-300 Ag '77 *

LEVINE, Robert
Publix, the Cleveland bookstore that could not go out of business, celebrates its 40 years. E. Batdorff. il pors Pub W 212:347-50 Ag 29 '77 *

LEVINSON, Eugene. See Sekuler, R. jt auth

LEVINSON, Harry
Oedipus in the board room; interview, ed by D. Goleman. bibl il por Psychol Today 11:44-6+ D '77

LEVINSON, Marc
AFSCME. Nation 225:208-10 S 10 '77

LEVINSON, Nancy
(ed) See Bateman, J. Super (market) script-writer

LEVINSON, Sanford
Specious morality of the law. Harpers 254:35-8+ My; 255:4-5 Jl '77

LEVINSTEIN, Henry
Infrared detectors. bibl il Phys Today 30:23-8 N '77

LEVITAN, Sar A.
Evaluating social programs. il Society 14:66-8 My '77

—and Alderman, K. C.
Military as an employer: past performance and future prospects; excerpt from Warriors at work. M Labor R 100:19-23 N '77

—and Taggart, Robert, 3d
Employment problems of disabled persons; excerpt from Jobs for the disabled. bibl il M Labor R 100:3-13 Mr '77

about

Federal hardship index? G. R. Rosen. por Duns R 110:63 D '77 *

LEVITATION
Maharishi over matter. K. L. Woodward and P. Abramson. Newsweek 89:98+ Je 13 '77

LEVITT, Harry
Cloudy side effects of sunny weather. il Parks & Rec 12:41 Ap '77

LEVITT, Theodore
As I see it: Big Mac theory of economic progress. il por Forbes 119:137-8 Ap 15 '77
Marketing and the corporate purpose; address, March 2, 1977. Vital Speeches 43:437-43 My 1 '77
Marketing when things change. il Harvard Bus R 55:107-13 N '77

LEVITT, William Jaird
Levittshahr will bring development housing to Tehran. D. Higgins. il Archit Rec 162:37 Ag '77 *
Profile. J. H. Ingersoll. il por House B 119:12+ Jl '77 *

LEVITT Corporation. See Construction industry

LEVITZ Furniture Corporation
Levitz redecorates its image. il por Bus W p59 Ag 8 '77

LEVODOPA. See Dopa

LEVSTIK, Frank R.
William T. Anderson: army officer, doctor, minister, and writer. il Negro Hist Bull 40:662-3 Ja '77

LEVY, Alan
Pollock and politics. Art N 76:96+ My '77
Sophia Loren: my 20 years with Carlo. pors McCalls 104:16+ Ag '77

LEVY, Bernard Henri
Trouble in Red City; tr by D. Betz. New Repub 177:23 O 8 '77

about

New Philosophes. M. S. Ross. Nat R 29:1361-2+ N 25 '77 *
Taking on Marx. K. L. Woodward and J. Friedman. il por Newsweek 90:68 Ag 22 '77 *

LEVY, David
Good try. il Sci Am 236:56+ Je '77 *

LEVY, Jerome
Fall shape-up for your skin; questions and answers. Harp Baz 110:104 S '77

LEVY, Joseph
Recreation renaissance; excerpt from Play behavior. Parks & Rec 12:16-20 D '77

LEVY, Natalie
Roadside eye-openers for the snapping. il Ret Liv 17:40-1 Ap '77

LEW, Marion
Santa Santa; story. Ladies Home J 94:88-9 D '77

LEWART, Cass R.
Build a legal in-flight airline receiver. il Pop Electr 11:61-3 My '77

LEWIN, Arie Y. and Wiles, J. G.
End of corporate enterprise? il pors Duns R 110:129-30+ O '77

LEWIN, Frank
Musical events. A. Porter. New Yorker 53:116-20 D 5 '77 *

LEWIN, Martin
Buffalo Slaughter; ed by L. R. Pearson. Am Lib 8:110 Mr '77

LEWIN, Nathan
Peculiar sense of justice. por Sat R 4:15-16+ My 28 '77

LEWIN, Roger. See Leakey, R. E. jt auth

LEWING, Paul
On-glaze brush decoration. il por Ceram Mo 25:55-8 N '77

LEWIS, Aaron. See Marcus, M. A. jt auth

LEWIS, Al Junior, murder trial. See Trials (murder)

LEWIS, Arthur H.
PW interviews; ed by B. A. Bergman. il por Pub W 212:14-15+ O 3 '77

LEWIS, Bernard
Anti-zionist resolution (cont) For Affairs 55:641-2 Ap '77
Right and left in Lebanon. New Repub 177:20-3 S 10 '77
Settling the Arab-Israeli conflict. Commentary 63:50-6 Je '77

LEWIS, C. Day
Adventures of the mind; excerpt from 1961 article. il Sat Eve Post 249:8 Jl '77

LEWIS, Clarence E.
Child looks at a tree. il Am For 83:30-3 Mr '77

LEWIS, Clive Staples
Lady stood on Perelandra. . .; excerpt from Perelandra. il Chr Today 21:10-12 Mr 4 '77

about

C. S. Lewis goes marching on. il por Time 110:92 D 5 '77 *
C. S. Lewis: The screwtape letters. L. S. Cunningham. Chr Cent 94:190-1 Mr 2 '77 *

LEWIS, Colby
Scouts survive island and vice versa. il Camp Mag 49:6-9 Ja '77

LEWIS, Edmonia
Edmonia Lewis arrives in Rome. C. P. Darcy. bibl f por Negro Hist Bull 40:688-9 Mr '77 *

LEWIS, Eleanor Parke (Custis)
George Washington's beautiful Nelly; story of the President and the granddaughter. D. Jackson. il por Am Heritage 28:80-5 F '77 *

LEWIS, Elma
Elma Lewis: keeping African culture alive in Boston. S. Quinn. il por Ms 5:14-15+ My '77 *

LEWIS, Flora
Europe's (almost) upbeat view of America. il N Y Times Mag p9-11+ Ag 7 '77

LEWIS, Gabriel
Soft-selling the treaties. S. J. Ungar. Atlantic 240:16 D '77 *

LEWIS, Harry
Live show daily at Hamburger Hamlet. A. Chamberlin. il pors Fortune 95:208-15+ Mr '77 *

LEWIS, Harry R. and Papadimitriou, C. H.
Efficiency of algorithms; with biographical sketches. il map Sci Am 238:12, 96-109 bibl(p 138+) Ja '78

LEWIS, Jeff. See Hiss, A. jt auth

LEWIS, Jerry D.
Santa Claus is alive and well. . . il por Ret Liv 17:34+ D '77

LEWIS, Jo Ann
Art will be considered just as important as the bricks. il por Art N 76:56-8 D '77
Modern Medici for public art. il Art N 76:36-7+ Ap '77

LEWIS, John
On to Washington. il pors Newsweek 90:25-6 S 5 '77 *
Realpolitik in Georgia: the fight for Young's seat. P. Kovler. Nation 224:400-1 Ap 2 '77 *

LEWIS, Jon C. and Kottke, B. A.
Endothelial damage and thrombocyte adhesion in pigeon atherosclerosis. bibl il Science 196:1007-9 My 27 '77

LEWIS, Linda
Domestic manners of the English. Atlantic 240:92+ N '77
Other people's houses. Atlantic 241:86-8 Ja '78

LEWIS, Margaret, and others
Experimental infarct sizing using computer processing and a three-dimensional model. bibl il Science 197:167-9 Jl 8 '77

LEWIS, Marilyn
Live show daily at Hamburger Hamlet. A. Chamberlin. il pors Fortune 95:208-15+ Mr '77 *

LEWIS, Marjorie
Why is poem a four-letter word? bibl SLJ 23:38-9 My '77

LEWIS, Mel
National Public Radio. W. Youngren. il por New Repub 177:23+ S 24 '77 *

LEWIS, Michael
Busy, purposeful world of a baby. bibl il por Psychol Today 10:53-4+ F '77

LEWIS, Milt
Don't buy it if you can build it or repair it. E. Morris. il por Ret Liv 17:45 Ap '77 *

LEWIS, Mort R.
Allan Nevins' triumph of will. il pors Am Hist Illus 11:26-33 Ja '77

LEWIS, Richard S.
Space prospect: factories and electric power. il Smithsonian 8:94-9 D '77

LEWIS, Roy S. and others
Strange xenon, extinct superheavy elements, and the solar neutrino puzzle. bibl Science 195: 209-10 Ja 14 '77

LEWIS, Shawn D.
Black women/white men: the other mixed marriage. il Ebony 33:37-9+ Ja '78
More than just handsome faces. il Ebony 32: 70-2+ Mr '77
Professional women: her fields have widened. il Ebony 32:114-16+ Ag '77
Who is Veronica Porche? il pors Ebony 32:60-2+ Jl '77
Why I'm not married. il Ebony 32:120+ S '77

LEWIS, Stephen G.
Stop fighting, start contracting. il Am City & County 92:67-9 Je '77

LEWIS, Tom
Part of my life in late August 1975 in the literal river of words; poem. Harpers 254:79 Mr '77

LEWIS, William H.
North Africa: the eye of the storm. Cur Hist 73:196-8+ D '77
U.S. arms embargo against South Africa; statement, July 20, 1977. Dept State Bull 77:320-2 S 5 '77

LEWITT, Sol
Sol Lewitt: the look of thought. D. B. Kuspit; rejoinder. Art in Am 65:5+ Ja '77 *

LEWITZKY, Bella
What a wild idea: Lewitzky and Gernreich design a dance. V. H. Swisher. il pors Dance Mag 51:75-7 Mr '77 *

LEWMAN, Mike, and Miller, Phillip
Supergraphics: student art that keeps on giving. il Sch Arts 77:38-40 D '77

LEWTY, Majorie
Winning of Kate; story; condensation of To catch a butterfly. Good H 185:209-12 O '77

LEXINGTON, Battle of, 1775
Paul Revere. B. A. Weisberger. il por Am Heritage 28:24-37 Ap '77

LEXITRON Corporation-Raytheon Company merger. See Corporations—Acquisitions and mergers

L'EXPRESS (periodical) See Periodicals—France

LEYLAND Motor Corporation, Ltd. See British Leyland Motor Corporation, Ltd

LEYS, Simon, pseud. See Ryckmans, P.

LHASA, Tibet
And on the roof of the world. L. Thomas. il U.S. News 83:37 N 14 '77

L'HEUREUX, John
Anatomy of bliss; story. Atlantic 239:66-7 Ap '77
Roman ordinary; story. Harpers 254:38-41 Mr '77
Success; story. Harpers 254:42-4 Mr '77

LHOTKA, Bonny Pierce
Watercolor page. il por Am Artist 41:76-9+ Ag '77

LIABILITY (law)
Abominable snow suits; claims for ski injuries. il Time 111:60-1 Ja 16 '78
Are lawyers, courts, big government dulling America's moral sense? G. E. Jones. U.S. News 83:84-5 S 26 '77
Business and the products liability crisis; legal aspects of no-fault insurance; address, October 27, 1976. J. O'Connell. Vital Speeches 43:278-80 F 15 '77
Can we afford to idiot-proof the woods? product liability of outdoor equipment. R. Starnes. Outdoor Life 160:12+ S '77
Dilemma in product liability. J. C. Perham. il Duns R 109:48-50+ Ja '77
Disaster damages; international airline-disaster litigation. J. K. Footlick and others. il Newsweek 89:111 Ap 18 '77
Ducking liability at sea; oil tanker accidents. S. Novick. il Environment 19:25-7+ Ja '77
GAO criticizes federal procurement agencies for their leniency with A-E errors and omissions; report entitled Procedures used for holding architects and engineers responsible for the quality of their design work. W. Hickman. Archit Rec 162:34 S '77
Growing criminal liability of executives; J. R. Park case. T. McAdams and R. C. Miljus. bibl f Harvard Bus R 55:36-7+ Mr '77
Legal risks and bold programming; liability for risk activities. J. Rankin. Parks & Rec 12: 47-8+ Jl '77
Liabilities of sitting on a bank board. il Bus W p86-7 S 26 '77
Minimizing defects in plans and specification; question of liability of architects and engineers. M. Stokes. Archit Rec 162:49 Jl '77
OSHA and the architect: a recent case lessens designer liability; liability for violations of the Construction Safety Standards. A. T. Kornblut. Archit Rec 162:63 N '77
Product liability; address, September 22, 1977. D. Angel. Vital Speeches 44:49-52 N 1 '77
Product liability costs may spur legislation. Aviation W 106:17 Ja 10 '77
Product liability—the search for solutions. il Nations Bus 65:24-6+ Je '77
Putting the issue of professional liability into perspective; with introd by C. E. Hamlin. A. T. Kornblut. Archit Rec 161:57 F '77
Responsibility for product innovation:how to be progressive, yet reduce your risk. H. J. Rosen. Archit Rec 162:14 mid-O '77
Tenerife case may alter liability rules. il Aviation W 106:32 Ap 4 '77
Treaty prerogatives in debate: Warsaw Convention amendments to raise carrier liability to air crash victims. Aviation W 107:29 Ag 1 '77
What went wrong? accident investigators Failure Analysis Associates. A. J. Mayer and D. Gram. il Newsweek 89:82 My 9 '77
See also
Damages
Government liability

LIABILITY insurance. See Insurance, Liability

LIBBEY, Elizabeth
On making his bed one morning; poem. New Yorker 53:63 Ag 15 '77

LIBBY, Bill
(ed) See Allison, B. Hot blood down in Dixie
(ed) See Pearson, D. Hot blood down in Dixie
(ed) See Petty, R. Hot blood down in Dixie

LIBEL and slander
Blood and money is target of $20-million libel suit. M. Reuter. Pub W 212:35 O 3 '77
Court dismisses $5-million libel claim against Holt. S. Wagner. Pub W 212:27-8 Jl 25 '77
Humorists: in jest or in jail? cases in Great Britain. P. Campbell. il Sat R 4:16+ Je 11 '77
See also
Trials (libel)

LIBERAL arts education. See Education, Humanistic

LIBERALISM
Bring back hell fire. A. Tonelson. New Repub 176:18-19 F 26 '77
Carter and compassion. M. Greenfield. Newsweek 90:104 D 19 '77
Carter and the evolution of liberalism. R. J. Bresler. Intellect 106:22-3 Ag '77
Congress: Liberals at bay. G. R. Rosen. il Duns R 110:40-4 S '77
Cultural counterrevolution. R. J. Bresler. Intellect 106:115 O '77
Liberals' dilemma: a professor's stump speech that worked. D. P. Moynihan. New Repub 176:57-60 Ja 22 '77
New religion for liberals. H. Sidey. il Time 109:37 My 23 '77
Not much cheer for liberals; policies of J. Carter. il Time 109:15-16 My 16 '77
Prophet of reason; J. Locke. P. W. Schmidtchen. il por Hobbies 82:134-6+ Ap '77
Think positive? W. T. Brookes. U.S. News 83: 116 O 17 '77
Three tales of a city. P. Steinfels. Commonweal 104:360-1+ Je 10 '77
Will the liberals buck Carter? G. R. Rosen. por Duns R 110:37 Ag '77
See also
Conservatism

LIBERALISM (religion)
Altar/throne clash updated; excerpt from address. J. J. Petuchowski. Chr Today 21:20+ S 23 '77

LIBERATION theology
Beyond masochism: a white male primal scream. R. C. Morgan. Chr Cent 94:1141-3 D 7 '77
Evangelical's duty to the Latin American poor. H. B. Kuhn. Chr Today 21:67-8 F 4 '77; Reply. 21:23-4 Je 3 '77
Liberation theology. G. R. Bucher. bibl il Intellect 105:278-80 F '77
More on liberation theology; Latin America. H. B. Kuhn. Chr Today 22:66-7 N 4 '77

LIBERATOR (periodical)
Claude McKay as an artist. S. Warren. bibl f por Negro Hist Bull 40:685-7 Mr '77

LIBERIA
See also
Public health—Liberia

LIBERMAN, Alexander
Alexander Liberman at Storm King. C. Ratcliff. il Art in Am 65:100-1 N '77 *

LIBERMAN, Sandu
Strictly a realist. Vasari. il Art N 76:18+ Summ '77 *

LIBERTARIANISM. See Liberty

LIBERTY
Failure of libertarianism. J. Tuccille. Nat R 29: 489+ Ap 29 '77
Fair versus free. M. Friedman. Newsweek 90:70 Jl 4 '77
Struggle for freedom; excerpts from address. A. I. Solzhenitsyn. por Intellect 105:302-3 Mr '77
Why I am a civil libertarian. R. L. MacBride. Sat Eve Post 249:34-5+ O '77

LIBERTY—*Continued*
Wilson to Carter: a 60-year American crusade for freedom. il U.S. News 82:18-19 Mr 14 '77
See also
American Civil Liberties Union
Anarchism and anarchists
Civil rights
Democracy
Equality
Free speech
Freedom of the press
Intellectual liberty
Liberalism
Religious liberty

LIBERTY of the press. See Freedom of the press

LIBICH, Suzanna
(tr) See Gottstein, K. Nuclear energy for the third world

LIBRAIRIE Hachette (firm) See Publishers and publishing—France

LIBRARIANS
Better utilization of personnel. J. C. MacCampbell. Lib J 102:1718-20 S 1 '77
Cavities and conscience pangs: candy can cause both; image of librarians in television commercials. F. J. Dempsey. il Am Lib 8:231 My '77
Hire the handicapped librarian! W. A. Zerface. bibl il por Wilson Lib Bull 51:656-60 Ap '77
News report 1976. K. Nyren. il Lib J 102:174-6+ Ja 15 '77
Some early women librarians in New England. E. McCauley. bibl il Wilson Lib Bull 51:648-55 Ap '77
What's in a name? L. L. Shapiro. SLJ 24:95 O '77
See also
Childrens librarians
Collective bargaining—Librarians
College librarians

Anecdotes, facetiae, satire, etc.

Asian zodiac for librarians. A. Luster. il Am Lib 8:166 Mr '77
Functional immediacy for herniated specialists. W. Miller. il Am Lib 8:181 Ap '77

Certification

Canadian caution. L. M. Bewley. Lib J 102:1727 S 1 '77
Certification and competence. R. L. Burr. Lib J 102:1728-9 S 1 '77
Certification debate—a preview. J. Berry. Lib J 102:527 Mr 1 '77
Certification: more study needed. D. R. Dowell. bibl Lib J 102:1720-1 S 1 '77
Mandatory certification—a proposal that lost. M. J. Reagan. Lib J 102:1723-4 S 1 '77

Education

See Library schools and education

Placement

See Librarians—Selection and appointment

Political activities

Stroke the legislators. F. H. Pletz. Am Lib 8:575-6 N '77

Qualifications

Library work without an M.L.S. R. E. Grady. Lib J 102:1726 S 1 '77
See also
College librarians—Qualifications
Librarians—Certification

Recruiting

LC Recruit/Intern Program: women moving up. Lib J 102:2118 O 15 '77

Salaries

Making more money as a librarian; views of librarians in the $35,000-$60,000 bracket. Am Lib 8:578-9 N '77
Placements & salaries 1976: a year of adjustment. C. L. Learmont and R. L. Darling. il pors Lib J 102:1345-51 Je 15 '77
See also
Librarians—Taxation

Selection and appointment

Calif. selection center eyes entry level skills. Lib J 102:1706-7 S 1 '77
Californians peg entry level Librarian I tasks. Lib J 102:2298+ N 15 '77
Downgrading menaces federal librarians' security. L. R. Pearson. Am Lib 8:175 Ap '77
Placements & salaries 1976: a year of adjustment. C. L. Learmont and R. L. Darling. il pors Lib J 102:1345-51 Je 15 '77
See also
Librarians—Recruiting

Taxation

Some thoughts on a librarian's income tax. Am Lib 8:62-3 F '77

Trade unions

See Librarians unions

Training

See Library schools and education

LIBRARIANS, Professional ethics for
Ethics Committee interprets code, asks for comments. Am Lib 8:500-1 O '77

LIBRARIANS in literature
Writing the library whodunit; Dewey decimated. C. A. Goodrum. il Am Lib 8:194-6 Ap '77

LIBRARIANS unions
Who do you think will fight for your raises? A. Henninger. Am Lib 8:579 N '77
See also
Collective bargaining—Librarians

LIBRARIANSHIP as a profession
Alternative info careers eyed in Syracuse. D. R. Smith. por Lib J 102:1712 S 1 '77
Professionalism; symposium; with editorial comment. Lib J 102:1699, 1715-31 S 1 '77
What's my line? workshop on Alternative Careers in Information and Library Services. E. P. Mitchell. Am Lib 8:417 S '77

LIBRARIES
Action line; questions and answers. See issues of American libraries
See also
Blind, Libraries for the
College libraries
Librarians
Newspapers—Library news
Presidential libraries
Prison libraries
School libraries

Acquisitions

Out of control—indefinitely. L. N. Gerhardt. SLJ 24:63 O '77
Publishers, librarians ponder BISG study of expected lower library acquisitions. Pub W 211:32+ Mr 28 '77
Third World acquisitions: a report on the workshop at LC. A. Pieratt and H. B. Neikirk. Lib J 102:978 My 1 '77
See also
College libraries—Acquisitions

Administration

See Library administration

Advertising

See Library publicity

Anecdotes, facetiae, satire, etc.

Hooper and the non-user. K. Nyren. Lib J 102:776-7 Ap 1 '77

Architecture

See Library architecture

Audio-visual materials

See Libraries and audio-visual materials

Automation

Database vendors in a price war? Lib J 102:665 Mr 15 '77
Developing a computerized organization file. J. E. Wegener and J. A. Haskett. il Lib J 102:2323-5 N 15 '77
Library catalog in a computerized environment; adaptation of address, October 1975. S. M. Malinconico; reply with rejoinder. A. D. Hogan. Wilson Lib Bull 51:724-5 My '77
Missouri science library nixes online service; the Linda Hall Library, Kansas City, Mo; with views by T. D. Gillies. Lib J 102:1547 Ag '77
More libraries switch to COM catalogs. Lib J 102:672 Mr 15 '77
Opening minds to closing catalogs, or, When can we throw out the cards? METRO seminar. A. Plotnik. Am Lib 8:594-5 D '77
Training in new technology: OCLC, data bases. Lib J 102:443 F 15 '77
Wanted: a minicomputer serials control system. R. De Gennaro. bibl Lib J 102:878-9 Ap 15 '77
See also
College libraries—Automation

Bibliographical control

See Bibliographical control

Book collections

See also
Libraries—Childrens collections
Libraries—Paperback book collections

Book losses

See also
Library protection systems
Library thefts

Book selection

See Book selection

Branches and stations

Branch library in the city. . options for the future; symposium; with editorial comment. il Lib J 102:145, 161-73 Ja 15 '77
Prefabricated and portable library units offer quick and easy extension of service. A. G. Bushman. il Am Lib 8:546-8 N '77
Ways to up city branch use charted by Ohio study; report by the Public Library of Columbus & Franklin County. Lib J 102:2208 N 1 '77

LIBRARIES—*Continued*

Business services

Politics for progress: Libraries & information industries: legislation for joint development. M. R. Owens. por Lib J 102:1819-22 S 15 '77

Caricatures and cartoons

Taxpayer's-eye view of library jargon. C. Slack. il Am Lib 8:554-5 N '77

Censorship

Boys and girls and sex and libraries; question of censorship and restricted circulation policy at the Oklahoma County Libraries System; adaptation of address; October 1976; with editorial comment. D. H. Meyers. bibl il por Lib J 102:433, 457-63 F 15 '77

Media censorship and printist librarians; interview, ed by D. Boyle. D. Roberts. por Am Lib 8:542-5 N '77

Tears and ivory towers: California libraries during the McCarthy era. W. E. Benemann. bibl il Am Lib 8:305-9 Je '77

See also

Library Bill of Rights

School libraries—Censorship

Childrens collections

Case for The five Chinese brothers. S. G. Lanes. il SLJ 24:90-1 O '77

Why is poem a four-letter word? childrens poetry anthologies. M. Lewis. bibl SLJ 23:38-9 My '77

See also

United States—Education, Office of—Educational Materials Review Center

Circulation, loans, etc.

Boys and girls and sex and libraries; question of censorship and restricted circulation policy at the Oklahoma County Libraries System; adaptation of address; October 1976; with editorial comment. D. H. Meyers. bibl il por Lib J 102:433, 457-63 F 15 '77

Retrieving overdue materials in court. V. E. Beck. Lib J 102:2321-2 N 15 '77

University of Illinois annual survey: public libraries show 12-percent spending jump. il Am Lib 8:391 Jl '77

See also

College libraries—Circulation, loans, etc.

Interlibrary loans

Libraries—Fines

Conservation and restoration of materials

See Libraries—Technical processes

Cooperative service

See Library cooperation

Cultural programs

Authors & artists as speakers: suggestions for hassle-free visits; excerpt from How to do a dozen (and more) odd jobs in library service. J. Botham and W. C. Morris. il por SLJ 24:27-9 D '77

How Denver brings history to life; Denver Public Library's TimeAlive! program. il Sunset 159:58 Ag '77

Equipment and supplies

See Library furniture and equipment

Federal aid

California's rich harvest; LSCA-funded projects. J. Berry. Lib J 102:1323 Je 15 '77

Carter budget: at last, better news for book, library and reading programs. S. Wagner. Pub W 211:32-4 Mr 7 '77

Education funding: a look at bills before Congress. S. Wagner. Pub W 211:36-7 Je 27 '77

Federal library funding. N. Savage. il Lib J 102:177 Ja 15 '77

For a big federal fix; views of R. Wedgeworth. J. Berry. Lib J 102:965 My 1 '77

Grants and how to get them: an update. S. Case. Am Lib 8:556-8 N '77

House-Senate conferees agree on education funds. S. Wagner. Pub W 212:46 Ag 1 '77

House-Senate group agrees on urban library funding. S. Wagner. Pub W 212:35-6 O 3 '77

LSCA in Massachusetts: Bureau under fire anew. Lib J 102:1545 Ag '77

Okla. audit says too much LSCA goes to systems. Lib J 102:2114 O 15 '77

Pennies from heaven. Wilson Lib Bull 52:289 D '77

Senators sponsor bills to save city libraries. S. Wagner. Pub W 211:26+ Mr 21 '77

State agency $$ efficiency stressed in COSLA study. Lib J 102:435+ F 15 '77

Threats to state agency $$ role shaping up. Lib J 102:1090+ My 15 '77

Wanted in 50 states; necessity of more aid to public libraries. K. Nyren. Lib J 102:743 Ap 1 '77

What good is Washington doing libraries? examination of report; Evaluation of the effectiveness of Federal funding of public libraries. R. Waters. bibl il Am Lib 8:566-8 N '77

See also

School libraries—Federal aid

Fiction collections

Launching the SF collection. N. Barron. Wilson Lib Bull 52:56-60 S '77

Film programs

See Libraries and motion pictures

Finance

Budget clashes threaten school & public libraries. SLJ 24:11 S '77

Budget woes persist in libraries; relief in proposed job legislation. SLJ 23:11 My '77

Buffalo slaughter; ed by L. R. Pearson. M. Lewin. Am Lib 8:110 Mr '77

Co-op options, $$ roles debated at ASLA. N. Savage. Lib J 102:1104+ My 15 '77

Fee dilemma. J. Berry. Lib J 102:651 Mr 15 '77

Libraries' decay speaks volumes. P. Hamill. il Wilson Lib Bull 52:48-50 S '77

Library dollar. See occasional issues of Library journal

Money, honey. Wilson Lib Bull 52:120-1 O '77

Money; symposium; with introd by W. D. Ford. il Am Lib 8:549-52+, 621-2 N, D '77

Rush to user fees: alternative proposals. F. M. Blake and E. L. Perlmutter. bibl Lib J 102:2005-8 O 1 '77

Special report: director's diary of a crisis; bookmobile budget of the Kearney, Neb, Public Library. R. Norman. Wilson Lib Bull 51:566-7 Mr '77

To charge or not to charge: a rationale. J. Linford. Lib J 102:2009-10 O 1 '77

Wonderful news in NYC, optimism in Boston. Am Lib 8:231-2 My '77

See also

Intergovernmental tax relations

Libraries—Federal aid

Libraries—State aid

Anecdotes, facetiae, satire, etc.

Hooper and the Nixon whiplash; fees for library service. K. Nyren. Lib J 102:991-3 My 1 '77

Fines

Overdues overdone. G. A. Carpenter. bibl Lib J 102:2137-8 O 15 '77

There is an alternative to fines. J. W. Griffith. SLJ 23:50 Ap '77

Furniture

See Library furniture and equipment

History

Library of Assurbanipal, King of the world; collection of Assyrian cuneiform tablets. L. Arksey. bibl il Wilson Lib Bull 51:832-40 Je '77

Information services

See Libraries—Reference services

Instruction in use

Future of reference service: death by complexity? J. Rosenblum. Wilson Lib Bull 52:300-1+ D '77

See also

College libraries—Instruction in use

School libraries—Instruction in use

International aspects

International. il Am Lib 8:409-12, 473-4 S, O '77

International library news. il Wilson Lib Bull 51:796-7 Je '77

See also

United States—Government Advisory Committee on International Book and Library Programs

Laws and legislation

See Library laws and legislation

Management

See Library administration

Manuscript collections

See also

College libraries—Manuscript collections

Microform collections

Making big ones out of little ones: current trends in micrographics. W. R. Hawken. il Lib J 102:2127-31 O 15 '77

Music collections

Live from the library; program of the Free Library of Philadelphia's Fleisher Collection. A. Milner. il Am Lib 8:75-6 F '77

Paperback book collections

Le$$ costly, more popular; paperback book collections in the Oklahoma County Libraries System. P. Little. il por Lib J 102:451-6 F 15 '77

The pull of paperback displays. H. H. Laskey. il SLJ 23:31-5 F '77

LIBRARIES—*Continued*

Periodical collections

Escalating journal prices: time to fight back. R. De Gennaro. bibl il Am Lib 8:69-74 F '77
New look at free magazines. C. E. Wall. il Am Lib 8:85-9 F '77
Periodical prices: 1975-77 update. F. F. Clasquin. il Lib J 102:2011-15 O 1 '77
School librarian recommends free magazines. M. C. Offerman. Am Lib 8:89 F '77

Phonograph and phonograph record collections

Diagnosis: slipped discography; R. H. Halsey's Classical music recordings for home and library. K. Furie. il Wilson Lib Bull 51:755-9 My '77
Lyons collection; Miami Dade Library music collection. J. Waxman. Am Rec G 40:6-7 Mr '77

Photocopying services

Clearance Center forms amid photocopying uncertainty. S. Wagner. Pub W 212:19+ Ag 8 '77
Copyright dilemma; report of conference at the Graduate Library School of Indiana University. L. X. Besant. Lib J 102:1337-9 Je 15 '77
Copyright, resource sharing, and hard times: a view from the field. R. De Gennaro. bibl Am Lib 8:430-5 S '77
Get it right; Copyright warnings required. Wilson Lib Bull 52:285 D '77
King report pegs photocopying volume; question of library royalty payments. Lib J 102:2381 D 1 '77
Librarian looks at the new copyright law. E. G. Holley. bibl il Am Lib 8:247-51 My '77
Library groups balk at new photocopying guidelines. S. Wagner. Pub W 212:20+ O 31 '77
Library urged to display copyright warning notices. S. Wagner. Pub W 212:24 S 5 '77
Living in the gap of ambiguity; an attorney's advice to libraries on the copyright law. L. I. Flacks. il Am Lib 8:252-7 My '77
More copyright information. Am Lib 8:624-5 D '77
NCLIS to propose center for periodical copying. S. Wagner. Pub W 211:21-2 My 2 '77
New Interlibrary loan form unveiled. W. R. Eshelman. Wilson Lib Bull 52:115-16 O '77
Publishers v. libraries, a real possibility. W. D. Nelson. Wilson Lib Bull 52:285-6 D '77

Photographic collections

Special report: minding your P.Q; photographic quotient. P. Segal. il Wilson Lib Bull 51:630-2 Ap '77

Public relations

Branches, service, and survival. M. Braverman. il por Lib J 102:163-5 Ja 15 '77
Discovering the public. J. Berry. Lib J 102:1799 S 15 '77
Giraffe factor. K. Nyren. Lib J 102:1979 O 1 '77
How a levy was won in the West; the Portland-Multnomah County Library. R. McCrank and L. McCrank. bibl il Am Lib 8:560-5 N '77
Library bond campaign to bank on; Vigo County Public Library, Terre Haute, Ind. E. N. Howard. Am Lib 8:622 D '77
See also
Library surveys

Reference services

Future of reference service: death by complexity? J. Rosenblum. Wilson Lib Bull 52:300-1+ D '77
Moon selects target: U.S. information policy; address, June 21, 1977. E. Moon. por Am Lib 8:381 Jl '77
Questions, anyone? C. A. Anthony. Am Educ 13:13-18 O '77
Social security $$ fuel N.C. library info center; Wake County Public Libraries System. Lib J 102:148 Ja 15 '77
What's new at the library? Lots. J. L. Lippert. Good H 184:229 Mr '77
See also
Libraries—Business services
Reference books

Automation

See Libraries—Automation

Registration

Special report: one for the books: a card trumps the system; southern California. C. M. Weisenberg. Wilson Lib Bull 51:720-1 My '77

Religious collections

Popular religious books for public libraries. D. Marsh. bibl il Lib J 102:1243-7 Je 1 '77

Return of books

See Libraries—Circulation, loans, etc.

Science fiction collections

See Libraries—Fiction collections

Security measures

See Library protection systems

Services to business

See Libraries—Business services

Services to children

Boys and girls and sex and libraries; question of censorship and restricted circulation policy at the Oklahoma County Libraries System; adaptation of address, October 1976; with editorial comment. D. H. Meyers. bibl il por Lib J 102:433, 457-63 F 15 '77
Exemplary media programs; excerpt from School and public library media programs for children and young adults. D. P. Baker. il por SLJ 23:23-7 My '77
For kids & YA's; story festival, disco & sex. il Lib J 102:1448 Jl '77
Moonshine; question of rights of the young to access to information. E. Moon; L. N. Gerhardt. SLJ 24:9 S; 5 N '77
Piscataway's puppet program. L. S. Hunter. il pors SLJ 23:32-4 My '77
Practically speaking. See issues of School library journal
Special report: a children's learning fair; project of Jackson County, Ore, Public Library. V. C. Munn. il Wilson Lib Bull 52:122-3 O '77
What you want the future to be . . . ; adaptation of address, June 16, 1977. F. W. Summers. bibl por SLJ 24:80-2 O '77
See also
Libraries—Childrens collections
Story telling

Services to the blind

Library-based blind service fought by nat'l blind group. J. L. Kopischke. Lib J 102:148-9 Ja 15 '77; Reply with rejoinder. B. Beach. 102:1221-2 Je 1 '77
Montana not NFB target; new battle in Nebraska; efforts to remove library service programs for the blind from jurisdiction of state library agencies. Lib J 102:536 Mr 1 '77
Service to blind in Mass.: libraries urged to run show. Lib J 102:2297 N 15 '77
See also
Blind, Libraries for the

Services to the handicapped

Iowa PL tangles with the feds—and wins; Rudd Public Library. Wilson Lib Bull 52:288 D '77
We can grow! D. Young. SLJ 23:44 My '77
See also
Handicapped, Libraries for the

Services to youth

Exemplary media programs; excerpt from School and public library media programs for children and young adults. D. P. Baker. il por SLJ 23:23-7 My '77
In the YA corner. See issues of School library journal
Keeping ed tech in the picture. L. N. Gerhardt. SLJ 23:7 Ap '77
Moonshine; question of rights of the young to access to information. E. Moon; L. N. Gerhardt. SLJ 24:9 S; 5 N '77
Packing 'em in at the Spotswood PL. il Wilson Lib Bull 52:293 D '77

Special collections

See also
College libraries—Special collections
Libraries—Music collections
Libraries—Photographic collections

State aid

California ups library aid to $5.3 million. Lib J 102:2304-5 N 15 '77
NCLIS $$ study urges more state aid. Lib J 102:1442-3 Jl '77
Oregon LA wins six-year state aid battle. il Lib J 102:1802 S 15 '77
State aid to systems challenged in N.Y. Lib J 102:1548 Ag '77
State funding blueprint sketched in Pennsylvania. Lib J 102:1439 Jl '77
Strength & weakness visible at the state level. Lib J 102:1336 Je 15 '77
Upping the states' ante for libraries. P. I. Dalton. Am Lib 8:621-2 D '77

Statistics

Book buying power drops, says Ohio study. Lib J 102:1998 O 1 '77
Public library building in 1977. H. R. Galvin and B. N. Asbury. il Lib J 102:2402-9 D 1 '77
Statistics of large U.S. and Canadian libraries. Wilson Lib Bull 52:20-1 S '77
University of Illinois annual survey: public libraries show 12-percent spending jump. il Am Lib 8:391 Jl '77
See also
College libraries—Statistics

Technical processes

Iowa's processing center skirts bankruptcy. Lib J 102:1981 O 1 '77
Preservation: a national plan at last? report of National Preservation Program Planning Conference. P. W. Darling. il Lib J 102:447-9 F 15 '77
See also
Cataloging

LIBRARIES—Technical processes—*Continued*

Anecdotes, facetiae, satire, etc.

Bee wing case: a preservation (tragedy) travesty; National Preservation Program Planning Conference. F. Patton and P. W. Darling. Lib J 102:771-5 Ap 1 '77

Trustees, boards, committees, etc.

Advice for the new trustee negotiator. P. Harris. por Wilson Lib Bull 52:237-40 N '77

Use studies

See Library surveys

Video art collections

Video art: not for visionaries only. D. Boyle. il Am Lib 8:349-50 Je '77

Volunteer workers

Volunteers in libraries: guards, PR, outreach. Lib J 102:1996 O 1 '77

Alabama

Alabama Regional Library for the Blind and Physically Handicapped. A. G. Bushman. il Am Lib 8:303-4 Je '77

Developing statewide services for young adults. J. L. Atkinson. SLJ 24:96 O '77

Asia, Southeastern

Scenes from a southeast Asian sabbatical. R. B. Palmer. il por Wilson Lib Bull 51:853-5 Je '77

Bolivia

Born again in the Andes. A. Plotnik. il Am Lib 8:409-12 S '77

California

Calif. selection center eyes entry level skills. Lib J 102:1706-7 S 1 '77

California ups library aid to $5.3 million. Lib J 102:2304-5 N 15 '77

Californians peg entry level Librarian I tasks. Lib J 102:2298+ N 15 '77

California's rich harvest; LSCA-funded projects. J. Berry. Lib J 102:1323 Je 15 '77

Home-town Salinas shares its Steinbeck memories; John Steinbeck Library exhibition. il Sunset 158:40 Mr '77

Mandatory certification—a proposal that lost. M. J. Reagan. Lib J 102:1723-4 S 1 '77

Sex and violence in the library: scream a little louder, please. C. Easton. il Am Lib 8:484-8 O '77

Special report: libraries and the fourth estate—a survey. E. Rancier. Wilson Lib Bull 51:722+ My '77

Special report: one for the books: a card trumps the system. C. M. Weisenberg. Wilson Lib Bull 51:720-1 My '77

Tears and ivory towers: California libraries during the McCarthy era. W. E. Benemann. bibl il Am Lib 8:305-9 Je '77

See also

California Library Association
San Francisco Public Library

Canada

Design concepts to complete in your mind; Metropolitan Toronto Library. A. G. Bushman. il Am Lib 8:426-8 S '77

Statistics of large U.S. and Canadian libraries. Wilson Lib Bull 52:20-1 S '77

See also

Canadian Library Association
Ontario Library Association

Colorado

See also

Denver Public Library

Florida

Florida county library faces tight budget; Leon County Public Library, Tallahassee. Lib J 102:2114+ O 15 '77

Lyons collection; Miami Dade Public Library music collection. J. Waxman. Am Rec G 40: 6-7 Mr '77

Georgia

Georgia launches first of the state library conferences. K. Nyren. Lib J 102:2307-8 N 15 '77

Georgia librarians outline needs at first Governor's Conference. il SLJ 24:9 N '77

See also

Atlanta Public Library

Hawaii

Trouble in Paradise: Hawaii auditor's report scores lack of co-op; views of C. Tanimura. Lib J 102:1330+ Je 15 '77

Illinois

Illinois maps collection development plan. Lib J 102:1233 Je 1 '77

Metamorphosis: library emerges from fire station cocoon; Schaumburg Township Public Library. A. G. Bushman. il Am Lib 241-2 My '77

See also

Chicago Public Library
Illinois Regional Library for the Blind and Physically Handicapped, Chicago
Illinois State Library, Springfield

Indiana

Developing a computerized organization file; project of the Monroe County Public Library. J. E. Wegener and J. A. Haskett. il Lib J 102: 2323-5 N 15 '77

Library bond campaign to bank on; Vigo County Public Library, Terre Haute, Ind. E. Howard. Am Lib 8:622 D '77

Iowa

Iowa PL tangles with the feds—and wins; Rudd Public Library. Wilson Lib Bull 52:288 D '77

Iowa's processing center skirts bankruptcy. Lib J 102:1981 O 1 '77

Massachusetts

LSCA in Massachusetts: Bureau under fire anew. Lib J 102:1545 Ag '77

MLA backs Mass. Bureau in its try for more clout. Lib J 102:749 Ap 1 '77

Mass. reorganization try: Bureau seeks more clout. Lib J 102:435+ F 15 '77

Massachusetts mess. J. Berry. Lib J 102:2195 N 1 '77

Retrieving overdue materials in court. V. E. Beck. Lib J 102:2321-2 N 15 '77

Service to blind in Mass: libraries urged to run show. Lib J 102:2297 N 15 '77

See also

Boston Public Library
Massachusetts—Library Extension, Bureau of

Michigan

Stroke the legislators. F. H. Pletz. Am Lib 8: 575-6 N '77

See also

Detroit—Libraries
Detroit Public Library

Missouri

See also

Kansas City, Mo. Public Library

Nebraska

Library-based blind service fought by nat'l blind group. J. L. Kopischke. Lib J 102:148-9 Ja 15 '77; Reply with rejoinder. B. Beach. 102: 1221-2 Je 1 '77

Network of academic libraries proposed in Nebraska. Lib J 102:670-1 Mr 15 '77

Special report: director's diary of a crisis; bookmobile budget of the Kearney Public Library. R. Norman. il Wilson Lib Bull 51:566-7 Mr '77

Nevada

Lamar Marchese: when planning a program, do it with style; film program of the Clark County Library. il por Wilson Lib Bull 51: 642-3 Ap '77

New England

NELINET gets some OCLC responsibilities. Lib J 102:1444 Jl '77

Some early women librarians in New England. E. McCauley. bibl il Wilson Lib Bull 51: 648-55 Ap '77

New Jersey

Ocean Co. cablecasts: programs for all ages. SLJ 23:20+ F '77

Packing 'em in at the Spotswood PL. il Wilson Lib Bull 52:293 D '77

Piscataway's puppet program. L. S. Hunter. il pors SLJ 23:32-4 My '77

Special report: as others see us; Tenafly, N.J. questionnaire. F. E. Andrews. Wilson Lib Bull 52:124-7 O '77

What publishers should know about the public library: a book editor's firsthand report; visit to the Orange Public Library. P. Johnson, Jr. il pors Pub W 211:40-2 Mr 28 '77

New York (state)

Budget woes persist in libraries; relief in proposed job legislation. SLJ 23:11 My '77

Buffalo slaughter; ed by L. R. Pearson. M. Lewin. Am Lib 8:110 Mr '77

Politics for progress:

Federal and state library legislation: a united strategy. M. R. Owens. por Lib J 102:988-90 My 1 '77

Libraries & information industries: legislation for joint development. M. R. Owens. por Lib J 102:1819-22 S 15 '77

State aid to systems challenged in N.Y. Lib J 102:1548 Ag '77

Storytime for toddlers: program of the Greenburgh Public Library, Elmsford. J. K. Markowsky. bibl il por SLJ 23:28-31 My '77

See also

Brooklyn Public Library
New York (city)—Libraries
New York Public Library

LIBRARIES—*Continued*

North Carolina

Patron is not the public. T. Hays and others. bibl il Lib J 102:1813-18 S 15 '77
Social security $$ fuel N.C. library info center; Wake County Public Libraries System. Lib J 102:148 Ja 15 '77

Ohio

Book buying power drops, says Ohio study. Lib J 102:1998 O 1 '77
Cooperation in Ohio: study pegs shortcomings. Lib J 102:1334-5 Je 15 '77
Ohio adds up costs of 1977 winter freeze. Lib J 102:1545 Ag '77
Ohio continuing education: shortcomings pegged; views of D. Luse. Lib J 102:2204 N 1 '77
Ohio user survey pegs inner city use; Public Library of Columbus & Franklin County. Lib J 102:1704 S 1 '77
Solar nexus: library pioneers in tapping the sun's energy; Troy-Miami County Public Library. il Am Lib 8:188-90 Ap '77
Ways to up city branch use charted by Ohio study; report by the Public Library of Columbus & Franklin County. Lib J 102:2208 N 1 '77
Work of love: Ohio community pulls together to win bond issue; advertising campaign of the Marion Public Library. il Am Lib 8:576 N '77
See also
Cleveland Public Library

Oklahoma

Boys and girls and sex and libraries; question of censorship and restricted circulation policy at the Oklahoma County Libraries System; adaptation of address; October 1976; with editorial comment. D. H. Meyers. bibl il por Lib J 102:433, 457-63 F 15 '77
Le$$ costly, more popular; paperback book collections in the Oklahoma County Libraries System. P. Little. il por Lib J 102:451-6 F 15 '77
Oases in Oklahoma; Open Access Satellite Educatino Services, a joint project of the Oklahoma County Libraries System and the South Oklahoma City Junior College. P. L. Little and J. R. Gilliland. pors Lib J 102:1458-61 Jl '77
Okla. audit says too much LSCA goes to systems. Lib J 102:2114 O 15 '77
Regional centers—sharing service; Tulsa City-County Library System. P. Woodrum. il por Lib J 102:165-6 Ja 15 '77

Oregon

How a levy was won in the West; the Portland-Multnomah County Library. R. McCrank and L. McCrank. bibl il Am Lib 8:560-5 N '77
Special report: a children's learning fair; project of Jackson County Public Library. V. C. Munn. il Wilson Lib Bull 52:122-3 O '77
See also
Oregon Library Association

Pennsylvania

Democratic process flourishes at Governor's Conference. L. R. Pearson. il Am Lib 8:593 D '77
Relating common solutions: two libraries by Mitchell/Giurgola; Tredyffrin Township Public Library, Stratfford; with introd by C. K. Hoyt. il Archit Rec 162:93-8 Ag '77
State funding blueprint sketched in Pennsylvania. Lib J 102:1439 Jl '77
See also
Philadelphia Free Library

Scotland

Legacy of a Scottish lord: Innerpeffray. G. Thomson. il Wilson Lib Bull 51:844-7 Je '77

Southwestern States

See also
Southwestern Library Association

Spain

See also
Madrid—Libraries

Tennessee

Branches for the need to know; Memphis Shelby County Public Library and Information Center. L. C. Wallis. il Lib J 102:166-8 Ja 15 '77
ILL policy directory: making sharing easier. R. L. Barclay. Lib J 102:2322-3 N 15 '77

Texas

See also
Houston Public Library

United States

Community education and public libraries: cooperation or conquest? L. D. Fleming. bibl por Wilson Lib Bull 52:319-23 D '77
Effect of appearance on requests for help in libraries. H. W. Kroll and D. K. Moren. il Am Lib 8:489 O '77
I ching on libraries. J. Berry. Lib J 102:2101 O 15 '77
Library life. Am Lib 8:122, 481 Mr, O '77
Mission statement for public libraries: guidelines for public library service; excerpt from text; with comments of librarians. Am Lib 8:615-20 D '77
New public library mission. J. Berry. Lib J 102:2379 D 1 '77
News report 1976. K. Nyren. il Lib J 102:174-6+ Ja 15 '77
PLA drafts new public library mission. Lib J 102:2460-1 D 15 '77
Practicing librarian. Lib J 102:2135-9, 2321-5 O 15, N 15 '77
Program alert. See occasional issues of Library journal
SLJ's 1977 news roundup. B. M. Cheatham. il SLJ 24:17-23 D '77
Unlock the liberry. B. Kaufman. il Read Digest 110:47-8 My '77
Will the national inventory lead from the slough of despond to the celestial city? E Castagna. il Am Lib 8:491-2 O '77
See also
American Library Association
Council on Library Resources, Inc
Indians of North America—Libraries
Libraries and state
National Librarians Association
Special Libraries Association
United States—National Commission on Libraries and Information Science

Virginia

Preschool craft activities; programs at the Fairfax County Public Library. M. I. Lane. il SLJ 23:43 My '77

Washington (state)

See also
Seattle Public Library

Western States

Western agency heads regroup & replace WILCO; establishment of the Western Council of State Librarians. Lib J 102:1444-6 Jl '77

Wisconsin

Threats to state agency $$ role shaping up. Lib J 102:1090+ My 15 '77
See also
Milwaukee Public Library

LIBRARIES, Ancient. See Libraries—History

LIBRARIES, Church
Granite is forever; Granite Mountain Genealogical Vault. il Am Heritage 28:81 Je '77
Tracking down your kinfolk; using Mormon Church libraries. il Sunset 158:36 Je '77

LIBRARIES, College. See College libraries

LIBRARIES, Government
Downgrading menaces federal librarians' security. L. R. Pearson. Am Lib 8:175 Ap '77

LIBRARIES, Institution
See also
Prison libraries

LIBRARIES, Newspaper. See Newspaper and periodical libraries

LIBRARIES, Periodical. See Newspaper and periodical libraries

LIBRARIES, Prison. See Prison libraries

LIBRARIES, Remodeled. See Buildings, Remodeled

LIBRARIES, School. See School libraries

LIBRARIES, Special
See also
Special Libraries Association

LIBRARIES, Thefts from. See Library thefts

LIBRARIES, Traveling. See Bookmobiles

LIBRARIES, University. See College libraries

LIBRARIES and audio-visual materials
Exemplary media programs; excerpt from School and public library media programs for children and young adults. D. P. Baker. il por SLJ 23:23-7 My '77
Libraries and technology—some future concerns; excerpt from Managing multi-media libraries. W. B. Hicks and A. M. Tillin. pors SLJ 23:27-32 Ap '77
Media minded. D. Boyle. See issues of American libraries
NCLIS and ACET conduct Project Mediabase. SLJ 23:14-15 Ap '77
Purchase AV equipment with care. H. Deutsch. SLJ 23:48 Ap '77
See also
Libraries—Photographic collections
Libraries—Video art collections

LIBRARIES and authors
Authors & artists as speakers: suggestions for hassle-free visits; excerpt from How to do a dozen (and more) odd jobs in library service. J. Botham and W. C. Morris. il por SLJ 24:27-9 D '77
Librarian looks at the new copyright law. E. G. Holley. bibl il Am Lib 8:247-51 My '77

LIBRARIES and business. See Libraries—Business services

LIBRARIES and foreign population
Modifying library education for ethnic imperatives; service to Spanish speaking persons. A. D. Trejo. bibl Am Lib 8:150-1 Mr '77

LIBRARIES and intellectual liberty
Intellectual freedom: justification for librarianship. G. R. Shields. bibl Lib J 102:1823-5 S 15 '77
Library Bill of Rights vs. the Racism and Sexism Awareness Resolution. Z. Horn. Lib J 102:1254-5 Je 1 '77
Resolution on Racism & Sexism Awareness revisited. E. J. Josey. Wilson Lib Bull 51:727-8 My '77
Selection and soapboxes: an ideological primer. E. Fain. Wilson Lib Bull 52:136-9 O '77
See also
American Library Association—Intellectual Freedom Committee
Freedom to Read Foundation
Libraries—Censorship
Library Bill of Rights

LIBRARIES and Learning Resources, Office of. See United States—Education, Office of—Libraries and Learning Resources, Office of

LIBRARIES and motion pictures
Lamar Marchese: when planning a program, do it with style; film program of the Clark County, Nev, Library. il por Wilson Lib Bull 51:642-3 Ap '77
Voyage of discovery for librarians; documentary film study at the Flaherty seminars of the International Film Seminars. D. Boyle. Am Lib 8:635-6 D '77
See also
School libraries and motion pictures

LIBRARIES and publishers
Baker & Taylor program will bring librarians and publishers together; New Books Showcase. D. Maryles. Pub W 211:56-7 Ja 10 '77
Copyright dilemma; report of conference at the Graduate Library School of Indiana University. L. X. Besant. Lib J 102:1337-9 Je 15 '77
Librarians & publishers: an idea exchange through library promotion. P. J. Van Orden. por SLJ 24:24-6 D '77
New cure for encyclopedic miasma. W. R. Eshelman. Wilson Lib Bull 51:714-15 My '77
Out of control—indefinitely. L. N. Gerhardt. SLJ 24:63 O '77
Prepayment dilemma: a consumer's guide. Am Lib 8:571-2 N '77
Publishers and librarians let windows do the talking on Fifth Avenue; Mid-Manhattan branch. J. Giusto. il Pub W 212:57-8 N 7 '77
Publishers v. libraries, a real possibility. W. D. Nelson. Wilson Lib Bull 52:285-6 D '77
What publishers should know about the public library: a book editor's firsthand report; visit to the Orange, N. J. Public Library. P. Johnson, Jr. il pors Pub W 211:40-2 Mr 28 '77
See also
Royalties

LIBRARIES and radio
CB radio in the library. P. Partovi. il por Lib J 102:2135-6 O 15 '77

LIBRARIES and schools
See also
School libraries

LIBRARIES and Spanish speaking people. See Libraries and foreign population

LIBRARIES and state
Carter underscores pre-election stand. J. Carter. Am Lib 8:289 Je '77
Iowa PL tangles with the feds—and wins; Rudd Public Library. Wilson Lib Bull 52:288 D '77
See also
Libraries—Federal aid
Libraries—State aid
State library agencies

LIBRARIES and television
Ocean Co. cablecasts: programs for all ages. SLJ 23:20+ F '77

LIBRARIES and the public. See Libraries—Public relations

LIBRARIES for the blind. See Blind, Libraries for the

LIBRARIES for the handicapped. See Handicapped, Libraries for the

LIBRARY administration
Better utilization of personnel. J. C. MacCampbell. Lib J 102:1718-20 S 1 '77
Libraries and technology—some future concerns; excerpt from Managing multi-media libraries. W. B. Hicks and A. M. Tillin. pors SLJ 23:27-32 Ap '77
Library administrators: time to show them the door? Wilson Lib Bull 51:636-8 Ap '77
Library councils could spearhead co-op. D. A. Kittel. Lib J 102:440+ F 15 '77
What you want the future to be . . . ; adaptation of address, June 16, 1977. F. W. Summers. bibl por SLJ 24:80-2 O '77
See also
College library administration
Libraries—Trustees, boards, committees, etc.
School library administration

LIBRARY advertising. See Library publicity

LIBRARY agencies, State. See State library agencies

LIBRARY architecture
Architectural issue; special issue. il Lib J 102:2393-411 D 1 '77
Facilities & design:
Barrier free; Alabama Regional Library for the Blind and Physically Handicapped. A. G. Bushman. il Am Lib 8:303-4 Je '77
Design concepts to complete in your mind; Metropolitan Toronto Library. A. G. Bushman. il Am Lib 8:426-8 S '77
From shambles to showplace; Chicago Public Library Cultural Center. D. Schabel. il Am Lib 8:602-4 D '77
Harvard's underground understatement. E. P. Mitchell. il Am Lib 8:114-16 Mr '77
Metamorphosis: library emerges from fire station cocoon. A. G. Bushman. il Am Lib 241-2 My '77
On the ground floor of a new trend; Columbia University's new Augustus Long Health Sciences Library. A. G. Bushman. il Am Lib 8:80 F '77
Prefabricated and portable library units offer quick and easy extension of service. il Am Lib 8:546-8 N '77
Solar nexus: library pioneers in tapping the sun's energy; Troy-Miami County Public Library. il Am Lib 8:188-90 Ap '77
Relating common solutions: two libraries by Mitchell/Giurgola; Tredyffrin Township Public Library, Stratfford, Pennsylvania and the University of Washington Law Library; with introd by C. K. Hoyt. il Archit Rec 162:93-8 Ag '77

LIBRARY assistants
Library work without an M.L.S. R. E. Grady. Lib J 102:1726 S 1 '77

Education

Library training program for native Americans; Paraprofessional Training of Aides for American Indian Information Centers. D. Hall. Wilson Lib Bull 51:751-4 My '77

LIBRARY associations
Proudly, British Library Association joins centenarian club. K. C. Harrison. Am Lib 8:473-4 O '77
See also
American Library Association
Association of American Library Schools
Association of Research Libraries
California Library Association
Canadian Library Association
Educational Film Library Association
International Federation of Library Associations
Massachusetts Library Association
Medical Library Association
Mountain-Plains Library Association
Music Library Association
National Librarians Association
Ontario Library Association
Oregon Library Association
Special Libraries Association
Urban Libraries Council

LIBRARY Bill of Rights
IFC/CSD documents in question. L. N. Gerhardt and others. SLJ 23:118-19 Mr '77
Library Bill of Rights vs. the Racism and Sexism Awareness Resolution. Z. Horn. Lib J 102:1254-5 Je 1 '77
Resolution on Racism & Sexism Awareness revisited. E. J. Josey. Wilson Lib Bull 51:727-8 My '77

LIBRARY budgets. See Libraries—Finance

LIBRARY buildings. See Library architecture

LIBRARY cards. See Libraries—Registration

LIBRARY catalogs. See Catalogs, Library

LIBRARY censorship. See Libraries—Censorship

LIBRARY conferences
American libraries datebook. See issues of American libraries
Calendar. See issues of Library journal
Calendar. See issues of School library journal
Calendar. See issues of Wilson library bulletin
Conference report. See occasional issues of Library journal
Democratic process flourishes at Governor's Conference. L. R. Pearson. il Am Lib 8:593 D '77
Georgia librarians outline needs at first Governor's Conference. il SLJ 24:9 N '77
Resource sharing in libraries; 1976 Pittsburgh conference. K. Nyren; discussion. Lib J 102:299 F 1 '77
Summer conferences, courses, institutes, workshops. SLJ 23:19-20 Ap '77
See also
American Library Association—Meetings, 1977
Library institutes and workshops
White House Conference on Library and Information Services (proposed)

LIBRARY cooperation
Co-op option, $$ roles debated at ASLA. N. Savage. Lib J 102:1104+ My 15 '77
Copyright, resource sharing, and hard times: a view from the field. R. De Gennaro. bibl Am Lib 8:430-5 S '77
Detroit library network. N. Seabrooks. il Lib J 102:1123-7 My 15 '77
Library cooperation. See occasional issues of Library journal
Trouble in Paradise: Hawaii auditor's report scores lack of co-op; views of C. Tanimura. Lib J 102:1330 Je 15 '77
See also
Interlibrary loans
Library networks

LIBRARY education. See Library assistants—Education; Library schools and education

LIBRARY employees
Better utilization of personnel. J. C. MacCampbell. Lib J 102:1718-20 S 1 '77
Seattle zeroes in on staff development needs. Lib J 102:1701 S 1 '77
Tasks approach to library personnel roles grows. Lib J 102:2197 N 1 '77
See also
Librarians
Library assistants
United States—Library of Congress—Employees

LIBRARY equipment. See Library furniture and equipment

LIBRARY exhibits
Library display. See issues of Wilson library bulletin
See also
Show windows

LIBRARY extension
See also
Bookmobiles
Libraries—Branches and stations
Libraries—Cultural programs

LIBRARY fees. See Libraries—Finance

LIBRARY finance. See Libraries—Finance

LIBRARY furniture and equipment
Annual buyers' guide 1977; ed by B.-L. Fox and others. Lib J 102:1590-4+ Ag '77; Same. SLJ 24:48-52+ S '77
Buyers' guide; ed by T. W. McConkey. See first issue of each month of Library journal
Product showcase. il SLJ 24:44 S; 97 O; 37 N; 41 D '77
See also
Bookends and bookracks

LIBRARY information networks. See Library networks

LIBRARY institutes and workshops
ALA/ISAD institute on the national network. K. Nyren. il Lib J 102:761-3 Ap 1 '77
Opening minds to closing catalogs, or, When can we throw out the cards? METRO seminar. A. Plotnik. Am Lib 8:594-5 D '77
Seven Springs Institute: state agency heads face the future. K. Nyren. Lib J 102:444-6 F 15 '77
Special report: SALALM in Gainesville. J. R. Freudenthal. Wilson Lib Bull 52:24 S '77
Summer conferences, courses, institutes, workshops. SLJ 23:19-20 Ap '77
Technology & the catalog; tradition vs. the new wave; ALA institute. Lib J 102:666 Mr 15 '77
Third world acquisitions: a report on the workshop at LC. A. Pieratt and H. B. Neikirk. Lib J 102:978 My 1 '77
What's my line? workshop on Alternative Careers in Information and Library Services. E. P. Mitchell. Am Lib 8:417 S '77
Yes, Virginia, is there a national bibliographic network? ALA institute. A. Plotnik. Am Lib 8:176+ Ap '77

LIBRARY instruction. See Libraries—Instruction in use

LIBRARY journal
LJ's annual awards. Lib J 102:2459 D 15 '77

LIBRARY laws and legislation
ALA Washington notes. E. D. Cooke and C. C. Henderson. See issues of Wilson library bulletin to June 1977
ALA Washington notes. E. D. Cooke and H. W. Sprouse. See issues of Wilson library bulletin, September 1977-
Brademas compromise wins LSCA extension. Am Lib 8:469 O '77
House-Senate group agrees on urban library funding. S. Wagner. Pub W 212:35-6 O 3 '77
Is the library an educational institution? A. Ladenson. il por Wilson Lib Bull 51:576-81 Mr '77
LSCA extended, with new provisions for urban public libraries. W. D. Nelson. Wilson Lib Bull 52:213 N '77
Politics for progress:
Federal and state library legislation: a united strategy. M. R. Owens. por Lib J 102:988-90 My 1 '77
Libraries & information industries: legislation for joint development. M. R. Owens. por Lib J 102:1819-22 S 15 '77
Stroke the legislators. F. H. Pletz. Am Lib 8: 575-6 N '77
See also
Librarians—Certification

LIBRARY loans. See Interlibrary loans

LIBRARY management. See Library administration

LIBRARY museums. See Museums

LIBRARY networks
ALA/ISAD institute on the national network. K. Nyren. il Lib J 102:761-3 Ap 1 '77
Modernizing OCLC's governance. N. D. Stevens. Lib J 102:2216-19 N 1 '77
NELINET gets some OCLC responsibilities. Lib J 102:1444 Jl '77
Network of academic libraries proposed in Nebraska. Lib J 102:670-1 Mr 15 '77
Public libraries, the Library of Congress, and the national bibliographic network; adaptation of address, February 1977. M. J. Freedman. il Lib J 102:2211-15 N 1 '77
Regional centers—sharing service; Tulsa City-County Library System. P. Woodrum. il por Lib J 102:165-6 Ja 15 '77
Resource sharing in libraries; 1976 Pittsburgh conference. K. Nyren; discussion. Lib J 102:299 F 1 '77
SWLA/MPLA joint conference. Lib J 102:323-4 F 1 '77
Yes, Virginia, is there a national bibliographic network? ALA institute. A. Plotnik. Am Lib 8:176+ Ap '77

LIBRARY news. See Newspapers—Library news

LIBRARY of Congress. See United States—Library of Congress

LIBRARY of Congress catalog cards. See Catalog cards

LIBRARY of Congress subject headings. See Subject headings

LIBRARY orientation. See Libraries—Instruction in use

LIBRARY personnel. See Librarians; Library assistants; Library employees

LIBRARY planning
Giraffe factor. K. Nyren. Lib J 102:1979 O 1 '77
More local library input sought for Ill. 5-year plan. Lib J 102:536 Mr 1 '77

LIBRARY promotion. See Library publicity

LIBRARY protection systems
Library material security systems: a school district's experience. D. Shirley. il SLJ 23:38-41 Ap '77
Security (title varies) Lib J 102:1805-6, 2202 S 15, N 1 '77

LIBRARY publicity
Packing 'em in at the Spotswood PL. il Wilson Lib Bull 52:293 D '77
Work of love: Ohio community pulls together to win bond issue; advertising campaign of the Marion Public Library. il Am Lib 8:576 N '77
See also
College library publicity
Newspapers—Library news

LIBRARY schools and education
Accreditation: participation wanted. J. Berry. Lib J 102:301 F 1 '77
CLENE: a success story. B. Conroy. il por Lib J 102:1453-5 Jl '77
Death at an early age: library schools in Oregon and California in jeopardy. W. R. Eshelman. Wilson Lib Bull 51:794 Je '77
Kansas City story: capital recovery through continuing education. B. M. Nichols. por Lib J 102:1456-7 Jl '77
Modifying library education for ethnic imperatives. A. D. Trejo. bibl Am Lib 8:150-1 Mr '77
New in education. Lib J 102:443-4 F 15 '77
Ohio continuing education: shortcomings pegged; views of D. Luse. Lib J 102:2204 N 1 '77
Practice makes perfect; fieldwork courses. M. C. Tietjen. il Wilson Lib Bull 52:61-3 S '77
Preparing YA librarians—questions & answers. J. V. Rogers. SLJ 23:51 Ap '77
YA library training—let's talk about it. S. Steinfirst. SLJ 23:51 F '77
See also
American Library Association—Accreditation, Committee on
Association of American Library Schools
Library assistants—Education
Library institutes and workshops
Oregon. University, Eugene—School of Librarianship

LIBRARY science

Bibliography

Professional reading. See issues of Library journal
Professional reading. See issues of School library journal

Periodicals

Alternative library periodicals. J. P. Danky and M. Fox. il Wilson Lib Bull 57:763-8 My '77
See also
American libraries (periodical)
Library journal

Study and teaching

See Library schools and education

LIBRARY seminars. See Library institutes and workshops

LIBRARY Services and Construction Act. See Library laws and legislation
LIBRARY Services and Contruction Act funds. See Libraries—Federal aid
LIBRARY staffs. See Library employees
LIBRARY statistics. See Libraries—Statistics
LIBRARY surveys
Ohio user survey pegs inner city use; Public Library of Columbus & Franklin County. Lib J 102:1704 S 1 '77
Patron is not the public. T. Hays and others. bibl il Lib J 102:1813-18 S 15 '77
Special report: as others see us; Tenafly, N.J. questionnaire. F. E. Andrews. Wilson Lib Bull 52:124-7 O '77
State agency $$ efficiency stressed in COSLA study. Lib J 102:435+ F 15 '77
Ways to up city branch use charted by Ohio study; report by the Public Library of Columbus & Franklin County. Lib J 102:2208 N 1 '77
YA survey: help wanted. L.-J. Roberts. SLJ 24:47 S '77
See also
College library surveys
LIBRARY thefts
Great Mozart-Beethoven caper; theft of music manuscripts from the German State Library. P. Moor. il Hi Fi 27:72-7 Mr '77
Libraries hit by book and art thefts. Lib J 102: 1446 Jl '77
Now it's a wave of thefts in historic documents. il U.S. News 83:51-2 S 5 '77
See also
Library protection systems
LIBRARY trustees. See Libraries—Trustees, boards, committees, etc.
LIBRARY user fees. See Libraries—Finance
LIBRARY workers. See Library employees
LIBRARY workshops. See Library institutes and workshops
LIBRETTISTS
See also
Beaumarchais, P. A. C. de
Forzano, G.
Gilbert, W. S.
Librettos
Scribe, A. E.
LIBRETTOS
Beyond Figaro. B. Fischer-Williams. il Opera N 41:26-8 Mr 5 '77
Debussy's House of Usher revisited. R. Orledge. bibl f il Mus Q 62:536-53 O '76
Out of The borough; G. Crabbe's poem as the inspiration for B. Britten's opera Peter Grimes. G. Schmidgall. il por Opera N 42:8+ D 10 '77
Scribe factory. H. Heinsheimer. por Opera N 41:16-19 Ja 29 '77
Tale of turmoil; adaptation of V. Hugo's play Le roi s'amuse into Verdi's opera Rigoletto. G. R. Marek. il por Opera N 42:10-14 D 3 '77
LIBYA
See also
Investments, Libyan

Foreign relations

Egypt

See Egypt—Foreign relations—Libya

Panama

Foothold for Kaddafi? K. Willenson and R. Moreau. por Newsweek 89:41-2+ Ap 25 '77

United States

See United States—Foreign relations—Libya
LIBYAN Desert
Onslaught on the Nile; shifting dunes. F. El-Baz. il UNESCO Courier 30:23-4+ Jl '77
LICATA, Joseph W. and others
Initiating structure for educational change. Educ Digest 43:21-4 S '77
LICE
See also
Plant lice
LICENSE plates, Automobile. See Automobiles—License plates
LICENSES
German hunting: it's the tradition that counts; hunting license regulations in West Germany. G. H. Haas. il Int Wildlife 7:38-43 N '77
How licensing hurts consumers. Bus W p 127+ N 28 '77
What is a deer management permit? special hunting permits. P. Kelsey. il map Conservationist 32:35-7 N '77
See also
Architects—Licenses and registration

Anecdotes, facetiae, satire, etc.

License: physicians. R. Lipez. Progressive 41:66 My '77
LICENSES, Nuclear reactor. See Atomic power—Laws and regulations
LICENSING of patents. See Patents—Licensing
LICHTENBERG, Allan J. See Schipper, L. jt auth
LICHTENSTEIN, Grace
Battle over the mighty Colorado. il map N Y Times Mag p 10-13+ Jl 31 '77; Same abr. Read Digest 111:49-50+ N '77
How women are faring at the Air Academy. il N Y Times Mag p 104-6+ S 11 '77
Inner gamesman. por Psychol Today 11:86+ N '77
Playing with the stars. il Esquire 87:108-9+ My '77
(ed) See Larrabee, S. B. Trekking on Everest: making a living from wanderlust
LICHTENSTEIN, Roy
Roy Lichtenstein: ceramic sculpture. C. W. Glenn. il Ceram Mo 25:40-5 My '77 *
LICHTIG, Meyer
Shalom. . .a gut yontiff. . .and a Merry Christmas. il por Ret Liv 16:35 D '76
LICKING (animals)
Licking behavior: evidence of hypoglossal oscillator. Z. Wiesenfeld and others. bibl il Science 196:1122-4 Je 3 '77
LICKS, Salt. See Salt licks
LIDDY, G. Gordon
Serving time in America. il por Esquire 88:138-40+ D '77
about
Good soldier Liddy. R. Boeth and E. Clark. il por Newsweek 90:44 S 19 '77 *
LIDS, Glass container. See Glass containers
LIE detectors and detection
Bitter beercott; dispute over polygraph exams at Adolph Coors Co. il Time 110:15 D 26 '77
Dirty little secret of lie detectors. J. Kwitny. il Esquire 89:73-6+ Ja '78
Telling lies and spotting liars; study by Paul Lavrakas and Richard Maier. S. Bush. Psychol Today 11:152+ D '77
LIEB, Charles
Clearance Center forms amid photocopying uncertainty. S. Wagner. Pub W 212:19+ Ag 8 '77 *
LIEBER, Charles S.
Test detects liver damage in alcoholics. Sci N 112:55+ Jl 23 '77 *
LIEBER, James B.
American travesty. por Nation 224:393-400 Ap 2 '77
LIEBER, Stephen
What bear market? il por Forbes 120:38+ D 1 '77 *
LIEBERMAN, Edward
Case closed. New Yorker 53:28-30 Je 13 '77 *
LIEBERMAN, Jethro K.
Commentary (cont) Bus W p74 Ag 29 '77
LIEBERMAN, M. A.
United States uranium resources—an analysis of historical data. bibl il Science 192:431-6; 196: 604+ Ap 30 '76, My 6 '77
LIEBERMAN, Myron
Administrative team: a step forward or backward? Educ Digest 43:4-5 S '77
How a mediator can help you bargain. Educ Digest 42:29-31 F '77
LIEBERMAN, William S.
Trends of the Twenties. il Art N 76:39-44 O '77
LIEBERMANN, Rolf
Liebermann's fractured Ring; Paris Opera. R. McMullen. il Hi Fi 27:MA34-5 My '77 *
LIEBERSON, Goddard
Cool conscience of a hot industry. R. Gelatt. il pors Sat R 4:28-9 Jl 23 '77 *
LIEBERTHAL, Mary Louchheim
On the Spanish easel. il Sat R 5:24-5 O 29 '77
LIEBIG, Veronica. See Pollack, E. D. jt auth
LIEBMAN, Charles Seymour
American Jews: still a distinctive group. Commentary 64:57-60 Ag '77
LIEDER. See Songs, German
LIENECK, Marjorie A. and others
Literary composite specifications as an intermediate result of the American characteristics spectrum. Engl J 66:59-63 D '77
LIEPA, Alex
Serving the Christian booksellers. por Pub W 212:64 S 26 '77
LIEPE, Katherine
Reviews. J. Pikula. Dance Mag 51:44-5 My '77 *
LIES. See Lying
LIETZKE, Bruce
Lietzke blitzkrieg. J. Jares. por Sports Illus 46:56-7 F 21 '77 *
LIFE
Demystification of life. R. J. Henle. Commonweal 104:457-60 Jl 22 '77
Despairing optimist . . : pursuit of happiness and the quality of life; defining joie de vivre. R. Dubos. Am Scholar 46:424+ Aut '77
History in books pot-pourri of collected reflections. P. W. Schmidtchen. il Hobbies 82:134-7+ Je '77
Last lecture; address, October 20, 1976. H. Skolimowski. Vital Speeches 43:177-81 Ja 1 '77
New LSD: life-span development. A. Rosenfeld. Sat R 5:32+ O 1 '77
When do you hit your prime? J. Newman. Read Digest 111:103-5 Ag '77
See also
Conduct of life
Death

LIFE (biology)
See also
Biosphere
Longevity

LIFE, Length of. See Longevity

LIFE after death. See Future life

LIFE expectancy. See Longevity

LIFE in the theatre; drama. See Mamet, D.

LIFE insurance. See Insurance, Life

LIFE insurance agents. See Insurance agents

LIFE insurance companies. See Insurance companies

LIFE masks. See Masks (sculpture)

LIFE on Mars
Ambiguities of Mars. Sci Am 236:48+ F '77
Attraction of life on Mars. L. Morris. Chr Today 21:56-7 Mr 4 '77
Biology stress for Mars 1984 debated. C. Covault. il Aviation W 107:53+ Jl 25 '77
Life on Mars. D. L. Chandler. il Atlantic 239:29-34+ Je '77
Life on Mars is still a question. Sci N 112:196-7 S 24 '77
Martian muddle: DNA the dry way? Sci N 111:276-7 Ap 30 '77
Martian organics and glow discharges. Sci N 112:183 S 17 '77
New thoughts on Mars; results of Viking experiments. il Time 109:83-4 Ja 24 '77
Of Mars. . .and realistic goals. W. Bennett. Sci Digest 81:20-2 Mr '77
One man's Mars: no Martians. Sci N 111:149-50 Mr 5 '77
Possible surface reactions on Mars: implications for Viking biology results. C. Ponnamperuma and others. bibl il Science 197:455-7 Jl 29 '77
Question of life. il Space World N-1-157:29 Ja '77
Report from Mars; excerpt from Until the sun dies. R. Jastrow. il Natur Hist 86:48-53 bibl (p96-7) Mr '77
Search for life on Mars. N. H. Horowitz. il Sci Am 237:52-61 bibl(p 163) N '77
Viking to Mars: the search for life on Mars. bibl il Space World N-6-162:24-32 Je '77
Viking's search for life: another mystery. Sci N 111:116-17 F 19 '77

LIFE on other planets
Extraterrestrials—who are they? Where are they? D. Steeno. il Space World N-2-158:41-2 F '77
Searching for extraterrestrial civilizations. T. B. H. Kuiper and M. Morris. bibl il Science 196:616-21 My 6 '77
Seeking other worlds; C. Sagan. D. Gelman and others. il pors Newsweek 90:46-7+ Ag 15 '77
See also
Interstellar communication
Life on Mars

Anecdotes, facetiae, satire, etc.

Miss Universe. C. Sagan. il N Y Times Mag p32+ O 23 '77

LIFE preservers
New styles for staying afloat. B. McKeown. il Pop Mech 148:52-3+ Jl '77
Overboard, and after . . . you can take it with you. H. Searls. il. Yachting 142:64-6 D '77

LIFE saving. See Rescue work

LIFE saving equipment
See also
Life preservers

LIFE Saving Service. See United States—Coast Guard—History

LIFE sciences
Life sciences. Sci N 111:233 Ap 9 '77
One and a half cheers for social science: challenges by the physical sciences. A. Etzioni. Psychol Today 11:168 D '77
See also
Biology

LIFE span. See Longevity

LIFE span (animals) See Age (animals)

LIFE-span development. See Life

LIFE Spring workshop. See Self realization

LIFESTYLE. See Conduct of life

LIFSHIN, Lyn
Photograph 1949; poem. Ms 5:64 Je '77

LIFT (aerodynamics)
Propulsive lift concepts flight tested. D. E. Fink. il Aviation W 107:44-5+ S 19 '77

LIFT bridges. See Drawbridges

LIFTING and carrying
See also
Weight lifting

LIFTON, Betty Jean
My search for my roots. Seventeen 36:132-3+ Mr '77
Why adoptees search for their parents. il Seventeen 36:145 O '77

LIGASES. See Synthetases

LIGHT, Larry
Cracks in AT&T's monopoly. Nation 225:690-2 D 24 '77
Offshore reactors. il Nation 225:205-8 S 10 '77

LIGHT
See also
Color
Lasers
Photochemistry
Photography—Light
Photons
Polarization (light)
Sunlight

Physiological effects

Photoreceptor outer segments: accelerated membrane renewal in rods after exposure to light. J. C. Besharse and others. bibl il Science 196:536-8 Ap 29 '77
See also
Plants, Effect of light on
Ultraviolet rays—Physiological effects

Speed

Reflecting on superluminal speed. Sci N 112:390 D 10 '77

LIGHT airplanes. See Airplanes, Light

LIGHT and darkness in the Bible
Seeing in the dark. E. Schaeffer. Chr Today 21:36-7 S 23 '77

LIGHT bulbs. See Electric lamps, Incandescent

LIGHT communication systems
Detectors for lightwave communication. H. Melchior. bibl il Phys Today 30:32-9 N '77
Infrared systems for wireless stereo. A. Makosinski. il Pop Electr 12:70+ O '77
Light talk in Chicago. il Chemistry 50:20 Mr '77
Light-wave communications. W. S. Boyle. il Sci Am 237:40-8 bibl(p 140) Ag '77
Observation of optical bistability confirms prediction. H. R. Leuchtag. bibl il Phys Today 30:17+ D '77
Optical phone lines in use in Chicago. Sci N 111:375 Je 11 '77

LIGHT detectors. See Detectors

LIGHT emitting diodes. See Diodes

LIGHT filters
Are filters for fools? il Mod Phot 41:102-7 O '77
Be gone dull filters: a visual dictionary of special-effect nostrums. H. Keppler. il Mod Phot 41:108-11 O '77
Ed Scully on color. il Mod Phot 41:44+ Jl '77
Filter foul-ups & how to avoid them. J. Schneider. il Mod Phot 41:8+ O '77
Filter gap: what you can't buy you can make—but beware of filter overkill; motion pictures. T. Galluzzo. il Mod Phot 41:38+ O '77
Infrared made easier. il Mod Phot 41:82-5+ F '77
Instant pictures. W. Andrews and D. L. Miller. il Mod Phot 41:57-8+ F '77
More than you or anyone else ever really wanted to know about filters. D. B. Eisendrath. il Mod Phot 41:112-23+ O '77
Offbeat; color polarizers. N. Rothschild. il Pop Phot 80:8+ Je '77
Offbeat; use of filters in color printing. N. Rothschild. bibl il Pop Phot 81:6+ O '77
Protechniques. E. Meyers. il por Pop Phot 80:67+ Mr '77
Red-green-blue? multiple exposures with color filters. N. Rothschild. il Pop Phot 81:98-9+ S '77
Tools & techniques; how to organize and carry filters. C. W. Kennedy. il Pop Phot 80:50+ My '77

LIGHT in art
Elizabeth Osborne: painting with light. E. Medoff. il por Am Artist 41:34-9+ S '77
Zen-science of light. M. Wortz. il Art N 76:200+ N '77

LIGHT meters. See Exposure meters

LIGHT poles. See Street lighting fixtures

LIGHT production in animals and plants. See Bioluminescence

LIGHT quantum. See Photons

LIGHT sensitization
Phototoxic keratoconjunctivitis from coal-tar pitch volatiles. E. A. Emmett and others. bibl il Science 198:841-2 N 25 '77

LIGHT standards. See Street lighting fixtures

LIGHT switches. See Electric switches

LIGHT verse. See Poetry

LIGHTHOUSES
Open again—the Point Reyes light. il Sunset 159:32 O '77
Sentinel in the sound; Execution Rocks Lighthouse. F. Klar. il Sea Front 23:361-4 N '77

LIGHTING
See also
Daylight
Electric lighting
Skylights
also subhead Lighting under various subjects, e.g. Offices—Lighting

LIGHTING, Architectural and decorative
All lighting is high—everything is on switch dimmers. il Sunset 159:108-9 Ag '77
Inviting lighting. Ladies Home J 94:154+ S '77; Same. Redbook 149:202 S '77
Let there be light: remodelings that bring the outdoors in. il House & Gard 149:108-13 Je '77

LIGHTING, Architectural and decorative—*Cont.*
Light up your life. Redbook 148:201 Ap '77; Same. Ladies Home J 94:178+ Ap '77
Lights up, energy down. E. Meehan. il House & Gard 149:82+ S '77
See your apartment in a new light. J. R. Cary. House B 119:83-4+ D '77

LIGHTING, Christmas. See Christmas decorations

LIGHTING, Colored
See also
Christmas tree lights

LIGHTING, Fluorescent. See Electric lamps, Fluorescent

LIGHTING, Outdoor
America shines; lights as seen from space. H. W. Brandli and E. I. Johnson. il Environment 19:6-9 D '77
Let there be darkness; light pollution near observatory sites. S. P. Maran. Natur Hist 86:88+ Ap '77
Light up the night. J. Cornell. Am Home 80:96+ Ap '77
See also
Lighting fixtures
Street lighting
Street lighting fixtures

LIGHTING fixtures
Lighting up. J. Roy. il Am Home 80:16 Jl '77
Low-voltage yard lighting. R. Capotosto. il Pop Sci 210:114-17 Ap '77
Product reports 78. il Archit Rec 162:165-77 mid-O '77
Yard light that's easy to make. il Mech Illus 73:114-15+ O '77
You can make your own low-voltage light fixtures. il Pop Sci 210:150+ Ap '77
See also
Street lighting fixtures

LIGHTING timers. See Timing devices

LIGHTNER, Otto C.
Americana page. por Hobbies 82:100-1 Je '77 *

LIGHTNING
Ball lightning. B. H. Bailey. bibl il Weatherwise 30:99-105 Je '77
Bolts from the blue. R. E. Orville. il Natur Hist 86:66-73 bibl(p93) Je '77
Bolts from the heavens; theories of J. W. Follin. il Time 110:105 D 19 '77
Lightning—a preliminary reassessment. H. M. Mogil and others. bibl il maps Weatherwise 30:192-9 O '77
Super lightning detected by satellite. Sci N 112:15 Jl 2 '77
Supervolts. Sci Am 237:105-6 S '77
See also
Golf—Lightning hazards
Thunderstorms

LIGHTNING protection
Lightning may be on the way. D. Martindale. il Farm J 101:H4 mid-Mr '77
Lightning protection. J. Darr. il Radio-Electr 48:81-2 Mr '77
Lightning safety. Weatherwise 30:200 O '77
Lightning safety. D. Martindale. il Outdoor Life 159:133-4 Je '77

LIGNITE
Why utilities are fired up over lignite; Texas plants. il Bus W p78-9 N 28 '77

LIJIMA, Sumio. See Cowley, J. M. jt auth

LIKELY, Wadsworth
Battle of the books. Sat R 4:31 Ja 22 '77
Nuclear primer. Sat R 4:8 Ja 22 '77

LIKENS, Gene E. See Bormann, F. H. jt auth

LIKUD Party. See Political parties—Israel

LI'L Abner (comic strip) See Comics (books, strips, etc)

LILIENTHAL, David Eli
Lost megawatts flow over nation's myriad spillways. il Smithsonian 8:82-9 S '77; Same abr. with title Let's put our rivers back to work! Read Digest 112:25-8+ Ja '78

LILIES
Consider the lilies of the terrace. A. Green. il Horticulture 55:44-5 N '77
Easy elegance of hardy lilies. il Bet Hom & Gard 55:140-3 S '77
See also
Day lilies

LILIES, Kafir. See Kafir lilies

LILLER, William
Story of AM Herculis. il Sky & Tel 53:351-5 My '77

LILLY, John Cunningham
Cetacean brain. il Oceans 10:4-7 Jl '77

LILY; opera. See Kirchner, L.

LIM, Ramon, and others
Glia maturation factor: effect on chemical differentiation of glioblasts in culture. bibl il Science 195:195-6 Ja 14 '77

LIMA, Peru

Social life and customs

Liberation à la limeña; tapadas worn by women. V. C. Holmgren. il Américas 29:12-13 Je '77

LIMA beans. See Beans

LIMAN, Ellen
Space savers; excerpt from The spacemaker book. See issues of American home, June 1977-

LIMB regeneration. See Regeneration (biology)

LIMBIC system
Brain and emotions. J. Greenberg. il por Sci N 112:74-5 Jl 30 '77
Limbic system interrelations: functional division among hippocampal-septal connections. T. W. Berger and R. F. Thompson. bibl il Science 197:587-9 Ag 5 '77

LIME
Promesol 30: a liquid way to lime fields? B. Gergen. il Suc Farm 75:K12 Ap '77

LIME spreaders
Build your own lime spreader; excerpt from Build it better yourself. il Org Gard & Farm 24:146-8 Mr '77

LIMELIGHT Gallery, New York. See Photography—Galleries and museums

LIMITATION of arms. See Disarmament

The **LIMITED Stores, Inc.** See Chain stores

LIMNOLOGY
See also
Eutrophication

LIMOŃ, José
Frost in the Rio Grande Valley. A. D. Treviño. Engl J 66:69 Mr '77 *

LIMÓN, José, Dance Company. See José Limón Dance Company

LIMULUS eye. See Eye (crustaceans)

LINCK, Penelope W.
Life insurance for your wardrobe. il pors House & Gard 149:44+ O '77

LINCOLN, Abraham
See also
Lincoln Memorial, Washington, D.C.

Assassination

Assassins! J. W. Booth. B. Z. Spencer. il por Sat Eve Post 249:72 Jl '77

Drama

Will the real Abraham Lincoln please stand up? T. A. Grinins. Plays 36:71-4 F '77

Portraits

Lincoln in death: bigger than life. H. Holzer il pors Hobbies 82:115-16 My '77

LINCOLN, Joan
Exhibition/sale—how does it happen? il Ceram Mo 25:44-6 D '77

LINCOLN Center for the Performing Arts, New York

Avery Fisher Hall

House that hi-fi built. R. Hodges. il Pop Electr 11:20+ Mr '77

Juilliard School

Artist life; master classes at Juilliard's American Opera Center by T. Gobbi. D. J. Soria. il por Hi Fi 27:MA6-7+ Ag '77
Juilliard American Opera Center: Chabrier's The reluctant king. il Hi Fi 27:MA13 Mr '77
Karajan at Juilliard; classes in conducting. D. J. Soria. il pors Hi Fi 27:MA5+ Ap '77
Musical events:
Falstaff. A. Porter. New Yorker 53:130-2 My 9 '77
Onward and upward with the arts; progress of pianist R. McCabe. H. D. Ruttencutter. New Yorker 53:42-4+ S 19 '77
Report: U.S. premiere of Le Roi malgré lui by the Juilliard American Opera Center. R. Jacobson. Opera N 41:29 Ja 22 '77
Schwarzkopf-Legge master classes. D. J. Soria. pors Hi Fi 27:MA5-6+ Mr '77
Search for perfection; Schwarzkopf-Legge master classes. R. Jacobson. il pors Opera N 41:24-7 Ja 22 '77

Opera House

Viewpoint; ballet at the New York Metropolitan Opera. R. Jacobson. Opera N 41:7 Je '77

Vivian Beaumont Theater

Papp's curtain at Lincoln Center. por Time 109:66 Je 20 '77
Why Joe Papp made his exit. J. Kroll. il por Newsweek 89:57 Je 27 '77

LINCOLN-Dickey dams project. See Dams

LINCOLN Experimental Satellites. See Communications satellites

LINCOLN Memorial, Washington, D.C.
Long labor of making nation's favorite statue. M. Richman. il Smithsonian 7:54-61 bibl(p 152) F '77

LIND, Jenny
Selling the Swedish Nightingale. R. Hume. il pors Am Heritage 28:98-107 O '77 *

LINDA Hall Library, Kansas City, Mo.
Missouri science library nixes online service; with views by T. D. Gillies. Lib J 102:1547 Ag '77

LINDAU, William E.
Whenever somebody says I'm too old. Ret Liv 17:37+ Ap '77

LINDAUER, Lois L.
Busy woman's diet plan. il Ladies Home J 94:77 Ap '77

LINDBERGH, Alika
Fond monkey business in France. il pors Time 109:88 My 23 '77 *
Lindberghs liberate monkeys from constraints. R. Chelminski. il pors Smithsonian 7:58-65 bibl(p 126) Mr '77 *

LINDBERGH, Anne (Morrow)
Anne Morrow Lindbergh reminisces about life with Lindy; interview, ed by A. Whitman. il pors N Y Times Mag p 16-18+ My 8 '77
Falling in love; excerpt from Bring me a unicorn. il pors McCalls 104:118-19+ Je '77
Hero's wife remembers; interview, ed by R. A. Thrush. il por Good H 184:74+ Je '77

LINDBERGH, Charles Augustus, 1902-1974
Lindbergh on his flight; excerpt from The Spirit of St Louis. il N Y Times Mag p 15 My 8 '77

about

America's First Ladies honor Charles Lindbergh. il Good H 184:72 Je '77 *
Anne Morrow Lindbergh reminisces about life with Lindy; interview, ed by A. Whitman. A. M. Lindbergh. il pors N Y Times Mag p 16-18+ My 8 '77 *
Eagle lands again. E. Keerdoja. il por Newsweek 89:8 My 2 '77 *
Falling in love; excerpt from Bring me a unicorn. A. M. Lindbergh. il pors McCalls 104: 118-19+ Je '77 *
Flight that opened an era: a master stroke of skill, daring. L. D. Lyman. il Sci Digest 81: 32-3 My '77 *
Flight to remember. R. F. Dempewolff. il por map Pop Mech 147:81-3+ My '77 *
Hero's wife remembers; interview, ed by R. A. Thrush. A. M. Lindbergh. il por Good H 184: 74+ Je '77 *
Lindbergh alone; condensation. B. Gill. il pors Read Digest 110:225-8+ My '77 *
Lindbergh: the heroic curiosity; Time essay. L. Morrow. il por Time 109:86-7 My 23 '77 *
Lindbergh was of the twenties. J. Chamberlain. il por Nat R 29:608-10+ My 27 '77 *
Lucky Lindy. il por Sr Schol 109:10-11 My 5 '77 *
Price of fame. A. Whitman. il pors N Y Times Mag p 12-15 My 8 '77 *
Showing Lindbergh the air and space museum. M. Collins. il Sat R 4:30-1+ Ap 16 '77 *
They almost grounded Lindy. il por Time 110:24 N 28 '77 *
Thirty-three hours that changed the world. E. K. Gann. il por Sat R 4:7-10 Ap 16 '77 *

LINDBERGH, Scott
Fond monkey business in France. il pors Time 109:88 My 23 '77 *
Lindberghs liberate monkeys from constraints. R. Chelminski. il pors Smithsonian 7:58-65 bibl(p 126) Mr '77 *

LINDBERGH flight. See Aviation—Transatlantic flights—History

LINDE, Ronald Keith
Acquisition-hungry Envirodyne leaps into steel. il por Bus W p96+ S 12 '77 *

LINDEMAN, Leslie
Little America's Cup: U.S. keeps it. il Yachting 142:209-10 O '77

LINDEMAN, Raymond Laurel
Raymond Lindeman and the trophic-dynamic concept in ecology. R. E. Cook. bibl Science 198:22-6 O 7 '77 *

LINDEMANN, B. and Driessche, W. van
Sodium-specific membrane channels of frog skin are pores: current fluctuations reveal high turnover. bibl il Science 195:292-4 Ja 21 '77

LINDEMEYER, Nancy and others
Easy-to-master stitchery painting. il Bet Hom & Gard 55:84-7+ My '77

LINDEN, Ronald
Ass. prof, GS-7. Nat R 29:818 Jl 22 '77 *

LINDER, Robert D.
East Germany: a vexing issue. Chr Today 22:54-5 N 18 '77

LINDERFELT, Klas August
Wayward bookman. W. A. Wiegand. bibl il Am Lib 8:134-7, 197-200 Mr-Ap '77 *

LINDERMAN, Lawrence
Picking winners. por Esquire 88:177-8+ D '77

LINDFORS, Viveca
Sons and mothers. il por Horizon 20:58 N '77 *

LINDGREN, Henry Clay. See Insel, P. M. jt auth

LINDISFARNE Association. See Collective settlements

LINDNER, Carl Henry
Carl Lindner's singular financial empire. C. J. Loomis. il pors Fortune 95:126-30+ Ja '77 *

LINDNER, Richard
Eros with skin of steel; retrospective by the Chicago Museum of Contemporary Art. M. Stevens. il Newsweek 89:66+ My 23 '77 *

LINDQUIST, Donald
Operation Trojan donkey. Nat R 29:1234-6 O 28 '77

LINDQUIST, Jennie D.
Obituary
Horn Bk 53:374 Je '77. V. Haviland

LINDSAY, G. Caroll
Man and nature. il Conservationist 31:4-11 N '76

LINDSAY, Gilbert
Dynamics of black local politics: an interview with G. Lindsay; ed by J. Elliot. por Negro Hist Bull 40:718-20 Jl '77

LINDSAY, John Vliet
Exile in his own city. H. Stein. il por N Y Times Mag p 10-11+ Ja 8 '78 *

LINDSAY, Sally (Price)
Spinnakers: the eternal trade-off. il Yachting 141:100-2 My '77

LINDSAY, Steele
Hook and eye appeal. Writer 90:12-14+ My '77

LINDSAY, Ted
Welcome back, Scarface. P. Gammons. il pors Sports Illus 47:86+ O 31 '77 *

LINDSELL, Harold
After three days and three nights. . . Chr Today 21:14-16 Ap 1 '77
Billy Graham's mission to Manila. il Chr Today 22:36-7 D 30 '77
Harold Lindsell reports from Taiwan. Chr Today 21:15-17 Ag 26 '77
Mystery at Bethlehem. il Chr Today 22:22-5 D 9 '77
Where did I come from? a question of origins. Chr Today 21:16-18 Je 17 '77

about

Battle for the Bible: renewing the inerrancy debate. D. W. Dayton. il Chr Cent 93:976-80 N 10 '76; Discussion. 94:198-9 Mr 2 '77 *

LINDSEY, Alton A.
Sighting at Pine Knot. il Natur Hist 86:40+ N '77
Time and the mountain. il Nat Parks & Con Mag 51:4-7 N '77

LINDSEY, Hal
PW interviews; ed by J. Kirsch. por Pub W 211:30-2 Mr 14 '77

LINDSEY, Karen
Sexual harassment on the job. il Ms 6:47-8+ N '77

LINDSEY, Robert
Anatomy of a reporter's murder. il por N Y Times Mag p 11-14+ F 20 '77
New battles over school budgets. il N Y Times Mag p 17-19+ S 18 '77
New tycoons of hollywood. il N Y Times Mag p 12-16+ Ag 7 '77
To be young, rich—and a spy. il pors N Y Times Mag p 18+ My 22 '77
White/Caucasian—and rejected. il pors N Y Times Mag p42-7+ Ap 3 '77

LINDSKOOG, Kathryn
Roots. Chr Cent 94:251 Mr 16 '77
That man in question. Chr Cent 94:934 O 19 '77

LINDSLEY, E. F.
Adventures in alternate energy (cont) il Pop Sci 211:62+ N '77

LINDSLEY, Mark
Get rid of fall litter with lawn vacs and blowers. il Pop Sci 211:70+ O '77

LINDSTROM, Jane
How will you know unless I tell you? Read Digest 110:43-4+ Ap '77

LINE, Les
Field & stream naturally. il por Field & S 82: 42-3 Jl; 48 Ag; 100 S; 36 O; 110 N '77
Mystery goose; excerpt from To behold a bird. il Field & S 81:82+ Mr '77

LINE (art)
Line can be beautiful. F. J. Kraft. il Sch Arts 76:51 F '77

LINEN, James Alexander, 1912-
Letter from the publisher; retirement of J. A. Linen. il por Time 110:2 Ag 29 '77 *

LINEN, Household
See also
Bedding
Sheets
Table linen

LINERS. See Ocean liners

LINES, Fishing. See Fishing tackle

LINEUPS, Police. See Crime and criminals—Identification

LINFORD, John
To charge or not to charge: a rationale. Lib J 102:2009-10 O 1 '77

LING, Joseph T.
Resource-conservation; address, April 27, 1977. Vital Speeches 43:541-4 Je 15 '77

LING-Temco-Vought, Inc. See LTV Corporation

LINGERIE. See Underwear

LINGG, Ann M.
Heart of a king. por Opera N 42:18-19 Ja 7 '78
Metropolitan mirror. il Opera N 41:32 F 26; 49 My; 42:51 D 3 '77

LINGUISTICS
See also
Sociolinguistics

LINHSIEN, China
Canal a million farmers built; Red Flag Canal. H. Forman. il Horticulture 55:30-5 My '77

LINK, Edwin A.
Link. R. B. Parke. il por Flying 101:260 S '77 *

LINN, Robert
Modified fast; interview. il por Good H 185:292+ N '77
about
No-food diet. S. C. Cowley and P. J. Seth. il por Newsweek 90:74 Jl 11 '77 *
Protein fad. P. Bonventre and S. Agrest. il por Newsweek 90:71 D 19 '77 *

LINNAEUS, Carolus
Dr Garden's wonderfully scented and almost imaginary namesake; excerpt from Species of eternity. J. Kastner. il Horticulture 55:64 N '77 *

LINNEMAN, Robert E. and Kennell, J. D.
Shirt-sleeve approach to long range plans. bibl f il Harvard Bus R 55:141-50 Mr '77

LINOWES, David Francis
Can our democratic government survive? address, September 9, 1977. Vital Speeches 44: 15-19 O 15 '77
International business and morality; address, March 25, 1977. Vital Speeches 43:475-8 My 15 '77
Snooping into your private life: can anything be done about it? interview. por U.S. News 82:35-6 My 2 '77

LINOWITZ, Sol Myron
Administration officials testify on the Panama Canal treaties; statement, September 8, 1977 Dept State Bull 77:537-9 O 17 '77
New Panama Canal treaties—in our national interest; address, October 18, 1977. Dept State Bull 77:806-11 D 5 '77
Should Senate OK Panama treaties? interview. pors U.S. News 83:33-4 D 12 '77
U.S. negotiators brief press on new Panama Canal treaties; transcript of briefing, August 12, 1977. Dept State Bull 77:526-32 O 17 '77
U.S.-Panama statement of understanding; transcript of press briefing, October 14, 1977. Dept State Bull 77:631-4 N 7 '77
Why a new Panama Canal treaty? address, August 19, 1977. Dept State Bull 77:520-5 O 17 '77
about
Ceding the Canal—slowly. il pors Time 110:8-13 Ag 22 '77 *

LINSCOTT, Eloise Hubbard
Centuries of song in her garage. J. W. Steinbergh. il Ms 6:22 S '77 *

LINTON, Calvin D.
Rage for chaos. Chr Today 21:22-5 My 6 '77

LINTON, David
Battle of Whiskey Run. il Parks & Rec 12:64-7+ S '77

LINVILL, John G. and Hogan, C. L.
Intellectual and economic fuel for the electronics revolution. bibl il Science 195:1107-14 Mr 18 '77

LION Theater Company. See Theater, Experimental

LIONS
Case of the murderess cat; ed by J. Carmichel. L. Games. il Outdoor Life 159:58-9+ Mr '77
Elsa the lioness. il Sat Eve Post 249:51 Jl '77
Locked in the lion's jaws; experience of T. Fitzjohn. A. Shapiro. il Read Digest 110:82-6 My '77
Paddington Press and Bantam Books reveal the startling existence of white lions; interview, ed by R. Dahlin. J. Marqusee. il Pub W 211: 31-2 My 9 '77
White lions. C. Panati and others. il Newsweek 89:96+ My 9 '77

LIONS, Mountain. See Pumas

LIP-reading. See Deaf—Means of communication

LIPATTI, Dinu
Is Dinu Lipatti beyond reproach? J. Agee. il Harpers 255:69-73 S '77 *

LIPCHITZ, Jacques
Lipchitz, legacy. E. Edwards. il Art N 76:166-8 Summ '77 *

LIPEZ, Richard
End game. See issues of Progressive
I do not like thee, Dr Seuss the reason why I can't deduce; poem. Atlantic 240:91 Ag '77
New big one. Atlantic 241:88-9 Ja '78
One last fling at Coobies Bay. Atlantic 239:92+ My '77
—and Demarest, Christopher
Putting one over on OPEC. il Atlantic 240:75-9 N '77

LIPIDS
See also
Liposomes
Phosphatides

LIPMAN, Harvy
Workfare and welfare. Nation 225:141-4 Ag 20 '77

LIPMAN, Samuel
Music. Commentary 63:72-5 Mr; 62-6 My; 64:8, 57-61 Jl; 55-60 N '77

LIPOPROTEINS
See also
Blood—Proteins

LIPOSOMES
Liposome accumulation in regions of experimental myocardial infarction. V. J. Caride and B. L. Zaret. bibl il Science 198:735-8 N 18 '77
Liposome-cell interaction: transfer and intracellular release of a trapped fluorescent marker. J. N Weinstein and others. bibl il Science 195:489-92 F 4 '77

LIPPARD, Lucy R.
Artist's book goes public. Art in Am 65:40-1 Ja '77
New landscape art. il Ms 5:68-73 Ap '77
Talking pictures, silent words: Yvonne Rainer's recent movies. bibl il Art in Am 65:86-90 My '77
You can go home again: Five from Louisiana. il Art in Am 65:22-3+ Jl '77

LIPPERT, Catherine Beth, and Measell, J. S.
Greentown glass: Indiana Tumbler and Goblet Company. bibl il Antiques 111:774-81 Ap '77

LIPPINCOTT, J. B, Company-Harper & Row, Publishers, Inc merger. See Publishers and publishing—Acquisitions and mergers

LIPPINCOTT, T. Procter
Discussion. See occasional issues of Senior scholastic including World week

LIPPS, Jere H.
Stonington Island: America's most southerly ghost town. il Oceans 10:42-5 My '77

LIPSCOMB, William Nunn, 1919-
Boranes and their relatives. bibl il Science 196: 1047-55 Je 3 '77

LIPSET, Seymour Martin, and Schneider, William
Carter vs. Israel: what the polls reveal. Commentary 64:21-9 N '77
Emerging national consensus. New Repub 177: 8-9 O 15 '77

LIPSHUTZ, Robert Jerome
Getting ready for Begin. J. M. Wall. Chr Cent 94:643-4 Jl 20 '77 *

LIPSON, Eden Ross
From Russia, with opulence. il N Y Times Mag p48-9+ Ja 16 '77

LIPSON, Greta B.
Folk play: a new technique. Clearing H 50:354-7 Ap '77

LIPSYTE, Robert
I am the greatest! condensation. il pors Read Digest 110:211-18+ Mr '77

LIPTON, Gary
Getting involved. il Opera N 42:46-7 N '77

LIPTON, James
Here be dragons. Read Digest 111:241-2+ N '77

LIPUMA, Tommy
George Benson & Tommy LiPuma: the in flight sessions; interview, ed by D. Heckman. il pors Hi Fi 27:134-6 F '77

LIQUEFACTION of coal. See Coal liquefaction

LIQUEFIED natural gas
Australia: set to spend billions on liquefied gas. map Bus W p43-4 Mr 14 '77
Importation of liquefied natural gas. E. Drake and R. C. Reid. il map Sci Am 236:22-9 bibl(p 148) Ap '77
Liquefied natural gas imports. K. H. Hohenemser. Environment 19:4+ D '77

Transportation

Dilemma called LNG. D. Pauly and others. il Newsweek 80:77 Jl 18 '77
Liquefied natural gas: bombs floating in our harbors; California. H. Rubin. Nation 225: 557-9 N 26 '77

LIQUEFIED petroleum gas
Why propane fuel is harder to get. il Bus W p34 F 21 '77

LIQUEURS
Concerning wine & food; cognacs and cordials. R. L. Balzer. Holiday 57:14-15 N '76
Help for the hyperactive host. il Esquire 88: 174-5 D '77
Sugar and spice liqueurs; with recipes. A. D. Blue. il House & Gard 149:136+ D '77
See also
Cookery—Liquors

LIQUID chromatography. See Chromatographic analysis

LIQUID drops. See Drops

LIQUID fertilizers and manures
Why farmers prefer nitrogen solutions. N. Reeder. Farm J 101:32 Ap '77

LIQUID helium. See Helium, Liquid

LIQUID protein diet. See Diet

LIQUIDATION
Alchemist; I. Jones, professional liquidator. E. Dyson. por Forbes 119:34 Ja 15 '77
Biggest liquidator of them all; Federal Deposit Insurance Corp. il Forbes 119:55+ F 15 '77
Tishman liquidates a problem—and itself. Bus W p26-7 N 7 '77

LIQUIDITY (economics)
See also
Banks and banking—Finance

LIQUIDITY, International
See also
International Monetary Fund

LIQUOR industry
Growing feud at American Distilling. D. G. Santry. por Bus W p 106 D 12 '77
How Bacardi put a new kick in rum sales; Bacardi Imports Inc. il Bus W p 142-4 Mr 21 '77
Publicker: can the ailing distiller be turned around? por Duns R 110:26-7 N '77
Revolution in drinking reshapes the liquor industry. il U.S. News 82:71-3 Mr 21 '77
Surprising changes in American drinking habits. C. G. Burck. Read Digest 110:163-4+ F '77
See also
Brown-Forman Distillers Corporation
Heublein, Inc
Seagram, Joseph E, and Sons (firm)

Marketing

Whiskey distillers put up their dukes. C. G. Burck. il Fortune 96:154-8+ S '77

Scotland

Dour outlook for Scotch whisky. il Bus W p51+ Ag 15 '77
Scotch on the rocks. J. Ross-Skinner. il Duns R 109:66-8+ Ap '77

LIQUOR laws and regulations

New Jersey

Government regulation: a smooth ride to the bank. J. McLaughlin. Nation 224:679-82 Je 4 '77

LIQUOR problem
See also
Alcohol and the clergy
Alcohol and women
Alcoholism
Temperance

LIQUOR traffic
See also
Bars and barrooms

LIQUORS
How to survive a liquor store. A. Fraser. Mademoiselle 83:200-1 Je '77
See also
Cocktails
Cookery—Liquors
Liqueurs
Rum
Tequila
Vodka
Whiskey

LIQUORS as gifts
Sparkling Christmas spirits. E. Fried. il Harp Baz 111:98-9+ D '77
Yuletide spirits to give. A. Fraser. Mademoiselle 83:70 D '77

LISBON, Portugal

Description

Return to Lisbon. H. Koenig and G. Koenig. il Trav/Holiday 148:58-63+ N '77
Transit-lover's tour of Lisbon. il Sunset 159:40+ S '77
Traveler's camera. C. Purcell. il Pop Phot 81:34+ O '77

LISCIOTTI, Larry
Hustler meets an artist. M. DelNagro. il pors Sports Illus 46:52+ Je 27 '77 *

LISH, Gordon
Chicanery topples international chili king in Houston invitational! il Esquire 88:92+ N '77
Chopped liver for gentiles. il Esquire 87:80-2 Mr '77

LISITRANO, Larry F.
Three-dimensional design: the environment. bibl il Sch Arts 76:26-8 Ap '77

LISLE, Harvey
Soil fertility in the orchard. il Org Gard & Farm 24:93-5 Je '77

LISSAU, Steve
Jaws of jaws. il Oceans 10:31-3 N '77
Marketing the shark. il Oceans 10:34-6 N '77

LISTENING
Listen! (It's an art you can learn) Changing T 32:20 Ja '78

LISTENING; drama. See Albee, E.

LISTON, Melba
Whatever happened to Melba Liston? il pors Ebony 32:122 Je '77 *

LISTON, William T.
Stage. Commonweal 104:564-6 S 2 '77

LISTS. See Records

LISZT, Franz
How do you like your Liszt? H. Goldsmith. por Hi Fi 27:95 F '77 *
Hungarian rhapsodies nos. 1-16 and no. 19. R. Kammerer. Am Rec G 40:28 N '76 *
Sonata in B minor; Aquitane recording. L. Radcliffe. Am Rec G 41:35-6 D '77 *
Transcendental etudes. D. Garvelmann. il por Am Rec G 40:32-5 D '76 *

LITCHFIELD, Conn.

Historic houses, sites, etc.

See Historic houses, sites, etc.—Connecticut

LITCHFIELD Historical Society
Paintings of Ralph Earl at the Litchfield Historical Society. L. F. Ballard, Jr. il Antiques 112:959-63 N '77

LITERACY. See Illiteracy

LITERARY agents
Best way to get an agent; comments by editors and publishers. Writer 90:22-5 O '77
Engel's millions; book producer. A. Myers. il por Writers Digest 57:35-6 O '77
Garage sale; the story of B. Briskin. J. Briskin. por Writers Digest 57:48+ D '77
Matchmakers. il Forbes 119:29 Mr 15 '77
Michelle Lapautre. H. R. Lottman. por Pub W 211:25-6 My 30 '77
Selling the German market: literary agents. H. R. Lottman. il Pub W 212:57-8+ S 12 '77
What can an agent do for you? D. Tritsch. Writers Digest 57:28 My '77
What my agent does for me. W. J. Slattery. Writers Digest 57:29 My '77
You ought to be in pictures. E. S. Stevens. Writers Digest 57:43-5 O '77

LITERARY characters. See Characters in literature

LITERARY clubs and societies
AAP aids Iranian writers in plea for association. M. Reuter. Pub W 212:16+ Ag 15 '77
More than wit flourished at the Round Table: there were creative blocks too, says HBJ book; Algonquin Round Table; interview, ed by R. Dahlin. J. R. Gaines. il Pub W 211:89+ Je 13 '77
See also
Authors League of America, Inc
PEN Club

LITERARY collaboration. See Authorship—Collaboration

LITERARY critics and criticism
Fear and trembling at Yale. G. Graff. Am Scholar 46:467-78 Aut '77
Flirting with guilt and tyranny. E. Larsen. il Harpers 225:95-8+ D '77; Reply. G. Lyons. Nation 226:24-6 Ja 7 '78
Literary ups and downs; Times literary supplement verdicts. C. Michener. il Newsweek 89:72 F 7 '77
Reviewing the reviewers. L. Ehrenkrantz. Intellect 106:246-8 D '77
Sanctification of literature. H. Fisch. Commentary 63:63-9 Je '77
See also
Book reviewers and reviewing
Trilling, L.

Bibliography

William H. Pritchard on literary criticism. W. H. Pritchard. New Repub 177:34-6 D 3 '77

LITERARY fantasies. See Fantasies, Literary

LITERARY Guild of America
Literary banquet; fiftieth-anniversary dinner. New Yorker 53:37-8 N 14 '77

LITERARY periodicals. See Literature—Periodicals

LITERARY prizes
Bouquet of spring prizes. M. Reuter. Pub W 211:16 My 30 '77
Industry gives $100,000 to new Readers Book Awards. M. Reuter. Pub W 212:108 S 26 '77
Year in review: literary prizes and awards. il Pub W 211:48-51 F 14 '77
See also
American Academy and Institute of Arts and Letters
Childrens literature—Awards, prizes, etc.
National Book Awards
Poetry—Awards, prizes, etc.
Scientific literature for children—Awards, prizes, etc.

LITERARY property. See Copyright

LITERARY recreations
Flip-strip sonnet, the lipogram and other mad modes of wordplay. M. Gardner. il Sci Am 236:121-6 F '77

LITERARY research
Brute indeed! working on the second edition of A short-title catalogue of books printed in England, Scotland, & Ireland and of English books printed abroad 1475-1640. New Yorker 53:30-2 Mr 28 '77
Home away from home for writers; Allen Room of the New York Public Library. N. Emergy. il Pub W 211:39-40 Ja 17 '77
How much is enough? W. C. Lee. Writers Digest 57:34+ D '77

LITERARY societies. See Literary clubs and societies

LITERATURE
In a bold hand; excerpts from works of six American women authors. il Sat Eve Post 249:34-5 Jl '77
Post sampler; excerpts from works of famous authors. il Sat Eve Post 249:42+ Jl '77
See also
Anthologies
Authorship

LITERATURE—See also—*Continued*
Best sellers
Biography
Books and reading
Characters in literature
Childrens literature
Creation (literary, artistic, etc)
Fiction
Humor
Literary critics and criticism
Poetry
Realism in literature
Symbolism in literature
Young adults literature
also literature of special subjects, e.g. Religious literature; *also* national literature, e.g. English literature

Anecdotes, facetiae, satire, etc.

Posh bars of Anchorage; book flap literature. R. Rosenblatt. New Repub 176:33-4+ Ja 15 '77

Appreciation and interpretation

Flirting with guilt and tyranny. E. Larsen. il Harpers 225:95-8+ D '77
On Margate sands: literature and ideas. J. Hollis. Intellect 105:362-5 Ap '77

Bibliography

Literature (cont) G. Doherty and P. C. Doherty. America 136:81-2 Ja 29 '77

Competitions

1977 Scholastic Awards. il Sr Schol 109:9-12+ My 19 '77
Prize offers. See issues of Writer
See also
Fiction—Competitions
Scholastic Magazine Awards

Periodicals

Little magazine: grow or die. G. Lyons. Nation 225:85-6 Jl 23 '77

Prizes

See Literary prizes

Study and teaching

But what good will it do? R. Rosenblatt. New Repub 176:37-9 Ja 29 '77
Multicultural literature to teach; symposium, comp by S. Koch. Engl J 66:57-70 Mr '77
Nobel prize winning world literature. M. J. Moran. Engl J 66:59-60 S '77
Quo vadis literature? ERIC/RCS report. H. O'Donnell. bibl Engl J 66:94-6 F '77
Reader's experience; symposium. il Engl J 66:32-51 F '77
Response to literature. A. R. Petrosky. bibl Engl J 66:96-8 O '77
Vocational English. B. G. Rowell. Clearing H 50:241-2 F '77
See also
English literature—Study and teaching

Aids and devices

G.B. Shaw and I are Leos. J. Sweet. il Engl J 66:62-3 O '77
Teaching ideas; symposium. il Engl J 66:60-76 F '77
Viewpoints on literature. C. Kuykendall. il Engl J 66:86-90 F '77

Technique

See also
Fiction—Technique

Themes

American nonfiction: dreams and nightmares; utopian thought. D. Rosen. Engl J 66:54 S '77
Coming of age in Shakespeare; sexual maturation in adolescents. M. Garber. Yale R 66:517-33 Je '77
Crime and punishment: matricide and the woman question. D. Kiremidjian. bibl f Am Imago 33:403-33 Wint '76
J. K. Huysmans: a study in decadence. E. Hartnett. Am Scholar 46:367-76 Summ '77
Kawps; police in literature. D. Roberts. Engl J 66:66-7 S '77
Lest I steal: the morality of theft. A. T. Barbeau. bibl Intellect 105:281-2 F '77
Poem of the pampas; gaucho theme of R. Güiraldes' Don Segundo Sombra. E. A. Echevarria. il Americas 29:2-5 Ap '77
Turn of the screw and The exorcist; demoniacal possession and childhood purity. B. Beit-Hallahmi. bibl Am Imago 33:296-303 Fall '76
Who's turning what into movies? M. Tuchman. il Esquire 87:72-4+ Ap '77
See also
Africans in literature
Bible in literature
Blacks in literature
Business in literature
Childrens literature—Themes
Chinese in literature
Confession in literature
Crime in literature
Death in literature
Eskimos in literature
French in literature
Homosexuality in literature
Indians (American) in literature
Indians (East Indian) in literature
Italians in literature
Jesus Christ in literature
Jews in literature
Librarians in literature
Mental illness in literature
Mexican Americans in literature
Minorities in literature
Politics in literature
Prisons in literature
Psychology in literature
Religion in literature
Reptiles in literature
Russians in literature
Sex role in literature
Sports in literature
Success in literature
Western States in literature
Women in literature

LITERATURE, Influence of
See also
Childrens literature, Influence of

LITERATURE, Medieval
See also
Poetry, Medieval

LITERATURE, Primitive
See also
Folklore

LITERATURE, Regional

Study and teaching

Ethnic and regional literature: making connections with composition. S. Burns and L. Burns. il Engl J 66:34-6 Mr '77

LITERATURE, Underground. See Underground literature

LITERATURE and art. See Art and literature

LITERATURE and communism. See Communism and literature

LITERATURE and motion pictures. See Motion pictures and literature

LITERATURE and music. See Music and literature

LITERATURE and opera. See Music and literature

LITERATURE and psychoanalysis. See Psychoanalysis and literature

LITERATURE and religion. See Religion and literature

LITERATURE and science
Poetic responses to the Copernican revolution. M. M. Byard. il Sci Am 236:120-9 bibl(p 142) Je '77
Visible college in British science. M. Green. Am Scholar 47:105-17 Wint '77
See also
Science fiction

LITERATURE and society
Author James Michener on future of this country. J. A. Michener. il pors U.S. News 83:60-1 S 12 '77
Nobel lecture. S. Bellow. Am Scholar 46:316-25 Summ '77
Novel in a changing society; excerpt from Literature in the marketplace; tr by G. Bisset. P. Gerdin. por Pub W 212:20-2 N 28 '77

LITERATURE and state
Voice of the South; poet J. Dickey. P. Axthelm. pors Newsweek 89:25 Ja 31 '77
See also
United States—National Foundation on the Arts and the Humanities

LITERATURE and television. See Television and literature

LITFIN, A. Duane
Perils of persuasive preaching. Chr Today 21:14-17 F 4 '77

LITHIUM
Lithium ion entry through the sodium channel of cultured mouse neuroblastoma cells: a biochemical study. E. Richelson. bibl il Science 196:1001-2 My 27 '77

LITHIUM carbonate
Lithium: effects on subjective functioning and morphine-induced euphoria. D. R. Jasinski and others. bibl il Science 195:582-4 F 11 '77

LITHOGRAPHS
How did an Indian chief really look? lithographic copies of Charles Bird King portraits. H. J. Viola. il Smithsonian 8:100-2+ Je '77
Winter in the country; Currier & Ives lithographs. Am Hist Illus 12:38-41 D '77

LITHOGRAPHS, Publishing of. See Publishers and publishing—Art

LITHOGRAPHY
Revolution in hand-drawn lithography. M. Hunter. il Am Artists 41:52-9+ O '77

LITHOPS
Stone plants are sheer camouflage. il Sunset 158:225 Je '77

LITHOSPHERE. See Earth—Surface

LITIGATION. See Actions and defenses

LITIGATION insurance. See Insurance, Litigation
LITRONIX, Inc. See Electronic industries—United States
LITTER. See Refuse and refuse disposal
LITTER (bedding)
TRU recycles manure into odorless bedding. il Suc Farm 75:no4 D12 Mr '77
LITTKE, Lael J.
You remind me of Lloyd; story. Seventeen 36:156-7 My '77
LITTLE, Joanne
Joan Little case. Newsweek 89:9 F 14 '77 *
LITTLE, Joanne, murder trial. See Trials (murder)
LITTLE, Paul L.
Le$$ costly, more popular. il por Lib J 102:451-6 F 15 '77
—and Gilliland, J. R.
OASES in Oklahoma. pors Lib J 102:1458-61 Jl '77
LITTLE, Steve
They're kicking up a real storm. J. Jares. il pors Sports Illus 47:26-9 N 7 '77 *
LITTLE, Brown and Company. See Publishers and publishing—United States
LITTLE Brown Jug (race) See Harness racing
LITTLE DIOMEDE Island. See Diomede Islands
LITTLE League baseball. See Baseball, Childrens
LITTLE League football. See Football, Childrens
LITTLE magazines. See Literature—Periodicals
LITTLE ROCK, Ark.
So this is Little Rock. D. Dahl. il Ret Liv 17:44-5 My '77

Education

See Education—Arkansas
LITTLE Tree (Cherokee Indian) See Carter, F.
LITTLEFIELD, Edmund Wattis
General Electric's very personal merger. L. Kraar. il pors Fortune 96:186-92+ Ag '77 *
LITTLETON, Harvey
Gallé: transcendence in glass and wood. il Craft Horiz 37:32-6+ Ag '77
LITTON Industries, Inc
Litton's Israel sale awaiting Defense Dept. approval. Aviation W 106:204 Mr 21 '77
Task teams for rapid growth; Microwave Cooking Products Division. W. W. George. il Harvard Bus R 55:71-80 Mr '77
LITURGIES
See also
Bible—Liturgical use
LITZ, Francis J.
Saint. New Yorker 53:24-6 Je 27 '77 *
LITZ, Katherine
Performance can have a dangerous connotation. por Dance Mag 51:131 My '77
LIU, Alvin Y. and others
Nucleotide sequences from a rabbit alpha globin gene inserted in a chimeric plasmid. bibl il Science 196:192-5 Ap 8 '77
LIU, Chin P.
Sprouts. New Yorker 53:16-17 Ag 1 '77 *
LIU, Lin-gun
First occurrence of the garnet-ilmenite transition in silicates. bibl il Science 195:990-1 Mr 11 '77
LIVE bait. See Bait
LIVE virus vaccines. See Vaccines
LIVER

Diseases

Fascioliasis: role of proline in bile duct hyperplasia. H. Isseroff and others. bibl il Science 198:1157-9 D 16 '77
Ratio of plasma alpha amino-*n*-butyric acid to leucine as an empirical marker of alcoholism: diagnostic value. M. Y. Morgan and others. il Science 197:1183-5 S 16 '77
Test detects liver damage in alcoholics. Sci N 112:55+ Jl 23 '77
See also
Hepatitis
Reye's syndrome
LIVER as food
See also
Cookery—Meat
LIVER fluke disease. See Liver—Diseases
LIVER regeneration. See Regeneration (biology)
LIVERMORE, Norman B. Jr
Open letter to Secretary Andrus. por Am For 83:30+ Jl '77
LIVERMORE, Calif.

Religious institutions and affairs

See California—Religious institutions and affairs
LIVESTOCK
Learning from the animals. R. Rodale. il Org Gard & Farm 24:60-4 O '77
Livestock news (cont) Farm J 101:LK1 Mr; LK1 Ap; LK1 N '77
See also
Goats
Horses
Poultry
Ruminants
Swine

Care

Antidote kits save poisoned livestock; Wisconsin program. Farm J 101:G3 S '77

Marketing

Livestock charts: take the guesswork out of selling. G. Johnston. il Suc Farm 75:H18 D '77
Livestock marketing: are you stuck in a one-buyer rut? L. Kruse. il Suc Farm 75:23-31 D '77

Statistics

How good are USDA livestock and meat reports? Suc Farm 75:H8-9 D '77

Watering

Your stock water: how good is it? D. Seim. Farm J 101:H2 mid-F '77
LIVESTOCK, Weight and measurements of
See also
Swine, Weight and measurements of
LIVESTOCK associations
See also
National Cattlemen's Association
LIVESTOCK barns. See Barns and stables
LIVESTOCK industry

Export-import trade

Growing market for U.S. producers. G. Vincent. il Suc Farm 75:44 O '77
LIVGREN, Kerry
Sound of fame and fortune. E. Miller. il pors Seventeen 36:245+ Ag '77 *
LIVING. See Conduct of life; Life
LIVING, Cost of. See Cost of living
LIVING Aquatic Resources Management, International Center for. See Aquaculture
LIVING fossils
Chemical evidence for separating the psilotaceae from the filicales. G. Cooper-Driver. bibl il Science 198:1260-2 D 23 '77
LIVING rocks. See Lithops
LIVING rooms
Living rooms: room for living? Redbook 148:198-9 Ap '77
One big room where we could cook and socialize; living-room-kitchen. il House & Gard 149:146-9 My '77
One room—two personalities. il Bet Hom & Gard 55:14 Jl '77
Summerize your living room. J. Cornell. il Am Home 80:100+ Ap '77
24 hour room. il Am Home 80:52-3 My '77
LIVING wills
Legislation and the living will. R. A. McCormick and A. E. Hellegers. America 136:210-13 Mr 12 '77
LIVINGSTON, Douglas
Sunrise; poem. Chr Today 21:18 Ap 1 '77
LIVINGSTON, Gordon S.
Search for a stranger. Read Digest 110:85-9 Je '77
LIVINGSTON, Myra Cohn
Writing poetry for children. Writer 90:25-8 Je '77
LIVINGSTON, Robert R.
Battle takes shape early for the '78 election. il por U.S. News 83:65-6 S 12 '77 *
LIZARDS
Circadian organization in lizards: the role of the pineal organ. H. Underwood. bibl il Science 195:587-9 F 11 '77
Ionochromic behavior of gecko visual pigments. F. Crescitelli. bibl il Science 195:187-8 Ja 14 '77
Lizard in beetle's clothing. il Sci N 111:54 Ja 22 '77
Natural selection for juvenile lizards mimicking noxious beetles. R. B. Huey and E. R. Planka. bibl il Science 195:201-3 Ja 14 '77
Refractoriness in female lizard reproduction: a probable circannual clock. H. S. Cuellar and O. Cuellar. bibl il Science 197:495-7 Jl 29 '77
Value of virgin birth. C. J. Cole. il Natur Hist 87:56-63 bibl(p 108) Ja '78
See also
Iguanas
LIZARDS, Fossil
Earliest diapsid reptile identified; petrolacosaurus. Sci N 112:7 Jl 2 '77
Petrolacosaurus, the oldest known diapsid reptile. R. R. Reisz. bibl il Science 196:1091-3 Je 3 '77
LLAMADAS festival. See Festivals—Uruguay
LLAMAS, A. and others
Amygdaloid projections to prefrontal and motor cortex. bibl il Science 195:794-6 F 25 '77
LLAMBIAS DE AZEVEDO, Alfonso
Raúl Cattelani, Uruguayan printmaker. il Américas 29:29-31 Ag '77
LLORDS, Daniel
Perspectives. N. M. Stoop. il por Dance Mag 51:98 S '77 *
LLOSA, Mario Vargas. See Vargas Llosa, M.
LLOYD, Alan
Fight on! And on and on; excerpt from The great prize fight. il pors Sports Illus 47:54-60+ Jl 25 '77

LLOYD, Frank
Act of alteration. G. Henry. Art N 76:115-16 My '77 *
Straw man in the Rothko case. J. H. Merryman. il por Art N 75:32-4 D '76; 76:32-3+ Mr '77 *

LLOYD, Freeman
Cricket and Katrine. B. Tarrant. il pors Field & S 82:154-6 My '77 *

LLOYD, Marcia
Workshop: wet forming in leather. il Craft Horiz 37:49-51 Je '77

LLOYD GEORGE, David, 1st Earl Lloyd George of Dwyfor. See Lloyd George of Dwyfor, D. L. G.

LLOYD GEORGE of Dwyfor, David Lloyd George, 1st Earl
David Lloyd George: land, the budget, and social reform. B. B. Gilbert. bibl f Am Hist R 81:1058-66 D '76 *

LLOYD'S, London
On becoming a member of Lloyd's. A. Tobias. Esquire 88:17-18 D '77
Ye olde negative sell; underwriting by Americans. il Forbes 120:127+ N 15 '77

LOAD (electric plants) See Electric plants—Load

LOADING and unloading
Balloons to move cargo ship-to-shore. Aviation W 107:70 Jl 4 '77

LOAN associations. See Savings and loan associations

LOAN companies. See Finance companies

LOANS
See also
Credit
Interest (economics)
Mortgages
Student loans

LOANS, Art. See Art loans

LOANS, Bank
Bert Lance's bind; National Bank of Georgia. M. Ruby and others. il por Newsweek 90:69-70+ Jl 18 '77
Big banks' money sale. D. Pauly and P. E. Simons. il Newsweek 89:65+ Je 6 '77
Fewer strings on bank loans. Bus W p 103 F 21 '77
For budget chief: a money problem all his own; B. Lance's National Bank of Georgia. il por U.S. News 83:65 Jl 25 '77
Good old boy network; Atlanta bank loans to J. Carter campaign; with White House response by J. Powell. R. Reeves and B. M. Hager. New Repub 177:6+ S 10 '77
I can get for you wholesale; banks undercutting their own prime rate. il Forbes 119:23-4 My 1 '77
Loan demand leaves bankers still flush. il Bus W p26 Ja 9 '78
Outlook for borrowers: plenty of money but it'll cost more. il U.S. News 83:82-4 O 31 '77
Problems, perspectives and responsibilities; address, March 15, 1977. D. Rockefeller. Vital Speeches 43:357-60 Ap 1 '77
Send Lance back to banking; questionable loans incurred as head of National Bank of Georgia. por New Repub 177:10-12 Ag 6 '77
See also
Agricultural credit

Finance

Banks find ways to boost lending. Bus W p44+ O 31 '77

Guaranty

New market for SBA loans. Bus W p54 Jl 4 '77
On getting the most out of Uncle Sam. Forbes 119:84+ My 15 '77

Brazil

Brazilian gamble. il Bus W p72-6+ D 5 '77

China

First Chicago reaches to win Peking's favor. por Bus W p36 O 17 '77

Europe, Eastern

New sophistication in East-West banking. il Bus W p40 Mr 7 '77

Indonesia

Lesson for bankers who lend to LDCs. Bus W p32+ Ap 4 '77

Korea, South

South Korea: Seoul tries out Europe as U.S. loans dry up. Bus W p37 Mr 7 '77

Malaysia

Oil beckons the international bankers. map Bus W p52 My 16 '77

Mexico

Mexican solution for companies in debt; Bank of America's loan to Fundidora de Monterrey. Bus W p42 F 14 '77

Peru

Debt-ridden Peru looks for scapegoats. Bus W p31+ S 5 '77
Turkey, Peru take banks to brink. il Time 110:33 S 5 '77
Why the banks bailed out Peru. il Bus W p 117-18 Mr 21 '77

Russia

German bankers win a big one. il Bus W p33 Je 20 '77

Taiwan

First Chicago reaches to win Peking's favor. por Bus W p36 O 17 '77

Turkey

Turkey, Peru take banks to brink. il Time 110:33 S 5 '77

Underdeveloped areas

Are the LDCs in over their heads? H. van B. Cleveland and W. H. B. Brittain. il For Affairs 55:732-50 Jl '77
Bankers milk the third world. J. Aronson and E. Stein, Jr. Progressive 41:49-51 O '77
Rescuing the LDCs. D. O. Beim. For Affairs 55:717-31 Jl '77
Shaky mountain of debt. il Time 109:63-4 Je 13 '77

Venezuela

Bankers try again for a Venezuela loan. Bus W p35 F 7 '77

Zaire

Bankers' stakes in Zaire. R. Kramer. map Nation 224:521-4 Ap 30 '77
Lesson for bankers who lend to LDCs. Bus W p32+ Ap 4 '77
Pulling Zaire out of a financial hole. Bus W p89 Ja 31 '77
Why a Nashville bank is deep in Zaire; Commerce Union Bank. il Bus W p 111+ Je 20 '77

LOANS, British

Bolivia

True coin of freedom; question of British loan to the State Mining Corporation of Bolivia. Nation 225:194-5 S 10 '77

LOANS, Foreign

Italy

Europe's sickest man; question of International Monetary Fund loan. M. Ledeen. New Repub 176:8-10 F 12 '77

Portugal

Portugal: a hard test for the IMF. S. W. Sanders. il Bus W p35 Ja 9 '78

Turkey

Austerity now—and hopes for IMF aid. Bus W p53+ O 17 '77

LOANS, Interlibrary. See Interlibrary loans

LOANS, Personal
Bargains for borrowers—last chance for easy loans? il U.S. News 82:71-2 My 30 '77
Best places to borrow money. L. David. il Mech Illus 73:56+ My '77
Do long-term car loans make sense for you? R. A. Dickelman. Bet Hom & Gard 55:34 S '77
Dollars and sense; auto loans. G. Mahon. Mademoiselle 83:122 O '77
How to save on an auto loan. il Consumer Rep 42:198-200 Ap '77
If you want a bank loan—new tests you have to pass. il U.S. News 83:65-6 Ag 22 '77
Q&A about money. J. S. Dennis. por Ret Liv 16:57 D '76
See also
Banks and banking—Overdrafts

LOANS, Saudi Arabian
IMF: no sign of that Saudi money. Bus W p36 My 2 '77
Will the IMF let the Saudis buy in? B. Nussbaum. por Bus W p 154 My 16 '77

LOBBYING. See Lobbyists and lobbying

LOBBYISTS and lobbying
Bard of oil; Rep R. Krueger's efforts on behalf of the petroleum industry lobby. T. Newsweek 89:75-6 Je 20 '77
California agencies get lobbyists for the people. Consumer Rep 42:185-6 Ap '77
Carter's health plans; labor's push for national health insurance. E. Marshall. New Repub 177:10-12 D 10 '77
Combating the energy lobbyists. J. M. Wall. Chr Cent 94:395 Ap 27 '77
Commanding voice in airline reform; M. M. Schuman. por Bus W p 170+ N 14 '77
Congress: Liberals at bay. G. R. Rosen. il Duns R 110:40-4 S '77
Cooking up a nutrition lobby. C. Holden. Science 198:36 O 7 '77
Expatriates may keep a tax break; efforts of Tax Equity for Americans Abroad. il Bus W p31 O 31 '77
Fishbowl approach to agency lobbying; recent U.S. Court of Appeals decision. Bus W p31-2 My 23 '77

LOBBYISTS and lobbying—*Continued*
Fragile pact to beat the Arab boycott; Business Roundtable—B'nai B'rith Anti-Defamation League agreement. Bus W p25-6 Mr 28 '77
Good ol' boy; C. E. Walker. T. Nicholson and J. Walcott. il por Newsweek 90:83-4 D 5 '77
Growing clout of do good lobbies. G. R. Rosen. il Duns R 109:44-7+ Ap '77
Hearts and minds; reactions to energy proposals. T. Mathews and others. il por Newsweek 89:30 My 2 '77
Hidden army of Washington lobbyists. T. J. Foley. il U.S. News 83:29-32 Jl 25 '77
How to send revolution through the mail. M. Rockwood. il Ms 6:85-8 Ja '78
Lobbying rules for nonprofits: new option sets specific limits. J. Walsh. Science 196:40+ Ap 1 '77
Lobbying the Carter UFO; energy bill. il Time 109:74-5 Je 20 '77
McCall's family lobby. A. O'Shea. McCalls 104: 64 My; 70 Jl; 74 Ag '77; 105:42 Ja '78
New corporate clout in the capital. Time 110:63 Jl 4 '77
Ocean mining: former negotiator now lobbies for Kennecott. D. Shapley. Science 196:964-5 My 27 '77
Politics of persuasion; interviews with women lobbyists, ed by S. P. Koslow. il Mademoiselle 83:58+ F '77
Reporter at large; C. E. Walker, lobbyist for corporate clients on the energy bill. E. B. Drew. New Yorker 53:32-6+ Ja 9 '78
Sky full of Learjets; gas industry and gas consumer lobbies. il Time 110:14 O 17 '77
Spotty scorecard for Carter's lobbyists. il Bus W p88+ N 14 '77
Thirty-one favors; dairy lobby's campaign against new ice cream standards. N. Wade. New Repub 177:15-17 N 5 '77
Tongsun Park's White House connection. A. Latham. il Esquire 88:78+ D '77
Unglued alliance on the Arab boycott; Business Roundtable and B'nai B'rith Anti-Defamation League. Bus W p43-4 S 12 '77
Who's who in the lobby; energy lobby. T. Mathews and J. Walcott. il Newsweek 89:18+ Je 27 '77
Women's voice in Washington; Women's Lobby, Inc. A. O'Shea. McCalls 105:115 O '77
Working the state house: home turf for the lobbyist. J. Wennersten. Nation 225:307-8 O 1 '77
Writing an official is a Capital idea. Sr Schol 109:22-3 F 24 '77
See also
Common Cause (organization)
New Directions (organization)
Pressure groups

Laws and legislation

ACLU, AAP oppose lobbying law dues disclosure. S. Wagner. Pub W 212:14 Ag 22 '77

LOBEL, Arnold, and others
Children's book illustrators play favorites. il Wilson Lib Bull 52:165-73 O '77

LOBEL, Michael
Yes plugs in at the Garden: equipment. il Hi Fi 27:129-31 D '77

LO BELLO, Nino
Across the Neva. il Travel 147:50-1 Ap '77
Mount McKinley National Park. il Travel 147: 52-7 Ap '77

LOBO STERNBERG, Ricardo da Silveira
Gifts; poem. Nation 225:535 N 19 '77

LOBOS, Arminda Villa-. See Villa-Lobos, A.

LOBOS, Heitor Villa-. See Villa-Lobos, H.

LOBROVICH, Mitch
Sawdust steaks in your future? Sci Digest 82: 79-80 N '77

LOBSENZ, Norman M.
Why some husbands stay faithful. Read Digest 111:98-101 O '77
—See Lasswell, M. jt auth

LOBSTER cactus. See Cactus

LOBSTER culture. See Shellfish culture

LOBSTER fisheries. See Shellfish fisheries

LOBSTER yachts. See Yachts and yachting

LOBSTERS
Developmental neuroethology: changes in escape and defensive behavior during growth of the lobster. F. Lang and others. il Science 197:682-5 Ag 12 '77
Lobster proportions dictate behavior. il Sci N 112:118-19 Ag 20 '77
See also
Cookery—Shellfish

LOCAL control of schools. See School management and organization

LOCAL finance
Deep freeze, drought hit local budgets. il Am City & County 92:13 Mr '77
Dramatic upturn in state and local spending. il Fortune 95:10 Mr '77
State and local spending is bolstering G.N.P. il Fortune 96:24 N '77
See also
Municipal finance

LOCAL government
Cutting the cost of local government; overstaffing. R. A. Smardon. Harvard Bus R 55: 8+ Mr '77
See also
Annexation (municipal government)
City manager plan
Municipal government
Public administration
Town meetings

Bibliography

Books (cont of) Book reviews. See issues of American city & county

United States

See also
National Conference on Alternative State and Local Public Policies

LOCAL service airlines. See Airlines—Local service

LOCAL taxation
Cities where taxes are highest—and lowest. il U.S. News 82:66 Je 6 '77
State, local taxes still heading up. il U.S. News 83:82 N 14 '77
See also
Assessment

LOCAL transit
Bikes get boost from mass transit. il Am City & County 92:48 Ja '77
Getting transit on track. G. M. Chamberlain. Am City & County 92:98 D '77
Is rail transit worth the expense? A. Swardson. Bus W p72 O 31 '77
Negative energy impact of modern rail transit systems. C. A. Lave; B. Hannon. bibl Science 195:595-6 F 11 '77; Discussion. 197:7, 938+ Jl 1, S 2 '77
People mover projects get ready to go. il Am City & County 92:54 My '77
Private people-mover. V. E. Smay. il Pop Sci 210:151 Je '77
Urban transit at the crossroads; rail transit. il Am City & County 92:31-4 D '77
What price transit accessibility? il Am City & County 92:18 O '77
See also
Buses
Detroit—Transit systems
New York (city)—Transit systems
Pittsburgh—Transit systems
Railroads, Elevated
Railroads, Single rail
San Francisco Bay Region—Transit systems

Federal aid

Anatomy of a boondoggle; Urban Mass Transit Administration funding of personal rapid transit system in Morgantown, W.Va. T. Armbrister. il Read Digest 111:133-6 Ag '77
Billions for transit seen in new federal legislation. H. V. Semling. Am City & County 92:20-1 Mr '77
Dark tunnel ahead for mass transit. il Bus W p 121+ Ap 18 '77
Diverting the Highway Fund. M. Gerrard Environment 19:4-5 Je '77
Road funds under transit attack. Am City & County 92:29 Jl '77

LOCATION, Target. See Target location

LOCATION in business and industry
Ailing cities spread the welcome mat for business. il U.S. News 83:75-7 D 19 '77
Business has the jitters in Quebec. H. E. Meyer. il Fortune 96:238-42+ O '77
Business loves the sunbelt and vice versa. G. Breckenfeld. map Fortune 95:132-7+ Je '77
Canada: business warns Quebec. il Bus W p44 My 23 '77
Denver: the new Houston? T. J. Murray. il map Duns R 110:54-8 O '77
Don't let industry move away. D. J. Springate. il por Am City & County 92:68-9 Ap '77
English-speaking rush to leave Quebec. il Bus W p62+ Ag 22 '77
Equality in industry for U.S. blacks. E. D. Jackson. por Nations Bus 65:91 D '77
Global cities of tomorrow. D. A. Heenan. bibl f Harvard Bus R 55:79-92 My '77
Going where the money is; bank trust operations. Forbes 119:62 Mr 15 '77
How a company helps its state attract business; Massachusetts. V. Louviere. Nations Bus 65: 75 S '77
More than a suburb, less than a city; Orange County, Calif. il map Bus W p76-7 S 5 '77
Moving in; Avis' move to New York City. New Yorker 53:38-40 D 5 '77
New Hampshire: mecca for industry. J. C. Perham. map Duns R 109:80-2+ Je '77
New layer of structural unemployment: older blue-collar workers. il map Bus W p 142+ N 14 '77
New York's loss is Fairfield County's gain. il Bus W p 121-2 Ap 25 '77
See also
Atomic power plants—Location
Petroleum refineries—Location
Steel works—Location

LOCATIONS, Motion picture. See Motion pictures—Setting and scenery

LOCH Ness monster
In pursuit of the Loch Ness monster. J. Stewart-Gordon. il Read Digest 110:120-4 F '77
Loch Ness: the lake and the legend. W. S. Ellis. il map Nat Geog 151:758-79 Je '77

LOCHER, David
Christmas before now; poem. America 137:455 D 24 '77
Summer straw & blue; poem. America 137:23 Jl 16 '77
That far, in Peru; poem. America 137:431 D 17 '77

LOCKE, Edward
Wing and the talon: poem. Yale R 67:69-70 O '77

LOCKE, John
Prophet of reason. P. W. Schmidtchen. il por Hobbies 82:134-6+ Ap '77 *

LOCKER rooms
Locker-room lib; women sportswriters in locker rooms. D. K. Shah and J. Whitmore. il Newsweek 91:86 Ja 16 '78
Locker room mystique. C. Whelton. il Horizon 21:64-9 Ja '78

LOCKERBIE, D. Bruce
Laughter without joy: the burlesque of our secular age. Chr Today 22:14-16 O 7 '77

LOCKERETZ, William
Can we take the chemicals out of the Corn Belt? Horticulture 55:14+ S '77

LOCKHEED Aircraft Corporation
Aerospace labor woes continue. Aviation W 107:15 D 19 '77
Anderson to succeed Haack as Lockheed's chief executive. Aviation W 107:24 Ag 8 '77
Bad debt that was profitable for everybody. L. G. Martin. Fortune 96:203 O '77
Can Roy Anderson make people forget Lockheed's problems? il por Bus W p74-7+ O 10 '77
How Lockheed got back its wings. L. Kraar. il por Fortune 96:198-202+ O '77
IAM strikes Lockheed's installations in California. Aviation W 107:24-5 O 17 '77
Is Lockheed's bribery saga over? il Bus W p27 My 30 '77
Labor, management adamant in Lockheed strike positions. J. M. Lenorovitz. Aviation W 107:23-4 D 12 '77
Loan guarantee cost Lockheed $30 million. Aviation W 107:20 O 3 '77
Lockheed contract offer rejected by machinists. Aviation W 108:22 Ja 2 '78
Lockheed details offer to machinists. Aviation W 107:21-2 N 28 '77
Lockheed employes return to jobs. J. M. Lenorovitz. Aviation W 108:17 Ja 9 '78
Lockheed looks to international markets, but not coproduction. Aviation W 107:23-4 O 31 '77
Lockheed payments changes approved. Aviation W 106:73 Ap 25 '77
Lockheed report details payments. D. E. Fink. Aviation W 106:50 Je 13 '77
Lockheed strike continued despite union member rift. J. M. Lenorovitz. Aviation W 107:21-2 D 5 '77
Lockheed: up from the ashes. T. J. Murray. il por Duns R 109:53-5+ Mr '77
Lockheed's great dilemma. il por Time 110:40+ Ag 22 '77
Lockheed's 70-day mission to Tokyo; excerpt from Lockheed sales mission: seventy days in Tokyo. A. C. Kotchian. il Sat R 4:7-12 Jl 9 '77
Renegotiation hearing cites Lockheed. Aviation W 106:24-5 Je 20 '77
Why Lockheed's strike is a holy war. il Bus W p31 D 19 '77

LOCKHEED Missiles and Space Company
Lockheed eyes ocean power plant. il Am City & County 92:40 O '77

LOCKS and keys
Foil car thieves with Digistart, the electronic security lock. J. Fortuna. il Pop Electr 11:48-9 Ap '77
Installing door and window locks. D. Raffel. il House & Gard 149:80+ Mr '77

LOCKWOOD, Allison
Pantsuited pioneer of Women's lib, Dr Mary Walker. il pors Smithsonian 7:113-14+ Mr '77

LOCOMOTION
See also
Animal locomotion

LOCOMOTIVE engineers
Casey Jones would be proud; a young woman engineer. S. Duckens. il pors Ebony 32:53-4+ Mr '77

LOCOMOTIVES
Big engine that couldn't: an Amtrak woe. il U.S. News 82:72 F 21 '77
Is GM's locomotive derailing Amtrak? il Bus W p32 F 7 '77

LOCTITE Corporation
True grip. Forbes 120:136 O 15 '77

LOCY, Sharon
Joy on Sunday; story. McCalls 105:218-19 N '77

LODAHL, Marlene Boskind-. See Boskind-Lodahl, M.

LOEB, G. E. and others
Long-term unit recording from somatosensory neurons in the spinal ganglia of the freely walking cat. bibl il Science 197:1192-4 S 16 '77

LOEHR, George, and Loehr, Valerie
Deer Island, Maine. il map Travel 147:24-9+ My '77

LOEHR, Valerie. See Loehr, G. jt auth

LOETTERLE, Fred. See Kusachi, S. jt auth

LOEVINGER, Lee
Is there intelligent life in Washington? address, September 16, 1976. Vital Speeches 43:173-7 Ja 1 '77

LOEWENDAHL, Evelyn
Three simple stretches that will change your life; excerpt from The power of positive stretching. il Good H 185:16 N '77

LOEWENFELDT, Paula von. See Speers, T. W. jt auth

LOEWENTHAL, Paul G. M.
Caribbean; incentives for American investment; address, April 20, 1977. Vital Speeches 43:468-70 My 15 '77

LOEWI & Company. See Brokers

LOFTAS, Tony
Great ornamental fish rip-off. il Int Wildlife 7:28-32 Jl '77

LOFTS, Norah (Robinson)
Queen Elizabeth at 51; excerpt from Queens of England. por Ladies Home J 94:67-8+ Jl '77

LOFTS, Converted. See Apartments, Remodeled

LOFTUS, Elizabeth F.
Follies of affirmative action. Society 14:21-4 Ja '77

LOG cottages, Converted. See Houses, Remodeled

LOG splitting machines. See Wood cutting machines

LOGAN, Andy
Around City Hall (cont) New Yorker 52:101-8 F 7; 53:112-20+ Mr 14; 91-8 Ap 4; 114-20+ My 2; 96-103 My 30; 84-90 Je 27; 72-7 Jl 18; 64-72 Ag 15; 71-6+ S 5; 142-8+ O 3; 134+ O 31; 203-11 N 21; 54-6 D 26 '77

LOGAN, Ben
Year the Christmas presents didn't come. il Good H 185:48+ D '77

LOGAN, Charles H.
Recidivism and the effectiveness of prison and parole. bibl Intellect 105:424-6 Je '77

LOGAN, William
Fever; poem. Nation 225:730 D 31 '77
Ice; poem. New Yorker 53:28 Ja 2 '78
In December, thirty-one moons; The desert of reminiscence; Anamnesis; Monocular; poems. Poetry 131:125-9 D '77
Language against fear. Poetry 130:221-9 Jl '77
Lizard in his medium; poem. New Yorker 53:111 O 3 '77
Totenlieder; Object; Three lives; Moth disturbs the night; poems. Poetry 130:201-7 Jl '77

LOGAN International Airport. See Boston—Airports

LOGGERHEAD turtles. See Turtles

LOGGERS. See Lumberjacks

LOGGING. See Lumbering

LOGIC
See also
Fallacies (logic)
Reasoning

LOGIC, Symbolic and mathematical
Computer corner. D. Larsen and others. Radio-Electr 48:78-9+ S '77
The jump proof and its similarity to the toppling of a row of dominoes. M. Gardner. il Sci Am 236:128+ My '77

LOGIC analyzers. See Testing instruments

LOGIC probes. See Testing instruments

LOGOS. See Trade marks and trade names

LOGOS (theology)
Whose signature? changing the word of God. E. Shaeffer. Chr Today 22:26+ N 18 '77

LOGSDON, Gene
Country living. See issues of Organic gardening and farming
Onions are a twelve-month vegetable. il Org Gard & Farm 24:168+ Mr '77
—See Berry, W. jt auth

LOGUE, John
Welfare state at the crossroads. Progressive 41:34-7 S '77

LOGUE, John J.
Carter's ocean opportunity. Commonweal 104:265-9 Ap 29 '77

LOGUIDICE, Frank A.
Transfer stations compact waste collection distances. il Am City & County 92:73-4 Ag '77

LOHENGRIN; opera. See Wagner, R.

LOHR, John F.
Krill. il Oceans 10:54-5 My '77
—and Castleman, Michael
Scotia Sea: waterway of the future. il Oceans 10:36-41 My '77

LOIRE Valley
Loire: once over lightly; touring the châteaux. P. L. Buckley. Nat R 29:681-2+ Je 10 '77

LOIS, George
Art director who has a way with words also has a book coming from Abrams; interview, ed by R. Dahlin. il Pub W 211:55+ Ja 17 '77

LOKE, Margarett
Pleasant art of peasant art. il N Y Times Mag p46-9 D 11 '77

LOLLEY, Richard N. and others
Cyclic GMP accumulation causes degeneration of photoreceptor cells: simulation of an inherited disease. bibl il Science 196:664-6 My 6 '77

LOMAX, Margaret I. and others
Cloned ribosomal RNA genes from chloroplasts of euglena gracilis. bibl il Science 196:202-5 Ap 8 '77

LOMBARDI, John
Plastic punks. il Psychol Today 11:121+ N '77

LOMBARDI, Joseph R. and Vandenbergh, J. G.
Pheromonally induced sexual maturation in females: regulation by the social environment of the male. bibl il Science 196:545-6 Ap 29 '77

LOMBARDO, Guy
Father New Year. H. Saal. por Newsweek 90: 126 N 14 '77 *

LOMBLOT, Roland
On the track of the invaders; with report by B. Starr. Time 109:30 My 2 '77 *

LOMEDICO, Peter T. and Saunders, G. F.
Cell-free modulation of proinsulin synthesis. bibl il Science 198:620-2 N 11 '77

LONDON, Clement B. G.
Carnival à la Trinidad and Tobago. bibl il Américas 29:19-24 F '77

LONDON, Jack
Piece of steak; story. Sat Eve Post 249:40-1 Jl '77

about

Jack London: the man who invented himself. A. Sinclair. il pors Am Heritage 28:98-107 Ag '77 *

LONDON, Perry
Experiments on humans: where to draw the line? il Psychol Today 11:20 N '77

LONDON
See also
Thames River

Airports

Concorde curfew urged at Heathrow. Aviation W 106:52 Ap 25 '77
U.K. noise study assesses Concorde operations impact. Aviation W 106:34 My 2 '77

Architecture

Triumph of style: one man's home and his collections; Sir John Soane's Museum. P. Goldberger. il Smithsonian 8:100-4+ bibl(p 147-8) Ap '77

Art

London. W. Feaver. See issues of Art news
See also
London—Galleries and museums

Banks

Bank of England's fall from grace: it can take London's bankers with it. il Bus W p60-64+ Mr 14 '77
Falling-out among City partners; consortium bankers. Bus W p48-9 O 24 '77
S. G. Warburg: the exceptional survivor. por Bus W p62 Mr 14 '77

Clubs

Sunset in clubland. C. Whipple and A. Collings. Newsweek 90:67 N 21 '77

Crime

Contemporary crime in historical perspective: a comparative study of London, Stockholm, and Sydney. T. R. Gurr. bibl f il Ann Am Acad 434:114-36 N '77

Description

Where to take your parents in London. D. Leon. il por House & Gard 149:58+ F '77

Education

Question of fault; race problems in London schools. T. J. Cottle. Progressive 41:34-6 O '77

Festivals

See Festivals—England

Finance

Closed currency club; Sarabex Ltd. charges against London banks and brokers. il Bus W p 114+ O 24 '77

Galleries and museums

Triumph of style: one man's home and his collections; Sir John Soane's Museum. P. Goldberger. il Smithsonian 8:100-4+ bibl(p 147-8) Ap '77
See also
Tate Gallery, London
Victoria and Albert Museum

Hospitals

Good death; St Christopher's Hospice. G. F. Will. Newsweek 91:72 Ja 9 '78

Music

Promenade. A. Porter. New Yorker 53:160+ O 17 '77
See also
Opera—Great Britain

Newspapers

And in Britain, too? Daily mail's charges against British Leyland Motor Corp. il Newsweek 89: 74+ My 30 '77
Mystical poetry in a court of law; conviction of D. Lemon, editor of Gay news, in London. T. Beeson. Chr Cent 94:838-9 S 28 '77
On trial for blasphemy; Gay news trial. Time 110:54 Jl 25 '77
Sir Jimmy's cross-Channel fiefdom; J. M. Goldsmith's purchase of Beaverbrook chain shares. il por Time 109:51-2 Ap 18 '77
Taken for a camel ride? Daily mail's charges against British Leyland Motor Corporation. Time 109:67-8 My 30 '77
See also
Observer (London)
Sunday times, London
Times, London

Parks and playgrounds

Afternoon in London's Syon Park. il Sunset 158:214+ Je '77

Riots

Bit of hell in Notting Hill. il Time 110:28 S 12 '77
Violence in Lewisham. T. Beeson. Chr Cent 94: 803-4 S 21 '77

Tate Gallery

See Tate Gallery, London

Theater

Letter from London:
A. Bennett's Old country. M. Panter-Downes. New Yorker 53:196-7 N 14 '77
P. Gems' Dusa, Fish, Stas & Vi. M. Panter-Downes. New Yorker 53:97-8 Mr 7 '77
See also
National Theatre (Great Britain)

LONDON boat show. See Boats—Exhibitions

LONDON Book Fair. See Book fairs

LONDON Festival Ballet. See Ballet—Great Britain

LONDON summit conference, 1977. See International conferences

LONDON Sunday times. See Sunday times, London

LONDON times. See Times, London

LONDON. University. See Colleges and universities—Great Britain

LONE Mountain College, San Francisco
Tunbridge in San Francisco. C. Pierre. Mademoiselle 83:86+ O '77

LONELINESS
Being single: how to stop waiting and start living; dealing with loneliness and solitude. M.-E. Banashek. Mademoiselle 83:95+ Jl '77
43 ways to get unlonely. M. Cantwell and A. Gross. Mademoiselle 83:122-3 D '77
Loneliness can kill you; views of J. J. Lynch. il Time 110:45 S 5 '77
Self as sybarite; Singles survival guide to metropolitan Washington. R. Rosenblatt. il Harpers 254:12+ Mr '77

LONEY, Glenn M.
Wahnfried restored. il Opera N 41:14-15 F 19 '77
(ed) See O'Horgan, T. Tom O'Horgan

—and MacKay, Patricia
America's past is alive and outdoors. Chr Cent 94:661-2 Jl 20 '77

LONG, Brett
Hostess with the mostest. il por Seventeen 36:208-9 Ap '77 *

LONG, Denise
What do you do when you grow up? J. Kaplan. il pors Sports Illus 47:38 Jl 4 '77 *

LONG, Michael E.
Air-safety challenge. il Nat Geog 152:206-35 Ag '77
Consider the sponge. il Nat Geog 151:392-407 Mr '77
Flight of the Gossamer Condor. il por Nat Geog 153:130-40 Ja '78

LONG, Robert, and Rodgers, H. A.
Get the noise out of your system. il Hi Fi 27: 64-9 Jl '77
New products at half time. il Hi Fi 27:60-5 My '77
—See Rodgers, H. A. jt auth

LONG, Russell Billiu
Sen. Russell Long: he can influence your life for years to come; interview. il pors Nations Bus 65:22-7 Ag '77

LONG, Russell Billiu—*Continued*

about

Cleverest senator. G. F. Will. Newsweek 89:122 My 16 '77 *
Lord of the manor. T. Mathews and others. il pors Newsweek 90:46-8 N 21 '77 *
Master of the maze. por Time 110:20 N 7 '77 *
No long delay needed. A. Cherlin. New Repub 177:13-15 D 17 '77 *
Senator to watch in energy bargaining. por U.S. News 83:75 N 7 '77 *
Son of Kingfish. New Repub 177:2+ D 24 '77 *

LONG, Sidney
Second look: Namesake. Horn Bk 53:477-8 Ag '77

LONG BEACH, Calif.
Saving the Queen; Queen Mary. E. Keerdoja and D. Gram. il Newsweek 91:7 Ja 9 '78

LONG ISLAND
See also
Architecture, Domestic—Long Island
Birds—Long Island
Gardens—Long Island

Banks

See Banks and banking—New York (state)

Industries

See also
Fruit industry

LONG ISLAND furniture. See Furniture, American

LONG ISLAND Railroad
Mugging of a garden; question of defoliation along Long Island Railroad rights of way. U. Roze. il Horticulture 55:18-23 Jl '77

LONG range navigation. See Loran

LONG underwear. See Underwear

LONGET, Claudine
Andy and Claudine; interview, ed by B. Messenger. A. Williams. il por Ladies Home J 94:40+ Je '77 *

LONGET, Claudine, murder trial. See Trials (murder)

LONGEVITY
Can blackness prolong life? melanin experiments of L. M. Edelstein. il pors Ebony 32:124-7 Je '77
Can we live forever? E. K. Pye. por Sat Eve Post 249:35+ Mr '77; Same abr. Sci Digest 82:14-15 S '77
How long will you live? L. Norment. il Ebony 32:44-6+ O '77
How long will you live? P. Passell. Sat Eve Post 249:53 Mr '77
Matter of life or death; healthy habits that prolong life. A. Silberman. Read Digest 110: 185-9 Mr '77
Our allotted lifetimes. S. J. Gould. Natur Hist 86:34+ Ag '77
Will you live to be 100? quiz. D. S. Woodruff. il Sr Schol 110:10-11 N 17 '77
Your life expectancy now. il U.S. News 83:70 N 7 '77
See also
Aging
Centenarians
Old age

Anecdotes, facetiae, satire, etc.

Some prefer old age to the alternative. P. Ryan. Smithsonian 8:120 Ja '78

LONGEVITY (animals) See Age (animals)

LONGHORN cattle. See Cattle—Breeds

LONGITUDE Lane cannon hoax. See Hoaxes

LONGSHOREMEN
See also
Collective bargaining—Longshoremen
Collective labor agreements—Longshoremen
International Longshoremen's Association
Strikes—United States—Longshoremen

LONGWALL mining. See Coal mines and mining

LONGWOOD Gardens. See Gardens—Pennsylvania

LOOMIS, Carol J.
Carl Lindner's singular financial empire. il pors Fortune 95:126-30+ Ja '77
Down the chute with Peabody coal. il Fortune 95:228-33+ My '77
Three-year deadline at David's bank. il por Fortune 96:70-6+ Jl '77

LOOMIS, Robert D.
Robert D. Loomis of Random House wins fourth Roger Klein Award for creative editing; interview, ed by M. Reuter. por Pub W 211:25+ My 9 '77

LOOMS
Build a loom for weaving fun. E. Waltner and W. Waltner. bibl il Pop Mech 147:118-21+ F '77
Hand lift sling looms. M. Kren. il Sch Arts 76:18-19 F '77
Tapestry weaving on the frame loom; excerpt from Weaving: design and expression. N. Belfer. il Sch Arts 77:48-53 O '77

LOONEY, Douglas S.
College football (cont) Sports Illus 47:57-8+ O 24 '77
Down and out can be upsetting. il Sports Illus 47:24-5 O 17 '77
Generation gap: half a length. il Sports Illus 46:20-1 Je 27 '77
Green Speed was red hot to trot. il Sports Illus 47:22-3 S 12 '77
Harness racing (cont) Sports Illus 46:62+ Je 13; 47:52 Ag 8; 48-50 Ag 22; 58+ O 3 '77
He's not pretty, he's just persistent. il pors Sports Illus 46:40-2+ My 9 '77
If only luck will be a lady. il pors Sports Illus 46:40-1+ Je 13 '77
It's all downhill from here. il Sports Illus 48: 22-5 Ja 2 '78
Out on the verge, but far from foolish. il por Sports Illus 46:16-17 Mr 14 '77
Reverie between the acts. il Sports Illus 46: 20-1 Je 20 '77
Suppression of his aggression. il pors Sports Illus 46:28-31 F 21 '77
TV/radio. Sports Illus 47:68 D 5 '77
They were dressed to kill. il Sports Illus 47:20-3 O 31 '77
They're paying through the nose. il Sports Illus 48:18-21 Ja 2 '78
Whoops and saddles in Helena. il Sports Illus 47:22-4 Ag 29 '77
Wrestling (cont) Sports Illus 46:56+ Mr 28 '77

LOOP Current. See Ocean currents

LOOP nebula. See Nebulae

LOOTING. See Pillage

LOOTS, Barbara Kunz
Chins on a window; poem. Ladies Home J 94: 20 Jl '77

LOPEZ, Barry
Alaskan tragedy. map Harpers 255:30-3 S '77
Wood I-beams. il Pop Sci 211:92 D '77

LÓPEZ, Eugenio, Jr
Great escape? C. Whipple and others. il pors Newsweek 90:62 O 17 '77 *

LÓPEZ PORTILLO, José
Mexico's President: no easy way to stop migration; interview, ed by C. J. Migdail. il por U.S. News 83:28-30 Jl 4 '77

about

Mexican foreign policy. G. W. Grayson. bibl f Cur Hist 72:97-101+ Mr '77 *
Mexico's government in crisis. S. Bizzarro. bibl f Cur Hist 72:102-5+ Mr '77 *
Road back to confidence. il por map Time 109: 32-6 F 21 '77 *

Visit to the United States, 1977

Mexico's new president comes to Washington to mend some fences. por U.S. News 82:36 F 21 '77
President Lopez Portillo of Mexico visits the United States; text of joint communique, February 17, 1977. Dept State Bull 76:234-5 Mr 14 '77

LOPICCOLO, Joseph
From psychotherapy to sex therapy. bibl Society 14:60-8 Jl '77

LOPIPARO, Jerome J.
Aggression on TV could be helping our children. Intellect 105:345-6 Ap '77

LOPOPOLO, Toni
Moonlighting in a bookstore: learning lessons at first hand. il por Pub W 212:123-5 S 26 '77

LOQUASTO, Santo
Setting the stage. J. Kroll. il por Newsweek 89:84 Mr 21 '77 *

LORAAMM, Lherif, P.
Porcelaneous sculptors; the marine lettered olive snail; with biographical sketch. il Sea Front 23:296-303, 319 S '77

LORAINE, John A.
Time for doctors to take a stand on nuclear proliferation. Bull Atom Sci 33:6-7 O '77

LORAL Corporation. See Electronic industries—United States

LORAN
Loran-C in every pot? M. Meisels. map Motor B & S 140:12+ D '77

LORD, Jack
Aloha 'oe. il por Holiday 58:42-5+ Ap '77

LORD, Jim
If you get lost in the wilderness. il Conservationist 31:35 My '77

LORD, Walter
Ordeal at Vella Lavella; survivors of sunken U.S.S. Helena; excerpt from Lonely vigil. il map Am Heritage 28:30-43 Je '77

LORD Byron; opera. See Thomson, V.

LORD Byron Hotel. See Rome (city)—Hotels, restaurants, etc.

LORD Jim (literary character) See Characters in literature

LORDE, Audre
Coniagui women; poem. New Yorker 53:84 N 28 '77

about

Comment. S. M. Gilbert. Poetry 129:296-301 F '77 *

LORDS Day. See Sunday

LORD'S Prayer
His new prayer; Anglican rewording. W. F. Buckley, Jr. Nat R 29:1453 D 9 '77

LORDS Supper
Communion as a culinary art. W. H. Willimon. Chr Cent 94:829-30 S 21 '77

LORE, Richard, and Flannelly, Kevin
Rat societies; with biographical sketches. il Sci Am 236:18, 106-11+ My '77

LOREN, Sophia
Sophia Loren: my 20 years with Carlo. A. Levy. pors McCalls 104:16+ Ag '77

LORENTZ, Adrien
PW interviews; ed by P. Holt. por Pub W 211:138 My 23 '77

LORENZ, Konrad Zacharias
Lorenz observed. G. E. Allen. il Natur Hist 86:78-82+ Je '77 *

LORENZO, Frank
Reform with caution; excerpts from address, February 17, 1977. Aviation W 106:9 Mr 28 '77

LORET, Jean Marie
Son of Hitler? por Time 110:45 N 14 '77 *

LORING, John
American prints from Fuses to Fizzles. il Art in Am 65:31-4 Ja '77

LORRAINE, Walter
(ed) Art of the picture book. Wilson Lib Bull 52:144-73 O '77
(ed) See Sendak, M. Interview with Maurice Sendak

LORSIGNOL, Eric
How the French do it. por Forbes 119:114+ Mr 15 '77 *

LORTZING, Albert
Zar und Zimmermann. Review
Hi Fi 27:MA28 S '77 *

LOS ALAMITOS, Calif.

Education

See Education—California

LOS ALAMOS Scientific Laboratory. See Atomic research laboratories

LOS ANGELES
Found: a place in the sun; 1984 Olympics site. W. O. Johnson. il Sports Illus 77:64+ N 7 '77
How to transplant & survive; getting a job and living in Los Angeles and San Francisco. D. Duke and others. il Mademoiselle 83:205+ Ap '77

Airports

Los Angeles—the other airports. Sunset 159:42 Ag '77

Art

Los Angeles. See issues of Art news
See also
Los Angeles—Monuments, statues, etc.

Blacks

SLA holocaust. E. Keerdoja and J. Huck. il Newsweek 89:9 Je 27 '77

Bookstores

See Booksellers and bookselling—California

City planning

Welcome to downtown L.A. J. Pastier. il Horizon 20:10-19 O '77

Crime

Finally on the side of the law; F. Williams of Baretta. il pors Ebony 33:74-6+ N '77
Fingering a .22-cal. killer; arrest of J. Ullo. Time 110:29+ S 26 '77
L.A. strangler. il Time 110:24 D 19 '77
Roman Polanski's tawdry troubles. il por Time 109:22 Mr 28 '77
Strangler. D. A. Williams and P. Brinkley-Rogers. il Newsweek 90:36 D 19 '77
Strangler's grip. D. A. Williams and others. il Newsweek 91:24-6 Ja 9 '78

Description

For visitors to Los Angeles, the movie experience. il Sunset 159:54-71 S '77
L.A: at home in the land of instant gratification. E. Kendall. Vogue 167:196+ O '77
Los Angeles. il Bet Hom & Gard 55:233+ N '77

Education

Children meet artists; field trips to artists' studios by Los Angeles students. E. Levin. il Sch Arts 76:20-2 Je '77

Foreign population

Koreans in business. E. Bonacich and others. bibl il Society 14:54-9 S '77

Galleries and museums

See also
George C. Page Museum of La Brea Discoveries

Gardens

It just won't work in Los Angeles. il Sunset 158:90-3 Mr '77

Hospitals

St Vincent Medical Center, Los Angeles; with introd by W. Marlin. il Archit Rec 162:113, 126-8 Ag '77

Housing

Hanging out with the L.A. rockers. il Time 109:81-2+ Ap 25 '77

Monuments, statues, etc.

But will they like it in Chicago? the Los Angeles Triforium. Vasari. il Art N 76:20+ O '77

Music

Debuts & reappearances. Hi Fi 27:MA30-1 F; MA21-2 Mr; MA24-6 Je; MA27 O; MA17-19 N '77
See also
Los Angeles Philharmonic Orchestra

Newspapers

See also
Los Angeles herald-examiner
Los Angeles times

Police

L.A.'s controversial cop; E. M. Davis. J. K. Footlick and M. Kasindorf. il por Newsweek 90:55 Ag 29 '77

Politics and government

Dynamics of black local politics: an interview with G. Lindsay; ed by J. Elliot. G. Lindsay. por Negro Hist Bull 40:718-20 Jl '77

Stores

L.A.'s dramatic Blue Whale; Pacific Design Center. il Sunset 159:48-9 O '77

Theater

Liveliest theater in town; Los Angeles Actors' Theater. D. Sullivan. il por Horizon 20:87+ N '77

Transportation

Commuter vans catch on at corporations; test program in Los Angeles. il Bus W p54-5 F 28 '77

LOS ANGELES (periodical)
California's magazine war. il Time 110:68 Ag 29 '77
How Los Angeles magazine thrives on rivalry. por Bus W p38 Mr 7 '77

LOS ANGELES Actors Theater. See Los Angeles—Theater

LOS ANGELES Art Center College of Design. See Art schools

LOS ANGELES County, Calif.

Education

Freeway madness; reassignment of teachers on basis of race by Los Angeles Unified School District. R. Kirk. Nat R 30:34 Ja 6 '78

Police

Cops for the love of it; executives in the Sheriff's Reserves. M. Wellemeyer. il Fortune 95:41+ Ap '77

Public health

New, fast help for the injured; paramedic teams. M. Spiegel. il Mech Illus 73:56+ O '77

Sanitary affairs

Centrifuges capture sludge solids. il Am City & County 92:44 Je '77
Los Angeles County loses landfill fight. il Am City & County 92:30 Je '77

LOS ANGELES Dance Festival. See Dance festivals

LOS ANGELES herald-examiner
Fixit goes west; J. G. Bellows appointed editor. por Time 110:112+ D 5 '77

LOS ANGELES Philharmonic Orchestra
Los Angeles Sym: Mahler's Eighth; performance June 12. il Hi Fi 27:MA17-19 N '77
Musician of the month: Zubin Mehta; interview, ed by D. Webster. Z. Mehta. por Hi Fi 27:MA8-9 N '77

LOS ANGELES Shakespeare Festival. See Shakespeare festivals

LOS ANGELES times
PW interviews; literary critic of the Los Angeles times; ed by J. Kirsch. R. Kirsch. por Pub W 212:10-11 D 12 '77
Word from Mamma Buff. L. Weymouth. il pors Esquire 88:154-7+ N '77

LOSING. See Failure (psychology)

LOS PADRES National Forest. See National forests

LOST cats. See Cats

LOST children. See Missing persons

LOST cities, Imaginary. See Geographical myths

LOST dogs. See Dogs

LOST persons. See Missing persons

LOST pets. See Pets

LOST wax process
Great Saddles of the West: an interview with Paul Rossi; ed by K. Mayer. P. Rossi. il Am Artist 41:64-7+ Ag '77

LOSTROM, Martha
Boating business. See issues of Yachting
LOTHROP, Eaton S. Jr
Time exposure. See every other issue of Popular photography
LOTTERIES
Lottery; New York State million dollar lottery drawing. New Yorker 53:30-1 S 26 '77
On lotteries; state lotteries. R. Bellico. il Progressive 41:24-5 Ap '77
LOTTMAN, Eileen
Novelizations: are the plums drying up? il Pub W 212:31-3 O 10 '77
LOTTMAN, Herbert R.
Despite aura of censorship, first Moscow Book Fair has positive results. il Pub W 212:46-53 O 3 '77
(ed) Germany and the German book business. il Pub W 212:9-14+ S 12 '77
International notes. Pub W 211:30 Mr 21 '77
International scene (cont) Pub W 211:42-4 Ja 10; 55-6 Je 13; 89-93 Je 27 '77
Letter from Paris. Pub W 211:24-5 Ap 4 '77
Michelle Lapautre. por Pub W 211:25-6 My 30 '77
Opportunities for downright business apparent at successful eighth biennial. il Pub W 211:20-4 My 30 '77
Paris dateline. Pub W 212:76 Jl 18 '77
Report on Scandinavia. il maps Pub W 211:39-42+ My 9 '77
What looked like a quiet fair was actually a record-setting event. il Pub W 212:28-35 N 7 '77
(ed) See Baensch, R. E. Robert E. Baensch: the global man at Harper & Row
—and Wagner, Susan
ICBA meeting focuses on bookseller problems. il Pub W 212:55-6+ Jl 4 '77
LOTUS (sports car) See Sports cars
LOUD, William, family
Loud family. M. Montagno and P. Cole. il Newsweek 90:6+ Jl 11 '77
LOUDSPEAKERS
Amplifier/speaker interface—a new concept. L. Feldman. il Radio-Electr 48:64-6 F '77
Barcus-Berry's mysterious glass plate; Audio Plate. Hi Fi 28:32 Ja '78
Big sound from those new mini-speakers. W. J. Hawkins. il Pop Sci 211:98-9 D '77
Great phase-coherency bandwagon. P. Mitchell. Hi Fi 27:76-80 O '77
How external speakers can improve mobile CB performance. S. R. Davis. il Pop Electr 11:54-7 Mr '77
Loudspeaker guidelines. H. Fantel. Esquire 88:147-8+ O '77
Loudspeakers without boxes. P. W. Mitchell. il Hi Fi 27:50-5 Je '77
Medium-priced loudspeakers. il Consumer Rep 42:215-17 D '77
Pros and cons of multi-way speaker systems. J. Hirsch. il por Pop Electr 12:22+ S '77
Speaker system measurements—is phase response important? J. D. Hirsch. il Pop Electr 11:24+ Je '77
Speaking of speakers. C. Graham. il Am Rec G 40:57-8 My '77
Super-speaker; AudioPlate produced by Barcus-Berry, Inc. T. Nicholson and others. il Newsweek 89:71-2 Je 6 '77

Design

Computer technology transforms speaker design. H. A. Rodgers. il Hi Fi 27:74-5 O '77
They're still inventing hi-fi loudspeakers H. H. Fantel. il Pop Sci 211:58+ S '77

Purchasing

Ten loudspeaker shopping tips. E. J. Foster. Hi Fi 27:48 Je '77

Testing

How to interpret loudspeaker tests. E. J. Foster. il Hi Fi 27:46-9 Je '77
In the loudspeaker testing lab; measurement techniques. E. Torick. il Hi Fi 27:69-73 O '77
Julian Hirsch audio reports:
Acoustic Research model AR-16 speaker system. il Pop Electr 11:26+ F '77
Speakerlab model S7 speaker system. kit. J. Hirsch. Pop Electr 12:36+ S '77
Technics model SB-6000A linear phase speaker system. il Pop Electr 11:30+ Je '77
Low-priced loudspeakers. il Consumer Rep 42:406-9 Jl '77
New equipment reports:
AR-15: a good speaker for a small room. il Hi Fi 28:47-8 Ja '78
And in this corner . . . David; Visonik D-50 system. il Hi Fi 27:52-3 O '77
Baron has a wide domain; KLH model 355. il Hi Fi 27:50-1 O '77
Bertagni's biggest Geostatic. il Hi Fi 27:39-40 Je '77
Cizek: a new—and welcome—name in speakers. il Hi Fi 27:37-8 Je '77
Custom-fitted accuracy from AR's 10π. il Hi Fi 27:55-6 Jl '77
Ditton 66: a sweet-sounding speaker. il Hi Fi 27:70 S '77
EPI's 200: simple, basic—and musical. il Hi Fi 27:53-4 O '77
ESS/Heil's Power Ring Tempest. il Hi Fi 27:54-5 O '77
Genesis does its thing again—simply and with elegance; Model 3. il Hi Fi 28:60 Ja '78
Jennings Vector 1: phasing virtues and a foam halo. il Hi Fi 27:38-9 Je '77
Koss Model Two turns the tables. il Hi Fi 27:41 Je '77
Paradox TA-12: leviathan so sweetly sings. il Hi Fi 27:57-8 Mr '77
Phase Linear's master illusionist. il Hi Fi 27:42 Je '77
Stereopillow, a novel way to listen—and relax. il Hi Fi 27:64-5 Mr '77
Technics SB-6000A lets you dream you're conducting. il Hi Fi 27:49-50 O '77
New tests for loudspeakers. R. Hodges. il Pop Electr 12:22+ N '77
Outstanding loudspeaker; Dahlquist DQ-10. C. Graham. Am Rec G 40:52-3 O '77
LOUGHBOROUGH Conference. See Childrens literature—Conferences
LOUIE, Elaine
Singular stores. il N Y Times Mag p 118-19 O 23 '77
LOUIS, Arthur M.
Brazil's coffee with sugar billionaire. il pors Fortune 96:82-8 Jl '77
Charles Pilliod was the odd man in at Goodyear. il pors Fortune 95:280-3+ My '77
In the grip of hands-on management. il por Fortune 95:170-8 Mr '77
LOUIS, Murray
From the inside. See occasional issues of Dance magazine

about

Dance Magazine Awards 1977. il pors Dance Mag 51:30-5 Jl '77 *
LOUIS, Murray, Dance Company. See Murray Louis Dance Company
LOUIS Falco Dance Company. See Dance companies
LOUISE; opera. See Charpentier, G.
LOUISIANA
See also
Crime and criminals—Louisiana
Forests and forestry—Louisiana
Music festivals—Louisiana
Opera—Louisiana
Shore protection—Louisiana

Plantations

See Plantations

Politics and government

See also
Politics, Corruption in—Louisiana
LOUISIANA furniture. See Furniture, American
LOUISIANA Museum of Modern Art, Humlebaek. See Art galleries and museums—Denmark
LOUISIANA Offshore Oil Port Inc. See Petroleum shipping terminals
LOUISIANA-Pacific Corporation
Swinging with Louisiana-Pacific. por Forbes 119:55 F 1 '77
LOUISIANA. State University, Baton Rouge

Rural Life Museum

Giving it back to their employer; museum donated by I. and S. Burden. D. Kirkpatrick. il Ret Liv 17:48-9 N '77
LOUISIANA Superdome. See Stadiums
LOUISVILLE

Banks

Now, mom-and-pop coal mines. S. Chace. il Forbes 120:69+ Jl 1 '77

Education

What Louisville has taught us about busing. R. M. Williams. il Sat R 4:6-8+ Ap 30 '77

Police

256 indictments, $3 million in recovered goods. il U. S. News 83:68 N 7 '77

Race question

Anecdotes, facetiae, satire, etc.

In the swim. M. Mayer. Progressive 41:24 Je '77
LOURIA, Donald B. See Chowdhury, P. jt auth
LOUSEWORTS
Of dams and Kate Furbish; threat to Maine's rare plants by proposed Dickey-Lincoln Dams project. R. Saltonstall, Jr. il por Liv Wildn 40:52-3 Ja '77
LOUTCHANSKY, Jacob
Superannuated sculpture. M. Ronnen. il por Art N 76:97-8 F '77 *
LOUVESTRE, Mary
Woman who saved the Union Navy. G. A. Foster. il Ebony 33:131-2+ D '77 *

LOUVIERE, Vernon
Panorama of the Nation's business. See issues of Nation's business to April 1977
People in business. il Nations Bus 65:64 My; 59 Je; 36-7 Jl; 57-8 Ag; 75 S; 64 O '77

LO-VACA Gathering Company. See Gas industry

LOVDAL, Michael L.
Making the audit committee work. il Harvard Bus R 55:108-14 Mr '77
—and others
Public responsibility committees of the board. Harvard Bus R 55:40-2+ My '77

LOVE, Ruth B.
Let's reward for success—not failure. Educ Digest 42:20-1 Ja '77

about

To the Oakland School District, with Love. C. Pogash. por Ms 5:19 My '77 *

LOVE
Are black youth more romantic about love? J. Wright. il Ebony 32:164-6+ O '77
Beyond sex: the joy of touching; affection. A. Gross. Mademoiselle 83:115-16+ D '77
Breakup: how he feels when it's over. V. Billings. Seventeen 36:94-5 Jl '77
How romantic are you? il House & Gard 149:117+ Mr '77
Learning to love again; excerpt. M. Krantzler. il Good H 185:130-1+ S '77
Love: giving of self or meeting the self's needs? America 136:501-3 Je 4 '77
Mastroianni talks about real-life love; interview, ed by C. B. Pepper. M. Mastroianni. Vogue 167:122+ O '77
Modern romance: a whole new way to be in love. A. Gross and A. Lovell. Mademoiselle 83:154-5+ N '77
On human love. M. B. Martin. Nat R 29:998 S 2 '77; Reply. D. K. Mano. 29:1237 O 28 '77
Pleasure and pain of that first crush. A. Bayer. il Seventeen 36:144-5+ My '77
Six styles of loving; studies of T. E. Lasswell. por Intellect 105:294-5 Mr '77
Speaking of love. E. Jong. por Newsweek 89:11 F 21 '77

Anecdotes, facetiae, satire, etc.

Arithmetic of love. D. K. Mano. il Nat R 29:954-5 Ag 19 '77

LOVE (theology)
Christian marital love: a reappraisal. D. M. Thomas. il New Cath World 220:296-300 N '77
Climbing out of the existential ditch. P. A. Siddons. Chr Today 21:8-9 Ag 12 '77
Frost came too soon. E. Schaeffer. Chr Today 22:32-3 N 4 '77
Is self-love biblical? J. Piper. il Chr Today 21:6-9 Ag 12 '77; Discussion. 22:9+ O 7 '77
Love makes the world go round; Dante's Divine comedy. N. Tischler. Chr Today 21:22-3 Ag 26 '77
Love, power and justice. P. B. Henry. il Chr Cent 94:1088-92 N 23 '77
Odd men out. G. McCauley. America 136:inside back cover Ja 22 '77
So what's new? commandment of love. T. H. Stahel. America 136:404-inside back cover Ap 30 '77
Works of compassion in Christ's name. Chr Today 22:28-30 D 9 '77

LOVE, Maternal
Bad love. A. T. Fleming. por Newsweek 90:9 Ag 1 '77

LOVE letters
For Valentine's Day: immortal love letters; comp by A. P. Fraser. il por N Y Times Mag p 16-18 F 13 '77

LOVEJOY, Arthur Oncken
Arthur O. Lovejoy. L. S. Feuer. Am Scholar 46:358-66 Summ '77 *

LOVEJOY, C. Owen, and others
Paleodemography of the Libben site, Ottawa County, Ohio. bibl il Science 198:291-3 O 21 '77

LOVEJOY, Elijah Parish
Martyrdom of Elijah P. Lovejoy. D. W. Blight. il Am Hist Illus 12:20-7 N '77 *

LOVELACE, Alan M.
Bold space program. Aviation W 106:11 F 28 '77

LOVELACE, Leroy
Teacher who gets results. J. Seligmann and S. Monroe. il por Newsweek 90:67 S 12 '77 *

LOVELOCK, James Ephraim
Gaia: the harmony of our sphere. F. Hapgood. Atlantic 240:100-4 D '77 *

LOVETT, Robert W.
Business sits for its portrait. Harvard Bus R 55:160+ Jl '77

LOVI, George
Rambling through [the month] skies. See issues of Sky & telescope
Stars for [the month] See issues of Sky and telescope

LOVING, Rush, Jr
Here comes another Kaiser. il pors Fortune 95:156-60+ F '77
Pros and cons of airline deregulation. il Fortune 96:208-12+ Ag '77

LOVINS, Amory B.
Energy strategy: the road not taken? bibl f il por For Affairs 55:65-96; 637-40, 896-900 O '76, Ap-Jl '77
Energy: the soft path. Science 196:1384 Je 24 '77

about

Soft technology energy debate: Limits to growth revisited? A. L. Hammond. Science 196:959-61 My 27 '77 *
Thinking soft. A. J. Mayer. il por Newsweek 90:108+ N 14 '77 *

LOW fat diet. See Diet

LOW sodium cookery. See Cookery

LOWE, Arbon Jack
Museum of Modern Art of Latin America. il Américas 29:S1-S12 Mr '77

LOWE, Betsy
Opossum. il Conservationist 31:42 Mr '77

LOWE, Bobby
Perils of doing your duty. il Time 109:13-14 Je 6 '77 *

LOWE, Janet
Ladies and gentlemen, start your engines. il Seventeen 36:100+ Ap '77

LOWE, Susan J. See Green, C. P. jt auth

LOWELL, Percival
Mars; excerpt, reprint from 1895 issue. Atlantic 239:32-3 Je '77

LOWELL, Robert
Dead in Europe; Christmas Eve under Hooker's statue; poems; reprints. Commonweal 104:786 D 9 '77

about

Appreciation of Robert Lowell. H. Carruth. por Harpers 225:110-12 D '77 *
Aspects of Robert Lowell. J. Druska. Commonweal 104:783-8 D 9 '77 *
Death of an elfking. P. Elmen. por Chr Cent 94:1057-60 N 16 '77 *
Obituary
Commonweal 104:772 D 9 '77. J. Deedy
Pub W 212:110+ S 26 '77
Robert Lowell, 1917-1977. R. Fitzgerald. il New Repub 177:10-12 O 1 '77 *
Robert Lowell and John Ashbery: the difference between poets. A. Kazin. il Esquire 89:20+ Ja '78 *
Self-examined life. por Time 110:80 S 26 '77 *
Sense of mortality. J. Kroll. il pors Newsweek 90:81-2 S 26 '77 *
Soldier Lowell, 1917-1977. C. Tucker. Sat R 5:64 O 29 '77 *

LOWELL, Mass.

Education

See Education—Massachusetts

National Cultural Park (proposed)

See National parks and reserves—Massachusetts

LOWENS, Irving
Holland Festival: an American emphasis. Hi Fi 27:MA38-40 F '77
Kennedy Center: the first five years. il Hi Fi 27:MA16-17 F '77
1976 Bach International Piano Competition. il por Hi Fi 27:MA24-5 Jl '77
Salzburg of the North. il Hi Fi 28:MA30-1+ Ja '78

LOWENSTEIN, Allard Kenneth
Murder of Robert Kennedy: suppressed evidence of more than one assassin? il por Sat R 4:6-10+ F 19 '77

LOWENTHAL, David
Magnificent amateur; adaptation of address; with excerpt from introduction to Man and nature. il pors Am For 83:8-11+ S '77

LOWER Manhattan. See New York (city)

LOWE'S Companies, Inc.
$660,000 farewell; profit sharing. H. Johnson. il pors Ebony 32:47-8+ F '77

LOWINSKY, Edward Elias
Laurence Feininger 1909-1976: life, work, legacy. bibl il por Mus Q 63:327-66 Jl '77

LOWRANCE, William W.
NAS surveys of fundamental research 1962-1974, in retrospect. bibl Science 197:1254-60 S 23 '77

LOWREY, Bette
Meet Mrs America. J. Miller. por New Repub 176:19-21 Ap 9 '77 *

LOWRY, Betty
On hearing that a cat has been to see the queen; poem. Horn Bk 53:83 F '77

LOYALTY investigations
Aftermath of a witch hunt: New York's subversive teachers; reinstatement of teachers dismissed in 1950's. I. Adler and B. M. Zelman. Nation 224:434-6 Ap 9 '77
Oppenheimer case: a study in the abuse of law; 1950's investigation by Atomic Energy Commission. H. P. Green. il pors Bull Atom Sci 33:12-16+ S '77

LOYND, Richard Birkett
In the grip of hands-on management. A. M. Louis. il por Fortune 95:170-8 Mr '77 *

LOYOLA, Ignatius of, Saint
Ignatian heritage for today's college. T. S. Healy. America 137:304-6 N 5 '77 *
LUAU. See Cookery, Hawaiian
LUBLIN, Joann
Mary Shane: baseball's new motor mouth. por Ms 6:24-5 O '77
LUBOVE, Roy
New Deal and national health. bibl f Cur Hist 72:198-200+ My '77
LUBOVITCH, Lar
Lar Lubovitch: choreographer in search of meaning; interview, ed by J. Gruen. il por Dance Mag 51:44-7 F '77
LUBRICANTS. See Lubrication and lubricants
LUBRICATION and lubricants
Lubricants made with Teflon. J. Smith. Yachting 142:84 Jl '77
N-nitrosodiethanolamine in synthetic cutting fluids: a part-per-hundred impurity. T. Y. Fan and others. bibl il Science 196:70-1 Ap 1 '77
See also
Automobiles—Lubrication and lubricants
Marine engines—Lubrication
Oils and fats
Quaker State Oil Refining Corporation
LUCAS, Bill
Management kingpin of the Atlanta Braves. il pors Ebony 32:52-4+ Jl '77 *
LUCAS, Christopher
Heavenly food of Japan. il Read Digest 110:38-40+ My '77
High adventure in ancient Afghanistan. il Read Digest 111:184-90 Ag '77
Island of the gods. il map Read Digest 110:188-9+ F '77
LUCAS, George
Movie movie gang. il por Time 109:61 My 30 '77 *
LUCAS, Hugh
Neutron bomb . . . destroy the enemy, not his camp. il Pop Mech 148:112-15+ N '77
LUCCHESI, John C. See Hughes, M. B. jt auth
LUCE, Charles Franklin
Catharsis time again at Con Ed. il por Time 110:46 Jl 25 '77 *
LUCE, Clare (Boothe)
Equality begins at home. por Sat Eve Post 249: 16-17+ O '77
High human price of detente. Nat R 29:1289-91 N 11 '77
Is the Republican Party dead? Nat R 29:326-7 Mr 18 '77
LUCE, Henry Robinson, 1898-1967
No-fault society. T. Griffith. Atlantic 239:26+ My '77 *
Time Inc.'s internal war over Vietnam; excerpt from The powers that be. D. Halberstam. il pors Esquire 89:94-100+ Ja '78 *
LUCENTINI, Mauro
Italian communism at home and abroad: the new class. Commentary 62:48-50 N '76; 63:24+ Mr '77
LUCEY, Patrick Joseph
How absurd federal rules victimize the states. por Nations Bus 65:43-6 My '77
LUCIA di Lammermoor; opera. See Donizetti, G.
LUCIANO, Kathy
I thought I had to be perfect. il McCalls 104: 102+ Jl '77
LUCINA, Mary
Memorial Day; poem. Chr Cent 94:506 My 25 '77
My sixth grade teacher; poem. Chr Cent 94:84 F 2 '77
LUCK, Robert F. and others
Chemical insect control—a troubled pest management strategy. bibl il BioScience 27:606-11 S '77
LUCK
Five ways to improve your luck; excerpt from The luck factor. M. Gunther. Read Digest 110: 77-80 My '77
How to make your luck work for you; excerpt from Chase, chance and creativity, the lucky art of novelty. J. Austin. il House & Gard 149:172+ N '77
LUCULLUS Circle. See Gastronomy
LUDLUM, David M.
Balloon to cross the ocean in 1859: the Atlantic. il por Weatherwise 30:154-7 Ag '77
Snowfall season of 1975-76. maps Weatherwise 30:18-21 F '77
Weather of Independence (title varies) (cont) il maps Weatherwise 30:114-19 Je '77
LUDLUM, Robert
Ludlum conspiracy. L. Block. por Writers Digest 57:25-6 S '77 *
Popularity. P. S. Nathan. Pub W 211:36 F 21 '77 *
LUDTKE, Melissa
Baseball. Sports Illus 47:44-5 Jl 11; 72-3 Ag 29 '77
TV/radio (cont) Sports Illus 46:42 F 14; 52 Mr 21; 47:98 O 10; 50 N 7 '77
LUDVIGSEN, Karl E.
Alcohol comes back to power your car. il Mech Illus 74:46+ Ja '78
Road test. il Motor T 29:52-4+, 72-4+ Je '77
LUDVIGSON, Susan Bartels
Trying to change the subject; poem. Nation 224:791 Je 25 '77
LUDWIG, Daniel Keith
Small change for a billionaire. por Bus W p 128 Mr 21 '77 *
LUECKE, Jane Marie
Dominance syndrome. Chr Cent 94:405-7 Ap 27 '77
LUEDTKE, Peggy Powers
Catastrophe model: can it see crises? il por Sci Digest 81:68-70 F '77
Hydrogen. por Sci Digest 82:68-72 O '77
LUERS, William H.
Inter-American relations in an era of change; statement, March 24, 1977. Dept State Bull 76:347-50 Ap 11 '77
LUETJE, Carolyn
Early childhood: the crucial years for learning. Parents Mag 52:18 Ag '77
School before school can be the answer. il Parents Mag 53:37+ Ja '78
LUFFMAN, Charles E.
Watercolor techniques of J.M.W. Turner. il Am Artist 41:36-9+ Je '77
LUFKIN, Tex.

Newspapers

See Newspapers—Texas
LUFTHANSA. See Airlines—Germany, West
LUFTIG, Don
Sex test; quiz, excerpt from WNBC television program. Read Digest 111:78-80 S '77
LUGAR, Richard Green
Energy; address, May 2, 1977. Vital Speeches 43: 520-2 Je 15 '77
LUGGAGE
Consumer's guide to: traveling gear. il Mech Illus 73:38 Ap '77
Molded luggage. il Consumer Rep 42:548-50 S '77
Soft-sided luggage. Consumer Rep 42:322-4 D '77
See also
Packing of luggage
LUGGAGE handling, Airline. See Airlines—Luggage handling
LUJÁN MUÑOZ, Jorge
Key to the past. il Américas 29:42-3 O '77
LUKACS, John Adalbert
Caveat lector. Nat R 29:946-8+ Ag 19 '77
Sans caviare. il Nat R 29:450-2 Ap 15 '77

about

Hitler and the revisionists. W. F. Buckley, Jr. Nat R 29:1072-3 S 16 '77 *
LUKAS, J. Anthony
White House press club. il N Y Times Mag p22+ My 15 '77
LUKAS, Jeffrey H. and Siegel, J. M.
Cortical mechanisms that augment or reduce evoked potentials in cats. bibl il Science 198:73-5 O 7 '77
LULLY, Jean Baptiste
Window on Lully's operatic world. P. H. Lang. il por Hi Fi 27:95-6 O '77 *
LULU; opera. See Berg, A.
LUMBER
Buying lumber. McCalls 104:62 Je '77
Lumber-buying tips for weekend carpenters. il Bet Hom & Gard 55:82-4 Mr '77

Drying

Kiln-dry your lumber with solar heat. il Pop Mech 147:273 My '77

Prices

What made lumber prices zoom. Bus W p27-8 Mr 14 '77
LUMBER industry
Giant battle in redwood country; controversy surrounding expansion of Redwood National Park. il Bus W p30-1 Ap 25 '77
Lumbermen vs. environmentalists: growing fight over what to do with nation's forests. il U.S. News 83:62-4 Ag 22 '77
Productivity in sawmills increases as labor input declines substantially. J. Duke and C. Huffstutler. bibl il M Labor R 100:33-7 Ap '77
Redwood protest; loggers demonstration against major expansion of Redwood National Park. S. Fraker and G. C. Lubenow. il map Newsweek 89:30 Ap 25 '77
Twilight of the great cedars; western red cedar. D. J. Chasan. il Audubon 79:50-5 N '77
What made lumber prices zoom. Bus W p27-8 Mr 14 '77
See also
Weyerhaeuser Company

Alaska

Alaska's interior forests: in the eye of the storm. D. T. Hoopes. il Am For 83:16-19+ Je '77

LUMBERING
Capitol Hill lag could narrow chances of salvaging Redwood Park. Nat Parks & Con Mag 51:21 N '77
Crisis in the Canoe country; Boundary Waters Canoe Area; with editorial comment. M. L. Heinselman. il maps Liv Wildn 40:3, 12-24 Ja '77
How to sell stumpage. D. S. Thomas. il Am For 83:36-42 D '77
North country forests get six-month reprieve; Boundary Waters Canoe Area. Nat Parks & Con Mag 51:26 Mr '77
Passionate suitors for a wild paradise; Boundary Water Canoe Area. W. O. Johnson. il por Sports Illus 47:8, 50-2 O 10 '77
Redwood Park: costly, sorry abortion. P. L. Fradkin. Audubon 79:121-2 Mr '77
Redwoods: as the worm turns; with letter by N. B. Livermore, Jr. J. B. Craig. il Am For 83:28-31+ Jl '77; Discussion. 83:4+ O '77
See also
Clearcutting
Lumberjacks

Machinery

New tree puller increases yield 20%. E. Kerr. il Pop Sci 210:12 My '77

LUMBERING machinery. See Lumbering—Machinery

LUMBERJACKS
Axes to grind; disputes between American and Canadian loggers. L. Langway and C. Foreman. il Newsweek 90:92 S 12 '77

LUMINESCENCE
See also
Bioluminescence
Thermoluminescence

LUMINOUS bacteria. See Bacteria, Luminous

LUMMIS, William Rice
Battle for the shrinking millions. il por Time 110:64+ Jl 4 '77 *

LUMPECTOMY. See Breast—Cancer—Surgery

LUMPKINS, Babranda
Don't call me egghead! Seventeen 36:74 S '77

LUNA flights. See Space flight to the moon—Luna flights

LUNAR distances. See Astronomical distances

LUNAR eclipses. See Eclipses, Lunar

LUNAR geology
Lunar surface chemistry: a new imaging technique. C. G. Andre and others. bibl il Science 197:986-9 S 2 '77
Studying near-earth resources. J. R. Arnold. Aviation W 107:9 S 19 '77

Conferences

See Moon—Conferences

LUNAR materials
Luna 24: shaking up the moon-watchers. Sci N 112:390 D 10 '77
Lunar soil: iron and titanium bands in the glass fraction. E. Wells and B. Hapke. bibl il Science 195:977-9 Mr 11 '77
U.S. scientists study Soviet moon sample. Space World N-8-164:29-30 Ag '77

LUNAR research. See Moon

LUNAR seismology. See Seismology

LUNAR soils. See Lunar materials

LUNCHEONS
See also
Brunches

LUNCHES
Floatable feast. J. Hemingway. il por Esquire 87:156-7 Ap '77
Hi mom, what's for lunch? See occasional issues of Parents' magazine
Hot lunches to go. il Bet Hom & Gard 55:94 F '77
Lunch-box specials. il Good H 185:160-2+ S '77
Take a bag to lunch. il Seventeen 36:164-5 S '77
See also
Brunches
Buffet meals
School lunches

LUNCHES, Business. See Business entertaining

LUNCHES, Business (tax deductions) See Income tax—Deductions

LUND, Doris Herold
Survival of Scott Helt. Good H 184:91+ F '77

LUND, Helen
Dear FIC, can you tell me. . .? Ret Liv 17:50+ N '77

LUND, K. T.
Black boy; R. Wright's novel. Engl J 66:59-60 Mr '77

LUND, Robert
Detroit listening post. See issues of Popular mechanics

LUND, Robert D.
Men behind the Car of the Year. il pors Motor T 29:36 F '77 *

LUNDSTEEN, Sara W.
On developmental relations between language-learning and reading. Educ Digest 42:49-52 Ap '77

LUNG cancer. See Cancer

LUNGER, Norman
(comp) Big debate over abolishing mandatory retirement at 65. Ret Liv 17:20-3 D '77

LUNGS
See also
Cardiopulmonary system
Respiration

Diseases

See also
Cystic fibrosis
Emphysema
Pneumonia
Tuberculosis

Dust diseases

Breathless cotton workers; byssinosis or brown lung disease. J. Schinto. Progressive 41:27-9 Ag '77

Metabolism

See Metabolism

LUNT, Alfred
Alfred the great. R. Boeth. il por Newsweek 90:59 Ag 15 '77 *
Obituary
Nation 225:221-2 S 10 '77. H. Clurman

LUNT, Storer B.
Obituary
Pub W 212:112 S 26 '77

LUPO, Sam
Death stalked the ice; ed by D. Richey. il Outdoor Life 160:74-5+ O '77

LUPUS erythematosus
Induction of suppressor T cells in systemic lupus erythematosus by thymosin and cultured thymic epithelium. S. Horowitz and others. bibl il Science 197:999-1001 S 2 '77
Little-known diseases. A. Belson. Fam Health 9:42-4+ My '77
Prevention of autoimmunity in experimental lupus erythematosus by soluble immune response suppressor. R. S. Krakauer and others. bibl il Science 196:56-9 Ap 1 '77
Radioimmunoassay for antibodies to cytoplasmic ribosomes in human serum. D. Koffler and others. bibl il Science 198:741-3 N 18 '77
Sign of the wolf. Time 110:58 Jl 25 '77

LUPUS nephritis. See Kidneys—Diseases

LURES, Fishing. See Fishing lures, flies, etc.

LURIA, Salvador Edward
Goals of science; adaptation of address, December 1976. il Bull Atom Sci 33:28-33 My '77; Same. Current 194:23-31 Jl '77

LURIE, Alison
Beatrix Potter: more than just Peter Rabbit. il por Ms 6:42-3+ S '77
Fairy tales for a liberated age. il Horizon 19:80-5 Jl '77

LURIE, Diana
(ed) See Bacall, L. Three independent views
(ed) See Farrell, S. Three independent views
(ed) See Sills, B. Three independent views

LURIE, Sidney B.
Market trends. por Forbes 119:136-7 Mr 15; 120:172 O 15 '77

LU SAN, Ruth I.
When Judy died; story. Ms 5:77-80 F '77

LUSCHIKOV, V. I.
Ultracold neutrons. bibl il Phys Today 30:42-3+ Je '77

LUSE, David
Ohio continuing education: shortcomings pegged. Lib J 102:2204 N 1 '77 *

LUSIS, Andrei Robertovich
Honorable schoolboy. Time 110:26 N 14 '77 *

LUST. See Desire

LUSTER, Arline
Asian zodiac for librarians. il Am Lib 8:166 Mr '77

LUSTER glazes. See Glazes and glazing (ceramics)

LUSTIG, Alvin
Alvin Lustig's graphic design draws well at AIGA retrospective exhibit. P. Doebler. il Pub W 211:72 Ap 4 '77 *

LUSTIG, Arnost
PW interviews; ed by J. F. Baker. por Pub W 211:6-7 F 21 '77

Die **LUSTIGEN** Weiber von Windsor; opera. See Nicolai, O.

LUTE music
See also
Phonograph records—Lute music

LUTEN, C. J.
100 years of Bayreuth. Am Rec G 40:10-12 N '76
Two new Meistersingers. il Am Rec G 40:8-9 Mr '77

LUTEOTROPIN
Proclactin-like immunoreactivity: localization in nerve terminals of rat hypothalamus. K. Fuxe and others. bibl il Science 196:899-900 My 20 '77

LUTHERAN Church
See also
Catholic Church—Relations—Lutheran Church
Lutheran Social Service
Lutheran World Federation

LUTHERAN Church in Africa
View from Tanzania; Lutheran World Federation. G. H. Muedeking. Chr Today 21:34-5 Jl 29 '77
LUTHERAN Church in South Africa
Lutherans and apartheid. W. Bockelman. Chr Cent 94:647-8 Jl 20 '77
LUTHERAN Church in the United States
America's newest denomination; Association of Evangelical Lutheran Churches. Chr Today 21:36 Ja 7 '77
Expelled; J. Tietjen expelled from the LCMS. Chr Today 22:40-1 O 21 '77
Lutheran women and creative worship. A. J. Lesher. il Chr Cent 94:697-8+ Ag 3 '77
Missouri Synod aftermath. E. E. Plowman. il por Chr Today 21:36-7 Ag 26 '77
Missouri's compromise. J. E. Adams. Chr Cent 94:709-10 Ag 17 '77
Season for binding together; English vs Missouri Synods. M. E. Marty. Chr Cent 94:51-3 Ja 26 '77
LUTHERAN Social Service
Religious tension in Saint Cloud; refusal of United Way funds to agencies making abortion referrals. J. M. Wall. Chr Cent 94:1019-20 N 9 '77
LUTHERAN World Federation
Lutherans and apartheid. W. Bockelman. Chr Cent 94:647-8 Jl 20 '77
View from Tanzania. G. H. Muedeking. Chr Today 21:34-5 Jl 29 '77
LUTTWAK, Edward N.
China behind the guided tour. Read Digest 110: 211-14+ Ap '77
Churchill and us. Commentary 63:44-9 Je '77
Defense reconsidered. Commentary 63:51-8 Mr '77
Seeing China plain. Commentary 62:27-33 D '76; 63:10+ Mr '77
Strange case of George F. Kennan. Commentary 64:30-5 N '77
Third alternative. New Repub 176:13-14 F 26 '77
LUTZ, George Lee
Our dream house was haunted. P. Hoffman. il Good H 184:119+ Ap '77 *
LUTZ, Kathleen Connors
Our dream house was haunted. P. Hoffman. il Good H 184:119+ Ap '77 *
LUTZ, Richard A. and Rhoads, D. C.
Anaerobiosis and a theory of growth line formation. bibl il Science 198:1222-7 D 23 '77
LUTZE, Lothar-Erwin
Spies with many secrets. il pors Time 110:25 D 26 '77 *
LUTZE, Renate
Spies with many secrets. il pors Time 110:25 D 26 '77 *
LUWUM, Janani, Abp
Death in Uganda. Chr Cent 94:212 Mr 9 '77 *
Death of an archbishop. por Time 109:31 F 28 '77 *
Idi Amin's holy war. R. Carroll and C. Harrison. il por Newsweek 89:35-6 F 28 '77 *
Making headway painfully in Uganda. F. Kivengere. Chr Today 21:20-1 Ap 15 '77 *
Murder in Uganda. W. P. Wood. America 136: 216-19 Mr 12 '77 *
Terror and death in Uganda. A. H. Matthews. por Chr Today 21:49-51 Mr 18 '77 *
LUX, H. D. See Eckert, R. jt auth
LUXENBERG, Stan
Keep trade free. New Repub 177:13-15 S 3 '77
LUXON, Benjamin
Musical events; performances of Die schöne Müllerin. A. Porter. New Yorker 53:93-4 F 28 '77 *
LUXOR, Egypt
Temples
See Temples—Egypt
LUXURIES
Americans: splurging in big ways, cutting back in small ones. il U.S. News 82:26-7 Ap 25 '77
LUXURY
See also
Leisure class
LWEIT, Sarah. See Tietze, C. jt auth
LYCABETTUS Press. See Publishers and publishing—Greece
LYDON, Christopher
Jimmy Carter revealed: he's a Rockefeller Republican. Atlantic 240:50-7 Jl '77
LYING
Lies, lies, lies. A. Brandt. Atlantic 240:58-60+ N '77
Manners of deceit and the case for lying. F. du P. Gray. Esquire 88:134-5+ D '77
Truth about children's lies. S. Warren. Educ Digest 42:51-3 Mr '77
See also
Lie detectors and detection
LYKES Corporation
Hard lesson Youngstown taught Lykes. il Bus W p83+ O 3 '77
See also
Youngstown Sheet & Tube Company
LYKES Corporation-LTV Corporation merger. See Corporations—Acquisitions and mergers
LYLE, Ron
Ron Lyle's last fight? R. Boeth and D. Gram. il pors Newsweek 91:29-30 Ja 16 '78 *
LYLES, Jean Caffey
Letting go: everybody has the right to be wrong. Chr Cent 94:451-3 My 11 '77
LYMAN, Lauren D.
Flight that opened an era: a master stroke of skill, daring. il Sci Digest 81:32-3 My '77
LYME, Conn.
Public health
See Public health—Connecticut
LYME arthritis. See Arthritis
LYMPHATIC system
Diseases
See also
Hodgkin's disease
LYMPHOCYTES
Collagenase production by rheumatoid synovial cells: stimulation by a human lymphocyte factor. J.-M. Dayer and others. bibl il Science 195:181-3 Ja 14 '77
Functional specificity of thymus-dependent lymphocytes. W. E. Paul and B. Benacerraf. bibl il Science 195:1293-300 Mr 25 '77
Induction of suppressor T cells in systemic lupus erythematosus by thymosin and cultured thymic epithelium. S. Horowitz and others. bibl il Science 197:999-1001 S 2 '77
Lymphocyte-defined loci in cattle. W. R. Usinger and others. bibl il Science 196:1017-18 My 27 '77
Selective display of histamine receptors on lymphocytes. W. Roszkowski and others. bibl il Science 195:683-5 F 18 '77
LYMPHOCYTIC choriomeningitis. See Meningitis
LYMPHOMAS. See Tumors
LYNCH, Dudley
Two-way cable TV protects America's safest town. il Pop Sci 211:70-1 Jl '77
LYNCH, Etta. See Rodgers, N. jt auth
LYNCH, Jack
Courage and the art of wolf maintenance. J. March. il pors Audubon 79:80-2+ N '77 *
LYNCH, James Joseph
Loneliness can kill you. il Time 110:45 S 5 '77 *
LYNCH, Janet
(ed) Trends in decorating; interviews. il Harp Baz 110:112+ S '77
What single women fear the most. Harp Baz 110:93+ Mr '77
LYNCH, John
Gentleman Jack gets back. por Time 109:27 Je 27 '77 *
LYNCH, John J.
Ultimum verbum—promitto! Nat R 29:887+ Ag 5 '77
LYNCH, Joseph T.
Environmental conservation officer. il por Conservationist 32:28-31 N '77
LYNCH, Patricia Kathleen
Women: the next endangered species? bibl Mademoiselle 83:32+ My '77
LYNCH, Peg
Historical tape recordings. L. Dumont. il pors Hobbies 82:58-9 Je '77 *
LYND, Staughton, 1929-
Touch of class. J. Lelyveld. il por N Y Times Mag p70 Ag 14 '77 *
LYNDE, Donna
Weaving a swing chair. il Design (US) 78:20-1 mid-Summ '77
LYNDON B. Johnson Space Center. See United States—Lyndon B. Johnson Space Center
LYNES, Russell
Architect was told world trade so he planned big. il Smithsonian 8:42-9 Ja '78
Cooper-Hewitt and its concern for American taste. il Smithsonian 8:69-77 bibl(p 160-1) N '77
LYNN, Barry W.
Big cop-out. Nation 225:678-82 D 24 '77
LYNN, James T.
Stop these secret tax hikes! Read Digest 11: 197-8+ N '77
LYNN, Kenneth S.
Welcome back from the raft, Huck honey! Am Scholar 46:338-47 Summ '77
LYNN, Loretta
Singer Loretta Lynn tells why country music thrives. pors U.S. News 83:71 O 24 '77
about
Country's angels. R. Blount, Jr. il pors Esquire 87:62-7+ Mr '77 *
LYNN, Marcia
Breast cancer cures without mastectomy. il Parents Mag 52:40-1+ My '77
LYNN, Walter R.
Engineering and society programs in engineering education. bibl Science 195:150-5 Ja 14 '77
LYNNE, Jill
Jill Lynne. A. Williams. il por Pop Phot 80: 88-91+ Mr '77 *

LYNXES
Canada lynx. E. A. Fountain, Jr. il Conservationist 31:2 N '76
LYON, Edwin
Edwin Lyon, an Anglo-American sculptor in the Mississippi River valley. H. P. Bacot and B. B. Lambdin. bibl il por Antiques 111:554-9 Mr '77 *
LYON, Matthew
Ragged Mat, the Democrat. L. Gragg. il Am Hist Illus 12:20-5 My '77 *
LYON, Nancy
Cholesterol. . .is just one heart threat. il Sci Digest 81:28-31 Ap '77
LYONS, Gene
[Column] Nation 224:120-2, 248-50, 378-9, 628-30; 225:85-6, 405-8 Ja 29, F 26, Mr 26, My 21, Jl 23, O 22 '77; 226:24-6 Ja 7 '78
Eavesdropping on the quotidian. Nation 224:248-50 F 26 '77
Inside the volcano. il Harpers 254:41-6+ Je '77
Literary licentiousness. Nation 224:378-80 Mr 26 '77
Other Carters. il pors N Y Times Mag p 14-16+ S 18 '77
Pieces of a Vietnam war story. Nation 224:120-2 Ja 29 '77
Tradition of the not so new. Nation 224:628-30 My 21 '77
LYONS, Harriet
(ed) See Schapiro, M. Woman's art: it's the only goddam energy around
LYONS, Len
(ed) See Hancock, H. Herbie Hancock's fifth incarnation
LYONS, Nick
Versatile flyfisherman. il pors Outdoor Life 160:74-7+ D '77
—See Tanzer, H. jt auth
LYONS Opera Company. See Opera—France
LYRIC Opera of Chicago
Callas remembered. C. Cassidy. il pors Opera N 42:12-14 N '77
Lyric: losing its Italian accent. K. Monson. il Hi Fi 27:MA28-9 Mr '77
Lyric Opera: accent on spectacle; performances of Tosca, Love for three oranges, and Khovanshchina. K. Monson. il Hi Fi 27:MA32-3+ Ap '77
Musical events:
L'Elisir d'amore and Idomeneo. A. Porter. New Yorker 53:210-11 N 7 '77
Report:
Elisir d'amore and Idomeneo. G. McElroy and J. W. Stedman. Opera N 42:36+ D 17 '77
Tosca and The love for three oranges. G. McElroy and J. W. Stedman. il Opera N 41:36 F 12 '77
Seria side of opera; production of Mozart's Idomeneo. W. Bender. il Time 110:86+ O 17 '77
LYSERGIC acid diethylamide. See LSD
LYSIS
Lysis of human cultured lymphoblastoid cell by cell-induced activation of the properdin pathway. A. N. Theofilopoulos and L. H. Perrin. bibl il Science 195:878-80 Mr 4 '77
See also
Bacteriolysis
LYSTAD, Mary
Adolescent image in American books for children. Educ Digest 43:50-2 N '77
LYTTELTON Theatre. See National Theatre (Great Britain)
LYTTLE, Joe
Red-hot coal. il por Newsweek 89:55 Ap 25 '77 *

M

M-10 machine guns. See Machine guns
MAB (Man and the Biosphere) program. See Unesco
MAF. See Missionary Aviation Fellowship
MARV (maneuverable reentry vehicle) See Guided missiles
MAST (Military Assistance to Safety and Traffic) See Helicopters in rescue work
MBA (Masters of Business Administration) schools. See Business schools and colleges
MBAs (Masters of Business Administration) See Business schools and colleges—Graduates
MBB (firm) See Messerschmitt-Boelkow-Blohm (firm)
MBFR (Mutual and Balanced Force Reduction) talks See Disarmament—Conferences
MBTA. See Massachusetts Bay Transportation Authority
MCA, Inc-Coca-Cola Bottling Company of Los Angeles merger. See Corporations—Acquisitions and mergers
MECCA (Milwaukee Exposition Convention Center Arena) See Stadiums
MG (sports car) See Sports cars
MHD. See Magnetohydrodynamics
MIF (melanocyte-stimulating hormone release-inhibiting factor) See Metabolism inhibiting substances
MIRA. See Monterey Institute for Research in Astronomy
MIT. See Massachusetts Institute of Technology, Cambridge
MIT Press. See University presses
MJS (Mariner Jupiter-Saturn) mission. See Space flight—Voyager flights
MLA. See Modern Language Association of America; Music Library Association
MLS (microwave landing system) See Airplanes—Landing
MMS (multimission modular spacecraft) See Artificial satellites
MMT additives. See Gasoline—Additives
MODE (Mid-ocean Dynamics Experiment) See Oceanographic research
MOMA. See Museum of Modern Art, New York
MOS (metal oxide semiconductor) devices. See Semiconductors
MOSFET (metal oxide semiconductor field-effect transistor) See Transistors
MS Read-a-thon (reading program)
Meet the MS Read-a-thon; address, May 23, 1977. J. Brothers. Vital Speeches 43:623-6 Ag 1 '77
MSG. See Monosodium glutamate
MSRB. See United States—Municipal Securities Rulemaking Board
MAASS, David A.
Maass vision. il Outdoor Life 161:74-81 Ja '78 *
MAASS, Ted
New mass market line uses innovative sales strategy; interview, ed by J. Giusto. Pub W 212:13-14 N 28 '77
MAAZEL, Lorin
On making the first symphonic direct-to-disc LP; excerpt from Concert stage; interview. ed by L. Marcus. il por Hi Fi 27:70-2 Jl '77
about
Beethoven by Maazel. il Sat R 4:38 Ap 2 '77 *
MACADAMS, Cynthia
Who you are now; excerpt from introduction to Emergence. K. Millett. il pors Vogue 167:302+ O '77 *
MCADAMS, Tony, and Miljus, R. C.
Growing criminal liability of executives. bibl f Harvard Bus R 55:36-7+ Mr '77
MCAFEE, Jerry
Gulf Oil goes back to what it knows best. il por Bus W p78+ Ja 31 '77 *
MACALADY, Donald Lee, and others
Sunlight-induced bromate formation in chlorinated seawater. bibl il Science 195:1335-7 Mr 25 '77
MCALISTER, Elizabeth
Keep the faith. il por Newsweek 90:30 S 5 '77 *
MCALISTER, Harold A.
Binary-star speckle interferometry. il Sky & Tel 53:346-50 My '77
MCALLASTER, Elva
Expedition; poem. Chr Today 22:11 D 30 '77
MCALLISTER, Lester G.
Visit to Ulster. Chr Cent 94:213-15 Mr 9 '77
MCALLISTER, William
Perhaps we all should pray; Golden Jason. Audubon 79:143 Mr '77
MACAO
Macau. B. Berger. il Travel 147:32-5+ F '77
See also
Hotels, motels, etc.—Macao
MCARDLE, Andrea
Annie; interview. New Yorker 53:29-30 Mr 14 '77
Close-up; interview, ed by E. Miller. il por Seventeen 36:46+ Jl '77
about
Little Orphan Annie lives! C. M. Dobrish. il pors Parents Mag 52:40-1+ Ag '77 *
Triumphant orphan. il por Newsweek 89:55 My 2 '77 *
MACARONI products
See also
Cookery—Macaroni products
Mueller, C. F, Company
MACARTHUR, Douglas
MacArthur; excerpt from screenplay. H. Barwood and others. il pors map Sr Schol 110:14-17 D 15 '77 *
MCARTHUR, Frank
North by kicker. M. Clevenger. il map Motor B & S 139:64-5+ Mr '77 *
MCATEER, J. Davitt, and Galloway, L. T.
Coal: still a disaster area. Nation 225:273-5 S 24 '77
MACAULAY, David
Great moments in architecture; excerpt. il Atlantic 240:71-6 D '77
MACAULAY, Jacqueline
Stereotyping child welfare. il Society 14:47-51 Ja '77

MCAULIFFE, Kate
Girl who hated Christmas. il Good H 185:72+ D '77
MCAULIFFE, Kevin
Clay feet in Connecticut. Progressive 41:43-4 N '77
MCAULIFFE, Michael
Richard J. Daley—a personal memoir. Commonweal 104:80-1 F 4 '77
MCAVITY, Thomas A. Jr
REITs redux. il por Forbes 120:63-4 O 1 '77 *
MCAVOY, Leo H.
Needs of the elderly: an overview of the research. bibl il Parks & Rec 12:31-4+ Mr '77
MACBETH; drama. See Shakespeare, W.—Plays
MCBRIDE, Chris
White lions. C. Panati and others. il Newsweek 89:96+ My 9 '77 *
MCBRIDE, Gail
What sunlight does to your skin. il Fam Health 9:36-9 Je '77
MCBRIDE, Lloyd
Activism takes over at the USW. il por Bus W p77-8 Je 6 '77 *
McBride apparent victor in Steelworkers contest. L. Bornstein and others. M Labor R 100:84 Ap '77 *
No go for Oilcan Eddie. por Time 109:67 F 21 '77 *
Steel: the ins have it. T. Nicholson and others. pors Newsweek 89:76 F 21 '77 *
Steelworkers' election grows to a national issue. il pors Bus W p69-71 Ja 24 '77 *
Steelworkers go for McBride. Bus W p31 F 21 '77 *
Struggle in steel. K. Bode. New Repub 176:10-13 F 5 '77 *
MCBRIDE, Patricia
Patricia McBride; interview, ed by T. Tobias. il pors Dance Mag 51:47-62 Ag '77
MCBRIDE, Raymond A. and others
Rous sarcomas in chickens: enhanced growth coexisting with concomitant immunity. bibl Science 197:1079-82 S 9 '77
MACBRIDE, Roger Lea
Why I am a civil libertarian. Sat Eve Post 249: 34-5+ O '77
MACBRIDE, Sean
Namibia moves towards independence. il map UNESCO Courier 30:16-20 N '77
New morality for a new world. por Bull Atom Sci 33:22-3 S '77
MCBRIEN, Richard P.
Case for Catholic education. Commonweal 104: 41-4, 246 Ja 21, Ap 15 '77
Church and catechesis. il por New Cath World 220:82-3 Mr '77
MCCABE, Bruce
HUP, MIT share warehousing facilities to reduce costs and improve service. il Pub W 211:58+ Mr 28 '77
MCCABE, Robert E.
Renaissance in Detroit. il Lib J 102:1128-31 My 15 '77
MCCAHILL, Tom
Mail for McCahill; questions and answers. See issues of Mechanix illustrated
MCCAHON, Jim F. and Robertson, M. K.
Nuclear South Pacific: can it be averted? il Bull Atom Sci 33:26-7 Ap '77
MCCALL, Bruce
[Column] (cont) Car & Dr 22:22 Mr; 20 Ap; 22-3 Je; 23:16 O '77; 21 Ja '78
Mementos and memories of the 1936 Cairo World's Fair. il Esquire 88:95-100 Jl '77
MCCALL, Cheryl
Who's afraid of bulging biceps? A call to arms for women athletes. il Ms 5:26+ My '77
MCCALL, Robert B.
Childhood IQ's as predictors of adult educational and occupational status. bibl il Science 197: 482-3 Jl 29 '77
MCCALL twins. See Siamese twins
MCCALL'S (periodical)
McCall's world; results of subscriber questionnaire. McCalls 105:12 O '77
MACCAMPBELL, James C.
Better utilization of personnel. Lib J 102:1718-20 S 1 '77
MCCANN, David
David; Morning light; poems. Poetry 130:1-2 Ap '77
MCCANN, Donnarae, and Richard, Olga
Picture books for children. il Wilson Lib Bull 52:77-9, 178-9, 256-7, 338-9 S-D '77
MCCANN, Edna
Thoughts for the new year; excerpt from The heritage book 1978. Good H 186:127-8 Ja '78
MCCARNEY, Robert
King of the referendum. por Time 109:19 Je 13 '77 *
MCCARRAN-Walter Act. See Immigration and emigration law
MCCARTHY, Abigail (Quigley)
Circles: a Washington story; condensation of a novel. Redbook 149:199-221 Je '77
[Column] See occasional issues of Commonweal
Houston retrospective. Commonweal 105:8-12 Ja 6 '78
New peril. Commonweal 104:40+ Ja 21 '77
MCCARTHY, Colman
After the floods. Progressive 41:44-7 D '77
Double disaster in Appalachia. America 136: 536-9 Je 18 '77
MCCARTHY, Eugene Joseph
Get a horse. New Repub 177:10-11 Jl 9 '77
Kennedy's betrayal; interview, ed by L. R. Obst. il por N Y Times Mag p90+ N 13 '77
Note on the new equality. Commentary 64:53-5 N '77
Philip Hart. New Repub 176:6+ Ja 15 '77
Sins of omission. Harpers 254:90-2 Je '77

about

McCarthy decade. il New Repub 177:5-6+ D 10 '77 *
MCCARTHY, Francis J.
Functions of an insurance company; address, February 26, 1977. Vital Speeches 43:394-8 Ap 15 '77
MCCARTHY, Jo Ann
Jo Ann McCarthy of Pittsburgh Ballet Theatre; interview, ed by N. M. Stoop. il pors Dance Mag 51:56-9 D '77
MCCARTHY, Joe
Lost battalion. il por Am Heritage 28:86-95 O '77
MCCARTHY, Joseph Raymond
On the screen: Joe McCarthyoid. M. J. Sobran, Jr. il Nat R 29:335-6 Mr 18 '77 *
Remember Paul Hughes. W. F. Buckley, Jr. Nat R 29:403 Ap 1 '77 *
Tail Gunner Joe. W. F. Buckley, Jr. Nat R 29: 350 Mr 18 '77 *
MCCARTHY, Martha N.
How can I best manage my classroom? Educ Digest 43:20-3 N '77
MCCARTHY, Patrick
Claudel reconsidered. America 136:392-3 Ap 30 '77
French Catholicism faces the left. America 137:350-3 N 19 '77
MCCARVER, Tim
Odd couple, but winning combination. L. Keith. il pors Sports Illus 47:16 Ag 29 '77 *
MCCASLIN, Robert
Toy that could change the toy business. il pors Bus W p60+ Je 20 '77 *
MCCAUGHAN, Ed, and Baird, Peter
Mexico's chaotic economy. Progressive 41:12 Mr '77
MCCAULEY, Elfrieda
Some early women librarians in New England. bibl il Wilson Lib Bull 51:648-55 Ap '77
MCCAULEY, George C.
Word. See issues of America
MCCAULL, Julian
Research in a box. il Environment 19:31-7 Ap '77
World economy. il Environment 19:34-44 N '77
MCCLATCHY, J. D.
Breakfast table; poem. Nation 225:636 D 10 '77
Comment. Poetry 131:169-75 D '77
Dialects of the tribe. Poetry 130:41-53 Ap '77
Suffering the cut; Scenes from another life; poems. Poetry 130:28-32 Ap '77
Variations on a line; poem. Yale R 67:70 O '77
MCCLEARY, Elliot H.
Chronic pain. il Fam Health 9:26-9+ Ag '77
MCCLELLAN, Gary
Build AM/FM frequency display. il Radio-Electr 49:21-4+ Ja '78
MCCLELLAN, Jim, and Anderson, D. E.
Lips that sink ships. Progressive 41:47-9 My '77
MCCLELLAND and Stewart-Bantam Ltd. See Publishers and publishing—Canada
MCCLEMENTS, W. and Skalka, A. M.
Analysis of chicken ribosomal RNA genes and construction of lambda hybrids containing gene fragments. bibl il Science 196:195-7 Ap 8 '77
MCCLENAHAN, Nelle
Do we ever? poem. McCalls 104:48 My '77
MCCLENDON, Edwin J.
Is local control of education dead or dying? Educ Digest 42:22-3 Ap '77
MCCLINTOCK, Jack
Edith Project. Harpers 254:21-4 Mr '77
MCCLINTON, Katharine Morrison
Royal Doulton series ware. il Hobbies 82:116-17+ Je '77
Silver miniatures. il Hobbies 82:118-20 N '77
MCCLORY, Robert
Excerpts from debate on Federal Elections Campaign Act Amendments, April 1, 1976. Cong Digest 56:83+ Mr '77
MCCLOY, John Jay
Hall of Fame for Business Leadership. M. Ways. por Fortune 95:121 Ja '77 *
MCCLURE, James A.
Excerpts from statement, and remarks on temporary alien workers in agriculture, May 25 and August 5, 1977. Cong Digest 56:241+ O '77
MCCLURE, Michael
Poem with a gift. Atlantic 239:97 Mr '77
MCCLURE'S magazine
Reconsideration. R. Stinson. New Repub 177:37-9 Jl 9 '77
MCCLUSKEY, Audrey, and McCluskey, John
Frederick Douglass on ethnology: a commencement address at Western Reserve College, 1854. bibl il por Negro Hist Bull 40:746-9 S '77

MCCLUSKEY, Harold
Riddled by isotopes. M. Clark and P. S. Greenberg. il por Newsweek 89:49 Mr 21 '77 *

MCCLUSKEY, John. See McCluskey, A. jt auth

MACCOBY, Michael
Age of the gamesman. il Time 109:57-8 F 14 '77 *
Gamesman. L. Langway. il por Newsweek 89:70 Ja 24 '77 *

MCCOMB, Dave
Tempest: an endangered species? il Yachting 141:60+ My '77

MCCOMB, Marshall Francis
Case of the senile judge. por Newsweek 89:36 Ja 24 '77 *

MCCONEGHEY, Howard
Art education, art therapy, art. bibl il Sch Arts 77:52-5 S '77

MCCONKEY, Clarence
Forgetting the holocaust. Chr Cent 94:669-70 Jl 20 '77

MCCONKEY, James
Fireflies; story. New Yorker 53:34-5 Jl 18 '77

MCCONKEY, Thomas W.
(ed) Buyers' guide. il Lib J 102:999 My 1 '77

MCCONNEL, Patricia
$50 writer's office. il Writers Digest 57:25 Ap '77

MCCONVILLE, Edward M.
Why Sol Stetin stepped down. por Nation 225: 621-4 D 10 '77

MCCOOK, John James
Hoboes told all to 1890s scholar. R. Bruns. il por Smithsonian 8:141-2+ N '77 *

MCCORD, Jean
(ed) See Manley, P. Phyllis Manley combines two worlds
(ed) See Wakeham, D. Duane Wakeham: sharing a way of seeing

MCCORMACK, Mike
Energy and the future of America. Intellect 105:314-17 Ap '77
Excerpts from address on nuclear energy production, March 19, 1976. Cong Digest 56:44+ F '77
Legislating the Nation's science business. il Phys Today 30:23-6 Ag '77

MCCORMACK, Shirley. See Clark, J. H. jt auth

MCCORMACK, Thomas J.
Prices, printings and profits: how to draw the bottom line; adaptation of address. il Pub W 212:34-41 Ag 15 '77

about

All things bright and exuberant: St Martin's Press is 25 years old. M. Reuter. il pors Pub W 212:30-3 Ag 8 '77 *

MCCORMICK, A. G. and Carter, Sharon
Neuroses. Vogue 167:139-40+ Mr '77

MCCORMICK, Brooks
Five International Harvesters in one. H. Seneker. il por Forbes 119:60+ Ap 15 '77 *

MCCORMICK, Richard A.
Conscience, theologians and the magisterium. il New Cath World 220:268-71 N '77

—and Hellegers, A. E.
Legislation and the living will. America 136: 210-13 Mr 12 '77

MCCORMICK, Robert Rutherford
Is there an exorcist in the house? P. W. Sturm. pors Forbes 120:61-2+ S 1 '77 *

MCCORMICK & Company
Sugar and spice and nearly everything nice. Forbes 120:56-7 Ag 15 '77

MCCOSKER, John E.
Flashlight fishes; with biographical sketch. il Sci Am 236:24, 106-12+ bibl(p 150) Mr '77
Fright posture of the plesiopid fish calloplesiops altivelis: an example of Batesian mimicry. bibl il Science 197:400-1 Jl 22 '77

MCCOURT, James
Kaye Wayfaring in Avenged; story. New Yorker 53:27-31 Ja 9 '78

MCCOVEY, Willie
I'll come home to you, said Willie. R. Fimrite. por Sports Illus 46:69-70+ My 2 '77 *

MCCOY, Elin
Amateur archaeology: the joy of the dig. il House & Gard 149:50+ Mr '77

MCCOY, John Gardner
Turncoat banker? P. Sturm. por Forbes 120:80 Jl 15 '77 *

MCCOY, Shirley
Revisiting America's canals. il Travel 148:60-5 Jl '77

MCCOY, Tim
High eagle: the many lives of Colonel Tim McCoy; interview, ed by D. Ponicsan. il pors Am Heritage 28:52-62 Je '77

MCCRACKEN, Gary F. and Bradbury, J. W.
Paternity and genetic heterogeneity in the polygynous bat, phyllostomus hastatus. bibl il Science 198:303-6 O 21 '77

MCCRACKEN, James
Rarest of birds. P. Andrews. il pors Horizon 21: 56-61 Ja '78 *

MCCRACKEN, James A.
Write your own history. Read Digest 111:7-9+ Ag '77

MCCRACKEN, Paul Winston
Sustaining orderly economic growth; excerpts from testimony before the Senate Budget Committee. por Intellect 105:208-10 Ja '77
Tax reduction is the best spur to job creation; interview. por U.S. News 82:56-7 F 21 '77
What makes America? address, February 7, 1977. Vital Speeches 43:311-14 Mr 1 '77

MCCRACKEN, Samuel
War against the atom. bibl f Commentary 64: 33-47 S; 20+ D '77

MCCRACKEN, William Patterson, 1888-1969
They almost grounded Lindy. il por Time 110:24 N 28 '77 *

MCCRANK, Lawrence. See McCrank, R. jt auth

MCCRANK, Ruth, and McCrank, Lawrence
How a levy was won in the West. bibl il Am Lib 8:560-5 N '77

MCCRAW, Jim
Road test. il Hot Rod 30:52-4+ Ap; 109-10+ Je '77
Up on two wheels. See issues of Hot Rod

MCCRAW, Thomas K.
Controversial world of the regulatory agencies. Am Heritage 28:40-7 Ap '77

MACCREADY, Paul Beattie, 1925-
Flight of the Gossamer Condor. M. E. Long. il por Nat Geog 153:130-40 Ja '78 *
Flying bike that won $86,000. il por U.S. News 83:92 O 31 '77 *
Gossamer wings. il Sci Am 237:74+ O '77 *
On Gossamer wings, one of those things. S. Moses. il por Sports Illus 47:19-21 Ag 1 '77 *
The winner. P. Wahl. il por Pop Sci 212:56-8+ Ja '78 *

MCCREE, Wade Hampton, 1920-
Uncle Sam's lawyer. J. K. Footlick and D. Camper. il por Newsweek 90:97 D 5 '77 *

MCCRORY, Wallace W.
(ed) Guide to good family health. il Parents Mag 52:65 N '77

MCCUE, Michael, and Wilson, Evie
Elderly books for youngerly readers (title varies) See issues of Wilson library bulletin

MCCULLAGH, James C.
Closer look at amaranth. Org Gard & Farm 24: 57-8 O '77
Crow; poem. Org Gard & Farm 24:53 My '77
For Uncle Lou who uses his hands; poem. Org Gard & Farm 24:141 Mr '77
Hints for encouraging fall; poem. il Org Gard & Farm 24:144 N '77
Solar greenhouse: heat and food wave of the future. Org Gard & Farm 24:53-4 D '77
Tinkering man. il por Org Gard & Farm 24: 139-41 Mr '77

MCCULLERS, Carson (Smith)
Sucker; story. Sat Eve Post 249:62-3 O '77

MCCULLOUGH, Colleen
About the author. M. Reuter. Pub W 211:27 Mr 7 '77 *

MCCULLOUGH, David G.
American adventure of Louis Agassiz. il por Audubon 79:2-17 Ja '77

MCCULLY, Helen
Microwave kitchen. See issues of House beautiful
Nobody ever tells you these things; questions and answers. See issues of House beautiful

MCCUNE, Shirley, and others
Teacher education: a new set of goals. Am Educ 13:24-5 Je '77

MCCURDY, Harold
Meditation; poem. America 137:323 N 12 '77

MCCUTCHEN, C. W.
Spinning rotation of ash and tulip tree samaras. bibl il Science 197:691-2 Ag 12 '77

MCDANIEL, Charles-Gene
Tut lives. Progressive 41:35-6 Jl '77

MCDANIEL, Jean
Cardoon, cardoni—whatever you call it, it's good. il Org Gard & Farm 24:148-50 F '77

MCDANIEL, Paul R.
Provide more incentives for investment by business; interview. por U.S. News 83:34-6 Jl 25 '77

MCDANIEL, Thomas R.
Principles of classroom discipline: toward a pragmatic synthesis. bibl Clearing H 51:149-52 D '77

MCDERMOTT, Ashley T. and DiCicco, Dennis
Ninth Riverside convention. il pors Sky & Tel 54:100-4 Ag '77

MCDERMOTT, Barry
Al, you went out in style. il por Sports Illus 46:20-3 Ap 4 '77
Back to Bruce in a moment. First, this commercial. il pors Sports Illus 47:42-4+ S 26 '77
Baseball. Sports Illus 47:54+ Jl 18 '77
Basketball. il Sports Illus 47:50-2 Jl 11 '77
College basketball (cont) Sports Illus 46:38+ Ja 31; 47-8 Mr 7 '77
College football. Sports Illus 48:48 Ja 2 '78
Dunkers are strutting their stuffs. il Sports Illus 46:20-2+ Mr 14 '77
Easy times the hard way. Sports Illus 47:54-62+ Ag 8 '77
Golf (cont) Sports Illus 46:50+ Ja 17; 47:50-1 Ag 8; 80-1 Ag 29; 67-8 S 12 '77

MCDERMOTT, Barry—*Continued*
It's veni, vidi, vici for Vitas. il pors Sports Illus 47:24-7 Ag 15 '77
Nevada-Las Vegas rolled with its fast break. il Sports Illus 46:16-18 Mr 28 '77
Sixteen sweetest fight for a kiss. il Sports Illus 46:28-9 Mr 21 '77
Streaks of San Francisco. il Sports Illus 46:26-9 Ja 31 '77
Tennis. Sports Illus 46:56+ My 9; 47:74+ O 17 '77
That trip to Vegas was no honeymoon. il Sports Illus 46:22-3+ F 21 '77

MCDERMOTT, Edwin J.
National catechetical directory: what it is, what it isn't. America 136:76-9 Ja 29 '77

MCDERMOTT, J. Ray & Company-Babcock & Wilcox merger. See Corporations—Acquisitions and mergers

MCDERMOTT, John M.
New voice for American theology. America 137:374-6 N 26 '77

MCDERMOTT, Robert
Measures of the heart; story. Redbook 148:101 F '77

MCDERMOTT, Thomas Charles, 1927-
Human dimension in productivity; address, January 19, 1977. Vital Speeches 43:306-9 Mr 1 '77

MCDIVITT, James A.
Astronauts & UFOs—the whole story! J. E. Oberg. il por Space World N-2-158:4-28 F '77 *

MACDONALD, A. B.
(ed) See Sutton, F. Only law

MACDONALD, Cynthia
World's fattest dancer; poem. New Yorker 53:52 N 7 '77

about

Comment. R. Holland. Poetry 129:289-90 F '77 *

MACDONALD, David
Canada: to be or not to be. il Read Digest 111:66-70 Ag '77
—See Wills, H. jt auth

MACDONALD, Duncan
Dormant no more, Duncan is erupting. K. Moore. il por Sports Illus 46:34-7 F 14 '77 *

MCDONALD, H. Dermot
Lusts of modern theology. Chr Today 22:18-20 O 21 '77

MACDONALD, John
Defending Yuri Orlov. New Yorker 53:29-31 S 19 '77 *

MCDONALD, John Kennely. See Schwabe, C. jt auth

MCDONALD, Laughlin
Has the Supreme Court abandoned the Constitution? il Sat R 4:10-12+ My 28 '77; Same with title Supreme Court today. Current 194:32-9 Jl '77

MCDONALD, Lawrence P.
Should U.S. do business with Cuba? interview. pors U.S. News 82:73-4 Mr 7 '77

about

Plunder on the right. K. Bode. New Repub 177:11-12 N 12 '77 *

MACDONALD, Nesta
Isadora reexamined; excerpt from Isadora Duncan. il pors Dance Mag 51:51-66 Jl; 42-6 Ag; 60-3 S; 79-81 O; 45-7 N; 71-3 D '77

MACDONALD, Peter
U.S. Indians demand a better energy deal. por Bus W p53 D 19 '77 *

MACDONALD, Ralph
Ralph MacDonald—modern musical all-rounder. J. S. Roberts. il pors Hi Fi 27:97-100 Ag '77 *

MACDONALD, Ray Woodward
How Ray Macdonald's growth theory created I.B.M.'s toughest competitor. B. Uttal. il pors Fortune 95:94-9+ Ja '77 *

MCDONALD, Stanley
Big catch. il pors Forbes 120:76 D 15 '77 *

MCDONALD, Steveson A.
Easiest seed germinator yet. il Org Gard & Farm 25:67-8 Ja '78

MCDONALD, T. J.
Last hurrah? The perpetual motion of the political machine. Intellect 106:30-2 Ag '77

MCDONALD-Halliday Enterprises. See Real estate business

MCDONALD Observatory. See Astronomical observatories

MACDONALD-Raintree, Inc. See Publishers and publishing—United States

MCDONALD'S Corporation
Fred L. Turner of McDonald's; growth company. por Forbes 119:95 F 15 '77
McDonald's blends new products with savvy merchandising. Bus W p56-60 Jl 11 '77
McDonald's grinds out growth. il por Duns R 110:50-2 D '77
Rituals at McDonald's. C. P. Kottak. il por Natur Hist 87:74-83 bibl(p 109) Ja '78
Still the champion. il Time 109:77 Ap 25 '77

MCDONNELL, Christine
Second look:
Yearling. Horn Bk 53:344-5 Je '77

MCDONNELL, Nancy
Northern Ireland's guerrillas of peace; interview, ed by R. S. Kennedy and P. Klotz-Chamberlin. il por Chr Cent 94:746-51 Ag 31 '77

MCDONNELL Douglas Corporation
Budget crunch threatens the F-15. Bus W p32 Mr 28 '77
DC-9-55 development aid sought. B. Miller. Aviation W 106:24 Ap 4 '77

MCDONOUGH, George E.
For Christ the Lord; poem. Chr Today 21:18 Ja 7 '77
Spirit of God; poem. Chr Today 22:27 O 7 '77
Wanderer; poem. Chr Cent 94:1223 D 28 '77

MCDONOUGH, John J, collection. See Art—Private collections

MCDONOUGH, William J.
First Chicago reaches to win Peking's favor. por Bus W p36 O 17 '77 *

MACDOUGAL, B. N.
Look at the man Liz found. il pors Sat Eve Post 249:62-3+ N '77

MACDOUGAL, Gary Edward
Financial controls help a valve maker expand. il por Bus W p47-8 Ag 1 '77 *

MACDOUGALL, J. D. and Kerridge, J. F.
Cubanite: a new sulfide phase in CI meteorites. bibl il Science 197:561-2 Ag 5 '77

MACDOWELL Colony, Peterboro, N.H.
In search of a novel at MacDowell. L. Franks. il por N Y Times Mag p72+ My 1 '77
Where artists do as they please—and, mostly, work. W. F. Claire. il Smithsonian 8:44-51 Jl '77

MACE, David R.
Making marriage work (cont of) Marriage lines. See issues of Parents' magazine & better homemaking

MACE, Myles L.
(ed) From the boardroom. See issues of Harvard business review

MCELROY, George
Quiet revolution. il Opera N 42:14-18 Jl '77

MACELROY, Robert David
Colonizing Mars: the age of planetary engineering begins. A. L. Robinson. il Science 195:668 F 18 '77 *

MCELROY, William David
Global age: roles of basic and applied research; address, February 23, 1977. Science 196:267-70 Ap 15 '77

MCELWAIN, Virginia
Consumer's guide to nursery shopping. il Horticulture 55:40-3 O '77
Guide to dwarf fruits. Horticulture 55:28-30+ S '77

MACELWAIN, Wade
Misunderstood morays; with biographical sketch. il Sea Front 23:96-100, 126 Mr '77

MCELWAINE, Sandra
Farmer's wife. il pors Ladies Home J 94:70-1+ Ag '77
Travel: Belgium. il Vogue 167:150+ D '77

MCENDARFER, Ed
Two wood-fired kilns: a natural-draft, brick design. il por Ceram Mo 25:36-8 D '77

MCENEANEY, Eamon
Cornell's wild Irish rose. J. Marshall. Sports Illus 46:63-4+ Je 6 '77 *

MACEOIN, Gary
President Carter's choices. Commonweal 104:616-18 S 30 '77

MACERA, Pablo
Living legacy of the Andes. il UNESCO Courier 30:38-45 Ag '77

MCEUEN, John
To Russia with rock; interview, ed by E. Dowling. il pors Sr Schol 110:2-5 N 3 '77

MCEVOY, Marian
California comers. il N Y Times Mag p60-3 Ja 8 '78

MCFADDEN, Cyra
Dancing school recital; story. McCalls 104:142-3 F '77
Semantic spinach. N Y Times Mag p51+ N 20 '77
Serial; story, excerpt from novel. il Sat Eve Post 249:54-5 D '77

MCFADDEN, Mary
Dinner plans from Mary McFadden. Vogue 167:146-7 D '77

about

Mary life: spectacular. J. Robinson. il Vogue 167:186-92+ D '77 *

MCFADDIN Ranch, Texas. See Ranches

MCFALL, Russell Whitney
Space-age treadmill. por Forbes 120:59-60 Ag 1 '77 *

MCFEE, Oonah
Wireless communication; story. Redbook 149:136 O '77

MCFERRAN, Douglass D.
Castaneda plot. America 136:162-4 F 26 '77

MACFLECKNOE, Sir Joseph
The muse doth protest; poem. Nat R 29:254 Mr 4 '77

MCGAHERN, John
Sierra Leone; story. New Yorker 53:28-34 Ag 22 '77
Wine breath; story. New Yorker 53:36-40 Ap 4 '77

MCGARRIGLE, Anna
Kate and Anna McGarrigle: not afraid to be corny; interview, ed by G. Christgau. pors Ms 5:36+ Mr '77
about
Music people. E. Miller. pors Seventeen 36:134 Ag '77 *
Musical paradox of Kate & Anna McGarrigle. il pors Hi Fi 27:117-18 My '77 *

MCGARRIGLE, Kate
Kate and Anna McGarrigle: not afraid to be corny; interview, ed by G. Christgau. pors Ms 5:36+ Mr '77
about
Music people. E. Miller. pors Seventeen 36:134 Ag '77 *
Musical paradox of Kate & Anna McGarrigle. il pors Hi Fi 27:117-18 My '77 *

MCGARRIGLE, Nancy B.
Manager of S.C. elderly housing project wins national award. por Aging 266:19 D '76 *

MACGARRY, Brian
Rhodesia: putting the record straight. America 137:239-40 O 15 '77

MCGAVRAN, Donald
Intensity of belief: a pragmatic concern for church growth; interviews, ed by D. E. Kucharsky. C. P. Wagner; A. Johnston. pors Chr Today 21:10-14 Ja 7 '77 *

MCGAW, Howard F.
Reference books for teachers. Clearing H 51:63-4 O '77

MCGEE, Gale William
Report on human rights in the Americas; statement, September 15, 1977. Dept State Bull 77: 573-5 O 24 '77

MCGEE, Robert T.
Is constancy outmoded? Clearing H 50:250-2 F '77

MCGEE, Vonetta
After the break up. pors Ebony 32:77 Ag '77 *

MCGEHEE, Edward G.
Case of civil disobedience. Chr Cent 94:1217-23 D 28 '77; Same abr. Progressive 41:24-5 D '77

MCGEHEE, Fielding M. 3d
Checking on the contractors. Progressive 41:8-9 S '77

MCGEHEE, Milly
Auburn in Natchez. bibl il Antiques 111:546-53 Mr '77

MCGEORGE, John
Tinkering man. J. C. McCullagh. il por Org Gard & Farm 24:139-41 Mr '77 *

MCGERR, Patricia
Listen to your heart; story. Good H 184:128-9 Ap '77

MCGHEE, Dorothy
Apple picker blues. New Repub 177:15-16 O 29 '77
Secret killers. Progressive 41:26 Ag '77
Workplace hazards: no women need apply. Progressive 41:20-5 O '77

MCGHEE, Edward, pseud
Canaries. Sat R 5:35 O 29 '77

MCGHEE, K. H.
Relieve summertime pavement blowups. il Am City & County 92:38-9 Jl '77

MCGILL, William J.
Anne Sexton and God. Commonweal 104:304-6 My 13 '77

MCGILL, William James
Science and the law; address, September 20, 1977. Vital Speeches 44:28-32 O 15 '77; Excerpts. Science 198:275 O 21 '77

MCGILVRAY, Scott
Getting the garden and gardener ready for spring. il Horticulture 55:43-5 Mr '77
How to water your garden less and enjoy it more. il Horticulture 55:24-7 Je '77

MACGINITIE, Walter H.
When should we begin to teach reading? Educ Digest 42:60-2 F '77

MCGINNIS, Leo G.
International economic outlook; address, April 20, 1977. Vital Speeches 43:478-80 My 15 '77

MCGINNIS, Lila Sprague
No greater love; story. il Good H 184:126-7 Mr '77

MCGINNIS, Ronald L.
Educational funeral; poem. Negro Hist Bull 40: 721 Jl '77

MCGINNIS, Terri
Ask the vet; questions and answers. See issues of Family health incorporating Today's health

MCGINTY, Brian
Friend of the wilderness. il pors map Am Hist Illus 12:4-9+ Jl '77
Land divided, the world united. il map Am Hist Illus 12:10-19 My '77

MCGINTY, Dennis J. See Baker, T. L; Siegel, J. M. jt auths

MCGINTY, John Milton
Two messages from AIA President McGinty. W. F. Wagner, Jr. Archit Rec 162:13 N '77 *

MCGLEISH, Wayland, pseud
Bangkok's seeds of revolt. America 136:520-2 Je 11 '77
Letter from Seoul. map America 136:99-101 F 5 '77

MCGONEGAL, Ro
Captain Jack will make it fly tonight. il Hot Rod 30:40-1+ Je '77

MCGOVERN, Ann
Half a kingdom; story; excerpt. il Ms 6:71-4 Jl '77

MCGOVERN, George Stanley
Memo to the White House. Harpers 255:33-5 O '77
Pluralist structures or interest groups? Society 14:13-15+ Ja '77
Russians are coming—again. Progressive 41:17-23 My '77
Talk with Castro. il pors N Y Times Mag p20+ Mr 13 '77
about
Feeling left out. E. Marshall. New Repub 176: 12-13 My 21 '77 *
George McGovern had a problem. K. Daly. Farm J 101:Dairy 16, Hog 24 O '77 *
McGovern vs. the farmers: South Dakota's water showdown. H. Gardner. il Nation 224:456-61 Ap 16 '77 *

MCGOWAN, Alan
New York blackout. Environment 19:48-9 Ag '77

MCGOWAN, Ann
Ann McGowan: design in color and black-and-white; interview, ed by Y. E. Benedek. il por Pop Phot 80:94-5+ F '77

MCGRATH, Joseph P.
Bentleg solution. Nat R 29:668-9 Je 10 '77

MCGRATH, Nancy
Learning with the heart. il N Y Times Mag p 100+ S 25 '77

MACGRAW, Ali
Ali & Steve; interview, ed by V. Scott. pors Ladies Home J 94:76+ N '77

MACGREGOR, Roger
One for the road. il por Forbes 120:100 O 1 '77 *

MACGREGOR, Ronald J.
To build a brain. J. A. Miller. il por Sci N 111:156-7 Mr 5 '77 *

MACGREGOR Yacht Corporation. See Boatbuilding

MCGUFFEY, William Holmes
Schoolmaster to a nation. H. C. Jacobs. il por Sat Eve Post 249:62-3+ Ap '77 *

MCGUFFEY Readers. See Readers (books)

MACGUINEAS, Carol
Uncommon goal. il Opera N 42:22-6+ N '77

MCGUIRE, Al
Conversation with chairman Al; interview, ed by L. Keith. il Sports Illus 47:34-7 N 28 '77
about
Al, you went out in style. B. McDermott. il por Sports Illus 46:20-3 Ap 4 '77 *
Final fling of Al McGuire. P. Axthelm. il por Newsweek 89:75 Mr 28 '77 *

MCGUIRE, E. Patrick
Economics (cont) Craft Horiz 37:17 F; 13 Ap; 9 Ag '77

MCGUIRE, John Richard
California fire report. Am For 83:6 O '77
There's more to reclamation than planting trees. il Am For 83:14-19 Jl '77

MCGUIRE, Phillip
Judge William H. Hastie civilian aide to the Secretary of War, 1940-1943. por Negro Hist Bull 40:712-13 My '77

MCGUIRE, Willard
(ed) See Haley, A. Interview with Alex Haley

MCHARG, Ian
Ian McHarg: champion for design with nature. C. Holden. por Science 195:379-82 Ja 28 '77 *

MCHENRY, Donald Franchot
Security Council favors U.N. membership for Vietnam; statement, July 19, 1977. Dept State Bull 77:283 Ag 29 '77
U.S. supports U.N. membership of Djibouti; statement, July 7, 1977. Dept State Bull 77: 226 Ag 22 '77

MACHIAVELLI, Niccolò
Mandrake Review
New Yorker 53:91 D 12 '77 *

MACHINE guns
Significant little gun; Ingram M-10. A. St George. il por Esquire 88:69-72+ Ag '77

MACHINE politics. See Boss rule

MACHINE tool industry

Securities

Machine-tool stocks may soon be hot again. E. Konrad. il Fortune 95:69-70+ Ja '77

MACHINE tools
See also
Drilling and boring machinery
Vises

MACHINERY
See also
Agricultural (machinery)
Bearings (machinery)
Bulldozers (machines)
Coal mining machinery
Construction equipment
Woodworking machinery

Stands, tables, etc.

Table for routers & sabers. R. Capotosto. il Mech Illus 73:162+ My '77

MACHINERY in art
Boilers can be beautiful. M. Reay. il Sch Arts 77:10-11 N '77

MACHINERY industry
See also
Agricultural machinery industry
Machine tool industry

Securities

After a pause, a new move ahead for machinery stocks; interview, ed by A. Hershman. J. Mackin. por Duns R 109:109-10+ Mr '77

Wages and hours

Record wage increases generated for nonelectrical machinery workers. C. Day. M Labor R 100:73-5 Ap '77

MACHINERY sheds. See Sheds

MACHINISTS union. See International Association of Machinists and Aerospace Workers

MCHUGH, Heather
Latitude; poem. Mademoiselle 83:86 D '77
On time; poem. New Yorker 53:179 O 17 '77

MCINNES, William Charles
Working together: an educational model. America 137:300-3 N 5 '77

MACINNIS, Joseph B.
In pursuit of the narwhal. il Int Widlife 7:36-41 My '77

MCINTIRE, Carl
On the beach, on the brink. Chr Today 21:48+ S 23 '77 *

MCINTOSH, F. B.
Environment and business aviation; excerpts from address. Aviation W 107:11 O 10 '77

MCINTOSH, Frank H.
High fidelity pathfinders. N. Eisenberg. por Hi Fi 27:64+ O '77 *

MCINTOSH, Mescal
Second coming. B. Brenner. Chr Today 21:43-4 Ja 21 '77 *

MCINTYRE, Frank O.
Ahead of Cronkite. Sci Digest 81:59 Mr '77

MCINTYRE, James T. Jr
Minding the store. D. A. Williams and R. Thomas. por Newsweek 90:30 S 19 '77 *
OMB goes back to its budgeting. por Bus W p24-5 Ja 9 '78 *
Technician as budget boss. il por Time 111:34 Ja 9 '78 *

MCINTYRE, Loren
Brazil's wild frontier. il map Nat Geog 152: 684-719 N '77

MACIOTI, Manfredo
Science policy visit to Israel. il Bull Atom Sci 33:10-21 Mr '77

MCISAAC, George S.
What's coming in labor relations? bibl f Harvard Bus R 55:22-3+ S '77

MACK, Barbara
Exotic vacations: inexpensive and accessible. il Harp Baz 110:18+ F '77
Great spots for your family vacation. il Harp Baz 110:4+ Jl '77

MACK, Bernard
Two years in Cuban jails. J. Huck. il por Newsweek 89:29 Je 27 '77 *

MCKAY, Claude
Claude McKay as an artist. S. Warren. bibl f por Negro Hist Bull 40:685-7 Mr '77 *

MCKAY, Heather
It was hard, but easy. J. Kaplan. il por Sports Illus 46:44-5 F 7 '77 *

MACKAY, Patricia. See Loney, G. M. jt auth

MCKAY, Robert L.
Promising mañana. por Forbes 120:62 Ag 1 '77 *

MACKAY, William
Amateur hour. il Time 110:94 N 14 '77 *
Amateur surgeons. M. Clark and D. Shapiro. il por Newsweek 90:125 N 14 '77 *

MCKEAN, Hugh F, collection. See Glassware—Collectors and collecting

MCKEE, Gladys
Happy ending love song; poem. Good H 185:224 S '77

MCKEE, Lonette
Lonette McKee; interview, ed by M. Cantwell. il pors Mademoiselle 83:198-9+ Ap '77

MCKEE, Myron
Law-and-order principal. P. Haslanger. Progressive 41:45 N '77 *

MCKEEN, William
Chicago. il Sat Eve Post 249:62-3 My '77

MCKELVEY, Vincent Ellis
McKelvey ousted as director of Geological Survey. D. Shapley. Science 197:1264 S 23 '77 *

MCKELVY, John E. Jr
Warm water to the north. il map Yachting 141: 67-9 Mr '77

MCKENNA, Bernard H.
What's wrong with standardized testing? il Todays Educ 66:35-42+ Mr '77
—and Quinto, Frances
7 good alternatives to group testing. Parents Mag 52:64-5 S '77

MCKENNEY, Thomas L.
How did an Indian chief really look? H. J. Viola. il Smithsonian 8:100-2+ Je '77 *

MACKENZIE, Sir Alexander
First crossing; excerpt from Winner take all. D. Lavender. il por Am West 14:4-11+ S '77 *

MACKENZIE, John P.
Dark doings among the judges. Sat R 4:18-19 My 28 '77

MCKENZIE, Julie N.
Company. New Yorker 53:26-7 Je 13 '77 *

MCKENZIE, Leo J.
Bishop for Philadelphia. America 136:543-4 Je 18 '77

MACKENZIE, R. A. F.
Sufferings of Job. America 136:242 Mr 19 '77

MACKENZIE, Ross
Carter strikes out in Virginia. Nat R 29:1425-6 D 9 '77
Howlin' Henry's surprise win. Nat R 29:778 Jl 8 '77

MACKENZIE River (Canada)
Interaction of two great rivers helps sustain the earth's vital biosphere. R. Campbell. il map Smithsonian 8:38-51 S '77

MCKEON, Nancy
Power of women consumers. Harp Baz 111:153+ N '77

MCKEOWN, Bill
All outdoors. See issues of Popular mechanics

MCKEOWN, Tom
Other lives; poem. Commonweal 104:555 S 2 '77

MACKEY, James A. and others
Effectiveness of teacher education. Educ Digest 43:32-5 N '77

MACKEY, Michael C. and Glass, Leon
Oscillation and chaos in physiological control systems. bibl il Science 197:287-9 Jl 15 '77

MACKIE, George O. See Anderson, P. A. V. jt auth

MCKIMMEY, James
What you do know can hurt you. Writer 90: 18-20 Je '77

MACKIN, John
After a pause, a new move ahead for machinery stocks; interview, ed by A. Hershman. por Duns R 109:109-10+ Mr '77

MCKINLEY, Fred
AC/DC trout flies. il Field & S 81:52-4+ F '77

MCKINLEY, James
Outdoors. Esquire 88:51+ S '77

MCKINLEY National Park. See Mount McKinley National Park

MCKINNEY, John A.
At Johns-Manville, it's back to basics. il por Bus W p76+ O 31 '77 *

MCKINNEY, Joseph C. Bp
Rejoice in the Lord always. . .the Lord is near. il New Cath World 220:6-9 Ja '77

MCKINNEY, Joseph F.
Tyler: unsung, prosaic and very profitable. por Duns R 109:21-2+ Mr '77 *

MCKINNEY, Stewart B.
Excerpt from remarks on national health insurance, February 22, 1977. Cong Digest 56: 209+ Ag '77

MACKINTOSH, Allan R.
Magnetism of rare-earth metals. bibl il Phys Today 30:23-30 Je '77

MACKINTOSH, Barry
George Washington Carver and the peanut. il pors Am Heritage 28:66-73 Ag '77

MACKINTOSH, Prudence
Merry Christmas in your house; merry chaos in mine. il por Redbook 150:80+ D '77

MACKLIN, Elizabeth
Three views of a woman inhaling; poem. New Yorker 53:36 Ag 22 '77

MACKSON, Richard
Of frogs and hats and bats; promotional days; photographs. Sports Illus 47:36-41 Jl 18 '77

MCKUSICK, Victor A. and Ruddle, F. H.
Status of the gene map of the human chromosomes. bibl il Science 196:390-405 Ap 22 '77

MCLAIN, Denny
Hard-luck heroes. E. Keerdoja. il pors Newsweek 90:5+ Ag 1 '77 *

MACLAINE, Shirley
Shirley MacLaine on the move. il pors Time 109:54 Mr 7 '77 *

MCLAUGHLIN, Charles
Pilobolus: six mavericks in search of their own style. il Horizon 20:23-7 N '77

MCLAUGHLIN, John
Government regulation. Nation 224:679-82 Je 4 '77
Political suicide in New Jersey. Nation 225: 593-6 D 3 '77

MCLAUGHLIN, Robert
Giving it back to the Indians. il map Atlantic 239:70-4+ F '77

MCLAUGHLIN, Robert J.
When a good try was not enough. Bus W p36-7 O 10 '77 *
MACLAURY, Bruce King
New set of exiles. por Forbes 119:67 F 1 '77 *
MACLAY, Elise
Green winter; excerpt. il Read Digest 110:106-9 Mr '77
I don't hear as well as I used to; Insights; This changing world; I keep forgetting things; My husband of so many years; Baskets; poems; excerpt from Green winter. McCalls 104:87, 236 F '77
MACLEAN, Fitzroy
Princesses for ransom: abduction in the grand style. il pors Horizon 19:82-7 Mr '77
MCLEAN, Malcom P.
Batten the hatches. por Forbes 120:156 O 15 '77 *
MACLEAN, Norman
Outdoors. Esquire 88:22+ O '77
MACLEAR, Frank
Head aches. il Motor B & S 141:90-3 Ja '78
MACLEISH, Archibald
Comment. R. Siegel. Poetry 130:102-7 My '77 *
MACLEISH, Kenneth
Leonardo da Vinci: a man for all ages. il Nat Geog 152:296-329 S '77
Mont Saint Michel. il map Nat Geog 151:820-31 Je '77
MACLELLAN, Esther and Schroll, C. V.
Test for a witch; drama. Plays 37:65-70 O '77
MCLEOD, Alan M. See Beale, A. V. jt auth
MACLEOD, Donald I. A. See Conner, J. D. jt auth
MCLOUGHLIN, John
American characters: John McLoughlin. D. Lavender. por Am Heritage 28:64-5 Je '77 *
Fort Vancouver. J. A. Hussey. bibl il por Am West 14:12-19+ S '77 *
MCLOUTH Steel Corporation
Tale of woe. Forbes 119:54 My 15 '77
MCLUCAS, John Luther
Requiem for a bureaucrat. Aviation W 106:23 Ap 25 '77
MCLURE, Charles E. Jr and Surrey, S. S.
Integration of income taxes: issues for debate. il Harvard Bus R 55:169-81 S '77
MCMAHON, A. M.
Computer communications; address, May 3, 1977. Vital Speeches 43:529-32 Je 15 '77
MCMAHON, Alexander
HEW's half-measure. E. Marshall. New Repub 176:8-10 My 7 '77 *
MCMAHON, Eugene J.
Why a constitutional convention is needed. America 137:12-14 Jl 2 '77
MCMAHON, Morgan E.
Restoring antique radios—how to get it started. il Radio-Electr 48:58-9 Ag '77
MCMANUS, Patrick F.
[Column] See issues of Field & stream
MCMANUS, Robert J. and Schneider, Jan
Shipwrecks, pollution & the law of the sea. Nat Parks & Con Mag 51:10-15 Je '77
MACMANUS, Yvonne
Paperback historical romance. Writer 90:33-5 Ap '77
MCMASTERS, A. J.
Boats & boating. See issues of Mechanix illustrated
MCMILLAN, Elizabeth, and Wymard, Eleanor
Marxism: its inadequacy as challenge to man-woman relationships. bibl il New Cath World 220:148-51 My '77
MACMILLAN, H. R, Planetarium, Vancouver. See Planetariums
MACMILLAN, Kenneth
Kenneth MacMillan's Requiem. H. Koegler. il por Dance Mag 51:56-8 Ap '77 *
MCMILLAN, Priscilla Johnson
Making of a marriage and of an assassin told in Harper & Row book for October; interview, ed by R. Dahlin. il pors Pub W 212: 46+ Jl 11 '77
Marina & Lee; excerpt. il pors Ladies Home J 94:175-82+ O; 122-3+ N '77
MACMILLAN Bloedel, Ltd
MacMillan Bloedel retreats to the woods. il por Bus W p28-9 Mr 7 '77
MCMILLEN, Joanne
How we turned our students on to organic gardening. il Org Gard & Farm 24:120+ F '77
MCMILLIAN, John G.
Cinderella's pipeline. A. J. Mayer and W. J. Cook. il por map Newsweek 90:87+ S 12 '77 *
MCMILLIN, Larry
Training model for junior high school communication aides. Engl J 66:52-3 Ap '77
MCMORRIS, Samuel C.
Smoking addiction. Current 189:33-8 Ja '77
MCMULLAN, James
Rigors of spring; reproductions of paintings. il Sports Illus 46:32-6 Mr 7 '77
MCMULLEN, Richard E.
Three leaves; poem. Commonweal 104:397 Je 24 '77
Trying to sleep; poem. Commonweal 104:168 Mr 18 '77
MCMULLEN, Roy
Beaubourg: a model or a portent. il Sat R 4: 52-5 Ja 22 '77
Boulez' IRCAM: amnesia in Nibelheim. il por Hi Fi 27:80-4 Ap '77
MCMURRAY, Patricia E. and Breslin, J. B.
Inaugural impressions. America 136:102-4 F 5 '77
MCMURTRY, Larry
Sky hunger. il Holiday 58:38-41+ Ap '77
MCNAIR, Bruce. See Goldenberg, R. jt auth
MCNALLY, Robert
Echolocation: cetaceans' sixth sense. il Oceans 10:27-33 Jl '77
To kill a whale. il Oceans 10:62-5 Ja '77
MCNAMARA, Joseph
Carter/Knox team wins a big one. J. Samson. pors Field & S 82:41+ S '77 *
MCNAMARA, Robert Strange
Dimensions of poverty; address, January 14, 1977. Vital Speeches 43:450-3 My 15 '77
How to defuse the population bomb; adaptation of address. il Time 110:93-4+ O 24 '77
Pittance for international aid; excerpt from address, October 4, 1976. il Bull Atom Sci 33: 36-8 N '77
World Bank head calls for special efforts to relieve poverty; excerpt from address, September 1977. UN Chron 14:40 O '77

about

Bureaucrats redux. B. Brower. map Harpers 254:25-6 Mr '77 *
House built on sand. J. Miller. New Repub 177: 19-21 S 3 '77; Reply. H. B. Hough. 177:5+ O 8 '77 *
Last question of summer. J. Lelyveld. il N Y Times Mag p47 S 4 '77 *
MCNASPY, Clement J.
Paraguay's lost paradise. il America 136:72-4 Ja 29 '77
Twelve stalwart women; Ursulines. America 136:373-5 Ap 23 '77
MACNAUGHTON, Donald Sinclair
Washington notebook. S. Booker. Ebony 33:25 D '77 *
MCNEELY, James D. and others
Student suicide epidemic. il Todays Educ 66: 70-3 S '77
MACNEIL, Neil
House shall chuse their Speaker. . . il Am Heritage 28:26-31 F '77
Whisperings in the press gallery; reply. Harpers 254:113+ Mr '77
MACNEIL, Richard D.
Opening minds and entryways at cultural centers. bibl il Parks & Rec 12:41-4 N '77
MACNEIL, Robert
Should US scientists trade data with USSR? Sci Digest 81:30-7+ Je '77
MCNEILL, John
Leveling of John McNeill. D. Berrigan. Commonweal 104:778-83 D 9 '77 *
MCNERNEY, Walter J.
Needed: a new direction for our medical system; interview. il por U.S. News 82:39-40+ Mr 28 '77
Voluntary health insurance. Cur Hist 73:9-12+ Jl '77
MCNICHOLS, Charles W. See Manley, T. R. jt auth
MCNIFF, Veronica
Fans can help you make energy savings. il House & Gard 149:88+ S '77
Give your house an energy update. House & Gard 149:38 Jl '77
MCNULTY, Faith
How to raise a woodchuck. il Audubon 79:50-5 Mr '77
MCNULTY, Henry P.
Memoir of Christmas in China. il House & Gard 149:74+ D '77
Tea teasers. il House & Gard 149:121+ F '77
Wonderful offbeat whiskey drinks. il House & Gard 149:154+ S '77
MACNUTT, Francis S.
Prayer for healing. il New Cath World 220:34-5 Ja '77
MCNUTT, Kristen W.
Office diet. il Harp Baz 110:90-1+ Je '77
MCPARTLAND, Jimmy
Our local correspondents. W. Balliett. il por New Yorker 53:80-6 S 5 '77 *
MCPETERS, W. Liddon
Estate planning for business owners. il por Nations Bus 65:67-8+ Je '77
MCPHEE, John
Encircled river; excerpt from Coming into the country. il por map Liv Wildn 41:44-60 Jl '77
Keel of Lake Dickey; reprint from May 3, 1976 issue of New Yorker. il map Liv Wildn 40:4-19+ O '76
Reporter at large (cont) New Yorker 53:47-8+ My 2; 88+ My 9; 43-4+ Je 20; 58-80 Je 27; 33-6+ Jl 4; 30-40+ Jl 11 '77

about

Well-done Alaska. il por Time 110:78+ D 5 '77 *

MCPHERSON, Aimee Semple
American characters. W. B. Hamilton. il por Am Heritage 28:62-3 O '77 *
MCPHERSON, Britt
Where and how to stow it. il por Yachting 141:98-9+ My '77
MCPHERSON, Don
Know your ABC. il Sat Eve Post 249:90+ My '77
MCPHERSON, Elizabeth
You can too build your own house. il Ms 5:49-51+ Je '77
MCPHERSON, Larry
Toast of Tompkinsville. W. F. Reed. il por Sports Illus 47:95-6+ D 19 '77 *
MACPHERSON, Myra
Cornelia Wallace: her struggle to save her troubled marriage. pors Ladies Home J 94:28+ F '77
Keeping up with Betty Ford. il por McCalls 105:206-7+ N '77
MCPHERSON, William
PW interviews; ed by S. Wagner. por Pub W 212:10-11 Ag 8 '77
MCQUADE, Walter
There's a saving grace in the new office lighting. il Fortune 96:151-4 D '77
Those annual physicals are worth the trouble. il Fortune 95:164-70+ Ja '77
Toughest hotel in the world to get into. il por Fortune 95:229-30 Mr '77
MCQUEEN, Steve
Ali & Steve; interview, ed by V. Scott. A. MacGraw. pors Ladies Home J 94:76+ N '77
MCQUILKIN, J. Robertson
Public schools: equal time for evangelicals. il Chr Today 22:8-11 D 30 '77
MCQUILLAN, M. Brendan
Spirit breathes where he wills. New Cath World 220:44-5 Ja '77
MCRAE, Bill
Camping with big game. il Field & S 82:58-60+ My '77
Girl learns to hunt. il pors Field & S 82:40-1+ O '77
MCRAE, Colleen
Girl learns to hunt. B. McRae. il pors Field & S 82:40-1+ O '77 *
MACRAE, Denis
Jazzing up your slide show. Pop Phot 80:114+ Je '77
MACRAMÉ
Macramé: a sampler becomes a handbag. S. La Pierre. il Design (US) 78:28-9 mid-Wint '77
MCREYNOLDS, Karman
French tarragon: hard-to-find herb. il Org Gard & Farm 24:88-9 N '77
MCROBERTS, Kenneth
Quebec and the Canadian political crisis. bibl f Ann Am Acad 433:19-31 S '77
MACROPHAGES
Angiotensin converting enzyme: induction by steroids in rabbit alveolar macrophages in culture. J. Friedland and others. bibl il Science 197:64-5 Jl 1 '77
Elastase release from human alveolar macrophages: comparison between smokers and nonsmokers. R. J. Rodriguez and others. bibl il Science 198:313-14 O 21 '77
Interferon: an inducer of macrophage activation by polyanions. R. M. Schultz and others. bibl il Science 197:674-6 Ag 12 '77
Macrophage tumor killing: influence of the local environment. J. B. Hibbs, Jr and others. bibl il Science 197:279-82 Jl 15 '77
Modulation of macrophage tumoricidal capability by components of normal serum: a central role for lipid. H. A. Chapman, Jr and J. B. Hibbs, Jr. bibl il Science 197:282-5 Jl 15 '77
Spotting invaders: which cells decide? Sci N 111:358 Je 4 '77
MACROPHOTOGRAPHY
Underwater, try macro. M. T. O'Keefe. il Pop Phot 81:90-1+ Ag '77
See also
Photomicrography
MACRORIE, Ken
Good works. Educ Digest 43:30-1 D '77
MACSHANE, Frank
Breath of satire in Chile. Nation 225:535-6 N 19 '77
MCSHANE, Yolande
Candid camera. il por Time 110:29 S 5 '77 *
No privacy? Newsweek 90:47 S 5 '77 *
MCSHINE, Kynaston
Earthbound and sublime. K. Evett. New Repub 176:29-30 Mr 5 '77 *
MCVEIGH, John J.
Hobby scene; questions and answers. See issues of Popular electronics including Electronics world
MCVEY, Marcia
Early childhood education, California-style. Educ Digest 43:14-16 D '77
MCWILLIAMS, Bernard F.
Married priests: one more try. America 136:416 My 7 '77
MCWILLIAMS, Mark L.
Power nomograph. il Pop Electr 12:69 O '77
MCWILLIAMS, Wilson Carey
Sadat initiative. Commonweal 104:806-8 D 23 '77

MACY, R. H, and Company
Cavorting in The Cellar. R. Kent. il Horizon 20:78-80 D '77
New Macy's greets Christmas; renovation of New York City store. il por Time 110:60 D 5 '77
MAD (periodical)
The Mad generation. A. Hiss and J. Lewis. il N Y Times Mag p 14-16+ Jl 31 '77
MADAGASCAR
Madagascar's mysterious meteorite. Sci N 112:102 Ag 13 '77
Meteorite fall reported in Madagascar. Sci N 112:86 Ag 6 '77

Foreign relations

France

See France—Foreign relations—Madagascar

Native races

Problem with simple folk; Tsimihety. P. J. Wilson. Natur Hist 86:26-8+ D '77
MADAMA Butterfly; opera. See Puccini, G.
MADAME Jumel; opera. See Wolf, A.
MADAME Tussaud's (waxworks) See Waxworks—Great Britain
MADDEN, Susan Brooks
Button up! SLJ 24:39 N '77
Reflections on corrections. il por Wilson Lib Bull 51:519-21 F '77
MADDIN, Robert
—and others
How the Iron Age began; with biographical sketches. il Sci Am 237:15, 122-31 O '77

about

From bronze to steel. Sci Am 236:61 My '77 *
MADDOCKS, Melvin
Inner life of a wealthy warrior. il pors Sports Illus 46:54-6+ My 23 '77
MADDOX, Robert J.
Doughboys in Siberia; excerpt from Unknown war with Russia. il Am Hist Illus 12:10-21 Ag '77
Teddy Roosevelt & the Rough Riders. il pors map Am Hist Illus 12:8-19 N '77
MADEIRA
Madeira. J. Anderson. Sat R 5:30 O 29 '77
MADEIRA wine. See Wine
MADELEY, John
Diego Garcia: a test of rights. America 136:461-2 My 21 '77
Rich world, poor world. Commonweal 104:423-4 Jl 8 '77
MADEMOISELLE (periodical)
Starting here . . . Mlle's 14 guest editors. il Mademoiselle 83:97-102 Ag '77
12 terrific women; winners of Mademoiselle awards. il Mademoiselle 83:144-7 F '77
MADEWELL, J. F. and Sexton, R. E.
Space stations for the international future. bibl il Space World N-9-165:4-40 S '77
MADHUBUTI, Haki R.
Big momma; Blackwoman; poems. Ebony 32:30 Ag '77
MADIGAN, John
Second City scold. il por Time 110:47-8 D 19 '77 *
MADISON, Robert J.
Low-fire porcelain for casting. il por Ceram Mo 25:38-9 N '77
MADISON, Ind.
Midwest gets Main Street Projects. il Am City & County 92:22-3 N '77
MADISON, Wis.

Education

There are no other children; special children in library media centers; Lapham Elementary School. E. T. Dresang. il SLJ 24:19-23 S '77

Music

See also
Opera—Wisconsin

Newspapers

Madison Connection. il Time 111:61 Ja 9 '78
See also
Strikes—United States—Newspapers

Politics and government

How Madison's radical mayor has mellowed with age; P. Soglin. T. Schultz. il pors N Y Times Mag p49+ Ap 17 '77

Strikes

See also
Strikes—United States—Newspapers
MADISON Civic Opera Association. See Opera—Wisconsin
MADISON Square Garden. See New York (city)—Madison Square Garden
MADISON Square Garden Corporation-Gulf and Western Industries, Inc merger. See Corporations—Acquisitions and mergers
MADNESS in motion pictures. See Motion pictures—Plots, themes, etc.
MADNICK, Stuart E.
Trends in computers and computing: the information utility. bibl il Science 195:1191-9 Mr 18 '77

MADRICK, Jeffrey
Inside Wall Street. See issues of Business week

MADRID
Reporter in Europe. J. Kramer. New Yorker 53:98+ Mr 21 '77

Description

Madrid: soul of the new Spain. H. Koenig and G. Koenig. il Travel 148:26-33 O '77

Libraries

Treasury of Hispanic lore. S. W. Byrd. il Améri-cas 29:10-13 Mr '77

MADRIGALS
See also
Phonograph records—Madrigals

MADSON, Chris
Claybird sharks. il Outdoor Life 160:84-5+ N '77

MADSON, John
Bee gums and long sweet'nin'. il Audubon 79: 32-7 S '77
Pheasants beyond autumn. il Outdoor Life 160: 64-6+ D '77
Secret life of the cottontail deer. il Outdoor Life 159:92-4+ Je '77

MAEROFF, Gene I.
Unfavored gifted few. il N Y Times Mag p30-2+ Ag 21 '77

MAFIA
America's newest crime syndicate—the Mexican Mafia. N. M. Adams. Read Digest 11:97-102 N '77
Chop-shop war; Mob murders in Chicago. R. Steele and C. J. Harper. Newsweek 90:22 Ag 15 '77
Cigar for the Mafia; C. Galante. il por Time 109:15 Mr 7 '77
Fingering a .22-cal. killer; arrest of J. Ullo in Los Angeles. Time 110:29+ S 26 '77
From mob to supermob; C. Marcello. L. Velie. por Read Digest 112:49-54 Ja '78
Has the Mafia penetrated the F.B.I? N. Gage. il N Y Times Mag p 14-16+ O 2 '77
How the Mafia invades business. O. Kelly. il U.S. News 82:21-2+ Je 13 '77
Mafia: big, bad and booming. il Time 109:32-3+ My 16 '77
Mafia's new godfather; C. Galante. por Read Digest 110:141-4 Je '77
Method acting; FBI infiltration of the International Longshoremen's Association. Time 109: 32+ F 7 '77
Mixing business and pleasure. il Time 109:16 My 30 '77
New Mafia killer: a silenced .22. il Time 109:22 Ap 18 '77
Pack tackles the Mob. D. Gelman and others. il Newsweek 89:85-6 Mr 28 '77
Putting heat on the Sunbelt Mafia; work of the Investigative Reporters and Editors Association. il Time 109:21-2 Mr 28 '77
Trouble in Las Vegas East; casino gambling in Atlantic City, N.J. il Time 111:14-15 Ja 16 '78
Victim no. 21; murder of Mafia lawyer, G. Gallina in New York City. Time 110:39 N 21 '77
Your Mafia cost of living. il Esquire 87:80-1+ F '77

Anecdotes, facetiae, satire, etc.

Galante can have it. R. Baker. N Y Times Mag p8 Mr 13 '77

MAGALIS, Elaine
Murder in Argentina. Chr Cent 94:1030-3 N 9 '77

MAGALLANES, Nicholas
Musical events. A. Croce. New Yorker 53:81-2 My 16 '77 *

MAGAZINE articles. See Periodical articles

MAGAZINE covers. See Periodical covers

MAGAZINE fiction. See Fiction in periodicals and newspapers

MAGAZINE illustration. See Illustration

MAGAZINE publishing. See Publishers and publishing—Periodicals

MAGAZINE stands, racks, etc.
Wall mounted magazine rack. il Bet Hom & Gard 55:74 O '77

MAGAZINES. See Periodicals

MAGAZINES, Childrens. See Childrens periodicals

MAGDALENA Bay
Where the whales put on a whale of a show; gray whales. R. F. Jones. il Sports Illus 46: 34-6+ Mr 28 '77

MAGDALENE, Mary, Saint. See Mary Magdalene

MAGEE, Sister M. Thomas
And gladly teach. Engl J 66:10-12 N '77

MAGELLAN, Strait of
Inside Cape Horn; excerpts. H. Roth. il Motor B & S 140:56-7+ Jl '77
Strait of Magellan: the ultimate passage. D. Connelly. il Sea Front 23:2-8 Ja '77

MAGELLANIC penguins. See Penguins

MAGGIO Musicale Fiorentino. See Music festivals—Italy

MAGIC
See also
Conjuring
Witchcraft

MAGIC Fishbone Bookshop, Carmel, Calif. See Booksellers and bookselling—California

MAGIC flute; opera. See Mozart, J. C. W. A.

MAGICIANS
See also
Diaconis, P.
Vaughn, J.

MAGIDA, Phylis
If pandas scream, an earthquake is coming! il Int Wildlife 7:36-9 S '77
Lure of the salt lick. il Int Wildlife 7:37 Mr '77

MAGILL, Dan
Georgia's on his mind. K. Hannon. il por Sports Illus 46:52-3 My 30 '77 *

MAGLEBY, Karl L. See Zengel J. E. jt auth

MAGMA tap power plants. See Steam power plants

MAGNETIC fields
Pulsed power from explosions. D. E. Thomsen. il Sci N 112:281+ O 29 '77

Measurement

Measuring minute magnetics; use of squids. D. E. Thomsen. il Sci N 111:234-5 Ap 9 '77

Physiological effects

Free-flying birds and geomagnetism. Sci N 111: 342 My 28 '77
Geomagnetic disturbance and the orientation of nocturnally migrating birds. F. R. Moore. bibl il Science 196:682-4 My 6 '77
Migrating birds respond to Project Seafarer's electromagnetic field. R. P. Larkin and P. J. Sutherland. bibl il Science 195:777-8 F 25 '77

MAGNETIC fields (cosmic physics)
Evidence for 10^{12}-gauss field on neutron star; Hercules X-1. B. G. Levi. il Phys Today 30: 19 Je '77
See also
Sun—Magnetic properties

MAGNETIC moments
New measurement of magnetic-moment anomaly tests QED. J. T. Scott. il Phys Today 30:17+ Mr '77
New measurement of muon magnetism. il Sci N 111:357-8 Je 4 '77

MAGNETIC poles. See Magnetism, Terrestrial

MAGNETIC resonance
See also
Nuclear magnetic resonance

MAGNETIC suspension vehicles
Super super trains of Europe. il Mech Illus 73: 90 Mr '77

MAGNETIC tape. See Tape, Magnetic

MAGNETIC trains. See Magnetic suspension vehicles

MAGNETISM
Magnetism of rare-earth metals. A. R. Mackintosh. bibl il Phys Today 30:23-30 Je '77

Physiological effects

See Magnetic fields—Physiological effects

MAGNETISM, Terrestrial
Polarity transition records and the geomagnetic dynamo. K. A. Hoffman. bibl il Science 196: 1329-32 Je 17 '77
See also
Auroras

MAGNETOCARDIOGRAPHY. See Cardiography

MAGNETOHYDRODYNAMICS
Giant magnet flow to Soviets; U.S.-USSR joint program to advance MHD technology. Aviation W 106:17 Je 27 '77

MAGNETOS
Magnetos—the spark of life; marine engines. il Motor B & S 140:46 Ag '77

MAGNETOSPHERE. See Atmosphere, Upper

MAGNETS
Powerful magnets find aerospace role. P. J. Klass. il Aviation W 107:66-7+ Ag 8 '77
Two magnets set records for field intensity. B. G. Levi. Phys Today 30:20 D '77

MAGNEY, John
Project Seafarer: Michigan's war against the Navy. Progressive 41:22-4 Jl '77

MAGNIN, Joseph, Company. See Clothing industry—United States

MAGOON, Robert
Mighty Magoon rides again. T. West. il por Motor B & S 140:51-3+ Jl '77 *
Revved up to ride on an ocean of trouble. R. Kennedy. il por Sports Illus 46:30-2+ Je 27 '77 *

MAGRIEL, Paul
Playing X-22. New Yorker 53:40-1 D 5 '77 *

MAGRUDER, Mary. See Magruder, R. jt auth

MAGRUDER, Richard, and Magruder, Mary
Blue Ridge of Georgia. il Travel 147:36-41+ F '77
Guanajuato. il Travel 148:38-43 O '77
Home on wheels. il Travel 147:58-63 Je '77
Houston. il Travel 147:36-9 My '77

MAGUIRE, Andrew
Excerpts from the debate on Federal Elections Campaign Act Amendments, April 1, 1976. Cong Digest 56:82+ Mr '77
MAGUIRE, Daniel C.
Unequal but fair. Commonweal 104:647-52 O 14 '77
MAGUIRE, Gerald L.
Excerpt from statement on retirement age policy, March 16, 1977. Cong Digest 56:278+ N '77
MAGUIRE, John W.
Using lunch time for effective community relations. Clearing H 51:5-6 S '77
MAGUIRE, Meg
Shortcut downtown for state resources. il Parks & Rec 12:22-5+ Je '77
Urban recreation study: doing it right. il Parks & Rec 12:28-31+ Ap '77
MAGUIRE, Robert
(tr) See Różewicz, T. Méliès
MAGUIRE, William M. See Meyer, G. E. jt auth
MAHAPATRA, Jayanta
Shadows; Ash; poems. Poetry 130:18-20 Ap '77
about
Comment. D. Allen. Poetry 130:350-2 S '77 *
MAHLENDORF, Ursula
Mörike's Mozart on the way to Prague. bibl f Am Imago 33:304-27 Fall '76
MAHLER, Gustav
Boulez and Mahler. B. H. Haggin. New Repub 176:25-7 Mr 12 '77 *
Die drei Pintos; RCA Red Seal recording. Hi Fi 27:110+ Jl '77 *
Fine new Mahler Ninth; Giulini recording; with discography of major works of Bruckner and Mahler. J. Diether. il por Am Rec G 40:24-6 Jl '77 *
Haitink's Mahler: much to commend; Des Knaben Wunderhorn. J. Diether. il Am Rec G 41:21-2+ N '77 *
Des Knaben Wunderhorn; Philips recording. A. Chipman. Hi Fi 27:94 D '77 *
Das Lied von der Erde. J. Diether. Am Rec G 40:21-2 Ap '77 *
Los Angeles Sym: Mahler's Eighth. il Hi Fi 27: MA17-19 N '77 *
Mahler everyone loves. S. Lipman. Commentary 64:55-60 N '77 *
Mahler marathon; New York Philharmonic September-October festival. P. J. Smith. por Hi Fi 27:MA20-1 F '77 *
Symphony no. 3. G. S. Fox. Am Rec G 40: 25-6 My '77 *
Symphony no. 4 in G. G. S. Fox. Am Rec G 40: 22-3 Ap '77 *
Weber/Mahler hybrid; Die drei Pintos; Bertini recording. N. F. Karlins. Am Rec G 40:37-9 Jl '77 *
MAHLMANN, Lewis
Nutcracker Prince; drama. Plays 37:81-4 D '77
MAHOGANY, Mountain. See Mountain mahogany
MAHON, Gigi
Dollars and sense. Mademoiselle 83:42+ S; 122 O; 22+ N; 26 D '77
MAHONEY, Brooke W. See Mittenthal R. A. jt auth
MAHONING River
Safe water or jobs? A classic confrontation; Mahoning River Valley and the steel industry. il U.S. News 82:47 F 7 '77
MAHOOD, Wayne
And they lived unhappily ever after. Clearing H 50:373-4 Ap '77
MAHRE, Phil
Starting out with a chaser. A. Verschoth. il pors Sports Illus 46:54-6 Ja 17 '77 *
They doubled the pleasure. W. O. Johnson. il pors Sports Illus 46:12-15 Mr 14 '77 *
MAHRE, Steve
They doubled the pleasure. W. O. Johnson. il pors Sports Illus 46:12-15 Mr 14 '77 *
MAIDENEK concentration camp. See Concentration camps—Poland
MAIDENHAIR ferns. See Ferns
MAIER, Cornell C.
Into the promised land. por Forbes 120:30-1 Jl 15 '77 *
MAIL advertising. See Advertising, Direct mail
MAIL censorship. See Postal censorship
MAIL chutes
Roomier place for the mail. il Sunset 159:132 O '77
MAIL order business
Buying hardcover books. il Consumer Rep 42:505-13 S '77
Buying quilt fabrics by mail. il Bet Hom & Gard 55:79+ Ap '77
Food gifts by mail. il Sunset 159:120+ N '77
Gourmet tips for mail-order menus. J. Wilson. il House & Gard 149:149+ S '77
If you're mail-ordering gifts. . . Changing T 31:4 D '77
Mail order buying. E. Orr. Motor T 29:52-4 Ap; 68-72 My '77
Mail-order maps; topographic maps. S. Netherby. Field & S 82:174 S '77
More food gifts by mail. Sunset 159:130 D '77
Publisher's letter; question of advertising ethics in nursery mailorder business. R. J. Fibkins. Horticulture 55:96 F '77
Sale away; mail ordering. A. Wilson. Seventeen 36:59 S '77
Shop by mail and love it. S. Auerbach. Am Home 80:19 N '77
Shopping by mail; with catalog list. M. Gough. House B 119:48+ S '77
Special delivery. P. Sadowsky; G. Steves. il Am Home 80:46-7+ N '77
See also
Sears, Roebuck and Company
MAIL order catalogs. See Catalogs, Commercial
MAIL service. See Postal service
MAIL service, Railway. See Railway mail service
MAILBOXES
Target: the checks in your mailbox. H. Gluck. il Ret Liv 16:25-6+ D '76
MAILER, Norman
Of a small and modest malignancy, wicked and bristling with dots. Esquire 88:125-48 N '77
Our man at Harvard. il Esquire 87:110-12 Ap '77
about
Celebrity monger. Nation 225:485-6 N 12 '77 *
MAILING lists
Missing names and the missions. E. E. Plowman. Chr Today 21:51-3 S 23 '77
MAIN, Jeremy
They don't make 'em like they used to. Read Digest 110:167-8+ Mr '77
Who's a good credit risk? Read Digest 110:197+ My '77
MAIN Street Project. See National Trust for Historic Preservation
MAINA, William, and French, Beverlee
Health info for all: San Diego meet. Lib J 102: 1552-3 Ag '77
MAINE
Cold; Maine winters. J. N. Cole. il N Y Times Mag p71 Ja 30 '77; Same abr. with title Cold comforts. Read Digest 112:157-60 Ja '78
U.S. journal: Maine; activities of M. J. Dodge III. C. Trillin. New Yorker 53:112+ O 10 '77
Way of life called Maine. E. A. Starbird. il map Nat Geog 151:726-57 Je '77
See also
Architecture, Domestic—Maine
Botany—Maine
Camps—Maine
Deer Island
Environmental policy—Maine
Forests and forestry—Maine
Hospitals—Maine
Isle Au Haut
Land tenure—Maine
Music festivals—Maine
St John River

Antiquities

Rock art and the power of shamans; petroglyphs of the Abnaki Indians. D. R. Snow. il Natur Hist 86:42-9 bibl(p 100) F '77

Description and travel

Rugged, fragile Maine. J. T. Starr. il Am For 83:14-17+ My '77

Parks and reserves

As Baxter Park burns, so burns Maine. A. Gauvin. il maps Audubon 79:146-53 S '77; Reply. J. L. Baxter, Sr. 79:128 N '77

Photographs

Timeless summers in old-time Maine; work of C. S. Emmons. D. Seiberling. il pors N Y Times Mag p 18-19+ Jl 24 '77

Restaurants

See Restaurants—United States

Transportation, Department of

Man can create a marsh. F. Graham, Jr. Audubon 79:140 S '77
MAINE. University, Orono

Library

Special report: book return lag? Try promos; radio promotions. C. Huntley. Wilson Lib Bull 52:294-5 D '77
MAINES, Mahin D. and Kappas, Attallah
Metals as regulators of heme metabolism. bibl il Science 198:1215-21 D 23 '77
MAINPRIZE, D. and Mann, P.
Educating adolescents with emotional and delinquency problems. bibl Clearing H 50:403-5 My '77
MAINSTREAMING (education) See Children, Handicapped—Education; Handicapped—Education
MAIRS, Robert L.
Gulf Stream analyses. map Yachting 142:36+ D '77
That October storm. il Yachting 141:82-3+ Mr '77
Weather forecasting for the racing sailor. il map Yachting 142:66-9+ Ag '77

MAIZE, Kennedy P.
Great Kern County mouse war. il Audubon 79: 158-60 N '77
How to buy at a farm auction. il Org Gard & Farm 24:114-18 My '77
MAIZE. See Corn
MAJESKI, Bill
Dracula returns; drama. Plays 36:25-36 My '77
Midnight ride of. . .who? drama. Plays 36:63-8 Ap '77
Not-so-wide world of sports; drama. Plays 37: 71-6, 83 N '77
Old-time melodrama—modern style; drama. Plays 37:17-26 O '77
MAJOR, Mike
Photography story without photos. America 137: 192-4 O 1 '77
MAJOR Religious Superiors, Inter-American Conference of. See Inter-American Conference of Major Religious Superiors
MAJORS, Farrah Fawcett-. See Fawcett-Majors, F.
MAJORS, Johnny
That orange shirt means something. J. Underwood. il Sports Illus 46:68-72+ Mr 28 '77 *
MAKAGIANSAR, Makaminan
Rubens: a 400th anniversary tribute. il UNESCO Courier 30:4 Je '77
UNESCO and world problems of communication. il UNESCO Courier 30:4-10 Ap '77
MAKAH Indian village excavation. See Washington (state)—Antiquities
MAKARIOS III, Abp
Obituary
Chr Today 21:39 Ag 26 '77. J. D. Douglas
Passing of the dark priest. il por Time 110: 32+ Ag 15 '77 *
Politician-priest. R. Carroll and P. Martin. il por Newsweek 90:32 Ag 15 '77 *
MAKAROVA, Natalia
Makarova: the sublime paradox; interview, ed by O. Maynard. il por Dance Mag 51:59-74 Ap '77
about
Dance Magazine Awards 1977. il pors Dance Mag 51:30-5 Jl '77 *
MAKE-up
Beauty: color '77; new products. B. Morris. il Vogue 167:282-91+ O '77
Daytime glow—nighttime dazzle. il Redbook 150: 126-9 N '77
Elizabeth Taylor. il pors Good H 185:118-20 O '77
Eyes; excerpts from Adrien Arpel's three week makeover. A. Newman. il Ladies Home J 94: 22+ D '77
Fall beauty news. il Vogue 167:318-23 S '77
Great new looks from top designers. il Harp Baz 110:146-53 O '77
How to individualize your make-up. Harp Baz 110:116-19 F '77
How to wake up your makeup. Seventeen 36: 120 S '77
Making eyes. il Redbook 148:96-7 F '77
Many faces of Eve. il Am Home 80:62 Mr '77
Nobody's perfect. M. Lynch. il Ladies Home J 94:108-11 My '77
Romantic faces of fall. il McCalls 104:166-71 S '77
Round-the-clock focus on eyes. il Good H 185: 144-7 N '77
Step-by-step guide to a new you. il Good H 186:90-3 Ja '78
Transforming faces; interview, ed by A. Penny. W. Bandy. il N Y Times Mag p 129-31 S 25 '77
Way Bandy's makeup book; excerpt from Designing your face. W. Bandy. il Good H 185: 121-5 O '77
See also
Beauty, Personal
MAKHLOUF, Sharbel, Saint. See Sharbel Makhlouf, Saint
MAKI, Fumihiko
Growing of grids. il Archit Rec 161:107-12 Ap '77 *
MAKLAN, David Mark
How blue-collar workers on 4-day workweeks use their time; excerpt from The four-day workweek. bibl il M Labor R 100:18-26 Ag '77
MAKOFSKY, David
Malpractice and medicine. bibl il Society 14:25-9 Ja '77
MAKOSINSKI, Arthur
Infrared systems for wireless stereo. il Pop Electr 12:70+ O '77
MAKSYMOWYCH, Roman, and Erickson, R. O.
Phyllotaxis in xanthium shoots altered by gibberellic acid. bibl il Science 196:1201-3 Je 10 '77
MAKUCK, Peter
Street lamps; poems. Nation 224:733 Je 11 '77
MALACOLOGY. See Mollusks
MALAGASY Republic. See Madagascar
MALAMUD, Bernard
Dubin's lives; story. New Yorker 53:38-50 Ap 18; 36-47 Ap 25 '77
Home is the hero; story; excerpt from novel. Atlantic 241:42-9+ Ja '78

MALARIA
Malaria makes a comeback. il Time 110:64 S 12 '77
Malaria: resurgence in research brightens prospects. T. H. Maugh, 2d. Science 196:413-14+ Ap 22 '77
Prevention and control
Editorial page; spraying for malaria. A. McGowan. Environment 19:inside cover, 44 O '77
Effective immunization of experimental monkeys against a human malaria parasite, plasmodium falciparum. W. A. Siddiqui. bibl il Science 197:388-9 Jl 22 '77
See also
Antimalarials
Malaria—Vaccines
Vaccines
Malaria, herpes vaccines: progress. Sci N 112:55 Jl 23 '77
MALARIAL parasites. See Plasmodium (parasite)
MALATESTA, Peter
For big fish only. M. Cimons. New Repub 177: 14-15 Jl 9 '77 *
MALAYSIA
Letter from Malaysia. R. Shaplen. New Yorker 53:109-31 Ap 18 '77
Malaysia: youthful nation with growing pains. W. S. Ellis. il map Nat Geog 151:634-67 My '77
See also
Government ownership—Malaysia
Loans, Bank—Malaysia
Singapore
Water pollution—Malaysia
Industries
See also
Petroleum industry—Malaysia
Politics and government
Singapore/Malaysia: sweatshop for the world. K. Bird and F. Y. Teng. Nation 225:242-4 S 17 '77
MALCOLM, Andrew H.
Family's affair with Japan. il N Y Times Mag p36-8 Jl 10 '77; Same abr. Read Digest 111: 145-8 D '77
MALCOLM, Janet
Photography (cont) New Yorker 53:107-11 O 10 '77
MALCOLM, Sarah, pseud
I am a second-generation lesbian; excerpt from We are everywhere: a celebration of lavender culture. Ms 6:13-16 O '77
MALDONADO, Rita M.
Why Puerto Ricans migrated to the United States in 1947-73. bibl il M Labor R 99:7-11 S '76; 100:34-5 Ag '77
about
Sorrentino, Maldonado, Klein Award winners M Labor R 100:2 Ap '77 *
MALE birth control clinics. See Birth control clinics
MALE models. See Models (persons)
MALENBAUM, Gloria Balaban-. See Balaban-Malenbaum, G.
MALESKA, Eugene T.
Will Weng's farewell puzzle. W. Weng. pors N Y Times Mag p73 F 27 '77 *
MALFORMATIONS. See Deformities
MALI
See also
Timbuktu
MALIBU, Calif.
Galleries and museums
Getty's little house on the highway. J. Didion. Esquire 87:30+ Mr '77
Getty's little palace in Malibu. J. Morgenstern. il Art N 76:72-5 Mr '77
J. Paul Getty's legacy: what is in store for the garden of the billionaire's whim? A. Eliot. il Horticulture 55:10-13 N '77
MALIN, Michael C. and Saunders, R. S.
Surface of Venus: evidence of diverse landforms from radar observations. bibl il Science 196: 987-90 My 27 '77
MALINCONICO, S. Michael
Another view from the Belgian front. Lib J 102:2484-5 D 15 '77
Library catalog in a computerized environment; adaptation of address, October 1975. bibl il Wilson Lib Bull 51:53-64, 724-5 S '76, My '77
MALINOVICH, Myriam Miedzian
On natural childbirth. Mademoiselle 83:30-1+ Mr '77
MALKIEL, Burton Gordon
Reports of the death of common stocks are greatly exaggerated. il Fortune 96:156-60+ N '77
MALKIN, Myron
Truckin' into orbit—with the space shuttle; interview. il por Sr Schol 110:4-5+ O 20 '77
MALLALIEU, H. B.
Voyage to Naxos; poem. Poetry 130:321-36 S '77
MALLARD ducks. See Ducks, Wild

MALLET, John
Glenys Barton at Wedgwood. il Ceram Mo 25: 28-30 O '77
MALLORY, G. Kenneth
Charles Scammon: whaler turned naturalist. il Oceans 10:40-4 Jl '77
MALLOZZI, Robert
High cost of whistling. T. Nicholson and others. pors Newsweek 89:75+ F 14 '77 *
MALLS, Shopping. See Shopping centers
MALOFF, Bruce L. and others
Membrane potential of mitochondria measured with microelectrodes. bibl il Science 195:898-900 Mr 4 '77
MALOFF, Saul
Dead writers: a parable. Commonweal 104:307-9 My 13 '77
Poetry and power. il por Commonweal 104:215-18 Ap 1 '77
Staying in touch. por Commonweal 104:371-4 Je 10 '77
Vladimir Nabokov: the emigre. por Commonweal 105:18-20 Ja 6 '78
MALONE, Bobby. See Maxon, R. C. jt auth
MALONE, John
Momentum mobili; story. Ms 5:58-61 My '77
MALONE, Michael
On one who wrote not wisely but to sell. Nation 224:597-8 My 14 '77
MALONE, Robert
Is there a robot in your future? Yes, there is. At least in a Harvest/HBJ spring paperback; interview, ed by R. Dahlin. il Pub W 212:30 D 5 '77
MALONEY, Elbert S.
Notices to boatmen. See issues of Motor boating & sailing
Pilot charts—and how to use them. il map Motor B & S 139:30+ My '77
Sailings: determining course and distance without a chart. map Motor B & S 139:84+ F '77
Sailings: useful applications. il Motor B & S 139:84+ Mr '77
MALONEY, Henry B.
In your head. Engl J 66:10-11 O '77
MALOTT, Robert Harvey
Myopia and multinationals; address, February 7, 1977. Vital Speeches 43:363-6 Ap 1 '77
about
Better management urged for company contributions. por Nations Bus 65:58 Ag '77 *
MALPIGHIAN vessels
Temporal control of urate oxidase activity in drosophila: evidence of an autonomous timer in Malpighian tubules. T. B. Friedman and D. H. Johnson. bibl il Science 197:477-9 Jl 29 '77
MALPRACTICE
Ethics, medical malpractice and the church. G. L. Haines. Chr Cent 94:1003-5 N 2 '77; Reply. T. E. Daniel. 94:1227-8 D 28 '77
Lawyers who sue lawyers. L. Scott. il N Y Times Mag p74-8 Je 26 '77
Malpractice and medicine. D. Makofsky. bibl il Society 14:25-9 Ja '77
Malpractice in the schools. J. C. Baratz and T. W. Hartle. Progressive 41:33-4 Je '77
Medical malpractice suits. D. Conrad. bibl f il Cur Hist 73:22-6+ Jl '77
Suing the teacher. Newsweek 90:101 O 3 '77
Why medical-malpractice furor is dying down. U.S. News 83:70-1 Jl 4 '77
MALPRACTICE liability insurance. See Insurance, Malpractice liability
MALRAUX, André
Malraux: engaged intellectual. E. Pawel. Nation 224:89-91 Ja 22 '77 *
Malraux mystery. G. Hartman. New Repub 176: 27-30 Ja 29 '77 *
MALTA
International Ocean Institute. E. M. Borgese. il Oceans 10:52-7 Ja '77
See also
Airlines—Malta
Investments, Foreign—Malta
Economic relations
Arab countries
See Arab countries—Economic relations—Malta
MALVIN, Richard L. and others
Angiotensin: physiological role in water-deprivation—induced thirst of rats. bibl il Science 197:171-3 Jl 8 '77
MALYA, Simoni
After literacy, what next? il UNESCO Courier 30:25-7 F '77
MAMET, David
American buffalo. Reviews
America 136:364 Ap 16 '77 *
Nation 224:313 Mr 12 '77 *
New Yorker 53:54+ F 28 '77 *
Sat R 4:37 Ap 2 '77 *
Time 109:54+ F 28 '77 *
Language equals action. S. Lawson. il pors Horizon 20:40-5 N '77 *
Life in the theatre. Reviews
America 137:423 D 10 '77 *
Nation 225:504 N 12 '77 *
New Yorker 53:115-16 O 31 '77 *
Time il 110:94 O 31 '77 *
Muzak man. J. Kroll. il por Newsweek 89:79 F 28 '77 *
Water engine. Review
Newsweek 91:69 Ja 16 '78 *
MAMILLAH district. See Jerusalem
MAMIYA, Richard T.
New freeways for the heart. G. Cant. il por Time 109:55-6 My 9 '77 *
MAMMALS
Minimum size of mammalian homeotherms: role of the thermal environment. C. R. Tracy. bibl il Science 198:1034-5 D 9 '77
Monogamous mammals: variations on a scheme. M. G. Riegel. il Sci N 112:76-8 Jl 30 '77
Our allotted lifetimes. S. J. Gould. Natur Hist 86:34+ Ag '77
See also
Bats
Cetacea
Marine mammals
Marsupials
Rodents
Ruminants
Whales
MAMMALS, Fossil
South American geochronology: radiometric time scale for middle to late Tertiary mammal-bearing horizons in Patagonia. L. G. Marshall and others. bibl il map Science 195:1325-8 Mr 25 '77
MAMMARY glands
See also
Breast
MAMMOGRAPHY
Are breast X-rays safe? P. Strax. il Parents Mag 52:48-9+ F '77
Breast X rays: who should take the risk? J. Chan. il McCalls 104:43-4 Mr '77
Cancer institute unilaterally issues new restrictions on mammography. B. J. Culliton. Science 196:853-5+ My 20 '77
Mammography. J. Rodgers. Ladies Home J 94: 88+ My '77
Mammography controversy: NIH's entrée into evaluating technology. B. J. Culliton. Science 198:171-3 O 14 '77
What every woman should know about breast X-ray; interview, ed by W. S. Ross. B. F. Byrd, Jr. Read Digest 110:116-20 Mr '77
MAMMON
Language of Mammon. L. H. Lapham. Harpers 254:12+ F '77
MAMMOTH Cave National Park
NPCA exposes concessioner's misrepresentation of profits. Nat Parks & Con Mag 51:23-4 S '77
MAMMOTHS
Frozen mammoths from Siberia bring the Ice Ages to vivid life. J. M. Stewart. il Smithsonian 8:60-9 bibl(p 134) D '77
MAMOU, La.
Run in Mamou; Mardi Gras celebration. H. Camp. Newsweek 89:10 Mr 14 '77
MAN
History in books: pot-pourri of collected reflections. P. W. Schmidtchen. il Hobbies 82:134-7+ Je '77
See also
Anthropometry
Civilization
Ethnology
Evolution
History
Human relations
Philosophical anthropology
Psychology
Attitude and movement
See also
Posture
Influence of environment
Environment factor: beauty/health hazard or helper? N. Simon. il Vogue 167:164-7+ Ag '77
Jensen: environment is a factor in IQ. Sci N 111:390 Je 18 '77
See also
Environmental health
Influence on nature
Are deserts man-made? M. El-Kassas. il UNESCO Courier 30:4-6 Jl '77
Despairing optimist. . . R. Dubos. Am Scholar 46:280-1+ Summ '77
Precarious balance upset; increase in aridification. V. A. Kovda. il map UNESCO Courier 30:11-14 Jl '77
Vermont's magnificent amateur; special issue; with editorial comment. Am For 83:4, 6+ S '77
See also
Environmental design

MAN—*Continued*

Migrations

Spread of the Bantu language. D. W. Phillipson. il maps Sci Am 236:106-14 bibl(p 148) Ap '77

Origin and antiquity

Puzzling out man's ascent; work of R. E. F. Leakey. il pors Time 110:64-7+ N 7 '77; Reply. Chr Today 22:34 D 9 '77
Where did I come from? a question of origins. H. Lindsell. Chr Today 21:16-18 Je 17 '77
See also
Man, Prehistoric

Periodicity

See Biology—Periodicity

MAN (theology)
Is man's purpose an enigma? W. W. Gasque. Chr Today 21:15-17 Jl 29 '77
Myth of the self-sufficient man; excerpt from address. M. N. Beck. Chr Today 21:12-16 S 23 '77
Nixon's Watergate—man's depravity; human nature and the image of God. D. M. Howard. Chr Today 21:12-14 Je 3 '77
See also
Fall of man

MAN, Erect position of. See Posture

MAN, Prehistoric
Bound for glory; discovery of Peking Man. R. C. Andrews. Sat Eve Post 249:19 Jl '77
Ecology of early man in Southern Africa. R. G. Klein. bibl il map Science 197:115-26 Jl 8 '77
Hominoid enamel prism patterns. D. G. Gantt and others. bibl il Science 198:1155-7 D 16 '77
Human evolution: hominoids of the miocene. G. B. Kolata. Science 197:244-5+ Jl 15 '77
Orthogenesis of the hominids: an exploration using biorthogonal grids. F. L. Bookstein. bibl il Science 197:901-4 Ag 26 '77
Pakistan fossils: new origins for man. map Sci N 111:244 Ap 16 '77
Ramaphithecus. E. L. Simons. il map Sci Am 236:28-35 My '77
Suid evolution and correlation of African hominid localities. T. D. White and J. M. Harris. bibl il maps Science 198:13-21 O 7 '77
Tooth patterns and the human-ape split. il Sci N 112:405 D 17 '77
See also
Cave drawings and paintings
Man—Origin and antiquity
Paleo-Indians
Piltdown forgery
Stone implements and weapons

Anecdotes, facetiae, satire, etc.

Ancestral voices. H. F. Ellis. New Yorker 53: 33-5 Mr 14 '77

MAN and nature. See Man—Influence on nature

MAN and superman; drama. See Shaw, G. B.

MAN and the Biosphere program. See Unesco

MAN of La Mancha; musical comedy. See Musical comedy, review, etc.—Reviews—Single works

MAN of the Year Awards (Motor trend) See Motor Trend Awards

MAN-powered airplanes. See Airplanes, Light

MAN with bags; drama. See Ionesco, E.

MANAGEMENT
Why things don't work any more. J. Diebold. por Newsweek 90:8-9 Jl 18 '77
See also
Art galleries and museums—Management
Business management
Communication in management
Farm management
School management and organization
United States—Navy—Management
Wildlife management

MANAGEMENT and Budget, Office of. See United States—Management and Budget, Office of

MANAGEMENT buyouts (business) See Employee ownership

MANAGEMENT consultants. See Business consultants

MANAGEMENT development programs. See Executives—Training

MANAGEMENT of children. See Children—Management and training

MANAGER plan, City. See City manager plan

MANAGERS, Baseball. See Baseball managers

MANAR, Hugh E. See Davis, W. W. jt auth

MANATEES
Precarious survival of the Florida manatee. J. E. Reynolds. 3d. il Oceans 10:50-3 S '77

MANCHESTER, Harland
Triumph of miniaturization: the transistor; excerpt from New trail blazers of technology. il Sci Digest 81:57-60 Ap '77

MANCOTT, Anatol
Chemical relevance—a heuristic approach (cont) Chemistry 50:24 Mr; 26 Ap; 28 My '77
Mathematics of first-order rate reactions. il por Chemistry 50:23-4 D '77

MANDANS Indians
Winter at Fort Clarke: Maximilian and Bodmer among the tribes of the Upper Missouri, 1833-1834; with reproductions of paintings; excerpt from People of the first man, ed by D. Thomas and K. Ronnefeldt. A. P. Maximilian. Am West 14:36-47 Ja '77

MANDARIN (restaurant) See San Francisco—Hotels, restaurants, etc.

MANDATORY retirement. See Retirement

MANDEL, Leon
[Column] (cont) Car & Dr 22:12+ Mr; 24 My; 16+ Je; 23:12 S '77

MANDEL, Marvin
Changing the rules. K. Bode. New Repub 177: 16-17 S 17 '77 *
Help from his friends. R. Boeth. il por Newsweek 90:20 S 5 '77 *
Mandel verdict: a warning to officials. il por U.S. News 83:46 S 5 '77 *
Trouble in the boys' club. A. Tyler. New Repub 177:16-19 Jl 30 '77 *
Verdict: bye-bye, Marvin. il por Time 110:20 S 5 '77 *

MANDELBAUM, Michael
Nuclear exporters cartel. bibl il Bull Atom Sci 33:42-50 Ja '77

MANDELONITRILE glucuronide. See Laetrile

MANDEL'SHTAM, Nadezhda
Nadezhda Mandelstam: memoir as prophecy. L. Basney. Chr Today 21:20-1 Jl 29 '77 *

MANDEL'SHTAM, Osip Emil'evich
Nadezhda Mandelstam: memoir as prophecy. L. Basney. Chr Today 21:20-1 Jl 29 '77 *

MANDLER, Walter
Schwalberg at large. B. Schwalberg. por Pop Phot 81:52+ Ag '77 *

MANDRAKE; drama. See Machiavelli, N.

MANEN, Carol-Ann, and Russell, D. H.
Ornithine decarboxylase may function as an initiation factor for RNA polymerase I. bibl il Science 195:505-6 F 4 '77

MANESS, Bill
Exercise: it ain't watcha do, it's the way that ya do it. il Fam Health 9:34-5 Ap '77

MANEUVERS, Military. See Military maneuvers

MANGANESE
Mining the wealth of the ocean deep. W. Wertenbaker. il N Y Times Mag p 14-16+ Jl 17 '77

MANGANESE additives. See Gasoline—Additives

MANGES, Clinton P.
How a Texas maverick lost one of his banks. il por Bus W p84+ Ja 24 '77 *

MANGIERI, Adolph A.
New no-camera printed circuit board methods. il Pop Electr 11:55-8 My '77
Wire-wrapping techniques for computer hobbyists. il Pop Electr 12:74-6+ D '77

MANGO melons. See Melons

MANGOSTEENS
Maltese fruit. R. Sokolov. Atlantic 240:32+ O '77

MANGROVE
Mangroves: trees that help build the land. L. E. Jerome. il Oceans 10:38-45 S '77
Tree nobody liked; red mangrove in Florida Gulf Coast area. R. Gore. il map Nat Geog 151:668-89 My '77

MANGROVE (dance company) See Dance companies

MANHATTAN. See New York (city)

MANHATTAN School of Music
Manhattan School: Wolf-Ferrari's I quattro rusteghi. il Hi Fi 27:MA30-2 Jl '77
Musical events:
Paul Bunyan. A. Porter. New Yorker 53: 124-6 +My 2 '77

MANHEIM, Ralph
(tr) See Handke, P. Left-handed woman

MANIC-depressive psychoses
From joy to depression: new insights into the chemistry of moods. M. Scarf. il N Y Times Mag p30-4+ Ap 24 '77; Same abr. with title What makes our moods? Read Digest 111: 45-7+ Ag '77
Lithium: effects on subjective functioning and morphine-induced euphoria. D. R. Jasinski and others. bibl il Science 195:582-4 F 11 '77
Manic depression—a chemical disorder? Chemistry 50:25 N '77

MANICURING
Handle with care. C. B. Abbott. il Am Home 80:32+ D '77
Nail file. B. Dubivsky. il N Y Times Mag p72+ F 27 '77
Shaping up your nails. il Seventeen 36:128 Jl '77
Two ways to terrific nails. il Redbook 149:134-5+ My '77
What to do, what to use for better nails; questions and answers. A. Shansky. il Harp Baz 110:58 F '77

MANIFEST destiny (United States) See Messianism, American

MANIFOLDS
Holley's system. G. Witzenburg. il Motor T 29:73-4+ N '77
Missing link; intake manifolds. G. Baskerville. il Hot Rod 30:48-9 My '77
Wide open. il Hot Rod 30:89-92+ Je '77

MANILA
Manila today. J. Ferri. il Trav/Holiday 149:40-3+ Ja '78

Religious institutions and affairs

Billy Graham's mission to Manila. H. Lindsell. il Chr Today 22:36-7 D 30 '77

MANIPULATION (psychology) See Behavior (psychology)

MANITOBA
See also
Winnipeg

MANKIEWICZ, Jane
Strategies, mostly kind; story. New Yorker 53: 38-42 Mr 28 '77

MANKIEWICZ, Joseph Leo
Careers of two major Hollywood directors unreel in a pair of spring titles. R. Dahlin. il por Pub W 212:40 N 21 '77 *

MANLEY, Frank
Retardation center; poem. Am Scholar 46:180 Spr '77

MANLEY, Michael Norman
Talk with Manley; excerpt from interview, ed by A. De Borchgrave. por Newsweek 89:38 F 28 '77

about

Cartel that never was. il Forbes 119:30-2 Mr 1 '77 *
Cuba's role in Jamaica. A. De Borchgrave. il por Newsweek 89:37-8 F 28 '77 *
Heavy manners in Jamaica. A. Bonner. Nation 224:80-4 Ja 22 '77 *
Jamaican limbo. F. Fitzgerald. Harpers 255:10+ Jl '77 *
Michael Manley: Jamaica's born-again socialist. B. Hale. por Chr Cent 94:1117-19 N 30 '77 *

MANLEY, Phyllis
Phyllis Manley combines two worlds; interview, ed by J. McCord. il por Am Artist 41:40-5+ Mr '77

MANLEY, T. Roger, and McNichols, C. W.
Scientists, engineers, and unions, revisited. il M Labor R 100:32-3 N '77

MANLEY, Will
Snowballs in the book drop. il Lib J 102:2138-9 O 15 '77

MANN, Dale
Politics of changing schools. Educ Digest 43:6-9 O '77

MANN, E. B.
It's a Daisy. il Field & S 82:64-9 O '77
Our endangered tradition. See issues of Field & stream

MANN, George V.
We need more beef dollars to counter nutrition myths. Farm J 101:Beef 20+ Ja '77 *

MANN, Heinrich
Heinrich Mann and Der Untertan. M. Kowal. Nation 225:346-8 O 8 '77 *

MANN, Hugo
A German expands in U.S. retailing. il Bus W p34-5 Ag 15 '77 *

MANN, James
End of youth culture. il U.S. News 83:54-6 O 3 '77; Same. Current 197:3-7 N '77

MANN, Murray Gell-. See Gell-Mann, M.

MANN, P. See Mainprize, D. jt auth

MANN, Peggy
(ed) European teens: would they like to be Americans? interviews. il Seventeen 36:96-7 Jl '77

MANN, Roger
Marriage-law controversy in Kenya. Chr Cent 94:457 My 11 '77
Missionaries, '70s style. Chr Cent 94:839-40 S 28 '77

MANN, Thomas
Achieving the impossible: Thomas Mann. H. Hatfield. Yale R 66:501-16 Je '77 *
Mann letters. L. Kriegel. Nation 225:309-11, 343-6 O 1-8 '77 *

MANN, Tom
Bassin' Mann; interview, ed by P. Miller. il pors Outdoor Life 159:55-7+ Mr '77

about

Tom Mann's best summer bass bets. K. Schultz. il Field & S 82:48+ Jl '77 *

MANNERS, J. Hartley
Peg o' my heart. Review
New Yorker 53:68 Mr 14 '77 *

MANNERS and customs
Memories that make families strong. G. Shipman. il por Parents Mag 52:30-1+ D '77
See also
Clothing and dress
Costume
Courtesy
Etiquette
Funeral rites and ceremonies
Hand shaking
Kissing
Popular culture
Rites and ceremonies
Salutations
Tattooing
Tipping
also subhead Social life and customs under names of countries, states, cities, etc. e.g. India—Social life and customs

MANNES, Marya
Five-minute cure. por Am Home 80:26-7 My '77

MANNING, Bayless Andrew
World affairs: a more cheerful perspective. Yale R 67:1-12 O '77

MANNING, Mary
Under the blanket; story. Atlantic 240:63-8 Jl '77

MANO, D. Keith
Book watch (cont) Esquire 87:16+ F; 34+ Mr; 20+ Ap; 54+ My '77
Gimlet eye. See occasional isssues of National review
Maitre d' meets his nemesis. il por Esquire 87: 104 Je '77

about

Gimlet eye of D. Keith Mano. D. G. Kehl. Chr Today 21:20-1 Je 17 '77 *

MANOFF, Robert Karl
Closing in on Mrs Gandhi. Nation 225:355-6 O 15 '77
Coup that failed. Nation 224:550-1 My 7 '77

MANPOWER
See also
Labor supply

MANPOWER and education. See Education and manpower

MANPOWER Department (Allegheny County, Pa)
See Allegheny County, Pa—Manpower Department

MANRICO (operatic character) See Characters in opera

MANROSS, Newton S.
This partition of the waters has served its end. New Repub 177:6-7 S 24 '77

MANSFIELD, John Worthington
American painting. S. B. Sherrill. por Antiques 112:1022+ D '77 *

MANSFIELD, Michael Joseph
Mansfield's mounting problems as envoy to Japan. J. N. Wallace. il por U.S. News 83:42 O 31 '77 *

MANSFIELD, Owen
If football is so tough, how come they call it a game? R. Blount, Jr. Esquire 88:52+ O '77 *

MANSFIELD, Ray
If football is so tough, how come they call it a game? R. Blount, Jr. Esquire 88:52+ O '77 *

MANTAS. See Rays (fishes)

MANTEIDAE
Misleading mantids. G. F. Rohrmann. il Natur Hist 86:66-71 bibl(p97) Mr '77

MANTIDS. See Manteidae

MANTLE, Mickey. See Ford, W. jt auth

MANTLE of the earth. See Earth—Internal structure

MANTURA, Andrew
Mediterranean enigma. il maps Oceans 10:24-7 Ja '77

MANTZ, Barbara
What are your rights to privacy? Bet Hom & Gard 55:36+ S '77

MANUAL labor. See Work

MANUFACTURERS agents
Selling a service in retailing; Sales Maids of America. P. Schwab. por Nations Bus 65:102 N '77

MANUFACTURERS Hanover Trust Company
Choosing strategies for business success; interview. G. Hauge. pors Nations Bus 65:32-5 Je '77
Lance alone; memo linking personal loan to correspondent relationship between Manufacturers and National Bank of Georgia. D. M. Alpern and others. por Newsweek 90:14-15 Ag 15 '77
Painful job: turning bankers into managers. il Bus W p49+ Mr 7 '77

MANUFACTURES
Can marketing and manufacturing coexist? B. P. Shapiro. bibl f Harvard Bus R 55:104-14 S '77; Discussion. 55:46-7+ N '77
See also
Industrial capacity

Statistics

Productivity and unit labor costs in 12 industrial countries. B. Boner and A. Neef. bibl il M Labor R 100:11-17 Jl '77
Ratios of manufacturing. il Duns R 110:92-3+ D '77

MANUFACTURING in space. See Space stations —Industrial use

MANUFACTURING processes
See also
Computers—Industrial use
Manufactures

MANURE handling. See Fertilizers and manures—Handling

MANURES. See Fertilizers and manures

MANUSCRIPTS
See also
Archives
Illumination of books and manuscripts
Music—Manuscripts

Collectors and collecting

See also
College libraries—Manuscript collections

MANUSCRIPTS, Celtic
See also
Book of Kells

MANUSCRIPTS, Coptic (papyri)
Nag Hammadi library scheduled by Harper & Row for February. P. Holt. Pub W 212:119 S 26 '77

MANUSCRIPTS, English
Scrope's last throw; discovery of Byron and Shelley manuscripts. R. Holmes. Harpers 254: 77-9+ Ap '77

MANUSCRIPTS, Hebrew
See also
Dead Sea Scrolls

MANUSCRIPTS, Illumination of. See Illumination of books and manuscripts

MANUSCRIPTS, Irish
See also
Book of Durrow

MANUSCRIPTS, Latin
See also
Book of Kells

MANZANITAS. See Bearberries

MAO, Tse-tung
China after Mao. O. E. Clubb. bibl Cur Hist 73:49-53+ S '77 *
Marxism as a political religion. il Nat R 29: 1427+ D 9 '77 *
Rise and fall of Mao's Empress. il pors Time 109:42-5 Mr 21 '77 *
Thought control in Mao's China; interview with Chinese intellectual, ed by W. Berkson. il Nat R 29:1173-7+ O 14 '77 *

Anecdotes, facetiae, satire, etc.
My Mao. V. Geng. New Yorker 53:32-4 Mr 21 '77

Funeral rites and ceremonies
Mao's funeral. B. J. Wattenberg. Harpers 254: 31-3 F '77 *

MAO, Tse-tung, Mme
Another top red's wife runs afoul of system. il pors U.S. News 83:55 N 7 '77 *
Comrade Chiang Ch'ing tells her story; excerpts from Comrade Chiang Ch'ing. R. Witke. il pors Time 109:46-8+ Mr 21 '77 *
Now it's China's cultural thaw. H. E. Salisbury. il pors N Y Times Mag p49+ D 4 '77 *
Rise and fall of Mao's Empress. il pors Time 109:42-5 Mr 21 '77 *

MAOISM. See Communism—China

MAP making. See Mapping Aerial

MAP making, Computerized. See Computers—Cartographic use

MAP reading
Highway map as a social studies resource. J. Ehemann. Clearing H 51:165-6 D '77

MAPCO Inc
Putting MAPCO on the map. J. Cook. Forbes 119:77-8 Je 15 '77

MAPLE
Canyon maple—a colorful mountaineer. P. A. Barker. il Am For 83:22-5 D '77
Should you try a Japanese maple? il Sunset 158: 175 F '77

MAPLE syrup
Gold in the trees. B. Mays. il Org Gard & Farm 24:128-9+ F '77
Inexpensive evaporator for backyard syrup making. L. E. Weeks, Jr. il Org Gard & Farm 24:138-41 F '77
World's best maple syrup. R. Traver. Esquire 87:156-8 My '77
See also
Cookery—Maple syrup

MAPPING, Aerial
Infrared photography maps non-point pollution; Toledo. il Am City & County 92:46-7 Ja '77

MAPS
Map innovations. . .by mail order. Sunset 159:56 S '77
Maps as gifts—wide choices. il Sunset 159:50+ D '77
See also
Booksellers and bookselling—Maps
Map reading
Topographic maps
Weather maps
World maps
also subhead Maps under names of continents, countries, cities, etc. e.g. Latin America—Maps

MAPS, Early

Collectors and collecting
Address book; dealers in antique prints and maps. S. Sunderlin. House B 119:22+ Jl '77

MAR, Laureen
Slugs, china, fire; poem. Mademoiselle 83:34 My '77

MARA, Bill
Mara. T. West. il Flying 101:116-17 S '77 *

MARACAIBO Symphony Orchestra. See Orchestras

MARAN, Stephen P.
Sky reporter (cont) Natur Hist 86:85-6+ F; 88+ Ap; 84-7 My; 88+ Ag; 106+ N '77

MARANOS
Catholics who celebrate Passover; Portugal. il Time 109:66 Ap 11 '77

MARANTZ, Kenneth
Picture book as art object: a call for balanced reviewing. il Wilson Lib Bull 52:148-51 O '77

MARATHON Oil Company
Marathon man sprints. por Forbes 119:70+ Ap 15 '77

MARATHON running. See Running

MARAVICH, Pete
Heavy truckin' on Bourbon Street. J. Papanek. il pors Sports Illus 47:26-7 D 5 '77 *

MARBACH, Joseph J.
Facial pain. M. Covell. Vogue 167:34+ Je '77 *

MARBLEHEAD, Mass.

Historic houses, sites, etc.
See Historic houses, sites, etc.—Massachusetts

MARBLES (game)
Marbles—another fun hobby. F. A. Burrows. Hobbies 82:117 Ap '77

MARBURY v. Madison decision. See United States—Supreme Court—Decisions

MARC, Robert E. and Sperling, H. G.
Chromatic organization of primate cones. bibl il Science 196:454-6 Ap 22 '77

MARCELLO, Carlos
From mob to supermob. L. Velie. por Read Digest 112:49-54 Ja '78 *

MARCH, John
Courage and the art of wolf maintenance. il pors Audubon 79:80-2+ N '77

MARCH, Melisand
Today is not a rehearsal; story. Ladies Home J 94:88-9 F '77

MARCHAIS, Georges
Death of Eurocommunism. T. Szulc. New Repub 177:21-2+ O 8 '77 *
Family feud on the left. pors Time 110:57 O 10 '77 *
Marchais plays it rough. Nat R 29:1161 O 14 '77 *

MARCHES (music)
See also
Phonograph records—Marches (Music)

MARCHESE, Lamar
Lamar Marchese: when planning a program, do it with style. il por Wilson Lib Bull 51:642-3 Ap '77 *

MARCHESI, Gustavo
Verdi's American correspondent. por Opera N 42:38+ D 3 '77

MARCHETTI, Victor L.
Marchetti asks U.S. to lift censorship of 1974 book. S. Wagner. Pub W 211:23 Ap 4 '77 *

MARCHINO, Michael, and Musil, R. K.
Food for peace or food for power? il Chr Cent 94:714-18 Ag 17 '77

MARCO Polo sings a solo; drama. See Guare, J.

MARCOS, Ferdinand E.
Billy Graham's mission to Manila. H. Lindsell. il Chr Today 22:36-7 D 30 '77 *
Carter's Far East strategy: new role for Philippine bases. L. Hansen. il por map U.S. News 83:29-30 Ag 29 '77 *
Carter's moral foreign policy and Philippine martial law. C. L. Hunt. bibl por Intellect 106:130-3 O '77 *
Ferdinand Marcos' new society. por Time 110:34 Ag 15 '77 *
Marcos and the Philippines; First Lady; Transplanting democracy. W. F. Buckley, Jr. Nat R 29:1512-13 D 23 '77 *
Marcos' yes and yes vote. il por Time 110:26 D 26 '77 *
New light on the Philippine dilemma. R. G. Soberano. il Chr Cent 94:624-7 Jl 6 '77 *
Other side of smiling. J. A. O'Hare. America 137:353-4 N 19 '77 *
Philippines: a nation in transition. S. Johnson. il por Read Digest 110:37-8+ Je '77; Reply. H. Kamm. 110:45 Je '77 *
Tortuous exculpation. Nation 225:581 D 3 '77 *

MARCOS, Imelda (Romualdez)
First Lady. W. F. Buckley, Jr. Nat R 29:1512-13 D 23 '77 *

MARCOVICCI, Andrea
Andrea Marcovicci talks scents; interview, ed by H. Brubach. il Mademoiselle 83:112-13+ D '77

MARCOVICH, Sharon J.
Busiest outdoor school. il Am Educ 13:28-30 My '77

MARCUM, Beverly A. and others
Polarity reversal in nerve-free hydra. bibl il Science 197:771-3 Ag 19 '77

MARCUM, Edwin
Taxes for the craftsman (title varies) (cont) Craft Horiz 37:12+ F '77

MARCUM, John A.
African front-line states. map Nation 225:492-5 N 12 '77

MARCUS, Adrianne
New Year's wish; poem. Nation 224:696 Je 4 '77
MARCUS, Joyce. See Marcus, S. jt auth
MARCUS, Leonard
How to organize a prize-giving institution. il Hi Fi 27:49-51+ D '77
(ed) See Maazel, L. On making the first symphonic direct-to-disc LP
MARCUS, Michael A. and Lewis, Aaron
Kinetic resonance Raman spectroscopy: dynamics of deprotonation of the Schiff base of bacteriorhodopsin. bibl il Science 195:1328-30 Mr 25 '77
MARCUS, Sheldon, and Marcus, Joyce
Utilizing sociodrama in the social studies curriculum. Clearing H 50:272-3 F '77
MARCUS, Stanley E.
Revolution in sculpture: a look at David Smith. il por Intellect 105:265-8 F '77
MARCUS, Yoel
Israel's self-inflicted wounds. il pors N Y Times Mag p26-9+ Ap 24 '77
MARCUSSON, Chuck
Chuck Marcusson has a way with fish; ed by M Wiley. por Yachting 141:98 Je '77
MARDEN, Philip. See Beck, A. M. jt auth
MARDI Gras. See Carnival
MAREK, George R.
Barnum of the opera. il Opera N 41:10-12+ Ja 29 '77
Earth spirit. il pors Opera N 41:16-17+ Ap 2 '77
Tale of turmoil. il por Opera N 42:10-14 D 3 '77
MAREK, Richard
Richard Marek talks about his first list through Putnam, set to debut next March; interview, ed by R. Dahlin. Pub W 211:50 Ap 25 '77
MAREK, Richard, Publishers, Inc. See Publishers and publishing—United States
MAREK'S disease. See Poultry—Diseases and pests
MARET-HAVENS, Elizabeth
Developing an index to measure female labor force attachment. bibl il M Labor R 100:35-8 My '77
MARGARET, Princess of Great Britain
Life & loves of Princess Margaret. N. Dempster. por Ladies Home J 94:30+ D '77 *
MARGIN buying. See Stocks—Margin buying
MARGINAL land. See Land
MARGOLIS, Art
Art's TV shop. il Pop Electr 11:99-100 Ap '77
MARGULIES, Walter P.
Make the most of your corporate identity. il Harvard Bus R 55:66-74 Jl '77
MARGULIS, Lynn
Gaia: the harmony of our sphere. F. Hapgood. Atlantic 240:100-4 D '77 *
MARIA Theresa, Empress of Austria
Heart of a king. A. M. Lingg. por Opera N 42:18-19 Ja 7 '78 *
MARIANI, John
Flirting. il Redbook 148:24+ F '77
Two-career crisis. Am Home 80:10+ O '77
MARIE Emmanuel, Sister
Gospel truths of religious writing. Writers Digest 57:20-1+ D '77
Mr Jake and speed-reading. il Engl J 66:64-5 O '77
MARIENTHAL, George
Energy and defense; excerpt from testimony before the Senate Armed Services Subcommittee on Military Construction and Stockpiles. Aviation W 107:7 D 5 '77
MARIGOLDS
Marigolds—sun flowers for your skin. Org Gard & Farm 24:120 S '77
MARIJUANA
All the evidence on pot isn't in! S. L. Kuhne. por Seventeen 36:32 Ap '77
Can marijuana cure glaucoma? il pors Ebony 32:108+ S '77
Fix for pain? use of heroin and marijuana for terminal cancer patients. M. Clark and others. il Newsweek 91:41 Ja 2 '78
Great Yosemite gold rush; crash of airplane carrying thousands of pounds of marijuana. G. Rowell. Audubon 79:135 S '77
Reverse uncertainty. Sci Am 236:64 Mr '77
See also
THC

Laws and legislation

Carter's grass-roots appeal. il Time 110:8 Ag 15 '77
Conservatives and marijuana. W. F. Buckley, Jr. Nat R 29:687 Je 10 '77
Easing the pot laws. J. Seligmann and L. Howard. il Newsweek 89:76 Mr 28 '77

Mexico

Busted in Mexico; Americans. D. Harris. il pors N Y Times Mag p26-30+ My 1 '77
MARIJUANA smuggling. See Smuggling
MARIKO Sanjo Dance Company. See Dance companies

MARIN County, Calif.

Education

See Education—California

Water supply

See Water supply—California
MARINARO, Vincent C.
Recluse. il Outdoor Life 160:84-5+ Jl '77
MARINAS
From the people who brought you full employment; insurance coverage of boatyard and marina workers. B. O'Donovan. il Motor B & S 139:81-3+ Je '77
Siege of the Province Lands; question of proposed CeeJay Marina in Provincetown Harbor. W. O. Johnson. il map Audubon 79:22-35 My '77
MARINE accidents
See also
Boats—Fires and fire prevention
Boats and boating—Accidents
Collisions at sea
Shipwrecks
MARINE ambulances. See Ambulance service
MARINE aquariums. See Aquariums
MARINE archeology. See Archeology, Submarine
MARINE batteries. See Storage batteries
MARINE biology
Biological consequences of the 1975 El Niño. T. J. Cowles and others. bibl il maps Science 195:285-7 Ja 21 '77
Life beneath the Antarctic ice. il Sci N 112:421 D 24 '77
See also
Benthos
Fresh water biology
Marine ecology
Marine fauna
Marine microbiology
Marine sediments
Plankton
Spawning

Bibliography

Bookshelf. See issues of Oceans

Study and teaching

Go chase a shark; fishing and tagging by high school students. S. M. H. Connett. il Yachting 141:74-6 Mr '77
MARINE CB. See Citizens band radio on ships, boats, etc.
MARINE charts. See Nautical charts
MARINE cookery. See Cookery, Marine
MARINE Corps. See United States—Marine Corps
MARINE deposits. See Marine sediments
MARINE ecology
Living sea. A. Fisher. il Int Wildlife 7:4-11 My '77
Wind caller; Torres Strait. B. Nietschmann. il map Natur Hist 86:10-12 Mr '77
MARINE electronics. See Boats—Electronic equipment
MARINE engines
Center consoles: powering. J. Martenhoff. il Motor B & S 139:101-2 Je '77
Engine guide; special section. il Motor B & S 140:65-8+ D '77
Laying up marine engines. B. Gladstone. il Motor B & S 140:93-7 N '77
Power play; gas or diesel. A. G. Hammitt. il Motor B & S 139:50-1+ F '77
Surveying your engine installation. C. Miller. il Motor B & S 139:85-7 Mr '77
Two screws are better than one. D. Bradley. Motor B & S 139:18+ Ap '77
See also
Diesel engines, Marine
Motor boat engines
Outboard motors

Cooling

Flushing a cooling system. P. Zweig. Yachting 141:106 Mr '77

Filters

Fuel filtration. D. Hart. il Motor B & S 140:20+ Ag; 13+ O '77

Fuel

See also
Gasoline

Fuel feeding

Most dangerous leak of all; fuel lines. C. M. Stephens. il Motor B & S 140:82-5 N '77

Ignition

See also
Magnetos

Lubrication and lubricants

Functions and makeup of lubricants. W. D. Dysart. il Motor B & S 139:79-80 Mr '77
Trouble shooting by test tube; testing lube oil. J. Peck. il Motor B & S 140:71-3 D '77

MARINE engines—*Continued*

Maintenance and repair

Gasoline-engine troubleshooting. il Motor B & S 139:133-6 Je '77

Get in line! engine/shaft alignment problems. J. Harden. il Yachting 141:82-5 Je '77

10 great engine get-home tips. . O Moore. il Motor B & S 140:54-5 D '77

MARINE farming. See Aquaculture

MARINE fauna

Bizarre world of undersea lights. G. S. Fichter. il Int Wildlife 8:12-15 Ja '78

See also

Corals

Foraminifera

Marine invertebrates

Marine mammals

Sea anemones

Sea serpents

Sea snakes

Sponges

MARINE fires. See Boats—Fires and fire prevention

MARINE flora

See also

Seaweed

MARINE instruments. See Nautical instruments

MARINE invertebrates

Chemical communication of marine invertebrates. P. J. Scheuer. bibl il BioScience 27: 664-8 O '77

MARINE mammals

Navy's natural divers: United States Navy Marine Mammal Training Program. C. Barton. il Oceans 10:34-9 Jl '77

See also

Cetacea

Dolphins (mammals)

Manatees

Seals (animals)

Walruses

Whales

Laws and legislation

All-porpoise war; limiting kill of porpoises caught by tuna fishermen. G. M. Prather. Nat R 29:439+ Ap 15 '77

Dolphins and/or tuna: an update on the problems of purse seining for yellowfin. S. M. Minasian. il Oceans 10:60-3 N '77

Magnificent mammals. V. B. Scheffer. il Environment 19:16-20+ O '77

Open season on wildlife laws; Marine Mammal Protection Act's regulation of porpoise kill by tuna industry. il Nat Parks & Con Mag 51:20-1 My '77

Troubled waters; effect of laws protecting porpoises in tuna fishing areas. il Forbes 119:56 Ap 1 '77

United States ratifies Convention for Conservation of Antarctic Seals. Dept State Bull 76:135 F 14 '77

What price porpoises? Marine Mammal Protection Act and tuna fishermen. A. J. Mayer and J. Huck. il Newsweek 89:58 F 7 '77

MARINE microbiology

Microbial life in the deep sea. H. W. Jannasch and C. O. Wirsen. il Sci Am 236:42-52 bibl(p 142) Je '77

MARINE mineral resources

See also

Ocean mining

Salt

MARINE navigation. See Navigation

MARINE paint. See Paint

MARINE painting

Carl Evers. N. Meglin. il por Am Artist 41:62-5 Jl '77

Conversation with Marshall Joyce; interview, ed by C. Movalli. M. Joyce. il por Am Artist 41: 90-5+ F '77

See also

Ships in art

MARINE photography. See Photography—Marines

MARINE police. See Police

MARINE pollution

Are your beaches polluted? R. Nader. Ladies Home J 94:24 Ag '77

Living sea. A. Fisher. il Int Wildlife 7:4-11 My '77

Polychlorinated biphenyls: penetration into the deep ocean by zooplankton fecal pellet transport. D. L. Elder and S. W. Fowler. bibl il Science 197:459-61 Jl 29 '77

Sunlight-induced bromate formation in chlorinated seawater. D. L. Macalady and others. bibl il Science 195:1335-7 Mr 25 '77

What can we do about marine pollution? views of Dr E. D. Goldberg. D. Behrman. il UNESCO Courier 30:27-8 Ja '77

See also

Oil pollution of rivers, harbors, etc.

Oil pollution of the sea

Waste disposal in the ocean

Measurement

Project CEPEX. M. R. Reeve and M. A. Walter. il Sea Front 23:365-73 N '77

Chesapeake Bay

Chlamydiae (with phages), mycoplasmas, and rickettsiae in Chesapeake Bay bivalves. J. C. Harshbarger and others. bibl il Science 196: 666-8 My 6 '77

Vibrio cholerae, vibrio parahaemolyticus, and other vibrios: occurrence and distribution in Chesapeake Bay. R. R. Colwell and others. bibl il map Science 198:394-6 O 28 '77

Mediterranean Sea

Campaign to cleanse the Mediterranean; United Nations Environment Program. il Bus W p32-3 O 31 '77

United to protect the Mediterranean; United Nations Environment Program. P. S. Thacher. il Oceans 10:58-61 Ja '77

San Francisco Bay

Water quality: Oceanic Society monitors San Francisco Bay. S. R. Krenzelok. Oceans 10: 65 Mr '77

MARINE propellers. See Propellers

MARINE radar. See Radar in navigation

MARINE radio equipment. See Boats—Radio equipment

MARINE research. See Oceanographic research

MARINE resources

New wave in oceanography. D. Behrman. il UNESCO Courier 30:16-17+ Ja '77

Policy for ocean resource development. W. S. Gaither. Science 196:383 Ap 22 '77

Power from the sea: fact or fancy. J. A. Maxtone Graham. il Pop Mech 147:192-6 Mr '77

Resources of continental margins: perspectives on a program for their management. C. N. K. Mooers and J. M. Hall. il Oceans 10:61-3 Mr '77

See also

Fisheries

MARINE rope. See Rope

MARINE sanitation devices. See Boats—Toilet facilities

MARINE science. See Oceanography

MARINE sediments

Azaarenes in recent marine sediments. M. Blumer and others. bibl il Science 195:283-4 Ja 21 '77

Estimates of cenozoic oceanic sedimentation rates. T. A. Davies and others. bibl il Science 197:53-5 Jl 1 '77

Interstitial nitrate profiles and oxidation of sedimentary organic matter in the eastern equatorial Atlantic. M. L. Bender. bibl il Science 198: 605-9 N 11 '77

Isoleucine epimerization for dating marine sediments: importance of analyzing monospecific foraminiferal samples. K. King and C. Neville. bibl il Science 195:1333-5 Mr 25 '77

North Atlantic ice-rafting: a major change at 75,000 years before the present. W. F. Ruddiman. bibl il maps Science 196:1208-11 Je 10 '77

Oxygen isotopic analysis of the size fraction between 62 and 250 micrometers in Caribbean cores P6304-8 and P6304-9. C. Emiliani. bibl il Science 198:1255-6 D 23 '77

Sea-floor data link glaciation to earth's orbital motion. G. B. Lubkin. il Phys Today 30:17+ My '77

Tiny building blocks of oceanic history; photo story. il UNESCO Courier 30:18-23 Ja '77

MARINE snails. See Snails

MARINE surveying. See Hydrographic surveying

MARINE turtles. See Turtles

MARINE zoology. See Marine fauna

MARINEL, Inna

Looking back years with Pavlova, a memoir. il por Dance Mag 52:42-3 Ja '78

MARINER flights. See Space flight to Mercury

MARINER Jupiter-Saturn mission. See Space flight—Voyager flights

MARINO, Joseph D.

Economical multi-mission spacecraft for the shuttle era. il Space World N-3-159: 20-3 Mr '77

MARION, Ia.

Marion, Iowa: a hometown scrapbook. il Sat R 5:17-19 N 26 '77

MARION, Ohio, Public Library. See Libraries—Ohio

MARION Federal Penitentiary. See Prisons—Illinois

MARION Rice's Denishawn Dancers. See Dance companies

MARIS, Roger

Record almost broke him. R. Telander. il pors Sports Illus 46:60-4+ Je 20 '77 *

MARISAT. See Communications satellites—Maritime use

MARITAL infidelity. See Adultery

MARITIME history. See Shipping—History

MARITIME law
Carter's options for cargo preference. Bus W p22 Jl 4 '77
House sinks the cargo bill; Energy Transportation Security Act of 1977. Time 110:14-15 O 31 '77
ILO tightens standards for maritime safety; standards for flag of convenience ships. J. P. Goldberg. bibl M Labor R 100:25-30 Jl '77
Payoff charges on cargo bill. il Time 110:53-4 Ag 15 '77
Proposal that would boost oil prices further; cargo preference legislation. il Nations Bus 65:66-8 O '77
Red tape may capsize river rafts; invoking the Jones Act to ban foreign-made rafts. il Bus W p38 Mr 21 '77
Ships and chauvinism; congressional squabble over oil-cargo-preference bill. A. J. Mayer. il Newsweek 90:82 O 17 '77
Tanker bill sinks or swims with Carter; requiring 30% of imported oil be hauled in American-flag tankers. il Bus W p26-7 My 30 '77
Washington report. M. P. Crain. See issues of Yachting
See also
Boats and boating—Laws and regulations
Pilots and pilotage
Rule of the road at sea
Territorial waters
United Nations Conference on Carriage of Goods by the Sea, 1978 (proposed)
United Nations Conference on the Law of the Sea
MARITIME meteorology. See Meteorology, Maritime
MARITIME museums. See Naval museums
MARITIME photography. See Photography—Marines
MARITIME surveying. See Hydrographic surveying
MARK, Charles Christopher
Government and the arts. por Am Artist 41:4+ Je '77
MARK, R. K. and Stuart-Alexander, D. E.
Disasters as a necessary part of benefit-cost analyses. bibl Science 197:1160-2 S 16 '77
MARK Twain, pseud. See Clemens, S. L.
MARK Controls Corporation. See Valves—Manufacture
MARKANDAYA, Kamala
Nectar in a sieve. M. R. Oran. Engl J 66:62-3 Mr '77 *
MARKEGARD, David
One-touch diode tester. il Pop Electr 12:75 Jl '77
MARKEL, Helen
(ed) See Brisson, F. My wife, Roz
MARKET Facts Inc. See Market research
MARKET gardening. See Truck farming
MARKET research
Forecasting with trade-off analysis; Market Facts Inc. J. C. Perham. il Duns R 109:87-8+ Mr '77
MARKETING
Can marketing and manufacturing coexist? B. P. Shapiro. bibl f Harvard Bus R 55:104-14 S '77; Discussion. 55:46-7+ N '77
From sales obsession to marketing effectiveness. P. Kotler. il Harvard Bus R 55:67-75 N '77
Marketing and the corporate purpose; address, March 2, 1977. T. Levitt. Vital Speeches 43: 437-43 My 1 '77
Marketing when things change. T. Levitt. il Harvard Bus R 55:107-13 N '77
New breed of consumer: growing challenge to business. il U.S. News 83:45-6 Jl 25 '77
See also
Advertising
Auctions
Communication in marketing
Consumers
Cooperative associations
Customer service
Distribution of goods
Franchise system
Mail order business
also subhead Marketing, under various subjects, e.g. Water, Bottled—Marketing

History

Moving the merchandise. il Forbes 120:P150-7 S 15 '77

International aspects

Coming marketing internationale; address, May 18, 1977. J. G. Keane. Vital Speeches 43:532-6 Je 15 '77
MARKETING consultants
Other MCA new star in consumer marketing; Marketing Corp. of America. Duns R 110:23+ O '77
MARKETING Corporation of America. See Marketing consultants
MARKETING research. See Market research

MARKETS
Finding bargains at auctions & flea markets. T. Pyle. il Mech Illus 73:76-8 Ag '77
See also
Boston—Markets
New York (city)—Markets
MARKETS, Farmers
Agriculture in Appalachia is looking brighter. D. O. Cunnion. Org Gard & Farm 24:149-51 D '77
Farmer's market with a sense of community; Las Cruces, N.Mex. T. L. Gettings. il Org Gard & Farm 24:155-6 Ag '77
Fine art of eating in Trinidad and Tobago. P. C. Richman. il Holiday 58:40-1+ Ja '77
Our far-flung correspondents; England. C. Trillin. New Yorker 53:149-52+ N 21 '77
MARKETS, Outdoor. See Street trades
MARKETS for authors. See Authors and publishers
MARKFIELD, Wallace
My college essay. il pors N Y Times Mag p30 Ja 16 '77
MARKHAM, James M.
Spain—after 40 years of fear. il N Y Times Mag p 18-20+ Je 5 '77
War that won't go away. il N Y Times Mag p33+ O 9 '77
MARKHAM, Margaret
Annual medical examination. Harp Baz 110:129+ F '77
Does pollution affect your nerves? Harp Baz 110:127+ Mr '77
How to choose your doctor. bibl Harp Baz 110: 126-7+ F '77
MARKHAM, Pamela
New exercise splash. il House & Gard 149:28+ Jl '77
Taking the bore out of chores; exercising around the house. il House & Gard 149:51 N '77
MARKING (students) See Grading and marking (students)
MARKISH, Simon
Example of Isaac Babel; tr. by D. Fanger and H. Shukman. Commentary 64:36-45 N '77
MARKO, Harold M.
S.O.S: no help, thank you. por Duns R 109:19-20 Ja '77 *
MARKOFF, John
NASA and the Pentagon. Nation 226:16-18 Ja 7 '78
MARKOV, Albert
Albert Markov, violin; debut recital at Alice Tully Hall. Hi Fi 27:MA33 F '77 *
MARKOV, M. A.
Have we learned to think in a new way? il Bull Atom Sci 33:20-3 N '77
MARKOVA, Dame Alicia
Conversations with Markova; interview, ed by D. Vaughan. il pors Dance Mag 51:56-62 Je '77

about

Alicia Markova: her appearances in America. A. Fay. il pors Dance Mag 51:47-55 Je '77 *
MARKOVITZ, Diane C. and Fernstrom, J. D.
Diet and uptake of aldomet by the brain: competition with natural large neutral amino acids. bibl il Science 197:1014-15 S 2 '77
MARKOW, Jack
Cartooning. See alternate issues of Writers digest
MARKOWSKI, Eugene
Hypnotic geometry. F. Hartt. Art N 76:100+ O '77 *
MARKOWSKY, Juliet Kellogg
Storytime for toddlers. bibl il por SLJ 23:28-31 My '77
MARKS, Andrea M.
Truth about teenage food fads. il por Parents Mag 52:44-5+ Mr '77
MARKS, Bruce
Ballet West's Don Quixote. J. Anderson. il Dance Mag 51:36-8 Jl '77 *
Bruce Marks and Toni Lander: breaking ground at Ballet West. J. Cumming. il pors Dance Mag 51:62-5 D '77 *
MARKS, Emily
Detailing slabs with slip impressions. il por Ceram Mo 25:33-6 F '77
MARKS, Frederick Howe
Too sacred to survive? il por Int Wildlife 8:20-5 Ja '78
MARKS, Jane
Some practical and sensible advice for breaking the bickering habit. Seventeen 36:136-7+ N '77
Working vacations in the wilds. McCalls 104:69 My '77
MARKS, Joe
6 scientists working hard on the hardwoods. il Am For 83:16-19+ N '77
MARKS & Spencer, Ltd
Marks & Sparks trades up. Time 110:97 N 28 '77
MARLBORO Festival of Music. See Music festivals—Vermont
MARLBORO Man. See Advertising characters

MARLBOROUGH Gallery, Inc
Act of alteration; indictment of Marlborough Gallery head F. Lloyd. G. Henry. Art N 76:115-16 My '77
Impact of the Rothko case. M. N. Carter. il por Art N 76:78-80 O '77
Straw man in the Rothko case. J. H. Merryman; discussion. Art N 76:32-3+ Mr '77
MARLENE Industries Corporation. See Clothing industry—United States
MARLER, Peter, and Peters, Susan
Selective vocal learning in a sparrow. bibl il Science 198:519-21 N 4 '77
MARLEY, Bob
Reggae way to salvation. J. Bradshaw. il pors N Y Times Mag p24-8+ Ag 14 '77 *
MARLEY, Kemper A.
Bolles file. il por Newsweek 89:32 Ja 31 '77 *
MARLIN Firearms Company. See Firearms industry
MARLIN fishing
Bitten from the records; marlin caught by N. Green off Australia. M. Sloan. il Motor B & S 139:52-5+ Mr '77
Black art of Black Bart. J. Elder. il por Motor B & S 140:61-3+ Jl '77
Frankenheimer; marlin fishing off Baja California. O. Moore. il pors Motor B & S 141:100-3+ Ja '78
Great Barrier marlin! Australia. J. Troy. il Field & S 81:130-5 F '77
Like a neon shadow in the sea; blue marlin in the Caribbean; with reproductions of paintings. S. Meltzoff. il Sports Illus 47:22-9 Jl 25 '77
Marvin as in marlin; black marlin; interview, ed by R. Vaughan. L. Marvin. il pors Motor B & S 139:72-5+ My '77
MARLING, Karal Ann
New Deal ceramics: the Cleveland workshop. il por Ceram Mo 25:25-31 Je '77
MARLING, William
High on icy rime and powdered sugar. il Fortune 95:51+ Ja '77
MARLINS
Marlins. G. Beardsley. il Sea Front 23:273-9 S '77
MARLOWE, Chris
Big Cy wasn't one bit shy. J. Jares. por Sports Illus 46:88+ My 23 '77 *
MARMER, Nancy
Art & politics '77. il Art in Am 65:64-6 Jl '77
MARMOTS
You can't sneak up on a marmot. J. J. Knap. il Int Wildlife 7:42-7 My '77
MARON, Davida
Consumers challenge legal monopoly. Intellect 105:333-5 Ap '77
MAROTEAUX-Lamy syndrome. See Metabolism, Disorders of
MAROTTA, Tom
Romania, Romania! il Craft Horiz 37:18-19+ Ap '77

about

Viewpoint. J. Deschin. il pors Pop Phot 80:36+ Mr '77 *
MAROULIS, Peter J. and Bandy, A. R.
Estimate of the contribution of biologically produced dimethyl sulfide to the global sulfur cycle. bibl il map Science 196:647-8 My 6 '77
MARQUA, Nancy Lill
RIF for teenagers. SLJ 23:45 My '77
MARQUARDT, Hildegard, and others
Mutagenic activity of nitrite-treated foods: human stomach cancer may be related to dietary factors. bibl il Science 196:1000-1 My 27 '77
MARQUSEE, John
Paddington Press and Bantam Books reveal the startling existence of white lions; interview, ed by R. Dahlin. il Pub W 211:31 My 9 '77
MARRA, Dorothy Brandt
Goodbye to litter; drama. Plays 36:53-7 F '77
MARRANOS. See Maranos
MARRIAGE
Are you ready for marriage? S. V. Didato. Harp Baz 110:51+ Je '77
Can this marriage be saved? D. C. Disney. See issues of Ladies' home journal
Christian marital love: a reappraisal. D. M. Thomas. il New Cath World 220:296-300 N '77
Church and erotic love in marriage. J. G. Milhaven. New Cath World 220:264-7 N '77
Commuter marriages—latest product of women's changing status. il U.S. News 83:109-10 O 24 '77
Crisis couples face at forty; excerpt from Passages. G. Sheehy. Read Digest 110:73-6 Mr '77
Emotional pain of mastectomy. J. Gaylin. Psychol Today 10:98+ Ap '77
Equality begins at home. C. B. Luce. por Sat Eve Post 249:16-17+ O '77
First aid for a failing marriage; excerpt from Total joy. M. Morgan. Sat Eve Post 249:48+ Ap '77
Focus: marriage. Seventeen 36:54-5 Je '77
How children can hurt a marriage. M. Lasswell and N. Lobsenz. McCalls 104:161+ S '77
How her job saved their marriage; interview, ed by M. L. Kotz. B. L. Pryor. il pors Good H 184:48+ My '77
How to have a closer, happier marriage; excerpt from Stop running scared! H. Fensterheim and J. Baer. Good H 186:40+ Ja '78
How to have the marriage you want; What makes a good marriage? il Redbook 150:114-15+ N '77
How to stay married and avoid divorce. M. S. Miller. Am Home 80:62-4 N '77
I canceled the wedding of my dreams. il Good H 184:24+ My '77
Liberation almost ruined my marriage. il Good H 185:24+ Ag '77
Love vs. privacy. M. Lasswell and N. M. Lobsenz. McCalls 104:46+ Ag '77
Making marriage work (cont of) Marriage lines. D. R. Mace. See issues of Parents' magazine & better homemaking
Marriage as a subversive activity. W. H. Willimon. il Chr Today 21:15-17 F 18 '77
Marriage: the traditional alternative. D. Sloan and L. Africano. Harp Baz 110:121+ My '77
My fake husband: notes on a very strange marriage. Ms 5:60-1+ Mr '77
New housewife blues; views of M. Morgan. il por Time 109:62-4+ Mr 14 '77; Same abr. with title Secrets of a total woman. Read Digest 111:91-4 Jl '77
Perfect union; monogamy. J. B. Cumming, Jr. il Esquire 87:68-70 F '77
Sometimes I wish I weren't married. J. Viorst. il Redbook 149:34+ Ag '77
State of the union. D. Ephron. il Esquire 87:63-7 F '77
Staying married; excerpt from Staying together: marriages that work. P. O'Brien. Good H 184:126-7+ My '77
To have and to hold from this day . . . to the next. C. Musello. Ms 6:57+ N '77
Two-career couples: how they make it work; interviews, ed by M.-E. Banashek. il Mademoiselle 83:168-9+ S '77
Varieties of intimacy; excerpt from No-fault marriage. M. Lasswell and N. M. Lobsenz. Read Digest 111:115-18 N '77
Walking the tightrope. E. Schaeffer. Chr Today 21:33-4 F 4 '77
Way we weren't; excerpt from Loose change. S. Davidson. il Esquire 87:83-7+ Mr '77
When your love affair turns into marriage; interviews with seven couples, ed by A. Lake. il Redbook 148:72+ F '77
You and your marriage. J. Wax. Vogue 167:152+ My '77

See also

Adultery
Celibacy
Childlessness
Divorce
Eugenics
Family
Husbands
Interracial marriage
Polygamy
Remarriage
Separation (law)
Wife beating
Wives

Annulment (canon law)

Catholic annulments: a dehumanizing process. S. J. Kelleher. il Commonweal 104:363-8 Je 10 '77; Reply. R. F. Carney. Commonweal 104:479 Jl 22 '77

Caricatures and cartoons

Marriage-go-round. Read Digest 110:112-13 Je '77

Catholic Church

Church and marriage: twin families for growth. G. B. Wilson. America 137:480-3 D 31 '77
MARRIAGE (canon law)

See also

Marriage—Annulment (canon law)
MARRIAGE, Education for. See Family life, Education for
MARRIAGE contracts
Marriage contract renewed. H. Cody; H. Sadis. pors Ms 6:21 Jl '77
MARRIAGE counseling
Baby talk; E. Whelan's counseling service. B. Carter. il pors Newsweek 90:73 Ag 8 '77
Can this marriage be saved? D. C. Disney. See issues of Ladies' home journal
Making marriage work. D. R. Mace. Parents Mag 52:30 My '77
Marriage counseling for unwed couples. A. Gross. N Y Times Mag p52+ Ap 24 '77
Marriage: minefields on the way to paradise. P. Yancey. il Chr Today 21:24-7 F 18 '77
MARRIAGE customs and rites

Africa

Zulu king weds a Swazi princess. V. Wentzel. il Nat Geog 153:46-61 Ja '78

Papua New Guinea

Fertility rites and sorcery in a New Guinea village; Gimi people. G. Gillison. il map Nat Geog 152:124-46 Jl '77

MARRIAGE law
See also
Community property

Kenya

Marriage-law controversy in Kenya. R. Mann. Chr Cent 94:457 My 11 '77

United States

Negro: by definition; state laws prohibiting interracial marriage. R. Poe. bibl Negro Hist Bull 40:668-70 Ja '77

MARRIAGE of Figaro; opera. See Mozart, J. C. W. A.

MARRIED women

Anecdotes, facetiae, satire, etc.

How did I get to be 40? excerpt from How did I get to be 40. . .& other atrocities. J. Viorst. Read Digest 110:90-1 Je '77

Education

See Education of women

Employment

Almost half of all children have mothers in the labor force. A. S. Grossman. bibl il M Labor R 100:41-4 Je '77
Are you trying to be super-woman? N. Love. il Am Home 80:56+ Ap '77
Bazaar's guide for every working mother; symposium. Harp Baz 110:176-9+ O '77
Behind the sharp increase in two-breadwinner families. il U.S. News 82:54-6 F 7 '77
Can power wreck your marriage? M. Stevens. Harp Baz 111:153+ N '77
Can you work and be a good mother? L. Salk. Harp Baz 110:88-9+ Ag '77
Especially for working mothers. M. P. Rowe. Parents Mag 52:26-7 Je; 24 Jl; 34+ S; 54 N '77; 53:10 Ja '78
Everyone works; children helping working mothers; interviews, ed by C. Jessup and G. Chipps. il Am Home 80:38-9 F '77
Future for working women; ed by R. J. Leaper; excerpt from Women and the American economy: a look to the 1980's. J. Kreps. por Ms 5:56-7 Mr '77
Help wanted: news and cues for working mothers. Parents Mag 52:38-9 Ap '77
How I stopped being the little woman. D. Smith. il McCalls 104:70+ Ap '77
How to make money without taking a job. McCalls 104:76+ Jl '77
How working couples work it out. S. Streshinsky. il Redbook 149:103+ Je '77
How you going to get 'em back in the kitchen? You aren't; views of E. Ginzberg. J. A. Briggs. il por Forbes 120:177-80+ N 15 '77
I felt guilty leaving my family for work. il Good H 185:26+ O '77
I thought I had to be perfect; experiences of a working mother. K. Luciano. il McCalls 104:102+ Jl '77
Labor force participation of married women, March 1976. B. L. Johnson and H. Hayghe. il M Labor R 100:32-6 Je '77
My husband and I are equal partners; working part time. M. N. Dudley. McCalls 104:46+ F '77
My job vs. my husband's pride. C. Bocardo. McCalls 105:57+ N '77
New working mothers; interviews. il Harp Baz 110:180-5 O '77
Reentry ripoff: one housewife's exposé. E. Zanar. il Ms 6:83-6+ O '77
Special issue on working mothers. Parents Mag 52:33-7+ Ap '77
Two-career crisis. J. Mariani. Am Home 80:10+ O '77
Way we were. T. Schwartz. il Newsweek 91:59 Ja 16 '78
What the books don't tell working mothers. D. Gorak. il por Redbook 148:77+ Mr '77
When mommy goes to work. . . S. W. Olds. il Fam Health 9:38-40 F '77
When mothers are also managers. il Bus W p155-6+ Ap 18 '77
See also
Part time employment

Law

See Women—Legal status, laws, etc.

Occupations

Giving birth to a business; arts and crafts shop. R. A. Petit. il por Redbook 148:57+ F '77
Myth of the liberated housewife. L. B. Francke. Harp Baz 110:101+ F '77
Should a career woman have children? E. M. Whelan. Harp Baz 110:101+ F '77

MARRIS, Robin
Is Britain an awful warning to America? New Repub 177:23-5+ S 17 '77
Present state of capitalism. New Repub 176:39-41 My 21 '77

MARROW
Simultaneous effects of erythropoietin and colony-stimulating factor on bone marrow cells. G. Van Zant and E. Goldwasser. bibl il Science 198:733-5 N 18 '77

Transplantation

Little boy who cheated death. A. Lake. il por Good H 185:96+ S '77

MARS (planet)
Colonizing Mars: the age of planetary engineering begins. A. L. Robinson. il Science 195:668 F 18 '77
Mars as a member of the solar system. bibl il Space World N-5-161:4-11 My '77
Mars; excerpt, reprint from 1895 issue. P. Lowell. Atlantic 239:32-3 Je '77
Mars—the ultimate suburb. . .but right now it's slightly chilly. il Chemistry 50:3 My '77
Pinning down the Viking landers. Sci N 112:199 S 24 '77
Prime meridian of Mars and the longitudes of the Viking landers. M. E. Davies. bibl Science 197:1277 S 23 '77
Sense of Mars. J. Eberhart. il Chemistry 50:7-16 N '77
What the exploration of Mars tells us about earth. S. I. Rasool and others. il Phys Today 30:23-30+ Jl '77
See also
Life on Mars
Space flight to Mars

Atmosphere

Atmosphere of Mars. C. B. Leovy. il Sci Am 237:34-43 bibl(p 154) Jl '77
Long-range Martian forecast. il Sky & Tel 54:468-9 D '77
Mars and earth: origin and abundance of volatiles. E. Anders and T. Owen. bibl il Science 198:453-65 N 4 '77
Mars: microwave detection of carbon monoxide. R. K. Kakar and others. bibl il Science 196:1090-1 Je 3 '77
Occultation of ε Geminorum by Mars: evidence for atmospheric tides? J. L. Elliot and others. bibl il Science 195:485-6 F 4 '77
Viking: Mars goes into hiding. Sci N 111:229 Ap 9 '77

Crust

See Mars (planet)—Surface

Exploration

Equipment

Martian surface dig stalled. Aviation W 107:22 S 12 '77

Maps

Mars of many colors. J. Eberhart. il Sci N 112:326-8 N 12 '77

Observations

Mars centennial; work of C. Flammarion. K. L. Franklin. il Sci Digest 82:66-9 S '77
Mars, Jupiter, and Saturn for the coming year. R. C. Victor. il Sky & Tel 53:125-6 F '77
Venus and Mars in the morning sky. R. C. Victor. il Sky & Tel 53:375 My '77
Venus, Mars, and the moon come together. il Sky & Tel 54:150-2 Ag '77

Photographs

Erosion on Mars detailed by Viking. il Aviation W 107:51 Jl 25 '77
Looking down on Mars. il Space World N-4-160:28-33 Ap '77
Mars album (cont) Sci N 111:186-7; 112:205 Mr 19, S 24 '77

Satellites

See Satellites

Surface

From this trench on Mars came. . .? il Space World N-1-157:27 Ja '77
Mars on earth. il Sci Digest 81:80-1 F '77
Planetary comparisons. B. M. French. il Space World N-1-157:30-1 Ja '77
Report from Mars; excerpt from Until the sun dies. R. Jastrow. il Natur Hist 86:48-53 bibl (p96-7) Mr '77
Skin of Mars; crust. J. Eberhart. il map Sci N 112:140-1 Ag 27 '77
Viking sampler arm activities resume. J. M. Lenorovitz. il Aviation W 106:54-6 Ja 24 '77

Temperature and radiation

Cold winter for Viking too. il Sci N 111:84 F 5 '77
Midnight on the red planet. J. Eberhart. il Sci N 112:329 N 12 '77
Viking lander sees frost on Mars. il Sci N 112:228 O 8 '77
Vikings to earth: it's cold up here! J. K. Beatty. il Sky & Tel 53:417-20 Je '77

MARS, Photography of. See Astronomical photography

MARSCHNER, Peter Erich
Wanted. P. Whittell. il pors Motor B & S 140:71-2 Ag '77 *

MARSEILLES

History

Marseilles-Fos. M.-L. Welker. il map Oceans 10:46-51 Ja '77

MARSEILLES-Fos port complex. See Ports—France

MARSH, Ben

Rose-colored map. il Harpers 255:80-2 Jl '77

MARSH, Corinna

College entrants bored; poem. Nat R 29:442 Ap 15 '77

Handle with prayer; poem. Nat R 29:1366 N 25 '77

With all my getting; poem. Nat R 29:1432 D 9 '77

MARSH, Dave

Clean sound of music. il Esquire 87:94-6 My '77

MARSH, Douglas

Popular religious books for public libraries; Popular religious books: a selected bibliography. il Lib J 102:1243-50 Je 1 '77

MARSH, George Perkins

Quotes from George Perkins Marsh. por Am For 83:12-13 S '77

about

Magnificent amateur; adaptation of address; with excerpt from introduction to Man and nature. D. Lowenthal. il pors Am For 83:8-11+ S '77 *

MARSH, Jeffrey

Creation according to cosmology. Commentary 64:65-6 O '77

Science and defense policy. Commentary 63:67-70 Ap '77

MARSH, Ngaio

Birth of a sleuth. Writer 90:23-5 Ap '77

about

Murder most tidy. J. M. White. il New Repub 177:36-8 Jl 30 '77 *

MARSH, Peter

By the yellow lake; story. New Yorker 53:24-9 Ag 8 '77

Our last breakfast on Saint Augustine's Farm; story. New Yorker 53:46-52 N 5 '77

MARSH, Richard. See Jones, B. jt auth

MARSH, Spencer

Loving wisdom of TV's Edith Bunker; excerpt from Edith the good. il Good H 185:48+ Ag '77

MARSH, Stanley, 3d

Panhandle pop. J. Lelyveld. il por N Y Times Mag p94 My 8 '77 *

Site for tired eyes. F. Deford. il por Sports Illus 46:84-8+ Ap 18 '77 *

MARSH, Thomas O.

How biocriminology's clues show diets relationship to violence! por Sci Digest 82:17-19 Jl '77

MARSH ecology

Mangroves: trees that help build the land. L. E. Jerome. il Oceans 10:38-45 S '77

MARSH Manufacturing, Inc. See Game birds—Breeding

MARSH plants

Salt-marsh plant geratology. M. Hardisky and R. J. Reimold. bibl il Science 198:612-14 N 11 '77

MARSHALL, Alexandra

Gus in bronze; novel; condensation. Redbook 150:229-51 N '77

MARSHALL, Andrew Walter

Defense miscalculations. E. Aerie. Nation 225:78-81 Jl 23 '77 *

MARSHALL, Colin Marsh

Avis: back on the main road, gathering speed. por Duns R 109:18-19 Ja '77 *

MARSHALL, F. Ray. See Marshall, Ray

MARSHALL, Garry

Candy store. M. Orth and M. Kasindorf. il por Newsweek 89:74-5 Mr 7 '77 *

MARSHALL, George

On Bob Marshall's landmark article. il por Liv Wildn 40:28-30 O '76

MARSHALL, Ingram

Marshall's Fragility Cycles; sonic performance environments. J. La Barbara. Hi Fi 27:MA15 My '77 *

MARSHALL, Janet Chase-. See Chase-Marshall, J.

MARSHALL, Joe

Bud thrives in the mud. il Sports Illus 48:16-17 Ja 2 '78

Feeling fit to hurt a lot of feelings. il pors Sports Illus 46:40-2+ Mr 28 '77

First and foremost for now. il Sports Illus 47:21 S 26 '77

Hollywood or bust for Off-Broadway Joe. por Sports Illus 46:26-7 Ap 25 '77

Lacrosse (cont) il Sports Illus 46:63-4+ Je 6 '77

New charge for the Chargers. il Sports Illus 47:20-2 Ag 22 '77

New generation of blues fans. il Sports Illus 46:24-6+ My 9 '77

Plainly, Jane has a penchant for the pentathlon. il pors Sports Illus 47:32-7 N 21 '77

Pro football (cont) il Sports Illus 46:63-4 Mr 7; 68+ Ap 18; 60+ My 16; 47:78+ O 24; 90+ O 31; 67-8 D 12 '77

Say hello to the fearsome threesome. il Sports Illus 47:26-8+ O 17 '77

That crushmas spirit. il Sports Illus 48:14-15 Ja 2 '78

Tony D comes to big D. il pors Sports Illus 47:38-43+ S 19 '77

Too tall, too mean, too much. il Sports Illus 48:14-16 Ja 9 '78

Track & field. Sports Illus 46:46-7 Ja 31; 77-9 Je 13 '77

Upending the upstarts. il Sports Illus 47:22-5 N 7 '77

Vince, you wouldn't believe it. il Sports Illus 47:24-6+ N 21 '77

When Irish guys are miling. il Sports Illus 46:14-17 F 7 '77

MARSHALL, John, 1755-1835

Mr Chief Justice; excerpt from television script. il Sr Schol 110:19-22 S 22 '77 *

MARSHALL, John F. and Ungerstedt, Urban

Striatal efferent fibers play a role in maintaining rotational behavior in the rat. bibl il Science 198:62-4 O 7 '77

MARSHALL, John S. See Nelson, J. C. jt auth

MARSHALL, Julie

Educational Paperback Association seeks larger share of the education market; report of symposium. il Pub W 211:82+ Mr 7 '77

MARSHALL, Larry G. and others

South American geochronology: radiometric time scale for middle to late tertiary mammal-bearing horizons in Patagonia. bibl il map Science 195:1325-8 Mr 25 '77

MARSHALL, Mel

Field cooking without utensils. il Outdoor Life 160:111-12 Jl '77

Tackle repairs in the field. il Outdoor Life 159:155-6 Mr '77

MARSHALL, Ray

Disputes between White House and labor—what can be done; interview. il por U.S. News 82:55-7 Je 6 '77

Excerpt from testimony on legislation to raise the Federal minimum wage, March 24, 1977. Cong Digest 56:140+ My '77

Undocumented worker; address, May 13, 1977. Vital Speeches 43:551-3 Jl 1 '77

about

How jobs fit into Carter's welfare plan. il por Nations Bus 65:64-6 N '77 *

Man Carter counts on to bolster ties with labor. il por U.S. News 83:87-8 O 10 '77 *

Marshall becomes Secretary of Labor. L. Bornstein and others. M Labor R 100:79 Mr '77 *

Ray Marshall: watch him create controversy. pors Bus W p66-7 F 7 '77 *

MARSHALL, Robert

Problem of the wilderness; reprint from February 1930 issue of Scientific monthly. bibl f il por Liv Wildn 40:31-5 O '76

about

On Bob Marshall's landmark article. G. Marshall. il por Liv Wildn 40:28-30 O '76 *

MARSHALL, Roger

Perfect set-up. il Yachting 141:86-9 My '77

MARSHALL, Sheila L.

April's rebellion; drama. Plays 36:43-8, 73 Ap '77

Treasure without measure; drama. Plays 37:16, 65-70 N '77

Year Santa forgot Christmas; drama. Plays 37:51-5 D '77

MARSHALL, Thurgood

Washington notebook. S. Booker. Ebony 32:29 F '77 *

MARSHALL Field & Company

Why profits shrink at a grand old name. il Bus W p66-9+ Ap 11 '77

MARSHALL Field & Company-Carter Hawley Hale Stores, Inc merger. See Department stores—Acquisitions and mergers

MARSHALL Islands

See also

Eniwetok

MARSHALL Plan. See Economic assistance, American—Europe, Western—History

MARSHES

See also

Bogs

Marsh ecology

MARSHES, Tide

Life in a salt marsh. R. Allen. il Int Wildlife 7:26-9 Mr '77

Man can create a marsh. F. Graham, Jr. Audubon 79:140 S '77

Meanders in the marsh. G. Reiger. il Audubon 79:4-15 S '77

MARSILY, G. de, and others

Nuclear waste disposal: can the geologist guarantee isolation? bibl il Science 197:519-27 Ag 5 '77

MARSTON, R. M.

XR-2206 IC function generator circuits. il Radio-Electr 48:36-8+ Ap; 66-9 My '77

MARSUPIALS
Sticking up for marsupials. S. J. Gould. il Natur Hist 86:22+ O '77
See also
Kangaroos
Opossums
MARTENHOFF, Jim
Center consoles for fun and fish. il Motor B & S 139:95+ Je '77
Guide to: stern-drive cruisers. il Motor B & S 140:82-5 S '77
Navigate with the smart stick. il Motor B & S 139:87+ Ap '77
Personal touch. il Motor B & S 141:71-2 Ja '78
MARTENS, Alexander U.
Paperback market: how it differs from America. tr by T. Weyr. il Pub W 212:70+ S 12 '77
MARTENS, Anne Coulter
Case of the silent dog; drama. Plays 36:15-24, 45 Mr '77
Fit to be tied; drama. Plays 37:27-37 O '77
MARTHA Graham Dance Company
Ancestral footsteps; Lunt-Fontanne Theatre performances May 16-June 11. R. Baker. il Dance Mag 51:51-4 S '77
Close-up, the dissolve, and Martha Graham; three films. J. Mueller. Dance Mag 52:94-5 Ja '78
Dance; Primitive mysteries. N. Goldner. Nation 224:697-8 Je 4 '77
Dancing:
Primitive mysteries and Plain of prayer. A. Croce. New Yorker 53:104 Je 13 '77
Martha Graham premieres; four-week season at the Lunt-Fontanne. J. Maskey. il Hi Fi 27: MA10 S '77
Spotlight on: Tim Wengerd; interview, ed by L. Draegin. T. Wengerd. il pors Dance Mag 51:55-9 S '77
MARTHA Movement (organization) See Womens clubs and societies
MARTHALER, Berard L.
Sounds of silence. New Cath World 220:33 Ja '77
MARTHA'S VINEYARD
Islands cast adrift. map Newsweek 89:23 Ap 4 '77
Last question of summer; Lucy Vincent Beach. J. Lelyveld. il N Y Times Mag p47 S 4 '77
See also
Architecture, Domestic—Martha's Vineyard

Bookstores

See Booksellers and bookselling—Massachusetts
MARTIAL arts. See Hand-to-hand fighting; Hand-to-hand fighting, Oriental
MARTIAN seismology. See Seismology
MARTIN, Aubrey
Calling spring gobblers. il Field & S 81:86-9+ F '77
MARTIN, Ben L.
Parable of the talents. il Harpers 256:12+ Ja '78
MARTIN, Beth Congdon-. See Congdon-Martin, B.
MARTIN, Billy (baseball manager)
No time for champagne. P. Axthelm. il por Newsweek 90:47 Ag 8 '77 *
MARTIN, Charles Allen, pseud
(introd) See Narayan, J. P. India my India!
MARTIN, Diane
Can adults live with their parents? America 136:482-3 My 28 '77
MARTIN, Glenn Luther
Martin. R. P. Hallion. il por Flying 101:248-9 S '77 *
MARTIN, Hacker
Flintlock rifles—new as tomorrow. J. Carmichel. il Outdoor Life 161:60-3+ Ja '78
MARTIN, Harold O.
Are medium tripods our ideal? il Mod Phot 41:134-9+ N '77
Rokuo Kawakami: simplicity revived. il Mod Phot 41:100-5 My '77
MARTIN, James G.
Excerpt from address on national health insurance, April 1976. Cong Digest 56:213+ Ag '77
Should saccharin be banned? interview. pors U.S. News 82:59-60 Ap 4 '77
MARTIN, James S. Jr, and Young, A. T.
Viking to Mars: profile of a space expedition. il pors Space World N-4-160:4-27 Ap '77
MARTIN, Jill
Bread and wine; I. Silone's novel. Engl J 66:65-6 Mr '77
MARTIN, Jim
Dig yourself a shallow well. Org Gard & Farm 24:81-2 Jl '77
MARTIN, Joan
I hate you! . . . love, Jeff. Writers Digest 57:22 D '77
MARTIN, John Bartlow
Commonwealth's choice. il Harpers 225:17-20 D '77
Immodest proposal: Nikita to Adlai; excerpt from Adlai Stevenson and the world. il por Am Heritage 28:88-9 Ag '77
MARTIN, Joseph, Jr
United States discusses disarmament in U.N. General Assembly debate; statement, November 1, 1976. Dept State Bull 76:17-22 Ja 10 '77
MARTIN, Larry D. and Stewart, J. D.
Teeth in Ichthyornis (class: aves) bibl il Science 195:1331-2 Mr 25 '77
—and others
Cheetah-like cat in the North American Pleistocene. bibl il Science 195:981-2 Mr 11 '77
MARTIN, Lee R.
Diving the Sea of Cortez. il Oceans 10:16-19 Mr '77
MARTIN, Linda Grant
Bad debt that was profitable for everybody. Fortune 96:203 O '77
MARTIN, Luann Habegger
Dilemmas of national service for youth. Chr Cent 94:228+ Mr 9 '77
MARTIN, Malachi B.
Out of this world (cont) Nat R 29:388, 615, 831, 998, 1242 Ap 1, My 27, Jl 22, S 2, O 28 '77
Priestly ordination. il Nat R 29:206-7 F 18 '77
MARTIN, Maria
Maria Martin: the brush behind Audubon's birds. M. Williams and P. Elliott. il Ms 5:14-15+ Ap '77 *
MARTIN, Millicent
Company. New Yorker 53:26-7 Je 13 '77 *
MARTIN, Parthena, and Consroe, Paul
Cannabinoid induced behavioral convulsions in rabbits (cont) bibl Science 197:1301-2 S 23 '77
MARTIN, Paul
Benefits of fasting. il Chr Cent 94:298-301 Mr 30 '77
Train your eyes; better your score. il Sci Digest 81:7-9 Mr '77
MARTIN, Peter W.
What's in a name? Plenty. Nation 226:6-7 Ja 7 '78
MARTIN, Richard J. See Gewirtz, G. jt auth
MARTIN, Robert K.
Sacred conversations. Poetry 130:36-40 Ap '77
MARTIN, Steve
Comedians. por Time 110:98 O 31 '77 *
Silly putty. M. Orth. por Newsweek 89:59 Ja 31 '77 *
MARTIN, Thérèse. See Teresa of the Child Jesus, Saint
MARTIN, William Frederick
Who says athletes are dumb? il Forbes 120:55+ D 1 '77 *
MARTIN Beck Theatre (building) See New York (city)—Theater
MARTIN Processing, Inc. See Conglomerate corporations
MARTINDALE, David
Lightning safety. il Outdoor Life 159:133-4 Je '77
19,000 tornadoes later. . .profile of terrible triangle, 45-year drought cycle. il map Sci Digest 81:11-15 My '77
Sweaty palms in the control tower. bibl il por Psychol Today 10:70-2+ F '77
MARTINDALE, Meredith
Benjamin Franklin's residence in France: the Hôtel de Valentinois in Passy. bibl il Antiques 112:262-73 Ag '77
MARTINE, Suzanne
Living alone & loving it. il por Mademoiselle 83:202-3+ S '77 *
MARTINEZ, Alfredo Ramos. See Ramos Martinez, A.
MARTINEZ, Mary
Underground Church. Nat R 29:944 Ag 19 '77
MARTINEZ, Romeo
Images from the Paris Salon. il Pop Phot 81: 134-7+ D '77
MARTINEZ, Rubén Berríos
Independence for Puerto Rico: the only solution. For Affairs 55:561-83 Ap '77
MARTINEZ, Tomás
Gambling, goods, and games. il Society 14:79-81 S '77
MARTINEZ-HERNANDEZ, Antonio, and others
Glutamine synthetase: glial localization in brain. bibl il Science 195:1356-8 Mr 25 '77
MARTINEZ-PARDO, Rafael. See Bowers, W. S. jt auth
MARTINI, Nino
Obituary
Opera N por 41:32 F 19 '77
MARTINI (cocktail) See Cocktails
MARTINIQUE
If your ship stops in Martinique. il Sunset 158:38 Mr '77
Other Martinique. J. O'Reilly. il House & Gard 149:76+ D '77
MARTINS, Peter
Peter Martins; interview, ed by T. Tobias. il pors Dance Mag 51:34-46 Je '77
about
Dance Magazine Awards 1977. il pors Dance Mag 51:30-5 Jl '77 *
Peter Martins, choreographer. il Horizon 21:92 Ja '78 *

MARTINS

Anecdotes, facetiae, satire, etc.

Purple martins, the ingrates, don't read their own paper. M. Hamman. Smithsonian 8:144 My '77

MARTY, Martin E.
Confusion among the faithful. il Sat R 40:10-11 Je 25 '77
God's almost chosen people. il Am Heritage 28:4-7 Ag '77
M.E.M.O. See issues of Christian century
Martin E. Marty: opposing the Zeitgeist. Chr Cent 94:5 Ja 5 '77
Science versus religion: an old squabble simmers down. il Sat R 5:29-32+ D 10 '77
Season for binding together. Chr Cent 94:51-3 Ja 26 '77

about

Yes, there are semi-evangelicals. J. Bayly. Chr Today 21:23 Jl 29 '77 *

MARTZ, Karl
Karl Martz retrospective. il por Ceram Mo 25: 27-34 My '77 *

MARUSI, Augustine Raymond
Some fun at last. por Forbes 120:112 D 1 '77 *

MARVIN, Lee
Marvin as in marlin; black marlin; interview, ed by R. Vaughan. il pors Motor B & S 139:72-5+ My '77

MARVIN, Mary
Zucchini milk—a new discovery. il Org Gard & Farm 24:100+ Jl '77

MARX, Groucho
At the circus go west; E. Fleming vs. Arthur Marx. R. Rosenblatt. il por New Repub 176:60-2 My 21 '77 *
Comedy's king leer. C. Michener. il pors Newsweek 90:78-9 Ag 29 '77 *

MARX, Karl
Greening of Karl Marx. R. Stromberg. Nat R 29: 991+ S 2 '77 *

MARX, Leo
Comments: aging of America. Am Hist R 82: 595-9 Je '77

MARX, Wesley
Huntington Beach: disaster waits impatiently in wings; excerpt from Acts of God, acts of man. Audubon 79:126-8 Mr '77

MARXISM. See Communism; Socialism

MARXISM and religion. See Socialism and religion

MARXIST Social Scientists, Union of. See Socialism—United States

MARY, Virgin
Many Advents, one Mary. A. McCarthy. Commonweal 104:810+ D 23 '77
Mary's assumption, God's promise fulfilled. R. Kress. America 137:71-4 Ag 13 '77
No match; Mary, Mother of God. G. McCauley. America 137:inside back cover D 24 '77

MARY Columba Offerman, Sister. See Offerman, M. C.

MARY Magdalene, Saint
Red-haired saint. J. T. Baker. il Chr Cent 94: 328-32 Ap 6 '77 *

MARY Richards (television character) See Women in television

M. Thomas Magee, Sister. See Magee, M. T.

MARYHILL Museum of Fine Arts, Maryhill. See Art galleries and museums—Washington (state)

MARYLAND
See also
Air pollution—Maryland
Architecture, Domestic—Maryland
Baltimore County
Booksellers and bookselling—Maryland
Chesapeake and Ohio Canal National Historical Park
Chesapeake Bay
Education—Maryland
Express highways—Maryland
Gardens—Maryland
Historic houses, sites, etc.—Maryland
Housing—Maryland
Landscape protection—Maryland
Opera—Maryland
Potomac River
Smith Island
Trials—Maryland
Wye Island

Parks and reserves

Evolution of a people's park; Glen Echo Park. M. Travaglini. il Am Educ 13:22-4 My '77
From the echoes of Chautauqua; Creative Education Program and the Children's Experimental Workshop at Glen Echo Park. M. Travaglini. il Am Educ 13:17-21 My '77

Politics and government

See also
Politics, Corruption in—Maryland

Religious institutions and affairs

Where are all the churches? Columbia. il U.S. News 83:75-6 D 26 '77

MARYLAND Ballet. See Ballet companies

MARYLAND furniture. See Furniture, American

MARYLAND Institute for Emergency Medical Services. See Baltimore—Hospitals

MARYLES, Daisy
(ed) Bookselling and marketing. See issues of Publishers weekly
Currents. Pub W 212:24-5 Ag 22 '77
—and Giusto, Joann
Currents: PW's annual survey of Christmas buying trends. Pub W 212:36-7 D 12 '77

MARZORATI, Gerald
Guernica will hang in the Prado as Picasso wished. il por Art N 76:65-7 My '77
MOMA's tower in the sky. il Art N 76:54-6 Ap '77

MARZULLO, Vito
Arrangement. J. Lelyveld. il por N Y Times Mag p 138 Mr 27 '77 *

MASATOMI, Hiroyuki
Too sacred to survive? F. H. Marks. il por Int Wildlife 8:20-5 Ja '78 *

MASCARAS. See Cosmetics

MASCULINITY (psychology)
New sexual pyramid; The club. K. Durbin. il Mademoiselle 83:142+ F '77

MASDEN, H. Daniel
Community college that would not freeze. Educ Digest 42:34-5 Ap '77

MASELLO, Sonia E.
Mother believed where there's a will, there has to be a way. House B 119:78 O '77

MASER, Werner
Son of Hitler? por Time 110:45 N 14 '77 *

MASERS
Water vapor maser turn-on in the HII region W3 (OH) A. D. Haschick and others. bibl il Science 198:1153-5 D 16 '77

MASIA, Seth
How to load a pack. il Outdoor Life 159:149-50 F '77
How to pitch your tent. il Outdoor Life 159:133-4 My '77

MASKED dance dramas, Korean. See Folk drama, Korean

MASKEY, Jacqueline
Dance. See issues of High fidelity and Musical America

MASKING stimuli. See Stimulus and response

MASKS (sculpture)
Decoding the message of African sculpture; mask carvings. O. Balogun. il UNESCO Courier 30:12-15+ My '77
How to make Paris craft masks. S. Sundick. il Design (US) 78:22 Summ '77

Photographs

Masks from 20 countries; African carvings. il UNESCO Courier 30:16-20 My '77

MASLAND, Richard Lambert
New hope for epileptics—but we still have a long way to go; interview. il por U.S. News 83:53-4 S 5 '77

MASLOW, Jonathan Evan
Puerto Rico, the 51st state? New Repub 177:12-14 Jl 2 '77
Reports & comment: Puerto Rico. il Atlantic 240:6+ Jl '77
Sporting life. Sat R 5:56-7 O 29; 49-51 N 26; 70-1 D 10 '77

MASON, B. J.
Has the weather gone mad? New Repub 177:21-3 Jl 30 '77

about

Cold shower for climatologists. N. Wade. Science 197:647 Ag 12 '77 *

MASON, Bert. See Fuller, V. jt auth

MASON, Daniel Gregory
Grand, glorious & unknown. D. Garvelmann. Am Rec G 40:17-19 O '77 *

MASON, Don
Agent OO-art; interview, ed by Vasari. por Art N 76:20+ Ja '77

MASON, Flo
Retired schoolteacher is mover and shaker as VISTA volunteer in Alaska. por Aging 266: 18-19 D '76 *

MASON, Jerry
Joys and the fears of childhood caught in Ridge Press/Grosset & Dunlap book; interview, ed by R. Dahlin. Pub W 211:221-2 My 23 '77

MASON, John
Traveling telephones. il Pop Sci 212:62-5 Ja '78

MASON, Rosemary
Amnesia; poem. Chr Cent 94:404 Ap 27 '77

MASONRY
See also
Bricklaying

MASONRY flooring. See Flooring

MASS
Listen, your holiness; Tridentine Mass. M. Smith. America 137:286 O 29 '77

MASS (music)
Notes on two Roman manuscripts of the early sixteenth century. R. Sherr. bibl f il Mus Q 63:48-73 Ja '77
Problems of transmission in Obrecht's Missa Je ne demande. T. Noblitt. bibl f il Mus Q 63: 211-23 Ap '77
See also
Phonograph records—Mass (music)
MASS (physics)
Conservation of mass and mole relationships. E. M. Hauck. il por Chemistry 50:25-6 Je '77
MASS media
Children's literature & mass media. A. P. Nilsen. il por SLJ 23:106-9 Mr '77
Media. N. Ephron. See issues of Esquire to July 1977
Media. R. Reeves. Esquire 88:40-1 Ag; 30+ S; 20+ O; 53-4 N; 68+ D '77; 89:38+ Ja '78
Spiro redux; news media criticized in Network. D. Brudnoy. Nat R 29:338-9 Mr 18 '77
See also
Accuracy in Media (organization)
Gossip in mass media
Motion pictures
New York (city)—Mass media
Periodicals
Radio broadcasting
Television broadcasting
Women in the mass media industry

International aspects
Now, a new international information order? H. I. Schiller. Intellect 106:42-3 Ag '77
World debate on information: flood-tide or balanced flow? symposium. il UNESCO Courier 30:4-33 Ap '77

Moral and religious aspects
Mass media's mythic world: at odds with Christian values. W. F. Fore. bibl Chr Cent 94: 32-8 Ja 19 '77
Perfidious printer. P. W. Schmidtchen. il Hobbies 82:134-6 Jl '77

Multiple ownership
America's press: too much power for too few? A. P. Sanoff. il U.S. News 83:27-33 Ag 15 '77
Another publisher expands into broadcasting; Ziff Corporation's acquisition of Rust Craft Greeting Cards Inc. il Bus W p87 N 21 '77
Bagging the broadcast limit; R. H. Park's broadcasting and newspaper operations. por Bus W p50 Jl 25 '77
Busting the media trusts. K. Phillips. Harpers 255:23-4+ Jl '77
Challenging media monopolies; newspaper-broadcast complexes. D. Carmody. il N Y Times Mag p21-4 Jl 31 '77
Crimping the air power of the press; FCC ruling against newspaper-broadcasting stations crossownerships. Bus W p33 Mr 14 '77
Divestiture debate; newspaper-television-radio combinations. Newsweek 89:43 Mr 14 '77
Time to sell? publishing and broadcasting operations. Forbes 120:32-3 Jl 1 '77
See also
Outlet Company

Political aspects
Busting the media trusts. K. Phillips. il Harpers 255:23-4+ Jl '77
Commentaries: media power; symposium. bibl il Society 15:10-25 N '77
Mass media and the 1976 Presidential campaign. H. Mowlana. Intellect 105:244-5 F '77
Sins of omission. E. McCarthy. Harpers 254:90-2 Je '77

Social aspects
Against consensus. R. Whittemore. Harpers 255: 15-17 Jl '77
Believing the Rocky Mountain news. J. M. Wall. Chr Cent 94:267-8 Mr 23 '77
Entertainment—the great leveler. il Forbes 120:P41-8+ S 15 '77
Hero, the harlot, and the glorified horse as mythic Americans. C. J. Deming and B. J. Wahlstrom. bibl Intellect 105:439-41 Je '77
Newspeak generation. R. Whittemore. Harpers 254:16+ F '77
Power of media elite. S. Rothman. Intellect 106:10 Jl '77
Power to the eloquent. J. Hitchcock. Yale R 66:374-87 Mr '77
MASS media and science
Science, the media and the paranormal. Sci N 112:118 Ag 20 '77
MASS spectroscopy. See Spectrum analysis
MASS transit. See Local transit
MASSACHUSETTS
See also
Architecture, Domestic—Massachusetts
Booksellers and bookselling—Massachusetts
City planning—Massachusetts
Criminal justice, Administration of—Massachusetts
Ecology—Massachusetts
Education—Massachusetts
Gardens—Massachusetts
Historic houses, sites, etc.—Massachusetts
Landscape protection—Massachusetts
Libraries—Massachusetts
Martha's Vineyard
Music—Massachusetts
Music festivals—Massachusetts
Nantucket Island
National parks and reserves—Massachusetts
Opera—Massachusetts
Prisons—Massachusetts
Public health—Massachusetts
Public welfare—Massachusetts
School libraries—Massachusetts
Tuckernuck Island

Hotels, motels, etc.
See Hotels, motels, etc.—United States

Industries
How a company helps its state attract business. V. Louviere. il Nations Bus 65:75 S '77

Legislature
Adopting an orphan. Time 109:19 My 30 '77

Library Extension, Bureau of
Massachusetts Bureau chief ousted by commissioners. Lib J 102:2302-3 N 15 '77

Politics and government
Hard times liberal: M. S. Dukakis. W. A. Henry. 3d. New Repub 176:20-3 Ja 15 '77
Joe Kennedy comes of age. H. Gorey. il pors N Y Times Mag p6-11+ My 29 '77

Restaurants
See Restaurants—United States
MASSACHUSETTS Bay Transportation Authority
When Boeing gets into the streetcar business. il Bus W p 127+ S 12 '77
MASSACHUSETTS Horticultural Society
Culture & notes; awards for contributions to field of horticulture. Horticulture 55:70-1 My '77
Five great gardens. K. Bast. il Horticulture 55: 28+ Mr '77
MASSACHUSETTS Institute of Technology, Cambridge
MIT's new coarse guide. Newsweek 89:57 My 30 '77

Press
See University presses
MASSACHUSETTS Library Association
MLA backs Mass. Bureau in its try for more clout. Lib J 102:749 Ap 1 '77
MASSAGE
How to get tension out, energy up; shiatsu; Oriental finger-pressure technique. il Mademoiselle 83:134-5 D '77
How to massage your spouse. G. Downing. il Sat Eve Post 249:66-9 O '77
MASSAGE showers. See Shower baths
MASSAQUOI, Hans J.
Alex Haley in Juffure. il pors Ebony 32:31-3+ Jl '77
Alex Haley: the man behind Roots. il pors Ebony 32:33-6+ Ap '77
Should parents spare the rod? il Ebony 33:68-70+ Ja '78
MASSE, Richard F. and Broussard, Camille
Land exchange. il map Parks & Rec 12:26-9+ D '77
MASSELINK, Ben
Boys! Throw your voices! story. Sat Eve Post 249:70-1 Ap '77
MASSENET, Jules
Le Cid; recording. Am Rec G 40:30-1 F '77 *
Esclarmonde. Reviews
Hi Fi 27:MA16-17 Mr '77 *
Opera N 41:28 Ja 22 '77 *
Esclarmonde. D. Arthur. il Am Rec G 40:24-5 Mr '77 *
Massenet in 'Frisco. D. Arthur. il Am Rec G 40:54-5 N '76 *
MASSERA, José Luis
Academy steps up human rights drive. Sci N 111:293-4 My 7 '77 *
MASSEY, Bob
Broker profile; interview. por Motor B & S 140: 117 D '77
MASSEY, Clarence
$20,000 for a hat? il por Ret Liv 17:44 Ap '77
MASSEY-Ferguson Ltd
Massey-Ferguson's pile of problems. il Bus W p30-1 Je 20 '77
You can't go fast without taking some bumps. il por Forbes 119:57-8 My 15 '77
MASSIE, Robert K.
1921 SALT talks—and you are there. il pors N Y Times Mag p38-40+ O 2 '77
about
Advance guard. il por Time 109:85 F 14 '77 *
Arbitration ends dispute of Atheneum and Robert Massie. M. Reuter. Pub W 211:24 Ja 31 '77 *

MASSINE, Leonide
Conversation with Leonide Massine; interview, ed by R. Hardin. il pors Dance Mag 51:68-70 D '77

MASSMAN, Gordon
Halloween pumpkins; poem. Esquire 87:24 Mr '77

MASSON, Charles, Jr
Romantic bouquets. il House & Gard 149:40 Jl '77

about

Let the flowers speak. il pors House & Gard 149:74-7 Jl '77 *

MASSON, Jeff. See Merwin, W. S. jt trs

MASSON, Walter
Spaghetti squash makes an unusual vegetable. il Org Gard & Farm 24:72-3 Je '77

MAST, Gerald
From 400 blows to Small change. New Repub 176:23-5 Ap 2 '77

MASTECTOMY. See Breast—Cancer—Surgery

MASTER registers (proposed) See United States—Library of Congress—Catalogs

MASTERS, Hilary
Hurricane of death; story; excerpt from Post. Sports Illus 47:100-4 N 28 '77

MASTERS, Kim
ETS's star chamber. New Repub 176:13-14 F 5 '77

MASTERS, William Howell, and Johnson, V. E.
Sex after sixty-five; excerpt from Human sexual inadequacy. il Sat Eve Post 249:48-52 Mr '77

MASTERS of Business Administration schools. See Business schools and colleges

MASTERS Track and Field. See Running

MASTERSON, Dan
Outing; Lawn; poems. Poetry 130:34-5 Ap '77

MASTERY learning. See Learning, Psychology of

MASTITIS
Control mastitis without drugs? C. S. Machan. il Farm J 101:Dairy 9+ S '77
Growing problem of coliform mastitis. Farm J 101:Dairy 8 D '77
How much is mastitis costing you? Farm J 101:Dairy 8 Je '77

Diagnosis

Whip disease with nutrition? R. E. Wanner. il Farm J 101:Dairy 10+ Ja '77

MASTODONS
Bone bonanza: early bird and mastodon. il Sci N 112:198 S 24 '77

MASTROIANNI, Marcello
Mastroianni talks about real-life love; interview, ed by C. B. Pepper. Vogue 167:122+ O '77

MASTROIANNI, Umberto
Neglected sculptor at Spoleto U.S.A. J. Gruen. il Art N 76:122+ S '77 *

MASTROVITO, Rene C.
Facts about hypnosis. il Seventeen 36:159 My '77

MASTS and rigging
Elements of mast design. il Motor B & S 139:64-5 My '77
Know your rigging:
Anatomy of wire rope. P. Dean. il Motor B & S 139:48-9+ F '77
Masthead weight and stability. J. Teale. Motor B & S 141:52+ Ja '78
Re-rigging (cheaply) with Norseman fittings. B. Lauren. il Motor B & S 139:129-31 Je '77
Simple, light, and adjustable; rigging on the Blitz. J. Rousmaniere. il Yachting 141:62+ My '77
Unstep your own mast. J. Dillon. il Motor B & S 140:118-19 O '77
See also
Sails

MATA, Eduardo
Symphony appointment raises questions. J. Ardoin. por Hi Fi 27:MA32-3 My '77 *

MATADORS. See Bullfighters

MATCHETT, William H.
Fireweed; poem. New Yorker 53:46 My 16 '77

MATERIALISM
See also
Wealth

MATERIALS
See also
Automobiles—Materials
Building materials

Handling

See Materials handling

MATERIALS handling
Automated stackers used by construction equipment dealer to speed parts retrieval. il Archit Rec 162:120 Jl '77

MATERNAL deprivation
Early separation—it's a problem; views of Rose Grobstein. K. Turok. Psychol Today 10:30 Ap '77

MATERNAL love. See Love, Maternal

MATERNITY benefits
Maternity bills: who pays? S. Auerbach. Am Home 80:20+ Je '77
Pregnancy exclusion not sexually biased. C. Polhemus. M Labor R 100:73-6 Mr '77
Working woman: labor pains. L. C. Pogrebin. il Ladies Home J 94:46+ Ap '77

MATHEMATICAL ability
Johann Dase and some other mental calculators. J. Ashbrook. Sky & Tel 54:365 N '77

MATHEMATICAL analysis
Comparison of Fourier analysis and feature analysis in pattern-specific color aftereffects. M. A. Green and others; discussion. bibl il Science 198:207-10 O 14 '77

MATHEMATICAL induction. See Logic, Symbolic and mathematical

MATHEMATICAL instruments
See also
Slide rules

MATHEMATICAL physics
Theory of the rainbow. H. M. Nussenzveig. il Sci Am 236:116-27 bibl(p 148) Ap '77

MATHEMATICAL recreations
How logical are you? excerpt from mathematical magic show. M. Gardner. Read Digest 112:139-40 Ja '78
How to program calculators for fun and games. il Pop Electr 11:39-46 Je '77
Incredible tale of the 37-year puzzle. D. Huff. il por Pop Sci 211:26+ O '77
Mathematical games. M. Gardner. See issues of Scientific American
Mathematical games: are they bona fide research? G. B. Kolata. Science 197:546 Ag 5 '77

MATHEMATICIANS
See also
Diaconis, P.
Erdös, P.

MATHEMATICS
See also
Arithmetic
Combinatorial analysis
Logic, Symbolic and mathematical
Numbers, Theory of
Numerical calculations

Study and teaching

Aftermath of the new math: its originators defend it. G. B. Kolata. Science 195:854-7 Mr 4 '77
Back to 2 plus 2: counterrevolution in math. G. W. Pinney. Nation 224:625-7 My 21 '77
Courses that women can count on; colleges offering math-anxiety classes. E. J. Pascoe. il McCalls 104:68 Jl '77
Math anxiety. B. Donady and S. Tobias. Educ Digest 43:49-52 D '77
Math mystique: fear of figuring. Time 109:36 Mr 14 '77
New math and its aftermath. D. Rappaport. Educ Digest 42:6-9 Ja '77
Numeration systems—a white elephant in elementary school. D. Rappaport. Educ Digest 42:56-7 Ap '77
Position paper on basic math skills. Educ Digest 43:45-8 D '77
Smorgasbord for an IQ of 150; Study of Mathematically Precocious Youth program at Johns Hopkins. il Time 109:64 Je 6 '77
Success in math. D. Z. Iams. Clearing H 50:362-3 Ap '77
What to do about basic skills in math. R. Taylor. Todays Educ 66:32-3 Mr '77
Young prodigies take off under special program; Study of Mathematically Precocious Youth at Johns Hopkins. D. Nevin. il por Smithsonian 8:76-81 bibl(160) O '77

Aids and devices

Effects of the fraction ruler manipulative for teaching computation of fractions. D. P. Schiller. il Clearing H 50:300-3 Mr '77

Anecdotes, facetiae, satire, etc.

Pi in the face; math anxiety. R. Baker. N Y Times Mag p 12 S 18 '77

MATHER, Cotton
Battling the red death. M. Musser. il por Am Hist Illus 12:30-6 N '77 *

MATHERS, Michael
Michael Mathers: the professionals. N. Canavor. il Pop Phot 81:142-51+ D '77 *

MATHEWS, Clarence
Unforgettable Clarence Mathews. B. N. Butler. il Read Digest 111:139-42 D '77 *

MATHEWS, Harry
Flip-strip sonnet, the lipogram and other mad modes of wordplay. M. Gardner. il Sci Am 236:121-6 F '77 *

MATHEWS, John
With education in Washington. See issues of Education digest

MATHEWS, Joseph Wesley
Harry, Joe and Al: the authenticity of death. G. Forshey. Chr Cent 94:1022-4 N 9 '77 *

MATHIAS, Charles McCurdy, 1922-
Dying party? interview. pors U.S. News 83:24-5 Ag 29 '77

MATHIAS, Elizabeth. See Borrello, M. A. jt auth

MATHIAS, Rex
Republican sentiment in Australia. Chr Cent 94:630 Jl 6 '77
Uniting church: new days, new ways. il Chr Cent 94:786-7 S 14 '77

MATHIS, Philip M.
Justifying science in an era of vocationalism. Educ Digest 42:32-5 My '77

MATHUR, Raghu P.
Educate teenagers to become people. Clearing H 51:170-2 D '77

MATING behavior. See Sexual behavior—Animals

MATISSE, Henri
Earthly paradise. M. Stevens. il Newsweek 90:100-1 S 19 '77 *
Final flowering of Henri Matisse, invincible artist. J. Russell. il Smithsonian 8:72-9 S '77 *
Masterful cutouts. il Horizon 20:27 S '77 *
Matisse cutouts. B. Forgey. il por Art N 76:66-9 D '77 *
No better religion; show of cutouts at the National Gallery in Washington. L. Prothro. Nat R 30:41-2 Ja 6 '78 *
Puvis de Chavannes: the alternative. P. Schneider. bibl il Art in Am 65:94-8 My '77 *
Sultan and the scissors; show of Matisse cutouts. R. Hughes. il Time 110:96-7 S 19 '77 *

MATLACK, Bruce
Trailer maintenance. Yachting 142:128-30 D '77

MATOVCIK, Lisa M. See Anderson, G. R. jt auth

MATRICIDE in literature. See Literature—Themes

MATRIMONY. See Marriage

MATRIX management. See Business management

MATSON, Peter H.
Unfinished house. Am Home 80:24 D '77

MATSUSHITA Electric Company, Ltd
Matsushita attacks its American problem; Quasar Electronics Corp. il Bus W p28 F 21 '77
$1,300 Christmas toy made in Japan; competition between Sony and Matsushita; videotape recorders. P. J. Schuyten. il Fortune 96:178-80+ S '77

MATTEL, Inc
Mattel's successful retreat. il Bus W p43 My 16 '77

MATTER
See also
Critical point
Mass (physics)
Surfaces

MATTER, Interstellar
Bok globules. R. L. Dickman. il Sci Am 236:66-70+ bibl(p 142) Je '77
Cellulose between the stars: excelsior; work of Fred Hoyle and N. C. Wickramasinghe. Sci N 112:133 Ag 27 '77
Consequences of meeting a dense interstellar cloud. Sky & Tel 54:193 S '77
Gone with the wind; with views of R. Weymann. D. E. Thomsen. il Sci N 112:106-7 Ag 13 '77
Heaviest (99) space molecule yet; cyanotriacetylene. Sci N 111:260-1 Ap 23 '77
Intergalactic gas: toward a closed universe. il Sci N 112:36 Jl 16 '77
Sodium cloud of Io. il Sky & Tel 54:479-80 D '77
Star dust. E. P. Ney. bibl il Science 195:541-6 F 11 '77
Structure of the interstellar medium; synthetic photography from radio wavelengths of interstellar gases. C. Heiles. Sci Am 238:74-84 Ja '78

MATTERN, Douglas
With humanity as pawns. il Commonweal 104:329-31 My 27 '77

MATTERN, Evelyn
Heads, hearts and justice. America 136:389-91 Ap 30 '77

MATTHAU, Walter
Matthau, the magnificent; interview, ed by L. Smith. por Ladies Home J 94:40+ Je '77

MATTHEWS, Clifford, and others
Deuterolysis of amino acid precursors: evidence for hydrogen cyanide polymers as protein ancestors. bibl il Science 198:622-5 N 11 '77

MATTHEWS, D. A. and others
Dihydrofolate reductase: X-ray structure of the binary complex with methotrexate. bibl il Science 197:452-5 Jl 29 '77

MATTHEWS, Douglas G.
Control sewer corrosion with H_2O_2. Am City & County 92:65 F '77

MATTHEWS, James
Death in detention in South Africa. P. Irish. Chr Cent 94:8 Ja 5 '77 *

MATTHEWS, Kathy
How to be your own boss; excerpt from On your own: 99 alternatives to a 9 to 5 job. il Sat Eve Post 249:52-3+ N '77

MATTHEWS, Ruth Inglis
Movies. See issues of Consumers' research magazine

MATTHEWS, Samuel W.
What's happening to our climate? il Read Digest 110:88-92 Mr '77

MATTHEWS, Victor
Fox in wolf's clothing. il por Forbes 120:152+ N 15 '77 *

MATTHIAE, Paolo
Ebla. il UNESCO Courier 30:6-12 F '77

MATTHIAS, Bernd T.
Attractive mystery in superconductivity. Sci N 111:229 Ap 9 '77 *
—See Vandenberg, J. M. jt auth

MATTHIAS, John
Pointless and poignant. Poetry 129:340-55 Mr '77
about
Comment. R. B. Shaw. Poetry 129:234-5 Ja '77 *

MATTHIESSEN, Barbara Heggie
La Scala: the most famous opera house in the world. il Travel 148:44-9 O '77
Oxford. il Travel 147:24-31+ Ap '77

MATTHIESSEN, Peter
Track on the beach. il Audubon 79:68-9+ Mr '77

MATTIS, David L.
Digital frequency readout for shortwave receivers. il Pop Electr 11:49-51+ F '77

MATTLIN, Everett. See Beaudoin, J. T. jt auth

MATTRESSES

Purchasing

Bedding down. Seventeen 36:74 F '77
How to buy a good night's sleep. E. Cole. il McCalls 104:116+ S '77

MATURA, Mustapha
Rum an Coca-Cola. Reviews
Nation 225:540 N 19 '77 *
New Yorker 53:105-6 N 7 '77 *

MATURATION (biology)
Pheromonally induced sexual maturation in females: regulation by the social environment of the male; house mice. J. R. Lombardi and J. G. Vandenbergh. bibl il Science 196:545-6 Ap 29 '77
Socially induced inhibition of genetically determined maturation in the platyfish, xiphophorus maculatus. J. J. Sohn. bibl il Science 195:199-201 Ja 14 '77

MATURIN, Larry, and Curtiss, Roy, 3d
Degradation of DNA by nucleases in intestinal tract of rats. bibl il Science 196:216-18 Ap 8 '77

MATURITY
Adult at eighteen? excerpt from How to stop worrying about your kids. J. D. Sanderson. Read Digest 110:136-9 Mr '77
Adult life cycles and teaching. D. Roberts. bibl f il Engl J 66:38-41 S '77
All of life's a stage. K. L. Woodward and P. Brinkley-Rogers. Newsweek 89:83 Je 6 '77
Climb to maturity: how the best and brightest came of age; excerpt from Adaptation to life. G. E. Vaillant. il Psychol Today 11:34-5+ S '77
Don't be adultish! interview, ed by D. Goleman. A. Montagu. il Psychol Today 11:46-7+ Ag '77
How to be 30 and love it; symposium. Harp Baz 110:132-3+ O '77
Kids afraid to grow up. C. Best and W. Best. il Parents Mag 52:58-9+ O '77
Thirty: not a dirty word anymore. M. Wolynski. Vogue 167:150+ O '77
Turning thirty with The graduate; motion picture, Rocky, compared. M. W. Foley. America 137:78-80 Ag 13 '77

Anecdotes, facetiae, satire, etc.

Revitalization of Clay Filter: yet another passage. N. Ephron. il Esquire 87:28+ Ap '77

MATURITY in literature. See Literature—Themes

MATUSA, Paula
Corruption and catastrophe: DePalma's Carrie. il Film Q 31:32-8 Fall '77

MATUSOW, Barbara
Art on TV: an unhappy marriage. Art N 76:26+ F '77

MATZ, Mary Jane
Flesh-and-blood angel. por Opera N 41:18-19 My '77

MAUGHAM, Kay
Little girl who became Farrah Fawcett-Majors. il pors Good H 185:128-9+ Ag '77

MAUI (island)
Hot time on a cool volcano. H. Sutton. il map Sat R 4:52-4 Mr 5 '77
Maui is in the chips. R. W. Johnston. il maps Sports Illus 46:44-7 Ja 24 '77

MAULDIN, Bill
Best gets better; editorial cartoons. H. Mitgang. il Art N 76:92-3 O '77 *

MAULDIN, Raleigh C.
Texas natives. D. Snell. il pors Horticulture 55:38-51 Ap '77 *

MAULDIN, William Henry. See Mauldin, B.

MAUNDER, E. Walter
Case of the missing sunspots. J. A. Eddy. il Sci Am 236:80-8 My '77 *

MAURA, Sister
Born of Mary; poem. America 137:455 D 24 '77

MAUREEN Murphy, Sister. See Murphy, M.

MAURER, Charles E.
How they're extracting oil from tar sands. il Pop Sci 210:80-3+ My '77
MAURER, Harry
Is it the future? Will it work? il por Nation 225:6-10 Jl 2 '77
Jews and leftists tremble. Nation 224:170-3 F 12 '77
—See Peraza, M. jt auth
MAURICE Béjart's Ballet of the 20th Century
Actual Maurice Bejart's imaginary Moliere. N. M. Stoop. il Dance Mag 51:50-5 Ap '77
Bejart's Notre Faust. il Hi Fi 27:MA10-11 Jl '77
Béjart's three queen bees; performance at the Uris Theatre, New York City. H. Saal. il Newsweek 89:93 Ap 4 '77
Maurice Béjart's Ballet of the 20th Century; season at the Uris, March 22-April 3. R. Baker. il Dance Mag 51:41-7 Jl '77
Twentieth Century Ballet: transatlantique. W. Terry. il por Sat R 4:44-5 Mr 19 '77
MAURITIUS
Foreign relations
France
See France—Foreign relations—Mauritius
MAURIZI, Dennis
Alexander Wilson. il pors Conservationist 31:2-7 My '77
MAURO, Carol
It serves them right. Ms 6:22 N '77
MAURY, Inez
My mother the mail carrier; story; excerpt. Ms 5:85-8 Mr '77
MAUSER, Ferdinand F.
Losing something in the translation. Harvard Bus R 55:14+ Jl '77
MAVROGENES, Nancy A.
101 ways to react to books. Engl J 66:64-6 My '77
MAWSON, Sir Douglas
This accursed land; excerpt from Mawson's will. L. Bickel. il por map Read Digest 111: 199-202+ Jl '77 *
MAX, Peter
America my love. . . ; interview, ed by J. Muchovej. il por Am Home 80:33+ F '77
about
Border dispute. Art N 76:34+ N '77 *
MAXEY, Julie
Not for children only. N Y Times Mag p90+ Ap 24 '77
Starring children. il N Y Times Mag p34-9+ Ag 21 '77
MAXIM, Larry
Photography story without photos. M. Major. America 137:192-4 O 1 '77 *
MAXIMILIAN, Alexander Philipp, Prinz von Wied-Neuwied. See Wied-Neuwied, M. A. P.
MAXIMILLIAN I, Emperor of the Holy Roman Empire
Raiser Max: first among the Hapsburgs. H. R. Trevor-Roper. il pors Horizon 19:68-81 Mr '77 *
MAXON, Robert C. and Malone, Bobby
Influence of peer groups on secondary school students. bibl Clearing H 50:191-3 Ja '77
MAXSON, Gloria
Complacent; poem. Chr Cent 94:1140 D 7 '77
Green wilderness; poem. Chr Cent 94:911 O 12 '77
Last census; poem. Chr Cent 94:1054 N 16 '77
MAXSON, Linda R. and others
Immunological resolution of a diploid-tetraploid species complex of tree frogs. bibl il Science 197:1012-13 S 2 '77
MAXTONE GRAHAM, James A.
Power from the sea; fact or fancy? il Pop Mech 147:192-6 Mr '77
Right sort of puzzle. il Horizon 19:94-5 Mr '77
MAXWELL, Elsa
Callas remembered. D. J. Soria. pors Opera N 42:15-16+ N '77 *
MAXWELL, Jessica
What your eyes tell you about your health. il Esquire 89:54-7 Ja '78
MAXWELL, John
Henry C. Pitz: picture maker. il por Am Artist 41:58-65+ My '77
MAXWELL, Nicole
Medical secrets of the Amazon. il por Américas 29:2-8 Je '77
MAXWELL, Paul C.
Maxwell and Sheahen chosen as Congressional fellows. pors Phys Today 30:71 Jl '77 *
MAXWELL, Willie
Seventh son. D. M. Alpern and V. E. Smith. il por Newsweek 90:21 Jl 4 '77 *
MAY, Derwent
Meanwhile, in Portugal. . . Sat R 5:22 O 29 '77
MAY, Elizabeth E.
Canada's moth war. bibl il map Environment 19:16-24 Ag '77
MAY, Ernest R.
Comments: aging of America. Am Hist R 82:600-3 Je '77
MAY, Jerome
Current foldback protects power supply and load. il Pop Electr 11:59-60 F '77
How computers detect and correct transmission errors. il Pop Electr 11:70-2 Je '77
MAY, Robert M. See Beddington, J. R; Diamond, J. M. jt auths
MAY flies
Amazing mayfly. B. Dalrymple. il Outdoor Life 159:65-7+ My '77
MAYAS
Earliest Maya. N. Hammond. il maps Sci Am 236:116-23 bibl(p 150) Mr '77
Oldest dates for Mayan origins; Cuello excavations. Sci N 112:4 Jl 2 '77
Ritual enemas. P. T. Furst and M. D. Coe. il Natur Hist 86:88-91 bibl(p97) Mr '77
Unraveling a Mayan mystery. R. J. Trotter. il map Sci N 111:74-5+ Ja 29 '77
See also
Chichén Itzá
MAYER, Ben
Projection blinking: a way toward discovery. il por Sky & Tel 54:246-9 S '77
MAYER, Charles S.
Russian and Soviet Painting: from the Church to the czars to the Ministry of Culture. il Art N 76:68-70 Summ '77
MAYER, Jean
Baby foods grow up. il Fam Health 9:36-7+ O '77
Battle over vitamin C. il Fam Health 9:26-8 Ap '77
Let's subtract additives. Fam Health 9:42-3 D '77
Saccharin ban: weighing the risks. il Fam Health 9:38-9+ Jl '77
Should you starve yourself thin? il Fam Health 9:24-6 F '77
Surefire ways to ruin your summer vacation. il Fam Health 9:22-4 Ag '77
Thirst quenchers. il Fam Health 9:32-4+ Je '77
3 musts that keep diabetics on the go. il Fam Health 9:30-2 My '77
Where can we get reliable facts about good nutrition? il Fam Health 9:32-3+ Ja '77
Why the feud over high-fiber foods? il Fam Health 9:32-4 Mr '77
—See Rawitscher, M. jt auth
MAYER, Kay
(ed) See Rossi, P. Great Saddles of the West: an interview with Paul Rossi
MAYER, Martin
Asolo Opera: uncommonly professional; Sarasota. il Hi Fi 27:MA28-9 Ag '77
Closet conservatives. Am Scholar 46:230+ Spr '77
(ed) See Plishka, P. Today's choice
MAYER, Milton
Fiasco. Progressive 41:26 F '77
In the swim. Progressive 41:24 Je '77
Whole old ball game. Progressive 41:25 S '77
MAYER, Peter
Pocket Books means to pull surprises out of its new kangaroo pouch; interview, ed by R. Dahlin. Pub W 211:64 F 7 '77
MAYER, Ralph
Technical page; questions and answers. See issues of American artist
MAYER, Timothy S.
Nothing undone. New Yorker 53:21-3 Ag 29 '77 *
MAYER, William
Modern American music makes a breakthrough. il Horizon 20:52-8 S '77
MAYERSVILLE, Miss.
Lady mayor of Mayersville; V. Blackwell. il pors Ebony 33:53-6+ D '77
MAYFLIES. See May flies
MAYHEW, Leonard
(tr) See Truffaut, F. Kind word for critics
MAYHEW, Margaret
Marriage to a stranger; story. Good H 185:181-4 Jl '77
MAYLEAS, Davidyne
Remarriage: survival manual; excerpt from Rewedded bliss: love, alimony, incest, ex-spouses, and domestic blessings. il Vogue 167:64+ N '77
MAYNARD, Edward
Dr Maynard and his primer. C. Worman. il Hobbies 81:142-3 F '77 *
MAYNARD, Fredelle
Turning failure into success. Read Digest 111: 123-6 D '77
MAYNARD, Harry
PS buyer's guide to turntables. il Pop Sci 211: 86-8+ N '77
Record cleaners—new devices reduce wear and noise. il Pop Sci 210:79-81+ Je '77
MAYNARD, Joyce
Good skate. il pors N Y Times Mag p70-1 Mr 6 '77
(ed) See Parton, D. Dolly
MAYNARD, Olga
Dance in Yugoslavia. il Dance Mag 51:67-82 My '77
(ed) See Makarova, N. Makarova: the sublime paradox

MAYNES, Charles William
Department discusses U.S. participation in international organizations; statement, June 15, 1977. Dept State Bull 77:100-3 Jl 18 '77
New hopes for human rights; address, September 9, 1977. Dept State Bull 77:556-61 O 24 '77
U.S. approach to the United Nations: new directions; address, July 13, 1977. Dept State Bull 77:284-91 Ag 29 '77
United States reiterates support for the independence of Namibia and Zimbabwe at Maputo conference; statement, May 21, 1977. Dept State Bull 77:58-9 Jl 11 '77
MAYO, John S.
Role of microelectronics in communication; with biographical sketch. il Sci Am 237:19, 192-3+ bibl(p260+) S '77
MAYONNAISE
From Julia Child's kitchen. J. Child. il McCalls 104:64+ Mr '77
Mayonnaise (and things that look like it) il Consumer Rep 42:148-51 Mr '77
MAYOR, A. Hyatt
Hunt for the fishing lady. il Antiques 112:113 Jl '77
MAYOR, Gilbert H. and others
Aluminum absorption and distribution: effect of parathyroid hormone. bibl il Science 197:1187-9 S 16 '77
MAYORS
See also
United States Conference of Mayors
Women mayors
MAYS, Benjamin Elijah
Last of the great schoolmasters. L. Bennett, Jr. il pors Ebony 33:72-4+ D '77 *
MAYS, Bruce
Gold in the trees. il Org Gard & Farm 24:128-9+ F '77
MAYTAG Company
Man who keeps those Maytag repairmen lonely; S. O. Swanger. E. Faltermayer. il pors Fortune 96:192-5+ N '77
MAZALESKI, Stanley C.
Price of blowing the whistle. H. Dudar. il pors N Y Times Mag p41-2+ O 30 '77 *
MAZDA (automobile) See Automobiles, Foreign
MAZET, Horace S.
Gentle giants: the phlegmatic whale shark. il Oceans 10:42-5 N '77
MAZLISH, Bruce
Psychobiography of everyday life. R. W. Noland. Nation 224:570-2 My 7 '77 *
MAZONOWICZ, Douglas
First hunters. il Field & S 82:130+ My '77
MAZUR, Jeffrey G.
Build this 10 function digital clock. il Radio-Electr 48:36-9 Ag; 40-2 S '77
Pink noise generator tests your hi-fi. il Radio-Electr 49:43-5 Ja '78
MAZZANTI, Deborah Szekely
Find your best self by using more sense; excerpt from Secrets of The Golden Door. il Fam Health 9:36-9 D '77
MAZZARO, Jerome
Lesson; Autumn landscape; The visit; Quadrille; poems. Poetry 131:69-72 N '77
MAZZEI, Renato
Yardstick gives way to meterstick. Clearing H 51:92 O '77
MAZZOCCO, Robert
Houses; poem. New Yorker 53:40 F 21 '77
MAZZOLENI, Ester
Con istinto: Ester Mazzoleni; interview, ed by L. Rasponi. por Opera N 42:32-4+ Ag '77
MBABI-KATANA, Solomon
Song for every season. il UNESCO Courier 30:26-8 My '77
M'BOW, Amadou Mahtar
Acropolis in danger. il por UNESCO Courier 30:4-6 F '77
Signposts for 1982: introduction to Unesco's Medium-Term Plan. il UNESCO Courier 30:6-10+ Mr '77
MEAD, Bernard F. Jr
Recreation semantics 101. Parks & Rec 12:26-8+ O '77
MEAD, Carver A. See Sutherland, I. E. jt auth
MEAD, Lawrence
Distance racing; ed by J. Rousmaniere. Yachting 141:38+ F '77
MEAD, Lawrence M.
Health policy: the need for governance. bibl f Ann Am Acad 434:39-57 N '77
MEAD, Leonard
1980 front-wheel-drive GM compacts. il Motor T 29:47-50 My '77
MEAD, Margaret
No fear of flying. J. Lelyveld. il por N Y Times Mag p 131 My 1 '77 *
MEAD, Margaret, 1901-
American society and its cities. Current 190:3-9 F '77
Five-million-dollar birthday present; interview, ed by R. Metraux. il por Redbook 149:29+ Je '77
Grandparents as educators. il Sat Eve Post 249:54-9 Mr '77
[Monthly column] See issues of Redbook
(ed) See Carter, R. Rosalynn Carter and Margaret Mead: a meeting of minds

about

Lecture. New Yorker 53:24-5 Mr 7 '77 *
Margaret Mead at seventy-five. J. Houston. por Sat R 4:6+ F 5 '77 *
MEAD, Walter J.
Economic appraisal of President Carter's energy program. bibl Science 197:340-5 Jl 22 '77
MEADE, James Edward
1977 Nobel Prize in economics. C. P. Kindleberger. pors Science 198:813-14+ N 25 '77 *
MEADOW, Susan Goldin-. See Goldin-Meadow, S.
MEADOWLANDS Race Track. See Race tracks
MEADOWLANDS sports complex. See New Jersey —Meadowlands sports complex
MEADOWS, Edward
Decadence of economic theory. Nat R 30:23-5+ Ja 6 '78
Economist's economist. Nat R 29:725 Je 24 '77
Pistol-whipped. il Nat R 29:1311-12 N 11 '77
MEADOWS
Sunrise, moonrise. S. Shaw. il Nat Wildlife 15:44-7 F '77
MEADS, Donald Edward
Quality certain, satisfaction guaranteed. por Forbes 119:64 My 1 '77 *
MEALS
Collection of cool summer meals. il McCalls 104:138-44+ Jl '77
Fish for compliments. il Fam Health 9:38-40+ O '77
Marvelous meals for less money. J. Neary. por Parents Mag 52:38-9+ Mr '77
More than just food; excerpt from Hidden art. E. Schaeffer. Chr Today 21:18-19 Je 3 '77
Roast pork with winter vegetables. E. W. Manning. il Farm J 101:56-7 Ja '77
See also
Breakfasts
Brunches
Buffet meals
Christmas meals
Cookery
Diet
Dinners and dining
Entertaining
Lunches
Snacks
Thanksgiving dinners
Wedding meals
MEANMOUTH bass. See Bass
MEANS, Bruce
Snakebite! What to know—what to do. C. Elliott. il Outdoor Life 160:84-7+ S '77 *
MEANY, George
George Meany speaks out on inflation, jobs, Carter; interview. por U.S. News 83:85-6 S 12 '77
Unions are better today; interview, ed by N. Kotz. N Y Times Mag p42-4 S 4 '77

about

AFL-CIO's growing troubles. B. J. Widick. Nation 225:168-71 S 3 '77 *
Annual sunbath. K. Bode. New Repub 176:12-14 Mr 12 '77 *
Big union blues: labor caught in Meany's grip. B. J. Widick. Nation 226:10-13 Ja 7 '78 *
Can labor's tired leaders deal with a troubled movement? N. Kotz. il por N Y Times Mag p8-11+ S 4 '77 *
Emancipation from Meany. B. J. Widick. Nation 224:368-72 Mr 26 '77 *
George and Jimmy show. K. Bode. il New Repub 176:28-30+ My 21 '77 *
Labor's call on Carter. T. Nicholson and T. Joyce. il por Newsweek 89:60-1 Mr 7 '77 *
Meany draws up his shopping list; with report on Bal Harbour, Fla. executive council meeting by P. Taubman. il por Time 109:43-4 Mr 7 '77 *
Meany faction. C. McWilliams. Nation 224:165 F 12 '77 *
Meany rejects prenotification of wage increases. L. Bornstein and others. M Labor R 100:84 Ap '77 *
Meany's veto. Nation 224:515-16 Ap 30 '77 *
Take George Meany seriously—please! A. Leggat. Am City & County 92:79 Ap '77 *
Who speaks for labor? Nation 224:418 Ap 9 '77 *
MEARES, Portia
Ode to October. il Am For 83:42-4 O '77
MEASELL, James S. See Lippert, C. B. jt auth
MEASLES
Alarming comeback for measles. il Time 109:67-8 Je 6 '77

Preventive inoculation

Measles: an epidemic. J. Seligmann. il Newsweek 89:73 F 21 '77
MEASLES, German. See Rubella

MEASUREMENT
Missing link; use of paper chains to study measuring. R. Harring. Educ Digest 42:48-9 Ja '77
See also
Cookery—Measurements
MEASURES. See Weights and measures
MEASURING instruments
See also
Micrometers
MEAT
See also
Cookery—Meat
Sausage

Grading

New beef grades: what do they mean? il Bet Hom & Gard 55:150+ Ap '77
USDA plans to tighten up on meat grading. Farm J 101:B4 N '77

Packaging

Boxed beef: no bargain? Farm J 101:Beef 29 O '77
Wrapping meat for your freezer. il Bet Hom & Gard 55:98 O '77

Preservation

Household worries; sodium nitrite as meat preservative and diaminoanisole sulfate as hair dye component. P. Gwynne and J. B. Copeland. il Newsweek 90:109 O 31 '77
Update on nitrite; use in curing of meat. J. Carper. il Am Home 80:16 S '77

Smoking

See Food—Smoking

Tenderizing

Papain meat tenderizers: objectionable for all and hazardous for some. B. T. Hunter. Consumers Res Mag 60:36 S '77
MEAT, Dried
Chinese jerky is moister and less brittle than cowboy jerky; beef jerky. Sunset 159:126 Jl '77
MEAT, Freezing of. See Freezing of food
MEAT, Frozen
Can cattlemen survive in the merchandising jungle? Tama Beef Producers Marketing Association. E. Ainsworth and W. Kester. il Farm J 101:Beef 7-10 Ag '77
Tama Beef: ahead of its time? W. Kester. Farm J 101:Beef 32 O '77
When is a steak not a steak? Consumer Rep 42:64-5 F '77
MEAT grinders. See Kitchen utensils and appliances
MEAT industry
Buy into your own packing plant; Morgan Colorado Beef Company. W. Kester. il Farm J 101: Beef 6-8+ D '77
Henry G. Parks gives his rules for success. J. Saddler. il pors Ebony 32:100-2+ Mr '77
Packer sees heavy meat output early in '77. Farm J 101:Hog 15 Ja '77
Shakedown in the packing business. W. Kester. map Farm J 101:Beef 16+ D '77
See also
Cattle industry
Monfort of Colorado, Inc

Advertising

BIC is working to sell excess beef on TV; Beef Industry Council. Farm J 101:LK7 Ap '77
Improving beef's unhealthy image. Bus W p26 Jl 4 '77
Is the checkoff a necessary evil? B. Eftink. Suc Farm 75:no3 B1 F '77
Look back at the checkoff. B. Eftink. il Suc Farm 75:15 S '77
National Cattlemen's Association to join in new checkoff efforts. Farm J 101:Beef 2 O '77
Think big on research and promotion; pork producers. J. Russell. il Farm J 101:Hog 7 O '77
Two vital decisions for cattlemen. W. Kester. il Farm J 101:Beef 28 Ja '77
We need more beef dollars to counter nutrition myths; views of Dr G. V. Mann. Farm J 101: Beef 20+ Ja '77
What happened to the beef referendum? R. C. Black. Farm J 101:B1 S '77
What next for beef promotion? W. Kester. Farm J 101:Beef 7 S '77
Who will defend the good name of beef? L. Palmer. Farm J 101:36 Je '77

Export-import trade

Beef management; increased exports could help balance trade. B. Eftink. il Suc Farm 75:no3 A8 F '77
U.S. cattlemen plead for protection. il Bus W p37 O 3 '77
Why you'll be selling more meat overseas. il Suc Farm 75:38 O '77

Laws and regulations

Protection from bankrupt packers. R. D. Wennblom. Farm J 100:LK4 D '76

Marketing

Carving out new meat markets. J. Russell. Farm J 101:LK4 Ap '77
Cheap protein is moving in on your markets. Farm J 101:Hog 39 S '77
See also
Butchers
MEAT industry workers
See also
Strikes—United States—Meat industry workers
MEAT loaf, pies, etc. See Cookery—Meat
MEAT packing industry. See Meat industry
MEATBALLS. See Cookery—Meat
MEATLESS meals. See Vegetarianism
MECH, L. David
Where can the wolf survive? il map Nat Geog 152:518-37 O '77
Wolf-pack buffer zones as prey reservoirs. bibl Science 198:320-1 O 21 '77
MECHANICAL banks. See Banks, Coin
MECHANICAL drawing
Careers in art. P. Savino. il Sch Arts 76:11 Ap '77
See also
Architectural drawing
MECHANICAL engineers
What went wrong? accident investigators Failure Analysis Associates. A. J. Mayer and D. Gram. il Newsweek 89:82 My 9 '77
MECHANICAL equipment of buildings
Building automation: what it does, what its benefits are, how the economics fare. D. E. Ross. il Archit Rec 161:147-50 Ap '77
Product reports 78. il Archit Rec 162:149-54 mid-O '77
MECHANICAL models. See Automatons
MECHANICAL musical instruments. See Musical instruments, Mechanical
MECHANICAL puzzles. See Puzzles
MECHANICS (persons)
See also
Automobile mechanics (persons)
Motorcycle mechanics (persons)
MECHANICS, Household
Ask Rufus; questions and answers. See issues of Mechanix illustrated
Fall home value ideas; symposium. il Pop Sci 211:138+ O '77
Home improvement ideas for the house fixer:
Build your own patio in sand. D. Raffel. il House & Gard 149:42+ Jl '77
Cover-up tactics with graphics. D. Raffel. il House & Gard 149:90+ N '77
5 easy steps to rewire a lamp. D. Raffel. il House & Gard 150:44+ Ja '78
Fixing up leaks. D. Raffel. il House & Gard 149:38+ Ag '77
Fixing up your window box. D. Raffel. House & Gard 149:62+ Je '77
How to make plants mobile; dollies. D. Raffel. il House & Gard 149:68+ D '77
Installing door and window locks. D. Raffel. il House & Gard 149:80 Mr '77
Preparing your house for paint. D. Raffel. House & Gard 149:76 S '77
Replacing an electrical switch. D. Raffel. House & Gard 149:68 Ap '77
Stopping drafts, saving energy. D. Raffel. il House & Gard 149:96+ O '77
Tips for spring painters. D. Raffel. House & Gard 149:94+ My '77
Homeowners' clinic; questions and answers. W. C. Lammey. See issues of Popular mechanics
Housepower clinic; questions and answers (cont) E. Powell. il Pop Sci 210:136+ F; 166 My; 211: 152-4 S '77
McCall's handywoman:
Almost indispensible tool: staple guns. il McCalls 104:45 Jl '77
Art of antiquing. il McCalls 105:60 N '77
Buying lumber. McCalls 104:62 Je '77
Caulking: easy and inexpensive way to save fuel. il McCalls 104:146 S '77
Hanging curtain and traverse rods. McCalls 104:110 My '77
Installing ceramic tile. il McCalls 104:118 F '77
Installing decorative beams. McCalls 105:142 Ja '78
Ladders. il McCalls 104:84 Mr '77
Patching and sealing a driveway. il McCalls 104:94 Ap '77
Rust removal & prevention. il McCalls 104:44 Ag '77
Ms. fix-it. J. Roy. See issues of American home
Q&A about home repairs. D. Pawelek. Ret Liv 17:18+ N; 16-17 D '77
Shop talk. A. Lees. See issues of Popular science
Tips tools & techniques. See issues of Better homes & gardens
See also
Plumbing

Bibliography

Here's how to remodel by the book. House B 119:99 S '77
How to select a how-to book. J. Roy. il Am Home 80:16 N '77

MECHANICS, Human. See Human mechanics

MECHLIN, Stuart. See Bonanno, E. jt auth

MEDALS
See also
Caldecott Medal
Franklin Mint Corporation
Newbery Medal
North American Forest Fire Medal

MEDAWAR, Jean S. See Medawar, P. B. jt auth

MEDAWAR, Sir Peter Brian and Medawar, J. S.
Revising the facts of life; excerpt from The life science: current ideas of biology. Harpers 254:41-8+ F '77

MEDDERS, Stanley
Morro Bay kangaroo rat: rodent in danger. il map Nat Parks & Con Mag 51:10-12 D '77

MEDIA centers. See Instructional materials centers

MEDIC Alert bracelets. See Identification tags, bracelets, etc.

MEDICAID
Abortion and the Supreme Court:
Anti-abortion view. S. Callahan. Current 198:21-3 D '77
Egalitarian view. M. C. Segers. Current 198:17-21 D '77
House passes bill cracking down on Medicare and Medicaid abusers. Ret Liv 17:57-8 N '77
Survey shows medicaid money is misspent. Aging 274:32 Ag '77
20 states face cuts in medicaid payments; Califano asks Congress to amend rules. il Ret Liv 17:39 Ag '77
See also
Abortion—State aid

MEDICAID fraud. See Fraud

MEDICAL assistants. See Health workers

MEDICAL botany. See Botany, Medical

MEDICAL care
Doctoring isn't just for doctors; self-care. R. C. Yeager. Read Digest 111:237-8+ D '77
Emergency medicine. H. Perlstadt and L. J. Kozak. il Society 14:41-6 Ja '77
Health care in America: an overview; symposium. Cur Hist 72:193-5+ My '77
Health care: the problem is profits. B. Winter. Progressive 41:16-19 O '77
Health economics and preventive care. M. M. Kristein and others. bibl il Science 195:457-62 F 4 '77
Improving health care in America; symposium. bibl Cur Hist 73:1-31+ Jl '77
It's an emergency! P. Bonventre and others. il Newsweek 90:105+ N 21 '77
Medical-welfare complex; symposium. bibl il Society 14:25-54 Ja '77
New era in health care: medical devices you use at home. K. Anderson. il Pop Mech 148:86-8+ D '77
Quality of life; address, May 21, 1977. E. D. Eddy. Vital Speeches 43:593-5 Jl 15 '77
Rationed care; address, June 19, 1977. R. E. Palmer. Vital Speeches 43:700-2 S 1 '77
Rx: a peer review system for physicians; quality of medical care. J. Fine. il Bull Atom Sci 33:38-43 S '77
What's wrong with U.S. health care? J. A. Califano, Jr. il Read Digest 111:122-6 O '77
See also
Aged—Medical care
Ambulance service
Ambulances
Burn care units
Children—Medical care
Coal miners—Medical care
Communications satellites—Medical use
Government investigations—Medical care
Health facilities
Home care services
Hospitals
Indians of North America—Medical care
Medicine—Practice
Mental health care
Nurses and nursing
Physicians
Poor—Medical care
Prisoners—Medical care
Telephone in medical care

Planning

See Health planning

Colombia

Inequality in Colombia. D. K. Zschock. bibl f il Cur Hist 72:68-72+ F '77

Dominican Republic

Rx for village health; rural health program. K. Chernush. il Américas 29:7-12 S '77

Great Britain

See also
Great Britain—National Health Service

Underdeveloped areas

See Underdeveloped areas—Medical care

MEDICAL care, Cost of
Abortion and the Supreme Court:
Anti-abortion view. S. Callahan. Current 198:21-3 D '77
Anatomy of health care costs. E. Marshall. New Repub 176:22-3 Mr 12; 16-19 Mr 19; 11-15 Ap 16; 22-5 My 28; 177:9-12 Jl 2; 9-11 O 29 '77
Business looks at health care costs; address, November 18, 1976. J. H. Perkins. Vital Speeches 43:211-15 Ja 15 '77
Curbing the cost of health. Bus W p82 Ap 4 '77
Federal involvement in health care after 1945. L. R. Judd. bibl f il Cur Hist 72:201-6+ My '77
Future of health care; address, October 13, 1977. E. K. Rose. Vital Speeches 44:115-17 D 1 '77
Great health care rip-off. R. Claiborne. Sat R 5:10-13+ Ja 7 '78
Health care, U.S.A. il Sr Schol 109:2-4+ Ap 21 '77
Health-cost crisis. M. Clark and others. il Newsweek 89:84+ My 9 '77
Health costs containment; address, August 9, 1977. W. E. Ryan. Vital Speeches 43:753-6 O 1 '77
Health policy: the need for governance. L. M. Mead. bibl f Ann Am Acad 434:39-57 N '77
High cost of health. H. Flieger. U.S. News 82:88 F 14 '77
Hot seat; J. Califano of HEW. G. F. Will. Newsweek 89:96 Mr 7 '77
How business can help cut health-care costs. il Nations Bus 65:16-20 F '77
Is your doctor overcharging you? W. A. Nolen. McCalls 105:169+ N '77
Malpractice and medicine. D. Makofsky. bibl il Society 14:25-9 Ja '77
Medical inflation: the system is the sickness. G. A. Sliver. Nation 225:210-12 S 10 '77
Michigan's clamp on doctor bills; Blue Cross and Blue Shield plan. Bus W p34 D 19 '77
Nader group finds wide variations in medicare fees for common surgery; the Health Research Group. Ret Liv 17:15 Ap '77
New medical technology: is it worth the price? A. T. Brett. il U.S. News 82:43-5 My 23 '77
Physician, heal thyself. . .or else! il Forbes 120:40-6 O 1 '77
Uproar over medical bills; with interview with W. J. McNerney. J. Mann. il U.S. News 82:35-40 Mr 28 '77
See also
Hospital care—Cost

MEDICAL care, Prepaid. See Insurance, Health—United States

MEDICAL care, Rural
Country doctor; work of G. Duckworth in Mound City, Kan. C. Remsberg. il por Fam Health 9:36-9+ Ap '77
Rx for village health; rural health program in Dominican Republic. K. Chernush. il Américas 29:7-12 S '77

MEDICAL care, State
Are national health services systems converging? Predictions for the United States. O. W. Anderson. bibl f Ann Am Acad 434:24-38 N '77
Coming: an overhaul of health programs. il U.S. News 82:76 F 28 '77
Federal involvement in health care after 1945. L. R. Judd. bibl f il Cur Hist 72:201-6+ My '77
Uncle Sam's dangerous prescriptions. M. S. Evans. Nat R 29:1368 N 25 '77
See also
Great Britain—National Health Service
Medicaid
Medicare

Pennsylvania

Social and political forces affecting the mental health system; address, October 17, 1977. R. M. Daly. Vital Speeches 44:139-41 D 15 '77

MEDICAL colleges
See also
California. University—San Francisco Campus—School of Medicine
Harvard University—Medical School
Northwestern University, Evanston, Ill.—Medical School
Rush Medical College, Chicago
United States—Uniformed Services University of the Health Sciences, Bethesda, Md.

Accreditation

. . . and meanwhile in the Caribbean. J. Walsh. Science 198:1019 D 9 '77
See also
United States—Advisory Committee on Accreditation and Institutional Eligibility

Admission

Contretemps on Capitol Hill. J. Walsh. Science 198:1018-19 D 9 '77
Doctored program; case of R. G. Clancy at the University of California, Davis. il por Time 110:89 O 10 '77
Federal money talks; transfer of students from foreign schools. Time 110:94 O 3 '77
Four medical schools draw the line on capitation. B. J. Culliton. Science 197:1066 S 9 '77
Other Bakke; R. G. Clancy case. por Newsweek 90:46 O 24 '77

MEDICAL colleges—Admission—*Continued*
Pushy parents; question of law requiring medical schools to admit American transfers from abroad. K. Keegan. New Repub 177:11 S 3 '77
U.S. foreign medical students: after the Guadalajara clause. J. Walsh. Science 197:346-8 Jl 22 '77
See also
Bakke, Allan, case

Federal aid

Coercion of medical schools. P. H. Abelson. Science 197:1137 S 16 '77

Tuition

See Medical education—Cost

MEDICAL deductions. See Income tax—Deductions

MEDICAL delusions
Eye myths. J. Eden. Harp Baz 110:115 Ag '77
New old wives' tales. A. Frank and S. Frank. Mademoiselle 83:46 D '77
22 myths & realities about your body. C. Dreifus. il Seventeen 36:125-9+ Je '77

MEDICAL devices. See Medical instruments and apparatus

MEDICAL education
Is a relapse ahead for minority medical education? K. Abarbanel. Educ Digest 42:24-7 Mr '77
See also
Medical colleges
Medical students

Cost

Future doctors balk at the bill. L. J. Carter. Science 197:1062-3 S 9 '77

MEDICAL electronics
Impact of integrated electronics in medicine. R. L. White and J. D. Meindl. bibl il Science 195:1119-24 Mr 18 '77
Red-hot coal; dorsal column stimulator used in paraplegic pain syndrome. il por Newsweek 89:55 Ap 25 '77

MEDICAL ethics
Acquiring new information while retaining old ethics. V. Herbert. bibl Science 198:690-3 N 18 '77
Ethics, medical malpractice and the church. G. L. Haines. Chr Cent 94:1003-5 N 2 '77; Reply. T. E. Daniel. 94:1227-8 D 28 '77
Experiments on humans: where to draw the line? P. London. il Psychol Today 11:20+ N '77
Jackson Pollock's drawings under analysis; question of psychiatric ethics. B. Carter. il Art N 76:58-60 F '77
Karen Ann a year later. E. Keerdoja. Newsweek 89:10 Mr 21 '77
Laying the Pollock case to rest. A. Frankenstein. Art N 76:94+ O '77
Performing abortions; excerpt from In necessity and sorrow: life and death in an abortion hospital. M. Denes. discussion. Commentary 62:4+ D '76; 63:18+ Ja; 22+ F '77
Social imperatives of medical research. L. Eisenberg. bibl Science 198:1105-10 D 16 '77
Some thoughts on clinical trials, especially problems of multiplicity. J. W. Tukey. bibl Science 198:679-84 N 18 '77
See also
Medical research—Experimentation on man

MEDICAL examinations. See Physical examinations

MEDICAL facilities. See Health facilities

MEDICAL fakers. See Quacks and quackery

MEDICAL fees. See Medical care, Cost of

MEDICAL geography
Cancer and geographic risks. il Sci N 111:38 Ja 15 '77
Cancer mortality in U.S. counties with petroleum industries. W. J. Blot and others. bibl Science 198:51-3 O 7 '77
Stalking the wild crab. J. L. Fox. maps Chemistry 50:50-1 Ja '77
Want to live longer? Look to your rocks! Sci Digest 82:58-60 Ag '77

MEDICAL hypnosis. See Hypnotism—Therapeutic use

MEDICAL instruments and apparatus
New era in health care: medical devices you use at home. K. Anderson. il Pop Mech 148:86-8+ D '77
See also
Hospitals—Equipment and supplies
Medical electronics
Sphygomomanometers

MEDICAL instruments and apparatus industry
Healthy outlook for medical devices. A. Hershman. il Duns R 109:66-8 Ja '77
Salesmen in the operating room. il Forbes 120:33 D 1 '77
See also
Becton, Dickinson & Company

MEDICAL insurance. See Insurance, Health

MEDICAL jurisprudence
Criminalist—the forensic scientist. R. L. Epstein. il Intellect 105:258-60 F '77
See also
Forensic hematology
Insanity—Jurisprudence
Malpractice

MEDICAL laboratories
Why MetPath lost its bid to be no. 2; clinical laboratory testing business. il por Bus W p27 Ag 22 '77

MEDICAL laws and legislation
Governmental interference with medical care; excerpts from address. D. X. Freedman. por Intellect 106:100-1 S '77
Physician, heal thyself. M. Clark and others. il Newsweek 90:74 Ag 8 '77
See also
Medical policy

MEDICAL Library Association
MLA in Seattle: change & controversy. C. Stock. Lib J 102:1807+ S 15 '77

MEDICAL literature
Diagnosis by the book; Symptoms: the complete home medical encyclopedia. Time 109:84 Mr 7 '77

MEDICAL news
Checkup on medicine. See issues of Science digest, May 1977-
Family doctor. A. E. Nourse. See issues of Good housekeeping
Health. M. Weber. See issues of Vogue
Health & medicine. P. Lehmann. Harp Baz 110:186-9+ S '77
Health harvest. E. J. Padus. See issues of Organic gardening and farming
Health matters. See issues of Family health incorporating Today's health
Healthwatch. See issues of Mademoiselle
Latest in health and medicine (cont) U.S. News 82:84 F 21; 59 Mr 21; 82 Ap 25; 78 Je 6; 83:60 Jl 11; 39 Ag 22; 86 S 26; 63 O 31; 82 D 5 '77
Medical news. il Sat Eve Post 249:107 O; 95 N '77
News from the world of medicine. See issues of Reader's digest
Parents alert. Parents Mag 52:26+ N; 36+ D '77
World progress report. A. Wolff. See occasional issues of Saturday review
Your family's health. D. R. Zimmerman. See issues of Ladies' home journal

MEDICAL policy
Bitter pill for U.S. hospitals. il Time 109:32 My 2 '77
Carter proposes setting strict controls on what hospitals can charge patients. Ret Liv 17:11-12 Je '77
Carter team promises national health plan soon. E. M. Leeper. il BioScience 27:777-8 D '77
Carter's first shot in war on medical costs. il U.S. News 82:79 My 9 '77
Carter's stab at health care. il Forbes 119:53-4 My 15 '77
Curbing the cost of health. Bus W p82 Ap 4 '77
Emergency medicine. H. Perlstadt and L. J. Kozak. il Society 14:41-6 Ja '77
Future of health care; address, October 13, 1977. E. K. Rose. Vital Speeches 44:115-17 D 1 '77
Health care in America: an overview; symposium. Cur Hist 72:193-5+ My '77
Health-cost crisis. M. Clark and others. il Newsweek 89:84+ My 9 '77
Health costs containment; address, August 9, 1977. W. E. Ryan. Vital Speeches 43:753-6 O 1 '77
Health policy: the need for governance. L. M. Mead. bibl f Ann Am Acad 434:39-57 N '77
Improving health care in America; symposium. bibl Cur Hist 73:1-31+ Jl '77
9% flaw in Carter's hospital plan. I. Pave. Bus W p36 My 9 '77
Physician, heal thyself. . .or else! il Forbes 120:40-6 O 1 '77
Race to cut medical costs. A. Hershman. il Duns R 109:48-53+ My '77
Radical cure for high medical costs. C. Peters. por Newsweek 89:11 Mr 28 '77
Rationed care; address, June 19, 1977. R. E. Palmer. Vital Speeches 43:700-2 S 1 '77
Science is no gentlemen's club: lessons of the swine flu debacle. G. A. Silver. Nation 224:166-9 F 12 '77
Uproar over medical bills; with interview with W. J. McNerney. J. Mann. il por U.S. News 82:34-40+ Mr 28 '77
See also
Health planning
Medical care, State
United States—Health, Education and Welfare, Department of

MEDICAL radiography. See Radiography, Medical

MEDICAL records
Health records and privacy: what would Hippocrates say? C. Holden. Science 198:382 O 28 '77
Health records face a privacy challenge; Du Pont challenges NIOSH on claim to undisputed access. il Bus W p38 O 31 '77

MEDICAL records—*Continued*
Patients' rights in medical privacy. Sci N 111:71 Ja 29 '77
What are your rights to medical records & prescriptions? M. L. Schildkraut. Good H 185:204 Jl '77

MEDICAL research
Biomedicine. Sci N 111:28, 40, 60, 88, 170, 205, 233, 267, 346, 360; 112:10, 40, 58, 105, 121, 200, 217, 248, 265, 280, 317, 376, 392, 424 Ja 8-22, F 5, Mr 12, 26, Ap 9, 23, My 28-Je 4, Jl 2, 16-23, Ag 13-20, S 24-O 1, 15-29, N 12, D 3-10, 24 '77
Clinical trials: methods and ethics are debated. G. B. Kolata. Science 198:1127-31 D 16 '77
Harvard and Monsanto: the $23-million alliance. B. J. Culliton. pors Science 195:759-63 F 25 '77
Medical research: statistics and ethics; papers from Birnbaum Memorial Symposium. bibl Science 198:677-705 N 18 '77
Social imperatives of medical research. L. Eisenberg. bibl Science 198:1105-10 D 16 '77
See also
Albert and Mary Lasker Foundation
Animal experimentation
Cancer research
Colleges and universities—Research
Diabetes research
Laboratory animals
Leprosy research
Pharmaceutical research
Virus research
Women in medicine

Experimentation on man

EPA rules out human cancer tests. W. D. Metz. Science 198:711 N 18 '77
Electroshock experiment at Albany violates ethics guidelines. R. J. Smith. Science 198:383-6 O 28 '77; Discussion. 198:1099-100 D 16 '77
Experiments on humans: where to draw the line? P. London. il Psychol Today 11:20+ N '77
Human experimentation rules debated. Sci N 111:230-1 Ap 9 '77
Lesson of retrolental fibroplasia. W. A. Silverman. il Sci Am 236:100-7 bibl(p 142) Je '77
SUNY at Albany admits research violations. R. J. Smith. Science 198:708 N 18 '77
See also
United States—National Commission for the Protection of Human Subjects of Biomedical and Behavioral Research

MEDICAL Research Council (Great Britain)
Medical research in England: new director seeks to boost morale. N. Wade. por Science 198:1021-2 D 9 '77

MEDICAL schools. See Medical colleges

MEDICAL self care. See Medical care

MEDICAL service. See Medical care

MEDICAL societies
See also
American Academy of Family Physicians
American Medical Association

MEDICAL students
David Hartman's impossible dream; graduate of Temple University School of Medicine. A. Rankin. il por Read Digest 110:78-82 Ap '77
Federal money talks; transfer of students from foreign schools. Time 110:94 O 3 '77
Four medical schools draw the line on capitation. B. J. Culliton. Science 197:1066 S 9 '77
Pushy parents; question of law requiring medical schools to admit American transfers from abroad. K. Keegan. New Repub 177:11 S 3 '77
Rumanian solution; American students. il Time 109:80+ Je 20 '77
U.S. foreign medical students: after the Guadalajara clause. J. Walsh. Science 197:346-8 Jl 22 '77

MEDICAL supplies
What's in your medicine cabinet? And what should be. G. Lang. il Ret Liv 17:35-7 My '77
Where's the aspirin? E. Zelig. il Am Home 80:30 Jl '77
See also
Baxter Travenol Laboratories, Inc
Hospital supply industry
Hospitals—Equipment and supplies
Medical instruments and apparatus

MEDICAL technology
Medical technology: too much of a good thing? il Forbes 119:67-8 Je 1 '77
New medical technology: is it worth the price? A. T. Brett. il U.S. News 82:43-5 My 23 '77
Physicians + physicists=far-out medicine; work of Johns Hopkins University's Applied Physics Laboratory. D. Lampe. il Fam Health 9:48-50 S '77
See also
Technology transfer

MEDICAL workers. See Black health workers; Health workers

MEDICARE
House passes bill cracking down on Medicare and Medicaid abusers. Ret Liv 17:57-8 N '77
Nader group finds wide variations in medicare fees for common surgery; the Health Research Group. Ret Liv 17:15 Ap '77
Rendezvous with a machine; medicare's kidney program. E. Marshall. New Repub 176:16-19 Mr 19 '77
See also
Medicaid

MEDICI, Giuseppe
Montedison: the new chief no one wants. por Bus W p30-1 Ag 1 '77 *

MEDICI, Marino de
(ed) See Vance, C. R. Secretary Vance interviewed by Il Tempo correspondent

MEDICINAL plants. See Botany, Medical

MEDICINE
Biostatistics in medicine. L. Thomas. Science 198:675 N 18 '77
Medical mailbox; questions and answers. C. SerVaas. See issues of Saturday evening post
Need for a new medical model: a challenge for biomedicine. G. L. Engel. bibl Science 196:129-36 Ap 8 '77
See also
Acupuncture
Anesthesia
Communications satellites—Medical use
Health
Osteopuncture
Quacks and quackery
Space medicine
Surgery
Telecommunication in medicine
Women in medicine
also headings beginning Medical

Bibliography

Scientific, technical, medical, & business books (cont) Lib J 102:567+, 2227-8+ Mr 1, N 1 '77

Caricatures and cartoons

Rx-rated. Read Digest 111:96-7 S '77

Instruments and apparatus

See Medical instruments and apparatus

Laws and legislation

See Medical laws and legislation

Practice

Governmental interference with medical care; excerpts from address. D. X. Freedman. por Intellect 106:100-1 S '77
Health for your whole life. E. Switzer. il Vogue 167:368-9+ S '77
Holistic health: revolution or revivalism? il Forbes 120:44 O 1 '77
Rx: a peer review system for physicians. J. Fine. il Bull Atom Sci 33:38-43 S '77
See also
Malpractice
Medical ethics
Physicians
Physicians and patients
Quacks and quackery

Social aspects

See also
Family medicine

Study and teaching

See also
Medical colleges
Medical students

Russia

Medicine: a decade behind; U.S.-Soviet comparison. M. Clark and others. il Newsweek 90:60+ O 10 '77

Taiwan

Medical mailbox; C. Chung and the Acupuncture Research Clinic of Taipei. C. SerVaas. il Sat Eve Post 249:138-9 D '77

United States

America's doctors: a profession in trouble. A. T. Brett. il U.S. News 83:50-2+ O 17 '77
Medicine: a decade behind; U.S.-Soviet comparison. M. Clark and others. il Newsweek 90:60+ O 10 '77
Profiles; views of L. Thomas. J. Bernstein. por New Yorker 53:27-32+ Ja 2 '78
See also
American Academy of Family Physicians
American Medical Association
Medical policy

History

Belly-my-grizzle; herbal medicine. S. Klaw. il por Am Heritage 28:96-105 Je '77
Physical toughness of colonial Americans. H. F. Rankin. Intellect 106:15 Jl '77

MEDICINE, Preventive
Health economics and preventive care. M. M. Kristein and others. bibl il Science 195:457-62 F 4 '77
Prevention guide to safeguarding your health and your life; symposium. Harp Baz 110:94-101+ Ap '77

MEDICINE, Preventive—*Continued*
Prevention or cure? Behind the shift in health care. T. Brett. il U.S. News 82:62 Ap 4 '77
See also
Heart—Diseases—Prevention
MEDICINE, Primitive
See also
Medicine men
MEDICINE, Psychosomatic
Emotional stress and sudden death. G. Engel. bibl il Psychol Today 11:114-15+ N '77
Holistic health: revolution or revivalism? il Forbes 120:44 O 1 '77
Link between your emotions and health; interview. C. N. Shealy. Harp Baz 110:131+ F '77
Loneliness can kill you; views of J. J. Lynch. il Time 110:45 S 5 '77
Mind as healer, mind as slayer; excerpt. K. R. Pelletier. il por Psychol Today 10:35-7+ F '77
Mysterious placebo: how mind helps medicine work. N. Cousins. il Sat R 5:8-12+ O 1 '77; Discussion. 5:6 Ja 7 '78
One chance in 500 to live; self-induced cure of ankylosing spondylitis. N. Cousins. por Sat Eve Post 249:52-4+ My '77; Same with title Anatomy of an illness (as perceived by the patient) Sat R 4:4-6+ My 28 '77; Same abr. Read Digest 110:130-4 Je '77; Discussion. Sat R 4:5-6 Jl 23 '77
Will power and your health. A. Etzioni. Intellect 105:429 Je '77
MEDICINE, State. See Medical care, State
MEDICINE, Tropical. See Tropics—Diseases and hygiene
MEDICINE, Veterinary. See Veterinary medicine
MEDICINE and geography. See Medical geography
MEDICINE and sports. See Sports medicine
MEDICINE and state. See Medical policy
MEDICINE cabinet supplies. See Medical supplies
MEDICINE men
Rock art and the power of shamans. D. R. Snow. il Natur Hist 86:42-9 bibl(p 100) F '77
MEDICINES. See Drugs
MEDICINES, Patent, proprietary, etc.
Complete guide to over-the-counter cough and cold remedies. Good H 184:184+ F '77
Latest news on how to fight the common cold. M. L. Schildkraut. Good H 185:261-2 N '77
Medical quacks: today's merchants of menace. R. D. Duncan. Ret Liv 17:25-6+ F '77
Standard cyclopedia of recipes, 1901; ed by C. Simmons. il N Y Times Mag p71 Ja 23 '77
MEDIEVAL civilization. See Civilization, Medieval
MEDIEVAL poetry. See Poetry, Medieval
MEDITATION
Meditation without mystery; excerpt from The varieties of the meditative experience. D. Goleman. il Psychol Today 10:54-6+ Mr '77
Two faces of meditation. E. Schur; L. LeShan. il Parents Mag 52:70-1+ N '77
See also
Transcendental meditation
MEDITERRANEAN Region
Mediterranean; symposium. il maps Oceans 10:22-57 Ja '77
See also
Balearic Islands
Cruising—Mediterranean Region
Malta
MEDITERRANEAN Sea
Mediterranean engima; origins. A. J. Mantura. il maps Oceans 10:24-7 Ja '77
See also
Marine pollution—Mediterranean Sea
Suez Canal
MEDLEY, Donald M.
Researcher looks at process-based teacher evaluation. Educ Digest 43:32-5 D '77
MEDNICK, Sarnoff A.
Schizophrenia: a cruel chain of events. R. J. Trotter. por Sci N 111:394-5 Je 18 '77 *
MEDOFF, Eve
Charles Santore: idea and image. il por Am Artist 41:66-71+ F '77
Elizabeth Bloom: art and nature. il Am Artist 41:62-7 Je '77
Elizabeth Osborne: painting with light. il por Am Artist 41:34-9+ S '77
MEDVEDEV, Roi Aleksandrovich
Loyal opposition. il por Newsweek 89:48 Je 20 '77
MEDVEDEV, Zhores Aleksandrovich
Documentation of alleged Soviet mishap. map Sci N 112:37 Jl 16 '77 *
MEE, Charles L. Jr
Guernica: an act of war, a work of art. il por Horizon 19:88-96 My '77
In my own time. por Horizon 19:94-5 Ja; 90-2 Mr '77
Who started the cold war? il pors Am Heritage 28:8-23 Ag '77
MEE, Suzi
Brighton Beach line; poem. Poetry 130:82 My '77
MEEDER, Verona
My pupil, Amy Carter. il por McCalls 104:126-7+ Je '77
about
Amy's new teacher. Chr Today 21:38-9 Ja 7 '77 *
MEEHAN, Elizabeth A.
Lights up, energy down. il House & Gard 149:82+ S '77
MEEHAN, Francis X.
Love and sexuality in Catholic tradition. America 137:230-4 O 15 '77
MEEHAN, John E.
His-and-hers cosmetics team. il pors Bus W p140 S 12 '77 *
MEEHAN, Paula Kent
His-and-hers cosmetics team. il pors Bus W p140 S 12 '77 *
Redken Labs: business is beautiful. il por Duns R 110:30-1 Jl '77 *
MEEHAN, Thomas
Unreal, hilarious world of Neil Simon. il pors Horizon 21:70-4 Ja '78
MEEK, George
Brazilian students spearhead development. il Américas 29:6-8 F '77
MEEK, Jay
Repechages on the last morning; Last book; poems. Yale R 67:65-7 O '77
MEEKER, John J.
Backyard melon patch. il Org Gard & Farm 24:78-81 Je '77
End of summer is not the end of your garden. il Org Gard & Farm 24:57-9 Ag '77
Fishing for good vegetables. il Org Gard & Farm 24:86-7 D '77
Garden honey pot. il Org Gard & Farm 25:142-5 Ja '78
Herbs in a small place. il por Org Gard & Farm 24:53-6 N '77
Winter squash from Asia. il Org Gard & Farm 24:64-7 Jl '77
MEEKING, Basil
Theological roots for Catholic ecumenical activity. bibl il New Cath World 220:164-7 Jl '77
MEEKS, M. Douglas
(tr) See Moltmann, J. American dream
MEERBOTT, Josef
Production throwing in Taiwan. il por Ceram Mo 25:45-50 Mr '77
MEET Miss Stone-age! drama. See Olfson, L.
MEETINGS
See also
Conferences
Corporations—Meetings
Stockholders meetings
MEFLUIDIDE. See Growth inhibiting substances (plants)
MEGALITHIC monuments
Ancient Europe is older than we thought. C. Renfrew. il map Nat Geog 152:614-23 N '77
MEGALOPOLIS. See Metropolitan areas
MEGLIN, Nick
Illustrators Workshop: an original approach to teaching tomorrow's artists. il Am Artist 41:42-7+ My '77
Jack Davis cover story. il Am Artist 41:34-7+ Ap '77
Jim Spanfeller: the illustrator as instructor. il Am Artist 41:46-9+ Mr '77
Special sports issue. il Am Artist 41:2+ Jl '77
MEGNA, Stephanie
Going Greek isn't great! por Seventeen 36:28 N '77
MEHEGAN, David
Attack and counterattack. J. Simon. Esquire 88:20+ D '77 *
MEHRINGER, Peter J. Jr, and others
Pollen influx and volcanic ash. bibl il map Science 198:257-61 O 21 '77
MEHTA, Martha
Charting the grandperson galaxy. Educ Digest 42:22-5 Ja '77
MEHTA, Ved
Department of amplification (cont) New Yorker 53:67-8+ My 9 '77
Letter from New Delhi. New Yorker 53:119-22+ O 17 '77
Our local correspondents: naturalized citizen no. 9845165. New Yorker 53:68-78 Ag 29 '77
Reporter at large. New Yorker 52:56-60+ F 14 '77
about
Talking with Ved Mehta. J. F. Baker. Sat R 4:35 Ja 22 '77 *
MEHTA, Zubin
Musician of the month: Zubin Mehta; interview, ed by D. Webster. por Hi Fi 27:MA8-9 N '77
about
New York concert season. B. H. Haggin. New Repub 177:23-4 S 3 '77 *
MEIER, Hugo A.
Thomas Jefferson and the growth of American technology. por Intellect 106:192 N '77

MEIER, Richard
Living in a work of art. M. Stevens. il Newsweek 89:59 My 30 '77 *
1977 Reynolds prize goes to Richard Meier. il Archit Rec 161:35 Je '77 *

MEIER, Richard L.
Multinationals as agents of social development. il Bull Atom Sci 33:30-2+ N '77

MEILAENDER, Gilbert, Jr
Glory of singing mountain; story. Chr Today 21:26 My 6 '77
Still forbidden fruit. il Chr Today 21:16-19 Ja 21 '77

MEINDL, James D.
Microelectronic circuit elements; with biographical sketch. il Sci Am 237:14, 70-81 bibl(p258) S '77
—See White, R. L. jt auth

MEINERS, Roger E. See Clarkson, K. W. jt auth

MEINTS, Russel H. See Tonelli, Q. jt auth

MEIR, Golda
Golda Meir; interview, ed by J. N. Eisenhower; excerpt from Special people. il por Ladies Home J 94:87+ Mr '77

MEISEL, Tony
Condition report. il Motor B & S 141:56+ Ja '78

MEISELS, Manfred
Electronic world of Manfred Meisels (cont of) Electronics. il por Motor B & S 139:20+ My; 18-19+ Je; 140:13+ Jl; 28+ S; 23-4 N '77; 141: 25+ Ja '78

MEISLER, Stanley
After Franco's forty years. il Nation 224:461-4 Ap 16 '77
Reports & comment: Spain. por Atlantic 239:14+ My '77
Spain's new democracy. il For Affairs 56:190-208 O '77

MEISSEN porcelain. See Pottery, German

MEISSNER, Paul
Computers: a seeing-eye watching you. il Sci Digest 81:64-7 Je '77

Die MEISTERSINGER; opera. See Wagner, R.

MEKONG River
Commission welcomes new agreement on development of Mekong River basin. UN Chron 14: 32 My '77

MELAMID, Aleksandr
Art on the line. M. A. Tighe. il New Repub 176:24-6 Ap 16 '77 *
Dissidence as a way of art. G. Glueck. il pors N Y Times Mag p33-5 My 8 '77 *

MELANESIA
See also
Fiji
Lauthala (island)
Solomon Islands

MELANIN
Can blackness prolong life? experiments of L. M. Edelstein. il pors Ebony 32:124-7 Je '77
Measuring melanin in the brain. Sci N 112:6-7 Jl 2 '77

MELANOCYTE-stimulating hormone release-inhibiting factor. See Metabolism inhibiting substances

MELANSON, Jim
At the crest of the air waves: syndicated radio. il Hi Fi 27:135-6+ O '77
Countdown to Monday: charting the top 100; Billboard, Cashbox, and Record world. il Hi Fi 27:106-9 My '77

MELATONIN
Melatonin: daily cycle in plasma and cerebrospinal fluid of calves. L. Hedlund and others. bibl il Science 195:686-7 F 18 '77
Melatonin induction of gonadal quiescence in pinealectomized Syrian hamsters. L. Tamarkin and others. bibl il Science 198:953-5 D 2 '77

MELBA, Dame Nellie
Melba. A. Porter. pors Hi Fi 28:86-9 Ja '78 *
Melba's farewell concert. W. R. Moran. il pors Hi Fi 27:86-9 Jl '77 *

MELBOURNE, Fla.
Make money by computer. E. Watkins and J. Burger. il Am City & County 92:57-8 Ap '77

MELCHER, C. L. and Zimmerman, D. W.
Thermoluminescent determination of prehistoric heat treatment of chert artifacts. bibl il Science 197:1359-62 S 30 '77

MELCHERT, James
Our legacy of crafts; address, June 1977. Craft Horiz 37:45 Ag '77

MELCHIOR, C. L. See Myers, R. D. jt auth

MELCHIOR, Hans
Detectors for lightwave communication. bibl il Phys Today 30:32-9 N '77

MELE, Linda
Common scents. Seventeen 36:110 Ag '77

MELENDY, H. Brett
(comp) Historic Hawaii. il Am West 14:55 S '77

MELIA, Jinx
Jinx Melia: crusader for homemakers. L. David. il por Good H 184:154+ Je '77 *

MELLAS, Nicholas
Locked up with fear. J. L. Kaplan. il Nation 225:530-2 N 19 '77 *

MELLEN, Joan
On Lina Wertmuller. il por Society 14:82-4 Ja '77

MELLEN, Polly Allen
Three days in Morocco. il por Vogue 167:188+ My '77

MELLON, Paul
Anglomania. Nat R 29:786 Jl 8 '77 *

MELLON, Paul, collection of British art. See Yale University—Center for British Art

MELLOW, James R.
Many faces of art. il Sat R 5:38-40 N 26 '77

MELNICK, Joseph L. and others
Viral hepatitis; with biographical sketches. il Sci Am 237:18, 44-52 bibl(p 154) Jl '77

MELODRAMA
Joining of words and music in late romantic melodrama. E. F. Dravitt. bibl f il Mus Q 62:571-90 O '76

MELONS
Backyard melon patch. J. Meeker. il Org Gard & Farm 24:78-81 Je '77
Give melons a head start; muskmelons. D. E. Stebbins. il Org Gard & Farm 24:98-9 F '77
Instant fruit—it's hard to ask more; vine peach or mango melon. B. Fisher. il Org Gard & Farm 24:74-5 Je '77
Melons ripe for the picking J. Yaeger. Org Gard & Farm 24:156-8 My '77
Plant cantaloupes now and feast later! N. Bubel. il Org Gard & Farm 24:168-70+ Je '77
Unlikely story—container melons. il Sunset 158: 260-1 My '77
See also
Cookery—Fruit
Watermelons

MELSON, Gail
Segregating the home into male and female territories. Intellect 106:186-7 N '77

MELTZER, Allan H.
It takes long-range planning to lick inflation. il Fortune 96:96-100+ D '77

MELTZOFF, Andrew N. and Moore, M. K.
Imitation of facial and manual gestures by human neonates. bibl il Science 198:75-8 O 7 '77

MELTZOFF, Stanley
Like a neon shadow in the sea. il Sports Illus 47:22-9 Jl 25 '77

MELVILLE, Herman
Darwin and Melville: why a tortoise? J. Franzosa. bibl f Am Imago 33:361-79 Wint '76 *

MELVILLE Corporation. See Chain stores

MELVIN, A. Gordon
Natural history. See issues of Hobbies

MELYAN, Helene
Gift for mama. Read Digest 110:118-20 My '77

MEMBRANE electrodes. See Electrodes

MEMBRANES (biology)
Asymmetric structure of the purple membrane. A. E. Blaurock and G. I. King. bibl il Science 196:1101-4 Je 3 '77
Bifunctional intercalators: relationship of antitumor activity of diacridines to the cell membrane. R. M. Fico and others. bibl il Science 198:53-6 O 7 '77
Covalent labeling of the tetrodotoxin receptor in excitable membranes. R. J. Guillory and others. bibl il Science 196:883-5 My 20 '77
Drug tolerance in biomembranes: a spin label study of the effects of ethanol. J. H. Chin and D. B. Goldstein. bibl il Science 196:684-5 My 6 '77
Duchenne dystrophy: alteration in muscle plasma membrane structure D. L. Schotland and others. bibl il Science 196:1005-7 My 27 '77
Fluidity in the membranes of adult and neonatal human erythrocytes. M. Kehry and others. bibl il Science 195:486-7 F 4 '77
Freeze-fractured purple membrane particles: protein content. K. A. Fisher and W. Stoeckenius. bibl il Science 197:72-4 Jl 1 '77
Ion channels in nerve membranes. G. Ehrenstein; reply with rejoinder. M. W. P. Strandberg. bibl Phys Today 30:13+ Je '77
Lateral transport of a lipid probe and labeled proteins on a cell membrane. J. Schlessinger and others. bibl il Science 195:307-9 Ja 21 '77
Membrane asymmetry. J. E. Rothman and J. Lenard. bibl il Science 195:743-53 F 25 '77
Membrane currents examined under voltage clamp in cultured neuroblastoma cells. W. H. Moolenaar and I. Spector. bibl il Science 196: 331-3 Ap 15 '77
Osmotically induced changes in electrical properties of plant protoplast membranes. R. H. Racusen and others. bibl il Science 198:405-7 O 28 '77
Permeation of manganese, cadmium, zinc, and beryllium through calcium channels of an insect muscle membrane. J. Fukuda and K. Kawa. bibl il Science 196:309-11 Ap 15 '77
Photoreceptor outer segments: accelerated membrane renewal in rods after exposure to light. J. C. Besharse and others. bibl il Science 196: 536-8 Ap 29 '77
Plasma membrane: rapid isolation and exposure of the cytoplasmic surface by use of positively charged beads. B. S. Jacobson and D. Branton. bibl il Science 195:302-4 Ja 21 '77

MEMBRANES (biology)—*Continued*
Puzzling role of cell surfaces. D. I. Meyer and M. M. Burger. bibl il pors Chemistry 50:36-41 Ja '77
Size limit of molecules permeating the junctional membrane channels. I. Simpson and others. bibl il Science 195:294-6 Ja 21 '77
Topological asymmetry of phospholipids in membranes. L. D. Bergelson and L. I. Barsukov. bibl il Science 197:224-30 Jl 15 '77
See also
Epithelium

MEMBRANES (technology)
Carrier-mediated photodiffusion membranes. J. S. Schultz. bibl il Science 197:1177-9 S 16 '77
Lateral diffusion in planar lipid bilayers. P. F. Fahey and others. bibl il Science 195:305-6 Ja 21 '77
Oxygen-enriching membrane cuts gas-heating bills. B. H. Berry. il Pop Sci 210:189 Mr '77
Synthetic peptides form ion channels in artificial lipid bilayer membranes. S. J. Kennedy and others. bibl il Science 196:1341-2 Je 17 '77

MEMOIRS. See Autobiography

MEMORIAL Day
Vets' reunions. . .with a purpose. M. C. Leeds. Ret Liv 17:48+ My '77

MEMORIAL pictures. See Pictures

MEMORIAL services
Last sayonara; World War II anniversary services in Japan. il Time 109:36+ Je 13 '77

MEMORIALS
See also
Lincoln Memorial, Washington, D.C.
Mount Rushmore National Memorial
Sepulchral monuments

MEMORIZING
In praise of regurgitation. W. M. Hastings. Intellect 105:349-50 Ap '77

MEMORY
Bridging a gap between men and monkeys; impairing memory of sound by cutting auditory association cortex. J. H. Dewson, 3d. por Intellect 105:215-16 Ja '77
Does sleep help you study? E. Hoddes. Psychol Today 11:69 Je '77
Memory for lists of sounds by the bottle-nosed dolphin: convergence of memory processes with humans? R. K. R. Thompson and L. M. Herman. bibl il Science 195:501-3 F 4 '77
Memory formation: evidence for a specific neurochemical system in the amygdala. M. Gallagher and others. bibl il Science 198:423-5 O 28 '77
Reading disability: an information-processing analysis. F. J. Morrison and others. bibl il Science 196:77-9 Ap 1 '77
Spatial memory. D. S. Olton. il Sci Am 236:82-4+ bibl(p 142) Je '77
Unsolved marvel of memory; excerpt from Mechanics of the mind. C. Blakemore. il N Y Times Mag p42-6+ F 6 '77
See also
Recognition (psychology)

MEMORY circuits, Integrated. See Electronic circuits, Integrated

MEMORY devices (computers) See Computers—Memory systems

MEMPHIS, Tenn.
Place of good abode. C. Mulford. il Trav/Holiday 149:44-7 Ja '78

Religious institutions and affairs

Reconciliation in Memphis. R. R. Holton. Commonweal 104:38-9 Ja 21 '77
Reconciliation in Memphis: a diocese prepared. A. Kirk. America 136:146-8 F 19 '77
Rome vs. Memphis. Commonweal 104:355-6 Je 10 '77

Water supply

Memphis water meter replacement cuts annual utility costs $175,000. Am City & County 92:46 F '77

MEMPHIS is gone; drama. See Hobson, R.

MEMPHIS-Shelby County, Tenn, Public Library and Information Center. See Libraries—Tennessee

MEN
Great male cop-out from the work ethic. il Bus W p 156+ N 14 '77
Men (cont) Ms 6:26-7 Ag; 14-15 N '77
Men at home:
Exploding the myth of casual sex. C. Gilbert. Am Home 80:12 O '77
Father's instincts. R. F. Koubek. Am Home 80:18+ Je '77
How not to do it yourself. C. Scarborough. il por Am Home 80:24+ S '77
Role models. R. Baker. Am Home 80:8 N '77
Sex and tennis: mismatched pair. D. Sheahan. il Am Home 80:27 Ag '77
Unfinished house; building a weekend retreat. P. H. Matson. Am Home 80:24 D '77
Whole-earth gourmet. E. O'Bryan. il Am Home 80:64-5 Jl '77
Men most likely. . .Mlle's top twelve sex objects. il Mademoiselle 83:163 My '77
See also
Beauty, Personal—Men
Christmas gifts for men
Cookery by men
Fathers
Great men and women
Husbands
Photography of men
Sex differences
Single men
Widowers

Health and hygiene

See also
Beauty, Personal—Men

Psychology

Abortion and men; excerpt from The ambivalence of abortion. L. B. Francke. il Esquire 89:58-60 Ja '78
Climb to maturity: how the best and brightest came of age; excerpt from Adaptation to life. G. E. Vaillant. il Psychol Today 11:34-5+ S '77
How men are changing. D. Gelman and others. il Newsweek 91:52-6+ Ja 16 '78
Now that men can cry. . . W. Sheed. N Y Times Mag p38-40+ O 30 '77
Woody Allen: schlemiel as sex maniac. R. Wetzsteon. il pors Ms 6:14-15 N '77

Anecdotes, facetiae, satire, etc.

Menopause that refreshes. G. Nachman. por Newsweek 89:19 Ap 18 '77

Sexual behavior

See Sexual behavior

MEN and women. See Women and men

MENABILLY (historic house) See Historic houses, sites, etc.—England

MENAKER, Daniel
Health Department lists restaurant violations. New Yorker 53:43 O 10 '77
Scrolls; story. Atlantic 240:104-6 D '77
Winter—up close and personal. New Yorker 53:36-8 O 31 '77

MENCKEN, Henry Louis
Rediscovering Mencken. J. Epstein. Commentary 63:47-52 Ap '77 *

MENDELSON, Edward
Poetry of John Fuller. New Repub 176:32-5 My 28 '77

MENDES, Guy
Appalachia revisited. il Craft Horiz 37:28-40+ Je '77

MENDEZ, Charlotte
Gaiety and dreaming; story. Ms 6:64-5 Ag '77

MENDOCINO Coast Hospital, Fort Bragg, Calif. See Hospitals—California

MENEFEE, Robert S.
We motivate mechanics for high-production maintenance. il por Am City & County 92:51-2 Mr '77

MENEGATTI, Beppe
Belcanto duet. C. Faria. il pors Opera N 41:16-19 Je '77 *

MENEN, Aubrey
Behind the roses 'round the door. il Horticulture 55:61-5 Ap '77
Expatriate living in decadent Rome: it still beats home. il por Smithsonian 8:38-43 bibl(p 101) Ag '77
Krishna: god as a troublesome youth. il Horizon 19:54-65 Ja '77
Rise and fall of the Roman house plant. il Horticulture 55:26-9 D '77

MENGELBERG, Willem
Beethoven: Symphonies (9); Fidelio Overture, Op. 72c; Philips recording. H. Goldsmith. il por Hi Fi 27:78-80 D '77 *
Heroic voices from pioneer days; 1928 recording of Strauss's Ein Heldenleben on Victrola. R. D. Darrell. pors Hi Fi 27:90-1 Ap '77 *

MENGELE, Josef
Wiesenthal's last hunt. il pors Time 110:36+ S 26 '77 *

MENGISTU, Haile Mariam
Farewell to American arms. il por Time 109:36-7 My 9 '77 *

MENHADEN
Menhaden in Maine. J. Hay. il Liv Wildn 40:48-9 O '76

MENINGITIS
Virus-induced behavioral alteration of mice; lymphocytic choriomeningitis. J. Hotchin and R. Seegal. bibl il Science 196:671-4 My 6 '77

MENINGOENCEPHALITIS. See Encephalitis

MENK, Louis Wilson
How to get the trains back on the tracks; interview. por U.S. News 82:73 F 21 '77

MENKUS, Belden
Are Jews still expecting the Messiah? Chr Today 21:25 Ag 26 '77

MENNEAR-DUBAS, Susan
Autumn ought-to's. il Fam Health 9:28-31 S '77
Sea rescue. il Fam Health 9:40-3 Ag '77

MENNINGER, Karl Augustus
Doing true justice. America 137:6-9 Jl 2 '77
Whatever happened to sin? il Sat Eve Post 249:58-9+ Ap '77
MENNONITES
Collecting: Amish quilts. B. S. Janos. il House B 119:24+ Mr '77
Energy conservation in Amish agriculture. W. A. Johnson and others. bibl il Science 198: 373-8 O 28 '77
MENOPAUSE
Estrogen: the rewards and the risks. P. Weideger. McCalls 104:70+ Mr '77
Estrogens: can they hold back the clock? M. Steinmann. il Fam Health 9:24-7 My '77
Menopause: it's a disease, says insurance company. B. Canon. Ms 5:22 Mr '77
MENOTTI, Gian Carlo
Menotti's two worlds. J. Gruen. il Opera N 41: 12-17 My '77 *
Newest U.S. immigrant: Spoleto. il por Time 109:72+ Je 6 '77 *
Spoleto comes to Charleston. J. Kroll. il por Newsweek 89:56-7+ Je 6 '77 *
Spoleto U.S.A. G. Glueck. il por N Y Times Mag p20-2+ My 22 '77 *
MENS hair styles. See Hairdressing
MENS shirts. See Shirts
MENSAH, Gottfried B. Osei- . See Osei-Mensah, G. B.
MENSTRUATION
Intelligent woman's guide to sex. K. Durbin. Mademoiselle 83:50+ Je '77
Menstruation: what's normal, what's not. N. A. Comer. Mademoiselle 83:182-3+ Ag '77
Olfactory synchrony of menstrual cycles. Sci N 112:5 Jl 2 '77
Premenstrual symptoms: a reinterpretation. D. N. Ruble. bibl il Science 197:291-2 Jl 15 '77
Putting an end to monthly misery. M. Newton. por Fam Health 9:10+ Jl '77

Disorders

What to do about menstrual discomfort; dysmenorrhea. W. A. Nolen. McCalls 104:54+ Ag '77
MENSTRUATION, Cessation of. See Menopause
MENTAL chronometry. See Time perception
MENTAL depression. See Depression, Mental
MENTAL development of children. See Children—Growth and development
MENTAL healing
Her hands may heal. L. Davis. Vogue 167:105 My '77
MENTAL health. See Mental hygiene
MENTAL Health, National Association for. See National Association for Mental Health, Inc
MENTAL health associations
See also
National Association for Mental Health, Inc
MENTAL health care
Beyond the cities. J. Witt. il MH 60:4-6 Wint '77
Social and political forces affecting the mental health system; address, October 17, 1977. R. M. Daly. Vital Speeches 44:139-41 D 15 '77

Citizen participation

Process to close the gap. G. J. Hunt. MH 61: 9-11 Spr '77
MENTAL health centers
New role for crisis centers. R. H. Nelson. il MH 61:12-13 Summ '77
Paraprofessionals in a multiservice community mental health center; Sound View-Throgs Neck Community Mental Health Center in Bronx, N.Y. M. B. Ahmed and A. Birenbaum. il Intellect 106:149-51 O '77
MENTAL health education. See Mental hygiene—Study and teaching
MENTAL health laws
See also
Mentally ill children—Civil rights
MENTAL health workers. See Health workers
MENTAL hospitals. See Hospitals, Psychiatric
MENTAL hygiene
Assessing one's sanity. I. R. Hyatt. bibl Intellect 106:147-8 O '77
Rosalynn Carter and Margaret Mead: a meeting of minds; interview, ed by M. Mead. R. Carter. pors Redbook 149:123+ O '77
Seven basic emotional problems & what you can do about them. N. Lande and A. Slade. Harp Baz 110:98-9+ Ap '77
What's new (cont) MH 60:16-17 Wint; 61:12-13 Spr '77
See also
Boredom
Child mental health
Maturity
Mental health care
Psychiatric social work
Psychology, Industrial
Psychotherapy
School children—Adjustment
United States—President's Commission on Mental Health

Bibliography

Books. G. L. Usdin. See issues of MH

Study and teaching

American family: it ain't what it used to be. R. T. Williams. il MH 60:24-7 Wint '77
See also
Health workers—Training

Israel

Calling Dr Stress. L. Miller. il por Psychol Today 11:93-4+ S '77
MENTAL illness
See also
Neuroses
Paranoia
Schizophrenia

Causes

For better mental health, get a better job; study by Frederic Ilfeld and Leonard Pearlin. S. Bush. Psychol Today 11:152 D '77

Nutritional aspects

Anecdotes, facetiae, satire, etc

Chickenphrenia seen as mental-health hazard. M. Bannon. Psychol Today 11:96 Jl '77

Prevention

Preventing emotional illness. J. Greenberg. por Sci N 112:202-3 S 24 '77
Prevention: begin at the beginning. J. Carver. MH 60:7-10 Wint '77

Therapy

See also
Psychopharmacology
Psychotherapy
MENTAL illness in literature
People in crisis. L. Tierney. Engl J 66:64-5 S '77
MENTAL illness in motion pictures. See Motion pictures—Plots, themes, etc.
MENTALLY handicapped
Right brain: surviving retardation. Sci N 112: 229-30 O 8 '77
See also
Church work with the handicapped

Care and treatment

New attempt to help the deinstitutionalized. C. Holden. Science 198:903 D 2 '77

Civil rights

He didn't know half . . . ; conviction of W. J. Spence for murder; Durham, N.C. B. Jacobs. Progressive 41:42 N '77

Education

Adult education for the mildly retarded; College for Living program. A. M. Dahms and others. Educ Digest 43:53-5 N '77

Institutional care

Living in a work of art; Bronx Developmental Center, New York City. M. Stevens. il Newsweek 89:59 My 30 '77
1977 Reynolds prize goes to Richard Meier; design of the Bronx Development Center, New York. il Archit Rec 161:35 Je '77
Saying, showing, shaping; gymnastic program of the Syracuse Developmental Center, N.Y. D. Blatchley and C. Gove. il Parks & Rec 12:38-40 N '77

Recreation

Time to listen. C. Sherril and L. Ruda. il Parks & Rec 12:30-3+ N '77
See also
Sports for the handicapped
MENTALLY handicapped children
See also
Brain damaged children
Camps for the handicapped
Slow learning children

Civil rights

Battle over children's rights. D. Ferleger. bibl il por Psychol Today 11:88-91 Jl '77
MENTALLY ill
Sex and violence in the library: scream a little louder, please. C. Easton. il Am Lib 8:484-8 O '77
Toward a more caring society; excerpts from address, August 25, 1977. R. S. Carter. il por MH 61:3-5 Summ '77
See also
Church work with the handicapped

Care and treatment

Advice to the patient's family—take it easy. D. Cohen. Psychol Today 10:46a My '77
Are they closing the mental hospitals too soon? R. M. Williams. bibl il por Psychol Today 10:124-7+ My '77
Growing controversy over putting mental patients on the street. U.S. News 83:90-1 O 24 '77

MENTALLY ill—Care and treatment—*Continued*
Intravenous naloxone administration in schizophrenia and affective illness. G. C. Davis and others. bibl il Science 197:74-6 Jl 1 '77
See also
Hospitals, Psychiatric
Mentally ill—Home care

Civil rights

Helping patients to vote; mentally ill. W. G. Lee. il MH 61:14-16 Summ '77
Kenneth Donaldson's fight for freedom. R. Steinzor. Progressive 41:48-50 Ap '77
Taking civil commitment out of the dark ages. J. Parry. il MH 61:18-20 Spr '77
See also
Mentally ill children—Civil rights

Home care

Trials of living with a schizophrenic; work of Clare Creer and J. K. Wing. D. Cohen. Psychol Today 10:102 My '77

Legal status, laws, etc.

See Mentally ill—Civil rights

MENTALLY ill children
See also
Autism

Civil rights

Kids in mental hospitals. J. K. Footlick and others. il Newsweek 90:116+ D 12 '77

Education

See also
Special classes and special schools

MENTALLY retarded. See Mentally handicapped
MENTALLY retarded children. See Mentally handicapped children
MENTALLY superior
See also
Children, Gifted
Honor students
MENTMORE Towers, Buckinghamshire. See Historic houses, sites, etc.—England
MENUHIN, Yehudi
PW interviews; ed by J. F. Baker. il por Pub W 211:12-13 Ap 25 '77

about

Menuhins of Highgate. R. Gelatt. il por Sat R 4:54-5 Ap 16 '77 *
Portrait of a prodigy. S. Lipman. Commentary 64:57-61 Jl '77 *
MENUS
Feast yourself slim; food served at The Greenhouse health resort, Texas. il House & Gard 149:102 Jl '77
Feel good food; diet menu at Rancho la Puerta health resort; with recipes. il House & Gard 149:173-5+ My '77
Gourmet tips for mail-order menus. J. Wilson. il House & Gard 149:149+ S '77
[Month] menus; with recipes. See issues of Sunset
See also
Breakfasts
Brunches
Buffet meals
Dinners and dining
Lunches
Meals
Thanksgiving dinners
MENZEL, Donald H.
Donald Howard Menzel. L. Goldberg. il pors Sky & Tel 53:244-51 Ap '77 *
Obituary
Phys Today por 30:96+ My '77. O. Gingerich
MENZIES, Robert T. and Seals, R. K. Jr
Ozone monitoring with an infrared heterodyne radiometer. bibl il Science 197:1275-7 S 23 '77
MEO, Tommaso, and others
Glyoxalase I polymorphism in the mouse: a new genetic marker linked to H-2. bibl il Science 198:309-10 O 21 '77
MERCADANTE, Saverio
Il bravo. Review
Opera N 41:40-1 Ap 2 '77 *
MERCADO, Carol
How to make a million before you're 34; interview, ed by D. Kaye and F. Ruffin. pors Redbook 149:60+ My '77
MERCE Cunningham Dance Company
Dance. N. Goldner. Nation 224:186-8 F 12 '77
Dance. M. Hodgson. il Am Home 80:19 Mr '77
Field for dancing; Merce Cunningham and Dance Company at the Minskoff Theatre. R. Baker. Dance Mag 51:24+ Ap '77
Wackiness in Travelogue; Sounddance. J. Maskey. il Hi Fi 27:MA10-11 My '77
MERCEDES Benz (automobile) See Automobiles, Foreign
MERCENARY troops
See also
Foreign enlistment
MERCER, Henry Chapman
DIY—a Yankee tradition. A. Lees. il Pop Sci 210:158-60 Ap '77 *
MERCER, Marilyn
How to control your sweet tooth. il McCalls 104:112+ Jl '77
MERCER, Tammy Lee
At tackle, Ms Tammy Lee Mercer. J. E. Maslow. por Sat R 5:49-51 N 26 '77 *
MERCHANDISE, Quality of. See Quality of products
MERCHANT; drama. See Wesker, A.
MERCHANT marine
See also
Shipping
MERCIER, Jean F.
Children's books celebration draws SRO crowds. il Pub W 212:46-8 N 14 '77
New generation of writers and artists brings fresh vision to children's books. Pub W 211: 99-100 F 28 '77
(ed) See Karl, J. PW interviews
(ed) See Zindel, P. PW interviews
MERCIER, Louis
Encyclopedia of practical photography. il Pub W 213:36-7 Ja 2 '78
MERCURY (planet)
See also
Space flight to Mercury
MERCURY poisoning
Money problems that mercury wrought; compensation paid by Chisso Corp. for Minamata disease. il Bus W p38 Je 27 '77
Pollution postscripts; Minamata disease and Kepone poisoning. E. Keerdoja. il Newsweek 89:12 Ap 4 '77
MERCURY pollution of rivers, lakes, etc.
Mercury dispersal from lode sources in the Kuskokwim River drainage, Alaska. H. Nelson and others. bibl il map Science 198:820-4 N 25 '77
See also
Mercury poisoning
MERCURY pollution of the air. See Air pollution
MEREDITH, Don
Ol' Don may be a new Danderoo. W. Leggett. il Sports Illus 47:42 O 3 '77 *
MEREDITH Monk/The House (dance company)
See Dance companies
MERGERS. See Corporations—Acquisitions and mergers
MERIDEN Britannia Company. See Britannia ware
MÉRIMÉE, Prosper
Meteo Falcone. B. J. Khalil. Engl J 66:66-7 Mr '77 *
MERINGUE
Elusive dacquoise. C. Claiborne and P. Franey. il N Y Times Mag p48 Ja 23 '77
MERKIN, Daphne
Looking back. Commentary 64:63-5 Jl '77
MERLO, Harry Angelo
Swinging with Louisiana-Pacific. por Forbes 119:55 F 1 '77 *
MERMAN, Ethel
What's happening; interview, ed by G. Shalit. il por Ladies Home J 94:8 My '77
MERMON, Dick
Steelhead of the East. il por Field & S 81:42-4+ Mr '77
MERRIAM, Eve
Jacques Prévert, 1900-1977. New Repub 177: 25-8 Jl 9 '77
Star words; excerpt from Ab to Zogg: a lexicon for science-fiction and fantasy readers. il N Y Times Mag p 147 S 25 '77
MERRICK, David
David Merrick talks about the stage. . . movies. . .TV. il pors U.S. News 83:62 Jl 18 '77
MERRILL, James
Lenses; poem. Nation 225:187 S 3 '77
O; poem. Poetry 131:1-18 O '77
Palm Beach with Portuguese Man-of-War; poem. New Yorker 52:34 Ja 17 '77
MERRILL, Reba
Yes, I can! interview, ed by J. Halloran. il pors Am Home 80:30-1 Ap '77
MERRILL Lynch, Pierce, Fenner and Smith, Inc
Anatomy of a sweet investment; sugar futures. A. Tobias. Esquire 88:12+ S '77
Banking challenge to margin checking; Colorado complaint. Bus W p56 D 12 '77
MERRILL, Lynch & Company, Inc
Merrill Lynch: the bull in banking's shop. il Bus W p50-4+ Ag 8 '77
Merrill Lynch's dual assault on the banks. il Bus W p23-4 Jl 4 '77
MERRIMAC and Monitor, Battle of. See United States—History—Civil War, 1861-1865—Naval operations
MERRITT, Carole
Negro boy Alfred. T. Schwartz and H. Camp. por Newsweek 90:29 Jl 4 '77 *
MERRITT, John C.
Can marijuana cure glaucoma? il pors Ebony 32:108+ S '77 *
MERRITT, John I. 3d
Naturalists across the Rockies. bibl il pors Am West 14:4-9+ Mr '77
MERROW, John
Gay sex in the schools. Parents Mag 52:66+ S '77

MERRY-go-rounds
Old wheel takes a new turn; art class carousel. R. Reinke. il Sch Arts 76:6 Mr '77
MERRY widow; operetta. See Lehár, F.
MERRYMAN, John Henry
Are museum trustees and the law out of step? excerpt from The art world; ed by B. Diamonstein. Art N 76:174 N '77
Bernard Buffet's Refrigerator and the integrity of the work of art. il Art N 76:38-42 F '77
California royalty bill: milestone or mistake? pors Am Artist 41:60 F '77
Straw man in the Rothko case. il por Art N 75:32-4 D '76; 76:33+ Mr '77
MERSAND, Joseph
European and ethnic presence in American literature. bibl f il Engl J 66:42-5 Mr '77
Profession in perspective. Engl J 66:6-9 S '77
MERSZEI, Zoltan
Dow's strategy for an unfriendly new era. A. L. Morner. il por Fortune 95:312-15+ My '77 *
MERTHAN, Lawrence
Tongsun Park's White House connection. A. Latham. il Esquire 88:78+ D '77 *
MERTON, Thomas
Cargo cults of the South Pacific; with introd by N. B. Stone. il America 137:94-9 Ag 27 '77
MERVOSH, Edward
Economic diary. Bus W p21 Mr 21 '77
MERWIN, William Stanley
Briefcase; poem. Atlantic 239:81 My '77
Coin; poem. New Yorker 52:38 Ja 17 '77
Ford; story. New Yorker 53:37 Mr 28 '77
Green water tower; poem. New Yorker 53:44 D 5 '77
Happens every day; poem. Nation 225:502 N 12 '77
Harbor. New Yorker 53:37 My 16 '77
Island city; poem. Nation 224:218 F 19 '77
(tr) Story of the ants and grasshoppers; poem; excerpt from the Tzeltal Nation 225:444 O 29 '77
Strawberries; poem. Nation 225:190 S 3 '77
Tidal lagoon; Red house; Line of trees; poems. Nation 224:760 Je 18 '77
Warm pastures; poem. Nation 225:249 S 17 '77
(tr) See Jalāl al-Dīn, R. Ghazal
—and Masson, Jeff
(tr) My husband; poem; excerpt from the Siddhahemasabdanusasana. Nation 224:506 Ap 23 '77
(tr) When hundreds of prayers at last; Lush clouds in; poems; excerpts from the Amarusataka. Nation 224:506 Ap 23 '77
MESA VERDE National Park
Cliff dwellers of the Mesa Verde. D. Smith. il Am Hist Illus 12:4-9+ O '77
MESCAL
See also
Tequila
MESKIL, Paul S.
Mafia's new godfather. por Read Digest 110:141-4 Je '77
MESON accelerators. See Acceleraters (electrons, etc)
MESOZOIC period. See Paleontology—Mesozoic
MESSENGER, Betty
(ed) See Williams, A. Andy and Claudine
MESSER, Thomas M.
Sending the best of America abroad; F. Ferretti. il Art N 76:62-5 Summ '77 *
MESSERSCHMITT, Willy
Messerschmitt. P. Garrison. Flying 101:275 S '77 *
MESSERSCHMITT-Boelkow-Blohm (firm)
Germans ponder industry consolidation; MBB and VFW-Fokker. R. R. Ropelewski. Aviation W 107:18-19 Ag 15 '77
MESSIAEN, Olivier
Vingt regards sur l'enfant Jesus. D. Garvelmann. por Am Rec G 40:21-2 Ag '77 *
MESSIAH
Are Jews still expecting the Messiah? B. Menkus. Chr Today 21:25 Ag 26 '77; Discussion. 22:7-9 N 18 '77
MESSIANISM, American
America: experiment or destiny? with discussion. A. Schlesinger, Jr. bibl f Am Hist R 82:505-30 Je '77. Same abr. Am Heritage 28:12-17 Je '77
MESSINESI, Despina
Travel. See issues of Vogue
METABOLISM
Pulmonary metabolism during diving: conditioning blood for the brain. P. W. Hochachka and others. bibl il Science 198:831-4 N 25 '77
See also
Bacteria—Metabolism
Drugs—Metabolism
Energy metabolism
METABOLISM, Disorders of
Biochemical identification of homogentisic acid pigment in an achronotic Egyptian mummy. F. F. Stenn and others. bibl il Science 197:566-8 Ag 5 '77
Biogenic amine synthesis defect in dihydropteridine reductase deficiency. S. H. Koslow and I. J. Butler. bibl il Science 198:522-3 N 4 '77
Circling mice: clue to human disorder; histidinemia. Sci N 111:86 F 5 '77
Erythrocyte carbonic anhydrase I: inherited deficiency in humans. A. G. Kendall and R. E. Tashian. bibl il Science 197:471-2 Jl 29 '77
Hyperphenylalanemia: effect on brain polyribosomes can be partially reversed by other amino acids. J. V. Hughes and T. C. Johnson. bibl il Science 195:402-4 Ja 28 '77
Identification of retinoyl complexes as the autofluoroscent component of the neuronal storage material in Batten disease. L. S. Wolfe and others. bibl il Science 195:1360-2 Mr 25 '77; Reply with rejoinder. E. C. Nelson and B. A. Halley. 198:527-8 N 4 '77
Manic depression—a chemical disorder? Chemistry 50:25 N '77
Mucopolysaccharidosis in a cat with arylsulfatase B deficiency: a model of Maroteaux-Lamy syndrome. P. F. Jezyk and others. bibl il Science 198:834-6 N 25 '77
Niemann-Pick disease experimental model: sphingomyelinase reduction induced by AY-9944. N. Sakuragawa and others. bibl il Science 196:317-19 Ap 15 '77
Purine nucleoside phosphorylase deficiency: altered kinetic properties of a mutant enzyme. I. H. Fox and others. bibl il Science 197:1084-6 S 9 '77
See also
Acidosis
Anorexia nervosa
Cystic fibrosis
Cystinuria
Diabetes
Gangliosidosis
Lesch-Nyhan syndrome
Phenylketonuria
Porphyria
Prader-Willi syndrome
METABOLISM inhibiting substances
Fatty acids and their prostaglandin derivatives: inhibitors of proliferation in aortic smooth muscle cells. J. J. Huttner and others. bibl il Science 197:289-91 Jl 15 '77
Pineal vasotocin: release into cat cerebrospinal fluid by melanocyte-stimulating hormone release-inhibiting factor. S. Pavel and others. bibl il Science 197:179-80 Jl 8 '77
METAL casting (sculpture) See Casting (sculpture)
METAL coloring. See Metals—Coloring
METAL construction
See also
Steel construction
METAL etching
Forming and etching as a plating process. J. R. Gianatasio and A. M. Grutter. il Sch Arts 77:30-3 D '77
METAL industry
Killing of a wild river; pollution by Molybdenum Corporation of America, or MolyCorp. D. Kline. Field & S 82:104+ S '77
Let the record show; question of the ownership of Bonanza gold mine in Nicaragua by Asarco, Inc. Nation 225:291-2 O 1 '77
Middlemen of metal; metal service centers. M. Wellemeyer. il Fortune 95:162-7 Mr '77
See also
Amax Inc
Steel industry

Finance

Instead of spending, a shrinking plant. il Bus W p 106+ O 17 '77
Metals. il Forbes 121:113-14 Ja 9 '78
METAL molecules. See Molecules
METAL poisoning
See also
Lead poisoning
METAL sculpture
Provocative portal; question of steel sculpture by I. Noguchi. Vasari. il Art N 76:30-1 F '77
See also
Bronzes
Casting (sculpture)
METAL service centers. See Metal industry
METAL turning lathes. See Lathes
METAL work
See also
Art metal work
Britannia ware
Ironwork
Metals—Coloring
METAL working tools. See Tools
METALLURGY
See also
Alloys
Steel metallurgy
Uranium metallurgy
METALS
See also
Alkali metals
Alloys
Earths, Rare
Intermetallic compounds
Trace elements
also names of metals, e.g. Copper

METALS—*Continued*

Coloring

Workshop: titanium: metal of many colors. J. B. Ward. il Craft Horiz 37:20-1+ Ag '77

Fatigue

Exoelectrons. E. Rabinowicz. il Sci Am 236:74-82 bibl(p 132) Ja '77

Finishing

See also
Metals—Coloring

Prices

Aerospace metals prices bulge upward. W. C. Wetmore. il Aviation W 106:112-14 Je 6 '77
See also
Metals, Nonferrous—Prices

Stockpiling

See Stockpiling

METALS, Nonferrous

Prices

Faster ups and downs in nonferrous prices. il Bus W p37-8 Je 13 '77
Why metals markets have started rising. il Bus W p29-30 F 7 '77

Stockpiling

See Stockpiling

METALS in the body
See also
Nickel in the body

METAPHYSICS
See also
Cosmology

METASTASIS
Concomitant elevations in serum sialyltransferase activity and sialic acid content in rats with metastasizing mammary tumors. R. J. Bernacki and U. Kim bibl il Science 195:577-80 F 11 '77
Metastasis results from preexisting variant cells within a malignant tumor. I. J. Fidler and M. L. Kripke. bibl il Science 197:893-5 Ag 26 '77

METCALF, Lee
Excerpts from testimony on the Executive Reorganization Act, February 8, 1977. Cong Digest 56:109+ Ap '77

METCALFE, Edna
Trimming the tree. il Sat Eve Post 249:74-7+ D '77

METEORITE craters. See Craters

METEORITES
Antarctica: a deep-freeze storehouse for meteorites. W. A. Cassidy and others. bibl il map Science 198:727-31 N 18 '77
Cubanite: a new sulfide phase in CI meteorites. J. D. MacDougall and J. F. Kerridge. bibl il Science 197:561-2 Ag 5 '77
Did asteroid impacts help shape earth? Sci N 112:341 N 19 '77
Innisfree meteorite. il Sky & Tel 53:339 My '77
Innisfree meteorite: after—and before—the fall. il Sci N 111:212 Ap 2 '77
Kirin meteorites. T. Y. Ouyang. il Sci N 111:92-4 F 5 '77
Madagascar's mysterious meteorite. Sci N 112:102 Ag 13 '77
Meteorite fall reported in Madagascar. Sci N 112:86 Ag 6 '77
Meteorite impact ejecta: dependence of mass and energy lost on planetary escape velocity. J. D. O'Keefe and T. J. Ahrens. bibl il Science 198:1249-51 D 23 '77
Meteorite on ice. Newsweek 91:50 Ja 16 '78
Netschaëvo: a new class of chondritic meteorite. R. W. Bild and J. T. Wasson. bibl il Science 197:58-62 Jl 1 '77
Primordial noble gases in chondrites: the abundance pattern was established in the solar nebula. L. Alaerts and others. bibl il Science 198:927-30 D 2 '77
2nd largest U.S. meteorite; Old Woman meteorite. il Sci N 111:406 Je 25 '77
Strange xenon, extinct superheavy elements, and the solar neutrino puzzle. O. K. Manuel and D. D. Sabu; R. S. Lewis and others. bibl Science 195:208-10 Ja 14 '77

METEOROLOGICAL instruments
See also
Anemometers

METEOROLOGICAL optics
See also
Halos (meteorology)
Rainbow

METEOROLOGICAL research
What's happening to our climate? S. W. Matthews. il Read Digest 110:88-92 Mr '77
See also
Artificial satellites—Meteorological use
Rain making
Weather control

METEOROLOGICAL services
Balmy days for weathermen. L. Smith. il map Duns R 110:64-5+ N '77
It's an ill blizzard; private weather services. il Forbes 120:54-5 Jl 15 '77

METEOROLOGY
See also
Atmospheric pressure
Auroras
Computers—Meteorological use
Cyclones
Dew
Hail
Hurricanes
Ice on rivers, lakes, etc.
Rain and rainfall
Snow
Storms
Sun and meteorology
Television in meteorology
Thunderstorms
Tornadoes
United States—National Weather Service
Winds
also headings beginning Meteorological; Weather

International aspects

Testing at Wallops to calibrate U.S./Soviet meteorological data. Aviation W 107:20 Jl 4 '77

Study and teaching

Today's weather: courtesy of 12-year-olds; Meyers school, Lake Tahoe, Calif. P. Zauner. il Sci Digest 81:81-2 Ap '77

METEOROLOGY, Aeronautic
Customized weather: the private forecasters. K. A. Leibell. Flying 100:61 My '77
Getting the picture. G. C. Larson. il Flying 100:78+ Je '77
See also
Mountain waves
Radar meteorology

METEOROLOGY, Maritime
Weather course:
Air masses and fronts; ed by M. Pyzel. H. B. Kaster. il Motor B & S 140:70-2+ S '77
Anticyclones. il maps Motor B & S 141:108-10 Ja '78
Atmospheric pressure. il Motor B & S 140:56-7+ D '77
Terrain effects; ed by M. Pyzel. H. B. Kaster. il map Motor B & S 140:54-6 Ag '77
Thunderstorms. il map Motor B & S 140:68-70+ O '77
Weather forecasting for the racing sailor; Olympic Trials, 1976. R. L. Mairs. il map Yachting 142:66-9+ Ag '77
What your weatherman doesn't tell you; interview, ed by J. Cameron. G. Flittner. il map Motor B & S 139:76-8+ My '77

METEOROLOGY, Military
See also
Weather control—Military use

METEORS
Dazzling Czechoslovakian fireball. D. W. Dunham. il map Sky & Tel 54:475-8 D '77
Good year for Perseids. il Sky & Tel 54:435-9+ N '77
Perseids and two other August showers. il Sky & Tel 54:127-8 Ag '77
Three meteor showers to observe in November. il Sky & Tel 54:407-8 N '77

METER (standard of length) See Metric system

METER, Musical. See Musical meter and rhythm

METERS
See also
Dwell meters
Electric meters
Exposure meters
Micrometers
Parking meters
Radiometers
Water meters

METHADONE
Methadone and motherhood. J. Schinto. Progressive 41:40-2 Mr '77
Methadone Jones. D. M. Alpern and others. il Newsweek 89:29 F 7 '77

METHANE
Pilot plant will turn garbage into gas. R. Ceppos. il Pop Sci 211:40 Ag '77

METHANOGENIC microorganisms. See Microorganisms

METHANOL
Methanol conversion for your car? E. F. Lindsley. il Pop Sci 211:90-1+ Ag '77

METHODIST colleges and universities. See Church colleges and universities

METHOTREXATE
Dihydrofolate reductase: X-ray structure of the binary complex with methotrexate. D. A. Matthews and others. bibl il Science 197:452-5 Jl 29 '77

METHOXYPSORALEN. See Psoralens

METHUEN, Inc. See Publishers and publishing—Canada

METHVIN, David
Surprising success. por Forbes 119:120 Mr 15 '77 *

METHVIN, Eugene H.
After Brezhnev? The Kremlin's succession crisis. Read Digest 110:103-6 My '77
Crime in America—a turnaround at last? Read Digest 110:61-5 Je '77
Why can't do-nothing bureaucrats be fired? Read Digest 111:119-22 N '77

METHYL sulfide
Estimate of the contribution of biologically produced dimethyl sulfide to the global sulfur cycle. P. J. Maroulis and A. R. Bandy. bibl il map Science 196:647-8 My 6 '77

METHYLATION
Biomethylation of toxic elements in the environment. W. P. Ridley and others. bibl il Science 197:329-32 Jl 22 '77
Methylation of selenium in the aquatic environment. Y. K. Chau and others; discussion. bibl Science 195:594-5 F 11 '77

METHYLDOPA
Diet and uptake of aldomet by the brain: competition with natural large neutral amino acids. D. C. Markovitz and J. D. Fernstrom. bibl il Science 197:1014-15 S 2 '77

METHYLPHENIDATE
Family that fought back; use of ritalin in Taft, Calif. schools. J. N. Bell. il McCalls 104:26+ My '77
Methylphenidate in hyperkinetic children: differences in doses effects on learning and social behavior. R. L. Sprague and E. K. Sleator. bibl il Science 198:1274-6 D 23 '77

METPATH Inc. See Medical laboratories

METRAUX, Rhoda
(ed) See Mead, M. Five-million-dollar birthday present

METRAZOLE. See Pentylenetetrazole

METRIC Board (United States) See United States—Metric Board

METRIC system
Art program and the metric systems. T. A. Hatfield. il Sch Arts 76:60-1 Mr '77
Conversion without representation. G. C. Larson. Flying 100:28 F '77
Fishing moves to metrics. B. Stearns. Outdoor Life 159:82-3 Ap '77
Gridiron of the future? conversion of football fields to metric system. il Sr Schol 110:9 D 1 '77
How soon will we measure in metric? K. F. Weaver. il Nat Geog 152:287-94 Ag '77
Inevitable metric advance. R. Elwell. Educ Digest 42:17-20 Mr '77
Metrics ahead: how you can cope; excerpt from Metric. . .in a nutshell. R. A. Hopkins. il Sci Digest 81:44-8+ F '77
Metrics: gaining some yardage—er, meterage. il Sr Schol 110:8+ D 1 '77
Prepare now for the metric system. S. Baxter. Am City & County 92:63 Jl '77
Top retailer plans for metric conversion; Sears. V. Louviere. por Nations Bus 65:75 S '77
U.S. metric conversion: rough road ahead. M. A. Guillen. il Sci N 112:42-3 Jl 16 '77
See also
United States—Metric Board

Anecdotes, facetiae, satire, etc.

Yardstick gives way to meterstick. R. Mazzei. Clearing H 51:92 O '77

Bibliography

Metrics: do the books measure up? S. Weir. il por SLJ 24:30-1 N '77

METROPOLITAN areas
Slowdown for strip cities: reversal of century-old trend. il maps U.S. News 82:39-42 Mr 7 '77
See also
City planning
Houston, Tex.—Metropolitan area
Urban renewal

METROPOLITAN government
See also
Twin Cities Metropolitan Council

METROPOLITAN libraries. See Libraries

METROPOLITAN Life Insurance Company
Metropolitan Life's failure as a swinger. il por Bus W p78+ N 21 '77

METROPOLITAN Museum of Art, New York
Annenberg controversy. G. Glueck. por Art N 76:63-4 My '77
Annenberg *interruptus*; cancellation of proposed Fine Arts Center of the Annenberg School of Communications. por Time 109:64 Mr 28 '77
French interiors; Wrightsman rooms. S. B. Sherrill. Antiques 112:818+ N '77
Help wanted at the Met. L. S. Gordon. il N Y Times Mag p 13-15+ Je 26 '77
Highlights of the Irwin Untermyer Collection at the Metropolitan Museum of Art. S. B. Sherrill. il Antiques 112:814+ N '77
Hoving years; interview, ed by M. N. Carter. T. P. F. Hoving. pors Art N 76:37-40 Ja '77
Touch; exhibition for the blind. New Yorker 53:22 S 5 '77
Who should manage museums? with views of museum administrators. P. M. Kadis. il por Art N 76:46-51 O '77

Cloisters

Strike up the shawm; Waverly consort at the Cloisters. H. Saal. il Newsweek 91:55 Ja 2 '78

Costume Institute

From Russia, with opulence. E. R. Lipson. il N Y Times Mag p48-9 Ja 16 '77
Ruffles and flourishes; Vanity fair-exhibit. S. C. Cowley. il por Newsweek 91:56-7 Ja 2 '78
Russian costume. S. B. Sherrill. il Antiques 111:266+ F '77
Vanity fair; interview, ed by J. Onassis. D. Vreeland. il N Y Times Mag p 150-2+ D 11 '77

METROPOLITAN Opera Association
Metropolitan mirror. A. M. Lingg. il Opera N 42:51 D 3 '77
Viewpoint; agreement between Metropolitan Opera and its orchestra musicians. R. Jacobson. Opera N 42:6 O '77

METROPOLITAN Opera Ballet
Met: a new ballet look. W. Terry. il Sat R 4:44-5 F 5 '77

METROPOLITAN Opera Company
At long last, Lulu. H. Saal. il Newsweek 89:105-6 Ap 11 '77
La Boheme telecast live from the Met. P. J. Smith. Hi Fi 27:MA27 Jl '77
Classical music: performance of Le Prophète. B. H. Haggin. New Repub 176:27-8 My 28 '77
Composers' revisions; decision to use first version of G. Verdi's Don Carlo. B. H. Haggin. New Repub 177:28-30 N 5 '77
Dialogues at the Met, finally. W. Bender. il Time 109:75 F 21 '77
False prophet, true martyrs; Prophète and Dialogues of the Carmelites. R. Jacobson. il Opera N 41:30-2 Mr 19 '77
Fidès tradition; performances of Le Prophète. G. Jellinek. il Opera N 41:20-1 Ja 29 '77
Fools' approval. B. H. Haggin. New Repub 176:21-3 Je 11 '77
Lulu. H. E. Phillips. Nat R 29:733-4 Je 24 '77
Lulu and the Cinderella from Idaho. W. Bender. il por Time 109:96 Mr 28 '77
Metropolitan Opera:
  Dialogues of the Carmelites. C. L. Osborne. il Hi Fi 27:MA21-2 Je '77
  Five new productions. Hi Fi 27:MA23-7 F '77
  Lucia di Lammermoor. Hi Fi 27:MA16 Ap '77
  Met's Lulu. il Hi Fi 27:MA26-7+ Jl '77
  New productions of Esclarmonde and La forza del destino. il Hi Fi 27:MA16-17 Mr '77
  Die Walküre, Le Prophète, Salome. il Hi Fi 27:MA27-9 My '77
  Die Zauberflöte. Hi Fi 27:MA16-17 Ap '77
Met's Prophète: raising the hull. W. Bender. il Time 109:50 Ja 31 '77
Music:
  Lulu and La forza del destino. D. Hamilton. Nation 224:444-6 Ap 9 '77
  Pelléas et Mélisande. D. Hamilton. Nation 225:541-2 N 19 '77
Music; Metropolitan Opera's new Rigoletto. B. H. Haggin. New Repub 178:28-9 Ja 7 '78
Music; performance of Boris Godunov and Eugene Onegin. New Repub 177:21-3 N 26 '77
Music to my ears:
  Lulu. I. Kolodin. il Sat R 4:37-8 Ap 30 '77
Musical events:
  La Bohème. A. Porter. New Yorker 53:141-3 Ap 18 '77
  Lulu. A. Porter. New Yorker 53:125-31 Ap 4 '77
  Poulenc's Dialogues des Carmélites. A. Porter. New Yorker 53:107-10 F 21 '77
  Le Prophète. A. Porter. New Yorker 52:95-100 F 7 '77
  Rigoletto. A. Porter. New Yorker 53:175-8 N 21 '77
  Tannhäuser. A. Porter. New Yorker 53:79-81 Ja 9 '78
New Rigoletto. H. Saal. il Newsweek 90:126 N 14 '77
Opera season. E. Calder and K. Moses. Am Rec G 40:62 Mr; 62 My '77
Playing Rigoletto up front. W. Bender. il Time 110:116 N 14 '77
Prophetic Prophète. I. Kolodin. il Sat R 4:47-8 Mr 5 '77
Rehearsals; rehearsal of G. Meyerbeer's Le Prophète. New Yorker 52:24-6 Ja 24 '77
Rehearsals; Tannhäuser. New Yorker 53:20-2 D 26 '77

METROPOLITAN Opera Company—*Continued*
Report:
Esclarmonde, La forza del destino and Aida. il Opera N 41:28 Ja 22 '77
Five revivals: Die zauberflöte, Faust, Lucia di Lammermoor, Tosca, and Salome. il Opera N 41:27-8 F 26 '77
Lulu; Bohème; Forza del destino; Die Walküre. R. Jacobson. Opera N 41:28-30 My '77
Opening week of the 94th season: Boris Godunov, Pelléas et Mélisande and Eugene Onegin. R. Jacobson. Opera N 42:42+ D 3 '77
Rigoletto and La Traviata. R. Jacobson il Opera N 42:34-6 Ja 7 '78
Samson et Dalila; Andrea Chenier; Tosca; and Lulu. il Opera N 41:30 Je '77
Reverence and rashness at the Met. I. Kolodin. Sat R 5:64 D 10 '77
Sensuous, new Tannhäuser. W. Bender. il Time 111:54 Ja 2 '78
Small Beer; performance of Le Prophète. il Newsweek 89:71 Ja 31 '77
Supers: world of the extras at the Met. L. Rubinstein. il por Opera N 42:12-16 O '77
What's up at the Met: a capsule guide to the 1977-78 season. il Opera N 42:24-5 O '77

History

What might have been: unrecorded Metropolitan Opera performances. J. B. Steane. il Opera N 42:26-9 Ag '77

METROPOLITAN Opera Guild
Metropolitan mirror. A. M. Lingg. il Opera N 42:51 D 3 '77
Metropolitan Opera Guild; annual luncheon 1977. il Opera N 41:4-5 F 19 '77
Viewpoint. L. D. Lovett. Opera N 42:6 Ag '77

METROPOLITAN Opera House, New York
From Pavlova to ABT. W. Terry. il pors Opera N 41:10-14 Je '77
See also
Lincoln Center for the Performing Arts, New York—Opera House

METROPOLITAN Opera on the air. See Radio broadcasting—Opera

METROPOLITAN Opera Orchestra
Viewpoint; agreement between Metropolitan Opera and its orchestra musicians. R. Jacobson. Opera N 42:6 O '77

Anecdotes, facetiae, satire, etc.

Pitfalls. L. Dreyer. il Opera N 42:26+ O '77

METZ, Christian
Segmentation. B. Henderson. Film Q 31:57-65 Fall '77 *

METZ, Robert K. Jr
Blue dun bonanza. S. Paulakavich. por Outdoor Life 159:31 Je '77 *

METZENBAUM, Howard Morton
Forgotten minority? por Forbes 120:105 Ag 15 '77 *

METZLER, Paula Wilens
In nature's laboratory. il pors Conservationist 32:30-3+ Jl '77

MEVES, Eric
Watts up must come down? bibl il Parks & Rec 12:29-31 O '77

MEWSHAW, Michael
Staying power and the glory. Nation 224:469-72 Ap 16 '77

MEXICAN AMERICANS
Jim, what are you? excerpt from TV series, As we see it. Sr Schol 110:16+ O 6 '77
Keeping the old: a celebration at Norma and Marino De Leon's. L. W. Eckhardt. il pors Redbook 150:94+ D '77
Remember Tierra Amarilla: Chicano power in the feudal West. P. Nabokov. il por Nation 225:336-40 O 8 '77
These proud Americans; Mexican-American migrant workers. L. Dunn and J. Ullman. il Sat Eve Post 249:42-4+ S '77
U.S. journal: San Antonio; Communities Organized for Public Service. C. Trillin. il New Yorker 53:92-4+ My 2 '77

Crime

See also
Mafia

Education

Culture, poverty and educational problems of Mexican Americans. C. S. Henkin and A. B. Henkin. bibl Clearing H 50:316-19 Mr '77
Se habla español; the story of the Chicano Education Project; Colorado. J. Earle. Todays Educ 66:76-7 N '77

MEXICAN AMERICANS in literature
Frost in the Rio Grande Valley; poem by J. Limoń. A. D. Treviño. Engl J 66:69 Mr '77

MEXICAN AMERICANS in poetry. See Mexican Americans in literature

MEXICAN architecture. See Architecture, Mexican

MEXICAN art. See Art, Mexican

MEXICAN cookery. See Cookery, Mexican

MEXICAN Mafia. See Mafia

MEXICAN painting. See Painting, Mexican

MEXICAN pottery. See Pottery, Mexican

MEXICANS in the United States
Earnings gap. C. McWilliams. Nation 224:356 Mr 26 '77
Illegal aliens; refugees from hunger. G. M. Anderson. America 136:68-72 Ja 29 '77
Labor functions of illegal aliens. A. Portes. bibl il Society 14:31-7 S '77
North of the border—who needs whom? J. Flanigan. il Forbes 119:37-41 Ap 15 '77
See also
El Paso, Tex.—Foreign population
Mexican Americans

MEXICO
Mexico for retirement? J. H. Budd. il Ret Liv 17:37-9 Mr '77
Mexico, 1977; symposium. bibl f map Cur Hist 72:97-127+ Mr '77
Time bomb in Mexico. C. J. Migdail. il map U.S. News 83:27-8 Jl 4 '77
See also
Acapulco
Americans in Mexico
Architecture, Domestic—Mexico
The Arts—Mexico
Automobile touring—Mexico
Birds—Mexico
Birth control—Mexico
Campeche
Camping—Mexico
Crime and criminals—Mexico
Criminal justice, Administration of—Mexico
Cruising—Mexico
Education—Mexico
Gas, Natural—Mexico
Guanajuato
Housing
Hunting—Mexico
Isla Mujeres
Loans, Bank—Mexico
Mexico (city)
Music festivals—Mexico
Narcotic laws and legislation—Mexico
Presidents—Mexico
Prisons—Mexico
Publishers and publishing—Mexico
Restaurants—Mexico
Rio Grande
Seaside resorts—Mexico
Sonoran Desert
Villages—Mexico
Women—Mexico
Yucatán

Antiquities

Aztec treasure house; Olmec artifacts; excerpt from El Dorado and other pursuits. E. Connell. il Harpers 255:80-4 O '77
See also
Monte Albán

Boundaries

U.S. and Mexico complete transfer of territory; announcement. May 26, 1977. maps Dept State Bull 77:10-12 Jl 4 '77

Civilization

Matter of life and death; Aztec myths and Christian beliefs; excerpt from The labyrinth of solitude. O. Paz. il UNESCO Courier 30:20-1+ Ag '77

Commerce

United States

See United States—Commerce—Mexico

Description and travel

Cool Mexican hill towns from the 15th century. J. O'Reilly. il House & Gard 149:43-5 Ag '77
Mexico's vacation centers. il Bet Hom & Gard 55:220+ S '77
Riding the U.S./Mexico borderland. W. Oleksy. il map Ret Liv 17:33-6+ Mr '77

Economic conditions

Income inequality in Mexico. D. Felix. bibl f Cur Hist 72:111-14+ Mr '77
Inside the volcano. G. Lyons. il Harpers 254:41-6+ Je '77
Mexico's chaotic economy. E. McCaughan and P. Baird. Progressive 41:12 Mr '77
Population growth and economic development: the case of Mexico. A. J. Coale. bibl f For Affairs 56:415-29 Ja '78

Economic policy

Echeverria's economic policy. C. P. Blair. bibl f Cur Hist 72:124-7+ Mr '77

Economic relations

United States

See United States—Economic relations—Mexico

Foreign relations

Mexican foreign policy. G. W. Grayson. bibl f Cur Hist 72:97-101+ Mr '77

United States

See United States—Foreign relations—Mexico

MEXICO—*Continued*

History

Conquest, 1519-1540

Campeche: buccaneer's battleground. N. Navarro and R. Bushnell. il Oceans 10:22-5 S '77

American Punitive Expedition, 1916

See United States—History—Punitive Expedition to Mexico, 1916

Industries

Tequila; Mexican mescal. N. K. Walton. il Américas 29:15-18 Ja '77

See also
Automobile industry—Mexico
Fisheries—Mexico
Petroleum industry—Mexico
Steel industry—Mexico

Native races

See Indians of Mexico

Photographs

William Henry Jackson in Mexico. W. C. Jones. il por Am West 14:10-21 Jl '77

Politics and government

Mexico's government in crisis. S. Bizzarro. bibl f Cur Hist 72:102-5+ Mr '77
Road back to confidence. il por map Time 109: 32-6 F 21 '77

See also
Presidents—Mexico

Population

Mexico's population pressures. M. Alisky. bibl f Cur Hist 72:106-10+ Mr '77
Population growth and economic development: the case of Mexico. A. J. Coale. bibl f For Affairs 56:415-29 Ja '78

Religious institutions and affairs

See also
Catholic Church in Mexico

Social conditions

Borders: Texas-Chihuahua. R. Morris. New Repub 177:12 O 22 '77
Inside the volcano. G. Lyons. il Harpers 254: 41-6+ Je '77

See also
Women—Mexico

Social life and customs

See also
Indians of Mexico—Social life and customs

Treaties

United States

See United States—Treaties—Mexico

MEXICO (city)

Social life and customs

Sunday afternoon in Mexico City. C. Hartman. il Holiday 57:32-3 N '76

MEXICO, Gulf of

Anoxic, hypersaline basin in the northern Gulf of Mexico. R. F. Shokes and others. bibl il Science 196:1443-6 Je 24 '77
Gulf of Mexico; symposium. il Oceans 10:14-53 S '77

See also
Gulf States
Petroleum—Gulf Coast Region

MEYER, André
Passing the baton at Lezard Frères. W. Robertson. il pors Fortune 96:116-20+ N '77 *

MEYER, Charles R.
Magnificent tarpon. il Field & S 81:26-7+ Ap '77
Solar heating—no longer a novelty. il Ret Liv 17:26-8 O '77
Whaling and the art of scrimshaw; excerpt. il Conservationist 31:29-32 N '76

MEYER, D. Eugene
Student teaching: opportunity or ordeal. Clearing H 50:258-9 F '77

MEYER, David I. and Burger, M. M.
Puzzling role of cell surfaces. bibl il pors Chemistry 50:36-41 Ja '77

MEYER, Debbie
What do you do when you grow up. J. Kaplan. il pors Sports Illus 47:30-2 Jl 4 '77 *

MEYER, Fred, Inc
Fred Meyer's grocery S&Ls. il Bus W p76 Ja 24 '77

MEYER, Glenn E. and Maguire, W. M.
Spatial frequency and the mediation of short-term visual storage. bibl il Science 198:524-5 N 4 '77

MEYER, Herbert E.
Business has the jitters in Quebec. il Fortune 96:238-42+ O '77
Flourishing new business of recycling executives. il Fortune 95:328-30+ My '77
Little bit of England in Toronto. il Fortune 96: 217-18 N '77
$900 lesson in podium power. il pors Fortune 96:196-8+ Ag '77
This Communist internationale has a capitalist accent. il Fortune 95:134-7+ F '77

MEYER, Jaclyn
Cardinal Ritter Institute provides care with flair to St Louis elderly. il Aging 272:8-10 Je '77 *

MEYER, Jeff
Big dream: a feature film to call your own. T. Galluzzo. il pors Mod Phot 41:90+ N '77 *

MEYER, John R.
Head capsule transmission of long-wavelength light in the curculionidae. bibl il Science 196: 524-5 Ap 29 '77

MEYER, Karl E.
Television. See issues of Saturday review

MEYER, L. Donald
Sloping lot? Take your pick of these retaining walls. il Pop Sci 210:118-20+ Ap '77

MEYER, Larry L.
Two hundred years of California earth-quakes; excerpt from California quake. il Am West 14:4-9+ Ja '77

MEYER, Martin
IC multiplex decoder improves stereo FM performance. il Pop Electr 12:67-71 S '77

MEYER, Mary L.
Dealing with death. il America 137:109-11 Ag 27 '77

MEYER, Nicholas
Meyer and Kaplan: two into one will go; interview, ed by R. Dahlin. il pors Pub W 212:46 N 21 '77

MEYER, Peter
Mexican transfer. Harpers 255:26+ N '77
Short history of form 1040. il Harpers 254:22-4 Ap '77

MEYER, Susan E.
Eric Sloane's America. il por Am Artist 41:40-5+ Je '77

MEYER, Victoria Junco de. See Junco de Meyer, V.

MEYERBEER, Giacomo
At long last Meyerbeer's Le Prophète. D. Arthur. Am Rec G 40:29-30 Je '77 *
Barnum of the opera. G. Marek. il Opera N 41:10-12+ Ja 29 '77 *
Columbia reopens the Meyerbeer case. P. J. Smith. il Hi Fi 27:87-8 Mr '77 *
Fidès tradition; performances of Le Prophète at the Metropolitan Opera. G. Jellinek. il Opera N 41:20-1 Ja 29 '77 *
Meyerbeer revealed: discovering the composer through his own words. R. Breuer. il Opera N 41:38-43 Ja 29 '77 *
Pathbreaker: analyzing Le Prophète. J. Thomson. Opera N 41:34+ Ja 29 '77 *
Le Prophète. Reviews
Hi Fi 27:MA28-9 My '77 *
Nation 224:157-8 F 5 '77 *
New Repub 176:27-8 My 28 '77 *
New Yorker 52:95-100 F 7 '77 *
Newsweek il 89:71 Ja 31 '77 *
Opera N 41:22+ Ja 29 '77 *
Sat R 4:47-8 Mr 5 '77 *
Time il 109:50 Ja 31 '77 *
Prophetic words; ed by P. La Cerra. P. Scudo. il Opera N 41:30-2 Ja 29 '77 *
Rehearsals; rehearsal of Le Prophète at the Metropolitan Opera. New Yorker 52:24-6 Ja 24 '77 *
Scribe factory. H. Heinsheimer. por Opera N 41:16-19 Ja 29 '77 *
Viewpoint. R. Jacobson. Opera N 41:6 Ja 29 '77 *

MEYERHOFF, M. and Rechnitz, G. A.
Antibody binding measurements with hapten-selective membrane electrodes. bibl il Science 195:494-5 F 4 '77

MEYERS, Arthur S.
Keeping up; a checklist. Am Lib 8:77 F '77

MEYERS, Duane H.
Boys and girls and sex and libraries; adaptation of address, October 1976. bibl il por Lib J 102:457-63 F 15 '77

MEYERS, Edward
Protechniques. See issues of Popular photography

MEYERS, Gerald Carl
New driver for the Laggard. il por Time 110: 113 N 7 '77 *

MEYERS, John A.
Letter from the publisher. See issues of Sports illustrated

MEYERS, Perla
It's salad, it's easy & it's dinner. il Mademoiselle 83:208-9 S '77
7-salad buffet. il pors House & Gard 149:132-3+ Je '77

MEZEY, Alison
Makeovers for the dancing life. pors Seventeen 36:124-5 O '77 *

MEZHAKOFF-KORIAKIN, Igor
(tr) See Akhmadulina, B. Tale about rain in several episodes

el MEZRAB, Jane Elizabeth (Digby) See Ellenborough, J. E. D. L. Countess of

MEZZOTINT engraving. See Engraving

MIALE, Walter
(ed) See Warnke, P. Real Paul Warnke

MIAMI, Fla.
Architecture
Apogee 1 Townhouses, Miami, Florida. il Archit Rec 161:112-13 mid-My '77
Crime
Cuban exiles: Miami, haven for terror. Nation 224:326-31 Mr 19 '77
Economic conditions
Miami: saved again. P. Berman. il Forbes 120: 37-41 N 1 '77
Foreign population
Brigade 2506; survivors of the Bay of Pigs. E. Keerdoja. il Newsweek 90:20 D 12 '77
Cuban exiles: Miami, haven for terror. Nation 224:326-31 Mr 19 '77
JFK, Castro—and controversy; B. Moyers' documentary The CIA's secret army. D. Gelman. il pors Newsweek 90:85 Jl 18 '77
Galleries and museums
Lipchitz legacy; the Metropolitan Museum and Art Centers and the proposed museum in the Dade County government center. E. Edwards. Art N 76:166-8 Summ '77
Music
See also
Opera—Florida
MIAMI BEACH, Fla.
Architecture
Those were the days, my friend; art deco architecture and design. H. Sutton. il Sat R 5:66-7 D 10 '77
Description
It should have been called Miami Beaches. P. Savage-Rich. Sat Eve Post 249:89+ Ap '77
Education
Studying death; Miami Beach Senior High School course. M. Sheils. il Newsweek 89:43 Mr '77
Hotels, restaurants, etc.
Ebb tide at Miami Beach. il Time 110:83-4 D 19 '77
Mickey Mouse haunts Miami Beach hotels. Bus W p24+ Ag 1 '77
Religious institutions and affairs
FM gabbai; J. Goldblum. M. Singer. Atlantic 240:98-100 O '77
MIAMI BEACH, Fla, Youth Center. See Recreation centers
MIAMI-Dade Community College, Miami, Fla.
Roots; using the telecast in black studies course. M. Rein and J. M. Elliot. il por Negro Hist Bull 40:664-7 Ja '77
MIAMI-Dade Public Library. See Libraries—Florida
MIANUS River
Photographs
Splendor of autumn. A. Eisenstaedt. Horticulture 55:36-43 S '77
MICA
Evidence for superheavies in mica looks weaker. G. B. Lubkin. il Phys Today 30:17+ Ja '77
MICE
Ectoparasitic mites on rodents: application of the island biogeography theory? with reply by B. O'Connor and others. A. M. Kuris and A. R. Blaustein. bibl Science 195:596-8 F 11 '77
Experimental triggering of reproduction in a natural population of microtus montanus. N. C. Negus and P. J. Berger. bibl il Science 196: 1230-1 Je 10 '77
Nude mouse: a new experimental model for pneumocystis carinii infection. P. D. Walzer and others. bibl il Science 197:177-9 Jl 8 '77
Phenolic plant compounds functioning as reproductive inhibitors in microtus montanus. P. J. Berger and others. bibl il Science 195:575-7 F 11 '77
Virus-induced behavioral alteration of mice; lymphocytic choriomeningitis. J. Hotchin and R. Seegal. bibl il Science 196:671-4 My 6 '77
See also
Dormice
Control
Great Kern County mouse war. K. P. Maize. il Audubon 79:158-60 N '77
Extermination
See Mice—Control
MICHAELIS, Gladys J.
Kabuki, a dance-drama art form of Japan. il Dance Mag 51:83-7 My '77
MICHAELS, Christopher
Blessing of the snows. il Field & S 82:54-5+ D '77
MICHAELS, Leonard
Berkeley memoir. New Repub 177:13-16 O 22 '77
MICHAELS, William
Broadcaster who fell from Grace with the Seers. pors Forbes 119:48-9 Ap 1 '77 *
MICHAELSON, Martin
Freedom of information. Nation 224:614-18 My 21 '77
MICHAELSON, Wes
Wes Michaelson: a call for repentance. Chr Cent 94:7 Ja 5 '77
MICHAILOVSKAIA, Kiri
My name is Asya. C. Reamer. Engl J 66:62 Mr '77 *
MICHALS, Duane
Masters of the darkroom; how Duane Michals creates his mystical masterpieces; excerpt from Darkroom. il Pop Phot 81:136-41+ O '77
MICHENER, James Albert
American family. il Ladies Home J 94:87+ D '77
Author James Michener on future of this country. il pors U.S. News 83:60-1 S 12 '77
He painted the West. il Read Digest 110:182-7 My '77
MICHIE, Mary M.
Encounter with an African potter. il pors Ceram Mo 25:32-5 D '77
Lamu door carving. il Design (US) 78:26 mid-Wint '77
MICHIGAN
See also
Agriculture—Michigan
Architecture, Domestic—Michigan
Berrien County
Booksellers and bookselling—Michigan
Crime and criminals—Michigan
Education—Michigan
Environmental policy—Michigan
Finance—Michigan
Fishing—Michigan
Housing—Michigan
Lakes—Michigan
Libraries—Michigan
Opera—Michigan
Organic farming—Michigan
Public health—Michigan
Recreation—Michigan
Shiawassee County
Wildlife sanctuaries—Michigan
Zoology—Michigan
Politics and government
State scientific advisers: the effort in Michigan. L. J. Carter; reply. D. G. Yerg. Science 195: 130-1 Ja 14 '77
Washing dirty laundry in Detroit; D. Riegle story in the Detroit News. N. Ephron. Esquire 87:42-4 F '77
Religious institutions and affairs
Second coming; Colonial Village Church in Flint. B. Brenner. Chr Today 21:43-4 Ja 21 '77
MICHIGAN, Lake
See also
Indiana Dunes National Lakeshore
MICHIGAN Audubon Society
To drill or not to drill; controversy surrounding proposed oil lease of Bernard W. Baker Sanctuary. J. G. Mitchell. il Audubon 79:78-85 Ja '77
MICHIGAN Opera Theatre. See Opera—Michigan
MICHIGAN State University, East Lansing
Aquatic farms clean up waste water; water-recycling experiment. B. Seaquist. il Pop Sci 211:88-9 S '77
Creation at Michigan State. Sci Am 237:87 D '77
MICKELSON, Sig
Free flow of information; address, January 21, 1977. Vital Speeches 43:314-17 Mr 1 '77
MICKEY Mouse (cartoon) See Motion pictures—Animated cartoons
MICROBIAL genetics
Bacterial genetics: action at a distance on DNA. G. B. Kolata. il Science 198:41-2 O 7 '77
Construction of chimeric phages and plasmids containing the origin of replication of bacteriophage lambda. D. D. Moore and others. bibl il Science 198:1041-6 D 9 '77
Expression in escherichia coli of a chemically synthesized gene for the hormone somatostatin. K. Itakura and others. bibl il Science 198:1056-63 D 9 '77
Expression of murine sarcoma virus genes in uninfected rat cells subjected to anaerobic stress. G. R. Anderson and L. M. Matovcik. bibl il Science 197:1371-4 S 30 '77
Gene transfer as a mechanism of microbial evolution. D. Reanney. bibl il BioScience 27:340-4 My '77
Genetic structure of the replication origin of bacteriophage lambda. M. E. Furth and others. bibl il Science 198:1046-51 D 9 '77
Intergeneric transfer of genes involved in the rhizobium-legume symbiosis. P. E. Bishop and others. bibl il Science 198:938-40 D 2 '77
Naturally occurring plasmid carrying genes for enterotoxin production and drug resistance. C. L. Gyles and others. bibl il Science 198: 198-9 O 14 '77
One strand equivalent of the escherichia coli genome is transcribed: complexity and abundance classes of mRNA. W. E. Hahn and others. bibl il Science 197:582-5 Ag 5 '77

MICROBIAL genetics—*Continued*
Overlapping genes: more than anomalies? G. B. Kolata. Science 196:1187-8 Je 10 '77
Packaging the message; viruses. il Chemistry 50:22-3 Mr '77
Physical structure of the replication origin of bacteriophage lambda. K. Denniston-Thompson and others. bibl il Science 198:1051-6 D 9 '77
Probability of establishing chimeric plasmids in natural populations of bacteria. B. R. Levin and F. M. Stewart. bibl il Science 196:218-20 Ap 8 '77
Superstrain of oil-eating microbes; work of A. M. Chakrabarty. K. Cottrell. il Sea Front 23:28-31 Ja '77
Suppression of the temperature-sensitive phenotype of a mutant of reovirus type 3. R. F. Ramig and others. bibl il Science 195:406-7 Ja 28 '77
Viral integration and excision: structure of the lambda *att* sites. A. Landy and W. Ross. il il Science 197:1147-60 S 16 '77
Viral messenger structure: some surprising new developments. J. L. Marx. il Science 197:853-5+ Ag 26 '77

MICROBIOLOGY
Van Leeuwenhoek: father of microbiology. J. W. M. La Rivière. il por UNESCO Courier 30:34-6 Je '77
See also
American Society for Microbiology
Marine microbiology
Microorganisms

MICROCHANNEL plate electron multipliers. See Photoelectric multipliers

MICROCIRCUITS. See Electronic circuits, Integrated; Microelectronics

MICROCIRCUITS, Manufacture of. See Electronic circuits—Manufacture

MICROCLIMATOLOGY
Microclimatology. T. T. Francis. il Org Gard & Farm 24:107-10 F '77

MICROCOMPUTERS. See Computers—Miniaturization

MICROELECTRONICS
Bell concept may meet military needs; polychip-DIP. P. J. Klass. il Aviation W 107:107+ S 26 '77
Chip carrier offers microcircuit gains. P. J. Klass. il Aviation W 106:49-51 Ja 24 '77
Customized microcircuit costs cut. P. J. Klass. il Aviation W 107:78-9 D 12 '77
Is it good-bye to the op amp? Cheaper, faster microcircuit. D. Scott. Pop Sci 211:88 O '77
Microcircuit speed increase sought. il Aviation W 107:59 O 24 '77
Microelectronics; symposium. il Sci Am 237:62-94+ bibl(p258+) S '77
Microstructure fabrication. R. W. Keyes. bibl il Science 196:945-9 My 27 '77
National facility for making submicron structures. A. L. Robinson. Science 197:448 Jl 29 '77
New microcircuits resist radiation. P. J. Klass. il Aviation W 107:58-9+ O 10 '77
Physical limits in semiconductor electronics. R. W. Keyes. bibl il Science 195:1230-5 Mr 18 '77
Use of large-scale microcircuits pushed. P. J. Klass. il Aviation W 107:49-51 Ag 29 '77
See also
Electronic circuits, Integrated

MICROFILM, Computer Output. See Computers—Input-Output equipment

MICROFLUOROMETRY. See Fluorimetry

MICROFORM reading machines
Making big ones out of little ones: current trends in micrographics; microform reader-printers. W. R. Hawken. il Lib J 102:2127-31 O 15 '77

MICROFORMS
See also
Libraries—Microform collections

MICROLERT. See Radio apparatus and instruments, Portable

MICROMETERS
Homemade filar micrometers. J. Polman. il Sky & Tel 53:391-6 My '77

MICROMOSAICS. See Mosaics

MICRONESIA
See also
Trust Territory of the Pacific Islands

MICROORGANISMS
Dawn of life; archae-bacteria or methanogens. il Time 110:56 N 14 '77
Electronic voyage through an invisible world: scanning electron microscope. K. F. Weaver. il Nat Geog 151:274-90 F '77
Methanogens: a third branch of life. il Sci N 112:310-11 N 12 '77
Oldest life; methanogens. P. Gwynne. il Newsweek 90:81 N 14 '77
Phylogeny: are methanogens a third class of life? T. H. Maugh, 2d. Science 198:812 N 25 '77
See also
Microbiology
Plankton

MICROORGANISMS, Pathogenic
Found: the Philly killer, perhaps; Legionnaires' disease. Time 109:47 Ja 31 '77
Legion fever: failed investigation may be successful after all. B. J. Culliton. Science 195:469-70 F 4 '77
Out of control? death of two workers at the Center for Disease Control. J. Seligmann and D. Shapiro. il Newsweek 89:46 Mr 14 '77
Tracking the killer fever; Legionnaires' disease. M. Clark. il Newsweek 89:78-9 Ja 31 '77
See also
Bacteria, Pathogenic
Mycoplasmas

MICROPALEONTOLOGY
Archean microfossils showing cell division from the Swaziland System of South Africa. A. H. Knoll and E. S. Barghoorn. bibl il Science 198:396-8 O 28 '77
Out of earth's past: biological roots. il Sci N 111:343 My 28 '77
See also
Algae, Fossil
Chitinozoa

MICROPHONES
If you can't afford more mikes . . . try binaural. J. Woram. il Hi Fi 27:130-2 S '77
Julian Hirsch audio reports:
Shure Model 516EQ microphone. J. Hirsch. il Pop Electr 12:39-40 O '77
Product test reports:
MURA model PRX-100 PRM CB microphone. il Pop Electr 11:93-4 My '77
Shure model 526T communication microphone. il Pop Electr 11:85-6 Ap '77

MICROPHOTOGRAPHY
Shadow photography-a new technique for studying small biological subjects. BioScience 27:224 Mr '77

MICROPROCESSORS
Brain for a house. por House B 119:14+ S '77
How to interface microprocessors. R. Tenny. il Pop Electr 12:66-70 D '77
Microelectronics. J. Schefter. il Pop Sci 212:52-5 Ja '78
Microprocessors. J. Free. il Pop Sci 210:90-3 Mr '77
Microprocessors. H. M. D. Toong. il Sci Am 237:146-7+ S '77
Minute microprocessor has more brainpower than a small computer. V. E. Smay. il Pop Sci 210:26 Je '77
New processor from National that can function as a programmable calculator or as a number cruncher for your microcomputer. K. Savon. il Radio-Electr 48:80-1 N '77
Smart instruments: microprocessors not the whole story. A. L. Robinson. Science 195:1315-18+ Mr 25 '77
Update on microprocessor developments. H. Chamberlin. il Pop Electr 12:110-11 S '77
Z-80. W. Barden, Jr. il Radio-Electr 48:78-9 N '77

Automotive use

See Automobiles—Electronic equipment

MICROSCOPES and microscopy
Gold-dust twins; technique for visualizing the tracks of moving cells on a gold-coated glass microscope slide. il Sci Am 237:102+ S '77
See also
Electron microscopes and microscopy
Microtomes
Photomicrography
X ray microscopes and microscopy

MICROSOMES
Prelytic damage of red cells in filtrates from peroxidizing microsomes. M. K. Roders and others. bibl il Science 196:1221-2 Je 10 '77

MICROSURGERY
Microsurgery for pituitary tumors. Sci N 112:71 Jl 30 '77
Preventing strokes; surgical bypass of the internal carotid artery. Newsweek 89:79 Ja 31 '77

MICROTOMES
Simple light attachment for better microtome illumination. L. Y. Yatsu. il BioScience 27:744 N '77

MICROTUBULES. See Cell organelles

MICROTUS. See Mice

MICROWAVE cookery
Meals from the microwave. il Ladies Home J 94:154 O '77
Microwave cooking. il Bet Hom & Gard 55:190 My; 70, 98 Jl; 157 Ag; 218 N '77
Microwave cooking: how good? How easy? il Redbook 149:114-15+ Ag '77
Microwave kitchen. H. McCully. See issues of House beautiful
Old-fashioned steamed pudding—quickly in a microwave. il Sunset 159:170 D '77
Shellfish moist and tender from a microwave. Sunset 158:198 Je '77
Wave of the future. il Seventeen 36:158-9+ S '77

MICROWAVE Cooking Products Division. See Litton Industries, Inc

MICROWAVE landing systems. See Airplanes—Landing

MICROWAVE ovens
Home works; what's cooking with today's ranges—from conventional to de luxe. il Redbook 148:130+ Mr '77
Institute report:
Microwave ovens. il Good H 185:166+ Ag '77
Microwave ovens. il Consumer Rep 42:10-13 D '77
Microwaving—20 years after the revolution. N. Craig. House B 119:104+ Ap '77

Manufacture

See also
Litton Industries, Inc

MICROWAVES
See also
Masers

Medical use

See also
Breast—Cancer—Diagnosis

MIDAS-International Corporation
Midas touch. il por Time 109:43 Mr 14 '77

MIDDELBURG, Netherlands
Spanish wool and Dutch rebels: the Middelburg incident of 1574. W. D. Phillips, Jr and C. R. Phillips. bibl f il map Am Hist R 82:312-30 Ap '77

MIDDLE age

Anecdotes, facetiae, satire, etc.

How do you know when you're 40? J. Viorst. il N Y Times Mag p66-7 F 6 '77
Life begins at forty to fifty. J. Leo. Time 109:91 My 23 '77
Menopause that refreshes. G. Nachman. por Newsweek 89:19 Ap 18 '77
Middle-aged spread. F. Lamport. il McCalls 105:216-17 N '77

Sexual behavior

Is there sex after 40? college students' views of parents' sex lives. O. Pocs and others. il Psychol Today 11:54-6+ Je '77

MIDDLE Ages
See also
Civilization, Medieval
Feudalism
Troubadours

History

Bibliography

Reviews of books: medieval. See issues of American historical review

MIDDLE Atlantic States. See Atlantic States

MIDDLE classes
Middle class poor. S. Fraker and others. il Newsweek 90:30-1+ S 12 '77
Squeeze on the middle class; with interview with M. Janowitz. il U.S. News 82:50-1 My 2 '77

MIDDLE EAST
See also
Arab Countries
Bahrein
Central Treaty Organization
Housing—Middle East
Israel
Jordan
Kurds
Lebanon
Public health—Middle East
Suez Canal
Syria
United Nations—Armed Forces—Forces in the Middle East
United Nations—Middle East
United Nations Relief and Works Agency for Palestine Refugees in the Near East

Antiquities

See also
Bible—Antiquities

Commerce

United States

See United States—Commerce—Middle East

Description and travel

Anecdotes, facetiae, satire, etc.

Follow me, Cy. New Repub 176:47 Mr 26 '77

Economic conditions

Profitless confrontation in the Mideast. America 136:90 F 5 '77

Foreign relations

American stake in Israel; a lesson in international relations. E. V. Rostow. Commentary 63:32-46 Ap '77; Discussion. 64:16+ Jl '77

Egypt

See Egypt—Foreign relations—Middle East

Russia

See Russia—Foreign relations—Middle East

United States

See United States—Foreign relations—Middle East

History

See also
Israel-Arab War, 1948-1949

Bibliography

Reviews of books: Near East. See issues of American historical review

Industries

See also
Petroleum industry—Middle East

Maps

Map section. Sr Schol 110:28 O 20 '77

Politics and government

For U.S. a race against time in the Mideast. il por map U.S. News 82:19-20 F 28 '77
1977: year of opportunity in the Middle East? address, December 8, 1976. T. F. Eagleton. Vital Speeches 43:201-4 Ja 15 '77
See also
Jewish-Arab relations

MIDDLE EASTERN Cookery. See Cookery, Middle Eastern

MIDDLE EASTERN dancing. See Dancing, Middle Eastern

MIDDLE Fork River, Idaho. See Salmon River (Idaho)

MIDDLE school teachers. See Teachers

MIDDLE schools

Curriculum

Focus: middle and junior high schools; symposium, ed by A. R. Gere. il Engl J 66:25-51 Ap '77
Teaching ideas: educating the in-betweener; symposium. Engl J 66:55-72 Ap '77

MIDDLE WESTERN States
See also
Agriculture—Middle Western States
Botany—Middle Western States
Frontier and pioneer life—United States
Great Plains
Organic farming—Middle Western States
Reclamation of land—Middle Western States

Description and travel

Revisiting America's canals. S. McCoy. il Travel 148:60-5 Jl '77

History

See also
Great Plains—History

Industries

To the heartland, with cameras; film production. il Time 110:71+ S 19 '77

Maps

Close-up: U.S.A. il Nat Geog 151:supp(folded map) F '77

MIDDLEBROOK, David
David Middlebrook. il Ceram Mo 25:54-5 Mr '77 •

MIDDLETON, Drew
Reports & comment: the volunteer army in review. il Atlantic 240:6+ D '77

MIDDLETON, Thomas H.
Light refractions. See issues of Saturday review

MIDGLEY, John
More heat than light. Harpers 254:30+ My '77

MIDLAND, Mich.
Outrageous Mr Cherry and the underachieving nukes; controversy surrounding construction of nuclear power plant in Midland, Mich. F. Graham, Jr. il por Audubon 79:50-67 S '77; Discussion. 79:128-30 N '77

MIDLAND Glass Company. See Glass industry

MIDNIGHT ride of...Who? drama. See Majeski, B.

MID-OCEAN Dynamics Experiment. See Oceanographic research

MIDSUMMER marriage; opera. See Tippett, M.

MIDSUMMER night's dream; ballet. See Ballet reviews—Single works

MIDSUMMER night's dream; drama. See Shakespeare, W.—Plays

MIDWAY Airlines. See Airlines—Local service

MIDWAY Airport. See Chicago—Airports

MIDWEST. See Middle Western States

MIDWESTERNERS
See also
Chicagoans

MIDWIVES
Midwives vs. doctors: who can deliver a baby? Nurse-midwives. M. Barnett. Nation 225:10-12 Jl 2 '77
Rebirth for midwifery. il Time 110:66 Ag 29 '77

MIES VAN DER ROHE, Ludwig
Enduring splendor of Mies van der Rohe. A. L. Huxtable. il por N Y Times Mag p70-1+ F 27 '77 •
Prince and the puritan; exhibition of furniture at the Museum of Modern Art. D. Davis. il Newsweek 89:77-77A Mr 28 '77 •

MIETTINEN, Jorma K.
Enhanced radiation warfare. bibl il Bull Atom Sci 33:32-7 S '77

MIFFLIN, Lawrie
Will competitive sports hurt your child? Harp Baz 110:90+ My '77

MiG airplanes. See Airplanes, Military—Russia

MIGNONETTES
It's dowdy, it's weedy, but also it's fragrant. Sunset 158:266 Ap '77

MIGRAINE. See Headache

MIGRANT labor
These proud Americans; Mexican-American migrant workers. L. Dunn and J. Ullman. il Sat Eve Post 249:42-4+ S '77
Tough tomatoes; mechanical harvesting in California. P. Barnett. Progressive 41:32-6 D '77
What about the Okies? California migrations during the Depression. G. Haslam. il Am Hist Illus 12:28-39 Ap '77
See also
United Farm Workers

Europe, Western

How Europe handles its migrant workers. Bus W p88 Je 13 '77

South Africa

Bulldozer remedy: apartheid at bay; squatters camps for migrant workers. A. Silk. Nation 25:298-304 O 1 '77

MIGRATION, Internal
Fresh look at drift from big cities. il U.S. News 82:71 Ap 25 '77
Immobile society. Time 110:107-8 N 28 '77
Look where America is growing fastest; rural settings. L. Palmer. il Farm J 101:52-4+ Ja '77
Mobility. C. Fischer and A. Stueve. Society 14:8-10 Ja '77
Population redistribution, migration, and residential preferences. G. F. De Jong and R. R. Sell. bibl f il Ann Am Acad 429:130-44 Ja '77
Race and desegregation; symposium. il Society 14:32-48 My '77
Return of the native; the move to small towns. S. Schiefelbein. Sat R 5:10-11 N 26 '77
Rights of movement. G. L. Houseman. bibl Society 14:16-19 Jl '77
Slowdown for strip cities: reversal of century-old trend. il maps U.S. News 82:39-42 Mr 7 '77
What shifts in population will mean for industry. il map U.S. News 82:60-2 My 30 '77
Who's moving to the sun and why. C. Seebohm. il map House & Gard 150:76+ Ja '78
Why more and more people are coming back to cities. il U.S. News 83:69-71 Ag 8 '77
See also
Cities and towns—Growth
Labor mobility

History

Farmers' frontier; excerpt from The American farm: a photographic history. M. Conrat and R. Conrat. il Am West 14:22-33 Mr '77

MIGRATION of man. See Man—Migrations

MIGRATORY workers. See Migrant labor

MIHAJLOV, Mihajlo
Meaning of Mihajlov. T. Fleming. America 137:145-7 S 17 '77 *

MIHALY, Mary E.
Speak for yourself! Seventeen 36:142-3+ O '77

MIHALY, Orestes J.
Disclosure rules hit the advisers. por Bus W p55-6 D 12 '77 *

MIKÉ, Valerie, and Good, R. A.
Old problems, new challenges. bibl Science 198:677-8 N 18 '77

MIKI, Takeo
Future of democracy in Japan; address, June 10, 1977. Vital Speeches 43:659-61 Ag 15 '77

MIKLOWITZ, Gloria D.
To the rescue. il pors Seventeen 36:102 Je '77

MIKOLAS, Mark
Mediums unite: super 8 reborn as video tape. il Mod Phot 41:46+ My '77

MIKVA, Abner Joseph
Will the liberals buck Carter? G. R. Rosen. por Duns R 110:37 Ag '77 *

MILAN, Italy

Crime

Kidnapped; P. Lazzaroni. C. B. Pepper. il pors N Y Times Mag p42-6+ N 20 '77

Description

La Scala: the most famous opera house in the world. B. H. Matthiessen. il Travel 148:44-9 O '77

La Scala

See Opera—Italy

Newspapers

Cultural terrorism: the Italian press as public-relations organ for the Communist Party; the Corriere della sera. M. A. Ledeen. Harpers 255:99-100 S '77

MILAN fashion shows. See Fashion shows

MILANOV, Zinka
Most beautiful voice in the world; interview, ed by R. Jacobson. il Opera N 41:8+ Ap 9 '77

MILES, Benny
How an elementary teacher does it. Todays Educ 66:76-7 Ja '77

MILES, Carlotta G.
Helping parents help their children. Educ Digest 43:57-9 D '77

MILES, Charles
Indian relics. See issues of Hobbies

MILES, Dick
Table tennis (cont) il Sports Illus 46:73-4+ Ap 18 '77; 48:38-9 Ja 2 '78

MILES, Elizabeth B.
Elizabeth B. Miles collection of English silver. il Antiques 112:114-19 Jl '77

MILES, Josephine
Parent; poem. New Yorker 53:126 My 9 '77

MILES, L. E. M. and others
Blind man living in normal society has circadian rhythms of 24.9 hours. bibl il Science 198:421-3 O 28 '77

MILES, Phillip S.
Nurse shark: unlikely terror of the sea. il Oceans 10:37-8 N '77

MILES Laboratories, Inc-Bayer AG merger. See Corporations—Acquisitions and mergers—International aspects

MILESKO-PYTEL, Diana
Changing the specifications for engineers. il Am Educ 13:27-31 Ja '77

MILETI, Dennis S.
Forecast: future shock. il Time 109:83 Ja 24 '77 *

MILFORD, Nancy
Kenya. il Holiday 57:36-9+ N '76

MILFORD Track trail. See Trails—New Zealand

MILGO Electronic Corporation-Racal Electronics Ltd merger. See Electronic industries—Acquisitions and mergers

MILGRAM, Jerome H.
Jerry Milgram. J. Rousmaniere. il por Yachting 141:104+ Je '77 *

MILHAUD, Darius
La mère coupable. il Opera N 41:26-8 Mr 5 '77 *

MILHAVEN, John Giles
Church and erotic love in marriage. New Cath World 220:264-7 N '77
Love: giving of self or meeting the self's needs? America 136:501-3 Je 4 '77

MILITARISM
Toy theory of western history. M. E. D. Koening. il Bull Atom Sci 33:16-18 O '77

MILITARY academies. See United States—Armed Forces—Education

MILITARY aeronautics. See Aeronautics, Military

MILITARY airplanes. See Airplanes, Military

MILITARY architecture
See also
Navy yards and naval stations

MILITARY art and science
Battlefield of the 1990s: it's not sci-fi it's real. U.S. News 83:48-50 Jl 4 '77
Military technology and social structure; impact on underdeveloped areas. M. H. Kaldor. il Bull Atom Sci 33:49-53 Je '77
One-star shop talk; exchange of lectures by Russian and American Army officers. Nation 225:485 N 12 '77
See also
War
War games

MILITARY assistance

Africa

Red herring? Cuban and Russian involvement in Africa. Nat R 29:536-7 My 13 '77

Africa, Southern

How a Ugandan bishop views Africa's upheaval; excerpts from interview. F. Kivengere. por U.S. News 82:30 Ap 4 '77

Ethiopia

U.S.-Soviet struggle to control the Horn of Africa. D. Mullin. il map U.S. News 83:43-5 Ag 29 '77

Somalia

U.S.-Soviet struggle to control the Horn of Africa. D. Mullin. il map U.S. News 83:43-5 Ag 29 '77

Zaïre

ABC's of fighting in Zaïre. il map U.S. News 82:45-6 Ap 25 '77
Little help from his friends. il Time 109:41 Ap 25 '77
Proxy war in Zaïre. R. Carroll and others. il Newsweek 89:32-3 Ap 25 '77

MILITARY assistance, American
Aid, human rights link reappraised. Aviation W 106:18 Ap 11 '77
Department discusses security assistance programs; statement, April 21, 1977. L. W. Benson. Dept State Bull 76:485-9 My 16 '77
Foreign aid authorizing bills transmitted to the Congress; text of letters, March 28, 1977. J. Carter. Dept State Bull 76:490-1 My 16 '77

MILITARY assistance, American—*Continued*
House votes military aid plan allotting major shares to Israel. Aviation W 106:20 My 30 '77
Military aid, human rights face study. K. Johnsen. Aviation W 106:59 F 7 '77
President Carter signs Security Assistance Act; statement, August 5, 1977. J. Carter. Dept State Bull 77:361 S 12 '77
Proliferating arms industry: America exports its know-how. M. T. Klare. Nation 224:173-8 F 12 '77

Africa

Russia's ruthless reach into Africa. D. Reed. map Read Digest 111:169-74 N '77

Ethiopia

Fifteen-year war: Ethiopia, Eritrea & U.S. policy. D. Connell. il map Nation 224:337-40 Mr 19 '77

Far East

U.S. economic and security assistance programs in East Asia; statement, March 10, 1977. R. C. Holbrooke. Dept State Bull 76:322-6 Ap 4 '77

Indonesia

U.S. diplomacy and human rights: the cruel case of Indonesia. A. S. Kohen. Nation 225:553-7 N 26 '77

Israel

Staunch friends at arms length. il Time 109: 30-1 Ja 31 '77

Japan

Boost in Japan's military funding pressed by GAO. H. J. Coleman. Aviation W 106:24 Je 27 '77

Korea, South

Transfer of defense articles to the Republic of Korea; message, October 21, 1977. J. Carter. Dept State Bull 77:852-4 D 12 '77

Somalia

Crossed wires. A. De Borchgrave. il por Newsweek 90:42-3 S 26 '77

Zaïre

Coca-colonialism. M. Kempton. Progressive 41:35 Ag '77
Our man Mobutu. R. Morris. New Repub 176: 10-11 My 7 '77

MILITARY assistance, Cuban

Africa

Castro in Africa—challenge to Carter? U.S. News 82:32 Mr 28 '77
Cuban connections. F. Willey and others. il Newsweek 90:73 N 28 '77
Cubans, Cubans everywhere. il map Time 109: 33-4 Mr 28 '77
Cubans in Africa. G. A. Geyer. New Repub 176: 11-13 Ap 2 '77
U.S. toughens stance on renewing Cuban ties. map U.S. News 83:50 D 19 '77

Ethiopia

Cuban connection. K. Labich and L. E. Nelson. il Newsweek 89:51-2 Je 6 '77
Cubans in Ethiopia. G. Legum. New Repub 176: 15-16 Je 11 '77

MILITARY assistance, Moroccan

Zaïre

Africa's policeman; excerpts from interview, ed by A. De Borchgrave. Hassan II. por Newsweek 89:58+ My 16 '77

MILITARY assistance, Russian

Africa

Russia's ruthless reach into Africa. D. Reed. map Read Digest 111:169-74 N '77

Ethiopia

Horning in. C. Legum. New Repub 177:18-21 O 1 '77
Soviet arms airlift to Ethiopia violates air space of Pakistan. Aviation W 107:17 D 19 '77

Somalia

Horning in. C. Legum. New Repub 177:18-21 O 1 '77
Ivan, go home. il U.S. News 83:76 S 26 '77
Shifting sands on the Horn. map Time 110:34+ Ag 22 '77
Somalia: sending Moscow a message. E. Peer. il Newsweek 90:37-8 Ag 29 '77
Trouble on the Horn. A. De Borchgrave. il map Newsweek 89:45 Je 27 '77

MILITARY avionics. See Avionics

MILITARY bases
Activities of foreign economic interests, military bases condemned. UN Chron 14:12-14 Ag '77
Carter's Far East strategy: new role for Philippine bases. L. Hansen. il por map U.S. News 83:29-30 Ag 29 '77
Don't mourn lost military bases; aid to affected communities by the Office of Economic Adjustment. il Am City & County 92:26 S '77
Military bases on Guam declared incompatible with Charter purposes. UN Chron 14:35-9 Ja '77
Our Philippine bases: Marcos would raise the ante. P. W. Stanley. Nation 224:561-2 My 7 '77
See also
Guided missile bases
Navy yards and naval stations

MILITARY budget. See United States—Defense, Department of—Appropriations and expenditures

MILITARY budgets, International. See Armed Forces—Appropriations and expenditures

MILITARY cemeteries. See National cemeteries

MILITARY communications satellites. See Communications satellites—Military use

MILITARY Currency, Allied. See World War, 1939-1945—Military currency

MILITARY desertion. See United States—Armed Forces—Desertion

MILITARY dictators. See Dictators

MILITARY discharges
Bad paper vets. D. Bradley. Progressive 41:31-3 Ap '77
Big cop-out: Carter and the veterans. B. W Lynn. Nation 225:678-82 D 24 '77
Still the back of the bus: Vietnam pardon, stage II; review of less than honorable discharges. J. Colhoun. il Nation 224:594-6 My 14 '77
Upgrading bad paper vets. Progressive 41:61-7 Jl '77

MILITARY education
See also
Military schools

United States

See also
Inter-American Defense College, Washington, D.C.
United States Air Force Academy, Colorado Springs
United States Coast Guard Academy, New London, Conn.
United States Military Academy, West Point
United States Naval Academy, Annapolis

MILITARY electronics. See Electronics—Military use

MILITARY expenditures. See United States—Defense, Department of—Appropriations and expenditures

MILITARY expenditures, International. See Armed Forces—Appropriations and expenditudes

MILITARY exports. See Munitions—Export-import trade

MILITARY facilities. See Military bases

MILITARY hospitals. See Hospitals, Military

MILITARY-industrial complex
To arms! To arms! F. Getlein. Commonweal 104:68-9 F 4 '77

MILITARY installations. See Military bases

MILITARY intelligence
Dig deeper, Jimmy! Soviet weapon developments. R. Hotz. Aviation W 106:7 My 9 '77
Fort Huachuca: where spies cavort; meeting of the National Military Intelligence Association T. Miller. Nation 224:108-10 Ja 29 '77

MILITARY maneuvers
A-10 survivability in attack role shown during simulated combat. D. E. Fink. il Aviation W 106:88-9+ Je 20 '77
Dogfights in the desert; Air Force air-combat maneuvers. R. Boeth and P. S. Greenberg. il Newsweek 90:30 Ag 8 '77
Joint combat exercise tests tactics. D. E. Fink. il Aviation W 106:24-5 My 23 '77
No-win war at Dogbone Lake; simulated aerial dog fighting by the Air Force and Navy. il U.S. News 84:56-7 Ja 9 '78
Orange v. blue in Bavaria; Carbon Edge Nato exercise. il Time 110:42-3+ O 3 '77
See also
War games

MILITARY officers. See Israel—Armed Forces—Officers

MILITARY officers, Retired. See Retired military personnel

MILITARY pay. See United States—Armed Forces—Pay, allowances, etc.

MILITARY pensions. See Pensions, Military

MILITARY personnel, Retired. See Retired military personnel

MILITARY policy
See also subhead Military policy under names of countries, e.g. Russia—Military policy

MILITARY propaganda films. See Motion pictures—Propaganda films

MILITARY reconnaissance
See also
Aerial reconnaissance

MILITARY research
Building blocks of weapons development. K. Tsipis. Bull Atom Sci 33:41 Ap '77
Science and the military. bibl il Bull Atom Sci 33:10-22+ Ja '77
Senate unit hits in-house defense research Aviation W 106:26 My 23 '77

MILITARY research—*Continued*
U.S. military R&D through Soviet eyes. M. A. Milstein and L. S. Semejko. bibl il Bull Atom Sci 33:32-8 F '77
See also
Aeronautic research

History

Eisenhower's other warning; excerpts from address, April 26, 1976. H. F. York. por Phys Today 30:9+ Ja '77
Military research and development: a postwar history. H. F. York and G. A. Greb. bibl il Bull Atom Sci 33:12-22+ Ja '77

MILITARY satellites. See Artificial satellites—Military use

MILITARY schools
How can the armed services help cover college costs? M. Daly and E. Sweeney. il Bet Hom & Gard 55:38+ Mr '77
See also
United States Air Force Academy, Colorado Springs
United States Coast Guard Academy, New London, Conn.
United States Military Academy, West Point
United States Naval Academy, Annapolis

MILITARY service, Compulsory
Bring back the draft? il U.S. News 82:55-8 F 14 '77
Draft: both sides of debate; interviews. S. Nunn; W. Proxmire. pors U.S. News 82:59-60 F 14 '77
Draft: service or coercion? J. Castelli. America 137:103-5 Ag 27 '77
Let's play taps for an all male Army! universal draft for men and women. Y. B. Burke. il Sat Eve Post 249:12-13+ O '77
Mercenaries or conscripts. il New Repub 176:5-6 F 5 '77
Minimal coercion: the plan to revive the draft. D. Cortright. Progressive 41:25-8 Je '77
National service for all Americans now; address, April 19, 1977. F. J. Schober, Jr. Vital Speeches 43:702-4 S 1 '77
See also
Conscientious objectors

Draft resisters

After the pardon. S. Fraker and others. il Newsweek 89:28-9 Ja 31 '77
Big cop-out: Carter and the veterans. B. W. Lynn. Nation 225:678-82 D 24 '77
Carter's first act touches off a storm; pardon for draft evaders. U.S. News 82:22 Ja 31 '77
Discriminatory pardon. J. Colhoun. Progressive 41:13 My '77
First small step; pardon. Nation 224:131-2 F 5 '77
Keeping his first promise; J. Carter's pardon of Vietnam draft evaders. Time 109:15 Ja 31 '77
Leap of faith, a leap of action; excerpt from Once to every man. W. S. Coffin. por Chr Cent 94:938-44 O 19 '77
Pardon everyone? report entitled Reconciliation after Vietnam. J. B. Breslin. America 136:67 Ja 29 '77
Universal and unconditional; Toronto conference. J. Elbert. Chr Cent 94:134-5 F 16 '77

History

See also
Draft riot, 1863

MILITARY service, Voluntary
Bring back the draft? il U.S. News 82:55-8 F 14 '77
Draft: both sides of debate; interviews. S. Nunn; W. Proxmire. pors U.S. News 82:59-60 F 14 '77
Mercenaries or conscripts. il New Repub 176:5-6 F 5 '77
Military as an employer: past performance and future prospects; excerpt from Warriors at work. S. A. Levitan and K. C. Alderman. M Labor R 100:19-23 N '77
Minimal coercion: the plan to revive the draft. D. Cortright. Progressive 41:25-8 Je '77
Pat on the back for the all-volunteer Army. U.S. News 83:42 O 10 '77
Rating the volunteer Army; Rand Corp study. R. V. L. Cooper. il Time 110:34+ O 10 '77
Reports & comment: the volunteer army in review. D. Middleton. il Atlantic 240:6+ D '77
Secretary of the Army Clifford Alexander . . . wants you; interview, ed by J. Landman. C. Alexander. il por Sr Schol 110:16-17+ N 3 '77

MILITARY strategy. See Strategy

MILITARY training
See also
Military maneuvers
Military schools
United States—Reserve Officers Training Corps

Anecdotes, facetiae, satire, etc.

Orientation. J. Mort. New Yorker 53:33 Ap 4 '77

MILITARY transport airplanes. See Airplanes, Military transport

MILJUS, Robert C. See McAdams, T. jt auth

MILK
Gonadotropin-releasing hormone in milk. T. Baram and others. bibl il Science 198:300-2 O 21 '77
Serum complement-like opsonic activities in human, animal, vegetable, and proprietary milks. M. E. Miller and R. G. Ganges. bibl il Science 196:1115-17 Je 3 '77
Zinc binding: a difference between human and bovine milk. C. D. Eckhert and others. bibl il Science 195:789-90 F 25 '77
See also
Milkshakes

Flavor and odor

What are we selling? C. S. Machan. Farm J 101:Dairy 20 Ag '77

Marketing

Kids are giving milk the cold shoulder. C. S. Machan. Farm J 101:Dairy 5 Je '77
More milk, less demand spell trouble. C. S. Machan. Farm J 101:Dairy 8 Ag '77
What are we selling? C. S. Machan. Farm J 101:Dairy 20 Ag '77
You're perched on a population bomb. E. Ainsworth. Farm J 101:Dairy 12 Je '77

Prices

California consumer groups win fight on milk prices. Consumer Rep 42:136 Mr '77
Milk pricing. J. R. Borcherding. il Suc Farm 75:D1-4+ D '77
Protein pricing for all dairymen? Farm J 101:Dairy 16 Ag '77
Two milk duds; question of increase in milk price supports. E. Yoffe. New Repub 177:9 Jl 23 '77
Yes, we have no undue enhancement; USDA investigating dairy co-op price enhancement. Farm J 101:Dairy 19 F '77

Production

Get more milk from your cows. C. S. Machan. Farm J 101:Dairy 1-2 F '77
Give her the fuel for top production. il Farm J 101:Dairy 10-11 F '77
Mystique of high herd averages. C. Machan. Farm J 101:Dairy 20 F '77

Protein content

Protein pricing for all dairymen? Farm J 101:Dairy 16 Ag '77

MILK, Dried
Bottle-baby disease; boycott of Nestle products in attempt to stop promotion of infant formula in underdeveloped countries. B. L. Benderly. Ms 6:20 D '77

MILK, Human
Zinc binding: a difference between human and bovine milk. C. D. Eckhert and others. bibl il Science 195:789-90 F 25 '77
See also
Breast feeding

MILK, Powdered. See Milk, Dried

MILK fever. See Cows—Diseases and pests

MILK industry
Ice cream: dairymen imperiled by FDA's recipe. N. Wade. Science 197:844-5+ Ag 26 '77
Thirty-one favors; dairy lobby's campaign against new ice cream standards. N. Wade. New Repub 177:15-17 N 5 '77

Advertising

How dairymen differ on promotion; Wisconsin study. il Farm J 101:Dairy 12+ O '77

MILK production. See Milk—Production

MILKEN, Michael R.
High risks—and rewards—in high-yield bonds; interview, ed by A. Hershman. por Duns R 109:121+ Je '77

MILKING machines

Equipment

Are automatic detachers for you? C. S. Machan. il Farm J 101:Dairy 7-8 My '77
Now: automatic detachers for stall barns. C. S. Machan. il Farm J 101:Dairy 1-2+ Ag '77

MILKING parlors
Rotary parlors—a 5-year report. N. Reeder. il Farm J 101:Dairy 8-9+ Ja '77

MILKSHAKES
Milk refreshers. il Bet Hom & Gard 55:172 Ap '77
Shakes; milkshake-making contest. New Yorker 53:32-3 Mr 28 '77

MILKWEED bugs
Antiallatotropins: inhibition of corpus allatum development. W. S. Bowers and R. Martinez-Pardo. bibl il Science 197:1369-71 S 30 '77

MILKY Way
Milky Way's tiny heart. il Sky & Tel 54:267-8 O '77
Searching for extraterrestrial civilizations. T. B. H. Kuiper and M. Morris. bibl il Science 196:616-21 My 6 '77

MILKY Way, Photography of the. See Astronomical photography

MILLAN, Manny, and Szabo, Al
Down a crazy river; photographs. Sports Illus 46:38-42 My 2 '77
MILLAR, T. B.
From Whitlam to Fraser. For Affairs 55:854-72 Jl '77
MILLARD, John R.
Propagation and how to live with it; excerpt from The Raytheon guide to single-sideband marine radio. il Motor B & S 139:82 Mr '77
MILLAY, Norma
Foster parents; story. Ladies Home J 94:69-70 O '77
MILLER, Alfred W. See Hackle, S. G. pseud.
MILLER, Ann M.
Advent meditation: Christmas letter. Chr Cent 94:1157 D 14 '77
MILLER, Arnold
Chaos in the coal fields. T. Nicholson and C. J. Harper. il por Newsweek 89:45+ My 23 '77 *
Chaos in the mines. il pors Time 109:69-70 Je 13 '77 *
Close horse race in the mines. il por Time 109:54 F 7 '77 *
Falling apart under Miller. P. Primack. Nation 224:714-17 Je 11 '77 *
Miner apparent victor in UMW race. L. Bornstein and others. M Labor R 100:53 Ag '77 *
Miller's UMW win settles very little. il Bus W p31-2 Je 27 '77 *
Miners' post-election blues. P. Primack. Nation 225:37-8 Jl 9 '77 *
Muddle in the mines. S. T. Atlas and J. B. Copeland. Newsweek 89:73-4 Je 27 '77 *
No peace in the pits. por Time 109:65 Je 27 '77 *
Turmoil in the UMW. T. Nicholson and T. Joyce. Newsweek 89:68-9 F 28 '77 *
Wildcat strikes: preview of turmoil in coal fields. F. W. Frailey. il U.S. News 83:65-7 S 5 '77 *
MILLER, Arthur
Archbishop's ceiling. Reviews
Commonweal 104:431-2 Jl 8 '77 *
MILLER, Arthur Selwyn
Bringing rationality to elections. Current 189:5-7 Ja '77
Carter and the CIA. Progressive 41:9-10 My '77
Congress: a great beached whale. Progressive 41:22-5 F '77
Unlimited nuclear risk. Progressive 41:8-9 Jl '77
MILLER, Barton Charles
Black art of Black Bart. J. Elder. il por Motor B & S 140:61-3+ Jl '77 *
MILLER, Clark
Military pension mess. Progressive 41:12-13 My '77
Stacking the B-1 deck. Progressive 41:7-8 Mr '77
MILLER, Conrad
Alternator charging circuit; excerpt from Your boat's electrical system. il Motor B & S 139:99-101 F '77
Living with a diesel. il Yachting 142:82-5 O '77
Surveying your engine installation. il Motor B & S 139:85-7 Mr '77
MILLER, David
Who'll produce feeder pigs? interview. il pors Farm J 101:Hog 13+ Ag '77
MILLER, David L. See Andrews, W. jt auth
MILLER, Diane (Disney)
Mouse that roared. il por Sat Eve Post 249:50 Jl '77
MILLER, Donald E.
Returning to the fold: disbelief within the community of faith. Chr Cent 94:810-13 S 21 '77
MILLER, Doris P.
Case for filmstrips: producing filmstrips in the classroom. il Engl J 66:70-2 O '77
MILLER, Dorothy A.
Evolution of primate chromosomes. bibl il Science 198:1116-24 D 16 '77
MILLER, Ed
High fidelity pathfinders. N. Eisenberg. por Hi Fi 27:52+ F '77 *
MILLER, Edwin
Spotlight. See issues of Seventeen
MILLER, Eldon
Big change in the affairs of State. L. Keith. il por Sports Illus 47:24-6+ D 12 '77 *
MILLER, Elizabeth
Out to protect a vital resource. MH 61:15-17 Spr '77
MILLER, Fish Bait. See Miller, W. M.
MILLER, Fred
Input output: instruments and accessories. il Hi Fi 27:138+ F; 135-6 Mr; 115-17 Je; 138+ Jl '77
Studio circuit. il Hi Fi 27:127-30 Mr '77
MILLER, George William
Not impossible goal; address, January 27, 1977. Vital Speeches 43:339-44 Mr 15 '77
Strange mixture; excerpt from interview, ed by J. Walcott. por Newsweek 91:54 Ja 9 '78

about

Adroit switch at money central; Miller: nice guy in a hard job. il pors Time 111:28-30 Ja 9 '78 *
Bill Miller at the Fed—what it adds up to. il pors U.S. News 84:49-50 Ja 9 '78 *
Changing the guard at the Fed. Nation 226: 4 Ja 7 '78 *
Economy: new look? M. Ruby and others. il pors Newsweek 91:48-56 Ja 9 '78 *
Miller: images of Jimmy. A. J. Mayer and others. il pors Newsweek 91:50-1 Ja 9 '78 *
New act, old woes at the Fed. il por Time 111: 40+ Ja 16 '78 *
Outsider Carter chose for the Fed. por Bus W p21-2 Ja 9 '78 *
MILLER, Gloria Bley
Secrets of successful stir-frying; excerpt from 1,000 recipe Chinese cookbook. Redbook 149: 140+ S '77
MILLER, Gus
Gus Miller story (cont) D. Rose. il Yachting 141:50+ F '77 *
MILLER, H. L.
Canadian's bells make the welkin ring. il pors Hobbies 82:118-19 S '77
MILLER, Hank
Teaming up on white water. D. Houser. pors Outdoor Life 160:35 S '77 *
MILLER, Harriet Evelyn
Must people retire at 65? interview. por U.S. News 83:37-8 Ag 22 '77
MILLER, Helen Louise
Balky bike; drama. Plays 36:49-57 Mr '77
Party line; drama. Plays 36:15-24 My '77
Red carpet Christmas; drama. Plays 37:1-14 D '77
Runaway toys; drama. Plays 37:39-44 D '77
Thanksgiving truce; drama. Plays 37:17-28 N '77
Visitor to Mount Vernon; drama. Plays 36:75-82 F '77
MILLER, J. Irwin
Blame not the socialistic college professor. . .; excerpt from address. por Forbes 120:48 Ag 1 '77
MILLER, James Nathan
Awful truth about our federal dams. il Read Digest 110:92-6 Je '77
Bitter battle of the waterways. Read Digest 111:83-7 S '77
Great Alaskan land battle. il Read Digest 111: 128-34 D '77
They're giving us gas, all right. New Repub 176:15-17 F 12 '77
Unholy trinities that undermine America. Read Digest 110:61-7 Mr '77
Who will win the battle of Alaska? map Read Digest 112:88-93 Ja '78
MILLER, James S.
Therapies ministers use. Chr Cent 94:504-8 My 25 '77
MILLER, Jerry
Cutting your postal costs down to size. il Ret Liv 17:42-3 Jl '77 *
MILLER, Johnny
His putter has the sputters. D. Jenkins. il por Sports Illus 46:55-6+ Ja 24 '77 *
MILLER, Jonathan
Ancient submariner. New Repub 177:16-19 N 12 '77
Conflicting signals. New Repub 177:10-11 Jl 23 '77
Cuban hustle. il por New Repub 177:11-14 O 8 '77
House built on sand. New Repub 177:19-21 S 3 '77
Meet Mrs America. por New Repub 176:19-21 Ap 9 '77
MILLER, Judith
Americans in Arabia: keys of the Kingdom. map Progressive 41:44-7 Ap '77
Gary Weissman's catch-22. Progressive 41:10 Ap '77
Popular power in Cuba. Progressive 41:33-4 Jl '77
MILLER, Julian Malcolm
Obituary
Phys Today por 30:66-7 Je '77. G. Friedlander
MILLER, Julie Ann
[Articles on the life sciences] See issues of Science news
Artificial organs and beyond. il Sci N 112:154-6 S 3 '77
—See Douglas, J. H. jt auth
MILLER, Kenneth E.
New Music Circle. Hi Fi 27:MA30+ S '77
MILLER, Leon A.
Q&A about taxes (cont) por Ret Liv 17:48 Ja; 66+ F; 13 Ag; 14-15 S; 12-13 D '77
10 questions retirees ask most about the new tax laws. il por Ret Liv 17:22-5 Mr '77
MILLER, Louis
Calling Dr Stress; interview, ed by J. R. Moskin. il por Psychol Today 11:93-4+ S '77
MILLER, Louis Howard. See Desowitz, R. S. jt auth
MILLER, Louis J.
In the vein of Abstract Expressionism. il Sch Arts 77:14-15 N '77
Prints from twine. il Design (US) 78:26 Spr '77
MILLER, Lowell
Selling of soccer-mania. il N Y Times Mag p 12-13+ Ag 28 '77

MILLER, Mary Susan
America's teacher of the year. por Ladies Home J 94:40+ Ap '77
Battle for the little red schoolhouse. il Ladies Home J 94:60+ N '77
Farrah factor. por Ladies Home J 94:34+ Je '77
How to stay married and avoid divorce. Am Home 80:62-4 N '77
Journal contest winner finds a new life. por Ladies Home J 94:68 Mr '77
Teen suicide. Ladies Home J 94:68+ F '77
What do you want to be when your kids grow up? il Am Home 80:52-3+ S '77

MILLER, Michael E. and Ganges, R. G.
Serum complement-like opsonic activities in human, animal, vegetable, and proprietary milks. bibl il Science 196:1115-17 Je 3 '77

MILLER, Michael Vincent
Intimate terrorism. bibl il por Psychol Today 10:78-80+ Ap '77

MILLER, Nory, and Marlin, William
2 learning places by Metz Train Olson & Youngren. il Archit Rec 162:90-3 Jl '77

MILLER, Peter
Behold the new fisherperson. il Outdoor Life 159:56-9+ F '77
Boca brookies. il Outdoor Life 160:88-93+ O '77
Great put-and-take controversy. il Outdoor Life 159:61-3+ Ap '77
Outdoor prints. il Outdoor Life 159:72-7+ Je '77
Record bass: the quest is getting frantic. il Outdoor Life 160:94-7+ S '77
(ed) See Mann, T. Bassin' Mann

MILLER, Philip. See Lewman, M. jt auth

MILLER, Philip L.
Muzio on Edison discs. Am Rec G 40:13 F '77

MILLER, Robert F. and others
Amacrine cells in necturus retina: evidence for independent γ-aminobutyric acid- and glycine-releasing neurons. bibl il Science 198:748-50 N 18 '77

MILLER, Ronald W.
Historic preservation in Natchez, Mississippi. il Antiques 111:538-45 Mr '77

MILLER, Sharon
Teaming up on white water. D. Houser. pors Outdoor Life 160:35 S '77 *

MILLER, Sigmund S.
Early warning signals of common diseases; excerpt from Symptoms: the complete home medical encyclopedia. Good H 184:223-5 Mr '77

MILLER, Steven. See Alpert, H. jt auth

MILLER, Stewart E.
Photons in fibers for telecommunication. bibl il Science 195:1211-16 Mr 18 '77

MILLER, Tom
Fort Huachuca: where spies cavort. Nation 224:108-10 Ja 29 '77

MILLER, W. J. and Neathery, M. W.
Newly recognized trace mineral elements and their role in animal nutrition. bibl BioScience 27:674-9 O '77

MILLER, Walter B.
Rumble this time. il por Psychol Today 10:52-4+ My '77

MILLER, William
Functional immediacy for herniated specialists. il Am Lib 8:181 Ap '77

MILLER, William D.
Cemetery at Holly Springs. America 137:194-5 O 1 '77

MILLER, William J.
President Carter versus Parkinson's law. Read Digest 110:59-60 Ap '77

MILLER, William Lee
Forgive us our daily press. Chr Cent 94:39-41 Ja 19 '77
Yankee from Georgia. il N Y Times Mag p 16-20+ Jl 3 '77

MILLER, William Moseley
Literary banquet; interview. New Yorker 53:37-8 N 14 '77

MILLER, Woody, and others
Detroit: a bite at a time. il Am Lib 8:315+ Je '77

MILLER-Wohl Company. See Chain stores

MILLER-Wohl Company-Amcena Corporation merger. See Chain stores—Acquisitions and mergers

MILLETT, Kate
Who you are now; excerpt from introduction to Emergence. il pors Vogue 167:302+ O '77

MILLHONE, John P.
Conservation: the Minnesota plan; excerpts from address, September 28, 1977. Science 198:1207 D 23 '77

MILLIAMETERS. See Ammeters

MILLICHAP, Joseph R.
George Catlin's life amongst the Indians. il pors Am Hist Illus 12:4-9+ Ag '77

MILLIGAN, Estelle
Quilts; poem. Ms 6:58-9 O '77

MILLIKEN, William Grawn
Navy project goes aground in Michigan. por Bus W p28 Ap 11 '77 *
Seafarer: project still homeless as Milliken says no to Navy. L. J. Carter. Science 197:964-8 S 2 '77 *

MILLIKEN and Company. See Textile industry—United States

MILLS, Charles Wright
Reconsideration. M. Dickstein. New Repub 176:36-7 Ja 29 '77 *
Richard Hofstadter, C. Wright Mills, and the critical ideal. R. Gillam. Am Scholar 47:69-85 Wint '77 *

MILLS, Harlan D.
Software engineering. bibl il Science 195:1199-205 Mr 18 '77

MILLS, James C.
Why nice men go to prostitutes. Redbook 148:96+ Mr '77

MILLS, Joan
Glimpse of glory. il Read Digest 111:164-7 Jl '77
In (reverent, loving, thankful) praise of books! il Read Digest 111:150-2 O '77
You belong to me. il Read Digest 110:189-90 Je '77

MILLS, Nicolaus
Picture of success. Yale R 66:347-63 Mr '77

MILLS, Wilbur Daigh
Maggie and Wilbur. R. Rosenblatt. New Repub 176:37 My 7 '77 *
Wilbur's return. E. Keerdoja and D. Camper. il pors Newsweek 90:13 D 19 '77 *

MILLS, Flour. See Flour mills

MILLSTEIN, Gilbert
Auto fantasies. N Y Times Mag p80-1 Je 26 '77
Cats I have known and loathed. il por N Y Times Mag p 110 Mr 13 '77
Mess of mopeds. N Y Times Mag p 110 S 18 '77

MILMAN, Gregory. See Ghangas, G. S. jt auth

MILNE, Alan Alexander
King John's Christmas; poem, excerpt from Now we are six. Sat Eve Post 249:17 D '77

MILNER, Arthur
Live from the library. il Am Lib 8:75-6 F '77

MILO
Pre-irrigated milo can top corn. V. Ehmke. il Suc Farm 75:no3 F21 F '77

MILONE, Karen
Cover. M. Schiller. Am Artist 41:6+ Ja '77; Correction. 41:5 Mr '77 *

MILSTEIN, M. A. and Semejko, L. S.
U.S. military R&D through Soviet eyes. bibl il Bull Atom Sci 33:32-8 F '77

MILSTEIN, Nathan
Nathan Milstein: Brahmin with violin; interview, ed by E. Kerner. il pors Hi Fi 27:84-8 N '77

MILSTEIN, Seymour
Milstein's shake-up at United Brands. por Bus W p40 S 19 '77 *
United Brands shifts to a shirtsleeve boss. por Bus W p37 F 14 '77 *

MILSTIEN, Julie B. and others
Bacteriophages in live virus vaccines: lack of evidence for effects on the genome of rhesus monkeys. bibl il Science 197:469-70 Jl 29 '77

MILTON, John, 1608-1674
Argument for Milton's Dalila. J. Colony. Yale R 66:562-75 Je '77

MILTON, John P.
Images of Alaska; photographs. Liv Wildn 41:24-9 Jl '77

MILTON, Joyce
Genetic roulette. Nation 225:361-5 O 15 '77
Splice of life. Sat R 5:26+ O 15 '77
Unanswered questions on reviewing for YA's. SLJ 23:127 Mr '77

MILTON, Mass.

Historic houses, sites, etc.

See Historic houses, sites, etc.—Massachusetts

MILWAUKEE

Galleries and museums

American furniture at the Milwaukee Art Center. K. M. Jones. il Antiques 111:974-83 My '77

Music

Debuts & reappearances. Hi Fi 27:MA25 Ap; MA34-6 Jl '77
See also
Milwaukee Symphony Orchestra
Opera—Wisconsin

Sanitary affairs

Milwaukee turns solid waste into new resources. il Am City & County 92:66-7 Ag '77

MILWAUKEE Art Center. See Milwaukee—Galleries and museums

MILWAUKEE County, Wis.

Unemployment

See Unemployment—Wisconsin

MILWAUKEE Exposition Convention Center Arena. See Stadiums

MILWAUKEE Public Library
Wayward bookman; question of embezzlement by Milwaukee public librarian and ALA president K. A. Linderfelt. W. A. Wiegand. bibl il Am Lib 8:134-7, 197-200 Mr-Ap '77

MILWAUKEE Symphony Orchestra
Milwaukee Sym: Richter prem. por Hi Fi 27: MA34-6 Jl '77
Milwaukee Sym: Trimble premiere; Panels VIII for orchestra. Hi Fi 27:MA25 Ap '77

MIME
Off Broadway; Mummenschanz. E. Oliver. New Yorker 53:85-6 Ap 11 '77
Reviews:
Mummenschanz. R. Philp. Dance Mag 51:91 Jl '77
Richard Morse Mime Theatre performances in October. R. Philp. Dance Mag 52:26 Ja '78

MIMICRY (biology)
Aggressive chemical mimicry by a bolas spider. W. G. Eberhard. bibl il Science 198:1173-5 D 16 '77
Batesian mimicry: selective advantage of color pattern. J. G. Sternburg and others. bibl il Science 195:681-3 F 18 '77
Fright posture of the plesiopid fish calloplesiops altivelis; an example of Batesian mimicry. J. E. McCosker. bibl il Science 197:400-1 Jl 22 '77
How to mimic an eel: look mean; calloplesiops altivelis. il Sci N 112:71 Jl 30 '77
Lizard in beetle's clothing. il Sci N 111:54 Ja 22 '77
Misleading mantids. G. F. Rohrmann. il Natur Hist 86:66-71 bibl(p97) Mr '77
Natural selection for juvenile lizards mimicking noxious beetles. R. B. Huey and E. R. Pianka. bibl il Science 195:201-3 Ja 14 '77

MIMOSA pudica. See Sensitive plants

MIMS, Forrest M. 3d
Experimenter's corner. See issues of Popular electronics including Electronics world

MINAMATA disease. See Mercury poisoning

MINASIAN, Stanley M.
Dolphins and/or tuna: an update on the problems of purse seining for yellowfin. il Oceans 10:60-3 N '77

MINCKLER, Leon S.
Conscience of a forester. Am For 83:10-11 Mr '77

MIND and body
How to overcome self-doubt and think your way to total confidence; ed by C. Seebohm. W. T. Gallwey. il House & Gard 149:22+ D '77
Marvelous new route to total body awareness; excerpt from The body has its reasons. T. Berthérat and C. Bernstein. Mademoiselle 83: 165+ My '77
Playing the inner game of working, living; interview. W. T. Gallwey. por Mademoiselle 83:203+ Ap '77
See also
Consciousness
Hypnosis
Medicine, Psychosomatic
Meditation
Parapsychology
Psychology, Physiological
Sleep

MINDANAO
See also
Davao, Philippines

MINDELL, Joseph
Don't be a monomaniac. il por Forbes 120:52-3 Jl 1 '77 *

MINDS eye. See Visualization

MINER, Jan
And now a word from your media-reality gap. . .Jan Miner and her alter ego Madge. S. Braudy. por Ms 5:54-5 Mr '77 *

MINER, Margaret. See Cohen, T. jt auth

MINERAL licks. See Salt licks

MINERAL rights. See Mining law

MINERAL waters
See also
Water, Bottled

MINERALOGY
See also
Meteorites
Precious stones

MINERALS, Clay. See Clay

MINERALS in diet
See also
Iron in diet

MINERALS in soils. See Soils—Mineral content

MINERALS in the body
See also
Cadmium in the body
Trace elements

MINERALS policy

United States

See Mines and mineral resources—United States

MINERS
See also
Coal miners
National Union of Mineworkers
United Mine Workers of America
Uranium miners

MINES, Samuel
Bite by bite, count yourself thin. il Read Digest 112:176-8+ Ja '78

MINES and mineral resources
See also
Coal mines and mining
Manganese
Ocean mining
Oil shales
Prospecting
Quarries and quarrying
Space mineral resources
Space mining

Law

See Mining law

Alaska

Alaska wilderness: Congress debates resources "lock up". L. J. Carter. il Science 198:474-8 N 4 '77

Canada

See also
Coal mines and mining—Canada
Mining industry and finance—Canada

South Africa

See also
Diamond mines and mining—South Africa

United States

Minerals and mining: major review of federal policy is in prospect. L. J. Carter. Science 198: 809-11 N 25 '77
See also
Iron mines and mining—United States

MINGO County, W. Va.

Housing

See Housing—West Virginia

MINI-track racing. See Automobile racing

MINIATURE automobiles. See Automobile models

MINIATURE cameras. See Cameras

MINIATURE cities. See Models of cities, towns, etc.

MINIATURE electronic equipment
See also
Electronic circuits, Integrated

MINIATURE furniture. See Furniture, Miniature

MINIATURE houses. See House models

MINIATURE objects
Design on a small scale; work of Robert Cull. S. Doherty. il Sch Arts 76:80 F '77
Kitchen little; miniatures by L. R. Page and M. F. Cochran. il por House & Gard 149: 96-7+ F '77
Miniaturia. S. A. Parvin. See issues of Hobbies
Silver miniatures. K. M. McClinton. il Hobbies 82:118-20 N '77
See also
Models (patents)
Models of cities, towns, etc.

Exhibitions

1977 National Cone Box Show; miniature ceramic objects. il Ceram Mo 25:46-7 O '77

MINIATURE painting
India's miniature paintings. W. Rodger. Hobbies 82:152-3 D '77

MINIATURE rooms. See Rooms, Miniature

MINIATURE roses. See Roses

MINIATURE stores. See Store models

MINIATURE towns. See Models of cities, towns, etc.

MINIATURE trees. See Trees, Dwarf

MINICHIELLO, Raffaele
Skyjacker in exile. E. Keerdoja. Newsweek 89: 18 Ap 18 '77 *

MINIMAL brain dysfunction
See also
Hyperactive children

MINIMAL competency tests. See Educational tests and measurements

MINIMUM wage

United States

Automatic escalator for the minimum wage? il Nations Bus 65:70-3 My '77
Carter melts a bit on the minimum wage. Bus W p30 My 30 '77
Congress raises the minimum wage. U.S. News 83:89 O 31 '77
Congress votes minimum wage increase over next 4 years. Ret Liv 17:48 D '77
Lifting the minimum wage. il Time 110:75 O 31 '77
Minimum employment. Nat R 29:1218 O 28 '77
New wage floor? T. Nicholson and J. B. Copeland. il Newsweek 90:88 S 19 '77
This month's feature: controversy over new federal minimum wage proposals. Cong Digest 56: 131-60 My '77
What a higher minimum wage will mean for workers, business. il U.S. News 83:100-1 S 26 '77
Would the teenwage cut unemployment? il Bus W p 106-8 S 19 '77
Youth differential. M. S. Evans. Nat R 29:888 Ag 5 '77

MINING industry and finance

Taxation

Tax showdown on yellowcake road; New Mexico bill to tax coal and uranium mining industries. Bus W p33+ Mr 14 '77

Bolivia

True coin of freedom; question of British loan to the State Mining Corporation of Bolivia. Nation 225:194-5 S 10 '77

Canada

New trials for rich but troubled Javelin. Bus W p31-2 Jl 4 '77

South Africa

See also
Anglo American Corporation of South Africa, Ltd

United States

Rosario's riches; Rosario resources. il Forbes 119:69-70 Je 1 '77
Shifting stockpile strategy; nonferrous metals. Bus W p57 S 26 '77
See also
Continental Copper & Steel Industries, Inc
Cyprus Mines Corporation

MINING law
Mineral rights raise new dust; federal lands. Bus W p48 O 3 '77
See also
Coal mines and mining—Laws and legislation

MINING leases
Mineral rights raise new dust; federal lands. Bus W p48 O 3 '77
Phosphate fate will determine Idaho high country's fate; leases for proposed open-pit mining. E. Chaney. Audubon 79:123-6 Mr '77
U.S. Indians demand a better energy deal; Council of Energy Resource Tribes. por Bus W p53 D 19 '77

MINING machinery
See also
Coal mining machinery

MINISTERS of the gospel. See Clergy

MINITAREE Indians. See Hidatsa Indians

MINK, Patsy (Takemoto)
Department discusses approach to environmental issues; statement, March 31, 1977. Dept State Bull 76:385-7 Ap 18 '77

about

For a troubled situation. . . try Mink. por Sci Digest 81:75 Ap '77 *
Science and technology at State: recognizing the problem. J. Walsh. Science 196:148-50 Ap 8 '77 *

MINK farming. See Fur farming

MINNEAPOLIS
Their elm forest is doomed, but Twin Cities are ready. F. Graham, Jr. Audubon 79:136-9 Jl '77

Buildings

Impressive new government center around a grand atrium space; Hennepin County Government Center. il Archit Rec 161:101-6 Mr '77

City planning

See also
Twin Cities Metropolitan Council

Hospitals

Hennepin County Medical Center, Minneapolis; with introd by W. Marlin. il Archit Rec 162:113-21 Ag '77

Music

Debuts & reappearances. il Hi Fi 27:MA24 Ag '77

MINNEAPOLIS Symphony Orchestra. See Minnesota Orchestra

MINNELLI, Liza
Invitation to dance. W. Terry. Sat R 5:44 O 1 '77 *
Liza & Marty show. M. Orth and P. S. Greenberg. il pors Newsweek 90:49 S 5 '77 *

MINNERS, Howard A.
Tropical medicine—new vigor. Science 196:1275 Je 17 '77

MINNESOTA Fats
Minnesota Fats. New Yorker 53:23-4 Jl 4 '77 *

MINNESOTA
Mondale's Minnesota. W. B. Furlong. il pors Horizon 20:66-74 O '77
See also
Agriculture—Minnesota
Air pollution—Minnesota
Camps—Minnesota
Education—Minnesota
Energy policy—Minnesota
Opera—Minnesota
Organic farming—Minnesota
Quetico-Superior Region
St Croix National Scenic Riverway
Wildlife management—Minnesota
Winona, Lake (Minnesota)

Electric utilities

See Electric utilities

Politics and government

Two feminists tell how they work; interview, ed by G. Steinem. K. Horbal. pors Ms 6:52+ Jl '77

Religious institutions and affairs

Religious tension in Saint Cloud; refusal of United Way funds to agencies making abortion referrals. J. M. Wall. Chr Cent 94:1019-20 N 9 '77

MINNESOTA Dance Theatre. See Dance companies

MINNESOTA Mining and Manufacturing Company
Resource-conservation; address, April 27, 1977. J. T. Ling. Vital Speeches 43:541-4 Je 15 '77
What do corporations do? P. Weiss. New Repub 176:25-6+ My 21 '77

MINNESOTA Opera Company. See Opera—Minnesota

MINNESOTA Orchestra
Minn. orch: Hovhaness premiere; Symphony no. 29. Hi Fi 27:MA24 Ag '77
Salute to the Minneapolis Symphony. R. Gelatt. Sat R 5:54-5 O 29 '77

MINNESOTA School for the Deaf. See Deaf—Education

MINNESOTA. University, Minneapolis
Buried bookstore saves energy, saves space, saves the view; Williamson Hall. S. J. Marcovich. il Pop Sci 211:96-7 S '77

Libraries

Minnesota library profile; views of R. H. Hopp. il por Lib J 102:1238-9+ Je 1 '77

MINNETAREE Indians. See Hidatsa Indians

MINNOWS
Changing bowls. B. A. Branson. bibl il Environment 19:25-30 Ap '77
Kepone-induced scoliosis and its histological consequences in fish. J. A. Couch and others. bibl il Science 197:585-7 Ag 5 '77

MINOR, Audax, pseud
Race track. See issues of New Yorker

MINOR, Gregory C.
Excerpts from testimony on nuclear reactor safety, February 18, 1976. Cong Digest 56:59+ F '77

MINOR, Robert N.
Study guide to non-Christian religions. il Chr Today 21:16-19 Jl 8 '77

MINOR league baseball. See Baseball, Professional

MINOR planets. See Asteroids

MINORITIES
American underclass. il Time 110:14-18+ Ag 29 '77
Ethnic conflict in the world today; symposium, ed by M. O. Heisler. bibl f Ann Am Acad 433:1-160 S '77
How unhappy minorities upset Europe's calm. il U.S. News 82:37-9 Ja 31 '77
In U.S.S.R. minority problems just won't wither away. J. N. Wallace. il map U.S. News 82:53-4 F 14 '77
Race certification. E. Marshall. New Repub 177:18-20 O 15 '77
Soviet Union: major ethnic groups. il map Sr Schol 110:15 N 3 '77
See also
Assimilation (sociology)
Discrimination
Minority business enterprises
Minority women
Self determination, National
United Nations—Sub-Commission on Prevention of Discrimination and Protection of Minorities

Civil rights

In the vanguard of U.S. push toward rights for all—. il U.S. News 83:31-2 O 31 '77
Rights explosion splintering America? D. C. Bacon. il U.S. News 83:29-30+ O 31 '77; Same with title Rights explosion. Current 198:28-33 D '77
See also
Bakke, Allan, case

Education

Changing the specification for engineers; program for prospective minority students at the Illinois Institute of Technology. D. Milesko-Pytel. il Am Educ 13:27-31 Ja '77
Enlarging the American dream; educating minority women. D. Hart. il Am Educ 13:10-16 My '77
Freedom from quotas; bills proposing to end quotas. M. S. Evans. Nat R 29:1497 D 23 '77
Is a relapse ahead for minority medical education? K. Abarbanel. Educ Digest 42:24-7 Mr '77
Program at Fermilab for minority students. J. C. Davenport and others. il Phys Today 30:9+ Je '77
See also
Bakke, Allan, case
Public schools—Desegregation

MINORITIES—*Continued*

Employment

Carter's score on minority hiring; appointments to public office. il U.S. News 82:59-61 Ap 25 '77
Unions divided; question of Bakke case effect on occupational discrimination. K. Bode. New Repub 177:20-2 O 15 '77
See also
United States—Equal Employment Opportunity Commission

MINORITIES in literature
American ethnic studies. L. Fischer. Engl J 66:58-9 S '77
Focus: multicultural literature; symposium. il Engl J 66:24-52 Mr '77
Multicultural literature to teach; symposium, comp by S. Koch. Engl J 66:57-70 Mr '77

MINORITY business enterprises
Business prospects in the inner city. R. N. Farmer. Intellect 105:263-4 F '77
Business, too, tests reverse discrimination. Associated General Contractors' suits. il Bus W p40-1 N 14 '77
EDA holds firm against set-aside challenges; minority business enterprise clause in Round II Local Public Works Act. Am City & County 92:13 D '77

MINORITY women
Enlarging the American dream. D. Hart. il Am Educ 13:10-16 My '77

MINORS, Employment of. See Children—Employment

MINOW, Newton N.
Bringing JFK up to date. por Newsweek 89:13 My 30 '77

MINSKY, Richard, and Seidler, Peter
Book of the century: Fuller's Tetrascroll. il pors Craft Horiz 37:18-21+ O '77

MINSTRELS
See also
Troubadours

MINT (United States) See United States—Mint

MINTON, Lynn
McCall's movie guide for puzzled parents. See issues of McCall's
Star is reborn. por McCalls 105:182+ N '77

MINTS
See also
Franklin Mint Corporation
United States—Mint

MINTZ, Marge, and Szajman, Rena
Art of preserving natural materials. il Design (US) 78:2-4 Summ '77

MINTZ, Mary Wyche
Flying home; R. Ellison's short story. Engl J 66:67-8 Mr '77

MINTZ, Morton, and Cohn, Victor
Hawking the estrogen fix. Progressive 41:24-5 S '77

MIOCENE period. See Paleobotany—Miocene; Paleontology—Miocene

MIRACLES
See also
Faith cure

MIRAGE (airplane) See Airplanes, Military—France

MIRANDA, Gary
Arrowhead; poem. Atlantic 239:62 My '77
Choosing; poem. New Yorker 53:83 Ap 4 '77
Horse chestnut; poem. Atlantic 240:48 S '77
Must-be-admired things; Survivor; poems. Poetry 130:14-16 Ap '77
Thickets of sleep; Collision; poems. Poetry 131:133-5 D '77

MIRANDA decision. See United States—Supreme Court—Decisions

MIRE, Joseph
Incomes policy in Austria under a voluntary partnership. bibl il M Labor R 100:13-17 Ag '77

MIRENDA, Rose
How to create a family food plan that's right for you. il por Parents Mag 52:38-9+ Mr '77

MIRÓ, Joan
Homage to Catalonia; with introd by M. F. Schmertz. il Archit Rec 161:85-92 Mr '77 *
Miró's latest works. E. White. il por Horizon 19:88-96 Jl '77 *

MIRROR frames
Full-length mirror you can make. R. Capotosto. il Mech Illus 73:68-70 Je '77

MIRROR glass construction. See Glass construction

MIRROR tile laying. See Tile laying

MIRRORS
It's both mirror and mailbox. il Sunset 159:116 D '77
See also
Mirror frames
Telescopes—Mirrors

MIRRORS, Burning. See Burning mirrors

MIRSKY, Jeannette
Discovering ancient treasures in Caves of the thousand Buddhas; excerpt from Sir Aurel Stein. il por map Smithsonian 8:94-6+ My '77

MISCH, Robert Jay
What's your wine IQ? House B 119:84+ N '77

MISCHE, Patricia M.
Parenting in a hungry world. il New Cath World 220:238-43 S '77

MISCONDUCT in office
See also
Politics, Corruption in

MISHKIN, Julie
Voices you hear might be your own; poem. Nation 225:27 Jl 2 '77

MISNER, Paul
Theology behind the Wall. Commonweal 104:620-2 S 30 '77

MISOGYNY
Intelligent woman's guide to sex; use of brutality toward women in record advertising. J. Coburn. Mademoiselle 83:58 Ag '77
Really socking it to women; misogyny. il Time 109:58-9 F 7 '77

MISS Margarida's way; drama. See Athayde, R.

MISS Universe contests. See Beauty contests

MISSILE bases. See Guided missile bases

MISSILES, Guided. See Guided missiles

MISSING in action servicemen. See Vietnamese war, 1957-1975—Casualties

MISSING persons
Another Hoffa case? E. A. Bramlet. R. Steele and M. Kasindorf. il por Newsweek 89:23 Mr 14 '77
Vegas vanishing act; dsippearance of E. A. Bramlet. por Time 109:21 Mr 14 '77
Who wouldn't help a lost child? You, maybe. H. Takooshian and others. bibl il pors Psychol Today 10:67-8+ F '77

MISSING ships
See also
Bermuda Triangle

MISSIONARIES
Brazil expels a missionary. R. Barbosa. Chr Cent 94:710-11 Ag 17 '77
Missionary's lot. M. Montagno and others. il Newsweek 89:88+ Ap 4 '77
Where the action isn't; interview. B. Bell. il por Chr Today 22:28-9 O 7 '77
See also
Missions
Wycliffe Bible Translators, Inc

MISSIONARY Aviation Fellowship
Missing names and the missions. E. E. Plowman. Chr Today 21:51-3 S 23 '77

MISSIONS
More for missions. Chr Today 21:52 Mr 4 '77
Pluralism and consensus: why mainline church mission budgets are in trouble. R. G. Hutcheson, Jr. Chr Cent 94:618-24 Jl 6 '77; Discussion. 94:955-7 O 19 '77

Bibliography

Excitement for missions. C. B. Murphey. Chr Today 22:34 D 30 '77

Africa

Missionaries, '70s style. R. Mann. Chr Cent 94:839-40 S 28 '77

Asia

See also
Evangelistic work—Asia

Brazil

Beyond Babel; work of Summer Institute of Linguistics Bible translators. il Time 111:65 Ja 9 '78
Vanishing breed in Brazil; Summer Institute of Linguistics. Chr Today 22:43-4 D 30 '77

Ethiopia

Ethiopia: pulling out. Chr Today 21:41-2 Je 17 '77

MISSISSIPPI
See also
Education—Mississippi
Historic houses, sites, etc.—Mississippi
Hunting—Mississippi
Newspapers—Mississippi
Opera—Mississippi
Tombigbee River

Race question

Turning point; Philadelphia. J. Lelyveld. N Y Times Mag p94 Ap 10 '77

Religious institutions and affairs

Black bishop for Mississippi; installation of J. L. Howze. G. V. Murray. America 137:32 Jl 16 '77

MISSISSIPPI Queen (steamboat) See Steamships and steamboats

MISSISSIPPI River

Regulation

Destroying tomorrow today; the Army Corps of Engineers wants the Mississippi River. J. Nedelman. Horticulture 55:8+ O '77
Lock & Dam 26: $400 million boondoggle or vital public interest program? G. L. Vincent. il Suc Farm 75:no5 24-5 Mr '77

MISSISSIPPI River shipping. See Inland water transportation

MISSOULA, Mont.
Education
See Education—Montana
MISSOURI
See also
Education—Missouri
Fishing—Missouri
Land—Missouri
Opera—Missouri
Ozark Mountains
Politics and government
Missouri sponsors Silver Haired Legislation Project. il Aging 268:15-17 F '77
MISSOURI Synod of the Lutheran Church. See Lutheran Church in the United States
MISSOURI. University, Columbia
6 scientists working hard on the hardwoods. J. Marks. il Am For 83:16-19+ N '77
Kansas City campus
Campus crunch; restriction against college facilities for religious use. M. Allison. Chr Today 22:41-2 O 21 '77
MISTAKES. See Errors, Popular
MR Puntila and his chauffeur Matti; drama. See Brecht, B.
MISTLETOE
Dwarf mistletoe. A. R. Breisch. il Conservationist 32:47 N '77
MITCHELL, Barbara
Antarctica: a special case? il Oceans 10:56-9 My '77
MITCHELL, Carleton
Never waste a calm, but. . . il por map Yachting 142:61-4 N; 56-9+ D '77
MITCHELL, Cary
NASA launches a new experiment to explore how plants react to stress. il pors Horticulture 55:10-13 S '77
MITCHELL, Clarence M. 1911-
Washington notebook. S. Booker. Ebony 32:30 Ap '77 *
MITCHELL, Daniel J. B.
Labor content of imports and exports. M Labor R 100:48-50 Mr '77
MITCHELL, Diana
Children's literature in the junior high? Of course. il Engl J 66:62-4 Ap '77
MITCHELL, Frederick
Markets & careers; interview, ed by H. Chapnick. il por Pop Phot 81:74+ Ag '77
MITCHELL, George P.
George Mitchell and his edifice complex. L. Minard. il por Forbes 120:81-2+ Jl 1 '77 *
MITCHELL, Gertrue E.
Glimpses of education in Poland and Romania. il Am Educ 13:16-24 Ap '77
MITCHELL, James
Encyclopedists; interview. New Yorker 53:36-7 O 3 '77
MITCHELL, Jim
Building a vineyard in Rhode Island wine country. R. Vaughan. il pors Horticulture 52:20-4+ S '77 *
MITCHELL, John G.
Baiter Award. Audubon 79:168 N '77
Big Cypress: tomorrow has arrived. il map Audubon 79:20-31 S '77
One of our rigs is missing. Audubon 79:149-51 N '77
To drill or not to drill. il Audubon 79:78-85 Ja '77
Ursus horribilis in extremis. il Am Heritage 28:16-29 O '77
Where have all the *tuttu* gone? il Audubon 79: 2-15 Mr '77
MITCHELL, John Newton
Nos. 24171-157 and 01489-163(B) il pors Time 110: 11 Jl 4 '77 *
MITCHELL, Joni
Joni Mitchell's Hejira. Hi Fi 27:138-9 Mr '77 *
MITCHELL, Langdon Elwyn
New York idea. Reviews
Nation 224:476-7 Ap 16 '77 *
New Yorker 53:81-2 Ap 4 '77 *
Newsweek il 89:110-11 Ap 11 '77 *
Sat R 4:50-1 Jl 9 '77 *
Time il 109:88 Ap 11 '77 *
MITCHELL, Lolly
Building a vineyard in Rhode Island wine country. R. Vaughan. il pors Horticulture 55:20-4+ S '77 *
MITCHELL, Margaretta K.
After ninety; excerpts. por Pop Phot 81:126+ O '77
MITCHELL, Martha (Beall)
Here's to the crazy ladies. E. Goodman. por Ms 5:22 My '77 *
MITCHELL, Peter W.
Great-phase-coherency bandwagon. Hi Fi 27:76-80 O '77
Loudspeakers without boxes. il Hi Fi 27:50-5 Je '77
MITCHELL, Robert A.
Women and world religions. America 136:123-5 F 12 '77
MITCHELL, Roger
For the children at U.S. Grant School, Sheboygan, Wisconsin; poem. Redbook 150:66 D '77
MITCHELL, Susan
Night tree; poem. New Yorker 52:44 F 14 '77
MITCHELL, William LeRoy
Designer's designer. G. Witzenburg. il pors Motor T 29:72-4+ Jl '77 *
Men behind the Car of the Year. il pors Motor T 29:37 F '77 *
MITCHELL, William S.
Safeway: selling nongrocery items to cure the supermarket blahs. il por Bus W p52-6+ Mr 7 '77 *
MITCHELL, Hutchins Inc. See Investment advisers
MITCHELL, Hutchins Inc-Paine Webber Inc merger. See Brokers—Acquisitions and mergers
MITCHELL Energy & Development Corporation. See Petroleum industry—United States
MITCHISON, G. J.
Phyllotaxis and the Fibonacci series. bibl il Science 196:270-5 Ap 15 '77
MITER boxes, gages, etc.
DeWalt's power miterbox. M. McClintock. il Pop Mech 147:124 F '77
Miter box that's powered! J. Capotosto. il Mech Illus 73:134-6 Mr '77
9 ways to miter by hand. R. E. Thomas and S. Walton. il Pop Mech 148:100-1+ Jl '77
MITES
Ectoparasitic mites on rodents: application of the island biogeography theory? with reply by B. O'Connor and others. A. M. Kuris and A. R. Blaustein. bibl Science 195:596-8 F 11 '77
MITFORD, Jessica
Funeral salesmen. McCalls 105:190+ N '77
If you think your family is crazy. . .; or, Taking tea with Hitler; excerpt from A fine old conflict. il por Ms 6:63-6+ S '77
Memoirs of a not-so-dutiful daughter; excerpt from A fine old conflict. il pors N Y Times Mag p35-7+ Ap 17 '77
Anecdotes, facetiae, satire, etc.
Our hearts were young and red. M. E. Kinsley. New Repub 177:43 O 8 '77
MITFORD, Unity Valkyrie
British anti-Semitism, then and now. D. R. Katz. New Repub 176:21 F 5 '77 *
Not their finest hour. D. Pryce-Jones. il New Repub 176:12-16 My 14 '77 *
MITGANG, Herbert
Bill Mauldin: the best gets better. il Art N 76: 92-3 O '77
Eden: a memoir. Nation 224:100-1 Ja 29 '77
MITOCHONDRIA
Genetic and translational capabilities of the mitochondrion. A. Tzagoloff. bibl BioScience 27:18-23 Ja '77
Membrane potential of mitochondria measured with microelectrodes. B. L. Maloff and others. bibl il Science 195:898-900 Mr 4 '77
Reye's syndrome: patient serum alters mitochondrial function and morphology in vitro. J. R. Aprille. bibl il Science 197:908-10 Ag 26 '77
Thyroid hormone action: the mitochondrial pathway. K. Sterling and others. bibl il Science 197:996-9 S 2 '77
MITOSIS (biology) See Cell division
MITTENTHAL, Richard A. and Mahoney, B. W.
Getting management help to the nonprofit sector. Harvard Bus R 55:95-103 S '77
MITTERRAND, François
Death of Eurocommunism. T. Szulc. New Repub 177:21-2+ O 8 '77 *
Family feud on the left. pors Time 110:57 O 10 '77 *
Marchais plays it rough. Nat R 29:1161 O 14 '77 *
Le nouveau régime. A. Berger. New Repub 176: 18-20 Je 18 '77 *
MITTLER, Gene A.
Evaluating teaching and learning in art. il Clearing H 50:252-5 F '77
MIXED pan. See Plants, Potted
MIXERS, Concrete. See Concrete mixers
MIXERS, Food. See Kitchen utensils and appliances
MIXES, Beverage. See Beverage mixes
MIXON, Jim
Jim Mixon; the man they didn't eat for breakfast. E. Kerr. por Am For 83:12-13+ My '77 *
MIXTEC Indians. See Indians of Mexico
MNEMONICS
It's hard enough to say it, let alone to remember it. M. Olmert. il Smithsonian 8:172 O '77
MNYUKH, Yuri
To shrink a scientist. F. Coleman. il por Newsweek 90:35-6 Ag 8 '77

MOBIL Oil Corporation
This man was made possible by a grant from Mobil Oil; H. Schmertz. M. Gerrard. il Esquire 89:62-4+ Ja '78
To drill or not to drill; controversy surrounding proposed oil lease of Michigan Audubon Society's Bernard W. Baker Sanctuary. J. G. Mitchell. il Audubon 79:78-85 Ja '77
What makes Mobil run? il Bus W p80-5 Je 13 '77

MOBILE, Ala.
Antiques; symposium, ed by W. Garrett. il Antiques 112:459-95 S '77

MOBILE home parks
Finding a good mobile home park. Changing T 31:39-42 S '77

MOBILE homes
Concrete homes that can be moved. J. M. Cruver. il Mech Illus 73:32 N '77
Mobile homes. S. Mead and K. Petersen. il Bet Hom & Gard 55:100-3 Ap '77

MOBILE libraries. See Bookmobiles

MOBILE Quarantine Facility. See Quarantine

MOBILE recreation centers. See Recreation centers

MOBILES
Alexander Calder: casting seeds into the wind. B. Bristow. Chr Today 21:38+ S 9 '77
Christmas mobile. il Design (US) 79:30-1 N '77
Existentialist on mobilist; excerpt from The art world; ed by B. Diamonstein. J. P. Sartre. il por Art N 76:158+ N '77
How to make a ceramic mobile. il Sunset 158:164+ My '77
Poetry in motion. S. E. Staller. il Design (US) 78:12-13 mid-Wint '77
Star of David (Mogen David) mobiles. il Design (US) 79:18 N '77

MOBILIZATION for Survival (organization) See Peace societies

MOBLEY, Tony A. See Panik, M. A. jt auth

MOBUTU, Joseph Désiré. See Mobutu, S. S.

MOBUTU, Sese Seko
Mobutu speaks out; excerpts from interview, ed by A. de Borchgrave. il por Newsweek 89:49-50+ Ap 18 '77

about

ABC's of fighting in Zaïre. il map U.S. News 82:45-6 Ap 25 '77 *
Going like 60. Nation 224:548-9 My 7 '77 *
Mobutu's victory. L. Griggs. il por Time 109:43 My 9 '77 *
New war in Africa? J. Pringle. il map Newsweek 89:37-8 Mr 28 '77 *
Our man Mobutu. R. Morris. New Repub 176:10-11 My 7 '77 *
Signs of support. il Time 109:28 Ap 18 '77 *
Things are looking bad for Mobutu. il por Time 109:38+ Ap 11 '77 *

MOCCASINS
First American footwear. C. Miles. il Hobbies 82:146-8 O '77
Moccasins and sandals. C. S. Miles. il Hobbies 82:146-8 Ja '78

MOCCIA, Richard D. and others
Increasing frequency of thyroid goiters in coho salmon (oncorhynchus kisutch) in the Great Lakes. bibl il Science 198:425-6 O 28 '77

MOCKINGBIRDS
Mocker still thrives in Brooklyn. J. P. Reilly. il por Conservationist 31:8-9 My '77

MODEL airplane engines. See Airplane models—Engines

MODEL United Nations. See United Nations—Study and teaching

MODELING
Dough; Aztec-inspired sculpture. New Yorker 53:28-9 F 21 '77
Glad tidings: wreaths of plenty; dough sculptures. il Ladies Home J 94:94-5+ D '77
How doughs your garden grow? bread dough sculptures. C. K. Sills. il Design (US) 78:18-19 mid-Wint '77
Parge away! plaster modeling. N. C. Clark. il Design (US) 78:24-5 mid-Wint '77
Sculpture lids for gift jars; baker's clay. il Sunset 159:80-1 D '77
Sculpture out of the oven...the artworks end up as dinner rolls. il Sunset 158:94-5 Mr '77

See also

Wax modeling

MODELS
Lipstick cases, typewriter parts melded into motorcycle art. S. Parker. il por Design (US) 79:14-16 Fall '77

See also

Circus, Miniature
Economic models
House models
Miniature objects
Railroad models
Ship and boat models
Zoological models

MODELS (patents)
Patent model by John Henry Belter. R. Roth. bibl il Antiques 111:1038-40 My '77

MODELS (persons)
More than just handsome faces; black male models. S. D. Lewis. il Ebony 32:70-2+ Mr '77
Nobody's perfect; seven models. il Seventeen 36:130-3 O '77
Off camera with seven super sales stars. R. Graham. il House B 119:72-3+ Ag '77
Successful black models in Europe. E. W. Johnson. il Ebony 32:156-9 Ag '77

See also

Cain, M.
Cleveland, P.
Sokal, Y.

MODELS of cities, towns, etc.
Britain in miniature; Tucktonia. T. Holloway. il Travel 147:50-3 Je '77
Lastville, a miniature town. S. A. Parvin. il Hobbies 82:123+ D '77

MODERN architecture. See Architecture, Modern

MODERN art. See Art, Modern

MODERN Art Museum, New York. See Museum of Modern Art, New York

MODERN design. See Design

MODERN furniture. See Furniture

MODERN Language Association of America
Academia nuts; convention. W. Cole. Sat R 4:30 F 19 '77
Multifarious horses of instruction. D. Grumbach. il Commonweal 104:87-9 F 4 '77
Those doctoral dilemmas; annual convention. A. Swan and E. McGrath. il Time 111:57 Ja 9 '78
U.S. journal: Manhattan. C. Trillin. New Yorker 53:84+ Mr 7 '77

MODERN languages. See Languages, Modern

MODERN music. See Music

MODERN theology. See Theology

MODERNIZATION. See Social change

MODERNIZATION of houses. See Houses, Remodeled

MODERT, Jo
Book reviewing for city newspapers. Writer 90:20-2+ Ja '77

MODIFIED airplanes. See Airplanes, Remodeled

MODRAS, Ronald
Devil, demons & dogmatism. il Commonweal 104:71-5 F 4 '77

MODULAR construction
Small is more. il Sunset 158:84-7 Mr '77

MODULATION, Pulse-width. See Pulse techniques (electronics)

MOE, Richard L. and Silva, P. C.
Antarctic marine flora: uniquely devoid of kelps. bibl il Science 196:1206-8 Je 10 '77

MOLLENDICK, Jake
Why Wichita. T. West. il Flying 101:254 S '77

MOELLER, Bill, and Moeller, Janet
Living aboard; excerpt. Yachting 142:143-5 Jl '77

MOELLER, Janet. See Moeller, B. jt auth

MOELLERING, Ralph L.
Canada's pipeline battle. il Chr Cent 94:982-5 O 26 '77

MOEN, Roger L. See Fletcher, E. A. jt auth

MOERS, Ellen
Prehumous classics. Am Scholar 47:118+ Wint '77

MOFFETT, Judith
Passage; Moving parts; Relay; Fadeout; Twinings orange pekoe; poems. Poetry 131:29-38 O '77
(tr) See Gullberg, H. Balloons

MOFFETT, Kenworth
Dublin. il Art N 76:215-16+ N '77

MOGADISHU raid. See Police—Germany, West

MOGIL, H. Michael and others
Lightning—a preliminary reassessment. bibl il maps Weatherwise 30:192-9 O '77

MOHAMMED Reza Pahlevi, Shah of Iran
I'm not the Judas; excerpts from interview, ed by W. E. Schmidt. il por Newsweek 89:47-8 Ja 24 '77
Shah on war and peace; excerpts from interview, ed by A. de Borchgrave. por map Newsweek 90:69-71 N 14 '77
Tough talk on oil, arms, investments; interview, ed by R. Taggiasco. por Bus W p36+ Ja 24 '77

Visit to the United States, 1977

Greetings for the Shah. il por Time 110:15+ N 28 '77
Iran a quarter-century back. Nat R 29:1478 D 23 '77
Promise to fight against an oil-price hike. il por U.S. News 83:44 N 28 '77
When Persians collide. il Newsweek 90:65 N 28 '77

MOHAMMEDANISM. See Islam

MOHAR, Laurence A.
Canyon lands of the Colorado Plateau. il Holiday 58:34-5+ Ap '77

MOHAWK, Richard, and Skyhorse, Paul, murder trial. See Trials (murder)

MOHAWK Rubber Company. See Tire industry

MOHLENBROCK, Robert H.
Forest of the Swamp Fox. il map Am For 83: 34-7 Mr '77
MÖHLER, H. and Okada, T.
Benzodiazepine receptor: demonstration in the central nervous system. bibl il Science 198: 849-51 N 25 '77
MOHR, Charles
Not-so-cool Jody Powell. il por N Y Times Mag p20-1+ My 15 '77
Time Inc.'s internal war over Vietnam; excerpt from The powers that be. D. Halberstam. Esquire 89:116+ Ja '78 *
MOHR, Howard
Minnesota farmer speaks; poem. Org Gard & Farm 24:51 Ag '77
MOHR, Milton Ernst
Quotron's fast climb up from the depths. il por Bus W p 110 Je 27 '77 *
MOISTURE
See also
Soil moisture
Water vapor
MOISTURE control in buildings. See Dampness in buildings
MOISTURIZERS. See Cosmetics
MOL, Caroline, and East, Ben
Death did not rattle. il Outdoor Life 159:88-9+ Ap '77
MOLBERG, A. Luther
Taking time to care. il MH 60:19-23 Wint '77
MOLDED luggage. See Luggage
MOLDED salads. See Salads
MOLDINGS (architecture)
How to create an effect with stock moldings. il Bet Hom & Gard 55:68 D '77
Wood moldings add the final touch. il Bet Hom & Gard 55:64 N '77
MOLDS (botany)
See also
Slime molds
MOLE, Arthur S.
Mole's other masterpieces. il por Am Heritage 28:92-3 Je '77 *
MOLECULAR asymmetry. See Stereochemistry
MOLECULAR biology
Application of genetic and cellular manipulations to agricultural and industrial problems. B. B. Hoskins and others. bibl BioScience 27: 188-91 Mr '77
Molecular graphics: application to the structure determination of a snake venom neurotoxin. D. Tsernoglou and others. bibl il Science 197: 1378-81 S 30 '77
Response regulator model in a simple sensory system; adaptation of address D. E. Koshland, Jr. bibl il Science 196:1055-63 Je 3 '77
See also
Genetic code
MOLECULAR evolution. See Evolution
MOLECULES
Molecular metal clusters; insights to chemisorption. E. L. Muetterties. bibl il Science 196: 839-48 My 20 '77
Size limit of molecules permeating the junctional membrane channels. I. Simpson and others. bibl il Science 195:294-6 Ja 21 '77
MOLECULES, Interstellar. See Matter, Interstellar
MOLESTERS, Child. See Child molesters
MOLIÈRE, Jean Baptiste Poquelin
Tartuffe. Reviews
Nation 225:348-9 O 8 '77 *
New Repub 177:24-5 N 12 '77 *
New Yorker 53:109 O 3 '77 *
Time il 110:108 O 10 '77 *
Le MOLIERE imaginaire; ballet. See Ballet reviews—Single works
MOLINARI, Angelo
Racing scene. M. Crook. Yachting 141:52+ My '77 *
MOLINARI, R. L. and others
Winter intrusions of the Loop Current. bibl il maps Science 198:505-7 N 4 '77
MOLINOFF, Daniel D.
Life with father. il N Y Times Mag p 12-17 My 22 '77
MOLL, L. and Kuypers, H. G. J. M.
Premotor cortical ablations in monkeys: contralateral changes in visually guided reaching behavior. bibl il Science 198:317-19 O 21 '77
MOLLE, T. J. C.
Realign your FM receiver. il Radio-Electr 48: 50-2+ O '77
MOLLER, Marc. See Phillips, S. jt auth
MOLLIE and the invisible giant; dramatization. See Boiko, C.
MOLLISON, James
Pollock and politics. A. Levy. Art N 76:96+ My '77 *
MOLLIVER, Mark E. See Coyle, J. T. jt auth
MOLLUSKS
Chlamydiae (with phages), mycoplasmas, and rickettsiae in Chesapeake Bay bivalves. J. C. Harshbarger and others. bibl il Science 196: 666-8 My 6 '77
On a reef, darkly; conchologist G. Vermeij. il K. Brower. Read Digest 110:125-8 F '77
See also
Clams
Gastropods
Mussels
Mussels, Fresh water
Nautilus
Nervous system—Mollusks
Octopuses
Shells (conchology)
Slugs
Snails
Squids

Growth

See Growth (mollusks)

Reproduction

See Fishes—Reproduction
MOLLY; drama. See Gray, S.
MOLNÁR, Ferenc
Guardsman. Reviews
Time il 109:62 Je 20 '77 *
MOLNAR, Peter, and Tapponnier, Paul
Collision between India and Eurasia; with biographical sketches. il maps Sci Am 236:20, 30-41 bibl(p 148) Ap '77
MOLNAR, R. E.
Crocodile with laterally compressed snout: first find in Australia. bibl il Science 197:62-4 Jl 1 '77
MOLNAR, Thomas
Failure of Marxist scholarship. Nat R 29:1430-2 D 9 '77
MOLOKAI (island)
After Damien; Kalaupapa leper colony. G. Cant. il Time 110:114-16+ S 19 '77
Hellish spot in heavenly surroundings. B. Gilbert. il maps Audubon 79:30-47 Mr '77
Is this the year to discover Molokai? il map Sunset 159:122-5 O '77
MOLOKAI leper colony. See Leprosy and lepers
MOLTING
Ecdysis: neural orchestration of a complex behavioral performance. J. R. Carlson and D. Bentley. bibl il Science 195:1006-8 Mr 11 '77
Pets; shedding of dog and cat fur. M. Siegal. House B 119:34+ Je '77
MOLTING hormone. See Ecdysone
MOLTMANN, Jürgen
American dream; tr by M. D. Meeks. Commonweal 104:490-6 Ag 5 '77

about

Power of the Spirit. J. J. O'Donnell. America 137:53-5 Jl 30 '77 *
MOLTON, Warren Lane
Emboldened Baptists: bidding for the world. Chr Cent 94:616-17 Jl 6 '77
MOLTZ, Howard, and Leidahl, Lois C.
Bile, prolactin, and the maternal pheromone. bibl il Science 196:81-3 Ap 1 '77
MOLUCCAN terrorists. See Terrorists, South Moluccan
MOLYBDENUM Corporation of America. See Metal industry
MOLYCORP Inc. See Metal indcstry
MOMATIUK, Yva, and Eastcott, John
Still Eskimo, still free. il map Nat Geog 152: 624-47 N '77
MOMENT, Gairdner B.
Roots and the biologist. BioScience 27:589 S '77
MONACO
Lace and velvet. C. Fenyvesi. New Repub 177: 13-15 N 5 '77

Description and travel

Princess Grace's Monaco. . . ; interview, ed by J. Winslow. Grace Patricia. il por Holiday 58:36-9+ Ja '77
MONADNOCK, Mount
Someone is always on Monadnock. S. Sherman. il Nat Wildlife 15:26-9 Ag '77
MONAHAN, Jane
Latin America's rebel priests. Progressive 41:43-6 My '77
MONARCH butterflies. See Butterflies
MONARCHS. See Kings and rulers
MONARCHY
See also
Great Britain—Kings and rulers
Kings and rulers
MONASTERIES
See also
Abbeys
MONASTERIES, Buddhist
Adventureland: the Himalayas; visiting Tibetan Buddhist monasteries in Ladakh. G. Baeyens. il Vogue 167:180+ My '77
MONDALE, Eleanor
My new life as the Vice-President's daughter. il pors Seventeen 36:112+ Je '77

MONDALE, Joan (Adams)
Artists and taxes. il Ceram Mo 25:73-5 O '77
In what ways can the government assist American artists? il por Am Artist 41:12 S '77

about

House that Joan Mondale decorated. S. B. Conroy. il pors Art N 76:56-7+ Summ '77 *
Joan Mondale highlights crafts in vice-presidential mansion. il por Craft Horiz 37:46 Je '77 *
Second lady. D. K. Goodwin. il por Ladies Home J 94:56+ Je '77 *
Second Lady's lunch. New Yorker 53:30-1 My 30 '77 *
Vice Presidential home on Naval Observatory hill. M. Elfin. il pors Smithsonian 8:62-9 S '77 *

MONDALE, Walter Frederick
Family in trouble. Psychol Today 10:39 My '77
Framework for Middle East peace: shaping a more stable world; address, June 17, 1977. Dept State Bull 77:41-6 Jl 11 '77
How Mondale sees his relationship with Carter; interview. il pors U.S. News 82:62-4 Mr 28 '77
Privacy to all the facts and options; excerpts from interview, ed by B. Angelo. il pors Time 109:33-4+ My 23 '77
Vice President Mondale visits Europe and Japan; remarks and addresses, with transcript of news conference, January 23-February 2, 1977. Dept State Bull 76:181-97 Mr 7 '77
Vice President Mondale visits Europe and meets with South African Prime Minister Vorster; statements, with transcript of news conference. May 3, 16-18, 20-21, 1977. Dept State Bull 76:659-66 Je 20 '77

about

Activist Veep at work. il U.S. News 82:18 Je 27 '77 *
Andy outstrips Fritz; stand on human rights. Nat R 29:654 Je 10 '77
Assistant president. T. Mathews and others. il pors Newsweek 89:24-6 Ap 18 '77 *
Blitz by Fritz. P. Goldman and others. por Newsweek 90:34+ O 17 '77 *
Breaking the ice; meeting with B. J. Vorster in Vienna. S. Fraker and others. pors Newsweek 89:16-17 My 30 '77 *
Have-clout, will-travel Veep. il Time 109:32 My 23 '77 *
Mondale v. Vorster: tough talk. il pors Time 109:34+ My 30 '77 *
Mondale's Minnesota. W. B. Furlong. il pors Horizon 20:66-74 O '77 *
Night Carter took over the party; excerpt from Convention. R. Reeves. il pors N Y Times Mag p32-8 F 20 '77 *
Remaking of the Vice President. B. Brower. il pors N Y Times Mag p38+ Je 5 '77; Same abr. Read Digest 111:113-17 D '77 *
Second lady. D. K. Goodwin. il por Ladies Home J 94:56+ Je '77 *
Social science and Presidential choices. I. L. Horowitz. bibl Society 14:21-3 My '77 *
Veep with clout. por U.S. News 82:30 Ja 31 '77 *
Vice Presidential home on Naval Observatory hill. M. Elfin. il pors Smithsonian 8:62-9 S '77 *
What ever happened to Fritz? por Time 110:15 O 10 '77 *
What U.S. is up to in Africa; meeting with B. J. Vorster in Vienna. il pors U.S. News 82:31 My 30 '77 *
Where's Fritz? R. Boeth and others. il por Newsweek 90:31 O 10 '77 *
White House watch. J. Osborne. il New Repub 176:10+ Ja 22; 10-13 Ap 23 '77 *

Visit to Europe, Western, 1977

Letter to a vice president. W. Rademaekers. il Time 109:39-41 Ja 24 '77
Mondale's mission—Europe in six days. il pors U.S. News 82:20-1 F 7 '77
Mondale's new era. M. R. Benjamin and M. Elfin. il pors Newsweek 89:30+ F 7 '77
Up, up and away with Fritz. M. Elfin. il por Newsweek 89:35-6 F 7 '77
Veep on the fly. M. R. Benjamin and others. il por map Newsweek 89:27-9 Ja 31 '77
Vice President Mondale visits Europe and Japan; remarks and addresses, with transcript of news conference, January 23-February 2, 1977. Dept State Bull 76:181-97 Mr 7 '77
With dash and panache. S. Talbott. il pors Time 109:28+ F 7 '77

Visit to Japan, 1977

Vice President Mondale visits Europe and Japan; remarks and addresses, with transcript of news conference, January 23-February 2, 1977. Dept State Bull 76:181-97 Mr 7 '77

MONDSCHEIN, Paula
In touch with their feelings; opera, children and education; interview, ed by S. Wadsworth. il pors Opera N 42:30-1+ N '77

MONET, Claude
Looking at paintings. B. Dunstan. il Am Artist 41:54-5 Ap '77 *

MONETARY Fund. See International Monetary Fund

MONETARY policy
Monetary policy instrumentation and the relationship of central banks and governments. J. T. Woolley. bibl f il Ann Am Acad 434:151-73 N '77

MONETTE, Paul
Wedding letter; poem. Poetry 129:278-83 F '77

MONEY, John William
Destereotyping sex roles. bibl il Society 14:25-8 Jl '77

MONEY
See also
Bank notes
Capital
Credit
Inflation (finance)
Interest (economics)
Investments
Monetary policy
Paper money
Wealth

History

See also
World War, 1939-1945—Military currency

International aspects

See also
Asiadollar market
Eurodollar market
Foreign exchange
International Monetary Fund

Psychological aspects

Capitalist paradox. L. H. Lapham. il Harpers 254:31-4+ Mr '77
Language of Mammon. L. H. Lapham. Harpers 254:12+ F '77

Arab countries

Petro-dollar pinch tightens. il U.S. News 82:22 My 9 '77
Why the Arabs hang on to sterling; British offer of securities in exchange for sterling. Bus W p80-1 Mr 14 '77

Austria

Austerity: a way to avoid devaluation. il por Bus W p32-3 Ja 9 '78

Canada

Canada's weak dollar both helps and hurts. Bus W p29-30 Ag 22 '77
Canada's weak dollar yields little profit. il Bus W p58 N 21 '77
Timetable to end wage-price controls. il Bus W p44 O 31 '77
See also
Canada—Monetary policy

France

France: borrowing to aid the franc. il Bus W p59 My 16 '77
Hedging against the franc's fall. il Bus W p70-2 Ja 31 '77
High-yielding currency hedge; use of floating rate by multinationals. il Bus W p67 F 21 '77
See also
France—Monetary policy

Germany, West

Betting on a stronger mark; R. J. Reynolds Industries debt refinancing. il Bus W p 196 N 14 '77
Strong D-mark, pressure on exports. Bus W p68-9 D 12 '77
U.S. companies flee the mark. il Bus W p78 My 23 '77

Great Britain

Floating pound makes big waves. Bus W p 196+ N 14 '77

Hawaii

Early Hawaiian money. G. Rayner. Hobbies 82:131 Ap '77

Japan

Eurobond hedge against a rising yen. Bus W p86 Ap 11 '77
Hot money floods the yen. il Bus W p 152 D 12 '77
How a rising yen could help the U.S. il Bus W p42 O 24 '77
Pressures on Japan to keep the yen rising. il Bus W p28 Mr 7 '77
$6 billion that Japan is squirreling away. il Bus W p 194 N 14 '77

Latin America

See also
Paper money—Latin America

Russia

Hard currency problems spur Soviet export push. E. Kozicharow. Aviation W 106:17-18 Ap 11 '77

Spain

Hedging on the peseta. il Bus W p71-2 My 2 '77

MONEY—*Continued*

Sweden

Pressure on Sweden's krona. il Bus W p72 Je 13 '77

Switzerland

What stopped the Swiss franc. il Bus W p42 Mr 21 '77

Turkey

Stung by Turkey's foreign exchange crisis. il Bus W p55 Jl 4 '77

United States

Behind the dollar's latest slump. il U.S. News 83:22-3 Ag 8 '77
Case for overthrowing the government; address; June 17, 1977. J. M. Snyder. Vital Speeches 43:717-20 S 15 '77
Coping with a tumbling dollar. S. Rose. il Fortune 96:272-4+ O '77
Dippy dollar. M. Ruby and others. il Newsweek 90:79 D 5 '77
Dollar slump. A. J. Mayer. il Newsweek 90:60 Ag 8 '77
Dollar's decline creates growing fears. il Bus W p51 Jl 25 '77
Dollar's sharp slide—what it means to you. il U.S. News 83:88-90 N 7 '77
Droopy dollar. New Repub 177:5-6+ D 24 '77
Exchange-rate jitters. M. Friedman. il Newsweek 90:74 S 5 '77
Face-off on dollar strategy. il por Bus W p20-1 Ag 8 '77
Flare-up at yawning gap. il Time 110:66-7 Ag 8 '77
Foreign investors thrash the dollar. il Bus W p92-4 O 31 '77
Free-falling dollar. M. Ruby and others. il Newsweek 90:77-8 D 26 '77
Free-falling U.S. dollar. il Time 110:40-1 D 26 '77
Gold and the dollar. P. A. Samuelson. Newsweek 90:70 O 31 '77
How a weak dollar hurts the stock market. il Bus W p 106-7 S 12 '77
Lower dollar may be a plus. il Bus W p100+ Ag 15 '77
Propping the dollar at last. il Time 111:38-40 Ja 16 '78
Push on the U.S. to support the dollar. E. Mervosh. Bus W p200 N 14 '77
Rising interest rates revive the dollar. il Bus W p35-6 O 17 '77
Sagging dollar may raise oil prices. il Bus W p42 N 14 '77
Saving the sick dollar. M. Ruby and others. il Newsweek 91:62+ Ja 16 '78
Show of support for the dollar. il Bus W p28-9 Ja 16 '78
Sick dollar's rising toll. R. A. Rossi. il U.S. News 84:33 Ja 9 '78
Turnabout to boost the dollar. il Bus W p30-1 D 26 '77
U.S. companies flee the mark. il Bus W p78 My 23 '77
When a declining dollar helps the investor. il Bus W p 131-2+ D 26 '77
See also
Coins
Paper money—United States
United States—Mint

MONEY, Counterfeit. See Counterfeits and counterfeiting
MONEY as gifts
Great ways to give money. Y. Chun. il Good H 185:212+ D '77
MONEY lending. See Loans, Personal
MONEY management. See Budget, Household; Finance, Personal
MONEY markets
Calmer outlook for the money markets. il Fortune 95:44+ My '77
High yields pull U.S. corporate cash abroad. il Bus W p79-80 Ja 16 '78
See also
Asiadollar market
Eurodollar market
Foreign exchange
MONEY raising campaigns. See Fund raising
MONEY rates. See Interest (economics)
MONEY supply
Arthur Burns: how good a job? G. R. Rosen. il por Duns R 110:68-71+ D '77
Burns-Carter not-quite fight. por Time 110-108+ N 7 '77
Faulting the Fed on money. il Time 110:86 S 26 '77
Fed's view of the economy. S. H. Wildstrom. Bus W p29 Je 6 '77
Fire under Burns. M. Ruby and others. il por Newsweek 90:91-2 O 24 '77
Has the Fed made a costly blunder? W. Wolman. Bus W p34 Ag 15 '77
How velocity can fool the money watchers. il Bus W p98-9 My 30 '77
Is the Federal Reserve building future inflation today? W. Wolman. il Bus W p 110+ S 26 '77
Money madness. Nat R 29:1347 N 25 '77
Money supply seems manageable. Bus W p60-1 Ag 1 '77
Why the Fed can't control money growth. il Bus W p94+ N 7 '77
MONFORT of Colorado, Inc
Taming the cattle cycle. il Forbes 119:81+ Ap 15 '77
MONGOLIA
Mongolia. J. M. Kane. il Travel 147:26-9+ Je '77
MONGOLIAN gerbils. See Gerbils
MONGOLISM
I'm gonna miss you; G. Gray. J. P. Blank. Read Digest 111:233-4+ N '77
MONGOLOIDS. See Mongolism
MONITOR (warship)
Monitor mission. P. Gwynne and E. Clark. il Newsweek 90:54 Ag 15 '77
MONITOR receivers. See Radio receivers
MONITOR and Merrimac, Battle of. See United States—History—Civil War, 1861-1865—Naval operations
MONJAN, Andrew A. and Collector, M. I.
Stress-induced modulation of the immune response. bibl il Science 196:307-8 Ap 15 '77
MONK, Meredith
And taking to the streets. A. Smith. il pors Ms 6:46-9+ D '77 *
Dancing. A. Croce. New Yorker 52:79 Ja 24 '77 *
MONK seals. See Seals (animals)
MONKEYS
Animals that kill their young; langurs; study by S. B. Hrdy. il Time 111:64 Ja 9 '78
Bacteriophages in live virus vaccines: lack of evidence for effects on the genome of rhesus monkeys. J. B. Milstien and others. bibl il Science 197:469-70 Jl 29 '77
Bridging a gap between men and monkeys; impairing memory of sound by cutting auditory association cortex. J. H. Dewson, 3d. por Intellect 105:215-16 Ja '77
Fond monkey business in France; work of S. Lindbergh and A. Lindbergh. il pors Time 109:88 My 23 '77
Lindberghs liberate monkeys from constraints; Verlhiac Primate Center. R. Chelminski. il pors Smithsonian 7:58-65 bibl(p 126) Mr '77
Who loves you? work of S. J. Suomi on the emotional development of rhesus monkeys. J. Greenberg. il por Sci N 112:139+ Ag 27 '77
See also
Baboons
Orangutans

Food and feeding

Insulin, glucagon, and glucose exhibit synchronous, sustained oscillations in fasting monkeys. C. J. Goodner and others. bibl il Science 195:177-9 Ja 14 '77
Poison in a monkey's Garden of Eden; howler monkeys in Costa Rican forests. K. E. Glander. il Natur Hist 86:34-41 bibl(p96) Mr '77
MONMOUTH County, N.J.

Education

See Education—New Jersey
MONNET, Jean
What Jean Monnet wrought. Z. For Affairs 55:630-5 Ap '77 *
MONOCOTYLEDONS
What are monocots and dicots? il Sunset 158:250 My '77
MONOCULAR deprivation. See Sensory deprivation
MONOCYTES. See Leukocytes
MONOGAMY. See Marriage
MONOGAMY in animals. See Animals—Habits and behavior
MONONGAHELA River
New life for the Monongahela. P. W. Weiser. il Parks & Rec 12:25a-27a F '77
MONOPOLIES
See also
Competition
Trusts, Industrial
MONORAIL railroads. See Railroads, Single rail
MONOSODIUM glutamate
Monosodium glutamate administration to the newborn reduces reproductive ability in female and male mice. W. J. Pizzi and others. bibl il Science 196:452-4 Ap 22 '77
MONOSSON, Adolf F.
Would you buy a used computer from this man? por Forbes 119:104 Mr 15 '77 *
MONROE, Harriet
Miss Monroe, Mr Pound, and the boorzoi. J. Parisi. Poetry 131:39-51 O '77 *
MONROE County, Mich.
Michigan sewer project beats all but weather. il Am City & County 92:75 My '77
MONROE County Public Library, Bloomington, Ind. See Libraries—Indiana
MONSANTO Company
Harvard and Monsanto: the $23-million alliance. B. J. Culliton. pors Science 195:759-63 F 25 '77
Meeting the greater competition of tomorrow. J. W. Hanley. pors Nations Bus 65:37-40 Mr '77

MONSMA, Stephen V.
Oval office: three models for a Christian. Chr Today 21:28-9 Ja 21 '77

MONSON, Karen
Lyric Opera: accent on spectacle. il Hi Fi 27: MA32-3+ Ap '77
Out of music, chaos? il por Hi Fi 27:MA28-30 N '77

MONSOONS
Somali Current: recent measurements during the southwest monsoon. J. G. Bruce. bibl maps Science 197:51-3 Jl 1 '77

MONSTERS
See also
Animals, Mythical
Deformities
Sea serpents

MONT SAINT MICHEL, France
Mont Saint Michel. K. MacLeish. il map Nat Geog 151:820-31 Je '77

MONTAGE
People and places merge in montage. R. Moore. il Sch Arts 77:12-13 N '77

MONTAGU, Ashley
Don't be adultish! interview, ed by D. Goleman. il Psychol Today 11:46-7+ Ag '77

about

Ashley Montagu—he likes to dance. D. Goleman. por Psychol Today 11:50 Ag '77 *

MONTAGUE, George T.
Scriptural response to the report on Human sexuality. America 137:284-5 O 29 '77

MONTAGUE, Louise
Straight talk about the living-together arrangement. Read Digest 110:91-4 Ap '77

MONTALCINI, Rita Levi-. See Levi-Montalcini, R.

MONTALE, Eugenio
Reconsideration. R. Fraser. New Repub 176:36-8 F 5 '77

MONTALVO, Protasio
Mayor who came out of the cellar. il por Time 110:28 Ag 1 '77 *

MONTANA
See also
Agriculture—Montana
Blacks—Montana
Camping—Montana
Education—Montana
Environmental policy—Montana
Flathead River
Hunting—Montana
Poplar River
Recreation—Montana
Skis and skiing—Montana
Wilderness areas—Montana

Description and travel

Sky hunger. L. McMurtry. il Holiday 58:38-41+ Ap '77

MONTANE voles. See Mice

MONTAÑÉS, Roger
Maritime history of Cuba; tr by R. Fagin. il Oceans 10:16-21 S '77

MONTE ALBÁN, Mexico
Monte Albán, city of the gods; Zapotec and Mixtec antiquities discovered by A. Caso. L. Elliott. il Read Digest 110:202-4+ My '77

MONTE BELLO Open Space Preserve. See California—Parks and reserves

MONTE CARLO Grand Prix. See Automobile racing

MONTEDISON, S.p.A. See Chemical industries—Italy

MONTEIRO, Lois A.
Immigrants without care. bibl il Society 14:38-42 S '77

MONTEIRO, Thomas
Sources of school-community conflict in black communities. il Intellect 106:155-6 O '77

MONTEMEZZI, Italo
L'amore dei tre re: like no other Italian opera; RCA recording. C. L. Osborne. il por Hi Fi 27:67-70 Ag '77 *
Winning hand; Montemezzi: L'amore dei tre re. D. Arthur. Am Rec G 41:24-6 N '77 *

MONTENEGRO
Montenegro: Yugoslavia's black mountain. B. Hodgson. il map Nat Geog 152:662-83 N '77

MONTEREY Historic Car Races. See Automobile racing

MONTEREY Institute for Research in Astronomy
Alternative astronomy: experiment in self-sufficiency blossoms. A. L. Hammond. il Science 197:1267-71+ S 23 '77
If you want an observatory, go build your own. D. E. Thomsen. il Sci N 112:323+ N 12 '77

MONTEVERDI, Claudio
Madrigals. W. L. Purcell. Am Rec G 40:26 Mr '77 *

MONTEVIDEO, Uruguay

Social life and customs

Night of nights in Montevideo; Llamadas festival. C. Páez Vilaró. il Américas 29:58-9 N '77

MONTEZUMA National Wildlife Refuge. See Wildlife sanctuaries—New York (state)

MONTGOMERY, Charles F.
Classics and collectibles. il Art N 76:126-9+ N '77
—and Ward, G. W. R.
Iron candlestands: made where, when, and by whom? bibl il Antiques 112:282-4 Ag '77

MONTGOMERY, Charlotte
Speaker for the house. See issues of Good housekeeping

MONTGOMERY, Cyrus
Decades are for goal-setting. il por Ret Liv 17:64-5 S '77

MONTGOMERY, G. Franklin
Product technology and the consumer; with biographical sketch. il Sci Am 237:10, 47-53 D '77

MONTGOMERY, John Warwick
Do we have the right to die? Chr Today 21:49-50 Ja 21 '77
Dr Johnson as apologist. Chr Today 21:62-3 Ap 15 '77

MONTGOMERY, Ala.

Blacks

Day the black revolution began; Montgomery bus boycott, 1975. L. Bennett, Jr. il pors Ebony 32:54-6+ S '77

MONTGOMERY County, Md.

Education

See Education—Maryland

MONTGOMERY County, Ohio
Everyone's in the act. H. Flieger. U.S. News 82:88 F 21 '77

MONTHLY labor review (periodical)
Sorrentino, Maldonado, Klein Award winners; 1976. M Labor R 100:2 Ap '77

MONTICELLO (historic house)
Jefferson's country. D. A. Tice. il por Am For 83:24-7 My '77

MONTMARTRE. See Paris

MONTOYA, Frank, family
Family that fought back; use of ritalin in Taft, Calif. schools. J. N. Bell. il McCalls 104:26+ My '77

MONTREAL

Art

Report from Toronto & Montreal. A. Goldin. il Art in Am 65:35-45+ Mr '77

Galleries and museums

Exhibitions in sight; remodeling of the Montreal Museum of Fine Arts. B. Wasserman. il Sch Arts 76:48-51 Ap '77

MONTREAL Book Fair. See Book fairs

MONTREAL Museum of Fine Arts. See Montreal—Galleries and museums

MONTY Python (comedy team)
New Python book a treat for both film and design buffs. P. Doebler. il Pub W 212:78+ O 3 '77

MONUMENTS
See also
Sepulchral monuments
Statue of Liberty
Washington, D.C.—Monuments, statues, etc.
also subhead Monuments, statues, etc. under names of cities, e.g, Hartford, Conn.—Monuments, statutes, etc.

MONUMENTS, Megalithic. See Megalithic monuments

MONUMENTS, National. See National monuments

MONUMENTS, Natural. See Natural monuments

MONZON, Carlos
Star bows out, a star bows in. P. Putnam. il pors Sports Illus 47:20-1 Ag 8 '77 *

MOODIE, Craig W.
Miracle of the reborn bells. il por Read Digest 111:9-12+ N '77

MOODS
From joy to depression: new insights into the chemistry of moods. M. Scarf. il N Y Times Mag p30-4+ Ap 24 '77; Same abr. with title What makes our moods? Read Digest 111: 45-7+ Ag '77

MOODY, Patricia A.
American grammatical revolution. Educ Digest 42:58-61 Ap '77

MOODY, Raymond A. Jr
City of light, realm of shadow; excerpt from Reflections on life after life. Read Digest 111: 151-4 Jl '77
Is there life after death? il Sat Eve Post 249: 66-7+ My '77

MOOERS, Christopher N. K. and Hall, J. M.
Resources of continental margins: perspectives on a program for their management. il Oceans 10:61-3 Mr '77

MOOG, Florence. See Black, B. L. jt auth

MOOG, Robert A.
Electronic muse. por Forbes 120:70 S 1 '77 *

MOOLENAAR, Wouter H. and Spector, Ilan
Membrane currents examined under voltage clamp in cultured neuroblastoma cells. bibl il Science 196:331-3 Ap 15 '77

MOON, Eric
Moon selects target: U.S. information policy; address, June 21, 1977. por Am Lib 8:381 Jl '77
Moonshine; question of rights of the young to access to information. SLJ 24:9 S; 5 N '77

MOON, George E.
Men behind the Car of the Year. il pors Motor T 29:38 F '77 *

MOON, Sun Myung
Divine principle and the Second Advent. S. M. Heim. por Chr Cent 94:448-51 My 11 '77 *
Moon trek: many enterprises. Chr Today 22:43 O 21 '77 *
Science, sin, and sponsorship. I. L. Horowitz. por Atlantic 239:98-102 Mr '77; Discussion. 239:22-3+ Je '77 *
Sun Myung Moon and the Unification Church. L. A. Belford. Intellect 105:336-7 Ap '77 *

MOON
Sun, moon, and planets this month. R. C. Victor. See issues of Sky and telescope
What's new on the moon? B. M. French. il Sky & Tel 53:164-9 Mr; 257-61 Ap '77
Whole moon catalog; computer data intercomparative system. J. Eberhart. il Sci N 111: 300-2 My 7 '77
See also
Eclipses, Lunar
Space flight to the moon

Conferences

Rockfest 8: still breaking new ground. Sci N 111:199 Mr 26 '77

Exploration

Equipment

Lunar science stations cease functioning. il Space World N-12-168:28-31 D '77
Science packages on moon shut down; ALSEP. il Sci N 112:213 O 1 '77

Observations

Venus, Mars, and the moon come together. il Sky & Tel 54:150-2 Ag '77

Photographs

Some photographs of young moons. il Sky & Tel 53:440 Je '77

Surface

Planetary comparisons. B. M. French. il Space World N-1-157:30-1 Ja '77

MOON distances. See Astronomical distances

MOONEY, Al
Mooney. G. Baxter. il Flying 101:258 S '77 *

MOONEY Grove Park. See California—Parks and reserves

MOONIES (movement) See Unification Church (movement)

MOONLIGHTING. See Supplementary employment

MOONQUAKES. See Seismology

MOONS. See Satellites

MOOR, Paul
Berlin Festival: liberal chic. il Hi Fi 27:MA36-7 Ap '77
Great Mozart-Beethoven caper. il Hi Fi 27:72-7 Mr '77
Zimmermann's The soldiers. il Hi Fi 28:MA35-6 Ja '78

MOORACHIAN, Rose
(ed) Adult books for young adults. See issues of School library journal

MOORBATH, Stephen
Oldest rocks and the growth of continents; with biographical sketch. il maps Sci Am 236:24, 92-104 bibl(p 150) Mr '77

MOORCROFT, Marilyn
Floundering with Grass. il por Commonweal 104: 435-8 Jl 8 '77

MOORE, Archie
Youthful Plimpton vs the wily Moore. G. Plimpton. il pors Sports Illus 47:38-40+ O 24 '77 *

MOORE, Arthur Cotton
Washington architect Arthur Cotton Moore. W. Marlin. il Archit Rec 162:84-95 D '77 *

MOORE, Charles Willard
Great architect looks at California architecture. il Mademoiselle 83:100-1+ Ap '77
—and Oliver, R. B.
Magic, nostalgia and a hint of greatness in the workaday world of the Building types study. il Archit Rec 161:117-37 Ap '77

about

More than meets the eye. P. Goldberger. il N Y Times Mag p46-7+ Ja 16 '77 *
Two houses by Charles Moore. M. F. Schmertz. il Archit Rec 161:109-16 Je '77 *

MOORE, David D. and others
Construction of chimeric phages and plasmids containing the origin of replication of bacteriophage lambda. bibl il Science 198:1041-6 D 9 '77

MOORE, Donald J.
Hope in Jerusalem. America 137:236-9 O 15 '77

MOORE, Elizabeth A. See Moore, J. W. jt auth

MOORE, Frank
How much less is Moore? il por Time 110:15 D 12 '77 *

MOORE, Frank R.
Geomagnetic disturbance and the orientation of nocturnally migrating birds. bibl il Science 196:682-4 My 6 '77

MOORE, Gerald
Deflowering of the Endangered Species Act. il Horticulture 55:36-9 My '77
Sudden stillness. il Read Digest 111:33-5+ Jl '77

MOORE, Gregory S.
Tired logician; poem. Esquire 88:24 Ag '77
Under the Hart Bridge; poem. Esquire 87:14 Mr '77

MOORE, Harold W.
Bioactivation as a model for drug design bioreductive alkylation. bibl il Science 197:527-32 Ag 5 '77

MOORE, Henry Spencer
Bringing bold splendor to the city. il Horizon 19:72-9 My '77 *
Confronting Henry Moore. R. A. Schwab. il por Intellect 106:241-4 D '77 *

MOORE, Honor
Theater. Ms 6:29-30 N '77
Theater will never be the same. il por Ms 6:36-9+ D '77

MOORE, Joanna
Tatum O'Neal: a child once again. R. D. Le Blanc. por Good H 184:56+ Je '77 *

MOORE, John
Goosed. il Flying 100:18+ My '77

MOORE, John H.
Racism and fishing rights. Nation 225:236-8 S 17 '77

MOORE, John W. and Moore, E. A.
Computers: the move to micro. Sci Digest 82: 60-70+ Jl '77

MOORE, Kenneth E.
Reign in Spain. Commonweal 104:460-3 Jl 22 '77

MOORE, Kenny (sports writer)
All their minds were on one track. il Sports Illus 46:24-6+ F 28 '77
Call him Kid Cool. por Sports Illus 47:56-8+ D 19 '77
Creating a Flemish masterpiece. il Sports Illus 46:28-30+ Ap 4 '77
Cup turned into a coup. il Sports Illus 47:16-21 S 12 '77
Cure for an Olympian headache. il Sports Illus 46:18-20+ Ja 17 '77
Dormant no more, Duncan is erupting. il Sports Illus 46:34-7+ F 14 '77
Enigma wrapped in glory. il por Sports Illus 46:66-72+ Je 27 '77
Gentle radical who runs scared. il pors Sports Illus 47:32-7 O 24 '77
Gideon Ariel and his magic machine. il por Sports Illus 47:52-60 Ag 22 '77
Good times and good time at L.A. il Sports Illus 46:24-6+ Je 20 '77
Grasshoppers beware, here they come! il Sports Illus 47:28-30+ D 5 '77
Mac adds a few new twists. il Sports Illus 46: 14-17 Ja 24 '77
Night for stars, both born and reborn. il Sports Illus 46:32-4 My 23 '77
Road racing. Sports Illus 47:48 Jl 18 '77

about

Letter from the publisher. J. A. Meyers. por Sports Illus 46:4 Je 27 '77 *

MOORE, M. Keith. See Meltzoff, A. N. jt auth

MOORE, Marianne
These sporting poets; Marianne Moore's meeting with Muhammad Ali; interview, ed by G. Plimpton. il pors Harpers 254:76-9+ My '77

MOORE, Mary Tyler
Farewell, Mary Richards; interview, ed by K. D. Fury. il por Ladies Home J 94:39-40+ Mr '77

about

Fond farewell to the finest, funniest show on television; with introd by Nora Ephron. il pors Esquire 87:74-9 F '77 *

MOORE, Oliver
One of a kind. il pors Motor B & S 140:58-60+ Jl '77
Stern-driving Lake Superior. il Motor B & S 141:68-9+ Ja '78

MOORE, Paul, Bp, 1919-
Ex cathedra. por Forbes 119:148 Ap 15 '77 *

MOORE, Richard E.
Toxins from blue-green algae. bibl il BioScience 27:797-802 D '77

MOORE, Rosanna
Collage comedy and action. il Sch Arts 76:20-2 F '77
People and places merge in montage. il Sch Arts 77:12-13 N '77
Study of design. il Design (US) 78:27 Spr '77
Wooden Indian. il Sch Arts 76:68 Mr '77

MOORE, Sally
(ed) See Hite, S. Hite report and female sexuality

MOORE-BETTY, Maurice
Creams of the crop. il por House & Gard 149: 96-7+ Ag '77
Fowl play: 6 new ways to make a chicken go farther. il pors House & Gard 149:122-3+ F '77

MOOREFIELD, Story
North, south, east and west side story. il Am Educ 13:12-16 Ja '77; Same abr. Educ Digest 42:10-13 My '77

MOORER, Thomas Hinman
Clash of views over Canal security. pors U.S. News 83:27 O 24 '77

MOORES, Frank Duff
I am a worried Canadian; address; December 9, 1976. Vital Speeches 43:162-5 Ja 1 '77

MOOSE, Richard M.
Concern expressed on recent events in South Africa; statement, October 26, 1977. Dept State Bull 77:897-9 D 19 '77

MOOSE
Moose on the loose! J. Wood. il Nat Wildlife 15:4-11 O '77

MOOSE hunting
High-country moose; Besa River, British Columbia. S. Netherby. il Field & S 81:150+ F '77
No bull moose hunt. E. A. Bauer. il Outdoor Life 160:64-6 N '77

MOPEDS
Boom in Mopeds touches off a furor. il U.S. News 83:74 O 17 '77
Driven by mo-ped madness. D. Hurford. il Sports Illus 47:24-7 Ag 8 '77
How to motorize your bicycle. B. Hartford. il Pop Mech 148:112-13 D '77
Moped decision. il Sunset 159:86-7 D '77
Moped madness. il Time 110:66 Jl 4 '77
Moped moment. L. Langway. il Newsweek 89: 56+ My 23 '77
Moped revolution. A. Hiss and J. Lewis. il N Y Times Mag p96-7 My 15 '77
Mopeds; 100+ mpg, but how safe, or legal? G. Stone. il Pop Sci 211:66-9+ Jl '77
Mopeds: somewhere between a Rolls and a tricycle. L. Dearborn and W. Dasheff. il Ms 6: 27-30 S '77
Onrush of mopeds: 150 mi. to the gal. il Bus W p33+ Je 20 '77

Anecdotes, facetiae, satire, etc.

Mess of mopeds. G. Millstein. N Y Times Mag p 110 S 18 '77

Maintenance and repair

How to maintain your moped. E. A. Sloane. il Pop Mech 148:114-15+ O '77

MORA, F. and Myers, R. D.
Brain self-stimulation: direct evidence for the involvement of dopamine in the prefrontal cortex. bibl il Science 197:1387-9 S 30 '77

MORA, Roland R.
Bringing the veterans back into the system. por Nations Bus 65:66-7 N '77 *

MORAINE Valley Community College, Palos Hills, Ill.
Learning to move, moving to learn; classes for teachers of physical education to the handicapped. M. Nelson. il Parks & Rec 12:34-5+ N '77

MORAL conditions
See also
Motion pictures—Moral and religious aspects
Television broadcasting—Moral and religious aspects
also subhead Moral conditions under names of countries, states, cities, etc, e.g. Cleveland —Moral conditions

MORAL education
But you can't do that! It's not fair! S. E. Davison. Educ Digest 42:36- 7 My '77
Lawrence Kohlberg: why Johnny can be good without being religious. R. Beechick. il Chr Today 22:12-14 D 30 '77
Mind bending in the schools stirs growing protests. il U.S. News 83:43-4 Jl 4 '77
Moral development: implications for pedagogy. R. H. Hersh and D. P. Paolitto. Educ Digest 42:13-16 Ja '77
Parenting in a hungry world. P. M. Mische. il New Cath World 220:238-43 S '77
Reading, writing, and. . .right from wrong? B. Clouse. Chr Today 22:14-17 D 30 '77
Schoolmaster to a nation; W. H. McGuffey. H. C. Jacobs. il por Sat Eve Post 249:62-3+ Ap '77
See also
Values—Study and teaching

MORAL theology. See Christian ethics

MORALE, National

Europe, Western

Fresh worry for U.S.—a Europe beset by stagnation, self-doubt and violence. J. Fromm. il U.S. News 83:38-40+ O 17 '77

France

Le mal français: is there a reason for being Cartesian? A. Burgess. il N Y Times Mag p46-8+ My 29 '77

Germany, West

West Germany: a pessimistic giant. J. Fromm. il U.S. News 83:39-40 O 17 '77

Great Britain

Prince Philip: the new battle of Britain. . .and how to win it; interview, ed by G. Bull. Philip. pors Sat R 4:8-10+ Je 11 '77

South Africa

Back to the laager? P. Younghusband. il Newsweek 90:45-6 O 3 '77

United States

American spirit—as Lawrence Welk sees it. L. Welk. il pors U.S. News 82:69 Ja 24 '77
America's mood: a wave of uneasiness over the future. il maps U.S. News 83:37-8+ S 19 '77
America's mood—on the upbeat. il U.S. News 82:19 My 30 '77
America's mood; symposium. il Time 109:8-13 Ja 24 '77
Hail, blithe spirits. C. Tucker. Sat R 4:64 Jl 9 '77
Moral equivalents and other bugle calls; Time essay. S. Kanfer. Time 109:25 My 2 '77
New confidence. il U.S. News 82:24-6+ Je 13 '77
New Year's mellow mood. il Time 111:46-7 Ja 2 '78

MORALES, Cristóbal de
Selected works. P. Althouse. Am Rec G 40:22-3 Ag '77 *

MORALES, Ricardo
Incident. T. Branch and J. Rothchild. il pors Esquire 87:58+ Mr '77 *

MORALITY and religion. See Christian ethics

MORALS and law. See Law and ethics

MORALS and war. See War and morals

MORAN, Edmundo
Witness to justice. America 136:410-14 My 7 '77

MORAN, Edward
Adventures in alternate energy. See issues of Popular science
Solar battery for passive heating. il Pop Sci 210:94+ Je '77

MORAN, James
Venison stew. il por Bet Hom & Gard 55:184 S '77

MORAN, Mary Jo
Nobel prize winning world literature. Engl J 66: 59-60 S '77
Not without laughter; L. Hughes novel. Engl J 66:58 Mr '77

MORAN, Moore
Him in San Francisco; poem. America 137:161 S 24 '77

MORAN, Richie
Cornell's wild Irish rose. J. Marshall. Sports Illus 46:63-4+ Je 6 '77 *

MORAN, W. R.
Melba's farewell concert. il pors Hi Fi 27:86-9 Jl '77

MORAND, Paul
Coco Chanel and the Duke of Westminster; excerpt from L'allure de Chanel, tr by A. Foulke. Vogue 167:18+ My '77

MORANDO, Jana
Smash-up! T. Morando. il por Good H 184:102+ Je '77 *

MORANDO, Theo
Smash-up! il por Good H 184:102+ Je '77

MORAVEK, Glenn
Alone with the ringneck. il Field & S 82:72-4+ Ag '77

MORAVIAN Church
Another century of intercession; hourly intercession. Chr Today 21:35-6 F 18 '77

MORAY eels. See Eels

MORE, Sir Thomas, Saint
Saint for this season. America 136:66 Ja 29 '77 *

MOREAU, Jeanne
Reviews; Lumière. C. Porter. por Film Q 30:53-7 Spr '77 *

MOREHOUSE, Laurence E.
How to do more by taking it easy; excerpt from Maximum performance. il Good H 184: 202-3 Ap '77
How to perform better at almost everything; interview, ed by C. Seebohm. il por House & Gard 149:88-9 Jl '77

MOREHOUSE, Ward, and Sigurdson, Jon
Science, technology and poverty. bibl f il Bull Atom Sci 33:21-6+ D '77

MORELAND, Evelyn
Now she can smile. por Newsweek 89:56 Ap 25 '77 *

MORELL, Susan Fulop
G is for chicken. il Read Digest 111:25-6+ N '77

MOREN, Deborah K. See Kroll, H. W. jt auth

MORENO, Cesar Fernandez-. See Fernandez-Moreno, C.

MORGAN, Berry
Christmas bush; story. New Yorker 53:43-5 O 17 '77
Headrag; story. New Yorker 53:20-3 Ag 8 '77

MORGAN, Charles
Sunnyside. il por Am For 83:26-9 Ap '77

MORGAN, Charles, Jr
Can Chuck Morgan keep Jimmy Carter honest? T. Branch. Esquire 87:14+ F '77 *
MORGAN, Clyde
International exchange: the 2nd World Festival of Black Art and Culture. il Dance Mag 51:90 Jl '77
MORGAN, Dan
U.S. agripower and a hungry world. Current 191:30-7 Mr '77
MORGAN, Edward P.
Never for Mundey. Progressive 41:9 My '77
Wilson Center immerses scholars in think tank. il pors Smithsonian 8:76-83 Ag '77
MORGAN, Frederick
As it was; poem. Atlantic 239:65 Ap '77
Eternity, I; poem. Am Scholar 47:104 Wint '77
Ghost; poem. Nation 225:310 O 1 '77
Hideyoshi; poem. Nation 224:407 Ap 2 '77
Message; poem. America 136:517 Je 11 '77
Suspiria; poem. Commonweal 104:777 D 9 '77
MORGAN, Henry M. See Foulkes, F. K. jt auth
MORGAN, Jack
Winner by any name. P. Axthelm. il por Newsweek 90:73 N 7 '77 *
MORGAN, James
Horse right here. New Repub 177:26-8 Jl 23 '77
MORGAN, Jane Hale. See Jones, C. S. jt auth
MORGAN, Janet L. and others
Quantitation of cytoplasmic tubulin by radioimmunoassay. bibl il Science 197:578-80 Ag 5 '77
MORGAN, Jim
Insulation: making your house snug. House & Gard 149:102+ My '77
MORGAN, John
End; poem. New Yorker 53:81 F 28 '77
Our civilization; poem. New Repub 177:35 Ag 6 '77
MORGAN, John M. and Routtenberg, Aryeh
Angiotensin injected into the neostriatum after learning disrupts retention performance. bibl il Science 196:87-9 Ap 1 '77
MORGAN, Judith
Compleat island collector's private gazetteer of places offbeat, if not outlandish. il Sat R 5: 22-3 Ja 7 '78
—and Morgan, Neil
California's north coast. il map Nat Geog 152:330-63 S '77
MORGAN, Lael
In Alaska, another wolf kill up against the wall. il Nat Wildlife 15:6-8 Ag '77
Women who chose the great outdoors; interview, ed by N. H. Clark. por Harp Baz 110: 148+ Ap '77
MORGAN, Lee Laverne
U.S. international economic policy and its administration; address, May 24, 1977. Vital Speeches 43:618-21 Ag 1 '77
MORGAN, Len
Flying the three-holer. il Flying 101:68-73+ O '77
Only fools run out of fuel. il Flying 101:56-7+ O '77
MORGAN, Marabel
First aid for a failing marriage; excerpt from Total joy. Sat Eve Post 249:48+ Ap '77

about

Does total woman add up? A. T. Fleming. Vogue 167:76 Ag '77 *
New housewife blues. il pors Time 109:62-4+ Mr 14 '77; Same abr. with title Secrets of a total woman. Read Digest 111:91-4 Jl '77 *
MORGAN, Marsha Y. and others
Ratio of plasma alpha amino-*n* butyric acid to leucine as an empirical marker of alcoholism: diagnostic value. il Science 197:1183-5 S 16 '77
MORGAN, Mary
We're both 16 years old! il por Redbook 148:22+ Ap '77
MORGAN, Neil
Daft with island love. Sat R 5:19-20 Ja 7 '78
—See Morgan, J. jt auth
MORGAN, Oliver J. See Natale, S. M. jt auth
MORGAN, Robert
Huckleberry bald; poem. Yale R 66:405 Mr '77
MORGAN, Robert C.
Beyond masochism: a white male primal scream. Chr Cent 94:1141-3 D 7 '77
MORGAN, Robert P.
Music of Edgard Varèse. il por Hi Fi 27:78-82 F '77
Recordings of Edgard Varèse. Hi Fi 28:82-3 F '77
MORGAN, Robin
Alice Paul: mother of the ERA. por Ms 6:112 O '77
Politics of body-image. il Ms 6:47-9 S '77
What do our masochistic fantasies really mean? excerpt from Going too far: the personal chronicle of a feminist. Ms 5:66-8+ Je '77

about

Comment. J. Parini. Poetry 130:301-3 Ag '77 *

MORGAN, Ted
Honk, honk, if you love Mary Hartman, Mary Hartman. il Read Digest 110:57-9+ F '77
United States versus the princes of porn. il pors N Y Times Mag p 16-17+ Mr 6 '77
Victor Hugo's wayward daughter. il pors Horizon 19:34-41 Ja '77
MORGAN, Thomas W.
Pervasive importance of USAF's space mission; interview, ed by E. Ulsamer. il por Space World N-5-161:12-16 My '77
MORGAN Colorado Beef Company. See Meat industry
MORGAN Guaranty Trust Company building. See New York (city)—Buildings
MORGAN Horse Farm. See Horse breeding
MORGANTOWN, W.Va.
Anatomy of a boondoggle; Urban Mass Transit Administration funding of personal rapid transit system. T. Armbrister. il Read Digest 111:133-6 Ag '77
MORGELLO, Clem
Editorial. See issues of Dun's review
MORGENSTERN, Joseph
Getty's little palace in Malibu. il Art N 76:72-5 Mr '77
We get you to places you can't get to. il por Horizon 20:17-23 D '77
MORGENSTERN, Oskar
Obituary
Science 197:649 Ag 12 '77. D. Shapley
MORGENTHAU, Hans Joachim
Old superstitions, new realities. New Repub 176: 50-2+ Ja 22 '77; Same with title On making foreign policy. Current 191:48-56 Mr '77
MORGENTHAU, Henry, 1856-1946
Assimilationist dilemma: Ambassador Morgenthau's story; adaptation of address, December 1976. B. W. Tuchman. Commentary 63: 58-62 My '77; Discussion. 64:12+ Ag '77 *
MORGENTHAU, Ruth Schachter
Developing states in Africa. bibl f Ann Am Acad 432:80-95 Jl '77
MORGUES
Succurrere vitae. J. Agee. il Harpers 225:88-90+ D '77
MÖRIKE, Eduard Friedrich
Mörike's Mozart on the way to Prague. U. Mahlendorf. bibl f Am Imago 33:304-27 Fall '76 *
MORIN, Lawrence P. and others
Estradiol shortens the period of hamster circadian rhythms. bibl il Science 196:305-7 Ap 15 '77
MORINE, David
We can work with you. il Am For 83:10-12 N '77
MORINIGO, Marcos A.
Spanish overseas. UNESCO Courier 30:62-3 Ag '77
MORISON, Robert S.
Nation fails to arouse teenagers against cigarette risks. il Intellect 105:298-9 Mr '77
MORISON, Samuel Eliot
Historian and publisher. A. A. Knopf. pors Am Heritage 28:100-6 Ap '77 *
MORISON, Samuel Eliot, award. See American heritage (periodical)
MORISOT, Berthe
Berthe Morisot: paintings from a private place. W. P. Scott. il pors Am Artist 41:66-71+ N '77 *
MORISSEAU, James J.
Where does your school tax money go? New York City's Educational Priorities Panel. il Parents Mag 52:36+ S '77
MORISSON, Jim
(ed) See Samples, J. Record bass that made Junior Samples a TV star
MORITZ VON HESSEN, Tatiana, Princess. See Tatiana, M. von H.
MORLAN, Don B.
Television programming: an image in a looking glass. bibl il Intellect 106:234-6 D '77
MORLAND, Howard
Overrated. il Flying 101:23+ Jl '77
MORLEY, Eileen, and Silver, Andrew
Film director's aproach to managing creativity. il por Harvard Bus R 55:59-70 Mr '77
MORLEY, Robert
The play's still the thing. il Sat R 4:12-13 Je 11 '77
MORLEY, Roger Hubert
Young Atlantan for American Express. por Bus W p31-2 Mr 14 '77 *
MORMONS and Mormonism
Mormon connection? The defeat of the ERA in Nevada. L. C. Wohl. Ms 6:68-70+ Jl '77
Mormon Utah: where a church shapes the life of a state; with interview with S. W. Kimball. il U.S. News 83:59-61 D 19 '77
Mormons: from persecution to power. R. W. Paul. il Am Heritage 28:74-83 Je '77
Tracking down your kinfolk; using Mormon Church libraries. il Sunset 158:36 Je '77
See also
Polygamy

MORMONS and Mormonism—*Continued*

Book of Mormon

Mormon manuscript claims: another look. E. E. Plowman. il Chr Today 22:38-9 O 21 '77
Mormon mystery. il Time 110:69 Jl 11 '77
Who really wrote the book of Mormon? E. E. Plowman. il Chr Today 21:32-4 Jl 8 '77

MORMONS and Mormonism, Black
Unjustifiable denial of priesthood to black Mormons. E. E. Wells. bibl il Negro Hist Bull 40:725-7 Jl '77

MORNER, Aimée L.
Castle in Peoria. il Fortune 95:171-2 Ap '77
Dow's strategy for an unfriendly new era. il por Fortune 95:312-15+ My '77
For Sohio, it was Alaskan oil—or bust. il por Fortune 96:172-6+ Ag '77
Junk aid for small business. il Fortune 96:204-7+ N '77
Product is born. il Fortune 95:124-9+ F '77

MOROCCAN cookery. See Cookery, Moroccan

MOROCCO

Description and travel

Three days in Morocco. P. A. Mellen. il por Vogue 167:188+ My '77

Foreign relations

See also
Military assistance, Moroccan

Algeria

See Algeria—Foreign relations—Morocco

MORPHINE
Lithium: effects on subjective functioning and morphine-induced euphoria. D. R. Jasinski and others. bibl il Science 195:582-4 F 11 '77
Morphine and enkephalin: analgesic and epileptic properties. G. Urca and others. bibl il Science 197:83-6 Jl 1 '77
Morphine lowering of self-stimulation thresholds: lack of tolerance with long-term administration. R. Esposito and C. Kornetsky. bibl il Science 195:189-91 Ja 14 '77
Speed heals; combining morphine with amphetamine. Newsweek 89:65 Ap 11 '77
Stereospecific and nonstereospecific effects of (+)-and(−) - morphine: evidence for a new class of receptors? Y. F. Jacquet and others. bibl il Science 198:842-5 N 25 '77

MORPHIS, Audrey
Principal who cared. por Clearing H 50:263-5 F '77

MORPHOGENESIS
Molecular determination of morphogenesis. R. A. Raff. bibl il BioScience 27:394-401 Je '77
See also
Neurogenesis

MORPHOLOGY
See also
Homology (biology)

MORRESI, Angelo C. See Cheremisinoff, P. N. jt auth

MORRIS, Bernadine
Beauty: color '77. il Vogue 167:282-91 O '77
Renaissance of haute couture. il N Y Times Mag p76-8+ F 27 '77

MORRIS, Carl. See Efron, B. jt auth

MORRIS, David
Winter bass. il Outdoor Life 160:78-81+ N '77

MORRIS, David J.
Solar cells find their niche in everyday life on earth. il Smithsonian 8:38-45 O '77

MORRIS, Desmond
People watching; excerpt from Manwatching—a field guide to human behavior. il Good H 186:100-1+ Ja '78
Secrets of man's unspoken language; excerpt from Manwatching: a field guide to human behavior. Read Digest 112:55-8 Ja '78

MORRIS, Ed
Don't buy it if you can build it or repair it. il por Ret Liv 17:45 Ap '77

MORRIS, Gay
La Loie. il pors Dance Mag 51:36-41 Ag '77

MORRIS, George B. Jr
Excerpt from testimony on retirement age policy, March 16, 1977. Cong Digest 56:285+ N '77

MORRIS, James Humphry. See Morris, Jan

MORRIS, Jan
Good-by to Britain, good-by British. il Horizon 19:40-1 Mr '77
Patriotism of the Scots. il Horizon 20:42-9 S '77
Takeoff for disaster. il Horizon 19:24-33 Ja '77
When an artist feels anxiety. il pors Horizon 20:16-22 N '77

MORRIS, Joan
Musical events. A. Porter. New Yorker 53:120+ Mr 21 '77 *

MORRIS, John G.
Shooting the presidents. il Pop Phot 81:79-81+ Ag '77
What happened at the press photographers convention. il Pop Phot 81:148-9+ O '77

MORRIS, John N.
Hours you keep; Halloween; Map problems; The Christmas letter; poems. Poetry 129:265-9 F '77
In there; poem. New Yorker 53:133 S 26 '77

about

Comment. R. B. Shaw. Poetry 129:235-6 Ja '77 *

MORRIS, John S.
Year's turning; poem. America 137:141 S 17 '77

MORRIS, Leon
Attraction of life on Mars. Chr Today 21:56-7 Mr 4 '77
Christianity is Christ. Chr Today 22:66-7 D 9 '77
Word and the words. Chr Today 21:40+ Je 3 '77

MORRIS, Lois Faith
Thinking about things. Engl J 66:57-8 S '77

MORRIS, M. See Kuiper, T. B. H. jt auth

MORRIS, Norval
From an expert—some ideas on what's needed to fight crime; interview. il pors U.S. News 82:61-3 Je 20 '77

MORRIS, Philip D.
Disciples of Christ-Roman Catholic dialogue. il New Cath World 220:196-201 Jl '77

MORRIS, Richard B.
Birth of the Constitution—our next big celebration? interview. por U.S. News 83:63-4 Jl 4 '77
Meet the men who were Presidents before Washington. il Smithsonian 8:92-4+ Ja '78
We the people of the United States: the bicentennial of a people's revolution. bibl f Am Hist R 82:1-19 F '77

MORRIS, Richard S.
Northeast versus the Sunbelt. Current 189:22-5 Ja '77

MORRIS, Roger
Borders. New Repub 177:12-13 O 22; 12-13 D 17 '77
Jimmy Carter's ruling class. Harpers 255:37-45 O '77

about

Word about Suetonius. New Repub 176:12 Mr 12 '77 *

MORRIS, Scot
(ed) See DeVore, I. New science of genetic self-interest

MORRIS, William C. See Botham, J. jt auth

MORRIS, Willie
Yazoo City: south toward home. il Time 110:13-14 Ag 1 '77

MORRISON, Bryan T.
Introduction to gyrator theory. il Pop Electr 12:58-9 Jl '77

MORRISON, David
Diameters of minor plants. il Sky & Tel 53:181-3 Mr '77

MORRISON, Frederick J. and others
Reading disability: an information-processing analysis. bibl il Science 196:77-9 Ap 1 '77

MORRISON, James
Serving Illinois inmates. il Wilson Lib Bull 51:522-5 F '77

MORRISON, Karl R.
Table top photography rediscovered. il Sch Arts 76:28-9 Je '77

MORRISON, Philip
Books. See issues of Scientific American
—and Morrison, Phylis
Annual survey of children's books on science and technology. Sci Am 237:26+ D '77

MORRISON, Phylis. See Morrison, Philip, jt auth

MORRISON, Toni
Song of Solomon; story; excerpt from novel. Redbook 149:237-60 S '77

MORRISON, Van
Van Morrison makes another good album. . . So? Period of transition. L. Baines. por Hi Fi 27:118-19 Je '77 *

MORRISON-Knudson Company, Inc
Giant garage sale. Forbes 120:192 N 15 '77
Morrison-Knudsen's foray into coal mining. il Bus W p52+ Je 20 '77

MORRISSEY, Daniel
Bishops play monopoly. Commonweal 104:528-30 Ag 19 '77

MORRISSEY, Robert B.
Energy: estimates and issues. America 136:523-4 Je 11 '77

MORRISTOWN, N.J.
Morristown's owls control city rats. Am City & County 92:30 O '77

MORRO Bay Region
Morro Bay kangaroo rat: rodent in danger. S. Medders. il map Nat Parks & Con Mag 52:10-12 D '77

MORRO, El. See El Morro National Monument

MORROW, Duncan
Of cowbells & common sense: the importance of park safety. il Nat Parks & Con Mag 51:16-18 My '77
—See Purkerson, L. L. jt auth

MORROW, Elizabeth Cutter
Pint of judgment; story. Sat Eve Post 249:62-3 D '77

MORROW, Lance
America after Viet Nam. il Horizon 19:42-7 Jl '77
Essay on the unfairness of life. Horizon 20:34-7 D '77
What is education? Who is educated? il Horizon 20:35-9 S '77; Same. Current 196:53-60 O '77

MORSE, Daniel E. and others
Hydrogen peroxide induces spawning in mollusks, with activation of prostaglandin endoperoxide synthetasé. bibl il Science 196:298-300 Ap 15 '77

MORSE, Douglass H.
Feeding behavior and predator avoidance in heterospecific groups. bibl BioScience 27:332-9 My '77
Resource partitioning in bumble bees: the role of behavioral factors. bibl il Science 197:678-80 Ag 12 '77

MORSE, Jonathan
Talking the developer's language: the financial analysis. il Archit Rec 162:56-7 D '77

MORSE, Margaret
(ed) Four experts give you a short course in china. House & Gard 149:20+ Je '77

MORSE, Philip McCord
Team approach to energy planning. por Bull Atom Sci 33:68-9 Mr '77

MORSE, Philip S. See Barmore, J. M. jt auth

MORSE, Richard, Mime Theatre. See Mime

MORSE, Roger A.
So you want to keep bees. il Conservationist 31:48 My '77

MORSE, Samuel French
Fee-fi-fo; poem. Horn Bk 53:641 D '77

MORSE, William C.
Drastic change in roles of schools. por Intellect 105:382-3 My '77

MORT, John
Orientation. New Yorker 53:33 Ap 4 '77

MORTALITY
Common death trends in early tribes. Sci N 111:358-9 Je 4 '77
Crowding, death rates linked in humans. Sci N 112:341 N 19 '77
When moved abruptly: death rates rise for nursing home patients. Aging 275:34 S '77
See also
Death

MORTENSEN, Barbara B.
Dental myths and misconceptions. Fam Health 9:14 D '77

MORTGAGE banks
Talent for finance, an eye on the tax code; Sonnenblick-Goldman Corp. il Bus W p56-7 Ag 1 '77

MORTGAGE bonds
Private sector apes Ginnie Mae. il Bus W p 110+ Jl 25 '77

MORTGAGE futures. See Commodity exchanges

MORTGAGE insurance companies. See Insurance companies

MORTGAGE interest deductions. See Income tax —Deductions

MORTGAGES
Boom in second mortgages. H. Rudnitsky. Forbes 120:58-9 Ag 1 '77
Great New York mortgage fire sale. Bus W p73-4 F 7 '77
Home buying is made easier. F. Casey. il Mech Illus 73:52+ F '77
How much house can you afford? M. Daly. il Bet Hom & Gard 55:56+ Je '77
How to shop for money when you're shopping for a house. P. Gross. por House & Gard 149:58+ O '77
If you are looking for a cut-rate mortgage—. U.S. News 82:40 Mr 21 '77
An interview with Anthony Frank—new thoughts on old mortgages. A. Frank. por Forbes 119:62 Ja 15 '77
It's coming on fast—the variable interest rate loan. il Sunset 159:90-1+ Jl '77
New money in old homes; second mortgages. D. Pauly and V. Smith. il Newsweek 90:80 D 5 '77
Pay ahead on your mortgage? il Changing T 31:15-17 Jl '77
Philadelphia solution to redlining; Philadelphia Mortgage Plan. il Bus W p54+ My 9 '77
Q&A about investments. S. Shulsky. por Ret Liv 17:52 Mr '77
Second mortgages entice the big banks. il Bus W p49 My 9 '77
Second mortgages: home-owners discover a hidden asset. il U.S. News 83:91-2 S 26 '77
VRMs go vroom in California. Forbes 119:110+ Ap 15 '77
Why Fannie, Ginnie, and Freddy can't do it. S. Rose. il Fortune 95:111+ Mr '77
See also
Federal Home Loan Mortgage Corporation
Federal National Mortgage Association
United States—Federal Home Loan Bank Board
United States—Federal Housing Administration

MORTICIANS. See Undertakers and undertaking

MORTISE and tenon joints. See Joints (carpentry)

MORTON, Beatrice K.
Listening: first steps in developmental drama. Engl J 66:68-73 My '77

MORTON, Bruce, and others
(ed) See Brzezinski, Z. Presidential assistant Brzezinski interviewed on Face the nation

MORTON, Dana
Swimmer's style. il pors Seventeen 36:182-3 Ap '77 *

MORTON, Gail
Ardent suitor. J. K. Footlick. il pors Newsweek 90:59 Jl 4 '77 *

MORTON, Gary
House where Lucille Ball lives! il pors Good H 185:132-5 S '77 *

MORTON, Herbert C.
Look at factors affecting the quality of working life; excerpt from Public economics and the quality of life, ed by L. Wingo and A. W. Evans. M Labor R 100:64-5 O '77

MORTON, Ree
Obituary
Art in Am il por 65:14 Jl '77. S. Burton

MORTUARY art. See Sepulchral monuments

MOSAIC viruses. See Viruses, Plant

MOSAICS
Great collection of tiny artistry—how it was made; Arthur Gilbert's micromosaics. M. Zucker. il Smithsonian 8:84-91 My '77
Mosaic mural. D. Oliver. il Sch Arts 76:33 Je '77
Spontaneous mosaics; egg shell mosaics. M. K. Gerstman. il Design (US) 78:10-11 mid-Summ '77

MOSAICS (biology)
Courtship of patchwork flies. J. A. Miller. il Sci N 111:107+ F 12 '77

MOSBY, Aline
(ed) See Chagall, M. Chagall at 90: when you have love, you work. That is my life

MOSCONE, George
Grudge match. C. J. Harper and G. C. Lubenow. por Newsweek 90:22 Ag 1 '77 *

MOSCOW
City around Red Square: Moscow. J. J. Putman. il map Nat Geog 153:2-24+ Ja '78
Snow is a friend. Time 109:16-17 F 14 '77

Art

Moscow. J. E. Bowlt. Art N 76:109-11 O '77

Education

English studies in the Soviet Union: a specialized language school in Moscow. P. E. Zevin. bibl f il Engl J 66:14-16 N '77

Music

See also
Opera—Russia

Theater

Moscow's underground hit; The master and Margarita. F. Coleman. il Newsweek 89:42 Je 13 '77

MOSCOW International Book Fair. See Book fairs

MOSCOW Olympics. See Olympic games, 1980

MOSCOW talks, March 1977. See Vance, C. R.—Visit to Russia, 1977

MOSELEY, Kent S.
Discipline alternative. Educ Digest 42:26-8 Ja '77

MOSELEY, Merritt W. Jr
News from the China-watchers. New Yorker 52:29 Ja 17 '77

MOSER, Charlotte
Deep in the art of Texas. il Ms 65:33-5 F '77
Houston (cont) il Art N 76:92-4 F; 94+ Ap; 92-4 O; 101-2 D '77
Houston's new cultural decision makers. il Art N 76:74-6 F '77
New Mexico: open land and psychic elbow room. il Art N 76:74-8 D '77

MOSER, Don
Better days still elude an old friend. il Nat Geog 151:360-91 Mr '77
Time of the angel: the U-2, Cuba, and the CIA. il Am Heritage 28:4-15 O '77

MOSES, Forrest
Forrest Moses: a man and his sanctuary; interview, ed by M. C. Nelson. il por Am Artist 41:44-9+ Ap '77

MOSES, Montrose J. and others
Mouse chromosome translocations: visualization and analysis by electron microscopy of the synaptonemal complex. bibl il Science 196:892-4 My 20 '77

MOSES, Sam
A. J, you're amazing. il por Sports Illus 46:16-19 Je 6 '77
Bull's-eye for the black dart. il Sports Illus 46:28-9 Ap 11 '77
Double-teaming the Talladega jinx. il Sports Illus 47:12-13 Ag 15 '77
If you can't prove it you ain't it. il pors Sports Illus 47:50-2+ O 17 '77
It was a piece of cake for Baker. il Sports Illus 46:26-7 Mr 21 '77
Land of Peter Pan. Sports Illus 47:34-6+ O 10 '77

MOSES, Sam—*Continued*
Man in the fiber glass mask. il por Sports Illus 46:36-8+ Je 27 '77
Motor sports (cont) Sports Illus 47:52-3 Jl 4; 108 O 10; 100+ N 14 '77
Nothin' could be finah. il Sports Illus 46:16-19 F 28 '77
On Gossamer wings, one of those things. il por Sports Illus 47:19-21 Ag 1 '77
Only way to go is up. il Sports Illus 46:24-6+ Je 6 '77
Pro skiing. Sports Illus 48:43-4 Ja 2 '78
Skateboards. Sports Illus 47:68+ N 21 '77
Skiing. Sports Illus 46:64-5 Mr 21 '77
Suddenly Mario is the magician again. il por Sports Illus 46:22-3 My 30 '77
Teaching them a lesson in timing. il Sports Illus 46:30-1 My 23 '77
MOSES David. See Berg, M. D.
MOSHÉ, Nancy Cornblath-. See Cornblath-Moshé, N.
MOSHER, Charles Adams
Blast-off for Swigert, reentry for Mosher. J. Walsh. Science 197:967 S 2 '77 *
MOSKIN, J. Robert
(ed) See Miller, L. Calling Dr Stress
MOSKOS, Charles C. Jr
Growing up Greek American. il por Society 14:64-71 Ja '77
MOSKOWITZ, Michael Ann
Special report: films and independent schools: a declaration of cooperation. il por Wilson Lib Bull 52:223-6 N '77
MOSLEY, Jean Bell
Summer I learned to see. il Read Digest 111: 88-90 Ag '77
MOSLEY, Sir Oswald Ernald, 6th Bart
British anti-Semitism, then and now. D. R. Katz. New Repub 176:21 F 5 '77 *
MOSQUITO control
Deadly mosquitoes dealt knockout blow; Houston. il Am City & County 92:53 Mr '77
Seeds that kill and eat mosquitoes. R. B. Dobbs. Org Gard & Farm 24:83 Ag '77
See also
Malaria—Prevention and control
MOSQUITOES
Malevolent mosquito. R. Conniff. il Read Digest 111:153-7 Ag '77
MOSQUITOES as carriers of infection
Venereal transmission of La Crosse (California encephalitis) arbovirus in aedes triseriatus mosquitoes. W. H. Thompson and B. J. Beaty. bibl il Science 196:530-1 Ap 29 '77
See also
Malaria
MOSS, Bill
Clever engineering shapes new tent designs. B. H. Berry. il por Pop Sci 211:128-30 O '77 *
Tents by Moss. S. Netherby. il por Field & S 82:128-9+ D '77 *
MOSS, Cynthia
Law of the jungle (revised): do you know that the king of beasts is a permissive father? il Ms 6:65-7 Ja '78
MOSS, Frank Edward
Senate reform too modest—Moss, Goldwater protest. por BioScience 27:9-10 Ja '77
MOSS, Frank T.
Sport fishermen. See issues of Yachting to August 1977
MOSS, Howard
Animal flowers; poems. il New Yorker 53:36-7 My 30 '77
Four birds; poem. New Yorker 53:40 Mr 28 '77
Gravel; poem. New Yorker 53:29 Ag 15 '77
Incomplete and disputed sonatas; poem. New Yorker 53:23 Ja 2 '78
Listening to jazz on a summer terrace; poem. New Yorker 53:34 Jl 25 '77
Standards; poem. New Yorker 53:35 S 19 '77
MOSS, Jerry
Independent that could: A&M records. T. Everett. il pors Hi Fi 27:132-4 Ap '77 *
MOSS, John Emerson
Will brokers continue to manage money? D. G. Santry. por Bus W p98 Ag 15 '77 *
MOSS, Laurence I.
Getting to know each other. pors Forbes 120:62 Ag 1 '77 *
MOSS, Ralph W.
Sunshine of your life. il Sci Digest 82:10-18 O '77
MOSS, Robert
Anglocommunism? Commentary 63:27-33 F; 8 My; 64:18-19 Jl '77
Britain's Ascot of the Left. Nat R 29:1238-40 O 28 '77
Fellow-traveling in Mozambique. Nat R 29:1495-6 D 23 '77
Let's look out for no. 1! il N Y Times Mag p31+ My 1 '77
—and Arostegui, Martin
Rocky road to democracy. Nat R 29:663-7 Je 10 '77
MOSS, Stanley
Fact song. Nation 225:184 S 3 '77
MOSSAD. See Intelligence service—Israel
MOSSE, George L.
On Nazism; interview, ed by M. A. Ledeen; excerpt from Nazism: a historical and comparative analysis of National socialism. bibl il Society 14:69-73 My '77
MOST, Bruce W.
Parent against parent. Nation 224:559-61 Mr 7 '77; Same with title Epidemic of child-stealing. Current 194:40-4 Jl '77
MOST, Harry Rutherford
Today's best book profits are in professional publishing. Pub W 211:39 Mr 21 '77
MOSTEL, Zero
Conquering Zero. J. Kroll. il por Newsweek 90: 71-2 S 19 '77 *
MOSTELLER, Dee
Roots of America's current major airframe and engine manufactuers. il Flying 101:240-7 S '77
MOTH orchids. See Orchids
MOTHER earth news
Writing or rewriting articles for the Mother earth news; excerpt. J. Shuttleworth. Writer 90:21-4 Je; 20-2+ Jl '77
MOTHER love. See Love, Maternal
MOTHER of us all; opera. See Thomson, V.
MOTHERCARE Ltd. See Specialty stores—Great Britain
MOTHERHOOD. See Mothers
MOTHERLESS families. See Single parent families
MOTHERS
How do you really feel about having children? questionnaire. il Redbook 149:117-19+ S '77
How to beat the after-the-baby blues. J. L. Lippert. Good H 184:228 My '77
I am the mother of eight, a housewife, a feminist—and happy: Jane Broderick's story; interview, ed by J. Lazarre. J. Broderick. il por Ms 5:51-5+ My '77; Discussion. 6:7-8+ S '77
Life with mother; famous people pay tribute to their mothers. il Ladies Home J 94:112-16+ My '77
Lovelier than roses on the vine. M. Hedin. McCalls 104:137+ My '77
Motherhood; address, July 16, 1977. S. L. Blumenfeld. Vital Speeches 43:661-6 Ag 15 '77
Problem may lie in the eye of the mother; seeking help for children from mental health professionals. J. Horn. Psychol Today 11:144-5 D '77
Professional mom; interview. J. Bear. il por Am Home 80:24-5+ My '77
Redbook's young mothers in a changing world; excerpt from Redbook's the young mothers. M. Mead. Redbook 149:33-4+ S '77
Should a career woman have children? E. M. Whelan. Harp Baz 110:101+ F '77
Starring mothers; mothers of cast members of Annie. A. Quindlen. il N Y Times Mag p50-1+ Ag 21 '77
What do you want to be when your kids grow up? M. S. Miller. il Am Home 80:52-3+ S '77
Young mother's story. See issues of Redbook
See also
Childbirth
Love, Maternal
Maternal deprivation
Single parent families
Stepparents

Employment

See Married women—Employment

Poetry

Ah, momma; poem; excerpt from Things that I do in the dark. J. Jordan. Redbook 150:74 D '77
MOTHERS, Unmarried
I refused to give up my baby; unwed teen-age mothers. L. David. il Seventeen 36:162-3+ Je '77
Lingering pain of surrendering a child. A. Baran and others. il Psychol Today 11:58-60+ Je '77
Make-believe world of teen-age maternity. L. Fosburgh. il N Y Times Mag p29-30+ Ag 7 '77
Seventeen's not so sweet when you're on your own—with a baby; interviews, ed by E. Stone. Parents Mag 52:55+ O '77
Tragedy of Joanne Bashold; neglect of infant. A. Adelson. il pors Good H 184:124-5+ Mr '77
Tragedy of Joanne; J. Bashold's neglect of infant. R. Severo. il pors Sr Schol 109:23-6+ Mr 24 '77
See also
Teen-age pregnancy
MOTHERS and children. See Parent-child relationship
MOTHERS and daughters. See Parent-child relationship
MOTHERS and sons. See Parent-child relationship
MOTHERS DAY gifts. See Gifts
MOTHERS discussion groups. See Discussion groups
MOTHERWELL, Robert
American in Paris. H. Kramer. il pors N Y Times Mag p 16-17+ Je 19 '77 *
Art. L. Alloway. Nation 226:29-30 Ja 7 '78 *

MOTHERWELL, Robert—*Continued*
Motherwell atelier. A. A. Cohen. il por Vogue 167:230-3+ Mr '77 *
Paris' prodigal son returns; retrospective at the Museum of Modern Art of the City of Paris. R. Hughes. il por Time 110:50-1 Jl 18 '77 *

MOTHS
Are you what you eat? il Chemistry 50:22 My '77
Batesian mimicry: selective advantage of color pattern. J. G. Sternburg and others. bibl il Science 195:681-3 F 18 '77
My useful friend, the cinnabar moth. V. H. Davis. Org Gard & Farm 24:89-90 My '77
See also
Caterpillars
Codling moths

MOTION aftereffects. See After images

MOTION in art. See Action in art

MOTION perception
Perception of moving targets. R. Sekuler and E. Levinson. il Sci Am 236:60-4+ Ja '77

MOTION picture acting
Reflections on the face in film. L. Shaffer. il Film Q 31:2-8 Wint '77

MOTION picture actors and actresses
Reel life heroes; excerpts from articles, 1938-1956. il Sat Eve Post 249:58-9 Jl '77
Spotlight. E. Miller. See issues of Seventeen
Year of the actress. C. Michener and M. Kasindorf. il por Newsweek 89:56-64+ F 14 '77
See also
Academy Awards (motion pictures)
Children as actors and actresses
Screen Actors Guild
also names of Motion picture actors and actresses, e.g. J. Crawford

Photographs

Bridge to the past; cast of Bridge too far pictured in their youth. il Ladies Home J 94:34 Jl '77

Political activities

Politics under the palms. B. Burlingham. il pors Esquire 87:47-52+ F '77

MOTION picture adaptations
Book, movie people gear up for the upcoming Raggedy Ann & Andy animated musical feature. il Pub W 211:112 F 28 '77
Hollywood and American literature: the American novel on the screen. H. Jay. Engl J 66:82-6 Ja '77
Humiliation in Hollywood; film version of The last tycoon. S. Koch. il Harpers 254:102-4 Mr '77
Out of Pandora's box; silent film of Lulu. D. Newlin. por Opera N 41:20+ Ap 2 '77
Rights and permissions. P. S. Nathan. See issues of Publishers weekly
Semi-tough goes to the movies. D. Jenkins. il Sports Illus 47:78-82+ N 7 '77

MOTION picture advertising. See Motion picture industry—Advertising

MOTION picture authorship
Béla Balázs in German exile. J. Ralmon. bibl il por Film Q 30:12-19 Spr '77
Faulkner filmography. B. F. Kawin. bibl il Film Q 30:12-21 Summ '77
Four-letter screenwriter; Slap shot writer, N. Dowd. J. Maslin. il por Newsweek 89:68-9 Mr 7 '77
Sylvester Stallone's rocky road to Rocky; interview, ed by P. Perry. S. Stallone. il pors Writers Digest 57:29-30 Jl '77
You ought to be in pictures. E. S. Stevens. Writers Digest 57:43-5 O '77

MOTION picture awards
See also
Academy Awards (motion pictures)

MOTION picture cameras
Complete shopping guide to super single 8 sound cameras. D. Sutherland. il Pop Phot 81:120-1+ O '77
Equipment report:
Beaulieu 5008-S multispeed super 8 sound camera. T. Galluzzo. il Mod Phot 41:65-8+ Mr '77
Bell & Howell Filmosonic 1237 XL super 8 sound camera. il Mod Phot 41:45-6 S '77
Canon auto zoom 512XL super 8 camera. T. Galluzzo. il Mod Phot 41:42+ F '77
Canon 514XL-S. T. Galluzzo. il Mod Phot 41:42+ My '77
Elmo 350SL super 8 sound camera. il Mod Phot 41:95-6+ N '77
Eumig 880 PMA super 8. T. Galluzzo. il Mod Phot 41:44-5 O '77
Fujica ZXM500 single 8 sound camera. T. Galluzzo. il Mod Phot 41:56+ D '77
Minolta XL-660 super 8 sound camera. T. Galluzzo. il Mod Phot 41:26+ Jl '77
First look: Kodak Ektasound 260. L. Drukker. il Pop Phot 81:121 S '77
Focus-free sound emerges; Elmo's 350SL. T. Galluzzo. il Mod Phot 41:38+ My '77
Good things in small packages: a case for the compact super 8. T. Galluzzo. il Mod Phot 41:40+ S '77
Guide to current XL cameras. Pop Phot 80:114-15 My '77
Movie cameras and projectors. L. Drukker. il Pop Phot 80:126-7+ Je '77
Take underwater movies from above the waves. I. Berger. il Pop Mech 147:18 Ap '77

Purchasing

Movie cameras. Consumer Rep 42:257-8 D '77

Sound equipment

Home-movie sound that sounds good. D. Sagarin. il Pop Mech 149:66-7 Ja '78

Testing

Test of time: is your camera and projector on the button? T. Galluzzo. il Mod Phot 41:54+ D '77

MOTION picture cameras, Instant print
At long last, Land's instant movies. il Time 109:66+ My 9 '77
From Polaroid: instant-color movies. L. Drukker. il Pop Phot 80:244 Je '77
How Polavision really works. D. Leavitt. il Pop Phot 81:103-7+ O '77
Inside Polaroid's instant-movie system. E. H. Ortner. il Pop Sci 211:96-8+ Ag '77
Instant movies; Polavision. E. H. Ortner. il Pop Sci 211:42 Jl '77
Instant movies: shoot now, see now; Polavision. H. Fantel. il Pop Mech 148:94-5+ Ag '77
Land's new wonder; Polavision. L. Langway and others. il por Newsweek 89:75+ My 9 '77
Moving instant: Polaroid movies from camera to screen in less than two min. T. Galluzzo. il Mod Phot 41:20+ Jl '77
Schwalberg at large; Polavision movies. B. Schwalberg. il Pop Phot 81:42+ Jl '77

MOTION picture cartoons. See Motion pictures—Animated cartoons

MOTION picture censorship
See also
Motion pictures—Moral and religious aspects

MOTION picture critics and criticism
Kind word for critics; excerpt from The films in my life; tr by L. Mayhew. F. Truffaut. Harpers 255:95+ O '77
See also
Motion picture reviews

MOTION picture directors
Cost of freedom; the director's function. S. Kauffmann. New Repub 177:26-8 O 1 '77
Finders keepers; casting directors. J. Maslin and M. Kasindorf. il Newsweek 89:92+ Mr 14 '77
See also
Altman, R.
Angelopoulos, T.
Antonioni, M.
Bergman, I.
Bertolucci, B.
Bresson, R.
Buñuel, L.
Cassenti, F.
Coppola, F. E.
DePalma, B.
Fassbinder, R. W.
Fellini, F.
Flaherty, R.
Godard, J. L.
Herzog, W.
Lucas, G.
Mankiewicz, J. L.
Oshima, N.
Pechter, W. S.
Peckinpah, S.
Poitier, S.
Polanski, R.
Resnais, A.
Rohmer, E.
Ross, H.
Russell, K.
Scola, E.
Scorsese, M.
Smith, H.
Spielberg, S.
Tanner, A.
Truffaut, F.
Vertov, D.
Watkins, P
Wenders, W.
Wertmüller, L.
Women motion picture directors

MOTION picture festivals
Conspirator in Berlin. P. Bogdanovich. Esquire 88:96+ D '77
Festival rites; New York Film Festival. D. Ansen. il Newsweek 90:102+ O 17 '77
Film festival: fifteenth New York Film Festival. H. Clurman. Nation 225:378-80, 412-14 O 15-22 '77
Film; second International Craft Film Festival. D. Hare. Craft Horiz 37:6+ D '77
Film; the American Film Festival. D. Hare. Craft Horiz 37:6+ O '77
Films that probe beneath the surface; New York Film Festival. J. M. Wall. Chr Cent 94:899-901 O 12 '77
In its way a great leap forward; International Ski Film Festival. A. Verschoth. il Sports Illus 47:60 O 17 '77

MOTION picture festivals—*Continued*
Personality plus; New York Film Festival. C. L. Westerbeck, Jr. Commonweal 104:757-8 N 25 '77
Quick cuts; New York Film Festival. F. Rich. Time 110:84 O 10 '77
West coast; San Diego Underwater Film Festival. A. Vance. il Pop Phot 80:70+ F '77
Year's top educational films; nineteenth annual American Film Festival. D. Boyle. il Am Lib 8:451-2 S '77
See also
Cannes International Film Festival

MOTION picture films
Mediums unite: super 8 reborn as video tape. M. Mikolas. il Mod Phot 41:46+ My '77

MOTION picture industry
See also
Motion picture production and direction
Women in the motion picture industry

Advertising

All the ads fit to print; ban on advertising of pornographic movies in newspapers. il Time 110:80 S 12 '77
Madison Avenue likes showbiz. il Bus W p 120 D 5 '77

Communist activities

After the blacklist; Hollywood Ten. E. Keerdoja. il Newsweek 89:10-10B Ja 24 '77

Finance

Cash-rich movie companies. il Bus W p 114-18+ My 16 '77
Is it worth making blockbuster films? il Bus W p36 Jl 11 '77
Star wars explosion. il Time 109:64 Je 27 '77
Who killed Hollywood? A. Trustman. il Atlantic 241:64-8+ Ja '78

Africa

Awakening African cinema. F. Bebey. il UNESCO Courier 30:30-3 My '77

Germany, West

Watching on the Rhine. S. Kauffmann. New Repub 177:24-5 Ag 20 '77

United States

After 50 years of talkies—change comes over the movie industry. il U.S. News 83:71-2 O 10 '77
Attack of the killer B's. M. Jefferson and M. Kasindorf. il Newsweek 90:52 Ag 1 '77
Big movie apple; shooting feature movies in New York City. M. Orth. il Newsweek 90:79+ D 12 '77
Case histories of business management: Hollywood artistic division; American Zoetrope. F. Coppola. il Esquire 88:190+ N '77
Current cinema. P. Kael. New Yorker 53:89 F 28 '77
Desperation in Hollywood: actor Jack Lemmon's view. J. Lemmon. il pors U.S. News 83:44 Ag 22 '77
For visitors to Los Angeles, the movie experience. il Sunset 159:64-71 S '77
New tycoons of Hollywood. R. Lindsey. il N Y Times Mag p 12-16+ Ag 7 '77
Politics under the palms. B. Burlingham. il pors Esquire 87:47-52+ F '77
To the heartland; with cameras; film production in the Midwest. il Time 110:71+ S 19 '77
Who killed Hollywood? A. Trustman. il Atlantic 241:64-8+ Ja '78
Will it be Paramount? Fourth television network. il Horizon 19:78-9 Jl '77
See also
Columbia Pictures Industries
Twentieth Century-Fox Film Corporation

MOTION picture locations. See Motion pictures—Setting and scenery

MOTION picture music. See Motion pictures—Music

MOTION picture novels. See Motion pictures and literature

MOTION picture photography
Film craft (cont of) Focus on film. L. Drukker. il por Pop Phot 81:22+ Jl; 56+ Ag '77
Film style and technology in the forties. B. Salt. il Film Q 31:46-57 Fall '77
How to make time in the movies. D. Sutherland. il Pop Phot 81:118-20+ S '77
Movie making. T. Galluzzo. See issues of Modern photography
See also
Motion pictures, Amateur
Photography of sports

Apparatus and supplies

New items of interest. T. Galluzzo. il Mod Phot 41:43 O '77
See also
Lenses, Photographic
Light filters
Motion picture cameras
Motion picture cameras, Instant print

Focusing

Auto focus? It's all done with mirrors. T. Galluzzo. il Mod Phot 41:40 Je '77
Focus-free sound emerges; Elmo's 350SL. T. Galluzzo. il Mod Phot 41:38+ My '77
Unsharp images—your lens, or is focusing the real villain? T. Galluzzo. il Mod Phot 41:42+ Ap '77

Lighting

Rated XL. D. Sutherland. il Pop Phot 80:112-15+ My '77

Processing

Process home movies at home? J. Lachky. il Mod Phot 41:46+ Je '77

Study and teaching

Filmmaker's eye (cont) N. R. Seider. il Pop Phot 80:106-7+ F; 116-17+ My '77

MOTION picture photography, Submarine
West coast; San Diego Underwater Film Festival. A. Vance. il Pop Phot 80:70+ F '77

MOTION picture plots. See Motion pictures—Plots, themes, etc.

MOTION picture premieres
Bobby Zarem, superflack. S. C. Cowley. il pors Newsweek 89:58-9 Ja 31 '77
Super flack muscles in; B. Zarem, arranger of premieres. il por Time 109:42-3 Ja 31 '77

MOTION picture production and direction
Big dream: a feature film to call your own; work of J. Meyer. T. Galluzzo. il pors Mod Phot 41:90+ N '77
Big movie apple; shooting feature movies in New York City. M. Orth. il Newsweek 90:79+ D 12 '77
Day on the Bergmanstrasse; filming of The serpent's egg. L. Janos. il por Time 109:78-9 F 14 '77
Drama defines dance: The turning point. N. M. Stoop. il pors Dance Mag 51:42-50 O '77
Fellini's unlovable Casanova. P. Schwartzman. il N Y Times Mag p22-4+ F 6 '77
Film director's approach to managing creativity; A. Penn's Night moves. E. Morley and A. Silver. il por Harvard Bus R 55:59-70 Mr '77
How they filmed a classic; excerpt from Making of the Wizard of Oz. A. Harmetz. il Read Digest 111:73-4+ N '77
I believe in this: a letter from Roberto Rossellini; with introd and ed by P. H. Wood. R. Rossellini. New Repub 177:27-30 Jl 2 '77
Look, Gideon—: a talk with Lina Wertmüller; ed by G. Bachmann. L. Wertmüller. pors Film Q 30:2-11 Spr '77
Making of Julia. S. Ferris. il por Horizon 20:86-90+ O '77
Messy fight for the final cut; 1900. il Time 109:70-1 My 2 '77
Onward and upward with the superman. il Time 110:64-5 Ag 1 '77
Rocky comes to Dubuque; location shooting of F.I.S.T. F. Maier. il pors Newsweek 89:28 Je 27 '77
Semi-tough goes to the movies. D. Jenkins. il Sports Illus 47:78-82+ N 7 '77
Somewhere over the rainbow this fall will be books on Oz from Knopf and Random House; interview, ed by R. Dahlin. V. Wilson. il Pub W 212:51 Jl 25 '77
Star wars; the year's best movie. il Time 109:54-6+ My 30 '77; Same abr. with title How Star wars was made. il Read Digest 111:162-3+ S '77
Tatum on location; filming of International Velvet. G. Clarke. il por Time 110:94+ O 31 '77
Television's little dramas. H. Gold. il Harpers 254:88-93 Mr '77
Truckin' with the big Iguana; filming of Convoy. il por Time 110:73-4 Jl 4 '77
Watching the Apocalypse; filming Apocalypse now. M. Orth. il pors Newsweek 89:57-8+ Je 13 '77
Watching Wiseman watch. D. Eames. il por N Y Times Mag p96-102+ O 2 '77
See also
Motion picture directors
Motion pictures—Setting and scenery

MOTION picture projection

Sound accompaniment

Add sound to your home movies. A. Jaremko. il Radio-Electr 48:45-8+ Ag '77

MOTION picture projectors
Equipment report:
Bauer T60 stereosound super 8 projector. T. Galluzzo. il Mod Phot 41:42+ Je '77
Eumig R 2000. il Mod Phot 41:46-7 Ap '77
Kodak Ektasound 285 moviedeck projector. T. Galluzzo. il Mod Phot 41:66+ Ag '77
First look:
Elmo ST-600; Elmo ST11200HD; Eumig R 2000. L. Drukker. il Pop Phot 81:152-3+ D '77
Movie cameras and projectors. L. Drukker. il Pop Phot 80:126-7+ Je '77
Movie projectors. Consumer Rep 42:253-4 D '77

MOTION picture projectors—*Continued*

Testing

Test of time: is your camera and projector on the button? T. Galluzzo. il Mod Phot 41:54+ D '77

MOTION picture reviews

Best and the worst. J. Kroll. il Newsweek 91: 58-9 Ja 9 '78
Current cinema. Chr Cent 94:517, 635, 792 My 25, Jl 6, S 14 '77
Current cinema. P. Gilliatt. See issues of New Yorker, March 28, 1977 to September 19, 1977
Current cinema. P. Kael. See issues of New Yorker to March 21, 1977; September 26, 1977-
Family movie guide. J. Ripp. See issues of Parents' magazine & better homemaking
Film. See issues of Ms.
Film. D. Brudnoy. Nat R 29:839-40 Jl 22 '77
Films. R. Hatch. See occassional issues of Nation
Films. S. Kauffmann. See occasional issues of New republic
Films. M. Ronan. See occasional issues of Senior scholastic including World week
Films/TV. R. A. Blake. See issues of America
Goings on about town. See issues of New Yorker
Looking and listening. See issues of Retirement living
McCall's movie guide for puzzled parents. See issues of McCall's
Movies. J. Crist. See issues of Saturday review to August 6, 1977
Movies. D. Davis. See issues of American home
Movies. W. S. Pechter. See alternate issues of Commentary to May 1977
Movies. R. Reed. See issues of Vogue
Movies. A. M. Schlesinger, Jr. il Sat R 5:46+ O 29; 62-3 D 10 '77; 46 Ja 7 '78
Movies. J. Simon. il Nat R 29:1375-7 N 25; 1443-4 D 9 '77; 30:38+ Ja 6 '78
Movies. K. Turan. See alternate issues of Progressive
On screen. L. Quart. Intellect 105:399; 106:78, 159, 245 Je, Ag, O, D '77
On the screen. M. J. Sobran, Jr. Nat R 29: 392+, 505-6, 622-3, 1061-2 Ap 1, 29, My 27, S 16 '77
Reviews. See issues of Film quarterly
Screen. C. L. Westerbeck, Jr. See issues of Commonweal
Spotlight. E. Miller. See issues of Seventeen
What's happening. G. Shalit. See issues of Ladies' home journal

Single works

Aguirre, the Wrath of God
Nation 224:508 Ap 23 '77
New Repub 176:23-4 Ap 16 '77
New Yorker il 53:127-8 Ap 11 '77
Time il 109:92-3 My 16 '77
Airport '77
Sat R 4:52 Ap 16 '77
Time 109:78 My 2 '77
All this and World War II
Time 109:59 Ja 31 '77
American friend
Commonweal 104:725-6 N 11 '77
Nation 225:380 O 15 '77
New Repub 177:27-8 O 1 '77
New Yorker 53:174-9 O 17 '77
Newsweek 90:71+ O 3 '77
Annie Hall
America 136:431 My 7 '77
Chr Cent 94:593-4 Je 22 '77
Commonweal 104:306-7 My 13 '77
Esquire 87:72-6+ My '77
Nat R 29:622-3 My 27 '77
Nation 224:540 Ap 30 '77
New Repub 176:22 My 14 '77
New Yorker 53:136+ Ap 25 '77
Newsweek 89:78 My 2 '77
Sat R il 4:38-9 il My 14 '77
Time 110:69-71 S 26 '77
Time il 109:70 Ap 25 '77
Vogue il 167:22 Je '77
Another man, another chance
Time il 110:70+ D 19 '77
Apocalypse now
Newsweek 89:57-8+ Je 13 '77
Au hasard, Balthazar
Film Q il 31:19-31 Fall '77
Audrey Rose
Sat R il 4:35 Ap 30 '77
Time 109:78 My 2 '77
Augustine of Hippo
New Yorker 53:118-19 Je 6 '77
Bad news bears in breaking training
Commonweal 104:533 Ag 19 '77
Newsweek 90:77+ Ag 8 '77
Sports Illus 47:55 S 12 '77
Best way
New Repub 177:24 Jl 30 '77
Between the lines
America 136:528 Je 11 '77
Ms 6:31-4 Ag '77
Nation 224:633 My 21 '77
New Yorker 53:126 My 9 '77
Newsweek il 89:108 My 9 '77
Sat R 4:39 My 14 '77
Time il 109:89 My 9 '77
Black and white in color
America 136:527-8 Je 11 '77
Nation 224:700 Je 4 '77
New Repub 176:23 Je 18 '77
New Yorker 53:109-10 My 23 '77
Sat R il 4:40 My 28 '77
Time il 109:91-2 My 16 '77
Black Sunday
America 136:383 Ap 23 '77
Mademoiselle 83:26+ Je '77
New Repub 176:22 Ap 9 '77
New Yorker 53:118+ Ap 4 '77
Newsweek il 89:73 Ap 4 '77
Sat R il 4:34-5 Ap 30 '77
Sports Illus 46:66 Ap 11 '77
Time il 109:68 Ap 4 '77
Bobby Deerfield
Am Home 80:12 D '77
Mademoiselle il 83:14 N '77
New Repub 177:20-2 O 22 '77
New Yorker 53:130-3 O 3 '77
Newsweek il 90:71 O 3 '77
Sat R 5:46 N 26 '77
Time il 110:83-4 O 10 '77
Vogue 167:50 O '77
Bound for glory
America 136:135-6 F 12 '77
Progressive 41:53 My '77
Psychol Today 10:22 Mr '77
Bridge too far
Commonweal 104:432-3 Jl 8 '77
New Yorker 53:90-1 Je 20 '77
Newsweek 89:65+ Je 20 '77
Sat R il 4:40-1 Je 25 '77
Time il 109:92 Je 13 '77
Brothers
America 136:384 Ap 23 '77
Newsweek 89:76 Ap 4 '77
Time 109:82 Ap 18 '77
By the blood of others
New Yorker 53:110+ S 19 '77
Carrie
Film Q il 31:32-8 Fall '77
Chac
New Yorker 53:68-70 S 5 '77
Choirboys
Newsweek 91:59 Ja 2 '78
Time 111:82 Ja 16 '78
Close encounters of the third kind
America 137:445 D 17 '77
Atlantic 241:90-1 Ja '78
Nat R 29:1500-2 D 23 '77
Nation 225:668-9 D 17 '77
New Repub 177:20-2 D 10 '77
New Yorker 53:174-8+ N 28 '77
Newsweek il 90:88-9+ N 21 '77
Sat R 5:80 D 10 '77
Sat R 5:46 Ja 7 '78
Sr Schol il 110:TE5 D 15 '77
Time il 110:102-3+ N 7 '77
Convoy
Time il 110:73-4 Jl 4 '77
Cookies
Time 109:89 Mr 21 '77
Cousin Angélica
Nation 224:698+ Je 4 '77
New Repub 176:26 My 28 '77
New Yorker 53:109 My 23 '77
Sat R 4:47 Jl 23 '77
Time il 109:76 Je 6 '77
Cría!
Nation 224:698 Je 4 '77
New Yorker 53:117 Je 6 '77
Sat R 4:47 Jl 23 '77
Time il 109:76 Je 6 '77
Cross of iron
America 136:528 Je 11 '77
New Repub 176:26 My 28 '77
New Yorker 53:110-11 My 23 '77
Newsweek il 89:73 My 23 '77
Sat R il 4:45 Je 11 '77
Time il 109:94 Je 13 '77
Darby O'Gill and the little people
Nat R 29:952-3 Ag 19 '77
Deep
Commonweal 104:499-500 Ag 5 '77
New Yorker 53:83 Jl 4 '77
Newsweek il 89:60 Je 27 '77
Sat R il 4:46 Jl 23 '77
Sr Schol 109:36-7 Mr 24 '77
Time il 109:60 Je 27 '77
Demon seed
Time 109:78 My 2 '77
Devil probably
Nation 225:379 O 15 '77
Domino principle
Sat R 4:42 Ap 2 '77
Time 109:93-4 My 16 '77
Duellists
Vogue 167:50 Ag '77
Eagle has landed
America 136:383-4 Ap 23 '77
New Repub 176:24 Ap 16 '77
New Yorker 53:121-2 Ap 4 '77
Newsweek 89:73+ Ap 4 '77
Time il 109:68 Ap 11 '77
Edvard Munch
Craft Horiz 37:16+ F '77
Film Q 30:38-46 Wint '76
Effi Briest
New Repub 176:20-1 Je 25 '77
New Yorker 53:81-2 Je 27 '77

MOTION picture reviews—Single works—*Cont.*
L'Empire des Sens. See In the realm of the senses
Les enfants du paradis
Nation 224:283-5 Mr 5 '77
Enforcer
Ms il 5:32+ Mr '77
New Yorker 52:86-8 Ja 24 '77
Equus
America 137:314 N 5 '77
Nat R 29:1444 D 9 '77
New Repub 117:24-6 N 5 '77
New Yorker 53:120-2 N 7 '77
Newsweek il 90:125 O 24 '77
Time il 110:91 O 31 '77
Exorcist II: the heretic
America 137:57 Jl 30 '77
New Yorker 53:70-1 Jl 18 '77
Newsweek 89:61-2 Je 27 '77
Time 110:54 Jl 4 '77
Fellini's Casanova
America 136:170 F 26 '77
Commentary 63:69-71 My '77
Commonweal 104:240-1 Ap 15 '77
Commonweal 104:277-8 Ap 29 '77
Film Q il 30:24-31 Summ '77
Mademoiselle 83:118+ Ap '77
N Y Times Mag il p22-4+ F 6 '77
Nation 224:252-3 F 26 '77
New Repub 176:28-9 Mr 5 '77
Newsweek il 89:60-1 Ja 24 '77
Psychol Today 11:26+ Je '77
Sat R 4:40-1 F 19 '77
Time il 109:70 F 21 '77
Film about a woman who...
Art in Am 65:86-90 My '77
First love
Newsweek 90:78 N 14 '77
Time il 110:85 N 14 '77
Fraternity row
Sat R 4:41 Jl 9 '77
Freaky Friday
Newsweek il 89:72 F 28 '77
Sr Schol 109:30 F 10 '77
Fun with Dick and Jane
New Repub 176:20 F 26 '77
New Yorker 53:90-1 F 28 '77
Newsweek 89:90-2 F 21 '77
Progressive 41:53-4 My '77
Sat R 4:41 F 19 '77
Time il 109:78 F 7 '77
Gauntlet
Newsweek il 91:59 Ja 2 '78
General
Film Q il pors 31:38-45 Fall '77
Goalie
New Repub 176:26-7 Ja 29 '77
Goodbye girl
New Repub 177:22 D 17 '77
Newsweek il 90:109 D 5 '77
Time il 110:110-11 N 28 '77
La grande bourgeoise
New Repub 177:24-5 S 10 '77
New Yorker 53:45 Ag 8 '77
Newsweek 90:81 Ag 8 '77
Time il 110:61+ Ag 15 '77
Greased lightning
New Yorker 53:66-7 Ag 22 '77
Newsweek 90:77 Ag 15 '77
Sports Illus 47:39 Ag 15 '77
Time il 110:61 Ag 15 '77
Greatest
Newsweek 89:63 My 30 '77
Sports Illus il 46:45 My 30 '77
Time il 109:76 Je 6 '77
Handle with care
New Yorker 53:150-4 O 24 '77
Time il 110:88+ N 7 '77
Heroes
Newsweek 90:78 N 14 '77
Time il 110:86+ N 21 '77
High anxiety
New Yorker 53:70+ Ja 9 '78
Newsweek il 91:58 Ja 2 '78
High Street
Nation 225:58+ Jl 9 '77
New Repub 177:18 Jl 23 '77
Hour of the wolf
Film Q 30:23-34 Wint '76
I never promised you a rose garden
America 137:112 Ag 27 '77
New Yorker 54:45 Ag 8 '77
Newsweek il 90:57 Jl 25 '77
Time 110:69 Jl 25 '77
Illusion travels by streetcar
New Yorker 53:65 Ag 29 '77
In search of Noah's ark
Newsweek il 89:56 Ja 31 '77
In the realm of the senses
Film Q il 30:58-61 Wint '76
New Repub 177:26 Jl 2 '77
Psychol Today 10:18+ F '77
Island of Dr Moreau
Sr Schol il 109:25 My 5 '77
Sr Schol il 110:12 S 22 '77
Time il 110:87 Jl 18 '77
Islands in the stream
America 136:244 Mr 19 '77
New Repub 176:20 Mr 19 '77
New Yorker 53:125-9 Mr 14 '77
Newsweek 89:94+ Mr 14 '77
Sat R il 4:40-1 Mr 19 '77
Sr Schol 109:36 My 19 '77
Time il 109:89 Mr 21 '77
It
Commonweal 104:790-1 D 9 '77
Jabberwocky
Nation 224:633-4 My 21 '77
New Yorker 53:124-5 My 9 '77
Sat R 4:44 Je 11 '77
Time il 109:89 My 9 '77
Jacob the liar
Nation 224:606 My 14 '77
Sat R 4:41 My 28 '77
Time il 109:92-3+ Je 13 '77
Jail bait
New Repub 176:22-3 Je 4 '77
Jaws
Society 14:78-81 My '77
Jeanne Dielman
Film Q 30:2-8 Summ '77
Jonah who will be 25 in the year 2000
Film Q il 30:36-42 Spr '77
Julia
America 137:268-9 O 22 '77
Atlantic 240:96-8 N '77
Horizon il 20:86-90+ O '77
Mademoiselle 83:76 Mr '77
Ms il 6:53-5 O '77
Nat R 29:1375-7 N 25 '77
Nation 225:475-6 N 5 '77
New Repub 177:32-3 O 15 '77
New Yorker 53:94+ O 10 '77
Newsweek il 90:78-82+ O 10 '77
Sat R il 5:46+ O 29 '77
Sr Schol il 110:21-2 D 15 '77
Time il 110:83 O 10 '77
Kentucky fried movie
Time il 110:76 Ag 29 '77
King Kong
America 136:87-8 Ja 29 '77
Commonweal 104:85-6 F 4 '77
New Repub 176:25 Ja 15 '77
Progressive 41:51-2 Mr '77
Sat R il 4:41 F 5 '77
Kristina talking pictures
Art in Am 65:86-90 My '77
Lacemaker
Nation 225:413 O 22 '77
Time il 110:88 N 7 '77
Last remake of Beau Geste
Commonweal 104:532 Ag 19 '77
Mademoiselle 83:28 O '77
New Yorker 53:78-9 Jl 25 '77
Time 110:58 Ag 8 '77
Last tycoon
Atlantic 239:92-4 F '77
Commonweal 104:51-2 Ja 21 '77
Harpers il 254:102-4 Mr '77
Mademoiselle il 83:171-3 F '77
Sr Schol 109:30 F 10 '77
Late show
America 136:244 Mr 19 '77
Nation 224:315 Mr 12 '77
New Repub 176:24 Mr 12 '77
New Yorker 52:109-10+ F 7 '77
Newsweek il 89:88+ F 21 '77
Psychol Today il 10:24 My '77
Sat R 4:41 Mr 19 '77
Time il 109:78 F 7 '77
Let joy reign supreme
New Repub 177:32-3 S 17 '77
New Yorker 53:108 S 19 '77
Newsweek 90:73 O 3 '77
Little girl who lives down the lane
Time 110:76 Ag 29 '77
Little night music
Vogue 167:220 S '77
Looking for Mr Goodbar
America 137:314 N 5 '77
Nat R 29:1443 D 9 '77
New Yorker 53:147-50 O 24 '77
Newsweek 90:126 O 24 '77
Sat R il 5:62-3 D 10 '77
Time il 110:104 O 24 '77
Time 110:68-9 S 26 '77
Lumière
Commonweal 104:114 F 18 '77
Commonweal 104:149-50 Mr 4 '77
Film Q 30:53-7 Spr '77
MacArthur
America 137:56 Jl 30 '77
Nat R 29:1061-2 S 16 '77
New Repub 177:24 Jl 30 '77
Newsweek 90:77-8 Jl 4 '77
Sat R il 4:40-1 Jl 9 '77
Time il 110:54 Jl 4 '77
Man on the roof
Nation 224:446 Ap 9 '77
Time il 109:79+ Ap 18 '77
Man who loved women
Nat R 30:40 Ja 6 '78
Nation 225:510 N 12 '77
New Repub 177:20 O 22 '77
New Yorker 53:125-6 D 5 '77
Newsweek il 90:96 O 31 '77
Sat R 5:46 N 26 '77
Time 110:84 O 10 '77

MOTION picture reviews—Single works—*Cont.*
Marathon man
Nat R 29:554-5 My 13 '77
March or die
New Repub 177:22-3 S 3 '77
New Yorker 53:68 Ag 22 '77
Time il 110:56 Ag 22 '77
Marquise of O
Commonweal 104:21-3 Ja 7 '77
Film Q il 30:50-3 Spr '77
Mikey and Nicky
Sat R 4:49 Ja 22 '77
Time il 109:59 Ja 31 '77
Mr Billion
Time 109:93+ Mr 28 '77
Mr Klein
Time 110:88+ N 14 '77
Mohammad, Messenger of God
Newsweek il 89:89 Mr 21 '77
Time il 109:16-17 Mr 21 '77
Mother Küsters goes to heaven
New Repub 176:22 Je 4 '77
New Yorker 53:118+ Mr 28 '77
Time 109:93 Mr 28 '77
Nasty habits
America 136:332+ Ap 9 '77
Commonweal 104:258 Ap 29 '77
New Repub 176:20 F 26 '77
New Yorker 53:115-18 F 21 '77
Newsweek 89:86-7 Mr 28 '77
Sat R 4:41 Ap 2 '77
Time 109:73 Ap 25 '77
Network
Chr Cent 94:178-9 F 23 '77
Nat R 29:338-9 Mr 18 '77
New York, New York
Commonweal 104:467-8 Jl 22 '77
Mademoiselle il 83:28 S '77
New Repub 177:18-19 Jl 23 '77
New Yorker 53:82 Jl 4 '77
Newsweek 89:80-4+ My 16 '77
Newsweek il 89:61 Je 27 '77
Progressive 41:39 S '77
Sat R 4:47 Jl 23 '77
Time il 109:61 Je 27 '77
Nickelodeon
Mademoiselle 83:32+ Mr '77
New Yorker 52:99-100 Ja 17 '77
Night porter
Film Q 30:35-8 Wint '76
1900
America 137:403 D 3 '77
Commonweal 104:820 D 23 '77
Commonweal 105:16-18 Ja 6 '78
Nat R 29:1503 D 23 '77
Nation 225:444-5 O 29 '77
Nation 225:573-4 N 26 '77
New Repub 177:20-1 N 26 '77
New Yorker 53:148-54+ O 31 '77
Newsweek il 90:101-2 O 17 '77
Progressive 41:50-1 N '77
Time 109:70-1 My 2 '77
Time il 110:99 O 17 '77
1976 minus one
Commentary 63:75-7 Mr '77
Numéro deux
Film Q 30:61-3 Wint '76
Oh, God!
Chr Cent 94:1085 N 23 '77
Chr Today 22:23-4 D 30 '77
Newsweek 90:126 O 24 '77
Sr Schol 110:32 N 17 '77
Time 110:90 O 31 '77
One on one
Newsweek il 90:78 S 5 '77
Sports Illus 47:48 Jl 11 '77
Sr Schol il 110:47 O 20 '77
Time il 110:69 Jl 25 '77
One sings, the other doesn't
America 137:269 O 22 '77
Ms il 6:26+ Ja '78
New Repub 177:26-7 O 8 '77
New Yorker 53:75-8 N 14 '77
Orca
Oceans 10:68 S '77
Time 110:59+ Ag 8 '77
Ossessione
New Yorker 53:70 Je 13 '77
Other side of midnight
New Repub 177:22-3 S 3 '77
New Yorker 53:84-6 Jl 11 '77
Newsweek 89:64 Je 13 '77
Time il 109:73 Je 20 '77
Outlaw blues
Times il 110:61 S 5 '77
Outrageous
New Yorker 53:93-4 S 12 '77
Newsweek 90:75-6 Ag 22 '77
Time il 110:60 S 5 '77
Padre padrone
Nation 225:378-9 O 15 '77
Nation 226:30 Ja 7 '78
New Yorker 53:127-30 O 3 '77
Newsweek il 91:81 Ja 16 '78
Time il 111:82 Ja 16 '78
Pardon mon affaire
Sat R il 4:44 Je 11 '77
Time il 110:88 Jl 18 '77
Pete's dragon
Time il 110:105+ D 5 '77
Phantom President
New Repub 176:64-5 Ja 22 '77
Piece of the action
Newsweek il 90:96 O 31 '77
Time 110:90 N 14 '77
Pink panther strikes again
New Yorker 52:98 Ja 17 '77
Sat R 4:50 Ja 22 '77
Pipe dreams
Time il 109:59 Ja 31 '77
Providence
Commonweal 104:181-2 Mr 18 '77
Film Q il 30:21-4 Summ '77
Film Q il 31:10-18 Fall '77
Nation 224:188-9 F 12 '77
New Repub 176:18-19 F 12 '77
New Yorker 52:53-5 Ja 31 '77
Newsweek 89:72-3 F 28 '77
Psychol Today 10:18 Ap '77
Sat R il 4:42 Mr 5 '77
Time 109:70+ F 21 '77
Vogue 167:200+ Ap '77
Rebellion in Patagonia
Commonweal 104:403-4 Je 24 '77
New Yorker 53:98-100 My 16 '77
Sat R 4:41 My 28 '77
Red poster
Film Q il 31:48-51 Wint '77
Rocky
America 136:87-8 Ja 29 '77
America 137:78-80 Ag 13 '77
Newsweek il 89:70-2+ Ap 11 '77
Sr Schol il 109:27 Ja 13 '77
Seventeen por 36:118-19+ F '77
Rollercoaster
New Yorker 53:90-1 Je 20 '77
Sat R il 4:46-7 Jl 23 '77
Sr Schol il 110:31 O 6 '77
Time il 110:55+ Jl 11 '77
Roseland
America 137:362 N 19 '77
Commonweal 104:757-8 N 25 '77
Nation 225:412 O 22 '77
New Yorker 53:126-9 D 5 '77
Newsweek 90:125 O 24 '77
Time 110:101 O 17 '77
Salò, 120 days of Sodom
Nation 225:380 O 15 '77
New Repub 177:24 O 29 '77
Sandakan 8
Commonweal 104:659-60 O 14 '77
Ms 6:49 O '77
New Repub 177:24 S 10 '77
New Yorker 53:60+ Ag 15 '77
Satan's brew
New Yorker 53:62-3 Ag 15 '77
Saturday night fever
New Yorker 53:59-60 D 26 '77
Newsweek il 90:65 D 19 '77
Time il 110:69-70 D 19 '77
Scenes from a marriage
Chr Cent il 94:535-40 Je 1 '77
Semi-tough
New Repub 177:22-3 D 17 '77
New Yorker 53:184-8 D 12 '77
Newsweek il 90:98 N 28 '77
Sports Illus il 47:78-82+ N 7 '77
Time il 110:85 N 21 '77
Sensual man
New Yorker 53:66 Ag 22 '77
Sentinel
Newsweek il 89:72 F 28 '77
Time 109:78 F 28 '77
Serpent's egg
Horizon il 20:16-22 N '77
Short eyes
Nation 225:381 O 15 '77
New Repub 177:24-5 O 29 '77
New Yorker 53:127-8+ S 26 '77
Time il 110:84 O 10 '77
Shout at the devil
Sr Schol il 109:28 Ja 27 '77
Silver Streak
New Yorker 52:98-9 Ja 17 '77
Sat R 4:49-50 Ja 22 '77
Slap shot
America 136:244 Mr 19 '77
Mademoiselle 83:42+ My '77
Ms il 6:31+ Jl '77
Nat R 29:392+ Ap 1 '77
New Repub 176:20-1 Mr 19 '77
New Yorker 53:91-5 Mr 7 '77
Newsweek 89:68-9 Mr 7 '77
Sat R 4:41-2 Ap 2 '77
Sports Illus 46:42 Mr 7 '77
Time il 109:73-4 Mr 14 '77
Small change
Film Q il 30:42-5 Spr '77
New Repub 176:23-5 Ap 2 '77
Smokey and the bandit
Time 109:73 Je 20 '77
Sorcerer
New Yorker 53:70-1 Jl 18 '77
Newsweek il 90:77 Jl 4 '77
Progressive 41:38 S '77
Time il 110:55 Jl 11 '77
Special day
Am Home 80:12 D '77
New Yorker 53:173-4 O 17 '77
Time 110:96+ O 3 '77

MOTION picture reviews—Single works—*Cont.*
Spy who loved me
Newsweek 90:77 Ag 8 '77
Time 110:58 Ag 8 '77
Star is born
Ms 5:39-40 My '77
New Repub 176:24-5 Ja 15 '77
Sat R il 4:41-2 F 5 '77
Star wars
America 136:568 Je 25 '77
Chr Cent 94:1044-5 N 9 '77
Chr Cent il 94:666-8 Jl 20 '77
Chr Today il 21:28-9 S 23 '77
Commonweal 104:433 Jl 8 '77
Ladies Home J 94:12 Ag '77
Nat R 29:839-40 Jl 22 '77
Nation 224:794 Je 25 '77
New Repub 176:22 Je 18 '77
New Yorker 53:69-70 Je 13 '77
New Yorker 53:123 S 26 '77
Newsweek 89:81 Je 13 '77
Newsweek il 89:60-1 My 30 '77
Newsweek il 90:77 Ag 29 '77
Read Digest 111:162-3+ S '77
Sat R il 4:40 Jl 9 '77
Sat R 5:80 D 10 '77
Sr Schol il 110:28 S 8 '77
Time 111:72 Ja 2 '78
Time il 109:54-6+ My 30 '77
Time il 109:64 Je 27 '77
Strongman Ferdinand
New Yorker 53:77-8 Jl 25 '77
Stroszek
Commonweal 104:624-5 S 30 '77
Nation 225:157 Ag 20 '77
New Repub 177:25 Ag 20 '77
New Yorker 53:74+ Jl 25 '77
Newsweek 90:77 Ag 15 '77
Sunshine boys
Sat Eve Post 249:14-15 Mr '77
Superman
Time il 110:64-5 Ag 1 '77
Telefon
Newsweek 91:59 Ja 2 '78
Time 110:72 D 26 '77
That obscure object of desire
Nat R 29:1503-4 D 23 '77
Nation 225:444 O 29 '77
Nation 225:572-3 N 26 '77
New Yorker 53:128-30 D 19 '77
Newsweek il 90:109 D 5 '77
O Thiasos
Film Q il 30:46-50 Spr '77
Thieves
New Yorker 53:91-2 F 28 '77
Sat R 4:41 F 19 '77
Time il 109:78 F 28 '77
Three women
America 136:431-2 My 7 '77
Commonweal 104:369 Je 10 '77
Film Q il 31:10-18 Fall '77
Intellect 106:159 O '77
Ms il 5:22+ Je '77
Nation 224:572-3 My 7 '77
New Repub 176:26-7 Ap 30 '77
New Yorker 53:133-5 Ap 18 '77
Newsweek 89:64 Ap 18 '77
Progressive 41:37-8 Jl '77
Psychol Today 11:14+ Ag '77
Sat R il 4:51-2 Ap 16 '77
Time 109:78+ My 2 '77
Truck
New Yorker 53:123-7 S 26 '77
Turning point
America 137:362 N 19 '77
Dance Mag 51:104-6 D '77
Dance Mag il 51:42-50 O '77
Ms il 6:29-30 Ja '78
Nat R 29:1502 D 23 '77
New Repub 177:22-3 N 19 '77
New Yorker 53:183-6, 212+ N 21 '77
Newsweek il 90:97-8 N 28 '77
Seventeen il pors 36:134-5+ N '77
Time il 110:111-12 N 28 '77
Vogue il 167:34 D '77
Twilight's last gleaming
Time il 109:72 F 21 '77
Uncle Vanya
New Yorker 53:132-3 Ap 18 '77
Union maids
New Yorker 53:97-8 My 16 '77
Valentino
Am Home 80:12 D '77
Dance Mag 51:60-1 D '77
Film Q il 31:19-24 Wint '77
New Yorker 53:119-20 N 7 '77
Newsweek il 90:102 O 17 '77
Time il 110:98 O 17 '77
Vogue il 167:149+ Ag '77
Victory march
Commentary 63:75-7 Mr '77
We all loved each other so much
America 136:569 Je 25 '77
Film Q il 31:45-7 Wint '77
Nation 224:766 Je 18 '77
New Repub 176:22 Je 18 '77
New Yorker 53:117-18 Je 6 '77
Sat R 4:47 Jl 23 '77
Welcome to L.A.
Commonweal 104:214-15 Ap 1 '77
Nation 224:380-1 Mr 26 '77
New Repub 176:22-3 Ap 2 '77
New Yorker 53:112-14 Mr 21 '77
Newsweek il 89:88 F 21 '77
Sat R 4:41-2 Mr 19 '77
Which way is up?
Newsweek 90:78+ N 14 '77
Time il 110:111-12 N 28 '77
Why does Herr R. run amok?
Nation 225:602 D 3 '77
Wild duck
New Yorker 53:124 My 9 '77
Sat R 4:45 Je 11 '77
Winstanley
Film Q 30:18-23 Wint '76
Woman's decision
America 137:217-18 O 8 '77
New Yorker 53:108-10 S 19 '77
Women
Nation 225:413-14 O 22 '77
Wonderful crook
Nation 224:380 Mr 26 '77
New Repub 176:20 F 26 '77
New Yorker 53:114-15 Mr 21 '77
Psychol Today 10:24 Ap '77
Time il 109:68+ Ap 11 '77
World's greatest lover
Newsweek il 91:58 Ja 2 '78
Time il 110:72 D 26 '77
You light up my life
Time 110:98+ O 3 '77

MOTION picture sets. See Motion pictures—Setting and scenery

MOTION picture sound recording
Birth of the talkies. P. Andrews. Sat R 5:40+ N 12 '77
Focus on film. L. Drukker. il por Pop Phot 81:22+ Jl '77
More is less: comedy and sound; sound added to Keaton's The general. P. Warshow. il pors Film Q 31:38-45 Fall '77
Shoot for the best film sound you can get! T. Galluzzo. il Mod Phot 41:64+ Ag '77
Sound that shook Hollywood. G. Flatley. il N Y Times Mag p34-7+ S 25 '77
Sync sound when no one's talking? Listen to this. Mod Phot 41:46 O '77

MOTION picture theaters
Afternoon at the New Yorker. P. Bogdanovich. il Esquire 89:28+ Ja '78
See also
New York (city)—Radio City Music Hall

MOTION pictures
See also
Academy Awards (motion pictures)
Advertising mediums—Motion pictures
Black motion pictures
Characters in motion pictures
Television broadcasting—Motion pictures
Television motion pictures
also headings beginning Motion picture

Advertising

See Motion picture industry—Advertising

Animated cartoons

Animation. G. Bregman. il Sch Arts 77:20-1 D '77
Book, movie people gear up for the upcoming Raggedy Ann & Andy animated musical feature. il Pub W 211:112 F 28 '77
Gene slips us a Mickey. G. Shalit. il Ladies Home J 94:8+ D '77
Mouse that roared. D. D. Miller. il por Sat Eve Post 249:50 Jl '77

Reviews—Single works

Allegro non troppo
Time il 110:100 O 3 '77
Raggedy Ann & Andy
Time 109:84 My 2 '77
Wizards
Newsweek 89:110+ My 9 '77

Art films

Film; second International Craft Film Festival. D. Hare. Craft Horiz 37:6+ D '77

Reviews—Single works

American potter
Craft Horiz 37:12+ Ap '77
Potters at work
Craft Horiz 37:12+ Ap '77

Bibliography

Film books (title varies) See issues of Film quarterly

Biographical films

Peter Watkins's Edvard Munch; art of film biography. J. A. Gomez bibl f il pors Film Q 30:38-46 Wint '76

Comedy

More is less: comedy and sound; sound added to Keaton's The general. P. Warshow. il pors Film Q 31:38-45 Fall '77

MOTION pictures—*Continued*

Conservation and restoration

Restoring Enthusiasm; interview, ed by L. Fischer. P. Kubelka. il Film Q 31:35-6 Wint '77

Dance films

Ballet history by Ballet for All. J. Mueller. Dance Mag 51:91 Ag '77
Close-up, the dissolve, and Martha Graham; three films. J. Mueller. Dance Mag 52:94-5 Ja '78
Dance in the earliest motion pictures; paper prints. J. Mueller. Dance Mag 51:99 F '77
Harald Kreutzberg's dances of death. J. Mueller. il por Dance Mag 51:28 Ap '77
Mail-order dance; J. Mueller. W. Terry. il Sat R 5:44-5 O 15 '77

Reviews—Single works

Appalachian spring
  Dance Mag 51:107 D '77
Bix pieces
  Dance Mag 51:99 S '77
Children of Theatre Street
  Dance Mag il 51:63-5 S '77
Entr'acte
  Dance Mag 51:102-3 Jl '77
Relâche
  Dance Mag 51:102-3 Jl '77
Walkaround time
  Dance Mag 51:94-5 Je '77
Sue's leg: remembering the thirties
  Dance Mag 51:99 S '77

Distribution

Star wars sparks a war with producers; investigation of block booking charges. il Bus W p30 Ag 29 '77

Editing

Motion pictures—Sound editing

Educational aspects

See Motion pictures in education

History and criticism

Béla Balázs in German exile. J. Ralmon. bibl il por Film Q 30:12-19 Spr '77
50 years of the talkies; special section. il Sat R 5:36-40+ N 12 '77
Film style and technology in the forties. B. Salt. il Film Q 31:46-57 Fall '77
Sound that shook Hollywood. G. Flatley. il N Y Times Mag p34-7+ S 25 '77

Horror films

Of heroes and devils: the supernatural on film. P. Leggett. il Chr Today 22:19-21 N 18 '77

Moral and religious aspects

Of heroes and devils: the supernatural on film. P. Leggett. il Chr Today 22:19-21 N 18 '77
Too close encounter. Commonweal 105:3-4 Ja 6 '78
What are they doing to our children. E. P. Frank. il Good H 185:99+ Ag '77
What teens think of violence and sex on TV and in movies; symposium, ed by E. Miller. Seventeen 36:158-9+ Je '77
  See also
Pornography
Violence in motion pictures

Music

Interview with Richard Rodney Bennett; ed by J. Caps. R. R. Bennett. il por Hi Fi 27:58-62 Je '77
Sound for the silver screen. I. Kolodin. Sat R 5:44+ N 12 '77
  See also
Phonograph records—Motion picture music

Philosophy

Segmentation. B. Henderson. Film Q 31:57-65 Fall '77

Plots, themes, etc.

Art of dreaming in Three women and Providence: structures of the self. M. Kinder. il Film Q 31:10-18 Fall '77
Corruption and catastrophe: DePalma's Carrie. P. Matusa. il Film Q 31:32-8 Fall '77
Hour of the Wolf; the case of Ingmar B; theme of paranoia. L. Buntzen and C. Craig. bibl f il por Film Q 30:23-34 Wint '76
Look, Gideon—: a talk with Lina Wertmüller; ed by G. Bachmann. L. Wertmüller. pors Film Q 30:2-11 Spr '77
Madness in film. R. Coles. il Horizon 21:18-22 Ja '78
Money in focus. S. Kauffmann. New Repub 176:42-3 My 21 '77
Narrative point of view: the rhetoric of Au hasard, Balthazar. N. Browne. il Film Q 31:19-31 Fall '77
Nuclear debate at the gut level. S. H. Day, Jr. Bull Atom Sci 33:56-8 Mr '77
Nuclear debate in film; with filmography. J. Dowling, Jr. il Bull Atom Sci 33:52-4 F '77
Turning thirty with The graduate; motion picture, Rocky, compared. M. W. Foley. America 137:78-80 Ag 13 '77
Vladimir Propp in Hollywood; analysis of plots according to fairy tale models. J. L. Fell. bibl il Film Q 30:19-28 Spr '77
Who's turning what into movies? M. Tuchman. il Esquire 87:72-4+ Ap '77
Wim Wenders: a worldwide homesickness. M. Covino. il Film Q 31:9-19 Wint '77
  See also
Aviation in motion pictures
Blacks in motion pictures
Children in motion pictures
Cities and towns in motion pictures
Jews in motion pictures
Prisons in motion pictures
Surrealism in motion pictures
Women in motion pictures

Anecdotes, facetiae, satire, etc.

Turning news into movies: the making of the deal. il Esquire 87:67-71 Ap '77

Political films

Lina Wertmüller as political visionary. N. P. Hurley. Chr Cent 94:726-8 Ag 17 '77
Unlikely hero, guaranteed villain; Marathon man. G. M. Young, Jr. Nat R 29:554-5 My 13 '77
Winstanley; interview, ed by V. Glaessner. K. Brownlow. il Film Q 30:18-23 Wint '76

Propaganda films

Hair-raising brass propaganda; American Security Council film, The price of peace and freedom. A. Kanegis. Nation 225:486-7 N 12 '77

Psychological aspects

Art of dreaming in Three women and Providence: structures of the self. M. Kinder. il Film Q 31:10-18 Fall '77

Psychological films

Mind, medium and metaphor in Harry Smith's Heaven and earth magic. N. Carroll. bibl il Film Q 31:37-44 Wint '77

Rating

CU readers rate the movies. See issues of Consumer reports
Movies. R. I. Matthews. See issues of Consumers' research magazine

Religious films

Schaeffer on film and in person; views on How should we then live? R. Cleath. Chr Today 21:50 Ap 1 '77

Science fiction films

Special effects

See Motion pictures—Special effects

Setting and scenery

After 50 years of talkies—change comes over the movie industry. il U.S. News 83:71-2 O 10 '77

Short subject films

Refreshing shorts. Horizon 21:92 Ja '78

Reviews

Cine-opsis. J. Varlejs. See issues of Wilson library bulletin

Reviews—Single works

Speaker
  Am Lib 8:371-6 Jl '77
  Am Lib 8:405-6 S '77
  Am Lib 8:502-5 O '77
  Am Lib il 8:337 Je '77
  Lib J 102:1227 Je 1 '77
  Lib J 102:1573-80 Ag '77; Discussion. 102:2289 N 15 '77
  SLJ 24:10 N '77
  SLJ 24:9 D '77
  Wilson Lib Bull 51:794-5 Je '77
  Wilson Lib Bull 52:51-5 S '77

Silent films

More is less: comedy and sound; sound added to Keaton's The general. P. Warshow. il pors Film Q 31:38-45 Fall '77
Out of Pandora's box; silent film of Lulu. D. Newlin. por Opera N 41:20+ Ap 2 '77

Social aspects

America at the movies A. Schlesinger, Jr. il Sat R 5:36-7 N 12 '77
Awakening African cinema. F. Bebey. il UNESCO Courier 30:30-3 My '77
Jaws in retrospect. M. S. Dworkin. il Society 14:78-81 My '77
Sons of Star wars. T. Schwartz. il Newsweek 90:77 Ag 29 '77

Sound editing

Enthusiasm: from kino-eye to radio-eye. L. Fischer. bibl il por Film Q 31:25-34 Wint '77
Restoring Enthusiasm; interview, ed by L. Fischer. P. Kubelka. il Film Q 31:35-6 Wint '77

MOTION pictures—*Continued*

Sound recording

See Motion picture sound recording

Special effects

City in the sky; science fiction effects in Close encounters of the third kind. Time 110:105 N 7 '77

Dream wizards; Star wars effects. il Newsweek 89:61+ My 30 '77

We get you to places you can't get to. J. Morgenstern. il por Horizon 20:17-23 D '77

Wizard of special effects; D. Trumbull's work on Close encounters. J. Kroll and M. Kasindorf. il por Newsweek 90:99 N 21 '77

Sports films

Cine-opsis; hunting films. J. Varlejs. il Wilson Lib Bull 51:810-11 Je '77

Here come the jocks. J. Kroll. il Newsweek 89: 68-9 Mr 7 '77

Reviews—Single works

Fangio
Car & Dr 23:7 O '77

Pumping iron
America 136:136 F 12 '77
Newsweek il 89:61 Ja 24 '77
Time 109:79 Ja 24 '77

Study and teaching

Voyage of discovery for librarians; documentary film study at the Flaherty seminars of the International Film Seminars. D. Boyle. Am Lib 8:635-6 D '77

Titling

Subtitles for TV and films; captions for the hearing-impaired. il Am Educ 13:18-22 Mr '77

Travel films

Shooting on the run: how to make a vacation film. J. Kealy. il por Pop Phot 81:126-7+ Ag '77

Unauthorized reprints

Film pirates. D. Pauly and others. il Newsweek 90:90+ O 17 '77

Westerns

High eagle: the many lives of Colonel Tim McCoy; interview, ed by D. Ponicsan. T. McCoy. il pors Am Heritage 28:52-62 Je '77

West that wasn't. C. L. Sonnichsen. il Am West 14:8-15 N '77

France

From 400 blows to Small change. G. Mast. New Repub 176:23-5 Ap 2 '77

Germany

Béla Balázs in German exile. J. Ralmon. bibl il por Film Q 30:12-19 Spr '77

Germany, West

Fassbinder: the poetry of the inarticulate. P. Thomas. il Film Q 30:2-17 Wint '76

Germans are coming! The Germans are coming! W. Herzog and R. W. Fassbinder. D. Denby. il pors Horizon 20:88-90+ S '77

New visionary in German films; W. Herzog. R. Eder. il pors N Y Times Mag p24-6+ Jl 10 '77

Wenders. S. Kauffman. New Repub 176:26-7 Ja 29 '77

Great Britain

Peter Watkins's Edvard Munch; art of film biography. J. A. Gomez. bibl f il pors Film Q 30:38-46 Wint '76

Winstanley; interview, ed by V. Glaessner. K. Brownlow. il Film Q 30:18-23 Wint '76

United States

Entertainment this fall. M. Stasio. il Harp Baz 110:36 S '77

Film style and technology in the forties. B. Salt. il Film Q 31:46-57 Fall '77

Movies; not-yet-released productions. J. Crist. il Sat R 4:14+ Ag 6 '77

Summer films: pictures without people. P. C. Rule. America 137:33-4 Jl 16 '77

Summer sweepstakes. M. Orth and M. Kasindorf. il Newsweek 90:74-5 Ag 22 '77

See also

Motion picture industry—United States

MOTION pictures, Amateur

Focus on film; home movies. L. Drukker. il por Pop Phot 80:74+ My '77

Stars in their eyes; work of M. Elias. E. R. Walsh. por Ret Liv 17:31+ Ag '77

MOTION pictures, Childrens. See Motion pictures for children

MOTION pictures, Documentary

Film; work of the Center for Southern Folklore in Memphis, Tenn. D. Hare. Craft Horiz. 37:7+ Je '77

Helen Van Dongen: an interview; ed by B. Achtenberg. H. Van Dougen. bibl il pors Film Q 30:46-57 Wint '76

Let's shoot a documentary: fear. N. R. Seider. il Pop Phot 80:116-17+ Mr '77

Traveler's camera: travel films. C. Purcell. Pop Phot 80:40+ My '77

See also

Motion pictures—Short subject films

Reviews

About books and films. Org Gard & Farm 24: 52-3 F '77

Single works

California Reich
Film Q 30:37 Summ '77

China
Film Q 30:9-12 Summ '77

Enthusiasm
Film Q il 31:25-36 Wint '77

F for fake
Nation 224:316 Mr 12 '77
New Repub 176:24-5 Mr 12 '77

Harlan County, U.S.A.
America 136:135 F 12 '77
Commonweal 104:149-50 Mr 4 '77
Ms il 5:32-4 Ap '77
Nation 224:158 F 5 '77
New Repub 176:18 F 12 '77
New Yorker 52:84-6 Ja 24 '77
Sat R il 4:39-42 Mr 5 '77

Hidden events
Smithsonian 8:80-7 N '77

Hitler—a career
Chr Today 22:50+ O 21 '77
Newsweek 90:78 S 5 '77
Time 110:43 Ag 29 '77

Hollywood on trial
Film Q il 30:32-4 Summ '77

Homage to Chagall: the colours of love
Sat R 4:41 Je 25 '77

How should we then live?
Chr Today 21:50 Ap 1 '77

Memory of justice
Chr Cent 94:361-3 Ap 13 '77
Commentary 62:65-7 D '76; discussion. 63: 15-16+ Mr '77
Ms il 5:37-8 F '77

Underground
Film Q il 30:34-7 Summ '77

Volcano: an inquiry into the life of Malcolm Lowry
Time il 110:92+ N 7 '77

We're not the jet set
New Repub 177:26-7 Jl 2 '77

Study and teaching

See Motion pictures—Study and teaching

MOTION pictures, Experimental

Films of Gunvor Nelson. J. M. Gill. bibl il Film Q 30:28-36 Spr '77

MOTION pictures, Silent. See Motion pictures—Silent films

MOTION pictures and children

See also

Children in motion pictures
Motion pictures—Moral and religious aspects
Motion pictures for children

MOTION pictures and libraries. See Libraries and motion pictures; School libraries and motion pictures

MOTION pictures and literature

New Python book a treat for both film and design buffs. P. Doebler. il Pub W 212:78+ O 3 '77

Novelizations: are the plums drying up? books from motion pictures and television programs. E. Lottman. il Pub W 212:31-3 O 10 '77

Theater/film. S. Kauffmann. New Repub 177: 24-6 N 5 '77

See also

Motion picture adaptations

MOTION pictures and morals. See Motion pictures—Moral and religious aspects

MOTION pictures and television

TV's impact on the movies—as a noted director sees it. il por U.S. News 83:62 N 21 '77

MOTION pictures for children

Children's film: conspiracy of mediocrity. D. Boyle. il Am Lib 8:267-8 My '77

Family movie guide. J. Ripp. See issues of Parents' magazine & better homemaking

MOTION pictures in education

Audiovisual materials; 16mm sound films. W. J. Cuttill. See issues of Today's education

Film and television research. R. Beach. bibl Engl J 66:90-3 Mr '77

Hollywood and American literature: the American novel on the screen. H. Jay. Engl J 66: 82-6 Ja '77

Poetry and film for the classroom. R. Armour. Engl J 66:88-91 Ja '77

Short film; ed by R. Fulginiti (cont) Engl J 66: 90-3 S '77

See also

Educational Film Library Association
Motion pictures in sex education
School libraries and motion pictures

MOTION pictures in sex education

Sex films; sexual attitude reassessment workshops. R. T. Francoeur. bibl il Society 14:33-7 Jl '77

MOTION pictures on airplanes. See Airlines—Passenger service

MOTION sickness
Motion sickness: an evolutionary hypothesis. M. Treisman. bibl Science 197:493-5 Jl 29 '77
Motion sickness—blame it on evolution; theory of Michel Treisman. J. Gaylin. Psychol Today 11:26+ D '77
See also
Seasickness

MOTIVATION (education)
Ascendancy of the Fonz. W. C. Williams. bibl Clearing H 50:333-7 Ap '77
Medicine pots—a motivation operation. L. L. Clark. il Sch Arts 76:32-3 F '77

MOTIVATION (psychology)
Diets work better in a crowd. D. Cohen. il Psychol Today 10:96 Ap '77
Industry's greatest energy shortage; address, June 6, 1977. R. W. Bunke. Vital Speeches 43:637-40 Ag 1 '77
Learning to give up; views of M. E. P. Seligman. A. Rosenfeld. il Sat R 4:36-7 S 3 '77
We motivate mechanics for high-production maintenance; Fort Worth, Tex. R. S. Menefee. il por Am City & County 92:51-2 Mr '77
See also
Risk taking (psychology)

MOTOR boat engines
Balance of power. N. Warren. il Motor B & S 141:74-6+ Ja '78
Inside the stern drives. E. F. Lindsley. il Pop Sci 210:106-8+ My '77
You and your engine. M. Crook. See issues of Yachting
See also
Outboard motors

MOTOR boat racing
Betty Cook is one hard-driving lady; Bacardi Trophy Race. T. West. il por Motor B & S 140:64-5+ S '77
Big race on Lake Havasu. Sunset 159:56 N '77
How to take the world's outboard championship. B. McKeown. il Pop Mech 147:96-7+ F '77
No flinching allowed; drag boat racing. B. Newman. il Sports Illus 47:50-1 Ag 1 '77
Out on the verge, but far from foolish; B. Cook's victory in the Bushmills Grand Prix. D. S. Looney. il por Sports Illus 46:16-17 Mr 14 '77
Power play at Parker; 9-Hour Enduro. B. Yates. il Motor B & S 140:61-3+ Ag '77
Racing scene. M. Crook. See issues of Yachting
Taking a thrashing—and giving one; Key West offshore powerboat race. C. Phinizy. Sports Illus 47:66-7 N 21 '77
See also
Hydroplane racing

MOTOR boating speed records. See Boat speed records

MOTOR boating & sailing (periodical)
Way we were; 70th anniversary. R. Burnham. il Motor B & S 140:73-82 Jl '77

MOTOR boats
Marvellous Molly and her Johnson 10. E. Walden. il Yachting 141:80-1 My '77
New boats in Yachting. See occasional issues of Yachting
Powerboats. il Motor B & S 141:152-70 Ja '78
Powerboats for 1978. il Yachting 142:137-8+ O '77
Refuge ducks are swamped by powerboats, politicians; Ruby Lake National Wildlife Refuge. G. Laycock. Audubon 79:152-3 N '77
Trailer boating; special section. il Motor B & S 141:67-9+ Ja '78
See also
Cruisers (pleasure boats)
Fishing boats
Hydrofoils
Outboard motor boats

Design

Racing scene; Evinrude Award presented to A. Molinari. M. Crook. Yachting 141:52+ My '77
Racy retirement; boats designed by D. Aronow. S. Reier. il por Forbes 120:98 Ag 15 '77
Yachting eyes: Aquasport 426. J. Smith. il Yachting 141:84-6 Ap '77
Trim-tab steering. R. Campoli. il Motor B & S 139:34 F '77

Testing

Performance test:
Egg harber 33. D. Hart. il Motor B & S 139:46-7+ F '77
Reinell 8-meter. D. R. Hart. il Motor B & S 140:24-6+ Ag '77
Sea Ray. D. Hart. il Motor B & S 140:24+ Jl '77
Powerboat testing. D. Hart. Motor B & S 140:14+ Jl '77

MOTOR buses. See Buses

MOTOR clubs. See Automobile clubs

MOTOR cortex. See Brain

MOTOR cycles. See Motorcycles

MOTOR development of infants. See Infants—Growth and development

MOTOR driven cameras. See Cameras

MOTOR fuels
See also
Automobile engines—Fuel
Diesel fuels
Gasoline

Taxation

See also
Gasoline—Taxation

MOTOR home touring. See Automobile touring

MOTOR homes. See Campers, Truck

MOTOR learning
Basal ganglia cooling disables learned arm movements of monkeys in the absence of visual guidance. J. Hore and others. bibl il Science 195:584-6 F 11 '77

MOTOR oils, Automotive. See Automobiles—Lubrication and lubricants

MOTOR responses
Long-term unit recording from somatosensory neurons in the spinal ganglia of the freely walking cat. G. E. Loeb and others. bibl il Science 197:1192-4 S 16 '77
Premotor cortical ablations in monkeys: contralateral changes in visually guided reaching behavior. L. Moll and H. G. J. M. Kuypers. bibl il Science 198:317-19 O 21 '77
See also
Licking (animals)

MOTOR Trend Awards
Announcing Motor Trend's Truck of the Year; Ford Econoline van. il Motor T 29:84+ D '77
Announcing Motor Trend's Truck of the Year nominees. il Motor T 29:50-1 N '77
Motor Trend Man of the Year Awards to Thomas A. Murphy and E. M. "Pete" Estes. pors Motor T 29:34+ F '77
Motor Trend's 1978 Domestic Car of the Year; nominees. il Motor T 30:46-7 Ja '78
1977 Motor Trend Car of the Year Award: the candidates. il Motor T 28:66-7 D '76
1977 Motor Trend Car of the Year: Chevrolet's Caprice Classic. il Motor T 29:26-8 F '77
1977 Motor Trend Import Car of the Year. J. Christy. Motor T 29:42-6 Mr '77
1977 Motor Trend Import Car of the Year; Mercedes Benz 280E. il Motor T 29:38-9 Ap '77
1978 Import Car of the Year; Toyota Celica. il Motor T 30:21-3+ Ja '78
1978 Motor Trend Import Car of the Year; nominees. B. Hall. il Motor T 29:34-7+ D '77

MOTOR truck industry. See Truck industry

MOTOR trucks. See Trucks

MOTOR vehicle engines

Fuel consumption

914-mpg car wins super-mileage contest. D. Scott. il Pop Sci 211:100-1 D '77
Talk about mileage. . .would you believe 1000 mpg? Super Mileage Project. S. M. Gallager. il Pop Mech 148:80-1 D '77

MOTOR vehicle fleets, Municipal
We motivate mechanics for high-production maintenance; Fort Worth, Tex. R. S. Menefee. il por Am City & County 92:51-2 Mr '77

MOTOR vehicle industries. See Automobile industry; Bus industry; Truck industry

MOTOR vehicle insurance. See Insurance, Motor vehicle

MOTOR vehicles
Imports & motorsports. B. Hartford. See issues of Popular mechanics
Vehicles. B. Behme. See issues of Field & stream 106+ N '77
See also
Automobiles
Buses
Electric vehicles
Jeep automobiles
Mopeds
Motorcycles
Recreational vehicles
Snowmobiles and snowmobiling
Station wagons
Trucks
Vans

Four wheel drive

New diesel pickups and bigger 4WD's. H. Shuldiner. il Outdoor Life 160:54+ O '77
Nobody beats the odds forever; repairing four-wheel-drive vehicles in the wilderness. B. Kilpatrick. il Field & S 82:90+ O '77

Laws and regulations

See also
Automobiles—Laws and regulations

Lighting

See also
Snow removal equipment—Lighting

Maintenance and repair

Nobody beats the odds forever; repairing four-wheel-drive vehicles in the wilderness. B. Kilpatrick. il Field & S 82:90+ O '77

MOTOR vehicles—*Continued*

Radio equipment

See also
Radiotelephone on motor vehicles

Safety devices and measures

Fire extinguishers. B. Behme. il Field & S 82: 130+ Je '77

MOTOR vehicles, All terrain
Monster vehicle to star in movie. J. Scagnetti. il Pop Sci 210:83 Mr '77

MOTOR vehicles, Municipal
Make gasoline losses evaporate; computerized control over fuel records; Bloomington, Minn. H. G. Wurdelman. il Am City & County 92: 39-40 Ja '77
See also
Motor vehicles fleets, Municipal
Trucks, Municipal

MOTOR yachts. See Yachts and yachting

MOTORBIKES. See Motorcycles

MOTORBOATS. See Motor boats

MOTORCYCLE brakes. See Brakes, Motorcycle

MOTORCYCLE engines
Five easy pieces; Honda 750F2. J. McCraw. il Hot Rod 30:87-90+ D '77

Maintenance and repair

How to keep the fuel flowing. C. Gromer. il Pop Mech 147:25 Ap '77

MOTORCYCLE helmet laws. See Motorcycling—Laws and legislation

MOTORCYCLE mechanics (persons)

Training

If you like working on bikes, why not make a living at it? with list of schools. C. Gromer. il Pop Mech 148:58+ D '77

MOTORCYCLE models. See Models

MOTORCYCLE racing
Hell on two wheels; Daytona 200; photographs; with report by S. Moses. il Sports Illus 46: 30-5 Mr 14 '77
It was a piece of cake for Baker; Daytona 200. S. Moses. il Sports Illus 46:26-7 Mr 21 '77
Racing on the ragged edge—why do they do it? a close look at G. Nixon. R. R. Olney. il pors Pop Mech 148:88-90 Ag '77

MOTORCYCLE riding. See Motorcycling

MOTORCYCLES
Big bikes come back. W. Thoms. il Mech Illus 73:46-7 My '77
Cars and bikes together: a shopper's sampler. il Car & Dr 23:40+ Ag '77
Evil sorcerer; twin-engined Honda. J. McCraw. il Hot Rod 30:52-4+ My '77
Motorcycling. R. Hill. See issues of Popular science
So you want a motorcycle. R. Huntington. il Consumers Res Mag 60:12-15 Mr '77
Up on two wheels:
Bad company; Harley-Davidson XLCR Cafe Racer. J. McCraw. il Hot Rod 30:99-100+ Jl '77
Highway 11; Yamaha's 1100CC. J. McCraw. il Hot Rod 30:96-7+ N '77
Kawasaki 900cc. J. McCraw. il Hot Rod 30: 103-7 Mr '77
Lonely at the top; Kawasaki KZ1000. il Hot Rod 30:95+ Ag '77
Middleweight contender; Suzuki GS 550. J. McCraw. il Hot Rod 30:113-14+ Ap '77
Right-on rocket; Yamaha RD400. J. McCraw. il Hot Rod 30:84-7 F '77
Shaft 'em! Yamaha's XS750. J. McCraw. il Hot Rod 30:30+ My '77
Supersuzi; Suzuki GS400B. J. McCraw. il Hot Rod 30:95-6+ O '77
Yes you can! Honda 400CC. J. McCraw. il Hot Rod 30:99-100+ S '77
Where the highway ends: motorcycles and Mother Nature; Honda MR175 and the Yamaha XT500D. J. Jordan. il Car & Dr 22:125-7 Je '77
Your motorcycle. il Pop Mech 147:24+ F; 25 Ap; 148:58+ D '77
See also
Mopeds
Motorcycling

Maintenance and repair

See also
Motorcycle engines—Maintenance and repair
Motorcycle mechanics (persons)

Photographs

Hot rod gallery. il Hot Rod 30:92-3 Jl '77

Shock absorbers

Air shocks for motorcycles. il Pop Sci 210:128 F '77

Testing

Big brother, little brother: Honda's CB750F2 and CB400F. J. McCraw. il Hot Rod 30:114+ Je '77
Great displacement race. E. A. Sloane. il Pop Mech 147:86-8+ My '77
Two wheels against four! Kawasaki KZ1000 vs. Firebird Trans-Am. S. Thompson. il Car & Dr 23:35-6+ Ag '77
We test the no. 1 motorcycle; Honda CJ-360T. W. Thoms. il Mech Illus 73:41-3 N '77
We try out a very hairy bike. W. E. Baker. il Mech Illus 73:68+ S '77

Transmission

Constant-mesh transmission selects gear ratios automatically. R. Hill. il Pop Sci 210:68+ Ap '77

MOTORCYCLES, Antique

Collectors and collecting

From crud to chrome. R. Bahr. il Pop Mech 148:76-8+ Jl '77

MOTORCYCLES, Steam
2-wheel clean machine. il Mech Illus 73:114 D '77

MOTORCYCLING
How it works: why a motorcycle isn't half a car. L. J. K. Setright. il Car & Dr 23:36-7 Ag '77
How to body English your bike and be a better rider. B. Hampton. il Pop Mech 147:24+ F '77
How to corner like a pro. B. Hampton. il Pop Mech 148:88-9+ S '77
Varoom! Goes the preacher; Stan George. D. Kloss. il Ret Liv 17:42+ Mr '77
See also
Motorcycle racing

Laws and legislation

Make motorcyclists wear helmets? interviews. B. Kelley; G. Wirwahn. il pors U.S. News 83:39-40 Jl 18 '77

MOTORHOMES. See Campers, Truck

MOTORISTS. See Automobile drivers

MOTOROLA, Inc
How to avoid charges of job discrimination. V. Louviere. il Nations Bus 65:69 Mr '77
Motorola's fast catch-up in microprocessors. Bus W p66 Ag 29 '77

MOTOROLA Inc.-Codex Corporation merger. See Electronic industries—Acquisitions and mergers

MOTORS, Electric. See Electric motors

MOTORS, Outboard. See Outboard motors

MOTT, Michael
Juniper; Crossing the line; poems. Poetry 129: 314-16 Mr '77

MOTT, Sir Nevill Francis
1977 Nobel Prize in physics. M. L. Cohen and L. M. Falicov. bibl pors Science 198:713-15 N 18 '77 *
Nobel Prizes: seven in '77. pors Sci N 112:260-1 O 22 '77 *
Physicists share in Nobel Prizes in three disciplines. G. B. Lubkin. pors Phys Today 30: 77-8 D '77 *

MOUFLON. See Mountain sheep

MOULINEX (firm) See Household appliances industry—France

MOUND CITY, Kan.
Country doctor; work of G. Duckworth. C. Remsberg. il por Fam Health 9:36-9+ Ap '77

MOUNDS and mound builders
Four Ukrainian archaeologists present their latest finds; Scythian burial mound excavations by Institute of Archaeology of the Academy of Sciences of the Ukrainian S.S.R. il UNESCO Courier 29:17-22 D '76

MOUNT, Ellis. See Crockett, E. S. jt comp

MOUNT, Ferdinand
Sick man of Europe. Nat R 29:727-30 Je 24 '77

MOUNT, William Sidney
Of fiddles and fiddlers (and friends) I. Lowens. il Hi Fi 27:89-90 Mr '77 *

MOUNT ETNA. See Etna, Mount

MOUNT EVEREST. See Everest, Mount

MOUNT KILIMANJARO climbs. See Mountaineering

MOUNT MCKINLEY National Park
Mount McKinley National Park. N. Lo Bello. il Travel 147:52-7 Ap '77

MOUNT MONADNOCK. See Monadnock, Mount

MOUNT RAINIER. See Rainier, Mount

MOUNT RAINIER climbs. See Mountaineering

MOUNT RAINIER National Park
Mountain; day hikes and climbing Mount Rainier. il map Sunset 159:60-7 bibl (p58) Jl '77
Time and the mountain. A. A. Lindsey. il Nat Parks & Con Mag 51:4-7 N '77

MOUNT RUSHMORE National Memorial
Carving the American colossus. E. M. Halliday. il por Am Heritage 28:18-27 Je '77

MOUNT SHASTA. See Shasta, Mount

MOUNT USU (volcano) See Volcanoes

MOUNT VERNON
Housekeeping at Mount Vernon. J. Warren. Chr Cent 94:851-2 S 28 '77

MOUNTAIN agriculture. See Hill farming
MOUNTAIN climbing. See Mountaineering
MOUNTAIN farming. See Hill farming
MOUNTAIN lion hunting. See Puma hunting
MOUNTAIN lions. See Pumas
MOUNTAIN mahogany
Mountain-mahogany makes music. J. E. Dealy. il por Am For 83:24-7 Je '77
MOUNTAIN-Plains Library Association
SWLA/MPLA joint conference. Lib J 102:323-4 F 1 '77
MOUNTAIN railroads
Allegheny Portage Railroad. il Nat Parks & Con Mag 51:25 Jl '77
MOUNTAIN resorts. See Resorts
MOUNTAIN sculpture
Heap big heap; statue of Chief Crazy Horse. E. M. Halliday. il Am Heritage 28:24-5 Je '77
Moving a mountain; K. Ziolkowski's Crazy Horse project. D. A. Williams and F. Maier il por Newsweek 90:28+ Ag 29 '77
MOUNTAIN sheep
Fecund mouflon. R. Valdez and L. V. Alamia. il Natur Hist 86:72-7 bibl(p 119) N '77
MOUNTAIN sheep hunting
Hunt your own sheep; Western States. C. J. Farmer. il Field & S 82:60-1+ S '77
MOUNTAIN sickness. See Altitude, Influence of
MOUNTAIN waves
Mountain wave weather in New York City. S. D. Gedzelman. il maps Weatherwise 30:202-6 O '77
MOUNTAINEERING
Challenging Hidden Peak; climb by R. Messner and P. Habeler in the Himalayas. L. Elliott. il Read Digest 111:102-7 D '77
Climbing Kilimanjaro. D. W. George. il Mademoiselle 83:188+ N '77
Ecstasy on the rocks; beginners' expedition in West Milford, N.J. B. Graustark. il Newsweek 90:64 Jl 18 '77
Heart of Mt Shasta. P. T. Parker. il Am For 83:32-4 O '77
High on icy rime and powdered sugar; Grand Teton winter climb. W. Marling. il Fortune 95:51+ Ja '77
High road to failure; climbing Mount K2 in the Karakoran Himalaya; excerpt from In the throne room of the mountain gods. G. Rowell. il Sports Illus 46:92-6+ My 2 '77
Mountain; day hikes and climbing Mount Rainier. il map Sunset 159:60-7 bibl(p58) Jl '77
Mounting a mole hill; Mount Hassell, Australia. M. Hassell. Seventeen 36:66-7 Jl '77
Profiles; Y. Chouinard. J. Bernstein. New Yorker 52:36-40+ Ja 31 '77
Scaling Chilkoot even today is a fearful ordeal. J. Hope. il Smithsonian 7:106-13 bibl(p 154+) F '77
Someone is always on Monadnock. S. Sherman. il Nat Wildlife 15:26-9 Ag '77
See also
Everest, Mount

Anecdotes, facetiae, satire, etc.

Down! T. Strasser. New Yorker 52:28-9 Ja 24 '77
Hangin' on; mountain climbing in Maine. M. Evans. il Seventeen 36:174 Mr '77

Equipment and supplies

How to hike straight up. J. Whittaker. il por Pop Mech 147:97-9+ Ap '77
Ingenious new gear for rock climbing. T. Morrisey. il Pop Sci 211:40+ S '77
MOUNTAINS
Range of precipitates? T. Benfey. il Chemistry 50:2 S '77
See also
Mountain waves
Seamounts
also names of mountain ranges and peaks, e.g. Etna, Mount
MOUNTCASTLE, V. B. See Yin, T. C. T. jt auth
MOUNTER, Julian
Great Kenya wildlife ripoff. J. Samson. il Field & S 82:48-9+ D '77 *
MOUNTING (taxidermy) See Taxidermy
MOUNTING of pictures. See Pictures—Mounting
MOUNTINGS, Telescope. See Telescope mountings
MOUNTS, Gary B.
Small company manages to take itself public. il por Bus W p88-9 Ja 31 '77 *
MOUR, Stanley I.
Censorship and the schools: a different perspective. bibl f il Engl J 66:18-20 F '77
MOURNING. See Grief
MOURNING dove shooting
Stalk a spooky dove. R. Tinsley. il Field & S 82:34+ Ag '77
MOURNING pictures. See Pictures
MOUSSAKA. See Cookery, Greek
MOUSSE. See Desserts
MOUSSORGSKY, Modest Petrovich. See Musorgskii, M. P.
MOUSTAFINE, Mara. See Rosen, S. J. jt auth
MOUTH
See also
Gums
Teeth

Cancer

See Cancer

Care and hygiene

Message by mouth. L. Beech. Sr Schol 109:16 My 5 '77

Surgery

See Oral surgery
MOVALLI, Charles
(ed) See Beatty, F. Frank Beatty: the peripatetic pastellist
(ed) See Cirino, A. Conversation with Antonio Cirino
(ed) See Göerschner, T. Conversation with Ted Göerschner
(ed) See Hensche, H. Teaching color relationships: a conversation with Henry Hensche
(ed) See Joyce, M. Conversation with Marshall Joyce
(ed) See Peters, C. W. Looking for patterns: a conversation with Carl W. Peters
MOVEMENT, Psychology of
See also
Communication, Nonverbal
Motor learning
Muscular sense
MOVEMENT in art. See Action in art
MOVEMENT of animals. See Animal locomotion
MOVEMENT of cells. See Cells—Motility
MOVEMENTS of man. See Human mechanics
MOVIES. See Motion pictures
MOVING
Household moving. Consumer Rep 42:366-8 D '77
How to make your best move. C. Seebohm. il House & Gard 149:144-5+ O '77
Making your own move. Sunset 158:114+ Je '77
Moving? Here's how to pack up. J. M. Stewart. Bet Hom & Gard 55:220+ Ap '77
See also
Migration, Internal
Moving and storage companies

Psychological aspects

Change of scene can be fatal; nursing-home patients. S. Bush. Psychol Today 10:32 F '77
Home—how to take it along when you move. A. J. Waterhouse. House B 119:72+ O '77
Moving. J. D. Bucher. il Redbook 149:60+ Jl '77
Moving can be fun. S. Bush. Psychol Today 11:28 Jl '77
Moving without tears. J. Weiner. Parents Mag 52:50+ F '77
Uprooted! C. Callahan. Seventeen 36:160-1+ Je '77
Vulnerable age—when moving brings special problems; research by Michael Inbar. D. Cohen. il Psychol Today 10:28+ Mr '77
MOVING and storage companies
Moving? Here's what you should know. il Good H 185:208 Ag '77
MOVING of structures, etc.
Houses to go—for a song; house moving. R. L. Williams. il House B 119:10+ Ap '77
MOVING pictures. See Motion pictures
MOWER, A. Glenn, Jr
Implementing United Nations covenants. bibl il Society 15:76-80 N '77
MOWING machines
See also
Lawn mowers
MOWLANA, Hamid
Mass media and the 1976 Presidential campaign. Intellect 105:244-5 F '77
MOWRY, George E.
Comments: America: experiment or destiny? Am Hist R 82:527-30 Je '77
MOYERS, Bill D.
Grinch who stole Castro. il por Time 109:50 Je 13 '77 *
JFK, Castro—and controversy. D. Gelman. il pors Newsweek 90:85 Jl 18 '77 *
Television; CIA's secret army. P. Sourian. Nation 225:155-7 Ag 20 '77 *
MOYNIHAN, Daniel Patrick
Liberals' dilemma. New Repub 176:57-60 Ja 22 '77
Party & international politics. Commentary 63:56-9 F '77
Politics of human rights. Commentary 64:19-26 Ag '77; Same abr. Read Digest 111:229-30+ D '77; Reply. Commentary 64:8 O '77

about

5 freshman senators who are moving into the spotlight. pors U.S. News 82:24-5 F 7 '77 *
Moynihan fires one. W. F. Buckley, Jr. Nat R 29:844-5 Jl 22 '77 *
Pat makes the dean's list. T. Mathews and J. J. Lindsay. por Newsweek 90:19 Jl 18 '77 *
Social science and Presidential choices. I. L. Horowitz. bibl Society 14:21-3 My '77 *

MOYNIHAN, Daniel Patrick—about—*Continued*
Speech. New Yorker 53:18-19 Ja 2 '78 *
Tax credits for tuition payments. America 136: 474 My 28 '77 *
War between the states. W. F. Buckley, Jr. Nat R 29:905 Ag 5 '77 *

MOYNIHAN, Richard
Inside look at a new, hot municipal bond fund; interview, ed by A. Hershman. por Duns R 110:141-4+ O '77

MOZAMBICAN refugees. See Refugees, Mozambican

MOZAMBIQUE
Mozambique: fragile independence. H. J. De Blij. bibl il map Focus 27:9-16 N '76
See also
Guerrillas—Mozambique
Hunting—Mozambique
United Nations—Mozambique

Foreign relations

Rhodesia

Dealing or double-dealing. il por map Time 110:49 D 12 '77
Mozambique's porous front. J. Pringle. il map Newsweek 89:36+ Ap 25 '77
Talk-talk, fight-fight. K. Willenson and others. il Newsweek 90:62+ D 12 '77

Russia

See Russia—Foreign relations—Mozambique

Politics and government

Fellow-traveling in Mozambique; M. Kaufman's reports in the New York times. R. Moss. Nat R 29:1495-6 D 23 '77
Our man in Maputo; views of M. T. Kaufman. Nat R 29:1413 D 9 '77

MOZART, Johann Chrysostom Wolfgang Amadeus
La clemenza di Tito. Reviews
Opera N il por 42:20-2+ S '77 *
Don Giovanni. Reviews
Hi Fi 27:MA6-7+ D '77 *
Hi Fi il 27:MA38-9 O '77 *
Flute and piano concertos; Galway, Serkin and Casadesus recordings. B. Hastings and R. Kammerer. Am Rec G 40:28 Jl '77 *
Idomeneo. Reviews
Opera N il por 42:20-2+ S '77 *
Time 110:86+ O 17 '77 *
Magic flute. Reviews
Hi Fi 27:MA29-30 Jl '77 *
Opera N il 41:16-23 Ja 22 '77 *
Marriage of Figaro. Reviews
Hi Fi 27:MA27 F '77 *
Newsweek il 90:117 O 10 '77 *
Opera N il 41:16+ Mr 5 '77 *
Mörike's Mozart on the way to Prague. U. Mahlendorf. bibl f Am Imago 33:304-27 Fall '76 *
Mozart: Symphonies nos. 22, 24-27, 39, 40. C. T. Veilleux. Am Rec G 40:34-5 Je '77 *
Notes on The flute. S. Hughes. il Opera N 41: 12-14 Ja 22 '77 *
Perilous path to soprano superstardom; recordings of Mozart recitals by S. Sass and M. Price. D. Harris. pors Hi Fi 27:89-90 Ap '77 *
Piano concerto no. 24 in C minor, K. 491; Piano concerto no. 14 in E-flat major, K. 449. E. Belov. Am Rec G 40:25 Ap '77 *
Piano concertos nos. 14 and 23; Supraphon recording. D. M. Martin. Am Rec G 41:38-9 D '77 *
Rampal plays Mozart; flute concertos. N. F. Karlins. Am Rec G 40:28-9 Mr '77 *
Requiem mass. P. Althouse. il Am Rec G 40: 27-8 Mr '77 *
Der Schauspieldirektor; Lo sposo deluso. R. V. Lucano. il Am Rec G 40:29-30 N '76 *
Symphonies nos. 23, 28, 30, 31 and 38, performed by the Concertgebouw Orchestra under J. Krips. L. M. Smoley. Am Rec G 40:41-2+ S '77 *
Various concertos performed by the Vienna Philharmonic conduced by Karl Bohm. L. M. Smoley. Am Rec G 40:38-9 O '77 *
Zaïde. W. Botsford. Am Rec G 40:31 N '76 *
Die Zauberflöte. Reviews
Hi Fi 27:MA16-17 Ap '77 *

MROSOVSKY, N.
Hibernation and body weight in dormice: a new type of endogenous cycle. bibl il Science 196: 902-3 My 20 '77

MS (periodical)
No comment olympics: the Ms first annual awards for surrealism in everyday life; comp by A. Northrop and G. Steinem. il Ms 6: 48-50+ Jl '77
Special 5th anniversary issue. G. Steinem. il Ms 6:47 Jl '77

MUCKRAKING
Reconsideration. R. Stinson. New Repub 177:37-9 Jl 9 '77

MUCOPOLYSACCHARIDOSIS. See Metabolism, Disorders of

MUCUS
Stimulation by immune complexes of mucus release from goblet cells of the rat small intestine. W. A. Walker and others. bibl il Science 197:370-2 Jl 22 '77

MUD rooms. See Rooms

MUD turtles. See Turtles

MUDIE, Colin. See Mudie, R. jt auth

MUDIE, Rosemary, and Mudie, Colin
Design: the scientific art; excerpt from Power yachts. Yachting 142:112+ N '77
Rough-water powerboat design; excerpt from Power yachts. il Yachting 142:162+ O '77

MUEHL, William
Myth of self-evident truths. Chr Cent 94:1000-2 N 2 '77

MUELLER, C. F, Company
Marts of trade; NYU Law School's acquisition and sale of C.F. Mueller Company. J. Brooks. New Yorker 53:48-53 D 26 '77

MUELLER, Del
Is it possible to teach peace? Educ Digest 43: 43-5 S '77

MUELLER, Elaine
Good-by, Walden Pond; story. Redbook 149:130 S '77

MUELLER, Erwin Wilheim
Obituary
Phys Today por 30:70-1 Ag '77. T. T. Tsong

MUELLER, George E.
Profiting from the revolution in technology; interview. il pors Nations Bus 65:44-9 Ag '77

MUELLER, Jo
Solar home in the Northland. il Mech Illus 74: 36-7+ Ja '78

MUELLER, John
Films. See issues of Dance magazine

about

Mail-order dance. W. Terry. il Sat R 5:44-5 O 15 '77 *

MUELLER, Larry
Finger on accuracy. il Outdoor Life 159:170 Mr '77
How we put sport back into chuck hunting. il Outdoor Life 159:80-1+ Ap '77
When it's hot. . .it's hot. il Outdoor Life 160: 78-9+ Ag '77

MUELLER, Lavonne
Language as art and art as language. bibl il Engl J 66:49-53 O '77

MUELLER, Lisel
Possessive case; poem. New Yorker 53:45 O 17 '77

about

Comment. D. Allen. Poetry 130:346-7 S '77 *

MUELLER, Majorie J. See Blank, J. P. jt auth

MUELLER, Robert Kirk
Hidden agenda. bibl f Harvard Bus R 55:40-1+ S '77

MUELLER, Ronald O. See Asbury, J. G. jt auth

MUELLNER, Steven L.
Thomas Gifford: the bestsell factor. por Writers Digest 57:50-1 Jl '77

MUETHING, G. and others
Low-cost digital logic analyzer. il Pop Electr 11:40-6 F '77

MUETTERTIES, E. L.
Molecular metal clusters. bibl il Science 196: 839-48 My 20 '77

MUFF, Russell
Spray-painting pros and cons. il Motor B & S 139:111-13 Ap '77

MUFFINS. See Bread

MUFTI, Abdul Majib
International development of energy: excerpts from address. il Intellect 105:206 Ja '77

MUGGERIDGE, Malcolm
Cheery doomsayer; interview, ed by W. Murchison. Nat R 29:1050-1 S 16 '77
Compleat New Yorker; E. B. White. il Harpers 254:94+ Mr '77
—and Vidler, Alec
Paul: ambassador to the world. il Sat Eve Post 249:6+ O '77

MUHAMMAD Ali. See Ali, M.

MUHAMMAD, Askia
Civil war in Islamic America. Nation 224:721-4 Je 11 '77

MUHAMMAD Daoud Audeh. See Abu Daoud

MUHAMMAD, Wallace D.
Conversion of the Muslims. il por Time 109:59 Mr 14 '77 *
Second resurrection. K. L. Woodward and N. Davis. por Newsweek 90:67 Ag 22 '77 *

MUHLFELD, Edward D.
24-carat gold; Flying's fiftieth birthday issue. Flying 101:3 S '77

MUHLFELD, Liz
Aquaculture: newest hope to expand food lifeline. il Sci Digest 81:37-9 Ap '77

MUIR, Edwin
Reconsideration. R. B. Shaw. New Repub 176: 39-41 Je 18 '77 *

MUIR, John
Friend of the wilderness. B. McGinty. il pors map Am Hist Illus 12:4-9+ Jl '77 *

MUIR Woods National Monument
Touch, listen, and smell; nature trails for the blind. E. B. Goodman. il Nat Parks & Con Mag 51:14-15 Jl '77
MUKTANANDA, Baba
Master of Ganeshpuri. P. Zweig. il Harpers 254:85-8+ My '77 *
MULCHING
Frames and mulches: self help for vegetables. il House & Gard 149:160-1 Ap '77
Mulching in March. M. Franz. il Org Gard & Farm 24:152+ Mr '77
Mulching with weeds. N. Bubel. il Org Gard & Farm 24:78-81 Ap '77
Potato races under mulch. J. Ruttle. il Org Gard & Farm 24:160-2 My '77
MULDOON, Robert David
Consternation and confusion from Carter's foreign policy; excerpts from address, April 19, 1977. por U.S. News 82:23 My 9 '77

Visit to the United States, 1977

New Zealand Prime Minister visits Washington; statement, November 9, 1977. Dept State Bull 77:840-1 D 12 '77
MULDOWNEY, Shirley
Cha Cha waltzed home. B. Newman. il por Sports Illus 47:26-7 Jl 18 '77 *
MULE deer hunting. See Deer hunting
MULFORD, Carolyn
Place of good abode. il Trav/Holiday 149:44-7 Ja '78
MULHERN, Frank
Old diseases are still a threat to your industry. Farm J 101:Dairy 14+ F '77 *
MULL, Gary
New boats for the SORC. Yachting 141:100+ F '77
MULL (island)
See also
Tobermory, Scotland
MULLANEY, James
April's skies. il Sci Digest 81:68-9 Ap '77
In the depths of space: an exciting cosmic hunt. il Sci Digest 81:41-3 F '77
Look up! The sky tonight provides great viewing. il Sci Digest 81:31-3 Mr '77
Our sun's future. il Sci Digest 82:30-2 N '77
Ufology: uneasy awareness of something gives a new status to investigations. il Sci Digest 82:26-32 Jl '77
Ultimate trip for summer nights. il Sci Digest 81:41-4 Je '77
MULLEN, Jim
Client to designer. T. Gibbs. il Yachting 142:100+ Ag '77 *
MULLEN, John
Colonel Pierce and the peach tree; excerpt from In a year of Our Lord. il Read Digest 111:187-9+ Jl '77
MULLEN, M. G.
Almost magical bean. il Org Gard & Farm 24:75-7 Ap '77
MULLER, H. N. 3d
Man from Putney. il por Am For 83:18-21+ S '77
MULLER, Jörg
Changing city; excerpt; reproductions of paintings, with introd by C. Breslin. Natur Hist 86:86 Je '77
There was a little town; reproductions of paintings; excerpt from The changing countryside. il Read Digest 111:45-7 S '77
MÜLLER, Lothar
Vanadium; memoir of Auschwitz; excerpt from *Il sistema periodico* (The periodic table) tr by G. Jochnowitz. P. Levi. Commentary 63:65-9 Mr '77 *
MULLER, Nancy C. and Oak, Jacquelyn
Noah North (1809-1880) bibl il Antiques 112:939-45 N '77
MULLER, Richard A.
Radioisotope dating with a cyclotron. bibl il Science 196:489-94 Ap 29 '77
—and others
Quarks with unit charge: a search for anomalous hydrogen. bibl il Science 196:521-3 Ap 29 '77
MULLIGAN, Bill
Plant watch. il Am Home 80:8 O; 40 N; 21 D '77
MULLIGAN, Joseph E.
Church investments: challenging G&W. Chr Cent 94:64-7 Ja 26 '77
MULLIN, Elizabeth
Coastal Zone Management; Federal Coastal Zone Management Act. il Environment 19:2-3 N '77
MULLIN, Laurence
Evening on Ravenhill Road. America 137:189-91 O 1 '77
MULLINS, Jack
Captain Jack will make it fly tonight. R. McGonegal. il Hot Rod 30:40-1+ Je '77 *
MULROY, Thomas W. and Rundel, P. W.
Annual plants: adaptations to desert environments. bibl BioScience 27:109-14 F '77
MULTIFLORA roses. See Roses
MULTIMEDIA. See Audio-visual materials
MULTIMETERS. See Electric meters
MULTINATIONAL collective bargaining. See Collective bargaining—Multinational bargaining
MULTINATIONAL corporations. See Corporations, International
MULTIPLE art
Multiple view. I. von Zahne. bibl Art in Am 65:41-3 Ja '77
MULTIPLE cropping. See Double cropping
MULTIPLE Employer Benefit Trusts. See Nonwage payments
MULTIPLE exposure photography. See Photography, Trick
MULTIPLE jobholding. See Supplementary employment
MULTIPLE personality. See Personality, Disorders of
MULTIPLE sclerosis. See Sclerosis, Multiple
MULTIPLE sclerosis reading program. See MS Read-a-thon (reading program)
MULTIPLE stars. See Stars, Multiple
MULTIPURPOSE rooms. See Rooms
MULTIVIBRATORS
Flip-flops and decade counters. F. M. Mims. il Pop Electr 11:75-6 F; 96-8 Mr '77
MULTNOMAH County, Ore, Library. See Libraries—Oregon
MUMBY, Edward
Not ready for the rocking chair. J. R. Hanley. il por Ret Liv 17:40-1 Jl '77 *
MUMFORD, George S.
AN Ursae Majoris—another AM Herculis? il Sky & Tel 54:194-6 S '77
MUMFORD, William Taylor
Diary of the Vicksburg siege. il Am Hist Illus 12:46-8 D '77
MUMMENSCHANZ mime troupe. See Mime
MUMMIES
Biochemical identification of homogenistic acid pigment in an ochronotic Egyptian mummy. F. F. Stenn and others. bibl il Science 197:566-8 Ag 5 '77
Egyptian way of death; excerpt from Book II of The history. Herodotus. il Sr Schol 109:17 Ap 7 '77
Sick mummy—real or imagined? il Chemistry 50:24-5 Ap '77
MUNCH, Edvard
Peter Watkins's Edvard Munch. J. A. Gomez. bibl f il pors Film Q 30:38-46 Wint '76 *
MUNDELL, William D.
Gem stone; In mingling wood; Weather change; poems. Am For 83:27 S '77
Maker of weather; poem. Am For 83:29 Ap '77
MUNDEY, Jack
Never for Mundey; visa refused. E. P. Morgan. Progressive 41:9 My '77 *
MUNDLE, Rob
America's Cup news (cont) Yachting 141:168-9 Je '77
MUNDY, Gregory R. and others
Direct resorption of bone by human monocytes. bibl il Science 196:1109-11 Je 3 '77
MUNICH

City planning

Munich; pedestrian malls. W. Von Eckardt. il New Repub 177:25-6 D 17 '77

Description

Munich. I. C. Kuhn. il Trav/Holiday 148:52-7 D '77

Music

See also
Opera—Germany, West
MUNICH Festival. See Music festivals—Germany, West
MUNICIPAL administration. See Municipal government
MUNICIPAL art. See Art, Municipal
MUNICIPAL bond funds. See Investment trusts
MUNICIPAL bonds
Bonds of Texas. Forbes 119:136 My 15 '77
Cut bond interest fees. il Am City & County 92:53-4 Ag '77
Investing in tax-exempts. bibl il Bus W p 127-9+ Jl 25 '77
Municipal bonds: investors can't get enough of them. L. Snyder. il Fortune 96:89-90+ N '77
Municipal research is a growth industry. J. Madrick. Bus W p81 Mr 14 '77
Mutual funds that pay tax-free income. il Changing T 31:6-9 Mr '77
NYC decision encourages bond market. Am City & County 92:10+ Ja '77
New York—more trouble ahead. Forbes 120:94-5 D 15 '77
Voters say yes to spending for essentials, no to frills. U.S. News 83:104-5 N 21 '77
Why municipals are the best bond buy. il Bus W p70 Ja 31 '77
Why tax-exempts are today's better buy. Bus W p 110 Ap 4 '77
See also
United States—Municipal Securities Rulemaking Board

MUNICIPAL bonds—*Continued*

Laws and regulations

See Securities—Laws and regulations

Yields

Why municipal-bond yields are plunging. Bus W p43 S 19 '77

MUNICIPAL buildings

See also

Public works facilities

MUNICIPAL contracts

Force account under contractor attack; with editorial comment. il Am City & County 92:13, 156 S '77

MUNICIPAL dumps

First steps taken to ban open dumps. il Am City & County 92:52 S '77

See also

Filling (earthwork)

MUNICIPAL employees

See also

American Federation of State, County, and Municipal Employees

New York (city)—Employees

Strikes—United States—Municipal employees

Trade unions—Municipal employees

Pensions

Municipal pension plans: provisions and payments. P. M. Doyle. il M Labor R 100:24-31 N '77

MUNICIPAL engineering

Chilling cost of winter damage. il Bus W p37 Mr 21 '77

MUNICIPAL-federal fiscal relations. See Intergovernmental fiscal relations

MUNICIPAL-federal tax relations. See Intergovernmental tax relations

MUNICIPAL finance

Better news for states, cities—and some taxpayers, too. il U.S. News 83:77-8 Jl 4 '77

For results, get citizens involved early; Brighton, Colo. R. A. Hellbusch. Am City & County 92:50 Ja '77

It's up to the cities to save themselves. G. Breckenfeld. il Fortune 95:194-8+ Mr '77

Macro theoretical approaches to public policy analysis: the fiscal crisis of American cities. H. Teune. bibl f Ann Am Acad 434:174-85 N '77

Policy options for beleaguered cities. A. K. Campbell and J. V. Burkhead. Intellect 105: 208 Ja '77

Put punch in fiscal reporting; Niagara Falls, N.Y. G. M. Chamberlain. Am City & County 92:144 My '77

Spurring S&L loans for the inner city; Federal Home Loan Bank Board. il Bus W p86+ Ap 25 '77

See also

Municipal bonds

Municipal contracts

New York (city)—Finance

MUNICIPAL Finance Officers Association of United States and Canada

Finance officers fight taxable bonds. Am City & County 92:25 Jl '77

MUNICIPAL garages. See Garages, Municipal

MUNICIPAL golf courses. See Golf courses

MUNICIPAL government

Municipal bureaucracies and municipal power. J. R. Hudson. Intellect 105:396-8 Je '77

Municipal departments must work together; views of W. V. Donaldson. por Am City & County 92:52 Ja '77

Surprising trend: you can beat city hall; citizens taking their governments to court. U.S. News 83:67-8 Ag 8 '77

See also

Annexation (municipal government)

Boss rule

City manager plan

Computers—Municipal use

Councilmen

Municipal officers

Municipal services

National League of Cities

also subhead Politics and government under names of cities, e.g. San Francisco—Politics and government

MUNICIPAL Hemeroteca. See Madrid—Libraries

MUNICIPAL improvement

Beyond beautification: cities with souls. J. L. S. Jennings, Jr and N. Sánchez. il Américas 29:50-7 N '77

Instant urban renewal; mural on building walls in Stamford, Conn. R. Kahn. il Design (US) 78:2-4 mid-Summ '77

Key to a beautiful America: renewed personal pride; interview. P. F. Noonan. il por U.S. News 82:39-40 Je 13 '77

See also

All-America cities

Ann Arbor, Mich.—Municipal improvement

Brooklyn—Municipal improvement

Buffalo, N.Y.—Municipal improvement

Business districts

City planning

Playgrounds

Trees in cities

Urban renewal

Water fronts

MUNICIPAL liability. See Government liability

MUNICIPAL liability insurance. See Insurance, Liability

MUNICIPAL motor vehicles. See Motor vehicles, Municipal

MUNICIPAL officers

From city desk to City Hall: the odyssey of an erstwhile journalist. O. Elliott. il pors N Y Times Mag p30-1+ Ag 28 '77

See also

Councilmen

Municipal Finance Officers Association of United States and Canada

Public works officers

MUNICIPAL public works equipment. See Public works equipment

MUNICIPAL recreation. See Recreation

MUNICIPAL Securities Rulemaking Board. See United States—Municipal Securities Rulemaking Board

MUNICIPAL services

Clustering services, mustering cooperation; new Department of Human Services in New Rochelle, N.Y. J. E. Curtis. il Parks & Rec 12: 68-9+ S '77

Cooperative department streamlines city services; New Rochelle, N.Y. J. E. Curtis. il Am City & County 92:67 Ap '77

Why things don't work any more. J. Diebold. por Newsweek 90:8-9 Jl 18 '77

MUNICIPAL Signal Association, International. See International Municipal Signal Association

MUNICIPAL taxation. See Local taxation

MUNICIPAL trucks. See Trucks, Municipal

MUNICIPAL utilities. See Public utilities

MUNITIONS

America's top arms merchants; table. M. T. Klare. Bull Atom Sci 33:20-1 Je '77

Let's change the way the Pentagon does business. J. S. Gansler. il Harvard Bus R 55: 109-18 My '77

Who's who in arms. R. K. Musil. Progressive 41:13 N '77

See also

Firearms industry

Military-industrial complex

Export-import trade

Arms export curbs expected to bend. C. Brownlow. il Aviation W 106:85+ Je 6 '77

Arms sales plan sent to Congress; Mixed impact seen in arms sales policy. Aviation W 107:16-17 S 19 '77

Arms sales unlimited. M. Klare. Progressive 41: 9-11 D '77

Carter approves arms sales. Aviation W 106:21 Ap 4 '77

Carter as arms merchant. R. Carroll and S. Sullivan. il map Newsweek 90:31-2 Ag 8 '77

Carter moves to expand Africa arms sales. Aviation W 107:24 Ag 1 '77

China pushes a trade decision. il Bus W p75 N 21 '77

Congress presses arms sales control. E. Kozicharow. Aviation W 107:17-18 Ag 8 '77

Controlling arms transfers: an instrument of U.S. foreign policy; address, June 27, 1977. L. W. Benson. Dept State Bull 77:155-9 Ag 1 '77

Cutting back on the arms trade. Nation 224: 418 Ap 9 '77

Europe's booming arms trade. il Fortune 96: 170-3 N '77

Export curb, NATO goal clash. C. Brownlow. Aviation W 106:12-13 My 30 '77

Exporting death to Ireland; arms purchased with American donations. D. Fisher. Commonweal 104:356-8 Je 10 '77; Discussion. 104:500-2 Ag 5 '77

Exports increase as proportion of military business for U.S. Aviation W 107:60-1 O 31 '77

Final Carter export policy year away. Aviation W 107:14 S 12 '77

Foreign arms sales hampered defense capability, GAO says. Aviation W 107:57-8 Ag 22 '77

Foreign military sales funding passed. K. Johnsen. Aviation W 107:19 Ag 1 '77

How not to limit the arms trade; cancelling promised sale of CBU-72 bombs to Israel. New Repub 176:5 F 26 '77

How we practice arms restraint. M. T. Klare. Nation 225:268-9+ S 24 '77

Korean arms buys from U.S. detailed. Aviation W 107:13 D 19 '77

Limited action against apartheid; UN imposition of mandatory arms embargo on South Africa. il Time 110:35-6 N 14 '77

Loneliness is an enemy; proposed arms embargo of South Africa. il Time 110:36-7 N 7 '77

Merchants of death revisited. E. Taylor. il Horizon 19:82-7 Ja '77

MUNITIONS—Export-import trade—*Continued*
Message to Pretoria. R. Steele and others. il Newsweek 90:30-1 N 7 '77
Mood in South Africa: defiance, bitterness, anger; with interview with B. J. Vorster. K. M. Chrysler. il U.S. News 83:38-40 N 21 '77
Navy's foreign military sales burgeon. il Aviation W 106:126+ Ja 31 '77
New arms export policy; excerpts from address. T. V. Jones. Aviation W 107:9 Ag 8 '77
Policy decision near on arms sales. Aviation W 106:20 Ap 18 '77
Policy is born; foreign arms sales. J. Osborne. New Repub 176:10-12 Je 18 '77
President Carter announces policy on transfers of conventional arms; statement, May 19, 1977. J. Carter. Dept State Bull 76:625-6 Je 13 '77
Proliferating arms industry: America exports its know-how. M. T. Klare. Nation 224:173-8 F 12 '77
Report warns on danger of Iran sales corruption. E. Kozicharow. Aviation W 107:22-3 D 12 '77
Revised figures boost Soviets' third world military deliveries. Aviation W 107:24 Ag 22 '77
Russia arms Peru. T. Szulc. New Repub 176:18-19 F 19 '77
State dept. control asked on arms export efforts. il Aviation W 106:34-5 Ap 25 '77
Study finds arms policy missing goals. K. Johnsen. Aviation W 107:19-20 O 17 '77
Taking the wind out of arms sales. New Repub 176:6+ Je 11 '77
Those controversial planes for Iran . . .; AWACS. il U.S. News 83:36 Ag 15 '77
U.N. Security Council condemns South Africa's apartheid policy and imposes a mandatory arms embargo; statements, with text of resolutions, October 31 and November 4, 1977. A. J. Young. Dept State Bull 77:859-66 D 12 '77
U.S. arms embargo against South Africa; statement, July 20, 1977. W. H. Lewis. Dept State Bull 77:320-2 S 5 '77
U.S. retains unilateral arms restraints; report on question and answer session. K. Johnsen. Aviation W 107:20-2 D 12 '77
U.S. security assistance policy for Latin America; statement, April 5, 1977. T. A. Todman. Dept State Bull 76:444-6 My 2 '77
Very promising man; American arms sales. Nation 225:388-9 O 22 '77
Vote for continued arms sales abroad. il Nations Bus 65:16 Ag '77
Voting the embargo; UN vote on South Africa. K. Willenson and others. il Newsweek 90:62 N 14 '77
Vulcan was a piker. Nation 225:548 N 26 '77
Why Carter will have a tough time trying to curb arms sales. il U.S. News 83:39-40 Ag 1 '77

Finance

Aerospace & defense. il Forbes 121:61-2+ Ja 9 '78

Arab countries

Arabs diversify into the arms business. Bus W p31-2 O 31 '77

MUNITIONS industries. See Munitions
MUNITIONS trade. See Munitions—Export-import trade

MUÑIZ, Mando
Staying at the top of his class. P. Putnam. il pors Sports Illus 46:20-2 Ja 31 '77 •

MUNK, Arthur W.
Whither religion? a plea for a return to sanity and a genuine creativity. bibl Intellect 106:249-50 D '77

MUNN, Vella C.
Special report: a children's learning fair. il Wilson Lib Bull 52:122-3 O '77

MUNNECKE, Tom
First West Coast Computer Faire. il Pop Electr 12:74-5 S '77

MUÑOZ, Aurelia
Muñoz of Barcelona. E. Arenal. il Craft Horiz 37:58-61+ D '77 •

MUÑOZ, Jorge Luján. See Luján Muñoz, J.

MUÑOZ, Juan
Chilean flamingo court and dance; with biographical sketch. il Natur Hist 86:9, 72-8 D '77

MUNRO, Alice
Beggar maid; story. New Yorker 53:34-40 Je 27 '77
Providence; story. Redbook 149:98-9 Ag '77
Royal beatings; story. New Yorker 53:36-44 Mr 14 '77

MUNRO, Eleanor C.
Money for art's sake. il Atlantic 239:75-8 Ap '77
(ed) See Cheever, J. Not only I the narrator, but I John Cheever

MUNRO, Ross Howard
China's bureaucratic nightmare: rationing for 900 million people. il U.S. News 83:35-6 D 12 '77

about

China without gee whiz. il por Time 110:99 N 7 '77 •

MUNROW, David John
Art of the Netherlands; Seraphim recording. S. T. Sommer. Hi Fi 27:92-4 Ag '77 •

MUNSON, Glenn
Increase your wood power. il Org Gard & Farm 24:95-100 O '77

MUNSON, Richard
Public power: its time has come. Progressive 41: 26-9 My '77

MUNVES, James
Annual report. il New Yorker 53:32-3 Mr 7 '77
Black holes. New Yorker 53:32-3 Ap 11 '77

MUONS. See Particles (nuclear physics)
MUPPETS. See Puppets and puppet plays

MURAL painting and decoration
Art room mural. E. Hayhurst. il Sch Arts 76: 13 Je '77
Bicentennial mural. M. L. Cox. il Sch Arts 76:32 Ap '77
Cheating the philistines; rediscovery and renovation of mural by A. Gorky. Vasari. il por Art N 76:20-2 S '77
Deck the walls. il Bet Hom & Gard 55:226 N '77
Group painting project; Thomas Johnson Elementary School, Baltimore. il Sch Arts 76:49 Mr '77
Home improvement ideas for the house fixer: cover-up tactics with graphics. D. Raffel. il House & Gard 149:90+ N '77
How to paint your own flower borders and trompe l'oeil gazebo. il House & Gard 149: 106+ Ap '77
Jack Beal's history of American labor; murals in the new Labor Department building. B. Forgey. il Art N 76:38 Ap '77
Labor Department mural: a complicated voyage; J. Beal's murals. B. Carter. il por Art N 76: 40-1 My '77
Los Cuatro: Mexico's majestic artists. E. C. Roberts. il Américas 29:38-45 Je '77
Printed mural. M. Foster. il Sch Arts 77:48-50 D '77
Puvis de Chavannes: the alternative. P. Schneider. bibl il Art in Am 65:94-8 My '77
Ramos Martínez, Mexican muralist. G. R. Small. il por Américas 29:19-22 Ap '77
See also
Cave drawings and paintings
Mosaics

Conservation and restoration

Shahn's Bronx P.O. murals: the perils of public art. C. Baldwin. il Art in Am 65:15-16+ My '77

MURAL painting and decoration, Exterior
American time line; Bicentennial mural at Altadena Elementary School, Pasadena, Calif. E. Levine. il Sch Arts 76:30-2 Je '77
Art as big as all outdoors il Horizon 21:23-9 Ja '78
Big picture on barn painting. il Parks & Rec 12:32-3 My '77
Broadway babies; Alex Katz's Times Square mural. Vasari. il Art N 76:19-20 S '77
Instant urban renewal; mural on building walls in Stamford, Conn. R. Kahn. il Design (US) 78:2-4 mid-Summ '77
Mona Lisa, revised; collage at the Red Rocks Campus of the Community College of Denver. T. M. Jenkins. il Design (US) 78:23 Summ '77
New canvases for art; Wisconsin barns funded by National Endowment for the Arts. il House B 119:10+ Ag '77
Rural murals in dairyland; barn murals in Wisconsin. il Time 109:71 My 16 '77

MURASE, Miyeko
Recent arrival in the ranks of great collectors. il Smithsonian 8:84-91 Je '77

MURCHISON, Brian
Two years in Africa. Todays Educ 66:87+ Ja '77

MURCHISON, William
(ed) See Muggeridge, M. Cheery doomsayer

MURDER
Anatomy of a reporter's murder; D. F. Bolles. R. Lindsey. il por N Y Times Mag p 11-14+ F 20 '77
And then there were sixty; execution of Teferi Benti. il Time 109:37 F 14 '77
Arrest in Birmingham; charging R. E. Chambliss with 1963 church bombing. R. Boeth and V. E. Smith. il pors Newsweek 90:32+ O 10 '77
Blow-up; murder of O. Letelier. K. Lynch. Nat R 29:320 Mr 18 '77
Chop-shop war; Mob murders in Chicago. R. Steele and C. J. Harper. Newsweek 90:22 Ag 15 '77
City under siege; Son of Sam case. P. Axthelm. il Newsweek 90:18+ Ag 15 '77
Civil war in Chinatown; San Francisco. D. A. Williams and others. il Newsweek 90:39 S 26 '77
Climbing the tower; Austin, Texas site of 1966 murders by C. Whitman. H. Crews. Esquire 88:38-9 Ag '77
David Berkowitz story. Commonweal 104:547-8 S 2 '77
Deadly messenger of God; E. LeBaron. il por Time 110:31 Ag 29 '77
Death of a wireman; murder of F. Chin. il por Time 109:19 F 21 '77

MURDER—*Continued*
Diamonds and death; murder of P. Jaroslawicz. R. Steele and S. Agrest. il por Newsweek 90:35-6 O 10 '77
Fingering a .22-cal. killer; arrest of J. Ullo in Los Angeles. Time 110:29+ S 26 '77
Has the Mafia penetrated the F.B.I.? N. Gage. il N Y Times Mag p 14-16+ O 2 '77
Hunting the Son of Sam. T. Mathews and others. il map Newsweek 90:18-21 Jl 11 '77
Hunting the Son of Sam; New York City killer. P. Axthelm and A. Lallande. il Newsweek 89:86 Je 20 '77
Killer captured; Son of Sam case. R. Rosenblatt. New Repub 177:40-1 Ag 20 '77
Killing excuse; wives' murdering husbands because of abuse. il por Time 110:108 N 28 '77
L.A. strangler. il Time 110:24 D 19 '77
Letelier/Moffitt murder: this is how it was done. S. Landau and R. Stavins. por Nation 224:358-60 Mr 26 '77
Letelier-Moffitt mystery. J. Stein. Progressive 41:36-9 N '77
Man hunt for Son of Sam goes on. il Time 110:13-15 Ag 15 '77
Murder at Jupiter; political corruption and construction workers' union in Lake Charles, La. K. Y. Tomlinson. il Read Digest 111:115-19 Jl '77
Nazi of New Rochelle; case of F. Cowan. T. Mathews and S. Agrest. il por Newsweek 89:30 F 28 '77
New life of Reilly. E. Keerdoja. il por Newsweek 90:6 Jl 25 '77
New Mafia killer: a silenced .22. il Time 109:22 Ap 18 '77
The night TV cried wolf; Son of Sam coverage. C. Tucker. Sat R 5:56 O 1 '77
Notes and comment; press treatment of Son of Sam story. New Yorker 53:21-2 Ag 15; 19-22 S 5 '77
Nun on trial for infanticide; case of Sister Maureen. C. Breslin. il por Ms 5:68-71+ Mr '77
On an unsolved mystery; 1948 murder of G. Polk in Greece. H. E. Salisbury. Progressive 41:24-5 My '77
Our dream house was haunted; scene of the De Feo murders and home of the G. L. Lutzes. P. Hoffman. il Good H 184:119+ Ap '77
Repentance, retreat and murder; case of Sheik Zahaby. il Time 110:32 Jl 18 '77
Ron Lyle's last fight? R. Boeth and D. Gram. il pors Newsweek 91:29-30 Ja 16 '78
Sam told me to do it. . .Sam is the devil. il pors Time 110:22-3+ Ag 22 '77
Season of savagery and rage; F. W. Cowan's shooting spree in New Rochelle, N.Y. il Time 109:23-4 F 28 '77
Seventh son; shooting of Rev W. Maxwell in Alexander City, Ala. D. M. Alpern and V. E. Smith. il por Newsweek 90:21 Jl 4 '77
Shoot-out in the Dirgue; Ethiopia. il Newsweek 89:48 F 14 '77
Shy murderers. M. Lee and others. bibl il Psychol Today 11:68-70+ N '77
Sick world of Son of Sam. P. Axthelm and others. il pors Newsweek 90:16-20+ Ag 22 '77
Silent one; case of D. Lang. J. K. Footlick and E. Sciolino. Newsweek 90:89+ N 7 '77
Sister Maureen: not guilty and not free. C. Breslin. Ms 6:22 Jl '77
Six million dollar murder; murder of M. V. Jackson. L. S. Connor. il por Sat Eve Post 249:54-5+ N '77
Son of Sam is not sleeping. il Time 110:61 Jl 11 '77
Son of Sam—the killer who terrorized New York. il por Read Digest 111:155-60 N '77
Strange murder of Homer G. Phillips. E. T. Clayton. il Ebony 32:160-2+ S '77
Strangler; Los Angeles murders. D. A. Williams and P. Brinkley-Rogers. il Newsweek 90:36 D 19 '77
Strangler's grip; Los Angeles. D. A. Williams and others. il Newsweek 91:24-6 Ja 9 '78
Terror in Spring Mill; murder of M. Jackson. il por Time 109:42 My 23 '77
They all trusted their killer; child killings in Oakland County Mich. il Time 109:20 Ap 4 '77
Through the looking-glass; conviction of R. Williams overturned. Nat R 29:428 Ap 15 '77
Town that lives in terror; child murders in Birmingham, Mich. in Oakland County. B. Davidson. il Good H 185:136-7+ S '77
Tracing of Beretta A47469; condensation. N. M. Adams. il Read Digest 112:203-6+ Ja '78
Trash-bag murders; case of D. D. Hill and P. W. Kearney in California. D. A. Williams and J. Huck. il pors Newsweek 90:22 Jl 18 '77
Twenty-eight, and counting. . .; arrest of mass murderers P. Kearney and D. Hill. il pors Time 110:49 Jl 18 '77
Understanding lethal violence. M. L. Simpson. Intellect 105:379-80 My '77
Victim no. 21; murder of Mafia lawyer, G. Gallina in New York City. Time 110:39 N 21 '77
Why men dominate women; female infanticide and overpopulation. M. Harris. il N Y Times Mag p46+ N 13 '77
Will he stand trial? D. Berkowitz. D. M. Alpern and S. Agrest. il por Newsweek 90:27-8 Ag 29 '77
Witness to justice; murder of R. Grande. E. Moran. il America 136:410-14 My 7 '77
See also
Trials (murder)

History

Murder in the Middle Ages. Sci Am 237:87 D '77

MURDER in literature. See Literature—Themes

MURDERERS. See Murder

MURDOCH, Keith Rupert. See Murdoch, R.

MURDOCH, Rupert
After a rash of take-overs, new worries about press lords. il por U.S. News 82:54-6 Ja 24 '77 •
How Murdoch does it. D. Gelman and others. il pors Newsweek 89:90-1 My 30 '77 •
Murdoch watch. Time 109:49 My 30 '77 •
New York's battleground. il Time 109:43-4 Ja 24 '77 •
Of many things. J. O'Hare. America 136:40 Ja 22 '77 •
Trials of Murdoch. D. Gelman. il por Newsweek 89:78 Ja 24 '77 •

MURGER, Henri
Drawn from life. S. Hughes. il Opera N 42:12-14+ D 24 '77 •
Woe to the vanquished; Vie de Bohème. J. Kestner. il Opera N 41:14-17 Mr 19 '77 •

MURIE, Margaret E.
Return to the Sheenjek. il por map Liv Wildn 41:4-12 Jl '77

MURINE lupus nephritis. See Kidneys—Diseases

MURINE sarcoma virus. See Tumor viruses

MURPHEY, Cecil B.
Accusing finger, the helping hand. Chr Today 21:30-1 Je 17 '77
Excitement for missions. Chr Today 22:34 D 30 '77
More psychological insights. Chr Today 21:20-5 S 9 '77
They count, too. Chr Today 22:30-1 O 21 '77

MURPHY, Calvin
Calvin discovers Murphy's law. C. Kirkpatrick. il por Sports Illus 47:14-15 Ag 15 '77 •

MURPHY, Ed
Distrusting reality. G. J. Hazlitt. il Art N 76:91-2 O '77 •

MURPHY, Ellen
Lines from a primitive; poem. Commonweal 104:135 Mr 4 '77
Watching the Olympics; poem. Commonweal 104:504 Ag 5 '77

MURPHY, Francis X.
Whatever happened to Xavier Rynne? J. Lelyveld. il por N Y Times Mag p 122 O 9 '77 •

MURPHY, Gerald D.
Early California gears up for the olive war. por Duns R 110:22-3 S '77 •

MURPHY, Jane M.
Psychiatric labeling in cross-cultural perspective. bibl il Science 191:1019-28; 196:484+ Mr 12 '76, Ap 29 '77

MURPHY, Jim
Optical template for easier wood-turning. il Pop Sci 210:186 Ap '77

MURPHY, John
Packing for a vacation trip. il Ret Liv 17:47-8 Jl '77

MURPHY, Louis. See Verner, Z. jt auth

MURPHY, Sister Maureen
Nun on trial for infanticide. C. Breslin. il por Ms 5:68-71+ Mr '77 •
Sister Maureen: not guilty and not free. C. Breslin. Ms 6:22 Jl '77 •

MURPHY, Morgan Francis
Excerpt from statement on illegal aliens, August 1977. Cong Digest 56:249+ O '77

MURPHY, Richard W.
European pleasures. il Horizon 19:28-33 Jl '77

MURPHY, Thomas Aquinas
Unemployment; address, February 9, 1977. Vital Speeches 43:329-33 Mr 15 '77
We are losing the freedom to decide; address, August 6, 1977. Vital Speeches 43:714-17 S 15 '77

about

Motor Trend Man of the Year Awards to Thomas A. Murphy and E. M. "Pete" Estes. pors Motor T 29:34+ F '77 •

MURPHY, Thomas P.
Venture capital. See second issue of each month of Forbes

MURRAY, Bain
Aki means new music in Cleveland. il Hi Fi 28:MA24-5+ Ja '78

MURRAY, Betsy Benjamin-. See Benjamin-Murray, B.

MURRAY, Jack
Writing for the martial arts market. il Writers Digest 57:29-30 Je '77

MURRAY, Sir James Augustus Henry
Arbiter of words. il por Horizon 20:30-1 O '77 *
Natural curiosity. D. Grumbach. Sat R 5:30 N 12 '77 *
MURRAY, Jim
Jim Murray: king of sports. W. Cieplik. por Writers Digest 57:23-4 Ag '77 *
MURRAY, Joan
Building inspector; poem; excerpt from Egg tooth. Ms 5:64 Je '77
MURRAY, John
Bermuda Triangle mystery; drama. Plays 36:1-14 My '77
Break that record! drama. Plays 37:15-30 D '77
Romantic robots; drama. Plays 37:1-15 N '77
Super-duper market; drama. Plays 37:81-3 N '77
Terror of Bigfoot; drama. Plays 36:1-12 Ap '77
That's a good question! drama. Plays 36:1-18 F '77
MURRAY, John E.
Lawyers—computers—and power; address, April 20, 1977. Vital Speeches 43:487-90 Je 1 '77
MURRAY, John F.
O'Phelan drinking; story. New Yorker 53:40-6 O 3 '77
MURRAY, Kate
Kate Murray: pharmacist/magazine publisher; On the line magazine. D. Duke. por Mademoiselle 83:78 O '77 *
MURRAY, Linda
Sexual boredom. il Fam Health 9:22-6 Je '77
MURRAY, Madalyn (Mays) See O'Hair, M. M. M.
MURRAY, Philip
Helbi-Gami: the serpent bridegroom; poem. Poetry 130:12-13 Ap '77
MURRAY, Polly
Mrs Murray's mystery disease. E. Keiffer. il por Good H 184:80+ Mr '77 *
MURRAY, Robert
People who fly: Robert Murray. S. Wilkinson. il pors Flying 100:54-5+ Je '77 *
MURRAY, Thomas E., family
Golden clan; excerpt. J. Corry. il N Y Times Mag p 16-19+ Mr 13 '77
MURRAY, Thomas M.
Spring training. il Sat Eve Post 249:72-3+ Ap '77
MURRAY Louis Dance Company
Dance; troupes of Alwin Nikolais and Murray Louis at the Beacon Theater. J. Maskey. il Hi Fi 27:MA12-13 Je '77
Murray and Nik; performances at New York's Beacon Theater. H. Saal. il Newsweek 89:43 F 21 '77
Nik and Murray at the Beacon. L. Small. il Dance Mag 51:22-3+ My '77
MURRES. See Auks
MURRY, George V.
Black bishop for Mississippi. America 137:32 Jl 16 '77
MURTHA, John Patrick, 1932-
Should U.S. limit steel imports? interview. pors U.S. News 83:77-8 O 24 '77
MUSCATINE, L. and Porter, J. W.
Reef corals: mutualistic symbioses adapted to nutrient-poor environments. bibl il BioScience 27:454-60 Jl '77
MUSCLE
Bounds on "bound water": transverse nuclear magnetic resonance relaxation in barnacle muscle. K. R. Foster and others; discussion. bibl Science 198:1180-2 D 16 '77
Gap junctions: their presence and necessity in myometrium during parturition. R. E. Garfield and others. bibl il Science 198:958-60 D 2 '77
Localization of cyclic GMP and cyclic AMP in cardiac and skeletal muscle: immunocytochemical demonstration. S. H. Ong and A. L. Steiner. bibl il Science 195:183-5 Ja 14 '77
Potassium accumulation in muscle: a test of the binding hypothesis. L. G. Palmer and J. Gulati; reply with rejoinder. G. I. Ling. bibl il Science 198:1281-4 D 23 '77
Stuff that holds you together. I. Ross. il Mech Illus 73:82+ F '77
See also
Electromyography
Heart—Muscle
Muscular sense

Diseases

See also
Dystrophy, Muscular
Myasthenia gravis

Innervation

Degenerating nerve fiber products do not alter physiological properties of adjacent innervated skeletal muscle fibers. T. N. Tiedt and others. bibl il Science 198:839-41 N 25 '77
Denervated skeletal muscle fibers develop discrete patches of high acetylcholine receptor density. P. K. Ko and others. bibl il Science 196:540-2 Ap 29 '77
Partial denervation affects both denervated and innervated fibers in the mammalian skeletal muscle. A. Cangiano and others. bibl il Science 196:542-5 Ap 29 '77

Proteins

Return of myosin heads to thick filaments after muscle contraction. N. Yagi and others. bibl il Science 197:685-7 Ag 12 '77
MUSCLE cells. See Cells
MUSCLE contraction
Return of myosin heads to thick filaments after muscle contraction. N. Yagi and others. bibl il Science 197:685-7 Ag 12 '77
MUSCLE fibers. See Muscle
MUSCLE men. See Body building
MUSCOVY ducks. See Ducks
MUSCULAR dystrophy. See Dystrophy, Muscular
MUSCULAR sense
Perception of impossible limb positions induced by tendon vibration. B. Craske. bibl il Science 196:71-3 Ap 1 '77
MUSELLO, Christine
To have and to hold from this day... to the next. Ms 6:57+ N '77
MUSEUM directors
Help wanted at the Met. L. S. Gordon. il N Y Times Mag p 13-15+ Je 26 '77
Hoving years; interview, ed by M. N. Carter. T. P. F. Hoving. pors Art N 76:37-40 Ja '77
Marcia's not there to take artistic chances; interview, ed by J. N. Gifford. M. Tucker. il por Ms 5:30+ Ap '77
Privilege and passion of directing museums; interview, ed by J. Gruen. R. Strong. il por Art N 76:58-62+ Ja '77
Scramble for museum sponsors: is curatorial independence for sale? L. Rosenbaum. il Art in Am 65:10-14 Ja '77
View from the castle. S. D. Ripley. Smithsonian 8:6 O '77
See also
Agee, W.
Drexler, A.
Freudenheim, T.
Houlihan, P.
Jordan, W. B.
Kutner, J.
Messer, T.
Mollison, J.
Turner, E. H.
Wittmann, O.
Women museum directors
MUSEUM education
Classroom in the cactus; Arizona-Sonora Desert Museum. J. Stocker. il Am Educ 13:6-11 D '77
MUSEUM of African Art. See Washington, D.C.—Galleries and museums
MUSEUM of Broadcasting. See New York (city)—Galleries and museums
MUSEUM of Contemporary Crafts, New York
Objects: USA Johnson collection given to MCC. Craft Horiz 37:39+ Ag '77
Open windows; question of acquisition of the Museum of Contemporary Crafts building by the Museum of Modern Art. B. Rockefeller. por Craft Horiz 37:43 Je '77
MUSEUM of Fine Arts, Boston. See Boston Museum of Fine Arts
MUSEUM of International Folk Art, Santa Fe. See Santa Fe, N. Mex.—Galleries and museums
MUSEUM of Modern Art, New York
MOMA plans expansion—including an apartment tower. il Archit Rec 162:37 S '77
MOMA's construction project: reflections on a glass tower. L. Rosenbaum. il Art in Am 65:10-13+ N '77
MOMA's survival plan: more harm than good? T. Trucco. il Art N 76:90-1 S '77
MOMA's tower in the sky. G. Marzorati. il Art N 76:54-6 Ap '77
Modern art museum opens in New York; excerpt from The art world; ed by B. Diamonstein. Art N 76:152+ N '77
Museum of Modern Art. R. Smith. il Art in Am 65:93-6 S '77
Open windows; question of acquisition of the Museum of Contemporary Crafts' building. B. Rockefeller. por Craft Horiz 37:43 Je '77
Pie in the sky? major building program. il Horizon 20:81 O '77
Pushing future directions in modern design; Department of Architecture and Design. B. Diamonstein. il por Art N 76:43-5 S '77
Spanish acquisition? Guernica. E. Keerdoja. il Newsweek 90:16 O 31 '77
MUSEUM of Modern Art of Latin America. See Washington, D.C.—Galleries and museums
MUSEUM of Natural History, New York. See American Museum of Natural History, New York
MUSEUM of the American China Trade, Milton, Mass. See Historic houses, sites, etc.—Massachusetts
MUSEUM of the City of New York
Early nineteenth-century parlor at the Museum of the City of New York. S. B. Sherrill. il Antiques 111:442+ Mr '77

MUSEUM stores
Cleopatra's choice. L. Nooger. il Am Home 80: 13 N '77
Museums find a new patron: the retail market. il Bus W p 135-6 O 24 '77
Shopping boom at your local museum. T. Trucco. il Art N 76:56-60 O '77

MUSEUM trustees. See Art galleries and museums—Trustees, boards, committees, etc.

MUSEUM workers
Viewpoint: women at ICP. J. Deschin. il Pop Phot 81:28+ S '77

MUSEUMS
See also
Agricultural museums
Art galleries and museums
Childrens museums
Historical museums
Indians of North America—Museums
Natural history museums
Naval museums
Photography—Galleries and museums
Science museums
Waxworks
also names of museums, e.g. National Gallery of Canada; *also* subhead Galleries and museums under names of cities, e.g. Denver—Galleries and museums

Architecture

Homage to Catalonia; Center for the Study of Contemporary Art/Joan Miró Foundation; with introd by M. F. Schmertz. il Archit Rec 161: 85-92 Mr '77
Parkin wins Canadian National Gallery competition. il Archit Rec 162:39 S '77
Spaces for anthropological art; Museum of Anthropology, University of British Columbia in Vancouver; with introd by M. F. Schmertz. il Archit Rec 161:103-10 My '77

Educational aspects

See Museum education

Management

See also
Art galleries and museums—Management

Work with children

See also
Art galleries and museums—Work with children
Museum education

England

See Museums—Great Britain

Great Britain

Museum of old buildings is established in England; Avoncroft Museum of Buildings. M. Burns. il Archit Rec 161:34 My '77
Wine and spirit labels in Harvey's Wine Museum; Bristol, England. J. Banister. il Antiques 112:278-81 Ag '77
See also
Waxworks—Great Britain

Netherlands

Keeper of the library past; Netherlands Library Museum and Archives. N. D. Stevens. il Wilson Lib Bull 51:841-3 Je '77

United States

See Museums

MUSEUMS, Remodeled. See Buildings, Remodeled

MUSEUMS and schools
Art museum and the school. B. Y. Newsom. il Am Educ 13:12-16 D '77
See also
Museum education

MUSGRAVE, Thea
Musician of the month: Thea Musgrave; interview, ed by S. Fleming. por Hi Fi 27:MA6-7+ S '77

about

Mistress Musgrave. H. Heinsheimer. por Opera N 42:44-6 S '77 •
Voice of Ariadne. Reviews
Hi Fi il 28:MA20-1 Ja '78 •
Nation 225:411-12 O 22 '77 •
New Yorker 53:163-5 O 24 '77 •
Newsweek il 90:117 O 10 '77 •
Sat R 5:64 D 10 '77 •
Time il 110:72 O 10 '77 •

MUSHROOM processing industry. See Food industry

MUSHROOMS
Shaggy mane—the safe fall mushroom. S. Hawn. il Field & S 81:150 Mr '77
See also
Cookery—Mushrooms

MUSIC
Artist life. D. J. Soria. See issues of High fidelity and Musical America
Here & there. See issues of High fidelity and Musical America
Music (cont) il Ms 5:36+ Mr; 6:27-8 N '77
New music. J. La Barbara. il por Hi Fi 27:MA14-15 My; MA14-15 Je '77
See also
Bands (music)
Christmas music
Church music
Composition (music)
Computers—Musical use
Concerto and concertos
Copyright—Music
East and West in music
Embellishment (music)
Jazz music
Libraries—Music collections
Mass (music)
Melodrama
Motion pictures—Music
Musical intervals and scales
Musical meter and rhythm
Muzak Corporation
Opera
Oratorio
Orchestral music
Orchestras
Radio broadcasting—Music
Religion and music
Rock music (songs, etc)
Television broadcasting—Music
Vocal music

Acoustics and physics

Acoustics of the singing voice. J. Sundberg. il Sci Am 236:82-4+ bibl(p 150) Mr '77

Analysis, appreciation

Modest proposal. Am Rec G 40:4+ Je '77
Music: a bridge through time. E. Schaeffer. Chr Today 21:22 Je 17 '77
Turning on to Beethoven & Co. J. Rockwell. Esquire 88:116+ D '77
See also
Opera—Appreciation

Appreciation

See Music—Analysis, appreciation

Bibliography

Book reviews. P. J. Smith. See alternate issues of High fidelity and Musical America
Book section. Am Rec G 41:45-8+ N '77
Books. il Hi Fi 27:152-3 F; 148+ Mr; 137 Je; 167 O '77
Folios. E. Bretton. See issues of High fidelity and Musical America
Quarterly book-list, comp by C. Bryant. See issues of Musical quarterly
Reviews of books. See issues of Musical quarterly

Collectors and collecting

Centuries of song in her garage; E. H. Linscott's collection of New England folk songs. J. W. Steinbergh. il Ms 6:22 S '77

Competitions

AMSA competition—something different; award presentation at American Music Scholarship Association piano competition by L. Hollander. J. Wierzbicki. il por Hi Fi 27:MA28-9 O '77
Damn good shot; Van Cliburn piano competition winner, S. De Groote. il por Horizon 20:33 D '77
Fifth Van Cliburn Piano Competition. A. Satz. il pors Hi Fi 28:MA16-18 Ja '78
Karajan Orchestra Competition; second prize won by Boston University Concert Orchestra. T. Eckert, Jr. il por Hi Fi 27:MA34-5+ Ap '77
1976 Bach International Piano Competition. I. Lowens. il por Hi Fi 27:MA24-5 Jl '77
Second Arthur Rubinstein Piano Competition. M. Bookspan. il Hi Fi 27:MA37-8 Ag '77
Sydney International Piano Competition. S. Fleming. il Hi Fi 27:MA36-8 D '77

Composition

See Composition (music)

Conferences

Commentary: the IMS at Berkeley. J. Peyser. Mus Q 63:545-8 O '77
International Musicological Congress; IMS conference in Berkeley. B. Schwarz. il Hi Fi 27: MA27-9 D '77
See also
International Congress of Organists

Copyright

See Copyright—Music

Economic aspects

See also
Music and state
Music as a profession

History and criticism

Ives's position in social and musical history. S. Blum. bibl f il Mus Q 63:459-82 O '77
Notes on two Roman manuscripts of the early sixteenth century. R. Sherr. bibl f il Mus Q 63:48-73 Ja '77
See also
Opera—History and criticism
Romanticism in music

MUSIC—*Continued*

Instruction and study

Boulez's IRCAM: amnesia in Nibelheim; Institut de Recherche et Coordination Acoustique/ Musique. R. McMullen. il pors Hi Fi 27:80-4 Ap '77
Motown blues; Detroit's music education program. I. Kolodin. Sat R 4:14 S 3 '77
Music education and the human brain. T. A. Regelski. Educ Digest 43:44-7 O '77
Music lessons: get the most for your money. M. L. Schildkraut. il Good H 184:204 Ap '77
Music lessons your child will like. il Changing T 31:17-19 S '77
Parent's guide to music lessons. D. M. Paananen. Bet Hom & Gard 55:64+ S '77
Teaching: Nadia Boulanger. S. R. Hoover. Am Scholar 46:496-502 Aut '77
See also
Music schools
Piano—Instruction and study

Anecdotes, facetiae, satire, etc.

Playing up to Toscanini. R. Severo. N Y Times Mag p79 Ja 16 '77

Manuscripts

Great Mozart-Beethoven caper; theft of music manuscripts from the German State Library. P. Moor. il Hi Fi 27:72-7 Mr '77
Laurence Feininger 1909-1976: life, work, legacy; cataloger and transcriber of Catholic Church music. E. E. Lowinsky. bibl il por Mus Q 63:327-66 Jl '77
Notes on two Roman manuscripts of the early sixteenth century. R. Sherr. bibl f il Mus Q 63:48-73 Ja '77

Motion pictures

See Motion pictures—Music

Notation

See Musical notation

Performance

See also
Embellishment (music)

Periodicals

See also
High fidelity and Musical America (periodical)

Philosophy and aesthetics

See also
Romanticism in music

Recording and reproducing

See Sound—Recording and reproducing

Scholarships and fellowships

AMSA competition—something different; award presentation at American Music Scholarship Association piano competition by L. Hollander. J. Wierzbicki. il por Hi Fi 27:MA28-9 O '77

Scores

Bibliography

Books of music. Am Rec G 40:60 My '77

Study and teaching

See Music—Instruction and study

Theory

See also
Musical intervals and scales
Musical meter and rhythm

Australia

Australia: an embarrassment of cultural energy. J. Culshaw. il Hi Fi 27:17+ My '77

California

See also
San Francisco—Music

Canada

See also
Vancouver, British Columbia—Music

Colorado

See also
Boulder, Colo.—Music
Denver—Music

England

History

Ears of an untoward make: Pope and Handel. M. R. Brownell. bibl f il Mus Q 62:554-70 O '76

France

See also
Paris—Music

History

L'Affilard's published Sketchbooks; with views on early 18th century musical style. E. Schwandt. bibl f il Mus Q 63:99-113 Ja '77
Facts and fiction about overdotting. F. Neumann. bibl f il Mus Q 63:155-85 Ap '77
Félicien David 1810-1876 and French romantic orientalism. P. Gradenwitz. bibl f il por Mus Q 62:471-506 O '76
Turkish affect in the land of the Sun King; French music from about 1625 to 1700. M. R. Obelkevich. bibl il Mus Q 63:367-89 Jl '77

Great Britain

Pistol-whipped; New Wave rock and British youth. E. Meadows. il Nat R 29:1311-12 N 11 '77

Italy

See also
Florence—Music

Massachusetts

Aston Magna: Bach Brandenburgs; performance in Great Barrington. il Hi Fi 27:MA26-7 O '77

Minnesota

See also
Minnesota Orchestra

Pennsylvania

See also
Pittsburgh—Music

Russia

Last days in Russia; Borodin Quartet; tr by A. Vergun. R. Dubinsky. il Hi Fi 27:MA10-11+ N '77
To Russia with rock; Nitty Gritty Dirt Band; interview, ed by E. Dowling. J. McEuen. il pors Sr Schol 110:2-5 N 3 '77

Southern States

Gonna shout, gonna shine; Southern gospel music. B. Overton. il Sat Eve Post 249:22-4+ N '77

Texas

In the heart of honky-tonk rock; Austin. il Time 110:86+ S 19 '77

United States

Concert and opera. I. Kolodin. il Sat R 4:20-2 Ag 6 '77
Getting it together '77. J. Rockwell. Vogue 167:300+ O '77
Music, youth, racial equality; views of pianist André Watts. A. Watts. il por U.S. News 82:69 Je 6 '77
Varèse in New York: from Ecuatorial to Intégrales; excerpt from Varèse: a looking glass diary, v2. L. Varèse. il pors Hi Fi 27:73-7 F '77
See also
Jazz music
Music, American
Opera—United States
also subhead Music under names of cities, e.g. Boulder, Colo.—Music

Venezuela

See also
Music and state—Venezuela

Western States

Messiah sing-alongs—bring your own score, join in. il Sunset 159:72 D '77

MUSIC, African
See also
Folk music, African

MUSIC, American
Art gone astray. G. Lees. Hi Fi 27:16+ F '77
Arthur Fiedler discusses the future of American music. A. Fiedler. pors U.S. News 82:44 Mr 7 '77
At a nation's heart; ethnicity of sounds in jazz. G. Lees. Hi Fi 27:22+ Mr '77
Holland Festival: an American emphasis. I. Lowens. Hi Fi 27:MA38-40 F '77
Modern American music makes a breakthrough. W. Mayer. il Horizon 20:52-8 S '77
Music U. $. A. G. Lees. See issues of High fidelity and Musical America
Music West; festivals of American music in the San Francisco Bay area. R. Commanday. il Hi Fi 27:MA32-4 Mr '77
Of fiddles and fiddlers (and friends): William Sidney Mount's Cradle of Harmony. I. Lowens. il Hi Fi 27:89-90 Mr '77
See also
Composers, American
Jazz music
Phonograph records—American music
Songs, American

MUSIC, Balinese
Bali Hoo; Barong dances and music. J. Culshaw. il Hi Fi 27:19+ Jl '77

MUSIC, Baroque
See also
Phonograph records—Baroque music

MUSIC, Black. See Black music

MUSIC, Brazilian
Brazil is alive & well & sneaking into your record collection. J. S. Roberts. il Hi Fi 27:124+ Je '77

MUSIC, Cataloging of. See Cataloging

MUSIC, Christmas. See Christmas music

MUSIC, Church. See Church music

MUSIC, Czech
See also
Phonograph records—Czech music

MUSIC, Electronic
Marshall's Fragility Cycles; sonic performance environments. J. La Barbara. Hi Fi 27:MA15 My '77
Synthe-sounds '77; concert presented by the Los Angeles chapter of the National Academy of Recording Arts and Sciences. D. Heckman. il Hi Fi 28:122+ Ja '78
Tudor at The Kitchen; six-day series of electronic music. J. La Barbara. il por Hi Fi 27: MA14-15 My '77
See also
Musical instruments, Electronic

MUSIC, Experimental
Aki means new music in Cleveland. B. Murray. il Hi Fi 28:MA24-5+ Ja '78
Bucknell Univ:
Cage, et al; New Music—four views. il Hi Fi 27:MA20-1 Mr; MA34 Jl '77
Graz: Styrian Autumn. Austria's avant-garde music festival. H. Koegler. Opera N 41:31 F 19 '77
IRCAM—underground and underway. A. Frankenstein. il Hi Fi 28:MA28-9+ Ja '78
New music. J. La Barbara. See issues of High fidelity and Musical America
Towards an aesthetic of experimental music. C. Ballantine. bibl f Mus Q 63:224-46 Ap '77
See also
Phonograph records—Music, Experimental

Instruction and study
See Music—Instruction and study

MUSIC, French
See also
Music—France
Songs, French

MUSIC, German
See also
Phonograph records—German music
Songs, German

MUSIC, Gospel. See Gospel music

MUSIC, Hungarian
See also
Phonograph records—Hungarian music

MUSIC, Incidental
See also
Phonograph records—Incidental music

MUSIC, Japanese
See also
Phonograph records—Japanese music

MUSIC, Jewish
See also
Phonograph records—Jewish music

MUSIC, Latin American
Music. See issues of Américas

MUSIC, Medieval
See also
Phonograph records—Medieval music

MUSIC, Mexican
See also
Phonograph records—Mexican music

MUSIC, Modern. See Music

MUSIC, Oriental
See also
Phonograph records—Oriental music

MUSIC, Popular (songs, etc)
Kate and Anna McGarrigle: not afraid to be corny; interview, ed by G. Christgau. A. McGarrigle; K. McGarrigle. pors Ms 5:36+ Mr '77
Natalie Cole: producers' puppet, father's daughter, or the new queen of R&B? interview, ed by J. S. Roberts. N. Cole. il pors Hi Fi 27: 125+ F '77
Queen of the Cajun sound; Creole or Zydeco music of Queen Ida. N. R. Spitzer. il por Ms 6:27-8 N '77
Ralph MacDonald—modern musical all-rounder. J. S. Roberts. il pors Hi Fi 27:97-100 Ag '77
Songsmith nobody knows; H. Warren. E. Calder. il por Am Rec G 40:4-7+ Jl '77
See also
Blues (songs, etc)
Country music
Disco music
Gospel music
Phonograph records—Music, Popular (songs, etc)
Rock music (songs, etc)

History
Pop gets juiced. S. Demorest. il Sat R 4:26-7 Jl 23 '77

MUSIC, Recording of. See Sound—Recording and reproducing

MUSIC, Renaissance
See also
Phonograph records—Renaissance music

MUSIC, Spanish American. See Music, Latin American

MUSIC, Turkish
Turkish affect in the land of the Sun King; French music from about 1625 to 1700. M. R Obelkevich. bibl il Mus Q 63:367-89 Jl '77

MUSIC and children
From the mouths of babes; music education in Birmingham, England. J. Culshaw. Hi Fi 28:64 Ja '78
Music lessons your child will like. il Changing T 31:17-19 S '77
Opera and education; symposium. il Opera N 42:22-6+ N '77

MUSIC and literature
Drawn from life; adaptation of Puccini's opera La Bohème from H. Mürger's novel Scènes de la vie de Bohème. S. Hughes. il Opera N 42:12-14+ D 24 '77
Out of The borough; G. Crabbe's poem as the inspiration for B. Britten's opera Peter Grimes. G. Schmidgall. il por Opera N 42:8+ D 10 '77
Tale of turmoil; adaptation of V. Hugo's play Le roi s'amuse into Verdi's opera Rigoletto. G. R. Marek. il por Opera N 42:10-14 D 3 '77
Woe to the vanquished; Mürger's Vie de Bohème. J. Kestner. il Opera N 41:14-17 Mr 19 '77
Zeroing in; adaptation of Kirchner's opera Lily from S. Bellow's Henderson, the rain king. H. Heinsheimer. il por Opera N 41:12-15 Ap 16 '77

MUSIC and motion pictures. See Motion pictures—Music

MUSIC and religion. See Religion and music

MUSIC and state

Venezuela
Oil dollars go into music; funding by Venezuelan government of Maracaibo Symphony Orchestra. D. Hawes. por Hi Fi 27:MA33+ N '77

MUSIC and youth
Getting involved; La Bohème performed by teenagers at Fieldston School in the Bronx. G. Lipton. il Opera N 42:46-7 N '77
Little league composer; K. Noda's opera, The canary. L. Henning. il Opera N 42:49 N '77

MUSIC as a profession
Making it in the musicbiz: myth & reality. J. S. Roberts. il Hi Fi 27:111-14 Je '77

MUSIC boxes
Build this electronic music box. R. A. Chamberlin. il Radio Electr 48:31-4+ Je '77

MUSIC clubs. See Musical societies

MUSIC collections. See Music—Collectors and collecting

MUSIC contests. See Music—Competitions

MUSIC copyright. See Copyright—Music

MUSIC critics and criticism
Fools' approval. B. H. Haggin. New Repub 176:21-3 Je 11 '77
Music critic in Paris in the nineteen-twenties: some personal recollections. R. Myers. il Mus Q 63:524-44 O '77
New higher criticism. B. H. Haggin. New Repub 177:30-2 O 1 '77
Prophetic words: opera by Meyerbeer measured by his contemporary, ed by P. La Cerra. P. Scudo. il Opera N 41:30-2 Ja 29 '77

MUSIC directors. See Conductors (music)

MUSIC Division of the Library of Congress. See United States—Library of Congress—Music Division

MUSIC education. See Musical education

MUSIC festivals

Austria
Bregenz:
Donizetti's Favorita; Weber's Oberon. H. Koegler. Opera N 42:46-7 O '77
Festival of Richard Strauss; Vienna State Opera. P. J. Smith. Hi Fi 27:MA39-40 Ag '77
Graz:
Styrian Autumn. Austria's avant-garde music festival. H. Koegler. Opera N 41:31 F 19 '77
Lavish Onegin, a new Giovanni; performances in Munich and Salzburg. D. Harris. il Hi Fi 28:MA32-4 Ja '78
News from Vienna; six operas of Richard Strauss performed by the Vienna State Opera. R. Jacobson. il Opera N 41:32-5 Mr 12 '77
Salzburg:
Opera performances at the Hellbrunn Palace Festival. J. H. Sutcliffe. il Opera N 42: 46 O '77
Salzburg and the spirit of Shangri-la; Salzburg Easter Festival. I. Kolodin. il Sat R 4:41-2+ My 14 '77

California
Music West; festivals of American music in the San Francisco Bay area. R. Commanday. il Hi Fi 27:MA32-4 Mr '77

Canada
Ottawa:
Opera performances at the Festival Canada in the National Arts Centre. R. Jacobson. Opera N 42:60-1 O '77
Success story; festival Canada of the National Arts Centre in Ottawa. D. Seabury. il Opera N 42:20-2 Jl '77

MUSIC festivals—*Continued*

Colorado

Aspen experience; Aspen Festival. S. Clark. il Hi Fi 27:MA33-5 D '77

Colorado:

Colorado Opera Festival in Colorado Springs and Central City; Aspen Music Festival's opera productions. G. Giffin. Opera N 42:64+ O '77

Musical playground; Aspen Music Festival. C. Michener. il Newsweek 90:34-5 Ag 15 '77

England

Glyndebourne:

Opera festival. F. G. Barker. Opera N 42:56 O '77

Glyndebourne's Giovanni & Covent Garden's Fanciulla. E. Greenfield. il Hi Fi 27:MA38-9 O '77

Europe

Operaphiles' Baedeker 1977; summer opera festivals. T. P. Lanier. il Opera N 41:20-2+ My '77

Finland

Salzburg of the North; Savonlinna Opera Festival. I. Lowens. il Hi Fi 28:MA30-1+ Ja '78

Germany, West

Bayreuth:

101st year. J. H. Sutcliffe. Opera N 42:52-3 O '77

Berlin Festival: liberal chic. P. Moor. il Hi Fi 27:MA36-7 Ap '77

ISCM World Music Days; Bonn festival held by the International Society for Contemporary Music. E. Schwartz. il Hi Fi 27:MA34-5+ S '77

Lavish Onegin, a new Giovanni; performances in Munich and Salzburg. D. Harris. il Hi Fi 28:MA32-4 Ja '78

Mixed bag: famous Wagner interpreters; 100 years of Bayreuth recordings. C. J. Luten. il Am Rec G 40:10-12+ O '77

Munich:

Bavarian State Opera's summer festival. H. E. Reed. Opera N 42:42 D 24 '77

100 years of Bayreuth; Deutsche Grammophon. C. J. Luten. Am Rec G 40:10-12 N '76

Wahnfried restored; cite of Bayreuth Festival. G. Loney. il Opera N 41:14-15 F 19 '77

Illinois

Out of music, chaos? Ravinia Festival. K. Monson. il por Hi Fi 27:MA28-30 N '77

Iowa

Indianola:

Opera festival at the Des Moines Metro. M. A. Feldman. Opera N 42:64 S '77

Place to grow; Des Moines Metro Summer Festival of Opera. M. A. Feldman. il por Opera N 41:20-2 Je '77

Ireland

Wexford:

Italian opera buffa performed at the Theatre Royal. B. Still. Opera N 42:41 D 24 '77

Israel

Bernstein in Israel; Bernstein Festival. G. Paz. il por Hi Fi 27:MA32-3 S '77

Fidelio; performances at the Israel Festival. Hi Fi 27:MA19+ N '77

Tel Aviv:

Israel Festival. M. Bookspan. Opera N 42:58+ O '77

Italy

Florence:

Operas at the Maggio Musicale. W. Weaver. il Opera N 42:50 S '77

Siena:

Opera performances at the Accademia Chigiana's annual festival. W. Weaver. Opera N 42:70+ N '77

Louisiana

Jazz in April in New Orleans; New Orleans Jazz & Heritage Festival. il Sunset 158:98+ Ap '77

Maine

Bowdoin's contemporary music festival. S. Cerf. il Hi Fi 27:MA28-9 Ap '77

Massachusetts

ISCM World Music Days; October 1976 festival held in Boston. S. Carlin. il Hi Fi 27:MA30-1+ Ap '77

Music; Festival of Contemporary Music at Tanglewood. D. Hamilton. Nation 225:221 S 10 '77

Tanglewood: Berlioz and Bartók; final two Friday concerts of 1977 season. il Hi Fi 27:MA20 D '77

Mexico

First Casals concerts; Primeras Jornadas Internacionales Casals. S. Fleming. il pors Hi Fi 27:MA36-7 My '77

Netherlands

Amsterdam:

Operas at the Holland Festival. G. Loney. Opera N 42:60 S '77

Holland Festival: an American emphasis. I. Lowens. Hi Fi 27:MA38-40 F '77

New York (state)

Caramoor: Bremen band et al. il Hi Fi 27:MA17 N '77

Caramoor; festival and house of Walter and Lucie Rosen. N. Hazelton. Nat R 29:1062+ S 16 '77

Indigenous music; Newport Jazz Festival-New York. N. Hentoff. Nation 225:158 Ag 20 '77

It's that jazz time again; Newport-New York Festival. R. Palmer. il N Y Times Mag p86-7 Je 12 '77

Jazz; Association for the Advancement of Creative Musicians. W. Balliett. New Yorker 53:92-7 Je 20 '77

Jazz; Newport Jazz Festival-New York. W. Balliett. New Yorker 53:80-6+ Jl 18 '77

Katonah:

Operas at the Caramoor festival. S. Wadsworth. Opera N 42:77-8 N '77

Ohio

Aki means new music in Cleveland; Biennial of New Music. B. Murray. il Hi Fi 28:MA24-5+ Ja '78

Pennsylvania

Pittsburgh:

Pennsylvania Opera Festival. R. Croan. Opera N 42:48 D 3 '77

Rhode Island

Sociable music among the very rich; Newport Music Festival. C. Suttoni. il Hi Fi 27:MA21-3 N '77

Scotland

Orkney Islands:

Davies' opera, The martyrdom of St Magnus, performed at the St Magnus Festival. N. Goodwin. Opera N 42:60+ S '77

See also

International Festival of Music and Drama, Edinburgh

Switzerland

Zurich:

Opera performances at the June Festival. E. V. Epstein. Opera N 42:47-8 O '77

United States

Bluegrass in blossom. R. Wolmuth. il Time 110:45 Jl 4 '77

Reports: U.S. festivals. il Opera N 42:62-4+ O '77

Summer crop of maestros. I. Kolodin. por Sat R 4:48-9 S 17 '77

Summer festivals. Hi Fi 27:MA20-3 Ap; MA16+ My '77

U.S. calendar. See issues of Opera news

Vermont

Marlboro on the road; Music from Marlboro touring orchestra. B. Paolucci. il Hi Fi 27:MA21-3 D '77

Washington, D.C.

ASOL Festival of Youth Orchestras. L. Sears. il Hi Fi 27:MA24-6 D '77

MUSIC for children

See also

Phonograph records—Childrens records

MUSIC from Marlboro (orchestra) See Chamber orchestras

MUSIC halls (variety theaters, etc)

See also

Cabarets

Discotheques

New York (city)—Radio City Music Hall

MUSIC history. See Music—History and criticism

MUSIC in art

Still-life paintings of William Michael Harnett; their reflections upon nineteenth-century American musical culture. C. J. Oja. bibl f il Mus Q 63:505-23 O '77

MUSIC in religion. See Religion and music

MUSIC in the Bible. See Bible—Music

MUSIC industry. See Music trade

MUSIC lessons. See Music—Instruction and study

MUSIC libraries

See also

Libraries—Music collections

MUSIC Library Association

Music LA convention. R. K. Burns. Lib J 102:870-1 Ap 15 '77

MUSIC on airplanes. See Airlines—Passenger service

MUSIC schools
See also
Cincinnati. University—College-Conservatory of Music
Curtis Institute of Music, Philadelphia
Idyllwild School of Music and the Arts
Manhattan School of Music
Rochester, University, Rochester, N.Y.—Eastman School of Music

History

New light on the Accademia degli Elevati of Florence. E. Strainchamps. bibl f il Mus Q 62:507-35 O '76

MUSIC scores. See Music—Scores

MUSIC trade
Arp & Friend, Inc; electronic synthesizer sales. J Ellis. il pors Hi Fi 28:114-16 Ja '78

MUSIC writing. See Composition (music)

MUSICAL appreciation. See Music—Analysis, appreciation

MUSICAL clubs. See Musical societies

MUSICAL comedies, revues, etc. See Musical comedy, revue, etc

MUSICAL comedy, revue, etc.
Musicals and the unquiet American. G. Rogoff. il Sat R 4:48-9 Je 11 '77
PW interviews; author of Show boat: the story of a classic American musical; ed by R. Dahlin. M. Kreuger. por Pub W 213:8-9 Ja 2 '78
See also
Industrial shows
Phonograph records—Musical comedy, revue, etc.

Reviews

Goings on about town. See issues of New Yorker
Musical theatre. Am Rec G 40:63 My; 49 O '77

Single works

Act
America 137:423 D 10 '77
New Yorker 53:103 N 7 '77
Newsweek il 90:49 S 5 '77
Newsweek il 90:99 N 14 '77
Sat R 5:44 O 1 '77
Time 110:61 N 14 '77
Annie
America 136:467 My 21 '77
Dance Mag 51:20 Ag '77
N Y Times Mag il p39 My 15 '77
Nation 224:602 My 14 '77
New Yorker 53:89-91 My 2 '77
Newsweek 89:112 Ap 11 '77
Newsweek 89:52-3 My 2 '77
Parents Mag il 52:40-1+ Ag '77
Sat R il 4:48-9 Je 11 '77
Time 109:87-8 My 2 '77
Beatlemania
Time 110:54-5 Ag 8 '77
Castaways
New Yorker 53:78 F 21 '77
Club
Mademoiselle il 83:142-3+ F '77
Ms 5:34+ Mr '77
Cockeyed tiger
New Yorker 52:65 Ja 24 '77
Comedy with music
New Yorker 53:93-4 O 17 '77
Fiddler on the roof
Nat R 29:394-5 Ap 1 '77
Hair
Newsweek 90:117 O 17 '77
Time il 110:94+ O 17 '77
Happy end
Nation 224:603 My 14 '77
New Yorker 53:59 My 9 '77
Sat R 4:49 Je 11 '77
Time il 109:89 Je 13 '77
I love my wife
Dance Mag 51:20-2 Ag '77
New Yorker 53:92 Ap 25 '77
Time il 109:87 My 2 '77
Ipi-Tombi
New Yorker 52:63 Ja 24 '77
Time il 109:55-6 Ja 24 '77
Jockeys
Dance Mag 51:92 Jl '77
King and I
Dance Mag 51:20 Ag '77
New Yorker 53:83 My 23 '77
Newsweek 89:101+ My 16 '77
Man of La Mancha
New Yorker 53:100 S 26 '77
New York City street show
New Yorker 53:59+ My 9 '77
Nightclub cantata
Ms 5:18+ Je '77
Nation 224:124-5 Ja 29 '77
New Repub 176:24+ F 5 '77
New Yorker 52:64 Ja 24 '77
Psychol Today il 10:22+ My '77
On the lock-in
New Yorker 53:59 My 9 '77
Party with Betty Comden and Adolph Green
Nation 224:573-4 My 7 '77
New Yorker 53:77 F 21 '77
Newsweek il 89:57 F 21 '77
Time 109:57 F 21 '77
Present tense
New Yorker 53:94+ O 17 '77
She loves me
Time il 109:88 Ap 11 '77
Side by side by Sondheim
Nation 224:573-4 My 7 '77
New Yorker 53:89 My 2 '77
New Yorker 53:26-7 Je 13 '77
Time il 109:88 My 2 '77
Unsung Cole
Newsweek 90:70 Ag 1 '77
Time 110:61 Jl 4 '77
Your arms too short to box with God
America 136:60 Ja 22 '77
Dance Mag 51:39-40 My '77
Time il 109:55 Ja 24 '77

MUSICAL composition. See Composition (music)

MUSICAL conferences. See Music—Conferences

MUSICAL criticism. See Music critics and criticism

MUSICAL education
Modest proposal. Am Rec G 40:4+ Je '77
On education. C. B. Fowler. See issues of High fidelity and Musical America
See also
Music—Instruction and study
Music and children
Music and youth
Music schools
Stringed instruments—Instruction and study

MUSICAL festivals. See Music festivals

MUSICAL form
See also
Concerto and concertos

MUSICAL instrument industry. See Music trade

MUSICAL instruments
Musical instruments. il Consumers Res Mag 60:25-9 O '77
Piano aboard: the sound of music on the water. D. Hollmann. il Yachting 141:195-7 Ap '77
See also
Music trade
also names of musical instruments, e.g. Piano

Instruction and study

See Music—Instruction and study

MUSICAL instruments, Electronic
Arp & Friend, Inc; electronic synthesizer sales. J. Ellis. il pors Hi Fi 28:114-16 Ja '78
Build Cabonga, an electronic percussion synthesizer. J. Barbarello. il Pop Electr 12:39-42 Ag; 76-80 S '77
Electronic muse; Moog synthesizer. por Forbes 120:70 S 1 '77
Product test reports:
Aries system 300 electronic music synthesizer. il Pop Electr 12:98-102 S '77
Three different drummers; drum synthesizers. il Hi Fi 28:127 Ja '78
Tom Oberheim's magical music machines; performance synthesizers. D. Heckman. il Hi Fi 27:127-30 Ap '77

Equipment

Build the V-4 VCO for electronic music. J. Barbarello. il Pop Electr 11:42-4 Mr '77
Input output: instruments and accessories. See issues of High fidelity and Musical America
Look at an interesting circuit that adds a vibrato effect to musical passages. K. Savon. il Radio-Electr 48:70-1+ S '77
Yes plugs in at the Garden: equipment. M. Lobel. il Hi Fi 27:129-31 D '77

Manufacture

See Music trade

MUSICAL instruments, Mechanical
Honk, tweet, blare: sounds of the fair; M. Fournier collection of fairground organs. R. Chelminski. il por Smithsonian 8:78-83 Ja '78

MUSICAL instruments in art. See Music in art

MUSICAL intervals and scales
Berg's master array of the interval cycles. G. Perle. bibl f il Mus Q 63:1-30 Ja '77

MUSICAL meter and rhythm
Words into music; rhythmic influence of language on music. G. Lees. Hi Fi 27:18+ Ap '77

MUSICAL notation
Facts and fiction about overdotting. F. Neumann. bibl f il Mus Q 63:155-85 Ap '77
Musecom II; musical notation computer. D. Heckman. il Hi Fi 27:106 Ag '77
See also
Embellishment (music)

MUSICAL societies
American Composers Alliance; April 4 Variations '77 concert. Hi Fi 27:MA24 Ag '77
Jazz plays the suburbs; jazz societies. R. E. Messinger. McCalls 104:69 F '77
New Music Circle; performance of modern music in St Louis. K. E. Miller. Hi Fi 27:MA30+ S '77
See also
International Musicological Society
International Society for Contemporary Music

MUSICAL taste. See Music—Analysis, appreciation

MUSICAL Theatre Lab. See John F. Kennedy Center for the Performing Arts, Washington, D.C.—Musical Theatre Lab

MUSICH, Aimée
Life insurance for your wardrobe. P. W. Linck. il pors House & Gard 149:44+ O '77 *

MUSICIANS
A-team west: L.A.'s most valuable players; studio musicians. D. Heckman. il Hi Fi 27:142-7 Jl '77
Artist life. D. J. Soria. See issues of High fidelity and Musical America
Debuts & reappearances. See issues of High fidelity and Musical America
Here & there. See issues of High fidelity and Musical America
Musician of the month. See issues of High fidelity and Musical America
New music. J. La Barbara. See issues of High fidelity and Musical America
Universal language; ideas of five music celebrities. il Sat Eve Post 249:32 Jl '77
Young artists 1977. il Hi Fi 27:MA16-20 Jl '77
See also
Black musicians
Children as musicians
Collective labor agreements—Musicians
Composers
Conductors (music)
Jazz musicians
MacDowell Colony, Peterboro, N.H.
Music as a profession
Orchestras
Pianists
Women musicians

MUSICIANS, Jewish
Indigenous music; the *klezmorim*. N. Hentoff. Nation 226:28-9 Ja 7 '78

MUSICIANS, Rumanian
See also
Lipatti, D.

MUSICIANS, Russian
See also
Rostropovich, M.

MUSICOLOGY
See also
International Musicological Society

MUSIL, Robert K.
Vietnam: a new numbers game. Progressive 41:32-3 S '77
Who's who in arms. Progressive 41:13 N '77
—See Marchino, M. jt auth

MUSKELLUNGE
Muskellunge; reproduction of painting. E. Kenney. il Conservationist 31:24-5 Mr '77

MUSKELLUNGE fishing
Fish that takes 1,000 casts. H. Bradshaw. il Outdoor Life 160:80-1+ Jl '77
How to catch a muskie—maybe. J. Bashline. il Field & S 81:78-82 F '77
Magic of musky fishing. H. E. Herrick, Jr. il Conservationist 31:26-7 Mr '77
Muskie man; L. Rudsenske. J. Elder. il por Motor B & S 139:60-1+ Je '77
Musky fishing. J. Brabant. il por Conservationist 31:21-3 Mr '77

MUSKIE, Edmund Sixtus
Muskie calls for CETA renewal. Am City & County 92:18 Ap '77 *

MUSKIE fishing. See Muskellunge fishing

MUSKIES (fishes) See Muskellunge

MUSKINGUM Watershed. See Watersheds

MUSKMELONS. See Melons

MUSLIMS
See also
Islam

MUSLIMS, Black. See Black Muslims

MUSLIMS in Egypt
Repentance, retreat and murder; case of Sheik Zahaby. il Time 110:32 Jl 18 '77

MUSLIMS in the United States
Allah was on our side; Washington, D.C. siege by Hanafi Muslims. J. T. Clemons. Chr Cent 94:319-20 Ap 6 '77
Behind the siege of terror in Washington. il map U.S. News 82:19-21+ Mr 21 '77
Civil war in Islamic America. A. Muhammad. Nation 224:721-4 Je 11 '77
From faith to faith; Hanafi sect. Chr Today 21:48-9 Ap 1 '77
From the concrete floor: thoughts while being held hostage; Washington, D.C. siege by Hanafi Muslims. C. Fenyvesi. New Repub 176:16-17 Mr 26 '77
Is there a treatment for terror? effects of Washington, D.C. seige by Hanafi Muslims. M. Belz and others. il Psychol Today 11:54-6+ O '77
Seizing hostages: scourge of the '70s; Washington, D.C. seige by Hanafi commandos. T. Mathews. il por Newsweek 89:16-20+ Mr 21 '77
38 hours; trial by terror; Washington, D.C. siege by Hanafi Muslims. il pors map Time 109:14-20 Mr 21 '77
Why two sects are at odds; Hanafi and Black Muslims. il por U.S. News 82:22 Mr 21 '77

MUSON, Howard
(ed) See Vaillant, G. E. Lessons of the Grant Study

MUSORGSKII, Modest Petrovich
At last, Mussorgsky's Boris Godunov. D. Hamilton. il Hi Fi 28:83-7 Ja '78 *
Boris Godunov. Reviews
Hi Fi 27:MA26 Je '77 *
New Repub 177:21-2 N 26 '77
Boris Godunov; Seraphim recording. W. Botsford. Am Rec G 40:30-1 Mr '77 *
Pictures at an exhibition: London Philharmonic Orchestra conducted by J. Pritchard. G. S. Fox. Am Rec G 40:34-5 N '76 *
Pictures at an exhibition; Scherzo in B flat, performed by Michel Beroff. G. S. Fox. Am Rec G 40:30 Mr '77 *

MUSSELS
How mussels get attached. A. Tamarin. il Natur Hist 86:42-7 bibl(p94) My '77
Mussel's secret formula. H. Danforth. il Sea Front 23:210-14 Jl '77
See also
Cookery—Shellfish

MUSSELS, Fresh water
Pond clam. W. S. Bousquet. il Conservationist 31:45 N '76

MUSSER, Mary
Battling the red death. il por Am Hist Illus 12:30-6 N '77

MUSSIO, John King, Bp
Talking to God. New Cath World 220:49-50 Ja '77

MUSTANGS. See Horses

MUT, Temple of. See Temples—Egypt

MUTAGENIC substances
Fire retardant may pose cancer hazard. Sci N 111:23 Ja 8 '77
Metal mutagens and carcinogens affect RNA synthesis rates in a distinct manner. D. J. Hoffman and S. K. Niyogi. bibl il Science 198:513-14 N 4 '77
Mutagenic activity of quercetin and related compounds. L. F. Bjeldanes and G. W. Chang. bibl il Science 197:577-8 Ag 5 '77
Saccharin and other sweeteners: mutagenic properties. R. P. Batzinger and others. bibl il Science 198:944-6 D 2 '77
See also
Caffeine

MUTATION (biology)
Adenine and adenosine are toxic to human lymphoblast mutants defective in purine salvage enzymes. M. S. Hershfield and others. bibl il Science 197:1284-7 S 23 '77
Cats and commerce. N. B. Todd. il maps Sci Am 237:100-6 bibl(p 163) N '77
Evidence for abnormal heart induction in cardiac-mutant salamanders (ambystoma mexicanum) L. F. Lemanski and others. bibl il Science 196:894-6 My 20 '77
Genetic rescue of a lethal null activity allele of 6-phosphogluconate dehydrogenase in drosophila melanogaster. M. B. Hughes and J. C. Lucchesi. bibl il Science 196:1114-15 Je 3 '77
HLA variants of cultured human lymphoid cells: evidence for mutational origin and estimation of mutation rate. D. Pious and C. Soderland. bibl il Science 197:769-71 Ag 19 '77
Mechanism of suppression in drosophila: control of sepiapterin synthase at the purple locus. J. J. Yim and others. bibl il Science 198:1168-70 D 16 '77
Mutant of paramecium defective in chemotaxis. J. Van Houten. bibl il Science 198:746-8 N 18 '77
Return of hopeful monsters; theories of R. Goldschmidt. S. J. Gould. Natur Hist 86:22+ Je '77
See also
Evolution

MUTATION (viruses)
Suppression of the temperature-sensitive phenotype of a mutant of reovirus type 3. R. F. Ramig and others. bibl il Science 195:406-7 Ja 28 '77

MUTUAL and Balanced Force Reduction Talks. See Disarmament—Conferences

MUTUAL funds. See Investment trusts

MUTUALISM (biology) See Symbiosis

MUZAK Corporation
Anniversary present; thirtieth anniversary of the Hensel Muzak franchise. New Yorker 53:40-1 O 17 '77

MUZIO, Claudia
Muzio on Edison discs. P. L. Miller. Am Rec G 40:13 F '77 *

MUZIO, Emanuele
Verdi's American correspondent. G. Marchesi. por Opera N 42:38+ D 3 '77 *

MUZOREWA, Abel T. Bp
Man of peace seeks to rule. J. M. Wall. bibl Chr Cent 94:611-12 Jl 6 '77 *

MUZZLE Loading Annual International Competition. See Shooting—Competitions

MUZZLE-loading rifles. See Rifles

MY life; drama. See Jacker, C. L.

MYASTHENIA gravis
Myasthenia gravis: cleansing the blood. il Sci N 112:391 D 10 '77
Myasthenic immunoglobulin accelerates acetylcholine receptor degradation. I. Kao and D. B. Drachman. bibl il Science 196:527-9 Ap 29 '77

MYCOBACTERIUM
In vitro growth of mycobacterium lepraemurium, an obligate intracellular microbe. A. M. Dhople and J. H. Hanks. bibl il Science 197:379-81 Jl 22 '77
MYCOPLASMAS
Pathogenic mycoplasmas: cultivation and vertebrate pathogenicity of a new spiroplasma. J. G. Tully and others. bibl il Science 195: 892-4 Mr 4 '77
MYDANS, Carl
Sri Lanka's Royal Botanic Gardens: a laboratory in a paradise. il Horticulture 55:58-65 Mr '77
MYERS, Arthur
Engel's millions. il por Writers Digest 57:35-6 O '77
MYERS, Barbara W.
Shark in miniature: keeping a horn shark in a home aquarium. il Oceans 10:39-41 N '77
MYERS, Barton
Toronto townhouse: a year-round garden. N. Skurka. il N Y Times Mag p52-3 Ag 21 '77 *
MYERS, Bob
Competition. il Motor T 29:108-9 Jl '77
MYERS, Charles E. and others
Adriamycin: the role of lipid peroxidation in cardiac toxicity and tumor response. bibl il Science 197:165-7 Jl 8 '77
MYERS, Dale Dehaven
Rockwell engineer tackles energy R&D. il por Bus W p65 S 26 '77 *
MYERS, Debra Francine (Jackson)
Dr Myers and Dr Myers. il pors Ebony 33:107-8+ N '77 *
MYERS, Douglas C.
Zap new life into dead Ni-Cd batteries. il Pop Electr 12:60-1 Jl '77
MYERS, Jack
Night inside the hunter; poem. Esquire 87:120 F '77
MYERS, Lou
Summer with no end; story. New Yorker 53: 27-31 Jl 18 '77
MYERS, Neil
Child in an orchard; poem. Mademoiselle 83:195 My '77
MYERS, Norman
Operation tsetse fly. il Int Wildlife 7:33-5 My '77
Selling of the zebra. il map Int Wildlife 8:26-31 Ja '78
MYERS, R. D. and Melchior, C. L.
Alcohol drinking: abnormal intake caused by tetrahydropapaveroline in brain. bibl il Science 196:554-6 Ap 29 '77
—See Mora, F. jt auth
MYERS, Robert John
Citizen Bailar. New Repub 177:6 Jl 23 '77
MYERS, Robert Julius
Retiring at 65: an arbitrary cut-off that started with three men. il Duns R 110:31-2 O '77 *
MYERS, Rollo
Music critic in Paris in the nineteen-twenties: some personal recollections. il Mus Q 63:524-44 O '77
MYERS, Woodrow Augustus, Jr
Dr Myers and Dr Myers. il pors Ebony 33:107-8+ N '77 *
MYERSON, Bess
[Column] por Redbook 148:96+ Ap; 149:74+ Je; 150:113+ N '77
MYERSON, Jacob Meyer
U.S. discusses its preparations for the U.N. Water Conference; statement, January 4, 1977. Dept State Bull 76:203-5 Mr 7 '77
U.S. supports U.N. resolution against the practice of torture; statement, December 3, 1976. Dept State Bull 76:77-80 Ja 24 '77
MYERSON, Joel, and others
Magnification in striate cortex and retinal ganglion cell layer of owl monkey: a quantitative comparison. bibl il Science 198:855-7 N 25 '77
MYKING, Lynn M.
Old four legs: the living fossil. il Sea Front 23:334-41 N '77
MYNDERSE, Jon S. and others
Antileukemia activity in the oscillatoriaceae: isolation of Debromoaplysiatoxin from lyngbya. bibl il Science 196:538-40 Ap 29 '77
MYOCARDIAL infarction. See Heart—Diseases
MYOCARDIUM. See Heart—Muscle
MYOMETRIUM. See Muscle
MYOPIA
How to save your child's good sight. E. Friedman. il Parents Mag 52:46-7+ F '77
MYOSIN. See Muscle—Proteins
MYRDAL, Alva
Heroine among the last survivors. C. L. Mee, Jr. il por Horizon 19:90-2 Mr '77 *
MYRDAL, Gunnar. See Myrdal, K. G.
MYRDAL, Karl Gunnar
Problem of widespread poverty. Current 197: 18-23 N '77
Swedish view of welfare in America; excerpt from address, October 28, 1976. Current 190: 15-18 F '77
Worried America; adaptation of address. Chr Cent 94:1161-6 D 14 '77

MYSTERY stories. See Detective and mystery stories
MYSTICISM
Flirting with mysticism; excerpt from Loose change: three women of the sixties. S. Davidson. il Ms 5:57-9+ Ap '77
Tao of physics: reflections on the cosmic dance. F. Capra. il Sat R 5:21-3+ D 10 '77

Hinduism

Freedom to be strange; New York Supreme Court ruling on Hare Krishna indoctrination. il Time 109:81 Mr 28 '77
Sharing a son with Hare Krishna. J. Wax. il pors N Y Times Mag p40-2+ My 1 '77
MYTHOLOGY
See also
Geographical myths

Study and teaching

Professor with a thousand faces. D. Newlove. il pors Esquire 88:99-103+ S '77
MYTHOLOGY, Greek

Study and teaching

Gods and goddesses: exploring Greek mythology. Engl J 66:57 S '77
MYTHOLOGY, Scythian
Three vases recount the legend of King Targitaus. D. S. Raevsky. il UNESCO Courier 29: 14-16 D '76
MYTHOLOGY in art
Three vases recount the legend of King Targitaus. D. S. Raevsky. il UNESCO Courier 29: 14-16 D '76
MYTHS. See Mythology

N

N-bombs. See Neutron bombs
N-Serve. See Nitrapyrin
NAACP. See National Association for the Advancement of Colored People
NACS. See National Association of College Stores
NAE. See National Academy of Engineering; National Association of Evangelicals
NAM. See New American Movement (organization)
NAMH. See National Association for Mental Health, Inc
NARB. See National Association for Regional Ballet
NAS. See National Academy of Sciences
NASA. See United States—National Aeronautics and Space Administration
NATO. See Nato
NAWAPA. See North American Water and Power Alliance
NBA. See National Basketball Association; National Book Awards
NBAA. See National Business Aircraft Association
NBC. See National Broadcasting Company
NBCC. See National Book Critics Circle
NBS. See United States—Standards, National Bureau of
NCA. See National Cattlemen's Association
NCAA. See National Collegiate Athletic Association
NCARB. See National Council of Architectural Registration Boards
NCC. See National Council of Churches
NCCB. See National Citizens Commission for Broadcasting; National Conference of Catholic Bishops
NCI. See United States—National Cancer Institute
NCLIS. See United States—National Commission on Libraries and Information Science
NCOA. See National Council on the Aging
NCR Corporation
NCR corporate headquarters. il Archit Rec 162: 97-102 N '77
NCR'S new strategy puts it in computers to stay. il Bus W p 100-4 S 26 '77
NCSC. See National Council of Senior Citizens
NCSS. See National Council for the Social Studies
NCTE. See National Council of Teachers of English
NDELA (N-nitrosodiethanolamine) See Nitrosamines
NEA. See National Education Association
NEA (National Endowment for the Arts) See United States—National Foundation on the Arts and the Humanities
NEH (National Endowment for the Humanities) See United States—National Foundation on the Arts and the Humanities
NELINET (New England Library Network) See Libraries—New England

NFB. See National Federation of the Blind
NFO. See National Farmers Organization
NFPC. See National Federation of Priests' Councils
NHRA races. See Drag racing
NIEO (New International Economic Order) program. See Economic relations
NIH. See United States—National Institutes of Health
NIOSH. See United States—National Institute for Occupational Safety and Health
NISO (National Institute of Student Opinion) See Scholastic Research Center
NLA. See National Librarians Association
NLRB. See United States—National Labor Relations Board
NMR. See Nuclear magnetic resonance
NOAA. See United States—National Oceanic and Atmospheric Administration
NON. See National Organization for Non-parents
NORAD. See North American Air Defense Command
NOW. See National Organization for Women
NOW (negotiable order of withdrawal) accounts. See Banks and banking—Checking accounts
NPCA. See National Parks and Conservation Association
NPPA. See National Press Photographers Association
NRA. See National Rifle Association
NRC. See National Research Council; United States—Nuclear Regulatory Commission
NRPA. See National Recreation and Park Association
NSA. See United States—National Security Agency
NSB. See United States—National Science Board
NSC. See United States—National Security Council
NSF. See United States—National Science Foundation
NTIS. See United States—Commerce, Department of—National Technical Information Service
NTSB. See United States—National Transportation Safety Board
NYCLU (New York Civil Liberties Union) See American Civil Liberties Union
NYPL. See New York Public Library
NYSUT. See New York State United Teachers
NYU. See New York University
NAAS, Charles W.
Human rights in Iran; statement, October 26, 1977. Dept State Bull 77:894-6 D 19 '77
NABHAN, Gary Paul
Tierra (incognita) poem. Org Gard & Farm 24:67 S '77
Well-pump churns; poem. Org Gard & Farm 24:64 O '77
—and Felger, R. S.
Ancient crops for desert gardens. il Org Gard & Farm 24:34+ F '77
NABISCO, Inc
Cookie crumbles for Xox-Nabisco; West German market. il Bus W p46+ Je 13 '77
When the cookie nearly crumbled. il Forbes 119: 94+ Ap 15 '77
NABOKOV, Peter
Remember Tierra Amarilla. il por Nation 225: 336-40 O 8 '77
NABOKOV, Vladimir
Back door. C. Tucker. Sat R 4:80 Ag 6 '77 *
Gamesman. R. Boeth. il pors Newsweek 90:42+ Jl 18 '77 *
Mister Nabokov. H. Green. New Yorker 52:32-5 F 14 '77 *
Notes and comment. New Yorker 53:21 Jl 18 '77 *
Obituary
Nat R 29:820 Jl 22 '77. W. F. Buckley, Jr
Pub W 212:77-8 Jl 18 '77
Vladimir Nabokov: 1899-1977. R. Z. Sheppard. il pors Time 110:91-2 Jl 18 '77 *
Vladimir Nabokov: the emigre. S. Maloff. por Commonweal 105:18-20 Ja 6 '78 *
Wisdom in exile. A. Kazin. New Repub 177:12-14 Jl 23 '77 *
NACHMAN, Gerald
Menopause that refreshes. por Newsweek 89:19 Ap 18 '77
NACHT, Michael
United States in a world of nuclear powers. Ann Am Acad 430:162-74 Mr '77
NADAR (photographer)
Shows we've seen. H. V. Fondiller. il Pop Phot 80:49+ My '77 *
Vive Nadar. M. R. Weiss. il Sat R 4:44-7 F 19 '77 *
NADER, Laura
Studying up. il Psychol Today 11:132 S '77
NADER, Ralph
Ralph Nader reports. See issues of Ladies' home journal
Ralph Nader: You've got to make it work! interview, ed by J. Landman. pors Sr Schol 110:6-9+ N 17 '77
Sorry state of the labor press. Progressive 41: 29-31 O '77
Special report: the dangers of nuclear power. Fam Health 8:46-8+ Ag '76; 9:53 Ja '77
—and Green, M. J.
Nader's advice to big business: don't pay those high legal bills. N Y Times Mag p53+ N 20 '77
—and Spann, G. A.
Access to the courts. Nation 225:495-8 N 12 '77
about
Is Nader losing his clout? por U.S. News 83:18 D 19 '77 *
Meet Ralph Nader. Sr Schol 110:9 N 17 '77 *
Nader: success or excess? il por Time 110:76+ N 14 '77 *
Nadir is to Nader as lowest is to. . . G. V. Glass. Nat R 29:776-7 Jl 8 '77 *
Ralph's wrath. il pors Newsweek 90:90+ D 12 '77 *
NADJARI, Maurice
I have no regrets. il por N Y Times Mag p64-5+ Mr 27 '77
NADLER, Bob
Color darkroom. See issues of Popular photography
NADLER, Paul S.
Medium-sized companies: outflank the hungry bankers. Harvard Bus R 55:8+ My '77
NAEF, Weston J. See Ferrez, G. jt auth
NAFOXIDINE. See Estrogens
NAFTEL, Gary. See Taylor, L. R. jt auth
NAG Hammadi codices. See Manuscripts, Coptic (papyri)
NAGANO, Paul T.
(ed) See Jacques, M. Michael Jacques: a double career in art
NAGASAKI
Continuing body count at Hiroshima and Nagasaki. F. Barnaby. il Bull Atom Sci 33:48-51+ D '77
Physical and medical effects of the Hiroshima and Nagasaki bombs; report of Natural Science Group. Bull Atom Sci 33:54-6 D '77
NAGEL, Myra
Ceremonies are a part of camping. Camp Mag 49:35-6+ Mr '77
NAGORSKI, Zygmunt, Jr
Member of the CFR talks back. Nat R 29:1416-19 D 9 '77
NAGY, Ivan
Story of the migrating Magyar. W. Terry. il por Sat R 4:50-1 Ag 6 '77 *
NAHANNI River. See South Nahanni River
NAIK, Datta V.
Qualitative analysis of some inorganic anions by paper chromatography. il por Chemistry 50:27-8 My '77
NAIL polish removers
Nail polish removers. il Consumers Res Mag 60: 7-10 My '77
NAILS (anatomy)
Four troublesome nail problems; excerpt from Dr Zizmor's skin care book. J. Zizmor and J. Foreman. il Fam Health 9:36-7 F '77
Guide to nail care. L. Lamberg. Bet Hom & Gard 55:162+ Je '77
See also
Manicuring
NAIMAN, Adeline
What to do about sex bias in the curriculum. Am Educ 13:10-11 Ap '77
NAIROBI, Kenya
Nairobi: a city safari. S. M. Agins. il Travel 148:52-5 Jl '77
NAISMITH, Grace
Too many pregnancies, too early. Read Digest 111:150-2 N '77
NAJAR, Ridha
Voice from the third world. UNESCO Courier 30: 21-3 Ap '77
NAKAYAMA, Roy M.
Big chile; interview. ed by J. Neary. il pors Horticulture 55:68-70+ Mr '77
NAKED; drama. See Pirandello, L.
NALOXONE. See Narcotic antagonists
NAMATH, Joe Willie
Giving Joe a big hello. R. Fimrite. il por Sports Illus 47:8-11 Ag 15 '77 *
Hello, Hollywood Joe. J. K. Footlick and M. Kasindorf. il por Newsweek 90:66-7 Ag 22 '77 *
Hollywood or bust for Off-Broadway Joe. J. Marshall. por Sports Illus 46:26-7 Ap 25 '77 *
Rough start for freeway Joe. il pors Time 110: 55 O 3 '77 *
NAME calling. See Invective
NAMES, African
What's in a name? S. S. Walker. il Ebony 32: 74-6+ Je '77
NAMES, Geographical
Trees and forests in American place names. H. Clepper. Am For 83:20-2 Ag '77

NAMES, Personal
Game of the name. H. Sutton. Sat R 4:45-7 Ap 2 '77
How children's names affect their grades. M. L. Schildkraut. Good H 184:219 Je '77
Name dropping. Seventeen 36:56 My '77
Name game: handle or handicap? il por Sci N 111:23 Ja 8 '77
Name game; views of C. Andersen. il Time 110:65 S 26 '77
Nation without last names; Time essay. L. Morrow. Time 110:43 Jl 11 '77
See also
Athletes—Names
Blacks—Names
Nicknames

Anecdotes, facetiae, satire, etc.
Naming our second baby. P. Schwartz. il Good H 184:72+ F '77

NAMIAS, June
Hijacked at Entebbe—July 4, 1976; poem. Chr Cent 94:620 Jl 6 '77

NAMIBIA
See also
Books and reading—Namibia
Education—Namibia
Namibians
United Nations—Namibia
United Nations Council for Namibia
Uranium mines and mining—Namibia
Walvis Bay
Wildlife conservation—Namibia

Foreign relations

United States
See United States—Foreign relations—Namibia

Politics and government
Namibia moves towards independence. S. MacBride. il map UNESCO Courier 30:16-20 N '77
South-west Africa: building on a base of rich resources. il Bus W p75-7 F 14 '77

Race question
Namibia: conscience and independence. W. P. Wood. Chr Cent 94:529-31 Je 1 '77
South Africa and Namibia. R. Dale. bibl f Cur Hist 73:209-13+ D '77

Religious institutions and affairs
See also
Church and state in Namibia

NAMIBIANS
African Gulag. New Repub 177:5 S 10 '77

NAMLIK, Joe
Not ready for the rocking chair. H. I. Miller. por Ret Liv 17:40-1 Jl '77 *

NAMPA, Idaho

Education
See Education—Idaho

NAMPEYO, 1859?-1942
Nampeyo: Hopi potter. K. A. Way. il por Ceram Mo 25:51-3 Mr '77 *

NANCE, Robert
Art of sprouting aboard. Yachting 141:98 F '77
New thoughts on an old boat. il Yachting 141:74-7 Je '77

NANNES, Caspar
New teacher, pupil at Sunday school. por Chr Today 21:52-3 Ap 1 '77

NANTAHALA National Forest, N.C. See National forests

NANTUCKET Island
Islands cast adrift. map Newsweek 89:23 Ap 4 '77
Nantucket offers the perfect autumn vacation. D. Hardie. il House & Gard 149:43+ Ag '77
Okay, bring on the snow. H. Sutton. il Sat R 5:46-8 O 15 '77
See also
Fishing—Nantucket Island

Public health
See Public health—Massachusetts

NAONE, Dana
Two; poem. Nation 224:539 Ap 30 '77

NAPA Valley
Bottling poetry in Napa Valley. J. G. Dunne. Esquire 87:8+ F '77
Champagne touring in Napa. il Sunset 159:58+ O '77

NAPLES

Music
See also
Opera—Italy

NAPPING (sleep) See Sleep

NARANJO, Emilio
Remember Tierra Amarilla. P. Nabokov. il por Nation 225:336-40 O 8 '77

NARAYAN, Jaya Prakash
India, my India! excerpt. il pors N Y Times Mag p35-7+ Mr 27 '77

NARAYAN, Opendra, and others
Antigenic shift of visna virus in persistently infected sheep. bibl il Science 197:376-8 Jl 22 '77

NARCISO, Filipina
Long count to a guilty verdict. il pors Time 110:54 Jl 25 '77 *
Narciso-Perez case. A. Jones. Nation 225:584-8 D 3 '77 *

NARCISSISM. See Self love

NARCISSUS
Daffodils: think spring! planting bulbs. il Bet Hom & Gard 55:88-91 O '77

NARCOTIC addicts
Fair play for drunks; Labor Department's proposal of affirmative action for alcoholics and drug addicts. E. Marshall. New Repub 177:7 Jl 23 '77
Physician, heal thyself. M. Clark and others. il Newsweek 90:74 Ag 8 '77

Rehabilitation
See also
Methadone

NARCOTIC antagonists
Drugs to help addicts kick the heroin habit. H. J. Sanders. il Chemistry 50:22-3 S '77
Hyperalgesia induced by naloxone follows diurnal rhythm in responsivity to painful stimuli. R. C. Frederickson & others. bibl il Science 198:756-8 N 18 '77
Intravenous naloxone administration in schizophrenia and affective illness. G. C. Davis and others. bibl il Science 197:74-6 Jl 1 '77
Naloxone in chronic schizophrenia. J. Volavka and others. bibl il Science 196:1227-8 Je 10 '77
Pain relief by electrical stimulation of the central gray matter in humans and its reversal by naloxone. Y. Hosobuchi and others. bibl il Science 197:183-6 Jl 8 '77

NARCOTIC habit
Conditioned narcotic withdrawal in humans. C. P. O'Brien and others. bibl il Science 195:1000-2 Mr 11 '77

NARCOTIC laws and legislation

Mexico
Sierra Madre's amapola war. B. Diederich. il Time 109:37 F 21 '77
See also
Marijuana—Laws and legislation—Mexico

United States
See also
United States—Drug Enforcement Administration

NARCOTIC trade, Control of. See Narcotics, Control of

NARCOTIC traffic, Control of. See Narcotics, Control of

NARCOTICS
Coke and angel dust. Time 110:49-50 Jl 18 '77
See also
Cocaine
Endorphins
Enkephalins
Heroin
Marijuana
Morphine
Phencyclidine hydrochloride
United Nations—Commission on Narcotic Drugs

NARCOTICS, Control of
Bad, bad Leroy Barnes; drug dealing trial in New York City. il por Time 110:21 D 12 '77
Department discusses program to control narcotic drugs; statement, July 12, 1977. R. B. Oakley. Dept State Bull 77:242-5 Ag 22 '77
International cooperation to control dangerous drugs; remarks and message to Congress, August 2, 1977. J. Carter. Dept State Bull 77:380-2 S 19 '77
Let's end the dope war: a junkie view of the quagmire. E. Bunker. Nation 224:785-8 Je 25 '77
Mexican heroin flow continues unabated. C. Holden. Science 196:509 Ap 29 '77
Mexican jailbirds. Nation 225:645 D 17 '77
Mister Untouchable; N. Barnes. F. Ferretti. il pors N Y Times Mag p 15-17+ Je 5 '77
Narcotics control program in Bolivia; statement, October 14, 1977. K. M. Falco. Dept State Bull 77:826-7 D 5 '77
New kings of heroin. N. M. Adams. Read Digest 110:117-21 Ap '77
Sierra Madre's amapola war. B. Diederich. il Time 109:37 F 21 '77
Super dog of Scotland Yard; identifying concealed narcotics. J. Stewart-Gordon. il por Read Digest 110:201-2+ Mr '77
Taming a tough county; marijuana smuggling in Starr County, Tex. Time 109:58-9 My 2 '77
See also
Airplanes in narcotics control
United Nations—Commission on Narcotic Drugs
United States—Drug Enforcement Administration

NARCOTICS and youth
On the drug scene: new rival for heroin. il U.S. News 83:65 Ag 8 '77
Our 16-year-old son was on drugs. il Good H 184:28+ Je '77
Sexes equal in alcohol, drug use. Sci N 111:277-8 Ap 30 '77

NARCOTICS Commission, United Nations. See United Nations—Commission on Narcotic Drugs
NARCOTICS smuggling. See Smuggling
NARITA airport. See Tokyo—Airports
NAROPA Institute, Boulder, Colo. See Buddha and Buddhism—Study and teaching
NARRATION (rhetoric)
I's have it; first-person narration. L. Block. il Writers Digest 57:14-15+ Je '77
Narrative point of view: the rhetoric of Au hasard, Balthazar. N. Browne. il Film Q 31: 19-31 Fall '77
NARRATIVE writing. See Narration (rhetoric)
NARWHALS. See Whales
NASCIMENTO, Edson Arantes do. See Pelé
Die NASE; opera. See Shostakovich, D. D.
NASH, Margaret
Destruction of an African community. Chr Cent 94:985 O 26 '77
NASH, N. Richard
PW interviews; ed by A. W. Ehrlich. por Pub W 211:6-7 Je 6 '77
NASH, Ronald H.
Truth by any other name. Chr Today 22:17-19+ O 7 '77
NASHNER, Marjorie, and White, Mimi
Beauty and the breast: a 60% complication rate for an operation you don't need. il Ms 6:53-4+ S '77
NASHUA Corporation. See Office equipment industry
NASHVILLE, Tenn.

Banks

Why a Nashville bank is deep in Zaire; Commerce Union Bank. il Bus W p 111+ Je 20 '77

Hotels, restaurants, etc.

Place to be pampered in Nashville; Spence Manor. S. Schoch. il Fortune 95:199-200 Je '77

Housing

Custom tailored apartments in Nashville fit together like a high-rise jigsaw puzzle; Rokeby Condominium Apartments. il Archit Rec 162: 120-1 S '77
NASON, Connie
Teen taxidermist. M. Allen. il por Seventeen 36: 19+ Ag '77 *
NASTASE, Ilie
Nasty! E. Lax. il por Esquire 87:96-9+ Mr '77 *
NATALE, Samuel M. and Morgan, O. J.
Social scientists and moral theology. bibl il New Cath World 220:301-9 N '77
NATCHEZ, Miss.
Yankee pilgrim in the Old South. B. Sabol. il N Y Times Mag p38-40+ Ap 24 '77

Historic houses, sites, etc.

See Historic houses, sites, etc.—Mississippi

Social life and customs

Natchez lifestyle. B. Niles and A. Scharffenberger. il Am Home 80:35-7+ Mr '77
NATCHEZ Trace Parkway. See Express highways —Southern States
NATHAN, Abie
Peace crusader. E. Keerdoja and M. J. Kubic. il pors Newsweek 91:5 Ja 2 '78 *
NATHAN, Gay T.
Hamlet's letters. Engl J 66:60-1 O '77
NATHAN, James A.
American foreign policy: the limits of power in the absence of purpose. bibl il Intellect 106: 208-12 D '77
NATHAN, Leonard
Comment. W. Logan. Poetry 130:225-6 Jl '77 *
NATHAN, Paul S.
Rights and permissions. See issues of Publishers weekly
NATHANSON, Iric
Diminishing filibuster. Nation 225:422-4 O 29 '77
NATHANSON, James A. and Greengard, Paul
Second messengers in the brain; with biographical sketch. il Sci Am 237:20, 108-19 bibl(p 140) Ag '77
NATHANSON, Larry
New leaf. il Am Home 80:38 Jl '77
NATHANSON, Melvyn Bernard
Soviets renege on mathematician. C. Holden. Science 198:174 O 14 '77 *
NATHANSON, Robert B.
Disabled employee: separating myth from fact. Harvard Bus R 55:6-8 My '77
NATIONAL Academy for Fire Prevention and Control. See United States—Commerce, Department of—National Fire Prevention and Control Administration
NATIONAL Academy of Engineering
NAE elects 92 new members. Science 196:633 My 6 '77
NATIONAL Academy of Sciences
Academy seeks to aid eight foreign scientists. E. M. Leeper. BioScience 27:427-8 Je '77
Academy shifts emphases to keep up with the times; interview. P. Handler. por BioScience 27:241-4+ Ap '77
Academy steps up human rights drive. Sci N 111:293-4 My 7 '77
Academy study finds low energy growth won't be painful. P. M. Boffey. Science 195:380 Ja 28 '77
Academy to campaign publicly for oppressed scientists. N. Wade. Science 196:741-3 My 13 '77
Half of new Academy members represent the life sciences. BioScience 27:501 Jl '77
NAS elects 60 new members. Science 196:740 My 13 '77
National Academy of Sciences: how the elite choose their peers. P. M. Boffey. Science 196: 738-41 My 13 '77
National Academy of Sciences presents its annual awards; National academies elect members and associates. il Phys Today 30:73-4 Jl '77
Recombinant DNA Forum—stellar cast; gripping plot; but no new message. E. M. Leeper. il BioScience 27:317-19 My '77
Seafarer: NAS sees no basic hazard. Sci N 112: 101-2 Ag 13 '77
Song, signs and spite spice DNA talks. Sci N 111:165 Mr 12 '77
See also
National Research Council

Committee on Science and Public Policy

NAS surveys of fundamental research 1962-1974, in retrospect. W. W. Lowrance. bibl Science 197:1254-60 S 23 '77
NATIONAL Accelerator Laboratory
Program at Fermilab for minority students. J. C. Davenport and others. il Phys Today 30:9+ Je '77
Tevatron. R. R. Wilson. bibl il Phys Today 30: 23-7+ O '77
Tom Swift and his electric synchrotron. D. E. Thomsen. il Sci N 111:282-3 Ap 30 '77
NATIONAL Advisory Commission on Criminal Justice Standards and Goals. See United States—National Advisory Commission on Criminal Justice Standards and Goals
NATIONAL Aeronautic Association
Clubhouse. T. West. Flying 101:96 S '77
NATIONAL Aeronautics and Space Administration. See United States—National Aeronautics and Space Administration
NATIONAL Air and Space Museum. See Smithsonian Institution—National Air and Space Museum
NATIONAL Airlines
Extended Paris-Miami authority pushed. R. K. Ellingsworth. Aviation W 107:30-1 Jl 11 '77
National mounts intense Paris marketing. R. K Ellingsworth. il Aviation W 107:35-6 Jl 18 '77
NATIONAL Amateur Astronomers Convention. See Astronomy—Conferences
NATIONAL anthems. See National songs
NATIONAL Arboretum. See Washington, D.C.—National Arboretum
NATIONAL Archives and Records Service. See United States—General Services Administration —National Archives and Records Service
NATIONAL Assessment of Educational Progress
Teaching all to read: still an uphill battle. il U.S. News 82:61 Ja 24 '77
NATIONAL Association for Mental Health, Inc
As the delegate from Georgia said. . . ; address, November 19, 1976. R. Carter. MH 60:14 Wint '77
Commentary; annual meeting. P. Knauth. MH 60:2 Wint '77
Dedicated to a cause; work of R. Carter. B. Perry, Jr. il por MH 61:14 Spr. '77
NATIONAL Association for Regional Ballet
Ballet from the bleachers; benefit for the National Association for Regional Ballet. W. Terry. il Sat R 4:46-7 Je 11 '77
National Association for Regional Ballet festivals—1977. S. Shelton. il Dance Mag 51:46-9 D '77
NATIONAL Association for the Advancement of Colored People
NAACP and the Supreme Court: Walter F. White and the defeat of Judge John J. Parker, 1930. D. C. Hine. bibl il por Negro Hist Bull 40:753-7 S '77
Washington notebook; C. Mitchell's retirement. S. Booker. Ebony 32:30 Ap '77
NATIONAL Association of Area Agencies on Aging
New president elected for National Assn. of AAA's in Washington. por Aging 275:32 S '77
NATIONAL Association of Bank Women
Path up for women bankers; program designed by Simmons College. il Bus W p 105 Je 13 '77
NATIONAL Association of Broadcast Employees and Technicians
Technological strike at ABC. il Bus W p67+ Ag 8 '77
NATIONAL Association of College Stores
54th NACS convention: traffic increases handily at AAP Publishers Center. D. Maryles. il Pub W 211:231-3 My 23 '77
Publishers' booths will surround AAP center at NACS 54th annual convention. D. Maryles. il Pub W 211:60 Mr 28 '77

NATIONAL Association of Evangelicals
NAE: unity the base; thirty-fifth annual convention. Chr Today 21:57 Ap 1 '77

NATIONAL Audubon Society
Annual dinner, election set November 9-10. Audubon 79:138 S '77
Audubon action. R. Sayre. See issues of Audubon
Audubon concerns and action agenda. Audubon 79:160 S '77
Etc; statistical profile of members. L. Line. Audubon 79:inside cover Ja '77
Newsman is honored for his editorials; news notes. Audubon 79:120-1 Ja '77
Sanctuary fund drive tops million-dollar goal. Audubon 79:151-2 Mr '77
To honor an engineer; Joan Hodges Queneau Award. il Audubon 79:160 Ja '77
See also
Michigan Audubon Society

NATIONAL Audubon Society Christmas bird count. See Bird census

NATIONAL Ballet of Canada
Canadian Conference: classical and contemporary ballet—the next twenty-five years; text of first session. il Dance Mag 51:50-8 Mr '77
Canadian Conference: funding, criticism and music; excerpts from text of second session. il Dance Mag 51:84-7 Ap '77
Dance. D. Diether. il Am Rec G 40:49-51 O '77
Dance; review of current season. J. Maskey. il Hi Fi 27:MA11-12 D '77
National Ballet of Canada: Metropolitan Opera House, July 12-July 23, 1977. D. Vaughan. il Dance Mag 51:71-3 N '77
National Ballet of Canada: two views from the present:
Looking back. S. I. Odom. il Dance Mag 51:60-3 Mr '77
Looking forward. P. Doob. il Dance Mag 51:63-7 Mr '77
Perspectives:
Toronto season and Choreographic Workshop. S. L. Odom. il Dance Mag 51:69-70 S '77
Toronto: National Ballet of Canada's La Fille mal gardée. S. L. Odom. Dance Mag 51:112+ Mr '77

NATIONAL Bank of Georgia. See Atlanta—Banks

NATIONAL Baptist Convention of the U.S.A, Inc. See Baptists in the United States

NATIONAL Baseball Hall of Fame and Museum
Why are these stars on the outs? R. W. Creamer. Sports Illus 46:91 Ap 11 '77

NATIONAL Basketball Association
Help! cried the four—and got it; annual meeting. J. Papanek. Sports Illus 46:63-5 Je 27 '77

NATIONAL Biscuit Company. See Nabisco, Inc

NATIONAL Black Evangelical Association
NBEA: when the Bible bumps blackness. R. Koskela. Chr Today 21:58 My 6 '77

NATIONAL Book Awards
AAP lists 21 judges for National Book Awards. M. Reuter. Pub W 212:26 D 26 '77
Less pomp, more circumstance, please. J. B. Breslin. America 136:403-4 Ap 30 '77
Some criticism, some faint praise—but still struggling along. J. F. Baker. il Pub W 211:32-4 My 2 '77
Something acrid in the lion house. A. Plotnik. il Am Lib 8:351-2 Je '77
35 nominees cited for 1977 National Book Awards. M. Reuter. Pub W 211:26-7 Mr 28 '77
21 judges named for 1977 National Book Awards. Pub W 211:34 Ja 31 '77

NATIONAL Book Critics Circle
Book Critics Circle: the best awards. M. Reuter. il Pub W 211:35 My 2 '77
Critics Circle Award ceremonies again a sellout. J. F. Baker. il Pub W 211:253 Ja 24 '77
NBCC nominates 20 titles for third annual award. M. Reuter. Pub W 212:23 D 26 '77

NATIONAL Broadcasting Company
Changing priorities at stodgy NBC. il Bus W p42-3 Jl 4 '77
Happy days at no. 2. H. F. Waters. il por Newsweek 90:119+ N 14 '77
Mixed verdict on NBC nuclear waste documentary. L. J. Carter. Science 198:1232-3 D 23 '77
NBC as a Soviet megaphone; NBC coverage of 1980 Olympics. J. Hart. il Sat Eve Post 249:31 O '77
NBC is 50! (cont) L. Dumont. Hobbies 81:58+ F; 82:56-9 Mr; 58-9 Ap '77
NBC: Kremlin megaphone. J. Burnham. Nat R 29:257 Mr 4 '77
NBC: the trouble with blockbusters. il Forbes 119:27 F 15 '77
NBC's Moscow connection. Nat R 29:483 Ap 29 '77
NBC's new-look news. H. F. Waters and R. Cohen. il Newsweek 90:103 S 19 '77
NBC's preseason cast change. Bus W p30 S 5 '77
Pyrrhic victory? awarding TV rights to the Moscow Olympics to NBC. M. A. Kellogg and others. il Newsweek 89:98 F 14 '77
Twin logos; NBC dispute. E. Keerdoja. Newsweek 89:9 F 14 '77

NATIONAL budget. See Budget—United States

NATIONAL Bureau of Standards. See United States—Standards, National Bureau of

NATIONAL Business Aircraft Association
Environment and business aviation; excerpts from address. F. B. McIntosh. Aviation W 107:11 O 10 '77
NBAA focuses on new models. E. J. Bulban. il Aviation W 107:16-18 O 3 '77

NATIONAL CB Radio Posse. See Vigilance committees

NATIONAL Cancer Institute. See United States—National Cancer Institute

NATIONAL catechetical directory. See Catholic Church—Catechisms

NATIONAL Cathedral. See Washington, D.C.—Churches

NATIONAL Cattlemen's Association
At last, one voice for beef. W. Kester. Farm J 101:Beef 32 O '77
National Cattlemen's Association to join in new checkoff efforts. Farm J 101:Beef 2 O '77

NATIONAL cemeteries

France

All quiet on the Western Front. J. Klein. il Read Digest 111:227-8 N '77

United States

Sixty million graves: the VA cemetery extravaganza. J. H. Kay. Nation 224:209-12 F 19 '77

NATIONAL Center for Appropriate Technology
NCAT: appropriate technology with a mission. C. Holden. il Science 195:857-9 Mr 4 '77

NATIONAL Center for Education Statistics. See United States—Education, Office of—National Center for Education Statistics

NATIONAL Chamber of Commerce. See Chamber of Commerce of the United States of America

NATIONAL characteristics, American; National characteristics, Israeli, etc. See Americans; Israelis, etc.

NATIONAL Chess League. See Chess

NATIONAL Citizens Commission for Broadcasting
Fight for law and order. J. Lardner. New Repub 177:32-5 O 1 '77

NATIONAL Climate Program Act. See Environmental law

NATIONAL Coalition Against Censorship Conference. See Censorship—Conferences

NATIONAL Collegiate Athletic Association
Ethics, due process, diversity, and balance; address, March 25, 1977. S. Horn. Vital Speeches 43:463-8 My 15 '77
Shark gets a ruling with bite; J. Tarkanian vs NCAA. R. Telander. il por Sports Illus 47:26-7 O 10 '77
Words spoke louder than action; convention. J. Underwood. Sports Illus 46:48-9 Ja 31 '77

NATIONAL Commission for the Protection of Human Subjects of Biomedical and Behavioral Research. See United States—National Commission for the Protection of Human Subjects of Biomedical and Behavioral Research

NATIONAL Commission on Employment and Unemployment Statistics. See United States—National Commission on Employment and Unemployment Statistics

NATIONAL Commission on Libraries and Information Science. See United States—National Commission on Libraries and Information Science

NATIONAL Commission on New Technological Uses of Copyrighted Works. See United States—National Commission on New Technological Uses of Copyrighted Works

NATIONAL Commission on Supplies and Shortages. See United States—National Commission on Supplies and Shortages

NATIONAL Commission on the Observance of International Women's Year. See United States—National Commission on the Observance of International Women's Year

NATIONAL Commission on United Methodist Higher Education. See Church colleges and universities

NATIONAL committees (political)
See also
Democratic National Committee
Republican National Committee

NATIONAL Conference of Catholic Bishops
Bishop to bishop; report of address by J. L. Bernardin. America 137:390 D 3 '77
Bishop's bishop; J. R. Quinn. por Time 110:114 N 28 '77
Bishops keep tabs on science; Committee for Human Values. N. Wade. Science 196:1180 Je 10 '77
Bishops reply. Chr Today 21:31-2 Je 3 '77
Bishops rule. M. Montagno and S. Monroe. il Newsweek 89:119 My 16 '77
Church teaching, church listening. America 136:454 My 21 '77
Detroit, Chicago and Rome. Commonweal 104:323-4 My 27 '77
Gathering of bishops. A. P. Klausler. Chr Cent 94:499 My 25 '77

NATIONAL Conference of Catholic Bishops —*Continued*
Replying to A Call to Action. il Time 109:75 My 16 '77
Second Call to Action; bishops to address conclusions of Detroit meeting. J. Finn. Commonweal 104:269-72 Ap 29 '77

NATIONAL Conference of Catholic Charities
Faith, service and community. America 137:158 S 24 '77

NATIONAL Conference on Alternative State and Local Public Policies
Discontent in Denver. K. Bode. New Repub 177: 14-16 Jl 23 '77

NATIONAL Conference on Educational Issues That Impact on the Black Community. See Education—Conferences

NATIONAL Congress of Parents and Teachers
Putting the networks on notice; work of National PTA. J. C. Lyles. Chr Cent 94:556-7 Je 8 '77

NATIONAL consciousness. See Nationalism

NATIONAL Construction Industry Council
Commerce Department moves toward Office of Construction. W. Hickman. Archit Rec 161:37+ Ja '77

NATIONAL conventions, Democratic
According to Hoyle; reform of delegate system for Presidential nominating conventions. New Repub 177:5-6 S 3 '77
Night Carter took over the party; excerpt from Convention. R. Reeves. il pors N Y Times Mag p32-8+ F 20 '77
Other convention in Chicago; 1968; interview, ed by L. R. Obst. A. Peck. il N Y Times Mag p92+ N 13 '77
Real debate in '78? New Repub 177:8 Jl 2 '77

NATIONAL Corn Growers Association. See Agricultural societies

NATIONAL Council for Community Services to International Visitors
Operation welcome mat; COSERV. J. Osgood. McCalls 105:44 Ja '78

NATIONAL Council for the Social Studies
NCSS-1976. S. L. Jantzen. il Sr Schol 109:TE7-10 Ja 13 '77

NATIONAL Council of Architectural Registration Boards
NCARB: tough talk on recertification, ethics, and the testing of young architects. W. Wagner, Jr. Archit Rec 162:13 Ag '77; Reply with rejoinder. J. M. McGinty. 162:2, 13 N '77

NATIONAL Council of Churches
Church investments: challenging G&W. J. E. Mulligan. Chr Cent 94:64-7 Ja 26 '77
Credentials controversy; issue concerning L. Kinsolving's reporting. Chr Today 21:57-8 Mr 18 '77
Gospel according to. . . Chr Today 21:58-9 Ap 15 '77
NCC: actions and words; semi-annual meeting in New York. A. H. Matthews. Chr Today 22:57-9 D 9 '77
NCC and Carter; supporting the two Panama Canal treaties. Chr Cent 94:1084 N 23 '77
NCC: speaking in softer tones. A. H. Matthews. Chr Today 21:35-6 Je 3 '77
South Africa: God and liberation. Chr Today 22: 56-7 D 9 '77

NATIONAL Council of Senior Citizens
National leaders stress needed reforms at NCSC legislative conference. Aging 275:16-17 S '77

NATIONAL Council of Teachers of English
Doublespeaking. Time 110:33 D 5 '77
For the members. See issues of English journal
NCTE and English usage. R. C. Pooley. Engl J 66:18-19 D '77
Two reminiscences of the NCTE. T. C. Pollock. bibl f Engl J 66:6-9+ Ap '77
What we have learned: reminiscences of the NCTE; address. L. Rosenblatt. Engl J 66:8+ My '77

NATIONAL Council on the Aging
First Lady hosts discussion on the Nation's elderly; NCOA conference provides forum for national leaders; Washington, D.C. il por Aging 272:3-5 Je '77
Older Americans: a national resource; address; November 18, 1976. L. Hausman. Vital Speeches 43:189-92 Ja 1 '77

NATIONAL Council on the Arts. See United States—National Foundation on the Arts and the Humanities

NATIONAL courier (newspaper) See Religious newspapers and periodicals

NATIONAL cultural parks. See National parks and reserves

NATIONAL debt (United States) See Debts, Public—United States

NATIONAL defense
See also subhead Defenses under names of countries, e.g. Russia—Defenses

NATIONAL Education Association
NEA plans our future. R. Kirk. Nat R 29:1301 N 11 '77
NEA, state employees union reach accord. L. Bornstein and others. M Labor R 100:89 F '77
NEA's legislative program; 95th Congress. Todays Educ 66:81-3 Ja '77
Unions on the brink: death wish among the teachers. L. Weiner. Nation 225:276-7 S 24 '77

Association for Educational Communication and Technology

AECT, AASL, and school librarians. B. M. Cheatham. SLJ 24:45 S '77
AECT convention gets an A for action. P. Harper. il Wilson Lib Bull 51:798-800+ Je '77
Teeth for the professionally nameless; views of F. Henne. L. N. Gerhardt. SLJ 24:7 D '77

NATIONAL emblems. See Emblems, National

NATIONAL Endowment for the Arts. See United States—National Foundation on the Arts and the Humanities

NATIONAL Endowment for the Humanities. See United States—National Foundation on the Arts and the Humanities

NATIONAL enquirer (newspaper)
Enquiring. D. K. Mano. Nat R 29:209-10 F 18 '77
Here at the National enquirer. F. A. Woodress. il Writers Digest 57:24-6 Jl '77

NATIONAL Environmental Satellite Service. See United States—National Oceanic and Atmospheric Administration

NATIONAL Farmers Organization
NFO sets price goals. R. D. Wennblom. Farm J 101:37 Ja '77

NATIONAL Federation of Priests' Councils
Letter from Louisville. J. Ratigan. America 136:464-5 My 21 '77

NATIONAL Federation of the Blind
Library-based blind service fought by nat'l blind group. J. L. Kopischke. Lib J 102:148-9 Ja 15 '77; Reply with rejoinder. B. Beach. 102:1221-2 Je 1 '77
Montana not NFB target; new battle in Nebraska. Lib J 102:536 Mr 1 '77

NATIONAL Fire Prevention and Control Administration. See United States—Commerce, Department of—National Fire Prevention and Control Administration

NATIONAL forests
American people are being robbed! K. Wiegner. il Forbes 120:102+ O 15 '77
Battle of Marble Cone; Los Padres National Forest. P. S. Greenberg. il Newsweek 90:26-7 Ag 22 '77
Fight for a wildflower haven; proposed clear-cutting in the Nantahala National Forest. M. Prince. il Liv Wildn 41:45-7 Ap '77
Forest inferno in the West; Los Padres National Forest. il Time 110:21 Ag 22 '77
Forest of the Swamp Fox; Francis Marion National Forest, S.C. R. H. Mohlenbrock. il map Am For 83:34-7 Mr '77
Let's save our roadless areas! with editorial comment. D. Sumner. il Liv Wildn 40:3, 25-33 Ja '77
Lumbermen vs. environmentalists: growing fight over what to do with nation's forests. il U.S. News 83:62-4 Ag 22 '77
Three-for-three elk hunt; in Uncompahgre National Forest, Colo. R. Tinsley. il map Outdoor Life 159:70-1+ Je '77
Working forests. J. B. Craig. Am For 83:9 Jl '77

Waterways

Endangered fish of Kentucky streams; problems in Daniel Boone National Forest. B. A. Branson. il Natur Hist 86:64-9 bibl(p 101) F '77

NATIONAL Foundation on the Arts and the Humanities. See United States—National Foundation on the Arts and the Humanities

NATIONAL Front (Great Britain) See Political parties—Great Britain

NATIONAL Gallery of Art, Washington, D. C.
About art museums and the National Gallery; interview, ed by K. Kuh. J. C. Brown. il por Sat R 4:55-6+ Ap 16 '77
Moving in on the Met. G. Glueck. il por N Y Times Mag p20-2+ F 27 '77

NATIONAL Gallery of Canada, Ottawa
Parkin wins Canadian National Gallery competition. il Archit Rec 162:39 S '77

NATIONAL geographic (periodical)
Geographic faces life. T. Schwartz and J. Whitmore. il por Newsweek 90:111 S 12 '77
Tariff on truth; AIM criticism of article on Cuba. M. J. Sobran, Jr. Nat R 29:564-5 My 13 '77

NATIONAL Geographic Society
Shop talk; repairman B. Stimson of the National Geographic Society. N. Goldberg. il por Pop Phot 80:10+ Je '77

NATIONAL Guard (United States) See United States—National Guard

NATIONAL health insurance. See Insurance, Health

NATIONAL Health Service (Great Britain) See Great Britain—National Health Service

NATIONAL Heritage Trust (proposed) See United States—National Heritage Trust (proposed)

NATIONAL High Blood Pressure Education Program. See Hypertension

NATIONAL High School Rodeo. See Rodeos

NATIONAL Highway Traffic Safety Administration. See United States—National Highway Traffic Safety Administration

NATIONAL Hockey League-World Hockey Association merger. See Hockey, Professional—Acquisitions and mergers

NATIONAL Humanities Center
Breaking ground. M. E. Marty. Chr Cent 94:439 My 4 '77
New center for the humanities. C. Holden. Science 195:858 Mr 4 '77

NATIONAL Hunting and Fishing Day. See Special days, weeks, and months

NATIONAL Institute for Occupational Safety and Health. See United States—National Institute for Occupational Safety and Health

NATIONAL Institute of Arts and Letters. See American Academy and Institute of Arts and Letters

NATIONAL Institute of Building Sciences
Building Sciences Institute is launched, and has begun its work. il Archit Rec 162:125-8 N '77
NIBS issues a wide-ranging missions paper to define its strategies and operations. W. Hickman. Archit Rec 161:37 Ja '77

NATIONAL Institute of Law Enforcement and Criminal Justice. See United States—National Institute of Law Enforcement and Criminal Justice

NATIONAL Institute of Student Opinions. See Scholastic Research Center

NATIONAL Institute on Aging. See United States—National Institute on Aging

NATIONAL Institutes of Health. See United States—National Institutes of Health

NATIONAL Interfaith Conference on Religion and Architecture. See Religious conferences

NATIONAL Jewish Hospital and Research Center. See Denver—Hospitals

NATIONAL Labor Relations Act. 1935. See Labor laws and legislation—United States

NATIONAL Labor Relations Board. See United States—National Labor Relations Board

NATIONAL Lawyers Guild
People vs. the FBI. Nation 224:292-3 Mr 12 '77

NATIONAL League of Cities
League of cities' agenda missing key ingredient. G. M. Chamberlain. Am City & County 92:112 Mr '77
NLC echoes call for economic stimulus; meeting. Am City & County 92:12 Ja '77

NATIONAL Librarians Association
Home for professionals? J. Berry. Lib J 102:1435 Jl '77
Lock the loonies in a stereotype! P. Pollard. Lib J 102:1725-6 S 1 '77

NATIONAL Livestock and Meat Board
BIC is working to sell excess beef on TV; Beef Industry Council. Farm J 101:LK7 Ap '77

NATIONAL Livestock Feeders Association. See National Cattlemen's Association

NATIONAL Livestock Feeders Association-American National Cattlemen's Association merger. See Cattle industry—Acquisitions and mergers

NATIONAL Market System (proposed) See Stock exchanges

NATIONAL Medal of Science
National Medal of Science: fifteen winners. il Sci N 112:372-3 D 3 '77
President gives science medals. Science 198:1020 D 9 '77

NATIONAL Military Intelligence Association. See Military intelligence

NATIONAL minorities. See Minorities

NATIONAL Model United Nations. See United Nations—Study and teaching

NATIONAL monuments
Canyon lands of the Colorado Plateau. L. A. Mohar. il Holiday 58:34-5+ Ap '77
Kenai Fjords: treasure unveiled; with editorial comment. W. Williams. il maps Nat Parks & Con Mag 51:4-9 S '77
See also
Bandelier National Monument
El Morro National Monument
Fort Jefferson National Monument
Fort Union National Monument
Katmai National Monument
Muir Woods National Monument
Natural Bridges National Monument
Rainbow Bridge National Monument
Valley National Monument
White Sands National Monument

NATIONAL Multiple Sclerosis Society
See also
MS Read-a-thon (reading program)

NATIONAL Municipal League
See also
All-America cities

NATIONAL Museum of History and Technology. See Smithsonian Institution—National Museum of History and Technology

NATIONAL Museum of the Building Arts (proposed) See Washington, D.C.—Galleries and museums

NATIONAL observer (newspaper)
Death of whatzit. T. Schwartz and others. il Newsweek 90:66 Jl 11 '77

NATIONAL Oceanic and Atmospheric Administration. See United States—National Oceanic and Atmospheric Administration

NATIONAL Orchestral Association
National Orchestral Association; concert at Carnegie Hall. Hi Fi 27:MA23-4 My '77

NATIONAL Organization for Non-parents
NON—making the case for childlessness. S. Bush. Psychol Today 11:43 N '77

NATIONAL Organization for Women
ERA now? economic boycott in states that have failed to ratify the amendment. il Time 110:28 N 14 '77
What I learned marching with N.O.W. J. M. Shutt. por Farm J 101:F1 D '77

NATIONAL organizations. See Associations, institutions, etc.

NATIONAL Parents and Teachers Association. See National Congress of Parents and Teachers

NATIONAL park personnel
Sequoia star stomp; sky interpretation talks. J. Henry. il por Sky & Tel 53:262-5 Ap '77

NATIONAL park safety. See National parks and reserves—United States—Safety devices and measures

NATIONAL Park Service (United States) See United States—National Park Service

NATIONAL Parks and Conservation Association
Broad program. A. W. Smith. Nat Parks & Con Mag 51:2+ Ag '77
Getting involved (cont of) Memo to members. See issues of National parks & conservation magazine
NPCA at work. See issues of National parks & conservation magazine
Note about cities. A. W. Smith. Nat Parks & Con Mag 51:2+ Jl '77
Two letters to the Administration. A. W. Smith. Nat Parks & Con Mag 51:2+ S '77

NATIONAL parks and reserves
See also
Natural areas
Recreation areas
Wild and scenic rivers
Wilderness areas

Conferences

500 attended Parks Conference; Conference on Scientific Research in the National Parks. BioScience 27:11 Ja '77

Transportation

Parks to the people & people to the parks. Nat Parks & Con Mag 51:22-3+ Ag '77

Alaska

Arctic splendor along the Noatak; combined kayaking and backpacking trip through the proposed Noatak National Preserve. il maps Nat Parks & Con Mag 51:4-9 Je '77
Gentle, welcoming wilderness; backpacking in the proposed Gates of the Arctic National Park; excerpt from Alaska: wilderness frontier. B. Norton. il Audubon 79:38-49 S '77
Guarding the great land: proposals of the Alaska Coalition for protecting a national heritage. il map Liv Wildn 41:20-3+ Jl '77
Lake Clark National Park: the Alps of Alaska. C. Brown. il map Nat Parks & Con Mag 51:4-9 Jl '77
See also
Katmai National Monument
Mount McKinley National Park

Arizona

See also
Grand Canyon National Park
Petrified Forest National Park

Arkansas

See also
Buffalo National River

California

See also
Muir Woods National Monument
Point Reyes National Seashore
Redwood National Park
Sequoia National Park
Valley National Monument
Yosemite National Park

Canada

Vacation discoveries in Canada's national parks. G. Bush. il Bet Hom & Gard 55:212+ My '77

Colorado

See also
Mesa Verde National Park
Rocky Mountain National Park

Florida

See also
Big Cypress National Preserve
Everglades National Park
Fort Jefferson National Monument

Georgia

See also
Cumberland Island National Seashore

NATIONAL parks and reserves—*Continued*

Hawaii

See also
Hawaii Volcanoes National Park

Indiana

See also
Indiana Dunes National Lakeshore

Israel

Synagogues & sea fans: Israel's national parks and nature reserves. E. Clark. il por map Nat Parks & Con Mag 51:13-20 Ap '77

Kentucky

See also
Mammoth Cave National Park

Kenya

On patrol with Africa's new park rangers; with interviews with D. S. Babu of Serengeti National Park and J. M. Kioko of Amboseli National Park. M. Gosnell. il pors Int Wildlife 7:4-13 S '77

Maine

See also
Acadia National Park

Maryland

See also
Chesapeake and Ohio Canal National Historical Park

Massachusetts

Lowell, Mass.—new birth for us all; National Cultural Park. J. H. Kay. Nation 225:245-7 S 17 '77

Minnesota

See also
St Croix National Scenic Riverway

Nepal

What I learned stalking Indian rhinos; Royal Chitawan National Park. A. Laurie. il Int Wildlife 7:6-16 Jl '77

Nevada

See also
Valley National Monument

New Mexico

See also
Bandelier National Monument
Carlsbad Caverns National Park
El Morro National Monument
Fort Union National Monument
White Sands National Monument

New Zealand

Islands in the mainstream of life; Hauraki Gulf Maritime Park Act. E. A. Scholer. il Parks & Rec 12:32-5 O '77

North Carolina

See also
Cape Hatteras National Seashore
Great Smoky Mountains National Park

Peru

How Peru saved Paracas. M. Wexler. il Int Wildlife 7:24-31 S '77

Tanzania

Dog days on the plains; wild dogs of Serengeti National Park. G. W. Frame and L. H. Frame. il Int Wildlife 7:48-55 S '77
On patrol with Africa's new park rangers; with interviews with D. S. Babu of Serengeti National Park and J. M. Kioko of Amboseli National Park. M. Gosnell. il pors Int Wildlife 7:4-13 S '77

Tennessee

See also
Great Smoky Mountains National Park

Texas

See also
Big Bend National Park
Big Thicket National Preserve

United States

Bumper to bumper in the wilderness. P. Stoler. il Time 110:38+ Jl 4 '77
Clean Air Act Amendments: fresh air for the national parks. Nat Parks & Con Mag 51:21-5 N '77
Commitment for recreation. C. D. Andrus. por Parks & Rec 12:15 Jl '77
Government bans sale of throwaway bottles in parks. Nat Parks & Con Mag 51:22 Jl '77
Graying of responsibility. Parks & Rec 12:19 O '77
Handy tips for park trips. bibl il Nat Parks & Con Mag 51:27-8 My '77
Impending leasing off coast; effects on eastern seashore parks. Nat Parks & Con Mag 51:22 F '77
More ASALH projects; black American representation. J. R. Picott. Negro Hist Bull 40: 736-7 S '77
National parks: success is causing a crisis. il U.S. News 82:36 Je 13 '77
Need for a boat; islands in the National Park System. G. Soucie. il Nat Parks & Con Mag 51:4-7 F '77
Our park system will be restored and protected. il Nat Parks & Con Mag 51:20-1 Mr '77
Proposal: Great Plains National Park; adaptation of address, November, 1976. il Nat Parks & Con Mag 51:4-9 Ag '77; Same with title Great Plains National Park. D. L. Allen. Current 197:13-17 N '77
Summary of NPCA survey of feral animals in the national park system. il Nat Parks & Con Mag 51:16-20 Jl '77
Washington scene; emerging options for preservation. B. S. Tindall. Parks & Rec 12:13+ D '77
Work in a national park. Nat Parks & Con Mag 51:27-9 N '77

See also
National forests
National monuments
United States—National Park Service
also names of national parks and reserves, e.g. Carlsbad Caverns National Park

Safety devices and measures

Great grizzly grapple. C. Cauble. il Natur Hist 86:74-81 bibl(p 117) Ag '77; Discussion. 86:132-3 O '77
Of cowbells & common sense: the importance of park safety. D. Morrow. il Nat Parks & Con Mag 51:16-18 My '77

Utah

Utah proposes blueprint for industrial development. Nat Parks & Con Mag 51:22+ Ap '77

See also
Arches National Park
Natural Bridges National Monument
Rainbow Bridge National Monument

Virgin Islands

See also
Virgin Islands National Park

Virginia

See also
Wolf Trap Farm Park for the Performing Arts

Washington (state)

See also
Mount Rainier National Park
Olympic National Park

Western States

Canyon lands of the Colorado Plateau. L. A. Mohar. il Holiday 58:34-5+ Ap '77

Wisconsin

See also
St Croix National Scenic Riverway

Wyoming

See also
Grand Teton National Park
Yellowstone National Park

NATIONAL Peach Council. See Fruit industry

NATIONAL planning (United States) See United States—Social policy

NATIONAL Press Photographers Association
What happened at the press photographers convention. J. G. Morris. il Pop Phot 81:148-9+ O '77

NATIONAL Presto Industries, Inc. See Household appliances industry

NATIONAL Railroad Passenger Corporation
Amtrak's $2 billion run into the red. il Bus W p70-1 My 2 '77
Big engine that couldn't: an Amtrak woe. il U.S. News 82:72 F 21 '77
Competitor asks: is this the way to run a railroad? J. L. Kerrigan. por Duns R 109:99-100+ Ap '77; Reply. P. H. Reistrup. 109:103-4+ My '77
Is GM's locomotive derailing Amtrak? il Bus W p32 F 7 '77
Time to get Amtrak on track. E. Selby and M. Selby. Read Digest 110:233-4+ Ap '77
Why rail passengers face more service cutbacks; Amtrak service. U.S. News 83:86 N 28 '77

NATIONAL Recreation and Park Association
Looking for trends in technical assistance; Park Practice Program. il Parks & Rec 12:52-3 My '77
NRPA in action. See issues of Parks & recreation
NRPA interview: Chris T. Delaporte tells what to expect from BOR; ed by B. Kravetz. C. T. Delaporte. il pors Parks & Rec 12:38-43 Ag '77
NRPA interview with Congressman Morris K. Udall; ed by B. Kravetz. M. K. Udall. il pors Parks & Rec 12:42-5 Mr '77
NRPA news. Parks & Rec 12:57 Mr '77
Special report: foundations for policy: delegate perspectives on the issues; proposed position papers. B. S. Tindall. Parks & Rec 12:78+ S '77
White House Conference hears NRPA position on handicapped. Parks & Rec 12:61 N '77

NATIONAL Recreation and Park Association —*Continued*

Meetings

Congress highlights. il Parks & Rec 12:35-59 Ja '77
1977 Congress for recreation and parks. il Parks & Rec 12:27-45 S '77

NATIONAL recreation areas. See Recreation areas

NATIONAL Religious Broadcasters (organization)
Religious broadcasters: pressing the issues; Washington Convention. A. H. Matthews. il Chr Today 21:56-9 F 18 '77

NATIONAL Research Council
End hunger by 2000—a possible dream. E. M. Leeper. BioScience 27:571-3 Ag '77
Our endangered children: it's a matter of money. J. Gaylin. Psychol Today 10:94 My '77

Transportation Research Board

Make mass transit more flexible—TRB. Am City & County 92:13 Mr '77

NATIONAL Rifle Association
For the NRA: a mandate; Cincinnati meeting. E. B. Mann. Field & S 82:14+ Ag '77
NRA revolution. J. Carmichel. il Outdoor Life 160:102-4+ S '77

NATIONAL SCCA Solo II Championship. See Automobile racing

NATIONAL School Lunch Program. See United States—Agriculture, Department of—Food and Nutrition Service

NATIONAL School of Administration, France
Reports & comment: France: the making of the elite. D. Cook. il Atlantic 240:16-18+ Jl '77

NATIONAL Science Board. See United States—National Science Board

NATIONAL Science Foundation. See United States—National Science Foundation

NATIONAL security. See Internal security

NATIONAL Security Agency. See United States—National Security Agency

NATIONAL Security Council. See United States—National Security Council

NATIONAL Semiconductor Corporation
Dog days at National Semiconductor. il Bus W p70+ F 28 '77
Running fast to stay in place. J. Grigsby. Forbes 120:58 D 15 '77

NATIONAL service, Non-military. See Service, Compulsory non-military

NATIONAL socialism
Not their finest hour: British aristocrats sympathetic to Hitler. D. Pryce-Jones. il New Repub 176:12-16 My 14 '77
On Nazism; interview, ed by M. A. Ledeen; excerpt from Nazism: a historical and comparative analysis of National socialism. G. L. Mosse. bibl il Society 14:69-73 My '77
SS revisited; promotion of book complimentary to the Waffen SS in Great Britain. F. Willey and J. Hopkins. il Newsweek 90:74+ N 28 '77

NATIONAL Socialist Party of America. See Nazis in the United States

NATIONAL Socialist White People's Party. See Nazis in the United States

NATIONAL songs

Russia

Up with Lenin. Time 110:26+ S 12 '77

NATIONAL Sporting Goods Show. See Sporting goods—Exhibitions

NATIONAL Standards Institute, American. See American National Standards Institute

NATIONAL Starch and Chemical Corporation-Unilever Group merger. See Corporations—International aspects—Acquisitions and mergers

NATIONAL Student Marketing Corporation. See Youth market

NATIONAL Student Marketing Corporation-Interstate National Corporation merger. See Corporations—Acquisitions and mergers

NATIONAL Stuttering Project (organization) See Stuttering

NATIONAL Symphony Orchestra
Maestro; M. Rostropovich. J. Lelyveld. il pors N Y Times Mag p 127 O 23 '77
Magnificent maestro; M. Rostropovich. il pors Time 110:82-6+ O 24 '77
Nat. Sym: Bicentennial prems. Hi Fi 27:MA37 F '77
Rostropovich in Washington; October concerts. I. Lowens. por Hi Fi 28:MA22 Ja '78
Slava as maestro. H. Saal and J. Whitmore. il pors Newsweek 90:69-70+ O 17 '77

NATIONAL Teacher of the Year Award. See Teachers—Awards, prizes, etc.

NATIONAL Technical Information Service. See United States—Commerce, Department of—National Technical Information Service

NATIONAL Theatre (Great Britain)
Always something to do at Britain's National Theatre. M. Green. il Smithsonian 8:66-73 Je '77
European pleasures: Britannia rules the stage. M. Gussow. il Horizon 19:34-7 Jl '77
Theater in London. J. Hepburn. New Repub 176:21-3 Je 25 '77
Theatre; recent productions. H. Clurman. Nation 225:92-4 Jl 23 '77
Triumph on the Thames: the National Theatre in London. W. Marlin. il Archit Rec 162:81-8 S '77

NATIONAL Transportation Safety Board. See United States—National Transportation Safety Board

NATIONAL Trust for Historic Preservation
In defense of Main Street. S. J. Ungar. Atlantic 240:24+ D '77
Midwest gets Main Street Projects. il Am City & County 92:22-3 N '77
Styles; Dutchess County. New Yorker 53:17-19 Ag 8 '77

NATIONAL Union of Mineworkers
True coin of freedom; question of British loan to the State Mining Corporation of Bolivia. Nation 225:194-5 S 10 '77

NATIONAL Urban League
Fallout between friends; J. Carter rebuked by V. Jordan. por Time 110:27-8 Ag 8 '77
Family squabble; V. Jordan's criticism of the Carter administration. P. Goldman and others. il pors Newsweek 90:16-18 Ag 8 '77

NATIONAL wealth. See Wealth

NATIONAL Weather Service. See United States—National Weather Service

NATIONAL wildlife (periodical)
Meet the people who read National wildlife; results of survey. J. Strohm. Nat Wildlife 15:38-9 O '77

NATIONAL Wildlife Federation
Conservationist of the Year; W. E. Towell. por Am For 83:4 Ap '77
Treasure of wildlife stamps; water bird designs and money raised for National Wildlife Federation. G. Reiger. il Field & S 82:114-16+ Je '77

NATIONAL wildlife photo contest. See Photography—Competitions

NATIONAL Women's Conference. See Women—Conferences

NATIONAL Women's Political Caucus
Women's movement under siege. il Time 110:64 S 26 '77

NATIONAL Zoological Park, Washington, D.C.
View from the castle; breeding programs with rare animals at the National Zoo's Front Royal Va. facility. S. D. Ripley. Smithsonian 7:6 Mr '77

NATIONALISM
Ethnic conflict in the world today; symposium, ed by M. O. Heisler. bibl f Ann Am Acad 433:1-160 S '77
On nationalism. J. Rossen. Progressive 41:26-7 N '77
See also
Autonomy
Self determination, National
also subhead Nationalism under names of continents, countries, etc, e.g. Canada—Nationalism

NATIONALIZATION of industry. See Government ownership

NATIONS
World in focus; facts and figures of nations; chart. Sr Schol 110:14-18 O 20 '77

NATIVE races
See also
Ethnology
also subhead Native races under names of continents, countries, etc, e.g. Oceania—Native races

NATIVITY groups. See Christmas cribs

NATIVITY of Christ. See Jesus Christ—Nativity

NATO
AWACS plan tests NATO cooperation. il Aviation W 106:88-9+ Je 6 '77
Address to North Atlantic Council, Brussels, January 24. W. F. Mondale. Dept State Bull 76:182-5 Mr 7 '77
Airborne warning crucial alliance issue. C. A. Robinson, Jr. il map Aviation W 107:39+ Ag 22 '77
Atlantic Treaty Association; text of letter, August 27, 1977. J. Carter. Dept State Bull 77:468 O 10 '77
Basic changes in NATO structure seen. il Aviation W 106:102-3 Je 6 77
Behind the Cape route theory: NATO flirts with South Africa. P. L. Smith. Nation 225:262-4 S 24 '77
British order Nimrod AEW development. D. A. Brown. Aviation W 106:15 Ap 4 '77
Carter's goal: more sharing of the NATO load. il Bus W p78-9 Ag 8 '77
Congress unit urges shift in European nuclear arms. E. Kozicharow. Aviation W 106:18 Ja 17 '77
Conventional force buildup emphasized. C. A. Robinson, Jr. il Aviation W 107:45-9+ Ag 15 '77
Decision on AWACS purchase expected to be delayed again. Aviation W 106:201 Mr 21 '77
Defense Dept. sustains effort to aid NATO standardization. Aviation W 106:32 Ap 25 '77
Differences still stymie NATO efforts. il Aviation W 106:41-2 Mr 21 '77
Export curb, NATO goal clash. C. C. Brownlow. Aviation W 106:12-13 My 30 '77

NATO—*Continued*
Force management key to effectiveness. C. A. Robinson, Jr. il map Aviation W 107:36-7+ Ag 29 '77
Grumman's chance to bag a NATO plane; E-2C Hawkeye. il Bus W p49+ Ap 18 '77
Increasing Soviet offensive threat spurs stronger Europe air arm. C. A. Robinson, Jr. il Aviation W 107:38-40+ Ag 1 '77
Military and political challenges of the 80's; address, May 10, 1977. J. Carter. Vital Speeches 43:482-4 Je 1 '77; Same with title President Carter attends economic, Berlin, and NATO meetings at London and with text of communique. J. Carter. Dept State Bull 76:597-602 Je 6 '77
NATO arms buildup urged to offset pact. Aviation W 106:23-4 Je 27 '77
NATO: Haig speaks out; excerpts from interview, ed by A. de Borchgrave. A. Haig. por Newsweek 91:39 Ja 9 '78
NATO leaders hike defense budgets. D. A. Brown. Aviation W 106:21-2 My 23 '77
NATO ministers cite wider force gap. Aviation W 107:19 D 12 '77
NATO modifies defense plans in spying case. Aviation W 108:22-3 Ja 2 '78
NATO: nobody wants standardized weapons. il Bus W p 178+ My 16 '77
NATO standardization advances. E. Kozicharow. Aviation W 107:8-10 D 19 '77
NATO studying new series of satellites. Aviation W 107:127-8 O 17 '77
NATO IIIB military communications satellite launched. il Space World N-8-164:26-7 Ag '77
NATO unit agrees to common AWACS. D. A. Brown. Aviation W 107:18 D 12 '77
NATO warned of gains in Soviet arms strength. Aviation W 106:22-3 My 23 '77
Needs of NATO; address, October 18, 1977. B. W. Rogers. Vital Speeches 44:136-9 D 15 '77
New Soviet threat to NATO. S. Nunn. Read Digest 111:73-7 Jl '77
Nightmare for NATO. A. De Borchgrave. il map Newsweek 89:36-8 F 7 '77
North Atlantic Council meets at Brussels; text of communique, December 10, 1976. Dept State Bull 76:9-12 Ja 3 '77
Probing NATO's northern flank. il Time 109:24+ Je 27 '77
Secretary Kissinger attends NATO ministerial meeting at Brussels and meets with British officials at London; statement, with texts of news conferences, December 7 and 10, 1976. H. A. Kissinger. Dept State Bull 76:1-9 Ja 3 '77
Senators find arms buildup in East Europe. Aviation W 106:21 Ja 31 '77
Short-term initiatives readied by NATO. Aviation W 107:54-5 Ag 15 '77
Standardization effort at pivotal stage. E. Kozicharow. Aviation W 106:105+ Je 6 '77
Strength sought at least cost. C. A. Robinson, Jr. il maps Aviation W 107:36-8+ Ag 8 '77
Strengthening NATO ties; excerpts from address. R. A. Basil. Aviation W 107:7 Ag 29 '77
To strengthen the American alliance: better training and equipment in NATO forces; address, May 11, 1977. H. Brown. Vital Speeches 43:522-5 Je 15 '77
U.S. allies urged to meet Soviet strategic advances; Atlantic Council report. Aviation W 108:61 Ja 9 '78
U.S. funds major standardization drive. C. A. Robinson, Jr. il, Aviation W 107:52-3+ S 12 '77
U.S. policy toward our NATO partners: traditional commitments and new directions; statement, May 23, 1977. A. A. Hartman. Dept State Bull 76:635-9 Je 13 '77
U.S. proposes NATO buy fewer E-3As. Aviation W 106:21 Mr 28 '77
Western alliance seeks to update nuclear capability. D. A. Brown. il maps Aviation W 107:12-15 Ag 1 '77

Military maneuvers
See Military maneuvers

NATURAL areas
At long last, we're planning for the future; biosphere reserves as part of the Man and the Biosphere program of Unesco. J. Doherty. il Int Wildlife 7:24-8 N '77
Biosphere reserve program in the United States. J. F. Franklin. bibl il map Science 195:262-7 Ja 21 '77
Why we need the biosphere program. T. L. Kimball. il por Int Wildlife 7:29 N '77
World of the birdless dog; preserving natural areas and wildlife conservation. B. Tarrant. il Field & S 82:156+ S '77
See also
Wilderness areas

Economic aspects
Joe Horvath is adding up your dollars of happiness. J. Skow. il por Outdoor Life 159:66-7+ Mr '77

Alaska
Alaska wilderness: Congress debates resources "lock up". L. J. Carter. il Science 198:474-8 N 4 '77

Illinois
Hunting for remnants of old Illinois. R. Thom. Audubon 79:139-40 S '77

Texas
See also
Big Thicket

Washington (state)
Elk in the shrub-steppe region of Washington: an authentic record; Arid Lands Ecology Reserve. W. H. Rickard and others. il Science 196:1009 My 27 '77

NATURAL Bridges National Monument
Natural Bridges. . .new paving makes it an easy Utah detour. il map Sunset 159:56 O '77

NATURAL childbirth. See Childbirth

NATURAL disaster warning systems. See Disaster warning systems

NATURAL disasters. See Disasters

NATURAL foods cookery. See Cookery—Organic food

NATURAL gas. See Gas, Natural

NATURAL gas industry. See Gas industry

NATURAL history
Natural sciences (cont) Sci N 111:28 Ja 8 '77
Naturalist at large. See issues of Natural history
Nature fakers and science. E. M. Reilly, Jr. il Conservationist 31:28-31 Ja '77
Nature's beauty gets its own show; Splendors of Nature at the Smithsonian Museum of Natural History. il Smithsonian 8:115-20 O '77
Wild world must be saved. Philip. il pors Sat Eve Post 249:26-9+ N '77
Wildlife omnibus. See issues of International wildlife
Wildlife omnibus. il Nat Wildlife 16:46-7 D '77
See also
Nature study
Phenology

Study and teaching
American adventure of Louis Agassiz. D. McCullough. il por Audubon 79:2-17 Ja '77
Whale-watchers; natural history study cruise off Baja California. G. Reiger. il Audubon 79:74-6+ My '77

Australia
Wind caller; Torres Strait. B. Nietschmann. il map Natur Hist 86:10-12+ Mr '77

Tibet
Wilds of Tibetan plateau: natural zoo. il Sci N 111:310 My 14 '77

NATURAL history museums
Classroom in the cactus; Arizona-Sonora Desert Museum. J. Stocker. il Am Educ 13:6-11 D '77
Near Tucson. . .caves to explain desert geology; Arizona-Sonora Desert Museum. il Sunset 159:50 O '77
See also
American Museum of Natural History, New York
George C. Page Museum of La Brea Discoveries, Los Angeles
New York State Museum, Albany
Ward's Natural Science Establishment, Rochester, N.Y.

NATURAL History Photographic Competition. See Photography—Competitions

NATURAL law
Natural law. K. Bockmühl. Chr Today 22:59-60 N 18 '77

NATURAL monuments
America, the mostest. A. Bernstein. il Am For 83:24-8 Mr '77
See also
Natural Bridges National Monument

NATURAL resources
See also
Conservation of resources
Forests and forestry
Marine resources
Peat
Power resources
Space mineral resources
United Nations—Committee on Natural Resources
Water resources development
Water supply

Bibliography
Reading about resources. M. Bush. See issues of American forests

Economic aspects
Joe Horvath is adding up your dollars of happiness. J. Skow. il por Outdoor Life 159:66-7+ Mr '77
Problem of exhaustible resources. S. F. Williams. il Nat R 29:1352-3+ N 25 '77

International aspects
Scarcity and strategy. G. Kemp. For Affairs 56:396-414 Ja '78

NATURAL resources—*Continued*

Alaska

Alaska: now that oil is flowing, what next? K. M. Chrysler. il map U.S. News 83:48-51 Jl 11 '77

See also

Conservation of resources—Alaska

Antarctic Regions

Antarctica: a special case? B. Mitchell. il Oceans 10:56-9 My '77

Antarctica's icy assets. P. Gwynne and others. il Newsweek 90:92-3+ O 3 '77

Heating up: global race for Antarctic's riches. J. F. McWethy. il U.S. News 82:62-6 F 28 '77

Parties of Antarctic Treaty meet in London; statement, September 19, 1977. R. C. Brewster. Dept State Bull 77:738-40 N 21 '77

Recommendation to protect Antarctic environment; statement, September 12, 1977. R. C. Brewster. Dept State Bull 77:576-7 O 24 '77

Scotia Sea: waterway of the future. J. F. Lohr and M. Castleman. il Oceans 10:36-41 My '77

Ivory Coast

Ivory Coast: political stability and economic growth. A. Taylor and others. bibl il maps Focus 27:1-15 Ja; 1-14 My '77

Mozambique

Mozambique: fragile independence. H. J. De Blij. bibl il map Focus 27:9-16 N '76

Rhodesia

Rhodesia (Zimbabwe): white minority rule in a black state. T. J. Kubiak. bibl il map Focus 27:1-8 N '76

Russia

Development of Soviet Asia. R. N. North. bibl f map Cur Hist 73:123-7+ O '77

Underdeveloped areas

See Underdeveloped areas—Natural resources

United States

See also

Water supply—United States

History

Eden ravished: the land, the pioneer attitudes, and conservation. H. Hague. bibl il Am West 14:30-3+ My '77

NATURAL selection

Darwin's mistake. T. Bethell. bibl Chr Today 21:12-15 Je 17 '77

Natural selection for juvenile lizards mimicking noxious beetles. R. B. Huey and E. R. Pianka. bibl il Science 195:201-3 Ja 14 '77

NATURAL wonders. See Natural monuments

NATURALISTS

Naturalist at large. See issues of Natural history

See also

Agassiz, L.

Muir, J.

NATURE

How much are nature's services worth? W. E. Westman. bibl Science 197:960-4 S 2 '77

See also

Man—Influence on nature

Natural history

Outdoor life

Seasons

Bibliography

Book reviews; ed by J. Taylor. See issues of Conservationist

Books. il Liv Wildn 40:36-42 O '76; 44-9 Ja; 41:34-6 Ap '77

Books in review. See issues of Natural history

Children's books for the trail. E. M. Graves. il Commonweal 104:726-7 N 11 '77

NATURE, Law of. See Natural law

NATURE and man. See Man—Influence on nature

NATURE Conservancy (organization)

Connecticut's last virgin forest. H. Black. il Am For 83:24-7+ N '77

Key to a beautiful America: renewed personal pride; interview. P. F. Noonan. il por U.S. News 82:39-40 Je 13 '77

Nature preservers; work of Nature Conservancy and G. Anable. B. Delatiner. McCalls 104:69 Jl '77

Partnership that pays off for the public; American Land Trust. il Nations Bus 65:46-8+ Jl '77

We can work with you. D. Morine. il Am For 83:10-12 N '77

NATURE conservation

See also

Forest conservation

Landscape protection

Natural areas

Shore protection

Stream conservation

Wildlife conservation

NATURE in art

Commitment to the past; work of S. Haden, A. Legros and A. Lepère. G. Weisberg. il Art N 76:150-2 Summ '77

Conversation with Antonio Cirino; interview, ed by C. Movalli. A. Cirino. il por Am Artist 41:58-63+ Ag '77

Elizabeth Bloom: art and nature. E. Medoff. il Am Artist 41:62-7 Je '77

Gallery of nature art; reproductions of paintings. See issues of Audubon

Maria Martin: the brush behind Audubon's birds. M. Williams and P. Elliott. il Ms 5:14-15+ Ap '77

Wayne Trimm's sketchbook. W. Trimm. See issues of Conservationist

See also

Animals in art

Birds in art

Leaves in art

NATURE literature

New naturalist books for children grow in environment provided by Sierra Club/Scribners. J. F. Mercier. il Pub W 211:44 Ap 18 '77

See also

Nature—Bibliography

NATURE photography

Camera trophies. T. Brakefield. Field & S 82:20 O '77

Eliot Porter on 35-mm; interview, ed by P. Caulfield. E. Porter. il por Pop Phot 81:108-17+ S '77

For love of wilderness; work of G. Braasch. N. Stevens. il Pop Phot 80:86-93 F '77

Mini-cameras for the outdoors. J. Tallon. il Field & S 82:40+ D '77

Nature photography is easy? H. Hansen. il Mod Phot 41:106-11+ My '77

Photo and word views of pioneer photographer Eliot Porter; interview, ed by J. Landman. E. Porter. il por Sr Schol 110:2-5 D 1 '77

Prizewinning photographs from the 1977 Natural History Photographic Competition. A. M. Cunningham. il Natur Hist 86:45-63 bibl(p 116) Ag '77

To meet the morning dew. H. Pfletschinger. il Int Wildlife 8:44-7 Ja '78

Winners of National wildlife's annual photo contest. il Nat Wildlife 15:24-33 Ap '77

See also

Blinds (camouflage)

Photography—Landscapes

Photography of animals

Photography of flowers, plants, trees, etc.

Photography of insects

NATURE reserves. See Natural areas

NATURE study

Child looks at a tree. C. E. Lewis. il Am For 83:30-3 Mr '77

Know more, see more. T. Trueblood. il Field & S 82:22+ D '77

Nature is my calendar; determining hunting and fishing seasons by natural signs. B. W. Dalrymple. il Outdoor Life 159:90-2+ Ap '77

To be an outdoorsman. S. Netherby. bibl il Field & S 82:160-2 Je '77

See also

Bird study

Camping—Educational aspects

Environmental education

Natural history museums

Outdoor education

Wildlife watching

NATURE trails. See Trails

NATURE'S Way (store) See Atlanta—Stores

NAUDÉ, Christian Frederic Beyers

Banning of Beyers Naudé. G. M. Bryan. Chr Cent 94:1020-1 N 9 '77 *

South African muzzle. A. Silk. Nation 225:581-4 D 3 '77 *

NAUGHTON, Brian A. and others

Hepatic regeneration and erythropoietin production in the rat. bibl il Science 196:301-2 Ap 15 '77

NAUSEA

See also

Motion sickness

NAUTICAL astronomy

See also

Navigation

NAUTICAL charts

Notices to boatmen. E. S. Maloney. See issues of Motor boating & sailing

Pilot charts—and how to use them. E. S. Maloney. il map Motor B & S 139:30+ My '77

NAUTICAL education

See also

Sailing—Study and teaching

NAUTICAL instruments

Night vision. D. Hart. il Motor B & S 140:26+ N '77

See also

Automatic pilot (boats)

NAUTICAL museums. See Naval museums

NAUTILUS

Still living fossil, the nautilus, glides through the ages. D. Faulkner. il Smithsonian 8:76-81 Je '77

NAVAHO blankets, rugs, etc. See Indian blankets, rugs, etc (American)

NAVAHO Indians

Students write about their artwork. M. Esping. il Sch Arts 76:36-8 F '77

NAVAJO Indians. See Navaho Indians

NAVAL Academy. See United States Naval Academy, Annapolis

NAVAL Air Development Center. See United States—Naval Air Development Center

NAVAL Air Systems Command. See United States—Naval Air Systems Command

NAVAL Air Test Center. See United States—Naval Air Test Center

NAVAL architecture

See also

Boatbuilding

Boats—Design

Hulls (naval architecture)

Keels

Yachts—Design

Study and teaching

Boat design at home; Yacht Design Institute home study course. il Yachting 142:146 Jl '77

NAVAL art and science

See also

Torpedoes

NAVAL Avionics Facility. See United States—Naval Air Systems Command—Naval Avionics Facility

NAVAL bases. See Navy yards and naval stations

NAVAL battles

When Argentina conquered California; naval battles fought by Argentine ship on voyage around the world. A. Alonso Piñeiro. il por Américas 29:34-7 Je '77

See also

United States—History—Revolution, 1775-1783—Naval operations

World War, 1914-1918—Naval operations

World War, 1939-1945—Naval operations

NAVAL education

See also

United States—Navy—Education

NAVAL history

See also

Cuba—History, Naval

NAVAL museums

Ship touring in San Diego; Maritime Museum. il Sunset 158:44 Je '77

NAVAL power. See Sea power

NAVAL radio communication. See Radio, Military

NAVAL Research, Office of. See United States—Naval Research, Office of

NAVAL Weapons Center. See United States—Naval Weapons Center

NAVARETTA, Cynthia

Guide to all the arts—for a modern Mona. Ms 6:87-90 D '77

NAVARRO, Nina, and Bushnell, Richards

Campeche: buccaneer's battleground. il Oceans 10:22-5 S '77

NAVASKY, Victor S.

Greening of Griffin Bell. por N Y Times Mag p41-2+ F 27 '77

NAVIES

See also

Sea power

also subhead Navy under names of countries, e.g. Russia—Navy

NAVIGATION

Chart your way to the fish. R. D. Stearns. il map Outdoor Life 160:133-4 S '77

Finding your position; celestial navigation; excerpt from Airborne. W. F. Buckley, Jr. il Motor B & S 140:67-71+ N '77

Rough log. T. Gibbs. Yachting 141:120 Ap '77

Sailings: determining course and distance without a chart. E. S. Maloney. map Motor B & S 139:84+ F '77

Sailings: useful applications. E. S. Maloney. il Motor B & S 139:84+ Mr '77

See also

Boats and boating

Hydrographic surveying

Lighthouses

Loran

Pilots and pilotage

Radar in navigation

Rule of the road at sea

Sailing

Seamanship

United States Power Squadrons, Inc

Aids and devices

By push button to Tahiti; electronic devices. M. Meisels. il Motor B & S 139:18-19+ Je '77

Calculator current predictions; tidal current. E. S. Maloney. il Motor B & S 140:14+ O '77

Calculator navigation. T. Gibbs. il Yachting 141:102-5 Ap '77

Electronic navigators. R. Schaefer. il Motor B & S 140:84-6+ O '77

Height of tide—by calculator! E. S. Maloney. il Motor B & S 140:16+ Jl '77

Navigate with the smart stick; slide rule. J. Martenhoff. il Motor B & S 139:87+ Ap '77

Push button navigators; calculators. E. Bergin and J. Buchanek. il Motor B & S 139:88-90+ My '77

State-of-the-art electronics; navigating station aboard Bay Bea. C. L. Hohenstein. il Yachting 142:40+ Ag '77

See also

Depth indicators

Nautical charts

Radio in navigation

Competitions

By the mark. B. Crabtree. See issues of Yachting to June 1977

NAVIGATION, Aerial. See Air navigation

NAVIGATION satellites. See Artificial satellites—Navigational use

NAVRATIL, James D. and Walton, H. F.

Ion exchange and liquid chromatography. bibl il pors Chemistry 50:18-20 Jl '77

NAVRATILOVA, Martina

She can beat Evert—but does she really want to? B. Collins. il pors N Y Times Mag p35-6+ Je 19 '77 *

NAVSTAR (artificial satellite) See Artificial satellites—Navigational use

NAVY yards and naval stations

Diego Garcia: a test of rights. J. Madeley. America 136:461-2 My 21 '77

For the U.S. Navy, a strategic setback in the Persian Gulf; eviction from Bahrain. D. Mullin. il map U.S. News 82:43-4 Je 6 '77

Hideout for Trident; proposed base in Palau. R. C. Aldridge. Progressive 41:11 F '77

Somewhere east of Suez; Diego Garcia. H. Jensen. il map Newsweek 89:56 Ap 18 '77

U.S. Navy and the AIA honor architecture at Annapolis and at naval bases around the country. il Archit Rec 161:39 F '77

Weighing anchor; facility in Bahrain. W. E. Schmidt. il map Newsweek 90:33 Jl 11 '77

When a supersub base invades a rural area in the Northwest; Bangor Trident base. il map U.S. News 83:41-2 Ag 1 '77

NAWAPA. See North American Water and Power Alliance

NAZARETH, Daniel

Artist life. D. J. Soria. pors Hi Fi 27:MA10+ D '77 *

NAZI war criminals. See World War, 1939-1945—War criminals

NAZIS in the United States

American Nazis: are they more than just a curiosity? il U.S. News 83:57-8 N 7 '77

Even for Nazis; Skokie, Ill. right-to-march controversy. Progressive 41:6-7 D '77

For all or for none; right-to-march case of the American Nazi Party in Skokie, Ill. Nation 225:354-5 O 15 '77

Neo-Nazi groups: artifacts of hate. il Time 109:25 F 28 '77

NAZISM. See National socialism

NAZZARO, Pellegrino

Italy: a new adventure. bibl f Cur Hist 73:160-4+ N '77

NEAL, Stephen Lybrook

Man who watches the Fed. G. R. Rosen. por Duns R 109:47 Ja '77 *

NEALIS, John R.

Remnants; poem. Conservationist 31:46 My '77

NEALSON, Kenneth H. See Ruby, E. G. jt auth

NEARSIGHTEDNESS. See Myopia

NEARY, Joan

Marvelous meals for less money. por Parents Mag 52:38-9+ Mr '77

When feelings clash. il Parents Mag 53:44+ Ja '78

NEARY, John

Earth log: eagle doctor of Tesuque. il pors Audubon 79:90-2+ Jl '77

Great Southwest water war. il Sat R 4:18-20+ S 3 '77

(ed) See Nakayama, R. M. Big chile

NEATHERY, M. W. See Miller, W. J. jt auth

NEATNESS

Tidies; excerpt from Eyes, etc. E. Clark. Atlantic 240:60-2 Jl '77

NEBRADA, Vicente

Ballet Internacional de Caracas and two of its dancers. N. M. Stoop. il pors Dance Mag 52:51-66 Ja '78 *

NEBRASKA

See also

Architecture, Domestic—Nebraska

Banks and banking—Nebraska

Irrigation—Nebraska

Libraries—Nebraska

Opera—Nebraska

Wildlife sanctuaries—Nebraska

Description and travel

Sod house frontier. J. Jordon and C. Jordon. il Travel 148:50-5 Ag '77

Restaurants

See Restaurants—United States

NEBRASKA. University, Omaha
Festival of education for older people; University of Nebraska at Omaha. S. Francke and B. Horacek. il Aging 275:24-5 S '77

NEBULAE
Disappearing nebula: a star turns on? il Sky & Tel 54:268-9 O '77
Laboratory exercises in astronomy: the Crab nebula. O. Gingerich. il Sky & Tel 54:378-82 N '77
New look at the Loop nebula. il Sky & Tel 53:112 F '77
Recent findings about planetary nebulae. Y. Terzian. il Sky & Tel 54:459-63 D '77
Structure in the Carina nebula and Eta Carinae. N. R. Walborn and T. E. Ingerson. il Sky & Tel 54:22-4 Jl '77

NECESSITIES
Question of 'I can't live without it.' S. Schraub. House B 119:66 O '77

NECK
Caring for your neck. E. Schoen. il House & Gard 149:30+ Ap '77

NECKLACES
Making a necklace with Indian corn kernels or beans. il Sunset 159:132+ N '77

NECKTIES
Ties that bind; neckties with corporate logos. il Forbes 119:90-1 F 15 '77

NEDELMAN, Jeffrey
Destroying tomorrow today: the Army Corps of Engineers wants the Mississippi River. Horticulture 55:8+ O '77

NEEDHAM, Gerald
Ambroise Vollard—impresario. il por Art N 76:78-80+ S '77
(tr) See Frèrebeau, M. What is Montmartre? Nothing! What should it be? Everything!

NEEDHAM, Hal
Man who loved stunt driving. K. Snedaker. il por Car & Dr 23:108-9 Jl '77 *

NEEDHAM, Joseph
I only hope that I live to see it. Horizon 19:12 Ja '77

NEEDHAM, Nancy R.
Internal security. Todays Educ 66:53 Ja '77

NEEDLE, June
Peace Corps planning in the world's parks. il Parks & Rec 12:16-21+ Ag '77

NEEDLEMAN, Philip, and others
Coronary tone modulation: formation and actions of prostaglandins, endoperoxides, and thromboxanes. bibl il Science 195:409-12 Ja 28 '77

NEEDLEPOINT embroidery. See Embroidery

NEEDLER, Martin C.
Omar Torrijos: the Panamanian enigma. por Intellect 105:242-3 F '77

NEEDLES. Phonograph. See Phonograph needles

NEEDLEWORK
Make-ahead presents: for all the family. il Seventeen 36:124-5+ N '77
Make it a Christmas to remember: with traditional American stitchery. N. Lindemeyer and C. Vaughan. il Bet Hom & Gard 55:86-103+ D '77
Pittsburgh center pinpoints the art of the needle; Center for the History of American Needlework. G. Bethel. Craft Horiz 37:42 Ag '77
60 glorious gifts to sew, knit, crochet, appliqué, quilt, etc. il Good H 185:164-8+ N '77
Stitching; excerpt from Designing in stitching and appliqué. N. Belfer. il Sch Arts 76:16-21 Mr '77
To the glory of God; needlework in the Washington National Cathedral. il Good H 185:120-3 D '77
Wildflowers—adapting floral designs for different types of needlework. N. Lindemeyer and G. Vaughan. il Bet Hom & Gard 55:64-76+ F '77
See also
Appliqué work
Crocheting
Embroidery
Knitting
Quilts
Samplers
Tapestry

Bibliography

Books. House B 119:30 O '77

NEEDS. See Necessities

NEEPER, Laurie
America's teacher of the year. M. S. Miller. por Ladies Home J 94:42+ Ap '77 *

NEES, Ruby T. See Prospero, J. M. jt auth

NEF, John U.
Early energy crisis and its consequences; with biographical sketch. il map Sci Am 237:16,140-2+ bibl(p 164) N '77

NEFF, John B.
Don't be a bottom-watcher. R. J. Flaherty. por Forbes 120:96-7 N 15 '77 *

NEGATIVE color films. See Photography—Films

NEGATIVE income tax
Jobs and income for the poor. R. I. Lerman. il Society 14:60-2 My '77
Welfare costs vs. the negative income tax. R. W. Haseltine. Intellect 106:141-2 O '77

NEGATIVE ions. See Ions

NEGATIVE numbers. See Numbers, Negative

NEGLIGENCE
See also
Liability (law)

NEGOTIABLE instruments
Hard Congressional look at credit cards. Bus W p96-7 F 7 '77
See also
Acceptances
Certificates of deposit

NEGROES. See Blacks

NEGUS, Norman C. and Berger, P. J.
Experimental triggering of reproduction in a natural population of microtus montanus. bibl il Science 196:1230-1 Je 10 '77

NEIGHBORHOODS
Bank's drive to rescue neighborhoods; Chemical Bank's program in New York city. V. Louviere. il Nations Bus 65:43 F '77
Great American melting pot. Holiday 58:24-6+ Ap '77
S&Ls will write a program for city neighborhood lending. D. Loomis. Archit Rec 161:34 Je '77

NEIKIRK, Harold B. See Pieratt, A. jt auth

NEIKIRK, William
Washington's new approach to antitrust action. pors Nations Bus 65:30-2 D '77

NEILL, Shirley Boes
Clearing the air in career education. il Am Educ 13:6-9+ Mr '77
Crisis counseling. il Am Educ 13:17-22 Ja '77
How to improve student writing. Educ Digest 42:44-7 Ja '77
New crisis in the classroom: energy. il Am Educ 13:15-21 Ag '77
(ed) See Hoyt, K. B. According to Hoyt

NEIMAN, LeRoy
LeRoy Neiman. N. Meglin. il por Am Artist 41:36-9 Jl '77 *

NEISSERIA
Conjugal transfer of the gonococcal penicillinase plasmid. B. I. Eisenstein and others. bibl il Science 195:998-1000 Mr 11 '77

NEIZVESTNY, Ernest
Equal time. Vasari. Art N 76:24-5 Summ '77 *

NELSEN, Hart M. and Potvin, R. H.
Rural church and rural religion: analysis of data from children and youth. bibl f il Ann Am Acad 429:103-14 Ja '77

NELSEN, Harvey W.
China's great wall: the People's Liberation Army. bibl Cur Hist 73:59-62+ S '77

NELSON, Ann
Summer business on Martha's Vineyard: how Bunch of Grapes makes it year-round. S. S. Steinberg. il por Pub W 212:44+ S 5 '77 *

NELSON, Anne
Women students v. male teachers. Nation 226:7-10 Ja 7 '78

NELSON, Bryan
Trial balloon; excerpt from Galapagos: islands of birds. il Audubon 79:42-3 My '77

NELSON, Bryce
Corn patch nobel laureate. Bull Atom Sci 33:48-50 O '77

NELSON, D. E. and others
Carbon-14: direct detection at natural concentrations. bibl il Science 198:507-8 N 4 '77

NELSON, Diana Furst, and Rubin, Philip
Radiation therapy. bibl il pors Chemistry 50:6-10 Jl '77

NELSON, Ed
Solar ponds—heat from a hole in the ground. il Pop Sci 211:80-1 D '77

NELSON, Gary L.
Finding and using the wild spices. il Org Gard & Farm 24:79-81 N '77
Why not homegrown paprika? il Org Gard & Farm 24:160+ Ap '77

NELSON, Gaylord Anton
Should saccharin be banned? interview. pors U.S. News 82:59-60 Ap 4 '77

NELSON, Gunvor
Films of Gunvor Nelson. J. M. Gill. bibl il Film Q 30:28-36 Spr '77 *

NELSON, Hans, and others
Mercury dispersal from lode sources in the Kuskokwim River drainage, Alaska. bibl il map Science 198:820-4 N 25 '77

NELSON, Horatio Nelson, Viscount
Life and loves of Lady Hamilton: A melodrama in several acts. F. V. Grunfeld. il pors Horizon 19:72-81 Ja '77 *

NELSON, James
Great wine at soda pop prices; rebottling wine; excerpt from The poorperson's guide to great cheap wines. il Sat Eve Post 249:10+ D '77

NELSON, James E.
Who gets the money? Educ Digest 42:54-6 Ja '77

NELSON, John S.
Church and catechesis. il por New Cath World 220:74-6+ Mr '77

NELSON, Jon
Summer business on Martha's Vineyard: how Bunch of Grapes makes it year-round. S. S. Steinberg. il por Pub W 212:44+ S 5 '77 *

NELSON, Judith C. and Marshall, J. S.
Vegetables at 8,000 feet. Org Gard & Farm 24:202 F '77

NELSON, Leona L.
Three successive crops from our corn patch. il Org Gard & Farm 24:69-71 F '77
Unusual varieties add spice to a garden. il Org Gard & Farm 24:162+ Mr '77

NELSON, Mary
Learning to move, moving to learn. il Parks & Rec 12:34-5+ N '77

NELSON, Mary Carroll
Creative pendulum of Mike Vogel: graphic artist and entrepreneur. il por Am Artist 41:70-5+ O '77
Taos art colony. Am Artist 42:27 Ja '78
Virginia Denn paints inscapes. il por Am Artist 41:50-3+ Mr '77
(ed) See Egri, T. Ted Egri: the survival of a sculptor
(ed) See Moses, F. Forrest Moses: a man and his sanctuary

NELSON, Mildred
Litterally spring; poem. McCalls 104:46 My '77

NELSON, Paula
Money talks. por McCalls 104:74+ F; 96+ Ap; 68+ Je; 76+ Jl; 105:46+ N '77
Why women can't save money. Harp Baz 110: 98+ Mr '77

NELSON, Peter
Steelheading sense. il pors Field & S 82:44-5+ O '77
Tent camp. il Outdoor Life 160:78-9+ D '77

NELSON, Ray
Weekend on 16 lbs. il Mech Illus 73:49+ Mr '77
World's largest radio telescope. il Pop Sci 210: 80-2+ Mr '77

NELSON, Ronald H.
New role for crisis centers. il MH 61:12-13 Summ '77

NELSON, Susan
How battered women can get help. Read Digest 110:21-3+ My '77

NELSON, W. Dale
Dateline: Washington. See issues of Wilson library bulletin

NELSON-REES, Walter A. and Flandermeyer, R. R.
Inter-and intraspecies contamination of human breast tumor cell lines HBC and BrCa5 and other cell cultures. bibl il Science 195:1343-4 Mr 25 '77

NEMATODES
Disruption of sex pheromone communication in a nematode. L. W. Bone and H. H. Shorey. bibl il Science 197:694-5 Ag 12 '77
Nematode caenorhabditis elegans: a new organism for intensive biological study. R. S. Edgar and W. B. Wood. bibl Science 198:1285-6 D 23 '77
Nematodes can steal 5 to 50 bu. of your corn yield. il Farm J 101:H2 Ag '77
Successful farming's guide to: nematodes. C. E. Sommers. il Suc Farm 75:no5 36-7 Mr '77; Same. 75:C36-7 D '77

NEMIKIN, Raisa
Of bombs and bishops. Time 109:59 Mr 14 '77 *

NEMIROFF, Martin J.
Natural life preservers. il por Time 110:73+ Ag 22 '77 *
Saving the drowned. S. Drake. il por Newsweek 90:79-80 Ag 22 '77 *

NEMY, Enid
Real Yasmine. il pors N Y Times Mag p80+ Ap 3 '77

NEOCLASSICISM (art)
See also
Architecture, Greek revival

NEO-GREEK architecture. See Architecture, Greek revival

NEO-IMPRESSIONISM. See Post-impressionism (art)

NEOLITHIC period. See Stone age

NEO-NAZIS in the United States. See Nazis in the United States

NEOPLASMS. See Tumors

NEOTENY
Neoplastic and possibly related skin lesions in neotenic tiger salamanders from a sewage lagoon. F. L. Rose and J. C. Harshbarger. bibl il Science 196:315-17 Ap 15 '77

NEPAL
Trek to Nepal's sacred Crystal Mountain; Dolpo province. J. F. Ziskin. il map Nat Geog 151: 500-17+ Ap '77
Young girl called Kumari: Nepal's current living goddess. D. O'Connor and P. O'Connor. il Ms 5:30 Mr '77
See also
National parks and reserves—Nepal

Politics and government

Nepal: despotism in tranquillity. P. Gupte. il Nation 224:781-4 Je 25 '77

NEPHRECTOMY. See Kidneys—Surgery

NEPOTISM
Nepotism question at General Motors; lawsuits charging E. M. Estes with furthering his sons' careers. por Bus W p41 S 19 '77

NEPTUNE (planet)
Reports on Neptune and Uranus. il Sky & Tel 53:429-30 Je '77

NERI, Manuel
Slouching mortality and inky galaxies. T. Albright. Art N 76:90+ Ja '77 *

NERPEL, Chuck
Driving impressions. il Motor T 29:83-5 S '77

NERUDA, Pablo
So is my life; poem; excerpt from Song of protest, tr by M. Algarin. Sat R 4:19 F 19 '77
Tides; poem; excerpt from A new decade: poems 1958-1967, tr by B. Belitt. Sat R 4:19 F 19 '77

about

Great bad men. S. Rodman. Nat R 29:340-1 Mr 18 '77 *
In my own time. C. L. Mee, Jr. por Horizon 19: 94-5 Ja '77 *

NERVE cells
Androgen concentration in motor neurons of cranial nerves and spinal cord. M. Sar and W. E. Stumpf. bibl il Science 197:77-9 Jl 1 '77
Bag cell control of egg laying in freely behaving aplysia. H. M. Pinsker and F. E. Dudek. bibl il Science 197:490-3 Jl 29 '77
Clockwise growth of neurites from retinal explants. A. M. Heacock and B. W. Agranoff. bibl il Science 198:64-6 O 7 '77
Early development of X-cells in kitten lateral geniculate nucleus. J. L. Norman and others. bibl il Science 198:202-4 O 14 '77
Glia maturation factor: effect on chemical differentiation of glioblasts in culture. R. Lim and others. bibl il Science 195:195-6 Ja 14 '77
Glial-neural interaction demonstrated by the injection of Na^+ and Li^+ into cortical glia. R. G. Grossman and A. Seregin. bibl il Science 195:196-8 Ja 14 '77
Glutamine synthetase: glial localization in brain. A. Martinez-Hernandez and others. bibl il Science 195:1356-8 Mr 25 '77
Ho-hum-cholinergic nerves are the culprit. il Sci N 111:359 Je 4 '77
Pontine reticular formation neurons: relationship of discharge to motor activity. J. M. Siegel and D. J. McGinty. bibl il Science 196: 678-80 My 6 '77
Schwann cells: mixing and matching. Sci N 112: 356-7 N 26 '77
Selective destruction of neurons by a transmitter agonist. R. M. Herndon and J. T. Coyle. bibl il Science 198:71-2 O 7 '77
Spinal neurons project to the dorsal column nuclei of rhesus monkeys. A. Rustioni. bibl il Science 196:656-8 My 6 '77
See also
Electrophysiology

NERVE fibers. See Nerve cells

NERVE growth promoting factor
NFG may hold the key—but to what? J. Arehart-Treichel. il por Sci N 111:330-1+ My 21 '77

NERVE regeneration. See Regeneration (biology)

NERVES
Licking behavior: evidence of hypoglossal oscillator. Z. Wiesenfeld and others. bibl il Science 196:1122-4 Je 3 '77
See also
Synapses

NERVIG, Marilyn
Concerned homemaker expresses her views on furniture flammability legislation. Consumers Res Mag 60:27+ Je '77

NERVOUS system
Circadian rhythm of synaptic excitability in rat and monkey central nervous system. C. A. Barnes and others. bibl il Science 197:91-2 Jl 1 '77
Mechanistic teleology and explanation in neuroethology; excerpt from Identified neurons and behavior of arthropods, ed by G. Hoyle. G. A. Horridge. bibl BioScience 27:725-32 N '77
Neurometrics. E. R. John and others. bibl il Science 196:1393-410 Je 24 '77
See also
Biological control systems
Brain
Chemoreceptivity
Electrophysiology
Muscle—Innervation
Neurogenesis
Psychology, Physiological
Reflexes
Spinal cord
Synapses

Coelenterates

Electrically coupled, photosensitive neurons control swimming in a jellyfish. P. A. V. Anderson and G. O. Mackie. bibl il Science 197:186-8 Jl 8 '77

Diseases

Basal ganglia cooling disables learned arm movements of monkeys in the absence of visual guidance. J. Hore and others. bibl il Science 195:584-6 F 11 '77
Little-known diseases; Tourette's syndrome. A. Belson. Fam Health 9:42-4+ My '77

NERVOUS system—Diseases—*Continued*
Nightmarish disease of screams and tics; Gilles de la Tourette syndrome. S. Bush. Psychol Today 11:34 Je '77
Regeneration of oligodendroglia during recovery from demyelinating disease. R. M. Herndon and others. bibl il Science 195:693-4 F 18 '77
Schwann cells: mixing and matching. Sci N 112:356-7 N 26 '77
Synthetic galactocerebrosides evoke myelination-inhibiting antibodies. S. Huruby and others. bibl il Science 195:173-5 Ja 14 '77
Unconventional viruses and the origin and disappearance of Kuru; Nobel Prize lecture, December 13, 1976. D. C. Gajdusek. bibl il maps Science 197:943-60 S 2 '77
See also
Brain—Diseases
Gangliosidosis
Huntington's chorea
Lesch-Nyhan syndrome
Neuritis, Multiple
Sclerosis, Multiple

Insects

Ecdysis: neural orchestration of a complex behavior performance. J. R. Carlson and D. Bentley. bibl il Science 195:1006-8 Mr 11 '77
Neuron duplications and deletions in locust clones and clutches. C. S. Goodman. bibl il Science 197:1384-6 S 30 '77

Mollusks

Bag cell control of egg laying in freely behaving aplysia. H. M. Pinsker and F. E. Dudek. bibl il Science 197:490-3 Jl 29 '77
Behavioral choice: neural mechanisms in pleurobranchaea. M. P. Kovac and W. J. Davis. bibl il Science 198:632-4 N 11 '77
Calcium-dependent depression of a late outward current in snail neurons. R. Eckert and H. D. Lux. bibl il Science 197:472-5 Jl 29 '77
Phenylethanolamine: a new putative neurotransmitter in aplysia. J. M. Saavedra and others. bibl il Science 195:1004-6 Mr 11 '77
Presynaptic electrical coupling in aplysia; effects on postsynaptic chemical transmission. R. Waziri. bibl il Science 195:790-2 F 25 '77
Structure of a molluscan cardioexcitatory neuropeptide. D. A Price and M. J. Greenberg. bibl il Science 197:670-1 Ag 12 '77
Tris buffer attenuates acetylcholine responses in aplysia neurons. W. A. Wilson and others. bibl il Science 196:440-1 Ap 22 '77

Rodents

Ultrasound emission in infant rats as an indicant of arousal during appetitive learning and extinction. A. Amsel and others. bibl il Science 197:786-8 Ag 19 '77

NERVOUS tension. See Stress (psychology)

NERVOUS tic. See Tic

NERVOUSNESS
Bazaar's health guide to your nerves; symposium. Harp Baz 110:124-9+ Mr '77

NESBITT, John A. and Hippolitus, Paul
Rehabilitating the employer. Parks & Rec 12: 36-7+ N '77

NESBITT, Patricia
Cistern for the garden. il Org Gard & Farm 24:88-9 Jl '77

NESSEN, Robert L.
Rich guy's loophole. New Repub 177:9-12 D 3 '77

NESSEN, Ronald H.
Poor Jody Powell. por Newsweek 89:9 Ja 31 '77

NESTLÉ Alimentana (firm) See Food industry—Switzerland

NESTS
'Dobe birds; mud nests of swallows. H. Borland. il Audubon 79:16-17 Mr '77

NETHERBY, Steve
Camping. See issues of Field & stream

NETHERLANDS
See also
Art—Netherlands
Ballet—Netherlands
Conglomerate corporations—Netherlands
Corporation law—Netherlands
Friesland
Industrial relations—Netherlands
Jews in the Netherlands
Middelburg
Museums—Netherlands
Music festivals—Netherlands
Opera—Netherlands
Terrorism—Netherlands
Wages—Netherlands

Commerce

Carnations from Kenya. . .; flower auctions in Holland. il Forbes 120:115-16 N 15 '77

Spain

See Spain—Commerce—Netherlands

Description and travel

Three to six-day Holland walks. il Sunset 158:78 Ap '77

Economic conditions

Dutch grope for a new social contract. il Bus W p46+ Ag 8 '77

Foreign relations

United States

See United States—Foreign relations—Netherlands

Industries

See also
Bulb industry—Netherlands
Philips of Eindhoven Companies

Politics and government

Turn to the right worries business. Bus W p47 D 26 '77

Race question

Dutch discord. E. Keerdoja. il Newsweek 90:27 N 14 '77

Social history

Tulipomania was no Dutch treat to gambling burghers. T. Berger. il Smithsonian 8:70-7 Ap '77

Social life and customs

Skating on the canals. F. V. Grunfeld. il Horizon 19:20-3 Mr '77

NETHERLANDS Antilles. See Netherlands West Indies

NETHERLANDS Library Museum and Archives. See Museums—Netherlands

NETHERLANDS WEST INDIES

Economic conditions

Caribbean; incentives for American investment; address, April 20, 1977. P. G. M. Loewenthal. Vital Speeches 43:468-70 My 15 '77

NETS, Fishing. See Fishing nets

NETSCHAËVO meteorite. See Meteorites

NETTLES
Take the sting out of stinging nettles. J. Jankowiak. il Org Gard & Farm 24:65-7 Ag '77

NETWORK intervention therapy. See Family psychotherapy

NETWORKS, Library. See Library networks

NETWORKS, Television. See Television industry

NEUHAUS, Max
Max Neuhaus: new sounds in natural settings. J. La Barbara. il por Hi Fi 27:MA13-15 O '77 *

NEUHAUS, Richard John
Freedom for ministry. Chr Cent 94:81-6 F 2 '77

NEUMAN, Matthias
Seminaries and the new conservatives. America 137:126-7 S 10 '77

NEUMANN, Frederick
Facts and fiction about overdotting. bibl f il Mus Q 63:155-85 Ap '77

NEUMANN, John Nepomucene, Saint
Bishop for Philadelphia. L. J. McKenzie. America 136:543-4 Je 18 '77 *
Saint. New Yorker 53:24-6 Je 27 '77 *
Saint they almost overlooked. il por Time 109:70+ Je 20 '77 *
We have a holy Bishop. J. W. Donohue. America 136:539-42 Je 18 '77 *

NEUMEIER, John
Hamburg's stylish dream of A dream. H. Koegler. il pors Dance Mag 51:48-50 N '77 *
John Neumeier's new tour de force: Legend of Joseph. H. Koegler. il Dance Mag 51:89 Je '77 *

NEUMEYER, Peter F.
Art of the word: significance in stories for young people. bibl Engl J 66:27-30 My '77

NEURALGIA, Trigeminal
Now she can smile; tic douloureux. por Newsweek 89:56 Ap 25 '77

NEURITES. See Nerve cells

NEURITIS, Multiple
Guillain-Barré: rare disease paralyzes swine flu campaign. P. M. Boffey. Science 195:155-9 Ja 14 '77; Reply. H. M. Gelfand. 195:728-9 F 25 '77

NEUROBLASTOMA. See Tumors

NEUROCHEMISTRY
Androgen concentration in motor neurons of cranial nerves and spinal cord. M. Sar and W. E. Stumpf. bibl il Science 197:77-9 Jl 1 '77
Cyclic nucleotides injected intracellularly into rat superior cervical ganglion cells. J. P. Gallagher and P. Shinnick-Gallagher. bibl il Science 198:851-2 N 25 '77
Efflux of cyclic nucleotides from rat pineal: release of guanosine 3', 5'-monophosphate from sympathetic nerve endings. M. Zatz and R. F. O'Dea. bibl il Science 197:174-6 Jl 8 '77
Neurophysin biosynthesis: conversion of a putative precursor during axonal transport. H. Gainer and Y. Sarne. bibl il Science 195: 1354-6 Mr 25 '77
Phenylethanolamine: a new putative neurotransmitter in aplysia. J. M. Saavedra and others. bibl il Science 195:1004-6 Mr 11 '77
Second messengers in the brain. J. A. Nathanson and P. Greengard. il Sci Am 237:108-19 bibl(p 140) Ag '77

NEUROCHEMISTRY—*Continued*
Structure of a molluscan cardioexcitatory neuropeptide. D. A. Price and M. J. Greenberg. bibl il Science 197:670-1 Ag 12 '77
See also
Brain—Analysis and chemistry
Electrophysiology

NEUROGENESIS
Neurogenesis in the adult rat: electron microscopic analysis of light radioautographs. M. S. Kaplan and J. W. Hinds. bibl il Science 197:1092-4 S 9 '77

NEUROLEPTIC drugs. See Tranquilizing drugs

NEUROLEPTICS. See Psychopharmacology

NEUROLOGY

Research

Biology. J. A. Miller. Sci N 112:40 Jl 16 '77
See also
Brain research

NEURONS. See Nerve cells

NEUROPHYSIN
Neurophysin biosynthesis: conversion of a putative precursor during axonal transport. H. Gainer and Y. Sarne. bibl il Science 195:1354-6 Mr 25 '77

NEUROPHYSIOLOGY. See Nervous system

NEUROPSYCHOPHARMACOLOGY. See Psychopharmacology

NEUROPTERA
See also
Ant lions

NEUROSCIENCE, Society for. See Society for Neuroscience

NEUROSES
Neuroses. A. G. McCormick and S. Carter. Vogue 167:139-40+ Mr '77
Psychoquiz: how neurotic are you? S. Feinstein. Harp Baz 110:229+ S '77
See also
Phobias

NEUROTOXINS. See Toxins and antitoxins

NEUROTRANSMITTER release. See Electrophysiology

NEUROTRANSMITTERS. See Neurochemistry

NEUSNER, Jacob
Who is Israel? il Nat R 29:714-16 Je 24 '77

NEUTRA, Richard Joseph
AIA Gold Medal goes to Neutra. W. Marlin. por Archit Rec 161:37 Ap '77 *

NEUTRINO beams. See Particle beams

NEUTRON bombs
Battle over the N-bomb; Lance Enhanced Radiation Warhead. M. R. Benjamin and L. H. Norman. il Newsweek 90:44-5 Jl 4 '77
Enhanced radiation warfare; with editorial comment. J. K. Miettinen. bibl il Bull Atom Sci 33:11, 32-7 S '77
Go ahead with neutron bomb? interviews. S. Nunn; M. O. Hatfield. il pors U.S. News 83:25-6 Jl 25 '77
Kill him, save it. F. Getlein. Commonweal 104:516-18 Ag 19 '77
Letter from Washington. R. Rovere. New Yorker 53:58-60 Ag 1 '77
Neutron bomb . . . destroy the enemy, not his camp. H. Lucas. il Pop Mech 148:112-15+ N '77
No neutron bombs for us, please: European letter to President Carter. B. Sørensen. Bull Atom Sci 33:7 D '77
People killer; question of appropriations spent on neutron warhead. Nation 225:34 Jl 9 '77; Reply with rejoinder. D. R. Cotter. 225:130-1 Ag 20 '77
Primer on enhanced radiation weapons. H. M. Agnew. Bull Atom Sci 33:6-8 D '77
Technology revolution in weaponry. J. H. Douglas. il Sci N 112:60-2 Jl 23 '77
Ultimate clean bomb. U.S. News 83:15 Jl 11 '77
Ultimate weapon. Progressive 41:5-6 Ag '77
Yellow light for the neutron bomb. il Time 110:29-30 Jl 25 '77

Anecdotes, facetiae, satire, etc.

Son of H-bomb. R. Baker. il N Y Times Mag p6 Jl 31 '77

NEUTRON generators. See Neutron sources

NEUTRON scattering. See Scattering (physics)

NEUTRON sources
Neutron generator aids cancer research. R. Ceppos. il Pop Sci 210:168 Je '77

NEUTRON stars
Evidence for 10^{12}-gauss field on neutron star; Hercules X-1. B. G. Levi. il Phys Today 30:19 Je '77

NEUTRON storage rings. See Accelerators (electrons, etc)

NEUTRONS
Recent advances in neutron physics. H. Feshbach and E. Sheldon. bibl il Phys Today 30:40-3+ F '77
Ultracold neutrons. V. I. Luschikov. bibl il Phys Today 30:42-3+ Je '77

NEVADA
See also
Libraries—Nevada
Public lands—Nevada
Taxation—Nevada
Valley National Monument
Wildlife sanctuaries—Nevada

Industries

New peaks of prosperity for Howard Hughes empire. il U.S. News 82:81-2 F 28 '77

Legislature

Mormon connection? The defeat of the ERA in Nevada. L. C. Wohl. Ms 6:68-70+ Jl '77
People's legislature. G. C. Lubenow. il Newsweek 89:13+ Ap 25 '77

NEVELSON, Louise
Night and silence, who is there? Mrs N's Palace, show at Manhattan's Pace Gallery. R. Hughes. il por Time 110:59-60 D 12 '77 *
Wood witch. M. Stevens. il por Newsweek 90:95-6 D 19 '77 *

NEVID, Jeffrey S.
Forget calories: think yourself thin; interview. Harp Baz 110:233+ S '77

NEVILLE, Colleen. See King, K. jt auth

NEVILLE, Mary Anne T.
In South Carolina, another transplant runs into trouble. il Nat Wildlife 15:10-11 Ag '77

NEVILLE, Phoebe
Phoebe Neville: going her own way. J. Anderson. il pors Dance Mag 51:40-3 F '77 *

NEVILLE, Richard
Has the first amendment met its match? il N Y Times Mag p 18 Mr 6 '77

NEVIN, David
Young prodigies take off under special program. il por Smithsonian 8:76-81 bibl(p 160) O '77

NEVIN, John J.
Is it really dumping? excerpts from interview, ed by F. Maier. pors Newsweek 89:58-9 Mr 28 '77
about
Troubled Zenith battles stiffer competition. il por Bus W p 128+ O 10 '77 *

NEVINS, Allan
Allan Nevins' triumph of will. M. R. Lewis. il pors Am Hist Illus 11:26-33 Ja '77 *

NEVINS, Francis, M. Jr
Murder like crazy. il New Repub 177:25-8 Jl 30 '77

NEW, Michael
Anniversary; story. Sat Eve Post 249:40-1 My '77

NEW American Movement (organization)
New hope for the NAM. H. C. Boyte. Progressive 41:10 O '77

NEW BRUNSWICK, Canada
Open-door policy. R. C. Paehlke. Environment 19:3-4 D '77

NEW CASTLE, Del.

Historic houses, sites, etc.

See Historic houses, sites, etc.—Delaware

NEW cities and towns

Federal aid

White paper calls New Town program poorly designed. D. Loomis. Archit Rec 161:38 Mr '77

United States

Two-way cable TV protects America's safest town; The Woodlands, Tex. D. Lynch. il Pop Sci 211:70-1 Jl '77
See also
Arcosanti, Ariz.

NEW Cleveland Opera Company. See Opera—Ohio

NEW Columbia encyclopedia. See Encyclopedias

NEW Deal. See United States—History—1933-1945

NEW Directions (organization)
Breeder, arms sales are targets of new lobby group. C. Holden. Science 195:160 Ja 14 '77
We citizens cannot sit back and relax: world security; address, April 20, 1977. R. W. Peterson. Vital Speeches 43:490-3 Je 1 '77

NEW ENGLAND
Glimpse of glory; seasons in New England. J. Mills. il Read Digest 111:164-7 Jl '77
See also
Agriculture—New England
Architecture, Domestic—New England
Art—New England
Booksellers and bookselling—New England
Crime and criminals—New England
Libraries—New England

Description and travel

New England's islands. B. Basch. il Travel 147:44-9 Ap '77
Reporter at large: memories of a day's walk from Massachusetts to Maine. A. Bailey. New Yorker 53:158+ N 21 '77
U.S. journal: New England. C. Trillin. New Yorker 53:101-2+ My 16 '77

NEW ENGLAND—*Continued*

History

Marats, Dantons, and Robespierres; Hartford Convention of 1814. C. Edward. il Am Hist Illus 12:10-16 Jl '77

NEW ENGLAND Booksellers Association. See Booksellers and bookselling—New England

NEW ENGLAND earthquakes. See Earthquakes—United States

NEW ENGLAND folk songs. See Folk songs, American

NEW ENGLAND Historic Genealogical Society
Genealogical artifacts; loan exhibition at the Ellis Memorial Antiques Show. S. B. Sherrill. il Antiques 112:616+ O '77

NEW ENGLAND Library Network. See Libraries—New England

NEW ENGLAND town meetings. See Town meetings

NEW GUINEA
See also
Papua New Guinea

NEW HAMPSHIRE
See also
Architecture—New Hampshire
Booksellers and bookselling—New Hampshire
Express highways—New Hampshire
Forests and forestry—New Hampshire
Monadnock, Mount
Taxation—New Hampshire

Description and travel

If you are susceptible to environment—New Hampshire is sure to get to you. il Mademoiselle 83:174 D '77

Industries

New Hampshire: mecca for industry. J. C. Perham. map Duns R 109:80-2+ Je '77
Wrong road taken? il Forbes 119:122+ Ap 15 '77

Parks and reserves

Up a Notch; routing Interstate Highway 93 through Franconia Notch State Park. il Time 110:51 D 26 '77

NEW HAMPSHIRE. University, Durham
From the mountains to the classrooms; Live, Learn, and Teach program. S. Eder and J. Williamson. il Am Educ 13:17-22 N '77

NEW HARMONY, Ind.
Growing up with a past. H. A. Wilson. Yale R 66:628-40 Je '77
New Harmony. I. C. Kuhn. il Travel 148:48-51+ S '77

Historic houses, sites, etc.

See Historic houses, sites, etc.—Indiana

NEW HAVEN, Conn.

Education

PR and the classroom teacher; informing parents of reading progress. N. P. Criscuolo. Educ Digest 42:46-7 Mr '77
Process for alternative education; High School in the Community and other alternative schools. L. Rich. il Am Educ 13:23-6 Mr '77

Music

Debuts & reappearances. il Hi Fi 27:MA25-6 Ap '77
See also
Opera—Connecticut

Police

Clay feet in Connecticut; case of police chief J. F. Ahern. K. McAuliffe. Progressive 41:43-4 N '77

NEW International Economic Order program. See Economic relations

NEW JERSEY
See also
Architecture, Domestic—New Jersey
Education—New Jersey
Environmental movement—New Jersey
Gardens—New Jersey
Historic houses, sites, etc.—New Jersey
Libraries—New Jersey
Liquor laws and regulations—New Jersey
Passaic River
Pine Barrens (New Jersey)
Port Authority of New York and New Jersey
Prisons—New Jersey
Water supply—New Jersey

Meadowlands sports complex

Miracle in the Meadows. R. Kennedy. il por Sports Illus 47:74-9+ S 12 '77

Parks and reserves

Resurrection of Fort Lee; Fort Lee Historic Park. C. J. Quadri, Jr and A. H. Vollmer. il Parks & Rec 12:30-1+ D '77

Politics and government

Political suicide in New Jersey: the GOP loses an easy one. J. McLaughlin. Nation 225:593-6 D 3 '77
Saving New Jersey; B. Byrne. W. F. Buckley, Jr. Nat R 29:1321 N 11 '77
Statehouse derby. R. Boeth and others. il pors Newsweek 90:42+ O 17 '77
Two tight gubernatorial races. il pors Time 110:25-6 N 7 '77
See also
Politics, Corruption in—New Jersey

NEW JERSEY. Stockton State College, Pomona
It's back to school for the systems approach. il Archit Rec 161:95-102 My '77

NEW left (politics) See Right and left (political science)

NEW LONDON, N.H.
New Hampshire buried under permacurse. J. Skow. New Yorker 53:36-7 F 21 '77

NEW math. See Mathematics

NEW MEXICO
See also
Architecture, Domestic—New Mexico
Art—New Mexico
Bandelier National Monument
Carlsbad Caverns National Park
Colorado Plateau
El Morro National Monument
Festivals—New Mexico
Fishing—New Mexico
Fort Union National Monument
Hunting—New Mexico
Opera—New Mexico
Red River (New Mexico)
Rio Arriba County
Taxation—New Mexico
Water supply—New Mexico
White Sands National Monument
Wildlife management—New Mexico

Electric utilities

See Electric utilities

Game and Fish, Department of

Game thieves: how they're destroying hunting. R. Starnes. il Outdoor Life 160:10+ Ag '77

History

New Mexico incident; murder of Albert J. Fountain and his son. W. H. Hutchinson. bibl il pors Am West 14:4-7+ N '77

NEW Museum. See New York (city)—Galleries and museums

NEW Music Circle. See Musical societies

NEW Opera Company. See Opera—Great Britain

NEW Opera Theatre. See Opera—New York (state)

NEW ORLEANS

Architecture

Shotgun houses. J. Vlach. il Natur Hist 86:50-7 bibl(p 100-1) F '77

Art

New Orleans. L. A. Glade. Art N 76:163-6 Summ '77
You can go home again: Five from Louisiana. L. R. Lippard. il Art in Am 65:22-3+ Jl '77

Banks

Along came Jones; First National Bank of Commerce. Forbes 120:72+ Jl 1 '77

Blacks

Shotgun houses. J. Vlach. il Natur Hist 86:50-7 bibl(p 100-1) F '77

Buildings

Saving old Orleans: architect protects the Vieux Carré. P. Brooks. il por Ms 6:21 Ag '77

Description

New Orleans. il Bet Hom & Gard 55:243-4 N '77
Not going all the way. S. Flythe, Jr. il Holiday 57:24-5+ N '76

Education

See also
New Orleans. University

History

Little adventures of Madeleine Hachard; role of Ursuline pioneers. P. Robbins. il Am Hist Illus 12:36-42 Jl '77

Mardi Gras

See Carnival

Music

Jazz in April in New Orleans; New Orleans Jazz & Heritage Festival. il Sunset 158:98+ Ap '77
See also
Opera—Louisiana

Sanitary affairs

Solid waste recovers land for industry use. il Am City & County 92:46-8 Ap '77

Water supply

Drinking water: health hazards still not resolved. N. Wade. Science 196:1421-2 Je 24 '77; Discussion. 197:320+ Jl 22 '77

NEW ORLEANS Opera Association. See Opera—Louisiana

NEW ORLEANS Superdome. See Stadiums

NEW ORLEANS. University

Pedestrian-idealist's approach to education; College Life Project. W. Barnwell. Chr Cent 94:944-8 O 19 '77

NEW products. See Products, New

NEW right (politics) See Right and left (political science)

NEW River

White water! New River Gorge, West Virginia. P. L. Buckley. Nat R 29:1007-8 S 2 '77

NEW ROCHELLE, N.Y.

Clustering services mustering cooperation; new Department of Human Services. J. E. Curtis. il Parks & Rec 12:68-9+ S '77

Cooperative department streamlines city services; New Rochelle, N.Y. J. E. Curtis. il Am City & County 92:67 Ap '77

Crime

See Crime and criminals—New York (state)

NEW School for Social Research, New York

Mother goes to school; Human Relations Work-Study Center. R. Gross. Parents Mag 52:18+ Ap '77

Students of the subjective. S. Helgesen. Harpers 254:26-7+ Je '77

NEW STANTON, Pa.

Industries

See Pennsylvania—Industries

NEW stock issues. See Stocks

NEW Wave rock. See Rock music (songs, etc)

NEW West (periodical)

California's magazine war. il Time 110:68 Ag 29 '77

NEW World. See America

NEW YORK (city)

Chances are one in a million; retiring in New York City. T. Davidson. por Ret Liv 17:26-7 Je '77

In praise of New York; adaptation of address. P. L. Berger. Commentary 63:59-62 F '77

Three ideas of New York. M. Greenfield. Newsweek 90:80 Ag 15 '77

Viewpoint; essentials of our civilization. R. Jacobson. Opera N 41:6 F 12 '77

See also

Bronx
Brooklyn
Ellis Island
Franklin Delano Roosevelt Island
Port Authority of New York and New Jersey
Queens
Staten Island

Air pollution

Toll in Manhattan; proposed tolls on East River and Harlem River bridges to help abate air pollution. R. Sandler and D. Schoenbrod. il Environment 19:5+ Ag '77

Airports

Airbus faces weight limitations. W. H. Gregory. Aviation 107:25-6 O 31 '77

Around City Hall; Concorde controversy. A. Logan. New Yorker 53:91-8 Ap 4; 86-90 Je 27 '77

Bull; attempting to load bull on airplane at Kennedy Airport. New Yorker 53:26-7 Mr 7 '77

Concorde JFK approval drive mounted. Aviation W 106:34 F 7 '77

Concorde JFK service to begin Nov. 22. W. C. Wetmore. il Aviation W 107:30-2 O 24 '77

Concordes begin service to N.Y. il Aviation W 107:14-15 N 28 '77

Court action nears on Concorde rights. R. K. Ellingsworth. Aviation W 106:29 Ap 18 '77

FAA monitors find Concorde quieter at Kennedy than Dulles. Aviation W 107:30 D 19 '77

Flushed; closing of Flushing Airport. S. Wilkinson. Flying 101:134 N '77

Ground laid for Concorde noise parley; British, French erupt over Concorde delay. Aviation W 106:27-8 Mr 14 '77

New York's Concorde stall. R. Hotz. Aviation W 106:9 Mr 14 '77

Skytrain ground plan approved over Port Authority objections; Laker Airways' proposal. Aviation W 107:25 Ag 29 '77

U.K, French carriers ready Concorde route-proving to JFK. Aviation W 107:31 O 3 '77

See also

Port Authority of New York and New Jersey

Anecdotes, facetiae, satire, etc.

On to the Manhathalon. A. R. Barber. N Y Times Mag p4 S 4 '77

Architecture

Born New Yorker sight-revels in places most people miss; architectural ornaments. G. Emerson. Vogue 167:144 Mr '77

Those were the days, my friend; art deco architecture and design. H. Sutton. il Sat R 5:66-7 D 10 '77

See also

City houses
New York (city)—Buildings

Art

Art (cont) L. Alloway. Nation 224:156, 669-70; 225:316-18 F 5, My 28, O 1 '77

Art world (cont) H. Rosenberg. New Yorker 53:108+ Ap 11; 123-8 My 16; 98-102 Je 20; 83-6 Ag 22; 155-8 O 24; 42-5 D 26 '77

Auctions: a N.Y.C. wrap-up and a forward look. L. Rosenbaum. Art in Am 65:33+ S '77

Is New York City vital to an artist's success? I. Karp; A. Emmerich. pors Am Artist 41:16-17 Ag '77

New York. B. Diamonstein. Art N 76:109-12 D '77

New York. G. Henry. il Art N 76:117 S '77

New York, New York; special issue. bibl il Art in Am 65:45-89 Jl; 65-111+ S '77

New York reviews. See issues of Art news

Paris/New York: who leads art? B. Rose. il Vogue 167:162-3+ Ap '77

Paris: tale of two cities; Paris-New York exhibit at the Beaubourg. J. Gruen. il Art N 76:109-11 S '77

Tale of two cities; Paris-New York exhibit at the Beaubourg. E. Peer. il Newsweek 89:64-5 Je 13 '77

See also

New York (city)—Galleries and museums

Auditoriums, convention facilities, etc.

See also

Lincoln Center for the Performing Arts
New York (city)—Madison Square Garden

Banks

Banking on New York; foreign banks. S. T. Atlas and P. L. Abraham. il Newsweek 90:93 S 19 '77

Bank's drive to rescue neighborhoods; Chemical Bank's program. V. Louviere. il Nations Bus 65:43 F '77

New York bankers say they didn't do it. il Bus W p50 S 19 '77

See also

Chase Manhattan Bank

Blacks

See also

New York (city)—Harlem

Bookstores

See Booksellers and bookselling—New York (state)

Bridges

Hardy Holzman Pfeiffer Associates plan restoration of markets under Manhattan's Queensborough Bridge. il Archit Rec 162:39 O '77

Toll in Manhattan; proposed tolls on East River and Harlem River bridges to help abate air pollution. R. Sandler and D. Schoenbrod. il Environment 19:5+ Ag '77

Budget

See New York (city)—Finance

Buildings

Brave new skyscraper; Citicorp Center. D. Davis. il Newsweek 90:84+ O 31 '77

Classy newcomer on the skyline; Citicorp Center. il Time 110:92-3+ D 19 '77

Local law 5; New York fire code for high-rise office buildings. D. Oliver. Nat R 29:387+ Ap 1 '77; Reply. J. T. O'Hagan. 29:717 Je 24 '77

Lush places; Morgan Guaranty Trust Company building. New Repub 176:68 My 21 '77

Not lively; but less dead; office building rental in New York City. H. Seneker. il Forbes 119:21-2 F 15 '77

Pastor Peterson makes a deal with Citicorp; St Peter's Lutheran Church. P. W. Bernstein. il pors Fortune 96:140-6+ N '77

Stunner on stilts; Citicorp Center. H. Sutton. il Sat R 4:24-7 Ag 6 '77

Tower of faith; Citicorp Center. Horizon 20:84 D '77

Tower of power; Olympic Tower. D. K. Shah and B. Carter. il Newsweek 91:63 Ja 9 '78

World's tallest building; the Woolworth building. S. Klaw. il pors Am Heritage 28:86-98 F '77

Buses

See New York (city)—Transit systems

Chinatown

New gangs of Chinatown. B. Rice. il Psychol Today 10:60-1+ My '77

NEW YORK (city)—*Continued*

Churches

Pastor Peterson makes a deal with Citicorp; St Peter's Lutheran Church. P. W. Bernstein. il pors Fortune 96:140-6+ N '77
Wood witch; L. Nevelson's sculpture in St Peter's Church in New York City. M. Stevens. il por Newsweek 90:95-6 D 19 '77
See also
Brooklyn—Churches
New York (city)—Religious institutions and affairs

City University

See New York (city). City University

Climate

Great blizzard of '88. N. Brandt. il Am Heritage 28:32-41 F '77
Mountain wave weather in New York City. S. D. Gedzelman. il maps Weatherwise 30:202-6 O '77
Our local correspondents. E. Kinkead. New Yorker 52:56-60+ Ja 31 '77

Clubs

Is there life in a swingers' club? Plato's Retreat. J. Leo. Time 111:53 Ja 16 '78
Tough is good for you; strenuous-exercise clubs. A. Penney. il N Y Times Mag p50+ Ag 14 '77
Uptown Racquet Club by architects Copelin, Lee and Chen; squash club; with introd by B. F. Gordon and C. K. Hoyt. il Archit Rec 161: 115-19 F '77
See also
New York Yacht Club
Women's City Club of New York

Courts

Courts and cops: enemies of battered wives? M. Rockwood. Ms 5:19 Ap '77
Games in kiddie court; Family Court. L. I. Barrett. il Time 110:27 Jl 11 '77

Crime

Around City Hall; question of federal aid after blackout looting. A. Logan. New Yorker 53: 64-72 Ag 15 '77
Bad, bad Leroy Barnes; drug dealing trial. il por Time 110:21 D 12 '77
Bastille Day 77; blackout looting. M. Edelson. Nat R 29:870 Ag 5 '77
City under siege; Son of Sam case. P. Axthelm. il Newsweek 90:18+ Ag 15 '77
David Berkowitz story. Commonweal 104:547-8 S 2 '77
Death of a wireman; murder of F. Chin. il por Time 109:19 F 21 '77
Diamonds and death; murder of P. Jaroslawicz. R. Steele and S. Agrest. il por Newsweek 90:35-6 O 10 '77
How they covered Sam; press coverage. D. M. Alpern and others. il Newsweek 90:77+ Ag 22 '77
Hunting the Son of Sam. P. Axthelm and A. Lallande. il Newsweek 89:86 Je 20 '77
Hunting the Son of Sam. T. Mathews and others. il map Newsweek 90:18-21 Jl 11 '77
Killer captured; Son of Sam case. R. Rosenblatt. New Repub 177:40-1 Ag 20 '77
Looting and liberal racism: blackout looting. M. Decter. Commentary 64:48-54 S '77; Discussion. 64:4+ N; 30+ D '77
Man hunt for Son of Sam goes on. il Time 110: 13-15 Ag 15 '77
Memory and a contrast; blackout looting. P. Steinfels. Commonweal 104:520+ Ag 19 '77
Mister Untouchable; N. Barnes. F. Ferretti. il pors N Y Times Mag p 15-17+ Je 5 '77
Mugging of New York. New Repub 177:5-6+ Jl 30 '77
Murder in Morningside Park; trial of M. Simon for murder of C. Houston. D. Gallagher. il pors N Y Times Mag p26-9+ Ag 28 '77
New York's looters: budding anarchy? G. E. Jones. U.S. News 83:14 Ag 1 '77
Night of terror; blackout and looting. il Time 110:12-22 Jl 25 '77
Night of the alienated; blackout looting. C. Tucker. il Sat R 4:56 S 3 '77
The night TV cried wolf; Son of Sam coverage. C. Tucker. Sat R 5:56 O 1 '77
Night the lights went on; urban poverty and the New York blackout. T. Powers. Commonweal 104:530-2 Ag 19 '77
Notes and comment; looting during blackout. New Yorker 53:15-17 Ag 8 '77
Notes and comment; press treatment of Son of Sam story. New Yorker 53:21-2 Ag 15; 19-22 S 5 '77
People in the dark; power failure. Nation 225: 100 Ag 6 '77
Plunderers; blackout looting. R. Boeth and others. il Newsweek 90:23-7 Jl 25 '77
Reporter at large. R. Harris. New Yorker 53: 56+ S 26 '77
Rip-off time; blackout looting. Nat R 29:869 Ag 5 '77
Sam told me to do it . . . Sam is the devil. il pors Time 110:22-3+ Ag 22 '77
Sick world of Son of Sam. P. Axthelm and others. il pors Newsweek 90:16-20+ Ag 22 '77
Son of Sam is not sleeping. il Time 110:61 Jl 11 '77
Son of Sam—the killer who terrorized New York. il por Read Digest 111:155-60 N '77
Tale of midnight; Son of Sam case. T. Powers. il Commonweal 104:594-6 S 16 '77
Tip of the iceberg; looting after blackout. il Ebony 32:132-3 S '77
Will he stand trial? D. Berkowitz. D. M. Alpern and S. Agrest. il por Newsweek 90:27-8 Ag 29 '77
Word from Washington; looting during blackout. F. Getlein. Progressive 41:14-15 O '77
See also
Brooklyn—Crime
Mafia

Anecdotes, facetiae, satire, etc.

Getting streetwise. D. K. Mano. Nat R 30:43-4 Ja 6 '78

Criminal justice, Administration of

Blackout justice. M. Sheils and others. il Newsweek 90:67-8 Ag 1 '77

Cultural Affairs, Department of

Brooklyn dropout in the thick of it; M. E. Segal. R. Gelatt. Sat R 4:40 Ap 2 '77
Why is New York called the Big Apple? Because everything about it is appealing. Vasari. Art N 76:26 Ap '77

Description

Big Apple's biggest bargain; sights to see on the Culture Bus. K. Simmon. il Travel 148:38-41+ S '77
Lower Manhattan takes on a new character. P. Goldberger. il Horizon 20:28-37 N '77
New York. Bet Hom & Gard 55:233+ O '77
Outsiders' inside guide to New York. il Mademoiselle 83:114-16+ Ag '77
Sunday. New Yorker 53:19-21 Ag 29 '77

Economic conditions

Counting losses in the rubble; effects of blackout looting. il Time 110:14+ Ag 1 '77
Impact; blackout aftermath. T. Nicholson and others. il Newsweek 90:29-30 Jl 25 '77
Picking up the pieces; economic impact of blackout. T. Nicholson and M. Reese. il Newsweek 90:60-1 Ag 1 '77
Steep price tag on the blackout. il Bus W p20-1 Ag 1 '77

Education

Failure richly rewarded. M. Kempton. Progressive 41:45 O '77
Learning with the heart; Rudolf Steiner School. N. McGrath. il N Y Times Mag p 100+ S 25 '77
Reading improvement through art; success story from the Big Apple. S. K. Corwin; reply. I. Seidenberg. Sch Arts 77:66 S '77
Role of interest groups in educational politics; New York City. F. Barbaro. bibl il Clearing H 51:136-42 N '77
Where does your school tax money go? Educational Priorities Panel. J. J. Morisseau. il Parents Mag 52:36+ S '77
See also
Bronx, N.Y.—Education
New School for Social Research, New York
New York (city). City University
Queens, N.Y.—Education
Staten Island—Education

Education, Board of

Aftermath of a witch hunt: New York's subversive teachers; reinstatement of teachers dismissed in 1950's. I. Adler and B. M. Zelman. Nation 224:434-6 Ap 9 '77

Electric power

Around City Hall; question of federal aid after blackout looting. A. Logan. New Yorker 53:64-72 Ag 15 '77
Bastille Day '77; blackout looting. M. Edelson. Nat R 29:870 Ag 5 '77
Blackout. J. A. Schnepper. Intellect 106:121 O '77
Blackout justice. M. Sheils and others. il Newsweek 90:67-8 Ag 1 '77
Bolt of lightning, then—; New York City blackout. il U.S. News 83:22-3 Jl 25 '77
Heart of darkness; blackout; symposium. il Newsweek 90:16-31 Jl 25 '77
Light on the blackout. Nat R 29:930-1 Ag 19 '77
Mugging of New York. New Repub 177:5-6+ Jl 30 '77
Must we try for blackout III? J. Wicklein. il Progressive 41:16-20 N '77
New York blackout. A. McGowan. Environment 19:48-9 Ag '77
New York blackout: weak links tie Con Ed to neighboring utilities. W. D. Metz. Science 197: 441-2 Jl 29 '77
New York's Con Ed counts its casualties. il Bus W p 19-20 Ag 1 '77
Night of terror; blackout and looting. il Time 110:12-22 Jl 25 '77

NEW YORK (city)—Electric power—*Continued*
Night of the transistor. D. M. Alpern. il Newsweek 90:58 Jl 25 '77
Notes and comment; blackout. New Yorker 53: 19-27 Jl 25 '77
People in the dark; power failure. Nation 225: 100 Ag 6 '77
Rip-off time; blackout looting. Nat R 29:869 Ag 5 '77
Seeing in the dark. E. Schaeffer. Chr Today 21: 36-7 S 23 '77
Shock of recognition. G. F. Will. Newsweek 90:80 Jl 25 '77
Steep price tag on the blackout. il Bus W p20-1 Ag 1 '77
When the news tickers fell silent; blackout. il Time 110:43 Jl 25 '77
Why the lights went out. map Time 110:24-5 Jl 25 '77

Anecdotes, facetiae, satire, etc.

Good explanation. I. Frazier. New Yorker 53:27 Ag 1 '77

Employees

New York City ties wage increases to productivity. L. Bornstein and others. M Labor R 100:75 O '77
Reporter at large. K. Auletta. New Yorker 53: 28-30+ Ag 1 '77; Reply with rejoinder. E. Handman. 53:134-8 O 3 '77

Finance

Are we all conservatives now? W. F. Buckley, Jr. Nat R 29:904 Ag 5 '77
Around City Hall (cont) A. Logan. New Yorker 53:112-20+ Mr 14; 64-72 Ag 15 '77
Back from brink again for New York City. U.S. News 82:87 Mr 21 '77
Bad news for Beame; SEC report. D. M. Alpern and others. il por Newsweek 90:18-19 S 5 '77
City built on sand. Nation 225:708 D 31 '77
Default. New Yorker 53:29-30 Mr 21 '77
Financial explosion hits New York City: the SEC report. P. D. Nigro. Intellect 106:180 N '77
Gnomes of Manhattan: how New York went for broke; SEC report. R. Lekachman. Nation 225:715-20 D 31 '77
Liberals' dilemma: a professor's stump speech that worked. D. P. Moynihan. New Repub 176:57-60 Ja 22 '77
Money hangover for New York's mayor. por Bus W p56-7 N 21 '77
Moynihan fires one. W. F. Buckley, Jr. Nat R 29:844-5 Jl 22 '77
NYC decision encourages bond market. Am City & County 92:10+ Ja '77
New face for New York; E. Koch. D. M. Alpern and others. il pors Newsweek 91:22-3 Ja 9 '78
New York bankers say they didn't do it. il Bus W p50 S 19 '77
New York City is still on the brink. W. Robertson. il Fortune 96:122-8+ Jl '77
New York City. . .now. Forbes 119:88 Ap 1 '77
New York draws up a four-part money plan. il Bus W p76 F 7 '77
New York—more trouble ahead. Forbes 120:94-5 D 15 '77
Reporter at large. K. Auletta. New Yorker 53:28-30+ Ag 1 '77; Reply with rejoinder. E. Handman. 53:134-8 O 3 '77
This way to the morass: a guide to New York City's fiscal crisis. E. M. Gramlich. il Intellect 106:226-30 D '77
Up the flagpole. Nat R 29:425-6 Ap 15 '77
What the SEC failed to do about New York. J. Patterson. Bus W p44 S 12 '77
Why New York faces the same old prospect: bankruptcy. J. Patterson and L. H. Young. il Bus W p86-8 Ja 16 '78

Anecdotes, facetiae, satire, etc.

Nine steps to fiscal solvency. G. Weales. N Y Times Mag p 123 Mr 27 '77

Fire Department

True soot; South Bronx firemen; excerpts from Firehouse. D. Smith and J. Freedman. il Esquire 87:97-9 My '77

Foreign population

Cosmopolitans from India. P. Saran. bibl il Society 14:65-9 S '77
Israelis of New York. J. Peron. il N Y Times Mag p 14-15+ Ja 16 '77
New greengrocers; Koreans. New Yorker 53:20-3 Jl 4 '77
See also
Queens, N.Y.—Foreign population

Galleries and museums

Art; exhibition, Tenth Street Days: the Co-ops of the 50s. L. Alloway. Nation 226:30 Ja 7 '78
Art; protest exhibition against Whitney biennial. L. Alloway. Nation 224:412 Ap 2 '77
Backing into sculpture; Hamilton Gallery of Contemporary Art; interview, ed by Vasari. P. Hamilton. Art N 76:21-2+ Mr '77
Birthday party; Museum of Broadcasting. New Yorker 53:55 N 21 '77
Brave New Museum. R. J. M. Olson. Art in Am 65:25+ N '77
Five years of A.I.R. M. Lebov. il Ms 6:22 Ja '78
Moving day; Hirschl & Adler's move to Knoedler's former gallery. Vasari. il Art N 76:19-20 O '77
New space for new art; New Museum. B. Rose. por Vogue 167:205 N '77
Other voices, other rooms: the rise of the alternative space. P. Patton. il Art in Am 65:80-9 Jl '77
Present tense: new art and the New York museum. A. Goldin and R. Smith. il Art in Am 65:92-104 S '77
Preserving broadcast history; Museum of Broadcasting. D. Boyle. il Am Lib 8:515-16 O '77
See it now; Museum of Broadcasting. il Horizon 19:38 My '77
See also
American Museum of Natural History, New York
Frick Collection
Marlborough Gallery, Inc.
Metropolitan Museum of Art, New York
Museum of Contemporary Crafts, New York
Museum of Modern Art, New York
Museum of the City of New York
Photography—Galleries and museums
Solomon R. Guggenheim Museum, New York
Whitney Museum of American Art, New York

Gardens

Shaping of a garden; design for garden of the Frick Collection. R. Page. il por House & Gard 149:34+ Jl '77
See also
Brooklyn Botanic Garden

Greenwich Village

Reporter at large; South Village. R. E. Harris. New Yorker 53:48-50+ Ap 25 '77
Team; Sixth Precinct Neighborhood Police Team. New Yorker 53:16-18 Ja 2 '78

Harbor

201; Fourth of July celebration. il Newsweek 90: 14-16 Jl 18 '77
See also
Statue of Liberty

Harlem

Growing up in Harlem. R. Bailey. Seventeen 36: 138-9+ N '77
To live in Harlem. . . F. Hercules. il Nat Geog 151:178-207 F '77; Same abr. Read Digest 110: 175-6+ Je '77

Highways

See Express highways—New York (state)

Historic houses, sites, etc.

New York City's proposed designation of historic district brings fiery debate—and uncertainty. C. K. Hoyt. il Archit Rec 161:35 Ap '77
Peking & Wavertree: refurbishing square-riggers at South Street Sea Port Museum. E. H. Fitzelle. il Oceans 10:4-10 My '77
See also
Bronx, N.Y.—Historic houses, sites, etc.

History

Ashes and blood: the New York City draft riots; Civil War years. A. Cook. il Am Hist Illus 12:30-40 Ag '77

Hospitals

Double miracle that's saving high risk newborns; unit at New York Hospital-Cornell Medical Center. C. M. Dobrish. il Parents Mag 52:35-7 Je '77
Saving preemies; techniques for treating respiratory-distress syndrome at New York's Columbia-Presbyterian Medical Center. M. Clark and D. Shapiro. il Newsweek 90:102 O 3 '77
$73,000 abandoned babies; boarder babies in New York City hospitals. S. Jacoby. il N Y Times Mag p55-61 Mr 6 '77

Hotels, restaurants, etc.

Algonquin at 75. A. W. Ehrlich. il N Y Times Mag p 126-7+ O 16 '77
Bitter *rijsttafel*; U.S. corporate contributors to the Ramayana restaurant. por Time 109: 58 F 14 '77
Cave at the club; wine cellar at the 21 Club. F. J. Prial. il N Y Times Mag p28-9 D 25 '77
Chef's table; Plaza's restaurants. New Yorker 53:27-8 Je 13 '77
Cook on the light side; Le Coup de fusil. il por House & Gard 149:172-3 O '77
Craft on commission; handwoven rug for Windows on the World restaurant. J. Wulke. il por Craft Horiz 37:30-1 Ap '77
Eating out in New York; Four Seasons, Le Moal, Woman's Exchange. N. S. Hazelton. Nat R 29: 623-4 My 27 '77
Eating out in New York; La Petite Ferme. L. Prothro. Nat R 29:734-5 Je 24 '77
Goings on about town. See issues of New Yorker
Igor's; Art Foods. New Yorker 53:22-3 Ja 9 '78

NEW YORK (city)—Hotels, restaurants, etc.—*Continued*
International chef: Shezan on the Plaza. L. Szathmary. por Travel 147:84 My '77
Joe Baum's food machine; World Trade Center restaurants. R. A. Sokolov. il por N Y Times Mag p64-5+ Mr 6 '77
Joe's in his heaven—his Window's on the World. C. Claiborne. il por Holiday 58:32-7+ Je '77
New York's best—1977; restaurants. Forbes 120: 26 D 15 '77
New York's hotel boom. L. Langway and P. E. Simons. il Newsweek 90:95-6 D 12 '77
Not for children only; restaurants. J. Maxey. N Y Times Mag p90+ Ap 24 '77
Stepping out; Harvey's Chelsea Restaurant. New Yorker 52:28-9 F 7 '77
Wien, Wien. . .; Biltmore Hotel. R. E. M. Whitaker. New Yorker 53:15-16 Ja 2 '78
Windows on the World; with introd by W. Wagner. il Archit Rec 161:111-18 My '77
See also
Night clubs

Anecdotes, facetiae, satire, etc.

Health Department lists restaurant violations. D. Menaker. New Yorker 53:43 O 10 '77

Housing

Great New York mortgage fire sale. Bus W p73-4 F 7 '77
High-density apartment conversion in New York City affords special design amenities; 240 East 26th Street. il Archit Rec 162:122-3 S '77
MOMA plans expansion—including an apartment tower. il Archit Rec 162:37 S '77
MOMA's construction project: reflections on a glass tower. L. Rosenbaum. il Art in Am 65: 10-13+ N '77
MOMA's survival plan: more harm than good? T. Trucco. il Art N 76:90-1 S '77
MOMA's tower in the sky. G. Marzorati. il Art N 76:54-6 Ap '77
Transformation of office tower to apartments creates luxurious living space in New York City; Turtle Bay Towers. il Archit Rec 162: 112-15 S '77
See also
Bronx, N.Y.—Housing
Queens, N.Y.—Housing

Housing Authority bonds

See Bonds, Housing authority

Industries

Ex cathedra. por Forbes 119:148 Ap 15 '77
New York's loss is Fairfield County's gain. il Bus W p 121-2 Ap 25 '77
See also
Diamond industry
Food industry
Motion picture industry—United States

Intellectual life

New York today: some artists comment; interviews, ed by D. B. Kuspit and others. il Art in Am 65:78-85 S '77

Anecdotes, facetiae, satire, etc.

Minutes of the meeting; New York Intellectuals and the State of the Culture, topic of conference at City University. P. Steinfels. Commonweal 104:8+ Ja 7 '77

Libraries

Fifth dimension of library service; Unpublished Library. S. Seward. bibl il por Wilson Lib Bull 51:741-5 My '77
Kiosks and Porta-branches. M. Byam. il Lib J 102:162-3 Ja 15 '77
Wonderful news in NYC, optimism in Boston. Am Lib 8:231-2 My '77
See also
Brooklyn Public Library
New York Public Library

Madison Square Garden

Yes plugs in at the Garden. J. S. Roberts; M. Lobel. il Hi Fi 27:125-31 D '77

Markets

4 A.M; Fulton Fish Market. New Yorker 53:32 Mr 14 '77
Hardy Holzman Pfeiffer Associates plan restoration of markets under Manhattan's Queensborough Bridge. il Archit Rec 162:39 O '77

Mass media

Night of the transistor. D. M. Alpern. il Newsweek 90:58 Jl 25 '77
When the news tickers fell silent; blackout. il Time 110:43 Jl 25 '77

Metropolitan Museum of Art

See Metropolitan Museum of Art, New York

Monuments, statues, etc.

See also
Statue of Liberty

Moral conditions

Altruism versus New York City; address, May 17, 1977. M. N. Buechner. Vital Speeches 43: 629-34 Ag 1 '77

Motion picture theaters

See Motion picture theaters

Music

BSO: Eugene Onegin (Ozawa); concert version. Hi Fi 27:MA31 F '77
Concert-ed efforts. D. Sargent. Vogue 167:60 Ag '77
Debuts & reappearances. See issues of High fidelity and Musical America
Jazz (cont) W. Balliett. New Yorker 53:98-104 F 21; 84-90 Ap 4; 120-2+ Je 6; 92-7 Je 20; 80-6+ Jl 18 '77; 60-9 Ja 9 '78
Music (title varies) B. H. Haggin. New Repub 177:25-7 Ja 15, 25-7 Mr 12, 27-8 My 28, 23-4 S 3, 21-3 N 26 '77; 178:27-9 Ja 7 '78
Music to my ears (cont) I. Kolodin. por Sat R 4:43-4 F 5; 47-8 Mr 19; 37-3 Ap 2; 5:52-3 O 29 '77
Musical events. A. Porter. See issues of New Yorker
Strike up the shawm; Waverly consort at the Cloisters. H. Saal. il Newsweek 91:55 Ja 2 '78
See also
Lincoln Center for the Performing Arts, New York
Manhattan School of Music
Metropolitan Opera Company
Metropolitan Opera House, New York
New York City Opera Company
New York Philharmonic-Symphony Orchestra
New York Pro Musica Antiqua (organization)

Music festivals

See Music festivals—New York (state)

Newspapers

It's passing strange; proposed publication of The trib. Nat R 29:1041 S 16 '77
New faces among the big-city dailies; The trib and the Philadelphia journal. il por Bus W p25 Ja 9 '78
Night the lights went on. T. Powers. Commonweal 104:530-2 Ag 19 '77
Punch's near miss; newspaper endorsements in Democratic mayoralty primary. K. Bode. New Repub 177:14-16 O 1 '77
Trib *redux*. Time 111:61 Ja 16 '78
Tribulations; New York's newest daily. il por Time 110:101-2 O 3 '77
See also
Daily news, New York
New York post
New York times

Night clubs

See Night clubs

Noise

Noise; public hearing to discuss garbage truck noise. New Yorker 53:44-5 N 7 '77

Office buildings

See New York (city)—Buildings

Parades

Inflation; inflating balloons for Macy's Thanksgiving Day parade. New Yorker 53:40-1 D 12 '77
Parade; Washington Heights. New Yorker 53: 39-40 O 17 '77

Parks and playgrounds

Forsythia; Central Park. New Yorker 53:31-2 S 12 '77
Play it where it lays; Frisbee golf in Central Park. P. J. O'Rourke. il N Y Times Mag p24-5 Je 12 '77
Pond; Central Park. New Yorker 53:23-4 S 5 '77
See also
New York (city)—Parks, Recreation and Cultural Affairs Administration
New York (city)—Washington Square

Parks, Recreation and Cultural Affairs Administration

Senior citizen cultural revolution. F. R. Jankovitz. il Aging 270:12-16 Ap '77

Photographs

N.Y, N.Y. il Horizon 21:75-7 Ja '78

Police

Cool-headed cop who saves hostages; F. Bolz of the New York Detective Bureau Hostage Negotiating Team. B. Gelb. il por N Y Times Mag p30-3+ Ap 17 '77
Courts and cops: enemies of battered wives? M. Rockwood. Ms 5:19 Ap '77
Mister untouchable; N. Barnes. F. Ferretti. il por N Y Times Mag p 15-17+ Je 5 '77
Team; Sixth Precinct Neighborhood Police Team. New Yorker 53:16-18 Ja 2 '78

NEW YORK (city)—*Continued*

Politics and government

Abzug: rage and asphalt glamour. L. I. Barrett. il pors Time 110:12-14 Jl 18 '77
Around City Hall (cont) A. Logan. New Yorker 52:101-8 F 7; 53:112-20+ Mr 14; 91-8 Ap 4; 114-20+ My 2; 96-103 My 30; 84-90 Je 27; 72-7 Jl 18; 64-72 Ag 15; 71-6+ S 5; 142-8+ O 3; 134+ O 31; 203-11 N 21; 54-6 D 26 '77
Bad news for Beame; SEC report. D. M. Alpern and others. il por Newsweek 90:18-19 S 5 '77
Beame's scenario: how to beat Bella. M. Carroll. il pors N Y Times Mag p32-5+ Je 26 '77
Cool man for a hot seat; E. Koch. L. I. Barrett. il por Time 110:22-3 O 3 '77
Embattled Abe; mayoralty primary. D. A. Williams and S. Agrest. il por Newsweek 89:30 My 30 '77
Exile in his own city; J. V. Lindsay. H. Stein. il por N Y Times Mag p 10-11+ Ja 8 '78
Forked tongue in New York; E. Koch. Nation 225:229 S 17 '77
From city desk to City Hall: the odyssey of an erstwhile journalist. O Elliott. il pors N Y Times Mag p30-1+ Ag 28 '77
In New York's mayor race: record field for a thankless job. il U.S. News 83:37 S 5 '77
In search of Bella Abzug. C. Winfrey. il pors N Y Times Mag p 14-16+ Ag 21 '77
Koch for New York City. New Repub 177:8-9 S 24 '77
Koch story. J. Corry. il pors N Y Times Mag p 15-17+ O 30 '77
Mob scene in New York; mayoral campaign. il por Time 110:21-2 S 5 '77
My candidate for mayor; J. Harnett. D. K. Mano. Nat R 29:787-8 Jl 8 '77
New face for New York; E. Koch. D. M. Alpern and others. il pors Newsweek 91:22-3 Ja 9 '78
Odd man out; R. Goodman. R. Steinberg. il por N Y Times Mag p 18-19+ O 30 '77
Political update: New York's finest—Bella, Ronnie, & Carol; B. Abzug, R. Eldrige, and C. Bellamy. L. Sherr. il pors Ms 6:60-1 S '77
Punch's near miss; newspaper endorsements in Democratic mayoralty primary. K. Bode. New Repub 177:14-16 O 1 '77
Rafshoon vs. Garth; mayoralty campaign managers. J. Lelyveld. il pors N Y Times Mag p78 Ag 21 '77
Raucous round 1 in New York; E. Koch and M. Cuomo. il pors Time 110:22+ S 19 '77
Survival of New York City; office of mayor. W. F. Buckley, Jr. Nat R 29:573 My 13 '77
Two for the seesaw; E. I. Koch and M. Cuomo. T. Mathews and S. Agrest. il por Newsweek 90:38 S 19 '77
What makes Andy (and Bobby) run? H. Stein. il pors N Y Times Mag p44-7+ N 6 '77

Poor

See also
New York (city)—Public welfare

Population

See also
Puerto Ricans in the United States

Primaries

See New York (city)—Politics and government

Public health

Big apple: better for your psyche. Sci N 111: 308-9 My 14 '77
City Medicares. Sci Am 236:52+ Ap '77

Public welfare

Do-it-yourself welfare. Sat Eve Post 249:30 O '77
How not to save a family: social worker's diary. M. Wagner. Ms 6:25-6+ D '77

Purchase, Department of

Souvenirs; pier auction of surplus equipment. New Yorker 53:29-30 Ap 25 '77

Race question

Looting and liberal racism; blackout looting. M. Decter. Commentary 64:48-54 S '77; Discussion. 64:4+ N; 30+ D '77

Radio City Music Hall

Remembering the mighty Wurlitzer. W. Terry. Sat R 5:48 Ja 7 '78
Save the Music Hall! J. Kroll. por Newsweek 91:15 Ja 16 '78
Shrine of showbigness goes down; Time essay. F. Trippett. il Time 111:37 Ja 16 '78

Recreation

Long-awaited well-respected community center; Webster Community Center. K. Kelly. il Archit Rec 162:95-8 O '77
Recreation at your doorstep; mobile recreation unit. C. Behrend. il Parks & Rec 12:54-5 Je '77
Urban alternative: making do with volunteers. R. Kraus. il Parks & Rec 12:35-7+ Mr '77
See also
New York (city)—Parks, Recreation and Cultural Affairs Administration
New York (state)—State Park and Recreation Commission for the City of New York

Religious institutions and affairs

Empty churches and nonbelievers; report called Catholic life in Yorkville. America 136:161 F 26 '77
Foresight of Felix Varela; establishment of Catholic churches in New York City. C. F. Benedí. il por Americas 29:9-12 Ap '77
World of our children; school founded by community of West Side Jews. P. Cowan. il N Y Times Mag p64-70 Ap 3 '77
Yorkville report. Commonweal 104:131-2 Mr 4 '77

Anecdotes, facetiae, satire, etc.

New bishop for New York. R. A. Blake. America 137:331-2 N 12 '77

Restaurants

See New York (city)—Hotels, restaurants, etc.

Riots

Notes and comment; riot in Washington Square Park. New Yorker 53:27-9 Mr 14 '77
See also
Draft riot, 1863

Sanitary affairs

College of hard knocks: my life as a garbageman. J. R. Coleman. il pors N Y Times Mag p32-4+ My 1 '77
Suffocating sea: sludge accumulation in New Jersey Bight. M. Seward. il Oceans 10:60-2 My '77

School Board

See New York (city)—Education, Board of

Social conditions

Street dwellers. A. M. Beck and P. Marden. il Natur Hist 86:78-85 bibl(p 119) N '77
See also
New York (city)—Harlem

Social life and customs

East-west blues: a New Yorker goes west. Mademoiselle 83:201+ Ap '77
Me and Mamie O'Rorke. H. Sutton. il Sat R 5:20-2 N 26 '77
Partygoing. New Yorker 53:43-5 N 28 '77

SoHo

Who said a warehouse is not a home? H. Sutton. il Sat R 4:48-9+ Jl 23 '77

Stores

Botanicas: Puerto Rican folk pharmacies. M. A. Borrello and E. Mathias. il Natur Hist 86: 64-73 bibl(p 116-17) Ag '77
Boutique Baedeker; childrens clothing stores. A. Skinner. N Y Times Mag p58+ Mr 13 '77
Chic on the cheap; Conran's. il Newsweek 90:83-4 N 7 '77
Grocery; afternoon prayers at L. Bistritzky's kosher grocery in New York City. New Yorker 53:29-30 My 23 '77
Impact; blackout aftermath. T. Nicholson and others. il Newsweek 90:29-30 Jl 25 '77
New greengrocers; Koreans. New Yorker 53:20-3 Jl 4 '77
New York: where to shop for your house within walking distance of the hotel. N. Richardson. il House & Gard 149:62+ S '77
On and off the avenue; boutiques. K. Fraser. New Yorker 53:91-8 Ap 11 '77
Singular stores; boutiques. il N Y Times Mag p 118-19 O 23 '77
Storehouses of ideas; window displays. N. Skurka. il N Y Times Mag p34-5 Jl 17 '77
Unusual gift. A. Penney. il N Y Times Mag p 157-60 D 4 '77
What's going on behind that plate-glass window? S. Tomkievicz. il Horizon 19:14-19 Mr '77
See also
Macy, R. H., and Company

Anecdotes, facetiae, satire, etc.

They do it all for me; exercise equipment from Hammacher Schlemmer. D. Wolters. Progressive 41:32 Mr '77

Streets

Encore for 42d Street. il Horizon 21:35 Ja '78
See also
Express highways—New York (state)

Terrorism

See Terrorism

Theater

Angel business. il Forbes 119:102+ Ap 15 '77
Bright promise in limbo. D. B. Wilmeth. Intellect 105:369 Ap '77
Dance funding; Beacon Theater. B. C. Bordelon. Dance Mag 51:24 Je '77

NEW YORK (city)—Theater—*Continued*
Goings on about town. See issues of New Yorker
How to lose less on Broadway. L. Snyder. il Fortune 95:147-8+ My '77
Off Broadway. E. Oliver. See occasional issues of New Yorker
Papp's curtain at Lincoln Center. por Time 109:66 Je 20 '77
Sex fantasy on Broadway; work of the Project. il Time 109:84 F 28 '77
Theatre. B. Gill. See occasional issues of New Yorker
Theatre. C. Hughes. See occasional issues of America
Theater; J. Papp's productions. S. Kauffmann. New Repub 177:24-5 Jl 9 '77
Three relics; Alma-Tadema Steinway at the Martin Beck Theatre. New Yorker 53:26-8 Je 20 '77
Why Joe Papp made his exit. J. Kroll. il por Newsweek 89:57 Je 27 '77

History

Yiddish idol; excerpt from Bright star of exile: Jacob Adler and the Yiddish theater. L. Rosenfeld. il pors N Y Times Mag p32-3+ Je 12 '77

Times Square

Broadway babies; Alex Katz's Times Square mural. Vasari. il Art N 76:19-20 S '77
Spectacolor; animated-light billboard. New Yorker 52:27-8 F 14 '77

Transit systems

Big Apple's biggest bargain, sights to see on the Culture Bus. K. Simmon. il Travel 148:38-41+ S '77
New way to go to work; Roosevelt Island's aerial tramway. C. A. Miller. il Mech Illus 73:52 Je '77

Transportation

City life's automotive pleasures. W. Weith. Car & Dr 22:20 Mr '77

Washington Square

Notes and comment; riot. New Yorker 53:27-9 Mr 14 '77

World Trade Center

Architect was told world trade so he planned big. R. Lynes. il Smithsonian 8:42-9 Ja '78
Around City Hall; G. Willig's climb. A. Logan. New Yorker 53:84 Je 27 '77
Case closed; New York City's suit against G. Willig. New Yorker 53:28-30 Je 13 '77
Joe Baum's food machine; World Trade Center restaurants. R. A. Sokolov. il por N Y Times Mag p64-5+ Mr 6 '77
Only way to go is up; G. Willig's ascent. S. Moses. il Sports Illus 46:24-6+ Je 6 '77
Striving for upward mobility; G. Willig's climb. il pors Time 109:27 Je 6 '77
Trade-Center stunts. E. Keerdoja. il pors Newsweek 90:18+ N 7 '77

NEW YORK (city). City University
Reports & comment: City University of New York. L. Van Dyne. il Atlantic 239:14-18 Je '77

Brooklyn College

Brouhaha in Brooklyn; question of Brooklyn College professor M. Selzer's involvement with the CIA. D. Ravitch. New Repub 176:18-21 Mr 12 '77; Discussion. 176:9 Mr 26; 7-8 Ap 2; 7+ My 7 '77

Department of Design

Brooklyn's just as good as anywhere else. Vasari. Art N 76:22-4 S '77

City College

Memoirs of a Trotskyist. I. Kristol. il por N Y Times Mag p42-3+ Ja 23 '77

NEW YORK (city) in art
Individual and mass identity in urban art: the New York case. D. B. Kuspit. bibl il Art in Am 65:66-77 S '77

NEW YORK (state)
See also
Architecture—New York (state)
Architecture, Domestic—New York (state)
Art galleries and museums—New York (state)
Banks and banking—New York (state)
Booksellers and bookselling—New York (state)
Botany—New York (state)
Canals—New York (state)
Colleges and universities—New York (state)
Crime and criminals—New York (state)
Education—New York (state)
Environmental movement—New York (state)
Express highways—New York (state)
Finance—New York (state)
Finger Lakes Region
Fishing—New York (state)
Forests and forestry—New York (state)
Historic houses, sites, etc.—New York (state)
Hospitals—New York (state)
Hudson River
Hunting—New York (state)
Law—New York (state)
Libraries—New York (state)
Mianus River
Music festivals—New York (state)
Newspapers—New York (state)
Opera—New York (state)
Organic farming—New York (state)
Oswego County
Paleontology—New York (state)
Prisons—New York (state)
Recreation—New York (state)
School libraries—New York (state)
Staten Island
Taxation—New York (state)
Thousand Islands
Trials—New York (state)
Water pollution—New York (state)
Water supply—New York (state)
Wildlife management—New York (state)
Wildlife sanctuaries—New York (state)

Environmental Conservation, Department of

Cape Vincent; Great Lakes Fisheries Research Station. W. A. Pearce. il Conservationist 31:19-20 Mr '77
Case for trapping. G. R. Parsons. il Conservationist 32:2-9 S '77
Environmental conservation officer. J. T. Lynch. il por Conservationist 32:28-31 N '77
Opportunity—an obligation; recent actions. J. J. DuPont. Conservationist 31:1 Mr '77

History

When New York feared the French; newly revealed documents of W. Bradford. il Am Heritage 28:84-5 O '77

Industries

New York's gentle industry; horses. A. Carl. il por Conservationist 31:10-15 My '77
See also
Fruit industry
Ice industry
Shellfish culture
Wine industry

History

Glory that was Troy, New York. L. Kraar. il Fortune 95:142-5 Ja '77
Shades of Adirondack iron; Salisbury Iron Mine. D. L. Tuttle. il Conservationist 31:33-5 Mr '77

Parks and reserves

Artpark hosts 73 craftspeople in 4th season. il Craft Horiz 37:42 Ag '77
Bordering on the surreal; summer 1977 at the Artpark in Lewiston. N. T. Willig. il Art N 76:196+ N '77
Canal—today; Erie Canal state parks. A. S. Smith. il Conservationist 32:26-7 N '77
Official avant-garde; Artpark in Lewiston. S. Helgesen. il Harpers 225:28-31 D '77
Whitman still walks; statue in Bear Mountain-Harriman State Park. W. H. Carr. il Conservationist 32:23 Jl '77

Politics and government

Liberals' dilemma; a professor's stump speech that worked. D. P. Moynihan. New Repub 176:57-60 Ja 22 '77
See also
Politics, Corruption in—New York (state)

State Museum

See New York State Museum, Albany

State Park and Recreation Commission for the City of New York

Shortcut downtown for state resources; State Park and Recreation Commission for the City of New York. M. Maguire. il Parks & Rec 12:22-5+ Je '77

Transportation, Department of

Light up for safety; regulations for snow plowing equipment. Am City & County 92:70 S '77

NEW YORK (state). State University
Changing stages of learning; address, October 26, 1977. G. M. Ambach. Vital Speeches 44:150-3 D 15 '77

Albany campus

Electroshock experiment at Albany violates ethics guidelines. R. J. Smith. Science 198:383-6 O 28 '77 Discussion. 198:1099-100 D 16 '77
SUNY at Albany admits research violations. R. J. Smith. Science 198:708 N 18 '77

College at Purchase

School for the dance by Gunnar Birkerts; with introd by M. F. Schmertz. il Archit Rec 161:85-90 F '77

NEW YORK Academy of Sciences
Science Academy presents children's book awards. Pub W 211:31 Ap 25 '77

NEW YORK Book Fair. See Book fairs

NEW YORK City artists. See Artists, American

NEW YORK City Ballet
Antic arts. C. Hughes. Holiday 57:12 N '76
Balanchine and the waltz; Vienna waltzes. J. Maskey. il Hi Fi 27:MA9+ O '77
Ballet for all seasons; The nutcracker. W. Terry. il Sat R 4:49-50 Mr 5 '77
Ballet is Balanchine. R. Garis. New Repub 177: 29-31 Ag 20 '77
Dance; performance of Bournonville divertissements. N. Goldner. Nation 224:250-2 F 26 '77
Dance; production of Vienna waltzes. N. Goldner. Nation 225:88+ Jl 23 '77
Dancing:
Bournonville divertissements. A. Croce. New Yorker 53:95-7 F 21 '77
Company members in performance at Brooklyn College. A. Croce. New Yorker 52: 79-81 Ja 24 '77
Higher and higher. A. Croce. il New Yorker 53:116-19 Mr 21 '77
Vienna waltzes. A. Croce. New Yorker 53: 73-5 Jl 11 '77
Emperor waltz; production of Vienna waltzes. H. Saal. il Newsweek 90:53 Jl 4 '77
Glorious unpredictability of George Balanchine; spring performances. J. Anderson. il Dance Mag 51:75-8 O '77
Musical events:
Midsummer night's dream. A. Croce. New Yorker 53:81-2 My 16 '77
NYC Ballet: on again; final performances of spring season. J. Maskey. il Hi Fi 27:MA10-11 My '77
Reviews. D. Vaughan. Dance Mag 51:119-23+ My '77
Two ballet theatres. B. H. Haggin. New Repub 177:28-31 Ag 6 '77
See also
School of American Ballet

NEW YORK City bums. See Tramps

NEW YORK City in motion pictures. See Cities and towns in motion pictures

NEW YORK City Marathon. See Running

NEW YORK City Opera Company
Brilliance on the brink; productions of Marriage of Figaro and Voice of Ariadne. H. Saal. il Newsweek 90:117 O 10 '77
Musgrave ritual; production of The voice of Ariadne. W. Bender. il Time 110:72 O 10 '77
Music:
Lily and Trilogy performances. D. Hamilton. Nation 224:600-2 My 14 '77
Voice of Ariadne. D. Hamilton. Nation 225: 411-12 O 22 '77
Musical events:
Ariadne auf Naxos, The pirates of Penzance, Mefistofele and Oedipus Rex. A. Porter. New Yorker 53:130+ Ap 25 '77
La fanciulla del west. A. Porter. New Yorker 53:211-12 N 7 '77
Lily. A. Porter. New Yorker 53:124-6+ My 2 '77
Louise. A. Porter. New Yorker 53:124-7 Mr 21 '77
T. Musgrave's The voice of Ariadne. A. Porter. New Yorker 53:163-5 O 24 '77
New York City Opera:
Lily. R. S. Brown. il Hi Fi 27:MA17-18 Ag '77
Musgrave's Voice of Ariadne. P. J. Smith. il Hi Fi 28:MA20-1 Ja '78
New productions of Barber and Dutchman. Hi Fi 27:MA28-9 F '77
Trilogy. P. J. Smith. Hi Fi 27:MA16-17 Ag '77
Opera season. Am Rec G 40:53-4 N; 57-8 D '76
Pageantry of a klutz's mind; production of Lily. W. Bender. il Time 109:78 Ap 25 '77
Rain king reigns again; production of Lily. H. Saal. il Newsweek 89:103 Ap 25 '77
Reports:
Fanciulla del west. R. Jacobson. Opera N 42:38 D 17 '77
Lily and Trilogy. R. Jacobson. il Opera N 41:30+ Je '77
Mefistofele, Die Fledermaus, La Traviata, Manon, and The marriage of Figaro. R. Jacobson. il Opera N 42:76-7 N '77
Musgrave's Voice of Ariadne. R. Jacobson. il Opera N 42:44+ D 3 '77

NEW YORK City street show; musical comedy. See Musical comedy, revue, etc.—Reviews—Single works

NEW YORK Civil Liberties Union. See American Civil Liberties Union

NEW YORK Dance Festival. See Dance festivals

NEW YORK Doll Hospital. See Dolls—Repairing

NEW YORK Film Festival. See Motion picture festivals

NEW YORK Hospital-Cornell Medical Center. See New York (city)—Hospitals

NEW YORK idea; drama. See Mitchell, L. E.

NEW YORK Lyric Opera. See Opera—New York (state)

NEW YORK Magazine Company. See Publishers and publishing—Periodicals

NEW YORK-Newport Jazz Festival. See Music festivals—New York (state)

NEW YORK Opera Theatre. See Opera—New York (state)

NEW YORK Philharmonic-Symphony Orchestra
Boulez and Mahler; performance of Mahler's Third Symphony. B. H. Haggin. New Repub 176:25-7 Mr 12 '77
Boulez signs off with Berlioz Damnation. por Hi Fi 27:MA25 S '77
Carter's symphony. I. Kolodin. por Sat R 4:37-8 Ap 2 '77
Convocation at the Philharmonic; celebration of black composers. I. Kolodin. il Sat R 5:42-3 O 15 '77
Departure; interview. P. Boulez. New Yorker 53:30-2 Je 6 '77
Lost souls; Star-child of G. Crumb. F. J. Spieler. Harpers 255:102+ S '77
Mahler marathon; New York Philharmonic September-October festival. P. J. Smith. por Hi Fi 27:MA20-1 F '77
Most visionary modernist; Boulez's conducting of Rituel. F. J. Spieler. Harpers 254:86-8 Je '77
Music; guest conductor A. Davis. B. H. Haggin. New Repub 177:23 N 26 '77
Music; performance of E. Carter's Symphony of Three Orchestras. D. Hamilton. Nation 224: 318 Mr 12 '77
Musical events:
Boulez conducting Rituel. A. Porter. New Yorker 52:64-8 Ja 31 '77
E. Carter's A Symphony of Three Orchestras. A. Porter. New Yorker 53:101-4 Mr 7 '77
G. Crumb's Star-child. A. Porter. New Yorker 53:126+ My 23 '77
Leonard Bernstein's Songfest. A. Porter. New Yorker 53:51-2 Ja 2 '78
N.Y. Phil: Carter premiere; Symphony of Three Orchestras. por Hi Fi 27:MA32 Je '77
N.Y. Phil: Crumb's Star-child. Hi Fi 27:MA26-7 Ag '77

NEW YORK post
How Murdoch does it. D. Gelman and others. il pors Newsweek 89:90-1 My 30 '77
How they covered Sam; press coverage. D. M. Alpern and others. il Newsweek 90:77+ Ag 22 '77
Mr Blood-and-guts; sensational style of S. Dunleavy. T. Schwartz. il por Newsweek 90:67 O 17 '77
My short, happy life as a gossip columnist. T. Schwartz. il pors Esquire 88:80-2+ Jl '77
New York's battleground. il Time 109:43-4 Ja 24 '77
Notes and comment; press treatment of Son of Sam story. New Yorker 53:21-2 Ag 15; 19-22 S 5 '77
Tale of midnight; Son of Sam case. T. Powers. il Commonweal 104:594-6 S 16 '77

NEW YORK Pro Musica Antiqua (organization)
Report:
Performances of The play of Daniel and The play of Herod. S. Wadsworth. Opera N 41:29 F 26 '77

NEW YORK Public Library
Home away from home for writers; Allen Room. N. Emery. il Pub W 211:39-40 Ja 17 '77

Branches

Branches, service, and survival. M. Braverman. il Lib J 102:162-3 Ja 15 '77
Publishers and librarians let windows do the talking on Fifth Avenue; Mid-Manhattan branch. J. Giusto. il Pub W 212:57-8 N 7 '77

NEW YORK review of books
Love among the brains: personal ads in New York review of books. M. Barton. Nat R 29: 840-1 Jl 22 '77

NEW YORK State Barge Canal. See Canals—New York (state)

NEW YORK State lottery. See Lotteries

NEW YORK State Museum, Albany
James Hall; champion of paleontology and engineer of the New York State Museum. D. W. Fisher. il pors Conservationist 31:12-16 N '76
Man and nature. G. C. Lindsay. il Conservationist 31:4-11 N '76

NEW YORK State United Teachers
N.Y. State United Teachers to vote on academic freedom resolution. SLJ 23:65 Mr '77

NEW YORK Stock Exchange. See Stock exchanges—New York Exchange

NEW YORK times
America's two best newspapers. T. Griffith. il Time 109:70-2 F 7 '77
Cutting velvet at the New York times. E. Shorris. il Harpers 255:102+ O '77
Ethics of bribery. Nation 224:260 Mr 5 '77
Kingdom and the cabbage. il pors Time 110: 72-5+ Ag 15 '77
New New York times. D. Gelman and others. Newsweek 89:84+ Ap 25 '77
Publishers assail N.Y. times for Moscow Fair editorial. M. Reuter. Pub W 212:27 Jl 25 '77

NEW YORK times—*Continued*
Punch's near miss; newspaper endorsements in New York City Democratic mayoralty primary. K. Bode. New Repub 177:14-16 O 1 '77
Taking on big business; S. Hersh's series on Gulf & Western. D. M. Alpern and others. il por Newsweek 90:81-2 Ag 8 '77
Yes, but what was His Holiness wearing? descriptions of interviewees. G. Weales. Nation 225:533-5 N 19 '77

NEW YORK times book review
Children's book page enhanced in revamped New York times book review; views of editor G. Woods. il por Am Lib 8:269-70 My '77
Computers star in expanded New York times best seller lists. D. Maryles. il Pub W 212:22 S 5 '77
New New York times book review to appear on April 3. A. W. Ehrlich. il Pub W 211:28 Mr 21 '77

NEW YORK Times Company
America's press: too much power for too few? A. P. Sanoff. il U.S. News 83:27-33 Ag 15 '77
New York times sues over Index. Pub W 211:28 Je 20 '77

NEW YORK times index. See Newspapers—Indexes

NEW YORK University
Make America smarter: the independent college; address, January 6, 1977. J. C. Sawhill. Vital Speeches 43:309-11 Mr 1 '77

Libraries

Open letter opens letters; question of access to Sean O'Casey letters. W. R. Eshelman. il Wilson Lib Bull 51:559-60 Mr '77

School of Law

Marts of trade; NYU Law School's acquisition and sale of C. F. Mueller Company. J. Brooks. New Yorker 53:48-54 D 26 '77

NEW YORK Yacht Club
Nineteenth-century silver in the New York Yacht Club. C. H. Carpenter, Jr. bibl il Antiques 112:496-505 S '77

NEW YORKER (periodical)
Compleat New Yorker; E. B. White. M. Muggeridge. il Harpers 254:94+ Mr '77
New Yorker lists at this season some books by its contributors published during the year. New Yorker 53:189 D 12 '77
There's a little Helen Hokinson in all of us. J. Dobbs. il Ms 5:16-17 F '77

NEW YORKER Theater, New York City. See Motion picture theaters

NEW ZEALAND
See also
Birds—New Zealand
Booksellers and bookselling—New Zealand
Fishing—New Zealand
Forests and forestry—New Zealand
Hospitals—New Zealand
Islands, Bay of
National parks and reserves—New Zealand
Trails—New Zealand

Description and travel

New Zealand. T. Talamini. Trav/Holiday 148:36+ D '77
Take us as we are. R. Baine. il Sat Eve Post 249:94-5 O '77

Military policy

Nuclear South Pacific: can it be averted? J. F. McCahon and M. K. Robertson. il Bull Atom Sci 33:26-7 Ap '77

NEW ZEALAND and the United States
See also
United States—Foreign opinion—New Zealand

NEWARK, N. J.

Blacks

Inner city vacation. D. E. Ritchie. Nat R 30:32-3 Ja 6 '78

Religious institutions and affairs

Inner city vacation. D. E. Ritchie. Nat R 30:32-3 Ja 6 '78

Sanitary affairs

Newark signs up for resource recovery. il Am City & County 92:21 O '77

NEWBERRY Crater Trails System, Ore. See Trails

NEWBERY, John
John Newbery: publisher with a radical idea. Z. Collier. il por Pub W 212:81-2 Jl 18 '77 *

NEWBERY Medal
Dillons win Caldecott Medal: Newbery goes to Mildred Taylor. il SLJ 23:65 Mr '77
Who reads the Newbery winners? Children's literary needs and reading tastes. J. Shackford. bibl il por SLJ 23:101-5 Mr '77

NEWBORN infants. See Infants, Newborn

NEWBURGER, David J.
Electric power: who pays for expansion? Environment 19:50-2 Je '77

NEWBURY, William K.
Managing your woods. il Horticulture 55:74-7 Mr '77

NEWCASTLE disease
BHT—from preservative to antiviral agent. il Chemistry 50:24-5 N '77
Butylated hydroxytoluene protects chickens exposed to Newcastle disease virus. M. Brugh, Jr. bibl il Science 197:1291-2 S 23 '77

NEWCOMBE, L. M.
Friendly southern Ontario. il Ret Liv 17:30-3 Jl '77

NEWELL, Ed. See Murphy, E.

NEWELL, George E.
Emerging self: a curriculum of self-actualization. bibl f Engl J 66:32-4 N '77

NEWFOUNDLAND
See also
Grand Banks (submarine plateau)

NEWHALL, Ray
CB scene. See issues of Popular electronics including Electronics world to August 1977

NEWKIRK, Thomas R.
Letter from England. Engl J 66:10-12 Mr; 15-16 Ap '77
—and others
What Johnny can't write: a university view of freshman writing ability; teacher interviews. bibl f Engl J 66:65-9 N '77

NEWLIN, Dika
Out of Pandora's box. por Opera N 41:20+ Ap 2 '77

NEWLOVE, Donald
Incredible paintings of Frank Frazetta. il por Esquire 87:86-94+ Je '77
Professor with a thousand faces. il pors Esquire 88:99-103+ S '77

NEWMAN, Adrienne
Eyes; excerpt from Adrien Arpel's three week makeover. il Ladies Home J 94:22+ D '77

NEWMAN, Albert J.
Oregon forest fire fighter receives heroism award. il por Am For 83:4 D '77 *

NEWMAN, Bruce
Baseball. Sports Illus 46:44+ Je 20 '77
Boating. il Sports Illus 47:50-1 Ag 1 '77
Cha Cha waltzed home. il por Sports Illus 47:26-7 Jl 18 '77
College basketball. Sports Illus 46:53-4 Mr 28 '77
Motor sports. Sports Illus 46:56+ Je 20 '77
Swimming. Sports Illus 47:72+ S 26 '77
TV/radio. Sports Illus 47:49 D 12 '77

NEWMAN, David
Best of Dubious. il Esquire 88:99-104 O '77

NEWMAN, Deborah
Prince and the pauper; dramatization of novel by S. L. Clemens. Plays 37:81-95 O '77
Wonderful world of Hans Christian Andersen; dramatization of fairy tales. Plays 36:39-45 Mr '77

NEWMAN, Edwin
Speaking out. Clearing H 51:52 O '77

NEWMAN, Edwin S.
Civil tongue; excerpt. Read Digest 110:189-90+ My '77
My college essay. il pors N Y Times Mag p29 Ja 16 '77

NEWMAN, Jill
When do you hit your prime? Read Digest 111:103-5 Ag '77

NEWMAN, John Henry, Cardinal
Letters of John Henry Newman. V. F. Blehl. America 137:184-6 O 1 '77 *

NEWMAN, Michael J. and Rood, R. T.
Implications of solar evolution for the earth's early atmosphere. bibl il Science 198:1035-7 D 9 '77

NEWMAN, Mildred
—and Berkowitz, Bernard
How to take charge of your life; excerpt. il por Ladies Home J 94:56 Ap '77
You can take charge of your life; excerpt from How to take charge of your life. Read Digest 111:118-20 O '77

about

Celebrity shrinks. S. Edmiston. il pors Esquire 88:53-6+ Ag '77 *

NEWMAN, Nancy
Magic moment; story. Redbook 150:116-17 N '77

NEWMAN, Paul
Paul Newman: at home with himself; interview, ed by E. James. il pors Sat Eve Post 249:50-3+ O '77

about

Pansy actors, meet drunken journalists, meet B. Yates. Car & Dr 22:12 F '77 *

NEWMAN, Randy
Randy Newman's latest outrageous triumph; Little criminals. K. Emerson. il por Hi Fi 27:134-5 D '77 *

NEWMAN, Robert
Good staff handbook should result from director and staff cooperation. Camp Mag 49:12-13+ Ap '77

NEWPORT, John F.
I like behavioral objectives because. . . Clearing H 51:182-3 D '77

NEWPORT, R.I.
Coney Island in Newport; commercialization surrounding America's Cup race. il Newsweek 90:72-3 S 5 '77

NEWPORT, R.I. Music Festival. See Music festivals—Rhode Island

NEWPORT-New York Jazz Festival. See Music festivals—New York (state)

NEWPORT News Shipbuilding & Dry Dock Company. See Tenneco Inc

NEWQUIST, Roy
(ed) See Crawford, J. Joan Crawford's revealing last interviews

NEWS
How about the good news? T. Griffith. Time 110:42-3 Ag 8 '77
Manufacturing the news. N. Cousins. Sat R 4:4 Je 25 '77
Ten best censored stories of 1976; results of Project Censored. il Intellect 106:187-9 N '77
Too much with us. T. Powers. Commonweal 104:400-3 Je 24 '77
See also
Architectural news
Art news
Current events
Environmental news
Journalism
Medical news
Newsletters
Religious news
Reporters and reporting
Science news
Television broadcasting—News

NEWS agencies
CANA: an independent news agency for the Caribbean. H. N. J. Cholmondeley. il UNESCO Courier 30:10-11 Ap '77
Non-aligned countries pool their news; international cooperation. P. Ivacic. il UNESCO Courier 30:18-20 Ap '77
Unesco and news agency development. UNESCO Courier 30:6 Ap '77
See also
Newspapers—Syndicate service

NEWS commentators. See Television broadcasting—News

NEWS consultants. See Business consultants

NEWS in motion pictures. See Motion pictures—Plots, themes, etc.

NEWS letters. See Newsletters

NEWS media. See Mass media

NEWS photography. See Photography, Journalistic

NEWS releases. See Press releases

NEWS services. See News agencies

NEWSCASTERS. See Television broadcasting—News

NEWSLETTERS
Kitchen-table entrepreneurs. il Time 109:46+ My 30 '77
Pulitzer for Mildred A. Pappas; apartment house newsletter, the Ontario bulletin. N. Ephron. Esquire 87:18+ Mr '77
Southern newsletter delivers 12 new project leads per week; Consulting Opportunities newsletter. il Archit Rec 162:59 S '77
See also
Privacy journal

NEWSOM, Barbara Y.
Art museum and the school. il Am Educ 13:12-16 D '77
—and Silver, A. Z.
(ed) Indian art—living with the political realities; excerpt from The art museum as educator: a collection of studies as guides to practice and policy. il Art N 76:92-5 D '77

NEWSPAPER advertising. See Advertising, Newspaper

NEWSPAPER and periodical libraries
Treasury of Hispanic lore. S. W. Byrd. il Américas 29:10-13 Mr '77

NEWSPAPER-broadcasting multiple ownership. See Mass media—Multiple ownership

NEWSPAPER columns. See Newspapers—Sections, columns, etc.

NEWSPAPER consultants. See Business consultants

NEWSPAPER editorials. See Editorials

NEWSPAPER ethics. See Journalistic ethics

NEWSPAPER layout and topography
Newspapers take a big step in automation; New York Daily news and Westchester Rockland Newspapers, Inc. il Bus W p58-60 Jl 4 '77

NEWSPAPER libraries. See Newspaper and periodical libraries

NEWSPAPER publishers and publishing
After a rash of take-overs, new worries about press lords: 12 biggest newspaper chains—. il por U.S. News 82:54-6 Ja 24 '77
Death of a whatzit; Dow Jones' closing of the National observer. T. Schwartz and others. il Newsweek 90:66 Jl 11 '77
Harlot's prerogative. H. Fairlie. New Repub 176:21-5 Ap 30; 16-19 My 7 '77; Discussion. 176:7 Je 4 '77
Is there an exorcist in the house? Tribune Co. P. W. Sturm. pors Forbes 120:61-2+ S 1 '77
Vanishing home-town editor. T. Griffith. il Time 110:104 N 28 '77
See also
Computers—Newspaper publishing use
New York Times Company
Times Mirror Company

Acquisitions and mergers

Big money hunts for independent newspapers. il Bus W p56-60+ F 21 '77
Small-town moxie. Nation 224:580 My 14 '77

Antitrust cases

Press lord comes to Buffalo; antitrust suit by the Buffalo courier-express against the Buffalo evening news. R. T. Grieves and D. Strack. Nation 225:590-2 D 3 '77

Finance

Printing money. Time 109:52 F 21 '77

Securities

Big play in newspaper stocks may be over. L. Snyder. il Fortune 95:71-2+ Je '77

Canada

Toronto star goes on a multimedia binge. por Bus W p68-9 F 7 '77

Great Britain

See also
Trafalgar House, Ltd

History

Pretenders of Fleet Street. C. Cockburn. Harpers 225:114+ D '77

NEWSPAPER reporters. See Reporters and reporting

NEWSPAPER strikes. See Strikes—United States—Newspapers

NEWSPAPERS
See also
Advertising, Newspaper
Freedom of the press
Journalism
Journalistic ethics
News agencies
Newsletters
Newspaper layout and topography
Press law
Religious newspapers and periodicals

Advice columns

What my readers teach me. A. Landers. il por Read Digest 111:175-8 N '77

Book reviewers and reviewing

See Book reviewers and reviewing

Columns

See Newspapers—Advice columns; Newspapers—Sections, columns, etc.

Comic strips

See Comics (books, strips, etc)

Crime reporting

See Crime and the press

Editorials

See Editorials

Employees

Notes and comment; experience of a copyperson in 1941. New Yorker 53:25-6 Je 13 '77

Financial news

See Journalism, Commercial

Indexes

New York times sues over Index. Pub W 211:28 Je 20 '77

Laws and legislation

See Press law

Library news

Snowballs in the book drop: library column. W. Manley. il Lib J 102:2138-9 O 15 '77
Special report: libraries and the fourth estate—a survey; California. E. Rancier. Wilson Lib Bull 51:722+ My '77

Magazine sections

Once again, into the bank; selling reprint rights to Sunday newspaper magazine editors. F. J. O'Rourke. Writers Digest 57:54 S '77

Obituaries

See Obituaries

Political news

See Newspapers and politics

NEWSPAPERS—*Continued*

Sections, columns, etc.

$500,000 housewife; E. Bombeck. il pors Newsweek 91:60 Ja 2 '78
Gossip's good ole gal; L. Smith's column. D. Gelman. por Newsweek 89:77 F 28 '77
My short, happy life as a gossip columnist. T. Schwartz. il pors Esquire 88:80-2+ Jl '77
Savage fire: the importance of Bill Safire. R. Reeves. por Esquire 89:38+ Ja '78
Time to write; J. Graham's column on cancer in the Chicago daily news. il por Time 110:94+ N 14 '77
Why not write a newspaper column? human interest column with a moral punch-line. K. M. Head. Chr Today 21:29 Ag 26 '77
See also
Newspapers—Advice columns
Newspapers—Syndicate service

Anecdotes, facetiae, satire, etc.

Your action line. C. Portis. New Yorker 53:42-3 D 12 '77

Sunday supplements

See Newspapers—Magazine sections

Syndicate service

Syndicate wars. il Time 110:79-80 S 12 '77

Tabloid papers

More tabs to check at the checkout counter. D. Sandhage and W. Brohaugh. Writers Digest 57:27-8 Jl '77
See also
National enquirer

Alaska

Feud in Anchorage; Daily news vs the Times. il por Time 109:86-7 Mr 21 '77
She keeps Anchorage a two-paper town; Daily news. E. Munro. Ms 6:19 N '77

Arizona

See also
Phoenix, Ariz.—Newspapers

California

See also
Los Angeles times
Oakland, Calif—Newspapers

Colorado

Price of success; Crested Butte chronicle story on H Callaway. E. Keerdoja. il por Newsweek 89:5+ Ja 31 '77

France

Vive la Watergaffe! court ruling on French government's wiretapping of Le Canard enchaîné's newspaper offices. Time 109:44 Ja 24 '77

Great Britain

Fleet Street and the free press. L. Heren. il Sat R 4:24-5 Je 11 '77
Hard pressed. N. Beloff. New Repub 177:12-13 S 3 '77
See also
London—Newspapers
Sunday times, London
Times, London

Italy

See also
Milan, Italy—Newspapers

Mississippi

Other Carters; founders of the Delta democrat-times. G. Lyons. il pors N Y Times Mag p 14-16+ S 18 '77

New York (state)

Newspapers take a big step in automation; New York daily news and Westchester Rockland Newspapers, Inc. il Bus W p58-60 Jl 4 '77
See also
Buffalo, N.Y.—Newspapers
Ithaca, N.Y.—Newspapers
New York (city)—Newspapers
New York times

Pennsylvania

See also
Philadelphia—Newspapers

South Africa

Black journalists in Johannesburg; shutdown of The world in Johannesburg. A. Silk. Nation 225:454-6 N 5 '77
Notes and comment; arrest of P. Qoboza, editor of World. New Yorker 53:41-2 N 28 '77
Rewards of moderation; government suppression of Johannesburg's The world newspaper. New Repub 177:5-6 O 29 '77

Texas

Small-town moxie; Pulitzer prize to K. Herman of the Lufkin news. Nation 224:580 My 14 '77

United States

See also
Labor press
Strikes—United States—Newspapers
also names of newspapers, e.g. National observer

Wisconsin

See also
Madison, Wis.—Newspapers

NEWSPAPERS, Catholic. See Catholic press

NEWSPAPERS, Labor. See Labor press

NEWSPAPERS and politics
Punch's near miss; newspaper endorsements in New York City Democratic mayoralty primary. K. Bode. New Repub 177:14-16 O 1 '77
Torture tempest; question of newspaper reports charging mistreatment of Palestinian prisoners by the Israeli government. S. Kaplan. New Repub 177:16-17 Jl 23 '77

NEWSPAPERS in education
Does the use of newspapers in the classroom affect attitudes of students? study made in a Houston high school. Z. Verner and L. Murphy. il Clearing H 50:350-1 Ap '77

NEWSWEEK (periodical)
From Newsweek; From the author. M. Sheils; S. H. Elgin. il Engl J 66:16-19 My '77
Glimpse of the American right. Nat R 29:1346 N 25 '77
Looking at '77. E. Kosner. il Newsweek 90:3 D 26 '77

NEWTON, Huey Pierce
Huey Newton comes home. P. Goldman and others. il pors Newsweek 90:27 Jl 11 '77 *
Politics under the palms. B. Burlingham. il pors Esquire 87:47-52+ F '77 *
Welcome back, Huey. R. M. Brown. Chr Cent 94:679-80 Ag 3 '77 *

NEWTON, James E.
Underground railroad in Delaware. bibl il Negro Hist Bull 40:702-3 My '77

NEWTON, Michael
Woman, wife, mother. See occasional issues of Family health incorporating Today's health

NEWTON, Robert Russell
Ptruth about Ptolemy. Time 110:116 N 28 '77 *

NEWTON-JOHN, Olivia
Olivia Newton-John and her four-legged family. K. D. Fury. il por Ladies Home J 94:14 Ag '77 *

NEY, Edward P.
Star dust. bibl il Science 195:541-6 F 11 '77

NEY, James W.
I passed my A*C*T test. Engl J 66:10-12 D '77

NEYLAND, James
Carter family scrapbook; with photographs; excerpt from the Carter family scrapbook: an intimate close up of America's first family. il Good H 185:100-5+ Jl '77

NEYMAN, Jerzy
Public health hazards from electricity-producing plants. bibl il Science 195:754-8 F 25 '77

NEZ Percé Indians
Chief Joseph; Nez Perce War of 1877. W. A. Allard. il por map Nat Geog 151:408-34 Mr '77

NGUU, Mwelu
Encounter with an African potter. M. Michie. il pors Ceram Mo 25:32-5 D '77 *

NGUYEN-cao-Ky
Exiles of Indochina. E. Keerdoja. por Newsweek 89:14+ Ap 11 '77 *

NGUYEN-cong-Hoan
Why I escaped from Vietnam. por Newsweek 90:24-5 O 31 '77

NIAGARA FALLS, N.Y.
Private & public partnership: the desperate case of Niagara Falls. W. H. Wendel. Harvard Bus R 55:6-8 N '77
Put punch in fiscal reporting. G. M. Chamberlain. Am City & County 92:144 My '77

NICARAGUA
See also
Gold mines and mining—Nicaragua
Guerrillas—Nicaragua
Regional planning—Nicaragua

Description and travel

Nicaragua. E. L. Wheater. il Travel 148:40-5+ Jl '77

Foreign relations

United States

See United States—Foreign relations—Nicaragua

Politics and government

Nicaragua, a wholly owned subsidiary. S. Kinzer. New Repub 176:14-17 Ap 9 '77
Our man in Managua. J. R. Brockman. America 136:268-9 Mr 26 '77
Our S.O.B.s: the Somozas of Nicaragua; with editorial comment. P. Lernoux. il map Nation 225:68-9, 72-7 Jl 23 '77
Perils of quiet diplomacy. A. Riding. il Sat R 5:18-20+ N 12 '77
Somoza's reign of terror. por Time 109:29-30 Mr 14 '77

NICCOLLS, John. See Holland, R. T. jt author

NICE, France

Crime

See Crime and criminals—France

NICE, France—*Continued*

Music

See also
Opera—France

NICE Book Festival. See Book fairs

NICHOLAS, Saint
See also
Santa Claus

NICHOLAS II, Emperor of Russia
Last Tsar. M. L. L. Bibesco. il por Sat Eve Post 249:46-7 Jl '77 *

NICHOLAS, Cindy
She double-crossed the Channel. B. Newman. il por Sports Illus 47:72+ S 26 '77 *

NICHOLS, Betty M.
Kansas City story: capital recovery through continuing education. por Lib J 102:1456-7 Jl '77

NICHOLS, Mel
Life begins at 185 mph. il Car & Dr 23:52-4+ Ag '77

NICHOLS, Nichelle
Star trek's Lt. Uhura talks about the space program. il pors Space World N-10-166:14-19 O '77

NICHOLS, Peter, 1927?-
Chez nous. Reviews
Nation 225:570-1 N 26 '77 *
New Yorker 53:143 N 21 '77 *

NICHOLS, W. W. and others
Characterization of a new human diploid cell strain, IMR-90. bibl il Science 196:60-3 Ap 1 '77

NICHOLS, William C.
Making marriage work. Parents Mag 52:42 N '77; 53:26 Ja '78

NICHOLSON, Eddy Gene
Analysts disagree about Congoleum. D. G. Santry. por Bus W p93 O 31 '77 *

NICHOLSON, Thomas D.
Celestial events. See issues of Natural history

NICHOLSON, William
Second look: Clever Bill. S. G. Lanes. il Horn Bk 53:694-6 D '77 *

NICKEL, K. N. See Collins, J. jt auth

NICKEL cadmium batteries. See Storage batteries

NICKEL in the body
Legionnaires' disease: nickel levels. J. R. Chen and others. bibl il Science 196:906-8 My 20 '77

NICKEL industry

Canada

See also
International Nickel Company of Canada

NICKLAUS, Jack
Have a whale of a time. il Sports Illus 47:44-6+ O 10 '77

about

Accepting with pleasure his kind invitation. D. Jenkins. il por Sports Illus 46:24-6+ My 30 '77 *
Braw brawl for Tom and Jack. D. Jenkins. il pors Sports Illus 47:28-30+ Jl 18 '77 *

NICKNAMES
Trailing the alias; nicknames in the old West. W. Koop. Am West 14:32-5 Ja '77

NICOL, Charles
Reinvented word. il Harpers 255:95-6+ N '77

NICOL, Davidson
UNITAR seeks to serve United Nations and agencies in practical and useful manner. il por UN Chron 14:42-6 Mr '77

NICOLAI, Otto
Die lustigen Weiber von Windsor. Hi Fi 27:102-4 S '77 *
Die lustigen Weiber von Windsor. K. Moses. Am Rec G 40:44-5 S '77 *

NICOLAÏDIS, Stylianos, and Rowland, N. E.
Intravenous self-feeding: long-term regulation of energy balance in rats. bibl il Science 195: 589-91 F 11 '77

NICOLSON, Sir Harold
Sackville-West's Sissinghurst. A. Eliot. bibl il Horticulture 55:12-15 Jl '77 *

NICOR Inc. See Holding companies

NICOTIANA
Switching flowers on and off. il Sci N 112:39 Jl 16 '77

NICOTINE
Why do you smoke? J. Greenberg. il Sci N 111: 297-8 My 7 '77

NIEBUHR, Reinhold
Carter, Castro and Reinhold Niebuhr. J. Bingham. Chr Cent 94:775-6 S 14 '77 *

NIEKRO, Phil
He didn't knuckle under. por Sports Illus 47:56+ S 12 '77 *

NIELSEN, Carl
Considering Carl Nielsen; symphonies nos. 1-6. S. Clark. Am Rec G 40:27-30 My '77 *

NIELSEN, Peter E. and others
Plant crops as a source of fuel and hydrocarbon-like materials. bibl il Science 198:942-4 D 2 '77

NIELSEN rating system. See Television programs—Rating

NIEMANN-Pick disease. See Metabolism, Disorders of

NIEMEYER, Gerhart
Days and works (cont) Nat R 29:333 Mr 18 '77

NIEOULLON, André, and others
Interdependence of the nigrostriatal dopaminergic systems on the two sides of the brain in the cat. bibl il Science 198:416-18 O 28 '77

NIERENBERG, William A.
What physicists can do in Washington. il Phys Today 30:28-32+ Ag '77

NIETSCHMANN, Bernard
Bambi factor. Natur Hist 86:84+ Ag '77
Wind caller; with biographical sketch. il map Natur Hist 86:4, 10-12+ Mr '77

NIGERIA
Nigeria—a profile. map Dept State Bull 77:692-3 N 14 '77
See also
Architecture—Nigeria
Festivals—Nigeria
Investments, American—Nigeria
Investments, Foreign—Nigeria
Lagos
Rural planning—Nigeria

Economic conditions

But it still hurts. Forbes 120:26 Jl 15 '77

Economic relations

United States

See United States—Economic relations—Nigeria

Foreign relations

United States

See United States—Foreign relations—Nigeria

Politics and government

Nigeria's dissident superstar; Fela Anikulapo-Kuti. J. Darnton. il pors N Y Times Mag p 10-12+ Jl 24 '77

Religious institutions and affairs

See also
Evangelistic work—Nigeria

NIGHT birds. See Birds—Habits and behavior

NIGHT blindness. See Eye—Accommodation and refraction

NIGHT blooming plants. See Plants, Night blooming

NIGHT clubs
Extensions downtown; the Ramones at C.B. G.B.'s, New York City. New Yorker 53:27-8 F 28 '77
For big fish only; Pisces Club, Washington, D.C. M. Cimons. New Repub 177:14-15 Jl 9 '77
Indigenous music; Hopper's Jazz Club, New York city. N. Hentoff. Nation 224:126 Ja 29 '77
It serves them right; case of discriminatory seating. C. Mauro. Ms 6:22 N '77
Jazz lofts: a walk through the wild sounds. S. Crouch. il N Y Times Mag p40-2+ Ap 17 '77
New nightlife; jazz. P. Hamill. il Vogue 167:250+ N '77
Nightclubs for Christ. il Newsweek 89:98 Je 13 '77
See also
Discotheques

Fires and fire prevention

After the fire; Beverly Hills Supper Club. E. Keerdoja. il Newsweek 90:15 D 5 '77
Beverly Hills inferno. R. Steele. il Newsweek 89:34 Je 6 '77
Fire next time; Beverly Hills Supper Club. H. Bruno. il Newsweek 89:24+ Je 13 '77

NIGHT crawlers. See Earthworms

NIGHT driving, Automobile. See Automobile driving

NIGHT fishing. See Fishing

NIGHT flying. See Aviation—Night flying

NIGHT of the moonspell; opera. See Siegmeister, E.

NIGHT of the tribades; drama. See Enquist, P. O.

NIGHT shift; drama. See Goldsmith, M.

NIGHT sky. See Sky

NIGHT vision. See Eye—Accommodation and refraction

NIGHTCLUB cantata; revue. See Musical comedy, revue, etc.—Reviews—Single works

NIGHTCLUBS. See Night clubs

NIGRO, Peter D.
Financial explosion hits New York City: the SEC report. Intellect 106:180 N '77

NIGROSH, Leon I.
Designing in clay. il Sch Arts 76:52-4 F '77

NIJHOUT, Mary M. See Carter, R. jt auth

NIJIM, Basheer K.
Elusive boundaries of peace in the Holy Land. bibl f maps Intellect 106:202-5 D '77

NIKKEL, Salley
How to find 277,593 new friends. P. Zauner. il por Ret Liv 17:42-3 O '77 *
NIKLAS, Karl J. and Giannasi, D. E.
Flavonoids and other chemical constituents of fossil miocene zelkova (ulmaceae) bibl il Science 196:877-8 My 20 '77
Geochemistry and thermolysis of flavonoids. bibl il Science 197:767-9 Ag 19 '77
—See Giannasi, D. E. jt auth
NIKOLAIS, Alwin, Dance Theatre. See Alwin Nikolais Dance Theatre
NILAN, Patrick J.
Excerpt from statement on proposed revisions of the Hatch Act, February 23, 1977. Cong Digest 56:310+ D '77
NILE Hilton Hotel. See Cairo—Hotels, restaurants, etc.
NILGIRI Press. See Publishers and publishing—United States
NILSEN, Alleen Pace
Books for young adults. il Engl J 66:84-8 S '77
Children's literature & mass media. il por SLJ 23:106-9 Mr '77
NILSEN, Richard
Transformation of the tract home. il Org Gard & Farm 24:178-81 Ag '77
NIMEIRY, Jaafar. See Nimieri, G. M.
NIMETZ, Matthew
Department recommends extending MFN treatment for Romania; statement, July 18, 1977. Dept State Bull 77:278-82 Ag 29 '77
Funding for earthquake relief to Romania urged; statement, April 8, 1977. Dept State Bull 76: 474-6 My 9 '77
el NIMIERI, Gaafar Mohamed
Another African country turns from Russia to the U.S. D. Mullin. il por map U.S. News 83: 75-6 S 26 '77 *
NIMROD, Naomi. See Broner, E. M. jt auth
NIMS, John Frederick
Cardiological; poem. Poetry 128:256 F '77
NIN, Anaïs
Impressions of Tahiti, satori land. il Holiday 58:34-5+ Mr '77

about

Anaïs Nin: 1903-1977. A. Walker. por Ms 5:46 Ap '77 *
Obituary
Pub W 211:256 Ja 24 '77
9-Hour Enduro (race) See Motor boat racing
NINETEEN hundred and seventeen
1917. il Forbes 120:P1-8 S 15 '77
NINETEEN hundred and twenties
Life wasn't a cabaret; Trends of the Twenties exhibition. S. Spender. il N Y Times Mag p20-1+ O 30 '77
Music critic in Paris in the nineteen-twenties: some personal recollections. R. Myers. il Mus Q 63:524-44 O '77
Trends of the Twenties; Council of Europe's exhibition of European art. W. S. Lieberman. il Art N 76:39-44 O '77
Trends of the Twenties; exhibition in Berlin. R. Hughes. il Time 110:104-5 O 10 '77
NINETEEN hundred and forties
Film style and technology in the forties. B. Salt. il Film Q 31:46-57 Fall '77
NINETEEN hundred and sixties
Reconsiderations: the '60s. M. Cowley. New Repub 177:37-40 Ag 20 '77
Way we weren't; excerpt from Loose change. S. Davidson. il Esquire 87:83-7+ Mr '77
Where have all the flower children gone? C. M. Spring. Chr Cent 94:952-4 O 19 '77
Where the flowers have gone. P. Goldman and G. Lubenow. il Newsweek 90:24-5 S 5 '77
Winding down the '60s. M. Dickstein. Nation 224:632-3 My 21 '77
NINETEEN hundred and sixty-eight
The 60's come to a full boil: 1968; interviews, ed by L. R. Obst; excerpt from The sixties. il por N Y Times Mag p40-3+ N 13 '77
NINETEEN hundred and seventies
Sex in the seventies; interview, ed by L. Sanford. B. Guccione. pors Am Home 80:46-8+ F '77
Who erased the seventies? H. Junker. il Esquire 88:152-5+ D '77
NINETEEN hundred and seventy-six
1976-1977: time for a shock. B T. Feld. Bull Atom Sci 33:8-9 Ja '77
NINETEEN hundred and seventy-seven
Images 1977; photographs. Time 111:37-45 Ja 2 '78
Peace and its priorities: 1977. America 137:472 D 31 '77
Pictures of '77; special issue. Newsweek 90:10, 16-24+ D 26 '77
Sr's top ten of '77. il Sr Schol 110:4-6 D 15 '77
Year that was; 1977. P. A. Samuelson. Newsweek 91:52 Ja 2 '78
NINETEEN hundred and seventy-eight
Outlook '78: a pivotal year. il U.S. News 83: 16-17 D 26 '77

Anecdotes, facetiae, satire, etc.

Here it comes. . . W. F. Rickenbacker. Nat R 30:19-20 Ja 6 '78

NINETEEN hundred and eighty-five
1985: forecasting your lifestyle. Sci Digest 82:86-7 O '77
NINETEENTH century
See also
Italy—History—19th century
NINETEENTH century (periodical)
Those were the good old days? il por Forbes 119:8 F 15 '77
El NIÑO (ocean current) See Ocean currents
NIOBE, Regina di Tebe; opera. See Steffani, A.
NITRAPYRIN
Apply nitrogen this fall? using N-Serve with anhydrous. N. Reeder. il Farm J 101:22-3 N '77
NITRATES
Interstitial nitrate profiles and oxidation of sedimentary organic matter in the eastern equatorial Atlantic. M. L. Bender. bibl il Science 198:605-9 N 11 '77
NITRIFICATION inhibitors
Nitrification inhibitors—new tools for food production. D. M. Huber and others. bibl il BioScience 27:523-9 Ag '77
See also
Nitrapyrin
NITRITES
Mutagenic activity of nitrite-treated foods: human stomach cancer may be related to dietary factors. H. Marquardt and others. bibl il Science 196:1000-1 My 27 '77
See also
Sodium nitrite
NITROGEN

Fixation

Biological nitrogen fixation. W. J. Brill. il Sci Am 236:68-74+ bibl(p 150) Mr '77
Biological nitrogen fixation. G. N. Schrauzer. il por bibl Chemistry 50:13-16 Mr '77
Biological nitrogen fixation for food and fiber production. H. J. Evans and L. E. Barber. bibl il Science 197:332-9 Jl 22 '77
Future fertilizer: chemistry or biology? il Sci N 112:246 O 15 '77
Genetic engineering: the origin of the long-distance rumor. J. L. Marx. Science 198:388 O 28 '77
Nitrogen fixation: a piece of the action. Sci N 112:149-50 S 3 '77
Nitrogen fixation: prospects for genetic manipulation. J. L. Marx. il Science 196:638-41 My 6 '77
Symposium on nitrogen fixation. W. E. Newton. BioScience 27:281-2 Ap '77
See also
Bacteria, Nitrogen fixing
NITROGEN cycle
Nitrogen budget for an aggrading northern hardwood forest ecosystem. F. H. Bormann and others. bibl il Science 196:981-3 My 27 '77
NITROGEN fertilizers. See Fertilizers and manures
NITROGEN fixation. See Nitrogen—Fixation
NITROGEN storage tanks. See Tanks
NITROSAMINES
Beauty products cause cancer? NDELA contamination. Sci N 111:213-14 Ap 2 '77
Can bacon cause cancer? R. Wennblom. Farm J 101:Hog 7+ Ag '77
N-nitrosodiethanolamine in synthetic cutting fluids: a part-per-hundred impurity. T. Y. Fan and others. bibl il Science 196:70-1 Ap 1 '77
13-*cis*-Retinoic acid: inhibition of bladder carcinogenesis induced in rats by *N*-butyl-*N*-(4-hydroxybutyl)nitrosamine. C. J. Grubbs and others. bibl il Science 198:743-4 N 18 '77
Update on nitrite; use in curing of meat. J. Carper. il Am Home 80:16 S '77
NITROSO compounds
Quantitation of dimethylnitrosamine in the whole mouse after biosynthesis in vivo from trace levels of precursors. D. P. Rounbehler and others. bibl il Science 197:917-18 Ag 26 '77
NITROSODIETHANOLAMINE. See Nitrosamines
NITROUS oxide
Breath of death; use of laughing gas for oxygen at Suburban General Hospital in Norristown. Time 110:56 Ag 15 '77
NITTY Gritty Dirt Band (rock group) See Rock groups
NIVEN, David, Jr
America's single couples. il pors Harp Baz 110: 108-13 My '77 *
NIXON, Colin
Cardboard box; poem. Chr Cent 94:13 Ja 5 '77
Love song; poem. Chr Cent 94:1089 N 23 '77
NIXON, Gary
Racing on the ragged edge—why do they do it? R. R. Olney. il pors Pop Mech 148:88-90 Ag '77 *
NIXON, Joan Lowery
Clues to the juvenile mystery. Writer 90:23-6 F '77
One father, two fathers; story. Ms 5:52-5 Je '77

NIXON, Richard Milhous
Former President Nixon's message to Prime Minister Pham Van Dong; February 1, 1973. Dept State Bull 76:674-5 Je 27 '77
I gave 'em a sword; excerpts from televised interview with David Frost. por Newsweek 89: 40 My 16 '77

about

American foreign policy: the limits of power in the absence of purpose. J. A. Nathan. bibl il Intellect 106:208-12 D '77 *
Back with Dick. J. Osborne. New Repub 176:8-9 My 14 '77 *
Burden of Nixon. Nation 224:708 Je 11 '77 *
Camera never blinks; excerpt. D. Rather and M. Herskowitz. por Ladies Home J 94:109 Jl '77 *
Dirty linen sale. Nation 224:611-12 My 21 '77 *
Ellsberg: a punk talks back. D. Ellsberg. il por Newsweek 89:19 My 30 '77 *
Facing the music; interviews. New Repub 176: 2+ Je 4 '77 *
G&D buys hardcover rights to Nixon memoirs. M. Reuter. Pub W 211:40 Mr 14 '77 *
Henry . . . remember Lot's wife; Coming attractions. il por Time 109:41 My 23 '77 *
Kicking Nixon around the couch. il por Time 109:29-30 Ap 18 '77 *
Last Nixon show. D. M. Alpern and H. Bruno. il Newsweek 90:34 S 12 '77 *
Last syllable of recorded time. C. L. Westerbeck, Jr. Commonweal 104:339-40 My 27 '77 *
Letting go of Richard Nixon. R. M. Herhold. Chr Cent 94:582-3 Je 22 '77 *
My college diary; interview, ed by L. R. Obst. J. N. Eisenhower. il por N Y Times Mag p97-9 N 13 '77 *
Nixon: a President may violate the law. il U.S News 82:65-6 My 30 '77 *
Nixon at Colonus. R. Rosenblatt. New Repub 176:41-2 Je 18 '77 *
Nixon details agony of his final days. il por U.S. News 82:24 Je 6 '77 *
Nixon on his fall; final Nixon-Frost interview. P. Goldman and H. Bruno. il por Newsweek 89:28+ Je 6 '77 *
Nixon on TV: still more light on Watergate. il por U.S. News 83:81 S 12 '77 *
Nixon: once more, with feeling. il pors Time 109: 21-2+ My 16 '77 *
Nixon: pride in his diplomacy. pors U.S. News 82:35 My 23 '77 *
Nixon speaks. D. M. Alpern and others. il pors Newsweek 89:25+ My 9 '77 *
Nixon special. Nation 224:228 F 26 '77 *
Nixon talks. il pors Time 109:22-4+ My 9 '77 *
Nixon without Dietrich. F. Getlein. Commonweal 104:324-6 My 27 '77 *
Nixon's good guy. J. Osborne. New Repub 177: 8-9+ O 8 '77 *
Nixon's own final days. D. M. Alpern and H. Bruno. il pors Newsweek 89:18-19 My 30 '77 *
Nixon's two-front war. D. M. Alpern and H. Bruno. il por Newsweek 89:17-18 My 23 '77 *
Nixon's Watergate—man's depravity. D. M. Howard. Chr Today 21:12-14 Je 3 '77 *
No one knows how it feels; last Frost telecast. il por Time 109:11-12 Je 6 '77 *
Not even earplugs could help. il pors Time 109: 15-16 My 30 '77 *
Notes and comment. New Yorker 53:31-2 My 16; 27-8 My 23 '77 *
Notes on Nixon. W. F. Buckley, Jr. Nat R 29: 686-7 Je 10 '77 *
Now, another villain. Time 110:23 S 12 '77 *
Obituary; the same old Nixon. E. Knoll. Progressive 41:13 Jl '77 *
On the rebound. D. Gelman and others. il pors Newsweek 89:26-7 My 9 '77 *
Past imperfect, future imperative. F. Getlein. Commonweal 104:359-61 Je 10 '77 *
President and law; analysis of Nixon's statement in third interview with Frost. Nat R 29: 652+ Je 10 '77 *
Saturday night live! excerpt from Not above the law. J. Doyle. il pors N Y Times Mag p40+ My 15 '77 *
Sins of Washington; ABC's portrayal. D. Eisenhower. il por Newsweek 90:104 S 19 '77 *
Struggle to find sponsors for Nixon. pors Bus W p33-4 My 9 '77 *
Teamsters' Watergate connection. il Time 110: 28 Ag 8 '77 *
Unhappy warrior; interviews. M. Kondracke. New Repub 176:11-12 Je 4 '77 *
Watching Nixon; symposium. il pors Newsweek 89:28-9+ My 16 '77 *
Were we fair to Nixon? M. Greenfield. Newsweek 89:100 My 23 '77 *
What did Nixon say to Chou? W. F. Buckley, Jr. Nat R 29:572 My 13 '77 *
When the President does it. I. L. Horowitz. Nation 224:751-4 Je 18 '77 *
Why Nixon went on the witness stand. pors U.S. News 82:27-9 My 16 '77 *

Anecdotes, facetiae, satire, etc.

David and Pariah. H. Fairlie. il New Repub 176:43-5 My 21 '77

Archives

Nixon's tapes—someday. Newsweek 90:17 Jl 11 '77

Staff

President's men—where are they now? il U.S. News 82:29 My 16 '77

Visit to China, 1972

See also
Peking talks, 1972

NIYOGI, Salil K. See Hoffman, D. J. jt auth
NIZAMIAN, Harold A.
Details pay off when you sell teddy bears. P. Schwab. il por Nations Bus 65:92 D '77 *
NIZEL, Abraham E.
How to have sound teeth for life. por Parents Mag 52:41+ Mr '77
NKOMO, Joshua
Nkomo: war is the only course; interview, ed by D. Wood. por Time 110:36 Ag 8 '77
NO-brand products. See Unbranded merchandise
Nō drama. See Japanese drama
NO-fault auto insurance. See Insurance, Automobile
NO-fault insurance. See Insurance, Liability
NO man's land; drama. See Pinter, H.
Nō theater costumes. See Costume, Theatrical—Japan
NOAH'S Ark
Ararat ark wood dated at A.D. 700. Sci N 111: 198 Mr 26 '77
Ararat's mystery ship. A. Gaunt. il Sea Front 23:167-71 My '77
NOATAK National Preserve (proposed) See National parks and reserves—Alaska
NOATAK River
Our wild and scenic rivers. J. M. Kauffman. il map Nat Geog 152:52-9 Jl '77
NOBEL prizes
En-Nobeling Milton Friedman. R. Skole. Nation 224:68-70 Ja 22 '77
Faded laurel crown. C. Hitchens. Harpers 255: 114-17 N '77
Fresh debate over those Nobel prizes; Is peace in Northern Ireland becoming possible at last? il U.S. News 83:83-4+ O 24 '77
Good news from Norway. pors Chr Cent 94:973 O 26 '77
1977 Nobel laureates in science. il pors Chemistry 50:18-20 D '77
1977 Nobel Prize in chemistry. I. Procaccia and J. Ross. il por Science 198:716-17 N 18 '77
1977 Nobel Prize in economics. C. P. Kindleberger. pors Science 198:813-14+ N 25 '77
1977 Nobel Prize in physics. M. L. Cohen and L. M. Falicov. bibl pors Science 198:713-15 N 18 '77
Nobel experience. E. Warner. il Horizon 19:46-55 My '77
Nobel prize winning world literature. M. J. Moran. Engl J 66:59-60 S '77
Nobel prizes. Sci Am 237:82+ D '77
Nobelists at the frontiers. il Newsweek 90:86-7 O 24 '77
Six Nobelmen—and a Nobelwoman. il Time 110: 114 O 24 '77
Spain coming into her own: Aleixandre's Nobel Prize. A. Josephs. il por New Repub 177:25-7 D 24 '77
State & society. pors Phys Today 30:77-80 D '77
Two Peace Prizes from Oslo. il pors Time 110: 54 O 24 '77
Two women of Ulster; M. Corrigan and B. Williams of Community of Peace People. K. Willenson and A. Collings. il pors Newsweek 90:61 O 24 '77
NOBILE, Philip
Skirmish over Guernica. il Harpers 254:15+ Mr '77
NOBILITY
See also
Great Britain—Nobility
NOBLE, C. Norman
Advertising your church. Chr Today 22:30-1 N 18 '77
NOBLE, Dennis, and O'Brien, T. M.
That others might live: the saga of the U.S. Coast Guard. il Am Hist Illus 12:4-7+ Je '77
NOBLE, Elizabeth
Bend over backwards for your baby. il Fam Health 9:43-6 Jl '77
NOBLE, J. Kendrick, Jr
AAP 1976 statistics—using the figures. il Pub W 212:41-3 Jl 4 '77
Year in review. Pub W 211:45 F 14 '77
NOBLE gases. See Gases, Rare
NOBLITT, Thomas
Problems of transmission in Obrecht's Missa Je ne demande. bibl f il Mus Q 63:211-23 Ap '77
NOCERA, Joseph
I am not a crook. por Newsweek 90:14-15 D 19 '77
NOCTURNAL birds. See Birds—Habits and behavior
NODA, Ken
Little League composer. L. Henning. il por Opera N 42:49 N '77 *

NOEL-BAKER, Philip John
Peace or oblivion? por Bull Atom Sci 33:18-20 S '77

NOGUCHI, Isamu
Akari lamps by Noguchi. il Craft Horiz 37:36-7 D '77 *
Playscapes sculpture-playground in Atlanta. A. Bledsoe. il Sch Arts 76:22-5 Ap '77 *
Provocative portal. Vasari. il Art N 76:30-1 F '77 *

NOISE
See also
Airplanes—Noise
Audio system—Noise
Boats—Noise
New York (city)—Noise

Physiological effects
How to keep your sense of hearing. L. David. il Mech Illus 73:102+ Ap '77
Noise. L. S. Burns. il Horizon 20:66-9 S '77

Psychological effects
Noise to drive you crazy—jets and mental hospitals; study by W. C. Meecham and H. G. Smith. N. Napp. Psychol Today 11:33 Je '77

NOISE control
Problem with noise in an apartment; excerpt from Quieting: a practical guide to noise control. Consumers Res Mag 60:25 F '77
See also
New York (city)—Noise

Economic aspects
Court orders OSHA to consider economics; noise controls at Turner Division plant. Bus W p46+ O 3 '77

Laws and regulations
EPA's next target: noisy appliances. Bus W p 100+ O 10 '77
Growing furor over noise regulations. it Nations Bus 65:16-20+ O '77
Noise and the home mechanic; effects of California car law. Mech Illus 73:120 Ag '77

NOISE filters, Radio. See Radio filters

NOISE pollution
See also
New York (city)—Noise

NOISE-reduction systems. See Audio systems—Noise

NOLAN, James
Comment. E. Butscher. Poetry 130:169 Je '77 *

NOLAN, Kathleen
Kathleen Nolan: from sit-com star to SAG prexy; interview, ed by L. Farr. por Ms 5:105-6+ Mr '77

NOLAN, Paul T.
Broken jug; adaptation of play by H. Kleist. Plays 36:70-80 Mr '77
It's your move; drama. Plays 36:33-42 F '77

NOLAN, Richard L.
Controlling the costs of data services. il Harvard Bus R 55:114-24 Jl '77

NOLAN, Robert R. and Roper, S. S.
How to succeed in team teaching by really trying. il Today Educ 66:54-6+ Ja '77

NOLAND, Helen Warvel, and Banta, R. F.
George Rogers Clark: bluff over bullets. il pors map Sat Eve Post 249:54-7 O '77

NOLAND, Kenneth
Color, format and abstract art: an interview with Kenneth Noland; ed by D. Waldman. il por Art in Am 65:99-105 My '77

about
Art. L. Alloway. Nation 224:540-1 Ap 30 '77 *
Kenneth Noland: independence in the face of conformity. S. Polcari. il por Art N 76:153-5 Summ '77 *
Kenneth Noland; retrospective at the Guggenheim Museum. H. Rosenberg. New Yorker 53:98-102 Je 20 '77 *
Noland's garden of color; retrospective at the Guggenheim Museum. M. Stevens. il Newsweek 89:72 My 16 '77 *
Pure, uncluttered hedonism; retrospective show at the Guggenheim Museum. R. Hughes. il Time 109:69 My 2 '77 *

NOLAND, Richard W.
Psychobiography of everyday life. Nation 224:570-2 My 7 '77

NOLEN, William A.
Doctor's world. See issues of McCall's
Why I don't want my children home next summer. Read Digest 110:146-7 F '77

NOLING, Kim
Camp guides deaf teen to informed relationships. il Camp Mag 49:10-11+ My '77

NOLL, Chuck
Walk on the sordid side. W. O. Johnson. il por Sports Illus 47:10-15 Ag 1 '77 *

NOLTE, Nick
Nick Nolte: actor on the edge—of success; interview, ed by M. Cantwell. por Mademoiselle 83:200+ Ap '77
Nick Nolte's big splash; interview, ed by E. Miller. il pors Seventeen 36:198-9+ Ap '77

about
Nick Nolte surfaces. L. Hershey. por Ladies Home J 94:54+ Jl '77 *

NOMADS
See also
Hunters and gatherers

NOMELAND, Ronald
Breaking the silence. E. M. Gobble. Progressive 41:35 F '77 *

NOMENCLATURE. See subhead Nomenclature under various subjects, e.g. Botany—nomenclature

NOMINATIONS for office
Reform is wrecking the U.S. party system. E. C. Ladd, Jr. il Fortune 6:176-81+ N '77

NOMOGRAPHY (mathematics)
Power nomograph. M. L. McWilliams. il Pop Electr 12:69 O '77

NONAS, Richard
Richard Nonas: field works. J. Van Der Marck. il Art in Am 65:114-17 Ja '77 *

NONCONFORMITY. See Individualism

NON-GOVERNMENTAL Organizations of the United Nations. See United Nations—Non-governmental Organizations

NON-PARENTS, National Organization for. See National Organization for Non-Parents

NONPRESCRIPTION drugs. See Medicines, Patent, proprietary, etc.

NON-PROFESSIONAL library assistants. See Library assistants

NONPROFIT institutions. See Institutions, Non-profit

NON-PROLIFERATION treaty. See Atomic weapons and disarmament

NON-SUPPORT. See Desertion and non-support

NONTE, George C. Jr
Ultimate test for your gun. il por Pop Mech 148:152+ N '77

NONVERBAL communication. See Communication, Nonverbal

NONVERBAL thought. See Visualization

NONVIOLENCE
African leaders' commitment to justice. P. E. Brink. Chr Cent 94:1143-6 D 7 '77

NON-WAGE payments
Emerging scandal in medical coverage; Multiple Employer Benefit Trusts. il Bus W p22-3 Jl 4 '77
Hidden raises—those fringes keep on growing. il U.S. News 83:88-9 O 31 '77
How to keep big government from growing bigger. R. W. Packwood. por Duns R 110:69-70 Ag '77
How to make the most of your fringe benefits. M. Daly. Bet Hom & Gard 55:24+ N '77
One firm's family; IBM. A. J. Mayer and M. Ruby. il Newsweek 90:82-4+ N 21 '77
Workers can set their own wages—responsibly. E. E. Lawler. il por Psychol Today 10:109-10+ F '77
Your paycheck plus. D. Duke. Mademoiselle 83:152 Mr '77
See also
Profit sharing
Trade unions—Benefit funds

Taxation
Next: you'll pay taxes on your fringe benefits; interview. J. Kurtz. il por U.S. News 83:26-8 Jl 18 '77

NONWOVEN textile fabrics. See Textile frabrics, Nonwoven

NOODLE cookery. See Cookery—Macaroni products

NOOGER, Laura B.
Booklets. Am Home 80:13 S; 25 O; 11 D '77

NOONAN, Patrick F.
Key to a beautiful America: renewed personal pride; interview. il por U.S. News 82:39-40 Je 13 '77

NORDAN, Lewis
Rat song; story. Harpers 256:59-65 Ja '78

NORDBLOM, Rodger
Open letter to fellow developer, Jimmy Carter; address, January 28, 1977. Vital Speeches 43:290-2 Mr 1 '77

NORDQUIST, Robert E. and others
Antibody-induced antigen redistribution and shedding from human breast cancer cells. bibl il Science 197:366-7 Jl 22 '77

NOREPINEPHRINE
Norepinephrine-dopamine interactions and behavior. S. M. Antelman and A. R. Caggiula. bibl Science 195:646-53 F 18 '77
Suppression of sympathetic nervous system during fasting. J. B. Young and L. Landsberg. bibl il Science 196:1473-5 Je 24 '77

NORFOLK, Va.
Norfolk & Virginia Beach. E. Cheatham and P. Cheatham. il Travel 147:32-7+ Ap '77

Historic houses, sites, etc.
See Historic houses, sites, etc.—Virginia

NORFOLK & Western Railway
So near and yet so far . . . il Forbes 120:49 Jl 1 '77

NORFOLK pine. See Pine
NORGREN, Jill. See Shattuck, P. T. jt auth
NORIN Corporation mergers. See Corporations—Acquisitions and mergers
NORLYN, J. D. See Epstein, E. jt auth
NORMA; opera. See Bellini, V.
NORMALITY
You may be normal than you think! J. Bosveld. Sci Digest 81:47-8 My '77
NORMAN, Billie
He wouldn't do that—would he? Ret Liv 17:46 Jl '77
NORMAN, Geoffrey
Outdoors. il Esquire 88:24+ N; 40+ D '77; 89:16+ Ja '78
NORMAN, Howard A.
(tr) See Barton, P. Honey seller
NORMAN, James
Huichols: Mexico's people of myth and magic. il map Nat Geog 151:832-53 Je '77
NORMAN, Joyce L. and others
Early development of X-cells in kitten lateral geniculate nucleus. bibl il Science 198:202-4 O 14 '77
NORMAN, R. J. and others
Classical conditioning with auditory discrimination of the eye blink in decerebrate cats. bibl il Science 196:551-3 Ap 29 '77
NORMAN, Ron
Special report: director's diary of a crisis. il Wilson Lib Bull 51:566-7 Mr '77
NORMENT, Lynn
Delta State's irresistible force. il pors Ebony 32:86-8 F '77
How long will you live? il Ebony 32:44-6+ O '77
People who return from death. Ebony 33:135-6+ N '77
Pros and cons of living together. il Ebony 33:94-6+ D '77
Tomorrow's black woman: independent, smart, feminine. il Ebony 32:44-6+ Ag '77
NORRIS, Jim
Brief test. il Motor T 29:51-2+ F '77
(ed) Detroit report. See issues of Motor trend
Spare parts. il Motor T 29:138 Ap; 128 My; 136 Je; 112 Jl; 120 Ag; 104 S '77
NORRIS, Kenneth S.
Tuna sandwiches cost at least 78,000 porpoise lives a year, but there is hope. il Smithsonian 7:44-53 bibl(p 152) F '77
NORRIS, Leslie, 1921-
Flight of geese; story. New Yorker 53:46-9 O 10 '77
In the west country; story. New Yorker 53:44-7 N 14 '77
Shaving; story. Atlantic 239:42-5 Ap '77
Young Devon Shorthorn bull; poem. Atlantic 239:36 Mr '77
NORRIS, Ruby Lee
Invisible stories become visible. Engl J 66:76-8 N '77
NORRIS Industries, Inc
New image and soaring profits for Norris. il Duns R 109:20-1+ Je '77
NORSEMEN. See Northmen
NORTH, John
Card catalog to COM. il Lib J 102:2132-4 O 15 '77
NORTH, Lowell
Balance for Lowell. J. Rousmaniere. il pors Yachting 141:69 F '77 *
In their hour of triumph. J. Hersey. il Yachting 142:86-91+ S '77 *
One on one. R. Vaughan. il pors Motor B & S 140:78-80+ Ag '77 *
NORTH, Noah
Noah North (1809-1880) N. C. Muller and J. Oak. bibl il Antiques 112:939-45 N '77 *
NORTH, Robert N.
Development of Soviet Asia. bibl f map Cur Hist 73:123-7+ O '77
NORTH ADAMS, Mass.
Hoosuck: a community story; Windsor Mill art center in remodeled textile mill. M. Flad and H. Flad. il Craft Horiz 37:20-1+ Ap '77
NORTH AMERICA
See also
Airlines—International services—North America
Architecture, Domestic—North America
Birds—North America
Paleontology—North America

Antiquities

See also
Indians of North America—Antiquities

Maps

Map section. Sr Schol 110:24 O 20 '77
NORTH AMERICAN Air Defense Command
From golf balls to box cars, NORAD keeps track of what's awhirl above. il Sci Digest 82:79-80 Ag '77
NORTH AMERICAN Aircraft Group. See Rockwell International Corporation
NORTH AMERICAN Bait Farms, Inc. See Earthworm culture
NORTH AMERICAN Forest Fire Medal
Oregon forest fire fighter receives heroism award. il por Am For 83:4 D '77
NORTH AMERICAN International Ballet Festival. See Dance festivals
NORTH AMERICAN International Dance Festival. See Dance festivals
NORTH AMERICAN Snow Conference. See Snow and ice removal—Conferences
NORTH AMERICAN Soccer League. See Soccer
NORTH AMERICAN Water and Power Alliance
World's biggest ditch; water from Alaska into the U.S. map Forbes 119:112+ My 15 '77
NORTH Atlantic Council. See Nato
NORTH Atlantic Treaty Organization. See Nato
NORTH CAROLINA
To know where we have been; excerpt from The Bob Timberlake collection; reproductions of paintings, with text by C. Kuralt and editorial comment. B. Timberlake. il Audubon 79:inside cover, 48-61 My '77. Same abr. Read Digest 111:136-42 S '77
See also
Architecture, Domestic—North Carolina
Cape Hatteras National Seashore
Criminal justice, Administration of—North Carolina
Education—North Carolina
Great Smoky Mountains
Great Smoky Mountains National Park
Libraries—North Carolina
Opera—North Carolina
Prisons—North Carolina
Skis and skiing—North Carolina
Trials—North Carolina

Description and travel

North Carolina Piedmont. E. Cheatham and P. Cheatham. il Travel 147:48-53+ My '77

History

Great state of Franklin. il Sr Schol 109:6-8 Ap 21 '77
NORTH CAROLINA. Appalachian State University, Boone
In North Carolina, its working; teacher education centers sponsored by Appalachian State University and local schools. K. D. Jenkins. il Clearing H 50:268-71 F '77
NORTH CAROLINA Dance Theatre. See Dance companies
NORTH CAROLINA furniture. See Furniture, American
NORTH Country Book Express (firm) See Book wholesalers
NORTH DAKOTA
See also
Burleigh County

Politics and government

King of the referendum; R. McCarney. por Time 109:19 Je 13 '77
NORTH SEA
See also
Oil pollution of the sea—North Sea
Petroleum—North Sea Region
NORTHCOTT, Cecil
Passing of the old imperialisms. Chr Cent 94:268-9 Mr 23 '77
NORTHEASTERN States
See also
Historic houses, sites, etc.—Northeastern States

Economic conditions

Northeast verses the Sunbelt R. S. Morris. Current 189:22-5 Ja '77
NORTHERN IRELAND
Visit to Ulster. L. G. McAllister. Chr Cent 94:213-15 Mr 9 '77
See also
Belfast
Children—Northern Ireland
Cooperative associations—Northern Ireland
Peace movements—Northern Ireland
Strikes—Northern Ireland
Visitors, Foreign—Northern Ireland

Foreign relations

United States

See United States—Foreign relations—Northern Ireland

Politics and government

Conflict and cleavage in Northern Ireland. R. J. Terchek. bibl f Ann Am Acad 433:47-59 S '77
Death in Ireland. S. Cronin; discussion. Commonweal 104:28-9+ Ja 7 '77
Erosions of violence, hopes for peace. V. Schmid. il Chr Cent 94:258-9 Mr 16 '77
Everywhere but Ireland: success of the Peace People. A. Boyd. il Nation 224:453-6 Ap 16 '77
Irish paradox. D. O'Brien. il N Y Times Mag p96-8+ S 11 '77
Letter from Belfast: post-Elizabethan blues. T. P. O'Mahony. America 137:147-8 S 17 '77
Northern Ireland: chance for peace? il map Sr Schol 109:13-15 Ja 13 '77
Northern Ireland's guerrillas of peace; interviews, ed by R. S. Kennedy and P. Klotz-Chamberlin. B. Williams; N. McDonnell. il por Chr Cent 94:746-51 Ag 31 '77

NORTHERN IRELAND—Politics and government—*Continued*
On the road to Drogheda; rally in Ireland. J. Gilhooley. il Commonweal 104:178-80 Mr 18 '77
President Carter states policy on Northern Ireland; statement, August 30, 1977. J. Carter. Dept State Bull 77:410 S 26 '77
Royal blitz in a troubled realm; Queen Elizabeth's visit. il por Time 110:39 Ag 22 '77
Stopping violence in Northern Ireland; excerpts from address. J. Hume. por Intellect 105:374-5 My '77

Religious institutions and affairs

See also
Presbyterian Church in Northern Ireland
Protestants in Northern Ireland

NORTHERN lights. See Auroras

NORTHERN Telecom, Ltd. See Telephone apparatus industry—Canada

NORTHERN Telecom, Ltd mergers. See Corporations—Acquisitions and mergers—International aspects

NORTHMEN
Lost Norse mystery; disappearance of Greenland settlements in Middle Ages. F. Garner. il Oceans 10:4-9 Mr '77

NORTHROP, Ann
How to reach out to hungry America. il Ms 6:91-4 O '77
This may be the year to stay tuned. il Ms 6:44-5+ D '77
Why the Justice Department doesn't want you to know what happened between Otto Passman and Shirley Davis. il pors Ms 6:57-9 Ja '78
—and Steinem, Gloria
(comps) No comment Olympics: the Ms first annual awards for surrealism in everyday life. il Ms 6:48-50+ Jl '77

NORTHROP, John Knudsen
Meeting the press; B-49 Flying Wing; interview, ed by R. B. Parke, il por Flying 101:4 Jl '77

about
Northrop. R. B. Parke. il Flying 101:250 S '77 *

NORTHROP Corporation
Business as usual. il Forbes 119:79 Je 1 '77
Comeback of Tom Jones. D. Pauly and others. il por Newsweek 89:70 Ja 31 '77
Trials and tribulations. Forbes 120:35-6 N 1 '77

NORTHWEST Energy Company. See Pipeline companies

NORTHWEST Passage
Arctic almost killed me twice! first man to canoe across the Northwest Passage. T. Dauksza. il map Outdoor Life 159:88-91+ Je '77

NORTHWEST TERRITORIES, Canada
Berger report: northern frontier, northern homeland; excerpt from Northern frontier, northern homeland; with editorial comments. T. R. Berger. il por maps Liv Wildn 41:3, 4-33 Ap '77
First crossing: Alexander Mackenzie's quest for the Pacific; excerpt from Winner take all. D. Lavender. il por Am West 14:4-11+ S '77
Still Eskimo, still free; Inuit of Umingmaktok. Y. Momatiuk and J. Eastcott. il map Nat Geog 152:624-47 N '77

Description and travel

Camper travel idea. map Outdoor Life 159:173 F '77
New maps & guides to adventure canoeing. V. Landi. Outdoor Life 160:72+ Ag '77

NORTHWESTERN Mutual Life Insurance Company
Uncommon risk-taker. por Forbes 119:85-6 F 15 '77

NORTHWESTERN States
See also
Botany—Northwestern States
Forests and forestry—Northwestern States

Description and travel

Unexpected Pacific Northwest. R. S. Kane. il Harp Baz 110:16+ Ap '77

History

American characters: John McLoughlin; manager of Hudson's Bay Company. D. Lavender. por Am Heritage 28:64-5 Je '77
Cameras at sea; historical west coast maritime photography. R. A. Weinstein. il Am West 14:34-9 My '77
Fort Vancouver: fur trade capital of the Pacific Northwest. J. A. Hussey. bibl il por Am West 14:12-19+ S '77
See also
Oregon Trail

Industries

See also
Lumber industry

NORTHWESTERN University, Evanston, Ill.

Medical School

Future doctors balk at the bill. L. J. Carter. Science 197:1062-3 S 9 '77

NORTON, Boyd
Gentle, welcoming wilderness; excerpt from Alaska: wilderness frontier. il Audubon 79:38-49 S '77

NORTON, Clark
Before the fall. Progressive 41:48 D '77

NORTON, Eleanor Holmes
Woman who changed the South; a memory of Fannie Lou Hamer. por Ms 6:51+ Jl '77

about
Cleaning up a mess. D. A. Williams and others. il por Newsweek 91:26 Ja 16 '78 *
Eager new team tackles job discrimination. por Bus W p 116+ Jl 25 '77 *
Task for Eleanor Norton. Nation 224:645 My 28 '77 *
Troubled drive for efficiency at the EEOC. il Bus W p90-1+ D 19 '77 *

NORTON, Gay. See Freedman, J. jt auth

NORTON, Gretchen
Cheerleading doesn't deserve a bad image. por Seventeen 36:64 Je '77

NORTON, H. Wilbert
Effective evangelism: a matter of marketing? interview, ed by D. Kucharsky. il Chr Today 21:12-15 Ap 15 '77

NORTON, John Henry
Game any number can play. V. Kraft. il por Sports Illus 47:40-1 Ag 22 '77 *

NORTON, Ken
Make him 38 and one. P. Putnam. il pors Sports Illus 46:96+ My 23 '77 *
Win some, lose some, split the rest. P. Putnam. il pors Sports Illus 47:36-8+ N 14 '77 *

NORTON, O. Richard
Eight feet of solar spectrum. il Sky & Tel 54:176-9 S '77

NORTON, Thomas T. and others
Loss of Y-cells in the lateral geniculate nucleus of monocularly deprived tree shrews. bibl il Science 197:784-6 Ag 19 '77

NORTON Pottery (firm) See Potteries—History

NORTON Simon, Inc-Avis, Inc merger. See Corporations—Acquisitions and mergers

NORWAY
See also
Cruising—Norway
Espionage, Russian—Norway
Fishing—Norway
Publishers and publishing—Norway
Skis and skiing—Norway

Foreign relations

Russia

See Russia—Foreign relations—Norway

Industries

See also
Electronic industries—Norway
Petroleum industry—Norway

Politics and government

Load of problems for a new government. Bus W p57 S 12 '77

NORWEGIANS
See also
Lapps
Northmen

NORWINE, Jim
Question of climate. bibl il maps Environment 19:6-13+ N '77

NOSE
See also
Smell

NOSE; opera. See Shostakovich, D. D.

NOSSITER, Bernard Daniel
Commentary sees red. Nation 224:298-300 Mr 12 '77
Oil to the rescue. Progressive 41:38-9 Mr '77

NOSTALGIA
Rewards of nostalgia. C. Amen. Writer 91:29-31 Ja '78
That old feeling. J. Bosveld. Sci Digest 81:65-7+ Ap '77
Were the good old days really that good? A. R. Swinnerton. Ret Liv 17:34 Jl '77

NOT-so-wide world of sports; drama. See Majeski, B.

NOTABLE Books Council. See American Library Association—Reference and Adult Services Division

NOTABLES. See Celebrities

NOTATION (music) See Musical notation

NOTRE Dame Cathedral. See Paris—Notre Dame (cathedral)

NOTRE DAME. University, Notre Dame, Ind.
Graham scores at Notre Dame. A. H. Matthews. il por Chr Today 21:30-1 Je 3 '77
President at Notre Dame; commencement exercises. America 136:494 Je 4 '77
Prince of priests, without a nickel. il pors Time 109:74-5 My 2 '77

NOTRE Faust; ballet. See Ballet reviews—Single works

NOTTINGHAM
Music
See also
Opera—Great Britain
NOUGAT. See Confectionery
NOUNOUFAR (artist)
Armenian Grandma Moses. P. J. Thomajan. il por Ret Liv 17:50 My '77 *
NOURSE, Alan E.
Family doctor. See issues of Good housekeeping
NOVA SCOTIA
See also
Cape Breton Island
Fisheries
See Fisheries—Canada
NOVAE SELO, British Columbia. See Villages, Restored
NOVAK, Michael
Closet socialists. Chr Cent 94:171-4, 1045-6 F 23, N 9 '77
Death of Marx. il New Cath World 220:122-5 My '77
Evangelicals and activists. Chr Cent 94:469-70 My 13 '77
London economic summit. America 136:518-20 Je 11 '77
Michael Novak: Jimmy, be true to yourself. Chr Cent 94:3 Ja 5 '77
On the ordination of women. Commonweal 104: 425-7, 561-4, 591-3 Jl 8, S 2-16 '77
Trilateral connection. Atlantic 240:57-9 Jl '77
Trilateral reform and world justice. America 137: 106-9 Ag 27 '77
Trilateralism: a new world system. America 136:95-9 F 5 '77
about
Little knowledge. P. Steinfels. Commonweal 104:392+ Je 24 '77; Reply with rejoinder. M. Novak. 104:642-3+, 646+ O 14 '77 *
Socialism and sin. B. Douglass; discussion. Chr Cent 94:171-4, 567-9 F 23, Je 8 '77 *
NOVELISTS
First novelists; statements by the writers (cont) il Lib J 102:410-19, 1414-22, 2086-90 F 1, Je 15, O 1 '77
NOVELISTS, American
See also
Bellow, S.
Berger, T. L.
Caldwell, E.
Cheever, J.
Cozzens, J. G.
Didion, J.
Futrelle, J.
Heller, J.
Hemingway, E.
Jones, J.
Keeler, H. S.
Kosinski, J. N.
Kotker, Z.
Ludlum, R.
Nabokov, V.
Roth, P.
Stout, R.
Updike, J.
NOVELISTS, English
Prehumous classics; Victorian novelists and publishers. E. Moers. Am Scholar 47:118+ Wint '77
See also
Clark, A. A. G.
Clayton, R.
Cornwell, D. J. M.
Richardson, S.
Tolkien, J. R. R.
Trollope, A.
NOVELISTS, French
See also
Hugo, V. M.
Huysmans, J. K.
Murger, H.
NOVELISTS, Irish
See also
Joyce, J.
NOVELISTS, Russian
See also
Zamiatin, E. I.
NOVELLI, Diego
Reports & comment: Turin. G. Hodgson. il Atlantic 240:20+ Ag '77 *
NOVELS. See Fiction
NOVELS, Filmed. See Television adaptations
NOVICK, Richard P.
Present controls are just a start. por Bull Atom Sci 33:16+ My '77
NOVICK, Sheldon
Jaundiced eye. See issues of Environment to June 1977
Spectrum. See issues of Environment to May 1977
NOWADNICK, James
There is but one ocean; with biographical sketch. il Sea Front 23:130-40, 191 My '77

NOYCE, Robert N.
Large-scale integration: what is yet to come? il Science 195:1102-6 Mr 18 '77
Microelectronics; with biographical sketch. il Sci Am 237:14, 62-9 S '77
about
Good life beckons. il por Forbes 119:53 Ap 15 '77 *
Le NOZZE di Figaro; opera. See Mozart, J. C. W. A.
NOZZLES
Garden hoses and nozzles. il Consumers Res Mag 60:32-6 Ag '77
See also
Guided missiles—Nozzles
Space vehicles—Nozzles
NUBIAN ibex. See Ibex
NUCLEAR Antiproliferation Act of 1977. See Atomic power—Laws and regulations
NUCLEAR bombs. See Atomic bombs
NUCLEAR energy. See Atomic power
NUCLEAR exports. See Atomic power industry —Export-import trade
NUCLEAR fallout. See Radioactive fallout
NUCLEAR fission
Natural fossil nuclear reactor. il Bull Atom Sci 33:40-1 F '77
Power play. G. Hill; discussion. Nat Wildlife 15:38-9 F '77
NUCLEAR fuel reprocessing. See Reactor fuel reprocessing
NUCLEAR Fuel Services (firm) See Reactor fuel reprocessing
NUCLEAR fuels
APS fuel-cycle study finds nuclear technology sound. F. C. Bennett. il Phys Today 30:77-9 Jl '77
Ambassador Smith briefs press on INFCE conference; excerpt from remarks, October 21, 1977. G. C. Smith. Dept State Bull 77:664-5 N 14 '77
Nuclear fuel cycle: an appraisal. il Phys Today 30:32-5+ O '77
Organizing conference of the International Nuclear Fuel Cycle Evaluation meets in Washington; remarks with text of communique. October 19, 21, 1977. J. Carter. Dept State Bull 77:659-64 N 14 '77
See also
Plutonium
Uranium
NUCLEAR fusion
Carbon dioxide laser: fusion at last. Sci N 111: 166 Mr 12 '77
Fusion, sure—but for the long term. Forbes 121:154 Ja 9 '78
Fusions by electron beam produced at Sandia. Sci N 112:4 Jl 2 '77
Great nuclear fusion race. il Time 109:80-1 Je 6 '77
Lighting a sun on earth. P. Gwynne and others. il Newsweek 90:132+ N 21 '77
Nuclear fusion's promise grows. P. Raeburn. Sci Digest 82:8-10 Jl '77
Pair of laser beams tame the sun's basic energy. il Sci Digest 82:11-13+ Jl '77
Sandia and Kurchatov groups claim electron-beam fusion. G. B. Lubkin. il Phys Today 30:17-19 Ag '77
Tests show CO_2 laser is suitable for fusion. G. B. Lubkin. il Phys Today 30:19-20 S '77
Thermonuclear burn in laser fusion. Sci N 112: 21-2 Jl 9 '77
U.S. electron beam tests trigger fusion. W. C. Wetmore. il Aviation W 107:22-4 Jl 4 '77
NUCLEAR industry. See Atomic power industry
NUCLEAR magnetic resonance
Analysis of living tissue by phosphorus-31 magnetic resonance. C. T. Burt and others. bibl il Science 195:145-9 Ja 14 '77
Biological nuclear magnetic resonance spectroscopy. S. J. Opella. bibl il Science 198:158-65 O 14 '77
Bounds on "bound water": transverse nuclear magnetic resonance relaxation in barnacle muscle. K. R. Foster and others; discussion. bibl Science 198:1180-2 D 16 '77
Chemistry tool probes muscle cells. il Sci N 111: 71 Ja 29 '77
Damadian's supermagnet: how he hopes to use it to detect cancer. S. Renner-Smith. il pors Pop Sci 211:76-9+ D '77
NUCLEAR non-proliferation treaty. See Atomic weapons and disarmament
NUCLEAR physics
See also
Accelerators (electrons, etc)
Nuclear spin
Quantum electrodynamics
Particle beams
Particles (nuclear physics)
Scattering (physics)
Transmutation (chemistry)
NUCLEAR policy. See Atomic power
NUCLEAR pollution. See Radioactive pollution
NUCLEAR power plants. See Atomic power plants

NUCLEAR powered submarines. See Submarine boats, Atomic powered
NUCLEAR-powered warships. See Warships, Atomic powered
NUCLEAR reactions
Analyzing hydrogen with nuclear reactions. S. T. Picraux. bibl il Phys Today 30:42-3+ O '77
See also
Nuclear fission
Nuclear fusion
Positronium
NUCLEAR reactors
Breeder: French prototype shut down for repairs. W. D. Metz. il Science 195:972 Mr 11 '77
Breeder's progress: when a veto is not a veto. W. D. Metz. Science 198:710-11 N 18 '77
Breeding in light water: the test begins; Shippingport, Pa. il Sci N 112:164 S 10 '77
Breeding in the U.S. Sci Am 236:58 Mr '77
Carter's new plutonium policy: maybe less than meets the eye; effect on Clinch River breeder reactor. W. D. Metz. Science 196:405-7 Ap 22 '77
Comparative breeding characteristics of fusion and fast reactors. P. Fortescue. il Science 196: 1326-9 Je 17 '77
Engineer's memo stirs doubts on Clinch River breeder. D. Shapley. Science 197:350-2 Jl 22 '77
How states can go nuclear. F. C. Barnaby. il Ann Am Acad 430:29-43 Mr '77
Japan completes breeder reactor. Sci N 111:22 Ja 8 '77
Landscape of nuclear tombs; decommissioning. A. Parks. Progressive 41:30-1 D '77
Nuclear laser power up 100-fold. Sci N 112:69 Jl 30 '77
Possible reprieve for the fast breeder; Clinch River project. Bus W p31-2 Je 20 '77
Reactors that can sub for the fast breeder. il Bus W p24 Ag 8 '77
Security implications of alternative fission futures. H. A. Feiveson and T. B. Taylor; reply with rejoinder. R. C. Dahlberg. Bull Atom Sci 33:58-9 My '77
Superphénix: a full-scale breeder reactor. G. A. Vendryes. il Sci Am 236:26-35 Mr '77
TRB from Washington; House hearings on nuclear power; Clinch River project. New Repub 176:2+ Je 18 '77
Thorium option. Sci Am 236:57+ My '77
Two hurdles remain for breeder funding. Sci N 112:247 O 15 '77
Veto may kill liquid metal fast breeder. Sci N 112:312 N 12 '77
Why the breeder reactor is inevitable. T. Alexander. il Fortune 96:122-8+ S '77
See also
Reactor fuel reprocessing
Tokamaks

Cost

Economic issues of the fast breeder reactor program. B. G. Chow. bibl il Science 195:551-6 F 11 '77

Fuel

See Nuclear fuels

History

Birth of the atomic reactor. il Sci Digest 81:55-8 F '77

Laws and regulations

See Atomic power—Laws and regulations

Maintenance and repair

Nuclear denting plagues the utilities. Bus W p20-1 Jl 4 '77

Manufacture

See Atomic power industry

Safety devices and measures

Is nuclear energy acceptable? A. M. Weinberg. bibl Bull Atom Sci 33:54-60 Ap '77; Reply with rejoinder. D. Meek. 33:3-5 Je '77
Looking back on the Rasmussen report. F. Von Hippel. bibl il Bull Atom Sci 33:42-7 F '77
Reactor safety: Congress hears critics of Rasmussen report. P. M. Boffey; discussion. Science 194:476-80; 195:344+; 196:1387-9 O 29 '76, Ja 28, Je 24 '77
Reactor safety: independence of Rasmussen study doubted. D. Shapley. Science 197:29-30 Jl 1 '77
This month's feature: controversy over nuclear reactor safety. Cong Digest 56:34-64 F '77
NUCLEAR security measures. See Atomic power—Security measures
NUCLEAR spin
Proton spin surprise. il Sci N 112:196 S 24 '77
Second back bend helps explain nuclear band crossing. H. R. Leuchtag. il Phys Today 30: 17-19 S '77
NUCLEAR test ban. See Atomic weapons—Testing, Suspension of
NUCLEAR warfare. See Atomic warfare
NUCLEAR warships. See Warships, Atomic powered
NUCLEAR waste disposal. See Radioactive waste disposal
NUCLEAR wastes. See Radioactive wastes
NUCLEAR weapons. See Atomic weapons
NUCLEATION. See Condensation
NUCLEIC acids
Early chemical evolution of nucleic acids: a theoretical model. D. A. Usher. bibl il Science 196:311-13 Ap 15 '77
See also
DNA
RNA
NUCLEONS
Nucleon stability: a geochemical test independent of decay mode. J. C. Evans, Jr and R. I. Steinberg. bibl il Science 197:989-91 S 2 '77
NUCLEOPROTEINS
Hyperphenylalanemia: effect on brain polyribosomes can be partially reversed by other amino acids. J. V. Hughes and T. C. Johnson. bibl il Science 195:402-4 Ja 28 '77
See also
Interferon
NUCLEOTIDES
Cyclic nucleotides injected intracellularly into rat superior cervical ganglion cells. J. P. Gallagher and P. Shinnick-Gallagher. bibl il Science 198:851-2 N 25 '77
Defined dimensional changes in enzyme cofactors: fluorescent "stretched-out" analogs of adenine nucleotides. D. I. C. Scopes and others. bibl il Science 195:296-8 Ja 21 '77
Nucleotide sequence of a viral DNA. J. C. Fiddes. il Sci Am 237:54-67 D '77
Nucleotide sequences from a rabbit alpha globin gene inserted in a chimeric plasmid. A. Y. Liu and others. bibl il Science 196:192-5 Ap 8 '77
Nucleotide sequences from the rabbit beta globin gene inserted into escherichia coli plasmids. J. K. Browne and others. bibl il Science 195: 389-91 Ja 28 '77
Possible cyclic nucleotide regulation of calcium mediating myocardial contraction. A. Schwartz and others. bibl il Science 195:982+ Mr 11 '77
See also
Adenosine monophosphate
Guanosine monophosphate
NUCLEUS, Cellular. See Cell nuclei
NUCOR Corporation. See Steel industry—United States
NUDE photography. See Photography of the nude
NUDITY
Swimsuit optional zone; nude sunbathing at Black's beach in La Jolla Calif. B. Golden. Progressive 41:41-2 My '77
NUESTRO (periodical)
New voice for Latinos. il Time 109:52 Ap 18 '77
NULTY, Peter
When we'll start running out of oil. il map Fortune 96:246-50 O '77
NUMBER systems. See Numeration
NUMBERING systems
What numbers on checks, licenses, labels tell you. M. L. Schildkraut. Good H 184:226-7 Mr '77
NUMBERS, Negative
Concept of negative numbers and the difficulty of grasping it. M. Gardner. il Sci Am 236:131-4 Je '77
NUMBERS, Theory of
Einstein's world and the big numbers game. D. E. Thomsen. Sci N 112:157-8 S 3 '77
See also
Fibonacci numbers
NUMBERS betting. See Gambling
NUMEIRY, Jaafar. See Nimieri, G. M.
NUMERATION
Numeration systems—a white elephant in elementary school. D. Rappaport. Educ Digest 42:56-7 Ap '77
NUMERICAL calculations
How figures can fool you. J. H. Foegen. il Ret Liv 17:35-6 Jl '77
NUMISMATICS
Numismatics. G. Rayner. See issues of Hobbies
NUNN, Clyde Z.
Is there a crisis of confidence in science? Science 198:995 D 9 '77
NUNN, Sam
Draft: both sides of debate; interview. pors U.S. News 82:59-60 F 14 '77
Go ahead with neutron bomb? interview. il pors U.S. News 83:25-6 Jl 25 '77
New Soviet threat to NATO. Read Digest 111: 73-7 Jl '77
NUNS
Nun on trial for infanticide; case of Sister Maureen. C. Breslin. il por Ms 5:68-71+ Mr '77
Nuns as jailers; Bolivia. Commonweal 104:354 Je 10 '77
Sister Maureen: not guilty and not free. C. Breslin. Ms 6:22 Jl '77
See also
Sisterhoods

NUREEV, Rudolf
Nureyev as Valentino; interview, ed by J. Watters. por Ladies Home J 94:68+ My '77
about
Nureyev in Valentino. V. H. Swisher. il pors Dance Mag 51:60-1 D '77 *
Nureyev leaps into films as Valentino. W. Terry. il pors Sat R 4:29-32 Ap 30 '77 *
Nureyev's Valentino tango. J. Gruen. il por Vogue 167:148-9+ Ag '77 *
Rudolf and Laura; Nureyev at the Uris. J. Anderson. Dance Mag 51:33+ Je '77 *
Tamerlane of the performing arts. A. Bland. il pors Horizon 20:28-34 S '77 *

NURSE midwives. See Midwives

NURSE practitioners. See Nurses and nursing

NURSERIES
And baby makes 3. B. Niles. il Am Home 80: 50-1 F '77

NURSERIES (horticulture)
Consumer's guide to nursery shopping. V. McElwain. il Horticulture 55:40-3 O '77
In Hilo, tropical plant discovery. il Sunset 159: 44 Ag '77
It's spring in February. il map Sunset 158:72-5 F '77

Mail order business
See Mail order business

NURSERY schools
Do-it-yourself nursery school. K. A. Wright. il por Redbook 149:38+ Jl '77
Wonderful world of the two-year-old; program at St Andrew's Nursery School, Cherry Hill, N.J. P. Crawford. il Parents Mag 52:39-41 F '77
See also
Day care centers
Special classes and special schools

NURSES and nursing
1977—the year of the nurse; address, June 11, 1977. V. Collins. Vital Speeches 43:590-3 Jl 15 '77
Should nurses have same personal accountability as doctors for patient care? A nurse says yes; independent practitioners. Ret Liv 17:43 Ag '77
Supernurses; nurse practitioners. M. Clark and others. il Newsweek 90:64 D 5 '77
10,000 nurses speak out: a startling report on hospitals and doctors. il Fam Health 9:36-8 Ag '77

NURSES and patients
Pathology, adversity, and nursing. I. G. Zuckermann. bibl Society 14:52-4 Ja '77

NURSING (infant feeding) See Breast feeding

NURSING (suckling) See Suckling

NURSING home patients. See Sick, The

NURSING homes
High cost of caring; church-related retirement and convalescent facilities. Chr Today 21:53 Mr 4 '77
Psychomotor approach in the nursing home; dancing programs for the aged. L. R. Schoenfeld. il Dance Mag 51:82-4 O '77
Stand-up gardening at Shady Lane. E. Pearson. il Org Gard & Farm 24:106-8 My '77
When moved abruptly: death rates rise for nursing home patients. Aging 275:84 S '77

Administration
Nursing the nursing homes back to health. il por Bus W p66+ D 5 '77

Employees
Occupational pay and benefits examined in nursing homes. M Labor R 100:45 Ag '77

NUSSENZVEIG, H. Moysés
Theory of the rainbow; with biographical sketch. il Sci Am 236:116-27 bibl(p 148) Ap '77

NUSSMAN, Pat
Try small newspapers. Writers Digest 57:35 Mr '77

NUT industry
Billy Carter: frustrations of the small businessman; interview. B. Carter. il pors Nations Bus 65:28-32+ My '77
Rumblings in the nutshell; the peanut business. L. Smith. il Duns R 109:44-6 F '77
Selling Jimmy out; shares in peanut warehouse. D. Pauly and V. E. Smith. il por Newsweek 90:58 Ag 29 '77
There is good news in peanut country. U.S. News 82:24 Je 27 '77
Two-story cropping; Hammons Products Company, world's largest processor of black walnuts. J. D. Ritchie. il Org Gard & Farm 24:80+ S '77

NUT rolls. See Cake

NUT trees
Nut trees; symposium. il Org Gard & Farm 24: 78-99 S '77
Splice graft that works for nut trees too. G. Logsdon. il Org Gard & Farm 25:88-9 Ja '78
See also
Butternut trees
Chestnut trees
Pecan trees
Walnut trees

NUTCRACKER; ballet. See Ballet reviews—Single works

NUTCRACKER Prince; drama. See Mahlmann, L.

NUTRITION
Are you eating right? S. N. Wellborn. il U.S. News 83:39-43 N 28 '77
Food and nutrition. B. T. Hunter. Consumers Res Mag 60:104-12 O '77
4 keys to live-longer diets. P. Shriever. il Ret Liv 17:44-6 N '77
How to create a family food plan that's right for you. R. Mirenda. il por Parents Mag 52: 38-9+ Mr '77
Is super nutrition the cure-all for everything? interviews, ed by M.-E. Banashek and N. A. Comer. Mademoiselle 83:204-7 O '77
Nutrition in a nutshell. L. Beech. Sr Schol 109: 20 My 19 '77
Rediscovering the joy of good eating for good health. A. L. Goldberg. il Parents Mag 52: 37+ Mr '77
We need more beef dollars to counter nutrition myths; views of Dr G. V. Mann. Farm J 101: Beef 20+ Ja '77
What you eat today can decide your health tomorrow. H. Alpert. il Ret Liv 17:26-30 S '77
What's your nutrition I.Q? Consumer Rep 42: 78-80 F '77; Same abr. with title Test your nutrition I.Q. Read Digest 111:158-60 Ag '77
Where can we get reliable facts about good nutrition? J. Meyer. bibl il Fam Health 9:32-3+ Ja '77
Wild ways to feel better. R. Rodale. il Org Gard & Farm 25:54-7 Ja '78
See also
Aged—Nutrition
Athletes—Nutrition
Blacks—Nutrition
Breakfasts
Cancer—Nutritional aspects
Children—Nutrition
College students—Nutrition
Dancers—Nutrition
Diabetes—Nutritional aspects
Diet
Infants—Nutrition
Iron in diet
Mental illness—Nutritional aspects
Plants—Nutrition
Proteins
Reproduction—Nutritional aspects
Snacks
Trace elements
Vitamins
Women—Nutrition
Youth—Nutrition

NUTRITION policy
Toward a national nutrition policy. Sci N 111:22 Ja 8 '77
See also
United States—Congress—Senate—Nutrition and Human Needs, Select Committee on

United States
Food factor: diet; McGovern report. Vogue 167: 168 Ag '77

NUTRITION problems
See also
Underdeveloped areas—Nutrition problems

NUTRITION research
High-fiber diet's value questioned; work of John G. Reinhold. W. O'Reilly, Jr. Sci Digest 81:26-8 Ap '77

NUTS
Gift from the woods. D. Fisher and B. Fisher. il Org Gard & Farm 24:95-6 S '77
Good food in a nutshell. M. C. Goldman. il Org Gard & Farm 24:97-9 S '77
See also
Acorns
Cookery—Nuts
Nut industry
Nut trees
Peanuts

NUTS (machinery) See Bolts and nuts

NUTS in house decoration. See Fruits, vegetables, etc. in decoration

NUTTALL, Thomas
Innocent botanist who herbalized the West; excerpt from A species of eternity. J. Kastner. il por Horticulture 55:44-51 S '77 *
Naturalists across the Rockies. J. I. Merritt. bibl il pors Am West 14:4-9+ Mr '77 *

NWOKO, Demas
In search of a new African theatre. UNESCO Courier 30:29+ My '77

NYE, Joseph Samuel, 1937-
Department testifies on nonproliferation and nuclear export policies; statement, May 6, 1977. Dept State Bull 76:558-64 My 30 '77
Nuclear power without nuclear proliferation; address, October 3, 1977. Dept State Bull 77: 666-71 N 14 '77
Planning a safeguardable nuclear future; address, June 30, 1977. Dept State Bull 77:183-90 Ag 8 '77
Time to plan for the next generation of nuclear technology. il Bull Atom Sci 33:38-41 O '77

NYE, Joseph Samuel, 1937—*Continued*
U.S. nuclear exports to South Africa; statement, July 12, 1977. Dept State Bull 77:236-41 Ag 22 '77
United States policy on nuclear technology: combining energy and security; address, May 2, 1977. Dept State Bull 76:550-4 My 30 '77

NYERERE, Julius Kambarage
America and Southern Africa. For Affairs 55: 671-84 Jl '77
Nyerere: how much war? interview, ed by L. Griggs. por Time 109:25 Mr 14 '77

Visit to the United States, 1977

Tanzanian President Nyerere visits the U.S. Dept State Bull 77:275 Ag 29 '77

NYOIKE, Kimani Wa
Aid to developing countries: a third world trade unionist view. M Labor R 100:38-9 Mr '77

O

OAS. See Organization of American States

OAU. See Organization of African Unity

OBIS (Outdoor Biology Instructional Strategies) project. See United States—National Science Foundation

OCLC (Ohio College Library Center) See Library networks

OECD. See Organization for Economic Cooperation and Development

OH radicals. See Hydroxyl

OLA. See Oregon Library Association

OMB. See United States—Management and Budget, Office of

OPEC. See Organization of Petroleum Exporting Countries

OPIC. See Overseas Private Investment Corporation

OSHA. See United States—Occupational Safety and Health Administration

OSTP. See United States—Science and Technology Policy, Office of

OTA. See United States—Technology Assessment, Office of

OTEC (Ocean Thermal Energy Conversion) program. See United States—Energy Research and Development Administration—Ocean Thermal Energy Conversion Program

OAHU (island)
Other Oahu. il map Sunset 158:78-83 Mr '77
See also
Honolulu

OAK, Jacquelyn. See Muller, N. C. jt auth

OAK
See also
Acorns

OAK Park, Ill.

Housing

See Housing—Illinois

OAKES, John Bertram
Newsman is honored for his editorials. Audubon 79:120-1 Ja '77 *

OAKLAND, Calif.

Architecture

Preserving a neighborhood. T. H. Watkins. il Am Heritage 28:106-9 Je '77

Description

Oakland bike loop. il map Sunset 159:40-1 Ag '77

Education

Oakland school official restricts library book. SLJ 23:12 Ap '77
To the Oakland School District, with Love; Superintendent R. B. Love. C. Pogash. por Ms 5:19 My '77

Newspapers

Bitter family squabble puts Oakland's Tribune on the block. il Bus W p60 F 21 '77

Water supply

Wastewater reuse by the truckload; East Bay Municipal Utility District of Oakland. Am City & County 92:40 S '77

OAKLAND County, Mich.

Crime

See Crime and criminals—Michigan

Recreation

See Recreation—Michigan

OAKLAND tribune. See Oakland, Calif.—Newspapers

OAKLEY, June P.
Middle school student council. Clearing H 50: 296-7 Mr '77

OAKLEY, Robert Bigger
Department discusses human rights in Thailand; statement, June 30, 1977. Dept State Bull 77: 210-13 Ag 15 '77
Department discusses program to control narcotic drugs; statement, July 12, 1977. Dept State Bull 77:242-5 Ag 22 '77
Human rights in Indonesia; statement, October 18, 1977. Dept State Bull 77:848-52 D 12 '77
U.S. assistance programs in southeast Asia: statement, March 17, 1977. Dept State Bull 76:342-4 Ap 11 '77

OAKS, Dallin Harris
Title IX: administrative, legal and constitutional aspects; address, March 10, 1977. Vital Speeches 43:372-6 Ap 1 '77

OARSMANSHIP. See Rowing

OATES, Joyce Carol
All the good people I've left behind; condensation of novel. Redbook 149:235-51 My '77
Famine country; story. Yale R 66:534-50 Je '77
Footprints; poem. Nation 224:475 Ap 16 '77
Gala power black-out of New York City, July '77; poem. New Repub 177:36 S 17 '77
Skyscape; poem. New Repub 176:27 F 5 '77
Tattoo; story. Mademoiselle 83:144 Jl '77
That; poem. Nation 225:23 Jl 2 '77

about

Comment. R. Siegel. Poetry 130:107-9 My '77 *

OAXACA (state) Mexico
See also
Monte Albán

O'BANNON, Helen B.
Power—and the vote. F. Ruffin. por Redbook 149:81+ Ag '77 *

OBASANJO, Olusegun
Lt. Gen. Obasanjo of Nigeria visits the United States; exchange of remarks, October 11, 1977. Dept State Bull 77:694-5 N 14 '77

about

Rhetoric and reality. por Forbes 120:122 N 1 '77 *

Visit to the United States, 1977

Lt. Gen. Obasanjo of Nigeria visits the United States; exchange of remarks, October 11, 1977. J. Carter; O. Obasanjo. Dept State Bull 77: 693-5 N 14 '77

OBEDIENCE
Shocking obedience found in children. Sci N 112: 117-18 Ag 20 '77

OBELKEVICH, Mary Rowen
Turkish affect in the land of the Sun King. bibl il Mus Q 63:367-89 Jl '77

OBERACKER, Shirley C.
Christmas tale; drama. Plays 37:73-4 D '77

OBERAMMERGAU Passion Play
Script trouble at Oberammergau. il Time 110:74 Ag 29 '77

OBERG, Arthur
What we've gathered here against the winter. Poetry 130:162-7 Je '77

OBERG, James E.
Astronauts & UFOs—the whole story! il por Space World N-2-158:4-28 F '77
China in space. il Sci Digest 81:33-8 F '77
Notes on Soviet space astronomy. il Sky & Tel 53:92-6 F '77
Plesetsk—Russia's top secret military space center. il map Space World N-3-159:4-7 Mr '77
Soyuz and the moon. il Space World N-7-163:26-32 Jl '77

OBERHEIM, Thomas Elroy
Tom Oberheim's magical music machines. D. Heckman. il Hi Fi 27:127-30 Ap '77 *

OBESITY
Adipose tissue regeneration following lipectomy. I. M. Faust and others. bibl il Science 197: 391-3 Jl 22 '77
Barbara Cook: fat can set you free; interview, ed by L. C. Pogrebin. B. Cook. il pors Ms 6:50-2 S '77
Can acupuncture help you lose weight? Stop smoking? R. Blackmon and S. Sheppard. Vogue 167:148+ Mr '77
Did your mother make you fat? Ebony 32:59-60+ My '77
Drastic methods to lose weight; intestinal bypass surgery. M. Burgen. il Ebony 32:124-6+ O '77
Fat people's fight against job bias. il U.S. News 83:78-80 D 5 '77
For the very fat, sexual problems are largely logistic; study by Theodore Wise and Jacqueline Gordon. D. Cohen. Psychol Today 11:33 S '77
Jaw wiring: tough anti-obesity weapon. Sci N 112:23 Jl 9 '77
Never too thin to feel fat; interviews, ed by J. Thurman. Ms 6:48-9+ S '77
Obesity: a growing problem. G. B. Kolata. Science 198:905-6 D 2 '77
Selective blockade of hypothalamic hyperphagia and obesity in rats by serotonin-depleting midbrain lesions. D. V. Coscina and H. C. Stancer. bibl il Science 195:416-19 Ja 28 '77

OBESITY—*Continued*
Surgical removal of adipose tissue alters feeding behavior and the development of obesity in rats. I. M. Faust and others. bibl il Science 197:393-6 Jl 22 '77
Those food-related cues magnify your weight problem. A. R. Weiss. Sci Digest 81:33-4 Ap '77
To lose weight, I had my jaws wired shut. D. Jaworski and M. A. Rodgers. Good H 185:76+ Ag '77
When fat was in fashion. A. Hollander. il N Y Times Mag p36-7+ O 23 '77
See also
Prader-Willi syndrome
Weight (physiology)
Weight Watchers, Inc
OBEY, David Ross
Day in the life of Congressman David Obey. J. Landman. il pors Sr Schol 109:9-12 F 24 '77 *
OBEY Commission. See United States—Congress—House—Standards of Official Conduct, Committee on
OBITUARIES
Rest in prose: the art of the obituary. W. Haley. Am Scholar 46:206-11 Spr '77
OBJECTIVES in education. See Education—Aims and objectives
OBJECTS, Miniature. See Miniature objects
O'BOYLE, Bonnie
Dream machine. il Motor B & S 141:83-5 Ja '78
OBRAZTSOVA, Elena
Musician of the month: Elena Obraztsova; interview, ed by G. S. Bourdain. por Hi Fi 27: MA4-5 F '77
about
Dynamite U.S.S.R. E. Davidson. il pors Opera N 42:26-8+ S '77 *
Elena Obraztsova, mezzo-soprano; recital at Avery Fisher Hall. Hi Fi 27:MA33-4 F '77 *
OBRECHT, Jacob
Problems of transmission in Obrecht's Missa Je ne demande. T. Noblitt. bibl f il Mus Q 63: 211-23 Ap '77 *
O'BRIEN, Charles P. and others
Conditioned narcotic withdrawal in humans. bibl il Science 195:1000-2 Mr 11 '77
O'BRIEN, Conor Cruise
How the cruiser was grounded and Finn MacCool returned. H. Kenner. Nat R 29:874-7 Ag 5 '77 *
O'BRIEN, Darcy
Irish paradox. il N Y Times Mag p96-8+ S 11 '77
O'BRIEN, David J.
American historical experience. il New Cath World 220:114-15 My '77
Holy Cross case. il Commonweal 103:647-53; 104: 48 O 8 '76, Ja 21 '77
O'BRIEN, Dennis
Looking at America. Commonweal 104:502-4 Ag 5 '77
O'BRIEN, Edna
Christmas roses; story. Atlantic 240:56-8 D '77
about
Gathering. Review
New Yorker 53:77-8 Mr 21 '77 *
O'BRIEN, John Conway
Ethics in the academy. R. Kirk. Nat R 29:726 Je 24 '77 *
O'BRIEN, Patricia
Staying married; excerpt from Staying together: marriages that work. Good H 184:126-7+ My '77
O'BRIEN, Stephen J. and others
Enzyme polymorphisms as genetic signatures in human cell cultures. bibl il Science 195: 1345-8 Mr 25 '77
O'BRIEN, T. Michael. See Noble, D. jt auth
O'BRIEN, Tim
Calling home; story; excerpt from Going after Cacciato. Redbook 150:75-6 D '77
Fisherman; story; excerpt from Going after Cacciato. il . . . Esquire 88:92-3 O '77
about
Pieces of a Vietnam war story. G. Lyons. Nation 224:120-1 Ja 29 '77 *
O'BRYAN, Elizabeth
Crafty vacations. Am Home 80:42+ Ap '77
Whole-earth gourmet. il por Am Home 80:64-5 Jl '77
O'BRYANT, John D.
Boston after Louise Day Hicks. H. Husock. il por Nation 225:710-12 D 31 '77 *
OBSCENE language. See Words, Obscene
OBSCENITY (law)
AAP cautions Senate on pending obscenity law. S. Wagner. Pub W 212:29+ Jl 25 '77
Another round in the obscenity battle; case of J. L. Smith. W. D. Nelson. Wilson Lib Bull 51:466-7 F '77
Censorship and the schools: a different perspective; studying community standards in Jefferson County, Ky. S. I. Mour. bibl f il Engl J 66:18-20 F '77
Confusion worse confounded. L. H. Lapham. Harpers 254:12+ Ap '77
Current status of obscenity laws. F. F. Schauer. Intellect 106:99-100 S '77
Dirty movies! Dirty books! ideas of L. Parrish. C. Remsberg and B. Remsberg. il Good H 184:103+ Mr '77
Freedom of expression: too much of a good thing? excerpt from Too much of a good thing. J. Sparrow. Am Scholar 46:165-80 Spr '77
High court upholds criminal conviction of Smith for intrastate mailing. S. Wagner. Pub W 211: 42 Je 6 '77
Hustler and freedom. Nat R 29:252 Mr 4 '77
I say lock 'em up, spank them, and send them home; obscenity and the first amendment. M. J. Sobran, Jr. Nat R 29:712-13+ Je 24 '77
Judicial thicket: the Supreme Court and obscenity. M. Friedman. Nation 225:110-13 Ag 6 '77
Obscenity—forget it. C. Rembar. Atlantic 239: 37-41 My '77
Obscenity: new High Court ruling, AAP on Flynt. S. Wagner. Pub W 211:41-2 Mr 14 '77
Publishers and librarians protest child porn provision in New York law. SLJ 24:64 O '77
St Martin's wins round against N.Y. obscenity law; case of Show me! M. Reuter. Pub W 212:23-4 D 12 '77
Washington takes three actions on obscenity issues. S. Wagner. Pub W 212:16+ N 14 '77
When freedom is difficult to live with. J. J. Kilpatrick. Nations Bus 65:9-10 Ap '77
See also
Trials (obscenity)
United States—Commission on Obscenity and Pornography
OBSERVATIONS, Astronomical. See Astronomy—Observations
OBSERVATORIES
See also
Astronomical observatories
OBSERVER (London)
Oil to the rescue; purchase of The Observer by ARCO. B. D. Nossiter. Progressive 41:38-9 Mr '77
Under Observation. D. K. Shah and A. Collings. il por Newsweek 90:102-3 D 19 '77
OBSESSIVE-compulsive behavior. See Behavior (psychology)
OBST, David
David Obst, Random House describe co-venture. M. Reuter. Pub W 211:42 Mr 14 '77 *
OBST, Lynda Rosen
(ed) The 60's come to a full boil; 1968: interviews, excerpts from The sixties. il N Y Times Mag p40-3+ N 13 '77
(ed) See Eisenhower, D. Grandpa Ike
OBSTETRICS
Why I became a gynecologist; interviews with four gynecologists, ed by L. Waters. Ms 65: 54-5+ F '77
See also
Cesarean section
Midwives
O'CALLAGHAN, James F.
Ecuadorean Church: new spirit, old believers. America 136:559-62 Je 25 '77
O'CALLAGHAN, Marion
From Rhodesia to Zimbabwe. il UNESCO Courier 30:22-5 N '77
OCAMPO, Victoria
Victoria Ocampo's gift for world culture. J. Rigaud. il pors UNESCO Courier 30:64-6 Ag '77 *
OCCHIOGROSSO, Frank
Murder in the dark. New Repub 177:28-30 Jl 30 '77
OCCULT sciences
Attacking the new nonsense; Committee for the Scientific Investigation of Claims of the Paranormal. il Time 110:100 D 12 '77
Occult: on the edge of the unknown. M. Mead. il Redbook 148:68+ Mr '77
Pseudoscience—why it won't go away. J. Pfeiffer. il Horizon 19:89-90 Mr '77
Science, the media and the paranormal. Sci N 112:118 Ag 20 '77
Scientists combine to combat pseudoscience; Committee for the Scientific Investigation of Claims of the Paranormal. J. Pfeiffer. Psychol Today 11:38+ N '77
See also
Astrology
I ching (Book of changes)
Parapsychology
Spiritualism
OCCULTATIONS
May 14th occultation of Venus. D. W. Dunham. il Sky & Tel 53:376 My '77
Occultation observations reveal ring system around Uranus. F. C. Bennett. bibl il Phys Today 30:17+ Je '77
Occultation of ε Geminorum by Mars: evidence for atmospheric tides? J. L. Elliot and others. bibl il Science 195:485-6 F 4 '77
Photoelectric observing of occultations. D. S. Evans. il Sky & Tel 54:164-6 S; 289-92 O '77
See also
Eclipses
OCCULTISM. See Occult sciences

OCCUPANCY
See also
Squatters
OCCUPATIONAL diseases. See Diseases, Industrial
OCCUPATIONAL education. See Technical education; Vocational education
OCCUPATIONAL guidance. See Vocational guidance
OCCUPATIONAL health. See Industrial hygiene
OCCUPATIONAL mobility
Choosing a second career. il Bus W p 119-21+ S 19 '77
Extent of job search by employed workers. C. Rosenfeld. bibl il M Labor R 100:58-62 Mr '77
Getting out of the rat race: how some workers are doing it. il U.S. News 83:85-6 S 19 '77
Going up! New rules for women on the job. D. R. Crouch. il Redbook 149:102-3+ Ag '77
How to find a new career. il Mech Illus 73:30 O '77
Occupational mobility in the American labor force. D. Sommers and A. Eck. bibl f M Labor R 100:3-18 Ja '77
Occupational mobility of health workers. P. Wash. bibl il M Labor R 100:25-9 My '77
See also
Labor turnover
OCCUPATIONAL safety. See Industrial safety
OCCUPATIONAL Safety and Health, National Institute for. See United States—National Institute for Occupational Safety and Health
OCCUPATIONAL Safety and Health Administration. See United States—Occupational Safety and Health Administration
OCCUPATIONAL success. See Success
OCCUPATIONS
Best job bets for 1985. Sr Schol 109:5 F 10 '77
Career guides for the arts and humanities; guidebooks produced by the Technical Education Research Center. E. B. Roth. il Am Educ 13:14-15 Je '77
Cloudy side effects of sunny weather; hazards for outdoor workers. H. Levitt. il Parks & Rec 12:41 Ap '77
How to get a job; special section. il Esquire 88:51-77+ Jl '77
Jobs with the brightest future. il Changing T 31:6-11 S '77
100 best careers for the future. il Ebony 32:33-6+ Mr '77
Unlikely routes to the top; early positions of three celebrities; interviews, ed by T. Bay. Harp Baz 110:48-9+ Je '77
Update on jobs. L. David. Mech Illus 73:18 F '77
See also
Black women—Occupations
Blacks—Occupations
Music as a profession
Professions
Women—Occupations

Anecdotes, facetiae, satire, etc.

Alternative careers for liberal-arts majors. Esquire 88:68-9 Jl '77
OCCUPATIONS, Hazardous
See also
Asbestos workers
Chemical workers
OCEAN
Living sea. A. Fisher. il Int Wildlife 7:4-11 My '77
Oceanic microcosm of particles. D. Lal. bibl il maps Science 198:997-1009 D 9 '77
See also
Antarctic Ocean
Atlantic Ocean
Coasts
Icebergs
Indian Ocean
Marine biology
Marine fauna
Meteorology, Maritime
Oceanography
Pacific Ocean
Sea water
Territorial waters
Tide power
Waves

Economic aspects

See Marine resources
OCEAN-atmosphere interaction
Carbon dioxide question. G. M. Woodwell. il map Sci Am 238:34-43 Ja '78
OCEAN birds. See Sea birds
OCEAN bottom
Expedition FAMOUS. X. Le Pichon. il UNESCO Courier 30:30-2 Ja '77
Research dives probe the Galapagos Rift. Sci N 111:182 Mr 19 '77
See also
Benthos
Continental shelf
Marine sediments
Seamounts
Submarine geology
Submarine valleys

International aspects

See also
Seabed Treaty, 1972
OCEAN County Library, Toms River, N.J. See Libraries—New Jersey
OCEAN currents
Biological consequences of the 1975 El Niño. T. J. Cowles and others. bibl il maps Science 195:285-7 Ja 21 '77
Calculator current predictions; tidal current. E. S. Maloney. il Motor B & S 140:14+ O '77
California current eddy formation: ship, air, and satellite results. R. L. Bernstein and others. bibl il maps Science 195:353-9 Ja 28 '77
Deep western boundary current in the eastern Indian Ocean. B. A. Warren. bibl map Science 196:53-4 Ap 1 '77
Determining the general circulation of the oceans: a preliminary discussion. C. Wunsch. bibl il map Science 196:871-5 My 20 '77
Ocean surface currents mapped by radar. D. E. Barrick and others. bibl il Science 198:138-44 O 14 '77
Somali Current: recent measurements during the southwest monsoon. J. G. Bruce. bibl maps Science 197:51-3 Jl 1 '77
Winter intrusions of the Loop Current. R. L. Molinari and others. bibl il maps Science 198:505-7 N 4 '77
See also
Gulf Stream

Measurement

Hidden dynamos of Neptune's powerhouse; work of the POLYGON and MODE expeditions. K. N. Fedorov. il UNESCO Courier 30:24-7 Ja '77
OCEAN energy resources. See Marine resources
OCEAN farming. See Aquaculture
OCEAN fishing. See Salt water fishing
OCEAN in art
See also
Marine painting
OCEAN life. See Marine biology
OCEAN lifesaving. See Rescue work
OCEAN liners
Cruising the Caribbean. T. B. Lesure. il Trav/Holiday 148:44-51 N '77
5½-day mini cruise; a crossing on the QE2. D. Butwin. il House & Gard 149:110+ O '77
Saving the Queen; Queen Mary. E. Keerdoja and D. Gram. il Newsweek 91:7 Ja 9 '78
Ship that hunted itself; naval battle fought between liners Carmania and Cap Trafalgar during First World War. C. Simpson. il pors map Read Digest 111:188-92+ S '77
Top decks. S. Birnbaum. il Esquire 88:147-51 D '77

Food service

Cuisine for a queen; Queen Elizabeth 2. J. Villas. il Holiday 58:46-9+ Je '77

Launching

Smashing; christening of the Cunard Princess by Princess Grace of Monaco. New Yorker 53:28-9 Ap 11 '77
OCEAN mining
Administration gives views on proposed legislation on deep seabed mining; statement, April 27, 1977. E. L. Richardson. Dept State Bull 76:524-7 My 23 '77
Congress is itching to start ocean mining. il Bus W p29-30 Jl 11 '77
International struggle for a law of the sea. R. Hudson. il Bull Atom Sci 33:14-20 D '77
Law of the sea: rethinking U.S. interests. R. G. Darman. bibl f For Affairs 56:373-95 Ja '78
Legal order for the oceans. A. W. Smith. Nat Parks & Con Mag 51:2+ F '77
Mining the wealth of the ocean deep. W. Wertenbaker. il N Y Times Mag p 14-16+ Jl 17 '77
Ocean mining: former negotiator now lobbies for Kennecott. D. Shapley. Science 196:964-5 My 27 '77
Review of the Law of the Sea Conference and deep seabed mining legislation; statement, October 4, 1977. E. L. Richardson. Dept State Bull 77:751-6 N 21 '77
Sixth session of Law of Sea Conference might prove decisive, says Mr Zuleta; summary of address, March 28, 1977. B. Zuleta. por UN Chron 14:37-8+ My '77
OCEAN pollution. See Marine pollution
OCEAN resources. See Marine resources
OCEAN sounds
Voices of the surf; excerpts from The outermost house. H. Beston. il Read Digest 111:45-8 D '77
OCEAN temperature
Effects of the winter of 1976-1977 on the northwestern Sargasso sea. A. Leetmaa. bibl il Science 198:188-9 O 14 '77
Ocean thermal gradients—a practical source of energy? J. O. Henrie; E. J. Beck. bibl Science 195:206-7 Ja 14 '77

Measurement

See Thermometers and thermometry

OCEAN Thermal Energy Conversion Program. See United States—Energy Research and Development Administration—Ocean Thermal Energy Conversion Program

OCEAN travel
See also
Cruising
Ocean liners
Voyages
Voyages around the world

OCEAN trenches. See Submarine valleys

OCEAN waves. See Waves

OCEANIA

Description and travel

Travel: the South Pacific. L. Janos. il Sat Eve Post 249:111-18+ D '77

Native races

Cargo cults of the South Pacific; with introd by N. B. Stone. T. Merton. il America 137:94-9 Ag 27 '77

OCEANIC basalt. See Basalt

OCEANOGRAPHIC instruments
Deep ocean sampler. N. Smith. il Pop Sci 210:68 Mr '77
New device retrieves and houses deep-sea organisms. il BioScience 27:300 Ap '77

OCEANOGRAPHIC research
Expedition FAMOUS. X. Le Pichon. il UNESCO Courier 30:30-2 Ja '77
Hidden dynamos of Neptune's powerhouse; work of the POLYGON and MODE expeditions. K. N. Fedorov. il UNESCO Courier 30:24-7 Ja '77
Marine scientific research issue in the law of the sea negotiations. map Science 197:230-3 Jl 15 '77
Oases of life in the cold abyss; deep sea exploration of Galapagos Rift, west of Ecuador. J. B. Corliss and R. D. Ballard. il por map Nat Geog 152:440-53 O '77
Oceanography: geochemical tracers offer new insight. A. L. Hammond. il Science 195:164-6 Ja 14 '77
See also
Antarctic research
Artificial satellites—Oceanographic use
California. University—Scripps Institution of Oceanography
Underwater drilling
United States—Naval Research, Office of

OCEANOGRAPHIC submersibles
Alvin: window in the deep. K. J. Sulak. il Sea Front 23:113-19 Mr '77
Helgoland diary: sixteen days under the North Atlantic. L. Barr. il Oceans 10:16-21 Ja '77

OCEANOGRAPHY
Oceanography and the law of the sea. M. Ruivo. il UNESCO Courier 30:10-13 Ja '77
See also
Intergovernmental Oceanographic Commission
International Ocean Institute
Marine microbiology
Marine resources
Ocean-atmosphere interaction
Oceanographic research
Radar in oceanography
Tides

Bibliography

Bookshelf. See issues of Oceans
Science of the sea in books. Sea Front 23:120-1+ Mr '77

Conferences

New wave in oceanography. D. Behrman. il UNESCO Courier 30:16-17+ Ja '77

Exhibitions

Planet Ocean. J. M. Pereira. il Sci Digest 82:33-6 N '77

International aspects

U.S-France Cooperative Program in Oceanography. Dept State Bull 77:857-8 D 12 '77

OCEANS and International Environmental and Scientific Affairs, Bureau of. See United States—Oceans and International Environmental and Scientific Affairs, Bureau of

OCHRONOSIS. See Metabolism, Disorders of

OCHSNER, Jeffrey K. and others
Elevator space requirements in high-rise buildings. il Archit Rec 162:117-18 Jl '77

OCKENGA, Harold John
Interview on relocation. Chr Today 21:35 Mr 18 '77

O'CONNELL, Jeffrey
Business and the products liability crisis; address, October 27, 1976. Vital Speeches 43:278-80 F 15 '77
Yes or no for no-fault insurance. il America 137:261-5 O 22 '77

O'CONNELL, Kevin
Avoiding the reel winch hazard. il Motor B & S 141:116-17+ Ja '78

O'CONNOR, Barry, and others
Ectoparasitic mites on rodents: application of the island biogeography theory? reply. bibl Science 195:598 F 11 '77

O'CONNOR, David, and O'Connor, Premla
Young girl called Kumari: Nepal's current living goddess. il Ms 5:30 Mr '77

O'CONNOR, F. X. Jr
Enduring fragility. il Sat Eve Post 249:46-9 My '77

O'CONNOR, Flannery
Comic genius of Flannery O'Connor. M. True. America 137:167-9 S 24 '77 •

O'CONNOR, Marita
Splitting a one-bedroom apartment two ways. il pors Mademoiselle 83:204-5+ S '77 •

O'CONNOR, Premla. See O'Connor, D. jt auth

O'CONNOR, Thomas H.
History (cont) America 136:425-6 My 7 '77

O'CONNOR, Ulick
Pitch for the disabled. il por Sat Eve Post 249:14 O '77

O'CONNOR, William F.
Girl to marry; story. il Good H 184:106-7 Mr '77
Season of magic; story. Good H 185:146-7 O '77

OCTAGONAL houses. See Houses, Octagonal

OCTANE rating. See Gasoline—Anti-knock and anti-knock mixtures

OCTOBER
Ode to October. P. Meares. il Am For 83:42-4 O '77

OCTOPUSES
Hormonal inhibition of feeding and death in octopus: control by optic gland secretion. J. Wodinsky. bibl il Science 198:948-51 D 2 '77
Octopus's life; aging process impeded by optic gland removal. il Newsweek 90:81 D 12 '77

OCULAR dominance. See Dominance, Ocular

OCULOMETERS. See Eye, Instruments and apparatus for

ODDO, Sandra
For people who want to live in glass houses. il House & Gard 150:36+ Ja '78
Going places, finding things in Canada. il House & Gard 149:74+ Je '77
New York state wine. map House & Gard 149:184+ My '77
Solar energy and you. il House & Gard 149:76-7 Ag '77

O'DEA, Robert F. See Zatz, M. jt auth

O'DELL, John
Gun in a tree; story. il Field & S 81:56 Ap '77

ODELL, Peter
Nader of North Sea oil. por Forbes 120:81 D 15 '77 *

ODEN, Gloria C.
Bonsai. por Negro Hist Bull 40:716-17 Jl '77

ODMARK, Marion
Two older adult generations under one roof. il Ret Liv 17:27-8 Ja '77

ODOM, Bruce
Some are more equal. Nat R 29:1114-15 S 30 '77

ODOM, Selma I.
National Ballet of Canada: two views from the present. il Dance Mag 51:60-3 Mr '77
Spotlight on: Veronica Tennant. il por Dance Mag 51:68-70 Mr '77

ODOMIROK, Marion
(ed) International scene. il pors Pub W 212:85-114 S 19 '77

O'DONNELL, Holly
ERIC/RCS report. bibl Engl J 66:94-6 F '77

O'DONNELL, John J. (priest)
Power of the Spirit. America 137:53-5 Jl 30 '77

O'DONNELL, L. A.
Should we repeal 14B? America 136:354-5 Ap 16 '77

O'DONNELL, Laurence
Torch passes. por Forbes 120:82 D 15 '77 •

O'DONNELL, Sean
Rockall—the smallest British Isle. il map Sea Front 23:342-9 N '77

O'DONNELL, Walter E.
How to increase your inner energy. Read Digest 110:84-6 Mr '77

O'DONNELL, William T.
Bally: betting bit on gambling's future. por Duns R 109:19+ F '77 •
Jackpot for Bally? T. O'Hanlon. il Forbes 119:57-61 Ja 15 '77 •

O'DONOVAN, Bonnie
From the people who brought you full employment. il Motor B & S 139:81-3+ Je '77
Fun boats. il Motor B & S 139:84-7+ My '77
Remembrance of things past. il Motor B & S 140:70-2+ Jl '77

ODORS
Olfactory synchrony of menstrual cycles. Sci N 112:5 Jl 2 '77
Plants for night people; odoriferous flowering plants. R. Langer. il House & Gard 149:42+ S '77
Winter smells, winter dreams. J. Taylor. il Conservationist 32:48 N '77
See also
Perfumes
Pheromones

ODUBER QUIRÓS, Daniel
Costa Rica imbroglio. K. Bode. New Repub 176:12-16 My 28 '77 •

ODUM, Anker
Canadian sketchbook. il Int Wildlife 7:42-3 Mr '77
International sketchbook (cont) il Int Wildlife 7:18-19 My; 18-19 Jl; 22-3 N '77; 8:18-19 Ja '78

ODUM, Eugene P.
Emergence of ecology as a new integrative discipline. bibl Science 195:1289-93 Mr 25 '77
Odum urges: speed up worldwide data gathering now; interview, ed by E. M. Leeper. por BioScience 27:755-8 N '77

about
Odum: ecology's highest award. por Sci N 111: 263 Ap 23 '77 *

OEDIPUS; drama. See Seneca, L. A.

OERTER, Al
His past is slipping into the future. W. Bingham. pors Sports Illus 46:56+ Ap 25 '77 *

OERTLE, V. Lee
Elk hunting today—a comparison of 11 states. Outdoor Life 160:85+ Ag '77
Full-time RV living. il Outdoor Life 160:158+ N '77
Mule deer are where you find them. il map Outdoor Life 160:76-9+ Jl '77

OESTERREICHER, John M.
Challenge of the Holocaust. America 136:525-7 Je 11 '77
Covenant of Israel: old, new and one. il America 137:282-3 O 29 '77

OETTINGER, Elizabeth
Emily Post. por Am Heritage 28:38-9 Ap '77

OFF, Louis B.
Rebirth of Bambino. il Yachting 141:176+ Ap '77

OFF-road recreational vehicles. See Recreational vehicles

OFFENBACH, Jacques
Orphée aux enfers. Reviews
New Yorker 53:92-4 Je 27 '77 *
Tales of Hoffmann (Les contes d'Hoffmann) Reviews
Hi Fi 27:MA28 Mr '77 *

OFFENSES against property
See also
Stolen goods, Receiving of

OFFENSES against the person
See also
Rape

OFFERING; drama. See Edwards, G.

OFFERMAN, Sister Mary Columba
School librarian recommends free magazines. Am Lib 8:89 F '77

OFFICE building industry. See Construction industry

OFFICE buildings
American Express Operations Center. il Archit Rec 162:93-6 N '77
Commercial office buildings continue to rise in major downtown areas. il Archit Rec 162:34-5 Jl '77
Corporate slick; mirror glass architectural design. R. Jensen. il Horizon 20:70-3 N '77
Johns-Manville world headquarters buildings—a winner for J-M and TAC. M. F. Schmertz. il Archit Rec 162:89-100 S '77
Low profile for IBM; with introd by M. F. Schmertz. il Archit Rec 161:141-6 Ja '77
What's a high-style design firm like Gwathmey-Siegel doing designing speculative office buildings along freeways and in office campuses? W. F. Wagner, Jr. il Archit Rec 162: 108-15 D '77
See also
County buildings
Dayton, Ohio—Buildings
New York (city)—Buildings
San Francisco—Buildings

Fires and fire prevention

See also
Skyscrapers—Fires and fire prevention

Leasing and renting

See Offices—Leasing and renting

Location

See Location in business and industry

OFFICE buildings, Converted. See Apartment houses, Remodeled

OFFICE decoration
Make your office look successful. B. Howell. il Harp Baz 110:98-9+ Mr '77

OFFICE equipment and supplies
Office at home. il Consumers Res Mag 60:169-77 O '77
Product reports 78. il Archit Rec 162:17-19 mid-O '77
See also
Dictating machines
Word processing equipment

OFFICE equipment industry
David (Savin) vs. Goliath (Xerox): chalk one up for David; Savin Business Machines Corp. il Forbes 120:38+ S 1 '77
Lively old fox; Cummins-Allison. por Forbes 120:154 O 15 '77
See also
Addressograph Multigraph Corporation
International Business Machines Corporation

Finance

Information processing. il Forbes 121:110+ Ja 9 '78

Securities

High and low; status of Savin Business Machines Corp's and Nashua Corp's relationship with Ricoh Company. Time 110:61 O 17 '77

Japan

High and low; status of Savin Business Machines Corp's and Nashua Corp's relationship with Ricoh Company. Time 110:61 O 17 '77

OFFICE for the Gifted and Talented. See United States—Education, Office of—Gifted and Talented, Office for the

OFFICE furniture
Product reports 78. il Archit Rec 162:127-35 mid-O '77

OFFICE furniture industry
Systems concept buoys office furniture. il Bus W p48 F 21 '77

OFFICE machines. See Office equipment and supplies

OFFICE management
Shuffling too much paper? Here's how to reduce it; interview. L. Grossman. por U.S. News 82:53 Ap 18 '77
See also
United States—Commission on Federal Paperwork

OFFICE of Education. See United States—Education, Office of

OFFICE of the Special Representative for Trade Negotiations. See United States—Special Representative for Trade Negotiations, Office of the

OFFICE supplies. See Office equipment and supplies

OFFICE workers
See also
Secretaries

OFFICER, Charles B. and Ryther, J. H.
Secondary sewage treatment versus ocean outfalls: an assessment. bibl il Science 197:1056-60 S 9 '77

OFFICERS, Military. See Israel—Armed Forces—Officers

OFFICERS Training Corps. See United States—Reserve Officers Training Corps

OFFICES
Business begins at home. C. Jessup and G. Chipps. Am Home 80:63+ S '77
$50 writer's office. P. McConnel. il Writers Digest 57:25 Ap '77
Home and office: bridging the gap; Milan apartment of G. Aulenti. R. Reif. il por N Y Times Mag p64-5 F 13 '77
Home offices that work. il Am Home 80:60-2 S '77
Stolen spaces; home offices. B. Niles. il Am Home 80:60 My '77

Leasing and renting

Not lively; but less dead; office building rental in New York City. H. Seneker. il Forbes 119: 21-2 F 15 '77
Those empty offices begin to fill up again. il Bus W p22 Mr 28 '77

Lighting

Most subtle layering of architecture and light. il Archit Rec 161:131-6 F '77
There's a saving grace in the new office lighting. W. McQuade. il Fortune 96:151-4 D '77

OFFICIAL entertaining. See Government entertaining

OFFICIAL secrets
Can anyone keep a secret? disclosing CIA payments to King Hussein. D. M. Alpern and others. Newsweek 89:16 Mr 7 '77
See also
Government and the press
Security classification (government documents)

Anecdotes, facetiae, satire, etc.

Secret passion. R. Baker. il N Y Times Mag p8 Ag 21 '77

OFFICIALS and employees, International. See International officials and employees

OFFIT, Avodah K.
How your job can affect your sex life; interview. Harp Baz 110:89+ Ag '77

OFFSHORE boundaries. See Territorial waters

OFFSHORE gas well rigs. See Gas well drilling rigs

OFFSHORE nuclear power plants. See Atomic power plants

OFFSHORE oil fields. See Petroleum in submerged lands

OFFSHORE oil well drilling. See Oil well drilling, Submarine

OFFSHORE oil well rigs. See Oil well drilling rigs

OFFSHORE oil wells. See Oil wells, Submarine

OFFSHORE petroleum shipping terminals. See Petroleum shipping terminals

OFFSHORE power boat racing. See Motor boat racing

OIL pollution of the sea—Laws and legislation—
—Continued
President announces measures to control marine oil pollution; message to Congress, March 17 1977. J. Carter. Dept State Bull 76:422-3 Ap 25 '77
Shipwrecks, pollution & the law of the sea. R. J. McManus and J. Schneider. Nat Parks & Con Mag 51:10-15 Je '77

Atlantic Ocean

Argo's legacy: batch of oily pancakes. il Sci N 111:230 Ap 9 '77
Beware of Greeks bearing oil; tanker Argo Merchant. G. Reiger. Audubon 79:141-6 Mr '77
NASA monitoring helps NOAA in tracking oil spill in Atlantic. Aviation W 106:21 Ja 10 '77
They're murdering our oceans; tanker Argo Merchant. R. Starnes. il Outdoor Life 159:10+ My '77
Tragedy off Nantucket: sinking of the Argo Merchant. J. Hearst, Jr. il Motor B & S 139:30+ Mr '77

Buzzards Bay

Aftermath of an oil spill: a black seven years; effects of Buzzards Bay oil slick on fiddler crab population. il Sci N 112:84 Ag 6 '77

Chesapeake Bay

Just another oil spill; Chesapeake Bay. R. Reiger. Audubon 79:144-8 Ja '77

North Sea

Blowout at Bravo. E. Keerdoja. Newsweek 91:7 Ja 9 '78
Ordeal by oil. il Time 109:54-5 My 9 '77
Setback for offshore drilling. map U.S. News 82:33 My 9 '77
Taming Bravo 14. K. Willenson and J. Friedman. il Newsweek 89:47+ My 9 '77

OIL ports. See Petroleum shipping terminals
OIL refineries. See Petroleum refineries
OIL reserves. See Petroleum—Reserves
OIL sands
How they're extracting oil from tar sands. C. E. Maurer. il Pop Sci 210:80-3+ My '77
Tar sands hold potential for a new oil source; Extraction getting underway in Canada. Sci Digest 82:63 O '77
OIL shale industry
Shale-oil economics look more promising; western Colorado. il Bus W p39-40 S 19 '77
OIL shales
Oil shale: prospects on the upswing... again. T. H. Maugh, 2d. il Science 198:1023-7 D 9 '77
Whatever happened to the oil from shale? L. D. Meyers. il Mech Illus 73:154-5 N '77
See also
Oil shale industry
OIL spills. See Oil pollution of rivers, harbors, etc; Oil pollution of the sea
OIL supply. See Petroleum supply
OIL swindles. See Fraud
OIL tankers. See Tank ships
OIL well drilling
From coast to coast, an all-out race to find more oil. il U.S. News 82:30+ My 16 '77
No rush. E. Marshall. New Repub 177:13-14 Ag 20 '77
See also
Petroleum—Prospecting

Equipment and supplies

Equipment thefts start to drain oil drillers. il Bus W p23-4 Ja 9 '78
See also
Oil well drilling rigs
OIL well drilling, Submarine
Drilling for offshore oil. U.S. News 83:66 S 26 '77
See also
Petroleum in submerged lands
OIL well drilling rigs
No oil or booze anywhere in sight. il Forbes 119:86 Mr 15 '77
Oil drillers run out of rigs. il Bus W p30 Ap 4 '77

Manufacture

See Petroleum equipment industry
OIL well engineers. See Petroleum engineers
OIL wells, Submarine
Blowout at Bravo. E. Keerdoja. Newsweek 91:7 Ja 9 '78
Ordeal by oil; North Sea blowout. il Time 109:54-5 My 9 '77
Setback for offshore drilling; North Sea disaster. map U.S. News 82:33 My 9 '77
Taming Bravo 14; North Sea well. K. Willenson and J. Friedman. il Newsweek 89:47+ My 9 '77

OILS and fats
Jojoba. Audubon 79:150-1 My '77
Sperm whale oil and the jojoba shrub. R. Scogin. il Oceans 10:65-6 Jl '77
Whale and the wild jojoba. il Sea Front 23:267-72 S '77
OILS and fats, Edible
See also
Food—Fat content
OILSEED plants
See also
Jojoba
OJA, Carol J.
Still-life paintings of William Michael Harnett; their reflections upon nineteenth-century American musical culture. bibl f il Mus Q 63:505-23 O '77
O'JAYS (rock group) See Rock groups
OKADA, T. See Möhler, H. jt auth
OKANAGAN Helicopters Ltd
Okanagan shuttles miners in helicopter operation. R. G. O'Lone. Aviation W 107:25-6 Ag 15 '77
OKAZAKI, Kayo. See Inoué, S. jt auth
O'KEEFE, John D. and Ahrens, T. J.
Meteorite impact ejecta: dependence of mass and energy lost on planetary escape velocity. bibl il Science 198:1249-51 D 23 '77
O'KEEFE, M. Timothy
Underwater, try macro. il Pop Phot 81:90-1+ Ag '77
O'KEEFFE, Georgia
Georgia O'Keeffe at 90; interview, ed by M. L. Kotz. il pors Art N 76:36-45 D '77

about

Art of being O'Keeffe. il pors N Y Times Mag p44-5 N 13 '77 *
Georgia O'Keeffe; excerpt from The art world; ed by B. Diamonstein. il Art N 76:168+ N '77 *
Happy birthday, Georgia O'Keeffe. por Vogue 167:144 N '77 *
Under a western sky. A. Wallach. il pors Horizon 20:24-31 D '77 *
OKIES. See Migrant labor
OKLAHOMA
Dying in Oklahoma. R. Morris. New Repub 177:8-9 Jl 23 '77
See also
Hospitals—Oklahoma
Libraries—Oklahoma
Organic gardening—Oklahoma

Social history

Meadowlark sang; memories of an Oklahoma childhood. L. W. Bartley and S. J. Wolfe. il Am West 14:34-7 Mr '77
OKLAHOMA City. South Oklahoma City Junior College
OASES in Oklahoma; Open Access Satellite Education Services, a joint project of the Oklahoma County Libraries System and the South Oklahoma City Junior College. P. L. Little and J. R. Gilliland. pors Lib J 102:1458-61 Jl '77
OKLAHOMA County Libraries System, Oklahoma City. See Libraries—Oklahoma
OKRA
For a pleasant surprise, try okra. N. P. Farris. Org Gard & Farm 24:170+ F '77
OKUN, Arthur M.
Blueprint for a sound economy: an expert's advice to Carter; interview. il por U.S. News 82:51-3 Ja 24 '77
Debate: how to stop inflation. pors Fortune 95:116-20 Ap '77
Great stagflation swamp; address, October 6, 1977. Vital Speeches 44:120-5 D 1 '77

about

Jimmy in Wonderland. New Repub 178:2+ Ja 7 '78 *
OLANO, Mila, and Echevarri, Javier
Coarrangement of kingfishers. il Natur Hist 86:58-63 F '77
OLD, Lloyd J.
Cancer immunology; with biographical sketch. il Sci Am 236:15, 62-70+ bibl(p 146) My '77
OLD age
Battle against senility. T. L. Brink. il MH 61:10-11 Summ '77
Dealing with old age. D. H. Fischer. Current 194:45-8 Jl '77
My crabbed age. F. Baldwin. Read Digest 110:31-2 My '77
No telling how old is old. Time 110:28 O 10 '77
Portrait of the artist as an old man. L. Edel. Am Scholar 47:52-68 Wint '77
Senility? It's more likely depression, says psychiatrist. Ret Liv 17:15 Mr '77
See also
Aged
Aging
Centenarians
Retirement

Psychological aspects

See Aged—Psychology

OLD age and nutrition. See Aged—Nutrition
OLD age assistance
AoA funds major study of federal outlays for the elderly. Aging 270:4-5 Ap '77
How well do seniors eat? Title VII can help. R. M. Dow. Aging 274:12-14 Ag '77
Kosher meals a specialty at New York Luncheon Club; Brighton Older Adult Luncheon Club Title VII project. L. Feldman. il Aging 274:6-8 Ag '77
Look what states are doing for older folks. il Changing T 31:27-30 Jl '77
National network on aging provides disaster assistance to the nation's elderly. il Aging 270: 17-21 Ap '77
News of federal agencies. See issues of Aging
News of state and area agencies. See issues of Aging
President-elect warned: remember promises to seniors or catch the devil from momma. il Ret Liv 17:11-12 Ja '77
Senate committee reports a better-than-expected year for legislation aiding older Americans. Ret Liv 17:13-14 F '77
Washington memo. R. D. Westgate. See issues of Retirement living
See also
United States—Aging, Administration on
OLD age homes
See also
Nursing homes
OLD age in childrens literature. See Childrens literature—Themes
OLD age stereotypes. See Stereotype (psychology)
OLD Colony Building. See Chicago—Buildings
OLD country; drama. See Bennett, A.
OLD people. See Aged
OLD SALEM, N.C. See Winston-Salem, N.C.
OLD Testament. See Bible—Old Testament
OLD-time melodrama—modern style; drama. See Majeski, B.
OLDAK, Elliott B.
Condition report. il Motor B & S 139:68-9+ Mr '77
OLDENBURG, Claes
Chimney stack, upside-down; Batcolumn. il Horizon 19:71 My '77 *
Fair game. A. G. Artner. il Art N 76:158 Summ '77 *
Profiles. C. Tomkins. New Yorker 53:55-6+ D 12 '77 *
Public art's big hit: Oldenburg bats high in Chicago. B. Rose. il por Vogue 167:118-19+ Jl '77 *
OLDER, Julia
Bagged or braided, onions winter well. il Org Gard & Farm 24:126-7 Ag '77
Green bean bargain. il Org Gard & Farm 24: 67-8 Jl '77
OLDER Americans Month. See Special days, weeks, and months
OLDFIELD, Barney
Barney Oldfield. R. F. Snow. il por Am Heritage 28:66-7 F '77
OLDHAM, William G.
Fabrication of microelectronic circuits; with biographical sketch. il Sci Am 237:14, 110-14+ bibl(p258) S '77
OLDS, Sally Wendkos
How to live with a difficult man. il Ladies Home J 94:58+ Ap '77
How to survive a heart attack. il Fam Health 9:34-7 Ja '77
Is divorce contagious? Ladies Home J 94:81+ F '77
Is his money your money too? il Redbook 149: 120+ S '77
My belly button surgery. Fam Health 9:49-51 Ap '77
When mommy goes to work. . . il Fam Health 9:38-40 F '77
Write a query—get an assignment! Writer 90:15-19 Ag '77
OLDS, Sharon
Feared drowned; poem. Am Scholar 46:350 Summ '77
Love fossil; poem. Ms 5:65 Je '77
O'LEARY, Brian T.
Mining the Apollo and Amor asteroids. bibl il Science 197:363-6 Jl 22 '77
Project Columbus 1992. Bull Atom Sci 33:4-5 Mr '77
OLEKSY, Walter
Riding the U.S./Mexico borderland. il map Ret Liv 17:33-6+ Mr '77
OLENZAK, Karen Romnes
We banished the unhappy hour. il por Redbook 148:49+ Ap '77
OLFACTORY sense. See Smell
OLFSON, Lewy
Adventures of Tom Sawyer; dramatization of novel by S. L. Clemens. Plays 36:74-9 Ap '77
Meet Miss Stone-age! drama. Plays 36:71-5 My '77
Taming of the shrew; adaptation of play by W. Shakespeare. Plays 36:83-95 F '77
OLINKRAFT, Inc. See Paper industry
OLIVE processing industry. See Food industry
OLIVER, Bernard M.
Role of microelectronics in instrumentation and control; with biographical sketch. il Sci Am 237:19, 180-1+ bibl(p260) S '77
OLIVER, Daniel
Constitutional nonsense. Nat R 29:1493 D 23 '77
Local law 5. Nat R 29:387+, 717 Ap 1, Je 24 '77
OLIVER, David J. and Zelitch, Israel
Increasing photosynthesis by inhibiting photorespiration with glyoxylate. bibl il Science 196:1450-1 Je 24 '77
OLIVER, Diane E.
Mosaic mural. il Sch Arts 76:33 Je '77
OLIVER, Edith
Off Broadway. See occasional issues of New Yorker
OLIVER, John S. See Dayton, P. K. jt auth
OLIVER, King Joe
Jazz. W. Balliett. New Yorker 53:94-8+ Ap 25 '77 *
OLIVER, Mary
Lamps; poem. Am Scholar 46:192 Spr '77
Meat; poem. Commonweal 104:455 Jl 22 '77
Mussels; poem. Atlantic 240:83 O '77
You know how it feels; poem. Commonweal 104: 710 N 11 '77
OLIVER, Richard B. See Moore, C. W. jt auth
OLIVERA, Hector
Once in a lifetime. W. F. Rickenbacker. Nat R 29:897-8 Ag 5 '77 *
OLIVERO, Magda
Artist life; interview, ed by D. J. Soria. por Hi Fi 27:MA6-7 N '77
about
One of a kind. J. Ardoin. il por Opera N 42: 18-23 D 3 '77 *
OLIVIA Records (firm) See Women in the record industry
OLIVIER Theatre. See National Theatre (Great Britain)
OLIVINE
Shock-produced olivine glass: first observation. R. Jeanloz and others. bibl il Science 197:457-9 Jl 29 '77
OLIVOMYCIN. See Antibiotics
OLKOWSKI, Helga, and Olkowski, William
Easy plan for making hot compost. il Horticulture 55:46-8 Mr '77
Gardening without land. il Horticulture 55:34-6 F '77
OLKOWSKI, William. See Olkowski, H. jt auth
OLMEC antiquities. See Mexico—Antiquities
OLMERT, Michael
It's hard enough to say it, let alone to remember it. Smithsonian 8:172 O '77
Pope's library is brought to light after 200 years. il Smithsonian 8:70-7 Ja '78
—See Kass, P. jt auth
OLMSTED, Frederick Law, 1822-1903
Designs and documents. J. H. Kay. Sat R 4:27 My 14 '77 *
OLMSTED, Nancy. See Olmsted, R. jt auth
OLMSTED, Roger, and Olmsted, Nancy
Death and rebirth of a city: San Francisco, 1906. il Am West 14:10-25 Ja '77
OLSEN, John W. See Olsen, S. J. jt auth
OLSEN, Mimi Vang
Art of family living. L. C. Pogrebin. il Ms 5: 15-16+ Je '77 *
OLSEN, Paul E. and Galton, P. M.
Triassic-Jurassic tetrapod extinctions: are they real? bibl il Science 197:983-5 S 2 '77
OLSEN, Stanley J. and Olsen, J. W.
Chinese wolf, ancestor of new world dogs. bibl il Science 197:533-5 Ag 5 '77
OLSEN, Turee
ERIC/RCS report. bibl Engl J 66:88-91 Ap '77
OLSON, Carol
Three young clergywomen: how they're changing their churches. J. T. Freeman. il Redbook 149:24+ Je '77 *
OLSON, Donald W.
Non-responsive students? Check the classroom communication channels. Clearing H 51:160-2 D '77
OLSON, Lloyd, and others
Osceola teacher education center. Todays Educ 66:75-6+ Mr '77
OLSON, McKinley C.
Caution: smoke detectors may be dangerous to your health. Progressive 41:22-5 Ag '77
OLSON, Mark
Preparing for Transpac. Yachting 142:36+ Jl '77
OLSON, Roberta J. M.
Brave New Museum. Art in Am 65:25+ N '77
OLSON, Victoria Thomas
Pioneer conservationist A. P. Hill: he saved the redwoods. il pors Am West 14:32-40 S '77
OLSTEIN, Robert A.
Analysts who don't ignore bad news. J. Madrick. pors Bus W p81 Je 6 '77 *
OLTMANS, Willem
Assassination: now a suicide talks. il por Time 109:20 Ap 11 '77 *

OLTON, David S.
Spatial memory; with biographical sketch. il Sci Am 236:18, 82-4+ bibl (p 142) Je '77
OLTON, Richard C.
Slotted drains cut street ponding. il Am City & County 92:56 Ap '77
OLYMPIA Brewing Company. See Brewing industry
OLYMPIC Games
Big red machine. Y. Brokhin. il N Y Times Mag p22-4+ My 29 '77
It's a site for sore eyes; Squaw Valley as Olympic training site. A. Verschoth. il Sports Illus 47:46-7 Ag 22 '77
See also
International Olympic Committee
United States—President's Commission on Olympic Sports
OLYMPIC Games, 1976
Weather forecasting for the racing sailor; Olympic Trials, 1976. R. L. Mairs. il map Yachting 142:66-9+ Ag '77
OLYMPIC Games, 1980
Contract with the Kremlin; rights to televise Moscow Olympics. W. O. Johnson. il Sports Illus 46:14-19 F 21 '77
NBC as a Soviet megaphone; NBC coverage of 1980 Olympics. J. Hart. il Sat Eve Post 249:31 O '77
NBC: Kremlin megaphone. J. Burnham. Nat R 29:257 Mr 4 '77
NBC's Moscow connection. Nat R 29:483 Ap 29 '77
Olympic development clinics. J. Rousmaniere. il Yachting 50+ O '77
Olympics send Russians off on a profit-making spree. il U.S. News 83:55 D 5 '77
Pyrrhic victory? awarding TV rights to the Moscow Olympics to NBC. M. A. Kellogg and others. il Newsweek 89:98 F 14 '77
OLYMPIC Games, 1984
Found: a place in the sun; Los Angeles as Olympics site. W. O. Johnson. il Sports Illus 77:64+ N 7 '77
Anecdotes, facetiae, satire, etc.
On to the Manhathalon. A. R. Barber. N Y Times Mag p4 S 4 '77
OLYMPIC National Park
Walking beach in wild Washington. il map Sunset 158:76+ My '77
OLYMPIC Tower. See New York (city)—Buildings
OMAHA
Music
See also
Opera—Nebraska
O'MAHONY, T. P.
Letter from Belfast: post-Elizabethan blues. America 137:147-8 S 17 '77
New Archbishop for Armagh. America 137:235-6 O 15 '77
Requiem for a Cardinal. America 136:445-6 My 14 '77
OMANN, Geneva, and Lakowicz, J. R.
Pesticide uptake into membranes measured by fluorescence quenching. bibl il Science 197:465-7 Jl 29 '77
O'MARA, Richard
Juntas of Chile and Argentina: studies in government by terror. por Sat R 4:13-16 Ap 2 '77
OMEGA system (navigation) See Radio in navigation
OMELETS
Basque omelet sandwiches. il Sunset 159:114 Jl '77
Omelets and soufflés. il Bet Hom Gard 55:161-2 S '77
Vietnamese pork and shrimp omelet. Sunset 158:190 Je '77
OMNIMEDICAL Services Inc. See Hospitals—Diagnostic services
ON the lock-in; musical comedy. See Musical comedy, revue etc.—Reviews—Single works
ONASSIS, Aristotle Socrates
Jackie and Ari; excerpt from Onassis, an extravagant life. F. Brady. il pors Sat Eve Post 249:30+ D '77 *
ONASSIS, Christina
How Christina's doing. il por Time 110:69 Ag 8 '77 *
ONASSIS, Jacqueline Lee (Bouvier) Kennedy
(ed) See Vreeland, D. Vanity fair
about
Jackie and Ari; excerpt from Onassis, an extravagant life. F. Brady. il pors Sat Eve Post 249:30+ D '77 *
Mrs Onassis leaves Viking over assassination novel. M. Reuter. Pub W 212:36 O 24 '77 *
Tale of two Jackies. il pors Ladies Home J 94:28 O '77 *
ONCORNAVIRUSES. See Tumor viruses
ONDETTI, Miguel A. and others
Design of specific inhibitors of angiotensin-converting enzyme: new class of orally active antihypertensive agents. bibl il Science 196:441-4 Ap 22 '77

ONE eye, two eyes and three eyes; dramatization. See Lavin, R. C.
ONE-of-a-kind regatta. See Sailboat racing
ONE-room apartments. See Apartments
O'NEAL, Arthur Daniel, 1936-
Get moving! por Forbes 120:97 Jl 1 '77 *
O'NEAL, Tatum
Tatum on location. G. Clarke. il por Time 110:94+ O 31 '77 *
Tatum O'Neal: a child once again. R. D. Le Blanc. por Good H 184:56+ Je '77 *
O'NEIL, Bill
Helping your community as a police volunteer. il Ret Liv 17:23+ Ag '77
O'NEIL, Kitty
Fastest woman on earth. P. Bowie. il pors Sat Eve Post 249:42-3+ Mr '77 *
Rocket ride to glory and gloom. C. Phinizy. il por Sports Illus 46:26-31 Ja 17 '77 *
O'NEILL, Eugene Gladstone
Anna Christie. Reviews
Nation 224:538-9 Ap 30 '77 *
New Repub 176:22-3 My 7 '77 *
New Yorker 53:92 Ap 25 '77 *
Newsweek il 89:89 Ap 25 '77 *
Sat R 4:38-9 My 28 '77 *
Time il 109:84 Ap 25 '77 *
José, Jason, and Gene. S. Lawson. il pors Horizon 21:36-42 Ja '78 *
Touch of the poet. Reviews
New Yorker 53:59 Ja 9 '78 *
Newsweek il 91:71 Ja 9 '78 *
Time il 111:68 Ja 9 '78 *
Touch of the tragic. B. Gelb. il pors N Y Times Mag p43-5+ D 11 '77 *
O'NEILL, Gerard Kitchen
O'Neill summer study notes. Space World N-12-168:27 D '77
Progress toward space manufacturing. bibl il Space World N-1-157:14-22 Ja '77
about
Living in space. B. Achee. il Sci Digest 81:8-12 Ap '77 *
O'NEILL, Johanna
Double life; story. Seventeen 36:146-7 Je '77
O'NEILL, John P.
John O'Neill doesn't just paint birds. J. Fisher. il por Int Wildlife 7:30-7 N '77 *
O'NEILL, Thomas P. Jr
Old pol takes on the new President. M. Tolchin. il pors N Y Times Mag p6-9+ Jl 24 '77 *
Tip O'Neill—Speaker of the House. I. Ross. por Read Digest 111:137-41 N '77 *
What it's like to be Speaker of the House. il pors U.S. News 82:70-1 Je 6 '77 *
ONEONTA, N.Y.
Slotted drains cut street ponding. R. C. Olton. il Am City & County 92:56 Ap '77
ONG, S. H. and Steiner, A. L.
Localization of cyclic GMP and cyclic AMP in cardiac and skeletal muscle: immunocytochemical demonstration. bibl il Science 195:183-5 Ja 14 '77
ONIONS
Bagged or braided, onions winter well. J. Older. il Org Gard & Farm 24:126-7 Ag '77
Let us now praise the lowly onion. J. R. Baggett. il Horticulture 55:24-7 Ap '77
Onions are a twelve-month vegetable. G. Logsdon. il Org Gard & Farm 24:168+ Mr '77
Onions tie the gardening year together. R. L. Hawk. Org Gard & Farm 24:72-3 O '77
See also
Alliums
Cookery—Vegetables
ONO, R. Dana
Oriental art of abalone scrimshaw; with biographical sketch. il Sea Front 23:16-19, 62 Ja '77
ONSAGER, Lars
Obituary
Phys Today por 30:77 F '77
ONTARIO
See also
Toronto
Description and travel
Friendly southern Ontario. L. M. Newcombe. il Ret Liv 17:30-3 Jl '77
ONTARIO bulletin. See Newsletters
ONTARIO Library Association
Experts/critics discuss children's development. il SLJ 23:25 F '77
ONTOGENY
Hemoglobin ontogenesis: test of the gene excision hypothesis. T. Papayannopoulou and others. bibl il Science 196:1215-6 Je 10 '77
ONTOLOGY
See also
Perspective (philosophy)
OPAL, Chet B. See Carruthers, G. R. jt auth
OPALAK, John
Challenges of engraving. il Design (US) 78:14-16 Summ '77
Winifred Johnson Clive. il Design (US) 78:8-11 mid-Wint '77

OPAMPO. See Amplifiers
OP-ED articles. See Editorials
OPEL (automobile) See Automobiles, Foreign
OPELLA, Stanley J.
Biological nuclear magnetic resonance spectroscopy. bibl il Science 198:158-65 O 14 '77
OPEN-air museums
See also
Agricultural museums
OPEN-air theater. See Theater, Open-air
OPEN and closed shop
Open-shop construction picks up momentum. il Bus W p 108-9 D 12 '77
Right-to-work fad. S. Kupferberg. New Repub 178:20-3 Ja 7 '78
Should we repeal 14B? L. A. O'Donnell. America 136:354-5 Ap 16 '77
OPEN-heart surgery. See Heart—Surgery
OPEN-pit mining. See Strip mining
OPEN plan schools
Open space education: success or failure. M. Ediger. Clearing H 50:262-3 F '77
Reappraising the open classroom; British report on traditional vs. progressive teaching styles. F. M. Hechinger. Sat R 4:6+ Mr 19 '77
OPEN space planning. See Land utilization
OPENERS, Bottle. See Corkscrews
OPERA
Names, dates and places. See issues of Opera news
See also
Arias
Ballad opera
Characters in opera
Gilbert and Sullivan opera
Librettos
Melodrama
Phonograph records—Opera
Radio broadcasting—Opera
Television broadcasting—Opera

Appreciation

Opera and education; symposium. il Opera N 42:22-6+ N '77

Bibliography

Book reviews. P. J. Smith. See alternate issues of High fidelity and Musical America

Censorship

Virtue restored; censorship of Verdi's opera La Traviata in 1850's. D. Rosen. il Opera N 42:36+ D 24 '77

Conferences

Love-hate relationship; Central Opera Service's national conference, held in Houston. J. Ardoin. il por Opera N 42:10-11 D 17 '77

History and criticism

Barnum of the opera; Meyerbeer enthralling the Paris of Louis-Philippe. G. Marek. il Opera N 41:10-12+ Ja 29 '77
Drawn from life; adaptation of Puccini's opera La Bohème from H. Mürger's novel Scènes de la vie de Bohème. S. Hughes. il Opera N 42:12-14+ D 24 '77
Happy ending for a tragic finale; Rossini's Tancredi. P. Gossett. il por Opera N 42:34-5+ O '77
Notes on the Flute. S. Hughes. il Opera N 41:12-14 Ja 22 '77
Puccini on trial; enemies among his Italian critics. P. J. Zappa. por Opera N 42:28-30 D 17 '77
Le Trouvere: comparing Verdi's French revision with his original. D. Rosen. il Opera N 41:16-17 Ap 9 '77
Virtue restored; censorship of Verdi's opera La Traviata in 1850's. D. Rosen. il Opera N 42:36+ D 24 '77
What might have been: unrecorded Metropolitan Opera performances. J. B. Steane. il Opera N 42:26-9 Ag '77
Woe to the vanquished; Mürger's Vie de Bohème. J. Kestner. il Opera N 41:14-17 Mr 19 '77
See also
Opera—United States—History

Instruction and study

In touch with their feelings; opera, children and education; interview, ed by S. Wadsworth. P. Mondschein. il pors Opera N 42:30-1+ N '77
Portrait of the young opera singer. L. A. Remmey. il Hi Fi 27:MA21-3 Jl '77
Répétiteuse; coaching French opera repertory; interview, ed by D. Seabury. J. Reiss. il por Opera N 42:30-2 O '77
San Francisco/Affiliate Artists Opera Program. Hi Fi 27:MA38 Jl '77
Search for perfection; Schwarzkopf-Legge master classes. R. Jacobson. il pors Opera N 41:24-7 Ja 22 '77
See also
Lincoln Center for the Performing Arts, New York—Juilliard School
Manhattan School of Music

Production and direction

Boring the audience is unforgivable; F. Corsaro's theatrics. P. Andrews. il pors Horizon 20:58-65 O '77
Don Giovanni as the ideal sensualist; excerpt from Maverick: a director's personal experience in theater and opera. F. Corsaro. por Hi Fi 27:MA6-7+ D '77
False prophet, true martyrs; Prophète and Dialogues of the Carmelites. R. Jacobson. il Opera N 41:30-1 Mr 19 '77
Great directors:
Jean-Pierre Ponnelle. S. Von Buchau. il Opera N 42:12-16+ S '77
Jorge Lavelli, stage director. D. J. Soria. Hi Fi 27:MA7+ My '77
Liebermann's fractured Ring; Paris Opera. R. McMullen. il Hi Fi 27:MA34-5 My '77
Old pros: Tajo & Barbieri; interviews, ed by C. Faria. F. Barbieri; I. Tajo. il pors Opera N 41:8-13 F 26 '77
Rehearsals; rehearsal of G. Meyerbeer's Le Prophète at the Metropolitan Opera. New Yorker 52:24-6 Ja 24 '77
Rehearsals; Tannhäuser at the Metropolitan Opera. New Yorker 53:20-2 D 26 '77
Sarah Caldwell's new idea; Second hurricane performed by Opera New England. H. E. Phillips. il por Hi Fi 27:MA17-19 S '77
Supers: world of the extras at the Met. L. Rubinstein. il por Opera N 42:12-16 O '77
Ten commandments of Puccini; excerpt from Puccini, a self interpretation. L. Ricci. Opera N 42:18-19 D 17 '77
Tom O'Horgan; interview, ed by G. M. Loney. T. O'Horgan. il Opera N 41:15-17 Ap 16 '77

Statistics

U.S. opera survey 1976-77. M. F. Rich. il Opera N 42:52+ N '77

Stories

See Librettos

Study and teaching

See Opera—Instruction and study

Themes

See also
Women in opera

Alabama

Birmingham:
Birmingham Civic Opera's Tosca; Opera Alabama's Amahl and the night visitors. O. Roosevelt. Opera N 41:39 F 12 '77

Australia

Sydney:
Australian Opera's performances of Lucrezia Borgia and Fra Diavolo. J. Cargher. Opera N 42:63 S '77

Austria

News from Vienna:
Concert performance of Mozart's Mitridate at the Musikverein. G. Jellinek. Opera N 41:36 Mr 12 '77
Gottfried von Einem's Kabale und Liebe at the Staatsoper. J. Wechsberg. Opera N 41:36 Mr 12 '77
Managing the Vienna State Opera. J. Wechsberg. por Opera N 41:32 Mr 12 '77
Salzburg:
Festspielhaus productions of Mozart and Salieri and Iolanta. E. Blane. Opera N 42:44-5 D 24 '77
Vienna:
State Opera's performance of Norma. E. Blane. Opera N 41:45-6 My '77

Belgium

Brussels:
Opéra National's performance of Don Giovanni. L. Mueller. Opera N 41:30 Mr 5 '77

Brazil

Sao Paulo:
Salvator Rosa at the Teatro Municipal. L. Rasponi. Opera N 42:74 N '77

California

Andrew Imbrie's Angle of repose; San Francisco Opera Company season. A. Frankenstein. il Hi Fi 27:MA30-1+ Mr '77
Death takes a holiday; performance of The emperor of Atlantis by the Spring Opera Theater. H. Saal. il Newsweek 89:116-17 My 16 '77
Gilbert and Sullivan this spring in Davis, S.F, San Jose, Stanford. il Sunset 158:34+ Mr '77
In the Bay area: Angle of repose. D. Arthur. Am Rec G 40:58-9 D '76
Massenet in 'Frisco. D. Arthur. il Am Rec G 40:54-5 N '76
San Diego:
San Diego Opera's production of Menotti's Saint of Bleecker Street. D. Dierks. Opera N 41:30 F 26 '77
San Diego Opera: Merry Widow. S. Fleming. Hi Fi 28:MA21 Ja '78

OPERA—California—*Continued*
San Francisco:
Performance by the Opera Piccola, Spring Opera Company and Dominican College. S. Von Buchau. Opera N 41:36+ Je '77
San Francisco Opera Company's production of Turandot and Un ballo in maschera. S. Von Buchau. Opera N 42:40 Ja 7 '78
San Francisco Opera's performances of Adriana Lecouvreur, Idomeneo, and Katya Kabanova. S. Von Buchau. il Opera N 42:78-9 N '77
San Francisco Opera's productions of Ariadne auf Naxos, Aida, and Das Rheingold. S. Von Buchau. Opera N 42:34+ D 17 '77
Spring Opera Theater's triple bill: Emperor of Atlantis, Combat, and Savitri. S. Von Buchau. Opera N 42:42 Ag '77
San Francisco/Affiliate Artists Opera Program. Hi Fi 27:MA38 Jl '77
Spring Opera: a death-dealing triple bill; San Francisco production of Emperor of Atlantis. A. Frankenstein. il Hi Fi 27:MA30-1 O '77
Stars over San Francisco. H. Saal. il Newsweek 90:101-2 N 28 '77

Canada

Toronto:
Canadian Opera Company's productions of Wozzeck and Fille du régiment. U. Kareda. Opera N 42:39 D 17 '77
Canadian Opera's performance of Verdi's Don Carlos. R. Jacobson. il Opera N 42:66 N '77
Vancouver:
Vancouver opera's performances of Roi de Lahore, La fille du régiment, and Don Giovanni. F. B. St Clair. Opera N 42:35 D 10 '77

Colorado

Denver:
Central City Opera House Association's La Bohème. G. Giffin. Opera N 41:30 Ja 22 '77

Connecticut

Hartford:
Connecticut Opera Association's Barbiere. C. Farley. Opera N 41:38 F 12 '77
Hartt College of music's performance of Tales of Hoffmann. V. Kramer. Opera N 41:38 Mr 19 '77
Musical events:
Debussy's The fall of the House of Usher at Yale. A. Porter. New Yorker 53:130+ Mr 14 '77
New Haven:
Yale production of La chute de la maison Usher. S. Casale. Opera N 41:34-5 Ap 16 '77
Yale Symphony: Debussy's Fall of the House of Usher; performance at Yale. il Hi Fi 27:MA26-8 Je '77

Czechoslovakia

Bratislava:
Boris Godunov, Rusalka, La Bohème, and Resurrection. Q. Eaton. Opera N 42:45-6 D 24 '77

Denmark

Copenhagen:
Royal Theater's Der Rosenkavalier. E. Rosenberg. Opera N 41:30-1 F 19 '77

Florida

Asolo Opera; uncommonly professional; Sarasota. M. Mayer. il Hi Fi 27:MA28-9 Ag '77
Greater Miami Opera: Boris. il Hi Fi 27:MA26 Je '77
Miami:
Greater Miami Opera Association's performance of Boris Godunov. I. Davis. Opera N 41:29 Mr 26 '77
Sarasota:
Asolo Opera's production of The coronation of Poppea and Don Giovanni. B. Jones. Opera N 41:29-30 Mr 26 '77

France

Liebermann's fractured Ring; Paris Opera. R. McMullen. il Hi Fi 27:MA34-5 My '77
Lyons:
Lyons Opera's Lulu. D. Stevens. Opera N 41:39-40 F 5 '77
Nice:
Nice Opera's new production of Boito's Mefistofele. D. Stevens. Opera N 42:46 Ag '77
Opera season. Am Rec G 40:61-2 My '77
Paris:
Le Comte Ory at the Salle Favart; Paris Opera's new Ring cycle. D. Stevens. il Opera N 41:38-9 F 5 '77
Opéra Comique's performance of Pelléas et Mélisande and the Paris Opera's new production of Platée. D. Stevens. Opera N 42:26 Jl '77
Paris Opera's performances of La cenerentola. D. Stevens. Opera N 42:58 O '77
Paris Opera's performance of Zauberflöte. D. Stevens. il Opera N 42:46 Ag '77
Tours:
Grand Théâtre of Tours performing Mussorgsky's Marriage and Rimsky-Korsakov's Mozart and Salieri. D. Stevens. Opera N 41:40 F 5 '77

Georgia

Augusta Opera Co: Susannah. Hi Fi 27:MA28 S '77
Augusta Opera: Italian girl. il Hi Fi 27:MA29 Jl '77

Germany, East

Berlin (East Berlin):
East Berlin Staatsoper's production of Parsifal. J. H. Sutcliffe. Opera N 42:53-4 O '77
Komische Oper's performance of Mahagonny and East Berlin Staatsoper's performance of Margarete. J. H. Sutcliffe. Opera N 42:53-4 S '77
Staatsoper's new production of Arabella and Komische Oper's performance of The secret. J. H. Sutcliffe. Opera N 41:29-30 Mr 5 '77
Three one-acters presented in the Apollo-Saal of the Staatsoper. J. H. Sutcliffe. Opera N 42:41-2 D 24 '77
Dresden:
Performance of Kunad's Lithuanian pianos. J. H. Sutcliffe. Opera N 41:43-4 Ap 2 '77

Germany, West

Berlin (West Berlin)
Deutsche Oper's Ball of fat and Entführung aus dem Serail. J. H. Sutcliffe. Opera N 41:31 F 26 '77
Deutsche Oper's performance of I vespri siciliani. J. H. Sutcliffe. Opera N 41:30 Ap 16 '77
Bielefeld:
Tannhäuser. J. H. Sutcliffe. Opera N 41:45-6 Ap 2 '77
Düsseldorf:
Deutsche Oper am Rhein's performance of Palestrina. H. Koegler. Opera N 41:30-1 Ap 16 '77
Hamburg:
Lohengrin. J. H. Sutcliffe. il Opera N 41:28 Ap 16 '77
Rosenkavalier and Elisir d'amore. J. H. Sutcliffe. il Opera N 42:57 S '77
Staatsoper's productions of Frau ohne Schatten and Pelléas et Mélisande. J. H. Sutcliffe. il Opera N 42:43-4 D 24 '77
Zauberflöte. J. H. Sutcliffe. Opera N 42:27 Jl '77
Zimmermann's Die Soldaten; and Barbiere di Siviglia. J. H. Sutcliffe. il Opera N 41:29 Mr 5 '77
Hanseatic tricentennial; Hamburg celebrates the opening of its first opera house. H. Koegler. il Opera N 42:8-13 Ja 7 '78
Kassel:
Jenufa. J. H. Sutcliffe. Opera N 41:29 Ap 16 '77
Kiel:
Busoni's Arlecchino and Zenlinsky's Florentine tragedy. J. H. Sutcliffe. Opera N 42:54+ S '77
Munich:
Peter Beauvais' production of Arabella. H. E. Reed. Opera N 41:41 My '77
Polanski's Rigoletto by the Bavarian State Opera; Theater am Gärtnerplatz' Manon. H. E. Reed. il Opera N 41:40 F 12 '77
State Opera's performances of Otello and Alcina. H. E. Reed. Opera N 42:43 D 24 '77
Theater am Gärtnerplatz's performance of Nozze di Figaro and Die Trauung. H. E. Reed. Opera N 41:41-2 Je '77
Stuttgart:
Württembergische Staatstheater's new Rheingold. E. A. Reed. Opera N 42:30 D 10 '77
Zimmermann's The soldiers; Hamburg State Opera production. P. Moor. il Hi Fi 28:MA35-6 Ja '78

Great Britain

Glasgow:
Performance of Die Meistersinger by the Scottish Opera. N. Goodwin. Opera N 41:32 Mr 5 '77
Scottish Opera's performance of Jenufa. N. Goodwin. Opera N 41:41 My '77
Glyndebourne's Giovanni & Covent Garden's Fanciulla. E. Greenfield. il Hi Fi 27:MA38-9 O '77
In London opera, a new parsimony; three new productions. E. Greenfield. il Hi Fi 27:MA38-9 Je '77

OPERA—Great Britain—*Continued*
London:
English National Opera's performance of Blake's Toussaint and an English version of La Boheme. F. G. Barker. Opera N 42:33-5 D 10 '77
English National Opera's performances of Werther and Royal hunt of the sun. F. G. Barker. Opera N 41:39-40 My '77
Strauss' Eine Nacht in Venedig performed by the English National Opera; Royal Opera's performance of Ariadne. F. G. Barker. Opera N 41:31-2 Mr 5 '77
Tippett's opera The ice break performed at Covent Garden. F. G. Barker. Opera N 42:57 O '77
Troilus and Cressida at Covent Garden; Ginastera's Bomarzo by the New Opera Company in association with the English National Opera; and Smetana's Dalibor by the E.N.O. F. G. Barker. Opera N 41:28-9 F 19 '77
Musical events:
Covent Garden's performance of Tippett's The ice break and Welsh National Opera's performance of Tippett's The midsummer marriage. A. Porter. New Yorker 53:124-8 S 19 '77
English National Opera's production of D. Blake's Toussaint; or, The aristocracy of the skin. A. Porter. New Yorker 53:165-7 O 24 '77
Scottish Opera's production of Carmen. A. Porter New Yorker 53:102-5 S 26 '77
Nottingham:
Kent Opera's performance of Monteverdi's Orfeo. M. Dunmore. Opera N 41:29-30 F 19 '77
Opera season. Am Rec G 40:61-2 My '77
Tippett premiere: The ice break; Covent Garden. E. Greenfield. il Hi Fi 27:MA34-6 N '77
See also
D'Oyly Carte Opera Company

History

Quiet revolution; post-war opera boom. G. McElroy. il Opera N 42:14-18 Jl '77

Hawaii

Honolulu:
Hawaii Opera Theatre's performances of Les pecheurs de perles, Turandot and Barber of Seville. H. Driver. Opera N 41:36 My '77

Hungary

Budapest:
Hungarian Opera's performances of Mózes, Rodelinda, and Manon Lescaut. Q. Eaton. Opera N 42:46 D 24 '77

Illinois

See also
Lyric Opera of Chicago

Iowa

Des Moines Metro Summer Opera. C. Suttoni. il Hi Fi 27:MA35-7 O '77

Italy

Bologna:
Teatro Communale's production of Oberto, conte di San Bonifacio. W. Weaver. il Opera N 41:38 Mr 12 '77
Callas remembered: La Divina; golden years at La Scala. W. Legge. pors Opera N 42:8-11+ N '77
Florence:
Teatro Communale's revival of Guglielmo Tell. W. Weaver. Opera N 41:38 Mr 12 '77
La Scala: the most famous opera house in the world; Milan. B. H. Matthiessen. il Travel 148:44-9 O '77
Milan:
La Scala's Otello simultaneously transmitted on national television and radio. A. Andris-Michalaros. il Opera N 41:28 F 19 '77
Performance of Berg's Wozzeck at La Scala. A. Andris-Michalaros. Opera N 41:41 Je '77
Performance of Pelléas et Mélisande at La Scala. A. Andris-Michalaros. Opera N 42:50 Ag '77
Performances at La Scala; Norma, Beggar's opera, and Moses und Aron. A. Andris-Michalaros. il Opera N 41:40 Ap 2 '77
Naples:
Mayr's Medea in Corinto at the Teatro San Carlo. L. Rasponi. Opera N 41:40-1 Je '77
Palermo:
Performance of Bizet's Docteur Miracle, Offenbach's Monsieur Choufleuri, and Verdi's Traviata. L. Rasponi. Opera N 42:24+ Jl '77
Rome:
Rome Opera's performances of Fidelio and Anna Bolena. L. Rasponi. Opera N 41:39-40 Je '77
Teatro dell' Opera's performances of Il bravo, and Turandot. L. Rasponi. Opera N 41:40-1 Ap 2 '77
Scala Norma: televised opera's self-inflicted wound. J. Culshaw. il Hi Fi 27:14 Je '77
Turin:
Falstaff at the Teatro Regio. A. Andris-Michalaros. Opera N 41:28 F 19 '77
Venice:
La Fenice's Bastien et Bastienne and Torneo notturno. A. Andris-Michalaros. Opera N 41:31 F 26 '77
Verona:
Roméo et Juliette, Aida, and Cavalleria rusticana and Pagliacci performed at the Arena. A. Andris-Michalaros. Opera N 42:69 N '77

Kansas

Wichita:
Wichita Symphony's Madama Butterfly. J. Toms. Opera N 41:39 F 12 '77

Kentucky

Danville:
Regional Arts Center of Centre College presents the original 1847 version of Verdi's Macbeth with the Kentucky Opera Association. W. Weaver. Opera N 42:38 Ja 7 '78

Louisiana

New Orleans:
New Orleans Opera House Association's production of Andrea Chénier. B. Eggler. Opera N 41:32 Ja 22 '77
Shreveport:
Elie Siegmeister's Night of the moonspell. H. Snow. Opera N 41:38 F 12 '77
Siegmeister's Night of the moonspell; performance by Shreveport Symphony in Shreveport. il Hi Fi 27:MA19+ Ap '77

Maryland

Baltimore:
Baltimore Opera's Don Giovanni. C. Jahant. Opera N 41:36+ F 12 '77
Baltimore Opera's production of The flying Dutchman. C. Jahant. Opera N 41:34 Ap 16 '77

Massachusetts

Boston:
Glinka's Ruslan and Ludmila. R. Jacobson. Opera N 41:32 My '77
Gluck's Orfeo ed Euridice and Offenbach's Orpheus in the underworld at the Orpheum Theater. R. Jacobson. Opera N 42:40+ Ag '77
Glinka's grand fairy tale; production of Russlan and Ludmilla by the Opera Company of Boston. H. Saal. il Newsweek 89:62 Mr 21 '77
Musical events:
Opera Company of Boston productions of Gluck's Orpheus and Offenbach's Orphée aux enfers. A. Porter. New Yorker 53:91-4 Je 27 '77
Rigoletto performed by the Opera Company of Boston. A. Porter. New Yorker 53:132+ My 9 '77
Russlan and Ludmila performed by the Opera Company of Boston. A. Porter. New Yorker 53:105-6 Mr 28 '77
Russlan and Ludmilla—finally; Opera Company of Boston. B. Schwarz. il Hi Fi 27:MA32-3 Ag '77
Russlan, Ludmilla and Sarah; Opera Company of Boston production of Glinka opera. W. Bender. il Time 109:66 Mr 21 '77
Sarah Caldwell's new idea; Second hurricane performed by Opera New England. H. E. Phillips. il por Hi Fi 27:MA17-19 S '77

Michigan

Detroit:
Michigan Opera Theatre's production of Regina. R. Jacobson. Opera N 42:47 D 3 '77
Mozart's Magic flute at the Music Hall. J. Carr. Opera N 41:30 Mr 26 '77
East Lansing:
Opera Guild of Greater Lansing's performance of Don Giovanni. J. Carr. Opera N 41:30 F 26 '77
Michigan op: The magic flute. il Hi Fi 27:MA29-30 Jl '77
Michigan Opera Th: Regina; performance in Detroit. R. Jacobson. il Hi Fi 28:MA19-20 Ja '78
Musical events:
Michigan Opera Theatre's production of M. Blitzstein's Regina. A. Porter. New Yorker 53:162 O 24 '77

Minnesota

Minnesota Opera: Mahagonny; St Paul. il Hi Fi 27:MA27+ Ag '77
St Paul:
Minnesota Opera presents the staged premiere of Offenbach's Columbus. M. A. Feldman. Opera N 42:38-9 Ja 7 '78
Minnesota Opera's performance of Bach's Passion according to St Matthew. M. A. Feldman. Opera N 41:34 Ap 9 '77
Minnesota Opera's performance of Rise and fall of the city of Mahagonny. M. A. Feldman. Opera N 42:45 Ag '77

OPERA—*Continued*

Mississippi

Jackson:
Opera/South's premiere of Ulysses Kay's Jubilee. B. Eggler. Opera N 41:30 Ja 22 '77
Opera/South: Jubilee; performance in Jackson. il Hi Fi 27:MA19 Ap '77

Missouri

Kansas city:
Twentieth season of the Kansas City Lyric Opera. H. Haskell. Opera N 42:39 Ja 7 '78
Musical events:
Opera Theatre of St Louis. A. Porter. New Yorker 53:103-7 Je 20 '77
St Louis:
Performances by the Opera Theatre of Saint Louis. R. Jacobson. il Opera N 42:38 Ag '77
Setting an example; Kansas City Lyric Opera. H. Haskell. il por Opera N 42:48-9 S '77

Nebraska

Omaha:
Aida. L. J. Leff. Opera N 41:30 Ja 22 '77

Netherlands

Amsterdam:
Netherlands Opera's world premiere of Houdini. M. Feenstra. Opera N 42:30+ D 10 '77

New Mexico

Night at the opera; Santa Fe production of The Italian straw hat. M. Kasindorf. il Newsweek 90:54 Jl 18 '77
Santa Fe:
Italian straw hat; Fedora; Così fan tutte; Falstaff; Pelléas et Melisande. R. Jacobson. Opera N 42:62-4 O '77
Three masterpieces return; Santa Fe Opera production of Italian straw hat, Fedora, Così fan tutte. J. Ardoin. il Hi Fi 27:MA30-2 D '77

New York (state)

Bel Canto: Tsar and carpenter. Hi Fi 27:MA28 S '77
Binghamton:
English adaptation of Madama Butterfly performed by Tri-Cities. D. Koch. Opera N 41:35-6 Ap 9 '77
James as opera; New York Lyric Opera production of Washington Square. H. Saal. il Newsweek 90:100+ N 7 '77
Musical events:
Clarion Opera Group of New York's performance of F. Cavalli's Giasone. A. Porter. New Yorker 52:74-6 Ja 24 '77
New Opera Theatre's productions of D. Argento's A water bird talk and V. Ullmann's The Emperor of Atlantis. A. Porter. New Yorker 53:108+ Je 6 '77
I quattro rusteghi performed by the Manhattan School of Music. A. Porter. New Yorker 53:106+ Mr 28 '77
New York (city):
Bronx Opera Company performing Verdi's Traviata in English. R. Levine. Opera N 41:30 F 26 '77
New Opera Theatre at the Brooklyn Academy. S. Wadsworth. Opera N 41:36 Ap 16 '77
New York Opera Theatre's performances of A water bird talk and Emperor of Atlantis. R. Jacobson. Opera N 42:40 Ag '77
SUNY at Buffalo: Madame Jumel; University Opera Studio. il Hi Fi 27:MA18-19 Ap '77
Verismo Opera Company: Adriana Lecouvreur. il Hi Fi 27:MA29 S '77
White Plains:
Devil's disciple produced by the Hoff-Barthelson Music School. W. C. Schwartz. Opera N 42:36 Ja 7 '78
See also
Clarion Music Society, Inc
Manhattan School of Music
Metropolitan Opera Company
New York City Opera Company
Opera Orchestra of New York

North Carolina

Charlotte:
Charlotte Opera Association's performance of Turandot. J. M. White. Opera N 41:30 Mr 26 '77

Ohio

Cincinnati:
Cincinnati Opera's performance of Norma with Renata Scotto. R. Jacobson. il Opera N 42:64 S '77
Cincinnati Op: Scotto's Norma. por Hi Fi 27: MA26 O '77
Cleveland:
Community-based professional troupes, the New Cleveland Opera Company, and the Cleveland Opera Theater Ensemble. R. Finn. Opera N 42:37 Ja 7 '78

Pennsylvania

Philadelphia:
Opera Company of Philadelphia's performance of Die Walküre and The barber of Seville. M. de Schauensee. Opera N 41: 38-9 Mr 19 '77
Pittsburgh:
Pittsburgh Opera's first Falstaff. R. Croan. Opera N 42:36-7 Ja 7 '78
Pittsburgh opera's performance of Bartered bride. R. Croan. Opera N 41:47 Ap 2 '77
Pittsburgh Opera's Tosca and Norma. R. Croan. Opera N 41:38-9 F 12 '77
See also
Curtis Institute of Music, Philadelphia

Puerto Rico

San Juan:
Opera de San Juan's production of Espinosa's Macias. L. A. Catoni. Opera N 42: 80 N '77

Russia

Moscow:
Bolshoi Theater's production of The kidnapping of the moon and Stone guest. W. A. Fisher. Opera N 42:51-2 S '77

Scotland

See Opera—Great Britain

Spain

Barcelona:
Gran Teatro del Liceo's December performances. L. A. Catoni. Opera N 41:42-3 Ap 2 '77

Sweden

Stockholm:
Gottfried von Einem's Besuch der alten Dame. E. Redvall. Opera N 41:30-1 Mr 5 '77
Lulu and Fröcken Julie. E. Redvall. il Opera N 42:24 Jl '77
Royal Opera's productions of Die Meistersinger and Egisto. E. Redvall. il Opera N 42:40 D 24 '77

Switzerland

Geneva:
Carmen at the Grand Théâtre. L. Rasponi. Opera N 42:28 Jl '77
Der Freischütz at the Grand Théâtre. L. Rasponi. Opera N 41:30 F 19 '77
Performance of Götterdämmerung and La Bohème at the Grand Théâtre. L. Rasponi. Opera N 42:58-60 S '77

Texas

Dallas:
Dallas Civic Opera's Salome. J. Ardoin. Opera N 41:32 Ja 22 '77
Dallas Civic Opera's twenty-first season. J. Ardoin. il Opera N 42:39-40 Ja 7 '78
Houston:
Il barbiere di Siviglia. J. Ardoin. Opera N 41:32 Ja 22 '77
Houston Opera's performance of Peter Grimes. J. Ardoin. Opera N 41:34 Ap 9 '77
Houston Opera's production of Rossini's Tancredi. J. Ardoin. Opera N 42:36 D 17 '77
Houston Opera: Peter Grimes a high point. C. Cunningham. il Hi Fi 27:MA36 Je '77
Musical events:
Houston Grand Opera's production of Rossini's Tancredi. A. Porter. New Yorker 53: 205-6+ N 7 '77
San Antonio:
Performance of Wagner's Rienzi. J. Ardoin. Opera N 41:31 Mr 26 '77
Symphony appointment raises questions; conductor E. Mata and Dallas Civic Opera season. J. Ardoin. por Hi Fi 27:MA32-3 My '77
Wagner's Rienzi; performance in San Antonio. Q. Eaton. il Hi Fi 27:MA30+ Ag '77

United States

At last, opera makes it big with U.S. audiences. il U.S. News 82:64-6 Ap 18 '77
Boring the audience is unforgivable. P. Andrews. il pors Horizon 20:58-65 O '77
Metropolitan mirror. A. M. Lingg. il Opera N 41: 32 F 26; 49 My '77
Opera and education; symposium. il Opera N 42:22-6+ N '77
Opera's exciting new era: Frederica Von Stade's view. F. Von Stade. il pors U.S. News 83:52 N 7 '77
U.S. calendar. See issues of Opera news
U.S. opera forecast. il Opera N 42:33-5+ S '77
U.S. opera survey 1976-77. M. F. Rich. il Opera N 42:52+ N '77
See also
Central Opera Service
Metropolitan Opera Guild
Opera America (organization)

History

Verdi's American correspondent; E. Munzio. G. Marchesi. Opera N 42:38+ D 3 '77
Verdi's early U.S. premieres. M. Chusid. il Opera N 42:32-3 Ja 7 '78

OPERA—*Continued*

Virginia

Vienna:
Busoni's Doktor Faust performed at Wolf Trap Park. R. Jacobson. il Opera N 42:62 O '77
Wolf Trap: Faust & L'Egisto. Hi Fi 27:MA19-20 D '77

Western States

Opera in the West 1977. il Sunset 158:60-3 F '77

Wisconsin

Florentine Opera Company—ups & downs; Milwaukee performances; with comment by L. Kenngott. L. B. Johnson. il Hi Fi 27:MA34-6 Ag '77
Madison:
Manon performed by the Madison Civic Opera. C. R. Faust. Opera N 41:35 Ap 9 '77

OPERA, American
Eastman School-Lib. of Congress: The disappointment; performance of the first American ballad opera. il Hi Fi 27:MA14-15+ Mr '77
See also
Blitzstein, M.
Chadwick, G. W.
Copland, A.
Floyd, C.
Imbrie, A. W.
Kay, U.
Kirchner, L.
Siegmeister, E.
Thomson, V.

OPERA, Czech
See also
Janáček, L.
Smetana, B.

OPERA, English
See also
Walton, W. T.

OPERA, French
Le Trouvere: comparing Verdi's French revision with his original. D. Rosen. il Opera N 41:16-17 Ap 9 '77
See also
Bizet, G.
Chabrier, E.
Charpentier, G.
Debussy, C.
Lully, J. B.
Massenet, J.
Poulenc, F.
Saint-Saëns, C.

OPERA, German
German romantic opera and the problem of origins. A. S. Garlington, Jr. il Mus Q 63:247-63 Ap '77
See also
Kreutzer, K.
Nicolai, O.
Strauss, R.
Wagner, R.
Weber, K.M. von
Zimmermann, B. A.

OPERA, Italian
See also
Albinoni, T.
Bellini, V.
Cavalli, P. F.
Cimarosa, D.
Donizetti, G.
Giordano, U.
Montemezzi, I.
Peri, J.
Puccini, G.
Rossini, G.
Scarlatti, A.
Verdi, G.
Wolf-Ferrari, E.

OPERA, Russian
See also
Glinka, M. I.
Musorgskiĭ, M. P.
Prokof'ev, S. S.

OPERA Alabama (company) See Opera—Alabama

OPERA America (organization)
Viewpoint. R. Jacobson. Opera N 41:6 My '77

OPERA and children. See Music and children

OPERA and literature. See Music and literature

OPERA and poetry. See Music and literature

OPERA and youth. See Music and youth

OPERA audiences. See Audiences

OPERA auditions. See Singing—Competitions

OPERA broadcasts. See Radio broadcasting—Opera; Television broadcasting—Opera

OPERA characters. See Characters in opera; Women in opera

OPERA Comique. See Opera—France

OPERA Company of Boston. See Opera—Massachusetts

OPERA Company of Philadelphia. See Opera—Pennsylvania

OPERA critics and criticism. See Music critics and criticism

OPERA de San Juan. See Opera—Puerto Rico

OPERA festivals. See Music festivals

OPERA Guild of Greater Lansing. See Opera—Michigan

OPERA guilds
See also
Metropolitan Opera Guild

OPERA houses
Backstage at the Santa Fe Opera—reservations-only tours. il Sunset 159:30 Jl '77
Hanseatic tricentennial; Hamburg celebrates the opening of its first opera house. H. Koegler. il Opera N 42:8-13 Ja 7 '78
La Scala: the most famous opera house in the world; Milan. B. H. Matthiessen. il Travel 148:44-9 O '77
See also
Lincoln Center for the Performing Arts, New York—Opera House
Metropolitan Opera House, New York

OPERA New England (opera company) See Opera—Massachusetts

OPERA Orchestra of New York
Musical events:
Puccini's Edgar. A. Porter. New Yorker 53:129 My 9 '77
Smetana's Dalibor. A. Porter. New Yorker 52:76-8 Ja 24 '77
Op. Orch. of N.Y: Edgar: concert performance at Carnegie Hall. Hi Fi 27:MA24-6 S '77
Opera Orch. of N.Y: Dalibor. Hi Fi 27:MA24 My '77

OPERA Rara (firm) See Phonograph record industry—Great Britain

OPERA reviews
Opera. B. H. Haggin. New Repub 176:21-3 Je 3; 177:28-30 N 5 '77

Single works

See name of composer for full entry
Adriana Lecouvreur. F. Cilea
Aida. G. Verdi
Andrea Chénier. U. Giordano
Angle of repose. A. W. Imbrie
Barber of Seville. G. Rossini
Il barbiere di Siviglia. See Barber of Seville, above
La Boheme. G. Puccini
Boris Godunov. M. P. Musorgskiĭ
Il bravo. S. Mercadante
Carmen. G. Bizet
La Chute de la maison Usher. See Fall of the House of Usher, below
La clemenza di Tito. J. C. W. A. Mozart
Les contes d'Hoffmann. See Tales of Hoffmann, below
Dalibor. B. Smetana
Dialogues of the Carmelites. F. Poulenc
Don Carlo. G. Verdi
Don Giovanni. J. C. W. A. Mozart
Edgar. G. Puccini
Emperor of Atlantis. V. Ullmann
Esclarmonde. J. Massenet
Eugene Onegin. P. I. Tchaikovsky
Fall of the House of Usher. C. Debussy
Falstaff. G. Verdi
La fanciulla del West. G. Puccini
Fidelio. L. van Beethoven
Der fliegender Holländer. See Flying Dutchman, below
Flying Dutchman. R. Wagner
Force of destiny. See La forza del destino, below
La forza del destino. G. Verdi
Ice break. M. Tippett
Idomeneo. J. C. W. A. Mozart
Intermezzo. R. Strauss
Italian girl in Algiers. G. Rossini
Italian straw hat. N. Rôta
Jubilee. U. Kay
Judith. G. W. Chadwick
Lily. L. Kirchner
Lohengrin. R. Wagner
Lord Byron. V. Thomson
Louise. G. Charpentier
Lucia di Lammermoor. G. Donizetti
Lulu. A. Berg
Madama Butterfly. G. Puccini
Madame Jumel. A. Wolf
Magic flute. J. C. W. A. Mozart
Marriage of Figaro. J. C. W. A. Mozart
Die Meistersinger von Nürnberg. R. Wagner
La mère coupable. D. Milhaud
Midsummer marriage. M. Tippett
Night of the moonspell. E. Siegmeister
Niobe, regina di Tebe. A. Steffani
Norma. V. Bellini
Le nozze di Figaro. See Marriage of Figaro, above
Orfeo ed Euridice. C. W. Gluck
Parsifal. R. Wagner
Paul Bunyan. B. Britten
Pelléas et Mélisande. C. Debussy
Peter Grimes. B. Britten
Porgy and Bess. G. Gershwin
Le Prophète. G. Meyerbeer
Pygmalion. J. P. Rameau
I quattro rusteghi. E. Wolf-Ferrari
Regina. M. Blitzstein
Reluctant king. See Le Roi malgré lui, below
Das Rheingold. R. Wagner

OPERA reviews—Single works—*Continued*
Rienzi. R. Wagner
Rigoletto. G. Verdi
Rise and fall of the city of Mahagonny. K. Weill
Le Roi malgré lui. E. Chabrier
Der Rosenkavalier. R. Strauss
Russlan and Ludmila. M. I. Glinka
Salome. R. Strauss
Samson and Dalilah. C. Saint-Saëns
Second hurricane. A. Copland
Soldiers. B. A. Zimmermann
Susannah. C. Floyd
Tales of Hoffmann. J. Offenbach
Tancredi. G. Rossini
Tannhäuser. R. Wagner
Tosca. G. Puccini
Toussaint; or, The aristocracy of the skin. D. Blake
La Traviata. G. Verdi
Il trittico. G. Puccini
Troilus and Cressida. W. Walton
Il Trovatore. G. Verdi
Voice of Ariadne. T. Musgrave
Die Walküre. R. Wagner
War and peace. S. S. Prokof'ev
Washington Square. T. Pasatieri
Water bird talk. D. Argento
Zar und Zimmermann. A. Lortzing
Die Zauberflöte. See Magic flute, above

OPERA singers
Buon appetito! a festa Verdi for opera luminaries. F. Tobey. il Opera N 42:8-11 D 24 '77
Fidés tradition: performances of Le Prophète at the Metropolitan Opera. G. Jellinek. il Opera N 41:20-1 Ja 29 '77
Musician of the month. See issues of High fidelity and Musical America
Names, dates and places. See issues of Opera news
Portrait of the young opera singer. L. A. Remmey. il Hi Fi 27:MA21-3 Jl '77
San Francisco/Affiliate Artists Opera Program. Hi Fi 27:MA38 Jl '77
Viewpoint; a place for the great singers of the near past. R. Jacobson. Opera N 41:5 F 26 '77
Viewpoint; young American opera singers. R. Jacobson. Opera N 41:4 Ap 9 '77
See also
British Actors' Equity Association
also names of opera singers, e.g. S. Verrett

OPERA/South (opera company) See Opera—Mississippi

OPERA Theatre of St Louis. See Opera—Missouri

OPERA workshops. See Opera—Instruction and study

OPERATIC characters. See Characters in opera

OPERATIC costume. See Costume, Theatrical

OPERATIC direction. See Opera—Production and direction

OPERATIC production and direction. See Opera—Production and direction

OPERATIC stage directors. See Opera—Production and direction

OPERATIC training. See Opera—Instruction and study

OPERATING managers. See Executives

OPERATION Head Start. See Project Head Start

OPERATIONAL amplifiers. See Amplifiers

OPERATIONAL gaming
On playing New Eleusis, the game that simulates the search for truth. M. Gardner. il Sci Am 237:18+ O '77

OPERATIONS, Surgical. See Surgery

OPERETTA
London: Strauss' Eine Nacht in Venedig performed by the English National Opera. F. G. Barker. Opera N 41:31-2 Mr 5 '77
Offenbach in New York. E. Calder. Am Rec G 40:53-4 N '76
See also
Melodrama

OPERETTA reviews

Single works

See name of composer for full entry
Merry widow. F. Lehár
Orphée aux enfers. J. Offenbach

OPHELIA DeVore School of Charm. See Charm—Study and teaching

OPHTHALMOLOGICAL apparatus and instruments. See Eye, Instruments and apparatus for

OPHULS, Marcel
Crimes against humanity. B. Rothenbuecher. Chr Cent 94:361-3 Ap 13 '77 *

OPIATE receptors. See Drug receptors

OPIATES. See Narcotics

OPINION, Public. See Public opinion

OPINION, Student. See Student opinion

OPINION, Teacher. See Teacher opinion

OPOSSUMS
Opossum. B. Love. il Conservationist 31:42 Mr '77

OPPENHEIMER, George
Hollywood's Garden of Allah. il Am Heritage 28:82-7 Ag '77

OPPENHEIMER, Julius Robert
Adventures of the mind; excerpt from 1958 article. il Sat Eve Post 249:8 Jl '77
about
I am become death. . .R. Rhodes. il pors Am Heritage 28:70-83 O '77 *
Oppenheimer case: a study in the abuse of law. H. P. Green. il pors Bull Atom Sci 33:12-16+ S '77 *

OPPENHEIMER and Company, Inc. See Brokers

OPTACON (optical-to-tactile converter) See Blind, Apparatus for the

OPTIC glands. See Glands

OPTICAL communication systems. See Light communication systems

OPTICAL glass. See Glass, Optical

OPTICAL illusions
Pincushion grid illusion. R. A. Schachar; discussion. il Science 198:960-2 D 2 '77
See also
Anamorphosis

OPTICAL industry
Retailing: eyes right; For Eyes Optical Co. D. Pauly and B. Keough. il por Newsweek 91:50+ Ja 2 '78
See also
Bausch and Lomb, Inc

France

New kind of bifocal for U.S. eyes; Essilor's progressive' lenses. il Bus W p34 Jl 18 '77

OPTICAL instruments
See also
Telescopes

OPTICAL scanners

Manufacture

Recognition Equipment revives itself. il por Bus W p88 S 5 '77

OPTICAL Society of America
Two Argonne scientists win Optical Society's Meggers Award. pors Phys Today 30:75 S '77

OPTICAL spectroscopy. See Spectrum analysis

OPTICAL transients. See Transients (dynamics)

OPTICS
See also
Fiber optics
Photographic optics

OPTICS, Physiological
See also
Vision

OPTIONS
See also
Put and call transactions
Stock purchase options

OPTIONS, Automobile. See Automobiles—Equipment

OPTIONS mutual funds. See Investment trusts

O'QUINN, Charlotte
Nursing an ambulance and a county. D. Lampe. il pors Fam Health 9:28-30 Je '77 *

L'ORACOLO; opera. See Leoni, F.

ORAL communication
Social and nonsocial speech. R. M. Krauss and S. Glucksberg. il Sci Am 236:100-5 bibl(p 138) F '77
Social speech—making the words fit the audience; work of Robert M. Krauss and Sam Glucksberg. D. Cohen. Psychol Today 10:98 My '77
See also
Public speaking

ORAL history
Nobody's special when they're poor. T. J. Cottle. Yale R 66:388-98 Mr '77
Taped talk: storing tomorrow's source materials. R. Hoopes. il Hi Fi 27:61-5 Ag '77

ORAL reading
See also
Books and reading—Reading aloud
Dramatic readings

ORAL surgery
President's operation; oral surgery for cancer performed on G. Cleveland. W. K. Keen. il Sat Eve Post 249:106+ Jl '77

ORAN, Mary R.
Nectar in a sieve; K. Markandaya's novel. Engl J 66:62-3 Mr '77

ORANGE, N.J, Public Library. See Libraries—New Jersey

ORANGE County, Calif.
More than a suburb, less than a city. il map Bus W p76-7 S 5 '77
Riviera in our own backyard; Orange Coast. R. Alleman. map Vogue 167:210+ O '77

ORANGE crate labels. See Labels

ORANGE desserts. See Desserts

ORANGE drink mixes. See Beverage mixes

ORANGE juice
Orange juice. Consumer Rep 42:70-2 D '77
Prices
Orange freeze heats futures prices. il Bus W p72 F 21 '77
ORANGE juice futures. See Commodity exchanges
ORANGES
Florida: frost-kissed oranges. R. Rauch. il Time 109:12 F 14 '77
Social history of a singular fruit. T. H. Watkins. il Am Heritage 28:84-7+ Ap '77
See also
Cookery—Fruit
Orange juice
ORANGUTANS
Hermits of the jungle; with editorial comment. P. S. Rodman. il map Int Wildlife 7:3, 20-5 My '77
Orang—endangered man of the forest. M. A. Rock. il Nat Parks & Con Mag 51:10-15 Ag '77
ORATORIO
Milan: Frank Martin's Le vin herbé at the Piccola Scala. A. Andris-Michalaros. Opera N 42: 50 Ag '77
Musical events; A. Scarlatti's Agar et Ismaele esiliati performed at Corpus Christi Church, New York City. A. Porter. New Yorker 53: 190+ D 12 '77
See also
Phonograph records—Oratorios
ORATORY
See also
Public speaking
Rhetoric
ORBEN, Robert
No laughing matter. P. Steinfels. Commonweal 104:434 Jl 8 '77 *
ORBITAL rendezvous (space flight)
Extra docking port saves Salyut flight. C. Covault. il Aviation W 107:11-12 D 19 '77
Failure to achieve rendezvous curtails Soviet Soyuz flight. Aviation W 107:25-6 O 17 '77
Not quite; Soyuz 25- Salyut 6 docking failure. il Newsweek 90:54 O 24 '77
ORBITS
See also
Artificial satellites—Orbits
Earth—Orbit
ORCHARDGRASS. See Grasses
ORCHARDS. See Fruit culture
ORCHESTRA festivals. See Music festivals
ORCHESTRAL conductors. See Conductors (music)
ORCHESTRAL music
Modern American music makes a breakthrough. W. Mayer. il Horizon 20:52-8 S '77
See also
Phonograph records—Orchestral music
ORCHESTRAS
ASOL Festival of Youth Orchestras; Washington, D.C. L. Sears. il Hi Fi 27:MA24-6 D '77
B. U. Orch. & Ch: Read's Prophet. il por Hi Fi 27:MA24 Je '77
Colorado Springs Symphony: Farberman's War cry. por Hi Fi 27:MA19-20 Mr '77
Debuts & reappearances. See issues of High fidelity and Musical America
Karajan Orchestra Competition; second prize won by Boston University Concert Orchestra. T. Eckert, Jr. il por Hi Fi 27:MA34-5+ Ap '77
Musical events: San Antonio Symphony's performance of Wagner's Rienzi. A. Porter. New Yorker 52:106-11 F 14 '77
Notes from the orchestra pit; women in symphony orchestras. H. Epstein. Ms 5:106+ Ap '77
Oil dollars go into music; funding by Venezuelan government of Maracaibo Symphony Orchestra. D. Hawes. por Hi Fi 27:MA33+ N '77
Rochester Philharmonic: Erb prem; Cello Concerto (1976) por Hi Fi 27:MA36 F '77
Russians came to browse in Hartford bookstore; visit of members of the Leningrad Philharmonic. T. Huntington. Pub W 211: 62-3 Mr 28 '77
Senior concert orchestra set for Carnegie Hall performance on May 18. il Ret Liv 17:17 My '77
Siegmeister's Night of the moonspell; performance by Shreveport Symphony in Shreveport, La. il Hi Fi 27:MA19+ Ap '77
Yale philharmonia; Penderecki; concert at Carnegie Hall. por Hi Fi 27:MA33-5 Je '77
Yale Sym. Westney: Ornstein cto. il por Hi Fi 27:MA25-6 Ap '77
See also
American Symphony Orchestra League
Chamber orchestras
National Orchestral Association
School orchestras
Stringed instruments
also names of orchestras, e.g. Boston Symphony Orchestra
Competitions
See Music—Competitions

ORCHIDS
Don't let orchids scare you. B. Gardner. Am Home 80:22+ F '77
Echoes at the Frick. New Yorker 53:27-8 Ap 11 '77
Flames in the jungle. S. Shaw. il Int Wildlife 7:44-7 N '77
Magic orchid. V. G. Stoddart. il Américas 29: 14-17 My '77
Moth in the orchid family; Phalaenopsis, the moth orchid. M. M. Whitson. Horticulture 55: 4 My '77
Orchid diplomacy; trip to Canton Fair in attempt to import orchids to U.S. W. K. Glikbarg. Horticulture 55:8-13 My '77
Orchids as art. il House & Gard 149:162-5 N '77
Orchids—exotics indoors. il House & Gard 149:32 Jl '77
San Salvador's urban orchids. P. Bernhardt. il Natur Hist 86:64-71 D '77
They're not rare or costly, just easy; Chinese ground orchid. il Sunset 158:154 F '77
Tips about orchids. J. Fanning. il House & Gard 149:288-9+ N '77
ORDER (philosophy)
Rage for chaos. C. D. Linton. Chr Today 21:22-5 My 6 '77
ORDER processing
Economics; order handling techniques for craftspeople E. P. McGuire. Craft Horiz 37:13 Ap '77
See also
Booksellers and bookselling—Order processing
ORDINATION
Church is full of wolves; ordination conducted by M. Lefebvre. il por Time 110:64 Jl 11 '77
Lefebvre's defiance. il por Newsweek 90:78 Jl 11 '77
Priestly ordination. M. B. Martin. il Nat R 29:206-7 F 18 '77
ORDINATION of homosexuals
Episcopal bishops: dealing with revolt. il Chr Today 22:46-9 N 4 '77
Homosexual rights and ordination. America 137: 346 N 19 '77; Discussion. 137:409 D 10 '77
ORDINATION of women
Anglican women priests in Australia? R. Mathias. Chr Cent 94:658 Jl 20 '77
Dissent, division and development. America 137: 229 O 15 '77
Episcopal bishops: dealing with revolt. il Chr Today 22:46-9 N 4 '77
Episcopal bishops eke out a fragile peace. K. Briggs. Chr Cent 94:996 N 2 '77
First women; Episcopal Church. Chr Today 21:42 Ja 21 '77
Lesbian priest; ordination of E. Barrett. por Time 109:58 Ja 24 '77
Matter preordained; Catholic Church. P. Steinfels. Commonweal 104:136 Mr 4 '77
More on a Dual-sex Eucharist. H. Cox. Commonweal 104:112-14 F 18 '77
More on Women in the Church. Commonweal 104:109-11 F 18 '77
On the ordination of women. M. Novak. Commonweal 104:425-7 Jl 8 '77; Discussion. 104: 556-64, 589-91 S 2-16 '77
Open letter to the apostolic delegate; response to Congregation for the Doctrine of the Faith's declaration. Commonweal 104:204-6 Ap 1 '77
Paul says no. Newsweek 89:77 F 7 '77
Pope Paul to women: keep out. por Time 109:65 F 7 '77
Vatican declaration; another view. D. Burrell. America 136:289-92 Ap 2 '77; Reply with rejoinder. D. L. Gelpi. 137:75-8 Ag 13 '77
Veteran out, a lesbian in. Chr Today 21:55-6 F 4 '77
Women, priesthood and the Vatican. J. R. Donahue. America 136:285-9 Ap 2 '77
Women priests: the door is opening. R. Mathias. Chr Cent 94:1006 N 2 '77
Women's ordination in the Mother Church; Catholic Church. S. Cunneen. Chr Cent 94: 256-8 Mr 16 '77
Women's ordination: the future of equality; Catholic Church. America 136:118-19 F 12 '77; Discussion. 136:157, 177-8 F 26-Mr 5 '77
See also
Women clergy
ORDNANCE
War of Longitude Lane; cannon hoax. W. Ripley. il Am Hist Illus 11:20-3 F '77
See also
United States—Army—Ordnance and ordnance stores
ORE deposits
Fluid inclusion assemblages of the stratiform Broken Hill ore deposit, New South Wales, Australia. R. W. T. Wilkins. bibl il Science 198:185-7 O 14 '77
See also
Prospecting
OREGON
Low-key Oregon: a model for the U.S? map U.S. News 83:60-1 D 5 '77
See also
Architecture, Domestic—Oregon
Fishing—Oregon
Forests and forestry—Oregon

OREGON—See also—*Continued*
Hells Canyon
Hunting—Oregon
Lake County, Oregon
Land tenure—Oregon
Paleobotany—Oregon
Willamette River

Description and travel

Oregon trails. E. Flick. il por Am For 83:36-7 My '77
Oregon's astonishing lava lands. il map Sunset 159:64-7 Ag '77
Oregon's magnificent Southwest. J. Ferri. il Travel 147:38-41+ Mr '77

History

American characters: John McLoughlin; manager of Hudson's Bay Company. D. Lavender. por Am Heritage 28:64-5 Je '77
Oregon yesterdays; with historic photographs by G. M. Weister. E. W. Buehler. Am West 14:41-53 S '77

Religious institutions and affairs

See also
Portland, Ore.—Religious institutions and affairs

OREGON Library Association
Oregon LA wins six-year state aid battle. il Lib J 102:1802 S 15 '77

OREGON Trail
For 300 miles, new exhibits mark the Oregon Trail. il map Sunset 158:54 Mr '77
Roads not taken; retracing the Oregon Trail by car. il map Sat Eve Post 249:90-3 Ap '77

OREGON. University, Eugene

School of Librarianship

Threat to library school stirs protest in Oregon. Lib J 102:1439 Jl '77

O'REILLY, Anthony John Francis
Heinz's O'Reilly winds down in Dublin. il Bus W p30-1 Jl 4 '77 *

O'REILLY, Jane
Bed/bath: new exposure. Vogue 167:245+ D '77
Clunks! Ms 6:66-7 Jl '77
Cool Mexican hill towns from the 15th century. il House & Gard 149:43-5 Ag '77
Glorious self-indulgence of the cruise life. il House & Gard 149:110+ O '77
On daring to be romantic. il House & Gard 149:110-15+ Mr '77
Other Martinique. il House & Gard 149:76+ D '77
75 easy ways to punch up your life. Mademoiselle 83:128-9+ Je '77

O'REILLY, William, Jr
High-fiber diet's value questioned. Sci Digest 81:26-8 Ap '77

ORENTREICH, Norman
How to clean & care for your skin; interview. Mademoiselle 83:174-7 Ag '77
Nerves and your skin; interview. Harp Baz 110:126+ Mr '77

ORFEO ed Euridice; opera. See Gluck, C. W.

ORFF, Carl
Carmina Burana; recording. G. S. Fox. Am Rec G 40:37-8 F '77 *

ORFILA, Alejandro José Luis
Can Latin America and the United States modernize their traditional special relationship? address, August 19, 1977. Vital Speeches 44:21-4 O 15 '77
Energy; adaptation of address, May 23, 1977. il Américas 29:6-12 O '77
Energy development in the Americas. Science 196:611 My 6 '77
Human rights in the Americas. Américas 29:18-20 My '77
New horizons for progress and freedom in the Americas; address, February 24, 1977. Vital Speeches 43:411-13 Ap 15 '77

ORFORD, N.H.
History in towns. A. D. Hodgson. il Antiques 112:712-25 O '77

ORGAN, Electronic
Build: portable mini-organ (cont) J. S. Simonton, Jr. il Radio-Electr 48:58-60 F '77
State of solid state; two rhythm generators. K. Savon. il Radio-Electr 48:78-80 Mr '77

ORGAN, Mechanical. See Musical instruments, Mechanical

ORGAN music
See also
Phonograph records—Organ music

ORGAN transplantation. See Transplantation of organs, tissues, etc.

ORGANIC farming
Hard questions, on and off the farm. J. Goldstein. il Org Gard & Farm 24:166+ O '77
Why do you work so hard on your homestead for nothing? G. Logsdon. il Org Gard & Farm 24:126-33 S '77

Conferences

People and places (cont of) Meetings and farm groups. See issues of Organic gardening and farming

Arkansas

Two homesteading newcomers to the Ozarks. T. Gettings. il Org Gard & Farm 24:111-15 F '77

California

Urban farm; Integral Urban House, Berkeley. K. Brower. il Atlantic 241:58-64 Ja '78

Kansas

Farming ten years ahead of his time. G. Logsdon. il Org Gard & Farm 24:104-6 F '77

Kentucky

Getting started in organic farming. J. Foote. il Org Gard & Farm 24:86-9 Mr '77

Michigan

Farm for the richest living of all. G. Logsdon. il Org Gard & Farm 24:143-7 N '77

Middle Western States

Can we take the chemicals out of the Corn Belt? Horticulture 56:14+ S '77

Minnesota

Dairy that delivers organic farm foods; Little Dutch Mill Dairy. C. Frye. il Org Gard & Farm 24:150+ S '77
How one farmer controls weeds naturally. C. Frye. il Org Gard & Farm 24:87-9 My '77

New York (state)

Three relics; Gericke's Organic Farm, Staten Island. New Yorker 53:28-9 Je 20 '77

Pennsylvania

Our retirement plans are working. T. Fenstermacher. il Org Gard & Farm 24:108-10 My '77

ORGANIC farming research. See Agricultural research

ORGANIC farms. See Farms, Organic

ORGANIC fertilizers. See Fertilizers and manures

ORGANIC foods snacks. See Snacks

ORGANIC gardening
Garden calendar. M. Franz. See issues of Organic gardening and farming
Hillside gardening without terraces; use of raised beds. R. Conrat. il Org Gard & Farm 24:61-2 Ap '77
Intensive gardening—less water and higher yields. J. Jeavons and R. Leler. il Org Gard & Farm 24:78-80 Jl '77
Organic living almanac. See issues of Organic gardening and farming
Planning the 1977 garden; symposium. il Org Gard & Farm 24:62-103 F '77
Raised beds for year-round gardening. N. A. Fisher. il Org Gard & Farm 24:140-1 Je '77
See also
Compost
Fruit culture
Vegetable gardening

Bibliography

About books; ed by J. Cox. See issues of Organic gardening and farming

Economic aspects

How much you can save by growing your own food. G. Logsdon. il Org Gard & Farm 24:56-9 Je '77

Study and teaching

How we turned our students on to organic gardening. J. McMillen. il Org Gard & Farm 24:120+ F '77

California

Earth rich on retirement income. P. Gunn. il Org Gard & Farm 24:110-11 My '77

Oklahoma

Gardening with the weather. S. K. Dark. il Org Gard & Farm 24:144-6 Jl '77

Utah

Retirement way of life. L. Tilton. il Org Gard & Farm 24:111-12 My '77

ORGANIC wastes, Utilization of. See Refuse, Utilization of

ORGANISTS
See also
Fox, V.
International Congress of Organists
Olivera, H.

ORGANIZATION
See also
Organizational behavior

ORGANIZATION for Economic Cooperation and Development
Move to divvy up the orders for ships. il Bus W p36-7 D 5 '77
Secretary Vance attends ministerial conference of the Organization for Economic Cooperation and Development; remarks, transcript of news conference, with texts of declaration and communique, June 23-24, 1977. C. R. Vance; W. M. Blumenthal. Dept State Bull 77:105-20 Jl 25 '77

ORGANIZATION for Economic Cooperation and Development—*Continued*
Slow, slow, slow; report. Time 11:39+ Ja 9 '78
Stoking the West's economic locomotive. E. Mervosh. Bus W p29 Jl 11 '77
Warm autumn for the West. P. A. Samuelson. Newsweek 90:80 Jl 18 '77
Widening split over growth policies. Bus W p37+ D 5 '77

ORGANIZATION of African Unity
Amin steals the OAU show. R. Carroll and J. Pringle. por Newsweek 90:30+ Jl 18 '77
Assembly welcomes OAU efforts to find African solutions. UN Chron 13:48 D '76
Glories of Gabon. J. Pringle. por map Newsweek 90:33 Jl 18 '77
Organization of African Unity and decolonization: present and future trends. G. L. Binaisa. bibl f Ann Am Acad 432:52-69 Jl '77
Secretary-General addresses OAU summit meeting. UN Chron 14:32 Jl '77
United States reemphasizes spirit of cooperation with OAU; statement, November 16, 1976. E. Poston. Dept State Bull 76:58 Ja 17 '77
Voting for the gun barrel; annual meeting. il Time 110:30+ Jl 18 '77

ORGANIZATION of American States
Energy; adaptation of address, May 23, 1977. A. Orfila. il Américas 29:6-12 O '77
Human rights: confrontation in Belgrade and another in Grenada; annual Foreign Ministers' meeting. il Time 109:6-8 Je 27 '77
New horizons for progress and freedom in the Americas; address, February 24, 1977. A. Orfila. Vital Speeches 43:411-13 Ap 15 '77
OAS and Europe. Américas 29:41 O '77
OAS chronicle. See issues of Américas
Our America; special section, ed by A. J. Lowe. il maps Américas 29:16-49 N '77
Secretary Vance attends OAS General Assembly at Grenada; statements, and transcript of news conference, arrival remarks; with text of resolution, June 14-17, 1977. C. R. Vance. Dept State Bull 77:69-72+ Jl 18 '77

General Assembly

Report on human rights in the Americas; statement, September 15, 1977. G. W. McGee. Dept State Bull 77:573-5 O 24 '77
Stalemate or catalyst? The Seventh General Assembly. F. X. Gannon. il Américas 29:2-6 S '77

ORGANIZATION of Petroleum Exporting Countries
Answering OPEC. D. Yergin. New Repub 176:45-7 Ja 22 '77
Can OPEC be broken up? influence of Saudi Arabia. J. Cook. il Forbes 119:48+ F 15 '77
Energy and the world economy; statement, January 5, 1977. J. L. Katz. Dept State Bull 76:61-7 Ja 24 '77
Is OPEC finally losing its grip? U.S. News 84:67 Ja 9 '78
Message from OPEC; excerpts from interview, ed by R. Thomas. W. M. Blumenthal. il por Newsweek 90:92 N 14 '77
Negotiating to heal OPEC's price split. Bus W p29-30 Je 27 '77
New oil prices: impact and response. R. Feitelson and G. Salomon. Intellect 105:327-9 Ap '77
New price jockeying at OPEC. il Bus W p24-5 My 30 '77
OPEC contributing to North-South dialogue, says Venezuela president. UN Chron 13:49-50 D '76
OPEC: where does the balance of power lie? interview. J. Akins. il por Forbes 120:34-6 O 1 '77
Oil and American power—three years later. R. W. Tucker; discussion. Commentary 63:6+ Ap '77
Oil glut slows OPEC's production. il Bus W p23-4 Ag 22 '77
Petro-dollar pinch tightens. il U.S. News 82:22 My 9 '77
President Ford responds to action by OPEC increasing oil prices; statement, December 17, 1976. G. R. Ford. Dept State Bull 76:67 Ja 24 '77
Push to control OPEC gas. il Bus W p72-4 Ja 9 '78
Sagging dollar may raise oil prices. il Bus W p42 N 14 '77
Saudis still reign over OPEC. Bus W p 19-20 Jl 18 '77
Strain on OPEC. M. R. Benjamin and others. il Newsweek 89:46-7 Ja 24 '77
U.S.-Saudi relations and the oil crises of the 1980s. D. A. Rustow. bibl f For Affairs 55:494-516 Ap '77
What price OPEC unity? Time 110:33 O 26 '77
Why an oil price rise is likely this year. S. E. Jackson. Bus W p35 Ja 16 '78

Conferences

Hold that line; OPEC meeting in Carabaleda, Venezuela. A. J. Mayer and others. il Newsweek 91:47-8 Ja 2 '78
OPEC closes ranks. Newsweek 90:64 Jl 25 '77
OPEC: no boost till June—if then. il Time 111:67 Ja 2 '78

ORGANIZATIONAL behavior
Do you have a compulsive personality? K. R. Gertz. Harp Baz 110:86+ Ag '77
Organization behavior as an aid to labor impasse resolution. G. Strauss. bibl M Labor R 100:49-52 Ap '77

ORGANIZATIONAL development. See Organizational change
ORGANIZATIONS. See Associations, institutions, etc.
ORGANIZATIONS, International. See International agencies
ORGANS, Donation of. See Donation of organs, tissues, etc.

ORGASM
Discover your own sexuality; interview. S. Hite. Harp Baz 110:100+ F '77
Women can reach orgasm as easily as men. S. Hite. Vogue 167:220 Mr '77

ORIENT. See Far East
ORIENT express. See Railroads—Europe
ORIENTAL (hotel) See Bangkok—Hotels, restaurants, etc.
ORIENTAL astronomy. See Astronomy, Oriental
ORIENTAL cookery. See Cookery, Oriental
ORIENTAL hand-to-hand fighting. See Hand-to-hand fighting, Oriental
ORIENTAL pottery. See Pottery, Oriental
ORIENTAL religions. See Religions
ORIENTAL rugs. See Rugs and carpets, Oriental
ORIENTAL sculpture. See Sculpture, Oriental
ORIENTAL vegetables. See Vegetables
ORIENTALISM in music. See East and West in music

ORIENTATION
Free-flying birds and geomagnetism. Sci N 111:342 My 28 '77
Geomagnetic disturbance and the orientation of nocturnally migrating birds. F. R. Moore. bibl il Science 196:682-4 My 6 '77
Migrating birds respond to Project Seafarer's electromagnetic field. R. P. Larkin and P. J. Sutherland. bibl il Science 195:777-8 F 25 '77
See also
Chemotaxis
Echolocation (physiology)

ORIENTATION, Military. See Military training

ORIENTEERING (sport)
They call it orienteering. M. Wexler. il map Nat Wildlife 15:12-16 Je '77

ORIGIN of man. See Man—Origin and antiquity
ORING, Lewis W. See Emlen, S. T. jt auth
ORION (constellation) See Constellations

ORISKANY Creek
Along the Oriskany. E. H. Dwight. il Conservationist 31:20-2 N '76

ORKIN, Ruth
Ruth Orkin. N. Stevens. il por Pop Phot 80:100-9+ Je '77 *

ORLAND, Calif.
Tiny town near collapse. J. Wilde. il Time 109:79 Mr 7 '77

ORLANDO Paladino; opera. See Haydn, F. J.

ORLEDGE, Robert
Debussy's House of Usher revisited. bibl f il Mus Q 62:536-53 O '76

ORLOFF, Neil
Payoff for business initiative on the environment. Harvard Bus R 55:8+ N '77

ORLOV, Yuri
Defending Yuri Orlov. New Yorker 53:29-31 S 19 '77 *

ORLOVSKY, Nikolai Sergeivitch. See Babaev, A. G. jt auth

ORME, Ted
Washington report. See issues of Motor trend

ORMONDE, Nick
Bankers aren't always right. il Am For 83:12-14 Je '77

ORNAMENTAL asparagus. See Asparagus
ORNAMENTAL cookery. See Cookery, Ornamental
ORNAMENTAL fishes. See Tropical fishes
ORNAMENTAL plants. See Plants, Ornamental
ORNAMENTS, Christmas tree. See Christmas decorations

ORNANO, Isabelle d'
Family Christmas in France. il por Harp Baz 111:100-1+ D '77

ORNANO, Michel
Duel over city hall. Time 109:31 Ja 31 '77 *

ORNE, Jerrold
Library building trends & their meanings. bibl il Lib J 102:2397-401 D 1 '77
—and Gosling, J. O.
Academic library building in 1977. il Lib J 102:2393-6 D 1 '77

ORNITHINE decarboxylase. See Decarboxylase
ORNITHOLOGY. See Bird study

ORNSTEIN, Allan C.
IQ tests and the culture issue. Educ Digest 42:9-11 Ap '77

ORNSTEIN, Leo
Yale Sym, Westney: Ornstein cto. il por Hi Fi 27:MA25-6 Ap '77 *

O'ROURKE, Frank J.
Once again, into the bank. Writers Digest 57: 54 S '77
O'ROURKE, P. J.
How P.J. became A.J. in just five days. il por Esquire 87:58-62+ F '77
Play it where it lays. il N Y Times Mag p24-5 Je 12 '77
ORPHANS and orphan asylums
Reaching out to orphans. M. McDonald. por Outdoor Life 159:140 My '77
See also
Adoption
ORPHÉE aux enfers; operetta. See Offenbach, J.
ORPHEUM concert hall, Vancouver. See Concert halls
ORR, Bobby
Wherever you find Orr, he glitters P. Gammons. il pors Sports Illus 46:20-1 Ja 24 '77 *
ORR, Ed
Aftermarket air. il Motor T 29:81-5 Je '77
Mail order buying. Motor T 29:52-4 Ap; 68-72 My '77
ORR, Lloyd D.
Profit in bottle laws. bibl il Environment 18: 33-40 D '76; 19:43 Ap '77
ORR, William
VHF antenna systems. il Motor B & S 140:51-3 N '77
ORTEGA, J. A. Campos-. See Campos-Ortega, J. A.
ORTHO Books (firm) See Publishers and publishing —Garden literature
ORTHODONTICS
Adult orthodontics. H. Brubach. il Mademoiselle 83:244+ O '77
ORTHODOX Church in America
Domesticating Orthodoxy. il Time 110:123-4 N 7 '77
ORTHODOX Eastern Church
See also
Catholic Church—Relations—Orthodox Eastern Church
Ecumenical movement
ORTHODOX Eastern Church, Russian
Russian Christianity: conflict and hope. D. Burkholz. il Chr Cent 94:627-9 Jl 6 '77
ORTHODOX Eastern Church in Greece
Casanova's law. C. Roberts. Commonweal 104: 486-8 Ag 5 '77
ORTHODOX Eastern Church in the United States
Visitor from the Middle East; Patriarch Elias IV of the Syrian Orthodoxy's See of Antioch. Chr Today 21:39-40 Ag 26 '77
ORTHOPEDIA
Amateur hour; alleged surgery performed by medical supply salesman W. MacKay at Smithtown General Hospital. il Time 110:94 N 14 '77
Amateur surgeons; alleged surgery performed by medical supply salesman W. MacKay at Smithtown General Hospital, N.Y. M. Clark and D. Shapiro. il por Newsweek 90:125 N 14 '77
Salesmen in the operating room. il Forbes 120: 33 D 1 '77
ORTHOPEDIC braces
Braced for the best; scoliosis, or curvature of the spine. C. Holtmann. por Seventeen 36:36 My '77
Convict and the boy; leather brace made for burn victim Kearey Allison by M. Leach. J. P. Blank and M. J. Mueller. il Read Digest 110:135-9 My '77
ORTHOPEDIC surgery. See Orthopedia
ORTNER, Everett H.
Through the viewfinder. See issues of Popular science
ORTON, Peter, and Stevens, Joyce
Survival in Boston. Educ Digest 42:19-21 Ap '77
ORTON, Vrest
Why Johnny can't read. Nat R 29:1006-7 S 2 '77
ORVILLE, Richard E.
Bolts from the blue; with biographical sketch. il Natur Hist 86:6, 66-73 bibl(p93) Je '77
OSAMU, Kataoka
Survivor's story: friends, please forgive us. Bull Atom Sci 33:52 D '77
OSANKA, Frank
What parents should know and do about kiddie porn. P. Bridge. il Parents Mag 53:42-3+ Ja '78 *
OSBORN, C. S.
Zero-zero=stupid-stupid. Flying 101:42+ O '77
OSBORN, D. Keith, and Osborn, J. D.
Television violence revisited. il Educ Digest 43:38-9 S '77
OSBORN, Earl D.
Osborn. J. W. Olcott. Flying 101:256-7 S '77 *
OSBORN, Janie D. See Osborn, D. K. jt auth
OSBORNE, Conrad L.
L'amore dei tre re: like no other Italian opera; RCA recording. il por Hi Fi 27:67-70 Ag '77
Spirit of the faydit. il Opera N 41:26-8 Ap 9 '77
Who can resist The mother of us all? il Hi Fi 27:92-4 Jl '77
OSBORNE, Edwin
Protecting the boat's plumbing. Motor B & S 140:120 O '77
OSBORNE, Elizabeth
Elizabeth Osborne: painting with light. E. Medoff. il por Am Artist 41:34-9+ S '77 *
OSBORNE, John, 1907-
White House watch. See occasional issues of New republic
OSBORNE, Kenan B.
Theology in 1977 and beyond. Chr Cent 94:92-3 F 2 '77
OSBORNE, W. E.
Build 3 low cost CB test meters. il Radio-Electr 48:40-1+ O '77
OSCARS (prizes) See Academy Awards (motion pictures)
OSCEOLA, Fla.
Education
See Education—Florida
OSCILLATORS
Build the V-4 VCO for electronic music. J. Barbarello. il Pop Elect 11:42-4 Mr '77
Portable 60-Hz clock oscillator. C. F. Smith. il Pop Electr 12:70 Jl '77
OSCILLOSCOPES
Create 3D scope patterns: build optical synthesizer. W. Sikonowiz. il Radio-Electr 48:33-6 D '77
Display quad signals on your scope. S. Dunifer. il Radio Electr 48:42-3 Je '77
Equipment reports:
Leader LBO-515 delayed-sweep dual trace oscilloscope. il Radio-Electr 48:26+ N '77
Guide to oscilloscopes. C. Hallmark. il Pop Electr 11:59-63 Je '77
Oscilloscopes. il Radio-Electr 48:57-8 N '77
Testing
Product test reports:
B&K precision model 1471B oscilloscope. il Pop Electr 11:94-5 My '77
Ballantine model 1010A oscilloscope. il Pop Electr 11:101 Mr '77
OSEI-MENSAH, Gottfried B.
Church in Africa: from adolescence to maturity; interview, ed by H. Lindsell. por Chr Today 21: 17-19 Ja 7 '77
O'SHAUGHNESSY, Helaine. See Friedman, S. M. jt auth
O'SHEA, Nancy
Fort Jefferson: confessions of a tour guide. il Nat Parks & Con Mag 51:20-2 S '77
OSHIMA, Nagisa
Review; L'Empire des sens. M. Silverman. il Film Q 30:58-61 Wint '76 *
OSIS, Karlis
What the dying see. J. White. Sci Digest 81: 71-2 F '77 *
OSMAN, John
Over lake & turf with Big Daddy. Time 109:20-1 Mr 7 '77
OSMEÑA, Sergio, 3d
Great escape? C. Whipple and others. il pors Newsweek 90:62 O 17 '77 *
OSMOLALITY. See Solution (chemistry)
OSMOND, George, family
Marie Osmond: I've got a brother for every mood; interview, ed by J. Wilkie. M. Osmond. il por Good H 184:52+ Mr '77
OSMOND, Marie
Marie; interview, ed by I. Silden. por Ladies Home J 94:52+ Mr '77
Marie Osmond: I've got a brother for every mood; interview, ed by J. Wilkie. il por Good H 184:52+ Mr '77
OSMOREGULATION
Chloride transport across isolated opercular epithelium of killifish: a membrane rich in chloride cells. K. J. Karnaky, Jr and others. bibl il Science 195:203-5 Ja 14 '77
OSNOS, Peter
Détente: a victim of mutual suspicion. il Bull Atom Sci 33:16-19 N '77
Polish road to communism. For Affairs 56:209-20 O '77
OSSETES
Ossetes: Scythians of the 20th century. V. I. Abaev. il UNESCO Courier 29:48-9 D '76
OSSINING, N.Y.
Taxation
See Taxation—New York (state)
OSSOFSKY, Jack
Excerpt from statement on proposed amendments to the Age Discrimination in Employment Act, September 14, 1976. Cong Digest 56: 274+ N '77
OSTEOPATHS
Country doctor; work of G. Duckworth in Mound City, Kan. C. Remsberg. il por Fam Health 9:36-9+ Ap '77
OSTEOPUNCTURE
Puncturing pain: Ronald Lawrence. P. Lehmann. Harp Baz 110:188 S '77
OSTLERE, Gordon
Aluminum wedding. il Horticulture 55:17 Je '77

O'SULLIVAN, Lily
So nice to know you; poem. Ladies Home J 94: 20 D '77

OSWALD, Lee Harvey
JFK: what the FBI found. R. Boeth and others. il pors Newsweek 90:28+ D 19 '77 *
Making of a marriage and of an assassin told in Harper & Row book for October; interview, ed by R. Dahlin. P. J. McMillan. il pors Pub W 212:46+ Jl 11 '77 *
Marina & Lee; excerpt. P. J. McMillan. il pors Ladies Home J 94:175-82+ O; 122-3+ N '77 *

OSWALD, Marina
Making of a marriage and of an assassin told in Harper & Row book for October; interview, ed by R. Dahlin. P. J. McMillan. il pors Pub W 212:46+ Jl 11 '77 *
Marina & Lee; excerpt. P. J. McMillan. il pors Ladies Home J 94:175-82+ O; 122-3+ N '77 *

OSWEGO County, N.Y.
Transfer stations compact waste collection distances. F. A. Loguidice. il Am City & County 92:73-4 Ag '77

OTAVALO, Ecuador
Looms of Otavalo. J. B. Casagrande. il Natur Hist 86:48-59 O '77

OTHERWISE engaged; drama. See Gray, S.

OTIS, Denise
Swedish treat: beautiful glass in a rustic landscape. il House & Gard 149:48+ Jl '77

O'TOOLE, Patricia
Six glorious weeks in Europe—on a buying spree. Vogue 167:254+ Mr '77

OTT, Elmer
Obituary
Camp Mag por 49:4 Je '77

OTTAWA

Description and travel

Canada's capital capital. L. Snyder. il Ret Liv 17:32-3 Jl '77

Galleries and museums

See also
National Gallery of Canada

National Arts Centre

Success story. D. Seabury. il Opera N 42:20-2 Jl '77

OTTAWA. University. See Colleges and universities—Canada

OTTEN, Jane
Gray chic. por Newsweek 90:13 D 5 '77
Start planning early to cushion the hardships of age; interview. por U.S. News 83:57-8 O 3 '77

—and Shelley, F. D.
As your parents grow older; excerpt from When your parents grow old. il Parents Mag 52:42+ Je '77

OTTERS
Otter. H. W. Trimm. il Conservationist 31:23-5 My '77

OTTO, Archduke of Austria
Peril of Soviet friendship pacts. por Sat Eve Post 249:21+ My '77
Southern Africa: race conflict or third world war? il Sat Eve Post 249:68-9 S '77
Trading with the Soviet Union. Sat Eve Post 249:38+ Mr '77

OUBRE, Edward P.
Hooked on barbed wire. Sat Eve Post 249:14-15 My '77

OUMANSKY, Valentina
Oumansky in queryland. V. H. Swisher. il por Dance Mag 52:75 Ja '78 *

OUMANSKY, Valentina, Dramatic Dance Ensemble. See Dance companies

OUR Father (prayer) See Lord's Prayer

OUR Lady of Good Counsel Church, Bedford-Stuyvesant. See Brooklyn—Churches

OUT-placement consultant services. See Business consultants

OUTBOARD motor boat racing. See Motor boat racing

OUTBOARD motor boats
Small outboard boats. il Consumer Rep 42: 125-8 D '77

OUTBOARD motors
Busting out the facts. D. Hart. il Motor B & S 139:62-5+ Je '77
Dollar-wise outboard buying; excerpt from Outboard motor handbook. N. Warren. il Motor B & S 139:96-7+ My '77
Here come the imported outboards! J. J. Whisler. il Mech Illus 73:120-1+ F '77
Little import outboards join the big leagues. B. McKeown. il Pop Mech 148:96-7 D '77
New boats & motors for 1978. B. Stearns. il Outdoor Life 161:85-8+ Ja '78
New import outboards join the little league. R. Gill. il Pop Mech 147:92-3+ Ap '77
New outboards: bigger than ever. D. Hart. il Motor B & S 140:22+ S '77
New outboards—new horsepower race. B. McKeown. il Pop Mech 148:96-7 O '77
1978 outboards: more macho. F. M. Paulson. il Field & S 82:92-4 D '77
Outboard scene for 1978. A. J. McMasters. il Mech Illus 73:46-7+ O '77
Outboards for 1978. il Yachting 142:86-8 O '77
'77 outboards. J. Roe. il Pop Sci 210:96-8 F '77
Winding up Black Max; Mercury engines compared. D. Hart. il Motor B & S 140:62-6+ N '77

Maintenance and repair

Springtime attention to your outboard. il Motor B & S 139:113-14 Ap '77

Purchasing

Transom power. D. Hart. il Motor B & S 140: 66-8+ D '77

Storage

Mothballing your outboard—do it the easy way with these new products. B. Stearns. il Pop Sci 211:42+ O '77

Testing

Mid-size outboards. B. Stearns. il Pop Sci 211: 116+ Jl '77
PM tests the outboard too hot to name. B. McKeown. il por Pop Mech 148:86-7+ S '77
PS test report: Mercury's 200-hp outboard. B. Stearns. il Pop Sci 211:8+ D '77
We try out an imported outboard. A. J. McMasters. il Mech Illus 73:60+ Jl '77

OUTCASTS in opera. See Characters in opera

OUTDOOR Biology Instructional Strategies project. See United States—National Science Foundation

OUTDOOR carpets. See Rugs and carpets, Outdoor

OUTDOOR Christmas decorations. See Christmas decorations, Outdoor

OUTDOOR cookery. See Cookery, Outdoor

OUTDOOR education
Classes for the courageous. J. W. Fears. il Seventeen 36:56-7 Je '77
High adventure: confronting the essentials. R. M. Tapply. il Parks & Rec 12:26-9+ Je '77
Indian summer for wayfarers; teaching Indian culture to children in natural areas. K. Kaltenbronn. il Parks & Rec 12:49-50 Je '77
Science and socialization out-of-doors; Doherty School Outing Club, Cincinnati. P. D. Dawson. Educ Digest 42:57-9 F '77
See also
Camping—Educational aspects
Conservation of resources—Study and teaching
Nature study
Outward Bound schools

OUTDOOR furniture. See Furniture, Outdoor

OUTDOOR life
All outdoors. B. McKeown. See issues of Popular mechanics
Bazaar's guide to the great outdoors; symposium. il Harp Baz 110:86-9+ Ap '77
Bird watcher nonpareil. J. J. Audubon. il Sat Eve Post 249:16 Jl '77
Christmas gift. R. Starnes. Outdoor Life 160: 10+ D '77
Hill country. G. Hill. See issues of Field & stream
Life outdoors. H. F. Waters and others. il Newsweek 90:56-7+ Jl 18 '77
Outdoor living. M. Davidson. il Parents Mag 52:59-61 Jl '77
Outdoors. See issues of Esquire
Outdoors. P. Barrett. See issues of Mechanix illustrated
Outdoors bulletins (cont) Mech Illus 73:142 Mr; 171 My; 90 Je '77
Women in the outdoors. il Outdoor Life 159:55 F '77
See also
Backpacks and backpacking
Camping
Country life
Hiking
Hunting
Mountaineering
Nature
Outdoor Women (organization)
Picnics
Sports
Walking
Wilderness survival

Anecdotes, facetiae, satire, etc.

[Column] P. F. McManus. See issues of Field & stream
Vermont, through a thermopane window. G. Wolff. il Esquire 87:48+ Ap '77
Who needs it? a guide to the great indoors. P. Axthelm. il Newsweek 90:67 Jl 18 '77

Bibliography

Books & comments. See issues of Field & stream
New books (cont) Outdoor Life 159:168 F; 160: 136 N '77

OUTDOOR life (periodical)
Outdoor life: Lamar Underwood, editor. J. Fry. por Outdoor Life 159:4 Mr '77
Update; new section. L. Underwood. Outdoor Life 160:26 O '77

OUTDOOR lighting. See Lighting, Outdoor

OUTDOOR living areas. See Decks, patios, terraces, etc.

OUTDOOR markets. See Street trades
OUTDOOR meals
Smoke an outdoor dinner. il Ebony 32:150+ My '77
Wining alfresco. D. Tobias. il Am Home 80:7 Jl '77
See also
Barbecue cookery
Picnics
OUTDOOR occupations. See Occupations
OUTDOOR recreation. See Recreation
OUTDOOR Recreation, Bureau of. See United States—Outdoor Recreation, Bureau of
OUTDOOR rooms. See Decks, patios, terraces, etc.
OUTDOOR survival. See Wilderness survival
OUTDOOR theater. See Theater, Open-air
OUTDOOR wall murals. See Mural painting and decoration, Exterior
OUTDOOR Women (organization)
Pushing for change. J. Fry. Outdoor Life 159:58 F '77
OUTER space. See Space, Outer
OUTER Space Committee. See United Nations—Committee on the Peaceful Uses of Outer Space
OUTHWAITE, Tony
Back in the U.S.A. Nat R 29:1125-6 S 30 '77
OUTLAWS
New Mexico incident; murder of Albert J. Fountain and his son. W. H. Hutchinson. bibl il pors Am West 41:4-7+ N '77
Only law; excerpts from 1926 articles, ed by A. B. Macdonald. F. Sutton. il por Sat Eve Post 249:62-3 Jl '77
OUTLET Company
Outlet Co: pouring broadcasting's cash flow into retailing acquisitions. Bus W p 100-1+ Ja 16 '78
OUTLETS, Factory. See Stores
OUTPATIENT services in hospitals. See Hospitals—Outpatient services
OUTPUT of workers. See Labor productivity
OUTWARD Bound schools
Outward Bound: the ultimate experience. S. Smolkin. Harp Baz 110:87+ Ap '77
OUYANG, Tzu-Yuan
Kirin meteorites. il Sci N 111:92-4 F 5 '77
OUZTS, Johnie M.
Oil makes Kewanee alluring to suitors. il Bus W p30-1 Mr 14 '77 *
OVA
Autoantibodies to zona pellucida: a possible cause for infertility in women. C. A. Shivers and B. S. Dunbar. bibl il Science 197:1082-4 S 9 '77
Transplantation
Embryo transfers practical for more dairymen. C. S. Machan. il Farm J 101:Dairy 16+ Ja '77
Now: calves from frozen embryos. G. Lorang. il Farm J 101:24-6+ Ag '77
OVEN FORK, Ky, mine disaster. See Coal mines and mining—Accidents and explosions
OVENS
See also
Microwave ovens
Stoves
Toaster ovens
OVER the counter drugs. See Medicines, Patent, proprietary, etc.
OVERALLS. See Clothing and dress—Work clothes
OVERBYE, Dennis
Out from under the cosmic censor: Stephen Hawking's black holes. il por Sky & Tel 54:84-9+ Ag '77
OVERDRAFTS, Bank. See Banks and banking—Overdrafts
OVERDRIVE (periodical)
Trucker militant; M. Parkhurst. H. Crews. il por Esquire 88:82-4+ Ag '77
OVERDUE books. See Libraries—Circulation, loans, etc; Libraries—Fines
OVEREATING. See Hyperphagia; Obesity; Weight (physiology)
OVERLAND journeys to the Pacific
First crossing: Alexander Mackenzie's quest for the Pacific; excerpt from Winner take all. D. Lavender. il por Am West 14:4-11+ S '77
Naturalists across the Rockies: 1834 journey of J. K. Townsend and T. Nuttall. J. I. Merritt. bibl il pors Am West 14:4-9+ Mr '77
Overland to California; memoirs, ed by G. C. Stein. il por Am Hist Illus 12:26-36 My '77
OVERPOPULATION. See Population—Overpopulation
OVERSEAS forces. See United States—Armed Forces—Forces in foreign countries
OVERSEAS Private Investment Corporation
Department discusses proposal to extend the authority of OPIC; statement, June 23, 1977. J. L. Katz. Dept State Bull 77:135-6 Jl 25 '77
Push to tap new resources. il Bus W p 18-19 Jl 18 '77
OVERSEAS Shipholding Group, Inc. See Shipping—United States
OVERSIGHT Subcommittee. See United States—Congress—House—Intelligence, Select Committee on—Oversight Subcommittee
OVERTON, Boyce
Gonna shout, gonna shine. il Sat Eve Post 249:22-4+ N '77
OVERWEIGHT. See Obesity
OVINGTON, Ray
Back to trout fishing fundamentals; excerpt from The trout and the fly. il Field & S 82:32-4+ My '77
OVIPOSITION
Bag cell control of egg laying in freely behaving aplysia. H. M. Pinsker and F. E. Dudek. bibl il Science 197:490-3 Jl 29 '77
OVRUT, Burt A. and Ovrut, Susan
Sahara: the growing giant. il Sci Digest 81:28-32 F '77
OVRUT, Susan. See Ovrut, B. A. jt auth
OVSHINSKY, Stanford R.
New promise of cheap solar energy. por Bus W p20-1 Jl 18 '77 *
OVULATION
Primate sex preference at ovulation. il Sci N 111:118-19 F 19 '77
OWEN, David
Illinois training program treats crafts seriously. il Aging 275:26-7 S '77
OWEN, David Anthony Llewellyn
Britain's Owen—a fresh start; excerpts from interview, ed by H. Nickel. il por Time 109:53-4 My 2 '77
Detente, Helsinki and human rights: the British view; address, March 3, 1977. Vital Speeches 43:369-72 Ap 1 '77
News conference by Secretary Vance and Foreign Secretary Owen, London, Aug. 12. Dept State Bull 77:345-50 S 12 '77
Rhodesia—proposals for a settlement; joint press conference, September 2, 1977. Dept State Bull 77:417-24 O 3 '77
Secretary Vance meets with Foreign Secretary Owen; remarks with the press, July 23, 1977. Dept State Bull 77:275-8 Ag 29 '77
about
Doctor's new practice. il por Newsweek 89:46 Mr 7 '77 *
Peace-plan safari. M. R. Benjamin and others. il pors Newsweek 90:35-6 S 5 '77 *
OWEN, Guy
Building characters from the ground up. Writer 90:17-19 Ja '77
OWEN, Howard R.
Your house is on fire! excerpt from Fire and you. Sat Eve Post 249:26 S '77
OWEN, Jean Z.
Likes attract: how to create likeable characters in your fiction. Writers Digest 57:31-2+ Je '77
OWEN, Nathan Richard
General Signal cashes in on federal dollars. por Bus W p 166+ Mr 21 '77 *
OWEN, Sam
Goodbye to the rubber diploma. il por Time 110:46 S 26 '77 *
School where students have to measure up. J. Greenwald. McCalls 104:58 Ap '77 *
OWEN, Tobias. See Anders, E. jt auth
OWENS, Bill
Working class. D. Davis. il Newsweek 90:75 O 10 '77 *
OWENS, Edgar L.
Appropriate technology. A. Von Lazar and K. Bode. New Repub 176:11-13 Je 11 '77 *
OWENS, Major R.
Politics for progress. por Lib J 102:988-90, 1819-22 My 1, S 15 '77
OWENS, Patrick
Attack and counterattack. J. Simon. Esquire 88:20+ D '77 *
OWENS, Ray C. See Cunningham, W. G. jt auth
OWENS, Virginia Stem
Price of praise. il Chr Today 22:14-16 N 18 '77
To see life steady and to see it whole. il Chr Today 21:18-21 Mr 4 '77
OWLS
Morristown's owls control city rats; barn owls. Am City & County 92:30 O '77
Night hunter; British barn owl. I. Smullen. il Int Wildlife 7:32-5 S '77
Receptive fields of auditory neurons in the owl. E. I. Knudsen and others. bibl il Science 198:1278-80 D 23 '77
OWNERSHIP. See Property
OWNERSHIP controversies. See Possession (law)
OXFORD English dictionary. See English language—Dictionaries
OXFORD. University
Oxford. B. H. Matthiessen. il Travel 147:24-31+ Ap '77
Sherry and skepticism: Oxford days; an American student at Balliol College. L. Wieseltier. Am Scholar 46:483-95 Aut '77

OXIDASES
Aldehyde oxidase compartmentalization in drosophila melanogaster wing imaginal disks. D. T. Kuhn and G. N. Cunningham. bibl il Science 196:875-7 My 20 '77
Herbivore-plant interactions: mixed-function oxidases and secondary plant substances. L. B. Brattsten and others. bibl il Science 196:1349-52 Je 17 '77

OXIDATION
Prelytic damage of red cells in filtrates from peroxidizing microsomes. M. K. Roders and others. bibl il Science 196:1221-2 Je 10 '77

OXIDATION, Physiological
Three hypolipidemic drugs increase hepatic palmitoyl-coenzyme A oxidation in the rat. P. B. Lazarow. bibl il Science 197:580-1 Ag 5 '77

OXIDATION ditches. See Sewage lagoons

OXYGEN

Isotopes

Oxygen and hydrogen isotopic ratios in plant cellulose. S. Epstein and others. bibl il Science 198:1209-15 D 23 '77
Oxygen isotopic analysis of the size fraction between 62 and 250 micrometers in Caribbean cores P6304-8 and P6304-9. C. Emiliani. bibl il Science 198:1255-6 D 23 '77

Physiological effects

Oxygen is toxic! I. Fridovich. bibl il BioScience 27:462-6 Jl '77

OXYGEN in the body
Natural life preservers; views of M. Nemiroff on the diving reflex. il por Time 110:73+ Ag 22 '77
Noninvasive, infrared monitoring of cerebral and myocardial oxygen sufficiency and circulatory parameters. F. F. Jobsis. bibl il Science 198:1264-7 D 23 '77
Reprieve from drowning; diving reflex. Sci Am 237:57-8 Ag '77
Saving the drowned; diving reflex during asphyxia. S. Drake. il por Newsweek 90:79-80 Ag 22 '77
See also
Anoxemia

OXYTOCIN
Pineal vasotocin: release into cat cerebrospinal fluid by melanocyte-stimulating hormone release-inhibiting factor. S. Pavel and others. bibl il Science 197:179-80 Jl 8 '77

OYAMA, Vance I.
Martian muddle: DNA the dry way? Sci N 111:276-7 Ap 30 '77 *

OYOTUNJI, S.C.

Blacks

See Blacks—South Carolina

OYSTER culture. See Shellfish culture
OYSTER plant. See Salsify
OYSTER shells. See Shells (conchology)

OZARK Mountains
American rustic: the Ozarks. R. L. Harmon. il Travel 148:42-5 Ag '77
Retiring to the Ozarks; So this is Little Rock. D. L. Goff; D. Dahl. il Ret Liv 17:44-5+ My '77

OZAWA, Seiji
Ives: Symphony no. 4; Central Park in the dark, conducted by S. Ozawa. W. D. Curtis. Am Rec G 40:32-4 O '77 *

OZICK, Cynthia
Does genius have a gender? pors Ms 6:56+ D '77
How to profit more from the teachings of Clara Schacht. . . Esquire 87:92-3+ My '77
Puttermesser: her work history, her ancestry, her afterlife; story. New Yorker 53:38-44 My 9 '77

OZICK, Shiphra Regelson
Passage to the New World. il por Ms 6:72-4+ Ag '77

OZONE
Energetic radiation belt electron precipitation: a natural depletion mechanism for stratospheric ozone. R. M. Thorne. bibl il Science 195:287-9 Ja 21 '77
FAA official claims new data minimize aircraft ozone impact. Aviation W 107:28 Ag 8 '77
Great ozone debate. E. Edelson. il Pop Sci 210:82-6 Je '77
Lasers shed light on ozone reaction. Chemistry 50:21 S '77
Ozone: a world plan of action. Sci N 111:166 Mr 12 '77
Ozone monitoring with an infrared heterodyne radiometer. R. T. Menzies and R. K. Seals, Jr. bibl il Science 197:1275-7 S 23 '77
Prediction of ozone loss down, and up. Sci N 111:372 Je 11 '77
Solar proton event: influence on stratospheric ozone. D. F. Heath and others. bibl il Science 197:886-9 Ag 26 '77
Vapor emission termed greater ozone threat. R. G. O'Lone. Aviation W 108:38-9 Ja 2 '78
Why ban fluorocarbons in aerosol sprays? interview. F. S. Rowland. Read Digest 110:35-6+ F '77

Physiological effects

Ozone irritation problem sparks various solutions. Aviation W 106:33 Ap 18 '77
Plague of ozone. L. Langway and others. Newsweek 89:97-8 My 16 '77

P

PAHO. See Pan American Health Organization
PBB (polybrominated biphenyls) See Diphenyl compounds
PBS. See Public Broadcasting Service
PCA International, Inc. See Photographic industry
PCB (polychlorinated biphenyls) See Diphenyl compounds
PCP. See Phencyclidine hydrochloride

PEN Club
P.E.N. lists 606 writers as victims of repression. M. Reuter. Pub W 212:18 N 14 '77

P4 laboratories. See United States—National Institutes of Health—Laboratories
pH. See Hydrogen ion concentration
P. H. Brennan Hand Delivery Service. See Postal service—United States
Ph.D. degrees. See Degrees, Academic
PIXE (proton-induced X-ray emission analysis) See Spectrum analysis
PLA. See American Library Association—Public Library Association
PLO. See Palestine Liberation Organization
POWs. See Prisoners of war
PROM (programmable read-only memory) See Electronic circuits, Integrated
PTA. See Parents and Teachers Associations
PURAC (Personal Use Radio Advisory Committee) See United States—Federal Communications Commission
PUSH. See People United to Save Humanity (organization)
PUT (programmable unijunction transistor) See Transistors
PVC pipes. See Pipes, Plastic

PAANANEN, Donna M.
Parent's guide to music lessons. Bet Hom & Gard 55:64+ S '77

PAARLBERG, Don
Land prices are running a fever! por map Farm J 101:17-19 Ap '77
New farm bill: how will it work out? por Farm J 101:28+ O '77

PABST, G. W.
Out of Pandora's box. D. Newlin. por Opera N 41:20+ Ap 2 '77 *

PABST Brewing Company-APL Corporation merger. See Corporations—Acquisitions and mergers

PACA, William, House, Annapolis. See Historic houses, sites, etc.—Maryland

PACE University, New York
Rest in Pace; takeover of Briarcliff College. M. Sheils and F. V. Boyd. il Newsweek 89:96 Ap 11 '77

PACEMAKER, Artificial (heart)
Pacemaker outpaced by new device that regulates heartbeat. Ret Liv 16:17 D '76

PACHECO, Ferdie
Ali's doctor: the greatest, in his own way. R. Blount, Jr. il Esquire 87:20+ Je '77 *

PACIFIC countries
See also
United Nations—Economic and Social Commission for Asia and the Pacific

Foreign relations

United States

See United States—Foreign relations—Pacific countries

PACIFIC Cultural Foundation. See Government publicity—Taiwan
PACIFIC Design Center. See Los Angeles—Stores
PACIFIC fleet. See United States—Navy
PACIFIC ISLANDS, Trust Territory of the. See Trust Territory of the Pacific Islands
PACIFIC Missile Test Center. See Proving grounds
PACIFIC Northwest. See Northwestern States

PACIFIC Ocean
High-frequency P_n phases observed in the Pacific at great distances. D. A. Walker. bibl il map Science 197:257-9 Jl 15 '77
Long waves in the eastern equatorial Pacific Ocean: a view from a geostationary satellite. R. Legeckis. bibl il Science 197:1179-81 S 16 '77
See also
Oceania

Discovery and exploration

Winning the pathless Pacific; first European voyagers. M. Shadbolt. il map Read Digest 111:98-105 Ag '77

PACIFIC Region

Description and travel

Pacific overture. . .; symposium. il Holiday 58: 29-46+ Mr '77

PACIFIC Trust Territory. See Trust Territory of the Pacific Islands

PACIFIC Western Airlines. See Airlines—Canada

PACIFICA (continent) See Continental drift

PACIFISM

Culture of appeasement. N. Podhoretz. Harpers 255:25-32 O '77

See also

Conscientious objectors

Nonviolence

PACINO, Al

Basic training of Al Pacino. M. Gussow. il pors N Y Times Mag p21-2+ Je 5 '77 *

PACK, Robert

Comment. D. Allen. Poetry 130:343-4 S '77 *

PACKAGED foods. See Convenience foods

PACKAGED mixes. See Beverage mixes

PACKAGES, Wrapping of. See Wrapping of packages

PACKAGING

Buy the product, not the package. Changing T 31:21-3 Ap '77

Japanese gift wraps use flowers, leaves, stems; tsutsumu. il Sunset 159:84 Ag '77

Truth and consequences; address, May 17, 1977. J. H. Alexander. Vital Speeches 43:565-9 Jl 1 '77

See also

Containers

Meat—Packaging

Pressure packaging

Seeds—Packaging

Tape, cartridges, cassettes, etc.—Packaging

PACKARD, Vance

People shapers; excerpt. Sat R 4:33-48 Ag 6 '77

PACKARD, William

Poetic devices. Writer 90:23-5+ Ag '77

PACKER, Alferd E.

Question of taste. por Newsweek 90:24 Ag 22 '77 *

PACKER, Kerry Francis Bullmore

Fending off vulgarity. il Time 110:45 Ag 8 '77 *

Sticky wicket. P. Webb. il Newsweek 90:36 Ag 8 '77 *

PACKING industry. See Meat industry

PACKING of luggage

Packing for a vacation trip. J. Murphy. il Ret Liv 17:47-8 Jl '77

PACKS

See also

Backpacks and backpacking

PACKWOOD, Robert W.

How to keep big government from growing bigger. por Duns R 110:69-70 Ag '77

Revitalizing of the Republican Party; address, March 5, 1977. Vital Speeches 43:453-6 My 15 '77

PADDLE tennis

Forest Hills Hilton; Tribuno World Championship. M. Donovan. il Sports Illus 46:74+ Ap 11 '77

Platform tennis, anyone? B. Tarshis. il House & Gard 149:42+ F '77

Racquets reach out. C. Wiseman. il Horizon 20:82-7 S '77

PADDLEFISH fishing

Incredible paddlefish; spoonbills in Missouri. G. Reiger. il Field & S 82:62+ N '77

PADHI, Bibhu Prasad

Sea breeze; poem. Poetry 129:270-1 F '77

PADS, Exercise. See Exercising equipment

PADULA, Alfred L. Jr

Claimsmen and the traders. Nation 225:390-3 O 22 '77

PADUS, Emrika J.

Health harvest. See issues of Organic gardening and farming to July 1977

PAEHLKE, Robert C.

Advanced island. See issues of Environment

Asbestos, maple trees, and Mounties. Environment 19:3-4 Ja '77

Overview: Canada. Environment 19:3-4 Ja; 5+ Mr; 2-3 My; 5+ Je; 2-3 Ag; 2-4 O '77

PÁEZ, VILARÓ, Carlos

Night of nights in Montevideo. il por Américas 29:58-9 N '77

PAFFENBARGER, Ralph Seal, 1922-

Coronary curb. Time 110:80 D 12 '77 *

PAGE, Benjamin B.

Right to health care. Cur Hist 73:5-8+ Jl '77

PAGE, Ernest R.

Black literature and changing attitudes: does it do the job? bibl f il Engl J 66:29-33 Mr '77

PAGE, George C. Museum of La Brea Discoveries. See George C. Page Museum of La Brea Discoveries, Los Angeles

PAGE, Greg

Can history repeat itself? il pors Ebony 33:104-6+ D '77 *

PAGE, James K. Jr

Phenomena, comment and notes. See issues of Smithsonian

PAGE, L. Rodman

Kitchen little. il por House & Gard 149:96-7 F '77 *

PAGE, Mary

Spending money on yourself can up your bank account. Vogue 167:236+ S '77

PAGE, Russell

Garden is a song of praise; interview, ed by C. Seebohm. il por House & Gard 149:92-7+ Jl '77

Shaping of a garden. il por House & Gard 149: 34+ Jl '77

PAGES, Congressional. See United States—Congress—Pages

PAGES from Parra; drama. See Parra, N.

PAGING devices, Radio. See Radio apparatus and instruments, Portable

PAGLIARO, John

Pags packs his bags. J. Papanek. il Sports Illus 47:56+ N 21 '77 *

PAHLEVI, Mohammed Reza, Shah of Iran. See Mohammed Reza Pahlevi

PAIN

Breaking out of the pain trap. J. Wang. bibl por Psychol Today 11:78-80+ Jl '77

Chronic pain; clinics. E. H. McCleary. il Fam Health 9:26-9+ Ag '77

Fix for pain? use of heroin and marijuana for terminal cancer patients. M. Clark and others. il Newsweek 91:41 Ja 2 '78

Heat and cold for treatment of pain. A. Frank and S. Frank. Mademoiselle 83:46+ F '77

New war on pain. M. Clark and others. il Newsweek 89:48-50 Ap 25 '77

Pain clinics. J. Greenwald. McCalls 104:46-7 Mr '77

Pain control with hypnosis. C. Holden. Science 198:808 N 25 '77

Pain: medical science begins to take it seriously. il U.S. News 83:61 Ag 1 '77

Solving the mysteries of pain. L. Cherry. il N Y Times Mag p 12-13+ Ja 30 '77

See also

Analgesia

Backache

Facial pain

Headache

Suffering

PAINE Webber Inc-Mitchell, Hutchins Inc merger. See Brokers—Acquisitions and mergers

PAINT

Easy texture for your walls. il Mech Illus 73: 78+ Ap '77

Exterior oil paints. il Consumer Rep 42:166-71 D '77

Interior semigloss paints; alkyd and latex types. Consumer Rep 42:479-83 Ag '77

Interior texture paints. il Consumer Rep 42:163-6 D '77

Porch-and-deck paints. il Consumer Rep 42: 176-9 D '77

Understanding paint chemistry; marine surface coatings. J. L. Duffett. il Motor B & S 139: 43-5 Ap '77

Variation in oil-color properties; questions and answers. R. Mayer. Am Artist 41:12 Je '77

See also

Primers (coating)

PAINT, Protective

Basement waterproofing paints. Consumer Rep 42:174-6 D '77

See also

Primers (coating)

PAINT industry

Thin coating of profit for paint makers. il Bus W p 106+ Ag 15 '77

PAINT pads. See Painting, Industrial and practical —Equipment and supplies

PAINT primers. See Primers (coating)

PAINT sprayers. See Spraying apparatus

PAINT spraying

Spray-painting pros and cons. R. Muff. il Motor B & S 139:11-13 Ap '77

PAINTED furniture. See Furniture, Painted

PAINTED pottery. See Pottery—Decoration

PAINTER, Mary

Hurst's remembrance '76. il Sch Arts 76:56-7 F '77

PAINTER, Marylyn

Fluorescent lights and hyperactivity in children: an experiment. Educ Digest 42:36-7 Ap '77

PAINTING

See also

Color

Impressionism (art)

Landscape painting

Marine painting

Miniature painting

Mural painting and decorating

Portrait painting

Post-impressionism (art)

Realism in art

Still life painting

Tempera painting

Textile painting

Water color painting

Competitions

See Art—Competitions

PAINTING—*Continued*

Study and teaching

Do your students paint with meaning and purpose? G. F. Horn. Sch Arts 77:4-5+ N '77

Doctor, lawyer, merchant, chief; career education through art. G. Gale. il Design (US) 78:23 mid-Summ '77

Ethnic circular painting. J. Dunstan. il Design (US) 78:20-1 Summ '77

Teaching color relationships: a conversation with Henry Hensche; interview, ed by C. Movalli. H. Hensche. il por Am Artist 41:34-9+ Mr '77

Technique

Conversation with Marshall Joyce; interview, ed by C. Movalli. M. Joyce. il por Am Artist 41:90-5+ F '77

In the vein of Abstract Expressionism. L. J. Miller. il Sch Arts 77:14-15 N '77

Painting with acrylics. R. Mayer. Am Artist 41:8 Ap '77

Pollock paints a picture; excerpt from The art world; ed by B. Diamonstein. R. Goodnough. il pors Art N 76:162+ N '77

Virginia Dehn paints inscapes. M. C. Nelson. il por Am Artist 41:50-3+ Mr '77

PAINTING, Abstract. See Art, Abstract

PAINTING, Amateur. See Art, Amateur

PAINTING, American

American painting; symposium. il Antiques 112:932-77 N '77

Art on the wild side; interview, ed by M. Berges. B. A. Bengston. il por Design (US) 78:6-9 Spr '77

Mortimer Wilson: romantic baroque in the Southwest; interview, ed by B. Cortright. M. Wilson, Jr. il por Am Artist 41:52-5+ Je '77

Phyllis Manley combines two worlds; interview, ed by J. McCord. P. Manley. il por Am Artist 41:40-5+ Mr '77

See also

Abstract Expressionism
Albright, I. L.
Beal, J.
Berninghaus, O. E.
Bloom, E. G.
Blumenschein, E. L.
Blunt, J. S.
Brown, B.
Catlin, G.
Cavallon, G.
Clive, W. J.
Close, C.
Couse, E. I.
Damitz, E.
Dehn, V.
Dering, W.
Dickinson, E.
Diebenkorn, R.
Dine, J.
Dunton, W. H.
Eakins, S. M.
Eakins, T.
Earl, R.
Egri, R.
Evans, D.
Fahlstrom, O.
Federal Art Project
Fox, L.
Golub, L.
Gordon, R.
Gorky, A.
Harnett, W. M.
Healy, G. P. A.
Helck, P.
Herreshoff, L.
Higgins, V.
Hofmann, H.
Homer, W.
Indiana, R.
Johns, J.
Johnson, L.
Jonson, J.
Katz, A.
Kitchen, T.
Koch, J. M.
Liberman, A.
Maass, D.
Mansfield, J. W.
Martin, M.
Motherwell, R.
Noland, K.
North, N.
O'Keeffe, G.
Osborne, E.
Phillips, B. G.
Pippin, H.
Pollock, J.
Portraits, American
Ramos, M.
Rauschenberg, R.
Reece, M.
Remington, F.
Rivers, L.
Rothko, M.
Schoonover, F.
Shahn, B.
Sharp, J. H.
Shelton, T. H.
Sloane, E.
Stallknecht, A.
Stern, M.
Stettheimer, F.
Stock, J. W.
Stuart, G.
Taos Society of Artists
Thiebaud, W.
Ufer, W
Weeks, J
Whitaker, F.
Wyeth, A.

Exhibitions

American art 1910-1940: a neglected vision. B. Forgey. il Art N 76:66-8 O '77

Corcoran Biennial: a generational split. G. F. Forgey. il Art N 76:106+ My '77

Earthbound and sublime; exhibition entitled The Natural Paradise: Painting in America 1800-1950 at the Museum of Modern Art. K. Evett. New Repub 176:29-30 Mr 5 '77

PAINTING, Automatic. See Automatism

PAINTING, Belgian

See also

Alechinsky, P.
Ensor, J.

PAINTING, British

Relentlessly personal vision of Lucian Freud; interview, ed by J. Gruen. L. Freud. il por Art N 76:60-3 Ap '77

See also

Hockney, D.
Rossetti, D. G.
Stubbs, G.
Turner, J. M. W.

PAINTING, Chinese

Exhibitions

Arcadians of Huhsien county. R. Hughes. il Time 111:26-7 Ja 9 '78

PAINTING, Dutch

Stones of madness; psychoanalytic study. J. J. Hartman and others. bibl f il Am Imago 33:266-95 Fall '76

See also

Rembrandt Harmenszoon van Rijn

PAINTING, Ethiopian

Painted churches of Lake Tana. B. Abbebe. il UNESCO Courier 30:13-17 F '77

PAINTING, European

Exhibitions

Art; exhibition of European paintings from Swiss collections at the Museum of Modern Art. L. Alloway. Nation 224:91-2 Ja 22 '77

European Master Paintings from Swiss Collections; exhibition at Museum of Modern Art. D. Leder. America 136:149-50 F 19 '77

PAINTING, Flemish

Looking at paintings. B. Dunstan. il Am Artist 41:62-3 D '77

See also

Rubens, P. P.

PAINTING, French

See also

Balthus
Bonheur, R.
Caillebotte, G.
Cézanne, P.
Courbet, G.
Degas, E.
Delacroix, E.
Ingres, J. A. D.
Morisot, B.
Poussin, N.
Puvis de Chavannes, P.
Renoir, A.
Rouault, G.
Seurat, G.
Signac, P.
Vernet, C. J.
Villon, J. pseud

Exhibitions

Exhibitions in sight; Wild Beasts: Fauvism and its Affinities. B. Wasserman. il Sch Arts 76:58-61 F '77

PAINTING, German

See also

Grosz, G.
Grünewald, M.
Lindner, R.
Zoffany, J.

PAINTING, Hindu. See Painting, Indian (East Indian)

PAINTING, Indian (East Indian)

Dark god at play: a portfolio of Rajput paintings. A. Menen. il Horizon 19:58-63 Ja '77

India's miniature paintings. W. Rodger. Hobbies 82:152-3 D '77

PAINTING, Industrial and practical
Tips for spring painters. D. Raffel. House & Gard 149:94 My '77
See also
Boats—Painting
House painting
Paint
Paint spraying
Varnish and varnishing

Equipment and supplies
New tools for spatter-free pad painting. il Pop Sci 210:48+ Ap '77

PAINTING, Israeli
See also
Berman, R.
Liberman, S.

PAINTING, Italian
See also
Bellini, G.
Leonardo da Vinci
Raphael
Titian

PAINTING, Japanese

Exhibitions
Tales told on screens; Cleveland Museum of Art. M. Stevens. il Newsweek 89:68-9 Ap 11 '77

PAINTING, Latin American
See also
Carreno, M.

PAINTING, Manuscript. See Illumination of books and manuscripts

PAINTING, Mexican
Los Cuatro: Mexico's majestic artists. E. E. Roberts. il Américas 29:38-45 Je '77
See also
Ramos Martínez, A.

PAINTING, Oriental
See also
Painting, Chinese
Painting, Japanese
Sumie

PAINTING, Pre-Raphaelite. See Pre-Raphaelites

PAINTING, Religious. See Christian art and symbolism

PAINTING, Russian
Art criticism of Pushkin, Gogol, Dostoevsky and Tolstoy. J. E. Bowlt. il Art N 76:86-8+ My '77
Momentous happening in Moscow; Costakis collection. il por Time 109:75-6 Ap 11 '77
See also
Chagall, M.
Glazunov, I.

Exhibitions
Art; exhibition of Russian and Soviet Painting. L. Alloway. Nation 224:604-5 My 14 '77
Art; Russian painting; 13th Century to the Present, exhibition. B. Rose. il Vogue 167:56+ Ap '77
Crucial room; interview with consultant for Metropolitan Museum exhibit. J. Bowlt. il New Yorker 53:29-31 My 2 '77
Equal time; reaction to Russian and Soviet Painting exhibition. Vasari. Art N 76:24-5 Summ '77
Lost horizons of Russian painting; exhibition at the Metropolitan Museum. J. Russell. il N Y Times Mag p23-5+ Ap 3 '77
Quid pro quo; Metropolitan Museum's exhibition of Russian and Soviet painting. R. Berenson. Nat R 29:680-1 Je 10 '77
Russian and Soviet Painting: from the Church to the Czars to the Ministry of Culture. C. S. Mayer. il Art N 76:68-70 Summ '77
Russian masters; Metropolitan Museum of Art display. M. Stevens. il Newsweek 89:77-8 Ap 25 '77
Russian paintings at the Met: an inside look at museum diplomacy. J. E. Bowlt. il Art in Am 65:74-9 My; 120-1 N '77

PAINTING, Scottish
See also
Alexander, C. J.

PAINTING, Spanish
Prado of the prairie. J. Kutner. il por Art N 76:74-7 My '77
See also
Miró, J.
Picasso, P.
Tàpies, A.

PAINTING, Swiss
See also
Bodmer, K.

PAINTING and literature. See Art and literature

PAINTING and photography. See Art and photography

PAINTING of Easter eggs. See Eggs, Decorated

PAINTING on textiles. See Textile painting

PAINTINGS

Appreciation
See Art—Appreciation

Collections
See Art—Private collections

Conservation and restoration
Raphael transfigured. il Time 109:65 F 14 '77

Exhibitions
Ruskin refuted; paintings by women artists exhibited at the Brooklyn Museum. R. Berenson. Nat R 29:1378-80 N 25 '77
Toward a complete history of art: Women Artists, 1550-1950. A. Frankenstein. il Art in Am 65:66-9 Mr '77
Woman as artist; Brooklyn Museum exhibition. G. Glueck. N Y Times Mag p48-50+ S 25 '77

Expertising
See Art—Expertising

PAINTINGS, Forgery of. See Forgery of works of art

PAINTS. See Paint

PAISLEY, Ian Richard Kyle
Evening on Ravenhill Road. L. Mullin. America 137:189-91 O 1 '77 *
Paisley led but few workers followed. il por Time 109:44 My 16 '77 *

PAK, Chung Hi. See Park, C. H.

PAKISTAN
Why Pakistan is uneasy about U.S. as an ally; with interview with Z. A. Bhutto, ed by J. N. Wallace. il map U.S. News 82:70-2 Mr 14 '77
See also
Paleontology—Pakistan

Antiquities
See also
Indus Valley—Antiquities

Foreign relations
United States
See United States—Foreign relations—Pakistan

Politics and government
Bhutto gets bounced. R. Steele and others. il por Newsweek 90:27-9 Jl 18 '77
Bhutto hangs on, but his troubles grow. il Time 109:38 My 2 '77
Bhutto's last card. R. Carroll and T. Clifton. il por Newsweek 89:57+ My 2 '77
Evil genius; Z. A. Bhutto. Time 110:51+ S 19 '77
Sir, the troops have come; army coup. pors Time 110:29-30 Jl 18 '77
Zia: so much mistrust; excerpts from interview, ed by E. Behr. Z. ul-Haq. il por Newsweek 90:28 Jl 18 '77
See also
Elections—Pakistan
Political campaigns—Pakistan

Riots
Rioting for a recount. M. Sheils and T. Clifton. il por Newsweek 89:39+ Ap 25 '77

PAL, Yash
Visitor to the village. il Bull Atom Sci 33:55-6 Ja '77

PALACES
New look at decorating Brighton style; Royal Pavilion at Brighton exhibition. il House & Gard 149:136-9 Ap '77
Prince and the puritan; Royal Pavilion at Brighton exhibition. D. Davis. il Newsweek 89:77-77A Mr 28 '77
Royal Pavilion; exhibition at the Cooper-Hewitt Museum. New Yorker 53:30-1 Mr 21 '77
See also
Versailles, Palaces of

PALACIOS, Argentina
Do you dig the Panama Canal treaty? il Sr Schol 110:12-13+ O 20 '77

PALAU, Luis
Caribbean crusade. J. C. Hefley. Chr Today 22:46-7 N 18 '77 *
Palau power in Latin America. il por Time 110:123 N 7 '77 *

PALAU (islands)
Hideout for Trident; proposed base in Palau. R. C. Aldridge. Progressive 41:11 F '77

PALEOBOTANY
Geochemistry and thermolysis of flavonoids. K. J. Niklas and D. E. Giannasi. bibl il Science 197:767-9 Ag 19 '77

Miocene
Chemistry of still-green fossil leaves. Sci N 111:391 Je 18 '77
Flavonoid and other chemical constituents of fossil miocene celtis and ulmus (succor creek flora) D. E. Giannasi and K. J. Niklas. bibl il Science 197:765-7 Ag 19 '77
Flavonoids and other chemical constituents of fossil miocene zelkova (ulmaceae) K. J. Niklas and D. E. Giannasi. bibl il Science 196:877-8 My 20 '77

PALEOBOTANY—*Continued*

Paleozoic

Evidence for a pollination-drop mechanism in Paleozoic pteridosperms. G. W. Rothwell. bibl il Science 198:1251-2 D 23 '77

Oregon

Flavonoids and other chemical constituents of fossil miocene zelkova (ulmaceae) K. J. Niklas and D. E. Giannasi. bibl il Science 196:877-8 My 20 '77

PALEOCEANOGRAPHY. See Paleontology

PALEOCLIMATOLOGY

Cold seas of 18,000 B.P. Sci N 112:358 N 26 '77
Devon Island ice cap: core stratigraphy and paleoclimate. R. M. Koerner. bibl il map Science 196:15-18 Ap 1 '77
Explosive cenozoic volcanism and climatic implications. D. Ninkovich and W. L. Donn; reply. J. P. Kennett and R. C. Thunell. bibl il Science 196:1231-4 Je 10 '77
Holocene woodlands in the southwestern deserts. T. R. Van Devender. bibl il map Science 198:189-92 O 14 '77
Paleoenvironment and human settlement in Japan and Korea. R. Pearson. bibl il maps Science 197:1239-46 S 23 '77

PALEOGEOGRAPHY

Paleogeographic reconstructions of coastal Aegean archaeological sites. J. C. Kraft and others. bibl il maps Science 195:941-7 Mr 11 '77

PALEO-INDIANS

Earlier Americans. Sci Am 236:61-2 Je '77

PALEONTOLOGICAL hoaxes. See Hoaxes

PALEONTOLOGY

Evolution's erratic pace. S. J. Gould. Natur Hist 86:12+ My '77
Reading the fossil record. il Time 110:69 N 7 '77

See also
Dinosaurs
Forests, Submerged
Man, Prehistoric

Cenozoic

Estimates of cenozoic oceanic sedimentation rates. T. A. Davies and others. bibl il Science 197:53-5 Jl 1 '77
Suid evolution and correlation of African hominid localities. T. D. White and J. M. Harris. bibl il maps Science 198:13-21 O 7 '77

Cretaceous

Teeth in Ichthyornis (class: aves) L. D. Martin and J. D. Stewart. bibl il Science 195:1331-2 Mr 25 '77

Mesozoic

Triassic-Jurassic tetrapod extinctions: are they real? P. E. Olsen and P. M. Galton. bibl il Science 197:983-5 S 2 '77

Miocene

Human evolution: hominoids of the miocene. G. B. Kolata. Science 197:244-5+ Jl 15 '77

Paleozoic

Arthropod invasion of land during late Silurian and Devonian times. L. Størmer. bibl il Science 197:1362-4 S 30 '77

Pennsylvanian

Earliest diapsid reptile identified; petrolacosaurus. Sci N 112:7 Jl 2 '77
Petrolacosaurus, the oldest known diapsid reptile. R. R. Reisz. bibl il Science 196:1091-3 Je 3 '77

Pleistocene

Cheetah-like cat in the North American Pleistocene. L. D. Martin and others. bibl il Science 195:981-2 Mr 11 '77
Early flakes from Sozudai, Japan: are they man-made? P. Bleed. bibl il Science 197:1357-9 S 30 '77
Frozen mammoths from Siberia bring the Ice Ages to vivid life. J. M. Stewart. il Smithsonian 8:60-9 bibl(p 134) D '77
Glacial-Holocene transition in deep-sea carbonates: selective dissolution and the stable isotope signal. W. H. Berger and J. S. Killingley. bibl il Science 197:563-6 Ag 5 '77
Great late Pleistocene extinction: a slothful tale. D. E. Thomsen. il Sci N 112:396-8 D 10 '77
Pleistocene avifaunas and the overkill hypothesis. D. K. Grayson. bibl Science 195:691-3 F 18 '77

Pre-Cambrian

Chitinozoans from the late Precambrian Chuar Group of the Grand Canyon, Arizona. B. Bloeser and others. bibl il Science 195:676-9 F 18 '77
Out of earth's past: biological roots. il Sci N 111:343 My 28 '77

Quaternary

Capsian escargotières. D. Lubell and others. bibl il Science 191:910-20 Mr 5 '76; Correction. 196:335 Ap 15 '77
Holocene woodlands in the southwestern deserts. T. R. Van Devender. bibl il map Science 198:189-92 O 14 '77

Tertiary

South American geochronology: radiometric time scale for middle to late Tertiary mammal-bearing horizons in Patagonia. L. G. Marshall and others. bibl il map Science 195:1325-8 Mr 25 '77

Africa, Sub-Saharan

Suid evolution and correlation of African hominid localities. T. D. White and J. M. Harris. bibl il maps Science 198:13-21 O 7 '77

Argentina

South American geochronology: radiometric time scale for middle to late Tertiary mammal-bearing horizons in Patagonia. L. G Marshall and others. bibl il map Science 195:1325-8 Mr 25 '77

Arizona

Chitinozoans from the late Precambrian Chuar Group of the Grand Canyon, Arizona. B. Bloeser and others. bibl il Science 195:676-9 F 18 '77

Australia

Crocodile with laterally compressed snout: first find in Australia. R. E. Molnar. bibl il Science 197:62-4 Jl 1 '77

California

Early man confirmed in America 40,000 years ago. Sci N 111:196 Mr 26 '77

Colorado

Bone bonanza: early bird and mastodon. il Sci N 112:198 S 24 '77

Japan

Early flakes from Sozudai, Japan: are they man-made? P. Bleed. bibl il Science 197:1357-9 S 30 '77

Kansas

Petrolacosaurus, the oldest known diapsid reptile. R. R. Reisz. bibl il Science 196:1091-3 Je 3 '77

New York (state)

James Hall; champion of paleontology and engineer of the New York State Museum. D. W. Fisher. il pors Conservationist 31:12-16 N '76

North America

Great late Pleistocene extinction: a slothful tale. D. E. Thomsen. il Sci N 112:396-8 D 10 '77

Ohio

Paleodemography of the Libben site, Ottawa County, Ohio. C. O. Lovejoy and others. bibl il Science 198:291-3 O 21 '77

Pakistan

Pakistan fossils: new origins for man. map Sci N 111:244 Ap 16 '77

Patagonia

See Paleontology—Argentina

Russia

See also
Paleontology—Siberia

Siberia

Frozen mammoths from Siberia bring the Ice Ages to vivid life. J. M. Stewart. il Smithsonian 8:60-9 bibl(p 134) D '77

South Africa

Archean microfossils showing cell division from the Swaziland System of South Africa. A. H. Knoll and E. S. Barghoorn. bibl il Science 198:396-8 O 28 '77

Southwestern States

Holocene woodlands in the southwestern deserts. T. R. Van Devender. bibl il map Science 198:189-92 O 14 '77

Wyoming

Cheetah-like cat in the North American Pleistocene. L. D. Martin and others. bibl il Science 195:981-2 Mr 11 '77

PALEOTEMPERATURE. See Paleoclimatology

PALEOZOIC period. See Paleontology—Paleozoic

PALERMO

Music

See also
Opera—Italy

PALESTINE

See also
Jews in Palestine

History

Recognizing Israel; address, December 28, 1976. C. M. Clifford. pors Am Heritage 28:4-7+ Ap '77

PALESTINE Liberation Organization

L'affaire Daoud: too hot to handle. il por Time 109:29-31 Ja 24 '77
Arch-terrorist who went scot-free; Abu Daoud. D. Reed. Read Digest 111:114-18 S '77
Bye-bye, PLO? R. Carroll and others. il Newsweek 91:39 Ja 16 '78

PALESTINE Liberation Organization—*Continued*
Bypassing the PLO? D. Holt and others. il por Newsweek 90:33 D 5 '77
Don't bank on it: the phantom of a West Bank PLO state. A. Dowty. New Repub 177:15-18 Ag 20 '77
Don't call it treason: the need to talk with the PLO. A. I. Waskow. Nation 224:178-80 F 12 '77
French recipe for cowardice; release of Abu Daoud. Nation 224:98-9 Ja 29 '77
Geneva: the Palestinian problem. il Time 110:51-2 O 10 '77
How to welcome President Sadat. il New Repub 176:5-6+ Ap 9 '77
Israel hangs tough. S. Fraker and others. il por Newsweek 90:36-7 Ag 22 '77
No to the P.L.O. il Time 110:26 S 12 '77
P.L.O: democracy gone wild. il Time 110:47 O 24 '77
PLO still hangs tough; excerpts from interview, ed by W. E. Schmidt. F. al-Kaddoumi. il por Newsweek 89:37 Mr 14 '77
Palestinians: a new unity. il Time 110:41-2 Ag 29 '77
Palestinians: still no. 1 block to Mideast harmony. il map U.S. News 83:20-1 D 5 '77
Proposal for a Palestinian state. E. R. F. Sheehan. il map N Y Times Mag p8-11 Ja 30 '77; Reply, C. Herzog. p 12 F 27 '77
Terrorist cross fire; releasing Abu Daoud. A. Deming and others. il por Newsweek 89:43+ Ja 24 '77
Time to take a gamble; interview, ed by W. Wynn. Hussein. il por Time 109:34 F 14 '77
Too casual diplomacy. New Repub 177:10-11 O 15 '77
Tough talk from a dove; excerpt from interview, ed by M. Bruzonsky. A. Eliav. Nation 225: 688-9 D 24 '77
Well-heeled guerrillas. il Time 110:34+ Jl 18 '77
What Vance will find: Mideast peace hopes on rise, but no quick breakthrough. D. Mullin. map U.S. News 82:34-5 F 21 '77
Why Breira? criticism of Israeli policy on question of negotiation with the PLO. J. Shattan. Commentary 63:60-6 Ap '77; Discussion. 63:4+ Je '77

PALESTINIAN Arabs
Assembly tells Israel to halt further removal of refugees from Gaza Camps; with text of resolution. UN Chron 13:32-3, 82-3 D '76
Bypassing the PLO? D. Holt and others. il por Newsweek 90:33 D 5 '77
Gloom in Israel, joy for the Arabs; American policy statement on Palestinian representation at peace talks. il Time 110:33-4 S 26 '77
Habash: Israel will fall; excerpts from interview, ed by D. Brelis. G. Habash. por Time 110:33 D 19 '77
Israeli lawyer who defends Arabs; F. Langer. L. Rivlin. Ms 6:21 O '77
Other Israelis. J. L. Ryan. Commonweal 104: 13-15 Ja 7 '77
Palestinian issue: anatomy of a slogan. B. Akzin. Intellect 106:198-200 D '77
Palestinians: a new unity. il Time 110:41-2 Ag 29 '77
West Bank: decade of occupation. il map Time 109:31+ Je 13 '77
West Bank today. M. J. Kubic. il map Newsweek 89:55 Je 13 '77

PALESTINIAN question. See Israel-Arab Wars, 1967-; Jewish-Arab relations

PALEY, Hiram
Solid waste disposal needs areawide solutions. por Am City & County 92:63 Mr '77

PALEY, Sarah
Miracle on 57th Street. Mod Phot 41:60 F '77

PALEY, William S.
Small change at CBS. pors Time 109:62-3 My 2 '77 *

PALLADIAN architecture. See Architecture, Italian

PALLADIO, Andrea
Most influential architect in history. A. L. Huxtable. il N Y Times Mag p22-5 Jl 17 '77 *
Palladio's splendid creations. F. Schulze. il por Art N 76:70-1 O '77 *
Three in one; Exhibition at the Cooper-Hewitt Museum. New Yorker 53:23 Jl 4 '77 *
Under Palladio's spell. G. Wills. Harpers 255: 75-7 Ag '77 *

PALLOTTINE Fathers. See Religious orders

PALM SPRINGS, Calif.
Oasis playground. L. Dennis and L. Dennis. il Trav/Holiday 148:26-31 N '77
Sunny world of Palm Springs. T. Schwartz and M. Kasindorf. il Newsweek 89:68-70 Mr 28 '77

PALM trees. See Palms

PALMDALE bulge. See Geology—California

PALMER, Alison
Alison Palmer: upsetting the Anglicans. T. Beeson. Chr Cent 94:1213-14 D 28 '77 *
To the rescue. Chr Today 22:49-50 N 4 '77 *

PALMER, Allison R.
Function of shell sculpture in marine gastropods: hydrodynamic destabilization in ceratostoma foliatum. bibl il Science 197:1293-5 S 23 '77

PALMER, Arnold
Crashing the party in Tulsa. W. Bingham. il Sports Illus 46:43 Je 20 '77 *

PALMER, John Derry
Human rhythms; excerpt from An introduction to biological rhythms. bibl il BioScience 27: 93-9 F '77

PALMER, Lawrence G. and Gulati, Jagdish
Potassium accumulation in muscle: a test of the binding hypothesis. bibl il Science 194:521-3; 198:1281-4 O 29 '76; D 23 '77

PALMER, Lilli
Curtain up at Shaw's corner; excerpt from Change lobsters—and dance. Read Digest 110: 173-4+ F '77

PALMER, Parker J.
Place called community. Chr Cent 94:252-6 Mr 16 '77

PALMER, Ray
Space world publisher dies. J. Oberg. por Space World N-11-167:4 N '77 *

PALMER, Richard Emery
AMA's health plan. por Newsweek 89:11 Je 6 '77
Rationed care; address, June 19, 1977. Vital Speeches 43:700-2 S 1 '77

PALMER, Robert
It's that jazz time again. il N Y Times Mag p86-7 Je 12 '77

PALMER, Robert B.
Scenes from a southeast Asian sabbatical. il por Wilson Lib Bull 51:853-5 Je '77

PALMER, Russell E.
Boss at 37. por Forbes 120:33 S 1 '77 *

PALMER, William
Exploring quality as definition. Engl J 66:46-8 D '77

PALMITER, George
Make the river do the work. B. East. il por Outdoor Life 160:78-81+ O '77 *

PALMS, Roger C.
Preaching for results. Chr Today 22:30-1 D 30 '77

PALMS
Easy to grow house plants: dwarf palm. E. McDonald. il House B 119:80 D '77
Jungle gems: bamboo and palm. R. Langer. il House & Gard 149:82+ Ap '77
Palm readings; date palms. R. Sokolov. il Natur Hist 86:114-17 O '77
This San Diego garden is a jungle of palms—more than 60 kinds; garden of Jim Wright. il Sunset 159:154-5 Ag '77

PALO ALTO, Calif.
Palo Alto sees golden glint in sludge; recovery of precious metals. Am City & County 92:23 Jl '77

Bookstores

See Booksellers and bookselling—California

Stores

Theatrical approach to shopping center remodeling; Stanford Shopping Center in Palo Alto, Calif; with introd by J. Nairn. il Archit Rec 161:105-8 Je '77

PALO ALTO Chamber Orchestra. See Chamber orchestras

PALOMINO, Carlos
Staying at the top of his class. P. Putnam. il pors Sports Illus 46:20-2 Ja 31 '77 *

PAMPHLETS
Best in booklets. See issues of House & garden incorporating Living for young homemakers
Booklets. House B 119:84+ My; 42+ O '77
Booklets. L. B. Nooger. Am Home 80:13 S; 25 O; 11 D '77
Booklets. P. Schiller. il Am Home 80:18 F; 17 Mr; 19 Ap; 12 My; 12 Jl '77
Booklets worth writing for. See issues of Good housekeeping
Ten most wanted government booklets. Good H 185:203 Jl '77
Things to write for; useful pamphlets, reports and circulars. See every other issue of Changing times
What to do about those annoying household pests. bibl il Consumers Res Mag 60:20-3 Ap '77

See also
Advertising mediums—Pamphlets
Government publications

Authorship

Thirty seconds to live. C. Schoenfeld. il Writers Digest 57:29 F '77

PAN AFRICAN Christian Leadership Assembly. See Religious conferences—Africa

PAN AM (airline) See Pan American World Airways

PANAMA
Panama—a profile. map Dept State Bull 77:511 O 17 '77

See also
Canals—Panama
Civil rights—Panama
Dams—Panama
Environmental policy—Panama
Fishing—Panama
Panama Canal Zone

PANAMA—*Continued*

Economic conditions

High economic hopes if ratification comes. Bus W p54-5 O 3 '77

Foreign relations

Libya

See Libya—Foreign relations—Panama

Politics and government

Omar Torrijos: the Panamanian enigma. M. C. Needler. por Intellect 105:242-3 F '77

Panic in a tropical playground. il Time 110:18 Ag 22 '77

Treaties

United States

See United States—Treaties—Panama

PANAMA, Isthmus of

This partition of the waters has served its end. N. S. Manross. New Repub 177:6-7 S 24 '77

PANAMA Canal

Canal as symbol. Progressive 41:11 O '77

Canal without rhetoric. Forbes 120:93 N 15 '77

Anecdotes, facetiae, satire, etc.

Where is it? R. Lipez. Progressive 41:66 N '77

History

How the big ditch was dug. il por Time 110:14+ Ag 22 '77

Land divided, the world united. B. McGinty. il map Am Hist Illus 12:10-19 My '77

Panama Canal question; address, July 29, 1977. M. P. Du Val, Jr. Vital Speeches 43:685-9 S 1 '77

Stormy history of the Panama Canal. il U.S. News 83:23-4 S 19 '77

Treaty rights acquired by the United States to construct the Panama Canal. bibl Dept State Bull 77:540-5 O 17 '77

PANAMA Canal Zone

Anglo-Saxon sentimentality. New Repub 177:5-8 S 24 '77

As U.S. and Panama head for showdown over Canal; with editorial comment. C. J. Migdail. il por map U.S. News 82:28-30, 76 My 2 '77

Canal. Commonweal 104:579-80 S 16 '77

Canal: interim notes. J. Burnham. Nat R 29:1351 N 25 '77

Canal politics. Nat R 29:1282 N 11 '77

Canal: time to go? A. Deming and others. il map Newsweek 90:28-32+ Ag 22 '77

Carter's high-risk move; Panama Canal treaties. U.S. News 83:18-19 S 12 '77

Ceding the Canal—slowly. il pors Time 110:8-13 Ag 22 '77

Church support for Canal treaties. J. M. Wall. Chr Cent 94:995 N 2 '77

Clarification, please. Newsweek 90:61-2 O 17 '77

Deal on the Canal. F. Willey and S. Sullivan. il por Newsweek 90:29-30 Ag 15 '77

Deputy Secretary Christopher discusses the Panama Canal treaties; address, November 11, 1977. W. M. Christopher. Dept State Bull 77:835-9 D 12 '77

Ditching the Panamanians. Nation 225:386-8 O 22 '77

Do you dig the Panama Canal treaty? opinions of Panamanian and Zonian students. A. Palacios. il Sr Schol 110:12-13+ O 20 '77

Eupeptic over progress in Panama. il Time 109:14-15 F 28 '77

Historic treaty with Panama: toughest test is still to come; with readers comments. il map U.S. News 83:25-7 Ag 22 '77

Justice and the Panama Canal. America 137:90 Ag 27 '77

Let's give it back. N. Von Hoffman. Progressive 41:49 N '77

Letter from Washington. R. H. Rovere. New Yorker 53:134-6 S 12 '77

Man, a plan, a Canal: Panama. New Repub 177:2+ S 3 '77

Military and Panama. W. F. Buckley, Jr. Nat R 29:1256-7 O 28 '77

New deals for the big ditch. il Time 110:28 Jl 25 '77

New Panama Canal treaties—in our national interest; address, October 18, 1977. S. M. Linowitz. Dept State Bull 77:806-11 D 5 '77

News directors interview President Carter; excerpts from transcript, September 15, 1977. J. Carter. Dept State Bull 77:568-9 O 24 '77

Now for the hard part. il Time 110:19-21 S 19 '77

Panama—a doomed treaty? with interview with O. Torrijos Herrera. il U.S. News 83:18-23 S 19 '77

Panama: a search for independence. E. B. Burns. bibl f Cur Hist 72:65-7+ F '77

Panama and Suez. V. S. Kearney. America 137:477-8 D 31 '77

Panama Canal:

Opposing argument. T. Wicker. Current 198:54-5 D '77

Why the U.S. should keep it. S. Thurmond. Current 198:52-4 D '77

Panama Canal treaties. il Américas 29:9-15 N '77

Panama Canal treaties and related materials, including text of treaties. bibl maps Dept State Bull 77:481-545 O 17 '77

Panama Canal treaties: statement, October 20, 1977. C. R. Vance. Dept State Bull 77:728-31 N 21 '77

Panama Canal treaty: it's no shoo-in. map Sr Schol 110:6+ O 20 '77

Panama Canal: use and ownership. P. A. Fitz-Gerald. America 137:473-6 D 31 '77

Panama Canal: what happens next. il Nations Bus 65:56-8+ O '77

Panama or Taiwan? J. Burnham. Nat R 29:1043 S 16 '77

Panama production. A. Deming and others. il map Newsweek 90:46-8 S 19 '77

Panama—sí. W. F. Buckley, Jr. Nat R 29:1132-3 S 30 '77

Panama: turn of the tide? D. M. Alpern and J. J. Lindsay. il Newsweek 91:19 Ja 2 '78

Path to 1980. J. Lelyveld. il pors N Y Times Mag p 110 O 2 '77

President Carter discusses Panama Canal treaties; remarks, question and answer session, October 22, 1977. J. Carter. Dept State Bull 77:720-8 N 21 '77

Proposed treaty; preliminary thoughts. Nat R 29:981-3 S 2 '77; Discussion. 29:1082+ S 30 '77

Reagan on the Canal; excerpts from interview, ed by G. C. Lubenow. R. Reagan. por Newsweek 90:50 S 19 '77

Reagan speaks out. P. Bonventre and others. por Newsweek 90:37-8 S 5 '77

Real message to U.S. in that Panama plebiscite. il por U.S. News 83:61-2 N 7 '77

Relinquishing the Canal. M. D. Kent. Chr Cent 94:755-6 Ag 31 '77

Secretary Vance and other administration officials urge ratification of Panama Canal treaties; statements, September 26-27, 29-30, 1977. C. R. Vance and others. Dept State Bull 77:615-29 N 7 '77

Secretary Vance attends OAS General Assembly at Grenada; statement, June 15, 1977. C. R. Vance. Dept State Bull 77:72 Jl 18 '77

Should Senate OK Panama treaties? interviews. S. M. Linowitz; J. Helms. pors U.S. News 83:33-4 D 12 '77

Stand up and be counted. R. Steele and H. Bruno. il Newsweek 90:26-7 S 12 '77

Storm over the Canal. il Time 110:28 Ag 29 '77

That troublesome Panama Canal treaty; Time essay. E. Warner. il Time 110:26-7 O 31 '77

Timid illusions about Panama. Nation 225:162-3 S 3 '77

Treaties can't shoot. Nat R 29:1036 S 16 '77

Vox pop on Panama. Newsweek 90:48+ O 24 '77

See also

Americans in the Panama Canal Zone

Science—Panama Canal Zone

Defenses

If U.S. had to defend the Panama Canal—; with comments from two former military chiefs. il map U.S. News 83:26-7 O 24 '77

Keeping the Canal pacts afloat. il Time 110:35+ O 24 '77

Right to intervene. Nat R 29:1347-8 N 25 '77

Why we should leave Panama. D. C. Armstrong. por Newsweek 90:32-3 N 28 '77

PANAMA Congress, 1826

Bolivar and the Congress of Panama. A. Uslar-Pietri. il por UNESCO Courier 30:28-32 F '77

PAN AMERICAN Day and Week

Pan American Day and Pan American Week, 1977; proclamation. J. Carter. Dept State Bull 76:350 Ap 11 '77

PAN AMERICAN Health Organization

PAHO at 75. H. R. Acuña. il Américas 29:2-4 N '77

PAN AMERICAN World Airways

Pan Am, American win popularity poll. L. Doty. Aviation W 107:38 S 19 '77

Pan Am chief favors capacity rules. R. G. O'Lone. Aviation W 106:32-3 My 9 '77

Pan Am: in the black—for now. il por map Bus W p52-6 S 5 '77

Pan Am Paris route reopening planned. Aviation W 107:30 D 19 '77

Pan American studies trijets for '80s fleet. Aviation W 107:31 O 3 '77

Pan Am's back. D. Pauly. il Newsweek 90:51-2 Ag 22 '77

747SP enhances route restructuring. L. Doty. il Aviation W 106:32-3 Je 27 '77

Standing by for London. P. L. Abraham. il Newsweek 90:65 S 26 '77

PANASENKO, Sharon M. and others

Five hundredfold overproduction of DNA ligase after induction of a hybrid lambda lysogen constructed in vitro. bibl il Science 196:188-9 Ap 8 '77

PANASSIÉ, Hugues
Profiles. W. Balliett. pors New Yorker 52:43-6+ F 14 '77 *
PANCAKE, B. D'J.
Trilobites; story. Atlantic 240:77-80 D '77
PANCAKES, waffles, etc.
Belgian waffles—deep and crisp. il Sunset 158:200 My '77
Blintzes—the dieter's downfall. M. J. Norton. il McCalls 104:97-8 F '77
Catered crepe. il Seventeen 36:104-5+ Jl '77
Crepe cult. C. Claiborne and P. Franey. N Y Times Mag p92 Je 12 '77
Crepe entrées. il Bet Hom & Gard 55:216-17 N '77
Crepe stack sandwich is chilled, nippy. il Sunset 159:162-3 D '77
Crisp golden waffles—a good send-off for a good day. il Parents Mag 52:44+ D '77
Crunchy and wholesome waffles. il Sunset 159:136 S '77
He cooks: whole wheat pancakes. il Bet Hom & Gard 55:144 F '77
Health waffles? Why not? Sunset 158:202 Mr '77
Here's our big Dutch Baby with a whole meal filling. il Sunset 159:203 O '77
How to make a perfect crepe. J. Gepin. il House B 119:157+ My '77
Legendary crepes suzette. C. Claiborne and P. Franey. il N Y Times Mag p66 Mr 6 '77
Magic crepe pan. G. Steves. il Am Home 80:72-4+ O '77
Pancake and crepe creations. il Bet Hom & Gard 55:145-6 Ap '77
Quick treats using crêpes. il Sunset 159:222 O '77
Set up a do-it-yourself crêpérie. il Sunset 158:188-9 My '77
PANCONTINENTAL mining (firm) See Uranium industry—Australia
PANCREAS
Hormone-induced cyclic guanosine monophosphate secretion from guinea pig pancreatic lobules. C. L. Kapoor and G. Krishna. bibl il Science 196:1003-5 My 27 '77

Diseases

Curare cure; treating pancreatitis. il Newsweek 89:74 My 2 '77
PANCREAS, Artificial
Artificial pancreas using living beta cells: effects on glucose homeostasis in diabetic rats. W. L. Chick and others. bibl il Science 197:780-2 Ag 19 '77
PANCREATIC cancer. See Cancer
PANCREATITIS. See Pancreas—Diseases
PANEL construction
Build these insulated shoji sliders; window panels. V. E. Smay. il Pop Sci 212:102 Ja '78
PANEL saws. See Saws
PANELING
How to do match-paneling. il Mech Illus 73:38+ Je '77
How to renew a room with paneling. il House & Gard 149:102+ Ap '77
New face for old paneling. W. Thoms. il Mech Illus 73:88+ F '77
New slant for paneled walls. R. Stepler. il Pop Sci 210:114-15 F '77
Paneled wall with an accent. R. Capotosto. il Mech Illus 73:74+ Ap '77
PANELS, Instrument. See Instrument panels
PANHANDLE Eastern Pipe Line Company
Light at the end of the pipeline. . . Forbes 119:31 F 1 '77
PANHANDLING. See Begging and beggars
PANICS. See Business depression
PANIK, Martin A. and Mobley, T. A.
Bottle and the tube: leisure for the convicted. Parks & Rec 12:28-30+ Mr '77
PANJWANI, Harry K.
Hyperactive children—problems of coping. Consumers Res Mag 60:21-2 S '77
PANORAMIC cameras. See Cameras
PANOS, Jim
Making of a travel agent. Holiday 58:80 Ap '77
PANOV, Galina
Strange case of the Panovs. pors Sat R 4:5 S 3 '77; Reply. R. Winckley. 5:5 N 12 '77 *
PANOV, Valery
Strange case of the Panovs. pors Sat R 4:5 S 3 '77; Reply. R. Winckley. 5:5 N 12 '77 '
PANSIES
Flowers that bloom in spite of frost. D. Schroeder. Org Gard & Farm 24:144 Ap '77
PANTALEONI, Helenka
Remember UNICEF. . .for the children's sake. il por Parents Mag 52:42 O '77
PANTER-DOWNES, Mollie
Letter from London (cont) New Yorker 53:96-8 Mr 7; 122-4 Ap 11; 52-3 Je 27; 196-7 N 14 '77
PANTHERS
See also
Pumas
PANTHERS clubs. See Gray Panthers (pressure group)
PANTOMIME
See also
Mime

PANTRIES
Pantry that can hold it all! il Bet Hom & Gard 55:190 O '77
PANTRY. See Pantries
PANTS
Booming market in counterfeit jeans; West Germany. il Bus W p37-8 Ag 8 '77
How Levi's cracked a ring of counterfeiters. il Bus W p27 S 5 '77

Prices

New cut for Levi's; discount jeans. L. Langway and P. S. Greenberg. il Newsweek 90:64 Jl 25 '77
PANTSUITS, Womens. See Clothing and dress
PANTY hose. See Hosiery
PANTZER, Katharine F.
Brute indeed! New Yorker 53:30-2 Mr 28 '77 *
PAOLITTO, Diana P. See Hersh, R. H. jt auth
PAOLUCCI, Bridget R.
Independent Schools Orchestra. il por Hi Fi 27:MA22-5 O '77
Marlboro on the road. il Hi Fi 27:MA21-3 D '77
PAOLUCCI, Ronald V.
Case for private industry. Aviation W 107:9 Jl; 25:7 Ag 1 '77
PAPADIMITRIOU, Christos H. See Lewis, H. R. jt auth
PAPAGEORGE, Tod
Winogrand's theater of quick takes. il N Y Times Mag p57-8+ O 16 '77
PAPAGEORGIOU, Photini S.
What to do about seasonal allergies. por Intellect 106:12-13 Jl '77
PAPAIN
Papain meat tenderizers: objectionable for all and hazardous for some. B. T. Hunter. Consumers Res Mag 60:36 S '77
PAPAL infallibility. See Popes—Infallibility
PAPALE, Vince
Recovering from a Rocky start. R. F. Jones. il pors Sports Illus 47:34-6+ O 3 '77 *
PAPANDREOU, Andreas
Victory without triumph. il pors Time 110:51 D 5 '77 *
PAPANEK, John
Back in business in Boston. il por Sports Illus 46:22-4+ Ja 24 '77
College football. Sports Illus 47:56+ N 21 '77
Golf. Sports Illus 47:44+ Jl 25; 45-7 Ag 1 '77
Heavy truckin' on Bourbon Street. il pors Sports Illus 47:26-7 D 5 '77
Horses. il Sports Illus 47:118+ O 10 '77
Nobody, but nobody, is going to hurt my teammates. Sports Illus 47:43-4+ O 31 '77
Pro basketball (cont) Sports Illus 46:54+ F 7; 62-3 F 28; 60+ Mr 14; 71-2 Ap 4; 64+ My 16; 63-5 Je 27; 47:72 O 24; 74+ N 7; 75+ D 12 '77; 48:81-2+ Ja 9 '78
Trouble? Call the bomb squad. il Sports Illus 47:24-5 D 19 '77
PAPAYANNOPOULOU, Th. and others
Hemoglobin ontogenesis: test of the gene excision hypothesis. bibl il Science 196:1215-16 Je 10 '77
PAPAYAS
See also
Papain
PAPER
Paper for superspies; can't-copy-paper. il Mech Illus 73:116 Jl '77
Revolution in paper; symposium, with introd by S. E. Meyer. il Am Artist 41:33-57 Ag '77
See also
Paper industry
Photographic paper

Taxation

AAP protests proposed solid waste tax on paper. S. Wagner. Pub W 213:13 Ja 2 '78
Paper industry argues against tax aimed at waste disposal problem. Pub W 213:51-2 Ja 2 '78
PAPER, Handmade. See Paper making
PAPER, Recycling of. See Refuse, Utilization of
PAPER beads. See Beads
PAPER chromatography. See Chromatographic analysis
PAPER cutting. See Paper work
PAPER flowers. See Flowers, Artificial
PAPER-hanging. See Wallpaper and wallpapering
PAPER industry
Annual API paper capacity survey indicates adequate growth probable for book grades. P. Doebler. il Pub W 212:62-3 N 7 '77
Enough paper, but prices up in 1977-78, BISG study says; 1979 shortages likely. P. Doebler. Pub W 211:74-6 F 7 '77
Machine and moldmade papers. M. Schiller. il Am Artist 41:45-8 Ag '77
Making it on its own; Olinkraft, Inc. por Forbes 119:78 Mr 1 '77
Paper industry argues against tax aimed at waste disposal problem. Pub W 213:51-2 Ja 2 '78

PAPER industry—*Continued*
Paper manufacturers face charges of price-fixing. S. Wagner. Pub W 212:106 S 26 '77
See also
APL Corporation
Fibreboard Corporation
Paper mills
Union Camp Corporation
Weyerhaeuser Company

Finance

How slow growth is remaking the paper industry. il Bus W p54-60 My 2 '77
Toughing out a slump in demand. il Bus W p52+ Ja 9 '78

Securities

Bad year for paper? Look at some special situations; interview, ed by R. Brady. D. S. Wilson. por Duns R 109:89+ F '77

Canada

See also
Reed International Ltd

PAPER making
Revolution in paper; symposium, with introd by S. E. Meyer. il Am Artist 41:33-57 Ag '77

PAPER mills
American community of hand papermakers. M. Schiller. Am Artist 41:39-42 Ag '77
Directory of papermakers/list of supplies. Am Artist 41:43-4 Ag '77
Where others fear to tread; Parsons & Whittemore Inc. il por Forbes 119:96+ My 15 '77

PAPER money
See also
World War, 1939-1945—Military currency

Latin America

Art of money. F. T. Peck. il Américas 29:21-8 My '77

United States

Two; the new two-dollar bill; interview. J. A. Conlon. New Yorker 53:23-5 Jl 18 '77
Whatever happened to: $2 bill. il U.S. News 82:61 Mr 21 '77

PAPER products
See also
Paper towels
Toilet paper

Prices

Sudden price war in paper products. il Bus W p50+ N 7 '77

PAPER sculpture
Person-ality box sculpture. D. L. Seaman. il Sch Arts 76:39 Je '77

PAPER towels
Paper towels. Consumer Rep 42:67 D '77

PAPER work
Angels, doves, geese got their start as 1¢ paper plates; Christmas decorations. il Sunset 159: 92-3 D '77
Art of cutting up; cloth and paper collages. N. Mandelbaum. il Ladies Home J 94:120-3+ O '77
Earthly paradise; H. Matisse exhibition. M. Stevens. il Newsweek 90:100-1 S 19 '77
Final flowering of Henri Matisse, invincible artist. J. Russell. il Smithsonian 8:72-9 S '77
Interpretations: an encounter with Rouault. L. R. Koch. il Sch Arts 76:23 F '77
Kirigami Christmas boxes. il Design (US) 79:10 N '77
Make-ahead presents: cut-and-paste jewelry. il Seventeen 36:128-9 N '77
Masterful cutouts; H. Matisse. il Horizon 20:27 S '77
Matisse cutouts. B. Forgey. il por Art N 76:66-9 D '77
No better religion; show of Matisse cutouts at the National Gallery in Washington. L. Prothro. Nat R 30:41-2 Ja 6 '78
Paper is the picture. il Am Artist 41:49-57 Ag '77
Puppets. S. Kusachi and F. Loetterle. il Design (US) 78:18-19 Summ '77
Sultan and the scissors; show of Matisse cutouts. R. Hughes. il Time 110:96-7 S 19 '77
See also
Paper sculpture
Papier-mâché

PAPER work, Office. See Office management

PAPERBACK book wholesalers. See Book wholesalers

PAPERBACK bookracks. See Bookends and bookracks

PAPERBACK books
Year in review: the paperback scene; Trade paperbacks in 1976. G. Stuttaford. Pub W 211: 41-3 F 14 '77
See also
Booksellers and bookselling—Paperback books
Libraries—Paperback book collections
Publishers and publishing—Paperback books

Advertising

See Books—Advertising

Bibliography

Best titles of 1977: LJ's small press roundup; with directory of publishers. B. Katz. Lib J 102:2467-76 D 15 '77
Fall trade paperbacks; Fall mass market paperbacks. Pub W 212:308-24 Ag 29 '77
PW forecasts; ed by B. A. Bannon. See issues of Publishers weekly
PW paperback best sellers. See issues of Publishers weekly
Paper power (cont) SLJ 23:85-6 Ap; 24:133-4 O '77
Paperback bookshelf. See every other issue of Changing times
Pick of the paperbacks; ed by M. Parish. il Engl J 66:90-3 O '77
Pick of the paperbacks (cont) L. Trout. Engl J 66:83-7 My '77
Sampler of boxed paperback sets. Pub W 212: 75+ Ag 1 '77
Softcover selections for seventy-seven. America 136:81-7 Ja 29 '77
Spring trade paperbacks; Spring mass market paperbacks. Pub W 211:282-97 Ja 24 '77
Summer trade paperbacks; Summer mass market paperbacks. il Pub W 211:40-9 Ap 4 '77

Marketing

It's easy to write and self-publish a consumer manual: the hard part is getting it to consumers. J. D. Bowers. Writers Digest 57:23-4 Ap '77
See also
Book wholesalers

PAPERWEIGHTS
Bryan-Kern paperweight. M. Wollett and B. Wollett. il Hobbies 82:99 O '77
Collecting: glass paperweights. N. Mines. il House B 119:28+ S '77
Paperweight passions. J. Goldman. Vogue 167:54 O '77

PAPERWORK, Commission on Federal. See United States—Commission on Federal Paperwork

PAPIER-MÂCHÉ
Artistic self-discovery through group reflection. R. Sarnoff. il Sch Arts 77:30-3 O '77
Papier-mâché realism. P. Route. il Sch Arts 76:10-12 Je '77

PAPILLOMAS. See Tumors

PAPOVAVIRUSES. See Tumor viruses

PAPP, Joseph
Antic arts. C. Hughes. il por Holiday 58:26 Ja '77 *
Papp's curtain at Lincoln Center. por Time 109: 66 Je 20 '77 *
Theater. S. Kauffmann. New Repub 177:24-5 Jl 9 '77 *
Why Joe Papp made his exit. J. Kroll. il por Newsweek 89:57 Je 27 '77 *

PAPPAS, Mildred A.
Pulitzer for Mildred A. Pappas. N. Ephron. Esquire 87:18+ Mr '77 *

PAPRIKA
Making paprika from homegrown peppers. S. K. Dark. Org Gard & Farm 24:116 Ag '77

PAPRIKA peppers. See Peppers

PAPUA NEW GUINEA
Fantom, yu pren tru bilong mi; popularity of Phantom comics. il Time 110:38 S 26 '77
See also
Ecology—Papua New Guinea

Native races

Fertility rites and sorcery in New Guinea village; Gimi people. G. Gillison. il map Nat Geog 152:124-46 Jl '77
Growing up as a Fore is to be in touch and free. E. R. Sorenson. il Smithsonian 8:106-10+ My '77

PARABLES
Bible parables bristle with modern pains—and hopes—in Seabury book by Berrigan; interview, ed by R. Dahlin. D. Berrigan. Pub W 211:72 Mr 14 '77

PARACAS National Marine Reserve. See National parks and reserves—Peru

PARACETAMOL
Aspirin. il Sci Digest 82:54-7 S '77
FDA urges new caveats for aspirin users. Ret Liv 17:60 S '77
Pained Bayer cries foul; ad refuting Tylenol's claims. il Bus W p 142 Jl 25 '77
Painkiller war. L. Langway and J. Whitmore. il Newsweek 90:79-80 Jl 18 '77
Relieving the analgesic headache; FDA study. il Time 110:70 Ag 1 '77

PARACHIN, Victor M.
Circulating saints. Chr Cent 94:396 Ap 27 '77

PARACHUTING
Sky sports: the thrill of flight. T. Crawford. Harp Baz 110:85+ My '77
Winging it on the way down; photographs. A. Keech. Sports Illus 46:36-9 My 23 '77

PARADES
See also
New York (city)—Parades

PARADISE. See Heaven

PARAGUAY
50-cycle politics. J. R. Brockman. map America 137:484-5 D 31 '77
See also
Political prisoners—Paraguay

Languages

Land-locked island of Paraguay; Guarani language. A. A. Roa Bastos. il UNESCO Courier 30:51-3+ Ag '77

Native races

See Indians of South America—Paraguay

Politics and government

Political murder in Paraguay. A. Cabral. il America 136:376-8 Ap 23 '77

Stroessner never sleeps. R. Moreau. il por Newsweek 89:31-2 F 21 '77

Religious institutions and affairs

See also
Catholic Church in Paraguay

PARALEGAL Training for Seniors (program) See Legal assistance to the aged

PARALYSIS
See also
Poliomyelitis

PARALYTICS
Joni's story; J. Eareckson. P. Yancey. il pors Sat Eve Post 249:75+ S '77
Paralytics: strangers in a strange land. K. Cone. il Chr Cent 94:589-92 Je 22 '77
Pitch for the disabled; C. Stevens. U. O'Connor. il por Sat Eve Post 249:14 O '77
Red-hot coal; dorsal column stimulator used in paraplegic pain syndrome. il por Newsweek 89:55 Ap 25 '77
See also
Cerebral palsied children

PARAMECIA
Mutant of paramecium defective in chemotaxis. J. Van Houten. bibl il Science 198:746-8 N 18 '77
Saltatory motility of uninserted trichocysts and mitochondria in paramecium tetraurelia. K. J. Aufderheide. bibl il Science 198:299-300 O 21 '77

PARAMEDICS. See Health workers

PARAMOUNT Picture Corporation. See Motion picture industry—United States

PARANOIA
Researchers find physical basis for some paranoia; views of Brendan Maher. M. Marcus. Psychol Today 11:38-40 O '77

PARANORMAL. See Occult sciences

PARANOY, Halcyon Q. pseud. See McCourt, J.

PARAPLEGICS. See Paralytics

PARAPROFESSIONAL social workers. See Social workers

PARAPSYCHOLOGY
I'm the Maharishi—fly me. J. Gaylin. Psychol Today 11:29+ Ag '77
Importance of psychical research for religion. L. S. Betty. bibl Intellect 106:168-70 O '77
Psychic power of Uri Geller. K. Toffler. il pors Sat Eve Post 249:58-9+ O '77
Seer of flying; transcendental meditation and supernatural powers. il Time 110:75 Ag 8 '77
See also
Dreams
Extrasensory perception

Periodicals

See also
Zetetic (periodical)

PARARAS-CARAYANNIS, George
International Tsunami Warning System; with biographical sketch. il Sea Front 23:20-7, 63 Ja '77

PARASITES
Airs, waters, and places: harmonious parasites. R. S. Desowitz. Natur Hist 86:34+ O '77
See also
Fleas
Mites
Plasmodium (parasite)
Protozoa, Pathogenic
Sarcocystis
Symbiosis
Trypanosomes

Insects

Cleptoparasitism and odor mimetism in bees: do nomada males imitate the odor of andrena females? J. Tengo and G. Bergstrom. bibl il Science 196:1117-19 Je 3 '77
Exotic forest saved by foreign sting. il Sci N 112:69 Jl 30 '77
North American egg parasite successfully controls a different host genus in South America. A. T. Drooz and others. bibl il Science 197:390-1 Jl 22 '77

PARASITIC diseases
Challenge of parasitic diseases. Bull Atom Sci 33:46-53 Mr '77
Strategy for the chemotherapy of infectious disease. S. S. Cohen. bibl Science 197:431-2 Jl 29 '77
See also
Schistosomiasis
Trypanosomiasis

PARASITIC plants
See also
Mistletoe

PARATHORMONE. See Parathyroid hormone

PARATHYROID hormone
Aluminum absorption and distribution: effect of parathyroid hormone. G. H. Mayor and others. bibl il Science 197:1187-9 S 16 '77
1,25-Dihydroxycholecalciferol and parathormone: effects on isolated osteoclast-like and osteoblast-like cells G. L. Wong and others. bibl il Science 197:663-5 Ag 12 '77

PARDAH. See Purdah

PARDEE, Arthur B. and Schneider, D. S.
Control of cell growth in cancer. il pors Chemistry 50:25-9 Ja '77

PARDO, Rafael Martinez-. See Martinez-Pardo, R.

PARDO, Richard
Our national bonsai collection. il Am For 83:14-17+ D '77
Two different worlds. il Am For 83:14-17+ Ap '77
Washington lookout. See issues of American forests

PARDON
See also
Forgiveness
Probation

PARDON of draft resisters. See Military service, Compulsory—Draft resisters

PARENT and child (law)
Baiting the hook; case of J. and U. Krownapple of the Children of God movement. J. M. Hopkins. Chr Today 22:40-1 D 30 '77
Joint custody. M. A. Kellogg. Newsweek 89:56-7 Ja 24 '77
Life with father; divorced fathers. D. D. Molinoff. il N Y Times Mag p 12-17 My 22 '77
Parent against parent; the child-stealing epidemic. B. W. Most. Nation 224:559-61 My 7 '77; Same with title Epidemic of child-stealing. Current 194:40-4 Jl '77
Rights of parents and children; conflicts of civil rights. T. R. Hayden. Current 190:24-31 F '77
See also
Adoption
Desertion and non-support
Mentally ill children—Civil rights

PARENT-child relationship
Adolescent in the house; teen-age daughter. J. Geniesse. McCalls 104:31+ Jl '77
Adult at eighteen? excerpt from How to stop worrying about your kids. J. D. Sanderson. Read Digest 110:136-9 Mr '77
Are you a daddy's girl? A. Koral. Seventeen 36:53 Mr '77
Are you trying to be too good a parent? interview, ed by F. Davis. R. Farson. il Redbook 148:88+ Ap '77
Brooke Hayward talks about her children; interview, ed by C. M. Dobrish. B. Hayward. il por Parents Mag 52:52-3 O '77
Can adults live with their parents? D. Martin. America 136:482-3 My 28 '77
Children's hour; Foundation for Child Development survey. K. L. Woodward. il Newsweek 89:90+ Mr 14 '77
Christmases with my father; excerpt from Act one. M. Hart. Redbook 150:63-4 D '77
Commentary; hugging of children. P. Knauth. MH 61:2 Spr '77
Day I found my father. S. Albert. Good H 184:156+ Je '77
Did you hug your child today? A. Silberman. Read Digest 110:143-6 F '77
Emotional inheritance: a dubious legacy. Sci N 111:326 My 21 '77
Everyone works; children helping working mothers; interviews, ed by C. Jessup and G. Chipps. il Am Home 80:38-9 F '77
Genealogy of the weakest child; views of M. Bowen. il Time 109:85 Ap 11 '77
Heirs of the Holocaust; children of survivors. H. Epstein. il por N Y Times Mag p 12-15+ Je 19 '77; Discussion. p 14+ Jl 24 '77
How to come to terms with your parents; interview. H. Halpern. Harp Baz 110:47+ Je '77
How to relate to your children. il Bus W p 117-19+ D 12 '77
I had to ask my mother to move out of our house; mother and daughter. il Good H 185:38+ N '77
In love and in trouble; mother's discovery of daughter's pregnancy. Good H 184:32+ Ap '77
Is there sex after 40? college students' views of parents' sex lives. O. Pocs and others. il Psychol Today 11:54-6+ Je '77
Isaac syndrome; ego identity development in father-son relationships. S. G. Shoham. bibl f Am Imago 33:329-49 Wint '76

PARENT-child relationship—*Continued*
Mother & daughter: mothers can't give the world . . . but they can try; excerpt from Anne Sexton: a self-portrait in letters. A. Sexton. por Mademoiselle 83:176-7+ O '77
Mothering. G. Carro. See issues of Ladies' home journal
My search for my roots. B. J. Lifton. Seventeen 36:132-3+ Mr '77
Our 16-year-old son was on drugs. il Good H 184:28+ Je '77
Papa mia. B. G. Harrison. il por Ms 5:30+ Je '77
Parenting: you learn, too. L. Wyse. Vogue 167:243 D '77
Parents' aloofness slows twins' progress. Sci N 111:390 Je 18 '77
Quintana. J. G. Dunne. Esquire 87:8+ Je '77
Search for a stranger; adopted child's search for a mother. G. S. Livingston. Read Digest 110:85-9 Je '77
Should you try to change your parents? L. Konner. il Seventeen 36:154-5+ O '77
Silent lives; children's relationship with deaf parents. L. Konner. il Seventeen 36:38+ Ap '77
Special issue on working mothers. Parents Mag 52:33-7+ Ap '77
Sudden stillness; father-daughter relationship. G. Moore. il Read Digest 111:33-5+ Jl '77
Summer with Alex; father and son's trip to Alaska. P. L. Fradkin. il por Audubon 79:36-41 My '77
Ten ways to help your child succeed. S. L. Woodard. il por Ebony 32:52-4+ O '77
Thirty: not a dirty word anymore. M. Wolynski. Vogue 167:150+ O '77
What do you still want—that you're not getting—from your father? A. T. Fleming. il Redbook 149:42+ Jl '77
What your kids really want. P. Theroux. il Am Home 80:36-7 My '77
When feelings clash. J. Neary. il Parents Mag 53:44+ Ja '78
When your teenager needs you the most: learning to talk openly about homosexuality; excerpt from What every parent should know about sex and the American teenager. M. M. Kappelman. il Fam Health 9:44-6 Ag '77
Why adoptees search for their parents. B. J. Lifton. il Seventeen 36:145 O '77
Why I don't want my children home next summer. W. A. Nolen. Read Digest 110:146-7 F '77
Will the child be normal? Ask mother. Sci N 112:213 O 1 '77
Write the truth, my son said. Write about me. B. G. Harrison. il Ms 6:14-18 Ja '78
Writer's daughter. J. Delton. Seventeen 36:86 Ag '77
Your father's daughter. G. Emerson. Vogue 167:303+ O '77
See also
Aged—Family relationships
Child abuse
Children—Management and training
Children of alcoholics
Children of divorced parents
Family life
Families Anonymous (organization)
Fathers
Generation gap
Mothers

PARENT education
How do you stop fighting with your children? Parent Effectiveness programs on PBS. G. Carro. il Ladies Home J 94:80 O '77
Winning play at home base; home visitation program for parents of preschoolers in Yakima, Wash. V. Hedrich. il Am Educ 13:27-30 Jl '77

PARENT participation in school management. See School management and organization—Parent participation

PARENT-teacher associations. See Parents and teachers associations

PARENT-teacher cooperation. See School and the home

PARENTE, William J.
Conservative response. America 137:313 N 5 '77

PARENTHOOD, Education for. See Parent education

PARENTS
Baby?. . .Maybe. E. Whelan. il Ms 5:26+ Ap '77
Death in the family. J. Seligmann and S. Agrest. il Newsweek 89:89 Je 20 '77
Help for bereaved parents; ideas of H. S. Schiff. J. Chan. McCalls 105:114 O '77
Parent test; excerpt. E. Peck and W. A. Granzig. Good H 185:104+ N '77
See also
Children
Family
Family life
Fathers
Parent education
School and the home
Stepparents

PARENTS and teachers associations
New PTA's. E. J. Pascoe. McCalls 104:68 My '77
Parents' PTA page (cont) Parents Mag 52:29 Mr; 25 Je; 12 S '77
See also
National Congress of Parents and Teachers

PARENTS and teachers conferences. See School and the home

PARIETAL lobe. See Brain

PARINGER, Lynn. See Scheffler, R. M. jt auth

PARINI, Jay
Coal train; poem. New Yorker 53:38 Je 6 '77
Small valleys of our living. Poetry 130:293-303 Ag '77
This reaping; poem. Atlantic 239:62 My '77

PARIS, Judy
Pop-top panache. por Writers Digest 57:16 S '77

PARIS

Art

Paris. M. Gibson. il Art N 76:101-2 Ap; 104 O; 123 D '77
Paris/New York: who leads art? B. Rose. il Vogue 167:162-3+ Ap '77
Paris: tale of two cities; Paris-New York exhibit at the Beaubourg. J. Gruen. il Art N 76:109-11 S '77
Tale of two cities; Paris-New York exhibit at the Beaubourg. E. Peer. il Newsweek 89:64-5 Je 13 '77

Bookstores

See Booksellers and bookselling—France

Cabarets

See Cabarets

Centre Beaubourg

See Paris—Georges Pompidou Center

Description

New Paris focus. M. R. Henry. Vogue 167:106-8+ Ap '77

Georges Pompidou Center

Beaubourg. W. Von Eckardt. New Repub 177:26-8 N 5 '77
Beaubourg: a model or a portent. R. McMullen. il Sat R 4:52-5 Ja 22 '77
Beaubourg: brave new world. M. Stevens. il Newsweek 89:66-7 F 7 '77
Beaubourg preview; interview, ed by E. Baker. P. Hulten. il Art in Am 65:100-2 Ja '77
Boulez' IRCAM: amnesia in Nibelheim; Institut de Recherche et Coordination Acoustique/Musique. R. McMullen. il por Hi Fi 27:80-4 Ap '77
Canaveral of sound; Institut de Recherche et de Coordination Acoustique/Musique. H. Saal and J. Friedman. il Newsweek 89:67-8 F 7 '77
Cultural colossus of Beaubourg. M. Blume. il Art N 76:36-9 Mr '77
European pleasures: six million visitors can't be wrong. R. W. Murphy. il Horizon 19:28-33 Jl '77
Exoskeletal art container is the rage, literally, and the delight of Paris. R. Chelminski. il Smithsonian 8:20-9 Ag '77
France's bold art coup. il Vogue 167:160-1+ Ap '77
France's new culture palace. H. Kramer. il N Y Times Mag p 13 Ja 23 '77
IRCAM—underground and underway. A. Frankenstein. il Hi Fi 28:MA28-9+ Ja '78
Moral message from La Grande France; boycott of Pompidou Center in protest to release of Abu Daoud. Art N 76:31 Mr '77
Paris celebrates: a new art center and the brothers Duchamp. F. Steegmuller. Atlantic 239:88-90 Je '77
Paris' new Meccano machine. il Time 109:81 F 7 '77
Le tour Babel. N. Silver. Harpers 254:90-1 Ap '77
$200 million erector set. A. Burgess. il N Y Times Mag p 14-15+ Ja 23 '77

Historic houses, sites, etc.

Benjamin Franklin's residence in France: the Hôtel de Valentinois in Passy. M. Martindale. bibl il Antiques 112:262-73 Ag '77

History

See also
Paris—Siege, 1870-1871

Hotels, restaurants, etc.

International chef; Brasserie Lowenbrau Munich. L. Szathmary. Travel 147:84 Mr '77
Putting on the Ritz. H. O. Dormann. il Holiday 58:8 Ja '77

Monuments, statues, etc.

See also
Eiffel Tower

Music

Music critic in Paris in the nineteen-twenties: some personal recollections. R. Myers. il Mus Q 63:524-44 O '77
See also
Opera—France

PARIS—*Continued*

Notre Dame (cathedral)

Medieval mystery; discovery of sculptured heads that once adorned facade. il Horizon 20:26-7 S '77

Politics and government

Duel over city hall; J. Chirac vs M. d'Ornano in mayoral race. Time 109:31 Ja 31 '77
M. le Maire de Paris; Mayor J. Chirac's challenge to V. Giscard d'Estaing. G. Ross. New Repub 176:17-19 Ap 9 '77
Paris is worth a race; J. Chirac running for Mayor. K. Willenson and others. pors Newsweek 89:53-4 Ja 31 '77

Pompidou Center

See Paris—Georges Pompidou Center

Siege, 1870-1871

Siege of Paris. G. Carson. il Natur Hist 86: 68-77 O '77

Social history

Empathy with the humanity of the streets; illustrations of turn of the century Paris by T. A. Steinlen. P. D. Cate. il Art N 76:56-9 Mr '77

Social life and customs

What is Montmartre? Nothing! What should it be? Everything! tr by G. Needham. M. Frèrebeau. il Art N 76:60-2 Mr '77

Stores

How to look beautiful in Paris. M. Russell. il N Y Times Mag p 132-3 N 27 '77

Theater

Theatre. H. Clurman. Nation 225:125-6 Ag 6 '77

PARIS Boat Show. See Boats—Exhibitions
PARIS fashion shows. See Fashion shows
PARIS International Air Show. See Aviation—Exhibitions
PARIS Opera. See Opera—France
PARIS Opéra Ballet. See Ballet—France
PARIS Salon. See Photography—Exhibitions

PARISH, Mrs Henry
Imagination, country style. il House & Gard 149:110-15 D '77 *

PARISH, Margaret
(ed) Pick of the paperbacks. il Engl J 66:90-3 O '77

PARISH, Nathaniel J. and Teglas, Csaba
1977 Housing and Community Development Act: some new tools for central-city revitalization. Archit Rec 162:61 D '77

PARISH management. See Church management

PARISHES
Church and the Cherry orchard. F. E. Fitzpatrick. America 136:266-7 Mr 26 '77

PARISI, Anthony J.
Commentary. Bus W p 101 F 14 '77
—See Ediger, D. jt auth

PARISI, Joseph
Miss Monroe, Mr Pound, and the boorzoi. Poetry 131:39-51 O '77

PARISMINA River. See Reventazón River

PARK, Chung Hee
Fearless and the humorless. N. Kim. Chr Cent 94:733-4 Ag 17 '77 *
Korea, Inc. T. Szulc. New Repub 176:20-2 Ja 29 '77 *
Korea stonewalls. New Repub 177:7-8 N 5 '77 *
South Korea with sympathy. M. Kondracke. New Repub 177:12+ S 17 '77 *
South Korean exposure. J. Stentzel. Nation 224: 77-80 Ja 22 '77 *

PARK, Edwards
Around the Mall and beyond. See issues of Smithsonian
Eye of Bill Garnett looks down on the commonplace and sees art. il por Smithsonian 8:74-81 My '77

PARK, John Robinson
Growing criminal liability of executives. T. McAdams and R. C. Miljus. bibl f Harvard Bus R 55:36-7+ Mr '77 *

PARK, Roy Hampton
Bagging the broadcast limit. por Bus W p50 Jl 25 '77 *

PARK, Tongsun
Talking with Tongsun Park; interview, ed by B. Krisher. pors Newsweek 90:36-8 O 3 '77

about

All about Koreagate. D. M. Alpern and others. il pors Newsweek 90:17+ Ag 1 '77 *
As the Korean bribery scandal unfolds—. il U.S. News 83:27 O 31 '77 *
Civil rights for Tongsun Park. Nation 225:261 S 24 '77 *
Korea stonewalls. New Repub 177:7-8 N 5 '77 *
Lid finally blows off Korean bribery scandal. il por U.S. News 83:28+ S 19 '77 *
New scandal in Congress. J. S. Lang. il por U.S. News 83:9-12 Ag 1 '77 *
Paper chase. D. A. Williams and N. Horrock. il Newsweek 89:33-4 Je 6 '77 *
Park stays put. Newsweek 90:44 S 19 '77 *
Park's lobby hobby. K. Willenson and others. il pors Newsweek 90:37 S 5 '77 *
Still waiting for harvest time. il por Time 110: 21-2 S 19 '77 *
Swindler from Seoul. Time 110:8+ Jl 4 '77 *
Tongsun Park's White House connection. A. Latham. il Esquire 88:78+ D '77 *

PARK administration. See Parks—Administration

PARK employees
Code to work by. C. W. Pezoldt. il Parks & Rec 12:32-4+ Ja '77

PARK End Tavern (restaurant) See Queens, N.Y. —Hotels, restaurants, etc.

PARK management. See Parks—Administration

PARK planning
Peace Corps planning in the world's parks. J. Needle. il Parks & Rec 12:16-21+ Ag '77
Recreation planning for energy conservation. S. M. Gold. il Parks & Rec 12:61-3+ S '77
Regional planning in the Ruhr Valley. G. G. Wynne. il map Parks & Rec 12:21-3 D '77
Uptown parks and air rights. W. Theobald. bibl Parks & Rec 12:31-3+ Ag '77

PARK SLOPE Branch Library. See Brooklyn Public Library—Branches

PARKE, Robert B.
Passing the flag. E. D. Muhlfeld. il pors Flying 101:1+ O '77 *

PARKE, Ross D. and Sawin, D. B.
Fathering: it's a major role. bibl il pors Psychol Today 11:108-9+ N '77

PARKE Bernet Group, Ltd. See Sotheby Parke Bernet Group, Ltd

PARKER, C. Wolcott, 2d
Technolitics; address, September 15, 1976. Vital Speeches 43:253-6 F 1 '77

PARKER, Clinton E.
Save water at highway rest stops. il Am City & County 92:63-4 Je '77

PARKER, Daniel
U.S. signs articles of agreement of Agricultural Development Fund; statement, December 22, 1976. Dept State Bull 76:71 Ja 24 '77

PARKER, Donn B.
Computer criminals; excerpt from address. Intellect 106:187 N '77

PARKER, Graham
Graham Parker: born to stand and fight; Stick to me. T. Goldstein. il por Hi Fi 28:128 Ja 78 *
Mighty mite. J. Maslin and M. MacPherson. por Newsweek 89:71-2 Ja 31 '77 *

PARKER, John Carson-. See Carson-Parker, J.

PARKER, John Johnston
NAACP and the Supreme Court: Walter F. White and the defeat of Judge John J. Parker, 1930. D. C. Hine. bibl il por Negro Hist Bull 40:753-7 S '77 *

PARKER, Peter T.
Heart of Mt Shasta. il Am For 83:32-4 O '77

PARKER, Steven
Lipstick cases, typewriter parts melded into motorcycle art. il por Design (US) 79:14-16 Fall '77

PARKER, Wes
Gold Glover snags a big role. W. Leggett. il por Sports Illus 46:48 My 9 '77 *

PARKER, William E.
Operational amplifier quiz. il Pop Electr 11:111 Mr '77

PARKER, Willie J. and Robinson, Conway
Boy who fired too soon; excerpt from Halt! I'm a federal game warden. il Read Digest 111: 170-4 S '77

PARKER Drilling Company. See Petroleum industry—United States

PARKES, Joseph P.
Deep down, around hope. America 137:444 D 17 '77
Home scene. America 136:423-5 My 7 '77

PARKES, M. See Pihl, R. O. jt auth

PARKHURST, Michael
Trucker militant. H. Crews. il por Esquire 88: 82-4+ Ag '77 *

PARKING, Automobile. See Automobile parking

PARKING garages. See Garages; Garages, Municipal

PARKING lots. See Automobile parking

PARKING meters
Free-pay meters ring up shopper smiles; Peoria, Ill. il Am City & County 92:93-4 My '77

PARKINSON, C. Northcote
Why writers need islands. il Sat R 5:33-4 Ja 7 '78

PARKMAN, Francis
Perspectives on the past. W. W. Hassler, Jr. Am Hist Illus 12:37 D '77 *

PARKS, Alexis
Landscape of nuclear tombs. Progressive 41:30-1 D '77

PARKS, Dennis
Dust glazing. il Ceram Mo 25:23-7 O '77

about

Tuscarora Pottery School. A. Schwartz. il pors Ceram Mo 25:36-41 Je '77 *

PARKS, Henry G. 1916-
Henry G. Parks gives his rules for success. J. Saddler. il pors Ebony 32:100-2+ Mr '77 *
PARKS, Rosa
Day the black revolution began. L. Bennett, Jr. il pors Ebony 32:54-6+ S '77 *
PARKS
See also
Amusement parks
National parks and reserves
Playgrounds
Recreation
Administration
EEI: a survival tool; economic equivalency index to measure leisure services. R. L. Wilder. il Parks & Rec 12:22-4+ Ag '77
Concessions
See Concessions (food, etc)
Equipment
Wood for all seasons; redwood park equipment. il Parks & Rec 12:34-5 My '77
Maintenance
Community maintenance for city parks; program in Seattle. B. L. Balshone. il Parks & Rec 12:34-6 Ag '77
Coping with a water shortage; care of grass in recreation facilities. J. R. Watson. il Parks & Rec 12:54-5+ Jl '77
Management approach to park maintenance; method, time-measurement. R. W. Harris. il Parks & Rec 12:32-4 D '77
Management
See Parks—Administration
Planning
See Park planning
United States
Parks for the year 2000. R. Dattner. il Am City & County 92:39-44 N '77
See also
Baton Rouge, La.—Parks and playgrounds
National parks and reserves—United States
New York (city)—Parks and playgrounds
San Francisco—Parks and playgrounds
Seattle—Parks and playgrounds
also subhead Parks and reserves under names of states, e.g. New York (state)—Parks and reserves
PARKS and recreation (periodical)
Questions & answers on how to write for Parks & recreation. Parks & Rec 12:60-1 Mr '77
PARKS Sausage Company. See Meat industry
PARKWAYS. See Express highways
PARLETT, Jim
Absence of light; poem. Atlantic 241:57 Ja '78
PARLIAMENT-Funkadelic (rock group) See Rock groups
PARLIN, Bradley W.
Immigrants, employers, and exclusion. Society 14:23-6 S '77
PARMENTER, Frances C.
Election Day weather—2 November 1976. map Weatherwise 29:301 D '76
PAROCHIAL schools, Catholic. See Catholic schools
PAROLE
Recidivism and the effectiveness of prison and parole. C. H. Logan. bibl Intellect 105:424-6 Je '77
Rethinking parole. G. F. Cole and S. M. Talarico. il Intellect 106:143-6 O '77
See also
Probation
PARQUET flooring. See Flooring
PARRA, Nicanor
Pages from Parra. Review
Nation 225:535-6 N 19 '77 *
PARRISH, Larry
Dirty movies! Dirty books! C. Remsberg and B. Remsberg. il Good H 184:103+ Mr '77 *
United States versus the princess of porn. T. Morgan. il pors N Y Times Mag p 16-17+ Mr 6 '77 *
PARRISH, Michael E.
Cold war justice: the Supreme Court and the Rosenbergs. bibl f Am Hist R 82:805-42 O '77
PARRISH, Wayne W.
Foreign airlines. il Flying 101:236-7 S '77
Ticket to anywhere. il Sat R 4:16+ Ap 16 '77
PARROT fever. See Psittacosis
PARRY, John
Taking civil commitment out of the dark ages. il MH 61:18-20 Spr '77
PARRY arcs. See Halos (meteorology)
PARSHALL, Phil
Bangladesh update. Chr Today 21:35 Ag 12 '77
PARSIFAL; opera. See Wagner, R.
PARSLEY
Parsley is much more than just pretty. N. Albright. il Org Gard & Farm 24:128+ Mr '77

PARSON and Jackson dolls. See Dolls
PARSONS, E. Spencer
American Baptists: now more inclusive. Chr Cent 94:721 Ag 17 '77
PARSONS, Ellen
Will it be okay? story; excerpt. Ms 6:61-4 Ja '78
PARSONS, Estelle
At the Parsonage. New Yorker 52:31 F 14 '77 *
PARSONS, Nancy
Wizard of whiz-bang; drama. Plays 36:46-8, 57 Mr '77
PARSONS, Ralph M, Company. See Construction industry
PARSONS, Stephanie
Girl who wouldn't grow up. J. P. Blank. il Read Digest 111:199-202+ O '77 *
PARSONS, Timothy R.
Test tubes in the sea. il UNESCO Courier 30:28-9 Ja '77
PARSONS and Whittemore, Inc. See Paper mills
PART time employment
Army of the partly employed. il Forbes 119:58 Mr 1 '77
Flexitime, flexiwork, flexijobs, & retiree job-sharing. H. Alpert. il Ret Liv 17:22-5 My '77
Full and part time: a review of definitions. J. N. Hedges and S. J. Gallogly. bibl il M Labor R 100:21-8 Mr '77
My husband and I are equal partners. M. N. Dudley. McCalls 104:46+ F '77
PART time teachers. See Teachers, Part time
PARTAIN, Lloyd E.
On human engineering. il Am For 83:32-3+ Je '77
PARTHENOGENESIS
Animal parthenogenesis. O. Cuellar. bibl il maps Science 197:837-43 Ag 26 '77
Value of virgin birth. C. J. Cole. il Natur Hist 87:56-63 bibl(p 108) Ja '78
Virgin birth and mixed mice. il Sci N 112:263 O 22 '77
PARTHENON
Acropolis: threat of destruction. il Time 109:55 Ja 31 '77
Parthenon in perspective. il map UNESCO Courier 30:18-19 O '77
PARTICIPATIVE management. See Employees representation in management
PARTICLE accelerators. See Accelerators (electrons, etc)
PARTICLE beam weapons. See Weapons
PARTICLE beams
Electron cooling offers high-luminosity antiproton beams. G. B. Lubkin. il Phys Today 30:17+ Ap '77
Telecommunication with neutrino beams. A. W. Sáenz and others. bibl il Science 198:295-7 O 21 '77
See also
Electrons—Beams
PARTICLES
Chainlike formation of particle deposits in fluid-particle separation. C. Tien and others. il Science 196:983-5 My 27 '77
Oceanic microcosm of particles. D. Lal. bibl il maps Science 198:997-1009 D 9 '77
PARTICLES (nuclear physics)
Ambivalent leptons. Sci Am 236:55-7 My '77
Discovery of the J particle: a personal recollection; Nobel Prize lecture, December 11, 1976. S. C. C. Ting. bibl il Science 196:1167-78 Je 10 '77
Does dibaryomania start here? Sci N 112:372 D 3 '77
Elementary particles: classical mechanics to the rescue? A. L. Robinson. Science 198:180-2 O 14 '77
Elusive quarks: hints of two from a Stanford experiment. W. D. Metz. Science 196:746-7 My 13 '77
Evidence grows for charged heavy lepton at 1.8-2.0 GeV. G. B. Lubkin. il Phys Today 30:17+ N '77
From the psi to charm the experiments of 1975 and 1976; Nobel Prize lecture, December 11, 1976. B. Richter. bibl il Science 196:1286-97 Je 17 '77
Fundamental particles with charm. R. F. Schwitters. Sci Am 237:56-70 bibl(p 152) O '77
Future of unified gauge theories; adaptation of address, February 8, 1977. S. Weinberg. bibl il Phys Today 30:42-3+ Ap '77
Hark, hark, a quark—maybe. Time 109:59 My 2 '77
High energy physics: a proliferation of quarks and leptons. A. L. Robinson. il Science 198:478-81 N 4 '77
Making fermions out of bosons. Sci Am 236:61+ Mr '77
More signs of a heavy lepton. Sci N 111:341 My 28 '77
Possible heavy lepton in Russia; New measurement of muon magnetism. il Sci N 111:357-8 Je 4 '77
Proliferating quarks. Sci Am 237:74 O '77
Quark; interview. M. Gell-Mann. New Yorker 53.22-3 Jl 18 '77

PARTICLES (nuclear physics)—*Continued*
Quarks: merely Joycean or the ultimate McCoy? M. Guillen. Sci Digest 81:38-41+ Mr '77
Quarks with unit charge: a search for anomalous hydrogen. R. A. Muller and others. bibl il Science 196:521-3 Ap 29 '77
Quest for the quark; work of William Fairbank and George LaRue. P. Gwynne. Newsweek 89:99 My 9 '77
Ripples in physics: apparent failure of muon conservation. Sci N 111:116 F 19 '77
Stanford group shows apparent evidence for quarks. G. B. Lubkin. bibl il Phys Today 30:17+ Jl '77; Discussion. 30:9+ D '77
Tachyons: faster than light. . .if they exist; excerpt from Smithsonian magazine, November 1976. J. S. Trefil. Sci Digest 81:38-40 F '77
Tri- again: evidence of heavy leptons. Sci N 111:325 My 21 '77
Upsilon and the fifth quark: a heavy resonance. il Sci N 112:100 Ag 13 '77
Upsilon particles at 9.4 and 10 GeV suggest new quark. G. B. Lubkin. il Phys Today 30:17+ O '77
See also
Neutrons
Nucleons
Scattering (physics)

Acceleration

Electron cooling offers high-luminosity antiproton beams. G. B. Lubkin. il Phys Today 30:17+ Ap '77
First 400-GeV results from Europe. Sci N 112:4-5 Jl 2 '77
See also
Accelerators (electrons, etc)

Anecdotes, facetiae, satire, etc.

Dileptomania: heavier and heavier. il Sci N 112:87 Ag 6 '77

Beams

See Particle beams

PARTIE, Dianne. See Frisch, A. jt auth

PARTIES. See Childrens parties; Entertaining

PARTITIONS
Easy-to-make kitchen divider. J. Capotosto. il Mech Illus 73:66 Jl '77
Partition wall has storage inside. il Sunset 158:186 Ap '77
Room divider—ingenuity. il Sunset 158:140 Je '77
They use hollow-core doors to make an art display. il Sunset 158:153 Mr '77
Two rooms from one; bedroom bed-wall unit. H. Wicks. il Pop Mech 148:96-9+ S '77

PARTNERSHIP
See also
Farm partnership
Joint adventures

PARTON, Dolly
Dolly; interview, ed by J. Maynard. por Good H 185:54+ S '77
about
Country's angels. R. Blount, Jr. il pors Esquire 87:62-7+ Mr '77 *
Hello Dolly. P. Axthelm. il por Newsweek 89:71 Je 13 '77 *
On the rock road with Dolly Parton. J. Vallely. por Time 109:72-3 Ap 18 '77 *
You've come a long way, Dolly. J. Hurst. il por Hi Fi 27:122-4 D '77 *

PARTOVI, Pat
CB radio in the library. il por Lib J 102:2135-6 O 15 '77

PARTRIDGE, C. R.
Unspoiling the spoiled child. il Todays Educ 66:67-9 S '77

PARTRIDGE, Eric Honeywood
Definition of Partridge. I. Shenker. pors N Y Times Mag p41-2 O 2 '77 *
Wit and wisdom of catch phrases. J. Simon. Esquire 88:46+ N '77 *
Word king. por Time 110:75-6 O 17 '77 *

PARTY affiliation. See Political parties—Membership

PARTY line; drama. See Miller, H. L.

PARTY with Betty Comden and Adolph Green; revue. See Musical comedy, revue, etc.—Reviews—Single works

PARVIN, Stuart A.
Miniaturia. See issues of Hobbies

PASADENA, Calif.

Education

American time line; Bicentennial mural at Altadena Elementary School. E. Levine. il Sch Arts 76:30-2 Je '77

PASAHOW, Edward
Elusive proteas. il Horticulture 55:30-7 Jl '77
Iris with the golden writing. il Horticulture 55:14-15 My '77

PASATIERI, Thomas
(ed) See Ponselle, R. From the Villa Pace
about
Washington Square. Review
Newsweek il 90:100+ N 7 '77 *

PASCA, T. M.
Observing foresters. il por Am For 83:24-7+ Ag '77

PASCAL, Jack
IBM way of life. M. Ruby and P. L. Abraham. il por Newsweek 90:84 N 21 '77 *

PASCOE, Robert D.
How's & why's of D/A and A/D converters. il Pop Electr 11:53-6 Ap '77

PASH, Donald N.
What's wrong with public broadcasting. il Hi Fi 27:MA19-21 O '77

PASSAGEWAYS. See Halls

PASSAIC River

Bridges

Sky hook lifts bridge from river; Union Avenue Bridge. il Am City & County 92:46 S '77

PASSAMAQUODDY Indians. See Indians of North America

PASSELL, Peter
How long will you live? Sat Eve Post 249:53 Mr '77
Second best; excerpts from The best, encore. il Esquire 87:72-4+ Mr '77

PASSENGER pigeons
Sighting at Pine Knot. A. A. Lindsey. il Natur Hist 86:40+ N '77

Stories

Hurricane of death; excerpt from Post. H. Masters. Sports Illus 47:100-4 N 28 '77

PASSENGER service on airlines. See Airlines—Passenger service

PASSIFLORA. See Passionflowers

PASSING game; drama. See Tesich S.

PASSION flowers. See Passionflowers

PASSION of Christ. See Jesus Christ—Passion

PASSION of Dracula; dramatization. See Hall, B. and Richmond, D.

PASSION plays
Passion according to the Yaquis. il UNESCO Courier 30:22-3 Ag '77
See also
Oberammergau Passion Play

PASSIONFLOWERS
Passionflower: exquisite tropical plant. I. Zucker. il Horticulture 55:52-3 N '77

PASSMAN, Otto Ernest
Why the Justice Department doesn't want you to know what happened between Otto Passman and Shirley Davis. A. Northrop. il pors Ms 6:57-9 Ja '78 *

PASSOVER
Woman's Passover Haggadah and other revisionist rituals. E. M. Broner and N. Nimrod. Ms 5:53-6 Ap '77

PASSPORTS
End to Meany's veto; amendment of the State Department Authorization Bill to grant visas to Communists. Nation 225:195-6 S 10 '77
Everything a traveler should know about passports and visas. M. Weiser. il Holiday 58:34-5 Ja '77
Expiration of area restrictions on use of passports. Dept State Bull 76:346 Ap 11 '77
Foggy bottom curtain; question of visa for H. Blanco. Nation 225:260 S 24 '77
Holiday in Havana; lifting U.S. ban on travel to Cuba. D. Pauly and P. E. Simons. il Newsweek 89:57 Mr 28 '77
Meany's veto; visas refused to delegates from Russian trade unions. Nation 224:515-16 Ap 30 '77
Never for Mundey; visa refused. E. P. Morgan. Progressive 41:9 My '77
Soviet side; McCarran-Walter Act. F. Willey and others. il Newsweek 89:30 F 21 '77

PASSY, France. See Paris

PAST, The
See also
Nostalgia

PAST tense; drama. See Zeman, J.

PASTA cookery. See Cookery—Macaroni products

PASTA makers. See Kitchen utensils and appliances

PASTAN, Linda
Arithmetic lesson: infinity; Egg; poems. Poetry 129:211-13 Ja '77
City; poem. New Yorker 53:135 Ap 18 '77
Funerary tower: Han dynasty; poem. Am Scholar 46:213 Spr '77
Return; My grandmother; poems; excerpt from The five stages of grief. Redbook 150:67, 73 D '77
Short history of Judiac thought in the twentieth century; poem. New Repub 177:35 Ag 6 '77
Terminal; poem. Am Scholar 46:457 Aut '77

PASTEELS, Jacques M. and Daloze, Désiré
Cardiac glycosides in the defensive secretion of chrysomelid beetles: evidence for their production by the insects. bibl il Science 197:70-2 Jl 1 '77

PASTEL drawing
Frank Beatty: the peripatetic pastellist; interview, ed by C. Movalli. il por Am Artist 41:66-9+ O '77

PASTEUR, Louis
Left-handed and right-handed molecules. G. B. Kauffman. bibl il por Chemistry 50:14-18 Ap '77 *
PASTIER, John
Welcome to downtown L.A. il Horizon 20:10-19 O '77
PASTON, Bryna N. and Tolins, Selma
Circus secret; drama. Plays 37:59-64 N '77
PASTORAL counseling
Burn-out: the hazard of professional people-helpers. G. R. Collins. Chr Today 21:12-14 Ap 1 '77
Minister's workshop. See every other issue of Christianity today
Therapies ministers use. J. S. Miller. il Chr Cent 94:504-8 My 25 '77; Discussion. 94:852-4 S 28 '77
PASTORAL training. See Theological education
PASTORE, Ann. See Pastore, A. R. Jr jt auth
PASTORE, Arthur Ralph, Jr
Washington's new museums. il Trav/Holiday 149:50-3 Ja '78
—and Pastore, Ann
Thurber's Bermuda. il Travel 147:32-7 Mr '77
PASTORS. See Clergy
PASTRY
Cream puffs and cherries on top. il Sunset 158:178 Je '77
Dutch treat—sausages baked in a pastry shell. il Sunset 158:180 Mr '77
For a winter parade or outing . . . a hot picnic that fits into your pocket; meat-filled pastries. il Sunset 159:26 D '77
How to line a flan ring; pastry crust. J. Pepin. il House B 119:112 F '77
Pastry overcoat idea; meat, poultry and fish. il Sunset 159:120-1 O '77
Perfect cream puffs. il Good H 184:92 My '77
Puff perfect. C. Claiborne and P. Franey. il N Y Times Mag p32-3 S 4 '77
Tarts and turnovers. il Bet Hom & Gard 55:161-2 S '77
Tea for two. . .with homemade strudel. J. Dannenbaum. il Am House 80:62-3+ F '77
Two delicious fila pastries. il Sunset 158:208 My '77
See also
Pie
Tarts
PASTURES
Sketch book visit to pastures. W. Trimm. il Conservationist 31:inside back cover My '77
See also
Grazing

Seeding

Six steps for sod seeding old pastures and hayfields. Suc Farm 75:no2 56 F '77
PATAGONIA
Behold, a multitude of penguins. G. H. Harrison. il Int Wildlife 7:36-9 Jl '77
PATCHING materials
Super patching it. H. Kelly. il Mech Illus 73:88 Mr '77
PATCHWORK
Easy patchwork tablecloth. il Bet Hom & Gard 55:56 Ap '77
How to make your own patchwork boxes. il House & Gard 149:70+ Mr '77
PATCHWORK quilts. See Quilts
PATEL, Y. C. and others
Somatostatin: widespread abnormality in tissues of spontaneously diabetic mice. bibl il Science 198:930-1 D 2 '77
PATENT lawyers
But what can it do? Bell Labs. por Forbes 120:104 O 1 '77
PATENT models. See Models (patents)
PATENT Office. See United States—Patent and Trademark Office
PATENTS
Build a better mousetrap. W. T. Messerly. il Suc Farm 75:no4 L 16 Mr '77
Can inventions make you rich? M. Grosswirth. il Mech Illus 73:30+ My '77
Long and rocky road to getting a patent. Changing T 31:31-3 D '77
See also
Lasers—Patents
United States—Patent and Trademark Office

Laws and regulations

Those cases that go on and on; rights to polypropylene patent. Time 109:46+ Je 27 '77
See also
Patents—Licensing

Licensing

Licensing furor in the EC. il Bus W p54-5 Jl 25 '77
Wild card gets wilder. T. P. Murphy. Forbes 120:204-5 N 15 '77
PATÉS. See Cookery—Poultry
PATHOGENIC microorganisms. See Microorganisms, Pathogenic
PATHS. See Trails
PATHS, Garden. See Garden walks
PATIENCE
See also
Hurry
PATIENTS, Nursing home. See Sick, The
PATIENTS and gynecologists. See Gynecologists and patients
PATIENTS and physicians. See Physicians and patients
PATIENTS and psychologists. See Psychologists and patients
PATIENTS rights. See Sick, The—Civil rights
Les **PATINEURS;** ballet. See Ballet reviews—Single works
PATIO doors. See Doors
PATIOS. See Decks, patios, terraces, etc.
PATOČKA, Jan
Jan Patočka. R. Jakobson. New Repub 176:26-8 My 7 '77 *
PATRI, Jennifer
Killing excuse. il por Time 110:108 N 28 '77 *
PATRICK, Ann Stover
Dream season; story. Seventeen 36:196-7 Ap '77
PATRICK, Anne E.
Be still and acknowledge that I am God. il New Cath World 220:42-3 Ja '77
PATRICK, Harry
Chaos in the mines. il pors Time 109:69-70 Je 13 '77 *
PATROL cars. See Automobiles, Police
PATROL work, Airplanes in. See Airplanes in patrol work
PATRON saints. See Saints
PATRONAGE, Art. See Art patronage
PATRONAGE, Political. See Political patronage
PATTERN in design. See Design, Decorative
PATTERN painting. See Art, Abstract
PATTERN perception
Vibrotactile pattern perception: extraordinary observers; use of Optacon. J. C. Craig. bibl il Science 196:450-2 Ap 22 '77
Visual search in the pigeon: hunt and peck method. D. S. Blough. bibl il Science 196:1013-14 My 27 '77
PATTERNS for embroidery. See Embroidery—Patterns
PATTERSON, Carolyn Bennett
New Zealand's Milford Track. il map Nat Geog 153:116-29 Ja '78
Rescuing the Rothschild. il Nat Geog 152:418-21 S '77
PATTERSON, Dow, family
Treasured offerings from Becky and Dow Patterson. S. Hearon. il pors Redbook 150:91+ D '77
PATTERSON, Floyd
Whatever happened to Floyd Patterson? il pors Ebony 33:44-6+ N '77 *
PATTERSON, Francine
Pursuit of reason. H. T. P. Hayes. il pors N Y Times Mag p21-3+ Je 12 '77; Reply. B. DeMott. Atlantic 240:86+ S '77 *
PATTERSON, Jerry E.
Art market. il Art N 76:113-14 O '77
PATTERSON, Lee Roy
Chaos in the mines. il pors Time 109:69-70 Je 13 '77 *
PATTERSON, Lois W.
Year-round Christmas tree. il Org Gard & Farm 144-5 D '77
PATTERSON, Michael M. and others
Classical nictitating membrane conditioning in the awake, normal, restrained cat. bibl il Science 196:1124-6 Je 3 '77
PATTERSON, Richard
Train robbery. il Am West 14:48-53 Mr '77
PATTERSON, Robert W. Jr
Let's not all leap on the coed bandwagon. il Camp Mag 49:36-9+ Ja '77
PATTERSON, Ronald P.
Broad-based publishing philosophy. por Pub W 212:65 S 26 '77
PATTERSON, Ronn Storro-. See Storro-Patterson, R.
PATTERSON, Russell
Setting an example. H. Haskell. il por Opera N 42:48-9 S '77 *
PATTERSON, Ruth
Arrow of God; C. Achebe's novel. Engl J 66:64-5 Mr '77
PATTERSON, Solom Pete
Inefficient stock. por Forbes 119:46 Ap 1 '77 *
PATTERSON, Walter C.
Overview: London report. Environment 19:41-3 Mr; 4+ Ap; 20+ My '77
PATTILLO, R. A. and others
Tumor antigen and human chorionic gonadotropin in CaSki cells: a new epidermoid cervical cancer cell line. bibl il Science 196:1456-8 Je 24 '77
PATTON, Edward L.
All about the pipeline; Alyeska Pipeline Service Company; interview. por U.S. News 82:36-7 Je 20 '77

about

One final squabble. por Forbes 119:140 Ap 15 '77 *

PATTON, Frank, and Darling, P. W.
Bee wing case: a preservation (tragedy) travesty. Lib J 102:771-5 Ap 1 '77

PATTON, George Smith, 1885-1945
Patton in Mexico: the Punitive Expedition. M. Blumenson. il pors Am Hist Illus 12:34-42 O '77 *

PATTON, Gerald R.
Single sideband: the high-performance CB. il Pop Mech 148:100-1+ N '77

PATTON, Phil
Other voices, other rooms: the rise of the alternative space. il Art in Am 65:80-9 Jl '77
Photography '77: a stocktaking. Art in Am 65:34-6 Ja '77

PAUGH, Tom
(ed) Update. il Outdoor Life 160:32, 36, 98, 102, 104 O; 54, 56, 58, 104, 108 N; 50, 54, 56, 108, 112 D '77; 161:42, 50, 100, 102, 104 Ja '78

PAUL, Saint
Paul: ambassador to the world. M. Muggeridge and A. Vidler. il Sat Eve Post 249:6+ O '77 *

Teachings

Paradoxes of prayer. F. E. Gaebelein. Chr Today 21:33-4 S 9 '77
Paul, apostle of love. L. Morris. Chr Today 21:76+ S 9 '77

Teaching

Spiritual lift no one is talking about; analysis of Paul's letters to the Corinthians. L. Samuel. il Chr Today 21:10-12 Ja 21 '77

PAUL VI, Pope
As Pope Paul VI reaches 80 . . . il por U.S. News 83:65 S 26 '77 *
Day in the life of the Pope. C. B. Pepper. pors N Y Times Mag p38-40+ Ap 10 '77 *
Dr Coggan and Paul VI. America 136:435 My 14 '77 *
Papabile Cardinal Benelli. D. O'Grady. Commonweal 104:488 Ag 5 '77 *
Paul says no. Newsweek 89:77 F 7 '77 *
Paul says no to women: keep out. por Time 109:65 F 7 '77 *
Pilgrim pope at 80. K. L. Woodward and L. Jenkins. il por Newsweek 90:73-4 O 3 '77 *
Pope's birthday. America 137:206 O 8 '77 *
Portrait of a Pope. Y. Karsh. por Sat Eve Post 249:28 Ap '77 *
Red hat for the right-hand man. por Time 109:49 Je 13 '77 *
Third summit: more hurdles. il pors Time 109:80 My 9 '77 *
Twilight papacy. il pors Time 110:76-7 O 10 '77 *
Why the Pope should resign. Commonweal 104:707-8 N 11 '77 *

PAUL, Alice
Alice Paul: mother of the ERA. R. Morgan. por Ms 6:112 O '77 *

PAUL, Anthony. See Barron, J. jt auth

PAUL, Henry E.
Henry E. Paul: an appreciation. G. T. Keene. il por Sky & Tel 53:177 Mr '77 *

PAUL, Iain C. See Chiang, C. C. jt auth

PAUL, James
Green bottle, the road, the dream; poem. Am Scholar 46:383 Summ '77

PAUL, Jim
Bananas in the bushes. P. Putnam. il por Sports Illus 47:32-5 S 12 '77 *

PAUL, Rodman W.
Mormons: from persecution to power. il Am Heritage 28:74-83 Je '77

PAUL, Ron
Reviews. J. Dunning. Dance Mag 51:36 Ap '77 *

PAUL, Steven M. and Axelrod, Julius
Catechol estrogens: presence in brain and endocrine tissues. bibl il Science 197:657-9 Ag 12 '77

PAUL, William E. and Benacerraf, Baruj
Functional specificity of thymus-dependent lymphocytes. bibl il Science 195:1293-300 Mr 25 '77

PAUL Bunyan; opera. See Britten, B.

PAUL Taylor Dance Company
Dance. M. Hodgson. il Am Home 80:19 Mr '77
Dance; performance of Aphrodisiamania. N. Goldner. Nation 225:700-1 D 24 '77
Dance; performances of Dust, Images, Esplanade and Polaris. N. Goldner. Nation 224:794+ Je 25 '77
Dancing. A. Croce. New Yorker 53:113-14 Je 20 '77
Eye witness; City Center performances May 31-June 5. T. Tobias. il Dance Mag 51:45-50 S '77
Terrific tempo of Paul Taylor. il Time 110:78-9 Jl 18 '77
Three by Paul Taylor; week at the New York City Center. J. Maskey. il Hi Fi 27:MA12+ O '77

PAULDEN, Sydney
Booming new way to get books to children in Britain: the school bookstore. il Pub W 211:95-6 F 28 '77

PAULEY, Jane
Barbara's heir. por Forbes 120:102 O 1 '77 *
Jane Pauley & Sandy Hill. A. L. Ball. pors Redbook 150:94+ N '77 *

PAULING, Linus
Nuclear fission is not the answer. por Bull Atom Sci 33:66 Mr '77
Pauling: just try to find the answer; interview. il por Sci Digest 82:54-7 Ag '77

PAULOWNIA
This princess heals disturbed land. S. B. Carpenter. il Am For 83:23 Jl '77

PAULSON, F. M.
Boating. See issues of Field & stream

PAULUS, Judith Ann. See Tenenbaum, S. jt auth

PAUST, Gil
Spin a fly. il Field & S 82:92+ Je '77

PAVAROTTI, Luciano
Mangia, mangia; celebrating the new Met production of La Bohème. R. Jacobson. il pors Opera N 41:8-13 Mr 19 '77 *

PAVE Penny system. See Airplanes, Military—Electronic equipment

PAVEL, S. and others
Pineal vasotocin: release into cat cerebrospinal fluid by melanocyte-stimulating hormone release-inhibiting factor. bibl il Science 197:179-80 Jl 8 '77

PAVEMENT markings. See Traffic markings

PAVEMENTS
Build bike paths to last concrete pavement. E. G. Robbins. il Am City & County 92:70 Ap '77
Can fabrics soften paving problems? il Am City & County 92:69-70 N '77
Crazy-quilt paving; using worn or broken bricks. il Sunset 158:246-7 My '77
Is pavement reinforcing worth its cost? concrete pavements; Wisconsin. R. C. Blum and C. E. Solberg. il Am City & County 92:59-61 D '77

See also
Bridges—Floors
Driveways
Sidewalks

Maintenance and repair

Chilling cost of winter damage. il Bus W p37 Mr 21 '77
Cold recycling of asphalt pavement meets conservation ethic; method used in Texas. W. S. Foster. Am City & County 92:36 N '77
Relieve summertime pavement blowups; pressure relief joints for concrete highways: Virginia. K. H. McGhee. il Am City & County 92:38-9 Jl '77

See also
Pavements—Surface treatment
Roads—Maintenance and repair

Surface treatment

Make new streets out of old. il Am City & County 92:41-4 Mr '77

Traffic lines

See Traffic markings

PAVLOVA, Anna
From Pavlova to ABT. W. Terry. il pors Opera N 41:10-14 Je '77 *
Looking back: years with Pavlova, a memoir. I. Marinel. il por Dance Mag 52:42-3 Ja '78 *

PAWEL, Ernst
Between survival and solvency. Nation 224:584-7 My 14 '77
Malraux: engaged intellectual. Nation 224:89-91 Ja 22 '77

PAWELEK, Dick
Q&A about home repairs. Ret Liv 17:18+ N; 16-17 D '77

PAXTON, James S. See Jones, R. E. jt auth

PAY differentials. See Wage differentials

PAY television. See Television broadcasting, Subscription

PAY television, Cable. See CATV system

PAYMENTS, Balance of. See Balance of payments

PAYNE, Ralph
Americanization of Japan. il Society 14:81-4 Jl '77

PAYNE, Stanley G.
Political transformation of Spain. Cur Hist 73:165-8+ N '77

PAYOLA. See Bribery

PAYSON, Charles Shipman
At Payson's place he's just plain Charlie. V. Kraft. il por Sports Illus 46:54+ Ap 18 '77 *

PAYTON, Walter
Payton runs all over the place. il por Sports Illus 47:26-7 N 28 '77 *
Running wild. il Time 110:90 D 19 '77 *
Sweetness is a Bear. P. Bonventre and S. Monroe. il por Newsweek 90:63 D 5 '77 *

PAZ, Gideon
Bernstein in Israel. il por Hi Fi 27:MA32-3 S '77

PAZ, Octavio
Matter of life and death; excerpt from The labyrinth of solitude. il UNESCO Courier 30: 20-1+ Ag '77
Spanish-American literature; address, December 4, 1976. New Repub 176:23-7 Ap 9 '77

PAZERESKIS, John
Electrolysis. il Yachting 142:53-5 D '77

PAZYRYK excavations. See Altai Mountains

PEABODY Book Shop, Baltimore. See Booksellers and bookselling—Maryland

PEABODY Coal Company
Down the chute with Peabody coal. C. J. Loomis. il Fortune 95:228-33+ My '77
What awaits Hills at Peabody. por Bus W p 18-19 Jl 4 '77

PEACE
In search of a lasting peace; excerpt from Unesco's Medium-Term Plan (1977-1982) UNESCO Courier 30:16-17 Mr '77
Macho obstacles to peace. A. M. Davidson. Bull Atom Sci 33:22-4 Je '77
Organized peace in southern France and Catalonia, ca. 1140-ca. 1233. T. N. Bisson. bibl f map Am Hist R 82:290-311 Ap '77
Peace and its priorities: 1977. America 137:472 D 31 '77
Peace crusader; work of A. Nathan. E. Keerdoja and M. J. Kubic. il pors Newsweek 91:5 Ja 2 '78
Peacetime. T. Powers. Commonweal 104:723-5 N 11 '77
See also
International relations
International security
Pacifism
Stockholm International Peace Research Institute
United Nations
United Nations—Special Committee on Peacekeeping Operations
War

PEACE conferences
See also
Israel-Arab Wars, 1967- —Peace and mediation

PEACE Corps. See United States—ACTION

PEACE movements

Northern Ireland

Everywhere but Ireland: success of the Peace People. A. Boyd. il Nation 224:453-6 Ap 16 '77
Is peace in Northern Ireland becoming possible at last? pors U.S. News 83:84+ O 24 '77
Northern Ireland: chance for peace? il map Sr Schol 109:13-15 Ja 13 '77
Northern Ireland's guerrillas of peace; interviews, ed by R. S. Kennedy and P. Klotz-Chamberlin. B. Williams; N. McDonnell. il por Chr Cent 94:746-51 Ag 31 '77
On the road to Drogheda. J. Gilhooley. il Commonweal 104:178-80 Mr 18 '77
Two Peace Prizes from Oslo; award to Community of Peace People. il pors Time 110:54 O 24 '77
Two women of Ulster; M. Corrigan and B. Williams of Community of Peace People. K. Willenson and A. Collings. il pors Newsweek 90:61 O 24 '77

PEACE People movement, Northern Ireland. See Peace movements—Northern Ireland

PEACE Resource Center. See Wilmington College, Wilmington, Ohio—Peace Resource Center

PEACE societies
Mobilizing for survival. Progressive 41:5-6 S '77
New coalition still is more of a courtship than a marriage: Mobilization for Survival. J. Walsh. il Science 198:384 O 28 '77

PEACE studies
Is it possible to teach peace? D. Mueller. Educ Digest 43:43-5 S '77
See also
Wilmington College, Wilmington, Ohio—Peace Resource Center

PEACEFUL nuclear explosive testing, Underground. See Atomic bombs—Testing, Underground

PEACH industry. See Fruit industry

PEACOCK, Mary, and Troy, Carol
(ed) How to have fun though dressed: a sneak preview of Rags. il pors Ms 5:67-70 My '77

PEANUT industry. See Nut industry

PEANUTS
George Washington Carver and the peanut. B. Mackintosh. il pors Am Heritage 28:66-73 Ag '77
Peanut power. J. Chan. il McCalls 104:64 F '77
Peanuts are my favorite crop. G. Solberg. il Org Gard & Farm 24:74-6 Mr '77

PEARCE, John Ed
Let's lower the obscenity level. Read Digest 111: 91-2 N '77

PEARCE, Laer. See Arnold, R. E. jt auth

PEARCE, William A.
Cape Vincent. il Conservationist 31:19-20 Mr '77

PEARL HARBOR, Attack on, 1941
Dec. 7, 1941; excerpt from Flames in the sky. P. Clostermann. il Flying 101:186-7 S '77
When isolationism died. New Repub 177:2+ D 10 '77

PEARL Lang Dance Company
Reviews; engagement at the 92nd Street Y. L. Small. Dance Mag 51:96+ Jl '77

PEARLMAN, Alan Robert
Arp & Friend, Inc. J. Ellis. il pors Hi Fi 28: 114-16 Ja '78 *

PEARLMAN, Sy
Sawyer brothers—their only crime was being poor. pors Good H 185:82+ Ag '77

PEARS
Seckels grow in the southwest. A. B. Yeager. Org Gard & Farm 24:176-8 Ap '77

PEARSALL, Bill
Adventure. Sports Illus 46:56+ Mr 14 '77

PEARSON, Allen D. and others
Tornado season of 1976. il maps Weatherwise 30:3-9+ F '77

PEARSON, David, 1934-
Hot blood down in Dixie; excerpt from King Richard, ed by B. Libby. il pors Sports Illus 46:64 F 21 '77
about
Pearson hits the road. B. Myers. il Car & Dr 22:128 My '77 *

PEARSON, Ethelyn
Stand-up gardening at Shady Lane. il Org Gard & Farm 24:106-8 My '77

PEARSON, John F.
Science worldwide. See issues of Popular mechanics

PEARSON, Richard
Paleoenvironment and human settlement in Japan and Korea. bibl il maps Science 197: 1239-46 S 23 '77

PEARSON, S. & Son, Ltd
Why Pearson is after Madame Tussaud's. il Bus W p57 D 12 '77

PEAS
Compost and mulch make peas aplenty. W. Yurkiewicz and G. Yurkiewicz. Org Gard & Farm 24:113 Mr '77
Peas twice a week. J. Cox. il Org Gard & Farm 24:95-7 F '77

PEAT
How about burning a bit o'peat? P. Egan. Sci Digest 82:60 O '77
Origins of sulfur in coal: importance of the ester sulfate content of peat. D. Casagrande and K. Siefert. bibl Science 195:675-6 F 18 '77

PEAT, Marwick, Mitchell and Company. See Accountants

PEBBLES
See also
Gravel

PECAN trees
All about pecans. P. Runnels. il Org Gard & Farm 24:87-91 S '77
How I graft pecans for profits and pleasure. L. Riotte. il Org Gard & Farm 25:90-1 Ja '78

PECHMAN, Joseph A.
Eliminate all preferences and reduce tax rates; interview. por U.S. News 83:37-8 Jl 25 '77

PECHTER, William S.
Movies. See alternate issues of Commentary to May 1977

PECK, Abe
Other convention in Chicago; 1968; interview, ed by L. R. Obst. il N Y Times Mag p92+ N 13 '77

PECK, Ellen, and Granzig, W. A.
Parent test; excerpt. Good H 185:104+ N '77

PECK, F. Taylor
Art of money. il Américas 29:21-8 My '77

PECK, Gregory
Gregory Peck remembers; interview, ed by M. Haskell. por Ladies Home J 94:52+ Jl '77

PECK, John
Trouble shooting by test tube. il Motor B & S 140:71-3 D '77

PECK, Steven
Steven Peck Jazz Dance Company; interview, ed by V. H. Swisher. il Dance Mag 51:78-9 Mr '77

PECK, Steven, Dance Company. See Dance companies

PECKARSKY, Peter
Flaherty's promise. New Repub 177:9-10 D 10 '77

PECKHAM, Stanton
Lively publishing scene in Boulder. il Pub W 211:49-51 Je 6 '77

PECKINPAH, Sam
Truckin' with big Iguana. il por Time 110:73-4 Jl 4 '77 *

PEDDLER dolls. See Dolls

PEDDLERS and peddling
See also
Street trades

PEDESTALS
How to build a basic pedestal. il Mech Illus 73: 70+ Jl '77

PEDESTRIAN bridges. See Bridges, Foot

PEDESTRIAN malls. See Business districts

PEDESTRIANS
Cross with a flag for safety; Laguna Beach, Calif. il Sunset 159:32 N '77

PEDIATRICS
See also
Sick children
PEDICULARIS. See Louseworts
PEDLEY, John Griffiths. See Humphrey, J. H. jt auth
PEDODONTISTS. See Dentists
PEELE, David
Exploring catalog country's great divide. bibl il Wilson Lib Bull 52:324-9 D '77
PEELERS (kitchen utensils) See Kitchen utensils and appliances
PEER groups. See Groups (sociology)
PEER review for research grants. See Research grants
PEERMAN, Dean
Cuba: no room for naysayers? il Chr Cent 94: 845-9 S 28 '77
PEETOOM, Adrian
Statistically significant genre teaching. Engl J 66:9-11 F '77
PEG o' my heart; drama. See Manners, J. H.
PEHL, Richard H.
Germanium gamma-ray detectors. bibl il Phys Today 30:50-4+ N '77
PEIRCE, Neal R.
What of national "town meetings"? Current 190: 21-3 F '77
about
Other end of the telescope. il por Time 109: 49 My 9 '77 *
PEKING (ship) See Sailing vessels
PEKING Book Fair. See Book fairs
PEKING duck. See Cookery—Poultry
PEKING Man. See Man, Prehistoric
PEKING talks, 1972
Thinking through the China problem; Shanghai communiqué. R. H. Solomon. bibl f For Affairs 56:324-56 Ja '78
U.S. and Peking agree: there's only one China, but—; excerpts from Shanghai communiqué. il U.S. News 83:50 Ag 22 '77
PELADEAU, Pierre
Hoagie City hero. por Time 110:47 D 19 '77 *
Pulpy Pierre. T. Schwartz. il por Newsweek 90:102 D 19 '77 *
Safari into darkest publishing. por Forbes 120: 108 D 1 '77 *
PELÉ
Happy families. M. J. Arlen. New Yorker 53: 104+ O 17 '77 *
Pelé, Pelé, Pelé. il pors Sports Illus 47:24-5 O 10 '77 *
Pelé's mission accomplished. il por Time 110: 62-3 S 12 '77 *
PELL, Claiborne
Should U.S. recognize Peking? interview. pors U.S. News 83:27-8 Ag 29 '77
PELLÉAS et Mélisande; opera. See Debussy, C.
PELLEGRINO, Victoria Y.
Your first-job strategy. Harp Baz 110:48+ Je '77
—See De Rosis, H. A. jt auth
PELLETED feed. See Feeds—Pelleted feed
PELLETIER, Georges, and others
Somatostatin: electron microscope immunohistochemical localization in secretory neurons of rat hypothalamus. bibl il Science 196: 1469-70 Je 24 '77
PELLETIER, Kenneth R.
Mind as healer, mind as slayer; excerpt. il por Psychol Today 10:35-7+ F '77
PELLETIER, S. William. See De Camp, W. H. jt auth
PELLMAR, T. C. and Wilson, W. A.
Synaptic mechanism of pentylenetetrazole: selectivity for chloride conductance. bibl il Science 197:912-14 Ag 26 '77
PELOSI, James J.
Silent treatment. E. Keerdoja. il por Newsweek 90:11 Ag 8 '77 *
PELTIER, Leonard
Leonard Peltier and the posse. B. Johansen. por Nation 225:304-7 O 1 '77 *
PELVIC examinations. See Gynecologic examinations
PEMBROOK, Linda
Birth control: what's new, safe and foolproof. il Parents Mag 52:74+ N '77
PEMCOR Inc. See Holding companies
PEMEX (firm) See Petroleum industry—Mexico
PEN Club. See PEN Club
PEN pals. See International correspondence
PEÑA, Américo
Political murder in Paraguay. A. Cabral. America 136:376-8 Ap 23 '77 *
PENAL institutions. See Prisons
PENAL law. See Criminal law
PENANCE
First confession: law and catechesis. T. F. Sullivan. il America 137:128-31 S 10 '77
First sacraments and the Synod on Catechetics. J. L. Cunningham. America 137:212-15 O 8 '77

PENDERECKI, Krzysztof
Musical events. A. Porter. New Yorker 53:120 Mr 21 '77 *
Yale Philharmonia: Penderecki. por Hi Fi 27: MA33-5 Je '77 *
PENDERGAST, Joseph W.
Mirage made real. por Forbes 120:82 D 15 '77 *
PENDERGRASS, Teddy
Teddy bear. J. Maslin. por Newsweek 89:86 Mr 7 '77 *
PENDERGRAST, Steve
Wall Street garden. New Yorker 53:31-2 My 30 '77 *
PENFIELD, Edward
Posters. il por Harpers 225:57-70 D '77
PENFIELD, N.Y.
Education
See Education—New York (state)
PENGUINS
Adelie and emperor penguins; ed by R. Chemey. F. S. Todd. il Oceans 10:20-5 My '77
Behold, a multitude of penguins. G. H. Harrison. il Int Wildlife 7:36-9 Jl '77
Lonely are the hunted; leopard seals, penguins and killer whales. F. Erize. il Int Wildlife 7: 14-16 S '77
Penguins and their neighbors. R. T. Peterson. il map Nat Geog 152:236-55 Ag '77
PENICK, Patsy
People on the cover. A. L. Ball. il por Redbook 150:2+ D '77 *
PENINSULA (hotel) See Hotels, motels, etc.—Hong Kong
PENINSULA Bookshop, Palo Alto, Calif. See Booksellers and bookselling—California
PENIS, Artificial
Functioning artificial penis. Sci N 111:246-7 Ap 16 '77
PENITENCE. See Repentance
PENITENTIARIES. See Prisons
PENLAND School of Crafts, North Carolina. See Art schools
PENMANSHIP
See also
Calligraphy
PENN, Arthur
Film director's approach to managing creativity. E. Morley and A. Silver. il por Harvard Bus R 55:59-70 Mr '77 *
PENN, Irving
Haute couture of decades past recollected by Penn and Vreeland in Viking book; interview, ed by R. Dahlin. il Pub W 211:44+ Ja 31 '77
Perspectives of Penn; interview, ed by O. Edwards. il N Y Times Mag p 18-19+ S 4 '77
about
Bad and the beautiful. M. Stevens. il Newsweek 90:72-3 S 26 '77 *
Notes on Irving Penn. H. Kramer. il New Repub 177:27-9 O 29 '77 *
Photo-luxe. T. B. Hess. il Vogue 167:330-3+ S '77 *
Small world in a room. O. Edwards. il Sat R 5:34-6 O 1 '77 *
PENN Central Company
Reincarnation of Penn Central; with editorial comment. P. Blustein. il Forbes 119:6, 50-4 My 1 '77
Shattered railroad becomes a land company. il Bus W p46+ Ja 24 '77
PENN Relays. See Running
PENNANT, Edmund
Talking to walls; poem. Commonweal 104:814 D 23 '77
PENNEKAMP Coral Reef State Park. See Florida—Parks and reserves
PENNELLA, Florence C.
Dance in Washington—it's happening. Dance Mag 51:92-3 Je '77
PENNER, Jonathan
Held in darkness; condensation of Going blind. Redbook 148:189-211 Mr '77
PENNEY, Alexandra
Beauty. il N Y Times Mag p94-5 Ap 24; 38-9 Jl 17; 40-1 Jl 31; 50+ Ag 14; 50-1 Ag 28; 123-4 S 11; 129-31 S 25; 100-1 O 9; 90-1 O 23; 157-8+ N 6; 150-1 D 4; 88+ D 18 '77; 58 Ja 8 '78
Dollars and scents. N Y Times Mag p50-1 Ag 28 '77
Foot facials and other helpful hints. il N Y Times Mag p40-1 Jl 31 '77
Making an impression. il N Y Times Mag p38-9 Jl 17 '77
New wave in hair. il N Y Times Mag p94-5 Ap 24 '77
New wave of permanents. il N Y Times Mag p 123-4 S 11 '77
Tough is good for you. il N Y Times Mag p50+ Ag 14 '77
PENNEY, J. C, Company
Encore needed. Forbes 119:55 Ja 15 '77
J.C. Penney's fashion gamble. il Bus W p66-9+ Ja 16 '78
PENNIES. See Coins

PENNINGTON, Howard
SSP: semi-submerged platform. il Oceans 10:32-4 Mr '77

PENNINGTON, James M.
Rock music—love ad infinitum, ad absurdum. Chr Today 21:20-1 Jl 8 '77

PENNINGTON, John
Cumberland, my island for a while. il por map Nat Geog 152:648-61 N '77

PENNINGTON, M. Basil
Spirituality for a world culture. il America 137:100-3 Ag 27 '77

PENNSYLVANIA
Making it happen in Pennsylvania. F. Ruffin. il Redbook 149:81+ Ag '77
See also
Air pollution—Pennsylvania
Allegheny County
Architecture, Domestic—Pennsylvania
Education—Pennsylvania
Environmental movement—Pennsylvania
Fayette County
Fishing—Pennsylvania
Gardens—Pennsylvania
Historic houses, sites, etc.—Pennsylvania
Hospitals—Pennsylvania
Hunting—Pennsylvania
Libraries—Pennsylvania
Mahoning River
Medical care, State—Pennsylvania
Music festivals—Pennsylvania
Opera—Pennsylvania
Organic farming—Pennsylvania
Reclamation of land—Pennsylvania
Trials—Pennsylvania
Water supply—Pennsylvania

Description and travel

Walk across America. P. G. Jenkins. il map Nat Geog 151:466-99 Ap '77

Industries

Volkswagen moves into Pennsylvania: start of a wholesale migration? New Stanton. il U.S. News 83:41 O 31 '77

Parks and reserves

Battle of Whiskey Run; community battle to save Woodland Park. D. Linton. il Parks & Rec 12:64-7+ S '77

Politics and government

Complaining about government may not be in vain; Governor's Action Center. D. W. Hyman. Intellect 105:377 My '77

Religious institutions and affairs

Strange visions in Shamokin; shadows resembling face of Jesus on tabernacle cloth at Holy Trinity Episcopal Church. il Time 109:52 My 30 '77

PENNSYLVANIA Academy of the Fine Arts, Philadelphia
Slapping wrists; question of admission fee policy and use of Pennsylvania Bicentennial Commission grant. A. Jarmusch. Art N 76:170+ Summ '77

PENNSYLVANIA Avenue. See Washington, D.C.—Streets

PENNSYLVANIA Ballet
Dance; Pennsylvania Ballet's engagement at the Brooklyn Academy of Music. J. Maskey. il Hi Fi 27:MA10-11 F '77
Reviews:
April season at the Brooklyn Academy of Music. R. A. Thom. Dance Mag 51:84-5 Ag '77
Brooklyn Academy of Music performances. M. Robertson. Dance Mag 52:26+ Ja '78

PENNSYLVANIA Dutch. See Pennsylvania Germans

PENNSYLVANIA Dutch cookery. See Cookery, American

PENNSYLVANIA German folk art. See Folk art

PENNSYLVANIA Germans
Pennsylvania Dutch country. H. Clepper. il Am For 83:30-5 D '77

PENNSYLVANIA Opera Festival. See Music festivals—Pennsylvania

PENNSYLVANIA Power and Light Company
Stepping aside; J. K. Busby's appointment of R. K. Campbell as president. il pors Forbes 119:58 F 1 '77

PENNSYLVANIAN period. See Paleontology—Pennsylvanian

PENNYWOODEN dolls. See Dolls

PENNZOIL Company
One of our rigs is missing; Geological Survey report on sinking of Pennzoil's Platform A. J. G. Mitchell. Audubon 79:149-51 N '77
Pennzoil spins off an exploration arm; Pennzoil Offshore Gas Operators Inc. Bus W p42 My 16 '77

PENNZOIL Offshore Gas Operators Inc. See Pennzoil Company

PENOBSCOT Bay Medical Center, Rockport. See Hospitals—Maine

PENOBSCOT Indians. See Indians of North America

PENS
Ball-point pens. il Consumers Res Mag 60:19+ Ap '77

PENSION Benefit Guaranty Corporation. See Pensions

PENSION fund frauds. See Fraud

PENSION Fund of the United Nations. See United Nations Joint Staff Pension Fund

PENSION funds and funding. See Pensions—Finance

PENSIONS
How to take it with you. S. Chace. Forbes 121:235-6 Ja 9 '78
Husbands and widowers win railroad annuity Court victory. Ret Liv 17:60 S '77
PBGC—a not-so-retiring agency. Forbes 119:28 Ja 15 '77
Seven points to check in your pension plan. Changing T 31:13-14 Mr '77
Spending your money; Individual Retirement Accounts for homemakers. S. Porter. Ladies Home J 94:31+ Mr '77
Study indicates growth of private pensions faces problems; work of Norman B. Ture and Barbara A. Fields. Aging 272:7 Je '77
See also
Civil service pensions
Municipal employees—Pensions
Social security
Trade unions—Benefit funds

Finance

California hearing spotlights pension funding problems. R. E. Praul. Ret Liv 16:11-12 D '76
Equitable alchemy; Teamsters' pension fund management under Equitable Life Assurance Society. il Time 110:52+ Jl 11 '77
Financing pensions. P. A. Samuelson. Newsweek 89:62 Ap 4 '77
Fitzsimmons, three others quit pension fund; Central States Pension Fund. L. Bornstein and others. M Labor R 100:57 My '77
Golden fleecing of union funds; Teamster pension funds. L. Velie. Read Digest 111:88-92 O '77
Inflation protection for retired employees. H. Heaton. il Harvard Bus R 55:8+ S '77
Pension-fund manager's cautious investment strategy; interview, ed by A. Hershman. por Duns R 109:125-6+ My '77
Pension funds still trail the averages. Bus W p34 Mr 21 '77
Pension funds test new territory. il Bus W p81-2 D 26 '77
Pension plan crisis looming; public employee pension plans; Michigan. Am City & County 92:27 D '77
Putting more pounds into U.S. property; British pension funds. il Bus W p57 O 10 '77
Real estate investment for pension funds. P. C. Aldrich and K. Upton. Harvard Bus R 55:14+ My '77
Risk vs. return in pension fund investment. I. Tepper. il Harvard Bus R 55:100-7 Mr '77
Sticky fingers; trusteeship of the Teamsters' Central States Pension Fund. Nation 224:355-6 Mr 26 '77
Those pension plans are even weaker than you think. A. F. Ehrbar. il Fortune 96:104-8+ N '77
Tying individual pension funds to the CPI. Bus W p82 D 26 '77
Unfunded pension liabilities a growing worry for companies. il Bus W p86-8 Jl 18 '77
Why some pension investment patterns are changing. S. A. Smerling. por Nations Bus 65:60-1 Ag '77
Your pension: will you get a fair shake? il U.S. News 83:68-9 Jl 25 '77

Laws and regulations

Challenges to profit sharing: the danger of social security on pensions; Employee Retirement Income Security Act; address, October 20, 1976. A. M. Wood. Vital Speeches 43:230-3 F 1 '77
Impact of pension reform act on older workers studied by NCOA. Ret Liv 17:13-14 My '77
Pensions land in divorce court. Bus W p 104+ N 7 '77
Time for a fairer shake. M. Stone. il U.S. News 83:76 Jl 11 '77
Vital pension funds that ERISA may kill; multiple-employer plans. P. Gall and G. Koretz. il Bus W p 124 N 28 '77

Taxation

IRS retreats from pension tax plan. Am City & County 92:38 O '77
If you get a lump-sum settlement when you leave your job—. il U.S. News 83:63-5 Ag 15 '77

PENSIONS, Military

Laws and regulations

Carter plans commission to review excessive military pension costs. Ret Liv 17:14 Ap '77
Double dippers. New Repub 176:6+ F 12 '77
Double dippers; retirement pay of veterans. Sat Eve Post 249:36+ N '77
Military pension mess. C. Miller. Progressive 41:12-13 My '77
President signs veterans' pension reform bills. Aging 266:35 D '76
Why the fuss over retired officers in federal jobs; double dipping. il U.S. News 82:39 F 7 '77

PENTATHLON
Plainly, Jane has a penchant for the pentathlon; J. Frederick. J. Marshall. il pors Sports Illus 47:32-7 N 21 '77

PENTECOST
Tongues, towers and fire. G. McCauley. il America 136:inside back cover My 21 '77

PENTECOSTAL churches
Pneuma '76: a call for unity. V. Synan. Chr Today 21:43-4 Ja 7 '77
See also
Assemblies of God

PENTECOSTAL movement

Conferences

See Religious conferences

PENTECOSTAL movement (Catholic)
Choice; case of Father J. Dollard of St Charles Borromeo in Livermore, Calif. C. Stephens. Chr Today 21:38 Jl 8 '77

PENTHOUSE (periodical)
Merchants of raunchiness. T. Griffith. il por Time 110:69+ Jl 4 '77
Sex in the seventies; interview, ed by L. Sanford. B. Guccione. pors Am Home 80:46-8+ F '77

PENTYLENETETRAZOLE
Synaptic mechanism of pentylenetetrazole: selectivity for chloride conductance. T. C. Pellmar and W. A. Wilson. bibl il Science 197:912-14 Ag 26 '77

PEOPLE (periodical)
Joining the People parade. il Bus W p71+ My 16 '77

PEOPLE/Dorothy Vislocky Dance Theatre. See Dance companies

PEOPLE mover. See Local transit

PEOPLE United to Save Humanity (organization)
You can pray if you want to; interview, ed by G. Arnold. J. L. Jackson. por Chr Today 21:12-16 Ag 12 '77

PEOPLE'S Development Corporation. See Community development corporations

PEOPLE'S Liberation Army. See China—Armed Forces

PEORIA, Ill.
Free-pay meters ring up shopper smiles. il Am City & County 92:93-4 My '77

PEOTONE, Ill.

Education

See Education—Illinois

PEPE, Barbara
Revolution per minute: woman's labels. Ms 6:67-8+ D '77

PEPER, Eric
Fly of the month. See issues of Field & stream

PÉPIN, Jacques
Finishing touches that make a meal a feast; excerpts from La technique. il McCalls 104:133-40 Ap '77
House beautiful chef. See issues of House beautiful

PEPPER, Art
Pepper and Gordon. M. A. Ullman. il pors New Repub 177:35-7 O 1 '77 *

PEPPER, Claude Denson
Excerpt from testimony on mandatory retirement legislation, June 2, 1977. Cong Digest 56:270+ N '77
Mandatory retirement; address, June 6, 1977. Vital Speeches 43:651-3 Ag 15 '77

about

Challenging the 65 barrier. il Time 110:67 Ag 8 '77 *
Champ of the elderly. por Time 110:25 O 10 '77 *

PEPPER, Curtis Bill
Day in the life of the Pope. pors N Y Times Mag p38-40+ Ap 10 '77
Kidnapped. il pors N Y Times Mag p42-6+ N 20 '77
(ed) See Mastroianni, M. Mastroianni talks about real-life love

PEPPERDINE University, Malibu, Calif.
School of soft knocks. R. Telander. il Sports Illus 46:100-4+ My 23 '77

PEPPERS
Big chile; interview, ed by J. Neary. R. M. Nakayama. il pors Horticulture 55:68-70+ Mr '77
Chiles mild to wild. il Sunset 159:82-5 S '77
Pick windowsill peppers all year long. J. D. Foraker. il Org Gard & Farm 24:88-90 Ag '77
Why not homegrown paprika? G. Nelson. il Org Gard & Farm 24:160+ Ap '77
See also
Cookery—Vegetables
Paprika

Drying

Surplus chile peppers? Dry them. Sunset 159:125 S '77

PEPPIATT, Michael
(ed) See Dubuffet, J. Warring complexities of Jean Dubuffet

PEPSICO, Inc
Profiting from Pepskis. il Time 109:39 Ja 31 '77

PEPTIC ulcers
Ulcer pains? possible relief with cimetidine. Time 110:67 Ag 29 '77
Ulcers: latest on how to detect, treat—and prevent them; interview. H. P. Roth. il por U.S. News 82:80-2 My 9 '77
Worrying about ulcers. G. Cant. il N Y Times Mag p70+ N 6 '77

PEPTIDASES
Angiotensin converting enzyme: induction by steroids in rabbit alveolar macrophages in culture. J. Friedland and others. bibl il Science 197:64-5 Jl 1 '77

PEPTIDES
Bombesin: potent effects on thermoregulation in the rat. M. Brown and others. bibl il Science 196:998-1000 My 27 '77
New precursor to natural painkillers. Sci N 112:6 Jl 2 '77
Sickle hemoglobin aggregation: a new class of inhibitors. J. R. Votano and others. bibl il Science 196:1216-19 Je 10 '77
Synthetic peptides form ion channels in artificial lipid bilayer membranes. S. J. Kennedy and others. bibl il Science 196:1341-2 Je 17 '77
Vasoactive intestinal polypeptide occurs in nerves of the female genitourinary tract. L. I. Larsson and others. bibl il Science 197:1374-5 S 30 '77
See also
Endorphins
Enkephalins

PEPTIDOGLYCAN. See Glycans

PERAZA, Maricela, and Maurer, Harry
Honduras: did the Church start something it can't stop? il Ms 6:12-15 Ag '77

PERCEPTION
See also
Anamorphosis
Consciousness
Extrasensory perception
Human information processing
Pattern perception
Space perception
Time perception
Visual perception
Word perception

PERCEPTION, Disorders of
See also
Hallucinations and illusions

PERCH
What they didn't tell you about the snail darter & the dam. S. G. Cook and others. il map Nat Parks & Con Mag 51:10-13 My '77

PERCH fishing
Best fishing for surfperch is now or soon in California, later up north. il Sunset 158:48+ F '77
Walleyes: find 'em—then it's easy; interview, ed by J. Gibbs. G. Lau. il pors Outdoor Life 159:104+ Je '77
Yellow perch. J. Fullum. il Conservationist 31:23 Ja '77

PERCOLATION, Soil. See Soil percolation

PERCUSSION Instruments
See also
Drum

PERCUSSION instruments, Electronic. See Musical instruments, Electronic

PERCY, Walker
PW interviews; ed by J. F. Baker. por Pub W 211:6-7 Mr 21 '77
Questions they never asked me. il pors Esquire 88:170-2+ D '77

about

Walker Percy: not just whistling Dixie. R. Ford. Nat R 29:558 My 13 '77 *

PERDUE, Inc. See Poultry industry

PEREGRINE falcons. See Falcons

PEREIRA, Joseph M.
Planet Ocean. il Sci Digest 82:33-6 N '77

PEREIRA, Thomas
Southern Neuse Racing Circuit. il Yachting 142:131-2 D '77

PERELMAN, Sidney Joseph
All precincts beware—paper tigress loose! New Yorker 53:28-31 Je 27 '77
Me thinks the lady doth propel too much. New Yorker 53:32-4 S 26 '77
Meanness rising from the suds. New Yorker 53:20-3 Ja 2 '78

PERELMAN, Sidney Joseph—*Continued*
Scram! You made the pants too short. New Yorker 53:38-41 O 24 '77
To yearn is subhuman, to forestall divine. New Yorker 53:32-4 My 23 '77

PERENNIALS (plants)
For next year's garden: plant ahead; perennial garden of John B. Leake family in Pennsylvania. il House & Gard 149:142-5 S '77
It's discovery time and planting time for perennials. Sunset 159:174 S '77
Perennial vegetables. K. Kraft and P. Kraft. il Horticulture 55:44-6 O '77
Shopping search for perennials, rock plants. Sunset 158:226+ Mr '77
See also
Sages (plants)

PERES, Shimon
Big bird in a land of hawks and doves. il por Time 109:34+ Ap 25 '77 *
Israeli innovator. K. Willenson and M. J. Kubic. il por Newsweek 89:39 Ap 18 '77 *
Jerusalem: the race for change. M. J. Kubic. il por Newsweek 89:29 F 21 '77 *
Prospect with Peres. D. Caploe. il Nation 224:587-90 My 14 '77 *
Rabin just makes it. R. Carroll and J. Kubic. il pors Newsweek 89:38+ Mr 7 '77 *
Step by step with Shimon Peres. por Time 109:24 Ap 18 '77 *

PERETTI, Elsa
Jewelry's new dazzle. S. C. Cowley and others. il pors Newsweek 89:64-5+ Ap 4 '77 *

PÉREZ, Carlos Andrés
President Pérez of Venezuela visits the United States; exchange of remarks, with texts of joint communiques, June 28, July 1, 1977. Dept State Bull 77:152-3 Ag 1 '77
Third world has given everything and received little; interview. il por U.S. News 83:53-4+ Jl 25 '77

Visit to the United States, 1977

Oil and *abrazos* in Washington. il Time 110:37 Jl 11 '77
President Pérez of Venezuela visits the United States; exchange of remarks, with texts of joint communiques, June 28, July 1, 1977. J. Carter; C. Pérez. Dept State Bull 77:151-4 Ag 1 '77

PEREZ, Leonora
Long count to a guilty verdict. il pors Time 110:54 Jl 25 '77 *
Narciso-Perez case. A. Jones. Nation 225:584-8 D 3 '77 *

PEREZ, Norah A.
Staying up late; story. Ms 5:80-3+ Ap '77

PERFECTION (psychology)
Perfectionists; houses of celebrities. P. O'Higgins. House B 119:90-1+ Ap '77

PERFORMANCE
How to perform better at almost everything; interview, ed by C. Seebohm. L. E. Morehouse. il por House & Gard 149:88-9 Jl '77

PERFORMANCE Handicap Racing Fleet System. See Yachts—Rating

PERFORMANCE synthesizers. See Musical instruments, Electronic

PERFORMING arts
Cross country. il Horizon 20:4 S; 4 O; 4 N; 4 D '77; 21:4+ Ja '78
Culture boom. il U.S. News 83:50-3 Ag 8 '77
Viewpoint. R. Jacobson. Opera N 42:4 D 24 '77
See also
Ballet
Dancing
Motion pictures
Music
Opera
Sex in the performing arts
Theater

Finance

Can the show go on? R. Brustein. il N Y Times Mag p8-9+ Jl 10 '77; Discussion. p50-1 Ag 7 '77

Study and teaching

See also
John F. Kennedy Center for the Performing Arts, Washington, D.C.—Musical Theater Lab

PERFORMING arts and children
See also
Young Audiences, Inc

PERFUME industry

Advertising

Promise him anything. S. C. Cowley and L. Whitman. il Newsweek 90:109+ O 17 '77

PERFUMES
Andrea Marcovicci talks scents; interview, ed by H. Brubach. A. Marcovicci. il Mademoiselle 83:112-13+ D '77
Dollars and scents. A. Penney. N Y Times Mag p50-1 Ag 28 '77
How to find the scent that suits you; quiz. il Mademoiselle 83:104-5 Jl '77
Meaning of perfume. il Vogue 167:248-55 My '77
Perfume—a woman's memories, and desires. J. Robinson. Vogue 167:260+ My '77
Power of perfume; interview. R. Henkin. Harp Baz 111:123 N '77
Ready-to-wear fragrance collections. il Harp Baz 110:104-5 Ap '77
Scent. M. R. Carter. See issues of Mademoiselle to July 1977
Uncommon scents. C. B. Abbott. il Am Home 80:65+ N '77
Whiff. Seventeen 36:26 N '77

Advertising

See Perfume industry—Advertising

Anecdotes, facetiae, satire, etc.

Common scents. L. Mele. Seventeen 36:110 Ag '77

PERFUMES for men
Scent: a man's view; views of Clovis Ruffin. il Mademoiselle 83:62 D '77
Vogue beauty report on men. Vogue 167:222+ D '77

Advertising

See Perfume industry—Advertising

PERGAMENT, Moses
The Jewish song. W. Simmons. Am Rec G 40:29 Jl '77 *

PERI, Jacopo
Euridice. R. V. Lucano. Am Rec G 40:29-30 Jl '77 *

PERICLES
Pericles as seen by Plutarch; excerpt from The rise and fall of Athens, tr by I. Scott-Kilvert. Plutarch. il UNESCO Courier 30:26-7 O '77 *

PERIDINIUM. See Dinoflagellates

PERILLA
Perilla ketone: a potent lung toxin from the mint plant, perilla frutescens britton. B. J. Wilson and others. bibl il Science 197:573-4 Ag 5 '77

PERIODIC Reports on Human Rights, Committee on. See United Nations—Commission on Human Rights

PERIODICAL articles
Article market. Writer 90:32-42+ Ag '77
Be a billboard artist; how to keep the reader's attention. B. Vachon. Writers Digest 57:26 Ap '77
Big as all outdoors; environmental writing. C. Schoenfeld. Writers Digest 57:21-3 S '77
Easiest article to sell; using quotes from celebrities. M. Weisinger. Writer 90:11-14+ S '77
Environmental markets. D. Sandhage and W. Brohaugh. Writers Digest 57:22-3 S '77
Getting published: an unraveled mystery; architectural articles; excerpt from Creative communications for a successful design practice. S. A. Kliment. Archit Rec 161:59+ F '77
Getting started. F. A. Dickson. Writers Digest 57:46+ O '77
Gospel truths of religious writing. M. Emanuel. Writers Digest 57:20-1+ D '77
Hook and eye appeal. S. Lindsay. Writer 90:12-14+ My '77
Horse markets. W. Brohaugh. il Writers Digest 57:31-3 Ag '77
Humor markets. W. Brohaugh. Writers Digest 57:31-4 O '77
I hate you! . . . love, Jeff; inspirational articles. J. Martin. Writers Digest 57:22 D '77
Make a big name with little markets. T. Schwarz. Writers Digest 57:21-2 Ap '77
Making crime pay. C. W. Sasser. Writers Digest 57:29-32 S '77
Nonfiction. A. Spikol. See issues of Writer's digest
Path to evangelicals is straight and narrow—but easy to follow. E. Houtz. Writers Digest 57:24-5 D '77
Personal article. E. Russell. Writer 90:14-17 F '77
Pop-top panache. J. Paris. por Writers Digest 57:16 S '77
Questions and answers on how to write for Parks & recreation. Parks & Rec 12:60-1 Mr '77
Rewards of nostalgia. C. Amen. Writer 91:29-31 Ja '78
Students write about their artwork. M Esping. il Sch Arts 76:36-8 F '77
Ten ways to build article sales. K. Cruzic. Writer 90:30-1 D '77
Thinking ahead; ideas for articles. F. A. Dickson. Writers Digest 57:28+ Je '77
Timing the submission. A. S. Harris, Jr. Writer 90:19-21+ Mr '77
Write a query—get an assignment! S. W. Olds. Writer 90:15-19 Ag '77
Writing for the aged: new vistas for the old. H. Alpert. Writers Digest 57:15+ Mr '77
Writing for the farm magazines. C. A. Radimer. il Writers Digest 57:25-7 Ag '77
Writing for the martial arts market. J. Murray. il Writers Digest 57:29-30 Je '77
Writing or rewriting articles for the Mother earth news; excerpt. J. Shuttleworth. Writer 90:21-4 Je; 20-2+ Jl '77
See also
Fiction in periodicals and newspapers

PERIODICAL articles—*Continued*

Competitions

Couple's article wins first $1,000 prize; Ruth and Lawrence McCrank. il Am Lib 8:293 Je '77

Library manuscripts wanted: $1,000 prize article competition. Am Lib 8:237 My '77

PERIODICAL cicadas. See Cicadas

PERIODICAL covers

Child's garden of memories; Good housekeeping covers; excerpt from Jessie Willcox Smith. S. M. Schnessel. il Good H 184:142-5 My '77

Cover. M. Schiller. Am Artist 41:6+ Ja '77; Correction. 41:5 Mr '77

Jack Davis cover story. N. Meglin. il Am Artist 41:34-7+ Ap '77

My life as an illustrator; with portfolio of magazine covers. N. Rockwell. il Sat Eve Post 249:73 Jl '77

Portfolio of Christmases past; Good housekeeping covers. il Good H 185:103-9 D '77

PERIODICAL fillers

Writing selected shorts; excerpt from How to write and sell fillers, light verse and short humor; with list of markets. S. Glasser. Writer 90:26-9 N '77

PERIODICAL libraries. See Newspaper and periodical libraries

PERIODICAL literature

Market update; ed by D. Sandhage. See issues of Writer's digest

Markets. See issues of Writer's digest

New York newsletter. J. P. Hayes. See issues of Writer's digest

On one who wrote not wisely but to sell; magazine freelancing. M. Malone. Nation 224:597-8 My 14 '77

25 top-paying magazine markets. Writer 90:29-31 Je '77

Where to sell manuscripts. See issues of Writer

See also

Fiction in periodicals and newspapers
Periodical articles

PERIODICAL reading

What I read. T. Powers. Commonweal 104:211-14 Ap 1 '77

PERIODICALS

See also

Freedom of the press
Journalism
Libraries—Periodical collections
Periodical reading
Religious newspapers and periodicals
Trade journals
also subhead Periodicals under various subjects, e.g. Indians of North America—Periodicals

Bibliographical control

See Bibliographical control

Bibliography

Alternative periodicals. J. P. Danky and M. Fox. il Wilson Lib Bull 51:481-5, 662-6, 763-8 F, Ap, My '77

Magazines. il Am Lib 8:154-5 Mr '77

Magazines; ed by W. Katz. See issues of Library journal

New look at free magazines. C. E. Wall. il Am Lib 8:85-9 F '77

School librarian recommends free magazines. M. C. Offerman. Am Lib 8:89 F '77

Illustration

See Illustration

Indexes

Price indexes for 1977: U.S. periodicals and serial services. N. B. Brown. il Lib J 102:1462-7 Jl '77

Letters to the editor

Forbes readers have their say—1917-1977; selection of letters to the editors. Forbes 120:244+ S 15 '77

Personal advertisements

See Advertising, Classified

Prices

Escalating journal prices: time to fight back. R. De Gennaro. bibl il Am Lib 8:69-74 F '77

Periodical prices: 1975-77 update. F. F. Clasquin. il Lib J 102:2011-15 O 1 '77

Price indexes for 1977: U.S. periodicals and serial services. N. B. Brown. il Lib J 102:1462-7 Jl '77

Prices of physics and chemistry journals. F. F. Clasquin and J. B. Cohen. bibl il Science 197:432-8 Jl 29 '77

Canada

Canada's environmental magazines. R. C. Paehlke. Environment 19:5+ Je '77

France

Empathy with the humanity of the streets; illustrations of turn of the century Paris by T. A. Steinlen in Chat noir. P. D. Cate. il Art N 76:56-9 Mr '77

Our man in Paris; P. Salinger, L'Express reporter. por Time 110:103 N 28 '77

Sir Jimmy's cross-Channel fiefdom; J. M. Goldsmith's purchase of L'Express shares. il por Time 109:51-2 Ap 18 '77

Great Britain

Of mice and men; popularity rating of pets by Which? magazine. il Newsweek 90:51 Ag 22 '77

Poland

Meaning of Brzezinski; opinions of Kultura; tr by O. Scherer. Nat R 29:612-13 My 27 '77

United States

California's magazine war; Los Angeles vs New West. il Time 110:68 Ag 29 '77

LC to run national periodicals center. Lib J 102:1708+ S 1 '77

Quartet of newcomers. Time 109:90 Je 20 '77

Serials-center derby enters the homestretch. A. Plotnik. Am Lib 8:287-8 Je '77

See also

Childrens periodicals
also names of periodicals, e.g. Saturday review

PERIODICALS, Catholic. See Catholic press

PERIODICALS, Reading of. See Periodical reading

PERIODICALS for men

See also

Esquire (periodical)
Hustler (periodical)
Penthouse (periodical)
Playboy (periodical)

PERIODICALS for women

See also

Good housekeeping (periodical)
Ladies' home journal
McCall's (periodical)
Mademoiselle (periodical)
Ms (periodical)
Rags (periodical)
Redbook (periodical)

PERIODICITY. See Biology—Periodicity; Botany—Periodicity; Cycles

PERIODONTAL disease. See Gums—Diseases

PERIODONTIA

Anecdotes, facetiae, satire, etc.

Latest indignity. J. B. Smith. Nat R 29:786-7 Jl 8 '77

PERIPHERAL equipment (computers) See Computers—Equipment

PERISSINOTTO, Giorgio

Mexican education: Echeverria's mixed legacy. bibl f Cur Hist 72:115-19+ Mr '77

PERKINS, Anne

Being old in Britain. Chr Cent 94:540-1 Je 1 '77

PERKINS, Courtland Davis

Stacking the B-1 deck. C. Miller. Progressive 41:7-8 Mr '77 *

PERKINS, John Harold

Business looks at health care costs; address, November 18, 1976. Vital Speeches 43:211-15 Ja 15 '77

PERLE, George

Berg's master array of the interval cycles. bibl f il Mus Q 63:1-30 Ja '77

PERLIS, Vivian

Schoenberg is alive! il Hi Fi 27:MA19-21 Ag '77

PERLMAN, Eric

Confrontation: Greenpeace Foundation puts itself on the line. il Oceans 10:58-61 Jl '77

PERLMUTTER, Amos

Begin's strategy and Dayan's tactics: the conduct of Israeli foreign policy. For Affairs 56:357-72 Ja '78

Israel's De Gaulle. il pors Newsweek 90:28-9 Ag 15 '77

PERLMUTTER, Edith L. See Blake, F. M. jt auth

PERLMUTTER, Nathan

And the nightingales sing. il Nat R 29:996+ S 2 '77

PERLMUTTER, Philip

Troubling future of ethnicity. Chr Cent 94:718-21 Ag 17 '77

PERLSTADT, Harry, and Kozak, L. J.

Emergency medicine. il Society 14:41-6 Ja '77

PERMANENT hair preparations. See Hair preparations

PERMANENT waves. See Hairdressing

PERMITS, Building. See Building laws and regulations

PEROT, H. Ross

H. Ross Perot's new game plan at EDS. il por Bus W p92+ Ap 11 '77 *

PEROVSKITE

Perovskite oxides: materials science in catalysis. R. J. H. Voorhoeve and others. bibl Science 195:827-33 Mr 4 '77

PEROXIDATION. See Oxidation
PEROXIDES
See also
Hydrogen peroxide
PERPICH, Rudolph George
Minnesota: Rudy's disappearing act. C. J. Harper. por Newsweek 89:46 Ap 11 '77 *
PERRAULT, Charles
Sleeping beauty; dramatization. See Thane, A.
PERREAULT, John
Art; pattern painting. L. Alloway. Nation 225: 698-9 D 24 '77 *
PERRICAUDET, Michael, and others
Excision and recombination of adenovirus DNA fragments in escherichia coli. bibl il Science 196:208-10 Ap 8 '77
PERRIER mineral water. See Water, Bottled
PERRIN, Luc H. See Theofilopoulos, A. N. jt auth
PERRIN, Noel
James Gould Cozzens. New Repub 177:43-5 S 17 '77
PERRY, Bill, Jr
Dedicated to a cause. il por MH 61:14 Spr '77
PERRY, Donald
Lives of a tree: the mysterious inner world of tropical plants. il Horticulture 55:30-5 O '77
PERRY, Mike
Springtime sailboat work. il Motor B & S 139: 99-101 Ap '77
PERRY, Paul
(ed) Sylvester Stallone's rocky road to Rocky
PERRY, Phillip M.
(ed) See Spencer, J. W. One self-publishing writer who made it big
PERRY, Robert H.
Guide to: 30-foot cruising sailboats. il Motor B & S 140:86-91 S '77
Non-linear comparisons. il Yachting 142:97-8 D '77
PERRY, Ronnie
Perry is doing admirably. J. Kaplan. il por Sports Illus 46:48-9 F 28 '77 *
PERRY, Russell H.
Country slicker's progress. por Forbes 120:67+ D 1 '77 *
PERRY, Susan
Growing grapes along the Rio Grande. Org Gard & Farm 24:130-2 My '77
PERSECUTION
Prospect of suffering; Christian persecutions. C. F. H. Henry. Chr Today 21:40+ F 4 '77
See also
Genocide
PERSEIDS. See Meteors
PERSHING, John Joseph
Patton in Mexico: the Punitive Expedition. M. Blumenson. il pors Am Hist Illus 12:34-42 O '77 *
PERSIAN cookery. See Cookery, Persian
PERSIAN GULF
See also
Bahrein
PERSIAN poetry

Translations into English

Ghazal; tr by W. S. Merwin and T. S. Halman. Rumi. Nation 224:190 F 12 '77
PERSICHETTI, Vincent
Persichetti perspective; String quartets nos. 1-4. W. Simmons. Am Rec G 40:6-8 My '77 *
PERSICO, Joseph E.
For energy solution: Teller gives us 5 years. por Sci Digest 82:37-9 Jl '77
1918: the plague year. il Sci Digest 81:76-9 Mr '77
Scientists urge President: stop reliance on coal and nuclear fuel. Sci Digest 82:8-9+ O '77
PERSIMMONS
Persimmon makes a fine umbrella. il Sunset 159: 203 D '77
PERSON, Ann (Potter)
Success is sweet and so is love: interview. ed by J. Muchovej. il pors Am Home 80:30-1+ F '77
PERSONAL advertisements. See Advertising, Classified
PERSONAL articles. See Periodical articles
PERSONAL beauty. See Beauty, Personal
PERSONAL computers. See Computers
PERSONAL Computing Expo. See Computers—Exhibitions
PERSONAL confidences. See Confidential communications
PERSONAL criticism. See Self evaluation
PERSONAL efficiency. See Efficiency
PERSONAL finance. See Finance, Personal
PERSONAL hygiene. See Hygiene
PERSONAL loans. See Loans, Personal
PERSONAL names. See Names, Personal
PERSONAL property. See Property
PERSONAL rapid transit. See Local transit
PERSONAL responsibility. See Responsibility
PERSONAL space
See also
Crowding stress
PERSONAL Use Radio Advisory Committee. See United States—Federal Communications Commission
PERSONALITY
Fragrance personalities. M. R. Carter. Mademoiselle 83:105 Mr '77
What your sleeping position reveals about you; interview, ed by N. A. Comer. S. Dunkel. il Mademoiselle 83:176-7+ Mr '77
What your sleep position reveals; excerpt from Sleep positions: the night language of the body. S. Dunkell. il Read Digest 11:137-9 Jl '77
See also
Charm
Human relations
Identity (psychology)
Idiosyncrasies
PERSONALITY, Disorders of
I'm Eve; struggle with a split personality; excerpt. C. C. Sizemore and E. S. Pittillo. il pors Ladies Home J 94:92+ My '77
See also
Schizophrenia
PERSONALITY tests. See Psychological tests
PERSONNEL management
How to reduce dependence on the boss; delegating authority. T. W. Zimmerer. Nations Bus 65:55-8 F '77
Humanizing the workplace: then and now; Hawthorne Studies in personnel management. il Society 15:112-15 N '77
One firm's family; IBM. A. J. Mayer and M. Ruby. il Newsweek 90:82-4+ N 21 '77
Organizing and staffing the personnel function. F. K. Foulkes and H. M. Morgan. Harvard Bus R 55:142-54 My '77
Should you work for a woman? R. Shapiro. Harp Baz 110:85+ Ag '77
Too old or not too old. B. Rosen and T. H. Jerdee. il Harvard Bus R 55:97-106 N '77
Want to be a better boss? interview. J. L. Hayes. il por U.S. News 82:68-70 Mr 21 '77
Where white-collar status boosts productivity; Eaton Corp. il Bus W p80+ My 23 '77
See also
Communication in management
Employees—Relocation
Factory management
Grievance procedures
Incentives in industry
Job satisfaction
Labor discipline
Layoff systems
Leadership
Library administration
Personnel records
Psychology, Industrial
PERSONNEL records
At IBM, privacy is a top priority. Bus W p 108 Ap 4 '77
PERSONNEL service in education
Counseling: potential superbomb against sexism. M. E. Verheyden-Hilliard. Am Educ 13:12-15 Ap '77
See also
Student counselors
PERSONS, Ad
Blue water stern-drive. B. O'Donovan. il por Motor B & S 140:71-2 O '77 *
PERSPECTIVE
See also
Anamorphosis
PERSPECTIVE (philosophy)
Living in a valley; historical perspective. O. Handlin. Am Scholar 46:301-12 Summ '77
PERSUASION (psychology)
Practical pointers for painstaking panhandlers; study by Chris Kleinke. N. Napp. Psychol Today 11:86 Ag '77
PERSUASION (rhetoric) See Rhetoric
PERTAMINA (firm) See Petroleum industry—Indonesia
PERTSCHUK, Michael
Crackdown ahead on advertising: what the government plans next; interview. pors U.S. News 83:70-2 O 17 '77
about
Carter's trustbusters. D. Pauly and J. B. Copeland. il por Newsweek 90:66 S 26 '77 *
Tough man for the FTC. A. J. Mayer and J. Bishop, Jr. il por Newsweek 89:61-2 Mr 7 '77 *
Washington's new approach to antitrust action. W. Neikirk. pors Nations Bus 65:30-2 D '77 *
PERU
See also
Agriculture—Peru
Birds—Peru
Cities and towns—Peru
Costume—Peru
Geology—Peru
Industrial relations—Peru
Loans, Bank—Peru
National parks and reserves—Peru
Women—Peru

PERU—*Continued*

Commerce

Russia

See Russia—Commerce—Peru

Economic policy

Peru runs out of credit: left-wing junta vs. the bankers. D. Freedman and C. Krauss. il Nation 225:466-8 N 5 '77

Politics and government

Dilemma in Peru. J. R. Brockman. America 137: 148-50 S 17 '77
Peruvian revolution in crisis. D. P. Werlich. Cur Hist 72:61-4+ F '77

PERUVIAN art. See Art, Peruvian

PEST control
Wildlife pests in your garden: solving the unsolvable problem. G. Logsdon. il Org Gard & Farm 24:91-6 Ag '77

PEST control operators
Just wait till next year for those pest control jobs; Integrated Pest Management. J. Goldstein. Org Gard & Farm 24:54+ S '77
Need an exterminator to fight household bugs? Changing T 31:31-2 Ap '77
Termite control: how not to get ripped off. R. Nader. Ladies Home J 94:14 My '77

PESTICIDE industry. See Chemical industries

PESTICIDE regulations. See Pesticides—Laws and legislation

PESTICIDES
Mix tanks make pesticide refills easy. G. Lepper. il Suc Farm 75:no4 L28 Mr '77
Pesticide treadmill. D. Zwerdling. il Nat Parks & Con Mag 51:15-19 S '77
See also
Herbicides
Insecticides
Spraying and dusting

Decomposition

Environmental degradation of 2,3,7,8-tetrachlorodibenzo-*p*-dioxin (TCDD); action of sunlight. D. G. Crosby and A. S. Wong. bibl il Science 195:1337-8 Mr 25 '77

Disposal

Incinerator ship deep-sixes poisons. B. Berry. il Pop Sci 211:105 N '77
See also
Herbicides—Disposal

Injurious effects

Baiter Award; National Peach Council's recommendation to use DBCP as form of birth control. J. G. Mitchell. Audubon 79:168 N '77
Chemical assault on our natural defenses. J. Cox. Org Gard & Farm 24:174-81 O '77
Industrial sterility; chemical workers exposed to DBCP. J. Seligmann and others. il Newsweek 90:69 Ag 29 '77
Pesticide uptake into membranes measured by fluorescence quenching. G. Omann and J. R. Lakowicz. bibl il Science 197:465-7 Jl 29 '77
Sterility scare sends OSHA scurrying. Bus W p45+ S 12 '77

Laws and legislation

Inconsistent with the label—what it means. Suc Farm 75:A3 Ja '77
New EPA policy on pesticides. Farm J 100:J4 D '76
Pesticide certification—where we are now. Suc Farm 75:no4 L45 Mr '77
Upstairs, downstairs at EPA; Senate report. F. Graham, Jr. Audubon 79:148-50 Mr '77; Reply. E. M. Kennedy. 79:100+ Jl '77

Safety devices and measures

Public gains access to pesticide safety data. R. J. Smith. Science 197:1346-7 S 30 '77
What Bergland really said about farm chemicals. Farm J 101:32 N '77
What it takes to become a certified applicator for pesticides. G. W. Beshore. Farm J 101:32 Ag '77

PESTICIDES and wildlife
Carlsbad's famous bats are dying off. M. Gosnell. il Nat Wildlife 15:28-33 Je '77
Pesticides and pollination. H. M. Caine. il Environment 19:28-33 N '77

PESTS
See also
Insects, Injurious and beneficial
Parasites

PET, Inc
Route to personal success in business; interview. B. F. Schenk. il pors Nations Bus 65:58-60+ N '77

PET food
See also
Dogs—Food and feeding

PET industries
Dog eat dog. Forbes 119:153-4 My 15 '77

PET sterilization. See Sterilization, Sexual—Animals

PETER, Carl J.
Ambiguity, criticism and promise. il New Cath World 220:187-90 Jl '77

PETER, Lily
Marvel of Big Creek. G. Purvis. por Outdoor Life 160:7 O '77 *

PETER Grimes; opera. See Britten, B.

PETER Rogers Associates. See Advertising agencies

PETERBORO, N.H.
See also
MacDowell Colony

PETERS, Anne
As bombs devour now one and now another; poem. America 136:367 Ap 23 '77

PETERS, B. Guy. See Heisler, M. O. jt auth

PETERS, Carl W.
Looking for patterns: a conversation with Carl W. Peters; interview, ed by C. Movalli. il por Am Artist 41:56-61+ D '77

PETERS, Charles
Radical cure for high medical costs. por Newsweek 89:11 Mr 28 '77

PETERS, Mary
Truth about those pulsating showers. il Mech Illus 73:36 Mr '77

PETERS, Nancy
Woman in her window; poem. Commonweal 105: 12 Ja 6 '78

PETERS, Susan. See Marler, P. jt auth

PETERS, Svetlana. See Stalina, S. I.

PETERS, Virginia. See Baylor, E. R. jt auth

PETERS, Walter
Multiplying dividends through stock swaps. J. Madrick. il Bus W p 126 Ap 18 '77 *

PETERS, William T.
HP-25 as a digital clock & timer. il Pop Electr 12:57-8 Ag '77

PETERSBURG, Va.

Historic houses, sites, etc.

See Historic houses, sites, etc.—Virginia

PETERSEN, Andrea
America's teacher of the year. M. S. Miller. por Ladies Home J 94:42+ Ap '77 *

PETERSEN, Svend. See Drake, J. jt auth

PETERSON, Carol Ann. See Gunn, S. L. jt auth

PETERSON, Doug
New boats for the SORC. Yachting 141:104 F '77

PETERSON, Ed
Quick & easy way to photograph art; interview. il Mod Phot 41:80-3+ Jl '77

PETERSON, Eugene H.
Eye of a needle; Whose image? Birth trauma; poems. Chr Today 21:21 F 4 '77
Let not man put asunder; Blind Bartimaeus; poems. Chr Today 22:23 O 7 '77
You lack one thing; poem. Chr Today 22:24 N 4 '77

PETERSON, Franklynn. See Kesselman, J. R. jt auth

PETERSON, Mendel L.
Reach for the New World. il Nat Geog 152:724-67, supp(folded map) D '77

PETERSON, Michael
Production trimming. il Ceram Mo 25:50-2 O '77

PETERSON, Ralph Edward
Pastor Peterson makes a deal with Citicorp. P. W. Bernstein. il pors Fortune 96:140-6+ N '77 *

PETERSON, Roger Tory
Dean of bird watchers; interview, ed by G. H. Harrison. il por Américas 29:33-9 My '77
Penguins and their neighbors. il map Nat Geog 152:236-55 Ag '77

about

Field guide to Roger Tory Peterson. J. Diffily. il por Am Artist 41:28-33+ Ap '77 *
Making of the world's number one bird watcher. G. H. Harrison. il pors Am For 83:18-21+ F '77 *

PETERSON, Russell Wilbur
We citizens cannot sit back and relax; address, April 20, 1977. Vital Speeches 43:490-3 Je 1 '77
What price plutonium? il Nat Parks & Con Mag 51:16-19 Ag '77

about

Congress' tough new technical consultant. por Bus W p64 D 12 '77 *
Russell Peterson says yes—he will head OTA. C. Holden. Science 198:903 D 2 '77 *
Will Russell Peterson be OTA's new direction? B. J. Culliton. por Science 198:592-3 N 11 '77 *

PETERSON, Sonja
Blessed be this day; story. il Good H 185:150-1 N '77

PETERSON, Susan
(ed) See Levine, M. Ceramics of Marilyn Levine

PETERSON, Tom
People who fly: Tom Peterson. G. Baxter. il por Flying 100:65-6+ My '77 *

PETERSON, William
Santa Fe Festival: eclecticism and a high-noon showdown. il Art N 76:78-9 D '77

PETIT, Philippe
Trade-Center stunts. E. Keerdoja. il pors Newsweek 90:18+ N 7 '77 *

PETIT, Ruth A.
Giving birth to a business. il por Redbook 148:57+ F '77

La **PETITE Ferme (restaurant)** See New York (city)—Hotels, restaurants, etc

PETITTI, Jack R.
Message from Las Vegas. il por Parks & Rec 12:56-8 My '77

PETRAKIS, Harry Mark
Great American melting pot. Holiday 58:24-5 Ap '77

PETRAS, Fred
40-channel roundup. il Radio-Electr 48:40-4+ F '77

PETREE, Richard W.
U.S. reiterates support for negotiated solution in Rhodesia; statement, December 14, 1976. Dept State Bull 76:54-5 Ja 17 '77

PETRICK, Paul J.
Fiberglass refinishing—the easy way; the hard way; excerpts from Fiberglass repairs. il Motor B & S 139:108-11 Ap '77
Laminating fiberglass over wood. il Motor B & S 140:100-4 D '77

PETRIE, Paul
Gardener; poem. Commonweal 104:296 My 13 '77

PETRIFIED Forest National Park
Forests of stone. C. Konopa. il Am For 83:8-11+ Je '77

PETROCHEMICAL industry. See Chemical industries

PETROFINA S. A. See Petroleum industry—Belgium

PETROGLYPHS
Dating the Salton Sea petroglyphs. Sci N 111:138 F 26 '77
Rock art and the power of shamans; petroglyphs of the Abnaki Indians. D. R. Snow. Natur Hist 86:42-9 bibl(p 100) F '77

PETROLACOSAURUS. See Lizards, Fossil

PETRÓLEOS Mexicanos (firm) See Petroleum industry—Mexico

PETROLEUM
See also
Oil shales

Conferences

See also
Organization of Petroleum Exporting Countries—Conferences

International aspects

Co-opting the third world elites: trilateralism goes to work. K. Bird. Nation 224:425-8 Ap 9 '77
Guess what? We've got an oil glut. L. Smith. il Duns R 110:58-60 S '77
Oil power in the Middle East. J. C. Campbell. bibl f For Affairs 56:89-110 O '77
West's tenuous oil lifeline. map Bus W p56 N 28 '77
Who gets to distribute that extra Saudi oil. Bus W p35-6 F 7 '77
See also
Organization of Petroleum Exporting Countries

Pipelines

See Petroleum pipelines

Prices

Answering OPEC. D. Yergin. New Repub 176:45-7 Ja 22 '77
Billion-barrel question. Time 109:68 My 30 '77
Can OPEC be broken up? influence of Saudi Arabia. J. Cook. il Forbes 119:48+ F 15 '77
Case for overthrowing the government; address; June 17, 1977. J. M. Snyder. Vital Speeches 43:717-20 S 15 '77
Department discusses international economic importance of enactment of the President's energy program; statement, May 17, 1977. J. L. Katz. Dept State Bull 76:640-2 Je 13 '77
Energy and the world economy; statement, January 5, 1977. J. L. Katz. Dept State Bull 76:61-7 Ja 24 '77
Energy crisis: production and politics. T. J. Reese. America 137:398-400 D 3 '77
Friction over Canadian oil prices. Bus W p31+ Jl 11 '77
Hold that line; OPEC meeting in Caraballeda, Venezuela. A. J. Mayer and others. il Newsweek 91:47-8 Ja 2 '78
I'm not the Judas; excerpts from interview, ed by W. E. Schmidt. Mohammed Reza Pahlevi. il por Newsweek 89:47-8 Ja 24 '77
Is OPEC finally losing its grip? U.S. News 84:67 Ja 9 '78
Message from OPEC; excerpts from interview, ed by R. Thomas. W. M. Blumenthal. il por Newsweek 90:92 N 14 '77
Negotiating to heal OPEC's price split. Bus W p29-30 Je 27 '77
New oil prices: impact and response. R. Feitelson and G. Salomon. Intellect 105:327-9 Ap '77
New price jockeying at OPEC. il Bus W p24-5 My 30 '77
OPEC closes ranks. Newsweek 90:64 Jl 25 '77
OPEC: no boost till June—if then. il Time 111:67 Ja 2 '78
OPEC: where does the balance of power lie? interview. J. Akins. il por Forbes 120:34-6 O 1 '77
Oil and American power—three years later. R. W. Tucker; discussion. Commentary 63:6+ Ap '77
Perspectives. S. Lens. Progressive 41:12 N '77
President Ford responds to action by OPEC increasing oil prices; statement, December 17, 1976. G. R. Ford. Dept State Bull 76:67 Ja 24 '77
Sagging dollar may raise oil prices. il Bus W p42 N 14 '77
Saudis still reign over OPEC. il Bus W p 19-20 Jl 18 '77
Strain on OPEC. M. R. Benjamin and others. il Newsweek 89:46-7 Ja 24 '77
Tough talk on oil, arms, investments; interview, ed by R. Taggiasco. Mohammed Reza Pahlevi. por Bus W p36+ Ja 24 '77
Unexpected demand frustrates the Saudi oil gamble. Bus W p29 F 21 '77
What price OPEC unity? Time 110:33 D 26 '77
Why an oil price rise is likely this year. S. E. Jackson. Bus W p35 Ja 16 '78
Why higher oil prices mean fewer jobs; theories of D. W. Jorgenson. S. Zucker. il por Bus W p 134+ S 12 '77

Prospecting

FASB ruling hurts oil exploration; successful-efforts accounting for oil and gas companies. Bus W p41-2 O 10 '77
From coast to coast, an all-out race to find more oil. il U.S. News 82:30+ My 16 '77
Lower 48. Time 110:50+ Ag 1 '77
Whatever happened to: Amazon oil boom: disappointing so far. il map U.S. News 82:46 Ap 18 '77
See also
Helicopters in the petroleum industry
Pennzoil Company

Refining

After Valdez: the problems may be just starting. il U.S. News 82:38 Je 20 '77
How they're extracting oil from tar sands. C. E. Maurer. il Pop Sci 210:80-3+ My '77

Reserves

Petroleum reserve at twice the speed. Bus W p38 Je 13 '77
Reserves: the new math. A. J. Mayer and others. il Newsweek 89:71-3 Je 27 '77
Salt domes; storage for oil reserves. S. T. Atlas and W. J. Cook. il Newsweek 90:55 Ag 22 '77
Salting away oil. B. Spanke. il Pop Sci 212:77 Ja '78
Second thoughts on oil stockpiles. il Bus W p36 D 5 '77
Sweet crude, sweet profits. Forbes 120:40 N 15 '77

Transportation

After Valdez: the problems may be just starting. il U.S. News 82:38 Je 20 '77
See also
Petroleum pipelines
Petroleum shipping terminals
Tank ships

Well drilling

See Oil well drilling

Alaska

See also
Petroleum pipelines—Alaska

Amazon River Region

Whatever happened to: Amazon oil boom: disappointing so far. il map U.S. News 82:46 Ap 18 '77

Arctic Regions

World's biggest moving job—icebergs! E. D. Fales, Jr. il Pop Mech 149:47-51 Ja '78

Canada

See also
Petroleum pipelines—Canada

Gulf Coast Region

Oil under the Gulf. C. T. Feazel. il Oceans 10:33-7 S '77

North Sea Region

Can the North Sea save Britain? J. Ross-Skinner. il Duns R 109:82-4+ My '77
Nader of North Sea oil; P. Odell. por Forbes 120:81 D 15 '77
North Sea oil: a mixed blessing for Britain. J. Ross-Skinner. il Duns R 110:82-3+ D '77
Oil comes to the Shetlands. P. Koenig. maps Audubon 79:129-33 Mr '77

PETROLEUM—North Sea Region—*Continued*
Oil platform builders are left high and dry; North Sea industry. il Bus W p38 My 30 '77
Problems beyond today's oil wealth. il Bus W p52-3 O 17 '77
Striking it rich in the North Sea. R. Gore. il map Nat Geog 151:518-49 Ap '77
What a little oil can do. A. Collings. il Newsweek 90:59+ O 17 '77
What North Sea oil won't do for Britain. R. Ball. il Fortune 95:138-42+ Ap '77

Red Sea Region

Middle East: driller discord in the Gulf of Suez. map Bus W p47 Mr 21 '77

Russia

Beware of Russians bearing gas. il Forbes 119:91+ Mr 15 '77

South America

See also
Petroleum—Amazon River Region

United States

Those slippery data. Time 109:58 Ap 18 '77

PETROLEUM, Synthetic
See also
Coal liquefaction

PETROLEUM as fuel
Why utility rates will keep going up. il Changing T 31:41-4 F '77

PETROLEUM chemicals
See also
Benzene

PETROLEUM digesting bacteria. See Oil pollution of rivers, harbors, etc.—Control

PETROLEUM engineering
See also
Oil well drilling

PETROLEUM engineers
Red, boots, coots and toots; taming runaway oil wells. K. Willenson and N. C. Proffitt. il por Newsweek 89:50 My 9 '77

PETROLEUM equipment industry
Oil platform builders are left high and dry; North Sea industry. il Bus W p38 My 30 '77
Surge in demand for offshore oil rigs. il Bus W p30+ N 7 '77
See also
Baker International Corporation

Export-import trade

Revving up oil output with the West's help. il Bus W p52 O 17 '77

PETROLEUM Exporting Countries, Organization of. See Organization of Petroleum Exporting Countries

PETROLEUM in submerged lands
Offshore drilling rights. P. J. Bernstein. Nation 224:75 Ja 22 '77
Opening up the canyon; sale of offshore oil leases on the East coast. maps Time 110:31 S 5 '77
See also
Oil well drilling, Submarine
Petroleum—Gulf Coast Region
Petroleum—North Sea Region
Petroleum—Red Sea Region

PETROLEUM industry
See also
Airplanes in the petroleum industry
Oil shale industry

Accounting

FASB: a single oil standard. Bus W p50 Ag 1 '77

Acquisitions and mergers

Double jeopardy; proposed purchase of Commonwealth Oil Refining Company by Ashland Oil, Inc. E. Dyson. Forbes 119:88+ Je 15 '77
Troubles compound for Commonwealth Oil; delay of sale to Ashland Oil. Bus W p26 S 5 '77

Antitrust cases

Collusion at the gas pump: independents they are not. D. Zielenziger. Nation 224:551-4 My 7 '77
First big test of a new antitrust law; price fixing lawsuits against oil companies. por Bus W p48+ S 12 '77
Wages of hoodwinking: little oil's slippery slope. D. Zielenziger. Nation 225:434-6 O 29 '77

Equipment and supplies

See also
Oil well drilling—Equipment and supplies

Export-import trade

Help wanted with the trade deficit. B. France and J. Pearson. Bus W p46 My 16 '77
Payoff charges on cargo bill. il Time 110:53-4 Ag 15 '77
Tanker bill sinks or swims with Carter; requiring 30% of imported oil be hauled in American-flag tankers. il Bus W p26-7 My 30 '77
See also
Organization of Petroleum Exporting Countries

Finance

Are they earning it or aren't they? il Forbes 119:88+ Ja 15 '77
Biggest rip-off; How big are big oil's profits? J. Carter's attack. il pors Time 110:24-7 O 24 '77
Carter's oil war; Big oil's big bucks. A. J. Mayer and others. il Newsweek 90:38-40 O 24 '77
Decline, with demand in doubt. il Bus W p 110+ O 17 '77
Energy. il Forbes 121:152-4 Ja 9 '78
Mr Carter confronts the oil industry. America 137:277 O 29 '77
Out of foresight. . .opportunity; investment in oil and gas drilling ventures. il Forbes 119:23 F 15 '77
Unfazed by a continuing glut. il Bus W p50-2 Ja 9 '78
Why the big refiners aren't expanding. il Bus W p69+ S 12 '77

History

How they kept the trust; Ida Tarbell's John D. Rockefeller; Standard Oil Company. R. Stinson. Nation 225:561-4 N 26 '77

International aspects

See Petroleum—International aspects

Marketing

See also
Society of Independent Gasoline Marketers of America

Public relations

This man was made possible by a grant from Mobil Oil; H. Schmertz. M. Gerrard. il Esquire 89:62-4+ Ja '78

Regulation

See Petroleum laws and regulations

Securities

American chance to buy more of BP. il Bus W p49+ Ap 25 '77
Oil buyouts—a sellers' market. il Forbes 120:76+ O 15 '77

Taxation

Tough oil tax in the energy plan. il Bus W p32 Ap 11 '77
Windfall windmills. Nat R 29:1476-7 D 23 '77

Wages and hours

Occupational wage levels cluster in petroleum refineries. C. Barsky. bibl il M Labor R 100:54-6 Je '77

Belgium

Petrofina's problems come by the barrel. Bus W p37 Ag 8 '77

Canada

Friction over Canadian oil prices. Bus W p31+ Jl 11 '77
Race against time; Dome Petroleum. W. Schmick. map Forbes 120:24-5 Ag 1 '77

Europe, Western

New policies to help the underdogs in oil. il Bus W p39 D 19 '77

Great Britain

Can the North Sea save Britain? J. Ross-Skinner. il Duns R 109:82-4+ My '77
Nader of North Sea oil; P. Odell. por Forbes 120:81 D 15 '77
State oil company takes a private loan; British National Oil Corp. il Bus W p48 Je 20 '77
See also
British Petroleum Company

Indonesia

Untangling what Pertamina owes—and to whom; controversy surrounding payment to B. Rapaport for rental of oil tankers. il Bus W p90 F 7 '77

Iran

I'm not the Judas; excerpts from interview, ed by W. E. Schmidt. Mohammed Reza Pahlevi. il por Newsweek 89:47-8 Ja 24 '77

Malaysia

Oil beckons the international bankers. map Bus W p52 My 16 '77

Mexico

Gas bonanza; Pemex' Mexican pipeline plan. S. T. Atlas and W. J. Cook. il map Newsweek 90:61-2 Ag 1 '77
Neighbor strikes it rich; Petróleos Mexicanos Pemex. il Forbes 120:88 Jl 1 '77
Pemex to Brown & Root; yankee, come in; American contractor for state oil company. il Forbes 120:28 Ag 15 '77
Pemex wants dollars for a new gas line. il Bus W p42 My 23 '77
Pressuring the U.S. over the price of gas; Pemex pipeline. map Bus W p32 Ja 9 '78

PETROLEUM industry—*Continued*

Middle East

Oil power in the Middle East. J. C. Campbell. bibl f For Affairs 56:89-110 O '77

Norway

Blowout at Bravo. E. Keerdoja. Newsweek 91:7 Ja 9 '78

Puerto Rico

See also
Commonwealth Oil Refining Company

Saudi Arabia

Can OPEC be broken up? J. Cook. il Forbes 119:48+ F 15 '77
OPEC: where does the balance of power lie? interview. J. Akins. il por Forbes 120:34-6 O 1 '77
Oil glut slows OPEC's production. il Bus W p23-4 Ag 22 '77
Strain on OPEC. M. R. Benjamin and others. il Newsweek 89:46-7 Ja 24 '77
U.S.-Saudi relations and the oil crises of the 1980s. D. A. Rustow. bibl f For Affairs 55:494-516 Ap '77
Who gets to distribute that extra Saudi oil. Bus W p35-6 F 7 '77

United States

Bitter *rijsttafel*; U.S. corporate contributors to the Ramayana restaurant. por Time 109:58 F 14 '77
Can't lose for winning; Crown Central Petroleum. Forbes 120:42-3 Jl 15 '77
Crime and no punishment; Home-Stake oil swindle. J. K. Galbraith. il Esquire 88:102+ D '77
From coast to coast, an all-out race to find more oil. il U.S. News 82:30+ My 16 '77
George Mitchell and his edifice complex; Mitchell Energy & Development Corp. L. Minard. il por Forbes 120:81-2+ Jl 1 '77
Go get it, fellows! il Forbes 119:25-7 Je 1 '77
New octane race quietly revs up. il Bus W p38-9 Ja 31 '77
No rush. E. Marshall. New Repub 177:13-14 Ag 20 '77
Oil industry under siege: how it plans to meet the challenge. il U.S. News 83:73-4+ O 31 '77
On sources of energy. W. F. Buckley, Jr. Nat R 29:1320-1 N 11 '77
Populism and petroleum. il Progressive 41:6-7 D '77
Pumping money; Sigmor Corp. il por Forbes 120:37 D 1 '77
Should we break up the oil companies? controversy surrounding horizontal and vertical divestiture. I. Ross. Read Digest 110:153-4+ Je '77
Spanking the sisters; views of J. M. Blair. Time 109:47-8 F 28 '77
Tesoro's $130 million burden. por Bus W p93-4 My 9 '77
U.S. energy crisis; horizontal divestiture; address, November 30, 1976. R. Warner, Jr. Vital Speeches 43:246-51 F 1 '77
Watch your language, fellows! Parker Drilling Co. Forbes 119:51 F 15 '77
Why chemical companies are nervous; expansion of ethylene production by oil companies. Forbes 120:68 D 15 '77
See also names of oil companies, e.g. Mobil Oil Company

History

Texas became Texas; excerpt from Early Texas oil. il Am Heritage 28:48-55 Ap '77

PETROLEUM industry lobby. See Lobbyists and lobbying

PETROLEUM laws and regulations
Oil industry under siege: how it plans to meet the challenge. il U.S. News 83:73-4+ O 31 '77
Socking it to big oil. il Time 110:68-9 Ag 8 '77
Teddy bared; Kennedy bill to prevent horizontal divestiture by oil companies. Nat R 29:1097-8 S 30 '77
See also
Oil and gas leases

PETROLEUM pipeline companies. See Pipeline companies

PETROLEUM pipelines
See also
Pipeline companies

Shipping terminals

See Petroleum shipping terminals

Alaska

Alaska: now that oil is flowing, what next? K. M. Chrysler. il map U.S. New 83:48-51 Jl 11 '77
Alaska oil. Audubon 79:155-6 S '77
Alaska pipeline. R. Gannon. il Pop Sci 210:90-3 Ap '77
Alaskan oil. P. H. Abelson. Science 196:13 Ap 1 '77
Alaskan oil still can't find a Midwest route. Bus W p44 N 28 '77
Alaska's line starts piping—at last. il Time 109:16-17 Je 27 '77
Alaska's oil flows south; with interview with E. L. Patton. K. M. Chrysler. il map U.S. News 82:35-8 Je 20 '77
Blast shuts the pipeline. il map Newsweek 90:75 Jl 18 '77
800 miles of pipeline 2-way energy conductor; assessing pipeline potential. Sci Digest 82:33 O '77
Filling the pipe. A. J. Mayer and W. J. Cock. il Newsweek 89:86+ Je 13 '77
For Sohio, it was Alaskan oil—or bust. A. L. Morner. il por Fortune 96:172-6+ Ag '77
Oil will soon flow, but where will it go? P. L. Fradkin. il Audubon 79:86-8+ Ja '77
Pipeline lessons. Progressive 41:6 S '77
Pipeline to nowhere? il Time 110:50 Ag 1 '77
Promises and betrayals: the trans-Alaska pipeline. R. A. Fineberg. Nation 225:293-7 O 1 '77
Still the wrong route; Trans Alaska pipeline. C. J. Cicchetti. il Environment 19:2-3 Ja '77
Taming of Alaska. R. Rau; discussion. Nat Wildlife 15:17 Ap '77
U.S.-Canada transit pipeline treaty transmitted to the Senate; message, March 30, 1977. J. Carter. Dept State Bull 76:425 Ap 25 '77

Canada

First and forgotten pipeline; the War Department's Canol project. P. L. Fradkin. il pors map Audubon 79:58-79 N '77

Egypt

Arab pipeline that's thirsty for oil; Sumed pipeline. il Bus W p39-40 N 7 '77

PETROLEUM pollution of waters. See Oil pollution of the sea

PETROLEUM ports. See Petroleum shipping terminals

PETROLEUM refineries
Why oil refiners are drowning in crude. il Bus W p37-8 Ag 15 '77

Environmental aspects

Cancer mortality in U.S. counties with petroleum industries. W. J. Blot and others. bibl Science 198:51-3 O 7 '77
Using cancer's rates to track its cause. map Bus W p69-70+ N 14 '77

Location

Boys from Buffalo Creek; proposed Pittston Company refinery in Eastport, Me. J. E. Chappell, Jr. Progressive 41:11 N '77

Wages and hours

See Petroleum industry—Wages and hours

PETROLEUM refining. See Petroleum—Refining

PETROLEUM shipping terminals
Alaskan oil still can't find a Midwest route. Bus W p44 N 28 '77
Can they head off the tankers at the pass? proposed Harbor Island superport off Texas coast. D. G. Schueler. Audubon 79:146-8 N '77
Go-ahead at last for an oil superport; Louisiana Offshore Oil Port Inc. map Bus W p38 Ag 15 '77
Valdez connection; question of Valdez as Alaska pipeline shipping terminal. P. L. Fradkin. maps Audubon 79:134-40 Mr '77

PETROLEUM supply
Adding to the gloom over world oil supplies; Workshop on Alternative Energy Strategies report. Bus W p25-6 My 30 '77
Another energy binge. M. Ruby and others. il Newsweek 89:67 F 28 '77
Days dwindle down for a precious fuel. F. Kendig. il Sci Digest 82:44-6 O '77
Drain Texas first—it's said with bitterness, partner. il U.S. News 82:29 My 9 '77
Guess what? We've got an oil glut. L. Smith. il Duns R 110:58-60 S '77
Guessing what's there. map Time 109:76-8 My 9 '77
How much more oil? P. H. Abelson. Science 198:451 N 4 '77
Looming gap; study by Workshop on Alternative Energy Strategies. A. J. Mayer. il Newsweek 89:48+ My 23 '77
Now, an oil glut. D. Pauly and W. J. Cook. il Newsweek 90:85+ S 19 '77
Oil will soon flow, but where will it go? P. L. Fradkin. il Audubon 79:86-8+ Ja '77
Running short, no matter what; report by the Workshop on Alternative Energy Strategies. Time 109:63 My 23 '77
Secretary Vance testifies on energy program; statement, May 4, 1977. C. R. Vance. Dept State Bull 76:564-6 My 30 '77
Shortage of intelligence; CIA report on oil supplies. Nat R 29:705 Je 24 '77
U.S.-Saudi relations and the oil crises of the 1980s. D. A. Rustow. bibl f For Affairs 55:494-516 Ap '77
What energy crisis? Current 198:42-3 D '77
Whatever happened to the energy crisis? J. J. Du Pont. Conservationist 31:1 Ja '77

PETROLEUM supply—*Continued*
When the oil runs out. G. Reiger. Field & S 82:22+ S '77
When we'll start running out of oil. P. Nulty. il map Fortune 96:246-50 O '77
Why oil refiners are drowning in crude. il Bus W p37-8 Ag 15 '77
World energy situation would be dominated by oil until end of century but coal likely to make significant comeback. il UN Chron 14:41-3 My '77

PETROLEUM swindles. See Fraud

PETROLEUM workers
See also
Petroleum industry—Wages and hours

PETROSKY, Anthony R.
(ed) Research roundup (cont) bibl Engl J 66:90-3 Mr; 96-8 O; 86-8 D '77

PETROV, Michel
(tr) See Rabbot, B. Letter to Brezhnev

PETROV, Petar Slanov
Bulgarian artist wins $1,000 for best poster design. UN Chron 14:50+ Ap '77 *

PETS
Hercule Pawret; J. Keane, finder of lost pets. il por Time 110:53 Ag 1 '77
Of mice and men; popularity rating of pets by Which? magazine. il Newsweek 90:51 Ag 22 '77
Olivia Newton-John and her four-legged family. K. D. Fury. il por Ladies Home J 94:14 Ag '77
Pet journal. See issues of Ladies' home journal
Pet set. D. L. Hunter. il Parents Mag 52:77 N; 50 D '77; 53:64+ Ja '78
Pet show; questions and answers. S. Stein. Am Home 80:77 D '77
Pets. See issues of Better homes and gardens
Pets. M. Siegal. House B 119:38+ Jl; 92 Ag; 36 S; 80 O; 42 N; 78 D '77
Understanding your pet. M. W. Fox. See issues of McCall's
Which pet is right for you. E. H. Hart. Am Home 80:28 N '77
Wild creatures and your children. M. W. Fox. McCalls 104:106+ Jl '77
See also
Travel with pets
Vivariums
also names of pets, e.g. Cats

Age

See Age (animals)

Anecdotes, facetiae, satire, etc.

Peeved at pets. J. Cronley. il Esquire 87:134-5 F '77

Care

Ask the vet; questions and answers. T. McGinnis. See issues of Family health incorporating Today's health
Grooming: the secret of good health. M. W. Fox. McCalls 105:158+ N '77
Pets and their care. il Ebony 32:119-20+ Jl '77
Rx for Fido, Fifi and friends. il Time 109:51 My 30 '77
Summer's special problems. M. W. Fox. McCalls 104:92+ Je '77

Caricatures and cartoons

Petpourri. il Read Digest 110:96-7 F '77

Equipment and supplies

Pet journal. K. Larson. il Ladies Home J 94:156 Mr '77
Pets; Christmas gifts for pets and pet owners. M. Siegal. House B 119:42 N '77

Habits and behavior

See Animals—Habits and behavior

Housing

See also
Kennels

Sexual behavior

See Sexual behavior—Animals

PETS and children. See Children and animals

PETS as gifts
Christmas dogs. R. Caras. il Ladies Home J 94:144 D '77
Pets; Christmas gifts. M. Siegal. House B 119:78 D '77

PETS in psychotherapy. See Psychotherapy

PETT, Saul
Unforgettable Bob Considine. il Read Digest 111:87-90 Jl '77

PETTERSON, Pelle
Being guided to Newport by a northern star. C. Phinizy. il por Sports Illus 46:38-40+ Mr 7 '77 *

PETTERSON, Richard B.
Marguerite Wildenhain. il por Ceram Mo 25:21-8 Mr '77

PETTERSSON, Allan
Music of Allan Pettersson. P. Rapoport. Am Rec G 40:23-4 Ag '77 *

PETTIGREW, Richard Allen
Fixing up the government (again) S. J. Ungar. Atlantic 240:16+ D '77 *

PETTINGELL, Phoebe
Comment. Poetry 131:165-9 D '77

PETTIT, George
Who'll produce feeder pigs? interview. il pors Farm J 101:Hog 13+ Ag '77

PETTY, Richard
Hot blood down in Dixie; excerpt from King Richard, ed by B. Libby. il pors Sports Illus 46:58-62+ F 21 '77
It's tough at the top; interview, ed by J. Norris. il pors Motor T 29:48-50+ Jl '77

about

King is not dead—dust off the throne! L. A. Taylor. il pors Motor T 29:98-9 S '77 *
Petty's hot as a firecracker. B. Myers. il Motor T 29:116-17 O '77 *
Visit with the king. B. Myers. il Car & Dr 22:120 My '77 *

PETTY, Roy. See Fuerst, J. S. jt auth

PETUCHOWSKI, Jakob J.
Altar/throne clash updated; excerpt from address. Chr Today 21:20+ S 23 '77

PETZAL, David E.
Buffalo Bill story. il Field & S 82:150-1+ My '77
Rifle that's yours. il Field & S 82:96-8 O '77

PEUGEOT (automobiles) See Automobiles, Foreign

PEUGEOT-Citroen (firm) See Automobile industry—France

PEVSNER, Sir Nikolaus
Pevsner choices among the fine English buildings. M. Green. il pors Smithsonian 7:96-103 bibl(p 154) F '77 *

PEW, Robert Anderson
Making it—Pew-family style. por Forbes 119:48+ Ja 15 '77 *

PEW, Thomas W. Jr
Route 66: ghost road of the Okies. il Am Heritage 28:24-33 Ag '77
Spectre of an American wasteland. il map Horticulture 55:40-53 Ag '77

PEWTER
See also
Britannia ware

PEYREFITTE, Alain
Gadfly in France. il por Horizon 20:56-7 O '77 *

PEZET, R. and Pont, V.
Elemental sulfur: accumulation in different species of fungi. bibl il Science 196:428-9 Ap 22 '77

PEZOLDT, Charles W.
Code to work by. il Parks & Rec 12:32-4+ Ja '77

PEZZI, Maria
Milan signals—where the action is; tr by G. Alhadeff. il Vogue 167:108-9+ Jl '77

PFAEFFLE, Gena
Black woman's guide to skin care. il McCalls 104:140-1+ F '77

PFAFF, William
Reflections (cont) New Yorker 52:66-70+ Ja 24; 53:87-92 My 16; 101-7 Je 6; 113-18+ S 19 '77

PFEIFFER, C. Boyd
All about fishing lines. il Outdoor Life 161:91-8 Ja '78

PFEIFFER, John Edward
How the establishment got established; excerpt from The emergence of society. il Horizon 19:62-7 Mr '77
Human species. il Horizon 19:92-3 Ja; 89-90 Mr '77

PFEIFFER, Norman
(ed) See Hardy, H. Recycling architectural masterpieces—and other buildings not so great

PFLETSCHINGER, Hans
Conjugation of snails, photographs. Natur Hist 86:104-7 Ag '77
To meet the morning dew. il Int Wildlife 8:44-7 Ja '78

PHAGES. See Bacteriophages

PHAGOCYTES and phagocytosis
See also
Immunity

PHALAENOPSIS. See Orchids

The **PHANTOM (comic strip)** See Comics (books, strips, etc)

PHANTOM Ranch, Arizona. See Ranches

PHARAON, Ghaith
Lance's mysterious rescuer. il por Time 111:45 Ja 9 '78 *
Surprising turn in saga of Bert Lance. pors U.S. News 84:36 Ja 9 '78 *
Texas-Saudi affair. il Forbes 120:88 O 1 '77 *

PHARMACEUTICAL industry. See Drug industry

PHARMACEUTICAL research
Bioactivation as a model for drug design bioreductive alkylation. H. W. Moore. bibl il Science 197:527-32 Ag 5 '77
Custom tailored chemicals: new drugs. il Sci N 111:213 Ap 2 '77
Design of specific inhibitors of angiotensin-converting enzyme: new class of orally active antihypertensive agents. M. A. Ondetti and others. bibl il Science 196:440-4 Ap 22 '77

PHARMACEUTICAL research—*Continued*
Drug design: developing new criteria. G. B. Kolata. Science 197:36-7 Jl 1 '77
Hidden cost of drug safety; FDA's regulations effect on drug industry research projects. il Bus W p80+ F 21 '77
Primate model for long-term study of intraventricularly or intrathecally administered drugs and intracranial pressure. J. H. Wood and others. bibl il Science 195:449-501 F 4 '77
Synthetic peptides form ion channels in artificial lipid bilayer membranes. S. J. Kennedy and others. bibl il Science 196:1341-2 Je 17 '77

PHARMACIES. See Drugstores

PHARMACISTS
Pharmacy in the year 2000; address, June 11, 1977. C. A. Rodowskas, Jr. Vital Speeches 43: 595-8 Jl 15 '77
Rx for choosing a pharmacist. F. Schumacher and G. Schumacher. il Fam Health 9:48-9 Je '77

PHARMACOLOGY
See also
Drug receptors
Psychopharmacology

PHASE rule and equilibrium
See also
Critical point

PHASE transitions
First occurrence of the garnet-ilmenite transition in silicates. L. G. Liu. bibl il Science 195: 990-1 Mr 11 '77

PHASWANA, Koketso
Teaching African literature: the case of Zimbabwe. bibl f il Engl J 66:46-8 Mr '77

PHEASANT shooting
Alone with the ringneck. G. Moravek. il Field & S 82:72-4+ Ag '77
Foxy pheasant. N. Strung. il Field & S 82:42-3+ O '77
He's a woods bird now; ringnecks. R. L. Henry. il Outdoor Life 160:82-3+ O '77
Make pheasants fly! C. Dickey. il Field & S 82: 39+ N '77
Pheasants beyond autumn. J. Madson. il Outdoor Life 160:64-6+ D '77
Unlimited pleasure. T. Trueblood. il Field & S 82:30+ O '77

PHEASANTS
Nepal's downhill flyers; Impeyan pheasants. R. L. Fleming, Jr. il Int Wildlife 7:46-7 S '77

PHEGLEY, Roger
Walk-on who has stepped up. L. Keith. il pors Sports Illus 47:87 D 19 '77 *

PHELAN, John J. Jr
Big Board and the National Market System. il por Duns R 110:97+ N '77

PHELPS, Edwin R.
From pariah to messiah: recent history of coal; address, February 28, 1977. Vital Speeches 43: 366-9 Ap 1 '77

PHENCYCLIDINE hydrochloride
On the drug scene: new rival for heroin. il U.S. News 83:65 Ag 8 '77
PCP: a terror of a drug. il Time 110:53 D 19 '77

PHENOL compounds. See Phenols

PHENOLOGY
Nature's own weather bureau. R. J. Hopp and M. T. Vittum. il Org Gard & Farm 24:127-9 Ap '77

PHENOLS
Phenolic plant compounds functioning as reproductive inhibitors in Microtus montanus. P. J. Berger and others. bibl il Science 195: 575-7 F 11 '77

PHENYLALANINE
See also
Dopa
Phenylketonuria

PHENYLALKANOIC acids
Stink of stinkpot turtle identified: ω-phenylalkanoic acids. T. Eisner and others. bibl il Science 196:1347-9 Je 17 '77

PHENYLETHANOLAMINE
Phenylethanolamine: a new putative neurotransmitter in aplysia. J. M. Saavedra and others. bibl il Science 195:1004-6 Mr 11 '77

PHENYLKETONURIA
Phenylketonuria: a new method for the simultaneous determination of plasma phenylalanine and tyrosine. R. S. Shen and C. W. Abell. bibl il Science 197:665-7 Ag 12 '77

PHEROMONES
Aphids foiled by false alarm. W. S. Bowers. il Chemistry 50:23 Jl '77
Bile, prolactin, and the maternal pheromone. H. Moltz and L. C. Leidahl. bibl il Science 196: 81-3 Ap 1 '77
Chemical communication of marine invertebrates. P. J. Scheuer. bibl il BioScience 27: 664-8 O '77
Cleptoparasitism and odor mimetism in bees: do nomada males imitate the odor of andrena females? J. Tengö and G. Bergstrom. bibl il Science 196:1117-19 Je 3 '77
Disruption of sex pheromone communication in a nemotode. L. W. Bone and H. H. Shorey. bibl il Science 197:694-5 Ag 12 '77
Language of scent. . and you. S. Bronson. il Sci Digest 81:59-63 F '77
Odor gives home team ants early lead. il Sci N 111:356-7 Je 4 '77
Pheromonally induced sexual maturation in females: regulation by the social environment of the male; house mice. J. R. Lombardi and J. G. Vandenbergh. bibl il Science 196:545-6 Ap 29 '77
Sesquiterpene progenitor, germacrene A: an alarm pheromone in aphids. W. S. Bowers and others. bibl il Science 196:680-1 My 6 '77
See also
Insect sex attractants

PHILADELPHIA

Architecture

Robin Hood Dell West: a new summer capital for Philadelphia's music lovers. il Archit Rec 161:129-32 Ja '77

Art

Philadelphia. F. Hartt. Art N 76:100+ O '77
Philadelphia (cont) A. Jarmusch. Art N 76:92-4+ Ja; 89+ Ap; 170+ Summ; 194-5 N '77

Anecdotes, facetiae, satire, etc.

Art plight: the Philadelphia triangle (cont) B. Richards; discussion. Art in Am 65:5 Ja '77

Banks

Fidelity's experiment with index funds. il Bus W p 107 F 14 '77
Philadelphia solution to redlining; Philadelphia Mortgage Plan. Bus W p54+ My 9 '77

Education

Championship season; Vaux Junior High school and Frederick Douglass elementary school chess teams. J. Lelyveld. il N Y Times Mag p86 Je 19 '77

Galleries and museums

See also
Pennsylvania Academy of the Fine Arts, Philadelphia

Historic houses, sites, etc.

Samuel Powel House in Philadelphia. B.-L. Adams. il Antiques 112:1156-63 D '77

Housing

Philadelphia solution to redlining; Philadelphia Mortgage Plan. Bus W p54+ My 9 '77

Libraries

See also
Philadelphia Free Library

Music

See also
Curtis Institute of Music, Philadelphia
Opera—Pennsylvania
Philadelphia Orchestra

Newspapers

Hoagie City hero; P. Péladeau, publisher of the Philadelphia journal. por Time 110:47 D 19 '77
New faces among the big-city dailies; the Trib and the Philadelphia journal. il por Bus W p25 Ja 9 '78
Pulpy Pierre; P. Peladeau's Philadelphia journal. T. Schwartz. il por Newsweek 90:102 D 19 '77
Safari into darkest publishing; Quebecor's plans for new Philadelphia journal. por Forbes 120: 108 D 1 '77
See also
Philadelphia inquirer

Police

Police story: two hard towns. il Time 110: 29-30 S 19 '77
Rizzo lives; investigations of brutality. Nation 225:324 O 8 '77
Roundhouse punches; brutality charges. D. M. Alpern and S. Agrest. il Newsweek 90:24 Jl 4 '77

Religious institutions and affairs

Bishop for Philadelphia; J. Neumann. America 136:543-4 Je 18 '77

Sanitary affairs

Fight over Jersey dumping heats up. il Am City & County 92:42 Ag '77

Schools

See Philadelphia—Education

Social conditions

Wife beating: a community to the rescue; station KYW-TV. E. J. Pascoe. McCalls 105:81 N '77

PHILADELPHIA, Miss.

Race question

See Mississippi—Race question

PHILADELPHIA Children's Hospital. See Children—Hospitals

PHILADELPHIA Free Library
Live from the library; program of the Free Library of Philadelphia's Fleisher Collection. A. Milner. il Am Lib 8:75-6 F '77
PHILADELPHIA inquirer
Philadelphia story; conflict of interest charges against reporter L. Foreman. T. Schwartz and L. Howard. il por Newsweek 90:48 N 14 '77
PHILADELPHIA journal. See Philadelphia—Newspapers
PHILADELPHIA Life Insurance Company mergers. See Corporations—Acquisitions and mergers
PHILADELPHIA Museum of Art
Slapping wrists; resignation of director E. H. Turner. A. Jarmusch. Art N 76:173-4 Summ '77
PHILADELPHIA Orchestra
Music to my ears; visit to Carnegie Hall. I. Kolodin. il por Sat R 4:46-7 Ja 22 '77
PHILADELPHIA Society. See Political clubs and associations
PHILIP II, King of Macedonia
Royal find. P. Gwynne. il Newsweek 90:86 D 5 '77 *
Treasures from a golden tomb. N. Gage and J. Gage. il por map N Y Times Mag p 14:19+ D 25 '77 *
PHILIP, Consort of Elizabeth II, Queen of Great Britain
Prince Philip: the new battle of Britain. . .and how to win it; interview, ed by G. Bull. pors Sat R 4:8-10+ Je 11 '77
Wild world must be saved. il pors Sat Eve Post 249:26-9+ N '77
PHILIPPINE Sea, Battles of the, 1944. See World War, 1939-1945—Campaigns and battles—Pacific
PHILIPPINES
Better days still elude an old friend. D. Moser. il Nat Geog 151:360-91 Mr '77
See also
Ballet—Philippines
Davao
Manila
Political prisoners—Philippines

Description and travel

Land of a hundred Hawaiis. A. Zich. Holiday 58:40-1+ Mr '77
Philippines. T. Talamini. Trav/Holiday 148:82 D '77

Foreign relations

United States

See United States—Foreign relations—Philippines

Politics and government

Carter's moral foreign policy and Philippine martial law. C. L. Hunt. bibl por Intellect 106:130-3 O '77
Ferdinand Marcos' new society. por Time 110:34 Ag 15 '77
Marcos and the Philippines; First Lady; Transplanting democracy. W. F. Buckley, Jr. Nat R 29:1512-13 D 23 '77
New light on the Philippine dilemma. R. G. Soberano. il Chr Cent 94:624-7 Jl 6 '77
Other side of smiling. J. A. O'Hare. America 137:353-4 N 19 '77
Philippines: a nation in transition. S. Johnson. il por Read Digest 110:37-8+ Je '77; Reply. H. Kamm. 110:45 Je '77
See also
Referendum—Philippines

Religious institutions and affairs

See also
Catholic Church in the Philippines
Evangelistic work—Philippines
PHILIPPINOS in the United States. See Filipinos in the United States
PHILIPS, Jesse
Still at the helm. por Forbes 119:72 Ja 15 '77 *
PHILIPS, Mack
House splicing. il Pop Sci 210:121-3 Ap '77
Sharpening jigs—use them like a pro. il Pop Sci 210:72+ My '77
PHILIPS Industries Inc. See Building fittings—Manufacture
PHILIPS of Eindhoven companies
Regional units support complex group. il Aviation W 106:307-15 Je 6 '77
PHILLIPS, Anthony G. See Van Der Kooy, D. jt auth
PHILLIPS, B. J.
New nightlife. il Vogue 167:259 N '77
PHILLIPS, Bert Greer
Bert Greer Phillips: Taos romantic. M. C. Nelson. il por Am Artist 42:32-5+ Ja '78 *
PHILLIPS, Carla Rahn. See Phillips, W. D. Jr, jt auth
PHILLIPS, Daniel
Daniel Phillips, violin; New York solo debut. Hi Fi 27:MA24-5 My '77 *
PHILLIPS, David P.
Motor vehicle fatalities increase just after publicized suicide stories. bibl il Science 196:1464-5 Je 24 '77
PHILLIPS, Gene D.
Tennessee Williams and the Jesuits. America 136:564-5 Je 25 '77
PHILLIPS, Harvey E.
Sarah Caldwell's new idea. il por Hi Fi 27:MA17-19 S '77
PHILLIPS, Homer G.
Strange murder of Homer G. Phillips. E. T. Clayton. il pors Ebony 32:160-2+ S '77 *
PHILLIPS, James D.
Shuttle payload at KSC. il Space World N-8-164-9-23 Ag '77
PHILLIPS, James Howard
Baiting laws are a mess. il Outdoor Life 159:63-5+ Je '77
How they cracked duck hunting's isle of shame. il Outdoor Life 161:64-5+ Ja '78
In Washington, the policy makers fret and sweat. il Nat Wildlife 15:12-13 Ag '77
Snow geese are coming! The snow geese are coming! il por Int Wildlife 7:21 N '77
Twilight for lead shot? il Outdoor Life 160:90-1+ Ag '77
Woodies on the wing again. il Outdoor Life 159:94-5+ My '77
PHILLIPS, John
Jerusalem of 1948 and its survivors today counterpoint in Dial Press/James Wade title; interview, ed by R. Dahlin. il Pub W 211:47-8 Ja 10 '77
PHILLIPS, John L.
Crating up the California dream. il Am Heritage 28:88-93 Ap '77
Triple Crown trainer. il pors N Y Times Mag p47-8+ N 13 '77
PHILLIPS, Johnny
Man himself. New Yorker 53:32-4 S 12 '77 *
PHILLIPS, Keith
No salt in the city. il Chr Today 21:12-15 My 20 '77
PHILLIPS, Kevin P.
Busting the media trusts. Harpers 255:23-4+ Jl '77
Controlling media output; excerpt from The media: the power and the glory. bibl Society 15:10+ N '77
PHILLIPS, Liz
Output. New Yorker 53:31-2 Ap 18 '77 *
PHILLIPS, O. A.
Keeping the faith. C. Fox. il pors Car & Dr 23:97-8+ Ag; 89-91 S '77 *
PHILLIPS, Steven
Justice for whom? il por Psychol Today 10:70-2+ Mr '77
—and Moller, Marc
Putting a price on death. il pors Psychol Today 10:70-2+ My '77
PHILLIPS, William D. Jr, and Phillips, C. R.
Spanish wool and Dutch rebels: the Middelburg incident of 1574. bibl f il map Am Hist R 82:312-30 Ap '77
PHILLIPS Petroleum Company
Who says athletes are dumb? il Forbes 120:55+ D 1 '77
PHILLIPSON, D. W.
Spread of the Bantu language; with biographical sketch. il maps Sci Am 236:20, 106-14 bibl(p 148) Ap '77
PHILO (firm) See Phonograph record industry
PHILOSOPHERS
Rockefeller University: no time for philosophers. J. Walsh. il Science 195:272-5 Ja 21 '77
See also
Von Hildebrand, D.
PHILOSOPHERS, Russian
See also
Chaadaev, P. I.
PHILOSOPHICAL anthropology
Beyond the human heartland. M. B. Martin. Nat R 29:1242 O 28 '77
History in books pot-pourri of collected reflections. P. W. Schmidtchen. il Hobbies 82:134-7+ Je '77
PHILOSOPHY
Reflections. H. Arendt. New Yorker 53:65-8+ N 21; 114+ N 28; 135-42+ D 5 '77
Whatever happened to philosophy? M. E. Marty. Sat R 5:31 D 10 '77
See also
Belief and doubt
Cosmology
Education—Philosophy
Evolution
Free will and determinism
History—Philosophy
Liberty
Mind and body
Mysticism
Order (philosophy)
Perspective (philosophy)
Political philosophy
Psychology
Science—Philosophy

Study and teaching

Arthur O. Lovejoy. L. S. Feuer. Am Scholar 46:358-66 Summ '77
Sherry and skepticism: Oxford days; an American student at Balliol College. L. Wieseltier. Am Scholar 46:483-95 Aut '77

PHILOSOPHY, American
Aging of America. C. V. Woodward. bibl f Am Hist R 82:583-603 Je '77
See also
Kripke, S.
Messianism, American
Transcendentalism (New England)

PHILOSOPHY, Czech
See also
Patočka, J.

PHILOSOPHY, Dutch
See also
Spinoza, B. de

PHILOSOPHY, French
New philosophers; criticism of Marxism by French philosophers. il Time 110:29-30 S 12 '77
New Philosophes. M. S. Ross. Nat R 29:1361-2+ N 25 '77
Taking on Marx; criticism by French philosophers. K. L. Woodward and J. Friedman. il por Newsweek 90:68 Ag 22 '77
See also
Descartes, R.

PHILOSOPHY, German
See also
Heidegger, M.

PHILOSOPHY, Greek
See also
Aristotle
Socrates

PHILOSOPHY, Jewish
See also
Buber, M.

PHILOSOPHY and religion
Barrier to Christian belief. D. E. Kucharsky. Chr Today 21:38-9 F 4 '77
Letters from Ernest; correspondence between E. Becker and H. Bates. il pors Chr Cent 94:217-27 Mr 9 '77
Philosophy: the roots of vain deceit. N. L. Geisler. Chr Today 21:8-12 My 20 '77

PHINIZY, Coles
Being guided to Newport by a northern star. il por Sports Illus 46:38-40+ Mr 7 '77
Boating (cont) Sports Illus 46:54-5 Mr 7; 48+ Mr 28; 47:48+ Ag 15; 66-7 N 21 '77
Cup of tea for Courageous. il Sports Illus 47:26-8+ S 26 '77
Day of reckoning is drawing nigh. il Sports Illus 47:24-6+ S 12 '77
Record run on the southern sea. il Sports Illus 46:22-4+ F 14 '77
Rocket ride to glory and gloom. il Sports Illus 46:26-31 Ja 17 '77
Sailing on a sea of perplexity. il Sports Illus 47:22-3 Ag 8 '77
Setting sail for the defense. il Sports Illus 46:30-5 Je 20 '77
Staging a battle royal on the briny. il por Sports Illus 47:18-20+ Jl 4 '77

about

Letter from the publisher. J. A. Meyers. por Sports Illus 46:4 Ja 17 '77

PHOBIAS
Agoraphobia: life ruled by panic. J. Baumgold. il N Y Times Mag p46-8+ D 4 '77
Commonest phobia of all; shutting out the world; agoraphobia; excerpt from Nothing to fear. F. Kent. il Fam Health 9:44-6+ O '77
Fighting the fear of flying. C. English. Time 109:34 Ap 11 '77
Housewife's disease; agoraphobia. B. Delatiner. Good H 184:84+ Je '77
Old enigma: scientists and therapists gain in understanding your phobias. M. Davidson and N. Ponnamperuma. Sci Digest 82:60-4 Ag '77
Panic of open spaces; agoraphobia. il Time 110:58 N 7 '77
Phobia dictionary. Harp Baz 110:125+ Mr '77
Phobias: new freedom from fear. E. B. Wilson. Harp Baz 110:125+ Mr '77
Stop running scared; excerpt. H. Fensterheim and J. Baer. Good H 185:116+ N '77
Taking the fear out of flying; work of T. W. Cummings. J. Gaylin. il Psychol Today 10:92 My '77
See also
School phobia

PHOBOS (satellite) See Satellites

PHOENIX, Ariz.
Arizona's suburbs of the sun. D. Jeffery. il supp (folded map) Nat Geog 152:486-517 O '77

Crime

Anatomy of a reporter's murder; D. F. Bolles. R. Lindsey. il por N Y Times Mag p 11-14+ F 20 '77
Bolles file; linking K. A. Marley to killing of D. Bolles. il por Newsweek 89:32 Ja 31 '77

Description

300 miles of horse trails circle Phoenix. il map Sunset 159:66+ O '77

Heard Museum

See Indians of North America—Museums

Newspapers

Pack tackles the Mob; Arizona republic's refusal to publish investigative journalists' series. D. Gelman and others. il Newsweek 89:85-6 Mr 28 '77

PHONIC method. See Reading—Study and teaching

PHONOGRAPH
Phonograph celebrates a birthday; symposium. il Sat R 4:18-22+ Jl 23 '77

Equipment

See also
Television receivers, Portable—Radio, phonograph and tape recorder combination

History

Along the memory trail; coin-slot phonograph; reprint from February 1934 issue of The music lover's guide. F. Dorian. Am Rec G 40:58-60 F '77
At the creation. R. R. Wile. bibl il por Am Rec G 40:6-10 F '77
Centennial of the phonograph. G. A. Stahl. bibl il por Chemistry 50:10-12 D '77
Echoing from the past. R. Gelatt. il Opera N 42:14-16 Ag '77
Edison concept; drawings of early phonographs; comp by R. R. Wile. Am Rec G 41:10-13 D '77
Edison's baby: from tinfoil to tape. I. Kolodin. il por Sat R 4:20-2 Jl 23 '77
First 100 years of the phonograph. H. Fantel. il por Pop Mech 148:87+ Ag '77
From a little cylinder. . . C. Graham. il Am Rec G 40:55-7 F '77
Genius to genius; correspondence with the Edison Laboratories; comp by R. R. Wile. J. Hofmann. Am Rec G 40:6-8 S '77
Hi-fi: the once and future phonograph. H. Fantel. il Opera N 41:28-9 Je '77
What hath Edison wrought? Am Rec G 40:4-5 F '77

Pickup

Easy way to test phono cartridges. L. Feldman. il Radio-Electr 49:51+ Ja '78
Julian Hirsch audio reports:
Ortofon Model MC20 phono cartridge and Model MCA-76 preamplifier. J. Hirsch. il Pop Electr 12:35-6 Ag '77
Stanton model 881S phono cartridge. J. Hirsch. il Pop Electr 12:34+ D '77
New equipment reports:
ADC's new pickup: idiosyncratic, but superb in sound; ZLM Deluxe. il Hi Fi 27:30 D '77
Dynavector 20-B—a computer-designed moving-coil pickup. il Hi Fi 27:60 Jl '77
Featherweight at the top of the Goldring line; G-900SE. il Hi Fi 28:61 Ja '78
One of Satin's super pickups. il Hi Fi 27:66-7 S '77
Pickering's Stereohedron—new shape for stereo. il Hi Fi 27:31-2 F '77
Stanton calibrates a new leader; Model 881S. il Hi Fi 27:62 N '77

Purchasing

Buyer's guide to record-playing equipment. il Hi Fi 27:64-8 Ap '77
How to judge record-playing equipment. E. J. Foster. il Hi Fi 27:60-3 Ap '77

Record changers

See Phonograph—Turntables

Testing

How to judge record-playing equipment. E. J. Foster. il Hi Fi 27:60-3 Ap '77
Julian Hirsch audio reports:
Empire model 698 record player. J. D. Hirsch. il Pop Electr 11:26+ Mr '77
Garrard model DD75 direct-drive record player. J. Hirsch. il Pop Electr 11:32-3 Ap '77
Thorens Model TD-126C record player. J. Hirsch. il Pop Electr 12:33-5 Ag '77

Tone arm

New equipment reports:
ADC's stylish, capable tone arm; LMF-1 and LMF-2. il Hi Fi 28:55-6 Ja '78

Turntables

Consumer's guide to record players & tape recorders. Mech Illus 73:34 D '77
Julian Hirsch audio reports:
Dual model 1245 automatic turntable. J. Hirsch. il Pop Electr 12:37-9 N '77
Julian Hirsch audio reports:
Measuring and interpreting turntable rumble. J. D. Hirsch. por Pop Electr 11:24+ Mr '77
Manual turntables. il Consumer Rep 42:662-5 N '77

PHONOGRAPH—Turntables—*Continued*
New equipment reports:
Dual CS-704, a very together turntable. il Hi Fi 27:61-2 Mr '77
Elac PC-870 has belt drive—and more. il Hi Fi 27:59 Jl '77
Empire 698: a classic revisited. il Hi Fi 27:47 Ap '77
Garrard's second-generation tangent-tracking automatic. il Hi Fi 27:32 F '77
Micro Seiki DDX-1000—lean and classic. il Hi Fi 27:51-2 Mr '77
PL-570, a luxury turntable from Pioneer. il Hi Fi 27:55-6 N '77
Rock-solid turntable from Kenwood. il Hi Fi 27:38 My '77
Sophisticated automation in Mitsubishi's premier turntable. il Hi Fi 28:48+ Ja '78
Thorens' latest semiautomatic features a plug-in arm; model TD-126 IIC. il Hi Fi 27:36+ D '77
PS buyer's guide to turntables. H. Maynard. il Pop Sci 211:86-8+ N '77
Radio-electronics tests:
Garrard GT-55 turntable. L. Feldman. il Radio-Electr 48:47-8 Mr '77
Record changers. il Consumer Rep 42:233-5 D '77
Silent partners. H. Fantel. il Opera N 41:34-5 F 12 '77
Turntables. il Consumers Res Mag 60:28-33 Je '77

PHONOGRAPH industry. See Audio equipment industry

PHONOGRAPH needles
Records and the vertical angle. R. Hodges. il Pop Electr 12:14+ S '77

PHONOGRAPH record cleaners. See Cleaning compositions

PHONOGRAPH record covers
Art of album art. il Horizon 20:32 D '77
Musical artform that doesn't make a sound has its cover story told in new A&W book; publication of The album cover album. R. Dahlin. il Pub W 211:59+ Mr 7 '77

PHONOGRAPH record industry
Boys in the band + 2: a 1977 retrospective; rock music trends; symposium. il Hi Fi 28:117-21 Ja '78
Caedmon, at 25, is expanding record sales in book outlets. J. Giusto. il Pub W 212:52-3 O 24 '77
Clive's comeback; C. Davis of Arista Records. G. Stokes. il pors N Y Times Mag p70+ Ap 24 '77
Denon/Reference/Gale recordings: art weds technology. H. A. Rodgers. Hi Fi 27:112-13 O '77
HNH & Quintessence: impressive debuts. K Furie. il Hi Fi 27:108-9 S '77
Independent that could: A&M records. T. Everett. il pors Hi Fi 27:132-4 Ap '77
Indigenous music; Philo. N. Hentoff. Nation 225:414 O 22 '77
K-Tel grows by selling other people's music. il por Bus W p62+ My 2 '77
Monster pop and the little classics. J. Rockwell. il Esquire 87:148-51 F '77
Peter Asher—producer power & a touch of class. S. Sutherland. il por Hi Fi 27:107-10 Je '77
Quintessence classical recordings. G. S. Fox. Am Rec G 41:43-7 D '77
Records for teachers: Educator Records. il Dance Mag 52:107 Ja '78
See also
CBS, Inc-Records Division
Women in the phonograph record industry

Advertising

Intelligent woman's guide to sex; use of brutality toward women in record advertising. J. Coburn. Mademoiselle 83:58 Ag '77

Periodicals

Countdown to Monday: charting the top 100; Billboard, Cashbox, and Record World. J. Melanson. il Hi Fi 27:106-9 My '77

Great Britain

Behind the scenes; Opera Rara. Hi Fi 27:58 O '77

Italy

Behind the scenes; Dischi Ricordi. Hi Fi 27:72+ My '77

PHONOGRAPH records
Classic and choice. il Time 109:98 My 23; 110:88+ S 19 '77
Classic and choice. W. Bender. il Time 109:82+ Ap 4 '77
Classical gems. H. Saal. il Newsweek 89:85-6 Mr 7 '77
Collections; various classical works. Am Rec G 40:33-40 Ag; 48-9 S; 41:37-9 N; 40-1 D '77
Concert records (cont) W. Sargeant. New Yorker 52:68-70 Ja 31; 53:104-7 Mr 7; 109-11 Mr 28; 118-21 Ap 11; 143-4+ Ap 18; 112-16 Je 6; 82-3 Jl 11; 61-2 Ag 1; 73-5 Ag 15; 168+ O 24; 187-90+ N 14; 178+ N 21; 124-7 D 19 '77
Denon/Reference/Gale recordings: art weds technology. H. A. Rodgers. Hi Fi 27:112-13 O '77
Eshpai, Popov and Boris who. . . ? works of minor composers. J. A. Smith. Am Rec G 40:5+ Mr '77
Favorite pioneer recording artists. J. Walsh. See issues of Hobbies
Guide to records. See issues of American record guide
Imports; classical recordings from foreign countries (title varies) C. Bauman. See issues of American record guide
Music: guide to bargain bins. S. Ditlea. il Am Home 80:14 My '77
New records in review. B. H. Haggin. See issues of Yale review
Pick of the classics. H. Saal. Newsweek 90:92 S 26 '77
Recent recordings. B. H. Haggin. New Repub 177:23-5 D 17 '77
Recommended recordings. Harpers 254:88 Je '77
Record reviews (cont) M. Bookspan. Consumer Rep 42:114-15, 172-3, 333, 430, 490 F-Mr, Je-Ag '77
Recorded music in review. W. F. Grueninger. See issues of Consumers' research magazine
Recorded oddities, novelties, and rarities. I. Kolodin. Sat R 4:42 S 3 '77
Recordings. A. Goldman. Esquire 88:44+ O; 8+ N; 60+ D '77
Recording music in review. (cont) W. F. Grueninger Consumers Res Mag 60:43 Mr '77
Recordings (cont of) Fresh faces and first encounters (cont) I. Kolodin. Sat R 4:42 F 19; 42 My 28; 48-9 Jl 9 '77
Recordings '78: a preview of industry releases. Hi Fi 27:28+ S '77
Records (cont) D. Hamilton. Nation 224:92-4, 253-4, 381-2, 509-10, 797-8; 225:318, 477-8, 602-4, 734 Ja 22, F 26, Mr 26, Ap 23, Je 25, O 1, N 5, D 3, 31 '77
Records and the vertical angle. R. Hodges. il Pop Electr 12:14+ S '77
Records 1977. D. Hamilton. Nation 225:666-7 D 17 '77
Reviews of records. See issues of Musical quarterly
Sounds. D. Sargent. See issues of Vogue
Spinoffs. M. Cooper. Am Rec G 40:48-9 D '76; 50-1 Mr '77
Spotlight. E. Miller. See issues of Seventeen
Time capsule; 78 rpm recordings. E. Birchenough. Am Rec G 40:8-10 Jl '77
Vanity labels. S. Ditlea. il Am Home 80:14 Jl '77
Year's best. Time 111:54 Ja 2 '78
See also
Booksellers and bookselling—Phonograph records
Libraries—Phonograph and phonograph record collections

Advertising

See Phonograph record industry—Advertising

American music

Foster: songs—vol. 2. P. L. Miller. Am Rec G 40:50 F '77
Good survey—but flawed: Piano music in America—vol. 2: 1900-1945. D. Gavelmann. il Am Rec G 40:9-11 My '77
Manchester (N.H.) circa 1850: you are there; Homespun America. I. Lowens. il Hi Fi 27:115 Ap '77
Year that was. Am Rec G 40:4+ Mr '77

Arias

Bach: arias; selected works. J. R. Oestreich. Am Rec G 40:12 Ag '77
Carlo Bergonzi sings Verdi: 31 tenor arias from 25 operas. D. Arthur. por Am Rec G 40:41-4 N '76
Gluck: opera arias. P. L. Miller. Am Rec G 40:17-18 Mr '77
Historical records:
Carlo Ferretti. A. F. Artsay. il por Hobbies 82:37+ Mr '77
Computerized Caruso. A. F. Artsay. il pors Hobbies 81:37+ F '77
Melba; Emil's five-disc collection of the London recordings. A. Porter. pors Hi Fi 28:86-9 Ja '78
Melba's farewell concert. W. R. Moran. il pors Hi Fi 27:86-9 Jl '77
Perilous path to soprano superstardom; recordings of Mozart recitals by S. Sass and M. Price. D. Harris. pors Hi Fi 27:89-90 Ap '77
Records:
Emma Carelli; Ester Mazzoleni individual releases. J. W. Freeman. Opera N 41:33 F 26 '77
Janet Baker, Bidù Sayão, and Frederica von Stade; individual releases. J. W. Freeman. Opera N 41:44 Ja 29 '77
Montserrat Caballé; Claudia Muzio, vol. 2; Elena Obraztsova; individual releases. J. W. Freeman. Opera N 41:33 Ja 22 '77
Rimsky-Korsakov; arias from The tsar's bride, Snow maiden, Sadko, and The invisible city of Kitzeh. P. L. Miller. Am Rec G 40:28 Ap '77

PHONOGRAPH records—*Continued*

Avant-garde music

See Phonograph records—Music, Experimental

Awards, prizes, etc.

Best records of 1977; annual High Fidelity/International Record Critics Awards; with remarks by L. Marcus. il Hi Fi 27:48-55 D '77
Top honors; classical gold albums. Am Rec G 40:3 O '77

Ballet music

Bartok: the Wooden Prince; Boulez recording. W. Botsford. Am Rec G 40:16 Jl '77
Khachaturian: Gayne ballet suites nos. 1, 2 and 3. M. Mark. il Am Rec G 40:19-20 Ag '77
On discs; Ravel's Daphnis and Chloë. J. D. Richardson. Dance Mag 51:90-1 Je '77
Piston: The incredible flutist. W. D. Curtis. Am Rec G 40:36-8 Je '77
Stravinsky: Le sacre du printemps. G. S. Fox. por Am Rec G 40:42-3 D '76
Stravinsky: Petrouchka conducted by D. Dutoit, recording. W. D. Curtis. Am Rec G 41:32-4 N '77

Band music

See also
Phonograph records—Marches (music)

Baroque music

De Lavigne: De Boismortier: Loeillet: Telemann: Bertoli: Handel. L. Gerber. Am Rec G 40:48 F '77

Brass instruments

See Phonograph records—Wind instruments

Canons, fugues, etc.

Bach: Goldberg variations; Sonata in B-flat major for clarinet and piano. E. Richmond. Am Rec G 40:14+ O '77
New set of Bach canons; Marlboro recording. A. Porter. por Hi Fi 27:84-5 My '77

Cantatas

Bach: Cantatas nos. 10, 135, and 24. E. Richmond. Am Rec G 40:17-18 S '77
Bach: Cantatas, vols. 15-16; Telefunken series. A. Porter. il Hi Fi 27:77-8 Ag '77
Most successful project; Bach's cantatas, Telefunken vols:15-16. E. Richmond. Am Rec G 40:14-15 Jl '77
Pergament: The Jewish song. W. Simmons. Am Rec G 40:29 Jl '77

Care

Clean sound of music. D. Marsh. il Esquire 87:94-6 My '77
Decontamination squad. R. Hodges. Pop Electr 11:18+ My '77
Keeping it clean: solutions for record care. H. Fantel. Opera N 41:38-9 Ap 2 '77
Record cleaners—new devices reduce wear and noise. H. Maynard. il Pop Sci 210:79-81+ Je '77

Catalogs

Diagnosis: slipped discography; R. H. Halsey's Classical music recordings for home and library. K. Furie. il Wilson Lib Bull 51:755-9 My '77
High fidelity weds Schwann. L. Marcus. Hi Fi 27:4 Mr '77

Cello music

Bloch: Schelomo; Schumann: Cello concerto, M. Rostropovich soloist. L. M. Smoley. Am Rec G 40:21-3 S '77
Geminiani: six cello sonatas. E. Belov. Am Rec G 40:16-17 Mr '77
Haydn: Cello concertos in C major and D major conducted by P. Makanowitzky. P. L. Althouse. Am Rec G 41:34 D '77
New voices for strings: fresh readings by young cellists. D. W. Moore. Am Rec G 41:6-7 N '77
Survey for cello & piano; Beethoven's complete cello sonatas; comparison of new and old recordings. D. W. Moore. Am Rec G 40:19-22 O '77

Chamber music

Couperin, Francois: Concerts royaux; Nouveaux concerts. W. L. Purcell. il Am Rec G 40:31-4 F '77
Fibich: Quintet in D major, op. 42; Trio in F minor. J. Ringo. Am Rec G 40:29-30 D '76
Heifetz chamber music collection. E. Belov. Am Rec G 41:40-1 D '77
Review of records; selected works of J. C. Bach, M. Haydn and W. A. Mozart performed by the St Paul Chamber Orchestra. G. Lazarevich. Mus Q 63:446-50 Jl '77
Telemann: Sinfonia in F major; Overture in C major Concerto in B flat major; Triple concerto in E major. E. Belov. Am Rec G 40:39 N '76
Vivaldi: Four seasons; two recordings. J. R. Oestreich and J. Diether. Am Rec G 40:35-6 Jl '77

Chants (Gregorian, plain, etc)

Guide to Gregorian chant. W. L. Purcell. il Am Rec G 40:45-6 Mr '77

Childrens records

Children's records. E. Conford. Am Rec G 40:50-1 N '76; 48-50 Mr '77

Choral music

Berlioz: Lélio ou le Retour à la vie. J. W. Barker. Am Rec G 41:12-14 N '77
Berlioz: Te deum; Columbia recording. J. W. Barker. il Am Rec G 41:21-2 D '77
Historic reissues; Schoenberg: Gurre-Lieder. G. S. Fox. Am Rec G 40:5-6+ Ag '77
Janáček: Choral works for female voices. W. D. Curtis. Am Rec G 40:37 S '77
Rachmaninoff: Bells, op. 35; Vocalise, op. 34, no. 14. J. Oestreich. Am Rec G 40:31-2 Mr '77
Their muses faced East and West; Janáček's Amarus and Suk's Under the apple tree. J. Ringo. Am Rec G 41:8-10+ N '77
Vocal/choral/etc. Am Rec G 40:49 N; 55-6 D 76; 39-40 Mr; 28-30 Ap; 47-8 My '77

Church music

Grandi: Music for San Marco, Venezia, San Giorgio, Ferrara, & Santo Maria Maggiore, Bergamo. J. W. Barker. Am Rec G 40:30 D '76

Clarinet music

Brahms: Clarinet quintet in B minor, op. 115. E. Belov. il Am Rec G 40:19 Ap '77

Collectors and collecting

Da capo. S. Smolian. il Am Rec G 40:52-3 D '76; 16-17+ Ap '77

Concert performances

Concert of the century: celebrating the 85th anniversary of Carnegie Hall. M. Cooper. il Am Rec G 40:26 D '76
For human rights; recording of benefit concert for Amnesty International. J. R. Oestreich. il Am Rec G 40:12-15 My '77

Concertos

Bach: Brandenburg Concertos (6) recorded by Leonhardt Consort. A. Chipman. Hi Fi 27:77 D '77
Bolling: Concerto for classic guitar and jazz piano. J. Ringo. Am Rec G 40:23-5 D '76
Brahms: Piano concerto no. 1, in D minor, op. 15. L. Gerber. Am Rec G 40:17 N '76
Elliott Carter: Double concerto for harpsichord and piano with two chamber orchestras. B. Archibald. Mus Q 63:287-9 Ap '77
Handel: the Complete concerti for keyboard and orchestra. J. W. Barker. Am Rec G 40:13-14 Ag '77
Heinz Holliger: now that's charisma; latest Philips disc. R. D. Darrell. il por Hi Fi 27:97 O '77
Mozart: Flute and piano concertos; Galway, Serkin and Casadesus recordings. B. Hastings and R. Kammerer. Am Rec G 40:28 Jl '77
Mozart: various concertos performed by the Vienna Philharmonic conducted by Karl Bohm. L. M. Smoley. Am Rec G 40:38-9 O '77
Reimann: Concerto for piano and 19 players. D. M. Garvelmann. Am Rec G 40:37-8 D '76
Vivaldi; current recordings. J. W. Barker. Am Rec G 40:32-3 Ag '77
See also
Phonograph records—Flute music
Phonograph records—Organ music
Phonograph records—Piano music
Phonograph records—Violin music

Country music

Country. N. Tosches. il Hi Fi 27:145 F '77; 28:132-3 Ja '78

Czech music

Flosman: Violin concerto no. 2. Válek: Symphony no. 10. D. W. Moore. Am Rec G 40:34-5 S '77

Dance music

On discs. J. D. Richardson. Dance Mag 51:90-1 Je '77
Records for teachers. Dance Mag 51:107 S '77; 52:107 Ja '78
See also
Phonograph records—Ballet music

Disco music

Disco fever. A. Goldman. il Esquire 88:60+ D '77

Experimental music

See Phonograph records—Music, Experimental

Flute music

Mozart: Rampal plays Mozart; flute concertos. N. F. Karlins. Am Rec G 40:28-9 Mr '77
Romantic flute. M. Mark. Am Rec G 40:37 Ag '77

Folk music

Indigenous music: Folk Music in America series. N. Hentoff. Nation 224:477-8 Ap 16 '77
Interesting reissues: jazz & folk. Am Rec G 50:56-7 N '76
Just folk. Am Rec G 40:45-6 D '76

PHONOGRAPH records—*Continued*

French music

Looking for new angles. P. L. Miller. Am Rec G 40:52 Je '77

German music

Wolf: Lieder vol. 2. D. Arthur. il Am Rec G 40: 44-5 My '77

Gilbert and Sullivan opera

Gilbert and Sullivan discography. R. Dyer. il Hi Fi 27:52-8 My '77
Gilbert and Sullivan: The grand duke or The statutory duel; recording performed by D'Oyly Carte. W. Botsford. Am Rec G 41:15 N '77

Harpsichord music

Bach: Italian concerto, Overture in the French style; performed by I. Kipnis. L. Gerber. Am Rec G 40:12-13 D '76
Bach: Partitas 1 and 2 performed by I. Kipnis. C. Greenleaf. Am Rec G 40:16-17 S '77
Benda: 3 concerti for harpsichord. Am Rec G 40:22-3 O '77
Reviews of records; Music for two harpsichords, by J. S. Bach. G. Herz. bibl f Mus Q 63:562-70 O '77

History

Echoing from the past; landmarks from the first 50 years of recorded opera. R. Gelatt. il Opera N 42:14-18+ Ag '77
Historical records. A. Favia-Artsay. See issues of Hobbies to April 1977

Hungarian music

Contemporary Hungarian brass chamber music. L. M. Smoley. Am Rec G 40:39-40 Ag '77

Incidental music

Their muses faced East and West; Janáček's Amarus and Suk's Under the apple tree. J. Ringo. Am Rec G 41:8-10+ N '77

Instrumental music

See also
Phonograph records—Chamber music

Japanese music

Japan: traditional vocal & instrumental music. W. L. Purcell. Am Rec G 40:42-3 Mr '77

Jazz music

Antic arts; Fantasy/Prestige/Milestone series. A. Zich. Holiday 58:10+ Je '77
Eclectic plus ethnic plus electric equals fusion. A. Goldman. Esquire 88:44+ O '77
Indigenous music:
Basie jam #2. N. Hentoff. Nation 224:222 F 19 '77
C. Bley album, Dinner music. N. Hentoff. Nation 225:126 Ag 6 '77
The devil is afraid of music/Barbara Lea. N. Hentoff. Nation 225:350 O 8 '77
Dizzy Gillespie: the development of an American artist, 1940-46. N. Hentoff. Nation 224:350 Mr 19 '77
George Lewis solo trombone record and Leroy Jenkins solo concert. N. Hentoff. Nation 225:574 N 26 '77
Intimate Ellington. N. Hentoff. Nation 224: 314-15 Mr 12 '77
Warren Vaché and Tommy Flanagan. N. Hentoff. Nation 225:509 N 12 '77
Woody Herman/The new thundering herd/ The 40th anniversary concert recorded live. N. Hentoff. Nation 224:636 My 21 '77
Interesting reissues: jazz & folk. Am Rec G 40:56-7 N '76
Jazz:
Reissues. W. Balliett. il New Yorker 53: 118+ S 12 '77
Young Louis Armstrong. W. Balliett. New Yorker 53:84 Ap 4 '77
Jazz; J. Hall's album, Commitment. M. Ullman. New Repub 177:23-5 N 19 '77
Jazz. D. Heckman and J. S. Wilson. Hi Fi 27: 144 Mr; 120 My; 142 S; 142 D '77; 28-139 Ja '78
Jazz. E. Summerlin. Am Rec G 40:41-2 Ag '77
Jazz. M. Ullman. New Repub 177:23-5 D 24 '77
John Coltrane & Eric Dolphy: the Vanguard years; three new releases. D. Heckman. pors Hi Fi 27:116-17 Ag '77

Jewish music

Pergament: The Jewish song. W. Simmons. Am Rec G 40:29 Jl '77

Keyboard instruments

German keyboard music of about 1700. G. Herz. Mus Q 63:570-2 O '77
Haydn: The complete keyboard solo music, v4. R. Kammerer. Am Rec G 40:31-2 D '76
Reviews of records: Orlando Gibbons: Keyboard music. H. L. Clarke. Mus Q 63:146-8 Ja '77

Lute music

Bakfark: Complete works for solo lute. J. Warren. Am Rec R 40:10-11 Je '77

Madrigals

Monteverdi: madrigals. W. L. Purcell. Am Rec G 40:26 Mr '77
Reviews of records: Orlando Gibbons: Madrigals and motets. H. L. Clarke. Mus Q 63:146-8 Ja '77

Marches (music)

Strike up the band; French military marches. M. Mark Am Rec G 40:50-1 F '77

Mass (music)

Beethoven: Missa solemnis, op. 123. P. L. Althouse. Am Rec G 40:13-15 D '76
Dufay, Guillaume: Missa se la face ay pale. W. L. Purcell. Am Rec G 40:27-8 D '76
See also
Phonograph records—Requiems

Medieval music

Dufay: Fifteen songs; Transformations. W. Purcell. Am Rec G 40:28-30 S '77
Instruments of the Middle Ages and Renaissance; Vanguard recording. J. W. Barker. Am Rec G 41:16-18 D '77
World of Gothic music. W. L. Purcell. il Am Rec G 40:43-5 Mr '77

Mexican music

Revueltas: Sensemayá; Redes; Caminos; Itinerarios; Janitzio. W. D. Curtis. Am Rec G 41: 29-30 N '77

Motion picture music

Poignant backdrop for cinematic horrors; Carrie. R. S. Brown. il Hi Fi 27:80 My '77
Theater and film. R. S. Brown. See issues of High fidelity and Musical America

Music, Experimental

And in a similar vein; Avant-garde woodwind quintet in the U.S.A; Vox recording. W. Simmons. Am Rec G 41:51-3 D '77
Lazarof: Spectrum; Concerto for flute and orchestra. J. Ringo. Am Rec G 41:18-19 N '77
Music in the modern manner; works of Babbitt, Smith, Bassett and Wuorinen. L. M. Smoley. Am Rec G 41:49-51 D '77
New music; avant-garde recordings. J. La Barbara. il Hi Fi 27:MA14-15 D '77

Music, Popular (songs, etc)

Brazil is alive & well & sneaking into your record collection. J. S. Roberts. il Hi Fi 27: 124+ Je '77
Carole Bayer Sager. por Hi Fi 27:128 Je '77
Carole King: optimistic craftsmanship; Simple things. D. Heckman. por Hi Fi 27:142+ O '77
Discussions; J. Talley's Blackjack choir. P. Lippincott. por Sr Schol 109:26-7 My 5 '77
James Taylor: no more kinks; JT album. S. Sutherland. por Hi Fi 27:136 S '77
Kate & Anna McGarrigle: Dancer with bruised knees. il pors Hi Fi 27:117-18 My '77
Linda Ronstadt breaks training; Simple dreams. S. Holden. por Hi Fi 27:150-1 N '77
Michael Franks is no three-chord composer; Sleeping gypsy. il Hi Fi 27:142+ Mr '77
New sound in review. Consumers Res Mag 60: 32 D '7
Pop/Rock. il Hi Fi 27:143 Ap; 122 My; 145 S '77
Popular records. D. Watt. New Yorker 53:66-8 Ag 8 '77
Post-Christmas pop. J. Maslin. il Newsweek 89:93-5 F 14 '77
Randy Newman's latest outrageous triumph; Little criminals. K. Emerson. il por Hi Fi 27:134-5 D '77
Records. See issues of High fidelity and Musical America
Top ten, or, the dregs of the sixties. A. Goldman. il Esquire 88:8+ N '77
Tops in pops. il Time 109:100+ My 23 '77
Tops in pops. J. Downs. il Time 109:79+ Ap 4 '77
Who is Leon Redbone & why is he singing all those oddball songs? Double time. L. Bangs. por Hi Fi 27:140+ Ap '77
See also
Phonograph records—Country music

Musical comedy, revue, etc.

Annie: original cast album. M. Galewski. Am Rec G 40:51+ O '77
Popular records. D. Watt. New Yorker 53:66-8 Ag 8 '77
Reviews of records; works by K. Weill. K. H. Kowalke. Mus Q 63:441-6 Jl '77
Side by side by Sondheim. M. Galewski. Am Rec G 40:52-4 F '77
Theater and film. R. S. Brown. See issues of High fidelity and Musical America
Three penny opera. M. Galewski. Am Rec G 40: 46-7 Mr '77

Opera

Again the silver rose: Der Rosenkavalier; Philips recording. R. V. Lucano. il Am Rec G 40:43-5 O '77
L'amore dei tre re: like no other Italian opera; RCA recording. C. L. Osborne. il por Hi Fi 27:67-70 Ag '77

PHONOGRAPH records—Opera—*Continued*
At last. Mussorgsky's Boris Godunov; Angel recording. D. Hamilton. il Hi Fi 28:83-7 Ja '78
At long last Meyerbeer's Le Prophète. D. Arthur. Am Rec G 40:29-30+ Je '77
Behind the scenes; Opera Rara. Hi Fi 27:58 O '77
Bolle: Oil of dog. J. Ringo. Am Rec G 40:15 N '76
Boris Godunov. W. Botsford. Am Rec G 40:30-1 Mr '77
Catfish Row revisited; Porgy and Bess performed by the Houston Grand Opera. E. Jablonski. il por Am Rec G 40:10-15 S '77
Catfish Row springs to life; RCA recording of Houston Grand Opera production of Porgy and Bess. D. Hamilton. il Hi Fi 27:92-4 S '77
Charpentier: Louise. D. Arthur. Am Rec G 40:29-30 F '77
Cimarosa: Il matrimonio segreto; Deutsche Grammophon recording. G. L. Mayer. il Am Rec G 41:25-7 D '77
Cimarosa's comic masterpiece; DG's recording of il matrimonio segreto. P. H. Lang. il Hi Fi 27:95-6 N '77
Columbia reopens the Meyerbeer case; recording Le Prophète. P. J. Smith. il Hi Fi 27:87-8 Mr '77
Concert records (cont) W. Sargeant. New Yorker 53:104-7 Mr 7; 109-11 Mr 28; 118-21 Ap 11; 143-4+ Ap 18; 112-16 Je 6; 82-3 Jl 11; 61-2 Ag 1; 73-5 Ag 15; 168+ O 24 '77
Connoisseur's Carmen. D. Arthur. Am Rec G 40:19-21 D '76
Donizetti: Gemma di Vergy; Columbia recording of concert performance. A. Porter. il Hi Fi 27:86-8 Je '77
Dvorak: Rusalka. B. Hastings. Am Rec G 40:30-2 S '77
Echoing from the past; landmarks from the first 50 years of recorded opera. R. Gelatt. il Opera N 42:14-18+ Ag '77
Gagliano: La Dafne. R. V. Lucano. Am Rec G 41:32 D '77
German wartime broadcasts. S. Lipman. Commentary 63:72-5 Mr '77; Discussion. 64:7-8 Jl '77
Handel: Semele. R. V. Lucano. Am Rec G 40:21-2 Mr '77
Haydn: La vera costanza. R. V. Lucano. il Am Rec G 40:14-16 Ag '77
Haydn: L infedelta delusa; Hungaroton recording. R. V. Lucano. Am Rec G 40:31-2 O '77
Haydn: L'infedeltà delusa; La vera costanza; recordings by Hungaroten and Philips. A. Porter. il Hi Fi 27:83-4+ Ag '77
Haydn's mad knight; Orlando Paladino. R. V. Lucano. il Am Rec G 41:16-17 N '77
Haydn's Orlando Paladino: a heroic-comic delight; Philips recording. P. H. Lang. il Hi Fi 27:107 D '77
In the opera house: how much does neatness count? recordings of Andrea Chénier and La forza del destino, conducted by J. Levine. K. Furie. il por Hi Fi 27:71-4 Ag '77
Janáček: Kátya Kabanova; London recording. D. Hamilton. Hi Fi 28:97-100 Ja '78
Johann Strauss II: Die Fledermaus. W. Botsford. Am Rec G 40:36-7 Mr '77
Kabalevsky: Colas Breugnon, opp. 24/90. Hi Fi 27:104-5 Ap '77
Kreutzer: Das Nachtlager in Granada. J. Ringo. Am Rec G 40:24-5 My '77
Like singing three Normas; M. Caballé records Donizetti's Gemma di Vergy. R. V. Lucano. il por Am Rec G 40:16-18 My '77
Massenet: Esclarmonde. D. Arthur. il Am Rec G 40:24-5 Mr '77
Massenet; Le Cid. Am Rec G 40:30-1 F '77
Mixed bag: famous Wagner interpreters; 100 years of Bayreuth. C. J. Luten. il Am Rec G 40:10-12+ O '77
Mozart: Der Schauspieldirektor; Lo sposo deluso. R. V. Lucano. il Am Rec G 40:29-30 N '76
Mozart: Zaïde. W. Botsford. Am Rec G 40:31 N '76
New life for Louise. C. L. Osborne. il Hi Fi 27:92-4 F '77
New Tosca. R. V. Lucano. il Am Rec G 40:42-3 Je '77
Nicolai: Die lustigen Weiber von Windsor. Hi Fi 27:102-4 S '77
Nicolai: Die lustigen Weiber von Windsor. K. Moses. Am Rec G 40:44-5 S '77
Nose: explosively imaginative music theater; Melodiya recording. C. L. Osborne. il Hi Fi 27:69-73 D '77
100 years of Bayreuth; Deutsche Grammophon. C. J. Luten. Am Rec G 40:10-12 N '76
Operatic Scarlatti. A. Porter. por Hi Fi 27:72-4 Je '77
Orff: Carmina Burana. G. S. Fox. Am Rec G 40:37-8 F '77
Outstanding effort; Giordano: Andrea Chénier; RCA recording. D. Arthur. il Am Rec G 40:29-31 O '77
Peri: Euridice. R. V. Lucano. Am Rec G 40:29-30 Jl '77
Ponselle legacy; survey of her recordings. G. Jellinek. por Opera N 41:30-1 Mr 12 '77
Prokofiev: The gambler. D. W. Moore. Am Rec G 41:26-7 N '77
Rachmaninoff: Francesca da Rimini; Columbia/Melodiya recording. J. R. Oestreich. Am Rec G 40:40 O '77
Records:
Charpentier: Louise. il Opera N 41:41 F 5 '77
Delius: Fennimore and Gerda. J. W. Freeman. il Opera N 41:41 F 12 '77
Donizetti: Gemma di Vergy. J. W. Freeman. il Opera N 41:32 Mr 26 '77
Gershwin: Porgy and Bess; RCA recording. J. W. Freeman. il Opera N 42:37 D 10 '77
Giordano: Andrea Chenier. J. W. Freeman. Opera N 41:48 My '77
Gounod: Faust. J. W. Freeman. il Opera N 42:52 D 3 '77
Kabalevsky: Colas Breugnon. il Opera N 41:33 Ja 22 '77
Meyerbeer: Le Prophète. J. W. Freeman. Opera N 41:44 Ja 29 '77
Mussorgsky: Boris Godunov. J. W. Freeman. il Opera N 42:84 N '77
Offenbach: Le vie parisienne. J. W. Freeman. il Opera N 41:37 Ap 16 '77
Perl: Euridice J. W. Freeman. il Opera N 41:37 Ap 9 '77
Puccini: Edgar. J. W. Freeman. Opera N 42:40 D 17 '77
Puccini: Suor Angelica. J. W. Freeman. Opera N 41:40 Mr 19 '77
Puccini: Tosca. J. W. Freeman. Opera N 41:37 Ap 9 '77
Rimsky-Korsakov: May night. J. W. Freeman. Opera N 41:48 My '77
Strauss: Der Rosenkavalier; Philips recording conducted by E. De Waart. J. W. Freeman. Opera N 42:56 Ag '77
Thomson: The mother of us all. J. W. Freeman. Opera N 41:40 Mr 19 '77
Verdi: La forza del destino. J. W. Freeman. il Opera N 41:40 Mr 12 '77
Verdi: Macbeth. J. W. Freeman. il Opera N 41:33 Mr 5 '77
Verdi: Otello. J. W. Freeman. Opera N 42:29 Jl '77
Verdi: Simon Boccanegra. J. W. Freeman. il Opera N 42:48 D 24 '77
Verdi: Il Trovatore. J. W. Freeman. il Opera N 42:41 Ja 7 '78
Wagner: Der fliegende Holländer; London recording. J. W. Freeman. il Opera N 42:70 O '77
Wagner: Rienzi. J. W. Freeman. Opera N 41:33 F 19 '77
Wagner: The Valkyrie. J. W. Freeman. il Opera N 41:33 F 19 '77
Weber/Mahler: Die drei Pintos. J. W. Freeman. Opera N 41:44 Je '77
Records. D. Hamilton. Nation 225:602-4 D 3 '77
Rimsky-Korsakov: May night. D. M. Moore. Am Rec G 40:44-5 Je '77
Rossini: Elisabetta, Regina d'Inghilterra. R. V. Lucano. Am Rec G 40:39-40 F '77
Rossini's romanticism of the soul; new recording of Elisabetta, Regina d'Inghilterra. A. Porter. Hi Fi 27:106-7 F '77
Scarlatti: La Griselda—excerpts. R. V. Lucano. il Am Rec G 40:32-4 My '77
Star-baritone's opera; Leoni: L'Oracolo. D. Arthur. Am Rec G 40:38-40 S '77
Strauss, R: Der Rosenkavalier, op. 59; Philips recording conducted by E. de Waart. Hi Fi 27:110-13 S '77
Tchaikovsky: Mazeppa; Melodiya recording. Am Rec G 40:56 O '77
Thomson: the mother of us all. B. Hastings. il Am Rec G 40:30-1 Ag '77
Two new Meistersingers. C. J. Luten. il Am Rec G 40:8-9 Mr '77
Verdi: La forza del destino. D. Arthur. Am Rec G 40:47-8 Je '77
Verdi: Macbeth. Hi Fi 27:92+ My '77
Verdi: overtures and preludes, complete. J. Oestreich. Am Rec G 40:44 F '77
Verdi: Il Trovatore; London recording conducted by R. Bonynge. K. Furie. Hi Fi 28:104-6 Ja '78
Verdi well-served; two Macbeth recordings. D. Arthur. il Am Rec G 40:40-2 My '77
Wagner: Der fligende Hollander; Die Walküre; recordings by London and Angel. K. Furie. Hi Fi 27:91-2 Ag '77
Wagner in English; Valkyrie. D. Arthur. Am Rec G 40:37-8 Mr '77
Wagner's masters get their due; two new recordings of Meistersinger. D. Hamilton. il Hi Fi 27:89-91 F '77
Wagner's Roman colossus; recording of Rienzi. D. Hamilton. il Hi Fi 27:91-3 Mr '77
Walton: Troilus and Cressida; EMI recording. C. L. Osborne. Hi Fi 28:106-8 Ja '78
Weber-Mahler: Die drei Pintos; RCA Red Seal recording. J. Noble. Hi Fi 27:110+ Jl '77
Weber/Mahler hybrid; Die drei Pintos; Bertini recording. N. F. Karlins. Am Rec G 40:37-9 Jl '77
What might have been: unrecorded Metropolitan Opera performances. J. B. Steane. il Opera N 42:26-9 Ag '77

PHONOGRAPH records—Opera—*Continued*
Who can resist The mother of us all? New World recording. C. L. Osborne. il Hi Fi 27: 92-4 Jl '77
Window on Lully's operatic world; Columbia's recording of Alceste. P. H. Lang. il por Hi Fi 27:95-6 O '77
Winning hand; Montemezzi: L'amore dei tre re. D. Arthur. Am Rec G 41:24-6 N '77
Wolf-Ferrari: Il segreto di Susanna. R. V. Lucano. il Am Rec G 40:45-6 My '77
See also
Phonograph records—Arias
Phonograph records—Gilbert and Sullivan operas

Operetta

Fine French frou-frou; Planquette's Les cloches de Corneville. W. Botsford. Am Rec G 40:35 N '76
Strauss, Johann, Jr. & Sr: Vienna waltzes. W. L. Purcell. Am Rec G 40:38 N '76

Oratorios

Another Messiah. R. V. Lucano. Am Rec G 40: 19-21 Mr '77
Bach: Christmas oratorio, BWV 248; recording. P. Althouse. Am Rec G 41:6-8 D '77
Bach: Christmas oratorio, s. 248; Handel: Messiah; Angel and Sine Qua Non recordings. K. Furie. il Hi Fi 28:90-1 Ja '78
Elgar: The dream of Gerontius. J. Diether. Am Rec G 40:32-3 S '77
Handel: Belshazzar; Telefunken recording. J. Noble. Hi Fi 28:94-7 Ja '78
Handel: Israel in Egypt. R. V. Lucano. Am Rec G 40:24-5 N '76
Handel: Judas Maccabeus. R. V. Lucano. Am Rec G 40:34 F '77
Twenty years of Messiah recordings. R. V. Lucano. il Am Rec G 40:6-9 D '76

Orchestral music

Berio: Nones; Allelujah II; Concerto for two pianos; London Symphony Orchestra. J. Ringo. Am Rec G 40:14-15 Ap '77
Bloch: Symphony for trombone and orchestra; Suite symphonique. W. Simmons. por Am Rec G 40:22-3 D '76
Chabrier; complete orchestral works. W. Curtis. il Am Rec G 40:18-19 Jl '77
Dvorak: The water-sprite, The noonday witch and Symphonic variations; Deutsche Grammophon recording. L. M. Smoley. il Am Rec G 41:28-32 D '77
Heroic voices from pioneer days; W. Mengelberg's 1928 recording of Strauss's Ein Heldenleben on Victrola. R. D. Darrell. pors Hi Fi 27:90-1 Ap '77
Holst: The planets—suite for large orchestra, op. 32. J. Diether. Am Rec G 40:27 N '76
J. S. Bach; Selected works: Fiedler recording. W. Botsford. Am Rec G 40:12-13 Jl '77
Making a dent into Weber. P. Althouse. Am Rec G 41:34-5 N '77
Mussorgsky: Pictures at an exhibition: London Philharmonic Orchestra conducted by J. Pritchard. G. S. Fox. Am Rec G 40:34-5 N '76
Rachmaninoff: Bells, op. 35; Vocalise, op. 34, no. 14. J. Oestreich. Am Rec G 40:31-2 Mr '77
Ravel: Orchestral works. W. D. Curtis. Am Rec G 40:25-6 Ag '77
Real Kurt Weill; London Sinfonietta's DG set of vocal and instrumental works. A. Porter. il por Hi Fi 27:77-9 My '77
Recordings of Edgard Varèse. R. P. Morgan. Hi Fi 27:82-3 F '77
Second time around; works by Brahms performed by the Berlin Philharmonic Orchestra conducted by H. von Karajan. P. L. Althouse. il por Am Rec G 40:24-6 O '77
Seon: old friends on a new label. R. D. Darrell. il Hi Fi 27:108-9 Mr '77
Strauss: Ein Heldenleben, op. 40. G. S. Fox. Am Rec G 40:41 D '76
See also
Phonograph records—Symphonic poems

Organ music

Handel: Concerti for organ and orchestra complete. J. W. Barker. Am Rec G 40:21-2 My '77
Handel: 16 organ concertos. P. Pfunke. por Am Rec G 40:23 Mr '77
Not-so-bland organs of Britain; new Vista releases. S. Cantrell. il Hi Fi 27:95-6 Jl '77

Oriental music

Javanese court gamelan; Shakuhachi, the Japanese flute; Ladakh: Nonesuch recordings. W. L. Purcell. Am Rec G 41:41-2 D '77

Periodicals

See also
American record guide (periodical)

Piano music

Beethoven: Piano sonata no. 23 in F minor op. 57 (Appassionata); Liszt: Piano sonata in B minor; performed by L. Berman. R. Kammerer. Am Rec G 40:14 N '76
Boulez: Piano sonata no. 1; Piano sonata no. 3-Trope; Messiaen: Canteyodjaya; Berio: Rounds; Holliger: Elis. D. W. Moore. il Am Rec G 40:48 My '77
Brahms: Piano concerto no. 1 in D minor; 2 recordings, A. Rubinstein and R. Kerer soloists. G. S. Fox. Am Rec G 40:23-4 S '77
Brahams: Piano trio, op. 8; Intermezzi, op. 117. D. W. Moore. Am Rec G 40:15 Ap '77
Brahms: Three intermezzi, D. Alexeev soloist; Variations and fugue on a theme by Handel, V. Cliburn soloist. D. M. Garvelmann. Am Rec G 40:24-6 S '77
Dvořák plain vs. Dvořák fancified; recordings of G minor piano concerts by S. Richter. H. Goldsmith. por Hi Fi 27:73-4 D '77
Edison recordings of Serge Rachmaninoff. R. R. Wile. Am Rec G 40:11-12 F '77
Ginastera: Piano concerto no. 2, op. 37; Quintet for piano and strings. G. S. Fox. Am Rec G 40:25-6 Je '77
Good survey—but flawed; Piano music in America—vol. 2: 1900-1945. D. Garvelmann. il Am Rec G 40:9-11 My '77
Grand, glorious & unknown: Beach: Concerto for pianoforte and orchestra; Mason: Prelude and fugue for piano and orchestra. D. Garvelmann. Am Rec G 40:17-19 O '77
Haydn: Piano works, v 1, R. Buchbinder soloist. R. Kammerer. Am Rec G 40:36 S '77
How do you like your Liszt? three new recordings of the First Piano Concerto. H. Goldsmith. por Hi Fi 27:95 F '77
Ives: Complete works for solo piano. D. Garvelmann. il Am Rec G 40:16-19 Ag '77
King of pianists; V. Horowitz. S. Lipman. Commentary 63:62-6 My '77
Liszt: Concerto for piano and orchestra no. 1 in E-flat major. D. M. Garvelmann. Am Rec G 40:35-6 D '76
Liszt: Sonata in B minor; Glazounov: Sonata no. 1 in B-flat minor; Aquitane recording. L. Radcliffe. por Am Rec G 41:35-6 D '77
Liszt: Transcendental etudes. D. Garvelmann. il por Am Rec G 40:32-5 D '76
Messiaen: Vingt regards sur l'enfant Jesus. D. Garvelmann. por Am Rec G 40:21-2 Ag '77
Mozart: Piano concerto in C; Haydn: Piano concerto in D. D. Gravelmann. por Am Rec G 40:35 Je '77
Mozart: Piano concerto no. 24 in C minor, K. 491; Piano concerto no. 14 in E-flat major, K. 449. E. Belov. Am Rec G 40:25 Ap '77
Mozart: Piano concertos nos. 14 and 23; Supraphon recording. D. R. Martin. Am Rec G 41: 38-9 D '77
Mussorgsky: Pictures at an exhibition: Scherzo in B flat, performed by Michel Beroff. G. S. Fox. Am Rec G 40:30 Mr '77
Rare treasures from the recent past; recordings from the International Piano Archives. D. Garvelmann; R. Kammerer and E. Richmond. Am Rec G 40:14-20 F '77
Survey for cello & piano; Beethoven's complete cello sonatas; comparison of new and old recordings. D. W. Moore. Am Rec G 40:19-22 O '77
Unknown recordings of Vladimir Horowitz; discography of unreleased recordings; with editorial comment by L. Marcus. C. Alder. pors Hi Fi 28:69-74 Ja '78
Villa-Lobos: Music for piano. D. Gravelmann. Am Rec G 40:49 Je '77

Poetry

See Phonograph records—Spoken records

Preludes (music)

Bach: Eighteen preludes. P. L. Althouse. il Am Rec G 40:10-12 D '76

Rating

Countdown to Monday: charting the top 100; Billboard, Cashbox, and Record World. J. Melanson. il Hi Fi 27:106-9 My '77

Recording

Behind the scenes. See issues of High fidelity and Musical America
Confessions of an allergic producer; producing classical music. J. Culshaw. il Hi Fi 27:22+ N '77
Direct-to-disc: recordings of real performances. H. A. Rodgers. il Hi Fi 27:122-3 Jl '77
Direct-to-disc revolution (?) R. Hodges. Pop Electr 13:16+ Ja '78
Herbie Hancock's fifth incarnation; interview at recording session of new album. H. Hancock. il pors Hi Fi 27:121-3 S '77
Mix to master to mother to disc: manufacturing a record. H. Cummings. il Hi Fi 27:143-5 N '77
On making the first symphonic direct-to-disc LP; excerpt from Concert stage; interview, ed by L. Marcus. L. Maazel. il por Hi Fi 27: 70-2 Jl '77
Resurrecting the Beatles: Star-Club to stereo; phonograph record made from tape of 1962 Hamburg performance. C. Repka. il Hi Fi 27: 101-3 Ag '77

PHONOGRAPH records—Recording—*Continued*
Studio circuit. D. Heckman. il Hi Fi 27:134-6 F '77
Studio circuit. F. Miller. il Hi Fi 27:127-30 Mr '77
Those limited-edition superdiscs. H. A. Rodgers. il Hi Fi 27:64-6 D '77
Through the microphone. R. Hodges. il Pop Electr 11:22+ Ap '77
Why records should never be flat. J. Culshaw. Hi Fi 27:19-20 O '77

Anecdotes, facetiae, satire, etc.

Toward a super-refined music reproducer. A. Kazdin. il Hi Fi 28:76-8 Ja '78

History

Edison recordings of Serge Rachmaninoff. R. R. Wile. Am Rec G 40:11-12 F '77
Muzio on Edison discs. P. L. Miller. Am Rec G 40:13 F '77
100 years of recording:
Acoustic era; with reproductions of paintings by J. Jonson. R. Long. Hi Fi 27:69-72 Ap '77
Cylinder era; with reproductions of paintings by J. Jonson. Hi Fi 27:67-70 F '77
Electrical era; with reproductions of paintings by J. Jonson. R. Long. Hi Fi 27:73-6 Jl '77
Electrical recording: the convert revolution. R. D. Darrell. il Hi Fi 27:79-85 Jl '77
Microgroove era; with reproductions of paintings by J. Jonson. R. Long. il Hi Fi 27:81-5 O '77
Recording that ended World War II; attempt to stop broadcast of recording of Hirohito's surrender speech; with text of speech. F. Bowers. il Hi Fi 27:87-90 O '77

Study and teaching

Learning to make records at Eastman. J. Arthur. il por Hi Fi 27:MA18-20 Je '77

Reissues

Heroic voices from pioneer days; W. Mengelberg's 1928 recording of Strauss's Ein Heldenleben on Victrola. R. D. Darrell. pors Hi Fi 27:90-1 Ap '77
Quintessence classical recordings. G. S. Fox. Am Rec G 41:43-7 D '77
Weingartner, Kleiber, De Sabata: a matter of record; symphony recordings. H. Goldsmith. pors Hi Fi 27:94-6 S '77

Religious music

Beethoven and Mozart: Masses in C; Bruckner's Te Deum. P. C. Pfunke. Am Rec G 40:20-1 S '77
Berlioz: Te deum; Columbia recording. J. W. Barker. il Am Rec G 41:21-2 D '77
Two settings for the same text; Bruckner: Te Deum; Verdi: Te Deum. P. L. Althouse. Am Rec G 40:19-20 Je '77
Vivaldi: various sacred works. P. L. Miller. Am Rec G 40:46+ O '77
See also
Phonograph records—Church music

Renaissance music

David Munrow: the art of the Netherlands; Seraphim recording. Hi Fi 27:92-4 Ag '77
Dufay: Fifteen songs; Transformations. W. Purcell. Am Rec G 40:28-30 S '77
Instruments of the Middle Ages and Renaissance; Vanguard recording. J. W. Barker. Am Rec G 41:16-18 D '77
Morales; Selected works. P. Althouse. Am Rec G 40:22-3 Ag '77

Requiems

Berlioz: Requiem, op. 5; two recordings. Hi Fi 27:93-4 Ap '77
Bruckner: Requiem in D minor. J. Diether. Am Rec G 40:19-20 N '76
Mozart: requiem mass. P. Althouse. il Am Rec G 40:27-8 Mr '77

Rhapsody (music)

Liszt: Hungarian rhapsodies nos. 1-16 and no. 19. R. Kammerer. Am Rec G 40:28 N '76

Rhythm and blues (songs, etc)

See Phonograph records—Rock music (songs, etc)

Rock music (songs, etc.)

Andrew Gold gets into the picture. por Hi Fi 27:146-7 F '77
The Band: Islands. il Hi Fi 27:113-14 My '77
Beach Boys: The Beach Boys love you. il Hi Fi 27:114 My '77
Beatles at the Hollywood Bowl; Beatles live! at the Star Club in Hamburg, Germany; 1962. S. Sutherland. Hi Fi 27:111 Ag '77
Billy Joel: up from Piano man. S. Elliott. pors Hi Fi 28:110-13+ Ja '78
Boys in the band + 2: a 1977 retrospective; rock music trends; symposium. il Hi Fi 28:117-21 Ja '78
Discussions. T. P. Lippincott. See occasional issues of Senior scholastic including World week
Dwight Twilley Band: British rockabilly comes of age; Twilley don't mind. K. Emerson. il Hi Fi 27:154 N '77
Elvis Costello: new wave rock classicist; My aim is true. S. Sutherland. por Hi Fi 27:138 D '77
Emerson, Lake & Palmer—gnomes + gongs + tanks; with discography. J. S. Roberts. il Hi Fi 27:121-4 O '77
Emerson, Lake and Palmer; Works. W. Simmons. Am Rec G 40:33-4 S '77
Foreigner: sixties rock yields seventies success. il Hi Fi 27:152-4 Jl '77
Former Traffic leader travels the solo route; Steve Winwood. S. Sutherland. por Hi Fi 27:140 S '77
Gong show; Shamal. il Sr Schol 109:35 Ap 21 '77
Graham Parker: born to stand and fight; Stick to me. T. Goldstein. il por Hi Fi 28:128 Ja '78
Gregg Allman: the fink has soul; Gregg Allman Band: playin' up a storm. L. Baines. por Hi Fi 27:110 Ag '77
Herbie Hancock's fifth incarnation; interview at recording session of new album. H. Hancock. il pors Hi Fi 27:121-3 S '77
Key to Stevie Wonder. D. J. Evearitt. Chr Today 21:30 F 18 '77
Kinks: Sleepwalker. il Hi Fi 27:115+ My '77
Mad, mad world of rock 'n' records. J. L. Collier. Read Digest 111:13+ O '77
Pink Floyd: Animals. Hi Fi 27:118+ My '77
Pop/Rock. il Hi Fi 27:143 Ap; 122 My; 145 S '77
R&B. J. S. Roberts. il Hi Fi 27:145 Mr; 130 Je; 160 N '77; 28-134 Ja '78
The Rumour: up from pub rock; Max. S. Sutherland. il Hi Fi 27:150 O '77
Steely Dan sans sarcasm. S. Sutherland. il pors Hi Fi 27:139-42 N '77
Van Morrison: A period of transition. por Hi Fi 27:118-19 Je '77

Sacred music

See Phonograph records—Religious music

Sonatas

Bach: Goldberg variations; Sonata in B-flat major for clarinet and piano. E. Richmond. Am Rec G 40:14+ O '77
Bach: sonatas for flute and harpsichord. J. Barker. Am Rec G 40:10-11 Mr '77
Brahms: Sonatas for cello and piano: nos. 1 and 2. W. D. Curtis. Am Rec G 40:14 Je '77
Foote: Sonata in G minor for violin & piano; Beach: Sonata in A minor for violin & piano. W. Simmons. Am Rec G 40:27-8 O '77
Handel: complete sonatas for wind instrument and basso continuo. J. W. Barker. Am Rec G 40:35 F '77
Of fiddles and fiddlers (and friends): Bach's violin-and-harpsichord sonatas. S. Fleming. Hi Fi 27:90-1 Mr '77
Powell: Sonata Teutonica. W. Simmons. Am Rec G 40:24-5 Ag '77
Quantz: Flute sonata no. 1 in A minor; Flute sonata no. 2 in B-flat major; Dutilleux: Sonatine; Muller-Zurich: Capriccio. J. Ringo Am Rec G 40:35-6 N '76
Reviews of records: Hindemith: The complete sonatas for brass and piano. W. Hilse. Mus Q 63:144-6 Ja '77

Songs

Fauré: songs; two recordings by Connoisseur Society and Musical Heritage. D. Hamilton. Hi Fi 27:80+ Ag '77
Haitink's Mahler: much to commend; Des Knaben Wunderhorn. J. Diether. il Am Rec G 41:21-2+ N '77
Ives. P. L. Miller. Am Rec G 40:36-7 F '77
Kirsten Flagstad sings from Norway. P. L. Miller. Am Rec G 40:47 F '77
Mahler: Des Knaben Wunderhorn; Philips recording. A. Chipman. Hi Fi 27:94 D '77
Rachmaninoff: songs. F. Crociata. Am Rec G 40:38 F '77
Recordings of songs about Alice. J. Walsh. il Hobbies 82:35-6+ O; 35-6 N; 35-6+ D '77; 35-6 Ja '78
Schumann: Frauenliebe und Leben, op. 42; Liederkreis; Jessye Norman's recording. P. L. Miller. Am Rec G 40:31-3 Jl '77
Songs of Strauss and Wolf. C. T. Veilleux. Am Rec G 40:46 Mr '77
Wolf: Songs, vol. 3; Deutsche Grammophon recording. D. Hamilton. Hi Fi 27:103-4+ D '77

Sounds

Music; sensuous sounds; Environments albums. S. Ditlea. il Am Home 80:19 F '77

Spoken records

Caedmon, at 25, is expanding record sales in book outlets. J. Giusto. il Pub W 212:52-3 O 24 '77
Master storyteller in search of a voice; Argo recordings of Chaucer's Knight's tale and Pardoner's tale. A. T. Gaylord. Hi Fi 27:74-6 Je '77

PHONOGRAPH records—Spoken records—*Cont.*
Recording that ended World War II; attempt to stop broadcast of recording of Hirohito's surrender speech; with text of speech. F. Bowers. il Hi Fi 27:87-90 O '77
Spoken words. Am Rec G 40:49-50 N; 54-5 D '76
See also
Talking books

String ensemble music

Dvorák: String quartet no. 6 in F major (American), op. 96; String quintet no. 3 in E flat major, op. 97. J. Diether. Am Rec G 40:20-1 N '76

String quartet music

Bartok: Six string quartets. D. W. Moore. il Am Rec G 40:12-14 Ap '77
Beethoven: the late quartets; performed by Quartetto Italiano. E. Belov. Am Rec G 41: 11-12 N '77
For modern strings. L. M. Smoley. Am Rec G 41:40-1 N '77
Persichetti perspective; String quartets nos. 1-4. W. Simmons. Am Rec G 40:6-8 My '77
Reviews of records: George Rochberg: String Quartet no. 1, Concord Quartet. B. Archibald. il Mus Q 62:613-15 O '76
Reviews of records: Martin Boykan: String Quartet no. 1 Contemporary Quartet. Elaine Barkin: String Quartet (1969) American Quartet. E. Cory. il Mus Q 62:616-20 O '76
Segerstam: String quartets nos. 4-7. P. Rapoport. Am Rec G 40:33-4 Jl '77
Shostakovich: Quartet no. 8 in C minor, op. 110; Quartet no. 15 in E-flat minor, op. 144. W. Simmons. por Am Rec G 40:40-1 D '76

Suites (music)

Sibelius: King Christian II suite; Swanwhite suite; Andante festivo. E. Richmond. Am Rec G 40:35-6 Mr '77
Sibelius: Lemminkäinen suite; Karelia suite. W. L. Purcell. il Am Rec G 40:37 My '77

Symphonic poems

Franck: Psyché. J. Ringo. Am Rec G 40:21 N '76
Historic reissues; Strauss, R: Ein Heldenleben. G. S. Fox. Am Rec G 40:5-6+ Ag '77

Symphonies

Again the mighty nine; Beethoven: The nine symphonies. G. S. Fox and M. Cooper. Am Rec G 40:23-5 F '77
All about Alwyn; Symphonies nos. 4 and 5. R. Tiedman. il por Am Rec G 40:4+ S '77
Beethoven: Symphonies (9); Fidelio overture, Op. 72c; Philips recording conducted by W. Mengelberg. H. Goldsmith. il por Hi Fi 27:78-80 D '77
Beethoven: symphonies (9); Philips recording. H. Goldsmith. Hi Fi 27:99-100 Jl '77
Beethoven: Symphony no. 6 in F major op. 68; Symphony no. 7 in A major op. 92. J. Waxman. Am Rec G 40:15 D '76
Beethoven: Symphony no. 7. G. S. Fox. Am Rec G 40:11-12 Je '77
Brahms by Böhm; 4 symphonies. P. L. Althouse. Am Rec G 40:26-9 F '77
Brahms: six symphonies and other orchestral works recorded on Vanguard. J. R. Oestreich. Am Rec G 41:22-4 D '77
Brahms: symphony no. 4 in E minor op. 98. J. Waxman. Am Rec G 40:12-13 Mr '77
Brian: Symphony no 6, sinfonia tragica; Symphony no 16. R. Tiedman. Am Rec G 40:16-18 Je '77
Bruckner: Symphony no. 4 in E flat major. S. Clark. Am Rec G 40:18-19 Je '77
Bruckner tradition moves on; recordings of Symphonies nos. 4, 7 and 8 conducted by Karl Böhm and Kurt Masur. A. Chipman. il Hi Fi 27:93-4 N '77
Considering Carl Nielsen: symphonies no. 1-6. S. Clark. Am Rec G 40:27-30 My '77
D'Indy; Symphony on a French mountain air. Franck: Symphonic variations and Les djinns. J. Waxman. Am Rec G 40:21-2 Je '77
Dvořák: Symphony no. 7 in D minor, op. 70. J. R. Oestreich. por Am Rec G 40:18-20 My '77
Elgar: Symphony no. 2 in E flat, London Philharmonic Orchestra conducted by Sir Adrian Boult. J. Diether. Am Rec G 40:27 O '77
Fine new Mahler Ninth; Giulini recording; with discography of major works of Bruckner and Mahler. J. Diether. il por Am Rec G 40:24-6 Jl '77
Franck: Symphony in D minor; Symphonic variation for piano and orchestra. J. Waxman. Am Rec G 40:24 Je '77
Furtwangler on Brahms; Symphony no. 1 in C minor, op. 68. G. S. Fox. Am Rec G 40:16-17 N '76
Haydn: Symphonies; Barenboim and Previn discs. J. W. Barker. Am Rec G 40:22-3 Jl '77
Ives: Symphony no. 4; Central Park in the dark, conducted by S. Ozawa. W. D. Curtis. Am Rec G 40:32-4 O '77
Kubelik and the mighty nine; Beethoven symphonies. G. S. Fox. Am Rec G 40:16-17 D '76
Magnificent Bruckner Eighth. S. Clark. por Am Rec G 40:6-9 Ap '77
Mahler: Das Lied von der Erde. J. Diether. Am Rec G 40:21-2 Ap '77
Mahler: Symphony no. 3. G. S. Fox. Am Rec G 40:25-6 My '77
Mahler: Symphony no 4 in G; Bruckner: Symphony no 3 in D minor. G. S. Fox. Am Rec G 40:22-3 Ap '77
Mozart: Symphonies nos. 22, 24-27, 39, 40. C. T. Veilleux. Am Rec G 40:34-5 Je '77
Mozart: Symphonies nos, 23, 28, 30, 31 and 38, performed by the Concertgebouw Orchestra under J. Krips. L. M. Smoley. Am Rec G 40: 41-2+ S '77
Music of Allan Pettersson. P. Rapoport. Am Rec G 40:23-4 Ag '77
New view of Shostakovich's somber Fourteenth. R. S. Brown. Hi Fi 27:71-2 Je '77
Schubert; new recordings of symphonies nos. 5, 8 and 9. Hi Fi 27:114+ O '77
Schubert: Symphonies no. 5 in B flat; no. 8 in B minor. J. R. Oestreich and P. Althouse. Am Rec G 40:34-5 My '77
Shostakovich: Symphony no. 14. J. Diether. Am Rec G 40:27-9 Ag '77
Sibelius: Symphony no. 1, conducted by P. Berglund. C. Bauman. Am Rec G 40:55 O '77
Sibelius: Symphony no. 1 in E minor, conducted by P. Berglund. E. Richmond. Am Rec G 41:31-2 N '77
Sibelius: Symphony no. 2 in D, Boston Symphony Orchestra, conducted by C. Davis. J. W. Barker. por Am Rec G 40:41-2 O '77
Tchaikovsky: Six symphonies and Manfred conducted by M. Rostropovich. J. R. Oestreich. pors Am Rec G 41:14-16 D '77
Tchaikovsky: Symphony no. 6 in B minor, Op. 74 Pathetique, Symphony no. 1 in G minor Op. 13 winter dreams. J. Waxman. il Am Rec G 40:42-4 F '77
Válek: Symphonies nos. 8 and 9. B. Pernick. Am Rec G 40:45-6 O '77
Weingartner, Kleiber, De Sabata: a matter of record; symphony recordings reissued. H. Goldsmith. pors Hi Fi 27:94-6 S '77

Test records

Easy way to test phono cartridges. L. Feldman. il Radio-Electr 49:51+ Ja '78

Trios, Instrumental

Haydn: Piano trios H xv, no. 13 in C minor, no. 16 in D, no. 17 in F. E. Belov. il Am Rec G 40:22-3 My '77

Trumpet music

Trumpet shall sound. J. Barker. Am Rec G 40:40 Mr '77

Violin music

Of fiddles and fiddlers (and friends): William Sidney Mounts's Cradle of Harmony. I. Lowens. il Hi Fi 27:89-90 Mr '77
Szymanowski: Violin concerto no. 1, op. 35; Prokofiev: Violin concerto no. 1, op. 19. W. Simmons. Am Rec G 40:43 D '76

Vocal music

Exciting voice; J. Gadski; Club 99 recordings. P. L. Miller. por Am Rec G 40:19-21 Jl '77
Real Kurt Weill; London Sinfonietta's DG set of vocal and instrumental works. A. Porter. il por Hi Fi 27:77-9 My '77
Vocal/choral/etc. Am Rec G 40:49 N; 55-6 D 76; 39-40 Mr; 28-30 Ap; 47-8 My 77
See also
Phonograph records—Cantatas
Phonograph records—Songs

Wind instruments

Gorgeous brass: New York brass choir. J. Ringo. Am Rec G 40:40-1 Mr '77

Woodwind instruments

And in a similar vein; Avant-garde woodwind quintet in the U.S.A; Vox recording. W. Simmons. Am Rec G 41:51-3 D '77

PHONOGRAPH records as gifts
Christmas special. M. Latour. Mademoiselle 83: 28+ D '77
Classics shopping list. S. Ditlea. Am Home 80: 12 D '77
Give music; Christmas gifts. D. Sargent. Vogue 167:98+ D '77
Indigenous gifts. N. Hentoff. Nation 225:702 D 24 '77
Musical offerings. H. Saal. il Newsweek 90:112+ D 12 '77
Turning to the classical side. W. Bender. il Time 110:64+ D 12 '77

PHOSPHATASES
See also
Adenosine triphosphatase

PHOSPHATE mines and mining
See also
Strip mining

PHOSPHATES
See also
Cytidine phosphates
Soils—Phosphorus content
PHOSPHATES in detergents. See Detergents
PHOSPHATIDES
Topological asymmetry of phospholipids in membranes. L. D. Bergelson and L. I. Barsukov. bibl il Science 197:224-30 Jl 15 '77
PHOSPHATIDYLINOSITOL
Phospholipid derivative of cytosine arabinoside and its conversion to phosphatidylinositol by animal tissue. C. R. H. Raetz and others. bibl il Science 196:303-5 Ap 15 '77
PHOSPHOLIPIDS. See Phosphatides
PHOSPHORESCENCE
See also
Bioluminescence
PHOSPHORUS nuclear magnetic resonance. See Nuclear magnetic resonance
PHOSVEL. See Insecticides
PHOTOACOUSTIC spectroscopy. See Spectrum analysis
PHOTOBACTERIUM. See Bacteria, Luminous
PHOTOCELLS. See Photoelectric cells
PHOTOCHEMICAL smog. See Smog
PHOTOCHEMISTRY
Carrier-mediated photodiffusion membranes. J. S. Schultz. bibl il Science 197:1177-9 S 16 '77
Photophysics and photochemistry. V. S. Letokhov. bibl il Phys Today 30:23-32 My '77
Psoralen-DNA photoreaction: controlled production of mono- and diadducts with nanosecond ultraviolet laser pulses. B. H. Johnston and others. bibl il Science 197:906-8 Ag 26 '77
Sunlight-induced bromate formation in chlorinated seawater. D. L. Macalady and others. bibl il Science 195:1335-7 Mr 25 '77
See also
Photosynthesis
PHOTOCOPYING law. See Copyright
PHOTOCOPYING machines and processes
AAP seeks bids to run copy payments center. S. Wagner. Pub W 212:28 Jl 11 '77
Article-copying service by NTIS takes off. H. E. Rosenfeld. Wilson Lib Bull 52:284 D '77
Jill Lynne; use of color copiers. A. Williams. il por Pop Phot 80:88-91+ Mr '77
NTIS plan draws fire at CONTU photocopying hearing. S. Wagner. Pub W 211:252+ Ja 24 '77
Photocopiers: new ones offer more for the money. L. Lane. il Farm J 101:M6 Ja '77
See also
Addressograph Multigraph Corporation
Libraries—Photocopying services
Xerox Corporation
PHOTODECOMPOSITION of pesticides. See Pesticides—Decomposition
PHOTODIODES. See Diodes
PHOTOELECTRIC cells
Techniques tomorrow; photocells. B. Sherman. Mod Phot 41:8+ Je '77
See also
Solar batteries

Control use

Build the Light Genie. M. Graden. il Pop Electr 11:57-9 Ap '77
PHOTOELECTRIC multipliers
Microchannel plates. B. Leskovar. bibl il Phys Today 30:42-9 N '77
PHOTOELECTRON spectroscopy. See Spectrum analysis
PHOTOELECTRONIC devices
See also
Photoresistors
PHOTOEMISSION spectroscopy. See Spectrum analysis
PHOTOGRAMS
Negatives from nature. K. Thomas. il Design (US) 78:12-13 Summ '77
Tips for summer photo fun; photograms and sungrams. G. Kolasa. Camp Mag 49:12-13 My '77
PHOTOGRAPH; drama. See Shange, N.
PHOTOGRAPHERS
First photographers of the Grand Canyon. G. Simmons and V. Simmons. il Am West 14:34-8+ Jl '77
Fresh visions through the camera's eye; executives. M. Wellemeyer. il Fortune 96:55+ N '77
Interview with Imogen Cunningham; ed by B. Conrad, 3d; excerpt from Interview with master photographers. I. Cunningham. il Art in Am 65:42-5+ My '77
New talent series. A. Grundberg. il por Mod Phot 41:140-1 N '77
See also
Avedon, R.
Benson, H.
Callahan, H.
Cohen, M.
De Meyer, A. Baron
Egar
Feininger, A.
Funk, R.
Gutmann, J.
Haas, E.
Heinecken, R.
Hine, L.
Jackson, W. H.
Laughlin, C. J.
Maxim, L.
Mole, A.
Penn, I.
Photography as a profession
Struss, K.
Vishniac, R.
Weister, G. M.
Weston, E.
Winogrand, G.
Women photographers

Applications for positions

See Applications for positions
PHOTOGRAPHERS, French
See also
Atget, E.
Nadar
PHOTOGRAPHERS, Japanese
See also
Domon, K.
Kawakami, R
PHOTOGRAPHERS agents
Protechniques; W. Hayum of Photo Media Ltd. E. Meyers. il por Pop Phot 80:68+ Ap '77
PHOTOGRAPHIC auctions. See Auctions
PHOTOGRAPHIC batteries. See Electric batteries
PHOTOGRAPHIC books. See Picture books
PHOTOGRAPHIC chemistry
Ed Scully on color; mixing and storing color processing kits. E. Scully. il Mod Phot 41:55-6+ Je '77
Offbeat. N. Rothschild. il Pop Phot 81:12+ S '77
See also
Photography—Developing and developers
Photography—Processing
PHOTOGRAPHIC copying. See Photography—Copying
PHOTOGRAPHIC enlargers. See Photography—Enlargers and enlarging
PHOTOGRAPHIC equipment. See Photography—Apparatus and supplies
PHOTOGRAPHIC exhibitions. See Photography—Exhibitions
PHOTOGRAPHIC films. See Photography—Films
PHOTOGRAPHIC filters. See Light filters
PHOTOGRAPHIC industry
Photo-electronics; early manufacturers of electronic flash units. E. Farber. il Pop Phot 80:62+ Ap '77
See also
Bell & Howell Company
Eastman Kodak Company
GAF Corporation
Polaroid Corporation

Marketing

Photo chain's fuzzy picture; PCA International, Inc. il Bus W p69-70 N 28 '77

Canada

Schwalberg at large; Ernst Leitz Canada. B. Schwalberg. por Pop Phot 81:52+ Ag '77
Techniques tomorrow: Leitz's Canadian operation. B. Sherman. Mod Phot 41:52+ Ag '77

Japan

Special report from Japan. A. Goldsmith. il Pop Phot 81:90-1+ S '77

Russia

From Russia with lens. J. S. Socha. il Mod Phot 41:109-10+ N '77
PHOTOGRAPHIC lenses. See Lenses, Photographic
PHOTOGRAPHIC literature
See also
Photography—Bibliography
Publishers and publishing—Photographic literature
PHOTOGRAPHIC Marketing Association show, Chicago. See Photography—Exhibitions
PHOTOGRAPHIC meters
See also
Exposure meters
PHOTOGRAPHIC optics
Techniques tomorrow; speckle, an image annoyance. Mod Phot 41:28+ Mr '77
See also
Lenses, Photographic
PHOTOGRAPHIC paper
As I see it; views of famous photographers. D. Vestal. por Pop Phot 81:46+ D '77
Editorial; let's save the fibre-base papers. A. Goldsmith. por Pop Phot 80:10 Ap '77
Films and paper. D. Leavitt. il Pop Phot 80:92+ Je '77
Great printing-paper crunch. D. Vestal. Pop Phot 80:91+ Ap '77
Tools & techniques; RC papers. C. W. Kennedy. il Pop Phot 81:28+ D '77
PHOTOGRAPHIC processing. See Photography—Processing
PHOTOGRAPHIC slides. See Slides (photography)

PHOTOGRAPHIC supplies. See Photography—Apparatus and supplies

PHOTOGRAPHIC supplies industry. See Photographic industry

PHOTOGRAPHS

Family of woman: 5 years in focus; comp by H. Lyons and B. Richer. il Ms 6:56-61 Jl '77

Friendly way to put photography to work; family photographs transferred to fabric. il Sunset 159:124-5 D '77

New talent series. A. Grundberg. il por Mod Phot 41:140-1 N '77

Photography '77: a stocktaking. P. Patton. il Art in Am 65:34-6 Ja '77

See also

Ambrotypes

Daguerreotypes

Slides (photography)

also subhead Photographs under various subjects, e.g. Insects—Photographs

Collections

Romance of old photos. D. Davis and M. Rourke. il Newsweek 89:40-3 F 21 '77

See also

Libraries—Photographic collections

Collectors and collecting

See Photography—Collectors and collecting

Conservation and restoration

Ed Scully on color; permanence of color images. E. Scully. Mod Phot 41:8+ My '77

Evaluation

See Photography—Criticism, interpretation, etc.

Exhibitions

See Photography—Exhibitions

Marketing

Markets & careers. H. Chapnick. See issues of Popular photography

Seeing pictures; K. Townend method of selling prints. J. Scully. il Mod Phot 41:8+ S '77

Traveler's camera; marketing travel pictures. C. Purcell. il Pop Phot 80:14+ Je '77

View point; photographic auctioneer and dealer; interview, ed by J. Deschin. D. Stulz. il por Pop Phot 81:117+ Ag '77

Mounting

See Photographs—Trimming, mounting, etc.

Reproducing

See Photography—Copying

Trimming, mounting, etc.

Color darkroom; dry-mounting color prints. B. Nadler. il Pop Phot 81:94+ O '77

Last word on mounting prize photos. A. Grundberg. il Mod Phot 41:163 N '77

PHOTOGRAPHS, Forgery of. See Forgery of works of art

PHOTOGRAPHY

How a camera helped a teenager discover herself. il por Sr Schol 110:6 D 1 '77

How to. See issues of Modern photography

My return to the view camera. L. Jacobs, Jr. il por Pop Phot 81:138-41+ D '77

Perspectives of Penn; interview, ed by O. Edwards. I. Penn. il N Y Times Mag p 18-19+ S 4 '77

Photography (cont) M. R. Weiss. Sat R 4:44-5+ Jl 23; 60-1 Ag 6; 5:40-1 O 15 '77

Pop photo snapshots. See issues of Popular photography

The street. . . M. O'Grady. il Mod Phot 41:84-9 My '77

Through the viewfinder. E. H. Ortner. See issues of Popular science

Tools & techniques. C. W. Kennedy. See issues of Popular photography

What's what. See issues of Modern photography

Why photography now? P. C. Bunnell. New Repub 177:25-7 O 29 '77

See also

Ambrotypes

Art and photography

Astronomical photography

Color photography

Computers—Photographic use

Creative photography

Daguerreotypes

Electronics in photography

Electrophotography

Lenses, Photographic

Macrophotography

Microphotography

Motion picture photography

Nature photography

Photograms

Photographers

Photomicrography

Slides (photography)

Space photography

Travel photography

United States—Centennial celebrations, etc.—Photographs and photography

Women photographers

Apparatus and supplies

Accessories. N. Rothschild. il Pop Phot 80:129-30 Je '77

Behind the scenes. See issues of Modern photography

Easiest closeup system ever! support device for object photographed. H. Keppler. il Mod Phot 41:80-3 Mr '77

Ed Scully on color; image-modifying attachments. E. Scully. Mod Phot 41:93-4+ O '77

Good grief! More gadgets. J. Schneider. il Mod Phot 41:110+ Ap '77

How to. See issues of Modern photography

Just out. J. P. Fesce. See issues of Popular photography

Keep those film cans! L. O. Rexrode. il Pop Phot 81:258 D '77

Lens tissue papers! J. Schneider. il Mod Phot 41:158-61 N '77

New wave of super dupers; Elinchrom slide duplicator. il Mod Phot 41:73 Ag '77

Nuts & bolts; packing photo gear. B. Pierce. por Pop Phot 80:22+ Mr '77

Photo technology: the way we were in 1937. B. Schwalberg. Pop Phot 80:80+ My '77

Schwalberg at large; viewfinder display. B. Schwalberg. Pop Phot 81:56+ D '77

Shop talk; Macbeth Color Checker. N. Goldberg. il Pop Phot 81:12+ Jl '77

Shop talk; using the Macbeth Color Checker to test electronic flash. N. Goldberg. il Pop Phot 81:16+ Ag '77

Tools & techniques. C. W. Kennedy. See issues of Popular photography

Well traveled camera: equipment for photographing antiquities. H. Keppler. il Mod Phot 41:33+ O '77

What's what. See issues of Modern photography

See also

Astronomical photography—Apparatus and supplies

Blinds (camouflage)

Camera bags, cases, etc.

Camera supports

Camera tripods

Cameras

Electric lamps, Photoflash

Exposure meters

Lenses, Photographic

Libraries—Photographic collections

Light filters

Photography—Electronic equipment

Photography—Enlargers and enlarging

Photography—Processing—Apparatus and supplies

Exhibitions

See Photography—Exhibitions

Maintenance and repair

See also

Camera repairmen

Testing

Modern tests. See issues of Modern photography

Bibliography

Annuals: some come loaded, some late, some lethargic. il Mod Phot 41:78-9 S '77

Book reviews in brief. See occasional issues of Popular photography

Books (cont) il Pop Phot 80:72+ My; 81:48+ Jl '77

Books in review. See occasional issues of Modern photography

Images and ideologies. G. Thornton. Art N 76:56+ N '77

Special section: photography books. Art in Am 65:31-7+ N '77

Time exposure; reference books on photographica. E. S. Lothrop, Jr. il Pop Phot 81:58+ Ag '77

Business methods

See Photography, Commercial

Cold weather conditions

Capturing winter with your camera. P. Miller. il Mech Illus 73:48-9 F '77

Collectors and collecting

Collectors beware! Which of these ambrotypes are fake? R. Busch. il Pop Phot 80:110-11+ My '77

Fine art of collecting photographs; excerpt from Collecting photographs: a guide to the new art boom. L. Dennis and L. Dennis. il Horizon 19:80-5 My '77

Greening of the black-and-white:

At the auctions. M. R. Weiss. il Sat R 4:32-4+ Ap 2 '77

Old photographs don't just fade away. W. Rodger. il Hobbies 81:152-3+ F; 82:152-3 Mr; 151-3 My '77

So you want to begin collecting photographs? excerpt from Collecting photographs: a guide to the new art boom. L. Dennis and L. Dennis il Pop Phot 81:87-9+ S '77

See also

Photographs—Collections

PHOTOGRAPHY—*Continued*

Competitions

Horticulture magazine's first annual photography contest. il Horticulture 55:34-43 N '77
1977 Scholastic Awards. il Sr Schol 109:9-12+ My 19 '77
Prizewinning photographs from the 1977 Natural History Photographic Competition. A. M. Cunningham. il Natur Hist 86:45-63 bibl(p 116) Ag '77
Seeing pictures; White House News Photographers Association competition. il Mod Phot 41:25+ My '77
What's happening to the picture press? Pictures of the Year photojournalism competition. A. Goldsmith. il Pop Phot 81:89-91+ Jl '77
Winners of National wildlife's annual photo contest. il Nat Wildlife 15:24-33 Ap '77
Winners: Redbook's fourth annual photography contest. Redbook 149:63+ Je '77
See also
Astronomical photography—Competitions

Conferences

Seeing pictures; views of professional photographers at the 21st Annual Wilson Hicks Conference. J. Scully. il Mod Phot 41:10+ Je '77

Copying

Instant pictures. W. Andrews and D. L. Miller. il Mod Phot 41:33 Jl; 29+ Ag; 64+ O '77
See also
Slides (photography)—Copying

Criticism, interpretation, etc.

Editors' pix and potshots. J. Scully and D. L. Miller. il Mod Phot 41:84-93 Ap '77
Seeing pictures. J. Scully. See issues of Modern photography

Darkroom technique

See Photography—Processing

Darkrooms

See Photography—Studios and darkrooms

Developing and developers

David Vestal's photo workbook: step-by-step black and white developing. D. Vestal. Pop Phot 81:83-4 Jl '77
Nuts & bolts; diluting D-76 with water. B. Pierce. Pop Phot 81:36+ Ag '77
Tools & techniques; ASA 400 films and general-purpose developers. C. W. Kennedy. il Pop Phot 81:64+ S '77

Dictionaries and encyclopedias

Encyclopedia of practical photography. L Mercier. il Pub W 213:36-7 Ja 2 '78

Drying (films and prints)

Hang it all! RC paper quick dried efficiently. A. Adair and M. Adair. il Mod Phot 41:112 My '77

Economic aspects

Protechniques; printing costs. E. Meyers. il Pop Phot 81:116+ Ag '77

Electronic equipment

All slaves are not created equal! P. White and J. Schneider. il Mod Phot 41:92-5+ F '77
Bounce light: the flash that flatters. D. Sagarin. il Pop Mech 147:198+ Ap '77
Build a digital camera shutter timer. R. S. Hedin. il Pop Electr 12:59+ Ag '77
Electronic flash. M. Frank. il Pop Phot 81:122+ Jl '77
Electronic flash units. il Consumer Rep 42:292-7 My '77
Instant photography; Kodak instant-flash units. D. Leavitt. il por Pop Phot 81:68+ D '77
Keppler on the SLR; flash units designed for SLRs. H. Keppler. il Mod Phot 41:60+ Ap '77
Lab report:
Sunpak Auto flash units. M. A. Frank. il Pop Phot 81:109-13+ Ag '77
Vivitar 283 flash. M. Frank. il Pop Phot 80:122-5+ Ap '77
Nuts & bolts; small flash units. B. Pierce. il Pop Phot 81:24+ O '77
Offbeat; electronic-flash units. N. Rothschild. Pop Phot 80:17+ Ap '77
Photo-electronics:
Synch-cord testing device. E. Farber. il por Pop Phot 81:80+ D '77
Phototronics. J. Bailey. il por Mod Phot 41:70+ D '77
Want flash-in-the-sky? Reach up and out with sure-footed Soligors. il Mod Phot 41:81 S '77
See also
Camera shutters—Control

History

Photo-electronics; beginnings of electronic flash. E. Farber. il por Pop Phot 80:8+ Mr '77

Testing

Shop talk; using the Macbeth Color Checker to test electronic flash. N. Goldberg. il Pop Phot 81:16+ Ag '77

Enlargers and enlarging

Add voltage regulation to a color photo enlarger. D. W. Schneider. il Pop Electr 12:63-5 N '77
Color darkroom; choosing an enlarger. B. Nadler. Pop Phot 80:32+ F '77
Kids and kameras: CV horizontal enlarger. D. Cyr. il Pop Phot 81:51+ Ag '77
Modern tests:
Beseler dichro 67 colorhead. il Mod Phot 41:170+ N '77
Beseler 67C enlarger. il Mod Phot 41:108-9 F '77
Nikor System 6 x 7 color enlarger. il Mod Phot 41:146 O '77
Schwalberg at large; prototype enlarger designed by E. J. Coppage. B. Schwalberg. il por Pop Phot 81:48+ S '77
View from Kramer; Vivitar VI enlarger. A. Kramer. il Mod Phot 41:12+ My '77

Equipment

See Photography—Apparatus and supplies

Exhibitions

Bad and the beautiful; works of I. Penn and Weegee. M. Stevens. il por Newsweek 90:72-3 S 26 '77
Bellocq's girls: exhibition at New York's Light Gallery. D. Davis. il Newsweek 89:89 Mr 14 '77
Big business: photography's newest patron; sponsorship of exhibitions. M. R. Weiss. il Sat R 4:44-5+ Jl 23 '77
Big show ends; PMA trade show. il Mod Phot 41:76-7 S '77
Big show, little news; Photographic Marketing Association show in Chicago. il Mod Phot 41:120-1 Je '77
Chicago's PMA show. il Pop Phot 81:122-5+ Jl '77
Color; W. Eggleston show at the Museum of Modern Art. J. Malcolm. il New Yorker 53:107-11 O 10 '77
Digging up the past. D. Davis. il Newsweek 90:116+ N 28 '77
Epitaph on film; elephant photographs by P. Beard at the International Center of Photography. R. Hughes. il Time 110:60 D 12 '77
Faces; The Great American Face; exhibit at the United Nations. New Yorker 53:25-6 Mr 7 '77
From Chicago's PMA show: the shape of photo products to come. A. Goldsmith. il Pop Phot 80:91-9+ Je '77
Images from the Paris Salon. R. Martinez. il Pop Phot 81:134-7+ D '77
Jerusalem: The Artist and the Photograph exhibition. M. Ronen. il Art N 76:98-101 F '77
Journalist of the plague years; work of P. Beard at the ICP. O. Edwards. il Sat R 5:43-5 Ja 7 '78
Medium is the message; Winogrand exhibit at the Museum of Modern Art. D. Davis. Newsweek 90:106+ N 7 '77
More big show; PHA trade show. il Mod Phot 41:94-5+ Jl '77
N.Y, N.Y. il Horizon 21:75-7 Ja '78
New products from Japan; '77 Japan Camera Show. il Pop Phot 80:58+ My '77
Notes on Irving Penn. H. Kramer. il New Repub 177:27-9 O 29 '77
Photography. M. R. Weiss. Sat R 4:60-1 Ag 6 '77
Photography (cont) il Art N 76:108-9 Ja; 110-11 F; 118 Ap; 126 My; 186 Summ; 116+ O; 230+ N '77
Seeing pictures; exhibits in Arles, France. J. Scully. il Mod Phot 41:14+ O '77
Shows we've seen. See issues of Popular photography
Small world in a room; I. Penn. O. Edwards. il Sat R 5:34-6 O 1 '77
What's what. See issues of Modern photography

Exposure

Art of color exposure. B. Schwalberg. il Pop Phot 80:116-21 Ap '77
Color darkroom; recalculation of exposure variation in magnification. B. Nadler. il Pop Phot 80:34+ My '77
Eye. R. Ergenbright. il Trav/Holiday 148:8+ N '77
Nuts & bolts. B. Pierce. Pop Phot 80:12+ F '77
Protechniques; exposures problems with automatic cameras. E. Meyers. Pop Phot 81:68+ O '77
Schwalberg at large; film speeds. B. Schwalberg. il Pop Phot 80:56+ Je '77
Who says you can't push color print film? il Mod Phot 41:78-81+ F '77
See also
Exposure meters

Films

Adox finds a new life in the Adriatic sun; Efke film. il Mod Phot 41:78 Ap '77
Amateur E6 Ektachromes. B. Schwalberg. il Pop Phot 81:112-17 O '77
Case for negative color. L. Bogen. il Mod Phot 41:90-3+ My '77
Color prints at Tri-X speed. D. Leavitt. il Pop Phot 81:82-9+ Ag '77

PHOTOGRAPHY—Films—*Continued*

David Vestal's photo workbook: B&W film and film speed. D. Vestal. Pop Phot 81:27 O '77

Ed Scully on color:

Process E-6 duplicating film. E. Scully. il Mod Phot 41:56+ Mr '77

Films and paper. D. Leavitt. il Pop Phot 80:92+ Je '77

Films to give you better snapshots. K. Werner. il Mech Illus 74:62+ Ja '78

Fujicolor F-II 400. D. Leavitt. il Pop Phot 80: 83-7+ Mr '77

Ilford HP5: How it compares to Tri-X. D. Leavitt. il Pop Phot 80:98-103+ My '77

Instant-picture film roundup. W. Andrews. il Mod Phot 41:124-7 O '77

Instant pictures:

Polaroid films. W. Andrews and D. L. Miller. Mod Phot 41:74+ Ap '77

Polaroid type 51 high-contrast film. W. Andrews and D. L. Miller. il Mod Phot 41:24+ Je '77

Polaroid's new black-and-white film. W. Andrews and D. L. Miller. il Mod Phot 41:56+ My '77

Kodacolor? Vericolor? What's the difference? M. Hershenson. il Mod Phot 41:118-19+ N '77

Kodak vs. Fuji: which fast color film does it all best? A. M. Gordon. il Mod Phot 41:88-93+ Ag '77

New super-fast color-print films. E. H. Ortner. il Pop Sci 211:100-1+ Jl '77

Offbeat; E-6 Ektachrome. N. Rothschild. il Pop Phot 80:39-40 F '77

On the road to better astronomical photographs. B. D. Wallis and R. W. Provin. il Sky & Tel 53:399-405 My '77

Photo fun with infrared. B. Berger. il Mech Illus 73:50 Ag '77

Pleasures of high-speed B&W films. B. Schwalberg. il Pop Phot 81:92-7+ Ag '77

Polaroid's new pro packs; type 668. W. Andrews and D. L. Miller. il Mod Phot 41:94-9+ My '77

35mm slide films: which look best . . . and when? A. Gordon and J. Schneider. il Mod Phot 41: 94-101+ S '77

Who says you can't push color print film? il Mod Phot 41:78-81+ F '77

Storage

Load film on the go. M. Adair and A. Adair. il Mod Phot 41:139 O '77

Focusing

Autofocus, as predicted; Konica C35AF. N. Goldberg. il Pop Phot 81:86+ D '77

Control of focus; depth of field. il Trav/Holiday 148:16+ D '77

First automatic-focus camera; Konica C35AF. S. Walton. il Pop Mech 148:66 D '77

Floating elements: do they really help? B. Sherman. il Mod Phot 41:78-9+ Jl '77

Konica opens new era with first production autofocusing 35mm. H. Keppler. il Mod Phot 41:70 N '77

Tools & techniques (cont) C. W. Kennedy. il Pop Phot 80:46+ Je '77

See also

Lenses, Photographic

Motion picture photography—Focusing

Galleries and museums

Critical focus; Museum of Holography. K. Poli. il por Pop Phot 80:6+ Mr '77

ICP fall '77 schedule. Pop Phot 81:82 S '77

ICP spring '77 schedule. Pop Phot 80:58 F '77

Miracle on 57th Street; New York. S. Paley. Mod Phot 41:60 F '77

Seeing pictures. J. Scully. il Mod Phot 41:8+ F '77

Shows we've seen; Focus Gallery tenth anniversary exhibition. J. Murray. il Pop Phot 80:57+ F '77

Time exposure. E. S. Lothrop, Jr. il Pop Phot 81:44+ Jl '77

Viewpoint:

Celebrities honor Limelight Gallery. J. Deschin. il Pop Phot 80:30+ My '77

Galerie Zabriskie in Paris. J. Deschin. il Pop Phot 81:18+ Jl '77

Prakapas gallery. J. Deschin. il pors Pop Phot 81:12+ O '77

Women at ICP. J. Deschin. il Pop Phot 81: 28+ S '77

Handbooks, manuals, etc.

Offbeat; Kodak master photoguide. N. Rothschild. il Pop Phot 81:12+ Ag '77

History

Digging up the past. D. Davis. il Newsweek 90:116+ N 28 '77

First photographers of the Grand Canyon. G. Simmons and V. Simmons. il Am West 14:34-8+ Jl '77

Gertrude Käsebier lost and found. M. A. Tighe. bibl il por Art in Am 65:94-8 Mr '77

Hold still—don't move a muscle: you're on Brady's camera! excerpt from Mathew Brady and his world. P. B. Kunhardt, Jr. il Smithsonian 8:58-67 bibl(p 101) Ag '77

Images of which history was made bore the Mathew Brady label; excerpts from Mathew Brady and his world. P. B. Kunhardt, Jr. il pors Smithsonian 8:24-35 Jl '77

Pop photo and its world-1937-77: a 40th-anniversary collage; symposium, ed by A. Goldsmith. Pop Phot 80:79-97+ My '77

Romance of old photos. D. Davis and M. Rourke. il Newsweek 89:40-3 F 21 '77

Time exposure. E. S. Lothrop, Jr. See every other issue of Popular photography

Timeless summers in old-time Maine; work of C. S. Emmons. D. Seiberling. il pors N Y Times Mag p 18-19+ Jl 24 '77

Industrial uses

See Photography in industry

Landscapes

Scenic landscape today. J. Scully and M. O'Grady. il Mod Phot 41:120-33+ N '77

Light

Can color shine on cloudy days? A. Grundberg. il Mod Phot 41:88-93 S '77

Instant photography; available-light. D. Leavitt. il por Pop Phot 80:66+ Je '77

Lights inside the camera? concurrent photon amplification. P. Wahl. il Pop Sci 211:49-50 Jl '77

1937 available light revisited. B. Schwalberg. il por Pop Phot 80:120-1+ My '77

Sun—the one light source that does it all. H. Shaman. il Pop Phot 80:82-5 F '77

Techniques tomorrow. B. Sherman. il Mod Phot 41:28+ N; 48+ D '77

Tools & techniques. C. W. Kennedy. il Pop Phot 81:26+ Jl '77

See also

Photography—Exposure

Lighting

All slaves are not created equal! P. White and J. Schneider. il Mod Phot 41:92-5+ F '77

Funnel flash makes bare bulb light for only 39¢. R. Jungman. il Mod Phot 41:102 F '77

Lights fantastic. R. Wolters. Writers Digest 57:11+ Mr '77

Nuts & bolts; incandescent bulbs or electronic flash? B. Pierce. il Pop Phot 80:16+ Je '77

See also

Motion picture photography—Lighting

Photography, Flashlight

Marines

Cameras at sea; historical west coast maritime photography. R. A. Weinstein. il Am West 14:34-9 My '77

Vagabond camera: the beach. R. G. Clancy. il Travel 148:68-9 Jl '77

News

See Photography, Journalistic

Periodicals

See also

Popular photography (periodical)

Portraits

After ninety; excerpts. M. Mitchell; I. Cunningham. por Pop Phot 81:126-35+ O '77

Friends of mine: Richmond Jones. A. Goldsmith. il por Pop Phot 80:100-9+ Mr '77

Gertrude Käsebier lost and found. M. A. Tighe. bibl il por Art in Am 65:94-8 Mr '77

Hold still—don't move a muscle: you're on Brady's camera! excerpt from Mathew Brady and his world. P. B. Kunhardt, Jr. il Smithsonian 8:58-67 bibl(p 101) Ag '77

How to sit for a camera portrait. V. E. Towns. House B 119:10+ F '77

How to take your own picture; self-timer. D. H. Bryan. il Mech Illus 73:62+ Je '77

Images of which history was made bore the Mathew Brady label; excerpts from Mathew Brady and his world. P. B. Kunhardt, Jr. il pors Smithsonian 8:24-35 Jl '77

Interview with Imogen Cunningham; ed by B. Conrad, 3d; excerpt from Interview with master photographers. I. Cunningham. il por Art in Am 65:42-5+ My '77

John Benton-Harris: Yankee eye on the English. P. Turner. il Mod Phot 41:128-37 O '77

Many faces of Yousuf Karsh; excerpt from Karsh portraits. Y. Karsh. il Read Digest 110:153-9 F '77

Michael Mathers: the professionals. N. Canavor. il Pop Phot 81:142-51+ D '77

Milton Rogovin: compassionate portraitist. S. Rice. il Mod Phot 41:116-21 S '77

Portraits. J. Scully and others. Mod Phot 41: 92-119 Je '77

Portraits at an exhibition; ed by D. Seiberling. N. Farb. N Y Times Mag p57-9 N 20 '77

Seeing pictures; four major books of portraits. J. Scully. il Mod Phot 41:27+ Ap '77

Tools & techniques. C. W. Kennedy. il por Pop Phot 80:32+ Mr '77

PHOTOGRAPHY—Portraits—*Continued*
Try self-portraits. R. M. Hattersley. il Pop Phot 80:110-13+ Je '77
Woman behind the credit: photo by Jill Krementz. D. K. Mano. il Esquire 87:16+ F '77
See also
Daguerreotypes
Photography of children
Photography of women

Printing processes

Case for negative color. L. Bogen. il Mod Phot 41:90-3+ My '77
Color darkroom. B. Nadler. See issues of Popular photography
David Vestal's photo workbook: contact-printing with RC paper. Pop Phot 81:28 O '77
Ed Scully on color:
Dignan Divided Color Print System. E. Scully. il Mod Phot 41:30+ S '77
Kids and kameras: toning black-and-white prints. D. Cyr. il por Pop Phot 81:56+ O '77
Lumigraphic print process. M. Sapiro. bibl il Sch Arts 77:28-35 S '77
Masters of the darkroom:
Eikoh Hosoe: how he controls the photographic process; excerpt from Darkroom. E. Hosoe. il por Pop Phot 81:102-7+ Jl '77
How Duane Michals creates his mystical masterpieces; excerpt from Darkroom. D. Michals. il Pop Phot 81:136-41+ O '77
Ralph Gibson: how he creates his fractional images; excerpt from Darkroom. R. Gibson. il por Pop Phot 80:110-15+ Mr '77
Offbeat; use of filters in color printing. N. Rothschild. bibl il Pop Phot 81:6+ O '77
Protechniques; printing costs. E. Meyers. il Pop Phot 81:116+ Ag '77
Turn your color flops into exciting images; print manipulation techniques. L. H. Bogen. il Pop Phot 81:116-17+ Jl '77
Working pro looks at Cibachrome. F. Ward. il por Pop Phot 80:112-15+ Ap '77

Processing

Color in your darkroom. M. Hershenson. il por Mod Phot 41:50+ O; 10+ N; 40+ D '77
Nuts & bolts; developing times. B. Pierce. Pop Phot 81:36+ D '77
David Vestal's photo workbook: Film processing in general. D. Vestal. Pop Phot 80:79-80 Je '77
Ed Scully on color:
E-6 processing. E. Scully. Mod Phot 41:46 F '77
Masters of the darkroom: how W. Eugene Smith shoots and prints; excerpt from Darkroom. W. E. Smith. il pors Pop Phot 80:76-81+ F '77
On the road to better astronomical photographs. B. D. Wallis and R. W. Provin. il Sky & Tel 53:484-91 Je '77
View from Kramer; tray processing sheet film. A. Kramer. Mod Phot 41:54+ Ap '77
See also
Motion picture photography—Processing

Apparatus and supplies

Check hypo, stop print curl and water waste; hypo-sniffer device. F. I. Gilpin. il Mod Phot 41:138-9 O '77
Color darkroom:
Cibachrome color print material and Falcon FRC resin coated print drying system. B. Nadler. il por Pop Phot 81:121+ Ag '77
Durst RCP 20 automatic color-print processing machine, Kodak Ektaprint 2 chemicals, and Ektacolor RC 74 color-printing paper. B. Nadler. il Pop Phot 81:54+ D '77
Full-frame negative carriers. B. Nadler. il Pop Phot 80:31-2+ Je '77
GraLab's 400 and Unicolor's programmable Bigger Ben timers. B. Nadler. il Pop Phot 81:34+ Jl '77
Tents or portable darkrooms. B. Nadler. il Pop Phot 81:56+ S '77
Unicolor film drum II and chemicals. B. Nadler. il Pop Phot 80:48+ Ap '77
Color in your darkroom:
Using a color analyzer. M. Hershenson. il por Mod Phot 41:10+ N '77
Darkroom. E. Meyers. il Pop Phot 81:123+ Jl '77
First look: Agnekolor processor. M. Frank. il Pop Phot 80:73+ Ap '77
Great news for stabilization printers! C. W. Kennedy. il Pop Phot 80:92-5+ Ap '77
Kids and kameras: Instafilm kit for making slides from negatives. D. Cyr. il Pop Phot 80:38+ Je '77
Print washer. il Mech Illus 73:128 Mr '77
Silicone seals sink in darkroom. J. W. Ward. il Mod Phot 41:94 Mr '77
View from Kramer; automatic color print processors. A. Kramer. il Mod Phot 41:85 D '77
See also
Thermometers and thermometry

Scholarships and fellowships

Viewpoint; photography awards program of the National Endowment for the Arts. J. Deschin. Pop Phot 80:30+ Ap '77

Scientific use

See also
Photomicrography

Self portraits

See Photography—Portraits

Societies

Protechniques; Association of Professional Color Laboratories meeting. E. Meyers. il Pop Phot 80:70+ My '77
See also
Royal Photographic Society of Great Britain, London

Studios and darkrooms

Build this organizer panel for your darkroom. W. Fitz. il Pop Mech 147:72 Mr '77

Study and teaching

Arles festival ponders future of B&W papers, photo collecting and color imagery. il Mod Phot 41:54+ O '77
Courses (cont) Mod Phot 41:67 My; 35 Jl '77
David Vestal's photo workbook:
B&W film and film speed; Contact-printing with RC paper. D. Vestal Pop Phot 81:27-8 O '77
The camera. D. Vestal. Pop Phot 80:67-8 My '77
Light meters & metering. D. Vestal. Pop Phot 81:69-70 Ag '77
Photographic seeing; Point & shoot photography; Film processing in general. D. Vestal. Pop Phot 80:79-80 Je '77
Step-by-step black & white developing. D. Vestal. Pop Phot 81:83-4 Jl '77
Festival of F-stops in France; Arles workshop; with photographs by E. Erwitt. N Y Times Mag p 10-11 Ag 14 '77
ICP spring '77 schedule. Pop Phot 80:58 F '77
Just wear a camera and a smile; Ansel Adams Gallery Workshop in nude photography. S. Freidberg. il Mod Phot 41:96-9+ F '77
Kids and kameras:
CV horizontal enlarger. D. Cyr. il Pop Phot 81:51+ Ag '77
Instafilm kit for making slides from negatives. D. Cyr. il Pop Phot 80:38+ Je '77
Snapshooter camera. D. Cyr. il por Pop Phot 80:58+ Mr '77
Toning black-and-white prints. D. Cyr. il por Pop Phot 81:56+ O '77
Navy school: photo career port of entry. E. Scully. il Mod Phot 41:18+ S '77
Photo education. il Mod Phot 41:83+ D '77
Pop photo on campus. M. Cipnic. il Pop Phot 80:92-5 Mr '77
Workshops. See occasional issues of Popular photography
See also
Society for Photographic Education

Terminology

Would you buy an AE SLR with SBCs in its LIC? J. Schneider. Mod Phot 41:36+ F '77

Therapeutic use

See Photography in psychotherapy

Brazil

Pioneer photographers of Brazil; excerpt from Pioneer photographers of Brazil, 1840-1920. G. Ferrez and W. J. Naef. il Society 14:74-6 My '77

Europe, Western

Letter from Paris. J. A. Fox. Pop Phot 80:62+ F '77

France

Letter from Paris (cont) J. A. Fox. Pop Phot 80:62+ F '77

Russia

Critical focus. K. Poli. il Pop Phot 81:8+ S '77

PHOTOGRAPHY, Aerial
Eye of Bill Garnett looks down on the commonplace and sees art. E. Park. il por Smithsonian 8:74-81 My '77
Looking in on us. D. Jordan. il Environment 19:6-11 Ag '77; Same with title Surveilling the earth. Current 198:34-41 D '77
Mole's other masterpieces. il pors Am Heritage 28:92-3 Je '77
See also
Aerial reconnaissance
Mapping, Aerial

PHOTOGRAPHY, Agricultural
Now—infrared can spot your crop problems. J. G. White. il Farm J 100:18-19+ D '76
Space scientist launches infrared photo service for farmers. J. D. Boyd. por Farm J 101:K2 F '77

PHOTOGRAPHY, Applied
Friendly way to put photography to work; family photographs transferred to fabric. il Sunset 159:124-5 D '77

PHOTOGRAPHY, Architectural. See Photography of buildings and structures

PHOTOGRAPHY, Artistic
As I see it. D. Vestal. por Pop Phot 81:30+ O '77
Doctored images. D. Davis and M. Rourke. il Newsweek 90:69+ Ag 15 '77
Images: forty years of evolution and revolution. C. Reynolds. Pop Phot 80:97+ My '77
Jill Lynne; use of color copiers. A. Williams. il por Pop Phot 80:88-91+ Mr '77
Photo-luxe; Irving Penn: time is luxury. T. B. Hess. il Vogue 167:330-3+ S '77
Shows we've seen; California Pictorialism. J. Murray. il Pop Phot 80:87-8+ Ap '77
Snapshot mastery. F. Ritchin. il Horizon 20:75-9 O '77
See also
Photography of the nude

PHOTOGRAPHY, Astronomical. See Astronomical photography

PHOTOGRAPHY, Close-up
Basics and variations of close-up photography. il Mod Phot 41:114-15 S '77
Easiest closeup system ever! support device for object photographed. H. Keppelr. il Mod Phot 41:80-3 Mr '77
How to get close, closer, closest with any zoom lens. R. Rothschild. il Pop Phot 80:96-9+ F '77
Shop talk. N. Goldberg. il Pop Phot 80:16+ F '77
See also
Macrophotography

PHOTOGRAPHY, Cold weather. See Photography—Cold weather conditions

PHOTOGRAPHY, Commercial
Images: forty years of evolution and revolution. C. Reynolds. Pop Phot 80:97+ My '77
Markets & careers; free-lance contract plan of S. Stibbens. H. Chapnick. il por Pop Phot 80:50+ Je '77
Seeing pictures; business considerations in publishing photographs. J. Scully. Mod Phot 41:10+ Ag '77
See also
Photographers agents
Photography, Fashion
Photography, Journalistic
Photography as a profession
Photography in advertising

PHOTOGRAPHY, Documentary
How it really was; excerpt from People from our side. D. H. Eber. il por Natur Hist 86:70-5 bibl(p 101) F '77
Ken Domon: a documentary pilgrimage: tr by M. Tsuji. T. Kishi. il Mod Phot 41:84-93 Mr '77

PHOTOGRAPHY, Fashion
Fashion from barons to guys. S. Eauclaire. il Mod Phot 41:104-5 D '77
Fashions in fashion photography. A. Knight. il Horizon 20:59-65 S '77
From rags to photographic riches; exhibit at the Brooklyn Museum. O. Edwards. il N Y Times Mag p 151-4 N 6 '77

PHOTOGRAPHY, Flashlight
Direct flash zaps back! A. Grundberg and M. O'Grady. il Mod Phot 41:72-7 Jl '77
Electronic flash landscapes. R. Busch. il Pop Phot 81:130-3+ D '77
See also
Electric lamps, Photoflash

Electronic equipment
See Photography—Electronic equipment

PHOTOGRAPHY, Industrial. See Photography in industry

PHOTOGRAPHY, Infrared
How much insulation do you need? thermography consultants. House & Gard 149:96 S '77
Infrared energy spies. il Chemistry 50:23-4 N '77
Infrared made easier. il Mod Phot 41:82-5+ F '77
Infrared photography maps non-point pollution; Toledo. il Am City & County 92:46-7 Ja '77

PHOTOGRAPHY, Journalistic
Future of photojournalism in books; excerpt from Photojournalism '76. H. Chapnick il Pop Phot 80:56+ Ap '77
He was there; work of A. Fellig. A. Quindlen. il pors N Y Times Mag p40-3 S 11 '77
Picture yourself tripling your income as a writer. J. E. Kelley. Writers Digest 57:26-8 F '77
Pictures. R. Wolters. See issues of Writer's digest
Say it better with pictures. P. Comen. Writers Digest 57:27 My '77
Shooting the presidents; White House photography. J. G. Morris. il Pop Phot 81:79-81+ Ag '77
Should photographers try to write? P. Seligman. Pop Phot 80:75+ F '77
Weegee the famous. J. Coplans. il por Art in Am 65:37-41 S '77
Weegee's brilliant flash of light. N. Ffrench-Frazier. il Art N 76:230+ N '77
See also
Israel-Arab War, 1948-1949—Photographs and photography
National Press Photographers Association
Photography of sports

History
Images of war: Jimmy Hare's photojournalism. E. M. Halliday. il por Am Heritage 28:74-81 Ag '77

PHOTOGRAPHY, Marine. See Photography—Marines

PHOTOGRAPHY, Medical
See also
Radiography, Medical

PHOTOGRAPHY, Nature. See Nature photography

PHOTOGRAPHY, Nude. See Photography of the nude

PHOTOGRAPHY, Pinhole
Instant pictures. W. Andrews and D. L. Miller. il Mod Phot 41:12+ D '77

PHOTOGRAPHY, Submarine
Images from the deep; work of D. Faulkner. D. Steigman. il Pop Phot 81:92-7+ S '77
Three critical aspects of underwater photography. D. Wallin. il Sea Front 23:204-9 Jl '77
Underwater, try macro. M. T. O'Keefe. il Pop Phot 81:90-1+ Ag '77
See also
Motion picture photography, Submarine

Apparatus and supplies
Underwater flash—bright light in a small package. C. P. Gilmore. il Pop Sci 210:63 F '77

PHOTOGRAPHY, Table top
Table top photography rediscovered. K. R. Morrison. il Sch Arts 76:28-9 Je '77

PHOTOGRAPHY, Theatrical
Nuts & bolts. B. Pierce. il Pop Phot 81:36+ S '77

PHOTOGRAPHY, Time-lapse
How to take your own picture; self-timer. D. H. Bryan. il Mech Illus 73:62+ Je '77

PHOTOGRAPHY, Travel. See Travel photography

PHOTOGRAPHY, Trick
Be gone dull filters: a visual dictionary of special-effect nostrums. H. Keppler. il Mod Phot 41:108-11 O '77
Red-green-blue? multiple exposures with color filters. N. Rothschild. il Pop Phot 81:98-9+ S '77

PHOTOGRAPHY and art. See Art and photography

PHOTOGRAPHY as a profession
Markets & careers. H. Chapnick. See issues of Popular photography
Seeing pictures; views of professional photographers at the 21st Annual Wilson Hicks Conference. J. Scully. il Mod Phot 41:10+ Je '77

PHOTOGRAPHY books. See Picture books

PHOTOGRAPHY by children. See Children as photographers

PHOTOGRAPHY in advertising
On assignment: photographing running horses for ad campaign; work of C. Seghers, 2d. R. Busch. il Pop Phot 81:118-19+ O '77

PHOTOGRAPHY in agriculture. See Photography, Agricultural

PHOTOGRAPHY in archeology
Well traveled camera: equipment for photographing antiquities. H. Keppler. il Mod Phot 41:33+ O '77

PHOTOGRAPHY in industry
Ted Horowitz; free-lance corporate/industrial photography. R. Busch. il por Pop Phot 81:98-105+ Ag '77

PHOTOGRAPHY in psychotherapy
Photographs help patients focus on their problems. B. Zakem. Psychol Today 11:22+ S '77

PHOTOGRAPHY of animals
Encounters in the wild; excerpt from Meet my psychiatrist. L. Blacklock. il Nat Wildlife 15:25-9 O '77
Epitaph on film; elephant photographs by P. Beard at the International Center of Photography. R. Hughes. il Time 110:60 D 12 '77
Focus on the sportsman's camera. T. Trueblood. il Field & S 82:12+ Jl '77
His business has gone to the dogs; F. Corder's pet photos. il pors Ebony 32:50-1+ My '77
How to shoot backyard game. A. Darrow. il Mech Illus 73:114-15 Ap '77
Journalist of the plague years; work of P. Beard at the ICP. O. Edwards. il Sat R 5:43-5 Ja 7 '78
On assignment: photographing running horses for ad campaign; work of C. Seghers, 2d. R. Busch. il Pop Phot 81:118-19+ O '77
Shooting wildlife with a camera. J. Tallon. il Pop Mech 147:74-6+ F '77
See also
Blinds (camouflage)

Anecdotes, facetiae, satire, etc.
Bear story; attempts to photograph a wild black bear. R. Whitehead il por Conservationist 32:16-18 S '77
Mountain goats never say cheese! P. F. McManus. Field & S 82:78+ Jl '77

PHOTOGRAPHY of buildings and structures
View point; country-inn project of L. Raymond. J. Deschin. il Pop Phot 81:22+ D '77

PHOTOGRAPHY of children
Casual camera; sure-fire photo tips for parents. N. Rudolph. il Parents Mag 52:10+ Je '77
Protechniques. E. Meyers. il Pop Phot 80:115+ F '77
See also
Children—Photographs
PHOTOGRAPHY of eclipses. See Astronomical photography
PHOTOGRAPHY of flowers, plants, trees, etc.
Flowers in the rough; wildflower photographer. N. K. Koran. il por Ret Liv 17:42 Ap '77
Focus on flowers; work of P. B. Kaplan. R. Busch. il por Pop Phot 80:116-25+ Je '77
Horticulture magazine's first annual photography contest. il Horticulture 55:34-43 N '77
PHOTOGRAPHY of insects
Buggy cosmopolis in your garden; identifying and photographing common insects. il Sunset 158:112-17 bibl(p291) My '77
It's a small world. D. Cavagnaro. il Nat Wildlife 15:36-41 Ag '77
Man's obsession reveals the riches of a hidden world; Dr S. Y. Lee. T. Green. il por Smithsonian 8:80-7 bibl(p 161) N '77
Micro macabre. D. Scharf. il Int Wildlife 7:18-23 S '77
See also
Insects—Photographs
PHOTOGRAPHY of men
As the lens turns: women photograph men; excerpt from Women photograph men. M. Haskell. il Ms 6:31-2+ S '77
PHOTOGRAPHY of nature. See Nature photography
PHOTOGRAPHY of plants. See Photography of flowers, plants, trees, etc.
PHOTOGRAPHY of sports
Letter from the publisher; horse racing. J. Meyers. il Sports Illus 46:4 Je 20 '77
Sports action challenges your camera eye; movies. il Mod Phot 41:62 D '77
PHOTOGRAPHY of the nude
Hipped on nudes; work of T. Eakins. il Horizon 21:35 Ja '78
Just wear a camera and a smile; Ansel Adams Gallery Workshop in nude photography. S. Freidberg. il Mod Phot 41:96-9+ F '77
Nude redefined; work of D. Holleley. M. R. Cipnic. il Pop Phot 81:112-15 Jl '77
Strongest way of seeing; work of E. Weston. il Horizon 20:82-6 N '77
PHOTOGRAPHY of weddings
Seeing pictures; exhibit at the International Center of Photography. J. Scully. il Mod Phot 41:15+ N '77
PHOTOGRAPHY of women
Bellocq's girls; exhibition at New York's Light Gallery. D. Davis. il Newsweek 89:89 Mr 14 '77
Who you are now; excerpt from introduction to Emergence. K. Millett. il pors Vogue 167:302+ O '77
PHOTOGRAPHY of works of art
Getting the big picture; use of giant Polaroid camera to photograph art works. il Time 110:82-3 S 26 '77
Quick & easy way to photograph art; interview. E. Peterson. il Mod Phot 41:80-3 Jl '77
PHOTOGRAPHY schools. See Photography—Study and teaching
PHOTOJOURNALISM. See Photography, Journalistic
PHOTOMICROGRAPHY
Micro macabre; photography of insects using the scanning electron microscope. D. Scharf. il Int Wildlife 7:18-23 S '77
PHOTONS
Detecting photons; symposium, with editorial comment. bibl il Phys Today 30:23-8+, 112 N '77
PHOTOPULOS, Bud
Replaceable you. por Newsweek 90:23 O 10 '77
PHOTORECEPTOR cells. See Rods and cones
PHOTORESISTORS
The photoresistor. F. M. Mims. il Pop Electr 11:90-1 Je '77
PHOTORESPIRATION. See Plants—Respiration
PHOTOSENSITIZATION. See Light sensitization
PHOTOSYNTHESIS
Greening of physical chemistry. D. E. Thomsen. il Sci N 111:188+ Mr 19 '77
Increasing crop production through more controlled photosynthesis. J. A. Bassham. bibl il Science 197:630-8 Ag 12 '77
Increasing photosynthesis by inhibiting photorespiration with glyoxylate. D. J. Oliver and I. Zelitch. bibl il Science 196:1450-1 Je 24 '77
Photosynthesis: limited yields, unlimited dreams. R. Radmer and B. Kok. bibl il BioScience 27:599-605 S '77
Photosynthetic solar energy: rediscovering biomass fuels. A. L. Hammond. Science 197:745-6 Ag 19 '77
Photosynthetic unit of hydrogen evolution; chlorella vulgaris. E. Greenbaum. bibl il Science 196:879-80 My 20 '77
PHOTOTYPESETTING
Market-wise; Compugraphic Corp. il Forbes 119:59-60 Mr 1 '77
PHUKET Island
Bangkok. C. D. B. Bryan. il Holiday 57:34-5+ N '76
PHYLLOTAXIS
Phyllotaxis and the Fibonacci series. G. J. Mitchison. bibl il Science 196:270-5 Ap 15 '77
Phyllotaxis in xanthium shoots altered by gibberellic acid. R. Maksymowych and R. O. Erickson. bibl il Science 196:1201-3 Je 10 '77
PHYSALIS. See Husk tomatoes
PHYSICAL apparatus and instruments
New products. See issues of Physics today
PHYSICAL astronomy. See Astrophysics
PHYSICAL distribution of goods. See Distribution of goods
PHYSICAL education and training
Frankly speaking: you deserve a gym break! M. B. Levenson. por Seventeen 36:36 O '77
It's a site for sore eyes; Squaw Valley as Olympic training site. A. Verschoth. il Sports Illus 47:46-7 Ag 22 '77
Look what's happening in gym class; programs of American Alliance for Health, Physical Education and Recreation. il Changing T 31:33-4 My '77
See also
T'ai chi ch'üan
PHYSICAL education for the aged
Exercise: it can be fun keeping fit. J. Brunner. il Ret Liv 17:20-1 Ja '77
Running for your life; Masters Track and Field. G. Leonard. Read Digest 110:43-4+ F '77
PHYSICAL education for the handicapped
Learning to move, moving to learn; classes for teachers of physical education at Moraine Valley Community College, Palos Hills, Ill. M. Nelson. il Parks & Rec 12:34-5+ N '77
PHYSICAL education for women
See also
Women athletes
PHYSICAL examinations
Annual medical examination. M. Markham. Harp Baz 110:129+ F '77
Do you really need a yearly medical checkup? survey of doctors. L. C. Deslauriers. il Fam Health 9:32-4 F '77
Off with your pants. H. D. Hoekstra. Ret Liv 17:34 My '77
Those annual physicals are worth the trouble. W. McQuade. il Fortune 95:164-70+ Ja '77
See also
Gynecologic examinations
PHYSICAL fitness
Are you in shape for hunting season? exercise for hunters. S. Netherby. il Field & S 82:148-9+ Ag '77
Family guide to fitness through fun. A. H. Bruckheim. por Parents Mag 52:68-9+ N '77
Farrah's way; interview, ed by E. Sabol. F. Fawcett-Majors. il por Vogue 167:128-9 Ap '77
Fitness programs: a fringe that's paying off for employers. il U.S. News 83:79 D 5 '77
From cycling to mountain climbing—using leisure time for fitness. il U.S. News 82:70-1 My 23 '77
How to keep fit without killing yourself. il Mademoiselle 83:158-9+ Je '77
It's fun to be fit. . . Vogue 167:132-49 Ap '77
Keeping fit: America tries to shape up. H. F. Waters and others. il Newsweek 89:78-9+ My 23 '77
Keeping fit, Carter style. il pors U.S. News 82:28 Ap 25 '77
Keeping fit in California. A. Penney. il N Y Times Mag p58 Ja 8 '78
Two cheers for the unfit. M. Greenfield. Newsweek 91:68 Ja 2 '78
See also
Exercise
Health
Health clubs
Physical education and training
Vitality
PHYSICAL geography
See also
Deserts
Paleogeography
PHYSICAL measurements
See also
Dimensional analysis
PHYSICAL sciences. See Life sciences
PHYSICALLY handicapped. See Handicapped
PHYSICIANS
Advisor speaks to aspiring physicians. M. B. Rock. Intellect 106:76-7 Ag '77
America's doctors: a profession in trouble. A. T. Brett. il U.S. News 83:50-2+ O 17 '77
Between guilt and gratification: abortion doctors reveal their feelings. N. Rosen. il N Y Times Mag p70-1+ Ap 17 '77
Brain drain said setting problems for health planners; international migration of physicians. UN Chron 14:33 My '77
Family doctor of the year 1977; R. E. Boyer. il pors Good H 185:98+ O '77
Famous physicians & medical researchers. W. Rodger. Hobbies 82:156+ D '77
Friendly new family doctors. il Time 110:72 Jl 4 '77

PHYSICIANS—*Continued*
Health employment and the Nation's health. C. E. Bishop. bibl f Cur Hist 72:207-10+ My '77
New breed of doctor: he'll know you better. Sci Digest 81:62-4 My '77
Supply of Federal physicians and dentists found adequate. M Labor R 100:50 My '77
10,000 nurses speak out: a startling report on hospitals and doctors. il Fam Health 9:36-8 Ag '77
See also
American Academy of Family Physicians
American Medical Association
Black physicians
Gynecologists
Malpractice
Medical education
Medicine
Osteopaths

Advertising

AMA digs in against ads; FTC case. Bus W p45+ S 19 '77
Dr Huckster. M. Clark and M. Lord. il Newsweek 91:70 Ja 9 '78

Anecdotes, facetiae, satire, etc.

Warning: your doctor may be hazardous to your health. E. Berman. Harp Baz 110:128+ F '77

Fees

See Medical care, Cost of

Health and hygiene

Impaired MDs now recognized as a peril to patients. M. Grosswirth. il Sci Digest 81:8-11+ Je '77
Menace of drunken doctors. D. Robinson. Ladies Home J 94:94+ Ap '77
Physician, heal thyself; drug addiction. M. Clark and others. il Newsweek 90:74 Ag 8 '77
When the magic runs out for doctors; views of Bernard Bressler. D. Cohen. Psychol Today 11:26-7 Jl '77

Legal status, laws, etc.

See Medical laws and legislation; Medical policy

Licenses

See Licenses

Supply and demand

Operators. Sci Am 236:43 Ja '77

PHYSICIANS and patients
Choosing a new doctor. R. L. Carl. Ret Liv 17:26-7 Ap '77
Dancers and medical science. R. Gelabert. il Dance Mag 51:74-5 D '77
Doctoring isn't just for doctors; self-care. R. C. Yeager. Read Digest 111:237-8+ D '77
Doctors chided for not giving clear instructions on taking medicines. Ret Liv 17:43 Ag '77
Health care and the patient's needs. M. W. Herman. bibl f Cur Hist 73:1-4+ Jl '77
How to choose your doctor. M. Markham. bibl Harp Baz 110:126-7+ F '77
How to make your doctor work for you. N. A. Comer. bibl Mademoiselle 83:106-9+ Jl '77
Is your doctor ripping you off? T. E. Evans. Ebony 32:45-6+ S '77
Need for caring in medical practice; excerpts from address. S. S. Bergen, Jr. por Intellect 105:213-14 Ja '77
Off with your pants. H. D. Hoekstra. Ret Liv 17:34 My '77
On helping the doctor help you. H. Steirman. Fam Health 9:4 My '77
Patient-doctor contracts. Intellect 105:383 My '77
Ten questions your doctor should answer. W. A. Nolen. McCalls 104:96+ Jl '77
What women don't know about the medicines they take. A. Lake. McCalls 104:117+ Je '77
See also
Gynecologists and patients

Anecdotes, facetiae, satire, etc.

Say aaaahrrrrgh. D. K. Mano. Nat R 29:1445-6 D 9 '77

PHYSICIANS liability insurance. See Insurance, Malpractice liability

PHYSICIANS records. See Medical records

PHYSICISTS
Changing career opportunities for physicists; Conference on Changing Career Opportunities for Physicists. G. B. Lubkin. por Phys Today 30:85-6 O '77
Consulting for fun and profit. C. Goodman. bibl il Phys Today 30:44-6+ S '77
We hear that. See issues of Physics today
See also
American Physical Society
Bardeen, J.
also names of physicists, e.g. J. R. Oppenheimer

PHYSICISTS in government. See Scientists in government

PHYSICS
Can physics develop reasoning? R. G. Fuller and others. bibl il Phys Today 30:23-8 F '77 *
Physical sciences. Sci N 111:30, 108, 125, 154, 281, 299; 112:73, 91, 120, 425 Ja 8, F 12-19, Mr 5, Ap 30-My 7, Jl 30-Ag 6, 20, D 24 '77
Physics without limits. D. E. Thomsen. il Sci N 112:186-7 S 17 '77
Wonders of physics that can be found in a cup of coffee or tea. J. Walker. il Sci Am 152+ N '77
See also
American Institute of Physics
American Physical Society
Astrophysics
Conservation laws (physics)
Critical phenomena (physics)
Field theory (physics)
Fluids
Mathematical physics
Radio programs—Science programs
Relativity (physics)

Apparatus and instruments

See Physical apparatus and instruments

Bibliography

Books. See issues of Physics today

Conferences

Booth sessions: a critical assessment. J. S. Risley. Phys Today 20:9+ Ap '77; Discussion. 30:9+ Ag '77

History

J. J. Thomson and the Bohr atom. J. L. Heilbron. il pors Phys Today 30:23-4+ Ap '77
Lambert: self-taught physicist. S. L. Jaki. bibl il por Phys Today 30:25-30+ S '77
Physics in 1976—a personal account. W. A. Fowler. il Phys Today 30:33-8+ Ap '77

Periodicals

Prices of physics and chemistry journals. F. F. Clasquin and J. B. Cohen. bibl il Science 197:432-8 Jl 29 '77

Philosophy

Is physics human? V. F. Weisskopf; discussion. Phys Today 30:79-80 Mr '77
Tao of physics: reflections on the cosmic dance. F. Capra. il Sat R 5:21-3+ D 10 '77

Research

Big science struggles with the problems of its own success. G. Bylinsky. il Fortune 96:60-6+ Jl '77
Key to the universe; excerpt. N. Calder. il Sci Digest 81:58-63+ Je '77
Search & discovery. See issues of Physics today
See also
Johns Hopkins University, Baltimore—Applied Physics Laboratory

PHYSICS and state. See Science and state

PHYSICS research. See Physics—Research

PHYSICS teachers
See also
American Association of Physics Teachers

PHYSIOGNOMY
See also
Face

PHYSIOLOGICAL effects of cold. See Cold—Physiological effects

PHYSIOLOGICAL oxidation. See Oxidation, Physiological

PHYSIOLOGICAL psychology. See Psychology, Physiological

PHYSIOLOGY
See also
Electrophysiology
Obesity
Psychology, Physiological
Stress (physiology)
Temperature, Animal and human
Weight (physiology)
Women—Anatomy and physiology
also subheads Physiology; Physiological effects under various subjects, e.g. Drugs—Physiological effects; *also* names of organs of the body, e.g. Heart

PHYSIQUE. See Body, Human

PIAGET, Jean
Can physics develop reasoning? R. G. Fuller and others. bibl il Phys Today 30:23-8 F '77 *
Piaget and Lamarck. F. J. Thomas. Educ Digest 43:47-9 N '77 *

PIALORSI, Frank
Some aspects of bilingualism for the English teacher. bibl Engl J 66:94-7 Ja '77

PIANISTS
Keyboard clash; pianists' criticism of Steinway pianos. A. Kuflik. Newsweek 90:109 S 12 '77
See also
Adni, D.
Ax, E.
Bachauer, G.
Berman, L.
Bottazzi, A. M. T. de
Brendel, A.
Buchbinder, R.

PIANISTS—See also—*Continued*
Cliburn, V.
De Groote, S.
Garner, E.
Gilels, E.
Hines, E.
Hollander, L.
Horowitz, V.
Jaimes, J.
Kerer, R.
Kuerti, A.
Lipatti, D.
Pollini, M.
Rachmaninoff, S.
Richter, S. T.
Rubinstein, A.
Sherman, R.
Somer, H.
Szidon, R.
Tazaki, E.
Tishman, N.
Vazsonyi, B.
Vera, A. M.
Weissenberg, A.

PIANKA, Eric R. See Huey, R. B. jt auth

PIANKA, Helen Dunlap-. See Dunlap-Pianka, H.

PIANO
Bach on the piano? Why not? comparison with other keyboard instruments. R. Tureck. il por Hi Fi 27:91-3 O '77
Julius Bauer art case grand piano. il Hobbies 82:153 N '77
Key to buying a piano. Bet Hom & Gard 55: 170+ O '77
Pianos big & little, new & used. Changing T 31: 35-7 Ag '77
Three relics; Alma-Tadema Steinway at the Martin Beck Theatre. New Yorker 53:26-8 Je 20 '77
See also
Player piano

Instruction and study

Onward and upward with the arts; progress of pianist R. McCabe at the Juilliard School. H. D. Ruttencutter. New Yorker 53:42-4+ S 19 '77

PIANO contests. See Music—Competitions

PIANO makers
Around the Mall and beyond; presenting two Steinways to the Smithsonian's Division of Musical Instruments. E. Park. il Smithsonian 7:32+ F '77
Keyboard clash; pianists' criticism of Steinway pianos. A. Kuflik. Newsweek 90:109 S 12 '77

PIANO music
See also
Phonograph records—Piano music
Tape recordings—Piano music

PIANO playing
See also
Embellishment (music)

PIANOCORDER. See Tape recorders and recording

PIATIGORSKY, Gregor
Heifetz Piatigorsky concerts; recording. E. Belov. Am Rec G 40:48-9 F '77 *

PIATIGORSKY, Joram, and Shinohara Toshimichi
Lens contaract formation and reversible alteration in crystallin synthesis in cultured lenses. bibl il Science 196:1345-7 Je 17 '77

PICASSO, Pablo
Exclusive portfolio of unpublished works. il por Sat R 5:12-16 N 12 '77

about

Ascent from Plato's cave. D. Leder. America 137:244-5 O 15 '77 *
Guernica: an act of war, a work of art. C. L. Mee, Jr. il por Horizon 19:88-96 My '77 *
Guernica will hang in the Prado as Picasso wished. G. Marzorati. il por Art N 76:65-7 My '77 *
Picasso in retrospect 1939-1900; excerpt from The art world; ed by B. Diamonstein. A. M. Frankfurter. il Art N 76:156+ N '77 *
Picasso's cries of children . . . cries of stones. P. Failing. bibl il Art N 76:55-8+ S '77 *
Picasso's legacy. R. Gelatt. il pors Sat R 5:8-10 N 12 '77 *
Skirmish over Guernica; Museum of Modern Art's refusal to return painting. P. Nobile. il Harpers 254:15+ Mr '77 *
Spanish acquisition? E. Keerdoja. il Newsweek 90:16 O 31 '77 *
Would you like to buy 118 stolen Picassos? Vasari. Art N 76:22+ Ja '77 *

PICCINI, Sandi
California co-op cuts bills in half. il por Aging 274:3-5 Ag '77 *

PICHARD, Sally U.
Tunnel your way to earlier crops! Org Gard & Farm 24:172 D '77

PICK, Diane
Water relays. Camp Mag 49:11+ F '77

PICK-N-PAY Super Markets Inc-First National Stores Inc merger. See Supermarkets—Acquisitions and mergers

PICKER, Jean (Sovatkin)
United States reaffirms support of UNHCR programs; statement, November 15, 1976. Dept State Bull 75:756-8 D 27 '76

PICKEREL fishing
Old snaggletooth! J. Dean. il Field & S 82:38+ Je '77

PICKERING, George
Meanwhile, back in Detroit. Commonweal 104:49-51 Ja 21 '77

PICKET Post Trail. See Trails

PICKETT, Robert S.
Tomorrow's family. bibl f Intellect 105:330-2 Ap '77

PICKLES and relishes
How to make tangy pickled vegetables. E. W. Manning. il Farm J 101:46-7 Ag '77
Pickle it! il Bet Hom & Gard 55:110-11 Ag '77
What to do with too much summer fruit? Consider chutney. il Sunset 159:152 S '77

PICKUP campers. See Campers, Truck

PICKUP trucks. See Trucks

PICKWICK Bookshops. See Booksellers and bookselling—California

PICNIC cookery. See Cookery, Outdoor

PICNIC tables. See Tables

PICNICS
Bach's lunch; excerpt. J. R. Stevens. il Ladies Home J 94:98+ Jl '77
Make-ahead meal to go. il Bet Hom & Gard 54:20 Ag '76
Picnic! il Seventeen 36:114 Jl '77
Picnic in a pocket; pita bread; with recipes. il Ladies Home J 94:88-9+ Jl '77
Rah-rah tailgate picnic! S. B. Huffman. il Ladies Home J 94:140-2+ O '77
Round the world picnics: eating out; with recipes. P. Sadowsky and G. Steves. il Am Home 80:33-5+ Jl '77
Sandwiches that turn a picnic into a feast. H. McCully. House B 119:82-3+ Ag '77
Totable feasts; recipes. il Bet Hom & Gard 55: 174 O '77
25 perfect picnic wines. P. Quimme. House B 119:81 Ag '77
Viking picnic. il Fam Health 9:34-7 Jl '77
Your own French country picnic. il Sunset 159: 102-3 Jl '77

PICRAUX, Samuel T.
Analyzing hydrogen with nuclear reactions. bibl il Phys Today 30:42-3+ O '77

PICTURE agents. See Photographers agents

PICTURE books
Future of photojournalism in books; excerpt from Photojournalism '76. H. Chapnick. il Pop Phot 80:56+ Ap '77
Joys and the fears of childhood caught in Ridge Press/Grosset & Dunlap book; publication of The family of children, photographic book; interview, ed by R. Dahlin. J. Mason. Pub W 211:221-2 My 23 '77
Markets & careers; photographic-book producer; interview, ed by H. Chapnick. R. Wenkam. il por Pop Phot 81:70+ S '77

Bibliography

Camera-eye on Christmas. M. R. Weiss. il Sat R 5:31-2 N 26 '77
Coffee table books, demitasse size. P. Andrews. il Sat R 5:32+ N 26 '77
Seeing pictures; four major books of portraits. J. Scully. il Mod Phot 41:27+ Ap '77

PICTURE books for children
Art of the picture book; symposium, ed by W. Lorraine. Wilson Lib Bull 52:144-73 O '77
Caldecott Award acceptance; illustration of Ashanti to Zulu; address, June 18, 1977. L. Dillon and D. Dillon. Horn Bk 53:415-21 Ag '77
Dr Seuss at 72—going like 60. D. Freeman. il por Sat Eve Post 249:8+ Mr '77
Fantastical world of Maurice Sendak. J. Culhane. il por Read Digest 110:104-8 F '77
See also
Caldecott Medal

Bibliography

Picture books for children. D. McCann and O. Richard. il Wilson Lib Bull 52:77-9, 178-9, 256-7, 338-9 S-D '77
Picturely books for children. B. Dill. See issues of Wilson library bulletin to June 1977

Book reviewers and reviewing

See Book reviewers and reviewing

PICTURE cards
See also
Advertising cards

PICTURE frames
Breaking the frame barrier. R. Boneno. il Design (US) 78:2-4 Spr '77
Build a floater picture frame. A. Nunes-Vais. il Pop Mech 147:103 Ap '77
It's inexpensive and ingenious; display frame. il Sunset 159:175 O '77
Make rustic picture frames from barn siding. J. A. Long. il Pop Mech 147:184+ F '77
Make your own acrylic frames. il Mech Illus 73: 106-8 Ag '77

PICTURE post cards. See Post cards
PICTURE windows. See Windows
PICTURES
Fine art of fleurage; pressed flower pictures. H. White. il por Horticulture 55:26-8 O '77
Washington memorial prints; with editorial comment by W. Garrett. D. T. Deutsch. bibl il por Antiques 111:323, 324-31 F '77
See also
Illustration
Framing
See Picture frames
Mounting
Mount on museum board, not masonite. R. Mayer. Am Artist 41:16 Mr '77
PICTURES, Framing of. See Picture frames
PICTURES, Patchwork. See Patchwork
PICTURES of the Year Competition. See Photography—Competitions
PIDO, Antonio J. A.
Brain drain Philippinos. bibl Society 14:50-3 S '77
PIE
American classic updated; apple pie. G. Steves. il Am Home 80:68-9 O '77
Apple pie the French way. il McCalls 104:125-6 Ap '77
Best banana pie. il Good H 186:54 Ja '78
Cold and creamy—lemon chiffon pie. il McCalls 104:81-2 Jl '77
Favorite holiday pies—simple and superb. il Parents Mag 52:106-7 N '77
He cooks: pumpkin gelatin pie. D. Tait. il por Bet Hom & Gard 55:74 Ag '77
It's upside down—apple and nuts. il Sunset 158:186 Mr '77
Lemon is the secret; two pies. il Sunset 158: 234 My '77
Make it apricot! il Bet Hom & Gard 55:146 Je '77
One way the French make apple pie. il Sunset 159:214 N '77
Perfect lemon meringue pie. il McCalls 104:173-4 Ap '77
Pie cookbook. il Good H 184:128-39 Mr '77
Shell game; pie crusts. il Ladies Home J 94:92-3+ Je '77
Sweet and tarte; chocolate sabayon pie; French apple tart. C. Claiborne and P. Franey. il N Y Times Mag p 102 Ap 17 '77
PIE, Meat. See Cookery—Meat
PIEDMONT Airline. See Airlines—Local service
PIEDMONT Driving Club. See Atlanta—Clubs
PIER 4 restaurant, Cape Cod. See Restaurants—United States
PIERATT, Asa, and Neikirk, H. B.
Third World acquisitions: a report on the workshop at LC. Lib J 102:978 My 1 '77
PIERCE, Bill
Nuts & bolts. See issues of Popular photography
PIERCE, David A.
Summer science program. il Sky & Tel 53:175-7 Mr '77
PIERCE, Donald E.
Do-it-yourself garden cart. il Org Gard & Farm 24:142-3 Je '77
PIERCE, Edith Lovejoy
Risk-taking; poem. Chr Cent 94:269 Mr 23 '77
Terminal; poem. Chr Cent 94:58 Ja 26 '77
PIERCE, John Robinson
Edward E. David, Jr, president-elect. il por Science 196:336-7 Ap 15 '77
Electronics: past, present, and future. il Science 195:1092-5 Mr 18 '77
PIERCE, Warren
Hollow-stemmed cover crops for soil aeration. il Org Gard & Farm 24:174-5 Je '77
PIERCY, Marge
Sage and rue; poem; excerpt from Living in the open. Org Gard & Farm 24:91 N '77
PIERRE, Clara
Tunbridge in San Francisco. Mademoiselle 83: 86+ O '77
PIERS, Maria W. and Helstein, Toni, J.
Play: the key to emotional growth. il por Parents Mag 52:67+ N '77
PIERSON, William H. Jr
Hammond-Harwood House: a colonial masterpiece. bibl il Antiques 111:186-93 Ja '77
PIES. See Pie
PIES, Meat. See Cookery—Meat
PIETREWICZ, Alexandra T. and Kamil, A. C.
Visual detection of cryptic prey by blue jays (cyanocitta cristata) bibl il Science 195:580-2 F 11 '77
PIETRI, Arturo Uslar. See Uslar-Pietri, A.
PIETROPINTO, Anthony
—and Simenauer, Jacqueline
Beyond the male myth: results of questionnaire; excerpt. il Ladies Home J 94:126-7+ O '77; Same abr. with title How men really feel about sex and love. Read Digest 112:83-6 Ja '78
about
Hite-ing back. il por Time 110:106 D 12 '77 •
Male sexuality: the amazing truth about all those myths. M.-E. Banashek. Mademoiselle 83:152-3+ N '77 •
PIEZOELECTRIC devices
See also
Acoustic surface wave devices
PIGALU (island)
Annobon: forgotten island of the Atlantic. G. L. Voss. il Sea Front 23:101-5 Mr '77
PIGEON shooting
Swing . . . swing . . . swing and you'll hit those doves. J. Carmichel. il Outdoor Life 160: 62-3+ Jl '77
See also
Mourning dove shooting
PIGEONS
Visual search in the pigeon: hunt and peck method. D. S. Blough. bibl il Science 196:1013-14 My 27 '77
See also
Passenger pigeons
PIGGYBACK transportation of airplanes. See Airplanes—Transportation
PIGMENTS (biology)
Asymmetric structure of the purple membrane; bacteriorhodopsin. A. E. Blaurock and G. I. King. bibl il Science 196:1101-4 Je 3 '77
Kinetic resonance Raman spectroscopy: dynamics of deprotonation of the Schiff base of bacteriorhodopsin. M. A. Marcus and A. Lewis. bibl il Science 195:1328-30 Mr 25 '77
See also
Hemes
Melanin
Visual pigments
PIGNONE, Mary Margaret
Concentrated ownership of land: a problem of stewardship and world hunger. bibl il New Cath World 220:254-9 S '77
PIGS. See Swine
PIHL, Robert Olander
—and Parkes, M.
Hair element content in learning disabled children. bibl il Science 198:204-6 O 14 '77
about
Lead, cadmium linked to learning problems. Sci N 112:262 O 22 '77 •
PIKE, Arlene Rosen
Turning the menace into magic. Parents Mag 52:38-9+ Je '77
PIKE
See also
Muskellunge
PIKE fishing
Day the pike put the move on Herman; use of suckerfish when pike ice fishing in Michigan. R. Rau. il Sports Illus 46:38-40+ F 28 '77
King of the North. E. A. Bauer. il map Outdoor Life 159:82-5+ My '77
PILCHER, Don
Bad clay. Ceram Mo 25:17+ Mr '77
about
Don Pilcher. il por Ceram Mo 25:37-9 Mr '77 •
PILCHER, Rosamunde
Day of the storm; story; excerpt from novel. Good H 186:143-6 Ja '78
Heart is home; story. Good H 185:100-1 Ag '77
This time be true; story; excerpt from Under Gemini. Good H 184:181-4 Je '77
PILEATED woodpeckers. See Woodpeckers
PILEGGI, Sarah
Another rabbit is in the lettuce patch. il Sports Illus 46:22-3 F 28 '77
Biggie among the smalls. Sports Illus 47:83-4 N 28 '77
Choking off criticism with one stroke. il por Sports Illus 46:28-30+ Ap 25 '77
Golf (cont) il Sports Illus 46:54+ Ap 4; 47:88-9 S 5 '77
No end with this end. il pors Sports Illus 47: 32-4+ D 12 '77
Now on the other hand. . il Sports Illus 47: 16-19 D 12 '77
Pleasure of being the world's strongest woman. il pors Sports Illus 47:60-4+ N 14 '77
78 victories and she's still counting. il Sports Illus 46:30-2+ Ap 11 '77
This sport is not on the level. il Sports Illus 46:22-4 F 7 '77
To the right, to the left, hold it! il Sports Illus 46:36-9 Je 13 '77
With a grip on glory and her game. il pors Sports Illus 46:30-3+ Je 6 '77
PILES (disease) See Hemorrhoids
PILFERING. See Stealing
PILGRIM (ship) See Sailing vessels
PILIPOWSKYJ, S. See Hamilton, G. D. jt auth
PILL (birth control) See Contraceptives
PILLAGE
Around City Hall; question of federal aid after blackout looting in New York City. A. Logan. New Yorker 53:64-72 Ag 15 '77
Bastille Day '77; blackout looting in New York City. M. Edelson. Nat R 29:870 Ag 5 '77

PILLAGE—*Continued*
Blackout; New York City. J. A. Schnepper. Intellect 106:121 O '77
Counting losses in the rubble; effects of blackout looting in New York City. il Time 110:14+ Ag 1 '77
Illicit artifacts: a booming business. J. A. Dorman. il Sci Digest 81:inside cover, 68 Je '77
Looting and liberal racism: blackout looting in New York City. M. Decter. Commentary 64:48-54 S '77; Discussion. 64:4+ N; 30+ D '77
Memory and a contrast; blackout looting. P. Steinfels. Commonweal 104:520+ Ag 19 '77
Mugging of New York. New Repub 177:5-6+ Jl 30 '77
New York's looters: budding anarchy? G. E. Jones. U.S. News 83:14 Ag 1 '77
Night of terror, New York City blackout and looting. il Time 110:12-22 Jl 25 '77
Night of the alienated; blackout looting in New York City. C. Tucker. il Sat R 4:56 S 3 '77
Night the lights went on; urban poverty and the New York blackout. T. Powers. Commonweal 104:530-2 Ag 19 '77
Notes and comment; looting during New York City blackout. New Yorker 53:15-17 Ag 8 '77
People in the dark; New York City power failure. Nation 225:100 Ag 6 '77
Picking up the pieces; economic impact of New York's blackout. T. Nicholson and M. Reese. il Newsweek 90:60-1 Ag 1 '77
Plunderers: blackout looting in New York City. R. Boeth and others. il Newsweek 90:23-7 Jl 25 '77
Rip-off time; blackout looting in New York City. Nat R 29:869 Ag 5 '77
Tip of the iceberg; looting after blackout in New York City. il Ebony 32:132-3 S '77
Word from Washington; looting during New York blackout. F. Getlein. Progressive 41:14-15 O '77

PILLIOD, Charles J. 1918-
Charles Pilliod was the odd man in at Goodyear. A. M. Louis. il pors Fortune 95:280-3+ My '77 *

PILLOWS
Children's art into stitchery pillows. il Sunset 159:120 D '77
On this pillow the doll has four places to go. il Sunset 158:108+ F '77

PILLSBURY Company
New face jolts Pillsbury; R. F. Good. il por Bus W p92+ My 2 '77
Shaking up a company for solid growth; interview. W. H. Spoor. il pors Nations Bus 65:34-6+ O '77

PILOBOLUS Dance Theater. See Dance companies

PILOT, Automatic. See Automatic pilot (boats)

PILOT charts. See Nautical charts

PILOT ejection seats, capsules, etc. See Airplanes—Escape devices

PILOT whales. See Dolphins (mammals)

PILOTING, Airplane. See Airplanes—Piloting

PILOTS, Aviation. See Air pilots

PILOTS and pilotage
Push-button piloting; use of a calculator. E. Bergin and J. Buchanek. il Motor B & S 140:68-70+ Ag '77

Competitions

See Navigation—Competitions

PILTDOWN forgery
Paleontological hoaxes. A. M. Keen. Natur Hist 86:24+ My '77

PIMENTEL, David, and others
Pesticides, insects in foods, and cosmetic standards. bibl il BioScience 27:178-85 Mr '77

PINBALL machines
Extensions downtown; use of pinball machines by Manhattan Cable Television's The game show. New Yorker 53:25-7 F 28 '77
Fun machines; sports games. R. Cantwell. il Sports Illus 47:24-9 Jl 4 '77
Pinball goes electronic. T. Buckley. il N Y Times Mag p30-1 Ja 23 '77
Pinball lives! il Newsweek 89:54 My 30 '77
Pinball redux: the hottest games. il Time 110:80-1 O 31 '77

PINBALL machines for the home
Newest rage: home pinball. il Mech Illus 73:46 Jl '77

PINCUS, Walter
What reforms for Congress? Current 191:6-13 Mr '77

PINE
Conservation of potassium in the pinus resinosa ecosystem. E. L. Stone and R. Kszystyniak. bibl il Science 198:192-4 O 14 '77
Year-round Christmas tree; potted Norfolk pine. L. W. Patterson. il Org Gard & Farm 24:144-5 D '77

PINE Barrens (New Jersey)
Greenlining of America would start in Pine Barrens. Nat Parks & Con Mag 51:18-21 D '77
Pine Barrens under pressure. P. J. Baxter and J. Goldstein. il map Parks & Rec 12:20-3+ O '77

PINEAL body
Circadian organization in lizards: the role of the pineal organ. H. Underwood. bibl il Science 195:587-9 F 11 '77
Efflux of cyclic nucleotides from rat pineal: release of guanosine 3',5'-monophosphate from sympathic nerve endings. M. Zata and R. F. O'Dea. bibl il Science 197:174-6 Jl 8 '77
Melatonin induction of gonadal quiescence in pinealectomized Syrian hamsters. L. Tamarkin and others. bibl il Science 198:953-5 D 2 '77
Timekeeping by the pineal gland. S. Binkley and others. bibl il Science 197:1181-3 S 16 '77

PINEAPPLE family. See Bromeliads

PIÑEIRO, Armando Alonso. See Alonso Piñeiro, A.

PINEL, John P. J. and others
Temporal lobe aggression in rats. bibl il Science 197:1088-9 S 9 '77

PIÑERO, Miguel
Eulogy for a small-time thief. Review
Nation 225:668 D 17 '77 *

PINES, Maya
St-st-st-st-st-st-stuttering. il N Y Times Mag p26+ F 13 '77

PINEVILLE, Ky, flood. See Floods—United States

PING pong. See Table tennis

PINHOLE photography. See Photography, Pinhole

PINK Floyd (rock group) See Rock groups

PINKERTON, Jamie Horace
Jamie Horace Pinkerton. T. J. Cottle. il America 136:370-3 Ap 23 '77 *

PINNACLE Books (firm) See Publishers and publishing—Paperback books

PINNEY, Gregor W.
Back to 2 plus 2. Nation 224:625-7 My 21 '77

PINNEY, Robert E. See Armstrong, D. G. jt auth

PINNIPEDIA
See also
Walruses

PINOCHET UGARTE, Augusto
After DINA. R. Moreau. il Newsweek 90:50 S 12 '77 *
Chile's referendum farce. Nation 226:2-4 Ja 7 '78 *
Junta wins in a landslide. il por Time 111:29 Ja 16 '78 *
Juntas of Chile and Argentina: studies in government by terror. N. E. Roman. por Sat R 4:12+ Ap 2 '77 *
Pinochet and human rights. W. F. Buckley, Jr. Nat R 29:350-1 Mr 18 '77 *

PINSHOW, Berry, and others
Terrestrial locomotion in penguins: it costs more to waddle. bibl il Science 195:592-4 F 11 '77

PINSKER, Harold M. and Dudek, F. E.
Bag cell control of egg laying in freely behaving aplysia. bibl il Science 197:490-3 Jl 29 '77

PINSKY, Mark
American Gulag. Progressive 41:9 N '77
Dawson boys. Progressive 41:40-1 My '77
Not-so-new South. il Nation 224:367-8 Mr 26 '77
Testing in the dark. Nation 225:41-4 Jl 9 '77
Trial of the 1950s. Progressive 41:36-7 F '77
Trial they never had. Nation 224:754-6 Je 18 '77

PINSKY, Robert
Lair; poem. New Yorker 53:157 O 17 '77

about

Comment. R. Howard. Poetry 129:228-9 Ja '77 *

PINSON, Barbara B.
To one-up with honors, one must be unimpressed in the right way. House B 119:76 O '77

PINSON, Penelope
Books for parents. See occasional issues of Parents' magazine

PINTA Island. See Galápagos Islands

PINTER, Harold
No man's land. Review
Commonweal 104:20-1 Ja 7 '77 *

PINTO, Andrew. See Berman, N. jt auth

PIONEER flights. See Space flight to Jupiter; Space flight to Saturn

PIONEER life. See Frontier and pioneer life

PIONEER Village (amusement park) See Amusement parks

PIOTROVSKY, Boris Borisovich
Scythian world. il UNESCO Courier 29:4-8 D '76

PIOUS, Donald, and Soderland, Carl
HLA variants of cultured human lymphoid cells: evidence for mutational origin and estimation of mutation rate. bibl il Science 197:769-71 Ag 19 '77

PIPELINE companies
Alaskan oil still can't find a Midwest route. Bus W p44 N 28 '77
Alyeska Pipeline's huge surplus sale; machines, materials, and construction camp facilities. il Bus W p35-6 Ja 31 '77
Cinderella's pipeline; Alcan Pipeline's winning route. A. J. Mayer and W. J. Cook. il por map Newsweek 90:87+ S 12 '77
Fight to pipe Alaska's gas; Northwest Energy Co. map Time 110:80 S 19 '77

PIPELINE companies—*Continued*
Irony of holding too much natural gas. Bus W p56+ Jl 25 '77
Man who won the pipeline; S. R. Blair's Alberta Gas Trunk Line Co. por Bus W p88-9 Ag 22 '77
One final squabble; Alyeska Pipeline Service Co. por Forbes 119:140 Ap 15 '77
See also
Panhandle Eastern Pipe Line Company
Texas Eastern Transmission Corporation
Williams Companies

Finance

Financing: the real test for Alcan pipeline. il map Bus W p 102+ N 28 '77

PIPELINES
See also
Coal pipelines
Gas, Natural—Pipelines
Petroleum pipelines

PIPER, John
Deciding what we deserve. Chr Today 22:12-15 O 21 '77
Is self-love biblical? il Chr Today 21:6-9 Ag 12 '77

PIPER, William Thomas, 1911-
Piper. J. W. Olcott. por Flying 101:256-7 S '77 *

PIPER Aircraft Corporation
Courts to rule on Piper control. Aviation W 107:71 S 12 '77
Piper counts on new trainer to boost market identification. D. M. North. il Aviation W 107:21-2 O 24 '77

PIPES, Richard Edgar
Our elite is unwilling to look facts in the face. por U.S. News 82:44-5 Je 27 '77
Why the Soviet Union thinks it could fight and win a nuclear war. bibl f Commentary 64:21-34 Jl; 20+ S '77

PIPES
Case of the disappearing pipes. T. H. Jones. il Mech Illus 73:104+ Ag '77
See also
Sewer pipes
Water pipes

Corrosion

See Corrosion and anti-corrosives

PIPES, Concrete
See also
Sewer pipes

PIPES, Plastic
Greenhouse frame, water wand; using polyvinyl chloride pipe. il Sunset 158:256+ My '77
See also
Sewer pipes
Water pipes, Plastic

PIPES, Tobacco. See Tobacco pipes

PIPPERT, Wesley G.
Carter at Sunday school. Chr Cent 94:446 My 11 '77
Viewing the family from the Oval Office. Chr Today 21:60-1 S 9 '77

PIPPIN, Horace
Exhibitions in sight. B. Wasserman. il por Sch Arts 77:34-7 D '77 *
Horace Pippin's personal spiritual journey. B. Forgey. il Art N 76:74-5 Summ '77 *
Pippin's folk heroes. M. Stevens. il Newsweek 90:59-60 Ag 22 '77 *

PIPPIN, R. Gene
In Herculaneum; poem. Poetry 130:17 Ap '77

PIRANDELLO, Luigi
Naked. Review
Time 110:61 N 14 '77 *

PIRANHAS
Piranha: minijaws of the Amazon. E. D'Aulaire and P. O. D'Aulaire. il Read Digest 111:11-14+ S '77

PIRATE radio stations. See Radio stations, Illegal

PIRATES
See also
Buccaneers
United States—History—Tripolitan War, 1801-1805

PIRATING of motion pictures. See Motion pictures —Unauthorized reprints

PIRELLI, Leopoldo
Italian economy at a crossroad; address, March 3, 1977. Vital Speeches 43:382-4 Ap 1 '77

PIRELLI/Lancia/Wonder Muffler Marquette 1000. See Automobile rallies

PIROPLASMOSIS
Dangerous nymphs of Nantucket; babesiosis. R. S. Desowitz and L. H. Miller. il Natur Hist 86:10+ bibl(p 110) D '77
Human babesiosis: reservoir of infection on Nantucket Island; discussion. bibl Science 195:506-7 F 4 '77

PIRSIG, Robert M.
Cruising blues and their cure. por Esquire 87: 65-8 My '77

PISAR, Samuel
Let's put detente back on the rails. il N Y Times Mag p31-3+ S 25 '77

PISCATAWAY, N.J. Public Libraries. See Libraries—New Jersey

PISIER, Marie France
Marie-France Pisier: French best; interview, ed by J. J. Buch. il pors Vogue 167:238-9+ My '77

PISTOL shooting. See Shooting

PISTOLS
New Mafia killer: a silenced .22. il Time 109:22 Ap 18 '77
Remington-Elliot ring trigger derringers. C. Worman. il Hobbies 82:154 Ja '78
Target pistols: how to pick a winner. J. Carmichel. il por Outdoor Life 159:54+ My '77
U.S. model 1841-43 pistol; Ames/Deringer pistols. C. Worman. il Hobbies 82:154 Jl '77
See also
Revolvers

PISTON, Walter
Fitting memorial: The incredible flutist. W. D. Curtis. Am Rec G 40:36-8 Je '77 *
Piston discography. W. D. Curtis. Am Rec G 40:38-40 Je '77 *

PISTON rings
Bridging the gap. il Hot Rod 30:88 F '77

PITA bread. See Bread

PITCHERS
Liberty Bell water pitcher. M. Wollett and B. Wollett. il Hobbies 82:99 Je '77

PITCHERS, Baseball. See Baseball players

PITCHFORD, Kenneth
Balcony scene; poem. Poetry 130:311-18 S '77
Water-bearer; poem; excerpt from The contraband poems. Ms 6:17-18 Jl '77

PITKIN, Anne
Good Friday poem. Nation 225:502 N 12 '77
Notes for continuing the performance; poem. Nation 225:57 Jl 9 '77
River: poem. Nation 225:476 N 5 '77

PITNEY-BOWES, Inc
Pressure to compromise personal ethics; results of studies at Pitney-Bowes and Uniroyal. il Bus W p 107 Ja 31 '77
Winning and holding employee loyalty; interview. F. T. Allen. pors. Nations Bus 65:40-2+ Ap '77

PITOT, Henry C.
Cancer—an overview. bibl il por Chemistry 50:11-17 Ja '77

PITSEOLAK, Peter
How it really was; excerpt from People from our side. D. H. Eber. il por Natur Hist 86:70-5 bibl (p 101) F '77 *

PITTILLO, Elen Sain. See Sizemore, C. C. jt auth

PITTS, James L.
Con: Alaska wolf kill. il Nat Wildlife 15:9 Ag '77

PITTS, James N. Jr, and others
Enhancement of photochemical smog by N,N'-diethylhydroxylamine in polluted ambient air. bibl il Science 197:255-7 Jl 15 '77

PITTS, Robert A.
Unshackle your comers. bibl f Harvard Bus R 55:127-36 My '77

PITTSBURGH

Bridges

Polymer surface revamps bridge; Smithfield street bridge. il Am City & County 92:32 Ap '77

Crime

Offside in Pittsburgh? investigation of football players for possible involvement in fraud against a job-training program. S. Fraker and S. Lesher. pors Newsweek 89:40 My 9 '77

Galleries and museums

Pittsburgh center pinpoints the art of the needle; Center for the History of American Needlework. G. Bethel. Craft Horiz 37:42 Ag '77

Music

Once in a lifetime; performance by H. Olivera in St Paul's Cathedral. W. F. Rickenbacker. Nat R 29:897-8 Ag 5 '77
See also
Opera—Pennsylvania

Transit systems

Busway aims for more transit riders. il Am City & County 92:23 Je '77

PITTSBURGH Ballet Theatre
Jo An McCarthy of Pittsburgh Ballet Theatre; interview, ed. by N. M. Stoop. J. A. McCarthy. il pors Dance Mag 51:56-9 D '77
Reviews: M. Béjart's Romeo and Juliet. N. M. Stoop. il Dance Mag 51:78-9 D '77

PITTSBURGH Conference on Analytical Chemistry and Applied Spectroscopy. See Chemistry —Conferences

PITTSBURGH Opera. See Opera—Pennsylvania

PITTSBURGH. University

Libraries

Pitt study pegs faulty acquisitions patterns. Lib J 102:1438 Jl '77

Stalking the wild job; or, A career library from the ground up; Career Planning Library at the University of Pittsburgh. R. J. Egelston. bibl il Wilson Lib Bull 52:330-5 D '77

Use of a university library collection: a progress report on a Pittsburgh study; with editorial comment. T. J. Galvin and A. Kent. Lib 102:2295, 2317-20 N 15 '77

PITTSTON Company

Boys from Buffalo Creek; proposed refinery in Eastport, Me. J. E. Chappell, Jr. Progressive 41:11 N '77

PITUITARY body

β-Endorphin and adrenocorticotropin are secreted concomitantly by the pituitary gland. R. Guillemin and others. bibl il Science 197:1367-9 S 30 '77

PITUITARY hormone releasing factors

Gonadotropin-releasing hormone in milk. T. Baram and others. bibl il Science 198:300-2 O 21 '77

PITUITARY hormones

Growth hormone: species-specific stimulation of erythropoiesis in vitro. D. W. Golde and others. bibl il Science 196:1112-13 Je 3 '77

See also

Gonadotropins

PITUITARY tumors. See Tumors

PITZ, Henry Clarence

Henry C. Pitz: picture maker. J. Maxwell. il por Am Artist 41:58-65+ My '77 *

PIUS IX, Pope

Was Vatican I rigged? il pors Time 110:92-3 N 14 '77 *

PIVEN, Frances Fox. See Cloward, R. A. jt auth

PIZZA. See Cookery, Italian

PIZZA Hut, Inc. See Restaurants—Chain and franchise operations

PIZZI, William J. and others

Monosodium glutamate administration to the newborn reduces reproductive ability in female and male mice. bibl il Science 196:452-4 Ap 22 '77

PIZZICA excavations. See Italy—Antiquities

PLACE, Jennifer, and Zeifer, Ellen

Making handmade paper. il Am Artist 41:34-8 Ag '77

PLACE, Mary Kay

Close-up; interview, ed by E. Miller. por Seventeen 36:92+ Ap '77

Guess who's for the ERA? ed by E. Wheeler. pors Ms 5:79 Ap '77

about

Happiest survivor of Mary Hartman. C. See. por McCalls 104:28+ Je '77 *

PLACE names. See Names, Geographical

PLACEBOS

Mysterious placebo: how mind helps medicine work. N. Cousins. il Sat R 5:8-12+ O 1 '77; Discussion. 5:6 Ja 7 '78

PLACENTIA, Calif.

Digitized mapping pays off for California city. il Am City & County 92:111 S '77

PLACES of retirement. See Retirement, Places of

PLAGENS, Peter

Ad Reinhardt, where are you now that we really need you? Art in Am 65:10-11 S '77

70 years of California modernism in 340 works by 200 artists. il Art in Am 65:63-9 My '77

PLAINS, Ga.

Billy Carter talks about all the money he's making; interview. B. Carter. il pors U.S. News 83:33-5 Ag 29 '77

Changing times in Plains. J. A. Williams. Read Digest 111:133-6 Jl '77

Pain in Plains. R. Boeth and others. il Newsweek 90:16-17 Ag 15 '77

Say goodbye to poor Plains. il Time 109:14-15 Ap 4 '77

Too much hoopla in Plains even for the Carters. il U.S. News 82:84-5 Ap 11 '77

Will celebrity spoil Plains, Ga? H. Seneker. il Forbes 119:29-30 Ja 15 '77

Religious institutions and affairs

See Georgia—Religious institutions and affairs

PLAINS

See also

Great Plains

PLANET Ocean exhibit. See Oceanography—Exhibitions

PLANETARIUMS

Communicating astronomy in Vancouver; H. R. MacMillan Planetarium. D. A. Rodger. il Sky & Tel 53:104-7 F '77

Eight feet of solar spectrum; Grace Flandrau Planetarium. O. R. Norton. il Sky & Tel 54:176-9 S '77

New West German planetarium; Stuttgart Planetarium. H. U. Keller. il Sky & Tel 54:375-7 N '77

PLANETARY engineering. See Environmental engineering

PLANETARY nebulae. See Nebulae

PLANETS

Brilliant disc-shaped star may be forming planets. il Space World N-9-165:41-2 S '77

Colorful groupings of the bright planets. il Sky & Tel 54:536-8 D '77

Companions of sunlike stars. H. A. Abt. il Sci Am 236:96-104 bibl(p 148) Ap '77

In the depths of space: an exciting cosmic hunt. J. Mullaney. il Sci Digest 81:41-3 F '77

Is the star MWC 349 forming a planetary system? Sky & Tel 54:363 N '77

[Month] stars. J. Stokley. See fourth issue of each month of Science news to December 24, 1977

Planetary system about to form; planet for a third nearby star? il Sci N 111:404-5 Je 25 '77

Stellar disk suggests planet formation. G. B. Lubkin. Phys Today 30:19 N '77

Sun, moon, and planets this month. R. C. Victor. See issues of Sky and telescope

See also

Life on other planets
Occultations
Satellites
Solar system

also names of planets, e.g. Uranus (planet)

Atmosphere

Climate and the planets. R. Goody. il Natur Hist 87:84-93 Ja '78

Sunny days on other worlds. J. Eberhart. il Sci N 111:380-2 Je 11 '77

Exploration

Next great leap into space. C. Sagan. il N Y Times Mag p 12-16+ Jl 10 '77

Planetary exploration. C. Sagan. por Newsweek 89:9 Je 20 '77

Voyaging to the outer planets. J. K. Beatty. il Sky & Tel 54:95-9 Ag '77

See also

Space flight—Voyager flights
Space flight to Jupiter
Space flight to Mars
Space flight to Mercury
Space flight to Saturn
Space flight to Venus

Observations

Bright planets in the predawn sky. R. C. Victor. il Sky & Tel 54:45 Jl '77

See also

Mars (planet)—Observations
Venus (planet)—Observations

PLANETS, Minor. See Asteroids

PLANKTON

Evolution of phosphorus limitation in lakes. D. W. Schindler. bibl il Science 195:260-2 Ja 21 '77

Hot plankton; uranium deposit creation by coccolith plankton. Newsweek 90:81 D 12 '77

Polychlorinated biphenyls: penetration into the deep ocean by zooplankton fecal pellet transport. D. L. Elder and S. W. Fowler. bibl il Science 197:459-61 Jl 29 '77

See also

Water bloom

PLANNING, Business. See Business planning

PLANNING, City. See City planning

PLANNING, Educational. See Educational planning

PLANNING, Land. See Land utilization

PLANNING, Library. See Library planning

PLANNING Research Corporation. See Business consultants

PLANQUETTE, Robert

Fine French frou-frou; Planquette's Les cloches de Corneville. W. Botsford. Am Rec G 40:35 N '76 *

PLANS (architecture) See Architecture—Designs and plans; Architecture, Domestic—Designs and plans

PLANT alkaloids. See Alkaloids

PLANT boxes. See Flower boxes, planters, etc.

PLANT breeding

April in the garden; hybrids. D. Fell. Horticulture 55:70-3 Ap '77

Energy limits crop improvement. Sci N 111:23 Ja 8 '77

Superseeds. J. Powell. il Sci Digest 81:35-8+ My '77

World's crop plant germplasm—an endangered resource. H. G. Wilkes. bibl il map Bull Atom Sci 33:8-16 F '77

See also

Corn—Breeding
Corn—Hybrids
Hybridization

PLANT buying. See Plants—Purchasing

PLANT cells and tissues
Mechanically induced wall appositions of plant cells can prevent penetration by a parasitic fungus. J. R. Aist. bibl il Science 197:568-71 Ag 5 '77
See also
Chloroplasts
Protoplasts
Stomata

Culture

Regeneration of Douglas fir plantlets through tissue culture. T. Y. Cheng and T. H. Voqui. bibl il Science 198:306-7 O 21 '77

PLANT conservation
See also
Rare plants

PLANT covers. See Plants, Protection of

PLANT cuttings. See Plant propagation

PLANT dyes. See Dyes and dyeing

PLANT ecology. See Botany—Ecology

PLANT enzymes. See Enzymes, Plant

PLANT evolution. See Plants—Evolution

PLANT genetics
Breeding crisis for our crops: is the gene pool drying up? H. G. Wilkes. map Horticulture 55:52-9 Ap '77
More efficient bread. Sci Digest 81:86 F '77
Plant genetics: increasing crop yield. P. R. Day. bibl Science 197:1334-9 S 30 '77
Somatic cell genetic manipulation in plants. P. R. Day and others. bibl BioScience 27:116-18 F '77
World's crop plant germplasm—an endangered resource. H. G. Wilkes. bibl il map Bull Atom Sci 33:8-16 F '77
See also
Plant breeding

PLANT growth. See Growth (plants)

PLANT growth regulators. See Growth inhibiting substances (plants)

PLANT growth regulators. See Growth promoting substances (plants)

PLANT holders. See Flower boxes, planters, etc.

PLANT hormones. See Hormones, Plant

PLANT hybrids. See Hybridization

PLANT lice
Aphids foiled by false alarm. W. S. Bowers. il Chemistry 50:23 Jl '77
Peptidoglycan in the cell wall of the primary intracellular symbiote of the pea aphid. E. J. Houk and others. bibl il Science 198:401-3 O 28 '77
Sesquiterpene progenitor, germacrene A: an alarm pheromone in aphids. W. S. Bowers. bibl il Science 196:680-1 My 6 '77

PLANT lore
Believe-it-or-not herbal. T. Gabriell. il Org Gard & Farm 24:82-4 N '77

PLANT mail order business. See Mail order business

PLANT membranes. See Membranes (biology)

PLANT names. See Botany—Nomenclature

PLANT nutrition. See Plants—Nutrition

PLANT propagation
Growing ferns from spores. il Sunset 159:154-5 Jl '77
Making your plants live forever. C. O. Foster. il Org Gard & Farm 24:65-7 O '77
Rooting section; propagation of cuttings. il Seventeen 36:115 Jl '77
Vine and dine. J. Farmer. Seventeen 36:59 O '77
See also
Grafting

PLANT proteins
Energy limits crop improvement. Sci N 111:23 Ja 8 '77

PLANT research. See Botanical research

PLANT roots. See Roots

PLANT shelves. See Shelves

PLANT stands. See Flower stands

PLANT succession
Inevitable forest; excerpt from A closer look. M. A. Godfrey. il Nat Wildlife 15:14-16+ Ag '77

PLANT therapy. See Gardening—Therapeutic use

PLANT viruses. See Viruses, Plant

PLANTATIONS
Furniture of the River Road plantations in Louisiana. J. J. Poesch. bibl il Antiques 111:1184-8 Je '77
Mini-holiday: Southern plantation houses in Louisiana and Mississippi. B. Jeffer. map Holiday 58:28-30 Ap '77
Restoration of San Francisco (St Frusquin), Reserve, Louisiana. H. W. Krotzer, Jr. il Antiques 111:1194-1203 Je '77
River Road plantations of Louisiana. W. N. Banks. bibl il Antiques 111:1170-83 Je '77

PLANTEGENEST, Gerald L.
Nicaragua of tomorrow. il map Américas 29:13-18 S '77

PLANTERS (farm machines)
Gear your planter for narrow rows. L. Reichenberger. Suc Farm 75:24 Ap '77
Get your planter ready—now. Suc Farm 75:no2 A3 F '77
No-till planters for better stands. il Farm J 101:K4 My '77
Plants 640 acres a day. E. Stout. il Farm J 101:B2 mid-F '77
Swing-back planters handle like dreams. G. Lepper. il Suc Farm 75:no3 26-7 F '77

Equipment

In-row subsoiling. K. Copeland. il Farm J 101:24-6 O '77
Instant refills buy Don Refert extra planting time. B. Gergen. il Suc Farm 75:no3 20-1 F '77
Mix-and-match planters. il Farm J 101:14-15 mid-Mr '77
Modified drills rival planters for accuracy. G. Lepper. il Suc Farm 75:23+ Ap '77
No-till drills for double-crop soybeans. G. Lepper. il Suc Farm 75:no4 39 Mr '77
One-trip planter cuts fuel bills in half. B. Coffman. il Farm J 101:A8 Mr '77
Planters for better stands with less tillage. il Farm J 101:30-1 Mr '77
Plants 9 acres an hour-in 21'' rows; soybean drills. B. Coffman. il Farm J 101:B8 Ap '77
Speed up fertilizer refills. il Farm J 101:20-3 F '77

PLANTERS (flower boxes) See Flower boxes, planters, etc.

PLANTING. See Gardening; Landscape gardening; Plants, Space arrangement of

PLANTING machinery. See Planters (farm machines)

PLANTING of corn. See Corn—Seeding

PLANTING of trees. See Tree planting

PLANTING plans and tables. See Vegetable gardening—Planting plans and tables

PLANTS
Fossil plants you can still grow. M. M. Whitson. il Horticulture 55:22-5 O '77
[Month] in your garden. See issues of Sunset
See also
Angiosperms
Annuals (plants)
Aquatic plants
Biomass energy
Botany
Bulbs
Ferns
Forage plants
Forcing (plants)
Hallucination and illusion producing plants
Herbs
Insectivorous plants
Perennials (plants)
Poisonous plants
Pollen
Rare plants
Roots
Seeds
Succulent plants
Tropical plants
Urban flora
Vegetation
Weeds
also names of plants, e.g. Ferns; *also* headings beginning Plant

Adaptation

See Adaptation (botany)

All-America Selections

Culture & notes; All-America Rose Selections. il Horticulture 55:62-3 Jl '77

Breeding

See Plant breeding

Collection and preservation

Art of preserving natural materials. M. Mintz and R. Szajman. il Design (US) 78:2-4 Summ '77
See also
Herbariums

Disease and pest resistance

Bacteria-plant cell surface interactions: active immobilization of saprophytic bacteria in plant leaves. V. O. Sing and M. N. Schroth. bibl il Science 197:759-61 Ag 19 '77
Helping plants hold the line. J. A. Miller. il Sci N 112:268-70 O 22 '77
Mechanically induced wall appositions of plant cells can prevent penetration by a parasitic fungus. J. R. Aist. bibl il Science 197:568-71 Ag 5 '77
See also
Alfalfa—Disease and pest resistance

Diseases and pests

See also
Insects, Injurious and beneficial

Dormancy

See Dormancy (plants)

PLANTS—*Continued*

Drought resistance

Drought discoveries. il Sunset 159:96-7 N '77
How to adjust for a dry year. C. E. Sommers. il Suc Farm 75:18 Ap '77

Electrophysiology

See Electrophysiology of plants

Evolution

Compound ovary with open carpels in winteraceae (magnoliales) evolutionary implications. J. F. Leroy. bibl il Science 196:977-8 My 27 '77
Ecology and evolution of flowering plant dominance. P. J. Regal. bibl Science 196:622-9 My 6 '77
Overlooked link: Darwin and his flowers; excerpt from Darwin and his flowers. M. Allan. il por Horticulture 55:12-21 O '77

Export-import problems

Orchid diplomacy; trip to Canton Fair in attempt to import orchids to U.S. W. K. Glikbarg. Horticulture 55:8-13 My '77
See also
Convention on International Trade in Endangered Species of Wild Fauna and Flora

Fertilization

See Fertilization of plants

Folklore

See Plant lore

Hardiness

See also
Plants—Drought resistance

Nitrogen fixation

See Nitrogen—Fixation

Nomenclature

See Botany—Nomenclature

Nutrition

What you should know if you foliar feed your soybeans. B. Coffman. il Farm J 101:20-1 My '77
See also
Eutrophication
Photosynthesis

Odors

See Odors

Potassium content

Conservation of potassium in the pinus resinosa ecosystem. E. L. Stone and R. Kszystyniak. bibl il Science 198:192-4 O 14 '77

Protection

See Plants, Protection of

Purchasing

Consumer's guide to nursery shopping. V. McElwain. il Horticulture 55:40-3 O '77

Reproduction

Gemmae: a role in sexual reproduction in the fern genus vittaria. V. D. Emigh and D. R. Farrar. bibl il Science 198:297-8 O 21 '77

Periodicity

See Botany—Periodicity

Respiration

Increasing photosynthesis by inhibiting photorespiration with glyoxylate. D. J. Oliver and I. Zelitch. bibl il Science 196:1450-1 Je 24 '77

Soilless culture

See Hydroponics

PLANTS, Aquatic. See Aquatic plants

PLANTS, Edible
Finding and using the wild spices. G. L. Nelson. il Org Gard & Farm 24:79-81 N '77
Lambs-quarters: a wild food worth discovering. il Bet Hom & Gard 55:196 My '77
Wild harvest. bibl il Field & S 82:10+ S '77
Wild ways to feel better. R. Rodale. il Org Gard & Farm 25:54-7 Ja '78
See also
Crops
Greens, Edible
Nettles
Tubers
Vegetables

PLANTS, Effect of climate on
Be your own weatherman. C. E. Sommers. il Suc Farm 75:19-24 My '77
Editorial; question of Department of Agriculture's world crop yield forecasts and abnormal weather patterns. C. Whipple. Horticulture 55:6 Ap '77

PLANTS, Effect of cold on. See Plants, Effect of temperature on

PLANTS, Effect of drought on. See Plants—Drought resistance

PLANTS, Effect of light on
Light and stomatical function: blue light stimulates swelling of guard cell protoplasts. E. Zeiger and P. K. Hepler. bibl il Science 196:887-9 My 20 '77
See also
Artificial light gardening
Photosynthesis

PLANTS, Effect of salts on
Growing crops on sand dunes? L. Wood. il Sea Front 23:228-32 Jl '77

PLANTS, Effect of stress on
NASA launches a new experiment to explore how plants react to stress. C. Mitchell. il pors Horticulture 55:10-13 S '77

PLANTS, Effect of temperature on
Cold-weather survival guide for houseplants. G. Abraham and K. Abraham. il Org Gard & Farm 25:166-71 Ja '78
Florida: frost-kissed oranges. R. Rauch. il Time 109:12 F 14 '77
Florida grits and bears it. T. Nicholson and A. Jaffe. il Newsweek 89:56-7 F 7 '77
Price impact of Florida's freeze. il Bus W p30-1 F 7 '77

PLANTS, Effect of wind on
Do plants shiver in the north wind? L. Hill. il Org Gard & Farm 24:92-4 O '77

PLANTS, Flowering of
Coadapted competitors: the flowering seasons of hummingbird-pollinated plants in a tropical forest. F. G. Stiles. bibl il Science 198:1177-8 D 16 '77
How to keep your holiday plants blooming. R. Langer. il House & Gard 149:30+ D '77
See also
Fruit-bud development
Plants, Night blooming

PLANTS, Food. See Plants, Edible

PLANTS, Fossil. See Paleobotany

PLANTS, Hallucinogenic. See Hallucination and illusion producing plants

PLANTS, Hanging. See Hanging plants

PLANTS, Indoor. See House plants

PLANTS, Marsh. See Marsh plants

PLANTS, Medical. See Botany, Medical

PLANTS, Night blooming
Plants for night people; odoriferous flowering plants. R. Langer. il House & Gard 149:42+ S '77

PLANTS, Ornamental
Grays—restful, luminous. il Sunset 158:255 My '77
See also
Ardisia
Coleus
Hanging plants

PLANTS, Photography of. See Photography of flowers, plants, trees, etc.

PLANTS, Poisonous. See Poisonous plants

PLANTS, Potted
Greenhouse; pot-et-fleur, or mixed pan. J. Kilborn. il Horticulture 55:50+ O '77
How to make plants mobile. D. Raffel. il House & Gard 149:68+ D '77
See also
Flower boxes, planters, etc.
House plants
Soils, Potting
Watering of plants

PLANTS, Protection of
Call it a cloche—or a portable plastic plant speeder-upper. il Sunset 158:186 F '77
Frost protection for spring crops. il Org Gard & Farm 24:98-103 Mr '77
How to cage tomatoes. il Bet Hom & Gard 55:172 Je '77
Tunnel your way to earlier crops! cloche gardening. S. U. Pichard. Org Gard & Farm 24:172 D '77
See also
Scarecrows

PLANTS, Rock. See Rock plants

PLANTS, Sex in
See also
Plants—Reproduction

PLANTS, Shade
Shade-loving plants and how to grow them. R. O'Harra. il Bet Hom & Gard 55:88-93 My '77

PLANTS, Space arrangement of
How planting accuracy pays. L. Reichenberger. il Suc Farm 75:no4 L12 Mr '77
I'm putting my garden to beds. G. Williams, Jr. Org Gard & Farm 24:69-73 My '77

PLANTS, Useful. See Botany, Economic

PLANTS, Watering of. See Watering of plants

PLANTS as energy sources. See Biomass energy

PLANTS as gifts
Almost instant plant gifts—cuttings in water, pebbles. il Sunset 159:176-7 D '77
Best plant gifts. B. Mulligan. il Am Home 80:21 D '77
Taking care of gift plants. Sunset 159:182 D '77

PLANTS as water purifiers. See Water purification
PLANTS for shady places. See Plants, Shade
PLANTS in cities. See Urban flora
PLANTS in house decoration
Keeping winter green; ideas of Renny Reynolds. E. Brown. il N Y Times Mag p86 D 18 '77
PLANTS in literature
See also
Shakespeare, W.—Natural history
PLASMA (ionized gases)
Energetic oxygen ions stream up to magnetosphere. W. A. Flanagan. bibl il Phys Today 30:17-19 N '77
See also
Solar wind
PLASMA confinement
Double your pleasure double your fun. D. E. Thomsen. il Sci N 111:61 Ja 22 '77
See also
Tokamaks
PLASMA membranes. See Membranes (biology)
PLASMAPHERESIS
Myasthenia gravis: cleansing the blood. il Sci N 112:391 D 10 '77
PLASMIDS
Conjugal transfer of the gonococcal penicillinase plasmid. B. I. Eisenstein and others. bibl il Science 195:998-1000 Mr 11 '77
Construction of chimeric phages and plasmids containing the origin of replication of bacteriophage lambda. D. D. Moore and others. bibl il Science 198:1041-6 D 9 '77
Novel screening procedure for recombinant plasmids. J. Telford and others. bibl il Science 195:391-3 Ja 28 '77
Nucleotide sequences from the rabbit beta globin gene inserted into escherichia coli plasmids. J. K. Browne and others. bibl il Science 195:389-91 Ja 28 '77
Rat insulin genes: construction of plasmids containing the coding sequences. A. Ullrich and others. bibl il Science 196:1313-19 Je 17 '77
Recombinant DNA: examples of present-day research; symposium. bibl il Science 196:159-221 Ap 8 '77
PLASMODIUM (parasite)
Control of gamete formation (exflagellation) in malaria parasites. R. Carter and M. M. Nijhout. bibl il Science 195:407-9 Ja 28 '77
PLASSON, Michel
Artist life. D. J. Soria. il por Hi Fi 27:MA8+ F '77 *
Man of Toulouse. H. Johnson. por Opera N 41:34-5 F 5 '77 *
PLASTER masks. See Masks (sculpture)
PLASTER modeling. See Modeling
PLASTER work (craft)
Balth and the beast. S. Butchkes. il pors Craft Horiz 37:28-31 Ag '77
Hand sculpture. A.-L. Sanger. il Sch Arts 77:54-5 O '77
Plaster techniques. V. G. Timmons. Sch Arts 76:41 Ap '77
Tackle your spackle for ingenious sculpture. N. Berman and A. Pinto. il Design (US) 79:18-19 Fall '77
PLASTIC flooring. See Flooring, Plastic
PLASTIC foams
Buoyancy in a bottle; triggered foam flotation system. S. Stapleton. il Motor B & S 139:72-4 Mr '77
New way to set posts. il Mech Illus 73:92 Mr '77
PLASTIC pipes. See Pipes, Plastic
PLASTIC sewer pipes. See Sewer pipes
PLASTIC surgery. See Surgery, Plastic
PLASTIC water pipes. See Water pipes, Plastic
PLASTIC worms. See Fishing lures, flies, etc.
PLASTICS
See also
Flooring, Plastic
Polypropylene
PLASTICS in automobiles. See Automobiles—Materials
PLASTICS industry
See also
APL Corporation
PLASTICS work
Plastic/leather. D. Aguado. il Craft Horiz 37:17 Je '77

Projects

How to custom design plastic cases for projects. J. Huff. il Pop Electr 12:81-4 S '77
Plastic cube with memory. il Mech Illus 73:153 O '77
PLATE, Thomas
Cops & robbers offshore. il map Motor B & S 140:51-3 O '77
Mysterious disappearance of Pirate's Lady. il por Motor B & S 140:57-60+ S '77
PLATE tectonics. See Geology, Structural
PLATFORM tennis. See Paddle tennis
PLATFORMS
Easy-to-build garage space-saver; storage platform. il Pop Mech 147:122 F '77
PLATO'S Retreat (club) See New York (city)—Clubs
PLATT, Richard B.
New method of metal casting: cold casting with epoxy and metal powders. il Am Artist 41:56-61+ Ap '77
PLATYFISHES
Socially induced inhibition of genetically determined maturation in the platyfish, xiphophorus maculatus. J. J. Sohn. bibl il Science 195:199-201 Ja 14 '77
PLAY
Capturing the play spirit of the child. B. Tyler. Educ Digest 42:32-5 F '77
Child's play: what every parent needs to know. J. Lever. il Ms 65:22 F '77
Play: the key to emotional growth. M. W. Piers and T. J. Helstein. il por Parents Mag 52:67+ N '77
See also
Games
Recreation
PLAY and other plays; drama. See Beckett, S.
PLAY houses. See Playhouses
PLAY schools
See also
Nursery schools
PLAY writing. See Drama—Technique
PLAYBOY (periodical)
Andy Young, Andy Young; interview. P. Goldman and E. Clift. Newsweek 89:34 Je 20 '77
LeRoy Neiman; sports illustrator. N. Meglin. il por Am Artist 41:36-9 Jl '77
Merchants of raunchiness. T. Griffith. il por Time 110:69+ Jl 4 '77
Sex in the seventies; interview, ed by L. Sanford. B. Guccione. pors Am Home 80:46-8+ F '77
Young survives another storm; Playboy interview. U.S. News 82:29 Je 20 '77
PLAYBOY Enterprises Inc
Another Playboy hutch cleaning. por Time 110:95 S 26 '77
Middle-aged rabbit. il por Forbes 119:29-32 Je 1 '77
Skinning the rabbit. D. Pauly and C. J. Harper. il por Newsweek 90:66+ S 26 '77
Thinning the staff fattens Playboy. Bus W p59+ S 26 '77
PLAYER piano
Digits on the ivories; Pianocorder. Hi Fi 27:56 S '77
PLAYGROUND apparatus. See Playgrounds—Equipment
PLAYGROUNDS
Do-it-yourself adventure playgrounds. N. Rudolph. il Parents Mag 52:38-9+ My '77
Playground blend; adventure playground planned by campers; Forest Acres Camp for Girls in Fryeburg, Me. C. Leigh. il Camp Mag 49:6-8 My '77
See also
Athletic fields

Equipment

Old West. il Parks & Rec 12:31 My '77
Playscapes sculpture-playground in Atlanta. A. Bledsoe. il Sch Arts 76:22-5 Ap '77
Plywood playthings for climbing, for sliding, for playing house. il Sunset 159:98-9 Jl '77
Reaching high point with a playground; construction of playground for the handicapped, High Point, Mich. P. Hogan. il Parks & Rec 12:26-9 N '77
PLAYGROUNDS, Home

Equipment

Play tower . . . easily built, inexpensive. il Sunset 159:116 S '77
See also
Playhouses
PLAYHOUSES
Knole Cottage. S. A. Parvin. il Hobbies 82:123-4 Ag '77
Playhouse is an old cable spool. il Sunset 158:156 Mr '77
Split-level playhouse. il Sunset 158:154 Ap '77
See also
Tree houses
PLAYING cards. See Cards
PLAYING fields. See Athletic fields
PLAYWRIGHTS, American. See Dramatists, American
PLAYWRITING. See Drama—Technique
PLAZA Hotel. See New York (city)—Hotels, restaurants, etc.
PLEAS (criminal procedure)
Justice for whom? plea bargaining. S. Phillips. il por Psychol Today 10:70-2+ Mr '77
PLEASANTS, Henry
André Previn comes home. pors Sat R 4:34-6 F 19 '77
PLEASURE
See also
Happiness
PLEISTOCENE period. See Geology, Stratigraphic—Pleistocene; Paleontology—Pleistocene

PLESETSK launch site. See Space vehicles—Launching sites

PLESHETTE, Suzanne
Suzanne Pleshette: the private life of TV's favorite wife; interview, ed by J. N. Bell. il por Good H 185:58+ N '77

PLESIOPIDS. See Fishes

PLESIOSAURS
At sea: plesiosaur merely a rotten whale? Sci N 112:68 Jl 30 '77
Creature feature: what was the New Zealand monster? J. Koster. il Oceans 10:56-9 N '77
South Pacific Nessie? carcass found by Japanese trawler. il Newsweek 90:77 Ag 1 '77

PLETCHER, David M.
United States relations with Latin America: neighborliness and exploitation. bibl Am Hist R 82:39-59 F '77

PLETZ, Frances H.
Stroke the legislators. Am Lib 8:575-6 N '77

PLEUROBRANCHAEA. See Gastropods

PLIERS
Pliers that do it in reverse. W. L. Burton. il Mech Illus 73:126-7 Ag '77

PLIMPTON, George
Un gran pedazo de carne. il pors Audubon 79: 10-25 N '77
Grand old hotels of the Orient. il Holiday 58: 42-3+ Mr; 36-7+ Ap '77
Ultimate confrontation (title varies); excerpt from Shadow box. il Sports Illus 47:98-104+ O 17; 38-40+ O 24 '77
(ed) See Ali, M. These sporting poets; Marianne Moore's meeting with Muhammad Ali
(ed) See Curry, B. I'm number 50!
(ed) See Moore, M. These sporting poets; Marianne Moore's meeting with Muhammad Ali

about

Playing X-22. New Yorker 53:40-1 D 5 '77 *

PLIO-PLEISTOCENE boundary. See Paleontology—Cenozoic

PLISHKA, Paul
Today's choice; interview, ed by M. Mayer. pors Opera N 41:8-11 Ja 22 '77

PLOGGER, Loretta M.
Egyptian souvenir spoons. il Hobbies 82:153 S '77

PLOMIN, Robert, and others
Assortative mating by unwed biological parents of adopted children. bibl il Science 196:449-50 Ap 22 '77

PLOTKIN, John
Seaweed: manure, mulch and fertilizer free from the sea. Org Gard & Farm 24:148-9 S '77

PLOTNICK, Robert. See Danziger, S. jt auth

PLOTNIK, Art
Editor walks those mean streets. il pors Am Lib 8:311+ Je '77
Opening minds to closing catalogs, or, When can we throw out the cards? Am Lib 8:594-5 D '77

PLOTS (drama, novel, etc)
Every writer needs a turquoise horse. L. Baker. Writer 90:14-17 Je '77
First things second. L. Block. Writers Digest 57:10+ Ag '77
Plot. A. Vivante. Writer 90:29-32 Ap '77
Where the action is. E. Jensen. Writers Digest 57:27-8 S '77
See also
Motion pictures—Plots, themes, etc.

PLOTSKY, Paul M. and others
Liquid chromatographic analysis of endogenous catecholamine released from brain slices. bibl il Science 197:904-6 Ag 26 '77

PLOWING. See Tillage

PLOWMAN, Edward E.
Believers in Romania: divided they stand. il pors Chr Today 21:18-21 My 20 '77

PLUGS (fishing lures) See Fishing lures, flies, etc.

PLUMB, J. H.
Collections of kings. il por Horizon 20:86-93 D '77

PLUMBING
ABCs of plastic pipe. A. S. Jetter. il Mech Illus 73:80+ Ap '77
Hooking up a new bath is easier than ever with a plumbing manifold. R. Day. il Pop Sci 210: 120-3 Mr '77
PS tests bathroom water-savers. E. Powell. il Pop Sci 211:120-2+ Ag '77
See also
Boats—Sanitation

Maintenance and repair

First aid for faucets. J. Roy. il Am Home 80: 18 Ag '77
How to fix a faucet that leaks. il Good H 184:162 Je '77
Keeping a clear kitchen sink drain. D. Raffel. House & Gard 149:54 F '77
Thousands fewer gallons; devices that save money and conserve water. il Sunset 158:110-11 Ap '77

PLUMMER, Bill
Few things come to him who waits. B. McDermott. por Sports Illus 47:54+ Jl 18 '77 *

PLUMMER, E. Ward, and Gustafsson, T.
Geometry of adsorbates on solid surfaces. bibl il Science 198:165-70 O 14 '77

PLURALISM (social sciences)
See also
Ethnicity

PLUTARCH
Pericles as seen by Plutarch; excerpt from The rise and fall of Athens, tr. by I. Scott-Kilvert. il UNESCO Courier 30:26-7 O '77

PLUTO (planet)
Methane frost on Pluto. Sky & Tel 53:172 Mr '77

PLUTONIUM
How states can go nuclear. F. C. Barnaby. il Ann Am Acad 430:29-43 Mr '77
Plutonium: how safe? interview, ed by D. Colligan. T. Taylor. por Sci Digest 81:60-4 Mr '77
Retention of plutonium and americium by rock. S. Fried and others. bibl il Science 196:1087-9 Je 3 '77
Toxicity of plutonium and some other actinides. J. T. Edsall. Bull Atom Sci 33:6-7 Ja '77; Reply. C. R. Richmond. 33:6 Ap '77

Isotopes

Plutonium hazard in respirable dust on the surface of soil. C. J. Johnson and others; reply with rejoinder. J. A. Hayden. Science 196:1126 Je 3 '77

PLUTONIUM recycling. See Reactor fuel reprocessing

PLYWOOD
How to buy plywood. il Pop Sci 210:122-3 F '77

PNEUMOCOCCI
Deadly strain. M. Clark. Newsweek 90:98 S 19 '77
Menace from South Africa; new strain of pneumonia. Time 110:113 S 19 '77

PNEUMONIA
Nude mouse: a new experimental model for pneumocystis carinii infection. P. D. Walzer and others. bibl il Science 197:177-9 Jl 8 '77
Pneumonia is still a killer. J. J. Fried. Read Digest 110:178-81 My '77

Vaccines

Shots for pneumonia. Time 110:84 N 7 '77
Vaccines to prevent pneumonia. Sci N 112:292 N 5 '77

POACHING
Game thieves: how they're destroying hunting. R. Starnes. il Outdoor Life 160:10+ Ag '77
Great Kenya wildlife ripoff; endangered elephants. J. Samson. il Field & S 82:48-9+ D '77
I was a big-time poacher; deer hunting. il Outdoor Life 159:74-7+ Ap '77
Poaching gators for fun and profit. H. Crews. il Esquire 87:54+ Ap '77
Selling of the zebra. N. Myers. il map Int Wildlife 8:26-31 Ja '78

POCKET Books, Inc. See Publishers and publishing—Paperback books

POCKET cameras. See Cameras

POCKETBOOKS. See Handbags

POCLAIN SA-J. I. Case Company merger. See Corporations—Acquisitions and mergers—International aspects

POCONO 500. See Automobile racing

POCS, Ollie and others
Is there sex after 40? il Psychol Today 11:54-6+ Je '77

PODGORNII, Nikolaĭ Viktorovich
Brezhnev's purge. F. Willey and F. Coleman. por Newsweek 89:43-4 Je 6 '77 *
Unhitching Podgorny from the Troika. por Time 109:35 Je 6 '77 *

PODHORETZ, Norman
Culture of appeasement. Harpers 255:25-32 O '77
Return of success. por Newsweek 90:11 Ag 29 '77

about

Toujours gai. Nat R 29:1160 O 14 '77 *

PODS in house decoration. See Fruits, vegetables, etc. in decoration

PODUSLO, S. E. and others
Antiserums to neurons and to oligodendroglia from mammalian brain. bibl il Science 197:270-2 Jl 15 '77

PODZOLS. See Soils, Podzol

POE, Edgar Allan
Tale of horror; story. Sat Eve Post 249:12 Jl '77

POE, Martin
Antibacterial synergism: a proposal for chemotherapeutic potentiation between trimethoprime and sulfamethoxazole (cont) bibl Science 197:1300-1 S 23 '77

POE, Richard
Negro: by definition. bibl Negro Hist Bull 40: 668-70 Ja '77

POESCH, Jessie J.
Furniture of the River Road plantations in Louisiana. bibl il Antiques 111:1184-8 Je '77

POETICS
Poetic devices. W. Packard. Writer 90:23-5+ Ag '77
Poetry. J. Jerome. See issues of Writers digest
Poet's workshop. F. Trefethen. See every other issue of Writer

POETKER, Joel S.
Techniques for assessing attitudes and values. bibl il Clearing H 51:172-5 D '77

POETRY
Heat—and some light—on poetry. J. F. Baker. il Pub W 211:34-5 My 2 '77
New poetry; excerpt from introduction to The crowned cannibals. E. L. Doctorow. Harpers 254:92+ My '77
Take five; writing cinquains. F. Miller. Seventeen 36:58 Mr '77
Weight of a few words. J. Fandel. Commonweal 104:791-4 D 9 '77
See also
Childrens poetry
Christmas poems
Free verse
Poetics
Poets
Teachers poems (by teachers)
also national poetry, e.g. Polish poetry; *also* subhead Poetry under various subjects, e.g. Whales—Poetry

Authorship

Adventures of the mind; excerpt from 1961 article. C. D. Lewis. il Sat Eve Post 249:8 Jl '77
Poetry. J. Jerome. See issues of Writers digest
Throwing some light on light verse. R. Armour. Writer 90:15-18 O '77
Writing poems to sell. D. D. Guyer. Writers Digest 57:52-3 S '77

Awards, prizes, etc.

Lenore Marshall Poetry Prize. W. Stafford. Sat R 4:34-5 S 3 '77

Bibliography

Books received. See issues of Poetry
Other voices, other tones. D. Hall. Atlantic 240:100+ O '77
Poetry; notes from a selfish reader. J. Thurman. bibl Ms 6:30+ N '77

Collections

See Anthologies

Periodicals

This month's special market list; poetry. Writer 90:31-42+ Mr '77
See also
Poetry (periodical)

Study and teaching

Cremation of Sam McGee and The Shooting of Dan McGrew; R. Service's ballads. L. Burke. Engl J 66:69-70 Mr '77
Frost in the Rio Grande Valley; poem by J. Limoń. A. D. Treviño. Engl J 66:69 Mr '77
On teaching poetry. R. Burroughs. il Engl J 66:48-51 F '77
Poems on various subjects, religious and moral; P. Wheatley's poetry. K. Holder. Engl J 66:68 Mr '77

Aids and devices

Found poetry. M. Karnish. Engl J 66:73-5 Ap '77
Poetry and film for the classroom. R. Armour. Engl J 66:88-91 Ja '77
Presenting poems in class? Try several readers. C. Ross. il Engl J 66:62-4 F '77
Reader as poet; a strategy for creative reading. C. B. Dilworth. bibl f il Engl J 66:43-7 F '77

Technique

See Poetics

POETRY (periodical)
Miss Monroe, Mr Pound, and the boorzoi. J. Parisi. Poetry 131:39-51 O '77

POETRY, Medieval
Christmas game; Sir Gawain and the Green Knight. E. D. Cuffe. America 137:465 D 24 '77

POETRY and art. See Art and literature

POETRY and communism. See Communism and literature

POETRY and music. See Music and literature

POETRY and opera. See Music and literature

POETRY and psychoanalysis. See Psychoanalysis and literature

POETRY and science. See Literature and science

POETRY and state. See Literature and state

POETS
New poetry; excerpt from introduction to The crowned cannibals. E. L. Doctorow. Harpers 254:92+ My '77
Poet's statements of faith. R. Hugo. il Atlantic 239:79-82 Ap '77
See also
Women poets

POETS, American
Poetry is dead, long live poetry. J. F. Cotter. bibl America 137:80-2 Ag 13 '77
See also
American poetry
Appleman, P.
Benedikt, M.
Berg, S.
Berryman, J.
Booth, P.
Brathwaite, E.
Corn, A.
Dennis, C.
Dickey, J.
Dickinson, E.
Dorn, E.
Feldman, I.
Francis, R.
Frost, R.
Galvin, B.
Gregor, A.
Grossman, A.
Hacker, M.
Hayden, R. E.
Hazo, S.
Hecht, A.
Hollander, J.
Howard, R.
Kees, W.
Lattimore, R.
Lazarus, E.
Lerman, E.
Levine, P.
Lorde, A.
Lowell, R.
Macdonald, C.
MacLeish, A.
Matthias, J.
Monroe, H.
Morgan, R.
Morris, J. N.
Mueller, L.
Nathan, L.
Nolan, J.
Oates, J. C.
Pack, R.
Pinsky, R.
Pound, E.
Raab, L.
Reznikoff, C.
St John, D.
Sexton, A.
Slavitt, D. R.
Stevens, W.
Stokes, T.
Stone, R.
Tate, J.
Urdang, C.
Wagoner, D.
Walcott, D.
Walker, D.
Warren, R. P.
Weiss, T.
Welch, J.
Whitman, W.
Wilbur, R.
Williams, W. C.
Woods, J.
Young, A.
Zukofsky, L.

POETS, Argentine
See also
Borges, J. L.
Squirru, R.

POETS, Australian
See also
Porter, P.

POETS, Chilean
See also
Neruda, P.

POETS, English
See also
Betjeman, J.
Browning, E. B
Byron, G. G. N. B.
Causley, C.
Chaucer, G.
Crabbe, G.
English poetry
Finlay, I. H.
Fuller, J
Hopkins, G. M.
Jennings, E.
Kirkup, J.
Muir, E.
Pope, A.
Rossetti, D. G.

POETS, French
See also
Chénier, A. M. de
Prévert, J.

POETS, Indian (East Indian)
See also
Mahapatra, J.

POETS, Irish
See also
Heaney, S.
Yeats, W. B.

POETS, Italian
See also
Dante Alighieri
Montale, E.

POETS, Latin American
See also
Latin American poetry
POETS, Polish
See also
Polish poetry
POETS, Russian
See also
Akhmadulina, B.
Mandel'shtam, O. E.
Russian poetry
POETS, South African
See also
Matthews, J.
POETS, Spanish
See also
Aleixandre, V.
Guillén, J.
POETS, Welsh
See also
Thomas, R. S.
POETS Laureate
See also
Betjeman, J.
POETS, Playwrights, Editors, Essayists, Novelists Club. See PEN Club
POGASH, Carol
Sinister companions: the left handed. Sci Digest 81:17-20 Je '77
Stress—new prison tests: sadism or therapy? il Sci Digest 81:64-7 F '77
POGREBIN, Letty Cottin
Art of family living. il Ms 5:15-16+ Je '77
Feminist goes to Israel. il Ms 6:69-72+ O '77
Have you ever supported equal pay, child care, or women's groups? The FBI was watching you. Ms 5:37-44+ Je '77
This year's best toy buys. il Ms 6:10+ D '77
Working woman. Ladies Home J 94:46+ Ap; 24+ Je; 39+ Jl; 31-2+ S; 30+ N '77
(ed) See Cook, B. Barbara Cook: fat can set you free
POGRUND, Benjamin
Anatomy of white power. il Atlantic 240:51-6+ O '77
Color line. New Repub 177:15-17 D 17 '77
POHICK Bay Regional Park. See Virginia—Parks and reserves
POINSETT, Alex
Annual progress report. il Ebony 33:25-8 Ja '78
Festac '77. il Ebony 32:33-6+ My '77
Is the U.S. short-changing Africa? il Ebony 33:85-6+ D '77
PUSH for excellence. il pors Ebony 32:104-6+ F '77
SBA scandals: whites bilk black fronts. il Ebony 32:75-6+ O '77
POINSETTIAS
Houseplant how-to. il Bet Hom & Gard 55:48 D '77
POINT REYES Lighthouse. See Lighthouses
POINT REYES National Seashore
Naturally. il Nat Parks & Con Mag 51:24-5+ F '77
POINTE DU SABLE, Jean Baptiste
Black man who founded Chicago. L. Bennett, Jr. il por maps Ebony 33:64-6+ N '77 *
POINTILLISM. See Post-impressionism (art)
POISON ivy
How to avoid the itch. il Camp Mag 50:23 S '77
How to stay well. Seventeen 36:56 Je '77
POISONING. See Poisons
POISONOUS animals
Poison!
Black widow. R. E. Arnold. Field & S 82:37 O '77
Cobras. R. E. Arnold. Field & S 82:114 D '77
Coral snake. R. E. Arnold. Field & S 82:128-9 My '77
Russels' viper. R. E. Arnold. Field & S 82:20 S '77
Sea snakes. R. E. Arnold. Field & S 82:130 N '77
Sting; Brazilian or Killer bees. R. E. Arnold. Field & S 81:104 Ap '77
POISONOUS fishes
Fish and food poisoning. B. L. Gordon. il Sea Front 23:218-27 Jl '77
Poison!
Jellyfish. R. E. Arnold. Field & S 82:150 Je '77
POISONOUS plants
Burgeoning cult of wild food nourishes fatal misconceptions. R. E. Arnold and L. Pearce. il Smithsonian 8:48-55 My '77
Deadly harvests and wildlife. J. V. Dennis. il por Conservationist 31:26-7 My '77
Pediatrician's advice to parents on poisonous garden plants. G. Hartman. il Horticulture 55:18-25 Ag '77
Please don't eat these plants. Bet Hom & Gard 55:176 Ap '77
Poison!
Foraging. R. E. Arnold. Field & S 81:134-5 F '77
Plantsmanship. R. E. Arnold. Field & S 82:124 Ag '77
Poison in a monkey's Garden of Eden. K. E. Glander. il Natur Hist 86:34-41 bibl(p96) Mr '77
Pretty poison. P. Brooks. il Fam Health 9:29-32 Jl '77
Watch out for these poisonous plants. N. Smith. il Nat Wildlife 15:46-7 O '77
See also
Poison ivy
POISONOUS snakes. See Snakes
POISONS
Chemical relevance—a heuristic approach (cont) A. Mancott. Chemistry 50:24 Mr; 26 Ap; 28 My '77
How to poison-proof your home; safeguard children. G. C. Schulz. Parents Mag 52:42-3+ My '77
Lifesaving news about the poisons in your home; poisoning of children. N. Rollins. il Good H 184:199-200 Ap '77
What to do if a child swallows poison. K. Pritchard. il McCalls 104:59 Ap '77
What to do in a poison emergency. Consumer Rep 43:42-5 Ja '78
See also
Antidotes
Botulism
Curare
Food poisoning
Lead poisoning
Toxins and antitoxins
Venom
POISONS, Industrial
Killing of a wild river; pollution by Molybdenum Corporation of America, or MolyCorp. D. Kline. Field & S 82:104+ S '77
See also
Carbon tetrachloride
Mercury poisoning
POITIER, Sidney
Sidney Poitier tells how to stay on top in Hollywood. L. Robinson. il pors Ebony 33:53-4+ N '77 *
POKER (game)
Amateur is burned at high stakes: World Series of Poker. E. Shrake. il Sports Illus 46:56+ My 30 '77
POLAND
See also
Astronomy—Poland
Civil rights—Poland
Concentration camps—Poland
Consumption (economics)—Poland
Contracts, Government—Poland
Education—Poland
Food supply—Poland
Government, Resistance to—Poland
Periodicals—Poland
Student demonstrations—Poland
Underground literature—Poland

Commerce

Trying to prop up Poland's shaky government. S. W. Sanders. il por Bus W p44 D 19 '77

Great Britain

See Great Britain—Commerce—Poland

Description and travel

Memories of Chopin; Zelazowa Wola and Warsaw. H. Bradshaw and V. Bradshaw. il Travel 147:46-9 Je '77

Economic conditions

Can Marxism stand prosperity? G. Smith. il Forbes 120:41-6 Jl 1 '77

Foreign relations

Russia

See Russia—Foreign relations—Poland

Politics and government

Poland: meat and potatoes. P. Martin. Newsweek 91:26 Ja 2 '78
Polish road to communism. P. Osnos. For Affairs 56:209-20 O '77
Reports & comment: Poland: a culture in hiding. F. Stein. il Atlantic 241:11+ Ja '78

Religious institutions and affairs

See also
Catholic Church in Poland

Social conditions

Reports & comment: Poland: a culture in hiding. F. Stein. il Atlantic 241:11+ Ja '78
POLANSKI, Roman
Roman Polanski's tawdry troubles. il por Time 109:22 Mr 28 '77 *
POLAR exploration
See also
Antarctic exploration
POLAR ice. See Ice—Polar Regions
POLAR Regions
See also
Antarctic Regions
POLAR research
See also
Antarctic research
Arctic research

POLARITY (biology)
Polarity reversal in nerve-free hydra. B. A. Marcum and others. bibl il Science 197:771-3 Ag 19 '77

POLARIZATION (light)
More about polarizers and how to use them, particularly for studying polarized sky light. J. Walker. il Sci Am 238:132-6 Ja '78
Studying polarized light with quarter-wave and half-wave plates of one's own making. J. Walker. il Sci Am 237:172-4+ D '77

POLARIZING filters. See Light filters

POLAROID Corporation
At long last, Land's instant movies. il Time 109:66+ My 9 '77
Land's new wonder; Polavision. L. Langway and others. il por Newsweek 89:75+ My 9 '77
Polaroid pulls out; South African market. Newsweek 90:80 D 5 '77

POLAROID Land cameras. See Cameras, Instant print

POLAROID Land films. See Photography—Films

POLAVISION motion picture cameras. See Motion picture cameras, Instant print

POLCARI, Stephen
Kenneth Noland: independence in the face of conformity. il por Art N 76:153-5 Summ '77

POLES, Wood. See Wood poles

POLHEMUS, Craig E.
Significant decisions in labor cases. See issues of Monthly labor review

POLI, Bruce
Books. il Pop Phot 81:48+ Jl '77

POLI, Kenneth
Critical focus (cont) il Pop Phot 80:10+ F; 6+ Mr; 6+ Je; 81:8+ Ag; 8+ S '77

POLICE
Deadly force—deciding when to shoot. J. Horn. Psychol Today 11:85 Ag '77
Police and military in the resolution of ethnic conflict. C. H. Enloe. bibl f Ann Am Acad 433:137-49 S '77
See also
Police dogs
Policewomen
Traffic police

Community relations

See Police—Public relations

Psychological aspects

See Police psychology

Public relations

Helping your community as a police volunteer; using retirees. B. O'Neil. il Ret Liv 17:23+ Ag '77
How one city slashed its crime rate; Santa Ana, Calif. il Am City & County 92:73-4 N '77
Law's a good neighbor; deputies visiting the elderly in Dallas County, Ala. il Aging 274:23 Ag '77

Alabama

Law's a good neighbor; deputies visiting the elderly in Dallas County. il Aging 274:23 Ag '77

California

How one city slashed its crime rate; Santa Ana. il Am City & County 92:73-4 N '77
Patrol car logs cut speeding accidents; tachographic recording devices; Hawthorne. il Am City & County 92:96 My '77
See also
Los Angeles—Police
Los Angeles County, Calif.—Police
San Francisco—Police

Canada

See also
Canada—Royal Canadian Mounted Police

Chile

See also
Secret service—Chile

Connecticut

See also
New Haven, Conn.—Police

Florida

Florida's underwater policemen; Florida Marine Patrol. R. Clancy. il Sea Front 23:140-3 My '77

Germany, West

Commandos thwart hijackers; rescue of 85 hostages on Lufthansa 737 in Somalia. R. R. Ropelewski. il Aviation W 107:14-16 O 24 '77
Germany's finger squads. R. Carroll and P. Martin. il Newsweek 90:64+ N 21 '77
Is the tide turning against terrorists? West German rescue of hostages in Mogadishu, Somalia. il U.S. News 83:22-4 O 31 '77
New war on terrorism; rescue of hostages by German commandos in Mogadishu, Somalia. A. Deming and others. il map Newsweek 90:48-50+ O 31 '77
Terror and triumph at Mogadishu; New breed of commando. il map Time 110:42-4 O 31 '77
War goes on. K. Willenson and others. il Newsweek 90:55-6 N 7 '77

Idaho

Boise police turn against their own. J. Roche. Ms 6:20 N '77

Ireland

Police brutality in Ireland. D. Fisher. Commonweal 104:230-1 Ap 15 '77

Kentucky

See also
Louisville—Police

New York (state)

See also
New York (city)—Police

Pennsylvania

See also
Philadelphia—Police

Russia

See also
Secret service—Russia

South Africa

South Africa: dirty tricks. il Newsweek 90:49 D 19 '77

Texas

See also
Houston, Tex.—Police

United States

In cities across the country, the sting goes on and on. T. Gest. il U.S. News 83:67-8 N 7 '77
Pinch must really sting; study by the Institute for Law and Social Research. il Time 110:59-60 S 26 '77
Your rights with the police; comp by M. Gunther. il Bet Hom & Gard 55:13+ Ap '77
See also
United States—Law Enforcement Assistance Administration

POLICE automobiles. See Automobiles, Police

POLICE brutality. See Police cruelty

POLICE chases
Think slow; safety instructor, R. Turner. Time 110:63 N 7 '77

POLICE cruelty
Police brutality in Ireland. D. Fisher. Commonweal 104:230-1 Ap 15 '77
Police story: two hard towns; Philadelphia and Houston. il Time 110:29-30 S 19 '77
Rizzo lives; investigations of brutality. Nation 225:324 O 8 '77
Roundhouse punches; brutality charges against Philadelphia's police. D. M. Alpern and S. Agrest. il Newsweek 90:24 Jl 4 '77
Wild bunch; Houston, Tex, force. J. K. Footlick. il Newsweek 89:80-1 Je 6 '77

POLICE dogs
Super dog of Scotland Yard; identifying concealed narcotics. J. Stewart-Gordon. il por Read Digest 110:201-2+ Mr '77
See also
Bloodhounds

POLICE in literature. See Literature—Themes

POLICE lineups. See Crime and criminals—Identification

POLICE operators, Telephone. See Telephone operators

POLICE psychology
Delicate art of handling terrorists. P. Goldman and others. il Newsweek 89:25-7 Mr 21 '77
How to play the waiting game. Time 109:18-19 Mr 21 '77
View from the 44th precinct; interview. T. Gallagher. Sat R 4:16-17 Mr 19 '77

POLICE television shows. See Television programs—Crime programs

POLICE volunteers. See Volunteer service

POLICEWOMEN
Boise police turn against their own. J. Roche. Ms 6:20 N '77
Careers: the lady is a cop. Seventeen 36:55 N '77

POLICIES, Insurance. See Insurance—Policies

POLING, Jim
Mistake. il Outdoor Life 159:74-5+ F '77; Same abr. Read Digest 110:117-20 Je '77

POLIOMYELITIS

Vaccines

Control of influenza and poliomyelitis with killed virus vaccines. J. Salk and D. Salk. bibl il Science 195:834-47 Mr 4 '77
Dead or alive? Sci Am 237:96+ S '77
Polio: Salk challenges safety of Sabin's live-virus vaccine. P. M. Boffey. Science 196:35-6 Ap 1 '77

POLIOMYELITIS virus in water. See Water—Microbiology

POLISARIO. See Guerrillas—Western Sahara

POLISH AMERICANS
Great American melting pot. B. Vinton. Holiday 58:25-6+ Ap '77

POLISH poetry

Translations into English

Méliès; excerpt from The Survivor and other poems; tr by M. Krynski and R. Maguire. T. Różewicz. New Repub 176:34 Mr 19 '77

POLISH visitors in the United States. See Visitors, Foreign—United States

POLITBURO. See Communist Party (Russia)—Political Bureau

POLITICAL advertising. See Advertising, Political

POLITICAL affiliation. See Political parties—Membership

POLITICAL asylum. See Asylum, Right of

POLITICAL attitudes

Ask Americans about their president: so far, so good. U.S. News 82:18-19 Mr 7 '77

Do not criticize government for all Nation's ills; excerpts from address. W. D. Carey. por Intellect 105:290-1 Mr '77

From special-interest groups: a mixed verdict on Carter. il U.S. News 82:20-1 My 30 '77

Great expectations. il Newsweek 89:20 Ja 24 '77

Jimmy Carter and the new reality. S. Lens. il por Chr Cent 94:10-14 Ja 5 '77

New era begins. il U.S. News 82:16-17 Ja 24 '77

Political structure of rural America. D. Knoke and C. Henry. bibl f il Ann Am Acad 429:51-62 Ja '77

Time poll:

High marks on his early exams; Carter administration. il pors Time 109:12-13 Ap 4 '77

Several A's, some F's for Jimmy. il por Time 109:15-16 Je 13 '77

Sliding down the polls. il por Time 110:10-12 D 26 '77

Verdict from experts on Jimmy Carter's first year. il pors U.S. News 84:16-19 Ja 9 '78

What Carter should do now—advice from four political experts. il U.S. News 83:23-4 N 7 '77

What people expect of Carter; national survey. il U.S. News 82:20-2 Ja 24 '77

Why Carter is still a mystery; with comment by J. W. Mashek. por U.S. News 83:26-8 O 17 '77

See also

High school students—Attitudes

Public opinion polls

Israel

Euphoric Israel. M. J. Kubic. il Newsweek 90:34 D 5 '77

Sniping at Begin. R. Carroll and M. J. Kubic. il Newsweek 91:31 Ja 9 '78

Italy

Conversations with Italians; interviews, ed by C. Fenyvesi. New Repub 178:18-19 Ja 7 '78

Russia

Russia's Revolution—as it looks from the inside; interview. R. Knight and J. N. Wallace. il U.S. News 83:46-50 O 24 '77

POLITICAL bosses. See Boss rule

POLITICAL campaigns

Battle takes shape early for the '78 election. il por U.S. News 83:65-6 S 12 '77

New GOP game plan. D. Holt and H. Bruno. Newsweek 91:25 Ja 16 '78

Outlook '78: Republicans fight for a bigger toe hold. U.S. News 83:35-7 D 26 '77

Trends to watch for in off-year elections. il U.S. News 83:25-6 N 7 '77

Working on the campaign trail. C. R. Arrington. il por Ret Liv 17:38+ O '77

See also

Campaign buttons, etc.

Campaign funds

Presidential campaigns

also subhead Politics and government under names of countries, states, cities, etc. e.g. Georgia—Politics and government

France

Center holds. il por Time 110:51-2 N 7 '77

French voters crank up for a fateful decision. A. de Segonzac. il U.S. News 83:67 S 12 '77

Le nouveau regime. A. Berger. New Repub 176:18-20 Je 18 '77

Paris in June. L. P. De Menil. New Repub 176:21 Je 18 '77

Political uncertainty in France. E. W. Fox and J. O. Safford, 3d. Cur Hist 73:149-52+ N '77

India

Ill winds batter Indira Gandhi. il por Time 109:34-5 Mr 21 '77

India's game of surprises. H. Jensen. il por Newsweek 89:41+ Mr 21 '77

Son also rises. F. Willey. il pors Newsweek 89:36 F 28 '77

Uniting against Indira. il por Time 109:37-8 Mr 7 '77

Israel

Big bird in a land of hawks and doves; S. Peres. il por Time 109:34+ Ap 25 '77

Go in peace. R. Carroll and M. J. Kubic. il por Newsweek 89:34 Mr 14 '77

Israel's disillusioned voters: the Knesset faces a shake-up. A. Wallfish. Nation 224:390-3 Ap 2 '77

Israel's Mr Clean; Prime Minister candidate, Y. Yadin vs the Labor Party. M. Kondracke. New Repub 176:6+ F 26 '77

Israel's self-inflicted wounds. Y. Marcus. il pors N Y Times Mag p26-9+ Ap 24 '77

Jerusalem: the race for change. M. J. Kubic. il por Newsweek 89:29 F 21 '77

Rabin's distress. M. Kondracke. New Repub 176:15-18 Mr 12 '77

Running out of giants. K. Willenson and M. J. Kubic. il Newsweek 89:55 My 16 '77

Japan

Japan's coming election: the Rashomon scenarios. E. Pond. Nation 224:775-8 Je 25 '77

Pakistan

Absentee candidate; Z. A. Bhutto. T. Clifton. Newsweek 90:46 O 3 '77

Spain

Finally a real campaign. il Time 109:36 Je 13 '77

Spain—after 40 years of fear. J. M. Markham. il N Y Times Mag p 18-20+ Je 5 '77

POLITICAL cartoons. See Caricatures and cartoons

POLITICAL clubs and associations

It happens every spring; 13th annual meeting of the Philadelphia Society. T. J. Wheeler. Nat R 29:548 My 13 '77

See also

Common Cause (organization)

Israel

Israel and its Bloc of Faithful; Gush Emunim. C. E. Brewster. Chr Cent 94:174-6 F 23 '77

POLITICAL contributions. See Campaign funds

POLITICAL conventions

See also

Constitutional conventions

National conventions, Democratic

POLITICAL corruption. See Politics, Corruption in

POLITICAL crimes and offenses

South Africa

South Africa—a police state? A banned monograph on inhumanity. S. Cohen. Nation 224:143-6 F 5 '77

POLITICAL defectors. See Defectors, Political

POLITICAL education. See Political science—Study and teaching

POLITICAL ethics

Ain't misbehaving; House code of ethics. Newsweek 89:16 Mr 14 '77

Bring back hell fire. A. Tonelson. New Repub 176:18-19 F 26 '77

Congress adopts ethics code, but skepticism still runs strong. U.S. News 82:79 Ap 11 '77

Dealing with Dada; consideration of morality in foreign policy. New Repub 176:5-6+ Mr 19 '77

Eccentricities of ethics. F. Getlein. Commonweal 104:228-9 Ap 15 '77

Ethics on Capitol Hill. Progressive 41:8-10 Ag '77

Facing the perfectionism backlash. J. M. Wall. Chr Cent 94:835-6 S 28 '77

Metaphysical dimensions of a door. T. H. Troeger. Chr Cent 94:557-9 Je 8 '77

Post-Watergate morality, a dubious legacy. I. Kristol. Read Digest 110:169-171 My '77

Power, fame and fortune too; ethics and the pay raise for Congressmen. New Repub 176:7-8 Mr 5 '77; Reply. M. Peretz. 176:6 Mr 12 '77

Regulating Congress: a citizens' committee is needed. J. Anderson. Current 189:11-16 Ja '77

Reporter at large: Congressional ethics. E. B. Drew. New Yorker 53:70-4+ Ag 22 '77

Rewriting the rule book. M. Greenfield. Newsweek 90:80 Ag 29 '77

Sexless orgies of morality. E. L. Richardson. por N Y Times Mag p33 Ja 23 '77

They are paying the price of virtue; code of ethics. il Time 109:12-13 Mr 7 '77

Wallowing, anyone? revelations of V. Lasky. Nat R 29:537-8 My 13 '77

See also

Government, Resistance to

Politics, Corruption in

Anecdotes, facetiae, satire, etc.

No plums for me! asking for favors. M. E. Marty. Chr Cent 94:71 Ja 26 '77

POLITICAL films. See Motion pictures—Political films

POLITICAL forecasting
8 experts size up U.S. future in a dangerous world; symposium. il U.S. News 82:43-6+ Je 27 '77
New era begins. il U.S. News 82:16-17 Ja 24 '77
Outlook '78:
In Congress, the mood will get even feistier. il U.S. News 83:33-4 D 26 '77
Republicans fight for a bigger toe hold. U.S. News 83:35-7 D 26 '77
Washington's star stargazer. M. A. Kellogg. il por N Y Times Mag p 12-13+ Ja 16 '77
See also
Public opinion polls

Anecdotes, facetiae, satire, etc.

Why President Carter wasn't re-elected. G. F. Will. Newsweek 89:96 F 21 '77

POLITICAL independence. See Autonomy; Nationalism; Self determination

POLITICAL indoctrination. See Indoctrination

POLITICAL leaders. See Politicians

POLITICAL leadership. See Leadership

POLITICAL liberty. See Liberty

POLITICAL literature
See also
World politics—Bibliography

POLITICAL machine. See Boss rule

POLITICAL novels. See Politics in literature

POLITICAL parties
Party & international politics. D. P. Moynihan. Commentary 63:56-9 F '77
See also
Campaign funds
Communist parties

Membership

Impact of the new politics. W. E. Miller and T. E. Levitin. Intellect 105:375 My '77

Canada

Socialist tides in Canada; British Columbia. G. Woodcock. Progressive 41:25-8 Jl '77

Europe

See also
Communist parties—Europe

Europe, Western

See also
Communist parties—Europe, Western

France

Anatomy of the French crisis; conflict between Communist and Socialist Parties. J. Burnham. Nat R 29:1224 O 28 '77
Center holds; leftist split. il por Time 110:51-2 N 7 '77
Death of Eurocommunism; collapse of Socialist-Communist alliance. T. Szulc. New Repub 177:21-2+ O 8 '77
Family feud on the left. pors Time 110:57 O 10 '77
France: a leftist split. E. Behr and C. Mitchelmore. Newsweek 90:51 O 3 '77
France: disarray on the left. A. Deming and E. Peer. il Newsweek 90:45-6 S 26 '77
French left: squabbling toward the election. N. Birnbaum. Nation 225:424-8 O 29 '77
From fete to fiasco; leftists. il Time 110:32+ S 26 '77
Left at City Hall; Reims. H. Muller. Time 110: 54+ N 28 '77
Marchais plays it rough; Socialist Party vs Communist Party. Nat R 29:1161 O 14 '77
See also
Communist Party (France)

Great Britain

Britain: testing a collaboration. R. Carroll and A. Collings. il por Newsweek 89:45-6 Ap 4 '77
Britain's new ultra-right; the National Front. P. Webb and M. MacPherson. il Newsweek 90:44 Ag 29 '77
Coloreds must go! National Front party; with report by E. Amfitheatrof. il Time 110:50+ D 12 '77
Violence in the streets; the National Front. B. Wicker. Commonweal 104:582-4 S 16 '77
See also
Labor Party (Great Britain)

India

Rebels' rally; I. Gandhi and the Congress Party. il por Time 111:30 Ja 16 '78

Israel

Israel's disillusioned voters: the Knesset faces a shake-up. A. Wallfish. Nation 224:390-3 Ap 2 '77
Israel's Mr Clean; Prime Minister candidate, Y. Yadin vs the Labor Party. M. Kondracke. New Repub 176:6+ F 26 '77
Israel's troubled choice. A. Deming and M. J. Kubic. il por Newsweek 89:33-4 F 28 '77
Likud's victory. B. J. Wattenberg. Harpers 255: 14-17 Ag '77
Rabin just makes it; Labor Party nominee. R. Carroll and J. Kubic. il pors Newsweek 89:38+ Mr 7 '77
Rabin on the razor's edge; nomination as Labor Party candidate. il por Time 109:32+ Mr 7 '77
Yadin jumps in; Democratic Movement for Change. por Time 110:52 O 31 '77

Italy

Italy: where Communists share power. J. Fromm. il U.S. News 83:41-2 O 17 '77
See also
Communist Party (Italy)

Spain

Spain: inching toward democracy; Popular Party. por Bus W p37 Mr 7 '77
See also
Communist Party (Spain)

United States

Reform is wrecking the U.S. party system. E. C. Ladd, Jr. il Fortune 96:176-81+ N '77
See also
Communist Party (United States)
Democratic Party
Nazis in the United States
Republican Party

History

Ideology and political culture from Jefferson to Nixon; with discussion. R. Kelley. bibl f Am Hist R 82:531-82 Je '77

POLITICAL patronage
New Washington power game. M. Greenfield. Newsweek 89:80 Ja 31 '77
Patronage: the power of appointment. Sr Schol 109:12+ Ja 27 '77
Politics and Federal D.A.'s. D. M. Alpern and others. il Newsweek 90:21 Jl 18 '77

History

Civil service: it brought an end to the infamous spoils system. il Duns R 110:21+ N '77

POLITICAL philosophy
New Philosophes. M. S. Ross. Nat R 29:1361-2+ N 25 '77
Political superstition and the intellectuals. A. Kazin. il Esquire 88:42+ N '77
Reconsideration; C. Wright Mills. M. Dickstein. New Repub 176:36-7 Ja 29 '77
See also
Conservatism
Democracy
Liberalism
Right and left (political science)
Socialism

POLITICAL polls. See Public opinion polls

POLITICAL pressure groups. See Pressure groups

POLITICAL prisoners
Rights—and wrongs. il Newsweek 89:54-5 Je 20 '77

Africa

African Gulag. New Repub 177:5 S 10 '77

Argentina

Letter from an Argentine prison. M. D. Wilde. Chr Cent 94:901-2 O 12 '77
Murder in Argentina; death of E. Käsemann. E. Magalis. Chr Cent 94:1030-3 N 9 '77
Physics in Argentina. N. Wade. Science 196: 1302 Je 17 '77

Chad

End of an ordeal; France's efforts to secure release of F. Claustre from rebels. il por Time 109:38 F 14 '77

Chile

Desaparecidos. H. Fairlie. New Repub 176:10-11 Ap 9 '77
Prayer under duress; imprisonment of English doctor in Chile. S. Cassidy. il Nat R 29:826-8 Jl 22 '77

Germany, East

Fixer. C. R. Whitney. il pors N Y Times Mag p46-50+ Mr 20 '77

India

India, my India! excerpt; with introd by C. A. Martin. J. P. Narayan. il pors N Y Times Mag p35-7+ Mr 27 '77

Indonesia

Human rights in Indonesia; statement, October 18, 1977. R. B. Oakley. Dept State Bull 77: 848-52 D 12 '77
Indonesia: devil's island; release of 10,000 prisoners from the island of Buru. R. Carroll. il map Newsweek 91:29 Ja 2 '78

Israel

Entebbe five. Newsweek 89:56 Ap 11 '77
Torture tempest; question of newspaper reports charging mistreatment of Palestinian prisoners. S. Kaplan. New Repub 177:16-17 Jl 23 '77

POLITICAL prisoners—*Continued*

Korea, South

Seoul: an acute sense of timing. B. Krisher. Newsweek 89:63-4 My 2 '77
South Korea: still guilty. Chr Today 21:42-3 Ja 21 '77

Paraguay

New hope for Paraguay's prisoners. R. Barbosa. Chr Cent 94:301-2 Mr 30 '77

Philippines

Great escape? C. Whipple and others. il pors Newsweek 90:62 O 17 '77
Quality of justice in Manila; case of B. S. Aquino. America 137:410 D 10 '77

Russia

Censuring the Soviets; vote by the World Psychiatric Association. il Time 110:36 S 12 '77
Defending Yuri Orlov; work of J. Macdonald. New Yorker 53:29-31 S 19 '77
Fate of families. N. Solzhenitsyna. il por Time 109:30 F 21 '77
Human-rights widows; prisoners' families. F. Coleman. il Newsweek 91:28-9 Ja 2 '78
Inside Russia's psychiatric jails. L. Thorne. il N Y Times Mag p26-7+ Je 12 '77
Mother courage: how Vladimir Bukovsky was saved. L. Thorne. il por N Y Times Mag p38-40+ F 27 '77
Prisoner of conscience: the Bukovsky file. L. Elliott. por Read Digest 111:93-7 Ag '77
Serbsky treatment; interview, ed by E. F. Torrey. V. Bukovsky. il por Psychol Today 11:38-9+ Je '77
Soviet psychiatric practices criticized; World Psychiatric Association. Sci N 112:164-5 S 10 '77
Statement by prisoner H. I. Butman to the chief of the Perm administration of corrective labor establishments (ITK-35) H. Butman. il Nat R 29:822-5 Jl 22 '77

South Africa

Biko on death; excerpts from interview. S. Biko. New Repub 178:11-13 Ja 7 '78
Biko's last days. S. Strasser and P. Younghusband. il Newsweek 90:74 N 28 '77
Death of a prisoner; S. Biko. por Time 110:35 S 26 '77
In a South African prison; P. Qoboza. R. Javers. Commonweal 104:808-9 D 23 '77
Inquest into a curious death; case of S. Biko. il Time 110:53 N 28 '77
No-fault verdict; S. Biko inquest. R. Carroll and P. Younghusband. il Newsweek 90:67+ D 12 '77
Steve Biko is dead. R. Carroll and P. Younghusband. il por Newsweek 90:41-2 S 26 '77

United States

America's oubliette; Puerto Rican nationalists in federal penitentiaries. Nation 224:548 My 7 '77

Yugoslavia

Another top red's wife runs afoul of system; J. B. Tito. il pors U.S. News 83:55 N 7 '77
Meaning of Mihajlov. T. Fleming. America 137:145-7 S 17 '77
Purging of Cinderella; Madame Tito. il por Newsweek 90:61 N 7 '77

POLITICAL psychology
How to think about politicians. W. Karp. il por Horizon 19:14-15 Ja '77
POLITICAL publicity. See Advertising, Political
POLITICAL reform
Bring back hell fire. A. Tonelson. New Repub 176:18-19 F 26 '77
Reform is wrecking the U.S. party system. E. C. Ladd, Jr. il Fortune 96:176-81+ N '77
POLITICAL refugees. See Refugees
POLITICAL reporting. See Press and politics
POLITICAL responsibility. See Responsibility
POLITICAL scandals. See Politics, Corruption in
POLITICAL science
See also
Authority
Citizenship
Civil rights
Communism
Democracy
Equality
Geopolitics
Legislation
Liberty
Nationalism
Nations
Political philosophy
Power (social sciences)
Public administration
Radicalism
Regionalism
Separation of powers
Socialism
Totalitarianism
Utopias

Bibliography

Jeane Kirkpatrick on politics. J. Kirkpatrick. New Repub 177:36-8 D 3 '77

Study and teaching

Education for citizenship. R. F. Butts. Educ Digest 43:25-7 O '77
Most valuable in-put; Student Congressional Council of Ohio's 16th District. E. Erlanger. il por Sr Schol 109:14 Mr 24 '77
Proper study of government; Institute for Political and Legal Education. C. H. Harrison. il Am Educ 13:10-14 Jl '77
Recommendations for strengthening civic education. Educ Digest 43:41-4 D '77
See also
Colorado. University, Boulder—Graduate School of Public Affairs

POLITICAL theory. See Political philosophy
POLITICIANS
Get a horse: a proposal to distract the rich from politics. E. McCarthy. New Repub 177:10-11 Jl 9 '77
Politician's art. H. Fairlie. Harpers 225:33-6+ D '77
Politics of promises. A. Etzioni. Read Digest 110:121-2 My '77
What the Carters are doing to wipe out divorce in Washington. J. L. Block. il Good H 184:109+ Je '77
See also
Boss rule
POLITICIANS wives
How her job saved their marriage; interview, ed by M. L. Kotz. B. L. Pryor. il pors Good H 184:48+ My '77
POLITICS
See also
Art and politics
The Arts and politics
Conservatism
Elections
Geopolitics
Lawyers in politics
Liberalism
Mass media—Political aspects
Television in politics
Women and politics
Women in politics
World politics
also headings beginning Political; *also* subhead Politics and government under names of continents, countries, etc. e.g. France—Politics and government

Poetry

See also titles of poems listed under Von Dreele, W. H.

POLITICS, Corruption in
Businessman and the government: corruption, yesterday and today. J. Brooks. il Am Heritage 28:66-73 Je '77
How prosecutors are nabbed. J. Lardner. New Repub 176:22-5 Ja 29 '77
In Washington, scandal has a long history. il U.S. News 83:12-13 Ag 1 '77
Public officials for sale; bribery, graft, kickbacks, etc. il U.S. News 82:36-8 F 28 '77
See also
Boss rule
Conflict of interests (public office)
Elections—Corrupt practices
Government investigations—Congressmen
Muckraking
Watergate case

Anecdotes, facetiae, satire, etc.

Last of the just. R. Baker. N Y Times Mag p 12 O 2 '77

Costa Rica

Costa Rica imbroglio. K. Bode. New Repub 176:12-16 My 28 '77
Costa Rica's Vescogate. M. R. Benjamin and others. por Newsweek 89:47 Je 13 '77

Hawaii

Rotten system; bribery case against Honolulu Mayor F. Fasi. T. Mathews and G. C. Lubenow. il pors Newsweek 90:47 N 14 '77

India

Closer to Indira. il por Time 110:29 S 5 '77
Closing in on Mrs Gandhi. R. K. Manoff. Nation 225:355-6 O 15 '77
Closing in on Sanjay. F. Willey and others. il por Newsweek 89:64 My 2 '77
Empress in distress; case of I. Gandhi. il por Time 110:37 O 17 '77
Family affairs; charges of financial corruption involving S. Gandhi. il por Newsweek 89:56 Ap 11 '77
India: a bungled arrest. R. Carroll and others. il por Newsweek 90:53-4 O 17 '77
India's net closes. H. Jensen. il pors Newsweek 90:46 S 12 '77
Letter from New Delhi. V. Mehta. New Yorker 53:119-22+ O 17 '77
Sanjay in the dock. K. Willenson and R. Ramanujam. il por Newsweek 90:45 S 5 '77

POLITICS, Corruption in—*Continued*

Israel

Israel's troubled choice. A. Deming and M. J. Kubic. il por Newsweek 89:33-4 F 28 '77

Japan

Japan's coming election: the Rashomon scenarios. E. Pond. Nation 224:775-8 Je 25 '77
Lockheed's 70-day mission to Tokyo; excerpt from Lockheed sales mission: seventy days in Tokyo. A. C. Kotchian. il Sat R 4:7-12 Jl 9 '77
Reports & comment: Japan; collusion between industry and politicians. F. Gibney. il por Atlantic 239:6-9+ Je '77

Korea, South

Korea, Inc. T. Szulc. New Repub 176:20-2 Ja 29 '77

Louisiana

Bell ringers; election fraud investigation of R. Tonry in Louisiana. S. Fraker and others. por Newsweek 89:30+ Ap 18 '77
Murder at Jupiter; political corruption and construction workers' union in Lake Charles, La. K. Y. Tomlinson. il Read Digest 111:115-19 Jl '77

Maryland

Changing the rules; case of Governor M. Mandel. K. Bode. New Repub 177:16-17 S 17 '77
Help from his friends; M. Mandel case. R. Boeth. il por Newsweek 90:20 S 5 '77
Mandel verdict: a warning to officials. il por U.S. News 83:46 S 5 '77
Trouble in the boys' club; trials of M. Mandel. A. Tyler. New Repub 177:16-19 Jl 30 '77
Verdict: bye-bye, Marvin. il por Time 110:20 S 5 '77

New Jersey

Government regulation: a smooth ride to the bank. J. McLaughlin. Nation 224:679-82 Je 4 '77

New York (state)

I have no regrets. M. Nadjari. il por N Y Times Mag p64-5+ Mr 27 '77

United States

See Politics, Corruption in

Wyoming

Prosecutor; 60 minutes television program's investigation of corruption. M. J. Arlen. New Yorker 53:166-73 N 28 '77

POLITICS and art. See Art and politics
POLITICS and blacks. See Blacks and politics
POLITICS and business. See Business—Political aspects
POLITICS and Christianity. See Church and politics
POLITICS and economics. See Economics and politics
POLITICS and education
Evaluation and politics in education. G. E. Sroufe. Educ Digest 43:20-3 D '77
Law, politics, and equal educational opportunity. D. L. Kirp. Educ Digest 43:32-5 S '77
Political role of educators. T. M. Black. Educ Digest 42:30-2 Mr '77
Politics without civics. F. M. Wirt. bibl il Society 14:46-8 My '77
Role of interest groups in educational politics; New York City. F. Barbaro. bibl il Clearing H 51:136-42 N '77
See also
Teachers—Political activities
POLITICS and language

Anecdotes, facetiae, satire, etc.

Scaling the heights of absurdity. R. Baker. N Y Times Mag p9 F 20 '77
POLITICS and newspapers. See Newspapers and politics
POLITICS and religion. See Religion and politics
POLITICS and the arts. See The Arts and politics
POLITICS and the press. See Press and politics
POLITICS in literature
Books; Washington, D.C. political novels. J. Kraft. New Yorker 53:140-6+ D 19 '77
Conspiracy of silence. J. Epstein. il Harpers 255:77-80+ N '77
If the left wins; French novel, The 180 days of Mitterrand. il Time 110:28 S 5 '77
Truth as fiction. M. Greenfield. Newsweek 90:78 Ag 1 '77

Anecdotes, facetiae, satire, etc.

Quick, write a novel. R. Reeves. Esquire 88:30+ S '77
POLIVKA, Grace
Dear high school English teacher. Engl J 66: 36-7 Ap '77
POLK, George W.
On an unsolved mystery. H. E. Salisbury. Progressive 41:24-5 My '77 *
POLK County, Fla.
Another kind of strip mining that's stirring up a storm. il map U.S. News 82:41-2 My 23 '77
POLL, Heinz
Ohio Ballet: Poll's ensemble tackles Taylor. J. Pikula. il Dance Mag 51:39-40 Jl '77 *
POLLACK, Emanuel D. and Liebig, Veronica
Differentiating limb tissue affects neurite growth in spinal cord cultures. bibl il Science 197:899-900 Ag 26 '77
POLLACK, Gerald H.
Cardiac pacemaking: an obligatory role of catecholamines? bibl il Science 196:731-8 My 13 '77
POLLACK, Henry N. and Chapman, D. S.
Flow of heat from the earth's interior; with biographical sketches. il maps Sci Am 237:20, 60-8+ bibl(p 140) Ag '77
POLLACK, Louis. See Edelson, B. I. jt auth
POLLACK, Merrill
Case of the vengeful twins. Esquire 87:105+ Je '77
POLLACK, Pamela D.
Cheer up to here: Christmas books '77. il SLJ 24:86-8 O '77
POLLAK, George, and others
Echo-detecting characteristics of neurons in inferior colliculus of unanesthetized bats. bibl il Science 196:675-8 My 6 '77
POLLARD, Mark
Planning your personal financial strategy. Archit Rec 161:59 Mr; 77 Ap '77
POLLEN
Incompatability on Brassica stigmas is overcome by treating pollen with cycloheximide. T. E. Ferrari and D. H. Wallace. bibl il Science 196:436-8 Ap 22 '77
POLLEN, Fossil
Pollen influx and volcanic ash. P. J. Mehringer, Jr and others. bibl il map Science 198:257-61 O 21 '77
POLLENS, David
My story; poem. Atlantic 239:61 My '77
POLLINATION. See Fertilization of plants
POLLINI, Maurizio
Maurizio Pollini, piano; Carnegie program. Hi Fi 27:MA26 S '77 *
POLLITT, Katha
Intimation; poem. New Repub 176:26 F 5 '77
Nettles; Onion; Potatoes; poems. Atlantic 239:63 F '77
Wild orchids; Whose sleeves? Moon and flowering plum; poems. New Yorker 53:34 Mr 14 '77
POLLOCK, Jackson
Another side of Jackson Pollock. C. F. Stuckey. bibl il por Art in Am 65:80-91 N '77 *
Jackson Pollock's drawings under analysis. B. Carter. il Art N 76:58-60 F '77 *
Laying the Pollock case to rest. A. Frankenstein. Art N 76:94+ O '77 *
Pollock and politics. A. Levy. Art N 76:96+ My '77 *
Pollock paints a picture; excerpt from The art world; ed by B. Diamonstein. R. Goodnough. il pors Art N 76:162+ N '77 *
POLLOCK, John Crothers, and Robinson, J. L., Jr
Reporting rights conflicts. bibl il Society 15:44-7 N '77
POLLOCK, Jonathan
Mystery no more: Madagascar's intriguing indris. il por Int Wildlife 7:12-16 Mr '77
POLLOCK, Oliver
Birth of the great American $. J. Gustaitis. il Am Hist Illus 12:17-19 Jl '77 *
POLLOCK, Sam
Would you buy a used hockey player from this man? J. Kirshenbaum. por Sports Illus 46:46-8+ Ap 18 '77 *
POLLOCK, Thomas Clark
Two reminiscences of the NCTE. bibl f Engl J 66:6-9+ Ap '77
POLLS, Public opinion. See Public opinion polls
POLLUTION
Environment (cont) Sci N 111:44; 112:185, 233, 392, 425 Ja 15, S 17, O 8, D 10, 24 '77
Week's watch. Time 109:51 Ap 4 '77
See also
Air pollution
Coke plants—Environmental aspects
Power plants—Environmental aspects
Radioactive pollution
Steam power plants—Environmental aspects
Water pollution

Control

Clean America; special section. il U.S. News 82:40-6+ F 7 '77
Fresh air-clean water exchange. F. H. Bormann and G. E. Likens. il Natur Hist 86:62-71 bibl(p 118) N '77
Resource-conservation; address, April 27, 1977. J. T. Ling. Vital Speeches 43:541-4 Je 15 '77
See also
Environmental movement
Industry and the environment
United States—Environmental Protection Agency
Water pollution—Control

POLLUTION—*Continued*

Economic aspects

New breed of pollutants: the dangers they carry. il U.S. News 82:42-6 F 7 '77
Pollution takes backseat to energy—maybe! S. S. Baxter. Am City & County 92:67 Mr '77
See also
Industry and the environment

Laws and legislation

Noisy environmental fight over a quiet wilderness; restrictions against snowmobiles and motorboats in Boundary Waters Canoe Area. H. R. Kennedy. il map U.S. News 83:61-2 O 31 '77
What's ahead in pollution control rules? D. Seim. Farm J 101:Beef 9 My '77
See also
Air pollution—Laws and legislation
Oil pollution of the sea—Laws and legislation
Water pollution—Laws and legislation

Measurement

Tracing toxic environmental chemicals. Sci N 111:134-5 F 26 '77

Physiological effects

Does pollution affect your nerves? M. Markham. Harp Baz 110:127+ Mr '77
Whatever happened to the cranberry crisis? J. F. Henahan. Atlantic 239:29-36 Mr '77; Discussion. 239:26-7 Je '77
See also
Environmental health
Water pollution—Physiological effects

Italy

Cleaning up Seveso; science, politics, and chaos. il Chemistry 50:21-2 N '77
Persistent poison; spread of dioxin pollution over Seveso. E. Keerdoja. map Newsweek 89:10 Je 13 '77
Poison that fell from the sky; dioxin poisoning following factory explosion; condensation. J. G. Fuller. il map Read Digest 111:191-6+ Ag '77
Reporter at large; TCDD explosion at Icmesa chemical plant. T. Whiteside. New Yorker 53:41+ Jl 25 '77
Seveso—one year later: aftermath of TCDD at Icmesa chemical plant. D. B. Richardson. il U.S. News 83:44-5 Ag 1 '77
Seveso: the questions persist where dioxin created a wasteland. J. Walsh. map Science 197:1064-7 S 9 '77

POLLUTION control bonds. See Bonds, Industrial development

POLLUTION control devices (automobiles) See Automobiles—Pollution control devices

POLLUTION control devices (refuse incinerators) See Refuse incinerators—Pollution control devices

POLLUTION control industries
Push to ease water rules. il Bus W p69+ Mr 21 '77
See also
General Signal Corporation
Research-Cottrell, Inc

POLLUTION policy. See Environmental policy

POLMAR, Norman
Russian bear has gone to sea. il Sat Eve Post 249:22-4+ Mr '77

POLO
Cowboy who showed 'em; C. Smith. R. Cantwell. il pors Sports Illus 46:68-72+ My 9 '77
Polo. il Sunset 158:100-1 Mr '77
Where and when to watch polo. Sunset 158:77 Mr '77

POLSGROVE, Carol
Making moonscapes for coal. Progressive 41:38 F '77
Paying for schools in Washington. Progressive 41:44 N '77
(ed) See Gardner, J. Conversation with John Gardner

POLUSHKIN, Maria
Great dumpling cookbook. il por Redbook 148:126-7+ Mr '77

POLYBROMINATED biphenyls. See Diphenyl compounds

POLYBUTYLENE pipes, water. See Water pipes, Plastic

POLYCHLORINATED biphenyls. See Diphenyl compounds

POLYCYCLIC hydrocarbons. See Hydrocarbons

POLYELECTROLYTES. See Electrolytes

POLYGAMY
Eternal triangles. D. K. Shah and J. Huck. il Newsweek 90:113+ N 21 '77
Reappraisal of polygamy in Africa. P. Bock. bibl il Intellect 105:435-6 Je '77

POLYGONAL buildings. See Buildings, Polygonal

POLYGRAPH. See Lie detectors and detection

POLYHEDRONS
See also
Pyramid (form)

POLYMERASE
Ornithine decarboxylase may function as an initiation factor for RNA polymerase I. C.-A. Manen and D. H. Russell. bibl il Science 195:505-6 F 4 '77

POLYMERS and polymerization
Polymer cuts cost of Rochester water. D. R. Lawson. il por Am City & County 92:97-8 S '77
Polymer pioneers. J. A. Sears. bibl il por Chemistry 50:6-10 S '77

POLYMORPHISM (biology)
Enzyme polymorphisms as genetic signatures in human cell cultures. S. J. O'Brien and others. bibl il Science 195:1345-8 Mr 25 '77
Glyoxalase I polymorphism in the mouse: a new genetic marker linked to H-2. T. Meo and others. bibl il Science 198:311-13 O 21 '77
Group-specific component: evidence for two subtypes of the Gc^1 gene. J. Constans and M. Viau. bibl il Science 198:1070-1 D 9 '77

POLYMORPHONUCLEAR leukocytes. See Leukocytes

POLYNESIA
See also
Easter Island
Tahiti

Discovery and exploration

Voyaging canoes and the settlement of Polynesia. B. R. Finney. bibl il maps Science 196:1277-85 Je 17 '77

POLYNESIAN explorers. See Explorers, Polynesian

POLYNOMIALS
Efficiency of algorithms. H. R. Lewis and C. H. Papadimitriov il map Sci Am 238:96-109 bibl(p 138+) Ja '78

POLYOMA virus. See Tumor viruses

POLYPEPTIDES. See Peptides

POLYPROPYLENE
Those cases that go on and on; rights to patent. Time 109:46+ Je 27 '77

POLYRIBOSOMES. See Nucleoproteins

POLYSACCHARIDES
How bacteria stick. J. W. Costerton and others. il Sci Am 238:86-95 Ja '78
Multistranded helix in xanthan polysaccharide. G. Holzwarth and E. B. Prestridge. bibl il Science 197:757-9 Ag 19' 77

POLYVINYL chloride pipes. See Pipes, Plastic

POMACENTRIDS. See Damselfishes

POMERANCE, Jo
Anti-test-ban coalition. bibl Bull Atom Sci 33:51-4 Ja '77

POMEROY, Wardell Baxter
New sexual myths. McCalls 105:102+ O '77

POMO Indians. See Indians of North America

POMPEII
Rise and fall of the Roman house plant; world's first indoor gardens unearthed in Pompeii. A. Menen. il Horticulture 55:26-9 D '77

POMPIDOU Center. See Paris—Georges Pompidou Center

POND, Elizabeth
Japan's coming election. Nation 224:775-8 Je 25 '77

POND, Peter
First crossing; excerpt from Winner take all. D. Lavender. il por Am West 14:4-11+ S '77 *

POND ecology. See Fresh water ecology

POND life. See Fresh water biology

PONDER, Leanne
Furniture mover; poem. Esquire 88:12 N '77

PONDS
How to diagnose a sick pond. il Farm J 101:H4-5+ D '77
Taking trout from beaver ponds. P. Barrett. il Mech Illus 73:8+ Jl '77
Vernal pools. D. M. Small. il Am For 83:30-3 My '77

PONG (game) See Electronic games

PONIATOFF, Alexander Matthew
High fidelity pathfinders. N. Eisenberg. il por Hi Fi 27:72-3 '77 *

PONICSAN, Darryl
(ed) See McCoy, T. High eagle: the many lives of Colonel Tim McCoy

PONIK the Terrible (sea monster) See Sea serpents

PONNAMPERUMA, Cyril Andrew, and others
Possible surface reactions on Mars: implications for Viking biology results. bibl il Science 197:455-7 Jl 29 '77

PONNAMPERUMA, Nirmali
Science court. il por Sci Digest 82:21-3 S '77
—See Davidson, M. jt auth

PONNELLE, Jean Pierre
Sensual stylist. S. Von Buchau. il por Opera N 2:12-16+ S '77 *
Stuttgart: Württembergische Staats-theater's new Rheingold. E. A. Reed. Opera N 42:30 D 10 '77 *

PONS, Lily
Lily Pons in retrospect; coloratura assoluta. P. L. Miller. Am Rec G 40:49-50 My '77 *

PONSELLE, Rosa
From the Villa Pace; ed by T. Pasatieri. il por Opera N 41:16-18 Mr 12 '77
Rosa Ponselle reminisces; interview, ed by J. A. Drake. il pors Hi Fi 27:75-8 Ap '77

about

Ponselle legacy; survey of her recordings. G. Jellinek. por Opera N 41:30-1 Mr 12 '77 *
Rosa: an eightieth birthday homage. W. Legge. il pors Opera N 41:10-15 Mr 12 '77 *
Viewpoint. R. Jacobson. Opera N 41:6 Mr 12 '77 *

PONT, V. See Pezet, R. jt auth

PONTI, Carlo
Sophia Loren: my 20 years with Carlo. A. Levy. pors McCalls 104:16+ Ag '77 *

PONTIAC, Mich.

Housing

See Housing—Michigan

PONTIAC'S Conspiracy, 1763-1765
Pontiac's conspiracy. A. Keller. il map Am Hist Illus 12:4-8+ My '77

PONTO, Jürgen
Big bank loses a powerful personality. por Bus W p48+ Ag 15 '77 *
Hit women. K. Willenson and T. Nater. il pors Newsweek 90:30 Ag 15 '77 *
Red roses from Roter Morgen. pors Time 110:30 Ag 15 '77 *

PONTY, Jean Luc
Fiddler on the rock. M. Orth and P. Brinkley-Rogers. il por Newsweek 90:109 S 12 '77 *

PONYTAIL plants. See Beaucarnea

POOL (game) See Billiards

POOLEY, Robert C.
NCTE and English usage. Engl J 66:18-19 D '77

POOLS. See Garden pools; Ponds; Swimming pools

POOR
See also
Poverty
Television and the poor

Health and hygiene

See also
Poor—Medical care

Housing

See also
Slums

Legal aid

See Legal aid

Medical care

Sterilizing the poor. S. M. Rothman. bibl Society 14:36-40 Ja '77
See also
Medicaid

Statistics

Hiding the other America; question of Congressional Budget Office poverty report. M. Harrington. New Repub 176:15-17 F 26 '77

India

Underappreciated India. N. Eberstadt. New Repub 176:14-16 Ja 15 '77

United States

American family; Duffy family of Arkansas. J. P. Blank. il Read Digest 111:107-12 Jl '77
American underclass. il Time 110:14-18+ Ag 29 '77
Americans dislike the poor; interview results. J. E. Tropman. Intellect 106:7-8 Jl '77
Middle class poor. S. Fraker and others. il Newsweek 90:30-1+ S 12 '77
Night the lights went on; urban poverty and the New York blackout. T. Powers. Commonweal 104:530-2 Ag 19 '77
Numbers game. M. Kempton. Progressive 41:49 My '77
Recounting the poor. T. M. Smeeding. bibl il Intellect 106:222-5 D '77
See also
Coxey's Army, 1894
Public welfare—United States

POOR laws

United States

See also
Public welfare—United States

POOR relief. See Public welfare

POP art. See Art, Modern

POP music. See Music, Popular (songs, etc)

POPCORN
Popcorn. il Sunset 158:108-9 Ap '77

POPE, Alexander, 1688-1744
Ears of an untoward make: Pope and Handel. M. R. Brownell. bibl f il Mus Q 62:554-70 O '76 *
Southern gentleman and Pope's Homer. R. S. Sugg, Jr. il Smithsonian 7:125-7+ F '77 *

POPE, Liston, Jr
Prize is life. Chr Cent 94:916-18 O 12 '77

POPE, Michael
(ed) See Farr, B. Bruce Farr talks about light displacement and the IOR

POPES
See also
Clement XI, Pope
Paul VI
Pius IX, Pope

Infallibility

Was Vatican I rigged? views of A. B. Hasler. il pors Time 110:92-3 N 14 '77

Primacy

Anglican/R. C. agreement? P. Hebblethwaite. Commonweal 104:106-8 F 18 '77
Anglicans and Roman Catholics on authority in the Church. H. J. Ryan. America 136:183-6 Mr 5 '77
Pope for Anglicans? il Time 109:44 Ja 31 '77
Power to the Pope; Anglican/Roman Catholic report. K. Woodward. Newsweek 89:56 Ja 31 '77
Understanding the Church's authority; Joint Anglican Roman Catholic International Commission. T. Beeson. Chr Cent 94:211-12 Mr 9 '77
Word about Rome, Keele, and Nottingham. J. D. Douglas. Chr Today 21:60-1 Ap 1 '77

POPLAR River
U.S, Canada to study river water quality. Dept State Bull 77:282-3 Ag 29 '77

POPOVERS. See Bread

POPP, Mariana
Africa—American style. il Ebony 33:86-8+ Ja '78

POPPIES
Poppy surprises. il Sunset 159:80-1 S '77

POPULAR culture
See also
Great Britain—Popular culture
United States—Popular culture

Study and teaching

Pop topics; popular culture courses in colleges. E. Tolkoff. il Seventeen 36:53 Ap '77

POPULAR errors. See Errors, Popular

POPULAR music. See Music, Popular (songs, etc)

POPULAR Party (Spain) See Political parties—Spain

POPULAR photography (periodical)
Editorial. A. Goldsmith. por Pop Phot 80:10 Ap; 8 My '77
Pop photo and its world—1937-77; a 40th-anniversary collage; symposium, ed by A. Goldsmith. Pop Phot 80:79-97+ My '77

POPULARITY
Popularity: how important is it? M. Rabe-Cochran. il Seventeen 36:49 Ap '77

POPULATION
See also
Africa, Central—Population
Birth control
Birth rate
Mexico—Population
United States—Population

Overpopulation

How to defuse the population bomb; adaptation of address. R. S. McNamara. il Time 110: 93-4+ O 24 '77
Profile of a world overflowing with people. il U.S. News 82:54-5 Mr 28 '77
Why men dominate women; female infanticide and overpopulation. M. Harris. il N Y Times Mag p46+ N 13 '77
See also
Population, Increase of

Statistics

Profile of a world overflowing with people. il U.S. News 82:54-5 Mr 28 '77

POPULATION, Increase of
Breast-feeding and population growth. J. Knodel. bibl il Science 198:1111-15 D 16 '77
Planning for how many people? R. T. Dennis; discussion. BioScience 24:4-5 Ja '77
Population bomb threat: a look at the facts. J. R. Kasun. Intellect 105:412-14 Je '77
Population explosion; excerpt from address, August 1977. Society 15:9 N '77
Tick, tick tick. New Repub 177:3+ D 3 '77
See also
Population—Overpopulation

POPULATION biology
Ecosystems analysis and population biology: lessons for the development of community ecology. T. C. Foin and S. K. Jain. bibl il BioScience 27:532-8 Ag '77
Harvesting natural populations in a randomly fluctuating environment. J. R. Beddington and R. M. May. bibl il Science 197:463-5 Jl 29 '77
Species turnover rates on islands: dependence on census interval. J. M. Diamond and R. M. May. bibl il Science 197:266-70 Jl 15 '77

POPULATION education
Including population problems in the curriculum. P. M. Hauser. Educ Digest 42:14-16 Mr '77

POPULATION forecasting
Failure in the West: a demographic insight. R. De Marcellus. America 137:278-80 O 29 '77
POPULATION genetics
Cats and commerce. N. B. Todd. il maps Sci Am 237:100-6 bibl(p 163) N '77
POPULATION growth. See Population, Increase of
POPULATION policy
Alternative views of moral priorities in population policy. A. J. Dyck. bibl BioScience 27: 272-6 Ap '77
POPULATIONS, Fish. See Fish populations
PORAC, Clare. See Coren, S. jt auth
PORCELAIN. See Pottery
PORCELLI, Carmine
Entertain beautifully on a budget. il Harp Baz 110:130-1+ Mr '77
Tom Tryon entertains. il por House B 119:102-3 Ap '77
PORCHES, Winterized. See Rooms
PORGY and Bess; opera. See Gershwin, G.
PORK
See also
Bacon
Cookery—Meat

Advertising

See Meat industry—Advertising
PORK barrel legislation. See United States—Appropriations and expenditures
PORK industry. See Meat industry
PORK-O-Rama Research Knoll, Inc. See Swine industry
PORKET, J. L.
Soviet model of industrial democracy. bibl f Ann Am Acad 431:123-32 My '77
PORNOGRAPHY
All the ads fit to print; ban on advertising of pornographic movies in newspapers. il Time 110:80 S 12 '77
Child pornography: outrage starts to stir some action. U.S. News 82:66 Je 13 '77
Child's garden of perversity. il Time 109:55-6 Ap 4 '77; Same abr. with title Kid sex pornography's all-time low. Read Digest 111: 45-8+ Jl '77
Coming of bold pornography; interviews, ed by W. Goodman. E. Van Den Haag; G. Talese. Current 190:32-8 F '77
Crackdown on porn. S. Fraker and others. il Newsweek 89:21-2+ F 28 '77
Exploited children. Chr Today 22:23 N 18 '77
Keeping a rein on sex business. il Changing T 32:21-3 Ja '78
Pornography—not sex but the obscene use of power. G. Steinem. Ms 6:43-5 Ag '77
There is no right to peddle pornography! E. Van Den Haag. Read Digest 111:48 Jl '77
What parents should know and do about kiddie porn; work of F. Osanka. P. Bridge. il Parents Mag 53:42-3+ Ja '78
What pornographers are doing to children: a shocking report. J. Densen-Gerber. Redbook 149:86+ Ag '77
See also
Obscenity (law)
United States—Commission on Obscenity and Pornography
PORPHYRIA
Bovine protoporphyria: the first nonhuman model of this hereditary photosensitizing disease. G. R. Ruth and others. bibl il Science 198:199-201 O 14 '77
PORPHYRINS
Porphyrin induction: equivalent effects of 5αH and 5βH steroids in chick embryo liver cells. J. K. Stephens and others. bibl il Science 197:659-60 Ag 12 '77
PORPOISES. See Dolphins (mammals)
PORSCHE (sports car) See Sports cars
PORT Aransas, Tex.
Can they head off the tankers at the pass? proposed Harbor Island superport off Texas coast. D. G. Schueler. Audubon 79:146-8 N '77
PORT Authority of New York and New Jersey
Concorde ban termed discriminatory. Aviation W 106:38 Je 13 '77
Concorde landing rights court hearing postponed. Aviation W 106:202 Mr 21 '77
Court clears Concorde JFK service. W. C. Wetmore. Aviation W 106:29 My 16 '77
Court ruling awaited in Concorde case. W. H. Gregory. Aviation W 106:24+ My 9 '77
Federal judge lifts ban on Concorde. Aviation W 107:34 Ag 22 '77
La grande crise over Concorde. il Time 109:40 Mr 21 '77
How the richest public agency lost its way. il Bus W p 110-11 D 12 '77
Nerve war in the sky; Concorde landing rights decision. A. J. Mayer and others. il Newsweek 89:68-9 Mr 21 '77
New York ban on Concorde continued. Aviation W 107:24 Jl 11 '77
Port Authority chastised for noise standard delay. Aviation W 107:30 S 26 '77
Port Authority delay attacked. Aviation W 107: 24 Jl 18 '77
Port Authority publishes new N.Y. noise rule. Aviation W 107:31 O 17 '77
Ports in a storm. B. Weberman. Forbes 120:120 D 1 '77
U.K, France ponder JFK Concorde action. Aviation W 106:29 Je 20 '77
PORT of New York Authority. See Port Authority of New York and New Jersey
PORT Orchard, Wash.
When a supersub base invades a rural area in the Northwest; Bangor Trident base. map U.S. News 83:41-2 Ag 1 '77
PORTABLE audio systems. See Audio systems, Portable
PORTABLE electric typewriters. See Typewriters, Electric
PORTABLE radio apparatus. See Radio apparatus and instruments, Portable
PORTABLE radio receivers. See Radio receivers, Portable
PORTABLE television receivers. See Television receivers, Portable
PORTER, Andrew (music critic)
Musical events. See issues of New Yorker
Real Kurt Weill. il por Hi Fi 27:77-9 My '77
PORTER, Cecelia Hopkins
Rheinlieder critics: a case of musical nationalism; 1840-1850. bibl f il Mus Q 63:74-98 Ja '77
PORTER, Charlotte M. See Coonen, L. P. jt auth
PORTER, David Dixon
Cruise of the USS Essex. R. J. Toner il por map Am Hist Illus 11:4-7+ Ja '77 *
PORTER, Eliot
Eliot Porter on 35-mm; interview, ed by P. Caulfield. il por Pop Phot 81:108-17+ S '77
Photo and word views of pioneer photographer Eliot Porter; interview, ed by J. Landman. il por Sr Schol 110:2-5 D 1 '77
PORTER, Gareth
Healing the wounds of war: justice, not charity, for Vietnam. Chr Cent 94:192-4 Mr 2 '77
Kissinger's double-cross for peace. Nation 224: 519-21 Ap 30 '77
PORTER, James W.
Pseudorca stranding. il Oceans 10:8-15 Jl '77
—See Muscatine, L. jt auth
PORTER, Katherine Anne
Never-ending wrong. il pors Atlantic 239:37-48+ Je '77
PORTER, Lynn
People on the cover. A. L. Ball. por Redbook 150:2 N '77 *
PORTER, Marina Oswald. See Oswald, M.
PORTER, Peter
Comment. J. Matthias. Poetry 129:350-3 Mr '77 *
PORTER, Sylvia
Spending your money; questions and answers. See issues of Ladies' home journal
PORTES, Alejandro
Labor functions of illegal aliens. bibl il Society 14:31-7 S '77
PORTES, Richard
East Europe's debt to the West: interdependence is a two-way street. bibl f il For Affairs 55:751-82 Jl '77
PORTFOLIOS, Personal. See Applications for positions
PORTILLO, José López. See López Portillo, J.
PORTIS, Charles
Your action line. New Yorker 53:42-3 D 12 '77
PORTLAND, Me.

Restaurants

See Restaurants—United States
PORTLAND, Ore.

Airports

Portland's airport—Oregon showcase; Portland International Airport. il Sunset 159:48 Ag '77

Architecture

In just two years, transformation. il Sunset 158: 100-3 Je '77

Art

How the seed money in Portland has grown. P. Failing. il Art N 76:58-61 My '77

Galleries and museums

Portland's starving grande dame; financial crisis at the Portland Art Museum. P. Failing. il Art N 76:85-8 O '77
See also
Western Forestry Center, Portland, Ore.

Religious institutions and affairs

Devilish destruction; vandalism in eight churches. Chr Today 21:58 S 23 '77
PORTLAND Art Museum. See Portland, Ore.—Galleries and museums
PORTLAND Ballet Company. See Ballet companies
PORTLAND Dance Theater. See Dance companies
PORTLAND International Airport. See Portland, Ore.—Airports

PORTLAND-Multnomah County, Ore, Library. See Libraries—Oregon

PORTMAN, John Calvin, 1924-
Architecture for people and not for things; excerpt from The Architect as developer. il Archit Rec 161:133-40 Ja '77

PORTRAIT drawing
Raphael Soyer: a realist without a slogan. J. Shaw-Eagle. il por Art N 76:187-8 N '77

PORTRAIT painting
Art of family living; work of M. V. Olsen. L. C. Pogrebin. il Ms 5:15-16+ Je '77
Ivan Albright: more than meets the eye. J. Van Der Marck. bibl il por Art in Am 65:92-9 N '77
Looking at paintings; work of J. A. D. Ingres. B. Dunstan. il Am Artist 41:74-5 Ag '77
Pomo Indian portraits of Grace Carpenter Hudson; excerpt from The painter lady. S. R. Boynton. il por Am West 14:20-9 S '77
Portrait of a New England town. F. S. Wight. il Art in Am 65:106-7 My '77

PORTRAITS
See also
Photography—Portraits

Exhibitions

Art; work of L. Golub. L. Alloway. Nation 224: 221-2 F 19 '77
Earthbound and sublime; exhibition, Modern Portraits: the Self and Others. K. Evett. New Repub 176:30-1 Mr 5 '77
Modern Portraits—an art exhibit that evokes the shock of recognition; Modern Portraits—the Self and Others. B. Brody. Psychol Today 10:25 F '77

PORTRAITS, American
American painting; symposium. il Antiques 112: 932-77 N '77
G.P.A. Healy and his Louisiana portraits. V. L. Glasgow. bibl il Antiques 111:1204-9 Je '77
Portrait painting in eighteenth-century Annapolis. C. J. Weekley. bibl il Antiques 111:345-53 F '77
Portraits in Lexington, Massachusetts. S. B. Sherrill. il Antiques 111:234+ F '77
Strictly realist; S. Liberman's portrait of N. A. Rockefeller. Vasari. il Art N 76:18+ Summ '77
See also
Carter, J.—Portraits
Washington, G.—Portraits

PORTRAITS, British
Ms Browning's spiritual face. Vasari. il Art N 76:34 N '77

PORTS
See also
Petroleum shipping terminals

France

Marseilles-Fos. M.-L. Welker. il map Oceans 10:46-51 Ja '77

PORTUGAL
Iberia; symposium. il Sat R 5:10-14+ O 29 '77
See also
Economic assistance, American—Portugal
Lisbon
Loans, Foreign—Portugal

Colonies

See also
Angola
Azores
Macao
Madeira

Description and travel

Autumn in Portugal. A. Rand. il Harp Baz 111: 16+ N '77
Portugal: poet kings and the sea. W. Barnstone. il Sat Eve Post 249:70-1 N '77

Economic policy

Portugal: a hard test for the IMF. S. W. Sanders. il Bus W p35 Ja 9 '78

Industries

Old guard returns to rebuild. il Bus W p36 Ag 29 '77

Politics and government

After Soares, Soares? F. Willey and E. Behr. il por Newsweek 90:47 D 19 '77
500 days of Mário Soares. il por Time 110:34 D 19 '77
Meanwhile, in Portugal . . . D. May. Sat R 5:22 O 29 '77
Portugal's crisis. G. W. Grayson. bibl f Cur Hist 73:169-73+ N '77
Soares' shaky political seesaw. por Time 110: 34 Ag 8 '77

Social conditions

Portugal's returnees; refugees from Mozambique. T. Land. Progressive 41:50 D '77

PORTUGUESE in the United States
See also
Rhode Island—Foreign population

PORZECANSKI, Arturo C.
Authoritarian Uruguay. Cur Hist 72:73-5+ F '77

POSEY, Lawton W.
Southern Presbyterian dilemma. Chr Cent 94: 142-5, 765-6 F 16, Ag 31 '77
Winter communion; poem. Chr Cent 94:1133 D 7 '77

POSEY, Sam
Down a dark hall at 185 m.p.h. il Read Digest 110:93-6 Mr '77

POSITIONS, Applications for. See Applications

POSITIONS, Sleep. See Sleep positions

POSITRONIUM
Flaw in the diamond of QED. Sci N 111:20 Ja 8 '77

POSLUSZNY, Usher. See Tomlinson, P. B. jt auth

POSNER, Bruce
Detroit takes EV seriously, but output on large scale is at least decade away. Sci Digest 82: 78-9 S '77

POSNER, Victor
Victor Posner: living on borrowed time. P. Blustein. por Forbes 120:23-4 S 1 '77 •

POSS, Stanley
Letters and comment: spaced out West. Yale R 66:472-80 Mr '77
Summer fun with Karl and Fred. Progressive 41:43-5 O '77

POSSESSION (law)
A friend's going to fly my plane. T. Benenson. Flying 100:24+ Ap '77
N.C. ruling menaces manuscript collections; document ownership case of B. C. West, Jr. vs North Carolina. M. U. Russell. Am Lib 8: 471-2 O '77

POSSESSIONS. See Property

POSSUMS. See Opossums

POST, Elizabeth L.
New Emily Post. See issues of Good housekeeping

POST, Emily (Price)
Emily Post. E. Oettinger. por Am Heritage 28: 38-9 Ap '77 •

POST, New York. See New York post

POST, Washington. See Washington post

POST cards
Picture postcard. S. Carver. See issues of Hobbies
Post cards from museums—used for art displays. il Sunset 159:142 N '77

Collectors and collecting

Power to the postcard. J. Goldman. Vogue 167:36 Jl '77

POST Company. See Washington Post Company

POST-Hold (foam) See Plastic foams

POST-impressionism (art)
Art; Neo-impressionism. L. Alloway. Nation 225:377-8 O 15 '77
Looking at paintings; pointillism of G. Seurat. B. Dunstan. il Am Artist 41:84-5 F '77

POST office buildings

Conservation and restoration

See Architecture—Conservation and restoration

POSTAGE stamp design
Stamp of approval J. Swanson and D. Curtis. il Sch Arts 76:50-1 Mr '77

Anecdotes, facetiae, satire, etc.

Inventors of the faith. M. E. Marty. Chr Cent 94:207 Mr 2 '77

POSTAGE stamps
Celebrating America's beauty; commemorative stamps. il Conservationist 31:36-7 Mr '77
1977 Christmas stamps were issued October 21. Hobbies 82:130 D '77
Treasure of wildlife stamps; water bird designs and money raised for National Wildlife Federation. G. Reiger. il Field & S 82:114-16+ Je '77
Universe of stamps. G. G. Young. il Sky & Tel 54:366-70 N '77
See also
Postage stamp design

Collectors and collecting

Stamps. H. Herst, Jr. See issues of Hobbies

POSTAL, Bernard, and Koppman, Lionel
Liberty stands on her words; excerpt from American Jewish landmarks: a travel guide and history. il por Ms 6:22 Ag '77

POSTAL censorship
Living the rest to God; dictatorships in Latin America. M. D. Wilde. Chr Cent 94:396-7 Ap 27 '77

POSTAL rates

United States

Citizen Bailar; proposed citizen's rate as sign of collapse of Postal Service. R. J. Myers. New Repub 177:6 Jl 23 '77
Cutting your postal costs down to size. J. Miller. il Ret Liv 17:42-3 Jl '77
Data services win on second-class mail. Bus W p23-4 Jl 18 '77

POSTAL rates—United States—*Continued*
From pillar to post. New Repub 176:6 F 26 '77
No rate change if page charges are voluntary. W. G. P. Peter. BioScience 27:12+ Ja '77
Postal service approves 34% hike for fourth class; book rates. S. Wagner. Pub W 212:76-7 Jl 18 '77
Save money on postage. il Changing T 31:20 O '77
Why the two-tier postal rate is unjustified. S. Zucker. Bus W p53 Jl 25 '77

POSTAL service
See also
Electronics in postal service
United Nations Postal Administration

United States

Their (dis)appointed rounds; P. H. Brennan Hand Delivery Service in competition with United States Postal Service in Rochester, N.Y. R. Brookhiser. il Nat R 29:1294-6 N 11 '77
See also
Railway mail service
United States Postal Service

POSTCARDS. See Post cards

POSTERS
Border dispute; question of installing P. Max's posters. Vasari. Art N 76:34+ N '77
Paul Davis: a personal vision; interview, ed by S. Bonhomme; with editorial comment. P. Davis. il Am Artist 41:7-9, 34-41+ My '77
Posters; E. Penfield's advertising posters for Harper's. E. Penfield. il por Harpers 225:57-70 D '77

POSTERS, Publishing of. See Publishers and publishing—Art

POSTON, Ersa Hines
United States reemphasizes spirit of cooperation with OAU; statement, November 16, 1976. Dept State Bull 76:58 Ja 17 '77

POSTON, J. Michael
Leucine 2,3-aminomutase: a cobalamin-dependent enzyme present in bean seedlings. bibl il Science 195:301-2 Ja 21 '77

POSTURE
How to beat backaches and pains in a new hot seat. il House & Gard 149:130 Mr '77
Posture; dancers' posture. R. Gelabert. il Dance Mag 51:85-7 O '77
Sitting pretty: science offers 4000 weighs it can help you! N. Carlisle and M. Carlisle. il Sci Digest 82:43-5 Jl '77
See also
Sleep positions

POT. See Marijuana

POT-et-fleur. See Plants, Potted

POTAMKIN, Victor H.
King of Cadillacs—and taxis. por Forbes 119:64 Ap 1 '77 *

POTASSIUM
See also
Plants—Potassium content

POTASSIUM in the body
Potassium accumulation in muscle: a test of the binding hypothesis. L. G. Palmer and J. Gulati; reply with rejoinder. G. I. Ling. bibl il Science 198:1281-4 D 23 '77

POTATO salads. See Salads

POTATOES
Potato races under mulch. J. Ruttle. il Org Gard & Farm 24:160-2 My '77
Potatoes redux. New Yorker 53:41-2 O 17 '77
Trenches and sawdust: huge potatoes from hard clay. D. Haenke. il Org Gard & Farm 24:80-1 Mr '77
See also
Cookery—Vegetables

Diseases and pests

Potato scab. Org Gard & Farm 24:36+ N '77

POTEMRA, Thomas A.
Aurora borealis: the greatest light show on earth. il Smithsonian 7:64-70 bibl(p 152+) F '77

POTOK, Chaim
The chosen, The promise, and My name is Asher Lev. A. D. Sgan. Engl J 66:63-4 Mr '77 *

POTOMAC River
Passage of the Potomac; excerpt from Notes on Virginia, with photographs by William A. Bake. T. Jefferson. il por Read Digest 110:194-9 Ap '77
Undiscovered Potomacs; north and south branches in Maryland and West Virginia. J. Bowen. il Travel 148:34-7+ O '77

POTOMACUS, pseud
Word from Washington. See issues of Progressive to August 1977

POTPOURRI
Sweet scents of summer. il Redbook 149:100+ Je '77
With potpourri or sachet, summer just stays with you. il Sunset 159:162 S '77

POTS and pans. See Kitchen utensils and appliances

POTT Industries Inc.- Houston Natural Gas Corporation merger. See Corporations—Acquisitions and mergers

POTTER, Beatrix
Beatrix Potter: more than just Peter Rabbit. A. Lurie. il por Ms 6:42-3+ S '77 *
Happy birthday, Peter Rabbit and friends. il Time 109:92 Ap 11 '77 *

POTTER, Richard C.
Booker T. Washington: a visit to Florida. por Negro Hist Bull 40:744-5 S '77

POTTER, Robert J.
Electronic mail. bibl il Science 195:1160-4 Mr 18 '77

POTTER, Russell M. and Rossman, G. R.
Desert varnish: the importance of clay minerals. bibl il Science 196:1446-8 Je 24 '77

POTTER, Van Rensselaer
Evolving ethical concepts. bibl BioScience 27:251-3 Ap '77

POTTERIES
Establishing a student-built pottery. S. Edwards. il Ceram Mo 25:37-9 F '77
Glenys Barton at Wedgwood. J. Mallet. il Ceram Mo 25:28-30 O '77
Production throwing in Taiwan. J. Meerbott. il por Ceram Mo 25:45-50 Mr '77
Siphnos potters. P. Turner. il map Ceram Mo 25:45-50 Ap '77

History

Early Bennington potteries; Fenton and Norton Potteries of Bennington, Vt. L. Vozar. il Ceram Mo 25:54-7 O '77
19th century Staffordshire; with excerpts from 1827 pamphlet. G. Elliott. Ceram Mo 25:29-36 Mr '77

POTTERS
Ceramactivities: people, places, and things. See issues of Ceramics monthly
Eight Independent Production Potters. il Ceram Mo 25:46-52 F '77
Eight Independent Production Potters. il Craft Horiz 37:44-50 F '77
Interior monologue: a potter's thoughts amidst work. C. Counts. Ceram Mo 25:19+ D '77
See also
Bacerra, R.
Bringle, C.
Duckworth, R.
Heino, O.
Kwong, E.
LaVerdiere, B.
Leach, B. H.
Martz, K.
Rubin, M.
Wildenhain, M.
Williams, G.

POTTERS clubs and societies. See Art clubs and societies

POTTERS materials. See Artists materials

POTTERY
Four experts give you a short course in china; ed by M. Morse. House & Gard 149:20+ Je '77
Low-fire porcelain for casting. R. J. Madison. il por Ceram Mo 25:38-9 N '77
See also
Ceramic sculpture
Glazes and glazing (ceramics)
Potteries

Bibliography

New books. See occasional issues of Ceramics monthly

Collectors and collecting

Address book; porcelain and pottery dealers specializing in collectors items. S. Sunderlin. House B 119:39-40 F '77
Collecting the crossed swords; Meissen porcelain M. D. Schwartz. il Art N 76:110 Ap '77
Collector's plates: an excellent way to meet the artists. il House B 119:51-6+ N '77

Competitions

Potter's pentathlon. R. Jolliffe and R. Richards. il por Ceram Mo 25:43-6 N '77

Conferences

Lead and cadmium release; WHO conference on ceramic foodware safety. il Ceram Mo 25:69+ D '77

Critics and criticism

See Art critics and criticism

Decoration

Detailing slabs with slip impressions. E. Marks. il por Ceram Mo 25:33-6 F '77
Judy Chicago: china painter. il Ceram Mo 25:34-5 Je '77
On-glaze brush decoration. P. Lewing. il por Ceram Mo 25:55-8 N '77
Oxidation glazes, slips, stains, and bodies for cone 6. R. Zakin. il Ceram Mo 25:33-43 Ap '77
Unmistakably Mexican; Mexican ceramic decorations. C. L. Ogorek. Design (US) 78:12-15 mid-Summ '77

Drying

See Pottery—Firing

POTTERY—*Continued*

Exhibitions

Approaches to function. il Ceram Mo 25:44 Ap '77
Arts and crafts in Detroit: 1906-1976. il Ceram Mo 25:43-5 F '77
Atlanta exhibition; 35 Artists in the Southeast. il Ceram Mo 25:24-6 My '77
Canadian exhibition; National Ceramics Exhibition, Calgary. il Ceram Mo 25:58-9 Mr '77
Ceramactivities: people, places, and things. See issues of Ceramics monthly
Ceramic Conjunction. il Ceram Mo 25:42-3 D '77
Craftforms. il Ceram Mo 25:64-6 F '77
Craftsman's Fair of the Southern Highlands. il Ceram Mo 25:40-2 F '77
Definition Clay L.A. E. Levin. il Ceram Mo 25:40-2 N '77
Eight Independent Production Potters. il Ceram Mo 25:46-52 F '77
Eight Independent Production Potters. il Craft Horiz 37:44-50 F '77
Exhibition at Dartmouth; Contemporary Clay: Ten Approaches. il Ceram Mo 25:26-9 F '77
Exhibition/sale—how does it happen? annual event of the potters' association Clay. J. Lincoln. il Ceram Mo 25:44-6 D '77
Exhibitions at Arizona State. il Ceram Mo 25:56-7 Ap '77
Functional Ceramics 1977. il Ceram Mo 25:38-43 S '77
Illinois Clayworks. il Ceram Mo 25:24-7 D '77
Into White. il Ceram Mo 25:36-7 N '77
Itinerary. See issues of Ceramics monthly
M.F.A. exhibition at Puget Sound. il Ceram Mo 25:30 S '77
May Show. il Ceram Mo 25:56-7 Mr '77
1977 National Cone Box Show. il Ceram Mo 25:46-7 O '77
Porcelain; exhibit at the Kaplan-Baumann Gallery, Los Angeles. il Ceram Mo 25:58 S '77
Pot shows in New Mexico, Colorado; Maxwell and Taylor Museums. il Sunset 158:49 My '77
Resident potters at Penland. il Ceram Mo 25:48-9 O '77
Rochester Folk Art Guild. il Ceram Mo 25:24-5 F '77
Texas Pottery: Caddo Indian to Contemporary. il Ceram Mo 25:28-32 Ap '77
Where to show. Ceram Mo 25:8+ S; 8+ O; 15+ N; 13+ D '77

Firing

Barbecue and fireplace firing. M. Poupeney. il Ceram Mo 25:59-62 Je '77
Sawdust injection firing; raku. W. L. Baker. il pors Ceram Mo 25:45-7 S '77

History

Comment: recent clay history. S. R. Thompson. Ceram Mo 25:19+ Je '77
Enduring fragility; eighteenth century European porcelain. F. X. O'Connor. il Sat Eve Post 249:46-9 My '77
Porcelain or china ware. il Hobbies 82:70-2 My '77

Marketing

Retail sales cooperative; Yellow Springs Pottery, near Dayton, Ohio. L. Eder. il por Ceram Mo 25:51-4 N '77

Philosophy

Interior monologue: a potter's thoughts amidst work. C. Counts. Ceram Mo 25:19+ D '77

Study and teaching

Don Reitz workshop. il pors Ceram Mo 25:50-5 S '77
Emphasis: planning for ceramics. V. G. Timmons. il Sch Arts 77:31-2 N '77
Establishing a student-built pottery. S. Edwards. il Ceram Mo 25:37-9 F '77
Hal Riegger: Bizen Kiln workshop. il Ceram Mo 25:35-9 My '77
Indiana State University. R. Bonham. il Ceram Mo 25:28-33 N '77
Potter of Penland. N. Schulman. il Craft Horiz 37:23-7 Je '77
Summer workshops 1977. il Ceram Mo 25:51-5+ Ap; 95 My '77
Tuscarora Pottery School. A. Schwartz. il pors Ceram Mo 25:36-41 Je '77
Wedgewood International Seminar. il Hobbies 82:117+ My '77
Workshop in Belgium. S. Hyman. il Ceram Mo 25:31-4 O '77

Projects

Bowl your students over with coiled clay. T. Dahood. il Design (US) 79:6+ Fall '77
Medicine pots—a motivation operation. L. L. Clark. il Sch Arts 76:32-3 F '77

Technique

Ceramic air cooler. Z. Kujundzic. il Ceram Mo 25:56-7 S '77
Ceramic dish hands you the soap. il Sunset 159:155 N '77
Clay whistle. R. A. Fromme. il Ceram Mo 25:60-3 Mr; 58-62 Ap '77
Constructing your own slab roller; excerpt from Getting into pots, a basic pottery manual. G. Wettlaufer and N. Wettlaufer. il Ceram Mo 25:30-2 F '77
Designing in clay. L. I. Nigrosh. il Sch Arts 76:52-4 F '77
Elly and Willy Kuch. S. Hyman. il pors Ceram Mo 25:50-7 My '77
Handbuilt fireplace facade. F. Simons. il Ceram Mo 25:59-61 N '77
How to make a ceramic mobile. il Sunset 158:164+ My '77
Light of Rudolph Staffel; interview, ed by P. Winokur and R. Winokur. R. Staffel. il por Craft Horiz 37:24-9+ Ap '77
Locking and sealing storage containers; ceramic containers for food storage. D. Hendley. il Ceram Mo 25:60-3 F '77
Making cranks for production firing. G. Wettlaufer and N. Wettlaufer. il Ceram Mo 25:64-6 S '77
Pots from slab and wheel-thrown sections. R. Benjamin. il Ceram Mo 25:58-61 O '77
Production trimming. M. Peterson. il Ceram Mo 25:50-2 O '77
Throw a head. M. Sapiro. il Sch Arts 77:20-7 O '77
Throw a ring-vase. M. Sapiro. il Sch Arts 76:22-7 Mr '77
Throwing a double-walled planter. P. Wood. il Ceram Mo 25:59-61 My '77
Vitrified bisque. R. Behrens. por Ceram Mo 25:62-3 O '77

See also

Glazes and glazing (ceramics)
Modeling
Raku pottery

Themes

Royal Doulton series ware. K. M. McClinton. il Hobbies 82:116-17+ Je '77

POTTERY, African
Encounter with an African potter. M. Michie. il pors Ceram Mo 25:32-5 D '77

POTTERY, American
Interview with Robert Winokur; ed by C. Sewalt. R. Winokur. il pors Ceram Mo 25:31-5 S '77
White House crafts & craftsmen; luncheon for Senators' wives, May 16, 1977. E. K. Canavier. il Ceram Mo 25:47-55 D '77

See also

American Ceramic Society
Indians of North America—Pottery
Potteries

History

Alkaline glazes and groundhog kilns: Southern pottery traditions. G. H. Greer. il Antiques 111:768-73 Ap '77
New Deal ceramics: the Cleveland workshop. K. A. Marling. il por Ceram Mo 25:25-31 Je '77

POTTERY, Chinese
China trade armorial porcelain in America. C. Le Corbeiller. bibl il Antiques 112:1124-9 D '77
Clay soldiers: the army of Emperor Ch'in; with editorial comment. A. Topping. il Horizon 19:2, 4-13 Ja '77

POTTERY, Danish
Profile—Niels Refsgaard; stoneware; interview, ed by S. G. Lewin. N. Refsgaard. il por House B 119:12+ Mr '77

POTTERY, English
American hotels on early Staffordshire. F. Stefano, Jr. bibl il Antiques 112:274-7 Ag '77
English domestic pottery. il Ceram Mo 25:20-3 D '77
Enoch Wood earthenware found in St Paul's Church, Burslem. P. D. Kingsbury. bibl il Antiques 112:122-7 Jl '77
19th century Staffordshire; with excerpts from 1827 pamphlet. G. Elliott. Ceram Mo 25:29-36 Mr '77
Royal Doulton series ware. K. M. McClinton. il Hobbies 82:116-17+ Je '77
Wedgewood International Seminar. il Hobbies 82:117+ My '77

POTTERY, European
Enduring fragility; eighteenth century European porcelain. F. X. O'Connor. il Sat Eve Post 249:46-9 My '77

POTTERY, French
French ceramist; M. Lévêque. C. Barth. il por Ceram Mo 25:48-50 N '77

POTTERY, German
Collecting the crossed swords; Meissen porcelain. M. D. Schwartz. il Art N 76:110 Ap '77
Elly and Willy Kuch. S. Hyman. il pors Ceram Mo 25:50-7 My '77
Meissen. il Ceram Mo 25:87+ D '77

POTTERY, Greek
Siphnos potters. P. Turner. il map Ceram Mo 25:45-50 Ap '77

See also

Vases, Greek

POTTERY, Indian (American) See Indians of North America—Pottery

POTTERY, Japanese
Film; Potters at work. D. Hare. Craft Horiz 37:12+ Ap '77
Japanese ash glazes. H. Sasaki. il por Ceram Mo 25:53-9 F '77
Japanese incense boxes. il Ceram Mo 25:22-7 N '77
Pottery by Japanese masters. C. Barth. il Design (US) 78:18-20 Spr '77
POTTERY, Mexican
Tin-glazed pottery of Puebla, Mexico. C. Wilcoxen. bibl il Antiques 111:794-8 Ap '77
Unmistakably Mexican; Mexican ceramic decorations. C. L. Ogorek. il Design (US) 78: 12-15 mid-Summ '77
POTTERY, Oriental
Far Eastern art in New York collections. il Ceram Mo 25:19-25 S '77
POTTERY, Raku. See Raku pottery
POTTERY, Taiwanese
Production throwing in Taiwan. J. Meerbott. il por Ceram Mo 25:45-50 Mr '77
POTTERY clay. See Clay
POTTERY critics and criticism. See Art critics and criticism
POTTERY industry. See Potteries
POTTERY kilns. See Kilns
POTTERY painting. See Pottery—Decoration
POTTERY sales. See Art sales
POTTERY studios. See Potteries
POTTING sheds. See Garden houses, shelters, etc.
POTTING soils. See Soils, Potting
POTTINGER, J. Stanley
Bakke case: how to argue about reverse discrimination. Ms 6:59-60 Ja '78
POTTS, James L.
Jailhouse law book. A. Wolff. Sat R 4:54 Mr 19 '77 *
POTVIN, Raymond H. See Nelson, H. M. jt auth
POUCHES (bags) See Bags
POULAIN, Nicolas
He built the Statue of Liberty. il Read Digest 110:27-32 Ap '77
POULENC, Francis
Certain grace. P. Bernac. il Opera N 41:28-32 F 5 '77 *
Dialogues of the Carmelites. Reviews
Hi Fi 27:MA21-2 Je '77 *
New Yorker 53:107-10 F 21 '77 *
Opera N 41:20+ F 5 '77 *
Sat R il 4:47-8 Mr 19 '77 *
Time il 109:75 F 21 '77 *
Monologue and dialogues. N. Rorem. il pors Opera N 41:10-16 F 5 '77 *
Voice of Poulenc; interview, ed by L. Rasponi. D. Duval. por Opera N 41:17-19 F 5 '77 *
POULTRY
Our far-flung correspondents; England. C. Trillin. New Yorker 53:149-52+ N 21 '77
See also
Carving (meat, etc)
Cookery—Poultry
Ducks
Geese

Breeding

See Poultry breeding

Diseases and pests

Avian muscular dystrophy: functional and biochemical improvement with diphenylhydantoin. R. K. Entrikin and others. bibl il Science 195: 873-5 Mr 4 '77
Marek's disease: effects of B histocompatibility alloalleles in resistant and susceptible chicken lines. W. E. Briles and others. bibl il Science 195:193-5 Ja 14 '77
See also
Newcastle disease

Smoking

See Food—Smoking
POULTRY, Freezing of. See Freezing of food
POULTRY breeding
Blue dun bonanza; raising roosters to supply feathers for fishing flies. S. Paulakavich. por Outdoor Life 159:31 Je '77
POULTRY industry
It takes a tough man to fowl a tender creek: pollution of Parker Creek by Perdue's Accomac plant in Virginia. G. Reiger. il Audubon 79: 142-5 N '77
POULTRY stuffing. See Cookery—Poultry
POUND, Ezra
Miss Monroe, Mr Pound, and the boorzoi. J. Parisi. Poetry 131:39-51 O '77 *

Anecdotes, facetiae, satire, etc.

Lunch with Uncle Ez. H. Bibesco. Atlantic 240: 55-8 Ag '77
POUNDCAKE. See Cake
POUPENEY, Mollie
Barbecue and fireplace firing. il Ceram Mo 25: 59-62 Je '77
POUSNER, Michael
New urban riots. por Newsweek 89:11 Je 27 '77
POUSSAINT, Alvin Francis
Black women/black men: has something gone wrong between them? interview. il pors Ebony 32:160-2 Ag '77
How to cope with tragedy. il Ebony 32:94-6+ F '77
POUSSAINT, Ann Ashmore
Black women/black men: has something gone wrong between them? interview. il pors Ebony 32:160-2 Ag '77
POUSSIN, Nicolas
Looking at paintings. B. Dunstan. il Am Artist 41:46-7 Je '77 *
POUST, Mary Ann
Conquering childhood heart disease. Parents Mag 52:16+ O '77
POVERTY
Birth into poverty. V. J. Genovesi. America 137: 459-60 D 24 '77
Theoretical framework for analyzing poverty as a subculture. J. J. Harris, 3d and W. R. Bentzen. bibl Clearing H 50:209-11 Ja '77
See also
Poor
Public welfare
POVERTY, Vow of
N.L.R.B. and the vow of poverty; taxation of members of religious orders teaching in Catholic schools. America 137:157 S 24 '77
Vow of poverty ruling modified. America 137:91-2 Ag 27 '77
POWDERED milk. See Milk, Dried
POWEL, Samuel, House. See Philadelphia—Historic houses, sites, etc.
POWELL, Barbara Schieffelin
Intensive education: the impact of time on learning. Educ Digest 42:6-9 Mr '77
POWELL, Enoch
Belt up, you big bore. por Time 109:44-5 F 7 '77 *
POWELL, Evan
Housepower clinic; questions and answers (cont) il Pop Sci 210:136+ F; 166 My; 211-152-4 S '77
POWELL, J. Enoch. See Powell, E.
POWELL, Jack
Great train chase. il map Motor B & S 139: 44-5+ Mr '77
POWELL, Jim
Cancer and your diet. Sci Digest 82:38-40 S '77
Marisat. il Sci Digest 82:56-8+ Jl '77
Superseeds. il Sci Digest 81:35-8+ My '77
Young at heart. il Sci Digest 82:66-9 N '77
POWELL, Jody. See Powell, J. L. Jr
POWELL, John
Sonata Teutonica. W. Simmons. Am Rec G 40: 24-5 Ag '77 *
POWELL, Joseph L. Jr
Carter and the press—as Jody Powell sees it: interview. il pors U.S. News 83:25-7 O 10 '77
Good old boy network; White House response. New Repub 177:9 S 10 '77

about

Dumb is not the word for it. Nation 225:290 O 1 '77 *
Jody faces life. D. M. Alpern and others. por Newsweek 90:119-20 S 19 '77 *
Not-so-cool Jody Powell. C. Mohr. il pors N Y Times Mag p20-1+ My 15 '77 *
President and press: honeymoon lingers on. il U.S. News 82:44 Ap 11 '77 *
President's boys. il pors Time 109:16-18+ Je 6 '77 *
Reports & comment: Washington. S. J. Ungar. por Atlantic 239:6+ Ap '77 *
POWELL, Ken
Build a field disturbance sensor for security. il Pop Electr 12:60-2 N '77
POWELL, Lew
Unsinkable Charleen: renegade muse of the South. Ms 6:62-3 D '77
POWELL, Lake
Boaters' wilderness. il map Sunset 158:102-7 Ap '77
Earth log: the trammeling of Rainbow Bridge. G. Reiger. il Audubon 79:114-15+ N '77
POWER, Taryn
Taryn Power; interview, ed by M. Cantwell. il pors Mademoiselle 83:190-3+ Ap '77
POWER (social sciences)
Job power: how to get ahead fast. M. Korda. Harp Baz 111:152+ N '77
Love, power and justice. P. B. Henry. il Chr Cent 94:1088-92 N 23 '77
Macho obstacles to peace. A. M. Davidson. il Bull Atom Sci 33:22-4 Je '77
Men & women: towards a new eroticism. K. Durbin. Mademoiselle 83:156-7+ N '77
Missing the people's message; address, October 24, 1977. P. Lesly. Vital Speeches 44:141-5 D 15 '77
New Washington power game. M. Greenfield. Newsweek 89:80 Ja 31 '77
Notes and comment; relationship of journalism to power. New Yorker 53:27-8 F 21 '77

POWER (social sciences)—*Continued*
On power; symposium. bibl f For Affairs 56:1-110 O '77
Power, dependence, and effective management. J. P. Kotter. bibl f Harvard Bus R 55:125-36 Jl '77; Discussion. 55:74 S '77
Power games in the corporation; excerpt from Men and women of the corporation. R. M. Kanter. il por Psychol Today 11:48-9+ Jl '77
Who's on top? 34 ways to find out who's got the power. il Mademoiselle 83:164-5 S '77
See also
Elite (social sciences)

POWER boat racing. See Motor boat racing

POWER boats. See Motor boats

POWER failures. See Electric power failures

POWER lawn mowers. See Lawn mowers

POWER lines. See Electric lines

POWER plants
See also
Atomic power plants
Electric plants
Hydroelectric plants
Steam power plants

Environmental aspects

Son of a gun, it's son of Kaiparowits! P. L. Fradkin. Audubon 79:146-8 My '77

POWER plants, Solar. See Solar energy

POWER pools. See Electric plants—Interconnection

POWER production, Electric. See Electric power production

POWER resources
Academy study finds low energy growth won't be painful. P. M. Boffey. Science 195:380 Ja 28 '77
Electrical equipment industry; energy needs; address, November 9, 1976. R. E. Kirby. Vital Speeches 43:186-9 Ja 1 '77
Energy (cont) Sci N 111:249; 112:185, 280, 345, 361 Ap 16, S 17, O 29, N 19-26 '77
Energy. J. Cook. il Forbes 120:P163-71 S 15 '77
Energy crisis:
Fact or fiction? T. J. Reese. America 137:373-4 N 26 '77
Production and politics. T. J. Reese. America 137:398-400 D 3 '77
Taxes and rebates; insulation tax credit. T. J. Reese. America 137:418-20 D 10 '77
Energy crisis: optimistic look. Sci Digest 81:85 Mr '77
Energy from the biomass; using organic "junk" for energy. J. K. Hanson. Current 190:39-42 F '77
Energy line. C. A. Miller. il Mech Illus 73:10 O; 8 N; 16 D '77
Energy: roots of the problem, seeds of the solution. J. F. Houlihan. il Intellect 106:237-40 D '77
Energy; symposium. Sci Digest 82:6-48+ O '77
Learning about energy the hard way. P. H. Abelson. Science 195:733 F 25 '77
Nightmare life without fuel; Time essay. I. Asimov. Time 109:33 Ap 25 '77; Same abr. with title Life without fuel. Read Digest 111:126-8 Ag '77
Overview: energy. K. H. Hohenemser. See issues of Environment
Pedal power; excerpts. il Org Gard & Farm 24:82-92 Je '77
Permanent energy shortage. Progressive 41:5-6 Ap '77
Solving the energy crisis: we're not even taking the first step; interview, ed by J. Cook. E. D. Kane. por Forbes 120:91+ N 1 '77
Unfreezing the future. C. J. Hitch. Science 195:825 Mr 4 '77
What to do about energy crisis—advice from five experts; symposium. il U.S. News 82:41-5 Ap 18 '77
Winter fuel outlook: another tight year. U.S. News 83:71-2 O 3 '77
Yes, there is an energy crisis. C. Byron. il Time 110:61-2 O 10 '77
See also
Atomic power
Biomass energy
Coal supply
Electricity supply
Energy policy
Fuel
Fuel supply
Geothermal resources
Marine resources
Petroleum supply
Solar energy
Tide power
United States—Energy, Department of
United States—Energy Research and Development Administration

Bibliography

Books on energy: a current checklist; comp by R. Dahlin and D. Maryles. Pub W 212:33-4+ O 31 '77

Caricatures and cartoons

Putting one over on OPEC. R. Lipez and C. Demarest. il Atlantic 240:75-9 N '77

Conferences

Opening the debate; Time Inc's energy conference. il Time 109:27-8+ Ap 25 '77

Conservation

Adventures in alternate energy:
Bill Rankins and David Wilson: solar window. E. Moran. il Pop Sci 210:24+ Mr '77
Clarence Kenney: wind power for home heating. E. F. Lindsley. il Pop Sci 211:62+ N '77
David and Cynthia Edney: solar-assisted heat pump. E. Moran. il Pop Sci 211:84+ O '77
Dennis L. Vories: all-seasons solar heater. E. Moran. il Pop Sci 211:52-3+ Ag '77
Energy house uses native materials. E. Moran. il Pop Sci 211:44+ Jl '77
Gene Feeney, fireplace grate for total heating. E. Moran. il Pop Sci 210:34-5 Je '77
John Des Chenes: corrugated-plate window collector. E. Moran. il Pop Sci 212:24+ Ja '78
Michael Hackleman: electric truck is wind-powered, too. E. Moran. il Pop Sci 210:78-9 Ap '77
O.W. Wood, solar + woodstove heats his water. E. Moran. il Pop Sci 210:48-9 My '77
Ronald W. Kock: tubular collector in a drain-down system. E. Moran. il Pop Sci 211:52+ D '77
Stephan Sieradzki: windmill on a boom. E. Moran. il Pop Sci 210:22-3 F '77
Thomas P. Powell: freestanding fireplace. E. Moran. il Pop Sci 211:10+ S '77
At the grass roots, a rush to save fuel. il U.S. News 82:17 My 2 '77
Cleanups and checkups that help you save household energy. L. Wick. House & Gard 149:86+ O '77
Close to home. A. J. Mayer. il Newsweek 89:25-6 My 2 '77
Energy behavior. P. C. Stern and E. M. Kirkpatrick. bibl il Environment 19:10-15 D '77
Energy management: a crisis in industry. H. L. Breckenridge. bibl f Intellect 105:352-4 Ap '77
Energy-saver's guide. S. Porter. Ladies Home J 94:52+ N '77
Going our own way—at 65 m.p.h; Time essay. F. Trippett. Time 110:95 N 21 '77
Here's my idea on how to save energy . . . Changing T 31:21-3 S '77
Home energy guide. H. Wicks and others. il Pop Mech 148:115+ S '77
How the energy shortage will change life in America; with interview with J. Schlesinger. il U.S. News 82:22-5 F 14 '77
How to save energy. A. J. Mayer and others. il Newsweek 89:70-1+ Ap 18 '77
How to save $300 a year on utility bills. il Good H 185:266+ O '77
How U.S. consumers view energy crisis; University of Texas study. S. C. Lopreato and W. Cunningham. Intellect 106:95+ S '77
How willing to pare? Time 109:63 Mr 7 '77
Job for energy misers. M. E. Marty. Chr Cent 94:463 My 11 '77
Just set 35 dials—computer will budget your home energy use. il Sci Digest 82:47-8 O '77
Keepers of the flame. L. H. Lapham. Harpers 255:7-9 Jl '77; Discussion. 255:4+ O '77
Lighting the way to energy savings. il Am City & County 92:63-4 Ag '77
Lobbyists for the people; church support of energy policy. J. M. Wall. Chr Cent 94:467-8 My 18 '77
Making your home energy-efficient. Sci Digest 82:64 O '77
Moral equivalents and other bugle calls; Time essay. S. Kanfer. Time 109:25 My 2 '77
New American dream. R. Rodale. il Org Gard & Farm 24:52-5 Ap '77
Passing of the age of affluence. T. Bender. Current 197:23-33 N '77
Plugging the leaks. Sci Am 236:57-8 Ap '77
Public opinion and energy use. P. H. Abelson. Science 197:1325 S 30 '77
Saving energy, saving dollars. J. L. Carter and others. il Redbook 150:118+ N '77
Shape of the future. S. Fraker and J. Bishop. Newsweek 89:28 F 14 '77
Solving the energy crisis. il Am Heritage 28:30-3 O '77
Stamp out energy guzzlers. A. Scharffenberger. il Am Home 80:96+ S '77
Tale of two suburbs: near Chicago and outside Cologne. P. Delaney; B. Seaman. il Time 109:23-4 My 2 '77
Tinkering man. J. C. McCullagh. il por Org Gard & Farm 24:139-41 Mr '77
Tips from the pros. D. Pauly. il Newsweek 89:78-9 Ap 18 '77
22 energy-miser tricks that cut your living costs. R. F. Dempewolff. il Pop Mech 148:88-91+ Jl '77
War, he said. A. J. Mayer. il Newsweek 90:40 D 26 '77

POWER resources—*Continued*
Washington scene: Park Project on Energy Interpretation. B. Kravetz. Parks & Rec 12:48+ S '77
We must save energy. But we must not develop a shortage psychology. C. Morgello. Duns R 109:132 Je '77
What to do about energy crisis—advice from five experts; symposium. il U.S. News 82:41-5 Ap 18 '77
What we're already doing to save energy. il Changing T 31:7-10 Ag '77
Whatever happened to the energy crisis? J. J. Du Pont. Conservationist 31:1 Ja '77
Yankee ingenuity plugs away at the energy problem. il U.S. News 83:78-9 O 10 '77
See also
Energy policy
Fuel—Conservation

Economic aspects

Economic impact; energy policy. M. Ruby and others. il Newsweek 89:20-2+ My 2 '77
Energy and the economy; address, May 18, 1977. D. D. Danforth. Vital Speeches 43:539-41 Je 15 '77
Energy costs: large portion of elderly's bill. Aging 274:13+ Ag '77
Energy problems and our cities: solving two problems jointly. F. G. Rohatyn. Current 196: 3-6 O '77
Energy, world resources and population trends; report of Pugwash Conference. Bull Atom Sci 33:37-8 D '77
For some firms, there's a bonanza ahead. il U.S. News 82:30 My 9 '77
Getting more energy. D. Pauly and others. il Newsweek 89:27-8 My 2 '77
$1 trillion—the cost of meeting U.S. energy needs. il U.S. News 82:19-20 My 2 '77
Our energy problem; address, May 23, 1977. J. E. Swearingen. Vital Speeches 43:569-72 Jl 1 '77
Our over-developed society; address, April 20, 1977. J. T. Connor. Vital Speeches 43:555-7 Jl 1 '77
Pollution takes backseat to energy—maybe! S. S. Baxter. Am City & County 92:67 Mr '77
Problem of exhaustible resources. S. F. Williams. il Nat R 29:1352-3+ N 25 '77
Will energy conservation throttle economic growth? with interview with J. R. Schlesinger. il Bus W p66-72+ Ap 25 '77

International aspects

International development of energy; excerpts from addresses. A. M. Mufti; G. Hoffman; F. N. Ikard. il Intellect 105:206-7 Ja '77

Laws and legislation

By any other name; Senate consideration. A. J. Mayer and W. J. Cook. Newsweek 90:87-8 S 19 '77
Carter fights back; trip to the Midwest and California. il pors U.S. News 83:19-21 O 31 '77
Carter's oil war; Big oil's big bucks. A. J. Mayer and others. il Newsweek 90:38-40 O 24 '77
Energy and politics. B. T. Feld. Bull Atom Sci 33:12 D '77
Energy fallback. R. Boeth and others. il por Newsweek 90:37 D 5 '77
Energy talkathon; Senate debate. T. Mathews and others. il por Newsweek 90:28-30 O 10 '77
Great energy debate—who gets the $25-billion pie? J. Berry. Forbes 120:33-4 D 15 '77
Gutting the energy bill. A. J. Mayer and W. J. Cook. il Newsweek 90:79-80 O 3 '77
Hard going for Carter's plan. il Time 110:48 S 26 '77
Impact of energy rift in White House. J. McWethy. il U.S. News 83:28 D 19 '77
Is America ready for democracy? il New Repub 177:5-6+ N 26 '77
Launching the energy blitz. il por Time 110: 12-14 O 31 '77
Low energy. E. Marshall. New Repub 177:8-9 N 5 '77
Mr Stay-at-Home. R. Boeth and others. il Newsweek 90:30 N 14 '77
New Cabinet whip; R. S. Strauss. M. A. Ruby and others. il por Newsweek 90:37 O 31 '77
Oil shortage: public doesn't believe it and won't pay to cure it. C. Morgello. Duns R 110:156 O '77
On the road. R. Boeth and others. il pors Newsweek 90:34-6 O 31 '77
Pending energy bills dangle many carrots. Sci N 112:261 O 22 '77
Political priorities; proposed effects of House energy bill. Nat R 29:1036+ S 16 '77
President's address on energy problems; November 8, 1977. J. Carter. Vital Speeches 44:98-100 D 1 '77
Recreational vehicles: gas curbs on off-road vehicles? H. Shuldiner. il Outdoor Life 160: 24+ D '77
Reporter at large; C. E. Walker, lobbyist for corporate clients on the energy bill. E. B. Drew. New Yorker 53:32-6+ Ja 9 '78
Score one for Jimmy; House passage of national energy program. D. M. Alpern and others. il por Newsweek 90:15-16 Ag 15 '77
Senate and energy. Commonweal 104:643-4 O 14 '77; Discussion. 104:766-7 N 25 '77
Solving the energy problem; address, October 19, 1977. F. N. Ikard. Vital Speeches 44:117-20 D 1 '77
Son of Kingfish. New Repub 177:2+ D 24 '77
Swinging from the floor. Nation 225:418-19 O 29 '77
To Jimmy from James. M. Friedman. Newsweek 90:99 O 17 '77
War, he said. A. J. Mayer. il Newsweek 90:40 D 26 '77
War without troops; the energy problem. New Repub 177:2+ D 17 '77
What's in, what's out of the energy bill. U.S. News 83:74-5 N 7 '77
Where the Carter plan stands. il Time 110:85-6 N 28 '77
Why Carter's energy program is bogged down in Congress. il U.S. News 83:76-8 O 10 '77
Why the energy program is in such a mess. K. R. Sheets. U.S. News 83:28 O 24 '77

Leases

See Mining leases; Oil and gas leases

Research

Energy conservation's impact on R&D. il Bus W p52-5+ Je 27 '77
How technology will reshape life in years ahead. J. McWethy and L. McKirgan. il U.S. News 83:62-6+ N 28 '77
Secrets of the Nazis. Newsweek 90:70 Jl 4 '77
Ten crazy ways to make energy . . . cheap! R. Sgarlata. il Sat Eve Post 249:56-7+ S '77
See also
United States—Energy, Department of
United States—Energy Research and Development Administration

Statistics

Scorecard on energy. il Duns R 109:54-7 Je '77

Study and teaching

Energy Week. il Sr Schol 110:TE22+ S 22 '77
Special report: a winning role for the school library; energy technology program at East Senior High School in West Seneca, N.Y. C. D. Gwitt. bibl il Wilson Lib Bull 52:295-8 D '77

Brazil

Unconventional energy sources: Brazil looks for applications. A. L. Hammond. Science 195: 862-3 Mr 4 '77

China

China's energy performance. V. Smil. il Cur Hist 73:63-7 S '77

Great Britain

Petrol, sweat & tears. B. Silcock. Sci Digest 82:42-3 O '77

Israel

Israel moves toward a new solar society. il Intellect 106:5-6 Jl '77

Latin America

Energy; adaptation of address, May 23, 1977. A. Orfila. il Américas 29:6-12 O '77
Energy development in the Americas. A. Orfila. Science 196:611 My 6 '77

Underdeveloped areas

See Underdeveloped areas—Power resources

Western States

Denver: the new Houston? T. J. Murray. il map Duns R 110:54-8 O '77
U.S. Indians demand a better energy deal; Council of Energy Resource Tribes. por Bus W p53 D 19 '77

POWER supplies for electronic apparatus. See Electronic apparatus and appliances—Power supply
POWER supply. See Power resources
POWER tools. See Electric tools
POWERS, Francis Gary
High-spying U-2. E. Keerdoja and W. J. Cook. il por Newsweek 89:11+ F 28 '77 *
Obituary
Nat R 29:933 Ag 19 '77
POWERS, John R.
Accent on Chicawgo. il Holiday 58:46-7+ S '77
POWERS, Roger W.
. . . helps beautify land. Camp Mag 49:8-9 Je '77
POWERS, Stefanie
Problems and pleasures of living together; interview, ed by I. Silden. pors Harp Baz 110: 114-15+ My '77
Stefanie & Bill; interview, ed by S. Decatur. il pors Ladies Home J 94:78+ N '77
POWERS, Thomas
Press. See occasional issues of Commonweal
POWERS, Separation of. See Separation of powers

POWILLS, Dorothy
Playing cards. See issues of Hobbies
POWLEDGE, Fred
Island fever. il Esquire 87:88-93+ Mr '77
Therapist as double agent. il Psychol Today 11:44-7 Jl '77
POWWOWS. See Indians of North America—Rites and ceremonies
POYNTER, Margaret
Peace Corps . . . where age can be an asset. il Ret Liv 17:42-3+ N '77
PRACTICE teaching. See Student teaching
PRADER-Willi syndrome
Eating disease. H. Bottel. Good H 184:176+ My '77
PRAIRIE chickens
Rites of spring. il Audubon 79:56-67 Mr '77
See also
Heath hens
PRAIRIE Provinces, Canada
North again; with reproductions of paintings by F. Golden. J. Madson. il Audubon 79:18-29 Mr '77
PRAIRIES
See also
Prairie Provinces, Canada
Steppes
PRAISE
Bitter-sweet compliment problem. R. E. Turner and C. Edgley. il Todays Educ 66:28-30+ Ja '77
See also
Appreciation
PRAKAPAS, Eugene
Viewpoint. J. Deschin. il pors Pop Phot 81:12+ O '77 *
PRAKAPAS Gallery, New York. See Photography—Galleries and museums
PRANG, Louis
Prang Christmas cards. L. Freeman. il Hobbies 82:118-19 D '77 *
You can thank Louis Prang for all those cards. L. Cheney. il por Smithsonian 8:120-5 bibl (p 135) D '77 *
PRATHER, Grace Marie
All-porpoise war. Nat R 29:439+ Ap 15 '77
PRATSON, Frederick J.
Texas rawhide in academia. Nat R 29:204-5 F 18 '77
PRATSON, Frederick John
Yankee heritage is secured without government aid. il Smithsonian 8:92-9 Je '77
PRATT, Nancy
Beware! Antiques fakery is thriving again. il House B 119:12+ Jl '77
PRATT and Whitney Aircraft Group. See United Technologies Corporation—Pratt and Whitney Aircraft Group
PRATTE, Guy P. Wyser-. See Wyser-Pratte, G. P.
PRAUL, R. E.
California hearing spotlights pension funding problems. Ret Liv 16:11-12 D '76
PRAYER
Another century of intercession. Chr Today 21:35-6 F 18 '77
Paradoxes of prayer. F. E. Gaebelein. Chr Today 21:33-4 S 9 '77
Prayer; symposium; with editorial comment. New Cath World 220:2-24+ Ja '77
Prayer under duress; imprisonment of English doctor in Chile. S. Cassidy. il Nat R 29:826-8 Jl 22 '77
Redeeming the time. E. Schaeffer. Chr Today 21:24 Ja 21 '77
Staying power. G. McCauley. America 137:inside back cover O 8 '77
See also
Meditation

Bibliography

Discipline of prayer. M. Boyd. Chr Cent 94:759-62 Ag 31 '77
PRAYER books
See also
Jews—Prayer books and devotions
PRAYER breakfasts
New church member in town; National prayer breakfast in Washington, D. C. January 27, 1977. E. Plowman. Chr Today 21:54-5 F 18 '77
PRAYERS
See also
Lord's Prayer
PREACHING
Perils of persuasive preaching. A. D. Litfin. Chr Today 21:14-17 F 4 '77
Preaching for results. R. C. Palms. Chr Today 22:30-1 D 30 '77
PREAKNESS (race) See Horse racing
PREAMPLIFIERS. See Amplifiers
PRE-CAMBRIAN period. See Geology, Stratigraphic—Pre-Cambrian; Paleontology—Pre-Cambrian
PRECIOUS stones
Gems and minerals. H. D. Brown. See issues of Hobbies
Gems of information. Mademoiselle 83:40+ N '77
See also
Gems
also names of precious stones, e.g. Diamonds

Collectors and collecting

Dig your own diamond or opal, topaz, or other precious stones; rockhounding. D. Robertson. il por Ret Liv 17:34-5 S '77
PRECIPITATION (meteorology)
See also
Hail
Rain and rainfall
Snow
PRECISION location strike system. See Target locations
PRECISION Valve Corporation. See Pressure packaging
PRECOOKED food, Frozen. See Food, Frozen
PREDATION (biology)
Feeding behavior and predator avoidance in heterospecific groups. D. H. Morse. bibl BioScience 27:332-9 My '77
Visual detection of cryptic prey by blue jays (cyanocitta cristata) A. T. Pietrewicz and A. C. Kamil. bibl il Science 195:580-2 F 11 '77
PREDATORY animals. See Animals, Predatory
PREDATORY birds. See Birds of prey
PREDMORE, Dorthy
Why we leave the hall light on all night. il Farm J 101:L15-16 Ap '77
PREFABRICATED furniture. See Furniture, Prefabricated
PREFABRICATION
See also
Buildings, Prefabricated
Houses, Prefabricated
PREFERRED stocks. See Stocks
PREFRONTAL cortex. See Brain
PREGEL, Boris
Obituary
Phys Today por 30:98-9 My '77. S. A. Korff
PREGELJ, Vladimir
When free trade means higher consumer prices. il Bus W p61-2 S 5 '77 *
PREGNANCY
Before the baby comes. il Parents Mag 52:20 Ja; 20 My; 28 Ag; 15 S '77; 53:21 Ja '78
Bend over backwards for your baby; good posture. E. Noble. il Fam Health 9:43-6 Jl '77
Birth defects: how to prevent them. N. H. Clark. Harp Baz 110:86-7+ Jl '77
Having a baby—1978. A. E. Nourse and others. Good H 186:68 Ja '78
Hormones taken during pregnancy affect the child's personality; study by June Reinisch. J. Gaylin. Psychol Today 11:31-2 O '77
How to have a healthy child. H. J. Burroughs. McCalls 105:82 N '77
Meeting sexual and emotional needs during pregnancy. M. Newton. Fam Health 9:15-16+ O '77
Mom, the cadet; Air Force Academy's ruling. il Time 110:14 N 28 '77
On popping pills and potions during pregnancy. M. Newton. Fam Health 9:20+ My '77
Pregnancy no-no's; substances that may be risky to unborn. G. Carro. il Ladies Home J 94:24 S '77
Sex during pregnancy; excerpt from Making love during pregnancy. E. Bing and L. Coleman. il Redbook 150:89-90+ N '77
See also
Abortion
Childbirth
Fetus
Teen-age pregnancy

Signs and diagnosis

Early test for pregnancy. M. Smith. McCalls 104:86 Je '77
Screening for twin pregnancy. L. Jovanovic and others. bibl il Science 198:738 N 18 '77
PREGNANCY, Complications of
Fat-containing uterine smooth muscle cells in toxemia: possible relevance to atherosclerosis? M. D. Haust and others. bibl il Science 195:1353-4 Mr 25 '77
Testing for toxemia. il Newsweek 89:79 Ja 31 '77
PREGNANCY in animals
How to pick a pregnancy tester; swine. J. Russell. il Farm J 101:Hog 12+ My '77
PREGNANCY tests. See Pregnancy—Signs and diagnosis
PREGNANT onion. See Sea-onions
PREGNANT schoolgirls. See Teen-age pregnancy
PREHISTORIC man. See Man, Prehistoric
PREHISTORIC monuments. See Megalithic monuments
PREJUDICE
Are you a secret bigot? S. Horwitz. il Seventeen 36:110-11+ F '77
Intelligent woman's guide to sex; anti-feminist bias. K. Durbin. Mademoiselle 83:173+ F '77
See also
Anti-Semitism
PRELUDES (music)
See also
Phonograph records—Preludes (music)
PREMATURE birth. See Childbirth

PREMATURE infants. See Infants, Premature
PREMAZON, Judith, and West, P. T.
Requiem or rebirth? From voucher to magnet. Clearing H 51:38-40 S '77
PREMIERES, Motion picture. See Motion picture premieres
PREMIUMS, Insurance. See Insurance—Rates and tables
PRENATAL care. See Pregnancy
PRENSKY, Sol D.
Inside basic electronics. See issues of Popular electronics including Electronics world
New, practical OP AMP circuits. il Pop Electr 11:47-8 F '77
PRENTICE, Ann E.
Lingo of library finance. il Am Lib 8:550-2 N '77
PRENTISS, Stan
19-inch color portables. il Pop Sci 210:128-30+ Ap '77
Step by step troubleshooting. il Radio-Electr 48:84+ S '77
PREPAID legal services. See Insurance, Litigation
PREPAID medical service. See Insurance, Health—United States
PREPARATION of manuscripts. See Authorship—Copy preparation
PREPARATORY schools. See Private schools
PREPAREDNESS, Military. See Great Britain—Military policy; United States—Military policy
PREPOSITIONS
See also
English language—Prepositions
PRE-RAPHAELITES
Dante Gabriel Rossetti and the double work of art. M. Amaya. il Art in Am 65:90-3 Mr '77
PRESBYTERIAN Church
See also
Catholic Church—Relations—Presbyterian Church
PRESBYTERIAN Church in Northern Ireland
Evening on Ravenhill Road; service conducted by I. R. K. Paisley. L. Mullin. America 137: 189-91 O 1 '77
PRESBYTERIAN Church in the United States
Cautious optimism for Southern Prebyterians. H. Wall. Chr Cent 94:646-7 Jl 20 '77
Out of the blue, a vote. Chr Today 21:52 F 18 '77
Pastoral training under tutors. Chr Today 22:61-3 O 7 '77
Presbyterian austerity. V. Jameson. Chr Cent 94:28 Ja 19 '77
Southern Presbyterian dilemma; proposed book of confessions. L. W. Posey. Chr Cent 94:142-5 F 16 '77; Discussion. 94:541-3, 765-6 Je 1, Ag 31 '77
United Presbyterians: a new sensitivity. J. M. Mulder. Chr Cent 94:695-6 Ag 3 '77
United Presbyterians: slowing the slide. G. C. Fuller. Chr Today 21:38 Jl 29 '77
Urge to merge; Southern and United Presbyterians meeting in Nashville. A. H. Matthews. Chr Today 21:35-6 Jl 29 '77

Anecdotes, facetiae, satire, etc.

Last Presbyterian. M. E. Marty. Chr Cent 94: 767 Ag 31 '77
Precision and the Presbyterians. M. E. Marty. Chr Cent 94:863 S 28 '77
PRESCHOOL children. See Children
PRESCHOOL education. See Education, Preschool
PRESCHOOL Screening Program, North Carolina. See Educational tests and measurements
PRESCRIPTION drugs. See Drugs
PRESENILE dementia. See Brain—Diseases
PRESENT, Gerald
Nuclear energy. il Sci Digest 82:20-5 O '77
Resetting biological clocks. Sci Digest 81:82 Je '77
PRESENT tense; revue. See Musical comedy, revue, etc.—Reviews—Single works
PRESENTS
See also
Gifts
PRESERVATION of architecture. See Architecture—Conservation and restoration
PRESERVATION of food. See Food preservation and preservatives
PRESERVATION of landmarks, scenery, etc. See Landscape protection
PRESERVATION of library materials. See College libraries—Technical processes; Libraries—Technical processes
PRESERVATION of photographs. See Photographs—Conservation and restoration
PRESERVATION of plants. See Plants—Collection and preservation
PRESERVES. See Jelly, jam, etc.
PRESERVING
See also
Canning and preserving
PRESIDENTIAL advisers
Carter's outside insiders; P. Caddell and G. M. Rafshoon. pors Bus W p94+ Je 27 '77
Immodest proposal; Cabinet choices, Presidential advisers and campaign issues. P. Steinfels. Commonweal 104:70 F 4 '77
Power people. R. Steele. il Newsweek 89:23-5 Ja 24 '77
See also
Carter, J.—Staff
Kirbo, C. H.
PRESIDENTIAL Advisory Board on Ambassadorial Appointments. See United States—Presidential Advisory Board on Ambassadorial Appointments
PRESIDENTIAL airplanes. See Airplanes, Government
PRESIDENTIAL campaigns
See also
Campaign buttons, etc.
Campaign funds
Campaign issues
National conventions, Democratic

1968

Kennedy's betrayal; interview, ed by L. R. Obst. E. McCarthy. il por N Y Times Mag p90+ N 13 '77
Last day of the RFK campaign; interview; ed by L. R. Obst. J. Witcover. il por N Y Times Mag p85+ N 13 '77
McCarthy decade. il New Repub 177:5-6+ D 10 '77

1972

Pluralist structures or interest groups? G. McGovern. Society 14:13-15+ Ja '77
TV's effect on American voters. T. E. Patterson and R. D. McClure. Intellect 105:217-18 Ja '77

1976

Bringing rationality to elections. A. S. Miller. Current 189:5-7 Ja '77
Mass media and the 1976 Presidential campaign. H. Mowlana. Intellect 105:244-5 F '77
Reporter in Washington, D. C. (cont) E. B. Drew. New Yorker 52:48+ Ja 17 '77
Sins of omission. E. McCarthy. Harpers 254:90-2 Je '77
Women behind the Presidential debates; League of Women Voters. M. McLaughlin. McCalls 104:65 F '77
PRESIDENTIAL candidates
See also
Presidential campaigns

Religion

Anecdotes, facetiae, satire, etc.

See what you could have had? M. E. Marty. Chr Cent 94:47 Ja 19 '77

1976

I voted for a man who... P. Fish. Mademoiselle 83:174+ F '77
PRESIDENTIAL Commission on Americans Missing and Unaccounted For in Southeast Asia. See United States—Presidential Commission on Americans Missing and Unaccounted For in Southeast Asia
PRESIDENTIAL elections. See Presidents—United States—Election
PRESIDENTIAL entertaining. See Government entertaining
PRESIDENTIAL libraries
It's Kennedy, by a nose. W. D. Nelson. Wilson Lib Bull 51:562 Mr '77
Presidential libraries: where history comes alive. K. Keating. il Bet Hom & Gard 54: 99-102 Ag '76
Presidential libraries: where tourists, scholars brush elbows. il U.S. News 83:23-5 Jl 11 '77
PRESIDENTIAL power. See Presidents—United States—Powers and duties
PRESIDENTIAL press corps. See Press and politics
PRESIDENTIAL retreats. See Presidents—United States—Homes
PRESIDENTIAL travel. See Presidents—United States—Travel
PRESIDENTS

Brazil

See also
Geisel, E.

Egypt

See also
Sadat, A.

Mexico

No-lose elections; administrations of three recent presidents. C. Untel. Nat R 29:1297-8 N 11 '77
See also
Echeverria Alvarez, L.
Lopez Portillo, J.

United States

Becoming great. D. K. Goodwin. New Repub 176:29+ Ja 22 '77
Carter: a popular President, but—the way honeymoons compare. il por U.S. News 82: 24 My 30 '77
Hidden Presidents: looking through their memoirs for involuntary truth. F. M. Brodie. il Harpers 254:61-6+ Ap '77; Discussion. 254:4+ Je '77
Little experience is... useful; making foreign policy. H. Sidey. il Time 109:13 Ap 18 '77

PRESIDENTS—United States—*Continued*
Nos. 37, 38 and 39, all onstage. H. Sidey. il Time 109:14 My 30 '77
Presidential suite; pieces by six presidents. il Sat Eve Post 249:70-1 Jl '77
Squandered national resource. R. L. Hardesty. por Newsweek 89:11 Mr 14 '77
This thankless office: William T. Sherman views the Presidency. W. T. Sherman. il por Am Hist Illus 11:46-8 Ja '77
Why it will be hard to stay just plain folks. il por U.S. News 82:23-5 Ja 24 '77
See also
Adams, J.
Coolidge, C.
Eisenhower, D. D.
Jackson, A.
Jefferson, T.
Johnson, L. B.
Nixon, R. M.
Roosevelt, F. D.
Roosevelt, T.
Vice-presidents—United States
Wilson, W.

Addresses, messages, etc.
See also
Carter, J.—Addresses, messages, etc.

Advisers
See Presidential advisers

Anecdotes, facetiae, satire, etc.
Fee enterprise system. G. Ace. Sat R 4:74 Ag 6 '77
Our misplaced President. A. Ward. il Am Heritage 28:84-5 Je '77
President's plumbing. R. Baker. N Y Times Mag p6 Ja 16 '77

Archives
See also
Presidential libraries

Brothers
See Presidents—United States—Families

Caricatures and cartoons
200 years of the great American freedom to complain; the American Presidency in Political Cartoons: 1776-1976. il Art in Am 65:99-105 Mr '77

Children
Amy Carter—latest in long line of White House youngsters. il U.S. News 82:25-7 Ja 31 '77

Correspondence
See also
Carter, J.—Correspondence

Election
Black vote; Joint Center for Political Studies survey. Society 14:8 Ja '77
Let us now praise (faintly) famous economists. J. K. Galbraith. Esquire 87:70-1+ My '77
Victory for teacher power: 1976 election. J. Ryor. Todays Educ 66:5 Ja '77
See also
Electoral College
Presidential campaigns

Families
First brothers. E. Keerdoja and E. Shannon. il Newsweek 90:26+ N 21 '77
See also
Presidents—United States—Children

Health
Cleveland, G.—Health

Homes
Camp David: where Carter goes to unwind. il U.S. News 83:82-3 S 12 '77
See also
Mount Vernon

Inaugural addresses
See also
Carter, J.—Inaugural Address

Inaugurations
TRB from Washington: I solemnly swear. New Repub 176:2 Ja 22 '77
See also
Carter, J.—Inauguration

Libraries
See Presidential libraries

Portraits
See also
Carter, J.—Portraits
Lincoln, A.—Portraits
Washington, G.—Portraits

Powers and duties
Is a President ever above the law? il U.S. News 82:66 My 30 '77
Laying on of hands. H. Fairlie. New Repub 177:17-19 Jl 2 '77
Presidency: its powers and limitations. U.S. News 82:46-8 My 9 '77
President and law; analysis of Nixon's statement in third interview with Frost. Nat R 29:652+ Je 10 '77
This month's feature: Congress and Executive Branch reorganization powers. Cong Digest 56:99-128 Ap '77
When the President does it: what the tapes really reveal; opinion of Presidential powers expressed in Nixon-Frost interviews. I. L. Horowitz. Nation 224:751-4 Je 18 '77
See also
War and emergency powers—United States

Press conferences
See also
Carter, J.—Press conferences

Press relations
Old defense: they all did it; views of V. Lasky. il por Time 110:20+ S 12 '77
Poor Jody Powell. R. H. Nessen. por Newsweek 89:9 Ja 31 '77
See also
Carter, J.—Press relations

Protection
If U.S. comes under nuclear assault—. O. Kelly. il U.S. News 83:19-20 S 5 '77

Public relations
See also
Carter, J.—Public relations

Relations with Congress
Congress: a great beached whale. A. S. Miller. Progressive 41:22-5 F '77
See also
Carter, J.—Relations with Congress

Religion
See also
Carter, J.—Religion

Retirement
When a president leaves office. il U.S. News 82:29-30 Ja 24 '77

Salaries, allowances, etc.
See also
Carter, J.—Salaries, allowances, etc.

Staff
See also
Carter, J.—Staff
Roosevelt, F. D.—Staff

Succession
Reforming the succession laws. S. Fuzest, Jr. Current 189:7-10 Ja '77

Taxes
See also
Carter, J.—Taxes

Term
Change in Presidential terms favored; single six-year term. il Nations Bus 65:16+ Ap '77

Transition periods
Changing of the guard. Sci N 111:21-2 Ja 8 '77
Ford's last days. T. Mathews and others. il por Newsweek 89:34-5 Ja 24 '77
In transition. New Repub 176:92 Ja 22 '77
July in January? M. Harrington. New Repub 176:60+ Ja 22 '77
Transition diary. L. Butler. il por Newsweek 89:26+ Ja 24 '77

Transportation
See also
Airplanes, Government

Travel
Into the wild blue yonder. H. Sidey. Time 111:11 Ja 9 '78
See also
Carter, J.—Travel

Travel—Anecdotes, facetiae, satire, etc.
Presidential catnip. R. Baker. N Y Times Mag p 10 N 13 '77

Wives
America's First Ladies honor Charles Lindbergh. il Good H 184:72 Je '77
First ladies out front; views on Equal Rights Amendment. il Time 110:25 D 5 '77
Six former First Ladies: what their lives are like now. il U.S. News 82:52-4 Je 20 '77

PRESIDENTS, College. See College presidents

PRESIDENT'S Commission on Mental Health. See United States—President's Commission on Mental Health

PRESIDENT'S Commission on Olympic Sports. See United States—President's Commission on Olympic Sports

PRESIDENT'S Commission on Personnel Interchange. See United States—President's Commission on Personnel Interchange

PRESLEY, Elvis
All shook up; Heartbreak kid. M. Orth; J. Kroll. il pors Newsweek 90:46-9 Ag 29 '77 *
Elvis. J. Bradshaw. il por Esquire 88:96-8 O '77; Same abr. with title Elvis: the man. Read Digest 112:72-5 Ja '78 *
Elvis. C. Forbes. Chr Today 21:32 S 23 '77 *
Elvis; interview, ed by N. Anderson. V. Presley. il pors Good H 186:80-1+ Ja '78 *
Elvis: the mystique. A. A. Conner. Read Digest 112:75-7 Ja '78 *
Heirs of Elvis. M. J. Sobran, Jr. Nat R 29:1185-6 O 14 '77 *
Last stop on the mystery train. J. Cocks. il pors Time 110:56-9 Ag 29 '77 *
Notes and comment. New Yorker 53:19 Ag 29 '77 *
Rebel who became a legend. S. B. Walton. il pors Sat Eve Post 249:56-7+ D '77 *
Unique appeal of Elvis Presley's music now carries over to books about him. R. Dahlin. Pub W 212:34 S 5 '77 *

PRESLEY, Vernon
Elvis; interview, ed by N. Anderson. il pors Good H 186:80-1+ Ja '78

PRESS, Frank
Intensified exploitation of shuttle urged; excerpts from testimony before the Senate Commerce science and transportation subcommittee; ed by C. Covault. Aviation W 106:21-2 Ap 18 '77
Physicists in Washington. Phys Today 30:80 Ag '77
Press decries technological optimists; excerpts from address, October 8, 1977. Science 198:1022 D 9 '77

—and Busbee, George
Intergovernmental science and technology. Science 196:943 My 27 '77

about

Day in the life of the science adviser. D. Shapley. Science 198:278-9 O 21 '77 *
Dr Press reviews China exchange. Sci Digest 82:80 Jl '77 *
Frank Press: Carter's man on science. J. H. Douglas. por Sci N 111:250-1 Ap 16 '77 *
Frank Press, long-shot candidate, may become science adviser P. M. Boffey. por Science 195:763+ F 25 '77 *
Frank Press outlines tasks as President's science advisor. F. C. Bennett. por Phys Today 30:69+ Je '77 *
Geophysicist next science adviser? Sci N 111:119 F 19 '77 *
President's scientist. il por Time 109:73 Ap 11 '77 *
Press meets the press. J. Walsh. Science 197:538 Ag 5 '77 *
Press named science adviser, busy on job. Sci N 111:215 Ap 2 '77 *
Science adviser Press: first hints of how he is doing. P. M. Boffey. por Science 196:412+ Ap 22 '77 *
Senate quizzes science adviser nominee. E. M. Leeper. por BioScience 27:367-8 My '77 *
Will science adviser suffer in shuffle? P. M. Boffey. Science 196:742 My 13 '77 *

PRESS
Fourth estate. Harpers 254:113-17 Mr; 90-2 Je; 255:99-100 S; 102+ O; 114+ D '77; 256:88-90+ Ja '78
Newswatch. T. Griffith. See occasional issues of Time
Press media; address, May 12, 1977. H. Simons. Vital Speeches 43:689-92 S 1 '77
See also
Freedom of the press
Government and the press
Vatican and the press
Vietnam War, 1957-1975—Press reports

Confidential communications

See Confidential communications—Press

PRESS, Catholic. See Catholic press
PRESS, Labor. See Labor press
PRESS agencies. See News agencies

PRESS agents
Bobby Zarem, superflack. S. C. Cowley. il pors Newsweek 89:58-9 Ja 31 '77
Super flack muscles in; B. Zarem. il por Time 109:42-3 Ja 31 '77

PRESS and business. See Business and the press
PRESS and crime. See Crime and the press
PRESS and government. See Government and the press

PRESS and politics
Commentaries: media power; symposium. bibl il Society 15:10-25 N '77
Cultural terrorism: the Italian press as public-relations organ for the Communist Party. M. A. Ledeen. Harpers 255:99-100 S '77
Forgive us our daily press. W. L. Miller. Chr Cent 94:39-41 Ja 19 '77
Getting your man; B. Lance case. T. Griffith. Time 110:79 O 17 '77
How politicians eat reporters for breakfast; G. Sperlin's Washington breakfasts. N. Ephron Esquire 87:26-7+ Je '77
Jimmy One Term and Johnny One Note. Time 110:100 N 7 '77
Media: truth or consequences? M. Novak. Chr Cent 94:317-18 Ap 6 '77
Myth of an adversary press. T. Bethell; discussion. Harpers 254:4+ Mr '77
News about Eurocommunism. M. Ledeen. Commentary 64:53-7 O '77
Notes and comment; relationship of journalism to power. New Yorker 53:27-8 F 21 '77
Reporting rights conflicts. J. C. Pollock and J. L. Robinson, Jr. bibl il Society 15:44-7 N '77
Savage fire: the importance of Bill Safire. R. Reeves. por Esquire 89:38+ Ja '78
Sins of omission. E. McCarthy. Harpers 254:90-2 Je '77
Time Inc.'s internal war over Vietnam; excerpt from The powers that be. D. Halberstam. il pors Esquire 89:94-100+ Ja '78
Turning the bird dogs loose; press coverage of Lance affair. Time 110:117 S 19 '77
Visions of hobnails; European criticism of West Germany's anti-terrorist measures. M. Ledeen. New Repub 177:17-19 N 19 '77
Was he hounded out? the story of B. Lance. D. Gelman and L. Howard. Newsweek 90:35 O 3 '77
White House press club. J. A. Lukas. il N Y Times Mag p22+ My 15 '77

Anecdotes, facetiae, satire, etc.

I cover Carter. G. W. S. Trow. New Yorker 53:28-9 Jl 25 '77

PRESS and the judiciary. See Government and the press
PRESS connection (newspaper) See Madison, Wis.—Newspapers

PRESS critics and criticism
Second City scold; critic, J. Madigan of Chicago's radio station, WBBM. il por Time 110:47-8 D 19 '77

PRESS law
Covering the courts; address, September 23, 1977. J. V. R. Bull. Vital Speeches 44:52-4 N 1 '77
Herbert's war; ruling in slander suit against CBS. Time 110:103 N 21 '77
See also
Confidential communications—Press

PRESS photography. See Photography, Journalistic

PRESS releases
News release as marketing tool. S. A. Kliment. Archit Rec 162:55 Jl '77
See also
Government and the press

PRESSED flowers and leaves. See Flowers, Dried

PRESSURE
Pressure: the dangerous friend; what makes guns work. J. Carmichel. il Outdoor Life 160:92-5+ Jl '77
See also
High pressure (science)
Vapor pressure

PRESSURE, Atmospheric. See Atmospheric pressure
PRESSURE canners. See Canning and preserving—Equipment and supplies

PRESSURE groups
Behind the fronts: phony consumer groups; industry-backed groups. D. H. Rothman. Nation 225:239-42 S 17 '77
Citizen-band lobbying. R Boeth and others. il Newsweek 90:45 D 5 '77
Clamshell Alliance: getting it together. H. Wasserman. Progressive 41:14-18 S '77
Clamshell reaction; protest against atomic power plant at Seabrook, N.H. by Clamshell Alliance. H. Wasserman. Nation 224:744-9 Je 18 '77
Confrontation at Seabrook; Clamshell Alliance. H. Wasserman. Progressive 41:11-12 Jl '77
From interest groups a catalogue of demands on Congress and Carter. il U.S. News 82:24-5 Mr 7 '77
From special-interest groups: a mixed verdict on Carter. il U.S. News 82:20-1 My 30 '77
Nader's invaders are inside the gates. J. Cameron. il Fortune 96:252-6+ O '77
New activists; conservative organizations. R. Boeth and others. il Newsweek 90:41 N 7 '77
New hope for the same old complaint; organizations against 55-mph speed limit. B. Yates. Car & Dr 23:16 Ja '78
Pluralist structures or interest groups? G. McGovern. Society 14:13-15+ Ja '77
Role of interest groups in educational politics; New York City. F. Barbaro. bibl il Clearing H 51:136-42 N '77
Seabrook saga; Clamshell Alliance. E. Keerdoja and P. Malamud. Newsweek 91:5 Ja 2 '78
Setback on energy; coalition of environmental and consumer groups. A. J. Mayer and J. B. Copeland. il Newsweek 89:93 My 16 '77
Troubled steel towns campaign for help; Steel Communities Coalition. Bus W p35 O 24 '77
See also
Clergy and Laity Concerned (organization)
Common Cause (organization)
Gray Panthers (pressure group)
Lobbyists and lobbying
New Directions (organization)

PRESSURE packaging
Aerosol ban has lost its sting. il Bus W p30-1 My 30 '77
Aquasol: aerosol spray without fluorocarbons. R. L. Stepler. il Pop Sci 211:54 S '77
Fluorocarbons out, new systems in. Sci N 111: 324-5 My 21 '77
Precision Valve: spray it again, Bob. por Duns R 110:14-15 Ag '77
Pressurized sprayer doesn't need a propellant. H. Shuldiner. il Pop Sci 211:16 Ag '77
Psst! aerosol! alternatives. P. Gwynne and others. il Newsweek 89:99 My 9 '77
Pump sprayer-mist without propellants. B. H. Berry. Pop Sci 210:33 Je '77
Son of aerosol; Aquasol. il Time 109:72 My 23 '77
Why ban fluorocarbons in aerosol sprays? interview. F. S. Rowland. Read Digest 110:35-6+ F '77

PRESSURE point massage. See Massage

PRESSURE suits
See also
Astronauts—Clothing

PRESTON, Dickson J.
Wye Island. il Am For 83:20-2+ N '77

PRESTON, James J.
Toward an anthropology of death. bibl f il Intellect 105:343-4 Ap '77

PRESTON, Paul. See Zimmerer, T. W. jt auth

PRESTRIDGE, E. B. See Holzwarth, G. jt auth

PRETZELS
German pretzels—chewy and big. il Sunset 159:230 O '77
Homemade soft pretzels. P. A. Ward. il Farm J 100:36 D '76

PREUS, Jacob A. O.
Missouri Synod aftermath. E. E. Plowman. il por Chr Today 21:36-7 Ag 26 '77 *

PREVENTION of accidents. See Accidents—Prevention

PREVENTION of crime. See Crime prevention

PREVENTION of cruelty to animals. See Animals—Treatment

PREVENTION of suicide. See Suicide—Prevention

PREVENTIVE medicine. See Medicine, Preventive

PRÉVERT, Jacques
Jacques Prévert, 1900-1977. E. Merriam. New Repub 177:25-8 Jl 9 '77 *

PREVIN, André
André Previn comes home. H. Pleasants. pors Sat R 4:34-6 F 19 '77 *

PRIAL, Frank J.
Wine. il N Y Times Mag p 102-4 Ap 24; 44-5 Jl 10; 30-1 Jl 24; 45-7 Ag 7; 61-2 Ag 21; 40-1 S 4; 70-1 S 18; 82+ O 2; 128-9 O 16; 92-3 O 30; 134-5 N 13; 154+ N 20; 142-5 D 11; 28-9 D 25 '77

PRIBILOF Islands
Green eggs by the thousands; collecting murre eggs on Walrus Island. V. B. Scheffer. il Audubon 79:112-13 S '77

PRICE, Charles
To hell with golf! Esquire 87:150-2 My '77

PRICE, David A. and Greenberg, M. J.
Structure of a molluscan cardioexcitatory neuropeptide. bibl il Science 197:670-1 Ag 12 '77

PRICE, Joe
Joe Price: serigraphs in light and tone. D. Wakeham. il por Am Artist 41:46-51+ O '77 *

PRICE, Jonathan
Video art: a medium discovering itself. il Art N 76:41-7 Ja '77

PRICE, Leontyne
America: to Leontyne Price, opportunities are growing. pors U.S. News 82:56 Mr 28 '77

PRICE, Margaret
Perilous path to soprano superstardom; recording of Mozart recitals. D. Harris. pors Hi Fi 27:89-90 Ap '77 *

PRICE, Priscilla Hadley
Time out of yesterday; story. Good H 184:120-1 My '77

PRICE, Raymond K. Jr
Now it's their turn. il Newsweek 89:34 My 16 '77

about

Nixon's good guy. J. Osborne. New Repub 177: 8-9+ O 8 '77 *

PRICE, Reynolds
Home: an American obsession. Sat R 5:9-14+ N 26 '77

PRICE, Richard, 1949-
Studs Lonigan in the Bronx; interview, ed by A. Auster and L. Quart. Nation 224:725-7 Je 11 '77

PRICE, Steve
You can catch bass after a front. il Field & S 82:44-5+ N '77

PRICE, T. Rowe
T. Rowe Price: he's got a little list. il Forbes 120:64 N 1 '77 *

PRICE cutting
See also
Dumping (commercial policy)

PRICE-earnings ratios. See Stocks—Price-earnings ratios

PRICE fixing, Resale. See Price maintenance by industry

PRICE indexes
Anatomy of price change:
Inflation slowed markedly during the third quarter. T. Nakayama and C. Howell. il M Labor R 100:49-52 D '77
Sharp first-quarter rise. V. Howell and others. bibl il M Labor R 100:3-8 Je '77
Price changes in 1976—an analysis. T. Nakayama and others. il M Labor R 100:14-24 F '77
Price data. See issues of Monthly labor review
Users find industrial price data satisfactory but urge some changes. D. J. Moeller. il M Labor R 100:58-9 D '77
See also
Index linking (economics)

PRICE maintenance by industry
Antitrust: a hot line to nab price fixers; Justice Department consumer project in Pittsburgh. Bus W p34 My 30 '77
First big test of a new antitrust law; price fixing lawsuits against oil companies. por Bus W p48+ S 12 '77
Paper manufacturers face charges of price-fixing. S. Wagner. Pub W 212:106 S 26 '77

PRICE marks
See also
Unit pricing

PRICE policies
Flexible pricing. il Bus W p78-81+ D 12 '77
Price rise in spite of spare capacity. il Bus W p 120-3+ Mr 21 '77
Problems in review. Harvard Bus R 55:20-2+ My '77
See also
Price maintenance by industry

PRICE regulation by government
See also
Wage-price policy

Canada

Friction over Canadian oil prices. Bus W p31+ Jl 11 '77

Germany, West

Preemptive jawboning astonishes business; auto makers. il Bus W p36-7 Mr 28 '77

PRICE supports, Agricultural. See Agricultural administration—United States

PRICE-wage policy. See Wage-price policy

PRICE Waterhouse and Company. See Accountants

PRICES
See also
Cost of living
Inflation (finance)
Wage-price policy
also subhead Prices under various subjects, e.g. Tin—Prices

Canada

See also
Price regulation by government—Canada

United States

Behind the bulge in industrial prices. il Bus W p26-8 Ap 25 '77
Despite inflation, your work buys more. il U.S. News 83:44 D 5 '77
Drive to keep prices from soaring higher. il U.S. News 82:23-5 Ap 25 '77
Galloping new inflation of fears. Time 109:38+ Mr 14 '77
How government itself keeps prices rising. il U.S. News 82:16-17 Ap 18 '77
Inflation is now too serious a matter to leave to the economists. D. Warsh and L. Minard; discussion. il Forbes 119:44-6 Ja 15 '77
Less scary side of the price story. il Fortune 95:48 My '77
Measuring the ripples of the price urge. il Bus W p35-6 Mr 21 '77
Price changes in 1976—an analysis. T. Nakayama and others. il M Labor R 100:14-24 F '77
What the thirteen sensitives are telling us. il Fortune 96:24 O '77
What to expect if prices keep going up. il U.S. News 82:22-3 My 30 '77
Will prices go crazy in '78? How living costs are headed higher in coming year. il U.S. News 84:20-2 Ja 9 '78
See also
Cost of living—United States

PRIDE and vanity
Seven deadly sins today; excerpt. H. Fairlie. New Repub 177:19-23 N 12 '77

PRIDEAUX, Tom
Garden talk of William Shakespeare. il Horticulture 55:24-7 N '77
Rich and rugged Thracian life seen in a glittering show. il Smithsonian 8:42-51 Je '77

PRIEST, Alice L.
Commentary. Bus W p25 Ag 29 '77

PRIESTS
See also
Cardinals
Celibacy
Clergy
Ex-nuns, priests, etc.
Ordination
Women priests

PRIESTS—*Continued*

Associations, institutions, etc.

See also
National Federation of Priests' Councils

Political activities

Latin America's rebel priests. J. Monahan. Progressive 41:43-6 My '77

PRIGOGINE, Ilya
Chemistry: the flow of life. por Newsweek 90: 87 O 24 '77 *
1977 Nobel laureates in science. il pors Chemistry 50:18-20 D '77 *
1977 Nobel Prize in chemistry. I. Procaccia and J. Ross. il por Science 198:716-17 N 18 '77 *
Nobel Prizes: seven in '77. pors Sci N 112:261 O 22 '77 *
Prigogine awarded chemistry prize. G. B. Lubkin. por Phys Today 30:79-80 D '77 *

PRIMACK, Phil
Born-again poverty program. Nation 224:431-4 Ap 9 '77
Falling apart under Miller. Nation 224:714-17 Je 11 '77
Great strip mine flood. Nation 224:691-2 Je 4 '77
Miners' post-election blues. Nation 225:37-8 Jl 9 '77

PRIMACY of the Pope. See Popes—Primacy

PRIMARIES
Legacy of Carter and Reagan: political reality overtakes the myth of the Presidential primaries. J. R. Beniger. bibl il Intellect 105:234-7 F '77

Texas

LBJ accused; 1948 Democratic Senatorial primary. D. A. Williams and L. Donosky. il pors Newsweek 90:27 Ag 8 '77
L.B.J: the softer they fall; 1948 primary. H. Sidey. il por Time 110:10 Ag 15 '77
Vote forever; 1948 primary. W. F. Buckley, Jr. Nat R 29:1013 S 2 '77

PRIMATES
Newly evolved repeated DNA sequences in primates. D. Gillespie. bibl il Science 196:889-91 My 20 '77
See also
Apes
Lemurs
Monkeys

Evolution

See Evolution

Sexual behavior

See Sexual behavior—Animals

Vision

See Vision (animals)

PRIMATES as laboratory animals. See Laboratory animals

PRIME rate. See Interest (economics)

PRIMERAS Jornadas Internacionales Casals. See Music festivals—Mexico

PRIMERS (coating)
Metal primer paints. Consumer Rep 42:180-1 D '77

PRIMERS, Rifle. See Detonators

PRIMITIVE and early church. See Church history—Primitive and early church

PRIMROSES
This article will lead you down the primrose path G. K. Fenderson. il Horticulture 55:50-5 Je '77

PRIMULAS. See Primroses

PRINCE, Alfred M.
Our last vaccine? Science 195:1287 Mr 25 '77

PRINCE, Martha
Fight for a wildflower haven. il Liv Wildn 41:45-7 Ap '77

PRINCE and the pauper; dramatization. See Newman, D.

PRINCE EDWARD Island
Advanced island. R. C. Paehlke. See issues of Environment

PRINCE Manufacturing Company. See Sporting goods industry

PRINCESS tree. See Paulownia

PRINCETON University
Annals of higher education; conflict between Concerned Alumni of Princeton and the University. E. J. Kahn, Jr. New Yorker 53:88+ My 23 '77
For the kid who has everything; Houseparties weekend. L. A. Walker. il Esquire 88:68-73 S '77

PRINCIPALS, School. See School superintendents and principals

PRINE, Arthur C. Jr
Must people retire at 65? interview. por U.S. News 83:37-8 Ag 22 '77

PRINN, Ronald G. and Barshay, S. S.
Carbon monoxide on Jupiter and implications for atmospheric convection. bibl il Science 198: 1031-4 D 9 '77

PRINT dryers. See Photography—Processing—Apparatus and supplies

PRINT makers. See Printmakers

PRINT sales. See Art sales

PRINT washers. See Photography—Processing—Apparatus and supplies

PRINTED circuits
New no-camera printed circuit board methods. A. A. Mangieri. il Pop Electr 11:55-8 My '77

PRINTED Matter bookstore, New York City. See Booksellers and bookselling—New York (state)

PRINTED textiles. See Textile fabrics

PRINTERS (computer) See Computers—Printout equipment

PRINTING
Printing. P. D. Doebler. Pub W 212:57-8+ D 5 '77
See also
Computers—Printing use
Proofreading
Typesetting

Design

See also
Type and typefounding

History

Finding things to say; J. Blumenthal, fine printer. New Yorker 53:29-31 S 12 '77

Private presses

See Private presses

PRINTING (photography) See Photography—Printing processes

PRINTING industry
Hand-crafted fine editions survive at Angelica. C. B. Grannis. il Pub W 211:71 Ap 4 '77

Great Britain

See also
De La Rue Company, Ltd

PRINTING paper (photography). See Photographic paper

PRINTMAKERS
Stamp of Whistler; late 19th-century printmakers. G. P. Weisberg. il Art N 76:66-8+ S '77

PRINTMAKING. See Prints—Technique

PRINTS
American prints from Fuses to Fizzles. J. Loring. il Art in Am 65:31-4 Ja '77
Commitment to the past; work of S. Haden, A. Legros and A. Lepère. G. Weisberg. il Art N 76:150-2 Summ '77
Jacob Kainen: vision and technique. B. Forgey. il Art N 76:86-7 F '77
New editions (cont) il Art N 76:108 F; 110-12+ Mr; 108 Ap; 99-100+ S '77
Raúl Cattelani, Uruguayan printmaker. A. Llambias de Azevedo. il Américas 29:29-31 Ag '77
Special prints section. il Art N 76:46-54+ Mr; 50-8+ S '77
See also
Block printing
Engraving
Etchings
Lithographs
Lithography
Photograms
Silk screen printing
Wood engravings

Bibliography

Prints and printmaking. D. Preiss; F. Johnson. il Am Artist 41:22-6+ O '77

Collectors and collecting

Address book; dealers in antique prints and maps. S. Sunderlin. House B 119:22+ Jl '77
Outdoor prints: a sporting chance for pleasure and profit. P. Miller. il Outdoor Life 159:72-7+ Je '77

Exhibitions

Backward look at American printmaking; Brooklyn Museum's 20th National Print Exhibition. G. Henry. il Art N 76:64-6 Mr '77
Stamp of Whistler. G. P. Weisberg. il Art N 76:66-8+ S '77

Purchasing

See Art sales

Study and teaching

Printing and evaluation. J. W. Burgner. il Sch Arts 76:36-8+ Je '77
See also
Lakeside Studio (firm)

Technique

Collagraph printmaking. D. Stoltenberg. il Sch Arts 77:10-17 D '77
Prints from twine. L. J. Miller. il Design (US) 78:26 Spr '77
Students print a calendar. T. Bilderback. il Sch Arts 77:18-19 D '77

Themes

Hunt for the fishing lady; English print. A. H. Mayor. il Antiques 112:113 Jl '77
See also
Birds in art

PRINTS, Drying of. See Photography—Drying (films and prints)

PRINTS, Photographic. See Photographs
PRINTS, Publishing of. See Publishers and publishing—Art
PRINTS in the home. See Art in the home
PRINZE, Freddie
Chico's last act. D. M. Alpern and others. il por Newsweek 89:25-6 F 7 '77 *
Freddie Prinze: too much, too soon. il pors Time 109:37 F 7 '77 *
PRIOR, Moody E.
Urban scene. Am Scholar 46:506-13 Aut '77
PRISON escapes. See Escapes
PRISON furloughs
Case is not closed; allegations of illegalities in M. G. Thevis's medical furlough. T. Mathews and others. il por Newsweek 90:51 N 7 '77
PRISON grievances. See Grievance procedures
PRISON guards. See Prisons—Officials and employees
PRISON industries. See Convict labor
PRISON labor. See Convict labor
PRISON libraries
Breaking in: library service to prisoners; symposium, ed by R. J. Rubin. bibl il por Wilson Lib Bull 51:496-533 F '77
Federal prison libraries: the quiet collapse. D. Suvak. bibl il por Lib J 102:1341-4 Je 15 '77
High Court reaffirms need for prison law libraries. W. D. Nelson. Wilson Lib Bull 51: 857-8 Je '77
PRISON psychology
Doing time. J. W. Dean, 3d. por Newsweek 90: 9 Jl 4 '77
Serving time in America. G. G. Liddy. il por Esquire 88:138-40+ D '77
Stress—new prison tests: sadism or therapy? C. Pogash. il Sci Digest 81:64-7 F '77
Stretch in jail—how would you handle it? views of Barbara Price. S. Bush. il Psychol Today 10:27+ Ap '77
PRISON recreation
Art in prison: a way out of the sewer. G. E. Wood. Nation 225:370-2 O 15 '77
Bottle and the tube; leisure for the convicted. M. A. Panik and T. A. Mobley. Parks & Rec 12:28-30+ Mr '77
Hosanna in a spot of hell; Soledad Prison concert by Andrae Crouch and the Disciples. J. Wilde. il por Time 111:14 Ja 9 '78
Stars behind bars. H. M. Heyn. il Sky & Tel 54:296 O '77
PRISON reform
In disgrace with fortune: prison reform today. D. Rothenberg. America 136:141-4 F 19 '77
PRISONERS
Annals of crime. S. Sheehan. New Yorker 53: 48-52+ O 24; 46-50+ O 31; 123-40+ N 7 '77
Debate over prisons. J. Q. Wilson. il Current 189:26-32 Ja '77
Handling prison grievances: the labor model in practice. T. S. Denenberg. M Labor R 100:53-6 Mr '77
United States and Mexico sign treaty on execution of penal sentences. Dept State Bull 75:750 D 27 '76
We simply sit . . . and wait. . . E. Knoll. Progressive 41:13 O '77
What happened to me is my fault. W. C. Spann. il por Good H 185:44+ O '77
See also
Convict labor
Escapes
Parole
Political prisoners
Prisons
Social work with delinquents and criminals
Women prisoners

Education

College for convicts; program at Attica. E. Cuddy. Progressive 41:53-5 F '77

Employment

See Convict labor

Furloughs

See Prison furloughs

Legal status, laws, etc.

Jailhouse law book; manual by J. L. Potts. A. Wolff. Sat R 4:54 Mr 19 '77

Medical care

Health hazards behind bars. O. R. T. Smith. America 136:144-6 F 19 '77

Psychology

See Prison psychology

Reading

Survey of inmates' reading habits; Orange County, Fla. C. L. Kirby. Wilson Lib Bull 51:503 F '77

Recreation

See Prison recreation

Rehabilitation

One of the luckier ones. R. J. Stout. Commonweal 104:463-5 Jl 22 '77
With the help of a friend; Amicus, Inc's work with prisoners in Minneapolis-St Paul. M. W. Fedo. America 136:463-4 My 21 '77

Treatment

Behind bars; visit to the United States Penitentiary at Marion; with editorial comment. T. Miller; discussion. Progressive 41:60-1 Mr '77
Crisis in the prisons: not enough room for all the criminals. il U.S. News 83:76-9 N 28 '77
Young Americans in Mexican jails. C. J. Migdail. il U.S. News 82:31-2 Je 27 '77
See also
Torture
PRISONERS, Discharged
Bottle and the tube: leisure for the convicted. M. A. Panik and T. A. Mobley. Parks & Rec 12:28-30+ Mr '77

Rehabilitation

Recidivism and the effectiveness of prison and parole. C. H. Logan. bibl Intellect 105:424-6 Je '77
PRISONERS, Political. See Political prisoners
PRISONERS, Women. See Women prisoners
PRISONERS as artists
Art in prison: a way out of the sewer. G. E. Wood. Nation 225:370-2 O 15 '77
PRISONERS as authors
Oxford University Press unlocks prison writing to show its integration in American culture. R. Dahlin. Pub W 212:41+ Ag 22 '77
PRISONERS of war
Pueblo postscript. E. Keerdoja. il pors Newsweek 91:11 Ja 16 '78
PRISONERS of war, Returned
Healthier adjustment for Vietnam POWs. Sci N 112:182 S 17 '77
PRISONERS of war in the United States
Captured by the Americans; German, Italians and Japanese World War II prisoners. M. H. Byrd. il Am Hist Illus 11:24-35 F '77
PRISONS
See also
Concentration camps
Prison reform
Prisoners
Probation
Reformatories
Women prisoners

Fires and fire prevention

Fire in the cells. J. K. Footlick. il Newsweek 90: 56 Jl 25 '77

Medical care

See Prisoners—Medical care

Officials and employees

To guard or be guarded; discrimination against women as prison guards. M Labor R 100:70-1 O '77

Bolivia

Nuns as jailers. Commonweal 104:354 Je 10 '77

California

Hosanna in a spot of hell; Soledad Prison concert by Andrae Crouch and the Disciples. J. Wilde. il por Time 111:14 Ja 9 '78
Inside. . .looking out; work of the Inmate Library Committee at the California Training Facility, Soledad. il Wilson Lib Bull 51:506-9 F '77

Canada

Transfer of sanctions treaties with Mexico and Canada; American prisoners in foreign jails; statement, July 13, 1977. B. M. Watson. Dept State Bull 77:208-10 Ag 15 '77

Cuba

Two years in Cuban jails; T. O'Hare and B. Mack. J. Huck. il por Newsweek 89:29 Je 27 '77

Illinois

Behind bars; visit to the United States Penitentiary at Marion; with editorial comment. T. Miller; discussion. Progressive 41:60-1 Mr '77
Locked up with fear: Stateville, Illinois Bastille. J. L. Kaplan. il Nation 225:530-2 N 19 '77
See also
Chicago—Prisons and reformatories

Massachusetts

Providing for prisoners in Massachusetts; library of the Massachusetts Correctional Institution at Bridgewater. S. J. Souza. il Wilson Lib Bull 51:526-9 F '77

Mexico

Busted in Mexico; Americans. D. Harris. il pors N Y Times p26-30+ Mr 1 '77
Mexican jailbirds. Nation 225:645 D 17 '77
Mexican transfer; treaty to return American prisoners. P. Meyer. Harpers 255:26+ N '77

PRISONS—Mexico—*Continued*
Transfer of sanctions treaties with Mexico and Canada; American prisoners in foreign jails; statement, July 13, 1977. B. M. Watson. Dept State Bull 77:208-10 Ag 15 '77
Yankees come home. il Time 110:25 D 19 '77
Young Americans in Mexican jails. C. J. Migdail. il U.S. News 82:31-2 Je 27 '77

New Jersey

Don't let them take me back! visits by juvenile offenders to Rahway State Prison. R. Tunley. il Read Digest 112:96-100 Ja '78

New York (state)

Annals of crime; Green Haven prison. S. Sheehan. New Yorker 53:48-52+ O 24; 46-50+ O 31; 123-40+ N 7 '77
College for convicts; program at Attica. E. Cuddy. Progressive 41:53-5 F '77

North Carolina

No wall, no bars, but barbed wire and work; Butner. il U.S. News 83:78 N 28 '77
Testing in the dark: Butner, the jinxed prison. M. Pinsky. Nation 225:41-4 Jl 9 '77

Russia

See also
Concentration camps—Russia

South Africa

Death in detention in South Africa. P. Irish. Chr Cent 94:8 Ja 5 '77

Tennessee

Ray's breakout. il pors Time 109:12-16 Je 20 '77
Ray's escape; breakout at Brushy Mountain State Prison. P. Goldman and others. il pors map Newsweek 89:22-4+ Je 20 '77

Texas

Bibliotherapy project in Texas. C. House. il por Wilson Lib Bull 51:530-3 F '77

United States

Crime in America—a turnaround at last? E. H. Methvin. Read Digest 110:61-5 Je '77
Crisis in the prisons: not enough room for all the criminals. il U.S. News 83:76-9 N 28 '77
Debate over prisons. J. Q. Wilson. il Current 189:26-32 Ja '77
Doing true justice. K. Menninger. America 137: 6-9 Jl 2 '77
See also
United States—Prisons, Bureau of

PRISONS in literature
Literature from prison. M. Bellinger. Engl J 66:62-3 S '77

PRISONS in motion pictures
Cine-opsis. J. Varlejs. il Wilson Lib Bull 51: 676-7, 772-3 Ap, My '77

PRITCHARD, Peter C. H.
Three, two, one tortoise; with biographical sketch. il map Natur Hist 86:4, 90-100 bibl(p 123) O '77

PRITCHARD, William H.
Poetry of Donald Davie. New Repub 177:24-8 O 22 '77
William H. Pritchard on literary criticism. New Repub 177:34-6 D 3 '77

PRITCHETT, Victor Sawdon
Family man; story. New Yorker 53:48-52 N 28 '77
Spanish bed; story. Atlantic 240:64-72 N '77

PRITZLAFF, Lois
Celosia: the annual with many uses. il Org Gard & Farm 24:84-5 Mr '77

PRIVACY
Love vs. privacy. M. Lasswell and N. M. Lobsenz. McCalls 104:46+ Ag '77
Where has all the privacy gone? M. Mead. por Redbook 148:44+ Ap '77

PRIVACY, Right of
Banking on privacy; checks printed on red paper. il Time 110:59 S 26 '77
Computer privacy. M. Davidson. Sci Digest 82: 42-4 S '77
Computers: a seeing-eye watching you. P. Meissner. il Sci Digest 81:64-7 Je '77
Day in the life of the science adviser; suppression of government booklet on how to invade other people's privacy. D. Shapley. Science 198:278-9 O 21 '77
Employees' rights; excerpt from Freedom inside the organization. D. W. Ewing. il Society 15: 104-11 N '77
Everybody is poking into your personal business. Changing T 31:21-3 D '77
Health records and privacy: what would Hippocrates say? C. Holden. Science 198:382 O 28 '77
Health records face a privacy challenge; Du Pont challenges NIOSH on claim to undisputed access. il Bus W p38 O 31 '77
No privacy? controversy surrounding the televising of a police film in Y. McShane case in Great Britain. Newsweek 90:47 S 5 '77
Patients' rights in medical privacy. Sci N 111: 71 Ja 29 '77
Press, privacy and the Constitution. F. Abrams. il N Y Times Mag p 11-13+ Ag 21 '77; Same with title What of the privacy explosion? Current 196:7-17 O '77; Discussion. N Y Times Mag p26+ S 18 '77
Privacy bill is tagged H.R. 1984. Sci Digest 82:78-9 Jl '77
Protecting your privacy. il Bus W p 103-6+ Ap 4 '77
Rights of parents and children; conflicts of civil rights. T. R. Hayden. Current 190:24-31 F '77
Turning you into movies. C. Rembar. Esquire 87:75+ Ap '77
Washington privacy; interview. R. E. Smith. New Yorker 53:28-30 My 30 '77
What are your rights to privacy? B. Mantz. Bet Hom & Gard 55:36+ S '77
See also
Confidential communications
United States—Privacy Protection Study Commission
Wiretapping

PRIVACY journal
Washington privacy; interview. R. E. Smith. New Yorker 53:28-30 My 30 '77

PRIVACY Protection Study Commission. See United States—Privacy Protection Study Commission

PRIVATE clubs. See Clubs

PRIVATE colleges and universities. See Colleges and universities

PRIVATE detectives. See Detectives

PRIVATE enterprise. See Free enterprise

PRIVATE flying
Being born at the right time. R. Bach. il Flying 101:302-4 S '77
Inheritance. R. B. Parke. il Flying 101:288-300 S '77
Sky's the limit. M. R. Rinehart. il por Sat Eve Post 249:93+ Jl '77
See also
Airplanes, Private
Airplanes in business

History

Day of the Cub. W. Langewiesche. Flying 101: 164-5+ S '77
Flying at Yale. W. F. Buckley, Jr. Flying 101: 6+ S '77

PRIVATE mail service. See Postal service

PRIVATE pension plans. See Pensions

PRIVATE placement of bonds. See Bonds—Marketing

PRIVATE presses
Fifth dimension of library service; self-publishing. S. Seward. bibl il por Wilson Lib Bull 51: 741-5 My '77
One self-publishing writer who made it big; interview. ed by P. M. Perry. J. W. Spencer. il por Writers Digest 57:40-1 F '77

PRIVATE property. See Property

PRIVATE schools
Back-to-basics school created by enterprise; Indian Creek School in Crownsville, Md. P. Schwab. il por Nations Bus 65:91 D '77
Crunch. S. W. Gilbert. Educ Digest 42:46-9 F '77
Heraldic embroidery from Miss Balch's in Providence; ed by K. M. Jones. il Antiques 112:754+ O '77
Is it true what they say about private schools? H. Cosell. Seventeen 36:138-9+ O '77
See also
Council for American Private Education

Finance

How to make our schools better; Tuition Tax Credit Act. G. Will. Newsweek 99:104 O 3 '77
School tax credits? D. Holt and others. il Newsweek 90:76 D 26 '77
Tax credits for tuition payments; views of D. P. Moynihan. America 136:474 My 28 '77
Time to cut strings; Moynihan-Packwood bill. America 137:470 D 31 '77

PRIVATE weather services. See Meteorological services

PRIVATE wire systems. See Telephone—Private wire systems

PRIVILEGES and immunities
See also
Diplomatic privileges and immunities

PRIZE fighting. See Boxing

PRIZES. See Rewards, prizes, etc.

PRO Musica (organization) See New York Pro Musica Antiqua (organization)

PRO Training Conference. See Religious conferences

PROAÑO, Leonidas, Bp
Ecuadorean Church: new spirit, old believers. J. F. O'Callahan. America 136:559-62 Je 25 '77 *

PROBATE law and practice
Probate: what it's really all about. B. Holder. Suc Farm 75:28 N '77
See also
Wills

PROBATION
Probation program planning for youthful offenders. H. Weinberg. il Intellect 106:58-61 Ag '77
PROBES, Testing. See Testing instruments
PROBLEM children
Homes for the unwanted. R. J. Stout. Chr Cent 94:849-51 S 28 '77
Unspoiling the spoiled child; immature character development. C. R. Partridge. il Todays Educ 66:67-9 S '77
See also
Hyperactive children
Juvenile delinquency
Runaways
School children—Adjustment

Education
Cedric Robinson; interview, ed by M. S. Clayton. C. Robinson. Todays Educ 66:35-6 Ja '77
Charlie Darwin was an underachiever. A. Franza. Engl J 66:12-14 Ap '77
Disruptive youth and the rights of others. K. A. Erickson. Todays Educ 66:40-1 Ja '77
Educating adolescents with emotional and delinquency problems. D. Mainprize and P. Mann. bibl Clearing H 50:403-5 My '77
Kevin's case. B. L. Sloane. il Engl J 66:31-5 Ap '77
Responding to student misbehavior. R. A. Gorton. Educ Digest 42:2-5 Ap '77
See also
Special classes and special schools
PROBLEM drinking. See Alcoholism
PROBLEM solving
Discovering your problem-solving style. D. W. Ewing. il por Psychol Today 11:68-70+ D '77
Hidden agenda of sequencing. P. M. Cunningham and J. W. Cunningham. Clearing H 50:320-1 Mr '77
Jumping to solutions: 12 exercises in creative problem-solving; excerpt from Creative growth games. E. Raudsepp. il Psychol Today 11:75-6+ D '77
See also
Thought and thinking
PROCACCIA, Itamar, and Ross, John
1977 Nobel Prize in chemistry. il por Science 198:716-17 N 18 '77
PROCEDURE (law)
Fools in court; *pro se* defenses. Time 109:44+ My 9 '77
See also
Civil procedure
Criminal procedure
Due process of law
PROCESS control
See also
Process control equipment industry
PROCESS control equipment industry
Quiet success of a talented engineer; H. Henderson of Henderson Industries. H. Johnson. il pors Ebony 32:72-4+ F '77
PROCESSING, Signal. See Signal processing
PROCESSORS, Food. See Kitchen utensils and appliances
PROCTER and Gamble Company
Bean bagged; Folger Company. Forbes 119:28 Ap 15 '77
PROCTOR, William
H.R. 41: the state demands church disclosures. Chr Today 22:15-17 N 4 '77
PROCUREMENT, Government. See Purchasing, Government
PROCUREMENT, Military. See United States—Army—Procurement
PRODIGAL son; ballet. See Ballet reviews—Single works
PRODUCE trade
Arabs buying more U.S. farm products. il Suc Farm 75:K9 N '77
Compromise speeds the Tokyo Round; agricultural concession between the U.S. and the European Community. Bus W p53-4 Jl 25 '77
Europe's farmers—tougher competitors than you think. R. C. Black. il Farm J 101:K1+ Ja '77
Farm exports rising to $24 billion record. il Suc Farm 75:A4 Ag '77
Farm imports: big competition? Suc Farm 75:32 Je '77
Freedom to trade; question of American markets for agricultural products and the GATT trading rules, address, December 6, 1976. D. L. Hume. Vital Speeches 43:244-6 F 1 '77
Global props for U.S. farm prices. il Bus W p74+ My 9 '77
Japan, still your best customer. . . S. Cain. il Suc Farm 75:60 N '77
Keep an eye on India, your swinging customer. il Farm J 101:D1 N '77
Marketing. L. Kruse and S. Cain. See issues of Successful farming
Sharp boost for your exports; Japan. R. C. Black. Farm J 101:H2 O '77
Successful farming's marketing section. G. Lepper and others. il Suc Farm 75:11-13 D '77
Taiwan next $1 billion farm customer? il Suc Farm 75:A4 My '77
See also
Corn—Export-import trade
Dairying—Export-import trade
PRODUCT diversification. See Diversification in industry
PRODUCT liability. See Liability (law)
PRODUCT safety. See Commercial products—Safety devices and measures
PRODUCTION
Myth of the big, bad multinational. L. A. Iacocca. por Newsweek 90:21 S 12 '77
Winter's toll in lost production. Bus W p32-3 F 21 '77
See also
Industrial capacity
Labor productivity
PRODUCTION, Agricultural
Build a chain of colleges. il Forbes 119:78 Je 1 '77
Eating ourselves out of house and home. J. B. Craig. Am For 83:6 My '77
Editorial; making science more human. S. Trachtman. Horticulture 55:14 F '77
1977 world food review: supply tight, outlook mixed. L. Simerl. Suc Farm 75:no2 42 F '77
See also
Crop yields
United Nations World Food Council
PRODUCTION, Theatrical. See Theater—Production and direction
PRODUCTION control
See also
Quality control
PRODUCTIVITY, Labor. See Labor productivity
PRODUCTS, Commercial. See Commercial products
PRODUCTS, New
Array of new products—with accent on saving energy. il U.S. News 82:63-5 Je 13 '77
Fall cleanup. Mech Illus 73:38 O '77
Good news. R. A. Dickelman. See issues of Better homes and gardens
Health & beauty update. R. Graham. See issues of House beautiful
It's new. See issues of Yachting
It's new now. See issues of Popular mechanics
March look at the new hardware; First New Earth Exposition. il Sunset 158:33 Mr '77
Marketplace (cont of) New products and processes. See issues of American city & county
New energy-saving products. il Pop Mech 148:126-7 O '77
New for you. See issues of House beautiful
New products. See issues of Motor trend
New products. See issues of Popular electronics including Electronics world
New products. See issues of Radio-electronics
New stuff. See issues of Hot rod
9 new products for home improvement. il Pop Mech 148:90-1 S '77
Product reports 78; special issue. il Archit Rec 162:5-15+ mid-O '77
Raft of new products for Christmas—or any time. il U.S. News 83:75-6+ N 14 '77
What's new. See issues of Popular science
See also
Design, Industrial

Marketing
Middletowns of marketing; nation's top test-marketing towns. R. Levy. il Duns R 110:41-3 Jl '77
PRODUCTS, Second quality. See Quality of products
PROFESSIONAL Air Traffic Controllers Organization
Air controllers get restive again. il Bus W p38 N 28 '77
PROFESSIONAL education
Professional schools: cram courses in tension and trauma. R. Lamb. il N Y Times Mag p49+ N 20 '77
See also
Business schools and colleges
Library schools and education
Medical education
Technical education
PROFESSIONAL ethics
Code to work by; recreation and park profession. C. W. Pezoldt. il Parks & Rec 12:32-4+ Ja '77
See also
Architects, Professional ethics for
Business ethics
Engineers, Professional ethics for
Foresters, Professional ethics for
Journalistic ethics
Legal ethics
Librarians, Professional ethics for
Medical ethics
Scientists, Professional ethics for
PROFESSIONAL women. See Business and professional women
PROFESSIONS
Is this any way to make a living? M. Friedman. Esquire 88:66-7+ Jl '77
See also
Black women—Occupations
Occupations
Women—Occupations

PROFESSIONS—*Continued*

Advertising

See also
Architects—Advertising
Lawyers—Advertising

PROFESSORS. See College teachers
PROFICIENCY tests. See Educational tests and measurements
PROFIT
See also
Corporations—Finance
PROFIT sharing
Challenges to profit sharing: the danger of social security on pensions; Employee Retirement Income Security Act; address, October 20, 1976. A. M. Wood. Vital Speeches 43:230-3 F 1 '77
Employee wrath hits profit-sharing plans. il Bus W p25+ Jl 18 '77
If you get a lump-sum settlement when you leave your job—. il U.S. News 83:63-5 Ag 15 '77
$660,000 farewell; profit sharing at Lowe's Companies. H. Johnson. il pors Ebony 32:47-8+ F '77
Turn to the right worries business; Netherlands. Bus W p47 D 26 '77
PROFITEERING
See also
Black markets
PROGRAMMING languages (computers) See Computer languages
PROGRESS
See also
Technological innovations
PROGRESSIVE Farmer Company. See Publishers and publishing—Periodicals
PROHIBITION of the Emplacement of Nuclear Weapons and Other Weapons of Mass Destruction on the Sea-bed and the Ocean Floor and in the Subsoil Thereof, Treaty on the. See Seabed Treaty, 1972
PROJECT ARTS program. See The Arts—Study and teaching
PROJECT FAMOUS (French-American Mid-ocean Undersea Survey) See Oceanographic research
PROJECT Head Start
Whatever happened to: Operation Head Start: still going strong. il U.S. News 83:67 Ag 22 '77
PROJECT HOPE. See Underdeveloped areas—Medical care
PROJECT: Knowledge 2000. See United States—Centennial celebrations, etc.—Science
The **PROJECT theater group.** See Theater, Experimental
PROJECTION, Television. See Television projection
PROJECTION of slides. See Slides (photography)—Projection
PROJECTORS
Slide projectors. Consumer Rep 42:255-6 D '77
Still projectors. il Pop Phot 81:125+ Jl '77
See also
Motion picture projectors
PROJECTS (teaching)
See also
United States—Centennial celebrations, etc.—School projects
PROKOF'EV, Sergeĭ Sergeevich
Gambler. D. W. Moore. Am Rec G 41:26-7 N '77 *
War and peace. Review
Mus Q 63:297-326 Jl '77 *
PROLACTIN. See Luteotropin
PROLETARIAN Socialism, League for. See Socialism—United States
PRO-LIFE, Pro-Family Coalition Conference. See Women—Conferences
PROLINE
Fascioliasis: role of proline in bile duct hyperplasia. H. Isseroff and others. bibl il Science 198:1157-9 D 16 '77
PROMENADE concerts, London. See London—Music
PROMETHIUM
Element number 61: illinium, florentium, cyclonium, and promethium. R. K. Bunting. por Chemistry 50:16-18 Je '77
PROMOTERS and promoting
See also
Impresarios
King, D.
Riordan, B.
Theatrical agencies
Watson, E.
PROMOTION, Sales. See Sales promotion
PROMOTION check-offs. See Milk industry—Advertising
PROMOTIONS, School. See Grading and marking (students)
PROMS, School. See Student activities
PRONENESS to accidents. See Accidents—Psychological aspects
PRONGHORN hunting
Double on antelope. E. A. Bauer. il Outdoor Life 159:60-3+ F '77
Waterhole pronghorns. C. J. Farmer. il Field & S 82:52-4+ Ag '77
PRONGHORNS
How antelope became a regulatory problem; halting railroad construction in Wyoming. Nations Bus 65:65-6 Ja '77
PRONOUNS
See also
English language—Pronouns
PRONZINI, Bill
Writing the mystery short-short. Writer 90:19-23 D '77
PROOF (law) See Evidence (law)
PROOFREADING
From typographer to novelist: one man's experience in switching keyboards. E. Cantor. il Pub W 213:44+ Ja 2 '78
PROPAGANDA
See also
Government publicity
Indoctrination
Motion pictures—Propaganda films
Radio broadcasting—Propaganda
PROPAGANDA, British
Propaganda in the Revolution of 1688-89. L. G. Schwoerer. bibl f il Am Hist R 82:843-74 O '77
PROPAGANDA, Chinese
Paper tigers; Quemoy's propaganda forays. F. Willey. il Newsweek 89:51 Mr 7 '77
PROPAGANDA, Dutch
Propaganda in the Revolution of 1688-89. L. G. Schwoerer. bibl f il Am Hist R 82:843-74 O '77
PROPAGATION of plants. See Plant propagation
PROPANE
See also
Liquefied petroleum gas
PROPELLERS
Don't give up the prop; boat propellers. il Motor B & S 139:87-9 F '77
Ever larger propellers; ship propellers. R. Burton. il Sea Front 23:144-51 My '77
Stainless-steel props—better performance, longer life. R. D. Stearns. il Pop Sci 210:38+ Je '77
Two screws are better than one. D. Bradley. Motor B & S 139:18+ Ap '77
See also
Airplanes—Propellers
PROPERDIN
Lysis of human cultured lymphoblastoid cells by cell-induced activation of the properdin pathway. A. N. Theofilopoulos and L. H. Perrin. bibl il Science 195:878-80 Mr 4 '77
PROPERTY
Role of property in an economic system. C. K. Wilber. bibl il New Cath World 220:226-9 S '77
See also
Airspace (law)
Community property
Joint tenancy
Land tenure
Possession (law)
Real property
Wills
PROPERTY appraisal. See Real property—Valuation
PROPERTY insurance. See Insurance, Property
PROPERTY rights. See Property; Real property
PROPERTY tax
See also
Real property tax
PROPHECIES
Bargain in futures. L. Conger. Writer 90:9-10 Ja '77
Le **PROPHÈTE:** opera. See Meyerbeer, G.
PROPORTION (art)
Dynamic symmetry of Ruth Egri. C. Collins. il por Am Artist 41:46-51+ D '77
PROPOSITIONAL revelation. See Revelation
PROPP, Vladimir
Vladimir Propp in Hollywood. J. L. Fell. bibl il Film Q 30:19-28 Spr '77 *
PROPRIETARY hospitals. See Hospitals
PROSE literature

Technique

Let variety spice your words. W. A. Spencer. Writer 90:26-7 Ag '77
PROSECUTORS, Public. See Public prosecutors
PROSPECTING
Greatest gold rush since the Depression is on now all over the West. il Sunset 158:52+ Je '77
See also
Airplanes in prospecting
Gas, Natural—Prospecting
Petroleum—Prospecting
PROSPERITY training. See Wealth
PROSPERO, Joseph M. and Nees, R. T.
Dust concentration in the atmosphere of the equatorial North Atlantic: possible relationship to the Sahelian drought. bibl il Science 196:1196-8 Je 10 '77
PROSTAGLANDINS
A.I. without heat detection; cow breeding. C. S. Machan. il Farm J 101:Dairy 1-2 S '77
Blood clotting: the role of the prostaglandins. J. L. Marx. il Science 196:1072-5 Je 3 '77; Reply. L. S. Wolfe and C. Pace-Asciak. bibl 197:210 Jl 15 '77

PROSTAGLANDINS—*Continued*
Conformations of prostaglandin F_{2a} and recognition of prostaglandins by their receptors. D. A. Langs and others. bibl il Science 197:1003-5 S 2 '77
Coronary tone modulation: formation and actions of prostaglandins, endoperoxides, and thromboxanes. P. Needleman and others. bibl il Science 195:409-12 Ja 28 '77
Fatty acids and their prostaglandin derivatives: inhibitors of proliferation in aortic smooth muscle cells. J. J. Huttner and others. bibl Science 197:289-91 Jl 15'77
PG, mysterious molecule, studied. Sci Digest 81:84 Mr '77
Prostaglandins can make AI work better. il Suc Farm 75:no4 D2-3 Mr '77

PROSTATE gland

Cancer

Diagnosis

Early detection. Time 111:56 Ja 16 '78

PROSTHESIS
Artificial organs and beyond. J. A. Miller. il Sci N 112:154-6 S 3 '77
See also
Joints, Artificial

PROSTITUTION
Prosecutor; 60 minutes television program's investigation of corruption in Wyoming. M. J. Arlen. New Yorker 53:166-73 N 28 '77
Prostitution: old problem, new conflicts. G. M. Anderson. America 136:350-4 Ap 16 '77
Why nice men go to prostitutes. J. C. Mills. Redbook 148:96+ Mr '77
Youth for sale on the streets. Time 110:23 N 28 '77

PROSTRATION, Heat. See Heatstroke

PROTEAS
Elusive proteas. E. Pasahow. il Horticulture 55: 30-7 Jl '77

PROTECTION against burglary. See Burglary protection

PROTECTION from lightning. See Lightning protection

PROTECTION of plants. See Plants, Protection of

PROTECTION of the President. See Presidents—United States—Protection

PROTECTIVE coatings
See also
Primers (coating)

PROTECTIVE mechanisms (biology) See Defense mechanisms (biology)

PROTECTIVE paint. See Paint, Protective

PROTEIN degradation. See Biodegradation

PROTEIN diet, Liquid. See Diet

PROTEIN evolution. See Evolution

PROTEIN synthesis. See Synthesis

PROTEINS
Cheap protein is moving in on your markets. Farm J 101:Hog 39 S '77
Freeze-fractured purple membrane particles: protein content. K. A. Fisher and W. Stoeckenius. bibl il Science 197:72-4 Jl 1 '77
High protein fasting: is it for you? M. L. Schildkraut. il Good H 184:227 My '77
Immunofluorescence localization of proteins of high molecular weight along intracellular microtubules. P. Sherline and K. Schiavone. bibl il Science 198:1038-40 D 9 '77
Inflammatory effects of endotoxin-like contaminants in commonly used protein preparations. L. Z. Bito. bibl il Science 196:83-5 Ap 1 '77
Posttranslational covalent modification of proteins. R. Uy and F. Wold. bibl il Science 198: 890-6 D 2 '77
Protein power. E. R. Trescher. il por House & Gard 149:36+ Mr '77
Protein: why you need it—how best to get it. P. Shriever. il Ret Liv 17:20-3 O '77
Your family's health; protein-sparing modified fast. D. R. Zimmerman. Ladies Home J 94: 96+ O '77
See also
Blood—Proteins
Cytochromes
Feeds—Protein content
Glycoproteins
Hemoproteins
Histones
Interferon
Lactoferrin
Milk—Protein content
Muscle—Proteins
Neurophysin
Tubulin

PROTESTANT churches
See also
Assemblies of God
Catholic Church—Relations—Protestant churches
Ecumenical movement
Protestantism

Clergy

See Clergy

Education

See also
Theological seminaries

Northern Ireland

See also
Presbyterian Church in Northern Ireland

Rumania

See also
Evangelical churches in Rumania

United States

Pluralism and consensus: why mainline church mission budgets are in trouble. R. G. Hutcheson, Jr. Chr Cent 94:618-24 Jl 6 '77
Protestants: away from activism and back to the basics. il U.S. News 82:58+ Ap 11 '77
See also
Lutheran Church in the United States
National Council of Churches
Presbyterian Church in the United States
Reformed Church in America

PROTESTANT churches and social problems. See Church and social problems

PROTESTANT churches and women. See Women and religion

PROTESTANT Episcopal Church
Born again in Darien; E. L. Fullam of St Paul's Episcopal Church. S. Heath. Sat R 4:14-15 S 17 '77
Case of woman trouble. il Time 110:80 O 17 '77
Crack in the Anglican dam; establishment of Anglican Church in North America at St Louis conference. S. M. Smith. Nat R 29:1166 O 14 '77
Episcopal bishops: dealing with revolt. il Chr Today 22:46-9 N 4 '77
Episcopal bishops eke out a fragile peace; question of women's ordination. K. Briggs. Chr Cent 94:996 N 2 '77
Episcopal Church: an endangered species. B. Gray. Chr Cent 94:1052-3 N 16 '77
Episcopal spirit of St Louis. Chr Today 22:60-1 O 7 '77
Episcopalians: words of caution. Chr Today 21:42-3 My 20 '77
Homosexual ordination: bishops feel the flak. Chr Today 21:51 Mr 4 '77
House divided. Newsweek 90:95 S 26 '77
Lesbian priest; ordination of E. Barrett. por Time 109:58 Ja 24 '77
New Oxford Movement. Nat R 29:1222 O 28 '77
Of bombs and bishops; Puerto Rican independence movement and the Episcopal Church. Time 109:59 Mr 14 '77.
Resisting a probe; Interchurch Center in New York. Chr Today 21:55-6 Mr 18 '77
Veteran out, a lesbian in. Chr Today 21:55-6 F 4 '77
Who defines religion; investigation of the National Commission on Hispanic Affairs. J. M. Wall. Chr Cent 94:523-4 Je 1 '77
Women of the cloth. il Newsweek 90:12+ O 24 '77

PROTESTANTISM
Protestantism. il Sr Schol 109:22-4+ Ap 7 '77
Protestants: away from activism and back to the basics. il U.S. News 82:58+ Ap 11 '77
Why the evangelical upswing? contrast with Protestant orthodoxy. D. Tinder. Chr Today 22:10-12 O 21 '77
See also
Evangelicalism

PROTESTANTS in Northern Ireland
Conflict and cleavage in Northern Ireland. R. J. Terchek. bibl f Ann Am Acad 433:47-59 S '77

PROTESTS, demonstrations, etc.
See also
Atomic power plants—Protests, demonstrations, etc. against
Atomic weapons—Protests, demonstrations, etc. against
Coxey's Army, 1894
Student demonstrations
Vietnamese War, 1957-1975—Protests, demonstrations, etc. against

Brazil

Grass-roots protests in Brazil. R. Barbosa. Chr Cent 94:1119-20 N 30 '77

Illinois

Even for Nazis; Skokie, Ill. right-to-march controversy. Progressive 41:6-7 D '77
For all or for none; right-to-march case of the American Nazi Party in Skokie, Ill. Nation 225:354-5 O 15 '77
See also
Chicago—Protests, demonstrations, etc.

India

Travels with Indira. R. Ramanuiam. Newsweek 90:67+ N 14 '77

Italy

Red blues. F. Willey and L. Jenkins. Newsweek 89:39 My 23 '77

Washington, D.C.

See Washington, D.C.—Protests, demonstrations, etc.

PROTHRO, Laurie
Delectations. Nat R 29:734-5 Je 24 '77
No better religion. Nat R 30:41-2 Ja 6 '78

PROTOCOL, Diplomatic. See Diplomatic etiquette
PROTON flares, Solar. See Solar flares
PROTON-induced X-ray emission analysis. See Spectrum analysis
PROTON spin. See Nuclear spin
PROTOPLASTS
Osmotically induced changes in electrical properties of plant protoplast membranes. R. H. Racusen and others. bibl il Science 198:405-7 O 28 '77
PROTOPORPHYRIA. See Porphyria
PROTOZOA
See also
Amebas
Dinoflagellates
Euglena
Foraminifera
Paramecia
Plasmodium (parasite)
Sarcocystis
Slime molds
Tetrahymena
Trypanosomes
Culture
Infectivity reacquisition by trypanosoma brucei brucei cultivated with tsetse salivary glands. I. Cunningham and B. M. Honigberg. bibl il Science 197:1279-82 S 23 '77
PROTOZOA, Pathogenic
Babesia rodhaini: requirement of complement for penetration of human erythrocytes. W. E. Chapman and P. A. Ward. bibl il Science 196: 67-70 Ap 1 '77
See also
Piroplasmosis
PROUT, Joe
Good supermarket is a great deal. il por Forbes 119:48-9 F 1 '77 *
PROVENCE, France
Gypsy carting in France. L. Dennis and L. Dennis. il Travel 147:58-63 Ap '77
PROVERBS
Anecdotes, facetiae, satire, etc.
Wise sayings revisited; excerpt from Power of positive nonsense. L. Rosten. Read Digest 111: 160-1 D '77
PROVERBS, African
Africa's proverbial wit and wisdom; proverbs as guides to raising children. Tanoé-Aka and others. il UNESCO Courier 30:22-5 My '77
PROVIDENCE, R. I.
Architecture
House for tomorrow: Harrison family house in Providence. B. Niles. il Am Home 80:44-5 Ag '77
Housing
Case history in Providence: the quota approach to housing; Valley View Homes housing project. J. S. Fuerst and R. Petty. Nation 224: 428-31 Ap 9 '77
PROVIDENCE College, Providence, R.I.
Holiday eve disaster; fire in dormitory. il Time 110:16-17 D 26 '77
PROVIDENCE of God. See God—Providence
PROVINCETOWN, Mass.
Off season Provincetown. S. M. Schnessel. il Travel 148:42-7 S '77
Siege of the Province Lands; question of proposed CeeJay Marina in Provincetown Harbor. W. O. Johnson. il map Audubon 79:22-35 My '77
PROVING grounds
Military studies closing of Eastern Test Range. Aviation W 107:16-17 S 12 '77
Missile testing capabilities expanded; Pacific Missile Test Center. il Aviation W 106:183+ Ja 31 '77
System to monitor, control Nellis range activity readied. Aviation W 107:50 Jl 25 '77
PROVOCATEURS, Agents. See Agents provocateurs
PROVOST, Robert
Why women need insurance, too. Parents Mag 52:20+ Ap '77
PROXMIRE, William
Draft: both sides of debate; interview. pors U.S. News 82:59-60 F 14 '77
Hurry up and wait. il Sat Eve Post 249:39-40 Ap '77
about
Patronizing Proxmire. Nation 224:66-7 Ja 22 '77 *
Tale of SRI's golden fleece. D. Shapley. Science 197:1165 S 16 '77 *
Tougher banking laws? G. R. Rosen. por Duns R 110:81 O '77 *
PRUDDEN, Bonnie
Exer-sex. il Ladies Home J 94:42+ Ag '77
PRUDENTIAL Insurance Company of America
Picking the bones of Colony Square; division of assets by Prudential Insurance Co. and Chase Manhattan Mortgage & Realty Trust. Bus W p39+ Ja 31 '77
PRUDHOMME, Don
Day in the life of a working-class champion. J. Scalzo. il por Hot Rod 30:30-2+ Jl '77 *
PRUDHOMME, W. J.
Build a state-of-the-art battery charge monitor. il Pop Electr 11:88-9 Je '77
Multiplayer LED racing game. il Pop Electr 11:77-9+ Mr '77
PRUITT, Kenneth R.
How they cracked duck hunting's isle of shame. J. Phillips. il Outdoor Life 161:64-5+ Ja '78 *
PRUNIER, Frederick
Growth power in hospital-supply stocks; interview, ed by A. Hershman. por Duns R 110: 105-6+ N '77
PRUNING
November in the garden. D. Fell. il Horticulture 55:46-7 N '77
This creative hedge pruner is by trade a sculptor. il Sunset 159:282 O '77
PRUNING apparatus and equipment
Pruning tools; Pruning saws. Consumer Rep 42:201-3 D '77
PRYBYLA, Jan S.
Chinese economy after the Gang of Four. bibl Cur Hist 73:68-72+ S '77
PRYCE-JONES, David
Bête noire of France's Left. il pors N Y Times Mag p54-5+ D 11 '77
Not their finest hour. il New Repub 176:12-16 My 14 '77
Other jubilee. New Repub 176:14-17 Je 25 '77
(tr) See Revel, J. F. Revel-ations
about
British anti-Semitism, then and now. D. R. Katz. New Repub 176:21 F 5 '77 *
PRYOR, Barbara (Lunsford)
How her job saved their marriage; interview, ed by M. L. Kotz. il pors Good H 184:48+ My '77
PRYOR, David Hampton
How her job saved their marriage; interview, ed by M. L. Kotz. B. L. Pryor. il pors Good H 184:48+ My '77 *
PRYOR, Karen
Orchestra conductors would make good porpoise trainers. il por Psychol Today 10:61+ F '77
PRYOR, Paul L.
Around the world on a budget. il por Ret Liv 17:26-31 My '77
PRYOR, Richard
New black superstar. il por Time 110:66-7 Ag 22 '77 *
Perils of Pryor. M. Orth. pors Newsweek 90: 60-1+ O 3 '77 *
Richard Pryor talks. L. Robinson. il pors Ebony 33:116-18+ Ja '78 *
PSEUDOHERMAPHRODITISM. See Hermaphroditism
PSEUDONEPHRITIS. See Kidneys—Diseases
PSEUDORABIES in swine. See Swine—Diseases and pests
PSEUDOSCIENCE. See Occult sciences
PSILOTACEAE
Chemical evidence for separating the psilotaceae from the filicales. G. Cooper-Driver. bibl il Science 198:1260-2 D 23 '77
PSITTACOSIS
New clue to Legionnaires' disease. Sci N 111: 39 Ja 15 '77
PSORALENS
Method for detecting 8-methoxypsoralen in the ocular lens. S. Lerman and R. F. Borkman. bibl il Science 197:1287-8 S 23 '77
Psoralen-DNA photoreaction: controlled production of mono- and diadducts with nanosecond ultraviolet laser pulses. B. H. Johnston and others. bibl il Science 197:906-8 Ag 26 '77
PSORIASIS
Glucocorticoid in inflammatory proliferative skin disease reduces arachidonic and hydroxyeicosatetraenoic acids. S. Hammarstrom and others. bibl il Science 197:994-6 S 2 '77
Polymorphonuclear leukocytes: possible mechanism of accumulation in psoriasis. G. S. Labarus and others. bibl il Science 198:1162-3 D 16 '77
PSYCHIATRIC ethics. See Medical ethics
PSYCHIATRIC patients. See Mentally ill
PSYCHIATRIC research
See also
National Association for Mental Health, Inc
PSYCHIATRIC social work
Crisis. R. M. Grinnell and N. S. Kyte. il MH 60:11-13 Wint '77
PSYCHIATRISTS
See also
American Psychiatric Association
Medical ethics
World Psychiatric Association
PSYCHIATRY
Ethics of psychiatry: who is sick? J. Greenberg. il Sci N 112:346-7 N 19 '77
How accurate is psychiatry? J. Greenberg. il Sci N 112:28-9 Jl 9 '77
See also
American Psychiatric Association
Child psychiatry
Forensic psychiatry
Neuroses
Rich, The—Psychiatric care
World Psychiatric Association

PSYCHIATRY—*Continued*

Anecdotes, facetiae, satire, etc.

Autobiographer manqué. H. F. Ellis. New Yorker 53:25-6 S 5 '77

Bibliography

Books. G. L. Usdin. See issues of MH

International aspects

U.S. refuses to back Soviets on dissidents and psychiatry. B. J. Culliton. Science 198:593 N 11 '77

PSYCHIC healing. See Mental healing

PSYCHICAL research. See Parapsychology

PSYCHOANALYSIS
See also
Dreams

PSYCHOANALYSIS and art

Jackson Pollock's drawings under analysis. B. Carter. il Art N 76:58-60 F '77

Stones of madness; Dutch paintings. J. J. Hartman and others. bibl f il Am Imago 33:266-95 Fall '76

PSYCHOANALYSIS and literature

Conrad's Lord Jim and the enigma of sublimation. J. Berman. bibl f Am Imago 33:380-402 Wint '76

Darwin and Melville: why a tortoise? J. Franzosa. bibl f Am Imago 33.361-79 Wint '76

John Donne's The good-morrow. D. Grunes. Am Imago 33:261-5 Fall '76

PSYCHOANALYSTS and patients. See Psychotherapists and patients

PSYCHOBIOGRAPHY. See Biography

PSYCHOHISTORY. See History—Psychological aspects

PSYCHOLINGUISTICS. See Language and languages—Psychology

PSYCHOLOGICAL films. See Motion pictures—Psychological films

PSYCHOLOGICAL literature

How to read how-to books; do-it-yourself therapy. S. Arieti. Psychol Today 11:142+ O '77
See also
Psychology in literature

PSYCHOLOGICAL societies
See also
American Psychological Association

PSYCHOLOGICAL stress. See Stress (psychology)

PSYCHOLOGICAL tests

Are you ready for marriage? S. V. Didato. Harp Baz 110:51+ Je '77

How liberated are you? quiz. J. Muchovej. il Am Home 80:57-8+ Mr '77

How to find the scent that suits you; quiz. il Mademoiselle 83:104-5 Jl '77

How to recognize a good relationship . . . and a bad one; quiz. A. Frisch and D. Partie. Mademoiselle 83:165-6 S '77

Murderous mind; results of tests administered to A. Eichmann. M. Selzer. il pors N Y Times Mag p35-7+ N 27 '77

Parent test; excerpt. E. Peck and W. A. Granzig. Good H 185:104+ N '77

Personal palette; color personality quiz; ed by V. E. Towns. D. Vance. House B 119:98-9+ F '77

Psychoquiz: how neurotic are you? S. Feinstein. Harp Baz 110:229+ S '77

Speak for yourself! M. E. Mihaly. Seventeen 36:142-3+ O '77

Techniques for assessing attitudes and values; students. J. S. Poetker. bibl il Clearing H 51:172-5 D '77
See also
Firemen—Psychological examinations
Intelligence tests

PSYCHOLOGISTS
See also
Piaget, J.
Rogers, C. R.

PSYCHOLOGISTS and patients

Ethics and the sensual psychologist. Sci N 112:293 N 5 '77

PSYCHOLOGY

(ed) Newsline. J. C. Horn. See issues of Psychology today

Unmanifest; views of D. Bakan. New Yorker 53:28-9 Ap 4 '77
See also
Advertising—Psychological aspects
Age (psychology)
Aggressiveness (psychology)
Assertiveness (psychology)
Athletes—Psychology
Attention
Behavior (psychology)
Behavior genetics
Belief and doubt
Change (psychology)
Child psychology
Color—Psychology
Consciousness
Criminal psychology
Disasters—Psychological aspects
Dreams
Environmental psychology
Ethnopsychology
Executives—Psychology
Humor—Psychological aspects
Hypnosis
Identity (psychology)
Imagination
Imitation
Infant psychology
Intimacy
Laughter—Psychological aspects
Maturity
Medicine, Psychosomatic
Memory
Men—Psychology
Mental healing
Motivation (psychology)
Moving—Psychological aspects
Noise—Psychological effects
Parapsychology
Perfection (psychology)
Persuasion (psychology)
Police psychology
Political psychology
Prison psychology
Problem solving
Psychotherapy
Recognition (psychology)
Rejection (psychology)
Self
Self love
Skis and skiing—Psychological aspects
Social psychology
Stereotype (psychology)
Strikes—Psychological aspects
Television broadcasting—Psychological aspects
Tennis—Psychological aspects
Violence
Women—Psychology

Bibliography

Behavior books: best of the year. Psychol Today 11:160+ D '77

PSYCHOLOGY, Applied
See also
Behavior modification

PSYCHOLOGY, Comparative

Flurry of fauna, filled with familiar faces; comparison between humans in organizations and animals in nature; views of Harold Morowitz. J. Horn. Psychol Today 11:29+ Je '77

PSYCHOLOGY, Educational
See also
Imagination
Intelligence levels
Learning, Psychology of
Teachers—Psychology

PSYCHOLOGY, Environmental. See Environmental psychology

PSYCHOLOGY, Forensic
See also
Forensic psychiatry

PSYCHOLOGY, Industrial

Company shrink. A. J. Mayer and P. E. Simons. il Newsweek 90:96 O 24 '77

Flurry of fauna, filled with familiar faces; comparison between humans in organizations and animals in nature; views of Harold Morowitz. J. Horn. Psychol Today 11:29+ Je '77

Oedipus in the board room; interview, ed by D. Goleman. H. Levinson. bibl il por Psychol Today 11:44-6+ D '77

Power games in the corporation; excerpt from Men and women of the corporation. R. M. Kanter. il por Psychol Today 11:48-9+ Jl '77

Programming mental health care for the world of work. S. H. Akabas and S. Bellinger. il MH 61:4-8 Spr '77

Stress. K. Slobogin. il N Y Times Mag p48-50+ N 20 '77
See also
Job satisfaction

PSYCHOLOGY, Pathological
See also
Autism
Hypochondria
Manic-depressive psychoses
Mental illness
Paranoia

PSYCHOLOGY, Physiological

Nerves: mind and body therapies. N. Lande and A. Slade. Harp Baz 110:128-9+ Mr '77
See also
Color sense
Emotions
Facial expression
Laterality
Left- and right-handedness
Memory
Mind and body
Muscular sense
Pain
Reinforcement (psychology)
Sex (psychology)
Sleep
Stress (psychology)

PSYCHOLOGY, Religious

Listening to B. F. Skinner. J. W. Woelfel. Chr Cent 94:1112-16 N 30 '77
See also
Experience (religion)

PSYCHOLOGY, Religious—*Continued*

Bibliography

More psychological insights. C. B. Murphey. Chr Today 21:20-5 S 9 '77

PSYCHOLOGY, Sex. See Sex (psychology)

PSYCHOLOGY in literature

Horatio Algers of the nightmare; J. Kosinski's characters. E. Stone. il por Psychol Today 11:59-60+ D '77

Psychological novelist as portable man; interview, ed by G. Sheehy. J. N. Kosinski. il por Psychol Today 11:52-3+ D '77

PSYCHOPHARMACOLOGY

Antischizophrenic drugs; chronic treatment elevates dopamine receptor binding in brain. D. R. Burt and others. bibl il Science 196:326-8 Ap 15 '77

Behavioral history as a determinant of the effects of *d*-amphetamine on punished behavior. J. E. Barrett. bibl il Science 198:67-9 O 7 '77

Brain peptides as psychiatric drugs. Sci N 112:182 S 17 '77

Curing the mind; beta-endorphin. S. Drake. il Newsweek 90:68-9 Ag 29 '77

β-Endorphin: endogenous opiate or neuroleptic? D. S. Segal and others. bibl il Science 198:411-14 O 28 '77

Mathematics underlying the rate-dependency hypothesis. F. A. Gonzalez and L. D. Byrd. bibl il Science 195:546-50 F 11 '77; Reply with rejoinder. P. B. Dews. 198:1182-3 D 16 '77

Preview of the choose your mood society. G. Bylinsky. il Fortune 95:220-4+ Mr '77

Psychoactive drugs: do you need them? L. Wingerson. Harp Baz 110:231+ S '77

See also

Antidepressants
Tranquilizing drugs

PSYCHOPHYSICS. See Psychology, Physiological

PSYCHOSES

See also

Depression, Mental
Manic-depressive psychoses
Paranoia

PSYCHOSOMATIC medicine. See Medicine, Psychosomatic

PSYCHOSURGERY

Psychosurgery at the crossroads. J. Greenberg. il Sci N 111:314-15+ My 14 '77

Surgery to the rescue. L. Silver and others. Progressive 41:23 D '77

PSYCHOTHERAPISTS

See also

Confidential communications—Psychotherapists

PSYCHOTHERAPISTS and patients

Celebrity shrinks; M. Newman and B. Berkowitz. S. Edmiston. il pors Esquire 88:53-6+ Ag '77

Psychotherapy and moral culture: a psychiatrist's field report. Yale R 66:321-46 Mr '77

Sex counts in therapy, too; women receiving outpatient treatment. D. Cohen. Psychol Today 10:90+ My '77

PSYCHOTHERAPY

Bazaar's guide to psychotherapy; symposium. Harp Baz 110:228-33+ S '77

On the nature of empathy. F. W. Kaslow. bibl Intellect 105:273-7 F '77

Psychotherapy and moral culture: a psychiatrist's field report. Yale R 66:321-46 Mr '77

Spending money on yourself can up your bank account; depression alleviated by psychotherapy. M. Page. Vogue 167:236+ S '77

Star treatment; excerpts. D. Stelzer. Ladies Home J 94:62+ O '77

Take two Milkbone and call me in the morning. J. Greenberg. il Sci N 112:237 O 8 '77

Thirty-year follow up: counseling fails. Sci N 112:357 N 26 '77

When to see a therapist. A. Etzioni. Psychol Today 10:16 Ap '77

Where were you in 1643? Past-lives therapy. il Time 110:53 O 3 '77

See also

Alcoholism—Therapy
Art therapy
Child psychotherapy
Dance therapy
Family psychotherapy
Hypnotism—Therapeutic use
Photography in psychotherapy
Psychopharmacology
Shock therapy

PTERIDOSPERMS. See Ferns, Fossil

PTOLEMY, Claudius

Claudius Ptolemy: fraud. Sci Am 237:79-81 O '77 *

Ptruth about Ptolemy. Time 110:116 N 28 '77 *

Scandal in heavens: renowned astronomer accused of fraud. N. Wade. il Science 198:707-8 N 18 '77 *

PUBLIC administration

Effective public management. J. L. Bower. bibl f Harvard Bus R 55:131-40 Mr '77

Local government; address, October 3, 1977. L. F. Harlow. Vital Speeches 44:70-3 N 15 '77

See also

Bureaucracy
Local government
Municipal government

Study and teaching

Education for the public service. R. C. Bobowski. il Am Educ 13:31-2 Ap '77

See also

Colorado. University, Boulder—Graduate School of Public Affairs
National School of Administration, France

PUBLIC beaches. See Beaches

PUBLIC Broadcasting Corporation. See Corporation for Public Broadcasting

PUBLIC Broadcasting Service

Public TV: stop the waste. M. Stone. U.S. News 83:84 O 3 '77

What's wrong with Public Broadcasting; music programs. D. Pash. il Hi Fi 27:MA19-21 O '77

PUBLIC buildings

Designing a cost-effective public building. Am City & County 92:41-4 F '77

Some positive thinking from the General Services Administration. W. F. Wagner, Jr. Archit Rec 162:13 D '77

See also

Art in public buildings
County buildings
Courthouses
Embassies (buildings)
Library architecture
Public works facilities

Fuel requirements

How to cut energy use in public buildings. G. Vanderweil and J. R. Haynes. il Am City & County 92:46-7 Jl '77

Lighting the way to energy savings. il Am City & County 92:63-4 Ag '77

PUBLIC comfort stations

Save water at highway rest stops; recycle and reuse system, Virginia. C. E. Parker. il Am City & County 92:63-4 Je '77

PUBLIC debt (United States) See Debts, Public—United States

PUBLIC documents. See Government publications

PUBLIC employees. See Government employees

PUBLIC figures. See Celebrities

PUBLIC health

Public health (cont) Sci N 111:89; 112:296 F 5, N 5 '77

See also

Environmental health
Health facilities
Health planning
Medical policy
Medicine, Preventive
Public comfort stations
Quarantine
Sewage disposal
World Health Organization

California

See also

Los Angeles County, Calif.—Public health
San Diego, Calif.—Public health

Connecticut

Diagnosing Lyme's malady. il Time 109:56 Je 13 '77

Mrs Murray's mystery disease; Lyme arthritis discovered. E. Keiffer. il por Good H 184:80+ Mr '77

Europe, Western

La rage in Europe; rabies. M. Clark and T. Nater. Newsweek 90:52 S 12 '77

Latin America

See also

Pan American Health Organization

Liberia

Nurse Hopkins, 30 years later. il pors Ebony 32:80+ Ap '77

Massachusetts

Dangerous nymphs of Nantucket; babesiosis. R. S. Desowitz and L. H. Miller. il Natur Hist 86:10+ bibl(p 110) D '77

Human babesiosis: reservoir of infection on Nantucket Island; discussion. bibl Science 195:506-7 F 4 '77

Michigan

Cancer in clusters; Hodgkin's disease in Breckenridge, Mich. M. Clark and others. il Newsweek 90:119 O 17 '77

Michigan's clamp on doctor bills; Blue Cross and Blue Shield plan. Bus W p34 D 19 '77

Middle East

Ancient scourge strikes again; cholera. Time 110:62 S 26 '77

Cholera epidemic. M. Clark and W. E. Schmidt. il Newsweek 90:94 S 26 '77

New York (state)

See also

New York (city)—Public health

PUBLIC health—*Continued*

Ohio

Local rein on health costs; Central Ohio River Valley Association for Health Planning & Resource Development. il Bus W p 114+ O 31 '77

Rhode Island

Immigrants without care; Portuguese in Rhode Island. L. A. Monteiro. bibl il Society 14:38-42 S '77

Russia

New/old flu; A/USSR/77. Time 111:53 Ja 2 '78

South Africa

Menace from South Africa; new strain of pneumonia. Time 110:113 S 19 '77

Texas

Nursing an ambulance and a county; San Jacinto County. D. Lampe. il pors Fam Health 9:28-30 Je '77
See also
Houston, Tex.—Public health

United States

See also
Indians of North America—Health and hygiene

PUBLIC health nurses and patients. See Nurses and patients

PUBLIC institutions
See also
Mentally handicapped—Institutional care

PUBLIC interest law firms. See Law partnership

PUBLIC interest lawyers as public officers. See Public officers

PUBLIC lands
See also
National parks and reserves
Wilderness areas

Alaska

Administration discloses 92-million-acre Alaskan land proposal. il Nat Parks & Con Mag 51:28-30 N '77
Alaska: develop or conserve? Issue is moving toward a showdown; Alaska National Interest Lands Conservation Act. M. Hornblower. il map Smithsonian 8:38-49 bibl(p 134) D '77
Alaska national interest lands. Nat Parks & Con Mag 51:27-9 Je '77
Alaska's dilemma of untapped wealth. il map Bus W p 120+ Je 20 '77
Alaska's interior forests: in the eye of the storm. D. T. Hoopes. il Am For 83:16-19+ Je '77
Are conservationists asking for too much? national interest lands. Nat Parks & Con Mag 51:26-9 S '77
Battle for the last frontier. N. King. il Nat R 29:722-4 Je 24 '77
Battle of Alaska. il Time 109:53-4 My 9 '77
Fragile giant. R. F. Jones. Sports Illus 47:94-5 D 12 '77
Great Alaskan land battle. J. N. Miller. il Read Digest 111:128-34 D '77
NPCA urges approval of Alaska National Interest Lands Conservation Act. il Nat Parks & Con Mag 51:21-4+ Jl '77
Race to save wild Alaska; the Alaska National Interest Lands Conservation Act and related legislation. R. Cahn. il Liv Wildn 41:13-19 Jl '77
Viewpoint. J. G. Deane. Liv Wildn 41:3 Jl '77
Who will win the battle of Alaska? J. N. Miller. map Read Digest 112:88-93 Ja '78

Nevada

Does the BLM belong in Nevada? V. L. Fischer. il Am For 83:18-21 D '77

United States

Land exchange; case study involving Disney's resort plans and government land. R. F. Masse and C. Broussard. il map Parks & Rec 12:26-9+ D '77
Lumbermen vs. environmentalists. il U.S. News 83:62-4 Ag 22 '77
Mineral rights raise new dust; federal lands. Bus W p48 O 3 '77
Relieving the pressures on the parks; question of providing outdoor recreational opportunities on other public lands. A. W. Smith. Nat Parks & Con Mag 51:2+ N '77
See also
Homesteads
National forests
National parks and reserves—United States
United States—Land Management, Bureau of

PUBLIC libraries. See Libraries

PUBLIC Library Association. See American Library Association—Public Library Association

PUBLIC offerings of stock. See Stocks—Marketing

PUBLIC officers
Do not criticize government for all nation's ills; excerpts from address. W. D. Carey. por Intellect 105:290-1 Mr '77
Georgians on my mind. M. Greenfield. Newsweek 91:88 Ja 16 '78
Macho of time; question of length of public officials' work day. New Repub 177:2+ Ag 20 '77
Professors, politics, and palaver. C. Holden. Science 197:742 Ag 19 '77
Public distrust and government service. T. E Kauper. por Intellect 106:2 Jl '77
Public interest lawyers: Carter brings them into the establishment. L. J. Carter. Science 196:961-4 My 27 '77
Public officials for sale; bribery, graft, kickbacks, etc. il U.S. News 82:36-8 F 28 '77
Scanning the want ads with President Ford's top officials. P. M. Boffey. Science 195:853 Mr 4 '77
Situations wanted—2,200 of them; former top officials of the Ford administration. il Time 109:16 Mr 7 '77
Six who help run a government they spent years trying to change. il U.S. News 82:80-1 My 23 '77
Stanford goes to Washington. P. M. Boffey. Science 196:631 My 6 '77
They never go from the White House to the poorhouse; officials of past administrations. il U.S. News 83:38-9 Ag 29 '77
Washington's glut of ex-bureaucrats. il Bus W p25-6 Ap 4 '77
Writing an official is a Capital idea. Sr Schol 109:22-3 F 24 '77
See also
Black public officers
Bureaucracy
Children of public officers
Conflict of interests (public office)
Congressmen
Government investigations—Public officers
Governors
International officials and employees
Municipal officers
Political ethics
Politicians
Public administration
United States—President's Commission on Personnel Interchange
Women public officers

Appointment, qualifications, etc.

Carter's score on minority hiring. il U.S. News 82:59-61 Ap 25 '77
How old school ties help Carter fill jobs. il U.S. News 83:24 Ag 1 '77
Jimmy Carter's ruling class. R. Morris. Harpers 255:37-45 O '77
Liberal lineup in Carter's sub-Cabinet. il Bus W p74+ My 2 '77
Nader's invaders are inside the gates. J. Cameron. il Fortune 96:252-6+ O '77
New faces of 1977. New Repub 176:5-6 F 12 '77
Outsiders move inside. R. Boeth. il Newsweek 91:22-4 Ja 2 '78
Really new faces; sub-Cabinet appointments. S. Fraker and others. il Newsweek 89:17-18 Mr 14 '77
When Carter fills jobs—his promises, his record. il U.S. News 83:38+ N 14 '77
Why Carter is having trouble taking full reins of government. il U.S. News 82:24-5 Mr 21 '77
Why not the second best? Carter appointments. Nation 225:483-4 N 12 '77

Archives

Public or private papers? The arrogance of the intelligence community. A. G. Theoharis. Intellect 106:118-20 O '77

Resignation

See also
Lance, T. B.—Resignation
Rabin, Y.—Resignation

Salaries, allowances, etc.

For top officials: big pay raises in the works. il U.S. News 82:19 F 7 '77
Pay hikes for top officials: who gets what. il U.S. News 82:54 F 28 '77

Wives

Jimmy Carter's Cabinet—the spouses behind the scene. il U.S. News 82:30-2 F 14 '77
See also
Politicians wives

PUBLIC officers wives. See Public officers—Wives

PUBLIC opinion
Leaving it to the experts. T. Griffith. Atlantic 240:30+ N '77
Search for poor, happy people; Gallup/Kettering Global Survey on Human Needs and Satisfactions. S. Bush. Psychol Today 10:34+ Ap '77
What people around the world say about hopes, fears, life today. il U.S. News 82:66-7 Ja 24 '77
See also
Political attitudes
Public opinion polls
Student opinion
Teacher opinion
United States—Foreign opinion

PUBLIC opinion—*Continued*

Asia

Dragon and the bear: Asian perceptions of a Sino-Soviet war. J. Kefner. map America 137: 162-4 S 24 '77

See also

United States—Foreign opinion—Asian

Cuba

See also

United States—Foreign opinion—Cuban

Europe, Western

See also

Germany, West—Foreign opinion—European

United States—Foreign opinion—European

Great Britain

See also

World War, 1939-1945—Public opinion

New Zealand

See also

United States—Foreign opinion—New Zealand

South Africa

See also

United States—Foreign opinion—South African

United States

American leadership—latest assessment. il U.S. News 82:33 Ap 18 '77

Americans dislike the poor; interview results. J. E. Tropman. Intellect 106:7-8 Jl '77

Do the American people know what they want? P. H. Weaver. Commentary 64:62-7 D '77

Emerging national consensus; public opinion on issue of reverse discrimination. S. M. Lipset and W. Schneider. New Repub 177: 8-9 O 15 '77

How U.S. consumers view energy crisis; University of Texas study. S. C. Lopreato and W. Cunningham. Intellect 106:95+ S '77

How willing to pare? energy conservation. Time 109:63 Mr 7 '77

Liberal me and conservative you; study by James M. Fields and Howard Schuman. D. Cohen. Psychol Today 10:38+ Ap '77

Nefertiti graffiti; visitors' comments at the Brooklyn Museum's 1973 Akhenaten and Nefertiti exhibition. Vasari. Art N 76:21+ Summ '77

People's verdict: guilty; Richard Nixon's televised interview with David Frost. D. M. Alpern and others. il Newsweek 89:31+ My 16 '77

Public opinion and energy use. P. H. Abelson Science 197:1325 S 30 '77

Quality of life in rural America. D. A. Dillman and K. R. Tremblay, Jr. bibl f Ann Am Acad 429:115-29 Ja '77

Rural-urban differences in attitudes and behavior in the United States. N. D. Glenn and L. Hill, Jr. bibl f il Ann Am Acad 429:36-50 Ja '77

So, you don't change your mind. . .much? attitudes of Americans toward other nations. il Sr Schol 109:18 Mr 10 '77

There's no shortage of gripes when lawmakers talk to voters. H. Kennedy; R. Shoup; J. Hogue. il U.S. News 83:17-19 Ag 29 '77

Vox pop on Panama. Newsweek 90:48+ O 24 '77

What does the public think of the schools? il Todays Educ 66:26-31 N '77

What worries the voters? il Time 110:14-15+ S 5 '77

Why Nixon went on the witness stand. pors U.S. News 82:27-9 My 16 '77

See also

Arab countries—Foreign opinion—American

Israel—Foreign opinion—American

Israel-Arab Wars, 1967- —Public opinion

Vietnam—Foreign opinion—American

Vietnamese War, 1957-1975—Public opinion

PUBLIC opinion polls

Pollsters—the fifth estate? proposal for White House evaluation of the polls. Nation 225:517 N 19 '77

Sweet nothings: Pat Caddell is whispering nonsense in President Carter's ear. H. Fairlie. New Repub 176:17-19 Je 11 '77

See also

Scholastic Research Center

PUBLIC ownership. See Government ownership

PUBLIC prosecutors

One woman's war against rape. M. Gross. por Good H 184:84+ Ap '77

Politics and Federal D.A.'s. D. M. Alpern and others. il Newsweek 90:21 Jl 18 '77

PUBLIC records

Bureaucrats above the law: double-entry intelligence files. A. Theoharis. Nation 225:393-7 O 22 '77

PUBLIC relations

See also

Business—Public relations

Drug industry—Public relations

Electric utilities—Public relations

Hospitals—Public relations

Libraries—Public relations

Petroleum industry—Public relations

Press agents

Press releases

Publicity

School and the community

PUBLIC relations consultants

Who's who among the agencies. A. Hershman. Duns R 110:65 S '77

PUBLIC safety. See Accidents—Prevention

PUBLIC schools

See also

Rural schools

also headings beginning School; e.g. School and the community

Attendance

See School attendance

Curriculum

Mind bending in the schools stirs growing protests. il U.S. News 83:43-4 Jl 4 '77

See also

High schools—Curriculum

Desegregation

As we see it; desegregation resolution drafted by Stockton, Calif. students; excerpt from television script. il Sr Schol 110:17-18+ S 22 '77

Boston desegregation: what went wrong? K. Clark. bibl Clearing H 51:157-9 D '77

Case against separate schools. D. G. Carter. bibl Clearing H 51:125-9 N '77

Day race relations changed forever; Brown v Board of Education; school desegregation decision. L. Bennett. il por Ebony 32:132-6+ Mr '77

Desegregation and equality—much remains to be done; findings of the Civil Rights Commission. il Todays Educ 66:22-5 Ja '77

Freeway madness; reassignment of teachers on basis of race by Los Angeles Unified School District. R. Kirk. Nat R 30:34 Ja 6 '78

Growing up white in D.C. schools. R. Jordan. Educ Digest 43:41-3 N '77

Integration: more preventive than cure; work of Steven R. Asher and Louise C. Singleton. Sci N 112:133 Ag 27 '77

Little Rock revisited. E. Keerdoja. il Newsweek 90:8 S 5 '77

Positive experience; Commission on Civil Rights report. J. W. Donohue. America 136:236-8 Mr 19 '77

Race and desegregation; symposium. il Society 14:32-48 My '77

Reschooling society. J. Featherstone. New Repub 176:40+ Ja 22 '77

School race problems: the states move in. il U.S. News 83:50 N 28 '77

Some are more equal; Supreme Court decisions affecting discrimination in education and political representation. B. Odom. Nat R 29:1114-15 S 30 '77

Students who work together like each other more. J. Horn. Psychol Today 10:95-6 Ap '77

Tale of two cities; Supreme Court decisions on the proper role of Federal judges in school-desegregation cases. M. Sheils and others. il Newsweek 90:54 Jl 11 '77

Teachers and race. M. Sheils and others. il Newsweek 90:114 N 7 '77

See also

School children—Transportation for integration

Finance

See Education—Finance

United States

City schools in crisis. M. Sheils and others. il Newsweek 90:62-4+ S 12 '77

PUSH for excellence; J. Jackson's program. A. Poinsett. il pors Ebony 32:104-6+ F '77

What's going on in schools & colleges. Changing T 31:29-30 S '77

See also

Education—United States

Education, Urban

High schools

Junior high schools

School year

Voucher plan in education

PUBLIC schools and religion

New Jersey mantra; Federal court ruling on transcendental meditation. J. W. Donohue. America 137:360 N 19 '77

Public schools can study religion. M. D. Grote. por Intellect 106:105-6 S '77

Public schools: equal time for evangelicals. J. R. McQuilkin. il Chr Today 22:8-11 D 30 '77

Religion in school: seeking alternatives to chaos. Chr Cent 94:291-2 Mr 30 '77

TM and the religion-in-school issue. E. R. Baltazar; discussion. Chr Cent 94:150-2 F 16 '77

TM grounded; Federal district court ruled the government-funded teaching of TM unconstitutional. il Chr Today 22:56 N 18 '77

PUBLIC schools and the community. See School and the community

PUBLIC service commissions
Utilities fight to escape a tax-credit trap. il Bus W p96+ D 5 '77
See also
Independent regulatory commissions
PUBLIC Service Company of New Mexico. See Electric utilities
PUBLIC Service Electric and Gas Company
No place to go but up? Forbes 120:172 N 15 '77
Offshore reactors: where not to put the nuke. L. Light. il Nation 225:205-8 S 10 '77
PUBLIC services. See Municipal services
PUBLIC speaking
How to speak in public. J. D. Scott. Read Digest 111:80+ D '77
No laughing matter; humor in executives' speeches; views of R. Orben. P. Steinfels. Commonweal 104:434 Jl 8 '77
See also
Elocution

Study and teaching

How to be a better public speaker; views of Sandy Linver. Nations Bus 65:66 Jl '77
$900 lesson in podium power; coaching executives at Communispond. H. E. Meyer. il pors Fortune 96:196-8+ Ag '77
PUBLIC television. See Television broadcasting, Public
PUBLIC transportation. See Local transit
PUBLIC utilities
Public utilities can serve more than one use. G. Dunbar and M. Lang. il pors Am City & County 92:49-50 N '77
Winter fuel outlook: another tight year. U.S. News 83:71-2 O 3 '77
See also
Electric utilities
Gas companies
Telephone companies

Finance

Still growing, but not so fast. il Bus W p 114 O 17 '77
Utilities. il Forbes 121:129-30+ Ja 9 '78

Rates

Match utility rates to system costs; Englewood, Ohio. R. J. Holland and J. Niccolls. il Am City & County 92:53-5 Ap '77
Time to review utility rates carefully. S. Baxter. Am City & County 92:83 Je '77

Regulation

See also
Electric utilities—Regulation

Securities

Utility stocks may lose some of their voltage. il Bus W p 152 My 16 '77
See also
Electric utilities—Securities

Security measures

Protect against sabotage, vandalism. S. Baxter. Am City & County 92:81 Ag '77

Statistics

Fifty largest utilities. il Fortune 96:172-3 Jl '77
PUBLIC utility commissions. See Public service commissions
PUBLIC welfare
Complaint heard 'round the world—inefficiency and high cost in welfare. U.S. News 83:49 Ag 8 '77
See also
United Nations—Commission for Social Development

Massachusetts

Workfare and welfare. H. Lipman. Nation 225:141-4 Ag 20 '77
Working on welfare. Time 109:12 Je 27 '77

New York (state)

See also
New York (city)—Public welfare

Sweden

Problem of widespread poverty. G. Myrdal. Current 197:18-23 N '77

United States

ABC's of Carter welfare plan—and the changes it would bring. il U.S. News 83:42-3 Ag 22 '77
Another go at the welfare mess: will it work? D. C. Bacon. U.S. News 83:45-9 Ag 8 '77
Burgeoning social service payload. N. Gilbert. il Society 14:63-5 My '77
Can't we do better? views on reforms. M. Stone. U.S. News 82:104 Ap 11 '77
Carter's welfare fight. G. R. Rosen. por Duns R 110:53 N '77
Carter's welfare plan: Nixon warmed over? R. Lekachman. Sat R 5:9 D 10 '77
Carter's welfare reform. Progressive 41:9-10 O '77
Carter's welfare reform: a piece of complicated gimmickry. E. Currie. Nation 225:230-3 S 17 '77
Copycat Carter; welfare reform. Nat R 29:594-5 My 27 '77
Don't save the cities: welfare is cheaper. N. Von Hoffman. New Repub 176:6+ Mr 12 '77
Go on welfare, give up your privacy? U.S. News 82:83 Ja 24 '77
Kneading the poor. Nat R 29:705-6 Je 24 '77
Making sense of welfare. M. Greenfield. por Newsweek 89:116 My 9 '77
No long delay needed; guaranteed income and the Carter program. A. Cherlin. New Repub 177:13-15 D 17 '77
Politics of welfare reform. N. Kotz. New Repub 176:16-21 My 14 '77
Problem of widespread poverty. G. Myrdal. Current 197:18-23 N '77
Problems with poverty programs. R. Wilhelm. il Intellect 106:7 Jl '77
Promised: an overhaul of welfare. il U.S. News 82:68 Ja 24 '77
Second chance. New Repub 177:7-8 Ag 20 '77
Social-welfare spending—can anyone bring it under control? il U.S. News 82:40-1 Mr 14 '77
Status of welfare reform in the United States. C. W. Anderson. bibl Intellect 106:137-40 O '77
Straight talk about welfare; adaptation of address, April 27, 1977. J. A. Califano, Jr. Read Digest 111:157-8 S '77
Strange attitude. M. Stone. U.S. News 83:68 S 5 '77
Swedish view of welfare in America; excerpt from address, October 28, 1976. G. Myrdal. Current 190:15-18 F '77
Tip sheet on Carter's welfare plan. N. Cornbalth-Moshé and C. Burris. Ms 6:55-6+ Ja '78
Tough road ahead for Carter's welfare reform. il U.S. News 82:48 My 16 '77
Very modest proposal. Nation 225:131-2 Ag 20 '77
Welfare: reading the fine print; reform plan. D. A. Williams and C. Ma. il Newsweek 90:23-4 Ag 22 '77
Welfare reform. P. A. Samuelson. Newsweek 90:64 Ag 29 '77
Welfare reform. D. A. Williams and C. Ma. Newsweek 90:18 Ag 8 '77
Welfare reform: Act I. Time 109:16-17 My 9 '77
Welfare reform; address, April 1, 1977. E. J. Garn. Vital Speeches 43:484-7 Je 1 '77
Welfare reform and compassion. J. M. Wall. Chr Cent 94:579-80 Je 22 '77
Welfare reform charade. Progressive 41:6-7 Ag '77
Welfare, work and the family. America 137:66 Ag 13 '77
What's in a name? Plenty. P. W. Martin. Nation 226:6-7 Ja 7 '78
When states tell people they must work for welfare. il U.S. News 83:81-2 Jl 18 '77
Which way out of the welfare mess? K. Y. Tomlinson. Read Digest 111:149-54 D '77
Working to reform welfare. il Time 110:6-8 Ag 15 '77
See also
Child welfare—United States
Food relief—United States
Legal Services Corporation
Negative income tax
Old age assistance
Unemployment—Relief measures

Utah

Workfare and welfare. H. Lipman. Nation 225:141-4 Ag 20 '77
PUBLIC welfare fraud. See Fraud
PUBLIC works
Biggest jobs program in decades—is it a boon or a boondoggle? il U.S. News 82:96-8 My 23 '77
Force account under contractor attack; with editorial comment. Am City & County 92:13, 156 S '77
Furbish lousewort is no joke; Endangered Species Act and public works projects. J. Wheelwright. New Repub 176:9-12 My 14 '77
In Milwaukee: if you don't work, you don't eat; Pay for Work Program. il U.S. News 82:82-3 Ap 4 '77
Update. il Am City & County 92:22+ Ja; 36 F; 37 Mr '77
Washington hotline (cont of) Update. See issues of American city & county
See also
Dams
Municipal engineering

Federal aid

Allocating Federal funds through local unemployment rates. K. A. Peterson. M Labor R 100:45-6 O '77
Business, too, tests reverse discrimination; Associated General Contractors' suits. il Bus W p40-1 N 14 '77
EDA holds firm against set-aside challenges; minority business enterprise clause in Round II Local Public Works Act. Am City & County 92:13 D '77
$4 billion barrel of pork? G. R. Rosen. por Duns R 109:71 My '77
4 billions more for public works: where the money goes. il U.S. News 82:105-6 My 9 '77
More public works funds on tap by May. il Am City & County 92:12 F '77

PUBLIC works—Federal aid—*Continued*
Public jobs that aren't there. il Bus W p 113 Je 13 '77
Public works funds place emphasis on wrong projects. S. S. Baxter. Am City & County 92:75 Ap '77
Some news in the right direction from Washington. W. Wagner. Archit Rec 162:13 O '77
When Washington tries to create jobs—. il U.S. News 83:79-82 N 7 '77

United States

See Public works

PUBLIC Works Committee. See United States—Congress—House—Public Works, Committee on

PUBLIC works equipment
Marketplace (cont of) New products and processes. See issues of American city & county
See also
Motor vehicles, Municipal
Refuse collection trucks
Snow removal equipment
Street cleaning apparatus

PUBLIC works facilities
Design public works shops to increase productivity. W. C. Jacobs. por Am City & County 92:91-2 S '77
Public utilities can serve more than one use. G. Dunbar and M. Lang. il pors Am City & County 92:49-50 N '77
We built our service center on a landfill; La Crosse, Wis. il Am City & County 92:89-90 S '77

PUBLIC works officers
Local government wins eight awards. il Am City & County 92:46+ Je '77
Man of the Year; interview. D. C. Tillman. il pors Am City & County 92:27-9 Ja '77

PUBLICITY
Persuaders: jobs in publicity. C. Calvert. Mademoiselle 83:214+ O '77
See also
Advertising
College library publicity
Government publicity
Library publicity
Press agents
Press releases

PUBLICITY, Political. See Advertising, Political

PUBLICKER Industries Inc. See Liquor industry

PUBLISHERS and authors. See Authors and publishers

PUBLISHERS and libraries. See Libraries and publishers

PUBLISHERS and publishing
PW interviews. See issues of Publishers weekly
See also
Authors and publishers
Best sellers
Book clubs
Books—Marketing
Computers—Publishing use
Copyright
Libraries and publishers
Literary agents
Newspaper publishers and publishing
Private presses
Proofreading
University presses
Women in publishing

Acquisitions and mergers

Authors Guild asks U.S. to halt sinister merger trend. S. Wagner. Pub W 211:21-2 Je 20 '77; Reply. A. Hatcher. 212:7 Ag 15 '77
Bennett Cerf remembers; excerpt from At Random. B. Cerf. por Pub W 212:26-9 Ag 22 '77
Bertelsmann Group acquires 51% interest in Bantam. M. Reuter. Pub W 212:71 S 19 '77
Harper & Row in an agreement to acquire Lippincott. M. Reuter. Pub W 213:12 Ja 2 '78
Harper & Row is planning to acquire T. Y. Crowell. M. Reuter. Pub W 211:40 Mr 14 '77
Howard & Wyndham of London to acquire Hawthorn Books; merger with W. H. Allen Publishing Inc subsidiary. M. Reuter. Pub W 212:20 O 31 '77
Justice Dept. looking at Times Mirror-Random House. S. Wagner. Pub W 211:25 Mr 21 '77
Lippincott reports Harper offer for all its shares. Pub W 212:17 D 5 '77
Times Mirror negotiating with RCA for Random House. Pub W 211:26 F 21 '77
Tyndale House subsidiary in United Kingdom merger. M. Reuter. Pub W 211:42-3 Mr 14 '77
Udall to probe mergers, including book publishing. S. Wagner. Pub W 211:21 My 9 '77

Advertising

See Books—Advertising

Anecdotes, facetiae, satire, etc.

Notes on the trade. Colophon. Pub W 212:16 D 26 '77

Antitrust cases

After the Consent Decree: the effect on the Traditional Market Agreement. P. D. Standish. Pub W 211:44-8 Ap 25 '77

Art

Ambroise Vollard—impresario. G. Needham. il por Art N 76:78-80+ S '77
Cover; publication of E. Kelly print by Tyler Graphics. M. Schiller. il Am Artist 41:6+ Ag '77
Creative pendulum of Mike Vogel: graphic artist and entrepreneur; founder of Dayspring Graphics. M. C. Nelson. il por Am Artist 41:70-5+ O '77
Goldilocks' cosmic teach-in; Universal Limited Art Editions' publication of R. B. Fuller's lithographs in Tetrascroll. M. Hoelterhoff. il pors Art N 76:19-21 Mr '77
Hundertwasser art book features cover done specially by the artist. P. Doebler. il Pub W 212:96 Ag 1 '77
Master printer of Bedford, N.Y; K. Tyler of Gemini Ltd and Tyler Graphics. J. Goldman. il pors Art N 76:50-4 S '77
Nancy Burkert art featured in two new editions. P. Doebler. il Pub W 212:99-100 Ag 1 '77
Rainbow of subjects and art styles brightens poster books this fall. R. Dahlin. il Pub W 212:82 Ag 1 '77
Soviet-produced art books make debut in U.S. P. Doebler. il Pub W 212:50 S 5 '77
See also
Lakeside Studio (firm)

Brazilian literature

Brazilian writers meet with foreign editors, publishers, translators. S. Congrat-Butlar. il Pub W 212:24+ N 28 '77

Childrens literature

Co-op ventures, paperbacks, of growing interest to children's book publishers. J. F. Mercier. Pub W 212:84 Jl 18 '77
Is it true boys have more fun? What every parent should know about children's books. S. Scofield. Redbook 149:214+ My '77
John Newbery: publisher with a radical idea. Z. Collier. il por Pub W 212:81-2 Jl 18 '77
Librarians & publishers: an idea exchange through library promotion. P. J. Van Orden. por SLJ 24:24-6 D '77
Notes on the children's book trade. J. Goldthwaite; discussion. SLJ 23:7 F '77; Harpers 254:6-7 Mr '77
Peering into the fog: the future of children's books. J. R. Townsend. Horn Bk 53:346-55 Je '77

Conferences

Smaller publishers get together on West Coast. R. Calkins. il Pub W 211:24-5 Ap 11 '77
State of the publishing industry; Stanford University conference. Intellect 105:302 Mr '77
Washington diarist; Annual Publishing Conference and Exposition. R. J. Myers. New Repub 177:50 N 26 '77

Detective and mystery stories

Story behind the books: two unusual mysteries from the U. of Chicago press; Judge Dee stories. A. Barret. Pub W 212:62 O 17 '77

Educational literature

Big test for test publishers. il Bus W p 114+ Je 27 '77
Jacaranda Wiley at 10 months: the feeling is up Down Under. Pub W 212:23 O 31 '77
See also
Association of American Publishers—School Division
Educational Paperback Association

Employees

See also
Strikes—United States—Publishers and publishing

Encyclopedias

New cure of encyclopedic miasma. W. R. Eshelman. Wilson Lib Bull 51:714-15 My '77
See also
Grolier, Inc

Facsimiles

See Book rarities—Facsimiles

Fantasies, Literary

Paperback fairy tale given a new life in the market; Ballantine Books' reissue of William Goldman's The princess bride. P. Doebler. il Pub W 211:74+ Mr 7 '77

Federal aid

AAP pleads for loans to small publishers. S. Wagner. Pub W 212:22 D 26 '77

Fiction

Paperback historical romance (title varies) J. A. Glass and Y. MacManus. Writer 90:33-5 Ap; 18 My '77
Tradition of the not so new; Fiction Collective. G. Lyons. Nation 224:628-30 My 21 '77

Finance

Financial briefs (cont of) Financial notes (cont) Pub W 211:30 Mr 28; 23-4 My 9 '77

PUBLISHERS and publishing—Finance—*Continued*
More financial know-how offered to those who don't have to read the bottom line; report of AAP seminar. J. F. Baker and P. D. Doebler. Pub W 211:29+ Mr 7 '77
Prices, printings and profits: how to draw the bottom line; adaptation of address. T. J. McCormack. il Pub W 212:34-41 Ag 15 '77
Subsidy publishing: stigma or sesame? N. Richardson. il Writers Digest 57:44-8 Jl '77

Garden literature

From garden products to garden books was an obvious step for Ortho. il Pub W 211:65-6 Ja 17 '77

International aspects

After the Consent Decree: a new era in the marketing of English-language books. G. Graham. Pub W 211:38-40 Ja 31 '77
Australia/Britain/U.S.A.—a new bookselling era begins. M. G. Zifcack. il Pub W 212:40-1 Jl 11 '77
Bernstein and Albert testify on censorship, currency; testimony before Commission on Security and Cooperation in Europe. S. Wagner. Pub W 211:39+ Je 6 '77
Brazilian writers meet with foreign editors, publishers, translators. S. Congrat-Butlar. il Pub W 212:24+ N 28 '77
British agent finds indigenous publishing, not American competition, the factor to watch in the world book market. M. Sissons. Pub W 211:41-2 F 21 '77
British are coming! N. Dunnan. Lib J 102: 2311-16 N 15 '77
14 Soviet publishers have useful visit in U.S; Protocol question. M. Reuter. il Pub W 212: 11-13 N 28 '77
International notes. H. R. Lottman. Pub W 211: 30 Mr 21 '77
International scene at ABA. H. R. Lottman. il Pub W 211:89-93 Je 27 '77
International scene; symposium, ed by M. Odomirok. il Pub W 212:85-114 S 19 '77
Look at Methuen, Inc—the only Canadian-owned American publishing firm. Pub W 212:19-20 N 21 '77
See also
Association of American Publishers—International Freedom to Publish Committee
Franklin Book Programs, Inc

Large print books

G. K. Hall releases more large print titles and, now, will sell them to the trade. R. Dahlin. Pub W 212:36 N 14 '77

Laws and legislation

Court dismisses $5-million libel claim against Holt. S. Wagner. Pub W 212:27-8 Jl 25 '77
Litigations. Pub W 211:43 Je 6; 28 Je 20 '77
Year in review: the view from Washington. S. Wagner. Pub W 211:37-8 F 14 '77

Legal literature

Butterworths. R. Kolbe. il Pub W 213:23-5 Ja 2 '78

Medical literature

See also
Association of American Publishers—Technical, Scientific and Medical Division

Order processing

Out of control—indefinitely. L. N. Gerhardt. SLJ 24:63 O '77

Paperback books

Ace to issue its first instant title on Amin. M. Reuter. Pub W 212:74+ Jl 18 '77
Avon buys The thorn birds for record $1.9 million. M. Reuter. Pub W 211:27-8 Mr 7 '77
Ballantine Books at quarter century:
Founders; interview, ed by T. Weyr. B. Ballantine; I. Ballantine. il pors Pub W 212: 30-3 D 12 '77
New regime; interview, ed by T. Weyr. R. Busch. il por Pub W 212:44-6 D 26 '77
Book boom: action in paperbacks. il Bus W p50-2 Jl 4 '77
Inaugural book is first full-color large-format instant production. P. Doebler. il Pub W 211:78+ F 7 '77
New Golconda in book publishing. I. Ross. il Fortune 96:110-14+ D '77
New mass market line uses innovative sales strategy; Dale Books; interview, ed by J. Giusto. T. Maass. Pub W 212:13-14 N 28 '77
Paper war. T. Schwartz and B. Graustark. Newsweek 89:86+ Mr 14 '77
Paperback fairy tale given a new life in the market; Ballantine Books' reissue of William Goldman's The princess bride. P. Doebler. il Pub W 211:74+ Mr 7 '77
Paperback historical romance (title varies) J. A. Glass and Y. MacManus. Writer 90:33-5 Ap; 18 My '77
Paperback market: how it differs from America; West Germany; tr by T. Weyr. A. U. Martens. il Pub W 212:70+ S 12 '77
Paperback revolution: where has it gone? adaptation of address, October 1977. O. Dystel. por Pub W 212:31-3 N 14 '77
Paperbacks: getting the giveaways. il SLJ 24: 24-5 S '77
Pinnacle Books to move to Los Angeles in August. M. Reuter. Pub W 211:20-1 My 2 '77
Pocket Books means to pull surprises out of its new kangaroo pouch; interview, ed by R. Dahlin. P. Mayer. Pub W 211:64 F 7 '77
Science fiction proves to be no fantasy for DAW books, five years old this month; interview, ed by R. Dahlin. D. A. Wollheim. Pub W 211:52 Ap 11 '77
Seal Books makes splash from new firm: McClelland and Stewart-Bantam Ltd. B. Slopen. il Pub W 211:25+ Ja 31 '77
Selling trade paperbacks in mass quantities is the new game plan at Avon Books. D. Maryles. il Pub W 211:56+ Ja 31 '77
What the booksellers said in the AAP/ABA mass market paperback survey. D. Maryles. Pub W 211:85 Mr 7 '77
See also
Educational Paperback Association
Harcourt Brace Jovanovich, Inc
Paperback books—Marketing

Periodicals

Business is business. A. Spikol. Writers Digest 57:12+ Mr '77
Data services win on second-class mail. Bus W p23-4 Jl 18 '77
Joining the People parade. il Bus W p71+ My 16 '77
Kate Murray: pharmacist/magazine publisher; On the line magazine. D. Duke. por Mademoiselle 83:78 O '77
Most profitable magazine in the U.S; Progressive Farmer Company's Southern living. il Forbes 119:30-1 Je 15 '77
Murdoch watch. Time 109:49 My 30 '77
New York's battleground. il Time 109:43-4 Ja 24 '77
On one who wrote not wisely but to sell; magazine freelancing. M. Malone. Nation 224:597-8 My 14 '77
Our curious business. C. Tucker. Sat R 5:64 N 12 '77
Trials of Murdoch. D. Gelman. il por Newsweek 89:78 Ja 24 '77
Washington diarist; Annual Publishing Conference and Exposition. R. J. Myers. New Repub 177:50 N 26 '77
Why the black ink is spurting at magazines. il Bus W p 142+ D 12 '77

Photographic literature

From the tiny to the enormous, two fall books offer rare views of earth as we don't know it. R. Dahlin. il Pub W 211:44 Je 20 '77
Haute couture of decades past recollected by Penn and Vreeland in Viking book; interview, ed by R. Dahlin. I. Penn. il Pub W 211:44+ Ja 31 '77
How to get your photo book into print. D. S. Gelatt. il Pop Phot 80:74-7+ Mr '77
Markets & careers; negotiating a photographic book contract. H. Chapnick. il Pop Phot 81: 76+ D '77
Viewpoint; T. Marotta. J. Deschin. il pors Pop Phot 80:36+ Mr '77

Public relations

See also
Show windows

Religious literature

Abingdon, don't abdicate! J. C. Lyles. Chr Cent 94:470-1 My 18 '77
Bishops play monopoly; intervention of National Conference of Catholic Bishops in distribution practices of H. Costello. D. Morrissey. Commonweal 104:528-30 Ag 19 '77
Fall religious issue; symposium, ed by P. F. Hewitt. il pors Pub W 212:63-102 S 26 '77
Heavenly profits; Fleming H. Revell Co. D. Pauly. il Newsweek 90:68-9 O 31 '77
Holy writ. M. Montagno and others. il Newsweek 90:58-9 Jl 25 '77
PW interviews; ed by G. Stuttaford. B. Graham. por Pub W 211:10-11 Je 20 '77
Publishing in an age of mergers. Chr Cent 94: 1051 N 16 '77
William R. Barbour, Jr, Revell president, talks about getting our books out there where the unbeliever action is; interview. W. R. Barbour, Jr. pors Pub W 211:55-8 Mr 14 '77
You've got to say one thing about God: He sells books. D. K. Mano. il Esquire 87:20+ Ap '77
See also
Bible—Publication and distribution

Science fiction

Del Rey Books to launch hardcover line in spring. M. Reuter. Pub W 212:17-18 D 5 '77
Illustrated science fiction books for adults put a new spring in the picture. R. Dahlin. il Pub W 213:32 Ja 2 '78

PUBLISHERS and publishing—Science fiction —*Continued*
Science fiction proves to be no fantasy for DAW books, five years old this month; interview, ed by R. Dahlin. D. A. Wollheim. Pub W 211:52 Ap 11 '77
Talk with Kirill Bulychev, first Russian SF writer to visit U.S; interview, ed by M. Reuter. K. Bulychev. Pub W 211:34 My 16 '77

Scientific literature

See also
Association of American Publishers—Technical, Scientific and Medical Division

Securities

Year in review: the view from Wall Street: publishing stocks again outperformed the market. J. K. Noble, Jr. Pub W 211:45 F 14 '77

Statistics

AAP 1976 statistics—using the figures. J. K. Noble, Jr. il Pub W 212:41-3 Jl 4 '77
1976 statistics title counts and average prices per volume; Highlights from the annual AAP report. C. B. Grannis. il Pub W 212:32-6+ Ag 22 '77
Year in review: U.S. book industry statistics: prices, sales, trends. il Pub W 211:52-6 F 14 '77

Study and teaching

Theory vs. marketable skills: what do we teach the neophyte? Harcourt Brace Jovanovich Publishing Laboratory. G. Astor. il por Pub W 212:30-2 S 5 '77
See also
Association of American Publishers—Education for Publishing Committee
Coalition of Publishers for Employment, Inc.

Technical literature

See also
Association of American Publishers—Technical, Scientific and Medical Division

Textbooks

See also
Association of American Publishers—School Division
Scholastic Magazines, Inc

Australia

Jacaranda Wiley at 10 months: the feeling is up Down Under. Pub W 212:23 O 31 '77
Sale of Rigby's shares heats up debate over foreign ownership. M. G. Zifcak. Pub W 212: 74-6 S 19 '77; Reply. G. M. Gold. Pub W 212:7-8 D 5 '77

Austria

Publishing German books outside Germany. il Pub W 212:45+ S 12 '77

Canada

Look at Methuen, Inc—the only Canadian-owned American publishing firm. Pub W 212: 19-20 N 21 '77
Safari into darkest publishing; Quebecor's plans for new Philadelphia journal. por Forbes 120:108 D 1 '77
Seal Books makes splash from new firm: McClelland and Stewart-Bantam Ltd. B. Slopen. il Pub W 211:25+ Ja 31 '77

Denmark

Report on Scandinavia. H. R. Lottman. il map Pub W 211:52+ My 9 '77

Finland

Report on Scandinavia. H. R. Lottman. il map Pub W 211:41-2+ My 9 '77

France

Ambroise Vollard—impresario. G. Needham. il por Art N 76:78-80+ S '77
Hachette looks for foreign sales. il Pub W 211: 38 My 2 '77
Letter from Paris. H. R. Lottman. Pub W 211: 24-5 Ap 4 '77
Paris dateline. H. R. Lottman. Pub W 212:76 Jl 18 '77

Germany, West

Frontier: three big publishing houses; tr by T. Wyer. K. Goeppert. Pub W 212:43-4 S 12 '77
People in publishing. H. R. Lottman. il Pub W 212:10-14+ S 12 '77

Great Britain

British are coming! N. Dunnan. Lib J 102:2311-16 N 15 '77
Butterworths. R. Kolbe. il Pub W 213:23-5 Ja 2 '78
Ernest Hecht, of London's Souvenir Press, a pocket publisher with best selling ideas. H. R. Lottman. il por Pub W 211:48-9 Mr 28 '77
John Newbery: publisher with a radical idea. Z. Collier. il por Pub W 212:81-2 Jl 18 '77
See also
Reed International Ltd

History

Prehumous classics; Victorian novelists and publishers. E. Moers. Am Scholar 47:118+ Wint '77

Greece

American in Greece succeeds as a one-man publisher: meet John Chapple; Lycabettus Press. M. Duggan. por Pub W 211:43-4 Ja 17 '77

Mexico

Mexican publishing: a struggle against illiteracy, poverty and piracy—but with powerful government support. H. R. Lottman. il Pub W 211:42-4 Ja 10 '77

Norway

Report on Scandinavia. H. R. Lottman. il map Pub W 211:60+ My 9 '77

Russia

Books in 151 languages; publications of foreign books in Soviet languages. B. I. Stukalin. il UNESCO Courier 30:33-4 N '77
14 Soviet publishers have useful visit in U.S; Protocol question. M. Reuter. il Pub W 212: 11-13 N 28 '77
Soviet-produced art books make debut in U.S. P. Doebler. il Pub W 212:50 S 5 '77

Scandinavia

Report on Scandinavia. H. R. Lottman. il maps Pub W 211:39-43+ My 9 '77

Sweden

Report on Scandinavia. H. R. Lottman. il map Pub W 211:67-8+ My 9 '77

Switzerland

Publishing German books outside Germany. il Pub W 212:45+ S 12 '77

Underdeveloped areas

See Underdeveloped areas—Publishers and publishing

United States

AIGA explores role of typesetting firms in in-house operations. P. Doebler. Pub W 211:76 Mr 7 '77
All things bright and exuberant: St Martin's Press is 25 years old. M. Reuter. il pors Pub W 212:30-3 Ag 8 '77
America's press: too much power for too few? A. P. Sanoff. il U.S. News 83:27-33 Ag 15 '77
Arbitration ends dispute of Atheneum and Robert Massie. M. Reuter. Pub W 211:24 Ja 31 '77
Best titles of 1977: LJ's small press roundup; with directory of publishers. B. Katz. Lib J 102:2467-76 D 15 '77
British Printing, Raintree form U.S. company. Pub W 211:30+ Ja 10 '77
Confessions of a book publisher; Scribners; address, April 12, 1977. C. Scribner, Jr. por Pub W 211:46-8 Je 6 '77
Dutton at 125: past, present and future of a noted publisher. T. Weyr. il Pub W 212:32-6 N 21 '77
Feminist Press: new waves in Old Westbury. L. Van Gelder. il Ms 5:22 Ap '77
G. K. Hall releases more large print titles and, now, will sell them to the trade. R. Dahlin. Pub W 212:36 N 14 '77
Kissinger signs with Little, Brown for memoirs. il por Pub W 211:28 F 21 '77
Letter from the Bay Area. P. Holt. il Pub W 212:49-51 O 17 '77
Life and letters . . . Aristides. Am Scholar 46: 432+ Aut '77
Lively publishing scene in Boulder. S. Peckham. il Pub W 211:49-51 Je 6 '77
Majority of publishers oppose clearinghouses. W. D. Nelson. il Wilson Lib Bull 52:118-19 O '77
Markets & careers; Scrimshaw Press; interview, ed by H. Chapnick. F. Mitchell. il por Pop Phot 81:74+ Ag '77
New approaches to old ideas made two western success stories; Nilgiri Press. P. Holt. il Pub W 211:44-5 My 16 '77
News from the Summit is of a fall list that includes a reporter's view of Dasher Carter. R. Dahlin. Pub W 211:48-9 F 21 '77
News of new publishers (cont) Pub W 211:32+ Ja 10; 42 F 7; 68-9 F 28; 24 Ap 4; 35-6 Ap 25; 40-1 Je 27; 212:18+ Ag 15; 22-3 N 21 '77
Notes on trade. Colophon. Pub W 212:10 Jl 11; 6 Ag 15; 8 S 12; 10 O 31 '77
Publishers assail N.Y. times for Moscow Fair editorial. M. Reuter. Pub W 212:27 Jl 25 '77
Regnery sues three over new Schreiber book. M. Reuter. Pub W 211:28 Ja 10 '77
Richard Marek talks about his first list through Putnam, set to debut next March; interview, ed by R. Dahlin. R. Marek. Pub W 211:50 Ap 25 '77
Roger W. Straus, Jr, president of Farrar, Straus & Giroux, reflects on his firm's 30-year pursuit of literary excellence; interview. R. W. Straus, Jr. pors Pub W 211:55-9 F 7 '77

PUBLISHERS and publishing—United States —*Continued*
Roy Benjamin on premiums, incentives, special sales and copublishing ventures: interview, ed by D. Maryles. R. Benjamin. il por Pub W 213: 26-31 Ja 2 '78
St Martin's wins round against N.Y. obscenity law; case of Show me! M. Reuter. Pub W 212:23-4 D 12 '77
Small press movement. M. Haldeman. bibl por Lib J 102:2477-81 D 15 '77
Sussman & Sugar resigns Grove Press account. M. Reuter. Pub W 212:24 Jl 4 '77
Today's best book profits are in professional publishing. H. R. Most. Pub W 211:39 Mr 21 '77
Trade news; ed by R. Dahlin. See issues of Publishers weekly
Trade winds. W. Cole. See issues of Saturday review
Traditional book in the electronic age; address, November 10, 1977. H. S. Bailey, Jr. il pors Pub W 212:24-9 D 5 '77
Week; ed by M. Reuter. See issues of Publishers weekly
Year in review: 1976; symposium; with introd by J. F. Baker. Pub W 211:35-45+ F 14 '77
See also
Association of American Publishers
Doubleday & Company, Inc
Grolier, Inc
Grosset and Dunlap, Inc
Harcourt Brace Jovanovich, Inc
Harper & Row, Publishers, Inc
Random House, Inc
Reader's Digest Association, Inc
Simon & Schuster, Inc
Time, Inc
University presses
Viking Press, Inc
Women in publishing
PUBLISHERS for Employment, Inc. See Coalition of Publishers for Employment, Inc
PUBLISHERS warehouses. See Warehouses
PUBLISHERS weekly (periodical)
PW names Brandt and Bannon to top posts. M. Reuter. Pub W 212:23 D 26 '77
PUBLISHING. See Publishers and publishing
PUBLISHING-broadcasting multiple ownership. See Mass media—Multiple ownership
PUBLIX Book Mart, Cleveland. See Booksellers and bookselling—Ohio
PUCCINI, Giacomo
La Bohème. Reviews
Hi Fi 27:MA27 Jl '77 *
Hi Fi 27:MA15 Ag '77 *
New Yorker 53:141-3 Ap 18 '77 *
Opera N il 41:19-20+ Mr 19 '77
Opera N il 42:12-14+ D 24 '77 *
The cloak. J. Kestner. il Opera N 41:24-6 F 26 '77 *
Edgar. Review
Hi Fi 27:MA24-6 S '77 *
La fanciulla del West. Review
New Yorker 53:211-12 N 7 '77 *
Forzano remembered; a Trittico librettist. Opera N 41:14 F 26 '77 *
Getting involved; La Boheme performed by teenagers at Fieldston School in the Bronx. G. Lipton. il Opera N 42:46-7 N '77 *
Madama Butterfly. Reviews
Opera N 42:6 D 17 '77 *
Opera N il 42:14-16 D 17 '77 *
Opera N il 42:20+ D 17 '77 *
Musical events; Opera Orchestra of New York's concert version of Edgar. A. Porter. New Yorker 53:129 My 9 '77 *
New Tosca. R. V. Lucano. il Am Rec G 40:42-3 Je '77 *
Puccini on trial; enemies among his Italian critics. P. J. Zappa. por Opera N 42:28-30 D 17 '77 *
Ten commandments of Puccini; excerpt from Puccini, a self interpretation. L. Ricci. Opera N 42:18-19 D 17 '77 *
Tosca. Review
Hi Fi il 27:MA15 Ag '77 *
Il trittico. Review
Opera N il 41:15-16+ F 26 '77 *
Woe to the vanquished; Mürger's Vie de Bohème. J. Kestner. il Opera N 41:14-17 Mr 19 '77 *
PUDDING cake. See Cake
PUDDINGS
Old-fashioned steamed pudding—quickly in a microwave. il Sunset 159:170 D '77
PUDDLE jumpers (toys) See Toys
PUEBLO architecture
Astronomy, architecture, and adaptation at Pueblo Bonito. J. E. Reyman; reply with rejoinder. R. A. Williamson. bibl Science 197: 618-20 Ag 12 '77
PUEBLO incident, 1968
Pueblo postscript. E. Keerdoja. il pors Newsweek 91:11 Ja 16 '78
PUEBLO Indians
Cliff dwellers of the Mesa Verde; Anasazi Indians. D. Smith. il Am Hist Illus 12:4-9+ O '77
Pueblo population explosion. Sci N 111:133 F 26 '77
See also
Hopi Indians

PUERTO RICAN terrorists. See Terrorists, Puerto Rican
PUERTO RICANS in the United States
America's oubliette; Puerto Rican nationalists in federal penitentiaries. Nation 224:548 My 7 '77
Botanicas: Puerto Rican folk pharmacies; spiritism in New York City. M. A. Borrello and E. Mathias. il Natur Hist 86:64-73 bibl(p 116-17) Ag '77
Of bombs and bishops; Puerto Rican independence movement and the Episcopal Church. Time 109:59 Mr 14 '77
Resisting a probe; Interchurch Center in New York. Chr Today 21:55-6 Mr 18 '77
Who defines religion; investigation of the National Commission on Hispanic Affairs. J. M. Wall. Chr Cent 94:523-4 Je 1 '77
PUERTO RICO
Independence for Puerto Rico: the only solution. R. B. Martinez. For Affairs 55:561-83 Ap '77
See also
Aged—Puerto Rico
Architecture—Puerto Rico
Immigration and emigration—Puerto Rico
Investments, American—Puerto Rico
Opera—Puerto Rico
United Nations—Puerto Rico
Villages—Puerto Rico

Economic conditions

Puerto Rico, the 51st state? J. E. Maslow. New Repub 177:12-14 Jl 2 '77
Puerto Rico: trouble in the showcase. S. Lens. Progressive 41:13-19 Ag '77
Reports & comment: Puerto Rico. J. E. Maslow. il Atlantic 240:6+ Jl '77

Economic policy

Puerto Rico sketches a new economic policy. il por Bus W p 153-4+ S 26 '77

Nationalism

America's oubliette; Puerto Rican nationalists in federal penitentiaries. Nation 224:548 My 7 '77

Politics and government

Commonwealth's choice. J. B. Martin. il Harpers 225:17-20 D '77
Puerto Rico, the 51st state? J. E. Maslow. New Repub 177:12-14 Jl 2 '77
Should Puerto Rico be a state? interviews. pors U.S. News 82:47-8 Ap 11 '77
Statehood for Puerto Rico? Progressive 41:9-10 Mr '77
PUFF pastry. See Pastry
PUGA, Robustiano
This bonus is a real incentive. por Bus W p54+ Mr 14 '77 *
PUGET Sound
See also
San Juan Islands
PUGWASH Conference on Science and World Affairs
Arms race: a call to action. Bull Atom Sci 33:6 N '77
Peace and security in a changing world; reports of working groups. Bull Atom Sci 33:33-9 D '77
PUIG, Margarita, and others
Endogenous opiate receptor ligand: electrically induced release in the guinea pig ileum. bibl il Science 195:419-20 Ja 28 '77
PULITZER prizes
Pulitzer prizes to Roots and editor of Book world. M. Reuter. Pub W 211:31 Ap 25 '77
Small-town moxie; K. Herman of the Lufkin news. Nation 224:580 My 14 '77
PULLEY, Jerry L. See Doerrer, P. W. jt auth
PULLIAM, Russ
Nottingham '77: evangelicals eye unity. Chr Today 21:44-5 My 20 '77
PULMONARY embolism. See Embolism
PULMONARY metabolism. See Metabolism
PULP mills. See Paper mills
PULSARS
Anglo-Australian team observes Vela pulsar optically. M. S. Rothenberg. il Phys Today 30: 17-18 Jl '77
Flashes of light from the Vela pulsar. il Sky & Tel 54:26-7 Jl '77
Laboratory exercises in astronomy—pulsars. K. J. Gordon. il Sky & Tel 53:178-80 Mr '77
PULSATING showers. See Shower baths
PULSE
You can take your pulse; micro-computer. Sci Digest 81:85 Je '77
PULSE-duration modulation. See Pulse techniques (electronics)
PULSE generators. See Signal generators
PULSE techniques (electronics)
Pulse-width modulation for hi-fi. L. Feldman. il Radio-Electr 48:59-61 S '77
PUMA hunting
Lion in the rain-rinsed morning. J. Curtis. il Atlantic 240:67-73 S '77
PUMAS
Cougar attacks: new crisis for the big cats. B. Saile. il map Outdoor Life 160:66-8+ Ag '77

PUMP Room (restaurant) See Chicago—Hotels, restaurants, etc.

PUMP sprayers, Aerosol. See Pressure packaging

PUMPKIN faces. See Halloween

PUMPS

Can a water pump help in a drought? One firm thinks so. Consumer Rep 42:621-2 N '77

Pumps for moving gray water. il Sunset 158:287 My '77

Would you believe. . .water pump runs on its own water; hydraulic ram pump. il Pop Mech 147:57 Ap '77

See also

Heat pumps

Sewage pumps

PUNCH (beverage)

Ice ring keeps these punches cold. il Sunset 158:200 Je '77

Parties with punch; wine punch. D. Tobias. Am Home 80:55 Je '77

PUNCH and Toby; drama. See Cochrane, L.

PUNIC wars

Burning question; firing of Roman fleet by burning mirror in Second Punic War. Sci Am 236: 64 Je '77

PUNISHMENT

Crime or punishment? Islamic law. il Time 110: 38 Jl 25 '77

Let the punishment fit the crime. P. Brickman. Psychol Today 10:29 My '77

Making punishment fit the crime. M. Greenfield. il Newsweek 90:144 N 21 '77

See also

Capital punishment

Corporal punishment

Prisons

School discipline

Torture

PUNISHMENT (psychology)

Behavioral history as a determinant of the effects of *d*-amphetamine on punished behavior. J. E. Barrett. bibl il Science 198:67-9 O 7 '77

PUNITIVE Expedition to Mexico, 1916. See United States—History—Punitive Expedition to Mexico, 1916

PUNK rock. See Rock music (songs, etc)

PUNK rock groups. See Rock groups

PUNKE, Harold H.

Crash and creativeness in education. Clearing H 50:306-8 Mr '77

PUNS and punning

Chaucerian crux; Troilus and Criseyde. W. Frost. Yale R 66:551-61 Je '77

PUPPET Opera. See Puppets and puppet plays

PUPPETS and puppet plays

Get into the act: build a puppet theater; make puppets too. P. Angell. il Pop Mech 147:128-30+ Mr '77

Magical, madcap Muppets; J. Henson. J. Culhane. il por Read Digest 111:23-5+ S '77

Not ready for the rocking chair: no retiring for Christmas; D. Rankin's personal story. H. S. Davenport. il por Ret Liv 17:32-4 D '77

Perspectives: Llords International performed May 31-June 26. N. M. Stoop. il por Dance Mag 51:98 S '77

Piscataway's puppet program. L. S. Hunter. il pors SLJ 23:32-4 My '77

Puppets. S. Kusachi and F. Loetterle. il Design (US) 78:18-19 Summ '77

Puppets, an educational experience. E. Divone. il Sch Arts 77:50-1 S '77

Puppets are fun. H. C. Randall. il Sch Arts 76:14-15 Je '77

Puppets in Los Angeles are serious (?) business; California events. il Sunset 159:80-3 Ag '77

Santa Claus hand puppet. il Design (US) 79: 28-9 N '77

What's happening; the Muppets. G. Shalit. il Ladies Home J 94:10 O '77

Wonderful product; Puppet Opera at the University of Arkansas at Little Rock. B. Thebom. il por Opera N 42:40-1 N '77

Texts

One eye, two eyes and three eyes; dramatization of fairy tale by the Brothers Grimm. R. C. Lavin. Plays 36:58-64 Mr '77

Punch and Toby; drama. L. Cochrane. Plays 36:76-8 My '77

Three billy goats Gruff; dramatization of folktale. D. C. Jones. Plays 37:16, 77-80 N '77

PUPPIES. See Dogs

PURCELL, Carl

Traveler's camera. See issues of Popular photography

PURCELL, Henry

Selected works conducted by P. Ledger. J. W. Barker. Am Rec G 41:27-9 N '77 *

PURCELL, Philip F.

Basic guide to pitfalls in foreign contracts. Archit Rec 161:69 Je '77

PURCHASE College. See New York (state). State University—College at Purchase

PURCHASING

See also

Consumption (economics)

Shopping and shoppers

See also subhead Purchasing under various subjects, e.g. Loudspeakers—Purchasing

PURCHASING, Cooperative

Join forces for big buying bargains; local governments. il Am City & County 92:71-2 S '77

PURCHASING, Government

COFPAES meeting indicates support to retain Brooks Law; COFPAES renews its costs and audits argument; Committee on Federal Procurement of Architect-Engineer Services. W. Hickman. Archit Rec 161:34, 75 Ap '77

Join forces for big buying bargains; local governments. il Am City & County 92:71-2 S '77

See also

United States—General Accounting Office

United States—General Services Administration

PURCHASING, Household

Competent cook's pantry. Redbook 149:164 My '77

Introducing: pushers that buy your products; food shoppers. Farm J 101:38 Ja '77

See also

Consumer education

PURCHASING, Military. See United States—Air Force—Procurement; United States—Army—Procurement; United States—Coast Guard—Procurement; United States—Navy—Procurement

PURCHASING, Municipal

See also

Municipal contracts

New York (city)—Purchase, Department of

PURCHASING departments

Big rip-off in purchasing. R. Levy. il Duns R 109:76-7+ Mr '77

PURDAH

Purdah in India: life behind the veil. D. W. Jacobson. il por map Nat Geog 152:270-86 Ag '77

PURDY, Susan

Glorious Easter eggs. il Ladies Home J 94:80+ Ap '77

PURIFICATION of water. See Water purification

PURKERSON, L. Lee, and Morrow, Duncan

Open tap for Taylor Slough. il Parks & Rec 12: 31a-34a F '77

PURPLE martins. See Martins

PURSES

Pocket wallets and credit card cases. il Consumers Res Mag 60:23-7 Ag '77

PURSUIT of happiness. See Happiness

PUSEY, Nathan Marsh

Four stories of theology; with editorial comment. T. H. Stahel. America 136:inside cover, 230-3 Mr 19 '77 *

PUSH for Excellence (program) See Student achievements

PUSH Pin Studios, Inc

Push Pin conspiracy. H. T. P. Hayes. il N Y Times Mag p 19-22 Mr 6 '77

PUSKARICH, Mike

UMW's turf slowly erodes. il por Bus W p74-5 D 19 '77 *

PUT and call transactions

How arbitrageurs hedge with options. D. G. Santry. Bus W p 120 O 17 '77

How to trade options. il Bus W p77-9+ Mr 7 '77

Many strategies of trading in puts. Bus W p78 Je 13 '77

One for the bears. D. Pauly. il Newsweek 89: 78+ Je 13 '77

Options-market fraud? The SEC is suspicious. il U.S. News 83:81 O 31 '77

Options race goes to the Amex. Bus W p76+ F 7 '77

Puts. A. Tobias. Esquire 88:30 N '77

Safety factor in buying options. il Bus W p74-5 D 26 '77

State of war in options trading; competition between Chicago Board Options Exchange and the American Stock Exchange. Bus W p60 Mr 7 '77

Suckers wanted. H. Seneker. il Forbes 120:31-2 D 15 '77

PUT and call transactions mutual funds. See Investment trusts

PUTMAN, John J.

City around Red Square: Moscow. il map Nat Geog 153:2-24+ Ja '78

West Germany: continuing miracle. il map Nat Geog 152:148-81 Ag '77

PUTNAM, Patrick F.

Bananas in the bushes. il por Sports Illus 47:32-5 S 12 '77

Boxing (cont) Sports Illus 46:96+ My 23; 47:72+ O 31 '77

Classic win for a precocious pup. il Sports Illus 46:18-19 Mr 14 '77

College football (cont) Sports Illus 47:62+ S 12 '77

College hockey. il Sports Illus 46:46+ F 7 '77

Day the gold turned green. il Sports Illus 46: 18-19 F 14 '77

How to get zapped and still be a champ. il pors Sports Illus 46:28-9 My 2 '77

PUTNAM, Patrick F.—*Continued*
Jeemy Young! Jeemy Young! Jeemy Young! il pors Sports Illus 46:22-3 Mr 28 '77
March of the hit paraders. il Sports Illus 47:22-5 S 26 '77
Once more to the well. il pors Sports Illus 47: 20-3 O 10 '77
Star bows out, a star bows in. pors Sports Illus 47:20-1 Ag 8 '77
Staying at the top of his class. il pors Sports Illus 46:20-2 Ja 31 '77
This was the start of something big. il pors Sports Illus 46:18-19 Ja 24 '77
Win some, lose some, split the rest. il pors Sports Illus 47:36-8+ N 14 '77

PUVIS DE CHAVANNES, Pierre
Puvis de Chavannes: the alternative. P. Schneider. bibl il Art in Am 65:94-8 My '77 •

PUZO, Mario
Las Vegas: city built by losers; excerpt from Inside Las Vegas. il Holiday 58:32-3+ Ap '77

PUZZLES
Mathematical games; M. Berrocal's interlocking sculpture as a puzzle. M. Gardner. il Sci Am 238:14-16+ Ja '78
Selection of games, puzzles and toys: sidelines that educate and entertain. D. Maryles. il Pub W 211:41-52 Mr 7 '77
Strategy puzzles you can make. D. Ashe and C. Scott. il Bet Hom & Gard 55:129 N '77
See also
Crossword puzzles

PYE, Edward Kendall
Can we live forever? por Sat Eve Post 249:35+ Mr '77; Same abr. Sci Digest 82:14-15 S '77

PYGMALION; opera. See Rameau, J. P.

PYGMIES
Pygmies go to war; Zaïre conflict. il Newsweek 89:60 My 2 '77

PYJAS, Stanislaw
Death in Cracow. F. Willey and P. Martin. Newsweek 89:50 My 30 '77 •

PYORRHEA. See Gums—Diseases

PYRAMID (form)
Crack in the pyramid. B. D. Miller. il Mech Illus 73:32-3 S '77
Strange truth about pyramid power. B. D. Miller. il Mech Illus 73:150-3 Ap '77

Anecdotes, facetiae, satire, etc.

Pointy-power. M. E. Marty. Chr Cent 94:239 Mr 9 '77

PYRAMID of Kukulcan. See Chichén Itzá

PYROELECTRIC effect in plants. See Electrophysiology of plants

PYROLYSIS
Pyrolysis—a true alternative for solid waste disposal. il Am City & County 92:81-2 S '77
Resource recovery in trouble again; Seattle pyrolysis project. il Am City & County 92:9 My '77
Sludge, garbage may fuel California sewage plant; Contra Costa County wastewater reclamation plant. R. B. Sieger and B. D. Bracken. il Am City & County 92:37-8 Ja '77

PYRROLIZIDINE alkaloids. See Alkaloids

PYTEL, Diana Milesko-. See Milesko-Pytel, D.

PYZEL, Mike
(ed) See Kaster, H. B. Weather course

Q

al-QADDAFI, Muammar
Libya's Qadhafi charges...; interview, ed by D. B. Richardson. por U.S. News 83:36-7 Ag 8 '77
about
Foothold for Kaddafi? K. Willenson and R. Moreau. por Newsweek 89:41-2+ Ap 25 '77 •
Revenge in the desert. pors map Time 110:20 Ag 1 '77 •

QOBOZA, Percy
Black journalists in Johannesburg. A. Silk. Nation 225:454-6 N 5 '77 •
In a South African prison. R. Javers. Commonweal 104:808-9 D 23 '77 •
Making of a man. L. Sloane. il por Newsweek 90:58 O 31 '77 •
Notes and comment. New Yorker 53:41-2 N 28 '77 •
Rewards of moderation. New Repub 177:5-6 O 29 '77 •
Words from a silenced World. il por Time 110:51 O 31 '77 •

QUACKS and quackery
Amateur hour; alleged surgery performed by medical supply salesman W. MacKay at Smithtown General Hospital. il Time 110:94 N 14 '77
Amateur surgeons; alleged surgery performed by medical supply salesman W. MacKay at Smithtown General Hospital, N.Y. M. Clark and D. Shapiro. il por Newsweek 90:125 N 14 '77
Health robbers offers an Rx for quack medicine. Consumer Rep 42:67 F '77
Medical quacks: today's merchants of menace. R. D. Duncan. Ret Liv 17:25-6+ F '77
Quackery. P. K. Burkhalter. Sci Digest 82:36-7+ S '77
Salesmen in the operating room. il Forbes 120: 33 D 1 '77

QUADRI, Charles J. Jr, and Vollmer, A. H.
Resurrection of Fort Lee. il Parks & Rec 12:30-1+ D '77

QUAHOGS. See Clams

QUAIL Botanical Gardens, San Diego County, Calif. See Botanical gardens

QUAIL breeding. See Game birds—Breeding

QUAIL shooting
John Bailey: keeper of the faith. B. Tarrant. il pors Field & S 82:168-72 O '77
Percentage quail hunting; excerpt from Charley Dickey's bobwhite quail hunting. C. Dickey. il Outdoor Life 160:61-3+ N '77

Anecdotes, facetiae, satire, etc.

Uncle Wesley and the cemetery quail. R. Starnes. Outdoor Life 159:10+ Ap '77

QUAILS
Altered yolk structure and reduced hatchability of eggs from birds fed single doses of petroleum oils. C. R. Grau and others. bibl il Science 195:779-81 F 25 '77
Creating your own quail covey. N. Sisley. il Field & S 81:28+ Mr '77
Improve the lot of quail; managing populations. B. Brister. il Field & S 81:109-10+ Ap '77
See also
Cookery—Game

QUAKER State Oil Refining Corporation
Quaker State's marketing coup. N. Howard. il Duns R 110:51-2 O '77

QUAKERS. See Friends, Society of

QUALIFICATIONS of librarians. See College librarians—Qualifications; Librarians—Qualifications

QUALITY control
Controlling just noticeable differences in quality. J. M. Kamen. Harvard Bus R 55:12+ N '77
Is quality out of control? W. D. Vinson and D. F. Heany. bibl f il Harvard Bus R 55:114-22 N '77

QUALITY of life. See Life

QUALITY of products
Handbook of buying issue. il Consumers Res Mag 60:1-224 O '77
Institute report:
Best-buy guide to toaster ovens. il Good H 185:164+ O '77
Buying and caring for back-to-school clothes. Good H 185:248 S '77
Buying guide to food processors. il Good H 185:230+ N '77
Buying guide to outdoor carpets. il Good H 184:158 My '77
Donut makers. il Good H 186:116 Ja '78
Fabulous fakes; imitation leather, wool, fur and metallic fabrics. Good H 185:228 D '77
Four ways to cut your home-heating costs. il Good H 185:240+ O '77
Hand-held hair dryers and stylers. il Good H 184:210+ My '77
How to buy your next pair of boots. il Good H 185:236 S '77
How to save $300 a year on utility bills. Good H 185:266+ O '77
Making yogurt the easy way; yogurt makers. il Good H 185:140+ Jl '77
Microwave ovens. il Good H 185:166+ Ag '77
Mini-fryers. il Good H 185:238 D '77
Now! A better, quicker way to clean carpets; steam cleaning machines. il Good H 185:188 N '77
Now they've put the panties in panty hose! il Good H 185:182+ S '77
Read me! care instructions on fabric labels. Good H 185:166 Jl '77
Tablecloths—how to buy, how to keep them beautiful. Good H 185:186 N '77
Tape it! A buying guide to those handy cassette recorders. R. F. McGillick. il Good H 184:182+ Ap '77
Wall coverings—how to choose, how to use. il Good H 184:160 Mr '77
Warmest bathrobes of all. Good H 185:184 D '77
When the label reads medicated: what it really means. il Good H 185:220+ S '77
Window shades. il Good H 184:160+ Je '77
1978 buying guide issue. il Consumer Rep 42:1-431 D '77
Speaker for the house. C. Montgomery. See issues of Good housekeeping
They don't make 'em like they used to. J. Main. Read Digest 110:167-8+ Mr '77
See also
Quality control

QUANTUM electrodynamics
Elegant inquiry into the electron. Sci N 111:101 F 12 '77
Evidence for fractional electric charge. il Sci N 111:276 Ap 30 '77
Flaw in the diamond of QED. Sci N 111:20 Ja 8 '77
New measurement of magnetic-moment anomaly tests QED. J. T. Scott. il Phys Today 30:17+ Mr '77

QUANTUM mechanical tunneling. See Tunneling (physics)

QUANTUM theory
Quantum mechanics of black holes. S. W. Hawking. il Sci Am 236:34-40 bibl(p 132) Ja '77
Quantum statistics and liquid helium-3—helium-4 mixtures. E. G. D. Cohen. bibl il Science 197:11-16 Jl 1 '77
Will supergravity unify quantum theory with general relativity? G. B. Lubkin. Phys Today 30:17-19 Je '77

QUARANTINE
Way of forestalling epidemics and rescuing their victims; Mobile Quarantine Facility. il Space World N-10-166:31 O '77

QUARKS. See Particles (nuclear physics)

QUARREL (periodical)
Quarterly report. . . T. H. Middleton. il Sat R 5:49 Ja 7 '78

QUARRELS
Bystanders' creed: don't meddle in family fights; study by R. Lance Shotland and Margret K. Straw. J. Gaylin. il Psychol Today 10:29-30 F '77
How much do I love thee? Let me count the change. . . ; family money quarrels. V. Grey. il Am Home 80:82-3 F '77
How to make love not war; counseling for unmarried couples. M. Fabe. Mademoiselle 83:119+ D '77
How to stop those same old family fights. W. W. Dyer. Read Digest 111:25-8 O '77
Some practical and sensible advice for breaking the bickering habit. J. Marks. Seventeen 36:136-7+ N '77
When a family fights over finances. M. Daly. Bet Hom & Gard 55:154+ Je '77

QUARRIES and quarrying
Asbestos: trouble in the air from Maryland rock quarry. L. J. Carter. map Science 197:237-40 Jl 15 '77
Environmental asbestos pollution related to use of quarried serpentine rock. A. N. Rohl and others. bibl il Science 196:1319-22 Je 17 '77; Reply with rejoinder. J. T. Hack. 197:716+ Ag 19 '77

QUARRY; ballet. See Ballet reviews—Single works

QUART, Leonard
On screen. Intellect 105:399; 106:78, 159, 245 Je, Ag, O, D '77
(ed) See Price, R. Studs Lonigan in the Bronx
(ed) See Wesker, A. Making the case for Shylock

QUARTERBACKS. See Football players

QUARTETS, Instrumental
Last days in Russia; Borodin Quartet; tr by A. Vergun. R. Dubinsky. il Hi Fi 27:MA10-11+ N '77

QUARTETS, String. See String quartets

QUARTETTO Italiano. See String quartets

QUASAR Electronics Corporation. See Television apparatus industry

QUASARS
Far-out quasars. Time 111:55-6 Ja 16 '78
Five new far-out quasars found. il Sci N 112:69-70 Jl 30 '77
Hole in the middle of the galaxy. D. E. Thomsen il Sci N 111:121+ F 19 '77
Quasar 3C273 ultraviolet spectrum. il Sci N 112:199 S 24 '77

QUASI-War. See United States—History—War with France, 1798-1800

QUATERNARY period. See Paleontology—Quaternary

I QUATTRO rusteghi; opera. See Wolf-Ferrari, E.

QUBE cable television system. See CATV system

QUEBEC (province)
See also
Laurentian Mountains

Economic conditions

Business has the jitters in Quebec. H. E. Meyer. il Fortune 96:238-42+ O '77
Canada: business warns Quebec. il Bus W p44 My 23 '77
English-speaking rush to leave Quebec. il Bus W p62+ Ag 22 '77
Lévesque checked. por Time 109:44 F 7 '77

Labor laws and legislation

See Labor laws and legislation—Canada

Languages

English spoken here; Stanbridge East, Quebec. R. Manning. il Newsweek 89:63 My 9 '77
Happy birthday, bonne chance; proposed language law. il Time 110:38 Jl 11 '77
Quebec's language problem. R. E. Santoni. Progressive 41:49-50 D '77
Separation threat fuels Quebec crisis. W. E. Greening. Chr Cent 94:754 Ag 31 '77

Nationalism

Canada's time of troubles. B. Hutchison. For Affairs 56:175-89 O '77
Cool it, Canada! E. M. Bronfman. por Newsweek 90:11 S 26 '77
France with love; R. Lévesque's visit. il por Newsweek 90:67 N 14 '77
Gallic mischief; visit of R. Lévesque to France. Nation 225:547 N 26 '77
House divided; with interviews with P. E. Trudeau and R. Lévesque. R. Carroll and R. Manning. il Newsweek 90:51+ D 5 '77
Independence for Quebec: the debate gets sharper; with interview with R. Lévesque. il map U.S. News 83:69-72 S 26 '77
Institution design and the separatist impulse: Quebec and the antebellum American South. M. V. Levine. bibl f Ann Am Acad 433:60-72 S '77
Mountie morass. il Time 110:45 N 14 '77
Quebec and the Canadian political crisis. K. McRoberts. bibl f Ann Am Acad 433:19-31 S '77
Quebec's Jews: caught in the middle. R. R. Wisse and I. Cotler. Commentary 64:55-9 S '77
Specter of separatism. S. Talbott. Time 110:31-2 D 26 '77
Taste of Quebec. E. Kohak. il Commonweal 104:76-8 F 4 '77

Politics and government

Canada and separatism. R. E. Santoni. Progressive 41:10 F '77
Canada: to be or not to be. D. MacDonald. il Read Digest 111:66-70 Ag '77
Canada: trouble above the border. R. H. Heindel. il por Intellect 105:226-7 F '77
I am a worried Canadian; address, December 9, 1976. F. D. Moores. Vital Speeches 43:162-5 Ja 1 '77
Is Canada falling apart? C. W. Gonick. Current 191:38-47 Mr '77
Obsession with unity. A. Astrachan. New Repub 177:21-3 Ag '20 '77; Same. Current 196:46-52 O '77
Oh! Canada! Lament for a divided country. M. Richler. map Atlantic 240:41-55 D '77
One Canada—or two? P. T. White. il map Nat Geog 151:436-65 Ap '77
Quebec; address, January 25, 1977. R. Lévesque. Vital Speeches 43:283-7 F 15 '77
Quebec in a quandary. il Sr Schol 109:18-20+ F 10 '77
Separation and Quebec. K. M. Glazier. bibl f Cur Hist 72:154-7+ Ap '77
Separation threat fuels Quebec crisis. W. E. Greening. Chr Cent 94:754 Ag 31 '77
We're a satellite; excerpts from interview, ed by A. de Borchgrave. R. Lévesque. il por Newsweek 90:54-5 D 5 '77
Why Quebec wants out—there are two nations here; interview, ed by K. M. Chrysler. R. Lévesque. il por U.S. News 83:70-2 S 26 '77

QUEBECOR Inc. See Publishers and publishing—Canada

QUEEN Elizabeth 2 (ship) See Ocean liners

QUEEN Ida
Queen of the Cajun sound. N. R. Spitzer. il por Ms 6:27-8 N '77 *

QUEEN Mary (ship) See Ocean liners

QUEEN Rachel. See Canevaro, B.

QUEENS, N.Y.
Around City Hall. A. Logan. New Yorker 53:84-90 Je 27 '77

Airports

See New York (city)—Airports

Education

Reshaping secondary education; International Baccalaureate program at Francis Lewis High School, Queens, N.Y. J. R. Adams. Educ Digest 43:2-4 D '77

Foreign population

Colombian outpost in New York City; Jackson Heights, Queens. E. M. Chaney. bibl il Society 14:60-4 S '77

Hotels, restaurants, etc.

Rockaway; Park End Tavern restaurant. New Yorker 53:31-2 Ap 4 '77

Housing

Town that refused to panic; integration of Laurelton section. J. Cook. McCalls 104:71 Jl '77

Restaurants

See Queens, N.Y.—Hotels, restaurants, etc.

QUEENSBOROUGH-59th Street Bridge. See New York (city)—Bridges

QUEIJO, Jon
Harvesting a nuisance. il Environment 19:25-9 Mr '77

QUEMOY (island)
Paper tigers. F. Willey. il Newsweek 89:51 Mr 7 '77
QUERCETIN
Mutagenic activity of quercetin and related compounds. L. F. Bjeldanes and G. W. Chang. bibl il Science 197:577-8 Ag 5 '77
QUERCITRIN
Diabetic cataracts and flavonoids. S. D. Varma and others. bibl il Science 195:205-6 Ja 14 '77
QUESTER, George Herman
Reducing the incentives to proliferation. Ann Am Acad 430:70-81 Mr '77
QUESTIONNAIRES
Class and style; poll of Ebony readers. il Ebony 33:33-6+ N '77
Democracy-in-action dept: Car and Driver 1978 Readers' Choice Poll. il Car & Dr 23:35-41 D '77
English classroom 1977; EJ readership survey. C. Gillis and others. il Engl J 66:55-8 Ja; 20-6 S '77
How do you like your job? il Psychol Today 11: 72-9 S '77
How do you really feel about having children? questionnaire. il Redbook 149:117-19+ S '77
How happy are you? il Good H 184:49-50 Mr '77
Money: the subject harder to talk about than sex. C. Tavris. Ms 6:63-7 N '77
Other dimension of your life: faith, values, morals. McCalls 105:27-8 Ja '78
What sex means to the man you love; questionnaire. il Redbook 149:43-50 Je '77
What's happening to the American family? il Bet Hom & Gard 55:125-8 S; 119-22 O '77
What's the right age for retirement? il Ret Liv 16:18 D '76; 17:22-5 Ap '77
QUESTOR Corporation
Era ends in big-league baseball. il por Nations Bus 65:38 Ap '77
QUETICO-Superior Region
Administration backs strong wilderness plan for BWCA. il Nat Parks & Con Mag 51:22-3 N '77
Crisis in the Canoe country; Boundary Waters Canoe Area; with editorial comment. M. L. Heinselman. il maps Liv Wildn 40:3, 12-24 Ja '77
Noisy environmental fight over a quiet wilderness; restrictions against snowmobiles and motorboats in Boundary Waters Canoe Area. H. R. Kennedy. il map U.S. News 83:61-2 O 31 '77
North country forests get six-month reprieve; Boundary Waters Canoe Area. Nat Parks & Con Mag 51:26 Mr '77
Passionate suitors for a wild paradise; Boundary Waters Canoe Area. W. O. Johnson. il por Sports Illus 47:8, 50-2+ O 10 '77
Quetico-Superior: international negotiators must head off pollution of borderland wilderness; Boundary Waters Canoe Area. Nat Parks & Con Mag 51:20-1+ O '77
QUIGG, Philip W.
One earth. See issues of Audubon
QUILTS
Baby sleeps on or rides in this sunshine quilt. il Sunset 159:170+ O '77
Buying quilt fabrics by mail. il Bet Hom & Gard 55:79+ Ap '77
Collecting: Amish quilts. B. S. Janos. il House B 119:24+ Mr '77
Design your own historical quilt. J. H. Finch. il Design (US) 78:2-6 mid-Wint '77
Five thousand dollar quilt. S. Wilcox. il Hobbies 81:114-15 F '77
Grandmother's flower garden to quilt as you go. N. Lindemeyer and others. il Bet Hom & Gard 55:104-5+ Ap '77
Mother Goose stitch 'n stuffs: nursery rhyme dolls and quilt. N. Lindemeyer. il Bet Hom & Gard 55:130-1 N '77
Quilts. il Hobbies 82:116-17 Jl '77
Quilts for now from long ago. C. K. Toth. il Good H 184:110-13 Ap '77
Ruffle up some charm. il House & Gard 149: 78-9+ Ag '77
Sew up a quick quilt. il Seventeen 36:42 N '77
QUIMME, Peter
Sweet & low: good dessert wine buys. House B 119:131+ O '77
Taking the cap off bottled water. il House & Gard 149:106+ Jl '77
QUINDLEN, Anna
He was there. il pors N Y Times Mag p40-3 S 11 '77
Hello, doggy! il N Y Times Mag p38-9 My 15 '77
Starring mothers. il N Y Times Mag p50-1+ Ag 21 '77
QUINLAN, Karen Anne
Karen Ann a year later. E. Keerdoja. Newsweek 89:10 Mr 21 '77 *
QUINN, Edward
(tr) See Küng, H. Finding sense when it makes no sense
QUINN, Jane M.
Elementary school level sex education. Educ Digest 42:29-32 Ja '77
QUINN, John Raphael, Abp
Bishops' bishop. por Time 110:114 N 28 '77 *
QUINN, Peter J.
Humane education: a forgotten mandate. Educ Digest 43:60-1 S '77
QUINN, Sally
Carter style—beanies, beer, and Jesus. Ms 6: 106 Ja '78
Joy of being 30. Harp Baz 110:133+ O '77
QUINN, Susan
Elma Lewis: keeping African culture alive in Boston. il por Ms 5:14-15+ My '77
QUINOLINE
Alcohol drinking: abnormal intake caused by tetrahydropapaveroline in brain. R. D. Myers and C. L. Melchoir. bibl il Science 196:554-6 Ap 29 '77
Chemical cause of alcoholism; THP in brain. Sci N 111:327 My 21 '77
QUINTERO, José
José, Jason, and Gene. S. Lawson. il pors Horizon 21:36-42 Ja '78 *
Touch of the tragic. B. Gelb. il pors N Y Times Mag p43-5+ D 11 '77 *
QUINTESSENCE (firm) See Phonograph record industry
QUINTETS, Wind. See Wind quintets
QUINTO, Frances
Teacher-made tests—an alternative to standardized tests. Todays Educ 66:52-3 Mr '77
—See McKenna B. H. jt auth
QUIRK, Paul J.
Origins of the transportation cartel. bibl il Intellect 105:442-4 Je '77
QUIRKS. See Idiosyncrasies
QUIRÓS, Daniel Oduber. See Oduber Quirós, D.
QUITO, Ecuador
Quito; church architecture and decoration of the Colonial period. J. R. Chiriboga; H. Crespo Toral. il map Americas 29:S1-12 Ap '77
QUIZZES. See Information tests
QUOTAS, Employment. See Minorities—Employment
QUOTATION
Quotesmanship. A. Spikol. Writers Digest 57: 11-12+ My; 12+ Je '77
QUOTATIONS
Quotable quotes. See issues of Reader's digest
See also
Proverbs
QUOTRON Systems, Inc. See Computer industry

R

RANN (Research Applied to National Needs) program. See United States—National Science Foundation
RASD. See American Library Association—Reference and Adult Services Division
RCA Corporation
Product is born: RCA's mobile communications system. A. L. Morner. il Fortune 95:124-9+ F '77
RCA off the roller coaster, onto the escalator? J. Grigsby. por Forbes 119:25-7 F 15 '77
RCA's new vista: the bottom line. il Bus W 38-44 Jl 4 '77
See also
Hertz
RDF. See Radio direction finders
RDS. See Respiratory distress syndrome
REIT. See Real estate investment trusts
RFE. See Radio Free Europe
RFI (radio frequency interference) See Radio interference
R.H. Macy and Company. See Macy, R. H. and Company
RIF (Reading is Fundamental) program. See Childrens reading; Young adults reading
R. J. Reynolds Industries, Inc. See Reynolds, R. J. Industries, Inc
RNA
Analysis of chicken ribosomal RNA genes and construction of lambda hybrids containing gene fragments. W. McClements and A. M. Skalka. bibl il Science 196:195-7 Ap 8 '77
Cell-free modulation of proinsulin synthesis. P. T. Lomedico and G. F. Saunders. bibl il Science 198:620-2 N 11 '77
Cloned ribosomal RNA genes from chloroplasts of euglena gracilis. M. I. Lomax and others. bibl il Science 196:202-5 Ap 8 '77
Cloning of yeast transfer RNA genes in escherichia coli. J. S. Beckmann and others. bibl il Science 196:205-8 Ap 8 '77
Human globin messenger RNA: importance of cloning for structural analysis. J. T. Wilson and others. bibl il Science 196:200-2 Ap 8 '77
Metal mutagens and carcinogens affect RNA synthesis rates in a distinct manner. D. J. Hoffman and S. K. Niyogi. bibl il Science 198:513-14 N 4 '77
New theory of protein evolution. il Sci N 111: 228 Ap 9 '77
One strand equivalent of the escherichia coli genome is transcribed: complexity and abundance classes of mRNA. W. E. Hahn and others. bibl il Science 197:582-5 Ag 5 '77

RNA—*Continued*
Three-dimensional structure of transfer RNA. A. Rich and S. H. Kim. il Sci Am 238:52-62 Ja '78
Viral messenger structure: some surprising new developments. J. L. Marx. il Science 197:853-5+ Ag 26 '77
RNA polymerase. See Polymerase
RNA tumor forming viruses. See Tumor viruses
ROM (read-only memory) See Electronic circuits, Integrated
ROTC. See United States—Reserve Officers Training Corps
RPV (remotely piloted vehicle) See Airplanes, Drone
RSV (research safety vehicles) See Automobiles, Experimental
RVs. See Recreational vehicles
RAAB, Lawrence
After Edward Hopper; poem. New Yorker 53:75 Jl 11 '77
about
Comment. J. D. McClatchy. Poetry 130:49-50 Ap '77 *
RABBIT hunting
Blunt hunt for cottontails. R. Tinsley. il Outdoor Life 159:82-3+ F '77
Happiness is. . .beagles and rabbits. D. M. Duffey. il Outdoor Life 160:196+ N '77
Which is the best all-round dog? D. M. Duffey. il Outdoor Life 159:78-81+ My '77
Anecdotes, facetiae, satire, etc.
Dog day afternoon. R. Starnes. Outdoor Life 159:10+ F '77
RABBITS
Cottontail rabbit. J. Dell. il por Conservationist 32:13-15 S '77
Understanding your pet. M. W. Fox. McCalls 104:60+ Mr '77
See also
Cookery—Game
Hares
RABBITT, Thomas
Casino beach; poem. Esquire 87:58 My '77
RABBOT, Boris
Letter to Brezhnev; tr by M. Petrov. il pors N Y Times Mag p48+ N 6 '77
RABE, David
Basic training of Pavlo Hummel. Reviews
Nation 224:602 My 14 '77 *
New Yorker 53:91 My 2 '77 *
Time 109:50 My 9 '77 *
RABIANSKI, Nancy Anne
How to encourage the unwilling reader of fiction. il Engl J 66:64-9 F '77
RABIES
La rage in Europe. M. Clark and T. Nater. Newsweek 90:52 S 12 '77
RABIN, Leah
Rabin's sudden exit. A. Deming and M. J. Kubic. il pors map Newsweek 89:37-8+ Ap 18 '77 *
RABIN, Yitzhak
Prime Minister Rabin of Israel visits Washington; exchange of remarks, March 7, 1977. Dept State Bull 76:311 Ap 4 '77
Rabin sums it up; excerpts from interview, ed by M. J. Kubic. il por Newsweek 90:51 Jl 4 '77
about
Israel's self-inflicted wounds. Y. Marcus. il pors N Y Times Mag p26-9+ Ap 24 '77 *
Jerusalem; the race for change. M. J. Kubic. il por Newsweek 89:29 F 21 '77 *
Rabin just makes it. R. Carroll and J. Kubic. il pors Newsweek 89:38+ Mr 7 '77 *
Rabin on the razor's edge. il por Time 109:32+ Mr 7 '77 *
Rabin's distress. M. Kondracke. New Repub 176:15-18 Mr 12 '77 *
Resignation
Rabin's sudden exit. A. Deming and M. J. Kubic. il pors map Newsweek 89:37-8+ Ap 18 '77
Sad downfall of Yitzhak Rabin. il por Time 109:23-4 Ap 18 '77
Visit to the United States, 1977
Go in peace. R. Carroll and M. J. Kubic. il por Newsweek 89:34 Mr 14 '77
Prime Minister Rabin of Israel visits Washington; exchange of remarks, March 7, 1977. J. Carter; Y. Rabin. Dept State Bull 76:310-11 Ap 4 '77
RABINOWICZ, Ernest
Exoelectrons; with biographical sketch. il Sci Am 236:16, 74-82 bibl(p 132) Ja '77
RABINOWITZ, Dorothy
Hostage mentality. Commentary 63:70-2 Je; 64:9 Ag '77
RABINOWITZ, Richard
Baseball in the mind. New Repub 177:24-5 Jl 23 '77
RABUCK, John. See Scannella, A. jt auth
RACAL Electronics Ltd-Milgo Electronic Corporation merger. See Electronic industries—Acquisitions and mergers
RACCOON hunting
Bluetick hounds: bawling and treeing. G. Norman. il Esquire 89:16+ Ja '78
RACCOONS
Raccoons; with reproduction of painting by H. W. Trimm. E. Suss. Conservationist 31:23-5 N '76
RACE discrimination
Teaching kids the new discrimination. M. Greenfield. Newsweek 90:80 Jl 4 '77
See also
Blacks—Segregation
Discrimination in education
Discrimination in employment
International Day for the Elimination of Racial Discrimination
Racism
United Nations—Committee on the Elimination of Racial Discrimination
United Nations—Sub-Commission on Prevention of Discrimination and Protection of Minorities
RACE horse training. See Horse training
RACE horses. See Horses, Race
RACE improvement. See Eugenics
RACE prejudice
See also
Anti-Semitism
RACE problems
See also
Church and race problems
Interracial marriage
Race relations
also subhead Race question under names of continents, countries, state, cities, etc, e.g. Sweden—Race question
RACE relations
Black man's burden. L. H. Lapham. il Harpers 254:15-16+ Je '77
Gone with the whip; Roots. M. J. Sobran, Jr. Nat R 29:276+ Mr 4 '77
RACE tracks
Going to watch at racetracks in the morning; Western States. il Sunset 159:26 O '77
Keeneland: coming out party for racing royalty. C. R. Koch. il Sat Eve Post 249:30-2+ Mr '77
They're paying through the nose; race horse sickness at Meadowlands. D. S. Looney. il Sports Illus 48:18-21 Ja 2 '78
Whole other horse race; Saratoga. K. Gilman. Vogue 167:58+ Ag '77
RACE tracks, Automobile. See Speedways
RACEMIC tartaric acid. See Tartaric acid
RACEMIZATION method of dating. See Amino acid dating
RACHMANINOFF, Sergei
Bells, op. 35; Vocalise, op. 34, no. 14. J. Oestreich. Am Rec G 40:31-2 Mr '77 *
Edison recordings of Serge Rachmaninoff. R. R. Wile. Am Rec G 40:11-12 F '77 *
Francesca da Rimini; Columbia/Melodiya recording. J. R. Oestreich. Am Rec G 40:40 O '77 *
Songs; recording. F. Crociata. Am Rec G 40:38 F '77 *
RACING
See also
Airplane racing
Automobile racing
Bicycle racing
Dog racing
Horse racing
Hydroplane racing
Motorcycle racing
Sailboat racing
Ski racing
Snowmobile racing
Yacht racing
RACING bicycles. See Bicycles
RACING car models. See Automobile models
RACING cars. See Automobiles, Racing
RACING form (periodical) See Daily racing form (periodical)
RACISM
Andy Young and the truth. J. L. Jackson. por Newsweek 90:9 Jl 11 '77
Anti-Zionist resolution. B. Lewis; reply with rejoinder. A. M. Elmessiri. For Affairs 55:641-2 Ap '77
Conferences
Anti-apartheid conference at Lagos calls for end of nuclear co-operation with South Africa; with text of declaration. il UN Chron 14:6-10 Ag '77
Assembly decides to convene in Ghana World Conference to Combat Racism. UN Chron 14:59-60 Ja '77
August 1978 proposed as tentative date for anti-racism conference; World Conference to Combat Racism and Racial Discrimination. UN Chron 14:50 Ap '77
Developments concerning apartheid; World Conference for Action Against Apartheid; statement, with text of declaration, August 25, 1977. A. J. Young, Jr. Dept State Bull 77:446-51 O 3 '77
Lagos conference described as landmark in long struggle to eradicate apartheid; World Conference for Action Against Apartheid. il UN Chron 14:29-31 Jl '77

RACKETEERING
See also
Mafia
RACKETS, Tennis. See Tennis rackets
RACKS, Bicycle. See Bicycle racks
RACKS, Clothes. See Clothes racks
RACKS, Cooling. See Kitchen utensils and appliances
RACKS, Knife. See Knife racks
RACKS, Magazine. See Magazine stands, racks, etc.
RACKS, Spice. See Spice racks
RACKS, Wine. See Wine racks
RACQUET clubs. See Sports clubs
RACQUETBALL
Racquetball: the hottest new game. P. Singerman. il Esquire 89:78-81 Ja '78
Racquets reach out. C. Wiseman. il Horizon 20:82-7 S '77
Served up, imperially, under glass; work of R. Kendler. M. Sharnik. il pors Sports Illus 46:44-6+ My 2 '77
RACUSEN, R. H. and others
Osmotically induced changes in electrical properties of plant protoplast membranes. bibl il Science 198:405-7 O 28 '77
RADAR
Economical X-band radar developed. K. J. Stein. il Aviation W 106:55-7 Ap 18 '77
See also
Automobiles—Radar equipment

Antenna and scanning mechanisms

Radar sentinel scans with 16,000 eyes. S. Renner-Smith. il Pop Sci 210:181 Je '77

Military use

See also
Airplanes, Military—Radar equipment
Guided missiles—Control
RADAR astronomy. See Radar in astronomy
RADAR defense networks
Fourth Sinai Support Mission report transmitted to the Congress; message, October 19, 1977. J. Carter. Dept State Bull 77:787 N 28 '77
Second Sinai Support Mission report transmitted to the Congress; message, January 11, 1977. G. R. Ford. Dept State Bull 76:134 F 14 '77
Third Sinai Support Mission report transmitted to the Congress; message, April 27, 1977. J. Carter. Dept State Bull 76:639 Je 13 '77
RADAR detectors. See Detectors
RADAR in astronomy
Galilean satellites of Jupiter: 12.6-centimeter radar observations. D. B. Campbell and others. bibl il Science 196:650-3 My 6 '77
RADAR in aviation
See also
Airplanes—Detection
Airplanes—Radar equipment
Airplanes, Military—Radar equipment
RADAR in earth sciences
Remote sensing: Brazil explores its Amazon wilderness; Project Radam. A. L. Hammond. il map Science 196:513-15 Ap 29 '77
RADAR in navigation
Radar for everyone. M. Meisels. il Motor B & S 140:90-2 O '77
Radar: the all-seeing eye. M. Meisels. il Motor B & S 140:61-3+ S '77
Techniques of radar navigation. J. West. il Motor B & S 141:98-9+ Ja '78
RADAR in oceanography
Ocean surface currents mapped by radar. D. E. Barrick and others. bibl il Science 198:138-44 O 14 '77
RADAR in traffic control
If somebody's finger has to be on the button, I want it to be mine. P. Bedard. Car & Dr 23:11 S '77
On civil disobedience: 55-mph speed limit; symposium. Car & Dr 23:37-8+ S '77; Discussion. 23:9+ D '77
RADAR meteorology
How to work weather radar. T. H. Block. il Flying 101:70-2 Ag '77
Ocean wave patterns under Hurricane Gloria: observation with an airborne synthetic-aperture radar. C. Elachi and others. bibl il Science 198:609-10 N 11 '77
Radar takes wing. G. C. Larson. il Flying 100:61 Mr '77
Versatile displays stressed at Reading. K. J. Stein. il Aviation W 106:85+ Je 27 '77
RADAR reflectors, Boat. See Boats—Equipment
RADAR simulators. See Simulators
RADCLIFFE College, Cambridge, Mass.
Daughters of the middle class; excerpt from We must march my darlings. D. Trilling. Harpers 254:31-6+ Ap '77
RADER, Lawrence A.
Investing in small companies: adventuresome—and profitable; interview, ed by A. Hershman. il por Duns R 110:93+ S '77
RADER, Stanley
Armstrong's Worldwide Church of God: musical chairs of change. J. M. Hopkins Chr Today 21:20-3 Ap 1 '77 *
RADIAL saws. See Saws
RADIAL velocity of stars. See Stars—Motion in line of sight
RADIATION
Casting light on material structures; synchrotron radiation. D. E. Thomsen. il Sci N 112:426-7 D 24 '77
Synchrotron radiation: large demand spurs new facilities. A. L. Robinson. il Science 197:148 Jl 8 '77
Uses of synchrotron radiation. E. M. Rowe and J. H. Weaver. il Sci Am 236:32-41 bibl(p 142) Je '77
See also
Blackbody radiation
Cosmic rays
Gamma rays
Solar radiation
Stars—Radiation
Ultraviolet rays

Physiological effects

Death by incompetence: the blowout at Yucca Flat; exposure to radiation after underground test accident. J. Harris. Nation 226:18-20 Ja 7 '78
Time for doctors to take a stand on nuclear proliferation. J. A. Loraine. Bull Atom Sci 33:6-7 O '77
See also
Ultraviolet rays—Physiological effects
RADIATION and cancer. See Cancer—Causes
RADIATION belts
Energetic radiation belt electron precipitation: a natural depletion mechanism for stratospheric ozone. R. M. Thorne. bibl il Science 195:287-9 Ja 21 '77
RADIATION workers
See also
Radioactivity—Accidents and injuries
RADIATORS
Flue radiator reclaims stack heat. E. Powell. il Pop Sci 210:154 Mr '77
Hide your bulky radiator with this easy-to-make cover. R. Lasson. il Pop Mech 147:154 Ap '77
RADICALISM
Absent left. J. Greenfield. Harpers 255:19-21+ S '77
Grand jury abuse; investigations of Seattle radicals. R. C. Kelley. Progressive 41:34-5 F '77
Politics under the palms. B. Burlingham. il pors Esquire 87:47-52+ F '77
Radical trashers; Italy's *autoriduttori*. il Time 109:32 F 28 '77
We did overcome; radical movements of the 1960s. S. Jacoby. il N Y Times Mag p62-4+ Ap 10 '77
Where the flowers have gone. P. Goldman and G. Lubenow. il Newsweek 90:24-5 S 5 '77
See also
New American Movement (organization)
Student militants
Weathermen (organization)

Jews

Why Breira? J. Shattan. Commentary 63:60-6 Ap '77; Discussion. 63:4+ Je '77
RADICALS (chemistry)
Free radical increases in cancer: evidence that there is not a real increase. H. M. Swartz and P. L. Gutierrez. bibl il Science 198:936-8 D 2 '77
NH_2O_2—not a mushroom molecule. il Chemistry 50:25-6 O '77
See also
Hydroxyl
RADICALS, Student. See Student militants
RADIMER, Carl A.
Writing for the farm magazines. Writers Digest 57:25-7 Ag '77
RADIO

Bibliography

DX listening. G. Hauser. Pop Electr 12:112-14 S '77

Emergency use

See also
Citizens band radio—Emergency use
Radio beacons

History

Ahead of Cronkite. F. O. McIntyre. Sci Digest 81:59 Mr '77
Nathan Stubblefield: the radio prophet of the Kentucky fields. H. Geller. il pors Hi Fi 27:79-83 N '77

Interference

See Radio interference

International aspects

See also
Radio broadcasting—International aspects
World Administrative Radio Conference

RADIO, Amateur
Amateur radio. H. S. Brier. il Pop Electr 11:87 F; 88 Ap '77
Get started in ham radio the easy home study way. A. R. Curtis. il Pop Mech 147:270-1 My '77

Equipment

Ham-only receiver gives more for less. il Pop Mech 148:63 Jl '77
Tiny new ham radios span the globe. A. R. Curtis. il Pop Mech 148:212+ O '77
Tiny portable ham radio packs 800 channels. A. R. Curtis. il Pop Mech 148:67 N '77
Two hot ham radios you'll want when you step up from CB. A. R. Curtis. il Pop Mech 147:109+ Je '77

RADIO, Military
Bids due soon on new Army radio family. Aviation W 107:71 Ag 8 '77
Navy project goes aground in Michigan; Seafarer. por Bus W p28 Ap 11 '77
Project Seafarer: Michigan's war against the Navy. J. Magney. Progressive 41:22-4 Jl '77
Seafarer fund drive spurred by Navy. il Aviation W 106:51-4 Ap 4 '77
Seafarer; NAS sees no basic hazard. Sci N 112:101-2 Ag 13 '77
Seafarer: project still homeless as Milliken says no to Navy. L. J. Carter. Science 197:964-8 S 2 '77

RADIO, Naval. See Radio, Military

RADIO, Shortwave
DX listening. G. Hauser. Pop Electr 12:93+ N '77
End that utility futility; DXing CW without knowing Morse code. H. L. Helms, Jr. il Pop Electr 12:53-5 Jl '77
English-language shortwave broadcasts; tables (cont) R. E. Wood. Pop Electr 11:103-6 Mr; 101-4 My; 12:114-17 S; 94-7 N '77
See also
Citizens band radio

Equipment

Digital frequency readout for shortwave receivers. D. L. Mattis. il Pop Electr 11:49-51+ F '77
Eavesdrop on the world with these hot new receivers. C. W. Prestia, Jr. il Pop Mech 148:61-3 Jl '77

RADIO, Single sideband
Propagation and how to live with it; excerpt from The Raytheon guide to single-sideband marine radio. J. R. Millard. il Motor B & S 139:82 Mr '77
Single sideband. G. West. il Motor B & S 139:26-7+ Mr '77

RADIO advertising
See also
Books—Advertising
College library publicity

RADIO advertising copy. See Advertising copy

RADIO amateurs. See Radio operators, Amateur

RADIO and libraries. See Libraries and radio

RADIO antennas
Antennas for 40-channels. R. Bitner. il Radio-Electr 48:45-6 F '77
Choosing a CB antenna for the road. L. Buckwalter. il Mech Illus 73:50+ My '77
Field tests reveal strange facts about locating your car's CB antenna. H. Friedman. il Pop Sci 211:90-1 D '77
For your home—install a CB base antenna. W. J. Hawkins. il Pop Sci 211:97-9 Jl '77
Maximize your CB firepower. A. R. Curtis. il Pop Mech 147:262-4 My '77
One-wavelength loop antennas. H. S. Brier. il Pop Electr 11:88 Ap '77
Tell the world you're on the air; CB antenna light. J. P. Greeves. il Pop Mech 147:178 Je '77
Useful indoor FM antenna. C. Graham. Am Rec G 40:44 Jl '77
VHF antenna systems; boat antennas. W. Orr. il Motor B & S 140:51-3 N '77
What you should know about CB antennas. M. R. Friedberg. il Radio-Electr 48:64-6+ O '77

Safety devices and measures

CB safety can save your life. Farm J 101:P8 N '77

Testing

Equipment reports:
Audiovox MA-30 electric CB/FM-AM-MPX antenna. il Radio-Electr 48:25-6 D '77
JFD electronics FM-500 amplified FM antenna. il Radio-Electr 48:102+ S '77

RADIO apparatus and instruments
Equipment reports:
Wawasee Electronics JBC-1000-SM catalyzer oscilloscope/RF wattmeter and SWR bridge. il Radio Electr 48:25-8 Je '77
New products. See issues of Popular electronics including Electronics world

Military use

See Radio, Military

Power supply

Power supplies. il Radio-Electr 48:50-1 N '77

RADIO apparatus and instruments, Portable
Big buzz in beepers. R. Levy. Duns R 110:72-3 N '77
Buy a beeper? il Changing T 31:11-12 Mr '77
Chorus of beepers. Time 109:66-7 My 2 '77
Keep in touch from anywhere; beepers. H. Fantel. il Pop Mech 147:98-100+ My '77
Mini lifesaver; Microlert. Time 110:57 D 5 '77
Pocket pagers. J. Free. il Pop Sci 211:78-9+ Jl '77

RADIO apparatus industry

Europe, Western

Europe: the CB craze hits Europeans hard. Bus W p47-8 Mr 21 '77

RADIO apparatus on aircraft. See Airplanes—Radio equipment

RADIO astronomy
Structure of the interstellar medium; synthetic photography from radio wavelengths of interstellar gases. C. Heiles. Sci Am 238:74-84 Ja '78
See also
Interstellar communication
Radio sources (astronomy)
Radio telescopes

RADIO audiences
Chasing foreign DX on the broadcast band. H. L. Helms. il Pop Electr 11:78-83 Je '77
DX listening (cont) G. Hauser. Pop Electr 11:102-3 Mr; 100-1 My; 12:112-14 S '77
End that utility futility; DXing CW without knowing Morse code. H. L. Helms, Jr. il Pop Electr 12:53-5 Jl '77
How to DX earth radio from outer space. G. Hauser. il Pop Electr 11:37-40 Ap '77

RADIO beacons
EPIRBs save lives. W. F. Rea, 3d. Yachting 141:197-8 My '77

RADIO broadcasting
At the crest of the air waves: syndicated radio. J. Melanson. il Hi Fi 27:135-6+ O '77
Broadcast systems for AM stereo. L. Feldman. il Radio-Electr 48:51-3 D '77
Second City scold; press critic. J. Madigan of Chicago's radio station, WBBM. il por Time 110:47-8 D 19 '77
See also
Computers—Radio broadcasting use

Baseball

See Radio broadcasting—Sports

Censorship

Censorship and man's right to know; radio news; address, December 17, 1976. K. R. Giddens. Vital Speeches 43:280-3 F 15 '77

Football

See Radio broadcasting—Sports

Government use

America gets on the party line; ask President Carter show. il por Time 109:10-11 Mr 14 '77
Dial-a-president. P. Goldman and T. M. DeFrank. il por Newsweek 89:14-16 Mr 14 '77
Good afternoon, Phyllis; the President's call-in. Nation 224:323-4 Mr 19 '77
TRB from Washington; President Carter's radio call-in, March 5, 1977. New Repub 176:2+ Mr 5 '77

Anecdotes, facetiae, satire, etc.

Hello. . .Jimmy? proposed radio call-in sessions; Time essay. P. Gray. Time 109:78 F 21 '77
Presidential call-in. W. Goodman. N Y Times Mag p 10 F 27 '77

History

Historical tape recordings:
Tribute to NBC engineer, G. Windham. L. Dumont. Hobbies 82:58-9+ Jl '77
Profiles; G. Ace. M. Singer. por New Yorker 53:41-6+ Ap 4 '77
Those old-time voices are big-time again; collecting old broadcasts. R. Angus. il Ret Liv 16:40-2 D '76

Illegal use

See also
Citizens band radio—Illegal use
Radio stations, Illegal

International aspects

Censorship and man's right to know; radio news; address, December 17, 1976. K. R. Giddens. Vital Speeches 43:280-3 F 15 '77
Free flow of information; address, January 21, 1977. S. Mickelson. Vital Speeches 43:314-17 Mr 1 '77
International broadcasting report transmitted to the Congress; message, March 22, 1977. J. Carter. Dept State Bull 76:423-4 Ap 25 '77

Laws and regulations

See Radio laws and regulations

RADIO broadcasting—*Continued*

Music

Dotage of American radio. G. Lees. Hi Fi 28:12+ Ja '78
Heyday of network radio. G. Lees. Hi Fi 27:19 D '77
Historical tape recordings:
Jessica Dragonette. L. Dumont. por Hobbies 82:58-9 Ag; 58-9 S; 58-9+ O '77
Making air waves: Concert-stage, classical music. Am Rec G 40:4 Ag '77
National Public Radio:
Folk Festival USA. W. Youngren. New Repub 177:25-8 S 10 '77
Jazz Alive. W. Youngren. il por New Repub 177:23+ S 24 '77
See also
Radio broadcasting—Opera

News

Anecdotes, facetiae, satire, etc.

Meanwhile, in Zanzibar... R. Baker. il N Y Times Mag p 12 F 6 '77

Opera

Historical tape recordings:
Lyric Theatre. L. Dumont. Hobbies 82:58-9+ Ja '78
Texaco-Metropolitan Opera network; listing of U.S. stations. Opera N 42:24 D 3 '77
Viewpoint; opera and J. Carter. R. Jacobson. Opera N 41:6 Ap 16 '77
Viewpoint; PBS telecasts with simultaneous FM stereo broadcasts. R. Jacobson. Opera N 42:5 Ja 7 '78
Viewpoint; Texaco-Metropolitan Opera performances. R. Jacobson. Opera N 42:7 D 3 '77

Programs

See Radio programs

Propaganda

Another White House move that's riling the Russians; broadcasting news to the peoples of Russia and Eastern Europe. il U.S. News 82:25 Ap 18 '77
Voices of America. A. Deming and others. il Newsweek 89:30 Ap 11 '77
See also
Radio Free Europe

Sports

Mary Shane: baseball's new motor mouth. J. Lublin. por Ms 6:24-5 O '77
TV/radio:
Getting inside their 'Skins; Washington Redskins in broadcasting. B. Newman. Sports Illus 47:49 D 12 '77
Quick bites of a sporting feast; Weekend Sports. W. Leggett. il por Sports Illus 46:55 Ap 25 '77
Sure cure for sore necks; World Team Tennis broadcasts. J. Jares. Sports Illus 47:70 Ag 29 '77

Tennis

See Radio broadcasting—Sports

Weather forecasts

VHF-FM weather service. G. V. West. il Yachting 142:211-15 S '77
See also
United States—National Weather Service

Ethiopia

Ethiopian casualties; Radio Voice of the Gospel nationalized. Chr Today 21:57-8 Ap 15 '77

Germany

German wartime broadcasts. S. Lipman. Commentary 63:72-5 Mr '77; Discussion. 64:7-8 Jl '77

Japan

History

Recording that ended World War II; attempt to stop broadcast of recording of Hirohito's surrender speech; with text of speech. F. Bowers. il Hi Fi 27:87-90 O '77

Russia

Another White House move that's riling the Russians; broadcasting news to peoples of Russia and Eastern Europe. il U.S. News 82:25 Ap 18 '77
Voices of America. A. Deming and others. il Newsweek 89:30 Ap 11 '77

United States

Dotage of American radio. G. Lees. Hi Fi 28:12+ Ja '78
See also
National Broadcasting Company

RADIO censorship. See Radio broadcasting—Censorship

RADIO circuits
CB: uncommon circuits for common problems. R. F. Scott. il Radio-Electr 49:48-50 Ja '78

RADIO City Music Hall. See New York (city)—Radio City Music Hall

RADIO communication, Naval. See Radio, Military

RADIO compass
See also
Radio direction finders

RADIO control
See also
Garage doors—Control

RADIO direction finders
Armchair inventor looks at the RDF. M. Meisels. il Motor B & S 141:25+ Ja '78
It's over yonder. G. Baxter. Flying 101:78 N '77
On the beam. M. Meisels. il Motor B & S 139:73-7+ Je '77
Portable DF. G. West. il Yachting 142:68-70+ Jl '77

RADIO filters
Julian Hirsch audio reports:
Burwen model DNF 1201A noise reducer. J. Hirsch. il Pop Electr 12:39-40 N '77
Product test reports:
Telco channel guard model XL-1000 TVI filter. il Pop Electr 11:84-5 Ap '77

RADIO Free Europe
Free flow of information; address, January 21, 1977. S. Mickelson. Vital Speeches 43:314-17 Mr 1 '77

RADIO frequency interference. See Radio interference

RADIO frequency signal generators. See Signal generators

RADIO in defense
See also
Radio, Military

RADIO in meteorology
See also
Radio broadcasting—Weather forecasts

RADIO in navigation
Omega. J. West. il Motor B & S 139:59-61+ Mr '77
See also
Loran
Radio beacons
Radio direction finders

RADIO in rescue work
See also
Radio beacons

RADIO industry
See also
Radio production and direction
Storer Broadcasting Company

RADIO interference
CB & sun spots. J. Walders. il Sci Digest 81:24-7 F '77
Citizen's-band radio: danger of air pollution? il U.S. News 82:76-7 Mr 7 '77
Don't let the good buddies bug you. A. R. Curtis. il Pop Mech 147:230+ Ap '77
Getting rid of RFI. L. Feldman. il Radio-Electr 48:43-6+ Mr '77
How to clear up your CB channels. D. O. Hull. il Farm J 101:A4+ mid-F '77
How to cope with CB skip. C. M. Stanbury. il Mech Illus 73:45+ Ap '77
Is that a CB you hear on your TV? Changing T 31:18 Ag '77
Soviet pulser. G. Hauser. Pop Electr 11:102-3 Mr '77

RADIO laws and regulations
New law for TV and radio? G. R. Rosen. por Duns R 109:65 Ap '77
Your right to bear radar detectors; radio transmissions under Communications Act of 1934. R. Taylor. Car & Dr 23:59-60 S '77
See also
Citizens band radio—Laws and regulations
United States—Federal Communications Commission

RADIO listeners. See Radio audiences

RADIO observatories. See Astronomical observatories

RADIO on boats. See Boats—Radio equipment

RADIO operators, Amateur
How to find 277,593 new friends. P. Zauner. il por Ret Liv 17:42-3 O '77

RADIO, phonograph and tape recorder combination. See Television receivers, Portable—Radio, phonograph and tape recorder combination

RADIO production and direction
At the crest of the air waves: syndicated radio. J. Melanson. il Hi Fi 27:135-6+ O '77
Historical tape recordings:
William M. Sweets. L. Dumont. il Hobbies 82:116-17+ N; 58-9 D '77

RADIO program transcriptions. See Tape recordings

RADIO programs
Those old-time voices are big-time again; collecting old broadcasts. R. Angus. il Ret Liv 16:40-2 D '76

Comedy

See Radio programs—Humorous programs

Conversation programs

Artist life; B. Sills guest hosts The listening room. D. J. Soria. il por Hi Fi 27:MA6-8 F '77
Talk radio—the callers want approval, not an argument; research by Robert Avery. D. Cohen. Psychol Today 11:27 S '77

RADIO programs—*Continued*

Humorous programs

Historical tape recordings:
Tribute to Peg Lynch; creator of Ethel & Albert show. L. Dumont. il pors Hobbies 82:58-9 Je '77

Production and direction

See Radio production and direction

Religious programs

Casting for news. A. H. Matthews. Chr Today 21:59-60 F 18 '77
Father Bill and the voices of the night; W. Ayres' Where's it all going program. T. Ichniowski. il America 136:50-2 Ja 22 '77
Threat to religious broadcasting: somebody is lying. Chr Today 21:41 Ja 7 '77
See also
National Religious Broadcasters (organization)

Science programs

A new radio astronomy. C. Sumners. il por Sky & Tel 53:344-5 My '77
Physics on the airwaves. H. L. Davis. Phys Today 30:96 D '77

RADIO receivers
Build a legal in-flight airline receiver; low-cost Varactor-tuned crystal set. C. R. Lewart. il Pop Electr 11:61-3 My '77
Computerized scanners: action at your fingertips. A. R. Curtis. il Pop Mech 148:68-70 Jl '77
See also
Campers, Truck—Radio equipment
Clock radios
Radio, Amateur—Equipment
Radio, Shortwave—Equipment

Maintenance and repair

Realign your FM receiver. T. J. C. Molle. il Radio-Electr 48:50-2+ O '77
Restoring antique radios—how to get started. M. E. McMahon. il Radio-Electr 48:58-9 Ag '77

Noise

See also
Radio filters

Testing

Deluxe receiver at best-buy price. C. Graham. Am Rec G 41:56-7 N '77
Julian Hirsch audio reports:
H.H. Scott Model R376 stereo receiver. J. Hirsch. il Pop Electr 12:35-6+ O '77
Heath Model AR-1515 AM stereo FM receiver. J. Hirsch. il Pop Electr 12:30-3 Ag '77
Lafayette model LR-3030 AM/stereo FM receiver. J. D. Hirsch. il Pop Electr 11:34+ Je '77
Realistic model STA-2000 stereo reeciver. J. Hirsch. il Pop Electr 12:33-6 Jl '77
Rotel Model RX-7707 AM/stereo FM receiver. J. Hirsch. il Pop Electr 11:29-32 Ap '77
Sherwood model S-7910 stereo receiver. J. D. Hirsch. il Pop Electr 11:29-31 Mr '77
Yamaha model CR-2020 AM/stereo FM receiver. J. Hirsch. il Pop Electr 13:26-9 Ja '78
Mid-priced stereo receivers. il Consumer Rep 42:590-7 O '77
New equipment reports:
Advent's 300 receiver: simple is beautiful. il Hi Fi 27:52-4 Mr '77
B&O's iconoclastic receiver. il Hi Fi 27:65-6+ Mr '77
Hitachi's unique (Series E) receiver. il Hi Fi 27:48-50 Ap '77
Realistic new look—clean and powerful. il Hi Fi 27:58+ Mr '77
Separate-looking receiver from Toshiba. il Hi Fi 27:68-9 S '77
Solid midpriced receiver from Sony; Sony STR-5800SD. il Hi Fi 27:53-5 N '77
Twistless receiver from JVC. il Hi Fi 27:57-8 Jl '77
Yamaha CR-820: Mr Clean in sound and style. il Hi Fi 27:35-7 My '77
Product test reports:
Tennelec model MPC-1 memoryscan monitor receiver. il Pop Electr 11:79+ Ap '77
YAESU model FRG-7 communication receiver. il Pop Electr 11:95-8 Je '77
Radio-electronics tests:
Fisher RS-1080 AM/FM stereo receiver. L. Feldman. il Radio-Electr 48:50-2 Jl '77
GTE Sylvania model 2600 stereo receiver. L. Feldman. il Radio-Electr 48:54-5 D '77
Heath AR-1515 AM/FM receiver. L. Feldman. il Radio-Electr 48:62-3+ O '77
Hitachi SR-903 stereo receiver. L. Feldman. il Radio-Electr 48:56-7+ Ag '77
Kenwood KR-7600AM/FM receiver. L. Feldman. il Radio-Electr 48:51+ Ap '77
Onkyo TX-8500 Am/Fm receiver. L. Feldman. il Radio-Electr 48:56-7+ D '77
Stereo receivers. il Consumers Res Mag 60:29-34 Mr '77
Television and radio. il Consumers Res Mag 60:38-47 O '77

Tuning

Digital tuners. D. Hoover. il Pop Sci 211:92-3+ N '77
FM tuner selectivity ratings and measurement. J. Hirsch. il por Pop Electr 11:28-9 Ap '77
How FM tuners work. J. Hirsch. il Pop Electr 12:48-51 D '77; 13:58-9 Ja '78
Interpreting FM tuner specs. E. J. Foster. il Hi Fi 27:72-3+ N '77
Is there a digital FM tuner? J. Hirsch. Pop Electr 12:29-30 Ag '77
Julian Hirsh audio reports:
Phase Linear model 5000 FM tuner. J. Hirsch. il Pop Electr 12:32-4 D '77
New equipment reports:
Another rare bird from Nakamichi; 630 tuner/preamplifier. il Hi Fi 28:45-7 Ja '78
Kenwood's 600-T—a supertunable supertuner. il Hi Fi 27:27-9 F '77
1978 stereo FM tuner buying directory. I. Berger. il Pop Electr 13:54-7 Ja '78
Radio-electronics tests:
Optonica ST-3535 tuner. L. Feldman. il Radio-Electr 48:54-6 Ag '77
Sherwood micro CPU-100 FM tuner. L. Feldman. il Radio-Electr 48:65-6 N '77
Yamaha CT-800 tuner. L. Feldman. il Radio-Electr 48:49-51 Ap '77
Two very good tuners. C. Graham. Am Rec G 40:54-6 S '77

RADIO receivers, Portable
Small radios. il Consumers Res Mag 60:21-6 N '77
Stay tuned with go-anywhere hear-anything portables. G. R. Patton. il Pop Mech 148:76-7+ Ag '77
See also
Television receivers, Portable—Radio, phonograph and tape recorder combination

RADIO reception
Mine ears have heard the glory of the coming of Big Brother. L. J. K. Setright. Car & Dr 23:142 N '77

RADIO repairmen

Wages and hours

Pay relationships of TV-radio and appliance repairers. S. L. King. il M Labor R 100:48-9 My '77

RADIO Shack stores. See Tandy Corporation

RADIO signals
Will sunspots affect CB communications? S. Leinwoll. il Pop Electr 11:51-4 Mr '77

RADIO sources (astronomy)
BL lacertae objects. M. J. Disney and P. Véron. il Sci Am 237:32-9 Ag '77
Cygnus A conundrum. S. P. Maran. il Natur Hist 86:84-7 My '77
Radio galaxies and quasars. L. C. Green. il Sky & Tel 54:384-9 N '77
See also
Pulsars
Quasars

RADIO stations
At the crest of the air waves: syndicated radio. J. Melanson. il Hi Fi 27:135-6+ O '77
Texaco-Metropolitan opera network; listing of U.S. stations. Opera N 42:24 D 3 '77
Weather radio: keep one jump ahead of disasters; National Weather Service. A. R. Curtis. il map Pop Mech 148:68-71 Ag '77
See also
National Broadcasting Company

RADIO stations, Illegal
Piracy on the airwaves. H. L. Helms. il Pop Electr 12:56-8 N '77

RADIO talk shows. See Radio programs—Conversation programs

RADIO telegraph

Equipment

Morse code automatic readout on a TV screen. G. R. Steber. il Pop Electr 11:64-5 My '77

RADIO telephone. See Radiotelephone

RADIO telescopes
Massachusetts dish for radio astronomy at 1 mm. G. B. Lubkin. il Phys Today 30:18-19 F '77
World's largest radio telescope. R. Nelson. il Pop Sci 210:80-2+ Mr '77

RADIO-television repairmen. See Television repairmen

RADIO transmitters
Another White House move that's riling the Russians. il U.S. News 82:25 Ap 18 '77

Identification

Automatic transmitter identification. G. Garcia. il Pop Electr 13:80-1 Ja '78

RADIO tuners. See Radio receivers—Tuning

RADIO waves
See also
Pulse techniques (electronics)

RADIOACTIVE dating
Radioisotope dating with a cyclotron. R. A. Muller. bibl il Science 196:489-94 Ap 29 '77

RADIOACTIVE dating—*Continued*
South American geochronology: radiometric time scale for middle to late Tertiary mammal-bearing horizons in Patagonia. L. G. Marshall and others. bibl il map Science 195: 1325-8 Mr 25 '77
Tritium-helium dating in the Sargasso Sea: a measurement of oxygen utilization rates. W. J. Jenkins. bibl il Science 196:291-2 Ap 15 '77
See also
Radiocarbon dating

RADIOACTIVE decontamination
Riddled by isotopes. M. Clark and P. S. Greenberg. il por Newsweek 89:49 Mr 21 '77

RADIOACTIVE fallout
See also
Atomic bomb shelters

Physiological effects

See Radioactivity—Physiological effects

Sweden

Airborne short-lived radionuclides of unknown origin in Sweden in 1976. L. E. De Greer. il map Science 198:925-7 D 2 '77

RADIOACTIVE pollution
Documentation of alleged Soviet mishap. map Sci N 112:37-8 Jl 16 '77
Lethal seepage of nuclear waste. R. Kaper. Nation 224:266-70 Mr 5 '77
Plutonium hazard in respirable dust on the surface of soil. C. J. Johnson and others; reply with rejoinder. J. A. Hayden. Science 196:1126 Je 3 '77
See also
Atomic power plants—Environmental aspects

RADIOACTIVE substances
See also
Americium
Nuclear fuels
Plutonium
Promethium

Security measures

Controlling weapons-grade fissile material. J. Rotblat. bibl il Bull Atom Sci 33:37-43 Je '77
Improved nuclear security proposed. Sci N 112:38 Jl 16 '77
Protecting nuclear material: combative research. M. A. Guillen. il Sci N 112:108-10 Ag 13 '77
What happens if . . . ? Terrorists, revolutionaries, and nuclear weapons. D. Krieger. Ann Am Acad 430:44-57 Mr '77

RADIOACTIVE tracers
Comparison radioactive and stable Tl+ diffusion in potassium chloride: demonstration of a transmutation effect. G. C. T. Wei and B. J. Wuensch. bibl il Science 197:159-61 Jl 8 '77
Transmutation products may influence radiotracer diffusion rates in an ionic solid. G. C. T. Wei and B. J. Wuensch. bibl il Science 197:157-9 Jl 8 '77

RADIOACTIVE waste disposal
Aslosh in waste. New Repub 177:2+ S 24 '77
Atom's global garbage. il Time 110:62+ O 31 '77
Canadian disposal of spent fuel. W. D. Metz. il Science 196:286 Ap 15 '77
Deep six hundred. Sci Am 236:54+ Je '77
Disposal of radioactive wastes from fission reactors. B. L. Cohen. il Sci Am 236:21-31 bibl (p 142) Je '77; Reply with rejoinder. R. Sclove. 237:7+ O '77
High-level and long-lived radioactive waste disposal. E. E. Angino. bibl il Science 198:885-90 D 2 '77
"Interim" policy for spent nuclear fuel. Sci N 112:278 O 29 '77
Lasers reduce nuclear waste. map Chemistry 50:24-5 My '77
Layaway plan for nuclear fuel rods; federal plan for dealing with spent fuel. il Bus W p25 Ag 22 '77
Lethal seepage of nuclear waste. R. Kaper. Nation 224:266-70 Mr 5 '77
New spent fuel policy unveiled. W. D. Metz. Science 198:591 N 11 '77
Nuclear fuel cycle: an appraisal. il Phys Today 30:32-5+ O '77
Nuclear waste. R. Paehlke. Environment 19:2-3 Ag '77
Nuclear waste disposal: can the geologist guarantee isolation? G. de Marsily and others. bibl il Science 197:519-27 Ag 5 '77
Nuclear wastes: popular antipathy narrows search for disposal sites. L. J. Carter. il Science 197:1265-6 S 23 '77
Nuclear wastes stymie West Germans. N. Hawkes. Science 195:962-3 Mr 11 '77
Problem of nuclear waste disposal. Cong Digest 56:42 F '77
Radioactive wastes: some urgent unfinished business. L. J. Carter. il Science 195:661-6+ F 18 '77; Reply. B. L. Cohen. 195:1280+ Mr 25 '77
Retention of plutonium and americium by rock. S. Fried and others. bibl il Science 196:1087-9 Je 3 '77
Some say it will kill you; Maxey Flats nuclear waste disposal site, Fleming County, Ky; reprint from Audubon, November 1976 issue. G. Laycock. il Redbook 148:102+ Ap '77
West Valley: the question is where does buck stop on nuclear wastes? L. J. Carter. Science 195:1306+ Mr 25 '77

RADIOACTIVE waste reprocessing. See Reactor fuel reprocessing

RADIOACTIVE wastes
Radioactive wastes: a comparison of U.S. military and civilian inventories. H. Krugmann and F. Von Hippel. bibl il Science 197:883-5 Ag 26 '77

RADIOACTIVITY
See also
Transmutation (chemistry)

Accidents and injuries

Riddled by isotopes. M. Clark and P. S. Greenberg. il por Newsweek 89:49 Mr 21 '77

Physiological effects

Continuing body count at Hiroshima and Nagasaki. F. Barnaby. il Bull Atom Sci 33: 48-51+ D '77
Physical and medical effects of the Hiroshima and Nagasaki bombs; report of Natural Science Group. Bull Atom Sci 33:54-6 D '77

Safety devices and measures

See also
Radioactive decontamination

RADIOCARBON dating
Accelerator technique improves radioisotope dating. M. S. Rothenberg. bibl il Phys Today 30:17-19 D '77
Ancient Europe is older than we thought. C. Renfrew. il map Nat Geog 152:614-23 N '77
Carbon-14 dating: new possibilities. Sci N 111: 405 Je 25 '77
Carbon-14: direct detection at natural concentrations; use of Van de Graaff accelerator. D. E. Nelson and others. bibl il Science 198: 507-8 N 4 '77
Dating the Salton Sea petroglyphs. Sci N 111: 138 F 26 '77
Early man confirmed in America 40,000 years ago. Sci N 111:196 Mr 26 '77
New dating game. Time 109:72 Je 27 '77
Radiocarbon dating using electrostatic accelerators; negative ions provide the key. C. L. Bennett and others. bibl il Science 198:508-10 N 4 '77

RADIOGRAPHY
See also
Radiography, Medical

RADIOGRAPHY, Medical
CAT fever. E. Marshall. New Repub 176:11-15 Ap 16 '77
CT scans: profiteers and gadgets fads. il Sci N 111:293 My 7 '77
Computerized tomography: taking sectional X rays. W. Swindell and H. H. Barrett. bibl il Phys Today 30:32-6+ D '77
Miracle machine; CAT, computerized axial tomography. J. R. Kesselman and F. Peterson. il Sci Digest 82:70-4 S '77
Miracle machine; computerized axial tomography. J. R. Kesselman and F. Peterson. il Fam Health 9:28-30+ Ja '77
See also
Angiography
Mammography

RADIOIMMUNOASSAY. See Biological assay

RADIOISOTOPE dating. See Radioactive dating

RADIOISOTOPES
See also
Americium
Neutron sources

RADIOLOGISTS
Radiologists agree to end plan that let them fix fees. Ret Liv 17:14 Ja '77

RADIOLOGY, Medical
See also
Radiography, Medical
Radiologists

RADIOMETERS
Ozone monitoring with an infrared heterodyne radiometer. R. T. Menzies and R. K. Seals, Jr. bibl il Science 197:1275-7 S 23 '77

RADIOTELEPHONE
State of solid state; National LM1812 ultrasonic transceiver. K. Sayon. il Radio-Electr 48:100-4 F '77
See also
Citizens band radio—Equipment

Testing

Product test reports:
Kenwood model TS-820 transceiver. il Pop Electr 11:90-3 My '77

RADIOTELEPHONE, Portable
Traveling telephones. J. Mason. il Pop Sci 212: 62-5 Ja '78
See also
Walkie-talkies

RADIOTELEPHONE on aircraft
Procurement concept results studied; airborne ultra-high frequency transceiver. P. J. Klass. il Aviation W 107:61+ Jl 4 '77

RADIOTELEPHONE on automobiles
High-speed voices; use of two-way radios in auto racing. J. Scalzo. il Motor T 30:64+ Ja '78
Keep in touch from anywhere. H. Fantel. il Pop Mech 147:98-100+ My '77
RADIOTELEPHONE on motor vehicles
Product is born; RCA's mobile communications system. A. L. Morner. Fortune 95:124-9+ F '77
RADIOTELEPHONE on ships, boats, etc.
Mayday now from any ocean: U.S. Coast Guard's new lifesaving service. N. Collins. Yachting 141:184-8 My '77
On the air. M. Meisels. il Motor B & S 140:78-80+ O '77
Single sideband update. G. V. West. Yachting 142:126-7 Ag '77
Your marine operator; Camden Marine facility. B. Witherill. Yachting 142:141-2 Jl '77
RADIOTHERAPY
See also
Breast—Cancer—Therapy
Cancer—Therapy
RADMER, Richard, and Kok, Bessel
Photosynthesis: limited yields; unlimited dreams. bibl il BioScience 27:599-605 S '77
RADNAY, John P.
Emersons: dubious payments American-style. A. Hershman. il por Duns R 109:73-5 Mr '77 *
RADOMES
Men who walk on bubbles. il Mech Illus 73:126 Mr '77
RADOSH, Ronald
Schlesinger and Kennedy. Nation 225:104-9, 148 Ag 6-20 '77
RADOSTA, John S.
Roar of pro golf's young lions. il N Y Times Mag p 17-18+ Ag 21 '77
RADWELL, Louis
Men at home. Am Home 80:59 Mr '77
RAE, Diane
Plan now. . . prevent accidents later. il Parents Mag 52:43+ My '77
RAEBURN, Ben
Story behind the book: An autobiography; interview, ed by R. Dahlin. Pub W 212:55 Jl 25 '77
RAEBURN, Paul
Nuclear fusion's promise grows. il Sci Digest 82:8-10 Jl '77
RAETZ, Christian R. H. and others
Phospholipid derivative of cytosine arabinoside and its conversion to phosphatidylinositol by animal tissue. bibl il Science 196:303-5 Ap 15 '77
RAEVSKY, Dimitri Sergeevich
Three vases recount the legend of King Targitaus. il UNESCO Courier 29:14-16 D '76
RAFF, Rudolf A.
Molecular determination of morphogenesis. bibl BioScience 27:394-401 Je '77
RAFFEL, Deanne
Home improvement ideas for the house fixer. See issues of House & Garden incorporating Living for young homemakers
RAFFLES Hotel. See Hotels, motels, etc.—Singapore
RAFFONE, Arnold. See Keller, A. J. jt auth
RAFSHOON, Gerald M.
Carter's outside insiders. pors Bus W p94+ Je 27 '77 *
Rafshoon vs. Garth. J. Lelyveld. il pors N Y Times Mag p78 Ag 21 '77 *
RAFT racing
Rafts; third annual Great Connecticut River Raft Race. New Yorker 53:25-6 Ag 15 '77
RAFT trips. See River trips; Running rapids
RAFTS
Red tape may capsize river rafts; invoking the Jones Act to ban foreign-made rafts. il Bus W p38 Mr 21 '77
RAGS (periodical)
How to have fun though dressed: a sneak preview of Rags; ed by M. Peacock and C. Troy. il pors Ms 5:67-70 My '77
RAHMAN, Ziaur
Voting with their guns. K. Bird. Nation 225:650-3 D 17 '77 *
RAHN, Eduardo
Oil dollars go into music. D. Hawes. por Hi Fi 27:MA33+ N '77 *
RAHNER, Karl
Making ready the way; excerpt from Meditations on hope and love. Chr Cent 94:1110-11 N 30 '77
We are all forerunners; excerpt from Meditations on hope and love. Chr Cent 94:1134 D 7 '77
RAHWAY State Prison, N.J. See Prisons—New Jersey
RAIL shooting
Stalking the swamp walkers. D. Walrod. il Field & S 82:34-5+ Jl '77
RAIL transit, Local. See Local transit
RAILINGS. See Hand railings
RAILINGS, Boat. See Boats and boating—Safety devices and measures
RAILROAD cars. See Railroads—Cars
RAILROAD engineers. See Locomotive engineers
RAILROAD mergers. See Railroads—Acquisitions and mergers
RAILROAD models
How to pick the best track gauge for your needs. il Pop Mech 148:106-7+ D '77
Model trains keep on shrinking. D. Barnett. il Mech Illus 73:72+ D '77

Electric equipment

Model railroad sound synthesizer. H. Wright. il Pop Electr 12:80-3 D '77

Electronic equipment

Electronic model railroading. D. W. Hansen. il Pop Mech 148:104-8+ D '77
RAILROAD rates. See Railroads—Rates
RAILROAD retirement benefits. See Pensions
RAILROAD ties. See Railroads—Ties
RAILROAD tracks. See Railroads—Track
RAILROAD travel
Across U.S. by train: a reporter's odyssey; aboard Amtrak's trains. F. W. Frailey. il U.S. News 83:87-8 N 28 '77
Coming across; transcontinental trip by steam engine; interview. R. E. M. Whitaker. New Yorker 53:26-7 Je 27 '77
Europe goes on a train-riding spree. C. S. Foltz, Jr. il U.S. News 83:60 Ag 8 '77
Making tracks: America's top train trips. D. Butwin. Am Home 80:39+ Ap '77
Murder of the Orient Express. P. Theroux. Holiday 58:22 Ap '77
Notes and comment. il New Yorker 52:23 Ja 17 '77
Old friend; Broadway Limited's seventy-fifth anniversary celebrated on the New York-Chicago run. R. E. M. Whitaker. New Yorker 53:28-30 S 26 '77
Tracking the Blue Train of Africa. Holiday 58:31 Ap '77
RAILROAD workers. See Railroads—Employees
RAILROADS

Accidents

See also
Railroads, Elevated—Accidents

Acquisitions and mergers

Falling dominoes? Burlington Northern, Inc.-St Louis-San Francisco Railway Company merger. map Forbes 119:81-2 My 15 '77

Cars

Why foreigners own the U.S. transit-car field. il Bus W p68+ O 31 '77
See also
Budd Company
GATX Corporation
Rohr Industries, Inc

Employees

Rails aim at crew size again. il Bus W p88 Je 27 '77
See also
Locomotive engineers
United Transportation Union

Federal aid

See Railroads and state

Freight rates

See Railroads—Rates

Freight service

See also
Florida East Coast Railway

History

See also
Railroads—United States—History

Locomotives

See Locomotives

Mergers

See Railroads—Acquisitions and mergers

Models

See Railroad models

Passenger service

See also
National Railroad Passenger Corporation

Passenger traffic

See also
Railroad travel

Rates

Helping recyclers get lower rail rates; fighting against railroads and ICC. Bus W p36 S 5 '77

Right of way

Mugging of a garden; question of defoliation along Long Island Railroad rights of way. U. Roze. il Horticulture 55:18-23 Jl '77
Walking the railroads. J. Eastman. Natur Hist 86:90-3 N '77
Washington scene; converting abandoned railroad rights-of-way to recreation uses. B. Kravetz. Parks & Rec 12:16+ O '77

RAILROADS—*Continued*

Ties

How I built a railroad tie garden. R. Wolf. il Org Gard & Farm 24:62-4 Ap '77
Landscaping with old railroad ties. il Sunset 158:66-9 F '77

Track

End of the line for little-used tracks. Bus W p30-1 My 23 '77

Trains

Irresistible great trains. Esquire 87:16+ My '77

Wages and hours

See also
Collective bargaining—Railroads

Africa, Southern

Tracking the Blue Train of Africa. Holiday 58:31 Ap '77

Canada

Drop camp by rail. R. Gower. il map Outdoor Life 159:70-1 F '77
See also
Canadian National Railways

Ecuador

By roller coaster to the sea. E. J. Townsend. il map Américas 29:14-18 Mr '77

Europe

Murder of the Orient express. H. Fantel. il map Pop Mech 147:71-5+ Ap '77
Murder of the Orient express. P. Theroux. Holiday 58:22 Ap '77

Europe, Western

Europe goes on a train-riding spree. C. S. Foltz, Jr. il U.S. News 83:60 Ag 8 '77
Europe's scenic train rides. J. Andrews. il Travel 147:54-9 Mr '77
Irresistible great trains. Esquire 87:16+ My '77

United States

How to get the trains back on the tracks; interview. L. W. Menk. por U.S. News 82:73 F 21 '77
Hundred years' war; controversy between barge and railroad transportation in Mississippi Valley. Forbes 119:54 Ja 15 '77
See also
Central Pacific Railroad
Chicago and North Western Transportation Company
Collective bargaining—Railroads
Consolidated Rail Corporation
Florida East Coast Railway
National Railroad Passenger Corporation
Norfolk & Western Railway
Penn Central Company
Railroads, Short line
Railway mail service
Union Pacific Railroad

History

Great race; excerpt from Hear that lonesome whistle blow. D. Brown. il Am West 14:4-15+ My '77
Man of mystery; J. Gould. M. Klein. il pors Am Hist Illus 12:10-18 O '77
Train robbery. R. Patterson. il Am West 14:48-53 Mr '77
Transcontinental railroad; excerpt from Hear that lonesome whistle blow. D. Brown. il Am Heritage 28:14-25 F '77

RAILROADS, Elevated
Elevated guideways can be good neighbors. J. R. Billing and H. N. Grouni. il Am City & County 92:87-8 S '77

Accidents

Death in the Loop. D. M. Alpern and others. il Newsweek 89:32+ F 14 '77

RAILROADS, Magnetic. See Magnetic suspension vehicles

RAILROADS, Mountain. See Mountain railroads

RAILROADS, Short line
Steaming through the Mother Lode. . .with meals and entertainment; Sierra Railroad Company. il Sunset 159:44+ S '77

RAILROADS, Single rail
Whatever happened to. .monorails: interest reviving. il U.S. News 83:72-3 D 12 '77

RAILROADS and state
How antelope became a regulatory problem; halting railroad construction in Wyoming. V. Louviere. Nations Bus 65:65-6 Ja '77
More federal aid for railroads? G. R. Rosen. por Duns R 109:51 F '77
See also
Consolidated Rail Corporation
National Railroad Passenger Corporation
Railway mail service
United States—Interstate Commerce Commission

RAILS (birds)
Bird that is loath to fly but roams afar all the same; excerpt from Rails of the world. S. D. Ripley. il Smithsonian 7:88-93 Mr '77

RAILWAY mail service
Notes and comment. R. E. M. Whitaker. New Yorker 53:27-8 S 19 '77

RAIN and rainfall
It's raining H_2SO_4. il Chemistry 50:24-5 O '77
See also
Droughts
Floods
Storms

RAIN forests
Coadapted competitors: the flowering seasons of hummingbird-pollinated plants in a tropical forest. F. G. Stiles. bibl il Science 198:1177-8 D 16 '77
Saving tropical forests. J. Arehart-Treichel. il Sci N 112:362-3 N 26 '77
Timely reprieve or a death sentence for the Amazon. R. Campbell. il Smithsonian 8:100-11 bibl(p 160-1) O '77

RAIN making
Bone-dry west prospects for snow; Colorado's emergency cloud-seeding program. Bus W p33-4 F 21 '77
Cloud-coaxers. P. Gwynne. il Newsweek 89:58 Mr 14 '77
Coaxing rain from clouds. . .when and where you want it. O. L. Smith. il Sci Digest 81:18-23 My '77
Rainfall results, 1970-1975: Florida Area Cumulus Experiment. W. L. Woodley and others. bibl il map Science 195:735-42 F 25 '77
Rainmakers. J. Schinto. il por Am West 14:28-33 Jl '77

RAINBOW
How to create and observe a dozen rainbows in a single drop of water. J. Walker. il Sci Am 237:138-42+ Jl '77
Theory of the rainbow. H. M. Nussenzveig. il Sci Am 236:116-27 bibl(p 148) Ap '77

RAINBOW Bridge National Monument
Earth log: the trammeling of Rainbow Bridge. G. Reiger. il Audubon 79:114-15+ N '77

RAINBOW trout. See Trout

RAINER, Pete
Movies. See issues of Mademoiselle

RAINER, Yvonne
Talking pictures, silent words: Yvonne Rainer's recent movies. L. R. Lippard. bibl il Art in Am 65:86-90 My '77 •

RAINIER, Mount
Mt. Rainier inside and out; photographs. il Am For 83:39-40 Mr '77
See also
Mount Rainier National Park

RAINIER, Mount, climbs. See Mountaineering

RAINWEAR. See Clothing, Waterproof

RAISED bed vegetable gardening. See Vegetable gardening

RAJASTHAN, India
Pageant of Rajasthan. R. Singh. il Nat Geog 151:218-43 F '77

RAJCHMAN, Jan A.
New memory technologies. bibl il Science 195:1223-9 Mr 18 '77

RAJNEESH, Bhagwan Shree (guru)
God Sir at Esalen East. il por Time 111:59 Ja 16 '78 •

RAJPUT painting. See Painting, Indian (East Indian)

RAKOSI, Carl
ZZZZZZ; poem. Nation 224:438 Ap 9 '77

RAKOWSKA-HARMSTONE, Teresa
Ethnicity in the Soviet Union. bibl f il Ann Am Acad 433:73-87 S '77

RAKU pottery
Sawdust injection firing. W. L. Baker. il pors Ceram Mo 25:45-7 S '77

RALL, David P.
What needs to be done to save the environment; interview. il por U.S. News 82:51-3 F 7 '77

RALLIES, Automobile. See Automobile rallies

RALMON, John
Béla Balázs in German exile. bibl il por Film Q 30:12-19 Spr '77

RALOFF, Janet
Water pollution: appearances can be deceiving. il Sci N 112:428-31 D 24 '77

RALPH, James A.
God's eye view. il Commonweal 104:587-8 S 16 '77

RALPH M. Parsons Company. See Construction industry

RAM, Jagjivan
Opposition strikes back. il por Time 109:37-8 F 14 '77 •

RAM Dass
Confessions of an American guru. C. Dowling. il pors N Y Times Mag p41-3+ D 4 '77 •

RAM pumps. See Pumps

RAMAN spectroscopy. See Spectrum analysis

RAMAPITHECUS. See Man, Prehistoric

RAMAYANA (restaurant) See New York (city)—Hotels, restaurants, etc.

RAMAZZINI, Bernardino
Health issues; ed by J. Waller and L. Whitehead; excerpts from De morbis artificum. Craft Horiz 37:8+ O '77

RAMEAU, Jean Philippe
Musical events; performance of La danse. A. Porter. New Yorker 53:63-5 D 26 '77 *
Pygmalion. Review
New Yorker 53:103-7 Je 20 '77 *

RAMEY, James W.
Alternative life-styles. bibl il Society 14:43-7 Jl '77

RAMEY, Phillip
Benjamin Britten. por Opera N 41:36-7 F 5 '77

RAMIG, Robert F. and others
Suppression of the temperature-sensitive phenotype of a mutant of reovirus type 3. bibl il Science 195:406-7 Ja 28 '77

RAMINGTON, John
Ode to Luther Sperberg. New Repub 177:34 Ag 6 '77

RAMIREZ SANCHEZ, Ilitch
Link to Carlos? S. Strasser and P. Martin. il por Newsweek 91:25 Ja 2 '78 *

RAMJET Propulsion of missiles. See Guided missiles—Propulsion systems

RAMKE, Bin
Secrets of the saints: first glimmerings; poem. Poetry 130:81 My '77

RAMONES (rock group) See Rock groups

RAMOS, Mel
Pop's master of cheesecake. T. Albright. Art N 76:208+ N '77 *

RAMOS MARTINEZ, Alfredo
Ramos Martinez, Mexican muralist. G. R. Small. il por Américas 29:19-22 Ap '77 *

RAMPAL, Jean Pierre
Mozart: Rampal plays Mozart; flute concertos. N. F. Karlins. Am Rec G 40:28-9 Mr '77 *

RAMPHAL, Shridath S.
Economic relations between developed and developing countries. M Labor R 100:37-8 Mr '77

RAMPS
Build your own folding car ramp. P. J. Howerton. il Pop Mech 148:64 O '77

RAMSEY, Bob
Cricket and Katrine. B. Tarrant. il pors Field & S 82:154-6 My '77 *

RAMSEY, Jarold
Pisgah; poem. Atlantic 239:79 Mr '77

RAMSEY theory. See Graph theory

RAN, Shulamit
Contemp. ch. players: Ran prem. por Hi Fi 27:MA20 My '77 *

RANCH life
See also
Cowboys

RANCHES
At Payson's place he's just plain Charlie; Florida hunting ranch. V. Kraft. il por Sports Illus 46:54+ Ap 18 '77
Farm & ranch vacations. G. Bush. il Bet Hom & Gard 55:114-17 Je '77
Fever tick crashes roundup, causes trouble on range; cattle roundup at Texas' El Chapote Ranch. D. Snell. il Smithsonian 8:58-65 O '77
Phantom Ranch: yesterday and a mile deep. M. Franklin. il Nat Parks & Con Mag 51:4-9 D '77
Settling down in Texas; bird hunting at McFaddin Ranch. V. Kraft. il Sports Illus 47:74+ N 21 '77
Site for tired eyes; Cadillac Ranch, Amarillo, Tex. F. Deford. il por Sports Illus 46:84-8+ Ap 18 '77
Western guest ranching; working dude ranches. S. W. Byers. il Travel 147:54-7+ My '77

RANCHO la Puerta, Tecate, Mexico. See Health resorts, watering places, etc.

RANCIER, Esther
Special report: libraries and the fourth estate—a survey. Wilson Lib Bull 51:722+ My '77

RAND, Abby
Autumn in Portugal. il Harp Baz 111:16+ N '77
Sí, sí! They ski in Spain. il Holiday 57:44-6 N '76
10 best resorts in the world. il Harp Baz 110:12+ Ag '77
10 best ski resorts in the world. il Harp Baz 111:8+ D '77

RANDAL, Jonathan C.
Beating the press. D. M. Alpern and others. il pors map Newsweek 90:54 Ag 29 '77 *

RANDAL, Judith
DNA debate. Progressive 41:11-12 My '77
DNA lobby. Progressive 41:12 O '77
Life from the labs: who will control the new technology? Progressive 41:16-20 Mr '77; Same with title Who will control new living organisms? Current 193:52-60 My '77
—See Hines, W. jt auth

RANDALL, Dudley
Black magic; poem. Ebony 32:30 Ag '77

RANDALL, Francis Ballard
Maoism is dead. il Nat R 29:258-63 Mr 4 '77
Soochow: the Venice of China. Art N 76:112+ S '77

RANDALL, Helen C.
Puppets are fun. il Sch Arts 76:14-15 Je '77

RANDALL, Jill Weinick. See Kepler, K. jt auth

RANDALL, Patrick J. See Campbell, B. A. jt auth

RANDALL, Ron
Zero-base budgeting. Nation 224:331-4 Mr 19 '77

RANDALL, Tony
Hong Kong. il pors Holiday 58:30-3+ Mr '77

RANDALL, Williard S. See Solomon, S. D. jt auth

RANDIG, George W.
Build a digital bicycle-speedometer. il Pop Electr 11:39-41 Mr '77

RANDLE, Lenny
Fighting side of baseball. R. Blount, Jr. Esquire 88:30+ Jl '77 *
One mindless moment. K. Hannon. por Sports Illus 46:44+ Je 6 '77 *

RANDOLPH, Asa Philip
Day they didn't march. L. Bennett, Jr. il Ebony 32:128-30+ F '77 *

RANDOLPH, Edmund, 1753-1813
New nation's first lawyer. P. W. Schmidtchen. il pors Hobbies 82:134-7+ Ag '77 *

RANDOLPH, Eleanor
Carter complex. pors Esquire 88:166-8+ N '77

RANDOLPH, John
(ed) See Ciuffa, A. A. Secrets from a heartland bass lab

RANDOM House encyclopedia. See Encyclopedias

RANDOM House, Inc
Bennett Cerf remembers; excerpt from At Random. B. Cerf. il por Pub W 212:28-31 Ag 15; 26-9 Ag 22 '77
David Obst, Random House describe co-venture. M. Reuter. Pub W 211:42 Mr 14 '77
Paying $1 million to sell a book; television commercials for The Random House encyclopedia. il Bus W p 102+ S 12 '77

RANDOM House, Inc-Times Mirror Company merger. See Publishers and publishing—Acquisitions and mergers

RANGE enhancers. See Sound—Apparatus

RANGES, Kitchen. See Stoves

RANKIN, Allen
David Hartman's impossible dream. il por Read Digest 110:78-82 Ap '77

RANKIN, B. J.
When developing horse sense, use common sense. Consumers Res Mag 60:41 My '77

RANKIN, Dorothy
Not ready for the rocking chair. H. S. Davenport. il por Ret Liv 17:32-4 D '77 *

RANKIN, Hugh F.
Physical toughness of colonial Americans. Intellect 106:15 Jl '77

RANKIN, Janna
Legal risks and bold programming. Parks & Rec 12:47-8+ Jl '77

RANKIN, Judy
With a grip on glory and her game. S. Pileggi. il pors Sports Illus 46:30-3+ Je 6 '77 *

RANKIN, Peter Dunn-. See Dunn-Rankin, P.

RANLY, Ernest W.
Constructing local theologies. Commonweal 104:716-19 N 11 '77

RANSEN, Irving Rocke
New kind of development. J. M. Davern. il Archit Rec 162:96-107 D '77 *

RANSOM, James E.
Submersible pumps speed sewage flow. il Am City & County 92:70 Je '77

RAO, M. S. See Reddy, J. K. jt auth

RAPE
Arguing about death for rape. Time 109:80 Ap 11 '77
Death penalty for rape? case of Coker v. Georgia. D. Leavy. Ms 6:20 Jl '77
Decriminalizing rape. New Repub 177:8 Ag 20 '77
Mallard reactions to rape—it's a matter of costs and benefits; study by David P. Barash. J. Gaylin. Psychol Today 11:49 N '77
One woman's war against rape. M. Gross. por Good H 184:84+ Ap '77
Rape and culture; controversial views of A. Simonson. il por Time 110:41 S 12 '77
Rape and death; Supreme Court decision on death penalty in rape cases. il Newsweek 90:48 Jl 11 '77
Rape: the crime against women. Ladies Home J 94:69 Mr '77
Roman Polanski's tawdry trouble. il por Time 109:22 Mr 28 '77
Self-defense; ideas of F. Storaska. E. R. Dobell. Seventeen 36:194-5+ Ap '77
Victims of rape. F. R. Scarpitti and E. C. Scarpitti. bibl il Society 14:29-32 Jl '77
See also
Trials (rape)

RAPHAEL (artist)
Raphael transfigured. il Time 109:65 F 14 '77 *

RAPHAEL, Bette-Jane
On my obsession about weight. Mademoiselle 83:78+ S '77
Whatever happened to Mary Richards? il por McCalls 104:20+ S '77

RAPID-American Corporation
Riklis money game. D. Pauly and J. Walcott. por Newsweek 90:81 N 7 '77

RAPID-American Corporation-Kenton Corporation merger. See Corporations—Acquisitions and mergers

RAPID reading. See Speed reading

RAPID transit. See Local transit
RAPID transit cars. See Railroads—Cars
RAPIDS, Running of. See Running rapids
RAPOPORT, Sandra E.
Abu Daoud and the law. Commentary 63:70-2 Mr '77
RAPPAPORT, Bruce
Untangling what Pertamina owes—and to whom. il Bus W p90 F 7 '77 *
RAPPAPORT, David
New math and its aftermath. Educ Digest 42: 6-9 Ja '77
Numeration systems—a white elephant in elementary school. Educ Digest 42:56-7 Ap '77
RAPPOPORT, Solomon. See Ansky, S. pseud
RAPPORT, David J. and Turner, J. E.
Economic models in ecology. bibl il Science 195:367-73 Ja 28 '77
RAPTORIAL birds. See Birds of prey
RARATONGA. See Rarotonga
RARE animals
Canadian sketchbook: animals in peril. A. Odum. il Int Wildlife 7:42-3 Mr '77
Critical crossroads; question of critical habitat of endangered species. il map Nat Parks & Con Mag 51:19-22 F '77
Endangered species. il Nat Parks & Con Mag 51:12-15 F; 17-19 Mr; 16-20 Je; 8-10 N; 10-12 D '77
Facing the fate of the dinosaur? il map Sr Schol 109:12-13 Ap 21 '77
New hope for endangered species; Parque Zoológico Nacional, Dominican Republic. J. Duval. il Américas 29:19-23 Ja '77
Rare deer: still time? Calamian deer; Rare ox: alive or dead? kouprey. il Int Wildlife 7:17 My '77
Ten steps forward. il Nat Wildlife 16:4-13 D '77
View from the castle; breeding programs with rare animals at the National Zoo's Front Royal Va. facility. S. D. Ripley. Smithsonian 7:6 Mr '77
Wolves and louseworts. P. Gwynne. il Newsweek 89:95 F 21 '77
See also
Alligators
Convention on International Trade in Endangered Species of Wild Fauna and Flora
Manatees
Orangutans
Seals (animals)
Wolves

Export-import trade

See Wildlife—Export-import trade
RARE birds
Rare birds, bold men; efforts of the New Zealand Wildlife Service. J. Rearden. il Int Wildlife 7:4-11 Mr '77
See also
Bluebirds
Cranes (birds)
Eagles
Falcons
Woodpeckers

Conferences

Endangered birds: tinkering for time; Symposium on Management Techniques for Preserving Endangered Birds. F. Graham, Jr. Audubon 79:137-41 N '77

Protection

See Birds—Protection
RARE book collections. See College libraries—Special collections
RARE book dealers. See Booksellers and bookselling—Book rarities
RARE books. See Book rarities
RARE earth metals. See Earths, Rare
RARE fishes
Big Bend gambusia: . . . and then there were three. J. M. Schlatter. il Nat Parks & Con Mag 51:8-10 N '77
Changing bowls. B. A. Branson. bibl il Environment 19:25-30 Ap '77
Endangered fish of Kentucky streams. B. A. Branson. il Natur Hist 86:64-9 bibl(p 101) F '77
Native fish in troubled waters; with reproductions of paintings by G. L. Schelling. G. Reiger. il Audubon 79:18-41 Ja '77
What they didn't tell you about the snail darter & the dam. S. G. Cook and others. il map Nat Parks & Con Mag 51:10-13 My '77
RARE insects
See also
Butterflies
RARE plants
Bureaucratus delayus; discussion. Nat Parks & Con Mag 51:27-8 F '77
Deflowering of the Endangered Species Act. G. Moore. il Horticulture 55:36-9 My '77
Of dams and Kate Furbish; threat to Maine's rare plants by proposed Dickey-Lincoln Dams project. R. Saltonstall, Jr. il por Liv Wildn 40:42-3 Ja '77
See also
Convention on International Trade in Endangered Species of Wild Fauna and Flora
RARE species protection laws. See Conservation of resources—Laws and legislation
RAROTONGA
Return to Rarotonga. L. Janos. il Sat Eve Post 249:113-14+ D '77
RASCOE, Judith
This side of Hollywood. il Atlantic 239:92-4 F '77
RASHEED, Suraiya, and others
Establishment of a cell line with associated Epstein-Barr-like virus from a leukemic orangutan. bibl il Science 198:407-9 O 28 '77
RASKIN, A. H.
Can anybody clean up the Teamsters? il por N Y Times Mag p31+ N 7 '76; 63 Ja 16 '77
Heresy of worker participation. Psychol Today 10:111 F '77
Uncertain triumph. il Sat R 4:40-1 Mr 5 '77
RASKIN, Marcus G.
Survival. bibl il Society 15:53-7 N '77
RASKIND, Richard. See Richards, R.
RASMUSSEN, Henry
Retrospect: excerpt from Survivors. il Motor T 29:51-4 S '77
about
Retrospect. F. M. H. Gregory. il Motor T 28: 101-4 D '76 *
RASMUSSEN, Wallace N.
Beatrice Foods puts it together. por Duns R 110:55-6+ D '77 *
RASOOL, S. Ichtiaque, and others
What the exploration of Mars tells us about earth. il Phys Today 30:23-30+ Jl '77
RASPBERRIES
How a lifetime organic gardener grows berries profitably. G. Logsdon. il Org Gard & Farm 24:74-7 D '77
Red raspberries. C. Fenyvesi. New Repub 177:15 Ag 20 '77
RASPONI, Lanfranco
(ed) See Chiara, M. Chiara's way
(ed) See Duval, D. Voice of Poulenc
(ed) See Mazzoleni, E. Con istinto: Ester Mazzoleni
(ed) See Tess, G. Con ardore
(ed) See Villa-Lobos, A. Brasileiro
RAT control
Morristown's owls control city rats. Am City & County 92:30 O '77
RAT poisons
Controlling pesky sewer rats. W. S. Foster. il Am City & County 92:85-6 Je '77
RATCLIFF, Carter
Alexander Liberman at Storm King. il Art in Am 65:100-1 N '77
American artist from loner to lobbyist. il Art in Am 65:10-12 Mr '77
New York fever. il Art in Am 65:46-9 Jl '77
Report from San Francisco. il Art in Am 65: 55-62 My '77
Wyeth, the art world and class unconsciousness. il Art in Am 65:15+ Ja '77
RATCLIFFE, Stephen
Waterfall; Summer rain; The view from Mono Pass; Pause, Pico Blanco; poems. Poetry 129: 207-10 Ja '77
(tr) See Campion, T. Epigrammatum liber primus; Epigrammatum liber secundus
RATES. See subhead Rates under various subjects, e.g. Advertising—Rates
RATHBUN, Frank
Conciseness in F major. Writers Digest 57:45-7 Ag '77
RATHER, Dan
PW interviews; ed by J. F. Baker. por Pub W 211:8-9 My 9 '77
—and Herskowitz, Mickey
Camera never blinks; excerpt. por Ladies Home J 94:109 Jl '77
about
Prosecutor. M. J. Arlen. New Yorker 53:166-73 N 28 '77 *
RATIGAN, James
Letter from Louisville. America 136:464-5 My 21 '77
RATING. See subhead Rating under various subjects, e.g. Television programs—Rating
RATIONALISM
Cult of anti-rationalism in education. R. Hoffman. Educ Digest 42:57-60 Ja '77
RATIONING, Consumer

China

China's bureaucratic nightmare: rationing for 900 million people. R. H. Munro. il U.S. News 83:35-6 D 12 '77
RATIOS, Financial. See Financial ratios
RATLIFF, William E.
Palo Alto Chamber Orchestra. il Hi Fi 27:MA31-2+ N '77
RATNER, Leigh S.
Ocean mining: former negotiator now lobbies for Kennecott. D. Shapley. Science 196:964-5 My 27 '77 *
RATS
Degradation of DNA by nucleases in intestinal tract of rats. L. Maturin and R. Curtiss, 3d. bibl il Science 196:216-18 Ap 8 '77

RATS—*Continued*
Paradoxical effects of amphetamine on preweanling and postweanling rats. B. A. Campbell and P. J. Randall. bibl il Science 195:888-91 Mr 4 '77
Rat: lapdog of the devil. T. Y. Canby. il map Nat Geog 152:60-87 Jl '77
Rat societies. R. Lore and K. Flannelly. il Sci Am 236:106-11+ My '77
Suckling as incentive to instrumental learning in preweanling rats. J. T. Kenny and E. M. Blass. bibl il Science 196:898-9 My 20 '77
Woodrat slights rattler venom. il Sci N 112: 406-7 D 17 '77
See also
Nervous system—Rodents

Extermination

See Rat control

Food and feeding

Fenfluramine and fluoxetine spare protein consumption while suppressing caloric intake by rats. J. J. Wurtman and R. J. Wurtman. bibl il Science 198:1178-80 D 16 '77
Homeostasis during hypoglycemia: central control of adrenal secretion and peripheral control of feeding. E. M. Stricker and others. bibl il Science 196:79-81 Ap 1 '77
Intravenous self-feeding: long-term regulation of energy balance in rats. S. Nicolaïdis and N. Rowland. bibl il Science 195:589-91 F 11 '77
Selective blockade of hypothalamic hyperphagia and obesity in rats by serotonin-depleting midbrain lesions. D. V. Coscina and H. C. Stancer. bibl il Science 195:416-19 Ja 28 '77
Surgical removal of adipose tissue alters feeding behavior and the development of obesity in rats. I. M. Faust and others. bibl il Science 197:393-6 Jl 22 '77

RATS, Kangaroo. See Kangaroo rats
RATTAN furniture. See Furniture
RATTLESNAKE venom. See Venom
RATTLESNAKES
Death did not rattle; bite of massasauga rattler. C. Mol and B. East. il Outdoor Life 158:88-9+ Ap '77
Woodrat slights rattler venom. il Sci N 112: 406-7 D 17 '77
RATTNER, Abraham
Devotion to stained glass. Vasari. il Art N 76:20+ My '77 *
RAU, Ron
Day the pike put the move on Herman. il Sports Illus 46:38-40+ F 28 '77
Return to Sage Lake. il Nat Wildlife 15:36-9 Ap '77
Three fast rounds in Saginaw. il Sports Illus 46: 44-6+ Mr 21 '77
RAUDENBUSH, Don
Switching regulators reduce power supply cost. il Pop Electr 11:60+ Ap '77
RAUDSEPP, Eugene
Jumping to solutions; excerpt from Creative growth games. il Psychol Today 11:75-6+ D '77
RAUSCH, James Steven, Bp
Excerpts from letter on U.S. African policy, April 7, 1976. Cong Digest 56:30-1 Ja '77
RAUSCHENBERG, Robert
Rauschenberg; interview. New Yorker 53:30-1 My 23 '77
Robert Rauschenberg: an audience of one; interview, ed by J. Gruen. il por Art N 76:44-8 F '77

about

Artist for all decades. B. Forgey. il por Art N 76:34-6 Ja '77 *
Rauschenberg: the artist as witness. B. Rose. il por Vogue 167:174-5+ F '77 *
Rauschenberg: the world is a painting. il Horizon 19:16-19 My '77 *
Reading Rauschenberg. C. F. Stuckey. il pors Art in Am 65:74-84 Mr '77 *
Souvenirs of an avant-garde; retrospective at the Museum of Modern Art. H. Rosenberg. New Yorker 53:123-8 My 16 '77 *
RAVEL, Maurice
On discs; Daphnis and Chloë. J. D. Richardson. Dance Mag 51:90-1 Je '77 *
Orchestral works. W. D. Curtis. Am Rec G 40:25-6 Ag '77 *
RAVEN, Peter H.
Destruction of the tropics. BioScience 27:649 O '77
RAVENAL, Earl C.
Toward nuclear stability. Atlantic 240:35-41 S '77
RAVENSBRUCK Concentration Camp. See Concentration camps—Germany
RAVINIA Festival. See Music festivals—Illinois
RAVITCH, Diane
Brouhaha in Brooklyn. New Repub 176:18-21 Mr 12 '77
Wasted decade. New Repub 177:11-13 N 5 '77
RAW materials
See also
Stockpiling

RAWITCH, Allen B. and others
Competition of Δ^9-tetrahydrocannabinol with estrogen in rat uterine estrogen receptor binding. bibl il Science 197:1189-91 S 16 '77
RAWITSCHER, Mary, and Mayer, Jean
Nutritional outputs and energy inputs in seafoods. bibl il Science 198:261-4 O 21 '77
RAWLINGS, Marjorie (Kinnan)
Second look:
Yearling. C. McDonnell. Horn Bk 53:344-5 Je '77 *
RAWLS, Wendell, Jr
Tenn-Tom and Senator Stennis. N Y Times Mag p46 My 8 '77
RAWSON, Michael. See Heezen, B. C. jt auth
RAY, David
Climbing Mt Hood; poem. Nation 225:374 O 15 '77
RAY, Dixy Lee
Dixy rocks the Northwest. il pors map Time 110:26-9+ D 12 '77 *
Surprises from Nation's two women governors. pors U.S. News 83:45 O 10 '77 *
Washington: lady with a chain saw. T. Mathews and P. S. Greenberg. por Newsweek 89:45 Ap 11 '77 *
RAY, Elizabeth
I can't type. E. Keerdoja. il por Newsweek 89:10 Je 13 '77 *
RAY, James Earl
Capture in the Cumberlands. il por map Time 109:10-12 Je 27 '77 *
Ray's breakout; Question of conspiracy. il pors Time 109:12-18 Je 20 '77 *
Ray's capture. P. Goldman and others. il por Newsweek 89:25+ Je 27 '77 *
Ray's escape. P. Goldman and others. il pors map Newsweek 89:22-4+ Je 20 '77 *
Saga of Jimmy Ray. T. Mathews and others. pors Newsweek 89:24-5 Je 20 '77 *
RAY, Karen
Braving a new world. il Seventeen 36:232 Ap '77
I want to be terrific. . Seventeen 36:58 N '77
RAY, Man
Obituary
Art in Am por 65:21+ My '77. M. Amaya
Mod Phot por 41:62 F '77
Pop Phot 80:50 F '77
Practical dreams of Man Ray (1890-1976) A. D. Coleman. il Art N 76:52 Ja '77 *
RAY, Paul Richard
Executive placement; address, November 16, 1976. Vital Speeches 43:204-6 Ja 15 '77
RAY Surguine & Company. See Book wholesalers
RAYMOND, Ellsworth
Could Russia survive a nuclear attack? Nat R 29:1363 N 25 '77
RAYMOND, Lilo
Lilo Raymond. A. Wille. il Pop Phot 81:92-101+ Jl '77 *
View point. J. Deschin. il Pop Phot 81:22+ D '77 *
RAYMOND International Inc-Kaiser Engineers Inc merger. See Construction industry—Acquisitions and mergers
RAYNER, Graham
Coin quiz. See issues of Hobbies
Numismatics. See issues of Hobbies
RAYNER, William P.
Delights of Turkey. il map N Y Times Mag p80+ S 18 '77
Special pleasures of renting a house of your own in St Martin. il House & Gard 149:62+ S '77
RAYPORT, Stephen. See Wald, G. jt auth
RAYS (fishes)
Manta rays and stingrays: the much maligned devilfish. G. Compton. il Oceans 10:4-9 Ja '77
RAYTHEON Company
Self-healing computer in development. il Aviation W 107:57-60 Ag 15 '77
RAYTHEON Company-Lexitron Corporation merger. See Corporations—Acquisitions and mergers
RAYWARD, W. Boyd
IFLA 1977 AETAT 50. il Am Lib 8:606-8+ D '77
RAZOR blades
Razor blades. il Consumers Res Mag 60:26-8 F '77
See also
American Safety Razor Company
RAZORS
Close shave. R. L. Stepler. il Pop Sci 211:12 Ag '77
Personal care equipment and supplies. il Consumers Res Mag 60:49-58 O '77

Manufacture

See also
American Safety Razor Company
Bic Pen Corporation
RE, Dorothy Wicker
Confessions of a cartoon editor. il Writers Digest 57:39-41 Je '77
REA, James B.
Ben Graham's last will and testament. P. Blustein. il por Forbes 120:43-5 Ag 1 '77 *
REA, W. F. 3d
EPIRBs save lives. Yachting 141:197-8 My '77
REACTIONS, Chemical. See Chemical reactions

REACTOR fuel reprocessing
Carter on nuclear power: defer reprocessing. Sci N 111:244-5 Ap 16 '77
Carter's new plutonium policy: maybe less than meets the eye. W. D. Metz. Science 196:405-7 Ap 22 '77
Carter's nuclear switch. D. M. Alpern and others. il Newsweek 89:22-4 Ap 18 '77
Case for the breeder reactor; controversy concerning use of plutonium-239. B. L. Cohen. Nat R 29:1044-5+ S 16 '77; Discussion. 29: 1206+ O 28 '77
Department testifies on nonproliferation and nuclear export policies; statement, May 6, 1977. J. S. Nye, Jr. Dept State Bull 76:558-64 My 30 '77
Fizzle in Carter's anti-atom blast. Bus W p30 My 23 '77
How the genie got out of the bottle. T. Szulc. Forbes 119:89-91 My 15 '77
Making nuclear bombs the quick, dirty way. Sci N 112:357-8 N 26 '77
Nuclear power without nuclear proliferation; address, October 3, 1977. J. S. Nye, Jr. Dept State Bull 77:666-71 N 14 '77
Planning a safeguardable nuclear future; address, June 30, 1977. J. S. Nye, Jr. Dept State Bull 77:183-90 Ag 8 '77
Possible reprieve for the fast breeder. il Bus W p31-2 Je 20 '77
President Carter announces decisions on nuclear power policy; statement, and remarks, with transcript of question and answer session, April 7, 1977. J. Carter. Dept State Bull 76: 429-33 My 2 '77
Program to contain nuclear knowhow. Bus W p31 Ap 11 '77
Putting brakes on the fast breeder; J. Carter's policy on plutonium recycling. il Time 109:57 Ap 18 '77
Reprocessing alternatives: the options multiply. W. D. Metz. il Science 196:284-7 Ap 15 '77
Reprocessing: how necessary is it for the near term? W. D. Metz. il Science 196:43-5 Ap 1 '77
Reprocessing race; France. il Time 111:22 Ja 9 '78
Setback for plutonium; British Nuclear Fuels, limited. W. C. Patterson. Environment 19:41-3 Mr '77
TRB from Washington. New Repub 176:2+ My 7; 2+ My 14; 2+ Je 18 '77
Too hot to handle; Nuclear Fuel Services reprocessing plant in West Valley, N.Y. R. Severo. il N Y Times Mag p 15-19+ Ap 10 '77
Turning that worthless white metal into gold. T. Stevenson. Sat R 4:10 Ja 22 '77
U.S, Japan sign determination for nuclear facility. Dept State Bull 77:460-2 O 10 '77
U.S. nuclear power may be on the wrong track. D. Ediger and A. Parisi. il Bus W p 142-3 Ap 18 '77
United States policy on nuclear technology: combining energy and security; address, May 2, 1977. J. S. Nye, Jr. Dept State Bull 76: 550-4 My 30 '77
West Valley: the question is where does buck stop on nuclear wastes? L. J. Carter. Science 195:1306+ Mr 25 '77
What price plutonium? R. W. Peterson. il Nat Parks & Con Mag 51:16-19 Ag '77

REACTORS, Nuclear. See Nuclear reactors

READ, Gardner
B.U. Orch. & Ch: Read's Prophet. il por Hi Fi 27:MA24 Je '77 *

READ, Nat B. Jr
How to be Santa Claus. il Sat Eve Post 249:60-1+ D '77
Legend vs. legend. il Sat Eve Post 249:58-9+ N '77

READ-only memories. See Electronic circuits, Integrated

READABILITY and readable books
Identifying high interest/low reading level books. B. S. Bates. bibl il SLJ 24:19-21 N '77

READER, John. See Brelis, D. jt auth

READERS (books)
Back to McGuffey. R. Kirk. Nat R 29:614 My 27 '77
Schoolmaster to a nation; W. H. McGuffey. H. C. Jacobs. il por Sat Eve Post 249:62-3+ Ap '77

READERS Book Awards. See Literary prizes

READER'S digest
Behind the lines; Jackson Hole editorial conference. Read Digest 111:6+ D '77
Reaching for the Reader's Digest. J. M. Allen. Writer 90:26-8+ Ap '77

READER'S Digest Association, Inc.
Harper, Reader's Digest to copublish Fords' memoirs. M. Reuter. il pors Pub W 211:25-6 Mr 21 '77

READINESS for school
See also
Reading readiness

READING, Kate
Bike hiking. Seventeen 36:68 S '77
Skiing on the cheap. Seventeen 36:22 N '77

READING, Pa.
U.S. journal: Reading, Pa; factory outlets. C. Trillin. New Yorker 53:103-4+ D 5 '77

READING
See also
Books and reading
Readers (books)
Speed reading
Television and reading

Readiness

See Reading readiness

Remedial teaching

Comprehension revisited. J. Cox. Engl J 66:66-7 O '77
Fresh look at secondary reading. N. P. Criscuolo and J. F. Rossman. bibl Clearing H 50: 366-8 Ap '77
Helping reluctant readers help themselves: interest inventories. W. J. Lamberg. bibl f il Engl J 66:40-4 N '77
Preparing volunteer tutors. D. J. Sawyer. bibl Clearing H 51:152-6 D '77

Study and teaching

Appalachian reading instruction: the pragmatic social factor. G. Giordano. Engl J 66:31-2 My '77
On developmental relations between language-learning and reading. S. W. Lundsteen. Educ Digest 42:49-52 Ap '77
PR and the classroom teacher; informing parents of reading progress; New Haven, Conn. public schools. N. P. Criscuolo. Educ Digest 42:46-7 Mr '77
Reading improvement through art; success story from the Big Apple. S. K. Corwin; reply. I. Seidenberg. Sch Arts 77:66 S '77
Reading made easy for beginners; phonics-teaching. S. M. Friedman and H. O'Shaughnessy. il Parents Mag 52:62-3+ S '77
Reading skills in the English class. R. H. White. il Clearing H 51:32-5 S '77
Talking about reading: back to basics? A. Chambers. Horn Bk 53:567-74, 700-8 O-D '77
Teaching English: a view from the middle. R. T. Vacca. bibl Engl J 66:42-6 Ap '77
Using parents as teaching partners; program in Montgomery County, Md. public schools. A. Breiling. Educ Digest 42:50-2 F '77
What do students say about reading instruction? C. Bruckerhoff. Clearing H 51:104-7 N '77
Why Johnny can't read; sans serif type. V. Orton. Nat R 29:1006-7 S 2 '77
See also
Readers (books)
Reading readiness

Aids and devices

Developing lifelong readers in the middle schools. J. M. Barmore and P. S. Morse. il Engl J 66:57-61 Ap '77
Training model for junior high school communication aides; reading center at West Junior High School, Nampa, Idaho. L. McMillin. Engl J 66:52-3 Ap '77

Anecdotes, facetiae, satire, etc.

Story behind the great reading caper. A. Schatz. Psychol Today 10:96+ My '77

Testing

Cloze procedures and dialect considerations. C. W. Bonds. bibl Clearing H 50:360-2 Ap '77
Teaching all to read: still an uphill battle; test scores from National Assessment of Educational Progress. il U.S. News 82:61 Ja 24 '77
Visual characteristics of words. P. Dunn-Rankin. il Sci Am 238:122-30 Ja '78

READING air show. See Aviation—Exhibitions

READING aloud. See Books and reading—Reading aloud

READING and television. See Television and reading

READING comprehension
Improving children's comprehension abilities. D. R. Tovey. Educ Digest 42:60-2 Mr '77
Improving reading and the teaching of science. J. B. Davis. bibl Clearing H 50:390-2 My '77

READING disability
Developmental dyslexia: two right hemispheres and none left. S. F Witelson. bibl Science 195:309-11 Ja 21 '77
Dyslexia: a hemispheric explanation. Sci N 111:55 Ja 22 '77
Reading disability: and information-processing analysis. F. J. Morrison and others. bibl il Science 196:77-9 Ap 1 '77
See also
Reading—Remedial teaching

READING is Fundamental program. See Childrens reading; Young adults reading

READING lists
See also
Childrens literature—Bibliography
Young adults literature—Bibliography

READING machines
See also
Microform reading machines

READING of maps. See Map reading

READING of periodicals. See Periodical reading

READING readiness
Another look at reading readiness. A. L. Kovalcik. Educ Digest 43:48-50 S '77
Should you teach your child to read? preparing the preschooler. S. A. Jackson. bibl Am Educ 13:27-9 O '77
When should we begin to teach reading? W. H. MacGinitie. Educ Digest 42:60-2 F '77

READING research
Visual characteristics of words. P. Dunn-Rankin. il Sci Am 238:122-30 Ja '78

READINGS, Dramatic. See Dramatic readings

READOUTS (information display) See Information display systems

REAGAN, Michael J.
Mandatory certification—proposal that lost. Lib J 102:1723-4 S 1 '77

REAGAN, Ronald
Dying party? interview. pors U.S. News 83:23-4 Ag 29 '77
Reagan on the Canal; excerpts from interview, ed by G. C. Lubenow. por Newsweek 90:50 S 19 '77
Ronald Reagan—Mr Conservative; interview, ed by D. Pawelek. il pors Sr Schol 110:10-13 D 15 '77

about

Anglo-Saxon sentimentality. New Repub 177:5-8 S 24 '77 *
Legacy of Carter and Reagan: political reality overtakes the myth of the Presidential primaries. J. R. Beniger. bibl il Intellect 105:234-7 F '77 *
Reagan speaks out. P. Bonventure and others. il por Newsweek 90:37-8 S 5 '77 *

REAL estate agents
Women who sell houses. L. K. Howe. McCalls 104:123+ Ag '77

REAL estate business
Big catch; McDonald-Halliday Enterprises. il pors Forbes 120:76 D 15 '77
Boom in recycled buildings. il Bus W p 100-1+ Jl 11 '77
Case for design quality in today's marketplace: four studies of collaboration between architects and developers that explore the arithmetic of excellence; symposium. il Archit Rec 162:81-128 D '77
Clouded Sky; Big Sky of Montana Realty. E. Keerdoja. il Newsweek 90:13 S 12 '77
George Mitchell and his edifice complex. L. Minard. il por Forbes 120:81-2+ Jl 1 '77
Housing: raising the roof. T. Nicholson and others. il Newsweek 89:77-8 Je 13 '77
One that got away; loss of Uris Building Corp. by British Land. G. Smith. il por Forbes 119:58+ Ap 1 '77
Pentagon City is a family affair; new development project of Rose Associates Inc. in Arlington, Va. il Bus W p25 Mr 7 '77
Real estate without tears. por Forbes 119:57-8 Je 1 '77
Super Bowl winner; Iranian investment in New Orleans land development. por Forbes 120:78 D 15 '77
$3-billion cram-down? L. Minard. il Forbes 119:74+ Ap 15 '77
Tishman liquidates a problem—and itself. Bus W p26-7 N 7 '77
Wild speculation in California homes. il Bus W p31+ My 2 '77
See also
Arlen Realty and Development Corporation
Computers—Real estate use
Great Southwest Corporation
House selling
Land trusts
Offices—Leasing and renting
Webb, Del E. Corporation

Acquisitions and mergers

Bidding race for Irvine Ranch. por Bus W p29 My 2 '77
Mrs Smith's bonanza; bidding war over the Irvine Ranch. T. Nicholson and J. Huck. por map Newsweek 89:54+ My 23 '77
Now comes the hard part; ownership of Irvine Company by Taubman-Allen-Irvine, Inc. il Forbes 120:34-5 Jl 1 '77

Finance

Talking the developer's language: the financial analysis. J. Morse. il Archit Rec 162:56-7 D '77

Great Britain

Britain: a real estate flop embarrasses Labor; effect of financial problems of Italian International Bank Ltd on Labor Party Properties Ltd. Bus W p42+ F 7 '77
One that got away; loss of Uris Building Corp. by British Land. G. Smith. il por Forbes 119:58+ Ap 1 '77

REAL estate investment
Bundy touch; Ford Foundation's real estate troubles. L. Minard. Forbes 120:105 N 1 '77
Equitable Life goes on a realty investment spree. il Bus W p 114+ N 7 '77
For sale: bad deals in land. Changing T 31:13-15 Ag '77
Foreign buyers snap up more U.S. farmland. D. Braun. Farm J 101:E2 D '77
Great American land buyer. il Suc Farm 75:8-9 Ap '77
Invasion of the American heartland: a report on how and why foreign investors are gobbling up choice U.S. farms. C. H. Stern. il Sat R 5:18-20+ O 15 '77
Land boom in the farm belt. Forbes 119:25-6 Ap 15 '77
Let's stop the big grab for farmland. R. C. Black. il Farm J 101:14-15+ S; 20-1+ O '77; Discussion. 101:C4 D '77
New money target: profitable real estate. il Bus W p52-8 Ag 1 '77
Nobody here but us Texans..; foreign investments in Houston. il Forbes 119:52-4 F 1 '77
Putting money in land. P. Nelson. por McCalls 105:46+ N '77
Putting more pounds into U.S. property; British pension funds. il Bus W p57 O 10 '77
Real estate investment for pension funds. P. C. Aldrich and K. Upton. Harvard Bus R 55:14+ My '77
Real estate: we'll see some firming in prices; interview. N. B. Ture. por U.S. News 83:53-4 D 26 '77
Rich guy's loophole; real estate tax shelter. R. L. Nessen. New Repub 177:9-12 D 3 '77
Risk capital. G. L. Vincent. il Suc Farm 75:32-3+ Ja '77
Tough competition for profits in real estate. il Bus W p 112+ D 26 '77
20 years a landlord & how it paid; investment in a single-family dwelling. R. H. Howard. il Changing T 31:40-2 O '77
Why Canadian dollars are migrating south. il Bus W p42+ N 28 '77

REAL estate investment trusts
Country cousin; Realty Refund Trust. por Forbes 119:44 Mr 15 '77
Land anyone? AG-Land Fund I. Forbes 119:35 F 1 '77
Let's fence out Ag-Land trusts. Farm J 101:36 mid-Mr '77
Picking the bones of Colony Square; division of assets by Prudential Insurance Co. and Chase Manhattan Mortgage & Realty Trust. Bus W p39+ Ja 31 '77
REIT breakthrough to the capital markets; Connecticut General Mortgage & Realty Investments. il Bus W p66-8 Ja 9 '78
REIT revival may have its pitfalls. il Bus W p64-5 Ja 9 '78
REITs begin the gradual process of regaining some of their former status in funding development. G. A. Christie. il Archit Rec 162:61 O '77
REITs: more casualties ahead. il Bus W p 106+ Je 13 '77
REITs rebuild their debt structures. il Bus W p 114+ Ap 4 '77
REITs redux; B. E. Saul. il por Forbes 120:63-4 O 1 '77
Sissy; Washington Real Estate Investment Trust. por Forbes 120:100 Ag 15 '77
Speculating in white elephants. H. Rudnitsky. il Forbes 120:79-86 D 1 '77
Stop that farmland investment fund! Continental Illinois National Bank-Merrill Lynch fund. D. Cohen. Farm J 101:G2 mid-F '77
Three-year deadline at David's bank; Chase Manhattan. C. J. Loomis. il por Fortune 96:70-6 +Jl '77
Who wins the Reit game? First Union Real Estate Investments. il Forbes 119:132-3+ My 15 '77

REAL Estate Settlement Procedures Act. See House buying—Laws and legislation

REAL estate tax. See Real property tax

REAL property
Front-end cost of building. Bet Hom & Gard 55:98 My '77
Get ready to battle for your property rights. L. Lane. il Farm J 101:K3-4+ mid-Mr '77
See also
Airspace (law)
Condominium (housing)
Easements
Joint tenancy
Land
Land tenure
Mortgages
Real estate investment

Taxation

See Real property tax

Valuation

How much is your house worth? il Changing T 31:21-3 Je '77
How much should you pay for this farm? D. Seim. il Farm J 100:20-1+ D '76
See also
American Institute of Real Estate Appraisers
Assessment

REAL property and taxation
Figure tax angles when buying or selling farmland. Suc Farm 75:42 D '77

REAL property and taxation—*Continued*
Look what Congress did to your farm values; valuation for estate tax purposes. L. Lane. Farm J 101:K4 mid-F '77
REAL property tax
Don't lose control of the local property tax. G. M. Chamberlain. Am City & County 92:124 Je '77
Homeowners brew a revolt. il Bus W p20-1 Mr 28 '77
How taxes crushed a suburban family; Ossining, N.Y. il Bus W p21-2 Mr 28 '77
Those wild, wild property taxes. il Time 110:53 S 12 '77
See also
Forests and forestry—Taxation
REALISM in art
Always controversial Monsieur Courbet. A. Werner. il por Am Artist 41:58-63+ S '77
Gregory Gillespie's dense reality; interview, ed by J. Gruen. G. Gillespie. il por Art N 76:78-81 Mr '77
Illusionistic realism. il Ceram Mo 25:59-63 S '77
It's the real thing; D. Hanson's lifelike figures. R. Bongartz. il pors Horizon 20:72-81 S '77
Realism, past and present; Eight Contemporary American Realists. A. Jarmusch. il Art N 76: 194-5 N '77
REALISM in literature
Flirting with guilt and tyranny. E. Larsen. il Harpers 225:95-8+ D '77; Reply. G. Lyons. Nation 226:24-7 Ja 7 '78
REALITY
See also
Knowledge, Theory of
REALTORS. See Real estate agents
REALTY Refund Trusts. See Real estate investment trusts
REAMER, Sister Carol
My name is Asya; K. Michailovskaya's book. Engl J 66:62 Mr '77
REANEY, Desmond F.
Introducing IRIS, the International Rights Information Service. Pub W 212:99-114 S 19 '77
REANNEY, Darryl
Gene transfer as a mechanism of microbial evolution. bibl il BioScience 27:340-4 My '77
REAPPORTIONMENT. See Apportionment (election law)
REARDEN, Jim
Hunt Alaska now. il Field & S 82:60-1+ Ag '77
Pro: Alaska wolf kill. il Nat Wildlife 15:8 Ag '77
Rare birds, bold men. il Int Wildlife 7:4-11 Mr '77
REARDON, Jack
Rhodesian patrol. Nat R 29:611 My 27 '77
REARDON, Susan, and Dickmann, Don
Cornbelt conifers. il por Am For 83:8-10 Ag '77
REASON
See also
Common sense
Rationalism
REASONER, Harry
(ed) See Carter, J. President Carter interviewed by ABC news correspondents
about
Showdown at ABC News. J. Greenfield. il pors N Y Times Mag p32-4+ F 13 '77 •
REASONING
Can physics develop reasoning? R. G. Fuller and others. bibl il Phys Today 30:23-8 F '77
Remedial reasoning. C. Weingartner. Eng J 66: 12-14 My '77
See also
Fallacies (logic)
Problem solving
Thought and thinking
REAY, Mary
Boilers can be beautiful. il Sch Arts 77:10-11 N '77
REAY, Nina
Gold rush days; drama. Plays 36:43-6 F '77
REBATES, Income tax. See Income tax—United States
REBECCA (dancer)
Technique is only half the game; Rebecca: a DanceMime Concert. J. Pikula. Dance Mag 51:43+ Ap '77 •
REBETA-BURDITT, Joyce
Cracker factory; story; condensation of novel. Redbook 148:237-59 Ap '77
REBHAN, Herman
Building a counterforce to multinational corporations. M Labor R 100:46-7 Mr '77
RECALL of automobiles. See Automobiles—Recall
RECEIVING stolen goods. See Stolen goods, Receiving of
RECEPTIONS
See also
Government entertaining
RECEPTOR-specific proteins. See Lectins
RECEPTORS, Drug. See Drug receptors
RECEPTORS, Neural
Antischizophrenic drugs: chronic treatment elevates dopamine receptor binding in brain. D. R. Burt and others. bibl il Science 196: 326-8 Ap 15 '77
Chemical clues to schizophrenia. Sci N 112:342 N 19 '77
Covalent labeling of the tetrodotoxin receptor in excitable membranes. R. J. Guillory and others. bibl il Science 196:883-5 My 20 '77
Denervated skeletal muscle fibers develop discrete patches of high acetylcholine receptor density. P. K. Ko and others. bibl il Science 196:540-2 Ap 29 '77
Dopamine receptor binding enhancement accompanies lesion-induced behavioral supersensitivity. I. Creese and others. bibl il Science 197:596-8 Ag 5 '77
Inducibility of transferrin receptors on Friend erythroleukemic cells. H. Y. Y. Hu and others. bibl il Science 197:559-61 Ag 5 '77
Myasthenic immunoglobulin accelerates acetylcholine receptor degradation. I. Kao and D. B. Drachman. bibl il Science 196:527-9 Ap 29 '77
Response to acetylcholine. H. A. Lester. il Sci Am 236:106-16+ F '77
See also
Hormone receptors
RECEPTORS, Visual. See Rods and cones
RECHNITZ, G. A. See Meyerhoff, M. jt auth
RECIPES. See Cookery
RECK, W. Emerson
For the blessings of the year. il Am Hist Illus 12:4-7+ N '77
RECLAMATION, Bureau of. See United States—Reclamation, Bureau of
RECLAMATION of land
New strip mining law protects prime farm land. R. D. Wennblom. il Farm J 101:J4 O '77
Researchers seek ways to grow corn after coal. Farm J 101:D1 Ag '77
Soil and coal: a cost-benefit inquiry. S. F. Singer. Science 198:255 O 21 '77
Strip mining and the environment. B. A. Branson. il Nat Parks & Con Mag 51:10-12 Ap '77
There's more to reclamation than planting trees. J. R. McGuire. il Am For 83:14-19 Jl '77
See also
Irrigation
United States—Reclamation, Bureau of
Wetlands

Appalachian Region

This princess heals disturbed land. S. B. Carpenter. il Am For 83:22-3 Jl '77

Middle Western States

Lush grazing where coal was mined. J. G. White. il Farm J 101:J2+ mid-F '77

Ohio

On human engineering; Muskingum Watershed Conservancy District. L. E. Partain. il Am For 83:32-3+ Je '77

Pennsylvania

Johnny Appleseed for our time; reforestation of strip-mined land by W. G. Jones. J. Daniel. il Read Digest 111:142-6 Ag '77
Modern Johnny Appleseed; work of W. G. Jones. J. Cassell. por Outdoor Life 159:31 Je '77

Russia

Winning battle against destruction; reclamation of Russian steppes. A. G. Babaev and N. S. Orlovsky. il UNESCO Courier 30:18-22 Jl '77

Western States

Spectre of an American wasteland; with editorial comment. T. Pew. il map Horticulture 55:16, 40-53 Ag '77
RECLAMATION of waste water. See Water reuse
RECOGNITION (international law)
Diplomatic recognition. Dept State Bull 77:462-3 O 10 '77
RECOGNITION (psychology)
Faces passed. L. Wainwright. N Y Times Mag p45+ D 18 '77
From piecemeal to configurational representation of faces. S. Carey and R. Diamond. bibl il Science 195:312-14 Ja 21 '77
Self-awareness: humans are not alone. il Sci N 111:340 My 28 '77
RECOGNITION Equipment Inc. See Optical scanners—Manufacture
RECOGNITION of words. See Word perception
RECOIL (shooting) See Shooting
RECOMPENSE (Christian ethics) See Christian ethics
RECONCILIATION
Prodigal father. G. McCauley. America 136:224-inside back cover Mr 12 '77
RECONNAISSANCE, Aerial. See Aerial reconnaissance
RECONNAISSANCE satellites. See Artificial satellites—Military use
RECONSTRUCTION (Civil War)
1877-1977: a Southern Centennial. il Sr Schol 109:5-8 Ja 13 '77
RECONSTRUCTIVE surgery. See Surgery, Plastic
RECORD changers. See Phonograph—Turntables

RECORD industry. See Phonograph record industry

RECORD Interiors Award Program. See Architectural record (periodical)

RECORD ownership controversies. See Possession (law)

RECORD Plant (studio) See Sound—Recording and reproducing

RECORD players. See Phonograph

RECORDING of music. See Sound—Recording and reproducing

RECORDING studio musicians. See Musicians

RECORDING studios. See Sound—Recording and reproducing

RECORDS

Book of lists; excerpt from The book of lists. I. Wallace and others. Ladies Home J 94:169-76 My '77

I've got a little list; excerpt from The book of lists. D. Wallechinsky and others. Read Digest 111:62-4 Ag '77

Listomania. T. Schwartz. il Newsweek 89:59 Je 6 '77

See also

Aviation records
Business records
Farm records
Fishing records
Hunting records
Medical records
Personnel records
Public records
School reports and records
Sports records
Tax records

Anecdotes, facetiae, satire, etc.

Revelations of a list-maker; tr by A. Reid. G. Cabrera Infante. New Yorker 53:32-5 S 19 '77

Preservation

See Archives

RECORDS, Ancient

From reckoning to writing; work of D. Schmandt-Besserat on the correlation between geometric objects and signs on Sumerian tablets. il Sci Am 237:58 Ag '77

Roots of writing; ancient recording system used in trade; studies of D. Schmandt-Besserat. il por Time 110:76 Ag 1 '77

RECORDS, World. See World records

RECOVERY of space vehicles. See Space vehicles—Recovery

RECREATION

Recreation renaissance; excerpt from Play behavior. J. Levy. Parks & Rec 12:16-20 D '77

See also

Aged—Recreation
Children—Recreation
Handicapped—Recreation
Hobbies
Leisure
Outdoor life
Playgrounds
Prison recreation
Sports
Student activities

Activities

Hundred pockets for festivity. E. R. Walsh. il Parks & Rec 12:51-3+ Je '77

Legal risks and bold programming; liability for risk activities. J. Rankin. Parks & Rec 12:47-8+ Jl '77

Programs are for people. F. Wallach. Parks & Rec 12:21 Je '77

Self-renewal takes new directions in hobbies, culture, back-to-school. il U.S. News 82:64-9 My 23 '77

See also

Boats and boating
Camps—Activities
Horsemanship

Bibliography

Books (cont) Parks & Rec 12:31 F '77

Conferences

Coming events. See issues of Parks & recreation

See also

National Recreation and Park Association—Meetings

Economic aspects

Boom in leisure—where Americans spend 160 billions. il U.S. News 82:62-3 My 23 '77

People are shelling out more than ever for a good time. il U.S. News 82:40-2 F 21 '77

Equipment and supplies

1977 Parks & recreation buyers' guide. il Parks & Rec 12:83-93+ Ja '77

Product news. il Parks & Rec 12:68+ Mr '77

See also

Sporting goods

Federal aid

Washington scene. B. Kravetz. Parks & Rec 12:16+ Je; 12-13 Ag '77

Finance

Public-commercial joint venture. J. L. Crompton. bibl Parks & Rec 12:20-3+ Jl '77

Periodicals

See also

Parks and recreation (periodical)

Research

See Recreation research

Study and teaching

Path to accreditation; college and university programs in recreation education. I. G. Shapiro. Parks & Rec 12:29-31+ Ja '77

Recreation semantics 101. B. F. Mead, Jr. Parks & Rec 12:26-8+ O '77

SPRE responds to BOR director on leisure curricula, research. Parks & Rec 12:46 D '77

Colombia

See also

Bogota, Colombia—Recreation

Colorado

Brainstorming and name forming; programs offered in Aurora. L. Johnson. Parks & Rec 12:36+ Je '77

Germany, West

Regional planning in the Ruhr Valley. G. G. Wynne. il map Parks & Rec 12:21-3 D '77

Michigan

Pool makes waves; Oakland County. il Parks & Rec 12:46 My '77

Reaching high point with a playground; construction of playground for the handicapped, High Point. P. Hogan. il Parks & Rec 12:26-9 N '77

Montana

Day care with a difference; Missoula, Montana's Summer Enrichment Program. L. A. Heywood. il Parks & Rec 12:16-19 Jl '77

New York (state)

Hundred pockets for festivity; Westbury programs. E. R. Walsh. il Parks & Rec 12:51-3+ Je '77

State government on the road. B. Conn. il Parks & Rec 12:59-60+ Je '77

See also

New York (city)—Recreation

Ohio

Opening the locks to the past; use of canals in recreation. M. L. Drake. il map Parks & Rec 12:22-7+ Mr '77

United States

How Americans pursue happiness; special section. il U.S. News 82:60-72+ My 23 '77

Life outdoors. H. F. Waters and others. il Newsweek 90:56-7+ Jl 18 '77

Planning for young adults. Am City & County 92:40 N '77

Recreation planning for energy conservation; urban recreation. S. M. Gold. il Parks & Rec 12:61-3+ S '77

Recreation review may stall PL 92-500 projects; coordination of wastewater treatment and open space and recreational planning. il Am City & County 92:13 O '77

Relieving the pressures on the parks; question of providing outdoor recreational opportunities on other public lands. A. W. Smith. Nat Parks & Con Mag 51:2+ N '77

Urban recreation study: doing it right. M. Maguire. il Parks & Rec 12:28-31+ Ap '77

Washington scene; converting abandoned railroad rights-of-way to recreation uses. B. Kravetz. Parks & Rec 12:16+ O '77

Washington scene; emerging options for preservation. B. S. Tindall. Parks & Rec 12:13+ D '77

Watts up must come down? using utility rights-of-way. E. Meves. bibl il Parks & Rec 12:29-31 O '77

See also

National Recreation and Parks Association
Parks—United States

RECREATION activities. See Recreation—Activities

RECREATION and state

NRPA interview with Congressman Morris K. Udall; ed by B. Kravetz. M. K. Udall. il pors Parks & Rec 12:42-5 Mr '77

Plea for mediocrity; recreation research in the federal government. W. F. LaPage. Parks & Rec 12:25-6+ Ag '77

See also

United States—Outdoor Recreation, Bureau of

RECREATION areas

Poor planning may prevail; Gateway National Recreation Area. Nat Parks & Con Mag 51:19 F '77

Recall for greenways; excerpt from The public benefits of cleaned water: emerging greenway opportunities. H. Deardorff. il Parks & Rec 12:39a-40a F '77

RECREATION areas—*Continued*
Success stories in multiple-use; recreation potential of wastewater treatment sites. T. L. Gilbert. il Parks & Rec 12:22a-24a F '77
See also
National parks and reserves
Parks

California

Leg stretching in Nightmare Gulch; Red Rock Canyon State Recreation Area. il Sunset 158: 44+ My '77

Georgia

Georgia's enchanted land has friends in Washington, D.C; proposed Chattahoochee River National Recreation Area. il Nat Parks & Con Mag 51:17-19 D '77

Washington (state)

Sand dunes, sagebrush. . .and sails? reservoir near O'Sullivan Dam. L. G. Alkire, Jr. Yachting 141:199-203 My '77

Western States

10 best west boating spots. R. Burnham. maps Motor B & S 139:91-3+ My '77

RECREATION buildings. See Recreation centers

RECREATION centers
Building type study: building for sport; with introd by B. F. Gordon and C. K. Hoyt. il Archit Rec 161:115-30 F '77
Designers go to poles; El Cariso Park and Golf course. il Parks & Rec 12:36 My '77
Different kind of youth center; Miami Beach, Fla. il Archit Rec 162:79-84 Jl '77
Long-awaited well-respected community center; Webster Community Center, Bronx, N.Y. K. Kelly. il Archit Rec 162:95-8 O '77
Recreation at your doorstep; mobile recreation unit. C. Behrend. il Parks & Rec 12:54-5 Je '77
Two cities get jump on solar energy. il Am City & County 92:30 Ap '77

RECREATION education. See Recreation—Study and teaching

RECREATION for the aged. See Aged—Recreation

RECREATION programs. See Recreation—Activities

RECREATION research
Modernizing evaluation techniques. A. P. Strobell. il Parks & Rec 12:30-1+ Je '77
Plea for mediocrity. W. F. LaPage. Parks & Rec 12:25-6+ Ag '77
Tuning up for high performance. J. G. Williams and C. R. Edginton. il Parks & Rec 12: 36-40+ O '77

RECREATION rooms
All-in-the-family room. Redbook 148:205 Ap '77; Same. Ladies Home J 94:178+ Ap '77
Great ideas for a family hobby room. il Pop Mech 148:108-9+ N '77

RECREATION surveys
EEI: a survival tool; economic equivalency index to measure leisure services. R. L. Wilder. il Parks & Rec 12:22-4+ Ag '77

RECREATION workers
Code to work by. C. W. Pezoldt. il Parks & Rec 12:32-4+ Ja '77
People. See issues of Parks & recreation
Women in recreation. D. R. Dunn. bibl il Parks & Rec 12:24-30 Jl '77

RECREATIONAL vehicle camping. See Camping

RECREATIONAL vehicle industry. See Truck industry

RECREATIONAL vehicle insurance. See Insurance, Motor vehicle

RECREATIONAL vehicle trips. See Automobile touring

RECREATIONAL vehicles
Choosing an RV. B. Behme. Field & S 82:124+ My '77
Full-time RV living: the great escape. . .or the great hassle? V. L. Oertle. il Outdoor Life 160:158+ N '77
Motorized camping: an outdoorsman's guide to RVs. H. Shuldiner. il Outdoor Life 159: 89-96 F '77
New RV scene: simply astonishing! F. K. Coffee. il Mech Illus 73:58+ F '77
RV roundup:
Self-propelled rigs. B. Behme. il Field & S 81:124+ Ap '77
Towables; camping trailers. B. Behme. il Field & S 81:122+ Mr '77
RVs that pay their own way. F. K. Coffee. il Mech Illus 73:84+ Je '77
Recreation roundup. H. Shuldiner. See issues of Popular science
Recreational vehicles. H. Shuldiner. See occasional issues of Outdoor life
Wedge comes to RVs. F. K. Coffee. il Mech Illus 74:31-3+ Ja '78
See also
Automobile trailers
Campers, Truck
Snowmobiles and snowmobiling
Vans

Bibliography

Build your own library. B. Behme. Field & S 81:100+ F '77

Fuel consumption

Recreational vehicles: gas curbs on off-road vehicles? H. Shuldiner. il Outdoor Life 160: 24+ D '77

Insurance

See Insurance, Motor vehicle

RECREATIONS, Literary. See Literary recreations

RECRUITING and enlistment. See United States—Armed Forces—Recruiting, enlistment, etc.

RECRUITING of athletes. See Athletes—Recruiting

RECRUITING of basketball players. See Basketball players—Recruiting

RECRUITING of employees
Employment practices in South Africa; remarks, October 5, 1977. C. R. Vance. Dept State Bull 77:685-6 N 14 '77
In hotter pursuit of MBAs. il Bus W p98 F 7 '77
See also
College librarians—Recruiting
Employment interviewing
Executives—Recruiting
Librarians—Recruiting

RECRUITING of football players. See Football players—Recruiting

RECRUITING of soccer players. See Soccer players—Recruiting

RECRUITING of students. See Colleges and universities—Student recruiting

RECRUITING of teachers. See Teachers—Recruiting

RECTUM

Diseases

See also
Hemorrhoids

RECYCLED buildings. See Buildings, Remodeled

RECYCLED water. See Water reuse

RECYCLING of waste. See Refuse, Utilization of

RED Army Faction. See Terrorists, German

RED blood cells. See Erythrocytes

RED carpet Christmas; drama. See Miller, H. L.

RED cedar, Western. See Arborvitae

RED clover. See Clover

RED crested cranes. See Cranes (birds)

RED mangrove. See Mangrove

RED River (New Mexico)
Killing of a wild river; pollution by Molybdenum Corporation of America, or MolyCorp. D. Kline. Field & S 82:104+ S '77

RED Rock Canyon State Recreation Area. See Recreation areas—California

RED Sea
Synagogues & sea fans. E. Clark. il por map Nat Parks & Con Mag 51:13-20 Ap '77
See also
Petroleum—Red Sea Region
Suez Canal

RED-shouldered hawks. See Hawks

RED tape. See Bureaucracy

RED wolves. See Wolves

REDBONE, Leon
Who is Leon Redbone & why is he singing all those oddball songs? L. Bangs. por Hi Fi 27: 140+ Ap '77 *

REDBOOK (periodical)
Between the lines; winners of Redbook's Young Writers' Contest; short stories. A. M. Smith. il Redbook 149:20 Ag '77
Redbook fiction, from the inside. J. Johnson. Writer 90:18-21 N '77

REDDY, Enuga S.
U.N.'s world campaign against apartheid. il map UNESCO Courier 30:5-8 N '77

REDDY, Helen
At home with Helen Reddy. il por Good H 186:102-5 Ja '78 *

REDDY, J. K. and Rao, M. S.
Transplantable pancreatic carcinoma of the rat. bibl il Science 198:78-80 O 7 '77

REDECORATING. See House decoration

REDEMPTION. See Salvation

REDFORD, Robert
Riddle of Robert Redford. B. G. Harrison. il por McCalls 104:42+ My '77 *
What makes Robert Redford run? W. Davidson. il pors Sat Eve Post 249:42-3 My '77 *

REDFORD Union School District. See Education—Michigan

REDGRAVE, Vanessa
Jane Fonda: her own woman at last? M. Drabble. il pors Ms 6:51-3+ O '77 *

REDISTRIBUTION of wealth. See Wealth

REDISTRICTING. See Apportionment (election law)

REDKEN Laboratories, Inc. See Cosmetics industry

REDLER, Bruce H. See Yoon, S. C. C. jt auth

REDLINING (insurance) See Insurance, Property

REDLINING (mortgages) See Mortgages

REDONDO Beach, Calif.
Education
See Education—California
REDUCING diet. See Diet
REDUCING exercises. See Exercise
REDUCTASES
Diabetic cataracts and flavonoids. S. D. Varma and others. bibl il Science 195:205-6 Ja 14 '77
Dihydrofolate reductase: X-ray structure of the binary complex with methotrexate. D. A. Matthews and others. bibl il Science 197:452-5 Jl 29 '77
REDWOOD
Pioneer conservationist A. P. Hill: he saved the redwoods. V. T. Olson. il pors Am West 14:32-40 S '77
Wood for all seasons; park equipment. il Parks & Rec 12:34-5 My '77
REDWOOD National Park
Capitol Hill lag could narrow chances of salvaging Redwood Park. Nat Parks & Con Mag 51:21 N '77
Giant battle in redwood country. il Bus W p30-1 Ap 25 '77
Logger outcry obscures slow death of ancient park redwoods. il Nat Parks & Con Mag 51:22-3 Je '77
Redwood Park: costly, sorry abortion. P. L. Fradkin. Audubon 79:121-2 Mr '77
Redwood protest; loggers demonstration against major expansion. S. Fraker and G. C. Lubenow. il map Newsweek 89:30 Ap 25 '77
Redwoods: as the worm turns; with letter by N. B. Livermore, Jr. J. B. Craig. il Am For 83:28-31+ Jl '77; Discussion. 83-4+ O '77
REECE, Maynard
First, you've got to know wildlife; interview, ed by B. Strohm. il Nat Wildlife 15:48-55 O '77
about
Maynard Reece paints—memories on canvas. G. H. Harrison. il pors Am For 83:24-7 Jl '77 *
REED, Cordell
Nuclear energy expert. il pors Ebony 32:64-6+ Je '77 *
REED, David
Arch-terrorist who went scot-free. Read Digest 111:114-18 S '77
Russia's ruthless reach into Africa. map Read Digest 111:169-74 N '77
Search for the missing tomcat. il Read Digest 110:79-83 Mr '77
Time runs out for South Africa. map Read Digest 110:85-90 F '77
REED, J. D.
Booktalk. Sports Illus 47:8 Ag 8 '77
Fads. Sports Illus 47:80+ D 12 '77
Rowing. Sports Illus 46:70 My 16 '77
Soccer (cont) Sports Illus 46:52-3 F 7; 66+ Mr 14; 84+ Ap 11; 47:48-9 Ag 8; 66+ O 24; 70+ D 12 '77
Taut duel for two old comrades. il Sports Illus 47:40-2+ D 12 '77
They hunger for success. il Sports Illus 46:64-8+ F 28 '77
about
Letter from the publisher. J. Meyers. por Sports Illus 46:4 F 28 '77 *
REED, Jay
Earth log: the Audubon road show. G. H. Harrison. il pors Audubon 79:102-3+ My 77 *
REED, Nathaniel P.
Offer too good to refuse. il Parks & Rec 12:15a-18a F '77
REED, Rex
Movies. See issues of Vogue
REED, Thomas C.
Challenges in the 1980s; address, January 17, 1977. Vital Speeches 43:268-71 F 15 '77
REED, William F. Jr
College football. il Sports Illus 47:72+ N 14 '77
Horse racing (cont) Sports Illus 46:68+ Ap 25 '77
Horses. Sports Illus 47:95-6+ D 19 '77
You'll never hush hush Charlotte now. il Sports Illus 46:20-1 Mr 28 '77
REED, Willis
Gospel according to Willis. T. Kornheiser. il por N Y Times Mag p43-4+ O 16 '77 *
REED & Barton Corporation. See Silverware—Manufacture
REED canary grass. See Grasses
REED International Ltd
Why Reed stopped acquiring. il Bus W p76-7 Jl 18 '77
REEDY, Gerard C.
Fiction (cont) America 136:421-3 My 7; 137:336+ N 12 '77
REEF fishes. See Fishes
REEFING (sails) See Sails
REEFS
See also
Coral reefs and islands
REEL-to-reel tape recorders. See Tape recorders and recording
REELS, Fishing. See Fishing tackle

REEMS, Harry
United States versus the princes of porn. T. Morgan. il pors N Y Times Mag p 16-17+ Mr 6 '77 *
REES, Martin J.
Unfolding universe. Current 190:51-9 F '77
REES, Richard Charles
Rich man, poor man. il Time 109:22+ Ja 24 '77 *
REES, Walter A. Nelson-. See Nelson-Rees, W. A.
REESE, Gustave
Obituary
Mus Q 63:579-81 O '77. E. H. Roesner
REESE, Jay Rodney
Recognition Equipment revives itself. il por Bus W p88 S 5 '77 *
REESE, Paul
Trials of a letter writer. K. Wenger. il por Nation 225:657-9 D 17 '77 *
REESE, Ronald W.
Build charge! digital electronic bugle-call generator. il Pop Electr 13:45-8 Ja '78
REESE, Thomas J.
Energy crisis. America 137:373-4, 398-400, 418-20 N 26-D 10 '77
REEVE, Michael R. and Walter, M. A.
Project CEPEX. il Sea Front 23:365-73 N '77
REEVES, Randall R.
Hunt for the narwhal: unicorn of the Arctic seas. il Oceans 10:50-7 Jl '77
REEVES, Richard
Did it really happen here? il Esquire 88:83-7 Jl '77
Media. Esquire 88:40-1 Ag; 30+ S; 20+ O; 53-4 N; 68+ D '77; 89:38+ Ja '78
Night Carter took over the party; excerpt from Convention. il pors N Y Times Mag p32-8+ F 20 '77
Prime-time President. il por N Y Times Mag p 17-19 My 15 '77
—and Hager, B. M.
Good old boy network. New Repub 177:6+ S 10 '77
REEVES, Troy Dale
Sarai poem. Chr Today 22:24 N 4 '77
REFEREES and refereeing (sports) See Football, Professional—Refereeing
REFERENCE and Adult Services Division. See American Library Association—Reference and Adult Services Division
REFERENCE books
From Winchell's 8th to Sheehy's 9th; interview, ed by A. Plotnik. E. P. Sheehy. il Am Lib 8:129-32 Mr '77
Manufacturer of BooKassettes seeks editorial ties in U.S. J. Giusto. Pub W 212:32 O 31 '77
Reference books for teachers. H. F. McGaw. Clearing H 51:63-4 O '77
See also
Booksellers and bookselling—Reference books
Encyclopedias
Bibliography
Current reference books. C. A. Bunge. See issues of Wilson library bulletin
Keeping up; a checklist; black reference books. A. S. Meyers. Am Lib 8:77 F '77
Questions, anyone? C. A. Anthony. Am Educ 13:13-18 O '77
Reference books of 1976; comp by a committee of the Reference and Adult Services Division. American Library Association; ed by L. Wishart. il por Lib J 102:873-7 Ap 15 '77
REFERENCE services. See Libraries—Reference services
REFERENDUM
Going to the people. il Time 110:18-19 N 21 '77
King of the referendum; R. McCarney of North Dakota. por Time 109:19 Je 13 '77
Voters say yes to spending for essentials, no to frills. U.S. News 83:104-5 N 21 '77
Chile
Chile's referendum farce. Nation 226:2-4 Ja 7 '78
Junta wins in a landslide. il por Time 111:29 Ja 16 '78
Philippines
Marcos' yes and yes vote. il por Time 110:26 D 26 '77
REFF, Theodore
Duchamp & Leonardo: L.H.O.O.Q.—alikes; adaptation of address, February 17, 1974. bibl il Art in Am 65:82-93 Ja; 5 My; 5 Jl '77
REFINERIES. See Petroleum refineries
REFINISHING of floors. See Floors—Maintenance and repair
REFINISHING of furniture. See Furniture—Finishing
REFLECTING telescopes. See Telescopes
REFLECTORS (safety devices)
Road emergency signals; warning devices. il Consumer Rep 42:533-7 S '77
REFLEXES
Natural life preservers; views of M. Nemiroff on the diving reflex. il por Time 110:73+ Ag 22 '77
Reprieve from drowning; diving reflex. Sci Am 237:57-8 Ag '77

REFLEXES—*Continued*
Saving the drowned; diving reflex during asphyxia. S. Drake. il por Newsweek 90:79-80 Ag 22 '77
REFORESTATION
Johnny Appleseed for our time; reforestation of strip-mined land by W. G. Jones. J. Daniel. il por Read Digest 111:142-6 Ag '77
Modern Johnny Appleseed; work of W. G. Jones. J. Cassell. por Outdoor Life 159:31 Je '77
Tillamook: a modern success story. B. Keil. il Am For 83:20-3+ Mr '77
See also
Forest planting
Forest reproduction
REFORM, Political. See Political reform
REFORM schools. See Reformatories
REFORMATORIES
Reflections on corrections; juvenile corrections institution library. S. B. Madden. il por Wilson Lib Bull 51:519-21 F '77
REFORMED Church in America
RCA's carefully managed synod. H. Hageman. Chr Cent 94:696-7 Ag 3 '77
REFORMED churches
Reformed Alliance: sliding with man? J. D. Douglas. Chr Today 21:53-4+ S 23 '77
REFRACTORY metals. See Alloys
REFRIGERATION and refrigerating machinery
See also
Refrigerators
REFRIGERATION on boats
Maintaining your ice supply. B. Fleischhauer. Motor B & S 140:100-2 Jl '77
REFRIGERATOR-freezers. See Refrigerators
REFRIGERATOR thermometers. See Thermometers and thermometry
REFRIGERATORS
Manual defrost switch can save energy. J. Cedarleaf. il Pop Sci 210:179 Ap '77
Solar powered refrigerator stores vital medicines. il Space World M-12-156:30 D '76
Top-freezer refrigerators. il Consumer Rep 43:23-9 Ja '78
REFSGAARD, Niels
Profile—Niels Refsgaard; interview. ed by S. G. Lewin. il por House B 119:12+ Mr '77
REFUGEES
Political refugees; question of liberalization of US immigration law. New Repub 177:6+ D 3 '77
See also
Asylum, Right of
Exiles
United Nations—High Commissioner for Refugees
United Nations Relief and Works Agency for Palestine Refugees in the Near East
REFUGEES, Arab
See also
Palestinian Arabs
United Nations Relief and Works Agency for Palestine Refugees in the Near East
REFUGEES, Cambodian
How much blood makes a bloodbath? M. Kondracke. New Repub 177:21-2 O 1 '77
REFUGEES, Haitian
Back where they came from. Nation 225:260-1 S 24 '77
REFUGEES, Hungarian
Home thoughts from abroad. P. Jonas. Harpers 254:20-1 Ap '77
REFUGEES, Indochinese
Indochinese refugees. K. Keegan. New Repub 177:11-12 Jl 23 '77
Recommendation to parole Indochinese refugees; statement, August 4, 1977. R. C. Holbrooke. Dept State Bull 77:411-13 S 26 '77
Reporter at large. R. Shaplen. New Yorker 53:33-6+ S 5 '77
U.S. opens its doors to the floating refugees; parole section of the Immigration and Nationality Act. U.S. News 83:21 Ag 15 '77
Vietnam's legacy; emergency plan to admit 15,000 to the United States. D. M. Alpern and others. Newsweek 90:18 Jl 18 '77
REFUGEES, Mozambican
Portugal's returnees. T. Land. Progressive 41:50 D '77
REFUGEES, Political. See Refugees
REFUGEES, South African
Urgent need to aid South African student refugees recognized. UN Chron 14:64-5 Ja '77
REFUGEES, Vietnamese
Human rights and Vietnam. Commonweal 104:515-16 Ag 19 '77
Refugees: seeking safe harbor. il Time 110:24+ Jl 4 '77
See also
Vietnamese in the United States
REFUGES, Wildlife. See Wildlife sanctuaries
REFUSE, Utilization of
Energy from the biomass; using organic "junk" for energy. J. K. Hanson. Current 190:39-42 F '77
Environmentalists say tattletale gray is beautiful—in paper products. il Ret Liv 17:13 Je '77
Garbage—refuse or resource? M. LaBreque. il Pop Sci 210:95-8+ Je '77
Milwaukee turns solid waste into new resources. il Am City & County 92:66-7 Ag '77
New life for tired tires. M. Spiegel. il Mech Illus 73:138+ F '77
One company's waste, another's wealth. L. Hastings. il Environment 19:38-40 O '77
Solid waste recovers land for industry use; New Orleans. il Am City & County 92:46-8 Ap '77
Source recovery gets off to slow start; Separation of office and Residential Trash project in San Luis Obispo County. Am City & County 92:26 Je '77
Stop fighting, start contracting; resource recovery. S. G. Lewis. il Am City & County 92:67-9 Je '77
Time to retire; C. Heidelberger's collection of used tires. il por Time 109:42 My 23 '77
Waste: the problem that won't go away. J. Kagan. il McCalls 104:66 Jl '77
See also
Filling (earthwork)
Refuse as fertilizer
Refuse as fuel
Salvage (waste)

Conferences

Help your city discover composting; Composting and Waste Recycling Conference. Org Gard & Farm 24:150-1 Mr '77

Economic aspects

Helping recyclers get lower rail rates; fighting against railroads and ICC. Bus W p36 S 5 '77
REFUSE and refuse collection
Container collection cuts refuse service costs; Cordele, Ga. il Am City & County 92:40 Jl '77
REFUSE and refuse disposal
California litter; question of beach litter. B. E. Bechtol and J. R. Williams. il Natur Hist 86:62-5 (bibl(p93) Je '77
How to set refuse collection routes. il Am City & County 92:51-3 N '77
Mechanical collection puts lid on refuse inflation; Sidney, Neb. M. Dils. il Am City & County 92:31-2 Ja '77
Practical ideas for refuse truck routing. il Am City & County 92:47-8 D '77
Profitable way to get rid of solid waste; North American Bait Farms experiment. V. Louviere. por Nations Bus 65:65 Ja '77
Solid waste disposal needs areawide solutions; Champaign County, Ill. H. Paley. por Am City & County 92:63 Mr '77
Transfer stations compact waste collection distances; Oswego County, N.Y. F. A. Loguidice. il Am City & County 92:73-4 Ag '77
Truth and consequences; address, May 17, 1977. J. H. Alexander. Vital Speeches 43:565-9 Jl 1 '77
Vacuum handles big litter problem; Virginia Beach, Va. Am City & County 92:42 O '77
Wastes around the world. P. K. De Joie. il Environment 19:32-7 O '77
See also
Keep America Beautiful, Inc
Los Angeles County, Calif.—Sanitary affairs
Milwaukee—Sanitary affairs
Municipal dumps
New Orleans—Sanitary affairs
New York (city)—Sanitary affairs
Newark, N.J.—Sanitary affairs
Philadelphia—Sanitary affairs
Pyrolysis
Radioactive waste disposal
Refuse as fuel
Refuse collection trucks
Refuse containers
Refuse incinerators
SCA Services Inc
St Louis—Sanitary affairs
Seattle—Sanitary affairs
Sewage disposal
Street cleaning

Apparatus

Garbage disposers. il Consumer Rep 42:298-302 My '77

Laws and regulations

Containing waste. E. A. Goldstein. bibl il Environment 19:42-4 O '77
Waste region, agency guides outlined. Am City & County 92:56 S '77
REFUSE as fertilizer
Three options to turn waste into resources. C. Golueke. il Org Gard & Farm 24:142+ S '77
REFUSE as fuel
Garbage: a fuel for the future; refuse recycling. J. Daniel. il Read Digest 111:66+ D '77
Garbage power. il Forbes 119:29-30 My 1 '77
Moving to garbage power. il Time 111:46 Ja 9 '78
Newark signs up for resource recovery; production of Eco-Fuel. il Am City & County 92:21 O '77
Pilot plant will turn garbage into gas. R. Ceppos. il Pop Sci 211:40 Ag '77

REFUSE as fuel—*Continued*
St Louis trash plan goes down the drain; a Union Electric Co. project. Bus W p30-1 F 28 '77
Union Electric gives up waste fuel plan; with editorial statement by W. L. Forestell. Am City & County 92:13+, 106 Ap '77
REFUSE collection. See Refuse and refuse disposal
REFUSE collection trucks
Garbage grabber collects trash fast. R. Chadakoff. il Pop Sci 211:139 D '77
How to pick your next garbage truck. il Am City & County 92:43-5 Ap '77
Noise; public hearing to discuss garbage truck noise in New York City. New Yorker 53:44-5 N 7 '77
Will truck regs quiet trash pickup? Am City & County 92:34 N '77
REFUSE collectors. See Sanitation workers
REFUSE containers
Refuse bins must pass stability test. il Am City & County 92:18 D '77
REFUSE incinerators
Co-disposal of sewage sludge and solid wastes—it works. D. B. Sussman. il por Am City & County 92:55-8 O '77
Incinerators vs. the 0.08 gr/scf particulate standard. W. S. Foster. Am City & County 92: 115 S '77

Pollution control devices

How to select electrostatic precipitators. R. L. Bump. il Am City & County 92:76-7 My '77
REGAL, Philip J.
Ecology and evolution of flowering plant dominance. bibl Science 196:622-9 My 6 '77
REGATTAS
Regatta results. See issues of Yachting
See also
Rowing
Sailboat racing
Yacht racing
REGELSKI, Thomas A.
Music education and the human brain. Educ Digest 43:44-7 O '77
REGENERATION (biology)
Adipose tissue regeneration following lipectomy. I. M. Faust and others. bibl il Science 197:391-3 Jl 22 '77
Biological regeneration and pattern formation; with biographical sketches. P. J. Bryant and others. il Sci Am 237:66-76+ bibl(p 154) Jl '77
Electricity and natural healing. il Sci N 112:343 N 19 '77
Hepatic regeneration and erythropoietin production in the rat. B. A. Naughton and others. bibl il Science 196:301-2 Ap 15 '77
Pattern regulation in epimorphic fields. V. French and others; reply. L. Glass. Science 198:321-2 O 21 '77
Regenerating afferents establish synapses with a target neuron that lacks its cell body. F. B. Krasne and S. H. Lee. bibl il Science 198:517-19 N '77
Regeneration: a potential for cancer aid is seen in research; excerpt from reprint from Smithsonian, January 1977. R. Bahr. il Sci Digest 81:42-4 Ap '77
Regeneration of oligodendroglia during recovery from demyelinating disease. R. M. Herndon and others. bibl il Science 195:693-4 F 18 '77
Skin batteries and limb regeneration. R. B. Borgens. il Natur Hist 86:84-9 bibl(p 123) O '77
REGENERATION (botany)
Regeneration of Douglas fir plantlets through tissue culture. T. Y. Cheng and T. H. Voqui. bibl il Science 198:306-7 O 21 '77
REGENSBURG, Germany
Other Bavaria: Gothic, gloriously untraveled; Regensburg and vicinity. D. Messinesi. il Vogue 167:243-4+ O '77
REGENSTREIF, Peter
Canada's foreign policy. Cur Hist 72:150-3+ Ap '77
REGGAE (Jamaican rock) See Rock music (songs, etc)
REGINA; opera. See Blitzstein, M.
REGIONAL Ballet, National Association for. See National Association for Regional Ballet
REGIONAL literature. See Literature, Regional
REGIONAL planning
See also
City planning
Rural planning
Shopping centers
Suburbs

California

See also
Lake Tahoe Regional Planning Agency

Colorado

Development pains. C. S. Unfug and L. Schwartz. bibl il Environment 19:28-34 Ja '77

Minnesota

See also
Twin Cities Metropolitan Council

Nevada

See also
Lake Tahoe Regional Planning Agency

Nicaragua

Nicaragua of tomorrow: a strategy for decentralization. G. L. Plantegenest. il map Américas 29:13-18 S '77

United States

See also
Tennessee Valley Authority

Vermont

Development pains. C. S. Unfug and L. Schwartz. bibl il Environment 19:28-34 Ja '77
REGIONALISM

India

Nation, region, and welfare: ethnicity, regionalism, and development politics in south Asia. J. Das Gupta. bibl f il Ann Am Acad 433: 125-36 S '77
REGISTERS (heat) See Heating equipment
REGISTRATION, Library. See Libraries—Registration
REGISTRATION of architects. See Architects—Licenses and registration
REGISTRATION of voters. See Voters, Registration of
REGISTRATION of works of art. See Art—Registration
REGISTRY of ships. See Ships—Registration and transfer
REGNERY, Henry, Company. See Publishers and publishing—United States
REGULA, Ralph Straus
Most valuable in-put. E. Erlanger. il por Sr Schol 109:14 Mr 24 '77 *
REGULATION of body temperature. See Temperature, Animal and human
REGULATION of industry by government. See Industry and state
REGULATORS, Temperature. See Temperature—Control
REGULATORS, Voltage. See Voltage regulators
REGULATORY commissions. See Independent regulatory commissions
REHABILITATION
See also
Prisoners—Rehabilitation
Prisoners, Discharged—Rehabilitation

Laws and legislation

Section 504: impact on AoA programs; Rehabilitation Act of 1973. Aging 275:14-16 S '77
REHABILITATION Act. See Rehabilitation—Laws and legislation
REHABILITATION of juvenile delinquents
See also
Reformatories
REHEARSALS, Dance. See Dance production
REHEARSALS, Opera. See Opera—Production and direction
REHNQUIST, William Hubbs
Justice Rehnquist's unappealing guides to action. D. L. Shapiro. Sat R 4:16 My 28 '77 *
REICH, Sheldon
Being not doing. Art N 76:132+ S '77
REICHEK, Morton A.
Scientist triumphant. New Repub 176:16-18+ Ja 15 '77
REICHELT, Paul A.
Desirability of involving adolescents in sex education planning. Educ Digest 42:38-40 Ap '77
REICHENBERGER, Larry. See Lepper, G. jt auth
REICHL, Ruth. See Subtle, S. jt auth
REICHLIN, Elinor
Faces of slavery. il Am Heritage 28:4-11 Je '77
REICHLIN, Seymour. See Jackson, I. M. D. jt auth
REID, Alastair
Academy; poem. New Yorker 53:34 Mr 21 '77
Borges in his poetry. New Repub 177:29-30 N 19 '77
PW interviews; ed by A. W. Ehrlich. por Pub W 212:6-7 O 17 '77
Sporting scene. New Yorker 53:80-93 F 21 '77
(tr) See Borges, J. L. Brunanburh, A.D. 937
(tr) See Borges, J. L. Hengist wants men
(tr) See Borges, J. L. Keeper
(tr) See Borges, J. L. Palace
(tr) See Borges, J. L. Talismans
(tr) See Borges, J. L. Tankas; Poem of quantity; Milonga of Manuel Flores; Susana Bombal; Elegy; Fifteen coins
(tr) See Borges, J. L. To the nightingale
(tr) See Cabrera Infante, G. Fabulas rasas
(tr) See Cabrera Infante, G. Revelation of a list-maker
REID, Robert C. See Drake, E. jt auth
REID, Ron
Baseball (cont) il Sports Illus 47:78-9 S 5 '77
College football (cont) Sports Illus 47:62+ O 31 '77
Ghost to the post. il Sports Illus 48:12-13 Ja 2 '78

REID, Ron—*Continued*
In the spirit of joy and some joy of the spirit. il Sports Illus 46:32-7 F 28 '77
Interest centers on the Central. il Sports Illus 47:32-3 N 14 '77
Pro football (cont) Sports Illus 47:91-2+ O 17 '77
Week; college football (cont) Sports Illus 47:72 S 19; 55-6+ S 26; 49-51 O 3; 90+ O 10; 66+ O 17 '77

REID, Walker M.
Cervantes at Chamizal. il Américas 29:19-24 S '77

REIDEL, Carl H.
Vermont I know. il Am For 83:30-3+ S '77

REIF, F.
Where are the leaders in higher education? Educ Digest 42:25-7 My '77

REIF, Rita
Design (cont) N Y Times Mag p64-5 F 13; 84-5 Mr 27; 74-5 My 15 '77

REIGER, George W.
Conservation. See issues of Field & stream
Earth log: the trammeling of Rainbow Bridge. il Audubon 79:114-15+ N '77
It takes a tough man to fowl a tender creek. il Audubon 79:142-5 N '77
Meanders in the marsh. il Audubon 79:4-15 S '77
Native fish in troubled waters. il Audubon 79: 18+ Ja '77
New frontier: planned or plundered? excerpt from address, December 8, 1976. Field & S 81:22+ Mr '77
Treasure of wildlife stamps. il Field & S 82:114-16+ Je '77
Whale-watchers. il Audubon 79:74-6+ My '77

REILLY, Edgar M. Jr
Nature fakers and science. il Conservationist 31:28-31 Ja '77

REILLY, J. Porter
Mocker still thrives in Brooklyn. il por Conservationist 31:8-9 My '77

REILLY, Peter
New life of Reilly. E. Keerdoja. il por Newsweek 90:6 Jl 25 '77 *

REILLY, William Patrick
Involvement of industry with Business and Office; address, August 11, 1977. Vital Speeches 43:756-60 O 1 '77

REIMANN, Aribert
Concerto for piano and 19 players. D. M. Garvelmann. Am Rec G 40:37-8 D '76 *

REIMOLD, Robert J. See Hardisky, M. jt auth

REIMS, France. See Rheims, France

REIN, Martin, and Elliot, J. M.
Roots. il por Negro Hist Bull 40:664-7 Ja '77

REINCARNATION
Where were you in 1643? Past-lives therapy. il Time 110:53 O 3 '77

Anecdotes, facetiae, satire, etc.

Spiritual energy crisis. R. Frank. Atlantic 240: 76-7 Jl '77

REINDEER
Deer that came in from the cold. B. Vogt. il Nat Wildlife 16:50-3 D '77

REINER, Steven
Stranger in Holy Land. il Atlantic 239:85-7 Ap '77

REINFORCED concrete. See Concrete, Reinforced

REINFORCEMENT (psychology)
Schedule control of behavior reinforced by electrical stimulation of the brain. R. J. Beninger and others. bibl il Science 196:547-9 Ap 29 '77
Trigeminal substrates of intracranial self-stimulation in the brainstem. D. Van Der Kooy and A. G. Phillips. bibl Science 196:447-9 Ap 22 '77

REINHARDT, John E.
Guiding philosophy for American informational and cultural programs abroad; address, May 28, 1977. Dept State Bull 77:5-8 Jl 4 '77
—See Christopher, W. M. jt auth

REINHARDT, John J.
How much leachate can we afford? il Am City & County 92:48-9 Jl '77

REINKE, Rosemary
Old wheel takes a new turn. il Sch Arts 76:6 Mr '77

REINSTATEMENT of employees. See Employees—Reinstatement

REINSURANCE. See Insurance—Reinsurance

REISCHAUER, Edwin Oldfather
American policy in Asia. Current 194:58-60 Jl '77
PW interviews; ed by J. F. Baker. por Pub W 211:6-8 Ap 18 '77

REISENAUER, Ann M. and others
Folate conjugase: two separate activities in human jejunum. bibl il Science 198:196-7 O 14 '77

REISMAN, Marty
Little night music. R. Kennedy. il pors Sports Illus 47:82-6+ N 21 '77 *

REISMAN, Michael
Diplomacy of the possible. Nation 224:554-8 My 7 '77

REISNER, Marc P.
DNA: will the future curse science's decisions today? il Sci Digest 82:62-5+ Jl '77

REISS, James
By the steps of the Metropolitan Museum of Art; poem. New Yorker 53:44 My 2 '77

REISS, Janine
Répétiteuse; interview, ed by D. Seabury. il por Opera N 42:30-2 O '77

REISSUES of phonograph records. See Phonograph records—Reissues

REISZ, Robert R.
Petrolacosaurus, the oldest known diapsid reptile. bibl il Science 196:1091-3 Je 3 '77

about

Earliest diapsid reptile identified. Sci N 112:7 Jl 2 '77 *

REITER, Thomas
Snapshot of the Virgin Islands; poem. Commonweal 104:391 Je 24 '77

REITZ, Donald
Don Reitz workshop. il pors Ceram Mo 25:50-5 S '77 *

REITZE, Arnold W. Jr
Harnessing the auto. bibl il Environment 19:6-15 Ap '77
An Otto for the automobile. bibl il Environment 19:32-42 My '77
Running out of steam. bibl il Environment 19: 34-40 Je '77
Stalled; question of developing low-emission vehicles. bibl il Environment 19:39-42 Ag '77

REJECTION (psychology)
Accepting rejection. A. Koral. il Seventeen 36: 51 Ap '77

REKERS, Ben
Spinoza: philosopher of intellectual freedom. il por UNESCO Courier 30:28-33 Je '77

RELATIVES
See also
Fathers
Grandparents
Mothers
Uncles

RELATIVITY (physics)
Einstein's world and the big numbers game. D. E. Thomsen. Sci N 112:157-8 S 3 '77
Time. . . and space. . .adding credence to Einstein's work. P. Young. Sci Digest 82:33-6 Ag '77
Time dilatation: precise confirmation. Sci N 112: 23 Jl 9 '77
Viking: quake questions and relativity refinements. il Sci N 111:36-7 Ja 15 '77
Will supergravity unify quantum theory with general relativity? G. B. Lubkin. Phys Today 30:17-19 Je '77
X-raying special relativity. Sci N 112:313 N 12 '77

RELAXATION
How to relax when you think you can't. E. Schoen. il House & Gard 149:34+ O '77
Turning off: the great energizer. N. Lande and A. Slade. Harp Baz 110:121+ Ag '77

RELAXIN. See Hormones, Sex

RELAY running. See Running

RELAY systems, Television. See Television relay systems

RELIANCE Electric Company
Reliance's route to steady growth. por Bus W p86-7 Mr 7 '77

RELICS and reliquaries
See also
Holy Shroud

RELIEF (sculpture)
Charles Biederman's abstract analogues for nature. D. B. Kuspit. bibl il Art in Am 65: 80-3 My '77
Mind bending with George Segal. A. Elsen. il por Art N 76:34-7 F '77
Tackle your spackle for ingenious sculpture. N. Berman and A. Pinto. il Design (US) 79: 18-19 Fall '77

RELIEF pitchers, Baseball. See Baseball players

RELIEF work
See also
Catholic Relief Services
Disaster relief
Food relief
Rumania—Relief work

RELIGION
Taking the world's temperature; interview. B. Graham. pors Chr Today 21:16-19 S 23 '77
Whither religion? a plea for a return to sanity and a genuine creativity. A. W. Munk. bibl Intellect 106:249-50 D '77
See also
Atheism
Business and religion
Children—Religious life
Christianity
Colleges and universities—Religious life
Creeds
Faith
Liberalism (religion)
Mysticism
Prayer
Public schools and religion
Religions
Revelation
Secularism
Spiritual life
Sunday

RELIGION—See also—*Continued*
Television programs—Religious programs
Theology
Women and religion
Youth—Religious life
also headings beginning Religious
also subhead Religious institutions and affairs under names of countries, states, cities, etc. e.g. Mississippi—Religious institutions and affairs

Bibliography

Books. See issues of Christianity today
Books that shape lives. See issues of Christian century
Briefly noted. See occasional issues of Christianity today
Criticism. See issues of Christian century
Criticism: Theology and philosophy; Church and ministry; Devotional reading. Chr Cent 94:477-9 My 18 '77
Critics' choices: selections for Religious Book Week. Commonweal 104:153-8 Mr 4 '77
Hard-cover revival. R. N. Ostling. il Time 109:81-2+ My 9 '77
New fall books for adults; New fall books for children. Pub W 212:78-92+ S 26 '77
Prayer books and politics. J. B. Breslin. America 136:194-6 Mr 5 '77
Reading for Lent. America 136:150-1 F 19 '77
Religion. J. B. Breslin. America 136:82-3 Ja 29 '77
Religion (cont) J. Gaffney. America 136:417+ My 7; 137:338-40 N 12 '77
Roundup of religious books. Pub W 211:59-71 Mr 14 '77
Study guide to non-Christian religions. R. N. Minor. il Chr Today 21:16-19 Jl 8 '77

Caricatures and cartoons

Rolling in the aisles. Sat Eve Post 249:14 Ap '77

Periodicals

See Religious newspapers and periodicals

Philosophy

See Philosophy and religion

Statistics

See Religious statistics

RELIGION and children. See Children—Religious life
RELIGION and communism. See Communism and religion
RELIGION and culture
See also
Christianity and culture
RELIGION and ecology
Stewards of the earth's resources: a Christian response to ecology. J. P. Dobel. Chr Cent 94:906-9 O 12 '77
RELIGION and education. See Public schools and religion
RELIGION and labor. See Church and labor
RELIGION and language
Philosophy: the roots of vain deceit. N. L. Geisler. Chr Today 21:8-12 My 20 '77
Stopping by the pit stop. G. Grindal. bibl il Chr Cent 94:453-7 My 11 '77

Anecdotes, facetiae, satire, etc.

Legitimate at last; reviewing the Supplement to the Oxford English Dictionary. M. E. Marty. Chr Cent 94:287 Mr 23 '77
Tower of Babel; technical jargon of church bureaucracy. A. R. Brouwer. Chr Cent 94:276-9 Mr 23 '77
RELIGION and law
Should this judge be benched? case of H. W. Goodwin. V. Vogelzang and E. E. Plowman. por Chr Today 22:56-7 N 4 '77
RELIGION and literature
Laughter without joy: the burlesque of our secular age. D. B. Lockerbie. Chr Today 22:14-16 O 7 '77
RELIGION and motion pictures. See Motion pictures—Moral and religious aspects
RELIGION and music
Music: offerings of creativity; interview, ed by C. Forbes. H. Best. por Chr Today 21:12-15 My 6 '77
Music speaks. . .but what language? D. P. Hustad. Chr Today 21:16-18 My 6 '77
Rock music—love ad infinitum, ad absurdum. J. M. Pennington. Chr Today 21:20-1 Jl 8 '77
RELIGION and philosophy. See Philosophy and religion
RELIGION and politics
Altar/throne clash updated; excerpt from address. J. J. Petuchowski. Chr Today 21:20+ S 23 '77
Carter and the religion factor. J. M. Wall. Chr Cent 94:739-40 Ag 31 '77
Christians for Israel; evangelical stand. K. L. Woodward and R. Mark. il Newsweek 90:126 N 28 '77
Dialoguing at the Smithsonian. M. E. Marty. Chr Cent 94:316-17 Ap 6 '77
Egypt, Israel, and Isaiah. Chr Today 22:26 D 30 '77
Israel and the evangelicals. J. M. Wall. Chr Cent 94:1083-4 N 23 '77
Love, power and justice. P. B. Henry. il Chr Cent 94:1088-92 N 23 '77
Priests/nuns/ministers in politics. J. Castelli. Commonweal 104:398-400 Je 24 '77
South Africa: God and liberation. Chr Today 22:56-7 D 9 '77
See also
Church and politics
Presidential candidates—Religion
Priests—Political activities
Socialism and religion
RELIGION and psychology. See Psychology, Religious
RELIGION and science
Bishops keep tabs on science; Committee on Human Values. N. Wade. Science 196:1180 Je 10 '77
God and science: new allies in the search for values; symposium. il Sat R 5:13-23+ D 10 '77
See also
Creation
Man—Origin and antiquity
RELIGION and sex. See Sex and religion
RELIGION and social problems. See Church and social problems
RELIGION and socialism. See Socialism and religion
RELIGION and society. See Religion and sociology
RELIGION and sociology
Altar/throne clash updated; excerpt from address. J. J. Petuchowski. Chr Today 21:20+ S 23 '77
Caring for the caretakers. H. B. Kuhn. Chr Today 21:41 Ag 12 '77
God-language in the Inaugural; American civil religion; symposium. Chr Cent 94:3-7 Ja 5 '77
James Reston: prophet of American civil religion. L. Sandon, Jr. Chr Cent 94:15-18 Ja 5 '77
Letters from Ernest; correspondence between E. Becker and H. Bates. il pors Chr Cent 94:217-27 Mr 9 '77
RELIGION and state. See Church and state
RELIGION in literature
Dostoyevsky and the Grand Inquisitor: a study in atheism. S. R. Sutherland. Yale R 66:364-73 Mr '77
The god in science fiction. R. Bradbury. il Sat R 5:36-8+ D 10 '77
John Updike's theological world. R. K. Johnston. por Chr Cent 94:1061-6 N 16 '77
See also
Bible in literature
Religion in poetry
RELIGION in poetry
Anne Sexton and God. W. J. McGill. Commonweal 104:304-6 My 13 '77
RELIGION in public schools. See Public schools and religion
RELIGIONS
Eastern cults and western culture: why young Americans are buying Oriental religions; excerpt from Turning East. H. Cox. bibl il por Psychol Today 11:36-40+ Jl '77; Discussion. 11:8+ O '77
Religions of the world:
Islam. il Sr Schol 109:6-8 Mr 24 '77
Protestantism. il Sr Schol 109:22-4+ Ap 7 '77
See also
Buddha and Buddhism
Christianity and other religions
Cults
Mormons and Mormonism
Shamanism
Sikhism
Zoroastrianism
RELIGIOUS advertising
Advertising your church. C. N. Noble. Chr Today 22:30-1 N 18 '77
Born again businessmen; Christian business directories. America 137:140 S 17 '77
Buying Christian: Christian business directories. A. B. Haines. Chr Cent 94:804-5 S 21 '77
Christian yellow pages. Chr Today 22:46-8 O 21 '77
God & mammon; Christian yellow pages. Time 110:114 N 28 '77
Selling of Jesus; Baptist General Convention of Texas evangelical ad campaign. M. Montagno and J. Huck. il Newsweek 89:48+ F 28 '77
Tribulations for Christian ads; lawsuits against business directories for born-again Christians. il Bus W p 148 S 19 '77
RELIGIOUS architecture. See Church architecture
RELIGIOUS art. See Christian art and symbolism
RELIGIOUS article stores. See Specialty stores
RELIGIOUS comic strips. See Comics (books, strips, etc)
RELIGIOUS conferences
African impatience for change; meeting at Bergamo East Conference Center. C. E. Brewster. il Chr Cent 94:382-4 Ap 20 '77

RELIGIOUS conferences—*Continued*
Anathemas and orthodoxy: a reply to Avery Dulles; Hartford Appeal. L. Gilkey. Chr Cent 94:1026-9 N 9 '77; Reply. A. Dulles. 94:1053-4 N 16 '77
Black theology: raising the questions; conference on Black Church and Black Community: Unity and Education for Action in Atlanta. G. S. Wilmore. Chr Cent 94:645-6 Jl 20 '77
By the company we keep. M. E. Marty. Chr Cent 94:1151 D 7 '77
Campaign for inerrancy; formation of The International Council on Biblical Inerrancy. Chr Today 22:51-2 N 4 '77
Charismatic renewal: up to date in Kansas City. D. X. Stump. America 137:164-6 S 24 '77
Charismatic time was had by all; Kansas City conference. il Time 110:43 Ag 8 '77
Charismatic unity in Kansas City. il Chr Today 21:36-7 Ag 12 '77
Charismatics: beyond sloppy agape; Kansas City Conference on Charismatic Renewal. J. C. Lyles. Chr Cent 94:707-8 Ag 17 '77
Chicago Call. D. Tinder. Chr Today 21:32-3 Je 3 '77
Chicago Call: an appeal to evangelicals; with editorial comment. Chr Today 21:27-9 Je 17 '77
Church roundup; convention highlights. Chr Today 21:37-8 Ag 12 '77
Crack in the Anglican dam; establishment of Anglican Church in North America at St Louis conference. S. M. Smith. Nat R 29:1166 O 14 '77
Encuentro in Washington. America 137:118 S 10 '77
Friendly spaces: ecclesiology and the architect; National Interfaith Conference on Religion and Architecture. J. C. Lyles. Chr Cent 94:806-8 S 21 '77
House divided; Episcopal Church convention. Newsweek 90:95 S 26 '77
NAE: unity the base; thirty-fifth annual convention of the National Association of Evangelicals in suburban Chicago. Chr Today 21:57 Ap 1 '77
NBEA: when the Bible bumps blackness. R. Koskela. Chr Today 21:58 My 6 '77
New chance for the bishops; Call to Action conference in Detroit. P. Steinfels. Commonweal 104:200+ Ap 1 '77
New voice for American theology; report of symposium celebrating American visit of H. U. von Balthasar. J. M. McDermott. America 137:374-6 N 26 '77
No need for the great wait; resolutions of the Detroit Call to Action conference. America 136:227-8 Mr 19 '77
Roots for evangelicals; Chicago Call. K. L. Woodward and F. Maier. il Newsweek 89:76 My 23 '77
Second Call to Action; bishops to address conclusions of Detroit meeting. J. Finn. Commonweal 104:269-72 Ap 29 '77
Spirituality for a world culture; meeting of monks and nuns in Petersham, Mass. M. B. Pennington. il America 137:100-3 Ag 27 '77
Tacking toward Vatican III; conference of Catholic theologians at Notre Dame. J. B. Breslin. America 136:545-7 Je 18 '77
Training for pros; Pro Training Conference. W. Spoelstra. Chr Today 21:53 Mr 18 '77
Up-to-date in Kansas City; charismatic conference. America 137:42 Jl 30 '77
When piety prevails; Chicago Call. Chr Today 21:22 Jl 29 '77
Women and World Religions; conference in Bethesda, Md. R. A. Mitchell. America 136:123-5 F 12 '77
See also names of conferences, e.g. National Conference of Catholic Bishops

Africa

Evangelicals in Africa; general assembly of the Association of Evangelicals of Africa and Madagascar. W. H. Fuller. il Chr Today 21:38 Ag 26 '77
Evangelicals together in Africa; Pan African Christian Leadership Assembly and All Africa Conference of Churches. Chr Today 21:45-6 Ja 21 '77

Brazil

Grass-roots protests in Brazil. R. Barbosa. Chr Cent 94:1119-20 N 30 '77
Internationalizing youth for Christ. P. Yancey. Chr Today 21:70-2 S 9 '77

Great Britain

Anglican evangelicals speak out; Nottingham statement. J. R. W. Stott. Chr Today 21:30-1 Jl 8 '77
Nottingham '77: evangelicals eye unity. R. Pulliam. Chr Today 21:44-5 My 20 '77

India

India: strategy for the jet age; All-India Congress on Mission and Evangelization. Chr Today 21:49 Mr 4 '77
Indian evangelicals: some issues in mission; Devlali letter. S. P. Athyal. Chr Today 21:60-1 Mr 18 '77

Israel

Hope in Jerusalem. D. J. Moore. America 137:236-9 O 15 '77

Scotland

Reformed Alliance: sliding with man? J. D. Douglas. Chr Today 21:53-4+ S 23 '77

Switzerland

See also
International Congress on World Evangelization

Tanzania

Lutherans and apartheid. W. Bockelman. Chr Cent 94:647-8 Jl 20 '77
View from Tanzania; Lutheran World Federation. G. H. Muedeking. Chr Today 21:34-5 Jl 29 '77

RELIGIOUS denominations. See Religions

RELIGIOUS education
Decompartmentalizing the church; with views on the intergenerational principal. D. E. Kucharsky. Chr Today 21:19 Ap 15 '77
See also
Bible—Study and teaching
Catechetics
Catholic Church—Education
Church colleges and universities
Filmstrips in religious education
Theological education

RELIGIOUS ethics
Promoting religious values in an age of violence and terror; excerpts from address. M. H. Tanenbaum. por Intellect 105:218-19 Ja '77

RELIGIOUS experience. See Experience (religion)

RELIGIOUS faith. See Faith

RELIGIOUS festivals. See Fasts and feasts

RELIGIOUS freedom. See Religious liberty

RELIGIOUS institutions and affairs
See also subhead Religious institutions and affairs under names of countries, states, cities, etc. e.g. Portland, Ore.—Religious institutions and affairs

RELIGIOUS journalism. See Journalism, Religious

RELIGIOUS leadership. See Christian leadership

RELIGIOUS liberty
Freedom to be strange; New York Supreme Court ruling on Hare Krishna indoctrination. il Time 109:81 Mr 28 '77
Moonies—religious converts or psychic victims? R. A. Walsh. America 136:438-40 My 14 '77
See also
Persecution

RELIGIOUS life. See Christian life; Spiritual life

RELIGIOUS literature
Continuing phenomenon of the religious best seller. G. C. Wharton. Pub W 211:82-3 Mr 14 '77
Religious publishing's second spring. Chr Cent 94:468 My 18 '77
See also
Christian literature
Devotional literature
Libraries—Religious collections
Publishers and publishing—Religious literature
Religion—Bibliography
Religious newspapers and periodicals

Authorship

See also
Journalism, Religious

Bibliography

Popular religious books: a selected bibliography. D. Marsh. il Lib J 102:1248-50 Je 1 '77

RELIGIOUS music
See also
Church music
Phonograph records—Religious music
Sacred Music Society of America

RELIGIOUS news
Casting for news; radio broadcasting of religious news. A. H. Matthews. Chr Today 21:59-60 F 18 '77
Events and people. See issues of Christian century
Religion's top stories of 1977. Chr Cent 94:1211-12 D 28 '77
Year that was; top religious news stories of 1976. Chr Today 21:41 Ja 21 '77

RELIGIOUS newspapers and periodicals
Improving Postal Service; postal reorganization bill, H.R. 7700. Chr Today 22:27 D 30 '77
Kaput Courier; National courier. Chr Today 21:69-70 S 9 '77
Religious markets. W. Brohaugh and others. il Writers Digest 57:25-8+ D '77
See also
Associated Church Press (organization)
Catholic press
Christian century (periodical)
Christianity today (periodical)
Evangelical Press Association
Journalism, Religious

RELIGIOUS newspapers and periodicals—*Cont.*
Bibliography
New periodicals. Chr Today 21:46 Ap 15; 51 My 6; 35 Je 17 '77
RELIGIOUS orders
Giving and getting taken; cases of Boys Town, Pallottine Fathers, and others. Chr Today 22:59-61 D 9 '77
See also
Carmelites
Inter-American Conference of Major Religious Superiors
Jesuits
Poverty, Vow of
Sisterhoods
RELIGIOUS persecution. See Persecution
RELIGIOUS psychology. See Psychology, Religious
RELIGIOUS radio programs. See Radio programs —Religious programs
RELIGIOUS schools. See Church schools
RELIGIOUS societies
Theology and gutsy exegesis; Evangelical Theological Society. Chr Today 21:41-2 Ja 21 '77
Wesleyan issues; thirteenth annual meeting. Chr Today 22:63 D 9 '77
See also
Campus Crusade for Christ (organization)
Fellowship of Catholic Scholars
RELIGIOUS statistics
Portrait of religious America. il U.S. News 82:56-7 Ap 11 '77
RELIGIOUS supply stores. See Specialty stores
RELOCATION of industries. See Location in business and industry
RELUCTANT king; opera. See Chabrier, E.
RELYEA, Harold C.
Reorganizing U.S. executive agencies. Current 189:17-21 Ja '77
REMAINDERS (books)
See also
Booksellers and bookselling—Remainders
REMARRIAGE
After divorce: who gets married again—and when? excerpt from The divorce experience: a new look at the world of the formerly married. M. Hunt and B. Hunt. il Redbook 149:106+ O '77
Many-splendored thing at any age. V. Buchan. il Ret Liv 17:44-5 Jl '77
My family, his family and my job. D. Hughes. McCalls 104:58+ Ag '77
Remarriage: survival manual; excerpt from Rewedded bliss: love, alimony, incest, ex-spouses, and other domestic blessings. D. S. Mayleas. Vogue 167:64+ N '77
Second time around it seems to work; study by Norval D. Glenn and Charles N. Weaver. D. Cohen. Psychol Today 10:34+ Mr '77
Anecdotes, facetiae, satire, etc.
Case for remarriage. . .among friends. J. Leonard. Ms 6:26-7 Ag '77
REMBAR, Charles
Obscenity—forget it. Atlantic 239:37-41 My '77
Turning you into movies. Esquire 87:75+ Ap '77
REMBRANDT Harmenszoon van Rijn
Looking at paintings. B. Dunstan. il Am Artist 41:46-7 S '77 *
REMEDIAL reading. See Reading—Remedial teaching
REMEDIAL teaching
See also
English language—Remedial teaching
Reading—Remedial teaching
REMINGTON, Frederic
Frederic Remington 1861-1909. il por Conservationist 31:10-18 Mr '77 *
He painted the West. J. A. Michener. il Read Digest 110:182-7 My '77 *
Remington & Russell; excerpt from Way west. P. H. Hassrick. il Am West 14:16-29 N '77 *
REMMEY, Louise Austin
Portrait of the young opera singer. il Hi Fi 27:MA21-3 Jl '77
REMODELED automobiles. See Automobiles, Remodeled
REMODELED buildings. See Buildings, Remodeled
REMODELED helicopters. See Helicopters, Remodeled
REMODELED houses. See Houses, Remodeled
REMODELING (architecture)
Architecture; question of downtown renovations. J. H. Kay. Nation 225:635-6 D 10 '77
Mapping and remapping: four projects by R. M. Kliment and Frances Halsband; with introd by G. Allen. il Archit Rec 161:103-10 F '77
Recycling architectural masterpieces—and other buildings not so great; Hardy Holzman Pfeiffer Associates; ed by M. Holzman and N. Pfeiffer; with introd by M. F. Schmertz. H. Hardy. il Archit Rec 162:81-92 Ag '77
Recycling the city. C. Wiseman. il Horizon 21:43-9 Ja '78
Urban unions reduce wages to stimulate housing rehab. D. Loomis. Archit Rec 161:36 Ja '77
See also
Apartment houses, Remodeled
Apartments, Remodeled
Buildings, Remodeled
Houses, Remodeled
School buildings, Remodeled
Shopping centers, Remodeled
REMOND, Charles Lenox
Charles Lenox Remond: the lost prince of abolitionism. L. Wallace. bibl il Negro Hist Bull 40:696-701 My '77 *
REMOTE control
See also
Computers—Control
Photoelectric cells—Control use
Television receivers—Control
REMOTE sensing systems
Developing countries emphasize remote sensing data utilization. Aviation W 106:21 My 9 '77
Remote sensing:
Brazil explores its Amazon wilderness. A. L. Hammond. il map Science 196:513-15 Ap 29 '77
Landsat takes hold in South America. A. L. Hammond. il Science 196:511-12 Ap 29 '77
Tools continue to improve. A. L. Hammond. il Science 196:515-16 Ap 29 '77
Remote sensing commitments urged. C. Covault. Aviation W 106:48-9+ My 16 '77
Remote-sensing of crop yields. S. B. Idso and others. bibl il Science 196:19-25 Ap 1 '77
REMSBERG, Bonnie
(ed) See Clatworthy, N. M. Case against living together
—See Remsberg, C. jt auth
REMSBERG, Charles
Country doctor. il por Fam Health 9:36-9+ Ap '77
(ed) See Clatworthy, N. M. Case against living together
—and Remsberg, Bonnie
American scandal: why some parents abuse teens. Seventeen 36:154-5+ My '77
Dirty movies! Dirty books! il Good H 184:103+ Mr '77
RENAISSANCE
Science and humanism in the Italian renaissance. E. Cochrane. bibl f Am Hist R 81:1039-57 D '76
RENAISSANCE Center. See Detroit—Buildings
RENAISSANCE Pleasure Faire. See Festivals—California
RENAULT (automobile) See Automobiles, Foreign
RENAULT (firm) See Automobile industry—France
RENDEZVOUS (space) See Orbital rendezvous (space flight)
RENÉ, Natalia Petrovna Roselavleva
Obituary
Dance Mag 51:92-3 Mr '77. S. J. Cohen
RENEGOTIATION Board. See United States—Renegotiation Board
RENEGOTIATION of government contracts. See Contracts, Government—Renegotiation
RENEWAL of the church. See Church renewal
RENFREW, Colin
Ancient Europe is older than we thought. il map Nat Geog 152:614-23 N '77
RENFRO, Sally Jo
Calling; poem. Atlantic 239:61 My '77
RENNER-SMITH, Susan
Vertical windmill generates kilowatts from monsoons. il Pop Sci 210:99 Je '77
RENNINGER, Katharine Steele
Watercolor page. il por Am Artist 41:30+ Mr '77
RENOIR, Auguste
Looking at paintings. B. Dunstan. il Am Artist 41:28-9 Mr '77 *
RENOIR, Pierre Auguste. See Renoir, A.
RENORMALIZATION (physics)
Critical phenomena: experiments show theory on right track. A. L. Robinson. il Science 196:861-3 My 20 '77
RENOVATING (architecture) See Remodeling (architecture)
RENSBERGER, Boyce
Critter nobody loves; excerpt from Cult of the wild. il Int Wildlife 7:12-16 N '77
Cult of the wild; excerpt. il Sci Digest 82:56-61 N '77
This is the end of the game. il N Y Times Mag p43+ N 6 '77
RENSCH, James
Why? Because it's relevant. bibl il Clearing H 50:203-5 Ja '77
RENT
See also
Apartments—Leasing and renting
Houses—Leasing and renting
Landlord and tenant
RENT control. See Rent laws
RENT laws
European experience with rent controls. E. J. Howenstine. bibl il M Labor R 100:21-8 Je '77
New ground swell behind rent-control laws. il Bus W p 106 O 24 '77

RENT laws—*Continued*
Why rent controls don't work. T. F. Eagleton. Read Digest 111:108-11 Ag '77
RENTING of apartments. See Apartments—Leasing and renting
RENTING of automobiles. See Automobiles—Leasing and renting
RENTMEESTER, Co
Everyone is getting into the pack; photographs. il Sports Illus 46:40-4 Ap 18 '77
REORGANIZATION of corporations. See Corporations—Reorganization
REOVIRUSES. See Viruses
REPAIR men. See Repairmen
REPAIR shops
See also
Automobile service stations
Electronic repair shops
Television repair shops
REPAIRING
Supporting the life style of retired men through community service: a two-way street; Fix-it Workshop and Handyman Projects. M. Goodman and B. Solomon. il Aging 266:7 D '76
See also
Mechanics, Household
Patching materials
also subheads Maintenance and; Repairing under various subjects, e.g. Pavements—Maintenance and repair
REPAIRMEN
Don't buy it if you can build it or repair it. E. Morris. il por Ret Liv 17:45 Ap '77
See also
Camera repairmen

Wages and hours

Pay relationships of TV-radio and appliance repairers. S. L. King. il M Labor R 100:48-9 My '77
REPARATION
Aiding victims of crime. U.S. News 83:65 Jl 4 '77
At last—help for innocent victims of crime. A. Rule. il Good H 185:84+ Jl '77
Federal payments to crime victims? interviews. P. W. Rodino, Jr; C. E. Wiggins. pors U.S. News 83:55-6 N 28 '77
Making the punishment fix the crime; Law Enforcement Assistance Administration program. D. Cohen. Psychol Today 11:22+ Jl '77
Restitution: attention for forgotten victims of crime. il Am City & County 92:50-1 Jl '77
REPARATIONS
See also
Vietnamese war, 1957-1975—Reparations
REPAS, George A.
Measure your fireplace for top performance. il Pop Sci 211:118-19 D '77
REPELLENTS, Insect. See Insect baits and repellents
REPENTANCE
Lent, repentance: a parable. D. L. Gelpi. America 136:223-4 Mr 12 '77
REPKA, Charles
Resurrecting the Beatles: Star-Club to stereo. il Hi iF 27:101-3 Ag '77
REPLACEMENT-cost accounting. See Corporations—Accounting
REPORT writing
Mystery of the business graduate who can't write; teaching specialized writing courses at business schools. il Nations Bus 65:60-2 F '77
Writing for business: the bucks start here. R. E. Heinemann. Writers Digest 57:19-23 O '77
REPORTERS and reporting
Harlot's prerogative. H. Fairlie. New Repub 176:21-5 Ap 30; 16-19 My 7 '77; Discussion. 176:7 Je 4 '77
Point of order. L. H. Lapham. Harpers 254: 13-14+ My '77
Unforgettable Bob Considine. S. Pett. il Read Digest 111:87-90 Jl '77
Who said science reporting was a piece of cake? D. E. Thomsen. Sci N 111:351 My 28 '77
See also
Confidential communications—Press
Crime and the press
Foreign correspondents
Interviewing
Journalists
News
Press and politics
Sports journalism
Television broadcasting—News
United States—Congress—Reporters and reporting
Vietnamese War, 1957-1975—War correspondents and photographers
War correspondents
REPORTS
See also
Corporation reports
Financial statements
Student themes and reports
REPORTS, Accounting, and Management Subcommittee. See United States—Congress—Senate—Government operations, Committee on—Reports, Accounting, and Management Subcommittee

REPOSSESSION of property. See Possession (law)
REPRESENTATIVE government and representation
See also
Democracy
REPRESENTATIVES, Congressional. See Congressmen
REPRODUCTION
Fecund mouflon. R. Valdez and L. V. Alamia. il Natur Hist 86:72-7 bibl(p 119) N '77
Refractoriness in female lizard reproduction: a probable circannual clock. H. S. Cuellar and O. Cuellar. bibl il Science 197:495-7 Jl 29 '77
See also
Artificial insemination, Human
Fertility
Fertility, Human
Fertilization (biology)
Fetus
Fishes—Reproduction
Insects—Reproduction
Parthenogenesis
Plants—Reproduction
Spawning
Sterility
Viruses—Reproduction

Nutritional aspects

Experimental triggering of reproduction in a natural population of microtus montanus. N. C. Negus and P. J. Berger. bibl il Science 196:1230-1 Je 10 '77
Phenolic plant compounds functioning as reproductive inhibitors in Microtus montanus. P. J. Berger and others. bibl il Science 195:575-7 F 11 '77
REPRODUCTIONS of works of art
Ars gratia artis? B. Wicker. Commonweal 104: 622-4 S 30 '77
Shopping boom at your local museum. T. Trucco. il Art N 76:56-60 O '77
Special section: reproducibles; symposium. Art in Am 65:31-43 Ja '77
REPRODUCTIVE organs. See Generative organs
REPRODUCTIVE periodicity. See Botany—Periodicity
REPTILES
See also
Alligators
Crocodiles
Eye (reptiles)
Iguanas
Lizards
Sexual behavior—Reptiles
Snakes
Turtles

Export-import trade

Snake smugglers. P. Gwynne and others. il Newsweek 89:81+ Ap 25 '77

Food and feeding

Polymorphism and geographic variation in the feeding behavior of the garter snake thamnophis elegans. S. J. Stevan. bibl il Science 197:676-8 Ag 12 '77

Reproduction

See Reproduction

Scales

See Scales (reptiles)
REPTILES, Fossil
See also
Crocodiles, Fossil
Lizards, Fossil
Plesiosaurs
REPTILES and Amphibians, Hall of. See American Museum of Natural History, New York
REPTILES in literature
Darwin and Melville: why a tortoise? J. Franzosa. bibl f Am Imago 33:361-79 Wint '76
REPUBLIC Financial Services Inc. See Insurance companies
REPUBLIC Steel Corporation
Republic's struggle to heat up its ovens. Bus W p42+ Ja 31 '77
REPUBLICAN National Committee
Everyone's second choice; W. E. Brock elected chairman. il por Time 109:19 Ja 24 '77
Now Republicans map a comeback. por U.S. News 82:56 Ja 31 '77
REPUBLICAN Party
Can the Republicans come back? G. R. Rosen. il Duns R 109:54-6+ My '77
Democracy's other component. New Repub 176: 7-8+ Ja 29 '77
Doing the Republican jostle. il Time 110:19-20 N 28 '77
Dying party? symposium. pors U.S. News 83:22-5 Ag 29 '77
GOP's comeback plan. R. Steele and others. Newsweek 89:17-18 Mr 28 '77
Is the Republican Party dead? C. B. Luce; J. Hart; E. Van Den Haag. Nat R 29:326-9+ Mr 18 '77
New GOP game plan. D. Holt and H. Bruno. Newsweek 91:25 Ja 16 '78
Operation Trojan donkey. D. Lindquist. Nat R 29:1234-6 O 28 '77

REPUBLICAN Party—*Continued*
Outlook '78: Republicans fight for a bigger toe hold. U.S. News 83:35-7 D 26 '77
Republican notes. Nat R 29:537 My 13 '77
Republican strategy: back to grass roots. P. L. Martin and W. R. Shoup. il U.S. News 82:34 My 16 '77
Republicans and the tide. Nat R 29:1158 O 14 '77
Revitalizing of the Republican Party; address, March 5, 1977. R. W. Packwood. Vital Speeches 43:453-6 My 15 '77
Save the G.O.P? M. Stone. U.S. News 82: 100 My 23 '77
Situations wanted—2,200 of them; former top officials of the Ford administration. il Time 109:16 Mr 7 '77
Sorry state of the GOP. K. Bode. New Repub 177:12-15 D 10 '77
Unmaking of the Republican Party. E. C. Ladd, Jr. il maps Fortune 96:90-5+ S '77; Reply. Nat R 29:1094+ S 30 '77
Unruh to the rescue. C. McWilliams. Nation 224: 613-14 My 21 '77
Washington's glut of ex-bureaucrats. il Bus W p25-6 Ap 4 '77
See also
Republican National Committee

History

I looked down into my open grave; E. G. Ross and impeachment of A. Johnson; excerpt from Profiles in courage. J. F. Kennedy. il Sr Schol 109:17-19 F 24 '77

REPURCHASE of stocks. See Stocks—Repurchase
REPUTATION
Your reputation: why you should worry about it. L. Schwarzbaum. Mademoiselle 83:206+ Ag '77
REQUIEM; ballet. See Ballet reviews—Single works
REQUIEMS
See also
Phonograph records—Requiems
RESCUE beacon. See Radio beacons
RESCUE of wildlife. See Wildlife conservation
RESCUE trucks. See Trucks in rescue work
RESCUE work
Preserving ancient skills; training Newfoundland dogs for sea rescues. il Time 110:72 S 5 '77
There's a girl on the tracks! life saved by E. Sanderson. W. R. Young. il Read Digest 110: 91-5 F '77
See also
Ambulance service
Artificial satellites—Use in rescue work
Drowning
Helicopters in rescue work
Ice accidents
Respiration, Artificial
Resuscitation
Search and rescue operations
Space rescue work
Submarine rescue work
Survival after airplane accidents, shipwrecks, etc.
Trucks in rescue work
United States—Civil Air Patrol
United States—Coast Guard
RESEARCH
Baconian imperative. J. A. Goldman. bibl il Intellect 105:430-2 Je '77
Global age: roles of basic and applied research; address, February 23, 1977. W. D. McElroy. Science 196:267-70 Ap 15 '77
One and one-tenth lives of a librarian/scholar; interview, ed by A. Plotnik. D. Kranzler. por Am Lib 8:65 F '77
Research or plagiarize? B. Chamberlain. Am Artist 41:18-19 Mr '77
See also
Advertising research
Aeronautic research
Animal experimentation
Atmospheric research
Botanical research
Chemical research
Colleges and universities—Research
Communication in science
Computers—Scientific use
Educational research
Fisheries—Research
Industrial research
Literary research
Medical research
Meteorological research
Military research
Nutrition research
Pharmaceutical research
Physics—Research
Power resources—Research
Reading research
Recreation research

Cost

Cost of basic research. B. Wallace. BioScience 27:83 F '77
Overhead headache. H. Schull. Science 195:639 F 18 '77

Federal aid

At our expense; government funding of recombinant DNA research. T. Galazen. Progressive 41:22 D '77
Carter aides lament research decline. P. M. Boffey. Science 197:32 Jl 1 '77
Carter revises the science budget. Sci N 111: 150 Mr 5 '77
Carter's budget: little biomedical growth; energy conservation pushed; Breeder and other long-term energy projects cut back. B. J. Culliton; L. J. Carter. Science 195:961-2 Mr 11 '77
Editorial page; public concern over scientific research. A. McGowan. Environment 19:inside cover. 44 N '77
Federal R&D budget squeezes ERDA fission and fusion. il Phys Today 30:69-72 Ap '77
Ford's farewell budget: science fares quite well. B. J. Culliton. il Science 195:374-6 Ja 28 '77
GAO reports on federally funded science programs. F. C. Bennett and B. C. Carr. il Phys Today 30:69-70+ Je '77
Of drooling dogs and periwinkles. J. Kellerman. por Newsweek 89:11 My 23 '77
R&D budget frozen in stability. D. S. Greenberg. Sci Digest 81:73-5 Ap '77
Report finds US academic research base is endangered. F. C. Bennett. Phys Today 30:61-2+ Ag '77
Research, development budget up 8%. il Aviation W 106:52-3 F 7 '77
Research management scandals provoke queries in Washington. D. Shapley. Science 198:804-6 N 25 '77
Research support grows in federal R&D budgets. E. M. Leeper. BioScience 27:161-3 Mr '77
Technology and jobs: the vital link is weakening. T. A. Vanderslice. por Duns R 110:25+ Jl '77
Transition budget: steady growth for R&D. il Sci N 111:52-4 Ja 22 '77
See also
Colleges and universities—Federal aid

Anecdotes, facetiae, satire, etc.

Bad study habits. R. Baker. il N Y Times Mag p 12 Je 5 '77

China

Stalled leap forward. il Time 110:75 Ag 1 '77

Russia

See also
Academy of Sciences of the USSR

Underdeveloped areas

See Underdeveloped areas—Research

United States

Big science struggles with the problems of its own success. G. Bylinsky. il Fortune 96:60-6+ Jl '77
See also
United States—National Science Foundation
RESEARCH Applied to National Needs program. See United States—National Science Foundation
RESEARCH centers, Industrial. See Industrial districts
RESEARCH-Cottrell, Inc
No growth can be fun. por Forbes 119:78 Ap 1 '77
RESEARCH fraud. See Fraud
RESEARCH grants
Peer review reviewed. N. Wade. Science 196: 149 Ap 8 '77
Peer review system: a vindication. Sci N 111:170 Mr 12 '77
See also
United States—National Science Foundation—Appropriations and expenditures
RESEARCH institutions
How technology will reshape life in years ahead. J. McWethy and L. McKirgan. il U.S. News 83:62-6+ N 28 '77
See also
Academy for Contemporary Problems, Columbus, Ohio
American Enterprise Institute for Public Policy Research
Brookings Institution
Institute for Policy Studies
Institute for the Future
Institute of Society, Ethics and Life Sciences
SRI International
System Development Corporation

Great Britain

Science in Europe: a Brookings-style think tank is proposed. N. Hawkes. Science 195: 659-60 F 18 '77
RESEARCH laboratories
See also
Atomic research laboratories
Bell Telephone Laboratories
Genentech Inc
Laboratories, Government
Sandia Laboratories
United States—National Institute of Health—Laboratories

RESEARCH libraries
See also
Association of Research Libraries
College libraries
RESEARCH papers. See Student themes and reports
RESEARCH parks, Industrial. See Industrial districts
RESEARCH safety vehicles. See Automobiles, Experimental
RESEARCH ships. See Ships, Research
RESEARCH Triangle Park, Durham, N.C. See Industrial districts
RESERVE Mining Company
PR man helps select author of book on pollution case. L. J. Carter. Science 195:468 F 4 '77
Stillness (however brief) at Silver Bay. J. G. Mitchell. il Audubon 79:129-34 S '77
RESERVE Officers Training Corps. See United States—Reserve Officers Training Corps
RESERVOIRS
Sand dunes, sagebrush. . .and sails? reservoir near O'Sullivan Dam in Washington. L. G. Alkire, Jr. Yachting 141:199-203 My '77
Underground reservoirs to control the water cycle. R. P. Ambroggi. il map Sci Am 236:21-7 My '77
RESIDENCE halls. See Dormitories
RESIDUES, Crop. See Crop residues
RESIGNATION
See also
Lance, T. B.—Resignation
Rabin, Y.—Resignation
RESIN-coated photographic paper. See Photographic paper
RESISTANCE to government. See Government, Resistance to
RESISTORS, Photo. See Photoresistors
RESNAIS, Alain
Moviemaker. F. Tuten. Vogue 167:200+ Ap '77 •
RESNICK, Joseph
Ode to a computer: John Wiley's print-out catalogue; poem. Pub W 212:55 O 10 '77
RESNICK, Richard B. and others
Acute systemic effects of cocaine in man: a controlled study by intranasal and intravenous routes. bibl Science 195:696-8 F 18 '77
RESOLUTIONS
Make New Year's resolutions in October. L. Konner. Seventeen 36:46-7 S '77
RESORPTION (physiology) See Absorption (physiology)
RESORTS
Falling leaves, falling prices; vacations in mountain resorts. J. Wood. il Sat Eve Post 249:90-2 S '77
Is time running out for Taylor-Hilgard? effect of Big Sky resort; with editorial comment. R. Tawney. il map Liv Wildn 40:3, 34-41 Ja '77
New England condo rondo; resorts for all seasons. S. M. Joynes. il Holiday 57:16+ N '76
Socialism with a southern face; State Resort Parks in Kentucky. J. Burnham. Nat R 29:1102 S 30 '77
Sun living on the rise. il House & Gard 150:76-83+ Ja '78
10 best resorts in the world. A. Rand. il Harp Baz 110:12+ Ag '77
See also
Health resorts, watering places, etc.
Ranches
Seaside resorts
Summer resorts
Winter resorts

Directories

Directory of timeshare resorts; condominium apartments and vacation homes. C. Burlingame. Holiday 58:16+ S '77
RESOURCE recovery. See Refuse, Utilization of
RESOURCES, Natural. See Natural resources
RESPIRATION
Impaired regulation of alveolar ventilation and the sudden infant death syndrome. D. C. Shannon and D. Kelly. bibl il Science 197:367-8 Jl 22 '77
RESPIRATION, Artificial
Natural life preservers; views of M. Nemiroff on the diving reflex. il por Time 110:73+ Ag 22 '77
Reprieve from drowning; diving reflex. Sci Am 237:57-8 Ag '77
Saving the drowned; diving reflex during asphyxia. S. Drake. il por Newsweek 90:79-80 Ag 22 '77
RESPIRATORY apparatus
See also
Skin diving—Equipment and supplies
RESPIRATORY distress syndrome
Saving preemies; techniques for treating respiratory-distress syndrome at New York's Columbia-Presbyterian Medical Center. M. Clark and D. Shapiro. il Newsweek 90:102 O 3 '77
RESPIRATORY organs

Diseases

Stave off winter ills. Changing T 31:9-10 N '77
TDI: the unacknowledged poison; toluene diisocyanate. V. Cox. Nation 224:530-2 Ap 30 '77
See also
Asthma
Cold (disease)
Influenza
Pneumonia
Sinusitis
RESPONSA. See Jewish law
RESPONSIBILITY
Are lawyers, courts, big government dulling America's moral sense? E. G. Jones. U.S. News 83:84-5 S 26 '77
War crimes; excerpt from Just and unjust wars. M. Walzer. New Repub 177:17-23 N 5 '77

Anecdotes, facetiae, satire, etc.

Mother hen; government vs personal responsibility. P. M. Sellinger. por Newsweek 90:9 S 5 '77
RESPONSIBILITY (law) See Liability (law)
REST
See also
Relaxation
Sleep
REST homes. See Nursing homes
REST Place Mill, High Falls, N.Y. See Historic houses, sites, etc.—New York (state)
REST rooms, Public. See Public comfort stations
RESTAK, Richard
Brain makes its own narcotics! il Sat R 4:6-11 Mr 5 '77
RESTAURANT management
Daring to start your own business. il Changing T 31:24-8 Je '77
RESTAURANTS
International chef. See issues of Travel
See also
Cabarets
Ice cream parlors

Architecture

Windows on the World; with introd by W. Wagner. il Archit Rec 161:111-18 My '77

Chain and franchise operations

America: out to eat. L. Langway and others. il Newsweek 90:86-7+ O 3 '77
Cautious approach to fast-food chains; stock analysis. J. Madrick. il Bus W p85 Mr 28 '77
Denny's takes its menu East. il por Bus W p 110+ S 19 '77
Emersons: dubious payments American-style. A. Hershman. il por Duns R 109:73-5 Mr '77
Fast-food chains take a beating on breakfast. Bus W p30-1 F 21 '77
Fast food shops. Mech Illus 73:20 My '77
Fast-food stars: three strategies for fast growth; McDonald's, Wendy's and Pizza Hut. il Bus W p56-60+ Jl 11 '77
Lessons not learned in school; Dunkin' Donuts. P. Berman. por Forbes 120:78 Jl 15 '77
Live show daily at Hamburger Hamlet. A. Chamberlin. il pors Fortune 95:208-15+ Mr '77
Promising mañana; Taco Bell. por Forbes 120:62 Ag 1 '77
Still the champion. il Time 109:77 Ap 25 '77
Supermarkets fight back. N. Howard. il Duns R 110:108-10 O '77
Travels in burgerland. M. Kasindorf. il Newsweek 90:90 O 3 '77
Want food fast? Here's fast food. P. Gray. il Time 110:42-3 Jl 4 '77
Wendy's: a unique strategy for growth. por Duns R 110:14-15+ Ag '77
Yumbo; fast food restaurants. A. Ward. Atlantic 239:87-8 My '77
See also
Kentucky Fried Chicken Corporation
McDonald's Corporation

Employees

See also
Waiters and waitresses

Finance

Recovering from too much growth. il Bus W p 114+ O 17 '77

Management

See Restaurant management

Australia

Delicious fish in Australia; local fish served in restaurants. il Sunset 158:60+ My '77

Canada

1978 Holiday guide to fine dining. R. L. Balzer. Holiday 58:40Y-40Z Je '77

China

Taste of China. G. Lang. il por N Y Times Mag p 108 My 1 '77

Europe, Western

My favorite European restaurants. J. Wechsberg. il Holiday 58:28-9+ Je '77

RESTAURANTS—*Continued*

France

Bordeaux is for wine lovers. . . and other romantics: Le Saint-James. L. Balzer. il Holiday 58:32-3+ Ja '77
International chef; La Pyramide restaurant, Vienne, France. D. Reynolds. Travel 147:70+ Ap '77
Magnificent brothers Troisgros. R. Chelminski. Sat R 5:72 D 10 '77
With love to La Belle France. H. McCully. il House B 119:164-8+ S '77

Hawaii

See also
Honolulu—Hotels, restaurants, etc.

Italy

Best restaurants in Italy: where and why. A. Gold and R. Fizdale. il Vogue 167:158-9+ Ag '77
Culinary ramblings in Italy; with recipes. C. Claiborne and P. Franey. il N Y Times Mag p 124+ N 13 '77

Mexico

International chef; Villa Montana in Morelia. D. Reynolds. il Travel 148:74 S '77
1978 Holiday guide to fine dining. R. L. Balzer. Holiday 58:40Z Je '77

Trinidad and Tobago

International chef; dinner at Trinidad Hilton. D. Reynolds. Trav/Holiday 148:20-1+ D '77

United States

Chef's chatter (cont) A. Ely. Holiday 57:54 N '76
Herb-laden delicacies at the end of a red-dirt road; Hilltop Herb Farm, Cleveland, Tex. G. Breckenfeld. il Fortune 96:281-2 O '77
International chef: Florida's Marco Lodge. D. Reynolds. Travel 147:73 Je '77
International chef; Pier 4 on Cape Cod. il Trav/Holiday 149:8 Ja '78
International chef; The restaurant in Anchorage, Alaska. R. L. Balzer. Trav/Holiday 148:13 N '77
1978 Holiday guide to fine dining. R. L. Balzar. Holiday 58:40C-40Y Je '77
Old-fashioned ice cream parlors in the gold country; California. il Sunset 159:28+ Ag '77
Slice of pie and a cup of coffee—that'll be fifteen cents, honey; diners. R. F. Snow. il Am Heritage 28:68-71 Ap '77
Three restaurants to try in Stowe; Vermont. M. Burros. House & Gard 149:76+ D '77
U.S. journal: Kentucky; stalking the barbecued mutton. C. Trillin. New Yorker 52:70+ F 7 '77
U.S. journal: Nebraska. C. Trillin. New Yorker 53:76-81 Ag 15 '77
You can eat like a lord in Portland; Seamen's Club in Maine. E. J. Tracy. il Fortune 96:189-90 D '77
See also subhead hotels, restaurants, etc. under names of cities, e.g. New York (city)—Hotels, restaurants, etc.

RESTITUTION, Correctional. See Reparation

RESTON, James Barrett, 1909-
(ed) See Kissinger, H. A. Secretary Kissinger interviewed for the New York times

about

James Reston: prophet of American civil religion. L. Sandon, Jr. Chr Cent 94:15-18 Ja 5 '77 *
Point of order. L. H. Lapham. Harpers 254:13-14+ My '77 *

RESTORATION of buildings. See Architecture—Conservation and restoration

RESTORATION of motion pictures. See Motion pictures—Conservation and restoration

RESTORATION of mural painting and decoration. See Mural painting and decoration—Conservation and restoration

RESTORATION of works of art. See Art—Conservation and restoration; Paintings—Conservation and restoration

RESTORED automobiles. See Automobiles, Restored

RESTORED houses. See Houses, Restored

RESTRAINT of trade
See also
Boycott
Price maintenance by industry

RESTRICTIONS on travel. See Travel regulations

RÉSUMÉS of employment. See Applications for positions

RESURRECTION
See also
Jesus Christ—Resurrection and ascension

RESUSCITATION
Heart attack emergency... D. Seim. il Farm J 101:P6-7 N '77
In a medical emergency, can you get help fast? Changing T 31:21-4 O '77
The life you save. . . ; cardio-pulmonary resuscitation. C. W. Baher. il N Y Times Mag p82+ My 1 '77
See also
Respiration, Artificial

RETAIL districts. See Business districts

RETAIL trade
See also
Carter Hawley Hale Stores, Inc
Cashiers
Chain stores
Christmas business
Company stores
Computers—Retail trade use
Department stores
Drugstores
Franchise system
Furniture stores
Gamble-Skogmo, Inc
Grocery trade
Kresge, S. S. Company
Mail order business
Outlet Company
Penney, J. C. Company
Sales
Sears, Roebuck and Company
Shopping centers
Specialty stores

Advertising

Challenge to ad discounts; effect on small retailers of rate structure used in newspaper and magazine advertising. il Bus W p 146 S 19 '77

Finance

Coming slowdown in retail spending. S. H. Wildstrom. Bus W p32 Je 13 '77
Consumers in a buying mood—big lift for business. il U.S. News 82:27-8 Je 6 '77
Ratios of retailing. il Duns R 110:80-1 S '77
Retail distribution. il Forbes 121:143-5 Ja 9 '78
Softgoods join the sales surge. il Bus W p52-3 S 26 '77
Struggling to stay ahead. il Bus W p26-7 Je 20 '77
What lies beyond retailing's mini-recession. il Fortune 96:14 Ag '77

Securities

Investors shop for specialty retailers. il Bus W p88 O 3 '77
Why analysts like catalog showrooms. D. G. Santry. il Bus W p 105 O 10 '77

Statistics

Fifty largest retailing companies. il Fortune 96:168-9 Jl '77

Great Britain

See also
Department stores—Great Britain
Marks & Spencer, Ltd
Specialty stores—Great Britain

RETAIL trade catalogs. See Catalogs, Commercial

RETAILING stocks. See Retail trade—Securities

RETAINING walls
Good-looking approach. il Sunset 158:181 Ap '77
Sloping lot? Take your pick of these retaining walls. L. D. Meyer. il Pop Sci 210:118-20+ Ap '77
Step-up walls for sandstone slope. il Sunset 158:120 Mr '77

RETAMAR, Roberto Fernandez. See Fernandez Retamar, R.

RETARDED children. See See Mentally handicapped children

RETARDED persons. See Mentally handicapped

RETINA
Amacrine cells in necturus retina: evidence for independent γ-aminobutyric acid- and glycine-releasing neurons. R. F. Miller and others. bibl il Science 198:748-50 N 18 '77
Neuronal architecture of on and off pathways to ganglion cells in carp retina. E. V. Famiglietti, Jr and others. bibl il Science 198:1267-9 D 23 '77
Siamese cats: abnormal responses of retinal ganglion cells. Y. M. Chino and others. bibl il Science 197:173-4 Jl 8 '77
Structural basis for on- and off-center responses in retinal bipolar cells. W. K. Stell and others. bibl il Science 198:1269-71 D 23 '77
See also
Rods and cones

Diseases and defects

See Eye—Diseases and defects

RETINITIS pigmentosa. See Eye—Diseases and defects

RETINOIC acid
13-cis-retinoic acid: inhibition of bladder carcinogenesis in the rat. M. B. Sporn and others. bibl il Science 195:487-9 F 4 '77
13-*cis*-retinoic acid: inhibition of bladder carcinogenesis induced in rats by *N*-butyl-*N*-(4-hydroxybutyl)nitrosamine. C. J. Grubbs and others. bibl il Science 198:743-4 N 18 '77

RETIRED military personnel
Double dippers; retirement pay of veterans. Sat Eve Post 249:36+ N '77

RETIRED military personnel—*Continued*

Employment

Carter plans commission to review excessive military pension costs. Ret Liv 17:14 Ap '77
Double dippers. New Repub 176:6+ F 12 '77
Washington memo. . . ; military retirees. R. D. Westgate. Ret Liv 17:62-3 S '77
Why the fuss over retired officers in federal jobs; double dipping. il U.S. News 82:39 F 7 '77

RETIRED Senior Volunteer Program. See United States—ACTION

RETIREMENT
Ax for forced retirement. Bus W p38-9 S 19 '77
Big debate over abolishing mandatory retirement at 65; comp by N. Lunger. Ret Liv 17:20-3 D '77
Big fight over retirement at age 65. U.S. News 83:30-2 O 3 '77
Breaking the 65 barrier; legislation on issue of mandatory retirement. I. Ross. Read Digest 112:141-5 Ja '78
Challenging the 65 barrier; proposal of C. Pepper. il Time 110:67 Ag 8 '77
Congress should think long and hard; mandatory retirement. M. S. Forbes, Jr. Forbes 120:25 O 1 '77
Do not go gently. . .; compulsory retirement. H. D. Shapiro. il N Y Times Mag p36-8+ F 6 '77
Forced retirement: an issue that's riling older Americans. il U.S. News 83:75-6 Jl 4 '77
Forced retirement: how common is it? D. R. Kittner. il M Labor R 100:60-1 D '77
Gray rights retirement fight. A. Colamosca. il Duns R 110:82-4+ O '77
House—359 to 4—passes bill changing mandatory retirement age for private and Federal employees. R. D. Westgate. il Ret Liv 17:55-6 N '77
Is it time to retire the retirement age? J. Chan. McCalls 104:71 Ag '77
Mandatory retirement. R. D. Westgate. il Ret Liv 17:18 Ap '77
Mandatory retirement; address, June 6 1977. C. Pepper. Vital Speeches 43:651-3 Ag 15 '77
Minority we all hope to join; question of mandatory retirement age. New Repub 177:7 O 8 '77
Must people retire at 65? interviews. A. C. Prine, Jr; H. Miller. pors U.S. News 83:37-8 Ag 22 '77
New retirement rules: their impact on business, workers; When do foreign workers retire? il U.S. News 83:71-3 N 7 '77
News & views; mandatory retirement age. il Ret Liv 17:58+ S '77
Now, the revolt of the old. il Time 110:18-20+ O 10 '77
Plan today for tomorrow's retirement. G. W. Weinstein. House B 119:10+ N '77
Planning seminars ease transition to retirement. il Aging 270:22-5 Ap '77
Q&A about retiring. T. Collins. See issues of Retirement living
Raising the mandatory retirement age: examining the consequences. R. F. Schier. il Intellect 106:214-16 D '77
Retiring at 65: an arbitrary cut-off that started with three men. il Duns R 110:31-2 O '77
Right to keep working? T. Nicholson and J. B. Copeland. Newsweek 90:79 Jl 18 '77
Round 2: Senate approves bill raising mandatory retirement age, but House-Senate bills differ. il Ret Liv 17:47-8 D '77
Seniliphobia; raising the mandatory retirement age. Nation 225:357 O 15 '77
This month's feature: Congress & revision of mandatory retirement age policy. Cong Digest 56:258-87 N '77
Washington memo. . . ; mandatory retirement. R. D. Westgate. Ret Liv 17:62 S '77
Washington memo: uproar over proposal to raise social security age. R. D. Westgate. Ret Liv 17:52-3 O '77
What I wish someone had told me about retirement; symposium. See issues of Retirement living
What's the right age for retirement? questionnaire on mandatory retirement laws. il Ret Liv 16:18 D '76; 17:22-5 Ap '77
When compulsory retirement at 65 is ended. . . B. D. Gelb. Harvard Bus R 55:6-8 Jl '77
See also
College teachers—Retirement
Executives—Retirement
Government employees—Retirement
Presidents—United States—Retirement
Retirement, Places of
Teachers—Retirement

Anecdotes, facetiae, satire, etc.

Is retirement what your wife makes it? M. G. Stoddard. Ret Liv 17:38 Ap '77

RETIREMENT, Places of
Be careful where you aim those binoculars! small town life. R. B. Douglas. il Ret Liv 17:28-9 Je '77
Chances are one in a million; retiring in New York City. T. Davidson. por Ret Liv 17:26-7 Je '77
Gazetteer. il Ret Liv 17:39+ S '77
Mexico for retirement? J. H. Budd. il Ret Liv 17:37-9 Mr '77
Retiring? a guide to cheapest cities. il U.S. News 83:36 Ag 22 '77
Retiring alone to the country; running Brook Farm guest house in Lenox, Mass. G. Gewirtz and R. J. Martin. pors Ret Liv 17:30-1 Je '77
Retiring along the 5-state Gulf Coast. J. B. Truscott. il Ret Liv 17:30-1+ Ja '77
Retiring to the Ozarks; So this is Little Rock. D. L. Goff; D. Dahl. il Ret Liv 17:44-5+ My '77
Where should you live in retirement? V. Hoven. il Ret Liv 16:20-2 D '76
You can't talk to the trees! remote country living in California's Sierras. G. Bergman. il Ret Liv 17:32-3 Je '77
See also
Retirement communities

RETIREMENT communities
Alone in a retirement community. L. Homer. il pors Ret Liv 17:29-30 Ag '77
Home economist, minister obtain FmHA loan to build retirement community; case of Billie Hagler and Rev. Gordon Blunt. Aging 270:21 Ap '77

RETIREMENT income
Budgets for retired couples rose moderately in 1976. M. L. McCraw. il M Labor R 100:53-6 O '77
How much income will your savings yield? il Changing T 31:24 D '77
Money plan for your retirement. S. Shulsky. il Ret Liv 17:30-7 N; 24-31 D '77
$660,000 farewell; profit sharing at Lowe's Companies. H. Johnson. il pors Ebony 32:47-8+ F '77
See also
Pensions

RETRIEVERS
Retrievers good and bad; duck hunting in Montana. N. MacLean. Esquire 88:22+ O '77

RETROLENTAL fibroplasia. See Eye—Diseases and defects

RETTIG, Nell
In quest of the snatcher. il map Audubon 79:26-49 N '77

RETURNS policy in bookselling. See Booksellers and bookselling—Returns policy

REUNIONS, Family. See Family reunions

REUPHOLSTERING. See Upholstery

REUSS, Henry Schoelkopf
Reviewing the American city; address, March 4, 1977. Vital Speeches 43:401-5 Ap 15 '77

REUTER, Madalynne
All things bright and exuberant: St Martin's Press is 25 years old. il pors Pub W 212:30-3 Ag 8 '77
Annual AAUP meeting focuses on two identity problems. il Pub W 212:56-60 Ag 1 '77
(ed) Week. See issues of Publishers weekly

—and Wagner, Susan
Seventh annual AAP meeting. il Pub W 211:54-9 Je 20 '77

REVEL, Jean François
Myths of Eurocommunism. bibl f For Affairs 56:295-305 Ja '78
Revel-ations; tr by D. Pryce-Jones; excerpt from La nouvelle censure. N Y Times Mag p 115-16 D 11 '77
about
Bête noire of France's Left. D. Pryce-Jones. il pors N Y Times Mag p54-5+ D 11 '77 *
Political superstition and the intellectuals. A. Kazin. Esquire 88:42+ N '77 *

REVELATION
Truth by any other name; propositional revelation. R. H. Nash. Chr Today 22:17-19+ O 7 '77

REVELL, Donald
Rodeo aesthetique; Animaux; Motel view; poems. Poetry 129:195-7 Ja '77

REVELL, Fleming H, Company. See Publishers and publishing—Religious literature

REVELLE, Roger R.
NAS panel is concerned over atmospheric CO_2 buildup. F. C. Bennett. por Phys Today 30:17-18 O '77 *

REVENGE
Don't get mad, get even; views of seven authors. il Esquire 87:100-5+ Je '77

REVENTAZÓN River
Grand fish at night: the ultimate action; tarpon fishing at the mouth of the Parismina River, Costa Rica. S. Apte. il Outdoor Life 160:66-7+ Jl '77

REVENUE, Municipal. See Local taxation

REVENUE Cutter Service. See United States—Coast Guard—History

REVERE, Paul
Paul Revere. B. A. Weisberger. il por Am Heritage 28:24-37 Ap '77 *

REVERE Copper and Brass, Inc
Staying on top. J. Cook. il Forbes 120:54+ Jl 1 '77

REVERSE discrimination. See Discrimination; Discrimination in employment

REVIEN, Leon
Train your eyes; better your score. P. Martin. il Sci Digest 81:7-9 Mr '77 *
REVIEW, Judicial. See Judicial review
REVIEWS of books. See Book reviews
REVIEWS of plays. See Drama reviews
REVIVALS
See also
Jesus movement
REVOLUTIONARY War (United States) See United States—History—Revolution, 1775-1783
REVOLUTIONISTS, Cambodian
Nation as concentration camp; Khmer Rouge in Cambodia; tr by N. King. S. Groueff. Nat R 29:988-90 S 2 '77
REVOLUTIONS
See also
France—History—Revolution, 1789-1799
United States—History—Revolution, 1775-1783
REVOLVERS
Colt single action army revolver. C. Worman. il Hobbies 82:142-3 Mr '77
Colt's model 1871-2 .44 open top revolver. C. Worman. il Hobbies 82:154-5 O '77
Elisha Collier and his guns. C. Worman. il Hobbies 82:142-3 Je '77
S&W .22 first model second issue revolvers. C. Worman. il Hobbies 82:154-5 D '77
Tracing of Beretta A47469; condensation. N. M. Adams. il Read Digest 112:203-6+ Ja '78
REVUELTAS, Silvestre
Sensemayá; Redes; Caminos; Itinerarios; Janitzio. W. D. Curtis. Am Rec G 41:29-30 N '77 *
REWALD, John
Cézanne's final decade. il Horizon 20:40-7 O '77
REWARDS, prizes, etc.
See also
Literary prizes
Teachers—Awards, prizes, etc.
Television awards
also names of awards, e.g. Noble Prizes; *also* names of organizations, societies, etc. granting awards, e.g. American Academy and Institute of Arts and Letters; *also* subhead Awards, prizes, etc. under various subjects, e.g. Science—Awards, prizes, etc.

Anecdotes, facetiae, satire, etc.

Best of Dubious. D. Newman. il Esquire 88:99-104 O '77
Esquire's dubious achievement awards for 1977. il Esquire 89:45-9 Ja '78
LJ's annual awards. Lib J 102:2459 D 15 '77
No comment Olympics: the Ms first annual awards for surrealism in everyday life; comp by A. Northrop and G. Steinem. il Ms 6:48-50+ Jl '77
Otto Awards. R. Baker. N Y Times Mag p6 F 13 '77
Thoughts from the dais: on receiving an honorary award. S. C. Florman. Harper 254:29-30 F '77
REXBURG, Idaho
Boom after the burst; Teton Dam aftermath. E. Keerdoja and P. S. Greenberg. il Newsweek 89:9 Je 6 '77
REXRODE, L. O.
Keep those film cans! il Pop Phot 81:258 D '77
REY, Werner K.
Another upheaval keeps Bally unsettled. il por Bus W p23-4 Ag 1 '77 *
Switzerland: a sudden takeover of a staid shoemaker; C. F. Bally. il Bus W p40-1 F 21 '77 *
REYES BASUALTO, Neftalí Ricardo. See Neruda, P.
REYE'S syndrome
Canada's moth war; efforts to halt spruce budworm spraying program due to increase in Reye's syndrome cases. E. E. May. bibl il map Environment 19:16-24 Ag '77
Reye's syndrome: patient serum alters mitochondrial function and morphology in vitro. J. R. Aprille. bibl il Science 197:908-10 Ag 26 '77
REYKJALIN, John. See Enea, H. jt auth
REYMAN, Jonathan E.
Astronomy, architecture, and adaptation at Pueblo Bonito. bibl il Science 193:957-62; 197: 619-20 S 10 '76, Ag 12 '77
REYNOLDS, Barbara
What have they done to the rain? M. Hope. Chr Cent 94:693-5 Ag 3 '77 *
REYNOLDS, Burt
Good ole Burt; cool-eyed Clint. R. Schickel. il pors Time 111:48-54 Ja 9 '78 *
REYNOLDS, Charles
Images: forty years of evolution and revolution. Pop Phot 80:97+ My '77
REYNOLDS, Doris
International chef. Travel 147:70+ Ap; 73 Je; 148:24-5 Ag; 74 S '77 (cont as) Trav/Holiday 148:20-1 D '77
REYNOLDS, John C. Jr
Science fiction in the 7-12 curriculum. bibl Clearing H 51:122-5 N '77
REYNOLDS, John E. 3d
Precarious survival of the Florida manatee. il Oceans 10:50-3 S '77
REYNOLDS, R. J, Industries, Inc
Betting on a stronger mark. il Bus W p 196 N 14 '77
REYNOLDS Metal Company
Perils—and profits—of pioneering. il Forbes 119:41 Ja 15 '77
REYNOLDS Securities, Inc-Dean Witter Organization Inc merger. See Brokers—Acquisitions and mergers
REZNIKOFF, Charles
His mind a psalter: the poetry of Charles Reznikoff. E. Warren. Chr Today 22:26-7 D 9 '77 *
Poet of exile. R. Alter. Commentary 63:49-55 F '77 *
REZNY, Abe
Interview with two practitioners. il pors Pop Phot 81:104-5+ S '77
RHAPSODY (music)
See also
Phonograph records—Rhapsody (music)
RHEA, John
Big, big ideas at the Pentagon. Progressive 41: 13-18 Ap '77
RHEE, Katherine C.
Bud grafting to make an old-fashioned orchard. il Org Gard & Farm 25:92-6 Ja '78
RHEIMS, France
Left at City Hall. H. Muller. Time 110:54+ N 28 '77
Das RHEINGOLD; opera. See Wagner, R.
RHEINGOLD Breweries. See Brewing industry
RHEINHEIMER, Kurt
Visit on a Tuesday afternoon; story. Redbook 149:62-3 Ag '77
RHEINLIEDER. See Songs, German
RHESUS monkeys. See Monkeys
RHETORIC
Camus on doublespeak. D. Lazere. Engl J 66: 24-6 O '77
Perils of persuasive preaching. A. D. Litfin. Chr Today 21:14-17 F 4 '77
See also
Elocution
Narration (rhetoric)
RHEUMATISM
See also
Arthritis
RHEUMATOID arthritis. See Arthritis
RHINOCEROS
Most preposterous beast. il Int Wildlife 7:4-16 Jl '77
RHIZOBIUM
Chemotaxis of rhizobium spp. to a glycoprotein produced by birdsfoot trefoil roots. W. W. Currier and G. A. Strobel. bibl il Science 196: 434-6 Ap 22 '77
RHOADES, Clare
Women who chose the great outdoors; interview, ed by N. H. Clark. por Harp Baz 110:86-7+ Ap '77
RHOADS, Donald C. See Lutz, R. A. jt auth
RHODA Morgenstern Gerard (television character) See Women in television
RHODE ISLAND
See also
Architecture, Domestic—Rhode Island
Criminal justice, Administration of—Rhode Island
Music festivals—Rhode Island
Public health—Rhode Island

Foreign population

Immigrants without care; Portuguese in Rhode Island. L. A. Monteiro. bibl il Society 14:38-42 S '77

Industries

See also
Wine industry

Legislature

Bill Bailey's Rhode Island blues. il por Time 109:70 Mr 21 '77
RHODEN, Bill
Chicago teacher makes his classes come alive. il pors Ebony 32:43-6+ Mr '77
Fruitful past but a shaky future. il Ebony 32: 60-2+ Ag '77
O'Jays: there's a message in their music. il por Ebony 32:90-2+ S '77
Stormin' Norman. il pors Ebony 32:127-8+ My '77
Ten worst things you can do to your health. il Ebony 33:30+ Ja '78
Ups and downs of Reggie Jackson. il pors Ebony 32:60-2+ O '77
RHODES, Dean
Media monster: Ponik the Terrible. Int Wildlife 7:17 S '77
RHODES, Eugene Manlove
New Mexico incident. W. H. Hutchinson. bibl il pors Am West 14:4-7+ N '77 *
RHODES, James Ford
Perspectives on the past. W. W. Hassler, jr. Am Hist Illus 11:50 F '77 *

RHODES, Lynwood Mark
American Indian pow-wow. il Travel 147:48-53 F '77

RHODES, Richard
I am become death. . .il pors Am Heritage 28: 70-83 O '77

RHODESIA
Rhodesia (Zimbabwe); white minority rule in a black state. T. J. Kubiak. bibl il map Focus 27:1-8 N '76
See also
Americans in Rhodesia
Guerrillas—Rhodesia
Immigration and emigration—Rhodesia
Terrorism—Rhodesia
United Nations—Rhodesia

Armed Forces

Military: a mission impossible. il Time 109: 29 Je 13 '77
On the line in Rhodesia. P. Younghusband. il Newsweek 90:34+ Jl 11 '77

Army

Enemy also have problems; excerpts from interview, ed by P. Younghusband. P. Walls. por Newsweek 90:37 Jl 11 '77
Smith's Yankee recruits. A. De Borchgrave. il Newsweek 90:40 S 12 '77
Why Americans are fighting on Rhodesia's front lines. S. Hempstone. il map U.S. News 82:31-2 My 23 '77

Commerce

United States

See United States—Commerce—Rhodesia

Economic relations

Rhodesia and her neighbors. R. W. Hull. Cur Hist 73:218-22+ D '77

Foreign relations

Botswana

Security Council missions recommend assistance for Botswana and Lesotho. UN Chron 14:44-5 My '77
U.S. abstains on Security Council resolution on Botswana complaint; statements, with text of resolution, January 13-14, 1977. W. W. Scranton; A. W. Sherer, Jr. Dept State Bull 76:117-19 F 7 '77

Mozambique

See Mozambique—Foreign relations—Rhodesia

Native races

See also
Rhodesia—Race question

Politics and government

Another Smith surprise. K. Willenson and I. Mills. il por Newsweek 90:47-8 D 5 '77
Avoiding disaster in Southern Africa. C. Legum. New Repub 176:11-13 F 12 '77
Back of the rising fear of race war in Rhodesia; with interview with I. Smith. map U.S. News 83:34-5 Ag 8 '77
Between freedom fighters and mercenaries. J. M. Swomley, Jr. Nation 226:13-16 Ja 7 '78
Brief encounters in a hopeless war. W. McWhirter. il Time 109:36+ My 30 '77
Britain's Owen—a fresh start; excerpts from interview, ed by H. Nickel. D. Owen. il por Time 109:53-4 My 2 '77
Carrot and stick. K. Willenson. il Newsweek 89:35+ Mr 7 '77
Casual confidence; excerpts from interview, ed by A. Collings. A. J. Young. il por Newsweek 90:39 S 12 '77
Chief's plan; interview, ed by A. de Borchgrave. J. S. Chirau. il por Newsweek 90:36 Jl 18 '77
Chimurenga and the chicken run. L. Griggs. il Time 109:29+ Mr 28 '77
Countdown in Rhodesia. W. F. Buckley, Jr. Nat R 29:1012-13 S 2 '77
Decision time; peace proposal. por Time 110:27-8 S 5 '77
Devil himself. C. Legum. il New Repub 177:17-19 D 17 '77
Goodbye to white Rhodesia? R. Carroll and others. il Newsweek 89:24+ F 21 '77
Ian Smith: a bit cynical; excerpts from interview, ed by H. A. Grunwald and W. McWhirter. I. D. Smith. por Time 109:46+ My 23 '77
Ian Smith's last stand? por Time 110:27-8 Ag 1 '77
Man of peace seeks to rule; A. T. Muzorewa. J. M. Wall. bibl Chr Cent 94:611-12 Jl 6 '77
Moment of truth draws nearer for Rhodesia; Who's who among black leaders. il map U.S. News 82:32-4 My 30 '77
Narrowing options for Rhodesia. T. Beeson. Chr Cent 94:133-4 F 16 '77
News conference by Secretary Vance and Foreign Secretary Owen, London, Aug. 12. D. Owen; C. R. Vance Dept State Bull 77:345-50 S 12 '77
Peace-plan safari. M. R. Benjamin and others. il pors Newsweek 90:35-6 S 5 '77
Promises, payoffs and evasions: a new plan for Ian Smith to veto. G. Wasserman. il Nation 225:458-61 N 5 '77
Rhodesia: a gingerly diplomacy. D. I. Fine. Nation 225:199-201 S 10 '77
Rhodesia: bracing for a larger state role. il Bus W p70+ F 14 '77
Rhodesia—proposals for a settlement; joint press conference, with text of proposals, September 1-2, 1977. D. Owen; A. Young, Jr. Dept State Bull 77:417-39 O 3 '77
Rhodesia: putting the record straight; report of the Rhodesian Justice and Peace Commission. B. MacGarry. America 137:239-40 O 15 '77
Secretary Kissinger attends NATO ministerial meeting at Brussels and meets with British officials at London; text of joint news conference, December 10, 1976. A. Crosland; H. A. Kissinger. Dept State Bull 76:6-9 Ja 3 '77
Secretary Vance meets with Foreign Secretary Owen; remarks with the press, July 23, 1977. C. R. Vance; D. A. L. Owen. Dept State Bull 77:275-8 Ag 29 '77
Separate peace? R. Carroll and others. il Newsweek 89:46+ F 7 '77
Smith changes his tune. Time 110:52 D 5 '77
Smith takes a dangerous new gamble; Military: a mission impossible. il por Time 109:24+ Je 13 '77
Smith's internal solution; interview, ed by A. de Borchgrave. I. Smith. il por Newsweek 90: 34-5 Jl 18 '77
Three soldier peacemakers. pors Time 110:40 N 7 '77
Tragic and fateful decision. por Time 109:43-4 F 7 '77
Twilight in white Rhodesia. J. B. Treaster. il map Atlantic 239:63-70+ My '77
Two sides of a stalemate; interviews, ed by D. Wood. K. Kaunda; J. Nkomo. pors Time 110: 35-6 Ag 8 '77
Uncertainty in Rhodesia. America 137:138-9 S 17 '77
White bastion: hanging tough; excerpts from interview, ed by J. Elson and L. Griggs. I. D. Smith. por Time 109:31 Mr 7 '77
Why Rhodesia? J. Burnham. Nat R 29:935 Ag 19 '77
See also
Elections—Rhodesia

Race question

Before the fall. C. Norton. Progressive 41:48 D '77
End of a chapter; victory of I. Smith in elections. il por Time 110:24+ S 12 '77
From Rhodesia to Zimbabwe. M. O'Callaghan. il UNESCO Courier 30:22-5 N '77
Growing peril of race war in Southern Africa. D. B. Richardson. il map U.S. News 82:22+ F 7 '77
Rhodesian excess. W. F. Buckley, Jr. Nat R 29:222-3 F 18 '77
Strange alliance. E. M. von Kuehnelt-Leddihn. Nat R 29:1300 N 11 '77
White tribe of Zimbabwe. X. Smiley. New Repub 177:19-21 Jl 30 '77

Religious institutions and affairs

Christian witness in Rhodesia. A. Cook. Chr Cent 94:444-5 My 11 '77
See also
Catholic Church in Rhodesia
Christians in Rhodesia
Church and state in Rhodesia

RHODOPSIN. See Visual purple

RHODOPSIN, Bacterial. See Pigments (biology)

RHÔNE-Poulenc, S.A. See Conglomerate corporations—France

RHÔNE wines. See Wine

RHUBARB
See also
Cookery—Rhubarb

RHYTHM
See also
Cycles
Language and languages—Rhythm

RHYTHM method. See Birth control

RIAD, Mahmoud
Secretary Vance reaffirms factors for Mideast conference; exchange of remarks, October 6, 1977. Dept State Bull 77:638-9 N 7 '77

RIASANOVSKY, Nicholas V.
On Lamennais, Chaadaev, and the romantic revolt in France and Russia. bibl f pors Am Hist R 82:1165-86 D '77

RIBAKOVE, Barbara
Put on those jogging shoes and run for your life! il Fam Health 9:48-9 F '77

RIBAVIRIN
Congenital anomalies induced in hamster embryos with ribavirin. L. Kilham and V. H. Ferm. bibl il Science 195:413-14 Ja 28 '77
Ribavirin: efficacy in the treatment of murine autoimmune disease. L. W. Klassen and others. bibl il Science 195:787-9 F 25 '77

RIBMAN, Ronald
Cold storage. Reviews
America 136:398 Ap 30 '77 *
New Yorker 53:102+ Ap 18 '77 *
Newsweek 89:90 Ap 25 '77 *
Time il 109:31 Ap 18 '77 *
RIBONUCLEIC acid. See RNA
RIBULOSE bisphosphate carboxylase. See Carboxylases
RICCARDO, John J.
Chrysler's plan to head off a cash shortage. por Bus W p83 O 24 '77 *
RICCI, Luigi
Ten commandments of Puccini; excerpt from Puccini, a self interpretation. Opera N 42:18-19 D 17 '77
RICCIUTI, Edward R.
Bird lovers. il Audubon 79:68-72+ S '77
RICE, Berkeley
New gangs of Chinatown. il Psychol Today 10:60-1+ My '77
—and Cramer, James
Comes the counterrevolution. il Psychol Today 11:56-7+ S '77
RICE, Charles Owen
McBride for Abel. Commonweal 104:166-7 Mr 18 '77
RICE, Dabney
Nerves are a real headache. Harp Baz 110:124+ Mr '77
RICE, Dorothy P.
Health facilities in the United States. bibl f il Cur Hist 72:211-14+ My '77
RICE, George P. Jr
Conversation and literature; address, September 14, 1977. Vital Speeches 43:749-53 O 1 '77
RICE, Ruth
Infant care: a touching story. E. McCoy. por House & Gard 149:68+ Mr '77 *
RICE, Shelley
Milton Rogovin: compassionate portraitist. il Mod Phot 41:116-21 S '77
Reconsideration. New Repub 177:35-7 O 29 '77
RICE
Interaction of Beggiatoa and rice plant: detoxification of hydrogen sulfide in the rice rhizosphere. M. M. Joshi and J. P. Hollis. bibl il Science 195:179-80 Ja 14 '77
Rice. Consumer Rep 42:88-92 D '77
See also
Cookery—Rice
RICH, Adrienne Cecile
Natural resources; poem. Ms 6:60-2 D '77
RICH, Alexander, and Kim, S. H.
Three-dimensional structure of transfer RNA; with biographical sketches. il Sci Am 238:12, 52-62 Ja '78
RICH, Frank
Woody Allen wipes the smile off his face. por Esquire 87:72-6+ My '77
RICH, Leslie
Process for alternative education. il Am Educ 13:23-6 Mr '77
RICH, Maria F.
U.S. opera survey 1976-77. il Opera N 42:52+ N '77
RICH, Peggy Savage-. See Savage-Rich, P.
RICH, Robert
Flags of convenience—or necessity? il Oceans 10:22-7 Mr '77
RICH, The
Blue bloods. C. Amory; J. Dymock; C. Vanderbilt, Jr. il Sat Eve Post 249:84-5 Jl '77
Get a horse: a proposal to distract the rich from politics. E. McCarthy. New Repub 177:10-11 Jl 9 '77
Golden clan; excerpt. J. Corry. il N Y Times Mag p 16-19+ Mr 13 '77
Hot new rich. il Time 109:72-6+ Je 13 '77
Psychiatric care
Poor rich. R. R. Grinker, Jr. bibl il Psychol Today 11:74-6+ O '77
RICH-field telescopes. See Telescopes
RICHARD, Olga. See McCann, D. jt auth
RICHARD Marek Publishers, Inc. See Publishers and publishing—United States
RICHARD Morse Mime Theatre. See Mime
RICHARD III; drama. See Shakespeare, William —Plays
RICHARDS, Gilbert Francis
Focusing on people and productivity; interview. il pors Nations Bus 65:40-2+ Jl '77
RICHARDS, Ivor Armstrong
In want; poem. Am Scholar 46:313-15 Summ '77
Nothing at all; poem. Am Scholar 47:14 Wint '77
RICHARDS, Lawrence O.
Church teaching: content without context. il Chr Today 21:16-18 Ap 15 '77
RICHARDS, M. C.
Black Mountain College: a golden seed. il Craft Horiz 37:21-2+ Je '77
RICHARDS, Renee
Only human. P. Axthelm. por Newsweek 90:77-8 S 12 '77 *
Transsexual chic: the packaging of Renee Richards. M. Seligson. il Ms 5:74-6+ F '77 *
RICHARDS, Robert. See Jolliffe, R. jt auth
RICHARDS, Veronica Jean
What are we doing at a football game? Seventeen 36:198+ Ag '77
RICHARDSON, Elliot Lee
Administration gives views on proposed legislation on deep seabed mining; statement, April 27, 1977. Dept State Bull 76:524-7 My 23 '77
Law of the Sea Conference: problems and progress; statement, July 20, 1977. Dept State Bull 77:389-91 S 19 '77
Review of the Law of the Sea Conference and deep seabed mining legislation; statement, October 4, 1977. Dept State Bull 77:751-6 N 21 '77
Sexless orgies of morality. il por N Y Times Mag p33 Ja 23 '77
about
Carter appointments: fresh moves on sea law, arms control. D. Shapley. Science 195:560-2 F 11 '77 *
RICHARDSON, Jack
Theater (cont) Commentary 63:74-5 Ap '77
RICHARDSON, John David
On discs. Dance Mag 51:90-1 Je '77
RICHARDSON, Nancy McCarthy
Going places, finding things in Britain. il House & Gard 149:58+ F '77
RICHARDSON, Nelson
Subsidy publishing: stigma or sesame? il Writers Digest 57:44-8 Jl '77
RICHARDSON, Penny. See Forman, D. C. jt auth
RICHARDSON, Sir Ralph
Profiles. K. Tynan. por New Yorker 53:45-6+ F 21 '77 *
RICHARDSON, Samuel
Examplar to her sex: Richardson's Clarissa. R. M. Brownstein. Yale R 67:30-47 O '77 *
RICHARDSON, William J.
Martin Heidegger: in memoriam. Commonweal 104:16-18 Ja 7 '77
RICHELSON, Elliott
Lithium ion entry through the sodium channel of cultured mouse neuroblastoma cells: a biochemical study. bibl il Science 196:1001-2 My 27 '77
RICHEY, David
How to catch trophy brook trout. il por Field & S 81:78-80+ Ap '77
Ice safety and rescue. il Outdoor Life 160:123-4 D '77
My God. I've gotten too close! il Outdoor Life 161:58-9+ Ja '78
(ed) See Lupo, S. Death stalked the ice
RICHEY, Herbert S.
Real cause of inflation; address, March 16, 1977. Vital Speeches 43:386-9 Ap 15 '77
RICHEY, Russell E. See Jones, D. G. jt auth
RICHLER, Mordecai
Oh! Canada! Lament for a divided country. il Atlantic 240:41-55 D '77
RICHMAN, Michael
Long labor of making nation's favorite statue. il Smithsonian 7:54-61 bibl(p 152) F '77
RICHMAN, Phyllis C.
Fine art of eating in Trinidad and Tobago. il Holiday 58:40-1+ Ja '77
RICHMOND, David. See Hall, B. jt auth
RICHMOND, Doug
No-fuss wire splicing. il Mech Illus 73:74 Mr '77
RICHMOND, Frederick William
Excerpts from remarks on nuclear energy production, June 22, 1976. Cong Digest 56:47+ F '77
Farmers and consumers can work together. Farm J 101:14 Ja '77
about
Artists' tax bills. B. Chamberlain. Am Artist 42:18+ Ja '78 *
Richmond bill: H.R.1042. C. B. Fowler. Hi Fi 27:MA16 N '77 *
RICHMOND, Julius B.
Califano takes Richmond. B. J. Culliton. Science 196:739 My 13 '77 *
RICHMOND, Va.
Education
Invisible stories become visible; creative writing program. R. L. Norris. Engl J 66:76-8 N '77
RICHMOND Corporation-American General Insurance Company merger. See Insurance companies—Acquisitions and mergers
RICHTER, Marga
Milwaukee Sym: Richter prem. por Hi Fi 27:MA34-6 Jl '77 *
RICHTER, Sviatoslav Teofilovitch
Dvořák plain vs. Dvořák fancified; recordings of G minor piano concerto. H. Goldsmith. por Hi Fi 27:73-4 D '77 *
RICKARD, W. H. and others
Elk in the shrub-steppe region of Washington: an authentic record. il Science 196:1009 My 27 '77
RICKENBACKER, Adelaide F
Adelaide F. Rickenbacker: a tribute. W. F. Rickenbacker. Nat R 29:272 Mr 4 '77 *
RICKENBACKER, William F.
Music. Nat R 29:897-8 Ag 5 '77

RICKOVER, Hyman George
Ancient submariner. J. Miller. New Repub 177: 16-19 N 12 '77 *
Unsinkable Hyman Rickover. il por Time 109: 21 My 23 '77 *
RICKRACK cactus. See Cactus
RICOH Company. See Office equipment industry —Japan
RIDDICK, Steven Earl
Feeling fit to hurt a lot of feelings. J. Marshall. il pors Sports Illus 46:40-2+ Mr 28 '77 *
RIDGWAY, Rozanne L.
Department comments on fishery agreements with EEC and Japan; statement, February 22, 1977. Dept State Bull 76:272-3 Mr 21 '77
Department reviews developments in international fisheries policy; statement, February 3, 1977. Dept State Bull 76:175-8 F 28 '77
RIDING, Alan
Perils of quiet diplomacy. il Sat R 5:18-20+ N 12 '77
RIDING. See Horsemanship
RIDLEY, W. P. and others
Biomethylation of toxic elements in the environment. bibl il Science 197:329-32 Jl 22 '77
RIEDER, Corinne H.
Work, women, and vocational education. il Am Educ 13:27-30 Je '77
RIEGLE, Donald Wayne, 1938-
Washing dirty laundry in Detroit. N. Ephron. Esquire 87:42-4 F '77 *
RIENKE, Deloris
Solar heating—no longer a novelty. Ret Liv 17:28-9+ O '77
RIENZI; opera. See Wagner, R.
RIES, Stanley K. and others
Triacontanol: a new naturally occurring plant growth regulator. bibl il Science 195:1339-41 Mr 25 '77
about
Alfalfa yields a mystery chemical that spurs plant growth, even in the dark. E. Driscoll. il por Horticulture 55:8+ Ag '77 *
RIESENBERG, Laura Brunton
Recombinant DNA—the containment debate. bibl il Chemistry 50:13-17 D '77
RIESMAN, David
Human rights: conflicts among our ideals; excerpts from address, June 5, 1977. Commonweal 104:711-15 N 11 '77
Prospects for human rights adaptation of address, June 5, 1977. bibl il Society 15:28-33 N '77
RIESSMAN, Frank
Paraprofessionals, poverty, and politics; interview, ed by I. L. Horowitz. bibl Society 14: 72-8 Ja '77
RIFKIN, Jeremy
No turning back; what path now? Sci Digest 81:28-9 Je '77
One small step beyond mankind. Progressive 41:21 Mr '77
—and Howard, Ted
Who should play God? excerpt. il Progressive 41:16-22 D '77
RIFLE cartridges. See Cartridges
RIFLE primers. See Detonators
RIFLE sights. See Firearms—Sights
RIFLE stocks. See Gunstocks
RIFLE targets. See Targets
RIFLES
Buck Rogers gun; laser sighted rifle. il Newsweek 90:56 Jl 25 '77
Confederate Tarpley; breechloading carbine. C. Worman. il Hobbies 82:154 S '77
Flintlock rifles—new as tomorrow. J. Carmichel. il Outdoor Life 161:60-3+ Ja '78
Lightweight rifle: how to shave pounds. J. Carmichel. il Outdoor Life 160:116-18+ N '77
Magnum seven. J. Carmichel. il Outdoor Life 159:112-14+ Je '77
Rifle from the Alamo. C. Worman. il Hobbies 82: 142-3 Ap '77
Rifle that's yours; custom made rifles. D. E. Petzal. il Field & S 82:96-8 O '77
Winchester; 1866 carbine. C. Worman. il Hobbies 82:154-5 Ag '77
See also
National Rifle Association
RIFLES, Air. See Air guns
RIFTS (geology) See Faults (geology)
RIGAUD, Jacques
Victoria Ocampo's gift for world culture. il pors UNESCO Courier 30:64-6 Ag '77
RIGBY'S Ltd. See Publishers and publishing—Australia
RIGGING. See Masts and rigging
RIGGS, Michael
Boston: hub city of American audio. il Hi Fi 27:79-83 Mr '77
RIGHT and left (political science)
Absent left. J. Greenfield. Harpers 225:19-21+ S '77
Bête noire of France's Left; J. F. Revel. D. Pryce-Jones. il pors N Y Times Mag p54-5+ D 11 '77
Elegy for the new left; Time essay. L. Morrow. il Time 110:67-8 Ag 15 '77
Fission on the right: Richard Viguerie's bid for power; the new right. A. Crawford. Nation 224:104-8 Ja 29 '77
Motherhood, apple pie and human rights: where the old left meets the new right. R. Steel. New Repub 176:14-15 Je 4 '77
Right on for the new right. il Time 110:24+ O 3 '77
Why the new right lost. J. Kirkpatrick. bibl f Commentary 63:34-9 F '77; Discussion. 63:14+ My '77
See also
Conservatism
Liberalism
Radicalism
RIGHT- and left-handedness. See Left- and right-handedness
RIGHT of privacy. See Privacy, Right of
RIGHT of property. See Property; Real property
RIGHT of way
See also
Electric lines—Right of way
Railroads—Right of way
RIGHT to bear arms. See Firearms—Laws and regulations
RIGHT to counsel
Miranda still stands; case of R. Williams. C. Panati and L. Howard. por Newsweek 89:80+ Ap 4 '77
RIGHT to labor
Right-to-work fad. S. Kupferberg. New Repub 178:20-3 Ja 7 '78
See also
Open and closed shop
RIGHT to Read program
OE allocates funds to Right to Read/RIF. SLJ 23:24 F '77
RIGHT to work. See Right to labor
RIGHT turn on red. See Traffic regulations
RIGHT wing (politics) See Conservatism
RIGHTS, Bill of (United States) See United States —Constitution—Bill of Rights
RIGHTS, Civil. See Civil rights
RIGHTS of artists. See Artists rights
RIGHTS of authors. See Authors rights
RIGHTS of employees. See Employees—Civil rights
RIGHTS of women. See Women—Equal rights
RIGNEY, Janet
(comp) Source material. For Affairs 55:664-70 Ap '77
RIGOLETTO; opera. See Verdi, G.
RIGSBEE, David
(tr) See Brodskiĭ, I. Thames at Chelsea
RIKHOFF, Jean
People, not plot. Writer 90:15-18 Mr '77
RIKLIS, Meshulam
Riklis money game. D. Pauly and J. Walcott. por Newsweek 90:81 N 7 '77 *
Riklis stock deal that may save Kenton. D. Santry. por Bus W p 190 N 14 '77 *
RILEY, Fen
Back to the farm. il pors House & Gard 149: 88-9+ F '77 *
RILEY, Jenifer
Back to the farm. il pors House & Gard 149: 88-9+ F '77 *
RIMSKY-KORSAKOV, Nicholay Andreyevich
May night. D. M. Moore. Am Rec G 40:44-5 Je '77 *
Musical events; operas. A. Porter. New Yorker 53:121+ D 19 '77 *
Rimsky-Korsakov; arias from The tsar's bride, Snow maiden, Sadko, and The invisible city of Kitzeh. P. L. Miller. Am Rec G 40:28 Ap '77 *
RINALDI, Dominic S.
Court dismisses $5-million libel claim against Holt. S. Wagner. Pub W 212:27-8 Jl 25 '77 *
RINEHART, Mary (Roberts)
Sky's the limit. il por Sat Eve Post 249:93+ Jl '77
RING galaxies. See Galaxies
RING-necked pheasant shooting. See Pheasant shooting
RING of the Nibelung; opera. See Wagner, R.
RINGER, Robert J.
Another Ringer. H. F. Waters. il por Newsweek 90:78 Jl 25 '77 *
RINGO, J. and others
Trichromatic vision in the cat. bibl il Science 198:753-5 N 18 '77
RINGS, Piston. See Piston rings
RINGWALD, George B.
International outlook (cont) Bus W p47 F 7 '77
RINGWORM
See also
Athlete's foot (disease)
RINKS, Skating. See Skating rinks
RINZLER, Carol Eisen
Push the proper button; story. Redbook 149:137 O '77
RINZLER, Ralph, and Seitel, Peter
Cajun fiddles, Hindustani veenas and dulcimers. il Smithsonian 8:142+ O '77

RIO ARRIBA County, N.Mex.
Remember Tierra Amarilla: Chicano power in the feudal west. P. Nabokov. il por Nation 225:336-40 O 8 '77
RIO DE JANEIRO
Farewell to flesh: Rio goes Hollywood; excerpt from Carnival in Rio. A. Goldman. il Esquire 89:66-72+ Ja '78
RIO GRANDE
Our wild and scenic rivers. N. T. Kenney. il map Nat Geog 152:46-51 Jl '77
Wilderness river. J. Lelyveld. il N Y Times Mag p 174 D 11 '77
RIORDAN, Bill
Promo wiz kidvid bid. F. DeFord. il por Sports Illus 46:30-3 F 7 '77 *
RIORDAN, J. F. and others
Arginyl residues: anion recognition sites in enzymes. bibl il Science 195:884-6 Mr 4 '77
RIO RICO, Mex. See Villages—Mexico
RIOTS
See also
Berlin (East Berlin)—Riots
Bermuda—Riots
Draft riot, 1863
Egypt—Riots
Istanbul—Riots
New York (city)—Riots
Pakistan—Riots
South Africa—Riots
United States—Riots
RIOTTE, Carl. See Riotte, L. jt auth
RIOTTE, Louise
Blackberry, king of the brambles. il Org Gard & Farm 24:190-2+ Mr '77
How I graft pecans for profit and pleasure. il Org Gard & Farm 25:90-1 Ja '78
—and Riotte, Carl
Dig it: lily pools. il Am Home 80:20-1 Jl '77
RIP Van Winkle; dramatization. See Thane, A.
RIPLEY, Sidney Dillon, 1913-
Bird that is loath to fly but roams afar all the same; excerpt from Rails of the world. il Smithsonian 7:88-93 Mr '77
View from the castle. See issues of Smithsonian
about
Cold-shower time at the Smithsonian. I. Ross. il pors Fortune 96:132-4+ S '77 *
Now, the venerable Smithsonian is a target of Congress. il por U.S. News 82:58+ Je 27 '77 *
Smithsonian; the nation's attic undergoing new federal scrutiny. C. Holden. por Science 196:857-60 My 20 '77 *
RIPLEY, Warren
War of Longitude Lane. il Am Hist Illus 11:20-3 F '77
RIPP, Allan
How to beat Johnny Carson to the punch. il Horizon 20:91-5 N '77
Jazz. il Horizon 19:50-5 Jl '77
Life on the run. il Horizon 20:32-8 O '77
RIPP, Judith
Family movie guide. See issues of Parents' magazine & better homemaking
RISE and fall of the city of Mahagonny; opera. See Weill, K.
RISEMAN, Mervin H.
Problems of American Jewish families. il por Intellect 105:385-6 My '77
RISK, Mirna
(tr) See Levi, P. Iron: a memoir
RISK
Adjusting for risk in business investments. R. F. Dowd. Intellect 105:355-6 Ap '77
See also
Insurance—Risks
RISK recreation activities. See Recreation—Activities
RISK taking (psychology)
Here be dragons. J. Lipton. Read Digest 111:241-2+ N '77
High cost of living safe; need for women to take risks. C. Calvert. Mademoiselle 83:189+ S '77
RISLEY, John S.
Booth sessions: a critical assessment. Phys Today 30:9+ Ap '77
RISSEL, Martin C.
Are you ready for winter? il Am City & County 92:67-70 S '77
RISSER, Barbara G.
Formula essay writing: a new approach. il Engl J 66:56-8 D '77
RIST, Ray C.
Imperatives of integration. il Society 14:32-4 My '77
RITALIN. See Methylphenidate
RITBLAT, John Henry
One that got away; loss of Uris Building Corp. by British Land. G. Smith. il por Forbes 119:58+ Ap 1 '77 *
RITCHER, Burton
From the psi to charm: the experiments of 1975 and 1976; Nobel Prize lecture, December 11. 1976. bibl il Science 196:1286-97 Je 17 '77

RITCHEY, Beverly
Position wanted: dvcee, 5 kids, no exp. McCalls 104:32+ Je '77
RITCHIE, Daniel E.
Inner city vacation. Nat R 30:32-3 Ja 6 '78
RITCHIE, James D.
In praise of blackberries. Org Gard & Farm 24:88 D '77
Two-story cropping. il Org Gard & Farm 24:80+ S '77
Ways with wild trees. il Org Gard & Farm 24:154+ F '77
RITCHIE, Ros
Learning to make records at Eastman. J. Arthur. il por Hi Fi 27:MA18-20 Je '77 *
RITCHIN, Frederick
Snapshot mastery. il Horizon 20:75-9 O '77
RITE Aid Corporation. See Drugstores
RITES and ceremonies
Carnival à la Trinidad and Tobago. C. B. G. London. bibl il Américas 29:19-24 F '77
See also
Festivals
Marriage customs and rites
Memorial services
RITTER, Christine C.
More on Deborah Sampson. il Am Hist Illus 12:28-9 N '77
RITTER, Ted
Gate start: a two-sided coin. il Yachting 142:54+ N '77
RITTER, Willis William
Feet-First Ritter under siege. il por Time 110:63 N 7 '77 *
RITUAL. See Rites and ceremonies
RITZ, César
Room at the Ritz. H. Sutton. il por Sat R 4:45-7 My 14 '77 *
RITZ (hotel) See Paris—Hotels, restaurants, etc.
RIVAL Manufacturing Company. See Household appliances industry
RIVALRY, Sibling. See Siblings
RIVAS, Yolanda E.
For Spanish readers. Horn Bk 53:190-2, 686-8 Ap, D '77
RIVENES, David
Big sky TV. P. S. Greenberg. pors Newsweek 89:9 Mr 28 '77 *
RIVENES, Ella
Big sky TV. P. S. Greenberg. pors Newsweek 89:9 Mr 28 '77 *
RIVER basin development. See Water resources development
RIVER boats. See Steamships and steamboats
RIVER channelization. See Channels (hydraulic engineering)
RIVER conservation. See Stream conservation
RIVER pollution. See Water pollution
RIVER rafting. See Running rapids
RIVER trips
Float trip camping. N. Strung. il Field & S 82:52-4+ My '77
Heigh-O the Dairy-O, the traveler in the Dells; Wisconsin River. L. McPherson. il Holiday 58:27+ Ap '77
Reporter at large; Salmon River in Alaska; excerpt from Coming into the country. J. McPhee. New Yorker 53:47-8+ My 2; 88+ My 9 '77; Same abr with title Encircled river. il por map Liv Wildn 41:44-60 Jl '77
River run to match your interest. Sunset 158:56+ Mr '77
River runs in a dry year? Western States. il Sunset 158:46+ Je '77
We rafted down Canada's notorious Nahanni. S. J. Krasemann. il Int Wildlife 7:48-55 Mr '77
See also
Canoe trips
Running rapids
RIVERS, Larry
Larry Rivers and George Segal: back in the U.S.S.R; interview, ed by E. C. Baker. il por Art in Am 65:104-12 N '77
about
New editions. S. Boorsch. il pors Art N 76:108 Ap '77 *
Russian Revolution: a wall-sized history. S. F. Starr. il Smithsonian 8:52-4 Jl '77 *
RIVERS
Ten streams of history: how are they now? famous trout streams. J. Gibbs. il Outdoor Life 159:60-5 Mr '77
Wild rivers, trout galore. E. A. Bauer. il map Nat Wildlife 15:42-7 Ag '77
See also
Mercury pollution of rivers, lakes, etc.
Water pollution
Wild and scenic rivers
also names of rivers, e.g. Monongahela River
Cleaning
See Cleaning of lakes, rivers, etc.

RIVERS—*Continued*

Regulation

Make the river do the work; renovation of log-choked and flood-prone St Joseph and Tiffin Rivers in Ohio; alternative to channelization. B. East. il por Outdoor Life 160:78-81+ O '77

See also

Dams

Mississippi River—Regulation

RIVERSIDE Center for the Arts, Harrisburg, Pa. See The Arts—Study and teaching

RIVERSIDE Telescope Makers Conference. See Astronomy—Conferences

RIVIÈRE, Jan Willem Maurits la

Van Leeuwenhoek: father of microbiology. il por UNESCO Courier 30:34-6 Je '77

RIVLIN, Alice (Mitchell)

Everyone's wild over Alice. il por Time 110: 66+ Jl 18 '77 *

RIYADH, Saudi Arabia

Town-in-town will house 8,000 in suburban Riyadh. il Archit Rec 162:37 D '77

RIYADH Inter-Continental. See Hotels, motels, etc.—Saudi Arabia

RIZZA, Peggy

Sorrowful mysteries; poem. New Repub 176:27-8 F 5 '77

RIZZO, Frank Lazzaro

Thoughts of Chairman Rizzo; excerpts from The sayings of Chairman Frank. Time 110:40 O 24 '77

about

Rizzo lives. Nation 225:324 O 8 '77 *

RIZZO, Peter J. and Cox, E. R.

Histone occurrence in chromatin from peridinium balticum, a binucleate dinoflagellate. bibl il Science 198:1258-60 D 23 '77

RIZZOLI International Bookstore and Gallery. See Booksellers and bookselling—Washington, D.C.

ROA BASTOS, Augusto Antonio

Land-locked island of Paraguay. il UNESCO Courier 30:51-3+ Ag '77

ROACHES. See Cockroaches

ROAD construction. See Highway engineering

ROAD emergency signals. See Signals and signaling

ROAD graders. See Graders (excavating machinery)

ROAD machinery

See also

Bulldozers (machines)

ROAD markings. See Traffic markings

ROAD traffic

Automatic control

See also

Traffic signals—Control

ROADS

See also

Highway engineering

Trails

Federal aid

See also

Express highways—Federal aid

Finance

Why your roads are going to pot. R. D. Wennblom. il Farm J 101:G1 Ja '77

Maintenance and repair

Road, bridge repairs to cost $2.8 billion. il Am City & County 92:18 My '77

Materials

See also

Asphalt

Safety devices and measures

Dispelling a highway safety myth; excerpt from address, December 1976. H. L. Anderson. il Am City & County 92:109 My '77

Widening

Roadblocks to beauty. K. Hartsen. il Conservationist 32:36 S '77

Southern States

See also

Express highways—Southern States

United States

Weak bridges: growing hazard on the highways. il U.S. News 84:72 Ja 9 '78

See also

Express highways

History

Route 66: ghost road of the Okies. T. W. Pew, Jr. il Am Heritage 28:24-33 Ag '77

ROADSIDE improvement

Road show for sculptors. il Newsweek 89:56-7 Ja 24 '77

Whatever happened to: billboard removal: states drag their feet. il U.S. News 82:68 F 14 '77

ROASTING. See Cookery—Meat; Cookery—Poultry

ROBARDS, Jason

José, Jason, and Gene. S. Lawson. il pors Horizon 21:36-42 Ja '78 *

Resurrection of Jason Robards. J. Bryson. il pors Esquire 89:50-3+ Ja '78 *

ROBB, Lynda Bird (Johnson)

Life with mother. pors Ladies Home J 94:117+ My '77

(ed) See Carter, C. White House baby

(ed) See Carter, R. Amy

ROBBERIES and assaults

Bank heist of the century; robbery of the Societé Générale bank in Nice. R. Daley. il Read Digest 110:84-90 Ap '77

Chicago's great bank heist; First National Bank. Time 110:20 N 28 '77

Francs a lot; hijacking of Bank of France coin shipment delivery truck. Time 110:41 Ag 8 '77

See also

Pillage

History

Train robbery. R. Patterson. il Am West 14: 48-53 Mr '77

ROBBINS, E. Guy

Build bike paths to last. il Am City & County 92:70 Ap '77

ROBBINS, Fred

(ed) See Fonda, J. Jane Fonda, the woman

ROBBINS, I. D.

Let's go, South Bronx! il Time 110:39 N 21 '77 *

ROBBINS, Michael S.

Quiz-game electronics. il Pop Electr 11:64-5 F '77

ROBBINS, Peggy

Andrew & Rachel Jackson. il pors Am Hist Illus 12:22-8 Ag '77

Civilian life during the siege of Vicksburg. il map Am Hist Illus 12:12-17+ D '77

Little adventures of Madeleine Hachard. il Am Hist Illus 12:36-42 Jl '77

ROBBINS, Thomas

Brainwashing & religious freedom. Nation 224: 518 Ap 30 '77

Deprogramming the brainwashed. Nation 224: 238-42 F 26 '77

ROBBINS, Tom

Five Ws for the counterculture. por Horizon 19:70 My '77 *

ROBBINS, Warren M.

African village on Capitol Hill. il Smithsonian 8: 55-6 Ag '77

ROBENS, Alfred, Baron Robens of Woldingham. See Robens of Woldingham, A.

ROBENS of Woldingham, Alfred, Baron

Is there any hope for Britain? interview, ed by G. Smith. por Forbes 119:65-6 My 15 '77

ROBERSON, Sam

Going motorhome full-time. il Ret Liv 17:27-30 F '77

ROBERT Bosch Corporation. See Automobile equipment industry—Germany, West

ROBERT Hall Stores. See United Merchants & Manufacturers, Inc

ROBERTO Adobe, San Jose. See Historic houses, sites, etc.—California

ROBERTS, Bill

Racing clinics; one-design. il Yachting 141:58+ Mr '77

ROBERTS, Clay

Freelance game warden. F. Davis. por Outdoor Life 160:30 N '77 *

ROBERTS, Cokie

Casanova's law. Commonweal 104:486-8 Ag 5 '77

Reports & comment: Turkey. Atlantic 240:14+ S '77

ROBERTS, Don

Adult life cycles and teaching. bibl f il Engl J 66:38-41 S '77

Kawps. Engl J 66:66-7 S '77

ROBERTS, Donald L.

Media censorship and printist librarians; interview, ed by D. Boyle. por Am Lib 8:542-5 N '77

ROBERTS, Estelle Caloia

Los Cuatro: Mexico's majestic artists. il Américas 29:38-45 Je '77

ROBERTS, Gordie

Young and restless. P. Gammons. il por Sports Illus 46:52+ Mr 14 '77 *

ROBERTS, James A. Jr, and Searcy, A. W.

Anomalous temperature dependence for a partial vapor pressure. bibl il Science 196:525-7 Ap 29 '77

ROBERTS, John H.

Build an audio compander. il Pop Electr 12:43-6 N '77

ROBERTS, John Storm

Emerson, Lake & Palmer—gnomes + gongs + tanks. il Hi Fi 27:131-4 O '77

Making it in the musicbiz: myth & reality. il Hi Fi 27:111-14 Je '77

R&B. il Hi Fi 27:145 Mr; 130 Je; 160 N '77; 28: 134 Ja '78 *

Ralph MacDonald modern musical all-rounder. il pors Hi Fi 27:97-100 Ag '77

Yes plugs in at the Garden. il Hi Fi 27: 125-8 D '77

(ed) See Cole, N. Natalie Cole: producers' puppet, father's daughter, or the queen of R&B?

ROBERTS, Leila-Jane
YA survey: help wanted. SLJ 24:47 S '77

ROBERTS, Oral
If Christ were alive today. por Ladies Home J 94:64+ D '77

about

Oral Roberts' gift adds to a hospital glut. il Bus W p35 O 31 '77 *

ROBERTS, Paul Craig
Econometrics and politics. Nat R 29:549-51 My 13 '77

ROBERTS, Raymond
King of the suggestion box. R. Lund. il pors Pop Mech 147:58+ Mr '77 *

ROBERTS, Rebecca
For my mother; poem. McCalls 104:34 My '77

ROBERTS, Richard E.
Career investigation and planning in the high school English curriculum. bibl Engl J 66:49-52 N '77

ROBERTS, Stephanie
I hereby resign as keeper of this house. . . love, mom. il por Ms 5:56-7 My '77

ROBERTSON, Andrew. See Chapra, S. C. jt auth

ROBERTSON, Anthony, and Gingle, A. R.
Axial bending in the early chick embryo by a cyclic adenosine monophosphate source. bibl il Science 197:1078-9 S 9 '77
—See Gingle, A. R. jt auth

ROBERTSON, D. E. and others
Mercury emissions from geothermal power plants. bibl il Science 196:1094-7 Je 3 '77

ROBERTSON, Dorothy
Dig your own diamond or opal, topaz, or other precious stones. il por Ret Liv 17:34-5 S '77

ROBERTSON, Elizabeth
Retired teachers share skills as Peace Corps volunteers in Ghana. il por Aging 268:18-20 F '77 *

ROBERTSON, Murray K. See McCahon, J. F. jt auth

ROBERTSON, Pat
If Christ were alive today. por Ladies Home J 94:68 D '77

ROBERTSON, Wyndham
Big board strategy for staying alive. il por Fortune 95:134-41+ Mr '77
New York City is still on the brink. il Fortune 96:122-8+ Jl '77
Passing the baton at Lazard Frères. il pors Fortune 96:116-20+ N '77

ROBES. See Clothing and dress

ROBESPIERRE, Maximilien François Marie Isidore de
Robespierre and the French Revolution. J. I. Shulim. bibl Am Hist R 82:20-38 F '77 *

ROBIN Hood Dell West Theater, Philadelphia. See Concert halls

ROBINSON, Arthur L.
Impact of electronics on employment: productivity and displacement effects. bibl il Science 195:1179-84 Mr 18 '77

ROBINSON, Barbara
Dearly beloved; story. McCalls 105:214-15 N '77
How do babies get born? story. McCalls 104:120-1 Je '77
Would you marry him again? story. McCalls 104:130-1 Jl '77

ROBINSON, Bill
Editor's page. See issues of Yachting

ROBINSON, Bill, 1943-
He's an irregular regular. J. Kaplan. por Sports Illus 46:62+ Ap 25 '77 *

ROBINSON, Cedric
Cedric Robinson; interview, ed by M. S. Clayton. Todays Educ 66:35-6 Ja '77

ROBINSON, Charles W.
Department discusses implementation of economic provisions of the final act of the Helsinki Conference; statement, January 14, 1977. Dept State Bull 76:108-13 F 7 '77

ROBINSON, Conway. See Parker, W. J. jt auth

ROBINSON, Davis Ashton
Blood and money is target of $20-million libel suit. M. Reuter. Pub W 212:35 O 3 '77 *

ROBINSON, Donald
Menace of drunken doctors. Ladies Home J 94:94+ Ap '77
(ed) See Klein, E. Skin cancer: the avoidable killer

about

How prosecutors are nabbed. J. Lardner. New Repub 176:22-5 Ja 29 '77 *

ROBINSON, Edward R.
Hymn for soldiers who have lain in the snow. Poetry 129:284 F '77

ROBINSON, Frank, 1935-
Indian tomahawked. J. Jares. il por Sports Illus 47:40+ Jl 4 '77 *

ROBINSON, Gladys Reed
Two old houseplant toughies: aspidistra and sansevieria. il Org Gard & Farm 24:170-3 O '77

ROBINSON, Glen O.
New communications. Current 195:37-52 S '77

ROBINSON, James D. 3d
Young Atlantan for American Express. por Bus W p31-2 Mr 14 '77 *

ROBINSON, James Lee, Jr. See Pollock, J. C. jt auth

ROBINSON, Jill
Gift of giving. Vogue 167:184+ D '77
I hate sex. Vogue 167:150+ Ag '77
Mary life: spectacular. il Vogue 167:188+ D '77
New nightlife: eating and drinking. Vogue 167:251 N '77
Perfume—a woman's memories. . .and desires. Vogue 167:260+ My '77
(ed) See Tomlin, L. Bunch of Lily

ROBINSON, John
Now's the time to recondition garden tools for an active spring. il Pop Sci 210:118-19 Mr '77

ROBINSON, John Arthur Thomas, Bp
New Testament dating game. il por Time 109:95 Mr 21 '77 *

ROBINSON, Louie
Desert fox. il pors Ebony 32:44-6+ Ap '77
Dr Bill Cosby. il pors Ebony 32:130-2+ Je '77
Keep him happy and you can keep him. il Ebony 32:52-3+ Ag '77
LeVar Burton's rise to fame. il pors Ebony 32:146-8+ O '77
Richard Pryor talks. il pors Ebony 33:116-18+ Ja '78
Sidney Poitier tells how to stay on top in Hollywood. il pors Ebony 33:53-4+ N '77
Two Centuries of Black American Art. il Ebony 32:33-6+ F '77

ROBINSON, Margaret A.
Dog story; story. Redbook 150:84 N '77
Greatest show on earth; story. Redbook 150:65-7 D '77
Loving aunts; story. Redbook 149:106 My '77
Nicest wedding ever; story. Redbook 149:68 Ag '77
Pictures and the possibility of love; story. Sat Eve Post 249:70-1 S '77
That's the way it is; story. Redbook 149:100-1 Ag '77

ROBINSON, Michael J.
Not-so-mighty tube. G. F. Will. Newsweek 90:84 Ag 8 '77 *

ROBINSON, Mike
Animal lover finds ideal career. il pors Ebony 32:104+ O '77 *

ROBINSON, Sally
Family vacation; story. Redbook 148:110-11 Mr '77

ROBINSON, Toni. See Bryden, E. L. jt auth

ROBINSON, Tri
Class project: rewrite history. J. Kraus. Educ Digest 43:36-7 S '77 *

ROBISON, James
How the B-1 bomber was brought down. Chr Cent 94:711-12 Ag 17 '77

ROBISON, Mary A.
Doctor's sons; story. New Yorker 53:27 Ag 22 '77
Kite and paint; story. New Yorker 53:63-4 N 21 '77
Sisters; story. New Yorker 53:31-2 Je 20 '77

ROBITSCHER, Jonas, and Williams, R. M.
Should psychiatrists get out of the courtroom? bibl il Psychol Today 11:84-6+ D '77

ROBLE, Raymond G.
Auroras; with biographical sketch. il Natur Hist 86:2, 60-7 bibl(p 122) O '77

ROBOTS. See Automatons

ROBSON, John E.
Let's do it. por Forbes 120:98 Jl 1 '77 *

ROCARD, Michel
French socialism and Europe. For Affairs 55:554-60 Ap '77

ROCHAMBEAU, Jean Baptiste Donatien de Vimeur, Comte de
En avant with our French allies to Yorktown victory. S. Stember. il Smithsonian 8:64-8+ My '77 *

ROCHELL, Carlton C.
Call the shots yourself. Am Lib 8:574-5 N '77

ROCHELLE, Larry
Quest: the search for meaning through fantasy. Engl J 66:54-5 O '77

ROCHESTER, N.Y.
Their (dis)appointed rounds; P. H. Brennan Hand Delivery Service in competition with United States Postal Service. R. Brookhiser. il Nat R 29:1294-6 N 11 '77

See also

Ward's Natural Science Establishment, Rochester, N.Y.

Education

Rochester school supt. wins AASL service award. por SLJ 23:14+ My '77

Music

Debuts & reappearances. il Hi Fi 27:MA36-7 F '77

Sanitary affairs

Polymer cuts cost of Rochester water. D. R. Lawson. il por Am City & County 92:97-8 S '77

ROCHESTER Philharmonic Orchestra. See Orchestras

ROCHESTER. University, Rochester, N.Y.

Eastman School of Music

Eastman School-Lib. of Congress: The disappointment; performance of the first American ballad opera. il Hi Fi 27:MA14-15+ Mr '77

Learning to make records at Eastman. J. Arthur. il por Hi Fi 27:MA18-20 Je '77

ROCK, James M.

No boomtown on the Kaiparowits Plateau: who made the decision and why? bibl il Intellect 105:248-50 F '77

ROCK, Maxine A.

Orang—endangered man of the forest. il Nat Parks & Con Mag 51:10-15 Ag '77

ROCK, Miriam B.

Advisor speaks to aspiring physicians. Intellect 106:76-7 Ag '77

ROCK bands. See Rock groups

ROCK carvings. See Petroglyphs

ROCK climbing. See Mountaineering

ROCK Creek Park. See Washington, D.C.—Parks and playgrounds

ROCK garden plants. See Rock plants

ROCK gardens. See Gardens, Rock

ROCK groups

The Band: Islands; recording. il Hi Fi 27:113-14 My '77

Bang! It's the Sex Pistols. T. Schwartz. il Newsweek 91:71 Ja 16 '78

Beach Boys: The Beach Boys love you; recording. il Hi Fi 27:114 My '77

Beatle beaters; ABBA. G. Smith. por Forbes 120:78 Jl 15 '77

Black & white of Wild Cherry. B. Bornino. il Hi Fi 27:125-6 Mr '77

Chicago. W. McKeen. il Sat Eve Post 249:62-3 My '77

Chocolate city and beyond; black group, Parliament-Funkadelic. K. Emersosn. il por Sat R 5:48-9 N 12 '77

Down at the clubhouse with Dr Buzzard's Original Savannah Band. R. Cromelin. il Hi Fi 27:131-3 Jl '77

Dwight Twilley Band: British rockabilly comes of age; Twilley don't mind. K. Emerson. por Hi Fi 27:154 N '77

ELP: 72,000 watts in the name; Emerson Lake & Palmer. il Time 109:102 Je 13 '77

Earth, Wind & Fire members build their dream homes. il pors Ebony 33:154-6+ D '77

Emerson, Lake & Palmer—gnomes + gongs + tanks; with discography. J. S. Roberts. il Hi Fi 27:131-4 O '77

Extensions, downtown; the Ramones at C.B.G.B.'s, New York City. New Yorker 53:27-8 F 28 '77

Fleetwood Mac: 10 years of crisis & comeback. J. Rockwell. il Hi Fi 27:131-3 F '77

Foghat: paying dues to the blues; benefit concert for blues collection of New York Public Library. il Sr Schol 110:23 D 1 '77

Foreigner: sixties rock yields seventies success. il Hi Fi 27:152-4 Jl '77

Kinks: Sleepwalker; recording. il Hi Fi 27:115+ My '77

O'Jays: there's a message in their music. B. Rhoden. il por Ebony 32:90-2+ S '77

Outrage called Kiss. C. Dowling. il N Y Times Mag p 18+ Je 19 '77

Pink Floyd: Animals; recording. Hi Fi 27:118+ My '77

Plastic punks. A. Burgess; J. Lombardi. il Psychol Today 11:120-2+ N '77

The Rumour: up from pub rock. S. Sutherland. il Hi Fi 27:150 O '77

Sex Pistols are here. il Time 111:62 Ja 16 '78

Sound of fame and fortune:

Boston. E. Miller. il pors Seventeen 36:244+ Ag '77

Kansas. E. Miller. il pors Seventeen 36:245+ Ag '77

Steely Dan sans sarcasm. S. Sutherland. il pors Hi Fi 27:139-42 N '77

To Russia with rock; Nitty Gritty Dirt Band; interview, ed by E. Dowling. J. McEuen. il pors Sr Schol 110:2-5 N 3 '77

Yes plugs in at the Garden:

Equipment. M. Lobel. il Hi Fi 27:129-31 D '77

Setup; work of stagehands and electricians. J. S. Roberts. il Hi Fi 27:125-31 D '77

Zeppelin flies. J. Maslin. il Newsweek 89:63 Je 20 '77

See also

Beatles (rock group)

Anecdotes, facetiae, satire, etc.

Don: the true story of a young person. G. Keillor. New Yorker 53:39-43 My 30 '77

ROCK hunting. See Rocks—Collectors and collecting

ROCK music (songs, etc)

All shook up; Heartbreak kid; E. Presley. M. Orth; J. Kroll. il pors Newsweek 90:46-9 Ag 29 '77

Anthems of the blank generation; punk rock. il Time 110:46-7 Jl 11 '77

Elvis. C. Forbes. Chr Today 21:32 S 23 '77

Flood of X-rated music hits airwaves, concert halls, record shops. il U.S. News 83:47+ O 31 '77

Focus on rock. bibl Seventeen 36:54-5 Ag '77

Heirs of Elvis. M. J. Sobran, Jr. Nat R 29:1185-6 O 14 '77

I know it's only rock 'n' roll, but I hate it. C. Stinnett. il Atlantic 240:26-7 Ag '77

Last stop on the mystery train. J. Cocks. il pors Time 110:56-9 Ag 29 '77

Making the punk scene. il Horizon 20:51 S '77

Pistol-whipped; New Wave and British youth. E. Meadows. il Nat R 29:1311-12 N 11 '77

Rebel who became a legend; E. Presley. S. B. Walton. il pors Sat Eve Post 249:56-7+ D '77

Reggae way to salvation; B. Marley. J. Bradshaw. il pors N Y Times Mag p24-8+ Ag 14 '77

Rock. J. Rockwell. il Sat R 4:22-3 Ag 6 '77

Rock bottom; punk rock. T. Schwartz and others. il Newsweek 89:80-1 Je 20 '77

Rock lives! J. Rockwell. il N Y Times Mag p61-4+ F 27 '77

See also

Disco music

Religion and music

Rock groups

Rock singers

Periodicals

See also

Rolling stone (periodical)

ROCK 'n' roll music (songs, etc) See Rock music (songs, etc)

ROCK paintings. See Cave drawings and paintings

ROCK plants

Shopping search for perennials, rock plants. Sunset 158:226+ Mr '77

ROCK quarries. See Quarries and quarrying

ROCK record industry. See Phonograph record industry

ROCK salt industry. See Salt industry

ROCK sculpture. See Mountain sculpture

ROCK singers

Hanging out with the L.A. rockers; their houses il Time 109:81-2+ Ap 25 '77

See also

Rock groups

also names of rock singers, e.g. L. Ronstadt

ROCK songs. See Rock music (songs, etc)

ROCKALL (Island)

Rockall—the smallest British Isle. S. O'Donnell. il map Sea Front 23:342-9 N '77

ROCKBURNE, Dorothea

Out in front. B. Rose. pors Vogue 167:152-3+ Je '77 *

ROCKEFELLER, Barbara

Open windows. por Craft Horiz 37:43 Je; 39 Ag '77

ROCKEFELLER, David

Problems, perspectives and responsibilities; address, March 15, 1977. Vital Speeches 43:357-60 Ap 1 '77

about

Jimmy Carter revealed: he' a Rockefeller Republican. C. Lydon. Atlantic 240:50-7 Jl '77 *

Three-year deadline at David's bank. C. J. Loomis. il por Fortune 96:70-6+ Jl '77 *

ROCKEFELLER, David, Jr

Industry without art. R. Rosenblatt. New Repub 177:41-2 Jl 2 '77 *

ROCKEFELLER, John Davison, 1839-1937

How they kept the trust. P. Stinson. Nation 225:561-4 N 26 '77 *

ROCKEFELLER, John Davison, 1839-1937, family

Professor Kissinger. F. Getlein. Commonweal 104:388-90 Je 24 '77

ROCKEFELLER, John Davison, 1937-

We're not laughing our way to the bank yet; interview. por U.S. News 82:40 My 23 '77

ROCKEFELLER, Nelson Aldrich, 1908-

Strictly a realist. Vasari. il Art N 76:18+ Summ '77 *

ROCKEFELLER Archive Center

House that holds Rockefeller riches (papers, not $$$) I. Shenker. il Smithsonian 8:90-7 S '77

ROCKEFELLER Brothers Fund

Unfinished agenda. A. W. Smith. Nat Parks & Con Mag 51:2+ Mr '77

Unfinished agenda—a special report. J. L. Fox. il Chemistry 50:22-4 Ap '77

ROCKEFELLER Foundation

Inflation protection for retired employees. H. Heaton. il Harvard Bus R 55:8+ S '77

ROCKEFELLER University, New York

Lab for orphans; medical research. Time 110:79 N 28 '77

Rockefeller University: no time for philosophers. J. Walsh. il Science 195:272-5 Ja 21 '77

ROCKETS

Astronomical use

Far-ultraviolet rocket survey of Orion. G. R. Carruthers and C. B. Opal. il Sky & Tel 53:270-5 Ap '77

History

Von Braun: space pioneering from V-2 warfare to the moon; excerpt from The rockets' red glare. W. Von Braun. Sci Digest 82:80-1 S '77

ROCKETS—*Continued*

Specifications

Leading U.S. international research rockets; tables. Aviation W 106:126 Mr 21 '77

ROCKETTES. See Dance companies

ROCKHOUNDS. See Rocks—Collectors and collecting

ROCKMORE, Milton
(ed) Are you sorry you had an abortion? interviews. il Good H 185:120-1+ Jl '77

ROCKS
Whatdunit; spontaneous movement of stones on dry lake beds. il Sci Am 236:56+ F '77
See also
Gravel

Age

See Geological time

Collectors and collecting

Dig your own diamond or opal, topaz, or other precious stones; rockhounding. D. Robertson. il por Ret Liv 17:34-5 S '77
Making money on rocks. V. L. Oertle. il Mech Illus 73:94+ N '77

ROCKS, Igneous
Ancient lithosphere: its role in young continental volcanism. C. Brooks and others; reply with rejoinder. F. Chayes. bibl Science 196:1234-5 Je 10 '77
Evidence for late tertiary volcanic activity in the northern Black Hills, South Dakota. J. G. Kirchner. bibl Science 196:977 My 27 '77
See also
Basalt

ROCKWELL, Al. See Rockwell, W. F.

ROCKWELL, John
Fleetwood Mac: 10 years of crisis & comeback. il Hi Fi 27:131-3 F '77
Getting it together '77. Vogue 167:300+ O '77
Monster pop and the little classics. il Esquire 87:148-51 F '77
Rock. il Sat R 4:22-3 Ag 6 '77
Rock lives! il N Y Times Mag p61-4+ F 27 '77
Turning on to Beethoven & Co. il Esquire 88:116+ D '77

ROCKWELL, Norman
John Wayne's America; reproductions of paintings. Good H 185:138-41 N '77
My life as an illustrator. il Sat Eve Post 249:73-9 Jl '77

ROCKWELL, Willard Frederick, 1914-
Japanese connection; address, October 10, 1977. Vital Speeches 44:61-4 N 1 '77

ROCKWELL International Corporation
B-1 cost-effectiveness claimed; study on B-1 cruise missile launchers. D. E. Fink. il Aviation W 107:14-16 D 12 '77
Company helps youngsters launch careers. V. Louviere. il Nations Bus 65:60 Je '77
Musical chairs. M. Kempton. Progressive 41:42 F '77
Rockwell seeks funding to complete two B-1s. D. E. Fink. il Aviation W 107:20-1 S 26 '77
Rockwell to submit R&D options for B-1. B. Miller. Aviation W 107:13-14 Jl 11 '77
Rockwell's bombshell; loss of the B-1 bomber program. D. Pauly and D. Gram. il Newsweek 90:61-2 Jl 11 '77
Sabreliner reorganization under way. E. J. Bulban. il Aviation W 107:68-9 S 12 '77
Three Rockwell aircraft divisions reorganized into new grouping; North American Aircraft Group. Aviation W 107:15-16 S 19 '77

ROCKWOOD, Marcia
How to send revolution through the mail. il Ms 6:85 Ja '78

ROCKY Mountain Airways. See Airlines—Local service

ROCKY Mountain Helicopters (firm) See Helicopter airlines

ROCKY Mountain National Park
Indian Peaks: park or playground? proposed addition. B. Vollmerhausen. il map Nat Parks & Con Mag 51:4-9 My '77

ROCKY Mountains
But it's always hot-spring time in the Rockies. C. Brown. il Smithsonian 8:90-7 bibl(p 161) N '77
Indian Peaks: park or playground? B. Vollmerhausen. il map Nat Parks & Con Mag 51:4-9 My '77

RODALE, Robert
With the editor. See issues of Organic gardening and farming

RODENT control
If they're killers, what good are they? poisonous snakes of India. Z. Whitaker and R. Whitaker. il Int Wildlife 7:12-16 My '77
See also
Mice—Control
Rat control

RODENTICIDES
See also
Rat poisons

RODENTS
Competition between seed-eating rodents and ants in desert ecosystems. J. H. Brown and D. W. Davidson. bibl il Science 196:880-2 My 20 '77
See also
Nervous system—Rodents
Sex differences—Rodents
also names of rodents, e.g. Rats

RODEOS
Glut of cowboys; Cheyenne's Frontier Days Rodeo. M. Kasindorf. il Newsweek 90:40+ Ag '77
Rodeo in the Astrodome; Houston. il House & Gard 150:156-7 Ja '78
Whoops and saddles in Helena; National High School Rodeo. D. S. Looney. il Sports Illus 47:22-4 Ag 29 '77

RODERICK, David Milton
Tough talk at big steel; excerpts from interview, ed by D. Pauly. por Newsweek 90:60-1 Ag 15 '77

RODERS, Mark K. and others
Prelytic damage of red cells in filtrates from peroxidizing microsomes. bibl il Science 196:1221-2 Je 10 '77

RODGER, David A.
Communicating astronomy in Vancouver. il Sky & Tel 53:104-7 F '77

RODGER, William
Autographs; ed by K. V. Hostick. See issues of Hobbies
Paintings, old prints, drawings, maps. See issues of Hobbies

RODGERS, Bill
Gentle radical who runs scared. K. Moore. il pors Sports Illus 47:32-7 O 24 '77 *

RODGERS, Dorothy, and Rodgers, Mary
Of two minds; questions and answers. See issues of McCall's

RODGERS, Harold A.
Direct-to-disc: recordings of real performances. il Hi Fi 27:122-3 Jl '77
Those limited-edition superdiscs. il Hi Fi 27:64-6 D '77
—and Long, Robert
Audio '78. il Hi Fi 27:74-84 S '77
—See Long, R. jt auth

RODGERS, Joann Ellison
Coping with allergies. Ladies Home J 94:44+ O '77
Healthwatch. Mademoiselle 83:56 Ag; 58+ S; 110 O; 102+ N; 50 D '77
How to prevent dog bites. il Ladies Home J 94:199-200 N '77
Mammography. Ladies Home J 94:88+ My '77

RODGERS, Mary. See Rodgers, D. jt auth

RODGERS, Mary Augusta. See Jaworski, D. jt auth

RODGERS, Nilah, and Lynch, Etta
Greatest gift. il Good H 185:79-82+ D '77

RODINO, Peter Wallace, 1909-
Federal payments to crime victims? interview. pors U.S. News 83:55-6 N 28 '77

RODMAN, Peter S.
Hermits of the jungle. il map Int Wildlife 7:20-5 My '77

RODMAN, Selden
Great bad man. Nat R 29:340-1 Mr 18 '77

RODOWSKAS, Christopher A. 1939-
Pharmacy in the year 2000; address, June 11, 1977. Vital Speeches 43:595-8 Jl 15 '77

RODRIGUEZ, Rafael and others
Elastase release from human alveolar macrophages: comparison between smokers and nonsmokers. bibl il Science 198:313-14 O 21 '77

RODRIGUEZ, Zhandra
Ballet International de Caracas and two of its dancers. N. M. Stoop. il pors Dance Mag 52:51-66 Ja '78 *

RODS, Curtain. See Curtain and drapery fixtures

RODS, Fishing. See Fishing tackle

RODS and cones
Chromatic organization of primate cones. R. E. Marc and H. G. Sperling. bibl il Science 196:454-6 Ap 22 '77
Cyclic GMP accumulation causes degeneration of photoreceptor cells: simulation of an inherited disease; retinitis pigmentosa. R. N. Lolly and others. bibl il Science 196:664-6 My 6 '77
Defective phagocytosis of isolated rod outer segments by RCS rat retinal pigment epithelium in culture. R. B. Edwards and R. B. Szamier. bibl il Science 197:1001-3 S 2 '77
Interactions between rod and cone systems in the goldfish retina. J. M. Shefner and M. W. Levine. bibl il Science 198:750-3 N 18 '77
Photoreceptor outer segments: accelerated membrane renewal in rods after exposure to light. J. C. Besharse and others. bibl il Science 196:536-8 Ap 29 '77
Rod photoreceptors detect rapid flickers. J. D. Conner and D. I. A. MacLeod. bibl Science 195:698-9 F 18 '77

ROE, Joann
San Juan Islands of Washington. il map Travel 148:26-31 Jl '77

ROEDER, Edward, and Berlow, Alan
John Flynt. Nation 225:201-5 S 10 '77

ROEDIGER, David R.
Elma Stuckey: a poet laureate of black history. bibl f Negro Hist Bull 40:690-1 Mr '77
ROEGEN, Nicholas Georgescu-. See Georgescu-Roegen, N.
ROESSLER, Carl
Color control: multihued fishes; excerpt from Underwater wilderness. il Oceans 10:6-13 S '77
ROGER Klein Award. See Editors and editing—Awards, prizes, etc.
ROGERS, Barbara Radcliffe
Fireplaces are for cooking, too. il Org Gard & Farm 24:132+ N '77
ROGERS, Bernard William
Needs of NATO; address, October 18, 1977. Vital Speeches 44:136-9 D 15 '77
ROGERS, C. Paul
Corvette's 25th: polo-white and powerglide only. il Motor T 29:62-4+ D '77
ROGERS, Carl Ransom
Beyond education's watershed. Educ Digest 43: 2-5 O '77
Personal power at work; excerpt from Carl Rogers on personal power. il por Psychol Today 10:60-2+ Ap '77

about

Carl Rogers: giving people permission to be themselves. C. Holden. por Science 198:31-3+ O 7 '77 *
Therapies ministers use. J. S. Miller. il Chr Cent 94:504-8 My 25 '77; Discussion. 94:852-4 S 28 '77 *
ROGERS, Fred
Christmas in Mr Rogers' neighborhood; interview, ed by B. White. por Sat Eve Post 249: 24+ D '77
ROGERS, JoAnn V.
Preparing YA librarians—questions & answers. SLJ 23:51 Ap '77
ROGERS, Paul G.
Rogers lists advantages of his DNA bill; interview, ed by E. M. Leeper. por BioScience 27: 591-3 S '77
ROGERS, Peter
Advertising: the best one-liners. il por Time 111:66 Ja 2 '78 *
ROGERS, Peter, Associates. See Advertising agencies
ROGERS, Vincent R. and Baron, Joan
Declining scores: two explanations. Educ Digest 42:2-7 F '77
ROGERS, William Dill
Latin America and today's world economy; address, December 6, 1976. Dept State Bull 75: 751-4 D 27 '76
ROGGENBUCK, Mary June
Twenty years of Harper's young people. Horn Bk 53:29-35 F '77
ROGOFF, Gordon
Theater. il Sat R 4:46-7 Mr 5; 46-7 Mr 19; 36-7 Ap 2; 36-7 Ap 30; 42-3 My 14; 38-9 My 28; 48-9 Je 11; 50-1 Jl 9; 57-8 Ag 6 '77
ROGOVIN, Milton
Milton Rogovin: compassionate portraitist. S. Rice. il Mod Phot 41:116-21 S '77 *
ROGUE River
Joy of white water. N. Proffitt. il Newsweek 90:60-1 Jl 18 '77
ROHATYN, Felix G.
Energy problems and our cities: solving two problems jointly. Current 196:3-6 O '77
ROHDE, Barbara
Experimenting with perspective. Writer 91:9-12+ Ja '78
ROHE, Ludwig Mies van der. See Mies van der Rohe, L.
ROHL, Arthur N. and others
Environmental asbestos pollution related to use of quarried serpentine rock. bibl il Science 196:1319-22; 197:716+ Je 17, Ag 19 '77
ROHLF, John A.
Your beef business (cont) Farm J 101:Beef 16 F; Beef 16 My; Beef 12 Je; Beef 24 Ag; Beef 24 S; Beef 20 D '77
ROHM & Haas Company
Rohm & Haas prunes back to chemicals. Bus W p34-5 O 31 '77
ROHMER, Eric
Reviews; Marquise of O. W. Johnson. il Film Q 30:50-3 Spr '77 *
Rohmer renewed. C. L. Westerbeck, Jr. Commonweal 104:21-3 Ja 7 '77 *
ROHMER, Richard H.
Nationalist themes produce a novel success. por Bus W p66 Mr 28 '77 *
ROHR Industries, Inc
Crucial year for Rohr's survival. por Bus W p86-7 F 28 '77
ROHRMANN, George F.
Misleading mantids; with biographical sketch. il Natur Hist 86:8, 66-71 bibl(p97) Mr '77
Le ROI malgré lui; opera. See Chabrier, E.
ROIPHE, Anne Richardson
Human drama in small cage. N Y Times Mag p52-3 Je 26 '77
Lost art of touching. il Ladies Home J 94:105+ My '77
My college essay. il pors N Y Times Mag p30 Ja 16 '77
Trouble at Sarah Lawrence. il N Y Times Mag p21-2+ Mr 20 '77
Who's afraid of lesbian sex? Vogue 167:150-1+ Ag '77
Why have more than one? N Y Times Mag p49-50+ Je 5 '77
ROLAMITE bearings. See Bearings (machinery)
ROLAND (missile) See Guided missiles
ROLE playing
Folk play: a new technique. G. B. Lipson. Clearing H 50:354-7 Ap '77
Try role playing. P. T. Furness. bibl Todays Educ 66:94-5 Ja '77
ROLLE, Esther
Esther Rolle talks about her roots; interview, ed by J. Wilkie. por Good H 185:50+ Jl '77
ROLLER coasters
Roller coaster: king of the park. R. Cartmell. il Smithsonian 8:44-50 bibl(p 101) Ag '77
Those roller rides in the sky. B. J. Phillips. il Time 110:36-7 Jl 4 '77
ROLLER skating rinks. See Skating rinks
ROLLING stone (periodical)
Rolling stone's new trip. T. Schwartz. il por Newsweek 90:65+ O 3 '77
ROLLINS, Norman G.
Money questions and answers. See issues of Good housekeeping
ROLLO, C. David, and Wellington, W. G.
Why slugs squabble; with biographical sketches. il Natur Hist 86:7, 46-51 bibl(p 118) N '77
ROLLS. See Bread
ROLLS Royce (automobile) See Automobiles, Foreign
ROLLS-Royce, Ltd
Rolls-Royce leaves JT10D turbofan development program. Aviation W 106:17 My 16 '77
ROLOFF, Jeff
Build 2650-based microcomputer system. il Radio Electr 48:31-5+ Ap; 45-8 My; 47-9+ Je '77
ROLPH, Hammond
Detente in Soviet policy; address, September 30, 1977. Vital Speeches 44:108-12 D 1 '77
ROMAN, Melvin
How do the children feel? Parents Mag 52:37+ Ap '77
ROMAN, Nicholas E. pseud
Juntas of Chile and Argentina: studies in government by terror. por Sat R 4:12+ Ap 2 '77
ROMANIA. See Rumania
ROMANO, John
Ann Beattie & the 60's. Commentary 63:62-4 F '77
Beckett without angst. Am Scholar 47:95-102 Wint '77
Joan Didion & her characters. Commentary 64: 61-3 Jl '77
Redemption according to Cheever. Commentary 63:66-9 My '77
ROMANO, Louis. See Featherstone, R. L. jt auth
ROMANOVICZ, Dwight K. See Hanker, J. S. jt auth
ROMANTIC love. See Love
ROMANTIC robots; drama. See Murray, J.
ROMANTICISM
On daring to be romantic. J. O'Reilly. il House & Gard 149:110-15+ Mr '77
On Lamennais, Chaadaev, and the romantic revolt in France and Russia. N. V. Riasanovsky. bibl f pors Am Hist R 82:1165-86 D '77
ROMANTICISM in art
Commitment to the past; work of S. Haden, A. Legros and A. Lepère. G. Weisberg. il Art N 76:150-2 Summ '77
Earthbound and sublime; exhibition entitled The Natural Paradise: Painting in America 1800-1950 at the Museum of Modern Art. K. Evett. New Repub 176:29-30 Mr 5 '77
ROMANTICISM in music
Félicien David 1810-1876 and French romantic orientalism. P. Gradenwitz. bibl f il por Mus Q 62:471-506 O '76
ROMBERG, G. Patrick, and others
Temperature exposure measured by the use of thermoluminescence. bibl il Science 197:1364-5 S 30 '77
ROME

Antiquities

See also
Great Britain—Antiquities, Roman
ROME (city)
On leaving Rome. J. V. Schall. Commonweal 104: 744-50 N 25 '77
Reporter in Europe. J. Kramer. il New Yorker 53:101-13 My 2 '77

Antiquities

See also
Catacombs

Foreign population

Expatriate living in decadent Rome: it still beats home. A. Menen. il por Smithsonian 8:38-43 bibl(p 101) Ag '77

Hotels, restaurants, etc.

Hotel in Rome with a name people remember; Lord Byron Hotel. W. Galling. il Fortune 92: 219-20 Ag '77

ROME (city)—*Continued*
Music
See also
Opera—Italy
Stores
European pleasures: shopping includes people-watching and pauses for coffee and fountains. il Horizon 19:38-41 Jl '77
ROMELING, W. B.
Watercolor page. il Am Artist 41:52-5+ D '77
ROMEO and Juliet; ballet. See Ballet reviews—Single works
ROMEO and Juliet; drama. See Shakespeare, W.—Plays
ROMERO BARCELÓ, Carlos
Should Puerto Rico be a state; interview. pors U.S. News 82:47-8 Ap 11 '77
about
Puerto Rico sketches a new economic policy. il por Bus W p 153-4+ S 26 '77 *
ROMERSTEIN, Herbert
Transnational threat. Nat R 29:1364-6 N 25 '77
ROMIGH, Libbie Stacey
Six for the middle. il Engl J 66:64-6 Ap '77
ROMULO, Carlos P.
News conference by Secretary Romulo and Under Secretary Cooper; September 10, 1977. Dept State Bull 77:599-605 O 31 '77
RONAN, Margaret
Films. See occasional issues of Senior scholastic including World week
RONEN, Rosie
Leisure on the kibbutz. Parks & Rec 12:56-8 Je '77
RONNEFELDT, Karin
(ed) See Weid-Neuwied, M. A. P. Winter at Fort Clark: Maximilian and Bodmer among the tribes of the Upper Missouri, 1833-1834
RONNEN, Meir
Jerusalem (cont) il por Art N 76:97-101 F '77
RONSON, Gerald M.
Last British tycoon? por Forbes 120:52+ O 1 '77 *
RONSTADT, Linda
Linda down the wind. il pors Time 109:58-62 F 28 '77 *
Linda Ronstadt breaks training; Simple dreams. S. Holden. por Hi Fi 27:150-1 N '77 *
RONY, Peter R. and others
Komputer korner (cont) il Radio-Electr 48:22-4 Ap; 24+ My '77
ROOD, Robert T. See Newman, M. J. jt auth
ROOF brackets. See Brackets
ROOF gardens. See Balcony gardens, roof gardens, etc.
ROOFING
Roofing. M. Cubisino. il McCalls 104:126-7 S '77
See also
Shingles
ROOFS
New air age in construction; air-supported roofs. W. McQuade. il Fortune 96:228-35 O '77
Raising the rooftop consciousness. J. W. Hudson. il Parks & Rec 12:32-5+ Ap '77
Unusual hypar roof shelters zoo animals. il Archit Rec 161:154 Ja '77
Maintenance and repair
Mask that peeling paint with soffit covers. E. F. Lindsley. il Pop Sci 211:120-2 N '77
ROOKMAAKER, H. R.
Obituary
Chr Today 21:39 Ap 15 '77
ROOM air conditioners. See Air conditioning equipment
ROOM dividers. See Partitions
ROOM furnishings. See Household furnishings
ROOM models. See Rooms, Miniature
ROOM painting. See Painting, Industrial and practical
ROOMS
Here's how to keep fit; what goes on behind the no-iron curtain; combination bedroom, bath and spa. il House & Gard 149:62-3 Jl '77
Live-in rooms; handy and handsome. il McCalls 104:144-7 F '77
Lowell Nesbitt's plus-planted swimroom. il Vogue 167:372-3 S '77
Mud room makes a grand entry. il Pop Mech 148:109 S '77
New rooms from attics and basements; excerpt from The spacemaker book. E. Liman. il Am Home 80:15 N '77
Private lines; settings for five celebrity telephone users. J. Macurdy. il House B 119:38-45 Ag '77
Room of your own. il McCalls 104:124-7 Mr '77
Simple Oriental drama; room by Craig Raywood. il House B 119:80-3 Mr '77
$2001 space odyssey; remodeled multi-purpose room. B. Niles. il Am Home 80:104-6 N '77
Winterizing a summer porch. R. D. Freed. il Mech Illus 73:90-2 N '77
See also
Attics
Bathrooms
Bedrooms
Childrens rooms
Dining rooms
Furniture, Arrangement of
Garden rooms
Guest rooms
House decoration
Kitchens
Laundries
Living rooms
Locker rooms
Nurseries
Recreation rooms
Sewing rooms
ROOMS, Miniature
New venture. S. A. Parvin. il Hobbies 81:120-1 F '77
ROOMS, Remodeled. See Houses, Remodeled
ROONEY, Francis Charles, 1921-
Melville steps into the billion-dollar class. por Bus W p58+ Ap 11 '77 *
ROONEY, Fred
More federal aid for railroads? G. R. Rosen. por Duns R 109:51 F '77 *
ROONEY, Rita
We're the lucky ones. il por McCalls 104:28+ S '77
ROOSA, Robert V.
Debts of the poor: preventing the crash. New Repub 176:42-5 Ja 22 '77
ROOSEVELT, Chris
Reflections on a super-spill. Oceans 10:64-5 Mr '77
ROOSEVELT, Eleanor (Roosevelt)
Eleanor and Franklin: the White House years; excerpt from screenplay. J. Costigan. il Sr Schol 109:14-17 Mr 10 '77 *
How Eleanor Roosevelt forgave the other woman; excerpt from Mother R: Eleanor Roosevelt's untold story. E. Roosevelt and J. Brough. il por Ladies Home J 94:84+ Ap '77 *
Last days of Eleanor Roosevelt; excerpt from Mother R. E. Roosevelt and J. Brough. pors Ladies Home J 94:113+ O '77 *
White House years. B. White. il por Sat Eve Post 249:16+ Mr '77 *
ROOSEVELT, Elliot, and Brough, James
How Eleanor Roosevelt forgave the other woman; excerpt from Mother R: Eleanor Roosevelt's untold story. il por Ladies Home J 94:84+ Ap '77
Last days of Eleanor Roosevelt; excerpt from Mother R. pors Ladies Home J 94:113+ O '77
ROOSEVELT, Franklin Delano, 1882-1945
Day they didn't march. L. Bennett, Jr. il Ebony 32:128-30+ F '77 *
Eleanor and Franklin: the White House years; excerpt from screenplay. J. Costigan. il Sr Schol 109:14-17 Mr 10 '77 *
Franklin D. Roosevelt and the coming of war with Germany. B. J. Bernstein. Intellect 105:360-1 Ap '77 *
How Eleanor Roosevelt forgave the other woman; excerpt from Mother R; Eleanor Roosevelt's untold story. E. Roosevelt and J. Brough. il por Ladies Home J 94:84+ Ap '77 *
President goes birding. J. L. Whitehead. il pors Conservationist 31:20-3 My '77 *
We can't do business with Stalin. W. A. Harriman and E. Abel. il Am Heritage 28:16-23 Ag '77 *
White House years. B. White. il por Sat Eve Post 249:16+ Mr '77 *
Staff
New Deal: born again; testimonial dinner for B. V. Cohen and T. G. Corcoran. T. Mathews and J. Doyle. il pors Newsweek 89:16-17 Mr 14 '77
Temps perdu; reunion of F. D. Roosevelt's New Deal staff. New Repub 176:2+ Mr 19 '77
Washington: rites of passage. H. Sidey. il Time 109:18 Mr 14 '77
ROOSEVELT, Theodore
Hunting with Teddy Roosevelt; ed by B. Vint. il por Field & S 82:166+ My '77
about
Perspectives on the past. W. W. Hassler, Jr. Am Hist Illus 12:50 Ag '77 *
Sighting at Pine Knot. A. A. Lindsey. il Natur Hist 86:40+ N '77 *
Teddy Roosevelt & the Rough Riders. R. J. Maddox. il pors map Am Hist Illus 12:8-19 N '77 *
ROOSEVELT Island. See Franklin Delano Roosevelt Island
ROOSEVELT Memorial (proposed) See Washington, D.C.—Monuments, statues, etc.
ROOSTER breeding. See Poultry breeding
ROOT, Leon
Aches & pains of the weekend athlete. Harp Baz 110:91+ My '77 *

ROOT, Trent C. Jr
Failure of scientists to communicate; address, October 25, 1977. Vital Speeches 44:133-6 D 15 '77

ROOT, William Pitt
Arctic: poem. Nation 225:472 N 5 '77
Sometimes heaven is a mean machine; poem. Nation 225:633 D 10 '77

ROOT cellars. See Basements and cellars

ROOT cuttings. See Plant propagation

ROOTS
Role of roots in the chemical economy of life on earth. E. Epstein. bibl il Bioscience 27:783-7 D '77
See also
Tubers

ROOTWORMS, Corn. See Corn rootworms

ROPE
Know your rigging: anatomy of wire rope. P. Dean. il Motor B & S 139:48-9+ F '77
See also
Knots and splices

ROPE jumping
Jump your way to health. D. Burg. il Am Home 80:24-5+ Ag '77

ROPER, Hugh Redwald Trevor-. See Trevor-Roper, H. R.

ROPER, L. V.
Plots brew in Kansas. B. Townsend. il por Writers Digest 57:30-1 Mr '77 *

ROPER, Susan Stavert. See Nolan, R. R. jt auth

ROREM, Ned
Monologue and dialogues. il pors Opera N 41:10-16 F 5 '77

ROSA, Nicholas
Endurance: the epic of Ernest Shackleton. il por Oceans 10:31-5 My '77

ROSARIO Resources Corporation. See Mining industry and finance—United States

ROSASCO, José Luis
Is today tomorrow? story. Americas 29:6-8 Ap '77

ROSC '77. See Art, European—Exhibitions

ROSE, Barbara
Art. See issues of Vogue
Cézanne: the autumn years. Sat R 5:44-5 N 26 '77
Painting and photography: the two-way street. il Vogue 167:236-7+ My '77
Rauschenberg: the artist as witness. il por Vogue 167:174-5+ F '77

ROSE, Daniel Asa
Small family with rooster; story. New Yorker 53:28-32 D 26 '77

ROSE, E. Kash
Future of health care; address, October 13, 1977. Vital Speeches 44:115-17 D 1 '77

ROSE, Francis L. and Harshbarger, J. C.
Neoplastic and possibly related skin lesions in neotenic tiger salamanders from a sewage lagoon. bibl il Science 196:315-17 Ap 15 '77

ROSE, Helen Cynthia
Children's museum and art carnival. il Sch Arts 76:62-3 F '77

ROSE, Joseph B.
Canadian efforts to stabilize collective bargaining in construction. il M Labor R 100:76-8 Ap '77

ROSE, Mark
Mark Rose on science fiction. New Repub 177:37-8 N 26 '77

ROSE, Mitchell
Reviews. J. Pikula. Dance Mag 51:75 Jl '77

ROSE, Sanford
Bank regulation: the reforms we really need. il Fortune 96:122-4+ D '77
Checkless banking is bound to come. il Fortune 95:118-21+ Je '77
Coping with a tumbling dollar. il Fortune 96:272-4+ O '77
More bang for the buck: the magic of electronic banking. Fortune 95:202-5+ My '77
Sponge iron in steel's future. il Fortune 95:106-10+ Ja '77
Why Fannie, Ginnie, and Freddy can't do it il Fortune 95:111+ Mr '77
Why the multinational tide is ebbing. il Fortune 96:110-14+ Ag '77

ROSE, Willie Lee
Comments: ideology and political culture. Am Hist R 82:577-82 Je '77

ROSE Associates Inc. See Real estate business

ROSE-breasted grosbeak. See Grosbeaks

ROSE designs. See Design, Decorative—Plant forms

ROSE hips
Rugosas: roses full of flavor. M. C. Goldman. il Org Gard & Farm 24:93-5 Mr '77

ROSEFSKY, Robert S.
Buyers guide to jewelry. Bet Hom & Gard 55:108+ Ap '77
8 ways to protect your investment in your home. Bet Hom & Gard 55:37+ Ap '77

ROSELLINI, Robert
Rosellini's Other Place. R. L. Balzer. il por Holiday 57:40-1+ N '76 *

ROSELLINI'S Other Place (restaurant) See Seattle—Hotels, restaurants, etc.

ROSEMOND, Jane
Stylish nostalgia of a farmhouse Christmas. J. B. Reiter and J. Macurdy. il por House B 119:90-5 D '77 *

ROSEN, Benson, and Jerdee, T. H.
Too old or not too old. il Harvard Bus R 55:97-106 N '77

ROSEN, David
Le Trouvere: comparing Verdi's French revision with his original. il Opera N 41:16-17 Ap 9 '77
Virtue restored. il Opera N 42:36+ D 24 '77

ROSEN, Deborah
American nonfiction: dreams and nightmares. Engl J 66:54 S '77

ROSEN, Gerald R.
Washington. See issues of Dun's review

ROSEN, Harold J.
Responsibility for product innovation: how to be progressive, yet reduce your risk. Archit Rec 162:14 mid-O '77

ROSEN, Lillie F.
ABT's star system. Progressive 41:51-2 Ap '77
Alvin Ailey: total dance theater. Progressive 41:36-7 Ag '77
Twyla Tharp: dance maverick. Progressive 41:51-2 D '77

ROSEN, Lois
(ed) Once over. Engl J 66:80-2 Mr; 80-1 Ap; 79-80 My; 76-7 S; 76-7 O; 80-2 N; 74-5 D '77

ROSEN, Marjorie
Coming attractions...from the folks who are taking over Hollywood. il Ms 6:50-3+ D '77
Farrah Fawcett-Majors makes me want to scream! il Redbook 149:102+ S '77
Film (cont) Ms 5:32+ Mr; 39-40 My '77; 6:29 Ja '78

ROSEN, Norma
Between guilt and gratification: abortion doctors reveal their feelings. il N Y Times Mag p70-1+ Ap 17 '77

ROSEN, Steven J.
Solutionist delusions. New Repub 177:14-16 N 26 '77

—and Moustafine, Mara
Does Washington have the means to impose a settlement on Israel? Commentary 64:25-32 O '77

ROSENBAUM, Lee
Artist-gallery contracts: scenes from a marriage. Art in Am 65:10-14 Jl '77
(comp) Artworld. See issues of Art in America
Auctions. Art in Am 65:33+ S '77
MOMA's construction project: reflections on a glass tower. il Art in Am 65:10-13+ N '77
Scramble for museum sponsors: is curatorial independence for sale? il Art in Am 65:10-14 Ja '77
Sotheby's and Christie's square off. Art in Am 65:16+ Mr '77

ROSENBAUM, Ron
Last secrets of Skull and bones. il Esquire 88:84-9+ S '77

ROSENBERG, Alex
Art market: what is its future? pors Am Artist 41:12-13 Ap '77

ROSENBERG, David
Job speaks; poem; excerpt. il New Repub 176:22 Ap 16 '77

ROSENBERG, Harold
Art world (cont) New Yorker 53:108+ Ap 11; 123-8 My 16; 98-102 Je 20; 83-6 Ag 22; 155-8 O 24; 42-5 D 26 '77

ROSENBERG, Julius and Ethel, case
Cold war justice: the Supreme Court and the Rosenbergs. M. E. Parrish, bibl f Am Hist R 82:805-42 O '77
Out, damned spot: Judge Kaufman and the Rosenberg case. V. Countryman. New Repub 177:15-17 O 8 '77

ROSENBERG, Max
Educators' quiz. See issues of Education digest

ROSENBERG, Norman David
Brighton beach; poem. il Oceans 10:11 My '77

ROSENBERG, Robert Michael
Lessons not learned in school. P. Berman. por Forbes 120:78 Jl 15 '77 *

ROSENBLATT, Albert M. and Rosenblatt, J. C.
Legal house of cards. Harpers 255:18-21 Jl '77

ROSENBLATT, Julia Carlson. See Rosenblatt, A. M. jt auth

ROSENBLATT, Louise
What we have learned: reminiscences of the NCTE; address. Engl J 66:8+ My '77

ROSENBLATT, Roger
Back of the book. See issues of New republic
Self as sybarite. il Harpers 254:12+ Mr '77

ROSENBLOOM, Jerry Samuel
How to handle your money: latest from an expert; interview. il pors U.S. News 83:67-8+ S 19 '77

ROSENBLUM, Joseph
Future of reference service: death by complexity? Wilson Lib Bull 52:300-1+ D '77

ROSENBLUM, Mort
Reporting from the third world. For Affairs 55:815-35 Jl '77

ROSENBLUM, Robert
Trouble in paradise; The Natural Paradise exhibition at the Museum of Modern Art. S. Schwartz. il Art in Am 65:103-5 Ja '77 *

ROSENDAHL, Charles
Rosendahl. A. E. Talbert. il Flying 101:112 S '77 *

ROSENE, Douglas L. and Van Hoesen, G. W.
Hippocampal efferents reach widespread areas of cerebral cortex and amygdala in the rhesus monkey. bibl il Science 198:315-17 O 21 '77

ROSENFELD, Albert
Controls on male fertility now seem within our research. il Smithsonian 8:36-43 Jl '77
Scienceletter. Sat R 4:34-5 Je 11; 38-9 Jl 9; 36-7 S 3; 5:32+ O 1; 46 N 26 '77
When man becomes as god: the biological prospect. il Sat R 5:14-20 D 10 '77

ROSENFELD, Lulla
Old and venerated theater tradition relived in upcoming Crowell book; interview, ed by R. Dahlin. il Pub W 211:51 Mr 28 '77
Yiddish idol; excerpt from Bright star of exile: Jacob Adler and the Yiddish theater. il pors N Y Times Mag p32-3+ Je 12 '77

ROSENFELD, Stanley Z.
Day in the life of a crew; photographs. Yachting 142:92-5 S '77

ROSENFIELD, Paul
Cooper's cohorts run down heart disease. il Sat Eve Post 249:18-20 S '77

Der **ROSENKAVALIER**; opera. See Strauss, R.

ROSENLUND, Barbara
Get the picture! Seventeen 36:30 Je '77

ROSENSTEIN, Eliezer
Worker participation in Israel: experience and lessons. bibl f Ann Am Acad 431:113-22 My '77

ROSENSTIEL, Paul
From wage hikes to job security. Nation 225:720-3 D 31 '77

ROSENSTOCK, Robert
U.S. gives views on U.S.S.R. proposal for world treaty on the non-use of force; statement, November 22, 1976. Dept State Bull 76:32-5 Ja 10 '77
U.S. supports establishment of U.N. Ad Hoc Committee on Drafting of Convention Against Taking of Hostages; statement, November 29, 1976. Dept State Bull 76:72-4 Ja 24 '77

ROSENTHAL, Barbara
Auto option. bibl il Environment 19:18-24 Je '77

ROSENTHAL, Gerald A. and others
Degradation and detoxification of canavanine by a specialized seed predator. bibl il Science 196:658-60 My 6 '77

ROSENTHAL, M. L.
Friend in hospital; poem. Nation 224:158 F 5 '77

about

Poetry of M. L. Rosenthal. E. Capouya. Nation 225:311-14, 409-11 O 1, 22 '77 *

ROSENTHAL, Richard G.
Killing in Babcock & Wilcox. E. J. Tracy. il pors Fortune 96:266-9 O '77 *

ROSENZWEIG, Norbert
Obituary
Phys Today por 30:80 O '77. J. E. Monahan

ROSES
All that's new, good & fragrant—roses. E. McDonald. il House B 119:70-1+ Je '77
Culture & notes. T. Hever. Horticulture 55:78-9 Je '77
Curious double life of rosa multiflora. R. Schery. il Horticulture 55:56-61 Je '77
Grow a color fest of floribunda roses. R. O'Harra and S. Coulter. il Bet Hom & Gard 55:120-1+ F '77
How to plant a rose. Bet Hom & Gard 55:158 F '77
Miniature roses. R. Langer. il House & Gard 149:78 My '77
Plantable box: a new way to start roses. E. Bonanno and S. Mechlin. il Horticulture 55:50-1 My '77
Rose care tips worth remembering. A. B. Ferrara. il Org Gard & Farm 24:95-7 Mr '77
Rugosas: roses full of flavor. M. C. Goldman. il Org Gard & Farm 24:93-5 Mr '77

All-America Selections

See Plants—All-America Selections

ROSIN. See Gums and resins

ROSINSKI, Jose
Journalist's ultimate track test. il por Motor T 29:92-5 Ag '77

ROSOVSKY, Henry
Yale's blues. M. Sheils. il por Newsweek 90:79 D 26 '77 *

ROSOW, Jerome M.
Quality of working life and productivity; address, April 28, 1977. Vital Speeches 43:496-8 Je 1 '77

RÖSRATH, Germany
Tale of two suburbs: near Chicago and outside Cologne. B. Seaman. il Time 109:24 My 2 '77

ROSS, Adalene
(ed) See Crosby, K. My 20 years with Bing

ROSS, Campbell
Presenting poems in class? Try several readers. il Engl J 66:62-4 F '77

ROSS, Diana
Diana Ross: a quartet of superstars. il pors Ebony 32:156-8 Mr '77 *

ROSS, Donald E.
Building automation. il Archit Rec 161:147-50 Ap; 143-4 My '77

ROSS, Edmund G.
I looked down into my open grave; excerpt from Profiles in courage. J. F. Kennedy. il Sr Schol 109:17-19 F 24 '77 *

ROSS, George
M. le Maire de Paris. New Repub 176:17-19 Ap 9 '77

ROSS, Herbert
Drama defines dance: The turning point. N. M. Stoop. il pors Dance Mag 51:42-50 O '77

ROSS, Irwin
Children needn't fear bugs and other creepy crawlers. House B 119:163+ O '77

ROSS, Irwin, 1919-
Barbara Jordan—new voice in Washington. por Read Digest 110:148-52 F '77
Breaking the 65 barrier. Read Digest 112:141-5 Ja '78
Cold-shower time at the Smithsonian. il pors Fortune 96:132-4+ S '77
New Golconda in book publishing. il Fortune 96:110-14+ D '77
Should we break up the oil companies? Read Digest 110:153-4+ Je '77
60 minutes—television's finest hour. il Read Digest 111:155-8 Jl '77
Tax practitioners act of 1976. il Fortune 95:103-6+ Ap '77
Tip O'Neill—Speaker of the House. por Read Digest 111-137-41 N '77

ROSS, John. See Procaccia, I. jt auth

ROSS, John E.
From this valley they say we are going. bibl BioScience 27:254-8 Ap '77

ROSS, Judith
Almost perfect person. Reviews
America 137:423 D 10 '77 *
New Yorker 53:103-4 N 7 '77 *

ROSS, Ken
Out in the open. Nation 225:526-30 N 19 '77

ROSS, Mitchell
New Philosophes. il Nat R 29:1361-2+ N 25 '77

ROSS, Nellie Tayloe
First U.S. woman governor celebrates her centennial during the bicentennial. il por Aging 268:13-14 F '77 *

ROSS, Richard
One way to get good workers. Nations Bus 65:39-40 S '77

ROSS, Roland
Water-frugal garden in Pasadena. il Sunset 159:76-7 Jl '77 *

ROSS, Sari
Stories from the sky god; dramatization of African folktale. Plays 36:33-8 Mr '77

ROSS, Wallace C.
Chartering—how bare is the boat? il Yachting 141:170-4 Mr '77

ROSS, Walter Sanford
(ed) See Byrd, B. F. Jr. What every woman should know about breast X-ray

ROSS, Wilma. See Landy, A. jt auth

ROSS-SKINNER, Jean
London letter. Duns R 109:127-8 Je; 110:8 Jl; 79-80 Ag; 103-4 S; 149-50 O; 111-12 N; 113-14 D '77

ROSS Ice Shelf Project. See Antarctic research

ROSSANT, Colette
Food. Vogue 167:88+ Ap '77

ROSSELLINI, Roberto
I believe in this: a letter from Roberto Rossellini; with introd and ed by P. H. Wood. New Repub 177:27-30 Jl 2 '77

ROSSEN, John
On nationalism. Progressive 41:26-7 N '77

ROSSETTI, Dante Gabriel
Dante Gabriel Rossetti and the double work of art. M. Amaya. il Art in Am 65:90-3 Mr '77 *

ROSSI, John
Help for people society often ignores. il pors U.S. News 83:47-8 Ag 1 '77

ROSSI, Mario
Southern fried Ford. il Hot Rod 30:98+ Je; 80+ Jl '77

ROSSI, Paul A.
Great Saddles of the West: an interview with Paul Rossi; ed by K. Mayer. il Am Artist 41:64-7+ Ag '77

ROSSINI, Gioacchino
Barber of Seville (Il barbiere di Siviglia) Review
Hi Fi 27:MA28 F '77 *
Elisabetta, regina d'Inghilterra. R. V. Lucano. Am Rec G 40.39-40 F '77 *
Happy ending for a tragic finale. P. Gossett. il por Opera N 42:34-5+ O '77 *
Italian girl in Algiers (L'Italiana in Algeri) Review
Hi Fi 27:MA29 Jl '77 *
Rossini's romanticism of the soul; recording. A. Porter. Hi Fi 27:106-7 F '77 *
Tancredi. Review
New Yorker 53:205-6+ N 7 '77 *

ROSSMAN, George R. See Potter, R. M. jt auth
ROSSMAN, Jean F. See Criscuolo, N. P. jt auth
ROSSMAN, Parker
(ed) See Church and the coming electronic revolution
ROSSMANN, Ingrid. See Rossmann, W. jt auth
ROSSMANN, William, and Rossmann, Ingrid
There's so much more in Detroit! Sat Eve Post 249:18+ N '77
ROSS'S geese. See Geese, Wild
ROSTEN, Leo
Astonishing Talmud. il Read Digest 111:103-6 S '77
Diversions. See every other issue of Saturday review
Wise sayings revisited; excerpt from Power of positive nonsense. Read Digest 111:160-1 D '77
ROSTEN, Norman
Mandelstam; poem. New Yorker 52:108 Ja 17 '77
ROSTENBERG, Adolph, Jr
Your skin. il House & Gard 149:103+ F '77
ROSTENKOWSKI, Daniel David
Excerpts from the debate on Federal Elections Campaign Act Amendments, April 1, 1976. Cong Digest 56:85+ Mr '77
ROSTOW, Eugene Victor
American stake in Israel. Commentary 63:32-46 Ap '77
Is reverse discrimination justified? interview. pors U.S. News 83:39-40 O 3 '77
ROSTOW, Walt Whitman
Balance of power and balance of trade. Society 14:16-20 Ja '77
Tough times ahead. por Intellect 105:377 My '77
ROSTROPOVICH, Mstislav
Bloch: Schelomo; Schumann: Cello concerto. L. M. Smoley. Am Rec G 40:21-3 S '77 *
Maestro. J. Lelyveld. il pors N Y Times Mag p 127 O 23 '77 *
Magnificent maestro. il pors Time 110:82-6+ O 24 '77 *
Rostropovich in midpassage. G. Feifer. pors Sat R 4:35-9 Mr 5 '77 *
Rostropovich in Washington; October concerts with the National Symphony. I. Lowens. por Hi Fi 28:MA22 Ja '78 *
Slava as maestro. H. Saal and J. Whitmore. il pors Newsweek 90:69-70+ O 17 '77 *
Tchaikovsky: Six symphonies and Manfred. J. R. Oestreich. pors Am Rec G 41:14-16 D '77 *
Washington's biggest vote-getter. D. R. Smith. il pors Sat Eve Post 249:38-9+ O '77 *
ROSWELL Park Memorial Institute, Buffalo, N.Y.
Academics in New York and California fight disclosure policies. B. J. Culliton. Science 196: 37-8 Ap 1 '77
ROSZKOWSKI, Waldemar, and others
Selective display of histamine receptors on lymphocytes. bibl il Science 195:683-5 F 18 '77
ROTA, Nino
Flesh-and-blood angel. M. J. Matz. il por Opera N 41:18-19 My '77 *
Italian straw hat. Review
Newsweek il por 90:54 Jl 18 '77 *
ROTARY engines. See Airplane engines; Automobile engines
ROTARY lawn mowers. See Lawn mowers
ROTARY threshing combines. See Harvesting machinery
ROTARY tillers. See Cultivators
ROTATION
Striatal efferent fibers play a role in maintaining rotational behavior in the rat. J. F. Marshall and U. Ungerstedt. bibl il Science 198: 62-4 O 7 '77
ROTATION of crops
Succession planting chart. E. E. Jantzen. il Org Gard & Farm 24:72-3 F '77
20 bu. more yield than continuous corn. N. Reeder. Farm J 101:C2 My '77
ROTBLAT, Joseph
Controlling weapons-grade fissile material. bibl il Bull Atom Sci 33:37-43 Je '77
ROTELLE, John E.
Bishops play monopoly. D. Morrissey. Commonweal 104:528-30 Ag 19 '77 *
ROTH, Arnold
Letter from the publisher. J. Meyers. Sports Illus 47:4 Ag 15 '77 *
ROTH, Edith Brill
Career guides for the arts and humanities. il Am Educ 13:14-15 Je '77
First and only treasure. il Am Educ 13:6-9 N '77
Many paths for gifts and talents. Am Educ 13:25-7 My '77
ROTH, Edwin M.
Parking-lot king. por Forbes 119:78 Ap 1 '77 *
ROTH, Hal
Inside Cape Horn; excerpts. il por map Motor B & S 139:40-3 Mr; 70-3+ Ap; 68-71+ My; 78-80+ Je; 140:56-7+ Jl; 50-3+ S; 64-7+ O; 86-7+ N; 44-8+ D '77; 141:86-9+ Ja '78
Toward Cape Horn; excerpts from Inside Cape Horn. il map Motor B & S 139:40-3 Mr; 70-3+ Ap '77

ROTH, Harold P.
Ulcers: latest on how to detect, treat—and prevent them; interview. il por U.S. News 82:80-2 My 9 '77
ROTH, Henry
On being blocked & other literary matters; interview, ed by J. S. Friedman. Commentary 64:27-38 Ag '77
ROTH, Joan
If I'm not on my milk crate, you can find me in my phone booth. il Ms 5:74-7 Mr '77
ROTH, Philip
Professor of desire; story; excerpt from novel. Harpers 255:35-42 Ag '77

about

Philip Roth: Sonny Boy or Lenny Bruce? P. K. Bell. Commentary 64:60-3 N '77 *
ROTH, Robert J.
Colleges challenge value-free education. America 136:324-6 Ap 9 '77
ROTH, Rodris
Patent model by John Henry Belter. bibl il Antiques 111:1038-40 My '77
ROTH, Sigmund
World tour of cheese inside the Cheese Shop. S. P. Torpey. il pors Bet Hom & Gard 55:52-3 Ag '77 *
ROTH, Walter L. and Farrington, G. C.
Lithium-sodium beta alumina: first of a family of co-ionic conductors? bibl il Science 196: 1332-4 Je 17 '77
ROTHCHILD, John
Piracy on the low seas. il N Y Times Mag p50+ My 22 '77
—See Branch, T. jt auth
ROTHENBERG, David
In disgrace with fortune: prison reform today. America 136:141-4 F 19 '77
ROTHENSTEIN, Richard
Sisters—oh, brother! il Seventeen 36:24+ Je '77
ROTHKO, Mark
Act of alteration. G. Henry. Art N 76:115-16 My '77
Impact of the Rothko case. M. N. Carter. il por Art N 76:78-80 O '77 *
New life for Rothko. il Horizon 21:63 Ja '78 *
Straw man in the Rothko case. J. H. Merryman; discussion. Art N 76:32-3+ Mr '77 *
ROTHMAN, David H.
Behind the fronts. Nation 225:239-42 S 17 '77
ROTHMAN, James E. and Lenard, John
Membrane asymmetry. bibl il Science 195:743-53 F 25 '77
ROTHMAN, Lilian
Health. il Bet Hom & Gard 55:46+ Ap '77
ROTHMAN, Sheila M.
Sterilizing the poor. bibl Society 14:36-40 Ja '77
ROTHMAN, Stanley
Power of media elite. Intellect 106:10 Jl '77
ROTHSCHILD, Emma
Is it time to end Food for Peace? N Y Times Mag p 15+ Mr 13 '77
ROTHSCHILD, Fritz A.
Herberg as Jewish theologian. Nat R 29:885-6 Ag 5 '77
ROTHSCHILD, Norman
Off beat. See issues of Popular photography
ROTHSCHILD, Philippe, Baron de
Rothschild, tapestry, Mouton, and Picasso. S. Drake. il Holiday 58:48-9+ Ja '77 *
ROTHSTEIN, Margaret
The why of teaching. il Todays Educ 66:50-2 Ja '77
ROTHSTEIN, Stanley William
The first supportive environment. Clearing H 50:357-9 Ap '77
ROTHWELL, Gar W.
Evidence for a pollination-drop mechanism in Paleozoic pteridosperms. bibl il Science 198: 1251-2 D 23 '77
ROTMAN, Charles B. and others
Coed camping—yes! il Camp Mag 49:33-4+ Mr '77
ROTORS (helicopters) See Helicopters—Rotors
ROTTENBERG, Isaac C.
Should there be a Christian witness to the Jews? Chr Cent 94:352-6 Ap 13 '77
ROUAULT, Georges
Interpretations: an encounter with Rouault. L. R. Koch. il Sch Arts 76:23 F '77 *
ROUECHÉ, Berton
Annals of medicine. New Yorker 53:97-8+ S 12 '77
Profiles; Hermann, Mo. New Yorker 53:37-40+ F 28 '77
ROUECHE, John E.
What is college level? or, Why can't college students read and write? Clearing H 50:332 Ap '77
ROUGH-legged hawks. See Hawks
ROUGH Riders. See United States—Army—Cavalry
ROUGHAGE in food. See Food—Fiber content
ROUNBEHLER, D. P. and others
Quantitation of dimethylnitrosamine in the whole mouse after biosynthesis in vivo from trace levels of precursors. bibl il Science 197: 917-18 Ag 26 '77
ROUND Island. See Bristol Bay

ROUNDUPS
Fever tick crashes roundup, causes trouble on range; cattle roundup at Texas' El Chapote Ranch. D. Snell. il Smithsonian 8:58-65 O '77
ROURKE, Violet Bigelow
Antiques; poem. Hobbies 82:142 O '77
ROUS sarcoma. See Cancer
ROUSCH, Ron
He bottles houses. il por Pop Mech 148:128+ D '77 *
Houses that live in glass bottles. V. DeMoss. il Design (US) 78:8-11 Summ '77 *
ROUSE, James Wilson
Boston's historic Faneuil Hall Marketplace. M. F. Schmertz. il Archit Rec 162:116-27 D '77 *
ROUSE, Robert
Going, going. il por Forbes 119:74 Ja 15 '77
ROUSMANIERE, John
Distance racing. See issues of Yachting
ROUSUCK, J. Wynn
Winter Market. il Craft Horiz 37:44-5+ Ap '77
ROUTE, Pearl
Papier-mâché realism. il Sch Arts 76:10-12 Je '77
ROUTE 66. See Roads—United States
ROUTING machines
What can you do with a router? R. J. DeCristoforo. il Mech Illus 73:134+ O '77

Equipment

PM tool test. H. Wicks. il Pop Mech 148:74 O '77
ROUTTENBERG, Aryeh. See Morgan, J. M. jt auth
ROVAC Corporation. See Air conditioning industry
ROVERE, Richard Halworth
Letter from Washington (cont) New Yorker 52: 72-4+ Ja 31; 53:108-14 Mr 7; 129-34 Ap 11; 136-8+ My 9; 108+ Je 13; 56-60 Ag 1; 131-6 S 12; 180+ O 17; 200+ N 14 '77; 54-8 Ja 2 '78
ROWAN, Roy
Peaceful Asia beckons investors. il Fortune 96: 188-94+ O '77
There's also some good news about South Korea. il Fortune 96:170-6 S '77
ROWE, Ann Pollard
Andean warp-patterned weaves. il Craft Horiz 37:38-40 D '77
ROWE, Bobby Louise
Concepts in sculpture for young people. il Sch Arts 77:62-3 O '77
ROWE, David Nelson
Dancer spots in the Far East. il Nat R 29:829-30 Jl 22 '77
ROWE, Ednor M. and Weaver, J. H.
Uses of synchrotron radiation; with biographical sketches. il Sci Am 236:18, 32-41 bibl(p 142) Je '77
ROWE, Mary Potter
Especially for working mothers. Parents Mag 52:26-7 Je; 24 Jl; 34+ S; 54 N '77; 53-10 Ja '78
ROWE, Wallace P.
Guidelines that do the job. por Bull Atom Sci 33:14-15 My '77
ROWELL, Bobby G.
Vocational English. Clearing H 50:241-2 F '77
ROWELL, Galen
Great Yosemite gold rush. Audubon 76:135 S '77
High road to failure; climbing Mount K2 in the Karakoran Himalaya; excerpt from In the throne room of the mountain gods. il Sports Illus 46:92-6+ My 2 '77
ROWELL, Vicki Lynn
Makeovers for the dancing life. pors Seventeen 36:122-3 O '77 *
ROWEN, James
Public control of public money. Progressive 41:47-52 F '77
ROWING
Clem cakes: breakfast of champions; Cornell's victory in the Intercollegiate Rowing Association Championship. il Sports Illus 46:70+ Je 13 '77
Crew of husky Huskies; Pac-8 Championships and Eastern Sprints. D. Levin. il Sports Illus 46:54-5 My 30 '77
Foreign affair ends a domestic dispute; Henley Regatta. D. Levin. il Sports Illus 47:18-19 Jl 11 '77
Nash had his crew rambling; University of Pennsylvania's victory in the Adams Cup race. J. D. Reed. Sports Illus 46:70 My 16 '77
ROWLAND, F. Sherwood
Why ban fluorocarbons in aerosol sprays? interview. Read Digest 110:35-6+ F '77
ROWLAND, Hillis
Canadian's bells make the welkin ring. H. L. Miller. il pors Hobbies 82:118-19 S '77 *
ROWLAND, Neil. E. See Nicolaïdis, S. jt auth
ROWLEY, John C.
Geothermal energy development. bibl il Phys Today 30:36-8 Ja '77
ROY, Joyce
Ms. fix-it. See issues of American home
ROY M. Huffington Inc. See Gas industry
ROYAL, Donn
Take advantage of free water. il Org Gard & Farm 24:87-8 Jl '77
ROYAL Appliance Manufacturing Company. See Vacuum cleaners—Manufacture
ROYAL Botanic Gardens, Peradeniya, Sri Lanka. See Botanical gardens
ROYAL Canadian Mounted Police. See Canada—Royal Canadian Mounted Police
ROYAL Chitawan National Park. See National parks and reserves—Nepal
ROYAL Crown Cola Company
Royal Crown Cola gets a lot more fizz. il Bus W p84-5 Mr 14 '77
ROYAL Danish Ballet
Perspectives:
Productions of The three musketeers and A folk tale. E. Aschengreen. Dance Mag 51: 70-1 S '77
ROYAL Doulton pottery. See Pottery, English
ROYAL Opera, Great Britain. See Opera—Great Britain
ROYAL Opera, Stockholm. See Opera—Sweden
ROYAL Pavilion, Brighton. See Palaces
ROYAL Photographic Society of Great Britain, London
Critical focus. K. Poli. il Pop Phot 80:10+ F '77
ROYAL Winnipeg Ballet
Reviews: Royal Winnipeg Ballet's 1976-77 season. C. Carter. Dance Mag 51:79 D '77
ROYALTIES
Haley's quest for Roots. por Forbes 119:24 F 15 '77
King report pegs photocopying volume; question of library royality payments. Lib J 102:2381 D 1 '77
ROYALTIES for artists. See Artists rights
ROYALTY. See Kings and rulers
ROYBAL, Edward R.
Excerpts from remarks on amnesty for illegal aliens, April 5 and August 5, 1977. Cong Digest 56:234+ O '77
ROYSE, Dick
How to pick a healthy pup; interview, ed by B. Tarrant. il Field & S 81:154+ Mr '77
ROZE, Uldis
Mugging of a garden. il Horticulture 55:18-23 Jl '77
ROZEMA, Dave
Rose has bloomed. M. Ludtke. il por Sports Illus 47:72-3 Ag 29 '77 *
RÓŻEWICZ, Tadeusz
Méliès; poem; excerpt from The Survivor and other poems; tr by M. Krynski and R. Maguire. New Repub 176:34 Mr 19 '77
White marriage. Reviews
Nation 224:539 Ap 30 '77 *
Newsweek il 89:115 My 9 '77 *
RUANE, William J.
Tortoise and the hare. por Forbes 119:56-7 F 1 '77 *
RUARK, James E.
Meeting the evangelical needs. por Pub W 212:66 S 26 '77
RUBBER, Recycling of. See Refuse, Utilization of
RUBBER industry
See also
Collective bargaining—Rubber industry
Goodrich, B. F, Company
Goodyear Tire and Rubber Company
Tire industry
Uniroyal, Inc
RUBBER plants
Plant crops as a source of fuel and hydrocarbon-like materials. P. E. Nielsen and others. bibl il Science 198:942-4 D 2 '77
Rubber tires from weeds; investigating guayule and other plants. E. C. Bendall. Pop Sci 210: 64 Ap '77
See also
Guayule
RUBBER sculpture. See Sculpture
RUBBINGS
Brass rubbing in Britain—17 places. il Sunset 158:34+ F '77
RUBELLA
Test to prevent birth defects; blood test for susceptibilty to rubella. M. R. Skrocki. McCalls 104:67 Jl '77
RUBENS, Sir Peter Paul
Creature comforts; exhibition in Antwerp's Royal Museum of Fine Arts. M. Stevens. il Newsweek 90:36-7 Ag 1 '77 *
Gain for Rubens. il Horizon 19:49 Jl '77 *
Rubens: fed upon roses. R. Hughes. il por Time 110:47-8 Ag 1 '77 *
Rubens' garden. A. Eliot. il Horticulture 55:52+ My '77 *
Rubens: in praise of beauty; symposium. il por UNESCO Courier 30:4-27+ Je '77 *
Rubens year—a celebration. R. Chelminski. il Smithsonian 8:46-55 bibl(p 160) O '77 *
Rubens year: carnival in Flanders. R. Dobson. il por Art N 76:176+ Summ '77 *
When fat was in fashion. A. Hollander. il N Y Times Mag p36-7+ O 23 '77 *
RUBENS' house. See Antwerp, Belgium—Historic houses, sites, etc.
RUBENSTEIN, Dave. See Fischler, S. jt auth

RUBENSTEIN, David
White House workaholic. D. A. Williams and others. il por Newsweek 91:16 Ja 2 '78 *
RUBENSTEIN, Joshua
Reconsideration. New Repub 178:38-40 Ja 7 '78
Socialist surrealism. Commentary 64:67-9 S '77
RUBENSTEIN, Marc
No, all aspirin and pain remedies are not alike. il Ret Liv 17:30-2+ Mr '77
RUBIN, Carl B.
Conflicting signals. J. Miller. New Repub 177: 10-11 Jl 23 '77 *
RUBIN, Ellis
Trials on TV. J. K. Footlick. il por Newsweek 90:70 O 10 '77 *
RUBIN, Hal. See Rubin, Harold
RUBIN, Harold
Auburn Dam: a faulty business. il Nation 224: 563-4 My 7 '77
Bread from scratch. Org Gard & Farm 25:136-9 Ja '78
Dennis Banks' extradition fight. il Chr Cent 94: 691-2 Ag 3 '77
Legal history of an Indian. por Nation 225:113-15 Ag 6 '77
Liquefied natural gas. Nation 225:557-9 N 26 '77
RUBIN, Jerry
Yippie for money. il pors Newsweek 90:29-30 S 5 '77 *
RUBIN, Larry
For a blind young poet after his reading; poem. America 136:139 F 19 '77
RUBIN, Leslie
South Africa: facts and fiction. il UNESCO Courier 30:8-14 N '77
RUBIN, Mel
Mel Rubin. il Ceram Mo 25:34-5 N '77 *
RUBIN, Philip. See Nelson, D. F. jt auth
RUBIN, Rhea Joyce
(ed) Breaking in: library service to prisoners. bibl il por Wilson Lib Bull 51:496-533 F '77
RUBIN, Robert E.
Killing in Babcock & Wilcox. E. J. Tracy. il pors Fortune 96:266-9 O '77 *
RUBIN, Stephen E.
Behind the Berman legend. il pors N Y Times Mag p33+ O 23 '77
RUBIN, Theodore Isaac
Problems of sexual freedom; interview. Harp Baz 110:94-5+ Mr '77
Psychiatrist's notebook. See issues of Ladies' home journal
RUBIN, William
Skirmish over Guernica. P. Nobile. il Harpers 254:15+ Mr '77 *
RUBINSTEIN, Alvin Z.
Soviet policy in Europe. bibl f Cur Hist 73:105-8+ O '77
RUBINSTEIN, Arthur, International Piano Master Competition. See Music—Competitions
RUBINSTEIN, Artur
Brahms: Piano concerto no. 1 in D minor. G. S. Fox. Am Rec G 40:23-4 S '77 *
RUBINSTEIN, Leslie
Supers. il por Opera N 42:12-16 O '77
RUBLE, Diane N.
Premenstrual symptoms: a reinterpretation. bibl il Science 197:291-2 Jl 15 '77
RUBY, Edward G. and Nealson, K. H.
Luminous bacterium that emits yellow light. bibl il Science 196:432-4 Ap 22 '77
RUBY Lake National Wildlife Refuge. See Wildlife sanctuaries—Nevada
RUCKELSHAUS, William Doyle
Effective public management. J. L. Bower. bibl f Harvard Bus R 55:131-40 Mr '77 *
RUDA, Lucy. See Sherrill, C. jt auth
RUDD, Mark
Aging radical comes home. pors Time 110:25 S 26 '77 *
Mark Rudd returns. T. Powers. il Commonweal 104:657-9 O 14 '77 *
Return of Mark Rudd. R. Boeth and others. il pors Newsweek 90:34 S 26 '77 *
RUDD, Ricky
Honor isn't hollow. S. Moses. por Sports Illus 47:100+ N 14 '77 *
RUDD, Ia, Public Library. See Libraries—Iowa
RUDDERS. See Boats—Steering gear
RUDDIMAN, W. F.
North Atlantic ice-rafting: a major change at 75,000 years before the present. bibl il maps Science 196:1208-11 Je 10 '77
RUDDLE, Frank H. See Leinwand, L; McKusick, V. A. jt auths
RUDKIN, David
Ashes. Reviews
America 136:149 F 19 '77 *
Commonweal 104:370-1 Je 10 '77 *
New Repub 176:20-1 F 19 '77 *
Sat R 4:46-7 Mr 19 '77 *
RUDLOE, Anne. See Rudloe, J. jt auth
RUDLOE, Jack
Out for blood. il Sports Illus 46:76-80+ Ap 25 '77
—and Rudloe, Anne
Our wild and scenic rivers. il map Nat Geog 152:20-9 Jl '77
RUDNER, Ruth
Walker's guide to the mountains of Québec. Mademoiselle 83:44-6 Jl '77

RUDNER, Sara
Dance. N. Goldner. Nation 225:507-8 N 12 '77 *
Dancing. A. Croce. New Yorker 53:115-16 Mr 28 '77 *
Reviews. S. Banes. Dance Mag 51:36 My '77 *
RUDOFF, Doris
Ceramics and flowers. il Sch Arts 77:26-7 S '77
RUDOLF Steiner School. See New York (city)—Education
RUDOLPH, Lloyd I. and Rudolph, S. H.
India's election: backing into the future. For Affairs 55:836-53 Jl '77
RUDOLPH, Nancy
Casual camera. il Parents Mag 52:10+ Je '77
Do-it-yourself adventure playgrounds. il Parents Mag 52:38-9+ My '77
RUDOLPH, Susanne Hoeber. See Rudolph, L. I. jt auth
RUDSENSKE, Lee
Muskie man. J. Elder. il por Motor B & S 139: 60-1+ Je '77 *
RUDY, Jerry W. and Cheatle, M. D.
Odor-aversion learning in neonatal rats. bibl il Science 198:845-6 N 25 '77
RUETHER, Rosemary Radford
Authentic marriage of contemplation and social witness. il New Cath World 220:22-3 Ja '77
Rosemary Radford Ruether: mystification or liberation? Chr Cent 94:4 Ja 5 '77
Time makes ancient good uncouth: the Catholic report on sexuality. Chr Cent 94:682-5 Ag 3 '77
RUEVENI, Uri
You are cordially invited to help save a life. J. Gaylin. il Psychol Today 10:108+ Mr '77 *
RUFA, Robert H.
Vagabond camera. il Travel 147:64-5+ Je '77
RUFENER, Carol
Good food, good company. Am Home 80:88 D '77
RUFFED grouse shooting. See Grouse shooting
RUFFER, Matthew
Little boy who cheated death. A. Lake. il por Good H 185:96+ S '77 *
RUFFIAN Handicap. See Horse racing
RUFFIN, Frances E.
Making it happen in [state] il Redbook 149:81+ Ag; 82+ S '77
—See Carter, J. L. jt auth
RUG making. See Rugs and carpets
RUG steam cleaning machines. See Cleaning machinery and appliances
RUGBY football
Slim pickings at the cabbage patch; U.S. national rugby team vs English team. C. Gammon. il Sports Illus 47:26-8+ O 24 '77
RUGGERI, Elizabeth
Feed your vegetables chicken. il Org Gard & Farm 24:76-7 Je '77
RUGGLES, Eugene
Opening; poem. New Yorker 52:38 Ja 24 '77
RUGOSA roses. See Roses
RUGS and carpets
Carpet bag. B. Niles. Am Home 80:94 Je '77
Craft on commission; handwoven rug for Windows on the World restaurant, New York. J. Wulke. il por Craft Horiz 37:30-1 Ap '77
Folk floors. R. Reif. il N Y Times Mag p84-5 Mr 27 '77
Hooking, looping and knotting: versatile fiber techniques for rugs and wall hangings; excerpt from Weaving; design and expression. N. Belfer. il Sch Arts 77:20-5 S '77
How to lay cushion-backed carpeting. Bet Hom & Gard 55:256-7 O '77
Revival of rug hooking. M. L. Spung. il Ret Liv 17:40 F '77
See also
Indian blankets, rugs, etc (American)

Care

Consider care when you buy carpeting. Redbook 148:116+ F '77

Equipment

See Cleaning machinery and appliances

Exhibitions

Art; Smithsonian's America underfoot exhibition. E. V. Warren. il House B 119:36+ My '77

Purchasing

Plush carpeting. Consumer Rep 42:307 D '77
Quality you can stand on. McCalls 104:113-14+ S '77
RUGS and carpets, Oriental
Oriental carpets; exhibit at the Museum of Fine Arts in Boston. S. B. Sherrill. il Antiques 112: 336+ S '77
Oriental rugs. il Changing T 31:45-7 My '77
Rug show with a frayed look; Chinese rugs. il Bus W p29 N 7 '77
RUGS and carpets, Outdoor
Institute report:
Buying guide to outdoor carpets. il Good H 184:158 My '77
RUHR Valley
Regional planning in the Ruhr Valley. G. G. Wynne. il map Parks & Rec 12:21-3 D '77

RUIVO, Mario
Oceanography and the law of the sea. il UNESCO Courier 30:10-13 Ja '77
RULE, Ann Stackhouse
At last—help for innocent victims of crime. il Good H 185:84+ Jl '77
Public is not helpless! Ladies Home J 94:70 Mr '77
RULE, Philip C.
Summer films: pictures without people. America 137:33-4 Jl 16 '77
RULE of law
See also
Judicial review
United States—Constitutional law
RULE of the road at sea
New international rules of the road. E. S. Maloney. il Motor B & S 140:67-9+ Jl '77
Rules of the road. E. S. Maloney. il Motor B & S 140:32+ S '77
Rules of the road: inching toward uniformity. T. Gibbs. Yachting 142:72-5 D '77
RULERS. See Kings and rulers
RUM
How Bacardi put a new kick in rum sales; Bacardi Imports Inc. il Bus p 142-4 Mr 21 '77
Rum: more romantic than ever. C. Churchill. Am Home 80:70+ Ag '77
RUM an Coca-Cola; drama. See Matura, M.
RUMANIA
See also
Civil rights—Rumania
Education—Rumania
Foreign students in Rumania
Visitors, Foreign—Rumania

Commerce

United States

See United States—Commerce—Rumania

Description and travel

Romania, Romania! T. Marotta. il Craft Horiz 37:18-19+ Ap '77

Relief work

Funding for earthquake relief to Romania urged; statement, April 8, 1977. M. Nimetz. Dept State Bull 76:474-6 My 9 '77

Religious institutions and affairs

Springtime after Romania's quake. E. E. Plowman. Chr Today 21:54-5 Ap 1 '77
Time of testing for Romania's churches. T. Beeson. Chr Cent 94:421-2 My 4 '77
See also
Baptists in Rumania
Evangelical churches in Rumania

Riots

Unrest erupts. Time 110:56+ O 24 '77
RUMI. See Jalāl al-Dīn, R.
RUMINANTS
Ruminant livestock research and development. T. C. Byerly. bibl il Science 195:450-6 F 4 '77
The **RUMOUR** (rock group) See Rock groups
RUMPUS rooms. See Recreation rooms
RUMSFELD, Donald
GOP whiz kid takes Searle's reins. por Bus W p29-30 My 2 '77 *
RUNAWAY toys; drama. See Miller, H. L.
RUNAWAYS
Runaways. M. Brenton. il Todays Educ 66:64-6 Mr '77
Youth for sale on the streets. Time 110:23 N 28 '77
RUNDEL, Philip W. See Mulroy, T. W. jt auth
RUNNELS, Patricia
All about pecans. il Org Gard & Farm 24:87-91 S '77
RUNNING
Addicted to perpetual motion. M. Wellemeyer. il Fortune 95:55+ Je '77
All their minds were on one track; mile and two mile runs at Jack in the Box Indoor Games in San Diego. K. Moore. il Sports Illus 46:24-6+ F 28 '77
Almost too warm for the swarm; Peachtree Road Race. Sports Illus 47:48 Jl 18 '77
Bill Rodgers took Manhattan . . .; New York City Marathon. W. Bingham. il Sports Illus 47:24-5 O 31 '77
Byrne, as in blazing. A. Verschoth. il por Sports Illus 46:92+ My 23 '77
El Caballo is off and running; Cuba's A. Juantorena. J. Kirshenbaum. il pors Sports Illus 47:26-31 Ag 29 '77
Cooper's cohorts run down heart disease; Tyler Cup Invitational and aerobic exercise. P. Rosenfield. il Sat Eve Post 249:18-20 S '77
Creating a Flemish masterpiece; International Cross-Country Championship in Düsseldorf. K. Moore. il Sports Illus 46:28-30+ Ap 4 '77
Dormant no more. Duncan is erupting; 5,000-meter runner, D. Macdonald. K. Moore. il por Sports Illus 46:34-7 F 14 '77
Enigma wrapped in glory; Finnish runner L. Viren. K. Moore. il por Sports Illus 46:66-72+ Je 27 '77
Everyone can do it! women marathon runners. J. Kaplan. Seventeen 36:66+ Mr '77
Feeling fit to hurt a lot of feelings; sprinter S. Riddick. J. Marshall. il pors Sports Illus 46:40-2+ Mr 28 '77
Fitness Rx. G. Sheehan. il Vogue 167:136-7 Ap '77
Gentle radical who runs scared; marathoner, B. Rodgers. K. Moore. il pors Sports Illus 47:32-7 O 24 '77
Grasshoppers beware, here they come! AAU senior women's cross country race. K. Moore. il Sports Illus 47:28-30+ D 5 '77
In Hawaii, jogging clinics, a big run; Honolulu Marathon. il Sunset 159:48 D '77
Life on the run; marathons. A. Ripp. il Horizon 20:32-8 O '77
New generation of blues fans; Drake Relays. J. Marshall. il Sports Illus 46:24-6 My 9 '77
Night for stars, both born and reborn; Jamaican Invitational. K. Moore. il Sports Illus 46:32-4 My 23 '77
Old order holds at Penn. A. Verschoth. il Sports Illus 46:26+ My 9 '77
Running for your life. Masters Track and Field. G. Leonard. Read Digest 110:43-4+ F '77
Running—the new high; ideas of E. Colt and R. O. Schuster. C. Seebohm. il House & Gard 149:89+ Jl '77
Twenty-six-point-two miles; New York City Marathon. New Yorker 53:45-7 N 7 '77
Women on the run. S. C. Cowley. il Newsweek 90:100 N 14 '77
See also
Jogging

Accidents and injuries

Jogger's ills; pseudonephritis. il Time 111:56 Ja 16 '78

Anecdotes, facetiae, satire, etc.

Loveliness of the long distance runner. E. Segal. New Repub 177:25-6 Jl 23 '77

Photographs

Everyone is getting into the pack; Boston Marathon; with report by W. Bingham. C. Rentmeester. il Sports Illus 46:40-5 Ap 18 '77
RUNNING clothes. See Clothing and dress—Sports clothes
RUNNING rapids
Down a crazy river; canoes and kayaks in Hudson River White Water Derby; photographs; with report by D. Levin. M. Manny and A. Szabo. Sports Illus 46:38-43 My 2 '77
I challenged the Deliverance river—and loved it! Chattooga. J. Janedis. il Redbook 148:55-6 Ap '77
Joy of white water; Rogue River, Ore. N. Proffitt. il Newsweek 90:60-1 Jl 18 '77
Just keep your head above water; Colorado River; photographs; with report by M. Ludtke. J. Blaustein. Sports Illus 47:24-9 Ag 1 '77
Maiden voyage; Middle Fork of Idaho's Salmon River. N. Scofield. il por Am Home 80:28-9 Jl '77
New rides for white-water action. D. Sturges. il Pop Mech 148:80-1+ Jl '77
Remember when rivers were free? P. Singerman. Esquire 87:22+ F '77
Teaming up on white water. D. Houser. pors Outdoor Life 160:35 S '77
Two women, three men on a raft. R. Schrank. il Harvard Bus R 55:100-8 My '77
White-water high; river rafting. J. George. il Read Digest 111:74-7 S '77
White-water high; Snake River. P. Wood. il N Y Times Mag p66-73 My 22 '77
White water! New River Gorge, West Virginia. P. L. Buckley. Nat R 29:1007-8 S 2 '77
Wilderness river; Lower Canyons of the Rio Grande. J. Lelyveld. il N Y Times Mag p 174 D 11 '77
RUOFF, A. L. and Wanagel, J.
High pressures on small areas. bibl il Science 198:1037-8 D 9 '77
RURAL aged. See Aged
RURAL churches. See Country churches
RURAL crime. See Crime and criminals—United States
RURAL development programs. See Community development
RURAL Electrification Administration. See United States—Agriculture, Department of—Rural Electrification Administration
RURAL life. See Country life; Farm life
RURAL Life Museum. See Louisiana. State University, Baton Rouge—Rural Life Museum
RURAL medical care. See Medical care, Rural
RURAL mental health care. See Mental health care
RURAL planning
See also
Community development

Nigeria

All resettled at Kainji? Kainji Dam resettlement. F. A. Salamone. il Intellect 106:231-3 D '77
RURAL population
Census shows changes in farm population. Farm J 101:42 Ja '77

RURAL schools
Myths of rural school and district consolidation. J. P. Sher and R. B. Tompkins. Educ Digest 42:45-8 Ap '77
RURAL sociology. See Sociology, Rural
RURAL-urban conflict. See City and country
RURAL water supply. See Water supply, Rural
RURAL youth. See Youth
RUSALKA; opera. See Dvorak, A.
RUSH, Margaret House
Religion and ERA battle in the Rockies. Chr Cent 94:164-5 F 23 '77
RUSH Medical College, Chicago
2 learning places by Metz Train Olson & Youngren; cool-hand collegiate. N. Miller. il Archit Rec 162:90-3 Jl '77
RUSHFORD, Greg
Carter's way with Congress. Nation 225:270 S 24 '77
RUSHING, Jane (Gilmore)
Raincrow; condensation of a novel. Redbook 149:173-95 Jl '77
Walnut grove; story; excerpt from novel. Redbook 150:197-219 D '77
RUSHMORE National Memorial. See Mount Rushmore National Memorial
RUSK, Dean
Energy: a new cause of war coming down the road. por U.S. News 82:43-4 Je 27 '77
RUSSELL, Andy
Build the LED target game. il Pop Electr 11: 50-2 Je '77
RUSSELL, Beverly
Good looks and good health. House & Gard 149: 30+ Je '77
1765 mill grinds into action. il House & Gard 149:36+ Je '77
RUSSELL, Charles Marion
Remington & Russell; excerpt from Way west. P. H. Hassrick. il Am West 14:16-29 N '77 *
RUSSELL, Diana E. H.
Crimes against women. Ms 5:81-3+ F '77
RUSSELL, Diane H. See Manen, C.-A. jt auth
RUSSELL, Dick
Casebook of the medical detective (cont) il Fam Health 9:40-1+ Ja '77
RUSSELL, Elsa
Personal article. Writer 90:14-17 F '77
RUSSELL, Francis
End of the myth. Nat R 29:938-41 Ag 19 '77
RUSSELL, John
Your hog business (cont) il Farm J 101: Hog 28 Ja; Hog 16 F; Hog 28 My; Hog 20 Je; Hog 24 Ag; Hog 40 S; Hog 16 D '77
RUSSELL, John, 1919-
David Smith's art is best revealed in natural settings. il por Smithsonian 7:68-75 bibl(p 126-7) Mr '77
Final flowering of Henri Matisse, invincible artist. il Smithsonian 8:72-9 S '77
Lost horizons of Russian painting. il N Y Times Mag p23-5+ Ap 3 '77
Out of nowhere, he became the top art dealer in Paris. bibl(p 101) il por Smithsonian 8:68-75 Jl '77
RUSSELL, Ken
Ken Russell, again. M. Dempsey. il Film Q 31: 19-24 Wint '77 *
RUSSELL, Mary
Chez Kenzo, Chez Karl. il pors N Y Times Mag p 130-1 N 27 '77
How to look beautiful in Paris. il N Y Times Mag p 132-3 N 27 '77
RUSSELL, Mattie Underwood
N.C. ruling menaces manuscript collections. Am Lib 8:471-2 O '77
RUSSELL, Rosalind
My wife, Roz. F. Brisson. il pors McCalls 104: 194-5+ Ap '77 *
—and Chase, Chris
Memoirs of a gallant lady; excerpt from Life is a banquet. por Ladies Home J 94:87+ S '77
RUSSELL, Rosamond Bernier
Spain to U.S: art of Tàpies. Vogue 167:172+ My '77
RUSSELL, Van
Cruising gun. il Motor B & S 140:54-5 O '77
RUSSELS' viper. See Snakes
RUSSIA
In the mirror: a Soviet reflects on the Soviets; interview. A. F. Dobrynin. por Sr Schol 110: 13 N 3 '77
Russian Revolution turns 60; Time essay. L. Morrow. il Time 110:46+ N 14 '77
Russia's 60 years of communism: success or failure? special section. il map U.S. News 83: 42-54+ O 24 '77
Soviet Union, 1977; symposium. bibl f il maps Cur Hist 73:97-127+ O '77
Soviets at 60. R. Carroll and others. il por Newsweek 90:56-7+ N 14 '77
Through the mirror. J. Burnham. Nat R 29:1288 N 11 '77
See also
Aged—Russia
Agriculture—Russia
Air travel—Russia
Airlines—Russia
Airplanes, Military—Russia
Altai Mountains
Art—Russia
Art and state—Russia
Censorship—Russia
Cities and towns—Russia
City planning—Russia
Civil defense—Russia
Civil rights—Russia
Concentration camps—Russia
Costume—Russia
Courts—Russia
Crime and criminals—Russia
Espionage, Russian
Finance—Russia
Gambling—Russia
Gas, Natural—Russia
Georgia
Government and the press—Russia
Hospitals, Psychiatric—Russia
Hunting—Russia
Immigration and emigration—Russia
Immigration camps—Russia
Industrial relations—Russia
Investments, American—Russia
Investments, Russian
Irrigation—Russia
Jews in Russia
Leningrad
Loans, Bank—Russia
Medicine—Russia
Money—Russia
Mongolia
Moscow
Music—Russia
National songs—Russia
Natural resources—Russia
Opera—Russia
Petroleum—Russia
Photography—Russia
Political attitudes—Russia
Political prisoners—Russia
Public health—Russia
Publishers and publishing—Russia
Radio broadcasting—Russia
Reclamation of land—Russia
Science—Russia
Science and state—Russia
Secret service—Russia
Siberia
Space research—Russia
Sports—Russia
Ukraine
Visitors, Foreign—Russia
Water supply—Russia
Women—Russia
Wrangel Island
Yakutsk
Zoology—Russia

Air Force

Western alliance seeks to update nuclear capability. D. A. Brown. il maps Aviation W 107:12-15 Ag 1 '77

Anniversaries, etc.

Politburo loves a parade. il Time 110:48-9 N 21 '77

Antiquities

Scythians: nomad goldsmiths of the open steppes; symposium. il UNESCO Courier 29:4-49 D '76
See also
Ukraine—Antiquities

Appropriations and expenditures

See also
Russia—Armed Forces—Appropriations and expenditures

Armed Forces

Détente and the military balance. S. A. Garrett. bibl il Bull Atom Sci 33:10-20 Ap '77
New Soviet threat to NATO. S. Nunn. Read Digest 111:73-7 Jl '77
Senators find arms buildup in East Europe. Aviation W 106:21 Ja 31 '77
See also
Russia—Navy

Appropriations and expenditures

CIA's goof in assessing the Soviets; effect of defense spending on the Soviet economy. il Bus W p96-8+ F 28 '77
Defense miscalculations: dollarizing the Russian forces; criticism of CIA estimates by A. W. Marshall. E. Aerie. Nation 225:78-81 Jl 23 '77

Bibliography

Book reviews. Cur Hist 73:128 O '77

Climate

Soviet grain harvests: CIA study pessimistic on effects of weather. D. Shapley. Science 195: 377-8 Ja 28 '77

Commerce

Hard currency problems spur Soviet export push. E. Kozicharow. Aviation W 106:17-18 Ap 11 '77
Ready to spend on chemical plants. Bus W p56-7 S 12 '77
Soviets pushing exports to cut deficits. il Aviation W 106:187+ Je 6 '77

RUSSIA—Commerce—*Continued*
This Communist internationale has a capitalist accent; establishment of Soviet corporations in foreign countries. H. E. Meyer. il Fortune 95:134-7+ F '77
See also
Russia—Industries
Shipping—Russia

Europe, Western

New canals for Europe: Russia's invasion path? map U.S. News 82:81 Mr 21 '77
Trading with the Soviet Union. Otto. Sat Eve Post 249:38+ Mr '77

France

French exports seed future competition. il Bus W p34 My 23 '77

Great Britain

Soviets press to buy Rolls RB.211s for Il-86. Aviation W 106:22 Mr 7 '77

Peru

Russia arms Peru. T. Szulc. New Repub 176:18-19 F 19 '77

United States

See United States—Commerce—Russia

Constitution

Brezhnev's rising sun. il Time 109:41 Je 13 '77
Draft of the new Soviet constitution: excerpts. Cur Hist 73:129 O '77
Impending political struggle; provisions in new Russian constitution. Nat R 29:703-4 Je 24 '77
Konstitution. Nation 224:741 Je 18 '77
New draft constitution of the U.S.S.R; address, June 5, 1977. L. I. Brezhnev. Vital Speeches 43:546-51 Jl 1 '77
Proposed new Soviet constitution. Chr Today 21:23 Jl 8 '77

Cultural relations

Russian paintings at the Met: an inside look at museum diplomacy. J. E. Bowlt. il Art in Am 65:74-9 My; 120-1 N '77

Defenses

Across-the-board gains in Soviet forces detailed. E. Kozicharow. Aviation W 107:17-18 Ag 29 '77
Annual Red scare. Nation 224:67-8 Ja 22 '77
Arms control: the Russians are cheating! M. R. Laird. Read Digest 111:97-101 D '77
Arms race: is paranoia necessary for security? G. B. Kistiakowsky. il N Y Times Mag p52-4+ N 27 '77
Arms zealots. D. Yergin. il Harpers 254:64+ Je '77
Assessing Soviet intentions; excerpts from address. J. L. Buckley. Aviation W 107:7 Ag 22 '77
Congress told Soviets trailing technologically. Aviation W 107:55-6 S 5 '77
Could Russia survive a nuclear attack? E. Raymond. Nat R 29:1363 N 25 '77
DOD scrutinizes evolving air defenses of USSR. il Aviation W 107:16-18 D 5 '77
Dangers of a new Cold War. G. Arbatov. Bull Atom Sci 33:33-40 Mr '77
Defense reconsidered. E. N. Luttwak. Commentary 63:51-8 Mr '77
Deploying cruise missile may spur Soviet reaction. Aviation W 107:23 Jl 11 '77
Easy to fool. M. Kempton. Progressive 41:17 Ap '77
General goes zap; question of Gen. G. J. Keegan's comments on Russian weapons. M. Kondracke. New Repub 177:19-22 Jl 2 '77
International situation; address, January 18, 1977. L. I. Brezhnev. Vital Speeches 43:262-5 F 15 '77
Is it over, over there? A. G. J. Chalfont. il Nat R 29:200-3+ F 18 '77
Is there a present danger? M. Kondracke. New Repub 176:18-20 Ja 29 '77
It's budget time again: the Russians are coming! D. Cortright and R. L. Borosage. Nation 224:205-8 F 19 '77
Military leaders clash on Soviet threat. Aviation W 106:16 F 7 '77
NATO warned of gains in Soviet arms strength. Aviation W 106:22-3 My 23 '77
New assessment put on Soviet threat; address. G. J. Keegan, Jr. il por Aviation W 106:38-43+ Mr 28 '77
Nightmare for NATO. A. De Borchgrave. il map Newsweek 89:36-8 F 7 '77
Perils of détente. W. Laqueur. N Y Times Mag p 16+ F 27 '77
Practical power use urged on planners. H. J. Coleman. il Aviation W 107:18-21 Jl 18 '77
Russian bear besieged. il Sat Eve Post 249:76+ My '77
Russians are coming—again. G. McGovern. Progressive 41:17-23 My '77
Soviet defense evades economic strains. E. Kozicharow. Aviation W 107:55+ Ag 22 '77
Soviet strategic capabilities: the superpower balance. C. G. Jacobsen. Cur Hist 73:97-9+ O '77
Soviet strategic lead seen by 1980s; Soviet push scientist, engineer buildup. C. Brownlow; H. J. Coleman. Aviation W 106:18-20 F 14 '77
Threat: is there a present danger? the Carter administration and the Soviet. R. J. Bresler. Intellect 105:310-11 Ap '77
U.S. can still hold its own. . .for now; official report of the Joint Chiefs of Staff. U.S. News 82:61 F 14 '77
USAF simulates Soviet defense system. B. Miller. il Aviation W 106:43+ My 30 '77
Warnke in wonderland; U.S.-Soviet strategic relations. Nat R 29:250+ Mr 4 '77
See also
Guided missiles
Guided missiles—Defenses
Russia—Armed Forces
Russia—Navy

Economic conditions

CIA's goof in assessing the Soviets; effect of defense spending on the Soviet economy. il Bus W p96-8+ F 28 '77
Coming crisis in Russia—size-up by top government analysts. il U.S. News 83:23-4+ D 12 '77
How Russia and U.S. match up in output, living standards. il U.S. News 83:52-3 O 24 '77
Outlook bearish. Newsweek 90:43 Ag 22 '77
See also
Agriculture—Russia
Russia—Industries

Economic policy

Development of Soviet Asia. R. N. North. bibl f map Cur Hist 73:123-7+ O '77
Some observations on the plan-market relationship in centrally planned economies. A. Katsenelinboigen and H. S. Levine. bibl f il Ann Am Acad 434:186-98 N '77
Will Russia's ailing economy make it pull in its horns? il U.S. News 83:21 Ag 22 '77

Economic relations

See also
Russia—Commerce

Europe, Eastern

Recession, Communist style. J. Dornberg. il Duns R 109:82-6 Ap '77

Foreign relations

Coming crisis in Russia—size-up by top government analysts. il U.S. News 83:23-4+ D 12 '77
Detente in Soviet policy; address, September 30, 1977. H. Rolph. Vital Speeches 44:108-12 D 1 '77
International situation; address, January 18, 1977. L. I. Brezhnev. Vital Speeches 43:262-5 F 15 '77
Italian communism at home and abroad: the Soviet connection. M. Ledeen; discussion. Commentary 63:20-2+ Mr '77
Kremlin's unending quest for world domination. il U.S. News 83:54+ O 24 '77
Nature of Soviet power. R. Legvold. For Affairs 56:49-71 O '77
See also
Berlin question, 1945-
Military assistance, Russian

Africa

Africa, Soviet imperialism & the retreat of American power. B. Rustin and C. Gershman. Commentary 64:33-43 O '77
Russia: now a three-time loser in Africa. il map U.S. News 83:80+ N 28 '77
Soviet policy in Africa and the Middle East. J. C. Campbell. bibl f Cur Hist 73:100-4+ O '77
Soviets in Africa. K. Willenson and others. il map Newsweek 89:43+ Ap 4 '77
Turmoil in Africa—how Moscow capitalizes on strife. map U.S. News 82:29-30 Ap 4 '77
What the Russians are up to. il Time 109:39-40 Ap 4 '77

Africa, Northwest

Playing the Horn, Moscow style. map Time 109:37 My 9 '77

Asia

Soviet policy in Europe. A. Z. Rubinstein. Cur For Affairs 56:306-23 Ja '78

China

Dragon and the bear: Asian perceptions of a Sino-Soviet war. J. Kefner. map America 137:162-4 S 24 '77
Soviet quandary in Asia; Sino-Soviet relations. D. S. Zagoria. bibl f For Affairs 56:306-23 Ja '78

Cuba—History

See also
Cuban Missile Crisis, 1962

Denmark

Probing NATO's northern flank. il Time 109:24+ Je 27 '77

Ethiopia

Why the Kremlin threw its support to Ethiopia. il U.S. News 83:85 N 28 '77

RUSSIA—Foreign relations—*Continued*

Europe

Soviet quandary in Asia. D. S. Zagoria. bibl f Hist 73:105-8+ O '77

Europe, Eastern

Meaning of Brzezinski; opinions of Kultura; tr by O. Scherer. Nat R 29:612-13 My 27 '77

Europe, Western

Europe: the specter of Finlandization. W. Laqueur. Commentary 64:37-41 D '77

Finland

Europe: the specter of Finlandization. W. Laqueur. Commentary 64:37-41 D '77
Finlandization tactic. W. F. Buckley, Jr. Nat R 29:958-9 Ag 19 '77

France

See also
Brezhnev, L. I.—Visit to France, 1977

Germany, East

Peril of Soviet friendship pacts. Otto. por Sat Eve Post 249:21+ My '77

India

Russia also a loser in India's election. R. Knight. U.S. News 82:32 Ap 4 '77

Middle East

Shall I go to Cairo? W. F. Buckley, Jr. Nat R 30:48 Ja 6 '78
Soviet policy in Africa and the Middle East. J. C. Campbell. bibl f Cur Hist 73:100-4+ O '77
Why the PLO? The Soviets? Nat R 29:1216-17 O 28 '77

Mozambique

Great white fathers. K. Willenson and J. Pringle. il Newsweek 89:55 Ap 11 '77

Norway

Probing NATO's northern flank. il Time 109:24+ Je 27 '77

Poland

Polish road to communism. P. Osnos. For Affairs 56:209-20 O '77

Somalia

Booting out the Russians. K. Willenson and others. il map Newsweek 90:72-3 N 28 '77
Russians, go home! il map Time 110:48 N 28 '77

South Africa

South African nightmare. M. Friedman. Newsweek 90:94 N 28 '77

United States

See United States—Foreign relations—Russia

History

See also
Nicholas II, Emperor of Russia

17th century

Witchcraft trials in seventeenth-century Russia. R. Zguta. bibl f il Am Hist R 82:1187-207 D '77

20th century

From Revolution to superpower. il U.S. News 83:44-5 O 24 '77

Revolution, 1917-1921

Revolutionaries against the world; excerpt from The Russian revolution. L. Trotsky. il por Sat Eve Post 249:49 Jl '77
Russian Revolution turns 60; Time essay. L. Morrow. il Time 110:46+ N 14 '77

Revolution, 1917-1921—American participation

See Russia—History—Allied intervention, 1918-1920

Revolution, 1917-1921—Art and the Revolution

Russian Revolution: a wall-sized history. S. F. Starr. il Smithsonian 8:52-4 Jl '77

Revolution, 1917-1921—Foreign participation

See also
Russia—History—Allied intervention, 1918-1920

Allied intervention, 1918-1920

Doughboys in Siberia; American Expeditionary Force; excerpt from Unknown war with Russia. R. Maddox. il Am Hist Illus 12:10-21 Ag '77

Industries

Soviet-American trade: trick or treat! J. Barron. Read Digest 111:67-8+ O '77
See also
Automobile industry—Russia
Chemical industries—Russia
Computer industry—Russia
Photographic industry—Russia
Steel industry—Russia

Intellectual life

Ode to diversity. B. T. Feld. Bull Atom Sci 33:10-11 O '77
Ten days that shook me up in Russia. B. Gelb. N Y Times Mag p21+ S 18 '77
Word is freedom; interview, ed by J. R. Coyne, Jr. V. Bukovsky. il Nat R 29:378-82 Ap 1 '77

Languages

See also
English language in Russia

Military policy

Back to the Cold War. T. Powers. Commonweal 104:83-5 F 4 '77
Carter and Brezhnev: the game begins. il por Time 109:40-2 F 7 '77
Carter's intelligence chief sizes up world's trouble spots; interview. S. Turner. por U.S. News 82:24-6 My 16 '77
Détente and the military balance. S. A. Garrett. bibl il Bull Atom Sci 33:10-20 Ap '77
Detente in Soviet policy; address, September 30, 1977. H. Rolph. Vital Speeches 44:108-12 D 1 '77
Hiroshima echo. W. G. Kelsey. il Progressive 41:28-30 N '77
Kremlin's unending quest for world domination. il U.S. News 83:54+ O 24 '77
Latest round in debate over Russia's aims. U.S. News 82:18 F 28 '77
Nature of Soviet power. R. Legvold. For Affairs 56:49-71 O '77
Surprise attack by Russia: still unthinkable? with interview with H. Brown. R. Kelly. il U.S. News 83:18-24 S 5 '77
See also
Russia—Defenses
Strategy

Nationalism

Ethnicity in the Soviet Union. T. Rakowska-Harmstone. bibl f il Ann Am Acad 433:73-87 S '77
In U.S.S.R. minority problems just won't wither away. J. N. Wallace. il map U.S. News 82:53-4 F 14 '77

Navy

Russian bear has gone to sea. N. Polmar. il Sat Eve Post 249:22-4+ Mr '77
USSR submarines pose heavy threat. C. A. Robinson, Jr. il Aviation W 106:35-7+ Ja 24 '77

Politics and government

After Brezhnev? The Kremlin's succession crisis. E. H. Methvin. Read Digest 110:103-6 My '77
Letter to Brezhnev; tr by M. Petrov. B. Rabbot. il pors N Y Times Mag p48+ N 6 '77
Looking at the future; views of six Kremlin specialists. il Newsweek 90:60-1 N 14 '77
Reports & comment: Moscow: a chill in the air. D. K. Shipler. Atlantic 240:11-12+ S '77
Russia—beyond Brezhnev. W. Laqueur. Commentary 64:39-44 Ag '77
To Russia without love. New Repub 177:7-8+ N 19 '77
Veep in Moscow. por Time 110:40 O 17 '77
See also
Communism—Russia
Communist Party (Russia)
Russia—Constitution

Religious institutions and affairs

Witchcraft trials in seventeenth-century Russia. R. Zguta. bibl f il Am Hist R 82:1187-207 D '77
See also
Baptists in Russia
Christians in Russia
Orthodox Eastern Church, Russian

Social conditions

FYI: Pepsi, high fashion, and humor. il map Sr Schol 110:6+ N 3 '77
In Russia, it's wise to be ready for shocks and surprises. R. Knight. il U.S. News 82:73-5 Je 13 '77
Life in Russia—as the West moves in. R. Knight. il U.S. News 84:29-30 Ja 9 '78
Russia finally takes to the highways. R. Knight. il map U.S. News 82:52-5 Ja 31 '77
Russia's Revolution—as it looks from the inside; interview. R. Knight and J. N. Wallace. il U.S. News 83:46-50 O 24 '77
Russia's 25-billion-dollar drinking problem. U.S. News 83:47 S 26 '77
See also
Communism—Russia
Jews in Russia
Leningrad—Social conditions

Social history

On Lamennais, Chaadaev, and the romantic revolt in France and Russia. N.V. Riasanovsky. bibl f pors Am Hist R 82:1165-86 D '77
Science and values: the eugenics movement in Germany and Russia in the 1920s. L. R. Graham. bibl f Am Hist R 82:1133-64 D '77

RUSSIA—*Continued*

Social policy

Fuse is laid for a new revolution. B. Levin. il por U.S. News 83:66 O 24 '77

RUSSIA and the United States

Life on a cold rock; Siberian and Alaskan Eskimos of the Diomede Islands. F. Bruemmer. il map Natur Hist 86:54-65 bibl(p97) Mr '77

New kidney from Moscow. il Time 109:84 Mr 7 '77

One-star shop talk; exchange of lectures by Army officers. Nation 225:485 N 12 '77

Should US scientists trade data with USSR? symposium. il Sci Digest 81:30-7+ Je '77

Sputnik plus 20: the U.S. on top. M. R. Benjamin. il Newsweek 90:52-4+ O 10 '77

Web of relations: where détente is doing well; assorted joint projects. R. Knight. il U.S. News 82:26 Mr 28 '77

See also

United States—Foreign opinion—Russian

RUSSIA-United States cooperative science program. See Science—International aspects

RUSSIAN Academy of Sciences. See Academy of Sciences of the USSR

RUSSIAN art. See Art, Russian

RUSSIAN artificial satellites. See Artificial satellites—Cosmos missions; Artificial satellites, Russian

RUSSIAN artists. See Artists, Russian

RUSSIAN astronauts. See Astronauts

RUSSIAN authors. See Authors, Russian

RUSSIAN costumes. See Costume—Russia

RUSSIAN drama

See also

Moscow—Theater

RUSSIAN exiles. See Exiles

RUSSIAN fiction

Bibliography

Socialist surrealism. J. Rubenstein. Commentary 64:67-9 S '77

RUSSIAN Jews. See Jews in Russia

RUSSIAN literature

Mister Nabokov; Wellesley course taught by V. Nabokov. H. Green. New Yorker 52:32-5 F 14 '77

See also

Russian fiction

Russian poetry

RUSSIAN military assistance. See Military assistance, Russian

RUSSIAN minorities. See Minorities

RUSSIAN Orthodox Church. See Orthodox Eastern Church, Russian

RUSSIAN painting. See Painting, Russian

RUSSIAN poetry

Why Russian poets? B. Akhmadulina and Russian poetry. J. Brodsky. Vogue 167:112 Jl '77

Translations into English

Tale about rain in several episodes; poem; excerpt from Fever and other new poems; tr by G. Dutton and I. Mezhakoff-Koriakin. B. Akhmadulina. Vogue 167:113+ Jl '77

Thames at Chelsea; tr by D. Rigsbee. J. Brodsky. New Yorker 53:56 N 28 '77

RUSSIAN Revolution. See Russia—History—Revolution, 1917-1921

RUSSIAN scientists. See Scientists, Russian

RUSSIAN space stations. See Space stations, Russian

RUSSIAN space vehicles. See Space vehicles, Russian

RUSSIAN travel restrictions. See Travel regulations

RUSSIAN visitors in the United States. See Visitors, Foreign—United States

RUSSIANS

Soviet Union: major ethnic groups. il map Sr Schol 110:15 N 3 '77

Photographs

Portraits at an exhibition; ed by D. Seiberling. N. Farb. N Y Times Mag p57-9 N 20 '77

RUSSIANS in Canada

See also

Dukhobors

RUSSIANS in literature

My name is Asya; K. Michailovskaya's book. C. Reamer. Engl J 66:62 Mr '77

RUSSLAN and Ludmila; opera. See Glinka, M. I.

RUSSO, Tony, and Gregory, Donnelly

Gibson theories applied to integrated camps for mentally retarded. il Camp Mag 49:14-16+ Je '77

RUSSOTTO, Joseph S.

Doing it yourself is not always best. il Ret Liv 17:39+ F '77

RUST. See Corrosion and anticorrosives

RUST Craft Greeting Cards, Inc-Ziff Corporation merger. See Corporations—Acquisitions and mergers

RUSTIN, Bayard, and Gershman, Carl

Africa, Soviet imperialism & the retreat of American power. Commentary 64:33-43 O '77

RUSTIONI, Aldo

Spinal neurons project to the dorsal column nuclei of rhesus monkeys. bibl il Science 196: 656-8 My 6 '77

RUSTOW, Dankwart Alexander

U.S.-Saudi relations and the oil crises of the 1980s. bibl f For Affairs 55:494-516 Ap '77

RUSTPROOFING of automobiles. See Automobiles—Maintenance and repair

RUTH, George R. and others

Bovine protoporphyria: the first nonhuman model of this hereditary photosensitizing disease. bibl il Science 198:199-201 O 14 '77

RUTHERFORD, John E.

Put wallpaper on your walls? il Sch Arts 76:30-2 Mr '77

RUTHERFORD, Johnny

Countdown to a pot of gold; photographs. L. Stewart. il pors Sports Illus 46:34-8 My 16 '77 *

RUTHERFURD, Lucy Page (Mercer)

How Eleanor Roosevelt forgave the other woman; excerpt from Mother R: Eleanor Roosevelt's untold story. E. Roosevelt and J. Brough. il por Ladies Home J 94:84+ Ap '77 *

RUTIN

Tobacco protein may lead to heart disease. Sci N 112:214 O 1 '77

RUTTENBERG, Stanley H.

Development of third world would affect U.S. supply of raw materials. M Labor R 100:39-40 Mr '77

RUTTENCUTTER, Helen Drees

Onward and upward with the arts. New Yorker 53:42-4+ S 19 '77

RUTTER, Michael

Preventing emotional illness. J. Greenberg. por Sci N 112:202-3 S 24 '77 *

RYAN, Dennis P.

Crispus Attucks monument controversy of 1887. il Negro Hist Bull 40:656-7 Ja '77

RYAN, Herbert J.

Anglican-Roman Catholic dialogue. il New Cath World 220:168-72 Jl '77

Anglicans and Roman Catholics on authority in the Church. America 136:183-6 Mr 5 '77

RYAN, Jack

Restoration of Lightning Number One. il Yachting 141:134+ Ap '77

RYAN, Joseph L.

Other Israelis. Commonweal 104:13-15 Ja 7 '77

RYAN, Margaret

Arachne; poem. Mademoiselle 83:195 My '77

RYAN, Michael

Consider a move; poem. New Yorker 53:102 O 10 '77

Gangster dreams; poem. Atlantic 239:62 My '77

RYAN, Michael F. See Hillenbrand, R. jt auth

RYAN, Patrick

Dirty jobs that require more clean sweeps. Smithsonian 8:176 N '77

Get rid of the people, and the system runs fine. Smithsonian 8:140 S '77

It ticks and it talks—it may be too much. Smithsonian 8:140 D '77

Shorties don't always get short shrift in life. il Smithsonian 8:156 Ap '77

Some prefer old age to the alternative. Smithsonian 8:120 Ja '78

There's no such thing as a little boredom. Smithsonian 8:104 Jl '77

Warts still defy spunk water and more scientific cures. il Smithsonian 7:164 F '77

RYAN, Robert A.

Put the helm over! Yachting 141:182-4+ Ap '77

RYAN, Robert J. Jr

Department discusses CIEC and developing-country debt; statement, June 29, 1977. Dept State Bull 77:179-82 Ag 8 '77

RYAN, Tubal Claude

Ryan. P. Garrison. Flying 101:248-9 S '77 *

RYAN, William E.

Health costs containment; address, August 9, 1977. Vital Speeches 43:753-6 O 1 '77

RYCKMANS, Pierre

China's war on the mind; excerpt from Chinese shadows. il Sat R 4:14-16+ Je 25 '77

RYE

Rye helps worn-out backyards. Org Gard & Farm 24:174-5 S '77

Hybrids

See also

Triticale

RYERSON Polytechnical Institute, Toronto. See Colleges and universities—Canada

RYGH, Gerald L.

Christmas in Advent. Chr Cent 94:1133 D 7 '77

RYOR, John
Declining SAT scores. Todays Educ 66:6+ N '77
Integrating the handicapped; NEA resolution 77-33: education for all handicapped children. Todays Educ 66:24-6 S '77
U.S. Department of Education; the case for it Current 193:16-21 My '77
Victory for teacher power. Todays Educ 66:5 Ja '77

RYSANEK, Leonie
Salome and me; interview, ed by S. Von Buchau. il Opera N 41:20+ F 12 '77

RYTHER, John H. See Officer, C. B. jt auth

S

S&H Green Stamps. See Sperry and Hutchinson Company

S. Pearson & Son, Ltd. See Pearson, S, & Son, Ltd

SAB. See School of American Ballet

SAG. See Screen Actors Guild

SALALM (Seminar on the Acquisition of Latin American Library Materials) See Library institutes and workshops

SALT. See Strategic Arms Limitation Talks

SAMSO (Space and Missile Systems Organization) See United States—Air Force—Systems Command

SAS. See Scandinavian Airlines System

SAT. See College Entrance Examination Board—Scholastic Aptitude Test

SAW (surface acoustic wave) devices. See Acoustic surface wave devices

SBA. See United States—Small Business Administration

SCA Services Inc
Trash collector who cleaned house; SEC suit against SCA Services Inc. Bus W p25-6 Ag 22 '77

SCM Corporation
Long turnaround at SCM Corp. por Duns R 109:22-3 Ap '77
Streamlining the management at SCM; reorganizing Glidden-Durkee Div. il Bus W p96+ F 21 '77

SCR (silicon controlled rectifier) See Electric current rectifiers

SDS. See Students for a Democratic Society (organization)

SEC. See United States—Securities and Exchange Commission

SERI. See Solar Energy Research Institute (proposed)

SES (surface effect ships) See Air cushion vehicles

S. G. Warburg and Company. See London—Banks

SIDS (sudden infant death syndrome) See Infant mortality

SIGMA. See Society of Independent Gasoline Marketers of America

SIPI. See Scientists' Institute for Public Information

SIPRI. See Stockholm International Peace Research Institute

SIR Consorzio Industriale. See Chemical industries —Italy

SITE (Satellite Instructional Television Experiment) See Communications satellites—Educational use

SITE (Sculpture In the Environment) Inc. See Site, Inc

SLA. See Special Libraries Association; See Symbionese Liberation Army

SLR cameras. See Cameras, Single-lens reflex

SLR lenses. See Lenses, Photographic

SORC (Southern Ocean Racing Conference) See Yacht racing

S.O.S. Consolidated Inc. See Conglomerate corporations

SPRCCNY (State Park and Recreation Commission for the City of New York) See New York (state)—State Park and Recreation Commission for the City of New York

SRAM (short-range attack missile) See Guided missiles—Launching from airplanes

SRI International
Tale of SRI's golden fleece. D. Shapley. Science 197:1165 S 16 '77

S. S. Kresge Company. See Kresge, S. S, Company

SS troops. See National socialism

SSB radio. See Radio, Single sideband

SSP (semisubmerged stable platform) See Ships

SST (super sonic transport) See Airplanes, Supersonic

STARPAHC (space technology applied to rural Papago advanced health care) See Indians of North America—Medical care

STOL airplanes. See Airplanes, Short take-off and landing

SUNY (State University of New York) See New York (state). State University

SV40 virus. See Simian viruses

SWAPO. See Southwest Africa People's Organization

SWLA. See Southwestern Library Association

SWR meters. See Electric meters

SX-70 cameras. See Cameras, Instant print

SAAB (automobile) See Automobiles, Foreign

SAAB-Scania (firm)-Volvo Company merger. See Automobile industry—Acquisitions and mergers

SAAVEDRA, Juan M. and others
Phenylethanolamine: a new putative neurotransmitter in aplysia. bibl il Science 195:1004-6 Mr 11 '77

SABATA, Victor de
Weingartner, Kleiber, De Sabata: a matter of record. H. Goldsmith. pors Hi Fi 27:94-6 S '77 *

SABBATH
See also
Sunday

SABBATH labor. See Hours of labor

SABENA Belgian World Airlines. See Airlines—Belgium

SABER saws. See Saws

SABIN, Albert B.
Polio: Salk challenges safety of Sabin's live-virus vaccine. P. M. Boffey. Science 196:35 Ap 1 '77 *

SABINE, David B.
Ethan Allen and the Green Mountain Boys. il pors Am Hist Illus 11:8-15 Ja '77

SABOL, Blair
I love me—and why not. il Mademoiselle 83:147-8+ F '77
Yankee pilgrim in the Old South. il N Y Times Mag p38-40+ Ap 24 '77
(ed) See Fawcett-Majors, F. Farrah's way

SABOL, James W.
Selecting instructional materials. il Engl J 66:9-14 Ja '77

SABRELINER Division. See Rockwell International Corporation

SABRY, Zak. See Fremes, R. jt auth

SACCHARIDES
See also
Polysaccharides

SACCHARIN. See Sugar substitutes

SACCO-Vanzetti case
End of the myth. F. Russell. Nat R 29:938-41 Ag 19 '77
Massachusetts pays its debt. C. McWilliams. Nation 225:133-5 Ag 20 '77
Men and the symbols: Sacco and Vanzetti. E. Foner. il Nation 225:135-41 Ag 20 '77
Never-ending wrong. K. A. Porter. il pors Atlantic 239:37-48+ Je '77
That agony is our triumph. E. Knoll. Progressive 41:11 Ag '77

SACKS, Michael Paul
Sexual equality and Soviet women. bibl Society 14:48-51 Jl '77

SACKVILLE-WEST, Victoria Mary
Summer garden sampler; excerpt from A joy of gardening. il Horticulture 55:16-17 Jl '77
about
Sackville-West's Sissinghurst. A. Eliot. bibl il Horticulture 55:12-15 Jl '77 *

SACRAMENTO, Calif.

Architecture

Sunrise Apartments, Sacramento, California. il Archit Rec 161:122-3 mid-My '77

Gardens

Unexpected harvest: California gardens that raise community consciousness. R. L. Tracy. il Horticulture 55:46-9 Jl '77

SACRAMENTS
Our apostasy in worship. J. F. White. Chr Cent 94:842-5 S 28 '77
See also
Catholic Church—Eucharist
Confirmation (sacrament)
Penance

SACRED books
See also
Bible

SACRED Congregation for Catholic Education. See Congregation for Catholic Education

SACRED music. See Church music

SACRED Music Society of America
Report:
Licinio Refice's Cecilia. R. Jacobson. Opera N 41:28 F 26 '77

SACRIFICE, Human
Enigma of Aztec sacrifice. M. Harner. il map Natur Hist 86:46-51 bibl(p 100) Ap '77; Discussion. 86:20+ My '77
Who killed the bog men of Denmark? And why? theory of Tollund Man as victim of human sacrifice advanced by P. V. Glob. M. Shadbolt. il Read Digest 110:197-200+ Je '77

SADAT, Anwar
Anatomy of a bold action; interview, ed by M. Gart and W. Wynn. pors Time 111:30+ Ja 2 '78
Message to America. por Time 109:35 F 28 '77
News conference by Secretary Vance and President Sadat, Alexandria, August 2. Dept State Bull 77:329-33 S 12 '77
News conference by Secretary Vance and President Sadat, Cairo, February 17. Dept State Bull 76:211-14 Mr 14 '77
Peace with justice; address, November 20, 1977. Vital Speeches 44:100-5 D 1 '77; Excerpts. Newsweek 90:43 N 28 '77
President Sadat of Egypt visits Washington; exchange of remarks, April 4, 1977. Dept State Bull 76:435-6 My 2 '77
Reflections from Cell 54; excerpts from In search of identity. il Time 111:28-9 Ja 2 '78
Sadat: unique moment; interview, ed by W. E. Schmidt and P. Martin. pors Newsweek 90:54+ D 12 '77
Sadat: why Russia balks at peace; interview; ed by D. B. Richardson. por U.S. News 83:13 D 19 '77
What Sadat will seek from Carter; interview, ed by L. H. Young and R. Taggiasco. pors Bus W p96-9 Ap 4 '77

about

Actor with a will of iron. R. Ajemian. il pors Time 111:22+ Ja 2 '78 *
Assad: Sadat's folly; excerpts from interview; ed by A. de Borchgrave. H. Assad. il pors Newsweek 91:41-2+ Ja 16 '78 *
Bypassing the PLO? D. Holt and others. il por Newsweek 90:33 D 5 '77 *
Cairo: Sadat's bold gamble. B. Came. il por Newsweek 89:28-9 F 21 '77 *
Christmas summit. K. Willenson and others. il pors Newsweek 91:12-14 Ja 2 '78 *
Conference in Cairo. T. Mathews and others. il por Newsweek 90:20-2 D 19 '77 *
Four crises: a wife's view; interview, ed by W. Wynn. J. Sadat. por Time 111:33 Ja 2 '78 *
Goodbye, Arab solidarity. il por Time 110:38-40+ D 12 '77 *
Libya-Egypt clash—latest threat to Mideast peace; with interview with M. al-Qaddafi. il map U.S. News 83:36-8 Ag 8 '77 *
Long road to Geneva. A. Deming and others. pors Newsweek 90:27-9 Ag 15 '77 *
Man of the year. il pors Time 111:10-17 Ja 2 '78 *
Mideast: on to Cairo? R. Steele and others. il pors Newsweek 90:24-6+ D 5 '77 *
Mideast: phase 2. K. Willenson and others. il pors map Newsweek 91:28-31 Ja 9 '78 *
Morning after Ismailia. map Time 111:16-17 Ja 9 '78 *
Promises, promises. W. E. Schmidt. il Newsweek 90:51-2 N 28 '77 *
Revenge in the desert. pors map Time 110:20 Ag 1 '77 *
Rushing toward Cairo. il por map Time 110:26-8 D 19 '77 *
Sadat in trouble. Nat R 29:372 Ap 1 '77 *
Sadat's confidence restored. il pors Time 111:24+ Ja 16 '78 *
Sadat's darkest hour. R. Carroll and others. il por Newsweek 89:51-2 Ja 31 '77 *
Sadat's sorry state. M. Kondracke. New Repub 176:14-16 Mr 19 '77 *
Sadat's stormy wake. R. Steele and others. il Newsweek 90:51+ D 12 '77 *
Sound and the fury of the poor. il Time 109:29-30 Ja 31 '77 *
Summit: peeks behind the scenes. D. Halevy. il pors Time 111:18 Ja 9 '78 *
They are fated to succeed. H. Kissinger. il pors Time 111:34-5 Ja 2 '78 *
Two Mideast leaders on the hot seat. pors U.S. News 83:28 N 28 '77 *
What's holding up peace. il por U.S. News 84:24-5 Ja 9 '78 *
Will Sadat survive Egypt's mounting woes? il U.S. News 82:21-2 F 28 '77 *

Visit to Israel, 1977

Anatomy of a bold action; interview, ed by M. Gart and W. Wynn. A. Sadat. pors Time 111:30+ Ja 2 '78
Breakthrough in Middle East. il U.S. News 83:25-7 N 28 '77
Cronkite summit? D. M. Alpern and B. Carter. il por Newsweek 90:129 N 28 '77
Euphoric Israel. M. J. Kubic. il Newsweek 90:34 D 5 '77
Everything is open to negotiation; address, November 20, 1977. M. Begin. Vital Speeches 44:105-8 D 1 '77
Hope in the Middle East. New Repub 177:5-6 D 3 '77
Hussein: close ranks; excerpts from interview, ed by A. de Borchgrave. Hussein. por Newsweek 90:59-60+ D 12 '77
Israelis watch Begin: can he bend or must he go? M. Viorst. Nation 225:686-90 D 24 '77
Mohammed goes to the mountain. America 137:393 D 3 '77
Next step in Mideast; with report by Dennis Mullin. il por U.S. News 83:16-17 D 5 '77
Not-so-odd couple. P. Webb and M. J. Kubic. il pors Newsweek 90:49 N 28 '77
Notes and comment. New Yorker 53:37-8 D 5; 17 D 26 '77; 19 Ja 9 '78
Of many things. J. O'Hare. America 137:389 D 3 '77
Our ugly-Arab complex. M. Greenfield. Newsweek 90:110 D 5 '77
Peace with justice; address, November 20, 1977. A. Sadat. Vital Speeches 44:100-5 D 1 '77
Pharaoh in the promised land. G. F. Will. Newsweek 90:132 N 28 '77
Sadat in Israel. R. Steele and others. il pors maps Newsweek 90:36-40+ N 28 '77
Sadat in Jerusalem. Nat R 29:1406 D 9 '77
Sadat initiative. W. C. McWilliams. Commonweal 104:806-8 D 23 '77
Sadat: the hour of decision; Carter too played a part. il Time 110:38-41+ D 5 '77
Sadat's courage, Begin's desire. New Repub 177:8-9 N 26 '77
Sadat's historic trip. J. M. Wall. Chr Cent 94:1107-8 N 30 '77
Sadat's sacred mission. il pors Time 110:28-34+ N 28 '77
Support for Sadat. America 137:410-11 D 10 '77
TV goes into diplomacy; Time essay. L. Morrow. il Time 110:44 D 5 '77
Tales of the Mideast. M. J. Kubic and others. il por Newsweek 90:56 D 12 '77
Television. P. Sourian. Nation 225:670 D 17 '77
Triumph of the negative. Nation 225:578 D 3 '77
Unspoken ultimatum to the Arabs. Bus W p35 D 5 '77
Violent recoil. T. Mathews and others. il Newsweek 90:44 N 28 '77
Weekend in Jerusalem; photographs. Newsweek 90:27-8 D 5 '77
Wild gamble? T. Clifton. Newsweek 90:60 D 12 '77

Visit to the United States, 1977

Chemistry worked. il por Time 109:28 Ap 18 '77
How to welcome President Sadat. il New Repub 176:5-6+ Ap 9 '77
President Sadat of Egypt visits Washington; exchange of remarks, April 4, 1977. J. Carter; A. Sadat. Dept State Bull 76:434-6 My 2 '77
Small-town boy with shopping list. il por Time 109:42 Ap 11 '7

SADAT, Jehan
Four crises: a wife's view; interview, ed by W. Wynn. por Time 111:33 Ja 2 '78

SADD, Susan. See Tavris, C. jt auth

SADDLER, Jeanne
Henry G. Parks gives his rules for success. il pors Ebony 32:100-2+ Mr '77

SADDLERY
Great Saddles of the West: an interview with Paul Rossi; ed by K. Mayer. P. Rossi. il Am Artist 41:64-7+ Ag '77

SADDLES. See Saddlery

SADHU, Arun
Kondiba's daring dive. il Read Digest 111:11-12+ D '77

SADIS, Harvey
Marriage contract renewed. pors Ms 6:21 Jl '77

SADLOWSKI, Edward
Coming revolt in labor. S. Lens. Progressive 41:26-30 Ap '77 *
McBride apparent victor in Steelworkers contest. L. Bornstein and others. M Labor R 100:84 Ap '77 *
McBride for Abel. C. O. Rice. Commonweal 104:166-7 Mr 18 '77 *
No go for Oilcan Eddie. por Time 109:67 F 21 '77 *
Steel: the ins have it. T. Nicholson and others. pors Newsweek 89:76 F 21 '77 *
Steelworkers' election grows to a national issue. il pors Bus W p69-71 Ja 24 '77 *
Steelworkers go for McBride. Bus W p31 F 21 '77 *
Struggle in steel. K. Bode. New Repub 176:10-13 F 5 '77 *

SAENZ, A. W. and others
Telecommunication with neutrino beams. bibl il Science 198:295-7 O 21 '77

SAFARI. See Hunting—Africa

SAFECO Corporation. See Insurance companies

SAFEER Company. See Business consultants

SAFETY, Industrial. See Industrial safety

SAFETY at sea
See also
Navigation

SAFETY belts
See also
Automobiles—Safety belts

SAFETY devices and measures. See Accidents—Prevention

SAFETY latches
See also
Latches

SAFEWAY Stores, Inc
Safeway: selling nongrocery items to cure the supermarket blahs. il por Bus W p52-6+ Mr 7 '77

SAFFER, Margaret. See Yesberger, J. jt auth

SAFFIR, Leonard
New faces among the big-city dailies. il por Bus W p25 Ja 9 '78 *
Tribulations. il por Time 110:101-2 O 3 '77 *
SAFFORD, James O. 3d. See Fox, E. W. jt auth
SAFIRE, William
China: unraveling the new mysteries. il pors N Y Times Mag p33-4+ Je 19 '77
Doing a number on words. N Y Times Mag p95 F 13 '77
Full disclosure; story; excerpt from novel. Ladies Home J 94:113-15 Jl '77
Lancegate: why Carter stuck it out. il pors N Y Times Mag p37-9+ O 16 '77
about
Punder on the right. por Time 110:101 O 3 '77 *
Savage fire: the importance of Bill Safire. R. Reeves. por Esquire 89:38+ Ja '78 *
Word from Washington. F. Getlein. Progressive 41:12-13 D '77 *
SAFRAN, Claire
How today's couples are making it as parents. il Redbook 148:108-9+ Mr '77
—See Webb, M. jt auth
SAGAN, Carl
Carl Sagan on science. New Repub 177:30-3 D 3 '77
Cosmic calendar; excerpt from The dragons of Eden. il Read Digest 111:148-9 O '77
God and Norman Bloom. il Am Scholar 46:460-6 Aut '77
In praise of science and technology. New Repub 176:21-2+ Ja 22 '77; Same with title Role of science and technology. Current 192:47-53 Ap '77
Miss Universe. il N Y Times Mag p32+ O 23 '77
Next great leap into space. il N Y Times Mag p12-16+ Jl 10 '77
PW interviews; ed by J. F. Baker. por Pub W 211:8-9 My 2 '77
Planetary exploration. por Newsweek 89:9 Je 20 '77
about
Seeking other worlds. D. Gelman and others. il pors Newsweek 90:46-7+ Ag 15 '77 *
SAGAN, Miriam
Bag of waters; poem. Mademoiselle 83:106 N '77
SAGARIN, Dave
Home-movie sound that sounds good. il Pop Mech 149:66-7 Ja '78
SAGE Lake. See Lakes—Michigan
SAGER, Carole Bayer
Carole Bayer Sager—so much is so right. A. Swartley. por Hi Fi 27:128 Je '77 *
SAGES (plants)
Sage for spring cooking. R. Langer. House & Gard 149:12 Ap '77
SAGUARO. See Cactus
SAHARA Desert
Case study in survival; animal life. C. Grenot and R. Vernet. il UNESCO Courier 30:25-8 Jl '77
Expanding desert creates grim beauty but also threatens crucial cropland; Western Desert of Egypt. F. El-Baz. il Smithsonian 8:34-41 Je '77
Sahara: the growing giant. B. A. Ovrut and S. Ovrut. il Sci Digest 81:28-32 F '77
SAID, Abdul Aziz
Pursuing human dignity. bibl il Society 15:34-8 N '77
SAILBOAT building. See Boatbuilding
SAILBOAT masts. See Masts and rigging
SAILBOAT racing
Art of short course tactics. N. Fowler. il Yachting 141:46+ Je '77
Calendar of major sailing events. See issues of Yachting
College racing. G. Hall. See issues of Yachting
Getting away from it all; Star Bacardi Cup and Sunfish World Championships. E. Horan. il Yachting 141:81-3 Ap '77
Little America's Cup: U.S. keeps it; International Catamaran Challange Trophy. L. Lindeman. il Yachting 142:209-10 O '77
Long day's journey into night; Championship of Champions. J. Lamb. il Sports Illus 47:24-5 N 28 '77
Month in yachting; Kiel Week. M. Griffith. Yachting 142:206-7+ O '77
News from yachting centers. See issues of Yachting
Not yet ready to burn their bridges; college women's regatta in New York City. J. Lamb. il Sports Illus 46:55-6+ Je 6 '77
Notes from the classes (cont of) With the racing classes; ed by E. Horan. See issues of Yachting
Olympic development clinics. J. Rousmaniere. il Yachting 142:50+ O '77
One-of-a-kind comes full circle. B. Bavier. Yachting 141:52 Je '77
One-of-a-kind regatta. il Yachting 142:70-1 Ag '77
Reflections on the one-of-a-kind. D. Rose. il Yachting 142:42+ Ag '77
Singlehanders and the OOAK. D. Tillman. il Yachting 142:40+ D '77
Skûtsjesilen. M. Wiley. il Yachting 141:84-6 Mr '77
Testing the gate start. E. Adams. Yachting 141:48+ Je '77
Texas trailable tussle; Chrysler 22 class. il Yachting 141:96-7 Mr '77
12 days in a hobie . . . racing! catamarans. il Yachting 142:62-3 Jl '77
Weather forecasting for the racing sailor; Olympic Trials, 1976. R. L. Mairs. il map Yachting 142:66-9+ Ag '77
World away from Newport. E. Horan. il Yachting 142:58-62+ O '77
Yachting's big One-of-a-kind Regatta. J. Rousmaniere; E. Horan. il Yachting 142:44-9+ Jl '77
See also
Yacht racing

Crews

See Seamen

Photographs

Fireballs. G. Silk. il Yachting 141:88-91 Mr '77
SAILBOATS
Back to basics; Freedom 40 cat ketch. B. Robinson. il Yachting 141:72-5 Ap '77
Condition report:
C&C29. W. E. Tobin. il Motor B & S 139:26-7+ Je '77
DownEaster 32. G. Hammond. il Motor B & S 139:46-7+ My '77
Galway Blazer II; voyage around Antarctica. W. B. L. King. il Yachting 141:139-41 Je '77
Hotspur story; cutter. W. M. Eichbaum. il Yachting 141:151-4 Je '77
New boats in Yachting. See occasional issues of Yachting
New thoughts on an old boat; ketch, Tzu Hang. R. Nance. il Yachting 141:74-7 Je '77
Sailboats for 1978. il Yachting 142:107-8+ O '77
Sailboats. il Motor B & S 141:170-82 Ja '78
Tempest: an endangered species? D. McComb. il Yachting 141:60+ My '77
32 years of Thistles. J. Rousmaniere. il Yachting 141:79-81 Je '77
Voyage of Brendan. T. Severin. il map Nat Geog 152:770-97 D '77
See also
Catamarans
Cruisers (pleasure boats)
Masts and rigging
Sails
Trimarans
Yachts and yachting

Automobile trailer combination

New big boats you take in tow; trailerables. B. McKeown. il Pop Mech 147:74+ My '77

Chartering

See Sailboats—Leasing and renting

Design

New Tahiti built of steel. il Mech Illus 73:48-9+ S '77
Setting sail for Tahiti. S. Doherty. il Mech Illus 73:104+ D '77

Equipment

Rope traveler. D. Tillman. il Yachting 141:52+ F '77
Sailor's Bimini top; awning. T. L. Finnan. il Motor B & S 139:132 Je '77
Thoughts on midship travelers. B. Roberts. il Yachting 141:58+ Mr '77

Handling

Downwind control—not disaster! (cont) D. Deaver. il Yachting 141:82-4+ F '77
How to heave-to. R. Basham. il Yachting 142:123-5 D '77

Interior decoration

See Boat decoration

Leasing and renting

Renting a sailboat in Seattle. il Sunset 158:52 My '77

Maintenance and repair

Springtime sailboat work. M. Perry. il Motor B & S 139:99-101 Ap '77

Materials

See Boats—Materials

Purchasing

See Boats—Purchasing

Steering gear

See Boats—Steering gear

Testing

Test it yourself: sail. R. Stephens, Jr. il Motor B & S 141:128-9+ Ja '78
SAILBOATS, Model. See Ship and boat models
SAILBOATS, Remodeled
Rebirth of Bambino. L. B. Off. il Yachting 141:176+ Ap '77
Restoration of Lightning Number One. J. Ryan. il Yachting 141:134+ Ap '77
SAILCLOTH. See Sails—Materials

SAILE, Bob
Cougar attacks: new crisis for the big cats. il map Outdoor Life 160:66-8+ Ag '77
Trout truths. il por Outdoor Life 160:86-9 N '77

SAILFISH fishing
Bimini blues; Bimini Big Game Club's Members Tournament for billfish. O. Moore. il Motor B & S 140:76-7+ Ag '77
Pursuing Papa's marlin; Hemingway Billfish Tournament. R. F. Jones. il Sports Illus 47: 55-8+ Ag 1 '77

SAILING
Boats in blue: sailing at the U.S. Naval Academy. A. M. Hays. Yachting 141:158+ Je '77
See also
Cruising
Navigation
Sailboat racing
Seamen
Voyages
Yachts and yachting

Study and teaching

Family sailing; Annapolis sailing school. il Bet Hom & Gard 55:175-6+ Jl '77
How to improve your sailing skills. G. Jobson. il por Yachting 141:58+ Ap '77
Louise Burke; Naval Academy sailing coach. A. M. Hays. il pors Yachting 142:74-5 Jl '77

SAILING schools. See Sailing—Study and teaching

SAILING ships. See Sailing vessels

SAILING vessels
Backyard galleon. il Mech Illus 73:18 Mr '77
Million dollar dream; brig, Unicorn. M. Goodman and T. Wilson. il por Motor B & S 139:51-3+ Ap '77
Peking & Wavertree: refurbishing square-riggers at South Street Sea Port Museum. E. H. Fitzelle. il Oceans 10:4-10 My '77
Return of Pilgrim. G. Jones. il Sea Front 23: 331-3 N '77
See also
Sloops

SAILING yachts. See Yachts and yachting

SAILORS. See Seamen

SAILORS songs
Sea shanties. R. J. Schwendinger. il Am West 14:50-5 My '77

SAILPLANES. See Gliders (aeronautics)

SAILS
Add a sail for under $100. S. James. il Pop Mech 147:104-5+ Ap '77
Double-drum roller furling. R. R. Grams. il Motor B & S 140:106 Ag '77
End-of-season sail maintenance. J. Grant. il Motor B & S 140:116-17 O '77
Other ways to furl and reef. F. Hibberd. Yachting 141:32+ F '77
Racing clinic; offshore:
IOR sail inventory limits. B. Barton. il Yachting 141:56+ Mr '77
Problems in sail design. S. Haarstick. il Yachting 141:50+ Je '77
Rolling up the mainsail. T. Gibbs. il Yachting 141:30+ F '77
Shortening sail offshore; reefing. T. Jones. il Motor B & S 140:66-7+ S '77
Shorthanded sail shortening. G. H. Forrest. il Motor B & S 139:81-3 F '77
Spinnakers: the eternal trade-off. S. Lindsay. il Yachting 141:100-2 My '77

Materials

Triaxial sailcloth. J. Rousmaniere. il Yachting 142:94+ Jl '77

SAINT, William S. and Coward, E. W. Jr
Agriculture and behavioral science: emerging orientations. bibl Science 197:733-7 Ag 19 '77

ST ANDREWS Nursery School, Cherry Hill, N.J.
See Nursery schools

ST AUGUSTINE, Fla.
St Augustine: old Spain in the New World. Y. Gardozo. il Trav/Holiday 148:52-7 N '77

ST AUGUSTINE volcano, Alaska. See Volcanoes

ST CHRISTOPHER'S Hospice. See London—Hospitals

ST CLAIR, Jack B.
White hats and white coats; address, March 9, 1977. Vital Speeches 43:414-16 Ap 15 '77

ST CLOUD, Minn.

Religious institutions and affairs

See Minnesota—Religious institutions and affairs

ST CROIX Island
Scuba school. il Seventeen 36:163 Mr '77

ST CROIX National Scenic Riverway
Our wild and scenic rivers. D. S. Boyer. il Nat Geog 152:30-7 Jl '77

ST EMILION, France
St Emilion: warm, open and easy to like. F. J. Prial. il N Y Times Mag p45-7 Ag 7 '77

ST FRANCIS Hotel. See San Francisco—Hotels, restaurants, etc.

ST FRANCIS Yacht Club. See Yacht clubs

ST GEORGE, Andrew
Significant little gun. il por Esquire 88:69-72+ Ag '77

ST GERMAIN, Fernand Joseph
Bank reform loses a lot of momentum. il por Bus W p43 O 3 '77 •

SAINT Joan; drama. See Shaw, G. B.

ST JOHN, David
Shore; poem. New Yorker 53:46 My 9 '77

about

Comment. D. Allen. Poetry 130:344-6 S '77 •

ST JOHN, Jeffrey
Hemisphere of misunderstanding; address, September 19, 1977. Vital Speeches 44:5-9 O 15 '77

ST JOHN Island

History

St John: a trip through time. M. J. Goodban. il Nat Parks & Con Mag 51:16-18 F '77

ST JOHN River
Keel of Lake Dickey; canoe trip; reprint from May 3, 1976 issue of New Yorker; with editorial comment. J. McPhee. il map Liv Wildn 40:3, 4-19+ O '76
Maine: damned if you do. . .; Dickey-Lincoln project. D. Holt and others. il map Newsweek 91:21 Ja 2 '78
On dumping Dickey and saving the St John; with editorial comment. R. Saltonstall, Jr. Liv Wildn 40:3, 20-1 O '76

ST JOSEPH River
Make the river do the work. B. East. il por Outdoor Life 160:78-81+ O '77

ST LAURENT, Yves Mathieu
Yves Saint Laurent; interview; ed by P. O'Higgins. il House B 119:74-5+ F '77

about

All about Yves. A. Burgess. il pors N Y Times Mag p 118-21+ S 11 '77 •

ST LAWRENCE, Gulf of
Warm water to the north. J. E. McKelvy, Jr. il map Yachting 141:67-9 Mr '77

ST LAWRENCE River
Encore for the snow goose? G. Gruenefeld. il Int Wildlife 7:17-20 N '77
St Lawrence and the Thousand Islands; symposium. il Conservationist 31:2-32 Mr '77

ST LOUIS
Senior home security program aids St Louis elderly. il Aging 266:5 D '76

Air pollution

Downwind; SO_2 transport and transformation processes. K. H. Hohenemser. il Environment 19:2-4 Ap '77

Crime

Strange murder of Homer G. Phillips. E. T. Clayton. il pors Ebony 32:160-2+ S '77

Description

St Louis. il Bet Hom & Gard 55:239-40 N '77

Education

What's in this building, anyway? supergraphic project at Rosati-Kain High School. M. Scherer. il Design (US) 78:13-17 Spr '77

Electric power

St Louis trash plan goes down the drain; a Union Electric Co. project. Bus W p30-1 F 28 '77

Galleries and museums

See also
St Louis Art Museum

Hotels, restaurants, etc.

Place for your boardinghouse reach; Jefferson Avenue Boarding House. C. G. Burck. il Fortune 95:191-2 F '77

Housing

When tenants take over; Carr Square. il Time 110:22 Ag 29 '77

Music

New Music Circle; performance of modern music. K. E. Miller. Hi Fi 27:MA30+ S '77
See also
Opera—Missouri

Police

Off the force; Ed Fitzgerald. M. J. Albrecht. Progressive 41:42 My '77

Sanitary affairs

Union Electric gives up waste fuel plan; with editorial statement by W. L. Forestall. Am City & County 92:13+, 106 Ap '77

ST LOUIS Art Museum
Meissen. il Ceram Mo 25:87+ D '77

ST LOUIS-San Francisco Railway Company-Burlington Northern Inc. merger. See Railroads—Acquisitions and mergers

ST LUKE'S Chamber Ensemble. See Chamber orchestras

ST MAARTIN. See St Martin (island)

ST MAGNUS Festival. See Music festivals—Scotland

ST MARK'S Dance Company. See Dance companies

ST MARTIN (island)
Special pleasures of renting a house of your own in St Martin. W. P. Rayner. il House & Gard 149:62+ S '77

ST MARTIN'S Press. See Publishers and publishing—United States

SAINT MICHEL, Mont, France. See Mont Saint Michel, France

ST PAUL
Their elm forest is doomed, but Twin Cities are ready. F. Graham, Jr. Audubon 79:136-9 Jl '77

City planning

See also
Twin Cities Metropolitan Council

Music

Debuts & reappearances. il Hi Fi 27:MA27+ Ag '77
See also
Opera—Minnesota

ST PAUL Chamber Orchestra. See Chamber orchestras

ST PETER'S Lutheran Church. See New York (city)—Churches

ST PETERSBURG, Fla.

Education

Multi-image productions are magical motivators. C. M. Aborn. bibl il por SLJ 23:33-7 Ap '77

SAINT-SAËNS, Camille
Saint-Saëns et Dalila. W. Ashbrook. il Opera N 41:26-7 Ap 16 '77 *
Samson and Dalila. Reviews
Dance Mag 51:91 Jl '77 *
Opera N il 41:18+ Ap 16 '77 *

SAINT-STANISLAS, Sister Marie Madeleine Hachard. See Hachard, M. M.

ST STEPHEN'S crown. See Crowns

ST VALENTINES Day. See Valentines Day

ST VINCENT Medical Center. See Los Angeles—Hospitals

SAINTS
Patron saints. C. Greulich. Sat Eve Post 249:41+ Ap '77
Timely saints. A. McCarthy. Commonweal 104:169+ Mr 18 '77
See also
Beatification
Canonization
Hubert, Saint
Loyola, Ignatius of, Saint
Mary Magdalene, Saint
More, T.
Neumann, J. N.
Paul, Saint
Sharbel Makhlouf, Saint
Thomas Aquinas, Saint

SAITO, Hiroshi
We are being used as scapegoats; interview. Forbes 120:36 N 15 '77

SAKHAROV, Andreĭ Dmitrievich
Sakharov on human rights; excerpts from interview, ed by F. Coleman. il por Newsweek 89:31+ Mr 14 '77

about

Because we care about people. J. M. Wall. Chr Cent 94:187-8 Mr 2 '77 *
Daring to talk about human rights. por Time 109:38 F 7 '77 *
Letter to a friend. por Time 109:30-1 F 28 '77 *
Pilgrim of conscience. por Time 109:21 F 21 '77 *

SAKONNET Vineyard. See Wine industry

SAKSENA, Jogendra
Henna for happiness. il UNESCO Courier 30:18-22 F '77

SAKURAGAWA, Norio, and others
Niemann-Pick disease experimental model: sphingomyelinase reduction induced by AY-9944. bibl il Science 196:317-19 Ap 15 '77

SAKURAI, Syo, and others
3β-Hydroxy-5α-cholestan-6-one: a possible precursor of α-ecdysone biosynthesis. bibl il Science 198:627-9 N 11 '77

SALA, Martin A.
Core memories—how they work. il Radio-Electr 48:54-5 S '77

SALAD dressings
Garden fresh herbs: the secret in the salad. A. Hirsch. Org Gard & Farm 24:102-3 N '77

SALAD greens. See Greens, Edible

SALADS
Antipasto salad goes together in minutes, keeps. il Sunset 158:222 My '77
Anything goes with coleslaw. . .including fruits, nuts, cheese, ham. il Sunset 158:210 Ap '77
Chicken salad from Vietnam. il Sunset 158:206 Mr '77
Crispy Oriental shrimp salads. il Sunset 159:150 S '77
Easy-to-fix fruit salads. il Bet Hom & Gard 55:210-11 O '77
Five simple, elegant salads. J. Pepin. il House B 119:162 S '77
For super supper salads, try potatoes, rice, and pasta. R. Molter. il Parents Mag 52:72-3+ S '77
Fresh spinach salads. il Bet Hom & Gard 55:186 My '77
Harvest salads. il Bet Hom & Gard 55:119-20 Ag '77
Hearty salads make good meals. il Ebony 32:152+ O '77
It's salad, it's easy & it's dinner. P. Meyers. il Mademoiselle 83:208-9 S '77
Little table cooking is the salad secret. il Sunset 158:184 Mr '77
Molded salads. il Bet Hom & Gard 55:131-2 Je '77
Play it cool; rice salads. G. Steves. il Am Home 80:66-8 Ag '77
Potato salad winners. il Ladies Home J 94:86-7+ Ag '77
Salad arithmetic. il Seventeen 36:172-4 Je '77
Salad days. C. Claiborne and P. Franey. il N Y Times Mag p42 Jl 17 '77
Salad days. il Fam Health 9:40-3 Je '77
Salads with a new slant; vegetables. il House & Gard 150:104-5 Ja '78
7-salad buffet; vegetable salads. P. Meyers. il pors House & Gard 149:132-3+ Je '77
Substantial summer salads. il Bet Hom & Gard 54:105 Ag '76
Super salads for summer entertaining. il McCalls 104:150-1 Ag '77
These salads even travel well. il Sunset 159:180 N '77
26 super salads from around the world. il Good H 185:130-9+ Ag '77
Use thinnings for a thinning salad. il Sunset 158:202 My '77
Yes we have winter salads! il Redbook 148:128-9+ Mr '77

SALAMANDERS
Evidence for abnormal heart induction in cardiac-mutant salamanders (ambystoma mexicanum) L. F. Lemanski and others. bibl il Science 196:894-6 My 20 '77
Neoplastic and possibly related skin lesions in neotenic tiger salamanders from a sewage lagoon. F. L. Rose and J. C. Harshbarger. bibl il Science 196:315-17 Ap 15 '77; Reply with rejoinder. J. G. Windsor, Jr and others. 198:1280-1 D 23 '77
Woods are alive with salamanders. H. Ellis. il Nat Wildlife 15:42-5 O '77

SALAMONE, Frank A.
All resettled at Kainji? il Intellect 106:231-3 D '77

SALARIES
Is your salary up to par? il Changing T 31:24-7 N '77
Job strategies; 4 women who knew when to switch. bibl il Mademoiselle 83:150-1+ Mr '77
See also
Minimum wage
Wages
also subhead Salaries, allowances, etc. under various subjects, e. g. Teachers—Salaries, allowances, etc.

SALAS, Luis
LBJ accused. D. A. Williams and L. Donosky. il pors Newsweek 90:27 Ag 8 '77 *

SALEH, Jean
Inside story; interview, ed by C. Seebohm. il House & Gard 149:38+ My '77

SALEH, Mahmoud Abbas, and others
Polychlorobornane components of toxaphene: structure-toxicity relations and metabolic reductive dechlorination. bibl il Science 198:1256-8 D 23 '77

SALEM, Mass.

Galleries and museums

See also
Essex Institute, Salem, Mass.

Historic houses, sites, etc.

Historic houses owned by the Essex Institute in Salem, Massachusetts. G. W. R. Ward and B. M. Ward. bibl il Antiques 112:1130-47 D '77

SALEM, N.C. See Winston-Salem, N.C.

SALEM witchcraft. See Witchcraft

SALES, Richard W.
Two or three and God. Chr Cent 94:110-13 F 2 '77

SALES
Right time to buy anything. N. G. Rollins. il Good H 186:169 Ja '78
See also
Auctions

SALES agents. See Manufacturers agents

SALES catalogs. See Catalogs, Commercial

SALES incentives. See Incentives in industry

SALES Maids of America, Inc. See Manufacturers agents

SALES promotion
Improve distribution with your promotional mix. B. P. Shapiro. bibl f il Harvard Bus R 55:115-23 Mr '77
See also
Coupons
Industrial shows
SALESMEN and salesmanship
See also
Automobile salesmen
Manufacturers agents
Marketing
Sales promotion
Telephone selling
SALINAS, Enrique M. Jr
Texas piggy bank. D. Pauly and S. McGuire. il por Newsweek 90:86-7 S 12 '77 •
SALINAS, Calif
Libraries
See Libraries—California
SALINE water
Energy recovery from saline water by means of electrochemical cells. B. H. Clampitt and F. E. Kiviat; reply. A. F. Hadermann. il Science 197:598-9 Ag 5 '77
Salt fountain and other curiosities based on the different density of fluids. J. Walker. il Sci Am 237:142+ O '77
See also
Brine
Irrigation water—Salt content
Sea water
SALINGER, Pierre
Our man in Paris. por Time 110:103 N 28 '77 •
SALIS, Rodolphe
What is Montmartre? Nothing! What should it be? Everything! tr by G. Needham. M. Frèrebeau. il Art N 76:60-2 Mr '77 •
SALISBURY, Harrison E.
Americanization of Stalin's daughter. il por McCalls 104:75+ Ap '77
Now it's China's cultural thaw. il pors N Y Times Mag p49+ D 4 '77
On an unsolved mystery. Progressive 41:24-5 My '77
SALISBURY, England
Hometown in Britain. L. Halley. Sat R 5:22 N 26 '77
SALISBURY Iron Mine. See Iron mines and mining—United States
SALIT, Charles
PS guide to fire extinguishers. il Pop Sci 211:58+ D '77
SALIVA
New genetic marker in human parotid saliva (pm) S. Ikemoto and others. bibl il Science 197:378-9 Jl 22 '77
SALK, Darell. See Salk, J. E. jt auth
SALK, Jonas Edward
—and Salk, Darell
Control of influenza and poliomyelitis with killed virus vaccines. bibl il Science 195:835-47 Mr 4 '77
about
Polio: Salk challenges safety of Sabin's live-virus vaccine. P. M. Boffey. Science 196:35-6 Ap 1 '77 •
SALK, Lee
Can you work and be a good mother? Harp Baz 110:88-9+ Ag '77
Sharing Christmas with your children. Harp Baz 111:133+ D '77
Should your child be in therapy? Harp Baz 110:231+ S '77
You and your family; questions and answers. See issues of McCall's
SALLIE Mae. See Student Loan Marketing Association
SALMON, Paul Blair
Administrative team: a step forward or backward? Educ Digest 43:2-4 S '77
SALMON, Sydney E. See Hamburger, A. W. jt auth
SALMON-COX, Leslie. See Holzner, B. jt auth
SALMON
Detritus-based food webs: exploitation by juvenile chum salmon (oncorhynchus keta) J. Sibert and others. bibl il Science 196:649-50 My 6 '77
Help for salmon; work of R. A. Buck. D. Seamans. por Outdoor Life 160:100 Ag '77
Increasing frequency of thyroid goiters in coho salmon (oncorhynchus kisutch) in the Great Lakes. R. D. Moccia and others. bibl il Science 198:425-6 O 28 '77
Salmon for Hizzoner; stocking the Chicago River. R. Telander. il Sports Illus 46:60+ Mr 28 '77
See also
Cookery—Fish
SALMON fishing
About fishing and bears; encounter with brown bears while salmon fishing in Alaska. B. Brister. il Field & S 82:46-8+ Je '77
Coho salmon. D. Richey. il Outdoor Life 159:66-7 Je '77
Portland hitch on the Pinware; salmon fishing in Labrador. A. Cameron. il Field & S 81:62-4+ Ap '77
Seattle salmon fishing. il Sunset 158:92+ Ap '77
Tale of two rivers; salmon fishing in Canada and Norway. E. Zern. il Field & S 82:62-3 Jl '77
Update: trout/salmon; ed by J. Gibbs. il Outdoor Life 160:100 O; 102 N; 110 D '77; 161:106 Ja '78
SALMON River (Alaska)
Reporter at large; excerpt from Coming into the country. J. McPhee. New Yorker 53:47-8+ My 2; 88+ My 9 '77; Same abr with title Encircled river. il por map Liv Wildn 41:44-60 Jl '77
SALMON River (Idaho)
40-minute forward 40-year backward walk; trout fishing. T. Trueblood. il Field & S 81:8+ Ap '77
Maiden voyage; Middle Fork of Idaho's Salmon River. N. Scofield. il por Am Home 80:28-9 Jl '77
SALOME; opera. See Strauss, R.
SALOMON, George. See Feitelson, R. jt auth
SALOMON, Richard
Second thoughts on going public. il Harvard Bus R 55:126-31 S '77
SALON Nationale de la Photographie. See Photography—Exhibitions
SALONS, Beauty. See Beauty shops
SALPUKAS, Agis
Wall Street blues. il pors N Y Times Mag p42-4+ D 18 '77
SALSIFY
All the oysters don't grow in the ocean. J. Jankowiak. il Org Gard & Farm 24:156+ Ap '77
SALT, Barry
Film style and technology in the forties. il Film Q 31:46-57 Fall '77
SALT
Essence of life: salt. G. Young. il Nat Geog 152:380-401 S '77
Salt of the earth. I. Asimov. il Int Wildlife 7:30-6 Mr '77
Salt of the earth. R. Rodale. il Org Gard & Farm 24:52-5 Je '77
Season food the smart way—it could lengthen your life; effect of salt on health. S. L. Halpern. Vogue 167:80 O '77
See also
Brine
SALT and pepper grinders, shakers, etc.
Salt of the earth. il Ladies Home J 94:138+ My '77
SALT domes
Salt domes; storage for oil reserves. S. T. Atlas and W. J. Cook. il Newsweek 90:55 Ag 22 '77
Salting away oil. B. Spanke. il Pop Sci 212:77 Ja '78
SALT in the Bible. See Bible—Mineralogy
SALT in the body
See also
Animals, Effect of salt on
Osmoregulation
SALT industry
Shortage of salt to pour on the streets. il Bus W p34-5 F 14 '77
SALT Lake. See Great Salt Lake
SALT licks
Lure of the salt lick. P. Magida. il Int Wildlife 7:37 Mr '77
SALT marsh plants. See Marsh plants
SALT marshes. See Marshes, Tide
SALT talks. See Strategic Arms Limitation Talks
SALT water. See Saline water
SALT water aquariums. See Aquariums
SALT water fishing
Fighting chair. J. Hearst, Jr. See issues of Motor boating & sailing
Lure of surf fishing. P. Hellman. il N Y Times Mag p20-1+ O 2 '77
Magic of surf fishing. P. Smith. il Outdoor Life 160:82-3+ S '77
Sport fisherman. F. T. Moss. See issues of Yachting to August 1977
Update: salt water; ed by T. Paugh. il Outdoor Life 160:36 O; 56 N; 112 D '77; 161:102 Ja '78
See also
Bass fishing
Bluefish fishing
Bonefish fishing
Marlin fishing
Perch fishing
Sailfish fishing
Snook fishing
Swordfish fishing
Tarpon fishing
SALTCELLARS. See Salt and pepper grinders, shakers, etc.
SALTING (food preservation) See Food preservation and preservatives
SALTONSTALL, Richard, Jr
Of dams and Kate Furbish. il por Liv Wildn 40:42-3 Ja '77
On dumping Dickey and saving the St John. Liv Wildn 40:20-1 O '76
SALTS
See also
Plants, Effect of salts on
SALTS, Marine. See Sea water

SALUTATIONS
Greetings and salutations. Aristides. Am Scholar 47:16+ Wint '77
See also
Hand shaking
SALVADOR
See also
San Salvador (city)
Antiquities
Unraveling a Mayan mystery. R. J. Trotter. il map Sci N 111:74-5+ Ja 29 '77
Politics and government
El Salvador. S. Kinzer. New Repub 177:15-17 S 3 '77
El Salvador, a touchstone. Nation 224:164 F 12 '77
Religious institutions and affairs
See also
Catholic Church in Salvador
Church and social problems—Salvador
SALVAGE (airplanes)
Missing plane they had to find; recovering the F-14. C. Barton. il Pop Mech 147:69-73+ Je '77
Search for the missing tomcat; F-14 retrieved in North Atlantic. D. Reed. il Read Digest 110:79-83 Mr '77
SALVAGE (ships)
Buried but still a treasure; the Evangelista at Walker's Cay, Bahamas. B. Pearsall. il Sports Illus 46:56+ Mr 14 '77
Fit out for making money. H. Lake. il Pop Mech 147:101 F '77
See also
Treasure trove
SALVAGE (waste)
Ever see a worn-out paper clip? J. Brondfield. Read Digest 111:65-6+ N '77
See also
Automobiles—Wrecking
Refuse, Utilization of
SALVATION
Salvation according to Scripture: no middle ground. R. H. Gundry. Chr Today 22:14-16 D 9 '77
Update on Leonard Feeney. J. Deedy. Commonweal 104:5-7 Ja 7 '77
See also
Atonement
Covenants (theology)
SALYUT. See Space stations, Russian
SALZBERG, Ruth F.
Build a balloon—a 3-D project that flies. il Design (US) 78:10-12 Spr '77
SALZBURG
Music
See also
Opera—Austria
SALZBURG Easter Festival. See Music festivals—Austria
SALZBURG Festival. See Music festivals—Austria
SAM Davis Home, Smyrna. See Historic houses, sites, etc.—Tennessee
SAMARAS. See Fruit
SAMARITANS
Samaritans. S. Talmon. il Sci Am 236:100-8 Ja '77
SAMBAR, David
Very popular new issue. il por Forbes 120:188 N 15 '77 *
SAMBERG, James
Better look at binoculars. Field & S 82:20+ Ag '77
SAMIZDAT. See Underground literature
SAMPLERS
25 sensational samplers to stitch. il Good H 185: 128-33 O '77
SAMPLES, Junior
Record bass that made Junior Samples a TV star; interview. ed by J. Morison. il pors Outdoor Life 160:96-7 S '77
SAMPSON, Deborah. See Gannett, D. S.
SAMSON, Jack
Carter/Knox team wins a big one. pors Field & S 82:41+ S '77
Day of the elk. il Field & S 82:48-9+ O '77
Editorial. See issues of Field & stream
Great Kenya wildlife ripoff. il Field & S 82: 48-9+ D '77
SAMSON Agonistes; poem. See Milton, John
SAMSON and Dalila; opera. See Saint-Saëns, C.
SAMUEL, Leith
Spiritual lift no one is talking about. il Chr Today 21:10-12 Ja 21 '77
SAMUEL Eliot Morison Awards. See American heritage (periodical)
SAMUELS, John S. 3d
Outsider escalates a bank's family feud. por Bus W p44-5 N 14 '77 *
SAMUELS, Michael A.
Evolving African policy of the United States; address, August 18, 1977. Vital Speeches 43: 731-5 S 15 '77

SANACORE, Joseph
Reading supervisors—teachers have needs. bibl Clearing H 51:17-21 S '77
SAN ANDREAS fault. See Faults (geology)
SAN ANTONIO, Tex.
COPS comes to San Antonio. E. D. Yoes, Jr. Progressive 41:33-6 My '77
U.S. journal: San Antonio; Communities Organized for Public Service. C. Trillin. il New Yorker 53:92-4+ My 2 '77
Music
See also
Opera—Texas
Water supply
Meter tests cut water losses. il Am City & County 92:66 Ja '77
SAN ANTONIO Symphony. See Orchestras
SANASARDO, Paul, Dance Company. See Dance companies
SAN BERNARDINO County, Calif.
Articulated graders tackle county roads. il Am City & County 92:30 Ja '77
SANBORN-SKYLINE County Park. See California—Parks and reserves
SANCHEZ, Ilitch Ramirez. See Ramirez Sanchez, I.
SÁNCHEZ, Néstor. See Jennings, J. L. S. Jr, jt auth
SANCTIONS (international law)
Bill details proposed sanctions on countries aiding terrorists. Aviation W 107:27 O 31 '77
See also
Embargo
SANCTUARIES, Bird. See Bird sanctuaries
SAND camping. See Camping
SAND castles
Ultimate in sandcastling? work of T. Vander Pluym. il por Sunset 159:70-1 Jl '77
SAND dunes
Onslaught on the Nile; shifting dunes of the Libyan Desert. F. El-Baz. il UNESCO Courier 30:23-4+ Jl '77
See also
White Sands National Monument
SANDCASTLES. See Sand castles
SANDERLIN, Owenita
What's that about the poor little woman? handling money. il Ret Liv 17:25+ S '77
SANDERS, Andrew
Murray Stern: social surrealist. il por Am Artist 41:76-83+ F '77
SANDERS, Charles L.
Donna Summer. il pors Ebony 32:33-6+ O '77
SANDERS, Dale A.
Filmstrips. Chr Today 22:36 N 4; 42 D 9 '77
Return of the filmstrip. Chr Today 21:38+ F 18; 38-9 Mr 18 '77
SANDERS, Harland
How to make a million after you're 65. il por Sat Eve Post 249:46-7 Mr '77
SANDERS, Ivan
Human dialogues are born. Nation 224:504-7 Ap 23 '77
SANDERS, James W.
Island in the city. J. W. Donohue. America 136: 322-4 Ap 9 '77 *
SANDERS. See Sanding machines
SANDERSON, Everett
There's a girl on the track! W. R. Young. il Read Digest 110:91-5 F '77 *
SANDERSON, Ivan L.
Some California college store managers have drifted to textbook net pricing. Pub W 212:53 D 26 '77
SANDERSON, J. D.
Adult at eighteen? excerpt from How to stop worrying about your kids. Read Digest 110: 136-9 Mr '77
SANDHAGE, Doug
(ed) Market update. See issues of Writer's digest
SANDHAGE, Paula Arnett
Books. Writers Digest 57:46 Je; 54 Ag; 58 O '77
SANDIA Laboratories
Desert proving ground for solar energy. il U.S. News 83:99 N 14 '77
SAN DIEGO, Calif.
San Diego's greenbelt; San Pasqual. M. E. Trussell. il maps Am For 83:26-30 O '77
Wheelchair route to open San Diego for handicapped. Aging 274:26 Ag '77
Architecture
For convention-goers: a look at what's new in San Diego. il Archit Rec 161:42-3 My '77
Banks
In the shade of the FDIC: the tax-shelter farmers; failure of the U.S. National Bank. Nation 224:590-4 My 14 '77
Description
San Diego—the city that's still to good to be true. R. Alleman. il Vogue 167:236+ N '77

SAN DIEGO, Calif.—*Continued*

Gardens

This San Diego garden is a jungle of palms—more than 60 kinds; garden of Jim Wright. il Sunset 159:154-5 Ag '77

Music

See also
Opera—California

Parks and playgrounds

See also
San Diego, Calif. Zoological Park

Politics and government

Pete Wilson of San Diego. C. McWilliams. por Nation 224:305-7 Mr 12 '77

Public health

Health info for all: San Diego meet. W. Maina and B. French. Lib J 102:1552-3 Ag '77

SAN DIEGO, Calif. Zoological Park
Jungle walk in San Diego; botanical collection of San Diego Zoo. il Sunset 158:220-2 Je '77

SAN DIEGO Maritime Museum. See Naval museums

SAN DIEGO Opera Company. See Opera—California

SAN DIEGO Underwater Film Festival. See Motion picture festivals

SAN DIEGO Zoo. See San Diego, Calif. Zoological Park

SANDING machines
PM tool test: low-vibration sander. W. C. Leckey. il Pop Mech 148:167 O '77
Power sanding. J. Dillon. il Motor B & S 139:105-7 Ap '77

SANDINISTAS. See Guerrillas—Nicaragua

SANDISON, Hamish
California royalty bill: milestone or mistake? pors Am Artist 41:61 F '77

SANDLER, Bernice
Title IX: antisexism's big legal stick. il Am Educ 13:6-9 My '77

SANDLER, Jeffrey
Don't electrocute your car battery. il Pop Mech 148:68+ O '77
Shut-off timer for battery-powered appliances. il Pop Electr 12:48 Ag '77

SANDLER, Ross, and Schoenbrod, David
Toll in Manhattan. il Environment 19:5+ Ag '77

SANDON, Leo, Jr
James Reston: prophet of American civil religion. Chr Cent 94:15-18 Ja 5 '77
Pilgrimage to Plains. Chr Cent 94:145-6 F 16 '77

SANDPAPER
PS guide to sandpaper and other coated abrasives. R. Hill. il Pop Sci 211:106-9 Jl '77

SANDPIPERS
Little dun-colored bird; dunbin. il Audubon 79:2-3 S '77

SANDROFF, Ronni
Mother's day; story. McCalls 104:148-9+ My '77

SANDS, Leo
New band for kiddie-talkies. il Pop Electr 12:46-8 Ag '77

SANDSTROM, Mary
Nimble grandma in Santa's workshop. M. Baughman. il Ret Liv 16:36-7 D '76 *

SANDWICHES
Basque omelet sandwiches. il Sunset 159:114 Jl '77
College culinary catchall. il Bet Hom & Gard 54:33 Ag '76
Crepe stack sandwich is chilled, nippy. il Sunset 159:162-3 D '77
French-toasted sandwich. il Bet Hom & Gard 55:36 My '77
Sandwich breakfast? Why not. il Sunset 158:172 Je '77
Sandwiches that turn a picnic into a feast. H. McCully. House B 119:82-3+ Ag '77

SANDY, Stephen
Prefect; poem. Atlantic 240:45 Jl '77

SANDY soils. See Soils, Sandy

SANER, Reg
Milking the snowbank; Stitchwork; Neither lions ravens nor white toads; Clear night, small fire, no wind; poems. Poetry 131:73-7 N '77

SAN FERNANDO Valley

Housing

See Housing—California

SANFORD, Annette
Morning of the white shells; story. Redbook 150:70-3 D '77

SANFORD, Charlotte
Second sight. L. David. il por Ladies Home J 94:154+ Jl '77 *

SAN FRANCISCO
How to transplant & survive; getting a job and living in Los Angeles and San Francisco. D. Duke and others. il Mademoiselle 83:205+ Ap '77
November action in San Francisco; street entertainers. il Sunset 159:51-2 N '77
San Francisco blues. T. D. Allman; discussion. New Repub 176:39-40 Ja 29 '77

Airports

Don't drive to the S.F. airport? map Sunset 159:38+ D '77

Architecture

House with a heart; house of G. and A. Getty. il pors Vogue 167:322-7 O '77

Art

November street show in S.F; paintings on billboards. il Sunset 159:23-4 N '77
Report from San Francisco. C. Ratcliff. il Art in Am 65:55-62 My '77
San Francisco. T. Albright. See issues of Art news
San Francisco. A. Frankenstein. Art N 76:94+ O '77

Bookstores

See Booksellers and bookselling—California

Bridges

San Francisco's drawbridges will perform two days in April. il Sunset 158:70 Ap '77

Buildings

Most subtle layering of architecture and light; corporate offices of Crowley Maritime Corporation. il Archit Rec 161:131-6 F '77

Chinatown

Civil war in Chinatown. D. A. Williams and others. il Newsweek 90:39 S 26 '77

Churches

See also
San Francisco—Religious institutions and affairs

Crime

Local campaign against consumer fraud. il Bus W p66 Je 13 '77
Tracing of Beretta A47469; condensation. N. M. Adams. il Read Digest 112:203-6+ Ja '78

Description

San Francisco. Bet Hom & Gard 55:247-8 O '77

Earthquake and fire, 1906

Death and rebirth of a city: San Francisco, 1906. R. Olmsted and N. Olmsted. il Am West 14:10-25 Ja '77
922 Oak street: a personal remembrance of the San Francisco earthquake. D. Geissinger. il por Am West 14:26-31 Ja '77

Education

See also
Lone Mountain College, San Francisco

Gangs

See Gangs

Hotels, restaurants, etc.

Eat your way around the world on San Francisco's Clement Street. il map Sunset 159:36-8 S '77
Last meal to look forward to; Mandarin. C. A. Whittingham. il Fortune 96:191-2 S '77
Need money laundered? Then see Arnold Batliner; St Francis Hotel's coin laundry. J. D. Lewis. il por Ret Liv 17:16-17 Jl '77
U.S. journal: San Francisco: some thoughts on the International Hotel controversy. C. Trillin. New Yorker 53:116-20 D 19 '77

Housing

Urban living in San Francisco Bay Area enhanced by Albany Hill high-rise; Gateview at Albany Hill. il Archit Rec 162:116-19 S '77

Monuments, statues, etc.

Forgotten (?) sculptures in Golden Gate Park; bronze statues. il Sunset 159:36+ O '77

Music

Music West; festivals of American music. R. Commanday. il Hi Fi 27:MA32-4 Mr '77
See also
Opera—California

Parks and playgrounds

Forgotten (?) sculptures in Golden Gate Park; bronze statues. il Sunset 159:36+ O '77

Police

Police for hire; Patrol Special unit. il por Time 109:52 Ja 24 '77

Politics and government

Grudge match; referendum initiated by J. Barbagelata against Mayor G. Moscone. C. J. Harper and G. C. Lubenow. por Newsweek 90:22 Ag 1 '77
A walk on San Francisco's gay side. H. Gold. il N Y Times Mag p67-9+ N 6 '77

Recreation

See also
San Francisco—Parks and playgrounds

SAN FRANCISCO—*Continued*

Religious institutions and affairs

Temple trouble; accusations surrounding financial and disciplinary practices of J. Jones' People's Temple. K. L. Woodward and others. il por Newsweek 90:79 Ag 15 '77

Restaurants

See San Francisco—Hotels, restaurants, etc.

Social conditions

Gay power in San Francisco. S. Fraker and G. C. Lubenow. il Newsweek 89:25 Je 6 '77

Streets

Ten steepest streets in hilly San Francisco. il map Sunset 159:55 S '77

Transit systems

See also
San Francisco Bay Region—Transit systems

Water supply

Going dry. S. Fraker and W. J. Cook. il Newsweek 89:32 Ap 18 '77
Water rationing means dirty cars and quicker showers in California. il U.S. News 82:60 Ap 18 '77

SAN FRANCISCO Ballet
Balletic ramrod from Missoula; M. Smuin. W. Terry. il Sat R 4:50-1 S 17 '77
Bold new face; performances January 6-May 29. S. Von Buchau. il Dance Mag 51:38-41 S '77
Cinderella story. H. Saal. il Newsweek 89:71-2 My 9 '77

SAN FRANCISCO Bay
This is San Francisco Bay? il map Sunset 158:120-3 My '77
See also
Marine pollution—San Francisco Bay

SAN FRANCISCO Bay Region
Bay area aerial tour; chartering a small plane. il Sunset 159:26+ N '77
California co-op cuts bills in half; food cooperative for the elderly. il por Aging 274:3-5 Ag '77
You never know. New Yorker 53:29-31 Ap 11 '77

Education

How to improve student writing; Bay Area Writing Project and teachers workshops. S. B. Neill. Educ Digest 42:44-7 Ja '77

Transit systems

Troubled BART takes 1977 ASCE award. il Am City & County 92:39 My '77

SAN FRANCISCO Opera Company. See Opera—California

SAN FRANCISCO plantation, Reserve, La. See Plantations

SAN FRANCISCO Public Library
SFPL faces new demand for fiscal accountability. Lib J 102:2462 D 15 '77
Special report: rejoicing at the library; reading of James Joyce's Ulysses at the Ortega Branch. G. T. Hooper. il Wilson Lib Bull 51:718-19 My '77

SANGER, Alice-Lou
Hand sculpture. il Sch Arts 77:54-5 O '77

SANGER, Frederick
Amended dogma. Sci Am 236:50 My '77 *

SANGER, Margaret
Margaret Sanger. J. Alexander. il por Sat Eve Post 249:10-11+ My '77 *

SANITARY engineering
See also
Refuse and refuse disposal
Sewage disposal
Sewage disposal plants
Sewer cleaning
Sewerage
Snow and ice removal
Water supply engineering

SANITAS Service Corporation. See Service industries

SANITATION
See also
Barns and stables—Sanitation
Dayton, Ohio—Sanitary affairs
Detroit—Sanitary affairs
Farms—Sanitation
Hygiene
Los Angeles County, Calif.—Sanitary affairs
New York (city)—Sanitary affairs
Public comfort stations
Refuse and refuse disposal
Rochester, N.Y.—Sanitary affairs
Sewage disposal
Swimming pools—Sanitation
Virginia—Sanitary affairs

SANITATION, Household
See also
Plumbing

SANITATION workers
College of hard knocks: my life as a garbageman. J. R. Coleman. il pors N Y Times Mag p32-4+ My 1 '77
See also
Strikes—United States—Sanitation workers

SAN JACINTO County, Tex.

Public Health

See Public health—Texas

SAN JOSE, Calif.

City planning

San Jose. il Sunset 159:98-105 N '77

Education

Crisis counseling; program for students and parents at Yerba Buena High School. S. B. Neill. il Am Educ 13:17-22 Ja '77

Historic houses, sites, etc.

See Historic houses, sites, etc.—California

SAN JUAN, Puerto Rico

Music

See also
Opera—Puerto Rico

SAN JUAN BAUTISTA, Calif.
August is a good month to make the detour to San Juan Bautista. il Sunset 159:34-5 Ag '77

SAN JUAN Islands
San Juan Islands of Washington. J. Roe. il map Travel 148:26-31 Jl '77

SAN LUIS OBISPO County, Calif.
Quiet coast south of Big Sur; north coast of San Luis Obispo County. il map Sunset 159:40-1 O '77
Source recovery gets off to slow start; Separation of Office and Residential Trash project. Am City & County 92:26 Je '77

SAN PASQUAL, Calif. See San Diego, Calif.

SAN SALVADOR (city)
San Salvador's urban orchids. P. Bernhardt. il Natur Hist 86:64-71 D '77

SANSEVIERIA
Two old houseplant toughies: aspidistra and sansevieria. G. R. Robinson. il Org Gard & Farm 24:170-3 O '77

SANSKRIT poetry

Translations into English

My husband; poem; excerpt from the Siddhahemasabdanusasana; tr by W. S. Merwin and J. Masson. Nation 224:506 Ap 23 '77
When hundreds of prayers at last; Lush clouds in; poems; excerpts from the Amarusataka; tr by W. S. Merwin and J. Masson. Nation 224:506 Ap 23 '77

SANTA ANA, Calif.

Police

See Police—California

SANT'ANGELO, Giorgio
System for the simple life. il por House & Gard 149:150-3 O '77 *

SANTA BARBARA, Calif. fire. See Brush fires

SANTA BARBARA campus. See California. University—Santa Barbara campus

SANTA CATALINA Island
Backpackers on a cruise ship? They're off to explore Catalina. il Sunset 159:58+ S '77

SANTA CLARA County, Calif.
Swords and plowshares; project to sway companies from military contracts. S. H. Day, Jr. Bull Atom Sci 33:4-5 N '77

SANTA CLAUS
How I found the real Santa Claus. I. Hughes. il Good H 185:60+ D '77
How to be Santa Claus. N. B. Read, Jr. il Sat Eve Post 249:60-1+ D '77
Man who played Santa Claus. J. P. Hayes. il Good H 185:118-19+ D '77
Santa Claus is alive and well. . .; J. Yellig. J. D. Lewis. il por Ret Liv 17:34+ D '77
Santa lets his hair down; interview, ed by P. M. Jones. M. D. Kremer. il pors Sr Schol 110:2-3 D 15 '77
Santa's real story. M. Mead. il Redbook 150:33-4+ D '77
There is a Santa Claus. E. J. Kounitz. il Society 14:80-1 Ja '77
Yes, there is a Santa Claus. M. I. Levine and J. H. Seligmann. Harp Baz 111:132+ D '77

SANTA CRUZ, Calif.

Art

See Art—California

SANTA CRUZ campus. See California. University—Santa Cruz campus

SANTA FE, N.Mex.

Galleries and museums

Spanish America in today's New Mexico; Santa Fe's Museum of International Folk Art. il map Sunset 158:94-9 My '77

SANTA FE Festival of the Arts. See Festivals—New Mexico

SANTA FE Opera Company. See Opera—New Mexico
SANTA FE Opera House. See Opera houses
SANTA ROSA, Calif, Senior Skills Center. See Senior centers
SANTANA, Raul
Poetic journey with Rafael Squirru; excerpt from prologue to Números, veinte años de poesía. il Américas 29:45-6 S '77
SANTE, George
Build CB switcher for music between calls. il Radio-Electr 48:40-1 D '77
Build 30-MHz CB frequency counter. il Radio-Electr 48:43-5+ S '77
Preamplifier for long distance reception. il Radio-Electr 48:70-1+ My '77
SANTIAGO, Irene M.
Davao. il Travel 148:36-41 Ag '77
SANTIAGO, Chile
Flavor of Santiago. O. K. Gellona. il Américas 29:19-25 Mr '77
SANTO DOMINGO, Dominican Republic
Santo Domingo. T. Bross. il Trav/Holiday 149:54-7 Ja '78
Then and now; with photographs by E. H. Vokes. G. de Zéndegui. il Américas 29:9-11 Je '77
Trinidadian crowned Miss Universe. il Américas 29:23-5 O '77

Historic houses, sites, etc.

Hostal Nicolás de Ovando; two houses restored as a hotel. G. de Zéndegui. il Américas 29:21-8 Ag '77

Hotels, restaurants, etc.

Hostal Nicolás de Ovando; two houses restored as a hotel. G. de Zéndegui. il Américas 29:21-8 Ag '77
SANTONI, Ronald E.
Canada and separatism. Progressive 41:10 F '77
Quebec's language problems. il Progressive 41:49-50 D '77
SANTONS. See Figurines
SANTORE, Charles
Charles Santore: idea and image. E. Medoff. il por Am Artist 41:66-71+ F '77 *
SANTORINI (island) See Thera (island)
SANTOS-DUMONT, Alberto
Santos-Dumont. R. P. Hallion. il Flying 101:83 S '77 *
SAPIRO, Maurice L.
Armature for ceramic sculpture. il Ceram Mo 25:42-3 Je '77
Lumigraphic print process. bibl il Sch Arts 77:28-35 S '77
Throw a head. il Sch Arts 77:20-7 O '77
Throw a ring-vase. il Sch Arts 76:22-7 Mr '77
SAR, Madhabananda, and Stumpf, W. E.
Androgen concentration in motor neurons of cranial nerves and spinal cord. bibl il Science 197:77-9 Jl 1 '77
SARABEX Ltd. See Foreign exchange brokers
SARABYANOV, Dimitri
On the Russian avant-garde. il Art N 76:116-17 N '77
SARAH Lawrence College, Bronxville, N.Y.
Trouble at Sarah Lawrence. A. Roiphe. il N Y Times Mag p21-2+ Mr 20 '77; Discussion. p60-1 Ap 10 '77
SARAN, Parmatma
Cosmopolitans from India. bibl il Society 14:65-9 S '77
SARASOTA, Fla.
Candlelight and vintage years. M. H. Freedman. Aging 274:11 Ag '77

Music

See also
Opera—Florida
SARATOGA Campaign, 1777
Decision on the Hudson. A. C. Smith. il por Conservationist 32:23-5 S '77
Victory in 1777 that kept the American Revolution alive. il map U.S. News 83:81-2 O 10 '77
SARATOGA Horticultural Foundation
Useful improved plants for Californians. il Sunset 159:228-9 N '77
SARATOGA Race Track. See Race tracks
SARBANES, Paul Spyros
5 freshman senators who are moving into the spotlight. pors U.S. News 82:24-5 F 7 '77 *
SARCOCYSTIS
Sarcocystosis: a clinical outbreak in dairy calves. P. Frelier and others. bibl il Science 195:1341-2 Mr 25 '77
SARCOMA. See Cancer
SARGASSO Sea
Effects of the winter of 1976-1977 on the northwestern Sargasso Sea. A. Leetmaa. bibl il Science 198:188-9 O 14 '77
Tritium-helium dating in the Sargasso Sea: a measurement of oxygen utilization rates. W. J. Jenkins. bibl il Science 196:291-2 Ap 15 '77
SARGEANT, Frank
Bass methods for big bream. il Field & S 82:66-71 Jl '77
(ed) How experts solve fishing's 5 big problems; interviews. il Outdoor Life 159:90-3 My '77
SARGEANT, Winthrop
Concert records (cont) New Yorker 52:68-70 Ja 31; 53:104-7 Mr 7; 109-11 Mr 28; 118-21 Ap 11; 143-4+ Ap 18; 112-16 Je 6; 82-3 Jl 11; 61-2 Ag 1; 73-5 Ag 15; 168+ O 24; 187-90+ N 14; 178+ N 21; 124-7 D 19 '77
Profiles; Barry Tuckwell. por New Yorker 53:45-6+ Mr 14 '77
SARGENT, David
Sounds. See issues of Vogue
SARICK, Hy, and Sarick, Judy
Children's Book Store in Toronto. il Horn Bk 53:202-5 Ap '77
SARICK, Judy. See Sarick, H. jt auth
SARKIS, Elias
Lebanon: the chore of getting Beirut back in shape. il Bus W p42 F 28 '77 *
SARNE, Yosef. See Gainer, H. jt auth
SARNOFF, David
Bennett Cerf remembers; excerpt from At Random. B. Cerf. por Pub W 212:26-9 Ag 22 '77 *
SARNOFF, Robert
Artistic self-discovery through group reflection. il Sch Arts 77:30-3 O '77
SAROYAN, William
Eppe's of Paris. New Repub 176:23-5 Je 18 '77
How the barber finally got himself into a fable; story. Atlantic 240:55 N '77
Meditations on the letter Z. il Harpers 255:118-19 N '77
Oh death where is thy story line? New Repub 178:29-30 Ja 7 '78
Twenty is the greatest time in any man's life; story. Sat Eve Post 249:26-8 Mr '77
SARREL, Lorna J.
Introducing the Sarrels; interview, ed by A. L. Ball. pors Redbook 148:114+ Ap '77
—See Sarrel, P. M. jt auth
SARREL, Philip M.
Introducing the Sarrels; interview, ed by A. L. Ball. pors Redbook 148:114+ Ap '77
—and Sarrel, L. J.
Answers to questions about sex. pors Redbook 148:114-15+ Ap; 149:125+ My; 58+ Je; 28+ Ag; 112 S; 98+ O; 150:49+ N '77
SARRIS, Andrew
Spoiled children. il por Harpers 254:77-80 Je '77
SARTRE, Jean Paul
Existentialist on mobilist; excerpt from The art world; ed by B. Diamonstein. il por Art N 76:158+ N '77
SASAKI, Hitoshi
Japanese ash glazes. il por Ceram Mo 25:53-9 F '77
SASKATCHEWAN
See also
Poplar River
SASS, Sylvia
Artist life; interview, ed by D. J. Soria. por Hi Fi 27:MA6-7+ Jl '77
Sylvia Sass: remember the name; interview, ed by E. Davidson. por Opera N 41:28-9 Mr 19 '77

about

Perilous path to soprano superstardom; recording of Mozart recitals. D. Harris. pors Hi Fi 27:89-90 Ap '77 *
SASSER, Charles W.
Making crime pay. Writers Digest 57:29-32 S '77
SASSER, W. Earl. See Skinner, W. jt auth
SATALINO, Vicki. See Zipadelli, M. jt auth
SATAN. See Devil
SATELLITE antennas. See Antennas (electronics)
SATELLITE Business Systems Inc. See Communications satellites
SATELLITE DNA. See DNA
SATELLITE Instructional Television Experiment. See Communications satellites—Educational use
SATELLITE photographs of earth. See Earth—Photographs from space
SATELLITE search and rescue system. See Space rescue work
SATELLITE solar power stations. See Artificial satellites—Solar energy use
SATELLITES
Asaph Hall finds the moons of Mars. J. Ashbrook. il por Sky & Tel 54:20-1 Jl '77
Belt of satellites discovered around Uranus. il Sci N 111:180 Mr 19 '77
Centennial celebration for Phobos and Deimos. W. E. Brunk. il Chemistry 50:24-6 Jl '77
Cloud-gazing at 10. Eberhart. il Sci N 112:332-3 N 12 '77
Eclipses of Jupiter's satellites. il Sky & Tel 53:230-3 Mr '77
Eclipses of Iapetus by Saturn's rings. il Sky & Tel 54:190-1 S '77
Finding faint planetary satellites. S. Wheatcraft. il Sky & Tel 54:243-5 S '77
First actual look at Io's cloud. J. Eberhart. il Sci N 111:155 Mr 5 '77
Galilean satellites of Jupiter: 12.6-centimeter radar observations. D. B. Campbell and others. bibl il Science 196:650-3 My 6 '77

SATELLITES—*Continued*
Jovian moons: naked-eye observations. F. Schaaf. Sky & Tel 54:157 Ag '77
Martian moon shown in Viking mosaic; photograph. Aviation W 107:61 Ag 8 '77
New class of moons. Sci N 111:39 Ja 15 '77
New moon of Saturn, and an old one. il Sci N 111:69 Ja 29 '77
New satellite of Saturn? J. W. Fountain and S. M. Larson. bibl il Science 197:915-17 Ag 26 '77
Observing Saturn's moons Titan and Iapetus. il Sky & Tel 53:291 Ap '77
Phobos and Deimos. J. Veverka. il Sci Am 236:30-7 bibl(p 138) F '77
Phobos and Deimos: similar and yet....; Martian moons. il Sci N 112:295 N 5 '77
Sodium cloud of Io. il Sky & Tel 54:479-80 D '77
Striations on Phobos. il Sky & Tel 54:269 O '77
Zooming in on Phobos. il Sci Am 236:57 Ap '77
Zooming in on Phobos and Deimos. il Sky & Tel 54:469 D '77
See also
Artificial satellites
Moon

Photographs

Martian moon photographed by Viking. il Aviation W 106:42-3 Ap 11 '77

SATIACUM, Robert
Indian taker. E. Melton. il por Forbes 120:46 D 15 '77 *

SATIRE
See also
Caricatures and cartoons
also subhead Anecdotes, facetiae, satire, etc. under various subjects, e.g. Travelers—Anecdotes, facetiae, satire, etc.

SATROM, Thom
Dreamers who dared. il Sat Eve Post 249:64-5+ My '77

SATURDAY evening post
Man from Maine; C. H. K. Curtis. il por Sat Eve Post 249:4+ Jl '77
Special 250th anniversary issue; a sampling of treasures from its pages. Sat Eve Post 249: 4-8+ Jl '77

SATURDAY evening post covers. See Periodical covers

SATURDAY review
Back door. C. Tucker. Sat R 4:52 Je 25 '77
Confessions of a cartoon editor. D. W. Re. il Writers Digest 57:39-41 Je '77
Report to the readers. N. Cousins. Sat R 5:4 O 29 '77
Report to the readers. N. Cousins and C. Tucker. Sat R 4:4-5 Ap 16 '77
Saturday's child; sale of magazine to C. Tucker. T. Schwartz. pors Newsweek 89:89-90 Mr 21 '77

SATURDAY review Advertising Awards. See Advertising—Awards, prizes, etc.

SATURN (planet)
Mars, Jupiter, and Saturn for the coming year. R. C. Victor. il Sky & Tel 53:125-6 F '77
See also
Space flight—Voyager flights
Space flight to Saturn

Ring system

Asymmetry of Saturn's ring A. il Sky & Tel 53:357-8 My '77
Eclipses of Iapetus by Saturn's rings. il Sky & Tel 54:190-1 S '77

Satellites

See Satellites

Temperature and radiation

Detection of Lyman α emission from the Saturnian disk and from the ring system. H. Weiser and others. bibl il Science 197:755-7 Ag 19 '77

SATZ, Arthur
Fifth Van Cliburn Piano Competition. il pors Hi Fi 28:MA16-18 Ja '78

SAUBOLLE, Louis
Let's be practical. por Forbes 120:63 Ag 1 '77 *

SAUCES
Four sauces are cranberries plus. Sunset 159:208 N '77
Lavish sauces and simple desserts—so right together. il Parents Mag 52:77 O '77
Three cheers for sour cottage sauce. il Sunset 159:68-9 Jl '77

SAUD al Faisal, Prince of Saudi Arabia
Saud on war and oil; excerpts from interview, ed by A. de Borchgrave. pors Newsweek 90: 64 O 31 '77
Saudi Foreign Minister meets with President Carter; October 25, 1977. Dept State Bull 77: 766-7 N 28 '77

SAUDI ARABIA
See also
Americans in Saudi Arabia
Colleges and universities—Saudi Arabia
Hotels, motels, etc.—Saudi Arabia
Investments, Saudi Arabian
Loans, Saudi Arabian
Red Sea
Riyadh
Telephone—Saudi Arabia
Water supply—Saudi Arabia

Commerce

United States

See United States—Commerce—Saudi Arabia

Economic policy

Money is no object; planning for Asir province. por Forbes 120:97 Jl 1 '77
Saudi Arabia's growing petropower. il Time 110: 48-9 Jl 11 '77

Economic relations

Negotiating to heal OPEC's price split. Bus W p29-30 Je 27 '77
Saudis still reign over OPEC. il Bus W p 19-20 Jl 18 '77

Foreign relations

Co-opting the third world elites: trilateralism goes to work. K. Bird. Nation 224:425-8 Ap 9 '77
Oil power in the Middle East. J. C. Campbell. bibl f For Affairs 56:89-110 O '77
Why the Saudis act so peaceful. U.S. News 82:20 F 28 '77

Egypt

See Egypt—Foreign relations—Saudi Arabia

United States

See United States—Foreign relations—Saudi Arabia

Industries

Candles were a luxury; interview. G. Gosaibi. por Forbes 119:32 Je 1 '77
See also
Petroleum industry—Saudi Arabia

Politics and government

Failing king. R. Carroll. por Newsweek 89:34 F 28 '77

SAUERBRATEN. See Cookery—Meat; Cookery, German

SAUL, B. F. Real Estate Investment Trust. See Real estate investment trusts

SAUNA
Sauna and bath in just 66 square feet. il Sunset 158:102 F '77

SAUNDERS, Gayle
Getting into the real world. il Craft Horiz 37: 44-5 O '77

SAUNDERS, Grady F. See Lomedico, P. T. jt auth

SAUNDERS, James C. See Bock, G. R. jt auth

SAUNDERS, Joseph
Should US scientists trade data with USSR? por Sci Digest 81:34-7+ Je '77

SAUNDERS, R. Stephen. See Malin, M. C. jt auth

SAUNDERS, W. B.
Grain marketing for the next decade; address, September 12, 1977. Vital Speeches 44:37-9 N 1 '77

SAUSAGE
Bologna. Consumer Rep 42:96 D '77
My turn for the wurst; making sausages from pork and game meats. K. Green. Field & S 82:177-9+ N '77

SAUSAGE industry. See Meat industry

SAUTER, Van Gordon
Who shapes TV values? J. M. Wall. Chr Cent 94:131-2 F 16 '77 *

SAVAGE, Earl R.
Build a digital IC identifier/tester. il Radio-Electr 48:44-6 Je '77
Extra hands for the hobbyist. il Radio-Electr 48:56-7+ Jl '77
Hobby corner. See issues of Radio-electronics, October 1977-
Homebrew breadboard. il Radio-Electr 48:70-1 Ag; 72-3+ S '77; Correction. 48:69+ N '77

SAVAGE-RICH, Peggy
It should have been called Miami Beaches. Sat Eve Post 249:89+ Ap '77

SAVAGE Skulls (street gang) See Gangs

SAVAGES; drama. See Hampton, C.

SAVALAS, Telly
Public believes Kojak; interview, ed by B. Wilkins. Sat R 4:12 Mr 19 '77

about

Notes and comment. New Yorker 53:23-4 F 28 '77 *

SAVANNAH, Ga.

Description and travel

Not going all the way. S. Flythe, Jr. il Holiday 57:24-5+ N '76

Historic houses, sites, etc.

Living with antiques: the Bernard Constantine house in Savannah. il Antiques 111:1210-15 Je '77

SAVIN Business Machines Corporation. See Office equipment industry

SAVING and savings
Changing times saving & investment yardstick. il Changing T 31:41 Je; 25-8 O '77
House buying: how to dig up that down payment. Bet Hom & Gard 55:32+ Je '77
How much income will your savings yield? il Changing T 31:24 D '77
See also
Finance, Personal
Investments
SAVING the old homestead; drama. See Fay, M.
SAVINGS and loan associations
S&Ls: flying high in the golden state. T. J. Murray. il Duns R 109:92-4+ Ap '77
S&Ls will write a program for city neighborhood lending. D. Loomis. Archit Rec 161:34 Je '77
VRMs go vroom in California. Forbes 119:110+ Ap 15 '77
Finance
S&Ls find many reasons to be happy. il Bus W p41-2 N 28 '77
California
Point-of-sale system short-circuits in southern California; Glendale Federal Savings & Loan Assn. il Bus W p86-7 Ap 18 '77
S&Ls: flying high in the golden state. T. J. Murray. il Duns R 109:92-4+ Ap '77
SAVINGS and loan services. See Supermarkets—Banking services
SAVINGS banks
See also
Savings and loan associations
SAVINGS certificates. See Certificates of deposit
SAVINGS deposits
Saving for college the tax-free way; establishing a custodial savings account for a child. E. G. Pascoe. McCalls 105:112 O '77
Interest
How long will your nest egg last: V. Forsythe and B. Quint. il Bet Hom & Gard 55:40+ Jl '77
Savings account interest varies widely, California study shows. Ret Liv 17:11-12 Ja '77
SAVINO, Philip
Careers in art. il Sch Arts 76:4-5 F; 8-9 Mr; 10-11 Ap '77
SAVON, Karl
Automatic program search; new system for cassette decks. il Radio-Electr 48:52-3 Mr '77
Color TV:
What's new for '77. il Radio-Electr 48:55-7+ F '77
State of solid state. See issues of Radio-electronics
Today's semiconductors. il Radio-Electr 48:80 S '77
SAVONLINNA Opera Festival. See Music festivals—Finland
SAVORY, J. G.
Degradation of wood by fungi; excerpt from Deterioration of materials in a marine environment. il Motor B & S 140:47-8 Jl '77
SAVOURS, Ann
(ed) See Scott, R. F. Scott's last voyage
SAW horses. See Sawhorses
SAW sharpening. See Sharpening
SAWDUST
See also
Feeds—Sawdust
SAWDUST catchers. See Saws—Equipment
SAWFLIES
Chemical basis for feeding adaptation of pine sawflies neodiprion rugifrons and neodiprion swainei. T. Ikeda and others. bibl il Science 197:497-9 Jl 29 '77
SAWHILL, John Crittenden
Make America smarter; address, January 6, 1977. Vital Speeches 43:309-11 Mr 1 '77
Paralysis on the Potomac. Sat R 4:19-20 Ja 22 '77
Single most important thing: let prices go up; interview. por U.S. News 82:41-2 Ap 18 '77
SAWHORSES
Super horse. il Mech Illus 73:176 My '77
3 versatile sawhorses you can make. il Pop Mech 148:118-19+ O '77
SAWIN, Douglas B. See Parke, R. D. jt auth
SAWING
Taming the holy terror: a homily on living at peace with one's chain saw; excerpt from Barnacle Parp's chain saw guide. W. Hall. il Org Gard & Farm 24:138-42 O '77
See also
Miter boxes, gages, etc.
Wood cutting
SAWS
Basic cutting with a radial-arm saw. J. Marlow. il Pop Mech 148:112-14+ S '77
Carbide blades—performance at a price; circular saw. il Pop Mech 147:59-60+ My '77
Chain saws: electric vs gas. J. Capotosto. il Mech Illus 73:90+ Ap '77
How to make the most of a mini chain saw. il Bet Hom & Gard 55:8 Mr '77
Multi-use handsaw. E. J. Loiselle. il Pop Mech 149:99 Ja '78
New kind of chain for saws. B. Dalrymple. il Mech Illus 73:78 Mr '77
Pint-sized panel saw with a big bite. H. Wicks. il Pop Mech 147:113 Je '77
Portable jig (sabre) saws. il Consumers Res Mag 60:22-5 F '77
Saber saws. il Consumer Rep 42:147-52 D '77
Scroll saws. T. H. Jones. il Pop Sci 211:138+ O '77
Self-oiling, self-sharpening light chain saw. E. F. Lindsley. il Pop Sci 211:155 N '77
Small chain saws. il Consumer Rep 42:581-5 O '77
Smooth chainsaw. E. F. Lindsley. il Pop Sci 210:31 Ap '77
Stihl chain saw. M. McClintock. il Pop Mech 147:28 Ap '77
Tough electric saw for when the going's hard. E. F. Lindsley. il Pop Sci 210:186 My '77
Equipment
Catcher for flying sawdust. il Mech Illus 73:158 O '77
SAWS, Pruning. See Pruning apparatus and equipment
SAWYER, Charles
Dodging the spooks. Nation 225:325-8 O 8 '77
Writing on the party's terms. il Harpers 256:25+ Ja '78
SAWYER, Diane J.
Preparing volunteer tutors. bibl Clearing H 51:152-6 D '77
SAWYER, Lonnie, Jr
Sawyer brothers—their only crime was being poor. S. Pearlman. pors Good H 185:82+ Ag '77 *
SAWYER, Sandy
Sawyer brothers—their only crime was being poor. S. Pearlman. pors Good H 185:82+ Ag '77 *
SAWYER, Thomas K. and others
Pathogenic amoebas from brackish and ocean sediments, with a description of acanthamoeba hatchetti, n. sp. bibl il Science 196:1324-5 Je 17 '77
SAX, George David, family
Outsider escalates a bank's family feud; Sax family control of the Exchange National Bank of Chicago. por Bus W p44-5 N 14 '77
SAXBE, William Bart
Honeymoon is about over between India and Russia; interview. por U.S. News 82:41-2 Ja 24 '77
SAXENA, Surendra K.
Charnockite geotherm. bibl il map Science 198:614-17 N 11 '77
Entropy estimates for some silicates at 298°K from molar volumes. bibl il Science 193:1241-2; 198:207 S 24 '76, O 14 '77
SAXOPHONE players
See also
Davis, E.
Gordon, D.
SAYÃO, Bidú
La demoiselle elue; interview, ed by R. Jacobson. il pors Opera N 41:8-12 Mr 5 '77
SAYER, Leo
Music people; interview, ed by E. Miller. por Seventeen 36:88+ My '77
about
Sayer takes flight. T. Schwartz. il por Newsweek 90:89-90+ S 26 '77 *
SAYERS, Dorothy Leigh
Dorothy L. Sayers—for good work, for God's work. C. Forbes. Chr Today 21:16-18 Mr 4 '77 *
SAYERS, Tom
Fight on! And on and on; excerpt from The great prize fight. A. Lloyd. il pors Sports Illus 47:54-60+ Jl 25 '77 *
SAYINGS. See Proverbs
SAYLES, John
Golden State; story. Atlantic 239:70-4+ Je '77
Hoop; story. Atlantic 239:37-40 Mr '77
Writing dialogue. Writer 91:13-15 Ja '78
SAYRE, D. and others
Potential operating region for ultrasoft X-ray microscopy of biological materials. bibl il Science 196:1339-40 Je 17 '77
SAYRE, Roxanna
Audubon action. See issues of Audubon
SAYYAH, Victor
Insurer's spectacular rise. il por Bus W p69-70+ Je 6 '77 *
SCAB disease in potatoes. See Potatoes—Diseases and pests
SCAB disease of apples. See Apples—Diseases and pests
SCAFFOLDING
Scaffolding how-to. il Bet Hom & Gard 55:174 Je '77
SCAGNETTI, Jack
Auto insurance. il Motor T 29:93-8 D '77; 30:71-7 Ja '78
Let the sun shine in. il Motor T 29:82-6+ Jl '77
Monster vehicle to star in movie. il Pop Sci 210:83 Mr '77

SCALAPINO, Robert A.
Alliance with either China or Russia would be unwise. por U.S. News 82:46+ Je 27 '77
SCALDS. See Burns and scalds
SCALES, Junius
Trial of the 1950s. M. Pinsky. Progressive 41: 36-7 F '77 *
SCALES (reptiles)
Regional specialization of reptilian scale surfaces: relation of texture and biologic role. C. Gans and D. Baic. bibl il Science 195:1348-50 Mr 25 '77
SCALES (weighing instruments)
Kitchen scales. Consumer Rep 42:42-5 D '77
SCALIA, Antonin
Excerpts from testimony on proposals to reestablish the President's Executive Branch reorganization powers, March 1, 1977. Cong Digest 56:123+ Ap '77
SCALLOP fisheries. See Shellfish fisheries
SCALLOP shells. See Shells (conchology)
SCALLY, Sister Anthony
Woodson and the genesis of ASALH. il por Negro Hist Bull 40:653-5 Ja '77
SCALPING
Who invented scalping? J. Axtell. il Am Heritage 28:96-9 Ap '77
SCAMMON, Charles Melville
Charles Scammon: whaler turned naturalist. G. K. Mallory. il Oceans 10:40-4 Jl '77 *
SCANDALS, Political. See Politics, Corruption in
SCANDINAVIA
See also
Denmark
Finland
Industrial relations—Scandinavia
Publishers and publishing—Scandinavia
Sweden
Taxation—Scandinavia

Economic policy

See also
Economic assistance, Domestic—Scandinavia

Politics and government

Welfare state at the crossroads. J. Logue. Progressive 41:34-7 S '77
SCANDINAVIAN Airline System
SAS orders two Airbus A-300s. Aviation W 108: 28 Ja 9 '78
SCANDINAVIAN cookery. See Cookery, Scandinavian
SCANDINAVIANS
See also
Northmen

Anecdotes, facetiae, satire, etc.

Meet the Vikings. W. Breinholst. il Holiday 58: 42-3, 58+ Ja '77
SCANDURA, Joseph M.
Structural learning and open education. Clearing H 50:215-19 Ja '77; Same abr. Educ Digest 42:28-30 Ap '77
SCANNELLA, Anthony, and Rabuck, John
Planning and teaching for the middle school/junior high school. Engl J 66:55-6 Ap '77
SCANNERS (radio receivers) See Radio receivers
SCANNING electron microscope. See Electron microscopes and microscopy
SCANNING monitor receivers. See Radio receivers
SCARBOROUGH, Chuck
How not to do it yourself. il por Am Home 80: 24+ S '77
SCARBROUGH, Linda
For the birds. il Seventeen 36:42-3 Mr '77
SCARECROWS
Saluting a collection of happy scarecrows; exhibition in Winston-Salem, N.C. il Hobbies 82: 149 O '77
SCARF, Maggie
From joy to depression: new insights into the chemistry of moods. il N Y Times Mag p30-4+ Ap 24 '77; Same abr. with title What makes our moods? Read Digest 111:45-7+ Ag '77
I was a hooker for the CIA. New Repub 177: 17-19 S 3 '77
SCARFE, Alan
Romanian Baptists: notes of triumph. Chr Today 21:54-5 Mr 18 '77
SCARLATTI, Alessandro
La Griselda-excerpts. R. V. Lucano. il Am Rec G 40:32-4 My '77 *
Musical events; Agar et Ismaele esiliati performed at Corpus Christi Church, New York City. A. Porter. New Yorker 53:190+ D 12 '77 *
Operatic Scarlatti. A. Porter. por Hi Fi 27:72-4 Je '77 *
SCARPITTA, Salvatore
Esthetic transportation. C. Moser. il Art N 76: 92-4 O '77 *
SCARPITTI, Ellen C. See Scarpitti, F. R. jt auth
SCARPITTI, Frank R. and Scarpitti, E. C.
Victims of rape. bibl il Society 14:29-32 Jl '77
SCARR, Sandra
IQ, culture and adopted children. Sci N 112: 150 S 3 '77 *

SCARSDALE, N.Y.

Education

See Education—New York (state)
SCARUPA, Harriet Jackson
Robert Hayden poet laureate. il pors Ebony 33: 78-80+ Ja '78
SCARVES
How to tie up a summer wardrobe with scarves. il Seventeen 36:100-1 Jl '77
SCATTERING (physics)
Neutron scattering: new look at biological molecules. J. L. Marx. Science 198:481-3 N 4 '77
SCENERY, Preservation of. See Landscape protection
SCENERY, Stage. See Theater—Stage setting and scenery
SCENIC easements. See Easements
SCENIC rivers. See Wild and scenic rivers
SCENTED geraniums. See Geraniums
SCENTS. See Odors
SCENTS as deer bait. See Deer baits and repellents
SCHABEL, Donald
From shambles to showplace. il Am Lib 8:602-4 D '77
SCHACHT, Henry Brewer
Henry B. Schacht of Cummins Engine: big impression. por Forbes 119:95 F 15 '77 *
SCHACHTEL, Zeborah
Why a woman can't be a good boss—because no one will let you. C. Calvert. Mademoiselle 83:120+ Jl '77 *
SCHACHTER, Stanley
Chemistry of smoking. Time 109:48 F 21 '77 *
SCHAEFER, Robert
Electronic navigators. il Motor B & S 140:84-6+ O '77
SCHAEFFER, Edith
Witness stand. See issues of Christianity today
SCHAEFFER, Francis A.
Barrier to Christian belief. D. E. Kucharsky. Chr Today 21:38-9 F 4 '77 *
Schaeffer on film and in person. R. Cleath. Chr Today 21:50 Ap 1 '77 *
SCHAEFFER, Susan Fromberg
Confession in April; poem. Ms 5:84 Ap '77
SCHAEWEN, Deidi von
Wall flowers; photographs; excerpt from Walls. Harpers 255:66-7 S '77
SCHAFER, Larry A. and Hersh, E. M.
Immunotherapy of human cancer. bibl il Chemistry 50:11-15 Je '77
SCHALL, James V.
Future of the Christian clergy; address, January 7, 1977. Vital Speeches 43:271-4 F 15 '77
On leaving Rome. Commonweal 104:744-50 N 25 '77
SCHALLER, Lyle
Dr Schlesinger's threshing machine. Chr Cent 94:902-4 O 12 '77
SCHALLY, Andrew V.
1977 Nobel Prize in physiology or medicine. J. Meites. il pors Science 198:594-6 N 11 '77 *
Nobel prizes: seven in '77. pors Sci N 112:260-1 O 22 '77 *
SCHANK, John
Inventing the centerboard. T. Foote. il por Motor B & S 140:139-42 S '77 *
SCHAPIRO, Miriam
Canvassing our history; Women Artists: 1550-1950. il Ms 6:27-9 Jl '77
Woman's art: it's the only goddam energy around; interview, ed by H. Lyons. il por Ms 6:40-3+ D '77

about

Female Prometheus, David and Bathsheba. M. Wortz. il Art N 76:160-1 Summ '77 *
SCHARA, Ron
Maass vision. il Outdoor Life 161:74-81 Ja '78
SCHARF, David
Magnifications; excerpt. il Harpers 255:55-9 Jl '77
Micro macabre. il Int Wildlife 7:18-23 S '77
SCHAUFELE, William Everett, 1923-
Department discusses proposal for Zimbabwe Development Fund; statement, April 28, 1977. Dept State Bull 76:528-30 My 23 '77
U.S. relations in Southern Africa. Ann Am Acad 432:110-19 Jl '77
United States relations in Southern Africa; statement, April 16, 1977. Dept State Bull 76:464-71 My 9 '77
SCHAUFUSS, Peter
Making it to ballet's big time. W. Terry. il Sat R 4:40-1 S 3 '77 *
SCHAUMBURG, Frank David
PR man helps select author of book on pollution case. L. J. Carter. Science 195:468 F 4 '77 *
SCHAUMBURG Township, Ill, Public Library. See Libraries—Illinois
SCHEDULES, School. See School schedules
SCHEDULES of reinforcement. See Reinforcement (psychology)
SCHEEL, Henry A.
Are centerboards obsolete? il Yachting 141: 110+ Mr '77

SCHEELE, Roy
Counterpoise; poem. Commonweal 104:583 S 16 '77

SCHEER, Robert
Greening of a guerrilla. T. Griffith. por Time 109:56 Ap 4 '77 *

SCHEFF, S. and others
Progressive brain damage accelerates axon sprouting in the adult rat. bibl il Science 197: 795-7 Ag 19 '77

SCHEFFER, David J.
Britain's Bill of Rights. Nation 224:364-7 Mr 26 '77

SCHEFFER, Victor B.
Green eggs by the thousands. il Audubon 79: 112-13 S '77
Magnificent mammals. il Environment 19:16-20+ O '77

SCHEFFLER, Richard M. and Paringer, Lynn
Nation's health today. Cur Hist 72:193-5+ My '77

SCHEFLIN, Murray
You in the fur business? il por Forbes 119:110 My 15 '77 *

SCHEFTER, Jim
Microelectronics. il Pop Sci 212:52-5 Ja '78
Other story about the controversial B-1. il Pop Sci 210:109-12+ My '77
Project Voyager to Jupiter, Saturn, and beyond. il Pop Sci 211:92-5+ Ag '77

SCHEIB, Winfred H.
Writer in his heavenly house. Writer 90:27-9 Ja '77

SCHEINMAN, Pamela
(ed) See Akers, A. Adela Akers: the loomed plane

SCHELL, Francis
Prisoners of the ice. il Read Digest 112:66-71 Ja '78

SCHELL, Jessie
Family secrets; story. McCalls 104:124-9 Jl '77
Memoirs of a Mississippi misfit; story. McCalls 104:172-3 S '77

SCHELL, Orville, Jr
Reporter at large. New Yorker 53:40-2+ Mr 7; 74+ Mr 14 '77

SCHELLER, Richard H. and others
Chemical synthesis of restriction enzyme recognition sites useful for cloning. bibl il Science 196:177-80 Ap 8 '77
Clones of individual repetitive sequences from sea urchin DNA constructed with synthetic eco R1 sites. bibl il Science 196:197-200 Ap 8 '77

SCHELLING, George Luther
Native fish in troubled waters; reproductions of paintings. il Audubon 79:19-22+ Ja '77

SCHELLING, Thomas C.
Limits of non-proliferation. New Repub 176: 38-40 Ja 22 '77
Promise and the curse. il Sat R 4:26-30 Ja 22 '77

SCHENK, Boyd Frederick
Route to personal success in business; interview. il pors Nations Bus 65:58-60+ N '77

SCHERENBERG, Hans
Men behind the 280E. pors Motor T 29:50-1 Ap '77 *

SCHERER, Bill
Performance capabilities of 40-channel CB transceivers. il Pop Electr 11:47-9 Je '77

SCHERER, Margaret
What's in this building, anyway? il Design (US) 78:13-17 Spr '77

SCHERER, O.
(tr) Meaning of Brzezinski. Nat R 29:612-13 My 27 '77

SCHERER, Wilfred M.
Pros and cons of CB frequency-generation methods. il Pop Electr 11:46-51 Mr '77

SCHERR, Samuel
Open windows. por Craft Horiz 37:35 O; 43 D '77

SCHERY, Robert W.
Curious double life of rosa multiflora. il Horticulture 55:56-61 Je '77
What is the grass? il Horticulture 55:20-1+ Mr '77

SCHEUER, Paul J.
Chemical communication of marine invertebrates. bibl il BioScience 27:664-8 O '77

SCHIAVONE, Karen. See Sherline, P. jt auth

SCHIEFELBEIN, Susan
Norman Cousins. il por Sat Eve Post 249:32 My '77
Return of the native. Sat R 5:10-11 N 26 '77
Scholars at odds. Sat R 4:12 Je 25 '77

SCHIER, Richard F.
Raising the mandatory retirement age: examining the consequences. il Intellect 106:214-16 D '77

SCHIFF, Harriet Sarnoff
Help for bereaved parents. J. Chan. McCalls 105:114 O '77 *

SCHIFSKY, John P. See Hoffman, E. M. jt auth

SCHILLER, Bernt
Industrial democracy in Scandinavia. bibl f Ann Am Acad 431:63-73 My '77

SCHILLER, Diane Profita
Effects of the fraction ruler manipulative for teaching computation of fractions. il Clearing H 50:300-3 Mr '77

SCHILLER, Herbert I.
Now, a new international information order? Intellect 106:42-3 Ag '77

SCHILLER, Justin G. and Wapner, R. M.
Through the looking glass: notes on an antiquarian children's bookshop. il Horn Bk 53: 140-6 Ap '77

SCHILLER, Justin G, Ltd. See Booksellers and bookselling—Great Britain

SCHILLER, Lawrence
Hell's agent. R. Friedman. il Esquire 88:75-8+ O '77 *
Ringmaster at the circus. D. Gelman and others. il por Newsweek 89:77-8 Ja 31 '77 *

SCHILLER, Marlene
American community of hand papermakers. Am Artist 41:39-42 Ag '77
Machine and moldmade papers. il Am Artist 41:45-8 Ag '77

SCHILLER, Phyllis
Booklets. il Am Home 80:18 F; 17 Mr; 19 Ap; 12 My; 12 Jl '77

SCHILLER, Ronald
Awesome force that shaped our planet. maps Read Digest 112:112-16 Ja '78
Georgia on my mind. il map Read Digest 110: 152-6+ Mr '77
Three UFOs—how real were they? Read Digest 111:108-12 N '77

SCHINDLER, D. W.
Evolution of phosphorus limitation in lakes. bibl il Science 195:260-2 Ja 21 '77

SCHINTO, Jeanne
Alcohol for gasoline. Progressive 41:46-9 N '77
Breathless cotton workers. Progressive 41:27-9 Ag '77
Methadone and motherhood. Progressive 41:40-2 Mr '77
Rainmakers. il por Am West 14:28-33 Jl '77

SCHIPPER, Lee, and Lichtenberg, A. J.
Efficient energy use and well-being: the Swedish example. bibl Science 194:1001-13; 196:122+ D 3 '76; Ap 8 '77

SCHISTOSOMIASIS
Jirds are ideal models for schistosomiasis research. BioScience 27:68 Ja '77

SCHIZOPHRENIA
Blood bath; isolation of leu-endorphin by Frank Ervin and Roberta Palmour. Time 110:119 N 21 '77
Chemical clues to schizophrenia. Sci N 112:342 N 19 '77
Communication deviance in the families of schizophrenics: a comment on the misuse of analysis of covariance. J. A. Woodward and M. J. Goldstein. bibl Science 197:1096-7 S 9 '77
Genealogy of the weakest child; views of M. Bowen. il Time 109:85 Ap 11 '77
Naloxone in chronic schizophrenia. J. Volavka and others. bibl il Science 196:1227-8 Je 10 '77
Schizophrenia; a cruel chain of events. R. J. Trotter. por Sci N 111:394-5 Je 18 '77
Schizophrenia: sense and nonsense. E. F. Torrey. Psychol Today 11:157 N '77
Torque test for schizophrenia; tendency among youngsters to draw circles in a clockwise direction. Sci N 112:167 S 10 '77
Trial of living with a schizophrenic; work of Clare Creer and J. K. Wing. D. Cohen. Psychol Today 10:102 My '77

SCHLAFLY, Phyllis
Excerpt from statement on the ERA, April 1977. Cong Digest 56:189+ Je '77

about

End of an ERA? M. Kondracke. New Repub 176:14-16 Ap 30 '77 *
Kitchen crusader. S. Fraker and E. Sciolino. por Newsweek 90:35 Jl 25 '77 *
Should women be nicer than men? J. Lelyveld. il pors N Y Times Mag p 126 Ap 17 '77 *

SCHLAGER, Seymour I. and Ohanian, S. H.
Correlation between lipid synthesis in tumor cells and their sensitivity to humoral immune attack. bibl il Science 197:773-6 Ag 19 '77

SCHLAGETER, Robert W.
Cummer Gallery of Art. il Antiques 112:954-8 N '77

SCHLATTER, Janet M.
Big Bend gambusia: . . .and then there were three. il Nat Parks & Con Mag 51:8-10 N '77

SCHLEIERMACHER, Friedrich Ernst Daniel
Of tidy doctrine and truncated experience. R. K. Johnston. il Chr Today 21:10-14 F 18 '77 *

SCHLESINGER, Arthur, 1917-
America at the movies. il Sat R 5:36-7 N 12 '77
America: experiment or destiny? bibl f Am Hist R 82:505-22 Je '77; Same abr. Am Heritage 28:12-17 Je '77
Eurocommunism and detente. Current 196:42-5 O '77
Federal government and social rights. il Intellect 105:293-4 Mr '77
Movies. il Sat R 5:46+ O 29; 46 N 26; 62-3 D 10 '77; 46 Ja 7 '78

about

Once and future mandarin. J. Taft. il New Repub 177:16-19 N 26 '77 *

SCHLESINGER, Arthur, 1917—*Continued*
Schlesinger and Kennedy. R. Radosh. Nation 225:104-9 Ag 6 '77; Reply with rejoinder. A. Schlesinger, Jr. 225:147-8 Ag 20 '77 *

SCHLESINGER, James Rodney
Energy crisis is just beginning; interview. il por U.S. News 82:24-5 F 14 '77
Schlesinger: a good response; excerpts from interview, ed by R. Thomas and J. B. Copeland. Newsweek 89:22-3 My 9 '77
That man is energy Czar James R. Schlesinger and he has plans for all of us; interview. il pors Sr Schol 110:4-7+ S 8 '77
U.S. can squeeze out waste and still grow; interview, ed by A. J. Parisi and S. Jackson. por Bus W p70-1 Ap 25 '77

about

Back again. E. Marshall. New Repub 176:14-16 Ja 29 '77 *
Building an energy plan. M. Ruby and J. Bishop, Jr. il por Newsweek 89:59-60 Mr 7 '77 *
Energy czar. Nation 224:291-2 Mr 12 '77 *
Energy fallback. R. Boeth and others. il por Newsweek 90:37 D 5 '77 *
Energy squeeze coming for all Americans. por U.S. News 82:26 Ap 11 '77 *
Jim's overnight task force. por Time 109:60 F 21 '77 *
Legacy of James Schlesinger. R. J. Bresler and R. C. Gray. Intellect 105:228-9 F '77 *
Mao's funeral. B. J. Wattenberg. Harpers 254: 31-3 F '77 *
New Energy Department: where it goes from here. il por Nations Bus 65:44-6+ O '77 *
Score one for Jimmy. D. M. Alpern and others. il por Newsweek 90:15-16 Ag 15 '77 *
Superbrain's superproblem. il pors Time 109: 58-61+ Ap 4 '77 *
TRB from Washington. New Repub 176:2+ Je 18 '77 *
To Jimmy from James. M. Friedman. Newsweek 90:99 O 17 '77 *
White House point man. S. Fraker and J. Bishop. il por Newsweek 89:16 F 7 '77 *

SCHLESINGER, Leonard A. and Walton, R. E.
Process of work restructuring, and its impact on collective bargaining. M Labor R 100:52-5 Ap '77

SCHLESSINGER, J. and others
Lateral transport of a lipid probe and labeled proteins on a cell membrane. bibl il Science 195:307-9 Ja 21 '77

SCHLEYER, Hanns-Martin, kidnapping
Ambush in a civil war; kidnapping by Baader-Meinhof gang. il Time 110:37-8 S 19 '77
Germany: the terror. R. Carroll and P. Martin. il por Newsweek 90:55-6 S 19 '77
Life in a state of siege. il Time 110:34-5 S 26 '77
No more extensions. il por Time 110:53 O 24 '77
War without boundaries. il Time 110:28-31+ O 31 '77

SCHLITTEN, Don
Jazz. M. Ullman. New Repub 177:23-5 N 19 '77 *

SCHLITZ, Joseph, Brewing Company
Schlitz raids the competition. il por Bus W p54-5 N 21 '77

SCHLOSSBERG, Dan
Atlantic City gambles on casinos. il Travel 148: 50-1+ O '77
Summer in Colorado ski country. il Travel 147: 38-43 Ap '77

SCHLOSSER, Herbert Samuel
Happy days at no. 2. H. F. Waters. il por Newsweek 90:119+ N 14 '77 *

SCHLOSSER, Wolfhard. See Schmidt-Kaler, T. jt auth

SCHMANDT, Jurgen
Federal reorganization: science and technology. Science 197:425 Jl 29 '77

SCHMANDT-BESSERAT, Denise
From reckoning to writing. il Sci Am 237:58 Ag '77 *
Roots of writing. il por Time 110:76 Ag 1 '77 *

SCHMERTZ, Herbert
This man was made possible by a grant from Mobil Oil. M. Gerrard. il Esquire 89:62-4+ Ja '78 *

SCHMID, Vernon
Dance me the epic of Ireland; In from the Irish fog; Gallow waltz; poems. Chr Cent 94:747, 749, 750 Ag 31 '77
Erosions of violence, hopes for peace. il Chr Cent 94:258-9 Mr 16 '77

SCHMIDGALL, Gary
Imp of perversity. il Opera N 41:10-13 F 12 '77
Out of The borough. il por Opera N 42:8+ D 10 '77

SCHMIDT, C. James
How to win the budget battle on campus. Am Lib 8:569-70 N '77

SCHMIDT, Charles
Watercolor page. il por Am Artist 41:62-5+ O '77

SCHMIDT, Harry
Men who make the Blue Max run. J. Scalzo. il pors Hot Rod 30:24-6+ Ag '77 *

SCHMIDT, Helmut
Schmidt on terrorism; excerpts from interview, ed by R. M. Smith and P. Martin. por Newsweek 90:77 N 28 '77
Talk with Schmidt; excerpts from interview, ed by E. Behr and P. Martin. il Newsweek 89:50 Je 13 '77

about

Facing a Helmut problem. por Time 110:16 Jl 4 '77 *
Schmidt rides a new crest of confidence. por Bus W p46-7 D 5 '77 *
West Germany: a balance sheet. G. Braunthal. Cur Hist 73:156-9+ N '77 *

Visit to the United States, 1977

Federal German Chancellor Schmidt visits Washington: statement, July 14, 1977. Dept State Bull 77:178 Ag 8 '77

SCHMIDT, Julius
Julius Schmidt and his book about lunar eclipses. J. Ashbrook. il por Sky & Tel 53:173-4 Mr '77 *

SCHMIDT, Margaret Fox
Passions of Lady Jane Digby. il por Ms 5:78-80+ My '77

SCHMIDT, Michael
Comment. J. Silkin. Poetry 130:237-9 Jl '77 *

SCHMIDT, Siegfried
Swinging sergeant. il por Time 109:46 Ap 11 '77 *

SCHMIDT-KALER, Theodor, and Schlossor, Wolfhard
Super-wide-angle photographs of the Milky Way. il Sky & Tel 53:436-9 Je '77

SCHMIDTCHEN, Paul W.
History in books. See issues of Hobbies

SCHMIEDER, Allen A.
Most realistic future. Educ Digest 42:31-3 Ap '77

SCHMITT, Harrison H.
Starlawyers and shuttle. Aviation W 107:9 S 5 '77

SCHMITZ, Kenneth S. and Shaw, B. R.
Hydrodynamic evidence in support of spacer regions in chromatin. bibl il Science 197:661-3 Ag 12 '77

SCHMUCKER, Douglas L. and others
Age-related changes in the hepatic endoplasmic reticulum: a quantitative analysis. bibl il Science 197:1005-8 S 2 '77

SCHMÜCKER, Toni
Volkswagen's Herr Fix-it. il por Time 109:66+ My 16 '77 *

SCHNAPF, A.
Survey of the United States meteorological satellite program. il Weatherwise 30:180-91+ O '77

SCHNEEGAS, Kay
Learning to move, moving to learn. M. Nelson. il Parks & Rec 12:34-5+ N '77 *

SCHNEIDER, Barbara Hand
Reviving nearly lost crafts. House B 119:12+ Je '77

SCHNEIDER, Barry R.
Stonewalling on the arms control impact statements. Bull Atom Sci 33:5 Ja '77

SCHNEIDER, Bert
Politics under the palms. B. Burlingham. il pors Esquire 87:47-52+ F '77 *

SCHNEIDER, Bill
Last fight for the grizzly; excerpt from Where the grizzly walks. il Outdoor Life 161:55-8+ Ja '78
Will this grizzly attack? il Nat Wildlife 15:4-9 F '77

SCHNEIDER, D. W.
Add voltage regulation to a color photo enlarger. il Pop Electr 12:63-5 N '77

SCHNEIDER, David S. See Pardee, A. B. jt auth

SCHNEIDER, Jan. See McManus, R. J. jt auth

SCHNEIDER, Jason
Camera collector. See issues of Modern photography
Secrets of a good wood stove. bibl il Pop Sci 211:113-17+ N '77
—See Gordon, A. M; Kimata, H. jt auths

SCHNEIDER, John A.
Networks hold the line. Society 14:9+ S '77

SCHNEIDER, Louis E. and others
Experimental diabetes reduces circulating 1,25-dihydroxyvitamin D in the rat. bibl il Science 196:1452-4 Je 24 '77

SCHNEIDER, Mark L.
Human rights policy review; statement, October 25, 1977. Dept State Bull 77:829-33 D 5 '77

SCHNEIDER, Pierre
Puvis de Chavannes: the alternative. bibl il Art in Am 65:94-8 My '77

SCHNEIDER, Polly
Imaginary creatures. il Sch Arts 76:35 Je '77

SCHNEIDER, Stephen H.
Decision making with uncertain inputs; excerpt from The genesis strategy. BioScience 27:511 Ag '77

SCHNEIDER, William. See Lipset, S. M. jt auth

SCHNEIDERS, Greg
Friend at court? J. Deedy. Commonweal 104:2 Ja 7 '77 *

SCHNEIDERS, Sandra M.
Dimensions of the wheel. America 136:203-4 Mr 5 '77

SCHNELL, Donald E.
Leafy jaws: the plants that eat animals; excerpt from Carnivorous plants of the United States and Canada. il Sci Digest 81:7-10+ My '77

SCHNELL, Paul
Wood duck. il Conservationist 32:43 Jl '77
SCHNEPPER, Jeff A.
Big government or big brother? Intellect 105:376 My '77
Economic observer. Intellect 105:325, 395; 106:33, 121, 221 Ap, Je, Ag, O, D '77
Women and occupational segregation. il Intellect 105:415-17 Je '77
SCHNESSEL, S. Michael
Child's garden of memories; excerpt from Jessie Willcox Smith. il Good H 184:142-5 My '77
Off season Provincetown. il Travel 148:42-7 S '77
SCHNUR, Steven
Henry Adams at Nuremberg; story. Commentary 64:41-8 Jl '77
SCHOBER, Frank J. Jr
National service for all Americans now; address, April 19, 1977. Vital Speeches 43:702-4 S 1 '77
SCHOBER, Ralf, and others
Calcium-induced displacement of membrane-associated particles upon aggregation of chromaffin granules. bibl il Science 195:495-7 F 4 '77
SCHOCH, Susan
Place to be pampered in Nashville. il Fortune 95:199-200 Je '77
SCHODER, Marie Gutheil-. See Gutheil-Schoder, M.
SCHOEN, Elin
Caring for your neck. il House & Gard 149:30+ Ap '77
Fasting: is it a safe way to lose weight? House & Gard 149:130+ Mr '77
How to relax when you think you can't. il House & Gard 149:34+ O '77
New exercise. il House & Gard 149:158-9+ My '77
SCHOEN, Linda (Allen)
Bazaar's anti-acne guide. Harp Baz 110:54-5+ Jl '77
SCHOENBERG, Arnold. See Schönberg, A.
SCHOENBERG, Arnold, Institute, Los Angeles. See Arnold Schoenberg Institute, Los Angeles
SCHOENBORN, Roy V.
Name of the game: boxes. il Sch Arts 77:36-7 S '77
SCHOENBROD, David. See Sandler, R. jt auth
SCHOENFELD, Clay
Big as all outdoors. Writers Digest 57:21-3 S '77
Thirty seconds to live. il Writers Digest 57:29 F '77
SCHOENFELD, Linda Ruth
Psychomotor approach in the nursing home. il Dance Mag 51:82-4 O '77
SCHOENHOFF, Linda
Confessions of a home clutterer. Read Digest 111:20+ Ag '77
SCHOFER, Gill
Teachers should be dictators. Educ Digest 43:42-3 O '77
SCHOFIELD Barracks, Oahu (island) See United States—Army—Barracks and quarters
SCHOHARIE Aqueduct. See Aqueducts
SCHOLARS
Failure of Marxist scholarship. T. Molnar. Nat R 29:1430-2 D 9 '77
See also
Intellectuals
Woodrow Wilson International Center for Scholars
SCHOLARSHIPS and fellowships
Equal play, equal pay; women's sports scholarships. il Newsweek 90:83 S 5 '77
Fewer is finer except for some flaws; football scholarships. J. Underwood. il Sports Illus 47:28-31+ S 5 '77
See also
Music—Scholarships and fellowships
Student aid
SCHOLASTIC Aptitude Test. See College Entrance Examination Board—Scholastic Aptitude Test
SCHOLASTIC Institute of Student Opinion. See Scholastic Research Center
SCHOLASTIC Magazine Awards
Everything you ever wanted to know about the 1978 Scholastic Writing Awards. Sr Schol 110:TE10-11 D 15 '77
1977 Scholastic Awards. il Sr Schol 109:9-12+ My 19 '77
SCHOLASTIC Magazines, Inc
Scholastic Magazines forms new Text Division. M. Reuter. Pub W 212:36 O 3 '77
SCHOLASTIC Research Center
NISO poll (cont) Sr Schol 109:11 Ja 27; 16 Mr 24; 29 Ap 21; 2 My 5; 33 My 19; 110:15-16 S 22; 23 N 17; 9 D 15 '77
TV actress tops list of students' heroes; results of NISO poll no. 2; November 18, 1976 issue. il Sr Schol 109:15 F 10 '77
SCHOLDER, Fritz
Home in an adobe. R. Kent. il pors N Y Times Mag p46-7+ Ja 23 '77 *
SCHOLER, E. A.
Islands in the mainstream of life. il Parks & Rec 12:32-5 O '77
SCHOLZ, Tom
Sound of fame and fortune. E. Miller. il pors Seventeen 36:244+ Ag '77 *

SCHOMP, Gerald
St Brendan's fantastic voyage. il map Am Hist Illus 12:22-7 Ap '77
SCHON, Isabel
Heartfelt plea: note on books for children and adolescents from Spain. il Engl J 66:49-52 Mr '77
SCHÖNBERG, Arnold
Historic reissues. G. S. Fox. Am Rec G 40:5-6+ Ag '77 *
SCHÖNBERG, Arnold, Institute, Los Angeles. See Arnold Schoenberg Institute, Los Angeles
SCHOOL activities. See Student activities
SCHOOL administration. See School management and organization
SCHOOL administrators
Evaluation of administrative performance. R. L. Featherstone and L. Romano. Clearing H 50:412-15 My '77
The first supportive environment. S. W. Rothstein. Clearing H 50:357-9 Ap '77
Lonely at the top. P. W. Jackson. Educ Digest 43:10-13 S '77
See also
School superintendents and principals
Women school administrators
SCHOOL age
See also
Education, Compulsory
SCHOOL and social and economic problems
Including population problems in the curriculum. P. M. Hauser. Educ Digest 42:14-16 Mr '77
What about moral sensibility? R. Coles. Todays Educ 66:40-2 S '77
See also
Socially handicapped children—Education
SCHOOL and the community
Action learning: a model for in-service teacher education. L. C. Falkenstein. Clearing H 50:188-91 Ja '77
Building a human resources file: a model: Missoula Area Resource Center. K. Clay and J. J. Dietz. Clearing H 50:337-40 Ap '77
Sources of school-community conflict in black communities. T. Monteiro. il Intellect 106:155-6 O '77
Using lunch time for effective community relations. J. W. Maguire. Clearing H 51:5-6 S '77
What does the public think of the schools? il Todays Educ 66:26-31 N '77
See also
Community education
Community schools
School management and organization—Parent participation
SCHOOL and the home
Crisis counseling; program for students and parents at Yerba Buena High School in San Jose, Calif. S. B. Neill. il Am Educ 13:17-22 Ja '77
Developing self-concepts of urban children; Success program for parents of young children. K. R. Washington. Educ Digest 43:44-6 N '77
Education now; parents role in childrens' learning. F. M. Hechinger. Sat R 5:50 O 15 '77
Hearing from the teacher when nothing is wrong. D. W. England. Engl J 66:42-4 S '77
Helping parents help their children. C. G. Miles. Educ Digest 43:57-9 D '77
How parents are learning to help kids learn. M. P. Scott. il Bet Hom & Gard 55:10+ S '77
How to get the most out of parent-teacher conferences. D. Paananen. il Bet Hom & Gard 55:24+ Mr '77
How to help your kids in school. il Bet Hom & Gard 55:14+ N '77
Letter to parents. W. P. Cushman. il Engl J 66:45-8 O '77
PR and the classroom teacher; informing parents of reading progress; New Haven, Conn. public schools. N. P. Criscuolo. Educ Digest 42:46-7 Mr '77
Parent apathy: problem or symptom. R. A. Gorton. bibl Clearing H 51:93-4 O '77
Parent crunch: what should the teacher do? il Todays Educ 66:78-80 Ja '77
Parent involvement in the schools. S. Anselmo. bibl Clearing H 50:297-9 Mr '77
Parents and teachers speak out. il U.S. News 83:53-4 D 12 '77
Prep makes parents more intelligenter; early-intervention program for preschoolers and parents; Redford Union School District, Mich. J. Wagner. il Am Educ 13:9-12 O '77
Problem between home and school. C. Thompson. Todays Educ 66:37+ Ja '77
Saturday School; Parent-Child Early Education program, Ferguson-Florissant, Mo, School District. P. L. Williamson. il Am Educ 13:14-17 Mr '77; Same abr. Educ Digest 43:25-7 S '77
School as a resource for families. M. Hover. Clearing H 50:415-16 My '77
Ten ways to help your child succeed. S. L. Woodard. il por Ebony 32:52-4+ O '77
Using parents as teaching partners; reading program in Montgomery County, Md. public schools. A. Breiling. Educ Digest 42:50-2 F '77

SCHOOL and the home—*Continued*
Winning play at home base; home visitation program for parents of preschoolers in Yakima, Wash. V. Hedrich. il Am Educ 13:27-30 Jl '77
See also
Parents and teachers associations
SCHOOL art. See Art—Study and teaching
SCHOOL art exhibits. See Childrens art—Exhibitions
SCHOOL art galleries. See Art in the school
SCHOOL athletics
Croquet, anyone? athletic-injury awards in California. L. Langway and D. Gram. il Newsweek 90:72-3 S 5 '77
So your child wants to go out for the team. Changing T 31:34-6 O '77
See also
Basketball
Coaches (athletics)
Football, High school
Physical education and training
SCHOOL attendance
Declining enrollments: implications for the school curriculum. K. E. Eisenberger. Educ Digest 42:6-9 My '77
See also
School phobia
SCHOOL boards
Feminist surge hits school boards. B. Doran. Educ Digest 43:28-30 O '77
You & your school board: how to make your ideas count. M. Daly. il Bet Hom & Gard 55:206+ D '77
See also
New York (city)—Education, Board of
SCHOOL book fairs. See Book fairs
SCHOOL Bookshop Association. See School bookstores
SCHOOL bookstores
Booming new way to get books to children in Britain: the school bookstore. S. Paulden. il Pub W 211:95-6 F 28 '77
Letter from England: bookselling in schools; School Bookshop Association. A. Chambers. Horn Bk 53:217-21 Ap '77
SCHOOL buildings
Construction management, in a Miami test, saves $1.5 million. il Archit Rec 161:75-8 Ja '77
How school kids can survive tornadoes; National Oceanic and Atmospheric Administration study. K. J. Gilleland. il Farm J 101:J2+ Ap '77

Heating and ventilation

Our school-made solar project; Central Senior High School, Seat Pleasant, Md. J. Silver and K. Johnson. il por Todays Educ 66:62-4 S '77
See also
Schools—Fuel requirements

Security measures

Schools strike back against vandals. il U.S. News 83:66 Ag 8 '77
SCHOOL buildings, Converted. See Apartments, Remodeled
SCHOOL buildings, Remodeled
Modernization: everybody's doing it. B. E. Graves. Educ Digest 43:17-19 N '77
SCHOOL children
See also
Children, Gifted
High school students
Self government in education
Teachers and students

Adjustment

Helping parents help their children. C. G. Miles. Educ Digest 43:57-9 D '77

Anecdotes, facetiae, satire, etc.

First 12 days of school. E. Bombeck. il Read Digest 111:81-2 S '77

Grading and promotion

See Grading and marking (students)

Out of school activities

See Children—Recreation

Transportation for integration

Boston after Louise Day Hicks: no more mileage in busing. H. Husock. il por Nation 225: 710-12 D 31 '77
Back to busing—again. il Time 110:71 S 12 '77
Conflicting signals; Supreme Court decision in case of the National Association for the Advancement of Colored People against the Dayton Board of Education. J. Miller. New Repub 177:10-11 Jl 23 '77
What Louisville has taught us about busing. R. M. Williams. il Sat R 4:6-8+ Ap 30 '77

Anecdotes, facetiae, satire, etc.

Bentleg solution. J. P. McGrath. Nat R 29:668-9 Je 10 '77
SCHOOL counseling. See Personnel service in education
SCHOOL counselors. See Student counselors
SCHOOL decoration
Hurst's remembrance '76; sculpture to decorate school grounds. M. Painter. il Sch Arts 76:56-7 F '77
Supergraphics; student art that keeps on giving; project at Columbus East High School, Columbus, Ind. M. Lewman and P. Miller. il Sch Arts 77:38-40 D '77
What's in this building, anyway? supergraphic project at Rosati-Kain High School, St Louis. M. Scherer. il Design (US) 78:13-17 Spr '77
See also
Mosaics
Mural painting and decoration
Mural painting and decoration, Exterior
SCHOOL desegregation decision, 1954. See United States—Supreme Court—Decisions
SCHOOL discipline
Discipline; symposium. bibl Todays Educ 66: 32-7+ Ja '77
Let's talk sense about discipline. M. D. Thomas. Clearing H 50:309-12 Mr '77
New concept of discipline. K. Henson. Clearing H 51:89-91 O '77
Responding to student misbehavior. R. A. Gorton. Educ Digest 42:2-5 Ap '77
10 steps to good discipline. W. Glasser. il Todays Educ 66:60-3 N '77
See also
Classroom management
Corporal punishment
Student suspension and expulsion
SCHOOL employees
Alcoholics on the school staff. J. Cramer. Educ Digest 43:38-40 N '77
SCHOOL enrollment. See School attendance
SCHOOL excursions
Children meet artists; field trips to artists' studios by Los Angeles students. E. Levin. il Sch Arts 76:20-2 Je '77
How to keep your students from yawning at art museums. J. C. Vitale. Design (US) 79:10-11 Fall '77
Why the GLUB went mobile; Groton-Lowell Upward Bound Program, Mass. J. Helyar. il Am Educ 13:22-6 Ag '77
SCHOOL exhibitions
Fine arts festival. K. Herrmann. il Sch Arts 76: 47 Je '77
SCHOOL exhibitions, Traveling
Historical goodies crammed in old camelback trunks; West Virginia Heritage Trunk project. D. Sherwood. il Smithsonian 8:106+ Je '77
SCHOOL exhibits
See also
Childrens art—Exhibitions
SCHOOL finance. See Education—Finance
SCHOOL food service. See School lunches
SCHOOL furniture, equipment, etc.
Get equipment for your school—free! M. L. Schildkraut. Good H 184:228 Mr '77
SCHOOL grounds
Hurst's remembrance '76; sculpture to decorate school grounds. M. Painter. il Sch Arts 76:56-7 F '77
SCHOOL librarians
Ideal vs. actual roles focus of library study. SLJ 23:17-18 Ap '77
See also
American Library Association—American Association of School Librarians
SCHOOL libraries
Back to basics: its meaning for school media programs. M. Weber. bibl por SLJ 24:83-5 O '77
Practically speaking. See issues of School library journal
SLJ's 1977 news roundup. B. M. Cheatham. il SLJ 24:17-23 D '77

Bilingual collections

Special report: the bilingual library; Automotive High School, Brooklyn, N.Y. M. Bart. il por Wilson Lib Bull 51:475-6 F '77

Book selection

See Book selection

Censorship

Ban in Boston? Poem provokes dispute; Chelsea High. L. R. Pearson. Am Lib 8:472 O '77
Internal security. N. R. Needham. Todays Educ 66:53 Ja '77
Oakland school official restricts library book. SLJ 23:12 Ap '77
School board bans poem; defense committee sues; Chelsea High School library. SLJ 24:10 N '77

Federal aid

ALA testifies on school library/media aid. E. D. Cooke and H. W. Sprouse. Wilson Lib Bull 52:305+ D '77
ESEA IV-B hearings held. E. D. Cooke and H. W. Sprouse. Wilson Lib Bull 52:72 S '77
Federal funding update; ESEA extension. SLJ 24:11 S '77

Finance

Budget clashes threaten school & public libraries. SLJ 24:11 S '77

SCHOOL libraries—*Continued*

Instruction in use

Thirteen steps to library orientation. B. Kouns. SLJ 23:125 Mr '77

Why Susie can't use the library. B. Fast. Wilson Lib Bull 51:732-3 My '77

Services to the handicapped

There are no other children; special children in library media centers; Lapham Elementary School. E. T. Dresang. il SLJ 24:19-23 S '77

California

Los Alamitos schools win AASL/EBC award. il SLJ 23:11 My '77

Los Alamitos: the School Library Media Program of 1977; views of school system representatives. il SLJ 24:74-9 O '77

Hawaii

Trouble in Paradise: Hawaii auditor's report scores lack of co-op; views of C. Tanimura. Lib J 102:1330+ Je 15 '77

Illinois

Library birthday parties; Hawthorne School Learning Center, Wheaton. M. K. Bechtel. il SLJ 24:36 N '77

Kansas

Library material security systems: a school district's experience; Shawnee Mission Public School District. D. Shirley. il SLJ 23:38-41 Ap '77

Massachusetts

Special report: films and independent schools: a declaration of cooperation; Boston-area independent schools. M. A. Moskowitz. il por Wilson Lib Bull 52:223-6 N '77

New York (state)

Rochester school supt. wins AASL service award. por SLJ 23:14+ My '77

Special report: a winning role for the school library; energy technology program at East Senior High School in West Seneca. C. D. Gwitt. bibl il Wilson Lib Bull 52:295-8 D '77

Special report: the bilingual library; Automotive High School, Brooklyn, N.Y. M. Bart. il por Wilson Lib Bull 51:475-6 F '77

Texas

Ideal vs. actual roles focus of library study. SLJ 23:17-18 Ap '77

SCHOOL libraries and audio-visual materials

Multi-image productions are magical motivators. C. M. Alborn. bibl il por SLJ 23:33-7 Ap '77

SCHOOL libraries and motion pictures

Special report: films and independent schools: a declaration of cooperation; Boston-area independent schools. M. A. Moskowitz. il por Wilson Lib Bull 52:223-6 N '77

SCHOOL library administration

How to make something from nothing. S. D. Connolly and L. Wollin. il por Am Lib 8:572-3 N '77

SCHOOL library instruction. See School libraries—Instruction in use

SCHOOL library orientation. See School libraries—Instruction in use

SCHOOL library protection systems. See Library protection systems

SCHOOL Lunch Program, National. See United States—Agriculture, Department of—Food and Nutrition Service

SCHOOL lunches

Let's liven up school lunches. A. Stark. por Seventeen 36:42 S '77

Would you eat your child's school lunch? with comments by Jean Mayer. N. Benezra. il Fam Health 9:40-3+ S '77

See also

United States—Agriculture, Department of—Food and Nutrition Service

SCHOOL management and organization

Administrative team: a step forward or backward? P. B. Salmon; M. Lieberman. Educ Digest 43:2-5 S '77

Attitudes of principals toward participatory managerial practices. F. C. Wendel. il Clearing H 50:322-6 Mr '77

House plan in secondary schools. C. R. Kraegel. Clearing H 50:392-4 My '77

Is local control of education dead or dying? E. J. McClendon. Educ Digest 42:22-3 Ap '77

Myths of rural school and district consolidation. J. P. Sher and R. B. Tompkins. Educ Digest 42:45-8 Ap '77

Organizing clusters in a traditional building; Denonville Middle School, Penfield, N.Y. R. W. Barber. Clearing H 50:314-15 Mr '77

Sharing administrative decision making. A. F. Haynes, Jr and A. E. Garner. bibl Clearing H 51:53-7 O '77

See also

Ability grouping in education
School administrators
School boards
School discipline
School superintendents and principals
Student suspension and expulsion
Women school administrators

Anecdotes, facetiae, satire, etc.

More power to young administrators. T. E. Hightower. Educ Digest 42:36-7 F '77

On creating the Stepford instructorship. J. R. Dettre. Clearing H 51:120-2 N '77

Parent participation

Citizen advisory committees; Florida. G. E. Greenwood and others. Educ Digest 43:6-9 S '77

Parent power in the schools: can shared decision-making happen? G. Baisinger. por Parents Mag 52:25 Je '77

Where does your school tax money go? New York City's Educational Priorities Panel. J. J. Morisseau. il Parents Mag 52:36+ S '77

You & your school board: how to make your ideas count. M. Daly. il Bet Hom & Gard 55:206+ D '77

Student participation

As we see it; desegregation resolution drafted by Stockton, Calif. students; excerpt from television script. il Sr Schol 110:17-18+ S 22 '77

See also

Self government in education

Teacher participation

Initiating structure for educational change. J. W. Licata and others. Educ Digest 43:21-4 S '77

SCHOOL of American Ballet

School of American Ballet workshop: 1977. T. Tobias. Dance Mag 51:85+ Ag '77

SCHOOL orchestras

Independent Schools Orchestra; youth orchestra conducted by H. Bloch. B. R. Paolucci. il por Hi Fi 27:MA22-5 O '77

SCHOOL organization. See School management and organization

SCHOOL phobia

Fight your school fears. A. Koral. Seventeen 36:51 Ag '77

SCHOOL principals. See School superintendents and principals

SCHOOL projects, Bicentennial. See United States Centennial celebrations, etc.—School projects

SCHOOL public relations. See School and the community

SCHOOL reports and records

ETS's star chamber; Law School Admissions Test and the exemption of the Educational Testing Service from the Family Rights and Privacy act of 1974. K. Masters. New Repub 176:13-14 F 5 '77

Facts about Mr Buckley's amendment. L. Knight. Am Educ 13:6-9 Je '77

How to protect your children's school records. M. P. Scott. il Bet Hom & Gard 55:30+ F '77

Practitioner's guide to machete-swinging in the paperwork jungle: record keeping and individualized instruction. D. G. Armstrong and R. E. Pinney. il Clearing H 50:196-9 Ja '77

Yes! You can see your child's school records. N. G. Rollins. Good H 184:220 F '77

SCHOOL schedules

Making the most of the school day. C. W. Fowler. Educ Digest 43:28-9 D '77

SCHOOL signs. See Signs and signboards

SCHOOL subjects. See Courses of study

SCHOOL superintendents and principals

Lunch with the principal. D. Haarman. Educ Digest 43:60 O '77

Odd couple: the building principal and the visiting supervisor. B. Browning. Clearing H 50:352-3 Ap '77

Principal who cared; E. R. Brimhall. A. Morphis. por Clearing H 50:263-5 F '77

So you are the new principal? J. L. Colquit and E. Hendrix. bibl Clearing H 51:22-3+ S '77

When superintendents fail. C. W. Fowler. Educ Digest 42:18-20 My '77

See also

Women school superintendents and principals

SCHOOL supervision and supervisors

Lifeboat ethics and the first-year teacher. M. H. Brown and A. L. Willems. il Clearing H 51:73-5 O '77

Odd couple: the building principal and the visiting supervisor. B. Browning. Clearing H 50:352-3 Ap '77

Reading supervisors—teachers have needs. J. Sanacore. bibl Clearing H 51:17-21 S '77

SCHOOL surveys. See Educational surveys

SCHOOL vandalism. See Vandalism

SCHOOL verse

Spring poetry festival; ed by R. Calisch. il Engl J 66:42-60 My '77

SCHOOL violence. See Violence

SCHOOL visitations. See School and the home

SCHOOL-work plan. See Education, Cooperative

SCHOOL year
Whatever happened to: year-round schools—catching on. U.S. News 82:77-8 Je 20 '77

SCHOOLS
See also
Art schools
Catholic schools
Church schools
Correspondence schools and courses
Education
Nursery schools
Private schools
Rural schools
Vocational-technical schools

Finance
See Education—Finance

Fuel requirements
Energy and the schools. E. L. Boyer; K. C. Kryger; J. Silver and K. Johnson. bibl il Todays Educ 66:54-5+ S '77
New crisis in the classroom: energy. S. B. Neill. il Am Educ 13:15-21 Ag '77

Statistics
See Education—Statistics

England
See Schools—Great Britain

France
See also
Catholic schools—France
National School of Administration, France

Great Britain
In England now. D. J. M. Cornwell. pors N Y Times Mag p34-5+ O 23 '77

Switzerland
Gardening school, Swiss style; Gärtnerinnen-Schule Hünibach. R. Wolf. il Org Gard & Farm 25:160+ Ja '78

United States
See also
Education—United States
Public schools—United States

SCHOOLS, Experimental
Alternative education: at the crossroads. R. Byrne. Clearing H 50:348-9 Ap '77
Alternative schools: another view. J. M. Benjamin. Clearing H 50:312-13 Mr '77
Not so loudmouthed and foolish; views of H. Kohl. il por Time 109:66 Ja 24 '77
On finding some real alternatives. A. A. Glatthorn. il Todays Educ 66:68-71 N '77
Process for alternative education; High School in the Community and other alternative schools in New Haven, Conn. L. Rich. il Am Educ 13:23-6 Mr '77
See also
Open plan schools

SCHOOLS, Jewish. See Jews—Education

SCHOOLS, Medical. See Medical colleges

SCHOOLS and museums. See Museums and schools

SCHOOLS and politics. See Politics and education

SCHOONER racing. See Yacht racing

SCHOONOVER, Cortland
Frank Schoonover's frontier: excerpt from Frank Schoonover. il por Am West 14:38-47 Mr '77

SCHOONOVER, Frank Earl
Frank Schoonover's frontier; excerpt from Frank Schoonover. C. Schoonover. il por Am West 14:38-47 Mr '77 *

SCHOPF, J. William
AIBS nominee wins NSF award. por BioScience 27:497 Jl '77 *
NSF chooses Schopf as second Waterman Award recipient. por Phys Today 30:69 Ag '77 *
Out of earth's past: biological roots. il Sci N 111:343 My 28 '77 *

SCHOPP, Walter W.
Conference talk timer. il Pop Electr 11:62-3 F '77

SCHORK, John E.
No growth can be fun. por Forbes 119:78 Ap 1 '77 *

SCHORR, Daniel Louis
Is there life after TV? excerpt from Clearing the air. il por Esquire 88:105-7+ O '77

about

As Schorr sees it. H. F. Waters and N. Stadtman. por Newsweek 90:90+ O 31 '77 *
Dos and don'ts of television news. T. Griffith. Time 110:114 D 5 '77 *

SCHOTLAND, D. L. and others
Duchenne dystrophy: alteration in muscle plasma membrane structure. bibl il Science 196:1005-7 My 27 '77

SCHRAG, Peter
Education now. Sat R 5:53-4 N 12 '77

SCHRAMM, B. J.
RotorWay revolution. G. C. Larson. il pors Flying 100:56-61+ F '77 *

SCHRANK, Robert
Two women, three men on a raft. il Harvard Bus R 55:100-8 My '77

SCHRAUB, Susan Hope
Fine art of conversation. House B 119:74+ N '77

SCHRAUZER, G. N.
Biological nitrogen fixation. il por bibl Chemistry 50:13-16 Mr '77

SCHREIBER, Flora Rheta
Regnery sues three over new Schreiber book. M. Reuter. Pub W 211:28 Ja 10 '77 *

SCHREIBER, Marc
Mr Schreiber discusses achievements of United Nations in field of human rights; excerpts from address, April 7, 1977. il por UN Chron 14:39-40 My '77

SCHREIBER, Morris
Night campus. il Todays Educ 66:65-6 S '77

SCHREIBER, Norman
Pop photo snapshots. See issues of Popular photography, May 1977-

SCHREINER, Olive
Olive Schreiner—women of the Karroo. G. K. Kmetz. il por Ms 6:91-4 Ag '77 *

SCHROEDER, Becky
Young inventor sheds light on a tricky problem: interview. ed by A. Koral. por Seventeen 36:104 Ap '77

SCHROEDER, Dorothy
Flowers that bloom in spite of frost. Org Gard & Farm 24:144 Ap '77
My black walnut tree. il Org Gard & Farm 24:84-6 S '77

SCHROLL, Catherine V. See MacLellan, E. jt auth

SCHROTH, Milton N. See Sing, V. O. jt auth

SCHRUFER, George
Burn centers: the new miracle workers. G. Williams, 3d. il Fam Health 9:48-52 Jl '77 *

SCHUBECK, Thomas L.
Lenten lethargy and the invisible neighbor. America 136:274-5 Mr 26 '77

SCHUBERT, Franz Peter
Musical events; performances of Die schöne Müllerin. A. Porter. New Yorker 53:93-4+ F 28 '77 *
New recordings of symphonies nos. 5, 8 and 9. Hi Fi 27:114+ O '77 *
Reappraisal of Schubert's methods of composition. L. M. Griffel. bibl f il Mus Q 63:186-210 Ap '77 *
Schubert: the melody and the misery. I. Kolodin. por Sat R 5:42-3 O 1 '77 *
Symphonies-no. 5 in B flat; no. 8 in B minor. J. R. Oestreich and P. Althouse. Am Rec G 40:34-5 My '77 *

SCHUCK, Peter H.
Whisperings in the press gallery. Harpers 254:113-15 Mr '77

SCHUELER, Donald G.
Can they head off the tankers at the pass? Audubon 79:146-8 N '77

SCHUH, Dwight R.
(ed) See Kittredge, D. Elk that was king

SCHULBERG, Budd
(ed) See Grace Patricia. Other Princess Grace

SCHULER, Margaret
Christians for socialism. il New Cath World 220:152-4 My '77

SCHULIAN, John
Horse racing. Sports Illus 47:63-4 D 12 '77

SCHULLER, Gunther
Music. D. Hamilton. Nation 224:731-2 Je 11 '77 *

SCHULLER, Robert H.
If Christ were alive today. por Ladies Home J 94:62+ D '77

about

Finding the good at Garden Grove. B. Barr. il por Chr Cent 94:424-7 My 4 '77; Discussion. 94:764-5 Ag 31 '77 *
Profiles. C. Tomkins. por New Yorker 53:43-4+ My 23 '77 *

SCHULMAN, Norman
Potter of Penland. il Craft Horiz 37:23-7 Je '77

SCHULTZ, Bill
What Stanford does better than Harvard. il Esquire 88:118-19+ S '77

SCHULTZ, Dave
If I had a Hammer, I'd. . . P. Gammons. il por Sports Illus 46:49-50 F 14 '77 *

SCHULTZ, David L.
Recycled rubber stretches the imagination. il Design (US) 79:17 Fall '77

SCHULTZ, Dodi
Terror of child molestation. il Parents Mag 52:44-5+ F '77

SCHULTZ, Jerome S.
Carrier-mediated photodiffusion membranes. bibl il Science 197:1177-9 S 16 '77

SCHULTZ, June
Arts-In! What is it? il Sch Arts 76:18-21 Ap '77

SCHULTZ, Kenneth S.
Bass and the worm. il por Field & S 82:84-9 My '77
Fishing. See issues of Field & stream to March 1977
Meanmouth. il Field & S 82:84-5+ Je '77
Special kind of bream. il Field & S 82:52+ S '77
Treasure lives. il Field & S 82:114-22+ Ag '77

SCHULTZ, Morton J.
Car clinic; questions and answers. See issues of Popular mechanics

SCHULTZ, Philip
For the wandering Jews; poem. New Yorker 52:30 F 28 '77
Gift; poem. New Yorker 53:30 Ja 9 '78
Like wings; poem. New Yorker 52:32 F 7 '77

SCHULTZ, Richard M. and others
Interferon: an inducer of macrophage activation by polyanions. bibl il Science 197:674-6 Ag 12 '77

SCHULTZ, Terri
How Madison's radical mayor has mellowed with age. il pors N Y Times Mag p49+ Ap 17 '77

SCHULTZ, Theodore William
Hungry, crowded competitive world. il Bull Atom Sci 33:26-31 O '77

SCHULTZE, Charles Louis
Big surge ahead in business; interview. il pors U.S. News 82:23-4+ F 28 '77
Economic outlook and policy; address, October 4, 1977. Vital Speeches 44:66-70 N 15 '77
Public use of private interest; excerpt from Godkin lectures. Harpers 254:43-50+ My '77

about

CEA takes a backseat with Carter. il por Bus W p 114-15 Jl 25 '77 *
Jimmy Carter gets mixed marks in economics I. J. Cameron. il pors Fortune 95:98-102+ Je '77 *
Spenders vs. savers: split in the Cabinet. W. C. Bryant. il pors U.S. News 82:18 Ap 18 '77 *
Starring role for the CEA? il por Time 109:52 F 7 '77 *
Where Carter's team wants to intervene. il por Bus W p58+ Ap 4 '77 *
Who's calling the economic shots. Bus W p 117 Mr 28 '77 *

SCHULZ, Bruno
Father's last escape; story tr by C. Wieniewska. New Yorker 53:24-6 Ja 2 '78
Loneliness; story; tr by C. Wieniewska. New Yorker 53:43 N 14 '77
Sanatorium under the sign of the hour glass; story; tr by C. Wieniewska. New Yorker 53: 44-54 D 12 '77

SCHULZ, David A.
Sex and society in the seventies. bibl il Society 14:20-4 Jl '77

SCHULZ, Gene Church
How to poison-proof your home. Parents Mag 52:42-3+ My '77

SCHULZ, William
Crack! Roar! It's World Series time! il Read Digest 111:189-90+ O '77

SCHULZE, Franz
Consistently discriminating connoisseurship. F. Schulze. il Art N 76:64-7 Ap '77
Palladio's splendid creations. il por Art N 76: 70-1 O '77
Report from Chicago: restoration of the Trading Room. il Art in Am 65:58-9 N '77

SCHUMACHER, Ernest Friedrich
Taking the scare out of scarcity. Psychol Today 11:16 S '77; Same abr. Read Digest 111:168-9 D '77

about

Idea whose time has come? J. Ross-Skinner. il por Duns R 110:118-20+ O '77 *
Mr Small. S. Fraker and G. C. Lubenow. il por Newsweek 89:18 Mr 28 '77 *
Small is beautiful, and so is Rome. C. Fager. Chr Cent 94:325-8 Ap 6 '77 *

SCHUMACHER, Florence, and Schumacher, Gerald
Rx for choosing a pharmacist. il Fam Health 9:48-9 Je '77

SCHUMACHER, Gerald. See Schumacher, F. jt auth

SCHUMAN, Mary M.
Commanding voice in airline reform. por Bus W p 170+ N 14 '77 *

SCHUMAN, Wendy
Sisters: can they shape each other's lives? il Mademoiselle 83:172-3+ O '77

SCHUMANN, Robert Alexander
Frauenliebe und Leben, op. 42; Liederkreis; Jessye Norman's recording. P. L. Miller. Am Rec G 40:31-3 Jl '77 *

SCHUPF, Nicole. See Williams, C. A. Jr, jt auth

SCHUR, Edwin
Two faces of meditation; excerpt from The awareness trap. il Parents Mag 52:70+ N '77

SCHURR, George Michael
Hope of dying. Chr Cent 94:935-6 O 19 '77

SCHUSTER, Edgar H.
Back to basics: what does it really mean? Clearing H 50:237-9 F '77

SCHUSTER, Richard O.
Running—the new high; ideas of E. Colt and R. O. Schuster. C. Seebohm. il House & Gard 149:89+ Jl '77 *

SCHUYTEN, Peter J.
$1,300 Christmas toy made in Japan. il Fortune 96:179-80+ S '77

SCHWAB, Priscilla
People in business. il Nations Bus 65:100 N; 91-2 D '77

SCHWAB, Ruth A.
Confronting Henry Moore. il por Intellect 106: 241-4 D '77

SCHWABE, Christian, and McDonald, J. K.
Relaxin: a disulfide homolog of insulin. bibl il Science 197:914-15 Ag 26 '77

SCHWALBERG, Bob
Schwalberg at large. See issues of Popular photography

SCHWALBERG, Carol
España—littorally yours. il Sat Eve Post 249: 68-9 N '77
Ideal airport. Mademoiselle 83:42+ F '77

SCHWALM, Patricia A. and Starrett, P. H.
Infrared reflectance in leaf-sitting neotropical frogs. bibl il Science 196:1225-7 Je 10 '77

SCHWANDT, Erich
L'Affilard's published Sketchbooks. bibl f il Mus Q 63:99-113 Ja '77

SCHWANN catalogs. See Phonograph records—Catalogs

SCHWANN cells. See Nerve cells

SCHWARTZ, Alan U.
Danger: pendulum swinging. Atlantic 239:29-34 F '77

SCHWARTZ, Alvin
Children, humor, and folklore. il Horn Bk 53: 280-7, 471-6 Je; Ag '77

SCHWARTZ, Anne
Tuscarora Pottery School. il pors Ceram Mo 25:36-41 Je '77

SCHWARTZ, Arnold, and others
Possible cyclic nucleotide regulation of calcium mediating myocardial contraction. bibl il Science 195:982+ Mr 11 '77

SCHWARTZ, Bernard. See Wood, P. jt auth

SCHWARTZ, Bernard L.
Surplus labor. por Forbes 120:98 Jl 1 '77 *

SCHWARTZ, Brian B. and Foner, Simon
Large-scale applications of superconductivity. bibl il Phys Today 30:34-5+ Jl '77

SCHWARTZ, Dave
Mr Rent-a-wreck. M. Lamm. il pors Pop Mech 147:85+ Mr '77 *

SCHWARTZ, Douglas W.
Pueblo population explosion. Sci N 111:133 F 26 '77 *

SCHWARTZ, Ellen
Floating a line in space. Art N 76:52-3 Summ '77
Gaudier-Brzeska: a great unknown. il Art N 76:178+ N '77

SCHWARTZ, Elliott
ISCM World Music Days. il Hi Fi 27:MAE34-5+ S '77

SCHWARTZ, Gary
Amsterdam (cont) Art N 76:99-102 My '77
Haarlem. il Art N 76:96-7 F '77

SCHWARTZ, Gary E. See Hassett, J. jt auth

SCHWARTZ, Glenn E.
Day it snowed in Miami. Weatherwise 30:50+ Ap '77

SCHWARTZ, Harold L. 1921-
APL's bid for Pabst: a hasty try at growth by acquisition. por Bus W p85-6 Ja 9 '78 *
APL's big acquisition plans. por Bus W p92+ S 19 '77 *

SCHWARTZ, Jerry
Improve TV reception—install a tower. il Radio-Electr 48:70-1+ Ap '77

SCHWARTZ, Jonathan
Final notes; story. Mademoiselle 83:22 My '77

SCHWARTZ, Lewis. See Unfug, C. S. jt auth

SCHWARTZ, Loretta
Hungry women in America. il Ms 6:60-3+ O '77

SCHWARTZ, Lynne Sharon
Man who feared deep water; story. Redbook 149:114 Je '77

SCHWARTZ, Marvin D.
Antiques. See issues of Art news to Summer 1977
Antiques: questions from readers. See issues of American home

SCHWARTZ, Narda L.
Professional attitude. Lib J 102:1729-31 S 1 '77

SCHWARTZ, Norman
Substitute for substitutes. Educ Digest 43:36-7 N '77

SCHWARTZ, Paula
Naming our second baby. il Good H 184:72+ F '77
Treasure drawer; story. Seventeen 36:156-7 O '77

SCHWARTZ, Sanford
Joan Brown, long-distance painter. il Art in Am 65:88-9 Mr '77
Trouble in paradise. il Art in Am 65:103-5 Ja '77

SCHWARTZ, Sidney A.
Cold water survival. il Conservationist 31:6-7 Ja '77
To buy a fat pig. il por Conservationist 32:26-9 S '77

SCHWARTZ, Tony
My short, happy life as a gossip columnist. il pors Esquire 88:80-2+ Jl '77

SCHWARTZ, William J. and Gainer, Harold
Suprachiasmatic nucleus: use of ^{14}C-labeled deoxyglucose uptake as a functional marker. bibl il Science 197:1089-91 S 9 '77

SCHWARTZMAN, Paul
Fellini's unlovable Casanova. il N Y Times Mag p22-4+ F 6 '77

SCHWARZ, Boris
International Musicological Congress. il Hi Fi 27:MA27-9 D '77
Russlan and Ludmilla—finally. il Hi Fi 27: MA32-3 Ag '77

SCHWARZ, Ted
Make a big name with little markets. Writers Digest 57:21-2 Ap '77

SCHWARZBAUM, Lisa
Selling out. Mademoiselle 83:50+ Mr '77
Your reputation: why you should worry about it. Mademoiselle 83:206+ Ag '77

SCHWARZENEGGER, Arnold
Is all this muscle all that healthy? E. Kaye. il por Fam Health 9:20-4 D '77 *

SCHWARZER, Alice
(ed) See Beauvoir, S. de. Talking to a friend—an interview with Simone de Beauvoir

SCHWARZKOPF, Elisabeth
Music to my ears. I. Kolodin. il por Sat R 4:47 Ja 22 '77 *
Schwarzkopf-Legge master classes, singing classes at Juilliard. D. J. Soria. pors Hi Fi 27:MA5-6+ Mr '77 *
Search for perfection. R. Jacobson. il pors Opera N 41:24-7 Ja 22 '77 *

SCHWEBLER, Yuri
Plumb-bobs and waiting rooms. B. Forgey. Art N 76:168+ Summ '77 *

SCHWED, Peter
PW interviews; ed by A. W. Ehrlich. il por Pub W 212:268-9 Ag 29 '77

SCHWEID, Barry
(ed) See Vance, C. R. Secretary Vance interviewed by AP and UPI correspondents

SCHWEIKER, Richard Schultz
Excerpts from statement and remarks on bill designed to protect American workers from illegal alien employment, May 25 and August 29, 1977. Cong Digest 56:235+ O '77
about
Instant conservative. S. J. Ungar. Atlantic 240: 8+ S '77 *

SCHWEITZER, Gertrude
His kind of woman; story. Good H 185:108-9 Ag '77
Lost child; story. il Good H 184:203-6 Mr '77

SCHWENDINGER, Robert J.
Sea shanties. il Am West 14:50-5 My '77

SCHWINDT, Helen Dimos
All the President's women; or, What's a nice person like you doing in a job like this? il Ms 6:50-4+ Ja '78

SCHWINN Bicycle Company. See Bicycle industry

SCHWITTERS, Roy Frederick
Fundamental particles with charm; with biographical sketch. il Sci Am 237:15, 56-70 bibl (p 152) O '77

SCHWOERER, Lois G.
Propaganda in the Revolution of 1688-89. bibl f il Am Hist R 82:843-74 O '77

SCIENCE
Hazards of science; adaptation of address. L. Thomas. por Sci Digest 81:inside cover, 71 Mr '77
How fares basic science? W. D. Carey. Science 197:825 Ag 26 '77
Is there a crisis of confidence in science? C. Z. Nunn. Science 198:995 D 9 '77
Of Mars . . .and realistic goals. W. Bennett. Sci Digest 81:20-2 Mr '77
Off the beat (cont) Sci N 111:141, 351 F 26, My 28 '77
Outer limits; Encyclopaedia of ignorance. il Time 111:60 Ja 9 '78
Thomas S. Kuhn: revolutionary theorist of science. N. Wade. por Science 197:143-5 Jl 8 '77; Reply. R. J. Wurtman. 197:514 Ag 5 '77
See also
Biology
Communication in science
Life sciences
Medicine
Natural history
Physics
Religion and science
Technology

Awards, prizes, etc
Houssay Science Prize, 1976. il por Américas 29:32 My '77

Bibliography
Book reviews. See issues of Science
Books. See issues of Physics today
Books. See issues of Science news
Books. B. Ford. See issues of Science digest
Books. P. Morrison. See issues of Scientific American
Carl Sagan on science. C. Sagan. New Repub 177:30-3 D 3 '77
Library at large. See issues of Chemistry
Sci-tech books of 1976; comp by E. S. Crockett and E. Mount. il Lib J 102:543-53 Mr 1 '77
Scientific, technical, business and professional books. il Pub W 211:40-4+ Mr 21; 212:27-30+ O 17 '77
Scientific, technical, medical, & business books (cont) Lib J 102:567+, 2227-8+ Mr 1, N 1 '77
Significant science books: 1976-1977. Am Scholar 46:544-53 Aut '77

Conferences
Aerospace calendar. See issues of Aviation week & space technology
Calendar. See issues of Physics today
Science, sin, and sponsorship; International Conference on the Unity of the Sciences. I. L. Horowitz. por Atlantic 239:98-102 Mr '77; Discussion. 239:22-3+ Je '77
See also
Astronomy—Conferences
Gordon Research Conferences
Pugwash Conference on Science and World Affairs

Experiments
Amateur scientist. J. Walker. See issues of Scientific American, July 1977-

Fiction
See Science fiction

History
Calendar of science and technology. G. B. Kauffman. bibl il Chemistry 50:27-9 Mr '77
50 and 100 years ago. See issues of Scientific American
Poetic responses to the Copernican revolution. M. M. Byard. il Sci Am 236:120-9 bibl(p 142) Je '77
Protoscientific revolution; 12th-century cosmologists; with views of Tina Stiefel. Sci Am 238:68-9 Ja '78
Bibliography
History of science. Am Scholar 46:546-9 Aut '77

International aspects
Conditions of success in international enterprises in science and technology. L. Kowarski. Bull Atom Sci 33:44-8 S '77
Dr Press reviews China exchange. Sci Digest 82:80 Jl '77
Physicists report on progress in US-Soviet cooperation. il Phy Today 30:85+ O '77
Soviet-U.S. science agreements: Press presides over reappraisal. J. Walsh. Science 196:1064-6 Je 3 '77
U.S, France hold annual meeting of Cooperative Science Program; joint statement, May 2, 1977. Dept State Bull 76:523 My 23 '77
U.S.—Soviet exchange: politics lead science. Sci N 112:263 O 22 '77
U.S, U.S.S.R. renew agreement on science and technology; text of announcement, July 8, 1977. Dept State Bull 77:190 Ag 8 '77
U.S.-USSR scientific agreement renewed. Sci N 112:36 Jl 16 '77
U.S.-West European cooperation in science seems to be declining. J. Walsh. Science 198: 175-7 O 14 '77
See also
Oceanography—International aspects
United Nations—Committee on Science and Technology for Development

Juvenile literature
See Scientific literature for children

Methodology
Nature fakers and science. E. M. Reilly, Jr. il Conservationist 31:28-31 Ja '77

Moral aspects
See Science and ethics

Periodicals
In appreciation of page charges. H. L. Davis. Phys Today 30:120 Mr '77
No rate change if page charges are voluntary. W. G. P. Peter. BioScience 27:12+ Ja '77
Proposed anonymity for authors; letter. R. Wyatt. BioScience 27:5 Ja '77
See also
Bulletin of the atomic scientists
Environment (periodical)
Science (periodical)
Science news (periodical)

Philosophy
Objectivity of science. M. Black. bibl Bull Atom Sci 33:55-60 F '77
Reformation in science. F. Hapgood. Atlantic 239:107-10 Mr '77
See also
Physics—Philosophy

Research
See Research

Social aspects
Adventures of the mind; excerpt from 1958 article. J. R. Oppenheimer. il Sat Eve Post 249: 8 Jl '77
Baconian imperative. J. A. Goldman. bibl il Intellect 105:430-2 Je '77
Editorial; making science more human. S. Trachtman. Horticulture 55:14 F '77

SCIENCE—Social aspects—*Continued*
Editorial page; public concern over scientific research. A. McGowan. Environment 19:inside cover, 44 N '77
Failure of scientists to communicate; address, October 25, 1977. T. C. Root, Jr. Vital Speeches 44:133-6 D 15 '77
Goals of science; adaptation of address, December 1976. S. E. Luria. il Bull Atom Sci 33:28-33 My '77; Same. Current 194:23-31 Jl '77
On the uses of science. S. H. Day, Jr. Progressive 41:32-3 O '77
Science and progress. J. Rifkin and T. Howard. Progressive 41:20 D '77
Science & society (cont) Sci N 111:73, 153, 205; 112:104 Ja 29, Mr 5, 26, Ag 13 '77
Science and the citizen. See issues of Scientific American
Science, scientists and society; report of Pugwash Conference. Bull Atom Sci 33:39 D '77
Social studies of science: society crosses disciplinary lines. J. Walsh. Science 198:706-7 N 18 '77
See also
Technology—Social aspects

Study and teaching

Handicapped and science: moving into the mainstream. E. Walsh. Science 196:1424-6 Je 24 '77
Improving reading and the teaching of science. J. B. Davis. bibl Clearing H 50:390-2 My '77
Justifying science in an era of vocationalism. P. M. Mathis. Educ Digest 42:32-5 My '77
NSF science education: basic issues still unresolved. J. Walsh. Science 197:233+ Jl 15 '77
Piaget and Lamarck. F. J. Thomas. Educ Digest 43:47-9 N '77
Science education in China. BioScience 27:303 Ap '77
Unique Southwest educational program; Randall Aerospace-Marine Science Program, Washington, D.C. A. B. Finlayson. il Negro Hist Bull 40:658 Ja '77
See also
Biology—Study and teaching
Museum education

Terminology

Chinese words of science. A. Gottfurcht. il por Chemistry 50:17-19 Mr '77

Brazil

Instrument shortage slows Brazilian science. A. L. Hammond. Science 195:1316-17 Mr 25 '77

China

China after Mao: science seeks to be both red and expert. D. Shapley. Science 197:739-41 Ag 19 '77
More flowers, less cabbage. N. Wade. Science 198:176-7 O 14 '77
Role of science in China's development. D. Shapley. Science 198:1129 D 16 '77
Science in China: quakes, crops, lasers. il Sci N 111:295 My 7 '77

Europe, Western

European Science Foundation promotes joint activities. F. C. Bennett. Phys Today 30:101-2 Mr '77
Science in Europe (cont) N. Hawkes. Science 195:659-60, 962-3; 196:146-7, 636-7, 1067-8; 197: 141-3, 1167-9, 198:709-12, 1230-1 F 18, Mr 11, Ap 8, My 6, Je 3, Jl 8, S 16, N 18, D 23 '77

Great Britain

Visible college in British science. M. Green. Am Scholar 47:105-17 Wint '77

Israel

Science policy visit to Israel. M. Macioti. il Bull Atom Sci 33:10-21 Mr '77

Panama Canal Zone

American science in the Canal Zone. E. M. Leeper. BioScience 27:718 N '77

Russia

Science: peaks of excellence; U.S.- Soviet comparison. M. R. Benjamin. il Newsweek 90:54+ O 10 '77
See also
Science and state—Russia

Underdeveloped areas

See Underdeveloped areas—Science

United States

Science in Colorado: the second century begins. H. Lansford. il Science 195:477-9 F 4 '77
Science: peaks of excellence; U.S.- Soviet comparison. M. R. Benjamin. il Newsweek 90:54+ O 10 '77

Vietnam

Famous war general due to take over Vietnamese science. D. Shapley. il Science 198: 173-4 O 14 '77

SCIENCE (periodical)
Common censorship. N. Wade. Science 197:646-7 Ag 12 '77
Electronics: snapshot of a developing revolution; special issue of March 18, 1977. Sci N 111:184 Mr 19 '77
Science finally admitted to Congressional press gallery. C. Holden. Science 197:538 Ag 5 '77

SCIENCE, Freedom of
Human rights; AAAS Subcommittee on Infringements of Scientific Freedom in Foreign Countries. J. Edsall and J. Primack. Science 195: 245-6 Ja 21 '77

SCIENCE, Social. See Social sciences

SCIENCE and civilization
Science: no longer a sacred cow; Time essay. F. Trippett. il Time 109:72-3 Mr 7 '77
See also
Technology and civilization

SCIENCE and ethics
Ethos. J. P. Hailman. BioScience 27:715 N '77
What's right? Is increasingly faced by science. Sci Digest 81:83 Mr '77
See also
Bioethics

SCIENCE and industry. See Industrial research

SCIENCE and law
Science and the law; address, September 20, 1977. W. J. McGill. Vital Speeches 44:28-32 O 15 '77; Excerpts. Science 198:275 O 21 '77

SCIENCE and literature. See Literature and science

SCIENCE and mass media. See Mass media and science

SCIENCE and religion. See Religion and science

SCIENCE and society. See Science—Social aspects

SCIENCE and state
Brzezinski: role of science in society and foreign policy. N. Wade. Science 195:966-8 Mr 11 '77
Bureaucracy stifles US research community, NSB says; with editorial comment. F. C. Bennett. Phys Today 30:93-4 Ja '77
Campaign's science advisor sees: healthier outlook for creativity. W. K. Stuckey. il Sci Digest 81:12-19 F '77
DNA debate. J. Randal. Progressive 41:11-12 My '77
Danger for our research/technology: strangulation by bureaucratic red tape. D. S. Greenberg. il Sci Digest 81:20-3+ F '77
Federal reorganization: science and technology. J. Schmandt. Science 197:425 Jl 29 '77
For science policy—an opportunity. H. Feshbach. Phys Today 30:128 My '77
In praise of science and technology. C. Sagan. New Repub 176:21-2+ Ja 22 '77; Same with title Role of science and technology. Current 192:47-53 Ap '77
Intergovernmental cooperation in science. W. D Carey. Science 198:785 N 25 '77
Intergovernmental science and technology. F. Press. Science 196:943 My 27 '77
Isaac Asimov advises the President; here's the only road to save civilization. I. Asimov. il Sci Digest 81:8-12 F '77
Mediation: a better alternative to science courts. N. E. Abrams and R. S. Berry. Bull Atom Sci 33:50-3 Ap '77
Official circles. D. S. Greenberg. See issues of Science digest
Science advisory groups gearing up. C. Holden. Science 195:158 Ja 14 '77
Science and defense policy; physicist E. Teller, father of the hydrogen bomb. J. Marsh. Commentary 63:67-70 Ap '77
Science court. N. Ponnamperuma. il por Sci Digest 82:21-3 S '77
Science court experiment: criticisms and responses. A. Kantrowitz. bibl Bull Atom Sci 33:44-8+ Ap '77
Science in the Ford years: last things. W. D. Carey. Science 195:251 Ja 21 '77
Science in the White House: a new start; adaptation of address, March 3, 1977. L. M. Branscomb. Science 196:848-52 My 20 '77
Science: too much accountability. E. A. Shneour. Science 195:939 Mr 11 '77
Scientists and public policy, help or hindrance? excerpt from address, April 27, 1976. R. L. Garwin. Phys Today 30:9+ F '77
Scientists ask Congress to control DNA research. E. M. Leeper. BioScience 27:141-3 F '77
State & society. See issues of Physics today
Trumbull testifies on public participation. E. M. Leeper. BioScience 27:387-9 Je '77
What's ahead for science. E. M. Leeper. BioScience 27:222 Mr '77
See also
National Academy of Sciences—Committee on Science and Public Policy
Research—Federal aid
Science and law
Scientists in government
Technology and state
United States—Federal Coordinating Council of Science, Engineering and Technology
United States—National Science Foundation
United States—Science and Technology Policy, Office of

China

Gang of Four and Chinese science. J. Gardner. bibl il Bull Atom Sci 33:24-30 S '77

SCIENCE and state—*Continued*

Russia

To shrink a scientist; case of Y. Mnyukh. F. Coleman. il pors Newsweek 90:35-6 Ag 8 '77

SCIENCE and Technology, Committee on. See United States—Congress—House—Science and Technology, Committee on

SCIENCE and Technology for Development Conference, 1979 (proposed) See United Nations Conference on Science and Technology for Development, 1979 (proposed)

SCIENCE and Technology Policy, Office of. See United States—Science and Technology Policy, Office of

SCIENCE and the arts
Science and the arts; excerpt from Society, December 1976. R. D. Leighninger, Jr. il Sci Digest 81:61-4 Ap '77

SCIENCE and the humanities
Humanity in science: a perspective and a plea; address, February 24, 1977. J. Goodfield. bibl Science 198:580-5 N 11 '77
Science and humanism in the Italian renaissance. E. Cochrane. bibl f Am Hist R 81:1039-57 D '76
2 cultures—twenty years later. J. H. Douglas. Sci N 111:122-4 F 19 '77
Visible college in British science. M. Green. Am Scholar 47:105-17 Wint '77

SCIENCE as a profession
See also
Space science as a profession

SCIENCE citation index
Citation analysis and the quality of scientific productivity. S. M. Lawani. bibl BioScience 27:27-31 Ja '77

SCIENCE committees, Congressional. See United States—Congress—Committees

SCIENCE education. See Science—Study and teaching

SCIENCE fairs
Some student projects in astronomy; selected prize winners. il Sky & Tel 54:171-3 S '77

SCIENCE fellows, congressional. See Scientists in government

SCIENCE fiction
Jules Verne father of science fiction. E. Shrum. il Hobbies 82:152 S '77
Literature against the future. J. Stupple. Am Scholar 46:215-20 Spr '77
Tutankhamun and Star trek; address, July 29, 1977. C. L. Babcock. Vital Speeches 43:744-7 O 1 '77
See also
Publishers and publishing—Science fiction

Anecdotes, facetiae, satire, etc.

Orientation. J. Mort. New Yorker 53:33 Ap 4 '77

Authorship

Flying nonesuch; M. Caidin. D. R. Branch. il pors Writers Digest 57:41-3 Ag '77

Bibliography

Mark Rose on science fiction. M. Rose. New Repub 177:37-8 N 26 '77

Study and teaching

Science fiction in the 7-12 curriculum. J. C. Reynolds, Jr. bibl Clearing H 51:122-5 N '77

Technique

Character in science fiction; excerpt from Notes to a science fiction writer. B. Bova. Writer 90:17-19+ Ap '77

Themes

The god in science fiction. R. Bradbury. il Sat R 5:36-8+ D 10 '77

SCIENCE fiction collections in libraries. See Libraries—Fiction collections

SCIENCE in fiction. See Science fiction

SCIENCE in literature
See also
Science fiction

SCIENCE information. See Communication in science

SCIENCE literature. See Scientific literature

SCIENCE museums
Chemist's European travels. T. Benfey. il Chemistry 50:2-3 D '77

SCIENCE news
Phenomena, comment and notes. J. K. Page, Jr. See issues of Smithsonian
Science newsfront. See issues of Popular science
Science worldwide. J. F. Pearson. See issues of Popular mechanics
Search & discovery. See issues of Physics today
State & society. See issues of Physics today
Walrus. See issues of Chemistry
World progress report. A. Wolff See occasional issues of Saturday review
See also
Medical news

SCIENCE news (periodical)
. . . but the stars go on. E. G. Sherburne. Sci N 112:441 D 24 '77
[Jonathan Eberhart] K. Frazier. por Sci N 111:83 F 5 '77
Our own fight: a letter to our readers; denial of accreditation to the periodical press gallery. Sci N 111:323 My 21 '77

SCIENCE reporters and reporting. See Reporters and reporting

SCIENCE students
See also
Science Talent Search

SCIENCE Talent Search
Science Talent Search 1977. il Chemistry 50:22-3 My '77
Science Talent Search: top 40 winners. Sci N 111:87 F 5 '77
Young chemist wins Science Talent Search. Sci N 111:168 Mr 12 '77

SCIENCES, Occult. See Occult sciences

SCIENTIFIC apparatus and instruments
Coping with the high cost of instruments; Instrument shortage slows Brazilian science. T. H. Maugh; A. L. Hammond. Science 195:1316 Mr 25 '77
Guide to scientific instruments, 1977; comp by R. G. Sommer. il Science 197:9-169 S 20 '77
Products and materials. See issues of Science
See also
Astronomical instruments
Biological apparatus and supplies
Eye, Instruments and apparatus for
Oceanographic instruments
Physical apparatus and instruments

SCIENTIFIC associations. See Scientific societies

SCIENTIFIC creativity. See Creative ability

SCIENTIFIC education. See Science—Study and teaching

SCIENTIFIC errors. See Errors, Scientific

SCIENTIFIC exchanges. See Exchanges, Literary and scientific

SCIENTIFIC expeditions
Bush Negroes carry on tradition of rebel ancestors; A. Counter-D. Evans expeditions to Surinam. C. M. Turnbull. il Smithsonian 7:78-85 Mr '77
Earthwatch expeditions are the real thing. G. Goshgarian. Todays Educ 66:67-9 Mr '77
See also
Antarctic exploration
Botanical exploration

History

Early visions of imperial Brazil; illustrations produced by cultural and scientific missions. I. A. Striker. il Américas 29:S1-12 Ja '77
Naturalists across the Rockies: 1834 journey of J. K. Townsend and T. Nuttall. J. I. Merritt. bibl il pors Am West 14:4-9+ Mr '77

SCIENTIFIC illustration
Early visions of imperial Brazil; illustrations produced by cultural and scientific missions. I. A. Striker. il Américas 29:S1-12 Ja '77

SCIENTIFIC information. See Communication in science

SCIENTIFIC libraries
See also
Linda Hall Library, Kansas City, Mo.

SCIENTIFIC literature
Citation analysis and the quality of scientific productivity. S. M. Lawani. bibl BioScience 27:26-31 Ja '77; Discussion. 27:442-4 Jl '77
PW interviews; ed by J. F. Baker. C. Sagan. por Pub W 211:8-9 My 2 '77
See also
Information storage and retrieval systems—Science
Science—Bibliography

SCIENTIFIC literature for children

Awards, prizes, etc.

Science Academy presents children's book awards. Pub W 211:31 Ap 25 '77

Bibliography

Annual survey of children's books on science and technology. P. Morrison and P. Morrison. Sci Am 237:26+ D '77
Views on science books. S. Gagné. il Horn Bk 53:77-9, 336-9, 557-9 F, Je, O '77
Views on science books. H. C. Stubbs. il Horn Bk 53:195-7, 465-7, 691-3 Ap, Ag, D '77

SCIENTIFIC research. See Research

SCIENTIFIC research fraud. See Fraud

SCIENTIFIC societies
Attacking the new nonsense; Committee for the Scientific Investigation of Claims of the Paranormal. il Time 110:100 D 12 '77
Scientists combine to combat pseudoscience; Committee for the Scientific Investigation of Claims of the Paranormal. J. Pfeiffer. Psychol Today 11:38+ N '77
See also
American Association for the Advancement of Science
Astronomical societies
California Academy of Sciences, San Francisco
National Academy of Sciences
New York Academy of Sciences

SCIENTIFIC terms. See Science—Terminology

SCIENTISTS
See also
Biologists
Naturalists
Social scientists
Women scientists

Bibliography

Significant science books: 1976-1977; autobiography and biography. Am Scholar 46:544-5 Aut '77

Civil rights

AAAS workshop on scientific freedom and human rights. R. Chalk. Science 197:40-1 Jl 1 '77
Academy seeks to aid eight foreign scientists. E. M. Leeper. BioScience 27:427-8 Je '77
Academy steps up human rights drive. Sci N 111:293-4 My 7 '77
Academy to campaign publicly for oppressed scientists. N. Wade. Science 196:741-3 My 13 '77

Political activities

Protecting the whistle blowers. F. Von Hippel. bibl il Phys Today 30:9+ O '77

Supply and demand

Measuring the supply of scientific personnel. R. R. Trumble. M Labor R 100:47-8 O '77
See also
Brain drain

SCIENTISTS, Amateur
Amateur archaeology: the joy of the dig. E. McCoy. il House & Gard 149:50+ Mr '77
Amateur scientist. J. Walker. See issues of Scientific American, July 1977-
See also
Astronomers, Amateur

SCIENTISTS, Argentine
Physicist describes oppression of Argentine scientists. F. C. Bennett. Phys Today 30:61-2 Ag '77

SCIENTISTS, German
See also
Lambert, J. H.

SCIENTISTS, Professional ethics for
Code of the scientist and its relationship to ethics; address, May 27, 1977. A. Cournand. bibl Science 198:699-705 N 18 '77

SCIENTISTS, Russian
Moscow: meeting of the minds; Soviet and western scientists seminar. F. Coleman. il Newsweek 89:63 My 2 '77

SCIENTISTS in government
Carter remarks provide clues to attitude on science advice. J. Walsh. il por Science 196: 1300-1 Je 17 '77
Ecology interns report—new perspectives gained from Washington experience; Congressional internships through The Institute of Ecology. E. J. Christy and K. Weaver. il pors BioScience 27:631-3 S '77
FDA ready to turn corner. . . if it's still able. D. S. Greenberg. Sci Digest 81:71-2 Je '77
Frank Press: Carter's man on science. J. H. Douglas. por Sci N 111:250-1 Ap 16 '77
Frank Press, long-shot candidate, may become science adviser. P. M. Boffey. por Science 195: 763+ F 25 '77
Geophysicist next science adviser? Sci N 111: 119 F 19 '77
Maxwell and Sheahen chosen as Congressional fellows. pors Phys Today 30:71 Jl '77
1977-78 AAAS Congressional Science Fellows selected. Science 197:550-2 Ag 5 '77
Physicists and Washington; symposium; with editorial comment. il Phys Today 30:23-6+ Ag '77
Scientist/aide describes year on Capitol Hill. B. Diehn. BioScience 27:389-90 Je '77
Scientists on the Hill. B. M. Casper. il Bull Atom Sci 33:8-15 N '77
Senate quizzes science adviser nominee. E. M. Leeper. por BioScience 27:367-8 My '77
State scientific advisers: the effort in Michigan. L. J. Carter; reply. D. G. Yerg. Science 195: 130-1 Ja 14 '77
See also
United States—Science and Technology Policy, Office of

SCIENTISTS' Institute for Public Information
SIPI sells (out?) Environment magazine. D. Shapley. Science 198:1128-9 D 16 '77

SCIENTOLOGY
Scientology: filing on; Church of Scientology. Chr Today 21:61-2 F 4 '77
Scientology: parry and thrust. il Time 110:67 Jl 25 '77
Shaky Federal case against scientology. Chr Today 21:32-3 Ag 12 '77

SCILKEN, Marvin H.
What publishers should know about the public library: a book editor's firsthand report. P. Johnson, Jr. il pors Pub W 211:40-2 Mr 28 '77 *

SCINTILLATION autoradiography. See Autoradiography

SCLEROSIS, Multiple
EAE model: a tentative connection to multiple sclerosis. T. H. Maugh. Science 195:969-71 Mr 11 '77
MS mystery; relationship between multiple sclerosis and pet dogs. Time 110:44 S 5 '77
Multiple sclerosis: genetic link, viruses suspected. T. H. Maugh, 2d. Science 195:667+ F 18 '77
Multiple sclerosis: two or more viruses may be involved. T. H. Maugh, 2d. Science 195:768-71 F 25 '77
New tests for diagnosis of MS. T. H Maugh Science 195:970 Mr 11 '77

SCOBLE, Harry M. See Wiseberg, L. S. jt auth

SCOFIELD, Nanette
Maiden voyage. il por Am Home 80:28-9 Jl '77

SCOFIELD, Sandra
Is it true boys have more fun? What every parent should know about children's books. Redbook 149:214+ My '77

SCOGIN, Ron
Sperm whale oil and the jojoba shrub. il Oceans 10:65-6 Jl '77

SCOLA, Ettore
Reviews; We all loved each other so much! M. Seitz. il Film Q 31:45-7 Wint '77 *

SCOLIOSIS. See Spine—Abnormalities and deformities

SCOPES, David I. C. and others
Defined dimensional changes in enzyme cofactors: fluorescent "stretched-out" analogs of adenine nucleotides. bibl il Science 195:296-8 Ja 21 '77

SCOPES, Firearm. See Firearms—Sights

SCOREBOARDS
Take me out to the scoreboard. W. B. Furlong il Horizon 20:66-71 D '77

SCORES (music) See Music—Scores

SCORPIONS
Compressional and surface waves in sand: used by desert scorpions to locate prey. P. H. Brownell. bibl il Science 197:479-82 Jl 29 '77

SCORSESE, Martin
Liza & Marty show. M. Orth and P. S. Greenberg. il pors Newsweek 90:49 S 5 '77 *
Marty Scorsese: the movie brat. J. Kroll. por Newsweek 89:84 My 16 '77 *

SCOTCH whiskey. See Whiskey

SCOTCH whiskey industry. See Liquor industry—Scotland

SCOTIA Sea
Scotia Sea: waterway of the future. J. F. Lohr and M. Castleman. il Oceans 10:36-41 My '77

SCOTLAND
See also
Forests and forestry—Scotland
Investments, Scottish
Libraries—Scotland
Music festivals—Scotland
Shetland Islands
Tobermory

Industries

See also
Liquor industry—Scotland

Nationalism

Kilt bill; defeat of home rule for Wales and Scotland. F. Willey and M. MacPherson. il Newsweek 89:43+ Mr 7 '77
Labor runs afoul of a muddy loch; home rule bill. Time 109:31-2 Mr 7 '77
On hanging on to Scotland; devolution bill. A. Lejeune. Nat R 29:330-1 Mr 18 '77
Patriotism of the Scots. J. Morris. il Horizon 20:42-9 S '77

Religious institutions and affairs

See also
Church of Scotland
Free Church of Scotland
Religious conferences—Scotland

SCOTLAND, Church of. See Church of Scotland

SCOTOPIC vision. See Eye—Accommodation and refraction

SCOTT, Alison
New family triumvirate of writers welcomed by four publishers; interview, ed by R. Dahlin. por Pub W 212:107 S 12 '77

SCOTT, Bill
Prescription for a beat-up wilderness. il Nat Wildlife 15:12-16 Ap '77

SCOTT, Gavin
At home with the sweetlips and angelfish. il por Fortune 95:91+ Mr '77

SCOTT, George
Sometimes the ball just takes a funny bounce. R. Blount, Jr. il Esquire 88:17-18 Ag '77 *

SCOTT, George C.
Great Scott! B. Gelb. il pors N Y Times Mag p 10-12+ Ja 23 '77 *

SCOTT, Jack Denton
How to speak in public. Read Digest 111:80+ D '77

SCOTT, John
pHish pfinder? il Field & S 82:58+ Jl '77

SCOTT, Jonathan Lavon
Jonathan Scott of A&P: hunted head. por Forbes 119:94 F 15 '77 *

SCOTT, Justin
New family triumvirate of writers welcomed by four publishers; interview, ed by R. Dahlin. por Pub W 212:107 S 12 '77

SCOTT, Lael
Lawyers who sue lawyers. il N Y Times Mag p74-8 Je 26 '77
SCOTT, Leonard H.
Surrender of Detroit. il por map Am Hist Illus 12:28-36 Je '77
SCOTT, M. L. See Combs, G. F. Jr. jt auth
SCOTT, Michael P.
Education. Bet Hom & Gard 55:30+ F; 10+ S '77
Grooming. Bet Hom & Gard 55:86+ Je '77
Health. See issues of Better homes and gardens
SCOTT, Robert F.
Using PLL for CB frequency synthesizers. il Radio-Electr 48:47-9 F; 58-9 Mr; 43-5 Ap '77
SCOTT, Robert Falcon
Scott's last voyage; ed by A. Savours. il por Sat Eve Post 249:42-3+ N '77
SCOTT, Stanley DeForest, collection. See Engravings—Collectors and collecting
SCOTT, Stephen Decatur
(ed) See Wagner, L. Why I chose marriage over living together
SCOTT, Vernon
(ed) See MacGraw, A. Ali & Steve
SCOTT, William P.
Berthe Morisot: paintings from a private place. il pors Am Artist 41:66-71+ N '77
SCOTT-KILVERT, Ian
(tr) See Plutarch. Pericles as seen by Plutarch
SCOTTISH Opera Company. See Opera—Great Britain
SCOTTO, Renata
Revelation; interview, ed by C. Faria. il pors Opera N 42:12-16 D 17 '77
about
Cincinnati Op: Scotto's Norma. por Hi Fi 27: MA26 O '77 *
Mangia, mangia; celebrating the new Met production of La Bohème. R. Jacobson. il pors Opera N 41:8-13 Mr 19 '77 *
Viewpoint; Madama Butterfly. R. Jacobson. Opera N 42:6 D 17 '77 *
SCOTTS, Stephen Decatur
(ed) See Fields, T. Happy courage of Totie Fields
SCOTTSDALE, Ariz.
Scottsdale, Arizona. C. J. Burkhart. il Trav/Holiday 148:58-63+ D '77
SCOURING powders. See Cleaning compositions
SCOURS in calves. See Calves—Diseases and pests
SCOURS in swine. See Swine—Diseases and pests
SCOUTING, Baseball. See Baseball scouting
SCOUTING, Football. See Football scouting
SCOUTS and scouting
See also
Boy Scouts
Girl Scouts
SCOVILL Manufacturing Company
Scovill wins big by dropping out of brass. il Bus W p46+ My 2 '77
SCOVILLE, Herbert, Jr
SALT negotiations; with biographical sketch. il Sci Am 237:20, 24-31 bibl(p 140) Ag '77
Slowing the arms race. Bull Atom Sci 33:4-5 S '77
SCOVILLE, James G.
Has collective bargaining altered the salary structure of baseball? bibl il M Labor R 100: 51-2 Mr '77
SCRAMBLING (communication) See Speech scrambling
SCRANTON, William Warren
Ambassador Scranton's assessment of the 31st U.N. General Assembly; statement, December 22, 1976. Dept State Bull 76:68-70 Ja 24 '77
Human rights: let's mean what we say; statement, November 24, 1976. Dept State Bull 75: 745-9 D 27 '76
U.S. abstains on Security Council resolution on Botswana complaint; statement, January 13, 1977. Dept State Bull 76:117-18 F 7 '77
U.S. gives views in General Assembly debate on the Middle East; statement, December 9, 1976. Dept State Bull 76:37-9 Ja 17 '77
U.S. reaffirms commitment to self-determination and independence for Namibia; statement, December 2, 1976. Dept State Bull 76:43-4 Ja 17 '77
U.S. reiterates support for negotiated solution in Rhodesia; statement, December 13, 1976. Dept State Bull 76:53-4 Ja 17 '77
U.S. votes against U.N. resolution on question of Palestine; statement, November 23, 1976. Dept State Bull 76:41-2 Ja 17 '77
SCRAP metal industry
See also
Automobiles—Wrecking
Institute of scrap iron and steel
SCRAPIE
Latent form of scrapie virus: a new factor in slow-virus disease. J. Hotchin and R. Buckley. bibl il Science 196:668-71 My 6 '77
SCRATCHBOARD drawing
Architecture and scratchboard. M. A. Stafford. il Design (US) 78:30 mid-Wint '77

SCREEN Actors Guild
Kathleen Nolan: from sit-com star to SAG prexy; interview, ed by L. Farr. K. Nolan. por Ms 5:105-6+ Mr '77
SCREEN houses. See Garden houses, shelters, etc.
SCREEN painting, Japanese. See Painting, Japanese
SCREEN printing. See Silk screen printing
SCREEN writing. See Motion picture authorship
SCREENS (doors, windows, etc)
How to replace window screens. il Bet Hom & Gard 55:268-9 My '77
SCREENS (furniture)
Tricks with folding screens. E. Liman. il Am Home 80:15 Jl '77
SCREENS (sun)
Overhead wood heat screens roll out. il Sunset 158:175 My '77
Shade is good for you. il Sunset 158:208 Je '77
Shade stops afternoon sun. il Sunset 159:246 N '77
SCREENS, Boat. See Boats—Equipment
SCREW extractors. See Tools
SCRIBE, Augustin Eugène
Scribe factory. H. Heinsheimer. por Opera N 41:16-19 Ja 29 '77
SCRIBNER, Charles, Jr
Confessions of a book publisher; address, April 12, 1977. por Pub W 211:46-8 Je 6 '77
SCRIBNER, Richard A. and Shoaf M. L.
Four years of Congressional Science Fellows. il Phys Today 30:36-40 Ag '77
SCRIBNER'S, Charles, Sons (firm) See Publishers and publishing—United States
SCRIMSHAW
Oriental art of abalone scrimshaw. R. D. Ono. il Sea Front 23:16-19 Ja '77
Whaling and the art of scrimshaw; excerpt. C. R. Meyer. il Conservationist 31:29-32 N '76
SCRIMSHAW Press. See Publishers and publishing—United States
SCRIPPS Institution of Oceanography. See California. University—Scripps Institution of Oceanography
SCRIPT writing. See Television authorship
SCRIPT writing, Audio-visual. See Audio-visual script authorship
SCRIPTURE studies. See Bible—Study and teaching
SCRIPTURES. See Bible
SCROLL saws. See Saws
SCROLLS, Dead Sea. See Dead Sea Scrolls
SCUBA diving. See Skin diving
SCUDO, Paul
Prophetic words; ed by P. La Cerra. il Opera N 41:30-2 Ja 29 '77
SCULLY, Celia G.
Campus ministries: bread from heaven. Writers Digest 57:44 Ag '77
Harrah's Automobile Collection. il Trav/Holiday 148:36-7+ N '77
SCULLY, Ed
Ed Scully on color. See issues of Modern photography
SCULLY, Julia
Seeing pictures. See issues of Modern photography
SCULLY, Vincent, Jr
Yale Center for British Art. il Archit Rec 161:95-104 Je '77
SCULPTURE
Output; L. Phillips' sound sculpture entitled City Flow. il New Yorker 53:31-2 Ap 18 '77
Recycled rubber stretches the imagination; woven rubber sculpture. D. L. Schultz. il Design (US) 79:17 Fall '77
Sculpture. il Sch Arts 77:35-42 O '77
Sculpture cut to your taste. A. Ogden. House B 119:10+ Ap '77
See also
Animal sculpture
Bronzes
Casting (sculpture)
Ceramic sculpture
Chicago—Monuments, statues, etc.
Cleveland—Monuments, statues, etc.
Hartford, Conn.—Monuments, statues, etc.
Los Angeles—Monuments, statues, etc.
Masks (sculpture)
Mobiles
Mountain sculpture
Paper sculpture
Realism in art
Relief (sculpture)
San Francisco—Monuments, statues, etc.
Snow sculpture
Stone carving
Washington, D.C.—Monuments, statues, etc.
Wood carving

Exhibitions

Arcadia in the Bronx; Wave Hill sculpture exhibit. il Horizon 20:66-9 N '77
Earth probes; Probing the earth: contemporary land projects at Washington's Hirshhorn Museum. il Horizon 20:73 D '77

SCULPTURE—*Continued*

Study and teaching

Concepts in sculpture for young people. B. L. Rowe. il Sch Arts 77:62-3 O '77

Materials

See also
Papier-mâché

Projects

Contemplation of form. S. Corwin. il Sch Arts 77:18-19 O '77
Hand sculpture. A.-L. Sanger. il Sch Arts 77:54-5 O '77
Hurst's remembrance '76; sculpture to decorate school grounds. M. Painter. il Sch Arts 76:56-7 F '77
Sculpture on a large scale. V. Sloane. il Sch Arts 76:23 Je '77
Three construction projects with wood scraps. E. Levine. il Sch Arts 76:16-17 Je '77

Technique

See also
Lost wax process
Modeling

SCULPTURE, African
Decoding the message of African sculpture; mask carvings. O. Balogun. il UNESCO Courier 30:12-15+ My '77
See also
Chibanga, E.

Photographs

Masks from 20 countries; African carvings. UNESCO Courier 30:16-20 My '77

SCULPTURE, American
Ted Egri: the survival of a sculptor; interview, ed by M. C. Nelson. T. Egri. il por Am Artist 41:56-61+ Je '77
See also
Andre, C.
Borglum, G.
Calder, A.
De Staebler, S.
Di Suvero, M.
Fite, H.
French, D. C.
Fuller, M. V. W.
Gabo, N.
Gallagher, J.
Hanson, D.
Lewis, E.
Liberman, A.
Lyon, E.
Murray, R.
Noguchi, I.
Nonas, R.
Oldenburg, C.
Phillips, L.
Scarpitta, S.
Segal, G.
Singer, M.
Smith, D.
Vierthaler, B.
Winsor, J.
Young, J. L.
Ziolkowski, K.

SCULPTURE, Ancient
See also
Sculpture, Greek

SCULPTURE, Architectural. See Decoration and ornament, Architectural

SCULPTURE, British
See also
Moore, H. S.
Tucker, W.

SCULPTURE, Classical
See also
Sculpture, Greek

SCULPTURE, French
See also
Duchamp-Villon, R.
Dubuffet, J.
Gaudier-Brzeska, H.
Lipchitz, J.

SCULPTURE, Gothic
Medieval mystery; discovery of sculptured heads that once adorned facade of Notre Dame. il Horizon 20:26-7 S '77

SCULPTURE, Greek
Art is long, tax suits short; controversy surrounding Italian claims to a Greek statue in the J. Paul Getty Museum. il Time 110:22 D 12 '77
Youthful faces from a buried past. il UNESCO Courier 30:15-17 O '77

SCULPTURE, Israeli
See also
Loutchansky, J.

SCULPTURE, Italian
See also
Mastroianni, U.

SCULPTURE, Mexican
See also
Zuñiga, F.

SCULPTURE, Oriental

Exhibitions

Wood masterpieces: China and Japan. J. Brzostoski. il Craft Horiz 37:46-9+ Ap '77

SCULPTURE, Playground. See Playgrounds—Equipment

SCULPTURE, Roadside. See Roadside improvement

SCULPTURE, Rumanian
See also
Brancusi, C.

SCULPTURE, Russian
See also
Neizvestny, E.

SCULPTURE, Spanish
See also
Berrocal, M.

SCULPTURE in the Environment, Inc. See Site, Inc

SCULPTURE puzzles. See Puzzles

SCUPHAM, Peter
Comment. J. Silkin. Poetry 130:234-7 Jl '77 •

SCYTHIAN art. See Art, Scythian

SCYTHIAN mythology. See Mythology, Scythian

SCYTHIANS
Scythians: nomad goldsmiths of the open steppes; symposium. il UNESCO Courier 29:4-49 D '76
See also
Alani

SEA. See Ocean

SEA ambulance. See Ambulance service

SEA anemones
Berried anemone. R. V. Harrison. il Sea Front 23:194-7 Jl '77
Shrimps that dwell with anemones. N. Sefton. il Sea Front 23:32-7 Ja '77

SEA bass fishing. See Bass fishing

SEA birds
See also
Auks
Frigate birds

Protection

Notes and comment; rescue of oil-covered bird at Narragansett Pier, R.I. New Yorker 52:21-2 Ja 31 '77

SEA coasts. See Coasts

SEA food
Nutritional outputs and energy inputs in seafoods. M. Rawitscher and J. Mayer. bibl il Science 198:261-4 O 21 '77
See also
Cookery—Sea food
Fish as food
Shellfish as food

SEA food contamination. See Fish contamination

SEA food salads. See Salads

SEA hares
Bag cell control of egg laying in freely behaving aplysia. H. M. Pinsker and F. E. Dudek. bibl il Science 197:490-3 Jl 29 '77

SEA islands
Islands in the sun. M. Wexler. il Nat Wildlife 16:54-63 D '77
See also
Cumberland Island

SEA-level canal (Panama) See Canals—Panama

SEA monsters. See Sea serpents

SEA of Cortéz. See California, Gulf of

SEA-onions
Pregnant onion. F. E. Curtis. il Org Gard & Farm 24:76-7 My '77

SEA planes. See Seaplanes

SEA power
National strategy considerations in the Pacific Basin; address, June 27, 1977. W. G. Claytor, Jr. Vital Speeches 43:706-8 S 15 '77

SEA rescues. See Rescue work

SEA serpents
Media monster: Ponik the Terrible. D. Rhodes. Int Wildlife 7:17 S '77
See also
Loch Ness monster

SEA shells. See Shells (conchology)

SEA snails. See Snails

SEA snakes
Poison! Sea snakes. R. E. Arnold. Field & S 82:130 N '77

SEA songs
See also
Sailors songs

SEA sounds. See Ocean sounds

SEA turtles. See Turtles

SEA urchins
Biocrystals. S. Inoué and K. Okazaki. il Sci Am 236:82-4+ bibl(p 148) Ap '77
Clones of individual repetitive sequences from sea urchin DNA constructed with synthetic eco R1 sites. R. H. Scheller and others. bibl il Science 196:197-200 Ap 8 '77
Immune response in the sea urchin lytechinus pictus. K. A. Coffaro and R. T. Hinegardner. bibl il Science 197:1389-90 S 30 '77
Interspersion of short repetitive sequences studied in cloned sea urchin DNA fragments. A. S. Lee and others. bibl il Science 196:189-92 Ap 8 '77

SEA urchins—*Continued*
Sea urchin recruitment patterns and implications of commercial fishing. M. J. Tegner. and P. K. Dayton. bibl il Science 196:324-6 Ap 15 '77

SEA water
How salty is the ocean? D. G. Klim. il map Sea Front 23:152-8 My '77
Oceanography: geochemical tracers offer new insight. A. L. Hammond. il Science 195:164-6 Ja 14 '77

Pollution

See Marine pollution

SEA waves. See Waves

SEABED Treaty, 1972
Review conference calls for consideration of further measures to halt arms race on sea-bed. il UN Chron 14:18-19 Jl '77

SEABROOK, N.H, atomic power plant. See Atomic power plants—Location

SEABROOKS, Nettie
Detroit library network. il Lib J 102:11233-7 My 15 '77

SEABURY, Deborah
Success story. il Opera N 42:20-2 Jl '77
(ed) See Reiss, J. Répétiteuse

SEACAMP. See Camps—Florida

SEAFARER communication system. See Radio, Military

SEAFARING life
See also
Voyages

SEAFOOD. See Sea food

SEAGRAM, Joseph E, and Sons (firm)
Seagram antes $40 million. il por Bus W p68 Ag 22 '77
Seagram finds no. 3: Colgate's Beekman. por Bus W p26-7 Ja 24 '77
Soap? Whiskey? What's the difference? por Forbes 119:67 F 1 '77

SEAGRAVE, Sterling
Wise men from the south peer toward what may be limits of the universe. il Smithsonian 8:40-7 bibl(p 146) Ap '77

SEAGRAVES, Charles
Bromeliad boys at Nature's Way. il pors Horticulture 55:36-7 D '77

SEAL Books (firm) See Publishers and publishing—Canada

SEALE, Bobby G.
Party's over. pors Newsweek 90:29 S 5 '77 *

SEALFON, Peggy, and others
Holography—gimmick or new visual art? il Pop Phot 81:100-3+ S '77

SEALING
Dirge for the harp; work of B. Davies, director of the International Fund for Animal Welfare. D. Levin. il por Sports Illus 46:80+ Ap 18 '77
South Georgia island: the great southern fur rush. J. C. Simmons. il Oceans 10:46-51 My '77

SEALING compounds
See also
Caulking compounds

SEALS, Robert K. Jr. See Menzies, R. T. jt auth

SEALS (animals)
Andre the sociable seal; excerpt from A seal called Andre. H. Goodridge and L. Dietz. il Read Digest 110:134-8 Ap '77
Case of the missing monk seal; Caribbean monk seal. P. M. Knudtson. il Natur Hist 86:78-83 bibl(p 122-3) O '77
Celebration of the endearing harp seal is set for summer by Viking Penguin. R. Dahlin. il Pub W 212:40 N 7 '77
How to avoid shark attack (if you happen to be a Hawaiian monk seal) L. R. Taylor and G. Naftel. il Oceans 10:21-3 N '77
Lonely are the hunted; leopard seals, penguins and killer whales. F. Erize. il Int Wildlife 7:14-16 S '77
Pulmonary metabolism during diving: conditioning blood for the brain. P. W. Hochachka and others. bibl il Science 198:831-4 N 25 '77
Starting from scratch. il Int Wildlife 7:30-1 My '77
United States ratifies Convention for Conservation of Antarctic Seals. Dept State Bull 76:135 F 14 '77
See also
Sealing

SEAMAN, Barbara
Back to foam? excerpt from Women and the crisis in sex hormones. Ms 6:16-18 Ag '77

SEAMAN, Dick
Grand Prix racing in the thirties. J. Dugdale. il pors Car & Dr 23:105-6+ N '77 *

SEAMAN, Donald L.
Person-ality box sculpture. il Sch Arts 76:39 Je '77

SEAMANS, Robert C. 1918-
Ousted Seamans no fan of Schlesinger. P. M. Boffey. por Science 195:665 F 18 '77 *

SEAMANSHIP
Chapman's update. See issues of Motor boating & sailing
Cruising seamanship. See issues of Motor boating & sailing
Take the 20-minute skipper's test. il Motor B & S 141:114-15+ Ja '78
See also
Navigation

SEAMEN
Some thoughts for a new crew; sailboat racing. P. Wallio. il Yachting 142:40+ Jl '77

SEAMOUNTS
Emperor Seamounts: hotspot candidates. il Sci N 112:215 O 1 '77

SEAPLANE excursions. See Excursions

SEAPLANE schools. See Aviation schools

SEAPLANES
FBO on floats. J. A. Slocum. il Flying 101:46-9+ Ag '77
People who fly: Robert Murray. S. Wilkinson. por Flying 100:54-5+ Je '77
Spruce Goose: pterodactyl of World War II. C. Barton. il Pop Mech 148:83+ N '77
1200 passengers on three decks. . .a comeback for flying boats? il Pop Mech 148:84-5 N '77
See also
Airplanes, Amphibious

SEAPOWER. See Sea power

SEARCH and rescue operations
Prisoners of the ice; rescue of Italian couple swallowed by crevasse. F. Schell. il Read Digest 112:66-71 Ja '78
See also
Space rescue work

SEARCHES and seizures
Legal house of cards; unlawful searches of people and property. A. M. Rosenblatt and J. C. Rosenblatt. Harpers 255:18-21 Jl '77

SEARCY, Alan W. See Roberts J. A. Jr. jt auth

SEARLE, G. D, and Company
GOP whiz kid takes Searle's reins; D. H. Rumsfeld. por Bus W p29-30 My 2 '77
Unsnuffing Searle. L. Langway and others. il Newsweek 89:68+ Je 6 '77

SEARLS, Hank
Break in the reef; story; excerpt from Overboard. Yachting 141:81 Mr '77
Overboard, and after. . . you can take it with you. il Yachting 142:64-6 D '77

about

Sailing novelist. J. Rousmaniere. il por Yachting 141:80 Mr '77 *

SEARS, Ernest R.
More efficient bread. Sci Digest 81:86 F '77 *

SEARS, Jerry A.
Polymer pioneers. bibl il por Chemistry 50:6-10 S '77

SEARS, Lawrence
ASOL Festival of Youth Orchestras. il Hi Fi 27:MA24-6 D '77

SEARS, Paul Bigelow
Troubled waters. Natur Hist 86:112-15 N '77

SEARS, Roebuck and Company
At the top of the tower; E. R. Telling appointed chairman. il por Time 110:80 N 21 '77
Man who won't buy his shoes at Sears; E. R. Telling. E. J. Tracy and others. por Fortune 96:17 D '77
Telling changes. por Forbes 120:108 D 1 '77
Too big for miracles. P. Berman. il Forbes 119:26-8 Je 15 '77
Top retailer plans for metric conversion. V. Louviere. il Nations Bus 65:75 S '77
Vintner for Sears; E. R. Telling. L. Langway and C. J. Harper. il por Newsweek 90:78 N 21 '77
See also
Allstate Insurance Company

SEASAT. See Artificial satellites—Oceanographic use

SEASCAPE photography. See Photography—Marines

SEASCAPES. See Marine painting

SEASHORE
See also
Beaches
Coasts

SEASHORE houses. See Beach architecture

SEASHORE photography. See Photography—Marines

SEASHORE protection. See Shore protection

SEASICKNESS
Seasickness. D. Graul, Jr. Yatching 141:130+ Ap '77

SEASIDE resorts
Fly and fish; Pacific, Gulf of Mexico and the Caribbean. il Ebony 33:110-12+ Ja '78
From Little River to Georgetown: South Carolina's Grand Strand. L. M. Baker. il Travel 147:54-7 Je '77
See also
Miami Beach, Fla.
Port Aransas, Tex.

California, Lower

Now the jets get you quickly to Cabo San Lucas for the superb big-game fishing and so much else. il Sunset 159:82+ O '77

SEASIDE resorts—*Continued*

Caribbean Region

Anecdotes, facetiae, satire, etc.

One last fling at Coobies Bay. R. Lipez. Atlantic 239:92+ My '77

Mexico

Mexico's brand-new Ixtapa resort is off and running. il map Sunset 158:62+ Mr '77

Mexico's newest sunspots: Cancun & Ixtapa. B. Humeston. il Bet Hom & Gard 55:211-12+ S '77

On the road to Zihuatanejo. C. D. B. Bryan. il Holiday 58:32-5 S '77

Winter on a Mexican beach. il Mademoiselle 83:80-2+ D '77

Yugoslavia

Resort village on the coast of Yugoslavia; Bernardin. il Archit Rec 162:118-21 O '77

SEASON-all Industries, Inc. See Building materials industry

SEASONAL adjustments (economics) See Seasonal variations (economics)

SEASONAL labor

See also

Migrant labor

SEASONAL variations (economics)

Impact of the winter of 1977 on payroll employment. E. Dmytrow. il M Labor R 100:43-5 Ag '77

Seasonal maladjustment. il Bus W p 102+ O 24 '77

SEASONINGS

See also

Herbs

Salt

SEASONS

Earth almanac. See issues of Conservationist

Glimpse of glory; seasons in New England. J. Mills. il Read Digest 111:164-7 Jl '77

See also

Autumn

Spring

Summer

Winter

SEAT belts, Automobile. See Automobiles—Safety belts

SEAT PLEASANT, Md.

Education

See Education—Maryland

SEATRAIN Lines, Inc

Big-league TEGWAR. il Forbes 120:116+ O 15 '77

SEATS

See also

Airplanes—Seats

SEATTLE

Description

Those movers who shake Seattle. il Time 110:36 D 12 '77

Up by seaplane from Lake Union. il Sunset 158:56 F '77

Education

Arts are for learning. J. B. Gaines. il Todays Educ 66:72-4 N '77

Rainbow in industrial arts; Occupational Versatility program; Puget Sound Junior High. V. Hedrich. Educ Digest 42:53-6 F '77

Hotels, restaurants, etc.

Rosellini's Other Place. R. L. Balzer. il por Holiday 57:40-1+ N '76

Justice, Administration of

Grand jury abuse; investigations of Seattle radicals. R. C. Kelley. Progressive 41:34-5 F '77

Parks and playgrounds

Community maintenance for city parks. B. L. Balshone. il Parks & Rec 12:34-6 Ag '77

Downtown park quiets a freeway. il Am City & County 92:75-6 Je '77

Gasworks (ugh!) reborn as city park. G. Brynolson. il Smithsonian 8:116-18+ N '77

Sanitary affairs

Resource recovery in trouble again; pyrolysis project. il Am City & County 92:9 My '77

Transit systems

Seattle's rolling art galleries. il Sunset 159:46 D '77

SEATTLE Public Library

Seattle zeroes in on staff development needs. Lib J 102:1701 S 1 '77

Branches

Options to improve delivery. R. Dubberly. il Lib J 102:170-1 Ja 15 '77

SEAVER, George Thomas. See Seaver, T.

SEAVER, Harmon

In defense of my organic homestead. il por Org Gard & Farm 24:184+ O '77

SEAVER, Tom

How the franchise went West. il por Time 109:49 Je 27 '77 *

Notes and comment. New Yorker 53:19 Jl 4 '77 *

There goes the franchise. P. Axthelm. il pors Newsweek 89:62-4 Je 27 '77 *

Tom Seaver's farewell. A. B. Giamatti. Harpers 255:93-4+ S '77 *

Tom Terrific arms the Red arsenal. L. Keith. il por Sports Illus 46:22-4+ Je 27 '77 *

SEAWATER. See Sea water

SEAWEED

Antarctic marine flora: uniquely devoid of kelps. R. L. Moe and P. C. Silva. bibl il Science 196:1206-8 Je 10 '77

Antileukemia activity in the oscillatoriaceae: isolation of debromoaplysiatoxin from lyngbya. J. S. Mynderse and others. bibl il Science 196:538-40 Ap 29 '77

SEAWEED as fertilizer. See Fertilizers and manures

SEAWELL, William Thomas

Airline economic influence; excerpts from address. Aviation W 107:9 Jl 4 '77

about

Pan Am: in the black—for now. il por map Bus W p52-6 S 5 '77 *

SEBRELL, Alice

How a camera helped a teenager discover herself. il por Sr Schol 110:6 D 1 '77 *

SEBRING-Vanguard Citicar. See Automobiles, Electric

SECESSION

Islands cast adrift; Martha's Vineyard and Nantucket. map Newsweek 89:23 Ap 4 '77

SECKEL pears. See Pears

SECOND Advent

Anecdotes, facetiae, satire, etc.

Rapture-peddlers. M. E. Marty. Chr Cent 94:127 F 2 '77

SECOND hurricane; opera. See Copland, A.

SECOND marriages. See Remarriage

SECOND mortgages. See Mortgages

SECONDARY education. See Education, Secondary

SECONDARY stocks. See Stocks

SECRET codes. See Ciphers

SECRET service

See also

Intelligence service

Chile

After DINA; Central Nacional de Informaciónes (CNI) R. Moreau. il Newsweek 90:50 S 12 '77

Blow-up; murder of O. Letelier. K. Lynch. Nat R 29:320 Mr 18 '77

Letelier/Moffitt murder: this is how it was done. S. Landau and R. Stavins. por Nation 224:358-60 Mr 26 '77

Unwelcome good news; dissolution of DINA. Nat R 29:1040-1 S 16 '77

China

Enforcer from Fragrant Hill; Wang Tung-hsing. il por Time 110:27 S 5 '77

Confederate States of America

See United States—History—Civil War, 1861-1865—Secret service—Confederate States

Cuba

Cuba's role in Jamaica; DGI support. A. De Borchgrave. il por Newsweek 89:37-8 F 28 '77

Russia

Espionage: the dark side of détente; KGB agents in the United States. J. Barron. Read Digest 112:78-82 Ja '78

Inside the KGB. M. R. Benjamin and E. Clark. il Newsweek 89:16 Je 27 '77

United States

See also

United States—Central Intelligence Agency

Venezuela

Incident; investigating the Cuban connection to the Orlando Letelier murder in Venezuela. T. Branch and J. Rothchild. il pors Esquire 87:55-8+ Mr '77

SECRET societies

See also

Ku Klux Klan

South Africa

Broederbond's big brother act. il Time 110:61 N 21 '77

SECRETARIAT of the United Nations. See United Nations—Secretariat

SECRETARIES

Cinderella's revolt. Newsweek 90:99 O 17 '77

Frank talk from secretaries about their jobs and their pay. il U.S. News 82:75-6 Je 27 '77

God help the working girl. B. M. Stratton. Am Home 80:34 S '77

SECRETARIES—*Continued*
Secretary's manifesto. A. Butler. McCalls 105: 34+ Ja '78

Supply and demand

Suddenly, a new shortage of secretaries. il Bus W p84-5 Ag 8 '77

SECRETARIES of Agriculture (United States)
See also
Bergland, B. S.

SECRETARIES of Defense (United States)
Musical chairs. M. Kempton. Progressive 41:42 F '77
See also
Brown, H.

SECRETARIES of State (United States)
See also
Kissinger, H. A.

SECRETARIES of the Army (United States)
See also
Alexander, C. L. Jr

SECRETARIES of the Interior (United States)
See also
Andrus, C. D.

SECRETIONS
See also
Glands
Pheromones

SECRETS, Official. See Official secrets

SECRETS, Personal. See Confidential communications

SECRETS, Trade. See Trade secrets

SECTIONALISM
See also
Regionalism

SECTS
See also
Jehovah's Witnesses
Mennonites
Mormons and Mormonism
Samaritans
Unification Church (movement)

SECULARISM
Laughter without joy: the burlesque of our secular age. D. B. Lockerbie. Chr Today 22: 14-16 O 7 '77

SECURITIES
Help from an unexpected quarter; U.S. Treasury securities. B. Weberman. por Forbes 119:98 My 1 '77
High-yielding currency hedge; use of floating rate by multinationals. il Bus W p67 F 21 '77
Statistical spotlight. See issues of Forbes
What might hold interest rates down. J. Madrick. il Bus W p90 My 23 '77
See also
Banks and banking—Securities handling
Dividends
Security analysis
Stock exchanges
Stocks
also subhead Securities under various subjects, e.g. Fuel industry—Securities

Laws and regulations

Bad day in court for takeover laws; ruling on tender offer laws in case prompted by Great Western United Corp.'s bid to acquire Sunshine Mining Co. Bus W p44-5 S 19 '77
Disclosure rules hit the advisers; New York State registration requirements. por Bus W p55-6 D 12 '77
Municipals: a drive for fuller disclosure. Bus W p 101 S 19 '77
Will brokers continue to manage money? interpreting section 11(a); amendment to the Securities Exchange Act. D. G. Santry. por Bus W p98 Ag 15 '77
See also
United States—Municipal Securities Rulemaking Board

France

Government issues beckon investors. Bus W p48 Je 20 '77

Great Britain

Why the Arabs hang on to sterling; British offer of securities in exchange for sterling. Bus W p80-1 Mr 14 '77

Italy

Government issues beckon investors. Bus W p48 Je 20 '77

Japan

Hot money floods the yen. il Bus W p 152 D 12 '77

SECURITIES, Tax exempt
See also
Municipal bonds

SECURITIES and Exchange Commissison. See United States—Securities and Exchange Commission

SECURITIES Exchange Act. See Securities—Laws and regulations

SECURITY, Internal. See Internal security

SECURITY, International. See International security

SECURITY, Job. See Job security

SECURITY analysis
New era of expansion for small growth companies? interview, ed by A. Hershman. J. Westergaard. por Duns R 109:117-18+ Ap '77
Why the Arabs hang on to sterling; British offer of securities in exchange for sterling. Bus W p80-1 Mr 14 '77

SECURITY analysts. See Investment advisers

SECURITY and Cooperation in Europe, Commission on. See United States—Commission on Security and Cooperation in Europe

SECURITY classification (government documents)
First defeat; forcing T. Sorenson's resignation as C.I.A. nominee. D. M. Alpern and others. por Newsweek 89:30-1 Ja 31 '77
No rave reviews for Carter secrecy plan. R. J. Smith. Science 198:589 N 11 '77
Public or private papers? The arrogance of the intelligence community. A. G. Theoharis. Intellect 106:118-20 O '77
Secrecy lives. New Repub 177:9-10 N 26 '77
See also
Defense information, Classified

SECURITY Council of the United Nations. See United Nations—Security Council

SECURITY measures
See subhead Security measures under various subjects, e.g. Computers—Security measures

SECURITY systems
See also
Atomic power—Security measures
Camps—Security measures
Electronic alarm systems
Public utilities—Security measures
Radioactive substances—Security measures

SEDER. See Passover

SEDESTROM, Carol
Profile: Carol Sedestrom. H. Flad and M. Flad. por Craft Horiz 37:44 Je '77 *

SEDGWICK, John. See Fadiman, A. jt auth

SEDIMENTATION and deposition
Sedimentary polycyclic aromatic hydrocarbons: the historical record. R. A. Hites and others. bibl il Science 198:829-31 N 25 '77
See also
Detritus
Marine sediments

SEDITION Law, 1798. See Alien and Sedition Laws, 1798

SEE, Carolyn
Happiest survivor of Mary Hartman. por McCalls 104:28+ Je '77

SEEBOHM, Caroline
Good looks and good health. See occasional issues of House & garden incorporating Living for young homemakers

SEED, William
Children's emergencies; injuries and illnesses. Harp Baz 110:88-9 Jl '77

SEED catalogs. See Catalogs, Seed and plant

SEED drills. See Planters (farm machines)—Equipment

SEED germination. See Germination

SEED inoculation
Inoculating for free nitrogen. J. Ruttle. il Org Gard & Farm 24:137-8 Jl '77
Soybean inoculants not justified. Suc Farm 75: no3 34 F '77

SEED jewelry. See Jewelry

SEEDING
Interseeding and double cropping in a dry year. C. F. Marley. il Farm J 100:16-17 D '76
See also
Alfalfa—Seeding
Corn—Seeding

SEEDING machinery. See Planters (farm machines)

SEEDLINGS
Focus on seedling emergence. L. Reichenberger. il Suc Farm 75:no4 L5 Mr '77
Handling started seedlings. N. Bubel. il Org Gard & Farm 24:69-73 Mr '77

SEEDS
Electronic seed treatment: will it boost yields? G. W. Wormley. il Farm J 101:C1 Ag '77
Seed roundup; symposium. il Org Gard & Farm 25:58-68 Ja '78
Should you try magnetic seed treatment? il Farm J 101:24 My '77
See also
Germination
Grasses—Seed
Soybeans—Seed
Thistles—Seed

Dispersal

Spinning rotation of ash and tulip tree samaras. C. W. McCutchen. bibl il Science 197:691-2 Ag 12 '77

Packaging

May in the garden. D. Fell. Horticulture 55:56+ My '77

SEEDS in house decoration. See Fruits, vegetables, etc. in decoration

SEEFEHLNER, Egon
News from Vienna. J. Wechsberg. por Opera N 41:32 Mr 12 '77 *

SEEGAL, Richard. See Hotchin, J. jt auth

SEEGERS, Kathleen Walker
Slaying the paperwork monster. Read Digest 111:162-5 D '77
SEELEY, Franklin P.
Aluminum poles help light saltwater highways. il por Am City & County 92:35-6 Ja '77
SEELYE, John
Sayonara, Volkswagen. il New Repub 177:27-9 O 8 '77
Television. New Repub 176:23-6 Je 4 '77
SEEMAN, P. See Curran, M. jt auth
SEEMILLER, Dan
Affront of a backhand. D. Miles. il por Sports Illus 48:38-9 Ja 2 '78 *
SEFTON, Nancy
Shrimps that dwell with anemones; with biographical sketch. il Sea Front 23:32-7, 63 Ja '77
SEGAL, David S. and others
β-Endorphin: endogenous opiate or neuroleptic? bibl il Science 198:411-14 O 28 '77
SEGAL, Erich Wolf
Loveliness of the long distance runner. New Repub 177:25-6 Jl 23 '77
Oliver's story; condensation of novel. Ladies Home J 94:88-90 Mr; 114-15 Ap '77
SEGAL, George, 1924-
Capitalist decadent? ed by A. Newman. Art N 76:36 F '77
Larry Rivers and George Segal: back in the U.S.S.R; interview, ed by E. C. Baker. il por Art in Am 65:104-12 N '77

about

Beaux arts; exhibition. R. Berenson. Nat R 29: 342 Mr 18 '77 *
Color them masters; show at the Sidney Janis Gallery, New York City. M. Stevens. il Newsweek 89:80-1 F 14 '77 *
George Segal: on the verge of tragic vision. D. B. Kuspit. il Art in Am 65:84-5 My '77 *
Mind bending with George Segal. A. Elsen. il por Art N 76:34-7 F '77 *
SEGAL, Julius, and Segal, Zelda
Handling your anxieties. il Seventeen 36:146-7+ Mr '77
SEGAL, Margot
White Sands of New Mexico. il Travel 148:58-9 O '77
SEGAL, Martin E.
Brooklyn dropout in the thick of it. R. Gelatt. Sat R 4:40 Ap 2 '77 *
SEGAL, Philip
Special report: minding your P.Q. il Wilson Lib Bull 51:630-2 Ap '77
SEGAL, Stanton, and others
Transport interaction of cystine and dibasic amino acids in renal brush border vesicles. bibl il Science 197:169-71 Jl 8 '77
SEGAL, Zelda. See Segal, J. jt auth
SEGER, Bob
Reluctant rock star. J. Maslin and J. Lowell. por Newsweek 89:92 F 14 '77 *
SEGERS, Mary C.
Abortion and the Supreme Court: egalitarian view. Current 198:17-21 D '77
SEGERSTAM, Leif
String quartets nos. 4-7. P. Rapoport. Am Rec G 40:33-4 Jl '77 *
SEGHERS, Carroll, 2d
On assignment. R. Busch. il Pop Phot 81:118-19+ O '77 *
SEGONZAG, Adalbert de
Change in America—as seen by a veteran French newsman; interview. il por U.S. News 83:56-8 Jl 11 '77
French voters crank up for fateful decision. il U.S. News 83:67 S 12 '77
SEGREGATION, Social
See also
Blacks—Segregation
SEGREGATION in education
Segregation by sex; black boycott of policy prohibiting mingling of sexes in classrooms in Amite County, Miss. M. Sheils. il Newsweek 90:97 S 19 '77
Washington's segregated schools. E. Marshall. New Repub 177:15-17 Jl 9 '77
SEGREGATION in sports
Arthur Ashe: on politics & sports; interview, ed by E. Dowling. A. Ashe. il por Sr Schol 110: 4-6+ S 22 '77; Discussion. 110:7 D 1 '77
Athlete power over South Africa. il Sr Schol 110:8 S 22 '77
SEIBERLING, Dorothy
Timeless summers in old-time Maine. il pors N Y Times Mag p 18-19+ Jl 24 '77
(ed) See Farb, N. Portraits at an exhibition
SEIDER, Norman R.
Filmmaker's eye (cont) il Pop Phot 80:106-7+ F; 116-17+ Mr '77
Super 8 zoomsmanship. il Pop Phot 80:126-9+ Ap '77
SEIDLER, Peter. See Minsky, R. jt auth
SEIFERT, Edward
Carols; poem. America 137:455 D 24 '77
SEINGALT, Giacomo Girolamo Casanova de. See Casanova de Seingalt, G. G.
SEISMIC sea waves. See Tidal waves
SEISMOLOGICAL research
See also
Earthquake prediction
SEISMOLOGY
Earth as a seismic absorption band. D. L. Anderson and others. bibl il Science 196:1104-6 Je 3 '77
High-ferquency P_n phases observed in the Pacific at great distances. D. A. Walker. bibl il map Science 197:257-9 Jl 15 '77
Mars: a possible new quake and some new theories. Sci N 111:68-9 Ja 29 '77
Moonquakes: mechanisms and relation to tidal stresses. M. N. Toksöz. bibl il Science 196:979-80+ My 27 '77
Viking: quake questions and relativity refinements. il Sci N 111:36-7 Ja 15 '77
See also
Earth movements
SEITEL, Peter. See Rinzler, R. jt auth
SEITZ, Frederick
Rockefeller University: no time for philosophers. J. Walsh. il Science 195:272-5 Ja 21 '77 *
SEIZURES and searches. See Searches and seizures
SEKULER, Robert, and Ball, Karlene
Mental set alters visibility of moving targets. bibl il Science 198:60-2 O 7 '77
—and Levinson, Eugene
Perception of moving targets; with biographical sketches. il Sci Am 236:16, 60-4+ Ja '77
SELBIN, Joel
Unreal thinking about energy. Bull Atom Sci 33:54-5 S '77
SELBY, Earl, and Selby, Miriam
Time to get Amtrak on track. Read Digest 110: 233-4+ Ap '77
SELBY, Miriam. See Selby, E. jt auth
SELCHER, Wayne A.
Brazil's candidacy for major power status: short-term problems and long-term optimism. il Intellect 105:400-5 Je '77
SELDIN, Joseph J.
Ads insulting women. Nation 224:464-6 Ap 16 '77
SELECTION, Natural. See Natural selection
SELECTION of engineers. See Engineers—Selection and appointment
SELECTION of librarians. See Librarians—Selection and appointment
SELECTION of teachers. See Teachers—Selection and appointment
SELECTIVE service, Military. See Military service, Compulsory
SELENIUM
Methylation of selenium in the aquatic environment. Y. K. Chau and others; discussion. bibl Science 195:594-5 F 11 '77
SELENIUM in the body
Nutritional interrelationships of vitamin E and selenium. G. F. Combs, Jr and M. L. Scott. bibl il BioScience 27:467-73 Jl '77
Selenium supplements can be harmful. Sci Digest 81:83 Je '77
SELF, Charles, R. Jr
Wood stove you can weld. il Pop Sci 212:110+ Ja '78
SELF
Climbing out of the existential ditch. P. A. Siddons. Chr Today 21:8-9 Ag 12 '77
How to be happy with who you are; interview, ed by C. Seebohm. E. Fromm. il House & Gard 149:152-3+ Ap '77
Isaac syndrome; ego identity development in father-son relationships. S. G. Shoham. bibl f Am Imago 33:329-49 Wint '76
Who am I? Who am I? T. Howard. Chr Today 21:10-14 Jl 8 '77
See also
Consciousness
Identity (psychology)
Mind and body
SELF care, Medical. See Medical care
SELF concept. See Self perception
SELF confidence. See Self reliance
SELF consciousness
See also
Bashfulness
SELF control
Art of exercising self-control. J. S. Faier. Harp Baz 110:86+ Ag '77
Self-discipline called key to success; excerpt from address. R. A. Kroc. por Intellect 106: 185-6 N '77
SELF culture
Speckled ax. L. Conger. Writer 91:7-8 Ja '78
Students of the subjective; courses at New School for Social Research, New York. S. Helgesen. Harpers 254:26-7+ Je '77
SELF defense
See also
Hand-to-hand fighting
Hand-to-hand fighting, Oriental
SELF defense (law)
Killing excuse; wives' murdering husbands because of abuse. il por Time 110:108 N 28 '77
SELF defense for women
How to protect yourself. J. Wilson. Harp Baz 110:93+ Mr '77

SELF defense for women—*Continued*
New nightlife; self-defense; interview, ed by K. Madden. A. Wilson. il Vogue 167:259+ N '77
Self-defense; ideas of F. Storaska. E. R. Dobell. Seventeen 36:194-5+ Ap '77

SELF dependence. See Self reliance

SELF destruction. See Suicide

SELF determination, National
This land is whose land? M. Greenfield. Newsweek 89:92 Je 6 '77
See also
Autonomy

SELF discipline. See Self control

SELF education. See Self culture

SELF employed
How to be your own boss; excerpt from On your own: 99 alternatives to a 9 to 5 job. K. Matthews. il Sat Eve Post 249:52-3+ N '77
On changing jobs: from fulltime to freelance. H. Brubach. Mademoiselle 83:72-4 D '77
Raising your own small business; excerpt from Working for yourself. G. Hewitt. Org Gard & Farm 24:68-77 S '77

SELF estimate. See Self evaluation

SELF evaluation
Big deal. G. McCauley. America 137:inside back cover O 15 '77
Your declaration of independence. H. De Rosis and V. Y. Pellegrino. Harp Baz 110:98+ F '77
See also
Self perception
Students—Self evaluation

SELF fulfillment. See Self realization

SELF government. See Autonomy; Democracy

SELF government in education
Middle school student council; Fred S. Engle Middle School, West Grove, Pa. J. P. Oakley. Clearing H 50:296-7 Mr '77
Return of the EE 304s; honor code violators at West Point. il Time 110:29 S 19 '77

SELF image. See Self evaluation; Self perception

SELF improvement. See Self culture

SELF love
Is self-love biblical? J. Piper. il Chr Today 21:6-9 Ag 12 '77; Discussion. 22:9+ O 7 '77

SELF perception
How to take charge of your life; excerpt. M. Newman and B. Berkowitz. il por Ladies Home J 94:56 Ap '77
How your self-image controls your tennis game; excerpt from Love and hate on the tennis court. N. Cobb and others. il Psychol Today 11:46-7+ Je '77
I want to be terrific . . . K. Ray. Seventeen 36:58 N '77
Joy of being 30. S. Quinn. Harp Baz 110:133+ O '77
Mental labels and tattoos. I. R. Hyatt. il Intellect 106:74-5 Ag '77
Politics of body-image. R. Morgan. il Ms 6:47-9 S '77
Thinking positively about self. A. A. Hoekema. Chr Today 21:32-3 My 20 '77
Two faces of meditation; excerpt from The awareness trap. E. Schur. il Parents Mag 52:70+ N '77

SELF portraits. See Photography—Portraits; Portraits

SELF-publishing. See Private presses

SELF realization
Another Ringer. H. F. Waters. il por Newsweek 90:78 Jl 25 '77
Can a woman become liberated—and stay married? A. Silberman. Read Digest 111:71-4 Ag '77
Celebrity shrinks; M. Newman and B. Berkowitz. S. Edmiston. il pors Esquire 88:53-6+ Ag '77
Consuming self. America 136:498-501 Je 4 '77
Finding the way to self-fulfillment. P. Vaughn. por Parents Mag 52:68-9+ N '77
Fulfillment—it requires balanced satisfactions; study by Jeffrey Kane. J. Horn. Psychol Today 11:33+ S '77
God Sir at Esalen East; work of Bhagwan Shree Rajneesh in Poona, India. il por Time 111:59 Ja 16 '78
Guidance centers: where women can find themselves. J. Wilkins. Good H 184:152+ Je '77
Hey, rub-a-dub-dub; Life Spring and Theta Seminars programs. il Horizon 19:48 Jl '77
I love me—and why not. B. Sabol. il Mademoiselle 83:147-8+ F '77
Learning to live alone. S. Wright. Am Home 80:20 N '77
Metatalk. B. DeMott. Atlantic 240:89-90 S '77
Self as sybarite; Singles survival guide to metropolitan Washington. R. Rosenblatt. il Harpers 254:12+ Mr '77
Selling out. L. Schwarzbaum. Mademoiselle 83: 50+ Mr '77
What do you want to be when your kids grow up? M. S. Miller. il Am Home 80:52-3+ S '77
Whose shoes are you wearing? address, May 12, 1977. L. E. Dobriansky. Vital Speeches 43: 563-5 Jl 1 '77
You can take charge of your life; excerpt from How to take charge of your life. M. Newman and B. Berkowitz. Read Digest 111:118-20 O '77
See also
Erhard Seminars Training

Anecdotes, facetiae, satire, etc.
Man who couldn't find himself. J. Keefauver. Nat R 29:147 F 4 '77

SELF realization (religion) See Identification (religion)

SELF recognition. See Recognition (psychology)

SELF reliance
Power strategies: how to play the game—and win. A. Frisch and D. Partie. Mademoiselle 83: 166-7 My '77
Road less traveled. E. Kohák. il Harpers 225: 21-2+ D '77
Self-determination of success. L. A. Siebert. Nations Bus 65:42+ Mr '77
Three independent views; interviews, ed by D. Lurie. L. Bacall; S. Farrell; B. Sills. il pors Harp Baz 110:96-7+ F '77
What do boys think of independent girls? S. Abrahms. Seventeen 36:51 Jl '77
Your declaration of independence. H. De Rosis and V. Y. Pellegrino. Harp Baz 110:98+ F '77

SELF service garages. See Automobile service stations

SELF-steering gear (boats) See Boats—Steering gear

SELF-stimulation. See Stimulation (physiology)

SELIGMAN, Martin E. P.
Learning to give up. A. Rosenfeld. il Sat R 4: 36-7 S 3 '77 *

SELIGMAN, Paul
Should photographers try to write? Pop Phot 80:75+ F '77

SELIGMANN, Jean H. See Levine, M. I. jt auth

SELIGSON, Marcia
Transsexual chic: the packaging of Renee Richards. il Ms 5:74-6+ F '77

SELL, Ralph R. See De Jong, G. F. jt auth

SELLERS, Bettie
Chattahoochee River; Clean rags and kerosene; Mag; Evensong for Amanda; Ghost flowers; poems. America 136:80 Ja 29 '77

SELLERS, Robert V.
Results unrewarded. por Forbes 119:80 F 15 '77 *

SELLING by telephone. See Telephone selling

SELLINGER, Frank J.
Schlitz raids the competition. il por Bus W p54-5 N 21 '77 *

SELLINGER, Philip M.
Mother hen. por Newsweek 90:9 S 5 '77

SELVERSTONE, Robert, and Hacker, William
Human relations training. Camp Mag 49:9+ Ap '77

SELVIN, Nancy
Detailing slabs with slip impressions. E. Marks. il por Ceram Mo 25:33-6 F '77 *

SELYE, Hans
How to master stress: a guide for families today. il Parents Mag 52:25+ N '77
Secret of coping with stress; interview. il por U.S. News 82:51-3 Mr 21 '77; Same abr. with title To beat stress—learn how to live. Read Digest 111:161-3 Jl '77

SELZER, Michael
Murderous mind. il pors N Y Times Mag p35-7+ N 27 '77

about
Brouhaha in Brooklyn. D. Ravitch. New Repub 176:18-21 Mr 12 '77; Discussion. 176:9 Mr 26; 7-8 Ap 2; 7+ My 7 '77 *

SELZER, Richard
Discus thrower; story. Harpers 255:22-3 N '77
Secret; story. Sat Eve Post 249:22-4 S '77
Touched by something divine; excerpt from Mortal lessons. Read Digest 111:93-5 O '77

SEMEJKO, L. S. See Milstein, M. A. jt auth

SEMEN
Hyperosmolality in intraluminal fluids from hamster testis and epididymis: a micropuncture study. A. L. Johnson and S. S. Howards. bibl il Science 195:492-3 F 4 '77

SEMEN storage tanks. See Tanks

SEMICONDUCTOR industry. See Electronic industries

SEMICONDUCTOR testers. See Testing instruments

SEMICONDUCTORS
Amorphous-semiconductor devices. D. Adler. il Sci Am 236:36-48 bibl(p 146) My '77
Amorphous silicon: a new direction for semiconductors. A. L. Robinson. Science 197:851-3 Ag 26 '77
Chalcogenide glasses: a decade of dissension and progress. A. L. Robinson. Science 197:1068-70 S 9 '77
Hooray for arrays! L. Garner. il Pop Electr 12:80-1+ O '77
How to handle MOS devices without destroying them. L. Solomon. il Pop Electr 12:67-70 Ag '77

SEMICONDUCTORS—*Continued*
Intellectual and economic fuel for the electronics revolution. J. G. Linvill and C. L. Hogan. bibl il Science 195:1107-14 Mr 18 '77
Microelectronic circuit elements. J. D. Meindl. il Sci Am 237:70-81 bibl(p258) S '77
Solid state. L. Garner. See issues of Popular electronics including Electronics world
Solid-state electronics: scientific basis for future advances. J. A. Giordmaine. bibl il Science 195: 1235-40 Mr 18 '77
State of solid state. K. Savon. See issues of Radio-electronics
Today's semiconductors. K. Savon. il Radio-Electr 48:80 S '77
See also
Charge coupled devices (electronics)
Charge transfer devices (electronics)
Diodes
Electric current rectifiers
National Semiconductor Corporation
Transistors

Doping

Amorphous-silicon doping brightens solar-cell picture H. R. Leuchtag. il Phys Today 30:17-19 Ja '77

SEMIGLOSS paint. See Paint

SEMINARIANS
Living out the gospel in seminary life; Interdenominational Theological Center. G. S. Shockley. Chr Cent 94:90-1 F 2 '77

SEMINARIES. See Theological seminaries; Theological seminaries, Catholic

SEMINARS, Library. See Library institutes and workshops

SEMINARS, Motion picture. See Motion pictures —Study and teaching

SEMISUBMERGED stable platform (ship) See Ships

SEMISUBMERSIBLE hulls. See Hulls (naval architecture)

SEMLING, Harold V.
Washington hotline (cont of) Washington dateline. See issues of American city & county

SEMPERVIRENS Club. See Conservation associations

SENATE (United States) See United States—Congress—Senate

SENATE voting. See United States—Congress—Senate—Voting

SENATORS
5 freshman senators who are moving into the spotlight. pors U.S. News 82:24-5 F 7 '77
Six senators size up Carter's stand; views on issue of human rights. il U.S. News 82:21 Mr 14 '77
See also
United States—Congress—Senate

SENDAK, Maurice
Interview with Maurice Sendak; ed by W. Lorraine. il por Wilson Lib Bull 52:152-7 O '77

about

Fantastical world of Maurice Sendak. J. Culhane. il por Read Digest 110:104-8 F '77 *
Sendak receives honorary degree. il Horn Bk 53:485 Ag '77 *

SENECA, Lucius Annaeus
Oedipus. Review
New Yorker 53:112+ D 19 '77 *

SENEGAL

Description and travel

Senegal. L. Greenfield. il Trav/Holiday 148:38-43+ N '77

SENGERS, Anneke Levelt, and others
Critical-point universality and fluids. bibl il Phys Today 30:42-8+ D '77

SENILITY. See Old age

SENIOR centers
Arlington, Va. schoolhouse becomes center for elderly; Madison Activities Center for Frail Older Adults. Aging 272:5-6 Je '77
Taking senior citizens off the shelf; Santa Rosa Senior Skills Center. S. Brown. Educ Digest 42:45-7 My '77

SENIOR Citizen Internship Program. See Aged—Political activities

SENIOR Concert Orchestra of New York. See Orchestras

SENIOR Olympics. See Sports for the aged

SENIOR proms. See Student activities

SENIOR Scholastic Awards. See Scholastic Magazine Awards

SENIORITY, Employee
Blow to minorities; seniority systems decision by Supreme Court. H. Hill. il Commonweal 104:552-5 S 2 '77
Bona fide seniority and racial bias; Supreme Court decision. bibl M Labor R 100:48-9 Ag '77
Court strikes a blow for seniority. il Time 109:60 Je 13 '77
EEOC retreats after a senority ruling; Supreme Court decision. Bus W p28+ Je 20 '77
Seniority snags aerospace talks. il Bus W p45+ N 14 '77

SENNETT, Bill, and Gordon, Max
Italy's Communist paradox. Progressive 41:37-9 My '77

SENNETT, Tomas
Can color shine on cloudy days? A. Grundberg. il Mod Phot 41:88-93 S '77 *

SENSATIONALISM in news reporting. See Journalistic ethics

SENSE organs
See also
Ear
Eye

SENSES and sensation
See also
After images
Chemoreceptivity
Muscular sense
Pain
Smell
Taste
Touch
Vision

SENSING systems, Remote. See Remote sensing systems

SENSITIVE plants
Strange performer for the windowsill. I. Zucker. Horticulture 55:54 Ag '77

SENSITIVENESS
How to give and get emotional support. M. Lasswell and N. Lobsenz. McCalls 105:24+ Ja '78
Why do boys hide how they feel? il Seventeen 36:49 My '77

SENSITIVITY training. See Group relations training

SENSORS. See Detectors

SENSORY deprivation
Monocular deprivation: morphological effects on different classes of neurons in the lateral geniculate nucleus. L. J. Garey and C. Blakemore. bibl il Science 195:414-16 Ja 28 '77
Sensory deprivation helps social drinkers cut down; work of G. David Cooper and others. D. Cohen. Psychol Today 11:46+ N '77
Yugoslavs test man in isolation. il Sci N 111:183 Mr 19 '77

SENSUAL development of infants. See Infants—Growth and development

SENTENCES (grammar)
Let variety spice your words. W. A. Spencer. Writer 90:26-7 Ag '77

SENTENCES, Imposing of. See Criminal justice, Administration of

SEPARATION (chemistry)
See also
Chromatographic analysis

SEPARATION (law)
It's never too late to grab a chunk of life. E. Jackson. il Ebony 33:123-4+ N '77

SEPARATION (technology)
Chainlike formation of particle deposits in fluid-particle separation. C. Tien and others. il Science 196:983-5 My 27 '77
Hydrogen and oxygen from water. E. A. Fletcher and R. L. Moen. bibl il Science 197:1050-6 S 9 '77
See also
Isotope separation

SEPARATION anxiety. See Maternal deprivation

SEPARATION of powers
American system: keeping all the parts in balance. il U.S. News 82:65-6 My 9 '77

SEPARATISM. See Autonomy

SEPULCHRAL monuments
Social commentary from the cemetery. E. S. Dethlefsen and K. Jensen. il Natur Hist 86:32-9 bibl(p92) Je '77

Anecdotes, facetiae, satire, etc.

Talking tombstones. R. Baker. il N Y Times Mag p14 N 20 '77

SEQUOIA Fund. See Investment trusts

SEQUOIA National Park
Sequoia star stomp; sky interpretation talks. J. Henry. il por Sky & Tel 53:262-5 Ap '77

SEQUOIA String Quartet. See String quartets

SERBAN, Andrei
Andrei Serban's theater of terror and beauty. R. Eder. il pors N Y Times Mag p42-3+ F 13 '77 *
Serban takeover. L. Lerman. il por Vogue 167: 152-3 Ag '77 *
Theater. S. Kauffmann. New Repub 176:20-1 Je 11 '77 *

SERBAN, George
Liberated woman: identity crisis. Harp Baz 110: 232+ S '77

SEREBRENNIKOV, N.
Pas de deux; excerpt from Pas de deux or duet dance tr by E. Kraft. il Dance Mag 52:76-7 Ja '78

SEREGIN, Aleksandr. See Grossman, R. G. jt auth

SERENGETI National Park. See National parks and reserves—Tanzania

SERENY, Gitta
Champ of the cheap flight. il pors N Y Times Mag p 14+ S 4 '77

SERIALS, Bibliographical control of. See Bibliographical control

SERIALS, Television. See Television serials
SERIGRAPHY. See Silk screen printing
SERKIN, Rudolf
Music to my ears. I. Kolodin. il por Sat R 4: 46-7 Ja 22 '77 *
SERMONS
See also
Preaching
SEROCK, Kathy, and others
As children see old folks. il Todays Educ 66:70-3 Mr '77
SERPENTINE
Asbestos hazard on U.S. roads? use of asbestos-carrying crushed stone in Montgomery County, Md. il Am City & County 92:36 Ag '77
Environmental asbestos pollution related to use of quarried serpentine rock. A. N. Rohl and others. bibl il Science 196:1319-22 Je 17 '77; Reply with rejoinder. J. T. Hack. 197:716+ Ag 19 '77
SERRAO, John
Insects and spiders—how they spend the winter. il Conservationist 31:26-8 N '76
SERT, Josep Lluis
Homage to Catalonia; with introd by M. F. Schmertz. il Archit Rec 161:85-92 Mr '77 *
SERUMS
Antiserums to neurons and to oligodendroglia from mammalian brain. S. E. Poduslo and others. bibl il Science 197:270-2 Jl 15 '77
Influence of cadmium and other trace metals on human α_1-antitrypsin: an in vitro study. P. Chowdhury and D. B. Louria; reply with rejoinder. C. B. Glaser and others. bibl il Science 196:556-7 Ap 29 '77
Modulation of macrophage tumoricidal capability by components of normal serum: a central role for lipid. H. A. Chapman, Jr and J. B. Hibbs, Jr. bibl il Science 197:282-5 Jl 15 '77
SERVAAS, Beurt
South Africa: mirror image of the United States. il Sat Eve Post 249:62-7+ S '77
SERVAAS, Cory
Medical mailbox; questions and answers. See issues of Saturday evening post
Rx travel and play (cont) Holiday 57:8 N '76; 58:8 Mr; 10+ Ap; 14-15 Je '77
Time for a bran new diet. il Sat Eve Post 249:72-4 Mr '77
SERVICE, Robert
Cremation of Sam McGee and The Shooting of Dan McGrew. L. Burke. Engl J 66:69-70 Mr '77 *
SERVICE, Compulsory non-military
Dilemmas of national service for youth; with views on Andrew Young's Youth Initiatives Act of 1977. L. H. Martin. Chr Cent 94:228+ Mr 9 '77
SERVICE, Volunteer. See Volunteer service
SERVICE centers, Public works. See **Public works facilities**
SERVICE in industry. See Customer service
SERVICE industries
Sanitas: struggling out of bankruptcy. Bus W p27-8 Ap 4 '77
See also
Caterers and catering
Moving and storage companies

Management

As I see it: Big Mac theory of economic progress. T. Levitt. il por Forbes 119:137-8 Ap 15 '77
SERVICE stations. See Automobile service stations
SERVICEMEN
Police and military in the resolution of ethnic conflict. C. H. Enloe. bibl f Ann Am Acad 433: 137-49 S '77
See also
Trade unions—Servicemen

Pay, allowances, etc.

See United States—Armed forces—Pay, allowance, etc; United States—Army—Pay, allowances, etc.
SERVICEMEN (repairing) See Repairmen
SERVICEMENS benefits. See Veterans—Benefits
SERVICEMENS families
Prisoners of hope; relatives of MIAs J. Lelyveld. il N Y Times Mag p 110 Mr 20 '77
SERVICEMENS pensions. See Pensions, Military
SERVICES, Memorial. See Memorial services
SERVICEWOMEN
Let's play taps for an all male Army! universal draft for men and women. Y. B. Burke. il Sat Eve Post 249:12-13+ O '77
One way to avoid a new draft: recruit more women. il U.S. News 82:58 F 14 '77
Wave of the future? M. Stone. il U.S. News 83: 84 Jl 18 '77
See also
Women cadets
SERVING carts
Rolling tea cart. T. H. Jones. il Mech Illus 73:100-1+ F '77
SERVING trays. See Trays

SESAY, Lamin
Crime and development in Africa. Ann Am Acad 432:42-51 Jl '77
SESQUITERPENES. See Terpenes
SESSIONS, Roger
Musical events; setting of When lilacs last in the door-yard bloom'd. A. Porter. New Yorker 53:133-6+ My 16 '77 *
SET design. See Theater—Stage setting and scenery
SET theory
Structure in large sets: two proofs where there were none. G. B. Kolata. Science 195:767-8 F 25 '77
SETON, Elizabeth Ann (Bayley) Saint
Saint and women's lib. J. Deedy. Commonweal 104:418 Jl 8 '77 *
SETRIGHT, L. J. K.
[Column] See issues of Car and driver
SEURAT, Georges
Looking at paintings. B. Dunstan. il Am Artist 41:84-5 F '77 *
SEUSS, Dr, pseud. See Geisel, T. S.
SEVAREID, Eric
Eric Sevareid on today's morals, TV, war or peace, prosperity; interview. pors U.S. News 83:60-2 D 26 '77
Free press for a free people; excerpt from address, March 28, 1977. por Society 15:11+ N '77
about
He looked like God. D. M. Alpern and others. pors Newsweek 90:130 N 28 '77 *
Sign-off for Sevareid. il pors Time 110:111 D 12 '77 *
SEVEN deadly sins. See Sin
SEVENTEEN (periodical)
Here at Seventeen; teen-ager's experiences in internship program. G. Belson. Seventeen 36: 59-60 Ap '77
SEVERIN, Timothy
Voyage of Brendan. il map Nat Geog 152:770-97 D '77
SEVERO, Richard
Playing up to Toscanini. N Y Times Mag p79 Ja 16 '77
Too hot to handle. il N Y Times Mag p 15-19+ Ap 10 '77
Tragedy of Joanne. il pors Sr Schol 109:23-6+ Mr 24 '77
SEVERY, Merle
Celts. il Nat Geog 151:582-630, supp(folded map) My '77
SEVESO, Italy

Pollution

See Pollution—Italy
SEVIER, John
Great state of Franklin. il Sr Schol 109:6-8 Ap 21 '77 *
SEWAGE
See also
Water pollution

Measurement

How to determine wastewater flows. W. S. Foster. il Am City & County 92:61-2 Mr '77
SEWAGE as fertilizer
Sewage sludge and how to sell it. I. M. Knapp. il Am City & County 92:63-5 O '77
Sewage sludge and your garden. Org Gard & Farm 24:40+ S '77
SEWAGE disposal
Co-disposal of sewage sludge and solid wastes—it works. D. B. Sussman. il por Am City & County 92:55-8 O '77
EPA sets rules on ineligible sewers. Am City & County 92:13 Ag '77
Jury on land disposal of wastewater still out, Mr Costle; WPCF annual conference. S. Baxter. Am City & County 92:28 D '77
Palo Alto sees golden glint in sludge; recovery of precions metals. Am City & County 92:23 Jl '77
Treatment of effluents: modern methods of sewage disposal. J. A. Howell. il Oceans 10:63-7 My '77
See also
Sewage as fertilizer
Sewage lagoons
Waste disposal in the ocean
Water pollution
SEWAGE disposal plants
New classroom for environmental education. D. L. Hall. il Parks & Rec 12:36a-38a F '77
Push to ease water rules. il Bus W p69+ Mr 21 '77
Sludge, garbage may fuel California sewage plant; Contra Costa County wastewater reclamation plant. R. B. Sieger and B. D. Bracken. il Am City & County 92:37-8 Ja '77
Success stories in multiple-use; recreation potential of wastewater treatment sites. T. L. Gilbert. il Parks & Rec 12:22a-24a F '77
Tennis on a tank; Evergreen, Colo. J. S. Blair. il Parks & Rec 12:35a F '77

SEWAGE disposal plants—*Continued*

Automation

Make money by computer; wastewater system control; Melbourne, Fla. E. Watkins and J Burger. il Am City & County 92:57-8 Ap '77

Federal aid

EPA cuts sewage funding estimates. Am City & County 92:35 Mr '77

League of cities' agenda missing key ingredient. G. M. Chamberlain. Am City & County 92:112 Mr '77

Wastewater loans readied by EPA. Am City & County 92:28 S '77

Will monthly payments speed pollution cleanup? wastewater treatment facilities construction. il map Am City & County 92:83-6 O '77

SEWAGE irrigation

Retired mayor sparkplugs sewage treatment change; Winter Haven, Fla. il Am City & County 92:77 S '77

SEWAGE lagoons

Lagoons get secondary treatment OK. il Am City & County 92:41-2 D '77

Neoplastic and possibly related skin lesions in neontenic tiger salamanders from a sewage lagoon. F. L. Rose and J. C. Harshbarger. bibl il Science 196:315-17 Ap 15 '77; Reply with rejoinder. J. G. Windsor, Jr and others. 198:1280-1 D 23 '77

Oxidation ditch gives low-cost secondary treatment. il Am City & County 92:87-8 My '77

SEWAGE pumps

Submersible pumps speed sewage flow; Florence, Ky. J. E. Ransom. il Am City & County 92:70 Je '77

SEWAGE purification

AWT may be too expensive—GAO. il Am City & County 92:19 Mr '77

Albuquerque closes water-wastewater cycle. il Am City & County 92:60 Jl '77

Centrifuges capture sludge solids; Los Angeles County. il Am City & County 92:44 Je '77

Energy solution in China: biogas generation by anerobic fermentation. V. Smil. bibl il Environment 19:27-31 O '77

Recreation review may stall PL 92-500 projects; coordination of wastewater treatment and open space and recreational planning. il Am City & County 92:13 O '77

Save water at highway rest stops; recycle and reuse system, Virginia. C. E. Parker. il Am City & County 92:63-4 Je '77

Sludge dewatering—a task the right equipment makes easier. il Am City & County 92:49-52 O '77

Who controls rudderless regulatory ship-of-state? excerpt from address August 1976. J. C. Lamb. Am City & County 92:76+ Mr '77

See also

Sewage disposal plants

Water reuse

Aeration

Oxygen aeration adds treatment capacity, ups efficiency. il Am City & County 92:55-6 Ag '77

See also

Sewage lagoons

Biological treatment

Consumer's guide to composting toilets. il Org Gard & Farm 24:88-91 O '77

Living with a composting toilet. C. H. Stoner. il Org Gard & Farm 24:84-7 O '77

Toilet that takes no water; Clivus Multrum. J. Savage. il Mech Illus 73:102+ S '77

Waterless toilets. E. Moran. il Pop Sci 212:74-6 Ja '78

SEWAGE systems. See Sewerage

SEWAGE treatment plants. See Sewage disposal plants

SEWALT, Charlotte

(ed) See Winokur, R. Interview with Robert Winokur

SEWARD, Michael

Suffocating sea: sludge accumulation in New Jersey Bight. il Oceans 10:60-2 My '77

SEWARD, Stephen

Books as television best sellers; or, Give that TV addict a book! il Wilson Lib Bull 52:232-6 N '77

Fifth dimension of library service. bibl il por Wilson Lib Bull 51:741-5 My '77

SEWELL, Anna

Letter from England: a hope for benefit; Black beauty. A. Chambers. il Horn Bk 53:356-60 Je '77

SEWER cleaning

Equipment

Are high-pressure sewer cleaners safe? B. P. Fisco, Jr. il Am City & County 92:45 Jl '77

SEWER pipes

Cast-in-place pipe uses trench as form; concrete pipe. il Am City & County 92:59-60 N '77

PVC sewer pipe survives deep burial. il Am City & County 92:89-90 My '77

Plain-end pipe collars problem sewer connections. W. S. Foster. Am City & County 92:76 Ap '77

See also

Sewer cleaning

Corrosion

See Corrosion and anticorrosives

SEWERAGE

Michigan sewer project beats all but weather; Monroe County. il Am City & County 92:75 My '77

See also

Sewage disposal

Storm sewers

Maintenance and repair

Contract services stretch sewer maintenance budget; Gladstone, Mo. D. C. Anderson. il Am City & County 92:53 F '77

SEWERS. See Sewerage

SEWERS, Storm. See Storm sewers

SEWING

Great sewing machine projects you didn't know you could make. N. Lindemeyer and others. il Bet Hom & Gard 55:98-105+ Mr '77

Ideas for a golden summer. il Redbook 149:79-86 Jl '77

SEWING boxes

Easy-to-make sewing box. R. Gutter. il Mech Illus 73:129-31 O '77

SEWING centers. See Sewing rooms

SEWING equipment

For one who sews, 45 cents and up. il Sunset 159:112 D '77

SEWING machines

Sewing machines. il Consmers Res Mag 60:13-16 O '77

Manufacture

See also

Singer Company

SEWING rooms

Behind neat doors everything in sight. il Sunset 159:162 O '77

Sewing room you never have to close the door on. J. McCloskey. il Bet Hom & Gard 55:118-19 F '77

SEX (biology)

See also

Hermaphroditism

SEX (psychology)

Answers to questions about sex. P. M. Sarrel and L. J. Sarrel. pors Redbook 148:114-15+ Ap; 149:125+ My; 58+ Je; 28+ Ag; 112 S; 98+ O; 150:49+ N '77

From psychotherapy to sex therapy. J. LoPiccolo. bibl Society 14:60-8 Jl '77

Great news about men and sex; excerpt from The Redbook report on female sexuality. C. Tavris and S. Sadd. il Redbook 149:124-5+ O '77

Health, psychology, sex; questions and answers. R. Tyson and M. C. Tyson. pors House & Gard 149:36+ F; 50 Ap; 50+ Je '77

Health/sex/psychology; questions and answers. M. C. Tyson. por House & Gard 149:72+ O; 66+ N '77

How to conquer your sexual fears. J. D. Butts. il Ebony 32:141-2+ Jl '77

Sex and the black woman: they are now seeking advice. R. Tyson and J. Tyson. il por Ebony 32:103-4+ Ag '77

Sex therapy. D. Hogan. bibl il Society 14:38-42 Jl '77

Sexual boredom: what it means in a relationship. L. Murray. il Fam Health 9:22-6 Je '77

What do our masochistic fantasies really mean? excerpt from Going too far: the personal chronicle of a feminist. R. Morgan. Ms 5:66-8+ Je '77

Woody Allen: schlemiel as sex maniac. R. Wetzsteon. il pors Ms 6:14-15 N '77

See also

Femininity (psychology)

Sex role

Sublimation (psychology)

SEX, Change of. See Change of sex

SEX and law

See also

Prostitution

SEX and religion

Churches start facing up to the sexual revolution: abortions, married priests, homosexuals. il U.S. News 83:63-4 S 26 '77

Human sexuality; symposium. New Cath World 220:262-84+ N '77

It's not official, nor is it right; Human sexuality: new directions in American Catholic thought. Chr Today 21:22 Jl 8 '77

Love and sexuality in Catholic tradition; report of the Catholic Theological Society of America. F. X. Meehan. America 137:230-4 O 15 '77

Scriptural response to the report on Human sexuality. G. T. Montague. America 137:284-5 O 29 '77

Sex and the Catholic; Catholic Theological Society report. K. L. Woodward. Newsweek 90:78-9 Jl 11 '77

SEX and religion—*Continued*
Sexual challenge; report of the Catholic Theological Society of America. Time 109:40-59 Je 13 '77
Time makes ancient good uncouth: the Catholic report on sexuality. R. R. Ruether. Chr Cent 94:682-5 Ag 3 '77
UCC: a liberation stance on sexuality. W. F. Willoughby. Chr Cent 94:676-7 Ag 3 '77; Discussion. 94:815-16, 861-2, 1174 S 21-28, D 14 '77
See also
Homosexuality and Christianity
Homosexuality in the Bible
Sex in the Bible

Bibliography

Sexuality: a new candor in evangelical books. D. Tinder. il Chr Today 21:10-11 Mr 18 '77

SEX attractants (insects) See Insect sex attractants

SEX behavior. See Sexual behavior

SEX chromosomes. See Chromosomes

SEX crimes
See also
Child molesters
Incest
Rape

SEX determination and control
H-Y antigen and the genetics of sex determination. S. S. Wachtel. bibl Science 198:797-9 N 25 '77
See also
Amniocentesis
Sex reversal

SEX differences
Burning question circa 1869: Is there such a thing as sex? Ms 6:21 S '77
Child's play: what every parent needs to know. J. Lever. il Ms 5:22 F '77
Record breaking women. J. H. Douglas and J. A. Miller. il Sci N 112:172-4 S 10 '77
Theological anthropology of the man/woman relationship; excerpt from Sexual morality. P. Keane. il New Cath World 220:284+ N '77
Why men and women think differently. K. Lamott. il Horizon 19:40-5 My '77

Rodents

Bile, prolactin, and the maternal pheromone. H. Moltz and L. C. Leidahl. bibl il Science 196: 81-3 Ap 1 '77

SEX discrimination
Discrimination against whom? widowers seeking survivors' benefits. M Labor R 100:51-2 My '77
It serves them right; case of discriminatory seating in night clubs. C. Mauro. Ms 6:22 N '77
No comment. See issues of Ms.
U.S. journal: Tampa, Florida; discrimination against women at the University Club, Tampa, Fla. C. Trillin. New Yorker 53:101-7 Ap 11 '77
What insurance companies do to women; a new look. B. Myerson. por Redbook 149:74+ Je '77
See also
Discrimination in employment
Women—Employment

SEX discrimination in consumer credit
Credit rules that give women a fair shake; Equal Credit Opportunity Act. il Changing T 31:13-15 My '77
ECOA—in a nutshell. R. A. Lazarus. Ms 5:98 Mr '77
Equal Credit Opportunity Act: some good news, some not so good. L. C. Wohl. Ms 5:95-7 Mr '77
Giving yourself credit; four easy steps to establish your financial identity. P. Nelson. McCalls 104:106+ Mr '77
You become creditable; Equal Credit Opportunity Act and sex discrimination. W. Flanagan. Vogue 167:184+ Je '77

SEX discrimination in education
Anti-bias safeguards don't apply to teachers. C. M. Fields. Educ Digest 43:46-7 S '77
Bod and man at Yale; charges of sex discrimination for tolerating sexual coercion of female students by male teachers. il Time 110:52-3 Ag 8 '77
Counseling: potential superbomb against sexism. M. E. Verheyden-Hilliard. Am Educ 13:12-15 Ap '77
Cutting sex bias out of vocational education. P. Lehmann. Educ Digest 42:33-5 Mr '77
Road is paved with good intentions; Title IX and sex discrimination; address, January 25, 1977. E. Green. Vital Speeches 43:300-3 Mr 1 '77
Segregation by sex; black boycott of policy prohibiting mingling of sexes in classrooms in Amite County, Miss. M. Sheils. il Newsweek 90:97 S 19 '77
Teacher education: a new set of goals. S. McCune and others. Am Educ 13:24-5 Je '77
Title IX: administrative, legal and constitutional aspects; address, March 10, 1977. D. H. Oaks. Vital Speeches 43:372-6 Ap 1 '77
Title IX: antisexism's big legal stick. B. Sandler. il Am Educ 13:6-9 My '77
To the rescue; sex discrimination in education of paramedic L. Knop. G. D. Miklowitz. il pors Seventeen 36:102 Je '77
Toward a nonsexist school. il Am Educ 13:7-9 Ap '77
Update on sex bias cases. B. E. Sinowitz. Todays Educ 66:22-3 N '77
What to do about sex bias in the curriculum. A. Naiman. Am Educ 13:10-11 Ap '77
Women students v. male teachers: sexual harassment at Yale. A. Nelson. Nation 226: 7-9 Ja 7 '78
Women's Educational Equity Act. C. Hoffman. Am Educ 13:28-9 D '77

SEX discrimination in language
Increasingly visible female and the need for generic terms. R. S. Turner. Chr Cent 94: 248-52 Mr 16 '77
Maybe he isn't so bad after all. T. H. Middleton. Sat R 4:50 My 14 '77
Pondering the personal pronoun problem. T. H. Middleton. Sat R 4:59 Mr 5 '77
Words that make women disappear. A. Graham. Redbook 148:72+ Mr '77

Anecdotes, facetiae, satire, etc.

Sexless vocabulary for a sexist society. P. B. Horton. Educ Digest 42:36-8 Mr '77

SEX education
Adolescents, sex, and education. A. D. Hofmann. Educ Digest 43:24-7 N '77
Desirability of involving adolescents in sex education planning. P. A. Reichelt. Educ Digest 42:38-40 Ap '77
Elementary school level sex education; Washington, D.C. J. M. Quinn. Educ Digest 42:29-32 Ja '77
Let's put sex education back where it belongs—in the home. S. Gordon. il Good H 185:66+ O '77
S-e-x; China's program. H. Jensen and S. Liu. il Newsweek 91:48-9 Ja 16 '78
Sex-education controversy. J. S. Faier. Harp Baz 110:91+ Jl '77
Sex education: who needs it? J. D. Butts. il pors Ebony 32:96-8+ Ap '77
See also
Motion pictures in sex education

SEX education literature
Boys and girls and sex and libraries. D. H. Meyers. bibl il por Lib J 102:457-63 F 15 '77
St Martin's wins round against N.Y. obscenity law; case of Show me! M. Reuter. Pub W 212:23-4 D 12 '77

SEX hormones. See Hormones, Sex

SEX in business
Sex harassment; complaints of working women. L. C. Pogrebin. Ladies Home J 94:24+ Je '77
Sexual harassment on the job:
Help for the sexually harassed; the Alliance Against Sexual Coercion. R. Lefkowitz. Ms 6:49 N '77
How to spot it and how to stop it. K. Lindsey. il Ms 6:47-8+ N '77
UN's dirty little secret. M. Kelber. Ms 6:51+ N '77

SEX in drama. See Sex in the performing arts

SEX in literature
Coming of age in Shakespeare; sexual maturation in adolescents. M. Garber. Yale R 66: 517-33 Je '77
Shakespeare's Juliet and her nurse. E. S. Fliess and R. Fliess. bibl f Am Imago 33:244-60 Fall '76

SEX in motion pictures
See also
Motion pictures in sex education
Pornography

SEX in television
More sex less violence: TV's new pitch. J. Mann. il U.S. News 83:20-3 S 12 '77
What teens think of violence and sex on TV and in movies; symposium, ed by E. Miller. Seventeen 36:158-9+ Je '77
Where have you gone, Boccaccio? M. Greenfield. Newsweek 90:96 S 26 '77

SEX in the Bible
Scriptural response to the report on Human sexuality. G. T. Montague. America 137:284-5 O 29 '77

SEX in the performing arts
From the closet to the stage; The Project theater group. S. Bush and D. Goleman. Psychol Today 11:52 O '77
Sex fantasy on Broadway; work of. The Project il Time 109:84 F 28 '77

SEX in the theater. See Sex in the performing arts

SEX pheromones. See Pheromones

SEX pheromones (insects) See Insect sex attractants

SEX Pistols (rock group) See Rock groups

SEX ratio
Sex-ratio adjustment in the common grackle. H. F. Howe. bibl il Science 198:744-6 N 18 '77

SEX relations. See Sexual behavior

SEX reversal
Female fish produce mates when needed; anemone fish. Sci N 111:311 My 14 '77

SEX role
Can a woman become liberated—and stay married? A. Silberman. Read Digest 111:71-4 Ag '77
Changing male roles. J. Harrison. il Am Educ 13:20-6 Jl '77
Destereotyping sex roles. J. Money. bibl il Society 14:25-8 Jl '77
Equality now! For girls and boys; non-sexist schooling project of Women's Action Alliance. B. Sprung. il Parents Mag 52:44+ S '77
Genderisms; reinforcement of stereotypes by advertising. E. Goffman. il Psychol Today 11:60-3 Ag '77
Househusbands. L. C. Pogrebin. Ladies Home J 94:30+ N '77
How men are changing. D. Gelman and others. il Newsweek 91:52-6+ Ja 16 '78
Phallic imperialism: why economic recovery will not work for us. A. Dworkin. Ms 5:101-2+ D '76; Correction. 5:14 F '77
Preschool and the politics of sexism; excerpt from address, October 11, 1976. S. Greenberg. SLJ 23:126 Mr '77
Raising boys who know how to love. D. Singer and J. L. Singer. il pors Parents Mag 52:32+ D '77
Sex roles and how children learn them. R. T. Barnhouse. il New Cath World 220:280-3 N '77
Sexism: curing the disease vs. masking the symptoms; National Conference on Non-Sexist Early Childhood Education. P. D. Pollack; discussion. SLJ 23:52 Mr; 4 Ap '77
Talking to a friend—an interview with Simone de Beauvoir; ed by A. Schwarzer. S. de Beauvoir. por Ms 6:12-13+ Jl '77
Theological anthropology of the man/woman relationship; excerpt from Sexual morality. P. Keane. il New Cath World 220:284+ N '77
Why men dominate women. M. Harris. il N Y Times Mag p46+ N 13 '77
See also
Women and men

Caricatures and cartoons
Cartoon; playing house. C. Bretécher. il Ms 6:110 S '77

SEX role in literature
Bringing women into the curriculum. D. J. Zuersher. Educ Digest 42:38-40 F '77
Farewell to machismo; unpublished manuscripts of E. Hemingway. A. Latham. il pors N Y Times Mag p52-5+ O 16 '77
Non-sexist books. M. Bougere. il por Intellect 106:11 Jl '77

SEX role in television
Sexism's universal curriculum. K. Bonk and J. E. Gardner. il Am Educ 13:15-19 Jl '77

SEX role inversion. See Change of sex
SEX stereotypes. See Stereotype (psychology)
SEX surgery. See Generative organs—Surgery
SEX therapy. See Sex (psychology)
SEXISM. See Sex discrimination; Sex role
SEXIST language. See Sex discrimination in language

SEXTON, Anne
Mother & daughter: mothers can't give the world... but they can try; excerpt from Anne Sexton: a self-portrait in letters. por Mademoiselle 83:176-7+ O '77
Uncensored poet; excerpt from Anne Sexton: a self-portrait in letters; ed by L. G. Sexton and L. Ames. por Ms 6:52-3+ N '77
about
Anne Sexton and God. W. J. McGill. Commonweal 104:304-6 My 13 '77 *

SEXTON, Linda Gray
(ed) See Sexton, A. Uncensored poet

SEXTON, R. E. See Madewell, J. F. jt auth

SEXUAL behavior
Answers to questions about sex. P. M. Sarrel and L. J. Sarrel. pors Redbook 148:114-15+ Ap; 149:125+ My; 58+ Je; 28+ Ag; 112 S; 98+ O; 150:49+ N '77
Beyond the male myth; results of questionnaire; excerpt. A. Pietropinto and J. Simenauer. il Ladies Home J 94:126-7+ O '77; Same abr. with title How men really feel about sex and love. Read Digest 112:83-6 Ja '78
Church and erotic love in marriage. J. G. Milhaven. New Cath World 220:264-7 N '77
Cultural counterrevolution. R. J. Bresler. Intellect 106:115 O '77
Exploding the myth of casual sex. C. Gilbert. Am Home 80:12 O '77
For the very fat, sexual problems are largely logistic; study by Thomas Wise and Jacqueline Gordon. D. Cohen. Psychol Today 11:33 S '77
Great news about men and sex; excerpt from The Redbook report on female sexuality. C. Tavris and S. Sadd. il Redbook 149:124-5+ O '77
Hite report and female sexuality; interview, ed by S. Moore. S. Hite. Read Digest 110:121-3 Je '77
Hite-ing back. il por Time 110:106 D 12 '77
How now, fellatio! Why dost thou tarry? excerpt from Whistling girl. H. Lawrenson. Esquire 87:128+ My '77
How to keep sex from screwing up a friendship; platonic relationships. S. Haller. Mademoiselle 83:118+ D '77
How your job can affect your sex life; interview. A. K. Offit. Harp Baz 110:89+ Ag '77
I hate sex. J. Robinson. Vogue 167:150+ Ag '77
Intelligent woman's guide to sex. J. Coburn. See issues of Mademoiselle, August 1977-
Intelligent woman's guide to sex. K. Durbin. See issues of Mademoiselle to July '77
Is there life in a swingers' club? Plato's Retreat. J. Leo. Time 111:53 Ja 16 '78
Male sexuality: the amazing truth about all those myths; views of A. Pietropinto and J. Simenauer. M.-E. Banashek. Mademoiselle 83:152-3+ N '77
Meeting sexual and emotional needs during pregnancy. M. Newton. Fam Health 9:15-16+ O '77
New sexual myths. W. B. Pomeroy. McCalls 105:102+ O '77
Pleasures of sexual freedom. C. Breslin. Harp Baz 110:95+ Mr '77
Problems of sexual freedom; interview. T. I. Rubin. Harp Baz 110:94-5+ Mr '77
Sex at this moment. J. Robinson and others. Vogue 167:150-1+ Ag '77
Sex during pregnancy; excerpt from Making love during pregnancy. E. Bing and L. Coleman. il Redbook 150:89-90+ N '77
Sex in the seventies; interview, ed by L. Sanford. B. Guccione. pors Am Home 80:46-8+ F '77
Sex test; quiz, excerpt from WNBC television program. D. Luftig. Read Digest 111:78-80 S '77
Sex wars: is bed really a battlefield? ideas of R. Stoller. J. Chase-Marshall. Mademoiselle 83:167+ S '77
Sexual bond; symposium. il Society 14:20-68 Jl '77
Sociobiology and sex. il Time 110:63 Ag 1 '77
What makes a man a good lover? views of female celebrities, ed by E. Schoen. il Redbook 149:104-5+ Jl '77
What sex means to the man you love; questionnaire. il Redbook 149:43-50 Je '77
Why I feel sexier in the summer. M.-E. Banashek. Mademoiselle 83:162+ My '77
Why nice men go to prostitutes. J. C Mills. Redbook 148:96+ Mr '77
See also
Aged—Sexual behavior
Children—Sexual behavior
College students—Sexual behavior
College teachers—Sexual behavior
Homosexuality
Lesbianism
Middle age—Sexual behavior
Orgasm
Sex (psychology)
Teachers—Sexual behavior
Youth—Sexual behavior

Anecdotes, facetiae, satire, etc.
Sex and the lonely guy. B. J. Friedman. il Esquire 88:114-17+ O '77
Sex and the single hull. D. Bradley. il Motor B & S 140:14+ S '77

Animals
Animal rights: NIH cat sex study brings grief to New York museum. N. Wade; discussion. Science 195:131 Ja 14 '77
Ecology, sexual selection, and the evolution of mating systems. S. T. Emlen and L. W. Oring. bibl il Science 197:215-23 Jl 15 '77
Mating needs of animals; sexual behavior of pets. M. W. Fox. McCalls 104:90+ Ap '77
Primate sex preference at ovulation. il Sci N 111:118-19 F 19 '77
Son of Sisterhood in the pasture. J. Horn. Psychol Today 10:30 Mr '77

Birds
Female-female pairing in western gulls (larus occidentalis in southern California. G. L. Hunt, Jr and M. W. Hunt. bibl il Science 196:1466-7 Je 24 '77
Gay gulls of California. il Newsweek 90:86 D 5 '77
Lesbian gulls. il Time 110:106+ D 12 '77
Mallard reactions to rape—it's a matter of costs and benefits; study by David P. Barash. J. Gaylin. Psychol Today 11:49 N '77
Relative fecundity and parental effort in communally nesting anis, crotophaga sulcirostris. S. L. Vehrencamp. bibl il Science 197:403-5 Jl 22 '77
Sociobiology of rape in mallards anas platyrhynchos: responses of the mated male. D. P. Barash. bibl Science 197:788-9 Ag 19 '77
Species indentification in the North American cowbird: appropriate responses to abnormal song. A. P. King and M. J. West. bibl il Science 195:1002-4 Mr 11 '77
See also
Courtship of birds

SEXUAL behavior—*Continued*

Insects

Courtship of patchwork flies. J. A. Miller. il Sci N 111:107+ F 12 '77
Genetics of generation gap in insects. Sci N 111:278 Ap 30 '77
Local mate competition and parental investment in social insects. R. D. Alexander and P. W. Sherman. bibl Science 196:494-500 Ap 29 '77
Mating game: it's different if you fly; excerpt from The mating game. R. Burton. il Sci Digest 81:22-6+ Mr '77
Of cricket song and sex. W. Cade. il Natur Hist 87:64-73 bibl(p 108-9) Ja '78
Sexual calling behavior in primitive ants. B. Hölldobler and C. P. Haskins. bibl il Science 195:793-4 F 25 '77

Invertebrates

Homosexual rape and sexual selection in acanthocephalan worms. L. Abele and S. Gilchrist. bibl Science 197:81-3 Jl 1 '77

Reptiles

Snake chastity plug: his or hers? J. A. Miller. il Sci N 112:301 N 5 '77

SEXUAL desire. See Desire
SEXUAL deviation
See also
Homosexuality
Incest
SEXUAL dimorphism. See Dimorphism (biology)
SEXUAL diseases. See Venereal diseases
SEXUAL ethics
Diverging paths in Catholic sexual ethics. J. Gaffney. il New Cath World 220:276-9 N '77
New morality. Time 110:111-12+ N 21 '77
On female macho; Consumer guide to MIT men. J. Allen. Mademoiselle 83:88+ N '77
Sex harassment; complaints of working women. L. C. Pogrebin. Ladies Home J 94:24+ Je '77
See also
Adultery
Marriage
Prostitution
Sex and religion
Sex education
SEXUAL fantasy. See Fantasy
SEXUAL maturation. See Maturation (biology)
SEYCHELLES (islands)
Closing time in the Garden of Eden. J. Bradshaw. il Esquire 88:128-9+ O '77
SEYFARTH, Fritz
Cockroaches. il Motor B & S 139:28+ Mr '77
SEYFERT, Carl K. 1938-
Did asteroid impacts help shape earth? Sci N 112:341 N 19 '77 *
SEYFFERT, John D.
How Baltimore County keeps its residents high and dry. il por Am City & County 92:78-80 S '77
SGAN, Arnold D.
The chosen, The promise, and My name is Asher Lev; C. Potok's novels. Engl J 66:63-4 Mr '77
SGARLATA, Rob
Ten crazy ways to make energy. . .cheap! il Sat Eve Post 249:56-7+ S '77
SHACKFORD, Jane
Who reads the Newbery winners? bibl il por SLJ 23:101-5 Mr '77
SHACKLETON, Sir Ernest Henry
Endurance: the epic of Ernest Shackleton. N. Rosa. il por Oceans 10:31-5 My '77 *
SHAD
See also
Cookery—Fish
SHAD fishing
Canny container fish. P. Barrett. il Mech Illus 73:18+ Ap '77
Shad in the surf; Chesapeake Bay. N. Karas. il Field & S 81:96+ Ap '77
SHADBOLT, Maurice
Seven in the sea. il Read Digest 110:95-100 Ap '77
Who killed the bog men of Denmark? And why? il Read Digest 110:197-200+ Je '77
Winning the pathless Pacific. il map Read Digest 111:98-102 Ag '77
SHADE, Lucille
Grow watermelons in circles. il Org Gard & Farm 24:82-3 Mr '77
SHADE
See also
Screens (sun)
SHADE plants. See Plants, Shade
SHADE trees. See Tress
SHADES. See Window shades
SHADOW box; drama. See Cristofer, M.
SHAFFER, Lawrence
Reflections on the face in film. il Film Q 31:2-8 Wint '77
SHAFFER, Peter. See Berry, J. W. jt auth
SHAFFER, Peter, 1926-
Equus. Reviews
Chr Cent 94:472-6 My 18 '77 *
New Repub 177:24-6 N 5 '77 *
Psychol Today il 11:21-2 O '77 *
SHAGGYMANE mushrooms. See Mushrooms

SHAH, Keerti V. and others
Congenital transmission of a papovavirus of the stump-tailed macaque. il Science 195:404-6 Ja 28 '77
SHAH of Iran. See Mohammed Reza Pahlevi
SHAHN, Ben
Shahn's Bronx P.O. murals: the perils of public art. C. Baldwin. il Art in Am 65:15-16+ My '77 *
Viewpoint. J. Deschin. il pors Pop Phot 81: 12+ O '77 *
SHAKAL, Anthony F. and Toksöz, M. N.
Earthquake hazard in New England. bibl il map Science 195:171-3 Ja 14 '77
SHAKER folk art. See Folk art
SHAKER furniture. See Furniture, American
SHAKES (wood) See Shingles
SHAKESPEARE, William

Characters

Coming of age in Shakespeare; sexual maturation in adolescents. M. Garber. Yale R 66:517-33 Je '77
Shakespeare's Juliet and her nurse. E. S. Fliess and R. Fliess. bibl f Am Imago 33:244-60 Fall '76

Natural history

Garden talk of William Shakespeare. T. Prideaux. il Horticulture 55:24-7 N '77
Stalking the long purple. J. Janick. il Horticulture 55:28-31 N '77

Plays

Place and plot in Shakespeare. A. Kernan. Yale R 67:48-56 O '77

Hamlet

Hamlet's letters. G. T. Nathan. Engl J 66:60-1 O '77
Stalking the long purple. J. Janick. il Horticulture 55:28-31 N '77

Macbeth

Off Broadway; production at the New Federal. E. Oliver. New Yorker 53:84 My 23 '77

Midsummer night's dream

Stratford's reunion with the classics; Ontario Festival. T. E. Kalem. il Time 109:62 Je 20 '77

Richard III

Stratford's reunion with the classics; Ontario Festival. T. E. Kalem. il Time 109:62+ Je 20 '77

Romeo and Juliet

Shakespeare's Juliet and her nurse. E. S. Fliess and R. Fliess. bibl f Am Imago 33:244-60 Fall '76
Theatre; Circle in the Square production. B. Gill. New Yorker 53:83 Mr 28 '77

Taming of the shrew

Taming of the shrew; adaptation. See Olfson, L.

Staging and acting of plays

See also
Shakespeare festivals

Study and teaching

Hamlet's letters. G. T. Nathan. Engl J 66:60-1 O '77

SHAKESPEARE Festival, Stratford, Ontario
GBS: holy terrorist of iconoclasm; performance of Man and superman. T. E. Kalem. il Time 110:46 Ag 8 '77
Nothing undone. New Yorker 53:21-3 Ag 29 '77
Stratford's reunion with the classics. T. E. Kalem. il Time 109:62+ Je 20 '77
Success at Stratford. W. T. Liston. Commonweal 104:564-6 S 2 '77
SHAKESPEARE festivals
Black Swan Theater opens; Ashland, Ore. il Sunset 158:48+ Ap '77
Reaching everyman: Shakespeare in the streets; Los Angeles Shakespeare Festival. S. Greben. il Parks & Rec 12:39-40+ Ap '77
See also
Shakespeare Festival, Stratford, Ontario
SHAKING hands. See Hand shaking
SHAKLEE Corporation. See Food industry
SHALES, Oil. See Oil shales
SHALIT, Gene
What's happening. See issues of Ladies' home journal
SHAMANISM
Shamans and shamanism: epic journeys to a legendary land. G. M. Bongard-Levin and E. A. Grantovsky. il UNESCO Courier 29: 42-7 D '76
SHAMANS. See Medicine men
SHAMBERG, Michael
Video literacy: learning the language of television. il Horizon 21:85-8 Ja '78
SHAME
See also
Guilt

SHAMOKIN, Pa.

Religious institutions and affairs

See Pennsylvania—Religious institutions and affairs

SHAMPOOS

Shampoos. Consumer Rep 42:335-7 D '77

SHAMS, Feraidoon

Conflict in the African Horn. bibl f map Cur Hist 73:199-204+ D '77

SHAMYL, Imam

Princesses for ransom: abduction in the grand style. F. Maclean. il pors Horizon 19:82-7 Mr '77 *

SHANE, Mary

Mary Shane: baseball's new motor mouth. J. Lublin. por Ms 6:24-5 O '77 *

SHANGE, Ntozake

Ntozake Shange interviews herself. il por Ms 6:34-5+ D '77

about

Photograph. Review

New Yorker 53:48-9 Ja 2 '78 *

Shange's new song. il por Horizon 20:70 S '77 *

SHANGHAI Ballet. See Ballet—China

SHANGHAI Ballet Company. See Ballet—China

SHANGHAI communiqué. See Peking talks, 1972

SHANK, Russell

If elected I will . . . il por Lib J 102:880-7 Ap 15 '77

Russell Shank, ALA president-elect on target, became a librarian by a fluke; interview, ed by E. McCormick. pors Am Lib 8:365 Jl '77

SHANLEY, Paul

Set the captives free. J. Gramick. il New Cath World 220:292-5 N '77 *

SHANNON, D. C. and Kelly, D.

Impaired regulation of alveolar ventilation and the sudden infant death syndrome. bibl il Science 197:367-8 Jl 22 '77

SHANNON, Hugh

Profiles. W. Balliett. por New Yorker 52:36-42 Ja 17 '77 *

SHANSBY, J. Gary

When a family company outgrows the family. por Bus W p68-9 Ag 1 '77 *

SHANSKY, Albert

What to do, what to use for better nails; questions and answers. il Harp Baz 110:58 F '77

SHANTIES (songs) See Sailors songs

SHAPEY, Ralph

Contemporary Ch. Pl: Shapey. por Hi Fi 27: MA22 Ag '77 *

SHAPIRO, Arnold

Locked in the lion's jaws. il Read Digest 110: 82-6 My '77

SHAPIRO, Benson P.

Can marketing and manufacturing coexist? bibl f Harvard Bus R 55:104-14 S '77

Improve distribution with your promotional mix. bibl f il Harvard Bus R 55:115-23 Mr '77

SHAPIRO, Cecile, and Shapiro, David

Lakeside Studio: conserving the printmaking tradition. il por Art N 76:51-4 Mr '77

SHAPIRO, David, 1947-. See Shapiro, C. jt auth

SHAPIRO, David L.

Justice Rehnquist's unappealing guides to action. Sat R 4:16 My 28 '77

SHAPIRO, Eli

Where should you invest your money now? interview. il Changing T 31:6-10 My '77

SHAPIRO, Harvey D.

Do not go gently. . . il N Y Times Mag p36-8+ F 6 '77

SHAPIRO, Ira

Civil liberties and national security: the outlook in Congress. Intellect 105:230-3 F '77

SHAPIRO, Ira G.

Path to accreditation. bibl Parks & Rec 12:29-31+ Ja '77

SHAPIRO, Irving S.

American economy; address, August 28, 1977. Vital Speeches 43:738-41 O 1 '77

Why not zero based regulation? address, May 23, 1977. Vital Speeches 43:605-7 Jl 15 '77

SHAPIRO, Jane

Friends: when does caring become interference? Mademoiselle 83:174-5 O '77

(ed) Extraordinary Simon women. pors Ms 5:49-53+ F '77

SHAPIRO, Lillian Ladman

Best books for whom; or, Where have all the grown-ups gone? Wilson Lib Bull 51:803-4+ Je '77

What's in a name? SLJ 24:95 O '77

SHAPIRO, Ruth

Should you work for a woman? Harp Baz 110: 85+ Ag '77

Will an MBA make you a VIP? Harp Baz 110: 49+ Je '77

SHAPIRO, Susin

Psychology and the arts. il Psychol Today 10: 24 My '77

SHAPIRO, Zalman Mordecai

Mystery of Israel's bomb. D. Martin. il por Newsweek 91:26-7 Ja 9 '78 *

SHAPLEN, Robert

Letter from Indonesia. New Yorker 53:153-6+ D 12 '77

Letter from Malaysia. New Yorker 53:109-31 Ap 18 '77

Letter from Taiwan. New Yorker 53:72+ Je 13 '77

Reporter at large. New Yorker 53:33-6+ S 5 '77

SHARBEL Makhlouf, Saint

Special kind of equilibrium. America 137:276 O 29 '77 *

SHAREHOLDERS. See Stockholders

SHAREHOLDERS meetings. See Stockholders meetings

SHARK fisheries. See Fisheries

SHARK fishing

Hunters of the flats; shark fishing in the Bahamas. G. Drake, Jr. il Field & S 82:56-8+ Je '77

Out for blood; off Florida's Gulf Coast. J. Rudloe. il Sports Illus 46:76-80+ Ap 25 '77

SHARK meat as food. See Fish as food

SHARKS

Consider the shark; with reproductions of paintings by R. Ellis (cont) G. Soucie. Audubon 79:112-14 Ja '77

Go chase a shark; fishing and tagging by high school students. S. M. H. Connett. il Yachting 141:74-6 Mr '77

Shark; symposium, ed by J. Dillon. il Oceans 10:8-47 N '77

Two decades of shark research: a review. P. W. Gilbert. bibl il por BioScience 27:670-3 O '77

Jaws

See Jaws (fishes)

Teeth

See Teeth (fishes)

SHARKS, Fossil

Prehistoric jaws. il Sci Digest 81:74 F '77

SHARLET, Robert

Dissent and repression in the Soviet Union. bibl f Cur Hist 73:112-17+ O '77

SHARMAN, Ben A.

Problems facing international collective bargaining. M Labor R 100:36-7 Mr '77

SHARNIK, Morton

Boxing. Sports Illus 47:71-2 S 12 '77

Served up, imperially, under glass. il pors Sports Illus 46:44-6+ My 2 '77

SHARON, Ariel

Israel's Patton. M. R. Benjamin and M. J. Kubic. il por Newsweek 90:65 S 19 '77 *

SHARON, Nathan

Lectins; with biographical sketch. il Sci Am 236:18, 108-16+ bibl(p 142) Je '77

SHARON Steel Corporation. See Steel industry—United States

SHARON Steel Corporation-Foremost-McKesson, Inc merger. See Corporations—Acquisitions and mergers

SHARP, David Joshua

Self-definitions; Transformations; I will take me away; poems. Poetry 131:130-2 D '77

Voyage off and out; poem. Poetry 129:317 Mr '77

SHARP, Joseph Henry

Joseph Henry Sharp: dedicated observer. M. C. Nelson. il por Am Artist 42:28-31+ Ja '78 *

SHARP, Karen

Mothers can too! il por Redbook 149:54+ Je '77

SHARP, Mary Alice

Few silk purses from sows' ears. il Sat Eve Post 249:64-7 N '77

SHARP Corporation. See Electronic industries—Japan

SHARP-tailed grouse. See Grouse

SHARPE, Genell J. Subak-. See Subak-Sharpe, G. J.

SHARPE, Mary Alice

(ed) See Fawcett-Majors, F. Face looks vaguely familiar

SHARPENING

Knife sharpeners. il Consumers Res Mag 60:11-13 F '77

Saw sharpening tricks and techniques. R. Capotosto. il Pop Mech 147:116-18+ Je '77

Sharpening secrets of a pro. J. A. Juranitch. il Pop Sci 210:118-21 F '77

SHARPLESS family

Sharpless coat-of-arms. H. K. Eilers. il Hobbies 82:140-1 Ag '77 *

SHARRATT, John A. See Waitzkin, H. jt auth

SHASTA, Mount

Heart of Mt Shasta. P. T. Parker. il Am For 83:32-4 O '77

SHASTA Beverages Inc. See Soft drink industry

SHATRAW, Harriet Barrus

Green days of summer. il Conservationist 32:48 Jl '77

SHATTAN, Joseph

Why Breira? Commentary 63:60-6 Ap; 4+ Je '77

SHATTUCK, Petra T. and Norgren, Jill

Century of Pyrrhic victories. il Nation 225:12-16 Jl 2 '77

SHAUGHNESSY, Clark

Melding of men all suited to a T. R. Fimrite. il Sports Illus 47:90-100 S 5 '77 *

SHAVERS, Earnie B.

Importance of being Earnie, act 1. M. Sharnik. il por Sports Illus 47:71-2 S 12 '77 *

SHAVERS, Earnie B.—*Continued*
Once more to the well. P. Putnam. il pors Sports Illus 47:20-3 O 10 '77 *
You gotta have heart. P. Bonventre. il pors Newsweek 90:77 O 10 '77 *
SHAVERS, Electric. See Razors
SHAVING
See also
Barbers and barber shops
Razor blades
Razors
SHAW, Barbara Ramsay. See Schmitz, K. S. jt auth
SHAW, Bernard. See Shaw, G. B.
SHAW, Carolyn
Community-bound: a positive approach. Engl J 66:35-9 N '77
SHAW, Dale L.
Anti-hunting sentiment: can we fight it? il Field & S 82:56+ N '77
SHAW, David (reporter)
Hop on a bus, Gus. il Holiday 58:28-31 Ja '77
SHAW, Diana
Loneliness of a teenage feminist. il por Ms 6:112-13 N '77
SHAW, Eugene F.
Stumbling block: the paschal story. America 136:330 Ap 9 '77
SHAW, Evelyn
Can animals anticipate earthquakes? Natur Hist 86:14+ N '77
SHAW, George Bernard
Caesar and Cleopatra. Reviews
New Yorker 53:65 Mr 14 '77 *
Sat R 4:46-7 Mr 5 '77 *
Time il 109:71 Mr 7 '77 *
Curtain up at Shaw's corner; excerpt from Change lobsters—and dance. L. Palmer. Read Digest 110:173-4+ F '77 *
Man and superman. Review
Time 110:46 Ag 8 '77 *
Saint Joan. Reviews
Nation 226:27-8 Ja 7 '78 *
New Repub 178:24 Ja 7 '78 *
New Yorker 53:47 Ja 2 '78 *
Time il 110:71 D 26 '77 *
You never can tell. Review
New Yorker 53:117-18 O 31 '77 *
SHAW, James H. and Jordan, P. A.
Wolf that lost its genes; with biographical sketches. il Natur Hist 86:9, 80-8 bibl(p 111) D '77
SHAW, John
John Shaw, cabinetmaker of Annapolis. L. Bartlett. bibl il Antiques 111:362-77 F '77 *
SHAW, Robert
Cowgirls. il Esquire 88:80-3 O '77
SHAW, Robert B.
Coming out into the sun. Poetry 131:106-10 N '77
High notes and low. Poetry 129:233-9 Ja '77
Reconsideration. New Repub 176:39-41 Je 18 '77
SHAW, Robert Fletcher
Why nuclear energy! address, June 17, 1977. Vital Speeches 43:648-51 Ag 15 '77
SHAW, Susan
Flames in the jungle. il Int Wildlife 7:44-7 N '77
Sunrise, moonrise. il Nat Wildlife 15:44-7 F '77
SHAW-EAGLE, Joanna
Raphael Soyer: a realist without a slogan. il por Art N 76:187-8 N '77
Traces of the Brush. il Art N 76:84-8 S '77
Washington, D.C. il Art N 76:116 S '77
SHAW HEIGHTS, Colo.
Water supply
See Water supply—Colorado
SHAWLS
Super shawls! il Good H 186:96-8+ Ja '78
SHAWN, Ted
Look at Jacob's Pillow. J. Warren. Chr Cent 94:41-2 Ja 19 '77 *
SHCHARANSKY, Anatoly
AAP protests to Soviet on Shcharansky's arrest. M. Reuter. Pub W 211:14 My 30 '77 *
Charge of treason. F. Willey and F. Coleman. Newsweek 89:42+ Je 13 '77 *
SHEA, Kevin P.
Business of biological control. bibl il Environment 19:15-19 My '77
Endangered Species Act. bibl il Environment 19:6-15 O '77
Profile of a deadly pesticide. bibl il Environment 19:6-12 Ja '77
SHEAHAN, Denis
Sex and tennis: mismatched pair. Am Home 80:27 Ag '77
SHEAHEN, Thomas P.
Maxwell and Sheahen chosen as Congressional fellows. pors Phys Today 30:71 Jl '77 *
SHEALY, C. Norman
Link between your emotions and health; interview. Harp Baz 110:131+ F '77
SHEARER-IZUMI, Walter
Natural resources program at the United Nations University. Science 198:896-7 D 2 '77
SHEARN, Allen. See Davis, K. T. jt auth
SHEARN, Douglas
Super dog of Scotland Yard. J. Stewart-Gordon. il por Read Digest 110:201-2+ Mr '77
SHECHNER, Mark
Elusive Trilling. Nation 225:247-8+, 278-80 S 17, 24 '77
SHEDDING of fur. See Molting
SHEDS
Fuel shed stores flammables at a safe distance. A. Lees. il Pop Sci 211:138 D '77
Machine shed that's as big as a hangar. B. Coffman. il Farm J 101:D1 mid-F '77
See also
Garden houses, shelters, etc.
SHEED, Wilfrid
Now that men can cry . . . N Y Times Mag p38-40+ O 30 '77
Twin urges of James Baldwin. por Commonweal 104:404-7 Je 24 '77
SHEEDY, Alexandra
How can mom and dad do this to me? il Seventeen 36:242-3+ Ag '77
SHEEHAN, Edward R. F.
Proposal for a Palestinian state. il map N Y Times Mag p8-11 Ja 30 '77
SHEEHAN, George
Are you a runner? tips for women runners. il Vogue 167:136-7 Ap '77
SHEEHAN, Laurence
If you can type this you can make big money. Atlantic 239:106-7 Mr '77
My bird problem, and ours. il Atlantic 239:84-5 Je '77
Ump. il Atlantic 240:83-4 S '77
SHEEHAN, Susan
Annals of crime. New Yorker 53:48-52+ O 24; 46-50+ O 31; 123-40+ N 7 '77
SHEEHY, Eugene P.
From Winchell's 8th to Sheehy's 9th; interview, ed by A. Plotnik. il Am Lib 8:129-32 Mr '77
SHEEHY, Gail
Crisis couples face at forty; excerpt from Passages. Read Digest 110:73-6 Mr '77
(ed) See Kosinski, J. N. Psychological novelist as portable man
SHEEN, Fulton John, Abp
Bottom-line theology; interview, ed by D. Kucharsky. il Chr Today 21:8-11 Je 3 '77
SHEENJEK River
Return to the Sheenjek. M. E. Murie. il por map Liv Wildn 41:4-12 Jl '77
SHEEP
Diseases and pests
Antigenic shift of visna virus in persistently infected sheep. O. Narayan and others. bibl il Science 197:376-8 Jl 22 '77
SHEEP, Wild. See Mountain sheep
SHEEP industry
See also
American Sheep Producers Council
SHEERIN, John B.
Jewish-Catholic relations. il New Cath World 220:173-8 Jl '77
SHEETS
Awaken to spring. R. Weil. il House B 119:152-5 My '77
For bed and beyond: decorating with sheets. il Mademoiselle 83:164-7+ Mr '77
Personality sheets. P. Sadowsky. il Am Home 80:48-51+ Mr '77
Sheet savvy. E. Feldman. Am Home 80:23-4 Mr '77
Sheets play a dual role; Rita Moreno's decorating. J. Macurdy. il House B 119:58-61 Mr '77
SHEFNER, Jeremy M. and Levine, M. W.
Interactions between rod and cone systems in the goldfish retina. bibl il Science 198:750-3 N 18 '77
SHEHAN, Lawrence Joseph, Cardinal
Centrality of the Eucharist in the prayer life. il New Cath World 220:30-1 Ja '77
SHEILS, Merrill
From Newsweek. il Engl J 66:16-17 My '77
SHELBY, Carroll
Years of the snake. W. Wyss. il por Hot Rod 30:31-4+ Je '77 *
SHELDON, Charles
Soyuz program. il Space World N-7-163:4-26 Jl '77
SHELDON, Eric. See Feshbach, H. jt auth
SHELL craft. See Shellwork
SHELL work. See Shellwork
SHELLEDY, James E.
Prying out sources. Time 110:114 N 14 '77 *
SHELLENBERGER, Donald
Strong staff: the key ingredient. il Camp Mag 49:6-8+ Ap '77
SHELLEY, Florence D. See Otten, J. jt auth
SHELLEY, Percy Bysshe
Scrope's last throw. R. Holmes. Harpers 254:77-9+ Ap '77 *
SHELLFISH
See also
Crabs
Krill
Mollusks
Shrimps
Habits and behavior
See Fishes—Habits and behavior

SHELLFISH—*Continued*

Reproduction

See Fishes—Reproduction

SHELLFISH as food
House beautiful chef; how to enjoy a cooked hardshell crab. J. Pepin. il House B 119:112 Mr '77
See also
Cookery—Shellfish

SHELLFISH culture
Lobster aquaculture in New York: an experiment that failed. A. C. Jensen. il por map Conservationist 31:16-19 My '77
When scientists and oystermen cooperate; oyster culture and research in Brittany. C. Jones. il Sea Front 23:106-12 Mr '77

SHELLFISH fisheries
Crabbers, sooks and Jimmies; excerpt from Beautiful swimmers. W. W. Warner. il Read Digest 111:112-16 O '77
Hail, lobsterman . . . and farewell. J. Doherty. il Nat Wildlife 15:42-9 Ap '77
Reporter at large: scalloping. J. Stevenson. il New Yorker 53:46+ Ag 15 '77
Spiny lobster fishing in the Grenadines. J. E. Adams. il map Sea Front 23:322-30 N '77

SHELLHAAS, Judy
Techniques in building miniatures; interview, ed by S. A. Parvin. il Hobbies 82:120-1 My '77

SHELLS (conchology)
Anaerobiosis and a theory of growth line formation. R. A. Lutz and D. C. Rhoads. bibl il Science 198:1222-7 D 23 '77
Function of shell sculpture in marine gastropods: hydrodynamic destabilization in ceratostoma foliatum. A. R. Palmer. bibl il Science 197: 1293-5 S 23 '77
Natural history:
Scallops (title varies) A. G. Melvin. il Hobbies 82:144 My; 144-5 Je; 145+ Jl; 144-5+ Ag; 144-5 S; 144 O '77
True oysters. A. G. Melvin. il Hobbies 82: 144-5 N; 144-5 D '77; 144-5 Ja '78
Wing or pearl shells. A. G. Melvin. il Hobbies 81:139+ F; 82:145 Mr; 144-5 Ap '77
See also
Abalones

SHELLWORK
Shell game. J. M. Wood. il Design (US) 78:6-7 Summ '77

SHELTER Institute. See House construction—Study and teaching

SHELTERBELTS. See Windbreaks

SHELTERED housing program. See Aged—Housing

SHELTERS
See also
Garden houses, shelters, etc.

SHELTERS, Atomic bomb. See Atomic bomb shelters

SHELTON, Marlyn L.
1976 and 1977 drought in California: extent and severity. il map Weatherwise 30:139-46+ Ag '77

SHELTON, Richard
Prophet; poem. New Yorker 53:138 S 12 '77

SHELTON, Sally
United States and Mexico: a special relationship; remarks, September 21, 1977. Dept State Bull 77:811-14 D 5 '77

SHELTON, Thomas H.
Patient art of grantsmanship. M. N. Carter. il Art N 76:34-5 My '77 *

SHELVES
Clever, versatile utility-shelf hardware; for walls. M. Philips. il Pop Sci 211:148-9 O '77
Everything's in place on bolt-together plywood shelves. il Sunset 158:136 Ap '77
Paying attention to shelves in the kitchen. il Sunset 158:114 F '77
Plant shelves that swing. il Mech Illus 73:70-1+ F '77
Remodeling notebook. J. H. Ingersoll. il House B 119:30 Jl '77
They're useful and decorative. il Sunset 159: 157 O '77
See also
Bookcases

SHEN, Rong-sen, and Abell, C. W.
Phenylketonuria: a new method for the simultaneous determination of plasma phenylalanine and tyrosine. bibl il Science 197:665-7 Ag 12 '77

SHENANDOAH (airship) See Airships

SHENANDOAH River
Canoe cleanup campaign. B. Gooch. por Outdoor Life 160:30 N '77
Chemical plants leave unexpected legacy for two Virginia rivers; mercury pollution. L. J. Carter. map Science 198:1015-20 D 9 '77

SHENEFIELD, John H.
Carter's trustbusters. D. Pauly and J. B. Copeland. il por Newsweek 90:66 S 26 '77 *
Cracking the whip at the Justice Dept. por Bus W p43-4 S 19 '77 *
Lull before the antitrust storm. P. Sturm. por Forbes 120:25-6 Ag 15 '77 *
Washington's new approach to antitrust action. W. Neikirk. pors Nations Bus 65:30-2 D '77 *

SHENKER, Israel
Definition of Partridge. por N Y Times Mag p41-2 O 2 '77
House that holds Rockefeller riches (papers, not $$$) il Smithsonian 8:90-7 S '77
Life in the Talmud. il pors N Y Times Mag p44+ S 11 '77
Now, Jewish roots. N Y Times Mag p42-5 Mr 20 '77

SHEPHERD, George W. Jr
Does the Carter administration have a strategy for Southern Africa? il Chr Cent 94:782-6 S 14 '77

SHEPHERD, J. Barrie
Advent; poem. Chr Cent 94:1113 N 30 '77
Advent candles; poem. Chr Today 22:21 D 9 '77
Four-letter-word tree; Corkscrew; poems. Chr Cent 94:318, 324 Ap 6 '77
January; poem. Chr Cent 94:14 Ja 5 '77
September; poem. Chr Cent 94:837 S 28 '77
Star-crossing; poem. Chr Cent 94:1134 D 7 '77

SHEPHERD, Jack
New environment at Interior. il por N Y Times Mag p36+ My 8 '77

SHEPPARD, Robert
For candid wildlife pictures, build a blind. il Pop Phot 81:106-8+ Ag '77

SHEPPARD, Sally. See Blackmon, R. jt auth

SHEPPARD, Shaun
Kid from class 4-4. J. Lelyveld. N Y Times Mag p 127 Ap 24 '77 *

SHEPPARD, Suzanne Lefranc
More on government support of the arts. por Am Artist 41:17 N '77

SHER, Jonathan P. and Tompkins, R. B.
Myths of rural school and district consolidation. Educ Digest 42:45-8 Ap '77

SHERBET. See Ice cream, ices, etc.

SHEREIKIS, Richard
How you play the game: the novels of John R. Tunis. il Horn Bk 53:642-8 D '77

SHERER, Albert William, 1916-
U.S. abstains on Security Council resolution on Botswana complaint; statement, January 14, 1977. Dept State Bull 76:118 F 7 '77
U.S. gives views on U.S.S.R. proposal for world treaty on the non-use of force; statements, October 28 and 29, 1976. Dept State Bull 76: 30-2 Ja 10 '77
United States joins consensus on U.N. resolution on Benin; statement, with text of resolution, April 14, 1977. Dept State Bull 76:502-3 My 16 '77
U.S. joins Security Council appeal for assistance to Lesotho; statement, December 22, 1976. Dept State Bull 76:51 Ja 17 '77
U.S. reiterates support for negotiated solution in Rhodesia; statement, December 20, 1976. Dept State Bull 76:55 Ja 17 '77

SHERIDAN, Danny
Cashing in a sure thing. M. DelNagro. il Sports Illus 47:70+ D 5 '77 *
Picking winners. L. Linderman. por Esquire 88:177-8+ D '77 *

SHERIDAN, David
Second coal age promises to slow our dependence on imported oil. il Smithsonian 8:30-7 bibl(p 101) Ag '77

SHERLINE, Peter, and Schiavone, Karen
Immunofluorescence localization of proteins of high molecular weight along intracellular microtubules. bibl il Science 198:1038-40 D 9 '77

SHERMAN, Bennett
Techniques tomorrow. See issues of Modern photography

SHERMAN, Paul W.
Nepotism and the evolution of alarm calls. bibl il Science 197:1246-53 S 23 '77
—See Alexander, R. D. jt auth

SHERMAN, Russell
Musician who thinks for himself. D. Garvelmann. il por Am Rec G 40:32-5 D '76 *

SHERMAN, Steve
Someone is always on Monadnock. il Nat Wildlife 15:26-9 Ag '77

SHERMAN, William Tecumseh
This thankless office. il por Am Hist Illus 11: 46-8 Ja '77

SHERR, Lynn
Political update: New York's finest—Bella, Ronnie, & Carol. il pors Ms 6:60-1 S '77

SHERR, Richard
Notes on two Roman manuscripts of the early sixteenth century. bibl f il Mus Q 63:48-73 Ja '77

SHERRILL, Claudine, and Ruda, Lucy
Time to listen. il Parks & Rec 12:30-3+ N '77

SHERRILL, Robert G.
Raising hell on the highways. il N Y Times Mag p38-40+ N 27 '77

SHERRILL, Sarah B.
Current and coming. See issues of Antiques
Living with antiques. il Antiques 111:1002-5 My '77

SHERRIN, Ned
Company. New Yorker 53:26-7 Je 13 '77 *

SHERRY, Mary
Is state aid the saving grace of Catholic education? America 136:327-8 Ap 9 '77

SHERRY. See Wine

SHERTZ, Robert Harold
Deregulation: after the airlines, is trucking next? address, September 26, 1977. Vital Speeches 44:40-2 N 1 '77

SHERWIN, Judith (Johnson)
Imitation of death; poem. New Repub 176:27 F 5 '77
Noon; poem. Nation 225:470 N 5 '77
Statement; poem. Nation 225:606 D 3 '77

SHERWOOD, Dolly
Historical goodies crammed in old camelback trunks. il Smithsonian 8:106+ Je '77

SHERWOOD, Hugh C.
Credit: how to use it wisely. Harp Baz 110:50+ Je '77

SHETLAND Islands
Oil comes to the Shetlands. P. Koenig. maps Audubon 79:129-33 Mr '77

SHEVEY, Sandra
Buenos Aires: a great buy. il Harp Baz 110:12+ O '77

SHEVYAKOV, Yuri
City planning—Soviet style. Am City & County 92:110 My '77

SHEZAN on the Plaza (restaurant) See New York (city)—Hotels, restaurants, etc.

SHIATSU. See Massage

SHIAWASSEE County, Mich.
Put the jobless back to work. il Am City & County 92:85-6 My '77

SHICOFF, Neil
Zealot: Neil Shicoff; interview, ed by T. P. Lanier. por Opera N 42:34 D 3 '77

SHIELDS, Cornelius
Corny Shields wins Herreshoff trophy. R. N. Bavier. Yachting 141:62 Mr '77 *

SHIELDS, Gerald Robert
Intellectual freedom: justification for librarianship. bibl Lib J 102:1823-5 S 15 '77

SHIELDS, Nelson P.
Carter/Knox team wins a big one. J. Samson. pors Field & S 82:41+ S '77 *

SHIELDS, Pete. See Shields, N. P.

SHIFTERS, Automobile. See Automobiles—Transmission

SHINGLED walls. See Wall coverings

SHINGLES
Shakemaker lets you split your own. M. Robinson. il Pop Sci 210:156 Ap '77

SHINJUKU district. See Toyko

SHINKMAN, Paul G. and Bruce, C. J.
Binocular differences in cortical receptive fields of kittens after rotationally disparate binocular experience. bibl il Science 197:285-7 Jl 15 '77

SHINN, Richard Randolph
How your know-how can save private colleges. por Nations Bus 65:64 O '77

about

Metropolitan Life's failure as a swinger. il por Bus W p78+ N 21 '77 *

SHINN Historical Park. See California—Parks and reserves

SHINNECOCK Hills golf course, Southampton, N.Y. See Golf courses

SHINNICK-GALLAGHER, Patricia. See Gallagher, J. P. jt auth

SHINOHARA, Toshimichi. See Piatigorsky, J. jt auth

SHIP and boat models
Tank-testing Enterprise; model of racing yacht. A. M. Hays. il Yachting 141:66-8 F '77

Competitions

Around the mall and beyond; James Smithson Challenge Cup. E. Park. il Smithsonian 8:12+ N '77
Southern Neuse Racing Circuit; a sailboat model race. T. Pereira. il Yachting 142:131-2 D '77

SHIP building. See Shipbuilding

SHIP canals. See Canals

SHIP inspection. See Ships—Inspection

SHIP museums. See Naval museums

SHIP propulsion
See also
Propellers

SHIP simulators. See Simulators

SHIPBUILDING
Move to divvy up the orders for ships. il Bus W p36-7 D 5 '77
Torpedoing the Navy's ship plans. il Bus W p33 Ja 16 '78
See also
Congoleum Corporation
General Dynamics Corporation
Naval architecture

Europe, Western

Europe: failing to fend off Japan's shipbuilders. il Bus W p42-3 F 28 '77

Great Britain

Big ship order stranded in the yards; Polish order. il Bus W p46 D 26 '77

Japan

Europe: failing to fend off Japan's shipbuilders. il Bus W p42-3 F 28 '77

SHIPLER, David K.
Reports & comment: Moscow. Atlantic 240:11-12+ S '77

SHIPMAN, Gordon
Memories that make families strong. il por Parents Mag 52:30-1+ D '77

SHIPMENT of goods
See also
Delivery of goods

SHIPPING
Marine transport; symposium. il Oceans 10:20-55 Mr '77
See also
Containerization (freight)
Tank ships

History

Cameras at sea; historical west coast maritime photography. R. A. Weinstein. il Am West 14:34-9 My '77
China's ancient mariners. S. Steiner. il Natur Hist 86:48-63 bibl(p 110) D '77

Law

See Maritime law

Europe, Eastern

EC nations fight Communist tactics. il Bus W p69-70 D 12 '77

Europe, Western

EC nations fight Communist tactics. il Bus W p69-70 D 12 '77

Great Lakes

See Inland water transportation

Greece

How Christina's doing; Onassis fleet. il por Time 110:69 Ag 8 '77

Mississippi River

See Inland water transportation

Russia

Piracy or profit on the high seas? il Time 110:59 D 5 '77

Underdeveloped areas

See Underdeveloped areas—Shipping

United States

Help for shipping industry? U.S. News 83:65 Jl 4 '77
Old Glory sails again; Overseas Shipholding Group, Inc. il por Forbes 119:34-5 F 1 '77
Transport efficiency and future economic growth; a policy for Beaumont, Tex; address, January 12, 1977. A. L. Wilson. Vital Speeches 43:337-9 Mr 15 '77
See also
Seatrain Lines, Inc
United States Lines, Inc

SHIPPING, Inland water. See Inland water transportation

SHIPS
SSP: semi-submerged platform. H. Pennington. il Oceans 10:32-4 Mr '77
See also
Armored vessels
Hospital ships
Landing craft
Ocean liners
Sailing vessels
Salvage (ships)
Shipwrecks
Steamships and steamboats
Tank ships
Tugboats
Yachts and yachting

Corrosion

See Corrosion and anticorrosives

Design

See also
Hulls (naval architecture)

Food service

See also
Ocean liners—Food service

Inspection

Commerical vessel safety: Coast Guard inspection of United States Merchant Marine. J. Hunt. il Oceans 10:28-31 Mr '77

Loading and unloading

See Loading and unloading

Manufacture

See Shipbuilding

Photographs

Dockside; photographs. T. Thompson. Oceans 10:50-5 Mr '77

SHIPS—*Continued*

Registration and transfer

Flags of convenience—or necessity? R. Rich. il Oceans 10:22-7 Mr '77

U.S. tuna fleet fishes for foreigners; registry transfer due to new U.S. regulations that limit the kill of porpoises that swim with tuna. il Bus W p25 Ja 24 '77

Anecdotes, facetiae, satire, etc.

License. R. Lipez. Progressive 41:66 My '77

Safety devices and measures

ILO tightens standards for maritime safety; standards for flag of convenience ships. J. P. Goldberg. bibl M Labor R 100:25-30 Jl '77

See also

Ships—Inspection

Tank ships—Safety devices and measures

SHIPS, Atomic powered

See also

Warships, Atomic powered

SHIPS, Hospital. See Hospital ships

SHIPS, Research

Glomar Challenger. M. Blawis. il Oceans 10:6-7 N '77

SHIPS, Surface effect. See Air cushion vehicles

SHIPS in art

They owned the sea; reproductions of paintings. J. Stobart. Read Digest 110:146-51 Je '77

See also

Marine painting

SHIPWRECKS

Beware of Greeks bearing oil; tanker Argo Merchant. G. Reiger. Audubon 79:141-6 Mr '77

In praise of skepticism; loss of the Crystal Catfish II. J. Cartwright. il Motor B & S 140:21+ S '77

Oil tanker disasters. E. R. Gundlach. bibl il map Environment 19:16-20 D '77

Shipwrecked. H. Roth. il Motor B & S 140:50-3+ S '77

Shipwrecks, pollution & the law of the sea. R. J. McManus and J. Schneider. Nat Parks & Con Mag 51:10-15 Je '77

That others might live: the saga of the U.S. Coast Guard. D. Noble and T. M. O'Brien. il Am Hist Illus 12:4-7+ Je '77

Tragedy off Nantucket; sinking of the Argo Merchant. J. Hearst, Jr. il Motor B & S 139: 30+ Mr '77

Treasure of Tobermory Bay; Spanish galleon Florencia. E. Antrobus. il map Am For 83:20-3+ Je '77

See also

Archeology, Submarine

Bermuda Triangle

Collisions at sea

Salvage (ships)

Survival after airplane accidents, shipwrecks, etc.

Titanic (steamship)

SHIPYARDS

See also

Shipbuilding

SHIRK, Martha. See Glass, H. jt auth

SHIRLEY, Don

Library material security systems: a school district's experience. il SLJ 23:38-41 Ap '77

SHIRTS

More cotton in men's durable press shirts. il Consumers Res Mag 60:24-8 Mr '77

Work shirts personalized. il Sunset 159:74-5 Ag '77

SHISKIN, Julius

Too objective? por Forbes 120:76 Jl 15 '77 *

SHIVERS, C. Alex and Dunbar, B. S.

Autoantibodies to zona pellucida: a possible cause for infertility in women. bibl il Science 197:1082-4 S 9 '77

SHNEOUR, Elie A.

Science: too much accountability. Science 195: 939 Mr 11 '77

SHOAF, Mary L. See Scribner, R. L. jt auth

SHOCK, Nathan Wetherill

Nathan Shock first NIA science director. por Aging 274:21 Ag '77 *

SHOCK

See also

Electric shock

SHOCK absorbers

See also

Automobiles—Shock absorbers

Motorcycles—Shock absorbers

SHOCK collars, Dog. See Dogs—Equipment and supplies

SHOCK therapy

Case for shock therapy. D. Avery. Psychol Today 11:104 Ag '77

SHOCK waves

See also

Sonic boom

SHOCKLEY, Grant S.

Living out the gospel in seminary life. Chr Cent 94:90-1 F 2 '77

SHOCKLEY, Virgie F.

Versatile fig named celeste. il Org Gard & Farm 24:82-3 D '77

Yankee's love affair with collards. il Org Gard & Farm 24:62-4 Jl '77

SHOCKLEY, W. Ray

Textile industry; address, October 11, 1977. Vital Speeches 44:54-7 N 1 '77

SHOE industry

Bass' big turnaround. . .unaided. il Forbes 120:54 D 15 '77

This bonus is a real incentive; R. Puga's bonus pay at Suave Shoe Corp. il por Bus W p54+ Mr 14 '77

See also

Capezio Ballet Makers (firm)

Export-import trade

AFL-CIO rebuffed on shoe imports, situs picketing. L. Bornstein and others. M. Labor R 100: 64 Je '77

Carter's plan to stem imports. il U.S. News 82: 94 Ap 11 '77

President announces measures to assist U.S. shoe industry; statement, April 1, 1977. J. Carter. Dept State Bull 76:463 My 9 '77

ROC and Korea agree to curb shoe exports to U.S; announcement, June 14, 1977. Dept State Bull 77:202-3 Ag 15 '77

Yes and no on shoes. il Time 109:61-2 Ap 11 '77

Federal aid

Hope for the import victims. il Bus W p 17-18 Jl 4 '77

Where the shoe pinches. Forbes 120:53-4 D 15 '77

Wages and hours

Wages rise slowly, employment and output plummet in shoe factories. J. C. Bush. il M Labor R 100:53-4 Je '77

Switzerland

Another upheaval keeps Bally unsettled. il por Bus W p23-4 Ag 1 '77

Switzerland: a sudden takeover of a staid shoemaker; C. F. Bally. il Bus W p40-1 F 21 '77

SHOEMAKER, Carole

Waiting for Uncle Eddie; drama. Plays 37:31-8 D '77

SHOES, boots, rubbers, etc.

Buying a good pair of shoes. il Changing T 31: 45-7 F '77

Clothing and footware. il Consumers Res Mag 60:17-24 O '77

How to buy your next pair of boots. il Good H 185:236 S '77

See also

Moccasins

Anecdotes, facetiae, satire, etc.

Soft-shoe routine; sneakers. S. Kanfer. il N Y Times Mag p 12 Mr 6 '77

Repairing

How to sure-foot your waders. J. Cassell. il Outdoor Life 160:158 O '77

Spring retreads; waders. J. Fullum. il Conservationist 31:44 Mr '77

SHOHAM, S. Giora

Isaac syndrome. bibl f Am Imago 33:329-49 Wint '76

SHOJI, Kobe

Drip irrigation; with biographical sketch. il Sci Am 237:15, 62-8 N '77

SHOKES, Robert F. and others

Anoxic, hypersaline basin in the northern Gulf of Mexico. bibl il Science 196:1443-6 Je 24 '77

SHONA, John, pseud

Trying times for Zimbabwe Christians. Chr Cent 94:1226-7 D 28 '77

SHOOK, Patricia

What's new in my kitchen? Am Home 80:31 Jl '77

SHOOT apexes

Apical dichotomy demonstrated in the angiosperm flagellaria. P. B. Tomlinson and U. Posluszny. bibl il Science 196:1111-12 Je 3 '77

SHOOTING

How to tame recoil. P. Barrett. il Mech Illus 73:20+ F '77

Shooting. il Field & S 81:170-2+ Mr; 82:142-5 Ap; 84-6 Jl '77

Shooting. B. Brister. Field & S 81:120-4 F; 82: 114-16+ My; 134-9 Je; 102-5 Ag; 112-14+ S; 118-20+ N; 32+ D '77

There's safe fun in pistol shooting. P. Barrett. il Mech Illus 73:12+ Je '77

Which is your better shooting eye? eye dominance. J. R. Gregg. il Field & S 81:90+ Mr '77

See also

Archery

Decoys (hunting)

Duck shooting

Fowling

Game bird shooting

Hunting

National Rifle Association

Pheasant shooting

Pigeon shooting

Quail shooting

SHOOTING—See also—*Continued*
Rifles
Target practice
Targets
Trap shooting
Water bird shooting

Competitions

U.S. muzzleloaders go international; Fifth Muzzle Loading Annual International Competition. C. P. Smith. il Outdoor Life 159:134+ Mr '77

Study and teaching

Anecdotes, facetiae, satire, etc.

Catching flies and the art of wingshooting. R. Starnes. il Outdoor Life 160:8+ N '77

SHOOTING preserves
Improve the lot of quail; managing populations. B. Brister. il Field & S 81:109-10+ Ap '77

SHOOTING ranges
Trail walk—commando course for archers. G. Haman. il Pop Mech 147:280-1 My '77

SHOPLIFTING
Finding allies in the fight against shoplifting. T. J. Housel. il Nations Bus 65:64-6 S '77
Lie detectors to private eyes: antishoplifting battle heats up; pilfering employees. il U.S. News 83:61 N 28 '77
Tis the season to be wary. Time 110:22+ D 12 '77

SHOPPERS guides. See Consumer education

SHOPPING and shoppers
Buy the product, not the package. Changing T 31:21-3 Ap '77
Home centers: 1-stop shopping for Mrs Fixit; women making household repairs. S. Schraub. House B 119:48+ Ap '77
Right time to buy anything. N. G. Rollins. il Good H 186:169 Ja '78
See also
Christmas shopping
Purchasing, Household

Italy

European pleasures: shopping includes people-watching and pauses for coffee and fountains; Rome. il Horizon 19:38-41 Jl '77

SHOPPING bag ladies. See Tramps

SHOPPING centers
L.A.'s dramatic Blue Whale; Pacific Design Center. il Sunset 159:48-9 O '77
Mall; Bergen Mall in Paramus, N.J. New Yorker 53:19 D 26 '77
Malls at Water Tower Place. il Archit Rec 162:99-104 O '77
Suburbia's gift to the cities. E. Warner. il Horizon 20:14-25 S '77
Traffic-free areas magnet for people and business; excerpts from address, November 1976. N. T. Tiemann. Am City & County 92:76 Mr '77

SHOPPING centers, Remodeled
Theatrical approach to shopping center remodeling; Stanford Shopping Center in Palo Alto, Calif; with introd by J. Nairn. il Archit Rec 161:105-8 Je '77

SHOPPING malls. See Shopping centers

SHOPS. See Stores

SHORE, Jane
Witness; poem. New Repub 177:25 S 3 '77

SHORE birds
See also
Sandpipers
Sea birds

SHORE line changes. See Coast changes

SHORE lines
Shoreline forms and shoreline dynamics. R. Dolan and others. bibl il maps Science 197:49-51 Jl 1 '77
See also
Coast changes
Coasts

SHORE protection
Impending leasing off coast; effects on eastern seashore parks. Nat Parks & Con Mag 51:22 F '77
Inadequacy of law alone. C. Roosevelt. Oceans 10:65 N '77

Laws and legislation

Coastal Zone Management; Federal Coastal Zone Management Act. E. Mullin. il Environment 19:2-3 N '77

California

New Coastal Act will control California shore development. J. Nairn. Archit Rec 161:34 F '77

Louisiana

Here come the dredgers! Sneak attack on the wetlands; with editorial comment. P. J. Bernstein. il Nation 225:612-18 D 10 '77

SHOREY, H. H. See Bone, L. W. jt auth

SHORRIS, Earl
Cutting velvet at the New York times. il Harpers 255:102+ O '77
Gilmore's victory. il Harpers 254:16+ Ap '77

SHORT, Carroll Dale
Mine at Saragossa; story. Redbook 149:93 Ag '77

SHORT line railroads. See Railroads, Short line

SHORT men. See Stature

SHORT people. See Stature

SHORT stories
See name of author for full entry
About love and grasshoppers. M. Steele
About the gold wire bracelet. V. E. Wolff
Advancing Luna—and Ida B. Wells. A. Walker
All things wise and wonderful. J. Herriot
Anatomy of bliss. J. L'Heureux
And baby makes three. J. Smiley
Anniversary. M. New
Ark of larks. M. J. Amft
Attack on the queen. W. Kaufman
Aunt Adela. L. Becerra De Jenkins
Avelino Arredondo. J. L. Borges
Average waves in unprotected waters. A. Tyler
Bachelors. J. Falsey
Beautiful girl. A. Adams
Beggar maid. A. Munro
Beyond the dream. G. Vermandel
Birthday. V. E. Wolff
Bit of luck for Mabel. P. G. Wodehouse
Blessed be this day. S. Peterson
A book of common prayer. J. Didion
Boy knows the truth. I. B. Singer
Boyish lover. L. Colwin
Boys! Throw your voices! B. Masselink
Brain game. C. B. Cooney
Break in the reef. H. Searls
Breakfast at Brennan's. E. Leslie
Business talk. M. Apple
By the yellow lake. P. Marsh
Caballero of the law. B. Hecht
Calling home. T. O'Brien
Certain light. R. Leiter
Champ. T. C. Boyle
Chest. A. Vivante
Children are scared of the dark. B. Holland
Christmas bush. B. Morgan
Christmas roses. E. O'Brien
Circles: a Washington story. A. McCarthy
Collector of treasures. B. Head
Come back, my love. A. Glimm
Comfort. A. Gurganus
Coming and going. M. Granetz
Coming close to Donna. B. Hannah
Coming of age in Sonoma. R. C. Day
Cortes and Montezuma. D. Barthelme
Couch. W. D. Valgardson
Country people. R. L. Brown
Cousin Dot. I. English
Cracker factory. J. Rebeta-Burditt
Crisis. D. Barthelme
Crush on Doctor Dance. S. Hazzard
Dancing school recital. C. McFadden
Day in the pregnant life of . . . K. Stacey
Day of the storm. R. Pilcher
Day's work. B. Holland
Dearly beloved. B. Robinson
Decades. G. Sorrentino
Devil on horseback. V. Holt
Diplomatic relations. P. Theroux
Discus thrower. R. Selzer
Distant music. A. Beattie
Distant summer. J. Fowles
Doctor. M. Gallant
Doctor's sons. M. Robison
Dog in the alley, child in the sky. J. Irving
Double life. J. O'Neill
Draw a very big circle. M. Fineman
Dream season. A. S. Patrick
Dubin's lives. B. Malamud
Earthly possessions. A. Tyler
Egg race. J. Updike
Elka and Meir. I. B. Singer
Enchanted bride. A. Blake
Eulogy. H. Cerezo Dardón
Falconer. J. Cheever
Family man. V. S. Pritchett
Family secrets. J. Schell
Family vacation. S. Robinson
Famine country. J. C. Oates
Fantasies. S. A. Toth
Father's last escape. B. Schulz
Final notes. J. Schwartz
Finish line. S. Haller
Fireflies. J. McConkey
Fisherman. R. Collins
Fisherman. T. O'Brien
Fleeced. P. Gilliatt
Flight of geese. L. Norris
Flora. S. T. Warner
Foot-footing on. A. Tyler
For good. A. Adams
Ford. W. S. Merwin
Foster parents. N. Millay
Free and clear. L. Furman
Froggy green decision. G. Duncan
From two to three. M. Fineman
Full disclosure. W. Safire
Gaiety and dreaming. C. Mendez
Genevieve's birthday money. M. Franco
Getting to know you. M. F. Shyer
Ghost story. D. B. Baylor
Girl across the room. A. Adams
Girl skating. L. Colwin
Girl to marry. W. F. O'Connor
Glory of singing mountain. G. Meilaender

SHORT stories—*Continued*
Going on like this. J. R. Gardiner
Golden State. J. Sayles
Good-by, Walden Pond. E. Mueller
Good loser. E. Cullinan
Gorm. E. Leffland
Greatest show on earth. M. A. Robinson
Grounds. L. Cunningham
Guilt-gems. J. Updike
Gun in a tree. J. O'Dell
Gwilan's harp. U. K. Le Guin
Hand-me-downs. C. Sibley
Happiest day. M. Ellingson
Hard country friends. B. Wooley
Headrag. B. Morgan
Heart is home. R. Pilcher
Held in darkness. J. Penner
Henry Adams at Nuremberg. S. Schnur
Her son, the teen-aged ascetic. A. M. Green
Heuriger. M. C. Grey
His kind of woman. G. Schweitzer
Hitchhiker. R. Dahl
Hold her at that. H. P. Watts
Holding things together. A. Tyler
Home is the hero. B. Malamud
Hoop. J. Sayles
Hope. S. Spencer
House of angels. E. Leffland
House on twist road. M. Costigan
How do babies get born? B. Robinson
How the barber finally got himself into a fable. W. Saroyan
Ice age. M. Drabble
Idioms. E. Cullinan
Imperfect chords. P. Erbe
Imperfect listener. W. Stanton
In Miami, last winter. J. Kaplan
In the Miro District. P. Taylor
In the west country. L. Norris
Invitation to a wedding. C. R. Larson
Is today tomorrow? J. L. Rosasco
It's your move. S. F. Hartman
Jewish sons. A. H. Landau
Jim. C. A. Whitney
Joy on Sunday. S. Locy
Juvenile dice. A. Haley
Karma is a Chinaman. R. Coffey
Kaye Wayfaring in Avenged. J. McCourt
Key word. M. J. Gerber
Kindness. M. Gordon
Kindness of strangers. L. Furman
King of jazz. D. Barthelme
Kinky grass caper. R. T. Dodd
Kite and paint. M. Robison
Kramer & Son. A. Corman
Land of cotton. G. Sorrentino
Lassie come home. E. Knight
Last out. B. J. Bell
Last romantic. P. D. Boles
Laughingstock of Oat Hill. H. B. Fox
Laura, herself. M. Fineman
Left-handed woman. P. Handke
Letter to a grandson. C. Ford
Leveling. R. M. Griffin
Listen to your heart. P. McGerr
Little magic in the spring. M. Ellingson
Living room. M. Costigan
Loneliness. B. Schulz
Lonely dollhouse. I. L. Cusack
Lost child. G. Schweitzer
Louis Atkins: pest-control operator. S. George
Love and painting. J. Kaplan
Love is blind. J. Hecht
Lover's knot. M. J. Gerber
Love's own promise. C. Darcy
Loving aunts. M. A. Robinson
Magic moment. N. Newman
Man who feared deep water. L. S. Schwartz
Man who refused to watch the Academy Awards. D. Evanier
Marriage to a stranger. M. Mayhew
Matter of the heart. I. Stewart
Measures of the heart. R. McDermott
Mementos of our trip. P. Erbe
Memoirs of a Mississippi misfit. J. Schell
Million-dollar wound. J. Jones
Mine at Saragossa. C. D. Short
Mirages. A. Dillard
Miranda's star. L. Dowty
Mirror and the mask. J. L. Borges
Mrs Gage in her bed of pain with a nice cup of gin. W. Eastlake
Momentum mobili. J. Malone
Morning of the white shells. A. Sanford
Mother to daughter. S. Thaler
Mother yaws. T. Williams
Mother's day. R. Sandroff
Nicest wedding ever. M. A. Robinson
Night of the gifts. J. L. Borges
Nine bean rows. J. Stuart
No greater love. L. S. McGinnis
Okinawa's wife. S. Claiborne
Old-fashioned story. L. Colwin
Oliver's story. E. Segal
On a platform over the river. W. Kaufman
On the steps of the conservatory. D. Barthelme
On the water tower. M. Spanier
Once upon a time is enough. W. Stanton
O'Phelan drinking. J. F. Murray
Osage orange. A. Vivante
Our last breakfast on Saint Augustine's Farm. P. Marsh
Paradise Alley. S. Stallone
Partisan. D. Ely
Passion of Agatha McGee. J. Hassler
Perfect potions. E. Ibbotson
Perils of progress. B. Tarkington
Pete resists the man of his old room. B. Hannah
Picking up the tone. G. Kleege
Pictures and the possibility of love. M. A. Robinson
Piece of steak. J. London
Place of my own. M. F. Shyer
Players. D. DeLillo
Potter. M. Gallant
Prior claim. J. R. Gardiner
Problem of Li T'ang. G. Bush
Professor of desire. P. Roth
Promises to keep. R. Laker
Property of. A. Hoffman
Providence. A. Munro
Push the proper button. C. E. Rinzler
Puttermesser: her work history, her ancestry, her afterlife. C. Ozick
Question party. D. Barthelme
Qwertyuiop. S. T. Warner
Random voodoo. C. Collins.
Rat song. L. Nordan
Real estate. L. Furman
Red dress, yellow dress. K. Ungerer
Redemption. J. Gardner
Reflections from a black-eyed squint. A. A. Aidoo
Rich are different. S. Howatch
Roman ordinary. J. L'Heureux
Royal beatings. A. Munro
Rummage and loss. D. Black
Sanatorium under the sign of the hour glass. B. Schulz
Scrappy's miracle. T. Taylor
Scrolls. D. Menaker
Season of magic. W. F. O'Connor
Second time around. N. Johnson
Secret. R. Selzer
Seesaw. L. Furman
Serial. C. McFadden
Serious person. M. Gordon
Shaving. L. Norris
Shifting. A. Beattie
Sierra Leone. J. McGahern
Sisters. M. Gordon.
Sisters. M. A. Robison
Skaters on wood. L. Epstein
Small family with rooster. D. A. Rose
Some cold winter night. M. Costigan
Something to celebrate. M. Elmblad
Song of Solomon. T. Morrison
Spanish bed. V. S. Pritchett
Spell. G. Green.
Spider stories. E. Glaze
Squared-up petunia. M. Elmblad
Staying up late. N. A. Perez
Strategies, mostly kind. J. Mankiewicz
Success. J. L'Heureux
Such a lovely light. P. D. Boles.
Sucker. C. McCullers
Summer with no end. L. Myers
Take a lover. E. Jong
Tale of horror. E. A. Poe
Tales of the Swedish Army. D. Barthelme
Tattoo. J. C. Oates
Tell me where all past years are. L. S. Bernstein
Thank you, Allen French. M. Ellingson
That's the way it is. M. A. Robinson
Their day off. C. Flynt
This domain, that dominion. A. Leaton
This happy home. E. Fitzpatrick
This time be true. R. Pilcher
3 not-so-easy pieces: a sexual journal. C. Levine
Time out of yesterday. P. H. Price
Tin soldier. H. C. Andersen
To every thing there is a reason. . . C. Bittle
Today is not a rehearsal. M. March
Tomorrow. W. Faulkner
Torridge. W. Trevor
Touching bottom. B. W. Holmes
Treasure drawer. P. Schwartz
Trilobites. B. D'J. Pancake
Tuesday's heroine. M. Costigan
25 & married. T. Fitzpatrick, 3d
Twenty is the greatest time in any man's life. W. Saroyan
Two weddings and one divorce. I. B. Singer
Ulrike. J. L. Borges
Under the blanket. M. Manning
Under the family tree. M. Ellingson
Understanding heart. E. Allen
Undertow. S. Dybek
Undr. J. L. Borges
Unguided tour. S. Sontag
Unnamed but not unloved. G. Duncan
Verona: a young woman speaks. H. Brodkey
View of the mountain. R. Silman
Visit on a Tuesday afternoon. K. Rheinheimer
Walnut grove. J. G. Rushing
War stories. R. Stone
Way down upon the Swami River. P. De Vries
We are Norsemen. T. C. Boyle
Whitney's welcome. D. J. Leff
Widow's quilt. S. T. Warner
Winds of the morning. M. Brent
Wine breath. J. McGahern
Winning of Kate. M. Lewty

SHORT stories—*Continued*
Wireless communication. O. McFee
Would you marry him again? B. Robinson
Yochna and Shmelke. I. B. Singer
You are so lovely. S. M. Currey
You remind me of Lloyd. L. J. Littke
Zephyr. P. Duncan
Zombies. D. Barthelme
Zoysia grass. E. Clark
See also
Children's stories
Christmas stories
Detective and mystery stories—Single works

SHORT story
How to find your real story. S. L. Stebel. Writer 90:22-3 Mr '77
New traditions, old innovations; writing a Christmas story. L. Conger. Writer 90:9-10 D '77
Writing the confession story today. N. Stoyenoff. Writer 90:26-30 O '77
See also
Detective and mystery stories
Fiction in periodicals and newspapers

Study and teaching

Unlocking the box: an experiment in literary response. S. Howell. il Engl J 66:37-42 F '77

Aids and devices

Drama and the three stages in the teaching of literature. D. Donlan. il Engl J 66:74-6 F '77

SHORT story contests. See Fiction—Competitions

SHORT subject films. See Motion pictures—Short subject films

SHORTER, Frank
Now this is one way to travel light. J. Campbell. il por Sports Illus 46:69-70+ Mr 21 '77 *

SHORTHAND
See also
Stenographers

SHORTRIDGE, K. F. and others
Persistence of Hong Kong influenza virus variants in pigs. bibl il Science 196:1454-5 Je 24 '77

SHORTT, Terry
Many faces of birds. il Int Wildlife 7:26-9 My '77
Pterribly ptalkative ptarmigan and other zany birds. il Int Wildlife 8:32 Ja '78

SHORTWAVE radio. See Radio, Shortwave

SHOSTAK, Marjorie
Life before horticulture. il Horticulture 55:38-57 F '77

SHOSTAKOVICH, Dmitrii Dmitrievich
Music to my ears. I. Kolodin. por Sat R 4:43-4 F 5 '77 *
New view of Shostakovich's somber Fourteenth. R. S. Brown. Hi Fi 27:71-2 Je '77 *
Nose: explosively imaginative music theater; Melodiya recording. C. L. Osborne. il Hi Fi 27:69-73 D '77 *
Quartet no. 8 in C minor, op. 110; Quartet no. 15 in E-flat minor, op. 144. W. Simmons. por Am Rec G 40:40-1 D '76 *
Symphony no. 14. J. Diether. Am Rec G 40:27-9 Ag '77 *

SHOT
It's ok to ignore steel shot (if you don't mind losing your duck hunting) B. Brister. Field & S 82:112-14+ S '77
Lead shot; question of waterfowl mortality resulting from lead shot ingestion. Audubon 79:140 Jl '77
Twilight for lead shot? J. Phillips. il Outdoor Life 160:90-1+ Ag '77
Waterfowl hunters must give up lead shot. L. J. Carter. Science 198:1232 D 23 '77
Will steel shot work in your gun? J. Carmichel. il Outdoor Life 160:91-2+ Ag '77

SHOT putting
His past is slipping into the future; A. Oerter. W. Bingham. il pors Sports Illus 46:56+ Ap 25 '77

SHOTGUN houses. See Architecture, Domestic

SHOTGUN targets. See Targets

SHOTGUNS
Shotgunning for deer. J. Carmichel. il Outdoor Life 160:106-8+ O '77
Shotguns & loads: a practical guide. J. Carmichel. il Outdoor Life 160:86-92+ D '77
Shotguns go over & under. P. Barrett. il Mech Illus 73:10+ N '77

SHOW business. See Performing arts

SHOW windows
Duchamp's acephalic symbolism; analysis of bookstore window display called Lazy Hardware. C. F. Stuckey. bibl il Art in Am 65:94-9 Ja '77
Publishers and librarians let windows do the talking on Fifth Avenue; Mid-Manhattan branch. J. Giusto. il Pub W 212:57-8 N 7 '77
Storehouses of ideas; window displays, New York stores. N. Skurka. il N Y Times Mag p34-5 Jl 17 '77
What's going on behind that plate-glass window? S. Tomkievicz. il Horizon 19:14-19 Mr '77

SHOWER baths
Save $96 a year in the shower. A. Rosenblum. Good H 184:226 My '77
Shower heads. il Consumers Res Mag 60:17-20 N '77
Shower massagers: just a fancy way to get clean? il Consumer Rep 42:516-20 S '77
Truth about those pulsating showers. M. Peters. il Mech Illus 73:36 Mr '77

SHOWHOUSES. See House decoration

SHOWROOMS
Best Products Company; catalog showrooms designed by SITE, Inc; with introd by G. Allen. il Archit Rec 161:115-7, 124-30 Mr '77

Securities

See Retail trade—Securities

SHRAKE, Edwin
Cards. Sports Illus 46:56+ My 30 '77
Care to join our little old game? il Sports Illus 47:16-18+ Ag 15 '77
Shot of Lemons to cure the blues. por Sports Illus 46:32-4+ Ja 17 '77

SHREVEPORT, La.

Music

See also
Opera—Louisiana

SHREVEPORT Symphony Orchestra. See Orchestras

SHREWS
Loss of Y-cells in the lateral geniculate nucleus of monocularly deprived tree shrews. T. T. Norton and others. bibl il Science 197:784-6 Ag 19 '77
Ovarian hormone; lack of effect on reproductive structures of female Asian musk shrews. G. L. Dryden and J. N. Anderson. bibl il Science 197:782-4 Ag 19 '77

SHRIEVER, Placide
4 keys to live-longer diets. il Ret Liv 17:44-6 N '77
Protein: why you need it—how best to get it. il Ret Liv 17:20-3 O '77

SHRIMP salads. See Salads

SHRIMPS
Chemosensory tracking of scent trails by the planktonic shrimp acetes sibogae australis. P. Hamner and W. M. Hamner. bibl il Science 195:886-8 Mr 4 '77
Shrimps that dwell with anemones. N. Sefton. il Sea Front 23:32-7 Ja '77

SHRIVER, Donald W. Jr
Toward a public sense of pastoral care. Chr Cent 94:87-8 F 2 '77

SHRIVER, Eunice (Kennedy)
There is a moral dimension. Read Digest 111: 153-4 N '77

SHROUD, Holy. See Holy Shroud

SHROYER, David. See Carlson, F. jt auth

SHRUBS
See also
Hedges
also names of shrubs, e.g. Viburnums

Pruning

See Pruning

SHRUM, Edison
Collecting early law books. il Hobbies 82:80+ My '77
Historical solar energy devices. il Hobbies 82: 118-20 Ag '77
Jules Verne father of science fiction. il Hobbies 82:152 S '77
Strange monsters of farm and field. il Hobbies 82:113-15+ Jl '77

SHRUM, Robert
Let's have lunch. New Repub 177:9-10 Jl 9 '77

SHU, Frank Hsia-san
Shu and Hall win Astronomical Society prizes. pors Phys Today 30:95 My '77 *

SHUCARD, D. W. and others
Auditory evoked potentials as probes of hemispheric differences in cognitive processing. bibl il Science 197:1295-8 S 23 '77

SHUKMAN, Harry
(tr) See Markish, S. Example of Isaac Babel

SHULDINER, Herbert
Recreation roundup. See issues of Popular science
Recreational vehicles. See occasional issues of Outdoor life

SHULIM, Joseph I.
Robespierre and the French Revolution. bibl Am Hist R 82:20-38 F '77

SHULL, Harrison
University tenure problem. Science 194:137; 195: 440-1 O 8 '76, F 4 '77

SHULSKY, Sam
Money plans for your retirement. il Ret Liv 17: 30-7 N; 24-31 D '77
Q&A about investments. See issues of Retirement living

SHULTZ, Philip L.
Earth log: eagle doctor of Tesuque. J. Neary. il pors Audubon 79:90-2+ Jl '77 *

SHUNAMAN, Fred
New solderless coax connector. il Radio-Electr 48:54 F '77

SHUPP, Bruce D.
Understanding our bass population. il Conservationist 32:26-9 Jl '77
—and Georg, John
Those other fish. il pors Conservationist 31:32-4 My '77
SHURTLEFF, William
How to keep warm for pennies. . .Japanese style. il Org Gard & Farm 24:120-2+ Mr '77
—and Aoyagi, Akiko
Favorite tempeh recipes. il Org Gard & Farm 24:112+ Je '77
SHURTLIFF, Jay
Two wood-fired kilns: Smaug: a kiln of clay. il Ceram Mo 25:39-41 D '77
SHUSTER, Bud. See Shuster, E. G.
SHUSTER, E. G.
Are air bags worth the trouble? interview. il pors U.S. News 83:33-4 S 26 '77
SHUSTER, George Nauman
Obituary
Commonweal 104:100-1 F 18 '77. E. S. Skillin
SHUTT, Joyce M.
What I learned marching with N.O.W. por Farm J 101:F1 D '77
SHUTT, Steve
On the whole, it's the donut line. J. Kirshenbaum. il pors Sports Illus 46:26-9 F 7 '77 *
SHUTTERS
Flip, flip—and an eyesore view is forever hidden. il House B 119:46 Je '77
How to make fake shutters. R. S. Wilkes. il Mech Illus 73:162-3 N '77
Insulating shutters that work. C. G. Wing. il Org Gard & Farm 24:121-5 N '77
With just a pull, shutters let light in. il Sunset 159:98 D '77
SHUTTERS, Camera. See Camera shutters
SHUTTLE service, Airline. See Airlines—Shuttle service
SHUTTLEWORTH, John
Writing or rewriting articles for the Mother earth news; excerpt. Writer 90:21-4 Je; 20-2+ Jl '77
SHYER, Marlene Fanta
Getting to know you; story. Good H 184:120-1 Ap '77
Place of my own; story. Good H 184:112-13 F '77
SHYNESS. See Bashfulness
SIALIC acids
Concomitant elevations in serum sialyltransferase activity and sialic acid content in rats with metastasizing mammary tumors. R. J. Bernacki and U. Kim. bibl il Science 195:577-80 F 11 '77
Hepatic binding protein: the protective role of its sialic acid residues. R. J. Stockert and others. bibl il Science 197:667-8 Ag 12 '77
Surface molecules of hematopoietic stem cells: requirement for sialic acid in spleen colony formation. Q. Tonelli and R. H. Meints. bibl il Science 195:897-8 Mr 4 '77
SIALYLTRANSFERASE. See Transferases
SIAMESE language. See Thai language
SIAMESE twins
Successful separation; McCall twins. il Ebony 33:123-4+ D '77

Anecdotes, facetiae, satire, etc.

Personal habits of the Siamese twins. S. L. Clemens. il por Sat Eve Post 249:24+ Jl '77
SIBELIUS, Jean Julius Christian
King Christian II suite; Swanwhite suite; Andante festivo. E. Richmond. Am Rec G 40:35-6 Mr '77 *
Lemminkäinen suite; Karelia suite. W. L. Purcell. il Am Rec G 40:37 My '77 *
Symphony no. 1, conducted by P. Berglund. C. Bauman. Am Rec G 40:55 O '77 *
Symphony no. 1 in E minor, conducted by P. Berglund. E. Richmond. Am Rec G 41:31-2 N '77 *
Symphony no. 2 in D. Boston Symphony Orchestra, conducted by C. Davis. J. W. Barker. por Am Rec G 40:41-2 O '77 *
SIBERIA
See also
Altai Mountains
Paleontology—Siberia
Yakutsk, Russia

Description and travel

Reports & comment: Polus Kholodo: the coldest place. R. Chelminski. il Atlantic 240:4+ O '77

Native races

See also
Eskimos
SIBERIAN expedition, 1918-1920. See Russia—History—Allied intervention, 1918-1920
SIBERIAN explosion, 1908. See Explosions
SIBERT, J. and others
Detritus-based food webs: exploitation by juvenile chum salmon (oncorhynchus keta) bibl il Science 196:649-50 My 6 '77

SIBLEY, Celestine
Hand-me-downs; story; excerpt from Small blessings. Good H 185:90 Ag '77
SIBLEY, George
Desert empire. map Harpers 255:49-56+ O '77
SIBLINGS
Seven sisters tell you all about good looks, health, energy, their vital lifestyles. il pors Mademoiselle 83:56-71+ Jl '77
Sisters: can they shape each other's lives? W. Schuman. il Mademoiselle 83:172-3+ O '77
When should you have your next child? T. B. Brazelton. il Redbook 148:31+ F '77

Anecdotes, facetiae, satire, etc.

Sisters—oh, brother! R. Rothenstein. il Seventeen 36:24+ Je '77

Photographs

Sisters. A. S. Chwatsky. il Good H 185:88+ S '77
SIBSON, Robert E.
Why executives are not overpaid. il Nations Bus 65:51-4 N '77
SICILIAN cookery. See Cookery, Italian
SICILY
Sicilian carousel; excerpt. L. Durrell. il Sat Eve Post 249:72-3+ N '77
Sicily. D. Messinesi. il Vogue 167:129-30+ F '77
Surprise of Sicily. N. Hazelton. il Harp Baz 110:20+ Mr '77
See also
Taormina, Italy
SICK, The
Change of scene can be fatal; nursing-home patients. S. Bush. Psychol Today 10:32 F '77
See also
Gynecologists and patients
Physicians and patients
Sick children
Terminal care

Civil rights

Hospitals are no place for sick people. A. Kern and E. Keiffer. Good H 184:111+ My '77
When the patient says no; refusing permission to amputate; case of O. Simmons. Newsweek 89:77 Ja 24 '77
SICK children
Children's emergencies; injuries and illnesses. W. Seed. Harp Baz 110:88-9 Jl '77
SICKLE cell anemia
Sickle hemoglobin aggregation: a new class of inhibitors. J. R. Votano and others. bibl il Science 196:1216-19 Je 10 '77
SICKNESS
See also
Diagnosis
SIDDIQUI, Wasim A.
Effective immunization of experimental monkeys against a human malaria parasite, plasmodium falciparum bibl il Science 197:388-9 Jl 22 '77
SIDDONS, Philip A.
Climbing out of the existential ditch. Chr Today 21:8-9 Ag 12 '77
SIDE by side by Sondheim; revue. See Musical comedy, revue, etc.—Reviews—Single works
SIDE effects of drugs. See Drugs—Physiological effects
SIDE show; drama. See Dews, W.
SIDER, Ronald J.
Biblical perspective on stewardship. New Cath World 220:212-21 S '77
Sharing the wealth: the church as biblical model for public policy. il Chr Cent 94:560-5 Je 8 '77
SIDEWALKS
Short course on exposed aggregate; concrete sidewalk. il Parks & Rec 12:49-51 My '77
SIDEY, Hugh
Presidency. See occasional issues of Time
Real farmer in Carter's Cabinet. il pors Horticulture 55:28-31 Ap '77
SIDING (building)
Installing your own aluminum siding. T. H. Jones. il Mech Illus 73:60+ S '77
Remodeling notebook; aluminium siding. J. H. Ingersoll. House B 119:28+ N '77
Remodeling notebook; wood siding. J. H. Ingersoll. House B 119:32 Je '77
Re-siding—for more than a face-lift, choose the right type. M. Philips. il Pop Sci 211:118-22+ S '77
Siding. M. Cubisino. McCalls 104:125-6 S '77
SIDNEY, Neb.
Mechanical collection puts lid on refuse inflation. M. Dils. il Am City & County 92:31-2 Ja '77
SIEBERT, Lawrence Al
Self-determination of success. Nations Bus 65: 42+ Mr '77
SIEFERT, Kristine. See Casagrande, D. jt auth
SIEGAL, Mordecai
Pets. House B 119:38+ Jl; 92 Ag; 36 S; 80 O; 42 N; 78 D '77
SIEGEL, Gloria B.
Creative drama in the junior high. Engl J 66: 110-12 Ja '77

SIEGEL, Jerome M. and McGinty, D. J.
Pontine reticular formation neurons: relationship of discharge to motor activity. bibl il Science 196:678-80 My 6 '77
—See Lukas, J. H. jt auth

SIEGEL, Martin A.
Takeover target's defender. por Bus W p 160-2+ My 16 '77 *

SIEGEL, Micki
(ed) See Gabriel, A. I won $25,000 on a TV game show

SIEGEL, Robert
Bull; Them; Hog heaven; TV documentary; Knave of hearts; poems. Poetry 130:96-101 My '77
Emerson's smile. Poetry 130:102-14 My '77

SIEGEL, Rochelle
Afterward; poem. Nation 224:602 My 14 '77

SIEGEL, Ronald K.
Hallucinations; with biographical sketch. il Sci Am 237:15, 132-40 O '77

SIEGEL, Seymour
Biographical sketch. Nat R 29:880-1 Ag 5 '77

SIEGEL, Stanley
Hungry lion of talk. T. Schwartz. il por Newsweek 90:48 Ag 8 '77 *

SIEGER, R. B. and Bracken, B. D.
Sludge, garbage may fuel California sewage plant. il Am City & County 92:37-8 Ja '77

SIEGES
See also
Paris—Siege, 1870-1871

SIEGMEISTER, Elie
Night of the moonspell. Reviews
Hi Fi il 27:MA19+ Ap '77 *
Opera N 41:38 F 12 '77 *

SIEHL, George H.
Environment update: a review of environmental literature and developments in 1976. il por Lib J 102:981-7 My 1 '77

SIEMENS Ag (firm) See Electronic industries—Germany, West

SIEMENS Ag (firm)-Advanced Micro Devices, Inc merger. See Electronic industries—Acquisitions and mergers

SIEROTY, Alan Gerald
From bad to worse in California. A. Elsen. por Art N 76:53 O '77 *

SIERRA Nevada Mountains
You can't talk to the trees! remote country living. G. Bergman. il Ret Liv 17:32-3 Je '77

SIERRA Railroad Company. See Railroads, Short line

SIEVERTS, Frank Arne
Accounting for missing persons in Vietnam; statement, October 27, 1977. Dept State Bull 77:899-901 D 19 '77

SIFTERS, Garden. See Garden tools, equipment, and supplies

SIGHT. See Vision

SIGHTS for firearms. See Firearms—Sights

SIGHTSEEING trips. See Excursions

SIGLER, Paul B. and others
Cholera toxin crystals suitable for X-ray diffraction. bibl il Science 197:1277-9 S 23 '77

SIGLO de Oro Drama Festival, El Paso, Tex. See Drama festivals

SIGMOR Corporation. See Petroleum industry—United States

SIGN language
See also
Deaf—Means of communication

SIGNAC, Paul
Art. L. Alloway. Nation 225:377-8 O 15 '77 *

SIGNAL generators
All about RF signal generators. C. M. Gilmore. il Radio-Electr 48:49-51+ Ag; 56-8+ S; 67-9+ O '77
Build a pink noise generator for audio testing. D. Bohn. il Pop Electr 12:66 Jl '77
CB, VHF, and SSB radios; use of frequency synthesizer. G. West. il Motor B & S 139:26+ Ap '77
Equipment reports:
B & K model 2040 CB signal generator. il Radio-Electr 48:32+ F '77
Heath SG-1272 low distortion audio generator. il Radio-Electr 48:24+ O '77
Lunar electronics DX-555 signal generator/frequency counter. il Radio-Electr 48:32+ O '77
VIZ WR-549A pulse generator. il Radio-Electr 48:30+ My '77
Pink noise generator tests your hi-fi. J. G. Mazur. il Radio-Electr 49:43-5 Ja '78
Pros and cons of CB frequency-generation methods. W. M. Scherer. il Pop Electr 11:46-51 Mr '77
RF generators. il Radio-Electr 48:51-3 N '77
Using PLL for CB frequency synthesizers. R. F. Scott. il Radio-Electr 48:47-9 F; 58-9 Mr; 43-5 Ap '77
XR-2206 IC function generator circuits. R. M. Marston. il Radio-Electr 48:36-8+ Ap; 66-9 My '77
See also
Oscillators

SIGNAL processing
New technologies for signal processing; charge-transfer and surface acoustic-wave phenomena. R. W. Brodersen and R. W. White. bibl il Science 195:1216-22 Mr 18 '77
Role of microelectronics in communication. J. S. Mayo. il Sci Am 237:192-3+ bibl(p260+) S '77
See also
Charge coupled devices (electronics)

SIGNALS, Traffic. See Traffic signals

SIGNALS and signaling
Compulsory distress signals—what, where and maybe even if. T. Gibbs. Yachting 142:90 D '77
Cure for high decibels; communicating boat-handling directions. J. Cartwright. il Motor B & S 139:24+ My '77
Distress signalling: boats. E. S. Maloney. il Motor B & S 140:28+ N '77
Questions of distress; Coast Guard's signaling tests. T. Gibbs. Yachting 141:106+ F '77
Road emergency signals; warning devices. il Consumer Rep 42:533-7 S '77
See also
International Municipal Signal Association
Rule of the road at sea
Traffic signals

SIGNATURE writing machines
Sincerely yours, next . . . Sincerely yours, next . . ; prefabricated letters and automatic signature machine answering letters to J. Carter. M. Friedman. Sr Schol 109:8-9+ My 5 '77

SIGNATURES (writing)
See also
Signature writing machines

SIGNS and signboards
Sign that took three years to build; Stadley Rough School, Danbury, Conn. R. Farrell. il Sch Arts 76:46-7 Ap '77
This way out—from our mad jumble of signs. W. Von Eckardt. il Smithsonian 8:108+ D '77
See also
Billboards

SIGURDSON, Jon. See Morehouse, W. jt auth

SIKES, Robert L. F.
Clashing symbols. F. Getlein. Commonweal 104:101-3 F 18 '77 *

SIKHISM
Yogi Bhajan's synthetic Sikhism. il pors Time 110:70-1 S 5 '77

SIKONOWIZ, Walter
Create 3D scope patterns: build optical synthesizer. il Radio-Electr 48:33-6 D '77
2-digit electronic thermometer. il Radio-Electr 48:33-5+ S '77

SIKORSKY, Igor I.
Sikorsky. R. P. Hallion. il Flying 101:249 S '77 *
Turning your creativity into future success; adaptation of address. G. Bylinsky. il por Sci Digest 81:50-4 Mr '77 *

SIKORSKY Aircraft Division. See United Technologies Corporation—Sikorsky Aircraft Division

SILAGE
Anhydrous ammonia for corn silage. J. R. Borcherding and L. Reichenberger. il Suc Farm 75:24-7 Ag '77
Can stalks replace corn silage? B. Eftink. il Suc Farm 75:14 O '77
Cheapest way to finish quality beef; corn silage rations. C. Bickers. il Farm J 101:Beef 8-9 O '77
Feed sows silage? il Farm J 101:Hog 36 S '77
Get more production power from forage. il Suc Farm 75:no3 F44 F '77
Poor haylage: you can lose $15,000. Suc Farm 75:24 O '77
Program built on silage. J. D. Ritchie. il Farm J 101:Beef 24 Ja '77
Watch out for health problems when you feed only corn silage. C. Bickers. Farm J 101:Dairy 10 O; LK4 N '77

Storage

New way to store silage; Silopress system. J. White. il Farm J 101:Dairy 4-5, Beef 14-15 D '77

SILBER, John Robert
Need for elite education. Harpers 254:22-4 Je '77

about

Academic gore. N. Ephron. il por Esquire 88:76-8+ S '77 *
Texas rawhide in academia. F. J. Pratson. Nat R 29:204-5 F 18 '77 *

SILBERMAN, Arlene
Can a woman become liberated—and stay married? Read Digest 111:71-4 Ag '77
Did you hug your child today? Read Digest 110:143-6 F '77
Matter of life or death. Read Digest 110:185-9 Mr '77
Tests that cheat our children. Read Digest 111:127-30 Jl '77; Same. McCalls 104:191+ Ap '77

SILBERMAN, Cathleen Medwick
Hen. poem. Mademoiselle 83:34 My '77

SILCOCK, Bryan
Petrol, sweat & tears. Sci Digest 82:42-3 O '77

SILDEN, Isobel
(ed) See Fast, J. Problems and pleasures of living together
(ed) See Ingels, M. Problems and pleasures of living together
(ed) See Jong, E. Problems and pleasures of living together
(ed) See Osmond, M. Marie
(ed) See Powers, S. Problems and pleasures of living together

SILENT films. See Motion pictures—Silent films

SILENT night; drama. See Hollingsworth, L.

SILICATES
Asbestiform chain silicates: new minerals and structural groups. D. R. Veblen and others. bibl il Science 198:359-65 O 28 '77
Entropy estimates for some silicates at 298°K from molar volumes. S. K. Saxena; reply with rejoinder. S. Cantor. bibl il Science 198: 206-7 O 14 '77
See also
Serpentine

SILICON chips. See Electronic circuits, Integrated

SILICONE injections. See Injections, Hypodermic

SILK, Andrew
Black journalist in Johannesburg. Nation 225: 454-6 N 5 '77
Bulldozer remedy. Nation 225:298-304 O 1 '77
South Africa: post-diplomatic options. Nation 225:677 D 24 '77
South African muzzle. Nation 224:618-21 My 21; 225:581-4 D 3 '77
Where blacks have it good. Nation 225:144-7 Ag 20 '77

SILK, Dennis
Bug; poem. Harpers 255:82 Jl '77
Forlorn hope; Beginning; Epilogue for soldier Schweik; poems. Harpers 254:99 Mr '77

SILK, George
Fireballs; photographs. il Yachting 141:88-91 Mr '77

SILK screen printing
Joe Price: serigraphs in light and tone. D. Wakeham. il por Am Artist 41:46-51+ O '77
Silk screening for the impatient and the thrifty. il Sunset 159:116-17 N '77

SILKIN, Jon
Polarities. Poetry 130:230-9 Jl '77

SILKSCREEN printing. See Silk screen printing

SILKWORMS
2-Deoxy-α-ecdysone from ovaries and eggs of the silkworm, bombyx mori. E. Ohnishi and others. bibl il Science 197:66-7 Jl 1 '77

SILLS, Beverly
How we entertain in New York; ed by P. Pierce. il por McCalls 104:132-3+ Je '77
Three independent views; interview, ed by D. Lurie. por Harp Baz 110:97+ F '77
about
Artist life. D. J. Soria. il por Hi Fi 27:MA6-8 F '77 *
Beverly Sills is not the girl next door. J. Appleton. por Am Home 80:80-1 Ap '77 *
Bubbly widow. por Horizon 20:38 N '77 *

SILLS, Caryl Klein
Art appreciation: a practical approach. il Sch Arts 76:44+ Mr '77
How doughs your garden grow? il Design (US) 78:18-19 mid-Wint '77

SILLS, Mark R.
Freedom to sin; letter. Chr Cent 94:963-5 O 19 '77

SILMAN, Roberta
View of the mountain; story. McCalls 104:192-3 Ap '77

SILONE, Ignazio
Bread and wine. J. Martin. Engl J 66:65-6 Mr '77

SILVA, J. E. and Larsen, P. R.
Pituitary nuclear 3, 5, 3′-triiodothyronine and thyrotropin secretion: an explanation for the effect of thyroxine. bibl il Science 198:617-20 N 11 '77

SILVA, Paul C. See Moe, R. L. jt auth

SILVER, Adele Z. See Newsom, B. Y. jt ed

SILVER, Andrew. See Morley, E. jt auth

SILVER, George A.
Medical inflation. Nation 225:210-12 S 10 '77
Science is no gentlemen's club. Nation 224:166-9 F 12 '77

SILVER, Isidore
Self-image of a natural aristocracy. Nation 225: 44-51 Jl 9 '77

SILVER, Jerry, and Johnson, Kurt
Our school-made solar project. il pors Todays Educ 66:62-4 S '77

SILVER, Joan Micklin
Joan Micklin Silver: box office but no bankroll. E. Stone. il pors Ms 6:31-4 Ag '77 *

SILVER, Lani, and others
Surgery to the rescue. Progressive 41:23 D '77

SILVER, Nathan
House that modernism built. il Harpers 255:77+ Ag '77
Le tour Babel. Harpers 254:90-1 Ap '77

SILVER
See also
Silverware

SILVER BAY, Minn.
Stillness (however brief) at Silver Bay. J. G. Mitchell. il Audubon 79:129-34 S '77

SILVER Haired Legislation Project. See Aged—Legal status, laws, etc.

SILVER in water purification. See Water purification

SILVER trophies. See Trophies, Sport

SILVERMAN, Fred
Man with the golden gut. il pors Time 110:46-7+ S 5 '77 *

SILVERMAN, J. Herbert
Tasmania. il Travel 147:42-7 Mr '77

SILVERMAN, William A.
Lesson of retrolental fibroplasia; with biographical sketch. il Sci Am 236:18, 100-7 bibl(p 142) Je '77

SILVERS, Willys K. and Wachtel, S. S.
H-Y antigen: behavior and function. bibl il Science 195:956-60 Mr 11 '77

SILVERSMITHING
See also
Silverware

SILVERSMITHS
See also
Faris, W.
Leonard, J.

SILVERSTEIN, Bonnie
Douglas Allen: echoes of the Brandywine. il por Am Artist 41:44-9+ N '77

SILVERT, Kalman H.
Reasons for democracy; excerpt from The reason for democracy. il Society 14:25-31 My '77

SILVERWARE
Faneuil family silver cruet stand rediscovered. R. Feigenbaum. il Antiques 112:120-1 Jl '77
Wine and spirit labels in Harvey's Wine Museum. J. Banister. il Antiques 112:278-81 Ag '77
See also
Salt and pepper grinders, shakers, etc.
Spoons

Care

Guide to sterling silver care. Bet Hom & Gard 55:124 S '77

Collectors and collecting

Elizabeth B. Miles collection of English silver. E. B. Miles. il Antiques 112:114-19 Jl '77
Silver miniatures. K. M. McClinton. il Hobbies 82:118-20 N '77

Exhibitions

English silver in Boston; exhibition at the Museum of Fine Arts in Boston. S. B. Sherrill. il Antiques 11:658+ Ap '77

Manufacture

Crafts in industry; five jewelers join skills with Reed & Barton; ed by A. Gold, A. Fisch. il por Craft Horiz 37:10-15 Ag '77

SIMANIS, Joseph G.
British National Health Service in international perspective. bibl f Cur Hist 73:27-9+ Jl '77

SIME Darby (firm) See Conglomerate corporations—Malaysia

SIMENAUER, Jacqueline
—See Pietropinto, A. jt auth
about
Male sexuality: the amazing truth about all those myths. M.-E. Banashek. Mademoiselle 83:152-3+ N '77 *

SIMIAN viruses
Hybridization in situ of SV40 plaques: detection of recombinant SV40 virus carrying specific sequences of nonviral DNA. L. P. Villarreal and P. Berg. bibl il Science 196:183-5 Ap 8 '77

SIMIC, Charles
December trees; poem. New Yorker 53:52 D 12 '77

SIMMON, Kay
Big Apple's biggest bargain. il Travel 148:38-41+ S '77
Senior savings. il Travel 147:60-3+ Mr '77

SIMMONS, Beverley J. See Young, D. jt auth

SIMMONS, Charles
(ed) Standard cyclopedia of recipes, 1901. il N Y Times Mag p71 Ja 23 '77

SIMMONS, Ethel
Preserving summer flowers. il por Conservationist 32:19-22 S '77

SIMMONS, Freddie
Youngest landlord in Michigan. il pors Ebony 32:140+ S '77 *

SIMMONS, Georganna
Diving into the future; with biographical sketch. il Sea Front 23:38-42, 63 Ja '77

SIMMONS, George, and Simmons, V. M.
First photographers of the Grand Canyon. il Am West 14:34-8+ Jl '77

SIMMONS, James C.
South Georgia island: the great southern fur rush. il Oceans 10:46-51 My '77

SIMMONS, Virginia McConnell. See Simmons, G. jt auth

SIMMONS College, Boston
Path up for women bankers; program designed by Simmons College for the National Association of Bank Women. il Bus W p 105 Je 13 '77

SIMMS, D. L.
Burning question. Sci Am 236:64 Je '77 *

SIMON, Andrea
Extraordinary Simon women; interview, ed by J. Shapiro. por Ms 5:49-51 F '77

SIMON, Carly
Extraordinary Simon women; interview, ed by J. Shapiro. pors Ms 5:53+ F '77

SIMON, Debbie
Think you're ready for high school? Seventeen 36:52+ S '77

SIMON, Douglas
Cost of global stability. Intellect 106:182-3 N '77

SIMON, Herbert A.
What computers mean for man and society. bibl Science 195:1186-91 Mr 18 '77; Same with title Computers: changing man's view of himself. Current 193:39-51 My '77

SIMON, Joanna
Extraordinary Simon women; interview, ed by J. Shapiro. pors Ms 5:51-2 F '77

SIMON, John
The language. See issues of Esquire
Movies. il Nat R 29:1375-7, 1443-4, 1500-4; 30:38+ N 25-D 23 '77-Ja 6 '78

about

Count Dracula of Shubert Alley. por Time 110:34 D 26 '77 *

SIMON, Lucy
Extraordinary Simon women; interview, ed by J. Shapiro. por Ms 5:52-3 F '77

SIMON, Mark
Murder in Morningside Park. D. Gallagher. il pors N Y Times Mag p26-9+ Ag 28 '77 *

SIMON, Neil
Chapter two. Reviews
America 137:485 D 31 '77 *
Nation 225:699-70 D 24 '77 *
New Repub 178:25 Ja 7 '78 *
New Yorker 53:91 D 12 '77 *
Newsweek 90:86 D 19 '77 *
Time il 110:96 D 19 '77 *
Second thoughts. il por Horizon 20:73 D '77 *
Unreal, hilarious world of Neil Simon. T. Meehan. il pors Horizon 21:70-4 Ja '78 *

SIMON, Nissa
Backache: how not to have it. Vogue 167:142-4 My '77
Environment factor: beauty/health hazard or helper? il Vogue 167:164-7+ Ag '77
How sugar gets to your skin—and harms it. Vogue 167:108-9 My '77

SIMON, Paul, 1942?-
Paul Simon: the only living boy in New York. D. J. Evearitt. Chr Today 22:22-3 O 21 '77 *

SIMON, Richard, Family
Extraordinary Simon women; interviews, ed by J. Shapiro. pors Ms 5:49-53+ F '77

SIMON, Scott
End of the Panther trial. Progressive 41:9 Je '77

SIMON, Shirley
Learning to be thin. McCalls 105:81-2 O '77 *

SIMON, William Edward
Whither Simon? E. Keerdoja. il por Newsweek 90:10 Ag 29 '77 *

SIMON & Schuster, Inc
Advance guard; settlement of suit against R. Massie. il por Time 109:85 F 14 '77
Heller moves back to S&S for third novel. M. Reuter. Pub W 211:37 F 7 '77
PW interviews; chairman of the editorial board; ed by A. W. Ehrlich. P. Schwed. por Pub W 212:268-9 Ag 29 '77
Richard E. Snyder, president of Simon & Schuster, on his firm's explosive success and the present industry ferment; interview. R. E. Snyder. pors Pub W 211:32-8 Ap 11 '77

SIMONS, Elwyn L.
Ramaphithecus; with biographical sketch. il map Sci Am 236:15, 28-55 My '77

SIMONS, Frank
Handbuilt fireplace facade. il Ceram Mo 25:59-61 N '77

SIMONS, Howard
Press media; address, May 12, 1977. Vital Speeches 43:689-92 S 1 '77

SIMONS, Myron
Market comment. Forbes 120:216-17 N 15 '77
Market trends. por Forbes 119:92-3 Je 1; 120:134+ D 1 '77
Stock trends. Forbes 119:134 Mr 15; 120:168 O 15 '77

SIMONSON, Archie
Rape and culture. il por Time 110:41 S 12 '77 *
There goes the Judge. il por Time 110:26 S 19 '77 *

SIMONTON, John S. Jr
Build portable mini-organ (cont) il Radio-Electr 48:58-60 F '77

SIMPLICITY
Simplify! Simplify! excerpt from Walden. H. D. Thoreau. por Read Digest 111:175-7+ Ag '77

SIMPSON, Colin
Ship that hunted itself. il pors map Read Digest 111:188-92+ S '77

SIMPSON, Herbert M.
(ed) See Bettis, V. Valerie Bettis: looking back

SIMPSON, Ian, and others
Size limit of molecules permeating the junctional membrane channels. bibl il Science 195:294-6 Ja 21 '77

SIMPSON, Martin L.
Understanding lethal violence. Intellect 105:379-80 My '77

SIMPSON, Mary Scott
In the empyrean; poem. Chr Cent 94:1028 N 9 '77

SIMPSON, O. J.
Meet superstar O. J. Simpson: home is always where the heart is. P. Baum. il por Parents Mag 52:42-3+ F '77 *
O. J. Simpson's run to glory. D. Anderson. Read Digest 111:217-18+ N '77 *

SIMS, Edward H.
Airwar 1914-1918. il Flying 101:79-82 S '77
—See Fricker, J. jt auth

SIMS, Naomi
How to make a million before you're 34; interview, ed by D. Kaye and F. Ruffin. pors Redbook 149:60+ My '77

SIMSON, Earl L. and others
Axon-sparing brain lesioning technique: the use of monosodium-L-glutamate and other amino acids. bibl il Science 198:515-17 N 4 '77

SIMULATION games. See Operational gaming

SIMULATORS
Military use seen for visual simulators. D. A. Brown. il Aviation W 107:60-1+ D 5 '77
Radar simulator to be tested by USAF. il Aviation W 106:59+ My 23 '77
Training against ship disaster; tanker simulators. L. G. Feld. il Sea Front 23:280-6 S '77
USAF simulates Soviet defense system. B. Miller. il Aviation W 106:43+ My 30 '77
See also
Space flight simulators

SIN
Genuinely new, but. . . Chr Today 21:29 My 20 '77
Seven deadly sins today; excerpt. H. Fairlie. New Repub 177:17-20 S 10; 29-31 S 17; 18-21 S 24; 23-5 O 1; 18-21 O 8; 16-19 O 22; 20-3 O 29; 19-23 N 12 '77; Discussion. 177:9+ N 19 '77
Socialism and sin; capitalism vs socialism. B. Douglass; discussion. Chr Cent 94:171-4, 567-9 F 23, Je 8 '77
Whatever happened to sin? K. Menninger. il Sat Eve Post 249:58-9+ Ap 77
See also
Atonement
Fall of man
Temptation

SINAI, Allen L.
Sinai curve. Nat R 29:983-4 S 2 '77 *

SINAI (peninsula)
Creating facts in the desert. il map Time 109:26-7 F 28 '77

SINAI early warning system. See Radar defense networks

SINATRA, Frank
My way v. their way. il por Time 109:65 Ap 11 '77 *
Sinatra phenomenon. G. Lees. por Hi Fi 27:22+ O '77 *
Sinatra wants more of the Webb action. il Bus W p30-1 Ap 11 '77 *

SINCLAIR, Andrew
Jack London: the man who invented himself. il pors Am Heritage 28:98-107 Ag '77
What would you do if you met yourself? I'd shoot. Vogue 167:263 Mr '77

SINCLAIR, Clive
Littlest TV. il Time 110:61 O 17 '77 *

SINCLAIR, Ian David
Succeeding against government competition; interview. il por Nations Bus 65:84-90 D '77

SINCLAIR, John
Back to NORML. pors Newsweek 90:26 S 5 '77 *

SINCLAIR, Mary
Outrageous Mr Cherry and the underachieving nukes. F. Graham, Jr. il por Audubon 79:50-67 S '77 *

SINCLAIR, Ward E.
Turmoil in the miners' union. Progressive 41:29-32 Je '77

SINFELT, John H.
Heterogeneous catalysis: some recent developments. bibl il Science 195:641-6 F 18 '77

SING, Venancio O. and Schroth, M. N.
Bacteria-plant cell surface interactions: active immobilization of saprophytic bacteria in plant leaves. bibl il Science 197:759-61 Ag 19 '77

SINGAPORE
See also
Chemical industries—Singapore
Finance—Singapore
Hotels, motels, etc.—Singapore

Description and travel

Singapore. S. Fockler. il Trav/Holiday 148:40+ D '77

Politics and government

Singapore/Malaysia: sweatshop for the world. K. Bird and F. Y. Teng. Nation 225:242-4 S 17 '77

SINGAPORE—Politics and government—*Continued*
Singapore, where 1984 is now. H. Wasserman. map Progressive 41:34-8 Ap '77

SINGAPORE Handicraft Centre. See Art centers

SINGER, Alma
(tr) See Singer, I. B. Two weddings and one divorce

SINGER, Barnett
Provincial towns. Am Scholar 46:221-8 Spr '77

SINGER, Dorothy, and Singer, J. L.
Raising boys who know how to love. il pors Parents Mag 52:32+ D '77

SINGER, Isaac Bashevis
Boy knows the truth; story; tr by the author. New Yorker 53:48-53 O 17 '77
Elka and Meir; story; tr by J. Singer. New Yorker 53:36-42 My 23 '77
Two weddings and one divorce; story; tr by the author and A. Singer. New Yorker 53:28-33 Ag 29 '77
Yochna and Shmelke; story, tr by J. Singer. New Yorker 52:39-42 F 14 '77

SINGER, Isaac Merritt
Singer: making a business of Howe's invention. A. Hershman. il Duns R 109:28+ Je '77 *

SINGER, Jerome L. See Singer, D. jt auth

SINGER, Joseph
(tr) See Singer, I. B. Elka and Meir
(tr) See Singer, I. B. Yochna and Shmelke

SINGER, Mark
FM gabbai. Atlantic 240:98-100 O '77
Profiles; G. Ace. por New Yorker 53:41-6+ Ap 4 '77

SINGER, Max, and Bracken, Paul
Third-world poverty: don't blame us. Read Digest 110:114-17 F '77

SINGER, Maxine F.
Recombinant DNA debate. Science 196:127 Ap 8 '77

SINGER, Michael
Art out of nature which is about nothing but nature. B. Forgey. il por Smithsonian 8:62-4+ Ja '78 *

SINGER, Paris
Isadora reexamined; excerpt from Isadora Duncan. N. Macdonald. il pors Dance Mag 51:45-7 N '77 *

SINGER, S. Fred
Soil and coal: a cost-benefit inquiry. Science 198:255 O 21 '77

SINGER Company
Back to basics. por Forbes 119:72 Ja 15 '77
Singer: making a business of Howe's invention. A. Hershman. il Duns R 109:28+ Je '77
Stitch in time for Singer. R. Levy. il Duns R 109:69-71+ Je '77

SINGERMAN, Philip
Downward mobility. il Esquire 88:70-3 Jl '77
Outdoors. Esquire 87:22+ F '77
Racquetball: the hottest new game. il Esquire 89:78-81 Ja '78

SINGERS
Debuts & reappearances. See issues of High fidelity and Musical America
Hosanna in a spot of hell; Soledad Prison concert by Andrae Crouch and the Disciples. J. Wilde. il por Time 111:14 Ja 9 '78
People like honest sounds; Gaither Trio. S. B. Walton. il Sat Eve Post 249:46-7+ Ap '77
What you never knew about your favorite Christmas songs; interviews with singers, ed by J. Wilkie. il Good H 185:92+ D '77
Young artists 1977. il Hi Fi 27:MA16-20 Jl '77
See also
Black singers
Opera singers
Rock singers
also names of singers, e.g. T. Waits

SINGH, Arjan
Prince of cats. il por Nat Parks & Con Mag 51:4-9 Ap '77

SINGH, Raghubir
Pageant of Rajasthan. il Nat Geog 151:218-43 F '77

SINGING
Barbershop quartettes. B. Delatiner. il McCalls 104:46-7 Mr '77
Christians are singing people. E. Schaeffer. Chr Today 21:24-5 Ja 7 '77
See also
Voice

Competitions

Viewpoint; young American opera singers. R. Jacobson. Opera N 41:4 Ap 9 '77

Diction

Répétiteuse; coaching French opera repertory; interview, ed by D. Seabury. J. Reiss. il por Opera N 42:30-2 O '77

Expression

See Singing—Interpretation, phrasing, dynamics, etc.

Instruction and study

See Voice culture

Interpretation, phrasing, dynamics, etc.

Schwarzkopf-Legge master classes; singing classes at Juilliard. D. J. Soria. pors Hi Fi 27:MA5-6+ Mr '77
Sinatra phenomenon; singing techniques. G. Lees. por Hi Fi 27:22+ O '77

SINGING contests. See Singing—Competitions

SINGLAUB, John Kirk
General on the carpet. por Time 109:14-15 My 30 '77 *
Lost command. il por Newsweek 89:17 My 30 '77 *
When will the brass learn? Nation 224:676 Je 4 '77 *

SINGLE-lens reflex cameras. See Cameras, Single-lens reflex

SINGLE men
Bachelors '77. il Ebony 32:112-14+ Je '77
See also
Divorced fathers
Widowers

SINGLE parent families
Coping with behavior problems: one-parent household. R. Galdston. Parents Mag 52:97 O '77
Discrimination against whom? widowers seeking survivors' benefits. M Labor R 100:51-2 My '77
Father's instincts. R. F. Koubek. Am Home 80:18+ Je '77
Fathers with custody: the most rapidly increasing trend in single parenthood today; interviews, ed by R. Dougherty. il Parents Mag 52:56-7+ O '77
Life with father; divorced fathers. D. D. Molinoff. il N Y Times Mag p 12-17 My 22 '77
Mothers can too! K. Sharp. il por Redbook 149:54+ Je '77
Single father is doing well. J. Gaylin. Psychol Today 10:36+ Ap '77
Single mothers; excerpt from Lifelines. L. Caine. il Ladies Home J 94:104+ O '77
Single parenthood. B. King. Harp Baz 110:96+ Mr '77
What it's like for singles who adopt: four family stories; interviews, ed by G. Kopecky. il Ms 5:45-8+ Je '77
When fathers have to raise families alone—. il U.S. News 83:60-1 N 21 '77

SINGLE people
Intelligent woman's guide to sex. K. Durbin. Mademoiselle 83:24 Jl '77
Self as sybarite; Singles survival guide to metropolitan Washington. R. Rosenblatt. il Harpers 254:12+ Mr '77
Singlehood (cont) Am Home 80:26-7 Ap '77
Ways singles are changing U.S. il U.S. News 82:59-60 Ja 31 '77
See also
Celibacy
Church work with single people
Unmarried couples

SINGLE sideband radio. See Radio, Single sideband

SINGLE sideband radiotelephone on boats. See Radiotelephone on ships, boats, etc.

SINGLE women
Bachelorettes for 1977. il Ebony 32:164-6+ My '77
Bazaar's guide for the single woman; symposium. Harp Baz 110:92-9+ Mr '77
Being single: how to stop waiting and start living; dealing with loneliness and solitude. M.-E. Banashek. Mademoiselle 83:95+ Jl '77
Why I'm not married. S. D. Lewis. il Ebony 32:120+ S '77
See also
Divorcees
Mothers, Unmarried

SINGLETON, Carol
Carol Singleton; interview, ed by M. Cantwell. il pors Mademoiselle 83:194-7 Ap '77

SINGLETON, Judy
(ed) See Brown, M. Teaching LD adolescents
(ed) See Kessinger, D. I don't do this on purpose

SINGLETON, Ken
Beat feet but eyes right. L. Keith. il por Sports Illus 47:38+ Jl 25 '77 *

SINGULAR, Stephen
We want to make these kids neurotic. il N Y Times Mag p27+ Jl 10 '77

SINISTRALS. See Left- and right-handedness

SINK, James M, Associates. See Architectural firms

SINKS, Robert F.
Theology of divorce. Chr Cent 94:376-9 Ap 20 '77

SINKS
Easy-to-install sink. N. Smith. il Pop Sci 210:184 Ap '77

SINNOTT, R. W. See Cox, R. E. jt ed

SINO-Soviet relations. See Russia—Foreign relations—China

SINOWITZ, Betty E.
Update on sex bias cases. Todays Educ 66:22-3 N '77

SINTON, William M.
Uranus: the rings are black. bibl il Science 198:503-4 N 4 '77

SINUSITIS
What to do about sinus trouble. M. P. Scott. Bet Hom & Gard 55:84+ F '77
SIPE, Mike
Meet the green lacewing. il Org Gard & Farm 24:144+ Je '77
SIPHNOS (island)
Siphnos potters. P. Turner. il map Ceram Mo 25:45-50 Ap '77
SIR Gawain and the Green Knight. See Poetry, Medieval
SIR John Soane's Museum. See London—Galleries and museums
SIRACUSA, Ernest Victor
State department clientism. M. Holland and K. Bird. Nation 224:334-7 Mr 19 '77 *
SIRDOFSKY, Arthur
California's Renaissance Faire. il Travel 147: 40-1 My '77
SIRE, James W.
Human understanding of Saul Bellow. Chr Today 21:20+ Ja 21 '77
SIRLIN, Joyce. See Boskind-Lodahl, M. jt auth
SISK, Dorothy A.
What if your child is gifted? bibl Am Educ 13:23-6 O '77
SISK, John P.
Sexual stereotypes. Commentary 64:58-64 O '77
Tyranny of harmony. Am Scholar 46:193-205 Spr '77
SISLEY, Nick
Creating your own quail covey. il Field & S 81:28+ Mr '77
(ed) How the bass pros face tough weather; interviews with experts. il Field & S 82:46-7+ D '77
SISSINGHURST (castle) See Castles
SISSMAN, Louis Edward
Homage to Clotho: a hospital suite; Negatives; Under the rose: a granfalloon for Kurt Vonnegut, Jr; poems. New Yorker 53:34-5 Je 13 '77
SISSONS, Michael
British agent finds indigenous publishing, not American competition, the factor to watch in the world book market. Pub W 211:41-2 F 21 '77
SISTER cities. See Intercommunity cooperation
SISTERHOODS
Twelve stalwart women: Ursulines. C. J. McNaspy. America 136:373-5 Ap 23 '77
See also
Carmelites
Nuns
SISTERS. See Siblings
SISTERS and brothers. See Siblings
SITE, Inc
Best Products Company; catalog showrooms designed by SITE, Inc; with introd by G. Allen. il Archit Rec 161:115-7, 124-30 Mr '77
Disaster Site. il Horizon 19:87 My '77
SITES, James N.
Big government; address, June 28, 1977. Vital Speeches 43:711-14 S 15 '77
SITES, Historic. See Historic houses, sites, etc.
SITES, Industrial. See Location in business and industry
SITHYLEMENKAT Lake. See Lakes—Alaska
SITTING. See Posture
SITTS, Maxine
Academic librarians share their know-how. Am Lib 8:570 N '77
SITUATION comedy programs. See Television programs—Humorous programs
SIURU, William D. Jr
Scissor wings to snip the sonic boom. il Mech Illus 73:41-3 My '77
SIX year term for president. See Presidents—United States—Term
SIXTH fleet. See United States—Navy
SIZE
See also
Clothing and dress—Size
Earth—Size
SIZEMORE, Chris Costner, and Pittillo, E. S.
I'm Eve; excerpt. il pors Ladies Home J 94: 92+ My '77
SJÖGREN, Per A.
Per A. Sjögren: the pressing need for IPA; interview, ed by A. Johnson. por Pub W 212: 86+ S 19 '77
SKAGGS Companies. See Drugstores
SKAGIT River
Our wild and scenic rivers. D. S. Boyer. il map Nat Geog 152:38-45 Jl '77
SKALKA, A. M. See McClements, W. jt auth
SKALKA, Lois Martin
How to trace your own roots. il Ret Liv 17:34-5+ Je '77
SKALKA, Patricia
Ways to warm up this winter. il Fam Health 9:40-1 D '77
SKATEBOARDING
All aboard! J. Kaplan. il Seventeen 36:64 N '77
All aboard the skateboard. B. Surface. il Read Digest 111:135-8 D '77
$400 million on wheels. S. T. Atlas and D. Gram. il Newsweek 90:92+ N 14 '77
Thriller for the downhillers; Catalina Classic. S. Moses. il Sports Illus 47:68+ N 21 '77

Safety devices and measures

Skateboard safety. M. Smith. McCalls 104:68 F '77

Television broadcasting

See Television broadcasting—Sports
SKATERS
See also
Allen, L.
SKATING
Call him Kid Cool; speed skater E. Heiden. K. Moore. por Sports Illus 47:56-8+ D 19 '77
Skating on the canals; the Dutch on skates. F. V. Grunfeld. il Horizon 19:20-3 Mr '77

Competitions

Great, big wonderful whirl; Senior Ladies' U.S. championship. J. Bruce. il Sports Illus 46:53-4 F 14 '77

Study and teaching

Good skate; ice skating teacher and coach B. Williams. J. Maynard. il pors N Y Times Mag p70-1 Mr 6 '77
SKATING rinks
Coal Street Park by architects Bohlin and Powell; ice skating rink, Wilkes-Barre, Pa. il Archit Rec 161:124-7 F '77
How to make a back-yard skating rink. T. E. Mahl. il Pop Mech 148:74 N '77
It's revival time for roller skates; California rinks. il Sunset 159:42-3 D '77
SKEEL, Dorothy J.
What values are most important? il Todays Educ 66:62-4 Ja '77
SKEET shooting. See Trap shooting
SKELETAL muscle. See Muscle
SKELETAL remains. See Anthropometry
SKELETON (invertebrates)
Biocrystals. S. Inoué and K. Okazaki. il Sci Am 236:82-4+ bibl(p 148) Ap '77
SKELTON, C. L.
New family triumvirate of writers welcomed by four publishers; interview, ed by R. Dahlin. por Pub W 212:107 S 12 '77
SKELTON, Robin
Landmarks; poem. Poetry 131:148-58 D '77
SKEWER cookery. See Barbecue cookery
SKI clothes. See Clothing and dress—Sports clothes
SKI Film Festival, International. See Motion picture festivals
SKI lifts
Lift-line express. C. Breslin. il Esquire 87:91-3 F '77
SKI mountaineering. See Skis and skiing
SKI racing
Agony in the snow; American-Birkebeiner cross-country race. P. Bonventre and C. J. Harper. il Newsweek 89:56 Mr 14 '77
Jungle Jim and the rocky run; Aspen downhill race on World Pro Skiing circuit. S. Moses. il por Sports Illus 48:43-4 Ja 2 '78
Making like a giant in slaloms; NASTAR. S. Moses. Sports Illus 46:64-5 Mr 21 '77
Starting out with a chaser; I. Stenmark vs P. Mahre in World Cup competition. A. Verschoth. il pors Sports Illus 46:54-6 Ja 17 '77
Stem turn through the tulips; North American Grass Ski Championships. D. Levin. il Sports Illus 47:14-15 Jl 25 '77
They doubled the pleasure; Mahre twins in Sun Valley World Cup competition. W. O. Johnson. il pors Sports Illus 46:12-15 Mr 14 '77
SKI resorts. See Winter resorts
SKI waxing. See Skis and skiing—Maintenance and repair
SKIING. See Skis and skiing
SKIL Corporation. See Electric tools—Manufacture
SKILLED labor
Where the jobs go begging. il Bus W p34-5 O 10 '77
SKILLET cookery. See Cookery
SKIN
Moles, cysts and other skin problems. W. A. Nolen. McCalls 105:148+ O '77
Pale is pretty too! K. Canter. por Seventeen 36:64 Jl '77
See also
Sunburn

Care and hygiene

About face: do-it-yourself facials; skin-care products. Seventeen 36:104-5 Ag '77
Bazaar's complete guide for black skin & hair; questions and answers. il Harp Baz 110:156-9 O '77
Beauty collections '77: treatment. il Vogue 167: 294-5 O '77
Better-than-ever caring for skin. il Vogue 167: 324-5 S '77
Black woman's guide to skin care. G. Pfaeffle. il McCalls 104:140-1+ F '77
Cold weather and your skin. L. Lamberg. Bet Hom & Gard 55:59-60 F '77

SKIN—Care and hygiene—*Continued*
Common-sense beauty guide: skin. il Harp Baz 110-84-5 Je '77
Environment factor: beauty/health hazard or helper? N. Simon. il Vogue 167:164-7+ Ag '77
Everything you didn't want to ask about skin problems, but ought to know anyway. L. Beech. Sr Schol 109:26 Ap 7 '77
Facing up to winter. P. R. Jackson. House & Gard 149:22+ D '77
Fall shape-up for your skin; questions and answers. J. Levy. Harp Baz 110:104 S '77
How sugar gets to your skin—and harms it; refined carbohydrates and skin problems; ideas of W. M. Ringsdorf and E. Cheraskin. N. Simon. Vogue 167:108-9 My '77
How to clean & care for your skin; interviews with three dermatologists. R. Auerbach; N. Orentreich; J. Zizmor. Mademoiselle 83:174-7 Ag '77
How to stop the clock on wrinkles. M. Lynch. il Ladies Home J 94:84-7 F '77
Is your skin dying of thirst? M. Hill. il Am Home 80:46-7+ Jl '77
Jump into summer & hang loose! skin and hair care. il Mademoiselle 83:124-37 My '77
Let's face it; facials. A. Penney. il N Y Times Mag p88+ D 18 '77
Looking good. L. Beech. Sr Schol 110:20-1 N 17 '77
Marigolds—sun flowers for your skin. Org Gard & Farm 24:120 S '77
Miracle workers for your body. il Harp Baz 110:80-1 Ap '77
Miracle workers for your face. il Harp Baz 110:84-5 Ap '77
Nerves and your skin; interview. N. Orentreich. Harp Baz 110:126+ Mr '77
Salon facials: where to go. il Seventeen 36:80-1+ Ag '77
Saving face: help your skin stand up to winter. McCalls 105:94-5+ Ja '78
Scientific skin care. il Harp Baz 110:190-1 S '77
Skin game. il McCalls 105:40-1+ O '77
Springtime skin care for a more beautiful complexion. S. Beck. il Parents Mag 52:12 Mr '77
Take care of yourself. il Vogue 167:162-3 Je '77
Understanding skin care; excerpt from Skin care book. il Fam Health 9:28-9 My '77
Your skin. A. Rostenberg, Jr. il House & Gard 149:103+ F '77
See also
Beauty, Personal

Diseases

Glucocorticoid in inflammatory proliferative skin disease reduces arachidonic and hydroxyeicosatetraenoic acids. S. Hammarstrom and others. bibl il Science 197:994-6 S 2 '77
See also
Acne
Acrodermatitis enteropathica
Psoriasis
Warts

SKIN cancer. See Cancer
SKIN diving
At home with the sweetlips and angelfish; Indian Ocean off Kenya. G. Scott. il por Fortune 95:91+ Mr '77
Diving the Sea of Cortez. L. R. Martin. il Oceans 10:16-19 Mr '77

Equipment and supplies

Dream diver; scuba equipment. D. Abrahamson. il Motor B & S 140:73-5 Ag '77
It's a new scene for scuba divers. F. Bianco. il Mech Illus 73:58+ Ag '77

Safety devices and measures

What about the sharks? A master diving instructor offers some answers. J. D. Thurber. il Oceans 10:24-30 N '77

Study and teaching

Scuba school; St. Croix, U.S. Virgin Islands. il Seventeen 36:163 Mr '77

SKINNER, Andrea
Boutique Baedeker. N Y Times Mag p58+ Mr 13 '77
SKINNER, Burrhus Frederic
Between freedom and despotism; self government; excerpt from address. il por Psychol Today 11:80-2+ S '77

about

Listening to B. F. Skinner. J. W. Woelfel. Chr Cent 94:1112-16 N 30 '77 *
SKINNER, Dorothy M.
Satellite DNA's. bibl il BioScience 27:790-6 D '77
SKINNER, Jean Ross-. See Ross-Skinner, J.
SKINNER, Wickham, and Sasser, W. E.
Managers with impact: versatile and inconsistent; excerpt from Manufacturing in the corporate strategy. il Harvard Bus R 55:140-8 N '77
SKINNING of deer. See Game. Dressing of
SKINNING of fish. See Fish as food
SKIPPING rope. See Rope jumping

SKIRTS. See Clothing and dress
SKIS and skiing
Cross country to action. E. A. Bauer and others. il Outdoor Life 161:66-8 Ja '78
Skiing on the cheap. K. Reading. Seventeen 36:22 N '77
Skis that need no snow; grasskiing. il Mech Illus 73:106 S '77
Unloneliness of the long-distance skier. P. Wood. il N Y Times Mag p 19-22+ D 18 '77
See also
Helicopters in skiing
Ski lifts

Accidents and injuries

Abominable snow suits; claims for ski injuries. il Time 111:60-1 Ja 16 '78

Competitions

See also
Ski racing

Equipment

Cross-country skiing. P. Idleman. il Consumers Res Mag 60:27-30 N '77
Mile on skis. il Mademoiselle 83:114-16+ N '77

Maintenance and repair

There is both art and argument in the waxing of skis. il Sunset 159:70+ N '77

Photographs

Just an old snow job; ski mountaineering; with reports by J. Campbell and W. O. Johnson. il Sports Illus 47:52-60+ D 5 '77
Putting on a hill of a show; with report by W. O. Johnson. J. G. Zimmerman. Sports Illus 46:28-33 F 14 '77

Psychological aspects

Fear of skiing; excerpt from Inner skiing. W. T. Gallwey and R. Kriegel. il pors Psychol Today 11:78-9+ N '77

Study and teaching

It's all downhill from here; Vermont's Burke Mountain Academy. D. S. Looney. il Sports Illus 48:22-5 Ja 2 '78
Snow and slender skis; cross-country skiing taught at Royal Gorge Ski Touring, Inc. in California. S. Netherby. il Field & S 82:138+ N '77
Summer school for hot-dog skiers; World Freestyle Training Center at Heavenly Valley, South Lake Tahoe, Calif. P. Barmonde. il Pop Mech 147:74-5 Je '77

Waxing

See Skis and skiing—Maintenance and repair

California

Ski lessons for the very young. il Sunset 158:30 F '77
Snow and slender skis; cross-country skiing taught at Royal Gorge Ski Touring, Inc. S. Netherby. il Field & S 82:138+ N '77

Canada

Adventure in the high Bugaboos. P. A. Langan. il Fortune 96:25+ D '77
Expert-ski: heli-skiing in the Canadian Rockies. J. Gibb. il House & Gard 149:76+ D '77

Montana

Ski Montana—uncrowded, lots of powder. il Sunset 158:42+ F '77

North Carolina

Ski North Carolina. Y. Cardozo. il Trav/Holiday 148:46-51 D '77

Norway

On Holmenkollen Hill; annual ski festival. H. W. Wind. il New Yorker 53:58-60+ F 28 '77

Spain

Sí sí! They ski in Spain. A. Rand. il Holiday 57:44-6 N '76

United States

See Skis and skiing

Utah

Different slopes for different folks. J. Goodman. il Holiday 57:42-3+ N '76

Western States

Cross-country ski centers in the West. il Sunset 159:63+ D '77
New skiers are tourers, not downhillers; cross country skiing. il Sunset 159:90-5 N '77
SKJOLD, Norma Jane
We need a Red Cross for starving cattle. il por Farm J 100:10A-11 D '76
SKOGLUND, George A.
Excerpt from statement on mandatory retirement policy, February 14, 1977. Cong Digest 56:267+ N '77
SKOKIE, Ill.

Protests, demonstrations, etc.

See Protests, demonstrations, etc.—Illinois

SKOLE, Robert
En-Nobeling Milton Friedman. Nation 224:68-70 Ja 22 '77
SKOLIMOWSKI, Henryk
Last lecture; address, October 20, 1976. Vital Speeches 43:177-81 Ja 1 '77
SKOREK, Edward
Sole Pole for the Sol. J. Jares. il por Sports Illus 47:44-5 Ag 22 '77 *
SKORNIA, Harry J.
Great American teaching machine—of violence. Intellect 105:347-8 Ap '77
SKOW, John
Joe Harvath is adding up your dollars of happiness. il por Outdoor Life 159:66-7+ Mr '77
New Hampshire buried under permacurse. New Yorker 53:36-7 F 21 '77
(ed) See Sroda, G. King of worms
SKRDLA, J.
Make a stabilizer. il Motor B & S 140:103 Ag '77
SKULL and Bones (college society) See Yale University—Clubs
SKURKA, Norma
Design. See occasional issues of New York times magazine
SKURNIK, W. A. E.
Whither East Africa? Cur Hist 73:205-8+ D '77
SKY
April's skies. J. Mullaney. il Sci Digest 81:68-9 Ap '77
Here's what to look for in fall skies. J. Mullaney. il Sci Digest 82:89-91 O '77
Look up! The sky tonight provides great viewing. J. Mullaney. il Sci Digest 81:31-3 Mr '77
Morning sky configurations. il Sky & Tel 54:343-5 O '77
Stargazing urge. il Sci Digest 81:57-60 My '77
Ultimate trip for summer nights. J. Mullaney. il Sci Digest 81:41-4 Je '77
See also
Constellations
SKYCRANE helicopters. See Helicopters
SKYDIVING. See Parachuting
SKYHORSE, Paul, and Mohawk, Richard, murder trial. See Trials (murder)
SKYJACKING. See Airplane hijacking
SKYLAB. See Space stations
SKYLAB 2 (1st manned) mission. See Space stations—Skylab 2 (1st manned) mission
SKYLIGHTS
Daylighting design aids emerge as interest grows in the technique. il Archit Rec 161:152 Ja '77
If your skylight is sometimes too much. . .maybe it needs shade. il Sunset 158:116 F '77
Skylight turns the corner. il Sunset 158:150 Mr '77
SKYLINE to the Sea Trail, Calif. See Trails
SKYSCRAPERS
Brave new skyscraper; Citicorp Center in New York City. D. Davis. il Newsweek 90:84+ O 31 '77
Case against urban dinosaurs. W. G. Conway. il Sat R 4:12+ My 14 '77; Reply with rejoinder. P. Hammer. 4:10 S 17 '77
Elevator space requirements in highrise buildings. J. K. Ochsner and others. il Archit Rec 162:117-18 Jl '77

Fires and fire prevention

Bold new tactics for fighting high-rise fires. T. Dutton. il Pop Mech 148:67-71 S '77
SKYTRAIN. See Airlines—International services—Transatlantic
SLAB pottery technique. See Pottery—Technique
SLACK, Chuck
Taxpayer's-eye view of library jargon. il Am Lib 8:554-5 N '77
SLACKS. See Pants
SLADE, Afton. See Lande, N. jt auth
SLADEN, William J. L.
Adopt a swan for research. J. Cassell. por Outdoor Life 159:140 My '77 *
Snow geese are coming! The snow geese are coming! J. H. Phillips. il por Int Wildlife 7:21 N '77 *
SLANDER trials. See Trials (libel)
SLANG
Doing a number on words. W. Safire. N Y Times Mag p95 F 13 '77
See also
Gringo (term)
SLANSKY, Paul
Where have you gone, Sally Harmony? Esquire 88:129-32 Jl '77
—and Stein, Harry
Kicking Carter while he's up. il pors Esquire 87:59-61 Mr '77
SLATER, Charles
Mysterious disappearance of Pirate's Lady. T. Plate. il por Motor B & S 140:57-60+ S '77 *
SLATER, Elizabeth
Solzhenitsyn plans a publishing firm in Vermont. il por Pub W 211:38 F 7 '77
SLATER, Gail
Brought to you by . . . Educ Digest 43:36-7 D '77
SLATTERY, William J.
What Dick Powell taught me about writing. Writers Digest 57:4-5 Mr '77
What my agent does for me. Writers Digest 57:29 My '77
SLAUGHTER, Frank G.
How to be an expert on anything. Writer 90:11-13 Jl '77
SLAUGHTERING and slaughterhouses
How to spot the next numbers build-up; cattle and calves. il Farm J 101:Beef 12+ O; LK3-4 N '77
SLAVE flash units, Electronic. See Photography—Electronic equipment
SLAVERY
See also
Anti-slavery Society for the Protection of Human Rights

United States

Black conjugations; Black family in slavery and freedom, 1750-1925. J. D. Anderson. Am Scholar 46:384+ Summ '77
Faces of slavery. E. Reichlin. il Am Heritage 28:4-11 Je '77
Living with the peculiar institution; Time essay L. Morrow. il Time 109:76-7 F 14 '77
Negro boy Alfred. T. Schwartz and H. Camp. por Newsweek 90:29 Jl 4 '77
Slavery and the new history: a guide for the perplexed. W. T. Carlisle. bibl il Intellect 106:160-3 O '77
This one great evil; miscegenation prior to the Civil War. S. Hoffert. bibl il Am Hist Illus 12:37-41 My '77
See also
Abolitionists

Emancipation

Bull in the china shop; career of C. Sumner. D. W. Blight. il por Am Hist Illus 12:10-19 Ap '77

Fugitive slaves

See also
Underground railroad
SLAVITT, David R.
Poison; Night thoughts; poems. Poetry 131:90-2 N '77

about

Comment. H. Holland. Poetry 129:294-5 F '77 *
SLAYMAKER, S. R. 2d
Terrestrial tricks for low-water trout. il por Outdoor Life 160:78-9+ S '77
SLAYTON, Donald Kent
Profile: Slayton shapes up as 60-year-old astronaut. por Sci Digest 81:46-7 Mr '77 *
SLEATOR, Esther K. See Sprague, R. L. jt auth
SLEDDING, Dog. See Dog sleds and sledding
SLEEP
Appetitive and replacement naps: EEG and behavior. F. J. Evans and others. bibl il Science 197:687-9 Ag 12 '77
Does sleep help you study? E. Hoddes. Psychol Today 11:69 Je '77
Flurazepam effects on slow-wave sleep: stage 4 suppressed but number of delta waves constant. I. Feinberg and others. bibl il Science 198:847-8 N 25 '77
Health watch: the truth about sleep. Mademoiselle 83:98 Mr '77
Night is not for sleeping. S. Steinberg. il Vogue 167:272+ N '77
Reversal of cardiopulmonary failure during active sleep in hypoxic kittens: implications for sudden infant death. T. L. Baker and D. J. McGinty. bibl il Science 198:419-21 O 28 '77
Science of sleep. J. Arehart-Treichel. il Sci N 111:203-4+ Mr 26 '77
Sleep clinic's experts say most older people need less sleep than younger adults. il Ret Liv 17:11-12 F '77
Taking a nap: what it can do for you; ideas of F. J. Evans. C. Seebohm. il House & Gard 149:26+ F '77
Tracking the elusive sandman. J. Gaylin. il Psychol Today 10:101 Ap '77
What you should know about sleep disorders. M. P. Scott. il Bet Hom & Gard 55:20+ S '77
See also
Dreams
Insomnia
Sleep positions
Snoring
SLEEP positions
Way we sleep is the way we live; views of Samuel Dunkell. J. Gaylin. il Psychol Today 10:32+ My '77
What your sleep position reveals; excerpt from Sleep positions: the night language of the body. S. Dunkell. il Read Digest 111:137-9 Jl '77
What your sleeping position reveals about you; interview, ed by N. A. Comer. S. Dunkell. il Mademoiselle 83:176-7+ Mr '77
SLEEPING bags
Sleeping bags for backpacking. il Consumer Rep 42:355-9 Je '77
SLEEPING beauty; ballet. See Ballet reviews—Single works

SLEEPING beauty; dramatization. See Thane, A.
SLEEPING medicines. See Hypnotics
SLEEPING pills. See Hypnotics
SLEEPING sickness, African. See Trypanosomiasis
SLEEPLESSNESS. See Insomnia
SLEEPWEAR industry. See Clothing industry
SLEZAK, Ed
Some planning hints for the waterfront safety director. il Camp Mag 49:12-14+ F '77
SLICER-shredders. See Kitchen utensils and appliances
SLIDE duplicators. See Photography—Apparatus and supplies
SLIDE films. See Photography—Films
SLIDE projectors. See Projectors
SLIDE rules
Endangered species: the slide rule. Sci Digest 81:68-9 Mr '77
Navigate with the smart stick. J. Martenhoff. il Motor B & S 139:87+ Ap '77
SLIDE shows. See Slides (photography)—Projection
SLIDES (photography)
Five unusual slide techniques. A. Grundberg. il Mod Phot 41:72-7 Mr '77
Kids and kameras: Instafilm kit for making slides from negatives. D. Cyr. il Pop Phot 80:38+ Je '77

Copying

Ed Scully on color. E. Scully. il Mod Phot 41:36+ Ap '77
Instant pictures. W. Andrews and D. L. Miller. il Mod Phot 41:66+ S '77

Projection

Jazzing up your slide show. D. Macrae. Pop Phot 80:114-15+ Je '77
Using a slide projector to help plan your garden. il Sunset 159:144-5 Ag '77
SLIDING doors. See Doors
SLIME (toy) See Toys
SLIME molds
Do cellular slime molds form intercellular junctions? G. Johnson and others. bibl Science 197:1300 S 23 '77
Neither plant nor animal. D. Doeffinger. il Conservationist 31:38-9 Mr '77
SLIP covers
30-minute makeover. il House & Gard 149:104-5 F '77
SLIP decoration. See Pottery—Decoration
SLIPCOVERS. See Slip covers
SLIPEK, Edwin
How Best Products profits from SITE, Inc.'s designs. il Archit Rec 161:129-30 Mr '77
SLISKI, A. H. and others
Feline oncornavirus-associated cell membrane antigen: expression in transformed nonproducer mink cells. bibl il Science 196:1336-9 Je 17 '77
SLIVKA, Rose
Object as Poet. il Craft Horiz 37:26-39+ F '77
Our Aileen Osborn Webb. il por Craft Horiz 37:10-13 Je '77
SLOAN, Aubrey B. See Henry, R. C. jt auth
SLOAN, Bernard
Future doesn't work. por Newsweek 90:15 S 19 '77
SLOAN, Don, and Africano, Lillian
Marriage: the traditional alternative. Harp Baz 110:121+ My '77
SLOAN, Gary G.
Perils of paper grading. Engl J 66:33-6 My '77
SLOAN, Mike
Bitten from the records. il Motor B & S 139:52-5+ Mr '77
SLOAN-Kettering Institute for Cancer Research, New York
Laetrile at Sloan-Kettering: a question of ambiguity. N. Wade. Science 198:1231-4 D 23 '77
SLOANE, Barbara L.
Kevin's case. il Engl J 66:31-5 Ap '77
SLOANE, Eric
Eric Sloane's America. S. E. Meyer. il por Am Artist 41:40-5+ Je '77 *
SLOANE, Thomas O.
Readers theatre illusions and classroom realities. bibl f Engl J 66:73-8 My '77
SLOANE, Virginia
Sculpture on a large scale. il Sch Arts 76:23 Je '77
SLOBOGIN, Kathy
Stress. il N Y Times Mag p48-50+ N 20 '77
SLOCUM, Jerald A.
FBO on floats. il Flying 101:46-9+ Ag '77
Mooney the efficiency expert. il Flying 101:62-7 O '77
Murphy wins again. il Flying 100:68+ F '77
SLOCUM, Joshua
Joshua Slocum's magnificent voyage; excerpt from My country. P. Berton. il Read Digest 110:218-20+ F '77 *
SLOOP, Sally Clark
Wesley story. Am Educ 13:19 D '77

SLOOPS
Another one-design 40; North American 40 sloop. J. Rousmaniere. il Yachting 141:38+ Je '77

Materials

See Boats—Materials
SLOPEN, Beverley
Canadian Booksellers Association observes its 25th year with cautious confidence. Pub W 212:52 Jl 11 '77
Children and librarians are encouraged to browse in this successful Toronto shop. il Pub W 211:110-11 F 28 '77
Critical choices ahead as Montreal goes into third year. Pub W 211:65-6 Mr 21 '77
From Nigeria, guarded optimism; from Montreal, guarded pessimism. Pub W 211:29 My 16 '77
Seal Books makes splash from new firm: McClelland and Stewart-Bantam Ltd. il Pub W 211:25+ Ja 31 '77
SLOPES (physical geography)
Slope profiles of cycloidal form. B. J. Bridge and G. G. Beckman. bibl il Science 198:610-12 N 11 '77
SLOSS, Henry
Wedding at Vernazzano; poem. Poetry 131:21-3 O '77
SLOT machines, Electronic. See Electronic games
SLOTH. See Laziness
SLOTHS, Fossil
Great late Pleistocene extinction: a slothful tale. D. E. Thomsen. il Sci N 112:396-8 D 10 '77
SLOW crockery cookery. See Cookery
SLOW learning children
Duck boy. M. H. Kingston. il N Y Times Mag p54-5+ Je 12 '77
See also
Learning disabilities

Education

Medicine pots—a motivation operation. L. L. Clark. il Sch Arts 76:32-3 F '77
SLOW virus diseases. See Virus diseases
SLOWDOWN strikes. See Strikes
SLUDGE as fertilizer. See Sewage as fertilizer
SLUDGE disposal. See Sewage disposal
SLUDGE removal from sewage. See Sewage purification
SLUGS
Why slugs squabble. C. D. Rollo and W. G. Wellington. il Natur Hist 86:46-51 bibl(p 118) N '77
SLUMS
American underclass. il Time 110:14-18+ Ag 29 '77
No salt in the city; church and the ghetto. K. Phillips. il Chr Today 21:12-15 My 20 '77
SLUYTER, Eunice H.
Goal, a program and a community. il por Aging 272:13-17 Je '77
SLY fox; drama. See Gelbart, L.
SMALL, Dorothy May
Vernal pools. il Am For 83:30-3 My '77
SMALL, Frederick
Eagles Nest—classic lesson in wilderness politics. Audubon 79:128-31 Jl '77
SMALL, George Raphael
Ramos Martínez, Mexican muralist. il por Américas 29:19-22 Ap '77
SMALL, Robert C. Jr
Junior novel and the art of literature. il Engl J 66:56-9 O '77
SMALL arms. See Firearms
SMALL business
How to start your own business. P. Nelson. McCalls 104:81-2 S '77
Koreans in business; Los Angeles. E. Bonacich and others. bibl il Society 14:54-9 S '77
Overnight success stories; interviews. G. Chipps and C. Jessup. Harp Baz 110:49+ Je '77
Small businesses you can start on $6,000 and up. il Changing T 31:38-40 Ag '77
Starting a business: women show it's not just a man's world. il U.S. News 83:55-6 Ag 29 '77
Starting your own business: getting tougher but thousands still manage. il U.S. News 83:94-5 O 17 '77
See also
Cottage industries
Franchise system
Minority business enterprises
Self employed
Small business investment companies

Federal aid

See also
United States—Small Business Administration

Finance

How smaller firms are profiting from sales abroad. il Nations Bus 65:67-70+ D '77
New credit packages for the smaller borrower; competition for business loan customers. il Bus W p74-5 S 5 '77
New market for SBA loans. Bus W p54 Jl 4 '77

SMALL business—Finance—*Continued*
Now small business can pay its pollution tab. il Bus W p90 N 21 '77
Small businessman's struggle to stay afloat. U.S. News 83:47-8 S 12 '77

Management

See Business management

Securities

Investing in small companies: adventuresome—and profitable; interview, ed by A. Hershman. L. A. Rader. il por Duns R 110:93+ S '77

SMALL Business Administration. See United States—Small Business Administration

SMALL business insurance. See Insurance, Business

SMALL business investment companies
Top managers try venturing; AEA Investors. il por Bus W p 101-2 My 9 '77

SMALL claims courts
Could the small claims court settle your beef? Bet Hom & Gard 55:52+ Ap '77
Small claims courts. Consumer Rep 42:360-2 D '77

SMALL families. See Family, Size of

SMALL farms. See Farms, Small

SMALL presses. See Publishers and publishing

SMALL Tax Case Division. See United States—Tax Court

SMALL town life. See City and town life

SMALLMOUTH bass fishing. See Bass fishing

SMALLPOX
Red death on the Missouri; American Indian epidemic. K. C. Tessendorf. il Am West 14:48-53 Ja '77
WHO announces end to virulent smallpox. Sci N 112:407 D 17 '77

Preventive inoculation

Battling the red death. M. Musser. il por Am Hist Illus 12:30-6 N '77
Persistent pox. Sci Am 236:61 Mr '77
Smallpox: outbreak in Somalia slows rapid progress toward eradication. P. M. Boffey. map Science 196:1298-9 Je 17 '77
World safe from smallpox. Sci Digest 81:88 F '77

SMARDON, Raymond A.
Cutting the cost of local government. Harvard Bus R 55:8+ Mr '77

SMART-GROSVENOR, Vertamae. See Grosvenor, V. M.

SMAY, V. Elaine
Underground houses. bibl il Pop Sci 210:84-9+ Ap '77

SMEAD, Sandy
$20,000 for a hat? C. Massey. il por Ret Liv 17:44 Ap '77 *

SMEAL, Eleanor Cutri
Now, the president. F. Ruffin. por Redbook 149: 83 Ag '77 *

SMEEDING, Timothy M.
Recounting the poor. bibl il Intellect 106:222-5 D '77

SMELL
Differential sensitivity for smell: "noise" at the nose. W. S. Cain. bibl il Science 195:796-8 F 25 '77
How babies smell. M. R. Carter. Mademoiselle 83:104-5 F '77
Is something wrong with your sense of taste or smell? M. P. Scott. Bet Hom & Gard 55:8 My '77
Power of perfume; interview. R. Henkin. Harp Baz 111:123 N '77
Your sense of smell—it's nothing to sniff at. J. L. Lippert. il Good H 184:222 F '77
See also
Odors

SMERLING, Saul A.
Why some pension investment patterns are changing. por Nations Bus 65:60-1 Ag '77

SMETANA, Bedřich
Dalibor. Review
Hi Fi 27:MA24 My '77 *
Musical events; Opera Orchestra of New York's performance of Dalibor. A. Porter. New Yorker 52:76-8 Ja 24 '77 *

SMIL, Vaclav
China's energy performance. il Cur Hist 73:63-7 S '77
Energy solution in China. bibl il Environment 19:27-31 O '77
Intermediate energy technology in China. bibl il map Bull Atom Sci 33:25-31 F '77

SMILEY, Jane
And baby makes three; story. Redbook 149:231-4 My '77

SMILEY, Xan
White tribe of Zimbabwe. New Repub 177:19-21 Jl 30 '77

SMITH, Adam
Haggis & the Wealth of nations. E. Van Den Hagg. Nat R 29:268 Mr 4 '77 *

SMITH, Alan
Eschewing understatement, United Kingdom's Science attaché declares Tosca non grata. C. Holden. Science 196:1182-3 Je 10 '77 *

SMITH, Allie Murray
Growing up with Rosalynn Carter; excerpt from How Jimmy won. K. Stroud. il pors Good H 185:102-3+ Ag '77 *
Rosalynn Carter: my extraordinary mother. T. B. Feldman. il por McCalls 104:116+ My '77 *

SMITH, Amanda
And taking to the streets. il pors Ms 6:46-9+ D '77
Eliot Feld's animated cartoons. il por Dance Mag 51:63-5 Je '77

SMITH, Austin C.
Canal—today. il Conservationist 32:26-7 N '77
Decision on the Hudson. il por Conservationist 32:23-5 S '77

SMITH, B. Othanel
Curriculum: content and utility. Educ Digest 42:15-18 F '77

SMITH, Bettye L. Sebree
Alaskan original. S. Auerbach. pors Am Home 80:41-2 S '77 *

SMITH, Billy Mack
Boy who would be king. Nat R 29:552 My 13 '77

SMITH, Bob
Politicking. SLJ 24:40 D '77

SMITH, C. Ray
Classic purity. il N Y Times Mag p70-1 Ap 10 '77

SMITH, Cecil
Cowboy who showed 'em. R. Cantwell. il pors Sports Illus 46:68-72+ My 9 '77 *

SMITH, Charles F.
Portable 60-Hz clock oscillator. il Pop Electr 12:70 Jl '77

SMITH, Charles H. Jr
Business delegate to the ILO. Nations Bus 65: 32 O '77 *

SMITH, Clyde H.
Bates Wilson: wilderness curator. por Ret Liv 17:23 Ja '77
Ice inevitably wins; with photographs. Audubon 79:56-65 Ja '77

SMITH, Cyril Stanley
Weapons are the real problem. por Bull Atom Sci 33:69 Mr '77

SMITH, Cyrus P.
U.S. muzzleloaders go international. il Outdoor Life 159:134+ Mr '77

SMITH, D. Richard
Washington's biggest vote-getter. il pors Sat Eve Post 249:38-9+ O '77

SMITH, Dan Throop
Relief from double taxation of dividend income. Harvard Bus R 55:87-94 Ja; 168 My '77

SMITH, Dave
Apples in early October; Willows, pond glitter; Dreams in sunlit rooms; poems. Poetry 131: 24-28 O '77
Goshawk, antelope; poem. New Yorker 53:45 S 12 '77
Hath the drowned nothing to dream; poem. Nation 225:54 Jl 9 '77
Pond; poem. Nation 225:25 Jl 2 '77
Treehouse; August, on the rented farm; poems. New Yorker 53:40 Ag 29 '77

SMITH, David, 1906-1965
David Smith's art is best revealed in natural settings. J. Russell. il por Smithsonian 7:68-75 bibl(p 126-7) Mr '77 *
Revolution in sculpture: a look at David Smith. S. E. Marcus. il por Intellect 105:265-8 F '77 *

SMITH, David N.
Perils of Bert Lance. A. J. Mayer and others. il por Newsweek 90:62 Ag 8 '77 *

SMITH, Dean
Black Sox scandal. il por Am Hist Illus 11:16-24 Ja '77
Cliff dwellers of the Mesa Verde. il Am Hist Illus 12:4-9+ O '77

SMITH, Dennis, and Freedman, Jill
True soot; South Bronx firemen; excerpts from Firehouse. il Esquire 87:97-9 My '77

SMITH, Diana R.
Alternative info careers eyed in Syracuse. por Lib J 102:1712 S 1 '77

SMITH, Diane
How I stopped being the little woman. il McCalls 104:70+ Ap '77

SMITH, E. Newbold
Farthest North. il Yachting 141:68-72 My; 62-5 Je '77

SMITH, Elliott Varner
Bookstores of downtown San Francisco; photographs. il Pub W 211:42-3 Ap 18 '77

SMITH, Frank Kingston
Turbulent decade. il Flying 101:200-5+ S '77

SMITH, Fred
Environment and the economy: finding common ground. il por Duns R 110:83-4+ S '77

SMITH, Frederick Wallace
Breathing under water. R. J. Flaherty. il por Forbes 119:36-8 Mr 1 '77 *

SMITH, G. Royce
Book-giving made easy. Horn Bk 53:372-3 Je '77
about
ABA's Smith censures Furness and Today show. J. Giusto. Pub W 212:36+ O 24 '77 *

SMITH, Gaddis
U.S. vs. international terrorists. il Am Heritage 28:36-43 Ag '77

SMITH, Gary
Mourning doves; Swelter; Small boy, once lost and found; poems. Poetry 129:318-20 Mr '77
SMITH, George O.
Air/Space Museum: man's advances aloft dramatically chronicled. il Sci Digest 81:29-34 My '77
SMITH, Gerard Coad
Ambassador Smith briefs press on INFCE conference; excerpt from remarks, October 21, 1977. Dept State Bull 77:664-5 N 14 '77
Negotiating with the Soviets. N Y Times Mag p 18-19+ F 27 '77
SMITH, Gillian Bradshaw
Furry friends for Christmas; stuffed toys; excerpt from Adventures in toy-making. il Sat Eve Post 249:38-41+ D '77
SMITH, Harry
Mind, medium and metaphor in Harry Smith's Heaven and earth magic. N. Carroll. bibl il Film Q 31:37-44 Wint '77 *
SMITH, Harry K.
Hardest decision of them all. por Forbes 120: 50 D 1 '77 *
SMITH, Hedrick
Problems of a problem solver. il por N Y Times Mag p30+ Ja 8 '78
—and others
(ed) See Vance, C. R. Secretary Vance interviewed for the New York times
SMITH, Horace A.
Thomas Clap and the terrestrial comets. il Sky & Tel 53:420-2 Je '77
SMITH, Ian Douglas
Ian Smith: a bit cynical; excerpts from interview, ed by H. A. Grunwald and W McWhirter. por Time 109:46+ My 23 '77
Not much chance without U.S; interview. por U.S. News 82:34 My 30 '77
Rhodesia's future—as Ian Smith sees it now; interview. por U.S. News 83:35 Ag 8 '77
Smith's internal solution; interview, ed by A. de Borchgrave. il por Newsweek 90:34-5 Jl 18 '77
White bastion: hanging tough; excerpts from interview, ed by J. Elson and L. Griggs. por Time 109:31 Mr 7 '77

about

Another Smith surprise. K. Willenson and I. Mills. il por Newsweek 90:47-8 D 5 '77 *
Avoiding disaster in southern Africa. C. Legum. New Repub 176:11-13 F 12 '77 *
Boost for Ian Smith. M. R. Benjamin and others. il por Newsweek 90:38-40 S 12 '77 *
Carrot and stick. K. Willenson. il Newsweek 89:35+ Mr 7 '77 *
Dealing or double-dealing. il por map Time 110: 49 D 12 '77 *
Decision time. por Time 110:27-8 S 5 '77 *
Devil himself. C. Legum. il New Repub 177:17-19 D 17 '77 *
End of a chapter. il por Time 110:24+ S 12 '77 *
Ian Smith's last stand? por Time 110:27-8 Ag 1 '77 *
Separate peace? R. Carroll and others. il Newsweek 89:46+ F 7 '77 *
Smith changes his tune. Time 110:52 D 5 '77 *
Smith takes a dangerous new gamble. il por Time 109:24+ Je 13 '77 *
Tragic and fateful decision. por Time 109:43-4 F 7 '77 *
SMITH, J. August
Eshpai, Popov and Boris who. . . ? Am Rec G 40:5+ Mr '77
SMITH, J. Brian
Knowing when to leave. por Newsweek 90:13 O 3 '77
SMITH, Jack
Gadgets and gilhickies. See issues of Yachting
(ed) Designs. See issues of Yachting
SMITH, Jaclyn
Jaclyn Smith: the cool angel. C. Champlin. por McCalls 104:36+ Jl '77 *
SMITH, Jane Buckley
Health. Nat R 29:786-7 Jl 8 '77
SMITH, Janice Lee
On juggling a family, a home and a college education. Mademoiselle 83:32+ Ag '77
SMITH, Jeffrey E.
Learning to cope with the future. Educ Digest 42:38-40 Ja '77
SMITH, Jerry Lee
Another round in the obscenity battle. W. D. Nelson. Wilson Lib Bull 51:466-7 F '77 *
High court upholds criminal conviction of Smith for intrastate mailing. S. Wagner. Pub W 211:42 Je 6 '77 *
SMITH, Jessie Willcox
Child's garden of memories; excerpt from Jessie Willcox Smith. S. M. Schnessel. il Good H 184:142-5 My '77 *
SMITH, Joan
West Point log: the basic training of Joan Smith. M. Stamell. il pors Ms 6:48-51+ Ag '77 *
SMITH, Joan (Irvine)
Mrs Smith's bonanza. T. Nicholson and J. Huck. por map Newsweek 89:54+ My 23 '77 *
SMITH, John R. and others
Thyrotropin-releasing hormone: stimulation of colonic activity following intracerebroventricular administration. bibl il Science 196:660-2 My 6 '77
SMITH, Joseph, 1805-1844
Mormon manuscript claims: another look. E. E. Plowman. il Chr Today 22:38-9 O 21 '77 *
Mormon mystery. il Time 110:69 Jl 11 '77 *
Mormons: from persecution to power. R. W. Paul. il Am Heritage 28:74-83 Je '77 *
Who really wrote the Book of Mormon? E. E. Plowman. il Chr Today 21:32-4 Jl 8 '77 *
SMITH, Justin Harvey
Perspectives on the past. W. W. Hassler, Jr. il Am Hist Illus 12:44-6 N '77 *
SMITH, Lawrence H.
Employment prospects brighten a bit for some teachers in California. bibl M Labor R 100: 49-52 O '77
SMITH, Lee
Hard times come to steeltown. il Fortune 96:86-93 D '77
SMITH, Liz
(ed) See Matthau, W. Matthau, the magnificent

about

Gossip's good old gal. D. Gelman. por Newsweek 89:77 F 28 '77 *
SMITH, Lynn G. See Clanton, G. jt auth
SMITH, M. J. Sebastian
Cloister and the modern world. il Sat Eve Post 249:16+ Ap '77
SMITH, Maggie
Nothing undone. New Yorker 53:21-3 Ag 29 '77 *
SMITH, Marian
Listen, your holiness. America 137:286 O 29 '77
SMITH, Marilyn
Mom goes to law school. il Ms 6:16-18 S '77
SMITH, Mason
Glory be to man for dappled things. il Sports Illus 46:40-2+ My 23 '77
Marlboro man. il pors Sports Illus 46:58-62+ Ja 17 '77
SMITH, Mike
Codell, revisited. bibl il Weatherwise 30:112-13 Je '77
SMITH, Myra Okazaki, and others
Cerebral lateralization of haptic perception: interaction of responses to braille and music reveals a functional basis. bibl il Science 197:689-90 Ag 12 '77
SMITH, Ned
Wildlife sketchbook (cont) Nat Wildlife 15:22-3 Ap; 34-5 Je; 46-7 O '77
SMITH, O. L.
Coaxing rain from clouds . . . when and where you want it. il Sci Digest 81:18-23 My '77
SMITH, O. R. T. pseud
Health hazards behind bars. America 136:144-6 F 19 '77
SMITH, Otis M.
Boss of General Motors' legal staff. il pors Ebony 33:33-5+ D '77 *
SMITH, Parker
He hocked his house to get his own store. il por Forbes 119:48 F 1 '77 *
SMITH, Pat
Grand fish. il Outdoor Life 160:64-5 Jl '77
Magic of surf fishing. il Outdoor Life 160:82-3+ S '77
River that calls to the bold. il map Outdoor Life 160:69-73+ Ag '77
SMITH, Patrick J.
Book reviews. See alternate issues of High fidelity and Musical America
Festival of Richard Strauss. Hi Fi 27:MA39-40 Ag '77
SMITH, Patrick L.
Behind the Cape route theory. Nation 225:262-4 S 24 '77
SMITH, Peg
Alice in schoolroom land. Engl J 66:22-6 My '77
SMITH, Ralph E.
Sources of growth of the female labor force, 1971-75. il M Labor R 100:27-9 Ag '77
SMITH, Red. See Smith, Walter
SMITH, Rex L. and others
Nitrogen fixation in grasses inoculated with spirillum lipoferum. bibl il Science 193:1003-5; 195:1362. S 10 '76, Mr 25 '77
SMITH, Richard Joyce
Fighting for the wheel. por Time 109:57 Je 6 '77 *
SMITH, Richard P.
Think small for hares. il Outdoor Life 160:72-3+ N '77
SMITH, Robert
8 ways to stop snoring—sometimes. Fam Health 9:42-3 Ja '77
SMITH, Robert Ellis
Equal Employment Opportunity Commission and how to make it work. Ms 5:62-4+ F '77
Washington privacy; interview. New Yorker 53: 28-30 My 30 '77
SMITH, Robert G.
Russian paradoxes. il Intellect 105:373-4 My '77

SMITH, Roberta
About faces: the new work of Peter Campus. il Art in Am 65:85-7 Mr '77
1970s at the Whitney. il Art in Am 65:91-3 My '77
Winsor-built. il Art in Am 65:118-20 Ja '77
—See Goldin, A. jt auth

SMITH, Roger H. and Giusto, Joann
Approaching 50, Bookazine still stresses aggressive wholesaling with the personal touch. il Pub W 212:73-6 O 3 '77

SMITH, S. V. and Harrison, J. T.
Calcium carbonate production of the mare incognitum, the upper windward reef slope, at Enewetak Atoll. bibl il Science 197:556-9 Ag 5 '77

SMITH, Sheldon Moody
Crack in the Anglican dam. Nat R 29:1166 O 14 '77

SMITH, Shelley
America's single couples. il pors Harp Baz 110:108-13 My '77 *

SMITH, Sidney Adair
Arts in Mobile. il Antiques 112:482-91 S '77

SMITH, Susan Renner-. See Renner-Smith, S.

SMITH, Terence
Israel journal: 1972-1976: reflections on a troubled people. il Sat R 4:8-16+ F 5 '77
Peace Corps: alive but not so well. il N Y Times Mag p6-9+ D 25 '77

SMITH, Tony M.
Good news for the geese. il por Forbes 119:30-1 Ap 15 '77 *

SMITH, W. Eugene
Masters of the darkroom: how W. Eugene Smith shoots and prints; excerpt from Darkroom. il pors Pop Phot 80:76-81+ F 77

SMITH, Walter
Perfect beauty of a ninety-foot field. il Horizon 19:92-3 Mr '77

SMITH, William Jay
(tr) See Várady, S. Chairs above the Danube

SMITH and Wesson revolvers. See Revolvers

SMITH Barney, Harris Upham and Company Inc. See Brokers

SMITH College, Northampton, Mass.
My college diary; interview, ed by L. R. Obst. J. N. Eisenhower. il por N Y Times Mag p97-9 N 13 '77

SMITH-Corona Marchant. See SCM Corporation

SMITH Island
Chesapeake spring. J. Lelyveld. il N Y Times Mag p 110 Ap 3 '77

SMITHKLINE Corporation
Drug company workers like new schedules. R. T. Golembiewski and R. J. Hilles. M Labor R 100:65+ F '77

SMITHSONIAN Folklife Festival. See Festivals—Washington, D.C.

SMITHSONIAN Institution
Around the Mall and beyond. E. Park. See issues of Smithsonian
Smithsonian highlights. See issues of Smithsonian
This way out—from our mad jumble of signs; pictographs at the National Zoo and on the Mall. W. Von Eckardt. il Smithsonian 8:108+ D '77
View from the castle. S. D. Ripley. See issues of Smithsonian
Washington's new museums. A. R. Pastore, Jr. il Trav/Holiday 149:50-3 Ja '78
You'll find it in the Nation's attic. P. Bernstein. il Fortune 96:139-45 S '77
See also
Government investigations—Smithsonian Institution
National Zoological Park, Washington, D.C.
Woodrow Wilson International Center for Scholars

Appropriations and expenditures

Congress kills research money for Smithsonian scientists. C. Holden. Science 197:443 Jl 29 '77

Cooper-Hewitt Museum of Decorative Arts and Design, New York

Cooper-Hewitt and its concern for American taste; More Than Meets the Eye exhibit. R. Lynes. il Smithsonian 8:69-77 bibl(p 160-1) N '77
To celebrate the moment; exhibition at Cooper-Hewitt Museum. il Hobbies 82:119+ Ja '78

National Air and Space Museum

Air, space, and man in a museum. E. Keller. il Chemistry 50:13-16 O '77
Air/Space Museum: man's advances aloft dramatically chronicled. G. O. Smith. il Sci Digest 81:29-34 My '77
Millions of visitors and more coming. il U.S. News 82:59 Je 27 '77
Pure history. B. DeMott. il Atlantic 239:110-12 Mr '77
Showing Lindbergh the Air and Space Museum. M. Collins. il Sat R 4:30-1+ Ap 16 '77

National Museum of History and Technology

Atom smashers—50 years; exhibit at the National Museum. D. E. Thomsen. il Sci N 112:410-11 D 17 '77

SMITHTOWN General Hospital. See Hospitals—New York (state)

SMOG
Dioxirane: nonradical route to smog. il Sci N 112:340 N 19 '77
Enhancement of photochemical smog by N,N'-diethylhydroxylamine in polluted ambient air. J. N. Pitts, Jr and others. bibl il Science 197:255-7 Jl 15 '77
Hydroxyl radical reactivity with diethylhydroxylamine. R. A. Gorse, Jr and others. bibl il Science 197:1365-7 S 30 '77

SMOKE
See also
Cigarette smoke

SMOKE cooking. See Food—Smoking

SMOKE detectors. See Fire detectors

SMOKING
Case of the smoking baboons. il Sci Digest 82:14-15 Ag '77
Chemistry of smoking; studies by S. Schachter. Time 109:48 F 21 '77
Deadly new facts about women and smoking. M. L. Schildkraut. Good H 184:217-18 F '77
Elastase release from human alveolar macrophages: comparison between smokers and nonsmokers. R. J. Rodriguez and others. bibl il Science 198:313-14 O 21 '77
Hospitals begin crack-down on smokers. Sci Digest 81:84-5 Je '77
More young women are smoking, and they're smoking more. D. Cohen. Psychol Today 10:131 Ap '77
Reflections on tobacco smoke. W. F. Buckley, Jr. Nat R 29:1073 S 16 '77
Smoking addiction. S. C. McMorris. Current 189:33-8 Ja '77
Smoking and the pill. il Newsweek 89:65 Ap 11 '77
Those quit-smoking groups & how they work. Changing T 31:13-15 F '77
Toward a more fragrant world. S. H. Day, Jr. Bull Atom Sci 33:6-7 My '77
Two cheers for the unfit. M. Greenfield. Newsweek 91:68 Ja 2 '78
Unnatural history of tobacco. E. Eckholm. il Natur Hist 86:22-4+ Ap '77; Reply with rejoinder. H. R. Kornegay. 86:74-7 Je '77
Why do you smoke? J. Greenberg. il Sci N 111:297-8 My 7 '77
See also
Fetus, Effect of smoking on the

SMOKING accessories
See also
Tobacco pipes

SMOKING and youth
Nation fails to arouse teenagers against cigarette risks. R. S. Morison. il Intellect 105:298-9 Mr '77
Smoking in school; Suffern High School, New York. W. V. Woodward. Educ Digest 43:56-7 N '77

SMOKING of food. See Food—Smoking

SMOKING on airplanes
Right to smoke; CAB ban of cigar and pipe smoking on commercial airplanes. New Repub 177:8-9 D 10 '77

SMOKY Mountains. See Great Smoky Mountains

SMOKY Mountains National Park. See Great Smoky Mountains National Park

SMOLIAN, Steven
Da capo. il Am Rec G 40:52-3 D '76; 58-60 F; 16-17+ Ap '77

SMOLKIN, Shelley
Outward Bound: the ultimate experience. Harp Baz 110:87+ Ap '77

SMOOT, Bill
Giving up on the problem. Nation 225:81-4 Jl 23 '77

SMUGGLING
Border wars: busting the dope trade. G. C. Larson. il Flying 101:62-9+ N '77
Cigarette bootlegging: who says crime doesn't pay? J. Cook. il Forbes 120:43-5+ D 15 '77
Confessions of an animal trafficker; excerpt from The animal connection. J.-Y. Domalain. il Natur Hist 86:54-67 bibl(p94+) My '77
Crackdown on electronics smugglers. il Bus W p39 Mr 21 '77
Dark and violent world of the Mexican connection; behind America's marijuana high. D. Harris. il map N Y Times Mag p 15-18+ D 18 '77
Following the jade trail. il Time 111:24-5 Ja 9 '78
New connection; New England drug traffic. D. A. Williams and R. Manning. il map Newsweek 90:38 O 3 '77
New England connection; drugs. il Time 110:26 O 3 '77
Outlaw county; marijuana smuggling in Starr County, Tex. J. Lelyveld. il N Y Times Mag p 110 My 15 '77

SMUGGLING—*Continued*
Smuggling rare animals: latest global racket. il U.S. News 83:50 S 26 '77
Snake smugglers. P. Gwynne and others. il Newsweek 89:81+ Ap 25 '77
Taming a tough county; marijuana smuggling in Starr County, Tex. Time 109:58-9 My 2 '77
Tobacco Road; cigarette smuggling. il Time 110:82+ N 14 '77
Tricks that smugglers use—and how they get caught; interview. V. D. Acree. il por U.S. News 82:52-4 Mr 14 '77
We're not fools! cigarette smuggling and New York's sales tax. Forbes 119:118 Je 15 '77

SMUIN, Michael
Balletic ramrod from Missoula. W. Terry. il Sat R 4:50-1 S 17 '77 *

SMULLEN, Ivor
Night hunter. il Int Wildlife 7:32-5 S '77
Play it again, Sam. il Int Wildlife 7:38-40 Mr '77

SMYRNA, Tenn.
Historic houses, sites, etc.
See Historic houses, sites, etc.—Tennessee

SMYSER, Steve, and Gettings, T. L.
New opportunities in fish culture. il Org Gard & Farm 24:62-8 Mr '77

—and Weinsteiger, Richard
Easy-to-build insect traps. il Org Gard & Farm 24:112-14+ Jl '77

SMYTH, Paul
Box turtle; Elm leaf; They; Paperweight; poems. Poetry 130:337-41 S '77

SNACK food industry. See Food industry

SNACKS
Little league lunacy. J. Farmer. il Org Gard & Farm 24:120+ My '77
On the move: energy foods; with recipes. il Seventeen 36:174-5+ Ap '77
Quick treats using crêpes. il Sunset 159:222 O '77
Snack idea from southeast Asia; tortilla egg snacks. il Sunset 159:122 Ag '77

SNAIL darter. See Perch

SNAILS
Conjugation of snails; photographs; with introd by F. Hartmann. H. Pfletschinger. Natur Hist 86:104-7 Ag '77
Porcelaneous sculptors; the marine lettered olive snail. L. P. Loraamm. il Sea Front 23:296-303 S '77
Ram's horn snail. W. S. Bousquet. il Conservationist 31:45 My '77
See also
Cookery—Snails
Slugs

SNAKE River
White-water high. P. Wood. il N Y Times Mag p66-73 My 22 '77

SNAKE River Birds of Prey Natural Area. See Bird sanctuaries—Idaho

SNAKE stones. See Snakestones

SNAKE toxins. See Toxins and antitoxins

SNAKE venom. See Venom

SNAKEBITE. See Venom

SNAKES
Coral snake. R. E. Arnold. Field & S 82:128-9 My '77
If they're killers, what good are they? poisonous snakes of India. Z. Whitaker and R. Whitaker. il Int Wildlife 7:12-16 My '77
Polymorphism and geographic variation in the feeding behavior of the garter snake thamnophis elegans. S. J. Arnold. bibl il Science 197:676-8 Ag 12 '77
Regional specialization of reptilian scale surfaces: relation of texture and biologic role. C. Gans and D. Baic. bibl il Science 195:1348-50 Mr 25 '77
Russels' viper. R. E. Arnold. Field & S 82:20 S '77
See also
Cobras
Rattlesnakes
Sea snakes
Sexual behavior—Reptiles

SNAKESTONES
Magic of the snake-stone: does it cure? R. Caras il Sci Digest 82:53-5 Jl '77

SNAPPERS
See also
Cookery—Fish

SNEAKERS. See Shoes, boots, rubbers, etc.

SNEATH, William Scott
Managing for an uncertain future; address, November 19, 1976. Vital Speeches 43:196-9 Ja 15 '77

SNELL, David
Fever tick crashes roundup, causes trouble on range. il Smithsonian 8:58-65 O '77
Texas natives. il pors Horticulture 55:38-51 Ap '77
Why does a falling down goat not fall down? il Horticulture 55:36-9 O '77

SNELL, John Blashford. See Blashford-Snell, J.

SNEPP, Frank
Psst! Viet secrets? T. Mathews. il Newsweek 90:71 N 28 '77 *
RH edits book in secrecy to prevent CIA action. M. Reuter. Pub W 212:13 N 28 '77 *

SNITCH, Thomas H.
Idi Amin: more cunning than crazy. il Intellect 105:410-11 Je '77
Neither black nor white: South Africa as an African nation. il Intellect 106:126-9 O '77

SNOOK fishing
Snook: getting down to basics; Florida. V. Dunaway. il Field & S 81:28+ F '77

SNORING
8 ways to stop snoring—sometimes. R. Smith. Fam Health 9:42-3 Ja '77

SNOW, Brad
Reporter at large. J. McPhee. il New Yorker 53:58-80 Je 27 '77 *

SNOW, Charles Percy, Baron Snow of Leicester.
See Snow of Leicester, C. P. S.

SNOW, Dean R.
Rock art and the power of shamans; with biographical sketch. il Natur Hist 86:4, 42-9 bibl(p 100) F '77

SNOW, Richard F.
Barney Oldfield. il por Am Heritage 28:66-7 F '77
Hinckley fire. il Am Heritage 28:90-6 Ag '77

SNOW, Theodore P. Jr
Ultraviolet spectroscopy with Copernicus. il Sky & Tel 54:371-4 N '77

SNOW of Leicester, Charles Percy Snow, Baron
Interview. pors Sci Digest 82:22-5+ Jl '77
Literary legacy. il Sat R 4:14-15 Je 11 '77
Printed word; excerpt from address, April 1977. Writer 90:24-6 D '77
about
Visible college in British science. M. Green. Am Scholar 47:105-17 Wint '77 *

SNOW
Day it snowed in Miami. G. E. Schwartz. Weatherwise 30:50+ Ap '77
Ski season is off to a snowy start. il Bus W p59 D 12 '77
Snowfall season of 1975-76. D. M. Ludlum. maps Weatherwise 30:18-21 F '77
See also
Avalanches
Snowstorms
Anecdotes, facetiae, satire, etc.
White is not beautiful. G. Ace. Sat R 4:48 Ap 30 '77

SNOW and ice removal
Are you ready for winter? M. C. Rissel. il Am City & County 92:67-70 S '77
Blizzard of '77 teaches lessons for '78; Buffalo, N.Y. il Am City & County 92:61-2 Ag '77
Buffalo, N.Y.—digging out of the ice age. T. Fuller. il Newsweek 89:27 F 14 '77
Move more snow with motorgraders. D. Hurlugson. il Am City & County 92:73 Ap '77
Shortage of salt to pour on the streets. il Bus W p34-5 F 14 '77
Anecdotes, facetiae, satire, etc.
Jaundiced eye. S. Novick. Environment 19:inside cover Ja '77
Conferences
No de-icer shortage, snowfighters hear; North American Snow Conference. il Am City & County 92:17-18 Je '77

SNOW blowers, throwers, etc.
Facts (and myths) about snowthrower safety. E. F. Lindsley. il Pop Sci 211:142+ D '77

SNOW geese. See Geese, Wild

SNOW goose shooting. See Goose shooting

SNOW removal equipment
Lighting
Light up for safety; New York State Department of Transportation. Am City & County 92:70 S '77

SNOW sculpture
Snow, snow, snow. M. H. Stuckhardt. il Sch Arts 76:18-19 Je '77

SNOW slides. See Avalanches

SNOW storms. See Snowstorms

SNOW throwers. See Snow blowers, throwers, etc.

SNOW tires. See Tires, Automobile

SNOWDEN, Fred
Desert fox. L. Robinson. il pors Ebony 32:44-6+ Ap '77 *

SNOWDON, Anthony Charles Robert Armstrong-Jones, 1st Earl of
Life & loves of Princess Margaret. N. Dempster. por Ladies Home J 94:30+ D '77 *

SNOWFALL. See Snow

SNOWMOBILE industry
What's up, Irwin? purchase of Arctic Enterprises. por Forbes 120:78 D 15 '77

SNOWMOBILE racing
Grand Prix for snowmobiles; St Paul-Winnipeg race. il Time 109:82 F 7 '77

SNOWMOBILE racing—*Continued*
Race goes on in snow country. il Mech Illus 74:68 Ja '78
SNOWMOBILES and snowmobiling
Don't expect a peaceful winter retreat; snowmobiling in Grand Teton National Park. il Nat Parks & Con Mag 51:19+ My '77
New snowmos. . .more style and spunk. B. McKeown. il Pop Mech 148:88-9+ N '77
Picking out a snowmobile. B. Behme. il Mech Illus 73:52+ D '77
Recreational vehicles; new snowmobiles. H. Shuldiner. il Outdoor Life 160:20+ D '77
Snowmobiles: some second thoughts. B. Kilpatrick. Field & S 82:104+ D '77
What's happening to the snowmobile? B. Behme. il Mech Illus 73:62-3+ O '77
SNOWSLIDE. See Avalanches
SNOWSTORMS
Buffalo: camaraderie and tragedy. M. Knox. il Time 109:11-12 F 14 '77
Great blizzard of '88. N. Brandt. il Am Heritage 28:32-41 F '77
How Buffalo dented the Conrail budget. Bus W p32 F 21 '77
NOAA satellites track winter storms; photographs. Aviation W 106:50-1 F 21 '77
Record-breaking winter of 1976-77. A. J. Wagner. il maps Weatherwise 30:65-9 Ap '77
What it's like—living in a city drowning in snow; Buffalo, N.Y. il U.S. News 82:21 F 14 '77
Wild winter of 1976-77 in New York State. R. A. Wrightson. il Weatherwise 30:70-5 Ap '77
See also
Automobile driving—Storm hazards
SNYDER, Edward H.
Manhattan retailer. il por Forbes 120:46 D 15 '77
SNYDER, Gregory K.
Blood corpuscles and blood hemoglobins: a possible example of coevolution. bibl il Science 195:412-13 Ja 28 '77
SNYDER, John
Jazz. M. Ullman. New Repub 177:23-5 N 19 '77 *
SNYDER, Julian M.
Case for overthrowing the government; address; June 17, 1977. Vital Speeches 43:717-20 S 15 '77
SNYDER, Linda
Personal investing. See issues of Fortune
SNYDER, Louis
Canada's capital capital. il Ret Liv 17:32-3 Jl '77
SNYDER, Norman
View point. J. Deschin. il por Pop Phot 80:22+ F '77
SNYDER, Richard
Aging poet, on a reading trip to Dayton, visits the Air Force museum and discovers there a plane he once flew; poem. Commonweal 104: 231 Ap 15 '77
SNYDER, Richard Elliott
Richard E. Snyder, president of Simon & Schuster, on his firm's explosive success and the present industry ferment; interview. pors Pub W 211:32-8 Ap 11 '77
SNYDER, Solomon H.
Opiate receptors and internal opiates; with biographical sketch. il Sci Am 236:22, 44-56 bibl (p 150) Mr '77
SOANE, Sir John
Triumph of style: one man's home and his collections. P. Goldberger. il Smithsonian 8:100-4+ bibl(p 147-8) Ap '77 *
SOANE Museum. See London—Galleries and museums
SOAP
Toilet soaps. il Consumer Rep 42:128-30 Mr '77
Yogurt soap. Sci Digest 81:91 F '77
Your own soap bars—Christmas head start. il Sunset 159:150-2 N '77
SOAP dishes, trays, etc.
Ceramic dish hands you the soap. il Sunset 159: 155 N '77
SOAP opera comic strips. See Comics (books, strips, etc)
SOAP operas. See Television serials
SOARES, Mário
After Soares, Soares? F. Willey and E. Behr. il por Newsweek 90:47 D 19 '77 *
500 days of Mário Soares. il por Time 110:34 D 19 '77 *
Portugal's crisis. G. W. Grayson. bibl f Cur Hist 73:169-73+ N '77 *
Soares' shaky political seesaw. por Time 110:34 Ag 8 '77 *
SOBERANO, Rawlein G.
New light on the Philippine dilemma. il Chr Cent 94:624-7 Jl 6 '77
SOBIN, Julian M.
Coming leap forward in China trade. por Nations Bus 65:54-6 Jl '77
SOBOL, Harriet Langsam
My brother Steven is retarded; story; excerpt. Ms 6:67-70 S '77
SOBOSAN, Jeffrey G.
Clowns; poem. Chr Cent 94:1212 D 28 '77

SOBRAN, M. J. Jr
I say lock 'em up, spank them, and send them home. Nat R 29:712-13+ Je 24 '77
On the screen. Nat R 29:392+, 505-6, 622-3, 1061-2 Ap 1, 29, My 27, S 16 '77
Printed word. Nat R 29:1005-6, 1251-2, 1506 S 2, O 28, D 23 '77
SOCAL. See Standard Oil Company of California
SOCCER
Big kick behind soccer. il Bus W p94+ S 5 '77
Cosmos reach their goal; NASL championship. C. Gammon. il Sports Illus 47:14-17 S 5 '77
From kids to pros . . . soccer is making it big in U.S. il U.S. News 83:100-1 O 17 '77
Instilling tick-tick; U.S. clinics conducted by Brazilian coaches. J. D. Reed. Sports Illus 46: 52-3 F 7 '77
Laughing matter no longer; North American Soccer League. J. D. Reed. il Sports Illus 46:84+ Ap 11 '77
Lessons from a lower level; B level hometown soccer. J. Domini. il Sports Illus 47:72-6+ O 3 '77
Making soccer an American sport. P. Gardner. il Horizon 20:76-81 N '77
Mitey band of Warriors; Hartwick's victory in NCAA championships. J. D. Reed. il Sports Illus 47:70+ D 12 '77
Mmm, love that détente; Tampa Rowdies vs Leningrad Zenit. J. D. Reed. il Sports Illus 46: 66+ Mr 14 '77
New kick. P. Axthelm. il Newsweek 90:82-3 Jl 18 '77
No image for soccer. M. G. Cooke. New Repub 177:28-9 Jl 23 '77
Notes and comment; Cosmos. New Yorker 53:29 S 12 '77
Nothing but blue skies does Woosnam see; commissioner of the North American Soccer League. C. Gammon. il pors Sports Illus 46:38-40+ My 30 '77
Pelé's mission accomplished. il por Time 110:62-3 S 12 '77
Selling of soccer-mania. L. Miller. il N Y Times Mag p 12-13+ Ag 28 '77
Wallflowers in bloom; North American Soccer League. J. D. Reed. il Sports Illus 47:48-9 Ag 8 '77

Television broadcasting

See Television broadcasting—Sports
SOCCER, Childrens
At home with the Syosset Under-10 Travelling Team. J. E. Maslow. Sat R 5:56-7 O 29 '77
SOCCER players
See also
Banks, G.
Beckenbauer, F.
Pelé

Recruiting

Disturbing raid by the Cosmos; signing college players. J. D. Reed. il Sports Illus 47:66+ O 24 '77
SOCHA, John S.
From Russia with lens. il Mod Phot 41:109-10+ N '77
SOCIAL action
On rage remembered. A. M. Davidon. Progressive 41:18-19 Je '77
See also
Church and social problems
SOCIAL adjustment. See Adjustment, Social
SOCIAL agencies
Acquiescence of social work; excerpt from Radical social work. R. A. Cloward and F. F. Piven. Society 14:55-63 Ja '77
Family-help program that really works; Family Union of New York City. S. Bush. il Psychol Today 10:48+ My '77
SOCIAL aspects of education. See Educational sociology
SOCIAL aspects of science. See Science—Social aspects
SOCIAL behavior of animals. See Animals—Habits and behavior
SOCIAL behavior of insects. See Insects—Habits and behavior
SOCIAL change
Challenge of cultural transition in Sub-Saharan Africa. V. C. Uchendu. bibl f Ann Am Acad 432:70-9 Jl '77
Changing male roles. J. Harrison. il Am Educ 13:20-6 Jl '77
Cultural movements and ethnic change. D. L. Horowitz. bibl f Ann Am Acad 433:6-18 S '77
Dealing in futures; reprints. il Sat Eve Post 249:52-3 Jl '77
Identity and change: does development imply dependency? underdeveloped nations. W. M. Dyal, Jr and J. B. Donovan. il Américas 29: 13-18 Ap '77
On smallness. K. Kodner. Progressive 41:26-7 S '77
Spaciousness; change in patterns of living space. A. W. Smith. Nat Parks & Con Mag 51:2+ O '77
See also
Aviation—Social aspects

SOCIAL classes
Politics of envy. E. M. von Kuehnelt-Leddihn. Nat R 29:721 Je 24 '77
See also
Elite (social sciences)
Leisure class
Middle classes
Upper classes

SOCIAL conditions
Cheery doomsayer: an interview with Malcolm Muggeridge; ed by W. Murchison. M. Muggeridge. Nat R 29:1050-1 S 16 '77
See also
Social problems
also subhead Social conditions under names of countries, states, cities, etc. e.g. Leningrad—Social conditions

Bibliography

Self and society. J. P. Fitzpatrick. America 136: 86-7 Ja 29 '77

SOCIAL conflict
See also
Culture conflict

SOCIAL democracy. See Socialism

SOCIAL development of children. See Children—Growth and development

SOCIAL diseases. See Venereal diseases

SOCIAL drinking. See Drinking customs

SOCIAL education
See also
Family life, Education for
Group relations training
Human relations—Study and teaching
Sex education
Social sciences—Study and teaching

SOCIAL ethics
See also
Altruism
Bioethics
Crime and criminals
Political ethics
Sexual ethics

SOCIAL evolution. See Social change

SOCIAL forecasting
Author James Michener on future of this country. J. A. Michener. il pors U.S. News 83: 60-1 S 12 '77
Buckminster Fuller on minds instead of muscle. R. B. Fuller. il pors U.S. News 83:49 D 5 '77
Human ecology; address, March 25, 1977. C. E. Bishop. Vital Speeches 43:470-2 My 15 '77
Lifestyle of the future; address, May 19, 1977. T. J. Gordon. Vital Speeches 43:557-63 Jl 1 '77
Pharmacy in the year 2000; address, June 11, 1977. C. A. Rodowskas, Jr. Vital Speeches 43: 595-8 Jl 15 '77
Tomorrow's family. R. S. Pickett. bibl f Intellect 105:330-2 Ap '77
Top of the world is flat. H. J. Davidson. bibl f il Harvard Bus R 55:89-99 Mr '77
Unlucky generation. P. A. Samuelson. Newsweek 90:100 O 10 '77
We the people; address, February 27, 1977. P. J. Crow. Vital Speeches 43:456-7 My 15 '77
What life will be like in the 1980s. U.S. News 83:75-86 D 26 '77
Work in the year 2001. W. Abbott. Current 193-31-9 My '77

Anecdotes facetiae, satire, etc.

Catching the next trend. J. G. Dunne. il Esquire 87:10+ Ap '77

SOCIAL groups. See Groups (sociology)

SOCIAL history
See also
Cincinnati—Social history

SOCIAL insurance. See Social security

SOCIAL isolation
See also
Alienation (social psychology)
Loneliness

SOCIAL life and customs. See Manners and customs; *also* subhead Social life and customs under names of countries, states, etc, e.g. England—Social life and customs

SOCIAL organization
Breaking the shame barrier. B. Levin. il Horizon 19:88-9 Mr '77
How the establishment got established; excerpt from The emergence of society. J. Pfeiffer. il Horizon 19:62-7 Mr '77

SOCIAL perception
See also
Group relations training

SOCIAL policy
Social theory and public policy; symposium, ed by J. R. Hollingsworth. bibl f il Ann Am Acad 434:1-198 N '77
See also
Belgium—Social policy
United States—Social policy

SOCIAL problems
American society and its cities. M. Mead. Current 190:3-9 F '77
See also
Academy for Contemporary Problems, Columbus, Ohio
Church and social problems
Crime and criminals
Discrimination
Divorce
Family
Homosexuality
Juvenile delinquency
Liquor problem
Migrant labor
Prostitution
School and social and economic problems
Slums
Social action
Suicide
Technology—Social aspects

SOCIAL psychology
Alias Johnny Hooker; con games and social psychologists. A. C. Elms. Psychol Today 10: 17 F '77
See also
Behavior (psychology)
Empathy
Ethnopsychology
Family
Groups (sociology)
Human relations
Leadership
Political psychology
Prison psychology
Public opinion
Stereotype (psychology)
Violence

SOCIAL responsibility. See Responsibility

SOCIAL revolution
See also
Counterculture

SOCIAL role
See also
Sex role

SOCIAL science. See Social sciences

SOCIAL science research
Policy research. P. G. Brown. Society 14:8 Jl '77
Presidential decision making; symposium. Society 14:8-24 My '77
Studying up. L. Nader. il Psychol Today 11:132 S '77
See also
Criminal research

SOCIAL sciences
One and a half cheers for social science; challenges by the physical sciences. A. Etzioni. Psychol Today 11:168 D '77
See also
Economics
Geography
Political science
Power (social sciences)
Social scientists

Philosophy

Worried America; adaptation of address. G. Myrdal. Chr Cent 94:1161-6 D 14 '77

Research

See Social science research

Study and teaching

In a word, history. M. H. Dohan. il Am Educ 13:10-12 N '77
Should we teach about work in the social studies? P. K. Good and others. Educ Digest 42: 57-9 My '77
Social studies education with a purpose. L. L. Sommerfield. Clearing H 50:371-2 Ap '77
Teaching with a global perspective. G. M. Haniff. Current 194:17-22 Jl '77
Utilizing sociodrama in the social studies curriculum. S. Marcus and J. Marcus. Clearing H 50:272-3 F '77
See also
History—Study and teaching
National Council for the Social Studies
Population education

SOCIAL scientists
Born-again social scientists. B. Tyson. Society 14:15-16 My '77
See also
Mills, C. W.

SOCIAL security

United States

Can you still count on social security? il Bet Hom & Gard 55:6 Ag '77
Carter sends Congress his plan to reshuffle social security; debate begins on revisions. il Ret Liv 17:11-13 Jl '77
Carter's controversial social security cure. il Bus W p34+ My 23 '77
Discrimination against whom? widowers seeking survivors' benefits. M Labor R 100:51-2 My '77
Future funding of social security and the total dependency ratio. Y. P. Chen and K. W. Chu. bibl il M Labor R 100:53-5 F '77
How to pay for social security? interviews. W. J. Cohen; A. Ullman. pors U.S. News 83:37-8 Jl 4 '77
In the works: a fairer but costlier social security. U.S. News 82:85-6 Mr 21 '77

SOCIAL security—United States—*Continued*
Major changes in Supplemental Security Income Program to be implemented. Aging 268:6 F '77
My mother never worked; question of benefits for homemakers. B. Smith-Yackel. Ms 5:92-3 My '77
Pain in the paycheck. T. Mathews and H. W. Hubbard. il Newsweek 90:32-3 D 12 '77
Plan-of-the-week club. P. Goldman and others. il por Newsweek 89:16-17 My 23 '77
Rescuing social security. il Time 109:16 My 16 '77
Retire now, pay later. M. S. Evans. Nat R 29:1241 O 28 '77
Rush for disability pay proves a mounting burden for taxpayers. il U.S. News 83:104-6 O 17 '77
Salvaging social security. A. J. Mayer and M. Sniffen. il Newsweek 90:63-4 S 26 '77
Social security and social service; symposium. il Society 14:54-68 My '77
Social security deserters could face long-term woes. G. M. Chamberlain. Am City & County 92:108 F '77
Social security needs more than a quick fix. Fortune 95:97 Je '77
Social security overhaul: who'll pay the bill. il U.S. News 82:91-3 My 23 '77
Social security reform: a look at the problems. P. Henle. M Labor R 100:55-8 F '77
Social security time bomb is still ticking. G. Koretz. il Bus W p79+ Ja 9 '78
Social security—who will pay. U.S. News 83:82 N 7 '77
Social security's quick fix. M. Stone. U.S. News 83:104 N 28 '77
Social security's refinancing dilemma. Bus W p38-9 O 24 '77
Supreme Court eases social security rules; ruling on Social Security Act of 1972. Aging 274:27 Ag '77
Supreme Court strikes down a social security dependency requirement for widowers. Ret Liv 17:13-14 Ap '77
TRB from Washington. New Repub 176:2+ My 21 '77
Tax unfairly collected. Sat Eve Post 249:32 S '77
Time for decision on the social security dilemma. Nations Bus 65:52-4 O '77
Washington memo; key Republicans urge merger with Civil Service Retirement Fund to save social security. R. D. Westgate. Ret Liv 17:60-2 N '77
Washington memo: uproar over proposal to raise social security age. R. D. Westgate. Ret Liv 17:52-3 O '77
Will social security be there when you need it? Changing T 31:24-8 F '77
You can farm and still draw social security. C. F. Lein. Farm J 101:28 mid-F '77

SOCIAL Security Amendments of 1972. See Social security—United States

SOCIAL security taxes
Challenges to profit sharing: the danger of social security on pensions; Employee Retirement Income Security Act; address, October 20, 1976. A. M. Wood. Vital Speeches 43:230-3 F 1 '77
Checked your contribution lately? J. Berry. il Forbes 120:31-2 D 1 '77
For social security's ills: a choice of harsh remedies. il U.S. News 83:30-2 N 21 '77
New social security plan: what you will get—and lose. il U.S. News 83:89-90 D 26 '77
Saving social security. il Time 110:12-13 D 26 '77
Social security $$ fuel N.C. library info center; Wake County Public Libraries System. Lib J 102:148 Ja 15 '77
Social security earnings limitation is upped for '77; taxable base raised too. il Ret Liv 16:11-12 D '76
Social security time bomb is still ticking. G. Koretz. il Bus W p79+ Ja 9 '78
Social security: up, up and away! il Time 110:21-2 N 7 '77
Spreading the social security tax burden. il Nations Bus 65:16+ My '77..

SOCIAL service, Public. See Public welfare

SOCIAL status
What's in, what's out: the search for status; with interview with P. Blumberg. il por U.S. News 82:38-42 F 14 '77
See also
Students—Social and economic status
Youth—Social and economic status

SOCIAL stratification. See Social classes

SOCIAL structure. See Social organization

SOCIAL surveys
See also
Recreation surveys

SOCIAL thought
Impact of evolutionary thought on American culture in the 20th century. H. Cravens. bibl Intellect 106:83-6 Ag '77

SOCIAL values
Moral tales for a depraved age. T. Griffith. Atlantic 240:20-1 Jl '77
Myth of self-evident truths. W. Muehl. Chr Cent 94:1000-2 N 2 '77
New model me; program in Lakewood, Ohio high schools. F. Beatty. il Am Educ 13:23-6 Ja '77
No-fault society. T. Griffith. Atlantic 239:26+ My '77
Violinist Isaac Stern on American values today: interview. I. Stern il pors U.S. News 82:47 F 14 '77
What values are most important? D. J. Skeel. il Todays Educ 66:62-4 Ja '77
Who is shaping America's values? Chr Today 21:37 F 4 '77

SOCIAL welfare. See Public welfare

SOCIAL work
See also
Social agencies
United Way of America (organization)

SOCIAL work, Psychiatric. See Psychiatric social work

SOCIAL work with delinquents and criminals
When college students offer help to convicts; Vanderbilt Prison Project. il U.S. News 82:49 Ja 31 '77

SOCIAL workers
Acquiescence of social work; excerpt from Radical social work. R. A. Cloward and F. F. Piven. Society 14:55-63 Ja '77
Paraprofessionals, poverty, and politics; interview, ed by I. L. Horowitz. F. Riessman. Society 14:72-8 Ja '77

SOCIALISM
Greening of Karl Marx. R. Stromberg. Nat R 29:991+ S 2 '77
New philosophers; criticism of Marxism by French philosophers. il Time 110:29-30 S 12 '77
New Philosophes. M. S. Ross. Nat R 29:1361-2+ N 25 '77
Socialism and sin; capitalism vs socialism. B. Douglass; discussion. Chr Cent 94-171-4, 567-9 F 23, Je 8 '77
Taking on Marx; criticism by French philosophers. K. L. Woodward and J. Friedman. il por Newsweek 90:68 Ag 22 '77
See also
Collective settlements
Communism
Utopias

British Columbia

See Socialism—Canada

Canada

Socialist tides in Canada; British Columbia. G. Woodcock. Progressive 41:25-8 Jl '77

Cuba

Is it the future? Will it work? with the Venceremos in Cuba. H. Maurer. il por Nation 225:6-10 Jl 2 '77

Europe, Western

Europe: the collapse of the social democrats. S. Haseler. Commentary 64:42-6 D '77
Eurosocialism? M. Ledeen. New Repub 177:25 O 8 '77

France

Le nouveau regime. A. Berger. New Repub 176:18-20 Je 18 '77

Germany, East

Behind the Berlin wall: socialism with a German face. J. Steele. Nation 225:397-400 O 22 '77

Israel

Israel's other war. M. Friedman. Newsweek 90:57 Ag 22 '77

Sweden

Sweden's swing to the right overstated. M. Harrington. Current 190:18-20 F '77

United States

Let's start talking about socialism. J. Buell and T. De Luca. Progressive 41:24-7 Mr '77
Marxism and the Hispanic movement of the United States. A. M. Stevens-Arroyo. il New Cath World 220:126-8+ My '77
Marxism in America. M. Harrington. il New Cath World 220:118-21 My '77
Modern black movement and Marxism. M. S. Copeland. bibl il New Cath World 220:134-9 My '77
Summer fun with Karl and Fred; the Union of Marxist Social Scientists and the League for Proletarian Socialism. S. Poss. Progressive 41:43-5 O '77
What Henry heard; excerpts from address, February 1977. New Repub 176:20-1 Mr 26 '77
Why do we do this to ourselves? Sat Eve Post 249:36-7+ N '77
See also
Democratic Socialist Organizing Committee

SOCIALISM and religion
Christian-Marxist dialogue in America; symposium at Rosemont College. L. Swidler. Commonweal 104:138-9 Mr 4 '77

SOCIALISM and religion—*Continued*
Christian/Marxist dialogue; symposium; with editorial comment. il New Cath World 220:106-28+ My '77
Down the Marxist road with Harvey Cox; excerpt from On synthesizing Marxism and Christianity. D. Vree. Chr Today 21:12-14 Ag 26 '77
French Catholicism faces the left. P. McCarthy. America 137:350-3 N 19 '77
SOCIALIST International (organization)
Old comrades meet. M. Harrington. Harpers 254:26-8 F '77
SOCIALIST Workers Party (United States)
Disclosure and harassment; suit before the Federal Election Commission. Nation 224:516-17 Ap 30 '77
SOCIALLY handicapped children

Education

Jesse Jackson speaks out; interview, ed by M. S. Clayton. J. Jackson. il Todays Educ 66:42-6 Ja '77
Kid from class 4-4; S. Sheppard. J. Lelyveld. N Y Times Mag p 127 Ap 24 '77
Why the GLUB went mobile; Groton-Lowell Upward Bound Program, Mass. J. Helyar. il Am Educ 13:22-6 Ag '77
See also
Blacks—Education
Mexican Americans—Education
SOCIETA Generale Immobiliare (firm) See Construction industry—Italy
SOCIETIES
See also
Aged—Clubs and societies
Art clubs and societies
Associations, institutions, etc.
Forestry societies
Literary clubs and societies
Musical societies
Peace societies
Religious societies
Scientific societies
Secret societies
SOCIETIES, Insect. See Insect societies
SOCIETY. See subhead Social life and customs under names of countries, states, cities, etc. e.g. China—Social life and customs
SOCIETY, Primitive
See also
Cannibalism
Hunters and gatherers
Indians of South America—Culture
SOCIETY and architecture. See Architecture—Social aspects
SOCIETY and art. See Art and society
SOCIETY and law. See Sociological jurisprudence
SOCIETY and literature. See Literature and society
SOCIETY and religion. See Religion and sociology
SOCIETY and the individual. See Individual and society
SOCIETY for Neuroscience
Biology; summaries of papers. J. A. Miller. Sci N 112:344 N 19 '77
SOCIETY for Photographic Education
Photo educators bite the Big Apple—and find it's red! Mod Phot 41:61-2 Jl '77
SOCIETY Islands
See also
Tahiti
SOCIETY of Friends. See Friends, Society of
SOCIETY of Indepedent Gasoline Marketers of America
Collusion at the gas pump: independents they are not. D. Zielenziger. Nation 224:551-4 My 7 '77
Wages of hoodwinking: little oil's slippery slope. D. Zielenziger. Nation 225:434-6 O 29 '77
SOCIETY of Jesus. See Jesuits
SOCIETY of North American Goldsmiths. See Goldsmiths
SOCIOBIOLOGY. See Biology—Social aspects
SOCIOLINGUISTICS
Sacred trust. J. Simon. Esquire 88:44-5+ S '77
SOCIOLOGICAL jurisprudence
Putting a price on death; compensation awarded by legal systems of various countries. S. Phillips and M. Moller. il pors Psychol Today 10:70-2+ My '77
Treating people as equals; views of R. Dworkin. D. Beckwith. il por Time 110:54 S 5 '77
We've got too much law! J. K. Footlick. Read Digest 110:96-100 My '77
SOCIOLOGY
See also
Assimilation (sociology)
Economics
Equality
Family
Groups (sociology)
Human ecology
Human relations
Knowledge, Sociology of
Regionalism
Sociolinguistics

SOCIOLOGY, Christian
See also
Liberation theology
SOCIOLOGY, Jewish
See also
Jewish way of life
SOCIOLOGY, Religious. See Religion and sociology
SOCIOLOGY, Rural
New rural America; symposium; ed by F. Clemente. bibl f il Ann Am Acad 429:1-144 Ja '77
See also
Community development
Rural planning
SOCIOLOGY, Urban
Cities and political will. M. Tree. Current 190:9-10 F '77
New rural America; symposium; ed by F. Clemente. bibl f il Ann Am Acad 429:1-144 Ja '77
See also
Cities and towns
Urban renewal
SOCKETS, Automotive test. See Testing instruments
SOCRATES
Man for all reasons. P. W. Schmidtchen. il Hobbies 82:134-7+ D '77 *

Anecdotes, facetiae, satire, etc.

Under the agnus castus tree, by the banks of the old Ilissus. R. M. Strozier. il Atlantic 239:86-7 Je '77
SOD houses
Shelters on the plains. R. Welsch. il Natur Hist 86:48-53 bibl(p94) My '77
SODERLAND, Carl. See Pious, D. jt auth
SODERSTROM, Neil
Frame-and-bag backpacks. il Consumers Res Mag 60:7-12 Jl '77
Tents for family camping. il Consumers Res Mag 60:7-13 Ag '77
SODIUM
See also
Soils—Sodium content
SODIUM chloride. See Salt
SODIUM in the body
Cell membrane sodium pump as a mechanism for increasing thermogenesis during cold acclimation in rats. D. L. Guernsey and E. D. Stevens. bibl il Science 196:908-10 My 20 '77
SODIUM nitrite
Can bacon cause cancer? R. Wennblom. Farm J 101:Hog 7+ Ag '77
Household worries; sodium nitrite as meat preservative and diaminoanisole sulfate as hair dye component. P. Gwynne and J. B. Copeland. il Newsweek 90:109 O 31 '77
SODIUM vapor street lighting. See Street lighting
SOFAS
Easy-to-make modern sofa. il Mech Illus 73:64-5 Ag '77
SOFAS, Convertible. See Furniture, Convertible
SOFT contact lenses. See Contact lenses
SOFT drink industry
Graying of the soft-drink industry. in Bus W p68-72 My 23 '77
Shasta's difficult sales goal. il Bus W p 125 D 5 '77
See also
Coca-Cola Company
Royal Crown Cola Company

Acquisitions and mergers

Hard trading in soft drinks. il Forbes 120:35-6 D 15 '77
Thirst to acquire the soft-drink bottlers. Bus W p39-40 O 24 '77

Canada

Canada's diet sodas lose their saccharin. Bus W p46 O 17 '77
SOFTBALL
It's easy come, easy go; American Professional Slo-pitch League. il Sports Illus 46:66+ Je 13 '77
SOFTENING agents
Detergents, bleaches, softeners—when to use what. il Changing T 31:29-30 My '77
Guide to laundry aids; bleaches and fabric softeners. il Good H 184:216+ My '77
SOFTENING of water. See Water softening
SOFTWARE (computers) See Computer programming
SOGLIN, Paul
How Madison's radical mayor has mellowed with age. T. Schultz. il pors N Y Times Mag p49+ Ap 17 '77 *
SOHIO. See Standard Oil Company (Ohio)
SOHN, Joel J.
Socially induced inhibition of genetically determined maturation in the platyfish, xiphophorus maculatus. bibl il Science 195:199-201 Ja 14 '77
SOHO. See New York (city)—Soho
SOIL, Lunar. See Lunar materials

SOIL acidity
The why of liming soils. W. L. Carpenter. il Org Gard & Farm 24:143-4 Mr '77
See also
Lime
SOIL compaction. See Soil stabilization
SOIL conditioners
See also
Crop residues
SOIL conservation
No water or soil leaves these farms. C. E. Sommers. il Suc Farm 75:C40 D '77
Soil and oil. C. H. M. Van Bavel. Science 197: 213 Jl 15 '77
See also
Contour farming
Terraces (agriculture)
SOIL erosion. See Erosion
SOIL erosion prevention. See Erosion prevention and control
SOIL fauna
See also
Earthworms
SOIL fertility
Soil fertility in the orchard. H. Lisle. il Org Gard & Farm 24:93-5 Je '77
SOIL inoculation
See also
Seed inoculation
SOIL moisture
Will drouth ease in 1977? D. Seim. il Farm J 101:17+ F '77
SOIL percolation
Direct evidence of particle migration in the soil solution of a podzol. F. C. Ugolini and others. bibl il Science 198:603-5 N 11 '77
SOIL stabilization
Soil compaction: getting worse, but why? B. Coffman. il Farm J 101:24-6 D '77
SOILS
See also
Clay
Erosion

Calcium content

Promesol 30: a liquid way to lime fields? B. Gergen. il Suc Farm 75:K12 Ap '77

Composition

See also
Soils, Salts in

Mineral content

Calcium oxalate: occurrence in soils and effect on nutrient and geochemical cycles. W. C. Graustein and others. bibl il Science 198:1252-4 D 23 '77

Moisture

See Soil moisture

Phosphorous content

Apply manure on phosphate basis. Suc Farm 75:36 Ag '77
Detection and examination of anthrosols by phosphate analysis. R. C. Eidt. bibl il Science 197:1327-33 S 30 '77

Sodium content

Antidote for gray water; removing sodium from the soil. Sunset 158:219 Je '77
SOILS, Hardpan
Crippled acres become productive; fragipan soils. Farm J 101:D2 Ag '77
SOILS, Liming of. See Lime
SOILS, Podzol
Direct evidence of particle migration in the soil solution of a podzol. F. C. Ugolini and others. bibl il Science 198:603-5 N 11 '77
SOILS, Potting
Greenhouse; adding aggregates to potting soil. J. Kilborn. Horticulture 55:50-1 N '77
SOILS, Salts in
Salt of the earth. R. Rodale. il Org Gard & Farm 24:52-5 Je '77
SOILS, Sandy
Growing crops on sand dunes? L. Wood. il Sea Front 23:228-32 Jl '77
SOKAL, Yasmine
Real Yasmine. E. Nemy. il pors N Y Times Mag p80+ Ap 3 '77 *
SOKOL, Dan, and others
Using existing house wiring for computer remote control. il Pop Electr 12:60-5 D '77; 13: 60-2 Ja '78
SOKOLOV, Raymond A.
Cabbage fit for kings. il Sat Eve Post 249:100+ My '77
Joe Baum's food machine. il por N Y Times Mag p64-5+ Mr 6 '77
Maltese fruit. Atlantic 240:32+ O '77
Matter of taste. See issues of Natural history
Thinner with Skinner: a food critic's strategy for belly modification. il Psychol Today 11:98+ Je '77
Who needs a kitchen really? il Am Home 80:9 F '77
SOLANUM nigrum. See Garden huckleberries
SOLAR activity
Our sun's future. J. Mullaney. il Sci Digest 82:30-2 N '77
Solar activity increases. il Sky & Tel 54:339-41 O '77
See also
Solar flares
Sunspots
SOLAR air conditioning equipment. See Air conditioning equipment
SOLAR batteries
Amorphous-silicon doping brightens solar-cell picture. H. R. Leuchtag. il Phys Today 30:17-19 Ja '77
Dyes boost efficiency of solar concentrator. Sci N 112:313-14 N 12 '77
New promise of cheap solar energy; Energy Conversion Devices, Inc. por Bus W p20-1 Jl 18 '77
Photovoltaics: the semiconductor revolution comes to solar. A. L. Hammond. il Science 197:445-7 Jl 29 '77
Power your projects with solar energy! B. Green. il Pop Electr 12:41-7 D '77
Solar battery for passive heating. E. Moran. il Pop Sci 210:94+ Je '77
Solar cells find their niche in everyday life on earth. D. Morris. il Smithsonian 8:38-45 O '77
Stable semiconductor liquid junction cell with 9 percent solar-to-electrical conversion efficiency. K. C. Chang and others. bibl il Science 196:1097-9 Je 3 '77
Sun power for boats. L. Anders. il Mech Illus 73:114+ F '77
Turned on by the sun. M. Schultz. il Pop Mech 147:112-14+ F '77
SOLAR cells. See Solar batteries
SOLAR collectors
Adventures in alternate energy: Bill Rankins and Davis Wilson: solar window. E. Moran. il Pop Sci 210:24+ Mr '77
Concentrating solar collectors you can build. W. E. Miller, Jr. il Pop Sci 211:95 S '77
Do-it-yourselfers give solar energy a sharp boost. il U.S. News 83:96-7 O 17 '77
Historical solar energy devices. E. Shrum. il Hobbies 82:118-20 Ag '77
John Des Chenes; corrugated-plate window collector. E. Moran. il Pop Sci 212:24+ Ja '78
Low-cost solar collector. C. A. Miller. il pors Mech Illus 73:58+ D '77
Make your own solar collector! H. Kolbe. il Mech Illus 73:43-5 Mr '77
Solar collector for 85¢ a sq. ft. R. L. Stepler. il Pop Sci 211:51 S '77
SOLAR constant. See Solar radiation
SOLAR cooling/heating systems. See Air conditioning equipment
SOLAR drying apparatus. See Drying apparatus
SOLAR drying of crops. See Corn—Drying; Hay—Drying
SOLAR eclipses. See Eclipses, Solar
SOLAR energy
California's fight for the sun; attempt by gas industry to control solar energy. F. Branfman. Nation 224:749-51 Je 18 '77
Community solar and wind energy system. K. H. Hohenemser. Environment 19:3-4 Mr '77
Daylighting design aids emerge as interest grows in the technique. il Archit Rec 161:152 Ja '77
Desert proving ground for solar energy. il U.S. News 83:99 N 14 '77
Energy solution: solar or so long. G. Reiger. Field & S 82:10+ D '77
Energy: the sun and economics. A. H. Larson. il por Chemistry 50:12-13 Ap '77
For a new energy policy; toward using solar energy. B. Commoner. Current 191:17-22 Mr '77
Groups that can help you start using solar energy. Pop Mech 148:146 S '77
Growing rush to solar energy. il U.S. News 82: 69-71 Ap 4 '77
Here comes the sun. A. J. Mayer and others. il Newsweek 89:94-5 My 16 '77
International partnership for solar power. A. L. Hammond. Science 197:623 Ag 12 '77
Israel moves toward a new solar society. il Intellect 106:5-6 Jl '77
Let the sun shine in. J. Berger. Progressive 41: 43-6 F '77
Notes from the field: how architects, and their consultants, approach solar design. M. F. Gaskie. il Archit Rec 162:108-13 mid-Ag '77
Ocean thermal gradients—a practical source of energy? J. O. Henrie; E. J. Beck. bibl Science 195:206-7 Ja 14 '77
PM's guide to solar-energy systems. V. D. Chase. il Pop Mech 147:80-3+ Ap '77
Scientists urge President: stop reliance on coal and nuclear fuel; Go for development of uniform solar power. J. E. Persico. Sci Digest 82: 8-9+ O '77
Solar energy and electric utilities: should they be interfaced? J. G. Asbury and R. O. Mueller. bibl il Science 195:445-50 F 4 '77
Solar energy news notes. A. Salsberg. Pop Electr 12:4 Jl '77
Solar energy on trial in home and factory. il U.S. News 83:82 D 26 '77

SOLAR energy—*Continued*
Solar energy research: making solar after the nuclear model? A. L. Hammond and W. D. Metz. Science 197:241-4 Jl 15 '77
Solar energy: some hopes and some concerns. W. F. Wagner, Jr. Archit Rec 161:13 Je '77
Solar power plants: dark horse in the energy stable. R. S. Caputo. bibl il Bull Atom Sci 33:46-8+ My '77
Solar projects get local backing. il Am City & County 92:24 S '77
Solar thermal electricity: power tower dominates research. W. D. Metz. il Science 197:353-6 Jl 22 '77
Solar thermal energy: bringing the pieces together. W. D. Metz. Science 197:650-1 Ag 12 '77
Sunshine of your life. R. W. Moss. il Sci Digest 82:10-18+ O '77
Tinkering with sunshine: the prospects for solar energy. T. Kidder. il Atlantic 240:70-83 O '77
Toward a solar civilization. F. Von Hippel and R. H. Williams. bibl il Bull Atom Sci 33:12-15 O '77
Unconventional energy sources: Brazil looks for applications. A. L. Hammond. Science 195: 862-3 Mr 4 '77
Utilities offer site for nation's first solar power plant: Mojave Desert. il Intellect 106:98-9 S '77
When, not if, is now key to solar power. C. P. Gilmore. Sci Digest 81:42-5 Mr '77
See also
Artificial satellites—Solar energy use
Heliostats
United States—Energy Research and Development Administration—Ocean Thermal Energy Conversion Program

Bibliography

Guide to solar info. L. Gutowski. il Mech Illus 73:126-7 N '77
Reading up on energy. House & Gard 149:94 S '77

Laws and legislation

States expand tax incentives for solar energy users. il Ret Liv 17:49 D '77

SOLAR energy industry
Do-it-yourselfers give solar energy a sharp boost. il U.S. News 83:96-7 O 17 '77
Industry hides from the sun. H. Wasserman. il Nation 224:263-6 Mr 5 '77
New promise of cheap solar energy; Energy Conversion Devices, Inc. por Bus W p20-1 Jl 18 '77
Shadow on the sun. il Forbes 120:71-2 O 15 '77
Solar heat lights up a new industry. il Bus W p 142+ My 16 '77
Solar-power for California's desert. Bus W p23 Ja 24 '77

France

Selling sunshine to Saudis. por Forbes 120:110 D 1 '77

SOLAR Energy Research Institute
New Institute to make solar energy happen. Sci Digest 82:12-13 O '77
Solar Energy Research Institute: grumbles about a change in plans. P. M. Boffey. Science 196: 278-80 Ap 15 '77

SOLAR farm buildings. See Farm buildings—Heating and ventilation

SOLAR flares
Solar flares: link to thunderstorms. Sci N 111: 389 Je 18 '77
Solar proton event: influence on stratospheric ozone. D. F. Heath and others. bibl il Science 197:886-9 Ag 26 '77

SOLAR greenhouses. See Greenhouses

SOLAR halos. See Halos (meteorology)

SOLAR heat pumps. See Heat pumps

SOLAR heating
Add an energy-efficient room at the top. A. M. Watkins. il Pop Sci 210:140+ Mr '77
Dennis L. Vories: all-seasons solar heater. E. Moran. il Pop Sci 211:52-3+ Ag '77
Don't rush to solar heat. Changing T 31:8 Ag '77
Government money fuels solar heating. Bus W p29-30 My 23 '77
Growing rush to solar energy. il U.S. News 82: 69-71 Ap 4 '77
Our school-made solar project; Central Senior High School, Seat Pleasant, Md. J. Silver and K. Johnson. il pors Todays Educ 66:62-4 S '77
Our solar green-home; excerpt from The solar greenhouse book. D. Kruschke and K. Funk. il Org Gard & Farm 24:54-7 D '77
Owners tell all about life in solar-heated homes. V. D. Chase. il Pop Mech 148:84-7+ O '77
PM's guide to solar-energy systems. V. D. Chase. il Pop Mech 147:80-3+ Ap '77
PS update: the newest solar-heating equipment. R. Stepler. bibl il Pop Sci 211:85-9 Ag '77
Should you put your money on the sun? installing a heating system. P. Gross. House & Gard 149:44+ S '77
Solar energy and you. S. Oddo. il House & Gard 149:76-7 Ag '77
Solar heating—no longer a novelty. C. R. Meyer. il Ret Liv 17:26-8 O '77
Solar ponds—heat from a hole in the ground. E. Nelson. il Pop Sci 211:80-1 D '77
Solar power at home. il Sci Digest 82:18-19 O '77
Solar system for low-cost homes. il Farm J 101:22 Je '77
Two cities get jump on solar energy. il Am City & County 92:30 Ap '77
See also
Solar collectors
Solar houses

Control

Build a solar controller. J. M. Cogswell. il Pop Electr 12:69-70 Jl '77

SOLAR heating/cooling systems. See Air conditioning equipment

SOLAR heating industry. See Solar energy industry

SOLAR houses
Building a solar house. Sci Digest 81:44-5 Mr '77
Does solar heating really work? What owners say. il U.S. News 82:70-1 Ap 4 '77
Energy house uses native materials. E. Moran. il Pop Sci 211:44+ Jl '77
Hawaii's Energy House. il Sunset 158:142 Ap '77
How practical is solar heating? house designed by H. Wenning. il McCalls 105:168-73+ O '77
Solar heating—no longer a novelty. D. Rienke. Ret Liv 17:28-9+ O '77
Solar home in the Northland; Stevensville, Mich. J. Mueller. il Mech Illus 74:36-7+ Ja '78
Solar with style; house designed by Antoine Predock in New Mexico. il House & Gard 149: 130-3 S '77
Sun trap. A. Lees. il Pop Sci 211:118-19 N '77
Tall pipes of water heat and cool award-winning house; solar houses in California. il Sunset 159:112-15 N '77
Tomorrow's house? Sea Ranch, Calif. il Sunset 158:132-4 Ap '77
Two-story greenhouse is three-way heater for this Santa Fe adobe. il Sunset 158:146+ My '77
What size solar heating system is economical for a house? excerpt from Designing and building a solar house. D. Watson and F. N. Broberg. il Archit Rec 161:131-4 Mr '77
Will a solar home save you money? R. Frutkin. Sci Digest 82:70-1 N '77
World's most advanced solar home. P. Britton. il Pop Sci 211:92-6+ Jl '77

SOLAR irrigation. See Irrigation

SOLAR magnetic field. See Sun—Magnetic properties

SOLAR pool heaters. See Water heaters

SOLAR power. See Solar energy

SOLAR power plants. See Solar energy

SOLAR powered refrigerators. See Refrigerators

SOLAR prominences. See Sun—Prominences

SOLAR radiation
Implications of solar evolution for the earth's early atmosphere. M. J. Newman and R. T. Rood. bibl il Science 198:1035-7 D 9 '77
Sunny days on other worlds. J. Eberhart. il Sci N 111:380-2 Je 11 '77
See also
Burning mirrors
Solar heating
Solar wind
Sunspots
Ultraviolet rays

SOLAR swine houses. See Swine houses—Heating and ventilation

SOLAR system
Cratering in the solar system. W. K. Hartmann. il Sci Am 236:84-6+ bibl(p 132) Ja '77
New evidence supports supernova origin of solar system. G. M. Spruch. il Phys Today 30:17-19 My '77
Orbit established for Object Kowal. Sci N 112: 388-9 D 10 '77
Planetoid between Saturn and Uranus. il Sci N 112:311 N 12 '77
Puzzle in the sky; Object-Kowal. map Newsweek 90:141 N 21 '77
Sky centaur; Object-Kowal. il Time 111:60 Ja 9 '78
Tenth planet? C. Kowal's finding. Time 110:98 N 21 '77
Traumatic birth; formation of the solar system triggered by the concussion of a supernova. Sci Am 238:66+ Ja '78
Velikovsky; Worlds in collision. J. S. Trefil. por Sci Digest 82:75-7 S '77
See also
Planets

SOLAR wind
Waves in the solar wind. J. T. Gosling and A. J. Hundhausen. il Sci Am 236:36-43 bibl(p 150) Mr '77

SOLBERG, Clinton E. See Blum, R. C. jt auth

SOLBERG, Gordon
Peanuts are my favorite crop. il Org Gard & Farm 24:74-6 Mr '77

SOLDER and soldering
Basic and new soldering techniques. J. T. Frye. il Pop Electr 11:106-8 Je '77
Tricks of soldering/desoldering. F. Belt. il Radio-Electr 49:40-2+ Ja '78
SOLDERING apparatus
WAHL models 7700 and 7800 cordless soldering irons. il Pop Electr 12:86-7 Jl '77
SOLDIERS; opera. See Zimmermann, B. A.
SOLEDAD Prison. See Prisons—California
SOLES (fish)
See also
Cookery—Fish
SOLHEIM, Karsten B.
It all began with a garage sale. il por Sports Illus 47:67-8 S 12 '77 *
SOLICITOR General (United States) See United States—Justice, Department of
SOLID propellant boosters. See Space vehicles—Propulsion systems
SOLID state devices. See Semiconductors
SOLID wastes. See Refuse and refuse disposal
SOLIDS

Diffusion

See Diffusion

Fracture

See Fracture of solids

SOLIE, John E.
Aria structure and ritornello form in the music of Albinoni. bibl f il Mus Q 63:31-47 Ja '77
SOLIS-COHEN, Lita H.
Art in wrought from: the collection of James C. Sorber, West Chester, Pennsylvania. il Antiques 111:782-93 Ap '77
SOLITUDE
I love me—and why not. B. Sabol. il Mademoiselle 83:147-8+ F '77
See also
Loneliness

Anecdotes, facetiae, satire, etc.

Personal: alone is best. Vogue 167:183-4+ N '77
SOLKOFF, Joel
Paying farmers not to work. New Repub 177:19-21 S 17 '77
Strictly from hunger. New Repub 176:13-15 Je 11 '77
SOLLER, Patricia S.
Simple secrets of cooking fish. Redbook 149:116 Ag '77
SOLLID, Lynnette
Best present of all; dramatization of story by O. Houck. Plays 36:37-43 My '77
SOLOMON, Andy
On his kindness; poem. Atlantic 240:112 D '77
SOLOMON, Anthony
Protecting steel. New Repub 177:8-9 D 17 '77 *
SOLOMON, Bennie. See Goodman, M. jt auth
SOLOMON, Bill
Peculiar freedom. Nation 225:580 D 3 '77
SOLOMON, Bruce
Guess who's for the ERA? ed by E. Wheeler. pors Ms 5:78-9 Ap '77
SOLOMON, Jack
Art market: what is its future? pors Am Artist 41:12-13 Ap '77
SOLOMON, Jay
Art will be considered just as important as the bricks. J. A. Lewis. il por Art N 76:56-8 D '77 *
GSA head Jay Solomon sees his background in real estate development as good job experience for his new post. W. Hickman. Archit Rec 162:35 S '77 *
Some positive thinking from the General Services Administration. W. F. Wagner, Jr. Archit Rec 162:13 D '77 *
SOLOMON, Jolane, and others
Effect of delta-9-tetrahydrocannabinol on uterine and vaginal cytology of ovariectomized rats. bibl il Science 195:875-7 Mr 4 '77
Uterotrophic effect of delta-9-tetrahydrocannabinol in ovariectomized rats. bibl il Science 192:559-61; 195:905-6 My 7 '76, Mr 4 '77
SOLOMON, Leslie
Computer bits. il Pop Electr 11:109-11 Je; 12:88-9 Ag; 97-100 O; 118-21+ D '77
How to handle MOS devices without destroying them. il Pop Electr 12:67-70 Ag '77
SOLOMON, Neil
Dr Neil Solomon's calorie-free diet. Harp Baz 110:130-1+ F '77
NRG diet. il Good H 184:80+ My '77
Stay-warm diet. il Ladies Home J 94:100+ O '77
—and Dolinsky, Marsha
Dr. Solomon's healthy dollars-a-day diet. Harp Baz 110:131+ Mr '77

about

Dr Neil Solomon's youth diet: be beautiful forever. P. Lehmann. Harp Baz 110:137+ O '77 *
Eat and grow beautiful. M. Weber. il Ladies Home J 94:74+ My '77 *
SOLOMON, Phoebe
Woman; poem. Good H 185:204 S '77
SOLOMON, Richard H.
Thinking through the China problem. bibl f For Affairs 56:324-56 Ja '78
SOLOMON, Stephen D. and Randall, W. S.
Environmental balance sheet; excerpt from Building 6: the tragedy of Bridesburg. Nation 225:431-4 O 29 '77
SOLOMON R. Guggenheim Museum, New York
Guggenheim Museum. A. Goldin. il Art in Am 65:99-102 S '77
SOLOMON Islands
Ordeal at Vella Lavella; survivors of sunken U.S.S. Helena; excerpts from Lonely vigil. W. Lord. il map Am Heritage 28:30-43 Je '77
See also
United Nations—Solomon Islands
SOLOW, Robert M.
Requiem for a rebate. New Repub 176:11-13 My 7 '77
SOLTI, Sir Georg
Musical events. A. Porter. New Yorker 53:88+ My 30 '77 *
SOLUTION (chemistry)
Hyperosmolality in intraluminal fluids from hamster testis and epididymis: a micropuncture study. A. L. Johnson and S. D. Howards. bibl il Science 195:492-3 F 4 '77
See also
Electrolysis
SOLVENTS
Insecticide solvents: interference with insecticidal action. L. B. Brattsten and C. F. Wilkinson. bibl il Science 196:1211-13 Je 10 '77
SOLZHENITSYN, Aleksandr Isaevich
Struggle for freedom; excerpts from address. por Intellect 105:302-3 Mr '77

about

Solzhenitsyn plans a publishing firm in Vermont. E. Slater. il por Pub W 211:38 F 7 '77 *
SOLZHENITSYNA, Natalya
Fate of families. il por Time 109:30 F 21 '77
SOMALIA
See also
Guerrillas—Somalia
Military assistance, American—Somalia
Military assistance, Russian—Somalia

Foreign relations

Trouble on the Horn. A. De Borchgrave. il map Newsweek 89:45 Je 27 '77

Ethiopia

See Ethiopia—Foreign relations—Somalia

Russia

See Russia—Foreign relations—Somalia
SOMALILAND, French. See Afars and the Issas, French Territory of
SOMATOLOGY
See also
Anthropometry
SOMATOSTATIN. See Hypothalamic hormones
SOMER, Hilde
Ginastera: Piano concerto no. 2, op. 37; Quintet for piano and strings. G. S. Fox. Am Rec G 40:25-6 Je '77 *
SOMERVELL, Brehon Burke
First and forgotten pipeline. P. L. Fradkin. il pors map Audubon 79:58-79 N '77 *
SOMERVILLE, Hugh
America's Cup news. Yachting 141:190-1 Mr '77
British take the Admiral's Cup. il Yachting 142:52 O '77
SOMLYÓ, György
Tale of the double helix; Fairy tale of the cosmos; poems, tr by D. Hoffman. New Repub 176:30 Mr 26 '77
SOMMER, Nolan Ben
Challenges facing the multinational corporation; address, September 21, 1977. Vital Speeches 44:85-8 N 15 '77
SOMMER, Richard G.
(comp) Guide to scientific instruments, 1977. il Science 197:9-169 S 20 '77
SOMMERFELD, Linda L.
Social studies education with a purpose. Clearing H 50:371-2 Ap '77
SOMMERLAD, E. Lloyd
Unesco's first teleconference by satellite il UNESCO Courier 30:32-3 Ap '77
SOMMERS, Charles E.
Crop management. See issues of Successful farming
SOMMERS, Sam
Honor isn't hollow. S. Moses. por Sports Illus 47:100+ N 14 '77 *
SOMMERSTAD, C. R. See Hopp, M. A. jt auth
SOMOZA DEBAYLE, Anastasio
Nicaragua, a wholly owned subsidiary. S. Kinzer. New Repub 176:14-17 Ap 9 '77 *
Our S.O.B.s; with editorial comment. P. Lernoux. il map Nation 225:68-9, 72-7 Jl 23 '77 *
Perils of quiet diplomacy. A. Riding. il Sat R 5:18-20+ N 12 '77 *
Somoza's reign of terror. por Time 109:29-30 Mr 14 '77 *

SON of Sam. See Berkowitz, D.
SONATA and sonatas
See also
Phonograph records—Sonatas
SONDAY, Milton
Repeat. il Craft Horiz 37:52-4 Ag '77
SONDHEIM, Stephen
Side by side by Sondheim; recording. M. Galewski. Am Rec G 40:52-4 F '77 *
SONGS
See also
Christmas carols
Christmas music
Music, Popular (songs, etc)
National songs
Phonograph records—Songs
Rock music (songs, etc)
SONGS, American
Indian songs on Edison cylinders. J. Walsh. il Hobbies 82:35-6+ Ap; 35-7+ My; 35-6+ Je '77
See also
Folk songs, American
SONGS, Christmas. See Christmas carols; Christmas music
SONGS, French
Formidable achievement; G. Fauré's songs. P. L. Miller. Am Rec G. 40:5-9 Je '77
SONGS, German
Rheinlieder critics: a case of musical nationalism; 1840-1850. C. H. Porter. bibl f il Mus Q 63:74-98 Ja '77
SONGS, National. See National songs
SONGS of birds. See Birds—Song
SONGWRITERS' Hall of Fame. See Halls of Fame
SONIC boom
Concorde sonic booms as an atmospheric probe. N. K. Balachanadran and others. bibl il map Science 197:47-9 Jl 1 '77
SONNENBERG, Benjamin
Visionary and a master stylist helped shape modern PR. pors Duns R 110:29-30 S '77 *
SONNENBERG, Günter
Old lady and the terrorists. il Time 109:46 My 16 '77 *
SONNENBLICK-Goldman Corporation. See Mortgage banks
SONNENFELDT, Helmut
Russia, America and détente. For Affairs 56: 275-94 Ja '78
SONNICHSEN, C. L.
West that wasn't. il Am West 14:8-15 N '77
SONOMA County, Calif.
November is a good month to sample the four Valley of the Moon parks. il map Sunset 159: 42-3 N '77
Sonoma County nurseryman, farmers, craftsmen have Christmas offerings .il map Sunset 159:44 D '77
SONOMA Vineyards (firm) See Wine industry
SONORAN Desert
Saguaro—symbol of the desert. L. Line. il Field & S 82:48 Ag '77
SONS and fathers. See Parent-child relationship
SONS and mothers. See Parent-child relationship
SONSTEGARD, David A. and others
Surgical replacement of the human knee joint; with biographical sketches. il Sci Am 238:12, 44-51 bibl(p 138) Ja '78
SONTAG, Susan
Unguided tour; story. New Yorker 53:40-5 O 31 '77
SONY Corporation
$1,300 Christmas toy made in Japan; competition between Sony and Matsushita; videotape recorders. P. J. Schuyten. il Fortune 96:179-80+ S '77
Right to replay? suit against Betamax. il Time 109:64 Ap 11 '77
Technology versus tariffs; home video recorder. il Forbes 119:27-8 Ap 15 '77
SOOCHOW, China. See Wuhsien, China
SOPER, Cherrie L. and Blanch de Alcolea, Montserrat
Extremadura: cradle of conquistadors. il Américas 29:34-40 O '77
SOPHISTICATION
To one-up with honors, one must be unimpressed in the right way. B. B. Pinson. House B 119: 76 O '77
SOPWITH, Sir Thomas Octave Murdoch
Sopwith. R. B. Parke. por Flying 101:274 S '77 *
SORCERER'S apprentice finds a helping hand; drama. See Cheatham, V. R.
SORCERY. See Witchcraft
SØRENSEN, Bent
No neutron bombs for us, please. Bull Atom Sci 33:7 D '77
SORENSEN, Theodore Chaikin
CIA gauntlet. Nation 224:98 Ja 29 '77 *
Carter takes his lumps. il por Time 109:20+ Ja 31 '77 *
First defeat. D. M. Alpern and others. por Newsweek 89:30-1 Ja 31 '77 *
Sorensen caper. Nat R 29:134 F 4 '77 *
SORENSON, E. Richard
Growing up as a Fore is to be in touch and free. il Smithsonian 8:106-10+ My '77
SORENSON, Lewis
American doll artist. J. Chiara. il Hobbies 82: 38-9 N '77 *
SORGHUM
Growth regulator controls Johnson grass in soybeans; mefluidide. Farm J 101:M4 N '77
He double-crops sorghum, soybeans (irrigated) on sandy ground. il Suc Farm 75:no4 42 Mr '77
Sweet success with sweet sorghum. G. Logsdon. il Org Gard & Farm 24:150-4 My '77
See also
Milo
SORIA, Dorle J.
Artist life. See issues of High fidelity and Musical America
Greek sorceress. pors Opera N 42:15-16+ N '77
SORIA, Spain
Spain—after 40 years of fear. J. M. Markham. il N Y Times Mag p 18-20+ Je 5 '77
SORKIN, Dick
Guy with the edge. P. Axthelm. il por Newsweek 90:57 O 3 '77 *
SORORITIES, College. See College sororities
SORREL
See also
Cookery—Vegetables
SORRENTINO, Constance
Sorrentino, Maldonado, Klein Award winners. M Labor R 100:2 Ap '77 *
SORRENTINO, Gilbert
Decades; story. Esquire 88:94-6 Ag '77
Land of cotton; story. Harpers 255:73-6 N '77
SORROW. See Grief
SORROW beyond dreams; drama. See Handke, P.
SOSNOFF, Martin T.
Market trends (cont) por Forbes 119:90-1 Ap 1; 120:96-7 D 15 '77
Stock trends (cont) por Forbes 120:118-20 O 1 '77
SOTHEBY Parke Bernet Group, Ltd
Auctions: a N.Y.C. wrap-up and a forward look. L. Rosenbaum. Art in Am 65:33+ S '77
Gems among your junk? Heirloom Discovery Days. B. H. Schneider. McCalls 105:110 O '77
Sotheby's and Christie's square off. L. Rosenbaum. Art in Am 65:16+ Mr '77
Sotheby's gavels off some of its stock. il Bus W p27-8 Jl 11 '77
Treasure or trash? Heirloom Discovery Day. M. Kasindorf. il Newsweek 89:10 Mr 14 '77
SOTHEBY Parke Bernet, Inc. See Sotheby Parke Bernet Group, Ltd
SOTO, Gary
Cellar; poem. Poetry 129:254-5 F '77
Harvest; poem. Nation 224:413 Ap 2 '77
Little ones; poem. New Yorker 53:114 O 31 '77
Mitla; First; Tampamachoco; Drought; Antigua; Starlings; poems. Poetry 130:149-54 Je '77
Pockets; poem. Nation 224:568 My 7 '77
SOTTOSANTI, Joe
Canoe cleanup campaign. B. Gooch. por Outdoor Life 160:30 N '77 *
SOUCIE, Gary A.
Consider the shark (cont) Audubon 79:112-14 Ja '77
Need for a boat. il Nat Parks & Con Mag 51:4-7 F '77
SOUFFLES
Foolproof: 10 minute souffle. G. Steves. il Am Home 80:69+ My '77
From Julia Child's kitchen; strawberry soufflé. J. Child. il McCalls 105:68+ Ja '78
New role for soufflé; cheese soufflé. il McCalls 104:79-80 Ag '77
Omelets and soufflés. il Bet Hom & Gard 55: 161-2 S '77
Soufflé: how to make it rise to the occasion; with recipes. J. Pepin. il House B 119:100-1 Ap '77
Variations on a miracle. C. Claiborne and P. Franey. N Y Times Mag p76 O 30 '77
SOUL, David
Starsky & Hutch; interview, ed by M. Cohen. pors Ladies Home J 94:50+ Mr '77
SOUND
See also
Acoustics, Architectural
Noise

Apparatus

Build charge! digital electronic bugle-call generator. R. W. Reese. il Pop Electr 13:45-8 Ja '78
Equalizer kit tailors your hi-fi sound. W. J. Hawkins. il Pop Sci 210:150 Je '77
Expansively speaking. R. Hodges. il Pop Electr 11:20+ Je '77
Increase dynamic range for better hi-fi. L. Feldman. il Radio-Electr 48:46-8 Ap '77
Introducing equalization. il Hi Fi 27:115-16 Je '77
Julian Hirsch audio reports:
dbx model 128 dynamic range enhancer. J. Hirsch. il Pop Electr 13:31-2 Ja '78
New equipment reports:
Crown's synergistic equalizer. il Hi Fi 27: 63-4 S '77
Dynaco SE-10: all octaves are equal; graphic equalizer. il Hi Fi 27:40-1 My '77
Shure offers a critical ear; frequency equalizer. il Hi Fi 27:42 My '77

SOUND—Apparatus—*Continued*
New way to room equalization. L. Feldman. il Radio-Electr 48:42-4 My '77
Radio-Electronics tests:
Soundcraftmen PE2217 equalizer. L. Feldman. il Radio-Electr 48:67-9 F '77
Tomorrow's hi-fi gear. L. Feldman. il Radio-Electr 48:40-2+ Mr '77
What's out in semipro consoles. J. Woram. il Hi Fi 27:148-9 N '77
See also
Amplifiers
Headphones
Loudspeakers
Microphones
Phonograph

Measurement

See Sound measurement

Recording and reproducing

Binaural/biphonic sound. L. Feldman. il Radio-Electr 48:37-9+ Mr '77
Cashing in on charisma; Record Plant. il por Forbes 119:144 Ap 15 '77
Great phase-coherency bandwagon; loudspeakers. P. Mitchell. Hi Fi 27:76-80 O '77
Halloween at the Waldorf. R. Hodges. il Pop Electr 11:17+ F '77
If you can't afford more mikes. . .try binaural. J. Woram. il Hi Fi 27:130-2 S '77
Instruments I have miked. R. Hodges. il Pop Electr 12:22+ Jl '77
Making star tracks: Record Plant, Electric Lady, Mediasound; recording studios. F. Miller. Hi Fi 27:127-30 Mr '77
Recordings and the composer. C. Wuorinen. il Sat R 4:24-5 Jl 23 '77
See also
Audio systems
Motion picture sound recording
Muzak Corporation
Phonograph records—Recording
Tape recorders and recording
Television transmission—Sound transmission

SOUND engineering. See Audio engineering

SOUND equipment. See Sound—Apparatus

SOUND measurement
In the loudspeaker testing lab. E. Torick. il Hi Fi 27:69-73 O '77
See also
Decibels

SOUND production by animals
See also
Birds—Song

SOUND production by insects. See Insect sounds

SOUND sculpture. See Sculpture

SOUND technicians. See Electronic technicians

SOUND View-Throgs Neck Community Mental Health Center, Bronx, N.Y. See Mental health centers

SOUND waves
Noisy silence: natural infrasound can warn of impending disaster. J. T. Dennett. il Sci Digest 81:27-8 My '77

SOUNDERS. See Depth indicators

SOUNDING and soundings
See also
Depth indicators

SOUNDS
See also
Fish sounds
Ocean sounds
Phonograph records—Sounds

SOUPS
Chilly soups for summer. il Bet Hom & Gard 55:128 Je '77
Cold comfort. C. Clairborne and P. Franey. il N Y Times Mag p48 Ag 7 '77
Come for Christmas soup. il Sunset 159:76-7 D '77
Hearty, beany soups and stews. il Sunset 158: 169-70 Je '77
Mint and citrus consommé. il Sunset 159:246 O '77
Seeing red; soup recipes. P. Sadowsky and G. Steves. il Am Home 80:54-5+ F '77
Soups from vegetable scraps. L. Jones. il Org Gard & Farm 24:106-8 Jl '77
Soup's on. il Bet Hom & Gard 55:122-7+ F '77
Summer soup season; Flash foods—iced soups. A. Gold and R. Fizdale. Vogue 167:70, 124-5+ Jl '77
Surprise in these soups is the custard in the bottom. Sunset 158:202 Ap '77
Vegetable garden into creamy soup; recipes. il Sunset 159:138 Ag '77

SOURDOUGH. See Dough

SOURIAN, Peter
Television (cont) Nation 224:283-5, 442-3, 603-4; 225:155-7, 381-2, 670, 732-4 Mr 5, Ap 9, My 14, Ag 20, O 15, D 17, 31, '77

SOUTH. See Southern States

SOUTH AFRICA
South Africa—a profile. map Dept State Bull 77:862-3 D 12 '77
South Africa: mirror image of the United States. B. SerVaas. il Sat Eve Post 249:62-7+ S '77
Time for a bran new diet; South African research. C. SerVaas. il Sat Eve Post 249:72-4 Mr '77
See also
Bophuthatswana
Civil rights—South Africa
Economic assistance in South Africa
Good Hope, Cape of
Government and the press—South Africa
Housing—South Africa
Industrial relations—South Africa
Investments, American—South Africa
Investments, Foreign—South Africa
Labor and laboring classes—South Africa
Migrant labor—South Africa
Morale, National—South Africa
Newspapers—South Africa
Paleontology—South Africa
Police—South Africa
Political crimes and offenses—South Africa
Political prisoners—South Africa
Prisons—South Africa
Public health—South Africa
Secret societies—South Africa
Sports—South Africa
Terrorism—South Africa
Transkei
Trials—South Africa
United Nations—South Africa
Youth—South Africa

Commerce

If the world tries to block South Africa's trade—. il U.S. News 83:38 N 7 '77
South Africa: post-diplomatic options. A. Silk. Nation 225:677 D 24 '77

United States

See United States—Commerce—South Africa

Defenses

Behind the Cape route theory: NATO flirts with South Africa. P. L. Smith. Nation 225:262-4 S 24 '77

Economic policy

See also
Budget—South Africa

Foreign relations

Israel

See Israel—Foreign relations—South Africa

Lesotho

Council agrees on Lesotho aid following South Africa's closure of border posts. il UN Chron 14:5-9+ Ja '77
Security Council missions recommend assistance for Botswana and Lesotho. UN Chron 14: 44-5 My '77

Russia

See Russia—Foreign relations—South Africa

United States

See United States—Foreign relations—South Africa

History

South Africa's lonely ordeal. W. S. Ellis. il map Nat Geog 151:780-819 Je '77

Industries

See also
De Beers Consolidated Mines, Ltd
Diamond mines and mining—South Africa

Native races

See also
South Africa—Race question
Zulus

Politics and government

Back to the laager? P. Younghusband. il Newsweek 90:45-6 O 3 '77
Pretoria's siege mentality. Nation 225:450-1 N 5 '77
Sporadic troubles and uprisings but no racial war; interview. J. Vorster. il por U.S. News 83:39-40 N 21 '77
Time runs out for South Africa. D. Reed. map Read Digest 110:85-90 F '77
Vorster calls for elections. il por Time 110:39-40+ O 3 '77
White bastion: hanging tough; excerpts from interview, ed by J. Elson and P. Hawthorne. B. J. Vorster. por Time 109:30 Mr 7 '77
Why struggle for peace is losing in South Africa. il U.S. News 82:71-2 My 9 '77
See also
Elections—South Africa

Race question

Ambassador Young interviewed on Issues and answers; transcript of program, October 30, 1977; ed by B. Clark and others. A. J. Young. Dept State Bull 77:791-2+ D 5 '77
Anatomy of white power. B. Pogrund. il Atlantic 240:51-6+ O '77
Anti-apartheid conference at Lagos calls for end of nuclear co-operation with South Africa; with text of declaration. il UN Chron 14:6-10 Ag '77
Arguing with South Africa; Time essay. H. Grunwald. il Time 109:32+ Je 27 '77

SOUTH AFRICA—Race question—*Continued*
Asking for trouble in South Africa. G. W. Ball. Atlantic 240:43-51 O '77; Same abr. Read Digest 112:59-63 Ja '78
Athlete power over South Africa. il Sr Schol 110:8 S 22 '77
Big crackdown. R. Carroll and others. il Newsweek 90:57-8+ O 31 '77
Biko on death; excerpts from interview. S. Biko. New Repub 178:11-13 Ja 7 '78
Black journalists in Johannesburg; shutdown of The world in Johannesburg. A. Silk. Nation 225:454-6 N 5 '77
Bulldozer remedy: apartheid at bay; squatters camps for migrant workers. A. Silk. Nation 225:298-304 O 1 '77
Burning bridges between races; crackdown on dissent. il Time 110:46+ O 31 '77
Challenging the great white state; desegregation of Catholic schools in South Africa. il Time 109:46 F 7 '77
Church schools in South Africa. America 136:121 F 12 '77
Color line. B. Pogrund. New Repub 177:15-17 D 17 '77
Concern expressed on recent events in South Africa; statement, October 26, 1977. R. M. Moose. Dept State Bull 77:897-9 D 19 '77
Death of a prisoner; S. B. Biko. por Time 110:35 S 26 '77
Defiant Vorster; excerpts from interview, ed by R. Watson and P. Younghusband. B. J. Vorster. por Newsweek 90:32 N 7 '77
Defiant white tribe. il map Time 110:50-1+ N 21 '77
Developments concerning apartheid; World Conference for Action Against Apartheid; statement, with text of declaration, August 25, 1977. A. J. Young, Jr. Dept State Bull 77:446-51 O 3 '77
Digging in for a crisis ahead. il Time 109:50-3 My 2 '77
Dilemmas for U.S. policy in South Africa. S. W. Sanders. il Bus W p50 D 26 '77
Double standard. Nat R 29:1284 N 11 '77
I must keep this country safe; interview, ed by W. McWhirter. J. Kruger. pors Time 110:38 O 17 '77
In a South African prison; P. Qoboza. R. Javers. Commonweal 104:808-9 D 23 '77
Making of a man; P. Qoboza. L. Sloane. il por Newsweek 90:58 O 31 '77
Myopia in South Africa. M. Stone. U.S. News 83:112 N 14 '77
Neither black nor white: South Africa as an African nation. T. H. Snitch. il Intellect 106:126-9 O '77
Notes and comment; arrest of P. Qoboza, editor of World. New Yorker 53:41-2 N 28 '77
Problem at home and abroad; illegal aliens in the United States and race problems in South Africa. Sat Eve Post 249:32 S '77
Reducing investments in South Africa. R. E. Lambert. map America 136:130-2 F 12 '77
Rewards of moderation; government suppression of Johannesburg's The world newspaper. New Repub 177:5-6 O 29 '77
Rule by jackboot in South Africa. America 137:294 N 5 '77
South Africa and Namibia. R. Dale. bibl f Cur Hist 73:209-13+ D '77
South Africa: are there grounds for hope? G. P. Wiles. Chr Cent 94:400-4 Ap 27 '77
South Africa: facts and fiction. L. Rubin. il UNESCO Courier 30:8-14 N '77
South Africa: multinationals are caught in the middle again; European Community race discrimination in employment guidelines. il Bus W p49-50 O 24 '77
South Africa throws down a gauntlet to the world. il U.S. News 83:37-8 N 7 '77
South Africa: weary investing policy—until reform. il Bus W p67-8+ F 14 '77
South Africa: what is to be done. C. Ferguson and W. R. Cotter. bibl f For Affairs 56:253-74 Ja '78
South African muzzle: how one of its own got banned; B. Naudé. A. Silk. Nation 225:581-4 D 3 '77
South African reality. T. Powers. Commonweal 105:14-16 Ja 6 '78
South Africa's captive work-force. il UNESCO Courier 30:14-15 N '77
South Africa's gambling church. America 136:138 F 19 '77
South Africa's lonely ordeal. W. S. Ellis. il map Nat Geog 151:780-819 Je '77
Steve Biko is dead. Nation 225:356-7 O 15 '77
Steve Biko is dead. R. Carroll and P. Younghusband. il por Newsweek 90:41-2 S 26 '77
Steve Biko: liberator and martyr. T. W. Jennings. Chr Cent 94:997-9 N 2 '77
Stigma on South African sport. S. A. Ogouki. il UNESCO Courier 30:26-7 N '77
Time runs out for South Africa. D. Reed. map Read Digest 110:85-90 F '77
Tortured logic from South Africa; bishops' protest. America 137:371 N 26 '77
Where blacks have it good: Soweto looks at the U.S. A. Silk. Nation 225:144-7 Ag 20 '77
Why apartheid is worse. New Repub 177:5-6 N 12 '77
Why South Africa has a right to exist as a white African nation. R. F. Botha. por Intellect 106:34-6 Ag '77
Why white exodus picks up speed. U.S. News 82:72 My 9 '77
See also
Asians in South Africa
International Day of Solidarity with the Struggling People of South Africa
United Nations—South Africa
United Nations—Special Committee Against Apartheid

Religious institutions and affairs

See also
Catholic Church in South Africa
Church and state in South Africa
Lutheran Church in South Africa

Riots

Tragic turn to terrorism; riots following funeral of S. Biko. K. Willenson and P. Younghusband. il por Newsweek 90:50-1 O 10 '77

Social conditions

WHO reports on mental health care in South Africa. UN Chron 14:33-4 Ap '77

Territorial expansion

Security Council urged to take steps to preserve status of Walvis Bay. il UN Chron 14:23-4 O '77

SOUTH AFRICAN refugees. See Refugees, South African
SOUTH AFRICAN students in the United States. See Foreign students in the United States
SOUTH AFRICANS
Case for Africa's white tribe. P. J. Cillié. il Sat Eve Post 249:90-6+ Mr '77
Defiant white tribe. il map Time 110:50-1+ N 21 '77
SOUTH AMERICA
See also
Argentina
Aviation—South America
Birds—South America
Brazil
Cruising—South America
Guyana
Horn, Cape
Paraguay
Peru
Uruguay
Zoology—South America

History

Anita and Giuseppe Garibaldi: a love story on two continents. G. Arciniegas. il pors Américas 29:2-7 My '77

Native races

See Indians of South America

Politics and government

See Latin America—Politics and government
SOUTH AMERICAN cookery. See Cookery, South American
SOUTH AMERICAN Indians. See Indians of South America
SOUTH BEND, Ind.
New confidence. il U.S. News 82:24-5 Je 13 '77
SOUTH CAROLINA
See also
Architecture, Domestic—South Carolina
Blacks—South Carolina
Camping—South Carolina
Festivals—South Carolina
Historic houses, sites, etc.—South Carolina
Wildlife sanctuaries—South Carolina

Industries

Oompah in the Bible belt; Spartanburg, S.C. il Time 110:50-1 Jl 25 '77
SOUTH CAROLINA Educational Television Network. See Television stations, Educational
SOUTH DAKOTA
See also
Banks and banking—South Dakota
Criminal justice, Administration of—South Dakota
Geology—South Dakota
Irrigation—South Dakota
Mount Rushmore National Memorial

Description and travel

Black Hills & the Badlands. J. Ferri. il Travel 147:30-3 Je '77
SOUTH GEORGIA (island)
South Georgia island: the great southern fur rush. J. C. Simmons. il Oceans 10:46-51 My '77
SOUTH KOREA. See Korea, South
SOUTH MOLUCCAN terrorists. See Terrorists, South Moluccan

SOUTH Nahanni River
We rafted down Canada's notorious Nahanni. S. J. Krasemann. il Int Wildlife 7:48-55 Mr '77
SOUTH Oklahoma City Junior College. See Oklahoma City. South Oklahoma City Junior College
SOUTH Pole
See also
Antarctic exploration
SOUTH Sea Islands. See Oceania
SOUTH Street Seaport Museum. See New York (city)—Historic houses, sites, etc.
SOUTH VIETNAM. See Vietnam, South
SOUTH WEST AFRICA. See Namibia
SOUTHAMPTON, N.Y.
Golden clan; excerpt. J. Corry. il N Y Times Mag p 16-19+ Mr 13 '77
SOUTHERN, Terry
New editions. S. Boorsch. il pors Art N 76:108 Ap '77 *
SOUTHERN accent. See English language—Accents and accentuation
SOUTHERN AFRICA. See Africa, Southern
SOUTHERN ASIA. See Asia, Southern
SOUTHERN Baptist colleges and universities. See Church colleges and universities
SOUTHERN Baptist Convention. See Baptists in the United Staes
SOUTHERN Baptist Theological Seminary, Louisville, Ky.
Southern Baptist context. E. G. Hinson. Chr Cent 94:93-5 F 2 '77
SOUTHERN California Gas Company. See Gas companies
SOUTHERN cookery. See Cookery, American
SOUTHERN folklore. See Folklore—United States
SOUTHERN Hills golf course, Tulsa. See Golf courses
SOUTHERN living (periodical)
Most profitable magazine in the U.S. il Forbes 119:30-1 Je 15 '77
SOUTHERN Methodist University, Dallas

Meadows Museum and Sculpture Court

Prado of the prairie. J. Kutner. il por Art N 76:74-7 My '77
SOUTHERN Ocean Racing Conference. See Yacht racing
SOUTHERN Poverty Law Center. See Legal aid
SOUTHERN Presbyterian Church. See Presbyterian Church in the United States
SOUTHERN Regional Council, Inc
Reversing agricultural priorities. Society 14:5 S '77
SOUTHERN States
Carterland impressions. J. Burnham. Nat R 29:431-2 Ap 15 '77
Changing times in Plains. J. A. Williams. Read Digest 111:133-6 Jl '77
Poet James Dickey on Carter and the born-again South. J. Dickey. il pors U.S. News 82:67 Ap 18 '77
Stars in the southern sky; personalities share impressions of Dixie. il Holiday 57:26-7 N '76
Who's moving to the sun and why. C. Seebohm. il map House & Gard 150:76+ Ja '78
See also
Agriculture—Southern States
Architecture, Domestic—Southern States
Blacks—Southern States
Express highways—Southern States
Gulf states
Historic houses, sites, etc.—Southern States
Music—Southern States

Civilization

Questions they never asked me. W. Percy. il pors Esquire 88:170-2+ D '77
Selling off the Old South. J. Greene. il map Harpers 254:39-42+ Ap '77
Voice of the South; poet J. Dickey. P. Axthelm. pors Newsweek 89:25 Ja 31 '77
Yankee from Georgia; J. Carter. W. L. Miller. il N Y Times Mag p 16-20+ Jl 3 '77

Description and travel

Deep South—vistas of change. M. Gough. House B 119:48+ Mr '77
House touring in the South. N. Richardson. il House & Gard 149:84+ Mr '77
Mini-holiday: Southern plantation houses in Louisiana and Mississippi. B. Jeffer. map Holiday 58:28-30 Ap '77
Walk across America. P. G. Jenkins. il map Nat Geog 151:466-99 Ap '77

Economic conditions

New milestone in the shift to the sunbelt. il Nations Bus 65:69 My '77

History

Institution design and the separatist impulse: Quebec and the antebellum American South. M. V. Levine. bibl f Ann Am Acad 433:60-72 S '77
See also
Reconstruction (Civil War)
United States—History—Civil War, 1861-1865

Industries

Business loves the sunbelt and vice versa. G. Breckenfeld. map Fortune 95:132-7+ Je '77
Unions push south. T. Nicholson and others. map Newsweek 89:55 Ap 4 '77

Periodicals

See also
Southern living (periodical)

Social conditions

See also
Blacks—Social conditions

Social history

See also
Slavery—United States

Social life and customs

Yankee pilgrim in the Old South. B. Sabol. il N Y Times Mag p38-40+ Ap 24 '77
SOUTHERNERS
Southern men, Southern lies. G. Godwin. il Esquire 87:126-9 F '77
SOUTHLAND Royalty Company
Born again. Forbes 119:54 Mr 15 '77
SOUTHWEST AFRICA. See Namibia
SOUTHWEST AFRICA People's Organization
African Gulag. New Repub 177:5 S 10 '77
SOUTHWEST airlines
Southwest Airlines studies new markets. Aviation W 106:30 Ap 11 '77
SOUTHWEST Ballet Center (ballet company) See Ballet companies
SOUTHWEST monsoon. See Ocean currents
SOUTHWESTERN Bell Telephone Company. See American Telephone & Telegraph Company
SOUTHWESTERN Library Association
SWLA/MPLA joint conference. Lib J 102:323-4 F 1 '77
SOUTHWESTERN States
Who's moving to the sun and why. C. Seebohm. il map House & Gard 150:76+ Ja '78
See also
Camping—Southwestern States
Paleontology—Southwestern States
Water supply—Southwestern States

Industries

Business loves the sunbelt and vice versa. G. Breckenfeld. map Fortune 95:132-7+ Je '77

Photographs

Laura Gilpin: photographer of the Southwest; interview, ed by D. Vestal. L. Gilpin. il por Pop Phot 80:100-5 F '77
SOUVENIR Press. See Publishers and publishing—Great Britain
SOUZA, Sandra J.
Providing for prisoners in Massachusetts. il Wilson Lib Bull 51:526-9 F '77
SOVEREIGN immunity. See Government liability
SOVEREIGNTY
See also
Self determination, National
SOVIET Academy of Sciences. See Academy of Sciences of the USSR
SOVIET-AMERICAN Commission on Scientific and Technical Cooperation. See Science—International aspects
SOVIET minorities. See Minorities
SOVIET Russian poetry. See Russian poetry
SOVIET UNION. See Russia
SOW corporations. See Swine industry
SOWELL, Thomas
New light on black I.Q. il N Y Times Mag p56-8+ Mr 27 '77
SOWETO. See Johannesburg
SOYBEAN futures. See Commodity exchanges
SOYBEAN products
See also
Okara
Tempeh
Tofu
SOYBEANS
Branch-beans. il Org Gard & Farm 24:128-30 Jl '77
See also
Cookery—Vegetables

Cultivation

Closing in on narrow-row soybeans. G. Lepper. il Suc Farm 75:21-5+ Ap '77
Foliar fertilizers flunk big test on soybeans. B. Coffman. Farm J 100:29 D '76
Growth regulator controls Johnson grass in soybeans; mefluidide. Farm J 101:M4 N '77
He double-crops sorghum, soybeans (irrigated) on sandy ground. il Suc Farm 75:no4 42 Mr '77
Midwest soybean costs lowest in the nation. il map Farm J 101:B4 Ap '77

SOYBEANS—Cultivation—*Continued*
Stop tough weeds in soybeans. D. Seim. il Farm J 101:32+ Mr '77
Test shows the best way to incorporate soybean herbicides. B. Coffman. Farm J 101:C4 Ap '77

Diseases and pests

Drouth slows soybean diseases. Farm J 101:H1 Ja '77
Spray for soybean diseases? il Farm J 101:12-13 Je '77

Drying

Drying scheme for quality soybeans. il Suc Farm 75:41 O '77

Export-import trade

Soviet Union may be steadier soybean customer. Suc Farm 75:no3 F52 F '77

Marketing

How to handle the soybean roller coaster. R. N. Wisner. Farm J 101:H1 Ag '77
Soybean speculators: did they help farmers this time? il Farm J 101:22 S '77
Soybeans: two months of high livin'. D. Durchholz. il Suc Farm 75:C6-7 D '77

Prices

Strong soybean price influence from Brazil. Suc Farm 75:C21 D '77

Seed

Lectin release by soybean seeds. D. W. Fountain and others. bibl il Science 197:1185-7 S 16 '77
Soybean inoculants not justified. Suc Farm 75: no3 34 F '77

Seeding

How to get wheat off to plant soybeans earlier. G. Reynolds. il Farm J 101:M4-5 Ja '77
Plants 9 acres an hour—in 21'' rows; soybean drills. B. Coffman. il Farm J 101:B8 Ap '77

Yield

Drilled soybeans: up to 50% higher yields possible. Suc Farm 75:38 Ap '77
Farmers lower sights for soybean yields. B. Coffman. il Farm J 101:J6 S '77
60-bu. soybeans—what happened in 1976. B. Gergen. il Suc Farm 75:no5 26-7 Mr '77
What you should know if you foliar feed your soybeans. B. Coffman. il Farm J 101:20-1 My '77

SOYER, Raphael
Raphael Soyer: a realist without a slogan. J. Shaw-Eagle. il por Art N 76:187-8 N '77 *
SOYUZ-Apollo flight, 1975. See Space flight—Manned flights—Apollo-Soyuz flight, 1975
SOYUZ cosmonauts. See Astronauts
SOYUZ flights. See Space flight—Manned flights—Soyuz flights
SPACE
See also
Space vehicles—Electronic equipment
SPACE (architecture)
Elevator space requirements in high-rise buildings. J. K. Ochsner and others. il Archit Rec 162:117-18 Jl '77
Living big in less space. J. Tomchin and others. pors Am Home 80:43+ My '77
Space alive; house by Peter Eisenman. il House & Gard 150:70-5 Ja '78
Space savers; excerpt from The spacemaker book. E. Liman. See issues of American home, June 1977-
Your own space; interview, ed by B. Niles. E. Brickham. il por Am Home 80:39-41 My '77
SPACE, Outer
Assembly calls for high priority for moon treaty and remote sensing questions. UN Chron 13:33 D '76
Big is beautiful, too; Space Day gala of J. Brown. P. Goldman and M. Kasindorf. il por Newsweek 90:25-6 Ag 22 '77
Jerry Brown's space program. J. Lelyveld. por N Y Times Mag p55 Jl 17 '77
See also
United Nations—Committee on the Peaceful Uses of Outer Space

Exploration

See also
Planets—Exploration
SPACE age
Do you have a space-age mind? G. M. Spruch and L. Spruch. Read Digest 110:127-9 Mr '77
SPACE and Missile Systems Organization. See United States—Air Force—Systems Command
SPACE and time
See also
Relativity (physics)
SPACE astronomy
Notes on Soviet space astronomy. J. E. Oberg. il Sky & Tel 53:92-6 F '77
See also
Artificial satellites—Astronomical use
Rockets—Astronomical use

SPACE biology
Cell biology experiments conducted in space. G. R. Taylor. bibl BioScience 27:102-8 F '77
Four months under space-simulated conditions; Bios-3 experiment in Russia. B. Ivanov and G. Bogdanovsky. Space World N-8-164:24 Ag '77
Space biology symposium hears reports on gravity studies. BioScience 27:810 D '77
See also
Artificial satellites—Biological use
SPACE centers
NASA center work curtailed. C. Covault. Aviation W 107:14-15 O 31 '77
See also
Space vehicles—Launching sites
United States—John F. Kennedy Space Center
United States—Lyndon B. Johnson Space Center
SPACE chemistry. See Astrochemistry
SPACE colonies
Living in space; work of G. O'Neill. B. Achee. il Sci Digest 81:8-12 Ap '77
1975 NASA/Stanford study of space colonization. Space World N-1-157:32-4 Ja '77
Space colonies: one step closer. il Sci N 112:103 Ag 13 '77
SPACE Committee. See United Nations—Committee on the Peaceful Uses of Outer Space
SPACE communication. See Interstellar communication
SPACE flight
From Sputnik to shuttle; two decades in space, 1957-77. il U.S. News 83:62-5 O 3 '77
From Sputnik to Star Trek. J. Bergman. il Flying 101:317-21 S '77
Future flight: space. D. Bond. il Flying 101: 358-9 S '77
News from the world of space exploration. See issues of Space world
Pioneer 11 again crossing orbit of Jupiter. il Space World N-10-166:31-2 O '77
Sailing to Halley's comet. il Time 109:54 Mr 14 '77
Sailing with Halley's Comet—and other space spectaculars for the 1980s. J. F. Pearson. il Pop Mech 147:67-71 F '77
Shuttle payloads filled to August, 1981. C. Covault. il Aviation W 107:58-9 Ag 1 '77
Space shuttle priorities set for payloads. Aviation W 106:13 My 16 '77
Students in space? maybe! L. David. il Sci Digest 81:15-17 Mr '77
See also
Computers—Space flight use
Insurance, Space flight
Lasers—Space flight use
Space stations

Accidents

Backup Intelsat launch sought to replace spacecraft lost. Aviation W 107:24 O 10 '77
Camera records post-launch Atlas-Centaur blast. il Aviation W 107:60-1 N 21 '77
Delta explosion destroys ESA test satellite; photographs. Aviation W 107:43 O 3 '77
From the NASA oops! File. il Sky & Tel 54:466 D '77
Second satellite blow-up in 16 days. Sci N 112: 228-9 O 8 '77

International aspects

NASA, Soviets set early talks on new joint manned mission. Aviation W 107:53 O 31 '77
Soviets launch joint biological mission. Aviation W 107:22-3 Ag 8 '77
Soviets seek role in satellite rescue. C. Covault. Aviation W 106:23+ Mr 28 '77
Soviets urge joint mission decision. Aviation W 107:49+ D 5 '77
U.S, Soviets to discuss more biosat missions. R. G. O'Lone. il Aviation W 107:95+ S 26 '77
U.S, USSR sign manned space pact. Aviation W 106:27 My 23 '77
See also
Space flight—Manned flights—Apollo-Soyuz flight, 1975
United Nations—Committee on the Peaceful Uses of Outer Space

Manned flights

See also
Astronauts
Orbital rendezvous (space flight)
Space flight to the moon—Manned flights
Space stations—Skylab 2 (1st manned) mission

Apollo-Soyuz flight, 1975

EUV makes the grade; question of the extreme ultraviolet. S. P. Maran. Natur Hist 86:85-6+ F '77

Soyuz flights

Extra docking port saves Salyut flight. C. Covault. il Aviation W 107:11-12 D 19 '77
Failure to achieve rendezvous curtails Soviet Soyuz flight. Aviation W 107:25-6 O 17 '77
Not quite; Soyuz 25- Salyut 6 docking failure. il Newsweek 90:54 O 24 '77

SPACE flight—Manned flights—Soyuz flights—*Continued*

Second flight of The Hawk; mission of Soyuz 22. M. Cassutt. il Space World N-7-163:36-42 Jl '77

Soyuz and the moon. J. E. Oberg. il Space World N-7-163:26-32 Jl '77

Soyuz program. C. Sheldon. il Space World N-7-163:4-26 Jl '77

Military use

NASA and the Pentagon: the Air Force eyes a star war. J. Markoff. Nation 226:16-18 Ja 7 '78

Pervasive importance of USAF's space mission; interview, ed by E. Ulsamer. T. W. Morgan. il por Space World N-5-161:12-16 My '77

Will the next war be fought in space? E. Hymoff. il Pop Mech 148:47-51+ Jl '77

Will the Soviets wage war in space? E. Ulsamer. il Space World N-5-161:25-9 My '77

Philosophy

Time out; excerpt from address, May 9, 1977. H. B. Combs. Flying 101:369+ S '77

Physiological aspects

Women in space; shuttle simulation. P. Gwynne and P. S. Greenberg. il Newsweek 89:76-7 My 23 '77

See also

Space medicine

Safety devices and measures

See also

Space rescue work

Study and teaching

Project Parsec goes to Mars. R. Hillenbrand and M. F. Ryan. il Sky & Tel 54:464-5 D '77

Voyager flights

Earth's greatest hits; audio-visual record on Voyager. A. Druyan and T. Ferris. N Y Times Mag p 12-13 S 4 '77

First Voyager on trajectory to Jupiter. J. M. Lenorovitz. il Aviation W 107:20-1 Ag 29 '77

MJS '77: a space odyssey. C. E. Kohlhase. il Space World N-3-159:30-1 Mr '77

NASA bans sex from outer space; information disc designed for Voyagers. N. Wade. Science 197:1163-5 S 16 '77

Project Voyager to Jupiter, Saturn, and beyond. J. Schefter. il Pop Sci 211:92-5+ Ag '77

Space age grand tour. il Time 110:60 Ag 29 '77

Space odyssey; Voyager 2. P. Gwynne. il Newsweek 90:81 S 5 '77

Spacecraft set sail for distant planets—and beyond; unmanned Voyagers. il U.S. News 83:35 Ag 22 '77

Voyager controllers grappling with maneuverability problem. Aviation W 107:41 O 3 '77

Voyager: hard start on a long road. il Sci N 112:132 Ag 27 '77

Voyager: journey to the outer planets. il Space World N-11-167:5-14 N '77

Voyager launch virtually flawless. J. M. Lenorovitz. il Aviation W 107:20-2 S 12 '77

Voyager missions. P. H. Abelson. Science 197:1039 S 9 '77

Voyager: multiplanet mission has message. Sci N 112:86 Ag 6 '77

Voyager 1; on the catch-up trail. il Sci N 112:165-6 S 10 '77

Voyager 1 overtakes earlier spacecraft on Jupiter mission. Aviation W 108:48-9 Ja 9 '78

Voyager switch avoids delay in launch. Aviation W 107:20-1 Ag 15 '77

Voyager's message: record reviews. J. Eberhart. Sci N 112:211+ O 1 '77

Voyagers set for planet encounters. J. M. Lenorovitz. il Aviation W 107:65-7+ Jl 4 '77

World on a record. J. Eberhart. il Sci N 112:124-5 Ag 20 '77

SPACE flight simulators

Four months under space-simulated conditions; Bios-3 experiment in Russia. B. Ivanov and G. Bogdanovsky. Space World N-8-164:24 Ag '77

Need for spacelab simulation shown. C. Covault. il Aviation W 106:75-9+ Je 27 '77

Orbiter crews train in flight simulator. D. E. Fink. il Aviation W 106:44-5+ Ap 18 '77

Second exercise tests Spacelab plan. Aviation W 106:50-2 My 23 '77

Seven-day Spacelab simulation readied. C. Covault. il Aviation W 106:40-1+ My 9 '77

Spacelab simulation results evaluated. B. M. Elson. il map Aviation W 106:79-82 Je 13 '77

Women in space; shuttle simulation. P. Gwynne and P. S. Greenberg. il Newsweek 89:76-7 My 23 '77

SPACE flight to Jupiter

House approves Jupiter orbiter/probe; Jupiter mission approval saves planetary capability, 300 jobs. E. Kozicharow and C. Covault. Aviation W 107:20-2 Jl 25 '77

House unit cuts Jupiter mission funds. Aviation W 106:19 My 30 '77

Jupiter orbit mission survives House vote. Sci N 112:52-3 Jl 23 '77

Sun's magnetic field may reach outer limit of solar system; Pioneer 11 data. Space World N-8-164:28 Ag '77

See also

Space flight—Voyager flights

SPACE flight to Mars

Cold winter for Viking too. il Sci N 111:84 F 5 '77

Mars landing: like a final roll of dice. . . B. Biegon. il por Space World N-1-157:28 Ja '77

New thoughts on Mars; results of Viking experiments. il Time 109:83-4 Ja 24 '77

Report from Mars; excerpt from Until the sun dies. R. Jastrow. il Natur Hist 86:48-53 bibl(p96-7) Mr '77

Skin of Mars; crust. J. Eberhart. il map Sci N 112:140-1 Ag 27 '77

Viking: intellect and ingenuity triumphant. R. Calvin. il Space World N-6-162:4-8 Je '77

Viking: quake questions and relativity refinements. il Sci N 111:36-7 Ja 15 '77

Viking science: tantalizing Viking scientists: cautious. G. Alexander. il Space World N-6-162:9-17 Je '77

Viking to Mars: profile of a space expedition. J. S. Martin, Jr, and A. T. Young. il pors Space World N-4-160:4-27 Ap '77

Vikings at work again. Space World N-8-164:27 Ag '77

Anecdotes, facetiae, satire, etc.

Letter from a traveler. G. Ace. Sat R 4:56 F 19 '77

SPACE flight to Mercury

The now frontier linking earth and planets: Mariner 10 mission, Mercury II and III results. bibl il Space World N-5-161:17-24 My '77

SPACE flight to Saturn

Great Saturn quandary. J. Eberhart. il Sci N 112:249 O 15 '77

Pioneer 11: looking good for Saturn. il Sci N 111:391 Je 18 '77

SPACE flight to the moon

Soviets invite additional U.S. space cooperation. Aviation W 107:12-13 D 19 '77

Luna flights

Luna 24: shaking up the moon-watchers. Sci N 112:390 D 10 '77

U.S. scientists study Soviet moon sample. Space World N-8-164:29-30 Ag '77

Manned flights

Soyuz and the moon. J. E. Oberg. il Space World N-7-163:26-32 Jl '77

Apollo 11 flight

MFA booklet on the moon; microfilm copy of Apollo 11 booklet deposited during Apollo 15 mission; with facsimile of booklet. il Space World M-12-156:18-29 D '76

Apollo 15 flight

MFA booklet on the moon; microfilm copy of Apollo 11 booklet deposited during Apollo 15 mission; with facsimile of booklet. il Space World M-12-156:18-29 D '76

SPACE flight to Venus

Geomorphic degradations on the surface of Venus: an analysis of Venera 9 and Venera 10 data. C. P. Florensky and others. bibl il Science 196:869-71 My 20 '77

Pioneer Venus 1978. il Space World N-10-166:28-9 O '77

SPACE industrial processing. See Space stations—Industrial use

SPACE laboratories. See Space stations

SPACE law

Starlawyers and shuttle. H. Schmidt. Aviation W 107:9 S 5 '77

SPACE manufacturing. See Space stations—Industrial use

SPACE medicine

House calls in space: a doctor-astronaut's view. J. Kerwin. il por Space World N-3-159:26-9 Mr '77

See also

Space flight—Physiological aspects

SPACE mineral resources

Studying near-earth resources. J. R. Arnold. Aviation W 107:9 S 19 '77

SPACE mining

Mining the Apollo and Amor asteroids. B. O'Leary. bibl il Science 197:363-6 Jl 22 '77

Space mining offers metal depletion answer. Sci Digest 82:35-8 O '77

SPACE perception

Perceived lightness depends on perceived spatial arrangement. A. L. Gilchrist. bibl il Science 195:185-7 Ja 14 '77

SPACE photography

Specialized film lab plays key role as scientists probe secrets of Mars. il Space World N-10-166:20-3 O '77

See also

Earth—Photographs from space

SPACE probes
Soviets' Venus orbiter and lander detailed; photographs. Aviation W 107:52-4 Ag 22 '77
Voyager 2 boom appears operational. J. M. Lenorovitz. il Aviation W 107:19-21 S 5 '77

SPACE processing. See Space stations—Industrial use

SPACE programs. See Space research

SPACE rescue work
Soviets seek role in satellite rescue. C. Covault. Aviation W 106:23+ Mr 28 '77

SPACE research
Space sciences (cont) Sci N 111:58, 72, 106, 185, 267, 348; 112:11, 24, 72, 91, 200, 316, 409 Ja 22-29, F 12, Mr 19, Ap 23, My 28, Jl 2-9, 30-Ag 6, S 24, N 12, D 17 '77
Space technology; address, April 28, 1977. J. C. Toomay. Vital Speeches 43:602-5 Jl 15 '77
See also
Space flight

International aspects

NASA cites balance-of-payments gains. Aviation W 106:51-2 F 28 '77
Soviet-American cooperation in space: new prospects. Space World N-8-164:30+ Ag '77
See also
Space flight—International aspects
United Nations—Committee on the Peaceful Uses of Outer Space

China

China in space. J. Oberg. il Sci Digest 81:33-8 F '77

Europe, Western

See also
European Space Agency

Japan

Japan maps space program. Aviation W 107:19 Jl 25 '77

Russia

Expansion marks Soviet drive in space. Aviation W 106:63+ Mr 21 '77
Four months under space-simulated conditions: Bios-3 experiment. B. Ivanov and G. Bogdanovsky. Space World N-8-164:24 Ag '77

United States

Added funding spurs planetary studies. D. E. Fink. Aviation W 106:17-18 Ja 17 '77
Ambitious new goals for U.S. space program. il U.S. News 82:98-9 My 9 '77
Next 25 years: industrialization of space. J. Von Puttkamer. bibl il Space World N-10-166:4-13 O '77
Resources of space. H. Downs. il por Space World N-3-159:8-17 Mr '77
Unified policy on space readied. C. Covault. Aviation W 108:14-16 Ja 2 '78
See also
United States—National Aeronautics and Space Administration

SPACE Science, Office of. See United States—National Aeronautics and Space Administration—Space Science, Office of

SPACE science as a profession
All aboard the NASA ship; Symposium '77. il Ebony 32:96-8+ Je '77

SPACE sciences
Science as exploration; excerpts from address, February 1977. N. W. Hinners. Aviation W 106-7 F 14 '77
See also
Space science as a profession

SPACE shuttle. See Space vehicles

SPACE shuttle flights. See Space flight

SPACE shuttle simulators. See Space flight simulators

SPACE stations
NASA weighing space station approach. il Aviation W 106:42-3 Ap 18 '77
Space stations for the international future. J. F. Madewell and R. E. Sexton. bibl il Space World N-9-165:4-40 S '77
See also
Space colonies

Equipment

Advanced scanner results weighed. il Aviation W 106:42-5 F 21 '77

Industrial use

Materials processing in space planned. C. Covault. Aviation W 107:52-3 O 31 '77
Progress toward space manufacturing. G. K. O'Neill. bibl il Space World N-1-157:14-22 Ja '77
Project Columbus 1992. B. O'Leary. Bull Atom Sci 33:4-5 Mr '77
'77 NASA summer study: no show stoppers! C. Henson; G. O'Neill; M. Frazier. il Space World N-12-168:26-7 D '77
Shuttle opens the space frontier to U.S. industry; manufacturing in space. il Bus W p48-52+ Ag 22 '77
Space processing revised for attracting Europeans. C. Covault. Aviation W 106:18-19 F 21 '77
Space prospect: factories and electric power. R. S. Lewis. il Smithsonian 8:94-9 D '77
Work space in space. T. Nicholson and J. C. Jones. il Newsweek 90:67-8 Ag 15 '77

Skylab 2 (1st manned) mission

House calls in space: a doctor-astronaut's view. J. Kerwin. il por Space World N-3-159: 26-9 Mr '77

Spacelab missions (proposed)

Experiment plans pressed for Spacelab. Aviation W 106:45+ F 28 '77
NASA switches teams aiding Spacelab. Aviation W 107:60 Ag 8 '77
NASA to seek research bids in astrophysics. Aviation W 107:73+ N 28 '77
Skylab optics. Sky & Tel 53:427 Je '77
Spacelab. il Space World N-8-164:4-8 Ag '77
Spacelab 2 flight investigators selected. C. Covault. il Aviation W 107:47-8 S 5 '77

SPACE stations, Russian
Continuing Salyut operations expected. il Aviation W 108:20-1 Ja 2 '78
Extra docking port saves Salyut flight. C. Covault. il Aviation W 107:11-12 D 19 '77
Salyut 5 in rendezvous orbit. Aviation W 106: 25 Mr 28 '77
Sixth Salyut space station launched. Sci N 112: 229 O 8 '77
Soviets launch new Salyut; 15th spacecraft since Aug. 27. Aviation W 107:27 O 3 '77
Work level below average in Salyut 6. Aviation W 108:25 Ja 9 '78

SPACE suits. See Astronauts—Clothing

SPACE technology
Bold space program. A. M. Lovelace. Aviation W 106:11 F 28 '77
From Sputnik to shuttle; two decades in space, 1957-77. il U.S. News 83:62-5 O 3 '77
News from the world of space exploration. See issues of Space world
Special report: satellite technology serving earth; with editorial comment. il maps Aviation W 107:9, 40-2+ O 17 '77
See also
Technology transfer

SPACE travel. See Space flight

SPACE vehicle antennas. See Antennas (electronics)

SPACE vehicles
Another small step for man: shuttling into space. J. N. Wilford. il N Y Times Mag p24-5+ Ag 7 '77
Come ride the space shuttle; Orbiter. K. E. Kristofferson. il Read Digest 110:66-70 Je '77
Early shuttle experiment choices near. C. Covault. Aviation W 106:41 Ap 25 '77
Intensified exploitation of shuttle urged; excerpts from testimony before the Senate Commerce Science and Transportation Subcommittee; ed by C. Covault. F. Press. Aviation W 106:21-2 Ap 18 '77
Launching the shuttle. E. Keerdoja and others. il Newsweek 89:7-8A F 7 '77
Load factor of 75% seen for shuttle. C. Covault. Aviation W 106:22-3 F 28 '77
Manned shuttles; at hand: revolution in space travel. il U.S. News 83:28-30 Ag 8 '77
NASA evaluating major shuttle orbiter changes. C. Covault. Aviation W 107:26-7 O 10 '77
NASA in new shuttle marketing effort; India, Iran planning satcom launches from space shuttle. il Aviation W 107:40-1+ O 24 '77
Orbiter is first spacecraft designed for shuttle runs. M. Collins. il Smithsonian 8:38-47 bibl (p 134) My '77
Orbiter towed to Dryden for test; photographs. Aviation W 106:12-13 F 7 '77
Scientists in space—at least eventually; experiments for shuttle orbital flights. J. Walsh. Science 196:635 My 6 '77
Shuttle capabilities cut mission planning needs. C. Covault. Aviation W 106:39-41 My 30 '77
Shuttle payload at KSC. J. D. Phillips. il Space World N-8-164:9-23 Ag '77
Shuttle research test activities peaking. C. Covault. il Aviation W 106:83 Je 13 '77
Shuttle: the next step to the stars. B. T. Cummings. il Space World N-1-157:4-13 Ja '77
Space shuttle: high-flying Yankee ingenuity. E. Ulsamer. il Space World N-6-162:18-23 Je '77
Space shuttle research chief; I. T. Gillam, director of operations at Dryden Flight Research Center. il pors Ebony 32:124-6+ Ap '77
Space shuttle: three long trials. Sci N 111:343 My 28 '77
Space stations for the international future; shuttle/spacelab. J. F. Madewell and R. E. Sexton. bibl il Space World N-9-165:4-40 S '77
Truckin' into orbit—with the space shuttle; interview. M. Malkin. il por Sr Schol 110:4-5+ O 20 '77
We visit the space shuttle. R. G. Beason. il Mech Illus 73:54+ S '77
See also
Space stations

SPACE vehicles—*Continued*

Atomic power plants

Space nuclear power gains foreseen. il Aviation W 107:129-30 O 17 '77

Cost

Delay urged on funds for two orbiters. il Aviation W 106:87+ Je 13 '77
Jobs bill shuttle funds to aid development, test. Aviation W 106:18-19 My 9 '77
Shift of funds set for shuttle. C. Covault. Aviation W 106:14-15 F 7 '77
Shuttle criticism worries NASA. C. Covault. il Aviation W 106:12-16 Ap 11 '77
Space shuttle sticking closely to cost estimates, NASA says. il Aviation W 106:96 Je 13 '77

Crews

See Astronauts

Electronic equipment

Cures sought for parts contamination. B. Miller. il Aviation W 106:48-51 Ap 11 '77

Fuel tanks

Shuttle tanks undergo tests at Michoud; photographs. Aviation W 106:49 My 23 '77

Landing systems

Mars

See also
Mars (planet)—Exploration—Equipment

Launching sites

Plesetsk—Russia's top secret military space center. J. E. Oberg. il map Space World N-3-159: 4-7 Mr '77
Space shuttle and Vandenberg Air Force Base. R. C. Henry and A. B. Sloan. bibl il pors map Space World N-2-158:29-36 F '77

Maintenance and repair

Big savings seen in in-orbit servicing. il Aviation W 106:36-7+ My 30 '77

Nozzles

Upper stage nozzle unit test fired. il Aviation W 107:24 O 24 '77

Power supply

See also
Space vehicles—Atomic power plants

Propulsion systems

Low-cost satellite launcher developed by Germans. R. R. Ropelewski. il Aviation W 107: 42-3+ S 12 '77
Shuttle main engine problem diagnosed. C. Covault. il Aviation W 107:17-20 O 24 '77
Shuttle stage agreement made. Aviation W 106: 19 F 21 '77
UTC prepares for shuttle booster role. Aviation W 106:15 Ja 3 '77
See also
Lasers—Space flight use

Specifications

U.S. launch vehicles; international launch vehicles; tables. Aviation W 106:87-8 Mr 21 '77

Testing

Delay in shuttle engine activities being studied. C. Covault. Aviation W 107:26 O 3 '77
Engine tests raise confidence. Aviation W 107: 23 Ag 8 '77
Shuttle solids face full-duration firing. Aviation W 107:22 Jl 18 '77

Recovery

Booster recovery system drop tested. il Aviation W 106:15 Je 27 '77

Safety devices and measures

Space shuttle safety & rescue. N. E. Brown. bibl il Space World N-12-168:16-25 D '77

Specifications

Leading U.S. & international spacecraft; tables. Aviation W 106:85-6 Mr 21 '77

Testing

Beautiful drop for a new bird; space shuttle. il Time 110:64-5 Ag 22 '77
Boeing 747, orbiter tested on runway; photographs. Aviation W 106:14-15 F 21 '77
Cut in shuttle flight tests studied. Aviation W 107:23-4 Jl 25 '77
Enterprise flight evaluates controls; photographs. Aviation W 107:91-3 S 26 '77
Film strips detail free flight. il Aviation W 107: 16-17 S 12 '77
Free Enterprise; space shuttle lift off. R. Boeth and P. Gwynne. il Newsweek 90:14-15 Ag 22 '77
Maiden flight of the mated birds; testing of space shuttle orbiter Enterprise. il Time 109: 23 F 28 '77
NASA weighs payload changes for shuttle orbital test flights. Aviation W 107:20 O 24 '77
Orbiter experiences control problems. D. E. Fink. il Aviation W 107:16-17 O 31 '77
Orbiter flight plan expanded. D. E. Fink. il Aviation W 106:12-14 Je 27 '77
Orbiter nears final free flight tests. D. E. Fink. il Aviation W 107:24-5 O 3 '77
Orbiter readied for next test phase. D. E. Fink. Aviation W 106:19-20 Mr 7 '77
Orbiter responsive in free flight. D. E. Fink. il Aviation W 107:12-19 Ag 22 '77
Orbiter/747 cleared for ferry flight. J. M. Lenorovitz. il Aviation W 107:72-3 N 28 '77
Orbiter/747 open flight envelope. D. E. Fink. Aviation W 106:20-1 F 28 '77
Runway shifted for orbiter's next flight. D. E. Fink. Aviation W 107:22-3 Ag 29 '77
Second flight confirms Enterprise data. D. E. Fink. il Aviation W 107:22-3 S 19 '77
Shuttle orbiter begins flight tests; photographs. Aviation W 106:16-19 F 28 '77
Shuttle orbiter, carrier is readied for flight. D. E. Fink. il Aviation W 106:12-16 F 14 '77
Shuttle orbiter cleared for free flight. J. M. Lenorovitz. il Aviation W 107:20-1 Ag 1 '77
Shuttle orbiter passes critical milestone. D. E. Fink. il Aviation W 107:23-4 O 17 '77
Shuttle orbiter, 747 carrier move into flight phase. D. E. Fink. il Aviation W 106:16-18 F 21 '77
Shuttle orbiter, 747 complete initial flight test phase; photographs. Aviation W 106:36-9 Mr 14 '77
Shuttle orbiter test phase trimmed. J. M. Lenorovitz. Aviation W 107:18-19 Jl 4 '77
Shuttle test goal studies accelerated. C. Covault. Aviation W 106:20-1 Je 27 '77
Space shuttle in free flight. J. K. Beatty. il Sky & Tel 54:271-5 O '77
Space shuttle: on its own and s-m-o-o-t-h. il Sci N 112:117 Ag 20 '77
Space shuttle takes to the air. il Sci N 111:134 F 26 '77
Space shuttle: tests trimmed but delayed. Sci N 112:23 Jl 9 '77
Test bed for the shuttle. il Pop Mech 147:97 My '77

Transportation

Prairie schooner for space; transporting space shuttle orbiter Enterprise. il Time 109:80-1 F 14 '77

Water supply

Tough new coating channels shuttle's waste water; Tufram. S. Renner-Smith. il Pop Sci 210:190 Mr '77

SPACE warfare. See Space flight—Military use

SPACEK, Sissy
Year of the actress. C. Michener and M. Kasindorf. il por Newsweek 89:56-64+ F 14 '77 *

SPACELAB missions (proposed) See Space stations—Spacelab missions (proposed)

SPACEMEN. See Astronauts

SPACESUITS. See Astronauts—Clothing

SPACKLING compound crafts. See Plaster work (craft)

SPACKMAN, Robert R. Jr
Easy isometrics; excerpt from Exercise in the office. il Fam Health 9:48-51 My '77

SPACKMAN, W. M.
Few rude remarks about manners. Esquire 88: 134-5+ D '77

SPACKS, Barry
Imagining a unicorn; poem. Poetry 130:276-9 Ag '77
In memory of L. E. Sissman; poem. Atlantic 240:84 D '77
Working title; poem. Nation 225:662 D 17 '77

SPADY, William G.
Competency-based education. Educ Digest 42:21-4 My '77

SPAGGIARI, Albert
Bank heist of the century; robbery of the Société Générale bank in Nice. R. Daley. il Read Digest 110:84-90 Ap '77 *
To lose a thief. F. Willey and E. Peer. il por Newsweek 89:44 Mr 21 '77 *

SPAGHETTI cookery. See Cookery—Macaroni products

SPAGHETTI squash. See Squashes

SPAHR, Charles Eugene
For Sohio, it was Alaskan oil—or bust. A. L. Morner. il por Fortune 96:172-6+ Ag '77 *

SPAIN, Jayne Baker
Leading businesswoman's perspective on management; interview. il pors Nations Bus 65: 70-2+ Mr '77

SPAIN
Iberia; symposium. il Sat R 5:10-14+ O 29 '77
See also
Air traffic control—Spain
Andalusia
Archives—Spain
Art and state—Spain
The Arts—Spain
Balearic Islands
Banks and banking—Spain
Barcelona

SPAIN—See also—*Continued*
Calanda
Catalonia
Childrens literature—Spain
Cities and towns—Spain
Coruña
Estremadura
Festivals—Spain
Hotels, motels, etc.—Spain
Investments, Foreign—Spain
Jerez
Madrid
Money—Spain
Opera—Spain
Skis and skiing—Spain
Soria,

Colonies

City planning in the Spanish colonies. G. de Zéndegui. il map Américas 29:S1-12 F '77
Enduring heritage; influence of early Spanish settlers in Latin America. I. Vázquez de Acuña. il map Américas 29:30-3 O '77
See also
Canary Islands

Commerce
Netherlands

Spanish wool and Dutch rebels: the Middelburg incident of 1574. W. D. Phillips, Jr and C. R. Phillips. bibl f il map Am Hist R 82:312-30 Ap '77

Description and travel

España—littorally yours. C. Schwalberg. il Sat Eve Post 249:68-9 N '77
Paradores: Spain's castle hotels. E. Berman. il Harp Baz 110:12+ Je '77
Seduction in Spain. D. Messinesi. il Vogue 167:227-8+ N '77
Traveler's camera. C. Purcell. il por Pop Phot 81:30+ Jl; 64+ Ag '77

Economic policy

Pressing austerity in an ailing economy. il Bus W p48 Ag 15 '77

History
House of Austria, 1516-1700

Spanish wool and Dutch rebels: the Middelburg incident of 1574. W. D. Phillips Jr and C. R. Phillips. bibl f il map Am Hist R 82:312-30 Ap '77

Spanish American War, 1898

See United States—History—Spanish American War, 1898

Civil War, 1936-1939

Mayor who came out of the cellar; P. Montalvo's self-imposed 38-year imprisonment. il por Time 110:28 Ag 1 '77

Civil War, 1936-1939—Art and the war

Picasso's cries of children. . .cries of stones; series of etchings entitled The Dream and Lie of Franco. P. Failing. bibl il Art N 76:55-8+ S '77

Civil War, 1936-1939—Atrocities

Guernica—40 years later. il Time 109:57 My 2 '77

Industries

See also
Airplane industry—Spain

Politics and government

Democracy in Spain: can the impossible dream come true? H. Sutton. il Sat R 5:10-14+ O 29 '77
Political transformation of Spain. S. G. Payne. Cur Hist 73:165-8+ N '77
Reporter in Europe. J. Kramer. New Yorker 53:98+ Mr 21 '77
Reports & comment: Spain. S. Meisler. por Atlantic 239:14+ My '77
Skirmish over Guernica; Museum of Modern Art's refusal to return painting. P. Nobile. il Harpers 254:15+ Mr '77
Spain's new democracy. S. Mesler. il For Affairs 56:190-208 O '77
We're all Democrats now. Nat R 29:481 Ap 29 '77
See also
Communist Party (Spain)
Elections—Spain
Political campaigns—Spain
Political parties—Spain

Religious institutions and affairs

Spain strides toward democracy. T. S. Goslin. Chr Cent 94:615 Jl 6 '77

SPAIN and Latin America
Debunking the black legend; historical role of Spain in Latin America. R. Fernandez Retamar. il UNESCO Courier 30:54-5+ Ag '77

SPAKE, Amanda
Death on the reservation. Progressive 41:27-30 F '77

SPALDING, Albert
Spalding's baseball tour. C. Davidson. il Am Heritage 28:46-9 O '77 *

SPALDING Division. See Questor Corporation

SPANFELLER, Jim
Jim Spanfeller: the illustrator as instructor. N. Meglin. il Am Artist 41:46-9+ Mr '77 *

SPANIER, Muriel
On the water tower; story. Redbook 149:106 Jl '77

SPANISH AMERICAN art. See Art, Latin American

SPANISH AMERICAN history. See Latin America—History

SPANISH AMERICAN literature. See Latin American literature

SPANISH AMERICAN music. See Music, Latin American

SPANISH AMERICAN War. See United States—History—Spanish American war, 1898

SPANISH Americans in the United States. See Latin Americans in the United States

SPANISH art. See Art, Spanish

SPANISH Colonial art. See Art, American

SPANISH cookery. See Cookery, Spanish

SPANISH golfers. See Golfers

SPANISH language

Study and teaching

Learning Spanish the Fénix way. J. Wholey. Clearing H 51:130-5 N '77

Terms and phrases

Notes on the gringo. W. E. Hoy. Américas 29:15-16 Ag '77

SPANISH language in Latin America
Spanish overseas. M. A. Morínigo. UNESCO Courier 30:62-3 Ag '77

SPANISH literature
See also
Childrens literature—Spain

SPANISH painting. See Painting, Spanish

SPANISH SAHARA. See Western Sahara

SPANISH speaking people and libraries. See Libraries and foreign population

SPANISH-United States Council. See United States-Spanish Council

SPANISH wines. See Wine

SPANKE, Bill
Salting away oil. il Pop Sci 212:77 Ja '78

SPANKING. See Corporal punishment

SPANN, Girardeau A. See Nader, R. jt auth

SPANN, Gloria (Carter)
(ed) See Carter, L. Miss Lillian: my two sons

about

And the first sisters. T. Mathews and E. Shannon. il pors Newsweek 90:34 N 14 '77 *

SPANN, William Carter
What happened to me is my fault. il Good H 185:44+ O '77

SPANO, P. F. and others
Localization of nigral dopamine-sensitive adenylate cyclase on neurons originating from the corpus striatum. bibl il Science 196:1343-5 Je 17 '77

SPARANO, Vin T.
Have fun in the snow—but be careful! il Nat Wildlife 16:26-7 D '77

SPARE time. See Leisure

SPARK, Richard
Breaking the drug barrier. il N Y Times Mag p64-71 Mr 20 '77

SPARK plugs
How to read your sparkplugs. M. Schultz. il Pop Mech 149:78-81+ Ja '78

SPARKMAN, G. Temp
Baptists and baptism. Chr Cent 94:349-50 Ap 13 '77

SPARKPLUGS. See Spark plugs

SPARKS, Electric. See Electric sparks

SPARROW, John
Freedom of expression: too much of a good thing? excerpt from Too much of a good thing. Am Scholar 46:165-80 Spr '77

SPARROW hawks, American. See Falcons

SPARROWS
Selective vocal learning in a sparrow. P. Marler and S. Peters. bibl il Science 198:519-21 N 4 '77
Speaking of sparrows; house sparrows. M. Tomkies. il Read Digest 110:53-4+ My '77

SPARTANBURG, S.C.

Industries

See South Carolina—Industries

SPAS. See Health resorts, watering places, etc.

SPASMS
See also
Tic

SPASSKII, Boris Vasil'evich
Taut duel for two old comrades. J. D. Reed. il Sports Illus 47:40-2+ D 12 '77 *

SPAWNING
Hydrogen peroxide induces spawning in mollusks, with activation of prostaglandin endoperoxide synthetase. D. E. Morse and others. bibl il Science 196:298-300 Ap 15 '77

SPEAKERS. See Loudspeakers
SPEAKERS of the House of Representatives. See United States—Congress—House—Speakers
SPEAKING. See Elocution; Public speaking
SPEAR, Lois
Capital punishment—or suicide? Commonweal 104:742 N 25 '77
about
Sad footnote; Daniel R. Webster case. J. Deedy. Commonweal 104:772 D 9 '77 *
SPECIAL classes and special schools
Peotone flights school failure; special classes for kindergartners with learning disabilities. J. Bone. il Am Educ 13:32-5 Ja '77
We want to make these kids neurotic; Cornerstone Therapeutic Nursery in Yonkers. S. Singular. il N Y Times Mag p27+ Jl 10 '77
See also
Deaf—Education
SPECIAL Committee Against Apartheid. See United Nations—Special Committee Against Apartheid
SPECIAL Committee of Twenty-four on Colonialism. See United Nations—Special Committee on the Situation with Regard to the Implementation of the Declaration on the Granting of Independence to Colonial Countries and Peoples
SPECIAL Committee on Decolonization. See United Nations—Special Committee on the Situation with Regard to the Implementation of the Declaration on the Granting of Independence to Colonial Countries and Peoples
SPECIAL Committee on Peace-keeping Operations. See United Nations—Special Committee on Peace-keeping Operations
SPECIAL Committee on the Charter of the United Nations and on the Strengthening of the Role of the Organization. See United Nations—Special Committee on the Charter of the United Nations and on the Strengthening of the Role of the Organization
SPECIAL days, weeks, and months
Energy Week. il Sr Schol 110:TE22+ S 22 '77
Montana community honors young children; Week of the Young Child. il SLJ 24:13 S '77
National Hunting and Fishing Day. E. B. Mann. Field & S 82:12+ My '77
Proclamation for Older Americans Month. J. Carter. Aging 270:3 Ap '77
World Trade Week, 1977; a proclamation. J. Carter. Dept State Bull 76:440 My 2 '77
See also names of special days, weeks, and months, e.g. Memorial Day
SPECIAL education. See Special classes and special schools
SPECIAL effects. See Motion pictures—Special effects
SPECIAL effects light filters. See Light filters
SPECIAL interest groups. See Pressure groups
SPECIAL Libraries Association
Glee in Gotham. il Lib J 102:1581-3 Ag '77
SLA/ASIS Janus meet: costs of information scrutinized. N. Savage. Lib J 102:540-1 Mr 1 '77
SLA celebrates in the Big Apple. H. E. Rosenfeld. il Wilson Lib Bull 52:64-7 S '77
SLA in the City of Love. L. R. Pearson. Am Lib 8:417-18 S '77
SPECIAL Representative for Trade Negotiations, Office of the. See United States—Special Representative for Trade Negotiations, Office of the
SPECIALISTS
Building a human resources file: a model; Missoula Area Resource Center. K. Clay and J. J. Dietz. Clearing H 50:337-40 Ap '77
Leaving it to the experts. T. Griffith. Atlantic 240:30+ N '77
SPECIALTY stores
Botanicas: Puerto Rican folk phamacies; spiritism in New York City. M. A. Borrello and E. Mathias. il Natur Hist 86:64-73 bibl(p 116-17) Ag '77
On and off the avenue; New York City boutiques. K. Fraser. New Yorker 53:91-8 Ap 11 '77
Singular stores; boutiques. il N Y Times Mag p 118-19 O 23 '77
Vanity fair. P. McCabe. Harpers 255:83-5 Ag '77

Management

How to start a business of your own. G. Chipps and C. Jessup. bibl Redbook 149:66+ Jl '77

Great Britain

Some toddler! Mothercare. il Forbes 120:63 Ag 1 '77
SPECIATION. See Species
SPECIES
Evolution's erratic pace; speciation. S. J. Gould. Natur Hist 86:12+ My '77
Return of hopeful monsters; theories of R. Goldschmidt. S. J. Gould. Natur Hist 86:22+ Je '77
See also
Evolution

SPECIFICATIONS, Building. See Building—Contracts and specifications
SPECKLE interferometry. See Interferometry
SPECTACLES. See Eyeglasses
SPECTOR, Ilan. See Moolenaar, W. H. jt auth
SPECTOR, Malcolm
Legitimizing homosexuality. bibl il Society 14:52-6 Jl '77
SPECTROMETRY. See Spectrum analysis
SPECTROSCOPES
Spectroscope with a holographic grating. P. Delvo. il Sky & Tel 54:65-6 Jl '77
SPECTRUM, Solar
Eight feet of solar spectrum. O. R. Norton. il Sky & Tel 54:176-9 S '77
SPECTRUM, Ultraviolet
Quasar 3C273 ultraviolet spectrum. il Sci N 112:199 S 24 '77
SPECTRUM analysis
Coherent optical transients. R. G. Brewer. bibl il Phys Today 30:50-4+ My '77
Coherent Raman spectroscopy. M. D. Levenson. bibl il Phys Today 30:44-9 My '77; Reply with rejoinder. J. A. Koningstein. 30:15+ D '77
Geometry of adsorbates on solid surfaces; angle-resolved photoemission spectroscopy. E. W. Plummer and T. Gustafsson. bibl il Science 198:165-70 O 14 '77
High-resolution spectroscopy of atoms and molecules. T. W. Hänsch. bibl il Phys Today 30:34-6+ My '77
Introduction to spectroscopy:
Chemical applications of visible and ultraviolet absorption spectra. J. C. Davis, Jr. bibl il Chemistry 50:17-20 N '77
Ion cyclotron resonance: fourier transform mass spectrometry. T. H. Maugh, 2d. Science 195:1314-15 Mr 25 '77
Kinetic resonance Raman spectroscopy: dynamics of deprotonation of the Schiff base of bacteriorhodopsin. M. A. Marcus and A. Lewis. bibl il Science 195:1328-30 Mr 25 '77
Lateral diffusion in planar lipid bilayers. P. F. Fahey and others. bibl il Science 195:305-6 Ja 21 '77
Microwave spectroscopic imagery of the earth. D. H. Staelin and others. bibl il Science 197:991-3 S 2 '77
Photoacoustic spectroscopy comes of age. T. H. Maugh. Science 195:1317 Mr 25 '77
Proton-induced X-ray emission analysis of single human hair roots. E. C. Henley and others. bibl il Science 197:277-8 Jl 15 '77
Resonance electron spectroscopy detects single atoms. G. B. Lubkin. il Phys Today 30:17+ S '77
Spark discharge: application to multielement spectrochemical analysis. J. P. Walters. bibl il Science 198:787-97 N 25 '77
Surface science: a way to tell where the atoms are; angle-resolved photoelectron spectroscopy. A. L. Robinson. Science 196:1306-8 Je 17 '77
Zeeman effect: a unique approach to atomic absorption. T. H. Maugh. il Science 198:39+ O 7 '77
See also
Astronomical spectroscopy
Nuclear magnetic resonance
SPECTRUM analyzers. See Testing instruments
SPECULATION
See also
Arbitrage
Commodity exchanges
Hedging (finance)
Investments
Real estate investment
Stocks
SPEECH
See also
Conversation
Oral communication
Public speaking
SPEECH, Freedom of. See Free speech
SPEECH, Visible. See Deaf—Means of communication
SPEECH defects
See also
Stuttering
SPEECH processing systems
Introducing Speechlab: the first hobbyist vocal interface for a computer! H. Enea and J. Reykjalin. il Pop Electr 11:43-50 My '77
Speech processors. H. S. Brier. il Pop Electr 11:87 F '77
SPEECH reading. See Deaf—Means of communication
SPEECH scrambling
A secret revealed: X system; speech-encoding secrecy technique. B. H. Berry. Pop Sci 210:160 F '77
SPEECH therapy
St-st-st-st-st-st-stuttering; therapy methods of Dr R. Webster. M. Pines. il N Y Times Mag p26+ F 13 '77
SPEED

Measurement

See also
Speed indicators

SPEED (drugs) See Amphetamines
SPEED indicators
Mirrors shed light on traffic speed; the enoscope principle. W. S. Foster. Am City & County 92:70 Jl '77
See also
Speedometers
Tachometers
SPEED limits. See Traffic regulations
SPEED of light. See Light—Speed
SPEED reading
Mr Jake and speed-reading. Sister Marie Emmanuel. il Engl J 66:64-5 O '77
Anecdotes, facetiae, satire, etc.
On speed. D. K. Mano. Nat R 29:624-5 My 27 '77
SPEED records, Airplane. See Airplane speed records
SPEED records, Automobile. See Automobile speed records
SPEED records, Boat. See Boat speed records
SPEED skating. See Skating
SPEED traps, Radar. See Radar in traffic control
SPEEDOMETERS
Build a digital bicycle-speedometer. G. W. Randig. il Pop Electr 11:39-41 Mr '77
Speedometer as an endangered species. P. Bedard. Car & Dr 23:12 N '77
SPEEDWAYS
Ode to a race track that once was; VacaValley raceways. L. Mandel. Car & Dr 22:16+ Je '77
SPEER, Albert
Speer: Hitler knew; excerpts from interview, ed by A. Zarca. il pors Newsweek 90:56 S 19 '77
SPEER, Edgar B.
Hell with expanding. . .we won't even have the money to maintain; interview. il por Forbes 120:34-6 N 15 '77
Winter's child—and the cold hand of government; address, February 7, 1977. Vital Speeches 43:303-6 Mr 1 '77
SPEERS, T. W. and Loewenfeldt, Paula von
Fault at Diablo Canyon. Nation 225:333-6 O 8 '77
SPEIGHT, Jerry
Photography: an aid for compositional reference. il Sch Arts 76:24-7 F '77
SPELLMAN, A. B.
Role of the National Endowment. C. B. Fowler. Hi Fi 27:MA12+ Mr '77 *
SPELUNKERS. See Caves
SPENCE, Glen
What's that coming out of your shirt? Oh, it's just Jo-Jo. D. Levin. il por Sports Illus 46:44+ F 14 '77 *
SPENCE, William Junior
He didn't know half. . . B. Jacobs. Progressive 41:42 N '77 *
SPENCE Manor (hotel) See Nashville, Tenn.—Hotels, restaurants, etc.
SPENCER, Bella Z.
Assassins! il por Sat Eve Post 249:72 Jl '77
SPENCER, John Wallace
One self-publishing writer who made it big; interview, ed by P. M. Perry. il por Writers Digest 57:40-1 F '77
SPENCER, Scott
Hope; story. Ladies Home J 94:96-7 S '77
SPENCER, Warren H.
Tornadoes: enigma of spring. il Read Digest 110:15-16+ Ap '77
SPENCER, William A.
Let variety spice your words. Writer 90:26-7 Ag '77
SPENCER-CHURCHILL, Clementine Ogilvy (Hozier) Spencer-Churchill, Baroness. See Churchill, C. O. H. S.
SPENDER, Stephen
Life wasn't a cabaret. il N Y Times Mag p20-1+ O 30 '77
SPENDING. See Consumption (economics)
SPERLING, Edwardine
Your world; poem. Clearing H 50:273 F '77
SPERLING, Edwin K.
Thumbs down for the credit card—eventually. il Intellect 106:44-5 Ag '77
SPERLING, Godfrey, 1915-
How politicians eat reporters for breakfast. N. Ephron. Esquire 87:26-7+ Je '77 *
SPERLING, Harry G. See Marc, R. E. jt auth
SPERM. See Spermatozoa
SPERMATOZOA
Hooks and eyes of sperm and eggs. il Sci N 112:356 N 26 '77
See also
Semen
SPERRY, Elmer Ambrose
Sperry. R. P. Hallion. Flying 101:83 S '77 *
SPERRY and Hutchinson Company
Greening of S&H. il Forbes 120:36 Jl 1 '77
Whatever happened to S&H? por Duns R 109:18-19 Ja '77
SPERRY Rand Corporation
Conglomerate works. il Forbes 119:30 Ja 15 '77

SPEZZANO, Charles, and Waterman, Jill
First day of life. bibl il pors Psychol Today 11:110+ D '77
SPHERES
Gravitational compression of crystallized suspensions of polystyrene spheres. R. S. Crandall and R. Williams. bibl il Science 198:293-5 O 21 '77
SPHEROCENTRIC knee prosthesis. See Joints, Artificial
SPHINGOLIPIDOSIS. See Metabolism, Disorders of
SPHYGOMOMANOMETERS
Blood pressure measurement devices. S. N. Finkelstein. il Consumers Res Mag 60:7-10 F '77
Medical robot. il Time 110:96+ O 10 '77
SPICE cake. See Cake
SPICE racks
For the serious spice collector. il Sunset 159:88 S '77
SPICER, Carol
Live the Irish country life. il House & Gard 149:74+ Je '77
SPICES
See also
Curry
McCormick & Company
Paprika
SPIDER webs
Oh, what a tangled web. H. W. Levi. il Sci Digest 82:inside cover S '77
SPIDERS
Aggressive chemical mimicry by a bolas spider. W. G. Eberhard. bibl il Science 198:1173-5 D 16 '77
Poison! black widow. R. E. Arnold. Field & S 82:37 O '77
SPIEGEL, Herbert
Eyes have it. Time 110:53 D 19 '77
How hypnosis aids in passing over the threshold of consciousness. T. Bay. il por Sci Digest 81:45-8 Je '77 *
SPIEGEL, Steven L.
Carter and Israel. Commentary 64:35-40 Jl; 30-1 S '77
SPIELBERG, Steven
TV's impact on the movies—as a noted director sees it. il por U.S. News 83:62 N 21 '77
about
Aliens are coming! F. Rich. il por Time 110:102-3+ N 7 '77 *
Close encounter with Spielberg. J. Kroll. il pors Newsweek 90:98-9 N 21 '77 *
UFO's are coming! J. Kroll. il Newsweek 90:88-9+ N 21 '77 *
SPIELER, F. Joseph
Adrift among images. il Harpers 254:107+ Mr '77
Lost souls. Harpers 255:102+ S '77
Most visionary modernist. Harpers 254:86-8 Je '77
SPIES
See also
Agents provocateurs
Rosenberg, Julius and Ethel, case
Secret service
SPIKOL, Art
Nonfiction. See issues of Writer's digest
SPIN, Nuclear. See Nuclear spin
SPINACH
Our spinach loves winter. M. Susko. il Org Gard & Farm 24:68-9 O '77
SPINACH, Chinese. See Amaranths
SPINAL cord
Spinal neurons project to the dorsal column nuclei of rhesus monkeys A. Rustioni. bibl il Science 196:656-8 My 6 '77
SPINAL fluid. See Cerebrospinal fluid
SPINE
See also
Backache
Abnormalities and deformities
Braced for the best; scoliosis, or curvature of the spine. C. Holtmann. por Seventeen 36:36 My '77
Simple test for scoliosis. il Bet Hom & Gard 55:70+ Ag '77
Diseases
See also
Spondylitis
SPINELLI, Anthony R.
Dial-an-emperor. Nat R 29:440 Ap 15 '77
SPINKS, Leon
This was the start of something big. P. Putnam. il pors Sports Illus 46:18-19 Ja 24 '77 *
SPINKS, Leslie A.
Many shades of Webster. Writers Digest 57:38+ My '77
SPINNAKERS. See Sails
SPINNER, Thomas J. Jr
Guyana: old scars break open. Nation 225:723-4 D 31 '77

SPINNER dolphins. See Dolphins (mammals)
SPINNERS. See Fishing lures, flies, etc.
SPINNING tackle. See Fishing tackle
SPINOFF (technology) See Technology transfer
SPINOZA, Baruch. See Spinoza, Benedictus de
SPINOZA, Benedictus de
Spinoza: philosopher of intellectual freedom. B. Rekers. il por UNESCO Courier 30:28-33 Je '77 *
Why Spinoza was excommunicated. Y. Yovel. Commentary 64:46-52 N '77 *
SPIRAL arrangement of leaves. See Phyllotaxis
SPIRAL galaxies. See Galaxies
SPIRES, T. Grady
Tribute to Cornelius Van Til. Chr Today 22:20 D 30 '77
SPIRILLUM lipoferum. See Bacteria, Nitrogen fixing
SPIRIT, Holy. See Holy Spirit
SPIRITISM. See Spiritualism
SPIRITS. See Ghosts
SPIRITUAL healing. See Faith cure
SPIRITUAL life
Faith to face failure, or what's so great about success? V. C. Grounds. por Chr Today 22:12-13 D 9 '77
Metaphysical dimensions of a door. T. H. Troeger. Chr Cent 94:557-9 Je 8 '77
Total spiritual fitness—in 30 minutes a week. R. E. Gibson. Chr Cent 94:197-8 Mr 2 '77
Witness stand. E. Schaeffer. See issues of Christianity today
See also
Christian life

Bibliography

Right reading for right actions. D. Tinder. Chr Today 21:26-9 S 9 '77
SPIRITUALISM
Botanicas: Puerto Rican folk pharmacies; spiritism in New York City. M. A. Borrello and E. Mathias. il Natur Hist 86:64-73 bibl(p 116-17) Ag '77
See also
Levitation
SPIRITUALITY
See also
Mysticism
SPIROPLASMA. See Mycoplasmas
SPIROPLASMAVIRUSES. See Viruses, Plant
SPITZER, Nicholas R.
Queen of the Cajun sound. il por Ms 6:27-8 N '77
SPIVACK, Kathleen
January thaw; poem. Atlantic 239:44 Mr '77
SPIVACKE, Harold
Obituary
Mus Q 63:425-7 Jl '77. C. S. Smith
SPLICES. See Knots and splices
SPLINERS (woodworking machinery) See Jointers (woodworking machinery)
SPLIT equity. See Home ownership
SPLITTERS, Wood. See Wood cutting machines
SPOCK, Benjamin
[Column] See occasional issues of Redbook
We're both 16 years old! il por Redbook 148:22+ Ap '77
SPOHRER, Bill
Quest in the jungle. J. Underwood. il Sports Illus 48:86-90+ Ja 9 '78 *
SPOILING of children. See Children—Management and training
SPOILS system. See Political patronage
SPOKEN phonograph records. See Phonograph records—Spoken records
SPOLETO festival. See Festivals—Italy
SPOLETO festival U.S.A. See Festivals—South Carolina
SPONDYLITIS
One chance in 500 to live; self-induced cure of ankylosing spondylitis. N. Cousins. por Sat Eve Post 249:52-4+ My '77; Same with title Anatomy of an illness (as perceived by the patient) Sat R 4:4-6+ My 28 '77; Same abr. Read Digest 110:130-4 Je '77; Discussion. Sat R 4:5-6 Jl 23 '77
SPONGE iron. See Iron, Sponge
SPONGES
Consider the sponge. M. E. Long. il Nat Geog 151:392-407 Mr '77
SPONSORS, Advertising. See Television advertising
SPONZILLI, Alan N.
Surrealistic anatomy studies. il por Sch Arts 77:24-5 N '77
SPOONBILL fishing. See Paddlefish fishing
SPOONER, William Archibald
Spooner's other isms. Sci Am 236:49 Ja '77 *
SPOONS

Collectors and collecting

Egyptian souvenir spoons. L. M. Plogger. il Hobbies 82:153 S '77
Spooning around the world. B. Swanson. il Hobbies 82:120-2 S '77
SPOOR, William H.
Shaking up a company for solid growth; interview. il pors Nations Bus 65:34-6+ O '77
SPORKIN, Stanley
Sporkin the enforcer. M. Ruby and J. Walcott. il por Newsweek 90:94 O 24 '77 *
SPORN, Michael B. and others
13-cis-retinoic acid: inhibition of bladder carcinogenesis in the rat. bibl il Science 195:487-9 F 4 '77
SPORT fishing boats. See Fishing boats
SPORT trophies. See Trophies, Sport
SPORTING goods
Camping supplies and recreational equipment. il Consumers Res Mag 60:162-8 O '77
Can we afford to idiot-proof the woods? product liability of outdoor equipment. R. Starnes. Outdoor Life 160:12+ S '77
Give: sports; Christmas gifts. K. Gilman. Vogue 167:110 D '77
Here's PM's pick of the year's best gear. B. McKeown. il Pop Mech 148:20+ D '77
New equipment & ideas. See issues of Outdoor life to September 1977
Sportsman's shopper. See issues of Field & stream
Winter sports gear. Mech Illus 73:30 D '77
See also
Gymnastics—Equipment
Mountaineering—Equipment and supplies
Sporting goods industry
Track athletics—Equipment

Anecdotes, facetiae, satire, etc.

Operation case. G. Hill. Field & S 82:30-1 S '77
Zern. G. Hill. il Field & S 82:16+ O '77

Exhibitions

Special hats, high ribs, and other news; firearms at the National Sporting Goods Show. B. Brister. il Field & S 82:114-16+ My '77
SPORTING goods industry
Howard Head strikes again; Prince Manufacturing Co. por Forbes 119:76 Je 1 '77
It all began with a garage sale; Karsten Manufacturing Company, makers of golf clubs. B. McDermott. il por Sports Illus 47:67-8 S 12 '77
See also
Questor corporation
Uniroyal, Inc
SPORTS
For the record. See issues of Sports illustrated
Games (cont) R. Blount, Jr. Esquire 87:38+ F; 44+ Ap; 42-4 My '77
New nightlife; sports. B. J. Phillips. il Vogue 167:259 N '77
Rugged recreation for the brave and the strong. Changing T 31:21-3 Ag '77
Scorecard. See issues of Sports illustrated
Sports. R. Blount, Jr (title varies) See issues of Esquire
Sports. K. Gilman. il Vogue 167:60 Ap; 54 My; 28+ Je; 34+ Jl '77
Sports. J. Kaplan. See occasional issues of Seventeen
See also
Athletes
College athletics
Computers—Sports use
Photography of sports
Physical education and training
Radio broadcasting—Sports
Recreation
School athletics
Segregation in sports
Sports for children
Television broadcasting—Sports
Violence in sports
also names of sports, e.g. Lacrosse

Accidents and injuries

Aches & pains of the weekend athlete; views of L. Root. Harp Baz 110:91+ My '77
Be a good sport. E. Zelig. Am Home 80:28+ Je '77
How to keep fit without killing yourself. il Mademoiselle 83. 158-9+ Je '77
See also
Basketball, Professional—Accidents and injuries
Boxing—Accidents and injuries
Football, Professional—Accidents and injuries
Running—Accidents and injuries
Skis and skiing—Accidents and injuries
Sports medicine

Anecdotes, facetiae, satire, etc.

I hate sports. L. B. Francke. Harp Baz 110:91+ My '77

Awards, prizes, etc.

In the spirit of joy and some joy of the spirit; sports award banquet circuit. R. Reid. il Sports Illus 46:32-7 F 28 '77

Competitions

See also
Olympic Games
Skating—Competitions

SPORTS—*Continued*

Economic aspects

Troubled world of Mike Burke. S. Zion. il pors N Y Times Mag p30-2+ O 9 '77
What inflation is doing to the world of sports. il U.S. News 82:53-6 My 16 '77
Who are these guys? professional sports owners. R. Kennedy. il Sports Illus 46:50-8+ Ja 31 '77
Why the sports business ain't what it used to be. C. G. Burck. il Fortune 95:294-9+ My '77

Ethical aspects

See also
Baseball, Professional—Ethical aspects
College athletics—Ethical aspects
Football, College—Ethical aspects
Football, Professional—Ethical aspects
Hockey, Professional—Ethical aspects
Horse racing—Ethical aspects

International aspects

See also
Olympic Games

Medical aspects

See Sports medicine

Periodicals

See also
Sports illustrated (periodical)

Philosophy

Heavy going. A. Reid. New Yorker 53:80-93 F 21 '77

Psychological aspects

How to overcome self-doubt and think your way to total confidence; ed by C. Seebohm. W. T. Gallwey. il House & Gard 149:22+ D '77
Joy of deprogramming sport; Can/Am Hockey School in Guelph. R. Kahn. il Time 110:50 Ag 22 '77
See also
Skis and skiing—Psychological aspects
Tennis—Psychological aspects

Records

See Sports records

Social aspects

Locker room mystique. C. Whelton. il Horizon 21:64-9 Ja '78

Canada

See also
Football, Professional—Canada

Cuba

See also
Baseball—Cuba

England

See also
Cricket (game)
Rugby football

France

See also
Automobile racing—France

Japan

See also
Baseball, Professional—Japan

Russia

Big red machine. Y. Brokhin. il N Y Times Mag p22-4+ My 29 '77

South Africa

Athlete power over South Africa. il Sr Schol 110:8 S 22 '77
Stigma on South African sport. S. A. Ogouki. il UNESCO Courier 30:26-7 N '77

United States

From cycling to mountain climbing—using leisure time for fitness. il U.S. News 82:70-1 My 23 '77
Losersville, U.S.A; Atlanta. R. Blount, Jr. il por Sports Illus 46:74-7+ Mr 21 '77
Sports. B. Weber. See issues of Senior scholastic including World week
Their way. P. Axthelm. il Newsweek 90:63+ D 26 '77
See also
Recreation—United States
United States—President's Commission on Olympic Sports

SPORTS action games. See Games
SPORTS arenas. See Stadiums
SPORTS broadcasters. See Radio broadcasting—Sports; Television broadcasting—Sports
SPORTS calendars. See Calendars
SPORTS camps. See Camps
SPORTS cars

Aero-Vette. B. Hall. il Motor T 28:44-7 D '76
Back on the right track; 27 T roadster kit. G. Baskerville. il Hot Rod 30:90-1+ Ap '77
Corrida sports coupe spices Fiesta debut. il Motor T 29:32-3 Ag '77
Corvette's 25th: polo-shirt and powerglide only. C. P. Rogers. il Motor T 29:62-4+ D '77
Hypertourers: Ferrari 400 Auto, Bristol 412 and Aston Martin Lagonda. L. J. K. Setright. il Car & Dr 22:106-8+ Je '77
Introducing the 1979 DeLorean—the car and the company. K. Ludvigsen. il por Motor T 29:44-9+ S '77
Life begins at 185 mph: triple-Lamborghini Modena-to-Calais hundred-grand convoy. M. Nichols. il Car & Dr 23:52-4+ Ag '77
Luxury sports car performs like a racer; Porsche 928. J. Dunne. il Pop Sci 210:103 Je '77
Piecemeal; Sprint-TV. G. Baskerville. il Hot Rod 30:94+ Ap '77
Porsche re-introduces the sports car; Porsche 928. D. E. Davis, Jr and others. il Car & Dr 22:45-7+ Je '77
Short take:
 Automobili Intermeccanica Speedster replica; 1957 Porsche. L. Mandel. il Car & Dr 23:34-5 Ja '78
 Chevrolet Corvette. P. Bedard. il Car & Dr 22:37 Mr '77
 MGB. il Car & Dr 23:69 Ja '78
 Porsche 911S. D. Sherman. il Car & Dr 22:40 Mr '77
Triumph TR7 5-speed. J. Ethridge. il Motor T 29:85 Ag '77
25 years on the most wanted list! Corvette. K. Ludvigsen. il Pop Mech 148:72-4+ S '77
Vettes! special section. il Hot Rod 30:50-62+ S '77
Years of the snake; Cobra project. W. Wyss. il por Hot Rod 30:31-4+ Je '77

Design

John DeLorean builds a sports car: the DMC-12. P. Bedard. il Car & Dr 23:37-9+ Jl '77
Shape of Vettes to come: a sneak preview of the 1980s. il Motor T 28:49-50 D '76

Equipment

Vettalog. M. Davis. il Hot Rod 30:70-4 D '77

History

Keeping the faith:
 Ettore Bugatti, Bunny Phillips and the jewels of Molsheim; Bugattis. C. Fox. il pors Car & Dr 23:97-8+ Ag; 89-91 S '77
Retrospect:
 1925 Bentley 3 litre speed model. W. S. Jackson. il Motor T 29:113-19 My '77
 1963 Corvette Grand Sport. J. Christy. il Motor T 29:77-8+ D '77

Photographs

Corvette: everyman's sports car; Silver anniversary Corvette 1953-1978. il Motor T 29:51-6+ D '77
Hot rod gallery. Hot Rod 30:54 Jl '77
Vettes. Hot Rod 30:56-62+ S '77

Testing

At speed in the Porsche 928. B. Hartford. il Pop Mech 147:92+ Ja '77
Driving a legend; 1927 Bugatti. C. Fox. il Car & Dr 23:92-3+ S '77
Driving the Porsche 928 in Europe. B. Cahier. il por Motor T 29:65-6 Ag '77
Hot rod magazine rod test:
 Gone with the wind; 1968 Corvette. G. Baskerville. il Hot Rod 30:38-40 F '77
 Snake bit: 427 Cobra. G. Baskerville. il Hot Rod 30:67-9 Je '77
Luxotouring: starring the Jaguar XJ-S, Mercedes-Benz 450SLC and BMW 630CSi. S. Thompson and others. il Car & Dr 23:64-7+ D '77
PM owners report:
 Corvette. K. Ludvigsen. il Pop Mech 148:75+ S '77
PS car test & driving report:
 High-performance sports cars. J. Dunne and R. Ceppos. il Pop Sci 210:54+ Je '77
Peugette 104: bucks-down exoticar. R. Wakefield. il Car & Dr 23:111-13 N '77
Road test:
 Corvette. B. Yates. il Car & Dr 23:31-4 O '77
 Corvette '77. T. Swan. il Motor T 28:34-8 D '76
 Ferrari 308 GTB. il Car & Dr 22:71-2+ Mr '77
 Ferrari 308 GTB. J. Christy. il Motor T 29:57-60+ Ap '77
 Lotus Esprit. il Car & Dr 23:72+ Jl '77
 Porsche 928: eight for the road. K. Ludvigsen. il Motor T 29:72-4 Je '77
 Silver sleek; Corvette. C. J. Baker. il Hot Rod 30:58+ D '77
 Triumph TR7. J. Christy. il Motor T 29:88-91 D '77
Triumph TR7 5-speed. M. Jordan. il Car & Dr 23:69-70+ Ag '77
We test:
 New Porsches. R. G. Beason. il Mech Illus 73:48-9+ Je '77

SPORTS cars, Racing. See Automobiles, Racing
SPORTS cars, Remodeled. See Automobiles, Remodeled
SPORTS clothes. See Clothing and dress—Sports clothes
SPORTS clubs
Farewell to Forest Hills; West Side Tennis Club. B. Collins. il N Y Times Mag p48-50+ S 11 '77
Marin Tennis Club by Backen, Arrigoni & Ross; with introd by B. F. Gordon and C. K. Hoyt. il Archit Rec 161:115-16, 128-30 F '77
Me and Time Inc; Sports Illustrated Court Clubs. il por Forbes 120:81 D 15 '77
Splash in public squash. R. Levy. il Duns R 110:71-3+ S '77
Uptown Racquet Club by architects Copelin, Lee and Chen; squash club; with introd by B. F. Gordon and C. K. Hoyt. il Archit Rec 161: 115-19 F '77
Wimbledon wangle; debentures in All-England Lawn Tennis Ground Ltd. il Forbes 120:29 Jl 15 '77
SPORTS complex, Meadowlands. See New Jersey—Meadowlands sports complex
SPORTS equipment. See Sporting goods
SPORTS films. See Motion pictures—Sports films
SPORTS for children
So your child wants to go out for the team. Changing T 31:34-6 O '77
Will competitive sports hurt your child? mental and physical demands. L. Mufflin. Harp Baz 110:90+ My '77
See also
Baseball, Childrens
Football, Childrens
Golf, Childrens
Soccer, Childrens
SPORTS for the aged
Not ready for the rocking chair; Senior Olympics. J. R. Hanley. il por Ret Liv 17:40-1 Jl '77
Super-Seniors: age will be served; tournament tennis. il Time 109:68 Ap 18 '77
SPORTS for the blind
Fishing: the perfect sport for the blind. J. Bashline. il Field & S 82:42-3+ S '77
SPORTS for the handicapped
Pitch for the disabled; C. Stevens. U. O'Connor. il por Sat Eve Post 249:14 O '77
Saying, showing, shaping; gymnastic program of the Syracuse Developmental Center, N.Y. D. Blatchley and C. Gove. il Parks & Rec 12: 38-40 N '77
SPORTS for women
Bazaar's action sports health guide; symposium. il Harp Baz 110:84-91+ My '77
See also
Basketball
Bowling
Football, High school
Pentathlon
Running
Sailboat racing
Weight lifting
SPORTS gambling. See Gambling
SPORTS halls of fame
See also
National Baseball Hall of Fame and Museum
SPORTS illustrated (periodical)
Coby Whitmore; sports illustrator. M. Tinkelman. il por Am Artist 41:70-3 Jl '77
Letter from the publisher. J. A. Meyers. See issues of Sports illustrated
Robert Handville; sports illustrator. M. Tinkelman. il por Am Artist 41:56-61 Jl '77
Tom Allen; illustrator of fishing articles. N. Meglin. il por Am Artist 41:52-5 Jl '77
SPORTS Illustrated Court Clubs. See Sports clubs
SPORTS in art
Murray Stern: social surrealist; football works. A. Sanders. il por Am Artist 41:76-83+ F '77
Special sports issue; with introd by M. Schiller and editorial comment. N. Meglin; M. Tinkelman. il Am Artist 41:2+ Jl '77
See also
Fishing in art
Hunting in art
SPORTS in literature
How you play the game: the novels of John R. Tunis. R. Shereikis. il Horn Bk 53:642-8 D '77
SPORTS journalism
Editorially speaking. J. Dianna. il Hot Rod 30:7-8 Ag '77
Encountering the Yankees. R. Kahn. il Time 109:79 Je 6 '77
Everybody knew me Al; excerpt from Ring, a biography of Ring Lardner. J. Yardley. il Sports Illus 47:82-6+ Ag 29 '77
Jim Murray: king of sports. W. Cieplik. por Writers Digest 57:23-4 Ag '77
Locker-room lib; women sportswriters in locker rooms. D. K. Shah and J. Whitmore. il Newsweek 91:86 Ja 16 '78
SPORTS literature
See also
Fishing literature

SPORTS locker rooms. See Locker rooms
SPORTS medicine
Ali's doctor: the greatest, in his own way; F. Pacheco. R. Blount, Jr. il Esquire 87:20+ Je '77
Pricking up their ears; lactic acid blood testing to determine most efficient training pace. J. Kirshenbaum. il por Sports Illus 47:94+ O 31 '77
This strange and perilous joint; dealing with knee injuries. W. O. Johnson. il Sports Illus 47:84-8+ O 24 '77
SPORTS newscasters. See Television broadcasting—Sports
SPORTS officiating
See also
Football, Professional—Refereeing
SPORTS records
Gimmicks, gadgets, goodby records; swimming. J. Kirshenbaum. il Sports Illus 46:40-2+ Ap 25 '77
It was a day unlike any other day; A. Geiberger's tour record at the Danny Thomas Memphis Classic. C. Gillespie. il pors Sports Illus 46:50+ Je 20 '77
Kentuckian predicts new world records. J. Alsofrom. Sci Digest 81:14 Mr '77
Record almost broke him; R. Maris' home run record. R. Telander. il pors Sports Illus 46: 60-4+ Je 20 '77
Record breaking women. J. H. Douglas and J. A. Miller. il Sci N 112:172-4 S 10 '77
See also
Automobile speed records
Boat speed records
SPORTS uniforms. See Uniforms, Sports
SPORTS writing. See Sports journalism
SPORTSCASTERS. See Radio broadcasting—Sports; Television broadcasting—Sports
SPORTSMEN. See Athletes; Hunters
SPORTSWRITING. See Sports journalism
SPOTSWOOD, N.J, Public Library. See Libraries—New Jersey
SPRAGUE, Bob. See Bernhardt, M. jt auth
SPRAGUE, Richard Aurel
New man on two old cases. S. J. Ungar. por Atlantic 239:8+ F '77 •
Self-inflicted wounds. D. M. Alpern and others. pors Newsweek 89:18+ F 21 '77 •
Shrinking Sprague. por Time 109:24 F 14 '77 •
SPRAGUE, Robert L. and Sleator, E. K.
Methylphenidate in hyperkinetic children: differences in dose effects on learning and social behavior. bibl il Science 198:1274-6 D 23 '77
SPRAGUE, Susan W.
Storytime stretches with books. SLJ 24:42 S '77
SPRAY painting. See Paint spraying
SPRAYERS, Aerosol. See Pressure packaging
SPRAYING and dusting
4 steps to precision spraying. G. Lepper. il Suc Farm 75:no522-3 Mr '77
Spray day; dormant oil spray for fruit trees. M. Brandies. il Org Gard & Farm 24:90-2 Mr '77
Spray for soybean diseases? il Farm J 10:12-13 Je '77
See also
Fertilizers and manures—Spray applications
SPRAYING apparatus
Electrostatic sprayer reduces pesticide pollution in crops. E. Powell. il Pop Sci 211:10+ Jl '77
Faster spraying, fewer field trips. Farm J 101: A8 My '77
5 affordable paint sprayers. T. H. Jones. il Mech Illus 73:22+ Jl '77
Garden sprayers. Consumer Rep 42:196-201 D '77
Low-cost pre-plant spray rigs for accurate soil incorporation. il Farm J 101:22-3 Ap '77
New way to tank mix. il Farm J 101:18-19 My '77
Recirculating sprayers catch on. J. D. Boyd. il Farm J 101:22+ My '77
Spray and till before you plant. il Farm J 101: M6-7 Ap '77
Sprayers: the weakest link. G. Lepper and L. Reichenberger. il Suc Farm 75:35-7+ Ja '77
Winners: two ways to calibrate a sprayer. G. Lepper. il Suc Farm 75:no4 L22 Mr '77
SPRIESTERSBACH, D. C. and Farrell, W. J.
Impact of Federal regulations at a university. bibl Science 198:27-30 O 7 '77
SPRING, Charles M.
Where have all the flower children gone? Chr Cent 94:952-4 O 19 '77
SPRING
Awakening. J. P. Jackson. il Am For 83:8-11 Ap '77
61 days. R. F. Hall. il Conservationist 31:48 Mr '77
Spring: it's lethal and lovely. il Time 109:10-11 Ap 18 '77
Why we clean—and rejoice—in spring. C. Seebohm. il House & Gard 149:116-31+ Ap '77
See also
April

SPRING festivals. See Festivals
SPRING Opera Theater. See Opera—California
SPRING training (baseball) See Baseball, Professional
SPRING vacations. See Vacations
SPRINGATE, David J.
Don't let industry move away. il por Am City & County 92:68-9 Ap '77
SPRINGER, Morris
Ladies of easy virtue. il Opera N 42:24+ D 24 '77
SPRINGS
See also
Geysers
SPRINGS (mechanism)
See also
Automobiles—Springs and suspension
SPRINGWATER, Jacqueline
Visionary doing inspires Arcosanti. Craft Horiz 37:9 F '77
SPRINKLERS
Irrigates square fields. G. Lorang. il Farm J 101:F2 S '77
Programmed watering—what a way to grow. R. F. Graf and G. J. Whalen. il Pop Mech 148:92-3+ Jl '77
See also
Fire sprinklers
SPROUL, Robert C.
You can't tell a school by its name. Chr Today 22:18+ N 4 '77
SPROUSE, Harry W. See Cooke, E. D. jt auth
SPROUTING. See Germination
SPROUTS
Art of sprouting aboard. R. Nance. Yachting 141:98 F '77
Instead of just alfalfa, why not grow a crunchy mix of sprouts? il Sunset 158:156 F '77
Self-watering sprout grower. R. Edwards. il Org Gard & Farm 24:124+ D '77
Sprouts: self-starter food. J. Stern; B. Sabol. il Vogue 167:366-7+ S '77
See also
Cookery—Vegetables
SPRUCE
Diseases and pests
See also
Spruce budworms
SPRUCE budworms
Control
Canada's moth war; efforts to halt spruce budworm spraying program due to increase in Reye's syndrome cases. E. E. May. bibl il map Environment 19:16-24 Ag '77
SPRUCE Goose (seaplane) See Seaplanes
SPRUCE grouse. See Grouse
SPRUCH, Grace Marmor, and Spruch, Larry
Do you have a space-age mind? Read Digest 110:127-9 Mr '77
SPRUCH, Larry. See Spruch, G. M. jt auth
SPRUNG, Barbara
Equality now! For girls and boys. il Parents Mag 52:44+ S '77
SPUNG, Merle Lee
Revival of rug hooking. il Ret Liv 17:40 F '77
SPURR, Stephen H.
Political history of the Forest Service. Am For 83:15-16 F '77
SPUTNIK (artificial satellite) See Artificial satellites, Russian
SPY stories. See Detective and mystery stories
SQUARE dancing
Fun on the square. S. C. Cowley and M. Lord. il Newsweek 89:83 Mr 7 '77
Inaugural square dance. R. D. Abrahams. New Repub 176:21-2 F 26 '77
SQUARE riggers. See Sailing vessels
SQUARE root of soul (dramatic reading) See Dramatic readings
SQUARES (carpentry instruments) See Carpenters squares
SQUASH (game)
It was hard, but easy; Australians in American tournaments. J. Kaplan. il por Sports Illus 46:44-5 F 7 '77
Racquets reach out. C. Wiseman. il Horizon 20:82-7 S '77
Squash everyone? M. King. il Forbes 120:56-7 Ag 1 '77
Squash memories. R. M. Dorson. New Repub 177:29-31 Jl 23 '77
SQUASH clubs. See Sports clubs
SQUASHES
Consumer's guide to winter squash varieties. N. Bubel. il Org Gard & Farm 25:69-73 Ja '78
Spaghetti squash makes an unusual vegetable. W. Masson. il Org Gard & Farm 24:72-3 Je '77
Winter squash from Asia. J. Meeker. il Org Gard & Farm 24:64-7 Jl '77
See also
Cookery—Vegetables
SQUAT Theater (theater group) See Theater, Experimental
SQUATTERS
Bulldozer remedy: apartheid at bay; squatters camps for migrant workers. A. Silk. Nation 225:298-304 O 1 '77
Destruction of an African community. M. Nash. Chr Cent 94:985 O 26 '77
SQUAW VALLEY, Calif.
It's a site for sore eyes; Squaw Valley as Olympic training site. A. Verschoth. il Sports Illus 47:46-7 Ag 22 '77
SQUIDS
Jumbo squid. K. Straus. il Oceans 10:10-15 Mr '77
SQUIRREL hunting
Come summertime, the squirreling is easy. B. W. Dalrymple. il Outdoor Life 159:80-1+ Mr '77
Fox in the treetops. C. Elliott. il map Outdoor Life 160:70-1+ Jl '77
Study in gray . . . the rifleman's squirrel. B. Bell. il Outdoor Life 160:82-3+ N '77
24 facts that'll help you bag more squirrels. M. Hicks. il Outdoor Life 160:80-1+ S '77
SQUIRRELS
Nutty about squirrels. K. Leon. il por Seventeen 36:94+ My '77
See also
Cookery—Game
Ground squirrels
SQUIRRU, Rafael
Art and freedom. il Américas 29:2-5 F '77
Poetic journey with Rafael Squirru; excerpt from prologue to Números, veinte años de poesía. R. Santana. il Américas 29:45-6 S '77 *
SRI LANKA
See also
United Nations—Sri Lanka
Description and travel
Stop a week in Sri Lanka. G. Herndon. il map House & Gard 149:74+ Je '77
Politics and government
See also
Elections—Sri Lanka
Religious institutions and affairs
See also
Buddha and Buddhism
Royal Botanic Gardens, Peradeniya
See Botanical gardens
SRODA, George
King of worms; interview, ed by J. Snow. il Outdoor Life 159:84-6+ F '77
SROLE, Leo
Big apple: better for your psyche. Sci N 111:308-9 My 14 '77 *
SROUFE, Gerald E.
Evaluation and politics in education. Educ Digest 43:20-3 D '77
U.S. Department of Education; case against it. Current 193:22-30 My '77
STAATS, Elmer B.
(ed) Bicentennial conference on the United States Constitution: the shaping of public policy—issues and questions for discussion. Ann Am Acad 432:121-31 Jl '77
about
Top federal watchdog. por Duns R 109:42 F '77 *
STABILITY, Chemical. See Chemical stability
STABILITY of boats. See Boats—Stability and stabilizers
STABILIZATION processors. See Photography—Processing—Apparatus and supplies
STABILIZERS. See Airplanes—Stability and stabilizers; Boats—Stability and stabilizers
STABLER, Kenny
Gettin' nowhere fast. R. F. Jones. il pors Sports Illus 47:88-92+ S 19 '77 *
STABLES. See Barns and stables
STACEY, Karen
Day in the pregnant life of. . .; story. Redbook 149:115 Je '77
STACK, William B.
School counselor: role conflict. bibl Clearing H 50:341-4 Ap '77
STACKS (computers) See Computers—Memory system
STACY, Hollis
Stacy's not spacy anymore. J. Papanek. il por Sports Illus 47:44-7 Ag 1 '77 *
STADIUMS
Cloud over the Superdome. il Forbes 120:34 D 1 '77
How a loser is really a winner; Busch Memorial Stadium, St Louis. Nations Bus 65:110 N '77
Sports stadiums that don't burden the taxpayers. il Nations Bus 65:104-6+ N '77
Superdome named desire. il Time 111:68-9 Ja 16 '78
We had this nice big rectangle. So why not put a painting on it? R. Indiana's design for the basketball court of the Milwaukee Exposition Convention Center Arena. Vasari. il por Art N 76:24 D '77

STADTFELD, Curtis K.
Plowing: an inquiry. il Audubon 79:44-7 My '77

about

For reporting excellence—again. Audubon 79:146 Jl '77 *

STAELIN, D. H. and others
Microwave spectroscopic imagery of the earth. bibl il Science 197:991-3 S 2 '77

STAFFEL, Rudolph
Light of Rudolph Staffel; interview, ed by P. Winokur and R. Winokur. il por Craft Horiz 37:24-9+ Ap '77

STAFFORD, Mary Ann
Architecture and scratchboard. il Design (US) 78:30 mid-Wint '77

STAFFORD, William
Acoma mesa; poem. Nation 225:348 O 8 '77
At the conference on cold; poem. Nation 224:665 My 28 '77
Glance down; poem. Nation 225:602 D 3 '77
Lenore Marshall poetry prize. Sat R 4:34-5 S 3 '77
Little night stories; poem. Nation 224:507 Ap 23 '77
Slave on the headland; poem. New Yorker 53:24 Ag 1 '77
They carved an animal; poem. Am Scholar 46: 189 Spr '77
Watching a candle; Ways of seeing; On an unnamed mountain; poems. Nation 225:184 S 3 '77
Ways to say wind; poem. Am Scholar 47:51 Wint '77
Window to let pride out; poem. Nation 224:697 Je 4 '77

STAFFORDSHIRE pottery. See Pottery, English

STAFFS (canes, sticks, etc)
Walking sticks in a Southern collection. J. W. Stone, Jr. bibl il Antiques 111:338-44 F '77

STAGE lighting. See Theater—Stage lighting

STAGE scenery. See Theater—Stage setting and scenery

STAGECOACHES. See Coaches and coaching

STAGEHANDS. See Theater—Employees

STAGGERED hours. See Hours of labor

STAGHORN ferns. See Ferns

STAHEL, Thomas H.
Four stories of theology. America 136:230-3 Mr 19 '77

STAHL, Ben
Ben Stahl: teaching art through television. M. Corbino. il por Am Artist 41:24-7+ Mr '77 *

STAHL, G. Allan
Centennial of the phonograph. bibl il pors Chemistry 50:10-12 D '77

STAHR, Alden
Garden of children. Org Gard & Farm 25:102 Ja '78

STAIN removers. See Laundry products

STAINBROOK, Edward J.
Treating depression. por Intellect 105:299 Mr '77

STAINED glass. See Glass painting and staining

STAINS and staining
Exterior latex stains. il Consumer Rep 42:144-7 Mr '77
Wood stains. . .keys to a fine finish. A. J. Hand. il Pop Sci 211:131-5+ O '77
Working with stains. H. Wicks. il Pop Mech 148:120 D '77

STAIRCASES. See Stairways

STAIRWAYS
Stairs with flair. il Bet Hom & Gard 55:68 Jl '77

STAKMAN, Elvin Charles
Botanists capture distinguished service awards. pors BioScience 27:346 My '77 *

STALIN, Iosif
Who started the cold war? C. L. Mee, Jr; W. A. Harriman; E. Abel. il pors Am Heritage 28:8-23 Ag '77 *

STALINA, Svetlana Iosifovna
Americanization of Stalin's daughter. H. E. Salisbury. il por McCalls 104:75+ Ap '77 *

STALLER, Sondra E.
Poetry in motion. il Design (US) 78:12-13 mid-Wint '77

STALLKNECHT, Alice
Portrait of a New England town. F. S. Wight. il Art in Am 65:106-7 My '77 *

STALLONE, Sylvester
Blaze of talent; interview, ed by E. Miller. por Seventeen 36:118-19+ F '77
Paradise Alley; excerpt from novel. Vogue 167: 120 D '77
Sylvester Stallone's rocky road to Rocky; interview, ed by P. Perry. il pors Writers Digest 57:29-30 Jl '77

about

Mr Smith goes to Philadelphia: Capra and Stallone. L. Quart. Intellect 106:245 D '77 *
Rocky comes to Dubuque. F. Maier. il pors Newsweek 89:28 Je 27 '77 *
Rocky KO's Hollywood. M. Kasindorf. il pors Newsweek 89:70-2+ Ap 11 '77 *

STALVEY, Dorrance
College-Conservatory: Stalvey prem. por Hi Fi 27:MA24 Ap '77 *

STAMELL, Marcia
West Point log: the basic training of Joan Smith. il pors Ms 6:48-51+ Ag '77

STAMFORD, Conn.
Instant urban renewal; mural on building walls in Stamford, Conn. R. Kahn. il Design (US) 78:2-4 mid-Summ '77

STAMM, Fred W.
I will survive; ed by B. East. Outdoor Life 160: 80-1+ D '77

STAMM, Gustav M.
To Gustav Stamm, Sci/Di's founder. por Sci Digest 81:inside cover F '77 *

STAMMERING. See Stuttering

STAMP collecting. See Postage stamps—Collectors and collecting

STAMPS, Food. See Food relief—United States

STAMPS, Hand. See Hand stamps

STAMPS, Postage. See Postage stamps

STANBRIDGE East, Quebec. See Villages—Canada

STANCER, Harvey C. See Coscina, D. V. jt auth

STANCILL, James McN.
Search for a leveraged buyout. Harvard Bus R 55:8+ Jl '77

STANDARD Brands, Inc
GE alumni revamp Standard Brands. il por Bus W p41-2 My 16 '77
Ross Johnson of Standard Brands: showdown. por Forbes 119:94 F 15 '77

STANDARD of living
See also
Cost of living
Income
Luxuries

STANDARD Oil Company. See Petroleum industry—History

STANDARD Oil Company (Ohio)
For Sohio, it was Alaskan oil—or bust. A. L. Morner. il por Fortune 96:172-6+ Ag '77

STANDARD Oil Company of California
Serendipitous SoCal. Forbes 119:24 F 1 '77

STANDARDS. See Accounting—Standards; Education—Standards

STANDARDS, Color. See Color—Standards

STANDARDS, Engineering
See also
Building—Standards

STANDARDS, Labor. See Labor standards

STANDARDS, National Bureau of. See United States—Standards, National Bureau of

STANDARDS and Conduct, Select Committee on. See United States—Congress—Senate—Standards and Conduct, Select Committee on

STANDARDS Institute, American National. See American National Standards Institute

STANDISH, Peter D.
After the Consent Decree: the effect on the Traditional Market Agreement. Pub W 211: 44-8 Ap 25 '77

STANDS (furniture)
Easy-to-make typing table. T. H. Jones. il Mech Illus 73:154 O '77

STANDS, Christmas tree. See Christmas tree stands

STANFORD, Charles
How to convert a four banger for stopwatch functions. il Pop Electr 12:56-7 Ag '77

STANFORD Medical Center. See Hospitals—California

STANFORD Research Institute. See SRI International

STANFORD University, Palo Alto, Calif.
Stanford goes to Washington. P. M. Boffey. Science 196:631 My 6 '77

Graduate School of Business

What Stanford does better than Harvard. B. Schultz. il Esquire 88:118-19+ S '77

Libraries

Stanford & UC get $$ for broad-gauge co-op. Lib J 102:320 F 1 '77

STANG, Missy
Missy goes Surrealistic. G. Dostal. il por Sch Arts 77:22-3 N '77 *

STANHOPE, Philip Dormer, 4th Earl of Chesterfield. See Chesterfield, P. D. S.

STANLEY, Julian Cecil, 1918-
Smorgasbord for an IQ of 150. il Time 109:64 Je 6 '77 *
Young prodigies take off under special program. D. Nevin. il por Smithsonian 8:76-81 bibl(p 160) O '77 *

STANLEY, Peter W.
Our Philippine bases. Nation 224:561-2 My 7 '77

STANNOUS fluoride. See Fluorides

STANTON, Maura
Maple tree; poem. Esquire 88:94 N '77

STANTON, Walter Oliver
High fidelity pathfinders. N. Eisenberg. por Hi Fi 27:40+ Ap '77 *

STANTON, Will
Imperfect listener; story. Sat Eve Post 249:32-3 O '77
Keeping the home fires burning. il Good H 185: 78+ N '77
Once upon a time is enough; story. McCalls 104: 162-3 S '77
Showdown at generation gap. Read Digest 111: 134-6 O '77
STANTON, William K.
New talent series. A. Grundberg. il por Mod Phot 41:140-1 N '77 *
STAPLE guns
Almost indispensible tool: staple guns. il McCalls 104:45 Jl '77
STAPLETON, Constance
Art of staying old. il Am Home 80:6+ Mr '77
STAPLETON, James C. and Croft, John
Suggestions for ending classroom conflict. Educ Digest 42:28-9 Mr '77
STAPLETON, Jean
Being Edith. il Good H 185:48 Ag '77
STAPLETON, Ruth (Carter)
Christmas with the Carters. il por Ladies Home J 94:74+ D '77
Jimmy Carter's sister: how faith can heal; interview, ed by J. West. por McCalls 104:32+ Ap '77
Message of Easter. por Ladies Home J 94:107+ Ap '77
Walking people out of their past; interview. pors Chr Today 22:10-14 N 4 '77

about

And the first sisters. T. Mathews and E. Shannon. il pors Newsweek 90:34 N 14 '77 *
Hustling for the Lord. T. Schwartz and others. il pors Newsweek 90:61 D 5 '77 *
STAPLETON, Sid
Buoyancy in a bottle. il Motor B & S 139:72-4 Mr '77
Special delivery. il Motor B & S 139:82-3+ My '77
STAR Bacardi Cup Race. See Sailboat racing
STAR charts. See Astronomy—Charts, diagrams, etc.
STARBIRD, Ethel A.
Kauai. il map Nat Geog 152:584-613 N '77
New York's land of dreamers and doers. il map Nat Geog 151:702-24 My '77
Way of life called Maine. il map Nat Geog 151:726-57 Je '77
STARE, Fredrick J. and Whelan, E. M.
Dr Fredrick Stare rates the 10 top diets. Harp Baz 110:40-3 Jl '77
Safest diet for every woman on the pill. Harp Baz 110:120-1+ Ag '77
STARER, Robert
SUNY at Binghamton: Starer prem; The people, yes. por Hi Fi 27:MA18 Mr '77 *
STARK, Al
Case of the deadly hot peppers. Read Digest 111:207-8+ N '77
STARK, Anne
Let's liven up school lunches! por Seventeen 36: 42 S '77
Right combination. Seventeen 36:78 S '77
STARK, Craig
Selecting the best cassette tape for your recording needs. il Pop Electr 12:47-51 N '77
Tape recorder hygiene. il Pop Electr 12:56-7 Jl '77
STARNES, Richard
Starnes at large. See issues of Outdoor life
STARR, Douglas
Dust still falls on Derby despite a tough new law. Audubon 79:136-8 S '77
STARR, John T.
Rugged, fragile Maine. il Am For 83:14-17+ My '77
STARR, S. Frederick
Russian Revolution: a wall-sized history. il Smithsonian 8:52-4 Jl '77
Soviet painter poses a question. il por Smithsonian 8:101-4+ bibl(p 135) D '77

about

Wilson Center immerses scholars in think tank. E. P. Morgan. il pors Smithsonian 8:76-83 Ag '77 *
STARR County, Tex.

Crime

See Crime and criminals—Texas
STARRELS, John
United States and West Europe. bibl f Cur Hist 73:145-8+ N '77
STARRETT, Priscilla H. See Schwalm, P. A. jt auth
STARRY, Donn A.
Speak no evil. Nat R 29:764-5 Jl 8 '77 *

STARS
Deep-sky wonders. W. S. Houston. See issues of Sky and telescope
[Month] stars. J. Stokley. See fourth issue of each month of Science news to December 24, 1977

See also

Astrology
Astrophysics
Black holes (astronomy)
Constellations
Galaxies
Neutron stars
Occultations
Radio sources (astronomy)
Stellar winds

Clusters

Inside Messier 11. il Sky & Tel 53:427 Je '77
X-ray stars in globular clusters. G. W. Clark. il Sci Am 237:42-55 O '77

Evolution

As stars fall to ashes. D. E. Thomsen. il Sci N 111:364-5 Je 4 '77
Bok globules. R. L. Dickman. il Sci Am 236: 66-70+ bibl(p 142) Je '77
Brilliant disc-shaped star may be forming planets. il Space World N-9-165:42-3 S '77
Cloud collapsing, stars forming. il Sci N 112:359 N 26 '77
Disappearing nebula: a star turns on? il Sky & Tel 54:268-9 O '77
Infrared studies of star formation. M. W. Werner and others. bibl il Science 197:723-32 Ag 19 '77
Survey of galaxies sheds light on shape. il Sci N 111:86 F 5 '77
Water vapor maser turn-on in the HII region W3 (OH) A. D. Haschick and others. bibl il Science 198:1153-5 D 16 '77
Witnesses to a creation; MWC 349. il Time 109: 71 Je 27 '77

See also

Pulsars

Motion in line of sight

Whither thou goest. . ; recession velocities of remote spiral galaxies. Sky & Tel 53:111-12 F '77

Radial velocity

See Stars—Motion in line of sight

Radiation

EUV makes the grade; question of the extreme ultraviolet. S. P. Maran. Natur Hist 86:85-6+ F '77
STARS, Double
Binary-star speckle interferometry. H. A. McAlister. il Sky & Tel 53:346-50 My '77

See also

Stars, Eclipsing binary
STARS, Eclipsing binary
AN Ursae Majoris—another AM Herculis? G. S. Mumford. il Sky & Tel 54:194-6 S '77
CM Draconis: a very useful eclipsing system. il Sky & Tel 54:26 Jl '77
Story of AM Herculis. W. Liller. il Sky & Tel 53:351-4 My '77
STARS, Multiple
Companions of sunlike stars. H. A. Abt. il Sci Am 236:96-104 bibl(p 148) Ap '77
STARS, New
Giving cosmic rays their bounce. Sci N 111:309 My 14 '77
New evidence supports supernova origin of solar system. G. M. Spruch. il Phys Today 30:17-19 My '77
Nova Ophiuchi 1977. Sky & Tel 54:382-3 N '77
Nova Sagittae 1977. il Sky & Tel 53:163+ Mr '77
SS Cygni and the rapid burster. il Sky & Tel 54:364 N '77
Supernovae today. L. C. Green. il Sky & Tel 54:11-14 Jl '77
Supernovas. D. E. Thomsen. il Sci N 111:76-8 Ja 29 '77
Traumatic birth; formation of the solar system triggered by the concussion of a supernova. Sci Am 238:66+ Ja '78
STARS, Variable
Amateurs observe the new Trapezium variable. il Sky & Tel 53:319-20 Ap '77
Faint variable star. Sky & Tel 54:469 D '77
56-minute variable star; GD 428. Sky & Tel 54: 267 O '77
International flare-star campaign. Sky & Tel 54: 468 D '77

See also

American Association of Variable Star Observers
Stars, Eclipsing binary
START of something; drama. See Gersbach, J.
STARTING, Automobile. See Automobiles—Starting
STARVATION

See also

Anorexia nervosa
Famines

STASIO, Marilyn
Entertainment this fall. il Harp Baz 110:34+ S '77

STATE, The
Modern politics; state and society. G. Niemeyer. Nat R 29:333 Mr 18 '77

STATE aid to libraries. See Libraries—State aid

STATE and art. See Art and state

STATE and church. See Church and state

STATE and education. See Education and state

STATE and environment. See Environmental policy

STATE and federal relations. See Federal and state relations

STATE and industry. See Industry and state

STATE and libraries. See Libraries and state

STATE and literature. See Literature and state

STATE and medicine. See Medical policy

STATE and music. See Music and state

STATE and recreation. See Recreation and state

STATE and science. See Science and state

STATE and technology. See Technology and state

STATE and the arts. See The Arts and state

STATE and the individual. See Individual and state

STATE bonds
Voters say yes to spending for essentials, no to frills. U.S. News 83:104-5 N 21 '77

STATE colleges. See Colleges and universities, State

STATE courts. See Courts

STATE Department (United States) See United States—State, Department of

STATE employees
See also
American Federation of State, County, and Municipal Employees

Salaries, allowances, etc.

Academics in New York and California fight disclosure policies. B. J. Culliton. Science 196:37-8 Ap 1 '77

STATE fairs. See Fairs

STATE finance
Better news for states, cities—and some taxpayers, too. il U.S. News 83:77-8 Jl 4 '77
Dramatic upturn in state and local spending. il Fortune 95:10 Mr '77
Public control of public money; state-owned banks. J. Rowen. Progressive 41:47-52 F '77
State and local spending is bolstering G.N.P. il Fortune 96:24 N '77
See also
Finance—Alaska
Finance—Michigan
Finance—New York (state)
State bonds

STATE governments
Surprising trend: you can beat city hall; citizens taking their governments to court. U.S. News 83:67-8 Ag 8 '77
When states look for ways to help people—. il U.S. News 83:94-5 O 31 '77
See also
Governors
National Conference on Alternative State and Local Public Policies

STATE hospitals, Psychiatric. See Hospitals, Psychiatric

STATE laws. See Law—United States

STATE legislators. See Legislators

STATE legislatures
See also
Massachusetts—Legislature
Nevada—Legislature
Rhode Island—Legislature

STATE libraries
See also
Illinois State Library, Springfield

STATE library agencies
Montana not NFB target; new battle in Nebraska; efforts to remove library service programs for the blind from jurisdiction of state library agencies. Lib J 102:536 Mr 1 '77
Seven Springs Institute: state agency heads face the future. K. Nyren. Lib J 102:444-6 F 15 '77
State agency $$ efficiency stressed in COSLA study. Lib J 102:435+ F 15 '77
Threats to state agency $$ role shaping up. Lib J 102:1090+ My 15 '77
See also
American Library Association—Association of State Library Agencies

STATE lobbyists and lobbying. See Lobbyists and lobbying

STATE lotteries. See Lotteries

STATE medicine. See Medical care, State

STATE of the Union Message, 1977. See Ford, G. R.—State of the Union Message, January 12, 1977

STATE ownership. See Government ownership

STATE Park and Recreation Commission for the City of New York. See New York (state)—State Park and Recreation Commission for the City of New York

STATE parks and reserves
See also subhead Parks and reserves under names of states, e.g. California—Parks and reserves

STATE Resort Park system. See Kentucky—Parks and reserves

STATE rights. See Federal and state relations

STATE succession
See also
United Nations Conference of Plenipotentiaries on Succession of States in Respect of Treaties

STATE taxation. See Taxation, State

STATE universities. See Colleges and universities, State

STATE University of New York. See New York (state). State University

STATEN ISLAND

Education

Career education: success for the potential dropout; cooperative work program, Egbert Junior High School. A. J. Keller. Clearing H 51:70-2 O '77

STATES, Randy
Electronic flash landscapes. R. Busch. il Pop Phot 81:130-3+ D '77 *

STATES (United States)
States in focus; table. Sr Schol 109:11-12 Ja 13 '77
Surge in income—which states do best. il U.S. News 82:79 My 23 '77
U.S. in focus; facts about the states; chart. Sr Schol 110:35-6 O 20 '77
See also
State governments

STATES, Ideal. See Utopias

STATESMEN
World leaders who'll make news in coming year. il U.S. News 83:44-5 D 26 '77
See also
Dictators

STATEVILLE Correctional Center, Joliet. See Prisons—Illinois

STATEWIDE Preschool Screening Program, North Carolina. See Educational tests and measurements

STATHAKIS, George James
Excerpts from testimony on nuclear reactor safety, February 24, 1976. Cong Digest 56:60+ F '77

STATHAM, Robert R.
Tax outlook: hidden traps for business. il Nations Bus 65:22-4 N '77

STATION wagon engines. See Automobile engines

STATION wagons
Pontiac Firebird Type K. il Motor T 29:41-2 Je '77
Short take:
AMC Pacer wagon. M. Jordan. il Car & Dr 22:22 Ap '77
Buick Estate wagon. D. Abrahamson. il Car & Dr 23:101 Jl '77

Four wheel drive

See also
Station wagons, Foreign—Four wheel drive

Testing

PM owners report:
AMC Pacer station wagon. M. Lamm. il Pop Mech 147:92-3+ My '77
PS car test & driving report:
Compact wagons; Aspen and Pacer. il Pop Sci 210:34+ My '77
Road test:
Dodge Royal Monaco Brougham wagon. J. Christy. il Motor T 29:87-8+ Je '77
Two new station wagons; AMC Pacer and Pontiac Catalina Safari. il Consumer Rep 42:206-10 Ap '77
We test:
AMC's new Pacer wagon. B. Brender. il Mech Illus 73:80-1+ F '77

STATION wagons, Foreign

Four wheel drive

Wheels afield:
Subaru 4WD wagon. B. Kovacik. il Motor T 29:110+ N '77

Testing

Driving the Lambda Sond Volvo. B. Hartford. il Pop Mech 148:57+ Jl '77
Holy Conestoga, Sven, it's. . .Boss Wagon III! Volvo. M. Jordan. il Car & Dr 23:43-4+ D '77

STATISTICAL methods
Stein's paradox in statistics. B. Efron and C. Morris. il Sci Am 236:119-27 bibl(p 148) My '77
See also
United States—Labor Statistics, Bureau of

STATISTICS
See also
Average
Religious statistics
Seasonal variations (economics)
also subhead statistics under various subjects, e.g. United States—Statistics
STATUE of Liberty
He built the Statue of Liberty; F. A. Bartholdi. N. Poulain. il Read Digest 110:27-32 Ap '77
Liberty stands on her words; excerpt from American Jewish landmarks: a travel guide and history. B. Postal and L. Koppman. il por Ms 6:22 Ag '77
La statue colossale; report of lecture by M. Trachtenburg. New Yorker 53:15-16 Ag 1 '77
STATUES
See also
San Francisco—Monuments, statues, etc.
Statue of Liberty
STATUETTES. See Figurines
STATURE
Growing up tall; tall girls. A. Bayer. il Seventeen 36:186-7+ Ap '77
Short people—are they being discriminated against? il U.S. News 82:68-9 Mr 28 '77
Shorties don't always get short shrift in life. P. Ryan. il Smithsonian 8:156 Ap '77
STATUS, Social. See Social status
STATUS of Women, Commission on the. See United Nations—Commission on the Status of Women
STAVINS, Ralph. See Landau, S. jt auth
STAVRIANOS, Leften Slavros
Cuba: update on a revolution. Nation 224:270-4 Mr 5 '77
STEAD, Bette Ann
Why help women into careers? address, October 11, 1977. Vital Speeches 44:157-60 D 15 '77
STEAK. See Cookery—Meat
STEALING
Crime on the farm; rural property theft. J. K. Footlick and others. il Newsweek 90:101 O 3 '77
Equipment thefts start to drain oil drillers. il Bus W p23-4 Ja 9 '78
Guy with the edge; D. Sorkin's guilty plea in sports betting larceny case. P. Axthelm. il pors Newsweek 90:57 O 3 '77
I'm a friend of your son's. C. Green. il Ret Liv 17:32-3 S '77
Lie detectors to private eyes: antishoplifting battle heats up; pilfering employees. il U. S. News 83:61 N 28 '77
Now it's a wave of thefts in historic documents. il U.S. News 83:51-2 S 5 '77
Target: the checks in your mailbox. H. Gluck. il Ret Liv 16:25-6+ D '76
There are many ways to steal. Chr Today 22:28 N 4 '77
See also
Art thefts
Automobiles, Theft of
Boats, Theft of
Burglary and burglars
Embezzlement
Horse stealing
Library thefts
Poaching
Robberies and assaults
Shoplifting
Stolen goods, Receiving of
STEALING in literature. See Literature—Themes
STEAM juicers. See Canning and preserving—Equipment and supplies
STEAM motorcycles. See Motorcycles, Steam
STEAM power plants
Power source that has no limit; magma tap power plant. N. Carlisle. il Mech Illus 73:52-3+ Ag '77

Environmental aspects

Mercury emissions from geothermal power plants. D. E. Robertson and others. bibl il Science 196:1094-7 Je 3 '77
STEAM ships. See Steamships and steamboats
STEAMBOATS. See Steamships and steamboats
STEAMERS (kitchen utensils) See Kitchen utensils and appliances
STEAMING (cookery)
All steamed up about steamers. Am Home 80:13+ Mr '77
Best way to cook vegetables; with steamers. il McCalls 104:84+ Ag '77
STEAMSHIPS and steamboats
Beautiful white swan; campaign to save the Alexander Hamilton. New Yorker 53:29-30 F 21 '77
Luxury hotel designed to float down the Mississippi to New Orleans; Mississippi Queen. il Archit Rec 162:114-17 O '77
New Queen for the old Mississippi; Mississippi Queen. J. Hall. il map Pop Mech 148:57-61+ Ag '77
Three relics; final voyage of the Chauncey M. Depew. New Yorker 53:25-6 Je 20 '77
See also
Ocean liners

STEANE, John Barry
What might have been. il Opera N 42:26-9 Ag '77
STEARNS, Robert D.
Boating. See issues of Outdoor life
Chart your way to the fish. il map Outdoor Life 160:133-4 S '77
Stainless-steel props—better performance, longer life. il Pop Sci 210:38+ Je '77
STEBBINS, Doris E.
Give melons a head start. il Org Gard & Farm 24:98-9 F '77
STEBEL, S. L.
How to find your real story. Writer 90:22-3 Mr '77
STEBER, George R.
Morse code automatic readout on a TV screen. il Pop Electr 11:64-5 My '77
STECHER, Fred
Fingers in the sky. L. A. Taylor. por Motor T 29:117-18 O '77 *
STEDMAN, William Perry, 1923-
Department discusses consular services for Americans abroad; statement, July 14, 1977. il Dept State Bull 77:259-65 Ag 22 '77
Human rights in Panama; statement, October 11, 1977. Dept State Bull 77:652-5 N 7 '77
STEEGMULLER, Francis
Paris celebrates: a new art center and the brothers Duchamp. Atlantic 239:88-90 Je '77
STEEL, Danielle
New life poem. Good H 184:164 My '77
STEEL, Ronald
Motherhood, apple pie and human rights. New Repub 176:14-15 Je 4 '77
STEEL
Second phases in steel. W. R. Bandi. bibl il Science 196:136-42 Ap 8 '77
See also
Steel industry

Prices

Brake on steel price rises. il Bus W p 157-8 My 16 '77
Carter plan to aid steel—will it work? il U.S. News 83:67 D 19 '77
Cautious approval for U.S. reference prices. il Bus W p30 Ja 16 '78
European steelmen try U.S.-style protection. il Bus W p29-30 Ja 16 '78
First step in rescuing steel. il Bus W p34-5 N 28 '77
Mystery of steel prices. R. Lamb. il Fortune 95:158-60 Mr '77
Steel price increases jolt Carter's policy. il Bus W p21-2 Ag 8 '77
Steel prices go up without a word. Bus W p26 Ap 4 '77
Steel seeks more money, quick. il Time 111:65 Ja 2 '78
Too much, too soon? D. Pauly and R. Thomas. il Newsweek 89:88 My 16 '77
Trigger to curb dumping. Time 111:45-6 Ja 16 '78
Underselling Japanese steel. il Bus W p25-6 Jl 11 '77
Why government should stay out of steel pricing. E. Bickford. il por Nations Bus 65:40-2 Ja '77
STEEL Communities Coalition. See Pressure groups
STEEL construction
Parking deck saves money with tube columns and weathering steel. il Archit Rec 161:143-4 Je '77
STEEL framing. See Framing (building)
STEEL industry
See also
Collective bargaining—Steel industry
Collective labor agreements—Steel industry
Steel workers

Accounting

Court untangles Sharon Steel's books; inflated earnings. Bus W p34-5 My 9 '77

Acquisitions and mergers

LTV's play to cut its losses through a merger with Lykes; Jones & Laughlin and Youngstown Sheet. il Bus W p86+ Ja 9 '78
Lykes and LTV count on an antitrust break; Jones & Laughlin and Youngstown Sheet. il Bus W p64 N 21 '77
Mexican merger unsettles steelmakers. il Bus W p28 Je 6 '77

Antitrust cases

Lykes and LTV count on an antitrust break. il Bus W p64 N 21 '77

Export-import trade

Antitrust question about Japanese steel. Bus W p32+ D 19 '77
Big steel and big government. G. F. Will. Newsweek 90:124 D 12 '77
Heated campaign to fight steel imports. il Bus W p36 F 7 '77
How foreign steelmakers woo U.S. buyers. il Bus W p68-9 S 19 '77

STEEL industry—Export-import trade—*Cont.*
In the doldrums. D. Pauly and others. il Newsweek 90:60-1 Ag 15 '77
International reactions to the problems of steel trade; statement, September 20, 1977. W. G. Barraclough. Dept State Bull 77:742-50 N 21 '77
No fooling! address, April 1, 1977. L. W. Foy. Vital Speeches 43:435-7 My 1 '77
Protecting steel. New Repub 177:8-9 D 17 '77
Should U.S. limit steel imports? interviews. J. P. Murtha, Jr; C. Stern. pors U.S. News 83:77-8 O 24 '77
Specialty steel: help from temporary quotas. Bus W p78 S 19 '77
Steel: after the shutdowns and layoffs, what? with interviews with E. Speer and H. Saito. il Forbes 120:33-6 N 15 '77
Steel builds its dumping case. il Bus W p 128+ O 17 '77
Steel imports; address, September 21, 1977. J. D. Briggs. Vital Speeches 44:73-5 N 15 '77
Steel negotiator looks at election issues; foreign imports and the steel union; address, December 16, 1976. J. B. Johnston. Vital Speeches 43:238-43 F 1 '77
Testing our metal. New Repub 177:6+ O 22 '77
Underselling Japanese steel. il Bus W p25-6 Jl 11 '77
Why a key U.S. industry worries about its future. il U.S. News 82:60 Je 6 '77
Why steel's dumping cases may backfire. il Bus W p48 N 14 '77

Federal aid

Bailout. Newsweek 90:57-8 D 19 '77
Big steel and big government. G. F. Will. Newsweek 90:124 D 12 '77
Carter plan to aid steel—will it work? il U.S. News 83:67 D 19 '77
Growing conflict over rescuing steel. il Bus W p39-40 O 10 '77
Help is coming—but is it enough? il Bus W p58+ Ja 9 '78
How to help slumping steel. il Time 110:58-9 D 5 '77
What Washington may do for steel. Bus W p35-6 O 24 '77

Finance

Gleam is gone from steelmen's eyes. il Bus W p29-30 Ap 25 '77
Help is coming—but is it enough? il Bus W p58+ Ja 9 '78
In the doldrums. D. Pauly and others. il Newsweek 90:60-1 Ag 15 '77
Some reassurance for steel. il Time 110:63-4 O 24 '77
Steel. il Forbes 121:104+ Ja 9 '78
Steel: after the shutdowns and layoffs, what? with interviews with E. Speer and H. Saito. il Forbes 120:33-6 N 15 '77
Steel: biting the bullet. il Forbes 120:35-6 D 1 '77
Steel industry's woes hit close to home. map U.S. News 83:56 O 10 '77

International aspects

International reactions to the problems of steel trade; statement, September 20, 1977. W. G. Barraclough. Dept State Bull 77:742-50 N 21 '77
Sponge iron in steel's future. S. Rose. il Fortune 95:106-10+ Ja '77

Canada

Crossing the border; Dominion Bridge. J. Cook. il Forbes 120:85+ N 15 '77

Europe, Western

European steelmen try U.S.-style protection. il Bus W p29-30 Ja 16 '78
Take your (ugh!) pills, boys. por Forbes 120:120 N 1 '77

France

Creusot-Loire's tenuous U.S. prospects. il Bus W p214+ N 14 '77

Great Britain

See also
British Steel Corporation

Japan

We are being used as scapegoats; interview. H. Saito. Forbes 120:36 N 15 '77

Mexico

Mexican merger unsettles steelmakers. il Bus W p28 Je 6 '77
Mexican solution for companies in debt; Bank of America's loan to Fundidora de Monterrey. Bus W p42 F 14 '77

Russia

Snags that slow down Soviet steel. Bus W p82 S 19 '77

United States

Basic black; Carpenter Technology. Forbes 120:38 D 15 '77
Court untangles Sharon Steel's books; inflated earnings. Bus W p34-5 My 9 '77
Great iron ore squeeze. Forbes 120:58 S 1 '77
Hard times come to steeltown. L. Smith. il Fortune 96:86-93 D '77
If the steel industry is to survive. . .; interview. L. W. Foy. il por U.S. News 83:90+ N 21 '77
Nucor: one winner in troubled steel. D. G. Santry. il Bus W p 104 N 21 '77
Pygmy steelmaker struggles to survive; Alan Wood Steel Co. Bus W p27 Je 27 '77
Quandary of steel. Nation 225:484-5 N 12 '77
Soft as steel. Nat R 29:1284-5 N 11 '77
Steel companies announce layoffs. L. Bornstein and others. M Labor R 100:71 D '77
Steel fights Murphy's law. il Time 110:66+ S 19 '77
Steel's five big problems. il Nations Bus 65:26-8 N '77
Steel's sea of troubles. il Bus W p66-9+ S 19 '77
Victor Posner: living on borrowed time; chief executive of Sharon Steel. P. Blustein. por Forbes 120:23-4 S 1 '77
Wanted: prescription for steelmakers' ills; with interviews with J. P. Murtha and C. Stern. il U.S. News 83:76-8 O 24 '77
See also
Allegheny Ludlum Industries, Inc
Armco Steel Corporation
Bethlehem Steel Corporation
Inland Steel Company
Jones & Laughlin Steel Corporation
Kaiser Steel Corporation
McLouth Steel Corporation
United States Steel Corporation
United Steelworkers of America
Youngstown Sheet & Tube Company

STEEL metallurgy
Sponge iron in steel's future. S. Rose. il Fortune 95:106-10+ Ja '77

STEEL sculpture. See Metal sculpture

STEEL shot. See Shot

STEEL workers
Campbell faces up to hard times. . .again. M. King. il Forbes 120:57-64 N 15 '77
End for Steel City? closing of Youngstown Sheet & Tube Co. works. il Time 110:78 O 3 '77
Fear Valley, U.S.A; closing of Youngstown Sheet & Tube Company plant. R. W. Gibbons. Commonweal 104:720-2 N 11 '77
Hard times come to steeltown. L. Smith. il Fortune 96:86-93 D '77
Huge pink slip for an Ohio city; Youngstown Sheet & Tube Co. Bus W p39-40 O 3 '77
Steel blues; closing Youngstown Sheet & Tube Co. plant. D. Pauly and J. Lowell. il Newsweek 90:80+ O 3 '77
Steel companies announce layoffs. L. Bornstein and others. M Labor R 100:71 D '77
Steel negotiator looks at election issues: foreign imports and the steel union; address, December 16, 1976. J. B. Johnston. Vital Speeches 43:238-43 F 1 '77
See also
United Steelworkers of America

STEEL works

Coke plants

See Coke plants

Environmental aspects

Bethlehem's bind in Johnstown; air pollution moratorium request. il Bus W p40+ Ag 15 '77
EPA threatens to blacklist Kaiser; Fontana, Calif, plant. il Bus W p27 My 2 '77
EPA's big win; U.S. Steel Corp's water pollution. Time 109:63-4 Je 27 '77
Safe water or jobs? il U.S. News 82:47 F 7 '77

Location

Troubled steel towns campaign for help; Steel Communities Coalition. Bus W p35 O 24 '77

STEELE, Jonathan
Behind the Berlin Wall. Nation 225:397-400 O 22 '77

STEELE, Max
About love and grasshoppers; story. Redbook 149:126-7 My '77

STEELE, Timothy
Three notes toward definitions; poems. Poetry 130:218-20 Jl '77

STEELHEAD trout fishing. See Trout fishing

STEELWORKERS union. See United Steelworkers of America

STEELY Dan (rock group) See Rock groups

STEERE, Allen C. and others
Erythema chronicum migrans and Lyme arthritis: cryoimmunoglobulins and clinical activity of skin and joints. bibl il Science 196:1121-2 Je 3 '77

STEERE, William Campbell
Botanists capture distinguished service awards. pors BioScience 27:346 My '77 •

STEERING gear
See also
Automobiles—Steering gear
Boats—Steering gear

STEFANILE, Felix
Dawn; poem. Commonweal 104:205 Ap 1 '77

STEFANO, Frank, Jr
American hotels on early Staffordshire. bibl il Antiques 112:274-7 Ag '77
STEFFAN, Cecilia
What I've learned about raising geese. Org Gard & Farm 24:156-60 S '77
STEFFANI, Agostino
Niobe, regina di Tebe. Review
New Yorker 53:182-4+ N 28 '77 *
STEFFEK, Edwin F.
Double plot: multiply your vegetable harvest. il Pop Mech 147:100-1 Mr '77
STEFFENS, Lincoln
Reconsideration. R. Stinson. New Repub 177:37-9 Jl 9 '77 *
STEGEMAN, Janet A. See Stegeman, J. F. jt auth
STEGEMAN, John F. and Stegeman, J. A.
Cause célèbre of Caty Greene; excerpt from Caty. il por Am Hist Illus 12:8-16 Je '77
STEGNER, Page
Wynken, Blynken, and cod. Atlantic 240:39-45 Jl '77
STEGNER, Wallace
Literary life anything but romantic; excerpts from address. por Intellect 106:107 S '77
STEHL, R. H. and Lamparski, L. L.
Combustion of several 2,4,5-trichlorophenoxy compounds: formation of 2,3,7,8-tetrachlorodibenzo-p-dioxin. bibl il Science 197:1008-9 S 2 '77
STEHLING, Kurt R.
New age of airships may dawn. il Smithsonian 8:123-33 Ap '77
STEIF, William
Refuseniks of Kiev. il Sat R 4:20-1+ S 17 '77
STEIG, William
Amazing bone; story; excerpt. Ms 5:85-8 Ap '77
STEIGER Tractor Company. See Tractor industry
STEIGMAN, David
Images from the deep il Pop Phot 81:92-7+ S '77
Robert Funk. il Pop Phot 81:108-11 Jl '77
STEIMLE, Edmund Augustus
Four stories of theology; with editorial comment. T. H. Stahel. America 136:inside cover, 230-3 Mr 19 '77 *
STEIN, Andrew
What makes Andy (and Bobby) run? H. Stein. il pors N Y Times Mag p44-7+ N 6 '77 *
STEIN, Sir Aurel
Discovering ancient treasures in Caves of the Thousand Buddhas; excerpt from Sir Aurel Stein. J. Mirsky. il por map Smithsonian 8: 94-6+ My '77
STEIN, Elliot, Jr. See Aronson, J. jt auth
STEIN, Frieda, pseud
Reports & comment: Poland. il Atlantic 241:11+ Ja '78
STEIN, Gary C.
(ed) See Duval, I. H. Overland to California
STEIN, Gertrude
Gay genius and the gay mob. A. Kazin. Esquire 88:33-4+ D '77 *
Hemingway the painter. A. Kazin. por New Repub 176:21-8 Mr 19 '77 *
STEIN, Harry
Exile in his own city. il por N Y Times Mag p 10-11+ Ja 8 '78
How to make it in the water. il Esquire 88:58-65 Ag '77
Meet Reggie (Dr Jekyll) Jackson (Mr Hyde) il por Esquire 88:92-4+ Jl '77
What makes Andy (and Bobby) run? il pors N Y Times Mag p44-7+ N 6 '77
—See Slansky, P. jt auth
STEIN, Herbert
Ahead: you can look for more rather than less inflation; interview. il por U.S. News 83:19-20 Ag 22 '77
STEIN, Howard
Buying power for a strong market isn't there, says Dreyfus' Stein; interview, ed by R. Brady. por Duns R 109:79+ Ja '77
STEIN, Howard F. and Hill, R. F.
Limits of ethnicity. Am Scholar 46:181-9 Spr '77
STEIN, Jane
Fumbled help at the well; excerpt from Water: life or death. il Environment 19:14-17+ Je '77
Water for the wealthy. il Environment 19:6-14 My '77
STEIN, Jeffrey
Fort Lesley J. McNair. Nation 224:621-4 My 21 '77
Letelier-Moffitt mystery. Progressive 41:36-9 N '77
STEIN, Sara
Pet show: questions and answers. il Am Home 80:77 D '77
STEINBACK, Alice C.
Recording America: federal funds for photos & films. il Art in Am 65:19+ Ja '77
STEINBECK, John, 1902-1968
Home-town Salinas shares its Steinbeck memories. il Sunset 158:40 Mr '77 *
STEINBERG, Harry
Do hot lines really help? il Seventeen 36:150+ Ag '77
STEINBERG, Michael
Essay in virtuosity. il Opera N 41:32-5 Ap 2 '77
STEINBERG, Rafael
Odd man out. il por N Y Times Mag p 18-19+ O 30 '77
STEINBERG, Richard I. See Evans, J. C. jt auth
STEINBERG, Sally
Night is not for sleeping. il Vogue 167:272+ N '77
STEINBERG, Sybil S.
Summer business on Martha's Vineyard: how Bunch of Grapes makes it year-round. il por Pub W 212:44+ S 5 '77
(ed) See Koehn, I. PW interviews
(ed) See Latham, A. PW interviews
STEINBRENNER, George Michael, 1930-
Yankee Clipper. R. Fimrite. il pors Sports Illus 47:122-6+ O 10 '77 *
STEINEM, Gloria
Abortion alert. Ms 6:118 N '77
Anita Bryant's crusade. Progressive 41:37 Je '77
Hooked on television. Progressive 41:39 S '77
If the shoe doesn't fit, change the foot. Ms 5:76+ F '77
Pink-collar workers. Progressive 41:54 My '77
Pornography—not sex but the obscene use of power. Ms 6:43-4 Ag '77
Special 5th anniversary issue. il Ms 6:47 Jl '77
Where the women workers are. Ms 5:51-2 Mr '77
Women and unions. Progressive 41:34 Jl '77
(ed) See Bunch, C. Two feminists tell how they work
(ed) See Horbal, K. Two feminists tell how they work
—and others
Will women make Carter a one-term President? How do we like him so far? il Ms 6:43-7+ Ja '78
STEINER, A. L. See Ong, S. H. jt auth
STEINER, Karen
ERIC/RCS report. Engl J 66:90-3 N '77
STEINER, Rudolf, School. See New York (city)—Education
STEINER, Stan
China's ancient mariners; with biographical sketch. il Natur Hist 86:6, 48-63 bibl(p 110) D '77
STEINFELS, Peter
[Column] See issues of Commonweal
STEINFIRST, Susan
YA library training—let's talk about it. SLJ 23:51 F '77
STEINHART, Peter
Mighty, like a Furbish lousewort. Audubon 79: 121-5 My '77
STEINHART Aquarium, San Francisco. See Aquariums
STEINLEN, Théophile Alexandre
Empathy with the humanity of the streets. P D. Cate. il Art N 76:56-9 Mr '77 *
STEINMANN, Marion
Estrogens: can they hold back the clock? il Fam Health 9:24-7 My '77
STEIN'S paradox. See Statistical methods
STEINWAY and Sons. See Piano makers
STEINZOR, Rena
Kenneth Donaldson's fight for freedom. Progressive 41:48-50 Ap '77
STEIRMAN, Hy
As we see it. See issues of Family Health incorporating Today's Health
STELL, William K. and others
Structural basis for on- and off-center responses in retinal bipolar cells. bibl il Science 198: 1269-71 D 23 '77
STELLAFANE Convention. See Astronomy—Conferences
STELLAR evolution. See Stars—Evolution
STELLAR winds
Gone with the wind; with views of R. Weymann. D. E. Thomsen. il Sci N 112:106-7 Ag 13 '77
STELUX Manufacturing Company. See Watch industry—Hong Kong
STELZER, Dick
(ed) Star treatment; excerpts. Ladies Home J 94:62+ O '77
STEMBER, Sol
En avant with our French allies to Yorktown victory. il Smithsonian 8:64-8+ My '77
STEMPEL, Robert C.
Men behind the Car of the Year. il pors Motor T 29:37 F '77 *
STEMS (plants)
See also
Shoot apexes
STENCIL work
Crafty touch. P. Sadowsky. Am Home 80:85 O '77
How to stencil a floor. M. Stewart. il por House & Gard 149:54+ Je '77
Make-ahead presents: decorate with stencils. il Seventeen 36:126-7+ N '77
Stencil a rug. il Mademoiselle 83:118 Jl '77
Stencil your own cards. il Design (US) 79:33 N '77
See also
Furniture, Decorated

STENGEL, Casey
Life with Casey Stengel; excerpt from Whitey and Mickey: an autobiography of the Yankee years. W. Ford and others. il pors Sat Eve Post 249:44-5+ My '77 *

STENMARK, Ingemar
Starting out with a chaser. A. Verschoth. il pors Sports Illus 46:54-6 Ja 17 '77 *

STENN, Frederick F. and others
Biochemical identification of homogentisic acid pigment in an ochronotic Egyptian mummy. bibl il Science 197:566-8 Ag 5 '77

STENNIS, John Cornelius
Tenn-Tom and Senator Stennis. W. Rawls, Jr. N Y Times Mag p46 My 8 '77

STENOGRAPHERS
Careers: courting success; court reporter. Seventeen 36:62 S '77

STENSLAND, Anna Lee
Indian boyhood; C. A. Eastman's autobiography. Engl J 66:59 Mr '77
Indian presence in American literature. bibl f il Engl J 66:37-41 Mr '77

STENTZEL, James
Korea: the image problem. Nation 225:358 O 15 '77
Korea: time to trust the people. Nation 224:197-9 F 19 '77
South Korean exposure. Nation 224:77-80 Ja 22 '77

STEP Family Foundation
Mrs Greene's steps to successful family life. S. Edmiston. por Good H 185:70+ S '77

STEP stools. See Stools

STEPCHILDREN
See also
Step Family Foundation

STEPHAN, G. Edward
Territorial division: the least-time constraint behind the formation of subnational boundaries. bibl Science 196:523-4 Ap 29 '77

STEPHEN, E. L. and others
Swine influenza virus vaccine: potentiation of antibody responses in rhesus monkeys. bibl il Science 197:1289-90 S 23 '77

STEPHEN, George
Backyard bonanza. il por Time 109:78 Je 20 '77 *

STEPHENS, Carla
Choice. Chr Today 21:38 Jl 8 '77

STEPHENS, Charles M.
Most dangerous leak of all. il Motor B & S 140:82-5 N '77

STEPHENS, J. K. and others
Porphyrin induction: equivalent effects of 5αH and 5βH steroids in chick embryo liver cells. bibl il Science 197:659-60 Ag 12 '77

STEPHENS, Jackson Thomas
Jimmy Carter's Little Rock connection. il pors Bus W p88 Ap 11 '77 *

STEPHENS, Joanne
Super-dehydrator does much more. il Org Gard & Farm 24:108-9 Ag '77

STEPHENS, Raymond W. B.
Stephens wins Acoustical Society gold medal. por Phys Today 30:65 Je '77 *

STEPHENS, Roderick, Jr
Amateur's new boat survey. il Motor B & S 140:80-1+ S '77
Test it yourself: sail. il Motor B & S 141:128-9+ Ja '78

STEPHENS, Inc. See Investment banking

STEPHENSON, F. Richard, and Clark, D. H.
Ancient astronomical records from the Orient. il map Sky & Tel 53:84-91 F '77

STEPLER, Richard
Shop talk. See issues of Popular science
—See Houser, D. jt auth

STEPMOTHERS. See Stepparents

STEPPARENTS
Weaving together two families into one; excerpt from How to discipline—with love. F. Dodson. Fam Health 9:44-7+ S '77
Wicked stepmother doesn't live here any more. M. A. Hidalgo. il por Redbook 149:22+ Ag '77
See also
Step Family Foundation

STEPPES
Winning battle against destruction; reclamation of Russian steppes. A. G. Babaev and N. S. Orlovsky. il UNESCO Courier 30:18-22 Jl '77

STEPS. See Stairways

STEREO amplifiers. See Amplifiers

STEREO cartridges, Phonograph. See Phonograph—Pickup

STEREOCHEMISTRY
Left-handed and right-handed molecules: Louis Pasteur's resolution of racemic acid. G. B. Kauffman. bibl il por Chemistry 50:14-18 Ap '77
Molecular metal clusters. E. L. Muetterties. bibl il Science 196:839-48 My 20 '77

STEREOPHONIC pickup. See Phonograph—Pickup

STEREOPHONIC radio broadcasting. See Radio broadcasting

STEREOPHONIC radio receivers. See Radio receivers

STEREOPHONIC records. See Phonograph records

STEREOPHONIC sound systems. See Audio systems

STEREOPHONIC tape recorders. See Tape recorders and recording

STEREOTYPE (psychology)
Cavities and conscience pangs: candy can cause both; image of librarians in television commercials. F. J. Dempsey. il Am Lib 8:231 My '77
Genderisms; reinforcement of sex role stereotypes by advertising. E. Goffman. il Psychol Today 11:60-3 Ag '77
Hero, the harlot, and the glorified horse as mythic Americans. C. J. Deming and B. J. Wahlstrom. bibl Intellect 105:439-41 Je '77
Segregating the home into male and female territories. G. Melson. Intellect 106:186-7 N '77
Sexual stereotypes. J. P. Sisk. Commentary 64:58-64 O '77
Should you work for a woman? stereotyped female boss. R. Shapiro. Harp Baz 110:85+ Ag '77
Social communication in canids: evidence for the evolution of a stereotyped mammalian display. M. Bekoff. bibl il Science 197:1097-9 S 9 '77
Study finds children's books degrade older people. il Ret Liv 17:15 Mr '77

STERILITY
Autoantibodies to zona pellucida: a possible cause for infertility in women. C. A. Shivers and B. S. Dunbar. bibl il Science 197:1082-4 S 9 '77
Baiter Award; National Peach Council's recommendation to use DBCP as form of birth control. J. G. Mitchell. Audubon 79:168 N '77
Help for couples who can't conceive; views of Mary Harrison. A. Thompson. McCalls 104:72 Ag '77
Industrial sterility; chemical workers exposed to DBCP. J. Seligmann and others. il Newsweek 90:69 Ag 29 '77
New hope for the childless. E. D'Aulaire and P. O. D'Aulaire. Read Digest 111:197-200+ D '77
Sterility scare sends OSHA scurrying. Bus W p45+ S 12 '77

STERILIZATION (birth control) See Sterilization, Sexual

STERILIZATION, Sexual
And then there were none; Indian Health Service's sterilization practices. J. K. Larson. Chr Cent 94:61-3 Ja 26 '77
Lo, the poor and sterilized Indian; General Accounting Office report on practices of the Indian Health Service. B. Wagner. America 136:75 Ja 29 '77
My belly button surgery; laparoscopic tubal sterilization. S. W. Olds. Fam Health 9:49-51 Ap '77
Reversible sterilization. G. Largey. Society 14:57-9 Jl '77
Sterilization: now it's simpler, safer. Reversible? Maybe. M. L. Schildkraut. il Good H 186:163-4 Ja '78
Sterilizing the poor. S. M. Rothman. bibl Society 14:36-40 Ja '77
See also
Vasectomy

Animals

Birth control for dogs and cats. R. Caras. il Ladies Home J 94:148 F '77
Birth control for pets. B. Humeston. Bet Hom & Gard 55:272+ O '77
Neutering your pet. J. L. Lippert. Good H 184:226 Mr '77

STERILIZATION of animals. See Sterilization, Sexual—Animals

STERLING, Claire
Margaret Thatcher: Britain's next prime minister? il por Read Digest 110:172-6 My '77

STERLING, Kenneth, and others
Thyroid hormone action: the mitochondrial pathway. bibl il Science 197:996-9 S 2 '77

STERLING, Lionel N.
Controller expands his territory. por Bus W p90 Ag 15 '77 *

STERN, Aaron
Edith Project. J. McClintock. Harpers 254:21-4 Mr '77 *

STERN, Charles
Should U.S. limit steel imports? interview. pors U.S. News 83:77-8 O 24 '77

STERN, Christopher H.
Invasion of the American heartland. il Sat R 5:18-20+ O 15 '77

STERN, Edith
Edith Project. J. McClintock. Harpers 254:21-4 Mr '77 *

STERN, Elizabeth, and others
Steroid contraceptive use and cervical dysplasia: increased risk of progression. bibl il Science 196:1460-2 Je 24 '77

STERN, Frances Meritt
How to gear your mind to think yourself slim; interview, ed by C. Seebohm. House & Gard 149:22+ Ag '77

STERN, Fritz
Giant from afar: visions of Europe from Algiers to Tokyo. bibl f For Affairs 56:111-35 O '77
STERN, Gerald
96 Vandam; poem. New Yorker 53:26 Jl 4 '77
STERN, Isaac
Violinist Isaac Stern on American values today: interview. il pors U.S. News 82:47 F 14 '77
STERN, Judith S.
California diet. il Mademoiselle 83:214-15+ Ap '77
Junk food diet. Mademoiselle 83:178-9 Ag '77
Sprouts: self-starter food. il Vogue 167:366-7+ S '77
Two-week crash diet. Mademoiselle 83:137 D '77
STERN, Murray
Murray Stern: social surrealist. A. Sanders. il por Am Artist 41:76-83+ F '77 *
STERN, Paul C. and Kirkpatrick, E. M.
Energy behavior. bibl il Environment 19:10-15 D '77
STERN, Richard Martin
One way through the woods. Writer 90:11-13 F '77
STERN, Robert A. M.
Something borrowed, something new. il Horizon 20:50-7 D '77
about
Old house spreads its wing. il House & Gard 149:122-7 D '77 *
STERN drive engines. See Motor boat engines
STERNBERG, Ricardo de Silveira Lobo. See Lobo Sternberg, R. de S.
STERNBURG, J. G. and others
Batesian mimicry: selective advantage of color pattern. bibl il Science 195:681-3 F 18 '77
STEROIDS
Angiotensin converting enzyme: induction by steroids in rabbit alveolar macrophages in culture. J. Friedland and others. bibl il Science 197:64-5 Jl 1 '77
Does he or doesn't he? use of anabolic steroids by body builders. W. Ames. il Sports Illus 47:91-2+ D 5 '77
See also
Corticosteroids
Testosterone
STEROLS
See also
Cholesterol
STERRETT, Frances S.
Drinkable, but. . . bibl il Environment 19:28-36 D '77
—and Boss, C. A.
Careless Kepone. bibl map Environment 19:30-6 Mr '77
STETIN, Sol
Why Sol Stetin stepped down. E. M. McConville. por Nation 225:621-4 D 10 '77 *
STETTHEIMER, Florine
Autobiography of visual poems; adaptation of address. B. Zucker. il Art N 76:68-73 F '77 *
STEVEN Peck Dance Company. See Dance companies
STEVENS, Alex
Hat of August; poem. New Yorker 53:36 Ag 15 '77
Rare history; poem. New Yorker 53:52 N 14 '77
STEVENS, Alvin
Buying a Garden of Eden. il por Time 109:50 Je 27 '77 *
STEVENS, Claude
Pitch for the disabled. U. O'Connor. il por Sat Eve Post 249:14 O '77 *
STEVENS, E. Don. See Guernsey, D. L. jt auth
STEVENS, E. S.
You ought to be in pictures. Writers Digest 57:43-5 O '77
STEVENS, J. P, and Company
Labor victory. F. Gaillard. Progressive 41:8 N '77
New tactics in the textile war. D. Freedman. il Nation 225:618-21 D 10 '77
Organizing J. P. Stevens. F. Gaillard. Progressive 41:37 F '77
Recidivist. New Repub 177:2+ S 17 '77
Stevens digs its heels in deeper; boycott by Amalgamated Clothing & Textile Workers to force unionization. il Bus W p29 Mr 14 '77
Textile workers fight on: the battle against J.P. Stevens. A. Fishel. Ms 6:22 D '77
Touch of civil rights fervor; actions taken by Amalgamated Clothing and Textile Workers Union. il Time 109:44 Mr 14 '77
Trouble looming. P. D. Wellstone. New Repub 176:14-15 Mr 12 '77
U.S. injunction against Stevens? il Time 110:76 D 12 '77
When a union goes all out in a boycott drive—. il U.S. News 82:71-2 Je 20 '77
STEVENS, John R.
Community cookbook (cont) il Ladies Home J 94:104+ F; 98+ Ap; 68+ Je; 98+ Jl; 144+ O '77
STEVENS, Joyce. See Orton, P. jt auth
STEVENS, Maggi
Can power wreck your marriage? Harp Baz 111:153+ N '77
How to be an instant gourmet. Harp Baz 110:129+ Ag '77
STEVENS, Nancy
For love of wilderness. il Pop Phot 80:86-93 F '77
Ruth Orkin. il por Pop Phot 80:100-9+ Je '77
Young Audiences is twenty-five. il Hi Fi 27:MA12-15 F '77
STEVENS, Norman D.
Keeper of the library past. il Wilson Lib Bull 51:841-3 Je '77
Modernizing OCLC's governance. Lib J 102:2216-19 N 1 '77
STEVENS, Wallace
Books. J. Updike. New Yorker 53:128-30+ Mr 21 '77 *
Comment. P. Pettingell. Poetry 131:165-9 D '77 *
STEVENS-ARROYO, Antonio M.
Marxism and the Hispanic movement of the United States. il New Cath World 220:126-8+ My '77
STEVENS Institute of Technology, Hoboken, N.J.
Stevens Institute of Technology: after the strike, still unsettled. J. Walsh. il Science 196:280-3 Ap 15 '77
STEVENSON, Adlai Ewing, 1930-
Immodest proposal: Nikita to Adlai; excerpt from Adlai Stevenson and the world. J. B. Martin. il por Am Heritage 28:88-9 Ag '77 *
STEVENSON, F. L. See Holt, H. O. jt auth
STEVENSON, Florence
Lulu's last stand: Jack the Ripper. Opera N 41:36 Ap 2 '77
STEVENSON, James
Reporter at large. il New Yorker 53:46+ Ag 15 '77
STEVENSON, Tom
Gloom on the Monongahela. il Sat R 4:6-10 Ja 22 '77
STEVER, Horton Guyford
Departing Ford team establishes two new science groups. F. C. Bennett. Phys Today 30:69-70 F '77 *
R&D budget frozen in stability. D. S. Greenberg. Sci Digest 81:73-5 Ap '77 *
STEW
Beef stew Mexican style. il McCalls 104:113-14 Ap '77
Classic French veal stew. il McCalls 104:101-2 My '77
Hearty, beany soups and stews. il Sunset 158:169-70 Je '77
Hearty small-game stews. K. Green. il Outdoor Life 159:158 F '77
Hearty stews. il Bet Hom & Gard 55:153-4 O '77
Venison stew. J. Moran. il por Bet Hom & Gard 55:184 S '77
STEWARDESSES, Air. See Airlines—Flight attendants
STEWARDSHIP, Christian
Fairness in fundraising; Christian Stewardship Council code of ethical pursuit. Chr Today 21:24 Ag 26 '77
Stewardship and property; symposium; with editorial comment. bibl il New Cath World 220:210-32+ S '77
STEWART, Bruce
Some nuclear explosions will be necessary. Bull Atom Sci 33:51-4 O '77
STEWART, Frank M. See Levin, B. R. jt auth
STEWART, Ian
Gauss; with biographical sketch. il por Sci Am 237:20, 122-31 bibl(p 154) Jl '77
STEWART, Isobel
Matter of the heart; story. Good H 185:106 Jl '77
STEWART, J. D. See Martin. L. D. jt auth
STEWART, Jennifer
Princess Caroline turns twenty. il por McCalls 104:142-3+ My '77
STEWART, John Massey
Frozen mammoths from Siberia bring the Ice Ages to vivid life. il Smithsonian 8:60-9 bibl(p 134) D '77
STEWART, Jules
Leftist ground swell in Spain. Progressive 41:46-7 O '77
STEWART, Lane
Countdown to a pot of gold; photographs. il pors Sports Illus 46:34-8 My 16 '77
STEWART, Martha
Good eating country style. il pors House & Gard 149:134-5+ Je '77
How to stencil a floor. il por House & Gard 149:54+ Je '77
STEWART, Pamela
Above the tobacco fields of South Deerfield, Massachusetts; poem. New Yorker 53:134 Ap 11 '77
Vigil; poem. New Yorker 53:166 N 14 '77
STEWART, Paul L.
How to help a realtor sell your home. il Ret Liv 17:40-1+ My '77

STEWART-GORDON, James
Everybody is belly-dancing. il Read Digest 111:129-32 Ag '77
Harry Winston: ace of diamonds. il Read Digest 112:183-4+ Ja '78
In pursuit of the Loch Ness Monster. il Read Digest 110:120-4 F '77
Super dog of Scotland Yard. il por Read Digest 110:201-2+ Mr '77
World's first—and greatest—detective. il Read Digest 111:129-33 O '77

STEWS. See Stew

STIBBENS, Steve
Markets & careers. H. Chapnick. il por Pop Phot 80:50+ Je '77 *

STICKLEY, Gustav
Furniture of Gustav Stickley. C. L. Bohdan and T. M. Volpe. bibl il por Antiques 111:984-9 My '77 *

STICKS. See Staffs (canes, sticks, etc)

STIGLER, George
John Kenneth Galbraith's marathon television series. il Nat R 29:601-4 My 27 '77

STIGWOOD, Robert C.
Man to whom the angels flock. por Fortune 95:44 Je '77 *

STILBESTROLS
Cancer time bomb: did your mother take DES? J. Worthington. Ms 5:16-18 Mr '77
Carbon-14—labeled diethylstilbestrol synthesis by the McMurry method: concurrent formation of hexestrol. V. J. Feil and others. bibl Science 198:510-11 N 4 '77
Cattle drug: no evidence of cancer hazard. Sci N 111:102-3 F 12 '77
DES blamed for mothers' cancers. Sci N 112:422 D 24 '77
For stilbestrol: another round coming up. R. D. Wennblom. Farm J 101:E2 mid-Mr '77
Taking DES to court. il Time 109:44 My 9 '77

STILES, F. Gary
Coadapted competitors: the flowering seasons of hummingbird-pollinated plants in a tropical forest. bibl il Science 198:1177-8 D 16 '77

STILL life painting
Still-life paintings of William Michael Harnett; their reflections upon nineteenth century American musical culture. C. J. Oja. bibl f il Mus Q 63:505-23 O '77

STILWELL, Richard G.
Another General speaks; excerpts from interview, ed by B. Krisher. por Newsweek 89:51 Je 6 '77
Should U.S. withdraw troops from Korea? interview. pors U.S. News 82:27-8 Je 20 '77

STIMPFLE, Nedra
Soul brothers and sister Lou; K. Hunter's novel. Engl J 66:61 Mr '77

STIMSON, Burt
Shop talk. N. Goldberg. il Pop Phot 80:10+ Je '77 *

STIMULANTS
See also
Amphetamines
Coffee
Methylphenidate

STIMULATION (physiology)
Brain self-stimulation: direct evidence for the involvement of dopamine in the prefrontal cortex. F. Mora and R. D. Myers. bibl il Science 197:1387-9 S 30 '77
Development theory of environmental enrichment. R. A. Cummins and others. bibl il Science 197:692-4 Ag 12 '77
Endogenous opiate receptor ligand: electrically induced release in the guinea pig ileum. M. Puig and others. bibl il Science 195:419-20 Ja 28 '77
Hypothalamic stimulation facilitates contralateral visual control of a learned response. W. K. Beagley and T. L. Holley. bibl il Science 196:321-2 Ap 15 '77
Morphine lowering of self-stimulation thresholds: lack of tolerance with long-term administration. R. Esposito and C. Kornetsky. bibl il Science 195:189-91 Ja 14 '77
Trigeminal substrates of intracranial self-stimulation in the brainstem. D. Van Der Kooy and A. G. Phillips. bibl il Science 196:447-9 Ap 22 '77
Vestibular stimulation influence on motor development in infants. D. L. Clark and others. bibl il Science 196:1228-9 Je 10 '77

STIMULUS and response
Dopamine receptor binding enhancement accompanies lesion-induced behavioral supersensitivity. I. Creese and others. bibl il Science 197:596-8 Ag 5 '77
Masking of electrical by acoustic stimuli: behavioral evidence for tonotopic organization. C. J. Christopher and G. M. Gerken. bibl il Science 198:1276-8 D 23 '77
See also
Reflexes

STINGING nettles. See Nettles

STINGRAYS. See Rays (fishes)

STINGS, Insect. See Insect bites and stings

STINNETT, Caskie
And having writ, wrote on. Atlantic 239:20 Je '77
Dinner with the big boys. il Atlantic 239:26-7 Ap '77
Guestmanship. Atlantic 240:28 D '77
How Mombasa became the new place. il Sat R 4:11-12+ Ap 16 '77
I know it's only rock 'n' roll, but I hate it. Atlantic 240:26-7 Ag '77
Of man and islands. Sat R 5:20 Ja 7 '78
PW interviews; ed by A. Bester. il por Pub W 212:10-11 N 7 '77
Tidying up after an act of God. Atlantic 239:23-4 F '77

STINSON, Eddie
Stinson. T. West. il Flying 101:114 S '77 *

STINSON, Robert
How they kept the trust. il por Nation 225:561-4 N 26 '77

STIPP, John L.
Hidden revolution. il Commonweal 104:427-31 Jl 8 '77

STIR-frying. See Frying

STIRRERS (kitchen utensils) See Kitchen utensils and appliances

STITCHERY. See Embroidery; Needlework

STITT, R. M.
Build a digital IC tester. il Pop Electr 11:53-9 Je '77

STOBART, John
They owned the sea; reproductions of paintings. Read Digest 110:146-51 Je '77

STOCK, Carol
MLA in Seattle: change & controversy. Lib J 102:1807+ S 15 '77

STOCK, Joseph Whiting
Joseph Whiting Stock. S. B. Sherrill. il Antiques 111:642+ Ap '77 *

STOCK averages. See Stocks—Price indexes and averages

STOCK brokers. See Brokers

STOCK car racing. See Automobile racing

STOCK dividends. See Dividends

STOCK exchanges
Big Board and the National Market System. J. J. Phelan, Jr. il por Duns R 110:97+ N '77
Built-in drag on the stock market—secular inflation. J. Carson-Parker. Bus W p82-3 Mr 14 '77
Bulls, the bears and you; excerpt from The language of investing. il Harp Baz 110:99+ F '77
Buying power for a strong market isn't there, says Dreyfus's Stein; interview, ed by R. Brady. H. Stein. Duns R 109:79+ Ja '77
Fed is a risky trading indicator. Bus W p80 Mr 14 '77
Investment strategy for 1978. J. Fraser. U.S. News 83:91 D 26 '77
Market trends. M. T. Sosnoff. See issues of Forbes
Markets and investments. See issues of Business week
Random walk in stock-exchange seats. Fortune 96:90 Ag '77
Reading the stock tables. N. Verser. Redbook 149:64 My '77
Roller-coaster to nowhere. il Time 110:44-6+ Ag 29 '77
Wall Street's evolutionary revolution; address, April 21, 1977. R. W. Swinarton. Vital Speeches 43:507-11 Je 1 '77
What big investors see ahead for a restless stock market. U.S. News 82:43-4 My 2 '77
What the tape is telling us. Fortune 96:87 S '77
Why stock market is going down while business is going up. il U.S. News 83:29-30 S 5 '77
See also
Arbitrage
Computers—Investment use
Put and call transactions

International aspects

When a declining dollar helps the investor. il Bus W p 131-2+ D 26 '77

Regulation

See also
United States—Securities and Exchange Commission

American Exchange

Amex prepares to trade commodities. Bus W p89 O 3 '77
Bartering at the Big Board. il Sr Schol 110:25 O 6 '77
Options race goes to the Amex. Bus W p76+ F 7 '77
State of war in options trading; competition between Chicago Board Options Exchange and the American Stock Exchange. Bus W p60 Mr 7 '77
Wall Street blues; floor broker W. Tyrrell. A. Salpukas. il pors N Y Times Mag p42-4+ D 18 '77

STOCK exchanges—*Continued*

London Exchange

Bull market based on North Sea oil. il Bus W p40 S 5 '77
Compelling case for British equities. il Bus W p 104 My 9 '77

New York Exchange

Big Board and the National Market System. J. J. Phelan, Jr. il por Duns R 110:97+ N '77
Big Board strategy for staying alive. W. Robertson. il por Fortune 95:134-41+ Mr '77
Big Board's own national marketplace. il Bus W p34-5 D 5' 77
Big shake-out. M. Ruby and P. L. Abraham. il Newsweek 90:87+ O 17 '77
Comes the revolution! R. J. Flaherty. il Forbes 120:33-4 N 1 '77
Reviving the concept of a national market. Bus W p33-4 Ag 15 '77
SEC is forced to reprieve Rule 390. Bus W p37-8 O 17 '77

Tokyo Exchange

Japanese stocks still look good. J. Madrick. il Bus W p69 My 2 '77

STOCK fraud. See Fraud

STOCK margins. See Stocks—Margin buying

STOCK market. See Stock exchanges

STOCK market journalism. See Journalism, Commercial

STOCK option contracts. See Put and call transactions

STOCK option mutual funds. See Investment trusts

STOCK ownership, Employee. See Employees as stockholders

STOCK purchase options
Comeback for restricted stock plans. L. J. Brindisi, Jr. il Harvard Bus R 55:14+ S '77
Fortified bread. Forbes 119:26 Ap 15 '77
Stock options for outside directors. Harvard Bus R 55:47 Jl '77
Tax reform remodels the pay package; effect on executive's qualified stock option. il Bus W p48+ F 28 '77

STOCK tenders. See Stocks—Tender offers

STOCKDALE, John
Shows we've seen. N. Canavor. il Pop Phot 80:226 Je '77

STOCKER, Joseph
Classroom in the cactus. il Am Educ 13:6-11 D '77
Confessions of a bike bug. il Ret Liv 17:24-5+ O '77

STOCKERT, Richard J. and others
Hepatic binding protein: the protective role of its sialic acid residues. bibl il Science 197:667-8 Ag 12 '77

STOCKHOLDERS
Bittersweet victory for Gerber's directors; stockholders' suit over Anderson, Clayton bid. il Bus W p37 O 10 '77
Changing compensation package. J. Perham. il Duns R 110:50-2 S '77
Emerging solution to corporate governance. R. M. Estes. bibl f Harvard Bus R 55:20-3+ N '77
Flight from stocks speeds up. il Bus W p90-1 Je 20 '77
Investor profiles. il Bus W p85+ D 26 '77
Skittish investors—what will lure them back to stock market; interview. W. M. Batten. il por U.S. News 83:89-90 N 28 '77
Weep not for the individual investor. R. J. Farrell. Forbes 119:102-3 Ja 15 '77
Who owns American industry? the big shifts under way. il U.S. News 83:70-1 Jl 18 '77
See also
Employees as stockholders
United States—Congress—Senate—Judiciary, Committee on the—Citizen and Shareholders' Rights and Remedies Subcommittee

STOCKHOLDERS meetings
Dissidents gear up for annual meetings. J. Perham. il Duns R 109:74-5+ Ap '77

STOCKHOLM

Crime

Contemporary crime in historical perspective: a comparative study of London, Stockholm, and Sydney. T. R. Gurr. bibl f il Ann Am Acad 434:114-36 N '77

Music

See also
Opera—Sweden

STOCKHOLM International Peace Research Institute
Mounting prospects of nuclear war. F. Barnaby. il Bull Atom Sci 33:10-20 Je '77

STOCKING of streams, lakes, etc. See Fish culture

STOCKPILING
Aerospace metals prices bulge upward. W. C. Wetmore. il Aviation W 106:112-14 Je 6 '77
Copper producers gain Washington's ear. il Bus W p35-6 N 28 '77
Economic impact of the new restraints; buffer stockpiling. il Bus W p82-3 My 9 '77
In prospect: stockpiling goods to curb price boosts. il U.S. News 82:86 Ap 18 '77
Shifting stockpile strategy; nonferrous metals. Bus W p57 S 26 '77
U.S. seeks to replenish stockpile of materials. il Aviation W 106:114-15 Je 6 '77
When nations try to rig commodity prices—. W. S. Wingo. il U.S. News 82:67 My 30 '77
See also
Surplus products, Agricultural

STOCKS
Ben Graham's last will and testament. P. Bluestein. il por Forbes 120:43-5 Ag 1 '77
Don't be a bottom-watcher. R. J. Flaherty. por Forbes 120:96-7 N 15 '77
Don't be a monomaniac. il por Forbes 120:52-3 Jl 1 '77
1400 by 1979. por Forbes 120:53-4 O 15 '77
Hotter action in letter stock. Bus W p74 F 28 '77
Inefficient stock. por Forbes 119:46 Ap 1 '77
Inside Wall Street. J. Madrick. See issues of Business week
Is history repeating? interview, ed by R. Flaherty. T. M. Evans. Forbes 119:104+ Je 15 '77
Little risk in today's market. J. Fraser. U.S. News 82:81 Mr 28 '77
Market comment. L. O. Hooper. See issues of Forbes
Market trends. M. T. Sosnoff. See issues of Forbes
Money. A. Tobias. See issues of Esquire
New issues find a very weak market. Bus W p68-9 My 2 '77
(Old) new issues: the long-distance runners. il Forbes 119:74 F 15 '77
Peevish summer of '77. il Time 110:65-6 Ag 8 '77
Preferred position. B. Weberman. Forbes 120:128 N 1 '77
Questions investors should ask. J. Fraser. U.S. News 83:102 O 24 '77
Running against the tide; secondary stocks. J. Fraser. U.S. News 83:92 S 26 '77
Rush to issue preferred stock. Bus W p97 Je 27 '77
Spotting hot stocks in bankruptcy court. il Bus W p 103-4 N 21 '77
Stay with stocks that look cheap. J. Fraser. U.S. News 82:94 My 23 '77
Stock comments. H. H. Biel. See issues of Forbes
Stock trends. R. B. Hoey. See issues of Forbes
Stocks: next year has to be better than 1977; interview. T. Wilson. por U.S. News 83:50-2 D 26 '77
Streetwalker. R. J. Flaherty. Forbes 120:122 D 1 '77
T. Rowe Price: he's got a little list. il Forbes 120:64 N 1 '77
Taking stock. J. Fraser. U.S. News 82:93 Ap 25 '77
Wall Street (cont of) Wall Street beat. See issues of Dun's review
Ways to cut the risk when you invest. il Changing T 31:24-8 S '77
What bear market? il por Forbes 120:38+ D 1 '77
Why stocks remain cheap. J. Fraser. U.S. News 82:77 Je 20 '77
See also
Banks and banking—Securities handling
Dividends
Stock exchanges
Stock purchase options
Stockholders
also subhead Securities under various subjects, e.g. Insurance companies—Securities

Laws and regulations

See Securities—Laws and regulations

Margin buying

Why there's so much margin borrowing. L. Snyder. il Fortune 96:163-4+ O '77

Marketing

Art of selling stocks. J. Fraser. U.S. News 83:78 D 19 '77
Second thoughts on going public. R. Salomon. il Harvard Bus R 55:126-31 S '77
See also
Stocks—Repurchase

Price-earnings ratios

All quiet on the low-priced front? R. J. Flaherty and M. Latorraca. Forbes 119:25-8 F 1 '77
Bargain time for blue chips? il U.S. News 82:73 Ap 18 '77
How inflation swindles the equity investor. W. E. Buffett. il por Fortune 95:250-4+ My '77
Nifty fifty revisited. il Forbes 120:72-3 D 15 '77
Reports of the death of common stocks are greatly exaggerated. B. Malkiel. il Fortune 96:156-60+ N '77
Who's where in growth. il Forbes 121:191+ Ja 9 '78
Why the market acts the way it does. por Forbes 119:68 Mr 1 '77

STOCKS—*Continued*

Price forecasting

Investment strategy for 1978. J. Fraser. U.S. News 83:91 D 26 '77
New values in growth stocks. il Bus W p72-3 D 26 '77
Small companies can be bargains. il Bus W p73-4 D 26 '77

Price indexes and averages

And now for the Dow. il Sr Schol 110:22-5 O 6 '77
Bulls still make a persuasive case. J. Madrick. il Bus W p78 F 7 '77
Grand rally that wasn't. il Bus W p 146+ Mr 21 '77
How a weak dollar hurts the stock market. il Bus W p 106-7 S 12 '77
Index funds: queering Wall Street's money game. C. Welles. Nation 224:300-4 Mr 12 '77
Israeli election shakes up the Street. il Bus W p80 Je 6 '77
Money managers feel the inflationary chill. il Bus W p 106 F 14 '77
New case of jitters. D. Pauly and others. il Newsweek 90:59 Ag 8 '77
New glamour of lower-tier stocks. Bus W p76+ Jl 11 '77
Rally falters despite good news. il Bus W p68 My 2 '77
Right way to read the stock market averages; using the major indexes. Changing T 31:39-41 Ap '77
Roller-coaster to nowhere. il Time 110:44-6+ Ag 29 '77
Shooting holes in the January indicator. J. Madrick. il Bus W p71 Ja 31 '77
Street sells optimism short. il Bus W p32-3 Ag 15 '77
Survey of corporate performance (title varies) (cont) il Bus W p77-84+ Mr 21; 88+ My 16; 61-8+ Ag 15; 105-9+ N 14 '77
Wall Street: bad news is no news. il Time 110:82 D 19 '77
What ails the stock market? il U.S. News 83:26-7 N 14 '77
What is spooking Wall Street. il Bus W p26-7 Ap 11 '77
What the averages are saying. J. Fraser. U.S. News 83:65 Ag 15 '77
What's the score? Forbes 120:34 Jl 1 '77
Why Wall Street is skittish. il Bus W p30-1 My 9 '77

Prices

Bargains in the tax-selling season. il Bus W p 102 D 12 '77

Public offerings

See Stocks—Marketing

Repurchase

IBM buys itself. Time 109:50 Mr 7 '77
Now ad agencies are going private. il Bus W p76-7 Ja 24 '77
Repurchasing gets a new lease on life. Bus W p 110 Ap 4 '77
Tender offers that nobody opposes; Tandy Corp. buys itself. por Forbes 120:25-6 Jl 15 '77

Tender offers

Wall Street's tender trap. D. Pauly. il Newsweek 89:88 Ap 11 '77
See also
Corporations—Acquisitions and mergers

Laws and regulations

See Securities—Laws and regulations

Valuation

See Corporations—Valuation

Yields

Multiplying dividends through stock swaps; W. Peters of Unicorn Group. J. Madrick. il Bus W p 126 Ap 18 '77
Profits in collecting preferred dividends. il Bus W p 118+ O 17 '77
Trouble with stocks (cont) A. F. Ehrbar. il Fortune 96:89-90+ Ag '77

STOCKS, Gun. See Gunstocks

STOCKTON, Allen
Different strokes for all the folks. il Motor T 29:44-6 Jl '77

STOCKTON, Court
Bromeliad boys at Nature's Way. C. Seagraves. il pors Horticulture 55:36-7 D '77 *

STOCKTON, Dick
He's a first-class tourist. J. Underwood. il por Sports Illus 46:78+ My 23 '77 *
Little bit better than Lagos. C. Kirkpatrick. por Sports Illus 46:20-1 F 7 '77 *

STOCKTON, William
Healy sisters—clues to diabetes. il N Y Times Mag p88+ Je 12 '77
Pilots talk about air crashes; excerpt from Final approach. the crash of Eastern 212. il N Y Times Mag p41-2+ Ap 10 '77

STOCKTON, Calif.

Education

See Education—California

STOCKTON State College, Pomona. See New Jersey. Stockton State College

STOCKWELL, Eugene L.
(ed) See Ting, K. H. and Ting, Mrs K. H. Life of Christianity in China

STODDARD, Maynard Good
Is retirement what your wife makes it? Ret Liv 17:38 Ap '77

STODDARD, Sandol
Lazy gourmet afloat. Yachting 141:96-7+ My '77

STODDART, Veronica Gould
Roots and visions. il Américas 29:13-16 O '77

STOECKENIUS, Walther. See Fisher, K. A. jt auth

STOEHR, Taylor
Attitude of anarchism. Nation 224:437-40 Ap 9 '77
Cunning, fraud or flight. Nation 224:373-6 Mr 26 '77

STOEVER Glass and Company. See Brokers

STOKER, Bram
Dracula; dramatization. See Balderston, J. L. and Deane, H.
Passion of Dracula; dramatization. See Hall, B. and Richmond, D.

STOKES, Donald W.
Native dogwoods. il Horticulture 55:27-31 F '77

STOKES, Geoffrey
Clive's comeback. il pors N Y Times Mag p70+ Ap 24 '77

STOKES, McNeill
Minimizing defects in plans and specifications. Archit Rec 162:49 Jl '77

STOKES, Terry
Comment. R. Howard. Poetry 129:229-31 Ja '77

STOKESBURY, James L.
1943 invasion of Italy. il map Am Hist Illus 12:26-37 D '77

STOKLEY, James
[Month] stars. See fourth issue of each month of Science news to December 24, 1977

STOKOWSKI, Leopold
Letters from Stokowski; ed by D. J. Soria. il Hi Fi 28:MA6+ Ja '78

about

Century of music. H. Saal. por Newsweek 90:93-4 S 26 '77 *
Obituary
Hi Fi 27:53 D '77. L. Marcus
Sounds never heard before. il por Time 110:54-5 S 26 '77 *
Unforgettable Leopold Stokowski. A. Kostelanetz. por Read Digest 112:101-5 Ja '78 *

STOLEN goods, Receiving of
In cities across the country, the sting goes on and on. T. Gest. il U.S. News 83:67-8 N 7 '77
Sting's the thing; police-run fencing operations. E. Keerdoja and S. Lesher. Newsweek 89:11 F 28 '77

STOLIAR, Joan
Designer's perspective on technology and typography. il Pub W 212:63-4 Jl 4 '77

about

Copyrights for book designs. P. Doebler. il Pub W 212:59-60+ Jl 4 '77 *

STOLLER, Robert Jesse
Sex wars: is bed really a battlefield? Mademoiselle 83:167+ S '77 *
Transsexual riddle: an hypothesis. R. J. Trotter. il Sci N 111:236-8 Ap 9 '77 *

STOLTENBERG, Donald
Collagraph printmaking. il Sch Arts 77:10-17 D '77

STOLZ, Alan J. and Ball, A. B.
Legislative report. See issues of Camping magazine

STOMACH
Inside story; interview, ed by C. Seebohm. J. Saleh. il House & Gard 149:38+ My '77
Nervous stomach and what to do about it. L. Galton. Harp Baz 110:127+ Mr '77

Diseases

Wide-awake nightmares: headache and stomachache. M. Weber. Vogue 167:154 O '77
See also
Peptic ulcers

STOMACH cancer. See Cancer

STOMACH ulcers. See Peptic ulcers

STOMATA
Light and stomatal function: blue light stimulates swelling of guard cell protoplasts. E. Zeiger and P. K. Hepler. bibl il Science 196:887-9 My 20 '77

STOMATITIS virus, Vesicular. See Viruses

STONE, Christopher
Cashing in on charisma. por Forbes 119:144 Ap 15 '77 *

STONE, Clifford
Cutting garden: what to plant for fresh flowers all summer. il Horticulture 55:42-9 My '77

STONE, Earl L. and Kszystyniak, Richard
Conservation of potassium in the pinus resinosa ecosystem. bibl il Science 198:192-4 O 14 '77
STONE, Edward Durell
Buildings of the future—as a noted architect sees them; interview. il por U.S. News 83:55-6 Ag 15 '77
STONE, Elizabeth
Horatio Algers of the nightmare. il por Psychol Today 11:59-60+ D '77
Joan Micklin Silver: box office but no bankroll. il pors Ms 6:31-4 Ag '77
Psychology and the arts. il Psychol Today 10:18 Ap; 22+ My; 11:14+ Jl; 14+ Ag '77
STONE, Erika, and others
(ed) Family impact on a changing America; interviews. Parents Mag 52:54-7+ O '77
STONE, Greg
Detroit's war on car corrosion. il Pop Sci 212:84-7 Ja '78
Mopeds; 100+ mpg, but how safe, or legal? il Pop Sci 211:66-9+ Jl '77
Sun power makes window greenhouse self-ventilating. il Pop Sci 211:108-10 D '77
STONE, J. William, Jr
Walking sticks in a Southern collection. bibl il Antiques 111:338-44 F '77
STONE, John
Words; poem. Am Scholar 46:505 Aut '77
STONE, Judy
(ed) See Learned, M. Michael Learned: a woman in passage
STONE, Marty
His biggest pitch is yet to come. P. Gammons. il por Sports Illus 47:37-8 Ag 22 '77 *
STONE, Marvin Lawrence
Editor's page. U.S. News 82:88 Mr 14; 88 Mr 21 '77
STONE, Pat. See Wixon, V. jt auth
STONE, Robert
War stories; story. Harpers 254:63-6 My '77
STONE, Ruth
Comment. S. M. Gilbert. Poetry 129:296-301 F '77 *
STONE, William T.
Discovering the Western Caribbean. il maps Yachting 142:52-5 Jl; 54-7 Ag '77
STONE Age
See also
Stone implements and weapons

Great Britain

Getting the axe; stone axes from Neolithic sites. Sci Am 238:69 Ja '78
STONE Age monuments. See Megalithic monuments
STONE carving
James Washington: secrets in stone; interview, ed by R. Hackett. J. Washington, Jr. il por Am Artist 41:74-9+ N '77
STONE face. See Lithops
STONE implements and weapons
Functions of paleolithic flint tools. L. H. Keeley. il Sci Am 237:108-11+ N '77
Thermoluminescent determination of prehistoric heat treatment of chert artifacts. C. L. Melcher and D. W. Zimmerman. bibl il Science 197:1359-62 S 30 '77
See also
Stone Age
STONE plants. See Lithops
STONE quarries. See Quarries and quarrying
STONE sculpture. See Stone carving
STONER, Michael
Salting and brining. il Org Gard & Farm 24:117-18+ Ag '77
STONES, Dwight
Mouth that soars. F. DeFord. il pors Sports Illus 46:64-9+ My 30 '77 *
STONES, Flowering. See Lithops
STONES, Snake. See Snakestones
STONINGTON Island
Stonington Island: America's most southerly ghost town. J. H. Lipps. il Oceans 10:42-5 My '77
STOOLS
Step stools. il Consumer Rep 42:162-4 Mr '77
STOOP, Norma McLain
Dancevision: the T.V. beat. See issues of Dance magazine
Drama defines dance: The turning point. il pors Dance Mag 51:42-50 O '77
STOP watches
Consumer's guide to: stopwatches. il Mech Illus 73:18 My '77
How to convert a four banger for stopwatch functions. C. Stanford. il Pop Electr 12:56-7 Ag '77
STOPPARD, Tom
Dirty linen & New-found-land. Reviews
America 136:149 F 19 '77 *
Commonweal 104:180-1 Mr 18 '77 *
Nation 224:125 Ja 29 '77
New Yorker 52:63 Ja 24 '77 *
Time il 109:55 Ja 24 '77 *
Profiles. K. Tynan. New Yorker 53:41-6+ D 19 '77 *
STOPWATCHES. See Stop watches
STORAGE
See also
Garden houses, shelters, etc.
Storage in the home
also subhead Storage under various subjects, e.g. Bicycles—Storage
STORAGE batteries
Anatomy of marine batteries. il Motor B & S 139:43-6 Je '77
Batteries: should you charge or chuck 'em? nickel cadmium batteries. J. Bailey. il Mod Phot 41:20+ Mr '77
Build a state-of-the-art battery charge monitor. W. J. Prudhomme. il Pop Electr 11:88-9 Je '77
Electric cars: battery check-list. N. Gluckin. Sci Digest 82:12 S '77
Fisherman's battery. K. Schultz. Field & S 82:144-5 My '77
Need a battery? W. Woron. il Motor T 29:75-6+ Ap '77
No-fill, no-fuss batteries. R. Gorman. il Pop Sci 210:114-17+ Je '77
Non-electric battery stores energy from waste heat; water vapor battery. D. Scott. il Pop Sci 211:112 S '77
120 volts from a car battery. E. F. Lindsley. il Pop Sci 210:174 Ap '77
Storing electricity. R. Whitaker. il Environment 19:16-20+ Mr '77
See also
Electric batteries
Storage battery industry

Charging

Jumper cables: try these for starters. J. L. Lippert. il Good H 185:263 N '77
NiCad batteries. J. Darr. il Radio-Electr 48:75-6 N '77
Zap new life into dead Ni-Cd batteries. D. C. Myers. il Pop Electr 12:60-1 Jl '77
STORAGE battery chargers
Auto battery chargers. Consumer Rep 42:422-5 D '77
STORAGE battery industry

Acquisitions and mergers

Sweden: where acquisitions need union approval; ESB Inc's purchase of Tudor. il Bus W p43-4 F 28 '77
STORAGE cellars. See Basements and cellars
STORAGE containers. See Containers
STORAGE facilities in boats. See Boats—Equipment
STORAGE in the home
Clever kitchen storage. il Bet Hom & Gard 55:66 Ag '77
Odds and ends under the stairs. il Sunset 158:151 Ap '77
Overhead storage: four do-it-yourself units. D. Haupert and D. Ashe. il Bet Hom & Gard 55:94-5 N '77
Storage ideas from a hold-everything kitchen. J. McCloskey. il Bet Hom & Gard 55:100-1 Ag '77
Super scheme for attic storage. T. H. Jones. il Mech Illus 73:70+ Ap '77
Using all space under the stairs. il Sunset 158:137 Mr '77
See also
Cabinets (furniture)
Closets
Kitchen cabinets
Pantries
Storage walls
STORAGE platforms. See Platforms
STORAGE rings. See Accelerators (electrons, etc)
STORAGE tanks. See Tanks
STORAGE Technology Corporation. See Computer industry
STORAGE walls
Modular wall system you can build. R. Stepler. il Pop Sci 210:108-9+ Ap '77
Storage wall, desk wall, display wall. il Sunset 158:113 Mr '77
Super simple storage center. il Bet Hom & Gard 55:98 Je '77
Wall systems. R. Gorman. il Pop Sci 210:104-7 Ap '77
STORASKA, Frederic
Self-defense. E. R. Dobell. Seventeen 36:194-5+ Ap '77 *
STORE buildings. See Stores
STORE employees. See Department stores—Employees
STORE models
Dream come true. S. A. Parvin. il Hobbies 82:120-1 Ap '77
STORE windows. See Show windows
STORER, George
Broadcaster who fell from grace with the seers. pors Forbes 119:48-9 Ap 1 '77 *

STORER Broadcasting Company
Broadcaster who fell from grace with the seers. pors Forbes 119:48-9 Ap 1 '77
STORES
Building types study; bringing in the business; with introd by G. Allen. il Archit Rec 161:115-30 Mr '77
U.S. journal: Reading, Pa; factory outlets. C. Trillin. New Yorker 53:103-4+ D 5 '77
See also
Airports—Stores
Chain stores
Company stores
Department stores
Drugstores
Food stores
Furniture stores
Hardware stores
Museum stores
Retail trade
Shopping centers
Specialty stores
also subhead Stores under names of cities, e.g. Geneva, Switzerland—Stores
STORES, Cooperative. See Cooperative associations
STORES, Miniature. See Store models
STORES, Museum. See Museum stores
STORIES. See Childrens stories; Fairy tales; Parables
STORIES from the sky god; drama. See Ross, S.
STORIES of operas. See Librettos
STORM drainage systems. See Storm sewers
STORM King Art Center, Mountainville, N.Y. See Art galleries and museums—New York (state)
STORM King hydroelectric project. See Hydroelectric plants
STORM sewers
Slotted drains cut street ponding: Oneonta, N.Y. R. C. Olton. il Am City & County 92:56 Ap '77
STORM Trysail Club Race. See Yacht racing
STORM water sewers. See Storm sewers
STORM waves. See Waves
STORM windows. See Windows
STØRMER, Leif
Arthropod invasion of land during late Silurian and Devonian times. bibl il Science 197:1362-4 S 30 '77
STORMS
Storm on the river; excerpt from Where would you go? B. H. Lampman. il Read Digest 111: 33-4 Ag '77
That October storm. R. Mairs; J. Rousmaniere. il Yachting 141:82-3+ Mr '77
Year the weather went wild. T. Y. Canby. il maps Nat Geog 152:798-829 D '77
See also
Automobile driving—Storm hazards
Aviation—Storm hazards
Boats and boating—Storm hazards
Cyclones
Dust storms
Hurricanes
Snowstorms
Thunderstorms
Tornadoes
Typhoons
STORRO-PATTERSON, Ronn
Gray whale protection. il Oceans 10:45-9 Jl '77
STORROW, James Jackson
Obituary
Am For por 83:11 Ag '77
STORY machine; drama. See Asimov, I.
STORY telling
Legend in your own time. Seventeen 36:58 S '77
Merry yarn: your own kind of story. J. Clark. Camp Mag 49:21 My '77
Story time for toddlers; program of the Greenburgh Public Library, Elmsford, N.Y. J. K. Markowsky. bibl il por SLJ 23:28-31 My '77
Storytime stretches with books. S. W. Sprague. SLJ 24:42 S '77
STORY telling records. See Phonograph records—Childrens records
STOTT, Charles
Planning & development. Camp Mag 49:38-40 Mr; 17-18 Je '77
STOTT, John R. W.
Anglican evangelicals speak out. Chr Today 21: 30-1 Jl 8 '77
English-speaking West Africa. Chr Today 22: 38-9 D 9 '77
Evangelicals and Roman Catholics. Chr Today 21:30-1 Ag 12 '77
Is the incarnation a myth? Chr Today 22:34-5 N 4 '77
Unhooked Christians. Chr Today 22:40-1 O 7 '77
STOUT, Henry
Reporter at large. J. Stevenson. il New Yorker 53:46+ Ag 15 '77 *
STOUT, Joan A. and Turitz, Gilda
Outside. . .looking in. bibl il pors Wilson Lib Bull 51:499-505 F '77
STOUT, Rex
Murder Ink honors maitre d'tective Rex Stout. A. Goodwin. Pub W 212:50+ N 14 '77 *
Murder with dignity. A. Jaffe. il New Repub 177:41-3 Jl 30 '77 *
STOUT, Robert Joe
Homes for the unwanted. Chr Cent 94:849-51 S 28 '77
One of the luckier ones. Commonweal 104:463-5 Jl 22 '77
Our misfit children, young and old. Chr Cent 94:194-6 Mr 2 '77
STOVES
Ceramic cooktops: pretty but not practical. il Consumer Rep 42:586-9 O '77
Choosing the galley stove; excerpt from The galley book. J. Groene. Yachting 141:90-1 My '77
Complete wood stove story; with addresses of manufacturers. G. Reiger. Field & S 82:14+ N '77
Home works; what's cooking with today's ranges—from conventional to de luxe. il Redbook 148:130+ Mr '77
How to install a heating stove. B. Murphy. il Mech Illus 73:86+ N '77
Major kitchen appliances. il Consumers Res Mag 60:194-205 O '77
Secrets of a good wood stove. J. Schneider. bibl il Pop Sci 211:113-17+ N '77
They're cookin' with wood. D. Pauly and R. Manning. il Newsweek 91:53 Ja 2 '78
30-inch electric ranges. il Consumer Res Mag 60:27-33 My '77
Wood stove you can weld. C. Self. il Pop Sci 212:110+ Ja '78
See also
Camp stoves
Fireless cookers
STOVES on boats. See Boats—Equipment
STOWE, Harriet Elizabeth (Beecher)
Uncle Tom's Roots. M. Greenfield. il Newsweek 89:100 F 14 '77 *
STOWE, Vt.
Restaurants
See Restaurants—United States
STOYENOFF, Norma
Writing the confession story today. Writer 90:26-30 O '77
STRAATSMA, Bradley R.
Protecting your eyesight: an expert's advice; interview. il por U.S. News 82:79-81 Ap 25 '77; Same abr. with title What you should know about eye care. Read Digest 111:147-50 Ag '77
STRABISMUS
Katie's eyes are normal now. E. Larsen. il Parents Mag 52:37-9 Ag '77
STRACK, David. See Grieves, R. T. jt auth
STRAINCHAMPS, Edmond
New light on the Accademia degli Elevati of Florence. bibl f il Mus Q 62:507-35 O '76
STRAINS and stresses
Plastic-composite design cuts steel tonnage in Johns-Manville's new headquarters building. W. J. LeMessurier. il Archit Rec 162:127-8 S '77
See also
Deformation (mechanics)
STRAIT of Magellan. See Magellan, Strait of
STRAITS of Bosporus. See Bosporus
STRAND, Mark
Late hour; House in French village: for Elizabeth Bishop; For her; About a man; For Jessica, my daughter; poems. New Yorker 53: 44-5 O 10 '77
Night piece; poem. New Yorker 53:58 N 21 '77
Where are the waters of childhood? poem. New Yorker 53:48 D 12 '77
STRASSER, Todd
Down! New Yorker 52:28-9 Ja 24 '77
STRATEGIC Arms Limitation Talks
Advice from the former tenants; views of G. R. Ford and H. Kissinger. Nation 224:482-4 Ap 23 '77
After Moscow's frost, a thaw in Geneva; SALT II. il pors Time 109:6-7 My 30 '77
Arms control: the Russians are cheating! M. R. Laird. Read Digest 111:97-101 D '77
Assault on SALT. M. Kondracke. New Repub 177:19-21 D 17 '77
Behind the SALT fiasco. R. J. Barnet. Progressive 41:6-7 Je '77
Beyond SALT II—a missile test quota. S. D. Drell. bibl il Bull Atom Sci 33:34-42 My '77
Big defense issues on U.S. doorstep. J. Fromm. U.S. News 83:47 D 26 '77
Breaking the ice; SALT talks in Geneva. S. Fraker and others. pors Newsweek 89:16-17 My 30 '77
Brzezinski details administration's position. Z Brzezinski. il por Aviation W 106:34-5+ Ap 18 '77
Carter takes on the Russians. U.S. News 82: 21-3 Ap 11 '77
Carter to propose quick SALT agreement. Aviation W 106:19 F 14 '77

STRATEGIC Arms Limitation Talks—*Continued*
Carter v. Brezhnev: the SALT standoff; ABCs of the arms controversy. il pors Time 109: 10-14+ Ap 11 '77
Carter's arms budget is a signal to SALT. il Bus W p36 F 28 '77
Congressmen debate own role as advisers in SALT treaty. Aviation W 107:14 N 21 '77
Cruise missile halt considered. C. A. Robinson, Jr. il Aviation W 106:16-20 My 23 '77
Did we expect a dancing bear? Moscow visit of C. R. Vance. Nation 224:450-2 Ap 16 '77
Evaluating U.S. SALT bargaining strategies. L. Jensen. Intellect 106:26-9 Ag '77
Expiration of SALT pact scrutinized. Aviation W 107:19 Ag 8 '77
Explosive SALT. R. Hotz. Aviation W 106:7 Ap 11 '77
Fresh warning to Americans about U.S.-Soviet Arms talks; report of the Committee on the Present Danger. il U.S. News 83:59-60 Jl 18 '77
Hard-nosed but soft-headed: confirmation of P. Warnke as chief SALT negotiator. B. T. Feld. Bull Atom Sci 33:9 Ap '77
Jimmy's deadwood; collapse of the strategic arms negotiations in Moscow. J. Osborne. New Repub 176:8-10 Ap 9 '77
Let's not panic prematurely. B. T. Feld. Bull Atom Sci 33:8-9 My '77
Letter from Washington. R. H. Rovere. New Yorker 53:129 Ap 11 '77
Missile accuracies: overlooked program could undermine SALT. D. Shapley. il Science 196: 1185-6 Je 10 '77
Missile X becomes a hostage to SALT. Bus W p32+ Je 27 '77
Mission to Moscow; C. R. Vance's visit. R. Steele and others. il por Newsweek 89:20-2 Ap 4 '77
Negotiating with the Soviets. G. C. Smith. N Y Times Mag p 18-19+ F 27 '77
New math of SALT. M. R. Benjamin and others. il Newsweek 90:53-4 O 24 '77
Next SALT treaty with Soviets: ABC's of progress—and pitfalls. il U.S. News 83:29-30 N 14 '77
Options studied for expiration of SALT. E. Kozicharow. Aviation W 107:16-18 Ag 1 '77
Peppering SALT. Time 110:25 N 21 '77
Please pass the SALT; J. Carter's press conference, February 8, 1977. R. Steele and others. il por Newsweek 89:15-17 F 21 '77
Politics of arms control; President Carter's proposals. R. J. Bresler. Intellect 105:392-3 Je '77
President Carter discusses Cuba and SALT negotiations; transcript of remarks, May 30, 1977. J. Carter. Dept State Bull 77:9-10 Jl 4 '77
President Carter discusses Strategic Arms Limitation proposals; remarks, with transcript of question and answer session, March 30, 1977. J. Carter. Dept State Bull 76:409-14 Ap 25 '77
Presidential Assistant Brzezinski's news conference of April 1; transcript of news conference. Z. Brzezinski. Dept State Bull 76: 414-21 Ap 25 '77
Progress and problems in arms control negotiations; address, September 19, 1977. P. C. Warnke. Dept State Bull 77:772-7 N 28 '77
Proper perch for the dove; P. Warnke. por Time 109:23 F 14 '77
Quiet buildup to SALT II. Time 109:26-7 Ap 18 '77
Reading the Geneva barometer. Time 109:31 My 23 '77
Reporter at large. E. Drew. New Yorker 53:99-117 Ap 4 '77
SALT: a bargaining chip; FB-111H. M. R. Benjamin and S. Sullivan. il Newsweek 90:44-5 O 3 '77
SALT agreements face trouble in Congress. C. A. Robinson, Jr. il Aviation W 107:14-16 O 17 '77
SALT disaster coming? Nat R 29:1282-3 N 11 '77
SALT extension would raise Soviet first-strike questions. E. Kozicharow. il Aviation W 107: 22-3 Ag 15 '77
SALT negotiations. H. Scoville, Jr. il Sci Am 237:24-31 bibl(p 140) Ag '77
SALT: outgunned? Russian ICBMs. Newsweek 90:46 S 26 '77
SALT stalemate. B. T. Feld. Bull Atom Sci 33:7 N '77
SALT technology transfer curb cited. Aviation W 107:16 N 28 '77
SALT: toward a breakthrough. il Time 110:41-2 O 10 '77
SALT II and beyond. P. J. Ognibene. New Repub 176:16-18 F 5 '77
SALT updates. Nat R 30:16-17 Ja 6 '78
SALT — verifiability = O. J. Burnham. Nat R 30:22 Ja 6 '78
SALT violations confirmed. R. Hotz. Aviation W 107:9 D 12 '77
Secretary Vance and Soviet Foreign Minister Gromyko hold talks at Geneva; transcript of news conference, with joint communique, May 21, 1977. C. R. Vance; A. A. Gromyko. Dept State Bull 76:628-33 Je 13 '77
Secretary Vance visits Moscow and western Europe; remarks, transcripts of news conferences, with joint communique, March 27-30, April 1-2, 1977. C. R. Vance. Dept State Bull 76:389-409 Ap 25 '77
Senatorial saboteur; H. M. Jackson. Nation 225: 515-16 N 19 '77
Signs of change in Russia; interview. M. Toon. il pors U.S. News 84:27-8 Ja 9 '78
Skip step toward SALT II. il Newsweek 89:26 Mr 28 '77
Strategic force structure to face stiff debate. C. A. Robinson, Jr. il Aviation W 106:16-19 Ap 18 '77
TRB from Washington; J. Carter's press conference, February 8, 1977. New Repub 176:4+ F 19 '77
Test ban talks scrutiny urged. E. Kozicharow. Aviation W 107:12-13 N 21 '77
Testing Carter. R. Steele and others. il por Newsweek 89:26-30 Ap 11 '77
Toward nuclear stability. E. C. Ravenal. Atlantic 240:35-41 S '77
U.S. intent with regard to SALT I interim agreement; statement, September 26, 1977. P. C. Warnke. Dept State Bull 77:642-3 N 7 '77
U.S. sets new rules for detente; with interview with U. A. Johnson. pors U.S. News 82:24-6 Ap 4 '77
U.S. urged to set firm strategic goals. Aviation W 106:84 Je 27 '77
Unplugged leaks; H. M. Jackson and the progress of the Strategic Arms Limitation Talks. New Repub 177:2+ N 26 '77
Unsalted. Nat R 29:1158 O 14 '77
Vance in Moscow: a frank discussion. il por Time 109:23-4 Ap 4 '77
Wading into the stream. Time 110:36 O 3 '77
What the deadlock in arms talks is all about. il U.S. News 82:24-5 Ap 11 '77
What to hope for, and worry about, in SALT. F. C. Iklé. il por Fortune 96:176-9+ O '77
Wipe away those tears. il por New Repub 176:5-6+ Ap 16 '77

Anecdotes, facetiae, satire, etc.

Saline solution. R. Baker. N Y Times Mag p 12 Ap 3 '77

STRATEGIC materials

Stockpiling

See Stockpiling

STRATEGY
Dangerous delusion. E. R. Zumwalt, Jr. il pors Sat Eve Post 249:12-14 N '77
Obsessions with nuclear strategy. A. Wolfe. Nation 225:265-8 S 24 '77
Scarcity and strategy. G. Kemp. For Affairs 56: 396-414 Ja '78
Why the Soviet Union thinks it could fight and win a nuclear war. R. E. Pipes. bibl f Commentary 64:21-34 Jl '77; Discussion. 64:4+ S '77

STRATFORD, Ontario, Shakespeare Festival. See Shakespeare Festival, Stratford, Ontario

STRATOSPHERE. See Atmosphere, Upper

STRATTON, Barbara M.
God help the working girl. Am Home 80:34 S '77

STRAUS, Karen
Jumbo squid. il Oceans 10:10-15 Mr '77

STRAUS, Roger W. 1917-
Roger W. Straus, Jr, president of Farrar, Straus & Giroux, reflects on his firm's 30-year pursuit of literary excellence; interview. pors Pub W 211:55-9 F 7 '77

STRAUSFELD, N. J. and Campos-Ortega, J. A.
Vision in insects: pathways possibly underlying neural adaptation and lateral inhibition. bibl il Science 195:894-7 Mr 4 '77

STRAUSS, George
Organization behavior as an aid to labor impasse resolution. bibl M Labor R 100:49-52 Ap '77

STRAUSS, Johann, 1825-1899
Die Fledermaus. W. Botsford. Am Rec G 40:36-7 Mr '77 *
Vienna waltzes. W. L. Purcell. Am Rec G 40:38 N '76 *

STRAUSS, Levi, and Company
How Levi's cracked a ring of counterfeiters. il Bus W p27 S 5 '77
New cut for Levi's. L. Langway and P. S. Greenberg. il Newsweek 90:64 Jl 25 '77

STRAUSS, Lewis Lichtenstein
Oppenheimer case: a study in the abuse of law. H. P. Green. il pors Bull Atom Sci 33:12-16+ S '77 *

STRAUSS, Richard
Again the silver rose: Der Rosenkavalier; Philips recording. R. V. Lucano. il Am Rec G 40:43-5 O '77 *
Festival of Richard Strauss; Vienna State Opera. P. J. Smith. Hi Fi 27:MA39-40 Ag '77 *
Ein Heldenleben, op. 40. G. S. Fox. Am Rec G 40:41 D '76 *
Heroic voices from pioneer days; W. Mengelberg's 1928 recording of Ein Heldenleben on Victrola. R. D. Darrell. pors Hi Fi 27:90-1 Ap '77 *

STRAUSS, Richard—*Continued*
Historic reissues. G. S. Fox. Am Rec G 40:5-6+ Ag '77 *
Imp of perversity: Salome. G. Schmidgal. il Opera N 41:10-13 F 12 '77 *
Intermezzo. Reviews
Hi Fi 27:MA32 Jl '77 *
Der Rosenkavalier. Review
Opera N il 42:20+ Ja 7 '78 *
Der Rosenkavalier, op. 59; Philips recording conducted by E. de Waart. Hi Fi 27:110-13 S '77 *
Salome. Reviews
Hi Fi il 27:MA29 My '77 *
Opera N il 41:20+ F 12 '77 *

STRAUSS, Richard L.
Family church: any place for singles? Chr Today 21:12-14 Jl 29 '77

STRAUSS, Robert S.
Carter calls in a fence mender from Texas. il U.S. News 83:23 N 21 '77*
Collision course for Strauss. por Bus W p27-8 Je 6 '77 *
More about Strauss. J. Osborne. New Repub 178:8-10 Ja 7 '78 *
New Cabinet whip. M. A. Ruby and others. il por Newsweek 90:37 O 31 '77 *
Picking a winner. il por Time 109:49-50 Mr 7 '77 *
Resurrection. J. Osborne. New Repub 177:13-16 D 24 '77 *
Strauss's big test in Tokyo. S. W. Sanders. il por Bus W p48 D 5 '77 *

STRAUSSER, Helen R. See Lattime, E. C. jt auth

STRAVINSKY, Igor Fedorovich
Petrouchka conducted by C. Dutoit. Deutsche Grammaphon recording. W. D. Curtis. Am Rec G 41:32-4 N '77 *
Le sacre du printemps. G. S. Fox. por Am Rec G 40:42-3 D '76*

STRAWBERRIES
Building a 25-year strawberry bed. J. Vivian. il Org Gard & Farm 24:190+ F '77
How a lifetime organic gardener grows berries profitably. G. Logsdon. il Org Gard & Fam 24:74-7 D '77
My solution to the feathered berry thieves. R. E. Hampton. Org Gard & Farm 24:156 Je '77
Super strawberries: the organic convincers. C. B. Waldron. il Org Gard & Farm 24:186+ F '77
See also
Cookery—Fruit

STRAWN, Jarrett W.
Fine arts in college: a proposal for redesigning the curriculum. Am Artist 41:64-6 D '77

STRAX, Philip
Are breast X-rays safe? il Parents Mag 52:48-9+ F '77

STREAM conservation
Make the river do the work; renovation of log-choked and flood-prone St Joseph and Tiffin Rivers in Ohio; alternative to channelization. B. East. il por Outdoor Life 160:78-81+ O '77
Marvel of Big Creek. G. Purvis. por Outdoor Life 160:7 O '77
On dumping Dickey and saving the St John; with editorial comment. R. Saltonstall, Jr. Liv Wildn 40:3, 20-1 O '76
Preserving our wild and scenic rivers; symposium. il Nat Geog 152:2-59, supp (folded map) Jl '77

STREAM improvement. See Stream conservation

STREAMS. See Rivers

STREEP, Meryl
Close-up; interview, ed by E. Miller. por Seventeen 36:64 F '77
Interview: Meryl Streep on Julia; ed by M. Latour. Mademoiselle 83:76 Mr '77

STREET cars

Manufacture

See also
Boeing Company—Vertol division

STREET cleaning
How to get (and keep) streets cleaner. il Am City & County 92:51-4 Je '77
See also
Snow and ice removal

STREET cleaning apparatus
Sandy streets challenge Yuma sweepers. il Am City & County 92:55 Je '77

STREET entertainers. See Entertainers

STREET gangs. See Gangs

STREET lighting
500% more light with 47% less energy; high-pressure sodium lighting, Ft Wayne, Ind. il Am City & County 92:56 Mr '77
Lighting helps CBD sales; Tacoma Wash. il Am City & County 92:37 Jl '77

STREET lighting fixtures
Aluminum poles help light saltwater highways; use in Dade County, Fla. F. P. Seeley. il por Am City & County 92:35-6 Ja '77
High-mast lighting comes of age. il Am City & County 92:33-6 Jl '77
Street light standards anything but standard. W. S. Foster. Am City & County 92:72 F '77

STREET Machine Nationals. See Drag racing

STREET markings. See Traffic markings

STREET Rod Nationals. See Drag racing

STREET rods. See Automobiles, Remodeled

STREET sweepers. See Street cleaning apparatus

STREET sweeping. See Street cleaning

STREET trades
Gold in the streets. L. Langway and others. il Newsweek 91:56-7 Ja 9 '78
Madame Mercedes-Benz: merchant of Togo. E. J. Kiers. il Ms 5:112+ Ap '77

STREET trees. See Trees in cities

STREETER, Carole Sanderson
Immediacy; poem. Chr Today 22:17 N 4 '77
Love of darkness; poem. Chr Today 22:27 O 7 '77

STREETS
See also
Baltimore—Streets
Street trades

Lighting

See Street lighting

Maintenance and repair

See also
Pavements—Surface treatment

Safety devices and measures

See also
Traffic markings

STREICHER, Elizabeth
(ed) See Varnedoe, K. Max Klinger: a realm of privileged suspension

STREISAND, Barbra
Barbra Streisand: people who love power. M. Rosen. il por Ms 5:39-40 My '77 *

STRENGTH of materials
See also
Fracture of solids

STRESHINSKY, Shirley G.
How working couples work it out. il Redbook 149:103+ Je '77

STRESS (physiology)
Expression of murine sarcoma virus genes in uninfected rat cells subjected to anaerobic stress. G. R. Anderson and L. M. Matovcik. bibl il Science 197:1371-4 S 30 '77
Genetic predisposition and stress-induced hypertension. R. Friedman and J. Iwai; reply with rejoinder. M. Peters. bibl Science 198:80 O 7 '77
Stress and the heart. R. F. DeBusk. Intellect 106:190 N '77
Stress-illness link: not if but how. J. Greenberg. il Sci N 112:394-5+ D 10 '77
Stress-induced modulation of the immune response. A. A. Monjan and M. I. Collector. bibl il Science 196:307-8 Ap 15 '77
See also
Plants, Effect of stress on

STRESS (psychology)
Anti-tension diet and exercise plan. M. Mercer. McCalls 104:54+ F '77
Bazaars health guide to your nerves; symposium. Harp Baz 110:124-9+ Mr '77
Calling Dr Stress; Israel; interview, ed by J. R. Moskin. L. Miller. il por Psychol Today 11:93-4+ S '77
Coping with stress effectively. D. Hamburg. por Intellect 106:13-14 Jl '77
Emotional stress and sudden death. G. Engel. bibl il Psychol Today 11:114-15+ N '77
Fighting stress; biofeedback training for executives. L. Smith. il Duns R 109:59-61 Ja '77
Heart disease and life stress; identical twin studies by Einar Kringlen. Sci N 112:166 S 10 '77
How to cope with tragedy. A. F. Poussaint. il Ebony 32:94-6+ F '77
How to master stress: a guide for families today. H. Selye. il Parents Mag 52:25+ N '77
Link between your emotions and health; interview. C. N. Shealy. Harp Baz 110:131+ F '77
Lowering blood pressure. J. Arehart-Treichel. il Sci N 111:347 My 28 '77
Mind as healer, mind as slayer; excerpt. K. R. Pelletier. il por Psychol Today 10:35-7+ F '77
Secret of coping with stress; interview. H. Selye. il por U.S. News 82:51-3 Mr 21 '77; Same abr. with title To beat stress—learn how to live. Read Digest 111:161-3 Jl '77
Sigmund, here's a joke on you; laughter as a release of tension. D. Cohen. il Psychol Today 10:30+ Ap '77
Stress. K. Slobogin. il N Y Times Mag p48-50+ N 20 '77
Stress and the classroom teacher. R. Sylwester. Educ Digest 42:14-17 My '77
Stress in teaching and how to handle it. K. Styles and G. Cavanagh. bibl f Engl J 66:76-9 Ja '77
Stress—new prison tests: sadism or therapy? C. Pogash. il Sci Digest 81:64-7 F '77
Stress on the job. L. C. Pogrebin. Ladies Home J 94:31-2+ S '77

STRESS (psychology)—*Continued*
Stress: role in hypertension debated. J. L. Marx. Science 198:905-7 D 2 '77
Sweaty palms in the control tower. D. Martindale. bibl il por Psychol Today 10:70-2+ F '77
See also
Anxiety
Crowding stress

STRESSES. See Strains and stresses

STRETCHING exercises. See Exercise

STREUSEL (crumbs) See Crumbs (bread, cake, etc)

STRICKER, Edward M. and others
Homeostasis during hypoglycemia: central control of adrenal secretion and peripheral control of feeding. bibl il Science 196:79-81 Ap 1 '77

STRICKLAND, Anita
Looking for Mr Rightbar. Mademoiselle 83:170+ Je '77

STRIKER, Isabel A.
Early visions of imperial Brazil. il Américas 29:S1-12 Ja '77

STRIKES
See also
Collective labor agreements
Trade unions

Law

See Labor laws and legislation

Psychological aspects

Replaceable you. B. Photopulos. por Newsweek 90:23 O 10 '77

France

Labor disputes crippling major French airlines. Aviation W 107:35 D 12 '77
Paris in June. L. P. De Menil. New Repub 176:21 Je 18 '77
Trying to placate a hostile labor force. il Bus W p44 Ap 25 '77

Great Britain

Back to work at Leyland. il Time 109:80 Mr 28 '77
Britain's Ascot of the Left; strike at Grunwick film-processing company. R. Moss. Nat R 29:1238-40 O 28 '77
Unions break a truce; air-traffic controllers. D. Pauly and M. MacPherson. il Newsweek 90:68+ S 5 '77
Unions scuttle the social contract; walkout at the Grunwich Film Processing Laboratories. il Time 110:24+ Jl 18 '77
When firemen stop fighting. il Time 110:54 N 28 '77
Winter of discontent for British workers. il U.S. News 83:49 D 19 '77

Northern Ireland

Paisley led but few workers followed; general strike. il por Time 109:44 My 16 '77

United States

Strikes end labor's calm—with more unrest to come. il U.S. News 83:101-2 N 21 '77

Aerospace industries

Aerospace industry facing serious labor problems. R. G. O'Lone. Aviation W 107:25 O 10 '77
Aerospace labor disputes continue. J. M. Lenorovitz. Aviation W 107:22-3 O 31 '77
Aerospace labor woes continue. Aviation W 107:15 D 19 '77
IAM strikes Lockheed's installations in California. Aviation W 107:24-5 O 17 '77
Labor, management adamant in Lockheed strike positions. J. M. Lenorovitz. Aviation W 107:23-4 D 12 '77
Lockheed strike continued despite union member rift. J. M. Lenorovitz. Aviation W 107:21-2 D 5 '77
Seniority snags aerospace talks. il Bus W p45+ N 14 '77
Why Lockheed's strike is a holy war. il Bus W p31 D 19 '77

Air traffic controllers (persons)

Air controllers reach for the book; job slowdown. Bus W p37 D 26 '77

Airlines

Wien, pilots at impasse in strike over Boeing 737 crew size. Aviation W 106:70 Je 6 '77

Brewery workers

Bitter beercott; dispute over polygraph exams at Adolph Coors Co. il Time 110:15 D 26 '77

Coal miners

But life can be cruel. il Time 110:14-15 D 19 '77
Coal and the UMW are still at odds; wildcat coal strike. Bus W p29 Ag 29 '77
Coal miners walk out. il Time 110:72+ D 12 '77
Striking out of weakness? il Time 110:64+ O 24 '77
UMW is bargaining from weakness. J. Hoerr. Bus W p30 D 19 '77
Why a coal strike isn't what it used to be. il U.S. News 83:86 D 19 '77
Wildcat strikes: preview of turmoil in coal fields. F. W. Frailey. il U.S News 83:65-7 S 5 '77
Workers, strikers and unions. Nation 225:642-3 D 17 '77

College teachers

Stevens Institute of Technology: after the strike, still unsettled. J. Walsh. il Science 196:280-3 Ap 15 '77

Farmers

Behind the unrest on America's farms; Parity: what strike is all about. il U.S. News 83:69-70 D 26 '76
Carter and the farmers. New Repub 178:5-6 Ja 7 '78
Ends and beginnings. F. Getlein. Commonweal 105:4-5 Ja 6 '78
Furious farmers. Time 110:17 D 19 '77
Tractor rebellion. T. Nicholson and others. il Newsweek 90:57 D 19 '77

Government employees

Can public-employee unions be controlled? K. Y. Tomlinson. Read Digest 110:141-5 Ap '77
Strikes used to save money, AFSCME charges. Am City & County 92:13 Ap '77
See also
Strikes—United States—Municipal employees

Iron miners

Breaking steel's separate peace; testing the Experimental Negotiating Agreement. il Time 110:55 Ag 15 '77
Ore miners threaten steel's labor peace. Bus W p39-40 Ag 15 '77
Steel strike: another blow for a problem-ridden industry. il U.S. News 83:61-2 Ag 15 '77
Why a labor pact won't end steel's problems. J. Hoerr. Bus W p56-7 S 26 '77

Longshoremen

Contagious tie-up on the docks. il Bus W p33-4 O 24 '77
Container woes in dockland. il Time 110:53-4 O 17 '77
Off the waterfront. T. Nicholson and D. Witherspoon. il Newsweek 90:93 O 24 '77
Pinch on the docks. T. Nicholson and P. E. Simons. il Newsweek 90:77 N 21 '77
Strikes end labor's calm—with more unrest to come. il U.S. News 83:101-2 N 21 '77
That tricky trike strike. il Time 110:77 N 21 '77

Meat industry workers

Iowa beef becomes a test for management. Bus W p28-9 Mr 14 '77

Municipal employees

Day of reckoning for public sector strikes. S. S. Baxter. Am City & County 92:19 Ja '77

Newspapers

Peculiar freedom; Madison, Wis. B. Solomon. Nation 225:580 D 3 '77

Police

Anatomy of a police strike—winning public opinion. J. Horn. Psychol Today 10:92-4 F '77

Publishers and publishing

Harper & Row, District 65 agree on new contract. W. Gelles. il Pub W 211:154 My 23 '77
Harper & Row, District 65 brace for strike. M. Reuter. Pub W 211:21 My 9 '77
220 union members walk out at Harper & Row. M. Reuter. il Pub W 211:28-9 My 16 '77

Sanitation workers

Atlanta breaks union strike bid. Am City & County 92:27 Jl '77
Strikebreaker; M. Jackson of Atlanta. il por Newsweek 89:29-30 Ap 25 '77

Steel workers

See also
Strikes—United States—Iron miners

Teachers

Teacher strikes: at lowest ebb in years. U.S. News 83:84 S 19 '77

Television industry

Technological strike at ABC. il Bus W p67+ Ag 8 '77

STRINDBERG, August
Creditors. Review
Time 109:76 My 30 '77 •
Dance of death. Review
Time il 109:50 My 9 '77 •
Ghost sonata. Reviews
Nation 225:476-7 N 5 '77 •
Newsweek il 90:85 O 24 '77 •

STRING beans. See Beans
STRING quartets
Artist life; Quartetto Italiano. D. J. Soria. il Hi Fi 27:MA5+ Je '77
Bass part in Haydn's early string quartets. J. Webster. bibl il Mus Q 63:390-424 Jl '77
Chilingirian string quartet; New York debut. il Hi Fi 27:MA22 S '77
Fine Arts Quartet: Adler prem; Sixth string quartet. Hi Fi 27:MA21 S '77
Marriage Italian style; Quartetto Italiano. H. Saal. il Newsweek 89:85 Mr 7 '77
Sequoia String Quartet; Tully Hall debut. Hi Fi 27:MA36-7 Jl '77
See also
Phonograph records—String quartet music
STRING trimmers. See Lawn tools, equipment, and supplies
STRINGED instruments
See also names of stringed instruments, e.g. Violin
Instruction and study
String training on the Cape; music education program of the Barnstable, Mass. public school system. Mrs Conlon-Hoffman. il Hi Fi 28:MA14-15 Ja '78
STRIP-mined land, Reclamation of. See Reclamation of land
STRIP mining
Laws and legislation
Curbs on strippers celebrated. C. Holden. Science 197:743 Ag 19 '77
Impact of stiff new rules on strip mining. il U.S. News 83:43 Ag 1 '77
New strip mining law protects prime farm land. R. D. Wennblom. il Farm J 101:J4 O '77
Reform tempered with restraint. J. B. Craig. Am For 83:13 Ap '77
Strip mining and the environment. B. A. Branson. il Nat Parks & Con Mag 51:10-12 Ap '77
Strip mining: Carter makes the difference. Bus W p34+ F 21 '77
Strip mining: showdown near. U.S. News 82:47 Mr 14 '77
Appalachian Region
Great strip mine flood. P. Primack. Nation 224:691-2 Je 4 '77
Florida
Another kind of strip mining that's stirring up a storm; phosphate digging in Polk County. il U.S. News 82:41-2 My 23 '77
Idaho
Phosphate fate will determine Idaho high country's fate; leases for proposed open-pit minning. E. Chaney. Audubon 79:123-6 Mr '77
Kentucky
Making moonscapes for coal. C. Polsgrove. Progressive 41:38 F '77
Ohio
UMW's turf slowly erodes. il por Bus W p74-5 D 19 '77
West Virginia
After the floods; Tug Valley, West Virginia. C. McCarthy. Progressive 41:44-7 D '77
Double disaster in Appalachia; Tug Fork River flood. C. McCarthy. America 136:536-9 Je 18 '77
Western States
Spectre of an American wasteland; with editorial comment. T. Pew. il map Horticulture 55:16, 40-53 Ag '77
STRIPED bass fishing. See Bass fishing
STRIPER fishing. See Bass fishing
STRIPPING of furniture. See Furniture—Finishing
STRIPTEASE acts. See Burlesque
STROBEL, Gary A. See Currier, W. W. jt auth
STROBELL, Adah Parker
Modernizing evaluation techniques. il Parks & Rec 12:30-1+ Je '77
STROEH, J. Dietrich
What do you do when you're out of water? il Am City & County 92:49-50 D '77
STROESSNER, Alfredo
Stroessner never sleeps. R. Moreau. il por Newsweek 89:31-2 F 21 '77 *
STROHM, Bob
(ed) See Reece, M. First, you've got to know wildlife
STROHM, John
She brings back the good old days. il por Nat Wildlife 16:28-35 D '77
STROKE, George W.
Molecules in 3-D. il Time 109:81 F 14 '77 *
STROKE. See Cerebrovascular disease
STROLLERS (infants) See Baby carriages
STROM, Stephen E.
Survey of galaxies sheds light on shape. il Sci N 111:86 F 5 '77 *
STROMBERG, Roland N.
Greening of Karl Marx. Nat R 29:991+ S 2 '77
STRONG, Emily
Give them a reason to write: launching the informal school newspaper. Engl J 66:37-40 My '77
STRONG, Rodney D.
Happy ending in the vineyards. F. J. Prial. il por N Y Times Mag p61-2 Ag 21 '77 *
STRONG, Roy
Privilege and passion of directing museums; interview, ed by J. Gruen. il por Art N 76:58-62+ Ja '77
STRONTIUM
Isotopes
Ancient lithosphere: its role in young continental volcanism. C. Brooks and others; reply with rejoinder. F. Chayes. bibl Science 196:1234-5 Je 10 '77
STROUD, Kandy
Growing up with Rosalynn Carter; excerpt from How Jimmy won. il pors Good H 185:102-3+ Ag '77
Rosalynn's agenda in the White House. por N Y Times Mag p 19-20+ Mr 20 '77
STROUT, Cushing
Murder with manners. il New Repub 177:34-6 Jl 30 '77
STROUT, Richard L.
Henry the first. il New Repub 176:16-18 My 21 '77
STROZIER, Robert M.
Diary of me: Manhattan, 1976. il Atlantic 239:83-5 Ap '77
Under the agnus castus tree, by the banks of the old Ilissus. il Atlantic 239:86-7 Je '77
STRUCTURAL engineering
Designing brick masonry walls to avoid structural problems. C. T. Grimm. il Archit Rec 162:124-8 O '77
Engineering for architecture; special issue; with introd by W. F. Wagner, Jr. Archit Rec 162:7+ mid-Ag '77
Technical news and research (cont) il Archit Rec 161:151 Ja '77
See also
Strains and stresses
STRUCTURAL geology. See Geology, Structural
STRUCTURAL learning. See Learning, Psychology of
STRUCTURES, Moving of. See Moving of structures, etc.
STRUDEL. See Pastry
STRUGGLE for existence
Evolution in a time-varying environment. R. A. Armstrong and M. E. Gilpin. bibl il Science 195:591-2 F 11 '77
STRUM, Philippa
Selzer case. New Repub 176:7+ My 7 '77
STRUMPEL, Burkhard
Quality vs. quantity. Intellect 105:378 My '77
STRUNG, Norman
Endless fall. il Field & S 82:76-8+ S '77
Float trip camping. il Field & S 82:52-4+ My '77
Foxy pheasant. il Field & S 82:42-3+ O '77
Rain is catching time. il por Outdoor Life 159:96+ My '77
South of the border on a shoestring. il Field & S 81:158-9+ F '77
Trout—time of the push root. il Field & S 82:66-7+ Je '77
Whitetails & wild tales. il Field & S 82:42-3+ N '77
STRUSS, Karl
Stills of a cinematographer. il por Mod Phot 41:61 F '77 *
STUART, Alexander
Meanwhile, U.S. cigar makers are losing customers. Fortune 95:177 F '77
STUART, Dabney
Plowing it under; The top of the forest; poems. Poetry 131:141 D '77
STUART, Gilbert
By George, a Stuart! por Time 110:24+ N 28 '77 *
STUART, Jesse
Nine bean rows; story. Sat Eve Post 249:26-9 My '77
STUART, Michelle
New landscape art. L. R. Lippard. il Ms 5:68-73 Ap '77 *
STUART, Robert
Social responsibility of people in business. por Nations Bus 65:47-8 Ap '77
STUART-ALEXANDER, D. E. See Mark, R. K. jt auth
STUBBINS, Hugh Asher, 1912-
Brave new skyscraper. D. Davis. il Newsweek 90:84+ O 31 '77 *
STUBBLEFIELD, Nathan Bernard
Nathan Stubblefield: the radio prophet of the Kentucky fields. H. Geller. il pors Hi Fi 27:79-83 N '77 *
STUBBLEFIELD, Robert Lee
Lure of television—ways to unplug your kids; interview. U.S. News 83:24 S 12 '77

STUBBS, George
Helping Britain buy British. il Time 111:71 Ja 2 '78 *

STUBBS, Harry C.
Views on science books. il Horn Bk 53:195-7, 465-7, 691-3 Ap, Ag, D '77

STUCKER, Gilbert F.
World's thirst. il Nat Parks & Con Mag 51:14-19 O '77

STUCKER, Jan
Story of Mary C. Ms 5:66-7+ Ap '77

STUCKEY, Charles F.
Another side of Jackson Pollock. bibl il por Art in Am 65:80-91 N '77
Duchamp's acephalic symbolism. bibl Art in Am 65:94-9 Ja '77
Reading Rauschenberg. il pors Arts in Am 65:74-84 Mr '77

STUCKEY, Elma
Elma Stuckey: a poet laureate of black history. D. R. Roediger. bibl f por Negro Hist Bull 40:690-1 Mr '77 *

STUCKEY, William K.
Campaign's science advisor sees: healthier outlook for creativity. il Sci Digest 81:12-19 F '77

STUCKHARDT, Michael H.
Snow, snow, snow. il Sch Arts 76:18-19 Je '77

STUD extractors. See Tools

STUD farms. See Horse breeding

STUDEBAKER-Worthington, Inc
Studebaker: ready to move even higher? J. Madrick and D. G. Santry. il Bus W p92 Ap 25 '77

STUDENT achievements
Achievement values reinforcement in public schools. F. P. Bazeli. bibl Clearing H 51:78-80 O '77
Are 40 percent of our children really unsatisfactory? W. D. Hedges. bibl il Clearing H 50:417-22 My '77; Same abr. Educ Digest 43:31-3 O '77
Good works. K. Macrorie. Educ Digest 43:30-1 D '77
The more we spend, the less children learn; excerpt from Our children's crippled future: how American education has failed. F. E. Armbruster. il N Y Times Mag p9-11+ Ag 28 '77; Same abr. with title Why American education is failing. Read Digest 112:106-9 Ja '78
PUSH for excellence; J. Jackson's program. A. Poinsett. il pors Ebony 32:104-6+ F '77
Preaching pride; J. L. Jackson. M. Sheils and S. Monroe. por Newsweek 89:64 Je 27 '77
Ten ways to help your child succeed. S. L. Woodard. il por Ebony 32:52-4+ O '77
What is college level? Why can't college students read and write? J. E. Roueche. Clearing H 50:332 Ap '77
See also
Accountability (education)

STUDENT activities
Campus recreation. L. A. Heywood and R. B. Warnick. Educ Digest 42:33-5 Ja '77
For the kid who has everything; Houseparties weekend at Princeton. L. A. Walker. il Esquire 88:68-73 S '77
Taking a last, gaudy fling; high school senior proms. il Time 109:22 Je 13 '77

Anecdotes, facetiae, satire, etc.

Last mambo; high school dances. A. Ward. Atlantic 240:98-100 D '77

STUDENT aid
Carry that grant; Basic Educational Opportunity Grant. L. Luciano. Seventeen 36:61 S '77
Free choice for college students; constitutionality of public financial assistance to students attending church-related colleges. America 137:257 O 22 '77
Fund one, fund all. G. Wagner. Nat R 29:325 Mr 18 '77
Graduate student support; results of questionnaire. R. B. Hallock. il Phys Today 30:9 My '77
Public funds and college students; constitutionality of Tennessee state aid. America 136:514 Je 11 '77
Who gets the money? community college students. J. E. Nelson. Educ Digest 42:54-6 Ja '77
See also
Scholarships and fellowships
Student loans

STUDENT art. See Childrens art

STUDENT attitudes. See Students—Attitudes

STUDENT classification. See Ability grouping in education

STUDENT clothing. See Clothing and dress—Students

STUDENT councils. See Self government in education

STUDENT counselors
School counselor: role conflict. W. B. Stack. bibl Clearing H 50:341-4 Ap '77

STUDENT demonstrations

Italy

Big brawl in Bologna: against Italian Communist Party. il Time 110:47-8 O 3 '77

Poland

Death in Cracow; dissenter S. Pyjas. F. Willey and P. Martin. Newsweek 89:50 My 30 '77

United States

Case of civil disobedience; protest against gymnasium construction at Kent State University. E. G. McGehee. Chr Cent 94:1217-23 D 28 '77; Same abr. with title On civil disobedience. Progressive 41:24-5 D '77
Student strike at Columbia; interview, ed by L. R. Obst. J. S. Kunen. il N Y Times Mag p43+ N 13 '77

STUDENT employment
Jobs to help you pay for college. il Changing T 31:17-20 My '77
Why they hired the ones they did; views of interviewers. bibl Sr Schol 110:26 S 22 '77
Work it out; part time work. R. L. Russo. Seventeen 36:60 S '77
See also
Part time employment
United States—Youth Conservation Corps

STUDENT ethics
See also
Cheating in school work

STUDENT government. See Self government in education

STUDENT guidance. See Personnel service in education

STUDENT life
See also
College students
Student activities

STUDENT life insurance policies. See Insurance, Life—Policies

STUDENT Loan Marketing Association
New kind of collateral. il Forbes 120:71 D 1 '77

STUDENT loans
Banks cash in on collecting student loans. il Bus W p97 O 10 '77
I am not a crook. J. Nocera. por Newsweek 90:14-15 D 19 '77
Study now, pay never. J. Seligmann and others. il Newsweek 89:95 Mr 7 '77
Time of reckoning for student deadbeats. il U.S. News 83:21 Jl 18 '77
See also
Student Loan Marketing Association

STUDENT militants
Memoirs of a Trotskyist. I. Kristol. il por N Y Times Mag p42-3+ Ja 23 '77
Memory thereof. T. Powers. Commonweal 104:465-6 Jl 22 '77
See also
Students for a Democratic Society (organization)

STUDENT opinion
Do you dig the Panama Canal treaty? opinions of Panamanian and Zonian students. A. Palacios. il Sr Schol 110:12-13+ O 20 '77
Is there sex after 40? college students' views of parents' sex lives. O. Pocs and others. il Psychol Today 11:54-6+ Je '77
Meet the masters! comments about artists. K. Alexander. il Sch Arts 76:16-17 F '77
NISO poll (cont) Sr Schol 109:11 Ja 27; 16 Mr 24; 29 Ap 21; 2 My 5; 33 My 19; 110:15-16 S 22; 23 N 17; 9 D 15 '77
TV actress tops list of students' heroes; results of NISO poll no. 2; November 18, 1976 issue. il Sr Schol 109:15 F 10 '77
What teens think of violence and sex on TV and in movies; symposium, ed by E. Miller. Seventeen 36:158-9+ Je '77
See also
Students—Attitudes

STUDENT participation in school administration. See School management and organization—Student participation

STUDENT performance. See Student achievements

STUDENT radicals. See Student militants

STUDENT rating of teachers. See Teachers—Rating by students

STUDENT records. See School reports and records

STUDENT recruiting. See Colleges and universities—Student recruiting

STUDENT reports. See Student themes and reports

STUDENT residences. See Dormitories

STUDENT rights. See Students—Civil rights

STUDENT selection. See Colleges and universities—Admission

STUDENT self evaluation. See Students—Self evaluation

STUDENT suspension and expulsion
Discipline alternative; in-school suspension. K. S. Moseley. Educ Digest 42:26-8 Ja '77
Due process in discipline. C. E. Alberti. bibl Clearing H 51:12-14 S '77
End to expulsions? M. Sheils. il Newsweek 89:72 Mr 28 '77
Insuring procedural due process in expulsion cases. C. Hestor. Clearing H 50:256-7 F '77

STUDENT teachers
Student teacher as self. J. S. Johnson. Educ Digest 42:28-31 My '77

STUDENT teaching
Assessing your student teaching program. F. F. Funk and others. il Clearing H 51:108-12 N '77
Student teaching: opportunity or ordeal. D. E. Meyer. Clearing H 50:258-9 F '77

STUDENT themes and reports
Creative ways of book reporting. C. Heilmann. SLJ 23:49 F '77
Research paper redux. S. Howell. Engl J 66:52-5 D '77

Anecdotes, facetiae, satire, etc.

Literary composite specifications as an intermediate result of the American characteristics specturum. M. Lieneck and others. Engl J 66:59-63 D '77
My college essay; symposium. il pors N Y Times Mag p28-30 Ja 16 '77

STUDENT travel
Bermuda throws a party! vacations for college students. D. Byron. il Seventeen 36:162 F '77
How to run away from college. T. Janowitz. bibl Mademoiselle 83:130+ Ag '77
See also
School excursions

STUDENT tutors. See Tutors and tutoring

STUDENT volunteers. See Volunteer service

STUDENTS
August '77; back-to-school calendar. il Seventeen 36:222-3 Ag '77
See also
Black students
Clothing and dress—Students
College students
Foreign students in the United States
High school students
Honor students
Medical students
School management and organization—Student participation
Teen-age pregnancy
also headings beginning Student

Attitudes

New realists; college students. A. Astin. il por Psychol Today 11:50-1+ S '77; Same with title New mood on campus. Current 197:7-12 N '77
Nothing happened; college in the early seventies. F. Iseman. Esquire 88:74-5+ S '77
Today's students: more conservative, but not much; college students. J. Gaylin. Psychol Today 11:94+ Je '77
What the next generation is coming to; reaction of college students to old Excalibur automobile. L. Mandel. il Car & Dr 22:12+ Mr '77
Your reputation: why you should worry about it. L. Schwarzbaum. Mademoiselle 83:206+ Ag '77
See also
High school students—Attitudes

Testing

See Psychological tests

Civil rights

Contractual relationships between students and universities; University of Texas conference. Intellect 105:297-8 Mr '77
Defensive education; University of Texas conference. Intellect 105:297 Mr '77

Employment

See Student employment

Grading and promotion

See Grading and marking (students)

Rating

One way it can be; evaluation system at the Cambridge Alternative Public School, Mass. B. S. Engel. il Todays Educ 66:50-2 Mr '77
Printing and evaluation. J. W. Burgner. il Sch Arts 76:36-8+ Je '77
7 good alternatives to group testing. B. McKenna and F. Quinto. Parents Mag 52:64-5 S '77

Self evaluation

Personal meaning and personal learning as educational concepts. R. Griffin. Clearing H 50:227-30 Ja '77

Social and economic status

Influence of peer groups on secondary school students. R. C. Maxon and B. Malone. bibl Clearing H 50:191-3 Ja '77

Suicide

See Suicide

Volunteer service

See Volunteer service

STUDENTS, Mentally superior. See College students, Mentally superior

STUDENTS, Rating of. See Students—Rating

STUDENTS, Women. See College students, Women

STUDENTS and teachers. See Teachers and students

STUDENTS for a Democratic Society (organization)
Memory thereof. T. Powers. Commonweal 104:465-6 Jl 22 '77
Reunion and intimation: SDS around the campfire. T. Gitlin. Nation 225:400-4 O 22 '77

STUDIO musicians. See Musicians

STUDIOS
See also
Artists studios
Dance studios

STUDIOS, Pottery. See Potteries

STUDIOS, Recording. See Sound—Recording and reproducing

STUDY
See also
Concentrated study

STUDY tours. See Travel study courses

STUDY-work plan. See Education, Cooperative

STUFFED toys. See Toys

STUFFING. See Cookery—Meat; Cookery—Poultry

STUKALIN, Boris I.
Books in 151 languages. il UNESCO Courier 30:33-4 N '77

STUKANE, Eileen
Fathers can make good mothers, too. Harp Baz 110:179+ O '77

STULL, Richard
First year; Fame; Content; poems. Poetry 130:25-7 Ap '77

STULZ, Dale
View point; interview, ed by J. Deschin. il por Pop Phot 81:117+ Ag '77

STUMP, David X.
Charismatic renewal: up to date in Kansas City. America 137:164-6 S 24 '77

STUMPF, Walter E. and others
Heart: a target organ for estradiol. bibl il Science 196:319-21 Ap 15 '77

STUNT driving. See Automobile driving—Stunt driving

STUNT flying. See Aviation—Stunt flying

STUNT women
Fastest woman on earth; K. O'Neil. P. Bowie. il pors Sat Eve Post 249:42-3+ Mr '77

STUNTS
Around City Hall; G. Willig's World Trade Center climb. A. Logan. New Yorker 53:84 Je 27 '77
Case closed; New York City's suit against G. Willig for climbing World Trade Center. New Yorker 53:28-30 Je 13 '77
Only way to go is up; G. Willig's ascent of World Trade Center. S. Moses. il Sports Illus 46:24-6+Je 6 '77
Striving for upward mobility; G. Willig's World Trade Tower climb. il pors Time 109:27 Je 6 '77
They're climbing the walls; buildering. D. K. Shah and J. A. Foote. il Newsweek 90:86+ N 28 '77
Trade-Center stunts. E. Keerdoja. il pors Newsweek 90:18+ N 7 '77
Where is this horse going? diving horse stunts. S. Subtle. il Ms 5:78-9 Je '77

STUPPLE, James
Literature against the future. Am Scholar 46:215-20 Spr '77

STURGEON fishing
To kill a monster; San Francisco Bay. L. Green. il Field & S 81:64+ Mr '77

STURM, Paul W.
Nuclear power—where do we go from here? Forbes 119:91-2 My 15 '77

STURMTHAL, Adolf F.
Unions and industrial democracy. bibl f Ann Am Acad 431:12-21 My '77

STUTTAFORD, Genevieve
(ed) See Ginsberg, A. PW interviews
(ed) See Graham, B. PW interviews
(ed) See Woodiwiss, K. PW interviews

STUTTERING
Let's hear it for stutterers' lib! work of the National Stuttering Project. Time 110:98+ O 31 '77
St-st-st-st-st-st-stuttering; therapy methods of Dr R. Webster. M. Pines. il N Y Times Mag p26+ F 13 '77
Stammering and stuttering. A. Kazin. il Esquire 88:8+ O '77

STUTTGART, Germany

Music

See also
Opera—Germany, West

STUTTGART Ballet
After Cranko: the Stuttgart Ballet, Metropolitan Opera House, June 14-July 2, 1977. T. Tobias. il Dance Mag 51:67-70 N '77
Keeper of the flame; M. Haydee. H. Saal. il pors Newsweek 89:81 Je 27 '77
Kenneth MacMillan's Requiem. H. Koegler. il Dance Mag 51:56-8 Ap '77
Sleeping Beauty, old and new; performances June 14-July 2. J. Maskey. il Hi Fi 27:MA12-13 N '77

STUTTGART Planetarium. See Planetariums

STYLE, Musical
See also
Composition (music)

STYLE, Personal. See Individuality

STYLE in dress. See Fashion

STYLES, Ken, and Cavanagh, Gray
Stress in teaching and how to handle it. bibl f Engl J 66:76-9 Ja '77

STYLING, Automobile. See Automobiles—Design

STYLING dryers. See Hair dryers

STYLUSES, Phonograph. See Phonograph needles

STYRIAN Autumn (music festival) See Music festivals—Austria

SUÁREZ, Hugo Banzer. See Banzer Suárez, H.

SUÁREZ GONZÁLEZ, Adolfo
King's torero. R. Carroll and M. Acoca. il por Newsweek 89:39 Je 27 '77 *
Reports & comment: Spain. S. Meisler. por Atlantic 239:14+ My '77 *
Spain: inching toward democracy. por Bus W p37 Mr 7 '77 *
Spain: up the middle. R. Carroll and others. il por Newsweek 89:38-40 Je 27 '77 *
Spain's free election: now a move to join Europe? D. B. Richardson. il por U.S. News 82:30 Je 27 '77 *
Spain's new democracy. S. Meisler. il For Affairs 56:190-208 O '77 *
Voters say *si* to democracy. il pors Time 109:18-23 Je 27 '77 *

SUAVE Shoe Corporation. See Shoe industry

SUBAK-SHARPE, Genell J.
Expensive way to keep your teeth. il N Y Times Mag p56-9 Ap 10 '77

SUB-COMMISSION on Prevention of Discrimination and Protection of Minorities. See United Nations—Sub-Commission on Prevention of Discrimination and Protection of Minorities

SUB-COMPACT cars. See Automobiles

SUBCONSCIOUSNESS
See also
Hallucinations and illusions
Hypnosis

SUBJECT headings
Getting to it; a guest editorial; Library of Congress' black subject headings. S. Berman. Am Lib 8:77 F '77

SUBLIMATION (psychology)
Conrad's Lord Jim and the enigma of sublimation. J. Berman. bibl f Am Imago 33:380-402 Wint '76

SUBMARINE archeology. See Archeology, Submarine

SUBMARINE bases. See Navy yards and naval stations

SUBMARINE boats
Exploring the briny deep in your own submarine. J. Kornfeld. il por Sci Digest 81:53-7 Je '77
See also
Collisions at sea
Oceanographic submersibles

Safety devices and measures
See also
Submarine rescue work

SUBMARINE boats, Atomic powered
Inside subs; aboard the Thomas Jefferson. T. Buckley. il Esquire 87:81-4 Ap '77
N-boat standoff. R. L. Barkley. map Nat R 29:660-2 Je 10 '77
Soviet nuclear missile sub shown; photographs. Aviation W 107:15 S 12 '77

SUBMARINE geology
Visual observations of the sea floor subduction line in the middle-America trench. B. C. Heezen and M. Rawson. bibl il Science 196:423-6 Ap 22 '77
See also
Faults (geology)
Seamounts

SUBMARINE oil well drilling. See Oil well drilling, Submarine

SUBMARINE oil wells. See Oil wells, Submarine

SUBMARINE photography. See Photography, Submarine

SUBMARINE rescue work
Rescue from the heart of a typhoon; crew of drowned bomber saved by nuclear subs. C. Barton. il map Pop Mech 148:73-6+ D '77

SUBMARINE research vehicles. See Oceanographic submersibles

SUBMARINE salvage. See Salvage (ships)

SUBMARINE valleys
DSDP: hints at a larger Japan of old; Japan Trench. map Sci N 112:421 D 24 '77
Drilling into the Japan Trench. Sci N 112:279 O 29 '77

SUBMARINE warfare
See also
Anti-submarine warfare
Torpedoes

SUBMERGED forests. See Forests, Submerged

SUBMERGED lands
See also
Continental shelf
Petroleum in submerged lands

SUBMERSIBLES, Oceanographic. See Oceanographic submersibles

SUBRAHMANYAM, K.
Nuclear issue and international security. il Bull Atom Sci 33:17-21 F '77

SUB-SAHARAN AFRICA. See Africa, Sub-Saharan

SUBSIDIES
See also
Agricultural administration—United States
also subhead Federal aid under various subjects, e.g. School libraries—Federal aid

SUBSIDY publishing. See Publishers and publishing—Finance

SUBSOILERS (planters) See Planters (farm machines)—Equipment

SUBSTANTIA nigra. See Brain

SUBSTITUTE products
See also
Food substitutes

SUBTLE, Susan
Where is this horse going? il Ms 5:78-9 Je '77
—and Reichl, Ruth
Wax museums: the Mount Rushmore of pop culture. il Ms 6:72-3+ Ja '78

SUBURBAN General Hospital, Norristown. See Hospitals—Pennsylvania

SUBURBAN life
Survival in the suburbs. See issues of McCall's

SUBURBS
Gaining momentum: a drive to stop suburban sprawl. il U.S. News 82:82-4 Mr 21 '77

SUBVERSIVE activities
See also
Terrorism

SUBWAYS

Accidents
There's a girl on the tracks! life saved by E. Sanderson. W. R. Young. il Read Digest 110:91-5 F '77

SUCCESS
Children vs. your success drive. J. Curtis. Harp Baz 110:176+ O '77
Conspiracy of merit. M. Kinsley. New Repub 177:22-4 O 15 '77
Did fear of success fail? L. Shapiro. Ms 6:19 Jl '77
Faith to face failure, or what's so great about success? V. C. Grounds. por Chr Today 22:12-13 D 9 '77
Learning to give up; views of M. E. P. Seligman. A. Rosenfeld. il Sat R 4:36-7 S 3 '77
Make your first job really count. Changing T 31:31-3 Jl '77
Return of success. N. Podhoretz. por Newsweek 90:11 Ag 29 '77
Self-determination of success. L. A. Siebert. Nations Bus 65:42+ Mr '77
Turning failure into success. F. Maynard. Read Digest 111:123-6 D '77
When do you hit your prime? J. Newman. Read Digest 111:103-5 Ag '77
See also
Charm
Efficiency
Self realization
Self reliance

SUCCESS in literature
Picture of success; characters in American fiction. N. Mills. Yale R 66:347-63 Mr '77

SUCCESSION, Plant. See Plant succession

SUCCESSION planting. See Rotation of crops

SUCCULENT plants
Landscaping with the not-too-thirsty succulents. il Sunset 159:238-9 N '77
See also
Cactus
Echeveria
Lithops

SUCHOW, China. See Wuhsien, China

SUCKLING
First suckling response of the newborn albino rat: the roles of olfaction and amniotic fluid. M. H. Teicher and E. M. Blass. bibl il Science 198:635-6 N 11 '77
Suckling as incentive to instrumental learning in preweanling rats. J. T. Kenny and E. M. Blass. bibl il Science 196:898-9 My 20 '77

SUDAN

Foreign relations

United States

See United States—Foreign relations—Sudan

SUDARSKY, Igor
Igor's. New Yorker 53:22-3 Ja 9 '78

SUDDEN death in infants. See Infant mortality

SUDDEN infant death syndrome. See Infant mortality

SUDEK, Josef
Obituary
Mod Phot por 41:62 F '77
Shows we've seen. H. V. Fondiller. il Pop Phot 81:78+ S '77 *

SUETONIUS, pseud
Word about Suetonius. New Repub 176:12 Mr 12 '77 *

SUEZ Canal
Panama and Suez. V. S. Kearney. America 137:477-8 D 31 '77
Suez transformed. R. Burton. il Oceans 10:28-33 Ja '77

SUEZ-Mediterranean pipeline. See Petroleum pipelines—Egypt

SUFFERING
Faith in focus:
Dimensions of the wheel. S. M. Schneiders. America 136:203-4 Mr 5 '77
Suffering, responsibility and ethics: a Lenten reflection. J. A. Coleman. America 136:300-1 Ap 2 '77
Sufferings of Job. R. A. F. MacKenzie. America 136:242 Mr 19 '77
To fill up the sufferings of Christ. J. A. Tetlow. America 136:169 F 26 '77
Finding sense when it makes no sense; excerpt from On being a Christian, tr by E. Quinn. H. Küng. il Sat Eve Post 249:50-1+ Ap '77
Losing sight: a chronicle of affliction; excerpt from Eyes, etc. E. Clark. Commentary 63:36-47 My '77
Mistaken identity. G. McCauley. America 136: inside back cover Je 11 '77

SUFFERN, N.Y.

Education

See Education—New York (state)

SUFFIXES. See English language—Prefixes and suffixes

SUFFRAGE
See also
Voters, Registration of

United States

See also
Woman suffrage—United States

SUGA, Nobuo
Amplitude spectrum representation in the Doppler-shifted-CF processing area of the auditory cortex of the mustache bat. bibl il Science 196:64-7 Ap 1 '77

SUGAR
See also
Cookery—Sugar
Glucose

Physiological effects

How sugar gets to your skin—and harms it; refined carbohydrates and skin problems; ideas of W. M. Ringsdorf and E. Cheraskin. N. Simon. Vogue 167:108-9 My '77
Sugar: villain in disguise? J. E. Brody. Read Digest 111:163-5 O '77

Prices

Sticky slump. il Time 109:71 My 23 '77
Sugar's anguished plea for more Federal aid. il Bus W p60-1 Ag 8 '77
Tempest in the sugar pot. C. G. Burck. il Fortune 95:106-14+ F '77

SUGAR futures. See Commodity exchanges

SUGAR in the body
See also
Blood sugar

SUGAR industry

Export-import trade

Decisions on sugar imports and income supports announced; May 4, 1977. J. Carter. Dept State Bull 76:657-8 Je 20 '77
Washington's row over sugar imports. il Bus W p34-5 Mr 21 '77

United States

Sugar's anguished plea for more Federal aid. il Bus W p60-1 Ag 8 '77
Tempest in the sugar pot. C. G. Burck. il Fortune 95:106-14+ F '77

SUGAR pills. See Placebos

SUGAR substitutes
Another saccharin test. M. Clark and others. Newsweek 90:60 Jl 4 '77
Behind the saccharin uproar. W. Hines and J. Randal. Progressive 41:13-17 Je '77
Bitter reaction to an FDA ban; saccharin. il Time 109:60-1 Mr 21 '77
Canada's diet sodas lose their saccharin. Bus W p46 O 17 '77
Cancer and your sweet tooth; saccharin. New Repub 176:7-8 Mr 26 '77
Dispelling saccharin myths: the ban probably will stick. R. Field. Sci Digest 82:86-7 Ag '77
FDA postpones proposed ban on saccharin for two months. Ret Liv 17:41 Ag '77
FDA proposal to ban saccharin stirs tempest over its testing rules. Ret Liv 17:14-15 Ap '77
Fight over proposed saccharin ban will not be settled for months. B. J. Culliton. Science 196:276-8 Ap 15 '77
Fight starts to beat the ban on saccharin. U.S. News 82:49 Mr 28 '77
Great saccharin snafu. Consumer Rep 42:410-14 Jl '77
Has emotion tipped the scales on consumer safety? address, October 17, 1977. J. W. Hanley. Vital Speeches 44:92-5 N 15 '77
How good are the tests? saccharin studies. M. Clark and M. Gosnell. il Newsweek 89:67 Mr 21 '77
How much is enough? saccharin and the law; address, March 24, 1977. S. Gardner. Vital Speeches 43:457-9 My 15 '77
Hunting a safe sweetener. P. Gwynne and others. il Newsweek 89:95 Ap 4 '77
Lesson to be learned from saccharin mess? A. T. Brett. il U.S. News 82:80 Je 6 '77
Molecular aspects of sweetness. G. A. Crosby. il Chemistry 50:27 Jl '77
No mad scientists; proposed ban on saccharin. S. Kelman. New Repub 176:8+ Mr 26 '77
Nonnutritive sweeteners: taste-structure relationships for some new simple dihydrochalcones. G. E. DuBois and others. bibl il Science 195: 397-9 Ja 28 '77
Of rats and men; saccharin. A. Wolff. N Y Times Mag p88+ My 15 '77
Opting for cancer; Delaney amendment. il Org Gard & Farm 24:115+ Je '77
Reappraising saccharin—and the FDA. il Time 109:75-6 Ap 25 '77
Saccharin: a chemical in search of an identity. B. J. Culliton. Science 196:1179-80+ Je 10 '77; Reply. D. L. Arnold and others. bibl il 197: 320 Jl 22 '77
Saccharin and cancer: confounding data. Sci N 112:245-6 O 15 '77
Saccharin and other sweeteners: mutagenic properties. R. P. Batzinger and others. bibl il Science 198:944-6 D 2 '77
Saccharin ban. L. Langway. il Newsweek 89: 65+ Mr 21 '77
Saccharin ban: a sour reception. Sci N 111:182 Mr 19 '77
Saccharin ban: weighing the risks. J. Mayer. il Fam Health 9:38-9+ Jl '77
Saccharin can be sold—for now. il Bus W p38 Ap 25 '77
Saccharin's sour future. il Bus W p95+ Mr 28 '77
Should saccharin be banned? interviews. G. Nelson; J. G. Martin. pors U.S. News 82:59-60 Ap 4 '77
Sour taste of a sweetener ban. Time 109:76+ Mr 28 '77
Split decision; detailed proposals for banning saccharin. Newsweek 89:83 Ap 25 '77
Sweetener problem crystallizes. Sci N 112:388 D 10 '77
Why ban saccharin? M. Stone. il U.S. News 82:84 Ap 4 '77

Manufacture

Short 'n sweet; Cumberland Packing Co. makers of Sweet 'n Low. por Forbes 120:80 Jl 15 '77

SUGARMAN, Daniel A.
Gift of you. Good H 185:98+ D '77

SUGARS
See also
Polysaccharides

SUGG, Redding S. Jr
Southern gentleman and Pope's Homer. il por Smithsonian 7:125-30+ F '77

SUGGESTION
See also
Hypnosis

SUGGESTION systems
King of the suggestion box. R. Lund. il pors Pop Mech 147:58+ Mr '77

SUGIURA, Kanematsu
Laetrile at Sloan-Kettering: a question of ambiguity. N. Wade. Science 198:1231-4 D 23 '77 *

SUHOR, Charles
(ed) Professional publications (cont) Engl J 66:84-8 Mr; 81-2 My '77

SUICIDE
Chico's last act; F. Prinze. D. M. Alpern and others. il por Newsweek 89:25-6 F 7 '77
End of life. Chr Today 21:57 My 6 '77
Freddie Prinze: too much, too soon. il pors Time 109:37 F 7 '77
Motor vehicle fatalities increase just after publicized suicide stories. D. P. Phillips. bibl il Science 196:1464-5 Je 24 '77

SUICIDE—*Continued*
Some auto accidents are suicides in disguise; study by David Phillips. D. Cohen. Psychol Today 11:40+ O '77
Student suicide epidemic. J. D. McNeely and others. il Todays Educ 66:70-3 S '77
Suicide by auto; views of David Phillips. Time 110:62 Jl 11 '77
Suicide: let's separate fact from fiction. M. P. Scott and E. Kiester, Jr. Bet Hom & Gard 55:66+ Ap '77
Teen suicide. M. S. Miller. Ladies Home J 94:68+ F '77
Ties between news, suicides studied. il Sci Digest 81:87 Ap '77
Understanding lethal violence. M. L. Simpson. Intellect 105:379-80 My '77

Prevention

Death they whisper about. W. Coleman. Chr Today 21:38-9 S 23 '77
Preventing teenage suicide; excerpt from Too young to die. F. Klagsbrun. il Fam Health 9:21-3 Ap '77

SUIDS, Fossil. See Swine, Fossil
SUINN, Richard M.
Anxiety, stress, tension: how to turn them into creative energy; interview, ed by A. Gross. Mademoiselle 83:164+ My '77
SUITCASES. See Luggage
SUITES (music)
See also
Phonograph records—Suites (music)
SUITS (law) See Actions and defenses
SUITS, Womens. See Clothing and dress
SUK, Josef
Their muses faced East and West. J. Ringo. Am Rec G 41:8-10+ N '77 *
SULAK, Kenneth J.
Alvin: window in the deep; with biographical sketch. il Sea Front 23:113-19, 126-7 Mr '77
SULFA drugs. See Sulfonamides
SULFAMETHOXAZOLE
Antibacterial synergism: a proposal for chemotherapeutic potentiation between trimethoprim and sulfamethoxazole. M. Poe; discussion. bibl Science 197:1300-1 S 23 '77
SULFATE aerosols. See Aerosols
SULFATES
Household worries; sodium nitrite as meat preservative and diaminoanisole sulfate as hair dye component. P. Gwynne and J. B. Copeland. il Newsweek 90:109 O 31 '77
SULFIDES
Cubanite: a new sulfide phase in CI meteorites. J. D. MacDougall and J. F. Kerridge. bibl il Science 197:561-2 Ag 5 '77
See also
Gallium sulfide
Hydrogen sulfide
Methyl sulfide
SULFONAMIDES
Say good-bye to sulfa drugs? L. Schotsch. Farm J 101:Hog 11+ S '77
SULFUR
Elemental sulfur: accumulation in different species of fungi. R. Pezet and V. Pont. bibl il Science 196:428-9 Ap 22 '77
See also
Coal—Sulfur content
SULFUR bacteria
See also
Beggiatoa
SULFUR dioxide pollution of the air. See Air pollution
SULFUR industry

United States

Growing squeeze on sulfur. il Bus W p64-5 Ag 22 '77
SULFUR mines and mining

United States

See also
Sulfur industry—United States
SULFUR oxide pollution of the air. See Air pollution
SULFURIC acid
Sulfuric acid from cars: a problem that never materialized. T. H. Maugh, 2d. Science 198:280-4 O 21 '77
SULLAVAN, Margaret
Children of paradise. P. S. Prescott. il pors Newsweek 89:76-7 Mr 14 '77 *
Haywire; excerpt. B. Hayward. il por Ladies Home J 94:110-11 Jl '77 *
Hollywood hay days—every parent a star; excerpt from Haywire. B. Hayward. il pors Vogue 167:224-7+ Mr '77 *
Spoiled children. A. Sarris. il por Harpers 254:77-80 Je '77 *
SULLIVAN, Sir Arthur Seymour
Gilbert and Sullivan discography. R. Dyer. il Hi Fi 27:52-8 My '77 *
Secret diaries of Sir Arthur Sullivan. A. Jacobs. il pors Hi Fi 27:46-50 My '77 *

SULLIVAN, Dan
Liveliest theater in town. il por Horizon 20:87+ N '77
SULLIVAN, Daniel J.
Gene-splicing: the eighth day of creation. America 137:441-3 D 17 '77
SULLIVAN, Fred R.
Sullivan's sow. por Forbes 119:64-5 F 1 '77 *
SULLIVAN, James
Men on trees; poem. Commonweal 104:433 Jl 8 '77
SULLIVAN, Louis Henry
Report from Chicago: restoration of the Trading Room. F. Schulze. il Art in Am 65:58-9 N '77 *
SULLIVAN, Rosemary D.
Santons of Provence. il Hobbies 82:116-17+ D '77
SULLIVAN, Thomas F.
First confession: law and catechesis. il America 137:128-31 S 10 '77
SULLIVAN, William A. Jr
Troubled steel towns campaign for help. Bus W p35 O 24 '77 *
SULLIVAN, William H.
Carter's worst appointment. Nation 224:517 Ap 30 '77 *
SULPHATES. See Sulfates
SULZBERGER, Arthur Ochs
Business and the press; address, March 14, 1977. Vital Speeches 43:426-8 My 1 '77
Kingdom and the cabbage. il pors Time 110:72-5+ Ag 15 '77 *
SUM, Andrew M.
Female labor force participation: why projections have been too low. bibl il M Labor R 100:18-24 Jl '77
SUMED pipeline. See Petroleum pipelines—Egypt
SUMERIAN inscriptions. See Cuneiform inscriptions
SUMI painting. See Sumie
SUMIE
Sumi painting. E. Aaron. bibl il Am Artist 41:40-5+ S '77
SUMMA Corporation
Battle for the shrinking millions. il por Time 110:64+ Jl 4 '77
New peaks of prosperity for Howard Hughes empire. il U.S. News 82:81-2 F 28 '77
SUMMER, Donna
Disco fever. A. Goldman il Esquire 88:60+ D '77 *
Donna Summer. C. L. Sanders. il pors Ebony 32:33-6+ O '77 *
SUMMER
Green days of summer. H. B. Shatraw. il Conservationist 32:48 Jl '77
Here comes summer; special section. il Time 110:30-4+ Jl 4 '77
How to get the most mileage out of summer; an idea portfolio of food, tables, decorating, and energy savers. il House & Gard 149:50-75 Ag '77
25 things to do this summer. R. Hemming and H. Alpert. il Ret Liv 17:22-5 Je '77
Ultimate trip for summer nights. J. Mullaney il Sci Digest 81:41-4 Je '77
Why I feel sexier in the summer. M.-E. Banashek. Mademoiselle 83:162+ My '77
See also
August
Hot weather
Vacations

Anecdotes, facetiae, satire, etc.

Summertime. J. Viorst. il Redbook 149:114-15 Jl '77

Poetry

Eleven for summer. New Repub 177:25-8 S 3 '77
SUMMER camps. See Camps
SUMMER entertaining. See Entertaining
SUMMER flying. See Aviation—Summer flying
SUMMER Food Program for Children. See United States—Agriculture, Department of—Food and Nutrition Service
SUMMER houses. See Garden houses, shelters, etc.
SUMMER Institute of Linguistics. See Wycliffe Bible Translators, Inc
SUMMER meals. See Meals
SUMMER resorts
Summer in Colorado ski country; eight resorts. D. Schlossberg. il Travel 147:38-43 Ap '77
See also
Seaside resorts
SUMMER schools
See also
Idyllwild School of Music and the Arts
SUMMER soups. See Soups
SUMMERNATIONALS (drag race) See Drag racing
SUMMERS, Charles G. Jr
Splendor at the shore; photographs. Nat Wildlife 15:42-7 Je '77

SUMMERS, F. William
If elected I will. . . il por Lib J 102:880-7 Ap 15 '77
What you want the future to be. . .; adaptation of address, June 16, 1977. bibl por SLJ 24:80-2 O '77

SUMMERS, Martha
Learning disabilities. . .a puzzlement. Todays Educ 66:40-2 N '77

SUMMERS, William. See Summers, F. W.

SUMMIT Books (firm) See Publishers and publishing—United States

SUMMIT conferences. See International conferences

SUMMY, Jo Anne Moore
Journal contest winner finds a new life. M. S. Miller. por Ladies Home J 94:68 Mr '77 *

SUMNER, Charles
Bull in the China shop. D. W. Blight. il pors Am Hist Illus 12:10-19 Ap '77 *

SUMNER, David
Let's save our roadless areas! il Liv Wildn 40:25-33 Ja '77
What's next for Yosemite? il Nat Wildlife 15:34-7 O '77

SUMNERS, Carolyn
A new radio astronomy. il por Sky & Tel 53:344-5 My '77

SUN
Sun, moon, and planets this month. R. C. Victor. See issues of Sky and telescope
See also
Eclipses, Solar
Sunspots
also headings beginning Solar

Corona

See also
Solar wind

Influence on weather

See Sun and meteorology

Magnetic properties

Solar magnetism. H. Zirin. Natur Hist 86:100-4 D '77
Structure of the sun's magnetic field. Sky & Tel 53:357 My '77
Sun's magnetic field may reach outer limit of solar system; Pioneer 11 data. Space World N-8-164:28 Ag '77

Observations

Case of the setting sun. J. B. Irwin. il Sky & Tel 54:167-70 S '77

Prominences

Rapid changes in a solar prominence. D. Ammons. il Sky & Tel 54:531-2 D '77
See also
Solar flares

Rotation

Anomalous solar rotation in the early 17th century. J. A. Eddy and others. bibl il Science 198:824-9 N 25 '77
As the sun turns: a continuing story. il Sci N 112:374 D 3 '77

Spectrum

See Spectrum, Solar

SUN and meteorology
Sun and weather: things are popping. Sci N 112:423 D 24 '77
What's behind this winter. . .and what's ahead. map Sci N 111:100-1 F 12 '77

SUN baths
Playing it safe in the sun. L. Lynne. Bet Hom & Gard 55:34+ Jl '77
Summer sun—how to guard against dangers; interview. J. H. Herndon. il U.S. News 82:55 My 30 '77
Sun & you; symposium. Vogue 167:144-5+ Ap '77

SUN burn. See Sunburn

SUN Day (proposed)
Academics urged to join Sun Day observance. L. J. Carter. Science 198:472 N 4 '77

SUN dials. See Sundials

SUN glasses
Focus on sunglasses; quiz. il Fam Health 9:61+ My '77
Summer shades. il Esquire 88:97 Ag '77
Sunglasses—pretty and protective. S. Beck. il Parents Mag 52:28 My '77

SUN-heated pit houses. See Greenhouses

SUN light. See Sunlight

SUN-Mee Company. See Food industry

SUN Oil Company
Making it—Pew-family style. por Forbes 119:48+ Ja 15 '77

SUN screens. See Screens (sun)

SUN spots. See Sunspots

SUN tan. See Tan

SUN-times, Chicago. See Chicago sun-times

SUN Valley, Idaho
Earl has bought a pearl. W. O. Johnson. il por Sports Illus 47:93-4+ N 14 '77

SUNBATHING, Nude. See Nudity

SUNBURN
Summer sun—how to guard against dangers; interview. J. H. Herndon. il U.S. News 82:55 My 30 '77
What sunlight does to your skin. G. McBride. il Fam Health 9:36-9 Je '77
You & the sun & those tanning lotions. il Changing T 31:19-20 Je '77

Anecdotes, facetiae, satire, etc.

Sunburn index. R. Baker. N Y Times Mag p4 Ag 14 '77

SUNDAES. See Ice cream, ices, etc.

SUNDAY
Observing the Sabbath. Aristides. Am Scholar 46:159-63 Spr '77

SUNDAY dinners. See Dinners and dining

SUNDAY labor. See Hours of labor

SUNDAY legislation
See also
Hours of labor

SUNDAY schools
Decompartmentalizing the church; with views on the intergenerational principal. D. E. Kucharsky. Chr Today 21:19 Ap 15 '77

SUNDAY supplements. See Newspapers—Magazine sections

SUNDAY times, London
Torture tempest; question of newspaper reports charging mistreatment of Palestinian prisoners by the Israeli government. S. Kaplan. New Repub 177:16-17 Jl 23 '77

SUNDBERG, Johan
Acoustics of the singing voice; with biographical sketch. il Sci Am 236:22, 82-4+ bibl(p 150) Mr '77

SUNDERLIN, Sylvia
Address book. See issues of House beautiful

SUNDIALS
Chalice dial. O. R. Hagans. il Hobbies 82:127 D '77
Sundial at the San Diego zoo. il Sky & Tel 54:25 Jl '77

SUNDICK, Sherry
How to make Paris craft masks. il Design (US) 78:22 Summ '77

SUNFISH fishing
Bass methods for big bream; bluegill fishing. F. Sargeant. il Field & S 82:66-71 Jl '77
Flyrod bream: don't settle for runts; fishing for bluegills. L. Kreh. il por Outdoor Life 159:86-7+ Je '77
Is the bluegill America's favorite fish? G. H. Harrison. il Nat Wildlife 15:36-41 Je '77
Special kind of bream. K. Schultz. il Field & S 82:52+ S '77

SUNFISH World Championship. See Sailboat racing

SUNFLOWERS
Sunflowers make it big! M. C. Goldman. il Org Gard & Farm 24:146-8 D '77

SUNG, Betty Lee
Changing Chinese. bibl il Society 14:44-9 S '77

SUNGLASSES. See Sun glasses

SUNGRAMS. See Photograms

SUNKEN treasure. See Treasure trove

SUNLIGHT
Cloudy side effects of sunny weather; hazards for outdoor workers. H. Levitt. il Parks & Rec 12:41 Ap '77
What sunlight does to your skin. G. McBride. il Fam Health 9:36-9 Je '77
See also
Photosynthesis

Chemical action

See Photochemistry

SUNNYSIDE (historic house) See Historic houses, sites, etc—New York (state)

SUNOL Valley Regional Park. See California—Parks and reserves

SUNPIT greenhouses. See Greenhouses

SUNSCREEN preparations. See Cosmetics

SUNSET (periodical)
See also
Western Home Awards

SUNSET garden contest. See Gardening—Competitions

SUNSHADES. See Screens (sun)

SUNSHINE, Leo
Chewing for dollars. il por Time 110:107 N 28 '77 *

SUNSHINE. See Sunlight

SUNSHINE Act. See Information, Freedom of

SUNSHINE Mining Company-Great Western United Corporation merger. See Corporations—Acquisitions and mergers

SUNSPOTS
CB & sun spots. J. Walders. il Sci Digest 81:24-7 F '77
Case of the missing sunspots; the Maunder minimum. J. A. Eddy. il Sci Am 236:80-8 My '77
Droughts linked to sunspot cycle. il Chemistry 50:23-4 My '77
Length of the solar cycle. Sky & Tel 54:106 Ag '77
Will sunspots affect CB communications? S. Leinwoll. il Pop Electr 11:51-4 Mr '77

SUNSTROKE. See Heatstroke

SUNTAN. See Tan

SUNTAN preparations. See Cosmetics

SUOMI, Stephen J.
Who loves you? il por Sci N 112:139+ Ag 27 '77

SUPER Bowl. See Football, Professional

SUPER-duper market; drama. See Murray, J.

SUPER 8 cameras. See Motion picture cameras

SUPER 8 film. See Motion picture films

SUPER Valu Stores, Inc. See Grocery trade

SUPERCHARGERS
See also
Automobile engines—Superchargers

SUPERCONDUCTIVITY
Attractive mystery in superconductivity. Sci N 111:229 Ap 9 '77
Case of the vanishing superconductivity. G. B. Lubkin. Phys Today 30:17-28 Ap '77
John Bardeen: a study in the elusive nature of genius. por Sci Digest 81:55-7 Ap '77
Large-scale applications of superconductivity. B. B. Schwartz and S. Foner. bibl il Phys Today 30:34-5+ Jl '77

SUPERCONDUCTORS
Clustering hypothesis of some high-temperature superconductors. J. M. Vandenberg and B. T. Matthias. bibl il Science 198:194-6 O 14 '77
Ternary compounds: a promising way to make superconductors. A. L. Robinson. il Science 196:966-8 My 27 '77

SUPERDOME, New Orleans. See Stadiums

SUPERHEAVY chemical elements. See Transuranium elements

SUPERINTENDENTS, School. See School superintendents and principals

SUPERIOR, Lake
Stern-driving Lake Superior. O. Moore. il Motor B & S 141:68-9+ Ja '78

Water pollution
See Water pollution—Great Lakes

SUPERMARKET cashiers. See Cashiers

SUPERMARKET unit pricing. See Unit pricing

SUPERMARKETS
New nightlife; shopping; all-night supermarkets. E. Babitz. il Vogue 167:258-9 N '77
New store in town; Aldi-Benner. il Forbes 119: 64 Je 1 '77
See also
Albertson's Inc
Arden-Mayfair, Inc
Great Atlantic & Pacific Tea Company
Safeway Stores, Inc

Acquisitions and mergers
Pick-N-Pay picks up Finast's problems. Bus W p36 D 26 '77

Banking services
Fred Meyer's grocery S&Ls. il Bus W p76 Ja 24 '77
Point-of-sale system short-circuits in southern California; Glendale Federal Savings & Loan Assn. il Bus W p86-7 Ap 18 '77

Drug and cosmetic departments
Supermarkets versus the drugstores. il Forbes 120:78+ O 1 '77

Finance
Supermarkets fight back; competing with fast-food restaurants. N. Howard. il Duns R 110: 108-10 O '77
Unsuper markets. L. Langway and others. il Newsweek 91:65-6 Ja 16 '78

SUPERNATURAL
Danse macabre in Barbados. A. N. Forde. in Américas 29:29-31 My '77
See also
Ghosts
Occult sciences
Parapsychology

SUPERNATURAL motion pictures. See Motion pictures—Horror films

SUPERNOVAS. See Stars, New

SUPERPORTS. See Petroleum shipping terminals

SUPERSONIC air travel. See Air travel

SUPERSONIC airplanes. See Airplanes, Supersonic

SUPERSTITION
See also
Animal lore
Evil eye
Occult sciences
Witchcraft

SUPERTANKERS. See Tank ships

SUPERVISORS, School. See School supervision and supervisors

SUPPERS
See also
Buffet meals

SUPPLEMENTAL Security Income Program. See Social security—United States

SUPPLEMENTARY employment
Italy's secret economy: illegal cellar factories and moonlighting. il Time 110:46 Ag 22 '77
Multiple jobholding rate remained unchanged in 1976; moonlighters. K. Michelotti. il M Labor R 100:44-8 Je '77

SUPPLIES and Shortages, National Commission on. See United States—National Commission on Supplies and Shortages

SUPPORT (domestic relations)
See also
Alimony
Desertion and non-support

SUPRACHIASMATIC nucleus. See Brain

SUPREME Court law clerks. See United States—Supreme Court—Employees

SUPREME Court of the United States. See United States—Supreme Court

SUPREME Courts, State. See Courts

SURF. See Waves

SURF boards. See Surfboards

SURF fishing. See Salt water fishing

SURF riding
All aboard the tunnel express; photographs; with report by S. Moses. W. Bolster. Sports Illus 46:32-7 My 30 '77
One-on-one with the waves. M. Wellemeyer. il Fortune 96:75-6+ Ag '77
Ready for the ultimate sailing experience? Try windsurfing. G. P. Gilmore. il Pop Sci 210: 102-3 F '77
Surfing with the wind. il Mech Illus 73:118-19 Ap '77
Walkin' on water; windsurfing. M. Evans. Seventeen 36:186+ Ag '77
See also
Surfboards

SURFACE, Bill
All aboard the skateboard. il Read Digest 111: 135-8 D '77
How to profit from the new tax laws. N Y Times Mag p70-5 Mr 13 '77
Scout: sports' indefatigable spy. il Read Digest 111:53-4+ D '77

SURFACE acoustic wave devices. See Acoustic surface wave devices

SURFACE effect ships. See Air cushion vehicles

SURFACE effect vehicles. See Air cushion vehicles

SURFACE treatment of pavements. See Pavements—Surface treatment

SURFACES
Appearance of materials. T. B. Brill. bibl il por Chemistry 50:6-9 D '77
Calabi conjecture: a proof after 25 years. G. B. Kolata. Science 196:1308 Je 17 '77
Geometry of adsorbates on solid surfaces; angle-resolved photoemission spectroscopy. E. W. Plummer and T. Gustafsson. bibl il Science 198: 165-70 O 14 '77
Surface science: a way to tell where the atoms are. A. L. Robinson. Science 196:1306-8 Je 17 '77
Surface science: an X-ray probe for adsorbed molecules. A. L. Robinson. Science 197:34-6 Jl 1 '77

SURFBOARDS
Windsurfer you can build. H. Kelly. il Mech Illus 73:45-7+ Ag '77

SURFING. See Surf riding

SURFPERCH fishing. See Perch fishing

SURGEONS
See also
Mamiya, R.
White, R. J.

SURGERY
How to protect yourself against needless surgery; study funded by Social Security Administration. A. Rosenblum. Good H 185: 245-6 O '77
Operators. Sci Am 236:43 Ja '77
Statistics and ethics in surgery and anesthesia. J. P. Gilbert and others. bibl il Science 198: 684-9 N 18 '77
Touched by something divine; excerpt from Mortal lessons. R. Selzer. Read Digest 111:93-5 O '77

SURGERY—*Continued*
When the doctor says you need surgery. M. P. Scott. il Bet Hom & Gard 55:39-40+ N '77
See also
Amputation
Anesthesia
Cesarean section
Children—Surgery
Microsurgery
Orthopedia
Psychosurgery
Transplantation of organs, tissues, etc.
also subhead Surgery under names of organs and regions of the body, e.g. Heart—Surgery

Psychological aspects

See also
Children—Surgery—Psychological aspects

SURGERY, Cosmetic. See Surgery, Plastic

SURGERY, Oral. See Oral surgery

SURGERY, Plastic
Beauty and the breast: a 60% complication rate for an operation you don't need; breast implants. M. Nashner and M. White. il Ms 6:53-4+ S '77; Discussion. 6:4+ Ja '78
Cosmetic lib for men. J. Kelly. il N Y Times Mag p 119-20+ S 25 '77
New parts for old; reconstructive surgery. C. Duhe. Am Home 80:10+ Mr '77
Plastic-surgery boom. M. Clark and others. il Newsweek 89:73-4 Ja 24 '77
Plastic surgery: glamor yields to serious job of patching up. Sci Digest 82:36 Jl '77
Surgery to make you look better; cosmetic surgery. il Changing T 31:33-5 S '77

Personal narratives

On creating a new face through plastic surgery. M. G. Haddad. il Mademoiselle 83:53+ O '77

SURGICAL centers, Ambulatory. See Health facilities

SURGICAL instruments and apparatus industry
Salesmen in the operating room. il Forbes 120:33 D 1 '77

SURGICAL insurance. See Insurance, Health

SURGUINE, Ray
Ray and Mary Jane Surguine retire; interview, ed by P. Holt. il por Pub W 212:49 N 21 '77

SURGUINE, Ray, & Company. See Book wholesalers

SURINAM
See also
Blacks in Surinam

SURPLUS government property
Washington scene. B. Kravetz. Parks & Rec 12:12-13 Ag '77

SURPLUS products, Agricultural
All-too-normal granary. il Forbes 120:29-30 Jl 1 '77
Buffer food stocks. P. A. Samuelson. Newsweek 89:72 Je 6 '77
Bumper crop of controversy. il Bus W p48-9 Jl 25 '77
Golden glut. T. Nicholson and others. il Newsweek 90:64-5 Jl 4 '77
New wheat glut? D. Pauly and others. il Newsweek 89:84 Mr 14 '77
Suddenly the world has a glut of grain. il U.S. News 83:27 Ag 1 '77
World of extremes; address, April 27, 1977. M. Fribourg. Vital Speeches 43:527-9 Je 15 '77

SURREALISM
American Surrealist; D. Hare's Cronus series on display at the Guggenheim Museum. H. Rosenberg. New Yorker 53:155-8 O 24 '77
David Hare: American surrealist. K. Kuh. il Sat R 5:38-49 O 1 '77
Missy goes Surrealistic; work of M. Stang. G. Dostal. il por Sch Arts 77:22-3 N '77
Surrealism's automatic painting lesson. J. Wechsler. il Art N 76:44-7 Ap '77
Surrealistic anatomy studies. A. N. Sponzilli. il por Sch Arts 77:24-5 N '77

SURREALISM in motion pictures
Mind, medium and metaphor in Harry Smith's Heaven and earth magic. N. Carroll. bibl il Film Q 31:37-44 Wint '77

SURREY, Stanley S. See McLure, C. E. Jr, jt auth

SURVEYING
See also
Hydrographic surveying

SURVEYING, Aerial
See also
Mapping, Aerial

SURVEYING apparatus and instruments
See also
Electronics in surveying

SURVEYS
See also
College library surveys
Educational surveys
Library surveys

SURVIVAL; drama. See Kekana, F. D. and others

SURVIVAL (human ecology) See Human ecology

SURVIVAL, Wilderness. See Wilderness survival

SURVIVAL after airplane accidents, shipwrecks, etc.
Hypothermia, the chill that kills. A. H. Drummond. Jr. il Motor B & S 139:52-3+ F '77
I will survive; duck boat adrift in Chesapeake Bay; ed by B. East. F. W. Stamm. il Outdoor Life 160:80-1+ D '77
Ordeal at Vella Lavella; survivors of sunken U.S.S. Helena; excerpt from Lonely vigil. W. Lord. il map Am Heritage 28:30-43 Je '77
Seven in the sea; shipwreck off the coast of Fiji. M. Shadbolt. il Read Digest 110:95-100 Ap '77
Shipwreck! interview, ed by E. Keiffer. W. F. van Godtsenhoven. il Good H 184:51+ Ap '77
Will to survive. J. Cartwright. il Motor B & S 140:16+ N '77

SURVIVAL and emergency equipment
Blueprint for survival; boats. J. Cartwright. il Motor B & S 140:10 O '77
Checklist for survival; boats. M. Bailey. il Motor B & S 139:70-1+ Mr '77
Day pack and survival kit. J. W. Fears. il Outdoor Life 160:163-4 O '77
Survival—at bargain rates. il Pop Mech 147:169 Ap '77

SURVIVAL kits. See Survival and emergency equipment

SURVIVORS benefits. See Social security

SUSANNAH; opera. See Floyd, C.

SUSCE, Andrew
Curious case of an IRS agent. J. P. Hayes. Nation 225:17-18 Jl 2 '77 •

SUSHI. See Cookery, Japanese

SUSKO, Marilyn
Our spinach loves winter. il Org Gard & Farm 24:68-9 O '77

SUSMAN, Edward
I was a mother for six months. il por Good H 185:74+ Jl '77

SUSPENDED ceilings. See Ceilings

SUSPENSE stories. See Detective and mystery stories

SUSPENSION, Automobile. See Automobiles—Springs and suspension

SUSPENSION, Student. See Student suspension and expulsion

SUSPENSION bridges. See Bridges

SUSS, Elaine P.
Raccoon. Conservationist 31:23-5 N '76

SUSSMAN, David B.
Co-disposal of sewage sludge and solid wastes—it works. il por Am City & County 92:55-8 O '77

SUSSMAN & Sugar, Inc. See Advertising agencies

SUTER, David
Hammer and the sickle. il Harpers 255:70-1 N '77

SUTHERLAND, Grant R.
Fragile sites on human chromosomes: demonstration of their dependence on the type of tissue culture medium. bibl il Science 197: 265-6 Jl 15 '77

SUTHERLAND, Ivan E. and Mead, C. A.
Microelectronics and computer science; with biographical sketches. il Sci Am 237:20, 210-12+ bibl(p262) S '77

SUTHERLAND, John Andrew
Prehumous classics. E. Moers. Am Scholar 47: 118+ Wint '77 •

SUTHERLAND, Pamela J. See Larkin, R. P. jt auth

SUTHERLAND, Sam
Peter Asher—producer power & a touch of class. il por Hi Fi 27:107-10 Je '77

SUTHERLAND, Stewart R.
Dostoyevsky and the Grand Inquisitor: a study in atheism. Yale R 66:364-73 Mr '77

SUTHERLAND, Zena Bailey, and Hearne, Betsy
Search of the perfect picture book definition. il Wilson Lib Bull 52:158-60 O '77

SUTOWO, Ibnu
Bitter *rijsttafel*. por Time 109:58 F 14 '77 •

SUTTER Buttes
For the first time ever Sutter Buttes are open for wildlife adventurers. il map Sunset 159: 34-34A S '77

SUTTON, Denys
Paris-New York: a continuing romance. G. Henry. il Art N 76:60-2 D '77 •

SUTTON, Fred
Only law; excerpts from 1926 articles, ed by A. B. Macdonald. il por Sat Eve Post 249:62-3 Jl '77

SUTTON, Henry, pseud. See Slavitt, D. R.

SUTTON, Horace
Booked for travel. See issues of Saturday review (ed) Islands! il Sat R 5:17-20+ Ja 7 '78

SUTTON, Robert P.
Lessons learned: a practical lifestyle in the Med. il Yachting 142:72-6 Ag '77
Sea full of islands. il Yachting 141:70-3+ Mr '77

SUTTON, S. B.
How the Department got its start. il Horticulture 55:33-7 Ap '77
SUTTON, Sheryl
Reviews. S. Banes. Dance Mag 51:35 My '77 *
SUTTONI, Charles
Des Moines Metro Summer Opera. il Hi Fi 27: MA35-7 O '77
Sociable music among the very rich. il Hi Fi 27:MA21-3 N '77
SUVAK, Daniel
Federal prison libraries. bibl il por Lib J 102: 1341-4 Je 15 '77
SUVER, James D. and Brown, R. L.
Where does zero-base budgeting work? bibl f il Harvard Bus R 55:76-84 N '77
SUWANNEE River
Our wild and scenic rivers. J. Rudloe and A. Rudloe. il map Nat Geog 152:20-9 Jl '77
SVENSON, Peter
More on government support of the arts. por Am Artist 41:16 N '77
SVOBODA, Terese
Dust storm; poem. Nation 225:540 N 19 '77
SWADOS, Elizabeth
Girl with the incredible feeling; story; excerpt. Ms 6:73-6 O '77
about
Girl with an incredible feeling. por Horizon 19: 86 My '77 *
Serban's musical image-maker. R. Elder. il por N Y Times Mag p54-5 F 13 '77 *
SWAHILI language
Readers for new literates
After literacy, what next? Tanzanian folk tales in readers. S. Malya. il UNESCO Courier 30: 23-7 F '77
SWALLOWS
'Dobe birds. H. Borland. il Audubon 79:16-17 Mr '77
SWAN, Dick
Revolutionary new rod. J. Gibbs. il Outdoor Life 159:26+ Mr '77 *
SWAN, Henry
Can humans be "taught" to hibernate? A. Rosenfeld. Sat R 4:34-5 Je 11 '77 *
SWAN, Jon
Swans' way. N Y Times Mag p35-7 Mr 13 '77
SWAN, Tony
How to drive a small car. il Esquire 88:110-12+ O '77
Road test. il Motor T 28:34-8 D '76
SWAN lake; ballet. See Ballet reviews—Single works
SWANDER, Mary
Letter; In a dream; Song; poems. Poetry 129: 272-5 F '77
Oktoberfest; poem. Nation 224:472 Ap 16 '77
Winter, 1975; poem. Nation 224:310 Mr 12 '77
SWANGER, Sterling O.
Man who keeps those Maytag repairmen lonely. E. Faltermayer. il pors Fortune 96:192-5+ N '77 *
SWANK, J. Grant, Jr
Counseling is a waste of time. Chr Today 21:27 Jl 29 '77
SWANK, Inc. See Dress accessories—Manufacture
SWANN, Brian
Legend; poem. Nation 226:27 Ja 7 '78
Skids; poem. New Yorker 52:54 F 14 '77
Tourist; Art of the past; poems. Yale R 66:404 Mr '77
SWANS
Adopt a swan for research. J. Cassell. por Outdoor Life 159:140 My '77
SWANSEA, Charleen Whisnant
Unsinkable Charleen: renegade muse of the South. L. Powell. por Ms 6:62-3 D '77 *
SWANSON, Budington
Spooning around the world. il Hobbies 82:120-2 S '77
SWANSON, Joan, and Curtis, David
Stamp of approval. il Sch Arts 76:50-1 Mr '77
SWANSON, Marshall A.
Chaos and fear in Ethiopia. Chr Cent 94:580-1 Je 22 '77
SWAPPING. See Barter
SWAPS Stakes. See Horse racing
SWARTZ, Harold M. and Gutierrez, P. L.
Free radical increases in cancer: evidence that there is not a real increase. bibl il Science 198: 936-8 D 2 '77
SWAZILAND
See also
Swazis
SWAZIS
Rites and ceremonies
Zulu king weds a Swazi princess. V. Wentzel. il Nat Geog 153:46-61 Ja '78
SWEARINGEN, John Eldred, 1918-
Our energy problem; address, May 23, 1977. Vital Speeches 43:569-72 Jl 1 '77

SWEATERS
Fireside sweatering; with knitting instructions. A. B. Bradley. il Ladies Home J 94:124-5+ O '77
New looks in new yarns; family of sweaters. N. Lindemeyer and C. Vaughan. il Bet Hom & Gard 55:132-7+ O '77
28 enchanting children's sweaters to knit and crochet. il Good H 185:140-7+ S '77
Care
Life insurance for your wardrobe. P. W. Linck. il pors House & Gard 149:44+ O '77
SWEDEN
See also
Airlines—Sweden
Airplanes, Military—Sweden
Blacks in Sweden
Education—Sweden
Energy policy—Sweden
Immigration and emigration—Sweden
Money—Sweden
Opera—Sweden
Publishers and publishing—Sweden
Radioactive fallout—Sweden
Stockholm
Theater—Sweden
Trade unions—Sweden
United Nations—Sweden
Air Force
Viggen force change planned. Aviation W 106:21 Mr 28 '77
Armed Forces
Sweden nearing defense plan decision. R. R. Ropelewski. Aviation W 106:24-5 Ja 17 '77
Description and travel
Swedish treat: beautiful glass in a rustic landscape; touring southeastern Sweden. D. Otis. il House & Gard 149:48+ Jl '77
Economic conditions
Has Sweden had it? il Forbes 120:71-4+ N 1 '77
Sweden: new facts of life. S. T. Atlas and others. il Newsweek 90:52+ Ag 22 '77
Utopia in trouble. B. Kumm. Harpers 256:33-7 Ja '78
Industries
See also
Automobile industry—Sweden
Glass industry—Sweden
Politics and government
See also
Socialism—Sweden
Race question
Racial time bomb. Time 110:41 Ag 8 '77
Religious institutions and affairs
See also
Evangelistic work—Sweden
Social policy
Toward a multidimensional framework for the analysis of social policy. M. O. Heisler and B. G. Peters. bibl f Ann Am Acad 434:58-70 N '77
See also
Public welfare—Sweden
SWEDISH cookery. See Cookery, Swedish
SWEDISH poetry
Translations into English
Balloons; poem; tr by J. Moffett. H. Gullberg. New Yorker 53:188 D 12 '77
SWEENEY, Francis
Fool's errand. America 137:379 N 26 '77
Summer. America 136:563 Je 25 '77
SWEEPERS, Street. See Street cleaning apparatus
SWEEPING, Street. See Street cleaning
SWEET, Johanna
G.B. Shaw and I are Leos. il Engl J 66:62-3 O '77
SWEET, John Howard
Memo to our readers. U.S. News 82:3 Mr 14 '77
SWEET, William
Opposition to nuclear power in Europe. bibl f il map Bull Atom Sci 33:40-7 D '77
SWEET peas
Succeeding with sweet peas. D. E. Stebbins. Org Gard & Farm 24:92 Mr '77
SWEET tooth. See Food habits
SWEETENING agents. See Sugar substitutes
SWEETS, William McDowell
Historical tape recordings. L. Dumont. il Hobbies 82:116-17+ N; 58-9 D '77 *
SWENSON, Allan A.
Terrarium gardening. il Ladies Home J 94: 72+ O '77
SWENSON, G. R.
(ed) See Johns, J. What is pop art?

SWENSON, Mary Ann
Three young clergywomen: how they're changing their churches. J. T. Freeman. il Redbook 149:24+ Je '77 *

SWENSON, May
October; poem. New Yorker 53:45 O 31 '77
View to the north; poem. New Yorker 52:83 Ja 24 '77

SWETNAM, James
Self-discoveries in the Middle East. America 136:292-5 Ap 2 '77

SWIDLER, Arlene
In the presence of God my mother. New Cath World 220:20 Ja '77

SWIDLER, Leonard
Christian-Marxist dialogue in America. Commonweal 104:138-9 Mr 4 '77

SWIFT, A. Dean
Top retailer plans for metric conversion. V. Louviere. por Nations Bus 65: 75 S '77 *

SWIFT, Reuben
Reuben Swift, cabinetmaker of New Bedford. M. J. Bordes. bibl il Antiques 112:750-2 O '77 *

SWIFT, Susan
New faces on the big screen; interview, ed by E. Miller. pors Seventeen 36:122 Mr '77

SWIM bladders. See Fishes—Anatomy

SWIMBLADDERS. See Fishes—Anatomy

SWIMMING
Bottom was on top in very fast company; NCAA championships. J. Kirshenbaum. il Sports Illus 46:26-7 Ap 4 '77
Bottom was up to topping a Mark; East Germany-U.S. dual meet. J. Kirshenbaum. il Sports Illus 47:18-19 S 5 '77
But is it simon-pure? NAIA success of Canada's Simon Fraser University. J. Kirshenbaum. il Sports Illus 46:59-60 F 28 '77
Gimmicks, gadgets, goodby records. J. Kirshenbaum. il Sports Illus 46:40-2+ Ap 25 '77
How to make it in the water. H. Stein. il Esquire 88:58-65 Ag '77
She double-crossed the Channel; C. Nicholas. B. Newman. il por Sports Illus 47:72+ S 26 '77
They're bracing for Berlin; AAU long-course championships. J. Kirshenbaum. il Sports Illus 47:76+ Ag 29 '77

Safety devices and measures

How to drownproof your child. il Parents Mag 52:44-5 Jl '77
Some planning hints for the waterfront safety director; camps. E. Slezak. il Camp Mag 49: 12-14+ F '77

SWIMMING (animal locomotion) See Animal locomotion

SWIMMING games. See Games

SWIMMING pool heaters. See Water heaters

SWIMMING pools
Pool makes waves; Oakland County, Mich. il Parks & Rec 12:46 My '77
Space age swimming hole; Wet n' Wild in Orlando, Fla. F. Benson. il Parks & Rec 12:24-5+ O '77

Sanitation

Silver shines as pool purifier. il Am City & County 92:18 Ag '77

SWIMMING pools, Camp
Maintain free chlorine residual, pH balance in pool care. W. Treadwell. il Camp Mag 49:12-13 Je '77

SWIMMING pools, Home
Make a big splash in a small backyard. A. Scharffenberger. il Am Home 80:80-1 Mr '77
Not for swimming only. E. Brown. il N Y Times Mag p82-3 Je 12 '77
Sorting out the swimming pools. R. Wolkomir. il Mech Illus 73:44-5+ Jl '77
Yes, you can have a swiming pool. il Good H 184:246+ Mr '77

Equipment

One answer to the pool debris problem; fiberglass-screen cover. R. R. Grams. il Pop Mech 148:52 Ag '77

Maintenance and repair

Backyard pools: before you take the plunge. Bet Hom & Gard 55:92 Je '77
Success with a mind-boggling invention; poolsweep. P. Schwab. il por Nations Bus 65:92 D '77

SWIMSUITS. See Bathing suits

SWINARTON, Robert W.
Wall Street's evolutionary revolution; address, April 21, 1977. Vital Speeches 43:507-11 Je 1 '77

SWINDELL, William, and Barrett, H. H.
Computerized tomography: taking sectional X rays. bibl il Phys Today 30:32-6+ D '77

SWINDLERS and swindling. See Fraud

SWINE
Good feed from petroleum; annual meeting of the American Society of Animal Science. J. Russell. Farm J 101:Hog 21-2 S '77
Hog extra (cont) Farm J 101:Hog 1-2+ Ja; Hog 1-2+ F; Hog 1-2+ My; Hog 1-2+ Je; Hog 1-2+ Ag; Hog 1-2+ S; Hog 1-2+ O; Hog 1+ D '77
To buy a fat pig. S. A. Schwartz. il por Conservationist 32:26-9 S '77

Breeds

Why the swing to white sows? J. Russell. Farm J 101:Hog 8-9+ O '77

Care

As healthy as a. . .sow? Why not? il Suc Farm 75:no2 60 F '77
Start a pig as if it were sick. J. Russell. il Farm J 101:Hog 8-9+ Ja '77
TGE vaccination: these farmers say it pays; transmissible gastroenteritis. G. Johnston. il Suc Farm 75:H14 D '77
You can get along without shotgun treatment; excerpts from address. J. D. Coltrain. Farm J 101:Hog 7 Ja '77

Confinement methods

Breeding gilts in confinement can be successful. R. Brunoehler. il Suc Farm 75:no3 H10 F '77
Materials for confinement equipment: how do they compare? il Suc Farm 75:no3 H5 F '77
See also
Swine houses

Contamination by drugs, pesticides, etc.

Illegal drug residues. G. Johnston. il Suc Farm 75:25 My '77
Say good-bye to sulfa drugs? L. Schotsch. Farm J 101:Hog 11+ S '77

Diseases and pests

Decision time on pseudorabies. J. Russell. por Farm J 101:Hog 16 F '77
He fought pseudorabies and won. J. Russell. il Farm J 101:Hog 8-9+ Ag '77
New light on boar lameness. Farm J 101:Hog 19 Je '77
Pseudorabies case surprises experts. J. Russell. il Farm J 101:LK8 Ap '77
TGE vaccination: these farmers say it pays; transmissible gastroenteritis. G. Johnston. il Suc Farm 75:H14 D '77
Will this help you whip pig scours? lactobacillus paste. J. D. Ritchie. il Farm J 101:Hog 23 O '77
You can live with PRV! pseudorabies. J. Russell. il Farm J 101:Hog 12-13 S '77

Feeding

Don't skimp on feed to nursing sows. il Suc Farm 75:K8 S '77
Feed sows silage? il Farm J 101:Hog 36 S '77
Feeding tips that can make hogs profitable in '78. Suc Farm 75:H24 D '77
How to use records to improve profits. J. Russell. il Farm J 101:Hog 10-11 D '77
What's your sow-feeding IQ? il Farm J 101: Hog 30 S '77
See also
Swine feedlots

Identification

It's time for electronic ID. J. Russell. por Farm J 101:Hog 24 Ag '77

Marketing

Best hog marketing day: it changes with the season. il Suc Farm 75:32 S '77
Feed it or sell it? G. Johnston. Suc Farm 75: H12 D '77
His market hogs get individual treatment. il Suc Farm 75:no4 L40 Mr 77
How Mike Barton nets an extra $3 per hog. G. Johnston. il Suc Farm 75:H3 D '77
How to use grade and yield selling. J. Russell. il Farm J 101:Hog 12+ Je '77
Telephone feeder pig auction: a marketing hot line. R. Brunoehler. il Suc Farm 75:47 D '77
These pigs went to market. il Suc Farm 75:28-9 D '77
Winter losses temper hog build-up. il Farm J 101:Hog 24 My '77

Performance records and registration

Testing key to this breeding operation. J. D. Ritchie. il Farm J 101:Hog 16+ S '77

Prices

Ninety will get you fifteen. R. J. Fee. il Suc Farm 75:no3 H17 F '77
Pricecast (cont) Farm J 101:Hog 1 Ja; Hog 1 F; Hog 1 My; Hog 1 Je; Hog 1 Ag; Hog 1 S; Hog 1 O; Hog 1 D '77
Why did prices slide so fast? When will prices bottom? Is the hog cycle outdated? Suc Farm 75:no2 44 F '77

Size

See Swine, Weight and measurements of

SWINE, Effect of temperature on
What you should know about heat stress. il Farm J 101:Hog 27 My '77

SWINE, Fossil
Suid evolution and correlation of African hominid localities. T. D. White and J. M. Harris. bibl il maps Science 198:13-21 O 7 '77
SWINE, Weight and measurements of
One pork chop or two? R. J. Fee. il Suc Farm 75:no4 34 Mr '77
SWINE as carriers of infection
Persistence of Hong Kong influenza virus variants in pigs. K. F. Shortridge and others. bibl il Science 196:1454-5 Je 24 '77
SWINE auctions. See Auctions
SWINE breeding
Get more pigs from three-way cross. il Suc Farm 75:36 S '77
How English hogmen get top sow performance. R. Brunoehler. Suc Farm 75:no3 H24 F '77
How to beat the heat in breeding sows. Suc Farm 75:C5 Ag '77
Mismanagements: biggest cause of nonbreeder boars. Suc Farm 75:no3 H20 F '77
Pig Improvement Company: fresh approach to sow productivity. il Suc Farm 75:no3 H6 F '77
Simple way to schedule sows; tablet sheet. H. Pike. il Farm J 101:Hog 6 S '77
Testing key to this breeding operation. J. D. Ritchie. il Farm J 101:Hog 16+ S '77
See also
Swine—Breeds
SWINE cooperatives. See Agriculture, Cooperative
SWINE corporations. See Swine industry
SWINE farm management
Four-family operation that works. J. D. Ritchie. il Farm J 101:Hog 10-11 Ag '77
Hog management. R. J. Fee and G. Johnston. See issues of Successful farming
How he grew into hogs. J. Phillips. il Farm J 101:Hog 12-13 O; Same with title Hogs helped him make the leap into full time farming. 101:LK6-7 N '77
How to match capital and labor in the hog business. il Suc Farm 75:9 Ja '77
Low investment or low labor? D. Seim. il Farm J 101:Hog 10+ Ja '77
Make the most of feed; farrow-to-finish operations. J. D. Ritchie. il Farm J 101:Hog 24 S '77
Successful hog management (cont) il Suc Farm 75:no3 H1-3+ F '77
Two-year plan cuts back sows; doubles pig output. R. Fee. il Suc Farm 75:H22-3 D '77
You can't get big overnight. D. Wanner. il Farm J 101:Hog 20+ My '77
See also
Farm records
SWINE farms

Equipment

Get the most from your equipment dollar. G. Johnston. il Suc Farm 75:no3 H2-3 F '77
Scheduled maintenance—it can keep equipment operational. R. J. Fee. Suc Farm 75:no3 H1 F '77
See also
Swine—Confinement methods
SWINE farrowing cooperatives. See Agriculture, Cooperative
SWINE farrowing houses. See Swine houses
SWINE feedlots
Feed it or sell it? G. Johnston. Suc Farm 75: H12 D '77
Start small and grow. J. Russell. Farm J 101: Hog 23 My; LK8 N '77
Who'll produce feeder pigs? interviews. G. Pettit and D. Miller. il pors Farm J 101:Hog 13+ Ag '77
SWINE flu. See Influenza
SWINE houses
Get your hogs off the ground—go portable; confinement facilities. J. D. Ritchie. Farm J 101:Hog 9 F; LK6-7 Mr '77
Ideas that will help you plan your next farrowing house. C. S. Machan. il Farm J 101:Hog 18+ Ja '77
Remodeled farrowing unit: more advantages than just cost. J. Russnogle. il Suc Farm 75:H15 D '77
This compact setup offers flexibility and economy. S. M. Schwartz. il Farm J 101:Hog 18 O; LK2 N '77

Equipment

How to pick a pregnancy tester. J. Russell. il Farm J 101:Hog 12+ My '77
What you should know about heat stress; sprinkler systems. il Farm J 101:Hog 27 My '77

Floors

His hog operation founded on concrete. R. J. Fee. il Suc Farm 75:no3 H18 F '77
Homegrown feeding floors; concrete floors. il Farm J 101:Hog 28 S '77

Heating and ventilation

Now solar-heated prefabs. D. Seim. il Farm J 101:Hog 32-3 S '77
Reduce heat 10° to 15°: raise bigger, thriftier litters. E. Ainsworth. il Farm J 101:Hog 6-8 D '77
Save on energy by cutting air flow. B. Coffman. il Farm J 101:Hog 14+ O '77

Leasing and renting

Confinement leasing: makes $5 work like $50. il Suc Farm 75:H1 D '77
SWINE industry
Extra pay for quality hogs; Pork-O-Rama Research Knoll, Inc. B. M. Wilkinson. il Farm J 101:Hog 12-13 F '77
Hog operations will continue to grow. Farm J 101:LK5 Mr '77
What makes sow corporations work? E. Ainsworth. il Farm J 101:Hog 8-10 My '77
Your hog business (cont) il Farm J 101:Hog 28 Ja; Hog 16 F; Hog 28 My; Hog 20 Je; Hog 24 Ag; Hog 40 S; Hog 16 D '77
SWINE manure. See Fertilizers and manures
SWING, John Temple
Law of the sea at the brink. Oceans 10:4-5 S '77
SWING bands. See Bands (music)
SWING music. See Jazz music
SWINGS and swinging
Physics of swinging. Sci Am 236:60 Ap '77
SWINNERTON, A. R.
Were the good old days really that good? Ret Liv 17:34 Jl '77
SWISHER, Viola Hegyi
What a wild idea: Lewitzky and Gernreich design a dance. il pors Dance Mag 51:75-7 Mr '77
(ed) See Peck, S. Steven Peck Jazz Dance Company
SWISS Bank Corporation. See Banks and banking—Switzerland
SWISS chard. See Chard
SWISS cookery. See Cookery, Swiss
SWISS Credit Bank. See Banks and banking—Switzerland
SWISS Reinsurance Company. See Insurance companies—Switzerland
SWITCHEL. See Beverages
SWITCHES, Electric. See Electric switches
SWITCHING systems
See also
Telephone switching systems, Electronic
SWITZER, Ellen
Health for your whole life. il Vogue 167:368-9+ S '77
SWITZERLAND
See also
Alps
Art—Switzerland
Banks and banking—Switzerland
Festivals—Switzerland
Money—Switzerland
Music festivals—Switzerland
Opera—Switzerland
Publishers and publishing—Switzerland
Schools—Switzerland

Description and travel

In Switzerland—ride up, hike down. il Sunset 158:74+ Je '77

Industries

See also
Food industry—Switzerland
Shoe industry—Switzerland

Religious institutions and affairs

See also
Catholic Church in Switzerland
SWOMLEY, John M. Jr
Between freedom fighters and mercenaries. Nation 226:13-16 Ja 7 '78
SWORDFISH
Predators: the swordfish and the mako shark; excerpt from The book of sharks. R. Ellis. il Oceans 10:18-20 N '77
SWORDFISH fishing
Denizens of the dark; Florida. D. Levin. il Sports Illus 47:44-5+ Ag 15 '77
SWORDS
Art of the Japanese sword. R. Hughes. il Horizon 19:50-61 Mr '77
SYDNEY, Australia

Crime

Contemporary crime in historical perspective: a comparative study of London, Stockholm, and Sydney. T. R. Gurr. bibl f il Ann Am Acad 434:114-36 N '77

Music

See also
Opera—Australia
SYDNEY International Piano Competition. See Music—Competitions
SYDOW, Max von
Von Sydow; interview. New Yorker 52:24-5 Ja 17 '77
SYLWESTER, Robert
Stress and the classroom teacher. Educ Digest 42:14-17 My '77

SYMBIONESE Liberation Army
SLA holocaust. E. Keerdoja and J. Huck. il Newsweek 89:9 Je 27 '77
SYMBIOSIS
Dodo ecology. Sci Am 237:81-2 O '77
Intergeneric transfer of genes involved in the rhizobium-legume symbiosis. P. E. Bishop and others. bibl il Science 198:938-40 D 2 '77
Lives of a tree; the mysterious inner world of tropical plants. D. Perry. il Horticulture 55: 30-5 O '77
Nature's odd couples; dependency of hermit crabs on whelk shells and Calvaria major on dodos S. J. Gould. il Natur Hist 87:38-41 Ja '78
Peptidoglycan in the cell wall of the primary intracellular symbiote of the pea aphid. E. J. Houk and others. bibl il Science 198:401-3 O 28 '77
Plant-animal mutualism: coevolution with dodo leads to near extinction of plant. S. A. Temple. bibl Science 197:885-6 Ag 26 '77
Reef corals: mutualistic symbioses adapted to nutrient-poor environments. L. Muscatine and J. W. Porter. bibl il BioScience 27:454-60 Jl '77
Symbionts of sea fans & sea whips. L. P. Zann. il Oceans 10:10-15 Ja '77
Symbiosis runs wild on the backs of high-living weevils. J. L. Gressitt. il Smithsonian 7:135-6+ bibl(p 156) F '77
SYMBOLISM
See also
Ciphers
SYMBOLISM in art
Duchamp's acephalic symbolism; analysis of bookstore window display called Lazy Hardware. C. F. Stuckey. bibl il Art in Am 65:94-9 Ja '77
SYMBOLISM in literature
Plain and symbol. J. Jerome. Writers Digest 57: 55-7 D '77
SYMBOLISM of animals. See Animal lore
SYMBOLS
Fertility symbols on the Hadley chests. R. L. Greene. bibl il Antiques 112:250-7 Ag '77
SYME, Sherman Leonard
Stress: role in hypertension debated. J. L. Marx. Science 198:905-7 D 2 '77 *
SYMMETRY (art) See Proportion (art)
SYMMETRY (biology)
Asymmetric structure of the purple membrane. A. E. Blaurock and G. I. King. bibl il Science 196:1101-4 Je 3 '77
Membrane asymmetry. J. E. Rothman and J. Lenard. bibl il Science 195:743-53 F 25 '77
Topological asymmetry of phospholipids in membranes. L. D. Bergelson and L. I. Barsukov. bibl il Science 197:224-30 Jl 15 '77
See also
Laterality
SYMMS, Steven D.
Excerpts from debate on Federal Elections Campaign Act Amendments, April 1, 1976. Cong Digest 56:95 Mr '77
Excerpts from remarks on U.S. African policy, April 29, 1976. Cong Digest 56:19+ Ja '77
Federal voice in private land-use: two views. pors Nations Bus 65:19-20 Ag '77
Legalize laetrile as a cancer drug? interview. pors U.S. News 82:51-2 Je 13 '77
SYMONDS, Pringle Hart
Creation of a historic district in Annapolis. Antiques 111:146-7 Ja '77
SYMPATHY
Accusing finger, the helping hand. C. B. Murphey. Chr Today 21:30-1 Je 17 '77
See also
Empathy
SYMPATHY cards. See Greeting cards
SYMPHONIC poems
See also
Phonograph records—Symphonic poems
SYMPHONIES
See also
Phonograph records—Symphonies
SYMPHONY of the New World (orchestra)
Sym. of the New World, Friedman; concert at Carnegie Hall. Hi Fi 27:MA24-5 Mr '77
SYMPHONY orchestras. See Orchestras
SYMPTOMS. See Diagnosis
SYNAGOGUES
Spiraling arches shape a great space; Temple Beth El in West Palm Beach. il Archit Rec 161:111-14 F '77
See also
Chicago—Synagogues
SYNANON commune. See Collective settlements
SYNAPSES
Regenerating afferents establish synapses with a target neuron that lacks its cell body. F. B. Krasne and S. H. Lee. bibl il Science 198: 517-19 N 4 '77
Synapse formation between two clonal cell lines. C. N. Christian and others. bibl il Science 196:995-8 My 27 '77
SYNCH-cords. See Photography—Electronic equipment
SYNCHROTRON radiation. See Radiation
SYNCHROTRONS. See Accelerators (electrons, etc)
SYNDICATE material, Newspaper. See Newspapers—Syndicate service
SYNDICATED radio programs. See Radio production and direction
SYNDROMES
See also
Prader-Willi syndrome
Reye's syndrome
SYNERGISM
Antibacterial synergism: a proposal for chemotherapeutic potentiation between trimethoprim and sulfamethoxazole. M. Poe; discussion. bibl Science 197:1300-1 S 23 '77
SYNOD of Bishops, 1977
Display of unity. M. Hammond. Commonweal 104:774-6 D 9 '77
Fiddling in Rome. K. L. Woodword. il Newsweek 90:111 N 7 '77
Hopes for the coming Synod; with editorial comment. M. C. Bryce. America 137:inside cover, 215-17 O 8 '77
How to pass on the faith. K. L. Woodward and J. Whitmore. il Newsweek 90:69 O 10 '77
Roman holiday. Time 110:124 N 7 '77
Slumbering Synod. D. R. Campion. America 137:328-30, 355-8 N 12-19 '77
Spreading the word of God. America 137:297 N 5 '77
Twilight papacy. il pors Time 110:76-7 O 10 '77
SYNTHESIS
Cell-free modulation of proinsulin synthesis. P. T. Lomedico and G. F. Saunders. bibl il Science 198:620-2 N 11 '77
Correlation between lipid synthesis in tumor cells and their sensitivity to humoral immune attack. S. I. Schlager and S. H. Ohanian. bibl il Science 197:773-6 Ag 19 '77
Hypertension: increase of collagen biosynthesis in arteries but not in veins. K. Iwatsuki and others. bibl il Science 198:403-5 O 28 '77
Life that came in from the cold. Sci N 112: 277 O 29 '77
Mechanism of carbon isotope fractionation associated with lipid synthesis. M. J. DeNiro and S. Epstein. bibl il Science 197:261-3 Jl 15 '77
Natural product synthesis and vitamin B_{12}. A. Eschenmoser and C. E. Wintner. bibl il Science 196:1410-20 Je 24 '77
Neuronal circadian rhythm: phase shifting by a protein synthesis inhibitor. J. W. Jacklet. bibl il Science 198:69-71 O 7 '77
Neurophysin biosynthesis: conversion of a putative precursor during axonal transport. H. Gainer and Y. Sarne. bibl il Science 195:1354-6 Mr 25 '77
Phosphoribosylpyrophosphate synthesis in cultured human cells. P. J. Benke and D. Dittmar. bibl il Science 198:1171-3 D 16 '77
Quantitation of dimethylnitrosamine in the whole mouse ofter biosynthesis in vivo from trace levels of precursors. D. P. Roundbehler and others. bibl il Science 197:917-18 Ag 26 '77
SYNTHESIZED music. See Music, Electronic
SYNTHESIZERS, Electronic. See Musical instruments, Electronic
SYNTHETASES
Five hundredfold overproduction of DNA ligase after induction of a hybrid lambda lysogen constructed in vitro. S. M. Panasenko and others. bibl il Science 196:188-9 Ap 8 '77
Glutamine synthetase: glial localization in brain. A. Martinez-Hernandez and others. bibl il Science 195:1356-8 Mr 25 '77
SYNTHETIC food. See Food substitutes
SYNTHETIC fuels
Solving the energy crisis: we're not even taking the first step; interview, ed by J. Cook. E. D. Kane. por Forbes 120:91+ N 1 '77
SYNTHETIC photographs, Astronomical. See Astronomical photography
SYON Park. See London—Parks and playgrounds
SYOSSET, N.Y.

Education

See Education—New York (state)
SYRACUSE Ballet Theatre. See Ballet companies
SYRACUSE Developmental Center, N.Y. See Mentally handicapped—Institutional care
SYRACUSE University, Syracuse, N.Y.
ERIC clearinghouse goes to Syracuse, N.Y. Lib J 102:529 Mr 1 '77
SYRIA
See also
Jews in Syria

Antiquities

Ebla; Tell Mardikh excavations. P. Matthiae. il UNESCO Courier 30:6-12 F '77
Found: a lost kingdom; Ebla. map Sr Schol 109:33 F 24 '77
Older testament; Ebla texts. Sci Am 237: 101-2 S '77

SYRIA—*Continued*

Foreign relations

Assad: Sadat's folly; excerpts from interview; ed by A. de Borchgrave. H. Assad. il pors Newsweek 91:41-2+ Ja 16 '78
For Syria: a growing role in Middle East drama. D. Mullin. il por map U.S. News 82:79-80 Ap 18 '77
Peace, but not this year; excerpts from interview, ed by W. Wynn. H. Assad. por Time 109:32+ Ja 24 '77
Pressures mount on Syria's Assad—. D. Mullin. il por U.S. News 84:27-8 Ja 9 '78
Syria's Assad: Walking a tightrope. por U.S. News 83:22 D 12 '77

SYRIAN Orthodox Church in the United States. See Orthodox Eastern Church in the United States

SYRUPS
See also
Maple syrup

SYSTEM Development Corporation
Profiting from the revolution in technology; interview. G. E. Mueller. il pors Nations Bus 65:44-9 Ag '77

SYSTEMIC lupus erythematosus. See Lupus erythematosus

SYSTEMS building
Colombia will build shell housing with unfinished interiors at a Bogotá condominium. T. Berry. il Archit Rec 161:39 Ja '77

SYSTEMS engineering
Automated stackers used by construction equipment dealer to speed parts retrieval. il Archit Rec 162:120 Jl '77
Building automation: what it does, what its benefits are, how the economics fare. D. E. Ross. il Archit Rec 161:147-50 Ap '77
Give your house an energy update; how a systems engineer can help you. V. McNiff. House & Gard 149:38 Jl '77
See also
Computers—Engineering use

SYWULKA, Stephen R.
Guatemala remembers. Chr Today 21:55-6 Ap 1 '77

SZABO, Al. See Millan, M. jt auth

SZABO, Denis
Sociological criminology and models of juvenile delinquency and maladjustment. bibl f Ann Am Acad 434:137-150 N '77

SZAJMAN, Rena. See Mintz, M. jt auth

SZAMIER, R. Bruce. See Edwards, R. B. jt auth

SZATHMARY, Louis
International chef (cont) por Travel 147:8+ F; 84 Mr; 84 My; 148:16+ Jl; 64 O '77; 149:8 Ja '78

SZE, Nien Dak
Anthropogenic CO emissions: implications for the atmospheric CO-OH-CH_4 cycle. il Science 195:673-5 F 18 '77

SZECHWAN cookery. See Cookery, Chinese

SZETO, W. W. and others
Cloning of cauliflower mosaic virus (CLMV) DNA in escherichia coli. bibl il Science 196:210-12 Ap 8 '77

SZIDON, Roberto
Villa-Lobos: music for piano. D. Gravelmann. Am Rec G 40:49 Je '77 •

SZULC, Tad
CIA's electric kool-aid acid test. il Psychol Today 11:92-4+ N '77
How the genie got out of the bottle. Forbes 119:89-91 My 15 '77
Inside South Korea's C.I.A. il N Y Times Mag p41-2+ Mr 6 '77
Is paradise lost? il Sat R 5:18-20 O 1 '77
—and Yoffe, Emily
ITT under the gun. New Repub 177:18-22 Ag 6 '77

T

T cells. See Lymphocytes

TAC (The Architects Collaborative [firm]) See Architectural firms

TCDC. See United Nations Conference on Technical Co-operation among Developing Countries, 1978 (proposed)

TCDD (tetrachlorodibenzo-p-dioxin) See Dibenzodioxin

TDA Industries, Inc. See Building materials industry

TDI (toluene diisocyanate) See Isocyanates

TDRSS (tracking and data relay satellite system) See Communications satellites

TEAA (Tax Equity for Americans Abroad) See Lobbyists and lobbying

TGE (transmissible gastroenteritis) See Swine—Diseases and pests

THC
Cannabinoid induced behavioral convulsions in rabbits. P. Martin and P. Consroe; reply with rejoinder. D. M. Feeney. bibl Science 197:1301-2 S 23 '77
Cannabinoids inhibit testosterone secretion by mouse testes in vitro. S. Dalterio and others. bibl il Science 196:1472-3 Je 24 '77
Competition of Δ^9-tetrahydrocannabinol with estrogen in rat uterine estrogen receptor binding. A. B. Rawitch and others. bibl il Science 197:1189-91 S 16 '77
Effect of delta-9-tetrahydrocannabinol on uterine and vaginal cytology of ovariectomized rats. J. Solomon and others. bibl il Science 195: 875-7 Mr 4 '77
Inhibition of a lymphocyte membrane enzyme by Δ^9-tetrahydrocannabinol in vitro. J. H. Greenberg and others. bibl il Science 197:475-7 Jl 29 '77
Uterotrophic effect of delta-9-tetrohydrocannabinol in ovariectomized rats. J. Solomon and others; reply with rejoinder. A. B. Okey and G. P. Bondy. bibl Science 195:904-6 Mr 4 '77

THP (tetrahydropapaveroline) See Quinoline

TIE. See Institute of Ecology

TM. See Transcendental meditation

TRH (thyrotropin-releasing hormone) See Thyrotropin releasing factor

TRW, Inc
From auto cranks to space age. il Forbes 119: 31-2 Mr 15 '77
Pyramider spy case; A. Lee and C. Boyce. R. Steele and N. Horrock. il por Newsweek 89:29 Ap 18 '77
Stealing the company store; case of C. Boyce and A. D. Lee. il por Time 109:19 My 9 '77
To be young, rich—and a spy; A. D. Lee and C. J. Boyce. R. Lindsey. il pors N Y Times Mag p 18+ My 22 '77

TSA. See Taos Society of Artists

TU-144 (airplane) See Airplanes, Supersonic

TUC. See Trades Union Congress

TVA. See Tennessee Valley Authority

TVI. See Television interference

TWA. See Trans World Airlines

TZU Hang (ketch) See Sailboats

TABLE decoration
Butter lamb for the Easter Sunday breakfast table. il Sunset 158:200 Ap '77
18 centerpieces you can make to dress up any table for practically nothing. G. Wells. il Redbook 148:37-44 Mr '77
Holiday centerpieces . . . good enough to eat! il Good H 185:126-35+ D '77
Unconventional centerpieces. P. Pollock. il Bet Hom & Gard 55:112 Ag '77

TABLE linen
Easy patchwork tablecloth. il Bet Hom & Gard 55:56 Ap '77
Tablecloths—how to buy, how to keep them beautiful. Good H 185:186 N '77
Tabletop artistry; hand-painted cloths. M. Siple. il House B 119:134-5 N '77

TABLE manners. See Etiquette

TABLE setting
Of food and flowers. il House & Gard 149:152-7 My '77
Regal grace. il House B 119:130-3 N '77
Set for soup. P. Pollock. il Bet Hom & Gard 55:128 F '77
Table toppers you can make in minutes. P. Pollock. il Bet Hom & Gard 55:129 S '77

TABLE tennis
Affront of a backhand; U.S. Closed Championship. D. Miles. il por Sports Illus 48:38-9 Ja 2 '78
Little night music; M. Reisman, professional player. R. Kennedy. il pors Sports Illus 47: 82-6+ N 21 '77
One for all, but not all for one; World Table Tennis Championships. D. Miles. il Sports Illus 46:73-4+ Ap 18 '77

TABLE top photography. See Photography, Table top

TABLECLOTHS. See Table linen

TABLES
Build a drafting table that folds for easy storage. L. C. Sander. il Pop Mech 147:39+ My '77
Build an add-on barbecue table. R. Capotosto. il Pop Mech 147:107+ My '77
Butcher block table for working kitchens. R. Weinsteiger. il Org Gard & Farm 24:89-91 D '77
Chairside table you can make. D. Clayton. il Mech Illus 73:134-5 S '77
Create your own space-saving tables with folding-leg hardware. M. Philips. il Pop Sci 211: 146 O '77
Easy as child's play: a table-desk you can build in a day; excerpt from Things to do in a day. il Redbook 150:136+ N '77
Five-foot plate glass top makes buffet table unobtrusive. il Sunset 159:92+ S '77

TABLES—*Continued*
Good for 50 years of weather, picnics, and initial carving; picnic table. il Sunset 158:94-5 Je '77
Revolving worktable makes painting easier. R. C. Barnes. il Pop Mech 147:68+ Mr '77
Table top is either glass or wood. il Sunset 158: 122 Je '77
Trestle coffee table. R. Gutter. il Mech Illus 73:100+ N '77
See also
Pedestals
Stands (furniture)
TABLES, Accessory (machine work) See Machinery —Stands, tables, etc.
TABLES, Conversion. See Conversion tables
TABLETS (paleography)
Library of Assurbanipal, King of the world. L. Arksey. bibl il Wilson Lib Bull 51:832-40 Je '77
Writings on bamboo and wood; tablets found in tombs. W. S. Wong. bibl il Wilson Lib Bull 51:848-52 Je '77
TABLEWARE
White House showcase for crafts. J. B. Reiter and J. Macurdy. il pors House B 119:116-19 O '77
See also
Pottery
Table setting
TABLOID journalism. See Journalism
TABLOID papers. See Newspapers—Tabloid papers
TACHOMETERS
Patrol car logs cut speeding accidents; tachographic recording devices, Hawthorne, Calif. il Am City & County 92:96 My '77
TACHYONS. See Particles (nuclear physics)
TACKLE, Fishing. See Fishing tackle
TACO Bell (restaurant chain) See Restaurants—Chain and franchise operations
TACOMA, Wash.
Lighting helps CBD sales. il Am City & County 92:37 Jl '77
TACOS. See Cookery, Mexican
TACTICS
See also
War games
TACTILE vision substitution system. See Blind, Apparatus for the
TAFT, John
Grey eminences. New Repub 177:18-20 Ag 20 '77
Once and future mandarin. il New Repub 177: 16-19 N 26 '77
TAFT, Calif.
Education
See Education—California
TAFT-Hartley law. See Labor laws and legislation —United States—Taft-Hartley law
TAGGART, Kathleen Nelson
John Wornall House, Kansas City, Missouri. il Antiques 111:530-7 Mr '77
TAGGART, Robert, 3d. See Livitan, S. A. jt auth
TAGGING of fish. See Fish tagging
TAHITI
Paradise. . .and points beyond; Tahiti, Moorea and Bora Bora. L. Janos il Sat Eve Post 249:115-16+ D '77
Description and travel
Impressions of Tahiti, satori land. A. Nin. il Holiday 58:34-5+ Mr '77
Tahiti. A. L. Welsh and C. Hyde. il Trav/Holiday 148:28-32 D '77
TAHOE Regional Planning Agency. See Lake Tahoe Regional Planning Agency
T'AI chi ch'üan
Scholar who moonlights at T'ai chi ch'uan. il pors Ebony 32:44-6+ Jl '77
TAI language. See Thai language
TAILS
Ends and means. A. Odum. il Int Wildlife 7: 18-19 My '77
TAIPEI, Taiwan
Hotels, restaurants, etc.
World's greatest Chinese restaurant. A. Zich. Holiday 58:40-1+ Mr '77
TAIT, David
He cooks. il por Bet Hom & Gard 55:74 Ag '77
TAIT, Sunny
Gifts from the earth. il Org Gard & Farm 24: 119-20 D '77
TAIWAN
Letter from Taiwan. R. Shaplen. New Yorker 53:72+ Je 13 '77
See also
Civil rights—Taiwan
Government publicity—Taiwan
Investments, Foreign—Taiwan
Kaohiung
Loans, Bank—Taiwan
Medicine—Taiwan
Quemoy (island)
Taipei
Visitors, Foreign—Taiwan

Commerce
United States
See United States—Commerce—Taiwan
Description and travel
Taiwan. S. Fockler. Trav/Holiday 148:31-2 D '77
Foreign relations
United States
See United States—Foreign relations—Taiwan
Industries
See also
Potteries
Politics and government
Taiwan's future. M. Kondracke. New Repub 177:15-17 S 24 '77
Understanding Chiang Ching-kuo. W. F. Buckley, Jr. Nat R 30:48-9 Ja 6 '78
TAIWANESE Little League teams. See Baseball, Childrens
TAIWANESE pottery. See Pottery, Taiwanese
TAJO, Italo
Old pros: Tajo & Barbieri; interview, ed by C. Faria. il pors Opera N 41:8-13 F 26 '77
TAKADA, Kenzo
Chez Kenzo, chez Karl. M. Russell il pors N Y Times Mag p 130-1 N 27 '77 *
TAKAI, Toshio
Is it really dumping? excerpts from interview, ed by A. M. Field. pors Newsweek 89:58-9 Mr 28 '77
TAKAMINE, Jokichi
Jokichi Takamine (1854-1922) F. G. Creech. il por Chemistry 50:5-6 My '77 *
TAKEMITSU, Toru
Trendencies of Toru Takemitsu. I. Kolodin. por Sat R 4:39-40 F 19 '77 *
TAKOOSHIAN, Harold, and others
Who wouldn't help a lost child? You, maybe. bibl il pors Psychol Today 10:67-8+ F '77
TALAMINI, Tom
South Pacific il Trav/Holiday 148:28-32+ D '77
TALARICO, Susette M. See Cole, G. F. jt auth
TALBOT, Lee M.
Wildlife quotas sometimes ignored the real world. il Smithsonian 8:116-18+ My '77
TALE of two cities; dramatization. See Hackett, W.
TALENT agents. See Theatrical agencies
TALENTED children. See Children, Gifted
TALES from the Vienna woods; drama. See Horváth, O. von
TALES of Hoffmann; opera. See Offenbach, J.
TALESE, Gay
Coming of bold pornography; interview, ed by W. Goodman. Current 190:32-8 F '77
TALIAFERRO, Frances
Books in brief. Harpers 256:86-7 Ja '78
TALISMAN Motor Company. See Automobile industry—United States
TALK. See Conversation
TALK shows. See Radio programs—Conversation programs
TALKING books
Books that talk. D. Barnett. il Mech Illus 74: 97 Ja '78
Reading by listening; reading material on cassettes. H. Goldschlag. Ret Liv 17:44-5 D '77
TALL, Deborah
Ninth life; poem. Yale R 67:71 O '77
Touched three times. . . ; poem. Nation 224:604 My 14 '77
TALL people. See Stature
TALL women. See Stature
TALLADEGA 500. See Automobile racing
TALLEY, James
Discussions. P. Lippincott. por Sr Schol 109: 26-7 My 5 '77 *
TALLON, James
Mini-cameras for the outdoors. il Field & S 82:40+ D '77
TALLY, Ted
Terra nova. Reviews
Nation 225:638 D 10 '77 *
Time 110:96 D 19 '77 *
TALMEY, Allene
Books. See issues of Vogue
TALMON, Shemaryahu
Samaritans; with biographical sketch. il Sci Am 236:16, 100-8 Ja '77
TALMUD
Astonishing Talmud. L. Rosten. il Read Digest 111:103-6 S '77
Life in the Talmud. I. Shenker. il pors N Y Times Mag p44+ S 11 '77
TAMA Beef Producers Marketing Association. See Cattle industry
TAMALES. See Cookery, Mexican
TAMARIN, Arnold
How mussels get attached; with biographical sketch. il Natur Hist 86:4, 42-7 bibl(p94) My '77

TAMARKIN, Lawrence, and others
Malatonin induction of gonadal quiescence in pinealectomized Syrian hamsters. bibl il Science 198:953-5 D 2 '77

TAMING of the shrew; drama; adaptation. See Olfson, L.

TAMPA, Fla.

Clubs

U.S. journal: Tampa, Florida; discrimination against women at the University Club. C. Trillin. New Yorker 53:101-7 Ap 11 '77

Stores

Burdines Department Store holds up a mirror to passers-by; with introd by G. Allen. il Archit Rec 161:115-23 Mr '77

TAN, Henry K. and Andersen, J. C.
Human factor VIII: morphometric analysis of purified material in solution. bibl il Science 198: 932-4 D 2 '77

TAN
Sun lover's guide to beauty and health. il McCalls 104:122-5 Je '77
You & the sun & those tanning lotions. il Changing T 31:19-20 Je '77
See also
Sun baths

TANAKA, Kakuei
Reports & comment: Japan. F. Gibney. il por Atlantic 239:6-9+ Je '77 *

TANAKA, Toyoichi, and others
Phase separation of a protein-water mixture in cold cataract in the young rat lens. bibl il Science 197:1010-12 S 2 '77

TANANA, Frank
This guy Tanana's no second banana. R. Fimrite. il pors Sports Illus 47:38-43 Jl 11 '77 *

TANBERG Radiofabrikk (firm) See Electronic industries—Norway

TANCHO. See Cranes (birds)

TANCREDI; opera. See Rossini, G.

TANDEM bicycles. See Bicycles

TANDY, Charles David
Tender offers that nobody opposes. por Forbes 120:25-6 Jl 15 '77 *

TANDY, Jessica
Cards; interview. New Yorker 53:36-7 O 24 '77

TANDY Corporation
Radio Shack's rough trip. il Bus W p55 My 30 '77
Tender offers that nobody opposes. por Forbes 120:25-6 Jl 15 '77

TANENBAUM, Marc Herman
Promoting religious values in an age of violence and terror; excerpts from address. por Intellect 105:218-19 Ja '77

TANG, Lily C. See Cotzias, G. C. jt auth

TANGIER Island
How they cracked duck hunting's isle of shame; Pruitt's Paradise Inc. J. Phillips. il Outdoor Life 161:64-5+ Ja '78

TANGLEWOOD Music Festival. See Music festivals—Massachusetts

TANGO (dance)
Tango tangle. C. Fernandez Moreno. il UNESCO Courier 30:60-2 Ag '77

TANIMURA, Clinton
Trouble in Paradise. Lib J 102:1330+ Je 15 '77 *

TANK ship simulators. See Simulators

TANK ships
Carter's options for cargo preference. Bus W p22 Jl 4 '77
Dilemma called LNG. D. Pauly and others. il Newsweek 90:77 Jl 18 '77
House sinks the cargo bill; Energy Transportation Security Act of 1977. Time 110:14-15 O 31 '77
Payoff charges on cargo bill. il Time 110:53-4 Ag 15 '77
Proposal that would boost oil prices further; cargo preference legislation. il Nations Bus 65: 66-8 O '77
Ships and chauvinism; congressional squabble over oil-cargo-preference bill. A. J. Mayer. il Newsweek 90:82 O 17 '77
Small change for a billionaire; D. Ludwig's tanker sale. por Bus W p 128 Mr 21 '77
Supertankers—coming or going? J. Frye. il Sea Front 23:76-83 Mr '77
Tanker bill sinks or swims with Carter; requiring 30% of imported oil be hauled in American-flag tankers. il Bus W p26-7 My 30 '77
U.S. tankers: from duds to darlings. il Bus W p24 Ag 1 '77
What song the sirens sing. J. Y. Cousteau. Sat R 4:48+ F 19 '77
See also
Collisions at sea
Shipwrecks

Leasing and renting

Untangling what Pertamina owes—and to whom; controversy surrounding payment to B. Rappaport for rental of oil tankers. il Bus W p90 F 7 '77

Safety devices and measures

Cracking the tanker safety problem. J. Cameron. il Fortune 95:150-2 Ap '77
Demolition derby at sea. il Time 109:47-8 Ja 24 '77
Perhaps we all should pray; Golden Jason. W. McAllister. Audubon 79:143 Mr '77
Proposed tanker safety regulations need boost from public. Nat Parks & Con Mag 51:26-7 N '77
Reflections on a super-spill. C. Roosevelt. Oceans 10:64-5 Mr '77
Shipshape at last? oil tanker standards. Nat Parks & Con Mag 51:26 Je '77
Shipwrecks, pollution & the law of the sea. R. J. McManus and J. Schneider. Nat Parks & Con Mag 51:10-15 Je '77
They're murdering our oceans. R. Starnes. il Outdoor Life 159:10+ My '77
Those rusty tankers: the threat to our shores. P. J. Bernstein. Nation 224:73-7 Ja 22 '77
Training against ship disaster; tanker simulators. L. G. Feld. il Sea Front 23:280-6 S '77
U.S. Canada to insure safety of oil tanker traffic. Dept State Bull 77:307-9 S 5 '77
Valdez connection. P. L. Fradkin. maps Audubon 79:134-40 Mr '77
You say There ought to be a law. . . ? Oil tanker standards. Nat Parks & Con Mag 51: 23-5 Mr '77

TANKERS. See Tank ships

TANKERSLEY, W. H.
Role of business self-regulation in a changing world: address, October 11, 1977. Vital Speeches 44:125-8 D 1 '77

TANKS
Handle that nitrogen tank with care; semen storage tank. il Farm J 101:Dairy 10 S '77

TANNAHILL, R. Neal
America's *ostpolitik.* Commonweal 104:142-3 Mr 4 '77

TANNER, Alain
Reviews; Jonah who will be 25 in the year 2000. T. Gitlin. il Film Q 30:36-42 Spr '77 *

TANNHAUSER; opera. See Wagner, R.

TANOÉ-AKA, and others
Africa's proverbial wit and wisdom. il UNESCO Courier 30:22-5 My '77

TANSLEY, Brian W. and Boynton, R. M.
Line, not a space, represents visual distinctness of borders formed by different colors. bibl il Science 191:954-7; 197:1196 Mr 5 '76, S 16 '77

TANSY ragwort
My useful friend, the cinnabar moth. V. H. Davis. Org Gard & Farm 24:89-90 My '77
Pyrrolizidine alkaloids: their occurrence in honey from tansy ragwort (senecio jacobaea L.) M. L. Deinzer and others. bibl il Science 195: 497-9 F 4 '77

TANZANIA
Tanzania—a profile. map Dept State Bull 77:274-5 Ag 29 '77
Whither East Africa? W. A. E. Skurnik. Cur Hist 73:205-8+ D '77
See also
Illiteracy—Tanzania
National parks and reserves—Tanzania
Visitors, Foreign—Tanzania

Politics and government

Nyerere: how much war? interview. ed by L. Griggs. J. Nyerere. por Time 109:25 Mr 14 '77

Religious institutions and affairs

See also
Religious conferences—Tanzania

TANZANIAN folk literature. See Folk literature, Tanzanian

TANZER, Herbert, and Lyons, Nick
How to keep your pet from running your life; excerpt from Your pet isn't sick (he just wants you to think so) Redbook 149:254 My '77

TAORMINA, Italy
Taormina. A. J. Lazarus. il Travel 148:46-9 Ag '77

TAOS, N. Mex.

Art

See Art—New Mexico

TAOS Society of Artists
Taos art colony; special issue; with editorial comments. M. C. Nelson. Am Artist 42:6+, 27-63+ Ja '78

TAPE, Cassette. See Tape, Magnetic

TAPE, Magnetic
Cassette tapes for higher hi-fi. J. Free. il Pop Sci 210:50+ Je '77
Matching tapes to recorders. L. Feldman. il Pop Electr 12:63-6 S '77
Mysterious West. R. Hodges. il Pop Electr 12:20+ D '77
Selecting the best cassette tape for your recording needs. C. Stark. il Pop Electr 12:47-51 N '77
Those tiny new cassette systems—they're not all alike. C. Morgan. il Pop Mech 147:186+ Mr '77

Testing

What test reports don't tell you about blank cassettes. R. Angus. il Hi Fi 27:58-63 F '77

TAPE cartridges, cassettes, etc.
Elcaset has arrived. J. Hirsch. il Pop Electr 12:32 O '77
New shape in cassettes; Elcaset. A. J. Zuckerman. il Mech Illus 73:66+ F '77
Will the Elcaset make it? L. Zide. il Hi Fi 27:64-6 F '77

Packaging

Problem of packaging; size and shape of multi-cassette tape. M. Cooper. il Am Rec G 40:8-9+ O '77

TAPE decks. See Tape recorders and recording

TAPE recorders and recording
Automatic program search; new system for cassette decks. K. Savon. il Radio-Electr 48:52-3 Mr '77
Best buy cassette recorder; Realistic SCT-11. C. Graham. Am Rec G 40:43-4 Jl '77
Buyer's guide to cassette, elcaset, and open-reel equipment. il Hi Fi 27:52-60 Ag '77
Consumer's guide to: record players & tape recorders. Mech Illus 73:34 D '77
Creative recording with 4-channel tape recorders. L. Feldman. il Pop Electr 11:73-6 Je '77
Digits on the ivories; Pianocorder. Hi Fi 27:56 S '77
Increase dynamic range for better hi-fi. L. Feldman. il Radio-Electr 48:46-8 Ap '77
Incredible Pearlcorder SD adds sound to your slides and does plenty more. il Mod Phot 41:52 O '77
New hi-fi sound of cassette decks. J. Free. il Pop Sci 211:99-101+ Ag '77
Stalking the tape recorder; taping an interview. A. Spikol. Writers Digest 57:14+ Ag '77
Stereo cassette decks. il Consumer Rep 42:226-9 D '77
Stereo, hi-fi. Consumers Res Mag 60:183-93 O '77
Take your pick of tape decks. il Changing T 31:18-20 Jl '77
Tape it! A buying guide to those handy cassette recorders. R. F. McGillick. il Good H 184:182+ Ap '77
Tape recorder headroom explained. J. D. Hirsch. Pop Electr 11:23-4 F '77
Tape topics. R. Hodges. il Pop Electr 12:14+ Ag '77
Tape your interviews for radio. M. S. Bucki. Writers Digest 57:23-5 F '77
Taped talk: storing tomorrow's source materials. R. Hoopes. il Hi Fi 27:61-5 Ag '77
Taping off the air. H. Fantel. il Esquire 88:119-20+ Ag '77
See also
Ampex Corporation
Automobiles—Tape equipment
Campers, Truck—Tape equipment
Motion picture projection—Sound accompaniment
Phonograph records—Recording
Video recorders and recording

Equipment

Build an audio compander. J. Roberts. il Pop Electr 12:43-6 N '77
New equipment reports:
Russound's Rx for Gordian knot systems; SP-1. il Hi Fi 28:62 Ja '78

Maintenance and repair

Tape recorder hygiene. C. Stark. il Pop Electr 12:56-7 Jl '77

Testing

Julian Hirsch audio reports:
Akai model GX-27OD-SS four-channel tape recorder. J. Hirsch. Pop Electr 12:32+ S '77
Optonica model RT-3535 stereo cassette deck. J. Hirsch. il Pop Electr 13:29-31 Ja '78
Pioneer model CT-F8282 cassette deck. J. Hirsch il Pop Electr 11:24-6 F '77
Pioneer model RT-707 bidirectional tape deck. J. Hirsch. il Pop Electr 12:30-2 D '77
Sony Model El-5 Elcaset tape deck. J. Hirsch. il Pop Electr 12:34-5 O '77
Teac model PC-10 cassette recorder. J. Hirsch. il Pop Electr 11:36+ My '77
Mini tape recorders: small and super-small. il Consumer Rep 42:462-5 Ag '77
New equipment reports:
Akai's deck is stacked—in your favor. il Hi Fi 27:33+ F '77
At last: a random-access cassette deck—by Optonica. il Hi Fi 27:41-3 Ag '77
Fascinating budget cassette deck from Aiwa. il Hi Fi 27:50-2 Ap '77
Hitachi D-800: three heads in two, plus animation. il Hi Fi 27:45-6 Ag '77
Ultra-Tandberg cassette deck. il Hi Fi 27:39-40 Ag '77
Radio-electronics tests:
Bigston BSD-300 cassette deck. il Radio-Electr 48:69+ F '77
Dual C-939 cassette deck. L. Feldman. il Radio-Electr 49:58-9 Ja '78
Sony Elecaset EL-5 tape deck. L. Feldman. il Radio-Electr 48:57-9 Je '77
Step by step through our tape recorder tests. E. J. Foster. il Hi Fi 27:48-51 Ag '77

TAPE recorders and recording, Portable
Cassette recorder. il Consumers Res Mag 60:18-22 Ag '77
Choosing portable & mobile tape recorders. J. R. Horstman. il Pop Electr 12:43-5 Ag '77
New equipment reports:
Teac's entry in the road/home deck sweepstakes. il Hi Fi 27:29-31 F '77
New sound of shirt-pocket tape recorders. R. Gorman. il Pop Sci 211:8+ O '77
Taped talk: storing tomorrow's source materials. R. Hoopes. il Hi Fi 27:61-5 Ag '77

TAPE recordings
Tape deck. R. D. Darrell. See issues of High fidelity and Musical America
Tape your interviews for radio. M. S. Bucki. Writers Digest 57:23-5 F '77
See also
Automobiles—Tape equipment
Booksellers and bookselling—Tape recordings
Oral history
Talking books
Watergate tapes

Care

Tape recorder hygiene. C. Stark. il Pop Electr 12:56-7 Jl '77

Collectors and collecting

Historical tape recordings:
Tribute to collectors. L. Dumont. Hobbies 82:58-9+ My '77

History

Historical tape recordings. L. Dumont. See issues of Hobbies

Piano music

Unknown recordings of Vladimir Horowitz; discography of unreleased recordings; with editorial comment by L. Marcus. C. Alder. pors Hi Fi 28:69-74 Ja '78

TAPESTRY
Photorealism in a medieval medium. A. Knight. il por Horizon 20:58-9 D '77
Tapestry weaving on the frame loom; excerpt from Weaving: design and expression. N. Belfer. il Sch Arts 77:48-53 O '77

Exhibitions

Lausanne tapestry biennial; International Biennial of Tapestry; group discussion. il Craft Horiz 37:22-7+ O '77

TAPIES, Antoni
Spain to U.S: art of Tàpies. R. B. Russell. Vogue 167:172+ My '77 *

TAPOGNA, Paul
Roots spin-off; school project. Todays Educ 66:48 S '77

TAPPETT, Tom
Car care. See issues of Mechanix illustrated

TAPPLY, Horace G.
Taps tips. See issues of Field & stream

TAPPLY, Richard M.
High adventure: confronting the essentials. il Parks & Rec 12:26-9+ Je '77

TAPPONNIER, Paul. See Molnar, P. jt auth

TAR sands. See Oil sands

TARBELL, Ida Minerva
How they kept the trust. R. Stinson. Nation 225:561-4 N 26 '77 *

TARBOX, Lamont. See Wellstone, P. D. jt auth

TARGET drone airplanes. See Airplanes, Drone

TARGET location
USAF picks Lockheed team to develop targeting system; precision location strike system. B. M. Elson. Aviation W 107:23-4 Jl 11 '77

TARGET practice
Targets. See alternate issues of Outdoor life to May 1977
Ultimate test for your gun; bench-rest. G. Nonte. il por Pop Mech 148:152+ N '77

TARGET ranges. See Bombing and gunnery ranges

TARGET recognition attack multisensors. See Airplanes, Military—Electronic equipment

TARGET tracking
Mental set alters visibility of moving targets. R. Sekuler and K. Ball. bibl il Science 198:60-2 O 7 '77
Perception of moving targets. R. Sekuler and E. Levinson. il Sci Am 236:60-4+ Ja '77

TARGETS
Running-boar target for air-gun practice. P. Wahl. il Pop Sci 211:76 Ag '77
ZZ; Pro-Pigeon ZZ shotgun target. B. Brister. il Field & S 82:102-5 Ag '77

TARIFF
See also
General Agreement on Tariffs and Trade

Europe, Western

See also
European Economic Community

Israel

Cost of losing a tariff shelter. il Bus W p42-3 Jl 11 '77

TARIFF—*Continued*

Japan

Japan bows slightly to its trade critics. Bus W p32 O 31 '77

United States

Tariff hammer; effect on Latin America. Nation 225:675-6 D 24 '77
World trade: a round the protectionists won; increased duty liability on Japanese electronic products. Bus W p30 Ap 25 '77
Yes and no on shoes. il Time 109:61-2 Ap 11 '77
See also
United States—International Trade Commission

TARKANIAN, Jerry
Shark gets a ruling with bite. R. Telander. il por Sports Illus 47:26-7 O 10 '77 *

TARKINGTON, Booth
Perils of progress; story. Sat Eve Post 249:38-9 N '77

TARPLEY rifles. See Rifles

TARPON fishing
Grand fish. P. Smith. il Outdoor Life 160:64-5 Jl '77
Grand fish at night: the ultimate action; at the mouth of the Parismina River, Costa Rica. S. Apte. il Outdoor Life 160:66-7+ Jl '77
Magnificent tarpon; fishing off Punta Gorda Isles. C. R. Meyer. il Field & S 81:26-7+ Ap '77

TARRAGON
French tarragon: hard-to-find herb. K. McReynolds. il Org Gard & Farm 24:88-9 N '77

TARRANT, Bill
Gun dogs. See issues of Field & stream
Hunting the Soviet Union. il por Field & S 81:42-4+ Ap '77
Snow fever. il Field & S 82:39+ O '77

TARSHIS, Barry
Platform tennis, anyone? il House & Gard 149:42+ F '77

TARSHIS, Jerome
Bruce Conner is not Bruce Conner. il por Art N 76:80-2+ Ja '77
Far west's 20th-century art in East Coast review. il Smithsonian 8:56-61 My '77

TARTARIC acid
Left-handed and right-handed molecules: Louis Pasteur's resolution of racemic acid. G. B. Kauffman. bibl il por Chemistry 50:14-18 Ap '77

TARTS
Cherry plums in a tart—the pitting is easy. il Sunset 159:124 Jl '77
Hostess with the mostest; apricot cream tart. il por Seventeen 36:208-9 Ap '77
Pastry crisscrosses the top of this Guadeloupe tart. il Sunset 158:192 Je '77
Shimmering tart of purple plums. il Sunset 159:128 S '77
Tarts and turnovers. il Bet Hom & Gard 55:161-2 S '77

TARTUFFE; drama. See Molière, J. B. P.

TARVER, Stanley
Black rivers; poem. Negro Hist Bull 40:75[illegible] S '77

TASCHDJIAN, Claire L.
Story behind the book: The Peking Man is missing. B. A. Bannon. il por Pub W 212:70 O 3 '77 *

TASHIAN, Richard E. See Kendall, A. G. jt auth

TASMANIA

Bridges

See Bridges—Australia

Description and travel

Tasmania. J. H. Silverman. il Travel 147:42-7 Mr '77

TASTE
Annals of medicine; A. Coniglio's case of idiopathic hypogeusia. B. Roueché. New Yorker 53:97-8+ S 12 '77
Is something wrong with your sense of taste or smell? M. P. Scott. Bet Hom & Gard 55:8 My '77

TASTE (aesthetics) See Aesthetics

TATE, James
Comment. W. Logan. Poetry 130:221-3 Jl '77 *

TATE, Randy
Big-leaguer. J. Lelyveld. por N Y Times Mag p63 Ag 7 '77 *

TATE Gallery, London
Helping Britain buy British; acquisition of paintings by G. Stubbs. il Time 111:71 Ja 2 '78

TATIANA, Princess Moritz von Hessen
Tatiana von Hessen's summer solace. il por Vogue 167:154-7 Ag '77 *

TATTOOING
Cavorting creatures on the tattooed man of Pazyryk. il UNESCO Courier 29:34-5 D '76
Skin games; International Tattoo Artists Association convention. S. C. Cowley. il Newsweek 89:78-9 F '77

TATUM, George B.
Great houses from the golden age of Annapolis. bibl il Antiques 111:174-85 Ja '77

TAUBER, Catherine A. and others
Two genes control seasonal isolation in sibling species. bibl il Science 197:592-3 Ag 5 '77
—and Tauber, M. J.
Sympatric speciation based on allelic changes at three loci: evidence from natural populations in two habitats. bibl il Science 197:1298-9 S 23 '77

TAUBER, Maurice J. See Tauber, C. A. jt auth

TAUBMAN, A. Alfred
Bidding race for Irvine Ranch. por Bus W p29 My 2 '77 *

TAUBMAN-Allen-Irvine, Inc-Irvine Company merger. See Real estate business—Acquisitions and mergers

TAURUS, pseud
With Mrs Carter in Latin America. New Repub 176:13-14 Je 18 '77

TAVERNS. See Bars and barrooms

TAVOULAREAS, William Peter
Energy debacle. L. H. Lapham. Harpers 255:58-61+ Ag '77; Discussion. 255:6+ O '77 *

TAVRIS, Carol
Money: the subject harder to talk about than sex. Ms 6:63-7 N '77
Sexual lives of women over 60. Ms 6:62-5 Jl '77
—and Sadd, Susan
Great news about men and sex; excerpt from The Redbook report on female sexuality. il Redbook 149:124-5+ O '77

TAWNEY, Richard Henry
Reconsideration. J. Beatty. por New Repub 177:35-8 D 17 '77 *

TAWNEY, Robin
Is time running out for Taylor-Hilgard? il map Liv Wildn 40:34-41 Ja '77

TAX auditing
Auditors. D. K. Mano. Nat R 29:735-6 Je 24 '77
How to fight the I.R.S.—and win. J. Carper. il Am Home 80:16 My '77
If the IRS calls you in for a tax audit—il U.S. News 82:96-8 Ap 11 '77
Is the Internal Revenue Service unfair to artists? pro and con discussion. Am Artist 41:8-9 Mr '77
What are your rights with the IRS? M. Gunther. Bet Hom & Gard 55:78+ F '77

TAX collection
See also
Tax returns

TAX consultants
Helpers. T. Nicholson. Newsweek 89:72-3 Mr 21 '77
How to beat taxes. Forbes 119:120 Mr 15 '77
Pick a tax pro now for a happier '78. W. Flanagan. Vogue 167:238 D '77
You need a pro to figure your taxes. L. Lane. Farm J 101:17 mid-F '77

TAX courts
See also
United States—Tax Court

TAX credits
Add an employee—get tax credit. il Suc Farm 75:C32 D '77
Energy crisis; taxes and rebates; insulation tax credit. T. J. Reese. America 137:418-20 D 10 '77
How to get in on those energy benefits. F. Casey. il Mech Illus 73:50+ O '77
How to make our schools better; Tuition Tax Credit Act. G. Will. Newsweek 90:104 O 3 '77
New child-care tax credit: what will it do for you? S. Fingerhood. Ms 5:101-4 Ap '77
School tax credits? D. Holt and others. il Newsweek 90:76 D 26 '77
Share your child-care expenses with Uncle Sam. il Changing T 31:35-6 Je '77
Something for no one; A Ullman's jobs tax credit bill. il por Time 109:44+ Mr 7 '77
Subsidizing unemployment; employment tax credit. Nat R 29:654-5 Je 10 '77
Tax credits for tuition payments; views of D. P. Moynihan. America 136:474 My 28 '77
Tax gimmickry at its finest; tax credit proposals in jobs bill. M. Friedman. Newsweek 89:90 Ap 11 '77
Time to cut strings; Moynihan-Packwood bill for educational tax credits. America 137:470 D 31 '77
What the new estate and gift tax credits are all about. H. Guither. Suc Farm 75:47 N '77
See also
Investment tax credit

TAX deductions. See Income tax—Deductions

TAX Equity for Americans Abroad (organization) See Lobbyists and lobbying

TAX estimates. See Income tax—Estimates

TAX exemption. See Taxation, Exemption from

TAX forms
Form of reform. il Newsweek 90:68 O 31 '77
Why a simple tax form is causing trouble. U.S. News 82:87 F 21 '77

TAX laws and legislation (United States) See Taxation—United States

TAX planning
Born again: tax shelters '77. A. Hershman. il Duns R 109:55-7+ Ap '77
Cow-leasing generates cash to help you grow. E. Ainsworth. il Farm J 101:Dairy 1-2+ Ja '77

TAX planning—*Continued*
Gimme shelter. H. Seneker. il Forbes 120:27-9 Jl 15 '77
Hanging bookshelves on tax brackets. A. Tobias. Esquire 88:42+ Jl '77
How Congress landed on tax-loss farming. R. C. Black. il Farm J 101:18-19 F '77
How to make a tax-tight deferred sales contract; grain contracts. A. Brennecke. Suc Farm 75:K2 S '77
How to save on '77 taxes. U.S. News 83:99-102 O 24 '77
In the shade of the FDIC: the tax-shelter farmers. R. B. Taylor. Nation 224:590-4 My 14 '77
Key tax dates for '78. il U.S. News 84:61 Ja 9 '78
Long-range tax planning softens blow of net operating loss. il Suc Farm 75:8 N '77
Now aren't you glad you didn't go into a tax shelter? A. Tobias. il Esquire 89:12+ Ja '78
Rich guy's loophole; real estate tax shelter. R. L. Nessen. New Repub 177:9-12 D 3 '77
Seeking shelter of a Detroit bridge; Ambassador Bridge, between Detroit and Windsor, Ont. il Bus W p 24-5 N 7 '77
Stodgy old annuities take on a fresh allure. il U.S. News 83:91-2 O 10 '77
Surprising survival of tax shelters. il Bus W p 136+ D 26 '77
Tax-saving investments your family can make; tax shelters. M. Daly. il Bet Hom & Gard 55:193-4+ O '77
Taxes. J. Block. See issues of Vogue
Under way: crackdown on tax shelters. U.S. News 83:106-7 N 21 '77
Use tax planning when you support both parents. Suc Farm 75:K4 S '77
Ways to start saving on your '77 taxes. U.S. News 82:74-6 Je 20 '77
Year-end tactics that save taxes. il Changing T 31:15-17 N '77
Year-end tax planning: changes you should know about. P. Gross. House & Gard 149: 22-3+ N '77
See also
Estate planning

TAX records
It may pay to keep a diary on your vacation; business expenses. Farm J 101:B1 Ag '77
Keep tax records—here's why and how long. Farm J 101:29 My '77
What to keep for taxes. J. Block. Mech Illus 73:138 My '77

TAX reform (United States) See Income tax—United States; Taxation—United States

TAX returns
How to avoid the pitfalls in this year's tax return. U.S. News 82:80 Mr 7 '77
Need help with your tax return? Changing T 31:7-10 F '77
Taxes. M. Daly. Bet Hom & Gard 55:16+ F '77
When IRS gets your tax return—. il U.S. News 82:78-80 Mr 28 '77

Auditing

See Tax auditing

TAX shelters. See Tax planning

TAXATION
Where taxes are heaviest around world. il U.S. News 82:87 Ja 24 '77
See also
Americans in foreign countries—Taxation
Assessment
Automobiles—Taxation
Cigarettes—Taxation
Corporations—Taxation
Depreciation—Taxation
Income tax
Inheritance tax
Real property tax

International aspects

If you think taxes in U.S. are high—. il U.S. News 83:73 D 19 '77

California

From bad to worse in California; proposed bill exempting state museums from taxation of purchased or donated works of art. A. Elsen. por Art N 76:53 O '77

Germany, West

Multinationals rush to beat new taxes. il Bus W p52 O 10 '77

Great Britain

See also
Income tax—Great Britain

Nevada

Taxman cometh. S. T. Atlas and G. C. Lubenow. Newsweek 90:64+ Jl 11 '77

New Hampshire

Wrong road taken? il Forbes 119:122+ Ap 15 '77

New Mexico

Tax showdown on yellowcake road; New Mexico bill to tax coal and uranium mining industries. Bus W p33+ Mr 14 '77

New York (state)

How taxes crushed a suburban family; Ossining, N.Y. property tax. il Bus W p21-2 Mr 28 '77
We're not fools! cigarette smuggling and New York's sales tax. Forbes 119:118 Je 15 '77

Puerto Rico

Catch 936. il Forbes 120:96 N 1 '77

Scandinavia

Welfare state at the crossroads. J. Logue. Progressive 41:34-7 S '77

United States

Appeals for a different energy approach. il Nations Bus 65:18-19 S '77
By any other name; Senate consideration of energy legislation. A. J. Mayer and W. J. Cook. Newsweek 90:87-8 S 19 '77
Cake without bakers. Nat R 29:135 F 4 '77
Carter gives business a bigger tax break. il Bus W p34-5 F 7 '77
Carter's tax plan; special report. il Bus W p46-9+ Ag 29 '77
If Carter really wants a simple tax plan. . . il U.S. News 82:72-3 Ja 31 '77
Inflation is now too serious a matter to leave to the economists. D. Warsh and L. Minard; discussion. il Forbes 119:44-6 Ja 15 '77
Kemp & Co; proposals for tax cuts. M. S. Evans. Nat R 29:670 Je 10 '77
Needed—tax reform that will create jobs. J. Kemp. Read Digest 110:103-7 Ap '77
New tax laws: how they affect you. M. Daly. Bet Hom & Gard 55:8+ F '77
Stripping the stimulus; Tax Reduction Act of 1977. Time 109:64 My 16 '77
Taking aim at a disgrace. il Time 110:62-3 Jl 4 '77
Tax impact of new energy plan—who's helped, who's hurt. il U.S. News 82:73-4 My 2 '77
Tax law: more changes are due. map Nations Bus 65:18-20 Ja '77
Tax practitioners act of 1976. I. Ross. il Fortune 95:103-6+ Ap '77
Tax reduction is the best spur to job creation; interview. P. W. McCracken. por U.S. News 82:56-7 F 21 '77
Tax shenanigans. M. Friedman. Newsweek 90:55 D 19 '77
Throwing a bone; payroll-tax credit. Nat R 29: 195 F 18 '77
What it says—and what it means. il Newsweek 89:19 My 2 '77
What you need to know about the latest tax changes—. il U.S. News 82:81-2 My 16 '77
Where Carter is going wrong; interview. M. Friedman. il pors U.S. News 82:20-2 Mr 7 '77
See also
Forests and forestry—Taxation
Gasoline—Taxation
Income tax—United States
Inheritance tax
Intergovernmental tax relations
Local taxation
Social security taxes
Tariff—United States
Taxation, Exemption from
Taxation, State
Taxpayers associations
United States—Internal Revenue Service
United States—Tax Court
United States—Treasury, Department of the

TAXATION, Double
Coming tax reform: read the fine print. il Forbes 120:21-3 Ag 1 '77
Relief from double taxation of dividend income. D. T. Smith; discussion. Harvard Bus R 55:168+ Mr; 164+ My '77

TAXATION, Exemption from
Church schools and Form 990. America 136:122 F 12 '77
Last rights; parsonages not tax-exempt. Chr Today 21:60-1 My 6 '77
Small-town tax rebellion; ordination of Hardenburgh, N.Y. residents. D. Jacobs. McCalls 104: 69 F '77

TAXATION, Municipal. See Local taxation

TAXATION, State
Cities where taxes are highest—and lowest. il U.S. News 82:66 Je 6 '77
How new state taxes will bite business. il Bus W p30 Jl 18 '77
State, local taxes still heading up. il U.S. News 83:82 N 14 '77
Taxing the multistate company. il Bus W p36+ Ap 11 '77
See also
Income tax, State

TAXATION for education. See Education—Finance

TAXATION of bonds, securities, etc.
Finance officers fight taxable bonds. Am City & County 92:25 Jl '77
Why flower bonds wilted so much so fast. il Bus W p 148+ Mr 21 '77

TAXATION of works of art
Art is long, tax suits short; controversy surrounding Italian claims to a Greek statue in the J. Paul Getty Museum. il Time 110:22 D 12 '77
Artists' tax bills. B. Chamberlain. Am Artist 42:18+ Ja '78
From bad to worse in California; proposed bill exempting state museums. A. Elsen. il por Art N 76:53 O '77
Hirshhorn waltz. Vasari. Art N 76:27-8 Ja '77
Should the purchase of art be tax deductible? pro and con discussion. T. M. Rees; T. Crawford; reply. R. Blumberg. Am Artist 41:5+ Mr '77

TAXICAB drivers
Taxi jokes. New Yorker 53:35-6 O 3 '77

Anecdotes, facetiae, satire, etc.

Taxi rider. V. Canby. il N Y Times Mag p96-7 Ap 3 '77

TAXICABS
Buying back Belfast? IRA business activities. M. Dammerman. il Forbes 119:25-7 Mr 15 '77

Fares

Janie and the Mayor; M. Bilandic's role in cab fare hike in Chicago. D. A. Williams and F. Maier. il pors Newsweek 90:40 D 5 '77

TAXIDERMY
Teen taxidermist; C. Nason. M. Allen. il por Seventeen 36:19+ Ag '77

TAXONOMY. See Zoology—Classification

TAXPAYERS associations
Nation's taxpayers are getting angry—and getting organized. il U.S. News 82:69-70 Ap 25 '77

TAYLOR, Alice, and others
Ivory Coast: political stability and economic growth. bibl il maps Focus 27:1-15 Ja; 1-14 My '77

TAYLOR, Angela
Great-looking summer feet. il N Y Times Mag p92-6 Ap 17 '77
New bloom on you. il N Y Times Mag p84+ Ap 3 '77
Safe glow. N Y Times Mag p74 F 6 '77

TAYLOR, Buck
Quality hunting you can afford. il Outdoor Life 159:68-9+ My '77

TAYLOR, Calvin W.
Buildings may be hazardous to your health. Intellect 106:101-2 S '77

TAYLOR, Charles
Canning renaissance. il Sat Eve Post 249:26-9 O '77

TAYLOR, Cindy
Bowling 'em over; ed by B. Weber. il por Sr Schol 110:29 N 3 '77

TAYLOR, Edmond
Merchants of death revisited. il Horizon 19:82-7 Ja '77

TAYLOR, Edwin F.
Looking-glass world of testing. il Todays Educ 66:39-42+ Mr '77

TAYLOR, Eleanor Ross
Va. Sun. A.M. Dec. '73; poem. New Yorker 53:89 Jl 18 '77

TAYLOR, Elizabeth, 1912-
Blackwell's Children's Bookshop. il Horn Bk 53:206-8 Ap '77

TAYLOR, Elizabeth, 1932-
Elizabeth Taylor talks about her new love, her new life. .; interview, ed by D. Wigg. il pors Good H 184:100-3+ F '77

about

Elizabeth Taylor; new makeup look. il pors Good H 185:118-20 O '77 •
Elizabeth Taylor's surprising new life. N. Thimmesch. pors McCalls 104:16+ Jl '77 •
Farmer's wife. S. McElwaine. il pors Ladies Home J 94:70-1+ Ag '77 •
Look at the man Liz found. B. N. MacDougal. il pors Sat Eve Post 249:62-3+ N '77 •
National Velveeta. J. A. Latham. pors Esquire 88:101-4+ N '77 •

TAYLOR, G. Aiken
Is God as good as His word? Chr Today 21:22-5 F 4 '77

TAYLOR, Gary Addison
Public is not helpless. A. S. Rule. Ladies Home J 94:70 Mr '77 •

TAYLOR, Gerald R.
Cell biology experiments conducted in space. bibl BioScience 27:102-8 F '77

TAYLOR, James
No more kinks; JT. S. Sutherland. por Hi Fi 27:136 S '77 •

TAYLOR, James A.
Progeny of programmers: evangelical religion and the television age. il Chr Cent 94:379-82 Ap 20 '77

TAYLOR, James B. 1921-
In this corner . . . Fat Albert. por Forbes 120:106 D 1 '77 •

TAYLOR, James S.
Improve your classroom testing skills. Clearing H 50:381-5 My '77

TAYLOR, Jean. See Taylor, R. jt auth

TAYLOR, Joan
(ed) Book reviews. See issues of Conservationist
Winter smells, winter dreams. il Conservationist 32:48 N '77

—and Jenkins, Russell
Roadside beauty. il Conservationist 32:14-21 Jl '77

TAYLOR, Karen
If only luck will be a lady. D. S. Looney. il pors Sports Illus 46:40-1+ Je 13 '77 •

TAYLOR, Leighton R.
Megamouth: a new family of shark. il Oceans 10:46-7 N '77

—and Naftel, Gary
How to avoid shark attack (if you happen to be a Hawaiian monk seal) il Oceans 10:21-3 N '77

TAYLOR, Leon
(ed) See Levin, M. Martin Levin: the good humor man

TAYLOR, Les
Boxwood; poem. Poetry 131:142-3 D '77

TAYLOR, Leslie Ann
King is not dead—dust off the throne! il pors Motor T 29:98-9 S '77

TAYLOR, Malcolm
Camera collector. J. Schneider. il Mod Phot 41:20+ D '77 •

TAYLOR, Mark
Novels or war novels? Commonweal 104:566-71 S 2 '77

TAYLOR, Maxwell Davenport
Clash of views over Canal security. pors U.S. News 83:27 O 24 '77

about

Kennedy's cold war. T. Szulc. New Repub 177:19-21 D 24 '77 •

TAYLOR, Michael A.
Commercial vs. investment bankers. il Harvard Bus R 55:132-44 S '77

TAYLOR, Mickey
If only luck will be a lady. D. S. Looney. il pors Sports Illus 46:40-1+ Je 13 '77 •

TAYLOR, Mildred D.
Newbery Award acceptance; address, June 18, 1977. Horn Bk 53:401-9 Ag '77

about

Mildred D. Taylor. P. J. Fogelman. por Horn Bk 53:410-14 Ag '77 •

TAYLOR, Paul
Modern dance, Taylor-made. T. Tobias. il Horizon 21:50-5 Ja '78 •

TAYLOR, Paul, Dance Company. See Paul Taylor Dance Company

TAYLOR, Peter
In the Miro District; story. New Yorker 52:34-42+ F 7 '77

TAYLOR, Richard
Many-sided splendors. il House & Gard 149:58+ My '77

—and Taylor, Jean
Auto suggestions. il pors House & Gard 149:57-8+ S; 56+ N; 72+ D '77
Gas-saving baby cars. il pors House & Gard 149:104+ O '77

TAYLOR, Rick
From official Coast Guard files: accident report. Motor B & S 140:60-3 O '77

TAYLOR, Ronald B.
Burro or the bighorn? il Nat Parks & Con Mag 51:10-14 S '77
In the shade of the FDIC. Nation 224:590-4 My 14 '77

TAYLOR, Ross
What to do about basic skills in math. Todays Educ 66:32-3 Mr '77

TAYLOR, Stuart
Indians on the lawpath. il New Repub 176:16-21 Ap 30 '77

TAYLOR, Susan
Generation gap is wider than it needs to be. por Seventeen 96:78 My '77

TAYLOR, Theodore Brewster
Plutonium: how safe? interview, ed by D. Colligan. por Sci Digest 81:60-4 Mr '77
—See Feiveson, H. A. jt auth

TAYLOR, Theodore Langhans
Scrappy's miracle; story. Ladies Home J 94:44 My '77

TAYLOR, Verta
Good news about disaster. bibl il por Psychol Today 11:93-4+ O '77

TAYLOR-Hilgard Wilderness Study Area (proposed) See Wilderness areas—Montana

TAYLOR Wine Company. See Wine industry

TAZAKI, Etsuko
Etsuko Tazaki, piano; New York recital. por Hi Fi 27:MA26 My '77 •

TCHAIKOVSKY, Peter Ilyitch
BSO: Eugene Onegin (Ozawa); concert version at Carnegie Hall. Hi Fi 27:MA31 F '77 •
Eugene Onegin. Review
New Repub 177:22-3 N 26 '77 •

TCHAIKOVSKY, Peter Ilyitch—*Continued*
Mazeppa; Melodiya recording. Am Rec G 40:56 O '77 *
Six symphonies and Manfred conducted by M. Rostropovich. J. R. Oestreich. pors Am Rec G 41:14-16 D '77 *
Symphony no. 6 in B minor, Op. 74 Pathetique, Symphony no. 1 in G minor Op. 13 Winter Dreams; recordings. J. Waxman. il Am Rec G 40:42-4 F '77 *

TCHERKASSKY, Marianna
Closeup: Marianna Tcherkassky; interview, ed by H. Brubach. il pors Mademoiselle 83:56+ N '77

TEA (beverage)
Beware of coffee, tea, and cola beverages if you value good health. H. L. Abrams, Jr. Consumers Res Mag 60:21-2+ My '77
Herb tea gardening. il Sunset 158:262 Ap '77
Herb teas for the whole family. M. Wilbur. il Org Gard & Farm 24:110+ N '77
Herb teas: how safe? Consumers Res Mag 60:35-6 Mr '77
Iced tea into summer coolers. il Sunset 159:120 Ag '77
Package a gift of unusual teas. il Sunset 159:123 D '77
Producing your own homegrown teas. N. Bubel. il Org Gard & Farm 24:104-5+ N '77
Tea. il Consumer Rep 42:502-4 S '77
Tea anyone? J. L. Lippert. Good H 185: 50 O '77
Tea teasers. H. McNulty. il House & Gard 149:121+ F '77
Teapot tempest; suggesting wolfsbane and mistletoe tea as coffee substitutes. il Newsweek 89:55+ F 21 '77
That automatic pot brews tea, too. R. Field. Sci Digest 81:86-7 My '77
What your mother never told you about tea. G. Steves. il Am Home 80:60 F '77
See also
Caffeine

TEA carts. See Serving carts

TEACHER evaluation. See Teachers—Rating

TEACHER opinion
Teacher opinion poll. See issues of Today's education

TEACHER participation in school administration. See School management and organization—Teacher participation

TEACHER-pupil relations. See Teachers and students

TEACHER travel
See also
Travel study courses

TEACHERS
Leadership: the teacher's option. R. Drake. bibl Clearing H 50:291-3 Mr '77
Lifeboat ethics and the first-year teacher. M. H. Brown and A. L. Willems. il Clearing H 51:73-5 O '77
Question teachers ask. K. T. Henson. Clearing H 50:193-5 Ja '77
Reading supervisors—teachers have needs. J. Sanacore. bibl Clearing H 51:17-21 S '77
Relationship between work experience and occupational aspiration and attrition from teaching. J. W. Gosnell. bibl il Clearing H 51:176-9 D '77
Toward a new professionalism; the master teacher. L. R. Adler Clearing H 50:248-50 F '77
Why teachers are under fire; Parents and teachers speak out. P. Sanoff. il U.S. News 83:50-4+ D 12 '77
See also
Academic freedom
Art teachers
Collective bargaining—Teachers
College teachers
Dance teachers
English teachers
Law teachers
National Education Association
School and the home
School management and organization—Teacher participation
Teachers unions

Anecdotes, facetiae, satire, etc.

Pedagogical malpractice. M. E. Marty. Chr Cent 94:263 Mr 16 '77

Appointment

See Teachers—Selection and appointment

Awards, prizes, etc.

America's Teacher of the Year; M. Lee. M. S. Miller. por Ladies Home J 94:40+ Ap '77

Certification

History

Certification in the basics one hundred years ago. J. W. Velz. il Engl J 66:32-8 O '77

Civil rights

Teacher and the law. See issues of Today's education
Teacher rights in a changing society. R. G. Andree. Clearing H 50:398-401 My '77

Dismissal

What are teacher rights? Todays Educ 66:16-17 Ja '77

Education

Effectiveness of teacher education. J. A. Mackey and others. Educ Digest 43:32-5 N '77
IEP and personnel preparation. Am Educ 13:6-8 O '77
In North Carolina, its working; teacher education centers sponsored by Appalachian State University and local schools. K. D. Jenkins. il Clearing H 50:268-71 F '77
Preparing for bilingual education. L. J. Glickman. il Am Educ 13:31-2 Ag '77
Teacher education: a new set of goals. S. McCune and others. Am Educ 13:24-5 Je '77
See also
Student teachers
Student teaching

Education in service

Action learning: a model for in-service teacher education. L. C. Falkenstein. Clearing H 50:188-91 Ja '77
Concerns of jr. high school and middle school teachers: a framework for in-service programs. B. Underwood and R. Underwood. Clearing H 51:36-7 S '77
From the mountains to the classrooms; Live, Learn, and Teach program at the University of New Hampshire. S. Eder and J. Williamson. il Am Educ 13:17-22 N '77
Helping teachers teach the LD student. B. Jones. Todays Educ 66:46-8 N '77
Some requirements for successful in-service education. J. C. King and others. Educ Digest 43:14-16 S '77
Staff development: bright hope or empty promise. E. A. Dillon. Educ Digest 42:12-15 Ap '77
Using protocols in instructional supervision. J. G. Thornell. Clearing H 51:65-6 O '77

Legal status, laws, etc.

Teacher and the law. See issues of Today's education
Teacher rights in a changing society. R. G. Andree. Clearing H 50:398-401 My '77
Teachers' private lives and legal rights. T. J. Flygare. Educ Digest 42:26-8 F '77

Political activities

Aftermath of a witch hunt: New York's subversive teachers; reinstatement of teachers dismissed in 1950's. I. Adler and B. M. Zelman. Nation 224:434-6 Ap 9 '77
Victory for teacher power; 1976 election. J. Ryor. Todays Educ 66:5 Ja '77
See also
College teachers—Political activities

Psychology

Battered teacher. A. M. Bloch. Todays Educ 66:58-9+ Mr '77
Stress and the classroom teacher. R. Sylwester. Educ Digest 42:14-17 My '77
Stress in teaching and how to handle it. K. Styles and G. Cavanagh. bibl f Engl J 66:76-9 Ja '77
Teachers in role conflict: the hidden dilemma. S. K. Edgerton. Educ Digest 43:17-19 D '77

Qualifications

See also
Teachers—Certification

Rating

Researcher looks at process-based teacher evaluation. D. M. Medley. Educ Digest 43:32-5 D '77

Rating by students

Reaction to student evaluations. D. Edwards. Educ Digest 42:54-6 My '77
What do students say about reading instruction? C. Bruckerhoff. Clearing H 51:104-7 N '77

Recruiting

Recruitment and selection: a devilish process; quiz. L. D. Weller, Jr. Clearing H 50:406-7 My '77

Retirement

Retired teachers share skills as Peace Corps volunteers in Ghana. il por Aging 268:18-20 F '77

Salaries, allowances, etc.

New York City defers teacher pay increases. L. Bornstein and others. M Labor R 100:58 My '77

Selection and appointment

Recruitment and selection: a devilish process; quiz. L. D. Weller, Jr. Clearing H 50:406-7 My '77

TEACHERS—*Continued*

Sexual behavior

Education now. P. Schrag. Sat R 5:53-4 N 12 '77
Gay sex in the schools. J. Merrow. Parents Mag 52:66+ S '77

Anecdotes, facetiae, satire, etc.

Role models. R. Baker. N Y Times Mag p 10 Je 26 '77; Same. Am Home 80:8 N '77

Supply and demand

Employment prospects brighten a bit for some teachers in California. L. H. Smith. bibl M Labor R 100:49-52 O '77

Taxation

N.L.R.B. and the vow of poverty; taxation of members of religious orders teaching in Catholic schools. America 137:157 S 24 '77

Tenure

See also
Teachers—Dismissal

Transfer

Freeway madness; reassignment of teachers on basis of race by Los Angeles Unified School District. R. Kirk. Nat R 30:34 Ja 6 '78
Teachers and race. M. Sheils and others. il Newsweek 90:114 N 7 '77

TEACHERS, Part time
Two people, one job—how teachers do it. il U.S. News 82:80 Ap 4 '77

TEACHERS aides
Training model for junior high school communication aides; reading center at West Junior High School, Nampa, Idaho. L. McMillin. Engl J 66:52-3 Ap '77

TEACHERS and students
Battered teacher. A. M. Bloch. Todays Educ 66: 58-9+ Mr '77
Charlie Darwin was an underachiever. A. Franza. Engl J 66:12-14 Ap '77
Child no one knows. R. Goldenberg and B. McNair. Educ Digest 43:36-8 O '77
Focus: middle and junior high schools; symposium, ed by A. R. Gere. il Engl J 66:25-51 Ap '77
Students teach teachers. C. Buchanan. SLJ 24: 39 D '77
See also
Classroom management

TEACHERS assistants. See Teachers aides

TEACHERS centers. See Instructional materials centers

TEACHERS education. See Teachers—Education

TEACHERS poems (by teachers)
Spring poetry festival; ed by R. Calisch. il Engl J 66:42-60 My '77

TEACHERS resource centers. See Instructional materials centers

TEACHERS salaries. See Teachers—Salaries, allowances, etc.

TEACHERS strikes. See Strikes—United States—Teachers

TEACHERS unions
Bishops and the N.L.R.B; disputes between bishops and parochial school teachers' unions. America 137:65 Ag 13 '77
Catholic schools and unions. America 136:265 Mr 26 '77
Emancipating the schools. R. Kirk. Nat R 29:208 F 18 '77
Firm vote for teachers' unions; Catholic schools. America 137:206 O 8 '77
Freedom and parochial schools; NLRB and Catholic schools. R. Kirk. Nat R 29:441-2+ Ap 15 '77
Unions on the college campus: the struggle gets sharper. il U.S. News 83:59-60 Ag 22 '77
See also
American Federation of Teachers

TEACHING
Adult life cycles and teaching. D. Roberts. bibl f il Engl J 66:38-41 S '77
Classroom tips. J. T. Field. See issues of Today's education
Is constancy outmoded? R. T. McGee. Clearing H 50:250-2 F '77
Teaching as a performing art. M. D. Baughman. Clearing H 51:100 N '77
See also
Academic freedom
Classroom management
Group work in education
Individual instruction
Indoctrination
Motivation (education)
School discipline
School supervision and supervisors
Teachers—Rating
Team teaching
also subhead Study and teaching under various subjects, e.g. Skin diving—Study and teaching

Aids and devices

Materials and equipment. P. K. Komoski. See issues of Todays education
Missing link; use of paper chains to study measuring. R. Harring. Educ Digest 42:48-9 Ja '77
Open learning and guidelines for the design of instructional materials. D. C. Forman and P. Richardson. Educ Digest 42:41-4 Ap '77
Using hand calculators in schools. E. E. Hopkins. Educ Digest 42:44-5 F '77
See also
Audio-visual materials
Computers—Educational use
Instructional materials centers
Language arts—Study and teaching—Aids and devices
Memorizing
Motion pictures in education
Newspapers in education
Telephone in education
Television in education

TEACHING, Freedom of. See Academic freedom

TEACHING as a profession
Relationship between work experience and occupational aspiration and attrition from teaching. J. W. Gosnell. bibl il Clearing H 51:176-9 D '77

TEACHING machines
See also
Computers—Educational use

TEAGUE, W. Dorwin
Converting the iron jib to diesel. il Motor B & S 140:49-53 D '77
Phantom helmsman. il Motor B & S 139:74-5+ Ap '77

TEAK

Finishing

See Wood finishing

TEALE, John
Masthead weight and stability. Motor B & S 141:52+ Ja '78

TEAM Defense Project. See Legal aid

TEAM teaching
How to succeed in team teaching by really trying. R. R. Nolan and S. S. Roper. il Todays Educ 66:54+ Ja '77

TEAMSTERS union. See International Brotherhood of Teamsters, Chauffeurs, Warehousemen and Helpers of America

TEAS
Two teas. New Yorker 53:32-3 Ap 25 '77
Yankee hospitality . . . a Boston tea party. G. Steves. il Am Home 80:60-1+ D '77
See also
Tea (beverage)

TEASERS (fishing lures) See Fishing lures, flies, etc.

TECHNICAL assistance
See also
United Nations—Development Program

TECHNICAL assistance, American
See also
Appropriate Technology International (organization)

Underdeveloped areas

Technology transfer. P. H. Abelson and I. Tinker. Science 195:351 Ja 28 '77

TECHNICAL assistance, European

Latin America

OAS and Europe. Américas 29:41 O '77

TECHNICAL assistance in South Africa
States condemned for supporting foreign economic interests which exploit territories; with text of resolution. UN Chron 13:45-6, 81-2 D '76

TECHNICAL conferences
Assembly adopts resolutions on three United Nations technical conferences. UN Chron 14: 53-4 Ja '77

TECHNICAL Co-operation among Developing Countries Conference, 1978 (proposed) See United Nations Conference on Technical Co-operation among Developing Countries, 1978 (proposed)

TECHNICAL education
Technical advice. L. Luciano. Seventeen 36: 54 Ap '77
See also
Apprentices
Vocational-technical schools

TECHNICAL libraries
See also
Linda Hall Library, Kansas City, Mo.

TECHNICAL literature
See also
Technology—Bibliography

TECHNICAL processes in libraries. See Libraries—Technical processes

TECHNICAL writing
Technical writing: career opportunities. J. J. Franzman. bibl il por Chemistry 50:19-21 Ap '77

TECHNICIANS, Electronic. See Electronic technicians

TECHNIQUE (art) See Painting—Technique

TECHNICOLOR, Inc
Taking good care of himself. Forbes 120:34 O 15 '77

TECHNOLOGICAL forecasting
Backward, march! por Forbes 119:74 Ap 1 '77
How technology will reshape life in years ahead. J. McWethy and L. McKirgan. il U.S. News 83:62-6+ N 28 '77
Post-human intelligence; excerpt from Until the sun dies. R. Jastrow. Natur Hist 86:12-13+ Je '77
Technolitics; Latin America 2000 A.D; address, September 15, 1976. C. W. Parker, 2d. Vital Speeches 43:253-6 F 1 '77
What life will be like in the 1980s. U.S. News 83:75-86 D 26 '77

Anecdotes, facetiae, satire, etc.

Lion's roar. A. Burgess. il por Lib J 102:327-9 F 1 '77

TECHNOLOGICAL innovations
Communications. il Forbes 120:P139-46 S 15 '77
New companies that beat the odds. G. Bylinsky. il Fortune 96:76-80+ D '77
See also
Technology transfer

TECHNOLOGICAL research. See Industrial research

TECHNOLOGY
Appropriate technology in action—and inaction. J. Goldstein. il Org Gard & Farm 24:142-4 Ag '77
New weapons; technological breakthroughs. Nat R 29:931 Ag 19 '77
Press decries technological optimists; excerpts from address, October 8, 1977. F. Press. Science 198:1022 D 9 '77
Technology (cont) Sci N 111:60, 106, 154, 280, 348, 392, 410; 112:72, 152, 217, 296, 409 Ja 22, F 12, Mr 5, Ap 30, My 28, Je 18-25, Jl 30, S 3, O 1, N 5, D 17 '77
See also
Engineering
Inventions
Medical technology
National Center for Appropriate Technology
Space technology

Bibliography

Sci-tech books of 1976; comp by E. S. Crockett and E. Mount. il Lib J 102:543-53 Mr 1 '77
Scientific, technical, business and professional books. il Pub W 211:40-4+ Mr 21; 212:27-30+ O 17 '77
Scientific, technical, medical, & business books (cont) Lib J 102:567+, 2227-8+ Mr 1, N 1 '77

Conferences

See also
United Nations Conference on Science and Technology for Development, 1979 (proposed)
United Nations Conference on Technical Cooperation among Developing Countries, 1978 (proposed)

Economic aspects

DOD revises policy on export. E. Kozicharow. il Aviation W 107:12-13 S 12 '77
Technology and jobs: the vital link is weakening. T. A. Vanderslice. por Duns R 110:25+ Jl '77

History

50 and 100 years ago. See issues of Scientific American

International aspects

Assembly calls for wider exchange of information on technology. UN Chron 14:57-9 Ja '77
Giant magnet flown to Soviets; U.S-USSR joint program to advance MHD technology. Aviation W 106:17 Je 27 '77
Soviet technology for American companies. J. H. Douglas. Sci N 111:140-1 F 26 '77
Technological superiority required. M. R. Currie. Aviation W 106:7 F 7 '77
U.S.-Egypt Joint Working Group on Technology meets at Washington. Dept State Bull 75:754 D 27 '76
Worldwide view of technology. H. Hrubecky. por Intellect 106:14 Jl '77
See also
United Nations—Committee on Science and Technology for Development

Social aspects

A.T: the quiet revolution; application of appropriate technology. W. N. Ellis. il Bull Atom Sci 33:24-9 N '77
Bionic boom. R. Keyes. por Newsweek 89:9 F 7 '77
Human scene: growth: how big? How far? How risky? il Sr Schol 109:6-8+ Ja 27 '77
Idea whose time has come? appropriate technology; application of E. F. Schumacher's concepts. J. Ross-Skinner. il por Duns R 110:118-20+ O '77
Mr Small; theories of E. F. Schumacher. S. Fraker and G. C. Lubenow. il por Newsweek 89:18 Mr 28 '77
On smallness. K. Kodner. Progressive 41:26-7 S '77
Our love-hate affair with technology. C. Tucker. Sat R 5:80 D 10 '77
Small is dubious. S. C. Florman. Harpers 255: 10-12 Ag '77
Why less is more means more work for the techno-team. S. Thompson. Car & Dr 23:12+ Ag '77

Europe, Western

Science in Europe: low marks for high technology. N. Hawkes. Science 196:636-7 My 6 '77

Germany

Ersatz gasoline: forgotten archives yielding secret of how German army ran a war on fuel from low-grade coal. D. Lampe. Sci Digest 82: 65-7 O '77
Nazi coal conversion methods reviewed. C. Holden. Science 196:508-9 Ap 29 '77
Recycling Nazi secrets; making petroleum from coal. il Time 109:58 Ap 18 '77

Japan

Japanese science & technology:
The coming challenge. J. H. Douglas. il Sci N 112:378-81 D 3 '77
Computerizing Tokyo's traffic. J. H. Douglas. il map Sci N 112:412-14 D 17 '77

Latin America

Technolitics; Latin America 2000 A.D; address, September 15, 1976. C. W. Parker, 2d Vital Speeches 43:253-6 F 1 '77

Russia

Soviet technology focus reoriented. E. Kozicharow. Aviation W 106:51+ Ja 3 '77
We have buried them. New Repub 177:2+ O 22 '77

Underdeveloped areas

See Underdeveloped areas—Technology

United States

See Technology

TECHNOLOGY, Educational. See Educational technology

TECHNOLOGY and civilization
Shock of recognition; New York City blackout. Newsweek 90:80 Jl 25 '77
What of the world's future? T. A. Wertime. Current 194:49-57 Jl '77
See also
Institute for the Future

TECHNOLOGY and society. See Technology—Social aspects

TECHNOLOGY and state
Government-sponsored demonstrations of new technologies. W. S. Baer and others. bibl il Science 196:950-7 My 27 '77
In praise of science and technology. C. Sagan. New Repub 176:21-2+ Ja 22 '77; Same with title Role of Science and technology. Current 192:47-53 Ap '77
Science, technology, man and society; excerpt from Unesco's Medium-Term Plan (1977-1982) il UNESCO Courier 30:18-20 Mr '77

TECHNOLOGY assessment
Mammography controversy: NIH's entrée into evaluating technology. B. J. Culliton. Science 198:171-3 O 14 '77
See also
United States—Technology Assessment, Office of

TECHNOLOGY transfer
Challenges facing the multinational corporation; address, September 21, 1977. N. B. Sommer. Vital Speeches 44:85-8 N 15 '77
Issue of technology transfer is snag for 1979 U.N. meeting. J. Walsh. Science 198:35-8 O 7 '77
NASA tackles a down-to-earth job. E. M. Leeper. il BioScience 27:223 Mr '77
New medical techniques from space technology; vascular image processing. D. H. Blankenhorn. Intellect 106:189 N '77
Physicians + physicists=far-out medicine; work of Johns Hopkins University's Applied Physics Laboratory. D. Lampe. il Fam Health 9:48-50 S '77
Space technology—a way to help solve biomedical problems. il Space World N-3-159:24-5 Mr '77
Space technology; address, April 28, 1977. J. C. Toomay. Vital Speeches 43:602-5 Jl 15 '77
Technolitics; Latin America 2000 A.D; address, September 15, 1976. C. W. Parker, 2d Vital Speeches 43:253-6 F 1 '77
U.S.-Soviet exchange results; conference at Stanford University. Intellect 105:301 Mr '77

TECTONICS. See Geology, Structural

TEDESCO, Ted
We can learn from Europe's cities; address, September 26, 1976. Vital Speeches 43:209-11 Ja 15 '77

TEEN-age birth control. See Birth control
TEEN-age drinking. See Alcohol and youth
TEEN-age literature. See Young adults literature
TEEN-age marriage
See also
Teen-age pregnancy
TEEN-age mothers, Unmarried. See Mothers, Unmarried
TEEN-age pregnancy
In love and in trouble. Good H 184:32+ Ap '77
HEW and the sexual revolution: why teenagers get pregnant; contraception programs. M. Castleman. Nation 225:549-52 N 26 '77
Pregnant teens. T. Schwartz and others. Newsweek 89:54+ My 30 '77
Teenage pregnancy. C. P. Green and S. J. Lowe. Current 192:35-40 Ap '77
Teen-age sexuality:
There is a moral dimension. E. K. Shriver. Read Digest 111:153-4 N '77
Too many pregnancies, too early. G. Naismith. Read Digest 111:150-2 N '77
TEEN-age smoking. See Smoking and youth
TEEN-age suicide. See Suicide
TEEN-agers. See Adolescence; Youth
TEEN-agers, Runaway. See Runaways
TEENWAGE differential. See Wage differentials
TEETH
See also
Dentists
Gums

Care and hygiene

Ask the dentist; questions and answers. See issues of Family health incorporating Today's health to September 1977
Closeup on teeth. il Mademoiselle 83:146 My '77
Dental myths and misconceptions. B. B. Mortensen. Fam Health 9:14 D '77
How to keep your teeth clean, bright, and healthy. L. Lamberg. il Bet Hom & Gard 55:74+ N '77
Quick brushup. S. Mennear-Dubas. il Fam Health 9:56 Ag '77
Sound teeth for life. R. O. Cooley. il Parents Mag 52:28+ N '77
Tooth care that starts in the cradle; views of Stephen J. Moss. J. Chan. McCalls 105:41 Ja '78
See also
Dental caries—Prevention

Diseases

See also
Dental caries
TEETH (fishes)
Jaws of jaws; shark teeth and jaws. S. Lissau. il Oceans 10:31-3 N '77
TEETH, Fossil
Hominoid enamel prism patterns. D. G. Gantt and others. bibl il Science 198:1155-7 D 16 '77
Tooth patterns and the human-ape split. il Sci N 112:405 D 17 '77
TEFLON lubricants. See Lubrication and lubricants
TEGLAS, Csaba. See Parish, N. J. jt auth
TEGNER, Mia J. and Dayton, P. K.
Sea urchin recruitment patterns and implications of commercial fishing. bibl il Science 196:324-6 Ap 15 '77
TEHERAN, Iran
Levittshahr will bring development housing to Tehran. D. Higgins. il Archit Rec 162:37 Ag '77

City planning

City center for the Shah. il Horizon 20:71 S '77
TEHRAN, Iran. See Teheran, Iran
TEICHER, Martin H. and Blass, E. M.
First suckling response of the newborn albino rat: the roles of olfaction and amniotic fluid. bibl il Science 198:635-6 N 11 '77
TEILHARD DE CHARDIN, Pierre
Fresh look at the exile priest. il pors Time 109:53-4 F 28 '77 *
TEITELMAN, Michael
Should Dr Kissinger be seated? address, April 26, 1977. Nation 224:658-60 My 28 '77
TELANDER, Rick
At the other end of the rainbows. il por Sports Illus 46:50-2 Ap 25 '77
City game, country style. il Sports Illus 46:38-43 Mr 21 '77
Fishing. Sports Illus 46:60+ Mr 28 '77
Record almost broke him. il pors Sports Illus 46:60-4+ Je 20 '77
School of soft knocks. il Sports Illus 46:100-4+ My 23 '77
Shark gets a ruling with bite. il por Sports Illus 47:26-7 O 10 '77
TELECOMMUNICATION
Camelia report; teleconferencing systems. Sci Digest 82:48-53 S '77
Communications. il Forbes 120:P139-46 S 15 '77
Convergence of computing and telecommunications systems. D. Farber and P. Baran. Science 195:1166-70 Mr 18 '77
Photons in fibers for telecommunication. S. E. Miller. bibl il Science 195:1211-16 Mr 18 '77
Planning and policy: keys to our telephone network; address, February 4, 1977. G. L. Hough. Vital Speeches 43:344-7 Mr 15 '77
Role of microelectronics in communication. J. S. Mayo. il Sci Am 237:192-3+ bibl(p260+) S '77
Telecommunication with neutrino beams. A. W. Sáenz and others. bibl il Science 198:295-7 O 21 '77
See also
Communications satellites
Data transmission systems

Laws and regulations

Communications dog fight. G. R. Rosen. il Duns R 109:48-53 Je '77
The information economy and public policy. M. R. Irwin and S. C. Johnson. bibl Science 195:1170-4 Mr 18 '77
New communications. G. O. Robinson. Current 195:37-52 S '77
TELECOMMUNICATION in medicine
Health care via TV in a rural area; STARPAHC unit used on Papago Indian reservation in Ariz. il U.S. News 83:79-80 D 26 '77
See also
Communications satellites—Medical use
TELEMETER
See also
Remote sensing systems
TELEMETRY, Biological. See Biotelemetry
TELEPHONE
Hello central, give me heaven. R. Rosenblatt. New Repub 177:37-8 S 3 '77
Telephone services. Mech Illus 73:23 Ap '77
See also
Radiotelephone, Portable
Radiotelephone on motor vehicles

Apparatus and supplies

After-hour calls routed automatically; Code-a-phone answering device for emergencies; Raymond, Wash. il Am City & County 92:68 F '77
Build amplifier for hands-off telephone. J. Gilder. il Radio-Electr 48:60-1 My '77
Conversations; introduction of Dictaphone Corporation device. New Yorker 53:27-9 D 19 '77
Ma Bell stalls; FCC rules on interconnect modems. A. Salsberg. Pop Electr 11:4 Mr '77
Plug-in remote ringer. R. K. Atwood. il Radio-Electr 48:45-8 N '77
Pushbutton dialer with memory. D. Feinwell. il Radio-Electr 48:38-41+ Je '77
Turn-on appliances via long distance. J. Guilder. il Radio-Electr 48:39-42+ Ap '77

Directories

See Telephone directories

Emergency use

After-hour calls routed automatically; Code-a-phone answering device for emergencies; Raymond, Wash. il Am City & County 92:68 F '77
Chicago wires 911 into computer. Am City & County 92:38 Ag '77
Help! police operators in Detroit. D. Davis. il Newsweek 90:98+ D 5 '77
See also
Telephone in counseling

Government use

Antitrust: a hot line to nab price fixers; Justice Department consumer project in Pittsburgh. Bus W p34 My 30 '77

Private wire systems

Crossed wires over private-line rates. Bus W p36+ Je 20 '77

Rates

Are you paying too much for your phone? il Consumer Rep 43:50-3 Ja '78
Getting bludgeoned by a telephone; telephone rates in Europe. A. Kingery. Sat Eve Post 249:76 N '77
How to cut your phone bill. A. Rosenblum. Good H 186:165 Ja '78
Whole new way to figure AT&T's rates. il Bus W p86-8+ F 14 '77

Switching systems

See Telephone switching systems, Electronic

Wiretapping

See Wiretapping

Australia

ITT's strategy may benefit a competitor. Bus W p57+ S 12 '77

Europe, Western

Getting bludgeoned by a telephone; telephone rates. A. Kingery. Sat Eve Post 249:76 N '77

France

Setback in trying to Frenchify phones; Thomson-CSF. Bus W p68 N 21 '77

TELEPHONE—*Continued*

Saudi Arabia

Saudis say wrong numbers to the U.S. Bus W p20-1 Ja 9 '78
Wrong number; Americans lose telecommunications contract. D. Pauly and E. Shannon. Newsweek 90:78 D 26 '77

TELEPHONE, Automobile. See Radiotelephone on automobiles

TELEPHONE, Optical. See Light communication systems

TELEPHONE amplifiers. See Amplifiers

TELEPHONE answering machines. See Telephone—Apparatus and supplies

TELEPHONE apparatus industry

Canada

Northern Telecom's dive into the U.S. market. il Bus W p 144+ O 17 '77

Underdeveloped areas

See Underdeveloped areas—Telephone apparatus industry

TELEPHONE auctions. See Auctions

TELEPHONE bill paying service. See Telephone in business

TELEPHONE companies

Learning a lesson from David; address, February 17, 1977. R. W. Bunke. Vital Speeches 43:376-9 Ap 1 '77
When consumers tackle the phone companies—. il U.S. News 83:71 Jl 11 '77
See also
American Telephone & Telegraph Company
Collective labor agreements—Telephone companies

Accounting

Utilities fight to escape a tax-credit trap. il Bus W p96+ D 5 '77

Antitrust cases

Antitrust suit against Bell winds onward. D. Shapley. Science 198:278 O 21 '77
Cracks in AT&T's monopoly: Ma Bell shows her teeth. L. Light. Nation 225:690-2 D 24 '77
How courts will treat IBM, AT&T. A. Hershman. por Duns R 110:76-7+ D '77

Employees

Industry's greatest energy shortage; address, June 6, 1977. R. W. Bunke. Vital Speeches 43:637-40 Ag 1 '77

TELEPHONE directories

National directory of addresses and telephone numbers; interview, ed by R. Dahlin. S. R. Greenfield. Pub W 212:34 D 5 '77
Now, the green pages; National directory of addresses and telephone numbers. il Time 110:104 D 5 '77

TELEPHONE employees. See Telephone companies—Employees

TELEPHONE errors. See Errors, Popular

TELEPHONE in agriculture

Telephone feeder pig auction: a marketing hot line. R. Brunoehler. il Suc Farm 75:47 D '77
They irrigate by phone. W. Waltner and E. Waltner. il Farm J 101:MM1+ Mr '77

TELEPHONE in banking. See Telephone in business

TELEPHONE in business

Paying bills by telephone; services by banks and savings and loan associations. il Changing T 31:15-17 Je '77
See also
Telephone selling

TELEPHONE in counseling

212-686-3061; Help Line Center. D. K. Mano. Nat R 29:391-2 Ap 1 '77

TELEPHONE in education

You call us, they'll call you; the learning exchange. S. Croteau. Educ Digest 42:16-18 Ap '77

TELEPHONE in medical care

Cancer hot lines: lifesaving help by telephone. N. G. Rollins. Good H 184:222-3 Je '77

TELEPHONE information service

Do hot lines really help? H. Steinberg. il Seventeen 136:150+ Ag '77
Uncle Sam's toll-free hotlines. M. Pisaturo. il McCalls 104:85 Je '77

TELEPHONE numbers

Unlisted number. N. C. Grace. Atlantic 239:88-9 Ap '77

TELEPHONE operators

Help! police operators in Detroit. D. Davis. il Newsweek 90:98+ D 5 '77

TELEPHONE radio conversation programs. See Radio programs—Conversation programs

TELEPHONE rates. See Telephone—Rates

TELEPHONE selling

For whom the bell? FCC petition asking restraint of telephone soliciting. T. Nicholson and others. il Newsweek 90:89 O 17 '77
Watch out for these telephone sales pitches. L. Palmer. il Farm J 101:10-11 mid-Mr '77

TELEPHONE switching systems, Electronic

Northern Telecom's dive into the U.S. market. il Bus W p 144+ O 17 '77
Traveling telephones. J. Mason. il Pop Sci 212:62-5 Ja '78

TELEPHONE workers. See Telephone companies—Employees

TELEPHOTO lenses. See Lenses, Photographic

TELESAT Canada. See Communications satellites, Canadian

TELESCOPE lenses. See Lenses

TELESCOPE mountings

Porter's Folly mounting in Europe. R. Schlafke. il Sky & Tel 53:475-80 Je '77

TELESCOPE test instruments. See Testing instruments

TELESCOPES

Astronomers urge 25-meter telescope. il Sci N 111:247 Ap 16 '77
Better to see you with. D. E. Thomsen. il Sci N 112:318-20 N 12 '77
Cornell's 25-inch training telescope. J. R. Houck and G. E. Gull. il Sky & Tel 54:264-6 O '77
Easily transported 20-inch telescope. A. Grebner. il Sky & Tel 53:224-6 Mr '77
Easy-to-use rich-field telescope. C. P. Gilmore. il Pop Sci 210:72 Ap '77
First light for the ESO 3.6- meter telescope. S. Laustsen. il Sky & Tel 53:96-103 F '77
First tests of the Irénée du Pont telescope. H. W. Babcock. il Sky & Tel 54:90-4 Ag '77
Gleanings for ATM's; ed by R. E. Cox and R. W. Sinnott. See issues of Sky and telescope
Heavenly hardware. C. Panati and S. Begley. Newsweek 90:69+ Jl 25 '77
Large Maksutov with Newtonian and Cassegrain foci; with editorial comment. H. Louth. il Sky & Tel 53:139-45 F '77
MMT update. il Sky & Tel 54:9-10 Jl '77
New Catadioptric telescope. D. C. Dilworth. il Sky & Tel 54:425-30, 521-7 N, D '77
New kind of hobby telescope; rich-field instrument. C. J. Treagesser. il Mech Illus 73:83 Ag '77
Next generation telescope. il Sky & Tel 53:428 Je '77
Progress on the CFH reflector. il Sky & Tel 53:254-6 Ap '77
Soviet 6-meter altazimuth reflector. B. K. Ioannisiani. il map Sky & Tel 54:356-62 N '77
Soviet 6-meter telescope. Sky & Tel 53:111 F '77
Totable scope. il Mech Illus 74:94 Ja '78
See also
Radio telescopes

History

Herschel's large 20-foot telescope. J. Ashbrook. il Sky & Tel 54:174-5 S '77

Mirrors

Calculating a mirror's surface accuracy. R. W. Sinnott. bibl Sky & Tel 54:144-7 Ag '77
Foucault tester for short-focus mirrors. J. T. Carle. il Sky & Tel 53:481-2 Je '77
Foucault tester with digital readout. R. J. McKeon. il Sky & Tel 54:140-3 Ag '77
Size of the Newtonian diagonal. W. T. Peters and R. Pike. il Sky & Tel 53:220-3 Mr '77
Star tests of a rubber mirror. il Sky & Tel 53:429 Je '77

TELETYPE

Build the TVT-6: a low-cost direct video display. D. E. Lancaster. il Pop Electr 12:47-52 Jl; 49-55 Ag '77
Electronic bell for a TVT-II. D. J. Deutsch. il Pop Electr 12:46 Jl '77
Teletypewriter fundamentals for hams, SWL'ers & computer hobbyists. L. Kahaner. il Pop Electr 12:43-8 O '77

TELEVISION

New age of TV technology on the horizon. Sci Digest 81:88-9 My '77
TV for radio amateurs. A. Salsberg. Pop Electr 11:4 Je '77
See also
Video art

Police use

See Television in crime prevention

Reception

See Television reception

Transmitters and transmission

See Television transmission

TELEVISION, Cable. See CATV system

TELEVISION adaptations

Books as television best sellers; or, Give that TV addict a book! S. Seward. il Wilson Lib Bull 52:232-6 N '77
Rights and permissions. P. S. Nathan. See issues of Publishers weekly

TELEVISION advertising

ABC gets the feel of TV's no. 1 spot. il Bus W p33 My 9 '77

TELEVISION advertising—*Continued*
Cavities and conscience pangs: candy can cause both; image of librarians in television commercials. F. J. Dempsey. il Am Lib 8:231 My '77
Christianity's Hanafis; General Motors withdrawal of sponsorship of F. Zeffrelli's Jesus of Nazareth. M. E. Marty. Chr Cent 94:367 Ap 13 '77
Reinforcing the impact of TV commercials. il Bus W p40-1 Jl 18 '77
Struggle to find sponsors for Nixon. pors Bus W p33-4 My 9 '77
Those little eyes so helpless and appealing. R. Rosenblat. New Repub 176:33 Ap 23 '77
Why the huckster is no longer the heavy. K. E. Meyer. Sat R 4:44 My 14 '77
See also
Automobile industry—Advertising
Books—Advertising
Brokers—Advertising
Dairying—Advertising
Meat industry—Advertising

Anecdotes, facetiae, satire, etc.
Late, late, late movie. R. Baker. il N Y Times Mag p6 Jl 17 '77

Rates
See Advertising—Rates

TELEVISION alarm systems. See Electronic alarm systems

TELEVISION and children
Aggression on TV could be helping our children. J. J. Lopiparo. bibl f Intellect 105:345-6 Ap '77
Baretta's T-shirt; or, Youth must be served. M. J. Arlen. New Yorker 53:167-8+ N 14 '77
Brought to you by. . . G. Slater. Educ Digest 43:36-7 D '77
Christmas in Mr Rogers' neighborhood; interview, ed by B. White. F. Rogers. por Sat Eve Post 249:24+ D '77
Classroom's no longer prime time. S. Feinberg. Todays Educ 66:78-9 S '77; Same abr. Educ Digest 43:38-40 D '77
De-fusing the TV time bomb. Parents Mag 52: 38-9+ Je '77
Forget the message, worry about the medium; views of M. Winn. R. A. Blake. America 136: 276-7 Mr 26 '77
Great American teaching machine—of violence. H. J. Skornia. Intellect 105:347-8 Ap '77
Growing up cynical with TV; excerpt from Television: the first fifty years. J. Greenfield. Horizon 20:96 S '77
How TV can be good for children. B. G. Harrison. il McCalls 105:165+ O '77
Lure of television—ways to unplug your kids; interview. R. L. Stubblefield. U.S. News 83: 24 S 12 '77
Plug-in drug. M. Winn. Harp Baz 110:90+ Jl '77
Plug-in drug; excerpt. M. Winn. Sat Eve Post 249:40-1+ N '77
Ralph Nader reports: child power. R. Nader. Ladies Home J 94:72+ N '77
TV tyrant: how to liberate the children. G. Carro. il Ladies Home J 94:96 Ap '77
Television and the perception of reality. D. H. Cohen. Educ Digest 42:10-13 Mr '77
Television violence revisited. D. K. Osborn and J. D. Osborn. il Educ Digest 43:38-9 S '77
Those little eyes so helpless and appealing. R. Rosenblatt. New Repub 176:33 Ap 23 '77
Violence in America. B. Meyerson. Redbook 150:113+ N '77
What concerned parents can do about TV. E. Kaye. il McCalls 104:53 Ap '77
What TV does to kids. H. F. Waters. il Newsweek 89:62-5+ F 21 '77; Same abr. Read Digest 110:80-4 Je '77
See also
Television programs—Childrens programs

TELEVISION and copyright. See Copyright—Broadcasting rights

TELEVISION and libraries. See Libraries and television

TELEVISION and literature
Novelizations: are the plums drying up? books from motion pictures and television programs. E. Lottman. il Pub W 212:31-3 O 10 '77
See also
Television adaptations
Television and reading

TELEVISION and motion pictures. See Motion pictures and television

TELEVISION and politics. See Television in politics

TELEVISION and reading
Printed word; excerpt from address, April 1977. C. P. Snow. Writer 90:24-6 D '77

TELEVISION and the aged
AoA-funded TV series wins 2 Academy Awards; Getting on. il Aging 274:19 Ag '77
AoA supports two pilot TV programs for the elderly. il Aging 266:20 D '76
Media: TV entertainment leaders discuss image of elderly. il Aging 274:18-19+ Ag '77
Public TV focuses on older Americans. il Aging 275:8-10 S '77

TELEVISION and the poor
Drop-ins: mass media and the poor. N. P. Hurley. America 137:377-8 N 26 '77

TELEVISION and youth
Baretta's T-shirt; or, Youth must be served. M. J. Arlen. New Yorker 53:167-8+ N 14 '77
TV's new ABC's; youth oriented shows. H. F. Waters and M. Kasindorf. il Newsweek 90: 104+ D 5 '77
Tuesday night on the tube. il Time 110:94+ D 12 '77

TELEVISION antennas

Maintenance and repair
Step by step troubleshooting. S. Prentiss. il Radio-Electr 48:84+ S '77

TELEVISION apparatus
Build the hi-fi/tv audio-minder. C. Kobylarz. il Pop Electr 11:41-4 Ap '77
Build this digital on-screen TV clock. F. Blechman. il Radio-Electr 48:35-8 Jl '77
Build this video modulator. G. Dash. il Radio-Electr 48:33-5+ Ag '77
See also
Video recorders and recording

TELEVISION apparatus industry
Hotter competition in video recorders. il Bus W p36 Ap 25 '77
Matsushita attacks its American problem; Quasar Electronics Corp. il Bus W p28 F 21 '77
New hope for TV sound. R. Lanier. Hi Fi 27: 76-8 N '77
Tonight tomorrow? video tape recorder industry. S. T. Atlas and A. M. Field. Newsweek 90:69-70 O 31 '77
See also
Zenith Radio Corporation

Export-import trade
Agreement on importation of TV sets from Japan. Dept State Bull 76:684-5+ Je 27 '77
Free trade and the price of TV sets. Consumer Rep 43:20-1 Ja '78
Kickbacks in living color; charges against Japanese television manufcturers. il Time 109:63 Je 13 '77
Showdown on Japan's TV blitz; ITC tariff recommendation; with interviews with J. J. Nevin and T. Takai. A. J. Meyer and others. il Newsweek 89:58-9 Mr 28 '77
Tactics to outwit U.S. protectionists; Japan. il Bus W p36 Mr 28 '77
World trade: a round the protectionists won; increased duty liability on Japanese electronic products. Bus W p30 Ap 25 '77

Marketing
TV sales are booming, with Christmas ahead. il Bus W p62+ N 21 '77

TELEVISION audiences
Drop in TV viewing, but not in ad pricing. il Bus W p33-4 Ja 16 '78
TV's dropouts. Newsweek 90:123 D 12 '77
Year that rain fell up; drop in TV viewing. Time 111:69 Ja 9 '78

Caricatures and cartoons
Turned on. Read Digest 111:148-9 N '77

TELEVISION authorship
Eugene Orowitz makes good; interview, ed by L. Garton. M. Landon. por Writers Digest 57:27 Ap '77
Super (market) scriptwriter; interview, ed by N. Levinson. J. Bateman. il pors Writers Digest 57:38-9 Ap '77
You ought to be in pictures. E. S. Stevens. Writers Digest 57:43-5 O '77

TELEVISION awards
AoA-funded TV series wins 2 Academy Awards; Getting on. il Aging 274:19 Ag '77

TELEVISION broadcasting
The air (cont) M. J. Arlen. New Yorker 53:115-18+ O 3; 104+ O 17; 119-27 O 31; 167-8+ N 14; 166-73 N 28 '77
Television. J. Lardner. il New Repub 177:32-5 O 1; 29-31 N 12; 24-6 D 10 '77
See also
Communications satellites—Television broadcasting use
Television stations
Video recorders and recording

Advertising
See Television advertising

Anecdotes, facetiae, satire, etc.
TV news is good, even when the news is bad. J. Leonard. Vogue 167:221+ Mr '77

Baseball
See Television broadcasting—Sports

Basketball
See Television broadcasting—Sports

TELEVISION broadcasting—*Continued*

Bowling

See Television broadcasting—Sports

Boxing

See Television broadcasting—Sports

Censorship

Off color. J. Lelyveld. il N Y Times Mag p 174 N 6 '77
Who shapes TV values? J. M. Wall. Chr Cent 94:131-2 F 16 '77

Drama

Solid drama, not sitcoms. D. English. il Vogue 167:62 N '77
Vote against "documentary" dramas. K. E. Meyer. Sat R 4:46 F 5 '77

Educational programs

How do you stop fighting with your children? Parent Effectiveness programs on PBS. G. Carro. Ladies Home J 94:80 O '77

Football

See Television broadcasting—Sports

Golf

See Television broadcasting—Sports

Government use

Howard, Hughie and Jimmy. J. Seelye. New Repub 176:23-6 Je 4 '77
Prime-time President. R. Reeves. il por N Y Times Mag p 17-19 My 15 '77
Sell it on TV. New Repub 176:2+ Je 25 '77

International aspects

Kojak. . .the all-America image? il Sr Schol 110:14-15+ S 8 '77
TV imperialism. R. Reeves. Esquire 88:20+ O '77
Televising à la russe; failure of television agreement between BBC and Russia. J. Burnham. Nat R 29:1415 D 9 '77
Television's one-way traffic. H. Topuz. il UNESCO Courier 30:16-17 Ap '77
See also
World Administrative Radio Conference

Laws and regulations

See Television laws and regulations

Moral and religious aspects

Church and the coming electronic revolution; interview, ed by P. Rossman. B. Everist. Chr Cent 94:1167-8 D 14 '77
If the eye offend thee; church attacks on TV. il Time 110:53 S 26 '77
Memo to networks: clean up TV! Chr Today 22:42 D 30 '77
Speculative spectaculars; question of publicly televised executions. F. Getlein. Commonweal 104:4-5 Ja 7 '77
Where is TV heading? Chr Today 22:32 O 7 '77
See also
Sex in television
Television and children
Violence in television

Motion pictures

Television; classic films on public TV. P. Sourian. Nation 224:283-5 Mr 5 '77
See also
Television motion pictures

Anecdotes, facetiae, satire, etc.

Late, late, late movie. R. Baker. il N Y Times Mag p6 Jl 17 '77

Music

Laderman works are commissioned and aired on CBS. Hi Fi 27:MA35 Jl '77
Making music leap to life; music series on PBS. il Time 110:75 O 17 '77
Tuning in; Music series on Public Broadcasting Service. F. V. Boyd. il Newsweek 90:111 O 24 '77
U.N. Day concerts; 1976 television broadcast. J. Culshaw. il Hi Fi 27:14+ Ap '77
What's wrong with Public Broadcasting. D. Pash. il Hi Fi 27:MA19-21 O '77

News

ABC's wider world of news; appointment of R. Arledge. il por Time 190:79-80 My 16 '77
Art on TV: an unhappy marriage. B. Matusow. Art N 76:26+ F '77
As Schoor sees it. H. F. Waters and N. Stadtman. por Newsweek 90:90+ O 31 '77
Dos and don'ts of television news; CBS code. T. Griffith. Time 110:114 D 5 '77
Giggling newscasters. M. Kempton. Progressive 41:52 Mr '77
Giving ABC news athletic support. K. E. Meyer. Sat R 5:47 N 12 '77
He looked like God; E. Sevareid. D. M. Alpern and others. pors Newsweek 90:130 N 28 '77
Hoisting anchor; J. Chancellor leaving NBC's nightly newscast. H. F. Waters and others. il por Newsweek 90:98 D 12 '77
Is there life after TV? excerpt from Clearing the air. D. Schorr. il por Esquire 88:105-7+ O '77
Jane Pauley & Sandy Hill: this is your life. A. L. Ball. pors Redbook 150:94+ N '77
Local-news blues. H. F. Waters and R. Cohen. il Newsweek 91:82-3 Ja 16 '78
NBC forum. J. Nickerson. il Sr Schol 109:TE14-15 Mr 10 '77
NBC's new-look news. H. F. Waters and R. Cohen. il Newsweek 90:103 S 19 '77
New ABC's of news. D. M. Alpern and B. Carter. il por Newsweek 90:62 Ag 22 '77
News. M. J. Arlen. New Yorker 53:119-27 O 31 '77
News: women want it all; television reporters; interviews. ed by D. English. il Vogue 167:84 Mr '77
The night TV cried wolf; Son of Sam coverage. C. Tucker. Sat R 5:56 O 1 '77
Plot to get Barbara Walters; interview. ed by C. Chase. B. Walters. por Ladies Home J 94:84+ O '77
Prime time for TV newswomen. il Time 109: 85-6 Mr 21 '77
Public TV kills a news winner; Newsroom, program on KQED. J. Benet. Nation 225:588-90 D 3 '77
Revving up the television news. T. Griffith. por Time 110:58+ Ag 22 '77
Roone at the top; excerpts from interview ed by H. F. Waters. R. Arledge. por Newsweek 89:103-4 My 16 '77
Showdown at ABC News. J. Greenfield. il pors N Y Times Mag p32-4+ F 13 '77
Sign-off for Sevareid. il pors Time 110:111 D 12 '77
TV networks: centers of news power. il U.S. News 83:31 Ag 15 '77
Television's necessary neuters. T. Griffith. il Time 110:48 D 19 '77
Washington diarist: just for you, Barbara. M. M. Kondracke. New Repub 177:42 D 10 '77
See also
Television in politics

Anecdotes, facetiae, satire, etc.

Counseling anchorperson. R. Baker. N Y Times Mag p8 Mr 27 '77

Opera

La Bohème by the million. R. Gelatt. il Sat R 4:42-3 Mr 19 '77
La Boheme telecast live from the Met. P. J. Smith. Hi Fi 27:MA27 Jl '77
Love-hate relationship; Central Opera Service's national conference, held in Houston. J. Ardoin. il por Opera N 42:10-11 D 17 '77
Milan: La Scala's Otello simultaneously transmitted on national television and radio. A. Andris-Michalaros. Opera N 41:28 F 19 '77
Scala Norma: televised opera's self-inflicted wound. J. Culshaw. il Hi Fi 27:14 Je '77
TV:
Mozart's Nozze di Figaro, part of Great performances. R. Jacobson. Opera N 42: 72 O '77
Viewpoint; broadcasts from the Met. R. Jacobson. Opera N 41:5 Ja 22 '77
Viewpoint; opera and J. Carter. R. Jacobson. Opera N 41:6 Ap 16 '77
Viewpoint; PBS telecasts with simultaneous FM stereo broadcasts. R. Jacobson. Opera N 42:5 Ja 7 '78

Programming

Cleveland vs. Mary Hartman; protesting program time. J. H. Kraker. America 136:484-7 My 28 '77
Television programming: an image in a looking glass. D. B. Morlan. bibl il Intellect 106:234-6 D '77

Programs

See Television programs

Psychological aspects

Are you a secret TV addict? D. English. Vogue 167:184-5 F '77
Progeny of programmers: evangelical religion and the television age. J. A. Taylor. il Chr Cent 94:379-82 Ap 20 '77; Discussion. 94:788+ S 14 '77

Skateboarding

See Television broadcasting—Sports

Social aspects

As the world turns. R. Baker. N Y Times Mag p 12 O 30 '77
Comedienne Lucille Ball on the mess in television land. L. Ball. il pors U.S. News 83:58 S 26 '77
Hooked on television. G. Steinem. Progressive 41:39 S '77
Is there life after TV? excerpt from Clearing the air. D. Schorr. il por Esquire 88:105-7+ O '77
Kojak. .the all-America image? il Sr Schol 110:14-15+ S 8 '77
Not-so-mighty tube. G. F. Will. Newsweek 90: 84 Ag 8 '77

TELEVISION broadcasting—Social aspects—*Cont.*
Of a small and modest malignancy, wicked and bristling with dots. N. Mailer. Esquire 88:125-48 N '77
Plug-in drug; influence on family life; excerpt. M. Winn. Sat Eve Post 249:40-1+ N '77
Putting the networks on notice; work of National PTA. J. C. Lyles. Chr Cent 94:556-7 Je 8 '77
TV inhibiting creative ideas. E. Somers. Intellect 105:381-2 My '77
TV's drivel—and worse. M. Stone. U.S. News 83:108 N 21 '77
Television: a gold mine that's coming under heavy attack. il U.S. News 82:29-30 F 7 '77
Television: checking our stewardship. Chr Today 21:35 Ap 1 '77
Washington diarist: just for you, Barbara. M. M. Kondracke. New Repub 177:42 D 10 '77
Who shapes TV values? J. M. Wall. Chr Cent 94:131-2 F 16 '77
See also
Sex role in television programs
Television and children
Television and the aged
Television and the poor
Television and youth
Television broadcasting—Psychological aspects

Sports

Black eye for TV boxing; ABC telecasts of the U.S. Boxing Championships. P. Bonventre. pors Newsweek 89:81-2 My 2 '77
Contract with the Kremlin; rights to televise Moscow Olympics. W. O. Johnson. il Sports Illus 46:14-19 F 21 '77
Happy families; television interview with Pelé after retirement. M. J. Arlen. New Yorker 53:104+ O 17 '77
Joy of deprogramming sport. R. Kahn. il Time 110:50 Ag 22 '77
King-size scandal in the ring; United States Boxing Championships. por Time 109:64 My 2 '77
Mary Shane: baseball's new motor mouth. J. Lublin. por Ms 6:24-5 O '77
NBC as a Soviet megaphone; NBC coverage of 1980 Olympics. J. Hart. il Sat Eve Post 249:31 O '77
NBC: Kremlin megaphone. J. Burnham. Nat R 29:257 Mr 4 '77
NBC's Moscow connection. Nat R 29:483-4 Ap 29 '77
Promo wiz in kidvid bid; B. Riordan, promoter of first skateboard TV show. F. Deford. il por Sports Illus 46:30-3 F 7 '77
Pyrrhic victory? awarding TV rights to the Moscow Olympics to NBC. M. A. Kellogg and others. il Newsweek 89:98 F 14 '77
Some very wrong numbers; ABC's suspension of D. King's United States Championship boxing tournament. R. H. Boyle. il por Sports Illus 46:22-7 My 2 '77
Sportscasting time. T. H. Middleton. Sat R 5:58 O 29 '77
TV & sports—wedded with a golden hoop. J. M. Chandler. il por Psychol Today 10:64+ Ap '77
TV/radio:
At the Open, no news was bad news; ABC's golf telecast. W. Leggett. il Sports Illus 47:46 Jl 4 '77
Bushels of baskets on Sunday; professional and college basketball games. W. Leggett. Sports Illus 46:37 Ja 31 '77
Getting Inside their 'Skins; Washington Redskins in broadcasting. B. Newman. Sports Illus 47:49 D 12 '77
Idea that deserves no trophy; televising the Heisman Awards. D. S. Looney. il Sports Illus 47:68 D 5 '77
Its stand was less than grand; cancellation of Grandstand. W. Leggett. il Sports Illus 47:42 Ag 1 '77
Need to learn the ABCs; baseball playoff and World Series coverage. W. Leggett. il Sports Illus 47:52 O 24 '77
Ol'Don may be a new Danderoo; Monday night football. W. Leggett. il Sports Illus 47:42 O 3 '77
Remembrances of programs past. W. Leggett. il Sports Illus 47:80+ D 19 '77
Right up the viewers' alley; Bowling for dollars. M. Ludtke. il Sports Illus 46:52 Mr 21 '77
These people don't horse around; Kentucky Derby coverage. W. Leggett. il Sports Illus 46:62 My 23 '77
They've almost lost the game; Super Bowl game and preceding variety shows. W. Leggett. il Sports Illus 46:47 Ja 17 '77
They've boxed themselves in; network dealings with D. King. W. Leggett. por Sports Illus 47:68 S 19 '77
This program is a real eye-opener; R. Gandolf, sports newscaster on the CBS Morning News. M. Ludtke. il por Sports Illus 46:42 F 14 '77
Trashsport should be canned; Superstars and spinoffs. W. Leggett. il Sports Illus 46:65 Ap 18 '77
Trenchant words from a talking head; sportscaster J. Whitaker. W. Leggett. por Sports Illus 47:55 N 21 '77
Viewpoint; delayed telecasts in Hawaii. T. Horton. Sports Illus 47:6-7 O 17 '77
Winner takes what? Heavyweight Championships of Tennis. T. Schwartz. il Newsweek 89:68+ My 23 '77

Anecdotes facetiae, satire, etc.

Stow it till the commercial! E. Bombeck. il Read Digest 111:120-2 Jl '77

Study and teaching

Here's how to call the shots; B. Wolff's Sports Broadcasting course at St John's University, Jamaica, N.Y. W. Leggett. por Sports Illus 46:46 F 28 '77

Study and teaching

Video literacy: learning the language of television. M. Shamberg. il Horizon 21:85-8 Ja '78

Tennis

See Television broadcasting—Sports

Great Britain

See also
British Broadcasting Corporation

Israel

Television; views of W. Eytan of the Israel Broadcasting Authority. P. Sourian. Nation 224:603-4 My 14 '77

Italy

Scala Norma: televised opera's self-inflicted wound. J. Culshaw. il Hi Fi 27:14 Je '77
Two Christs in Italy; reactions to Jesus of Nazareth and Mistero buffo. M. Hammond. Commonweal 104:358-9 Je 10 '77

United States

See also
CBS, Inc
National Broadcasting Company
Television industry—United States

TELEVISION broadcasting, Public
New shows, bigger audiences—and growing problems; with editorial comment. il U.S. News 83:51-2, 84 O 3 '77
See also
Corporation for Public Broadcasting
Public Broadcasting Service

Finance

Public TV kills a news winner; Newsroom, program on KQED. J. Benet. Nation 225:588-90 D 3 '77

Laws and regulations

See Television laws and regulations

TELEVISION broadcasting, Subscription
Still pitching for pay-TV. il Bus W p 111-12+ Ap 11 '77
See also
CATV system

TELEVISION broadcasting for children. See Television programs—Childrens programs

TELEVISION censorship. See Television broadcasting—Censorship

TELEVISION characters. See Characters in television; Women in television

TELEVISION circuits
Focus troubles. J. Darr. il Radio-Electr 48:66+ Jl '77
High-voltage hold-down. J. Darr. il Radio-Electr 48:77-9 Ap '77

TELEVISION commentators. See Television broadcasting—News

TELEVISION commercials. See Television advertising

TELEVISION critics and criticism
Coddled critics. H. F. Waters and M. Kasindorf. Newsweek 90:78 Jl 4 '77
Helpful critics; promoting Lou Grant. Newsweek 91:65 Ja 2 '78
Upcoming books switch off television and sharpen up focus on its failings. R. Dahlin. Pub W 212:44 Ag 15 '77
See also
Television program reviews

TELEVISION games. See Electronic games

TELEVISION in agriculture
New on TV: a look inside your water well. il Farm J 101:C4 S '77
Sell livestock on big screen; videotaped cattle auction. il Farm J 100:LK2 D '76

TELEVISION in crime prevention
Candid camera; case of Y. McShane in Great Britain. il por Time 110:29 S 5 '77
No privacy? controversy surrounding the televising of a police film in Y. McShane case in Great Britain. Newsweek 90:47 S 5 '77

TELEVISION in education
Film and television research. R. Beach. bibl Engl J 66:90-3 Mr '77

TELEVISION in education—*Continued*
Roots; using the telecast in black studies course at Miami/Dade Community College, Miami, Fla. M. Rein and J. M. Elliot. il por Negro Hist Bull 40:664-7 Ja '77
School without schools; televising lessons during gas shortage closings in Columbus, Ohio. P. Bonventre and J. Lowell. il Newsweek 89:39 F 21 '77
Sexism's universal curriculum. K. Bonk and J. E. Gardner. il Am Educ 13:15-19 Jl '77
See also
Television broadcasting—Study and teaching
Television programs—Childrens programs
Television programs—Educational programs

TELEVISION in meteorology
Here's how to use your own TV to locate twisters; Weller method. R. Field. Sci Digest 81:14-16 My '77

TELEVISION in politics
Behind Cronkite's coup; bringing together A. Sadat and M. Begin. il por Time 110:47 N 28 '77
Cronkite summit? A. Sadat's Israeli trip. D. M. Alpern and B. Carter. il por Newsweek 90:129 N 28 '77
Not-so-mighty tube. G. F. Will. Newsweek 90:84 Ag 8 '77
Notes and comment; coverage of A. Sadat's visit to Israel. New Yorker 53:19 Ja 9 '78
TV goes into diplomacy; Sadat-Begin summit; Time essay. L. Morrow. il Time 110:44 D 5 '77
TV's effect on American voters; study of 1972 presidential campaign. T. E. Patterson and R. D. McClure. Intellect 105:217-18 Ja '77
Television; Sadat-Begin appearance on television. P. Sourian. Nation 225:670 D 17 '77
Women behind the Presidential debates; League of Women Voters. M. McLaughlin. McCalls 104:65 F '77

Anecdotes, facetiae, satire, etc.

Jimmy Carter show. R. Baker. N Y Times Mag p 12 D 18 '77

TELEVISION industry
See also
Women in the television industry

Finance

Television: a gold mine that's coming under heavy attack. il U.S. News 82:29-30 F 7 '77

Securities

TV network stocks get a bad review. il Bus W p42-3 S 19 '77

United States

Bad news for networks, good news for PBS. K. E. Meyer. Sat R 5:61 D 10 '77
Busting the media trusts. K. Phillips. Harpers 255:23-4+ Jl '77
Fresh crews over Sixth Avenue. Time 110:88 O 31 '77
Is a fourth TV network on the way? J. Perham. Duns R 109:59-60 Ap '77
Society's biggest engine. R. Reeves. Esquire 88: 53-4 N '77
TV imperialism. R. Reeves. Esquire 88:20+ O '77
TV networks: centers of news power. il U.S. News 83:31 Ag 15 '77
Why TV syndicators are striking it rich. il Bus W p76+ F 28 '77
Will it be Paramount? fourth television network. il Horizon 19:78-9 Jl '77
See also
American Broadcasting Companies
CBS, Inc
National Broadcasting Company
Storer Broadcasting Company
Strikes—United States—Television industry

TELEVISION interference
CB-related TVI—and what to do about it. R. Newhall. Pop Electr 11:100-1 Je '77
Product test reports:
Telco channel guard model XL-1000 TVI filter. il Pop Electr 11:84-5 Ap '77

TELEVISION laws and regulations
Bad news for networks, good news for PBS. K. E. Meyer. Sat R 5:61 D 10 '77
Boost for public TV. H. F. Waters and L. Howard. Newsweek 90:106 O 17 '77
Busting the media trusts. K. Phillips. Harpers 255:23-4+ Jl '77
New law for TV and radio? G. R. Rosen. por Duns R 109:65 Ap '77
See also
Television broadcasting—Censorship

TELEVISION motion pictures
Television's little dramas. H. Gold. il Harpers 254:88-93 Mr '77

TELEVISION networks. See Television industry

TELEVISION news. See Television broadcasting—News

TELEVISION performers
Actors get into the act; television actors as directors. L. Loughlin. il Am Home 80:18-19 F '77
See also names of television performers, e.g. C. Chase

TELEVISION production and direction
Actors get into the act; television actors as directors. L. Loughlin. il Am Home 80:18-19 F '77
Around the Mall and beyond; producing TV quiz show What in the world. E. Park. il Smithsonian 8:30-2+ Ap '77
Candy store; sitcom producer G. Marshall. M. Orth and M. Kasindorf. il por Newsweek 89: 74-5 Mr 7 '77
Maria Callas: a personal footnote; taping of BBC interview and concert. J. Culshaw. il por Hi Fi 27:46 D '77

TELEVISION program novels. See Television and literature

TELEVISION program reviews
Films/TV. R. A. Blake. See issues of America
Looking and listening. See issues of Retirement living
Spotlight. E. Miller. See issues of Seventeen
TV (cont) Ms 5:34+ My; 6:46+ O '77
Teleguide. See occasional issues of Senior scholastic including World week
Television. P. H. Hertz. See occasional issues of Senior scholastic including World week
Television. K. E. Meyer. See issues of Saturday review
Television. P. Terzian. Commonweal 104:722-3 N 11 '77

Single works

All creatures great and small
Sr Schol 109:TE12 Mr 10 '77
All that glitters
Sports Illus il 46:48 My 9 '77
Time il 109:68 Ap 25 '77
Amazing Howard Hughes
New Repub 176:23-6 Je 4 '77
American bandstand
Sr Schol 109:29-30 F 10 '77
American short story
Horizon il 20:85 D '77
Sat R 4:44 Ap 2 '77
Sr Schol 109:33 Ap 21 '77
As we see it
Sr Schol 110:17-18+ S 22 '77
Ascent of Mt Fuji
Sat R 5:47 Ja 7 '78
Baa baa black sheep
Flying il 100:46-51+ Je '77
Baretta
Ebony il 33:74-6+ N '77
Barney Miller
Sr Schol il 110:31 N 17 '77
Best of families
Newsweek il 90:108 O 24 '77
Sat R il 5:38-9 O 15 '77
Sr Schol il 110:TE5+ O 6 '77
Sr Schol il 110:47-8 O 20 '77
Time il 110:54 N 14 '77
Betty White show
Time il 110:74 S 12 '77
Captains courageous
Sr Schol il 110:TE17 N 17 '77
Carter country
Time il 110:94 S 19 '77
Charlie's angels
McCalls 104:36 Jl '77
Court-martial of George Armstrong Custer
Sr Schol 110:TE16 N 17 '77
Crockett's victory garden
Newsweek il 90:103 S 12 '77
Dance in America
Dance Mag 51:40 D '77
Dance Mag 52:92-3 Ja '78
Sat R 4:38-9+ Je 25 '77
Vogue 167:32 Je '77
David Copperfield
Sr Schol il 109:TE18-19 Ja 13 '77
Dick Cavett show
Nat R 29:1377-8 N 25 '77
Doctors
Seventeen il pors 36:77-8 N '77
Eleanor and Franklin: the White House years
America 136:243 Mr 19 '77
Sat Eve Post 249:16+ Mr '77
Emily, Emily
Sr Schol il 109:TE14 Ja 27 '77
Fernwood 2 night
Newsweek 90:79 Jl 11 '77
Time il 110:76 Ag 8 '77
Fitzpatricks
New Yorker 53:109-10+ O 17 '77
Forever Fernwood
Newsweek il 90:106 O 17 '77
Gathering
Sr Schol il 110:TE18 N 17 '77
Gong show
Newsweek il 89:40+ F 28 '77
Good morning America
Sat Eve Post il 249:45-7+ S '77
Hard times
Time il 109:57 My 16 '77
Have I got a Christmas for you
Sr Schol 110:TE6 D 1 '77
I, Claudius
New Repub il 177:29-31 N 12 '77
Time il 110:54 N 14 '77
In search of the real America
Nat R 29:197 F 18 '77

TELEVISION program reviews—Single works —*Continued*
Jesus of Nazareth
America 136:334+ Ap 9 '77
America 136:396-7 Ap 30 '77
Chr Cent il 94:373-4 Ap 20 '77
Chr Cent 94:701-2 Ag 3 '77
Chr Today 21:38 Ap 15 '77
Chr Today 21:24-5 My 20 '77
Commonweal 104:227-8 Ap 15 '77
Commonweal 104:358-9 Je 10 '77
Newsweek il 89:78-9 Ap 4 '77
Time il 109:72-3 Ap 4 '77
Last hurrah
Sr Schol 110:TE7 N 3 '77
Life and assassination of the Kingfish
New Repub 176:23-6 Je 4 '77
Life and times of Grizzly Adams
Sr Schol il 110:28-9 O 6 '77
Little women
Dance Mag 51:90 Mr '77
Lou Grant
New Yorker 53:112-14 O 17 '77
Newsweek 91:65 Ja 2 '78
Time il 110:94 S 19 '77
Love affair: the Eleanor and Lou Gehrig story
Sports Illus il 47:98 O 10 '77
Love boat
Newsweek il 91:65 Ja 2 '78
Man in the iron mask
Sr Schol il 109:26 Ja 13 '77
Mary Hartman, Mary Hartman
America 136:484-7 My 28 '77
Read Digest 110:57-9+ F '77
Mary Tyler Moore show
Esquire il 87:74-9 F '77
Nat R 29:448-9 Ap 15 '77
Nation 224:442-3 Ap 9 '77
Sat R il 4:49 Mr 19 '77
Time pors 109:37 Mr 14 '77
Minstrel man
Time 109:55 Mr 7 '77
Mr Chief Justice
Sat R il 4:44-5 S 17 '77
Mistero buffo
Commonweal 104:358-9 Je 10 '77
Muppet show
Ladies Home J il 94:10 O '77
Read Digest 111:23-5+ S '77
Newsroom
Nation 225:589-90 D 3 '77
Nixon interviews
Bus W p33-4 My 9 '77
Commonweal 104:324-6 My 27 '77
Commonweal 104:339-40 My 27 '77
Commonweal 104:359-61 Je 10 '77
Nat R 29:686-7 Je 10 '77
Nation 224:228 F 26 '77
Nation 224:708 Je 11 '77
Nation 224:751-4 Je 18 '77
New Repub 176:2+ Je 4 '77
New Repub 176:11-12 Je 4 '77
New Repub 176:41-2 Je 18 '77
New Yorker 53:31-2 My 16 '77
New Yorker 53:27-8 My 23 '77
Newsweek 89:28-9 My 16 '77
Newsweek 89:17-18 My 23 '77
Newsweek 89:18-19 My 30 '77
Newsweek 89:28+ Je 6 '77
Newsweek il 89:25+ My 9 '77
Newsweek il 90:34 S 12 '77
Sat R 4:35 Je 25 '77
Time il 109:21-2+ My 16 '77
Time il 109:15-16 My 30 '77
Time il 109:11-12 Je 6 '77
Time il pors 109:22-4+ My 9 '77
Time il por 109:41 My 23 '77
Time por 110:23 S 12 '77
U.S. News 82:35 My 23 '77
U.S. News 82:65-6 My 30 '77
U.S. News 82:24 Je 6 '77
U.S. News il por 83:81 S 12 '77
U.S. News pors 82:27-9 My 16 '77
Nutcracker
Sat R 5:60 D 10 '77
Our town
Sr Schol 109:TE9 My 19 '77
Over easy
Aging il 275:8-10 S '77
Pallisers
Nat R 29:336+ Mr 18 '77
Newsweek 89:74 Mr 7 '77
Sat R 4:51 Ja 22 '77
Time il 109:40-2 Ja 31 '77
Raid on Entebbe
Harpers 254:89-90 Mr '77
Rock follies
Newsweek il 89:79 Mr 21 '77
Roots
Chr Cent 94:200-2 Mr 2 '77
Chr Cent 94:279-80 Mr 23 '77
Chr Today 21:36-7 F 18 '77
Nat R 29:196 F 18 '77
Nat R 29:276+ Mr 4 '77
Negro Hist Bull 40:664-7 Ja '77
New Repub 176:2+ F 12 '77
New Repub 176:27-8 Mr 12 '77
Newsweek il 89:59 Ja 24 '77
Newsweek il 89:26 F 7 '77
Newsweek il 89:97-8 F 14 '77
Sr Schol il 109:TE22-3 Ja 13 '77
Sr Schol il 109:27-8 Ja 27 '77
Sr Schol il 109:38-9 Mr 24 '77
Time il 109:56 Ja 24 '77
Time il 109:96 F 7 '77
Time il 109:68-72+, 76-7 F 14 '77
Time il 109:72+ F 21 '77
Royal family
Sat R 5:50 O 29 '77
Saturday night
Horizon il 20:81-3 D '77
Ms il 6:46+ O '77
Newsweek il 90:80 N 28 '77
Sat Eve Post il 249:38-9+ My '77
Scenes from a marriage
America 136:202-3 Mr 5 '77
Chr Cent il 94:535-40 Je 1 '77
Sat R il 4:51 Mr 5 '77
Serpico
Chr Today 21:23-5 Mr 4 '77
Shades of Greene
Sat R 4:52 Jl 9 '77
Shields and Yarnell
Newsweek 89:85 Je 20 '77
Soap
Chr Today 22:42 D 30 '77
Commonweal 104:615+ S 30 '77
Commonweal 104:722-3 N 11 '77
New Yorker 53:124-5 O 3 '77
Newsweek il 89:92 Je 13 '77
Time 110:75 Jl 11 '77
Time 110:53 S 26 '77
Time il 110:72+ S 12 '77
Stanley Siegal show
Newsweek il por 90:48 Ag 8 '77
Tail Gunner Joe
Nat R 29:335-6 Mr 18 '77
Nat R 29:350 Mr 18 '77
This far by faith
Sr Schol 109:TE14 F 24 '77
3 girls 3
Newsweek 89:85 Je 20 '77
Trial of Aaron Burr
Sat R 4:44-5 S 17 '77
Trial of Lee Harvey Oswald
Newsweek il 90:64-5 O 3 '77
Time il 110:91 O 3 '77
Upstairs, downstairs
N Y Times Mag p60-4 My 8 '77
Time il 109:74 My 9 '77
Victory at Entebbe
Sat R 4:46 F 5 '77
Washington: behind closed doors
America 137:151 S 17 '77
Chr Cent 94:836-7 S 28 '77
New Yorker 53:115-18+ O 3 '77
Newsweek 90:54-5 S 5 '77
Newsweek il 90:104 S 19 '77
Progressive 41:14-15 N '77
Sat R 4:38-9 S 3 '77
Sat R 5:50 O 29 '77
Time 110:50 S 5 '77
Time il 110:92-3 S 19 '77
What in the world
Smithsonian 8:30-2+ Ap '77
What really happened to the class of '65?
Newsweek il 90:123 D 12 '77
Wodehouse playhouse
Sat R il 4:52 Jl 9 '77

TELEVISION programming. See Television broadcasting—Programming

TELEVISION programs
Another season for making whoopie. R. Rosenblatt. New Repub 177:54-6 S 17 '77
Decline of the western. C. Baldwin. Nat R 29: 679-80 Je 10 '77
Eyeballing the new season. H. F. Waters. il Newsweek 90:79 S 26 '77
More sex less violence: TV's new pitch. J. Mann. il U.S. News 83:20-3 S 12 '77
Playing with the facts. T. Griffith. il Time 110:92-3 S 19 '77
Some old, some new, a lot borrowed, a little blue; fall shows. il Time 110:48-9 S 5 '77
Sons of Roots: TV runs to serials. H. F. Waters and others. il Newsweek 90:52-3+ S 5 '77
TV. D. English. See issues of Vogue
TV's new ABC's; youth oriented shows. H. F. Waters and M. Kasindorf. il Newsweek 90: 104+ D 5 '77
Television. C. Gilbert. Am Home 80:14 S '77
Television. J. Lardner. New Repub 177:24-6 D 10 '77
Television; fall season. K. E. Meyer. il Sat R 4:65-7 Ag 6 '77
See also
Aviation in television
Sex role in television programs
Television adaptations
Television critics and criticism
Television program reviews
Television serials

Anecdotes, facetiae, satire, etc.

Confessions of a non-addict. P. Steinfels. Commonweal 104:328 My 27 '77
Me, Tarzanus; satire of I, Claudius. R. Baker. N Y Times Mag p6 Ja 8 '78

TELEVISION programs—*Continued*

Black programs

After Haley's comet. H. F. Waters. il por Newsweek 89:97-8 F 14 '77
Black experience; Roots. H. F. Waters. il Newsweek 89:59 Ja 24 '77
Why Roots hit home. il Time 109:68-71 F 14 '77

Childrens programs

All about Kidvid. H. F. Waters. il Newsweek 89:66 F 21 '77
Kid power. D. English. il Vogue 167:63 O '77
Turning the menace into magic. A. R. Pike. Parents Mag 52:38-9+ Je '77

Reviews—Single works

Mr Rogers' neighborhood
Sat Eve Post 249:24+ D '77
Music
Newsweek 90:111 O 24 '77
Time 110:75 O 17 '77

Christmas programs

Box that stole Christmas. R. Rosenblatt. New Repub 177:37-8 D 24 '77

Comedy

See Television programs—Humorous programs

Conversation programs

Cavett goes public. M. J. Sobran, Jr. Nat R 29:1377-8 N 25 '77

Anecdotes, facetiae, satire, etc.

Bored again; religious television talk shows. M. E. Marty. Chr Cent 94:1103 N 23 '77

Crime programs

How TV cops flout the law. S. Arons and E. Katsh. il Sat R 4:10-14+ Mr 19 '77
Serpico and the voyeurs of the moral war. L. Basney. il Chr Today 21:23-5 Mr 4 '77

Dance programs

Celebration; television production of ABT's Nutcracker. T. Tibias. il pors Dance Mag 51:50-3 D '77
Dancevision; Making television dance. Dance Mag 51:99 N '77
Dancevision: the T.V. beat. N. M. Stoop. See issues of Dance magazine
Eye on Tharp; Making television dance. il Horizon 20:81 O '77
On TV: America's dances and dancers. W. Terry. il Sat R 4:38-9+ Je 25 '77

Documentary programs

See Television programs, Documentary

Educational programs

Ben Stahl: teaching art through television; South Carolina Educational Television Network's Journey into art. M. Corbino. il por Am Artist 41:24-7+ Mr '77
See also
Television programs—Childrens programs

Game shows

Extensions downtown; use of pinball machines by Manhattan Cable Television's The game show. New Yorker 53:25-7 F 28 '77
Gambling, goods, and games. T. Martinez. il Society 14:79-81 S '77
I won $25,000 on a TV game show; $25,000 pyramid; ed by M. Siegel. A. Gibriel. il por Good H 184:154+ Mr '77

Humorous programs

Candy store; sitcom producer G. Marshall. M. Orth and M. Kasindorf. il por Newsweek 89:74-5 Mr 7 '77
Television's funniest show is on when you're asleep; Saturday night. S. Walton. il Sat Eve Post 249:38-9+ My '77
Tuesday night on the tube. il Time 110:94+ D 12 '77
What some women do for laughs on Saturday night. S. Weller. il Ms 6:46+ O '77

Production and direction

See Television production and direction

Rating

Rating game. H. R. Waters and others. il Newsweek 90:142-3 N 21 '77

Religious programs

Great alternative; Christian television programs. il Sat Eve Post 249:72-3 My '77
Rex Humbard's 25-25 vision. P. Geiger and N. Kennedy. il pors Chr Today 21:53-6 My 6 '77
Threat to religious broadcasting: somebody is lying. Chr Today 21:41 Ja 7 '77

Anecdotes facetiae, satire etc.

Bored again; religious television talk shows. M. E. Marty. Chr Cent 94:1103 N 23 '77

Sponsorship

See Television advertising

Titling

Subtitles for TV and films; captions for the hearing-impaired. il Am Educ 13:18-22 Mr '77

TELEVISION programs, Documentary

Cracks in the keystone; documentaries on contemporary education J. W. Donohue. America 137:242 O 15 '77
Media. Sci N 111:62, 142, 206, 271, 350 Ja 22, F 26, Mr 26, Ap 23, My 28 '77
Science on TV: update. Sci Digest 81:82 F '77
Sons of 60 minutes. T. Schwartz and A. R. Martin. il Newsweek 89:104+ My 16 '77

Reviews

Single works

Age of uncertainty
America 136:466-7 My 21 '77
N Y Times Mag p23-4+ My 15 '77
Nat R 29:601-4 My 27 '77
Newsweek 89:61-2 My 23 '77
Sat R 4:43 My 28 '77
Born again
Chr Today 21:21 Ag 12 '77
CIA's secret army
Nat R 29:792-3 Jl 8 '77
Nation 225:155-7 Ag 20 '77
Newsweek il 90:85 Jl 18 '77
Time 109:50 Je 13 '77
Canal Zone
America 137:218 O 8 '77
Nation 225:381-2 O 15 '77
N Y Times Mag il p96-102+ O 2 '77
Time il 110:103 O 10 '77
Crowded life
Sat R 5:47 Ja 7 '78
Danger! Radioactive waste
Science 198:1232-3 D 23 '77
Gentle giants of the Pacific
Sr Schol 110:TE5 D 1 '77
Giving birth: four portraits
Pop Phot 80:72+ F '77
Including me
Time il 110:109 S 19 '77
Miracle months
Time il 109:60-1 Mr 14 '77
National disaster survival test
Sr Schol il 109:TE15 Ap 21 '77
Parenthood game
Sr Schol il 109:TE15 Ja 27 '77
Royal heritage
Sat R il 4:33-4 Ap 30 '77
Six American families
Ms 5:34+ My '77
Sat R 4:39 Ap 30 '77
Sr Schol 109:37 Ap 7 '77
60 minutes
New Yorker 53:166-73 N 28 '77
Read Digest il 111:155-8 Jl '77
Time 109:60 My 2 '77
Tiger, tiger
Sr Schol il 109:TE14 Ap 21 '77
Treasures of the British crown
Horizon il 20:86-93 D '77
Volga
Sr Schol il 109:TE15 F 24 '77
Voyage of the Hokule'a
Sr Schol il 109:TE21 Ja 13 '77

TELEVISION projection

Projection TV—build your own for super-size pictures. J. Free. il Pop Sci 211:84-5+ N '77

TELEVISION ratings. See Television programs—Rating

TELEVISION receivers

Color TV:
What's new for '77. K. Savon. il Radio-Electr 48:55-7+ F '77
So what else is new in TV? R. D. Freed. il Mech Illus 73:62+ D '77

Circuits

See Television circuits

Control

Heathkit GR-2001: programmable color TV. A. Kleiman. il Radio-Electr 48:49-51+ My '77
Programmable color TV changes channels automatically. J. Free. il Pop Sci 210:30 Ap '77
TV remote control uses infrared signal. S. Prentiss. il Pop Sci 210:141 Je '77

Interference

See Television interference

Maintenance and repair

How to prevent TV damage from video game-playing. Consumer Rep 42:252 My '77
Service clinic. J. Darr. See issues of Radio-electronics
Step-by-step TV troubleshooters guide:
Faults in the horizontal and vertical sync circuits. J. Darr. il Radio-Electr 48:58-9+ Jl '77
See also
Television repair shops
Television repairmen

TELEVISION receivers—*Continued*

Manufacture

See Television apparatus industry

Prices

Troubled Zenith battles stiffer competition. il por Bus W p 128+ O 10 '77

Testing

Color TV consoles. Consumer Rep 42:250-3 D '77
19-inch color TV's. il Consumer Rep 43:13-17 Ja '78
Small black-and-white TV sets. Consumer Rep 42:158-61 Mr '77
TV receivers. il Consumers Res Mag 60:21-7 D '77
Television and radio. il Consumers Res Mag 60:38-47 O '77

TELEVISION receivers, Portable
Consumer's guide to: mini TVs. Mech Illus 73: 28 Mr '77
Littlest TV. il Time 110:61 O 17 '77
Mini TV that's also thin. C. A. Miller. il Mech Illus 73:29 N '77
19-inch color portables. S. Prentiss. il Pop Sci 210:128-30+ Ap '77
Tiny TV has 2-inch screen. J. R. Free. il Pop Sci 210:12 Mr '77
What's new: TV to go. V. Perlo. il Am Home 80:26 Jl '77

Radio, phonograph and tape recorder combination

Take-along entertainment you can carry in your hand. I. Berger. il Pop Mech 147:87-9 Ap '77

TELEVISION reception
Circular polarization minimizes TV ghosts. R. F. Scott. il Radio-Electr 48:38-40 N '77

TELEVISION relay systems
Balloon relay for Iranian TV program. R. H. Warren. il Pop Sci 210:113 My '77
See also
CATV system

TELEVISION repair shops
Art's TV shop. A. Margolis. il Pop Electr 11: 99-100 Ap '77

TELEVISION repairmen

Wages and hours

Pay relationships of TV-radio and appliance repairers. S. L. King. il M Labor R 100:48-9 My '77

TELEVISION script writing. See Television authorship

TELEVISION serials
Confessions of a soap addict. M. Edmondson. por Newsweek 90:3 Ag 22 '77
Great soap opera fan letters; excerpt from Letters from soap opera fans; comp by B. Adler. Good H 184:76+ Mr '77
Honk, honk, if you love Mary Hartman, Mary Hartman. T. Morgan. il Read Digest 110:57-9+ F '77
Soap gets in your eyes. R. La Guardia. il Sat Eve Post 249:40-1+ S '77
Soap opera teen; The doctors. J. Houlton. il pors Seventeen 36:77-8 N '77

Anecdotes, facetiae, satire, etc.

Confessions of a soap-opera addict. J. Kerr. il McCalls 104:36+ S '77

TELEVISION sets. See Television receivers

TELEVISION sound. See Television transmission —Sound transmission

TELEVISION stations
Big sky TV; Ma and Pa station KYUS, Miles City, Mont. P. S. Greenberg. pors Newsweek 89:9 Mr 28 '77
Time to sell? publishing and broadcasting operations. Forbes 120:32-3 Jl 1 '77
See also
American Broadcasting Companies
National Broadcasting Company

TELEVISION stations, Educational
Ben Stahl: teaching art through television; South Carolina Educational Television Network. M. Corbino. il por Am Artist 41:24-7+ Mr '77
Television; R. Kotlowitz of WNET. P. Sourian. Nation 225:732-4 D 31 '77

TELEVISION towers
Improve TV reception—install a tower. J. Schwartz. il Radio-Electr 48:70-1+ Ap '77

TELEVISION transmission
Radio hams use amateur bands for global TV. W. R. Haldane. Sci Digest 81:90-1 My '77

Sound transmission

New hope for TV sound. R. Lanier. Hi Fi 27: 76-8 N '77

TELEVISION workers
See also
National Association of Broadcast Employees and Technicians

TELEVISION writing. See Television authorship

TELFORD, John, and others
Novel screening procedure for recombinant plasmids. bibl il Science 195:391-3 Ja 28 '77

TELL MARDIKH excavations. See Syria—Antiquities

TELLER, Edward
For energy solution: Teller gives us 5 years. J. E. Persico. por Sci Digest 82:37-9 Jl '77 *
Science and defense policy. J. Marsh. Commentary 63:67-70 Ap '77 *

TELLICO Dam project. See Dams

TELLING, Edward Riggs
At the top of the tower. il por Time 110:80 N 21 '77 *
Man who won't buy his shoes at Sears. E. J. Tracy and others. por Fortune 96:17 D '77 *
Telling changes. por Forbes 120:108 D 1 '77 *
Vintner for Sears. L. Langway and C. J. Harper. il por Newsweek 90:78 N 21 '77 *

TEMIN, Howard Martin
Relationship of tumor virology to an understanding of nonviral cancers. bibl BioScience 27:170-6 Mr '77

TEMPEH
Calling all tempeh lovers. H. L. Wang and others. il Org Gard & Farm 24:108+ Je '77
See also
Cookery—Vegetables

TEMPER
See also
Anger

TEMPERA painting
Looking at paintings; Flemish painting. B. Dunstan. il Am Artist 41:62-3 D '77

TEMPERANCE
Catholics and temperance. J. H. Fichter; discussion. Commonweal 104:62-3 Ja 21 '77

TEMPERATURE
See also
Hot weather
Ocean temperature
Plants, Effect of temperature on

Control

Across U.S: conservation with a smile; thermostat at 65°. il U.S. News 82:12 F 7 '77

Measurement

See also
Thermometers and thermometry

Physiological effects

See also
Cows, Effect of temperature on
Fishes, Effect of temperature on
Heat—Physiological effects
Swine, Effect of temperature on

Regulation

See also
Thermostats

TEMPERATURE, Animal and human
Bombesin: potent effects on thermoregulation in the rat. M. Brown and others. bibl il Science 196:998-1000 My 27 '77
Cell membrane sodium pump as a mechanism for increasing thermogenesis during cold acclimation in rats. D. L. Guernsey and E. D. Stevens. bibl il Science 196:908-10 My 20 '77
Endothermy during terrestrial activity in large beetles. G. A. Bartholomew and T. M. Casey. bibl il Science 195:882-3 Mr 4 '77
Getting warm; nonshivering thermogenesis. J. A. Miller. il Sci N 111:42 Ja 15 '77
Hawaiian spinner; thermoregulatory behavior of the spinner dolphin. G. C. Whittow. il Sea Front 23:304-7 S '77
Rapid brain cooling in exercising dogs; function of the carotid rete. M. A. Baker and L. W. Chapman. bibl il Science 195:781-3 F 25 '77
See also
Hypothermia

TEMPERATURE changes, Global. See Global temperature changes

TEMPESTS (boats) See Sailboats

TEMPLATES
Mistakeproof template for plasterboard cutouts. H. Wicks. il Pop Mech 148:159 Ag '77

TEMPLE, Shirley. See Black, S. T.

TEMPLE, Stanley A.
Plant-animal mutualism: coevolution with dodo leads to near extinction of plant. bibl Science 197:885-6 Ag 26 '77

TEMPLE University Press. See University presses

TEMPLES
See also
Synagogues

China

Discovering ancient treasures in Caves of the thousand Buddhas; Tunhuang cave temples; excerpt from Sir Aurel Stein. J. Mirsky. il por map Smithsonian 8:94-6+ My '77

Egypt

Luxor's other temple; temple of Mut. il Time 110:64 O 17 '77

TEMPLES, Buddhist
See also
Borobudur, Java
Temples—China

TEMPLETON, Garry
Short, but not on hits. J. Kaplan. por Sports Illus 47:52-3 O 3 '77 *

TEMPLETON, John Marks
John Marks Templeton: serving God and hunting bargains. R. J. Flaherty. il por Forbes 119:72+ My 15 '77 *

TEMPLETON, Robert
First family portrait; reproductions of drawings. Good H 184:92-3 F '77

TEMPLETON Growth Fund. See Investment trusts

TEMPLETS. See Templates

TEMPORAL lobe. See Brain

TEMPORARY employment. See Employment, Temporary

TEMPTATION
Spider's web: deceptive beauty. E. Schaeffer. Chr Today 21:25-6 Jl 29 '77
See also
Jesus Christ—Temptation

TEMPURA. See Cookery, Japanese

TEN BOOM, Corrie, and others
Miracle of barracks 28. il por Sat Eve Post 249: 42-3+ Ap '77

TEN Commandments. See Commandments, Ten

TENAFLY, N.J, Public Library. See Libraries—New Jersey

TENANTS. See Landlord and tenant

TENDER offers. See Stocks—Tender offers

TENDERIZING of meat. See Meat—Tenderizing

TENDRILS
Experimental separation of sensory and motor functions in pea tendrils. M. J. Jaffe. bibl il Science 195:191-2 Ja 14 '77

TENENBAUM, Susan, and Paulus, J. A.
Legislation to watch—and work for—in the 95th Congress. Ms 5:99-102 F '77

TENER, Morton
Director's support key to CIT success. Camp Mag 49:5+ Ap '77

TENG, Fan Yew. See Bird, K. jt auth

TENG, Hsiao-ping
Comeback for Teng? K. Willenson and others. por Newsweek 89:51 Ja 24 '77 *
Comeback of a capitalist roader. il por Time 109:31-2 Ja 24 '77 *
Second comeback for Comrade Teng. il pors Time 110:23-4 Ag 1 '77 *
Teng: China's real boss. M. Smith. il por Newsweek 90:43-4 S 12 '77 *
Welcome home. il por Newsweek 90:34 Ag 1 '77 *

TENGö, Jan, and Bergstrom, Gunnar
Cleptoparasitism and odor mimetism in bees: do nomada males imitate the odor of andrena females? bibl il Science 196:1117-19 Je 3 '77

TENISON, Marika Hanbury
But can you eat the food? il Sat R 4:29-31+ Je 11 '77

TENNANT, Veronica
Spotlight on: Veronica Tennant. S. I. Odom. il por Dance Mag 51:68-70 Mr '77 *

TENNECO Inc
Settling for less on Navy contracts; General Dynamics Corp.'s Electric Boat Div. and Tenneco Inc.'s Newport News Shipbuilding & Dry Dock Co. il Bus W p27-8 Ap 11 '77
Tough way to make a living; expansion for Tennessee Gas Transmission Co. il Forbes 119: 46-8 Je 1 '77

TENNENBAUM, James I.
Season for insect stings—ways to protect yourself; interview. il U.S. News 82:73 My 9 '77

TENNESEN, Michael
California's kelp beds flourish again. il Nat Wildlife 15:12-16 O '77

TENNESSEE
See also
Great Smoky Mountains
Great Smoky Mountains National Park
Historic houses, sites etc—Tennessee
Prisons—Tennessee

History

Great state of Franklin. il Sr Schol 109:6-8 Ap 21 '77

TENNESSEE Gas Transmission Company. See Tenneco, Inc

TENNESSEE-Tombigbee Waterway Project. See Waterways—United States

TENNESSEE Valley Authority
Carter's mandate to transform TVA. por Bus W p29-30 S 5 '77
Critical TVA scholarship hard to come by. D. Shapley. Science 195:274 Ja 21 '77; Reply. C. Brewer. 195:726+ F 25 '77
Excerpts from statement on nuclear energy production, January 1977. A. J. Wagner. Cong Digest 56:54+ F '77
Little fish inspires big ideas; snail darter and the Tellico Dam project. E. M. Leeper. map BioScience 27:697-9 O '77
TVA: it ain't what it used to be. J. Branscome. il map Am Heritage 28:68-78 F '77
TVA today: former reformers in an era of expensive electricity. D. Shapley; discussion. Science 195:6, 243-5 Ja 7, 21 '77
What they didn't tell you about the snail darter & the dam; question of avoiding compliance with Endangered Species Act in Tellico Dam project. S. G. Cook and others. il map Nat Parks & Con Mag 51:10-13 My '77

TENNIEL, Sir John
Suppressed adventure of Alice surfaces after 107 years. il pors Smithsonian 8:50-7 bibl(p 134) D '77 *

TENNIS
According to Chairman Mao; U.S. tour of China. B. Collins. il Sports Illus 47:99-100 D 5 '77
Georgia's on his mind; tennis coach D. Magill. K. Hannon. il por Sports Illus 46:52-3 My 30 '77
Tennis tips:
Choosing a tennis racket. J. Heldman. il por Seventeen 36:34+ F '77
What to wear on the tennis court. J. Heldman. Seventeen 36:40+ Je '77
WTT reigns in Plains; Phoenix Racquets vs the Soviets. B. McDermott. il Sports Illus 46:56+ My 9 '77
Zing go the strings of our hearts; World Team Tennis. J. Jares. il Sports Illus 47:16-18+ Jl 25 '77
See also
Paddle tennis
Squash (game)
Table tennis

Equipment and supplies

Perfect tennis partner; ball throwing machines. J. Greenfield. il Esquire 87:110-11+ My '77
Tennis tips and products. F. Fochek. il Consumers Res Mag 60:13-15 Ap '77

History

White flannels, grass courts. J. Hart. New Repub 177:21-4 Jl 23 '77

Psychological aspects

How your self-image controls your tennis game; excerpt from Love and hate on the tennis court. N. Cobb and others. il Psychol Today 11:46-7+ Je '77
Playing the inner game of working, living; interview. W. T. Gallwey. por Mademoiselle 83:203+ Ap '77

Radio broadcasting

See Radio broadcasting—Sports

Study and teaching

Playing with the stars. G. Lichtenstein. il Esquire 87:108-9+ My '77

Television broadcasting

See Television broadcasting—Sports

Tournaments

After the last hurrah, a final murmur; Aetna World Cup. F. Deford. il Sports Illus 46:30-2+ Mr 21 '77
Ambush on the comeback trail; Colgate Series Championship. W. Bingham. il pors Sports Illus 47:34-5 N 14 '77
Ave atque vale; U.S. open. H. W. Wind. New Yorker 53:123-6+ O 10 '77
Borg's hot hand took all the tricks; Grand Slam of Tennis. C. Kirkpatrick. il pors Sports Illus 46:16-17 Ja 31 '77
Centenary; Wimbledon. H. W. Wind. New Yorker 53:56-66+ Jl 25 '77
Extra! Chrissie loses first set! Championship of the Virginia Slims tour. J. Jares. il por Sports Illus 46:24-5 Ap 4 '77
Family game; Muriel Ressler Memorial Mixed Doubles Tournament in Central Park. New Yorker 53:52-5 N 21 '77
Fantastico, Guillermo! U.S. Open. C. Kirkpatrick. il Sports Illus 47:12-17 S 19 '77
Farewell to Forest Hills. B. Collins. il N Y Times Mag p48-50+ S 11 '77
First she curtsied, then she bowed; T. Austin at Wimbledon. C. Kirkpatrick. il por Sports Illus 47:49-51 Jl 4 '77
Graham did not crack; National Collegiate Classic. J. Jares. por Sports Illus 46:48-9 Ja 17 '77
Hand that rocks the cradle; E. Goolagong in the World Invitational Tennis Classic. B. McDermott. por Sports Illus 37:74+ O 17 '77
He's a first-class tourist; WCT championship. J. Underwood. il por Sports Illus 46:78+ My 23 '77
Little bit better than Lagos; D. Stockton's victory in the U.S. Pro Indoor. C. Kirkpatrick. por Sports Illus 46:20-1 F 7 '77
Only human; R. Richards at the U.S. Open. P. Axthelm. il por Newsweek 90:77-8 S 12 '77
Only human; Wimbledon matches. P. Axthelm. il Newsweek 90:44 Jl 11 '77

TENNIS—Tournaments—*Continued*
Real grass, real class; Wimbledon. P. Axthelm. il Newsweek 90:54-5+ Jl 4 '77
South America takes it away; Argentina vs U.S. in Davis Cup play. W. Bingham. il Sports Illus 46:20-1 My 9 '77
Super-Seniors: age will be served. il Time 109: 68 Ap 18 '77
Tracy Austin tops Seventeen netters second annual Tennis Tournament of Champions. J. Heldman. il Seventeen 36:140-1+ S '77
Wimbledon was never better; Ginny fizz becomes Ginny tonic. C. Kirkpatrick. il pors Sports Illus 47:12-17 Jl 11 '77
Wimbledon: youth will be served. il Time 110: 72-3 Jl 11 '77

History

Little hanky-panky, but no fixes. J. Kramer and F. Deford. il Sports Illus 48:26-30+ Ja 9 '78
So everything was Jake. J. Kramer and F. Deford. il Sports Illus 48:50-8 Ja 2 '78
U.S. open tennis championships. il Sports Illus 47:35-6+ Ag 29 '77

TENNIS balls
Tennis balls. il Consumer Rep 42:131-3 Mr '77

TENNIS clothes. See Clothing and dress—Sports clothes

TENNIS clubs. See Sports clubs

TENNIS coaches
See also
Hines, H. 3d
Magill, D.

TENNIS courts
Tennis, folks? White House tennis court. J. Osborne. New Repub 177:11-12 N 26 '77
Tennis on a tank; Evergreen, Colo. J. S. Blair. il Parks & Rec 12:35a F '77

TENNIS players
Playing with the stars. G. Lichtenstein. il Esquire 87:108-9+ My '77
Sex and tennis: mismatched pair. D. Sheahan. il Am Home 80:27 Ag '77
Who's who in Seventeen's Tennis Tournament of Champions. il Seventeen 36:148+ Ap '77
See also
Ashe, A.
Austin, T.
Connors, J.
Evert, C.
Gerulaitis, V.
Goolagong, E.
Gottfried, B.
King, B. J.
Nastase, I.
Navratilova, M.
Stockton, D.
Vilas, G.
Wade, V.
Wightman, H. H.

Caricatures and cartoons

Remedial tennis. W. Eisner. il Esquire 88:78-9 Jl '77

TENNIS rackets
Can an exotic new racket improve your game? R. Nelson. il Pop Mech 147:94-6+ My '77
Choosing a tennis racket. J. Heldman. il por Seventeen 36:34+ F '77
Super racket. A. Fisher. il Pop Sci 210:44+ Mr '77

TENNSTEDT, Klaus
Body English from the story. W. Bender. por Time 109:64 Mr 7 '77 *
Summer crop of maestros. I. Kolodin. por Sat R 4:48-9 S 17 '77 *

TENNY, Ralph
How to interface microprocessors. il Pop Electr 12:66-70 D '77

TENSION (psychology) See Stress (psychology)

TENTS
Bright new shapes for the campground. B. McKeown. il Pop Mech 147:95-7 Je '77
Clever engineering shapes new tent designs. B. H. Berry. il por Pop Sci 211:128-30 O '77
Family tents. il Consumer Rep 42:424-9 Jl '77
How to pitch your tent. S. Masia. il Outdoor Life 159:133-4 My '77
Tent camp: perfect base for cold-weather action. P. Nelson. il Outdoor Life 160:78-9+ D '77
Tents by Moss. S. Netherby. il por Field & S 82:128-9+ D '77
Tents for family camping. N. Soderstrom. il Consumers Res Mag 60:7-13 Ag '77

TENURE, Academic. See College teachers—Tenure

TENURE of land. See Land tenure

TEPPER, Irwin
Risk vs. return in pension fund investment. il Harvard Bus R 55:100-7 Mr '77

TEQUILA
Tequila; Mexican mescal. N. K. Walton. il Américas 29:15-18 Ja '77

TERCHEK, Ronald J.
Conflict and cleavage in Northern Ireland. bibl f Ann Am Acad 433:47-59 S '77

TERESA of Lisieux, Saint. See Teresa of the Child Jesus

TERESA of the Child Jesus, Saint
Timely saints. A. McCarthy. Commonweal 104: 169+ Mr 18 '77

TERHORST, Jerald F.
Cheaper Ford. Nation 224:773 Je 25 '77 *

TERIET, Bernhard
Flexiyear schedules—only a matter of time? bibl f M Labor R 100:62-5 D '77

TERIYAKI. See Cookery, Japanese

TERKEL, Studs
Tipping is an art, not a science; excerpt from Talking to myself. Vogue 167:351-3 O '77

about

Interviewer. B. DeMott. il Atlantic 240:82-5 Jl '77 *

TERM papers. See Student themes and reports

TERMAN, Lewis Madison
Role of microelectronics in data processing; with biographical sketch. il Sci Am 237:14+, 162-4+ bibl(p260) S '77

TERMINAL buildings, Airport. See Airport buildings

TERMINAL care
Fix for pain? use of heroin and marijuana for terminal cancer patients. M. Clark and others. il Newsweek 91:41 Ja 2 '78
Heroic measures—giving the patient a choice; work at Los Angeles County-University of Southern California Medical Center. J. Gaylin. Psychol Today 11:149+ D '77
Home care for children with cancer; Univ. of Minnesota program. K. Leishman. McCalls 105:44-5 Ja '78
More comfortable death—home care for the dying child. J. Gaylin. Psychol Today 11:30+ Jl '77
See also
Terminal care facilities

TERMINAL care facilities
Good death; St Christopher's Hospice in London. G. F. Will. Newsweek 91:72 Ja 9 '78

TERMINALS (transportation)
See also
Airports
Petroleum shipping terminals

TERMITE control
How to cope with house-destroying termites. Bet Hom & Gard 55:258+ O '77

TERMITE exterminators. See Pest control operators

TERMITES

Extermination

See Termite control

TERPENES
Sesquiterpene antitumor agents: inhibitors of cellular metabolism. K. H. Lee and others. bibl il Science 196:533-6 Ap 29 '77

TERRA nova; drama. See Tally, T.

TERRACE gardens. See Balcony gardens, roof gardens, etc.

TERRACES (agriculture)
How I built a railroad tie garden. R. Wolf. il Org Gard & Farm 24:62-4 Ap '77
Terracing and contour farming to stop hillside erosion. G. Logsdon. il Org Gard & Farm 24: 64-7 Ap '77
Turning steep land into gardens. T. Gettings. il Org Gard & Farm 24:57-60 Ap '77

TERRACES (outdoor living areas) See Decks, patios, terraces, etc.

TERRARIUMS
Terrarium gardening. A. A. Swenson. il Ladies Home J 94:72+ O '77

TERRELL, John
Sociobiology. Sci Digest 82:58-61 S '77

TERRESTRIAL magnetism. See Magnetism, Terrestrial

TERRIEN, Samuel
Equus: human conflicts and the Trinity. Chr Cent 94:472-6 My 18 '77

TERRITORIAL expansion
See also
Indonesia—Territorial expansion
South Africa—Territorial expansion

TERRITORIAL waters
New U.S. lake in the Pacific; strategic implications of the 200-mile limit on Trust Territory. R. W. Gale. map Progressive 41:50-2 My '77
Reciprocal fisheries agreement with the United Kingdom; message to Senate, October 7, 1977. J. Carter. Dept State Bull 77:708-9 N 14 '77
There is but one ocean. J. Nowadnick. il Sea Front 23:130-40 My '77
U.S.-Canada maritime boundary and resource negotiations. Dept State Bull 77:896-7 D 19 '77
U.S, Canada to negotiate maritime issues; announcement, July 27, 1977. Dept State Bull 77: 282 Ag 29 '77
U.S. Cuba agree on maritime boundaries and fishery matters. map Dept State Bull 76:687 Je 27 '77

TERRITORIAL waters—*Continued*
U.S., Mexico sign fishery agreement; set provisional maritime boundaries. Dept State Bull 75:758-9 D 27 '76
See also
Fishery laws and legislation
United Nations Conference on the Law of the Sea

TERRITORIALISM (animals) See Animals—Habits and behavior

TERROR of Bigfoot; drama. See Murray, J.

TERRORISM
Allah was on our side; Washington, D.C. siege by Hanafi Muslims. J. T. Clemons. Chr Cent 94:319-20 Ap 6 '77
America's menacing misfits; taking of hostages by terrorists. Time 109:20 Mr 21 '77
Behind the siege of terror in Washington. il map U.S. News 82:19-21+ Mr 21 '77
Blast; bombing of the New York Public Library. New Yorker 53:35-6 O 24 '77
Civil war in Islamic America. A. Muhammad. Nation 224:721-4 Je 11 '77
Cuban exiles: Miami, haven for terror. Nation 224:326-31 Mr 19 '77
Delicate art of handling terrorists. P. Goldman and others. il Newsweek 89:25-7 Mr 21 '77
Forecast: more bombs ahead; Puerto Rican terrorists. J. Willwerth. il Time 110:39-40 O 24 '77
From the concrete floor: thoughts while being held hostage; Washington, D.C. siege by Hanafi Muslims. C. Fenyvesi. New Repub 176:16-17 Mr 26 '77
Hostage mentality. D. Rabinowitz. Commentary 63:70-2 Je '77; Discussion. 64:7-9 Ag '77
Is there a treatment for terror? effects of Washington, D.C. seige by Hanafi Muslims. M. Belz and others. il Psychol Today 11:54-6+ O '77
Koran in the crisis: unholy Muslim war; Washington, D.C. siege. J. S. Tinney. Chr Today 21:48 Ap 1 '77
Latest worry: terrorists using high technology; report of the National Advisory Committee on Criminal Justice Standards and Goals. U.S. News 82:69 Mr 14 '77
Living with a fearful memory; effects of the Washington, D.C. seige by Hanafi Muslims. C. Fenyvesi. por Psychol Today 11:61+ O '77
Nuclear sabotage. M. Flood; reply. J. Penkrot. Bull Atom Sci 33:6 Ja '77
Of many things. J. O'Hare. America 137:inside cover N 5 '77
Point of order. L. H. Lapham. Harpers 254:13-14+ My '77
Seizing hostages: scourge of the '70s; Washington, D.C. siege by Hanafi commandos. T. Mathews. il por Newsweek 89:16-20+ Mr 21 '77
Terrorism and censorship. il Time 109:57 Mr 28 '77
38 hours; trial by terror; Washington, D.C. siege by Hanafi Muslims. il pors map Time 109:14-20 Mr 21 '77
Why violent crime is now in fashion; interview. F. J. Hacker. il por U.S. News 82:57-8 F 28 '77
You can prepare for urban terror—but not prevent it. U.S. News 82:23 Mr 21 '77
See also
Airplane hijacking
Terrorists

History

U.S. vs. international terrorists. G. Smith. il Am Heritage 28:36-43 Ag '77

International aspects

Abu Daoud and the law. S. E. Rapoport. Commentary 63:70-2 Mr '77; Reply. S. Liskofsky. 63:10-11+ My '77
L'affaire Daoud: too hot to handle. il por Time 109:29-31 Ja 24 '77
Arch-terrorist who went scot-free; A. Daoud. D. Reed. Read Digest 111:114-18 S '77
Bill details proposed sanctions on countries aiding terrorists. Aviation W 107:27 O 31 '77
Businessmen and terrorism. A. J. Mayer and others. il Newsweek 90:82-4+ N 14 '77
Dealing with international terrorism; statement, September 14, 1977. J. E. Karkashian. Dept State Bull 77:605-9 O 31 '77
German Entebbe; Mogadishu. Nat R 29:1285-6 N 11 '77
Getting tough. K. Willenson and T. Nater. il Newsweek 90:51 O 31 '77
Incident; investigating the Cuban connection to the Orlando Letelier murder in Venezuela. T. Branch and J. Rothchild. il pors Esquire 87:55-8+ Mr '77
Is the tide turning against terrorists? il U.S. News 83:22-4 O 31 '77
Link to Carlos? Swiss capture of West German terrorist G. Kröcher-Tiedemann. S. Strasser and P. Martin. il por Newsweek 91:25 Ja 2 '78
Mind of Abu Daoud. R. Carroll. il Newsweek 89:45 Ja 24 '77
Mogadishu's aftermath. il Time 110:56 N 28 '77
More outrages. D. M. Alpern. il Newsweek 90:22-4 D 26 '77
Soul of terrorism. G. F. Will. Newsweek 90:112 O 31 '77
TRB from Washington: chain reaction. New Repub 176:2+ Ap 16 '77
Terror. New Repub 177:2+ O 29 '77
Terror. C. Johnson. bibl il Society 15:48-52 N '77
Terrorist cross fire; releasing Abu Daoud. A. Deming and others. il por Newsweek 89:43+ Ja 24 '77
Transnational threat. H. Romerstein. Nat R 29:1364-6 N 25 '77
U.S. business throws billions into a fight against terrorists. il U.S. News 83:24-6 N 21 '77
U.S. calls for responsible measures against international terrorism; statement, December 6, 1976. M. Leigh. Dept State Bull 76:75-7 Ja 24 '77
War without boundaries. il Time 110:28-31+ O 31 '77
What happens if. . . ? Terrorist, revolutionaries, and nuclear weapons. D. Krieger. Ann Am Acad 430:44-57 Mr '77
See also
United Nations—Ad Hoc Committee on International Terrorism

Argentina

Argentina today; address, June 28, 1977. R. C. Hill. Vital Speeches 43:612-15 Ag 1 '77
Argentine terror. W. F. Buckley, Jr. Nat R 29:286-7 Mr 4 '77

Bangladesh

Red Army's coup; Japanese hijacking. A. Deming and T. Clifton. il Newsweek 90:48 O 10 '77

Germany, West

Ambush in a civil war; H. M. Schleyer kidnapping by Baader-Meinhof gang. il Time 110:37-8 S 19 '77
Big bank loses a powerful personality; J. Ponto of Dresdner Bank. por Bus W p48+ Ag 15 '77
Germany: the terror; kidnapping of H. M. Schleyer by the Baader-Meinhof gang. R. Carroll and P. Martin. il por Newsweek 90:55-6 S 19 '77
Germany's terrorist lexicon. I. Dische. Nation 225:524-6 N 19 '77
Hit women; killing of J. Ponto. K. Willenson and T. Nater. il pors Newsweek 90:30 Ag 15 '77
Life in a state of siege. Time 110:34-5 S 26 '77
Red roses from Roter Morgen; murder of J. Ponto. pors Time 110:30 Ag 15 '77
Terrorism in Germany: groping for answers. il U.S. News 83:56 N 7 '77
Terrorism: why West Germany? Time essay. L. Morrow. Time 110:37-8 D 19 '77
Terrorists' revenge? murder of S. Buback. il por Newsweek 89:53 Ap 18 '77
Visions of hobnails; European criticism of West Germany's anti-terrorist measures. M. Ledeen. New Repub 177:17-19 N 19 '77
See also
Schleyer, Hanns-Martin, kidnapping

Italy

Don't let her suffer; Italian kidnapping cases. il Time 110:46 O 17 '77
Italy under the gun. R. Carroll and E. Behr. il Newsweek 90:32-3 Ag 1 '77
Kidnap epidemic. il Newsweek 90:61 O 17 '77
Radical trashers; *autoriduttori*. il Time 109:32 F 28 '77
Terrorism on trial in Italy; case of R. Curcio. il por Time 110:58 Jl 4 '77

Netherlands

Children in a school of terror; South Moluccan seizure of hostages. il Time 109:39 Je 6 '77
Children of terror; hostages seized by South Moluccans. R. Carroll and others. il map Newsweek 89:42-3 Je 6 '77
Commandos strike at dawn; raid on South Moluccan terrorists. il Time 109:32-4 Je 20 '77
Dutch Entebbe; rescue of South Moluccan captives. M. R. Benjamin and others. il Newsweek 89:40+ Je 20 '77
See also
Caransa, Maurits, kidnapping

Rhodesia

Anxious for a new start. il por Time 109:43-5 F 21 '77
Goodbye to white Rhodesia? R. Carroll and others. il Newsweek 89:24+ F 21 '77
Rhodesian patrol. J. Reardon. Nat R 29:611 My 27 '77

South Africa

Time for terror? P. Younghusband. il Newsweek 89:40 Je 27 '77

Spain

New visit from the old demons. il Time 109:42-3 F 7 '77
Week of the long knives. F. Willey and M. Acoca. il Newsweek 89:45-6 F 7 '77

Uganda

Year after Entebbe. E. Keerdoja and M. J. Kubic. il Newsweek 90:7 Jl 4 '77

United States

See Terrorism

TERRORISTS
Hijacking proposal; pilots' boycott of countries harboring terrorists. W. F. Buckley, Jr. Nat R 29:1384 N 25 '77
Tightening links of terrorism. il Time 110:45 O 31 '77

TERRORISTS, Cuban
Cuban exiles: Miami, haven for terror. Nation 224:326-31 Mr 19 '77
Incident; investigating the Cuban connection to the Orlando Letelier murder in Venezuela. T. Branch and J. Rothchild. il pors Esquire 87: 55-8+ Mr '77

TERRORISTS, German
Ambush in a civil war; H. M. Schleyer kidnapping by Baader-Meinhof gang. il Time 110: 37-8 S 19 '77
Attacking the terrorists. il Time 110:41 N 21 '77
Detour to Dubai. M. R. Benjamin and P. Martin. il Newsweek 90:62 O 24 '77
German terrorism; H. Böll accused of terrorist sympathy. J. Deedy. Commonweal 104:706 N 11 '77
Germany: the terror; kidnapping of H. M. Schleyer by the Baader-Meinhof gang. R. Carroll and P. Martin. il por Newsweek 90:55-6 S 19 '77
Germany's finger squads. R. Carroll and P. Martin. il Newsweek 90:64+ N 21 '77
Guilty as charged; sentencing of A. Baader. Time 109:43 My 9 '77
Is the tide turning against terrorists? West German rescue of hostages in Mogadishu. Somalia. il U.S. News 83:22-4 O 31 '77
Life in a state of siege. il Time 110:34-5 S 26 '77
Link to Carlos? Swiss capture of terrorist G. Kröcher-Tiedemann. S. Strasser and P. Martin. il por Newsweek 91:25 Ja 2 '78
New war on terrorism; rescue of hostages by German commandos in Mogadishu, Somalia. A. Deming and others. il map Newsweek 90:48-50+ O 31 '77
No more extensions; H. M. Schleyer kidnapping by Red Army Faction. il por Time 110:53 O 24 '77
Old lady and the terrorists; capture of G. Sonnenberg and V. Becker. il Time 109:46 My 16 '77
Peacetime; Baader-Meinhof gang. T. Powers. Commonweal 104:723-5 N 11 '77
Schmidt on terrorism; excerpts from interview, ed by R. M. Smith and P. Martin. H. Schmidt. por Newsweek 90:77 N 28 '77
Spreading brushfire. il Time 110:45-6 N 7 '77
War goes on. K. Willenson and others. il Newsweek 90:55-6 N 7 '77
War without boundaries. il Time 110:28-31+ O 31 '77

TERRORISTS, Japanese
Red Army's coup; airplane hijacking in Bangladesh. Newsweek 90:48 O 10 '77

TERRORISTS, Puerto Rican
Forecast: more bombs ahead; Puerto Rican terrorists. J. Willwerth. il Time 110:39-40 O 24 '77

TERRORISTS, South Moluccan
Children in a school of terror. il Time 109:39 Je 6 '77
Children of terror. R. Carroll and others. il map Newsweek 89:42-3 Je 6 '77
Commandos strike at dawn. il Time 109:32-4 Je 20 '77
Dutch discord. E. Keerdoja. il Newsweek 90:27 N 14 '77
Dutch Entebbe. M. R. Benjamin and others. il Newsweek 89:40+ Je 20 '77

TERRY, Clifford
Liberated arts. il Holiday 58:48-9+ S '77

TERRY, Luther Leonidas
Rx travel and play. Holiday 58:16 Ja '77

TERRY, Walter
Dance. See issues of Saturday review
From Pavlova to ABT. il pors Opera N 41:10-14 Je '77

TERTIARY period. See Geology, Stratigraphic—Tertiary; Paleontology—Tertiary

TERZIAN, Philip
Television. Commonweal 104:722-3 N 11 '77

TERZIAN, Yervant
Recent findings about planetary nebulae. il Sky & Tel 54:459-63 D '77

TESDATA Systems Corporation. See Computer industry

TESICH, Steven
Passing game. Reviews
America 137:486 D 31 '77 *
Nation 225:668 D 17 '77 *
Time 110:96 D 12 '77 *

TESLA, Nikola
American characters. N. Brandt. il por Am Heritage 28:44-5 Ag '77 *

TESORIERE, Kenneth
On the pit road stands an Eagle. il Car & Dr 22:61-4+ My '77

TESORO Petroleum Corporation. See Petroleum industry—United States

TESS, Giulia
Con ardore; interview, ed by L. Rasponi. il por Opera N 41:30-2 F 12 '77

TESSELLATIONS (mathematics)
Extraordinary nonperiodic tiling that enriches the theory of tiles. M. Gardner. il Sci Am 236: 110-12+ bibl(p 132) Ja '77

TESSENDORF, K. C.
Red death on the Missouri. il Am West 14:48-53 Ja '77

TEST for a witch; drama. See MacLellan, E. and Schroll, C. V.

TEST marketing. See Products, New—Marketing

TEST plots, Farm. See Field experiments (agriculture)

TEST records. See Phonograph records—Test records

TESTICLES
Cytochrome c: immunofluorescent localization of the testis-specific form. E. Goldberg and others. bibl il Science 196:1010-12 My 27 '77

Transplantation

Testicle transplant; case of twins Terry and Timothy Twomey. Newsweek 89:39 Je 6 '77

TESTICULAR feminization syndrome. See Hermaphroditism

TESTIMONIALS in advertising. See Advertising—Testimonials

TESTIMONY. See Witnesses

TESTING
See also
Psychological tests
also subhead Testing under various subjects, e.g. Loudspeakers—Testing

TESTING, Educational. See Educational tests and measurements

TESTING instruments
Antifreeze testers. Consumer Rep 42:425-6 D '77
Auto tune-up equipment; dwell tachometers and ignition-timing lights. Consumer Rep 42:419-22 D '77
Build a digital IC identifier/tester. E. R. Savage. il Radio Electr 48:44-6 Je '77
Build a digital IC tester. R. M. Stitt. il Pop Electr 11:53-9 Je '77
Build this $1 logic probe. A. F. Burr. il Radio-Electr 48:40-1 Ag '77
Build tone probe for testing digital IC's. L. Fort. il Radio-Electr 48:76-7 Mr '77
Build your own timing light from a kit. R. Hill. il Pop Sci 210:125 My '77
CB test instruments. F. Belt. il Radio-Electr 48:42-4 D '77
Circuit tester to catch—and miss—wiring errors. Consumer Rep 42:372 Jl '77
Dealing with the socket; troubleshooting electrical circuits in automobiles. T. Tappett. il Mech Illus 73:118+ S '77
Equipment reports:
B&K model 530 semiconductor tester. il Radio-Electr 48:26+ O '77
Heathkit IT-7400 digital IC tester. il Radio-Electr 48:22+ Ag '77
Hickok model 388 CB inline tester. il Radio-Electr 48:24+ Ag '77
Jerrold/Texscan VSM-5 spectrum analyzer. il Radio-Electr 48:34+ F '77
Polaris CT-751 Cobra curve tracer. il Radio Electr 48:26+ Jl '77
Sencore TF46 super cricket transistor and FET tester. il Radio-Electr 48:26-7 D '77
Switchcraft Q-Chek QC-1002 cable tester. il Radio-Electr 48:94-5 Mr '77
TeleMatic KC-720B CrysMate crystal tester. il Radio-Electr 48:22+ S '77
Telematic SG-785 ferret tuner substituter and digital pattern generator. il Radio-Electr 48:89-90 O '77
Foucault tester with digital readout. R. J. McKeon. il Sky & Tel 54:140-3 Ag '77
IC's for test instruments. L. Garner. il Pop Electr 12:77-81 Jl '77
Low-cost digital logic analyzer. G. Muething and others. il Pop Electr 11:40-6 F '77
Photo-electronics: synch-cord testing device. E. Farber. il por Pop Phot 81:80+ D '77
Pro names for home mechanics. il Mech Illus 74:102 Ja '78
Really basic voltage tester. R. D. Freed. il Mech Illus 73:22 Mr '77
Spectrum analyzer in hi-fi measurements. J. Hirsch. il Pop Electr 13:49-53 Ja '78
What you need to know about CB test gear. F. Belt. il por Radio-Electr 48:49-61 N '77
See also
Electric meters
Oscilloscopes
Signal generators

TESTING laboratories
Surge of business for independent labs. il Bus W p 116+ Ap 11 '77

TESTIS. See Testicles

TESTOSTERONE
Cannabinoids inhibit testosterone secretion by mouse testes in vitro. S. Dalterio and others. bibl il Science 196:1472-3 Je 24 '77

TESTS, Information. See Information tests

TETLOW, Joseph A.
Abba, father! New Cath World 220:40-1 Ja '77
Ashes in our mouths. America 137:402 D 3 '77
Grievous moral mischief. America 137:359 N 19 '77
To fill up the sufferings of Christ. America 136:169 F 26 '77

TETON Dam failure. See Dams—Failure

TETRACHLORODIBENZO-p-dioxin. See Dibenzodioxin

TETRAHYDROCANNABINOL. See THC

TETRAHYDROISOQUINOLINE. See Quinoline

TETRAHYDROPAPAVEROLINE. See Quinoline

TETRAHYMENA
Macronuclear subunits of tetrahymena thermophila are functionally haploid. F. P. Doerder and others. bibl il Science 198:946-8 D 22 '77

TETRAPODS, Fossil. See Paleontology

TEUNE, Henry
Macro theoretical approaches to public analysis: the fiscal crisis of American cities. bibl f Ann Am Acad 434:174-85 N '77

TEVATRON accelerator. See National Accelerator Laboratory

TEXACO-Metropolitan Opera radio broadcasts. See Radio broadcasting—Opera

TEXANS
Texan born again. L. Donosky. il Newsweek 90:45-6 D 12 '77

TEXAS
Making it happen in Texas. J. L. Carter and F. E. Ruffin. il Redbook 150:43+ D '77
See also
Architecture, Domestic—Texas
Art galleries and museums—Texas
Banks and banking—Texas
Big Bend National Park
Big Thicket
Big Thicket National Preserve
Botany—Texas
Courts—Texas
Crime and criminals—Texas
Education—Texas
Energy policy—Texas
Environmental movement—Texas
Express highways—Texas
Finance—Texas
Hospitals—Texas
Hunting—Texas
Irrigation—Texas
Music—Texas
Newspapers—Texas
Opera—Texas
Power resources—Texas
Prisons—Texas
Public health—Texas
Rio Grande
School libraries—Texas
Trials—Texas

Description and travel
Mini-holiday. B. Jeffer. il Holiday 58:58+ Je '77
Texas! The superstate. N. Proffitt. il map Newsweek 90:36-9+ D 12 '77

Electric utilities
See Electric utilities

History
Texas became Texas; excerpt from Early Texas oil. il Am Heritage 28:48-55 Ap '77

Industries
See also
Gas industry

Politics and government
See also
Primaries—Texas

Religious institutions and affairs
Selling of Jesus; Baptist General Convention of Texas evangelical ad campaign. M. Montagno and J. Huck. il Newsweek 89:48+ F 28 '77

Restaurants
See Restaurants—United States

Social life and customs
Christmas in the Southwest; symposium. il Redbook 150:99-120+ D '77
Outlaw places. P. Axthelm. il Newsweek 90:48 D 12 '77
This Christmas, their home is your home; symposium. Redbook 150:89+ D '77

TEXAS cookery. See Cookery, American

TEXAS Eastern Transmission Corporation
Waiting for the future. E. Bailey. il Forbes 120:50+ S 1 '77

TEXAS Instruments, Inc
Bubble memory finally arrives. il Bus W p72+ Mr 28 '77
Great digital watch shake-out. il Bus W p78+ My 2 '77
Texas Instruments shoots the moon. Forbes 119:29 Ap 1 '77

TEXAS International Airlines. See Airlines—Local service

TEXAS. University

Austin campus
What Johnny can't write: a university view of freshman writing ability; teacher interviews. T. R. Newkirk and others. bibl f Engl J 66:65-9 N '77

McDonald Observatory
See Astronomical observatories

TEXAS Utilities Company
Texas power companies converting from natural gas to coal, lignite. J. Walsh. il map Science 198:471-4 N 4 '77

TEXFI Industries Inc. See Textile industry—United States

TEXTBOOKS
Bringing women into the curriculum. D. J. Zuersher. Educ Digest 42:38-40 F '77
See also
Biology—Textbooks
Booksellers and bookselling—Textbooks
Readers (books)

TEXTILE arts. See Textile crafts

TEXTILE crafts
Clipboard: emphases: fibers and fabrics. V. G. Timmons. Sch Arts 77:26-8 D '77
Fiber. G. Kaufman. il Craft Horiz 37:15-16+ Je '77
Muñoz of Barcelona. E. Arenal. il Craft Horiz 37:58-61+ D '77
See also
Tapestry

Exhibitions
Fiberworks at the Cleveland Museum. il Craft Horiz 37:28-31 O '77
Knocked for a loop; Fiberworks. H. Cullinan. il Art N 76:119-20 D '77

TEXTILE design
Candace Wheeler, textile designer. W. H. Faude. bibl il por Antiques 112:258-61 Ag '77
Careers in art: fabric design. P. Savino. il Sch Arts 76:5 F '77
Egyptian influence; textiles. il House B 119:83-9 Ap '77
See also
Batik
Weaving

TEXTILE fabrics
Bring a room to bloom with a flowering of beautiful tulips. il House B 119:62-73 Mr '77
Buying quilt fabrics by mail. il Bet Hom & Gard 55:79+ Ap '77
Decorating by the yard. il Good H 184:142-7+ Mr '77
Double take. P. Sadowsky. il Am Home 80:66-7 O '77
For bed and beyond: decorating with sheets. il Mademoiselle 83:164-7+ Mr '77
Fresh breeze: new wallcoverings & fabrics that change the pace & pattern of today's rooms. R. Weil. il House B 119:100-5 O '77
Gray flannel room. il Ladies Home J 94:98-101+ S '77
I wanted a traditional air with the ripe, rich colors of today; work of designer John Leigh Spath. R. Weil. il House B 119:124-32 S '77
New fabrics for color energy. il House & Gard 149:150-1 My '77
New, tough electrically conductive fabric. V. E. Smay. Pop Sci 210:138 Mr '77
Patterns for living. il McCalls 104:144-7 My '77
Physics of textiles. L. R. G. Treloar. bibl il Phys Today 30:23-30 D '77
Rose is a rose . . . & so much more! il House B 119:57-71+ Je '77
Spring's new cover story. il House B 119:90-7 F '77
Style with stamina; upholstery fabrics. J. Macurdy and K. Mahoney. il House B 119:108-13 O '77
What's coming up in fabrics. il House & Gard 149:118-21 Mr '77
See also
Cotton fabrics
Tapestry

Care
Fabulous fakes. Good H 185:228 D '77
How to shop and care for a suit. il Consumers Res Mag 60:41 F '77
Read me! care instructions on fabric labels. Good H 185:166 Jl '77

Dyeing
See Dyes and dying

Fireproofing
See Fireproofing of textiles

History
Copperplate-printed Irish textile. D. S. Katzenberg. il Antiques 111:760-1 Ap '77

TEXTILE fabrics, Nonwoven
Can fabrics soften paving problems? il Am City & County 92:69-70 N '77

TEXTILE fabrics, Waterproof
Home water repellent treatment for fabrics. il Consumers Res Mag 60:34-6 F '77

TEXTILE fiber crafts. See Textile crafts

TEXTILE industry
See also
Weaving

Export-import trade

EC threat to textile exports; Hong Kong quota reduction. il Bus W p46 D 5 '77
Europe: textiles threaten to test an alliance. il Bus W p49-50 Ja 31 '77
President Carter's textile dilemma. Forbes 119: 25-8 Ap 1 '77
Textile industry; address, October 11, 1977. W. R. Shockley. Vital Speeches 44:54-7 N 1 '77
When free trade means higher consumer prices; study by V. Pregelj. il Bus W p61-2 S 5 '77

International aspects

Europe: textiles threaten to test an alliance. il Bus W p49-50 Ja 31 '77

Wages and hours

Occupational pay relationships and employment in textile mills. F. Porter. bibl il M Labor R 100:51-3 Je '77

Europe, Western

Textile producers demand protection. il Bus W p49-50 O 31 '77

United States

Drastic surgery at Texfi. il Bus W p 108+ Ag 15 '77
Star-studded polyester; Milliken & Co. industrial show. M. Orth. il Newsweek 89:75-6 Je 27 '77
Textile industry; address, October 11, 1977. W. R. Shockley. Vital Speeches 44:54-7 N 1 '77
See also
Amalgamated Clothing and Textile Workers Union
Cone Mills Corporation
Fieldcrest Mills, Inc
Stevens, J. P, and Company
United Merchants and Manufacturers, Inc

TEXTILE mills

Wages and hours

See Textile industry—Wages and hours

TEXTILE mills, Remodeled. See Buildings, Remodeled

TEXTILE painting
Dye painting with fiber reactive dyes. B. Benjamin-Murray. il Sch Arts 77:22-6 D '77

TEXTILE workers
Breathless cotton workers; byssinosis or brown lung disease. J. Schinto. Progressive 41:27-9 Ag '77
See also
Amalgamated Clothing and Textile Workers Union
Textile industry—Wages and hours

TEXTILE Workers Union of America-Amalgamated Clothing Workers of America merger. See Trade unions—Acquisitions and mergers

TEXTILES. See Textile fabrics

TEXTURE
See also
Food texture

TEXTURE paints. See Paint

TEXTURED walls. See Wall coverings

TEYLER'S Foundation, Haarlem, Netherlands. See Foundations, Charitable and educational

THACHER, Peter S.
United to protect the Mediterranean. il Oceans 10:58-61 Ja '77

THACKER, Julia
Snow letter; poem. Ms 5:65 Je '77

THACKRAY, John
Figures don't lie, but. . . .; Nation 224:582-4 My 14 '77

THAI language

Study and teaching

G is for chicken. S. F. Morell. il Read Digest 111:25-6+ N '77

THAILAND
School for elephants. D. D. Gray. il Int Wildlife 8:36-43 Ja '78
See also
Bangkok
Civil rights—Thailand
Guerrillas—Thailand
Investments, Foreign—Thailand
Phuket Island

Description and travel

Thailand. S. Fockler. il Trav/Holiday 148:36+ D '77

Foreign relations

United States

See United States—Foreign relations—Thailand

Politics and government

Bangkok's seeds of revolt. W. McGleish. America 136:520-2 Je 11 '77
Coup on cue. C. D. May and H. Jensen. il Newsweek 90:63 O 31 '77
War against the night; insurgency by Communist guerrillas. il map Time 109:33-4 Ja 31 '77

Religious institutions and affairs

Thailand's religious roots; Christianity and Buddhism. W. D. Carlsen. il Chr Today 22: 24-7 O 7 '77

THALAMUS
Early development of X-cells in kitten lateral geniculate nucleus. J. L. Norman and others. bibl il Science 198:202-4 O 14 '77
Monocular deprivation: morphological effects on different classes of neurons in the lateral geniculate nucleus. L. J. Garey and C. Blakemore. bibl il Science 195:414-16 Ja 28 '77
Postnatal development of the human lateral geniculate nucleus: relationship to a critical period for the visual system. T. L. Hickey. bibl il Science 198:836-8 N 25 '77

THALBERG, Irving
Humiliation in Hollywood. S. Kich. il Harpers 254:102-4 Mr '77 •

THALER, Susan
Mother to daughter; story. il Good H 185:142-3 N '77

THAMES River
Cleanly flows the Thames. T. Fishlock. il Int Wildlife 8:33-5 Ja '78
Thames: new life for a dead river. il U.S. News 83:47 Jl 4 '77

THANATOLOGY. See Death

THANE, Adele
Cinderella; dramatization of fairytale. Plays 36:14, 51-60 My '77
Dummling and the golden goose; dramatization of story by the Brothers Grimm. Plays 37:63-72 D '77
Rip Van Winkle; dramatization of story by W. Irving. Plays 36:58-66 F '77
Sleeping beauty; dramatization of fairy tale by C. Perrault. Plays 37:51-8 N '77

THANKS. See Thanksgiving

THANKSGIVING
Dinner and the proper frame of mind. L. Conger. Writer 90:9-10 N '77
Frozen yogurt, friends and a not-too-fat stomach: among the things I give thanks for. J. Viorst. il Redbook 150:34+ N '77
Price of praise. V. S. Owens. il Chr Today 22: 14-16 N 18 '77
See also
Gratitude

THANKSGIVING Day

Drama

Thanksgiving truce. H. L. Miller. Plays 37:17-28 N '77

History

For the blessings of the year. W. E. Reck. il Am Hist Illus 12:4-7+ N '77

THANKSGIVING dinners
Economics of a Thanksgiving dinner. il Sr Schol 110:12 N 17 '77
Holiday dinner at the White House. H. Haller. il Ladies Home J 94:110-11+ N '77
Other birds to be thankful for. il Redbook 150: 134-5+ N '77
Streamlined Thanksgiving. P. Sadowsky and G. Steves. il Am Home 80:44-5+ N '77

THANKSGIVING truce; drama. See Miller, H. L.

THARP, Twyla
Eye on Tharp. il por Horizon 20:81 O '77 •
Twyla Tharp and wide-angle lens; films entitled Sue's leg: remembering the thirties and The Bix pieces. J. Mueller. Dance Mag 51:99 S '77 •
Twyla Tharp: dance marverick. L. F. Rosen. Progressive 41:51-2 D '77 •
Twyla Tharp, in motion. E. Kendall. New Repub 176:19-20 F 12 '77 •

THARP, Twyla, Dance Company. See Dance companies

THATCHER, Margaret
How the conservatives would deal with Britain's troubles; interview. il por U.S. News 83:69-71 S 12 '77
Thatcher: we shall win; interview, ed by H. Nickel. por Time 110:44 S 19 '77

about

Margaret Thatcher: Britain's next Prime Minister? C. Sterling. il por Read Digest 110: 172-6 My '77 •
Travels with Mrs T. T. Fuller. il pors Newsweek 90:51 S 26 '77 •
Why Labor loses ground in Britain. R. A. Haeger. il U.S. News 83:68-71 S 12 '77 •

THAT'S a good question; drama. See Murray, J

THAYER, Frederick C.
Proliferation and the future: destruction or transformation? Ann Am Acad 430:133-46 Mr '77

THEATER
See also
Actors and actresses
Mime
Puppets and puppet plays
Trade unions—Theater
Women in the theater

Advertising

Madison Avenue likes showbiz. il Bus W p 120 D 5 '77

Costume

See Costume, Theatrical

Economic aspects

How to lose less on Broadway. L. Snyder. il Fortune 95:147-8+ My '77
Theater box offices boffo coast to coast. il Bus W p25 Je 6 '77

Employees

Yes plugs in at the Garden: setup. J. S. Roberts. il Hi Fi 27:125-31 D '77

History

See also
Theater—United States—History

Jews

Old and venerated theater tradition relived in upcoming Crowell book; interview, ed by R. Dahlin. L. Rosenfeld. il Pub W 211:51 Mr 28 '77
Yiddish idol; excerpt from Bright star of exile: Jacob Adler and the Yiddish theater. L. Rosenfeld. il pors N Y Times Mag p32-3+ Je 12 '77

Production and direction

Album of a play doctor. S. Kauffmann. Am Scholar 47:87-94 Wint '77
Andrei Serban's theater of terror and beauty. R. Eder. il pors N Y Times Mag p42-3+ F 13 '77
Annie; interview. A. McArdle. New Yorker 53: 29-30 Mr 14 '77
We open in Florence; production of The abdication. R. Wolff. il por N Y Times Mag p50-2+ D 4 '77
See also
John F. Kennedy Center for the Performing Arts, Washington, D.C.—Musical Theater Lab

Stage lighting

From the inside: light vs. lighting. M. Louis. Dance Mag 51:30-1 Je '77

Stage setting and scenery

Setting the stage; work of S. Loquasto. J. Kroll. il por Newsweek 89:84 Mr 21 '77

Africa

In search of a new African theatre. D. Nwoko. UNESCO Courier 30:29+ My '77

Canada

See also
Shakespeare Festival, Stratford, Ontario

Chile

Breath of satire in Chile; closing of the play Pages from Parra. F. MacShane. Nation 225: 535-6 N 19 '77

France

See also
Paris—Theater

Great Britain

The play's still the thing. R. Morley. il Sat R 4:12-13 Je 11 '77
See also
National Theatre (Great Britain)

Italy

See also
Florence—Theater

Japan

See also
Japanese drama
Kabuki

Korea

See also
Folk drama, Korean

Russia

See also
Moscow—Theater

Sweden

Theatre. H. Clurman. Nation 225:61-2 Jl 9 '77

United States

Antic arts. C. Hughes. il por Holiday 58:26 Ja '77
Entertainment this fall. M. Stasio. il Harp Baz 110:34+ S '77
Puppets in Los Angeles are serious (?) business; California events. il Sunset 159:80-3 Ag '77
Stars in their eyes; summer theater at Woodstock Playhouse in Woodstock, N.Y. S. Fischler and R. Friedman. il por Ret Liv 17:31-3 Ag '77
Theater. G. Rogoff. il Sat R 4:57-8 Ag 6 '77
Theatre today. D. B. Wilmeth. See alternate issues of Intellect
Theater USA. R. Eder. il Horizon 20:20-9 O '77
See also
Drama festivals
Los Angeles—Theater
New York (city)—Theater

History

Life upon the wicked stage; theater in colonial America. M. Klein. il Am Hist Illus 11:36-43 F '77

THEATER, Childrens
Children's theatre: they run the show; Chidren's Theatre Company. M. Smith. il House & Gard 149:44+ Je '77

THEATER, Experimental
Adrift among images; Einstein on the beach. F. J. Spieler. il Harpers 254:107+ Mr '77
From the closet to the stage; The Project theater group. S. Bush and D. Goleman. Psychol Today 11:52 O '77
Sex fantasy on Broadway; work of The Project. il Time 109:84 F 28 '77
Squat Theater. S. Kauffmann. New Repub 177: 18-19 D 3 '77
Theater: Lion Theater Company production called K: impressions of The trial by Franz Kafka. S. Kauffmann. New Repub 178:24-5 Ja 7 '78
Theatre; recent productions. H. Clurman. Nation 225:731-2 D 31 '77

THEATER, Open-air
America's past is alive and outdoors. G. Loney and P. MacKay. Chr Cent 94:661-2 Jl 20 '77
Stage in the garden. il Sunset 159:78-9 S '77

THEATER, Yiddish. See Theater—Jews

THEATER audiences. See Audiences

THEATER buildings
Triumph on the Thames: the National Theatre in London. W. Marlin. il Archit Rec 162:81-8 S '77
See also
Opera houses

Conservation and restoration

See Architecture—Conservation and restoration

THEATER critics and criticism. See Drama critics and criticism

THEATER festivals. See Drama festivals

THEATRE National de l'Opera-Comique. See Opera—France

THEATER photography. See Photography, Theatrical

THEATERS, Motion picture. See Motion picture theaters

THEATRICAL agencies
Everybody needs an agent. M. Orth. il Newsweek 89:90+ Ap 25 '77
Marvin Josephson: no business like 10% off the top. por Duns R 109:22-3 Ap '77
Sherpas of the subclause. il Time 109:79 Je 13 '77
Talent agency with a talent for growth; Marvin Josephson Associates Inc. J. Madrick. Bus W p92 Je 27 '77

THEATRICAL costume. See Costume, Theatrical

THEATRICAL directors
See also
Bobkoff, N.
Quintero, J.

THEATRICAL production and direction. See Theater—Production and direction

THEBOM, Blanche
Wonderful product. il por Opera N 42:40-1 N '77

THEFT. See Stealing

THEME parks. See Amusement parks

THEOBALD, William
Uptown parks and air rights. bibl Parks & Rec 12:31-3+ Ag '77

THEOFILOPOULOS, Argyrios N. and Perrin, L. H.
Lysis of human cultured lymphoblastoid cells by cell-induced activation of the properdin pathway. bibl il Science 195:878-80 Mr 4 '77

THEOHARIS, Athan G.
Bell limits FBI prosecutions. Nation 225:198-9 S 10 '77
Bureaucrats above the law. Nation 225:393-7 O 22 '77
Public or private papers? The arrogance of the intelligence community. Intellect 106:118-20 O '77

THEOLOGIANS
See also
Balthasar, H. U. von
Catholic Theological Society of America
Cox, H.
Henry, C. F. H.
Herberg, W.
Moltmann, J.
Schleiermacher, F. E. D.
Teilhard de Chardin, P.
Thomas Aquinas, Saint

Conferences

See Religious conferences

THEOLOGICAL conferences. See Religious conferences

THEOLOGICAL education
Pastoral training under tutors; requirements of the Presbyterian Church in America. Chr Today 22:61-3 O 7 '77
Theological education 1977; symposium with editorial comment. Chr Cent 94:76-7, 81-95+ F 2 '77

THEOLOGICAL seminaries
Impossible dream: can seminaries deliver? symposium. Chr Today 21:18-21 F 4 '77
Theological education 1977; symposium, with editorial comment. Chr Cent 94:76-7, 81-95+ F 2 '77
What seminaries don't believe; question of Jesus' bodily resurrection. Chr Today 22:29-31 N 4 '77
See also
Interdenominational Theological Center, Atlanta, Ga.
Southern Baptist Theological Seminary, Louisville, Ky.
Union Theological Seminary, New York

Faculties

See College teachers

Great Britain

Anglicans' bold scheme for theological education. T. Beeson. Chr Cent 94:525-6 Je 1 '77

THEOLOGICAL seminaries, Catholic
Seminaries and the new conservatives. M. Neuman. America 137:126-7 S 10 '77; Discussion. 137:177-8, 205 O 1-8 '77

THEOLOGICAL societies. See Religious societies

THEOLOGY
Anathemas and orthodoxy: a reply to Avery Dulles; Hartford Appeal. L. Gilkey. Chr Cent 94:1026-9 N 9 '77; Reply. A. Dulles. 94:1053-4 N 16 '77
Bottom-line theology; interview, ed by D. Kucharsky. F. J. Sheen. il Chr Today 21:8-11 Je 3 '77
Constructing local theologies. E. W. Ranly. Commonweal 104:716-19 N 11 '77
Creating a respect for theology. J. Daane. Chr Cent 94:89-90 F 2 '77
Divine Principle and the Second Advent; Unification Church doctrine. S. M. Heim. por Chr Cent 94:448-51 My 11 '77
Doctrinal hodgepodge in the churches. Chr Today 21:30-1 My 6 '77
Emergence of Asian theologies. S. P. Athyal. Chr Today 21:70+ S 23 '77
Four stories of theology; with editorial comment. T. H. Stahel. America 136:inside cover, 230-3 Mr 19 '77
Lusts of modern theology. H. D. McDonald. Chr Today 22:18-20 O 21 '77
Of tidy doctrine and truncated experience; relationalist and charismatic views of evangelical experiential theology. R. K. Johnston. il Chr Today 21:10-14 F 18 '77
Theology behind the Wall; East Germany. P. Misner. Commonweal 104:620-2 S 30 '77
Theology for the tent meeting; work of Evangelical C. F. H. Henry. por Time 109:82 F 14 '77
Who's catering the theological smorgasborg? M. C. Grant. Chr Cent 93:428-31 My 4 '77
See also
Catechetics
Catholic Theological Society of America
Chaos (theology)
Christianity
Congregation for the Doctrine of the Faith
Covenants (theology)
Creeds
Death of God theology
Devil
Faith
Fall of man
Free will and determinism
Incarnation
Jesus Christ
Liberation theology
Logos (theology)
Love (theology)
Man (theology)
Mysticism
Protestantism
Religion
Revelation
Salvation
Secularism

Bibliography

Theology; key books of '76. D. Tinder. il Chr Today 21:20-3 Mr 18 '77

Study and teaching

Theology in 1977 and beyond. K. B. Osborne. Chr Cent 94:92-3 F 2 '77
Two or three and God; extension theology. R. W. Sales. Chr Cent 94:110-13 F 2 '77
See also
Theological seminaries
Theological seminaries, Catholic

THEOLOGY in literature. See Religion in literature

THERA (island)
Easter on Atlantis. L. Halley. il Sat R 5:24+ Ja 7 '78

THERAPEUTICS
See also
Acupuncture
Gardening—Therapeutic use
Hypnotism—Therapeutic use
Osteopuncture
Psychotherapy
Shock therapy
also subhead Therapy under names of diseases, e.g. Cancer—Therapy

THERESA of the Child Jesus, Saint. See Teresa of the Child Jesus, Saint

THERMODYNAMICS
1977 Nobel Prize in chemistry. I. Procaccia and J. Ross. il por Science 198:716-17 N 18 '77
Steady state and ecological salvation: a thermodynamic analysis. N. Georgescu-Roegen. bibl il BioScience 27:266-70 Ap '77; Reply with rejoinder. J. Pournelle. 27:646-7 O '77
Thermodynamics and geometry. F. Weinhold; discussion. bibl il Phys Today 30:11+ Ja '77

THERMOGENESIS (biology) See Temperature, Animal and human

THERMOGRAPHY, Infrared. See Photography, Infrared

THERMOLUMINESCENCE
Temperature exposure measured by the use of thermoluminescence. G. P. Romberg and others. bibl il Science 197:1364-5 S 30 '77

THERMOLUMINESCENT dating. See Archeology—Methodology

THERMOMETERS and thermometry
Clock/thermometer sounds times and temperature alarms. J. Free. il Pop Sci 210:180 My '77
Getting a cold shoulder? water-temperature gauges for sports fishermen. J. Hearst, Jr. il Motor B & S 140:28 O '77
Light monitors tissue temperature. Sci N 112:7 Jl 2 '77
Power your projects with solar energy! B. Green. il Pop Electr 12:41-7 D '77
Refrigerator-freezer thermometers. il Consumer Rep 43:30-1 Ja '78
Thermometers; how do they measure up? darkroom thermometers. J. Bailey. il Mod Phot 41:84-7+ Ag '77
2-digit electronic thermometer. W. Sikonowiz. il Radio-Electr 48:33-5+ S '77

THERMONUCLEAR reactions. See Nuclear fusion

THERMOREGULATORY behavior. See Temperature, Animal and human

THERMOSTATS
Energy-saving thermostats. il Consumer Rep 42:602-5 O '77
New kind of thermostat. il Mech Illus 73:54+ D '77

THERMOTHERAPY
Heat and cold for treatment of pain. A. Frank and S. Frank. Mademoiselle 83:46+ F '77

THEROUX, Paul
Diplomatic relations; story. Redbook 149:110 My '77
Johore murders; story. Atlantic 239:93-4 Mr '77
Murder of the Orient Express. Holiday 58:22 Ap '77

THEROUX, Phyllis
What your kids really want. il Am Home 80:36-7 My '77

THETA Seminars. See Self realization

THEUS, Robert
Effects of divorce upon school children. bibl Clearing H 50:364-5 Ap '77

THEVIS, Michael George
Case is not closed. T. Mathews and others. il por Newsweek 90:51 N 7 '77 •

THEYARD, Harry
Harry Theyard: full of surprises. B. Fischer-Williams. por Opera N 41:26 Je '77 •

THICKET, Big. See Big Thicket

THICKNESS measurement
See also
Micrometers

THIEBAUD, Wayne
Wayne Thiebaud: outdistancing pop. T. Albright. il Art N 76:87-8+ F '77 •

THIELICKE, Helmut
But man fell on earth; excerpt from How the world began. il Chr Today 21:13-15 Mr 4 '77

THIEVES
See also
Burglary and burglars
Stealing

THIMMESCH, Nick
Elizabeth Taylor's surprising new life. pors McCalls 104:16+ Jl '77
(ed) See Humphrey, H. and Humphrey, M. Look at the fun we've had

THINK tanks. See Research institutions

THINKING. See Thought and thinking

THIRD fleet. See United States—Navy

THIRD world. See Underdeveloped areas

THIRST
Angiotensin: physiological role in water-deprivation—induced thirst of rats. R. L. Malvin and others. bibl il Science 197:171-3 Jl 8 '77
See also
Drinking (physiology)

THIRY, Jacques
Million dollar dream. M. Goodman and T. Wilson. il por Motor B & S 139:51-3+ Ap '77 *

THISTLES
Exotic looking and unthirsty; globe thistle. il Sunset 158:270 Ap '77

Seed

Case of the missing thistleseed; question of embargo by India. G. Reiger. Audubon 79:161 N '77

THISTLES (boats) See Sailboats

THOM, Mary. See Braudy, S. jt ed

THOM, Richard
Hunting for remnants of old Illinois. Audubon 79:139-40 S '77

THOMAJAN, P. J.
Armenian Grandma Moses. il por Ret Liv 17:50 My '77

THOMAS Aquinas, Saint
Diverging paths in Catholic sexual ethics. J. Gaffney. il New Cath World 220:276-9 N '77 *
What would St Thomas Aquinas do if faced with Karl Marx? address, 1974. H. Cámara. il por New Cath World 220:108-13 My '77 *

THOMAS, B. J.
Star is reborn. C. Forbes. Chr Today 21:17 Je 3 '77 *

THOMAS, Bill
Hiking holidays for teens. bibl il Parents Mag 52:20+ Ag '77

THOMAS, D. M.
Dream game; poem. Am Scholar 47:49-50 Wint '77
Vienna. Zürich. Constance; Orpheus in hell; poems. Am Scholar 46:479-82 Aut '77

THOMAS, Danny
Conversation with Marlo & Danny Thomas; interview, ed by K. D. Fury. pors Ladies Home J 94:36+ F '77

THOMAS, David Michael
Christian marital love: a reappraisal. il New Cath World 220:296-300 N '77

THOMAS, Davis
(ed) See Weid-Neuwied, M. A. P. Winter at Fort Clark: Maximilian and Bodmer among the tribes of the Upper Missouri, 1833-1834

THOMAS, Dawn F.
Maryland pioneers new concept in housing. il Aging 268:21-4 F '77

THOMAS, Dirk S.
How to sell stumpage. il Am For 83:36-42 D '77

THOMAS, Frederick J.
Piaget and Lamarck. Educ Digest 43:47-9 N '77

THOMAS, G. J. Jr, and others
Secondary structure of histones and DNA in chromatin. bibl il Science 197:385-8 Jl 22 '77

THOMAS, Jess
Blueprint for power. il Motor B & S 139:84-5+ Ap '77

THOMAS, Joe
Party became a lynching. J. Marshall. por Sports Illus 46:68+ Ap 18 '77 *
Really Joe, is all this necessary? J. Marshall. il por Sports Illus 47:90+ O 31 '77 *

THOMAS, Kay
Negatives from nature. il Design (US) 78:12-13 Summ '77

THOMAS, Keith R.
Experienced entrepreneur—at age 24. V. Louviere. por Nations Bus 65:76 S '77 *

THOMAS, Lewis, 1913-
Biostatistics in medicine. Science 198:675 N 18 '77
Enormous party. il House & Gard 149:86-9+ D '77
Hazards of science; adaptation of address. por Sci Digest 81:inside cover, 71 Mr '77
When outer space speaks. . . Read Digest 111: 181-2 Jl '77
about
Profiles. J. Bernstein. por New Yorker 53:27-32+ Ja 2 '78 *

THOMAS, Lowell, 1892-
And on the roof of the world. il U.S. News 83:37 N 14 '77

THOMAS, M. Donald
Let's talk sense about discipline. Clearing H 50: 309-12 Mr '77

THOMAS, M. V. and Gorman, A. L. F.
Internal calcium changes in a bursting pacemaker neuron measured with arsenazo III. bibl il Science 196:531-3 Ap 29 '77

THOMAS, Marlo
Conversation with Marlo & Danny Thomas; interview, ed by K. D. Fury. pors Ladies Home J 94:36+ F '77
Marlo Thomas: men, marriage & me; interview, ed by J. Ardmore. por Ladies Home J 94:40+ D '77
—and others
Four successful women talk about what they want—and can't have. pors Redbook 148:92-3+ F '77
about
People on the cover. A. L. Ball. il Redbook 148:3+ F '77 *

THOMAS, Michele
Down on the farm. il Seventeen 36:74+ My '77

THOMAS, Norman C.
Norman Thomas: successful failure. R. Baldwin. Nation 224:85 Ja 22 '77 *

THOMAS, Paul
Fassbinder: the poetry of the inarticulate. il Film Q 30:2-17 Wint '76

THOMAS, R. David
Wendy's: a unique strategy for growth. por Duns R 110:14-15+ Ag '77 *

THOMAS, Richard
Goodbye, John-Boy. Hello, Jimmy J. M. Ronan. il por Sr Schol 110:27 N 3 '77 *

THOMAS, Richard, family
Like father, like son. J. Ardmore. pors Good H 184:52+ F '77

THOMAS, Roger
Greening of a ball field. il Parks & Rec 12:26-7+ My '77

THOMAS, Ronald Stuart
Comment. J. Silkin. Poetry 130:230-2 Jl '77 *

THOMAS, Steven
Week that changed the world. il Sat Eve Post 249:64-7 Ap '77

THOMAS à Kempis
Thomas à Kempis: the imitation of Christ. L. S. Cunningham. Chr Cent 94:270 Mr 23 '77 *

THOMAS Cook and Son, Ltd. See Cook, Thomas, and Son, Ltd

THOMASSON, Dan, and West, Carl
Our multibillion-dollar Medicaid scandal. Read Digest 110:87-91 My '77

THOMPSON, Adele S.
Der Volksmarsch ist hier! il Am For 83:36-7 F '77

THOMPSON, Benjamin
Architect's choice. J. Davison. il N Y Times Mag p88-9 Ap 24 '77 *
Boston's historic Faneuil Hall Marketplace. M. F. Schmertz. il Archit Rec 162:116-27 D '77 *

THOMPSON, Constance
Problem between home and school. Todays Educ 66:37+ Ja '77

THOMPSON, Dean A. and Campbell, R. G.
Hunger in humans induced by 2-deoxy-D-glucose: glucoprivic control of taste preference and food intake. bibl il Science 198:1065-8 D 9 '77

THOMPSON, Donna Ashworth
I was given up for dead—twice! Good H 184: 102+ My '77

THOMPSON, Era Bell
Backstage. il por Ebony 33:22 N '77 *

THOMPSON, Eugene
Excerpt from testimony on the proposed Fair Labor Standards Amendments, March 16, 1977. Cong Digest 56:141+ My '77

THOMPSON, Jack
Mowed down by a Thompson. K. Hannon. por Sports Illus 47:70+ S 19 '77 *

THOMPSON, James R.
Dying party? interview. pors U.S. News 83:25 Ag 29 '77
about
Big Jim. K. Bode. New Repub 177:16-19 D 24 '77 *
Illinois: big man in a big hurry. F. Maier. por Newsweek 89:46 Ap 11 '77 *

THOMPSON, Katherine Denniston-. See Denniston-Thompson, K.

THOMPSON, Melissa A.
Excerpt from address on the ERA, April 18, 1977. Cong Digest 56:182+ Je '77

THOMPSON, Nancy Cromer
(ed) Multi-media. Engl J 66:100-4 F; 92-5 Ap; 96-101 N '77

THOMPSON, Phyllis
Jade; poem. New Yorker 53:111 My 23 '77

THOMPSON, Richard F. See Berger, T. W. jt auth

THOMPSON, Richard W.
Other side of the coin. Nat R 29:332 Mr 18 '77

THOMPSON, Roger K. R. and Herman, L. M.
Memory for lists of sounds by the bottle-nosed dolphin: convergence of memory processes with humans? bibl il Science 195:501-3 F 4 '77

THOMPSON, Steve
[Column] Car & Dr 23:12+ Ag; 14-15 O; 20 D '77

THOMPSON, Stuart R.
Comment. Ceram Mo 25:19+ Je '77

THOMPSON, Thomas
Nonfiction books: the new bestsellers. por Writers Digest 57:18-21 Ag '77
Richard the Lion-Hearted slept here. il N Y Times Mag p 16-19+ Je 26 '77
about
Blood and money is target of $20-million libel suit. M. Reuter. Pub W 212:35 O 3 '77 *

THOMPSON, Tim
Dockside; photographs. Oceans 10:50-5 Mr '77

THOMPSON, Wayne H. and Beaty, B. J.
Venereal transmission of La Crosse (California encephalitis) arbovirus in aedes triseriatus mosquitoes. bibl il Science 196:530-1 Ap 29 '77
THOMPSON, William Irwin
Visions of futures past. S. Helgesen. il Harpers 254:80-6 Mr '77 *
THOMPSON, William S.
Washington notebook. S. Booker. Ebony 32:29 My '77 *
THOMS, Wayne
Big bikes come back. il Mech Illus 73:46-7 My '77
Cars you can build from kits. il Mech Illus 73: 62+ Mr '77
THOMSEN, Dietrick E.
[Articles on the physical sciences] See issues of Science news
THOMSEN, Paul M. and Blank, J. P.
Helga's gift. il Read Digest 110:72-7 Je '77
THOMSON, Andrew W. J.
New focus on industrial democracy in Britain. bibl f Ann Am Acad 431:32-43 My '77
THOMSON, Gary
Legacy of a Scottish lord: Innerpeffray. il Wilson Lib Bull 51:844-7 Je '77
THOMSON, Joan
Pathbreaker: analyzing Le Prophète. Opera N 41:34+ Ja 29 '77
THOMSON, Sir Joseph John
J. J. Thomson and the Bohr atom. J. L. Heilbron. il pors Phys Today 30:23-4+ Ap '77 *
THOMSON, Samuel
Belly-my-grizzle. S. Klaw. il por Am Heritage 28:96-105 Je '77 *
THOMSON, Virgil
Lord Byron. Review
New Yorker 52:106-8 Ja 17 '77 *
Mother of us all. B. Hastings. il Am Rec G 40: 30-1 Ag '77 *
Who can resist The mother of us all? C. L. Osborne. il Hi Fi 27:92-4 Jl '77 *
THOMSON-CSF (firm) See Electronic industries—France
THOREAU, Henry David
Simplify! Simplify! excerpt from Walden. por Read Digest 111:175-7+ Ag '77

about

Transcendentalism and the expectation of dawn: Emerson and Thoreau. E. Ardura. il pors Américas 29:36-41 Ag '77 *
THORGAARD, Gary H.
Heteromorphic sex chromosomes in male rainbow trout. bibl il Science 196:900-2 My 20 '77
THORNBROUGH, Albert Adam
You can't go fast without taking some bumps. il por Forbes 119:57-8 My 15 '77 *
THORNE, Beth
Rebirth of Beth Thorne. J. L. Block. Good H 185:99+ Jl '77 *
THORNE, Ludmilla
Inside Russia's psychiatric jails. il N Y Times Mag p26-7+ Je 12 '77
Mother courage: how Vladimir Bukovsky was saved. il por N Y Times Mag p38-40+ F 27 '77
THORNE, Richard
Reviews. S. Banes. Dance Mag 51:32-3 Ap '77 *
THORNE, Richard Mansergh
Energetic radiation belt electron precipitation: a natural depletion mechanism for stratospheric ozone. bibl il Science 195:287-9 Ja 21 '77
THORNE, Robert Donald
Deutch and Thorne to fill two key DOE research posts. F. C. Bennett. pors Phys Today 30:93+ N '77 *
Robert Thorne: controversial nominee for energy R&D job. L. J. Carter. Science 198:34 O 7 '77 *
THORNELL, John G.
Using protocols in instructional supervision. Clearing H 51:65-6 O '77
THORNTON, Donald, family
Janitor and his six daughters prove we can. il por Ebony 32:33-4+ S '77 *
THORNTON, Jane Foster
Hamelin pays the piper; dramatization of The pied piper of Hamelin by R. Browning. Plays 36:33-41 Ap '77
THOROUGHBRED horses. See Horses, Race
THOUGHT, Visual. See Visualization
THOUGHT and thinking
How to think about politicians. W. Karp. il por Horizon 19:14-15 Ja '77
Reflections. H. Arendt. New Yorker 53:65-8+ N 21; 114+ N 28; 135-42+ D 5 '77
See also
Attention
Intellectual liberty
Problem solving
Reasoning
THOUSAND Islands
St Lawrence and the Thousand Islands; symposium. il Conservationist 31:2-32 Mr '77
THRACIAN art. See Art, Thracian
THRACIANS
Treasures of Thrace. J. Brzostoski. il Craft Horiz 37:32+ O '77
THREE billy goats Gruff; dramatization. See Jones, D. C.
3M Company. See Minnesota Mining and Manufacturing Company
THREE sisters; drama. See Chekhov, A. P.
THREE wheel automobiles. See Automobiles, Three wheel
THRESHER, Ronald E.
World under the reef; with biographical sketch. il Sea Front 23:66-75, 127 Mr '77
THRESHING combines. See Harvesting machinery
THRIFT
How to be cheap and keep your self-respect. C. Calvert. Mademoiselle 83:32+ Je '77
Once upon a dime. R. T. Allen. Read Digest 110:29-33+ Mr '77
THRIFT institutions
See also
Credit unions
THROMBIN
Formation of a serine enzyme in the presence of bovine factor VIII (antihemophilic factor) and thrombin. G. A. Vehar and E. W. Davie. bibl il Science 197:374-6 Jl 22 '77
THROMBOXANES
Coronary tone modulation: formation and actions of prostaglandins, endoperoxides, and thromboxanes. P. Needleman and others. bibl il Science 195:409-12 Ja 28 '77
THROUGH the looking glass. See Carroll, L. pseud
THROWERS, Snow. See Snow blowers, throwers, etc.
THROWING pots. See Pottery—Technique
THRUSH, Robin A.
(ed) See Lindbergh, A. M. Hero's wife remembers
THUJA. See Arborvitae
THUMBPRINTS. See Fingerprints
THUNDERBIRD American Indian Dancers. See Dance companies
THUNDERSTORMS
Solar flares: link to thunderstorms. Sci N 111: 389 Je 18 '77
Weather course: thunderstorms. il map Motor B & S 140:68-70+ O '77
See also
Aviation—Storm hazards
Lightning
THURBER, James
Thurber's Bermuda. A. Pastore and A. Pastore. il Travel 147:32-7 Mr '77 *
THURBER, John D.
What about the sharks? il Oceans 10:24-30 N '77
THURMAN, Judith
Film. il Ms 6:26 Ja '78
(ed) Never too thin to feel fat; interviews. Ms 6:48-9+ S '77
Poetry: notes from a selfish reader. bibl Ms 6:30+ N '77
(ed) See Varda, A. Varda: watch out. I do not authorize you to use me against other women
THURMOND, Strom
Panama Canal: why the U.S. should keep it. Current 198:52-4 D '77

about

Great nay-sayer. G. F. Will. Newsweek 90:84 S 5 '77 *
THUROW, Lester C.
Carter, the Fed and confidence. Nation 225: 166-8 S 3 '77
End tax breaks for capital gains? interview. pors U.S. News 83:71-2 D 19 '77
Myth of the American economy. por Newsweek 89:11 F 14 '77
Provide wage subsidies for hiring the jobless; interview. por U.S. News 82:60 F 21 '77

about

Jimmy in Wonderland. New Repub 178:2+ Ja 7 '78 *
THWAITES, John Anthony
Documenta 6: the medium was the message. il Art N 76:46-9 S '77
THYMUS-derived lymphocytes. See Lymphocytes
THYROID gland

Diseases

See also
Goiter
THYROID hormones
Pituitary nuclear 3, 5, 3′-triiodothyronine and thyrotropin secretion: an explanation for the effect of thyroxine. J. E. Silva and P. R. Larsen. bibl il Science 198:617-20 N 11 '77
Thyroid hormone action: the mitochondrial pathway. K. Sterling and others. bibl il Science 197:996-9 S 2 '77

THYROTROPIN releasing factor
Thyrotropin-releasing hormone: abundance in the skin of the frog, rana pipiens. I. M. D. Jackson and S. Reichlin. bibl il Science 198: 414-15 O 28 '77
Thyrotropin-releasing hormone: stimulation of colonic activity following intracerebroventricular administration. J. R. Smith and others. bibl il Science 196:660-2 My 6 '77
TIBBETTS, Arn M. and Tibbetts, Charlene
Vanished past of the American school. Clearing H 50:380 My '77
Whatever happened to the new English? Clearing H 51:183-8 D '77
—See Tibbetts, C. jt auth
TIBBETTS, Charlene, and Tibbetts, A. M.
How are English teachers reacting to declining college entrance scores? Engl J 66:13-16 D '77
—See Tibbetts, A. M. jt auth
TIBBITTS, Clark
Older Americans in the family context. Aging 270:6-11 Ap '77
TIBET
See also
Ladakh
Lhasa
Natural history—Tibet
Visitors, Foreign—Tibet
TIBETAN book of the dead. See Buddhist literature
TIC
Nerves: what makes you tic? M. Bernstein. Harp Baz 110:125+ Mr '77
TIC douloureux. See Neuralgia, Trigeminal
TICE, David A.
Jefferson's country. il por Am For 83:24-7 My '77
TICKET selling
Two on the fifty; letters to Purdue ticket seller J. S. Dienhart. B. Collins. il Sat Eve Post 249:40-1 O '77
TICKS
Fever tick crashes roundup, causes trouble on range; cattle roundup at Texas' El Chapote Ranch. D. Snell. il Smithsonian 8:58-65 O '77
TICONDEROGA, Fort. See Fort Ticonderoga
TICOR (firm) See Insurance companies
TIDAL currents. See Ocean currents
TIDAL flats
Tidal flats in the Hudson. R. R. Glunt. il por Conservationist 31:30-1 My '77
TIDAL marshes. See Marshes, Tide
TIDAL power. See Tide power
TIDAL waves
International Tsunami Warning System. G. Pararas-Carayannis. il Sea Front 23:20-7 Ja '77
TIDE power
Best energy source can be tides. J. E. Brown. Sci Digest 82:62+ O '77
TIDES
Height of tide—by calculator! E. S. Maloney. il Motor B & S 140:16+ Jl '77
TIDEWATER flats. See Tidal flats
TIDINESS. See Neatness
TIE-dyeing. See Dyes and dyeing
TIEDEMANN, Gabriele Kröcher-. See Kröcher-Tiedemann, G.
TIEDT, Thomas N. and others
Degenerating nerve fiber products do not alter physiological properties of adjacent innervated skeletal muscle fibers. bibl il Science 198:839-41 N 25 '77
TIEMANN, Norbert Theodore
Traffic-free areas magnet for people and business; excerpts from address, November 1976. Am City & County 92:78 Mr '77
TIEN, Chi, and others
Chainlike formation of particle deposits in fluid-particle separation. il Science 196:983-5 My 27 '77
TIEN, Joseleyne Slade
Unbound: the women of new China. bibl il Intellect 106:37-41 Ag '77
TIERNEY, Lani
People in crisis. Engl J 66:64-5 S '77
TIERNEY, Patricia O.
Hang-ups. Engl J 66:61-2 S '77
TIES (neckware) See Neckties
TIES, Railroad. See Railroads—Ties
TIETJEN, John Henry
Expelled. Chr Today 22:40-1 O 21 '77 *
TIETJEN, Mildred C.
Practice makes perfect. il Wilson Lib Bull 52: 61-3 S '77
TIETZE, Christopher, and Lewit, Sarah
Legal abortion; with biographical sketches. il maps Sci Am 236:16, 21-7 bibl(p 132) Ja '77
TIFFANY glass. See Glassware
TIFFIN River
Make the river do the work. B. East. il por Outdoor Life 160:78-81+ O '77
TIGERMAN, Stanley
To surreal with love. W. Marlin. il Archit Rec 162:89-94 O '77 *
TIGHE, Mary Ann
Art on the line. il New Repub 176:24-6 Ap 16 '77
Di Suvero in Grand Rapids: the public prevails. il Art in Am 65:12-13+ Mr '77
Gertrude Käsebier lost and found. bibl il por Art in Am 65:94-8 Mr '77
TILE drainage. See Drainage
TILE laying
DIY ceramic-tile floor. M. Bernstein. il Pop Sci 211:102-4 Jl '77
How to lay quarry or slate tile. Bet Hom & Gard 55:54 D '77
Laying your own ceramic tile. il Sunset 159: 106-7 Ag '77
McCalls' handywoman: installing ceramic tile. il McCalls 104:118 F '77
Mirror tiles—a quick face-lift for drab walls. M. Philips. il Pop Sci 211:151 O '77
New ceramic-tile countertop. . .right over the old one. il Pop Mech 148:114-15 D '77
TILL, Chris McD.
Same day delivery. il Parents Mag 52:37-9+ Jl '77
TILLAGE
Agriculture without tillage. G. B. Triplett, Jr and D. M. Van Doren, Jr. il Sci Am 236:28-33 Ja '77
Conservation tillage reduces fertilizer, pesticide losses. Suc Farm 75:no4 L48 Mr '77
Corn craftsmanship: picking your tillage. B. Brantley and C. E. Sommers. il Suc Farm 75: no5 28-30 Mr '77
Cultivating faster and bigger yields. J. Jankowiak. il Org Gard & Farm 24:80-2 F '77
How to plan fall tillage. Suc Farm 75:A8 O '77
Minimum tillage in the fall. il Farm J 101:A8 D '77
Plowing: an inquiry. C. K. Stadtfeld. il Audubon 79:44-7 My '77
System that works; no-till planting. B. Gergen. il Suc Farm 75:no4 24-7 Mr '77
See also
Contour farming
Terraces (agriculture)
TILLAMOOK Forest. See Forests and forestry—Oregon
TILLERS. See Cultivators
TILLERS, Boat. See Boats—Steering gear
TILLIN, Alma M. See Hicks, W. B. jt auth
TILLINGHAST, Charles Carpenter, 1911-
Dissenter's view. Aviation W 106:7 My 30 '77
More regulation or deregulation of the airlines? address, December 8, 1976. Vital Speeches 43: 206-9 Ja 15 '77
TILLINGHAST, Richard
Knife; poem. New Repub 177:26 S 3 '77
TILLMAN, Dick
Rope traveler. il Yachting 141:52+ F '77
Singlehanders and the OOAK. il Yachting 142: 40+ D '77
TILLMAN, Donald C.
Man of the year; interview. il pors Am City & County 92:27-9 Ja '77
TILLOTSON, Gordon
Tomatoes and bales. . .and bales. . .of hay. Org Gard & Farm 24:174+ Mr '77
TILMAN, Harold William
Rough log. T. Gibbs. por Yachting 141:96 Je '77 *
TILSHER, Warner G.
Lima as king bean. il Org Gard & Farm 24:72-5 Ap '77
TILTON, Lynn
Full-time goat dairy: how one family does it. il Org Gard & Farm 24:162+ O '77
Late crops for western gardening success. il Org Gard & Farm 24:69-71 Jl '77
Retirement way of life. il Org Gard & Farm 24: 111-12 My '77
TIMBER
See also
Lumber industry
TIMBER clearcutting. See Clearcutting
TIMBER cutting. See Lumbering
TIMBER wolves. See Wolves
TIMBERLAKE, Bob
To know where we have been; excerpt from The Bob Timberlake collection; reproductions of paintings; with text by C. Kuralt and editorial comment. il Audubon 79:inside cover, 48-61 My '77: Same abr. Read Digest 111:136-42 S '77 *
TIMBERLINE Lodge, Oregon (resort) See Winter resorts
TIMBUKTU, Mali
Fabulous Timbuktu. K.-F. Koch. il Natur Hist 86:68-72+ bibl(p96) My '77
TIME
See also
Chronology
Cycles

TIME (periodical)
Jack Davis cover story. N. Meglin. il Am Artist 41:34-7+ Ap '77
Letter from the publisher. R. P. Davidson. See issues of Time
Toward a just peace; Time magazine's plan. maps Time 110:49-50 D 5 '77

TIME, Inc
America's press: too much power for too few? A. P. Sanoff. il U.S. News 83:27-33 Ag 15 '77
Me and Time Inc; Sports Illustrated Court Clubs. il por Forbes 120:81 D 15 '77
Time Inc.'s internal war over Vietnam; excerpt from The powers that be. D. Halberstam. il pors Esquire 89:94-100+ Ja '78
Time Inc.'s money problems. Forbes 120:100 Ag 15 '77

TIME, Inc-Book-of-the-Month Club, Inc merger. See Corporations—Acquisitions and mergers

TIME, Use of
Future for working women; ed by R. J. Leaper; excerpt from Women and the American economy: a look to the 1980's. J. Kreps. por Ms 5:56-7 Mr '77
How blue-collar workers on 4-day workweeks use their time; excerpt from The four-day workweek. D. M. Maklan. bibl il M Labor R 100:18-26 Ag '77
Managing your time by managing yourself. C. L. Hamman. il Nations Bus 65:54-6 Ap '77
Ten tips to help you manage your time; excerpt from Getting things done: the ABC's of time management. E. C. Bliss. Read Digest 110: 185-6+ Ap '77
Tigers at the gates; waiting. R. Rosenblatt. New Repub 176:36-7 Ap 9 '77
Time: how to get the better of it. il Mademoiselle 83:134-7+ F '77
See also
Efficiency

Anecdotes, facetiae, satire, etc.

Time of your life. R. Baker. N Y Times Mag p 12 N 6 '77

TIME Computer, Inc. See Watch industry

TIME dilatation. See Relativity (physics)

TIME measurement
See also
Chronographs
Sundials

TIME perception
Augmenting mental chronometry: the P300 as a measure of stimulus evaluation time. M. Kutas and others. bibl il Science 197:792-5 Ag 19 '77

TIME sharing condominiums. See Condominium (housing)

TIMERS. See Timing devices

TIMERS, Darkroom. See Photography—Processing—Apparatus and supplies

TIMES, London
Right sort of puzzle; a guide to the crossword. J. A. Maxtone Graham. il Horizon 19:94-5 Mr '77

TIMES, Los Angeles. See Los Angeles times

TIMES, New York. See New York times

TIMES literary supplement, London
Literary ups and downs. C. Michener. il Newsweek 89:72 F 7 '77

TIMES Mirror Company
Big money hunts for independent newspapers. il Bus W p56-60+ F 21 '77

TIMES Mirror Company-Random House, Inc merger. See Publishers and publishing—Acquisitions and mergers

TIMES Square, New York City. See New York (city)—Times Square

TIMIDITY
See also
Bashfulness

TIMING devices
Conference talk timer. W. W. Schopp. il Pop Electr 11:62-3 F '77
Easy way to kill the lights; automatic shut-off. il Mech Illus 73:12 N '77
556 dual timer. il Pop Electr 12:82-3 Jl '77
Portable 60-Hz clock oscillator. C. F. Smith. il Pop Electr 12:70 Jl '77
Shut-off timer for battery-powered appliances. J. Sandler. il Pop Electr 12:48 Ag '77
Soft, medium, or hard boiled eggs? Consumers Res Mag 60:35 S '77
Timers and counters. L. Garner. il Pop Electr 11:66-9+ F '77
Timers, timers, timers. E. R. Savage. il Radio-Electr 48:70-1+ O '77
See also
Delay devices
Stop watches

TIMING lights. See Testing instruments

TIMMERMANN, Sandra
Lifetime learning and the arts—a new priority. Educ Digest 43:40-2 S '77

TIMMONS, Virginia G.
Clipboard. See issues of School arts
Emphasis: planning for ceramics. il Sch Arts 77:31-2 N '77

TIMOR (island)
Department testifies on East Timor; statement, July 19, 1977. G. H. Aldrich. Dept State Bull 77:324-6 S 5 '77
U.S. diplomacy and human rights: the cruel case of Indonesia. A. S. Kohen. map Nation 225:553-7 N 26 '77
See also
United Nations—Timor (island)

TIN

Prices

Shortage keeps tin prices hopping. il Bus W p38-9 O 3 '77
Tin prices shake off a speculative fever. il Bus W p44-5 Ap 18 '77

TINDALL, Barry S.
Washington scene. Parks & Rec 12:13+ D '77

TINDEMANS, Leo

Visit to the United States, 1977

Prime Minister Tindemans of Belgium visits Washington; statement, October 19, 1977. Dept State Bull 77:788-9 N 28 '77

TINDER, Donald
Choice evangelical books. il Chr Today 21:24-5 Mr 18 '77
Church and how it grew. Chr Today 21:10-18 S 9 '77
Right reading for right actions. Chr Today 21: 26-9 S 9 '77
Sexuality: a new candor in evangelical books. il Chr Today 21:10-11 Mr 18 '77
Theology. il Chr Today 21:20-3 Mr 18 '77
Why the evangelical upswing? Chr Today 22: 10-12 O 21 '77

TING, C. C. and others
Host control of tumor growth. bibl il Science 197:571-3 Ag 5 '77

TING, Kuang-hsun, Bp, and Ting, Mrs K. H.
Life of Christianity in China; interview. ed by E. L. Stockwell. il Chr Cent 94:168-71 F 23 '77

TING, Mrs Kuang-hsun. See Ting, K. H. Bp, jt auth

TING, Samuel C. C.
Discovery of the J particle: a personal recollection. bibl il Science 196:1167-78 Je 10 '77

TINKELMAN, Murray
Lorraine Fox: illustrator, painter, teacher, alchemist. il pors Am Artist 41:38-45+ D '77
Special sports issue. il Am Artist 41:2+ Jl '77

TINKER, Allen A.
1977 solar eclipse in Colombia. il maps Sky & Tel 53:267-9 Ap '77

TINNEY, James S.
Koran in the crisis: unholy Muslim war. Chr Today 21:48 Ap 1 '77
(ed) See Cleaver, E. Views of a regenerate radical

TINSLEY, Beatrice M.
Cosmological constant and cosmological change; adaptation of address, December 1976. bibl il Phys Today 30:32-8 Je '77

TINSLEY, Russell
Blunt hunt for cottontails. il Outdoor Life 159: 82-3+ F '77
Stalk a spooky dove. il Field & S 82:34+ Ag '77
Three-for-three elk hunt. il map Outdoor Life 159:70-1+ Je '77

TINSLEY, T. W.
Viruses and the biological control of insect pests. bibl il BioScience 27:659-61 O '77

TIPPET, Clark
Clark Tippet: I didn't have to kill anybody; interview, ed by N. M. Stoop. il pors Dance Mag 51:58-66 My '77

TIPPETT, Sir Michael
Ice break. Reviews
Hi Fi il 27:MA34-6 N '77 *
New Yorker 53:124-8 S 19 '77 *
Midsummer marriage. Review
New Yorker 53:124-8 S 19 '77 *
Musical events; Fourth symphony. A. Porter. New Yorker 53:128-30 O 31 '77 *

TIPPING
Q&A about money. J. S. Dennis. por Ret Liv 16:57 D '76
Tips on tipping; beauty operators. A. Penney. il N Y Times Mag p 150-1 D 4 '77

TIRE industry
Mohawk: a company that respects its limitations. N. Howard. il Duns R 110:47-8 O '77
See also
Goodrich, B. F. Company
Goodyear Tire and Rubber Company
Uniroyal, Inc

TIRES, Automobile
Elliptic tire stretches your gas mileage. H. Shuldiner. il Pop Sci 211:102-4 N '77
Goodyear rolls out a gas-saving tire. Bus W p28 Ag 8 '77

TIRES, Automobile—*Continued*
Tire insert—a flat you can drive on. R. L. Stepler. il Pop Sci 210:72 F '77
Tire primer. A. K. Dukes. Mademoiselle 83:74 N '77
Tires. il Changing T 31:31-4 Je '77
Tires. il Pop Mech 147:192-3+ My '77
Winter tires. W. Woron. il Motor T 30:56-9 Ja '78

TIRES, Recycling of. See Refuse, Utilization of

TIRES, Truck
Guide to off-road rubber. M. Schultz. il Pop Mech 147:110+ Mr '77
Now it's trucks on radial tires. P. M. Eckstein. il Mech Illus 73:86-7+ Jl '77

TIRREL, Ruth
Best plants for chasing bugs. il Org Gard & Farm 24:57-61 N '77

TISCHLER, Nancy M.
Love makes the world go round. Chr Today 21:22-3 Ag 26 '77

TISHMAN, Nina
Nina Tishman, piano; recital at Grace Rainey Rogers Auditorium. Hi Fi 27:MA26 My '77 *

TISHMAN Realty and Construction Company. See Real estate business

TISSUES
See also
Adipose tissues
Cells

Culture

Adenine and adenosine are toxic to human lymphoblast mutants defective in purine salvage enzymes. M. S. Hershfield and others. bibl il Science 197:1284-7 S 23 '77
Angiotensin converting enzyme: induction by steroids in rabbit alveolar macrophages in culture. J. Friedland and others. bibl il Science 197:64-5 Jl 1 '77
Clockwise growth of neurites from retinal explants. A. M. Heacock and B. W. Agranoff. bibl il Science 198:64-6 O 7 '77
Collagenase production by rheumatoid synovial cells: stimulation by a human lymphocyte factor. J.-M. Dayer and others. bibl il Science 195:181-3 Ja 14 '77
Defective phagocytosis of isolated rod outer segments by RCS rat retinal pigment epithelium in culture. R. B. Edwards and R. B. Szamier. bibl il Science 197:1001-3 S 2 '77
Differentiating limb tissue affects neurite growth in spinal cord cultures. E. D. Pollack and V. Liebig. bibl il Science 197:899-900 Ag 26 '77
Enzyme polymorphisms as genetic signatures in human cell cultures. S. J. O'Brien and others. bibl il Science 195:1345-8 Mr 25 '77
Establishment of a cell line with associated Epstein-Barr-like virus from a leukemic orangutan. S. Rasheed and others. bibl il Science 198:407-9 O 28 '77
Feline oncornavirus-associated cell membrane antigen: expression in transformed nonproducer mink cell. A. H. Sliski and others. bibl il Science 196:1336-9 Je 17 '77
Fragile sites on human chromosomes: demonstration of their dependence on the type of tissue culture medium. G. R. Sutherland. bibl il Science 197:265-6 Jl 15 '77
Glia maturation factor: effect on chemical differentiation of glioblasts in culture. R. Lim and others. bibl il Science 195:6 Ja 14 '77
Goblet cells in embryonic intestine: accelerated differentiation in culture. B. L. Black and F. Moog. bibl il Science 197:368-70 Jl 22 '77
Growth hormone: species-specific stimulation of erythropoiesis in vitro. D. W. Golde and others. bibl il Science 196:1112-13 Je 3 '77
HLA variants of cultured human lymphoid cells: evidence for mutational origin and estimation of mutation rate. D. Pious and C. Soderland. bibl il Science 197:769-71 Ag 19 '77
In vitro growth of imaginal disks from drosophila melanogaster. K. T. Davis and A. Shearn. bibl il Science 196:438-40 Ap 22 '77
Induction of acetylcholinesterase activity by β-ecdysone in a drosophila cell line. P. Cherbas and others. bibl il Science 197:275-7 Jl 15 '77
Inter-and intraspecies contamination of human breast tumor cell lines HBC and BrCa5 and other cell cultures. W. A. Nelson-Rees and R. R. Flandermeyer. bibl il Science 195:1343-4 Mr 25 '77
Lysis of human cultured lymphoblastoid cells by cell-induced activation of the properdin pathway. A. N. Theofilopoulos and L. H. Perrin. bibl il Science 195:878-80 Mr 4 '77
Phosphoribosylpyrophosphate synthesis in cultured human cells. P. J. Benke and D. Dittmar. bibl il Science 198:1171-3 D 16 '77
Primary bioassay of human tumor stem cells. A. W. Hamburger and S. E. Salmon. bibl il Science 197:461-3 Jl 29 '77
Simultaneous effects of erythropoietin and colony-stimulating factor on bone marrow cells. G. Van Zant and E. Goldwasser. bibl il Science 198:733-5 N 18 '77
Synapse formation between two clonal cell lines. C. N. Christian and others. bibl il Science 196:995-8 My 27 '77
Testing the commitment theory of cellular aging. R. Holliday and others. bibl il Science 198:366-72 O 28 '77
Tumor cell collagenase and its inhibition by a cartilage-derived protease inhibitor. K. E. Kuettner and others. bibl il Science 196:653-4 My 6 '77
See also
Plant cells and tissues—Culture

TITAN (satellite) See Satellites

TITANIC (steamship)
Woods Hole mulls Titanic expedition. B. J. Culliton. Science 197:848-9 Ag 26 '77

TITIAN
Looking at paintings. B. Dunstan. il Am Artist 41:60-1 O '77 *

TITLE VII Nutrition Program for the Elderly. See Old age assistance

TITLES, Job. See Job descriptions

TITO
Toast to Tito. T. Szulc. New Repub 177:17-18 S 24 '77 *

TITUS, Christopher A. and others
Komputer korner (title varies) il Radio-Electr 48:76-7 O '77

TITUS, John, and others
Komputer korner (title varies) (cont) il Radio-Electr 48:22+ F; 22+ Jl '77

TITUS, William R.
ABC's of a garden plan. Horticulture 55:42 Mr '77
Your own valuable space. il Horticulture 55:58-9 F '77

TIVEY, Hap
Zen-science of light. M. Wortz. il Art N 76:200+ N '77 *

TIZARD, Barbara
Adoption. D. Cohen. Psychol Today 11:128+ N '77 *

TLATELOLCO treaty. See Atomic weapons and disarmament

TOADS
Amphibious flycatcher. W. J. Betts. il Org Gard & Farm 24:120+ Ap '77

TOAST
Breakfast or dessert or wholesome snack—just fruit on toast. il Sunset 159:140 Ag '77
French toast the easy way. il Good H 185:70 N '77

TOASTER ovens
Best-buy guide to toaster ovens. il Good H 185:164+ O '77

TOASTERS
Toasters. il Consumers Res Mag 60:33-6 Ap '77

TOBACCO
Homogenized leaf curing keeps tobacco proteins from going up in smoke. BioScience 27:224 Mr '77
Tobacco protein may lead to heart disease. Sci N 112:214 O 1 '77
See also
Nicotiana
Nicotine
Smoking

TOBACCO chewing
Chaws. R. Blount, Jr. il Sports Illus 47:54-9+ Jl 4 '77

TOBACCO industry
Unnatural history of tobacco. E. Eckholm. il Natur Hist 86:22-4+ Ap '77; Reply with rejoinder. H. R. Kornegay. 86:74-7 Je '77
See also
Cigar industry
Cigarette industry

Advertising

See also
Cigarette industry—Advertising

United States

U.S. Tobacco: everything but cigarettes. por Duns R 110:26-8 N '77

History

When tobacco was king; colonial Virginia. E. L. Abel. il Am Hist Illus 11:10-19 F '77

TOBACCO mosaic virus. See Viruses, Plant

TOBACCO pipes
Carve your own dream pipe; briar. G. Graves. il Pop Mech 147:255-7 My '77
Some Indian pipes. C. Miles. il Hobbies 82:140-1+ My '77
Tobacco. C. Miles. il Hobbies 81:140-1+ F '77

TOBACCO smoke
See also
Cigarette smoke

TOBERMORY, Scotland
Treasure of Tobermory Bay; Spanish galleon Florencia. E. Antrobus. il map Am For 83:20-3+ Je '77

TOBEY, Fred
Buon appetito! il Opera N 42:8-11 D 24 '77

TOBIAS, Alice
You bet your vocabulary! drama. Plays 36:79-82 My '77

TOBIAS, Andrew
Money. See issues of Esquire

TOBIAS, Doris
Great white spirits. il House & Gard 149:182+ O '77
Movable drinks. il House & Gard 149:136+ Je '77
Wines. Am Home 80:6 F; 29 Ap; 55 Je; 7 Jl; 32+ S '77

TOBIAS, Sheila. See Donady, B. jt auth

TOBIAS, Tobi
Modern dance, Taylor-made. il Horizon 21:50-5 Ja '78

TOBIN, Wallace E.
Condition report. il Motor B & S 139:26-7+ Je; 140:42+ Ag; 40+ O; 22+ D '77

TOCCOA Creek dam failure. See Dams—Failure

TOCCOA FALLS Institute, Toccoa Falls, Ga.
Tragedy at Toccoa. E. E. Plowman. il Chr Today 22:48-50 D 9 '77

TODD, Frank S.
Adelie and emperor penguins; ed by R. Chemey. il Oceans 10:20-5 My '77

TODD, Garfield. See Todd, R. S. G.

TODD, Jan
Pleasure of being the world's strongest woman. S. Pileggi. il pors Sports Illus 47:60-4+ N 14 '77 *

TODD, Neil B.
Cats and commerce; with biographical sketch. il maps Sci Am 237:15, 100-7 bibl(p 163) N '77

TODD, Reginald Stephen Garfield
Former Premier calls for full UK, US commitment. il por UN Chron 14:25 Jl '77 *

TODD, Richard
Books. See issues of Atlantic

TODMAN, Terence A.
Approach to Latin American policy: creative developments; address, July 21, 1977. Dept State Bull 77:588-92 O 31 '77
Foundations of U.S. policy toward Latin America; address, October 18, 1977. Dept State Bull 77: 815-21 D 5 '77
Latin American development in an interdependent world; excerpt from address, May 29, 1977. Dept State Bull 77:440-5 O 3 '77
Leadership role for private enterprise in Latin America; address, June 27, 1977. Dept State Bull 77:464-8 O 10 '77
Trade and business in Inter-American relations; address, May 3, 1977. Dept State Bull 77:393-5 S 26 '77
U.S. business community and the Caribbean: partners in growth and development; excerpt from address, June 23, 1977. Dept State Bull 77:214-18 Ag 15 '77
U.S. security assistance policy for Latin America; statement, April 5, 1977. Dept State Bull 76:444-6 My 2 '77

about

Happy sounds on dictatorships. Nation 225:163-4 S 3 '77 *
Our man in Havana. F. Willey and L. E. Nelson. il Newsweek 89:44 My 9 '77 *

TOFFLER, Kris
Psychic power of Uri Geller. il pors Sat Eve Post 249:58-9+ O '77

TOFU
Tofu could lead to new market for your soybeans. Farm J 101:D1 O '77
Try making tofu—you'll like it. C. Bauer and J. Andersen. il Org Gard & Farm 24:100+ Ap '77

TOGNI, Alberto
Oh, those impetuous Swiss; Swiss Bank Corp. por Forbes 119:68 F 1 '77 *

TOGO, Fumihiko
Our bilateral economic relations; address, February 4, 1977. Vital Speeches 43:327-9 Mr 15 '77

TOGO
See also
Women—Togo

Industries

Madame Mercedes-Benz: merchant of Togo. E. J. Kiers. il Ms 5:112+ Ap '77

TOILET bowl cleaners. See Cleaning compositions

TOILET facilities on boats. See Boats—Toilet facilities

TOILET paper
Toilet tissues: softness, strength, or price? Consumer Rep 42:466-8 Ag '77

TOILET preparations
Beauty products cause cancer? NDELA contamination. Sci N 111:213 Ap 2 '77
Personal care equipment and supplies. il Consumers Res Mag 60:49-58 O '77
See also
Bath preparations
Cosmetics
Shampoos

Marketing

S. C. Johnson tries again on personal care. il por Bus W p54+ F 14 '77

TOILETS
Water-air toilets slash consumption. Am City & County 92:58 Ja '77

TOILETS, Composting. See Sewage purification—Biological treatment

TOILETS, Public. See Public comfort stations

TOKAMAKS
And still no JET yet. N. Hawkes. Science 196: 637 My 6 '77
Fusion gains ground with new tokamaks. Sci N 112:294 N 5 '77
JET arrives in England at subsonic speed. W. D. Metz. Science 198:711 N 18 '77

TOKELAU (islands)
See also
United Nations—Tokelau (islands)

TOKENS
From reckoning to writing; work of D. Schmandt-Besserat on the correlation between geometric objects and signs on Sumerian tablets. il Sci Am 237:58 Ag '77
Roots of writing; ancient recording system used in trade; studies of D. Schmandt-Besserat. il por Time 110:76 Ag 1 '77

TOKLAS, Alice B.
Gay genius and the gay mob. A. Kazin. Esquire 88:33-4+ D '77 *

TOKYO
Americanization of Japan. R. Payne. il Society 14:81-4 Jl '77
Shinjuku. P. Gluck. il Archit Rec 162:101-4 S '77

Airports

Narita Airport facing new hindrances. Aviation W 108:39 Ja 9 '78

Banks

$6 billion that Japan is squirreling away. il Bus W p 194 N 14 '77

Public buildings

See also
Embassies (buildings)

Street traffic

Computerizing Tokyo's traffic. J. H. Douglas. il map Sci N 112:412-14 D 17 '77

TOKYO Stock Exchange. See Stock exchanges—Tokyo Exchange

TOKSÖZ, M. Nafi, and others
Moonquakes: mechanisms and relation to tidal stresses. bibl il Science 196:979-80+ My 27 '77
—See Shakal, A. F. jt auth

TOLCHIN, Martin
Old pol takes on the new President. il pors N Y Times Mag p6-9+ Jl 24 '77

TOLEDO, Ohio

Galleries and museums

Consistently discriminating connoisseurship; Toledo Museum of Art. F. Schulze. il Art N 76:64-7 Ap '77

Water pollution

See Water pollution—Ohio

TOLEDO Museum of Art. See Toledo, Ohio—Galleries and museums

TOLERANCE, Immunological. See Immunological tolerance

TOLERANCE of pain. See Pain

TOLERANCE to drugs. See Drugs—Physiological effects

TOLINS, Selma. See Paston, B. N. jt auth

TOLKIEN, John Ronald Reuel
Answers about middle-earth. C. Forbes. il Chr Today 22:30-1 O 7 '77 *
HM's The Silmarillion sets new records. D. Maryles. il Pub W 212:106+ S 26 '77 *
Houghton Mifflin's fall title by J. R. R. Tolkien to excavate the founding of Middle-earth. R. Dahlin. Pub W 211:59 F 14 '77 *
Paradox of J. R. R. Tolkien. por Chr Today 21:35 S 9 '77 *
Reinvented word. C. Nicol. il Harpers 255:95-6+ N '77 *

TOLL, Stanley
Implementation strategy for values clarification. il Clearing H 50:385-9 My '77

TOLLEY, Howard B. Jr
Common Cause and campaign financing: reform liberals open up the system. il Intellect 106: 122-5 O '77

TOLLUND Man. See Denmark—Antiquities

TOLSTOI, Lev Nikolaevich, Graf
Portrait of the artist as an old man. L. Edel. Am Scholar 47:54-68 Wint '77 *

TOLSTOY, Leo. See Tolstoi, L. N.

TOLUENE diisocyanate. See Isocyanates

TOM Mann Bait Company. See Fishing lures, flies, etc.—Manufacture

TOMATILLOS
See also
Cookery—Vegetables

TOMATOES
Everything you always wanted to know about the tomato. D. Fell. il Horticulture 55:16-18+ F '77
How to cage tomatoes. il Bet Hom & Gard 55:172 Je '77
How to grow pots of tomatoes in your windowsill garden. S. K. Graham. il House & Gard 149:82+ N '77
May in the garden. D. Fell. Horticulture 55:56+ My '77
Reporter at large. T. Whiteside. New Yorker 52:36-42+ Ja 24 '77
Tomatoes and bales. . .and bales. . .of hay. G. Tillotson. Org Gard & Farm 24:174+ Mr '77
Tough tomatoes; mechanical harvesting in California. P. Barnett. Progressive 41:32-6 D '77
Up from catsup. R. Sokolov. Natur Hist 86:108+ Ag '77
See also
Cookery—Vegetables

Diseases and pests

Cucumber mosaic virus associated RNA 5: causal agent for tomato necrosis. J. M. Kaper and H. E. Waterworth. bibl il Science 196:429-31 Ap 22 '77
Editorial; cucumber mosaic virus and the 1972 tomato epidemic in Alsace. P. Trachtman. Horticulture 55:10-11 Jl '77

Preservation

See Vegetables—Preservation

TOMB robberies. See Pillage

TOMBIGBEE River
More on the corps; opposition to Tombigbee River Valley project. G. Reiger. Field & S 82:22+ My '77
Selling off the Old South. J. Greene. il map Harpers 254:39-42+ Ap '77

TOMBS
See also
Catacombs

China

Writings on bamboo and wood; tablets found in tombs. W. S. Wong. bibl il Wilson Lib Bull 51:848-52 Je '77
See also
Ch'in Shih-huang-ti—Tomb

Egypt

See also
Tutenkhamûn, King of Egypt—Tomb

Greece

Royal find; tomb of Philip II. P. Gwynne. il Newsweek 90:86 D 5 '77
Treasures from a golden tomb; Philip of Macedonia. N. Gage and J. Gage. il por map N Y Times Mag p 14-19+ D 25 '77

Russia

Horses for the hereafter; excavations at Arzhan. M. P. Gryaznov. il UNESCO Courier 29:38-41 D '76
Pazyryk, Altaian tombs excavated. M. P. Zavitukhina. il UNESCO Courier 29:30-3+ D '76

TOMBSTONES. See Sepulchral monuments

TOMCHIN, Julian, and others
Living big in less space. pors Am Home 80:43+ My '77

TOMKIES, Mike
Speaking of sparrows. il Read Digest 110:53-4+ My '77

TOMKIEWICZ, Micha, and Woodall, J. M.
Photoassisted electrolysis of water by visible irradiation of a *p*-type gallium phosphide electrode. bibl il Science 196:990-1 My 27 '77

TOMKINS, Calvin
Onward and upward with the arts. il New Yorker 53:43-6+ Mr 28 '77
Profiles; R. Bearden. por New Yorker 53:53-8+ N 28 '77
Profiles; P. Johnson. por New Yorker 53:43-4+ My 23 '77
Profiles; C. Oldenburg. New Yorker 53:55-6+ D 12 '77

TOMKINS, Frank S.
Two Argonne scientists win Optical Society's Meggers Award. pors Phys Today 30:75 S '77 •

TOMLIN, Lily
Bunch of Lily; interview, ed by J. Robinson. pors Vogue 167:148-9+ Je '77

about

Lily . . . Ernestine . . . Tess . . . Lupe . . . Edith Ann. . . il pors Time 109:68-72 Mr 28 '77 •
Lily Tomlin: funny lady. J. Kroll. il pors Newsweek 89:62-6 Mr 28 '77 •
Theatre; Appearing nitely. B. Gill. New Yorker 53:81 Ap 4 '77 •
Understanding Lily Tomlin; or, We're all in this alone. E. Stone. il Psychol Today 11:14+ Jl '77 •

TOMLINSON, Kenneth Y.
Can public-employee unions be controlled? Read Digest 110:141-5 Ap '77
Murder at Jupiter. il Read Digest 111:115-19 Jl '77
Which way out of the welfare mess? Read Digest 111:149-54 D '77

TOMLINSON, P. B. and Posluszny, Usher
Apical dichotomy demonstrated in the angiosperm flagellaria. bibl il Science 196:1111-12 Je 3 '77

TOMOGRAPHY, Axial. See Radiography, Medical

TOMPKINS, Barry
Quick bites of a sporting feast. W. Leggett. il por Sports Illus 46:55 Ap 25 '77 •

TOMPKINS, Rachel B. See Sher, J. P. jt auth

TOMPKINS, Warwick Miller
Obituary
Motor B & S 139:118 F '77

TON, Iosif
Believers in Romania: divided they stand. E. E. Plowman. il pors Chr Today 21:18-21 My 20 '77 •
Josif Ton's fight for rights. E. E. Plowman. il por Chr Today 21:40-1 My 20 '77 •

TONDER, Robert van
White roots: seeds of grievance. W. McWhirter. il por Time 110:54 N 21 '77 •

TONE arm, Phonograph. See Phonograph—Tone arm

TONELLI, Quentin, and Meints, R. H.
Surface molecules of hematopoietic stem cells: requirement for sialic acid in spleen colony formation. bibl il Science 195:897-8 Mr 4 '77

TONELSON, Alan
Bring back hell fire. New Repub 176:18-19 F 26 '77
Pitfalls of morality. New Repub 177:13-15 O 29 '77

TONER, Michael F.
Putting the Big Cypress together again. il map Nat Parks & Con Mag 51:4-9 Mr '77

TONER, Raymond J.
Cruise of the USS Essex. il por map Am Hist Illus 11:4-7+ Ja '77

TONING (photography) See Photography—Printing processes

TONRY, Richard
Bell ringers. S. Fraker and others. por Newsweek 89:30+ Ap 18 '77 •

TONSOR, Stephen J.
Second spring of American conservatism; adaptation of address. Nat R 29:1103-7 S 30 '77

TONTO (literary character) See Indians (American) in literature

TOOHEY, Barbara. See Biermann, J. jt auth

TOOL boxes, racks, etc.
Easy-to-make household carryalls. il Sunset 158:148 Mr '77

TOOL sheds, Garden. See Garden houses, shelters, etc.

TOOLS
ABCs of carving tools. T. H. Jones. il Mech Illus 73:126-7+ F '77
Basic tool box. J. Roy. il Am Home 80:16 Je '77
Basic tools. il Motor T 28:73-4 D '76
Equipment reports:
OK machine and tool WSU-30 wirewrapping tool. il Radio-Electr 48:24+ S '77
Extra hands for the hobbyist. E. R. Savage. il Radio-Electr 48:6-7+ Jl '77
Hot rod tool guide. C. J. Baker; J. McCraw. il Hot Rod 30:76-82+ Ag '77
Hot rod's tool kit guide. il Hot Rod 30:126 Mr '77
John Welch retooled for retirement—literally; dealer of antique tools. J. R. Wolkomir. Ret Liv 17:45+ Ag '77
New tools for electronics. R. D. Freed. il Mech Illus 73:124+ Je '77
New tools for your electronics workbench. I. Berger. il Pop Mech 147:115 Mr '77
PM tool test. See issues of Popular mechanics
PM's shop editors pick stocking stuffers. il Pop Mech 148:60+ N '77
Product test reports:
OK model WSU-30 wire-wrap tool. il Pop Electr 11:100 Mr '77
Vector Slit-N-Wrap wiring tool. il Pop Electr 11:98-9 Je '77
Removing broken bolts, studs, and screws. E. Hoffman. il Pop Sci 210:142-3 My '77
16 pages money saving backyard how-tos. C. J. Baker. il Hot Rod 30:82-4+ My '77
Striking and struck tools. A. Lees. il Pop Sci 211:112+ Jl '77
Tooling up for the task. Redbook 148:205 Ap '77
Tools for the home workshop. Consumers Res Mag 60:120-9 O '77
20 metalworking tools for dozens of home repairs. P. Angell. il Pop Mech 147:136-7+ Ap '77
Two tools you can make from scrap materials: Multi-use handsaw. E. J. Loiselle. il Pop Mech 149:99 Ja '78
Tap wrench. R. F. Bessmer. il Pop Mech 149:99 Ja '78

TOOLS—*Continued*
What you need to know about tools and handy gadgets. F. Belt. il Radio-Electr 49:33-42 Ja '78
Workshop mini-course. il Pop Mech 147:119 Je; 148:14 Ag; 8 N '77
See also
Garden tools, equipment, and supplies
also names of tools, e.g. Jigs

Collectors and collecting

Address book; antique tools. S. Sunderlin. House B 119:24 Je '77

Manufacture

See also
Electric tools—Manufacture

Storage

See also
Garden houses, shelters, etc.

TOOLS, Indian (American) See Indians of North America—Implements

TOOMAY, John C.
Space technology; address, April 28, 1977. Vital Speeches 43:602-5 Jl 15 '77

TOON, Malcolm
Signs of change in Russia; interview. il pors U.S. News 84:27-8 Ja 9 '78
Where is detente going? excerpts from interview, ed by F. Coleman. il Newsweek 90:48-9 Jl 25 '77

TOONG, Hoo-min D.
Microprocessors; with biographical sketch. il Sci Am 237:14, 146-7+ S '77

TOOTH decay. See Dental caries

TOPEL, Bernard Joseph, Bp
My God, my God, why have you forsaken me? New Cath World 220:12-13 Ja '77

TOPF, Nancy
Reviews. R. Baker. Dance Mag 51:28+ My '77 •

TOPKINS, Katharine
That college countdown. Seventeen 36:108-9+ F '77

TOPOFF, Howard R.
Pit and the antlion; with biographical sketch. il Natur Hist 86:4, 64-71 bibl(p 100-1) Ap '77

TOPOGRAPHIC maps
In search of Eden; using topographic maps to locate fishing sites. K. Schultz. il Field & S 81:58+ F '77
Joy of maps; backpacking trip in the Absaroka Primitive Area. W. Hjortsberg. il Esquire 88: 142-4 Ag '77
Mail-order maps. S. Netherby. Field & S 82:174 S '77

TOPOLOGY
Catastrophe model: can it see crises? P. P. Luedtke. il por Sci Digest 81:68-70 F '77
Catastrophe theory: the emperor has no clothes. G. B. Kolata. Science 196:287+ Ap 15 '77; Discussion. 196:1270+ Je 17 '77
Catastrophe theory: the first decade. L. A. Steen. il Sci N 111:218-19+ Ap 2 '77
See also
Graph theory

TOPPING, Audrey R.
Clay soldiers: the army of Emperor Ch'in. il Horizon 19:4-13 Ja '77

TOPPING, Seymour
How long can Africa's whites hold out? il N Y Times Mag p37-9+ N 13 '77

TOPPINGS, Whipped. See Icings

TOPSOIL erosion. See Erosion

TOPUZ, Hifzi
Television's one-way traffic. il UNESCO Courier 30:16-17 Ap '77

TORAL, Hernan Crespo. See Crespo Toral, H.

TOREL, Herman Geiger-. See Geiger-Torel, H.

TORGERSON, Randall E.
Farmer cooperatives. bibl f il Ann Am Acad 429:91-102 Ja '77

TORICK, Emil
In the loudspeaker testing lab. il Hi Fi 27:69-73 O '77

TORNADOES
Alaska tornadoes. T. Fathauer and W. J. Wilson. il maps Weatherwise 30:106-10 Je '77
Anticyclonic tornadoes. T. T. Fujita. bibl il Weatherwise 30:51-64 Ap '77
Codell, revisited. M. Smith. bibl il Weatherwise 30:112-13 Je '77
Good news about disaster; effects on residents of Xenia, Ohio. V. Taylor. bibl il por Psychol Today 11:93-4+ O '77
How school kids can survive tornadoes; National Oceanic and Atmospheric Administration study. K. J. Gilleland. il Farm J 101:J2+ Ap '77
19,000 tornadoes later . . profile of terrible triangle, 45-year drought cycle. D. Martindale. il map Sci Digest 81:11-15 My '77
Tornado forecasting. Sci Digest 81:86 Je '77
Tornado season of 1976. A. Pearson and others. il maps Weatherwise 30:3-9+ F '77
Tornadoes: enigma of spring. W. H. Spencer. il Read Digest 110:15-16+ Ap '77
What happens: cyclone whirl holds the key, not funnels. Sci Digest 81:16-17 My '77
Will cruel weather ever let up? il U.S. News 82:59-60 Ap 18 '77
Xenia sounds off to reduce tornado tragedies; warning system. il Am City & County 92:66 F '77

TORNAI, József
Mr T. S. Eliot cooking pasta; poem; tr by R. Wilbur. New Yorker 53:35 F 28 '77

TORONTO

Architecture

Toronto townhouse: a year-round garden; home of B. Myers. N. Skurka. il N Y Times Mag p52-3 Ag 21 '77
Wolf residence, Toronto, Ontario. il Archit Rec 161:50-3 mid-My '77

Art

Report from Toronto & Montreal. A. Goldin il Art in Am 65:35-45+ Mr '77

Bookstores

See Booksellers and bookselling—Canada

Hotels, restaurants, etc.

Little bit of England in Toronto; Windsor Arms. H. E. Meyer. il Fortune 96:217-18 N '77

Libraries

See Libraries—Canada

Music

See also
Opera—Canada

Underground areas

New kind of weatherproof city is evolving in Toronto; underground commercial development. il map Sunset 159:38 N '77

TORONTO Star Newspapers Ltd. See Newspaper publishers and publishing—Canada

TORPEDOES
Anechoic paint spurs torpedo guidance effort. Aviation W 107:21-2 Ag 15 '77

TORPEY, Sally P.
Great Italian bread from a real bread expert. il Bet Hom & Gard 55:62-3+ F '77

TORQUE wrenches. See Wrenches

TORRE, Susanna, and others
Rethinking closets, kitchens, and other forgotten spaces. il Ms 6:54-5 D '77

TORRES, Carlos Alberto
Who defines religion. J. M. Wall. Chr Cent 94: 523-4 Je 1 '77 •

TORRES, Liz
Liz Torres: I get my best material from the subways; interview, ed by S. Weller. il pors Ms 6:29-31 Ag '77

TORRES Strait
Wind caller. B. Nietschmann. il map Natur Hist 86:10-12+ Mr '77

TORREY, E. Fuller
Bureaucrat's new clothes: a cautionary tale. Psychol Today 11:95 Jl '77
Carter's little pills. Psychol Today 11:10+ D '77
Fantasy trial about a real issue. Psychol Today 10:24 Mr '77
Schizophrenia: sense and nonsense. il Psychol Today 11:157 N '77
(ed) See Bukovsky, V. Serbsky treatment

TORREY, Owen C. Jr
Pratt Project update. Yachting 142:30 Jl '77

TORRIJOS HERRERA, Omar
President Carter and General Torrijos sign Panama Canal treaties; remarks, September 7, 1977; with text of treaties. map Dept State Bull 77:482-3 O 17 '77
Torrijos: the U.S. has lied; excerpts from interview, ed by R. Moreau. por Newsweek 89:41 Ap 25 '77
We have two ways to go; interview, ed by J. Hannifin. Time 110:13 Ag 22 '77
We paid a price; interview. ed by R. Moreau. il por Newsweek 90:35 Ag 22 '77
What Panama's leader says about new Canal treaties; interview. por U.S. News 83:20-1 S 19 '77

about

As U.S. and Panama head for showdown over canal; with editorial comment. C. J. Migdail. il por maps U.S. News 82:28-30, 76 My 2 '77 •
Deal on the Canal. F. Willey and S. Sullivan. il por Newsweek 90:29-30 Ag 15 '77 •
Foothold for Kaddafi? K. Willenson and R. Moreau. por Newsweek 89:41-2+ Ap 25 '77 •
Omar Torrijos: the Panamanian enigma. M. C. Needler. por Intellect 105:242-3 F '77 •
Real message to U.S. in that Panama plebiscite. il por U.S. News 83:61-2 N 7 '77 •

Visit to Israel, 1977

Globe-trotter. M. J. Kubic. il por Newsweek 90: 47 O 10 '77

TORTOISES
Three, two, one tortoise; Pinta Island: P. C. H. Pritchard. il map Natur Hist 8(90-100 bibl(p 123) O '77
TORTOISES in literature. See Reptiles in literature
TORTS
See also
Government liability
TORTURE
Torture again. A. McCarthy. Commonweal 104: 743+ N 25 '77
Torture tempest; question of newspaper reports charging mistreatment of Palestinian prisoners by the Israeli government. S. Kaplan. New Repub 177:16-17 Jl 23 '77
U.S. supports U.N. resolution against the practice of torture; statement, with text of resolution, December 3, 1976. J. M. Myerson. Dept State Bull 76:77-80 Ja 24 '77
TOSCA; opera. See Puccini, G.
TOSCANINI, Arturo
Toscanini treatment; with list of recordings. C. J. Luten. Am Rec G 40:45-6 F '77 *
TOSCHES, Nick
Country. il Hi Fi 27:145 F '77; 28:132-3 Ja '78
George Jones: I'm never gonna sell pop. il pors Hi Fi 27:103-5 My '77
TOSTESON, Daniel C.
Tosteson new Harvard dean: Chicago bitter about his leaving. B. J. Culliton. Science 195: 160-2 Ja 14 '77 *
TOTALITARIANISM
Revel-ations; tr by D. Pryce-Jones; excerpt from La nouvelle censure. J. F. Revel. N Y Times Mag p 115-16 D 11 '77
TOTE bags. See Bags
TOTENBERG, Nina
Supreme embarrassment. por Newsweek 89:66 My 9 '77 *
TOTH, Linda Beth
Women's liberature. Engl J 66:63-4 S '77
TOTH, Robert Charles
Message from Moscow. A. Deming and others. il por Newsweek 89:14-16 Je 27 '77 *
TOTH, Susan Allen
Fantasies; story. Redbook 149:64-6 Ag '77
TOTMAN, Leland
Making milk. M. Kramer. il pors Atlantic 240: 80-4+ N '77 *
TOUCH
Beyond sex: the joy of touching. A. Gross. Mademoiselle 83:115-16+ D '77
Cerebral lateralization of haptic perception: interaction of responses to braille and music reveals a functional basis. M. O. Smith and others. bibl il Science 197:689-90 Ag 12 '77
Lost art of touching. A. Roiphe. il Ladies Home J 94:105+ My '77
Vibrotactile pattern perception: extraordinary observers; use of Optacon. J. C. Craig. bibl il Science 196:450-2 Ap 22 '77
TOUCH of the poet; drama. See O'Neill, E. G.
TOUR packagers. See Travel agencies and agents
TOURETTE syndrome. See Nervous system—Diseases
TOURING, Automobile. See Automobile touring
TOURIST trade
Beggar thy neighbor; overseas conventions. il Forbes 120:48 O 15 '77
Summer travel comes on strong. il Bus W p45 My 16 '77
See also
Travel—Economic aspects
Travel agencies and agents

Cuba

Holiday in Havana; lifting U.S. ban on travel to Cuba. D. Pauly and P. E. Simons. il Newsweek 89:57 Mr 28 '77

Europe, Western

Europe: full house. L. Langway and P. Malamud. Newsweek 89:67+ Je 27 '77

Greece

Art. L. Alloway. Nation 225:60-1 Jl 9 '77

Hawaii

Hawaii: the sun and fun islands. S. C. Cowley and G. C. Lubenow. il map Newsweek 91:30-3+ Ja 2 '78

United States

What? Me nonessential? il Forbes 119:79 Je 1 '77
Why foreign tourists flock to the U.S. il U.S. News 82:38 Je 27 '77
TOURISTS. See Travelers
TOURNAMENTS
See also
Basketball—Tournaments
Basketball, College—Tournaments
Boxing—Tournaments
Bridge (game)—Tournaments
Golf—Tournaments
Hockey, College—Tournaments
Tennis—Tournaments

TOURS, France

Music

See also
Opera—France
TOURS, European. See Europe, Western—Description and travel
TOURS, Package. See Air travel; Travel
TOUSSAINT, Donald Raymond
Funds requested for resumption of payment of dues to UNESCO; statement, February 17, 1977. Dept State Bull 76:241-2 Mr 14 '77
TOUSSAINT; or, The aristocracy of the skin; opera. See Blake, D.
TOVEY, Duane R.
Improving children's comprehension abilities. Educ Digest 42:60-2 Mr '77
TOWBOATS. See Tugboats
TOWELL, William Earnest
What's new at AFA. See issues of American forests
about
Conservationist of the Year. por Am For 83:4 Ap '77 *
TOWELS
See also
Paper towels
TOWERS
See also
Eiffel Tower
Television towers
Water towers
TOWN councilmen. See Councilmen
TOWN life. See City and town life
TOWN meetings
New England: rites of March. J. Bell. il Time 109:18-19 Mr 14 '77
TOWN planning. See City planning
TOWN that couldn't wake up; drama. See Boiko, C.
TOWNEND, Ken
Seeing pictures. J. Scully. il Mod Phot 41:8+ S '77
TOWNHOUSES. See City houses
TOWNHOUSES, Condominium. See Condominium (housing)
TOWNS, Victoria Erin
How to stop killing your house plants. House B 119:30-1+ Mr '77
TOWNS. See Cities and towns
TOWNSEND, Ben
Plots brew in Kansas. il por Writers Digest 57:30-1 Mr '77
TOWNSEND, Elizabeth Jane
By roller coaster to the sea. il map Américas 29:14-18 Mr '77
TOWNSEND, Irving
Once-again Prince. il Read Digest 110:126-8 My '77
TOWNSEND, James Bliss
Bomb from the blue; excerpt from The art world; ed by B. Diamonstein. il Art N 76:142-3 N '77
TOWNSEND, John Kirk
Naturalists across the Rockies. J. I. Merritt. bibl il pors Am West 14:4-9+ Mr '77 *
TOWNSEND, John Rowe
Peering into the fog: the future of children's books. Horn Bk 53:346-55 Je '77
TOWNSEND, Peter Wooldridge
Life & loves of Princess Margaret. N. Dempster. por Ladies Home J 94:30+ D '77 *
TOWNSEND, W. Camron
Uncle Cam visits the U.S.S.R. E. E. Plowman. il por Chr Today 22:61-2 D 9 '77 *
TOXAPHENE. See Insecticides
TOXEMIA of pregnancy. See Pregnancy, Complications of
TOXIC and inflammable goods. See Hazardous substances
TOXIC chemical elements. See Chemical elements
TOXIC substances. See Poisons
TOXIC Substances Control Act. See Chemicals Laws and legislation
TOXIC substances in industry. See Poisons, Industrial
TOXINS and antitoxins
Antileukemia activity in the oscillatoriaceae: isolation of debromoaplysiatoxin from lyngbya. J. S. Mynderse and others. bibl il Science 196: 538-40 Ap 29 '77
Cerebrospinal fluid production: stimulation by cholera toxin. M. H. Epstein and others. bibl il Science 196:1012-13 My 27 '77
Cholera toxin crystals suitable for X-ray diffraction. P. B. Sigler and others. bibl il Science 197:1277-9 S 23 '77
Covalent labeling of the tetrodotoxin receptor in excitable membranes. R. J. Guillory and others. bibl. il Science 196:883-5 My 20 '77
Inflammatory effects of endotoxin-like contaminants in commonly used protein preparations. L. Z. Bito. bibl il Science 196:83-5 Ap 1 '77

TOXINS and antitoxins—*Continued*
Laser fluorimetry: subpicogram detection of aflatoxins using high-pressure liquid chromatography. G. J. Diebold and R. N. Zare. bibl il Science 196:1439-41 Je 24 '77
Molecular graphics: application to the structure determination of a snake venom neurotoxin. D. Tsernoglou and others. bibl il Science 197:1378-81 S 30 '77
Perilla ketone: a potent lung toxin from the mint plant, Perilla frutescens britton. B. J. Wilson and others. bibl il Science 197:573-4 Ag 5 '77
Primary structure of cholera toxin β-chain: a glycoprotein hormone analog? A. Kurosky and others. bibl il Science 195:299-301 Ja 21 '77
Selective destruction of neurons by a transmitter agonist. R. M. Herndon and J. T. Coyle. bibl il Science 198:71-2 O 7 '77
Toxins from blue-green algae. R. E. Moore. bibl il BioScience 27:797-802 D '77

TOY boxes. See Toy chests

TOY chests
Step-by-step project scrapbook; toy-box van. il Bet Hom & Gard 55:60 S '77
These toyboxes please everybody. il Pop Mech 149:100-2 Ja '78

TOY dogs
Toy dogs. R. Caras. il Ladies Home J 94:128 Ag '77

TOY industry
Child's play; Knickerbocker Toy Co. il por Forbes 119:144 Ap 15 '77
Christmas is bringing mixed tidings for toys. il Bus W p59+ D 12 '77
Details pay off when you sell teddy bears; R. Dakin & Co. P. Schwab. il por Nations Bus 65:92 D '77
Great toy shortage. L. Langway and P. L. Abraham. il Newsweek 90:58+ D 19 '77
Toy that could change the toy business; George, toy van by Imaginetics International, Inc. il pors Bus W p60+ Je 20 '77
See also
Mattel, Inc

TOYOTA (automobile) See Automobiles, Foreign

TOYOTA Motor Company, Ltd. See Automobile industry—Japan

TOYS
Building blocks from milk cartons. il Sunset 159:100 D '77
CU takes a look at 16 ballyhooed toys. il Consumer Rep 42:636-41 N '77
Christmas amusement—toys made from scrub brushes. il Sunset 159:159 N '77
Furry friends for Christmas; stuffed toys; excerpt from Adventures in toy-making. G. B. Smith. il Sat Eve Post 249:38-41+ D '77
He turns kids' dreams into toys. J. Kraus. il por Ret Liv 17:33+ D '77
New toys: century old echoes. E. V. Warren. il House B 119:8+ D '77
On and off the avenue. New Yorker 53:99-100+ D 12 '77
On this pillow the doll has four places to go. il Sunset 158:108+ F '77
Puddle jumpers. D. M. Fox. il Parks & Rec 12:33 My '77
Say it with toys. M. Davidson. il Parents Mag 52:114-17+ N '77
Selection of games, puzzles and toys: sidelines that educate and entertain. D. Maryles. il Pub W 211:41-52 Mr 7 '77
Things to make by the batch for bazaars; stuffed animals and dolls. C. Vaughan and C. Deery. il Bet Hom & Gard 55:136-9+ S '77
This year's best toy buys. L. C. Pogrebin. il Ms 6:10+ D '77
Toy construction sets. il Consumers Res Mag 60:33-6 D '77
Toy that could change the toy business; George, toy van by Imaginetics International, Inc. il pors Bus W p60+ Je 20 '77
Ultimate yechhh; Slime. il Newsweek 90:61 Jl 11 '77
See also
Dolls
Playgrounds, Home—Equipment
Toy industry

Anecdotes, facetiae, satire, etc.
It says here . . .; assemblying toys on Christmas Eve. A. B. Heath. Nat R 30:30-1 Ja 6 '78

History
Trifles and treasures. A. Fraser. il Sat Eve Post 249:64-7+ D '77

Safety devices and measures
Parents' guide to toy safety. D. Fortino. Harp Baz 111:133+ D '77

TRACE elements
Hair element content in learning disabled children. R. O. Pihl and M. Parkes. Science 198:204-6 O 14 '77
Lead, cadmium linked to learning problems. Sci N 112:262 O 22 '77
Learning disabilities linked to elements. il Chemistry 50:21-2 D '77
Metals as regulators of heme metabolism. M. D. Maines and A. Kappas. bibl il Science 198:1215-21 D 23 '77
Newly recognized trace mineral elements and their role in animal nutrition. W. J. Miller and M. W. Neathery. bibl BioScience 27:674-9 O '77
Release of particles containing metals from vegetation into the atmosphere. W. Beauford and others. bibl il Science 195:571-3 F 11 '77
Trace elements and cancer. Sci N 111:38 Ja 15 '77

TRACE metals. See Trace elements

TRACERS, Radioactive. See Radioactive tracers

TRACHTENBERG, Marvin
La statue colossale. New Yorker 53:15-16 Ag 1 '77 *

TRACK athletics
Cracking down on the payoffs; payments to track stars. il Time 109:55-6 Je 13 '77
Cup turned into a coup; World Cup. K. Moore. il Sports Illus 47:16-21 S 12 '77
Good times and good time at L.A; AAU championships. K. Moore. il Sports Illus 46:24-6+ Je 20 '77
It was a hell of a win for the Devils; NCAA championships. il Sports Illus 46:77-9 Je 13 '77
Mac adds a few new twists; Sunkist Invitational. K. Moore. il Sports Illus 46:14-17 Ja 24 '77
1977 Adidas All-American high school track team. B. Weber and others. il Sr Schol 110:45 S 22 '77
Philly is Dwight's delight; Track Classic. J. Marshall. il Sports Illus 46:46-7 Ja 31 '77
Track at the middle distance. R. Berman. New Repub 177:19-21 Jl 23 '77
When Irish guys are miling; Milrose Games. J. Marshall. il Sports Illus 46:14-17 F 7 '77
See also
Jumping
Pentathlon
Running
Shot putting

Equipment
Sale; Olympic pole vault pits and high jump pits. New Yorker 52:27-8 F 7 '77

TRACKING (education) See Ability grouping in education

TRACKING and data relay satellite system. See Communications satellites

TRACKING and trailing
How the mountain men did it; tracking J. E. Ray. il Time 109:11 Je 27 '77
See also
Artificial satellites—Use in tracking and trailing

TRACKS, Railroad. See Railroads—Track

TRACT houses. See Architecture, Domestic

TRACT houses, Remodeled. See Houses, Remodeled

TRACTOR engines
Tailor power to the pull. Suc Farm 75:43 O '77
That old chore tractor—will it pay to rebuild it? B. Fogarty. Farm J 101:34 D '77

TRACTOR industry
Plowing ahead at Steiger Tractor. N. Howard. il Duns R 110:48 O '77
See also
Caterpillar Tractor Company

TRACTOR pulling contests. See Competitions

TRACTORS
Garden tractors. E. F. Lindsley. il Pop Sci 210:87-90 Je '77
Large inventory of big tractors helps you deal. B. Fogarty. Farm J 101:D2 Je '77
Lose traction to gain horsepower. G. Lepper. il Suc Farm 75:no3 F12 F '77
More drive wheels for all that power. il Farm J 101:D8 Ja '77
We test a $4,000 mower. il Mech Illus 73:56+ Mr '77

Equipment
Hitches to help you work up a seedbed faster. il Farm J 101:14-15 mid-F '77
Low-cost pre-plant spray rigs for accurate soil incorporation. il Farm J 101:22-3 Ap '77
Self-unloading haulers that . . . speed up corn harvest. il Farm J 101:L4 N '77
Spray and till before you plant. il Farm J 101:M6-7 Ap '77

Four-wheel drive
Timely planting makes four-wheel-drive pay. il Farm J 101:L12+ Ap '77

Maintenance and repair
Care and feeding of two-cylinder John Deere tractors. A. Voehringer. il Org Gard & Farm 24:76-80 Ag '77
Troubleshoot your garden tractor after a season's disuse. R. Ceppos. il Pop Sci 210:140 My '77

TRACTORS—*Continued*

Purchasing

Big tractor sales down—watch for price cuts. Farm J 101:B4 O '77

Trailers

See Trailers

TRACTORS, Used

Good buys in used tractors. B. Fogarty. il Farm J 101:51 Ag '77

TRACY, C. Richard

Minimum size of mammalian homeotherms: role of the thermal environment. bibl il Science 198: 1034-5 D 9 '77

TRACY, David

Reflections on the challenge of Marxism. il New Cath World 220:116-17 My '77

TRACY, Eleanor Johnson

Killing in Babcock & Wilcox. il pors Fortune 96:266-9 O '77

TRACY, Richard L.

Unexpected harvest. il Horticulture 55:46-9 Jl '77

TRADE. See Commerce

TRADE, Balance of. See Balance of trade

TRADE adjustment assistance. See Unemployment—Relief measures

TRADE agreements (labor) See Collective labor agreements

TRADE fairs. See Exhibitions

TRADE journals

Business and professional magazines for today's writers; with list of markets. Writer 90:27-8+ F '77

See also titles of trade journals, e.g. Publishers weekly

TRADE marks and trade names

For many firms: new names, new images. il U.S. News 83:55 Jl 4 '77

Marks for the marketplace. G. Carson. il Am Heritage 28:64-9 O '77

New logo for American Artist. D. Preiss. il Am Artist 41:37-8 F '77

Protecting a good name. il Time 110:89+ O 10 '77

Twin logos; NBC dispute. E. Keerdoja. Newsweek 89:9 F 14 '77

TRADE names. See Trade marks and trade names

TRADE Negotiations, Office of the Special Representative for. See United States—Special Representative for Trade Negotiations, Office of the

TRADE regulation. See Foreign trade regulation

TRADE schools. See Vocational-technical schools

TRADE secrets

How to protect corporate secrets. J. Perham. il Duns R 110:48-50+ Ag '77

TRADE shows. See Exhibitions

TRADE tokens. See Tokens

TRADE union leaders. See Trade unions—Officials

TRADE union mergers. See Trade unions—Acquisitions and mergers

TRADE unions

Unions and industrial democracy. A. F. Sturmthal. bibl f Ann Am Acad 431:12-21 My '77

See also

Collective bargaining

Collective labor agreements

Injunctions

Librarians unions

Open and closed shop

Strikes

Teachers unions

Acquisitions and mergers

Why Sol Stetin stepped down; merger of the Textile Workers Union of America with Amalgamated Clothing Workers. E. M. McConville. por Nation 225:621-4 D 10 '77

Actors

See also

British Actors' Equity Association

Benefit funds

Noninsured death benefits under union and company programs. A. P. Blostin. bibl il M Labor R 100:61-3 O '77

Conferences

Trade unions asked to put pressure on white southern African régimes; International Conference of Trade Unions Against Apartheid. il UN Chron 14:26-7 Jl '77

Construction workers

Fresh drive to put union label on more construction jobs. il U.S. News 82:79-80 F 28 '77

Murder at Jupiter; political corruption and construction workers' union in Lake Charles, La. K. Y. Tomlinson. il Read Digest 111:115-19 Jl '77

Running scared? Building unions hunt for recruits. il U.S. News 83:81-2 D 12 '77

Urban unions reduce wages to stimulate housing rehab. D. Loomis. Archit Rec 161:36 Ja '77

Discipline

Disciplinary latitude; court decision on intervention in disciplinary proceedings. A. L. Jacobson. M Labor R 100:68 D '77

Dues, fees, etc.

Labor organizations' fees and dues. C. W. Hickman. bibl il M Labor R 100:19-24 My '77

Teacher and the law; Abood v. Detroit Board of Education, decision concerning a service fee charged to non-members of unions. B. E. Sinowitz. Todays Educ 66:18+ S '77

Elections

Do representation elections need the NLRB? il Bus W p54+ Mr 21 '77

Farm labor

See also

United Farm Workers

Firemen

Unions and public sector supervisors: the case of fire fighters. H. N. Wheeler and T. A. Kochan. bibl f il M Labor R 100:44-8 D '77

Government employees

Can public-employee unions be controlled? K. Y. Tomlinson. Read Digest 110:141-5 Ap '77

Municipal bureaucracies and municipal power. J. R. Hudson. Intellect 105:396-8 Je '77

Public workers and public on a collision course; state and local workers. il U.S. News 82:82 Mr 14 '77

Restraining the public employee unions. J. J. Kilpatrick. Nations Bus 65:11-12 F '77

Scientists, engineers, and unions, revisited. T. R. Manley and C. W. McNichols. il M Labor R 100:32-3 N '77

See also

American Federation of Government Employees

Strikes—United States—Government employees

Trade unions—Municipal employees

History

See also

Trade unions—United States—History

International aspects

See also

Collective bargaining—Multinational bargaining

International Labor Organization

Law

See Labor laws and legislation

Membership

New chill in labor relations. il Bus W p32-3 O 24 '77

White-collar unions and the work humanization movement. E. M. Kassalow. bibl il M Labor R 100:9-13 My '77

Women and unions. G. Steinem. Progressive 41: 34 Jl '77

Membership drives

Battle that's brewing over changes in labor laws. il U.S. News 83:77-8 Jl 25 '77

Carter's detente; proposed reforms of the National Labor Relations Act. T. Nicholson and J. B. Copeland. Newsweek 90:64+ Jl 25 '77

Get ready to battle for your property rights. L. Lane. il Farm J 101:K3-4+ mid-Mr '77

Labor's new Southern strategy. il map Bus W p28-9 F 7 '77

Mixed results of labor-law reform. il Bus W p86 N 7 '77

NLRB licenses lying. D. Jacobs. Nation 225:176-7 S 3 '77

Running scared? Building unions hunt for recruits. il U.S. News 83:81-2 D 12 '77

Tough stand on paving the way for unions. il Nations Bus 65:18 N '77

Unions push south. T. Nicholson and others. map Newsweek 89:55 Ap 4 '77

Miners

See also

National Union of Mineworkers

Municipal employees

Clamor over municipal unions. R. M. Williams. il Sat R 4:12+ Mr 5 '77

Newspapers

See Labor press

Officials

Carter and the union chiefs—will the gulf widen? il por U.S. News 82:53-4 Je 6 '77

Coming revolt in labor. S. Lens. Progressive 41:26-30 Ap '77

Disenchanted. Newsweek 90:84 D 12 '77

New generation of leaders takes charge of the unions. il Duns R 109:32-3 Ja '77

Today's militant union leaders and what they're after. il U.S. News 82:91-2 Ap 11 '77

See also

Women trade union officials

TRADE unions—*Continued*

Organizing activities

See Trade unions—Membership drives

Pensions

See Pensions

Political activities

Annual sunbath: organized labor comes to terms with Jimmy Carter. K. Bode. New Repub 176:12-14 Mr 12 '77

Can labor's tired leaders deal with a troubled movement? N. Kotz. il por N Y Times Mag p8-11+ S 4 '77

Carter and the union chiefs—will the gulf widen? with interview with R. Marshall. il por U.S. News 82:53-7 Je 6 '77

Emancipation from Meany: new life for the unions. B. J. Widick. Nation 224:368-72 Mr 26 '77

Labor tests Carter with a picketing bill. Bus W p27 F 28 '77

More jobs at any cost: organized labor's top goal for 1977. il Nations Bus 65:23-6 F '77

Social contract with labor to limit wage gains would be full of loopholes. A. R. Weber. Duns R 109:9 Ja '77

Storm brews over union demands on Congress; AFL-CIO. il U.S. News 82:88-9 Mr 7 '77

Take George Meany seriously—please! A. Leggat. Am City & County 92:79 Ap '77

UAW's Doug Fraser looks ahead; interview. D. Fraser. Nation 225:171-6 S 3 '77

Unions and Carter: prospects for labor-law reform. W. B. Gould. Nation 224:466-8 Ap 16 '77

Who speaks for labor? defeats of commonsitus picketing bill and large increase in the minimum wage. Nation 224:418 Ap 9 '77

See also

Trade unions and communism

Publications

See also

Labor press

Servicemen

Cuba. . .courts. . . .coolies. M. Stone. U.S. News 82:84 Mr 28 '77

Drive to organize GI's picks up steam; with comments on European unions; with interviews with K. Blaylock and R. Beard. U.S. News 82:50 Mr 28 '77

If the Armed Forces were unionized. Nations Bus 65:16 Jl '77

Stop the battle: it's quitting time. M. Dammerman. il Forbes 120:54 N 1 '77

Union of soldiers. M. Uhl and T. Ensign. Progressive 41:46-8 Mr '77

Unorganizing GIs. T. Ensign and M. Uhl. Progressive 41:8-9 D '77

Textile workers

See also

Amalgamated Clothing and Textile Workers Union

Theater

Dance funding; New York musician, stagehand and technician unions. B. V. Bordelon. Dance Mag 51:24 Je '77

Chile

Waiting for Meany. Nation 225:644-5 D 17 '77

Germany, West

Labor's new thrust in Germany. Bus W p91+ F 7 '77

Great Britain

Britain: sink or swim. Nat R 29:1412-13 D 9 '77

Britain's Ascot of the Left; strike at Grunwick film-processing company. R. Moss. Nat R 29:1238-40 O 28 '77

Is there any hope for Britain? interview, ed by G. Smith. A. Robens of Woldingham. il por Forbes 119:65-6 My 15 '77

Rising rage of British labor. il Bus W p 109 D 12 '77

Roots of Britain's troubles. S. G. Slappey. il Nations Bus 65:77-80+ D '77

See also

British Actors' Equity Association

National Union of Mineworkers

Trades Union Congress

Israel

Worker participation in Israel: experience and lessons. E. Rosenstein. bibl f Ann Am Acad 431:113-22 My '77

Netherlands

Between harmony and conflict: industrial democracy in the Netherlands. W. Albeda. Ann Am Acad 431:74-82 My '77

Peru

Industrial community in Peru. W. F. Whyte and G. Alberti. Ann Am Acad 431:103-12 My '77

Sweden

Sweden: where acquisitions need union approval; ESB Inc's purchase of Tudor. il Bus W p43-4 F 28 '77

Unions know best. il Forbes 120:78 N 1 '77

United States

American labor's stake in a changing world economy; symposium. M Labor R 100:34-50 Mr '77

Collective bargaining: the American approach to industrial democracy. M. Derber. bibl f Ann Am Acad 431:83-94 My '77

Environmentalists try to win labor over. Bus W p 104 O 3 '77

Labor movement today. A. Blum. Intellect 106: 9 Jl '77

Labor tries to revitalize itself. il Bus W p38-9 S 12 '77

Labors creaking house. T. Nicholson and others. il Newsweek 90:83-4+ D 12 '77

Unions are better today; interview, ed by N. Kotz. G. Meany. N Y Times Mag p42-4 S 4 '77

Unions tee off on Carter's free trade stand. il U.S. News 82:84-5 Ap 18 '77

See also

American Federation of Labor and Congress of Industrial Organizations

Government investigations—Trade unions

Strikes—United States

United States—Labor policy

also names of unions, e.g. Amalgamated Meat Cutters and Butcher Workmen of North America

History

Coming revolt in labor. S. Lens. Progressive 41:26-30 Ap '77

Unemployment: new answers to a nagging problem. il Sr Schol 109:6-8+ F 10 '77

TRADE unions and communism

Meany's veto; visas refused to delegates from Russian trade unions. Nation 224:515-16 Ap 30 '77

Never for Mundey; visa refused. E. P. Morgan. Progressive 41:9 My '77

TRADE waste

Hazardous wastes may be valuable; sales or trades of waste products. Am City & County 92:22 Mr '77

See also

Wood waste

TRADE waste disposal

See also

Hazardous substances—Disposal

Waste disposal in the ocean

Water pollution

TRADE waste recycling. See Refuse, Utilization of

TRADEMARKS. See Trade marks and trade names

TRADER Vic, pseud. See Bergeron, V. J.

TRADES Union Congress

Buying time from the unions; vote to limit wage-increase demands. il Time 110:43 S 19 '77

Fragile victory; agreement to put off new wage demands. D. Pauly and A. Collings. Newsweek 90:93-4 S 19 '77

New focus on industrial democracy in Britain. A. W. J. Thomson. bibl f Ann Am Acad 431:32-43 My '77

Pay, inflation and unemployment; address, September 6, 1977. J. Callaghan. Vital Speeches 44:34-7 N 1 '77

TRADING. See Barter

TRADING companies

France

French banks turn traders. il Bus W p 148 N 21 '77

Japan

What Itoh got in absorbing Ataka. il Bus W p42 Jl 11 '77

TRADING stamps

See also

Sperry and Hutchinson Company

TRAFALGAR House, Ltd

Fox in wolf's clothing. il por Forbes 120:152+ N 15 '77

Trafalgar House: acquiring and reviving the grand old names. il Bus W p 105-6 Ja 16 '78

TRAFFIC, Airline. See Airlines—Traffic

TRAFFIC accidents

How did it happen? National Highway Traffic Safety Administration investigation teams. M. Schultz. il Pop Mech 148:80-2+ S '77

Motor vehicle fatalities increase just after publicized suicide stories. D. P. Phillips. bibl il Science 196:1464-5 Je 24 '77

16-day ordeal of John Vihtelic; surviving car crash in Gifford Pinchot National Forest, Ore. E. D'Aulaire and P. O. D'Aulaire. il Read Digest 110:142-6+ Mr '77

Some auto accidents are suicides in disguise; study by David Phillips. D. Cohen. Psychol Today 11:40+ O '77

Suicide by auto; views of David Phillips. Time 110:62 Jl 11 '77

TRAFFIC accidents—*Continued*
Trottier affair; R. Levesque's car accident in Montreal. K. Willenson and R. Manning. il por Newsweek 89:31 F 21 '77 *
Why do over-65s have second highest auto accident rate? Ret Liv 17:43 Ag '77
You won't play the piano anymore. R. T. Jones. il por Read Digest 111:103-7 N '77
See also
Automobile driving
Drinking and traffic accidents

Prevention

See Traffic safety

TRAFFIC control, Radar. See Radar in traffic control

TRAFFIC engineering
See also
Computers—Traffic control use
Radar in traffic control
also subhead Street traffic under names of cities, e.g. Albany, N.Y.—Street traffic

TRAFFIC lights. See Traffic signals

TRAFFIC markings
Stretching line striping budgets. il Am City & County 92:75-6 O '77

TRAFFIC police
Enforcers; highway patrolmen. B. Yates. il Car & Dr 23:53-4+ S '77

TRAFFIC regulations
As motorists start driving faster again—. il U.S. News 82:53 Je 13 '77
Contrary to what is written on the walls, speed saves. L. J. K. Setright. Car & Dr 23:110 S '77
How the rest of the world copes with traffic jams. il U.S. News 82:31-3 F 7 '77
New hope for the same old complaint; organizations against 55-mph speed limit. B. Yates. Car & Dr 23:16 Ja '78
On civil disobedience: 55-mph speed limit; symposium. Car & Dr 23:37-8+ S '77; Discussion. 23:9+ D '77
Raising hell on the highways; trucking. R. Sherrill. il N Y Times Mag p38-40+ N 27 '77
Right turn on red: it's all but unanimous. il U.S. News 83:50 Ag 1 '77
What this country needs is a good 20-mpg speed limit. P. Bedard. il Car & Dr 23:37-8 N '77
Whining is not the same as civil disobedience; 55-mph speed limit. L. Mandel. Car & Dr 23:12 S '77
See also
Automobile parking—Laws and regulations
Speed indicators
Traffic violations

TRAFFIC safety
Cross with a flag for safety; Laguna Beach, Calif. il Sunset 159:32 N '77
See also
Automobile driving
Traffic police
United States—National Highway Traffic Safety Administration

Laws and regulations

See Traffic regulations

TRAFFIC signals
See also
International Municipal Signal Association

Control

Traffic signal controllers. il Am City & County 92:75-8 Ag '77

TRAFFIC violations
Yellow boots on cars; Washington, D.C. il U.S. News 82:80 Mr 21 '77

TRAILER hitches. See Automobiles—Equipment

TRAILERABLE sailboats. See Sailboats—Automobile trailer combination

TRAILERABLE yachts. See Yachts—Automobile trailer combination

TRAILERS
Big self-unloading trailers. il Farm J 101:22-3 O '77
Giant wagons take big bites out of bottlenecks. G. Lepper. il Suc Farm 75:34-5 O '77
Homebuilt tilt trailer. il Mech Illus 73:89 Jl '77
Tailor-made to haul silage; tractor hookups. il Farm J 101:J5 Ag '77
See also
Automobile boat trailers
Automobile trailers

TRAILS
Gem of a trail sets the pace for a national system; Colorado Trail. E. A. Bauer. il Outdoor Life 159:82-4 Je '77
Grand Canyon high; hiking the Bright Angel Trail on the South Rim. M. Kasindorf. il Newsweek 90:59-60 Jl 18 '77
Historic trails to the wild country. V. Landi. il map Outdoor Life 159:84-5+ Je '77
On the trail of Wisconsin's Ice Age. A. LaBastille. il pors map Nat Geog 152:182-205 Ag '77
Oregon trails; the Newberry Crater Trails System. E. Flick. il por Am For 83:36-7 My '77
Skyline to the Sea hike from Castle Rock to Big Basin to the coast; California. il map Sunset 158:50-1 Je '77
300 miles of horse trails circle Phoenix. il map Sunset 159:66+ O '77
Walking the Picket Post Trail. il Sunset 158: 88+ Ap '77
See also
Appalachian Trail
Oregon Trail

Canada

Walker's guide to the mountains of Québec; trails and country inns. R. Rudner. Mademoiselle 83:44-6 Jl '77

New Zealand

New Zealand's Milford Track: walk of a lifetime. C. B. Patterson. il map Nat Geog 153:116-29 Ja '78

TRAIMAN, Stephen
Careers in audio: choosing a course. il Hi Fi 27:134-7 Jl '77
Quality portables for vacation entertainment. il Hi Fi 27:66-70 My '77

TRAIN, John
Bonds: false security. por Forbes 120:182 O 15 '77
Day Stanley Kroll quit; excerpt from The Midas touch. il por Forbes 120:66+ O 1 '77
Managing your money. por Forbes 120:134-5 N 1; 206 N 15; 130-1 D 1; 94-5 D 15 '77; 121:232-3 Ja 9 '78

TRAIN, Russell E.
Environmental cancer. Science 195:443 F 4 '77

TRAIN, Susan
Australia: Down Under is up. il por map Vogue 167:284+ S '77

TRAIN robberies. See Robberies and assaults

TRAIN travel. See Railroad travel

TRAINING airplanes. See Airplanes, Training

TRAINING devices. See Simulators

TRAINING for parenthood. See Parent education

TRAINING of animals. See Animals—Training

TRAINING of cats. See Cats—Training

TRAINING of dogs. See Dogs—Training

TRAINS, Model. See Railroad models

TRAMPS
Baldness experiment; Bowery bums and baldness. G. De Leon. il por Psychol Today 11: 62-3+ O '77
Hoboes told all to 1890s scholar; J. J. McCook. R. Bruns. il por Smithsonian 8:141-2+ N '77
If I'm not on my milk crate, you can find me in my phone booth: New York City's shopping-bag ladies. J. Roth. il Ms 5:74-7 Mr '77
Street dwellers; New York City. A. M. Beck and P. Marden. il Natur Hist 86:78-85 bibl (p 119) N '77

TRANQUILIZING drugs
Diazepam maintenance of alcohol preference during alcohol withdrawal. J. A. Deutsch and N. Y. Walton. bibl il Science 198:307-9 O 21 '77
Tranquilizers may sustain alcoholism. Sci N 112:277-8 O 29 '77
See also
Benzodiazepines

Receptors

See Drug receptors

TRANSACTIONAL analysis
Hang-ups. P. O. Tierney. Engl J 66:61-2 S '77

TRANS-ALASKA pipeline system. See Petroleum pipelines—Alaska

TRANSATLANTIC airline service. See Airlines —International services—Transatlantic

TRANSATLANTIC flights. See Aviation—Transatlantic flights

TRANSATLANTIC voyages. See Voyages

TRANSCEIVER circuits. See Radio circuits

TRANSCEIVERS. See Radiotelephone

TRANSCEIVERS, CB. See Citizens band radio—Equipment

TRANSCEIVERS on aircraft. See Radiotelephone on aircraft

TRANSCENDENTAL meditation
I'm the Maharishi—fly me. J. Gaylin. Psychol Today 11:29+ Ag '77
Maharishi over matter. K. L. Woodward and P. Abramson. il Newsweek 89:98+ Je 13 '77
New Jersey mantra; Federal court ruling on transcendental meditation in public schools. J. W. Donohue. America 137:360 N 19 '77
Seer of flying; supernatural powers. il Time 110: 75 Ag 8 '77
TM and the religion-in-school issue. E. R. Baltazar; discussion. Chr Cent 94:150-2 F 16 '77
TM grounded; Federal district court ruled the government-funded teaching of TM unconstitutional. il Chr Today 22:56 N 18 '77
TM's claims unsupported in experiments. J. White. Sci Digest 82:36-7 Ag '77

TRANSCENDENTALISM (New England)
Transcendentalism and the expectation of dawn: Emerson and Thoreau. E. Ardura. il pors Américas 29:36-41 Ag '77

TRANSCONTINENTAL railroad trips. See Railroad travel

TRANSFER of copyright. See Copyright—Transfer

TRANSFER of funds
See also
Computers—Banking use

TRANSFER of technology. See Technology transfer

TRANSFER pricing. See Price policies

TRANSFER RNA. See RNA

TRANSFER students, Medical. See Medical students

TRANSFERASES
Concomitant elevations in serum sialyltransferase activity in sialic acid content in rats with metatasizing mammary tumors. R. J. Bernacki and U. Kim. bibl il Science 195:577-80 F 11 '77
Hypoxanthine phosphoribosyltransferase: two-dimensional gels from normal and Lesch-Nyhan hemolyzates. G. S. Ghangas and G. Milman. bibl il Science 196:1119-20 Je 3 '77
Timekeeping by the pineal gland. S. Binkley and others. bibl il Science 197:1181-3 S 16 '77

TRANSFERS, Job. See Employees—Relocation

TRANSFIGURATION of Benno Blimpie; drama. See Innaurato, A.

TRANSFORMATION, Genetic. See Genetic transformation

TRANSIENTS (dynamics)
Coherent optical transients. R. G. Brewer. bibl il Phys Today 30:50-4+ My '77

TRANS INTERNATIONAL Airlines. See Airlines—Non-scheduled operations

TRANSISTORS
Microelectronic circuit elements. J. D. Meindl. il Sci Am 237:70-81 bibl(p258) S '77
The PUT. J. Darr. il Radio-Electr 48:68+ Je '77
VMOS—MOSFETs with muscle. L. Garner. il Pop Electr 11:76-8+ My '77

History
Triumph of miniaturization: the transistor; excerpt from New trail blazers of technology. H. Manchester. il Sci Digest 81:57-60 Ap '77

Testing
Yes, you can test your own transistors. A. Morgan. il Pop Mech 147:39+ Mr '77

TRANSIT cars. See Railroads—Cars

TRANSIT systems. See Local transit

TRANSKEI
Transkei's empty independence. H. Glass and M. Shirk. Progressive 41:28-31 Mr '77
See also
United Nations—Transkei

TRANSLATIONS and translating
Blind idiot: the problems of translation; adaptation of address, May 4, 1976. E. Fenton. Horn Bk 53:505-13, 633-41 O-D '77
Books in 151 languages; publications of foreign books in Soviet languages. B. I. Stukalin. il UNESCO Courier 30:33-4 N '77
See also
Translators

TRANSLATORS
Translators, at Montreal Congress, press for their professional rights; International Federation of Translators meeting. S. Congrat-Bautlar. il Pub W 212:36-9 Jl 11 '77

TRANSLOCATION of chromosomes. See Chromosomes

TRANSMISSIBLE gastroenteritis in swine. See Swine—Diseases and pests

TRANSMISSION, Automobile. See Automobiles—Transmission

TRANSMISSION, Motorcycle. See Motorcycles—Transmission

TRANSMUTATION (chemistry)
Comparison of radioactive and stable Tl+ diffusion in potassium chloride: demonstration of a transmutation effect. G. C. T. Wei and B. J. Wuensch. bibl il Science 197:159-61 Jl 8 '77
Transmutation products may influence radiotracer diffusion rates in an ionic solid. G. C. T. Wei and B. J. Wuensch. bibl il Science 197:157-9 Jl 8 '77

TRANSNATIONAL bargaining. See Collective bargaining—Multinational bargaining

TRANSPAC Race. See Yacht racing

TRANSPACIFIC airline service. See Airlines—International services—Transpacific

TRANSPARENCIES
See also
Slides (photography)

TRANSPLANTATION of organs, tissues, etc.
Overcoming transplant rejections. P. Lehmann. Harp Baz 110:187 S '77
See also
Brain—Transplantation
Cornea—Transplantation
Donation of organs, tissues, etc.
Heart—Transplantation
Kidneys—Transplantation
Marrow—Transplantation
Ova—Transplantation
Testicles—Transplantation

TRANSPLANTING of trees. See Tree planting

TRANSPORT, Biological. See Biological transport

TRANSPORT airplanes, Jet. See Airplanes, Jet

TRANSPORTATION
See also
Inland water transportation
Local transit
Shipping
also subhead Transportation under various subjects, e.g. Coal—Transportation

Federal aid
Irrigation, flood control, navigation and user taxes; address, May 6, 1977. J. D. Geary. Vital Speeches 43:536-9 Je 15 '77
See also
Local transit—Federal aid

Finance
Transportation. il Forbes 121:136-8 Ja 9 '78

Laws and regulations
Origins of the transportation cartel. P. J. Quirk. bibl il Intellect 105:442-4 Je '77
Transportation: the reins loosen. il Bus W p82-3 Ap 4 '77

Statistics
Fifty largest transportation companies. il Fortune 96:170-1 Jl '77

California
See also
Los Angeles—Transportation

Maine
See also
Maine—Transportation, Department of

New York (state)
See also
New York (city)—Transportation
New York (state)—Transportation, Department of

United States
Congealed traffic waits for the thaw; effect of weather. il Bus W p33-4 F 14 '77
See also
Roads—United States
United States—Transportation, Department of

TRANSPORTATION, Automotive
Auto option; bus vs. auto transportation for urban travel. B. Rosenthal. bibl il Environment 19:18-24 Je '77
See also
Trucking

TRANSPORTATION, Military
See also
Airplanes, Military transport
Landing craft

TRANSPORTATION research
See also
National Research Council—Transportation Research Board

TRANSPORTATION to airports. See Airports—Transportation problems

TRANSRACIAL adoption. See Adoption

TRANSSEXUALISM. See Change of sex

TRANSURANIUM elements
Evidence for superheavies in mica looks weaker. G. B. Lubkin. il Phys Today 30:17+ Ja '77
Superheavy elements: confirmation fails to materialize. A. L. Robinson. Science 195:473-4 F 4 '77

TRANS WORLD Airlines
Chicago-Los Angeles fare cut requested. Aviation W 106:65 Je 6 '77
TWA discount approval spurs quick response by competitors. Aviation W 107:27 Jl 18 '77
TWA plans to buy Bendix Omega unit. Aviation W 106:26 Ja 31 '77

TRAN-van-Dinh
Mandate of heaven; open letter to J. Carter. Chr Cent 94:29-30 Ja 19 '77
On Burma's heritage. Progressive 41:22-3 Mr '77
Zone of peace in the Indian Ocean. Chr Cent 94:524-5 Je 1 '77

TRAP shooting
Bloodless pigeon shoot. M. Wellemeyer. il Fortune 95:109+ My '77
Clay birds and the hunter. B. Brister. il Field & S 81:120-4 F '77
If you call him old folks, be prepared to duck; E. Gates. V. Kraft. por Sports Illus 47:34-6+ Ag 8 '77
1977 All-America Skeet Teams. il Field & S 82:112 Jl '77
What is International skeet, and why do other countries clean our clocks at it? B. Brister. il Field & S 82:134-9 Je '77

TRAP shooting—*Continued*

Anecdotes, facetiae, satire, etc.

Claybird sharks. C. Madson. il Outdoor Life 160: 84-5+ N '77

TRAPPING
Trapping: new angles on an old controversy. B. Gooch. il Ret Liv 17:41-2 F '77
Urban trapper. L. Pinck. por Outdoor Life 160:38 D '77

Laws and regulations

Bewildered by a lot of claptrap; Ohio vote on banning leghold traps. D. Levin. il Sports Illus 47:70+ N 7 '77
Case for trapping; regulation by New York's Department of Environmental Conservation. G. R. Parsons. il Conservationist 32:2-9 S '77
Editorial; voting on controversial trapping law in Ohio. M. G. Nichols. Field & S 82:6 N '77

TRAPS
Bewildered by a lot of claptrap; Ohio vote on banning leghold traps. D. Levin. il Sports Illus 47:70+ N 7 '77
What about leg hold traps? G. R. Parsons. il Conservationist 32:9 S '77

TRAPS, Insect. See Insect traps

TRAPSHOOTING. See Trap shooting

TRASH containers. See Refuse containers

TRAUBE, Klaus Robert
Case of the bugged physicist. il por Time 109:28 Mr 14 '77 *

TRÄUBLE, Hermann
Obituary
Phys Today por 30:62 Ap '77. U. Essmann

TRAUGH, Cecelia E.
Some thinking skills defined in historiographical terms. bibl Clearing H 51:76-7 O '77

TRAUSCHT, Michael
Brainwashing Moonies. Time 109:73 Ap 4 '77 *
Is deprograming legal? M. Montagno. il por Newsweek 89:44 F 21 '77 *

TRAUTH, Denise M. See Huffman, J. L. jt auth

TRAVAGLINI, Mark
From the echoes of Chautauqua. il Am Educ 13:17-21 My '77

TRAVEL
Air/sea circuit; packaged fly/cruise vacation trips. T. B. Lesure. il Travel 148:28-31+ S '77
Ask Holiday; questions and answers. E. Echols. See issues of Holiday
Best of everything; food service on trains, airplanes and ocean liners. R. E. M. Whitaker. New Yorker 53:29-32 D 19 '77
Booked for travel. H. Sutton. See issues of Saturday review
Compleat island collector's private gazetteer of places offbeat, if not outlandish. J. Morgan. il Sat R 5:22-3 Ja 7 '78
Getting away. S. Birnbaum. See issues of Esquire
Getting there. S. Birnbaum. Esquire 87:42+ Ap; 16+ My '77
Going places, finding things. See issues of House & garden incorporating Living for young homemakers
How to shake the travel jitters. D. Braun. il Farm J 101:47-9+ Mr '77
Ins and outs of holiday travel. K. Keating. Bet Hom & Gard 55:14+ D '77
It should have been called Miami Beaches. P. Savage-Rich. Sat Eve Post 249:89+ Ap '77
[Month] travel in and beyond the West. See issues of Sunset
New & now (cont) il Holiday 57:10 N '76; 58:20 Je; 14 S '77
Redbook traveler: great getaways North and South. R. S. Kane; M. Zellers. il Redbook 149:120+ O '77
Redbook traveler; symposium. il Redbook 148: 55-62 Ap '77
Roaming the globe. See issues of Travel
Tips for over-55s traveling abroad. G. Lang. il Ret Liv 17:31-6 Ap '77
Travel. D. Messinesi. See issues of Vogue
Travel bazaar. See issues of Harper's bazaar
Travel digest. See issues of Travel
Travel now. See issues of Vogue
Trip tips. Holiday 58:6 Mr '77
See also
Aged—Travel
Air travel
Automobile touring
Bus travel
Business travel
Congressmen—Travel
Cruising
Guidebooks
Luggage
Packing of luggage
Presidents—United States—Travel
Railroad travel
Student travel
Tourist trade
Vacations
World tours
also subhead Description and travel under names of countries, states, etc, e.g. Brazil—Description and travel

Bibliography

Books worth mentioning. il Travel 148:22 Ag; 27 S '77

Economic aspects

Around the world on a budget. P. L. Pryor. il por Ret Liv 17:26-31 My '77
Bad currency trip for tour packagers. il Bus W p22-3 Ja 9 '78
How to avoid the high cost of motels. L. David. il Mech Illus 73:54+ Ag '77
New ways to save on vacation. L. David. il Mech Illus 73:54-5+ Je '77
Rip-offs in faraway places. R. Gates. Changing T 31:37-8 D '77
Senior savings: foreign travel bargains. K. Simmon. il Travel 147:60-3+ Mr '77
Vacation bargains. Mech Illus 73:30 Jl '77
Vacationing on a budget. il Ebony 32:68-70+ Ap '77
When the traveling is easiest (and cheapest) Changing T 31:4 Mr '77
Where vacation bargains are. il U.S. News 82:48-51 Mr 14 '77
See also
Airlines—Fares

Health aspects

Rx travel and play (cont) Holiday 57:8 N '76; 58: 16 Ja; 8 Mr; 10+ Ap; 14-15 Je '77
Stay healthy while you travel. il Changing T 31:37-40 Jl '77

Periodicals

See also
Holiday (periodical)

TRAVEL (periodical)
See also
Travel/Holiday (periodical)
Traveler of the Year Award

TRAVEL agencies and agents
Agent commissions stir concern. R. K. Ellingsworth. Aviation W 106:24-5 F 14 '77
Airline commissions go sky-high. Bus W p31-2 F 7 '77
Bad currency trip for tour packagers. il Bus W p22-3 Ja 9 '78
Making of a travel agent. J. Panos. Holiday 58:80 Ap '77
Trip with your travel agent. Holiday 58:12-13 Ja '77
See also
Cook, Thomas, and Son, Ltd

TRAVEL and education. See Travel study courses

TRAVEL clubs
Man who would be Kipling; J. Blashford-Snell of the World Expeditionary Association. H. Sutton. il Sat R 4:44-5 My 28 '77
Vacations for adventurers only; World Expeditionary Association trips. il Mademoiselle 83: 116-18+ S '77

TRAVEL films. See Motion pictures—Travel films

TRAVEL guides. See Guidebooks

TRAVEL/Holiday (periodical)
Travel has a new logo! H. W. Shane. Trav/Holiday 148:24 N '77

TRAVEL literature
See also
Guidebooks

TRAVEL photography
Get the picture! B. Rosenlund. Seventeen 36:30 Je '77
Roadside eye-openers for the snapping. N. Levy. il Ret Liv 17:40-1 Ap '77
Shutter tripper. R. Ergenbright. il Travel 148: 20-1+ O '77 (cont as) Trav/Holiday 148:8+ N; 16+ D '77; 149:10+ Ja '78
Tired of taking ho-hum travel pictures? L. Dennis. il por Pop Phot 80:96-103+ Ap '77
Traveler's camera:
Canary Islands. C. Purcell. il Pop Phot 80: 42+ F '77
Lisbon. C. Purcell. il Pop Phot 81:34+ O '77
Marketing travel pictures. C. Purcell. il Pop Phot 80:14+ Je '77
Replacement of books by photography. C. Purcell. por Pop Phot 80:46+ Mr '77
Spain. C. Purcell. il Pop Phot 81:30+ Jl; 64+ Ag '77
Travel films. C. Purcell. Pop Phot 80:40+ My '77
Trinidad and Tobago. C. Purcell. il Pop Phot 81:64+ D '77
Vagabond camera; Carowinds amusement park. R. H. Rufa. il Travel 147:64-5+ Je '77
Well traveled camera:
Egypt. H. Keppler. il Mod Phot 41:46 Ag; 112+ N; 99-100 D '77
Equipment for photographing antiquities. H. Keppler. il Mod Phot 41:33+ O '77
Planning before a trip. H. Keppler. il Mod Phot 41:60+ Mr '77
See also
Motion pictures—Travel films

TRAVEL regulations
Off limits! prohibited zones for American and Russian tourists. maps Sr Schol 109:13 Mr 24 '77
Travel bars eased to off-limit countries. Ret Liv 17:40 Ag '77
See also
Passports

TRAVEL restrictions. See Travel regulations

TRAVEL study courses
Exploring the exotic East; teacher study tour of Asian schools. V. N. Kobayashi. Todays Educ 66:74-6 S '77
TRAVEL with children
Children's continent; Europe. P. Krasilovsky. il Sat Eve Post 249:90-1+ My '77
Westward ho! with all the Viorsts in tow. J. Viorst. il Redbook 148:57-9 Ap '77
TRAVEL with pets
Pet peeves. G. C. Larson. por Flying 101:27 Ag '77
TRAVELER of the Year Award
23rd annual Traveler of the Year Award: Pearl Bailey. por Travel 148:66-7 Jl '77
TRAVELERS
Untrapped tourist. T. Griffith. Atlantic 240:20+ S '77

Anecdotes, facetiae, satire, etc.

Boston straggler is a tour type not to be missed. E. Bombeck. il Smithsonian 8:128 Je '77
Hop on a bus, Gus: American package tours through Europe. D. Shaw. il Holiday 58:28-31 Ja '77
TRAVELERS checks
See also
American Express Company
TRAVELING bags. See Luggage
TRAVELING carnivals. See Carnivals
TRAVELING recreation centers. See Recreation centers
TRAVELS
Wandering gaucho; A. Baretta's five-year trip on horseback. A. J. Lowe. il pors Américas 29:26 Ja '77
See also
Overland journeys to the Pacific
Travel
TRAVER, Robert
Outdoors. Esquire 87:156-8 My '77
TRAVERS (race) See Horse racing
TRAVERSE rods (for curtains) See Curtain and drapery fixtures
La TRAVIATA; opera. See Verdi, G.
TRAVLOS, John
Putting the clock back 24 centuries. il UNESCO Courier 30:12-14 O '77
TRAVOLTA, John
Discomania. il pors Time 110:69-70 D 19 '77 *
From sweating to disco king. M. Orth. il pors Newsweek 90:63+ D 19 '77 *
TRAWLER yachts. See Yachts and yachting
TRAWLS and trawling
Trolling tactics. F. M. Paulson. il Field & S 82:134+ My '77
Who? Me use a downrigger? H. L. Lawrence. il Outdoor Life 160:88-90 Jl '77
TRAYNOR, James F.
Winter hawk. il por Conservationist 32:2-4 N '77
TRAYS
Quick & easy serving tray. J. Capotosto. il Mech Illus 73:102-3 Je '77
Salt Lake City Temple bread tray. M. Wollett and B. Wollett. il Hobbies 82:99 Ag '77
TREADWELL, William
Maintain free chlorine residual, pH balance in pool care. il Camp Mag 49:12-13 Je '77
TREASE, Geoffrey
Historical story: is it relevant today? il Horn Bk 53:20-8 F '77
TREASON
See also
Trials (treason)
TREASTER, Joseph B.
Reports & comment: Argentina: a state of fear. Atlantic 240:16+ N '77
Twilight in white Rhodesia. il map Atlantic 239:63-70+ My '77
TREASURE trove
Fortune to find a fortune; Atocha treasure. F. Casey. il Mech Illus 73:24 F '77
Guns of Atocha. R. F. Burgess. il Oceans 10:26-9 S '77
Reach for the New World. M. Peterson. il Nat Geog 152:724-67, supp(folded map) D '77
Treasure of Tobermory Bay; Spanish galleon Florencia. E. Antrobus. il map Am For 83:20-3+ Je '77
TREASURE without measure; drama. See Marshall, S. L.
TREASURY bill futures. See Commodity exchanges
TREASURY bills. See Securities
TREASURY Department (United States) See United States—Treasury, Department of the
TREASURY notes. See Securities
TREATIES
See also
American Convention on Human Rights
Antarctic Treaty, 1959
Seabed Treaty, 1972
United States—Treaties
Warsaw Convention
TREATMENT of prisoners. See Prisoners—Treatment
TREATS; drama. See Hampton, C.

TRECHOCK, Mark
After a photograph of Hans King; poem. Chr Cent 94:530 Je 1 '77
TREDYFFRIN Township Public Library, Stratford Pa. See Libraries—Pennsylvania
TREE, Marietta
Cities and political will. Current 190:9-10 F '77
TREE Communications (firm) See Design firms
TREE conservation
See also
Forest conservation
TREE conservation associations. See Conservation associations
TREE farming. See Forest management
TREE frogs and tree toads
Immunological resolution of a diploidtetraploid species complex of tree frogs. L. Maxson and others. bibl il Science 197:1012-13 S 2 '77
TREE harvesting machinery. See Lumbering—Machinery
TREE hoppers
Creature from outer space? M. G. Emsley. il Int Wildlife 7:44-7 Mr '77
TREE houses
Up a tree; excerpt from Housebuilding for children. L. Walker. il Am Home 80:36-7+ Jl '77
TREE planting
How to shade and landscape your house to save energy; planting shade trees. J. Fanning. il House & Gard 149:35-6 Ag '77
Ways with wild trees. J. D. Ritchie. il Org Gard & Farm 24:154+ F '77
See also
Forest planting
Reforestation
TREE research. See Botanical research
TREE rings
Tree-ring—drought relationships in the Hudson Valley, New York. E. R. Cook and G. C. Jacoby, Jr. bibl il Science 198:399-401 O 28 '77
Tree rings warn us; droughts in Western States. il Sunset 159:296 O '77
TREE shrews. See Shrews
TREE stands (hunting) See Hunting—Equipment and supplies
TREEHOPPERS. See Tree hoppers
TREES
Child looks at a tree. C. E. Lewis. il Am For 83:30-3 Mr '77
Energy-saving shade trees. il Bet Hom & Gard 55:196 Ap '77
Language of trees. B. Bristow. il Chr Today 21:16-17 Je 3 '77
Ten top shade trees. M. Franz. il Org Gard & Farm 24:130-2 Ag '77
Trees can cool and heat your house. Farm J 101:H2 S '77
See also
Bark
Christmas trees
Forest ecology
Forests and forestry
Fruit trees
Leaves
Nut trees
Tree planting
Tree rings
Windbreaks
Woodlots
also names of trees, e.g. Palms

Diseases and pests

See also
Trees—Wounds and injuries
Trees, Care of
also subhead Diseases and pests under names of trees, e.g. Elm—Diseases and pests

Fertilization

See Fertilization of plants

Growth

See Growth (plants)

Identification

Feininger's guide to identifying trees. A. Feininger. il Horticulture 55:32-49 Je '77

Planting

See Tree planting

Research

See Botanical research

Wounds and injuries

When to call the tree doctor. B. Stephen. il McCalls 104:55 Ap '77

Northwestern States

See Botany—Northwestern States

TREES, Artificial
Christmas fruit trees you make yourself. il Sunset 159:74-5 D '77

TREES, Care of
How to deal with bugs, blights, fungi. R. S. Foster. Am City & County 92:73 Jl '77
If you must deal with tree cavities. il Sunset 159:148 Ag '77
Spring priorities: spraying, planting, a boy with buckets. R. S. Foster. Am City & County 92:100 My '77
Three ways to fall-feed your trees. M. Franz. Org Gard & Farm 24:154+ O '77
Tree maintenance tips give budget-stretching ideas. R. S. Foster. Am City & County 92:69 Mr '77
See also
Trees—Wounds and injuries

TREES, Dwarf
Our national bonsai collection. R. Pardo. il Am For 83:14-17+ D '77
See also
Fruit trees, Dwarf

TREES, Fossil
See also
Petrified Forest National Park

TREES, Indoor. See House plants

TREES in cities
Different view of the forest. R. M. Brett. Am For 83:10+ D '77
Their elm forest is doomed, but Twin Cities are ready. F. Graham, Jr. Audubon 79:136-9 Jl '77
Urban forestry (cont) R. S. Foster. Am City & County 92:69 Mr; 100 My; 73 Jl; 114 S '77
Urban Tree Act stifled in House. Am City & County 92:21 N '77

TREFETHEN, Florence
Poet's workshop. See every other issue of Writer

TREFIL, James S.
Tachyons: faster than light . . . if they exist; excerpt from Smithsonian magazine, November 1976. Sci Digest 81:38-40 F '77
Velikovsky. por Sci Digest 82:75-7 S '77

TREFOIL, Birdsfoot. See Birdsfoot trefoil

TREICHEL, Joan Arehart-. See Arehart-Treichel, J.

TREISMAN, Michel
Motion sickness: an evolutionary hypothesis. bibl Science 197:493-5 Jl 29 '77

TREJO, Arnulfo D.
Modifying library education for ethnic imperatives. bibl Am Lib 8:150-1 Mr '77

TREJO, Ernesto
It's your name and it's also December; poem. Nation 224:662 My 28 '77

TRELLISES
Craftsman-era deck and trellis. il Sunset 158:158 My '77
Let a trellis give your yard a face-lift. R. Martens. il Farm J 101:H2-3 Mr '77
Trellis is the old swing set. il Sunset 158:216 Mr '77

TRELOAR, L. R. G.
Physics of textiles. bibl il Phys Today 30:23-30 D '77

TREMBLAY, Kenneth R. Jr. See Dillman, D. A. jt auth

TRENCHES, Ocean. See Submarine valleys

TRENKLE, Allen, and Willham, R. L.
Beef production efficiency. bibl il Science 198:1009-15 D 9 '77

TRENNERT, Robert A.
Walter Prescott Webb. Am West 14:57 Mr '77

TRESCHER, Eloise R.
Calcium: the backbone of minerals. por House & Gard 149:40+ D '77
Protein power. il por House & Gard 149:36+ Mr '77

TRESPASS
See also
Squatters

TRESTLE tables. See Tables

TREUER, Robert
Tree farmers. J. B. Craig. il pors Am For 83:8-11+ My '77 •

TREVIÑO, Albert D.
Frost in the Rio Grande Valley; analysis of poem by J. Limoń. Engl J 66:69 Mr '77

TREVOR, William
Torridge; story. New Yorker 53:36-45 S 12 '77

TREVOR-ROPER, Hugh Redwald
Raiser Max: first among the Hapsburgs. il por Horizon 19:68-81 Mr '77

TREZISE, Philip H.
If we don't lead, there isn't anybody else to do it. por U.S. News 82:47-8 Je 27 '77

TRIACETYLENE. See Acetylene

TRIACONTANOL
Alfalfa yields a mystery chemical that spurs plant growth, even in the dark. E. Driscoll. il por Horticulture 55:8+ Ag '77
This alcohol makes crops grow through night. Farm J 101:10 Je '77
Triacontanol: a new naturally occurring plant growth regulator. S. K. Ries and others. bibl il Science 195:1339-41 Mr 25 '77

TRIACS. See Electric current rectifiers

TRIAD Holding Corporation
Super-connector from Saudi Arabia; A. M. Khashoggi. L. Kraar. il por Fortune 95:108-14+ Je '77

TRIAL lawyers. See Lawyers

TRIALS
See also
Evidence (law)
Jury
Video recorders and recording—Court use
Witnesses

Germany, West

Guilty as charged; sentencing of A. Baader. Time 109:43 My 9 '77
See also
War crime trials

Great Britain

Mystical poetry in a court of law; conviction of D. Lemon, editor of Gay news, in London. T. Beeson. Chr Cent 94:838-9 S 28 '77
On trial for blasphemy; Gay news trial. Time 110:54 Jl 25 '77

Italy

Courageous Claudia fights back; rape trial. il por Time 109:53 Ap 25 '77
Terrorism on trial in Italy; case of R. Curcio. il por Time 110:58 Jl 4 '77

Maryland

Changing the rules; case of Governor M. Mandel. K. Bode. New Repub 177:16-17 S 17 '77
Help from his friends; M. Mandel case. R. Boeth. il por Newsweek 90:20 S 5 '77
Mandel verdict: a warning to officials. il por U.S. News 83:46 S 5 '77
Trouble in the boys' club; trials of M. Mandel. A. Tyler. New Repub 177:16-19 Jl 30 '77
Verdict: bye-bye, Marvin. il por Time 110:20 S 5 '77

New York (state)

Bad, bad Leroy Barnes; drug dealing trial. il por Time 110:21 D 12 '77

North Carolina

Heads, hearts and justice; Wilmington 10 and Joanne Little trials. E. Mattern. America 136:389-91 Ap 30 '77
Trial of the 1950s; J. Scales. M. Pinsky. Progressive 41:36-7 F '77
Trial they never had; Wilmington Ten trial. M. Pinsky. Nation 224:754-6 Je 18 '77
Who bombed Mike's Grocery? Wilmington Ten. il Time 109:83 My 23 '77
Wilmington Ten. V. E. Smith and S. Lesher. il Newsweek 89:21-2 F 21 '77

Pennsylvania

Entrance examination; U.S. probe into admissions practices of Philadelphia's medical and graduate schools. il por Time 109:14 Je 6 '77

South Africa

Biko's last days. S. Strasser and P. Younghusband. il Newsweek 90:74 N 28 '77
Inquest into a curious death; case of S. Biko. il Time 110:53 N 28 '77
No-fault verdict; S. Biko inquest. R. Carroll and P. Younghusband. il Newsweek 90:67+ D 12 '77

Texas

Pittsburg Fats dodges a silver bullet; football player E. Holmes' trial for possession of cocaine. R. Kennedy. il por Sports Illus 46:24-6+ Mr 7 '77

TRIALS (blasphemy)
Mystical poetry in a court of law; conviction of D. Lemon, editor of Gay news, in London. T. Beeson. Chr Cent 94:838-9 S 28 '77
On trial for blasphemy; Gay news trial in Great Britain. Time 110:54 Jl 25 '77

TRIALS (civil rights)
End of the Panther trial. S. Simon. Progressive 41:9 Je '77

TRIALS (espionage)
Pyramider spy case; A. Lee and C. Boyce. R. Steele and N. Horrock. il por Newsweek 89:29 Ap 18 '77
Stealing the company store; case of C. Boyce and A. D. Lee. il por Time 109:19 My 9 '77
See also
Rosenberg, Julius and Ethel, case

TRIALS (libel)
Herbert's war; ruling in slander suit against CBS. Time 110:103 N 21 '77
Walk on the sordid side; G. Atkinson's slander suit against C. Noll. W. O. Johnson. il por Sports Illus 47:10-15 Ag 1 '77

TRIALS (murder)
American travesty: Hurricane Carter's second trial. J. B. Lieber. por Nation 224:393-400 Ap 2 '77
Aspen affair; C. Longet case. il Time 109:22 Ja 24 '77
Birmingham clears its name; R. Chambliss case. Nation 225:578 D 3 '77
Blue Monday; sentences of two Houston policemen. Nation 225:421 O 29 '77
Dawson Five. D. A. Williams and V. E. Smith. il Newsweek 89:26 My 23 '77
Did TV make him do it? R. Zamora case. il Time 110:87+ O 10 '77

TRIALS (murder)—*Continued*
Heads, hearts and justice; Joanne Little trial. E. Mattern. America 136:389-91 Ap 30 '77
Juvenile justice; children on the witness stand at the Al Junior Lewis trial in Detroit. D. A. Williams and J. C. Jones. il Newsweek 89:22 Je 27 '77
Leonard Peltier and the posse: still fighting the Indian wars. B. Johansen. por Nation 225:304-7 O 1 '77
Long count to a guilty verdict; case of L. Perez and F. Narciso. il pors Time 110:54 Jl 25 '77
Murder in Morningside Park; trial of M. Simon for murder of C. Houston. D. Gallagher. il pors N Y Times Mag p26-9+ Ag 28 '77
Murder in Texas; trial of C. Davis. il Time 110: 101 N 14 '77
Narciso-Perez case: nurse hunting in Michigan. A. Jones. Nation 225:584-8 D 3 '77
Perils of doing your duty; testimony of B. Lowe in the Harry Aleman trial. il Time 109:13-14 Je 6 '77
Skyhorse and Mohawk: more than a murder trial. D. Blackburn. il Nation 225:682-6 D 24 '77
TV on trial; R. Zamora trial. Newsweek 90:104 S 12 '77
Texas gothic; T. C. Davis trial. R. Steele and M. Kasindorf. il por Newsweek 89:30 Ap 4 '77
Trials of TV; R. Zamora trial. J. K. Footlick. il por Newsweek 90:70 O 10 '77
Verdict on bloody Sunday; R. E. Chambliss murder trial. D. A. Williams and J. B. Cumming. Newsweek 90:63 N 28 '77
Verdict on Claudine. D. A. Williams and D. Gram. Newsweek 89:36 Ja 24 '77
Zamora case: TV gets a reprieve. Sci N 112:247 O 15 '77
See also
Sacco-Vanzetti case

TRIALS (obscenity)
Bad case makes worse law; trial of Hustler publisher, L. Flynt. il por Time 109:51-2 F 21 '77
Dirty book goes to jail; Hustler publisher L. Flynt. P. Bonventre and others. il por Newsweek 89:34 F 21 '77
First amendment hustle; trial of Hustler magazine publishers. Nation 224:99-100 Ja 29 '77
First amendment pixillation; A. Goldstein. Nat R 29:1349-50 N 25 '77
Has the first amendment met its match? R. Neville. il N Y Times Mag p 18 Mr 6 '77
Intelligent woman's guide to sex; L. Flynt's obscenity trial. K. Durbin. Mademoiselle 83: 94 My '77
Justice for Hustler. A. Kretchmer. Newsweek 89:13 F 28 '77
Obscenity: who's to say? Kansas trial of A. Goldstein and J. Buckley. R. Boeth and E. Sciolino. il por Newsweek 90:53 N 7 '77
United States versus the princes of porn. T. Morgan. il pors N Y Times Mag p 16-17+ Mr 6 '77

TRIALS (rape)
Courageous Claudia fights back; trial in Italy. il por Time 109:53 Ap 25 '77
Friendly forces go home! trial of Australian sailor Kevin Clark. R. Pullan. il Ms 5:19 F '77
Putting the victim's sex life on trial; study by Arnie Cann and others. S. Bush. Psychol Today 11:152 D '77

TRIALS (slander) See Trials (libel)

TRIALS (treason)
Charge of treason; case of A. Shcharansky. F. Willey and F. Coleman. Newsweek 89:42+ Je 13 '77

TRIALS (witchcraft)
Ergot reconsidered; Salem Witch trials. Chemistry 50:20 Mr '77
Witchcraft trials in seventeenth-century Russia. R. Zguta. bibl f il Am Hist R 82:1187-207 D '77

TRIB (proposed) See New York (city)—Newspapers

TRIBUNE Company. See Newspaper publishers and publishing

TRI CITIES Opera (Binghamton, Endicott, and Johnson City, N.Y) See Opera—New York (state)

TRICK photography. See Photography, Trick

TRICKS
See also
Conjuring

TRICYCLES
Tricycle. S. S. Wilson. il Org Gard & Farm 24: 91-2 Je '77
Tricycles. Consumer Rep 42:350-3 D '77

TRIDENT submarine bases. See Navy yards and naval stations

TRIDENTINE Mass. See Mass

TRIEN, Susan Flamholtz
When it's time for a bottle. il Parents Mag 52: 51+ O '77

TRIFLES (desserts) See Desserts

TRIGEMINAL neuralgia. See Neuralgia, Trigeminal

TRILATERAL Commission, Inc
Carter's Russia watchers: the Trilateralist straddle. A. Wolfe. Nation 225:712-15 D 31 '77
Trilateral commission: have capitalism and democracy come to a parting of the ways? S. Bowles. il Progressive 41:20-3 Je '77
Trilateral connection. J. Novak. Atlantic 240: 57-9 Jl '77
Trilateral world approach. Current 192:54-61 Ap '77
Trilateralism: a new world system. J. Novak. America 136:95-9 F 5 '77
Trilateralists at top—new foreign-policy elite. il U.S. News 82:31 F 21 '77
Where Jimmy went wrong. T. Branch. Esquire 87:28+ My '77

TRILLIN, Calvin
Day at the spaces. il Esquire 87:96-7 Ap '77
Our far-flung correspondents. New Yorker 53: 149-52+ N 21 '77
Reflections. il New Yorker 53:85-8+ Mr 21 '77
Temples of democracy. il Am Heritage 28:50-61 O '77
U.S. journal. See Occasional issues of New Yorker

TRILLING, Diana
Daughters of the middle class; excerpt from We must march my darlings. Harpers 254: 31-6+ Ap '77
Talking with Diana Trilling; interview, ed by J. Firth. por Sat R 4:22-3 My 28 '77

about

Legend of Lillian Hellman. A. Kazin. il Esquire 88:28+ Ag '77 *

TRILLING, Lionel
Elusive Trilling. M. Shechner. Nation 225:247-8+, 278-80 S 17, 24 '77 *

TRILLS. See Embellishment (music)

TRIM tabs, Boat. See Boats—Stability and stabilizers

TRIMARANS
Multihulls and other manias. D. Bradley. Motor B & S 140:8 Jl '77

TRIMBLE, George Simpson
Master tinkerer at Bunker Ramo. il por Bus W p 121-2 Ag 15 '77 *

TRIMBLE, Lester Albert
Milwaukee Sym: Trimble premiere. Hi Fi 27: MA25 Ap '77 *

TRIMETHOPRIM
Antibacterial synergism: a proposal for chemotherapeutic potentiation between trimethoprim and sulfamethoxazole. M. Poe; discussion. bibl Science 197:1300-1 S 23 '77

TRIMKNITS (firm) See Clothing industry—United States

TRIMM, Wayne
Boyers' birds. il pors Conservationist 31:28-32 Mr '77
Wards, a natural science treasure house. il Conservationist 32:2-7 Jl '77
Wayne Trimm's sketchbook. See issues of Conservationist

TRINIDAD and Tobago
Carnival à la Trinidad and Tobago. C. B. G. London. bibl il Américas 29:19-24 F '77
Fine art of eating in Trinidad and Tobago. P. C. Richman. il Holiday 58:40-1+ Ja '77
See also
Investments, Foreign—Trinidad and Tobago
Restaurants—Trinidad and Tobago

Description and travel

Traveler's camera. C. Purcell. il Pop Phot 81:64 D '77

Economic conditions

No place to hide. il Forbes 119:37 My 1 '77

Economic policy

Using oil wealth to industrialize. Bus W p39-40 Ag 22 '77

TRINITY
Image God. G. McCauley. America 136:inside back cover My 28 '77

TRIOLO, Tony
Letter from the publisher. J. Meyers. por Sports Illus 48:2 Ja 9 '78 *

TRIOS, Instrumental
Chung trio; performance at Fisher Hall. Hi Fi 27:MA23-4 Mr '77
More about the Dann Trio and Rudy Wiedoeft. J. Walsh. il pors Hobbies 82:35-6+ Jl '77
See also
Phonograph records—Trios, Instrumental

TRIP back down; drama. See Bishop, J.

TRIPLE Crown. See Horse racing

TRIPLETT, Glover B. Jr, and Van Doren, D. M. Jr
Agriculture without tillage; with biographical sketches. il Sci Am 236:16, 28-33 Ja '77

TRIPODS, Camera. See Camera tripods

TRIPOLITAN War. See United States—History—Tripolitan War, 1801-1805

TRIPPET, Robert Simons
Crime and no punishment. J. K. Galbraith. il Esquire 88:102+ D '77 *
TRIPS, Student. See School excursions
TRIS buffer. See Tromethamine
TRIS-BP. See Dibromopropyl phosphate
TRISHA Brown Dance Company. See Dance companies
TRITES, Robert T.
15-30,000-mile oils. Pop Sci 212:46+ Ja '78
TRITICALE
Cook's discovery; triticale; with recipes. il Sunset 158:222+ Ap '77
See also
Cookery—Grain
TRITSCH, Dina
What can an agent do for you? Writers Digest 57:28 My '77
Il TRITTICO; opera See Puccini, G.
TRIUMPH (sports car) See Sports cars
TROEGER, Thomas H.
Metaphysical dimensions of a door. Chr Cent 94:557-9 Je 8 '77
TROGNITZ, Willie
Wild Willie gets a new lease on life. P. Gammons. il por Sports Illus 47:28-30+ N 28 '77 *
TROILUS and Cressida; opera. See Walton, W. T.
TROILUS and Criseyde. See Chaucer, G.
TROLLING. See Trawls and trawling
TROLLOPE, Anthony
Time for a long, lazy Trollope ride; Time essay. G. Clarke. il por Time 109:55 My 16 '77 *
TROMBETTI, Joseph
Chef's table. New Yorker 53:27-8 Je 13 '77 *
TROMBONISTS
See also
Knepper, J.
TROMELIN (island)
No, man, it's my island. il map Time 110:32 D 26 '77
TROMETHAMINE
Tris bufferrattenuates acetylcholine responses in aplysia neurons. W. A. Wilson and others. bibl il Science 196:440-1 Ap 22 '77
TROPE, Mike
This agent's no secret. J. Marshall. il por Sports Illus 46:60+ My 16 '77 *
TROPHIES, Sport
Nineteenth-century silver in the New York Yacht Club. C. H. Carpenter, Jr. bibl il Antiques 112:496-505 S '77
See also
Football, College—Awards, prizes, etc.
TROPICAL fish aquariums. See Aquariums
TROPICAL fishes

Export-import trade

Great ornamental fish rip-off. T. Loftas. il Int Wildlife 7:28-32 Jl '77
TROPICAL medicine. See Tropics—Diseases and hygiene
TROPICAL plant research. See Botanical research
TROPICAL plants
Lives of a tree: the mysterious inner world of tropical plants. D. Perry. il Horticulture 55:30-5 O '77
Tropical flowers to give you a sunshine feeling when it's cold outside. il House & Gard 149:92+ O '77
TROPICAL rain forests. See Rain forests
TROPICS
Destruction of the tropics. P. H. Raven. BioScience 27:649 O '77

Diseases and hygiene

Tropical medicine—new vigor. H. A. Minners. Science 196:1275 Je 17 '77
See also
Trypanosomiasis
TROPMAN, John E.
Americans dislike the poor. Intellect 106:7-8 Jl '77
TROTSKY, Leon
Revolutionaries against the world; excerpt from The Russian revolution. il por Sat Eve Post 249:49 Jl '77

about

Talk with Trotsky. P. Berlinrut. Harpers 254:62-3+ F '77 *
TROTTA, Geri
India: three historic cities. il Travel 148:60-3 O '77
TROTTERS. See Horses, Race
TROTTIER, Edgar
Trottier affair. K. Willenson and R. Manning. il por Newsweek 89:31 F 21 '77 *
TROUBADOURS
Spirit of the faydit; troubadour-outcasts and Manrico, the hero of Il Trovatore. C. L. Osborne. il Opera N 41:26-8 Ap 9 '77
TROUBLE with tribbles; drama. See Gerrold, D.
TROUSERS. See Pants
TROUT, Lawana
Pick of the paperbacks (cont) Engl J 66:83-7 My '77
TROUT
Glory be to man for dappled things; B. Flick's brook trout research. M. Smith. il Sports Illus 46:40-2+ My 23 '77
Heteromorphic sex chromosomes in male rainbow trout. G. H. Thorgaard. bibl il Science 196:900-2 My 20 '77
Hiking to see the golden trout; Golden Trout Wilderness Study Area. Sunset 159:24+ Ag '77
Trout truths: learn here which trout are the largest, dumbest, most predatory; with views of R. Behnke. B. Saile. il por Outdoor Life 160:86-9 N '77
Visual pigment changes in rainbow trout in response to temperature. A. T. C. Tsin and D. D. Beatty. bibl il Science 195:1358-60 Mr 25 '77
See also
Cookery—Fish
TROUT fishing
AC/DC trout flies. F. McKinley. il Field & S 81:52-4+ F '77
Back to trout fishing fundamentals; excerpt from The trout and the fly. R. Ovington. il Field & S 82:32-4+ My '77
Boca brookies. P. Miller. il Outdoor Life 160:88-93+ O '77
Brute; fishing in Vermont. T. Vargish. il Nat R 29:507 Ap 29 '77
Care and feeding of a trout stream; Letort stream in Pennsylvania. A. Lee. il Sports Illus 46:30-2 Ja 31 '77
Catch and don't release; trout fishing in Lake Taupo, New Zealand. E. Zern. il Field & S 82:96+ Ag '77
Custom-caught big brown; trout fishing in California; ideas of B. Bringhurst. C. Garrison. il por Field & S 82:76+ Je '77
For big steelhead only; river fishing in Michigan. D. Bowring. il Field & S 82:46-7+ S '77
40-minute forward 40-year backward walk; trout fishing on the Middle Fork of the Salmon River, Idaho. T. Trueblood. il Field & S 81:8+ Ap '77
Great grandfather brown; brown trout of New Mexico's Rio Grande River. D. Kline. il Field & S 81:48-50+ Mr '77
Great put-and-take controversy; attitudes of trout fishermen toward stocking. P. Miller. il Outdoor Life 159:61-3+ Ap '77
Hang on for my life; boating accident while steelhead trout fishing. B. Knoll. il Outdoor Life 159:76-7+ My '77
Hemingway fished here. J. Harrison. il Esquire 88:38+ Jl '77
How now, brown trout? Pennsylvania; excerpt from Masters of the dry fly, ed by M. Migel. E. Zern. Field & S 82:90-3 My '77
How to catch trophy brook trout; Canada. D. Richey. il por Field & S 81:78-80+ Ap '77
Magic 40 degree mark; fishing in cold trout rivers. P. Barrett. il por Field & S 82:76-7+ My '77
Monster brown: new record—but will it last? J. Zumbo. il Outdoor Life 159:68-9+ Je '77
Neglected nomad of the saltwater; fishing for cutthroat trout from Alaska to California. C. H. Williams. il Field & S 82:54-6 Jl '77
On these two official wild trout streams you put your catch back; Hat Creek and Fall River, Calif. il map Sunset 158:68+ Je '77
100-year-old wet fly technique. J. Bashline. il Field & S 82:172+ My '77
Rain is catching time. N. Strung. il por Outdoor Life 159:96+ My '77
Recluse; brown trout. V. C. Marmaro. il Outdoor Life 160:84-5+ Jl '77
River that calls to the bold; Back River in the Northwest Territories, Canada. P. Smith. il map Outdoor Life 160:69-73+ Ag '77
Rocky Mountain high time of your life. V. Landi. il Outdoor Life 159:70-5+ My '77
Smith River steelheads; California. M. Fong. il Field & S 81:68-72 F '77
Spinning for trout. A. J. Acerrano. il Field & S 82:50-1+ D '77
Steelhead of the East; New York State. D. Mermon. il por Field & S 81:42-4+ Mr '77
Steelheading sense. P. Nelson. il pors Field & S 82:44-5+ O '77
Taking trout from beaver ponds. P. Barrett. il Mech Illus 73:8+ Jl '77
Ten streams of history: how are they now? famous trout streams. J. Gibbs. il Outdoor Life 159:60-5 Mr '77
Terrestrial tricks for low-water trout. S. R. Slaymaker, 2d. il por Outdoor Life 160:78-9+ S '77
Trout and the summer angler; Pennsylvania. R. L. Henry. il Field & S 82:20-1+ Jl '77
Trout fishing in the autumn. P. Barrett. il Mech Illus 73:18+ O '77

TROUT fishing—*Continued*
Trout—time of the push root. N. Strung. il Field & S 82:66-7+ Je '77
Trout truths: learn here which trout are the largest, dumbest, most predatory; with views of R. Behnke. B. Saile. il por Outdoor Life 160:86-9 N '77
Update: trout/salmon; ed by J. Gibbs. il Outdoor Life 160:100 O; 102 N; 110 D '77; 161:106 Ja '78
Wild rivers, trout galore. E. A. Bauer. il map Nat Wildlife 15:42-7 Ag '77

TROUTMAN, Benjamin I. Jr
Interdisciplinary approach to curriculum and instruction: from purpose to method. Clearing H 50:200-1 Ja '77

Il TROVATORE; opera. See Verdi, G.

TROW, George W. S.
Bobby Bison's energy budget for the eighties. New Yorker 53:38-9 O 3 '77
Gerry Plume does her own commercials. New Yorker 53:43-4 D 5 '77
I cover Carter. New Yorker 53:28-9 Jl 25 '77
I embrace the new candor. New Yorker 53:36-7 My 9 '77
Mrs Armand Reef likes to entertain. New Yorker 53:25-6 Jl 4 '77

TROWELS
Trowels: which ones for which jobs? il Bet Hom & Gard 55:230 Ap '77

TROWER, Peter
Reclaimed; poem. Poetry 129:250 F '77

TROY, Carol. See Peacock, M. jt ed

TROY, Jim
Great Barrier marlin! il Field & S 81:130-5 F '77

TROY, N.Y.
Glory that was Troy, New York. L. Kraar. il Fortune 95:142-5 Ja '77

TROY-Miami County, Ohio, Public Library. See Libraries—Ohio

TROYANOS, Tatiana
Musician of the month: Tatiana Troyanos; interview, ed by D. J. Soria. il por Hi Fi 27: MA6-8 Je '77

TRUCCO, Terry
MOMA's survival plan: more harm than good? il Art N 76:90-1 S '77
Shopping boom at your local museum. il Art N 76:56-60 O '77
Where are the women museum directors? il Art N 76:52-1 F '77

TRUCK and Coach Division. See General Motors Corporation—Truck and Coach Division

TRUCK campers. See Campers, Truck

TRUCK drivers
Driver; National Truck Driver of the Year; interview. O. L. Welk. New Yorker 52:23-5 Ja 31 '77
Raising hell on the highways. R. Sherrill. il N Y Times Mag p38-40+ N 27 '77
Trucker militant; M. Parkhurst. H. Crews. il por Esquire 88:82-4+ Ag '77

TRUCK driving
Sarge: our Socioprofile, Rolling Rorschach, Lend-a-truck. L. Mandel. il Car & Dr 23:95-6+ N '77

Competitions

MI's awards to truck drivers. . . il Mech Illus 73:123-4+ D '77

Anecdotes, facetiae, satire, etc.

Tuesday night with Cody, Jimbo and a fish of some proportion. H. Crews. Esquire 87:26+ F '77

TRUCK engines
See also
Diesel engines, Automotive

Fuel consumption

Now you can drive a V8, 7, 6, 5 or 4; Ford engine. il Mech Illus 73:19 Ag '77

Manufacture

See also
Cummins Engine Company

TRUCK farming

Economic aspects

Garden crops for extra income. il Org Gard & Farm 24:60-7 Je '77

TRUCK hijacking. See Robberies and assaults

TRUCK industry
Home on the asphalt trail; recreation vehicle industry. il Forbes 119:68-70 Je 15 '77
Oddball fire engine industry. R. Levy. il Duns R 109:52-5 Ja '77
Truck boom that won't stop. il Bus W p34+ Jl 11 '77
See also
International Harvester Company
Midas-International Corporation
Tractor industry
White Motor Corporation

Marketing

Going it alone in heavy trucks; Freightliner Corp. il Bus W p56+ Je 13 '77
White Motor sets Freightliner free; termination of marketing agreement. Bus W p30 Mr 7 '77

United States

See Truck industry

TRUCK tires. See Tires, Truck

TRUCKERS. See Truck drivers

TRUCKING
Big union that's haunted by its own success. U.S. News 83:75-6 Ag 8 '77
Raising hell on the highways. R. Sherrill. il N Y Times Mag p38-40+ N 27 '77
Routes and how to acquire them; Yellow Freight System. il Forbes 119:68+ My 15 '77
See also
Collective bargaining—Trucking
Leaseway Transportation Corporation

Laws and legislation

Deregulation: after the airlines, is trucking next? address, September 26, 1977. R. H. Shertz. Vital Speeches 44:40-2 N 1 '77
Trucking deregulation: rolling. il Bus W p 100+ D 5 '77

TRUCKS
Big self-unloading trucks. il Farm J 101:18-19 S '77
Big wheels rollin'; preview of Ford trucks. M. Jordan. il Car & Dr 23:77-80 S '77
Bigger boxes for little pickups. il Mech Illus 73:76+ Je '77
Cadillac what? L. Mandel. il Car & Dr 22:91-4+ F '77
Good and true truck. J. McKinley. Esquire 88: 51+ S '77
Lowering the cab to lift the payload. il Bus W p29 Mr 7 '77
Machinery management. G. Lepper and L. Reichenberger. See issues of Successful farming
Macho truck; pickups. B. Behme. il Field & S 82:78+ Ag '77
New Chevy, Dodge, GMC fuel-stretching diesel pickups. J. Dunne. il Pop Sci 211:77+ O '77
New diesel pickups and bigger 4WD's. H. Shuldiner. il Outdoor Life 160:54+ O '77
New rigs for rough action. B. McKeown. il Pop Mech 147:77+ Je '77
New trucks for '78. il Farm J 101:37 O '77
PM previews tomorrow's trucks. M. Lamm. il Pop Mech 148:81-3 Ag '77
Pick-em-ups go pretty. B. McKeown. il Pop Mech 148:112-13 O '77
Pickup trucks-do-all rigs for work and play. J. Dunne. il Pop Sci 210:103-5 Mr '77
Short take:
Ford Courier. L. Mandel. il Car & Dr 22:40 Je '77
3 ideas to speed unloading. il Farm J 101:40 N '77
Wheels afield. B. Kovacik. il Motor T 29:89+ My; 94-7 S '77
Wild horses; Dodge pickup. J. McCraw. il Hot Rod 30:49-50 N '77
See also
Campers, Truck
Vans

Awards, prizes, etc.

See also
Motor Trend Awards

Cabs

We drive a cab-under truck. R. G. Beason. il Mech Illus 73:120+ D '77

Camping equipment

Blazer Chalet. B. Kovacik. il Motor T 29:89-90+ Mr '77
Build PM's work-and-play camper. il Pop Mech 149:76-7 Ja '78
New add-ons for RVs. B. McKeown. il Pop Mech 148:91 Ag '77

Equipment

Endgates for fast unloading and versatile hauling. il Suc Farm 75:43 Je '77
Notable totables; hunter tops. il Mech Illus 73:140 Mr '77
Turning a pickup into a dump truck; Hy-Power Hoist. il Mech Illus 73:94 S '77

Periodicals

See also
Overdrive (periodical)

Photographs

Hot rod gallery (cont) il Hot Rod 30:60+ Je; 34 Jl; 110 O; 108 N '77
Pickups, vans & 4x4 highriders. il Hot Rod 30: 64-8 Jl '77

Testing

Datsun/Chevy. B. Kovacik. il Motor T 29:89+ My '77
Driving impression:
GMC's diesel pickup. G. Witzenburg. il Motor T 29:57-8 S '77

TRUCKS—Testing—*Continued*
Driving the Terra diesel pickup. M. Lamm. il Pop Mech 147:36 Je '77
Has Ford built the ultimate Bronco? B. Kovacik. il Motor T 30:60-3 Ja '78
International Suntanner; pickup with convertible roof. B. Kovacik. il Motor T 29:94-7 S '77
Road test:
Beat the devil; GMC Sprint Diablo Pickup. il Hot Rod 30:74+ S '77
Ford Bronco Ranger XLT. S. Thompson. il Car & Dr 23:37-9+ Ja '78
Fun truckin'; Chevrolet Silverado K-20, Dodge Power Wagon, and Ford F-150 Ranger XLT. il Hot Rod 30:112+ My '77
International Diesel Scout Traveler. il Car & Dr 22:94+ Je '77
3-truck test in Death Valley. il Mech Illus 73:37-9+ Jl '77

TRUCKS (dollies)
How to make plants mobile; dollies. D. Raffel. il House & Gard 149:68+ D '77

TRUCKS, Foreign
Bigger boxes for little pickups. il Mech Illus 73:76+ Je '77

Testing

PS car test & driving report:
Imported pickups. J. Dunne and R. Ceppos. il Pop Sci 211:36+ N '77
Small scale invasion. B. Kovacik. il Motor T 29:69-70+ S '77

TRUCKS, Municipal
Mobile concrete batchers save time, manpower and money; Baltimore. S. Cortese. il Am City & County 92:51-2 F '77
See also
Refuse collection trucks
Trucks in rescue work

TRUCKS, Remodeled
LUV. il Hot Rod 30:74+ N '77
Machine shop on wheels. il Farm J 101:G1 N '77
Steppin' out. il Hot Rod 30:88-90 Mr '77
See also
Vans, Remodeled

TRUCKS in rescue work
Ambulances and rescue vehicles. il Am City & County 92:95-8 O '77

TRUDEAU, Margaret (Sinclair)
Margaret Trudeau's own story; interview, ed by R. Leach. il pors Ladies Home J 94:60+ Jl '77

about

End of a storybook romance. il pors Time 109:40 Je 6 '77 *
Maggie and Wilbur. R. Rosenblatt. New Repub 176:37 My 7 '77 *

TRUDEAU, Pierre Elliott
Canadian and American friendship; address, February 22, 1977. Vital Speeches 43:322-4 Mr 15 '77
It's unthinkable; excerpts from interview, ed by A. de Borchgrave. il pors Newsweek 90:53-4 D 5 '77
Prime Minister Pierre-Elliott Trudeau of Canada visits Washington; exchange of toasts, February 21, 1977. Dept State Bull 76:256-8 Mr 21 '77
U.S.-Canada agreement on natural gas pipeline; joint statement, September 8, 1977. Dept State Bull 77:609-10 O 31 '77

about

End of a storybook romance. il pors Time 109:40 Je 6 '77 *
Margaret Trudeau's own story; interview, ed by R. Leach. M. S. Trudeau. il pors Ladies Home J 94:60+ Jl '77 *
Thorny issues for Trudeau, Carter. por U.S. News 82:17 F 28 '77 *

Visit to the United States, 1977

Musings from a neighbor. H. Sidey. il por Time 109:14 Mr 7 '77
Prime Minister Pierre-Elliott Trudeau of Canada visits Washington; exchange of toasts, February 21, 1977. J. Carter; P. E. Trudeau. Dept State Bull 76:255-8 Mr 21 '77

TRUE, Joseph
Joseph True and the piecework system in Salem. M. B. Clunie. bibl il Antiques 111:1006-13 My '77 *

TRUE, Michael
Comic genius of Flannery O'Connor. America 137:167-9 S 24 '77
People's parish. Commonweal 104:496-9 Ag 5 '77

TRUEBLOOD, Ted
[Column] See issues of Field & stream

TRUFFAUT, François
Kind word for critics; excerpt from The films in my life; tr by L. Mayhew. Harpers 255:95+ O '77

about

Bad case of satyriasis. A. Schlesinger, Jr. Sat R 5:46 N 26 '77 *
Engineer of fluid mechanics. J. Simon. Nat R 30:38+ Ja 6 '78 *
From 400 blows to Small change. G. Mast. New Repub 176:23-5 Ap 2 '77
Reviews; Small change. P. Thomas. il Film Q 30:42-5 Spr '77 *

TRUJILLO, Bertha
Lady in the bullring; interview, ed by M. Feiner. il pors Américas 29:25-7 S '77

TRULL, Elaine
Managing my home freezer. il por Org Gard & Farm 24:104-5 Jl '77

TRUMAN, Harry S.
Recognizing Israel; address, December 28, 1976. C. M. Clifford. pors Am Heritage 28:4-7+ Ap '77 *
Who started the cold war? C. L. Mee, Jr; W. A. Harriman; E. Abel. il pors Am Heritage 28:8-23 Ag '77 *

TRUMBULL, Douglas
We get you to places you can't get to. J. Morgenstern. il por Horizon 20:17-23 D '77 *
Wizard of special effects. J. Kroll and M. Kasindorf. il por Newsweek 90:99 N 21 '77 *

TRUMBULL, Richard
Proposed department of energy draws comment from the AIBS; letter. BioScience 27:345 My '77

about

Trumbull testifies on public participation. E. M. Leeper. BioScience 27:387-9 Je '77 *

TRUMPET music
See also
Phonograph records—Trumpet music

TRUSCOTT, J. B.
Retiring along the 5-State Gulf Coast. il Ret Liv 17:30-1+ Ja '77

TRUSSELL, Margaret Edith
Dan Diego's greenbelt. il maps Am For 83:26-30 O '77

TRUST. See Confidence

TRUST departments of banks. See Banks and banking—Trust departments

TRUST in God
On showing steadfast trust. E. Schaeffer. Chr Today 21:32-3 F 18 '77

TRUST Territory of the Pacific Islands
Getting the bugs out; question of independence. Nation 224:643-4 My 28 '77
Improbable welfare state. F. Butterfield. il map N Y Times Mag p55-6+ N 27 '77
New U.S. lake in the Pacific; strategic implications of the 200-mile limit on Trust Territory. R. W. Gale. map Progressive 41:50-2 My '77
Paradise with rough edges. D. DeVoss. il Time 111:18-19+ Ja 16 '78
Trusteeship Council welcomes recognition of need for unity in Micronesia. il UN Chron 14:20-2+ Jl '77
Wind shifts in the Pacific. il map Time 111:16-17 Ja 16 '78

TRUSTEES. See Trusts and trustees

TRUSTEES, Library. See Libraries—Trustees, boards, committees, etc.

TRUSTEES, Museum. See Art galleries and museums—Trustees, boards, committees, etc.

TRUSTEES of Reservations of Massachusetts. See Landscape protection—Massachusetts

TRUSTEESHIP Council. See United Nations—Trusteeship Council

TRUSTMAN, Alan
Who killed Hollywood? il Atlantic 241:64-8+ Ja '78

TRUSTMAN, Deborah
Watercolor; The fall; Clearing; Shelling; poems. Poetry 129:198-201 Ja '77

TRUSTS, Industrial
See also
Competition

International trusts

Bureaucratic imperialism; Justice Dept. investigation of foreign companies. Forbes 120:45 N 15 '77
Cartel that never was. il Forbes 119:30-2 Mr 1 '77
Corporate Patty Hearst; investigating Gulf's role in uranium cartel price fixing. D. Pauly. Newsweek 89:69 Je 27 '77
Darkening storm over Gulf; membership in uranium price-fixing cartel. il Time 109:62-3 Je 27 '77
Issues on trial in the Westinghouse lawsuits; suits charging failure to deliver on uranium supply contracts brought by electric utilities. Bus W p 125-6+ S 26 '77
More U.S. presssure on a uranium cartel; investigation of alleged price fixing. Bus W p26-7 Ag 29 '77
Uranium cartel's fallout. il Time 110:96+ N 21 '77
Why CIPEC's no OPEC. il Forbes 119:59-61 Je 1 '77

Law

Antitrusters aim overseas. il Bus W p 100+ Mr 14 '77
It's a snail's pace for four big antitrust cases; computers, telephones, cereals, and petroleum. U.S. News 83:40 Ag 15 '77

TRUSTS, Industrial—Law—*Continued*
Trial by Congress? Antitrust cases; views of G. Bell. por Time 109:71 My 23 '77
See also
Automobile industry—Antitrust cases
Computer industry—Antitrust cases
Foreign exchange brokers—Antitrust cases
Franchise system—Antitrust cases
Newspaper publishers and publishing—Antitrust cases
Petroleum industry—Antitrust cases
Steel industry—Antitrust cases
Telephone companies—Antitrust cases
United States—Federal Trade Commission
United States—Justice, Department of—Antitrust Division

United States

See also
United States—Federal Trade Commission
United States—Justice, Department of—Antitrust Division

History

Origins of the transportation cartel. P. J. Quirk. bibl il Intellect 105:442-4 Je '77

TRUSTS, Investment. See Investment trusts

TRUSTS and trustees
Fight to control a $2 billion estate; A. I. duPont trust's 24% interest in Florida National. D. G. Santry. il por Bus W p 108 S 26 '77
Give your money away—and enjoy it, too! Charitable remainder trusts. Changing T 31:15-17 D '77
No rest at 89; E. Ball, trustee of Alfred I. du Pont estate. por Time 110:69-71 O 10 '77
Strange case of Ed Ball; trustee of A.I. duPont estate. P. Berman. il por Forbes 119:63-6 F 15 '77
See also
Land trusts

Taxation

How a trust could save your life's work. M. Kilgore. il Farm J 101:D2 Ap '77

TRUSTWORTHINESS. See Confidence

TRUTH
See also
Honesty
Knowledge, Theory of

TRUTH in lending law. See Credit—Regulation

TRUTHFULNESS
See also
Lying

TRYON, Thomas, 1926-
Tom Tryon entertains. C. Porcelli. il por House B 119:102-3 Ap '77 *

TRYPANOSOMES
African trypanosomes: cultivation of animal-infective trypanosoma brucei in vitro. H. Hirumi and others. bibl il Science 196:992-4 My 27 '77
Infectivity reacquisition by trypanosoma brucei brucei cultivated with tsetse salivary glands. I. Cunningham and B. M. Honigberg. bibl il Science 197:1279-82 S 23 '77
Lab grows sleeping sickness parasite. il Sci N 111:261 Ap 23 '77
On the track of a shifty bug; trypanosoma brucei. il map Time 109:57 Ap 25 '77

TRYPANOSOMIASIS
Fly that would be king. R. S. Desowitz. il Natur Hist 86:76-83 bibl(p 101) F '77

TSAR and carpenter; opera. See Lortzing, A.

TSELENTIS, Raissa
1976 Bach International Piano Competition. I. Lowens. il por Hi Fi 27:MA24-5 Jl '77 *

TSERNOGLOU, Demetrius, and others
Molecular graphics: application to the structure determination of a snake venom neurotoxin. bibl il Science 197:1378-81 S 30 '77

TSETSE flies
Fly that would be king. R. S. Desowitz. il Natur Hist 86:76-83 bibl(p 101) F '77
Operation tsetse fly; livestock vs wildlife in United Nations tsetse fly control project. N. Myers. il Int Wildlife 7:33-5 My '77

TSIMIHETY (native race) See Madagascar—Native races

TSIN, Andrew T. C. and Beatty, D. D.
Visual pigment changes in rainbow trout in response to temperature. bibl il Science 195:1358-60 Mr 25 '77

TSIPIS, Kosta
Building blocks of weapons development. Bull Atom Sci 33:41 Ap '77
Cruise missiles; with biographical sketch. il Sci Am 236:16, 20-9 F; 237:13+ Ag '77
Science and the military. Bull Atom Sci 33:10-11 Ja '77

TSUJI, Minoru
(tr) See Kishi, T. Ken Domon: a documentary pilgrimage

TSUKUBA University. See Colleges and universities—Japan

TSUNAMI Warning System. See Tidal waves

TSURUTA, Dorothy Jane Randall
Bicentennial woman; Bicentennial woman II; poems. Negro Hist Bull 40:704 My '77

TSUTSUMU. See Packaging

TUBERCULOSIS
Last days of Eleanor Roosevelt; excerpt from Mother R. E. Roosevelt and J. Brough. pors Ladies Home J 94:113+ O '77

TUBERS
Finding and preparing edible wild roots. J. W. Fears. il Outdoor Life 159:129-30 Ap '77
See also
Potatoes

TUBULIN
Quantitation of cytoplasmic tubulin by radio-immunoassay. J. L. Morgan and others. bibl il Science 197:578-80 Ag 5 '77

TUCCILLE, Jerome
Failure of libertarianism. Nat R 29:489+ Ap 29 '77

TUCHMAN, Barbara W.
Assimilationist dilemma: Ambassador Morgenthau's story; adaptation of address, December 1976. Commentary 63:58-62 My; 64:16 Ag '77
On the altar of oil. New Repub 176:37-8 Ja 22 '77

TUCHMAN, Mitch
Who's turning what into movies? Esquire 87:72-4+ Ap '77

TUCKER, Carll
Back door. See issues of Saturday review, Je 25, 1977-
about
Report to the readers. N. Cousins. Sat R 5:4 O 29 '77 *
Saturday's child. T. Schwartz. pors Newsweek 89:89-90 Mr 21 '77 *

TUCKER, Donald L.
Scrutinizing another Carter appointment. por Bus W p42 O 3 '77 *

TUCKER, Frank H.
Frontiersmen of Nippon. il Intellect 106:251-3 D '77

TUCKER, Larry. See Hartley, G. L. jt auth

TUCKER, Marcia
Marcia's not there to take artistic chances; interview, ed by J. N. Gifford. il por Ms 5:30+ Ap '77
about
Brave New Museum. R. J. M. Olson. Art in Am 65:25+ N '77 *
New space for new art. B. Rose. por Vogue 167:205 N '77 *

TUCKER, Mary Louise
Clarence John Laughlin: phantoms and metaphors. il Mod Phot 41:100-9+ Ap '77

TUCKER, Robert W.
Beyond détente. Commentary 63:42-50 Mr; 14+ Jl '77
Oil and American power—three years later. Commentary 63:29-30 Ja; 8-9 Ap '77

TUCKER, William
Environmentalism and the leisure class. il map Harpers 225:49-56+ D '77

TUCKER, William, 1935-
William Tucker: meaning vs. matter. K. Baker. il Art in Am 65:102-3 N '77 *

TUCKERNUCK Island
Track on the beach. P. Matthiessen. il Audubon 79:68-9+ Mr '77

TUCKTONIA, Christchurch, England. See Models of cities, towns, etc.

TUCKWELL, Barry
Profiles. W. Sargeant. por New Yorker 53:45-6+ Mr 14 '77 *

TUCSON, Ariz.
Arizona's suburbs of the sun. D. Jeffery. il supp (folded map) Nat Geog 152:486-517 O '77

Foreign population

Manzo raid: sweeping up the aliens. M. Day. Nation 224:146-8 F 5 '77
Wetback scapegoats; indictment of workers at the Manzo Area Council. Nation 224:357 Mr 26 '77

TUDOR, David
Tudor at The Kitchen; six-day series of electronic music. J. La Barbara. il por Hi Fi 27:MA14-15 My '77 *

TUG FORK River flood. See Floods—United States

TUGBOATS
World's biggest moving job—icebergs! E. D. Fales, Jr. il Pop Mech 149:47-51 Ja '78

TUITION, College. See College education—Cost

TUITION, Medical school. See Medical education—Cost

TUITION, Private school. See Private schools—Finance

TUKEY, John W.
Some thoughts on clinical trials, especially problems of multiplicity. bibl il Science 198:679-84 N 18 '77

TULIN, Marshall
But will it last? por Forbes 120:33 Ag 15 '77 *

TULIPS
In praise of Darwin, Rembrandt, Mendel and other famous tulips; with photographs by D. Kessel. F. Endt. Horticulture 55:26-39 Ag '77
Tulipomania was no Dutch treat to gambling burghers. T. Berger. il Smithsonian 8:70-7 Ap '77

TULLIUS, F. P.
Newest consciousness. New Yorker 53:34-6 Mr 28 '77
TULLY, Joseph G. and others
Pathogenic mycoplasmas: cultivation and vertebrate pathogenicity of a new spiroplasma. bibl il Science 195:892-4 Mr 4 '77
TULSA, Okla.
Tulsa: the city that studhorse notes helped to build. il Forbes 120:148 N 15 '77

Hospitals

See Hospitals—Oklahoma
TULSA, Okla, City-County Library System. See Libraries—Oklahoma
TUMBLERS. See Drinking vessels
TUMLINSON, J. H. and others
Identification of the female Japanese beetle sex pheromone: inhibition of male response by an enantiomer. bibl il Science 197:789-92 Ag 19 '77
TUMOR cells
Correlation between lipid synthesis in tumor cells and their sensitivity to humoral immune attack. S. I. Schlager and S. H. Ohanian. bibl il Science 197:773-6 Ag 19 '77
Inter-and intraspecies contamination of human breast tumor cell lines HBC and BrCa5 and other cell cultures. W. A. Nelson-Rees and R. R. Flandermeyer. bibl il Science 195:1343-4 Mr 25 '77
Primary bioassay of human tumor stem cells. A. W. Hamburger and S. E. Salmon. bibl il Science 197:461-3 Jl 29 '77
TUMOR inhibiting substances. See Cancer inhibiting substances
TUMOR viruses
Cancer and viruses. A. J. Levine. bibl il por Chemistry 50:7-11 My '77
Congenital transmission of a papovavirus of the stump-tailed macaque. K. V. Shah and others. bibl il Science 195:404-6 Ja 28 '77
Expression of murine sarcoma virus genes in uninfected rat cells subjected to anaerobic stress. G. R. Anderson and L. M. Matovcik. bibl il Science 197:1371-4 S 30 '77
Oncornavirus: isolation from a squirrel monkey (saimiri sciureus) lung culture. R. L. Heberling and others. bibl il Science 195:289-92 Ja 21 '77
RNA tumor viruses. R. D. Cardiff. bibl il Chemistry 50:12-16 My '77
RNA tumor viruses: more insights. Sci N 111:247 Ap 16 '77
Relationship of tumor virology to an understanding of nonviral cancers. H. M. Temin. bibl BioScience 27:170-6 Mr '77
See also
Simian viruses
TUMORS
Double minute chromosomes and the homogeneously staining regions in chromosomes of a human neuroblastoma cell line. G. Balaban-Malenbaum and F. Gilbert. bibl il Science 198:739-41 N 18 '77
See also
Hodgkin's disease
Metastasis

Diagnosis

Angiogenesis: a marker for neoplastic transformation of mammary papillary hyperplasia. S. S. Brem and others. bibl il Science 195:880-2 Mr 4 '77

Immunological aspects

Host control of tumor growth. C. C. Ting and others. bibl il Science 197:571-3 Ag 5 '77

Personal narratives

Helen and the dragon; hystiocytic lymphoma. C. Whited. por Read Digest 110:74-9 F '77

Surgery

Microsurgery for pituitary tumors. Sci N 112:71 Jl 30 '77
TUNA fish
Bluefin tuna. C. S. Zawacki. il por Conservationist 32:34-6 Jl '77
Bluefin tuna: vulnerable giant. G. L. Beardsley. il Sea Front 23:9-15 Ja '77
Vanishing tuna. J. N. Cole. il Read Digest 110:132-5 Mr '77
TUNA fisheries. See Fisheries
TUNBRIDGE program. See Lone Mountain College, San Francisco
TUNGUSKA explosion. See Explosions
TUNING instruments and apparatus
Digital tuning; electronic tuners. F. Miller. il Hi Fi 27:132-3 D '77
See also
Audio systems—Tuning
Radio receivers—Tuning
TUNIS, John Roberts
How you play the game. R. Shereikis. il Horn Bk 53:642-8 D '77 •
TUNISIA
Tunisia. B. Dunne. il Trav/Holiday 149:26-33+ Ja '78
See also
Carthage, Africa
TUNLEY, Roul
Comeback of the small town. il Read Digest 111:143-7 O '77
Don't let them take me back! il Read Digest 112:96-100 Ja '78
TUNNELING (physics)
Life that came in from the cold. Sci N 112:277 O 29 '77
TUOLUMNE River
Tuolumne River: the drought in a microcosm. P. L. Fradkin. map Audubon 79:132-5 Jl '77
TUPOLEV, Andrei Nikolaevich
Tupolev. W. Gunston. Flying 101:272-3 S '77 •
TURAN, Kenneth
Movies. See alternate issues of Progressive
TURBEVILLE, Gus
Tuning in and turning on; address, September 15, 1977. Vital Speeches 43:747-9 O 1 '77
TURBINE blades. See Airplane engines, Jet—Blades
TURBINES
Twin-turbine softener knows when to regenerate; hydraulic turbine. R. Day. il Pop Sci 211:136-7+ O '77
TURBOCHARGERS. See Airplane engines—Superchargers; Automobile engines—Superchargers
TURBOFAN airplane engines. See Airplane engines, Jet
TURBULENCE
See also
Atmospheric turbulence
TURCK, Nancy
Arab boycott of Israel. bibl f For Affairs 55:472-93 Ap '77
TURCO, Lewis
Silo; poem. Nation 224:248 F 26 '77
Trolley; poem. Commonweal 104:551 S 2 '77
TURE, Norman B.
Real estate: we'll see some firming in prices; interview. por U.S. News 83:53-4 D 26 '77
TURECK, Rosalyn
Bach on the piano? Why not? il por Hi Fi 27:91-3 O '77
Rosalyn Tureck; interview. New Yorker 53:36-8 O 10 '77
TURF. See Lawns
TURGEON, Charlotte
Food for thought; questions and answers. Holiday 58:53+ Je '77
It happened in New Orleans. Holiday 58:14-15 Ja '77
Put a little glamour in your Christmas feast. il Sat Eve Post 249:132-4 D '77
Yogurt & the fountain of youth. il Sat Eve Post 249:18+ O '77
TURGEON, Gregoire
At home; poem. Poetry 130:79 My '77
TURIN, Italy

Music

See also
Opera—Italy

Politics and government

Reports & comment: Turin: nostalgic communism. G. Hodgson. il Atlantic 240:20+ Ag '77
TURIN, Shroud of. See Holy Shroud
TURITZ, Gilda. See Stout, J. A. jt auth
TURKEY
Reports & comment: Turkey: the reluctant westerners. C. Roberts. Atlantic 240:14+ S '77
Turkey: cross fire at an ancient crossroads. R. P. Jordan. il map Nat Geog 152:88-123 Jl '77
See also
Bosporus
Cruising—Turkey
Kurds
Loans, Bank—Turkey
Loans, Foreign—Turkey
Money—Turkey

Antiquities

Admiral Beaufort charted coasts for ships of the world. A. Friendly. il por map Smithsonian 8:68-70+ bibl(p 101) Ag '77
Wreck at Sheytan Deresi. G. F. Bass. il Oceans 10:34-9 Ja '77

Economic policy

Austerity now—and hopes for IMF aid. Bus W p53+ O 17 '77

Foreign relations

Cyprus

See Cyprus

Greece

See Greece—Foreign relations—Turkey

United States

See United States—Foreign relations—Turkey

TURKEY—*Continued*

Politics and government

Pas de deux; S. Demirel succeeded by B. Ecevit as Premier. por Time 111:30-1 Ja 16 '78
See also
Elections—Turkey

TURKEY as food. See Cookery—Poultry

TURKEY calling. See Bird calling

TURKEY hunting
At Payson's place he's just plain Charlie; Florida hunting ranch. V. Kraft. il por Sports Illus 46:54+ Ap 18 '77
Calling spring gobblers. A. Martin. il Field & S 81:86-9+ F '77
Clever footwork fools a clever bird. J. Carmichel. il Outdoor Life 159:86-7+ My '77
Fall gobblers are different. C. Elliott. il Outdoor Life 160:72-3+ O '77
Gunning for wild turkeys. J. Carmichel. il Outdoor Life 159:138-40+ Ap '77
Spring is turkey time; New York State. D. Knight. il Field & S 81:84-6+ Mr '77
Two clucks are enough. C. Elliott. il Outdoor Life 159:64-5+ F '77

TURKEYS, Wild
Turkey and the beech. W. W. Betts. Jr. il Nat Wildlife 15:18-23 O '77
See also
Turkey hunting

TURKISH cookery. See Cookery, Turkish

TURKISH music. See Music, Turkish

TURKISHER, K. Ch.
Monologue on an unpopular theme. Bull Atom Sci 33:48-51 F '77

TURNBULL, Agnes Sligh
Beyond the obvious. Writer 90:23-4 S '77

TURNBULL, Colin Macmillan
Bush Negroes carry on tradition of rebel ancestors. il Smithsonian 7:78-85 Mr '77

TURNBULL, William Watson
Power to the person. Educ Digest 43:28-31 N '77
about
Nadir is to Nader as lowest is to . . . G. V. Glass. Nat R 29:776-7 Jl 8 '77 *

TURNER, Alice K.
(comp) What your favorite authors are working on. il Ms 6:58-9+ D '77
(ed) See Corman A. PW interviews

TURNER, Billy
Triple Crown trainer. J. L. Phillips. il pors N Y Times Mag p47-8+ N 13 '77 *

TURNER, Evan H.
Slapping wrists. A. Jarmusch. Art N 76:173-4 Summ '77 *

TURNER, Evelyn
Black woman finds her roots. O. Coombs. Redbook 149:56+ O '77 *

TURNER, Frederick L.
Fred L. Turner of McDonald's: growth company. por Forbes 119:95 F 15 '77 *
McDonald's grinds out growth. il por Duns R 110:50-2 D '77 *

TURNER, Frederick William
Just what in the hell has gone wrong here anyhow? il pors Am Heritage 28:34-43 O '77
Second decade of Little big man. Nation 225:149-51 Ag 20 '77
Terror of the wilderness; excerpt from The cost of living. il Am Heritage 28:58-65 F '77

TURNER, James E. See Rapport, D. J. jt auth

TURNER, Jean
Printmaking with plywood: a simple and inexpensive method. il Design (US) 79:20 Fall '77

TURNER, Joseph Mallord William
Bound to the mast; exhibition at the Detroit Institute of Arts. M. Stevens. il Newsweek 91:60-1 Ja 9 '78 *
Fallacies of hope. Vasari. Art N 76:23+ Summ '77 *
Watercolor techniques of J.M.W. Turner. C. E. Luffman. il Am Artist 41:36-9+ Je '77 *
World's first Turner museum. Vasari. il Art N 76:30+ N '77 *

TURNER, Pamme
Siphnos potters. il map Ceram Mo 25:45-50 Ap '77

TURNER, Peter
John Benton-Harris: Yankee eye on the English. il Mod Phot 41:128-37 O '77

TURNER, Richard
Think slow. Time 110:63 N 7 '77 *

TURNER, Robert Edward, 3d
Benched from the bench. K. Hannon. il por Sports Illus 46:67-8 My 23 '77 *
Captain courageous. P. Bonventre. il por Newsweek 90:77 S 12 '77 *
Captain outrageous. P. Bonventre and R. Manning. il por Newsweek 90:45-6 Jl 11 '77 *
Defending the America's Cup. il por Time 110:84-5 S 19 '77 *
In their hour of triumph. J. Hersey. il Yachting 142:86-91+ S '77 *
Losersville, U.S.A. R. Blount, Jr. il por Sports Illus 46:74-7+ Mr 21 '77 *
Mouth of the South. P. Axthelm. il pors Newsweek 90:74-5+ S 19 '77 *
Mouth of the South at the helm. il por Time 110:44 Ag 8 '77 *
Staging a battle royal on the briny. C. Phinizy. il por Sports Illus 47:18-20+ Jl 4 '77 *
Tenacious Ted Turner. G. Hammond. Motor B & S 140:9 N '77 *
Why the gap hasn't closed. B. Robinson. il pors Yachting 142:58-60 N '77 *

TURNER, Roger
(comp) Heard what your grandchildren are saying about you? il Ret Liv 16:29+ D '76

TURNER, Ronny E. and Edgley, Charles
Bitter-sweet compliment problem. il Todays Educ 66:28-30+ Ja '77

TURNER, Rosa Shand
Increasingly visible female and the need for generic terms. Chr Cent 94:248-52 Mr 16 '77

TURNER, Stansfield
Carter's intelligence chief sizes up world's trouble spots; interview. por U.S. News 82:24-6 My 16 '77
about
Admirable Stansfield Turner. Suetonius. New Repub 176:10-12 Mr 12 '77 *
Admiral for superspook? il por Time 109:24 F 14 '77 *
Admiral for the CIA. D. M. Alpern and others. il por Newsweek 89:17-18 F 21 '77 *
Admiral of the covert seas. Nation 224:386 Ap 2 '77 *
Admiral Turner's fight. T. Mathews and N. Horrock. Newsweek 89:26 Je 20 '77 *
Appointments calendar. F. Getlein. Commonweal 104:133-4 Mr 4 '77 *
Backstage at the CIA. R. Boeth and others. il por Newsweek 90:27-8 S 12 '77 *
For new CIA chief, a big rebuilding job. il por U.S. News 82:24 F 21 '77 *
Inside story of battle to control spying. J. Fromm. pors U.S. News 83:27 Ag 8 '77 *
Intelligence superchief: Turner's new challenge. por U.S. News 83:22 Ag 15 '77 *
Old salt opens up the pickle factory. il por Time 109:22-5 Je 20 '77 *
Tale of two confirmations. Nation 224:290-1 Mr 12 '77 *
Turner disavows any intention to become intelligence czar. Aviation W 107:16 Ag 15 '77 *

TURNER, Ted. See Turner, R. E. 3d

TURNER, Tom E.
Pumping money. il por Forbes 120:37 D 1 '77 *

TURNER Division of Cleanweld Products, Inc. See Cylinders (engines, etc)—Manufacture

TURNER Museum of Colorado. See Denver—Galleries and museums

TURNING
How to turn dowels on your drill press. C. Baker. il Pop Mech 147:174 Je '77
See also
Lathes

TURNIPS
Turnips: the multipurpose vegetable. J. Jankowiak. il Org Gard & Farm 24:134+ S '77

TURNOVERS. See Pastry

TURNTABLES
See also
Phonograph—Turntables

TUROW, Scott
Tears and terror. J. K. Footlick. il por Newsweek 90:76 O 17 '77 *

TURTLES
Let's help the Atlantic loggerhead; with editorial comment. D. Haley. il map Nat Parks & Con Mag 51:12-15 F '77
NPCA sea turtle survey. il Nat Parks & Con Mag 51:23-4 Ap '77
Pet turtle industry working toward reprieve. BioScience 27:68 Ja '77
Rare albino turtle. J. R. Fletemeyer. il Sea Front 23:233 Jl '77
Stink of stinkpot turtle identified: ω phenylalkanoic acids. T. Eisner and others. bibl il Science 196:1347-9 Je 17 '77
Vest-pocket turtle; Illinois mud turtles. J. Cooper. il map Natur Hist 86:52-7 bibl(p 100) Ap '77
See also
Tortoises

TUSCARORA Pottery School, Nevada. See Pottery—Study and teaching

TUSSAUD'S (waxworks) See Waxworks—Great Britain

TUTEN, Frederic
Moviemaker. Vogue 167:200+ Ap '77

TUTENKHAMÛN, King of Egypt
Boy kings. P. W. Schmidtchen. il Hobbies 82:134-6 S '77 *
Tutankhamun and Star trek; address, July 29, 1977. C. L. Babcock. Vital Speeches 43:744-7 O 1 '77 *

Tomb

Art; Treasures of Tutenkhamun. E. V. Warren. il House B 119:34 Ap '77
Craft of King Tut's jewels. J. A. Black. il Craft Horiz 37:20-3 F '77

TUTENKHAMUN, King of Egypt—*Continued*
Dazzling legacy of an ancient quest; King Tut's gold. A. J. Hall. il Nat Geog 151:292-311 Mr '77
King Tut rises again. il Horizon 19:12-15 My '77
Treasures of a teenage god-king. il Sr Schol 109:8-10 Ap 7 '77
Treasures of King Tut; discovery of tomb by H. Carter. S. Flythe, Jr. il Sat Eve Post 249: 68-71+ My '77
Tut lives. C.-G. McDaniel. Progressive 41:35-6 Jl '77
Tutankhamun adventure; exhibition. J. Warren. Chr Cent 94:409-10 Ap 27 '77
View from the castle; contemplating Tut's treasures. S. D. Ripley. Smithsonian 7:6 F '77
Wonderful things; Treasures of Tutankhamun. S. Hochfield. il Art N 76:54-7 Ja '77
Young King Tut. L. Prothro. il Nat R 29:211 F 18 '77

TUTORS and tutoring
Bilingual teaching for newly arrived immigrant children; use of adult and peer tutors. J. J. Hassett. Clearing H 50:409-12 My '77
Preparing volunteer tutors. D. J. Sawyer. bibl Clearing H 51:152-6 D '77
Turning it around in education with student tutoring. A. H. Elliott. bibl il Clearing H 50: 285-90 Mr '77

TUTTLE, Donald L.
Charles Livingston Bull. il por Conservationist 32:8-13 Jl '77
Shades of Adirondack iron. il Conservationist 31: 33-5 Mr '77
Wedding of the waters. il pors Conservationist 32:10-15 N '77

TUTTLE, John
Reporter at large. J. Stevenson. il New Yorker 53:46+ Ag 15 '77 *

TWAIN, Mark, pseud. See Clemens, S. L.

TWELFTH night. See Epiphany

TWELVE Mile, Ind.
Living Christmas in the town park. J. Gillies. il Farm J 101:39-41 D '77

TWENTIETH century
See also names of years and decades, e.g. Nineteen hundred and sixties

TWENTIETH Century-Fox Film Corporation
Star is born; Star wars. il Newsweek 89:81 Je 13 '77
Star wars sparks a war with producers; investigation of block booking charges. il Bus W p30 Ag 29 '77
What makes Fox an inviting target. il Bus W p27-8 My 30 '77

21 Club (restaurant) See New York (city)—Hotels, restaurants, etc.

TWICHELL, David C. and others
Delaware River: evidence for its former extension to Wilmington Submarine Canyon. bibl il map Science 195:483-5 F 4 '77

TWIGHT, Charlotte
Big snoop strikes again. Nat R 29:269 Mr 4 '77

TWIN Cities Metropolitan Council
Government that links a whole region. il U.S. News 83:83 D 26 '77

TWIN-lens cameras. See Cameras, Twin-lens

TWINS
Biomedicine. J. Arehart-Treichel. Sci N 112:184 S 17 '77
Heart disease and life stress; identical twin studies by Einar Kringlen. Sci N 112:166 S 10 '77
Parents' aloofness slows twins' progress. Sci N 111:390 Je 18 '77
When you're having more than one; delivering twins. K. D. Anderson. Parents Mag 52:20 D '77
See also
Siamese twins

TWIRLING, Baton. See Baton twirling

TWIST drills. See Drilling and boring machinery

TWO dollar bills. See Paper money—United States

2,4,5-T. See Herbicides

TWO thousand two (year)
Flying in 2002. I. Asimov. il Flying 101:372 S '77

TWYLA Tharp Dance Company. See Dance companies

TYLER, Anne
Average waves in unprotected waters; story. New Yorker 53:32-6 F 28 '77
Earthly possessions; condensation of novel. Redbook 148:181-203 F '77
Foot-footing on; story. Mademoiselle 83:82 N '77
Holding things together; story. New Yorker 52: 30-5 Ja 24 '77
Trouble in the boys' club. New Repub 177:16-19 Jl 30 '77

TYLER, Bonnie
Capturing the play spirit of the child. Educ Digest 42:32-5 F '77

TYLER, Gus
Rentier economy would threaten manufacturing jobs. M Labor R 100:45-6 Mr '77

TYLER, Kenneth
Master printer of Bedford, N.Y. J. Goldman. il pors Art N 76:50-4 S '77 *

TYLER, Ralph W.
School and character development. il Todays Educ 66:72-3 Ja '77
Two new emphases in curriculum development. Educ Digest 42:11-14 F '77

TYLER, Tex.
New confidence. il U.S. News 82:25-6 Je 13 '77

TYLER Corporation. See Conglomerate corporations

TYLER Cup Invitational. See Running

TYLER Ecology Award. See Ecology—Awards, prizes, etc.

TYLER Graphics (firm) See Publishers and publishing—Art

TYMNET system. See Data transmission systems —Europe, Western

TYNAN, Kathleen
Jazzing into Cuba. il por Vogue 167:328-9+ S '77

TYNAN, Kenneth
Profiles; R. Richardson. por New Yorker 53:45-6+ F 21 '77
Profiles; T. Stoppard. New Yorker 53:41-6+ D 19 '77

TYNDALE House Publishers-Victory Press merger. See Publishers and publishing—Acquisitions and mergers

TYPE and typefounding
Why Johnny can't read; sans serif type. V. Orton. Nat R 29:1006-7 S 2 '77

TYPESETTING
AIGA explores role of typesetting firms in in-house operations. P. Doebler. Pub W 211:76 Mr 7 '77
See also
Computers—Printing use

TYPEWRITER stands. See Stands (furniture)

TYPEWRITERS, Automatic
Fastest typist in the world. il Mech Illus 73:8 F '77
See also
Computers—Print-out equipment

TYPEWRITERS, Electric
Portable electric typewriters. il Consumer Rep 42:656-61 N '77
Two electric ball-element typewriters. Consumers Res Mag 60:23-4 My '77

TYPEWRITING

Anecdotes, facetiae, satire, etc.

If you can type this you can make big money. L. Sheehan. Atlantic 239:106-7 Mr '77

TYPHOONS
Passage of Typhoon Pamela over Guam. G. D. Hamilton and S. Pilipowskyj. il map Weatherwise 30:147-53 Ag '77
Rescue from the heart of a typhoon; crew of downed bomber saved by nuclear subs. C. Barton. il map Pop Mech 148:73-6+ D '77

TYPING of manuscripts. See Authorship—Copy preparation

TYPING stands. See Stands (furniture)

TYRRELL, Robert Emmett, Jr
God and man in Bloomington. il por Time 109: 93-4 Mr 7 '77 *
Talking back. M. J. Sobran, Jr. Nat R 29:1506 D 23 '77 *

TYRRELL, Wilfred
Wall Street blues. A. Salpukas. il pors N Y Times Mag p42-4+ D 18 '77 *

TYSON, Brady
Born-again social scientists. Society 14:15-16 My '77

about

Do-it-yourself diplomacy. R. Carroll and E. Clift. pors Newsweek 89:36 Mr 21 '77 *

TYSON, Cicely
Cicely Tyson: reflections on a lone black rose. M. Angelou. il pors Ladies Home J 94:40-1+ F '77 *

TYSON, Graham
Dataproducts: it expects to match IBM. por Duns R 109:18-19 F '77 *

TYSON, Joanne. See Tyson, R. jt auth

TYSON, Mary Catherine
Health/sex/psychology; questions and answers. por House & Gard 149:72+ O; 66+ N '77
—See Tyson, R. jt auth

TYSON, Richard, and Tyson, Joanne
Sex and the black woman; they are now seeking advice. il por Ebony 32:103-4+ Ag '77

TYSON, Robert, and Tyson, M. C.
Health, psychology, sex; questions and answers. pors House & Gard 149:36+ F; 50 Ap; 50+ Je '77

TZAGOLOFF, Alexander
Genetic and translational capabilities of the mitochondrion. bibl il BioScience 27:18-23 Ja '77

U

U-2 (airplane) See Airplanes, Military—United States
UAL, Inc
New United pilot hiring plan stresses minorities, females. J. M. Lenorovitz. Aviation W 107:30-1 O 10 '77
Nothing to lose but their chains; United Airlines stand in favor of deregulation. Forbes 120:42 Ag 15 '77
United ponders transport buy. Aviation W 107:26 Ag 29 '77
United supports reforms for more flexible pricing. Aviation W 106:197+ Mr 21 '77
UAW. See United Automobile, Aerospace and Agricultural Implement Workers of America
UCAR Batterien (firm) See Electric battery industry—Germany, West
UCC. See United Church of Christ
UCLA Medical Center. See Hospitals—California
UDA. See Ulster Defense Association
UDAG (Urban Development Action Grant) program (proposed) See Urban renewal
UFO cult. See Cults
UFOs
Astronauts & UFOs—the whole story! J. E. Oberg. il por Space World N-2-158:4-28 F '77
Galileo of UFOlogy; J. A. Hynek. P. Gwynne and K. Ames. il por Newsweek 90:97 N 21 '77
Great UFO debate; pro and con. P. J. Klass; J. A. Hynek. Current 196:18-25 O '77
Three UFOs—how real were they? R. Schiller. Read Digest 111:108-12 N '77
UFOlogy: uneasy awareness of something gives a new status to investigations. J. Mullaney. il Sci Digest 82:26-32 Jl '77
UFO's just will not go away. D. Shapley. Science 198:1128 D 16 '77
Vast balloons create confusion. D. Lampe. Sci Digest 82:33-5 Jl '77
What were those 585 objects the USAF failed to identify—and why the cover-up? D. Berliner. il Sci Digest 82:24-8 Ag '77

Anecdotes, facetiae, satire, etc.

UFO menace. W. Allen. New Yorker 53:31-3 Je 13 '77
UMTA. See United States—Urban Mass Transportation Administration
UMW. See United Mine Workers of America
UN. See United Nations
UNCITRAL. See United Nations—Commission on International Trade Law
UNCTAD. See United Nations Conference on Trade and Development
UNDOF (United Nations Disengagement Observer Force) See United Nations—Armed Forces—Forces in the Middle East
UNDP. See United Nations—Development Program
UNEF (United Nations Emergency Force) See United Nations—Armed Forces—Forces in the Middle East
UNEP. See United Nations—Environment Program
UNESCO. See Unesco
UNFICYP (United Nations Peace-keeping Force in Cyprus) See United Nations—Armed Forces—Forces in Cyprus
UNHCR. See United Nations—High Commissioner for Refugees
UNIDO. See United Nations Industrial Development Organization
UNITA (National Union for the Total Independence of Angola) See Guerrillas—Angola
UNITAR. See United Nations Institute for Training and Research
UNRWA. See United Nations Relief and Works Agency for Palestine Refugees in the Near East
URW. See United Rubber, Cork, Linoleum and Plastic Workers of America
U.S. National Bank of Galveston. See Banks and banking—Texas
U.S. news & world report (periodical)
Memo to our readers; the Editor's page. J. H. Sweet. U.S. News 82:3 Mr 14 '77
Printing by computer: a USN&WR gamble pays off. il U.S. News 83:56-8 S 5 '77
Sincerely yours; H. Flieger's final editorial. H. Flieger. U.S. News 82:92 Mr 7 '77
USAF. See United States—Air Force
USDA. See United States—Agriculture, Department of
USGS. See United States—Geological Survey
USIA. See United States—Information Agency
USPS. See United States Power Squadrons, Inc
USS Essex (warship) See Warships—United States
USSR (Union of Soviet Socialist Republics) See Russia
UTC. See United Technologies Corporation
UTTAS (Utility Tactical Transport Aircraft System) See Helicopters—Military use
UCHENDU, Victor C.
Challenge of cultural transition in Sub-Saharan Africa. bibl f Ann Am Acad 432:70-9 Jl '77
UDALL, Morris King
Federal voice in private land-use: two views. pors Nations Bus 65:18+ Ag '77
NRPA interview with Congressman Morris K. Udall; ed by B. Kravetz. il pors Parks & Rec 12:42-5 Mr '77
Use tax dollars to elect Congress? interview. pors U.S. News 82:63-4 Ap 25 '77; Same. Current 194:3-5 Jl '77

about

Udall to probe mergers, including book publishing. S. Wagner. Pub W 211:21 My 9 '77 *
UELSMANN, Jerry N.
Shows we've seen. N. Canavor. il Pop Phot 80:27-8+ Je '77 *
UELTSCHI, Albert L.
Up, up and away! por Forbes 120:36 N 1 '77 *
UFER, Walter
Walter Ufer: passion and talent. T. Egri and K. Egri. il por Am Artist 42:64-7+ Ja '78 *
UGANDA
Whither East Africa? W. E. Skurnik. Cur Hist 73:205-8+ D '77
See also
Americans in Uganda
Civil rights—Uganda
Terrorism—Uganda

Commerce

United States

See United States—Commerce—Uganda

Foreign relations

United States

See United States—Foreign relations—Uganda

Politics and government

Amin: the wild man of Africa. il pors map Time 109:18-22+ Mr 7 '77
Amin's purge. A. Deming and others. il por Newsweek 89:25-6 Mr 14 '77
Coup or con job? il por Time 110:28 Jl 4 '77
Death in Uganda; Archbishop J. Luwum. Chr Cent 94:212 Mr 9 '77
Death of an archbishop; death of J. Luwum. por Time 109:31 F 28 '77
Henry Kyemba awaits the end of Idi Amin; interview, ed by G. Stuttaford. H. Kyemba. por Pub W 212:44 O 3 '77
Idi Amin: more cunning than crazy. T. H. Snitch. il Intellect 105:410-11 Je '77
Idi Amin's holy war. R. Carroll and C. Harrison. il por Newsweek 89:35-6 F 28 '77
Idi Amin's rule of blood. A. Deming and others. il pors map Newsweek 89:28-30+ Mr 7 '77
Idi's latest adventure. R. Watson and others. il Newsweek 90:43-4 Jl 4 '77
Murder in Uganda. W. P. Wood. America 136:216-19 Mr 12 '77
Power of irresponsibility; I. Amin. Nation 224:292 Mr 12 '77
Retreat from a collision course. il por Time 109:24 Mr 14 '77
Terror and death in Uganda; death of Archbishop Luwum. A. H. Matthews. por Chr Today 21:49-51 Mr 18 '77
Uganda: a helpless world wrings its hands. il por U.S. News 82:36 Mr 7 '77
Uganda after Idi Amin. W. P. Wood. America 137:51-3 Jl 30 '77

Religious institutions and affairs

Blessing of harassment. Chr Today 21:22 Je 3 '77
See also
Church and state in Uganda
Church of England in Uganda
UGARTE, Augusto Pinochet. See Pinochet Ugarte, A.
UGOLINI, F. C. and others
Direct evidence of particle migration in the soil solution of a podzol. bibl il Science 198:603-5 N 11 '77
UHL, Michael, and Ensign, Tod
Union of soldiers. Progressive 41:46-8 Mr '77 —See Ensign, T. jt auth
UHLMAN, Fred
Story behind the book: Reunion. R. Dahlin. Pub W 211:226 My 23 '77 *
UHNAK, Dorothy
Investigation; condensation of novel. Redbook 149:165-87 Ag '77
UKRAINE

Antiquities

Four Ukrainian archaeologists present their latest finds; Scythian burial mound excavations by Institute of Archaeology of the Academy of Sciences of the Ukrainian S.S.R. il UNESCO Courier il 29:17-22 D '76

UKRAINIAN poetry
Translations into English
Christmas in the Ukraine; Soviet version of Ukrainian Christmas carol Nova radist's stala. Nat R 30:18-19 Ja 6 '78
ULAM, Adam B.
Ample guilt, no policy. New Repub 176:26+ Ja 22 '77
ULCERS
See also
Peptic ulcers
ULENE, Art
Doctor's 20-day pleasure program for health; interview, ed by C. Seebohm. il por House & Gard 150:24+ Ja '78
ULLMAN, Albert Conrad
How to pay for social security? interview. pors U.S. News 83:37-8 Jl 4 '77
about
Most powerful committee in the House. G. R. Rosen. il por Duns R 109:46 Mr '77 *
Something for no one. il por Time 109:44+ Mr 7 '77 *
ULLMAN, Jackie. See Dunn, L. jt auth
ULLMAN, Leslie
Eventually, you; poem. Nation 225:86 Jl 23 '77
On vacation a woman mistakes her leg; poem. New Yorker 53:40 S 12 '77
ULLMAN, Michael A.
Jazz. New Repub 177:35-7 O 1; 23-5 N 19; 19-21 D 3; 23-5 D 24 '77
New directions. New Repub 176:45-7 My 21 '77
ULLMANN, Liv
Changing; excerpt. por McCalls 104:130-1+ F '77
Close-up; interview, ed by E. Miller. por Seventeen 36:82 Mr '77
Liv Ullmann on love and Bergman; excerpt from Changing. il Vogue 167:172-3+ F '77
Presenting Liv Ullmann; excerpt from Changing. por Read Digest 110:97-101 Je '77
Two women: Liv Ullmann & Erica Jong—an intimate conversation. pors Redbook 149:104-5+ Ag '77
What's happening; interview, ed by G. Shalit. il por Ladies Home J 94:21 Ap '77
ULLMANN, Viktor
Emperor of Atlantis. Reviews
Hi Fi il 27:MA30-1 O '77 *
New Yorker 53:111-12 Je 6 '77 *
Newsweek 89:116-17 My 16 '77 *
ULLO, Joseph
Fingering a .22-cal. killer. Time 110:29+ S 26 '77 *
ULLRICH, Axel, and others
Rat insulin genes: construction of plasmids containing the coding sequences. bibl il Science 196:1313-19 Je 17 '77
ULLRICH, R. L. and others
Cancer-causing radiation. il por Chemistry 50: 6-11 Ap '77
ULLYOT, Joan
Are women stronger than men? Harp Baz 110: 89+ My '77
ULPH, Owen
Dane Coolidge; western writer and photographer. bibl il por Am West 14:32-5 N '77
ULSAMER, Edgar
Laser-powered rockets and dark satellites. Space World N-5-161:30-2 My '77
Space shuttle: high-flying Yankee ingenuity. il Space World N-6-162:18-23 Je '77
Will the Soviets wage war in space? il Space World N-5-161:25-9 My '77
(ed) See Morgan, T. W. Pervasive importance of USAF's space mission
ULSTER Defense Association
Paisley led but few workers followed; general strike. il por Time 109:44 My 16 '77
ULTRASONIC waves
Lost da Vinci may yield its secret to ultrasonic science. D. Hellyer. il Sci Digest 82: 16-19 Ag '77
Ultrasound emission in infant rats as an indicant of arousal during appetitive learning and extinction. A. Amsel and others. bibl il Science 197:786-8 Ag 19 '77
ULTRAVIOLET astronomy
As stars fall to ashes. D. E. Thomsen. il Sci N 111:364-5 Je 4 '77
EUV makes the grade; question of the extreme ultraviolet. S. P. Maran. Natur Hist 86:85-6+ F '77
ULTRAVIOLET rays
See also
Spectrum, Ultraviolet
Physiological effects
Aposematic statement on nuclear war: ultraviolet radiation in the postattack environment. E. E. Koslow. bibl BioScience 27:409-13 Je '77
Light. N. Simon. il Vogue 167:164-6+ Ag '77
ULTRAVIOLET stars. See Stars—Radiation
ULYSSES in traction; drama. See Innaurato, A.

UMBRIA, Italy
Giovanni Urbani and restoration Italian-style. M. Gendel. il por Art N 76:146-8 Summ '77
UMINGMAKTOK. See Northwest Territories, Canada
UMPIRES and umpiring (sports) See Baseball, Childrens—Umpiring
UNBRANDED merchandise
No-brand groceries. il Time 110:80 N 21 '77
UNCLE Tom (literary character) See Blacks in literature
UNCLES
Anecdotes, facetiae, satire, etc.
Art of uncling. R. Baker. N Y Times Mag p8 O 16 '77
UNCOMMON women and others; drama. See Wasserstein, W.
UNCOMPAHGRE National Forest, Colo. See National forests
UNDERDEVELOPED areas
Against the New Economic Order. P. T. Bauer and B. S. Yamey. bibl f Commentary 63:25-31 Ap '77; Reply with rejoinder. J. Novak. 64: 4+ Jl '77
Assembly acts on economic co-operation; with text of resolution. UN Chron 14:55, 106-7 Ja '77
Developing countries emphasize remote sensing data utilization. Aviation W 106:21 My 9 '77
Development problems of the economically poor nations; report of Pugwash Conference. Bull Atom Sci 33:37 D '77
Dimensions of poverty; address, January 14, 1977. R. S. McNamara. Vital Speeches 43: 450-3 My 15 '77
Military technology and social structure. M. H. Kaldor. il Bull Atom Sci 33:49-53 Je '77
Pittance for international aid; excerpt from address, October 4, 1976. R. S. McNamara. il Bull Atom Sci 33:36-8 N '77
Signposts for 1982: introduction to Unesco's Medium-Term Plan. A. M. M'Bow. il UNESCO Courier 30:6-10+ Mr '77
Third world fantasies. W. Laqueur. Commentary 63:43-8 F '77
Transfer of resources to developing countries on assured basis urged. UN Chron 14:51-3 Ja '77
United States seeks improved U.N. programs to meet basic needs of world's poor; address, June 16, 1977. J. J. Gilligan. Dept State Bull 77:204-7 Ag 15 '77
World Bank head calls for special efforts to relieve poverty; excerpt from address, September 1977. R. S. McNamara. UN Chron 14: 40 O '77
See also
Community development
Contracts, Government—Underdeveloped areas
Debts, Public—Underdeveloped areas
Economic assistance, American—Underdeveloped areas
Economic assistance, Kuwaiti—Underdeveloped areas
Government and the press—Underdeveloped areas
Investments, American—Underdeveloped areas
Investments, Foreign—Underdeveloped areas
Loans, Bank—Underdeveloped areas
Technical assistance, American—Underdeveloped areas
United Nations Conference on Trade and Development
United Nations Negotiating Conference on a Common Fund
Agriculture
Hunger in the midst of plenty. J. J. DuPont. Conservationist 32:1 S '77
Hungry, crowded competitive world. T. W. Schultz. il Bull Atom Sci 33:26-31 O '77
Atomic power
Nuclear energy for the third world; tr by S. Libich. K. Gottstein. Bull Atom Sci 33:44-8 Je '77
Church and social problems
Saying God loves you to a starving man; interview, ed by D. Kucharsky. A. A. Whittaker. pors Chr Today 21:17-21 Ap 1 '77
Civil rights
Pursuing human dignity. A. A. Said. bibl il Society 15:34-8 N '77
Commerce
Commodities: a better idea? commodity-stabilization agreements. A. J. Mayer and R. Thomas. il Newsweek 89:57 Ap 4 '77
What the third world wants; Conference on International Economic Cooperation. il Bus W p80-1 My 9 '77
See also
Underdeveloped areas—Shipping
Communication
Communication—more than a one-way street; excerpt from Unesco's Medium-Term Plan (1977-1982) il UNESCO Courier 30:30 Mr '77
World debate on information: flood-tide or balanced flow? symposium. il UNESCO Courier 30:4-33 Ap '77

UNDERDEVELOPED areas—*Continued*

Ecology

Man and his environment; excerpt from Unesco's Medium-Term Plan (1977-1982) il UNESCO Courier 30:28-9+ Mr '77

Economic conditions

Experts see no physical limits to accelerated development of developing regions. UN Chron 13:59+ D '76

Economic relations

Conflict between North and South; Conference on International Economic Cooperation, Paris. il Time 109:30 Je 13 '77

Department discusses results of CIEC meeting; statement, June 21, 1977. R. N. Cooper. Dept State Bull 77:92-8 Jl 18 '77

Framework for a dynamic North-South dialogue; statement, July 8, 1977. A. J. Young. Dept State Bull 77:383-9 S 19 '77

Let's look out for no. 1! R. Moss. il N Y Times Mag p31+ My 1 '77

OPEC contributing to North-South dialogue, says Venezuela President. UN Chron 13:49-50 D '76

Package for the have-nots; Conference on International Cooperation and Development. Nation 224:739-40 Je 18 '77

Progress in Paris. il Newsweek 89:78 Je 13 '77

Requiem for the North-South conference; Conference on International Economic Cooperation. J. Amuzegar. bibl f For Affairs 56:136-59 O '77

Resumed Assembly session fails to agree on Paris conference achievements. il UN Chron 14:32-5 O '77

Secretary Vance attends ministerial meeting of the Conference on International Economic Cooperation; address, news conference, with text of communique, May 30, June 3, 1977. C. R. Vance; R. N. Cooper. Dept State Bull 76:645-52 Je 20 '77

Third world has given everything and received little; interview. C. A. Pérez. il por U.S. News 83:53-4+ Jl 25 '77

Trying to stabilize commodities; Conference on International Economic Cooperation. il Bus W p31-2 My 30 '77

Why so much worry about a world financial crisis. il U.S. News 82:84-5 F 14 '77

See also

Independent Commission on International Development Issues

United States

See United States—Economic relations—Underdeveloped areas

Education

Educational imperative; excerpt from Unesco's Medium-Term Plan (1977-1982) il UNESCO Courier 30:22-5 Mr '77

Equal chance for everyone; illiteracy and the problems of youth; excerpt from Unesco's Medium-Term Plan (1977-1982) il UNESCO Courier 30:26-7 Mr '77

Finance

Are the LDCs in over their heads? H. van B. Cleveland and W. H. B. Brittain. il For Affairs 55:732-50 Jl '77

Debts of the poor: preventing the crash. R. V. Roosa. New Repub 176:42-5 Ja 22 '77

Department discusses CIEC and developing-country debt; statement, June 29, 1977. R. J. Ryan, Jr. Dept State Bull 77:179-82 Ag 8 '77

Department discusses debt situations of developing countries and the role of private banks; statement, April 5, 1977. P. H. Boeker. Dept State Bull 76:441-4 My 2 '77

Department urges appropriation of funds for international financial institutions; statement, February 16, 1977. P. H. Boeker. Dept State Bull 76:198-201 Mr 7 '77

Rescuing the LDCs. D. O. Beim. For Affairs 55:717-31 Jl '77

Food relief

Place of U.S. food in eliminating world hunger. G. E. Brandow. bibl f il Ann Am Acad 429:1-11 Ja '77

World hunger and Christian conscience. H. B. Kuhn. Chr Today 21:68-9 My 6 '77

Housing

Urban housing policy for developing countries; report from the Colloquium on Urban Development Problems in Mexico City. M. Kilbridge. Archit Rec 161:37+ Ap; 37+ My '77

Journalism

Reporting from the third world. M. Rosenblum. For Affairs 55:815-35 Jl '77

Word war of the worlds; third world nations protesting Western coverage of their affairs. il Time 109:89 Je 20 '77

Medical care

New HOPE; history of S.S. Hope and plans for new Project HOPE. J. Cergol. il Américas 29:17-22 O '77

Natural resources

Push to tap new resources. il Bus W p 18-19 Jl 18 '77

Nutrition problems

Bottle-baby disease; boycott of Nestle products in attempt to stop promotion of infant formula in underdeveloped countries. B. L. Benderly. Ms 6:20 D '77

Power resources

Other energy crisis: firewood; excerpt from Losing ground: environmental stress and world food prspects. E. P. Eckholm. bibl il Focus 27:9-16 Mr '77; Same abr. with title Poor man's energy crisis. il UNESCO Courier 30:29-31 Jl '77; Same abr. with title Poor man's crisis: firewood. Sci Digest 82:59 O '77

Third world needs energy too. J. Raloff. il Sci N 112:234-5 O 8 '77

Third world's critical mass. K. Bird and D. Berick. Nation 224:236-8 F 26 '77

Publishers and publishing

Third world acquisitions: a report on the workshop at LC. A. Pieratt and H. B. Neikirk. Lib J 102:978 My 1 '77

Research

Linkages of R&D systems to contemporary societies. W. Morehouse and J. Sigurdson. il Bull Atom Sci 33:26-7 D '77

Science

Science and technology strategy for the LDC's. M. S. Wionczek. Science 196:837 My 20 '77

Science, technology, man and society; excerpt from Unesco's Medium-Term Plan (1977-1982) il UNESCO Courier 30:18-20 Mr '77

Self-help for third world scientists. M. W. C. Dharma-Wardana. il Bull Atom Sci 33:22-3 F '77

Some questions for the world jamboree; proposed U.N. conference. M. S. Wionczek. il Bull Atom Sci 33:29-32 D '77

Shipping

UNCTAD committee moves to combat port congestion in developing countries; Committee on Shipping. UN Chron 14:34 My '77

Social conditions

Man—the centre of development; excerpt from Unesco's Medium-Term Plan (1977-1982) il UNESCO Courier 30:21-2 Mr '77

Multinationals as agents of social development. R. L. Meier. il Bull Atom Sci 33:30-2+ N '77

Technology

A.T: the quiet revolution. W. N. Ellis. il Bull Atom Sci 33:24-9 N '77

Call issued for support of communication activities of developing countries. UN Chron 14:70-1 Ja '77

Identity and change: does development imply dependency? W. M. Dyal, Jr and J. B. Donovan. il Américas 29:13-18 Ap '77

Multinational investment and global purpose; address, June 17, 1977. L. A. Iacocca. Vital Speeches 43:720-4 S 15 '77

Science, technology, man and society; excerpt from Unesco's Medium-Term Plan (1977-1982) il UNESCO Courier 30:18-20 Mr '77

Some questions for the world jamboree; proposed U.N. conference. M. S. Wionczek. il Bull Atom Sci 33:29-32 D '77

See also

Appropriate Technology International (organization)

Technical assistance, American—Underdeveloped areas

United Nations Conference on Technical Cooperation among Developing Countries, 1978 (proposed)

Telephone apparatus industry

Great world telephone war. W. Guzzardi, Jr. il Fortune 96:142-7+ Ag '77

Water supply

Fumbled help at the well; excerpt from Water: life or death. J. Stein. il Environment 19:14-17+ Je '77

Youth

Equal chance for everyone; illiteracy and the problems of youth; excerpt from Unesco's Medium-Term Plan (1977-1982) il UNESCO Courier 30:26-7 Mr '77

UNDERGROUND areas

See also

Toronto—Underground areas

UNDERGROUND atomic testing. See Atomic bombs—Testing, Underground

UNDERGROUND films. See Motion pictures, Experimental
UNDERGROUND houses. See Houses, Underground
UNDERGROUND literature

Poland

Display of samizdat. il Time 110:55 D 12 '77
UNDERGROUND railroad
Underground railroad in Delaware. J. E. Newton. bibl il Negro Hist Bull 40:702-3 My '77
UNDERGROUND reservoirs. See Reservoirs
UNDERTAKERS and undertaking
Big government's needless interventions; FTC regulation of the funeral industry. J. J. Kilpatrick. Nations Bus 65:37-8 Ja '77
Consumer resistance; IFS Industries. Forbes 120:144 N 15 '77
Funeral salesmen. J. Mitford. McCalls 105:190+ N '77
UNDERWATER archeology. See Archeology, Submarine
UNDERWATER drilling
DSDP: hints at a larger Japan of old. map Sci N 112:421 D 24 '77
DSDP sets record, heads for Pacific. Sci N 111:375 Je 11 '77
Deep drilling in the Galapagos Rift. il Sci N 112:85 Ag 6 '77
Drilling into the Japan Trench. Sci N 112:279 O 29 '77
Unique volcanic subsea specimens. Sci N 111:102 F 12 '77
See also
Oil well drilling, Submarine
UNDERWATER motion picture photography. See Motion picture photography, Submarine
UNDERWATER photography. See Photography, Submarine
UNDERWATER research. See Oceanographic research
UNDERWATER thermometers. See Thermometers and thermometry
UNDERWATER treasure. See Treasure trove
UNDERWEAR
Long underwear. il Consumer Rep 43:46-9 Ja '78
Out from underwear. M. A. Kellogg and L. Whitman. il Newsweek 89:60-1 F 21 '77
Running short on long underwear. T. Buckley. il N Y Times Mag p62-3 F 20 '77
UNDERWOOD, Barbara, and Underwood, Robert
Concerns of jr. high school and middle school teachers: a framework for in-service programs. Clearing H 51:36-7 S '77
UNDERWOOD, Herbert
Circadian organization in lizards: the role of the pineal organ. bibl il Science 195:587-9 F 11 '77
UNDERWOOD, John
Baseball. il Sports Illus 46:46+ My 30 '77
College football (cont) Sports Illus 46:48-9 Ja 31 '77
Don't let 'em wear you down! il pors Sports Illus 47:46-8+ N 14 '77
Fewer is finer except for some flaws. il Sports Illus 47:28-31 S 5 '77
Maybe it's the luck of the Irish. il Sports Illus 47:20-2+ S 19 '77
Never too late for the Sooners. il Sports Illus 47:14-17 O 3 '77
Quest in the jungle. il Sports Illus 48:86-90+ Ja 9 '78
Setting up a showdown in Dallas. il Sports Illus 47:26-30+ D 19 '77
Shake down the thunder. il Sports Illus 48:6-9 Ja 9 '78
So it's two in a row for Bo. il Sports Illus 47:20-3 N 28 '77
Tennis. Sports Illus 46:78+ My 23 '77
That orange shirt means something. il Sports Illus 46:68-72+ Mr 28 '77
(ed) See Williams, T. I hope Rod Carew hits 400
UNDERWOOD, Lamar
Outdoor life: Lamar Underwood, editor. J. Fry. por Outdoor Life 159:4 Mr '77 *
UNDERWOOD, Robert. See Underwood, B. jt auth
UNDERWRITING. See Insurance
UNEMPLOYMENT
Danger: not enough young at work. il Time 109:64-5 My 30 '77
Unemployed youth: now a global worry. il Bus W p21-2 Ag 1 '77
See also
Employment
Labor supply

Psychological aspects

Replaceable you. B. Photopulos. por Newsweek 90:23 O 10 '77

Relief measures

CETA funds—a boon to North Carolina; employment programs for artists and musicians. C. B. Fowler. il Hi Fi 27:MA16-18 D '77
Don't just stand there! Do something! J. A. Briggs. il Forbes 120:29-31 O 1 '77
Fighting unemployment—six experts tell what's needed; interviews. il U.S. News 82:56-60 F 21 '77
How jobs fit into Carter's welfare plan. il por Nations Bus 65:64-6 N '77
How to find work for people on welfare. Bus W p30+ Ag 29 '77
Jobs and income for the poor. R. I. Lerman. il Society 14:60-2 My '77
Jobs and money—Carter's plan to save the cities. il U.S. News 83:37-8 N 28 '77
Jobs and public service. J. B. Craig. Am For 83:13 Ap '77
Jobs for all: Congressional will-o'-the-wisp. H. Ginsburg. Nation 224:138-43 F 5 '77
Jobs for youth; the Young Adult Conservation Corps. F. H. Armstrong. il Am For 83:30-3+ N '77
Lotsa bucks, but little bang? il Time 109:46 Ja 24 '77
More summer jobs for youths, but still not enough. il U.S. News 82:47-8 My 2 '77
Muskie calls for CETA renewal; countercyclical assistance program. Am City & County 92:18 Ap '77
Premium on youth. il Time 109:76+ Mr 21 '77
Put the jobless back to work; Shiawassee County, Mich. il Am City & County 92:85-6 My '77
Something for no one; A. Ullman's jobs tax credit bill. il por Time 109:44+ Mr 7 '77
Subsidizing unemployment; employment tax credit. Nat R 29:654-5 Je 10 '77
Tax gimmickry at its finest; tax credit proposals in jobs bill. M. Friedman. Newsweek 89:90 Ap 11 '77
Trade adjustment assistance: should it be modified? P. Henle. il M Labor R 100:40-5 Mr '77
Unemployed clean county's drain channels; CETA program in Calhoun, Mich. N. Reeder. Farm J 101:K1 O '77
Unemployment: new answers to a nagging problem. il Sr Schol 109:6-8+ F 10 '77
Waiting for jobs. Nation 224:484-5 Ap 23 '77
Washington tightens its grasp on CETA. Bus W p 120+ O 3 '77
What it takes to create jobs. Fortune 95:133 Mr '77
When Europe tailor-makes programs for millions out of work. A. Zanker. il U.S. News 82:61-2 F 21 '77
See also
Federal Art Project
Public works—Federal aid

Statistics

Analysis of unemployment in nine industrial countries. J. Moy and C. Sorrentino. bibl il M Labor R 100:12-24 Ap '77
Efforts to improve estimates of state and local unemployment. M. Ziegler. bibl f il M Labor R 100:12-18 N '77
Employment and unemployment during the first half of 1977. S. M. St Marie. il M Labor R 100:3-6 Ag '77
Inflated unemployment statistics. K. W. Clarkson and R. E. Meiners. Intellect 106:183-4 N '77
Method to measure flow and duration as unemployment rate components. R. S. Warren, Jr. bibl M Labor R 100:71-2 Mr '77
Reshaping a statistical program to meet legislative priorities. J. L. Norwood. il M Labor R 100:6-11 N '77
$16-billion problem; inadequacy of statistics for local areas. Forbes 120:58 Ag 15 '77
See also
United States—National Commission on Employment and Unemployment Statistics

Canada

Regional unemployment and job search in Canada. G. S. Barker. M. Labor R 100:42-3 O '77

Europe, Western

Europe's jobless: no end in sight? J. Ross-Skinner. il Duns R 110:54-6 Jl '77
Idle youth. D. Pauly. il Newsweek 89:53 My 23 '77
If you think U.S. has trouble finding jobs for young people... il U.S. News 83:101-2 N 28 '77
Jobless workers are turning restless. il Bus W p36-7 Ag 29 '77
When Europe tailor-makes programs for millions out of work. A. Zanker. il U.S. News 82:61-2 F 21 '77

Pennsylvania

See also
Allegheny County, Pa.—Manpower Department

United States

Beginning of wisdom about black unemployment. Fortune 96:175 O '77
Down and out; black youth. J. Lelyveld. il N Y Times Mag p 150 N 13 '77

UNEMPLOYMENT—United States—*Continued*
Employment and unemployment in 1976. R. W. Bednarzik and S. M. St Marie. bibl il M Labor R 100:3-13 F '77
Explosive issue of youth unemployment. il Bus W p64+ O 10 '77; Same with title Youth unemployment. Current 198:24-7 D '77
High unemployment could have a profund impact on free enterprise. A. R. Weber. por Duns R 109:11 Ap '77
Human right to a job. New Repub 177:2+ N 5 '77
Inflation & unemployment: the double whammy! il Sr Schol 110:13-16 N 17 '77
Is unemployment on the way out? il Forbes 121:221 Ja 9 '78
Jobless blacks; black youth. M. Stone. U.S. News 83:104 S 26 '77
Jobs: a look at the nation's most nagging problem. il U.S. News 82:54-62+ F 21 '77
More jobs don't mean less unemployment. il Bus W p29 Je 20 '77
Needed—tax reform that will create jobs. J. Kemp. Read Digest 110:103-7 Ap '77
New layer of structural unemployment; older blue-collar workers. il map Bus W p 142+ N 14 '77
Outcome of a spell of unemployment. S. H. Garfinkle. bibl f M Labor R 100:54-7 Ja '77
Rumblings in the volcano. New Repub 177:2+ Jl 30 '77
Specter of full employment. R. Lekachman. Harpers 254:35-40 F '77; Same. Current 192: 13-20 Ap '77; Discussion. Harpers 254:8+ Ap '77
Stagflation. M. J. Ulmer. New Repub 177:11-13 O 29 '77
Status quo economy. M. Harrington. Harpers 255: 34-5 S '77
Thirty years of full employment policies and growing unemployment; address, March 19, 1977. G. C. Wiegand. Vital Speeches 43:501-7 Je 1 '77
To be young, black and out of work; excerpt from Vocational Foundation Inc. report. il N Y Times Mag p38-40+ O 23 '77
Truth about unemployment. Forbes 119:97 F 15 '77
Unemployment; a strong economy without inflation; address, February 9, 1977. T. A. Murphy. Vital Speeches 43:329-33 Mr 15 '77
Why unemployment gains will be hard to come by. il Fortune 96:22+ N '77
Would the teenwage cut unemployment? il Bus W p 106-8 S 19 '77
Young blacks out of work: time bomb for U.S. D. Bacon. il U.S. News 83:22-5 D 5 '77
Young people without jobs—how real a problem. il U.S. News 82:94-6 My 9 '77
See also
Labor supply—United States

Wisconsin

In Milwaukee: if you don't work, you don't eat; Pay for Work Program. il U.S. News 82:82-3 Ap 4 '77

UNEMPLOYMENT compensation. See Insurance, Unemployment

UNEMPLOYMENT insurance. See Insurance, Unemployment

UNESCO
At long last, we're planning for the future; biosphere reserves as part of the Man and the Biosphere program. J. Doherty. il Int Wildl. 7:24-8 N '77
Call issued for support of communication activities of developing countries. UN Chron 14:70-1 Ja '77
Ceremony; appeal for funds to save the Acropolis. New Yorker 52:22-3 Ja 31 '77
Funds requested for resumption of payment of dues to UNESCO; statement, February 17, 1977. R. Toussaint. Dept State Bull 76:241-2 Mr 14 '77
Towards a new world order: Medium Term Plan (1977-1982); excerpts. il UNESCO Courier 30: 4+ Mr '77
Unesco and Latin America's cultural heritage. il UNESCO Courier 30:67-8 Ag '77
Unesco's role in alerting world opinion; position on racism in Southern Africa. UNESCO Courier 30:27 N '77
Why we need the biosphere program. T. L. Kimball. il por Int Wildlife 7:29 N '77
World debate on information: flood-tide or balanced flow? symposium. il UNESCO Courier 30:4-33 Ap '77
See also
Intergovernmental Oceanographic Commission

UNFUG, Charles S. and Schwartz, Lewis
Development pains. bibl il Environment 19:28-34 Ja '77

UNGAR, Sanford J.
Bleak house: frustration on Capitol Hill. il Atlantic 240:27-36+ Jl '77
Reports & comment: Chicago. il pors Atlantic 239:4+ Mr '77
Reports & comment: Washington (cont) Atlantic 239:6+ F; 6+ Ap; 240:4+ S; 16+ D '77
Shopping list for the FBI. por Newsweek 89:15 Ap 25 '77

UNGER, Kay
Living swell. il por Mademoiselle 83:158-61 F '77

UNGERER, Kathryn
Red dress, yellow dress; story. Esquire 87:76-8+ Mr '77

UNGERSTEDT, Urban. See Marshall, J. F. jt auth

UNHAPPINESS. See Happiness

UNICEF
$412 million for UNDP and Capital Fund; aid pledged to UNIDO, Children's Fund. il UN Chron 13:51-2 D '76
Remember UNICEF . . . for the children's sake. H. Pantaleoni. il por Parents Mag 52:42 O '77
UNICEF board approves $113.6 million for projects in developing nations. il UN Chron 14: 41-2 Jl '77

UNICORN (ship) See Sailing vessels

UNICORN Group (firm) See Investment advisers

UNIDENTIFIED flying objects. See UFOs

UNIFICATION Church (movement)
Brainwashing & religious freedom. T. Robbins. Nation 224:518 Ap 30 '77
Brainwashing Moonies; conservatorship strategy. Time 109:73 Ap 4 '77
Divine principle and the Second Advent. S. M. Heim. por Chr Cent 94:448-51 My 11 '77
Is deprograming legal? using conservatorship laws to obtain custody of young cultists. M. Montagno. il por Newsweek 89::44 F 21 '77
Letting go: everybody has the right to be wrong; deprogramming issue. J. C. Lyles. Chr Cent 94:451-3 My 11 '77
Moon trek: many enterprises. Chr Today 22:43 O 21 '77
Moonies—religious converts or psychic victims? R. A. Walsh. America 136:438-40 My 14 '77
Parents v. Moonies; conservatorship orders. J. K. Footlick and P. S. Greenberg. il Newsweek 89:83 Ap 25 '77
Rescue from a fanatic cult. C. H. Edwards. il Read Digest 110:129-33 Ap '77
Setback for what? deprogramming issue. Commonweal 104:232+ Ap 15 '77
Sun Myung Moon and the Unification Church. L. A. Belford. Intellect 105:336-7 Ap '77
Weekend with the Moonies. T. Donohoe. Intellect 105:338-9 Ap '77

UNIFORM donor cards. See Donation of organs, tissues, etc.

UNIFORMED Services University of the Health Sciences, Bethesda, Md. See United States—Uniformed Services University of the Health Sciences, Bethesda, Md.

UNIFORMS, Sports
Letter from the publisher; Marquette basketball uniforms designed by J. Campbell. J. Meyers. por Sports Illus 46:4 Ja 31 '77

UNILEVER Group-National Starch & Chemical Corporation merger. See Corporations—Acquisitions and mergers—International aspects

UNION agreements. See Collective labor agreements

UNION Avenue Bridge. See Passaic River—Bridges

UNION Camp Corporation
How Union Camp joined the billion-dollar club. il Bus W p68+ F 21 '77

UNION Carbide Corporation
Managing for an uncertain future; Union Carbide in 1996; address, November 19, 1976. W. S. Sneath. Vital Speeches 43:196-9 Ja 15 '77
Union Carbide's search for new markets. Bus W p78+ Ja 24 '77

UNION dues. See Trade unions—Dues, fees, etc.

UNION Electric Company
St Louis trash plan goes down the drain. Bus W p30-1 F 28 '77

UNION Labor Life Insurance Company. See Insurance companies

UNION membership. See Trade unions—Membership

UNION of Marxist Social Scientists. See Socialism—United States

UNION OF SOVIET SOCIALIST REPUBLICS. See Russia

UNION Pacific Corporation
Highball from a Harriman; J. H. Evans. il por Fortune 96:17 Ag '77
See also
Union Pacific Railroad

UNION Pacific Railroad
Great big railroad that could; with editorial comment. R. J. Flaherty. il Forbes 119:6, 37-40+ Je 1 '77
Great race; excerpt from Hear that lonesome whistle blow. D. Brown. il Am West 14:4-15+ My '77
Transcontinental railroad; excerpt from Hear that lonesome whistle blow. D. Brown. il Am Heritage 28:14-25 F '77

UNION shops. See Open and closed shop

UNION Theological Seminary, New York
Toward a public sense of pastoral care. D. W. Shriver, Jr. Chr Cent 94:87-8 F 2 '77

UNIONS, Labor. See Trade unions

UNIONS, Teachers. See Teachers unions

UNIPARENTALISM. See Parthenogenesis

UNIROYAL, Inc
Pressure to compromise personal ethics; results of studies at Pitney-Bowes and Uniroyal. il Bus W p 107 Ja 31 '77

UNIT pricing
Playing the numbers. J. S. King. Am Home 80:101 O '77

UNITED Airlines. See UAL, Inc

UNITED ARAB EMIRATES
See also
Americans in the United Arab Emirates

UNITED Automobile, Aerospace and Agricultural Implement Workers of America
Auto Workers' return to AFL-CIO hits a snag; with interview with D. A. Fraser. il U.S. News 82:68-9 My 30 '77
Job security and reduced work time. R. Wilhelm. Intellect 105:381 My '77
Jobs and the environment. R. F. Hall. il Conservationist 31:1 N '76
Labor on labor; Los Angeles convention. B. J. Widick. Nation 224:675-6 Je 4 '77
New stress on old solidarity. il Bus W p29-30 My 30 '77
No entangling alliances; proposed reaffiliation of the United Auto Workers Union and the AFL-CIO. B. J. Widick. Nation 225:388 O 22 '77
Piping in a new chief; D. Fraser. il por Time 109:67 My 30 '77
UAW elects its last Reuther-generation president. L. H. LeGrande. M Labor R 100:36-7 Ag '77
UAW's Doug Fraser looks ahead; interview. D. Fraser. Nation 225:171-6 S 3 '77
UAW's new chief: an ear to the young; D. A. Fraser. il por Bus W p 135+ My 16 '77

UNITED Biscuits (Holdings) Ltd. See Biscuit and cracker industry—Great Britain

UNITED Brands Company
Milstein's shake-up at United Brands. por Bus W p40 S 19 '77
United Brands shifts to a shirtsleeve boss. por Bus W p37 F 14 '77

UNITED Church of Christ
Disciples vote to resume union talks with UCC. H. E. Fey. Chr Cent 94:1021-2 N 9 '77
UCC: a libertarian stance on sexuality. W. F. Willoughby. Chr Cent 94:676-7 Ag 3 '77; Discussion. 94:815-16, 861-2, 1174 S 21-28, D 14 '77
UCC's covenants for churches in change. Chr Cent 94:1055 N 16 '77

UNITED Corporation-Baldwin, D. H, Company merger. See Corporations—Acquisitions and mergers

UNITED Farm Workers
Cesar's triumph. T. Nicholson and W. J. Cook. il Newsweek 89:70+ Mr 21 '77
Render unto Cesar. il por Time 109:81 Mr 21 '77
Trouble with Chavez: a union is not a movement. M. Yates. por Nation 225:518-20 N 19 '77
Truce ends 10-year jurisdictional dispute on farms. L. Bornstein and others. M Labor R 100:57-8 My '77

UNITED Fund of America (organization) See United Way of America (organization)

UNITED Managers, Inc. See Agricultural consultants

UNITED Merchants & Manufacturers, Inc
Death of a salesman; auctioning off the contents of all Robert Hall outlets. L. Langway and M. Reese. il Newsweek 90:64 Ag 15 '77
Rancorous bout with Chapter XI. Bus W p22-3 Ag 1 '77

UNITED Methodist Church
Should Methodists buy the church growth package? J. C. Lyles. Chr Cent 94:1214-15 D 28 '77
See also
Catholic Church—Relations—United Methodist Church

UNITED Methodist colleges and universities. See Church colleges and universities

UNITED Mine Workers of America
But life can be cruel. il Time 110:14-15 D 19 '77
Chaos in coal's labor relations. il Bus W p88+ N 28 '77
Chaos in the coal fields. T. Nicholson and C. J. Harper. il por Newsweek 89:45+ My 23 '77
Chaos in the mines; election campaigns. il pors Time 109:69-70 Je 13 '77
Close horse race in the mines. il por Time 109:54 F 7 '77
Coal and the UMW are still at odds; wildcat coal strike. Bus W p29 Ag 29 '77
Coal miners walk out. il Time 110:72+ D 12 '77
Dwindling benefits fuel a UMW strike threat. Bus W p 120+ Jl 25 '77
Election crisis in the coalfields. il Bus W p30-1 Je 13 '77
Internal politics splits Mine Workers convention. D. B. Hecker. M Labor R 100:58-61 Ja '77
King coal. J. Lelyveld. il N Y Times Mag p 111 Je 12 '77
Miller apparent victor in UMW race. L. Bornstein and others. M Labor R 100:53 Ag '77
Miller's UMW win settles very little. il Bus W p31-2 Je 27 '77
Miners' election no cure for a heap of troubles. il U.S. News 82:69-70 Je 13 '77
Miners' post-election blues. P. Primack. Nation 225:37-8 Jl 9 '77
Muddle in the mines. S. T. Atlas and J. B. Copeland. Newsweek 89:73-4 Je 27 '77
No peace in the pits. por Time 109:65 Je 27 '77
Separate peace in Western coal. il Bus W p41 D 5 '77
Soft-coal operators take a tough stance. Bus W p30 N 7 '77
Striking out of weakness? il Time 110:64+ O 24 '77
Turmoil in the miners' union. W. Sinclair. Progressive 41:29-32 Je '77
Turmoil in the UMW. T. Nicholson and T. Joyce. Newsweek 89:68-9 F 28 '77
UMW is bargaining from weakness. J. Hoerr. Bus W p30 D 19 '77
UMW is learning how to lose the West. il Bus W p 128+ Ap 18 '77
UMW's turf slowly erodes. il por Bus W p74-5 D 19 '77
Uncertain triumph. A. H. Raskin. il Sat R 4:40-1 Mr 5 '77
Unhealthy state of coalfield health care; 50 clinics. Bus W p38-9 Ag 15 '77
United mine workers: bad days in boom times. Nation 224:714-20 Je 11 '77
Why a coal strike isn't what it used to be. il U.S. News 83:86 D 19 '77
Wildcat strikes: preview of turmoil in coal fields. F. W. Frailey. il U.S. News 83:65-7 S 5 '77
Workers, strikers and unions. Nation 225:642-3 D 17 '77

UNITED NATIONS
Assembly approves resolution on medium-term plan. UN Chron 14:79+ Ja '77
Chances for progress on Middle East problem never better; excerpts from press conference, December 8, 1976. K. Waldheim. por UN Chron 14:88-9 Ja '77
Habitat plus one: what gives? actions by UN bodies. E. Carlson. Archit Rec 161:37+ Je '77
Human rights: let's mean what we say; statement, November 24, 1976. W. W. Scranton. Dept State Bull 75:745-9 D 27 '76
Mr Schreiber discusses achievements of United Nations in field of human rights; excerpts from address, April 7, 1977. M. Schreiber. il por UN Chron 14:39-40 My '77
News digest. See issues of UN chronicle
Next few weeks crucial for Middle East settlement, says Secretary-General; excerpt from transcript of press conference, September 19, 1977. K. Waldheim. UN Chron 14:45-7 O '77
Notes of the month. See issues of UN chronicle
Secretary-General's main weapons are reason, persuasion, says reappointed Mr Waldheim; address, December 8, 1976. K. Waldheim. UN Chron 14:86-7 Ja '77
Stakes high in Southern Africa, Mid-East, Cyprus; dangers of failure ominous—Secretary-General; address. K. Waldheim. UN Chron 14:5+ Ag '77
30-year struggle; with text of Universal Declaration of Human Rights. K. Vasak. UNESCO Courier 30:29-32 N '77
UN ruminations. J. Burnham. Nat R 29:987 S 2 '77
United Nations—a profile. il Dept State Bull 77:552-5 O 24 '77
United Nations, the superpowers, and proliferation. A. Bargman. Ann Am Acad 430:122-32 Mr '77
U.S. approach to the United Nations: new directions; address, July 13, 1977. C. W. Maynes. Dept State Bull 77:284-91 Ag 29 '77
See also
Food and Agriculture Organization of the United Nations
International Court of Justice, The Hague
International Day for the Elimination of Racial Discrimination
International Day of Solidarity with the Struggling People of South Africa
International Labor Organization
Unesco
World Health Organization

Ad Hoc Committee on International Terrorism

Committee on terrorism submits summary of views to Assembly. UN Chron 14:54 Ap '77

Ad Hoc Committee on the Drafting of an International Convention Against the Taking of Hostages

Hostages Committee recommends that work be continued during 1978. UN Chron 14:45 Ag '77
35-member group established to draft convention against taking hostages. UN Chron 14:81 Ja '77
U.S. supports establishment of U.N. Ad Hoc Committee on Drafting of Convention Against Taking of Hostages; statements, with text of resolution, November 29, December 10 and 15, 1976. R. Rosenstock; W. T. Bennett, Jr. Dept State Bull 76:72-5 Ja 24 '77

UNITED NATIONS—*Continued*

Ad Hoc Committee on the Indian Ocean

Great powers consulted regarding co-operation with Indian Ocean body. UN Chron 14:19 My '77

Zone of peace in the Indian Ocean. Tran-van-Dinh. Chr Cent 94:524-5 Je 1 '77

Ad Hoc Committee on the Restructuring of the Economic and Social Sectors of the United Nations System

Restructuring body focuses on three problem areas. UN Chron 14:43+ Ap '77

Ad Hoc Group on Equal Rights for Women

Secretary-General addresses women's group on rights; March 8, 1977. K. Waldheim. il UN Chron 14:51 Ap '77

Ad Hoc Intergovernmental Working Group on the Problem of Corrupt Practices

Group on practices of transnationals reaches agreement on major issues; Intergovernmental Working Group on the Problem of Corrupt Practices. UN Chron 14:31 Mr '77

Plenipotentiary talks favoured by Working Group. UN Chron 14:43 Jl '77

Administrative and Budgetary Committee

Assembly calls for strengthening of administrative management service. UN Chron 14:79 Ja '77

Eight appointed to administrative and budgetary bodies. UN Chron 13:56 D '76

Armed Forces

Forces in Cyprus

Mandate of Cyprus Peace-keeping Force extended until December; with text of resolution. il UN Chron 14:11-17 Jl '77

Secretary-General reports tension persists in Cyprus; mandate of Peace-keeping Force extended six months. il UN Chron 14:10-16+ Ja '77

U.N. Force in Cyprus extended for six months; UNFICYP; statement, with text of resolution, June 15-16, 1977. J. F. Leonard. Dept State Bull 77:133-4 Jl 25 '77

Forces in the Middle East

Assembly appropriates $92 million for Middle East Peace-keeping Forces. UN Chron 14:74-5 Ja '77

Mandate of Golan Heights Peace Force renewed for six months until May 1977. il UN Chron 13:24-5 D '76

U.N. Disengagement Observer Force in Israel-Syria sector extended; statement, May 26, 1977. J. F. Leonard. Dept State Bull 77:90-1 Jl 18 '77

U.N. Emergency Force in the Sinai extended for one year; statement, October 21, 1977. J. F. Leonard. Dept State Bull 77:866-7 D 12 '77

Assembly

See United Nations—General Assembly

Budget

See United Nations—Finance

Capital Development Fund

$412 million for UNDP and Capital Fund; aid pledged to UNIDO, Children's Fund. il UN Chron 13:51-2 D '76

Charter

U.S. gives views on U.S.S.R. proposal for world treaty on the non-use of force; statements, October 28, 29 and November 22, 1976. R. Rosenstock; A. W. Sherer, Jr. Dept State Bull 76:30-5 Ja 10 '77

See also

United Nations—Special Committee on the Charter of the United Nations and on the Strengthening of the Role of the Organization

Commission for Social Development

Social Commission acts on problems of crime prevention, youth, food and income distribution. il UN Chron 14:35-8 Mr '77

Commission on Human Rights

Growing role of mass media noted by committee. UN Chron 14:33-4 Mr '77

Human Rights Commission acts on situations in southern Africa and Israeli-occupied Territories. il UN Chron 14:44-8 Ap '77

Implementing United Nations covenants. A. G. Mower, Jr. bibl il Society 15:76-80 N '77

See also

United Nations—Sub-Commission on Prevention of Discrimination and Protection of Minorities

Commission on International Trade Law

Commission on Trade Law approves draft convention on sale of goods. UN Chron 14:44 Jl '77

UNCITRAL group considers draft on bills of exchange. UN Chron 14:47 Ag '77

Commission on Narcotic Drugs

Commission calls for greater control of psychotropic substances. UN Chron 14:38-40 Mr '77

Commission on the Status of Women

Draft convention on women's rights adopted. il UN Chron 14:66 Ja '77

Committee for Program and Co-ordination

Programme Committee urges shift of resources to transport sector. UN Chron 14:39-40 Jl '77

Committee of Twenty-four

See United Nations—Special Committee on the Situation with Regard to the Implementation of the Declaration on the Granting of Independence to Colonial Countries and Peoples

Committee on Disarmament

Conference of Committee on Disarmament continues meetings. UN Chron 14:34 Ap '77

Disarmament club at work. M. Fartash. il por Bull Atom Sci 33:57-62 Ja '77

Secretary-General hopes for progress at disarmament talks. K. Waldheim. UN Chron 14: 19 Mr '77

Committee on Human Rights

Human Rights Committee adopts guidelines for States' reports. il UN Chron 14:41-2 Ag '77

Implementing United Nations convenants. A. G. Mower, Jr. bibl il Society 15:76-80 N '77

S-G sees beginning of work of human rights body as important milestone. UN Chron 14:49 Ap '77

Committee on Natural Resources

World energy situation would be dominated by oil until end of century but coal likely to make significant comeback. il UN Chron 14: 41-3 My '77

Committee on Non-governmental Organizations

See United Nations—Council Committee on Non-governmental Organizations

Committee on Relations with the Host Country

Host Country urged to prevent acts against missions. UN Chron 14:83 Ja '77

Committee on Science and Technology for Development

Committee on Science, Technology drafts plans for 1979 conference. il UN Chron 14:24-5 Mr '77

Committee on Shipping

See United Nations Conference on Trade and Development

Committee on the Elimination of Racial Discrimination

Committee on Elimination of Racial Discrimination examines reports. UN Chron 14:35-6 il My '77

Committee takes decisions on Cyprus, West Bank of Jordan River situations. UN Chron 14:40-1 Ag '77

Committee on the Exercise of the Inalienable Rights of the Palestinian People

Chairman reports on contacts with West members of Security Council. UN Chron 14:19-20 Jl '77

Committee urges implementation of recommendations. il UN Chron 14:31 O '77

Israel, West nations of Security Council asked for positions. il UN Chron 14:21 My '77

U.S. votes against U.N. resolution on question of Palestine; statement, November 23, 1976. W. W. Scranton. Dept State Bull 76:41-2 Ja 17 '77

Committee on the Peaceful Uses of Outer Space

Significant progress made, says chairman of legal sub-committee. UN Chron 14:22 My '77

Sub-committee stresses importance to developing states of on-site training. UN Chron 14: 18+ Mr '77

Task force to study implications of proposed space conference. il UN Chron 14:33-4 Jl '77

UNITED NATIONS—*Continued*

Council Committee on Non-governmental Organizations

Consultative status urged for 18 non-govt. organizations. UN Chron 14:34 Mr '77
NGOs to be asked to report on 4-yr. span of activities. UN Chron 14:34 My '77

Delegates

Salaries, allowances, etc.

Assembly authorizes salary changes recommended by civil service body. UN Chron 14:75 Ja '77

Development Program

$412 million for UNDP and Capital Fund; aid pledged to UNIDO, Children's Fund. il UN Chron 13:51-2 D '76
Governing council seeks to make UNDP more responsive to changing needs of developing countries. il UN Chron 14:37-8 Ag '77
UNDP Governing Council approves $603 million aid for 15 countries and for global and regional projects. UN Chron 14:26-9 Mr '77
U.S. contributions to UNDP and other development funds; statement, November 2, 1977. M. Wells. Dept State Bull 77:872 D 12 '77
United States seeks improved U.N. programs to meet basic needs of world's poor; address, June 16, 1977. J. J. Gilligan. Dept State Bull 77:204-7 Ag 15 '77

Economic and Social Commission for Asia and the Pacific

Commission welcomes new agreement on development of Mekong River basin. UN Chron 14:32 My '77

Economic and Social Council

Challenge to the Economic and Social Council: advancing the quality of life in all its aspects; address, April 19, 1977. A. J. Young, Jr. Dept State Bull 76:494-502 My 16 '77
Framework for a dynamic North-South dialogue; statement, July 8, 1977. A. J. Young. Dept State Bull 77:383-9 S 19 '77
See also
United Nations—Commission for Social Development
United Nations—Committee for Program and Coordination
United Nations—Committee on Natural Resources
United Nations—Council Committee on Non-governmental Organizations

Meetings, 1976

Record of the month:
Council decides to place permanent headquarters of ECWA at Baghdad. UN Chron 13:53 D '76

Meetings, 1977

Record of the month:
Council acts on Ghana's withdrawal of offer to host anti-racism conference. UN Chron 14:32 Mr '77
ECOSOC calls for more aid for front-line African states. il UN Chron 14:29-36 Ag '77
NGOs to be asked to report on 4-yr. span of activities. UN Chron 14:34 My '77

Economic Commission for Africa

Conference of African ministers stresses self-help, stronger ECA role. UN Chron 14:41-2 Ap '77

Economic Commission for Europe

ECE to consider convening high-level meeting on protecting environment. il UN Chron 14:30-1 My '77

Economic Commission for Latin America

Caribbean countries move towards closer co-operation; Caribbean Development and Co-operation Committee. UN Chron 14:40 Ap '77
New unity and a new hope in the Western hemisphere: economic growth with social justice; statement, May 3, 1977. A. J. Young, Jr. Dept State Bull 76:567-76 My 30 '77

Economic Commission for Western Asia

Council decides to place permanent headquarters of ECWA at Baghdad. UN Chron 13:53 D '76
ECWA to assist in reconstruction of Lebanon. UN Chron 14:31 My '77

Employees

Sexual harassment on the job: UN's dirty little secret. M. Kelber. Ms 6:51+ N '77
See also
United Nations—Secretariat

Salaries, allowances, etc.

High pay at the U.N—it's drawing fire. il U.S. News 83:61 Ag 29 '77

Environment Program

Campaign to cleanse the Mediterranean. il Bus W p32-3 O 31 '77
International cooperation to protect the whales; UNEP and FAO. S. J. Holt. il Oceans 10:62-4 Jl '77
Mediterranean "Blue Plan" discussed at five-day environment meeting in Yugoslavia. UN Chron 14:32 Mr '77
Prescription for world survival. il Time 109:59 Je 13 '77
United States discusses environmental problems; statement, October 20, 1977. J. C. Kennedy. Dept State Bull 77:868-71 D 12 '77
United to protect the Mediterranean. P. S. Thacher. il Oceans 10:58-61 Ja '77

Finance

New scale of assessments approved; 28 states to pay more, 30 to pay less; with text of resolution. UN Chron 14:72, 104-6 Ja '77
1976-77 budget increased by $38 million to $783,932,900. UN Chron 14:73-4 Ja '77
See also
United Nations—Joint Inspection Unit
United Nations Joint Staff Pension Fund

General Assembly

Sessions (31st)

Ambassador Scranton's assessment of the 31st U.N. General Assembly; statement, December 22, 1976. W. W. Scranton. Dept State Bull 76:68-70 Ja 24 '77
Officers of thirty-first session of Assembly. il UN Chron 13:36-7 D '76
Peace in the Middle East; address, December 6, 1976. C. Herzod. Vital Speeches 43:170-3 Ja 1 '77
Record of the month:
Agencies asked to give urgent moral, material aid to colonial peoples. UN Chron 13:46-7 D '76
Angola admitted as 146th member state; minister says foreign policies based on non-alignment principles. UN Chron 13:12 D '76
Assembly action paves way for Agricultural Fund to attain target of $1,000 million; with text of resolution. UN Chron 14:44, 107 Ja '77
Assembly acts on disabled persons, narcotics, world social situation. UN Chron 14:67-9 Ja '77
Assembly acts on economic co-operation; with text of resolution. UN Chron 14:55, 106-7 Ja '77
Assembly acts on UNCTAD decisions on debt burdens, land-locked countries; with text of resolution. UN Chron 14:45-7, 113-15 Ja '77
Assembly adopts 4 resolutions on youth problems. UN Chron 14:67 Ja '77
Assembly adopts nine resolutions, two decisions on environment questions. UN Chron 14:47-9+ Ja '77
Assembly adopts resolutions on three United Nations technical conferences. UN Chron 14:53-4 Ja '77
Assembly adopts 10 resolutions calling for action against apartheid policies of South Africa; with text of resolution. UN Chron 13:38-45, 77-80 D '76
Assembly adopts two resolutions on World Food Council. UN Chron 14:44-5 Ja '77
Assembly appoints Mr Waldheim Secretary-General for second term. UN Chron 14:40 Ja '77
Assembly appropriates $92 million for Middle East Peace-keeping Forces. UN Chron 14:74-5 Ja '77
Assembly approves plan to transfer some offices from New York to Vienna. il UN Chron 14:77-8 Ja '77
Assembly approves resolution on medium-term plan. UN Chron 14:79+ Ja '77
Assembly approves statutes of Joint Inspection Unit. UN Chron 14:78 Ja '77
Assembly asks states to facilitate early independence; with text of resolution. UN Chron 14:33-4, 99-100 Ja '77
Assembly asks urgent aid for Cape Verde. UN Chron 13:54 D '76
Assembly authorizes salary changes recommended by civil service body. UN Chron 14:75 Ja '77
Assembly calls for high priority for moon treaty and remote sensing questions. UN Chron 13:33 D '76
Assembly calls for more funds for university. UN Chron 14:59 Ja '77
Assembly calls for resumption of Geneva peace talks not later than March this year with PLO participation; with texts of resolutions. UN Chron 14:17-19, 101-2 Ja '77
Assembly calls for sound investment in developing countries of resources of Pension Fund. UN Chron 14:76 Ja '77
Assembly calls for strengthening of administrative management service. UN Chron 14:79 Ja '77

UNITED NATIONS—General Assembly—Sessions (31st)—*Continued*

Assembly calls for wider exchange of information on technology. UN Chron 14:57-9 Ja '77

Assembly calls on Chile to end torture; reexamine basis of state of siege; with text of resolution. UN Chron 14:62-3, 107-8 Ja '77

Assembly commends activities of Office of Relief Co-ordinator. UN Chron 14:43 Ja '77

Assembly concerned at Paris Conference failure to achieve concrete results; Conference on International Economic Co-operation; with text of resolution. UN Chron 13:50-1, 82 D '76

Assembly condemns collaboration with southern Africa racist régimes. UN Chron 14:61 Ja '77

Assembly decides on States Succession Conference in Vienna in April-May 1977. UN Chron 13:56-7 D '76

Assembly decides to convene in Ghana a World Conference to Combat Racism. UN Chron 14:59-60 Ja '77

Assembly endorses call for Israeli withdrawal from occupied lands; with text of resolution. UN Chron 13:29-31+, 83 D '76

Assembly hopes Geneva talks will lead to independence with majority rule; with text of resolution. il UN Chron 14:30, 111-13 Ja '77

Assembly pays tribute to Simón Bolívar. UN Chron 14:27 Ja '77

Assembly rejects Indonesia integration claim; calls again for forces withdrawal; with text of resolution. UN Chron 14:32-3, 100 Ja '77

Assembly sends admission issue back to Council for reconsideration; admitting Viet Nam; with text of resolution. UN Chron 13:17-23, 83 D '76

Assembly supports armed struggle for freedom; with text of resolutions. il UN Chron 14:28-9, 109-11 Ja '77

Assembly suspends session; to consider economic questions on resumption. il UN Chron 14:84-5+ Ja '77

Assembly tells Israel to halt further removal of refugees from Gaza Camps; with text of resolution. UN Chron 13:32-3, 82-3 D '76

Assembly to hold special session on disarmament questions next year; with text of resolutions. UN Chron 14:21, 102-4; 115-16 Ja '77

Assembly welcomes OAU efforts to find African solutions. UN Chron 13:48 D '76

Call for continued negotiations between Greek and Turkish communities in Cyprus. il UN Chron 13:26-8 D '76

Call to halt illicit traffic in works of art. UN Chron 14:69+ Ja '77

Conference to mobilize support for Peoples of Namibia and Zimbabwe. UN Chron 14:31-3 Ja '77

Consensus adopted on Ganges waters dispute between Bangladesh, India. UN Chron 13:35-6 D '76

Criteria adopted for management of voluntary fund for Women's Decade; with text of resolution. UN Chron 14:65-6, 108-9 Ja '77

Destruction of Quneitra condemned; Assembly says Syria entitled to full compensation. UN Chron 14:20-6 Ja '77

Developed countries urged to carry out plan for redeployment of industries. UN Chron 14:50-1 Ja '77

Economic aid urged for Angola, Comoros, Mozambique, Sao Tome and Principe. UN Chron 14:41-2 Ja '77

France asked to implement plan for independence by summer this year; with text of resolution. UN Chron 14:34-5, 100-1 Ja '77

Further study urged of draft treaty on non-use of force. UN Chron 13:48-9 D '76

Host Country urged to prevent acts against missions. UN Chron 14:83 Ja '77

International Conference on Carriage of Goods by Sea to be convened in 1978. UN Chron 14:82 Ja '77

Judges salaries to be reviewed next four years; International Court of Justice. il UN Chron 14:80 Ja '77

Military bases on Guam declared incompatible with Charter purposes. UN Chron 14:35-9 Ja '77

More top-level posts urged for persons from developing countries and women; Secretariat staff; with text of resolution. UN Chron 13:55, 83-4 D '76

New scale of assessments approved; 28 states to pay more, 30 to pay less; with text of resolution. UN Chron 14:72, 104-6 Ja '77

1976-77 budget increased by $38 million to $783,932,900. UN Chron 14:73-4 Ja '77

1979 proclaimed International Year of the Child by assembly; with text of resolution. UN Chron 14:55-7, 115 Ja '77

Peace-keeping Committee gets extended mandate. UN Chron 14:19 Ja '77

Resumed Assembly session fails to agree on Paris conference achievements. il UN Chron 14:32-5 O '77

Samoa admitted to UN membership. il UN Chron 14:39 Ja '77

States condemned for supporting foreign economic interests which exploit territories; with text of resolution. UN Chron 13:45-6, 81-2 D '76

Techniques used to destabilize govts. condemned. UN Chron 14:27 Ja '77

35-member group established to draft convention against taking hostages. UN Chron 14:81 Ja '77

Transfer of resources to developing countries on assured basis urged. UN Chron 14:51-3 Ja '77

Urgent need to aid South African student refugees recognized. UN Chron 14:64-5 Ja '77

United States discusses disarmament issues in U.N. General Assembly debate; statements, with text of resolution, November 1, 18 and December 10, 1976. F. C. Iklé; J. Martin, Jr. Dept State Bull 76:17-29 Ja 10 '77

U.S. gives views in General Assembly debate on the Middle East; statement, with texts of resolutions, December 9, 1976. W. W. Scranton. Dept State Bull 76:37-40 Ja 17 '77

Sessions (32d)

Allocation of United Nations agenda items by committee. Dept State Bull 77:561-6 O 24 '77

Assembly adopts agenda with wide range of questions. il UN Chron 14:48-51+ O '77

Crucial test for Carter as world leader. il por U.S. News 83:23-4 S 26 '77

Record of the month:

Assembly opens new session; Admission of Viet Nam, Djibouti brings membership to 149. il UN Chron 14:5-10 O '77

Date recommended for special session on disarmament. UN Chron 14:28 O '77

Headquarters

Assembly approves plan to transfer some offices from New York to Vienna. il UN Chron 14:77-8 Ja '77

High Commissioner for Refugees

$16 million aid sought for refugees in southern Africa. UN Chron 14:28 Jl '77

United States reaffirms support of UNHCR programs; statement. November 15, 1976. J. Picker. Dept State Bull 75:756-8 D 27 '76

International Law Commission

Law Commission adopts articles on three priority questions. UN Chron 14:46 Ag '77

Joint Inspection Unit

Assembly approves statute of Joint Inspection Unit. UN Chron 14:78 Ja '77

Membership

Angola admitted as 146th member state; minister says foreign policies based on non-alignment principles. UN Chron 13:12 D '76

Assembly opens new session; Admission of Viet Nam, Djibouti brings membership to 149. il UN Chron 14:5-10 O '77

Assembly sends admission issue back to Council for reconsideration; admitting Viet Nam; with text of resolution. UN Chron 13:17-23, 83 D '76

Samoa admitted to UN membership. il UN Chron 14:39 Ja '77

Security Council again fails to support Viet Nam for United Nations membership. UN Chron 13:16+ D '76

Security Council recommendation paves way for action by Assembly; admitting Angola to membership. UN Chron 13:12-15+ D '76

Non-governmental organizations

NGOs. J. F. Green. bibl il Society 15:65-70 N '77

Opportunities for effective NGO action at United Nations discussed. UN Chron 14:42 Ap '77

Outer Space Committee

See United Nations—Committee on the Peaceful Uses of Outer Space

Publications

Bibliography

Documents; selected list. See issues of UN chronicle

Publications, official records. See issues of UN chronicle

Secretariat

More top-level posts urged for persons from developing countries and women; Secretariat staff; with text of resolution. UN Chron 13:55, 83-4 D '76

Secretary-General pays tribute to Secretariat. UN Chron 14:40-1 Ja '77

UNITED NATIONS—*Continued*

Security Council

Meetings, 1976

Record of the month:
Council agrees on Lesotho aid following South Africa's closure of border posts. il UN Chron 14:5-9+ Ja '77
Council expresses concern over serious situation in occupied Arab territories. il UN Chron 13:5-11+ D '76
Mandate of Golan Heights Peace Force renewed for six months until May 1977. il UN Chron 13:24-5 D '76
Secretary-General reports tension persists in Cyprus; mandate of Peace-keeping Force extended six months. il UN Chron 14:10-16+ Ja '77
Security Council again fails to support Viet Nam for United Nations membership. il UN Chron 13:16+ D '76
Security Council recommendation paves way for action by Assembly; admitting Angola to membership. UN Chron 13:12-15+ D '76
U.S. joins Security Council appeal for assistance to Lesotho; statement, with text of resolution, December 22, 1976. A. W. Sherer, Jr. Dept State Bull 76:51-2 Ja 17 '77

Meetings, 1977

Record of the month:
Council condemns Southern Rhodesia attack against Mozambique. il UN Chron 14:5-10+ Jl '77
Council debates Secretary-General's report on Middle East question. il UN Chron 14:16-23+ Ap '77
Council receives four draft resolutions on question of South Africa. il UN Chron 14:5-15+ Ap '77
Council sends mission to Benin to investigate attack on city; with text of resolution. il UN Chron 14:5-9+ Mr '77
Council strongly condemns act of armed aggression against Benin; with text of resolution adopted. il UN Chron 14:5-17 My '77
Council votes for appointment of UN representative; with text of resolution. il UN Chron 14:11-16 O '77
Council warns unilateral actions in Cyprus could endanger prospects of peaceful settlement; with text of resolution. il UN Chron 14:17-22 O '77
Israel, West nations of Security Council asked for positions. il UN Chron 14:21 My '77
Mandate of Cyprus Peace-keeping Force extended until December; with text of resolution. il UN Chron 14:11-17 Jl '77
Secretary-General reports to Council on first round of new Cyprus talks. il por UN Chron 14:17-18+ My '77
Security Council told main elements of Middle East issue remain difficult. UN Chron 14:14-15+ Mr '77
U.N. Security Council condemns South Africa's apartheid policy and imposes a mandatory arms embargo; statements, with text of resolutions, October 31, and November 4, 1977. A. J. Young. Dept State Bull 77:859-66 D 12 '77
U.S. abstains on Security Council resolution on Botswana complaint; statements, with text of resolution, January 13-14, 1977. W. W. Scranton; A. W. Sherer, Jr. Dept State Bull 76:117-19 F 7 '77

Space Committee

See United Nations—Committee on the Peaceful Uses of Outer Space

Special Committee Against Apartheid

Apartheid Committee pays tribute to deceased young African leader; Mr Biko left deep mark on South African scene, says Secretary-General. UN Chron 14:25-6 O '77
Committee told of mass South Africa arrests; UN investigation urged. UN Chron 14:20-1 Mr '77
Nordic initiatives on southern Africa very significant—chairman. UN Chron 14:24-5 My '77
United Nations marks Day for Elimination of Race Discrimination. il UN Chron 14:30-3 Ap '77

Special Committee on Decolonization

See United Nations—Special Committee on the Situation with Regard to the Implementation of the Declaration on the Granting of Independence to Colonial Countries and Peoples

Special Committee on Peace-keeping Operations

Peace-keeping Committee gets extended mandate. UN Chron 14:19 Ja '77
Renewed work on peace-keeping guidelines urged. UN Chron 14:23 Mr '77

Special Committee on the Charter of the United Nations and on the Strengthening of the Role of the Organization

Charter Committee completes first reading of study of states' views. UN Chron 14:52-3 Ap '77

Special Committee on the Situation with Regard to the Implementation of the Declaration on the Granting of Independence to Colonial Countries and Peoples

Activities of foreign economic interests, military bases condemned. UN Chron 14:12-14 Ag '77
Committee acts on visiting missions, implementation of declaration. UN Chron 14:19-20 Ag '77
Committee acts on visiting missions' reports on Caymans, US Virgin Islands. UN Chron 14:26-7 O '77
Committee ends debate on Rhodesia but defers decision to later stage. UN Chron 14:26-8 My '77
Committee of 24 adopts decisions on Bermuda, Solomons, Tokelau, Pitcairn. UN Chron 14:23-4 Jl '77
Committee urges settlement with full participation of people. UN Chron 14:11-12 Ag '77
Decolonization Committee adopts reports on small territories. UN Chron 14:15 Ag '77
Decolonization Committte begins work with consideration of Namibia question. UN Chron 14:21-3 Mr '77
Decolonization Committee condemns South Africa's occupation of Namibia. UN Chron 14:27-9 Ap '77
Former Premier calls for full UK, US commitment; question of Southern Rhodesia. il por UN Chron 14:25 Jl '77
Joint committee endorses plan for southern Africa conference. UN Chron 14:26-7 Ap '77
Rhodesia industry dominated by foreign economic interests: investments in Namibia uranium resources expected to rise. UN Chron 13:62+ D '76
Study of Puerto Rico, East Timor, Western Sahara questions deferred. il UN Chron 14:14-15 Ag '77

Special Committee to Investigate Israeli Practices Affecting the Human Rights of the Population of the Occupied Territories

Safeguards urged for protection of human rights in occupied territories. UN Chron 13:63-4 D '76

Study and teaching

Model U.N. New Yorker 53:35 My 9 '77

Sub-Commission on Prevention of Discrimination and Protection of Minorities

Sub-Commision seeks protection of gaoled persons, minority groups; Working Group on Slavery meets. UN Chron 14:43-4 Ag '77

Trusteeship Council

Trusteeship Council welcomes recognition of need for unity in Micronesia. il UN Chron 14:20-2+ Jl '77

Voting

Changing the United Nations. R. Hudson. Current 189:48-55 Ja '77

Womens participation

Sexual harassment on the job: UN's dirty little secret. M. Kelber. Ms 6:51+ N '77

Working Group on Slavery

See United Nations—Sub-Commission on Prevention of Discrimination and Protection of Minorities

Africa

Agencies asked to give urgent moral, material aid to colonial peoples. UN Chron 13:46-7 D '76
Operation tsetse fly; livestock vs wildlife in United Nations tsetse fly control project. N. Myers. il Int Wildlife 7:33-5 My '77

Africa, Southern

Activities of foreign economic interests, military bases condemned. UN Chron 14:12-14 Ag '77
Human Rights Commission acts on situations in southern Africa and Israeli-occupied territories. il UN Chron 14:44-8 Ap '77
Secretary-General speaks of Middle East, Uganda, Southern Africa, new United States spirit towards United Nations; excerpts from transcript of news conference, March 1, 1977. K. Waldheim. UN Chron 14:56-7 Ap '77
$16 million aid sought for refugees in southern Africa. UN Chron 14:28 Jl '77
Southern Africa at grips with racism; symposium. il maps UNESCO Courier 30:4-32 N '77

UNITED NATIONS—*Continued*

Angola

Angola admitted as 146th member state; minister says foreign policies based on non-alignment principles. UN Chron 13:12 D '76

Security Council recommendation paves way for action by Assembly. UN Chron 13:12-15+ D '76

Arab countries

Assembly endorses call for Israeli withdrawal from occupied lands; with text of resolution. UN Chron 13:29-31+, 83 D '76

Council expresses concern over serious situation in occupied Arab territories. il UN Chron 13:5-11+ D '76

Belize

Assembly asks states to facilitate early independence; with text of resolution. UN Chron 14:33-4, 99-100 Ja '77

Benin

Council sends mission to Benin to investigate attack on city; with text of resolution. il UN Chron 14:5-9+ Mr '77

Council strongly condemns act of armed aggression against Benin; with text of resolution adopted. il UN Chron 14:5-17 My '77

United States joins consensus on U.N. resolution on Benin; statement, with text of resolution, April 14, 1977. A. W. Sherer, Jr. Dept State Bull 76:502-3 My 16 '77

Bermuda

Committee of 24 adopts decisions on Bermuda, Solomons, Tokelau, Pitcairn. UN Chron 14:23-4 Jl '77

Botswana

Security Council missions recommend assistance for Botswana and Lesotho. UN Chron 14:44-5 My '77

U.S. abstains on Security Council resolution on Botswana complaint; statements, with text of resolution, January 13-14, 1977. W. W. Scranton; A. W. Sherer, Jr. Dept State Bull 76:117-19 F 7 '77

Cape Verde Islands

Assembly asks urgent aid for Cape Verde. UN Chron 13:54 D '76

Cayman Islands

Committee acts on visiting missions' reports on Caymans, US Virgin Islands. UN Chron 14:26-7 O '77

Cyprus

Call for continued negotiations between Greek and Turkish communities in Cyprus. il UN Chron 13:26-8 D '76

Committee takes decisions on Cyprus, West Bank of Jordan River situations. UN Chron 14:40-1 Ag '77

Council warns unilateral actions in Cyprus could endanger prospects of peaceful settlement; with text of resolution. il UN Chron 14:17-22 O '77

Secretary-General reports to Council on first round of new Cyprus talks. il por UN Chron 14:17-18+ My '77

See also

United Nations—Armed Forces—Forces in Cyprus

Denmark

Nordic initiatives on southern Africa very significant—chairman. UN Chron 14:24-5 My '77

Djibouti

Assembly opens new session: Admission of Viet-Nam, Djibouti brings membership to 149. il UN Chron 14:5-10 O '77

Djibouti attains independence, 27 June. UN Chron 14:25 Jl '77

U.S. supports U.N. membership of Djibouti; statement, July 7, 1977. D. F. McHenry. Dept State Bull 77:226 Ag 22 '77

Indonesia

Assembly rejects Indonesia integration claim; calls again for forces withdrawal; with text of resolution. UN Chron 14:32-3, 100 Ja '77

Israel

Anti-Zionist resolution. B. Lewis; reply with rejoinder. A. M. Elmessiri. For Affairs 55:641-2 Ap '77

Assembly tells Israel to halt further removal of refugees from Gaza Camps; with text of resolution. UN Chron 13:32-3, 82-3 D '76

Human Rights Commission acts on situations in southern Africa and Israeli-occupied territories. il UN Chron 14:44-8 Ap '77

Lebanon

See also

United Nations Trust Fund for Assistance to Lebanon

Lesotho

Council agrees on Lesotho aid following South Africa's closure of border posts. il UN Chron 14:5-9+ Ja '77

Security Council missions recommend assistance for Botswana and Lesotho. UN Chron 14:44-5 My '77

U.S. joins Security Council appeal for assistance to Lesotho; statement, with text of resolution, December 22, 1976. A. W. Sherer, Jr. Dept State Bull 76:51-2 Ja 17 '77

Middle East

Committee takes decisions on Cyprus, West Bank of Jordan River situations. UN Chron 14-40-1 Ag '77

Council debates Secretary-General's report on Middle East question. il UN Chron 14:16-23+ Ap '77

Secretary-General speaks of Middle East, Uganda, Southern Africa, new United States spirit towards United Nations; excerpts from transcript of news conference, March 1, 1977. K. Waldheim. UN Chron 14:56-7 Ap '77

Security Council told main elements of Middle East issue remain difficult. UN Chron 14:14-15 Mr '77

U.S. gives views in General Assembly debate on the Middle East; statement; with texts of resolutions, December 9, 1976. W. W. Scranton. Dept State Bull 76:37-40 Ja 17 '77

See also

United Nations—Armed forces—Forces in the Middle East

United Nations—Committee on the Exercise of the Inalienable Rights of the Palestinian People

Mozambique

Council condemns Southern Rhodesia attack against Mozambique. il UN Chron 14:5-10+ Jl '77

Namibia

Assembly supports armed struggle for freedom; with text of resolutions. il UN Chron 14:28-9, 109-11 Ja '77

Committee urges settlement with full participation of people. UN Chron 14:11-12 Ag '77

Decolonization Committee begins work with consideration of Namibia question. UN Chron 14:21-3 Mr '77

Decolonization Committee condemns South Africa's occupation of Namibia. UN Chron 14:27-9 Ap '77

Namibia moves towards independence. S. MacBride. il map UNESCO Courier 30:16-20 N '77

U.S. reaffirms commitment to self-determination and independence for Namibia; statements, with texts of resolutions, December 2, 10, and 20, 1976. W. W. Scranton; S. Hess. Dept State Bull 76:43-8 Ja 17 '77

See also

International Conference in Support of the Peoples of Zimbabwe and Namibia, 1977

Norway

Nordic initiatives on southern Africa very significant—chairman. UN Chron 14:24-5 My '77

Puerto Rico

Study of Puerto Rico, East Timor, Western Sahara questions deferred. il UN Chron 14:14-15 Ag '77

Rhodesia

Ambassador Young testifies on Rhodesian sanctions bill; statement, February 24, 1977. A. J. Young. Dept State Bull 76:271-2 Mr 21 '77

Assembly hopes Geneva talks will lead to independence with majority rule; with text of resolution. il UN Chron 14:30, 111-13 Ja '77

Committee ends debate on Rhodesia but defers decision to later stage. UN Chron 14:26-8 My '77

Committee urges settlement with full participation of people. UN Chron 14:11-12 Ag '77

Council condemns Southern Rhodesia attack against Mozambique. il UN Chron 14:5-10+ Jl '77

Council votes for appointment of UN representative; with text of resolution. il UN Chron 14:11-16 O '77

Former Premier calls for full UK, US commitment; question of Southern Rhodesia. il por UN Chron 14:25 Jl '77

Lynching Rhodesia; UN's May 27 resolution. Nat R 29:766 Jl 8 '77

On crushing Rhodesia. W. F. Buckley, Jr. Nat R 29:1195 O 14 '77

U.S. reiterates support for negotiated solution in Rhodesia; statement, with text of resolutions, December 13, 14 and 20, 1976. W. W. Scranton; R. Petree; A. W. Sherer, Jr. Dept State Bull 76:53-7 Ja 17 '77

U.S. supports expansion of sanctions against Rhodesia; statement, with text of resolution, May 27, 1977. J. F. Leonard. Dept State Bull 77:66-7 Jl 11 '77

See also

International Conference in Support of the Peoples of Zimbabwe and Namibia, 1977

UNITED NATIONS—*Continued*

Russia

Secretary-General visits USSR, Mongolia. il pors UN Chron 14:29-30 O '77

Solomon Islands

Committee of 24 adopts decisions on Bermuda, Solomons, Tokelau, Pitcairn. UN Chron 14:23-4 Jl '77

South Africa

Anniversary of Soweto incident observed. il UN Chron 14:27-8 Jl '77
Assembly adopts 10 resolutions calling for action against apartheid policies of South Africa; with text of resolution. UN Chron 13:38-45, 77-80 D '76
Council receives four draft resolutions on question of South Africa. il UN Chron 14:5-15+ Ap '77
Decolonization Committee condemns South Africa's occupation of Namibia. UN Chron 14:27-9 Ap '77
Lagos conference described as landmark in long struggle to eradicate apartheid. il UN Chron 14:29-31 Jl '77
Limited action against apartheid; UN imposition of mandatory arms embargo. il Time 110: 35-6 N 14 '77
Loneliness is an enemy; proposed arms embargo. il Time 110:36-7 N 7 '77
Message to Pretoria. R. Steele and others. il Newsweek 90:30-1 N 7 '77
Mood in South Africa: defiance, bitterness, anger; with interview with B. J. Vorster. K. M. Chrysler. il U.S. News 83:38-40 N 21 '77
Trade unions asked to put pressure on white southern African régimes; International Conference of Trade Unions Against Apartheid. il UN Chron 14:26-7 Jl '77
U.N. Security Council condemns South Africa's apartheid policy and imposes a mandatory arms embargo; statements, with text of resolutions, October 31, and November 4, 1977. A. J. Young. Dept State Bull 77:859-66 D 12 '77
United States urges peaceful change in South Africa; statements, November 3 and 9, 1976. S. Hess; R. P. Hupp. Dept State Bull 76:48-51 Ja 17 '77
Voting the embargo. K. Willenson and others. il Newsweek 90:62 N 14 '77

Sri Lanka

Zone of peace in the Indian Ocean. Tran-van-Dinh. Chr Cent 94:524-5 Je 1 '77

Sweden

Nordic initiatives on southern Africa very significant—chairman. UN Chron 14:24-5 My '77

Timor (island)

Assembly rejects Indonesia integration claim; calls again for forces withdrawal; with text of resolution. UN Chron 14:32-3, 100 Ja '77
Study of Puerto Rico, East Timor, Western Sahara questions deferred. il UN Chron 14: 14-15 Ag '77

Tokelau (islands)

Committee of 24 adopts decisions on Bermuda, Solomons, Tokelau, Pitcairn. UN Chron 14: 23-4 Jl '77

Transkei

Dissent on Transkei. Nat R 29:483-4 Ap 29 '77

Uganda

Secretary-General speaks of Middle East, Uganda, southern Africa, new United States spirit towards United Nations; excerpts from transcript of news conference, March 1, 1977. K. Waldheim. UN Chron 14:56-7 Ap '77

Underdeveloped areas

Governing council seeks to make UNDP more responsive to changing needs of developing countries. il UN Chron 14:37-8 Ag '77
World economy. J. McCaull. il Environment 19: 34-44 N '77

United States

Andy Young conundrum. Nat R 29:481 Ap 29 '77
Are Young's wings being clipped? por U.S. News 82:25 My 2 '77
Around two worlds in two days; visit of J. Carter. il pors Time 109:12-15 Mr 28 '77
Carter's point man; A. Young. R. Carroll and others. il por Newsweek 89:39-40 F 14 '77
Corridors of morality. J. Lelyveld. il por N Y Times Mag p 142 O 16 '77
Crucial test for Carter as world leader; proposals for the U.N. General Assembly's 32d session. il por U.S. News 83:23-4 S 26 '77
Department discusses U.S. participation in international organizations; statement, June 15, 1977. C. W. Maynes. Dept State Bull 77:100-3 Jl 18 '77
Diplomatic dissident; A. Young. Nation 224:516 Ap 30 '77
Do-it-yourself diplomacy. R. Carroll and E. Clift. pors Newsweek 89:36 Mr 21 '77
I don't mind being the lightning rod; excerpts from interview, ed by R. Watson and others. A. J. Young. il por Newsweek 89:30-1 Mr 28 '77
Irrelevant forum. S. Hess. New Repub 176:34+ Ja 22 '77
Mr Perseverance; C. Vance's negotiations on strategic arms and the Middle East. R. Watson and S. Sullivan. il por Newsweek 90:42+ O 10 '77
New tactics at U.N: it looks as if U.S. feud with third world is over—for now. U.S. News 83:37 O 17 '77
Our new voice at the U.N; A. Young. J. Lelyveld. il pors N Y Times Mag p 17-19+ F 6 '77
Outspoken Andy Young. R. Carroll and E. Clift. il por Newsweek 89:24-6+ Mr 28 '77
Point man, or unguided missile? A. Young. il por Time 109:27-8 Mr 21 '77
Report on 1976 U.S. participation in the U.N. transmitted to Congress; message, November 1, 1977. J. Carter. Dept State Bull 77:867-8 D 12 '77
S-G confers with President Carter during two-day visit to Washington. il pors UN Chron 14:16-17 Mr '77
Secretary-General speaks of Middle East, Uganda, southern Africa, new United States spirit towards United Nations; excerpts from transcript of news conference, March 1, 1977. K. Waldheim. UN Chron 14:56-7 Ap '77
Secretary Vance's activities at the United Nations. Dept State Bull 77:640-2 N 7 '77
U.N. myth; address, September 8, 1977. F. L. Dale. Vital Speeches 43:760-4 O 1 '77
Washington notebook; blacks serving on the U.S. delegation. S. Booker. Ebony 32:26 Jl '77

Vietnam

Assembly opens new session; Admission of Viet Nam, Djibouti brings membership to 149. il UN Chron 14:5-10 O '77
Assembly sends admission issue back to Council for reconsideration; with text of resolution. UN Chron 13:17-23, 83 D '76
Security Council again fails to support Viet Nam for United Nations membership. il UN Chron 13:16+ D '76
Security Council favors U.N. membership for Vietnam; statement, July 19, 1977. D. F. McHenry. Dept State Bull 77:283 Ag 29 '77

Virgin Islands

Committee acts on visiting missions' reports on Caymans, US Virgin Islands. UN Chron 14: 26-7 O '77

Western Sahara

Study of Puerto Rico, East Timor, Western Sahara questions deferred. il UN Chron 14: 14-15 Ag '77

Western Samoa

Samoa admitted to UN membership. il UN Chron 14:39 Ja '77

UNITED NATIONS Children's Fund. See Unicef

UNITED NATIONS Conference of Plenipotentiaries on Succession of States in Respect of Treaties

Assembly decides on States Succession Conference in Vienna in April-May 1977. UN Chron 13:56-7 D '76

UNITED NATIONS Conference of Plenipotentiaries on Territorial Asylum

Further talks urged on question of territorial asylum. UN Chron 14:41 Mr '77

UNITED NATIONS Conference on Carriage of Goods by the Sea, 1978 (proposed)

International Conference on Carriage of Goods by Sea to be convened in 1978. UN Chron 14: 82 Ja '77

UNITED NATIONS Conference on Desertification, 1977

Desertification. C. L. Rogers. il map Sci N 112:282-3+ O 29 '77
Lethal spread of the sands. P. Gwynne. il Newsweek 90:80 S 19 '77
Measures to combat world desert conditions approved at Nairobi conference. UN Chron 14: 36-9 O '77
Regional meetings held in preparation for Conference on Desertification. UN Chron 14:33 My '77
U.N. Conference on Desertification; statement. J. A. Joseph. map Dept State Bull 77:453-60 O 10 '77

UNITED NATIONS Conference on Human Settlements, 1976

Habitat plus one: what gives? E. Carlson. Archit Rec 161:37+ Je; 162:29+ Jl '77

UNITED NATIONS Conference on Science and Technology for Development, 1979 (proposed)

Committee on Science, Technology drafts plans for 1979 conference. il UN Chron 14:24-5 Mr '77
Issue of technology transfer is snag for 1979 U.N. meeting. J. Walsh. Science 198:35-8 O 7 '77
Science, technology and poverty. W. Morehouse and J. Sigurdson. bibl f il Bull Atom Sci 33: 21-6+ D '77
Some questions for the world jamboree. M. S. Wionczek. il Bull Atom Sci 33:29-32 D '77

UNITED NATIONS Conference on Technical Co-operation among Developing Countries, 1978 (proposed)
Committee recommends new dates for Argentina Conference on Co-operation. UN Chron 14:39 O '77

UNITED NATIONS Conference on the Law of the Sea
Administration gives views on proposed legislation on deep seabed mining; statement, April 27, 1977. E. L. Richardson. Dept State Bull 76:524-7 My 23 '77
Carter's ocean opportunity. J. J. Logue. Commonweal 104:265-9 Ap 29 '77
Congress is itching to start ocean mining. il Bus W p29-30 Jl 11 '77
Department discusses international approaches to problem of oil spills from vessels; statement, January 11, 1977. T. V. Learson. Dept State Bull 76:113-16 F 7 '77
For a law of the seas. R. Hudson. Current 198:44-51 D '77
International struggle for a law of the sea. R. Hudson. il Bull Atom Sci 33:14-20 D '77
Law of the sea at the brink. J. T. Swing. Oceans 10:4-5 S '77
Law of the sea: breaking the deadlock. J. I. Charney. bibl f For Affairs 55:598-629 Ap '77
Law of the Sea Conference: problems and progress; statement, July 20, 1977. E. L. Richardson. Dept State Bull 77:389-91 S 19 '77
Law of the Sea: rethinking U.S. interests. R. G. Darman. bibl f For Affairs 56:373-95 Ja '78
Legal order for the oceans. A. W. Smith. Nat Parks & Con Mag 51:2+ F; 2+ Ap '77
Marine scientific research issue in the Law of the Sea negotiations. map Science 197:230-3 Jl 15 '77
New composite text to be studied by next session of Sea Law Conference. il UN Chron 14:24-6 Ag '77
Ocean mining: former negotiator now lobbies for Kennecott. D. Shapley. Science 196:964-5 My 27 '77
Ocean scientists may wash hands of sea law treaty. D. Shapley. Science 197:645 Ag 12 '77
Oceanography and the law of the sea. M. Ruivo. il UNESCO Courier 30:10-13 Ja '77
President comments on new text in explanatory memorandum. il UN Chron 14:27-8 Ag '77
Review of the Law of the Sea Conference and deep seabed mining legislation: statement, October 4, 1977. E. L. Richardson. Dept State Bull 77:751-6 N 21 '77
Shipwrecks, pollution & the law of the sea. R. J. McManus and J. Schneider. Nat Parks & Con Mag 51:10-15 Je '77
Sixth session of Law of Sea Conference might prove decisive, says Mr. Zuleta; summary of address, March 28, 1977. B. Zuleta. por UN Chron 14:37-8+ My '77
Who owns the oceans? M. E. Goncalves. il UNESCO Courier 30:4-8 Ja '77

UNITED NATIONS Conference on Trade and Development
Assembly acts on UNCTAD decisions on debt burdens, land-locked countries; with text of resolution. UN Chron 14:45-7, 113-15 Ja '77
Fifth session of UNCTAD in Manila recommended. UN Chron 14:40 O '77
Government experts to deal with cotton trade problems. UN Chron 14:36 Jl '77
Rx for Carter: heed the poor nations. B. Jones. il Commonweal 104:9-12 Ja 7 '77
Time to pay our dues. Nation 224:322-3 Mr 19 '77
UNCTAD committee moves to combat port congestion in developing countries; Committee on Shipping. UN Chron 14:34 My '77

UNITED NATIONS Council for Namibia
Council for Namibia mission concludes successful four-day visit to Canada. il UN Chron 14:29-30 Ap '77
Council for Namibia to send mission to Canada. UN Chron 14:19-20 Mr '77
Council mission encouraged by positive response of specialized agencies. UN Chron 14:23 My '77
Namibia Day marked with special meeting. UN Chron 14:10 Ag '77
Security Council urged to take steps to preserve status of Walvis Bay. il UN Chron 14:23-4 O '77

UNITED NATIONS Day
U.N. Day concerts; 1976 television broadcast. J. Culshaw. il Hi Fi 27:14+ Ap '77
United Nations Day, 1977; a proclamation. J. Carter. Dept State Bull 77:549 O 24 '77

UNITED NATIONS Decade for Women
Criteria adopted for management of voluntary fund for Women's Decade; with text of resolution. UN Chron 14:65-6, 108-9 Ja '77

UNITED NATIONS Declaration on the Strengthening of International Security
Techniques used to destabilize govts. condemned. UN Chron 14:27 Ja '77

UNITED NATIONS Development Decade, 2d
Committee reviews first six years of Second Development Decade. UN Chron 14:38-9 Jl '77
Experts see no physical limits to accelerated development of developing regions. UN Chron 13:59+ D '76

UNITED NATIONS Disaster Relief Office
Assembly commends activities of Office of Relief Co-ordinator. UN Chron 14:43 Ja '77

UNITED NATIONS Educational, Scientific and Cultural Organization. See Unesco

UNITED NATIONS Emergency Force. See United Nations—Armed Forces—Forces in the Middle East

UNITED Nations Food and Agriculture Organization. See Food and Agriculture Organization of the United Nations

UNITED NATIONS General Assembly. See United Nations—General Assembly

UNITED NATIONS Group of Experts on the Economic and Social Consequences of the Arms Race and of Military Expenditures
Experts see $350 billion a year arms race damaging world development prospects. il UN Chron 14:41-4 O '77

UNITED NATIONS Industrial Development Organization
Developed countries urged to carry out plan for redeployment of industries. UN Chron 14:50-1 Ja '77
$412 million for UNDP and Capital Fund; aid pledged to UNIDO, Children's Fund. il UN Chron 13:51-2 D '76
Industrial Development Board sets $50 million target for new fund. UN Chron 14:35 Jl '77

UNITED NATIONS Institute for Training and Research
UNITAR seeks to serve United Nations and agencies in practical and useful manner. D. Nicol. il por UN Chron 14:42-6 Mr '77

UNITED NATIONS International Atomic Energy Agency. See International Atomic Energy Agency

UNITED NATIONS International Conference in Support of the Peoples of Zimbabwe and Namibia, 1977. See International Conference in Support of the Peoples of Zimbabwe and Namibia, 1977

UNITED NATIONS International Fund for Agricultural Development
Assembly action paves way for Agricultural Fund to attain target of $1,000 million; with text of resolution. UN Chron 14:44, 107 Ja '77
First loans likely this year, says commission chairman. il UN Chron 14:32 My '77
IFAD agreement expected to enter into force this year. UN Chron 14:39+ Ag '77
U.S. joins U.N. Fund for Agricultural Development; statement, October 4, 1977. A. J. Young. Dept State Bull 77:644 N 7 '77
U.S. signs articles of agreement of Agricultural Development Fund; statements, December 22, 1976. G. R. Ford; D. Parker. Dept State Bull 76:70-1 Ja 24 '77

UNITED NATIONS International Year for Disabled Persons, 1981 (proposed) See International Year for Disabled Persons, 1981 (proposed)

UNITED NATIONS International Year of the Child, 1979 (proposed) See International Year of the Child, 1979 (proposed)

UNITED NATIONS Joint Staff Pension Fund
Assembly calls for sound investment in developing countries of resources of Pension Fund. UN Chron 14:76 Ja '77

UNITED NATIONS Negotiating Conference on a Common Fund
Rich world, poor world. J. Madeley. Commonweal 104:423-4 Jl 8 '77
Wide consensus seemed to have been reached at conference. UN Chron 14:39-40 Ap '77

UNITED NATIONS Peace-keeping Force in Cyprus. See United Nations—Armed Forces—Forces in Cyprus

UNITED NATIONS Postal Administration
United Nations Postal Administration 25 years old; special stamp issued. il UN Chron 13:60-1 D '76

UNITED NATIONS receptions. See Government entertaining

UNITED NATIONS Regional Cartographic Conference for Asia and the Pacific
Training in mapping and surveying stressed at cartographic conference. UN Chron 14:33 Mr '77

UNITED NATIONS Relief and Works Agency for Palestine Refugees in the Near East
United States calls for support for UNRWA; statement, November 2, 1976. P. Bailey. Dept State Bull 75:755-6 D 27 '76

UNITED NATIONS Trust Fund for Assistance to Lebanon
Secretary-General appeals for more aid for Lebanon. UN Chron 13:52 D '76

UNITED NATIONS University, Tokyo
Assembly calls for more funds for university. UN Chron 14:59 Ja '77
Natural resources program at the United Nations University. W. Shearer-Izumi. Science 198:896-7 D 2 '77
U.N.U; interview. A. A. Kwapong. New Yorker 53:33-5 O 3 '77

UNITED NATIONS Water Conference
Politics of water. B. Handler. il Sat R 4:16-19 My 14 '77
UN confronts issue of clean water for human settlements. S. Watt. Archit Rec 161:37 F '77
United Nations Water Conference adopts plan of action in Argentina. il UN Chron 14:35-40 Ap '77
U.S. discusses its preparations for the U.N. Water Conference; statement, January 4, 1977. J. M. Myerson. Dept State Bull 76:203-5 Mr 7 '77
World's thirst. G. F. Stucker. il Nat Parks & Con Mag 51:14-19 O '77

UNITED NATIONS World Food Council
Assembly adopts two resolutions on World Food Council. UN Chron 14:44-5 Ja '77
Food Council adopts action plan to combat hunger, malnutrition. UN Chron 14:37 Jl '77

UNITED Nuclear Corporation. See Uranium industry

UNITED Presbyterian Church in the United States. See Presbyterian Church in the United States

UNITED Rubber, Cork, Linoleum and Plastic Workers of America
No give on either side in rubber talks. il Bus W p43-4 Mr 28 '77

UNITED Services Automobile Association. See Insurance companies

UNITED Services Life Insurance Company. See Insurance companies

UNITED STATES
America at age 201. il U.S. News 83:15 Jl 4 '77
America: to Leontyne Price, opportunities are growing. L. Price. por U.S. News 82:56 Mr 28 '77
Close-up of America:
Low-key Oregon: a model for the U.S? map U.S. News 83:60-1 D 5 '77
Sunny Florida: foreshadowing our future? impact of the aged. J. R. Wooten. map U.S. News 84:34-5 Ja 9 '78
Creative response to our crisis. A. Etzioni. Bull Atom Sci 33:24 F '77
Eric Sevareid on today's morals, TV, war or peace, prosperity; interview. E. Sevareid. pors U.S. News 83:60-2 D 26 '77
John Wayne's America; excerpt from America, why I love her; with reproductions of paintings by N. Rockwell. J. Wayne. il Good H 185:138-41+ N '77
New myths for the third century. America 136:42 Ja 22 '77
Our America; special section, ed by A. J. Lowe. il maps Américas 29:16-49 N '77
Our blessed land; excerpt from The foxes' union. J. J. Kilpatrick. Read Digest 111:193-4+ D '77
Road ahead. U.S. News 83:17 S 12 '77
Simmering struggles. il U.S. News 83:15 Jl 18 '77
What a year. G. F. Will. il Newsweek 90:10 D 26 '77
Who runs America: annual survey. il U.S. News 82:28-36+ Ap 18 '77
See also
Americans
Atlantic States
Great Plains
Southern States
States (United States)
also subhead United States under various subjects, e.g. Income tax—United States; Trade unions—United States

ACTION

ACTION volunteers work together in Hilo: Foster Grandparents and Retired Senior Volunteer Program. il Aging 272:11-12 Je '77
CPAs agree to audit a federal agency—free. Bus W p43-4 My 16 '77
My life in the Peace Corps: excerpt from Away from home: letters to my family. L. G. Carter. il por Good H 184:115-18+ Ap '77
National youth service; a test program. D. J. Eberly. Current 192:3-12 Ap '77
Peace Corps: alive but not so well. T. Smith. il N Y Times Mag p6-9+ D 25 '77
Peace Corps planning in the world's parks. J. Needle. il Parks & Rec 12:16-21+ Ag '77
Peace Corps. . .where age can be an asset. M. Poynter. il Ret Liv 17:42-3+ N '77
Retired schoolteacher is mover and shaker as VISTA volunteer in Alaska. por Aging 266:18-19 D '76
Retired teachers share skills as Peace Corps volunteers in Ghana. il por Aging 268:18-20 F '77
She shuns retirement; joins Peace Corps instead; work of M. L. Daniell. por Aging 274:22 Ag '77
Two new agency heads: study in contrasts. il pors U.S. News 82:60 Mr 14 '77
Two years in Africa; Peace Corps volunteer. B. Murchison. Todays Educ 66:87+ Ja '77
Whatever happened to: Peace Corps: ready for a comeback. il U.S. News 83:45-6 O 17 '77
White House likes its accounting freebie. Bus W p36-7 Ag 15 '77

Advisory Committee on Accreditation and Institutional Eligibility

More trouble for doctors and lawyers. il Bus W p 102 Ap 25 '77

Agency for Consumer Advocacy (proposed)

Case for a consumer protection agency. S. S. Epstein. Bull Atom Sci 33:6-7 S '77
Closer to creating a consumer agency. Bus W p32 Je 6 '77
Consumer agency: pro. M. Green. New Repub 176:14-16 Je 18 '77
Consumer protection: what's at issue. il Nations Bus 65:18-20+ Je '77
Idea whose time has passed. il Time 109:16 Je 13 '77
New agency for consumers—sizing up its chances. il U.S. News 82:46 My 30 '77
New interventionists. il Time 109:64 Ap 18 '77
President pushes consumer power. Bus W p45 Ap 18 '77
Pluralism run amok. S. Chapman. New Repub 176:36-9 My 21 '77
President's plan for a new consumer agency. U.S. News 82:62 Ap 18 '77
You can put in your nickel's worth. R. H. Karpatkin. Consumer Rep 42:440 Ag '77

Agency for International Communication (proposed)

New communication agency proposed by President Carter; message to Congress, October 11, 1977. J. Carter. Dept State Bull 77:683-5 N 14 '77
Reorganizing cultural and informational activities; joint statement, September 1, 1977. W. Christopher and J. E. Reinhardt. Dept State Bull 77:572 O 24 '77

Agency for International Development

Appropriate technology; Appropriate Technology International. A. Von Lazar and K. Bode. New Repub 176:11-13 Je 11 '77
Chile cover-up? alleged covert activities of Jesuit missionary R. Vekemans. Chr Today 21:40-1 Ag 26 '77

Aging, Administration on

AoA and Treasury launch joint project on direct deposit. Aging 275:5-6 S '77
AoA issues findings on I&R services. Aging 275:12-13 S '77
AoA supports $4 million joint study on crime. Aging 275:7 S '77
Corporation, AoA sign pact aimed at legal needs of aged; Legal Services Corporation. Aging 272:7 Je '77
Federal Council on Aging sets 1977 priorities. Aging 268:4-5 F '77
Federal Council on the Aging members sworn in at White House ceremony. Aging 266:4 D '76
Funding level for fiscal year 1977 highest in AoA's history; labor-HEW Appropriations Act. Aging 266:3 D '76
Nelson Cruikshank new Federal Council head. il por Aging 274:20 Ag '77
Section 504: impact on AoA programs; Rehabilitation Act of 1973. Aging 275:14-16 S '77
$26 million awarded to AoA training, multidisciplinary center, R&D, and model project programs. Aging 266:8-13 D '76

Agriculture, Department of

Editorial; question of world crop yield forecasts and abnormal weather patterns. C. Whipple. Horticulture 55:6 Ap '77
How good are USDA livestock and meat reports? Suc Farm 75:H8-9 D '77
Know what your cattle are worth; USDA's fabricated carcass report. W. Kester. il Farm J 101:Beef 4-5+ Je '77
New for scientists: RFP's from USDA, EIS's from NIH. E. M. Leeper. il BioScience 27:297-8 Ap '77
Organizing knowledge for small farmers. J. Goldstein. il Org Gard & Farm 25:146+ Ja '78
Pizen squad; USDA Board of Food and Drug Inspection. il pors Chemistry 50:18-21 S '77
Question of taste; naming of the Agriculture Department's employee cafeteria after A. E. Packer. por Newsweek 90:24 Ag 22 '77
Rupert Cutler: the environmentalist in the farmer's back yard. N. Wade. Science 196:505-7 Ap 29 '77
USDA plans to tighten up on meat grading. Farm J 101:B4 N '77

UNITED STATES—Agriculture, Department of—*Continued*
USDA's profound change: to help farmers naturally. J. Cox. por Org Gard & Farm 24:48-52 S '77
What Bergland really said about farm chemicals. Farm J 101:32 N '77
Yes, we have no undue enhancement; USDA investigating dairy co-op price enhancement. Farm J 101:Dairy 19 F '77
See also
United States—Forest Service

Animal and Plant Health Inspection

Keeping insects in the zoo. BioScience 27:72-3 Ja '77

Commodity Credit Corporation

How government programs may fit your grain marketing strategy. il Suc Farm 75:8 O '77

Farmers Home Administration

Farmers Home Administration: less farm, more home. Suc Farm 75:no5 9 Mr '77
Home economist, minister obtain FmHA loan to build retirement community; case of Billie Hagler and Rev. Gordon Blunt. Aging 270:21 Ap '77
Project loans for youth. J. Gillies. il Farm J 101:37-9 F '77

Food and Nutrition Service

Kosher meals a specialty at New York Luncheon Club; Brighton Older Adult Luncheon Club Title VII project. L. Feldman. il Aging 274:6-8 Ag '77
Strictly from hunger; WIC program. J. Solkoff. New Repub 176:13-15 Je 11 '77; Reply. B. Stultz and others. 177:6 Ag 6 '77
Summer food program: how your camp can join; questions and answers. W. G. Boling. Camp Mag 49:9+ My '77
Why Johnny doesn't eat; National School Lunch Program. P. Bonventre and E. Sciolino. il Newsweek 89:52 Mr 21 '77

Rural Electrification Administration

Over-powering at the REA. Forbes 119:29 Ap 15 '77
REA expansion plans bump into landowners. il Bus W p36+ O 31 '77

Air Force

NASA and the Pentagon: the Air Force eyes a star war. J. Markoff. Nation 226:16-18 Ja 7 '78

Appropriations and expenditures

B-1 no, cruise yes. S. Fraker and others. il por Newsweek 90:14-17 Jl 11 '77
Carter and the B-1 bomber. R. Freund. Chr Cent 94:53-4 Ja 26 '77
Carter's big decision: down goes the B-1, here comes the cruise. il por Time 110:8-12 Jl 11 '77
Cruise missile fund rise sought in revised budget. Aviation W 107:18 Ag 8 '77
STOL may lose out in the budget battle. Bus W p37-8 N 28 '77
USAF Force modernization stressed. il Aviation W 106:16-17 Ja 24 '77
See also
Airplanes, Military—Cost

Civil Reserve Air Fleet

Civil Reserve Air Fleet's funds pass in House unit. K. Johnsen. Aviation W 107:59 D 5 '77

Education

See also
United States Air Force Academy, Colorado Springs

Forces in Europe

Air Force doctrine, missions revised. D. A. Brown. il Aviation W 107:48-9+ Ag 8 '77
Increasing Soviet offensive threat spurs stronger Europe air arm. C. A. Robinson, Jr. il Aviation W 107:38-40+ Ag 1 '77

Maneuvers

See Military maneuvers

Procurement

Air Force studies AMST procurement. D. E. Fink. il Aviation W 106:60-1 My 9 '77

Systems Command

Pervasive importance of USAF's space mission; interview, ed by E. Ulsamer. T. W. Morgan. il por Space World N-5-161:12-16 My '77

Alcohol, Drug Abuse, and Mental Health Administration

New ADAMHA head expected to lead, not just coordinate. C. Holden. por Science 197:846 Ag 26 '77

American Revolution Bicentennial Administration

Rediscovery of America; American Revolution Bicentennial Administration. J. W. Warner. il por Sat Eve Post 249:12+ Ap '77

Anti-Communist movements

See Anti-Communist movements

Antiquities

Contract archeology: new source of support brings new problems. C. Holden. Science 196:1070-2 Je 3 '77
Who really discovered America? ideas of B. Fell. T. Fleming. il Read Digest 110:69-73 F '77
See also
Indians of North America—Antiquities

Appropriations and expenditures

Another spending gap haunts Washington. Bus W p42-3 S 12 '77
Can our democratic government survive? address, September 9, 1977. D. F. Linowes. Vital Speeches 44:15-19 O 15 '77
Carter dares his party. il U.S. News 82:19-20 Je 13 '77
Carter takes on the budget monster; with editorial comment. J. Cameron. il Fortune 95:81, 82-7+ Ja '77
Embarrassment of underspending. il Bus W p39-40 Mr 21 '77
Inflation, interest rates and the Fed; address, July 26, 1977. J. J. Balles. Vital Speeches 43:741-4 O 1 '77
Leaning against next year's wind; interview, ed by F. Kutchins. M. Friedman. il por Sat Eve Post 249:16+ My '77
More appropriations—more unemployment. O. G. Hatch. il Nat R 29:942-3 Ag 19 '77
Now, underruns. A. J. Mayer and R. Thomas. il Newsweek 89:83 Mr 14 '77
On limiting the size of government; proposal to decrease federal spending. P. Laxalt. il Nat R 29:437-8 Ap 15 '77
Path we dare not take. M. Friedman. Read Digest 110:110-14 Mr '77
Pork-barrel war between the states. il U.S. News 83:39-41 D 5 '77
President Carter and the honeymooners; non-enacted legislation supported by Democratic congressmen. J. Drake and S. Petersen. il Nat R 29:433-6+ Ap 15 '77
Road to recovery. Y. Brozen. il Nat R 29:264-7 Mr 4 '77
249 billions to prop incomes—where government money goes. il U.S. News 83:98-9 N 28 '77
See also
Budget—United States
also subhead Appropriations and expenditures under names of government departments, e.g. United States—Energy, Research and Development Administration—Appropriations and expenditures

Armed Forces

Armed Forces of today; address, February 14, 1977. G. S. Brown. Vital Speeches 43:324-7 Mr 15 '77
Our Armed Forces: ready—or not? il U.S. News 83:35-42 O 10 '77
See also
Trade unions—Servicemen
United States—Air Force
United States—Army
United States—Coast Guard
United States—Joint Chiefs of Staff
United States—Marine Corps
United States—Navy
United States—Reserve Officers Training Corps

Appropriations and expenditures

See United States—Defense, Department of—Appropriations and expenditures

Blacks

Judge William H. Hastie civilian aide to the Secretary of War, 1940-1943. P. McGuire. por Negro Hist Bull 40:712-13 My '77
See also
United States—Army—Blacks

Desertion

After the pardon. S. Fraker and others. il Newsweek 89:28-9 Ja 31 '77
Big cop-out: Carter and the veterans. B. W. Lynn. Nation 225:678-82 D 24 '77
Carter's first act touches off a storm: pardon for draft evaders. U.S. News 82:22 Ja 31 '77
Discriminatory pardon. J. Colhoun. Progressive 41:13 My '77
First small step; pardon. Nation 224:131-2 F 5 '77
Pardon everyone? report entitled Reconciliation after Vietnam. J. B. Breslin. America 136:67 Ja 29 '77
Still the back of the bus: Vietnam pardon, stage II; review of less than honorable discharges. J. Colhoun. il Nation 224:594-6 My 14 '77
Universal and unconditional; Toronto conference. J. Elbert. Chr Cent 94:134-5 F 16 '77

Discharges

See Military discharges

UNITED STATES—Armed Forces—*Continued*

Education

So far, so good; a report card on coed military academies. il U.S. News 83:26-9 Jl 11 '77
Women warriors. E. Keerdoja. il Newsweek 90: 12 S 19 '77
See also
United States—Navy—Education

Forces in Asia

Again it's a Europe first strategy for U.S. il map U.S. News 82:22-4 Je 20 '77
Asians' biggest worry: will Carter jettison them? il map U.S. News 83:51-4 Jl 18 '77
Concern about rights and troops. R. Graves. il Time 109:32+ Je 6 '77
Danger spots in the Far East. D. N. Rowe. il Nat R 29:829-30 Jl 22 '77

Forces in Europe

Again it's a Europe first strategy for U.S. il map U.S. News 82:22-4 Je 20 '77
U.S. strategic forces; address, March 16, 1977. R. E. Dougherty. Vital Speeches 43:584-90 Jl 15 '77

Forces in foreign countries

U.S. troops abroad: new beef-up begins. il map U.S. News 83:48-9 D 26 '77

Forces in Germany, West

See also
United States—Army—Forces in Germany, West

Forces in Korea, South

Korea: time to trust the people. J. Stentzel. Nation 224:197-9 F 19 '77
See also
United States—Army—Forces in Korea, South

Forces in Southeast Asia

Stability in Southeast Asia: a lot depends on U.S. leadership; interview. il U.S. News 83:43-4 O 31 '77

Forces in the Mediterranean Region

Independent U.S. support urged for military in Mediterranean. Aviation W 106:32 Ap 25 '77

Maneuvers

See Military maneuvers

Officers, Retired

See Retired military personnel

Pay, allowances, etc.

Military pay: what the furor is all about; with interview with R. F. Cocklin. il U.S. News 83:28-32 Ag 22 '77
See also
United States—Army—Pay, allowances, etc.

Procurement

See also
United States—Air Force—Procurement
United States—Army—Procurement
United States—Coast Guard—Procurement
United States—Navy—Procurement

Recruiting, enlistment, etc.

If all else fails... il Esquire 88:77 Jl '77
One way to avoid a new draft: recruit more women. il U.S. News 82:58 F 14 '77
Winning hearts and minds for the all-volunteer military force. T. Conrad. Progressive 41:28-31 S '77
See also
Military service, Compulsory
Military service, Voluntary

Retired military personnel

See Retired military personnel

Weapons systems

Inter-service weapons rivalry. R. F. Coulam. bibl il Bull Atom Sci 33:25-36 Je '77

Women

See Servicewomen

Arms Control and Disarmament Agency

Arms and the man; nomination of P. C. Warnke. T. Mathews and J. J. Lindsay. por Newsweek 89:29 F 14 '77
Arms control statement criticized. K. Johnsen. Aviation W 106:14-15 My 16 '77
Opposition to Warnke mounts in Senate. E. Kozicharow. Aviation W 106:21-2 F 14 '77
Proper perch for the dove; P. Warnke. il por Time 109:23 F 14 '77
Sixteenth annual report of ACDA transmitted to the Congress; text of letter, January 19, 1977. G. R. Ford. Dept State Bull 76:132-3 F 14 '77
Warnke problem. Nation 224:195-6 F 19 '77
What lies ahead in arms control? address, November 12, 1976. F. C. Iklé. Vital Speeches 43: 166-8 Ja 1 '77
Why not the best? M. Stone. U.S. News 82: 38 Mr 21 '77

Army

Needs of NATO; address, October 18, 1977. B. W. Rogers. Vital Speeches 44:136-9 D 15 '77
New-look Army. D. M. Alpern and T. Fuller. il Newsweek 89:20-1+ Mr 28 '77
Boss man of the Army; C. Alexander. il pors Ebony 32:33-6+ Je '77
Updating Willie and Joe. Time 109:26 My 23 '77

Air Corps

War to war. I. C. Eaker. il Flying 101:180-3 S '77

Appropriations and expenditures

Army turns to missile procurement. K. J. Stein. il Aviation W 106:20 Ja 24 '77

Barracks and quarters

Good-bye, gentleman-ranker; visiting Schofield Barracks, site of J. Jones' From here to eternity. J. Didion. Esquire 88:50+ O '77

Blacks

William T. Anderson: army officer, doctor, minister, and writer. F. R. Levstik. il Negro Hist Bull 40:662-3 Ja '77

Cavalry

Campaigning with Custer; excerpt from Life in Custer's cavalry: diaries and letters of Albert and Jennie Barnitz, 1867-68, ed by R. M. Utley. A. Barnitz and J. P. Barnitz. il pors Am West 14:4-9+ Jl '77
Teddy Roosevelt & the Rough Riders. R. J. Maddox. il pors map Am Hist Illus 12:8-19 N '77

Communications systems

See also
Radio, Military

Corps of Engineers

Bitter battle of the waterways. J. N. Miller. Read Digest 111:83-7 S '77
Boondoggle busted? Cross-Florida Canal. Nat Parks & Con Mag 51:21-2 Mr '77
Corps to guard environment. E. M. Leeper. BioScience 27:67 Ja '77
Coup de grâce for barge canal. G. Laycock. Audubon 79:147 Mr '77
Destroying tomorrow today: the Army Corps of Engineers wants the Mississippi River. J. Nedelman. Horticulture 55:8+ O '77
Here come the dredgers! Sneak attack on the wetlands; with editorial comment. P. J. Bernstein. il Nation 225:612-18 D 10 '77
Hired scapegoats. S. C. Florman. Harpers 254: 26-9 My '77
More on the Corps; opposition to Tombigbee River Valley project. G. Reiger. Field & S 82:22+ My '77
On dumping Dickey and saving the St John; with editorial comment. R. Saltonstall, Jr. Liv Wildn 40-3, 20-1 O '76

Corps of Engineers—Anecdotes, facetiae satire, etc.

Option. R. Lipez. Progressive 41:66 D '77

Education

See also
United States Military Academy, West Point

Forces in Europe

Helicopters play new role in Europe. D. A. Brown. Aviation W 107:62-3+ N 28 '77

Forces in Germany, West

G.I. watch on a deadly border. B. W. Mader. il Time 110:38 Jl 18 '77
Tough fight in West Germany; G.I. financial problems. il Time 110:17 D 26 '77

Forces in Korea, South

Another General speaks; excerpts from interview, ed by B. Krisher. R. G. Stilwell. por Newsweek 89:51 Je 6 '77
Careful response to an accident; North Korean attack on American helicopter. il map Time 110:36+ Jl 25 '77
Carter's Koreanization plan. New Repub 176:5-6 Je 11 '77
G.I.s at the DMZ: time to come home? il map Time 109:28-9 Je 6 '77
General on the carpet; J. K. Singlaub relieved of command. por Time 109:14-15 My 30 '77
Grim reminder from smoldering Korea; shooting down unarmed American helicopter. il U.S. News 83:50 Jl 25 '77
Korea: the image problem. J. Stentzel. Nation 225:358 O 15 '77
Letter from Seoul. W. McGleish. map America 136:99-101 F 5 '77
Lost command; Gen. J. K. Singlaub relieved of command. il por Newsweek 89:17 My 30 '77
New Korean conflict. K. Willenson and others. il map Newsweek 89:49+ Je 6 '77
Readers say: keep our troops in South Korea. il Nations Bus 65:42-3 O '77
Ripple effect in Korea. F. Gibney. For Affairs 56:160-74 O '77

UNITED STATES—Army—Forces in Korea, South —*Continued*
Should U.S. withdraw troops from Korea? interviews. J. C. Culver; R. G. Stilwell. pors U.S. News 82:27-8 Je 20 '77
Transfer of defense articles to the Republic of Korea; message, October 21, 1977. J. Carter. Dept State Bull 77:852-4 D 12 '77
When will the brass learn? J. K. Singlaub. Nation 224:676 Je 4 '77
Why Carter's withdrawal plan draws fire. map U.S. News 82:18 Je 6 '77
Why we can't leave Korea. D. S. Zagoria. il N Y Times Mag p 17-18+ O 2 '77
Withdrawal of U.S. ground forces from South Korea; statement, June 10, 1977. P. C. Habib. Dept State Bull 77:48-50 Jl 11 '77

Ordnance and ordnance stores

Modern GI Joe: you've come a long way, buddy. M. Schultz. il Pop Mech 148:77-9+ D '77

Pay, allowances, etc.

Tough fight in West Germany; G.I. financial problems. il Time 110:17 D 26 '77

Procurement

Tale of two cities; UTTAS contract awarded to Sikorsky. E. Shields. il Time 109:51+ F 14 '77

Recruiting, enlistment, etc.

See also
Military service, Voluntary

Weapons systems

See also
United States—Army—Ordnance and ordnance stores

Army Electronics Command

Army to relocate, reorganize some avionic activities. Aviation W 108:18-19 Ja 2 '78

Atomic Energy Commission

Oppenheimer case: a study in the abuse of law; 1950's investigation by Atomic Energy Commission. H. P. Green. il pors Bull Atom Sci 33:12-16+ S '77
See also
United States—Nuclear Regulatory Commission

Bibliography

Home scene. J. P. Parkes. America 136:423-5 My 7 '77

Bonneville Power Administration

Paradise lost; effect of forthcoming power shortage on the aluminum industry. il Forbes 119:32 F 1 '77

Border Patrol

Border crisis: illegal aliens out of control. O. Kelly. il U.S. News 82:33-8+ Ap 25 '77
On the track of the invaders; with report by B. Starr. Time 109:30 My 2 '77

Boundaries

Borders: Texas-Chihuahua. R. Morris. New Repub 177:12 O 22 '77
U.S. and Mexico complete transfer of territory; announcement, May 26, 1977. maps Dept State Bull 77:10-12 Jl 4 '77

Cabinet

Appointing men who care about equality. J. Steinem and others. Ms 6:45-6+ Ja '78
Bureaucrats redux; new Carter Cabinet. B. Brower. map Harpers 254:25-6 Mr '77
Cabinet government? Unlikely. New Repub 176:5 F 12 '77
Cabinet members tell what they own and what they owe. il U.S. News 82:28-9 Mr 7 '77
Carter to Cabinet: cut out frills. il U.S. News 82:29 F 14 '77
Carter's Cabinet. il Sr Schol 109:16-17 F 10 '77
Emerging under Carter: a Cabinet with real clout. il U.S. News 82:35-6 Mr 14 '77
Hail, hail, the gang's all here. Progressive 41: 5-6 F '77
Immodest proposal; Cabinet choices, Presidential advisers and campaign issues. P. Steinfels. Commonweal 104:70 F 4 '77
Jimmy Carter's Cabinet—the spouses behind the scene. il U.S. News 82:30-2 F 14 '77
Jimmy Carter's computer connection; selection of IBM directors for Cabinet. il Forbes 119: 27-8 Ja 15 '77
Jimmy Carter's ruling class. R. Morris. Harpers 255:37-45 O '77
Junior varsity. Suetonius. New Repub 176:12-14 F 19 '77
New Cabinet whip; R. S. Strauss. M. A. Ruby and others. il por Newsweek 90:37 O 31 '77
Peek in the wallet; disclosure reports. il Newsweek 89:21 Mr 7 '77
Presidents' starting lineup—the new team in Washington. il por U.S. News 82:20-1 Ja 31 '77
Putting promises into practice—Carter's Cabinet makes a start. il U.S. News 82:14-15 F 21 '77
Religion in the Cabinet. Chr Today 21:47-8 Mr 4 '77
Suprises and sparks on the Hill; Senate hearings for Jimmy Carter's nominees. il Time 109:14-15 Ja 24 '77
Two from Column B.; financial statements. il Time 109:13 Mr 7 '77

Capitol

Facade of power. D. A. Williams and C. Ma. il Newsweek 90:18 Jl 18 '77
Uproar over the west front. il U.S. News 83:57 Jl 18 '77

Cavalry

See United States—Army—Cavalry

Census

Census shows changes in farm population. Farm J 101:42 Ja '77

Centennial celebrations, etc.

Aging of America. C. V. Woodward. bibl f Am Hist R 82:583-603 Je '77
Bicentennial era; proposed creation of American Constitution Bicentennial Foundation; address, October 27, 1976. C. L. Andes. Vital Speeches 43:194-6 Ja 15 '77
View from the castle; re-creation of the Philadelphia Centennial Exposition of 1876. S. D. Ripley. il Smithsonian 8:6 Jl '77
Way I see it; comments on Bicentennial observances. B. Catton. por Am Heritage 28:79 F '77
See also
United States—American Revolution Bicentennial Administration

Art

Evaluating the Bicentennial exhibitions. A. Frankenstein. bibl Art in Am 65:10-11+ My '77

Business aspects

Bye-bye Bicentennial. E. Keerdoja. il Newsweek 89:18 Ap 18 '77

Photographs and photography

How proudly we hailed! T. Fleming. il Read Digest 111:63-72 Jl '77
Recording America: federal funds for photos & films. A. C. Steinback. il Art in Am 65:19+ Ja '77

School projects

American time line; Bicentennial mural at Altadena Elementary School, Pasadena, Calif. E. Levine. il Sch Arts 76:30-2 Je '77
Art in Westbrook. D. F. Axelsen. il Sch Arts 76:34 Je '77
Bicentennial mural. M. L. Cox. il Sch Arts 76: 32 Ap '77

Science

Redistribution of wealth means bloody politics; Project: Knowledge 2000 conference; excerpts from address. G. A. Almond. por Intellect 105: 205-6 Ja '77

Central Intelligence Agency

Admirable Stansfield Turner. Suetonius. New Repub 176:10-12 Mr 12 '77
Admiral for superspook? S. Turner. il por Time 109:24 F 14 '77
Admiral for the CIA; S. Turner nomination. D. M. Alpern and others. il por Newsweek 89: 17-18 F 21 '77
Admiral of the covert seas; S. Turner. Nation 224:386 Ap 2 '77
Admiral Turner's fight; planning for consolidation of U.S. intelligence operations under the CIA. T. Mathews and N. Horrock. Newsweek 89:26 Je 20 '77
Advice from the old boys. il Time 109:14 F 21 '77
Appointments calendar; nomination of S. Turner. F. Getlein. Commonweal 104:133-4 Mr 4 '77
Backstage at the CIA. R. Boeth and others. il por Newsweek 90:27-8 S 12 '77
Behind the purge at CIA. il U.S. News 83:37 N 21 '77
Bribery and human rights; secret CIA payments. N. Cousins. Sat R 4:4 Ap 2 '77
Brouhaha in Brooklyn; question of Brooklyn College professor M. Selzer's involvement with the CIA. D. Ravitch. New Repub 176:18-21 Mr 12 '77; Discussion. 176:9 Mr 26; 7-8 Ap 2; 7+ My 7 '77
CIA: an all-purpose football. M. Stone. U.S. News 83:88 D 19 '77
CIA and Cuba; question of Kennedy's participation in Castro assassination plots. W. F. Buckley, Jr. Nat R 29:792 Jl 8 '77
C.I.A. and the funny men. C. L. Bach. America 137:142-5 S 17 '77
CIA gauntlet; nomination of T. Sorensen. Nation 224:98 Ja 29 '77
CIA satellite data link study revealed. J. M. Lenorovitz. Aviation W 106:25-6 My 2 '77
CIA's apprentices. Nation 224:770-2 Je 25 '77
CIA's electric kool-aid acid test; LSD experimentation. T. Szulc. il Psychol Today 11:92-4+ N '77

UNITED STATES—Central Intelligence Agency —*Continued*

CIA's goof in assessing the Soviets; effect of defense spending on the Soviet economy. il Bus W p96-8+ F 28 '77
Carter and the CIA. A. S. Miller. Progressive 41: 9-10 My '77
Carter takes his lumps; T. Sorensen's withdrawal of CIA nomination. il por Time 109:20+ Ja 31 '77
Carter's intelligence chief sizes up world's trouble spots; interview. S. Turner. por U.S. News 82:24-6 My 16 '77
Carter's Oversight; Intelligence Oversight Board's review of CIA payments to Hussein. J. Osborne. New Repub 176:8-10 Mr 19 '77
Cloak, dagger and gown: CIA in academe. J. K. Larson. Chr Cent 94:931-3 O 19 '77
Cutting off the King's dole; covert payments to King Hussein and other leaders. il por Time 109:13 F 28 '77
Defense miscalculations: dollarizing the Russian forces. E. Aerie. Nation 225:78-81 Jl 23 '77
Deputies are forever; Deputy Director for National Intelligence. R. Morris. New Repub 176:15-17 Ap 23 '77
First defeat; forcing T. Sorenson's resignation as C.I.A. nominee. D. M. Alpern and others. por Newsweek 89:30-1 Ja 31 '77
For new CIA chief, a big rebuilding job. il por U.S. News 82:24 F 21 '77
Gary Weissman's catch-22. J. Miller. Progressive 41:10 Ap '77
Grinch who stole Castro; B. Moyers' documentary. il por Time 109:50 Je 13 '77
Gumshoe stampede. Nation 225:610-11 D 10 '77
Hussein flap: cui bono? CIA payoffs. Nat R 29: 313 Mr 18 '77
Hussein on his CIA money; excerpts from interview, ed by A. de Borchgrave. Hussein. il por Newsweek 89:16-18 Mr 7 '77
ITT under the gun. T. Szulc and E. Yoffe. New Repub 177:18-22 Ag 6 '77
If you can't beat them, join them. R. J. Smith. Science 198:810 N 25 '77
JFK, Castro—and controversy; B. Moyers' documentary The CIA's secret army. D. Gelman. il pors Newsweek 90:85 Jl 18 '77
Journalists as spooks; CIA use of newsmen of intelligence operations. H. Bray. Progressive 41:9-10 F '77
King's pay packet. D. M. Alpern and others. il por Newsweek 89:18-19 F 28 '77
Letter from Washington. R. H. Rovere. New Yorker 53:111-14 Mr 7 '77
Marchetti asks U.S. to lift censorship of 1974 book. S. Wagner. Pub W 211:23 Ap 4 '77
Old salt opens up the pickle factory. il Time 109:22-5 Je 20 '77
One man's files. G. C. Zahn. America 135:438-42 D 18 '76; Correction. 136:62 Ja 29 '77
Out in the cold; firing 200 officers. R. Boeth and D. C. Martin. il Newsweek 90:48 N 21 '77
Psst! Viet secrets? agent F. Snepp's account. T. Mathews. il por Newsweek 90:71 N 28 '77
RH edits book in secrecy to prevent CIA action; publication of Decent interval. M. Reuter. Pub W 212:13 N 28 '77
Shortage of intelligence; report on oil supplies. Nat R 29:705 Je 24 '77
Sorensen lesson. J. Burnham. Nat R 29:199 F 18 '77
Soviet grain harvests: CIA study pessimistic on effects of weather. D. Shapley. Science 195: 377-8 Ja 28 '77
Spies who hate us. Progressive 41:6-7 O '77
Spooked spooks at the CIA. il Time 110:22 N 28 '77
Stealing the company store. il por Time 109:19 My 9 '77
Television; B. Moyers' The CIA's secret army. P. Sourian. Nation 225:155-7 Ag 20 '77
Time of the angel: the U-2, Cuba, and the CIA. D. Moser. il Am Heritage 28:4-15 O '77
Tongsun Park's White House connection. A. Latham. il Esquire 88:78+ D '77
Weather modification; CIA report. N. Cousins. Sat R 4:4 F 5 '77
When spies talk shop. Nation 224:452-3 Ap 16 '77
Wiley withholds book with possible CIA link; Robert Moss' Chile's Marxist experiment; interview, ed by S. Wagner. D. Edwards. Pub W 211:37-8 F 7 '77
Working for the Company? journalists. il Time 110:60 S 26 '77

See also

Government investigations—Central Intelligence Agency

Anecdotes, facetiae, satire, etc.

I was a hooker for the CIA. M. Scarf. New Repub 177:17-19 S 3 '77

History

Birth of the CIA. T. Braden. il Am Heritage 28:4-13 F '77

Chamber of Commerce

See Chamber of Commerce of the United States of America

Civil Aeronautics Board

Bargains ahead for U.S. air travelers. il U.S. News 82:55-6 Mr 21 '77
CAB delays foreign permits. Aviation W 106:27 Ja 3 '77
CAB expands carrier access to Europe. R. K. Ellingsworth. Aviation W 107:29 S 19 '77
CAB plans new overbooking proposal. Aviation W 107:30 Ag 8 '77
CAB proposes Continental for South Pacific. Aviation W 106:31 My 16 '77
CAB regulatory shifts concern carriers. Aviation W 108:36-7 Ja 9 '78
CAB sets tighter conduct code. L. Doty. Aviation W 106:27 Ja 17 '77
CAB shifts interlocking relationships policy. Aviation W 106:25 Ja 3 '77
CAB to hear oral arguments on intercarrier equipment talks. Aviation W 107:30 Ag 15 '77
California agency clashes with CAB. Aviation W 106:25 Ja 10 '77
Carriers get domestic fill-up rights Aviation W 106:33 My 9 '77
Free flights; CAB and regulation of intrastate airlines. Nat R 29:779 Jl 8 '77
Latest plans for cheaper air fares. il U.S. News 82:67 Je 27 '77
McDonnell Douglas, Eastern oppose Boeing on carrier talks. Aviation W 107:35 O 10 '77
Midway case may reveal Carter policy. R. K. Ellingsworth. Aviation W 106:30 F 7 '77
Overbook plan reactions mixed. D. R. Griffiths. Aviation W 107:26+ D 12 '77
Pros and cons of airline deregulation. R. Loving, Jr. il Fortune 96:208-12+ Ag '77
Real ferment in low-fare flying. Bus W p58 S 26 '77
Right to smoke; CAB ban of cigar and pipe smoking on commercial airplanes. New Repub 177:8-9 D 10 '77
Scrutinizing another Carter appointment; D. L. Tucker. por Bus W p42 O 3 '77
Shifts in fare standards seen. R. K. Ellingsworth. Aviation W 107:24-5 Ag 29 '77
Shifts urged in discount tests. R. K. Ellingsworth. Aviation W 107:24-5 Ag 15 '77

Civil Air Patrol

Civil Air Patrol. P. Trenner. il Flying 101:191 S '77

Civil defense

See Civil defense

Civil Rights Commission

See United States—Commission on Civil Rights

Civil Service Commission

Inside look at our runaway bureaucracy; with interview with A. Campbell. J. S. Lang. il U.S. News 83:22-4+ O 3 '77

Civilization

Acting your age. T. Griffith. Atlantic 239:20 Mr '77
America—passing out of adolescence; excerpts from address. C. Hills. por Intellect 105:207-8 Ja '77
American dream; tr by M. D. Meeks. J. Moltmann. Commonweal 104:490-6 Ag 5 '77
Limits of ethnicity; address, June 25, 1977. I. Howe. New Repub 176:17-19 Je 25 '77; Same with title What role for ethnicity? Current 195: 13-17 S '77
Little man at Chehaw Station: the American artist and his audience. R. Ellison. Am Scholar 47:25-48 Wint '77
Two exhibitions on American culture. S. B. Sherrill. il Antiques 111:258+ F '77
Winding down the '60s. M. Dickstein. Nation 224: 632-3 My 21 '77

See also

United States—Social conditions

Climate

Big freeze: Forecast: unsettled weather ahead. il map Time 109:22-8 Ja 31 '77
Circulation and weather of 1976. A. J. Wagner. maps Weatherwise 30:22-31+ F '77
Climatic change. R. C. Cowen. Current 195:53-6 S '77
Deep freeze! Why it's so cold; Winter wasteland. R. Steele. il maps Newsweek 89:34-40+ Ja 31 '77
Makings of real disasters. il Time 109:13 F 21 '77
Simmer of '77. R. Boeth. il map Newsweek 90: 14-16 Ag 1 '77
Weather with a vengeance: heat, storm and flood. il Time 110:10-11 Ag 1 '77
Where all that sticky weather came from. il U.S. News 83:32 Ag 1 '77
Will cruel weather ever let up? Now it's floods, tornadoes. il U.S. News 82:59-60 Ap 18 '77
Winter to remember; 1976-77. il U.S. News 82:40-1 Ja 31 '77
Year the weather went wild. T. Y. Canby. il maps Nat Geog 152:798-829 D '77

UNITED STATES—*Continued*

Coast Guard

Case of red herring; seizure of two Russian trawlers. T. Mathews and R. Manning. il Newsweek 89:23+ Ap 25 '77
Coast Guard buy challenges Falcon Jet. E. J. Bulban. il Aviation W 107:53-8 Ag 29 '77
Coast Guard helicopter buy awaited. D. M. North. Aviation W 106:18-19 My 16 '77
Coast Guard will monitor CB. G. West. Yachting 142:126 D '77
Commercial vessel safety: Coast Guard inspection of United States Merchant Marine. J. Hunt. il Oceans 10:28-31 Mr '77
Crackdown on Russian poachers—a state of more to come. il map U.S. News 82:43-4 Ap 25 '77
Little stink about a lot of fish; violation of U.S. 200 mile fishing zone by Russian ships. il Time 109:42+ Ap 25 '77
Questions of distress; Coast Guard's signaling tests. T. Gibbs. Yachting 141:106+ F '77
Thin blue line. S. Fraker and others. il map Newsweek 89:25-6 Ap 25 '77
Tough new Coast Guard mission: policing today's vast 200-mile limit. R. Petrow. il map Pop Mech 148:72-5+ Ag '77
Valdez connection. P. L. Fradkin. maps Audubon 79:134-40 Mr '77
You say There ought to be a law. . . ? Oil tanker standards. Nat Parks & Con Mag 51:23-5 Mr '77

See also

United States Coast Guard Academy, New London, Conn.

History

That others might live: the saga of the U.S. Coast Guard; Life Saving and Revenue Cutter Services. D. Noble and T. M. O'Brien. il Am Hist Illus 12:4-7+ Je '77

Procurement

Senate unit schedules hearings on Coast Guard buy of Falcon. il Aviation W 106:23-4 Ja 3 '77

Commerce

Global props for U.S. farm prices. il Bus W p74+ My 9 '77
How a rising yen could help the U.S. il Bus W p42 O 24 '77
How foreign steelmakers woo U.S. buyers. il Bus W p68-9 S 19 '77
Labor content of imports and exports. D. J. B. Mitchell. M Labor R 100:48-50 Mr '77
Long, steep slide is over in foreign trade. S. Parker and others. il Fortune 95:24 Je '77
Secretary Kreps won't talk; sale of American computers to foreign governments. M. T. Klare. Nation 224:678-9 Je 4 '77
Two faces of foreign trade. M. King. il Forbes 120:46-52+ N 15 '77

See also

Balance of payments—United States
Balance of trade—United States
Export-import trade
Investments, American
Shipping—United States
United States—Interstate Commerce Commission

Africa

Building business with Africa. A. Colamosca. map Duns R 109:92-4 My '77

Arab countries

AAP urges end to Arab book boycott. M. Reuter. Pub W 212:22-3 Ag 8 '77
Anti-boycott legislation. E. M. Bronfman. New Repub 176:17-19 Je 4 '77
Arab boycott of Israel. N. Turck. bibl f For Affairs 55:472-93 Ap '77
Arabs buying more U.S. farm products. il Suc Farm 75:K9 N '77
Fragile pact to beat the Arab boycott; Business Roundtable—B'nai B'rith Anti-Defamation League agreement. Bus W p25-6 Mr 28 '77
How antiboycott law was hammered out. D. C. Bacon. il U.S. News 82:64 Je 20 '77
President Carter discusses boycott issue; remarks, February 9, 1977. J. Carter. Dept State Bull 76:266 Mr 21 '77
Secretary Vance discusses antiboycott legislation and nuclear nonproliferation; statement, March 1, 1977. C. R. Vance. Dept State Bull 76:267-71 Mr 21 '77
Unglued alliance on the Arab boycott; Business Roundtable and B'nai B'rith Anti-Defamation League. Bus W p43-4 S 12 '77

Brazil—History

Perspective on development: Brazil and the United States, 1976. G. Hawrylyshyn. il Américas 29:12-13 My '77

China

China pushes a trade decision. il Bus W p75 N 21 '77
China's new leaders start looking outward. il Bus W p46+ S 5 '77
Coming leap forward in China trade. J. M. Sobin. por Nations Bus 65:54-6 Jl '77
Lightbulbs for the lamps of China? il Forbes 119:45 Mr 1 '77
Rug show with a frayed look. il Bus W p29 N 7 '77
Surprise attack on trade with China; Work Glove Manufacturers Assn. Bus W p32 D 26 '77

Communist countries

Crackdown on electronics smugglers. il Bus W p39 Mr 21 '77
Enough rope to hang us? M. Stone. U.S. News 82:80 Je 20 '77

Cuba

Claimsmen and the traders: U.S. business squabbles over Cuba; reimbursement for expropriated properties. A. L. Padula, Jr. Nation 225:390-3 O 22 '77
Cuban hustle. J. Miller. il por New Repub 177:11-14 O 8 '77
Early-bird businessmen are flying to Cuba. il Bus W p 132+ Ap 18 '77
Help from Havana? Cuban tobacco. Forbes 120:69 N 15 '77
Probing the Cuba trade; visiting American businessmen. L. Langway and C. J. Harper. il Newsweek 90:66-7 Jl 4 '77
Should U.S. do business with Cuba? interviews. J. B. Bingham; L. P. McDonald. pors US. News 82:73-4 Mr 7 '77

Egypt

Proposed sales of military equipment to Egypt; statement, September 15, 1977. A. L. Atherton, Jr. Dept State Bull 77:650-2 N 7 '77

Europe, Western

Compromise speeds the Tokyo Round; agricultural concession between the U.S. and the European Community. Bus W p53-4 Jl 25 '77
Europe: a liability threat to U.S.-bound exports. il Bus W p42 Mr 14 '77
Trade war: the first skirmishes? T. Szulc. il Forbes 120:29-30 O 15 '77

Germany, West

How my no.2 corn became low no.3 overseas. L. Schaller and G. Wormley. il Farm J 101:17-19+ O '77

Great Britain

Britain's bric-a-brac boom. J. Ross-Skinner. il Duns R 109:76-9 Je '77

India

Case of the missing thistleseed; question of embargo by India. G. Reiger. Audubon 79:161 N '77
Keep an eye on India, your swinging customer. il Farm J 101:D1 N '77

Iran

Ambassador for sale; R. Helms of the Safeer Company. Nation 225:580 D 3 '77
Carter withdraws notice of AWACS sale to Iran. Aviation W 107:18 Ag 1 '77
Carter's way with Congress; sale of AWACS aircraft to Iran. G. Rushford. Nation 225:270 S 24 '77
Congressional criticism mounts against AWACS sale to Iran. Aviation W 107:22 Jl 18 '77
Further Iran arms bids face opposition. Aviation W 107:16 N 21 '77
GAO criticizes AWACS sale to Iran on justification basis. Aviation W 107:24-5 Jl 25 '77
Iran AWACS sale returned to Congress. Aviation W 107:18-19 S 12 '77
Proposed sale of AWACS to Iran; statement, July 28, 1977. C. R. Vance. Dept State Bull 77:245-7 Ag 22 '77
Report warns on danger of Iran sales corruption. E. Kozicharow. Aviation W 107:22-3 D 12 '77
Special rules for the Shah; proposed AWACS sale to Iran. New Repub 177:10 Jl 30 '77
Those controversial planes for Iran. . . ; AWACS. il U.S. News 83:36 Ag 15 '77

Israel

How not to limit the arms trade; cancelling promised sale of CBU-72 bombs. New Repub 176:5 F 26 '77

Japan

Agreement on importation of TV sets from Japan. Dept State Bull 76:684-5+ Je 27 '77
Animal airlift to feed the Japanese; live beef cattle. Bus W p28-9 My 23 '77
Antitrust question about Japanese steel. Bus W p32+ D 19 '77
At brink of trade war—Japan backs away. il U.S. News 83:38-9 D 12 '77
Big steel and big government. G. F. Will. Newsweek 90:124 D 12 '77
Cracking down on Japan. D. Pauly and others. il Newsweek 90:75+ N 21 '77
Europe fights Japanese imports; effect on U.S. J. Ross-Skinner. il Duns R 109:68-70+ F '77
Free trade and the price of TV sets. Consumer Rep 43:20-1 Ja '78

UNITED STATES—Commerce—Japan—*Continued*

Half a loaf. K. Willenson and others. Newsweek 90:41 D 19 '77
High cost of doing business with Japan. D. Kirk. il Sat R 4:20-6 Mr 19 '77
Japan rebuffed in first round. il Time 110:41 D 26 '77
Japan, still your best customer. . . S. Cain. il Suc Farm 75:60 N '77
Kickbacks in living color; charges against Japanese television manufacturers. il Time 109:63 Je 13 '77
Mansfield's mounting problems as envoy to Japan. J. N. Wallace. il por U.S. News 83:42 O 31 '77
Oil will soon flow, but where will it go? P. L. Fradkin. il Audubon 79:86-8+ Ja '77
Protectionist scare sobers the Japanese. Bus W p53-5 D 12 '77
Ready to deal. F. Willey and others. il Newsweek 90:69-70 D 12 '77
Sharp boost for your exports. R. C. Black. Farm J 101:H2 O '77
Showdown on Japan's TV blitz; ITC tariff recommendation; with interviews with J. J. Nevin and T. Takai. A. J. Mayer and others. il Newsweek 89:58-9 Mr 28 '77
Strauss's big test in Tokyo. S. W. Sanders. il por Bus W p48 D 5 '77
Tactics to outwit U.S. protectionists. il Bus W p36 Mr 28 '77
Underselling Japanese steel. il Bus W p25-6 Jl 11 '77
Ushiba: maneuvering room; excerpts from interview, ed by B. Krisher. N. Ushiba. il por Newsweek 91:32 Ja 9 '78
World trade: a round the protectionists won; increased duty liability on Japanese electronic products. Bus W p30 Ap 25 '77

Korea, South

Korean arms buys from U.S. detailed. Aviation W 107:13 D 19 '77
ROC and Korea agree to curb shoe exports to U.S; announcement, June 14, 1977. Dept State Bull 77:202-3 Ag 15 '77

Latin America

Tariff hammer. Nation 225:675-6 D 24 '77
Trade and business in Inter-American relations; address, May 3, 1977. T. A. Todman. Dept State Bull 77:393-5 S 26 '77
U.S security assistance policy for Latin America; statement, April 5, 1977. T. A. Todman. Dept State Bull 76:444-6 My 2 '77

Mexico

Gas bonanza; Pemex' Mexican pipeline plan. S. T. Atlas and W. J. Cook. map Newsweek 90:61-2 Ag 1 '77
Pemex wants dollars for a new gas line. il Bus W p42 My 23 '77
Pressuring the U.S. over the price of gas; Pemex' pipeline. map Bus W p32 Ja 9 '78

Middle East

Casualties of a cut in arms sales abroad. il Bus W p34-5 Ap 25 '77

Rhodesia

Ambassador Young testifies on Rhodesian sanctions bill; statement, February 24, 1977. A. J. Young. Dept State Bull 76:271-2 Mr 21 '77
Department urges passage of bill to halt importation of Rhodesian chrome; statements, February 10, 1977. J. L. Katz; C. R. Vance. Dept State Bull 76:170-4 F 28 '77
Door is closing on chrome. Bus W p29-30 F 21 '77
President signs bill restoring embargo on Rhodesian chrome; statement, March 18, 1977. J. Carter. Dept State Bull 76:333-4 Ap 11 '77
Rhodesian chrome. Nat R 29:373 Ap 1 '77

Rumania

Department recommends extending MFN treatment for Romania; statement, July 18, 1977. M. Nimetz. Dept State Bull 77:278-82 Ag 29 '77

Russia

Firm guilty in technology export case. Aviation W 106:55 F 21 '77
Innocents abroad; Kama River plant. W. F. Buckley, Jr. Nat R 29:168-9 F 4 '77
Politics and Soviet-American trade: the three questions. D. Yergin. For Affairs 55:517-38 Ap '77
Red tractors in the Midwest. il Time 110:44-5 Ag 22 '77
Revving up oil output with the West's help. il Bus W p52 O 17 '77
Soviet-American trade: trick or treat? J. Barron. Read Digest 111:67-8+ O '77
Soviet trade. D. Yergin. New Repub 176:16-17 Je 4 '77
We have buried them. New Repub 177:2+ O 22 '77
See also
Grain trade

Saudi Arabia

U.S.-Saudi relations and the oil crises of the 1980s. D. A. Rustow. bibl f For Affairs 55:494-516 Ap '77

South Africa

Loneliness is an enemy; proposed arms embargo. il Time 110:36-7 N 7 '77
Message to Pretoria. R. Steele and others. il Newsweek 90:30-1 N 7 '77
Myopia in South Africa. M. Stone. U.S. News 83:112 N 14 '77
Polaroid pulls out. Newsweek 90:80 D 5 '77
U.S. arms embargo against South Africa; statement, July 20, 1977. W. H. Lewis. Dept State Bull 77:320-2 S 5 '77
U.S. nuclear exports to South Africa; statement, July 12, 1977. J. S. Nye, Jr. Dept State Bull 77:236-41 Ag 22 '77

South America

See United States—Commerce—Latin America

Taiwan

ROC and Korea agree to curb shoe exports to U.S; announcement, June 14 1977. Dept State Bull 77:202-3 Ag 15 '77
Taiwan next $1 billion farm customer? il Suc Farm 75:A4 My '77

Uganda

Death and coffee in Uganda. J. M. Wall. Chr Cent 94:971-3 O 26 '77

Commerce, Department of

Bureaucratic brainstorm; corporate Social Performance Index. M. Stone. U.S. News 84:76 Ja 9 '78
Can the Commerce Department revolutionize federal policy on the arts? L. Wiener. por Am Artist 41:12 D '77
Commerce Department moves toward Office of Construction. W. Hickman. Archit Rec 161:37+ Ja '77
First lady of Commerce; J. M. Kreps. L. Langway and R. Thomas. il por Newsweek 89:61 F 7 '77
Halo game; proposal for corporate social performance lists. Nation 225:516-17 N 19 '77
Juanita Kreps: more active role for Commerce; interview. J. M. Kreps. il pors Nations Bus 65:30-4 S '77

Economic Development Administration

EDA holds firm against set-aside challenges; minority business enterprise clause in Round II Local Public Works Act. Am City & County 92:13 D '77

National Fire Prevention and Control Administration

Agency plans fire safety courses for architects; program of the National Academy for Fire Prevention and Control. W. Hickman. Archit Rec 162:33 mid-Ag '77
Municipal departments must work together; views of W. V. Donaldson. por Am City & County 92:52 Ja '77

National Technical Information Service

Article-copying service by NTIS takes off. H. E. Rosenfeld. Wilson Lib Bull 52:284 D '77
NTIS plan draws fire at CONTU photocopying hearing. S. Wagner. Pub W 211:252+ Ja 24 '77

Commercial policy

American labor's stake in a changing world economy; symposium. M Labor R 100:34-5 Mr '77
Begging to disagree. por Forbes 120:152 O 15 '77
Carter as arms merchant. R. Carroll and S. Sullivan. il map Newsweek 90:31-2 Ag 8 '77
Carter's plan to stem imports. il U.S. News 82:94 Ap 11 '77
Cautious approval for U.S. reference prices. il Bus W p30 Ja 16 '78
Challenge of selling a liberal trade policy. B. France and J. Pearson. Bus W p32 Je 20 '77
Commodities: a better idea? A. J. Mayer and R. Thomas. il Newsweek 89:57 Ap 4 '77
Controlling arms transfers: an instrument of U.S. foreign policy; address, June 27, 1977. L. W. Benson. Dept State Bull 77:155-9 Ag 1 '77
Controls on trade and technology; Pentagon puts stress on know-how. J. Walsh. Science 197:1261-4 S 23 '77
DOD revises policy on export. E. Kozicharow. il Aviation W 107:12-13 S 12 '77
Dangerous U.S. trade deficit. G. R. Rosen. il map Duns R 110:62-5 O '77
Decisions on sugar imports and income supports announced; May 4, 1977. J. Carter. Dept State Bull 76:657-8 Je 20 '77
Department testifies on International commodity agreements; statement, June 8, 1977. J. L. Katz. Dept State Bull 77:19-25 Jl 4 '77

UNITED STATES—Commercial policy—*Continued*
Echoes of OPEC in Bergland's commodity pricing scheme. il Bus W p76 Mr 14 '77
Enough rope to hang us? M. Stone. U.S. News 82:80 Je 20 '77
First step in rescuing steel. il Bus W p34-5 N 28 '77
Free trade or protection: a hot potato for Carter. W. S. Wingo. il U.S. News 82:66-7 F 14 '77
Growing conflict over rescuing steel. il Bus W p39-40 O 10 '77
Hard times for free traders. A. J. Mayer and others. il Newsweek 89:78+ Mr 14 '77
How we practice arms restraint. M. T. Klare. Nation 225:268-9+ S 24 '77
Importance of current trade negotiations on U.S. industry; Tokyo Round; address, October 13, 1977. N. Berkeley, Jr. Vital Speeches 44:75-8 N 15 '77
Improving U.S. prospects in global competition. R. E. Anderson. por Nations Bus 65:66-8 My '77
Is the U.S. going protectionist? No, but dangers do exist. W. E. Hoadley. Duns R 109:9 Mr '77
Labor's new push for protection. il Bus W p31-2 D 26 '77
Missing advocates. M. Friedman. Newsweek 90:67 Jl 25 '77
Perils of rising protectionism; Time essay. E. Warner. Time 109:65 Ap 18 '77
Policy is born; foreign arms sales. J. Osborne. New Repub 176:10-12 Je 18 '77
President announces measures to assist U.S. shoe industry; statement, April 1, 1977. J. Carter. Dept State Bull 76:463 My 9 '77
President Carter announces policy on transfers of conventional arms; statement, May 19, 1977. J. Carter. Dept State Bull 76:625-6 Je 13 '77
President Carter's textile dilemma. Forbes 119:25-8 Ap 1 '77
President signs 1977 amendments to Export Administration Act; statement, June 22, 1977. J. Carter. Dept State Bull 77:162-3 Ag 1 '77
Protectionist storm brews. il Bus W p 152+ Mr 21 '77
Protectionists gain more allies. E. Lewis. Bus W p99 D 19 '77
Protectionists test Carter. il Time 109:74-5 Mr 28 '77
Push for protection. T. Nicholson and J. B. Copeland. il Newsweek 90:81-2+ O 17 '77
ROC and Korea agree to curb shoe exports to U.S; announcement, June 14, 1977. Dept State Bull 77:202-3 Ag 15 '77
Rethinking free trade. H. P. Gray. New Repub 176:12-13 Mr 19 '77
Should U.S. curb imports? interviews. J. L. Kirkland; C. F. Bergsten. pors U.S. News 83:25-6 Ag 8 '77
Should U.S. limit steel imports? interviews. J. P. Murtha, Jr; C. Stern. pors U.S. News 83:77-8 O 24 '77
Specialty steel: help from temporary quotas. Bus W p78 S 19 '77
Stakes go higher in new trade talks. Bus W p22-3 Mr 7 '77
Taking the wind out of arms sales. New Repub 176:6+ Je 11 '77
Trade restrictions: the hidden sales tax. il Consumer Rep 43:18-22 Ja '78
Trigger to curb dumping; steel. Time 111:45-6 Ja 16 '78
Unions go all out for tougher curbs on imports. il U.S. News 83:83-4 D 19 '77
Unions tee off on Carter's free trade stand. il U.S. News 82:84-5 Ap 18 '77
U.S. commodity policy; address, October 3, 1977. C. F. Bergsten. Vital Speeches 44:57-61 N 1 '77
U.S. international economic policy and its administration; address, May 24, 1977. L. L. Morgan. Vital Speeches 43:618-21 Ag 1 '77
U.S. retains unilateral arms restraints; report on question and answer session. K. Johnsen. Aviation W 107:20-2 D 12 '77
U.S. seeks an auto cartel. Bus W p46+ My 16 '77
Very promising man; American arms sales. Nation 225:388-9 O 22 '77
Vote for continued arms sales abroad. il Nations Bus 65:16 Ag '77
Vulcan was a piker; arms. Nation 225:548 N 26 '77
Waging a case-by-case war. il Time 109:63-4 My 30 '77
What Washington may do for steel. Bus W p35-6 O 24 '77
Why Carter will have a tough time trying to curb arms sales. il U.S. News 83:39-40 Ag 1 '77
Zeroing in on dumping. Time 110:107-8 N 7 '77
See also
Tariff—United States
United States—International Trade Commission
United States—Special Representative for Trade Negotiations, Office of the

Commission on Civil Rights

Desegregation and equality—much remains to be done; findings. il Todays Educ 66:22-5 Ja '77
Positive experience. J. W. Donohue. America 136:236-8 Mr 19 '77

Commission on Electronic Fund Transfers

Banking by computer. il U.S. News 82:81-2 Mr 7 '77

Commission on Federal Paperwork

Commission on Federal Paperwork. P. H. Abelson. Science 197:1237 S 23 '77
Drive to cut paper work: one step forward, two steps back. il U.S. News 82:51-2 Ap 18 '77
Slaving the paperwork monster. K. Seegers. Read Digest 111:162-5 D '77

Commission on Obscenity and Pornography

Measuring the impact of erotica. G. Wills. bibl il Psychol Today 11:30-1+ Ag '77

Commission on Security and Cooperation in Europe

Bernstein and Albert testify on censorship, currency; testimony before Commission on Security and Cooperation in Europe. S. Wagner. Pub W 211:39+ Je 6 '77

Commodity Credit Corporation

See United States—Agriculture, Department of—Commodity Credit Corporation

Commodity Futures Trading Commission

Breaking the Hunts' grip on soybeans. pors Bus W p40-1 My 16 '77
Futures watchdog has a cloudy future. Bus W p37 O 24 '77
Hunts and the soybeans. M. Ruby and others. il pors Newsweek 89:77-8 My 9 '77
U.S. rule stifles a London market. Bus W p80-1 Je 6 '77
Why soybean prices blew the fuse. R. C. Black. il Farm J 101:18B+ Je '77
See also
Government investigations—Commodity Futures Trading Commission

Community Services Administration

Born-again poverty program. P. Primack. Nation 224:431-4 Ap 9 '77
Energy crisis funds to help poor and elderly households. Aging 274:17 Ag '77
Urban aid—banned in Boston; Urban Planning Aid of Cambridge, Mass. S. Blumenthal. Nation 224:70-2 Ja 22 '77

Comptroller of the Currency, Office of the

Bert, I'm proud of you. il pors Time 110:8-10 Ag 29 '77
Big showdown over banker Bert. il por Time 110:19-20 Ag 22 '77
Closer watch on bank takeovers. por Bus W p29 Ag 22 '77
Lance affair: an official report gives an inside look at banking. il por U.S. News 83:62-4 Ag 29 '77
Sticking up for Bert. J. Osborne. New Repub 177:8-10 S 3 '77

Congress

Congress: where the people speak. il U.S. News 82:49-51 My 9 '77
Message to the professions: Congress can and should correct its own problems; address, August 27, 1977. R. P. Griffin. Vital Speeches 44:82-5 N 15 '77
Unholy trinities that undermine America. J. N. Miller. Read Digest 110:61-7 Mr '77
Use tax dollars to elect Congress? interviews. K. Udall; L. P. Weicker, Jr. pors U.S. News 82:63-4 Ap 25 '77; Same. Current 194:3-7 Jl '77
Videoconferences via satellite: opening Congress to the people? L. J. Carter. il Science 197:31-3 Jl 1 '77
Why Congress doesn't work. A. S. King, Jr. por Newsweek 91:9 Ja 9 '78
See also
Congressmen
Congresswomen
Lobbyists and lobbying
Presidents—United States—Relations with Congress
Senators

Budget Office

Congress budget unit defines strategic arms options, costs. Aviation W 106:22 Ap 11 '77
Everyone's wild over Alice. il por Time 110:66+ Jl 18 '77
Hiding the other America; questions of Congressional Budget Office poverty report. M. Harrington. New Repub 176:15-17 F 26 '77

Committees

Capitol Hill staffs: hidden government in Washington. il U.S. News 82:37-40 Ap 4 '77
Congress and the cozy triangles: the case of energy. B. M. Casper. Bull Atom Sci 33:5 My '77

UNITED STATES—Congress—Committees—*Cont.*
Congressional science committees have a new look. F. C. Bennett. Phys Today 30:109-11 My '77
We've been asked: how a conference committee works. il U.S. News 83:80 N 21 '77
See also
United States—Congress—House—Committees

Employees

See also
Congressmen—Staff

History

I looked down into my open grave; E. G. Ross and impeachment of A. Johnson; excerpt from Profiles in courage. J. F. Kennedy. il Sr Schol 109:17-19 F 24 '77
See also
United States—Continental Congress

Joint Commission on Prescription Drug Use

Adverse drug reactions: monitoring needed of drugs on market. B. J. Culliton. Science 195: 159-62 Ja 14 '77
18-member panel to set up new prescription drug monitor system. il Ret Liv 17:14 Ja '77

Pages

Where the girls are. il Newsweek 89:16 My 16 '77

Powers and duties

This month's feature: Congress and Executive Branch reorganization powers. Cong Digest 56:99-128 Ap '77
See also
War and emergency powers—United States

Reorganization

What reforms for Congress? W. Pincus. Current 191:6-13 Mr '77
See also
Congressmen—Term

Reporters and reporting

Our own fight: a letter to our readers; denial of accreditation to the periodical press gallery. Sci N 111:323 My 21 '77
Science finally admitted to congressional press gallery. C. Holden. Science 197:538 Ag 5 '77
Whisperings in the press gallery; periodical correspondents banned from Congress. P. H. Schuck. Harpers 254:113-17 Mr '77; Discussion. 254:113+ Mr; 6+ Ap '77

Rules and practice

Staff member hits lack of Congress coordination. Aviation W 107:23 Ag 1 '77
See also
United States—Congress—Senate—Rules and practice

Salaries

See Congressmen—Salaries, allowances, etc.

Term of members

See Congressmen—Term

Voting

See also
United States—Congress—House—Voting
United States—Congress—Senate—Voting

94th Congress

Civil liberties and national security: the outlook in Congress. I. Shapiro. Intellect 105:230-3 F '77
President Carter and the honeymooners; non-enacted legislation supported by Democratic congressmen. J. Drake and S. Petersen. il Nat R 29:433-6+ Ap 15 '77

94th Congress—2d session

Tax practitioners act of 1976. I. Ross. il Fortune 95:103-6+ Ap '77

95th Congress

Legislation to watch—and work for—in the 95th Congress. S. Tenenbaum and J. A. Paulus. Ms 5:99-102 F '77
95th Congress: doing or dozing? il Sr Schol 109: 6-8 F 24 '77
Same old gang? M. Stone. U.S. News 82:88 Mr 14 '77
See also
Carter, J.—Relations with Congress

95th Congress—1st session

Behind the growing feud; Congress vs. President. G. Parshall. U.S. News 82:23 My 23 '77
Business and the new Congress—what lies ahead. map Nations Bus 65:16-20 Ja '77
Capitol Hill lag could narrow chances of salvaging Redwood Park. Nat Parks & Con Mag 51:21 N '77
Carter and Congress: seeds of more discord. U.S. News 83:21-2 N 21 '77
Carter sends Congress his plan to reshuffle social security; debate begins on revisions. il Ret Liv 17:11-13 Jl '77
Congress. il Time 109:10 F 28; 12-13 Mr 14; 20 Ap 11 '77
Congress adopts ethics code, but skepticism still runs strong. U.S. News 82:79 Ap 11 '77
Congress gives Carter mixed grades on first report card. il U.S. News 82:22-3 Mr 28 '77
Congress: Liberals at bay. G. R. Rosen. il Duns R 110:40-4 S '77
Congress plays the Carter game. il Bus W p32 Ag 22 '77
Congress: showdown ahead. il Time 110:18-19 N 7 '77
Congress that startled everybody. U.S. News 83: 14 D 19 '77
Congress waits for Carter's signal; regulatory reform. il Bus W p94-5 Ap 4 '77
Congressional threat to the World Bank; attaching conditions to U.S. contributions. Bus W p40-1 O 10 '77
Day in the life of Congressman David Obey. J. J. Landman. il pors Sr Schol 109:9-12 F 24 '77
Defiant Congress. il U.S. News 83:25 O 17 '77
Detente in the Capital. il por U.S. News 82:15-16 Je 27 '77
Flurry in the Capital. il U.S. News 83:15-16 Ag 15 '77
Gutting the energy bill. A. J. Mayer and W. J. Cook. il Newsweek 90:79-80 O 3 '77
Hard year's work. A. J. Mayer and others. il Newsweek 90:22-3+ D 19 '77
Home for Christmas. R. Boeth and others. il por Newsweek 90:75-6 D 26 '77
Is America ready for democracy? question of energy legislation. il New Repub 177:5-6+ N 26 '77
Is Congress becoming more practical? il Nations Bus 65:30-3 N '77
Major proposals before Congress affecting the elderly: June 30, 1977. Aging 274:38 Ag '77
Mounting discontent with first billion-dollar Congress. il U.S. News 82:23-6+ Mr 7 '77
95th, first session. Nat R 30:16-17 Ja 6 '78
Now it is up to Congress; dealing with J. Carter's energy plan. il Time 109:12-13 My 2 '77
On a collision course. il pors U.S. News 82:14-15 Ap 18 '77
Rebels on the Hill. R. Steele and H. W. Hubbard. il Newsweek 90:19+ Ag 8 '77
Recent major action in the Congress. Cong Digest 56:1-2 Ja; 33+ F; 65-6+ Mr; 97-8 Ap; 129-30 My; 161 Je; 257+ N '77
Same old gang. M. Stone. il U.S. News 82:88 Mr 14; 83:100 O 31 '77
Score one for Jimmy; House passage of national energy program. D. M. Alpern and others. il por Newsweek 90:15-16 Ag 15 '77
Ships and chauvinism: congressional squabble over oil-cargo-preference bill. A. J. Mayer. il Newsweek 90:82 O 17 '77
Some new laws you may have missed. il U.S. News 83:74 D 19 '77
Son of Kingfish. New Repub 177:2+ D 24 '77
Support for B-1 decision seen mixed in Congress. K. Johnsen. Aviation W 107:21-2 Jl 11 '77
Unfinished work of the 95th Congress. Todays Educ 66:80 S '77
What's wrong—and right—with Congress as seen by five freshmen. il U.S. News 82:34-5 Je 13 '77
Why Congress is ready to move; major tax legislation. il Bus W p62 Ag 29 '77
Worst Congress in years—or is it? T. J. Foley. U.S. News 83:25-6 S 26 '77

95th Congress—2d session

Outlook '78; in Congress, the mood will get even feistier. il U.S. News 83:33-4 D 26 '77
Toughest business battles in 1978. R. T. Gray. il Nations Bus 65:22-6+ D '77

House

Bleak house: frustration on Capitol Hill. S. J. Ungar. il Atlantic 240:27-36+ Jl '77
Plunder on the right; movement to impeach A. Young. K. Bode. New Repub 177:11-12 N 12 '77
Same old gang: chapter II. M. Stone. il U.S. News 83:100 O 31 '77
TRB from Washington; hearings on nuclear power. New Repub 176:2+ Je 18 '77
See also
Congressmen
Congresswomen

House—Aging, Select Committee on

What Congress is hearing about retirement. U.S. News 83:30-1 O 3 '77

House—Agriculture, Committee on—Forests Subcommittee

Larger equation for forestry. J. Weaver. por Am For 83:28-9+ N '77

UNITED STATES—Congress—*Continued*

House—Assassinations, Select Committee on

Are there new leads? suicide of witness G. de Mohrenschildt. D. M. Alpern and others. il por Newsweek 89:32+ Ap 11 '77
Assassination: now a suicide talks. il por Time 109:20 Ap 11 '77
Congress and the assassinations. G. Lardner, Jr. il Sat R 4:14-17 F 19 '77
New man on two old cases. S. J. Ungar. por Atlantic 239:8+ F '77
Self-inflicted wounds; H. B. Gonzalez-R. Sprague feud. D. M. Alpern and others. pors Newsweek 89:18+ F 21 '77
Shrinking Sprague. por Time 109:24 F 14 '77

House—Banking, Currency and Housing, Committee on—Domestic Monetary Policy Subcommittee

Man who watches the Fed. G. R. Rosen. por Duns R 109:47 Ja '77

House—Banking, Currency and Housing, Committee on—Financial Institutions Supervision, Regulation and Insurance Subcommittee

Bank reform loses a lot of momentum. il por Bus W p43 O 3 '77

House—Committees

Congress: House redistributes jurisdiction over energy. J. Walsh. il Science 195:562-3 F 11 '77
Washington scene; Committee assignments. B. Kravetz. Parks & Rec 12:14-16+ Mr '77

House—Education and Labor, Committee on

News and views; mandatory retirement age. il Ret Liv 17:58+ S '77

House—Energy, Ad Hoc Select Committee on

All it needs is Lud; Chairman T. L. Ashley. T. Mathews and others. il por Newsweek 89:24 My 9 '77

House—Ethics Committee

See United States—Congress—House—Standards of Official Conduct, Committee on

House—Intelligence, Select Committee on—Oversight Subcommittee

Spooking the press; CIA ties. Newsweek 91:30 Ja 16 '78
Who can be a paid spook? journalists and the CIA. il Time 111:12 Ja 9 '78

House—Interior and Insular Affairs, Committee on

NRPA interview with Congressman Morris K. Udall; ed by B. Kravetz. M. K. Udall. il pors Parks & Rec 12:42-5 Mr '77

House—Internal Security, Committee on

Investigative asymmetry proposed reestablishment of House Internal Security Committee. M. S. Evans. Nat R 29:997 S 2 '77

House—Public Works, Committee on

Industry cries overkill on clean-water rules. il Bus W p41 O 10 '77

House—Science and Technology, Committee on

Blast-off for Swigert, reentry for Mosher. J. Walsh. Science 197:967 S 2 '77

House—Speakers

House shall chuse their Speaker... N. McNeil. il Am Heritage 28:26-31 F '77

House—Standards of Official Conduct, Committee on

All about Koreagate. D. M. Alpern and others. il pors Newsweek 90:17+ Ag 1 '77
As the Korean bribery scandal unfolds—. il U.S. News 83:100 O 31 '77
Ethics committee size-up of probe: we are dealing with TNT here. U.S. News 83:11 Ag 1 '77
Fresh stirrings on Koreagate. il Time 110:19-20 S 5 '77
John Flynt: fox in the chicken coop. E. Roeder and A. Berlow. Nation 225:201-5 S 10 '77
Legislating ethics; Obey Commission. Nat R 29:314-15 Mr 18 '77
Memories of Ice Mountain; House Ethics Committee investigation of South Korea's attempts to bribe Congressmen. Time 110:16 O 31 '77
Park's lobby hobby. K. Willenson and others. il por Newsweek 90:37 S 5 '77
Patriarch's blessing; Koreagate influence-buying scandal. R. Steele and E. Shannon. il Newsweek 90:38 O 31 '77
Sordid example. M. Stone. U.S. News 83:68 Ag 1 '77

House—Voting

Ain't misbehaving; House code of ethics. Newsweek 89:16 Mr 14 '77
Congress's pay raise. U.S. News 83:32 Jl 11 '77
They are paying the price of virtue; code of ethics. il Time 109:12-13 Mr 14 '77

House—Ways and Means, Committee on

Most powerful committee in the House. G. R. Rosen. il por Duns R 109:46 Mr '77
Something for no one; A. Ullman's jobs tax credit bill. il por Time 109:44+ Mr 7 '77

Senate

By any other name; consideration of energy legislation. A. J. Mayer and W. J. Cook. Newsweek 90:87-8 S 19 '77
Canal debate begins. il Time 110:15-16 O 10 '77
The Club. M. Greenfield. Newsweek 90:118 O 10 '77
Debating abortion. J. Garn. Nat R 29:1299+ N 11 '77
Hooding the hawks; debate over nomination of P. Warnke. Nation 224:354-5 Mr 26 '77
Jimmy's oracle; R. C. Byrd. T. Mathews and J. J. Lindsay. por Newsweek 90:27 O 3 '77
Master of the maze; work of R. Long. por Time 110:20 N 7 '77
Panama Canal debate: Senate grasps the nettle. il U.S. News 83:30 O 10 '77
Senate and energy. Commonweal 104:643-4 O 14 '77; Discussion. 104:766-7 N 25 '77
Surprises and sparks on the Hill; Senate hearings for Jimmy Carter's nominees for the Cabinet. il Time 109:14-15 Ja 24 '77
Welcome home, Hubert! J. J. Lindsay. il por Newsweek 90:33 N 7 '77

See also

Government investigations

Senate—Aging, Special Committee on

Senate defeats by vote of 90 to 4 move to abolish Special Committee on Aging. il Ret Liv 17:13-14 Mr '77
Senate votes to retain Aging Committee. Aging 268:3 F '77

Senate—Budget, Committee on the

Mr Hayakawa goes to Washington. S. I. Hayakawa. il Harpers 256:39-43 Ja '78

Senate—Commerce, Committee on

FCC nomination causes some static; C. D. Ferris. il por Bus W p41-2 O 3 '77
Scrutinizing another Carter appointment; D. L. Tucker. por Bus W p42 O 3 '77

Senate—Committees

Senate reform too modest—Moss, Goldwater protest. F. E. Moss; B. Goldwater. por BioScience 27:10-11 Ja '77
Senate tunes up committee system. J. Walsh. Science 195:760 F 25 '77
Washington memo. R. D. Westgate. il Ret Liv 16:13 D '76
Washington scene: committee reform. B. Kravetz. Parks & Rec 12:18 My '77

Senate—Ethics Committee

See United States—Congress—Senate—Standards and Conduct, Select Committee on

Senate—Finance, Committee on

Cleverest senator; R. Long. G. F. Will. Newsweek 89:122 My 16 '77
Sen. Russell Long: he can influence your life for years to come; interview. R. B. Long. il pors Nations Bus 65:22-7 Ag '77

Senate—Government Operations, Committee on—Reports, Accounting, and Management Subcommittee

CPAs get another lashing. Bus W p76 Ja 31 '77
CPAs suggest the watchdogs they want. il Bus W p94+ My 23 '77
Figures don't lie, but. . . : auditing the auditors; FASB. J. Thackray. Nation 224:582-4 My 14 '77
More CPAs chime in on self-regulation. il Bus W p84+ Je 6 '77
Should CPAs be management consultants? staff study. il Bus W p70+ Ap 18 '77

Senate—Governmental Affairs, Committee on

Case against Lance—and his reply. il pors U.S. News 83:21-2 S 26 '77
Lance comes out swinging. il pors Time 110:12-18+ S 26 '77
Lance on the offense. R. Steele and others. il pors Newsweek 90:20-3+ S 26 '77

Senate—Governmental Affairs, Committee on—Anecdotes, facetiae, satire, etc.

How it might have gone. W. F. Buckley, Jr. Nat R 29:1194-5 O 14 '77

Senate—Hearings

See Government investigations

UNITED STATES—Congress—*Continued*

Senate—Intelligence, Select Committee on

Carter and Spyland. J. Osborne. New Repub 176:9-11 Je 11 '77
Carter takes his lumps; T. Sorensen's withdrawal of CIA nomination. il por Time 109:20+ Ja 31 '77
Civil liberties and national security: the outlook in Congress. I. Shapiro. Intellect 105:230-3 F '77
First defeat; forcing T. Sorenson's resignation as C.I.A. nominee. D. M. Alpern and others. por Newsweek 89:30-1 Ja 31 '77
Foreign agents in America—shady tactics and worse. il U.S. News 83:23-4 Jl 4 '77

Senate—Judiciary, Committee on the—Citizen and Shareholders' Rights and Remedies Subcommittee

Forgotten minority? por Forbes 120:105 Ag 15 '77

Senate—Judiciary, Committee on the—Criminal Laws and Procedures Subcommittee

AAP cautions Senate on pending obscenity law. S. Wagner. Pub W 212:29+ Jl 25 '77

Senate—Judiciary, Committee on the—Internal Security Subcommittee

Phasing out security. Nat R 29:427 Ap 15 '77

Senate—Nutrition and Human Needs, Select Committee on

Are you eating right? S. N. Wellborn. il U.S. News 83:39-43 N 28 '77
George McGovern had a problem. K. Daly. Farm J 101:Dairy 16, Hog 24 O '77
New dietary goals; recommendations of Select Committee on Nutrition and Human Needs report. House & Gard 149:101+ Jl '77
Open letter to Congress. H. Steirman. Fam Health 9:6 Ap '77

Senate—Rules and practice

Blitz by Fritz; ending the gas deregulation filibuster. P. Goldman and others. por Newsweek 90:34+ O 17 '77
Diminishing filibuster: squeeze play on the Senate floor; cloture. I. Nathanson. Nation 225: 422-4 O 29 '77
Energy talkathon. T. Mathews and others. il por Newsweek 90:28-30 O 10 '77
Filibuster ends, but not the gas war. il por Time 110:10-11+ O 17 '77
Night of the long winds; filbuster over natural gas rate controls. il por Time 110:12-14 O 10 '77
Senator Byrd: more than just a manager. por Bus W p38 O 17 '77

Senate—Select Committee to Study Governmental Operations with Respect to Intelligence Activities

Murder of President Kennedy. V. Cadden. il McCalls 104:119-20+ Mr '77

Senate—Standards and Conduct, Select Committee on

Behavior modification. E. Marshall. New Repub 177:9-11 N 12 '77

Senate—Voting

Two thirds. New Repub 177:2+ S 10 '77

Constitution

Bicentennial conference on the United States Constitution: the shaping of public policy—issues and questions for discussion; ed by E. B. Staats. Ann Am Acad 432:121-31 Jl '77
Birth of the Constitution—our next big celebration? interview. R. B. Morris. por U.S. News 83:63-4 Jl 4 '77

Amendments

Alice Paul: mother of the ERA. R. Morgan. por Ms 6:112 O '77
Berger v. Court; 14th Amendment decisions. J. K. Footlick. por Newsweek 90:75 N 14 '77
Berger's big book; 14th Amendment. W. F. Buckley, Jr. Nat R 29:1320 N 11 '77
Chains of the Constitution; the Fourteenth Amendment. E. Abrams. Commentary 64:84+ D '77
Constitutional shell game; Equal Rights Amendment. Nat R 29:1218 O 28 '77
Deadline time for ERA. New Repub 177:6+ D 17 '77
ERA in trouble. J. Miller. Progressive 41:8 My '77
ERA now? economic boycott in states that have failed to ratify the amendment. il Time 110:28 N 14 '77
End of an ERA? M. Kondracke. New Repub 176:14-16 Ap 30 '77
Equal Rights Amendment: what's it all about? E. D'Aulaire and P. O. D'Aulaire. Read Digest 110:98-102 F '77
Equal Rights: why the Amendment appears doomed. U.S. News 82:53 Mr 28 '77
Feminists' boycott; support for the ERA. Nation 225:548-9 N 26 '77
Fie on the 14th; views of R. Berger. Time 110: 101-2 N 14 '77
First ladies out front; views on Equal Rights Amendment. il Time 110:25 D 5 '77
Guess who's for the ERA? ed by E. Wheeler, B. Solomon and M. K. Place. pors Ms 5:78-9 Ap '77
Mormon connection? The defeat of the ERA in Nevada. L. C. Wohl. Ms 6:68-70+ Jl '77
Religion and ERA battle in the Rockies; Broomfield, Colo. M. H. Rush. Chr Cent 94:164-5 F 23 '77
Should women be nicer than men? views of P. Schlafly concerning the Equal Rights Amendment. J. Lelyveld. il pors N Y Times Mag p 126 Ap 17 '77
Stacking the deck on ERA. G. F. Will. por Newsweek 90:128 N 14 '77
This month's feature: controversy over the Equal Rights Amendment. Cong Digest 56: 162-92 Je '77
Time's up; ERA ratification deadline. Nat R 29:1344+ N 25 '77
Unmaking of an Amendment; Equal Rights Amendment. map Time 109:89-90 Ap 25 '77
We've been asked: how hard is it to amend the Constitution? il U.S. News 84:68 Ja 9 '78
We've been asked: is time running out on ERA's chances? map U.S. News 83:32 N 28 '77
Why a constitutional convention is needed; human Life Amendment. E. J. McMahon. America 137:12-14 Jl 2 '77
Why nice women should speak out for ERA. J. Carter. bibl Redbook 149:118+ O '77
Women against women; symposium. R. M. Williams. il Sat R 4:6-13+ Je 25 '77
Women vs women. S. Fraker and others. il Newsweek 90:34-5+ Jl 25 '77
See also
Presidents—United States—Term

Bill of Rights

Day the first amendment died; address, September 16, 1977. J. R. Bittner. Vital Speeches 44:24-8 O 15 '77
Do we have rights to everything? J. Houston. U.S. News 83:34 O 31 '77
I say lock 'em up, spank them, and send them home; obscenity and the first amendment. M. J. Sobran, Jr. Nat R 29:712-13+ Je 24 '77
Obscenity—forget it; the first amendment. C. Rembar. Atlantic 239:37-41 My '77

Constitutional law

Specious morality of the law. S. Levinson. Harpers 254:35-8+ My; 255:4-5 Jl '77
See also
United States—Supreme Court

Consumer Product Safety Commission

Banning Tris; chemically treated nightwear. il Newsweek 89:67 Ap 18 '77
Case of overkill in federal regulation. J. J. Kilpatrick. Nations Bus 65:11-12 Je '77
Concerned homemaker expresses her views on furniture flammability legislation; proposed flammable upholstered furniture law. M. Nervig. Consumers Res Mag 60:27+ Je '77
Cooperation; standards program for miniature electric Christmas tree lights and decorations. D. Chaucer. Consumers Res Mag 60:37-8 Jl '77
Flame-retardant ban dishevels an industry; childrens sleepwear chemical Tris-BP. il Bus W p45-6 Ap 18 '77
Tris—a sleepwear flame retardant banned. Consumers Res Mag 60:4 Je '77
Tris: confusion over another cancer hazard. Consumer Rep 42:415-16 Jl '77
What price safety? D. Pauly and J. Whitmore. il Newsweek 89:97 My 16 '77
What the Government can—and cannot—do to protect the public; interview. S. J. Byington. il por U.S. News 83:33-5 O 24 '77

Consumer Protection Agency (proposed)

See United States—Agency for Consumer Advocacy (proposed)

Continental Congress

Meet the men who were Presidents before Washington. R. B. Morris. il Smithsonian 8:92-4+ Ja '78

Copyright Office

AAP and authors differ on copyright termination. S. Wagner. Pub W 211:29-30 Ja 10 '77
Authors, publishers divide on divisibility doctrine. S. Wagner. Pub W 212:20+ O 17 '77

UNITED STATES—Copyright Office—*Continued*
Copyright workshop sees new forms, is cautioned on problems ahead. S. Wagner. Pub W 212:23-4 N 14 '77
Writers blast copyright registration concept. S. Wagner. Pub W 212:35 O 24 '77

Council of Economic Advisers

CEA takes a backseat with Carter. il por Bus W p 114-15 Jl 25 '77
Starring role for the CEA? il por Time 109:52 F 7 '77

Council on Environmental Quality

CEQ nominee learns judge not, lest ye be judged. L. J. Carter. Science 198:473 N 4 '77
Eating ourselves out of house and home. J. B. Craig. Am For 83:6 My '77
Executive office reorganization: OSTP and CEQ are still in. J. Walsh. Science 197:442-4 Jl 29 '77
Science units spared in shuffle. Sci N 112:54 Jl 23 '77
Speaking up for an imperiled CEQ. L. J. Carter. Science 197:240 Jl 15 '77

Council on International Economic Policy

White House eliminates export council. Aviation W 107:19 Ag 29 '77

Council on Wage and Price Stability

Bosworth: firm ideas for a drifting COWPS. por Bus W p28 Jl 11 '77
Fight on prices; appointment of B. P. Bosworth. il por Time 110:54-5 Ag 15 '77
Strong opposition to the Wage-Price Council. il Nations Bus 65:14-15 Je '77
Wage and price stability: this council is a real-life joke. D. Bollier and N. Waitzman. il Nation 225:456-8 N 5 '77

Courts

See Courts—United States

Cultural relations

Fifth U.S.-German cultural talks held at Washington; text of communique, April 27, 1977. Dept State Bull 76:556-7 My 30 '77
Guiding philosophy for American informational and cultural programs abroad; address, May 28, 1977. J. E. Reinhardt. Dept State Bull 77: 5-8 Jl 4 '77
See also
United States—Agency for International Communication (proposed)

Customs Service

See United States Customs Service

Declaration of Independence

British tried to discredit Declaration of Independence. R. Ginsberg. por Intellect 105:387 My '77

Defense, Department of

Brown vows to maintain military strength of U.S. Aviation W 106:25-6 Ja 17 '77
Controls on trade and technology; Pentagon puts stress on know-how. J. Walsh. Science 197: 1261-4 S 23 '77
DOD pressing for joint missile efforts. C. A. Robinson, Jr. il Aviation W 106:22-5 Mr 21 '77
DOD revises policy on export. E. Kozicharow. Aviation W 107:12-13 S 12 '77
DOD scrutinizes evolving air defenses of USSR. il Aviation W 107:16-18 D 5 '77
Defense Dept. sustains effort to aid NATO standardization. Aviation W 106:32 Ap 25 '77
Harold Brown and defense: from scientist to secretary. J. Walsh. por Science 195:463-6 F 4 '77
Meddling by Congress staff hit. C. A. Robinson, Jr. Aviation W 107:14-18 Jl 25 '77
See also
Secretaries of Defense (United States)
United States—Joint Chiefs of Staff
United States—Uniformed Services University of the Health Sciences, Bethesda, Md.

Advanced Research Projects Agency

Progress made on high-energy laser. P. J. Klass. Aviation W 106:16-17 Mr 7 '77

Appropriations and expenditures

Annual Red scare. Nation 224:67-8 Ja 22 '77
Arms acquisition reports show $19-billion drop in total costs. Aviation W 107:16-17 N 21 '77
Behind Carter's gamble on defense outlays. il U.S. News 82:17 Mr 7 '77
Big, big ideas at the Pentagon. J. Rhea. Progressive 41:13-18 Ap '77
Budget crunch threatens the F-15. Bus W p32 Mr 28 '77
Budget cuts Navy plans, bolsters Europe defense. Aviation W 108:18 Ja 2 '78
Carter and the big bomber; B-1 supersonic bomber. S. Fraker and others. il Newsweek 89:30+ Je 20 '77
Carter moves in on Pentagon budgeting. J. Canan. Bus W p55 N 21 '77
Carter strategic weapon funding backed in House. K. Johnsen. Aviation W 106:23-4 My 2 '77
Carter to consider Defense cuts; Ford budget for Defense getting Pentagon review. C. Brownlow. Aviation W 106:14-15 Ja 31 '77
Carter's arms budget is a signal to SALT. il Bus W p36 F 28 '77
Carter's goal: more sharing of the NATO load. il Bus W p78-9 Ag 8 '77
Caution marks Carter approach. C. Brownlow. Aviation W 106:21 Mr 21 '77
Conferees set defense ceilings. Aviation W 106: 15 My 16 '77
Congress initiates studies on cruise missile stress. K. Johnsen. Aviation W 107:18-19 Jl 25 '77
Cruise missiles, FB-111 stretch funding voted by Senate group. Aviation W 107:19-20 S 26 '77
DOD budget nearing passage. Aviation W 107:21 Jl 4 '77
DOD request keyed to extend military gains for third year. C. Brownlow. Aviation W 106:13-15 Ja 24 '77
Defense authorization passes Senate without serious debate. Aviation W 106:26-7 My 23 '77
Defense budget retains real growth. Aviation W 106:24-6 F 28 '77
Defense cut proposals draw opposition. C. Brownlow. Aviation W 106:22-3 F 7 '77
Discipline urged in budgetary process; statement to the Congressional Joint Committee on Defense Production. T. V. Jones. por Aviation W 107:46-7+ O 24 '77
Fiscal 1979 budget bids by services delayed. Aviation W 106:24 Je 20 '77
Foreign VIP's—another group of junketeers financed by U.S. taxpayers; visits of foreign military officers. G. Parshall and R. Barr. il U.S. News 83:30-1 S 19 '77
Fund curb hits Pentagon plans. il Aviation W 107:12-14 Ag 29 '77
House unit hikes Defense procurement; Congress budget unit defines strategic arms options, costs. K. Johnsen. Aviation W 106:21-2 Ap 11 '77
House unit overturns B-1, MX funding cuts. C. A. Robinson, Jr. Aviation W 107:21-2 O 3 '77
House unit votes major weapon funds. Aviation W 106:59 Je 6 '77
It's budget time again: the Russians are coming! D. Cortright and R. L. Borosage. Nation 224: 205-8 F 19 '77
LTV's campaign to save Vought; effect of defense budget cuts. il Bus W p24-5 Mr 7 '77
Laser-powered rockets and dark satellites. E. Ulsamer. Space World N-5-161:30-2 My '77
Minuteman production funds released. K. Johnsen. il Aviation W 107:23-4 O 24 '77
Missing billions. Nation 224:294-5 Mr 12 '77
Modest proposal; transfer of funds from military to social spending. Progressive 41:5-7 Mr '77
Nimble juggler; H. Brown. T. Mathews and L. H. Norman. il por Newsweek 91:20-1 Ja 9 '78
On consuming the surplus; excerpt from Toward socialism in America. H. Freeman. Progressive 41:20-1 F '77
Recess delays Defense actions. K. Johnsen. Aviation W 107:14-16 Ag 15 '77
Stabilizing defense budgets; excerpts from address. T. V. Jones. Aviation W 106:9 Ja 3 '77
Stunted growth in defense dollars. Bus W p40 D 26 '77
Technological superiority required. M. R. Currie. Aviation W 106:7 F 7 '77
Threat: is there a present danger? the Carter administration and the Soviet. R. J. Bresler. Intellect 105:310-11 Ap '77
What Carter will do with the B-1 money. Bus W p21-2 Jl 18 '77
See also
Military-industrial complex
United States—Air Force—Appropriations and expenditures
United States—Army—Appropriations and expenditures
United States—Marine Corps—Appropriations and expenditures
United States—Navy—Appropriations and expenditures

Economic Adjustment, Office of

Don't mourn lost military bases; aid to affected communities. il Am City & County 92:26 S '77

Procurement

Disciplined defense procurement urged. E. Kozicharow. Aviation W 107:20-1 O 3 '77
Let's change the way the Pentagon does business. J. S. Gansler. il Harvard Bus R 55:109-18 My '77
Overhaul of Defense Dept. procurement debated. E. Kozicharow. Aviation W 107:50-2 O 24 '77
Overseers urged for Defense programs. W. C. Wetmore. Aviation W 107:49 O 10 '77
Strengthening NATO ties; excerpts from address. R. A. Basil. Aviation W 107:7 Ag 29 '77
Top 100 Defense Dept. contractors; tables. Aviation W 106:51-3+ Mr 14 '77

UNITED STATES—*Continued*

Defenses

Arming for the 21st century. il por Time 109:14-21 My 23 '77
Arms race: is paranoia necessary for security? G. B. Kistiakowsky. il N Y Times Mag p52-4+ N 27 '77
Arms zealots. D. Yergin. il Harpers 254:64+ Je '77
Balancing the equations of terror. America 137:25 Jl 16 '77
Behind the furor over future arms. J. Fromm. il U.S. News 83:24 Jl 25 '77
Big defense issues on U.S. doorstep. J. Fromm. U.S. News 83:47 D 26 '77
Decision making in a nuclear-armed world. M. Brenner. Ann Am Acad 430:147-61 Mr '77
Defense planning and arms control; address, April 13, 1977. H. Brown. Vital Speeches 43:460-3 My 15 '77
Defense reconsidered. E. N. Luttwak. Commentary 63:51-8 Mr '77
For new CIA chief, a big rebuilding job. il por U.S. News 82:24 F 21 '77
Framework for national security decisionmaking; remarks, with transcript of question and answer session, July 29, 1977. H. Brown. Dept State Bull 77:297-303 S 5 '77
From the Joint Chiefs of Staff: a top-level size-up of U.S. strength—and weaknesses. il U.S. News 83:38-9 O 10 '77
General goes zap; question of Gen. G. J. Keegan's comments on Russian weapons. M. Kondracke. New Repub 177:19-22 Jl 2 '77
Is it over, over there? A. G. J. Chalfont. il Nat R 29:200-3+ F 18 '77
It's budget time again: the Russians are coming! D. Cortright and R. L. Borosage. Nation 224:205-8 F 19 '77
Muzzled defense study hearing sought. E. Kozicharow. Aviation W 107:54-5 S 5 '77
Our bewildered allies. Sat Eve Post 249:76+ My '77
Perils of détente. W. Laqueur. N Y Times Mag p 16+ F 27 '77
Practical power use urged on planners. H. J. Coleman. il Aviation W 107:18-21 Jl 18 '77
Real Paul Warnke; excerpts from interview, ed by W. Miale. P. Warnke. New Repub 176:22-5 Mr 26 '77
Russians are coming—again. G. McGovern. Progressive 41:17-23 My '77
Soviet strategic lead seen by 1980s. C. Brownlow. Aviation W 106:18 F 14 '77
Technology push urged to meet Soviet buildup. E. Kozicharow. Aviation W 107:15-16 D 5 '77
U.S. can still hold its own. . .for now; official report of the Joint Chiefs of Staff. U.S. News 82:61 F 14 '77
Warnke in wonderland; U.S.-Soviet strategic relations. Nat R 29:250+ Mr 4 '77
Weakened America. Sat Eve Post 249:76+ My '77
When trouble strikes—how U.S. crisis management works. il U.S. News 82:28-9 F 21 '77
Whiz kids: round two; shaping of defense policy. Sat Eve Post 249:34 Ap '77
With humanity as pawns. D. Mattern. il Commonweal 104:329-31 My 27 '77
See also
Airplanes, Military—United States
Civil defense
Guided missiles
North American Air Defense Command
Panama Canal Zone—Defenses
Sea power
Stockpiling
Submarine boats, Atomic powered
United States—Air Force
United States—Armed Forces
United States—Army
United States—Navy

Description and travel

Around the U.S. See issues of Travel
Last-minute tips for summer vacationers. il U.S. News 82:52-4 My 30 '77
U.S. journal. C. Trillin. See occasional issues of New Yorker
Vacationing on a budget. il Ebony 32:68-70+ Ap '77
See also
Automobile touring—United States
Railroad travel
also subhead Description and travel under names of sections, states, e.g. Arizona—Description and travel

Diplomatic and Consular Service

Amateur hour. T. Szulc. New Repub 176:20-2 My 28 '77
Department discusses consular services for Americans abroad; statements, July 14, 1977. B. M. Watson; W. P. Stedman, Jr. il Dept State Bull 77:248-65 Ag 22 '77
Great ambassador hunt. T. Mathews and H. Bruno. il Newsweek 89:37+ Ap 11 '77
Message from Secretary Vance to Department and Foreign Service; January 24, 1977. C. R. Vance. Dept State Bull 76:125-6 F 14 '77
Search for excellencies. il Time 109:14 Ap 4 '77
Secretary Kissinger pays tribute to the Foreign Service; remarks, January 19, 1977. H. A. Kissinger. Dept State Bull 76:127-9 F 14 '77
See also
Ambassadors

Great Britain

Our far-flung correspondents, Ambassador K. Brewster, Jr. J. Bainbridge. New Yorker 53:141-8+ D 12 '77

Japan

Mansfield's mounting problems as envoy to Japan. J. N. Wallace. il por U.S. News 83:42 O 31 '77

Discovery and exploration

See America—Discovery and exploration

Domestic Council

TRB from Washington; reports of the Domestic Council Committee on Illegal Aliens. New Repub 176:2+ F 26 '77

Drug Abuse Law Enforcement, Office for

See United States—Drug Enforcement Administration

Drug Enforcement Administration

New strategy against drug rings—dramatic story of a successful bust; central tactical units—CENTAC 1. O. Kelly. il U.S. News 83:64-6 O 31 '77

Economic conditions

American economy; address, August 28, 1977. I. S. Shapiro. Vital Speeches 43:738-41 O 1 '77
Assessing the cold's damage. Time 109:59 F 21 '77
Backlash from U.S. growth. il Bus W p 16-17 Jl 4 '77
Business roundup. See issues of Fortune
Coping with a tumbling dollar. S. Rose. il Fortune 96:272-4+ O '77
Economic diary. See issues of Business week
Economy. See issues of Dun's review
Economy. See issues of Forbes
Faster recovery without overheating. il Bus W p33 My 23 '77
Feeling the chill. M. Ruby and others. il Newsweek 89:70-1 F 14 '77
Ford's robust legacy. il Time 109:38 Ja 31 '77
Galbraithian guide to the economic folkways of Americans. J. K. Galbraith. por Fortune 96:97-8+ Ag '77
How Russia and U.S. match up in output, living standards. il U.S. News 83:52-3 O 24 '77
Is this why the economy is lagging? Farm J 101:72 Ja '77
Labor month in review. See issues of Monthly labor review
Myth of the American economy. L. C. Thurow. por Newsweek 89:11 F 14 '77
New case of jitters. D. Pauly and others. il Newsweek 90:59 Ag 8 '77
No recession is in sight. il Time 110:48 S 12 '77
Old-style winter disrupts the economy. il Bus W p44 Ja 31 '77
Our over-developed society; address, April 20, 1977. J. T. Connor. Vital Speeches 43:555-7 Jl 1 '77
Plain talk from Jerry; Economic report of the President. il Newsweek 89:61 Ja 31 '77
Present state of capitalism. R. Marris. New Repub 176:39-41 My 21 '77
Recession-recovery fluctuations. G. Katona. Intellect 106:6-7 Jl '77
Spring: good news it will bring. il U.S. News 82:17-19 Mr 28 '77
Sunny midyear outlook. il U.S. News 83:16-18 Jl 4 '77
Too much, too soon? D. Pauly and R. Thomas. il Newsweek 89:88 My 16 '77
Wealth of the Nation. il U.S. News 82:66-7 Mr 21 '77
What the tape is telling us. Fortune 96:87 S '77
Where the recovery stands now. il U.S. News 82:22-3 Ap 4 '77
Where U.S. stands as the 1980s approach. il U.S. News 83:48-9 Jl 25 '77
Year that was; 1977. P. A. Samuelson. Newsweek 91:52 Ja 2 '78
See also
Blacks—Economic conditions
Business conditions
Debts, Public—United States
Economic forecasting
Economic indicators
Inflation (finance)
Poor—United States
Prices—United States
Unemployment—United States
Wages—United States

Economic Development Administration

See United States—Commerce, Department of—Economic Development Administration

UNITED STATES—*Continued*

Economic history

Capitalism's last gasp. S. Lens. Current 195:27-36 S '77
How 80 years of inflation have shrunk your dollar. il U.S. News 83:19 Jl 4 '77
Prelude to the Federal Reserve: the currency panic of 1907. il Duns R 110:21 D '77
Red and the black; excerpts from articles, 1924-48. il Sat Eve Post 249:57 Jl '77
60 years of American business; a picture portfolio. il Forbes 120:P1-8+ S 15 '77
Sixty years of American business: the pursuit of happiness through the pursuit of profit. J. Brooks. Forbes 120:69-76+ S 15 '77
See also
Business depression, 1929-1939

Economic Opportunity, Office of

See United States—Community Services Administration

Economic policy

Back to the shop. Nation 224:610 My 21 '77
Big surge ahead in business; interview. C. L. Schultze. il pors U.S. News 82:23-4 F 28 '77
Blueprint for a sound economy: an expert's advice to Carter; interview. A. M. Okun. il por U.S. News 82:51-3 Ja 24 '77
Bridging the gap. M. Ruby and others. Newsweek 90:75-6 N 7 '77
Building a democratic economy. G. Alperovitz and J. Faux. Progressive 41:15-19 Jl '77; Same with title Changing American economy. Current 195:18-27 S '77
Carter business boom shaping up? with interview with B. Lance. U.S. News 82:15-18 F 7 '77
Carter tackles inflation. D. Pauly and R. Thomas. il Newsweek 89:80+ Ap 11 '77
Carter's bad start. il por Bus W p96-101 O 31 '77
Carter's Mr Inside; excerpts from interview, ed by L. Martz and R. Thomas. T. B. Lance. por Newsweek 89:86 Ap 11 '77
Carter's plan: criticized, but flexible. il Time 109:45-6 Ja 24 '77
Carter's pursuit of inconsistent goals. Bus W p56+ D 26 '77
Caught in the ice. Nation 224:194-5 F 19 '77
Check is in the mail—almost. A. J. Mayer and others. il Newsweek 89:55-6 F 7 '77
Cold comfort. G. F. Will. Newsweek 89:80 F 7 '77
Confidence in the future versus government spending. D. N. Balatsos. por Nations Bus 65:64-6 F '77
Continuing Keynesian economics. M. Edel. Society 14:17-19 My '77
Cost criterion for the regulators. il Bus W p36+ Mr 14 '77
Deceptive allure of national planning. T. Alexander. il Fortune 95:148-52+ Mr '77
Does future look bright for business? It does indeed; interview. J. M. Kreps. pors U.S. News 83:17-19 Ag 1 '77
Economic outlook and policy; address, October 4, 1977. C. L. Schultze. Vital Speeches 44:66-70 N 15 '77
Economy. See issues of Dun's review
Economy: new look? M. Ruby and others. il pors Newsweek 91:48-56 Ja 9 '78
Forecasts for the Carter years. J. Carlson. por Nations Bus 65:28+ Ja '77
Furl that reform banner, Mr President. Fortune 96:75 D '77
Government by what people? P. Steinfels. Commonweal 104:756+ N 25 '77
Government intervention; special issue. il pors Bus W p42-3+ Ap 4 '77
Great stagflation swamp; address, October 6, 1977. A. M. Okun. Vital Speeches 44:120-5 D 1 '77
How government itself keeps prices rising. il U.S. News 82:16-17 Ap 18 '77
Icy grip tightens. il Time 109:6-11 F 14 '77
Inventory of improbables. E. Marshall. New Repub 176:16-17 Ja 22 '77
Jimmy Carter gets mixed marks in economics. I. J. Cameron. il pors Fortune 95:98-102+ Je '77
Jimmy vs. the liberals. T. Mathews and others. il por Newsweek 89:44 My 16 '77
Jimmy's conciliatory gestures. il Time 110:20 N 21 '77
Keeping business on course: experts tell what's needed. il U.S. News 83:15-16 Ag 1 '77
Keeping them guessing; J. Carter's policies. il por Time 110:14-17 N 14 '77
Keynesian moves in as Treasury Secretary; interview. W. M. Blumenthal. por Bus W p34-5 Ja 31 '77
Let's get rid of families! C. S. Bell. por Newsweek 89:19 My 9 '77
National policy of human resource economics; excerpts from address. W. W. Wirtz. por Intellect 106:102 S '77
Not impossible goal: full employment and price stability; address, January 27, 1977. G. W. Miller. Vital Speeches 43:339-44 Mr 15 '77
Now a search for ways to keep business perking. il U.S. News 83:23-5 O 24 '77
Now it's government itself pushing prices higher and higher. il U.S. News 83:16-17 D 19 '77
Open letter to fellow developer, Jimmy Carter: climate for business expansion; address, January 28, 1977 R. Nordblom. Vital Speeches 43:290-2 Mr 1 '77
President Carter interviewed by European broadcast journalists; transcript of interview, May 2, 1977. J. Carter. Dept State Bull 76: 540-8 My 30 '77
President talks tough; interview. J. Carter. il pors U.S. News 82:19-23 Je 6 '77
President's economic package: on balance, a step forward. C. Morgello. por Duns R 109:96 F '77
Public use of private interest; excerpt from Godkin lectures. C. L. Schultze. Harpers 254:43-50+ My '77
Restraints on Carter's economic policy. il Bus W p62-6 Ja 24 '77
Retreat on the rebate. Progressive 41:7 Je '77
Road to recovery. Y. Brozen. il Nat R 29:264-7 Mr 4 '77
Shaky truce on money. il Bus W p22-3 N 7 '77
Signs of staggering. A. J. Mayer and others. il Newsweek 90:24-5 S 12 '77
Sizing up a hectic four months. il Time 109:64+ My 23 '77
Slings and arrows. D. Pauly and others. il Newsweek 89:85-6 Ap 18 '77
Some praise, growing worry: how business views Carter. il por U.S. News 83:61-4 S 19 '77
Sorry, no change. M. J. Ulmer. New Repub 176: 15-16 F 5 '77
Specter of full employment. R. Lekachman. Harpers 254:35-40 F '77; Same. Current 192:13-20 Ap '77; Discussion. Harpers 254:8+ Ap '77
Spenders vs. savers: split in the Cabinet. W. C. Bryant. il pors U.S. News 82-18 Ap 18 '77
Spur to business spending: idea White House has in mind. il U.S. News 82:82-3 F 14 '77
Status quo economy. M. Harrington. Harpers 255:34-5 S '77
Steel price increases jolt Carter's policy. il Bus W p21-2 Ag 8 '77
Stitch in time. P. A. Samuelson. Newsweek 90:94 S 19 '77
Strange mix of confidence and doubt. Time 109: 14 Je 13 '77
Sudden spring thaw. D. Pauly and others. il Newsweek 89:52+ Mr 28 '77
Sustaining orderly economic growth; excerpts from testimony before the Senate Budget Committee. P. W. McCracken. por Intellect 105: 208-10 Ja '77
TRB from Washington (cont) New Repub 176:2 Ja 15; 2+ Ja 29; 2+ Ap 9; 177-2+ O 15 '77; 178: 2+ Ja 7 '78
Tax cuts and federal spending needed to revive economic recovery in 1977. G. A. Christie. Archit Rec 161:83 Ja '77
Tax cuts versus spending. G. R. Rosen. por Duns R 109:67 Mr '77
Tell it like it is, Jimmy. il Forbes 119:153 Ap 15 '77
Unemployment and taxes; Humphrey-Hawkins bill. A. B. Laffer. il Nat R 29:148-50 F 4 '77
Well begun: Mr Carter passes up some ill-conceived advice. C. Morgello. Duns R 109:88 Ja '77
What makes America? address, February 7, 1977. P. W. McCracken. Vital Speeches 43:311-14 Mr 1 '77
When Arthur Burns speaks out—. A. Burns. U.S. News 82:45 My 2 '77
Where Carter is going wrong; interview. M. Friedman. il pors U.S. News 82:20-2 Mr 7 '77
Who runs policy? il Time 110:70+ N 21 '77
Who's calling the economic shots; C. L. Shultze vs W. M. Blumenthal. Bus W p 117 Mr 28 '77
Who's who in no 2. il Newsweek 89:62-3 Ja 31 '77
Year of the economy. M. Ruby and others. il Newsweek 90:40-1 N 21 '77
See also
Budget—United States
Economic assistance, Domestic
Energy policy
Inflation (finance)
Tariff—United States
Taxation—United States
United States—Appropriations and expenditures
United States—Council of Economic Advisers
United States—Council on International Economic Policy
United States—Domestic Council
Wage-price policy

Anecdotes, facetiae, satire, etc.

Case for fiscal irresponsibility. W. Howler. Nat R 29:605 My 27 '77

Economic relations

American labor's stake in a changing world economy; symposium. M Labor R 100:34-5 Mr '77

UNITED STATES—Economic relations—*Cont.*
International economic report transmitted to the Congress; message, January 18, 1977. G. R. Ford. Dept State Bull 76:129-32 F 14 '77
International economic situation; statement, April 6, 1977. R. N. Cooper. Dept State Bull 76:378-84 Ap 18 '77
New American imperialism? P. A. Samuelson. por Newsweek 89:98 My 16 '77
President Carter interviewed by European newspaper journalists; transcript of interview, April 25, 1977. J. Carter. Dept State Bull 76: 533-9 My 30 '77
See also
Balance of payments—United States
Economic assistance, American
United States—Commerce

Africa, Southern

Doing business with a blacker Africa. il Bus W p64-8+ F 14 '77

Asia, Southeastern

United States and ASEAN hold economic consultations in Manila; statement, transcript of joint press conference, and text of press release, September 8, 10, 1977. R. N. Cooper; C. P. Romulo. Dept State Bull 77:595-605 O 31 '77

Canada

Canada and the United States: a special relationship. R. H. Leach. bibl f Cur Hist 72:145-9+ Ap '77
Canada: trouble above the border. R. H. Heindel. il por Intellect 105:226-7 F '77
Cinderella's pipeline; Alcan Pipeline's winning route. A. J. Mayer and W. J. Cook. il por map Newsweek 90:87+ S 12 '77

Caribbean Region

Caribbean; incentives for American investment; address, April 20, 1977. P. G. M. Loewenthal. Vital Speeches 43:468-70 My 15 '77

China

What the Chinese told a visiting U.S. banker; interview. C. M. Berry. il por U.S. News 83: 53-4 Ag 22 '77

Europe, Western

Western Europe's economic crisis: the U.S. must lead the way out. G. Ackley. Duns R 110:9 Ag '77
Why Europe fears sag in business. K. S. Smith. il U.S. News 84:47-8 Ja 9 '78

Germany, West

Behind Germany's refusal to reflate its economy. G. T. Gibson. il Bus W p65 Jl 18 '77

Italy

Europe's sickest man; question of International Monetary Fund loan. M. Ledeen. New Repub 176:8-10 F 12 '77

Japan

Deteriorating U.S.-Japanese relations: several ways to reduce tensions. W. E. Hoadley. Duns R 110:9 D '77
Our bilateral economic relations: political and security relations; address, February 4, 1977. F. Togo. Vital Speeches 43:327-9 Mr 15 '77

Latin America

Latin America and today's world economy; address, December 6, 1976. W. D. Rogers. Dept State Bull 75:751-4 D 27 '76

Mexico

Mexico's President: no easy way to stop migration; interview, ed by C. J. Migdail. J. López Portillo. il por U.S. News 83:28-30 Jl 4 '77
United States and Mexico: a special relationship; remarks, September 21, 1977. S. Shelton. Dept State Bull 77:811-14 D 5 '77

Nigeria

Wooing of Nigeria: a courtship pays off. il map U.S. News 83:67-70 D 5 '77

Russia

See also
United States—Commerce—Russia

South Africa

South Africa: post-diplomatic options. A. Silk. Nation 225:677 D 24 '77

Underdeveloped areas

Dealing with the third world—will new U. S. strategy work? with interview with C. A. Pérez. il U.S. News 83:51-4+ Jl 25 '77
Development of third world would affect U.S. supply of raw materials. S. H. Ruttenberg. M Labor R 100:39-40 Mr '77
Rx for Carter: heed the poor nations. B. Jones. il Commonweal 104:9-12 Ja 7 '77

Education, Department of (proposed)

U.S. Department of Education: the case for it; the case against it. J. Ryor; G. E. Sroufe. Current 193:16-30 My '77
U.S. expected to propose new Education Department. S. Wagner. Pub W 212:27 D 26 '77

Education, Office of

Downgrading menaces federal librarians' security. L. R. Pearson. Am Lib 8:175 Ap '77
Drive for better schools—what the government plans; interview. E. L. Boyer. il por U.S. News 83:63-4 Jl 11 '77
Guide to OE-administered programs, fiscal year 1977; comp by C. Joffe. il Am Educ 13:36-43 Ja '77
Time of reckoning for student deadbeats. il U.S. News 83:21 Jl 18 '77

Appropriations and expenditures

OE allocates funds to Right to Read/RIF. SLJ 23:24 F '77

Educational Materials Review Center

First and only treasure. E. B. Roth. il Am Educ 13:6-9 N '77

Gifted and Talented, Office for the

Many paths for gifts and talents. E. B. Roth. Am Educ 13:25-7 My '77

Libraries and Learning Resources, Office of

OE library office staff face salary cuts. Lib J 102:855 Ap 15 '77

National Center for Education Statistics

National standardization of educational statistics. E. R. Kay. M Labor R 100:46-7 O '77

Energy, Department of

Birth of a superagency. M. Ruby and others. il Newsweek 90:59+ Jl 11 '77
Coming: a new energy department. U.S. News 82:65 Mr 14 '77
DOE sets interagency CO_2 research priorities. Sci N 112:375 D 3 '77
Department of Energy? M. Friedman. Newsweek 89:62 My 23 '77
Department of Energy: opposition rises as the plan leaks out. W. D. Metz. Science 197:1166-7 S 16 '77
Deutch and Thorne to fill two key DOE research posts. F. C. Bennett. pors Phys Today 30:93+ N '77
Energy czar; J. Schlesinger. Nation 224:291-2 Mr 12 '77
Energy reorganization is set to begin. Sci N 112:199 S 24 '77
MIT chemist, Schlesinger ally assumes energy research post. W. D. Metz. por Science 198: 1125-6 D 16 '77
National laboratories: focused goals and field work hinted under DOE. W. D. Metz. il Science 198:901-4 D 2 '77
New Cabinet agency takes on energy crisis. il U.S. News 83:18 Ag 15 '77
New Cabinet agency that Congress fenced in. Bus W p 126-8 O 17 '77
New Energy Department: where it goes from here. il por Nations Bus 65:44-6+ O '77
New Energy Department: who will champion research? F. C. Bennett. Phys Today 30:109-10 My '77
New era in energy regulation. J. J. DuPont. Conservationist 32:1 Jl '77
Proposed Department of Energy draws comment from the AIBS; letter. R. Trumbull. BioScience 27:345 My '77
Research status in DOE looking good. C. Holden. Science 197:648 Ag 12 '77
Robert Thorne: controversial nominee for energy R&D job. L. J. Carter. Science 198:34 O 7 '77
Rockwell engineer tackles energy R&D; D. D. Myers. il por Bus W p65 S 26 '77
Schlesinger's czardom takes shape. il Time 109: 56+ Mr 7 '77
See also
United States—Federal Power Commission

Energy Research and Development Administration

ERDA laboratories: Los Alamos attracts some special attention. J. Walsh. Science 196:743-5 My 13 '77
ERDA will continue to push frontier facilities: Kane. F. C. Bennett, por Phys Today 30:69-71 F '77
Electric vehicles (EV's) in your future... N. Gluckin. il Sci Digest 82:7-13+ S '77
Energy: estimates and issues. R. B. Morrissey. America 136:523-4 Je 11 '77
Geothermal energy: ERDA leaves it lay. S. Bierman and G. T. Hunt. Nation 225:487-9 N 12 '77
How ERDA is spending your money. C. A. Miller. il Mech Illus 73:48+ N '77

UNITED STATES—Energy Research and Development Administration—*Continued*
How ERDA's billions funnel to industry. il Bus W p54-5 Je 27 '77
Super sun power from mirrors; heliostat project in New Mexico. C. A. Miller. il Mech Illus 73:86+ S '77
Utilities offer site for nation's first solar power plant; Mojave Desert. il Intellect 106:98-9 S '77

Appropriations and expenditures

Battle over the N-bomb; Lance Enhanced Radiation Warhead. M. R. Benjamin and L. H. Norman. il Newsweek 90:44-5 Jl 4 '77
ERDA budget: from coal to fusion. Sci N 111:53 Ja 22 '77
Federal R&D budget squeeze ERDA fission and fusion. il Phys Today 30:69-72 Ap '77
Future car's future; federal electric-car contracts. il Forbes 120:12+ O 15 '77
People killer; question of appropriations spent on neutron warhead. Nation 225:34 Jl 9 '77; Reply with rejoinder. D. R. Cotter. 225:130-1 Ag 20 '77
Two hurdles remain for breeder funding. Sci N 112:247 O 15 '77

Emergency Decontamination Facility

Riddled by isotopes. M. Clark and P. S. Greenberg. il por Newsweek 89:49 Mr 21 '77

Ocean Thermal Energy Conversion Program

Lockheed eyes ocean power plant. il Am City & County 92:40 O '77
Ocean thermal energy: the biggest gamble in solar power. W. D. Metz. il Science 198:178-80 O 14 '77; Discussion. bibl 198:989-90+ D 9 '77

Environmental policy

See Environmental policy

Environmental Protection Agency

Against silence; indictments against Velsicol Chemical Corp. in pesticide coverup. Time 110:49 D 26 '77
Asbestos: trouble in the air from Maryland rock quarry. L. J. Carter. map Science 197:237-40 Jl 15 '77
Behind the uproar over those gas-mileage ratings. il U.S. News 83:32 S 26 '77
Carter reforms may change EPA ways. il Am City & County 92:26-7 N '77
Chemical producers must report to EPA. Sci N 112:423 D 24 '77
Drinking water: health hazards still not resolved. N. Wade. Science 196:1421-2 Je 24 '77; Discussion. 197:320+ Jl 22 '77
EPA: cleanup, not concrete; WPCF conference. Am City & County 92:15 N '77
EPA crackdown on water polluters ahead; views of officials. Am City & County 92:8 Ja '77
EPA cuts sewage funding estimates. Am City & County 92:35 Mr '77
EPA enforcement push shows little regard for local options. W. L. Forestell. Am City & County 92:88 Ja '77
EPA gets tough with air polluters. il Am City & County 92:10 Ja '77
EPA lists restricted farm chemicals. Farm J 101:A4 Je '77
EPA sets rules on ineligible sewers. Am City & County 92:13 Ag '77
EPA: the tricks of the trade-off. il Bus W p72-3 Ap 4 '77
EPA threatens to blacklist Kaiser; Fontana, Calif. plant. il Bus W p27 My 2 '77
EPA's big win; U. S. Steel Corp's water pollution. Time 109:63-4 Je 27 '77
EPA's new man; D. Costle. L. Langway and J. Bishop, Jr. por Newsweek 89:81 F 21 '77
EPA's next target: noisy appliances. Bus W p 100+ O 10 '77
Growing furor over noise regulations. il Nations Bus 65:16-20+ O '77
High noon at Clairton. J. G. Mitchel Audubon 79:128-136 Ja '77
If your drinking water gets tainted, you'll now be told; EPA standards. M. Zeldin. Audubon 79:127 My '77
In search of a final SO_2 plan; Ohio rules vs the EPA's. il Bus W p78+ S 26 '77
NAS: EPA effort needs some revising. Sci N 111:199 Mr 26 '77
New administration: EPA nominees seem acceptable to all sides. L. J. Carter. Science 195:852+ Mr 4 '77
New day at the EPA? interview, ed by J. Doherty. D. Costle. por Nat Wildlife 15:18-19 Ag '77
New EPA policy on pesticides. Farm J 100:J4 D '76
New end run around EPA air standards. il Bus W p64 O 31 '77
New U.S. pollution challenge: a deluge of dangerous chemicals; interview. D. M. Costle. por U.S. News 83:31-2 D 19 '77
Noise; public hearing to discuss garbage truck noise in New York City. New Yorker 53:44-5 N 7 '77
PennDOT curbs cutback asphalt use; EPA emissions offset ruling. il Am City & County 92:30 Ag '77
Pollution may kill VW's Rabbit plant; EPA ruling. il Bus W p26 Mr 7 '77
Public gains access to pesticide safety data. R. J. Smith. Science 197:1346-7 S 30 '77
Regulations, si; bureaucrats, no! T. Orme. Motor T 29:8-9+ D '77
Safe water or jobs? A classic confrontation; Mahoning River Valley and the steel industry. il U.S. News 82:47 F 7 '77
Taking the profit out of pollution. Bus W p27 D 19 '77
Toxic? To whom? Toxic Substances Control Act. J. A. Briggs. Forbes 120:66 S 1 '77
Upstairs, downstairs at EPA; Senate report on regulation of pesticides. F. Graham, Jr. Audubon 79:148-50 Mr '77; Reply. E. M. Kennedy. 79:100+ Jl '77
Washington won't fight: Detroit's chemical warfare. P. J. Bernstein. Nation 224:422-5 Ap 9 '77
Water pollution: appearances can be deceiving. J. Roloff. il Sci N 112:428-31 D 24 '77
When the public will buy a parking ban; implementing transportation control plans. il Bus W p58 Ag 22 '77
Will EPA do the job? Nat Parks & Con Mag 51:27-8 Jl '77

Equal Employment Opportunity Commission

Cleaning up a mess. D. A. Williams and others. il por Newsweek 91:26 Ja 16 '78
EEOC retreats after a seniority ruling; Supreme Court decision. Bus W p28+ Je 20 '77
Eager new team tackles job discrimination. por Bus W p 116+ Jl 25 '77
Equal Employment Opportunity Commission and how to make it work. R. E. Smith. Ms 5:62-4+ F '77
Task for Eleanor Norton. Nation 224:645 My 28 '77
Troubled drive for efficiency at the EEOC. il Bus W p90-1+ D 19 '77

Executive advisory bodies

See Executive advisory bodies

Executive departments

Bureaucrats: the real power? map U.S. News 82:59-60 My 9 '77
Carter's blueprint for reorganization. il Bus W p26-7 F 21 '77
Coping with corporate crime. Progressive 41:10-11 Ap '77
Cost criterion for the regulators. il Bus W p36+ Mr 14 '77
Eager new team tackles job discrimination. por Bus W p 116+ Jl 25 '77
Federal agencies—which are worst? U.S. News 83:42 N 14 '77
Fishbowl approach to agency lobbying; recent U.S. Court of Appeals decision. Bus W p31-2 My 23 '77
Government bureaucracy: too snarled to untangle? reorganization plans of J. Carter. il Sr Schol 109:6-8+ My 19 '77
Grand scale of federal intervention. Bus W p52-3+ Ap 4 '77
Happenings; government reorganization. J. Osborne. New Repub 177:9-12 D 17 '77
Liberal lineup in Carter's sub-Cabinet. il Bus W p74+ My 2 '77
Nader's invaders are inside the gates. J. Cameron. il Fortune 96:252-6+ O '77
OMB director Bert Lance seeks business help; interview, ed by R. L. Lesher. T. B. Lance. il pors Nations Bus 65:18-22+ My '77
Outsiders move inside. R. Boeth. il Newsweek 91:22-4 Ja 2 '78
Really new faces; sub-Cabinet appointments. S. Fraker and others. il Newsweek 89:17-18 Mr 14 '77
Spotty scorecard for Carter's lobbyists. il Bus W p88+ N 14 '77
Super agency? Not likely. D. S. Greenberg. Sci Digest 81:82-4 My '77
This month's feature: Congress and Executive Branch reorganization powers. Cong Digest 56: 99-128 Ap '77
Thoughts on reorganization. W. D. Carey. Science 198:129 O 14 '77
When Carter fills jobs—his promises, his record. il U.S. News 83:38+ N 14 '77
Who's who now in setting Carter's economic policy. il U.S. News 83:16-17 Ag 22 '77
Why Carter is having trouble taking full reins of government. il U.S. News 82:24-5 Mr 21 '77

Executive Office of the President

Carter's blueprint for reorganization. il Bus W p26-7 F 21 '77
Carter's painful reorganization plan. Bus W p52 Jl 25 '77
Carter's shuffle. J. Osborne. New Repub 177:11-13 Jl 30 '77

UNITED STATES—Executive Office of the President—*Continued*
Executive office reorganization: OSTP and CEQ are still in. J. Walsh. Science 197:442-4 Jl 29 '77
Remaking foreign policy; government reorganization. J. Osborne. il New Repub 177:12+ O 1 '77
Reorganization loses out to politics. L. Walczak. Bus W p22 Ag 1 '77
Ringing the changes. J. Osborne. New Repub 176:9-11 Je 25 '77
This month's feature: Congress and Executive Branch reorganization powers. Cong Digest 56:99-128 Ap '77
Who's riding high at the White House. il U.S. News 83:20-1 Jl 25 '77

Expenditures

See United States—Appropriations and expenditures

Federal Aviation Administration

Air controllers get restive again. il Bus W p38 N 28 '77
Editorial! FAA proposed ban on carrying weapons in airports. J. Samson. Field & S 82:4 S '77
FAA cuts collision avoidance options. il Aviation W 106:57-9 My 9 '77
FAA hit on regulatory reform safety role, collision avoidance. Aviation W 107:31-2 D 12 '77
FAA proficiency proposal hit. D. M. North. Aviation W 107:23-4 S 12 '77
FAA safety role seen boosted with airline regulatory reform. D. M. North. Aviation W 107:31 S 19 '77
FAA takes unified look at cabin fires. Aviation W 107:40 S 26 '77
Former FAA head urges more research on displays, controls. Aviation W 106:100 Ap 25 '77
Inquiry on unapproved parts for Boeing transports broadens. Aviation W 106:29 F 21 '77
New deal. R. L. Collins. Flying 100:42 My '77
On top: GAO study of FAA's development of an air traffic control system. R. L. Collins. Flying 100:17-18+ Ap '77

Appropriations and expenditures

FAA's budget underscored by aviation safety. Aviation W 106:56-7 F 7 '77

Flight service stations

Weather information: too little, too late. R. L. Collins. map Flying 100:59-60+ My '77

Federal Bureau of Investigation

Agent OO-art; FBI art crime agent; interview, ed by Vasari. D. Mason. por Art N 76:20+ Ja '77
Alabama judge is picked for FBI—the challenge he faces. F. M. Johnson, Jr. il U.S. News 83:20-1 Ag 29 '77
Bell limits FBI prosecutions. A. Theoharis. Nation 225:198-9 S 10 '77
Bureaucrats above the law: double-entry intelligence files. A. Theoharis. Nation 225:393-7 O 22 '77
Central crime computer project draws mixed reviews. D. Shapley. Science 197:138-41 Jl 8 '77
Defense fund; harassment of the FBI. W. F. Buckley, Jr. Nat R 29:793 Jl 8 '77
Do we want to trust the FBI? E. Knoll. il Progressive 41:11 S '77
FBI: back to square one. P. Bonventre and others. Newsweek 90:34-5 D 12 '77
FBI dirty tricks; revelations from Cointelpro files. il Time 110:30 D 5 '77
FBI five: a closer look; candidates for director. D. M. Alpern and others. il Newsweek 90:22 Jl 11 '77
FBI story on J.F.K.'s death; with report by H. Gorey. il Time 110:18+ D 19 '77
For business: advice from FBI on curbing crime. il U.S. News 83:69-70 N 14 '77
Fortress breached; indictment of J. J. Kearney. Nation 224:482 Ap 23 '77
Gilt-edged choice for the FBI. il pors Time 110:11-12 Ag 29 '77
Griffin Bell believes in law; prosecution of J. J. Kearney. Nation 224:547-8 My 7 '77
Gumshoe stampede. Nation 225:610-11 D 10 '77
Has the Mafia penetrated the F.B.I? murder of informants. N. Gage. il N Y Times Mag p 14-16+ O 2 '77
Have you ever supported equal pay, child care, or women's groups? The FBI was watching you; with excerpts from FBI files. L. C. Pogrebin. Ms 5:37-44 Je; 6:7-8+ O '77
Honorable schoolboy; domestic counterespionage; attempted recruiting of Russian exchange student A. R. Lusis. Time 110:26 N 14 '77
Hope for the FBI. Nation 225:164 S 3 '77
How the FBI spotted me. V. L. Bullough. Nation 225:51-2 Jl 9 '77
Infiltrating the underground; FBI capture of Weather Underground members. il Time 111:13 Ja 9 '78
Is the F.B.I. obsolete? address, May 18, 1977. C. M. Kelley. Vital Speeches 43:578-81 Jl 15 '77
JFK killing: FBI files raise questions, give no answers. il U.S. News 83:15 D 19 '77
JFK: what the FBI found. R. Boeth and others. il pors Newsweek 90:28+ D 19 '77
Judge for the FBI. R. Boeth and D. Camper. por Newsweek 90:26-7 Ag 29 '77
Leonard Peltier and the posse: still fighting the Indian wars. B. Johansen. por Nation 225:304-7 O 1 '77
Method acting; infiltration of the International Longshoremen's Association. Time 109:32+ F 7 '77
Most wanted; nomination of F. Johnson as FBI director. E. Yoffe. New Repub 177:10-11 S 3 '77
My forty years with the F.B.I. J. K. Galbraith. il por Esquire 88:122-6+ O '77
Mystery of Israel's bomb; investigation of missing uranium from processing plant in Apollo, Pa. D. Martin. il por Newsweek 91:26-7 Ja 9 '78
Narcisco-Perez case: nurse hunting in Michigan. A. Jones. Nation 225:584-8 D 3 '77
One man's files. G. C. Zahn. America 135:438-42 D 18 '76; Correction. 136:62 Ja 29 '77
Opening the JFK file. P. Bonventre and others. il Newsweek 90:34-5 D 12 '77
People vs. the FBI; suit by the National Lawyers Guild. Nation 224:292-3 Mr 12 '77
Perjury will out. Nation 224:612 My 21 '77
Reflections: crime in the F.B.I. R. Harris. New Yorker 53:30-2+ Ag 8 '77
Respect for law; prosecution of FBI agents. Nation 224:644 My 28 '77
Scientology: parry and thrust. il Time 110:67 Jl 25 '77
Shaky Federal case against scientology. Chr Today 21:32-3 Ag 12 '77
Shopping list for the FBI. S. J. Ungar. por Newsweek 89:15 Ap 25 '77
Still wanted; hunt for new director. Time 110:16 D 12 '77
Talent hunt at the FBI; candidates for director. il Newsweek 90:38 Jl 25 '77
Who defines religion; investigation of the National Commission on Hispanic Affairs. J. M. Wall. Chr Cent 94:523-4 Je 1 '77
See also
Government investigations—Federal Bureau of Investigation

Federal Communications Commission

CB rules changes for 1977. Pop Electr 11:45-6 Mr '77
Challenging media monopolies; newspaper-broadcast complexes. D. Carmody. il N Y Times Mag p21-4 Jl 31 '77
Citizen's-band radio: danger of air pollution. il U.S. News 82:76-7 Mr 7 '77
Communications dog fight. G. R. Rosen. il Duns R 109:48-53 Je '77
Court of Appeals upholds FCC on Comsat, hits procedures. Aviation W 107:25 O 24 '77
Crimping the air power of the press; FCC ruling against newspaper-broadcasting stations cross-ownerships. Bus W p33 Mr 14 '77
Day the first amendment died; address, September 16, 1977. J. R. Bittner. Vital Speeches 44:24-8 O 15 '77
Divestiture debate; newspaper-television-radio combinations. Newsweek 89:43 Mr 14 '77
FCC lofts a new satellite network; Satellite Business Systems. Bus W p37 Ja 31 '77
FCC nomination causes some static; C. D. Ferris. il por Bus W p41-2 O 3 '77
For whom the bell? petition asking restraint of telephone soliciting. T. Nicholson and others. il Newsweek 90:89 O 17 '77
How the FCC tunes in for CB enforcement. J. Walders. il Pop Sci 210:64-8 Je '77
New FCC rules; class D citizens band. il Radio-Electr 48:50 F '77
PURAC—a voice for CB'ers. F. Newhall. il Pop Electr 11:85-6 F '77
Threat to religious broadcasting: somebody is lying. Chr Today 21:41 Ja 7 '77
Uncle Charlie is snowed-in. R. Newhall. il Pop Electr 11:98-9 My '77
Who won? FCC decision on Western Electric and AT&T. Forbes 119:46 My 1 '77
Whole new way to figure AT&T's rates. il Bus W p86-8+ F 14 '77

Federal Contract Compliance, Office of

See United States—Labor, Department of—Federal Contract Compliance, Office of

Federal Coordinating Council of Science, Engineering and Technology

Departing Ford team establishes two new science groups. F. C. Bennett. Phys Today 30:69-70 F '77
No rate change if page charges are voluntary. W. G. Peter. BioScience 27:12+ Ja '77

Federal Council on the Aging

See United States—Aging, Administration on

Federal Deposit Insurance Corporation

See Federal Deposit Insurance Corporation

UNITED STATES—*Continued*

Federal Election Commission

Auditing the FEC. New Repub 177:8+ O 1 '77
Disclosure and harassment; suit of the Socialist Workers Party. Nation 224:516-17 Ap 30 '77
Good old boy network; Atlanta bank loans to J. Carter campaign; with White House response by J. Powell. R. Reeves and B. M. Hager. New Repub 177:6+ S 10 '77
Trojan horse at the FEC. New Repub 177:10-11 N 26 '77

Federal Grain Inspection Service

Federal grain inspection in high gear. Farm J 101:45 N '77
Who'll pay for grain inspection? Farm J 101:62 Mr '77

Federal Home Loan Bank Board

Spurring S&L loans for the inner city. il Bus W p86+ Ap 25 '77

Federal Housing Administration

HUD task force recommends preservation of FHA. D. Loomis. Archit Rec 162:35 Ag '77

Federal Information Center

Dear FIC, can you tell me...? H. Lund. Ret Liv 17:50+ N '77

Federal Mediation and Conciliation Service

Experienced hand for labor mediator. Bus W p27 Mr 28 '77

Federal Power Commission

Bad news for oilmen? por Forbes 120:70 S 1 '77
Electrocuting Con Edison. il Time 110:51 Ag 15 '77
Full disclosure that may be too full; Justice Department intervention in electric utilities' fuel price information case. Bus W p28+ Ag 8 '77

Federal Reserve banks

See Federal Reserve banks

Federal Reserve System

ABC's of how Federal Reserve works. il U.S. News 84:51-2 Ja 9 '78
Adroit switch at money central; Miller: nice guy in a hard job. il pors Time 111:28-30 Ja 9 '78
Arthur Burns: born again at 73. il pors Time 109:53-4+ Je 6 '77
Arthur Burns: how good a job? G. R. Rosen. il por Duns R 110:68-71+ D '77
Behind tightening bind on federal money managers. R. A. Rossi. U.S. News 83:97 N 28 '77
Bill Miller at the Fed—what it adds up to. il pors U.S. News 84:49-50 Ja 9 '78
Bond market falls into a Fed trap; raising the Federal funds rate. il Bus W p 187+ N 14 '77
Burns: a tough act to follow. Time 111:33 Ja 9 '78
Burns-Carter not-quite fight. por Time 110:108+ N 7 '77
Carter gets the message. il Forbes 120:119 D 1 '77
Carter, the Fed and confidence. L. C. Thurow. Nation 225:166-8 S 3 '77
Changing the guard at the Fed; appointment of G. W. Miller. Nation 226:4 Ja 7 '78
Creating a healthy financial climate for construction requires a delicate balance by the Administration and Federal Reserve. G. A. Christie. il Archit Rec 161:73 Ap '77
Economy: new look? M. Ruby and others. il pors Newsweek 91:48-56 Ja 9 '78
Faulting the Fed on money. il Time 110:86 S 26 '77
Fed is a risky trading indicator. Bus W p80 Mr 14 '77
Fed will lean to the left. il Bus W p 108-12+ N 21 '77
Fed worries the markets. il Bus W p32-3 Ja 31 '77
Fed's sudden tightening: has Burns gone too far? S. H. Wildstrom. por Bus W p43 N 14 '77
Fed's view of the economy. S. H. Wildstrom. Bus W p29 Je 6 '77
Fire under Burns. M. Ruby and others. il por Newsweek 90:91-2 O 24 '77
Has the Fed made a costly blunder? W. Wolman. Bus W p34 Ag 15 '77
Here comes the tax cut. il por Time 110:13-14 D 12 '77
Importance of being Arthur. H. Sidey. por Time 110:13 D 26 '77
Is the Federal Reserve building future inflation today? W. Wolman. il Bus W p 110+ S 26 '77
King Arthur. E. Marshall. New Repub 177:8-9 D 3 '77
Money & credit: signs of a tighter policy. Bus W p42 My 9 '77
New act, old woes at the Fed. il por Time 111:40+ Ja 16 '78
Nudging bankers to unbundle prices. Bus W p44 F 14 '77
Outsider Carter chose for Fed; G. W. Miller. il por Bus W p21-2 Ja 9 '78
Reappoint Burns? P. A. Samuelson. il Newsweek 90:81 N 21 '77
Show of support for the dollar. il Bus W p28-9 Ja 16 '78
Trying to make Texas a major money center. il Bus W p 105 Jl 25 '77
Why inflation persists. M. Friedman. il Newsweek 90:84 O 3 '77
Why the Fed can't control money growth. il Bus W p94+ N 7 '77
See also
Federal Reserve banks

Federal Trade Commission

AMA digs in against ads. Bus W p45+ S 19 '77
Big government's needless interventions; FTC regulation of the funeral industry. J. J. Kilpatrick. Nations Bus 65:37-8 Ja '77
Carter trustbusters take a tough new line. il U.S. News 83:39-40 Ag 15 '77
Carter's trustbusters; M. Pertschuk and J. H. Shenefield. D. Pauly and J. B. Copeland. il por Newsweek 90:66 S 26 '77
Cigarette makers balk at the FTC's demands. Bus W p44 My 16 '77
Crackdown ahead on advertising; what the government plans next; interview. M. Pertschuk. pors U.S. News 83:70-2 O 17 '77
Dr Huckster; advertising by physicians. M. Clark and M. Lord. il Newsweek 91:70 Ja 9 '78
Down the chute with Peabody coal. C. J. Loomis. il Fortune 95:228-33+ My '77
FTC broadens its attack on ads. Bus W p27-8 Je 20 '77
FTC challenge to the legal profession. Bus W p23 Ja 9 '78
FTC reviews its own consumer rules. Bus W p92 Mr 28 '77
FTC sues AMA over code of ethics. R. J. Smith. Science 197:1346 S 30 '77
Funeral salesmen. J. Mitford. McCalls 105:190+ N '77
ITT branches out. E. Marshall. New Repub 176:9-11 Ap 2 '77; Reply with rejoinder. R. B. Keane. 176:7+ My 21 '77
Merger notification business can live with. Bus W p40 O 17 '77
New teeth for the FTC? G. R. Rosen. il Duns R 109:61 Je '77
Tough man for the FTC. A. J. Mayer and J. Bishop, Jr. il por Newsweek 89:61-2 Mr 7 '77
Two years of the power rule; FTC amplifier power rule. Hi Fi 27:33 N '77
Washington's new approach to antitrust action. W. Neikirk. pors Nations Bus 65:30-2 D '77

Fiscal policy

See also
Budget—United States
United States—Appropriations and expenditures

Fish and Wildlife Service

Endangered species: review of law triggered by Tellico impasse. C. Holden. Science 196:1426-8 Je 24 '77
How they cracked duck hunting's isle of shame; Pruitt's Paradise Inc on Tangier Island. J. Phillips. il Outdoor Life 161:64-5+ Ja '78
In Washington, the policy-makers fret and sweat. J. H. Phillips. il Nat Wildlife 15:12-13 Ag '77
Uncle Sam says scram! efforts to reduce Canada geese population in Horicon Marsh refuges. B. Gilbert. il maps Audubon 79:42-55 Ja '77

Food and Drug Administration

Another saccharin test. M. Clark and others. Newsweek 90:60 Jl 4 '77
Antibiotics in feed: the first punch has been thrown. J. Russell. Farm J 101:Hog 20 Je '77
Are we losing our animal feed additives? G. Johnston. il Suc Farm 75:no3 19+ F '77
Behind the saccharin uproar. W. Hines and J. Randal. Progressive 41:13-17 Je '77
Biologist Kennedy to head FDA. Sci N 111:168 Mr 12 '77
Bitter pills for the FDA. M. Clark and others. il Newsweek 90:93+ Jl 18 '77
Bitter reaction to an FDA ban; saccharin. il Time 109:60-1 Mr 21 '77
Breaking the drug barrier. R. Spark. il N Y Times Mag p64-71 Mr 20 '77
Cancer and your sweet tooth; saccharin. New Repub 176:7-8 Mr 26 '77
Creative penmanship in animal testing prompts FDA controls; Good Laboratory Practice regulations. R. J. Smith. Science 198:1227-9 D 23 '77
Donald Kennedy to head FDA. B. J. Culliton. por Science 195:1307 Mr 25 '77
Drive to limit the antibiotics in animal feed. il Bus W p55-6 Ja 16 '78
Dubious drugs for pregnant women. M Cimons. McCalls 104:63 F '77

UNITED STATES—Food and Drug Administration —*Continued*
Eat with caution! FDA's second look at additives will take five more years. Sci Digest 82: 70-3 Ag '77
FDA enforcing new standards for blood donations. Ret Liv 17:14 Ja '77
FDA postpones proposed ban on saccharin for two months. Ret Liv 17:41 Ag '77
FDA proposal to ban saccharin stirs tempest over its testing rules. Ret Liv 17:14-15 Ap '77
FDA ready to turn corner. . .if it's still able. D. S. Greenberg. Sci Digest 81:71-2 Je '77
FDA reform: an idea whose time has come. R. J. Smith. Science 198:272-3 O 21 '77
FDA to limit drugs in animal feeds. B. J. Culliton. Science 196:510 Ap 29 '77
FDA to take a solid look at solid-weight labeling. Consumer Rep 42:313 Je '77
FDA urges new caveats for aspirin users. Ret Liv 17:60 S '77
Feasting on fat; liquid protein. L. Langway and others. il Newsweek 90:83 D 5 '77
Fight starts to beat the ban on saccharin. il U.S. News 82:49 Mr 28 '77
Freedom of choice and apricot pits; Time essay. F. Golden. il Time 109:54 Je 20 '77
Great saccharin snafu. Consumer Rep 42:410-14 Jl '77
Hidden cost of drug safety; FDA's regulations effect on drug industry research projects. il Bus W p80+ F 21 '77
How much is enough? saccharin and the law; address, March 24, 1977. S. Gardner. Vital Speeches 43:457-9 My 15 '77
How safe are the drugs you take? interview. D. Kennedy. il pors U.S. News 83:65-6 N 21 '77
Ice cream: dairymen imperiled by FDA's recipe. N. Wade. Science 197:844-5+ Ag 26 '77
Legislators aim at bureaucratic overkill, drug lag. Sci Digest 82:45 Ag '77
Lesson to be learned from saccharin mess? A. T. Brett. il U.S. News 82:80 Je 6 '77
New treatments vs. unknown risks A. A. Belson. Vogue 167:132-3+ Jl '77
No mad scientists; proposed ban on saccharin. S. Kelman. New Repub 176:8+ Mr 26 '77
Reappraising saccharin—and the FDA. il Time 109:75-6 Ap 25 '77
Relieving the analgesic headache. il Time 110: 70 Ag 1 '77
Saccharin and other health scares: what can you believe? N. G. Rollins. Good H 185:201-2 Jl '77
Saccharin ban. L. Langway. il Newsweek 89:65+ Mr 21 '77
Saccharin ban: weighing the risks. J. Mayer. il Fam Health 9:38-9+ Jl '77
Saccharin can be sold—for now. il Bus W p38 Ap 25 '77
Saccharin's sour future. il Bus W p95+ Mr 28 '77
Safety muddle at FDA. il Bus W p73-4 Ap 4 '77
Say good-bye to sulfa drugs? L. Schotsch. Farm J 101:Hog 11+ S '77
Screening for cancer; FDA use of the Ames test. M. Weinstock. Environment 19:2-4 D '77
Should saccharin be banned? interviews. G. Nelson; J. G. Martin. pors U.S. News 82:59-60 Ap 4 '77
Sour taste of a sweetener ban. Time 109:76+ Mr 28 '77
Split decision; detailed proposals for banning saccharin. Newsweek 89:83 Ap 25 '77
Strange case of the anti-aging drug; gerovital H3. S. J. Sansweet. McCalls 105:79-80 N '77
Thirty-one favors; dairy lobby's campaign against new ice cream standards. N. Wade. New Repub 177:15-17 N 5 '77
What an antibiotic ban will mean. J. Rohlf. Farm J 101:Beef 12 Je '77
What if you lose feed drugs? K. Daly. Farm J 101:Hog 16 Ag '77
What price safety? D. Pauly and J. Whitmore. il Newsweek 89:97 My 16 '77
Why ban saccharin? M. Stone. il U.S. News 82:84 Ap 4 '77

Food and Nutrition Service

See United States—Agriculture, Department of—Food and Nutrition Service

Foreign economic policy

See United States—Economic relations

Foreign opinion

Abroad—a sudden respect for Carter. il U.S. News 82:31-2 Ja 31 '77
American culture takes the world by storm. il U.S. News 82:54-6 Je 27 '77
Applause—and warnings—for U.S. from abroad. U.S. News 82:20 Mr 14 '77
Peace: Mideast solution soon? opinions of senior officials abroad. il por U.S. News 83:38-40 D 26 '77

Asian

In Asia—a reservoir of good will for Americans. L. Hansen. il U.S. News 83:25-6 S 5 '77

British

Actor Michael Caine finds marvelous equality in U.S. il pors U.S. News 84:66 Ja 9 '78

Cuban

Conversation with Castro. J. Armstrong. Chr Cent 94:743-4 Ag 31 '77

European

European teens: would they like to be Americans? interviews, ed by P. Mann. il Seventeen 36:96-7 Jl '77
Europe's (almost) upbeat view of America. F. Lewis. il N Y Times Mag p9-11+ Ag 7 '77
Reflections. W. Pfaff. il New Yorker 53:101-7 Je 6 '77
What Europe thinks of Russian threat and NATO. U.S. News 82:24 Je 20 '77

French

Change in America—as seen by a veteran French newsman. A. de Segonzac. il por U.S. News 83:56-8 Jl 11 '77

New Zealand

Consternation and confusion from Carter's foreign policy; excerpts from address, April 19, 1977. R. Muldoon. por U.S. News 82:23 My 9 '77

Russian

Helsinki check list: Russia keeps tabs. A. Beam. Nation 224:709-10 Je 11 '77

South African

How five South Africans view U.S. role. il U.S. News 83:47-8 Ag 29 '77

Foreign policy

See United States—Foreign relations

Foreign population

See also
Immigrants in the United States
Immigration and emigration—United States

Foreign relations

Address by President Carter to people of other nations; January 20, 1977. J. Carter. Dept State Bull 76:122-3 F 14 '77
Alternatives to political paranoia. F. M. Wilhoit. il por Intellect 105:289-90 Mr '77
America and the world: the next four years:
Beyond détente R. W. Tucker. Commentary 63:42-50 Mr '77; Reply with rejoinder. D. S. Lichtenstein. 64:14+ Jl '77
Confronting the problems. W. Laqueur. Commentary 63:33-41 Mr '77
Defense reconsidered. E. N. Luttwak. Commentary 63:51-8 Mr '77
American foreign policy: the limits of power in the absence of purpose. J. A. Nathan. bibl il Intellect 106:208-12 D '77
America's innocence abroad. T. D. Allman. il Harpers 255:57-60+ N '77
America's new strategy of containment. J. Chace. Harpers 256:46-8+ Ja '78
Ample guilt, no policy. A. B. Ulam. New Repub 176:26+ Ja 22 '77
As the Carter team sizes up the world. il U.S. News 83:49-50 Jl 18 '77
Balance of power and balance of trade. W. W. Rostow. Society 14:16-20 Ja '77
Can Jimmy Carterize foreign policy? il Time 109:24-7 Mr 28 '77
Carter and human rights. S. Karnow. il Sat R 4:6-11 Ap 2 '77; Same. Current 193:3-11 My '77
Carter at Notre Dame. W. F. Buckley, Jr. Nat R 29:740 Je 24 '77
Carter at sea. Nat R 29:371 Ap 1 '77
Carter decides to stay home. Time 110:17 N 14 '77
Carter sets a new style in foreign policy. B. France and J. Pearson. Bus W p30 Je 27 '77
Carter spins the world. il por Time 110:8-12+ Ag 8 '77
Carter's global blitz. R. Steele and others. map Newsweek 89:16-18 F 28 '77
Carter's morality play. il pors Time 109:10-11 Mr 7 '77
Carter's new world; commencement address at the University of Notre Dame, May 22, 1977. J. Osborne. New Repub 176:8+ Je 4 '77
Carter's new world order. U.S. News 82:17-18 Je 6 '77
Carter's patchwork doctrine. R. J. Barnet. Harpers 255:27-30+ Ag '77
Carter's world: too much, too soon? il U. S. News 82:15-17 F 28 '77
Change in America—as seen by a veteran French newsman; interview. A. de Segonzac. il por U.S. News 83:56-8 Jl 11 '77
Contagion of liberty. Nation 224:132-3 F 5 '77
Cyrus Vance sizes up 11 global issues. C. R. Vance. U.S. News 82:30 F 21 '77

UNITED STATES—Foreign relations—*Continued*
Decision making in a nuclear-armed world. M. Brenner. Ann Am Acad 430:147-61 Mr '77
Democratic foreign policy; address, May 22, 1977. J. Carter. Vital Speeches 43:514-17 Je 15 '77; Same with title Foreign policy based on America's essential character. Dept State Bull 76:621-5 Je 13 '77
Department discusses U.S. participation in international organizations; statement, June 15, 1977. C. W. Maynes. Dept State Bull 77:100-3 Jl 18 '77
Diplomacy of the possible: the pragmatism of human rights. M. Reisman. Nation 224:554-8 My 7 '77
Diplomatic recognition. Dept State Bull 77:462-3 O 10 '77
Do-it-yourself diplomacy. R. Carroll and E. Clift. pors Newsweek 89:36 Mr 21 '77
Do-it-yourself diplomacy. il por Time 109:26-7 Mr 21 '77
Editors and news directors interview President Carter; excerpts from question and answer session, August 26, 1977. J. Carter. Dept State Bull 77:397-401 S 26 '77
Editors and news directors interview President Carter; excerpts from transcript, July 15, 1977. J. Carter. Dept State Bull 77:200-1 Ag 15 '77
Editors and news directors interview President Carter; October 14, 1977. J. Carter. Dept State Bull 77:767-71 N 28 '77
Editors and news directors interview President Carter; remarks, with transcript of question and answer session, July 29, 1977. J. Carter. Dept State Bull 77:304-6 S 5 '77
8 experts size up U.S. future in a dangerous world; symposium. il U.S. News 82:43-6+ Je 27 '77
Fireside chat; excerpts from address, February 2, 1977. J. Carter. Dept State Bull 76:161 F 28 '77
Foreign policy by committee—can it really work? il U.S. News 82:27-30 F 21 '77
Graves of academe; policies of H. Kissinger. F. Getlein. Commonweal 104:36-8 Ja 21 '77
Guiding philosophy for American informational and cultural programs abroad; address, May 28, 1977. J. E. Reinhardt. Dept State Bull 77:5-8 Jl 4 '77
His legacy: realism and allure; H. Kissinger. J. Schecter. il Time 109:16+ Ja 24 '77
How moral can we get? J. Chace. il N Y Times Mag p38-40+ My 22 '77
Human rights: an important concern of U.S. foreign policy; statement, March 7, 1977. W. Christopher. Dept State Bull 76:289-19 Mr 28 '77
Human rights and foreign policy. T. Buergenthal and others. Intellect 106:179+ N '77
Human rights and foreign policy; address, with question and answer session, April 30, 1977. C. R. Vance. Dept State Bull 76:505-12 My 23 '77
Human rights as a national policy. J. M. Wall. Chr Cent 94:371-2 Ap 20 '77
Human rights policy review; statement, October 25, 1977. M. L. Schneider. Dept State Bull 77: 829-33 D 5 '77
Human rights: principle and realism; address, August 9, 1977. W. M. Christopher. Dept State Bull 77:269-73 Ag 29 '77
Human rights: sermons or substance. F. Ajami. Nation 224:389-90 Ap 2 '77
I have learned a lot; interview, ed by H. Grunwald and others. J. Carter. por Time 110:24-5 Ag 8 '77
Interview with President Carter by media representatives; April 15, 1977. J. Carter. Dept State Bull 76:459-61 My 9 '77
Interview with President Carter by media representatives; excerpt from transcript of interview, June 24, 1977. J. Carter. Dept State Bull 77:159-62 Ag 1 '77
Issue of human rights. W. Laqueur. Commentary 63:29-35 My '77
Kissinger years: morals and moralism. America 136:63 Ja 29 '77
Kraft flunks Carter; views on June 10 foreign policy statement. Nation 225:4-5 Jl 2 '77
Laying the foundation of a long-term policy; remarks, with transcript of question and answer session, January 10, 1977. H. A. Kissinger. Dept State Bull 76:81-7 Ja 31 '77
Learning from Idi Amin. M. Greenfield. il Newsweek 89:100 Mr 14 '77
Letter from Washington (cont) R. H. Rovere. New Yorker 53:108+ Je 13; 200+ N 14 '77
Limits of linkage; civil rights and foreign policy. T. Szulc. New Repub 176:17-19 Mr 5 '77
Loose talk; Carter and foreign affairs. J. Osborne. New Repub 176:12-13 Mr 26 '77
Magazine Publishers Association interviews President Carter; remarks, with excerpt from question and answer session, June 10, 1977. J. Carter. Dept State Bull 77:46-8 Jl 11 '77
Mr Carter's discovery of human rights. W. F. Buckley, Jr. Nat R 29:402 Ap 1 '77
Mr Stay-at-Home. R. Boeth and others. il Newsweek 90:30 N 14 '77
Moral policeman to the world? il U.S. News 82:17-19+ Mr 14 '77
Morality and foreign policy; excerpt from U.S. Foreign policy and Christian ethics. Chr Cent 94:778-81 S 14 '77
Morality at the water's edge. S. A. Garrett. il Commonweal 104:170-5 Mr 18 '77
Motherhood, apple pie and human rights. R. Steel. New Repub 176:14-15 Je 4 '77
My valedictorian address; January 10, 1977. H. A. Kissinger. Vital Speeches 43:265-7 F 15 '77
National Newspaper Association interviews President Carter; October 28, 1977. J. Carter. Dept State Bull 77:798-9 D 5 '77
New American imperialism? P. A. Samuelson. por Newsweek 89:98 My 16 '77
New hopes for human rights; address, September 9, 1977. C. W. Maynes. Dept State Bull 77:556-61 O 24 '77
New U.S. challenge to Russia; interview. Z. Brzezinski. il por U.S. News 82:35-6+ My 30 '77
Nuclear arms reduction; address, October 4, 1977. J. Carter. Vital Speeches 44:2-5 O 15 '77; Same. Dept State Bull 77:547-52 O 24 '77; Excerpts. por U.S. News 83:37 O 17 '77
Of human rights. . .and wrongs. B. Catton. por Am Heritage 28:44-5 O '77
Old superstitions, new realities. H. J. Morgenthau. New Repub 176:50-2+ Ja 22 '77; Same with title On making foreign policy. Current 191:48-56 Mr '77
On human rights and social obligations; symposium. bibl il Society 15:26-103 N '77
Party & international politics. D. P. Moynihan. Commentary 63:56-9 F '77
Passing of the Cold War generation. T. J. Knight. il Intellect 105:238-41 F '77
Peace, arms control, world economic progress, human rights: basic priorities of U.S. foreign policy; address, March 17, 1977. J. Carter. Dept State Bull 76:329-33 Ap 11 '77
Peace: Mideast solution soon? opinions of senior officials abroad. il por U.S. News 83:38-40 D 26 '77
Perspectives. S. Lens. See issues of Progressive
Plain talk about America's global role. il pors Time 109:8-10 Je 6 '77
Politics of human rights. D. P. Moynihan. Commentary 64:19-26 Ag '77; Same abr. Read Digest 111:229-30+ D '77; Discussion. Commentary 64: 4+ O '77
President Carter discusses foreign affairs priorities; remarks, February 16, 1977. J. Carter. Dept State Bull 76:265-6 Mr 21 '77
President Carter interviewed by AP and UPI correspondents; excerpts from transcript of interview, January 23, 1977. J. Carter. Dept State Bull 76:123-5 F 14 '77
President Carter interviewed by European broadcast journalists; transcript of interview, May 2, 1977. J. Carter. Dept State Bull 76:540-8 My 30 '77
President Carter interviewed by European newspaper journalists; transcript of interview, April 25, 1977. J. Carter. Dept State Bull 76:533-9 My 30 '77
President Carter interviewed by media representatives; excerpt from transcript of interview, March 4, 1977. J. Carter. Dept State Bull 76:316-17 Ap 4 '77
President Carter interviewed by newspaper farm editors; excerpt from remarks and question and answer session, September 30, 1977. J. Carter. Dept State Bull 77:681-3 N 14 '77
President Carter's call-in radio program of March 5; excerpts from transcript of program. J. Carter. Dept State Bull 76:314-16 Ap 4 '77
President Carter's news conference:
February 23, 1977. Dept State Bull 76:251-5 Mr 21 '77
March 9, 1977. Dept State Bull 76:305-9 Ap 4 '77
March 24, 1977. Dept State Bull 76:357-62 Ap 18 '77
April 15, 1977. Dept State Bull 76:457-9 My 9 '77
April 22, 1977. Dept State Bull 76:481-2 My 16 '77
May 12, 1977. Dept State Bull 76:604-7 Je 6 '77
May 26, 1977. Dept State Bull 76:653-7 Je 20 '77
June 13, 1977. Dept State Bull 77:1-4 Jl 4 '77
June 30, 1977. Dept State Bull 77:146-51 Ag 1 '77
July 12, 1977. Dept State Bull 77:174-8 Ag 8 '77
July 28, 1977. Dept State Bull 77:221-4 Ag 22 '77
August 23, 1977. Dept State Bull 77:376-9 S 19 '77
September 29, 1977. Dept State Bull 77:584-6 O 31 '77
October 27, 1977. Dept State Bull 77:718-20 N 21 '77

UNITED STATES—Foreign relations—*Continued*
President Carter's remarks at Clinton, Mass, town meeting; excerpts from remarks and question and answer session, March 16, 1977. J. Carter. Dept State Bull 76:334-5 Ap 11 '77
President Carter's remarks at Dobbins Air Force Base, Ga; excerpts from transcript of question and answer session, April 8, 1977. J. Carter. Dept State Bull 76:461-2 My 9 '77
President Carter's remarks at Yazoo City, Mississippi; excerpt from transcript of question and answer session, July 21, 1977. J. Carter. Dept State Bull 77:197-200 Ag 15 '77
President talks tough; interview. J. Carter. il pors U.S. News 82:19-23 Je 6 '77
Presidential assistant Brzezinski interviewed on Face the nation; transcript of program, October 30, 1977; ed by B. Morton and others. Z. Brzezinski. Dept State Bull 77:800-5 D 5 '77
President's address at the United Nations; March 17, 1977. J. Carter. Vital Speeches 43: 354-6 Ap 1 '77; Excerpts. U.S. News 82:21 Mr 28 '77; UN Chron 14:24-5 Ap '77
Push for human rights. A. Deming and others. il Newsweek 89:46-8+ Je 20 '77
Rebuffs at home, flak from abroad. Time 110:12+ Jl 11 '77
Reporter at large; human rights. E. B. Drew. New Yorker 53:36-8+ Jl 18 '77
Rising debate over Carter's global goals. il map Bus W p 112+ S 12 '77
Secretary interviewed at Foreign Policy Conference for Editors and Broadcasters; transcript of remarks, June 28, 1977. C. R. Vance. Dept State Bull 77:121-6 Jl 25 '77
Secretary Kissinger attends NATO ministerial meeting at Brussels and meets with British officials at London; statement, with texts of news conferences, December 7 and 10, 1976. H. A. Kissinger. Dept State Bull 76:1-9 Ja 3 '77
Secretary Kissinger emphasizes need for nonpartisan foreign policy; remarks, January 11, 1977. H. A. Kissinger. Dept State Bull 76:88-90 Ja 31 '77
Secretary Kissinger interviewed for the New York times; ed by J. Reston and others, January 20, 1977. H. A. Kissinger. Dept State Bull 76:102-7 F 7 '77
Secretary testifies on Administration's approach to foreign assistance; statement, February 24, 1977. C. R. Vance. Dept State Bull 76: 236-41 Mr 14 '77
Secretary Vance attends OAS General Assembly at Grenada; statements, and transcript of news conference, June 16, 1977. C. R. Vance. Dept State Bull 77:72-6 Jl 18 '77
Secretary Vance interviewed by AP and UPI correspondents; transcript of interview; ed by B. Schweid and others, February 3, 1977. C. R. Vance. Dept State Bull 76:147-54 F 21 '77
Secretary Vance interviewed by Il Tempo correspondent; ed by M. de Medici, June 18, 1977. C. R. Vance. Dept State Bull 77:85-90 Jl 18 '77
Secretary Vance interviewed for the New York times; transcript of interview, ed by H. Smith and others, February 9, 1977. C. R. Vance. Dept State Bull 76:162-9 F 28 '77
Secretary Vance interviewed on Face the Nation; transcript of interview, ed by G. Herman and others, February 27, 1977. C. R. Vance. Dept State Bull 76:245-50 Mr 21 '77
Secretary Vance interviewed on Issues and answers; ed by B. Clark and B. Dunsmore, June 19, 1977. C. R. Vance. Dept State Bull 77:78-83 Jl 18 '77
Secretary Vance interviewed on Meet the press; transcript of program, October 16, 1977. C. R. Vance. Dept State Bull 77:579-84 O 31 '77
Secretary Vance's news conference:
January 31, 1977. Dept State Bull 76:137-46 F 21 '77
March 4, 1977. Dept State Bull 76:277-83 Mr 28 '77
May 4, 1977. Dept State Bull 76:513-20 My 23 '77
July 29, 1977. Dept State Bull 77:227-34 Ag 22 '77
November 2, 1977. Dept State Bull 77:711-18 N 21 '77
Shot from Paris. D. Martin and others. il pors Newsweek 90:44 Jl 25 '77
Showing initiative. F. Willey and L. E. Nelson. il Newsweek 89:49-50 My 16 '77
Sir, the election is over. M. Stone. U.S. News 82:108 My 9 '77
Stalled abroad. U.S. News 83:14-15 S 5 '77
Strange case of George F. Kennan: from containment to isolationism. E. N. Luttwak. Commentary 64:30-5 N '77
TRB from Washington: grinning along. New Repub 177:2+ Jl 23 '77
Third alternative: divining the secret of Carter's foreign policy. E. N. Luttwak. New Repub 176: 13-14 F 26 '77
Toward a moral foreign policy. America 136: 208 Mr 12 '77
Toward world order. S. Hoffmann. New Repub 176:10-12 Mr 19 '77
U.S. and the world: new horizons. R. Steele. il por Newsweek 90:37 D 26 '77
United States in a world of nuclear powers. M. Nacht. Ann Am Acad 430:162-74 Mr '77
Uses of American power; excerpt from The lure of primacy and the logic of world order. S. Hoffmann. bibl f For Affairs 56:27-48 O '77
Vance and Brzezinski: peaceful coexistence or guerrilla war? M. Berger. il pors N Y Times Mag p 19+ F 13 '77
What Carter is up to. T. Mathews and others. il por Newsweek 89:32+ Mr 28 '77
What price candor? R. Steele and others. il por Newsweek 89:28+ Mr 21 '77
What U.S. stand on human rights? R. J. Barnet. Current 193:12-15 My '77
Where U.S. is gaining in the world; interview. C. R. Vance. il pors U.S. News 83:27-30 N 7 '77; Same. Dept State Bull 77:732-8 N 21 '77
Will a Carter foreign policy make a difference? D. V. Edwards. Intellect 105:319-21 Ap '77
World affairs: a more cheerful perspective. B. Manning. Yale R 67:1-12 O '77
World wonder and worries about U.S. foreign policy. J. Fromm. U.S. News 82:24 Mr 28 '77
Young mission. N. Cousins. Sat R 4:4 Jl 9 '77
Your diplomacy: free advice to Mr Carter. R. Morris. New Repub 176:17+ Ja 22 '77
Zbig and Wolfgang at dawn. H. Sidey. Time 110:17 D 19 '77
Zbiggy zpeaks; views of Z. Brzezinski. J. Osborne. New Repub 177:8-9 O 22 '77
Zbig's optimism in a hostile world; interview, ed by S. Cloud. Z. Brzezinski. por Time 110:18 Ag 8 '77
See also
Berlin question, 1945-
Carter, J.—Visit to seven countries, December 29, 1977-January 6, 1978
Committee on the Present Danger
Council on Foreign Relations
Economic assistance, American
Military assistance, American
Trilateral Commission, Inc
United Nations—United States
United States—Agency for International Communication (proposed)
United States—Diplomatic and Consular Service
United States—Economic relations
United States—Information Agency
United States—State, Department of
United States—Treaties

Anti-Communist measures

End to Meany's veto; amendment of the State Department Authorization Bill to grant visas to Communists. Nation 225:195-6 S 10 '77
Kennedy's cold war; the Taylor report. T. Szulc. New Repub 177:19-21 D 24 '77

Bibliography

Congressional documents relating to foreign policy. See occasional issues of Department of State bulletin

History

Containment: a reassessment. J. L. Gaddis. bibl f For Affairs 55:873-87 Jl '77; Reply with rejoinder. E. Mark. 56:430-41 Ja '78
Henry. . .remember Lot's wife; Coming attractions; Nixon interviews. il por Time 109:41 My 23 '77
Little experience is. . .useful. H. Sidey. il Time 109:13 Ap 18 '77
Nixon: pride in his diplomacy. pors U.S. News 82:35 My 23 '77
Tales of the K; second Nixon-Frost interview. P. Goldman and H. Bruno. il Newsweek 89: 43 My 16 '77
Unhappy warrior; Nixon interviews. M. Kondracke. New Repub 176:11-12 Je 4 '77
Who started the cold war? with introduction and discussion. C. L. Mee, Jr; W. A. Harriman; E. Abel. il pors Am Heritage 28:8-23 Ag '77
See also
United States—Treaties—History

Africa

Administration supports increased U.S. contributions to the African Development Fund; statement, April 18, 1977. A. J. Young. Dept State Bull 76:471-4 My 9 '77
Africa in a global perspective; address, October 27, 1977. A. Lake. Dept State Bull 77:842-8 D 12 '77
Africa isn't Vietnam. New Repub 176:5-6 My 14 '77
Africa, Soviet imperialism & the retreat of American power. B. Rustin and C. Gershman. Commentary 64:33-43 O '77
Anxious for a new start; visit of A. Young. il por Time 109:43-5 F 21 '77
Carter's point man; A. Young. R. Carroll and others. il por Newsweek 89:39-40 F 14 '77
Continent rediscovered. S. J. Ungar. Atlantic 240:4+ S '77
Evolving African policy of the United States; address, August 18, 1977. M. A. Samuels. Vital Speeches 43:731-5 S 15 '77
New multi-ring spectacle; A. Young's visit. il por Time 109:29-30 F 14 '77

UNITED STATES—Foreign relations—Africa—*Continued*

Present U.S. policy: text of the Kissinger statement; April 27, 1976. H. A. Kissinger. Cong Digest 56:7-9+ Ja '77
United States and Africa: building positive relations; address, with transcript of question and answer session, July 1, 1977. C. R. Vance. Dept State Bull 77:165-74 Ag 8 '77; Same. Vital Speeches 43:642-5 Ag 15 '77
United States policy in Africa. R. E. Bissell. bibl f Cur Hist 73:193-5+ D '77
What U.S. is up to in Africa; W. F. Mondale's meeting with B. J. Vorster in Vienna. il pors U.S. News 82:31 My 30 '77
Young at heart; A. Young's visit. J. Pringle. il por Newsweek 89:44 My 30 '77

Africa, North

U.S. walks a tightrope in the Sahara. S. W. Sanders. il Bus W p47 Ja 16 '78

Africa, Southern

African-American manifesto; Black Leadership Conference on Southern Africa, September 25, 1976. Current 190:43-50 F '77
African impatience for change; meeting at Bergamo East Conference Center. C. E. Brewster. il Chr Cent 94:382-4 Ap 20 '77
America and Southern Africa. J. K. Nyerere. For Affairs 55:671-84 Jl '77
American lifelines around southern Africa. Sat Eve Post 249:38 Mr '77
Are Young's wings being clipped? por U.S. News 82:25 My 2 '77
Avoiding disaster in southern Africa. C. Legum. New Repub 176:11-13 F 12 '77
Diplomatic dissident; A. Young. Nation 224:516 Ap 30 '77
Does the Carter administration have a strategy for Southern Africa? G. W. Shepherd, Jr. il Chr Cent 94:782-6 S 14 '77
Needed: a change in U.S. policy in Southern Africa. G. M. Houser. Chr Cent 94:244-6 Mr 16 '77
Risk in Rhodesia. Progressive 41:11 Mr '77
South Africa & liberal interventionism: Yankee, stay home! I. Wallerstein. Nation 225:489-92 N 12 '77
Southern Africa in the global context; statement, March 3, 1977. P. C. Habib. Dept State Bull 76: 318-21 Ap 4 '77
This month's feature: controversy over U.S southern African policy. map Cong Digest 56:3-6 Ja '77
United States & southern Africa. P. Walshe. map Commonweal 104:201-3 Ap 1 '77
United States reiterates support for the independence of Namibia and Zimbabwe at Maputo conference; statements, with text of declaration, May 19 and 21, 1977. A. J. Young; C. W. Maynes. Dept State Bull 77:55-65 Jl 11 '77
U.S. relations in Southern Africa. W. E. Schaufele, Jr. Ann Am Acad 432:110-19 Jl '77
United States relations in Southern Africa; statement, April 16, 1977. W. E. Schaufele, Jr. Dept State Bull 76:464-71 My 9 '77
Vorster's crocodile. F. Willey and others. il Newsweek 90:37-8 Ag 22 '77
Washington notebook. S. Booker. Ebony 33:30 N '77
Watch out! Here we come! J. Burnham. Nat R 29:659 Je 10 '77

Arab countries

Influence game; commercialization of influence. T. D. Allman. New Repub 176:25-7 Mr 26 '77

Asia

American policy in Asia. E. O. Reischauer. Current 194:58-60 Jl '77
America's role in consolidating a peaceful balance and promoting economic growth in Asia; address, June 29, 1977. C. R. Vance. Dept State Bull 77:141-5 Ag 1 '77
Asian biggest worry: will Carter jettison them? il map U.S. News 83:51-4 Jl 18 '77
Concern about rights and troops. R. Graves. il Time 109:32+ Je 6 '77
What Asian nations want most from Carter; interview, ed by J. N. Wallace and H. Tanakadate. T. Fukuda. por U.S. News 82:76-7 Mr 28 '77

Asia, Southeastern

Thailand and cold-war diplomacy. L. Howell. Chr Cent 94:817-18+ S 21 '77

Australia

See also
Fraser, M.—Visit to the United States, 1977

Belgium

See also
Tindemans, L.—Visit to the United States, 1977

Bolivia

United States-Bolivia joint communique, June 7, 1976. Cur Hist 72:128-9 Mr '77

Brazil

Secret War in Brazil; American role in 1964 coup. J. V. Kohl. Progressive 41:33-5 Ag '77
Why angry Brazil shaped up as Rosalynn's toughest challenge. J. Benham. il pors map U.S. News 82:44-5 Je 13 '77

Canada

Canada and the United States: a special relationship. R. H. Leach. bibl f Cur Hist 72: 145-9+ Ap '77
Canadian and American friendship; address, February 22, 1977. P. E. Trudeau. Vital Speeches 43:322-4 Mr 15 '77
Specter of separatism; possibility of US-Canada merger. S. Talbott. Time 110:31-2 D 26 '77
U.S., Canada exchange notes on nuclear cooperation; November 15, 1977. Dept State Bull 77:857 D 12 '77
U.S.-Canada maritime boundary and resource negotiation. Dept State Bull 77:896-7 D 19 '77
U.S., Canada to negotiate maritime issues; announcement, July 27, 1977. Dept State Bull 77: 282 Ag 29 '77
See also
International Joint Commission (United States and Canada)
Trudeau, P. E.—Visit to the United States, 1977
United States—Treaties—Canada

Chile

CIA's apprentices. Nation 224:772 Je 25 '77
Dancing on the graves. Nation 225:292 O 1 '77
Digging for justice. Nation 225:420-1 O 29 '77
Four years after the fall. T. Szulc. New Repub 177:14-16 S 10 '77
Letelier-Moffitt mystery. J. Stein. Progressive 41:36-9 N '77
Letter from a Chilean exile. L. Allende. Chr Cent 94:79-80 F 2 '77

Chile—History

Charles Horman; family's suit against U.S. government concerning death during 1973 coup. J. Deedy. Commonweal 104:738 N 25 '77
Guarding the secrets; testimony of R. Helms. Nation 225:482-3 N 12 '77
Helms cops a plea. R. Steele and others. por Newsweek 90:31 N 14 '77
Helms file. por Newsweek 90:31-2 O 10 '77
Spare that spook! case of R. M. Helms. New Repub 177:5+ N 19 '77
Up against Citizen Helms. J. K. Larson. Chr Cent 94:1108-10 N 30 '77

China

China and Panama: the connection. W. F. Buckley, Jr. Nat R 29:1072 S 16 '77
China ends an era. A. Deming and others. il Newsweek 90:32-3+ Ag 29 '77
Chinese puzzle that Vance will try to solve; with editorial comment. il U.S. News 83:48-50, 68 Ag 22 '77
Eternal China, eternal conspiracies. R. Elegant. il map Nat R 29:1167+ O 14 '77
Japanese solution? Nat R 29:1098 S 30 '77
Military-security relations between China and the United States; excerpt from China policy: Old problems and new challenges. A. D. Barnett. bibl f For Affairs 55:584-97 Ap '77
Open door policy. A. Deming and others. il por Newsweek 89:42 Ap 25 '77
Our next move on China. S. Karnow. il N Y Times Mag p7-9+ Ag 14 '77
Should U.S. recognize Peking? interviews. C. Pell; E. J. Garn. pors U.S. News 83:27-8 Ag 29 '77
Thinking through the China problem. R. H. Solomon. bibl f For Affairs 56:324-56 Ja '78
What the Chinese told a visiting U.S. banker; interview. C. M. Berry. il por U.S. News 83: 53-4 Ag 22 '77
Where China is headed; interview. G. Bush. il pors U.S. News 83:33-4 N 14 '77
Wide of the mark. C. Johnson. New Repub 177: 12-14 N 26 '77
See also
Vance, C. R.—Visit to China, 1977

China—History

U.S. and two Chinas: 40 years of turmoil. il U.S. News 83:48-9 Ag 22 '77
What did Nixon say to Chou? secret memorandum of conversation in 1972. W. F. Buckley, Jr. Nat R 29:572 My 13 '77
Word from Washington. F. Getlein. Progressive 41:12-13 S '77
See also
Peking talks, 1972

Communist countries

Culture of appeasement. N. Podhoretz. Harpers 255:25-32 O '77
Toujours gai; N. Podhoretz's article in Harper's magazine. Nat R 29:1160 O 14 '77

UNITED STATES—Foreign relations—*Continued*

Cuba

Absence of Castro. Nation 225:226-7 S 17 '77
Another fresh start. K. Willenson and S. Sullivan. il Newsweek 89:33-4 Mr 14 '77
Cuba...courts...coolies. M. Stone. U.S. News 82:84 Mr 28 '77
Cuban Interest Section opens in Washington; statement, September 1, 1977. P. Habib. Dept State Bull 77:572-3 O 24 '77
Cuba's developing policies. G. W. Grayson. bibl f Cur Hist 72:49-52+ F '77
New relationship. K. Willenson and S. Sullivan. Newsweek 89:47-8 Je 13 '77
Now: a U.S. rush to heal rift with Cuba. C. J. Migdail. il U.S. News 82:34 Mr 21 '77
President Carter discusses Cuba and SALT negotiations; transcript of remarks, May 30, 1977. J. Carter. Dept State Bull 77:9-10 Jl 4 '77
Repairing the 90-mile bridge. Nation 224:324-5 Mr 19 '77
Talk with Castro. G. S. McGovern. il pors N Y Times Mag p20+ Mr 13 '77
U.S. toughens stance on renewing Cuban ties. map U.S. News 83:50 D 19 '77
What Castro risks—and gains—in deal with Carter. C. J. Migdall. U.S. News 82:30 Je 20 '77
What if with one hand? J. Burnham. Nat R 29: 600 My 27 '77
Why it won't be easy to strike a U.S.-Cuba deal. il por map U.S. News 82:71-2 Mr 7 '77
See also
United States—Treaties—Cuba

Cuba—History

CIA and Cuba; question of Kennedy's participation in Castro assassination plots. W. F. Buckley, Jr. Nat R 29:792 Jl 8 '77
CIA's apprentices. Nation 224:770-2 Je 25 '77
Kennedy's cold war; the Taylor report. T. Szulc. New Repub 177:19-21 D 24 '77
Television; B. Moyers' The CIA's secret army. P. Sourian. Nation 225:155-7 Ag 20 '77
See also
Cuba—History—Invasion, 1961
Cuban Missile Crisis, 1962

Egypt

What Sadat will seek from Carter; interview, ed by L. H. Young and R. Taggiasco. A. Sadat. pors Bus W p96-9 Ap 4 '77
See also
Sadat, A.—Visit to the United States, 1977

Ethiopia

Ethiopia: how big a loss for U.S? il map U.S. News 82:38 My 9 '77
Farewell to American arms. il por Time 109:36-7 My 9 '77

Europe

U.S. policy toward our NATO partners: traditional commitments and new directions; statement, May 23 1977. A. A. Hartman. Dept State Bull 76:635-9 Je 13 '77

Europe, Eastern

Human rights and East-West relations. K. E. Birnbaum. bibl f For Affairs 55:783-99 Jl '77
Understanding the Communist threat; excerpt from address, July 1977. A. B. Bozeman. bibl Society 15:92-6 N '77

Europe, Western

America's *ostpolitik*. R. N. Tannahill. Commonweal 104:142-3 Mr 4 '77
Carter's blueprint for Europe; excerpts from interviews. J. Carter. U.S. News 82:22 My 16 '77
Europe breaks apart. M. Ledeen. Commentary 63:53-7 My '77
Europe's future. M. Ledeen. New Repub 177:8-9 Jl 2 '77
United States and West Europe. J. Starrels. bibl f Cur Hist 73:145-8+ N '77
See also
Mondale, W. F.—Visit to Europe, Western, 1977

France

See also
Barre, R.—Visit to the United States, 1977

France—History

Quasi-War; American war with France, 1798-1800. A. DeConde. il Am Hist Illus 12:4-9+ Ap '77

Germany, West

New troubles for old friends. il Time 109:26 Mr 28 '77
See also
Schmidt, H.—Visit to the United States, 1977

Great Britain

British American relations; address, March 11, 1977. J. Callaghan. Vital Speeches 43:360-3 Ap 1 '77
Jimmy and Britain. J. Osborne. New Repub 176:10-12 My 28 '77
See also
Callaghan, J.—Visit to the United States, 1977
United States—Diplomatic and consular service—Great Britain

Great Britain—History

Reflections. W. Pfaff. New Yorker 53:113-18+ S 19 '77

Greece

Turks, Greeks, Congress and Carter. il Time 109:50 My 16 '77

Hungary

Ancient symbol stirs a storm for Carter. St Stephen's crown. il U.S. News 83:44 N 21 '77
Kadar's crown; return of St Stephen's crown to Hungary. C. Fenyvesi. il New Repub 177:15-17 N 19 '77
Meaning of a crown; return of St Stephen's crown. Nation 225:516 N 19 '77
Return of an ancient symbol; Crown of St Stephen. il Time 111:25 Ja 9 '78

India

Notes and comment. New Yorker 53:43-4 N 7 '77

Iran

Carter's worst appointment; nomination of W. H. Sullivan as ambassador. Nation 224:517 Ap 30 '77
No wreath for Mr Baskerville: America in cahoots with the Shah. R. Baraheni. Nation 224:307-8 Mr 12 '77
Secretary Vance attends Spanish-U.S. Council meeting at Madrid and CENTO Council of Ministers meeting at Tehran; remarks, with news conference, statement and communiques, May 11-15, 1977. C. R. Vance. Dept State Bull 76:612-18 Je 6 '77
Shah on war and peace; excerpts from interview, ed by A. de Borchgrave. Mohammed Reza Pahlevi. por map Newsweek 90:69-71 N 14 '77
See also
Mohammed Reza Pahlevi, Shah of Iran—Visit to the United States, 1977

Israel

American Jews and Mr Carter. Commonweal 104: 773-4 D 9 '77
American stake in Israel. E. V. Rostow. Commentary 63:32-46 Ap '77; Discussion. 64:16+ Jl '77
America's continuing concerns in the Middle East; remarks, January 11, 1977. H. A. Kissinger. Dept State Bull 76:90-1 Ja 31 '77
Begin in Middle East perspective: new factor in an old equation. I. L. Gendzier. Nation 225: 102-4 Ag 6 '77
Begin the Begin. New Repub 176:5-6+ My 28 '77
Behind Carter's gamble in the Middle East. il U.S. News 83:30-1 O 17 '77
Carter and Israel. S. L. Spiegel. Commentary 64:35-40 Jl '77; Discussion. 64:29-31 S '77
Carter and the worried Jews. R. Steele and others. il por Newsweek 89:21-2 Je 27 '77
Carter, the world and the Jews. il por Time 109: 8-10 Je 27 '77
Christians for Israel; evangelical stand. K. L. Woodward and R. Mark. il Newsweek 90:126 N 28 '77
Crunch with Israel. M. Kondracke. New Repub 176:17-19 Ap 2 '77
Does Washington have the means to impose a settlement on Israel? S. J. Rosen and M. Moustafine. Commentary 64:25-32 O '77
Don't deliver Israel. New Repub 177:5+ Ag 6 '77
Geneva: push comes to shove. il Time 110:24-8+ O 17 '77
Getting ready for Begin. J. M. Wall. Chr Cent 94:643-4 Jl 20 '77
Hawk on a mission of peace; M. Begin. W. E. Farrell. il pors N Y Times Mag p9-11+ Jl 17 '77
How to save Israel in spite of herself. G. W. Ball. For Affairs 55:453-71 Ap '77; Discussion. 55:888-90; 56:221-5 Jl-O '77
Into the Mideast crunch. S. Fraker and others. Newsweek 90:17 Jl 18 '77
Israel and Munich. G. F. Will. il Newsweek 90:80 Jl 11 '77
Israel and the evangelicals. J. M. Wall. Chr Cent 94:1083-4 N 23 '77
Israel thumps the Bible. Nation 224:674 Je 4 '77
Israel's De Gaulle. A. Perlmutter. il pors Newsweek 90:28-9 Ag 15 '77
Israel's hardening line in the Middle East. D. Mullin. il por map U.S. News 83:59-61 Jl 4 '77
Jimmy woos the Jewish leaders. il por Time 110: 11-12 Jl 18 '77
Keeping up the pressure. A. Deming and others. il por Newsweek 89:14-15 Je 6 '77
On the hustings with Moshe Dayan. il pors Time 110:34 O 17 '77
Prospect with Peres; peace settlement. D. Caploe. Nation 224:587-90 My 14 '77

UNITED STATES—Foreign relations—Israel —*Continued*
Sending Israel a message. R. Steele and others. il map Newsweek 90:28-9 Jl 11 '77
Strained alliance. R. Steele and others. il pors Newsweek 90:26-7+ O 17 '77
Trying to sell Geneva. A. Deming and others. il por Newsweek 90:56 O 24 '77
U.S. position on Israeli settlements; statement, with text of resolution, October 28, 1977. A. J. Young. Dept State Bull 77:821-2 D 5 '77
U.S. responsibility toward peace and human rights; address, November 2, 1977. J. Carter. Dept State Bull 77:759-62 N 28 '77
Warning shot across Begin's bow. por Time 110:34 Jl 11 '77
Will the working paper work? il Time 110:46-7 O 24 '77
See also
Begin, M.—Visits to the United States, 1977
Rabin, Y.—Visit to the United States, 1977

Israel—History
Recognizing Israel; address, December 28, 1976. C. M. Clifford. pors Am Heritage 28:4-7+ Ap '77

Italy
See also
Andreotti, G.—Visit to the United States, 1976
Andreotti, G.—Visit to the United States, 1977

Japan
Tokyo has risen. M. Kondracke. New Repub 177:11-14 S 10 '77
See also
Fukuda, T.—Visit to the United States, 1977
Mondale, W. F.—Visit to Japan, 1977

Korea, North
Careful response to an accident; attack on American helicopter. il map Time 110:36+ Jl 25 '77
Grim reminder from smoldering Korea; shooting down unarmed American helicopter. il U.S. News 83:50 Jl 25 '77
Korea: danger phase. Nat R 29:764 Jl 8 '77

Korea, North—History
See also
Pueblo incident, 1968

Korea, South
All about Koreagate. D. M. Alpern and others. il pors Newsweek 90:17+ Ag 1 '77
As the Korean bribery scandal unfolds—. il U.S. News 83:27 O 31 '77
Civil rights for Tongsun Park. Nation 225:261 S 24 '77
Fresh stirrings on Koreagate. il Time 110:19-20 S 5 '77
Kissinger, Haig and the Koreans. Nation 225:227-8 S 17 '77
Korea: danger phase. Nat R 29:764 Jl 8 '77
Korea stonewalls. New Repub 177:7-8 N 5 '77
Lid finally blows off Korean bribery scandal. il por U.S. News 83:28+ S 19 '77
Memories of Ice Mountain; House Ethics Committee investigation of South Korea's attempts to bribe Congressmen. Time 110:16 O 31 '77
New scandal in Congress. J. S. Lang. il por U.S. News 83:9-12 Ag 1 '77
New wave of repression in South Korea. Chr Cent 94:420 My 4 '77
Park stays put. Newsweek 90:44 S 19 '77
Park's lobby hobby. K. Willenson and others. il por Newsweek 90:37 S 5 '77
Patriarch's blessing. R. Steele and E. Shannon. il Newsweek 90:38 O 31 '77
South Korea with sympathy. M. Kondracke. New Repub 177:12+ S 17 '77
South Korean exposure: bad news for President Park. J. Stentzel. Nation 224:77-80 Ja 22 '77
Still waiting for harvest time; indictment of T. Park. il por Time 110:21-2 S 19 '77
Swindler from Seoul. Time 110:8+ Jl 4 '77
System fixer; L. Jaworski heading investigation. Nation 225:98 Ag 6 '77
Talking with Tongsun Park; interview, ed by B. Krisher. T. Park. pors Newsweek 90:36-8 O 3 '77

Laos
See also
United States—Presidential Commission on Americans Missing and Unaccounted For in Southeast Asia

Latin America
Approach to Latin American policy: creative developments; address, July 21, 1977. T. A. Todman. Dept State Bull 77:588-92 O 31 '77
Are South American dictators serious about stepping down? il map U.S. News 83:47-8 N 28 '77
Foundations of U.S. policy toward Latin America; address, October 18, 1977. T. A. Todman. Dept State Bull 77:815-21 D 5 '77
Happy sounds on dictatorships; visit by T. Todman. Nation 225:163-4 S 3 '77
Inter-American relations in an era of change; statement, March 24, 1977. W. H. Luers. Dept State Bull 76:347-50 Ap 11 '77
Kissinger's legacy: a Latin American policy. F. P. Kessler. bibl f Cur Hist 72:76-8+ F '77
Lofty rhetoric and business interests: the real Latin American policy. A. Howard. Nation 225:365-70 O 15 '77
Moves on Latin America impact on export market. Aviation W 106:18 Mr 7 '77
Of many things; First Lady's trip through Latin America. J. O'Hare. America 136:inside cover Je 11 '77
Out on her own; R. Carter's trip to the Caribbean and Latin America. P. Goldman and others. il pors Newsweek 89:15-18 Je 13 '77
President Carter holds bilateral meetings with Western Hemisphere leaders; remarks, September 6-9, 1977. J. Carter. Dept State Bull 77:510+ O 17 '77
President Carter's choices. G. MacEoin. Commonweal 104:616-18 S 30 '77
President's closest emissary; visit of R. Carter. il pors Time 109:17+ Je 13 '77
Rosalynn takes a message home. il por Time 109:26 Je 20 '77
Rosalynn's turn at diplomacy family style. por map U.S. News 82:36 Je 6 '77
Russia arms Peru; effect on US-Latin American relations. T. Szulc. News Repub 176:18-19 F 19 '77
La senora de Carter hits the road. il por map Time 109:10 Je 6 '77
Spreading the Carter gospel. Time 110:30+ Ag 22 '77
Still forgotten continent. Nation 224:227-8 F 26 '77
Third world has given everything and received little; interview. C. A. Pérez. il por U.S. News 83:53-4+ Jl 25 '77
United States' policy toward Latin America; address, April 14, 1977. J. Carter. Vital Speeches 43:424-6 My 1 '77; Same with title President Carter's Pan American Day address. Dept State Bull 76:453-7 My 9 '77
United States relations with Latin America: neighborliness and exploitation; a consideration of nine books. D. M. Pletcher. bibl Am Hist R 82:39-59 F '77
U.S. security assistance policy for Latin America; statement, April 5, 1977. T. A. Todman. Dept State Bull 76:444-6 My 2 '77
Why angry Brazil shaped up as Rosalynn's toughest challenge. J. Benham. il pors map. U.S. News 82:44-5 Je 13 '77
Why Latin Americans are bitter about Carter. il U.S. News 82:33-4 Ap 4 '77
With Mrs Carter in Latin America. Taurus. New Repub 176:13-14 Je 18 '77
See also
United States—Treaties—Latin America

Libya
Why U.S. continues to suspect Qadhafi. U.S. News 83:38 Ag 8 '77

Luxembourg
Ambassadors are no joke. Nation 224:613 My 21 '77

Mexico
Borders: Texas-Chihuahua. R. Morris. New Repub 177:12 O 22 '77
Mexico's problems won't stop at the border. S. W. Sanders. il Bus W p44+ D 19 '77
Realities of U.S.-Mexican relations. R. R. Fagen. For Affairs 55:685-700 Jl '77
Secretary reaffirms continuity of U.S.-Mexican relations; remarks, November 30, 1975. H. A. Kissinger. Dept State Bull 75:749-50 D 27 '76
U.S.-Mexican border problems. A. Paredes and others. Intellect 106:98 S '77
United States-Mexico joint communique issued at Mexico City, June 11, 1976. Cur Hist 72:128 Mr '77
See also
López Portillo, J.—Visit to the United States, 1977
United States—Treaties—Mexico

Mexico—History
South of the border—a legacy of bitterness. il Forbes 119:43-8 Ap 15 '77
See also
United States—History—Punitive Expedition to Mexico, 1916

Middle East
Carter too played a part; Sadat-Begin summit. S. Talbott. Time 110:43 D 5 '77
Code words from an oracle. il Time 109:27-8 Mr 28 '77
Co-opting the third world elites: trilateralism goes to work. K. Bird. Nation 224:425-8 Ap 9 '77
Framework for Middle East peace: shaping a more stable world; address, June 17, 1977. W. F. Mondale. Dept State Bull 77:41-6 Jl 11 '77
Gloom in Israel, joy for the Arabs; American policy statement on Palestinian representation at peace talks. il Time 110:33-4 S 26 '77

UNITED STATES—Foreign relations—Middle East —*Continued*
Interview with Secretary Vance on February 8 by Egyptian and Syrian media representatives; transcript of interview, ed by A. Fawzi and G. Rifai. C. R. Vance. Dept State Bull 76: 224-8 Mr 14 '77
Interview with Secretary Vance on February 10 by Israeli media representatives; transcript of interview, ed by E. Nissan and others. C. R. Vance. Dept State Bull 76:228-34 Mr 14 '77
Is '77 the year? M. Kondracke. New Repub 176: 13-15 F 12 '77
Let's resolve the Middle East crisis—now! W. E. Griffith. Read Digest 110:73-7 Ap '77
Mideast impasse. W. F. Buckley, Jr. Nat R 29: 1194 O 14 '77
Oil and American power—three years later. R. W. Tucker; discussion. Commentary 63:6+ Ap '77
On the altar of oil. B. W. Tuchman. New Repub 176:37-8 Ja 22 '77
Peace in the Middle East: Mr Carter grasps that nettle. M. A. Bruzonsky. il por Nation 224: 489-92 Ap 23 '77
Sadat's confidence restored. il pors Time 111:24+ Ja 16 '78
Secretary Vance attends Spanish-U.S. Council meeting at Madrid and CENTO Council of Ministers meeting at Tehran; remarks, with news conference, statement and communiques, May 11-15, 1977. C. R. Vance. Dept State Bull 76: 612-18 Je 6 '77
Secretary Vance meets at London with Israeli foreign minister; remarks, May 11, 1977. C. R. Vance and Y. Allon. Dept State Bull 76: 607-9 Je 6 '77
Una selva oscura. Nat R 29:762-3 Jl 8 '77
West's tenuous oil lifeline. map Bus W p56 N 28 '77
Why the PLO? The Soviets? Nat R 29:1216-17 O 28 '77
Why U.S. takes tougher line on Mideast. D. Mullin. il U.S. News 83:35-6 O 3 '77
See also
Cairo conference, 1977
Vance, C. R.—Visit to the Middle East, February 1977

Namibia

U.S. reaffirms commitment to self-determination and independence for Namibia; statements, with texts of resolutions, December 2, 10, and 20, 1976. W. W. Scranton; S. Hess. Dept State Bull 76:43-8 Ja 17 '77
Vice President Mondale visits Europe and meets with South African Prime Minister Vorster; news conference at Vienna, May 20, 1977. W. F. Mondale. Dept State Bull 76:661-6 Je 20 '77

Netherlands—History

Dutch republic in John Adams' day; exhibition. S. B. Sherrill. il Antiques 111:26 Ja '77

New Zealand

See also
Muldoon, R. D.—Visit to the United States, 1977

Nicaragua

Nicaragua, a wholly owned subsidiary. S. Kinzer. New Repub 176:14-17 Ap 9 '77

Nigeria

Wooing of Nigeria: a courtship pays off. il map U.S. News 83:67-70 D 5 '77
See also
Obasanjo, O.—Visit to the United States, 1977

Northern Ireland

Carter's Irish initiative. America 137:138 S 17 '77
Welcome initiative. D. Fisher. Commonweal 104: 612-13 S 30 '77

Pacific Countries

National strategy considerations in the Pacific Basin; address, June 27, 1977. W. G. Claytor, Jr. Vital Speeches 43:706-8 S 15 '77

Pakistan

Why Pakistan is uneasy about U.S. as an ally; with interview with Z. A. Bhutto, ed by J. N. Wallace. il map U.S. News 82:70-2 Mr 14 '77

Panama

See also
United States—Treaties—Panama

Philippines

Carter's Far East strategy; new role for Philippine bases. L. Hansen. il por map U.S. News 83:29-30 Ag 29 '77
Carter's moral foreign policy and Philippine martial law. C. L. Hunt. bibl por Intellect 106:130-3 O '77
Our Philippine bases: Marcos woud raise the ante. P. W. Stanley. Nation 224:561-2 My 7 '77
U.S. Philippine officials hold discussions in Manila; joint press release, September 24, 1977. Dept State Bull 77:695 N 14 '77

Rhodesia

Department testifies on U.S. policy toward Rhodesia; statement, June 8, 1977. W. B. Edmondson. Dept State Bull 77:98-9 Jl 18 '77
Lynching Rhodesia; UN's May 27 resolution. Nat R 29:766 Jl 8 '77
Mondale v. Vorster: tough talk. il pors Time 109:34+ My 30 '77
Narrowing options for Rhodesia. T. Beeson. Chr Cent 94:133-4 F 16 '77
On crushing Rhodesia. W. F. Buckley, Jr. Nat R 29:1195 O 14 '77
Rhodesia: a gingerly diplomacy. D. I. Fine. Nation 225:199-201 S 10 '77
Rhodesian blackout? Nat R 29:426-7 Ap 15 '77
Vice President Mondale visits Europe and meets with South African Prime Minister Vorster; news conference at Vienna, May 20, 1977. W. F. Mondale. Dept State Bull 76:661-6 Je 20 '77

Russia

Ample guilt, no policy. A. B. Ulam. New Repub 176:26+ Ja 22 '77
Back to secret diplomacy? F. Willey and F. Coleman. il Newsweek 89:43 Ap 18 '77
Because we care about people; views on Sakharov letter. J. M. Wall. Chr Cent 94:187-8 Mr 2 '77
Behind Carter's gamble in the Middle East. il U.S. News 83:30-1 O 17 '77
Beyond détente. R. W. Tucker. Commentary 63: 42-50 Mr '77; Reply with rejoinder. D. S. Lichtenstein. 64:14+ Jl '77
Breaking the linkage; February 8 press conference of J. Carter. Nation 224:197 F 19 '77
Brezhnev's bluster. F. Willey and others. il por Newsweek 90:46 Jl 4 '77
Carter and the Kremlin—now a war of nerves. U.S. News 82:23-4 Ap 18 '77
Carter and the Russians: semi-tough. il pors Time 109:10-11 F 21 '77
Carter backs off; Belgrade conference on European security and cooperation. C. Whipple and others. Newsweek 90:48+ O 10 '77
Carter faces the Russians. New Repub 177:5-6 Jl 23 '77
Carter hour. Nat R 29:480 Ap 29 '77
Carter's plain talk. Nation 224:258-9 Mr 5 '77
Carter's strategy for dealing with Russia; excerpts from news conference, February 8, 1977. J. Carter. il por U.S. News 82:39 F 21 '77
Carter's world: too much, too soon? il U.S. News 82:15-17 F 28 '77
Case of red herring; Coast Guard seizure of two Russian trawlers. T. Mathews and R. Manning. il Newsweek 89:23+ Ap 25 '77
Churchill and us; question of policies toward military preparedness in pre-World War II Great Britain and in the United States today. E. N. Luttwak. Commentary 63:44-9 Je '77
Cold war? Nyet. But it's getting chilly. il por Time 110:10-11 Jl 18 '77
Congress concerned by test ban talks. Aviation W 108:54+ Ja 9 '78
Containment: a reassessment. J. L. Gaddis. bibl f For Affairs 55:873-87 Jl '77. Reply with rejoinder. E. Mark. 56:430-41 Ja '78
Crackdown on Russian poachers—a taste of more to come. il map U.S. News 82:43-4 Ap 25 '77
Dangerous delusion. E. R. Zumwalt, Jr. il pors Sat Eve Post 249:12-14 N '77
Dangers of a new Cold War. G. Arbatov. Bull Atom Sci 33:33-40 Mr '77
Daring to talk about human rights; State Department response to statement by A. Sakharov. por Time 109:38 F 7 '77
Détente: a victim of mutual suspicion. P. Osnos. il Bull Atom Sci 33:16-19 N '77
Détente and the military balance. S. A. Garrett. bibl il Bull Atom Sci 33:10-20 Ap '77
Detente party. J. Burnham. Nat R 29:319 Mr 18 '77
Détente: the new morality. F. Willey and others. il Newsweek 89:36-7+ F 14 '77
Display of anniversary amity. il Time 110:34-5 N 14 '77
Drawing the line. D. Fromkin. New Repub 176: 12-14 Je 4 '77
Dual messages to Washington. il por Time 109: 30+ F 14 '77
Eurocommunism and detente. A. Schlesinger, Jr. Current 196:42-5 O '77
Forked tongue; Carter administration statements on Russian human rights. New Repub 176:7-8 F 19 '77
High human price of detente. C. B. Luce. Nat R 29:1289-91 N 11 '77
Honorable schoolboy FBI's domestic counterespionage; attempted recruiting of Russian exchange student A. R. Lusis. Time 110:26 N 14 '77
How goes detente? Sr Schol 110:14+ N 3 '77
How to deal with the Russians; Time essay. L. Morrow. il Time 109:42-3 My 30 '77
Human rights and East-West relations. K. E. Birnbaum. bibl f For Affairs 55:783-99 Jl '77
Human rights: conflicts among our ideals; excerpts from address, June 5, 1977. D. Riesman. Commonweal 104:711-15 N 11 '77

UNITED STATES—Foreign relations—Russia —*Continued*
Immoralists. F. Getlein. Commonweal 104:196-8 Ap 1 '77
Is it over, over there? A. G. J. Chalfont. il Nat R 29:200-3+ F 18 '77
Is there a present danger? M. Kondracke. New Repub 176:18-20 Ja 29 '77
Jimmy, the Bible—and Brezhnev. il pors Time 110:12-13 Ag 1 '77
Let's put detente back on the rails. S. Pisar. il N Y Times Mag p31-3+ S 25 '77
Letter to a friend; J. Carter's letter to A. Sakharov. por Time 109:30-1 F 28 '77
Little stink about a lot of fish; violation of U.S. 200 mile fishing zone by Russian ships. il Time 109:42+ Ap 25 '77
Loyal opposition. R. Medvedev. il por Newsweek 89:48 Je 20 '77
Message from Moscow. A. Deming and others. il por Newsweek 89:14-16 Je 27 '77
Mr Perseverance; C. Vance's negotiations on strategic arms and the Middle East. R. Watson and S. Sullivan. il por Newsweek 90:42+ O 10 '77
Mr X^2; G. F. Kennan. H. Fairlie. New Repub 177:9-11 D 24 '77; Reply. Nation 226:4-5 Ja 7 '78
Nature of Soviet power. R. Legvold. For Affairs 56:49-71 O '77
New U.S. challenge to Russia; interview. Z. Brzezinski. il por U.S. News 82:35-6+ My 30 '77
Now a cold war over human rights. U.S. News 82:52 F 14 '77
Pitfalls of morality. A. Tonelson. New Repub 177:13-15 O 29 '77
Plan to lessen suspicions. H. M. Agnew. Bull Atom Sci 33:6-7 Mr '77; Same with title Truth in verification. Aviation W 106:7 My 16 '77
Polecats, beavers, and détente; U.S.-U.S.S.R. Agreement on Cooperation in the Field of Environmental Protection. G. Reiger. Field & S 81:20+ Ap '77
President Carter outlines the U.S.-Soviet relationship; remarks, July 21, 1977. J. Carter. Dept State Bull 77:193-7 Ag 15 '77; Same with title President Carter on the Soviet Union. Cur Hist 73:176-7+ N '77
President Carter's news conference of February 8. J. Carter. Dept State Bull 76:157-60 F 28 '77
Prospects for human rights; adaptation of address, June 5, 1977. D. Riesman. bibl il Society 15:28-33 N '77
Relations with the Soviet Union; address, November 14, 1977. P. C. Habib. Dept State Bull 77:854-6 D 12 '77
Reports & comment: Moscow: a chill in the air. D. K. Shipler. Atlantic 240:11-12+ S '77
Russia, America and détente. H. Sonnenfeldt. For Affairs 56:275-94 Ja '78
Secret speech: did Brezhnev come clean? Nat R 29:248+ Mr 4 '77
Showdown with Russia; human rights issue. U.S. News 82:17-18 Je 20 '77
Signal to the Soviets—and to Carter; excerpts from interview. P. Warnke. il por Time 109:28 Mr 21 '77
Signs of change in Russia; interview. M. Toon. il pors U.S. News 84:27-8 Ja 9 '78
Soviet Foreign Minister Gromyko visits Washington; communique, with joint statement, September 24, 1977. Dept State Bull 77:643-4 N 7 '77
Soviet official tells U.S.—don't push the issue too far; interview, ed by R. Knight. G. Arbatov. il por U.S. News 82:23-4+ Mr 14 '77
Soviets hit back on human rights il Time 109:22 Mr 14 '77
Too casual diplomacy. New Repub 177:10-11 O 15 '77
Tough talk on human rights—will it scuttle detente? il U.S. News 82:30+ Mr 7 '77
Trying to scare Carter. Nation 224:162 F 12 '77
U.S. sets new rules for detente; with interview with U. A. Johnson. pors U.S. News 82:24-6 Ap 4 '77
U.S.-Soviet relations. Dept State Bull 77:356-9 S 12 '77
Washington's favorite Russian. M. Kondracke. New Repub 177:19-21 N 19 '77
Where is detente going? excerpts from interview, ed by F. Coleman. M. Toon. il Newsweek 90:48-9 Jl 25 '77
Where U.S. is gaining in the world; interview. C. R. Vance. il pors U. S. News 83:27-30 N 7 '77; Same. Dept State Bull 77:732-8 N 21 '77
Zigzagging with the Russians. M. Stone. U.S. News 83:92 N 7 '77
See also
Strategic Arms Limitation Talks
Vance, C. R.—Visit to Russia, 1977

Russia—History

Dealing with the Russian leaders; work of W. Hyland. il por Time 110:28 N 21 '77
Who started the cold war? with introduction and discussion. C. L. Mee, Jr; W. A. Harriman; E. Abel. il pors Am Heritage 28:8-23 Ag '77
See also
Cuban Missile Crisis, 1962

Saudi Arabia

Arab brings a warning for Carter. por U.S. News 82:28 My 30 '77
High stakes in continuing Saudi stability. S. W. Sanders. il Bus W p47+ Ja 16 '78
Saudi Foreign Minister meets with President Carter; October 25, 1977. Dept State Bull 77:766-7 N 28 '77
Why U.S. and Saudi Arabia team up for peace in Mideast. il map U.S. News 83:57-8 Jl 25 '77
See also
Fahd, Prince of Saudi Arabia—Visit to the United States, 1977

South Africa

Africa: are we too smug? M. Stone. U.S. News 82:92 Je 6 '77
Ambassador Young interviewed on Issues and answers; transcript of program, October 30, 1977; ed by B. Clark and others. A. J. Young. Dept State Bull 77:791-2+ D 5 '77
Andy Young is at it again. R. Carroll and others. il por Newsweek 89:52 Je 6 '77
Asking for trouble in South Africa. G. W. Ball. Atlantic 240:43-51 O '77; Same abr. Read Digest 112:59-63 Ja '78
Breaking the ice; W. F. Mondale's meeting with B. J. Vorster in Vienna. S. Fraker and others. pors Newsweek 89:16-17 My 30 '77
Concern expressed on recent events in South Africa; statement, October 26, 1977. R. M. Moose. Dept State Bull 77:897-9 D 19 '77
Dilemmas for U.S. policy in South Africa. S. W. Sanders. il Bus W p50 D 26 '77
President discusses U.S. policy toward South Africa; excerpt from transcript of question and answer session, May 17, 1977. Dept State Bull 76:626-7 Je 13 '77
South Africa: are there grounds for hope? G. P. Wiles. Chr Cent 94:400-4 Ap 27 '77
South Africa warns U.S: don't move too fast. D. B. Richardson. U.S. News 83:46-7 Ag 29 '77
South Africa: what is to be done. C. Ferguson and W. R. Cotter. bibl f For Affairs 56:253-74 Ja '78
U.N. Security Council condemns South Africa's apartheid policy and imposes a mandatory arms embargo; statements, with text of resolutions, October 31 and November 4, 1977. A. J. Young. Dept State Bull 77:859-66 D 12 '77
United States urges peaceful change in South Africa; statements, November 3 and 9, 1976. S. Hess; R. P. Hupp. Dept State Bull 76:48-51 Ja 17 '77
Vice President Mondale visits Europe and meets with South African Prime Minister Vorster; news conference at Vienna, May 20, 1977. W. F. Mondale. Dept State Bull 76:661-6 Je 20 '77

Spain

See also
United States-Spanish Council

Sudan

Another African country turns from Russia to the U.S. D. Mullin. il por map U.S. News 83:75-6 S 26 '77

Syria

President Carter meets with President Asad of Syria at Geneva; exchange of remarks and toasts, May 9, 1977. J. Carter and H. Assad. Dept State Bull 76:593-7 Je 6 '77

Taiwan

Appointment in Peking; C. R. Vance's visit. il por Time 110:34-5 Ag 29 '77
China ends an era. A. Deming and others. il Newsweek 90:32-3+ Ag 29 '77
Chinese puzzle that Vance will try to solve; with editorial comment. il U.S. News 83:48-50, 68 Ag 22 '77
Getting to know you; Pacific Cultural Foundation's sponsoring of Taiwan junkets. A. Deming and others. il Newsweek 89:54-5 Ja 31 '77
Harold Lindsell reports from Taiwan. H. Lindsell. Chr Today 21:15-17 Ag 26 '77
Japanese solution? Nat R 29:1098 S 30 '77
Letter from Taiwan. R. Shaplen. New Yorker 53:72+ Je 13 '77
Our next move on China. S. Karnow. il N Y Times Mag p7-9+ Ag 14 '77
Should U.S. recognize Peking? interviews. C. Pell; E. J. Garn. pors U.S. News 83:27-8 Ag 29 '77
Taiwan's stake in the Vance trip. L. Hansen. il U.S. News 83:51 Ag 22 '77
Understanding Chiang Ching-kuo. W. F. Buckley, Jr. Nat R 30:48-9 Ja 6 '78
Visa time again on Taiwan. il Time 110:36 Ag 29 '77

Taiwan—History

U.S. and two Chinas: 40 years of turmoil. il U.S. News 83:48-9 Ag 22 '77

Tanzania

See also
Nyerere, J. K.—Visit to the United States, 1977

UNITED STATES—Foreign relations—*Continued*

Thailand

Thailand and cold-war diplomacy. L. Howell. Chr Cent 94:817-18+ S 21 '77

Turkey

Turks, Greeks, Congress and Carter. il Time 109:50 My 16 '77

Uganda

America's shaky truce with Amin. map U.S. News 82:28 Mr 14 '77
Dealing with Dada. New Repub 176:5-6+ Mr 19 '77
Limits of morality. I. Amin Dada. il por Newsweek 89:14-15 Mr 7 '77

Underdeveloped areas

New tactics at U.N: it looks as if U.S. feud with third world is over—for now. U.S. News 83:37 O 17 '77
North-South dialogue. Dept State Bull 77:235-6 Ag 22 '77
Third-world poverty: don't blame us. M. Singer and P. Bracken. Read Digest 110:114-17 F '77

Uruguay

State Department clientism: Siracusa, our man in Uruguay. M. Holland and K. Bird. Nation 224:334-7 Mr 19 '77

Venezuela

See also
Perez, C. A.—Visit to the United States, 1977

Vietnam

Dancing in the dark. W. F. Buckley, Jr. Nat R 29:631 My 27 '77
Extending a hand to Hanoi. il Time 109:30 F 28 '77

See also
United States—Presidential Commission on Americans Missing and Unaccounted For in Southeast Asia
Vietnamese War, 1957-1975—American participation

Zaire

Going like 60. Nation 224:548-9 My 7 '77

Foreign Service

See United States—Diplomatic and Consular Service

Forest Service

American people are being robbed! K. Wiegner. il Forbes 120:102+ O 15 '77
Forest Service is ready. J. B. Craig. Am For 83:6 Ag '77
In defense of my organic homestead. H. Seaver. il por Org Gard & Farm 24:184+ O '77
Indian Peaks: park or playground? proposed addition to Rocky Mountain National Park. B. Vollmerhausen. il map Nat Parks & Con Mag 51:4-9 My '77
Is time running out for Taylor-Hilgard? with editorial comment. R. Tawney. il map Liv Wildn 40:3, 34-41 Ja '77
Land exchange; case study involving Disney's resort plans and government land. R. F. Masse and C. Broussard. il map Parks & Rec 12:26-9+ D '77
Let's save our roadless areas! with editorial comment. D. Sumner. il Liv Wildn 40:3, 25-33 Ja '77
Observing foresters. T. M. Pasca. il por Am For 83:24-7+ Ag '77
Political history of the Forest Service. S. H. Spurr. Am For 83:15-16 F '77
Reorganization and the Forest Service: a sense of place. W. E. Towell. Am For 83:11 D '77
There's more to reclamation than planting trees. J. R. McGuire. il Am For 83:14-19 Jl '77
296 million acre myth; nonindustrial private commercial forestland. R. E. Jones and J. S. Paxton. Am For 83:6+ N '77

General Accounting Office

AWT may be too expensive—GAO. il Am City & County 92:19 Mr '77
Agencies quick to blunt GAO impact on F-16. Aviation W 106:23 Ap 18 '77
Airline fuel conservation effort hit in GAO report. Aviation W 107:36 S 12 '77
Boost in Japan's military funding pressed by GAO. H. J. Coleman. Aviation W 106:24 Je 27 '77
Coal option; report. Sci Am 238:64 Ja '78
F-16 survivability reassessment urged. Aviation W 106:19-20 Ap 11 '77
Foreign arms sales hampered defense capability, GAO says. Aviation W 107:57-8 Ag 22 '77
GAO criticizes AWACS sale to Iran on justification basis. Aviation W 107:24-5 Jl 25 '77
GAO criticizes federal procurement agencies for their leniency with A-E errors and omissions; report entitled Procedures used for holding architects and engineers responsible for the quality of their design work. W. Hickman. Archit Rec 162:34 S '77
GAO decision on NSF claim favors curriculum study group. J. Walsh. Science 197:234 Jl 15 '77
GAO hits British support for Harriers. H. J. Coleman. Aviation W 106:23 Ja 17 '77
GAO hits F-18 ejection seat selection. E. Kozicharow. Aviation W 106:24-5 Ap 18 '77
GAO reports on federally funded science programs. F. C. Bennett and B. C. Carr. il Phys Today 30:69-70+ Je '77
GAO space telescope study disputed. Aviation W 106:47 My 23 '77
GAO urges tighter scrutiny of RPV programs. Aviation W 106:50 Mr 7 '77
GAO wary of multinational F-16 pace. E. Kozicharow. Aviation W 107:20-1 Ag 22 '77
GAO: watching over Washington. il Duns R 109:38-43+ F '77
Kennedy, GAO criticize NSF; grant renewal is rejected. P. M. Boffey. Science 195:556-8 F 11 '77
Lo, the poor and sterilized Indian; report on practices of the Indian Health Service. B. Wagner. America 136:75 Ja 29 '77
Lockheed payments changes approved. Aviation W 106:73 Ap 25 '77
Lowered fare feasibility claimed in study by GAO. Aviation W 106:38 Mr 7 '77
Mixed impact seen in arms sales policy. Aviation W 107:17 S 19 '77

General Services Administration

Art will be considered just as important as the bricks; J. Solomon and GSA's Art-in-Architecture program. J. A. Lewis. il por Art N 76:56-8 D '77
Di Suvero in Grand Rapids: the public prevails. M. A. Tighe. il Art in Am 65:12-13+ Mr '77
GSA head Jay Solomon sees his background in real estate development as good job experience for his new post. W. Hickman. Archit Rec 162:35 S '77
Get involved with government—you can make it better. J. Eckerd. pors Nations Bus 65:61-3 Je '77
Labor Department mural: a complicated voyage; J. Beal's murals. B. Carter. il por Art N 76:40-1 My '77
Modern Medici for public art. J. A. Lewis. il Art N 76:36-7+ Ap '77
Some positive thinking from the General Services Administration. W. F. Wagner, Jr. Archit Rec 162:13 D '77
Washington scene; distribution of surplus federal personal property to eligible agencies. B. Kravetz. Parks & Rec 12:12-13 Ag '77

National Archives and Records Service

Archivists seek to split from GSA. Lib J 102:313 F 1 '77
Steal the Constitution? Not likely. U.S. News 83:52 S 5 '77

Geological Survey

Concept wins converts at Federal agency; flexible work schedules. O. Mueller and M. Cole. M Labor R 100:71-4 F '77
Geological Survey hits thematic mapper. C. Covault. Aviation W 107:20-1 Ag 8 '77
Leadership of the Geological Survey. P. H. Abelson. Science 198:11 O 7 '77
McKelvey ousted as director of Geological Survey. D. Shapley. Science 197:1264 S 23 '77
One of our rigs is missing; report on sinking of Pennzoil's Platform A. J. G. Mitchell. Audubon 79:149-51 N '77
35 percent of south Florida down the drain? Nat Parks & Con Mag 51:25 Mr '77

Gerontology Research Center

See United States—National Institutes of Health—Gerontology Research Center

Government

See United States—Politics and government

Government Advisory Committee on International Book and Library Programs

State Department action imperils advisory group. S. Wagner. Pub W 211:31 Ap 25 '77

Health, Education, and Welfare, Department of

Califano loses Fordham as assistant secretary. B. J. Culliton. Science 196:635 My 6 '77
Christopher Fordham named assistant secretary for health. B. J. Culliton. Science 196:148 Ap 8 '77
HEW and the sexual revolution: why teenagers get pregnant; contraception programs. M. Cattleman. Nation 225:549-52 N 26 '77
HEW vs. HUD; controversy over housing allowances. S. Kaplan. New Repub 177:15-16 Ag 6 '77

UNITED STATES—Health, Education, and Welfare, Department of—*Continued*
Hire the handicapped. S. Fraker and H. McGee. il Newsweek 89:39 My 9 '77
Hot seat; J. Califano. G. F. Will. Newsweek 89:96 Mr 7 '77
Hurrah for HEW; experiences of Kenilworth, Ill. school. Time 110:39 D 26 '77
Lips that sink ships; security investigations of HEW employees. J. McClellan and D. Anderson. Progressive 41:47-9 My '77
More blacks in colleges; integration order. il U.S. News 83:69 Jl 18 '77
One more plan to end fraud in welfare; interview. J. A. Califano, Jr. il pors U.S. News 84:41-4 Ja 9 '78
Politics of welfare reform. N. Kotz. New Repub 176:16-21 My 14 '77
Rights for the handicapped—new rules stir turmoil. il U.S. News 82:84 My 9 '77
Sec Califano announces major HEW reorganization. Aging 270:35-9 Ap '77
Section 504: impact on AoA programs. il Aging 275:14-16 S '77
Sweeping rules on employing the handicapped. Nations Bus 65:11-12 Jl '77
What's being done for 35 million handicapped. il U.S. News 83:58 Ag 29 '77
See also
Alliance for Arts Education
United States—Alcohol, Drug Abuse, and Mental Health Administration
United States—Education, Office of
United States—Human Development Services, Office of

Appropriations and expenditures

Taming a 148-billion-dollar federal giant: will anything work? il U.S. News 82:42-6 My 16 '77

Health Services Administration

And then there were none; Indian Health Service's sterilization practices. J. K. Larson. Chr Cent 94:61-3 Ja 26 '77
Death on the reservation; Indian Health Service. A. Spake. Progressive 41:27-30 F '77
Lo, the poor and sterilized Indian; General Accounting Office report on practices of the Indian Health Service. B. Wagner. America 136:75 Ja 29 '77

Historic houses, sites, etc.

See Historic houses, sites, etc.—United States

History

See also
Frontier and pioneer life—United States
Indians of North America—History
Northwestern States—History
Political parties—United States—History
Southern States—History
United States—Declaration of Independence
United States—Economic history
United States—Foreign relations—History
United States—Social history
United States—Treaties—History
Western States—History
also names of years, decades and centuries, e.g. Nineteen hundred and sixties; *also* subhead History under names of regions, states, cities, etc. e.g. New York (city)—History

Bibliography

Book reviews. Am Hist Illus 11:49-50 F; 12:49-50 Jl; 49-50 Ag; 50 O; 47 N '77
Reviews of books; United States. See issues of American historical review

Discovery and exploration

See America—Discovery and exploration

Drama

America's past is alive and outdoors. G. Loney and P. MacKay. Chr Cent 94:661-2 Jl 20 '77

Historiography

Perspectives on the past; work of J. F. Rhodes. W. W. Hassler, jr. Am Hist Illus 11:50 F '77

Periodicals

See also
American heritage (periodical)

Personal narratives

Conflict! personal accounts of wars. il Sat Eve Post 249:66-7 Jl '77

Study and teaching

Class project: rewrite history; ideas of T. Robinson. J. Kraus. Educ Digest 43:36-7 S '77

Colonial period, ca. 1600-1775

But was it history? P. W. Schmidtchen. il Hobbies 82:134-7+ N '77
Little adventures of Madeleine Hachard; role of Ursuline pioneers, in New Orleans. P. Robbins. il Am Hist Illus 12:36-42 Jl '77
Physical toughness of colonial Americans. H. F. Rankin. Intellect 106:15 Jl '77
Pontiac's conspiracy. A. Keller. il map Am Hist Illus 12:4-8+ My '77
See also
United States—Social life and customs—Colonial period, ca. 1600-1775

18th century

Ecoscene; introduction to eighteenth century customs in environmental education program, Greensboro, N.C. W. W. Davis and H. E. Manar. il Parks & Rec 12:26-8+ Ja '77
Paul Revere. B. A. Weisberger. il por Am Heritage 28:24-37 Ap '77

Revolution, 1775-1783

We the people of the United States: the bicentennial of a people's revolution. R. B. Morris. bibl f Am Hist R 82:1-19 F '77
Weather of Independence (title varies)
Burgoyne's northern campaign (cont) D. M. Ludlum. maps Weatherwise 29:288-90 D '76
Campaign for Philadelphia: July-November 1977. D. M. Ludlum. il maps Weatherwise 30:114-19 Je '74
See also
Clark's Expedition to the Illinois, 1778-1779
Valley Forge, Pa.

Revolution, 1775-1783—American forces

Ethan Allen and the Green Mountain Boys. D. B. Sabine. il pors Am Hist Illus 11:8-15 Ja '77

Revolution, 1775-1783—Campaigns and battles

George Rogers Clark: bluff over bullets; capture of British outposts in the Midwest. H. W. Noland and R. F. Banta. il pors map Sat Eve Post 249:54-7 O '77
Weather of Independence: Burgoyne's northern campaign (cont) D. M. Ludlum. maps Weatherwise 29:288-90 D '76
Weather of Independence: Campaign for Philadelphia: July-November 1977. D. M. Ludlum. il maps Weatherwise 30:114-19 Je '77
See also
Concord, Battle of, 1775
Fort Ticonderoga
Lexington, Battle of, 1775
Saratoga Campaign, 1777

Revolution, 1775-1783—French participation

Beaumarchais: Figaro's playwright. S. Hughes. il Opera N 41:13-15 Mr 5 '77
En avant with our French allies to Yorktown victory. S. Stember. il Smithsonian 8:64-8+ My '77

Revolution, 1775-1783—Naval operations

Battle of the Kegs; attempt to destroy British fleet in Philadelphia in January, 1778. D. H. Cross. il Am Hist Illus 12:40-1 Ap '77
John Barry, fighting Irishman; navy captain. B. Everett. il pors map Am Hist Illus 12:18-25 D '77

Revolution, 1775-1783—Personal narratives

Cause célèbre of Caty Greene; excerpt from Caty. J. F. Stegeman and J. A. Stegeman. il por Am Hist Illus 12:8-16 Je '77

Revolution, 1775-1783—Women

More on Deborah Sampson. C. C. Ritter. il Am Hist Illus 12:28-9 N '77

Constitutional period, 1789-1809

See also
Alien and Sedition Laws, 1798

War with France, 1798-1800

Quasi-War. A. DeConde. il Am Hist Illus 12:4-9+ Ap '77

19th century

Bull in the China shop; career of C. Sumner. D. W. Blight. il pors Am Hist Illus 12:10-19 Ap '77

Tripolitan War, 1801-1805

U.S. vs. international terrorists. G. Smith. il Am Heritage 28:36-43 Ag '77

War of 1812

Surrender of Detroit. L. H. Scott. il por map Am Hist Illus 12:28-36 Je '77

War of 1812—Naval operations

Cruise of the USS Essex; 32-gun frigate. R. J. Toner. il map Am Hist Illus 11:4-7+ Ja '77

Civil War, 1861-1865

See also
Draft riot, 1863
Reconstruction (Civil War)

UNITED STATES—History—*Continued*

Civil War, 1861-1865—Campaigns and battles

Civilian life during the siege of Vicksburg. P. Robbins. il map Am Hist Illus 12:12-17+ D '77
See also
Charleston, S.C.—Siege, 1863

Civil War, 1861-1865—Naval operations

Woman who saved the Union Navy; M. Louvestre's drawings of warship Merrimac. G. A. Foster. il Ebony 33:131-2+ D '77
See also
Monitor (warship)

Civil War, 1861-1865—Personal narratives

Diary of the Vicksburg siege. W. T. Mumford. il Am Hist Illus 12:46-8 D '77

Civil War, 1861-1865—Photographs

Images of which history was made bore the Mathew Brady label; excerpts from Mathew Brady and his world. P. B. Kunhardt, Jr. il pors Smithsonian 8:24-35 Jl '77

Civil War, 1861-1865—Secret service—Confederate States

Woman who saved the Union Navy; M. Louvestre's drawings of warship Merrimac. G. A. Foster. il Ebony 33:131-2+ D '77

1865-1898

Coxey's march on Washington, 1894. G. G Eggert. il pors Am Hist Illus 12:20-31 O '77
See also
Indians of North America—Wars

Spanish American War, 1898

Sam Waller: eyewitness to history. M. Jones. il pors Ebony 32:79-80+ F '77
Teddy Roosevelt & the Rough Riders. R. J. Maddox. il pors map Am Hist Illus 12:8-19 N '77

Punitive Expedition to Mexico, 1916

Patton in Mexico: the Punitive Expedition. M. Blumenson. il pors Am Hist Illus 12:34-42 O '77

1933-1945

Fork in the road; New Deal legislators. T. G. Corcoran and B. V. Cohen. E. Yoffe. New Repub 177:21-3 S 17 '77
New Deal and national health. R. Lubove. bibl f Cur Hist 72:198-200+ My '77
New Deal: born again; testimonial dinner for B. V. Cohen and T. G. Corcoran. T. Mathews and J. Doyle. il pors Newsweek 89:16-17 Mr 14 '77
Temps perdu; reunion of F. D. Roosevelt's New Deal staff. New Repub 176:2+ Mr 19 '77
Washington: rites of passage; gathering of New Deal staff. H. Sidey. il Time 109:18 Mr 14 '77

History, Naval

See also
United States—History—Revolution, 1775-1783 Naval operations
United States—History—Civil War, 1861-1865—Naval operations

House of Representatives

See United States—Congress—House

Housing and Urban Development, Department of

After the strip floods: relief is the real disaster; emergency housing for Mingo County, W.Va. R. E. Wise, Jr. il Nation 225:18-20 Jl 2 '77
Big boost for housing. il U.S. News 82:42 Mr 14 '77
Block grant rules land HUD in court. il Am City & County 92:16 S '77
Cities; meeting of New Yorkers to assist in the formation of Federal urban policies. New Yorker 53:38-40 N 14 '77
Core city fight for housing not over; Hartford Conn; with editorial comment. il Am City & County 92:33-4, 138 O '77
Erosion of aid to the cities. por Bus W p36 Ag 15 '77
HEW vs. HUD; controversy over housing allowances. S. Kaplan. New Repub 177:15-16 Ag 6 '77
HUD Secretary Harris puts priority on good design. D. Loomis. Archit Rec 161:34 F '77
HUD tightens block grant rules. Am City & County 92:13-14 D '77
Housing and community development: an act to bleed the cities. J. M. Baer. il Nation 224:274-6 Mr 5 '77
How much more federal aid can cities expect? interview. P. R. Harris. por U.S. News 83:63-4 D 12 '77
Jobs and money—Carter's plan to save the cities. il U.S. News 83:37-8 N 28 '77
Mayors call for help. il Time 110:12-13 D 12 '77
People fire in the ghetto ashes. W. G. Conway. il Sat R 4:15-16 Jl 23 '77
Secretary Harris picks top aides, seeks more housing funds. D. Loomis. Archit Rec 161:34 Ap '77
Urban unions reduce wages to stimulate housing rehab. D. Loomis. Archit Rec 161:36 Ja '77
Wanted: an agent for HUD's flood insurance. Bus W p48+ S 19 '77
Washington scene; survey of Community Development Block Grant program. B. Kravetz. Parks & Rec 12:16+ Je '77
White paper calls New Town program poorly designed. D. Loomis. Archit Rec 161:38 Mr '77
See also
United States—Federal Housing Administration

Human Development Services, Office of

Secretary Califano announces major OHD reorganization. Aging 275:3-4 S '77

Immigration and Naturalization Service

On a raid with U.S. agents: nabbing 29 illegals in one Illinois town. O. Kelly. il U.S. News 83:33-4 Jl 4 '77
Our local correspondents: naturalized citizen no. 9845165. V. Mehta. New Yorker 53:68-78 Ag 29 '77
Role of the Federal Immigration Agency. Cong Digest 56:231 O '77

Industries

Anatomy of U.S. industry's investment dilemma. il Bus W p 105-6+ O 17 '77
For some firms, there's a bonanza ahead; effects of energy policy. il U.S. News 82:30 My 9 '77
How the bellwether industries face 1978; special section. il Bus W p36-40+ Ja 9 '78
Industry leaders size up 1978. il U.S. News 83:26-7 D 26 '77
Panorama of the Nation's business. V. Louviere. See issues of Nation's business to April 1977
Patchwork kind of recovery. il Bus W p28-9 O 31 '77
Sizing up the winners and losers; effects of Carter energy program. il Time 109:78-9 My 9 '77
What shifts in population will mean for industry. il map U.S. News 82:60-2 My 30 '77
Who's where in the industry groups. il Forbes 121:170+ Ja 9 '78
See also
Labor and laboring classes—United States
also names of industries, e.g. Steel industry—United States; *also* subhead Industries under names of regions, states, cities, e.g. Middle Western States—Industries

History

60 years of American business; a picture portfolio. il Forbes 120:P1-8+ S 15 '77
Sixty years of American business: the pursuit of happiness through the pursuit of profit. J. Brooks. Forbes 120:69-76+ S 15 '77
See also
New York (state)—Industries—History

Information Agency

See also
United States—Agency for International Communication (proposed)

Intellectual life

Against consensus; intellectual tradition under siege. R. Whittemore. Harpers 255:15-17 Jl '77
Treason of the clerisy. C. Williamson, Jr. Harpers 256:88-90+ Ja '78

Intelligence Oversight Board

Carter's Oversight. J. Osborne. New Repub 176:8-10 Mr 19 '77
President names new members to Intelligence Oversight Board; statement, May 5, 1977. J. Carter. Dept State Bull 76:658 Je 20 '77

Interior, Department of the

Audubon talks with Andrus; interview, ed by G. Reiger. C. D. Andrus. Audubon 79:148-50 My '77
Down on the farm; regulations preventing ownership of more than 160 acres of federally watered land. A. J. Mayer and others. il Newsweek 90:67-8 S 5 '77
Energy, water, environment—a top official looks ahead; interview. C. D. Andrus. il por U.S. News 82:62-4 Je 27 '77
Fairness for farmers; question of enforcing limit on ownership of federally watered land. New Repub 177:2+ N 12 '77
Homestead Act hits home. il Time 110:20 O 17 '77
Inside the Interior's superior; C. B. Andrus. T. Trueblood. il por Field & S 82:16+ My '77
Interior Department: Andrus promises sweeping changes. L. J. Carter. por Science 196:507-10 Ap 29 '77
Interior redesign. R. Boeth and others. il por Newsweek 90:22 Ag 8 '77

UNITED STATES—Interior, Department of the —*Continued*
New environment at Interior; C. Andrus. J. Shepherd. il por N Y Times Mag p36+ My 8 '77
New man at Interior; with interview with C. D. Andrus. E. A. Bauer. il por Outdoor Life 159:106+ Mr '77
Offer too good to refuse; responsibility of the Interior Department for protection of wildlife. N. P. Reed. il Parks & Rec 12:15a-18a F '77
Refuge ducks are swamped by powerboats, politicians; Ruby Lake National Wildlife Refuge. G. Laycock. Audubon 79:152-3 N '77
Relieving the pressures on the parks; question of providing outdoor recreational opportunities on other public lands. A. W. Smith. Nat Parks & Con Mag 51:2+ N '77
U.S. Interior Department moves to enforce the law to break up big farms. Farm J 101:14 O '77
See also
United States—Bonneville Power Administration
United States—Fish and Wildlife Service
United States—Geological Survey
United States—Land Management, Bureau of
United States—National Park Service
United States—Reclamation, Bureau of

Appropriations and expenditures

Executive branch opens conservation budget process to public scrutiny. Nat Parks & Con Mag 51:24-5 N '77
NPCA-backed funding program to boost park staffs; Land and Water Conservation Fund. Nat Parks & Con Mag 51:25-8 Jl '77

Internal Revenue Service

Cracking down on the payoffs; payments to track stars. il Time 109:55-6 Je 13 '77
Curious case of an IRS agent; A. Susce. J. P. Hayes. Nation 225:17-18 Jl 2 '77
Good news for the geese. il por Forbes 119:30-1 Ap 15 '77
How to fight the I.R.S.—and win. J. Carper. il Am Home 80:16 My '77
IRS may be part of the problem. Bus W p60 Ag 29 '77
IRS retreats from pension tax plan. Am City & County 92:38 O '77
IRS theology; definition of church. Chr Cent 94:213 Mr 9 '77
If the IRS calls you in for a tax audit—il U.S. News 82:96-8 Ap 11 '77
Is the Internal Revenue Service unfair to artists? pro and con discussion. Am Artist 41:8-9 Mr '77
Strange case of the IRS questionnaire; address, May 3, 1977. R. E. Hanson. Vital Speeches 43:498-501 Je 1 '77
Tangling with an IRS code for professionals; rules of conduct for lawyers and accountants arguing tax cases. Bus W p84 F 14 '77
Under way: crackdown on tax shelters. U.S. News 83:106-7 N 21 '77
Vow of poverty ruling modified. America 137:91-2 Ag 27 '77
What are your rights with the IRS? M. Gunther. Bet Hom & Gard 55:78+ F '77
See also
United States—Tax Court

Anecdotes, facetiae, satire, etc.

Jesus and the tax collectors; defining church. M. E. Marty. Chr Cent 94:343 Ap 6 '77

International Trade Commission

Antitrust question about Japanese steel. Bus W p32+ D 19 '77
Protectionists test Carter. il Time 109:74-5 Mr 28 '77
Showdown on Japan's TV blitz; ITC tariff recommendation; with interviews with J. J. Nevin and T. Takai. A. J. Mayer and others. il Newsweek 89:58-9 Mr 28 '77
U.S. cattlemen plead for protection. il Bus W p37 O 3 '77

Interstate Commerce Commission

Get moving! por Forbes 120:97 Jl 1 '77
Helping recyclers get lower rail rates; fighting against railroads and ICC. Bus W p36 S 5 '77
Regulation's phantom benefits—ICC style. S. Zucker. il Bus W p83+ My 16 '77

John F. Kennedy Center for the Performing Arts

See John F. Kennedy Center for the Performing Arts, Washington, D.C.

John F. Kennedy Space Center

Cape preparations for shuttle pressed. C. Covault. il Aviation W 107:43-4 D 5 '77
Launching the shuttle. E. Keerdoja and others. il Newsweek 89:7-8A F 7 '77
Shuttle payload at KSC. J. D. Phillips. il Space World N-8-164:9-23 Ag '77
Spaceport reshaped for role in space shuttle era. il Space World N-10-166:24-7 O '77

Joint Chiefs of Staff

From the Joint Chiefs of Staff: a top-level size-up of U.S. strength—and weaknesses. il U.S. News 83:38-9 O 10 '77
U.S. can still hold its own . . . for now; official report. U.S. News 82:61 F 14 '77

Judicial Conference

See Judicial Conference of the United States

Justice, Department of

Attempt to control thought; complaint against American Institute of Real Estate Appraisers. J. J. Kilpatrick. Nations Bus 65:11-12 O '77
Bakke brief. J. K. Footlick and D. Camper. Newsweek 90:97 S 19 '77
Bakke brief. N. Lewin. New Repub 177:17-18 O 1 '77
Carter and Helms. J. Osborne. New Repub 177:10-13 N 19 '77
Carter's brief; question of J. Carter's influence on Bakke case brief. J. Osborne. New Repub 177:13-15 O 15 '77
Dangling justice. M. Stone. U.S. News 83:94 O 10 '77
Disappearing witnesses; Witness Security Program. il Time 110:41-2 S 12 '77
Early returns on Griffin Bell. Nation 224:260-1 Mr 5 '77
Flaherty's promise. P. Peckarsky. New Repub 177:9-10 D 10 '77
Griffin Bell opens the doors. P. Goldman and S. Lesher. il por Newsweek 89:20-1 F 28 '77
Griffin Bell's dilemma. Newsweek 90:35 D 19 '77
Helms cops a plea. R. Steele and others. por Newsweek 90:31 N 14 '77
Helms file. por Newsweek 90:31-2 O 10 '77
Helms makes a deal. il por Time 110:18+ N 14 '77
Helmsmen, what quarry? F. Getlein. Commonweal 104:740-1 N 25 '77
How Griffin Bell sees his role as Attorney General; interview. G. B. Bell. il pors U.S. News 82:67-8+ My 16 '77
Maze of school desegregation: litmus test for Griffin Bell. S. Gillers. Nation 224:688-91 Je 4 '77
New look at old crime problems. il U.S. News 82:48 Ja 31 '77
Plan to cut litigation; interview. ed by J. K. Lieberman and D. B. Moskowitz. G. B. Bell. por Bus W p60-2+ Je 6 '77
Secrecy lives; question of freedom of the press. New Repub 177:9-10 N 26 '77
Spare that spook! case of R. M. Helms. New Repub 177:5+ N 19 '77
They never laid a hand on him; R. Helms. Nation 225:514-15 N 19 '77
Uncle Sam's lawyer, Solicitor General W. H. McCree. J. K. Footlick and D. Camper. il por Newsweek 90:97 D 5 '77
Why the Justice Department doesn't want you to know what happened between Otto Passman and Shirley Davis; charge of sex discrimination after dismissal of congressional aide. A. Northrop. il pors Ms 6:57-9 Ja '78
See also
United States—Border Patrol
United States—Drug Enforcement Administration
United States—Federal Bureau of Investigation
United States—Immigration and Naturalization Service
United States—Law Enforcement Assistance Administration

Antitrust Division

After the Consent Decree: the effect on the Traditional Market Agreement. P. D. Standish. Pub W 211:44-8 Ap 25 '77
Antitrust: a hot line to nab price fixers; Justice Department consumer project in Pittsburg. Bus W p34 My 30 '77
Bureaucratic imperialism; investigation of foreign companies. Forbes 120:45 N 15 '77
Carter trustbusters take a tough new line. il U.S. News 83:39-40 Ag 15 '77
Carter's trustbusters; M. Pertschuk and J. H. Shenefield. D. Pauly and J. B. Copeland. il por Newsweek 90:66 S 26 '77
Cracking the whip at the Justice Dept. por Bus W p43-4 S 19 '77
Full disclosure that may be too full; intervention in electric utilities' fuel price information case. Bus W p28+ Ag 8 '77
Justice Dept. looking at Times Mirror-Random House. S. Wagner. Pub W 211:25 Mr 21 '77
Lull before the antitrust storm; department head nominee. P. Sturm. por Forbes 120:25-6 Ag 15 '77
Star wars sparks a war with producers; investigation of block booking charges. il Bus W p30 Ag 29 '77
Washington's new approach to antitrust action. W. Neikirk. pors Nations Bus 65:30-2 D '77

Labor, Department of

Apple picker blues: question of importing Jamaican pickers. D. McGhee. New Repub 177:15-16 O 29 '77

UNITED STATES—Labor, Department of—*Cont.*
Fair play for drunks; Labor Department's proposal of affirmative action for alcoholics and drug addicts. E. Marshall. New Repub 177:7 Jl 23 '77
Politics of welfare reform. N. Kotz. New Repub 176:16-21 My 14 '77
See also
United States—Labor Statistics, Bureau of
United States—Occupational Safety and Health Administration

Federal Contract Compliance, Office of

Legal cloud over affirmative action. Bus W p40+ D 26 '77

Labor policy

Disputes between White House and labor—what can be done; interview. R. Marshall. il por U.S. News 82:55-7 Je 6 '77
George and Jimmy show. K. Bode. il New Repub 176:28-30+ My 21 '77
George Meany speaks out on inflation, jobs, Carter; interview. G. Meany. por U.S. News 83:85-6 S 12 '77
Man Carter counts on to bolster ties with labor. il por U.S. News 83:87-8 O 10 '77
Marshall becomes Secretary of Labor. L. Bornstein and others. M Labor R 100:79 Mr '77
Ray Marshall: watch him create controversy. pors Bus W p66-7 F 7 '77
See also
Labor laws and legislation—United States
United States—National Labor Relations Board

Labor Statistics, Bureau of

Family spending habits. Society 14:5-6 S '77
New BLS method—no loose change. M Labor R 100:71-2 O '77
Too objective? por Forbes 120:76 Jl 15 '77
See also
United States—National Commission on Employment and Unemployment Statistics

Land Management, Bureau of

Does the BLM belong in Nevada? V. L. Fischer. il Am For 83:18-21 D '77
Eagle's fate and mine are one; Snake River Birds of Prey Natural Area. A. Zwinger. il map Audubon 79:50-80+ Jl '77
Last Idaho land rush: growth at any cost? E. Chaney. Audubon 79:154-7 N '77
Mustang roundup. D. A. Williams and P. S. Greenberg. il Newsweek 90:22 S 5 '77
Wild horse dilemma; Bureau of Land Management's Adopt-a-Horse program. il Sunset 158: 304 My '77

Law Enforcement Assistance Administration

Making the punishment fix the crime. D. Cohen. Psychol Today 11:22+ Jl '77
U.S. business throws billions into a fight against terrorists. il U.S. News 83:24-6 N 21 '77
See also
United States—National Institute of Law Enforcement and Criminal Justice

Library of Congress

ALA/ISAD institute on the national network. K. Nyren. il Lib J 102:761-3 Ap 1 '77
Advice? LC asks for and gets 35 years' worth from librarians. A. Plotnik. Am Lib 8:236 My '77
LC reorganization to use computer cataloguing. S. Wagner. Pub W 212:91-2 S 12 '77
LC to run national periodicals center. Lib J 102: 1708+ S 1 '77
Legislation introduced for Center for the Book. S. Wagner. il Pub W 211:25+ Ap 18 '77
NCLIS to propose center for periodical copying. S. Wagner. Pub W 211:21-2 My 2 '77
Preservation: a national plan at last? report of National Preservation Program Planning Conference. P. W. Darling. il Lib J 102:447-9 F 15 '77
Public libraries, the Library of Congress, and the national bibliographic network; adaptation of address, February 1977. M. J. Freedman. il Lib J 102:2211-15 N 1 '77
Robert Hayden poet laureate. H. J. Scarupa. il pors Ebony 33:78-80+ Ja '78
Serials-center derby enters the homestretch. A. Plotnik. Am Lib 8:287-8 Je '77
Task force gives blueprint for Library of Congress. S. Wagner. Pub W 211:30 F 21 '77
Task force recommends LC shake-up. W. D. Nelson. Wilson Lib Bull 51:625-6 Ap '77
Task force report: LC sketches present overhaul, future leadership. N. Savage. il Lib J 102:756-9 Ap 1 '77
See also
United States—Copyright Office

Anecdotes, facetiae, satire, etc.

Bee wing case: a preservation (tragedy) travesty; National Preservation Program Planning Conference. F. Patton and P. W. Darling. Lib J 102:771-5 Ap 1 '77

Catalog cards

See Catalog cards

Catalogs

New bibliographic tools proposed by LC; Master registers. Lib J 102:1701 S 1 '77

Employees

LC Recruit/Intern Program: women moving up. Lib J 102:2118 O 15 '77
LC staff rates TAP career program. Lib J 102: 1800 S 15 '77

Music Division

Eastman School-Lib. of Congress: The disappointment; performance of the first American ballad opera. il Hi Fi 27:MA14-15+ Mr '77

Lyndon B. Johnson Space Center

Launching the shuttle. E. Keerdoja and others. il Newsweek 89:7-8A F 7 '77

Management and Budget, Office of

Bert Lance's OMB plays a weaker role. il Bus W p23-4 Ag 29 '77
Budget unit asks caution in shift to private sector. K. Johnsen. Aviation W 107:16-17 N 28 '77
Business is wary about Carter's volunteer plan. Bus W p36-7 D 26 '77
Carter's painful reorganization plan. Bus W p52 Jl 25 '77
Don't underestimate Bert. P. Taubman. por Time 109:16 F 28 '77
Executive branch opens conservation budget process to public scrutiny. Nat Park & Con Mag 51:24-5 N '77
Happenings; government reorganization. J. Osborne. New Repub 177:9-12 D 17 '77
Minding the store; J. McIntyre. D. A. Williams and R. Thomas. por Newsweek 90:30 S 19 '77
OMB goes back to its budgeting; J. T. McIntyre named Director. por Bus W p24-5 Ja 9 '78
Remaking foreign policy; government reorganization. J. Osborne. il New Repub 177:12+ O 1 '77
Reorganization loses out to politics. L. Walczak. Bus W p22 Ag 1 '77
STOL may lose out in the budget battle. Bus W p37-8 N 28 '77
Technician as budget boss; appointment of J. T. McIntyre. il por Time 111:34 Ja 9 '78
We've been asked: why the OMB is so important. U.S. News 83:108 O 24 '77

Marine Corps

GAO hits British support for Harriers. H. J. Coleman. Aviation W 106:23 Ja 17 '77
Marines emphasize night air capability. il Aviation W 106:61-3 Ja 31 '77

Airplanes

See Airplanes, Military—United States

Appropriations and expenditures

Aircraft modernization plans pushed in Marine requests. Aviation W 106:21 Ja 24 '77

Procurement

Marines acquiring attack helicopters. W. C. Wetmore. il Aviation W 106:193-5 Ja 31 '77

Medical policy

See Medical policy

Metric Board

Metric Board slow to form. Sci Digest 81:85 F '77

Military bases

See Military bases

Military policy

Carter and Brezhnev: the game begins. il por Time 109:40-2 F 7 '77
Churchill and us; question of policies toward military preparedness in pre-World War II Great Britain and in the United States today. E. N. Luttwak. Commentary 63:44-9 Je '77
Collective security and confidence; excerpt from address. C. W. Duncan, Jr. Aviation W 107:7 S 12 '77
Détente and the military balance. S. A. Garrett. bibl il Bull Atom Sci 33:10-20 Ap '77
Drawing the line. D. Fromkin. New Repub 176:12-14 Je 4 '77
Hiroshima echo. W. G. Kelsey. il Progressive 41:28-30 N '77
Is there a present danger? M. Kondracke. New Repub 176:18-20 Ja 29 '77
Latest round in debate over Russia's aims. il por U.S. News 82:18 F 28 '77
Old superstitions, new realities. H. J. Morgenthau. New Repub 176:50-2+ Ja 22 '77; Same with title On making foreign policy. Current 191:48-56 Mr '77
Speak no evil; D. A. Starry called home. Nat R 29:764-5 Jl 8 '77
Strange case of George F. Kennan: from containment to isolationism. E. N. Luttwak. Commentary 64:30-5 N '77

UNITED STATES—Military policy—*Continued*
Surprise attack by Russia: still unthinkable? with interview with H. Brown. R. Kelly. il U.S. News 83:18-24 S 5 '77
U.S. urged to set firm strategic goals. Aviation W 106:84 Je 27 '77
What the President needs. N. Cousins. Sat R 4:4 F 19 '77
See also
Military assistance, American
Strategy
United States—Defenses
Vietnamese War, 1957-1975—American participation

Minerals policy

See Mines and mineral resources—United States

Mint

Last of the western mints—Denver, Carson City, and San Francisco. il Sunset 159:33 Jl '77

Monetary policy

What might hold interest rates down. J. Madrick. il Bus W p90 My 23 '77
See also
United States—Congress—House—Banking, Currency and Housing, Committee on—Domestic Monetary Policy Subcommittee
United States—Federal Reserve System

Moral conditions

Are lawyers, courts, big government dulling America's moral sense? G. E. Jones. U.S. News 83:84-5 S 26 '77
Crackdown on porn. S. Fraker and others. il Newsweek 89:21-2+ F 28 '77
How America looks to me now. E. H. Hunt. por Newsweek 89:15 Ap 4 '77
How Mormons cope with deterioration in morals; interview. S. W. Kimball. il por U.S. News 83:60-1 D 19 '77
New morality. Time 110:111-12+ N 21 '77
Public morality after Bert Lance. J. Castelli. America 137:280-2 O 29 '77
Where have all the flower children gone? C. M. Spring. Chr Cent 94:952-4 O 19 '77
Where have you gone, Boccaccio? M. Greenfield. Newsweek 90:96 S 26 '77
Worried America; adaptation of address. G. Myrdal. Chr Cent 94:1161-6 D 14 '77
See also
Crime and criminals—United States

Anecdotes, facetiae, satire, etc.

Minions of morality. R. Baker. il N Y Times Mag p 10 Je 19 '77

Municipal Securities Rulemaking Board

High noon in municipal bonds. il Forbes 120:58-61 O 15 '77

National Academy of Sciences

See National Academy of Sciences

National Advisory Commission on Criminal Justice Standards and Goals

Latest worry: terrorists using high technology. U.S. News 82:69 Mr 14 '77

National Aeronautics and Space Administration

All aboard the NASA ship; Symposium '77. il Ebony 32:96-8+ Je '77
Another small step for man: shuttling into space. J. N. Wilford. il N Y Times Mag p24-5+ Ag 7 '77
Frosch sees period of evolutionary exploration for NASA. F. C. Bennett. por Phys Today 30: 85+ S '77
How NASA went into the freight business. Bus W p52 Ag 22 '77
Landsat data use urged to aid developing nations. Aviation W 108:24-5 Ja 9 '78
Major reviews ordered of NASA advisory units. Aviation W 106:22 Ap 4 '77
NASA advances supersonic technology. C. Covault. Aviation W 106:16-17 Ja 10 '77
NASA and the Pentagon: the Air Force eyes a star war. J. Markoff. Nation 226:16-18 Ja 7 '78
NASA bans sex from outer space; information disc designed for Voyagers. N. Wade. Science 197:1163-5 S 16 '77
NASA chief designate selection keyed to issues facing agency. Aviation W 106:61 My 9 '77
NASA evaluating major shuttle orbiter changes. C. Covault. Aviation W 107:26-7 O 10 '77
NASA eyes climate research projects. C. Covault. il Aviation W 107:57-9 N 21 '77
NASA in new shuttle marketing effort. C. Covault. il Aviation 107:40-1 O 24 '77
NASA launch plans for 1977 detailed. Aviation W 106:63 Mr 21 '77
NASA mulls new fiscal 1979 efforts. C. Covault. il Aviation W 107:49+ Jl 18 '77
NASA nominee to stress applications. Aviation W 106:79-80 Je 20 '77
NASA patents cell control method; work of Clarence D. Cone, Jr. Sci N 112:134-5 Ag 27 '77
NASA plans for 1977. Sky & Tel 53:190 Mr '77
NASA schedules 25 launches in 1978. Aviation W 108:48 Ja 9 '78
NASA spurs agricultural aircraft effort. E. Kozicharow. il Aviation W 107:80+ S 26 '77
NASA switches teams aiding Spacelab. Aviation W 107:60 Ag 8 '77
NASA tackles a down-to-earth job. E. M. Leeper. il BioScience 27:223 Mr '77
NASA to end manned hypersonic effort. Aviation W 107:24 S 26 '77
NASA to seek research bids in astrophysics. Aviation W 107:73+ N 28 '77
NASA to stress planning on merits, future goals. Aviation W 106:55 Mr 28 '77
NASA to stress space, aircraft in Paris. Aviation W 106:53 F 28 '77
NASA urged to resume talksat R&D. il Sci N 111:231 Ap 9 '77
NASA urged to study satcom program. C. Covault. Aviation W 106:41-2 Mr 14 '77
New chief plans strengthened NASA space applications role. Aviation W 107:56 Jl 18 '77
Public satellite effort keyed to services, not hardware. Aviation W 107:54-5 O 24 '77
'77 NASA summer study: no show stoppers! C. Henson; G. O'Neill; M. Frazier. il Space World N-12-168:26-7 D '77
Shuttle criticism worries NASA. C. Covault. il Aviation W 106:12-16 Ap 11 '77
Space chief nominee stresses need for good science. D. Shapley. por Science 196:1301-3 Je 17 '77
Space highlights. il Sky & Tel 54:275 O '77
Star trek's Lt. Uhura talks about the space program. N. Nichols. il pors Space World N-10-166:14-19 O '77
Tech House: an experiment in future living; developed by NASA. il Consumers Res Mag 60: 41 Ag '77
Tighter technical scrutiny facing NASA programs. C. Covault. Aviation W 107:55 Jl 11 '77
Woods Hole's Frosch to be NASA nominee. Sci N 111:279 Ap 30 '77
Would you buy a rocket from this agency? J. Walsh. Science 198:385 O 28 '77
See also
Space centers
United States—John F. Kennedy Space Center

Anecdotes, facetiae, satire, etc.

How NASA got out of the red. J. Keefauver. Nat R 29:331 Mr 18 '77

Appropriations and expenditures

Budget revision to cover additional Landsat vehicle. Aviation W 106:23 F 28 '77
Few shifts expected in NASA request. C. Covault. il Aviation W 106:24-7 Ja 24 '77
Five-year space agency plan raises budget to $4.7 billion. Aviation W 106:47 Mr 7 '77
House approves Jupiter orbiter probe; Jupiter mission approval saves planetary capability, 300 jobs. E. Kozicharow and C. Covault. Aviation W 107:20-2 Jl 25 '77
House unit boosts space authorization. E. Kozicharow. Aviation W 106:17 Mr 14 '77
House unit cut threatens NASA planetary planning. C. Covault. Aviation W 106:13-14 My 9 '77
House unit cuts Jupiter mission funds. Aviation W 106:19 My 30 '77
Jobs bill shuttle funds to aid development, test. Aviation W 106:18-19 My 9 '77
NASA assessing budget slashes. C. Covault. Aviation W 106:12-13 My 16 '77
NASA funding increased by group in House. Aviation W 106:24-5 Mr 7 '77
NASA: new starts but no post-Viking. Sci N 111:53 Ja 22 '77
NASA reassessing cost, risk of transonic tunnel facility. Aviation W 106:43-4 F 28 '77
NASA study was bust, not boost, says Proxmire. R. J. Smith. Science 198:810-11 N 25 '77
Senate committee boosts NASA budget $4 million. Aviation W 106:16-17 Ap 11 '77
Senate unit votes key NASA funding. Aviation W 106:18-19 Je 27 '77
Shift of funds set for shuttle. C. Covault. Aviation W 106:14-15 F 7 '77
Shuttle fund boost urged in jobs bill. Aviation W 106:21 Mr 7 '77
Staff member hits lack of Congress coordination. Aviation W 107:23 Ag 1 '77
Zero-based budget to strain Congress. E. Kozicharow. il Aviation W 106:57+ Je 13 '77

Flight Research Center

Space shuttle research chief; I. T. Gillam, director of operations at Dryden Flight Research Center. il pors Ebony 32:124-6+ Ap '77

Space Science, Office of

Potential in space awaits funds. C. Covault. il Aviation W 106:59-61 Mr 21 '77

National Arboretum

See Washington, D.C.—National Arboretum

UNITED STATES—*Continued*

National Cancer Institute

Arthur Canfield Upton: new director of the NCI. B. J. Culliton. por Science 197:737-9 Ag 19 '77

Cancer Institute unilaterally issues new restrictions on mammography. B. J. Culliton. Science 196:853-5+ My 20 '77

Meanwhile, at NCI the search for director narrows. B. J. Culliton. Science 196:635 My 6 '77

New NCI group offers diverse advice on testing. BioScience 27:302 Ap '77

No-win war against cancer. A. L. Huebner. Progressive 41:26-8 O '77

Talk with the new head of the NCI; interview, ed by W. Barnhill. A. C. Upton. il por Fam Health 9:6+ O '77

Testing laetrile—sort of. Newsweek 89:39 Je 6 '77

Using cancer's rates to track its cause. map Bus W p69-70+ N 14 '77

National Commission for the Protection of Human Subjects of Biomedical and Behavioral Research

Still forbidden fruit; fetal research report. G. Meilaender, Jr. il Chr Today 21:16-19 Ja 21 '77

National Commission on Employment and Unemployment Statistics

Establishment of a new employment statistics review commission; with text of resolution. J. E. Bregger. bibl M Labor R 100:14-20 Mr '77

Federal hardship index? G. R. Rosen. por Duns R 110:63 D '77

Seeking a more meaningful gauge of joblessness. Nations Bus 65:68 N '77

National Commission on Libraries and Information Science

LC to run national periodicals center. Lib J 102:1708+ S 1 '77

NCLIS $$ study urges more state aid. Lib J 102:1442-3 Jl '77

NCLIS to propose center for periodical copying. S. Wagner. Pub W 211:21-2 My 2 '77

National library needs sketched by NCLIS. Lib J 102:1229 Je 1 '77

Serials-center derby enters the homestretch. A. Plotnik. Am Lib 8:287-8 Je '77

Three NCLIS studies on library needs aired. W. D. Nelson. Wilson Lib Bull 51:715-16 My '77

Will the national inventory lead from the slough of despond to the celestial city? E. Castagna. il Am Lib 8:491-2 O '77

National Commission on New Technological Uses of Copyrighted Works

AAP & authors clash over copy fee scheme. Lib J 102:1083 My 15 '77

AAP spells out clearinghouse plan for photocopying at CONTU meeting. S. Wagner. Pub W 211:28 Ap 11 '77

AAP to present plan for photocopying fees. S. Wagner. Pub W 211:27-8 Mr 28 '77

NTIS plan draws fire at CONTU photocopying hearing. S. Wagner. Pub W 211:252+ Ja 24 '77

New interlibrary loan form unveiled. W. R. Eshelman. Wilson Lib Bull 52:115-16 O '77

National Commission on Supplies and Shortages

TRB from Washington. New Repub 176:2+ F 26 '77

National Commission on the Observance of International Women's Year

Editor's notebook. J. M. Carter. il Good H 184:4 F '77

National Foundation on the Arts and the Humanities

Creating the livable city; Architecture/Environmental Arts Program of the National Endowment for the Arts. il Sunset 159:176 Jl '77

Dance funding. B. V. Bordelon. See issues of Dance magazine

Devolution at NEH; politics and the National Endowment for the Humanities. Nat R 29:932-3 Ag 19 '77

Federal pie; appointment of L. L. Biddle. por Horizon 20:72-3 D '77

How effective is the National Endowment for the Arts? Literature Program. S. Wagner. Pub W 212:45-8 Jl 25 '77

How the seed money in Portland has grown. P. Failing. il Art N 76:58-61 My '77

Humanist at the Humanities; nomination of J. Duffey as chairman of the National Endowment for the Humanities. New Repub 177:8+ Ag 20 '77

Joe Duffey's new job. Chr Cent 94:742 Ag 31 '77

NEA craft grants to workshops, exhibits. Craft Horiz 37:8 Ap '77

NEA grants go to 156 craftsmakers and artists. Craft Horiz 37:37+ Ag '77

NEA: will success spoil our biggest patron? M. N. Carter. il por Art N 76:32-40+ My '77

NEA's low marks in self-assessment; Artists in Schools program. M. N. Carter. il Art N 76:44-5 My '77; Reply. P. H. Bihler. 76:34 S '77

NEH gives 14 grants to 10 university presses. S. Wagner. Pub 212:18 N 21 '77

Nancy Hanks on craft grants; excerpt from address. N. Hanks. Craft Horiz 37:6 F '77

Nancy Hanks resigns NEA post. B. V. Bordelon. Dance Mag 51:4 N '77

New canvases for art; Wisconsin barns funded by National Endowment for the Arts. il House B 119:10+ Ag '77

On getting the public involved and interested in architecture; proposals for public education founded by the National Endowment for the Arts. W. F. Wagner, Jr. il Archit Rec 162:13 S '77

Populism vs. elitism. R. Steele and others. il pors Newsweek 90:39 O 31 '77

Recording America: federal funds for photos & films. A. C. Steinback. il Art in Am 65:19+ Ja '77

Richmond bill: H.R.1042. C. B. Fowler. Hi Fi 27:MA16 N '77

Rights and wrongs of scholarship; National Endowment for the Humanities. por Horizon 20:57 O '77

Role of the National Endowment; study by A. B. Spellman. C. B. Fowler. Hi Fi 27:MA12+ Mr '77

Scramble for museum sponsors: is curatorial independence for sale? L. Rosenbaum. il Art in Am 65:10-14 Ja '77

Small cultural disaster; search for new chairman. Nat R 29:1410 D 9 '77

Tax support for visual arts; National Council on the Arts. B. Chamberlain. Am Artist 41:14-15 Ap '77

Viewpoint; photography awards program. J. Deschin. Pop Phot 80:30+ Ap '77

National Guard

Whatever happened to: National Guard: facing a crisis. il U.S. News 83:72 N 21 '77

National Heritage Trust (proposed)

Administration will propose new conservation program soon. Nat Parks & Con Mag 51:23 S '77

Two letters to the Administration; question of proposal for a National Heritage Trust. A. W. Smith. Nat Parks & Con Mag 51:2+ S '77

National Highway Traffic Safety Administration

How did it happen? investigation teams. M. Schultz. il Pop Mech 148:80-2+ S '77

Ralph's wrath; R. Nader's attack on J. B. Claybrook over air bag decision. il pors Newsweek 90:90+ D 12 '77

National Institute for Occupational Safety and Health

Health records face a privacy challenge; Du Pont challenges NIOSH on claim to undisputed access. il Bus W p38 O 31 '77

How a stillborn child started a NIOSH study; case of employee at Wyeth Laboratories. il por Bus W p76-7 Ag 29 '77

National Institute of Building Sciences

See National Institute of Building Sciences

National Institute of Education

See also

Eric

National Institute of Law Enforcement and Criminal Justice

NAS and justice panels pan federal crime research effort. C. Holden. Science 197:236-7 Jl 15 '77

National Institute on Aging

Nathan Shock first NIA science director. por Aging 274:21 Ag '77

National Institutes of Health

Califano praises NIH, retains Frederickson as director. B. J. Culliton. il por Science 195:663 F 18 '77

Case of the 15 gardeners; racial discrimination suit. Nation 225:614 D 10 '77

Dialogue via satellite: NIH director meets students. E. M. Leeper. il BioScience 27:428-9 Je '77

Gene rules: violation and revisions. Sci N 112:420 D 24 '77

If they held a meeting there'd be no one to come. B. J. Culliton. Science 198:592 N 11 '77

Mammography controversy: NIH's entrée into evaluating technology. B. J. Culliton. Science 198:171-3 O 14 '77

NIH director stays, CDC director goes. Sci N 111:119 F 19 '77

UNITED STATES—National Institutes of Health —*Continued*
NIH seeks law on gene-splice research. N. Wade. Science 195:859 Mr 4 '77
New for scientists: RFP's from USDA. EIS's from NIH. E. M. Leeper. il BioScience 27:297-8 Ap '77
See also
United States—National Cancer Institute
United States—National Institute on Aging

Appropriations and expenditures

NIH budget on the decline. B. J. Culliton. Science 195:375 Ja 28 '77

Gerontology Research Center

Probing the aging process. J. Arehart-Treichel. il Sci N 111:26-7 Ja 8 '77

Laboratories

New P4 laboratories: containing recombinant DNA. J. L. Marx. il Science 197:1350-2 S 30 '77

National Labor Relations Board

Bishops and the N.L.R.B; disputes between bishops and parochial school teachers' unions. America 137:65 Ag 13 '77
Catholic schools and unions. America 136:265 Mr 26 '77
Do representation elections need the NLRB? il Bus W p54+ Mr 21 '77
Firm vote for teachers' unions; Catholic schools. America 137:206 O 8 '77
Freedom and parochial schools; NLRB and Catholic schools. R. Kirk. Nat R 29:441-2+ Ap 15 '77
Man who heads NLRB now; J. H. Fanning. il por Nations Bus 65:26+ S '77
N.L.R.B. and the vow of poverty; taxation of members of religious orders teaching in Catholic schools. America 137:157 S 24 '77
NLRB licenses lying. D. Jacobs. Nation 225:176-7 S 3 '77
Significant decisions in labor cases. C. Polhemus. See issues of Monthly labor review
U.S. injunction against Stevens? il Time 110:76 D 12 '77

National Oceanic and Atmospheric Administration

How school kids can survive tornadoes. K. J. Gilleland. il Farm J 101:J2+ Ap '77
NESS: National Environmental Satellite Service. J. C. Fine. il Sea Front 23:198-203 Jl '77
See also
United States—National Weather Service

Appropriations and expenditures

Seasat use boosts Satellite Service bid. Aviation W 106:55 F 7 '77

National Park Service

Great grizzly grapple. C. Cauble. il Natur Hist 86:74-81 bibl(p 117) Ag '77; Discussion. 86:132-3 O '77
Looking for trends in technical assistance; Park Practice Program. il Parks & Rec 12:52-3 My '77
Member deplores NPS fire policy; NPS resource specialist responds; letters to the editor. G. M. Schoepfle; D. B. Butts. il Nat Parks & Con Mag 51:27-8 Mr '77
NPCA-backed funding program to boost park staffs. Nat Parks & Con Mag 51:25-7 Jl '77
Park Service discloses ripoff operations in land of Old Faithful. Nat Parks & Con Mag 51:26-7 Ag '77
Two letters to the Administration; question of proposal for a National Heritage Trust. A. W. Smith. Nat Parks & Con Mag 51:2+ S '77
See also
National park personnel

Appropriations and expenditures

Deteriorating parks need funds, personnel more than ever. Nat Parks & Con Mag 51:21 Ap '77

National parks and reserves

See National parks and reserves—United States

National Science Board

Bureaucracy stifles US research community, NSB says; with editorial comment. F. C. Bennett. Phys Today 30:93-4, 112 Ja '77

National Science Foundation

Atkinson sees good relationship between NSF and White House; interview. R. C. Atkinson. por BioScience 27:447-50+ Jl '77
Carter reducing plan adds pounds. R. J. Smith. il Science 198:900 D 2 '77
Conflict of interest at NSF. Sci N 111:87 F 5 '77
Federal research helps improve local services; Research Applied to National Needs program. H. V. Semling. Am City & County 92:16 Ja '77
Measuring the supply of scientific personnel. R R. Trumble. M Labor R 100:47-8 O '77
More fingers in the RANN pie? R. J. Smith. Science 197:1347 S 30 '77
NSF chooses Schopf as second Waterman Award recipient. por Phys Today 30:69 Ag '77
NSF science education: basic issues still unresolved. J. Walsh. Science 197:233+ Jl 15 '77
New director forecasts fresh commitments for NSF. F. C. Bennett. por Phys Today 30:77+ Jl '77
OBIS and ACA—the impossible equation does match. D. Buller. il Camp Mag 49:10-11 Ap '77
Project CEPEX. M. R. Reeve and M. A. Walter. il Sea Front 23:365-73 N '77
Psychologist Atkinson to head NSF. Sci N 111: 215 Ap 2 '77
Test tubes in the sea; Controlled Ecosystem Pollution Experiment. T. R. Parsons. il UNESCO Courier 30:28-9 Ja '77
What's new in research? RANN grantees report. E. M. Leeper. BioScience 27:65-6 Ja '77

Appropriations and expenditures

Biology, social sciences up 14.4% in NSF budget. E. M. Leeper. BioScience 27:163-4 Mr '77
Kennedy, GAO criticize NSF; grant renewal is rejected. P. M. Boffey. Science 195:556-8 F 11 '77
NSF authorization coming up. C. Holden. Science 196:1423 Je 24 '77
NSF: pressures mount to provide grants for industrial researchers. P. M. Boffey. Science 196:142-3 Ap 8 '77
Peer review and the support of science. S. Cole and others. il Sci Am 237:34-41 O '77
Science Foundation seeks funding increase of 11%. Aviation W 106:53 F 7 '77
Social anthropologists learn to be scientific. G. B. Kolata. Science 195:770 F 25 '77; Discussion. 196:372+ Ap 22 '77

National Security Agency

Computer encryption and the National Security Agency connection. G. B. Kolata. il Science 197:438-40 Jl 29 '77
Cryptology: scientists puzzle over threat to open research, publication. D. Shapley and G. B. Kolata. Science 197:1345-9 S 30 '77
Telecommunications eavesdropping by NSA on private messages alleged. D. Shapley. Science 197:1061-4 S 9 '77

National Security Council

Life at Brzezinski U. R. Watson and others. il por Newsweek 89:55+ My 9 '77

National Transportation Safety Board

Charade. S. Wilkinson. por Flying 101:120 Jl '77
NTSB analyzes cargo aircraft crash; 1975 crash of Aerotransportes Entre Rios at Miami. Aviation W 108:52-3+ Ja 2 '78
NTSB cites heavy load in DHC-2 crash; Ketchum Air Service accident, September 12, 1975. Aviation W 108:78-9 Ja 9 '78

National Weather Service

Another frigid winter ahead? What a top authority says; interview. G. P. Cressman. por map U.S. News 83:43-4 N 7 '77
NOAA weather radio operating locations; table. Pop Electr 11:92-3 F '77
Weather radio: keep one jump ahead of disasters. A. R. Curtis. il map Pop Mech 148:68-71 Ag '77
What your weatherman doesn't tell you; interview, ed by J. Cameron. G. Flittner. il map Motor B & S 139:76-8+ My '77

Nationalism

See also
Messianism, American

Naval Air Development Center

Development Center plays many roles. il Aviation W 106:219-23 Ja 31 '77
Unit specializes in launch, landing aids. Aviation W 106:242-3 Ja 31 '77

Naval Air Systems Command

Naval Air Systems Command: advancing technology at sea; symposium, with editorial comment. il Aviation W 106:9, 28-38+ Ja 31 '77

Aircraft and Weapons System Division

Unit monitors technical performance. il Aviation W 106:188-9+ Ja 31 '77

Naval Avionics Facility

Avionics unit handles special needs. P. J. Klass. il Aviation W 106:212-13+ Ja 31 '77

Naval Air Test Center

Single-site tests expand Patuxent role. C. A. Robinson, Jr. il Aviation W 106:158+ Ja 31 '77
Test center studies fleet readiness. il Aviation W 106:152-3+ Ja 31 '77

UNITED STATES—*Continued*

Naval Research, Office of

Office of Naval Research. R. Trumbull. BioScience 27:43 Ja '77
Tale of two cities; ONR's oceanography research office in Bay St Louis, Miss. Science 197:1164 S 16 '77

Naval Weapons Center

Weapons Center studies new concepts. il Aviation W 106:171+ Ja 31 '77

Navy

Guardian of the Pacific; S. L. Gravely, Jr of the Third fleet. il pors Ebony 32:66-8+ S '77
National strategy considerations in the Pacific Basin; address, June 27, 1977. W. G. Claytor, Jr. Vital Speeches 43:706-8 S 15 '77
Navy stressing fleet readiness drive. E. H. Kolcum. Aviation W 106:241 Ja 31 '77
Navy's natural divers: United States Navy Marine Mammal Training Program. C. Barton. il Oceans 10:34-9 Jl '77
Project Seafarer: Michigan's war against the Navy. J. Magney. Progressive 41:22-4 Jl '77
Return of the natives to Kahoolawe; protesting Navy bombing. J. Wilde. il Time 110:32 Ag 8 '77
Special report: Sixth Fleet modernization (cont) C. A. Robinson, Jr. il Aviation W 106:43-8 Ja 17; 35-7+ Ja 24 '77
U.S. retains edge in Mediterranean Sea. C. A. Robinson, Jr. il Aviation W 106:43-8 Ja 17 '77
West's tenuous oil lifeline. map Bus W p56 N 28 '77
See also
Landing craft
Navy yards and naval stations
United States—Naval Air Systems Command
World War, 1939-1945—Naval operations

Appropriations and expenditures

DOD cuts Navy's new carrier. C. Brownlow. Aviation W 106:12-13 Ja 10 '77
House stifles smaller carrier plans of Navy. Aviation W 106:20-1 My 30 '77
Navy request stresses shift to V/STOL. E. H. Kolcum. il Aviation W 106:18-19 Ja 24 '77

Boats

See also
Warships—United States
Warships, Atomic powered

Communications systems

See also
Radio, Military

Education

Navy school: photo career port of entry. E. Scully. il Mod Phot 41:18+ S '77
See also
United States Naval Academy, Annapolis

History

See also
United States—History—War of 1812—Naval operations

Management

Matrix system enhances management. il Aviation W 106:41+ Ja 31 '77

Maneuvers

See Military maneuvers

Procurement

Budget squeeze boosts test, evaluation significance. il Aviation W 106:234-5+ Ja 31 '77
Hard choices confronting Navy. C. A. Robinson, Jr. Aviation W 106:14-16 Mr 28 '77
Navy pushes aircraft fleet readiness. Aviation W 106:196 Ja 31 '77
Rescue mission at Electric Boat; Navy contracts. il Bus W p34 O 31 '77
Settling for less on Navy contracts; General Dynamics Corp.'s Electric Boat Div. and Tenneco Inc.'s Newport News Shipbuilding & Dry Dock Co. il Bus W p27-8 Ap 11 '77
Technical aid guides material buys. K. J. Stein. il Aviation W 106:231-3 Ja 31 '77
Torpedoing the Navy's ship plans. il Bus W p33 Ja 16 '78

Weapons systems

Pentagon is working on it; anti-submarine warfare. R. C. Aldridge. Nation 224:711-14 Je 11 '77

Women

See Servicewomen

Nuclear Regulatory Commission

Looking back on the Rasmussen report; NRC's reactor safety study. F. Von Hippel. bibl il Bull Atom Sci 33:42-7 F '77
Outrageous Mr Cherry and the underachieving nukes; controversy surrounding construction of nuclear power plant in Midland, Mich; involvement of the AEC and NRC. F. Graham, Jr. il por Audubon 79:50-67 S '77; Discussion. 79:128-30 N '77
Real nuclear terrorists. Progressive 41:7 Ap '77

Occupational Safety and Health Administration

Court orders OSHA to consider economics; noise controls at Turner Division plant. Bus W p46+ O 3 '77
End to frivolous safety rules? U.S. News 82:70 My 30 '77
Eula Bingham: will she take the nonsense out of OSHA? pors Nations Bus 65:28-32 Ag '77
Furor spreads over safety rules for workers. il U.S. News 82:69-70 Ja 31 '77
Growing furor over noise regulations. il Nations Bus 65:16-20+ O '77
Industry's challenge on benzene; OSHA hearings on benzene links to leukemia. il Bus W p30+ Ag 22 '77
Making lead as costly as gold; new OSHA rule. il Bus W p26 Ja 24 '77
Marshall identifies safety administration problems. L. Bornstein and others. M Labor R 100:59-60 My '77
New hope for employers harassed by OSHA. J. J. Kilpatrick. Nations Bus 65:15-16 Mr '77
New set of incentives to make OSHA work. il Bus W p36 O 31 '77
OSHA and the architect: a recent case lessens designer liability; liability for violations of the Construction Safety Standards. A. T. Kornblut. Archit Rec 162:63 N '77
OSHA gets ready to analyze its rules. Bus W p30 Ag 8 '77
OSHA: hardest to live with. il Bus W p74+ Ap 4 '77
OSHA under fire. S. Kelman. New Repub 176:18-20+ My 21 '77
Problems with OSHA's cancer proposal. Bus W p38 O 24 '77
Rage over rising regulation. Time 111:48-50 Ja 2 '78
Safety agency issues coke emission standard. L. Bornstein and others. M Labor R 100:86-7 F '77
Searching for probable cause; requiring agency to submit reasons for certain company inspections. M. Labor R 100:53 N '77
Secret killers; regulation of chemicals used in industry. D. McGhee. Progressive 41:26 Ag '77
Sterility scare sends OSHA scurrying. Bus W p45+ S 12 '77
Stressing health over safety—a switch in on-the-job rules. il U.S. News 83:65-6 Jl 11 '77
Tougher rules to protect workers against cancer. U.S. News 83:115 O 17 '77
What benzene's link to leukemia will cost. il Bus W p35 My 9 '77
Whipping boy. S. J. Ungar. Atlantic 239:14-16 F '77

Oceans and International Environmental and Scientific Affairs, Bureau of

For a troubled situation. . .try Mink. por Sci Digest 81:75 Ap '77

Outdoor Recreation, Bureau of

BOR gives recreation for the handicapped a high priority. Parks & Rec 12:54 N '77
BOR looks at water quality. G. M. Kyle. il Parks & Rec 12:19a-21a F '77
NRPA interview: Chris T. Delaporte tells what to expect from BOR; ed by B. Kravetz. C. T. Delaporte. Parks & Rec 12:38-43 Ag '77
Urban recreation study: doing it right. M. Maguire. il Parks & Rec 12:28-31+ Ap '77

Paperwork Commission

See United States—National Commission on Federal Paperwork

Patent and Trademark Office

How the Department got its start; early agricultural administration by the Patent Office. S. B. Sutton. il Horticulture 55:33-7 Ap '77

Peace corps

See United States—ACTION

Photographs

Pilot's camera. J. Yarnell. il Flying 101:170-3 S '77

Politics and government

ABC's of how your government works. U.S. News 82:43-52+ My 9 '77
Administration under siege. New Repub 177:5-6 O 22 '77
As Carter gets down to brass tacks. il pors U.S. News 82:27-9 F 14 '77
Assessing the federal government. Current 191:3-6 Mr '77
Big government; address, June 28, 1977. J. N. Sites. Vital Speeches 43:711-14 S 15 '77
Big problems; issues facing Carter. D. M. Alpern and others. il Newsweek 89:29-32+ Ja 24 '77
Birth of the Constitution—our next big celebration? interview. R. B. Morris. por U.S. News 83:63-4 Jl 4 '77
Blowing in the wind. T. Bethell. il Harpers 254:25-6+ Ap '77
Bringing JFK up to date. N. N. Minow. pors Newsweek 89:13 My 30 '77

UNITED STATES—Politics and government —*Continued*

Can Jimmy Carter cope? P. Goldman and others. il por Newsweek 90:36-8 O 24 '77
Carter at home: rising pressure. il por U.S. News 82:21-3 My 23 '77
Carter: captain or engineer? Commonweal 104: 419-20 Jl 8 '77
Carter: man in motion. il pors Time 110:8-9 O 17 '77
Carter so far—a puzzle to many. J. W. Mashek. U.S. News 82:19 Ja 31 '77
Carter takes over. por U.S. News 82:11-12 Ja 31 '77
Carter up close. P. Goldman and others. il por Newsweek 89:32-5+ My 2 '77
Carter: will he change course? il pors U.S. News 83:18-21 D 26 '77
Carter's dog-day afternoons. il pors Time 110: 12-13 S 5 '77
Carter's first week. P. Goldman and others. il por Newsweek 89:23-4 F 7 '77
Carter's summer storms. U.S. News 83:15-16 Ag 29 '77
Change in America—as seen by a veteran French newsman; interview. A. de Segonzac. il por U.S. News 83:56-8 Jl 11 '77
Democracy's other component. il New Repub 176:7-8+ Ja 29 '77
Do the American people know what they want? P. H. Weaver. Commentary 64:62-7 D '77
Down the homestretch; Carter's promises: how many has he kept; with interview with C. H. Kirbo. il por map U.S. News 83:15-20 D 12 '77
Fireside chat; address, February 2, 1977. J. Carter. Vital Speeches 43:259-62 F 15 '77; Excerpts. Dept State Bull 76:161 F 28 '77
Fireside manner; February 2, 1977. P. Goldman and others. il Newsweek 89:22-4 F 14 '77
First six months; J. Carter as President. il por U.S. News 83:17-19 Jl 25 '77
Ford era—highlights of a pivotal 2½ years. il pors U.S. News 82:26-7 Ja 24 '77
Growing power of Stuart Eizenstat. por Bus W p42+ O 10 '77
How America looks to me now. E. H. Hunt. por Newsweek 89:15 Ap 4 '77
How Carter will differ from Ford—an expert's view; interview. M. W. H. Collins, Jr. il por U.S. News 82:17-18 Ja 31 '77
How Congress sizes up Carter as President. il pors U.S. News 83:17-20 Ag 8 '77
How Mondale sees his relationship with Carter; interview. W. F. Mondale. pors U.S. News 82: 62-4 Mr 28 '77
Hurry up and wait; problems to be solved by the government. W. Proxmire. il Sat Eve Post 249:39-40 Ap '77
I don't intend to lose; excerpts from interview, ed by M. Elfin and others. J. Carter. por Newsweek 89:36-7 My 2 '77
Impact of the new politics. W. E. Miller and T. E. Levitin. Intellect 105:375 My '77
Inaugural address of President Carter, January 20, 1977. J. Carter. Vital Speeches 43:258-9 F 15 '77
Inaugural issue—1977; special issue. il pors New Repub 176:5-6+ Ja 22 '77
It takes more than 100 days for a president to get a grip. il por U.S. News 82:26-7 My 9 '77
Jimmy Carter and the new reality. S. Lens. il por Chr Cent 94:10-14 Ja 5 '77
Jimmy the engineer. M. Greenfield Newsweek 89:104 Ap 25 '77
Just call him Mister. il Time 109:11-12 F 21 '77
Leading authority sizes up Carter's performance so far; interview. E. C. Hargrove. il pors U.S. News 82:23-4 My 2 '77
Letter from Washington. Cato. See issues of National review
Letter from Washington (cont) R. H. Rovere. New Yorker 52:72-4+ Ja 31; 53:108-14 Mr 7; 129-34 Ap 11; 136-8+ My 9; 108+ Je 13; 56-60 Ag 1; 131-6 S 12; 180+ O 17; 200+ N 14 '77; 54-8 Ja 2 '78
Lucky president. M. Stone. il U.S. News 83:80 Jl 25 '77
Mandate of heaven; open letter to J. Carter. Tran-van-Dinh. Chr Cent 94:29-30 Ja 19 '77
Need to act. T. Bethell. il Harpers 255:34-6+ N '77
New Washington. il pors Time 109:16-26 F 7 '77
New Washington power game. M. Greenfield. Newsweek 89:80 Ja 31 '77
Now, back to face the music; issues confronting J. Carter. il por Time 111:8-9 Ja 16 '78
Now, for the substance. il por Time 109:12-15 F 28 '77
Now it begins; Carter Presidency. P. Goldman and others. il pors Newsweek 89:16-17+ Ja 24 '77
Old gang. R. Baker. il N Y Times Mag p4 Ja 23 '77
Our far-flung correspondents. E. Drew. New Yorker 53:82-8 F 28 '77
Perspectives. S. Lens. See issues of Progressive
Presidency. H. Sidey. See occasional issues of Time
President learning. P. Goldman. por Newsweek 90:26 D 26 '77
Problems of a problem solver; President Carter's decision-making. H. Smith. il por N Y Times Mag p30+ Ja 8 '78
Real Carter emerges; 100-day benchmark. U.S. News 82:21-2 My 2 '77
Remaking of the Vice President. B. Brower. il pors NY Times Mag p38+ Je 5 '77; Same abr. Read Digest 111:113-17 D '77
Reporter at large. E. B. Drew. New Yorker 53: 112-14+ My 23; 156-62+ O 10 '77
Reports & comment: Washington: a town with a memory. W. Just. il Atlantic 241:6+ Ja '78
Road show goes West; J. Carter's visit to California. il pors Time 109:8-9 My 30 '77
Ronald Reagan—Mr Conservative; interview, ed by D. Pawelek. R. Reagan. il pors Sr Schol 110:10-13 D 15 '77
Skating deftly, but on thin ice; Carter administration. il Time 109:12-13 Mr 7 '77
Sowing seeds of real conflict. Time 109:12-13 Ap 18 '77
State of the Nation. R. J. Bresler. See alternate issues of Intellect
State of the Union 1977; address, January 12, 1977. G. R. Ford. Vital Speeches 43:226-30 F 1 '77; Same abr. Dept State Bull 76:97-101 F 1 '77
Stuart Eizenstat: an inside look at how the White House operates; interview, ed by R. L. Lesher. S. E. Eizenstat. il pors Nations Bus 65:36-41 Ag '77
TRB from Washington. See issues of New republic
Think positive? W. T. Brookes. U.S. News 83: 116 O 17 '77
Tougher tests coming. U.S. News 82:19 Ap 4 '77
Verdict from experts on Jimmy Carter's first year. il pors U.S. News 84:16-19 Ja 9 '78
Wait a minute. P. Goldman and others. il por Newsweek 90:29 N 7 '77
Warm words from Jimmy Cardigan; television address, February 2, 1977. il por Time 109:18 F 14 '77
Washington diarist. See issues of New republic, January 22, 1977-
Washington outlook. See issues of Business week
Washington report. F. Getlein. See issues of Commonweal
Watershed in Washington. il pors U.S. News 83:23-4 O 10 '77
What Ford thinks of Carter's style; interview. G. R. Ford. il pors U.S. News 83:20-2 Jl 4 '77
What of national "town meetings"? N. R. Peirce. Current 190:21-3 F '77
White House woes. il U.S. News 83:20-1 S 26 '77
Who runs America: annual survey. il U.S. News 82:28-36+ Ap 18 '77
Why I am a civil libertarian. R. L. MacBride. Sat Eve Post 249:34-5+ O '77
Why is Jimmy smiling? Why not? il pors Time 109:10-12 Ap 4 '77
With Jimmy from dawn to midnight. il por Time 109:14-19 Ap 18 '77
Word from Washington. See issues of Progressive

See also
Bureaucracy
Business—Political aspects
Conservatism
Democratic Party
Elections—United States
Federal and state relations
Liberalism
Lobbyists and lobbying
Political campaigns
Political parties—United States
Presidential campaigns
Presidents—United States—Relations with Congress
Republican Party
Right and left (political science)
Socialism—United States
State governments
Trade unions—Political activities
United States—Congress
United States—Constitution
Vice-presidents—United States
also subhead Politics and government under names of states, cities, etc. e.g. Madison, Wis. —Politics and government

Anecdotes, facetiae, satire, etc.

Is there intelligent life in Washington? address September 16, 1976. L. Loevinger. Vital Speeches 43:173-7 Ja 1 '77.
Mother hen. P. M. Sellinger. por Newsweek 90: 9 S 5 '77

Caricatures and cartoons

How cartoonists view the new administration—. il U.S. News 82:18-19 Mr 7 '77

Popular culture

American culture takes the world by storm. il U.S. News 82:54-6 Je 27 '77
Dracula lives! D. Ansen. il Newsweek 90:74-5+ O 31 '77

UNITED STATES—Popular culture—*Continued*
Fad, fashion, and style (cont'd) Sat R 4:43-5 Ap 30 '77
Fad, fashion, or style? W. M. Fine. il Sat R 4:52-3 F 5 '77
Plastic punks. A. Burgess; J. Lombardi. il Psychol Today 11:120-2+ N '77
Star trekking. J. Kroll. il Newsweek 90:48 D 26 '77
Who erased the seventies? H. Junker. il Esquire 88:152-5+ D '77

Population

End of youth culture: changes it will bring. J. Mann. il U.S. News 83:54-6 O 3 '77; Same. Current 197:3-7 N '77
Graying of America. A. Mayer and others. il Newsweek 89:50-2+ F 28 '77; Same abr. Read Digest 111:173-4+ Jl '77
Looking to the ZPGeneration. il Time 109:71-2 F 28 '77
Metamorphosis in the marketplace? R. Levy. il Duns R 109:65-7 F '77
New look at America today—evidence of major change. il U.S. News 82:64-5 My 16 '77
Profile of an aging America. il U.S. News 83:54 Ag 8 '77
Sunshine states show five-year population gain in new census survey. il Ret Liv 17:12 Ja '77
TRB from Washington; reports of the Domestic Council Committee on Illegal Aliens and the National Commission on Supplies and Shortages. New Repub 176:2+ F 26 '77
Trends in American marriage, childbirth, and retirement; excerpts from addresses. W. J. Cohen; C. F. Westoff. por Intellect 106:93-5 S '77
What's happening to us? il Sr Schol 110:10-13 S 8 '77
See also
Birth rate—United States
Migration, Internal
Puerto Ricans in the United States

Population policy

See Population policy

Presidential Advisory Board on Ambassadorial Appointments

Presidential Advisory Board on Ambassadorial Appointments; executive order; February 5, 1977. J. Carter. Dept State Bull 76:202-3 Mr 7 '77

Presidential Commission on Americans Missing and Unaccounted For in Southeast Asia

Bridgehead is won in Hanoi; work of the Woodcock delegation. S. Talbott. il por Time 109:17-18 Mr 28 '77
Presidential Commission to visit southeast Asia; statement, February 25, 1977. F. Z. Brown. Dept State Bull 76:258 Mr 21 '77
Presidential Commission visits Vietnam and Laos to seek information on missing Americans; remarks, transcript of news conference with text of Commission report, March 23, 1977. J. Carter; L. Woodcock. Dept State Bull 76:363-74 Ap 18 '77
Time for healing; Leonard Woodcock mission. F. Willey and S. Talbott. il por Newsweek 89: 38+ Mr 28 '77

President's Commission on Mental Health

Carter's little pills. E. F. Torrey. Psychol Today 11:10+ D '77
Mental health. C. Holden. Science 198:37 O 7 '77
Mental illness Rx: research, insurance. Sci N 112:198 S 24 '77
Not just for show. J. Greenberg. il Sci N 111: 396-7 Je 18 '77

President's Commission on Olympic Sports

Cure for an Olympian headache. K. Moore. il Sports Illus 46:18-20+ Ja 17 '77
Washington scene; report released. B. Kravetz. Parks & Rec 12:20+ Ap '77

President's Commission on Personnel Interchange

Unique job swap for executives. J. C. Perham. il Duns R 109:89-91 My '77

President's Council on Aging

See United States—Aging, Administration on

President's Council on Environmental Quality

See United States—Council on Environmental Quality

Prisons, Bureau of

Federal prison libraries: the quiet collapse. D. Buvak. bibl il por Lib J 102:1341 Je 15 '77

Privacy Protection Study Commission

Go on welfare, give up your privacy? U.S. News 82:83 Ja 24 '77
Privacy group recommends direct-mail measures. S. Wagner. Pub W 212:47-8 Ag 1 '77
Snooping into your private life: can anything be done about it? interview. D. F. Linowes. por U.S. News 82:35-6 My 2 '77
Striking back at the super snoops; Linowes Commission report. il Time 110:16-18+ Jl 18 '77
When private eyes poke into your affairs—. il U.S. News 82:34 F 7 '77

Public Health Service

See also
United States—Alcohol, Drug Abuse, and Mental Health Administration
United States—National Institutes of Health

Center for Disease Control

Found: the Philly killer, perhaps; Legionnaires' disease. Time 109:47 Ja 31 '77
Guillain-Barré rare disease paralyzes swine flu campaign. P. M. Boffey. Science 195:155-9 Ja 14 '77
Latest in health and medicine; more on Legionnaires' disease. il U.S. News 83:63 O 31 '77
Legion fever: failed investigation may be successful after all. B. J. Culliton. Science 195: 469-70 F 4 '77
NIH director stays, CDC director goes. Sci N 111: 119 F 19 '77
Out of control? death of two workers. J. Seligmann and D. Shapiro. il Newsweek 89:46 Mr 14 '77
Tracking the killer fever; Legionnaire's disease. M. Clark. il Newsweek 89:78-9 Ja 31 '77
War on germs. M. Clark. il Newsweek 90:98 S 19 '77
Way of forestalling epidemics and rescuing their victims; Mobile Quarantine Facility. il Space World N-10-166:31 O '77

Public opinion

See Public opinion—United States

Public works

See Public works

Race question

See also
Blacks
Church and race problems
also subhead Race question under names of regions, states, cities, e.g. Mississippi—Race question

Reclamation, Bureau of

Impending leasing off coast; effects on eastern seashore parks. Nat Parks & Con Mag 51:22 F '77
Pumping billions into the desert: the case against the Central Arizona Project. D. Hanson. il Audubon 79:133-45 My '77; Reply. B. Goldwater. 79:99-100 Jl '77
Torrent of litigation over Teton Dam. il Bus W p21-2 Ja 24 '77

Regulatory agencies

See Independent regulatory commissions

Religious institutions and affairs

American involvement in fringe religious cults. Intellect 105:299-300 Mr '77
Back to that oldtime religion. il Time 110:52-8 D 26 '77
Bottom-line theology; interview, ed by D. Kucharsky. F. J. Sheen. il Chr Today 21:8-11 Je 3 '77
Church roundup. Chr Today 21:37-8 Ag 12 '77
Churches start facing up to the sexual revolution: abortions, married priests, homosexuals. il U.S. News 83:63-4 S 26 '77
God's almost chosen people. M. E. Marty. il Am Heritage 28:4-7 Ag '77
Is America over-evangelized? D. W. Hillis. Chr Today 21:16-17 My 20 '77
Looking from the inside out; study by J. R. Hale. por Time 110:85 O 3 '77
New reformation aborning? Chr Today 22:24 O 21 '77
Police blotter; crime in church circles. Chr Today 22:64+ O 7 '77
Spirit of America; role of Christianity. M. B. Martin. Nat R 29:615 My 27 '77
Time of renewal for U.S. churches; with interview with P. L. Berger. il U.S. News 82: 54-8+ Ap 11 '77
Who is shaping America's values? Chr Today 21: 37 F 4 '77
See also
Appalachian Region—Religious institutions and affairs
Baptists in the United States
Catholic Church in the United States
Church and state
Evangelicalism

UNITED STATES—Religious institutions and affairs—*Continued*
Jehovah's Witnesses
Lutheran Church in the United States
Mormons and Mormonism
Orthodox Church in America
Orthodox Eastern Church in the United States
Presbyterian Church in the United States
Protestant churches—United States
Protestant Episcopal Church
United Church of Christ
also subhead Religious institutions and affairs under names of regions, states, cities; e.g. Georgia—Religious institutions and affairs

Renegotiation Board

Checking on the contractors. F. M. McGehee, 3d. Progressive 41:8-9 S '77
Stronger Renegotiation Board backed. K. Johnsen. Aviation W 106:20 Mr 14 '77

Reserve Officers Training Corps

How can the armed services help cover college costs? M. Daly and E. Sweeney. il Bet Hom & Gard 55:38+ Mr '77
Rebuilding the ROTC with women's help. U.S. News 83:30-1 Jl 11 '77

Riots

Those riot-torn cities—a look at progress 10 years later. il U.S. News 83:50-1 Ag 29 '77

History

Did it really happen here? 1967 urban riots. R. Reeves. il Esquire 88:83-7 Jl '77

Science and Technology Policy, Office of

Blind side of science policy. W. D. Carey. Science 196:1045 Je 3 '77
Executive office reorganization: OSTP and CEQ are still in. J. Walsh. Science 197:442-4 Jl 29 '77
Frank Press outlines tasks as President's science advisor. F. C. Bennett. por Phys Today 30:69+ Je '77
Mr Ford's vision of the White House Science Office. Sci Digest 81:18 F '77
President's scientist; F. Press. il por Time 109:73 Ap 11 '77
Press meets the press. J. Walsh. Science 197:538 Ag 5 '77
Press named science adviser, busy on job. Sci N 111:215 Ap 2 '77
Science units spared in shuffle. Sci N 112:54 Jl 23 '77
Senate panel wants OSTP to take the long view. L. J. Carter. Science 198:472 N 4 '77

Securities and Exchange Commission

Bad news for Beame. D. M. Alpern and others. il por Newsweek 90:18-19 S 5 '77
Big Board's own national marketplace. il Bus W p34-5 D 5 '77
Chairman Williams digs in at the SEC. il por Bus W p69+ My 30 '77
Corporate governance—new heat on outside directors? por Forbes 120:33 O 1 '77
Dean as a securities watchdog; H. M. Williams. por Time 109:61 Ap 11 '77
Disclosure rules survive. il Bus W p86 N 14 '77
Financial explosion hits New York City: the SEC report. P. D. Nigro. Intellect 106:180 N '77
Gauging bank profits by one bottom line. il Bus W p56-7 Jl 4 '77
Gnomes of Manhattan: how New York went for broke. R. Lekachman. Nation 225:715-20 D 31 '77
ITT's Hartford deal still worries the SEC; Lazard Frères stock sale arrangement. Bus W p26-7 Je 6 '77
Is forced disclosure inefficient? Forbes 119:78 Je 1 '77
Lance is rethinking the role of the SEC; possible addition of capital-formation policy planning. Bus W p36+ F 28 '77
Man for the markets; H. Williams. D. Pauly and others. por Newsweek 89:85-6 Mr 14 '77
Mining the dossiers; SEC files on corporate payments. il Newsweek 89:71+ My 30 '77
Mob scene in New York; mayoral campaign. il por Time 110:21-2 S 5 '77
New York bankers say they didn't do it. il Bus W p50 S 19 '77
Options-market fraud? The SEC is suspicious. il U.S. News 83:81 O 31 '77
Reviving the concept of a national market. Bus W p33-4 Ag 15 '77
SEC focuses on executive perks. Bus W p52+ Ap 18 '77
SEC gets slapped for double-dealing; stock fraud investigation of TDA Industries, Inc. Bus W p36 Je 20 '77
SEC is forced to reprieve Rule 390; NYSE rule. Bus W p37-8 O 17 '77
Sporkin the enforcer. M. Ruby and J. Walcott. il por Newsweek 90:94 O 24 '77
Talking back to the SEC. A. Hershman. il Duns R 109:78-80 Mr '77
Trash collector who cleaned house; SEC suit against SCA Services Inc. Bus W p25-6 Ag 22 '77
Wall Street's taste of freedom. il Bus W p91-3 Ap 4 '77
What the SEC failed to do about New York. J. Patterson. Bus W p44 S 12 '77
Which client secrets must a lawyer reveal? SEC suits against law firms involved in National Student Marketing Corporation's fraudulent takeover attempt of Interstate National Corp. il Bus W p 124+ Ag 15 '77

Senate

See United States—Congress—Senate

Small Business Administration

AAP pleads for loans to small publishers. S. Wagner. Pub W 212:22 D 26 '77
Big hand for Small Business? por Forbes 120:122 N 1 '77
Businesswomen get a champion at SBA. il pors Nations Bus 65:34-6 D '77
Junk aid for small business. A. L. Morner. il Fortune 96:204-7+ N '77
Pledge from Washington to help small business; interview. V. Weaver. pors Nations Bus 65:31-4 Jl '77
SBA can lend you money now. C. Bickers. Farm J 101:A8 O '77
SBA no! Time 110:28+ N 14 '77
Small business: Washington begins to take it more seriously. U.S. News 83:77-8 Ag 8 '77
You may qualify for pollution loans from SBA. C. Bickers. Farm J 101:33B Mr '77
See also
Government investigations—Small Business Administration

Social conditions

American family. J. A. Michener. il Ladies Home J 94:87+ D '77
American society and its cities. M. Mead. Current 190:3-9 F '77
Andy Warhol sketch of our soup can culture. A. Warhol. il pors U.S. News 82:57 Je 27 '77
Can Carter revitalize the American family? G. E. Jones. il U.S. News 82:35 F 28 '77
Can the American family survive? M. Mead. il Redbook 148:91+ F '77
Changing values. il Forbes 120:P125-32 S 15 '77
Cultural counterrevolution. R. J. Bresler. Intellect 106:115 O '77
Education, history, and the press; address, February 8, 1977. H. E. Foster. Vital Speeches 43:349-52 Mr 15 '77
End of youth culture: changes it will bring. J. Mann. il U.S. News 83:54-6 O 3 '77; Same. Current 197:3-7 N '77
Family under fire; address, March 23, 1977. M. D'Innocenzo. Vital Speeches 43:431-5 My 1 '77
How America lives. Ladies Home J 94:65-73 Mr '77
Impressions by the way. J. Burnham. Nat R 29:1178 O 14 '77
Moral tales for a depraved age. T. Griffith. Atlantic 240:20-1 Jl '77
Power to the eloquent. J. Hitchcock. Yale R 66:374-87 Mr '77
Squeeze on the middle class; with interview with M. Janowitz. il U.S. News 82:50-7 My 2 '77
Top of the world is flat. H. J. Davidson. bibl f il Harvard Bus R 55:89-99 Mr '77
Ways singles are changing U.S. il U.S. News 82:59-60 Ja 31 '77
We the people; address, February 27, 1977. P. J. Crow. Vital Speeches 43:456-7 My 15 '77
See also
Blacks
Child welfare—United States
Cities and towns—United States
Crime and criminals—United States
Divorce—United States
Labor and laboring classes—United States
Poor—United States
Recreation—United States
Social change
United States—Moral conditions
Violence
Youth—United States

Social conditions

also subhead Social conditions under names of regions, states, cities, etc. e.g. Washington, D.C.—Social conditions

Social history

Nobody's special when they're poor. T. J. Cottle. Yale R 66:388-98 Mr '77
Reconsiderations: the '60s. M. Cowley. New Repub 177:37-40 Ag 20 '77
Route 66: ghost road of the Okies. T. W. Pew, Jr. il Am Heritage 28:24-33 Ag '77
60 years of American business; a picture portfolio. il Forbes 120:P1-8+ S 15 '77
Worried America; adaptation of address. G. Myrdal. Chr Cent 94:1161-6 D 14 '77
See also
Business depression, 1929-1939
Oklahoma—Social history
Slavery—United States

UNITED STATES—*Continued*

Social life and customs

Great kissing epidemic; Time essay. il Time 109:66-7 F 7 '77
How you live; symposium, ed by B. Plumb. il Vogue 167:154-6+ Je '77
Miniguides: new nightlife; nine cities. Vogue 167:147-8+ N '77
Nation without last names; Time essay. L. Morrow. Time 110:43 Jl 11 '77
New nightlife; symposium. il Vogue 167:250-1+ N '77
Sharpshootin' chic takes over. B. Sabol. Vogue 167:165 My '77
What's in, what's out: the search for status; with interview with P. Blumberg. il por U.S. News 82:38-42 F 14 '77
See also
Christmas—United States
Collective settlements
Family reunions
also subhead Social life and customs under names of regions, states, cities, e.g. Southern States—Social life and customs

Colonial period, ca. 1600-1775

Life upon the wicked stage; theater in colonial America. M. Klein. il Am Hist Illus 11:36-43 F '77
See also
House decoration American
Williamsburg, Va.

Social policy

Bogus order of merit. New Repub 176:6+ Ap 2 '77
Carter and compassion. M. Greenfield. Newsweek 90:104 D 19 '77
Carter bears right. Nation 224:578-80 My 14 '77
Evaluating social programs. S. A. Levitan. il Society 14:66-8 My '77
Federal government and social rights. V. E. Jordan; A. Schlesinger. il por Intellect 105:293-4 Mr '77
Future is made, not predicted: technocratic planners vs. public interests. R. P. Appelbaum. bibl il Society 14:49-53 My '77
How the government affects family life. J. Chan. McCalls 104:63-4 My '77
Inventory of improbables. E. Marshall. New Repub 176:16-17 Ja 22 '77
Jimmy vs. the liberals. T. Mathews and others. il por Newsweek 89:44 My 16 '77
Mr Hayakawa goes to Washington. S. I. Hayakawa. il Harpers 256:39-43 Ja '78
Numbers game. M. Kempton. Progressive 41:49 My '77
Old people and public policy. A. Etzioni. Current 192:21-34 Ap '77
Presidential decision making; symposium. Society 14:8-24 My '77
Retreat of Democratic reform. R. J. Bresler. Intellect 106:213 D '77
Social contract with labor to limit wage gains would be full of loopholes. A. R. Weber. Duns R 109:9 Ja '77
Social cures, not palliatives; adaptation of address. B. Commoner. il Nat Parks & Con Mag 51:14-15 My '77
Toward a Swedenized America? Current 190:11-15 F '77
We citizens cannot sit back and relax: world security; address, April 20, 1977. R. W. Peterson. Vital Speeches 43:490-3 Je 1 '77
What are we planting? M. Stone. U.S. News 82:84 Je 13 '77
Why things don't work any more. J. Diebold. por Newsweek 90:8-9 Jl 18 '77
See also
Economic assistance, Domestic
Medical policy
Population policy
Public welfare—United States
United States—Domestic Council

Space and Missile Systems Organization

See United States—Air Force—Systems Command

Special Representative for Trade Negotiations, Office of the

Collision course for Strauss. por Bus W p27-8 Je 6 '77
More about Strauss. J. Osborne. New Repub 178: 8-10 Ja 7 '78
Picking a winner; R. Strauss appointed Special Representative. il por Time 109:49-50 Mr 7 '77
Resurrection; R. Strauss. J. Osborne. New Repub 177:13-16 D 24 '77

Standards, National Bureau of

Fiery debate over smoke-alarm efficiency: controversy surrounding claims made by Gillette and ADT concerning their photoelectric detectors. il Bus W p95-6+ S 26 '77
National Bureau of Standards: a fall from grace. G. B. Kolata. il Science 197:968-70 S 2 '77; Discussion. 198:8 O 7 '77
Product technology and the consumer. G. F. Montgomery. il Sci Am 237:47-53 D '77

Standards of Official Conduct, Committee on

Jaworski comes back. Time 110:8 Ag 1 '77

State, Department of

Amateur hour. T. Szulc. New Repub 176:20-2 My 28 '77
Carter's point woman; P. Derian. A. Deming and S. Sullivan. por Newsweek 89:70 My 16 '77
Junior varsity. Suetonius. New Repub 176:12-14 F 19 '77
Message from Secretary Vance to Department and Foreign Service; January 24, 1977. C. R. Vance. Dept State Bull 76:125-6 F 14 '77
President Carter visits the Department of State; remarks, with excerpts from question and answer session, February 24, 1977. J. Carter. Dept State Bull 76:259-65 Mr 21 '77
Publications. See issues of Department of State bulletin
Recommendation to parole Indochinese refugees; statement, August 4, 1977. R. C. Holbrooke. Dept State Bull 77:411-13 S 26 '77
Science and technology at State: recognizing the problem. J. Walsh. Science 196:148-50 Ap 8 '77
State Dept. control asked on arms export efforts. il Aviation W 106:34-5 Ap 25 '77
Vietnam's legacy; emergency plan to admit 15,-000 homeless Asians. D. M. Alpern and others. Newsweek 90:18 Jl 18 '77
See also
United States—Diplomatic and Consular Service
United States—Government Advisory Committee on International Book and Library Programs

Educational and Cultural Affairs, Bureau of

United States—Agency for International Communication (proposed)

Headquarters

Treasury of Americana by special invitation; top floor of the State Department. il U.S. News 83:69-70 O 24 '77

History

Recognizing Israel; address, December 28, 1976. C. M. Clifford. pors Am Heritage 28:4-7+ Ap '77

Statistics

Trivia treasure; statistics from Social indicators 1976. Time 111:15 Ja 9 '78
U.S. in focus; facts about the states; chart. Sr Schol 110:35-6 O 20 '77

Supreme Court

Another round in the obscenity battle; case of J. L. Smith. W. D. Nelson. Wilson Lib Bull 51:466-7 F '77
Arguing about death for rape; Last word. il Time 109:80+ Ap 11 '77
Burger vs. Warren: whose Court is better? Report card on Supreme Court. pors U.S. News 82:58+ Mr 7 '77
Cold war justice: the Supreme Court and the Rosenbergs. M. E. Parrish. bibl f Am Hist R 82:805-42 O '77
Court: don't spare the rod. il Time 109:58 My 2 '77
Court's tough agenda. J. K. Footlick and D. Camper. il Newsweek 90:75-6 O 17 '77
Death penalty for rape? case of Coker v. Georgia. D. Leavy. Ms 6:20 Jl '77
Do we have rights to everything? J. Houston. U.S. News 83:34 O 31 '77
Has the Supreme Court abandoned the Constitution? L. McDonald. il Sat R 4:10-12+ My 28 '77; Same with title Supreme Court today. Current 194:32-9 Jl '77
Imperial court; excerpt from Government by judiciary. R. Berger. il N Y Times Mag p38+ O 9 '77
In Supreme Court: fresh battles over individual rights. U.S. News 83:37 O 3 '77
Inside the Burger Court. J. K. Footlick and L. Howard. il pors Newsweek 89:101-2 Je 13 '77
Justices run nine little law firms at Supreme Court. R. L. Williams. il Smithsonian 7:84-93 bibl(p 154) F '77
New trial for states' rights; upcoming decisions. Bus W p38 O 10 '77
People's sense of powerlessness; excerpts from address. J. L. Buckley. por Intellect 106:95 S '77

Bakke case

See Bakke, Allan, case

Decisions

Access to the courts: the justices slam the door. R. Nader and G. A. Spann. Nation 225:495-8 N 12 '77
Advertisers-at-law. J. K. Footlick and L. Howard. por Newsweek 90:47-8 Jl 11 '77
After Gilmore; the death penalty. L. Denniston. New Repub 176:10-12 Ja 29 '77
Aid to nonpublic education. America 137:2-3 Jl 2 '77

UNITED STATES—Supreme Court—Decisions—*Continued*
Analyzing the Burger Supreme Court. G. Gunther. por Intellect 105:216-17 Ja '77
Arlington Heights case. America 136:90-1 F 5 '77
Bar's blushing maidens; decision allowing lawyers to advertise. N. Lewin. New Repub 177:17-19 S 17 '77
Berger v. Court; 14th Amendment decisions. J. K. Footlick. por Newsweek 90:75 N 14 '77
Blow to minorities; seniority systems decision. H. Hill. il Commonweal 104:552-5 S 2 '77
Case against separate schools. D. G. Carter. bibl Clearing H 51:125-9 N '77
Clues to the Supreme Court's future rulings. J. J. Kilpatrick. Nations Bus 65:11-12 Ag '77
Common sense on race; Arlington Heights, Ill. zoning refusal case. G. F. Will. Newsweek 89:80 Ja 24 '77
Conflicting signals; decision in case of the National Association for the Advancement of Colored People against the Dayton Board of Education. J. Miller. New Repub 177:10-11 Jl 23 '77
Court docket; gerrymander challenge by Hasidic Jews of Brooklyn. J. K. Footlick. Newsweek 89:97-8 Mr 14 '77
Court strikes a blow for seniority. il Time 109:60 Je 13 '77
Court switches franchising signals; Schwinn Bicycle Company ruling. Bus W p30 Jl 11 '77
Current status of obscenity laws. F. F. Schauer. Intellect 106:99-100 S '77
Danger: pendulum swinging; using the courts to muzzle the press. A. U. Schwartz. Atlantic 239:29-34 F '77
Day race relations changed forever; Brown v Board of Education; school desegregation decision. L. Bennett, Jr. il Ebony 32:132-6+ My '77
Deterrent to the deterrent argument; death penalty. Chr Cent 94:132-3 F 16 '77
Deviating into sense; Arlington Heights, Ill. zoning law. Nat R 29:136 F 4 '77
EEOC retreats after a seniority ruling. Bus W p28+ Je 20 '77
Farewell barrage from the Court. il Time 110:62-3 Jl 11 '77
Fie on the 14th; views of R. Berger. Time 110:101-2 N 14 '77
Free choice for college students; constitutionality of public financial assistance to students attending church-related colleges. America 137:257 O 22 '77
Full speed backward; ruling on corporal punishment. F. M. Hechinger. Sat R 4:14 My 28 '77
Growing criminal liability of executives; J. R. Park case. T. McAdams and R. C. Miljus. bibl f Harvard Bus R 55:36-7 Mr '77
High Court reaffirms need for prison law libraries. W. D. Nelson. Wilson Lib Bull 51:857-8 Je '77
High Court upholds criminal conviction of Smith for intrastate mailing. S. Wagner. Pub W 211:42 Je 6 '77
How liberals are making an end run around the Supreme Court; using state supreme courts. P. Oster. il U.S. News 82:50-1 Ja 31 '77
Husbands and widowers win railroad annuity Court victory. Ret Liv 17:60 S '77
In the works: a fairer but costlier social security. U.S. News 82:85-6 Mr 21 '77
Inside the Supreme Court: the momentous school desegregation decision; excerpt from The memoirs of Earl Warren. E. Warren. il por Atlantic 239:35-40 Ap '77
Intent, not impact; decision on Arlington Heights, Ill. zoning law. Time 109:52 Ja 24 '77
Judicial thicket: the Supreme Court and obscenity. M. Friedman. Nation 225:110-13 Ag 6 '77
Just leave it to the states. Time 109:46 Ap 4 '77
Keeping women in their place: the male chauvinist Court. C. H. Arber. Nation 225:654-7 D 17 '77
Kenneth Donaldson's fight for freedom. R. Steinzor. Progresive 41:48-50 Ap '77
Law, politics, and equal educational opportunity. D. L. Kirp. Educ Digest 43:32-5 S '77
License to beat children. Progressive 41:8 Je '77
Maze of school desegregation: litmus test for Griffin Bell. S. Gillers. Nation 224:688-91 Je 4 '77
Miranda still stands; case of R. Williams. C. Panati and L. Howard. por Newsweek 89:80+ Ap 4 '77
Mr Chief Justice; Marbury vs Madison decision; excerpt from television script. il Sr Schol 110:19-22 S 22 '77
94th Congress action on House & Senate campaign financing. Cong Digest 56:74-5 Mr '77
Nitpicking justice: unequal access to the courts. S. Gillers. il Nation 224:110-13 Ja 29 '77
Nixon's tapes someday. Newsweek 90:17 Jl 11 '77
No to Nixon's men; verdict on the convictions of John Ehrichman, H. R. Haldeman and John Mitchell. Time 109:13 Je 6 '77
Notes and comment; decision on school discipline. New Yorker 53:27 My 30 '77
Obscenity: new High Court ruling, AAP on Flynt. S. Wagner. Pub W 211:41-2 Mr 14 '77
Parochial decision. Newsweek 90:59 Jl 4 '77
Rape and death; decision on death penalty in rape cases. il Newsweek 90:48 Jl 11 '77
Recent developments in the law; cases involving Catholic schools; address, January 25, 1977. V. C. Blum. Vital Speeches 43:296-300 Mr 1 '77
Report card on Supreme Court; views of judges and lawyers. il U.S. News 82:60-6+ Mr 7 '77
Right not to speak; Wooley v. Maynard. C. McWilliams. Nation 225:69-70 Jl 23 '77
Right to refuse; rezoning refusal upheld by Supreme Court in Arlington Heights, Ill. case. J. K. Footlick and others. il Newsweek 89:77 Ja 24 '77
Ruling on the rod; decisions on school spankings. M. Sheils and F. V. Boyd. il Newsweek 89:65-6 My 2 '77
Setback in Arlington Heights; ruling on zoning. J. De Muth. America 136:167-8 F 26 '77
Significant decisions in labor cases. C. Polhemus. See issues of Monthly labor review
Significant labor decisions—an analysis. C. E. Polhemus. bibl f M Labor R 100:36-41 Ja '77
Some are more equal; Supreme Court decisions affecting discrimination in education and political representation. B. Odom. Nat R 29:1114-15 S 30 '77
Some surprises in High Court's conservative trend. il U.S. News 83:20-2 Jl 11 '77
Suburban iron curtain; decision on Arlington Heights, Ill. zoning law. Commonweal 104:99-100 F 18 '77
Supreme Court and civil rights. C. H. Falk. Current 191:13-16 Mr '77
Supreme Court eases social security rules. Aging 274:27 Ag '77
Supreme Court rules that attorneys may advertise, and speculation flourishes among the other professions. W. Hickman. Archit Rec 162:34 Ag '77
Supreme Court rulings during the 1976-77 term: some good news, some bad news and some maybe's. A. T. Kornblut. Archit Rec 162:63 Ag '77
Supreme Court scoreboard. Nat R 29:815 Jl 22 '77
Supreme Court strikes down a social security dependency requirement for widowers. Ret Liv 17:13-14 Ap '77
Supreme embarrassment; news leak describing action on appeals in the Watergate cover-up trial. J. K. Footlick and L. Howard. por Newsweek 89:66 My 9 '77
Tale of two cities; decisions on the proper role of Federal judges in school-desegregation cases. M. Sheils and others. il Newsweek 90:54 Jl 11 '77
Teacher and the law; Abood v. Detroit Board of Education **decision concerning a service** fee charged to non-members of unions. B. E. Sinowitz. Todays Educ 66:18+ S '77
Trivializing discrimination. N. Lewin. New Repub 176:19-21 Ap 2 '77; Discussion. 176:9 Ap 30 '77
Undercutting Miranda: the Burger way with suspects. A. Berlow. il Nation 224:498-500 Ap 23 '77
What the Supreme Court is really telling business. W. Guzzardi, Jr. il Fortune 95:147-54 Ja '77
Working on the Sabbath. Time 109:50-1 Je 27 '77
Zoning out low-income families in suburbia; Arlington Heights, Ill. J. S. Fuerst. Chr Cent 94:77-8 F 2 '77

Decisions—Abortion decisions

Abortion and fairness; medicaid funds. Progressive 41:9 S '77
Abortion and the Supreme Court:
Anti-abortion view. S. Callahan. Current 198:21-3 D '77
Egalitarian view. M. C. Segers. Current 198:17-21 D '77
Abortion funding where it stands now. U.S. News 83:22 Jl 11 '77
Abortion: the debate goes on; limiting medicaid funds. America 137:2 Jl 2 '77
Abortion: who pays? S. Fraker and others. il Newsweek 90:12-13 Jl 4 '77
High Court's abortion rulings: what they mean. il U.S. News 83:66 Jl 4 '77
Intelligent woman's guide to sex; **Supreme Court's decision on use of medicaid for abortions. J. Coburn. Mademoiselle 83:136+ S '77**
New abortion debate; decision on medicaid funding. Commonweal 104:451-2 Jl 22 '77
New abortion rulings (what they really mean) L. Prinz. McCalls 105:111 O '77
Of abortion and the unfairness of life; Time essay. L. Morrow. Time 110:49 Ag 1 '77
Politics of abortion; decision on medicaid funding. P. Steinfels. Commonweal 104:456 Jl 22 '77
Punitive and tragic; decision to deny public funds for abortion. Nation 225:3-4 Jl 2 '77

UNITED STATES—Supreme Court—Decisions—Abortion decisions—*Continued*

Rethinking abortion? Chr Today 21:48 Mr 4 '77

Supreme Court ignites a fiery abortion debate. il Time 110:6-8 Jl 4 '77

Unborn and the born again; Supreme Court decision on use of state funds to cover abortion costs. New Repub 177:5-6+ Jl 2 '77

Employees

Clerking for the Supremes. S. Kaplan. New Repub 177:25-6 O 15 '77

History

NAACP and the Supreme Court: Walter F. White and the defeat of Judge John J. Parker, 1930. D. C. Hine. bibl il por Negro Hist Bull 40:753-7 S '77

Tax Court

If you decide to take on the U.S. tax collector—small-case branch. il U.S. News 83:72+ Jl 11 '77

Taxing cases. J. Seligmann and L. Howard. il Newsweek 89:82 Ap 4 '77

Technology Assessment, Office of

Congress' tough new technical consultant; R. W. Peterson. por Bus W p64 D 12 '77

Continuing saga of the OTA. Science 197:1164-5 S 16 '77

Daddario resigns abruptly from OTA. P. M. Boffey. Science 196:1066 Je 3 '77

Impartial OTA future dubious; a launching pad for Kennedy? D. Gergen. Sci Digest 82:24-5+ S '77

OTA Council opts for big names. D. Shapley. Science 197:1348 S 30 '77

OTA: Daddario's exit heightens strife over Kennedy role. C. Holden. Science 197:27-8 Jl 1 '77

Office of Technology Assessment. P. H. Abelson. Science 196:1391 Je 24 '77

Russell Peterson says yes—he will head OTA. C. Holden. Science 198:903 D 2 '77

U.S. science and technology: a prescription for health. H. Brooks. Science 195:536 F 11 '77

Will Russell Peterson be OTA's new direction? B. J. Culliton. por Science 198:592-3 N 11 '77

Tennessee Valley Authority

See Tennessee Valley Authority

Territories and possessions

See also
Puerto Rico
Trust Territory of the Pacific Islands
Virgin Islands

Trade Negotiations, Office of the Special Representative for

See United States—Special Representative for Trade Negotiations, Office of the

Trade policy

See United States—Commercial policy

Transportation, Department of

Brock Adams—mystery man. T. Orme. Motor T 29:6+ Mr '77

Coming soon: gasoline at a dollar a gallon; interview. B. Adams. il pors U.S. News 83:43-5 Ag 15 '77

DOT delays bus specs for more study. il Am City & County 92:22 Ap '77

See also
United States—Federal Aviation Administration
United States—National Highway Traffic Safety Administration
United States—Urban Mass Transportation Administration

Appropriations and expenditures

Transportation Dept. cuts airport grants. Aviation W 106:22-3 Ja 24 '77

Treasury, Department of the

Axelson's gaffe; withdrawal of K. S. Axelson's nomination as Deputy Treasury Secretary. D. Pauly and R. Thomas. por Newsweek 89:70 Mr 21 '77

Forward trading that vexes Treasury; Treasury bill futures. il Bus W p60-1 Ag 22 '77

Trials of a T-man; W. M. Blumenthal. T. Mathews and others. il por Newsweek 90:40 O 17 '77

Will the penny soon be a thing of the past? il U.S. News 83:104-6 N 14 '77

See also
United States—Comptroller of the Currency, Office of the
United States—Internal Revenue Service
United States Customs Service

Treaties

Treaty information. See issues of Department of State bulletin

History

When Senators rejected treaties—. il U.S. News 83:19 S 12 '77

Canada

Transfer of sanctions treaties with Mexico and Canada; American prisoners in foreign jails; statement, July 13, 1977. B. M. Watson. Dept State Bull 77:208-10 Ag 15 '77

U.S.-Canada transit pipeline treaty transmitted to the Senate; message, March 30, 1977. J. Carter. Dept State Bull 76:425 Ap 25 '77

Cuba

Our man in Havana; T. Todman fishing rights mission. F. Willey and L. E. Nelson. il Newsweek 89:44 My 9 '77

U.S, Cuba agree on maritime boundaries and fishery matters. map Dept State Bull 76:686-7 Je 27 '77

Great Britain

Court judgments go international; treaty providing for reciprocal recognition and enforcement of judgments in civil cases. Bus W p50+ F 21 '77

Reciprocal fisheries agreement with the United Kingdom; message to Senate, October 7, 1977. J. Carter. Dept State Bull 77:708-9 N 14 '77

Japan

U.S, Japan sign determination for nuclear facility. Dept State Bull 77:460-2 O 10 '77

Latin America

President signs Latin American nuclear free zone treaty; Tlatelolco treaty; remarks, May 26, 1977. Dept State Bull 77:10 Jl 4 '77

Mexico

Mexican prison swap. D. Holt and others. il Newsweek 90:35-6 D 19 '77

Mexican transfer; treaty to return American prisoners. P. Meyer. Harpers 255:26+ N '77

Transfer of sanctions treaties with Mexico and Canada; American prisoners in foreign jails; statement, July 13, 1977. B. M. Watson. Dept State Bull 77:208-10 Ag 15 '77

United States and Mexico sign treaty on execution of penal sentences. Dept State Bull 75:750 D 27 '76

U.S, Mexico sign fishery agreement; set provisional maritime boundaries. Dept State Bull 75:758-9 D 27 '76

Yankees come home; transfer of convicts. il Time 110:25 D 19 '77

Panama

Anglo-Saxon sentimentality. New Repub 177:5-8 S 24 '77

As U.S. and Panama head for showdown over Canal; with editorial comment. C. J. Migdail. il por maps U.S. News 82:28-30, 76 My 2 '77

Bid for votes on Panama. il Bus W p41 S 12 '77

Canal. Commonweal 104:579-80 S 16 '77

Canal as symbol. Progressive 41:11 O '77

Canal debate begins. il Time 110:15-16 O 10 '77

Canal: interim notes. J. Burnham. Nat R 29:1351 N 25 '77

Canal politics. Nat R 29:1282 N 11 '77

Canal: time to go? A. Deming and others. il map Newsweek 90:28-32+ Ag 22 '77

Carter and the Canal. A. Deming and others. il Newsweek 89:43+ F 7 '77

Carter, Congress and the Canal. A. Deming and others. il Newsweek 90:49 Jl 4 '77

Carter's high-risk move. U.S. News 83:18-19 S 12 '77

Ceding the Canal—slowly. il pors Time 110:8-13 Ag 22 '77

Church support for Canal treaties. J. M. Wall. Chr Cent 94:995 N 2 '77

Clarification, please. Newsweek 90:61-2 O 17 '77

Controversial ditch. Nation 225:676 D 24 '77

Deal on the Canal. F. Willey and S. Sullivan. il por Newsweek 90:29-30 Ag 15 '77

Deputy Secretary Christopher discusses the Panama Canal treaties; address, November 11, 1977. W. M. Christopher. Dept State Bull 77:835-9 D 12 '77

Ditching the Panamanians. Nation 225:386-8 O 22 '77

Do you dig the Panama Canal treaty? opinions of Panamanian and Zonian students. A. Palacios. il Sr Schol 110:12-13+ O 20 '77

Editor's page. R. Manning. Atlantic 241:4-5 Ja '78

Eupeptic over progress in Panama. il Time 109:14-15 F 28 '77

Great nay-sayer; S. Thurmond. G. F. Will. il Newsweek 90:84 S 5 '77

High economic hopes if ratification comes. Bus W p54-5 O 3 '77

Historic treaty with Panama: toughest test is still to come; with readers comments. il map U.S. News 83:25-7 Ag 22 '77

If U.S. had to defend the Panama Canal—; with comments from two former military chiefs. il map U.S. News 83:26-7 O 24 '77

UNITED STATES—Treaties—Panama—*Continued*
Justice and the Panama Canal. America 137:90 Ag 27 '77
Keeping the Canal pacts afloat. il Time 110:35+ O 24 '77
Land divided, the world united. B. McGinty. il map Am Hist Illus 12:10-19 My '77
Let's give it back. N. Von Hoffman. Progressive 41:49 N '77
Letter from Washington. R. H. Rovere. New Yorker 53:134-6 S 12 '77
Man, a plan, a Canal: Panama. New Repub 177:2+ S 3 '77
Military and Panama. W. F. Buckley, Jr. Nat R 29:1256-7 O 28 '77
NCC and Carter. Chr Cent 94:1084 N 23 '77
New deals for the big ditch. il Time 110:28 Jl 25 '77
New Panama Canal treaties—in our national interest; address, October 18, 1977. S. M. Linowitz. Dept State Bull 77:806-11 D 5 '77
News directors interview President Carter; excerpts from transcript, September 15, 1977. J. Carter. Dept State Bull 77:568-9 O 24 '77
Now for the hard part. il Time 110:19-21 S 19 '77
Panama—a doomed treaty? with interview with O. Torrijos Herrera. il U.S. News 83:18-23 S 19 '77
Panama: a search for independence. E. B. Burns. bibl f Cur Hist 72:65-7+ F '77
Panama and Suez. V. S. Kearney. America 137: 477-8 D 31 '77
Panama Canal:
Opposing argument. T. Wicker. Current 198: 54-5 D '77
Why the U.S. should keep it. S. Thurmond. Current 198:52-4 D '77
Panama Canal debate: Senate grasps the nettle. il U.S. News 83:30 O 10 '77
Panama Canal question; address, July 29, 1977. M. P. Du Val, Jr. Vital Speeches 43:685-9 S 1 '77
Panama Canal treaties. il Américas 29:9-15 N '77
Panama Canal treaties and related materials, including text of treaties. bibl maps Dept State Bull 77:481-545 O 17 '77
Panama Canal treaties: conservationists fear squatters will cut forests. E. M. Leeper. il map BioScience 27:717-20 N '77
Panama Canal treaties; statement, October 20, 1977. C. R. Vance. Dept State Bull 77:728-31 N 21 '77
Panama Canal treaty: it's no shoo-in. map Sr Schol 110:6+ O 20 '77
Panama Canal: use and ownership. P. A. Fitz-Gerald. America 137:473-6 D 31 '77
Panama Canal: what happens next. il Nations Bus 65:56-8+ O '77
Panama—clarification of current talks; Department statement. Dept State Bull 77:629 N 7 '77
Panama or Taiwan? J. Burnham. Nat R 29:1043 S 16 '77
Panama production. A Deming and others. il map Newsweek 90:46-8 S 19 '77
Panama—sí. W. F. Buckley, Jr. Nat R 29:1132-3 S 30 '77
Panama: turn of the tide? D. M. Alpern and J. J. Lindsay. il Newsweek 91:19 Ja 2 '78
Path to 1980. J. Lelyveld. il pors N Y Times Mag p 110 O 2 '77
President Carter discusses Panama Canal treaties; remarks, question and answer session, October 22, 1977. J. Carter. Dept State Bull 77:720-8 N 21 '77
President Carter's news conference of October 13, 1977. J. Carter. Dept State Bull 77:630 N 7 '77
Proposed treaty: preliminary thoughts. Nat R 29:981-3 S 2 '77; Discussion. 29:1082+ S 30 '77
Reagan on the Canal; excerpts from interview, ed by G. C. Lubenow. R. Reagan. por Newsweek 90:50 S 19 '77
Reagan speaks out. P. Bonventre and others. por Newsweek 90:37-8 S 5 '77
Real message to U.S. in that Panama plebiscite. il por U.S. News 83:61-2 N 7 '77
Relinquishing the Canal. M. D. Kent. Chr Cent 94:755-6 Ag 31 '77
Right to intervene. Nat R 29:1347-8 N 25 '77
Secretary Vance and other administration officials urge ratification of Panama Canal treaties; statements, September 26-27, 29-30, 1977. C. R. Vance and others. Dept State Bull 77:615-29 N 7 '77
Secretary Vance attends OAS General Assembly at Grenada; statement, June 15, 1977. C. R. Vance. Dept State Bull 77:72 Jl 18 '77
Should Senate OK Panama treaties? interviews. S. M. Linowitz; J. Helms. pors U.S. News 83:33-4 D 12 '77
Soft-selling the treaties. S. J. Ungar. Atlantic 240:16 D '77
Stand up and be counted. R. Steele and H. Bruno. il Newsweek 90:26-7 S 12 '77
Storm over the Canal. il Time 110:28 Ag 29 '77
That troublesome Panama Canal treaty; Time essay. E. Warner. il Time 110:26-7 O 31 '77
Timid illusions about Panama. Nation 225: 162-3 S 3 '77
Torrijos: the U.S. has lied; excerpts from interview, ed by R. Moreau. O. Torrijos. por Newsweek 89:41 Ap 25 '77
Treaties can't shoot. Nat R 29:1036 S 16 '77
Two thirds. New Repub 177:2+ S 10 '77
U.S.-Panama statement of understanding; transcript of press briefing, October 14, 1977. S. M. Linowitz. Dept State Bull 77:631-4 N 7 '77
Vox pop on Panama. Newsweek 90:48+ O 24 '77
We paid a price; interview, ed by R. Moreau. O. Torrijos Herrera. il por Newsweek 90:35 Ag 22 '77
Why we should leave Panama. D. C. Armstrong. por Newsweek 90:32-3 N 28 '77

Panama—History

Treaty rights acquired by the United States to construct the Panama Canal. bibl Dept State Bull 77:540-5 O 17 '77

Russia

Convention on Migratory Birds transmitted to Senate; message, July 18, 1977. J. Carter. Dept State Bull 77:326-7 S 5 '77
Ratification recommended for treaties with U.S.S.R. restricting nuclear testing; statements, July 28, 1977. P. C. Warnke; P. C. Habib. Dept State Bull 77:310-14 S 5 '77
U.S-U.S.S.R. communique on antiballistic missile systems; treaty review, November 21, 1977. Dept State Bull 77:856 D 12 '77

Uniformed Services University of the Health Sciences, Bethesda, Md.

Congress rescues military med school. P. M. Boffey. Science 196:742 My 13 '77
Demise of military med school likely. B. J. Culliton. Science 195:1309 Mr 25 '77
On again, off again: military's medical school. D. S. Greenberg. Sci Digest 81:73 Je '77

Urban Mass Transportation Administration

Anatomy of a boondoggle; funding of personal rapid transit system in Morgantown, W.Va. T. Armbrister. il Read Digest 111:133-6 Ag '77
$22 million in DOT funds available for elderly. Aging 275:6 S '77
UMTA streamlines paperwork. il Am City & County 92:60 S '77

Veterans Administration

Sixty million graves: the VA cemetery extravaganza. J. H. Kay. Nation 224:209-12 F 19 '77
Two new agency heads: study in contrasts. il pors U.S. News 82:60 Mr 14 '77

Veterans Administration hospitals

Death knell for veterans' hospitals? il U.S. News 83:53 Ag 1 '77
VA hospital system under scrutiny. C. Holden. Science 198:36 O 7 '77

War Department

First and forgotten pipeline; the War Department's Canol project. P. L. Fradkin. il pors map Audubon 79:58-79 N '77

Water Resources Council

Water policy requires comment now; study. S. Baxter. Am City & County 92:28 O '77

Weather bureau

See United States—National Weather Service

Work Projects Administration

See also
Federal Art Project

Youth Conservation Corps

Who can keep up with these kids in the woods? M. Wexler. il Nat Wildlife 15:40-3 F '77
YCC: a recipe for youth development. B. E. Matthews and C. H. Yaple. il pors Conservationist 32:11-12 S '77

UNITED STATES Air Force Academy, Colorado Springs
How women are faring at the Air Academy. G. Lichtenstein. il N Y Times Mag p 104-6+ S 11 '77
Mom, the cadet; ruling on pregnancy. il Time 110:14 N 28 '77

UNITED STATES and France. See France and the United States

UNITED STATES and Latin America. See Latin America and the United States

UNITED STATES and Russia. See Russia and the United States

UNITED STATES Bracket Nationals. See Drag racing

UNITED STATES Chamber of Commerce. See Chamber of Commerce of the United States of America

UNITED STATES Coast Guard Academy, New London, Conn.
At Coast Guard Academy: coed ships. U.S. News 83:29 Jl 11 '77

UNITED STATES Conference of Mayors
Mayors form task force on urban elderly. Aging 268:7-8 F '77

UNITED STATES Customs Service
Border dispute; question of installing P. Max's posters. Vasari. Art N 76:34+ N '77
Bringing plants from abroad? il Sunset 158:258 Ap '77
Combat on the border; Night rider patrol on U.S.-Mexican border. il pors Ebony 32:104-6+ Ap '77
Customs and preclearance. H. W. Shane. Travel 148:6 O '77
Customs plans turbine aircraft buy. E. J. Bulban. il Aviation W 106:57-8 Ap 11 '77
Customs reorganization and modernization; address, May 17, 1977. B. Anderson. Vital Speeches 43:621-3 Ag 1 '77
Dealing with customs. U.S. News 82:51 Mr 14 '77
Ins and outs of customs duties. Changing T 31:4 Ap '77
Red tape may capsize river rafts; invoking the Jones Act to ban foreign-made rafts. il Bus W p38 Mr 21 '77
Souvenirs you shouldn't bring back. J. Greenwald. il McCalls 104:66-7 My '77
Tricks that smugglers use—and how they get caught; interview. V. D. Acree. il por U.S. News 82:52-4 Mr 14 '77

UNITED STATES—Egypt Joint Working Group on Technology, Research and Development. See Technology—International aspects

UNITED STATES embassy, Tokyo. See Embassies (buildings)

UNITED STATES Feed Grains Council
They want to. . .double your feed grain exports. R. C. Black. il Farm J 101:28-9 N '77

UNITED STATES flag. See Flags—United States

UNITED STATES-France Cooperative Program in Oceanography. See Oceanography—International aspects

UNITED STATES-France Cooperative Science Program. See Science—International aspects

UNITED STATES Golf Association
To the right, to the left, hold it! USGA's preparation of Southern Hills course for U.S. Open. S. Pileggi. il Sports Illus 46:36-9 Je 13 '77

UNITED STATES Grand Prix. See Automobile racing

UNITED STATES in art
Looking at America. D. O'Brien. Commonweal 104:502-4 Ag 5 '77
See also
Western States in art

UNITED STATES Information Agency. See United States—Information Agency

UNITED STATES-Japan air agreement. See Aviation—International aspects

UNITED STATES Life Saving Service. See United States—Coast Guard—History

UNITED STATES Lines, Inc
Batten the hatches. por Forbes 120:156 O 15 '77
Sullivan's sow. por Forbes 119:64-5 F 1 '77

UNITED STATES marshals
See also
Government investigations—United States marshals

UNITED STATES Military Academy, West Point
Forestry at West Point. J. J. Karnig. il Am For 83:24-5+ F '77
How women are faring at West Point and Annapolis. G. Lichtenstein. il N Y Times Mag p 107 S 11 '77
Return of the EE 304s; honor code violators. il Time 110:29 S 19 '77
Second chance; reinstated cadets. E. Keerdoja. il Newsweek 90:11 Ag 8 '77
Silent treatment; case of J. J. Pelosi. E. Keerdoja. il por Newsweek 90:11 Ag 8 '77
West Point faces life. S. Kinzer. New Repub 177:14-17 D 3 '77
West Point log: the basic training of Joan Smith. M. Stamell. il pors Ms 6:48-51+ Ag '77
West Point woman; ed by V. Eads. K. Kinzler. il por Seventeen 36:74+ Ap '77

UNITED STATES National Bank of San Diego. See San Diego, Calif.—Banks

UNITED STATES Naval Academy, Annapolis
Boats in blue: sailing at the U.S. Naval Academy. A. M. Hays. Yachting 141:158+ Je '77
How old school ties help Carter fill jobs. il U.S. News 83:24 Ag 1 '77
How women are faring at West Point and Annapolis. G. Lichtenstein. il N Y Times Mag p 107 S 11 '77
Louise Burke; Naval Academy sailing coach. A. M. Hays. il pors Yachting 142:74-5 Jl '77

UNITED STATES Postal Service
AAP acts on four fronts dealing with postal matters. S. Wagner. il Pub W 211:25+ Ja 17 '77
Citizen Bailar; proposed citizen's rate as sign of collapse of Postal Service. R. J. Myers. New Repub 177:6 Jl 23 '77
Congress begins hearings on postal recommendations. S. Wagner. Pub W 211:32+ My 16 '77
Improving Postal Service; postal reorganization bill, H.R. 7700. Chr Today 22:27 D 30 '77
In the black. D. Pauly and J. B. Copeland. Newsweek 89:83-4 F 21 '77
Mail service: better, but—excerpts from address, February 7, 1977. B. F. Bailar. por U.S. News 82:81 F 14 '77
Never on Saturday? findings of congressional commission. Time 109:77-8 Ap 25 '77
Soft answers by U.S. Postal Service turn away publishers' wrath. S. Wagner. Pub W 211:43-4 F 21 '77
Still trying to make the post office work. il por Bus W p 133+ Mr 21 '77
Their (dis)appointed rounds; P. H. Brennan Hand Delivery Service in competition with United States Postal Service in Rochester, N.Y. R Brookhiser. il Nat R 29:1294-6 N 11 '77
U.S. Postal Service: troubled giant heading for change; with interview with B. F. Bailar. il U.S. News 82:51-4 Ap 25 '77
See also
Postal rates—United States
Railway mail service

UNITED STATES Power Squadrons, Inc
People on the cover; USPS and their discrimination against women. A. L. Ball. Redbook 149:3 My '77

UNITED STATES Revenue Cutter Service. See United States—Coast Guard—History

UNITED STATES-Spanish Council
Secretary Vance attends Spanish-U.S. Council meeting at Madrid and CENTO Council of Ministers meeting at Tehran; remarks, with news conference, statement and communiques, May 11-15, 1977. C. R. Vance. Dept State Bull 76:610-12 Je 6 '77
United States-Spanish Council holds semiannual meeting; joint communique, September 30, 1977. Dept State Bull 77:680-1 N 14 '77

UNITED STATES Steel Corporation
EPA's big win. Time 109:63-4 Je 27 '77
High noon at Clairton. J. G. Mitchell. Audubon 79:128-36 Ja '77

UNITED STATES Tobacco Company. See Tobacco industry—United States

UNITED STATES Trust Company of New York
Chasing the coupon clippers. il por Forbes 119:56-7 My 1 '77

UNITED STATES-USSR Joint Commission on Scientific and Technical Cooperation. See Science—International aspects

UNITED STATES Yacht Racing Union
Pratt Project update; meeting of the USYRU Handicap Rule Committee. O. C. Torrey, Jr. Yachting 142:30 Jl '77

UNITED Steelworkers of America
Activism takes over at the USW. il por Bus W p77-8 Je 6 '77
Coke and cancer: it's up to the steelworkers. F. Goldsmith and D. Freedman. Nation 224:113-16 Ja 29 '77
Coming revolt in labor. S. Lens. Progressive 41:26-30 Ap '77
Election crisis in the coalfields. il Bus W p30-1 Je 13 '77
Hard line on lifetime security; can-manufacturing industry. il Bus W p33-4 O 31 '77
How lifetime security might work; USW bargaining program. Bus W p28 F 28 '77
Lifetime pay, come what may. Fortune 95:71 Ap '77
Lifetime security in steel? il Time 109:45 F 28 '77
McBride apparent victor in Steelworkers contest. L. Bornstein and others. M Labor R 100:84 Ap '77
McBride for Abel. C. O. Rice. Commonweal 104:166-7 Mr 18 '77
No go for Oilcan Eddie; election results. por Time 109:67 F 21 '77
Steel industry's expensive settlement. Bus W p28-9 Ap 25 '77
Steel: the ins have it. T. Nicholson and others. pors Newsweek 89:76 F 21 '77
Steelworkers' election grows to a national issue. il pors Bus W p69-71 Ja 24 '77
Steelworkers go for McBride. Bus W p31 F 21 '77
Steelworkers' vote: can a union have too much democracy? F. W. Frailey. U.S. News 82:69 F 21 '77
Steelworkers win enhanced employment security. L. Bornstein and others. M Labor R 100:62-3 Je '77
Struggle in steel; question of union president elections. K. Bode. New Repub 176:10-13 F 5 '77

UNITED Technologies Corporation
UTC prepares for shuttle booster role. Aviation W 106:15 Ja 3 '77

Pratt and Whitney Aircraft Group

IAM locals at P&W work under new labor contract. W. C. Wetmore. Aviation W 107:24 D 12 '77

Sikorsky Aircraft Division

Tale of two cities; UTTAS contract awarded to Sikorsky. E. Shields. il Time 109:51+ F 14 '77

UNITED Technologies Corporation-Babcock & Wilcox Company merger. See Corporations—Acquisitions and mergers

UNITED Transportation Union
For railroads, labor—some crucial bargaining. il U.S. News 82:97-8 My 16 '77

UNITED Way of America (organization)
Religious tension in Saint Cloud. J. M. Wall. Chr Cent 94:1019-20 N 9 '77
United Way: are the criticisms fair? il Changing T 31:29-31 O '77
Voluntarism in America: a realistic look ahead; address, May 23, 1977. J. W. Hanley. Vital Speeches 43:634-7 Ag 1 '77
Voluntarism in America; address, April 25, 1977. V. E. Jordan, Jr. Vital Speeches 43:493-5 Je 1 '77

UNITING Church in Australia
Uniting Church: new days, new ways. R. Mathias. il Chr Cent 94:786-7 S 14 '77

UNIVERSAL Declaration of Human Rights
30-year struggle; with text. K. Vasak. UNESCO Courier 30:29-32 N '77

UNIVERSAL Foods Corporation. See Food industry

UNIVERSAL Limited Art Editions (firm) See Publishers and publishing—Art

UNIVERSE
Collapsing universe; excerpt. I. Asimov. por Sci Digest 81:12-16+ Je '77
Key to the universe; excerpt. N. Calder. il Sci Digest 81:58-63+ Je '77
Unfolding universe; the 13,000,000,000-year bang. M. Rees. Current 190:51-9 F '77
See also
Cosmology
Creation
Galaxies

UNIVERSITIES. See Colleges and universities

UNIVERSITY Club. See Tampa, Fla.—Clubs

UNIVERSITY extension
Open learning and guidelines for the design of instructional materials. D. C. Forman and P. Richardson. Educ Digest 42:41-4 Ap '77

UNIVERSITY facilities. See College facilities

UNIVERSITY libraries. See College libraries

UNIVERSITY of London. See Colleges and universities—Great Britain

UNIVERSITY of Minnesota; University of Pittsburgh; etc. See Minnesota. University, Minneapolis; Pittsburgh. University; etc.

UNIVERSITY Opera Studio. See Opera—New York (state)

UNIVERSITY police force. See Colleges and universities—Security measures

UNIVERSITY presidents. See College presidents

UNIVERSITY presses
Academe's own printing houses. J. B. Breslin. America 136:302-3 Ap 2 '77
HUP, MIT share warehousing facilities to reduce costs and improve service. B. McCabe. il Pub W 211:58+ Mr 28 '77
NEH gives 14 grants to 10 university presses. S. Wagner. Pub W 212:18 N 21 '77
Temple University: starting a press in the 70s. M. English. por Pub W 212:37-40 Jl 4 '77
See also
Association of American University Presses

UNIVERSITY research. See Colleges and universities—Research

UNIVERSITY Savings Association-Entex, Inc merger. See Corporations—Acquisitions and mergers

UNIVERSITY students. See College students

UNIVERSITY teachers. See College teachers

UNMARRIED couples
America's single couples. il pors Harp Baz 110:108-21+ My '77
Assortative mating by unwed biological parents of adopted children. R. Plomin and others. bibl il Science 196:449-50 Ap 22 '77
Case against living together; interview, ed by C. Remsberg and B. Remsberg. N. M. Clatworthy. Seventeen 36:132-3+ N '77
How to make love not war; counseling for unmarried couples. M. Fabe. Mademoiselle 83:119+ D '77
Living together. C. B. Abbott; M. Pulik. il Am Home 80:35-6+ O '77
Living together. T. Schwartz and others. il Newsweek 90:46-50 Ag 1 '77
Marriage counseling for unwed couples. A. Gross. N Y Times Mag p52+ Ap 24 '77
New family groupings; interviews, ed by J. Neary. il Parents Mag 52:56-7+ O '77
New look at living together. J. Hassett. il Psychol Today 11:82-3 D '77
Pros and cons of living together. L. Norment. il Ebony 33:94-6+ D '77
Straight talk about the living-together arrangement. L. Montague. Read Digest 110:91-4 Ap '77
To have and to hold from this day. . .to the next. C. Musello. Ms 6:57+ N '77
What do you do. . .if your young people start living together? il Farm J 101:46-7+ N '77
Without benefit of clergy—or commitment. Chr Today 21:32-3 Mr 4 '77

Legal status, laws, etc.

How to protect your legal rights. J. Faier. Harp Baz 110:118-19+ My '77
Lover's guide to living together legally. R. Warner and T. Ihara. Ms 6:54-6+ N '77
What are your rights? C. B. Abbott. Am Home 80:36+ O '77

UNMARRIED mothers. See Mothers, Unmarried

UNMARRIED women. See Single women

UNPUBLISHED Library. See New York (city)—Libraries

UNRUH, Jesse Marvin
Unruh to the rescue. C. McWilliams. Nation 224:613-14 My 21 '77 *

UNSUNG Cole; revue. See Musical comedy, revue, etc.—Reviews—Single works

UNTEL, Carlos
No-lose elections. Nat R 29:1297-8 N 11 '77

UNTERECKER, John
Hospital; poem. Poetry 130:134-9 Je '77
Within, into, inside, under, within. . .; poem. Poetry 129:311-13 Mr '77

UNTERKOEFLER, Ernest L. Bp
Always pray and do not lose heart. il New Cath World 220:46-8 Ja '77

UNTERMEYER, Chase
From Peking to Lhasa—a 16-day journey through China. il U.S. News 83:35-7 N 14 '77

UNTERMYER Collection. See Metropolitan Museum of Art, New York

UPDIKE, John
Books. New Yorker 53:128-30+ Mr 21 '77
Dream and reality; poem. New Yorker 52:34 Ja 24 '77
Egg race; story. New Yorker 53:36-40 Je 13 '77
Guilt-gems; story. New Yorker 53:39-41 S 19 '77
Rats; poem. Atlantic 239:34 F '77

about

John Updike's theological world. R. K. Johnston. por Chr Cent 94:1061-6 N 16 '77 *

UPDIKE family
Updike coat-of-arms. H. K. Eilers. bibl il Hobbies 82:150-1 N '77

UPFIELD, Arthur W.
Murder in the outback. J. G. Cawelti. New Repub 177:39-41 Jl 30 '77 *

UPHOLSTERY
Concerned homemaker expresses her views on furniture flammability legislation; proposed flammable upholstered furniture law. M. Nervig. Consumers Res Mag 60:27+ Je '77
Great cover-up; reupholstering. J. Mark. il Pop Mech 148:128-30+ N '77
Upholstery in 6 easy lessons. D. Hardie. il House & Gard 149:66+ My '77
Upholstery upkeep. Bet Hom & Gard 54:31 Ag '76

UPHOLSTERY fabric. See Textile fabrics

UPHOLT, William B.
Superhelix densities of circular DNA's: a generalized equation for their determination by the buoyant method. bibl Science 195:891 Mr 4 '77

UPPER classes
Children of affluence; excerpt from Privileged ones: the well-off and the rich in America. R. Coles. il Atlantic 240:52-8+ S '77
Domestic manners of the English. L. Lewis. Atlantic 240:92+ N '77
See also
Rich, The

UPTON, Arthur Canfield
Talk with the new head of the NCI; interview, ed by W. Barnhill. il por Fam Health 9:6+ O '77

about

Arthur Canfield Upton: new director of the NCI. B. J. Culliton. por Science 197:737-9 Ag 19 '77 *

UPTON, King. See Aldrich, P. C. jt auth

UPWARD Bound (program) See Socially handicapped children—Education

URANIUM
Hot plankton; uranium deposit creation by coccolith plankton. Newsweek 90:81 D 12 '77

Prices

Corporate Patty Hearst; investigating Gulf's role in uranium cartel price fixing. D. Pauly. Newsweek 89:69 Je 27 '77
Darkening storm over Gulf; membership in uranium price-fixing cartel. il Time 109:62-3 Je 27 '77
Issues on trial in the Westinghouse lawsuits; suits charging failure to deliver on uranium supply contracts brought by electric utilities. Bus W p 125-6+ S 26 '77
More U.S. pressure on a uranium cartel; investigation of alleged pricefixing. Bus W p26-7 Ag 29 '77
Uranium cartel's fallout. il Time 110:96+ N 21 '77
Uranium pattern Westinghouse buys. Bus W p33 D 26 '77
Uranium thing; utilities suing Westinghouse over uranium contracts. A. J. Mayer and P. L. Abraham. il Newsweek 89:73 F 14 '77

Transportation

Uranium: the Israeli connection. il map Time 109:32-4 My 30 '77

URANIUM enrichment. See Uranium metallurgy
URANIUM industry
Little company with lots of uranium; United Nuclear Corp. il Forbes 119:45 Je 1 '77

Australia

Bird in the bush; Pancontinental Mining. M. Dammerman. por Forbes 119:31-2 Je 15 '77
URANIUM metallurgy
Captive market escapes; enriched uranium. M. Dammerman. Forbes 119:92+ My 15 '77
Enrichment by centrifugation; gas-centrifuge approach to separating uranium isotopes. Sci Am 237:52+ Ag '77
Government gambles on the centrifuge. il Bus W p 100-1 My 30 '77
Laser enrichment: a new path to proliferation? B. M. Casper. bibl il Bull Atom Sci 33:28-41 Ja '77; Discussion. 33:3 Ap; 54-6 Je '77
Laser enrichment of uranium: the proliferation connection. A. S. Krass. bibl il Science 196:721-31 My 13 '77
URANIUM miners
Manpower gap at uranium mines. il Bus W p32 N 7 '77
URANIUM mines and mining

Gabon

Natural fossil nuclear reactor. il Bull Atom Sci 33:40-1 F '77

Namibia

Namibia spells uranium. M. Bailey. Nation 224:525-7 Ap 30 '77

United States

United States uranium resources—an analysis of historical data. M. A. Lieberman; discussion. bibl Science 196:600-1+ My 6 '77
URANIUM ores
Natural fossil nuclear reactor. il Bull Atom Sci 33:40-1 F '77
URANUS (planet)
Reports on Neptune and Uranus. il Sky & Tel 53:429-30 Je '77
See also
Space flight—Voyager flights

Ring system

Discoverers provide details of Uranus rings. Space World N-8-164:25 Ag '77
Discovering the rings of Uranus. J. L. Elliot and others. Sky & Tel 53:412-16+ Je '77
Evidence of Uranus rings grows. il Aviation W 106:85 Ap 25 '77
Occultation observations reveal ring system around Uranus. F. C. Bennett. bibl il Phys Today 30:17+ Je '77
Resonances of Uranus. Sci Am 237:57 Ag '77
Rings around Uranus. S. P. Maran. Natur Hist 86:88+ Ag '77
Rings around Uranus. il Time 109:73 Ap 11 '77
Rings of Uranus. Sky & Tel 53:331 My '77
Rings of Uranus: news and views. il Sci N 112:52 Jl 23 '77
Strange rings of Uranus. il Sci N 111:245 Ap 16 '77
Uranus believed to be ringed by five belts. Aviation W 106:23 Ap 4 '77
Uranus: the rings are black. W. M. Sinton. bibl il Science 198:503-4 N 4 '77

Satellites

See Satellites
URBAN administration. See Municipal government
URBAN communes. See Collective settlements
URBAN Development Action Grant program (proposed) See Urban renewal
URBAN Development, Department of. See United States—Housing and Urban Development, Department of
URBAN ecology, Human. See Human ecology
URBAN economics
Insurance redlining: a new urban setback. J. De Muth. America 137:438-40 D 17 '77
URBAN education. See Education, Urban
URBAN flora
San Salvador's urban orchids. P. Bernhardt. il Natur Hist 86:64-71 D '77
See also
Trees in cities
URBAN forests. See Trees in cities
URBAN growth. See Cities and towns—Growth
URBAN homesteading
Homesteading in Hartford. E. V. Warren. il House B 119:10+ F '77
New urban pioneers: homesteading in the slums; People's Development Corporation. R. M. Williams. il Sat R 4:8-14 Jl 23 '77
People fire in the ghetto ashes. W. G. Conway. il Sat R 4:15-16 Jl 23 '77
URBAN housing. See Housing
URBAN League, National. See National Urban League

URBAN Libraries Council
Urban Libraries Council picks up members and steam. H. E. Rosenfeld. il Wilson Lib Bull 51:565 Mr '77
URBAN life. See City and town life
URBAN Mass Transportation Administration. See United States—Urban Mass Transportation Administration
URBAN planning. See City planning
URBAN poverty. See Poor—United States
URBAN recreation. See Recreation—United States
URBAN redevelopment. See Urban renewal
URBAN renewal
Energy problems and our cities: solving two problems jointly. F. G. Rohatyn. Current 196:3-6 O '77
Erosion of aid to the cities. por Bus W p36 Ag 15 '77
Hold harmless cities may get reprieve; Urban Development Action Grant program. Am City & County 92:35 Je '77
Saving our cities; special section. il Sat R 4:6-8+ My 14 '77
See also
Business districts
City planning
Urban homesteading
URBAN-rural conflict. See City and country
URBAN services. See Municipal services
URBAN sociology. See Sociology, Urban
URBAN transportation
See also
Local transit
United States—Urban Mass Transportation Administration
URBAN trees. See Trees in cities
URBANA Student Missionary Conference. See Inter-Varsity Christian Fellowship
URBANI, Giovanni
Giovanni Urbani and restoration Italian-style. M. Gendel. il por Art N 76:146-8 Summ '77 •
URBANIZATION
There was a little town; reproductions of paintings; excerpt from The changing countryside. J. Müller. il Read Digest 111:45-7 S '77
URBANIZED areas. See Metropolitan areas
URCA, Gideon, and others
Morphine and enkephalin: analgesic and epileptic properties. bibl il Science 197:83-6 Jl 1 '77
URDANG, Constance
Comment. W. Logan. Poetry 130:223-5 Jl '77 •
UREA
See also
Feeds—Urea
URGINEA maritima. See Sea-onions
URINARY organs
See also
Genito-urinary organs
URINE
See also
Cystinuria
URNS
Henry Clay's silver urn. il Antiques 112:112 Jl '77
URSULINES. See Sisterhoods
URUGUAY
See also
Montevideo

Economic policy

Authoritarian Uruguay. A. C. Porzecanski. Cur Hist 72:73-5+ F '77

Foreign relations

United States

See United States—Foreign relations—Uruguay

Politics and government

Authoritarian Uruguay. A. C. Porzecanski. Cur Hist 72:73-5+ F '77
URUGUAYAN prints. See Prints
USDIN, Gene L.
(ed) Books. See issues of MH
USE of time. See Time, Use of
USED automobiles. See Automobiles, Used
USED cameras. See Cameras, Used
USED car dealers. See Automobile dealers
USED computers. See Computers, Used
USEFUL Services Exchange. See Volunteer service
USHER, D. A.
Early chemical evolution of nucleic acids: a theoretical model. bibl il Science 196:311-13 Ap 15 '77
USHIBA, Nobuhiko
Ushiba: maneuvering room; excerpts from interview, ed by B. Krisher. il por Newsweek 91:32 Ja 9 '78
USINGER, William R. and others
Lymphocyte-defined loci in cattle. bibl il Science 196:1017-18 My 27 '77

USLANDER, Arlene S. and others
When kids explore sex; excerpt from Sex education for today's child. il Parents Mag 52: 44-5+ Ag '77

USLAR PIETRI, Arturo
Bolivar and the Congress of Panama. il por UNESCO Courier 30:28-32 F '77
Out of the tropics, and avant-garde art. il UNESCO Courier 30:30-8+ Ag '77

USTINOV, Peter
How I defeated the Germans; excerpt from Dear me. il Atlantic 240:67-9+ Ag '77

USTON, Kenneth
Hit me! T. Schwartz. il por Newsweek 89:58 Je 27 '77 *

USU, Mount (volcano) See Volcanoes

UTAH
See also
Air pollution—Utah
Arches National Park
Automobile touring—Utah
Birds—Utah
Colorado Plateau
Courts—Utah
Fishing—Utah
Great Salt Lake
Natural Bridges National Monument
Organic gardening—Utah
Powell, Lake
Public welfare—Utah
Rainbow Bridge National Monument
Skis and skiing—Utah

Description and travel

Last oasis; exploring the Escalante Canyon in Utah. E. Abbey. il Harpers 254:8+ Mr '77

Industries

Utah proposes blueprint for industrial development. Nat Parks & Con Mag 51:22+ Ap '77

Parks and reserves

Undulating ocean of sand; Coral Pink Sand Dunes State Reserve. il Sunset 158:42 Je '77

Religious institutions and affairs

See also
Mormons and Mormonism

UTAH International, Inc-General Electric Company merger. See Corporations—Acquisitions and mergers

UTAH State Hospital. See Hospitals, Psychiatric

UTAH. University, Salt Lake City
U of U is reason enough for a Salt Lake stopover. il Sunset 159:49 S '77

UTERUS
Uterotrophic effect of delta-9-tetrohydrocannabinol in ovariectomized rats. J. Solomon and others; reply with rejoinder. A. B. Okey and G. P. Bondy. bibl Science 195:904-6 Mr 4 '77
See also
Cervix

Muscle

See Muscle

UTILITIES, Public. See Public utilities

UTILITIES and Industries Corporation. See Conglomerate corporations

UTILITY holding companies. See Holding companies

UTILITY poles, Wood. See Wood poles

UTILITY rates. See Public utilities—Rates

UTILIZATION of land. See Land utilization

UTLEY, Robert M.
Perspectives on the past. Am Hist Illus 12:50 Je '77
(ed) See Barnitz, A. and Barnitz, J. P. Campaigning with Custer

UTOPIAS
On utopianism; excerpt from Visions of utopia. J. Egerton. Progressive 41:20-1 Jl '77

UTOPIAS in literature. See Literature—Themes

UTTAL, Bro
Exxon has its eye on more than oil. Fortune 95:166-8 Ap '77
Gene Amdahl takes aim at I.B.M. il por Fortune 96:106-10+ S '77
How Ray Macdonald's growth theory created I.B.M.'s toughest competitor. il pors Fortune 95:94-9+ Ja '77
I.B.M. reaches for a golden future in the heavens. il Fortune 95:172-6+ Je '77
Ride is getting scarier for theme park owners. il map Fortune 96:166-72+ D '77

UTZ, Thornton
Family at Thanksgiving; reproductions of paintings. Ladies Home J 94:109+ N '77

UY, Rosa, and Wold, Finn
Posttranslational covalent modification of proteins. bibl il Science 198:890-6 D 2 '77

UZZLE, Burk
Hell on two wheels; photographs. il Sports Illus 46:30-4 Mr 14 '77

V

VA. See United States—Veterans Administration

VA hospitals. See United States—Veterans Administration hospitals

VD. See Venereal diseases

VFW-Fokker (firm) See Aerospace industries—Europe, Western

VISTA (Volunteers in Service to America) See United States—ACTION

VMOS (vertical metal oxide semiconductor) transistors. See Transistors

VOM. See Voltohmmeters

VTN (firm) See Engineering construction companies

VTOL airplanes. See Airplanes, Vertical take-off and landing

VW (automobile) See Automobiles, Foreign

VACATION condominiums. See Condominium (housing)

VACATION houses
Arango house, Acapulco. il Archit Rec 161:64-7 mid-My '77
At home in half a barn; weekend home of the Winthrop Faulkners. N. Skurka. il N Y Times Mag p56-8 F 20 '77
Chapell residence, eastern Long Island. il Archit Rec 161:76-7 mid-My '77
Come up to comfort; weekend house on Long Island. il House & Gard 149:86-9 Ag '77
Delightful weekend retreat at the Sea Ranch. il Archit Rec 161:147-50 Ja '77
Easy living. B. Niles. il Am Home 80:46-9+ Je '77
Maxey residence, Wayne County, Pennsylvania. il Archit Rec 161:74-5 mid-My '77
PS leisure home of the month:
Atrium house—you build it in stages for progressive privacy. A. Lees. il Pop Sci 124-5+ O '77
Cool house for a hot climate. R. Gannon. il Pop Sci 212:90-3+ Ja '78
Fireproof retreat. A. Lees. il Pop Sci 211: 106-7 S '77
Hex cluster. il Pop Sci 210:144 Ap '77
King-post pagoda. A. Lees. il Pop Sci 210: 122 My '77
Octagon on piers. A. Lees. il Pop Sci 210: 132 F '77
Peak house on stilts. il Pop Sci 221:91+ Jl '77
Skewed-prow two-story. A. Lees. il Pop Sci 210:113+ Mr '77
Split-level twin shed. A. Lees. il Pop Sci 211:123 Ag '77
Sun cottage for all seasons. A. Lees. il Pop Sci 211:93 D '77
Sun trap. A. Lees. il Pop Sci 211:118-19 N '77
Two-phase split pavilions. A. Lees. il Pop Sci 210:102-3 Je '77
Private residence, eastern Long Island; weekend house. il Archit Rec 161:54-5 mid-My '77
Unfinished house; building a weekend retreat. P. H. Matson. Am Home 80:24 D '77
See also
Beach architecture

Leasing and renting

Directory of timeshare resorts; condominium apartments and vacation homes. C. Burlingame. Holiday 58:16+ S '77
New twists on vacation rentals. S. Birnbaum. Esquire 88:38+ S '77
Time-sharing: new way to buy a vacation home. il Changing T 32:40-2 Ja '78

VACATION houses, Condominium. See Condominium (housing)

VACATION travel clubs. See Travel clubs

VACATION villages
Club Med—everything you want. D. Messinesi. Vogue 167:98+ Je '77
Happy summer! Club Med at Cap Skirring, Senegal. il Vogue 167:208-9 My '77

VACATIONS
Big-city weekends: two on the town. Bet Hom & Gard 55:233+ O; 233+ N '77
Earthwatch expeditions are the real thing; search for shipwrecks near Palma de Mallorca. G. Goshgarian. Todays Educ 66:67-9 Mr '77
Falling leaves, falling prices; vacations in mountain resorts. J. Wood. il Sat Eve Post 249: 90-2 S '77
Farm & ranch vacations. G. Bush. il Bet Hom & Gard 55:114-17 Je '77
5 great do-it-yourself vacations. E. L. Rogers. il Pop Mech 147:101-3+ My '77
Great spots for your family vacation. B. Mack. il Harp Baz 110:4+ Jl '77
Great springtime vacations along the Gulf of Mexico. G. Bush. il Bet Hom & Gard 55: 173-4+ F '77
House exchanging: a way to go and stay awhile. H. Dennis. il Ret Liv 17:27-9 Jl '77

VACATIONS—*Continued*
How to avoid the high cost of motels. L. David. il Mech Illus 73:54+ Ag '77
Last-minute tips for summer vacationers. il U.S. News 82:52-4 My 30 '77
Learn-to-do-something-new vacations (cont) il Bet Hom & Gard 55:199-200+ Ap; 175-6+ Jl '77
Mini-holiday. B. Jeffer. See issues of Holiday
My vacation was nifty; diversions of football players. R. F. Jones. il Sports Illus 47:62-6+ Jl 11 '77
New ways to save on vacation. L. David. il Mech Illus 73:54-5+ Je '77
Or better yet—leave it all behind; winter vacations. Changing T 31:12-13 N '77
Psychiatrist's notebook; vacation blues. T. I. Rubin. Ladies Home J 94:70 Jl '77
Redbook traveler. il Redbook 148:37-44 F '77
Summer. F. Sweeney. America 136:563 Je 25 '77
Surefire ways to ruin your summer vacation. J. Mayer. il Fam Health 9:22-4 Ag '77
Tips for winter vacations. il U.S. News 83:39-42 N 7 '77
Try a campus vacation. F. Cross. il Read Digest 110:92-5 My '77
Vacation bargains. Mech Illus 73:30 Jl '77
Vacation planner; special section. il Am Home 80:38-42+ Ap '77
Vacations for adventurers only; World Expeditionary Association trips. il Mademoiselle 83:116-18+ S '77
Where to go. M. Worby. See issues of Outdoor life
Working vacations in the wilds. J. Marks. McCalls 104:69 My '77
See also
Travel

VACAVALLEY raceways. See Speedways

VACCA, Richard T.
Teaching English: a view from the middle. bibl Engl J 66:42-6 Ap '77

VACCINATION
Shot in time; vaccinations for adults. Mademoiselle 83:126 Jl '77
See also
Children—Diseases—Preventive inoculation
Influenza—Preventive inoculation
Measles—Preventive inoculation
Smallpox—Preventive inoculation
Whooping cough—Preventive inoculation

VACCINES
Anti-pneumonia shots and other new vaccines. Harp Baz 110:95 Ap '77
Bacteriophages in live virus vaccines: lack of evidence for effects on the genome of rhesus monkeys. J. B. Milstien and others. bibl il Science 197:469-70 Jl 29 '77
Our last vaccine? A. M. Prince. Science 195: 1287 Mr 25 '77
See also
Gonorrhea—Vaccines
Herpesvirus diseases—Vaccines
Influenza—Vaccines
Pneumonia—Vaccines
Poliomyelitis—Vaccines

VACHON, Brian
Be a billboard artist. Writers Digest 57:26 Ap '77

VACQUIER, Victor D.
Hooks and eyes of sperm and eggs. il Sci N 112:356 N 26 '77 *

VACUOLES
Gas vacuoles of blue-green algae. A. E. Walsby. il Sci Am 237:90-7 bibl(p 140) Ag '77

VACUUM
See also
American Vacuum Society

VACUUM apparatus
How to check vacuum systems. W. O. Koehler. il Pop Sci 212:106+ Ja '78

VACUUM cleaners
Cleaning appliances. il Consumers Res Mag 60:59-64 O '77
Penney's light weight vac. H. Wicks. il Pop Mech 148:46 D '77
Vacuum cleaners. Consumer Rep 42:308-15 D '77
What kind of vacuum cleaner do you need? il Redbook 148:114+ F '77

Manufacture

Royal: selling high-priced quality; Royal Appliance Manufacturing. N. Howard. il Duns R 110:52 O '77

VACUUM refuse collection. See Refuse and refuse disposal

VAGINAL spermicides. See Contraceptives

VAGINITIS
Infection inspection. P. Raber. Seventeen 36: 56 Mr '77

VAGRANCY
See also
Tramps

VAILLANT, George E.
Climb to maturity: how the best and brightest came of age; excerpt from Adaptation to life. il Psychol Today 11:34-5+ S '77
Lessons of the Grant Study; interview, ed by H. Muson. il por Psychol Today 11:42+ S '77

about
Living well is more than the best revenge. por Forbes 120:62-3 D 1 '77 *

VAITSES, Allan H.
Laminating fiberglass over wood. il Motor B & S 140:97-100 D '77

VALDERRAMA, Sara
Pilgrimage to La Tirana. il Américas 29:17-20 Ag '77

VALDES, Ching
Reviews: performances at the American Theatre Lab. S. Small. Dance Mag 51:34 Ag '77 *

VALDES, Rodrigo
Star bows out, a star bows in. P. Putnam. il pors Sports Illus 47:20-1 Ag 8 '77 *

VALDEZ, Raul, and Alamia, L. V.
Fecund mouflon; with biographical sketches. il Natur Hist 86:8, 72-7 bibl(p 119) N '77

VALDEZ, Alaska
Valdez connection. P. L. Fradkin. maps Audubon 79:134-40 Mr '77

VÁLEK, Jiří
Symphonies nos. 8 and 9. B. Pernick. Am Rec G 40:45-6 O '77 *

VALENTINA Oumansky Dramatic Dance Ensemble. See Dance companies

VALENTINE, Charles
$660,000 farewell. H. Johnson. il pors Ebony 32:47-8+ F '77 *

VALENTINE, William N. and others
Hereditary hemolytic anemia with increased red cell adenosine deaminase (45- to 70-fold) and decreased adenosine triphosphate. bibl il Science 195:783-5 F 25 '77

VALENTINES
Valentines. il Hobbies 81:116-17 F '77

VALENTINES Day

Drama

Cupivac. C. Boiko. Plays 36:47-52 F '77

VALENTINES Day cookery. See Cookery, Ornamental

VALENTINO, Rudolph
Nureyev leaps into film as Valentino. W. Terry. il pors Sat R 4:29-32 Ap 30 '77 *
Nureyev's Valentino tango. J. Gruen. il por Vogue 167:148-9+ Ag '77 *

VALENTINO
Festive Roman Christmas. il por Harp Baz 111: 102-3+ D '77

VALERIANI, G. See Arny, T. jt auth

VALGARDSON, W. D.
Couch; story. Sat Eve Post 249:52-3 Ap '77

VALIUM. See Tranquilizing drugs

VALLANZASCA, Renato
Love thief. K. Willenson. il por Newsweek 89: 46+ Mr 7 '77 *

VALLARTA, Manuel Sandoval
Obituary
Phys Today 30:70 D '77. R. Gall

VALLE, José Cecilio del
José Cecilio del Valle. il pors Américas 29:7-14 Ag '77 *

VALLEE, Bert Lester
Harvard and Monsanto: the $23-million alliance. B. J. Culliton. pors Science 195:759-63 F 25 '77 *

VALLEY FORGE, Pa.
Valley Forge: tragedy to triumph; winter, 1777-78. il U.S. News 83:57 D 26 '77

VALLEY National Monument
Burro or the boghorn? R. B. Taylor. il Nat Parks & Con Mag 51:10-14 S '77

VALLEYS
See also
Dells of the Wisconsin (valley)
Submarine valleys

VALUATION
See also
Art—Valuation
Assessment
Corporations—Valuation
Real property—Valuation

VALUE of college education. See College education, Value of

VALUE of education. See Education, Value of

VALUES
God and science: new allies in the search for values; symposium. il Sat R 5:13-23+ D 10 '77

Study and teaching

Achievement values reinforcement in public schools. F. P. Bazeli. bibl Clearing H 51:78-80 O '77
Colleges challenge value-free education; program developed by Fordham College. R. J. Roth. America 136:324-6 Ap 9 '77
Implementation strategy for values clarification. S. Toll. il Clearing H 50:385-9 My '77
Values education in the junior high school; ERIC/RCS report. T. Olsen. Engl J 66:88-91 Ap '77
Values; symposium. il Todays Educ 66:62-77 Ja; 28-30+ S '77

VALUES, Social. See Social values

VALVES
See also
Automobile engines—Valves

Manufacture

Financial controls help a valve maker expand; Mark Controls Corporation. il por Bus W p47-8 Ag 1 '77

VAN decoration
$50 van interior. il Hot Rod 30:68+ Mr '77
Van art. D. K. Hall. il Esquire 88:115-17 S '77
Winners in PM's paint-job photo contest. il Pop Mech 148:100-1+ S '77

VAN pools. See Automobile pools

VAN ALLEN, Bob
Magic is the balance of creativity & useability; converted garment-factory loft in Manhattan's SoHo; interview, ed by M. Gough and others. il por House B 119:140-5+ S '77

VAN BAVEL, Cornelius H. M.
Soil and oil. Science 197:213 Jl 15 '77

VAN BRUNT, Jennifer. See Harold, F. M. jt auth

VAN BUREN, Paul M.
Four stories of theology; with editorial comment. T. H. Stahel. America 136:inside cover, 230-3 Mr 19 '77 *

VANCASPEL, Venita
Where women should invest their money; interview. il por U.S. News 83:33-4 D 5 '77

VANCE, Cyrus Roberts
America's role in consolidating a peaceful balance and promoting economic growth in Asia; address, June 29, 1977. Dept State Bull 77:141-5 Ag 1 '77
Cyrus Vance sizes up 11 global issues. U.S. News 82:30 F 21 '77
Department urges passage of bill to halt importation of Rhodesian chrome; statement, February 10, 1977. Dept State Bull 76:170-2 F 28 '77
Employment practices in South Africa; remarks, October 5, 1977. Dept State Bull 77:685-6 N 14 '77
Goal of real peace; address, November 10, 1977. Dept State Bull 77:763-6 N 28 '77
Human rights and foreign policy; address, with question and answer session, April 30, 1977. Dept State Bull 76:505-12 My 23 '77
Interview with Secretary Vance on February 8 by Egyptian and Syrian media representatives; transcript of interview, ed by A. Fawzi and G. Rifai. Dept State Bull 76:224-8 Mr 14 '77
Interview with Secretary Vance on February 10 by Israeli media representatives; transcript of interview, ed by E. Nissan and others. Dept State Bull 76:228-34 Mr 14 '77
Message from Secretary Vance to Department and Foreign Service; January 24, 1977. Dept State Bull 76:125-6 F 14 '77
News conference of Secretary Vance and Secretary Blumenthal, May 8. Dept State Bull 76:586-93 Je 6 '77
Panama Canal treaties; statement, October 20, 1977. Dept State Bull 77:728-31 N 21 '77
Proposed sale of AWACS to Iran; statement, July 28, 1977. Dept State Bull 77:245-7 Ag 22 '77
Secretary discusses administration's objectives for Belgrade review conference on CSCE; statement, June 6, 1977. Dept State Bull 76:669-70 Je 27 '77
Secretary interviewed at Foreign Policy Conference for Editors and Broadcasters; transcript of remarks, June 28, 1977. Dept State Bull 77:121-6 Jl 25 '77
Secretary testifies on Administration's approach to foreign assistance; statement, February 24, 1977. Dept State Bull 76:236-41 Mr 14 '77
Secretary Vance and other administration officials urge ratification of Panama Canal treaties; statement, September 26, 1977. Dept State Bull 77:615-18 N 7 '77
Secretary Vance and Soviet Foreign Minister Gromyko hold talks at Geneva; transcript of news conference, with joint communique, May 21, 1977. Dept State Bull 76:628-33 Je 13 '77
Secretary Vance attends ministerial conference of the Organization for Economic Cooperation and Development; remarks and transcript of news conference, June 23-24, 1977. Dept State Bull 77:105-9+ Jl 25 '77
Secretary Vance attends ministerial meeting of the Conference on International Economic Cooperation; address, May 30, 1977. Dept State Bull 76:645-8 Je 20 '77
Secretary Vance attends OAS General Assembly at Grenada; statements, transcript of news conference and arrival remarks, June 14-17, 1977. Dept State Bull 77:69-76 Jl 18 '77
Secretary Vance attends Spanish-U.S. Council meeting at Madrid and CENTO Council of Ministers meeting at Tehran; remarks, with news conference, statement and communiques, May 11-15, 1977. Dept State Bull 76:610-18 Je 6 '77
Secretary Vance discusses antiboycott legislation and nuclear nonproliferation; statement, March 1, 1977. Dept State Bull 76:267-71 Mr 21 '77
Secretary Vance emphasizes importance of foreign assistance programs; statement, March 23, 1977. Dept State Bull 76:336-9 Ap 11 '77
Secretary Vance gives overview of foreign assistance programs; statement, March 2, 1977. Dept State Bull 76:284-9 Mr 28 '77
Secretary Vance interviewed by AP and UPI correspondents; transcript of interview; ed by B. Schweid and others, February 3, 1977. Dept State Bull 76:147-54 F 21 '77
Secretary Vance interviewed by Il Tempo correspondent; ed by M. de Medici, June 18, 1977. Dept State Bull 77:85-90 Jl 18 '77
Secretary Vance interviewed for the New York times; transcript of interview, ed by H. Smith and others, February 9, 1977. Dept State Bull 76:162-9 F 28 '77
Secretary Vance interviewed on Face the nation; transcript of interview, ed by G. Herman and others, February 27, 1977. Dept State Bull 76:245-50 Mr 21 '77
Secretary Vance interviewed on Issues and answers; ed by B. Clark and B. Dunsmore, June 19, 1977. Dept State Bull 77:78-83 Jl 18 '77
Secretary Vance interviewed on Meet the press; transcript of program, October 16, 1977. Dept State Bull 77:579-84 O 31 '77
Secretary Vance meets at London with Israeli foreign minister; remarks, May 11, 1977. Dept State Bull 76:607-9 Je 6 '77
Secretary Vance meets with Foreign Secretary Owen; remarks with the press, July 23, 1977. Dept State Bull 77:275-8 Ag 29 '77
Secretary Vance reaffirms factors for Mideast conference; exchange of remarks, October 6, 1977. Dept State Bull 77:637-8 N 7 '77
Secretary Vance testifies on energy program; statement, May 4, 1977. Dept State Bull 76:564-6 My 30 '77
Secretary Vance visits China and Japan August 20-27; exchanges of toasts, press conference, and remarks. Dept State Bull 77:365-74 S 19 '77
Secretary Vance visits Moscow and western Europe; remarks, transcripts of news conferences, with joint communique, March 27-30, April 1-2, 1977. Dept State Bull 76:389-409 Ap 25 '77
Secretary Vance's news conference:
January 31, 1977. Dept State Bull 76:137-46 F 21 '77
March 4, 1977. Dept State Bull 76:277-83 Mr 28 '77
May 4, 1977. Dept State Bull 76:513-20 My 23 '77
July 29, 1977. Dept State Bull 77:227-34 Ag 22 '77
November 2, 1977. Dept State Bull 77:711-18 N 21 '77
Secretary Vance's visit to the Middle East and London July 31-August 13; text of press conferences and remarks, with statement. Dept State Bull 77:329-54 S 12 '77
Secretary Vance's visit to the Middle East, February 14-21; remarks and texts of news conferences. Dept State Bull 76:209-23 Mr 14 '77
United States and Africa: building positive relations; address, with transcript of question and answer session, July 1, 1977. Dept State Bull 77:-165-74 Ag 8 '77; Same. Vital Speeches 43:642-5 Ag 15 '77
United States signs convention banning environmental warfare; statement, with text of joint US-USSR communique, May 17, 1977. Dept State Bull 76:633-4 Je 13 '77
Vance: the ball is in their court; excerpts from interview, ed by S. Talbott and C. Ogden. por Time 109:27 Ap 18 '77
Vance: we will speak out; excerpts from television interview. por U.S. News 82:18-19 Mr 14 '77
Where U.S. is gaining in the world; interview. il pors U.S. News 83:27-30 N 7 '77; Same. Dept State Bull 77:732-8 N 21 '77

about

After Moscow's frost, a thaw in Geneva; SALT II. il pors Time 109:6-7 My 30 '77 *
Breaking the ice; SALT talks in Geneva. S. Fraker and others. pors Newsweek 89:16-17 My 30 '77 *
Chinese puzzle that Vance will try to solve; with editorial comment. il U.S. News 83:48-50, 68 Ag 22 '77 *
Jet stream. Nation 225:196 S 10 '77 *
Mr Perseverance. R. Watson and S. Sullivan. il por Newsweek 90:42+ O 10 '77 *
Secretary Vance's activities at the United Nations. Dept State Bull 77:640-2 N 7 '77 *
Taiwan's stake in the Vance trip. L. Hansen. il U.S. News 83:51 Ag 22 '77 *
Vance and Brzezinski: peaceful coexistence or guerrilla war? M. Berger. il pors N Y Times Mag p 19+ F 13 '77 *
Vance v. Kissinger: a matter of style. C. Ogden. Time 109:19 Ap 11 '77 *

VANCE, Cyrus Roberts—*Continued*

Visit to China, 1977

Agreeing to disagree. il pors Time 110:24-6 S 5 '77
Appointment in Peking. il por Time 110:34-5 Ag 29 '77
No dealee. Nat R 29:1039 S 16 '77
No need to rush. A. Deming and R. M. Smith. il por Newsweek 90:16-17 S 5 '77
Secretary Vance visits China and Japan August 20-27; exchanges of toasts, press conference, and remarks. C. R. Vance; H. Huang. Dept State Bull 77:365-74 S 19 '77
Vance in China: big smiles, but what else? il por U.S. News 83:16-17 S 5 '77
Vance's aim: drive for a one China solution. R. P. Martin. U.S. News 83:26 Ag 29 '77

Visit to Russia, 1977

Carter takes on the Russians. U.S. News 82:21-3 Ap 11 '77
Carter v. Brezhnev: the SALT standoff. il pors Time 109:10-12+ Ap 11 '77
Did we expect a dancing bear? Nation 224: 450-2 Ap 16 '77
Jimmy's deadwood; collapse of the strategic arms negotiations in Moscow. J. Osborne. il New Repub 176:8-10 Ap 9 '77
Letter from Washington. R. H. Rovere. New Yorker 53:129 Ap 11 '77
Mission to Moscow. R. Steele and others. il por Newsweek 89:20-2 Ap 4 '77
Quiet buildup of SALT 11. Time 109:26-7 Ap 18 '77
Secretary Vance visits Moscow and western Europe; remarks, transcripts of news conferences, with joint communique, March 27-30, April 1-2, 1977. C. R. Vance. Dept State Bull 76:389-409 Ap 25 '77
Testing Carter. R. Steele and others. il por Newsweek 89:26-30 Ap 11 '77
Vance in Moscow: a frank discussion. il por Time 109:23-4 Ap 4 '77
Vance's Moscow mission: a bid to bolster detente. il por U.S. News 82:25 Mr 28 '77

Visit to the Middle East, February 1977

After the Vance mission: signs of hope. il pors Time 109:26-9 F 28 '77
For U.S. a race against time in the Mideast. il por map U.S. News 82:19-20 F 28 '77
Medieval maze. M. Kondracke. New Repub 176: 8+ Mr 5 '77
Personal touch. A. Deming and others. il Newsweek 89:27-8 F 21 '77
Secretary Vance's visit to the Middle East, February 14-21; remarks and texts of news conferences. C. R. Vance. Dept State Bull 76:209-23 Mr 14 '77
Time to meet the players. il por Time 109:38 F 21 '77

Anecdotes, facetiae, satire, etc.

Follow me, Cy. New Repub 176:47 Mr 26 '77

Visit to the Middle East, August 1977

After Vance trip: peace no closer in Mideast. D. Mullin. U.S. News 83:22 Ag 22 '77
Elusive Camelot. il por Time 110:28-30 Ag 22 '77
Israel hangs tough. S. Fraker and others. il por Newsweek 90:36-7 Ag 22 '77
Latest U.S. peace effort—will it save Egypt's Sadat? D. Mullin. il por map U.S. News 83:23-4 Ag 15 '77
Long road to Geneva. A. Deming and others. pors Newsweek 90:27-9 Ag 15 '77
Nutcracker suite. il Time 110:28-9 Ag 15 '77
Secretary Vance's visit to the Middle East and London July 31-August 13; text of press conferences and remarks, with statement. C. R. Vance. Dept State Bull 77:329-45+ S 12 '77

VANCE, Diana
Personal palette; ed by V. E. Towns. House B 119:98-9+ F '77

VAN CLEAVE, W. R. See Cohen, S. T. jt auth

VAN CLIBURN International Piano Competition. See Music—Competitions

VANCOUVER, British Columbia
For adventurer in Vancouver, B.C. il Sunset 158:40+ My '77

Architecture

Sleeping beauty in the Canadian West; the Orpheum theater, Vancouver. R. Gelatt. il Sat R 4:36-7 My 28 '77

Description

Vancouver and Victoria. J. Ferri. il Travel 147: 30+ My '77

Galleries and museums

See also
British Columbia. University, Vancouver—Museum of Anthropology

Music

Musical events; Orpheum concert hall. A. Porter. New Yorker 53:66-7 Jl 4 '77

VANCOUVER Opera Association. See Opera—Canada

VANCURA, William J.
High sensitivity SWR meter for low-power communications equipment. il Pop Electr 12:59-61 O '77

VANDALISM
Devilish destruction; vandalism on eight churches. Chr Today 21:58 S 23 '77
North, south, east and west side story; school vandalism and violence. S. Moorefield. il Am Educ 13:12-16 Ja '77; Same abr. Educ Digest 42:10-13 My '77
School strike back against vandals. il U.S. News 83:66 Ag 8 '77
Violence in our schools. L. David. il Good H 185: 129+ N '77

VAN DECASTLE, Robert Leon
Women's dreams. E. Howard. il Ladies Home J 94:50+ Je '77 *

VAN DEERLIN, Lionel
New law for TV and radio? G. R. Rosen. por Duns R 109:65 Ap '77 *

VAN DE GRAAF accelerators. See Accelerators (electrons, etc)

VANDENBERG, J. M. and Matthias, B. T.
Clustering hypothesis of some high-temperature superconductors. bibl il Science 198:194-6 O 14 '77

VANDENBERG Air Force Base. See Air bases

VANDENBERGH, John G. See Lombardi, J. R. jt auth

VAN DEN HAAG, Ernest
Coming of bold pornography; interview, ed by W. Goodman. Current 190:32-8 F '77
Haggis & the Wealth of nations. Nat R 29:268 Mr 4 '77
Is the Republican Party dead? Nat R 29:329+ Mr 18 '77
Reverse discrimination: a brief against it. Nat R 29:492-5 Ap 29 '77
There is no right to peddle pornography! Read Digest 111:48 Jl '77

VAN DER BENT, Ans Joachim
Fourteen years after Unity in mid-career. Chr Cent 94:565-7 Je 8 '77

VANDERBILT, Cornelius, Jr
Blue bloods. il Sat Eve Post 249:85 Jl '77

VANDERBILT, Gloria
Gloria Vanderbilt; interview, ed by M. Gough. il por House B 119:76-7+ F '77

VANDERBILT Prison Project. See Social work with delinquents and criminals

VANDERGRIFT, Kay E.
Are we selecting for a generation of skeptics? excerpt from address, November 4, 1976. SLJ 23:41-3 F '77

VAN DER KEMP, Gérald
Commoner with lordly air is bringing Versailles back to its days of glory. R. Wernick. il por Smithsonian 7:38-47 Mr '77 *

VAN DER KOOY, Derek, and Phillips, A. G.
Trigeminal substrates of intracranial self-stimulation in the brainstem. bibl il Science 196:447-9 Ap 22 '77

VAN DER MARCK, Jan
Ivan Albright: more than meets the eye. bibl il por Art in Am 65:92-9 N '77
Richard Nonas: field works. il Art in Am 65:114-17 Ja '77

VANDER PLUYM, Todd
Ultimate in sandcastling? il por Sunset 159:70-1 Jl '77 *

VANDERSLICE, Thomas Aquinas
Technology and jobs: the vital link is weakening. por Duns R 110:25+ Jl '77

VANDERWEIL, Gary, and Haynes, J. R.
How to cut energy use in public buildings. il Am City & County 92:46-7 Jl '77

VAN DE SANDE, J. H. and others
Reverse banding on chromosomes produced by a guanosine-cytosine specific DNA binding antibiotic: olivomycin. bibl il Science 195:400-2 Ja 28 '77

VAN DEVENDER, Thomas R.
Holocene woodlands in the southwestern deserts. bibl il map Science 198:189-92 O 14 '77

VAN DE WALLE, Etienne
Trends and prospects of population in tropical Africa. bibl f Ann Am Acad 432:1-11 Jl '77

VAN DONGEN, Helen
Helen Van Dongen: an interview, ed by B. Achtenberg. bibl il pors Film Q 30:46-57 Wint '76

VAN DOREN, David M. Jr. See Triplett, G. B. Jr, jt auth

VAN DUYN, Mona
At Père Lachaise; poem. New Yorker 53:44 Mr 28 '77

VAN DYKE, Dick
Carol Burnett & Dick Van Dyke: what alcoholism did to their lives. L. Fosburgh. pors Ladies Home J 94:34+ S '77 *

VAN DYNE, Cynthia
How a stillborn child started a NIOSH study. il por Bus W p76-7 Ag 29 '77 *

VAN DYNE, Larry
Reports & comment: City University of New York. il Atlantic 239:14-18 Je '77

VAN GELDER, Lindsy
Anita Bryant on the march. il por Ms 6:75-8+ S '77
Hot off the feminist presses: new journals. il Ms 6:95-8 N '77
Memo for the first National Women's Convention: countdown to Houston. il Ms 6:60-2+ N '77
VAN GOETHEM, Larry
Wisconsin: land of the gathering waters. il map Read Digest 111:208-12+ O '77
VAN HASSELT, Tony
Watercolor page. il por Am Artist 41:48-51+ Je '77
VAN HOESEN, Gary W. See Rosene, D. L. jt auth
VAN HOUTEN, Judith
Mutant of paramecium defective in chemotaxis. bibl il Science 198:746-8 N 18 '77
VANITIES (dressing tables) See Dressing tables
VAN LIER, Norm
Stormin' Norman. B. Rhoden. il pors Ebony 32:127-8+ My '77 *
VAN NOSTRAND, Albert Douglass
Teaching thinking on paper. il por Time 109: 74 Ap 18 '77 *
VAN NOTE, Craig
IWC slashes quotas, bans Eskimo hunt. Audubon 79:141-2 S '77
VAN ORDEN, Phyllis J.
Librarians & publishers: an idea exchange through library promotion. por SLJ 24:24-6 D '77
VANS
Is a van a good buy for your family? R. A. Dickelman. Bet Hom & Gard 55:18+ O '77
Maybe a van instead of a wagon. il Changing T 31:11-12 My '77
RV roundup. B. Behme. il Field & S 81:124+ Ap '77
There's no madness like nomadness. F. Trippett. il Time 110:55-7 S 5 '77
Viewpoint: Chevrolet travel van. R. Taylor. il Car & Dr 23:122-3+ N '77
Wheels afield. B. Kovacik. il Motor T 29:105-6 Ap; 50-2+ Ag '77
See also headings beginning Van

Equipment

Over easy; overhead van console installation. il Hot Rod 30:78+ Ap '77
Van bench/bed clears away for cargo. I. Glickstein. il Pop Sci 211:110-11 Jl '77
Vans. il Hot Rod 30:80-3 F '77

Four wheel drive

Getting the van off the road. B. Kovacik. il Motor T 29:105-6 Ap '77

Interior decoration

See Van decoration

Maintenance and repair

Van care for home mechanics. T. Tappett. il Mech Illus 73:92+ O '77

Photographs

Hot rod gallery. il Hot Rod 30:58 Ap; 64-5 Je; 95 Jl; 40 Ag; 106-7 S; 75 O '77
Pickups, vans & 4x4 highriders. il Hot Rod 30: 64-8 Jl '77

Testing

Bullnose; Ford E-150 van. il Hot Rod 30:93-5 F '77
Cross-country caravan; Plymouth Voyager vans. B. Kovacik. il Motor T 29:50-2+ Ag '77
PM owners report:
VW bus. M. Lamm. il Pop Mech 148:118-19+ N '77
PS car test & driving report:
Versatile vans. J. Dunne and R. Hill. il Pop Sci 210:34+ Mr '77
Three vans: Plymouth Voyager, Chevrolet Sportvan, Ford Club Wagon. il Consumer Rep 42:521-7 S '77
VANS, Remodeled
Designed by Hot Rod magazine; Denimachine. il Hot Rod 30:96-7 F '77
Do your own van conversion. R. Hill. Pop Sci 210:110-12+ Mr '77
Giveaway; grand prize in NSVA's Fifth Annual National Truck-in. il Hot Rod 30:38-9 D '77
Junkyard jamboree; locating and using parts for rods and vans. il Hot Rod 30:70-4+ F '77
Vantastic; customizing a van. J. Cashen. il Sat Eve Post 249:20-1+ Ap '77
VANS, Toy. See Toys
VAN SANT, C. L.
My sleeping family; poem. Chr Cent 94:380 Ap 20 '77
VAN SLYKE, Helen
Novelist's identity crisis. Writer 90:11-14 N '77
PW interviews; ed by J. F. Baker. il por Pub W 211:10-11 Ja 31 '77
VANT-HULL, Lorin L. See Hildebrandt, A. F.
VAN TIL, Cornelius
At the beginning, God; interview, ed by D. E. Kucharsky. por Chr Today 22:18-22 D 30 '77

about

Tribute to Cornelius Van Til. T. G. Spires. Chr Today 22:20 D 30 '77 *
VAN VLECK, John Hasbrouck
1977 Nobel laureates in science. il pors Chemistry 50:18-20 D '77 *
1977 Nobel Prize in physics. M. L. Cohen and L. M. Falicov. bibl pors Science 198:713-15 N 18 '77 *
Nobel prizes: seven in '77. pors Sci N 112: 260-1 O 22 '77 *
Physicists share in Nobel prizes in three disciplines. G. B. Lubkin. pors Phys Today 30:77-8 D '77 *
VAN ZANT, Gary, and Goldwasser, Eugene
Simultaneous effects of erythropoietin and colony-stimulating factor on bone marrow cells. bibl il Science 198:733-5 N 18 '77
VANZETTI, Bartolomeo
See also
Sacco-Vanzetti case
VAPOR pressure
Anomalous temperature dependence for a partial vapor pressure. J. A. Roberts, Jr and A. W. Searcy. bibl il Science 196:525-7 Ap 29 '77
VAPORS
See also
Water vapor
VÁRADY, Szabolcs
Chairs above the Danube; poem; tr by W. J. Smith. New Yorker 53:34 F 28 '77
VARDA, Agnès
Varda: watch out. I do not authorize you to use me against other women. . .; interview, ed by J. Thurman. por Ms 6:28 Ja '78
VARELA, Félix
Foresight of Féliz Varela. C. F. Benedi. il por Américas 29:9-12 Ap '77 *
VARÈSE, Edgard
Music of Edgard Varèse. R. P. Morgan. il por Hi Fi 27:78-82 F '77 *
Recordings of Edgard Varèse. R. P. Morgan. Hi Fi 27:82-3 F '77 *
Varèse in New York: from Ecuatorial to Intégrales; excerpt from Varèse: a looking glass diary, v2. L. Varèse. il pors Hi Fi 27:73-7 F '77 *
VARÈSE, Louise
Varèse in New York: from Ecuatorial to Intégrales; excerpt from Varèse: a looking glass diary, v2. il pors Hi Fi 27:73-7 F '77
VARGAS, Marjorie Fink
It's in the cards: a new deal for student writers. Engl J 66:48-51 S '77
VARGAS LLOSA, Mario
Vargas Llosa, visionary realist; interview, ed by T. Bridges. il pors Américas 29:2-5 O '77
VARGISH, Thomas
Brute. il Nat R 29:507 Ap 29 '77
VARIABLE-displacement engines. See Automobile engines
VARIABLE-rate mortgages. See Mortgages
VARIABLE stars. See Stars, Variable
VARIATION (biology)
See also
Mutation (biology)
VARIATION (music)
See also
Embellishment (music)
VARIATIONS, Seasonal. See Seasonal variations (economics)
VARIATIONS on America; ballet. See Ballet reviews—Single works
VARIETY stores
See also
Grant, W. T, Company
Kresge, S. S, Company
Woolworth, F. W, Company
VARILLA, Philippe Jean Bunau-. See Bunau-Varilla, P. J.
VARLEJS, Jana
Cine-opsis. See issues of Wilson library bulletin
VARMA, S. D. and others
Diabetic cataracts and flavonoids. bibl il Science 195:205-6 Ja 14 '77
VARNADO, S. L.
Eyes on the White House lawn. Nat R 29:496 Ap 29 '77
VARNEDOE, Kirk
Max Klinger: a realm of privileged suspension; ed by E. Streicher; excerpt from The graphic works of Max Klinger. il Art N 76:46-50 Mr '77
VARNEY, Carleton
Designer's guide to instant decorating. House B 119:46-7 Ag '77
VARNISH, Desert. See Desert varnish
VARNISH and varnishing
Plate-glass varnish; boats. G. Groene. il Motor B & S 139:101-4 Ap '77
VASAK, Karel
30-year struggle. UNESCO Courier 30:29+ N '77
VASARI, pseud
Vasari diary. See issues of Art news
VASECTOMY
Cobbler's tale; India's program. H. Jensen. il Newsweek 89:42 Ap 4 '77
Issue that inflamed India. L. Malkin. il Time 109:38-9 Ap 4 '77

VASECTOMY—*Continued*
Most kindest cut of all: vasectomy. H. Crews. Esquire 87:60+ My '77
Sperm autoantibodies in vasectomized rats of different inbred strains. P. E. Bigazzi and others. bibl il Science 197:1282-3 S 23 '77

VASES
Throw a ring-vase. M. Sapiro. il Sch Arts 76: 22-7 Mr '77
Two-in-one is lots more fun. P. R. Jackson. House & Gard 149:136+ N '77
See also
Urns

VASES, Greek
Greek art from the Atlantic depths; Sir William Hamilton's Greek vases. A. Birchall. il Horizon 19:66-71 Ja '77

VASOACTIVE peptides. See Peptides

VASOTOCIN. See Oxytocin

VASSAR College, Poughkeepsie, N.Y.
Recycling Main—a landmark at Vassar; with introd by M. F. Schmertz. il Archit Rec 162: 73-8 Jl '77

VATICAN and the press
Reporter at the Vatican. D. O'Grady. Commonweal 104:751-2+ N 25 '77

VATICAN Congregation for Catholic Education. See Congregation for Catholic Education

VATICAN Council, 1869-1870
See also
Popes—Infallibility

VATICAN Council, 2d
Ultimum verbum—promitto! J. J. Lynch. Nat R 29:887+ Ag 5 '77

VAUGHAN, David
American Ballet Theatre. il Dance Mag 51:71-4 O '77
(ed) See Markova, A. Conversations with Markova

VAUGHAN, J. G.
Multidisciplinary study of the taxonomy and origin of Brassica crops. bibl il BioScience 27: 35-40 Ja '77

VAUGHAN, Roger
Building a vineyard in Rhode Island wine country. il pors Horticulture 55:20-4+ S '77
Talking tuna. il por Motor B & S 139:66-9+ Je '77
(ed) See Marvin, L. Marvin as in marlin

VAUGHN, Dove
Goldfinger and Dove. il pors Ebony 32:88-90+ Ap '77 *

VAUGHN, Jack
Goldfinger and Dove. il pors Ebony 32:88-90+ Ap '77 *

VAUGHN, Patrica
Finding the way to self-fulfillment. por Parents Mag 52:68-9+ N '77

VAUX, Kenneth
Intending death: moral perspectives. il Chr Cent 94:56-60 Ja 26 '77

VÁZQUEZ DE ACUÑA, Isidoro
Enduring heritage. il map Américas 29:30-3 O '77

VAZSONYI, Balint
Balint Vazsonyi, piano; concerts at the YMHA. por Hi Fi 27:MA27 Mr '77 *

VEAL
See also
Cookery—Meat

VEAL stew. See Stew

VEATCHINE
Veatchine: coexistence of epimers in a crystal structure. W. H. De Camp and S. W. Pelletier. bibl il Science 198:726-7 N 18 '77

VEBLEN, David R. and others
Asbestiform chain silicates: new minerals and structural groups. bibl il Science 198:359-65 O 28 '77

VEBLEN, Thorstein Bunde
Veblen revisited. L. H. Lapham. Harpers 255:8+ N '77 *

VECSEY, Christopher
Black Catholics. Commonweal 104:332-6 My 27 '77

VEDERMAN, Ron. See Grundke, R. jt auth

VEECK, Bill
Bill Veeck: the happy hustler. Time 109:90 Ap 25 '77 *
Brains vs. bucks. P. Axthelm. il por Newsweek 89:65 My 30 '77 *

VEEMAN, Michele M. See Veeman, T. S. jt auth

VEEMAN, Terrence S. and Veeman, M. M.
Canadian agriculture today. bibl f Cur Hist 72: 162-5 Ap '77

VEGETABLE diet. See Vegetarianism

VEGETABLE dryers. See Drying apparatus

VEGETABLE gardening
Carrots to topiary to impatiens. il Sunset 159: 72-3 Jl '77
Double plot: multiply your vegetable harvest. E. F. Steffek. il Pop Mech 147:100-1 Mr '77
Down-to-earth guide to growing vegetables. B. Garrett. il Bet Hom & Gard 55:91-7 Mr '77
End of summer is not the end of your garden. J. Meeker. il Org Gard & Farm 24:57-9 Ag '77
Executive gardener. il Bus W p85-7+ My 2 '77
Frames and mulches: self help for vegetables. il House & Gard 149:160-1 Ap '77
Garden of children. A. Stahr. Org Gard & Farm 25:102 Ja '78
Garden of eatin. G. Logsdon. il Org Gard & Farm 25:192+ Ja '78
Gardens & game: do-it-yourself meals. S. Bashline. il Field & S 81:36+ F '77
Gourmet gardener. il House & Gard 149:98-9 Ag '77
Growing the big ones. M. C. Goldman. il Org Gard & Farm 24:140-3 Jl '77
High-altitude growing in California. F. Blanchard. il Org Gard & Farm 25:80-1 Ja '78
How to plan a raised bed garden. R. Wolf. il Org Gard & Farm 24:74-7 F '77
I'm putting my garden to beds. G. Williams, Jr. Org Gard & Farm 24:69-73 My '77
Just plow your problems into the garden. J. Wellenkamp. il Org Gard & Farm 25:158 Ja '78
Late crops for western gardening success. L. Tilton. il Org Gard & Farm 24:69-71 Jl '77
More vegetables in less space. R. S. Ele. il Org Gard & Farm 24:78-9 F '77
Perennial vegetables. K. Kraft and P. Kraft. il Horticulture 55:44-6 O '77
Planning an absentee garden. M. Johannsen. il Org Gard & Farm 24:92-4 F '77
Preserving in the garden. M. S. Hill. il Org Gard & Farm 24:104+ S '77
Springtime vegetable garden planner; symposium. il Horticulture 55:41-56 Mr '77
Starting vegetables early. T. Cruso. McCalls 104:82+ Mr '77
Swans' way. J. Swan. N Y Times Mag p35-7 Mr 13 '77
Unusual dishes from your garden. J. Goldstein. il Org Gard & Farm 24:142+ F '77
Vegetables at 8,000 feet. J. C. Nelson and J. S. Marshall. Org Gard & Farm 24:202 F '77
Vegetables in the front yard. M. Brandies. Org Gard & Farm 24:124-6 Ap '77
Well-dressed vegetable; Nice ways to beat the high cost of vegetables. il House & Gard 149: 104-7 Je '77
See also
Cold frames
Community gardens
Companion crops
Truck farming
also names of vegetables, e.g. Carrots

Anecdotes, facetiae, satire, etc.

Best laid garden plans go oft awry. T. Cooper. Horticulture 55:64 D '77
Perils of a first-time farmer. D. Henahan. il Read Digest 110:107-10 My '77

Economic aspects

Up the economic ladder with a spade and hoe. J. Goldstein. il Org Gard & Farm 24:30+ Jl '77

Planting plans and tables

Personal planting guide. J. U. Crockett. il Horticulture 55:41 Mr '77
Succession planting chart. E. E. Jantzen. il Org Gard & Farm 24:72-3 F '77

VEGETABLE industry. See Food industry

VEGETABLE juices
New and better way to preserve juice; use of steam juicer. il Org Gard & Farm 24:96-7 Jl '77

VEGETABLE oyster. See Salsify

VEGETABLE salads. See Salads

VEGETABLES
Exotic oriental vegetables. K. Kraft and P. Kraft. il Horticulture 55:22-4+ My '77
Expand your garden with oriental vegetables. J. Douglas. il Org Gard & Farm 24:78-81 D '77
Shopping adventures with vegetables. S. Oddo. il House & Gard 149:95+ Ag '77
See also
Cookery—Vegetables
Greens, Edible
Vegetable gardening
Vegetarianism
also names of vegetables, e.g. Potatoes

Drying

Surplus chile peppers? Dry them. Sunset 159:125 S '77

Harvesting

When to pick a perfect vegetable. W. Asa. Horticulture 55:24+ Jl '77

Preservation

Chinese greens—freezing or pickling. il Sunset 158:169 Mr '77
How to can tomatoes. il Bet Hom & Gard 55:83 Ag '77
Up from catsup. R. Sokolov. Natur Hist 86:108+ Ag '77

Seed

Culture & notes. Horticulture 55:86 Mr '77

Storage

Keeping fruits & vegetables fresh. il Changing T 31:34-6 Jl '77
Putting the harvest into storage. Sunset 159:164 S '77

VEGETABLES—Storage—*Continued*
Stocking the cold cellar. R. B. Yepsen, Jr. il Org Gard & Farm 24:109-10+ S '77
Storing your surplus vegetables. Bet Hom & Gard 55:250 O '77

Varieties

How fast-maturing vegetables cut garden problems. M. C. Goldman. il Org Gard & Farm 24:82-5 Ap '77
How to choose new varieties for your 1978 garden. M. C. Goldman. il Org Gard & Farm 25:74-9 Ja '78
Unusual varieties add spice to a garden. L. L. Nelson. il Org Gard & Farm 24:162+ Mr '77

VEGETABLES, Freezing of. See Freezing of food

VEGETABLES, Pickled. See Pickles and relishes

VEGETARIANISM
Going vegetarian? Be careful! il Changing T 31:31-3 N '77
Vegetarian buffet for eight. G. Lindley. il Redbook 150:134-5 D '77
Vegetarian who came to dinner. L. DeMauro. Am Home 80:36 S '77
Wise vegetarian. il Chemistry 50:21-2 Je '77

VEGETATION
Release of particles containing metals from vegetation into the atmosphere. W. Beauford and others. bibl il Science 195:571-3 F 11 '77

VEHAR, Gordon A. and Davie, E. W.
Formation of a serine enzyme in the presence of bovine factor VIII (antihemophilic factor) and thrombin. bibl il Science 197:374-6 Jl 22 '77

VEHICLES
See also
Bicycles
Electric vehicles
Motor vehicles
Wagons
Wheels

VEHRENCAMP, Sandra L.
Relative fecundity and parental effort in communally nesting anis, crotophaga sulcirostris. bibl il Science 197:403-5 Jl 22 '77

VEKEMANS, Roger
Chile cover-up? Chr Today 21:40-1 Ag 26 '77 *

VELASCO, Juan
Peruvian revolution in crisis. D. P. Werlich. Cur Hist 72:61-4+ F '77 *

VELIE, Lester
From mob to supermob. por Read Digest 112:49-54 Ja '78
Golden fleecing of union funds. Read Digest 111:88-92 O '77

VELIKOVSKY, Immanuel
Velikovsky. J. S. Trefil. por Sci Digest 82:75-7 S '77 *

VELIOTIS, P. Takis
Cost-cutter climbs all over Electric Boat. por Bus W p42+ N 14 '77 *

VELLA Lavella (island) See Solomon Islands

VELLELA, Tony
Renter's survival guide. Am Home 60:36 N '77

VELLUCCI, Alfred
Gene-splicing: Cambridge citizens OK research but want more safety. N. Wade. il por Science 195:268-9 Ja 21 '77 *

VELSICOL Corporation. See. Chemical industries

VELZ, John W.
Certification in the basics one hundred years ago. il Engl J 66:32-8 O '77

VENDING machine industry
Never volunteer! Vendo Co. por Forbes 120:106 D 1 '77
See also
Canteen Corporation

VENDO Company. See Vending machine industry

VENDORS, Street. See Street trades

VENDRYES, Georges A.
Superphénix: a full-scale breeder reactor; with biographical sketch. il Sci Am 236:22, 26-35 Mr '77

VENEERS and veneering
ABCs of veneering in easy photo steps. R. Capotosto. il Mech Illus 73:118 Mr '77
Flexible veneer—easy, inexpensive route to elegant furniture. H. J. Hobbs. il Pop Sci 210:124+ F '77
Veneering: enjoy beautiful wood on a budget. P. Angell. il Pop Mech 147:110-13 My '77

VENERA flights. See Space flight to Venus

VENERA spacecraft. See Space probes

VENEREAL diseases
Sexual liberation, V.D. and our children. V. Almon. America 137:169-72 S 24 '77
VD: the disease of the year. M.-E. Banashek. Mademoiselle 83:52+ Mr '77
See also
Gonorrhea

VENEZUELA
See also
Ballet—Venezuela
Loans, Bank—Venezuela
Music and state—Venezuela
Secret service—Venezuela

Foreign relations

Third world has given everything and received little; interview. C. A. Pérez. il por U.S. News 83:53-4+ Jl 25 '77

VENGEANCE. See Revenge

VENICE
Maladies of Venice: decay, delay and that old sinking feeling. D. J. Hamblin. il map Smithsonian 8:40-53 bibl(p 160) N '77

Music

See also
Opera—Italy

VENICE Biennale. See Art—Exhibitions

VENISON
See also
Cookery—Game

VENNINGEN, Jane Elizabeth (Digby) Baroness von. See Ellenborough, J. E. D. L. Countess of

VENOM
Death did not rattle; bite of massasauga rattler. C. Mol and B. East. il Outdoor Life 159:88-9+ Ap '77
Magic of the snake-stone: does it cure? R. Caras. il Sci Digest 82:53-5 Jl '77
Snakebite! What to know—what to do. C. Elliott. il Outdoor Life 160:84-7+ S '77
To save a child; rattlesnake venom victim at UCLA Medical Center. B. Dillman. il McCalls 105:104+ N '77
Woodrat slights rattler venom. il Sci N 112:406-7 D 17 '77

VENTILATION
Low- or no-power attic cooling. E. Powell. il Pop Sci 211:60+ Ag '77
New proof that outside venting saves fuel. E Powell. il Pop Sci 210:146+ F '77

VENTILATION (physiology) See Respiration

VENTILATORS
Attic fan to cool your house. il Mech Illus 73:90+ Ag '77

VENTURE capital. See Capital, Venture

VENTURES, Joint. See Joint adventures

VENUS (planet)

Atmosphere

Excitation of the Venus night airglow. G. M. Lawrence and others. bibl il Science 195:573-4 F 11 '77

Observations

Observing Venus near inferior conjunction. R. C. Victor. il Sky & Tel 53:207-8 Mr '77
Venus and Mars in the morning sky. R. C. Victor. il Sky & Tel 53:375 My '77
Venus, Mars, and the moon come together. il Sky & Tel 54:150-2 Ag '77
Venus passes inferior conjunction. il Sky & Tel 54:70-3 Jl '77

Surface

Geomorphic degradations on the surface of Venus: an analysis of Venera 9 and Venera 10 data. C. P. Florensky and others. bibl il Science 196:869-71 My 20 '77
Move over Olympus Mons—here comes Beta! J. Eberhart. il Sci N 111:313+ My 14 '77
Planetary comparisons. B. M. French. il Space World N-1-157:30-1 Ja '77
Possible lava flows on Venus. il Space World N-2-158:37-9 F '77
Surface of Venus: evidence of diverse landforms from radar observations. M. C. Malin and R. S. Saunders. bibl il Science 196:987-90 My 27 '77
Venus refined. J. Eberhart. il Sci N 111:252-3+ Ap 16 '77

VENUS probes. See Space probes

VENUTI, Joe
Jazz. M. Ullman. il por New Repub 177:19-21 D 3 '77 *

VERA, Ana-Maria
Mozart: Piano concerto in C; Haydn: Piano concerto in D. D. Gravelmann. por Am Rec G 40:35 Je '77 *

La VERA constanza; opera. See Haydn, F. J.

VERANDAS. See Decks, patios, terraces, etc.

VERBOSITY
Civil tongue; excerpt. E. Newman. Read Digest 110:189-90+ My '77
Conciseness in F major. F. Rathbun. Writers Digest 57:45-7 Ag '77

VERDI, Giuseppe
Aida. Review
Hi Fi 27:MA27 F '77 *
Carlo Bergonzi sings Verdi: 31 tenor arias from 25 operas. D. Arthur. por Am Rec G 40:41-4 N '76 *
Don Carlo. Review
New Repub 177:28-30 N 5 '77 *
Falstaff. Review
New Yorker 53:130-2 My 9 '77 *
La forza del destino. D. Arthur. Am Rec G 40:47-8 Je '77 *
La forza del destino (Force of destiny) Reviews
Hi Fi 27:MA17 Mr '77 *
Nation 224:445-6 Ap 9 '77 *
Opera N il 41:20+ Mr 12 '77 *

VERDI, Giuseppe—*Continued*
In the opera house: how much does neatness count? recordings of Andrea Chénier and La forza del destino, conducted by J. Levine. K. Furie. il por Hi Fi 27:71-4 Ag '77 *
Macbeth; recording. Hi Fi 27:92+ My '77 *
New dimensions: Rigoletto. F. G. Barker. Opera N 42:36-7 D 3 '77 *
Of prayers and curses; La forza del destino. W. Ashbrook. il Opera N 41:28-9 Mr 12 '77 *
Overtures and preludes, complete; recording. J. Oestreich. Am Rec G 40:44 F '77 *
Rigoletto. Reviews
New Repub 178:28-9 Ja 7 '78 *
New Yorker 53:132+ My 9 '77 *
New Yorker 53:175-8 N 21 '77 *
Newsweek 90:126 N 14 '77 *
Opera N il 42:25-6+ D 3 '77 *
Time 110:116 N 14 '77 *
Spirit of the faydit; troubadour-outcasts and Manrico, the hero of Il Trovatore. C. L. Osborne. il Opera N 41:26-8 Ap 9 '77 *
Tale of turmoil; adaptation of V. Hugo's play Le roi s'amuse into Verdi's opera Rigoletto. G. R. Marek. il por Opera N 42:10-14 D 3 '77 *
La Traviata. Review
Opera N il 42:30-2, 36+ D 24 '77 *
Le Trouvere: comparing Verdi's French revision with his original. D. Rosen. il Opera N 41:16-17 Ap 9 '77 *
Il Trovatore. Reviews
Hi Fi il 27:MA25-7 F '77 *
Opera N il 41:18+ Ap 9 '77 *
Opera N il 42:28-30 Ja 7 '78 *
Il Trovatore; London recording conducted by R. Bonynge. K. Furie. Hi Fi 28:104-6 Ja '78 *
Two settings for the same text; Bruckner: Te Deum; Verdi: Te Deum. P. L. Althouse. Am Rec G 40:19-20 Je '77 *
Verdi well-served; two Macbeth recordings. D. Arthur. il Am Rec G 40:40-2 My '77 *
Verdi's American correspondent; E. Muzio. G. Marchesi. por Opera N 42:38+ D 3 '77 *
Verdi's early U.S. premieres. M. Chusid. il Opera N 42:32-3 Ja 7 '78 *

VERGUN, Alexei
(tr) See Dubinsky, R. Last days in Russia

VERHEYDEN- HILLIARD, Mary Ellen
Counseling: potential superbomb against sexism. Am Educ 13:12-15 Ap '77

VERISMO Opera Company. See Opera—New York (state)

VERITY, Calvin William, 1917-
Diversification that offsets the slack in steel. il por Bus W p99+ D 12 '77 *

VERMANDEL, Janet Gregory
Beyond the dream; story. Good H 184:179-82 F '77

VERMEIJ, Geerat
On a reef, darkly. K. Brower. il Read Digest 110:125-8 F '77 *

VERMEULE, Emily
Parthenon is shrinking. il Atlantic 239:82-4+ My '77

VERMICULTURE. See Earthworm culture

VERMONT
Greening of Vermont. J. Eisen. Commonweal 104:7 Ja 7 '77
See also
Architecture, Domestic—Vermont
Education—Vermont
Environmental movement—Vermont
Fishing—Vermont
Forests and forestry—Vermont
Landscape protection—Vermont
Music festivals—Vermont
Regional planning—Vermont
Water pollution—Vermont

Description and travel
Leaf-taking in Vermont. P. Brooks. il House & Gard 149:10 O '77

Anecdotes, facetiae, satire, etc.
Vermont, through a thermopane window. G. Wolff. il Esquire 87:48+ Ap '77

History
Ethan Allen and the Green Mountain Boys. D. B. Sabine. il pors Am Hist Illus 11:8-15 Ja '77

Industries
See also
Potteries

Photographs
This is Vermont. Am For 83:22-6 S '77

Politics and government
Man from Putney; G. D. Aiken. H. N. Muller, 3d. il por Am For 83:18-21+ S '77

Restaurants
See Restaurants—United States

VERNAL pools. See Ponds

VERNE, Jules
Jules Verne father of science fiction. E. Shrum. il Hobbies 82:152 S '77 *

VERNER, Zenobia, and Murphy, Louis
Does the use of newspapers in the classroom affect attitudes of students? il Clearing H 50:350-1 Ap '77

VERNET, Claude Joseph
Battle of the blot. M. Gibson. il Art N 76:101-2 Ap '77 *

VERNET, Roland. See Grenot, C. jt auth

VERNON, James
Measure capacitance on a digital readout. il Radio-Electr 48:37-9 D '77

VERON, Philippe. See Disney, M. J. jt auth

VERRETT, Shirley
Shirley Verrett gambles on superstardom. G. Wills. il por N Y Times Mag p 15-16+ Ja 30 '77 *

VERSAILLES, Palaces of
Commoner with lordly air is bringing Versailles back to its days of glory; the chief curator, G. Van der Kemp. R. Wernick. il por Smithsonian 7:38-47 Mr '77

VERSCHOTH, Anita
Gymnastics fever. il Horizon 19:62-9 My '77
Movies. il Sports Illus 47:60 O 17 '77
Old order holds on Penn. il Sports Illus 46:26+ My 9 '77
Olympics. il Sports Illus 47:46-7 Ag 22 '77
Skiing. il Sports Illus 46:54-6 Ja 17 '77
Track & field. Sports Illus 46:92+ My 23 '77

VERSE. See Poetry

VERSER, Nancy
Reading the stock tables. Redbook 149:64 My '77

VERTA Mae, pseud. See Grosvenor, V. M.

VERTEBRATES, Fossil. See Paleontology

VERTOL Division. See Boeing Company—Vertol Division

VERTOV, Dziga
Enthusiasm: from kino-eye to radio-eye. L. Fischer. bibl il por Film Q 31:25-34 Wint '77 *

VERY large array radio telescopes. See Radio telescopes

VESAK, Norbert
Movement with meaning. R. Philp. Dance Mag 51:91 Jl '77 *

VESCO, Robert Lee
Costa Rica imbroglio. K. Bode. New Repub 176:12-16 My 28 '77 *
Costa Rica's Vescogate. M. R. Benjamin and others. por Newsweek 89:47 Je 13 '77 *
International Controls: the lively corpse. por Forbes 120:63-4 O 15 '77 *

VESELY, Melissa
Baseball glove that really fit. il Read Digest 110:108-11 Ap '77

VESICULAR stomatitis virus. See Viruses

VESILIND, Priit J.
Ohio—river with a job to do. il map Nat Geog 151:244-73 F '77

VESSELS, Armored. See Armored vessels

VESTA (asteroid) See Asteroids

VESTAL, David
As I see it. por Pop Phot 81:24+ Ag; 30+ O; 46+ D '77
David Vestal's photo workbook. Pop Phot 80: 67-8 My; 79-80 Je; 81:83-4 Jl; 69-70 Ag; 27-8 O '77
(ed) See Gilpin, L. Laura Gilpin: photographer of the Southwest

VESTMANNAEYJAR. See Heimaey (island)

VETERANS
Second-class heroes; Vietnam veterans. Nation 225:35-6 Jl 9 '77
Vets' reunions. . .with a purpose. M. C. Leeds. Ret Liv 17:48+ My '77
See also
Black veterans
Military discharges
United States—Veterans Administration
United States—Veterans Administration hospitals

Benefits
Use those veteran's benefits. il Changing T 31:43-4 O '77
See also
Pensions, Military

Employment
Bringing the veterans back into the system. por Nations Bus 65:66-7 N '77
Credit the vet. M Labor R 100:71 O '77

VETERANS, Disabled
Veterans. S. Kleinfield. Atlantic 240:89 D '77

VETERANS Administration. See United States—Veterans Administration

VETERANS Day
All quiet on the Western Front. J. Klein. il Read Digest 111:227-8 N '77

VETERANS hospitals. See Hospitals, Military

VETERANS pensions. See Pensions, Military

VETERINARIANS
Down on the farm. M. Thomas. il Seventeen 36:74+ My '77

VETERINARY medicine
All things wise and wonderful; excerpt. J. Herriot. il Read Digest 111:233-42+ O '77
Ask the vet; questions and answers. T. McGinnis. See issues of Family health incorporating Today's health

VETERINARY medicine—*Continued*
How to cut down on veterinary bills. B. Humeston. Bet Hom & Gard 55:240+ S '77
Ten tips to avoid drug troubles. Suc Farm 75:33 My '77
Ways to make water work for you; water medication systems. il Suc Farm 75:no5 34-5 Mr '77
See also
Birds of prey—Care
Veterinarians

Study and teaching

Schooling the animals' best friends. il Time 109:74+ Ap 18 '77

VETERINARY surgery
See also
Implantation, Subcutaneous

VEVERKA, Joseph
Phobos and Deimos; with biographical sketch. il Sci Am 236:16, 30-7 bibl(p 138) F '77

VIAU, M. See Constans, J. jt auth

VIBRIO
Vibrio cholerae, vibrio parahaemolyticus, and other vibrios: occurrence and distribution in Chesapeake Bay. R. R. Colwell and others. bibl il map Science 198:394-6 O 28 '77

VIBURNUMS
Virtuoso viburnums. P. Harper. il Horticulture 55:52-5 S '77

VICE
See also
Prostitution

VICE-PRESIDENTS

United States

See also
Mondale, W. F.

Homes

House that Joan Mondale decorated. S. B. Conroy. il pors Art N 76:56-7+ Summ '77
Sheep accounting. Vasari. Art N 76:29 F '77
Vice Presidential home on Naval Observatory hill. M. Elfin. il pors Smithsonian 8:62-9 S '77

VICKER, Ray
Clumsy fool—careful with that vase! il Read Digest 110:133-5 F '77

VICKERY, Jim Dale
Writer on the road. il por Writers Digest 57:20 Ap '77

VICKSBURG, Miss.

Siege, 1863

See United States—History—Civil War, 1861-1865—Campaigns and battles

VICTIMS of crime
AoA supports $4 million joint study on crime; reduce crimes against the elderly. Aging 275:7 S '77
Innocent victim myth. D. H. Bulkley. il Intellect 105:433-4 Je '77
New urban riots. M. Pousner. por Newsweek 89:11 Je 27 '77
Step-up in fight on crimes against elderly. il U.S. News 82:62 Je 13 '77
Victims of rape. F. R. Scarpitti and E. C. Scarpitti. bibl il Society 14:29-32 Jl '77

Compensation

See Reparation

VICTOR, Robert C.
Sun, moon, and planets this month. See issues of Sky & telescope

VICTORIA, Maximo Pedro
Physicist describes oppression of Argentine scientists. F. C. Bennett. Phys Today 30:61-2 Ag '77 *
Physics in Argentina. N. Wade. Science 196:1302 Je 17 '77 *

VICTORIA, British Columbia

Description

Vancouver and Victoria. J. Ferri. il Travel 147:30+ My '77

Hotels, restaurants, etc.

Tea at the Empress in Victoria. il Sunset 158:66 Je '77

VICTORIA and Albert Museum, London
Privilege and passion of directing museums; interview, ed by J. Gruen. R. Strong. il por Art N 76:58-62+ Ja '77

VICTORIAN furniture. See Furniture, Victorian

VICTOROFF, Victor M.
Psychiatrist discusses one solution. Fam Health 9:22-4 Ap '77

VICTORY Press-Tyndale House Publishers merger. See Publishers and publishing—Acquisitions and mergers

VIDAL, Gore
Good and bad of Gore Vidal. J. Simon. il Esquire 88:22-4 Ag '77 *
What makes Vidal run. J. Epstein. Commentary 63:72-5 Je '77 *

VIDARABINE
Antiviral drugs: possibilities against herpes. il Sci N 112:116 Ag 20 '77
Drug for treatment of herpes encephalitis. T. H. Metz. Science 197:973 S 2 '77
Drug for viruses; use of ara-A in treatment of herpes viruses. J. Seligmann and E. Clark. il Newsweek 90:80 Ag 22 '77
New drug effective against virus. il Chemistry 50:27 O '77
Viral antidote; adenine arabinoside. il Time 110:75 Ag 22 '77

VIDELA, Jorge Rafael
Hope from a clockwork coup. B. Hillenbrand. il por Time 109:45-6 Ap 11 '77 *

VIDEO art
About faces: the new work of Peter Campus. R. Smith. il Art in Am 65:85-7 Mr '77
Artists' video at the crossroads. B. Kurtz. il Art in Am 65:36-40 Ja '77
New music: Robert Ashley's videotapes of seven contemporary composers entitled Music with roots in the aether. J. La Barbara. il Hi Fi 27:MA14-15 Je '77
Video art: a medium discovering itself. J. Price. il Art N 76:41-7 Ja '77
See also
Libraries—Video art collections

VIDEO disc players. See Video recorders and recording

VIDEO discs. See Video records

VIDEO games. See Electronic games

VIDEO recorders and recording
Betamax: how well does it work? il Consumer Rep 42:291 My '77
Film craft. L. Drukker. il por Pop Phot 81:50+ S '77
Here at last—video-discs players. J. Free il Pop Sci 210:85-7+ F '77
Home video cassettes: a report from the front. Hi Fi 27:33+ N '77
Life with a video tape recorder. R. D. Freed. il Mech Illus 74:52+ Ja '78
New boom in videocassette recorders. D. Lachenbruch. il House & Gard 149:62+ N '77
New long-play video-cassette recorders. J. Free. il Pop Sci 211:81-3+ N '77
$1,300 Christmas toy made in Japan. P. J. Schuyten. il Fortune 96:179-80+ S '77
Right to replay? suit against Sony Corp.'s Betamax. il Time 109:64 Ap 11 '77
TV recorders: have the best of both shows. A. R. Curtis. il Pop Mech 148:98-9+ O '77
Technology versus tariffs; home video recorder. il Forbes 119:27-8 Ap 15 '77
Three video cassette recorders for your TV. il Pop Sci 210:46 Ap '77
War of the videotapes. R. Gelatt. Sat R 4:44-5 S 3 '77

Business use

TV that competes with the office grapevine. il Bus W p49+ Mr 14 '77

Court use

Trials of TV; R. Zamora trial. J. K. Footlick. il por Newsweek 90:70 O 10 '77
Trialvision. J. K. Footlick and L. Howard. il Newsweek 89:66-7 Mr 7 '77

Educational use

Film producers charge N.Y. BOCES with infringement of copyrights. SLJ 24:9 D '77
July conference focuses on off-air videotaping. SLJ 24:12 S '77
Tutored videotape instruction: a new use of electronics media in education. J. F. Gibbons and others. bibl il Science 195:1139-46 Mr 18 '77

Manufacture

See Television apparatus industry

Marketing

MCA vs. Sony; suit to prevent manufacture of Betamax video tape system. L. Marcus. Hi Fi 27:4 Ap '77

VIDEO records
Whatever happened to videodisc? D. Boyle. il Am Lib 8:97-8 F '77

VIDEO tape recorders and recording. See Video recorders and recording

VIDEO tape recordings
Mediums unite: super 8 reborn as video tape. M. Mikolas. il Mod Phot 41:46+ My '77
See also
Video art

VIDLER, Alec. See Muggeridge, M. jt auth

VIDOCQ, Eugène François
World's first—and greatest—detective. J. Stewart-Gordon. Read Digest 111:129-33 O '77 *

VIDOVIC, Jerry
Let's hear it for Croatia. J. Papanek. il por Sports Illus 47:44+ Jl 25 '77 *

VIENNA

Hotels, restaurants, etc.

International chef; coffee shop of the Vienna Hotel Inter-Continental. L. Szathmary. Travel 148:64 O '77

Music

See also
Opera—Austria

VIENNA State Opera. See Opera—Austria

VIENNA State Opera Ballet. See Ballet—Austria

VIENNA waltzes; ballet. See Ballet reviews—Single works

VIERTHALER, Bonnie
Recycled rubber stretches the imagination. D. L. Schultz. il Design (US) 79:17 Fall '77 *

VIETNAM
Cautious conquerors of Saigon. J. Shaw. il Time 109:45 My 16 '77
Life in the new Vietnam. R. Carroll and H. Jensen. il Newsweek 89:37+ My 23 '77
See also
Civil rights—Vietnam
Communism—Vietnam
Government and the press—Vietnam
Hanoi
Investments, Foreign—Vietnam
Mekong River
Science—Vietnam
United Nations—Vietnam

Foreign opinion

American

What right to judge? Nation 224:163-4 F 12 '77

Foreign relations

Viet overflight charges spur airline concern. Aviation W 107:31 Jl 11 '77

United States

See United States—Foreign relations—Vietnam

Politics and government

Monsters in our footsteps. Nation 224:388 Ap 2 '77

Reconstruction

Healing the wounds of war: justice, not charity, for Vietnam. G. Porter. Chr Cent 94:192-4 Mr 2 '77

Religious institutions and affairs

Visit in Viet Nam. H. Jantz. il Chr Today 21:49-51 F 18 '77

VIETNAM, North
See also
Economic assistance, American—Vietnam, North

VIETNAM, South
Liem's story; life before the fall of Saigon. L. B. Golsan. il Chr Cent 94:976-82 O 26 '77

VIETNAMESE-Cambodian conflict, 1977-. See Cambodian-Vietnamese conflict, 1977-

VIETNAMESE cookery. See Cookery, Vietnamese

VIETNAMESE in the United States
Braving a new world; Trang and Quynh Nguyen. K. Ray. il Seventeen 36:232 Ap '77
Exiles of Indochina. E. Keerdoja. il por Newsweek 89:14+ Ap 11 '77
Leap of faith. R. Kirk. Nat R 29:334 Mr 18 '77
Liem's story. L. B. Golsan. il Chr Cent 94:976-82 O 26 '77
Tutoring Vietnamese refugees. J. Koster. Todays Educ 66:32-4 N '77
Vietnamese in U.S: fleeing to California. il U.S. News 82:46 Je 13 '77

VIETNAMESE refugees. See Refugees, Vietnamese

VIETNAMESE War, 1957-1975

Aerial operations

Time of eagles. F. L. Harvey. il Flying 101:276-80 S '77

American participation

Culture of appeasement. N. Podhoretz. Harpers 255:25-32 O '77

Casualties

Accounting for missing persons in Vietnam; statement, October 27, 1977. F. A. Sieverts. Dept State Bull 77:899-901 D 19 '77
Department discusses MIA's in Vietnam and Laos; statement, July 27, 1977. R. C. Holbrooke. Dept State Bull 77:359-61 S 12 '77
Let them rest in peace; MIAs. Nation 224:293 Mr 12 '77
Prisoners of hope; relatives of MIAs. J. Lelyveld. il N Y Times Mag p 110 Mr 20 '77
See also
United States—Presidential Commission on Americans Missing and Unaccounted For in Southeast Asia

Destruction and pillage

See also
Vietnam—Reconstruction

Evacuation of civilians

Psst! Viet secrets? CIA agent F. Snepp's account. T. Mathews. il Newsweek 90:71 N 28 '77

Fiction

Pieces of a Vietnam war story; T. O'Brien. G. Lyons. Nation 224:120-2 Ja 29 '77

Missing in action

See Vietnamese War, 1957-1975—Casualties

News coverage

See Vietnamese War, 1957-1975—Press reports

Peace and mediation

Secret negotiation meetings

Former President Nixon's message to Prime Minister Pham Dong; February 1, 1973. R. M. Nixon. Dept State Bull 76:674-5 Je 27 '77
Kissinger's double-cross for peace: the broken promise to Hanoi. G. Porter. Nation 224:519-21 Ap 30 '77

Personal narratives

On the eve of the Tet offensive; interview, ed by L. R. Obst. R. Kovic. il por N Y Times Mag p40-2 N 13 '77
Psst! Viet secrets? CIA agent F. Snepp's account. T. Mathews. il por Newsweek 90:71 N 28 '77

Press reports

Time Inc.'s internal war over Vietnam; excerpt from The powers that be. D. Halberstam. il pors Esquire 89:94-100+ Ja '78

Prisoners and prisons

See also
Prisoners of war, Returned

Protests, demonstrations, etc. against

Hidden revolution. J. L. Stipp. Commonweal 104:427-31 Jl 8 '77
See also
Military service, Compulsory—Draft resisters

Public opinion

America after Viet Nam. L. Morrow. il Horizon 19:42-7 Jl '77

Reconstruction

See Vietnam—Reconstruction

Reparations

Healing the wounds of war: justice, not charity, for Vietnam. G. Porter. Chr Cent 94:192-4 Mr 2 '77

Strategy

Science advisers helped avert use of "nukes" in Vietnam. N. Wade. Science 195:968 Mr 11 '77

Veterans

See Veterans

War correspondents and photographers

PW interviews; ed by J. F. Baker. G. Emerson. por Pub W 211:8-9 Ja 10 '77

VIEUX Carré. See New Orleans

VIEUX Carré; drama. See Williams, T.

VIEW cameras. See Cameras

VIEWFINDERS. See Photography—Apparatus and supplies

VIGGEN (airplane) See Airplanes, Military—Sweden

VIGILANCE committees
Law and order comes to CB radio; National CB Radio Posse. S. Thompson. Car & Dr 23:20 D '77

VIGILANTES. See Vigilance committees

VIGO County, Ind, Public Library, Terre Haute. See Libraries—Indiana

VIGUERIE, Richard A.
Fission on the right. A. Crawford. Nation 224:104-8 Ja 29 '77 *

VIHTELIC, John
16-day ordeal of John Vihtelic. E. D'Aulaire and P. O. D'Aulaire. il Read Digest 110:142-6+ Mr '77 *

VIKING flights. See Space flight to Mars

VIKING Press, Inc
ABA's Smith censures Furness and Today show. J. Giusto. Pub W 212:36+ O 24 '77

VILARÓ, Carlos Páez. See Páez Vilaró, C.

VILLA-LOBOS, Arminda
Brasileiro; interview, ed by L. Rasponi. por Opera N 42:28-9 D 10 '77

VILLA-LOBOS, Heitor
Brasileiro; interview, ed by L. Rasponi. A. Villa-Lobos. por Opera N 42:28-9 D 10 '77 *
Music for piano. D. Gravelmann. Am Rec G 40:49 Je '77 *

VILLA Montana restaurant, Morelia. See Restaurants—Mexico

VILLAGES

Canada

English spoken here; Stanbridge East, Quebec. R. Manning. il Newsweek 89:63 My 9 '77

Chile

Pilgrimage to La Tirana; celebration of religious festival. S. Valderrama. il Américas 29:17-20 Ag '77

Gambia

Alex Haley in Juffure. H. J. Massaquoi. il pors Ebony 32:31-3+ Jl '77
To the roots of Roots; visiting Juffure. J. Pringle. il Newsweek 89:26-7 Mr 14 '77

Lebanon

Death of a village; Azziye. T. Clifton. il Newsweek 90:63 N 21 '77

Mexico

America's stepchildren; citizenship claims by Rio Ricans on U.S.-Mexican border. M. Kasindorf. il Newsweek 89:13 Ap 25 '77

Puerto Rico

Where Puerto Rico meets the sea; reefs surrounding La Parguera. P. L. Colin. il Sea Front 23:350-60 N '77

VILLAGES, Restored
British Columbia's Doukhobors; restoration of Novae Selo. il map Sunset 158:62 Je '77
See also
Greenfield Village and Henry Ford Museum, Dearborn, Mich.
Williamsburg, Va.

VILLARREAL, Luis Perez, and Berg, Paul
Hybridization in situ of SV40 plaques: detection of recombinant SV40 virus carrying specific sequences of nonviral DNA. bibl il Science 196: 183-5 Ap 8 '77

VILLAS, Guillermo
Fantastico, Guillermo! C. Kirkpatrick. il Sports Illus 47:12-17 S 19 '77 *

VILLAS, James
Art of eating out all alone. il por Esquire 88:101-2+ Jl '77
Cuisine for a queen. il Holiday 58:46-9+ Je '77

VILLIERS, Sir Charles
Stiff upper lip. il por Forbes 120:54+ S 1 '77 *

VILLON, Jacques, pseud
Paris celebrates: a new art center and the brothers Duchamp. F. Steegmuller. Atlantic 239:88-90 Je '77 *

VILLON, Raymond Duchamp-. See Duchamp-Villon, R.

VINCI, John
Report from Chicago: restoration of the Trading Room. F. Schulze. il Art in Am 65:58-9 N '77 *

VINCI, Leonardo da. See Leonardo da Vinci

VINDOLANDA excavations. See Great Britain—Antiquities, Roman

VINE peaches (melons) See Melons

VINEGAR
Bright, red, sweet-sour, aromatic, it's fresh strawberry vinegar. il Sunset 159:132 Jl '77
See also
Cookery—Vinegar

VINEYARDS. See Viticulture

VINSON, S. Bradleigh. See Hung, A. C. F. jt auth

VINSON, William D. and Heany, D. F.
Is quality out of control? bibl f il Harvard Bus R 55:114-22 N '77

VINT, Bill
(ed) See Roosevelt, T. Hunting with Teddy Roosevelt

VINTON, Bobby
Great American melting pot. Holiday 58:25-6+ Ap '77

VINYL floor coverings. See Flooring, Plastic

VINYL flooring. See Flooring, Plastic

VIOLA, Herman J.
How did an Indian chief really look? il Smithsonian 8:100-2+ Je '77

VIOLA, Thomas C.
Trash collector who cleaned house. Bus W p25-6 Ag 22 '77 *

VIOLA Farber Dance Company. See Dance companies

VIOLENCE
Battered teacher. A. M. Bloch. Todays Educ 66:58-9+ Mr '77
How biocriminology's clues show diet's relationship to violence! T. O. Marsh. por Sci Digest 82:17-19 Jl '77
Human species: the tribe that talks peace and makes war; the Yanomamo. J. Pfeiffer. il Horizon 19:92-3 Ja '77
Intelligent woman's guide to sex; use of brutality toward women in record advertising. J. Coburn. Mademoiselle 83:58 Ag '77
McCalls family lobby; family violence bills. A. O'Shea. McCalls 105:42 Ja '78
Majorities and minorities: a comparative survey of ethnic violence. C. Hewitt. bibl f il Ann Am Acad 433:150-60 S '77
Media mistreatment of women. H. Hyans. McCalls 105:43 Ja '78
North, south, east and west side story; school vandalism and violence. S. Moorefield. il Am Educ 13:12-16 Ja '77; Same abr. Educ Digest 42:10-13 My '77
Promoting religious values in an age of violence and terror; excerpts from address. M. H. Tanenbaum. por Intellect 105:218-19 Ja '77
TRB from Washington. New Repub 176:4+ Mr 26 '77
Understanding lethal violence. M. L. Simpson. Intellect 105:379-80 My '77
Unreported violence; within the family. Sci Digest 82:76 Ag '77
Violence in our schools. L. David. il Good H 185:129+ N '77
Violent American home. Sci N 111:158 Mr 5 '77
See also
Terrorism

Prevention

What to do about violence; public schools. J. E. Cole. Todays Educ 66:58-9 N '77

VIOLENCE in art
Murray Stern: social surrealist. A. Sanders. il por Am Artist 41:76-83+ F '77

VIOLENCE in motion pictures
Spreading fast: revolt against violence in movies. il U.S. News 82:58-9 Mr 14 '77

VIOLENCE in sports
Savagery on the playing fields. R. C. Yeager. il Read Digest 111:23-4+ Jl '77
See also
Basketball, Professional—Accidents and injuries
Basketball, Professional—Ethical aspects
Football, Professional—Ethical aspects

VIOLENCE in television
Aggression on TV could be helping our children. J. J. Lopiparo. bibl f Intellect 105:345-6 Ap '77
Antiviolence viewers strike back. U.S. News 82: 30 F 7 '77
Commentaries: on television violence. G. Gerbner; J. A. Schneider. Society 14:8-17 S '77
Did TV make him do it? R. Zamora case. il Time 110:87+ O 10 '77
Fight for law and order. J. Lardner. New Repub 177:32-5 O 1 '77
Great American teaching machine—of violence. H. J. Skornia. Intellect 105:347-8 Ap '77
Learning violence via TV. J. Bosveld. Sci Digest 81:27-30 Mr '77
Objections: violent and non-. D. English. Vogue 167:60 Ag '77
Putting the networks on notice; work of National PTA. J. C. Lyles. Chr Cent 94:556-7 Je 8 '77
TV: getting gun-shy? Sr Schol 110:11 O 6 '77
TV on trial; R. Zamora trial. Newsweek 90:104 S 12 '77
TV violence: are parents getting the message? Children are! C. Kimmel. por Parents Mag 52:29 Mr '77
Television violence: a call to arms. Sci N 111: 261-2 Ap 23 '77
Television violence revisited. D. K. Osborn and J. D. Osborn. il Educ Digest 43:38-9 S '77
Television's passing age. America 136:208-9 Mr 12 '77
Trials on TV; R. Zamora trial. J. K. Footlick. il por Newsweek 90:70 O 10 '77
Violence in America. B. Myerson. Redbook 150: 113+ N '77
Zamora case: TV gets a reprieve. Sci N 112:247 O 15 '77

VIOLENCE in the arts
Literary forecasts of violence. C. Brosman. il Intellect 105:218 Ja '77

VIOLIN

Construction

Of fiddles and fiddlers (and friends): William Sidney Mount's Cradle of Harmony. I. Lowens. il Hi Fi 27:89-90 Mr '77
Violin-making as American art. P. Kass and M. Olmert. il Smithsonian 8:106-10 bibl(p 131) S '77

VIOLIN making. See Violin—Construction

VIOLIN music
See also
Phonograph records—Violin music

VIOLINISTS
See also
Heifetz, D.
Heifetz, J.
Kremer, G.
Markov, A.
Menuhin, Y.
Phillips, D.
Ponty, J. L.
Venuti, J.

VIOLONCELLO. See Cello

VIORST, Judith
How did I get to be 40? excerpt from How did I get to be 40. . .& other atrocities. Read Digest 110:90-1 Je '77
How do you know when you're 40? il N Y Times Mag p66-7 F 6 '77

VIORST, Judith—*Continued*
How many dimes make a million dollars? Read Digest 111:166-8 N '77
[Monthly column] See issues of Redbook
Sometimes I hate my husband. Read Digest 110:19+ Mr '77

VIORST, Milton
Israelis watch Begin. Nation 225:686-90 D 24 '77

VIPERS. See Snakes

VIRAL genetics. See Microbial genetics

VIRAL hepatitis. See Hepatitis

VIRAL mutation. See Mutation (viruses)

VIRAZOLE. See Ribavirin

VIREN, Lasse
Enigma wrapped in glory. K. Moore. il por Sports Illus 46:66-72+ Je 27 '77 *

VIRGIN Mary. See Mary, Virgin

VIRGIN birth. See Parthenogenesis

VIRGIN ISLANDS
Is paradise lost? T. Szulc. il Sat R 5:18-20 O 1 '77
See also
Investments, American—Virgin Islands
St Croix Island
United Nations—Virgin Islands

VIRGIN Islands National Park
St John: a trip through time. M. J. Goodban. il Nat Parks & Con Mag 51:16-18 F '77

VIRGINIA
See also
Architecture, Domestic—Virginia
Blue Ridge Mountains
Chesapeake Bay
Education—Virginia
Express highways—Virginia
Forests and forestry—Virginia
Historic houses, sites, etc.—Virginia
Hunting—Virginia
Libraries—Virginia
Opera—Virginia
Potomac River
Shenandoah River
Tangier Island
Water pollution—Virginia
Water supply—Virginia

Industries
See also
Fruit industry

History
See also
Tobacco industry—United States—History

Parks and reserves
Pool party: catfish for 600; Pohick Bay Regional Park. R. G. Bowers. il Parks & Rec 12:38-40+ Mr '77

Politics and government
Carter strikes out in Virginia; gubernatorial race lost by H. Howell. R. Mackenzie. Nat R 29:1425-6 D 9 '77
Howell for Virginia. New Repub 177:6 O 29 '77
Howlin' Henry's surprise win; June 14 Democratic primary. R. Mackenzie. Nat R 29:778 Jl 8 '77
Statehouse derby. R. Boeth and others. il pors Newsweek 90:42+ O 17 '77
Two tight gubernatorial races. il pors Time 110: 25-6 N 7 '77

Sanitary affairs
Save water at highway rest stops; recycle and reuse system. C. E. Parker. il Am City & County 92:63-4 Je '77

VIRGINIA BEACH, Va.
Norfolk & Virginia Beach. E. Cheatham and P. Cheatham. il Travel 147:32-7+ Ap '77
Vacuum handles big litter problem. Am City & County 92:42 O '77

VIRTUE
Roots. K. Lindskoog. Chr Cent 94:251 Mr 16 '77

VIRUS diseases
Unconventional viruses and the origin and disappearance of kuru; Nobel Prize lecture, December 12, 1976. D. C. Gajdusek. bibl il maps Science 197:943-60 S 2 '77
See also
Cold (disease)
Herpesvirus diseases

VIRUS diseases in animals
See also
Newcastle disease
Scrapie

VIRUS research
Animal viruses: probes of cell function. G. B. Kolata. Science 196:417-18 Ap 22 '77
Microbiology; summaries of papers from the Gustav Stern Symposium on Perspectives in Virology. Sci N 111:120 F 19 '77
Persistent infections: the role of viruses. J. L. Marx. Science 196:151-2 Ap 8 '77
Virus transfer from surf to wind. E. R. Baylor and others. bibl il Science 198:575-80 N 11 '77
Water-to-air transfer of virus. E. R. Baylor and V. Peters. bibl il Science 197:763-4 Ag 19 '77

VIRUS vaccines. See Vaccines

VIRUSES
Persistent infections: the role of viruses; vesicular stomatitis virus. J. L. Marx. Science 196:151-2 Ap 8 '77
Suppression of the temperature-sensitive phenotype of a mutant of reovirus type 3. R. F. Ramig and others. bibl il Science 195:406-7 Ja 28 '77
Venereal transmission of La Crosse (California encephalitis) arbovirus in aedes triseriatus mosquitoes. W. H. Thompson and B. J. Beaty. bibl il Science 196:530-1 Ap 29 '77
Viruses and the biological control of insect pests. T. W. Tinsley. bibl il BioScience 27:659-61 O '77
See also
Bacteriophages
Herpesviruses
Influenza viruses
Simian viruses
Tumor viruses
Visna virus

Inactivation
BHT—from preservative to antiviral agent. Chemistry 50:24-5 N '77
Drinkers rejoice: a little wine may kill your virus. T. J. Maugh. Science 196:1074 Je 3 '77
Grape products: virus killers. Sci N 111:138 F 26 '77
See also
Interferon
Ribavirin
Vidarabine

Reproduction
How the virus builds itself; tobacco mosaic virus. il Sci N 111:103 F 12 '77

VIRUSES, Plant
Cucumber mosaic virus associated RNA 5: causal agent for tomato necrosis. J. M. Kaper and H. E. Waterworth. bibl il Science 196: 429-31 Ap 22 '77
Editorial; cucumber mosaic virus and the 1972 tomato epidemic in Alsace. P. Trachtman. Horticulture 55:10-11 Jl '77
How the virus builds itself; tobacco mosaic virus. il Sci N 111:103 F 12 '77
Spiroplasmavirus citri 3: propagation, purification, proteins, and nucleic acid. R. M. Cole and others. bibl il Science 198:1262-3 D 23 '77

VIRUSES in water. See Water—Microbiology

VISA charge card. See Credit cards

VISAS. See Passports

VISCARDI, Henry, 1912-
Help for people society often ignores. il pors U.S. News 83:48 Ag 1 '77 *

VISES
Benchtop vise for tricky holds. R. M. Gutter. il Pop Mech 147:60+ F '77
PM tool test: instant bench vise. H. Wicks. il Pop Mech 148:196 O '77

VISHNIAC, Roman
Viewpoint. J. Deschin. il Pop Phot 80:12+ Je '77 *
Vishniac's treasures, almost lost, surely will survive. H. Keppler. il Mod Phot 41:60 Jl '77 *

VISHNU
See also
Krishna

VISIBLE speech. See Deaf—Means of communication

VISION
All the news in sight; symposium. Harp Baz 110: 112-17+ Ag '77
Biomedicine. Sci N 111:296 My 7 '77
Cortical potentials associated with the detection of visual events. R. Cooper and others. bibl il Science 196:74-7 Ap 1 '77
Eye contact and face scanning in early infancy. M. M. Haith and others. bibl il Science 198:853-5 N 25 '77
How to save your child's good sight. E. Friedman. il Parents Mag 52:46-7+ F '77
How to spot vision problems in young children. Parents Mag 52:39 Ag '77
Look into my eyes: an infant's view. il Sci N 112:373 D 3 '77
Shedding light on vision. J. Arehart-Treichel. il Sci N 111:408-9 Je 25 '77
Train your eyes; better your score. P. Martin. il Sci Digest 81:7-9 Mr '77
See also
After images
Blindness
Color sense
Contact lenses
Dominance, Ocular
Eye
Eyeglasses
Flicker phenomena
Visual discrimination
Visual perception

VISION (animals)
Binocular differences in cortical receptive fields of kittens after rotationally disparate binocular experience. P. G. Shinkman and C. J. Bruce. bibl il Science 197:285-7 Jl 15 '77
Loss of Y-cells in the lateral geniculate nucleus of monocularly deprived tree shrews. T. T. Norton and others. bibl il Science 197:784-6 Ag 19 '77
Magnification in striate cortex and retinal ganglion cell layer of owl monkey: a quantitative comparison. J. Myerson and others. bibl il Science 198:855-7 N 25 '77
Trichromatic vision in the cat. J. Ringo and others. bibl il Science 198:753-5 N 18 '77
Visual sensitivity: significant within-species variations in a nonhuman primate. G. H. Jacobs. bibl il Science 197:499-500 Jl 29 '77

VISION (birds)
Stereopsis in the falcon. R. Fox and others. bibl il Science 197:79-81 Jl 1 '77

VISION (insects)
Head capsule transmission of long-wavelength light in the curculionidae. J. R. Meyer. bibl il Science 196:524-5 Ap 29 '77
Vision in insects: pathways possibly underlying neural adaptation and lateral inhibition. N. J. Strausfeld and J. A. Campos-Ortega. bibl il Science 195:894-7 Mr 4 '77

VISION (invertebrates)
Vision in annelid worms. G. Wald and R. Stephen. bibl il Science 196:1434-9 Je 24 '77

VISITOR to Mount Vernon; drama. See Miller, H. L.

VISITORS, Foreign
Friendship Force. P. Davis. Bet Hom & Gard 55:204+ N '77
Making friends abroad, down-home style; Friendship Force. il U.S. News 83:58 S 19 '77
See also
Visits of state

Africa, Southern
African leaders' commitment to justice. P. E. Brink. Chr Cent 94:1143-6 D 7 '77

Africa, West
English-speaking West Africa. J. R. W. Stott. Chr Today 22:38-9 D 9 '77

Asia, Southeastern
Travels with le Carré. H. D. S. Greenway. pors Newsweek 90:102 O 10 '77

China
According to Chairman Mao; U.S. tennis tour of China. B. Collins. il Sports Illus 47:99-100 D 5 '77
Albert reports on Peking visit, coming book exhibit. M. Reuter. il Pub W 212:19-20 O 17 '77
China behind the guided tour. E. N. Luttwak. Read Digest 110:211-14+ Ap '77
China: unraveling the new mysteries. W. Safire. il pors N Y Times Mag p33-4+ Je 19 '77
From Peking to Lhasa—a 16-day journey through China. C. Untermeyer. il U.S. News 83:35-7 N 14 '77
Open-door policy; C. Carter's visit. A. Deming and others. il por Newsweek 89:42 Ap 25 '77
Orchid diplomacy; trip to Canton Fair in attempt to import orchids to U.S. W. K. Glikbarg. Horticulture 55:8-13 My '77
Roots in China. a first encounter. L. Wong. il por Smithsonian 8:116-20 bibl(p 148) Ap '77
Seeing China plain. E. N. Luttwak; discussion. Commentary 63:4+ Mr '77

Cuba
Bowie's bean ball; failure to arrange US-Cuba baseball game. Nation 224:420 Ap 9 '77
Cuba: no room for naysayers? D. Peerman. il Chr Cent 94:845-9 S 28 '77
Ecumenical inspection; U.S. group. Chr Today 21:56 Ap 1 '77
Good neighbors mean good business. il Time 109:54 My 2 '77
Is it the future? Will it work? with the Venceremos in Cuba. H. Maurer. il por Nation 225:6-10 Jl 2 '77
Our men in Havana; basketball teams. E. Sciolino. il Newsweek 89:45+ Ap 18 '77
Probing the Cuba trade; visiting American businessmen. L. Langway and C. J. Harper. il Newsweek 90:66-7 Jl 4 '77
Secrets of the new Cuba. A. Walker. il por Ms 6:71-4+ S '77

Czechoslovakia
Dodging the spooks: an American journalist in Prague. C. Sawyer. Nation 225:325-8 O 8 '77

Egypt
Hava nagila in Egypt; Israeli correspondents in Cairo. W. Stewart. il Time 110:24 D 26 '77

Europe, Western
How to shake the travel jitters; Farm Journal tour. D. Braun. il Farm J 101:47-9+ Mr '77

Gambia
To the roots of Roots; visiting Juffure. J. Pringle. il Newsweek 89:26-7 Mr 14 '77

India
Miss Lillian's sentimental journey. il pors Time 109:17 F 28 '77

Ireland
Other Ireland. G. Bergman. Chr Cent 94:1006-7 N 2 '77

Israel
Feminist goes to Israel. L. C. Pogrebin. il Ms 6:69-72+ O '77
Journey through a land of doubts. M. Kalb. il N Y Times Mag p 12-13+ Jl 17 '77
Road to Tel Aviv. T. Powers. Commonweal 104:275-7 Ap 29 '77
Science policy visit to Israel. M. Macioti. il Bull Atom Sci 33:10-21 Mr '77
West Bank settlements. J. M. Wall. Chr Cent 94:1155-7 D 14 '77

Japan
Two different worlds; American Forestry Association tour of Alaska and Japan. R. Pardo. il Am For 83:14-17+ Ap '77

Latin America
Art and politics: from protest to myth: lecture tour. J. Canaday. il New Repub 178:25-7 Ja 7 '78
Notes on the gringo. W. E. Hoy. Américas 29:15-16 Ag '77

Northern Ireland
Journal from Northern Ireland. V. O. Baron. Chr Cent 94:757-9, 820-4 Ag 31, S 21 '77

Rumania
Believers in Romania: divided they stand; American visitors. E. E. Plowman. il pors Chr Today 21:18-21 My 20 '77

Russia
Art educators' odyssey, USSR. A. Hurwitz. il Sch Arts 76:56-8+ Ap '77
Capitalist decadent? ed by A. Newman. G. Segal. Art N 76:36 F '77
Critical focus. K. Poli. il Pop Phot 81:8+ S '77
Encounter in Moscow. L. Gersten. America 137:30-1 Jl 16 '77
Five times to Yakutsk; American photojournalist. D. Conger. il pors Nat Geog 152:256-69 Ag '77
Larry Rivers and George Segal: back in the U.S.S.R; interview, ed by E. C. Baker. L. Rivers; G. Segal. il por Art in Am 65:104-12 N '77
Rare look at wildlife in Russia. G. H. Harrison. il por map Int Wildlife 8:4-11 Ja '78
Russian paradoxes. R. G. Smith. Intellect 105:373-4 My '77
Ten days that shook me up in Russia. B. Gelb. il N Y Times Mag p21+ S 18 '77
Uncle Cam visits the U.S.S.R. E. E. Plowman. il por Chr Today 22:61-2 D 9 '77

Taiwan
Getting to know you; Pacific Cultural Foundation's sponsoring of Taiwan junkets. A. Deming and others. il Newsweek 89:54-5 Ja 31 '77
Harold Lindsell reports from Taiwan. H. Lindsell. Chr Today 21:15-17 Ag 26 '77
Taiwan's future. M. Kondracke. New Repub 177:15-17 S 24 '77

Tanzania
Tanzanian socialism: American impressions. W. Bockelman. Chr Cent 94:774 S 14 '77

Tibet
Inside the new Tibet. G. Bush. Newsweek 90:62+ N 7 '77

United States
End to Meany's veto; amendment of the State Department Authorization Bill to grant visas to Communists. Nation 225:195-6 S 10 '77
Foreign VIP's—another group of junketers financed by U.S. taxpayers; visits of foreign military officers. G. Parshall and R. Barr. il U.S. News 83:30-1 S 19 '77
14 Soviet publishers have useful visit in U.S; Protocol question. M. Reuter. il Pub W 212:11-13 N 28 '77
Host Country urged to prevent acts against missions. UN Chron 14:83 Ja '77
Polish farmers learn about free enterprise. V. Louviere. il Nations Bus 65:44 F '77
Share your home for the holidays. J. Walker. House B 119:8+ D '77
Travels with Mrs T: M. Thatcher's visit. T. Fuller. il pors Newsweek 90:51 S 26 '77
Why foreign tourists flock to the U.S. il U.S. News 82:38 Je 27 '77
See also
National Council for Community Services to International Visitors

VISITS of state
Meeting foreign leaders—a whirlwind pace. il pors U.S. News 83:20-2 Ag 1 '77

VISLOCKY, Dorothy, Dance Theatre. See Dance companies

VISNA virus
Antigenic shift of visna virus in persistently infected sheep. O. Narayan and others. bibl il Science 197:376-8 Jl 22 '77
Slow persistent infection caused by visna virus: role of host restriction. A. T. Haase and others. bibl il Science 195:175-7 Ja 14 '77

VISSER, Martin
Martin Visser on Gretel II. Yachting 141:126-8 F '77

VISTA. See United States—ACTION

VISUAL aids. See Audio-visual materials

VISUAL cortex. See Brain

VISUAL deprivation. See Sensory deprivation

VISUAL discrimination
Visual detection of cryptic prey by blue jays (cyanocitta cristata) A. T. Pietrewicz and A. C. Kamil. bibl il Science 195:580-2 F 11 '77

VISUAL perception
Spatial frequency and the mediation of short-term visual storage. G. E. Meyer and W. M. Maguire. bibl il Science 198:524-5 N 4 '77
Visual search in the pigeon: hunt and peck method. D. S. Blough. bibl il Science 196:1013-14 My 27 '77
See also
Space perception
Word perception

VISUAL pigments
Ionochromic behavior of gecko visual pigments. F. Crescitelli. bibl il Science 195:187-8 Ja 14 '77
Visual pigment changes in rainbow trout in response to temperature. A. T. C. Tsin and D. D. Beatty. bibl il Science 195:1358-60 Mr 25 '77

VISUAL purple
Cold studies specify light chemistry. il Sci N 112:183 S 17 '77

VISUAL target tracking. See Target tracking

VISUALIZATION
Language as art and art as language. L. Mueller. bibl il Engl J 66:49-53 O '77
Mind's eye: nonverbal thought in technology. E. S. Ferguson. bibl il Science 197:827-36 Ag 26 '77

VITALE, John C.
How to keep your students from yawning at art museums. Design (US) 79:10-11 Fall '77
How to read a painting. il Sch Arts 77:44-6 N '77

VITALITY
Anxiety, stress, tension: how to turn them into creative energy; interview, ed by A. Gross. R. Suinn. Mademoiselle 83:164+ My '77
Energy and how to have more of it. L. E. Lamb. Harp Baz 110:89+ My '77
How to do more taking it easy; excerpt from Maximum performance. L. E. Morehouse; L. Gross. il Good H 184:202-3 Ap '77
How to get tension out, energy up. il Mademoiselle 83:134-7 D '77
How to increase your inner energy. W. E. O'Donnell. Read Digest 110:84-6 Mr '77
Turning off: the great energizer. N. Lande and A. Slade. Harp Baz 110:121+ Ag '77

VITAMINS
Vitamin update. E. Darden. Parents Mag 52:43+ Mr '77
See also
APL Corporation

Vitamin A acid

See Retinoic acid

Vitamin B_{12}

Leucine 2,3-aminomutase: a cobalamin-dependent enzyme present in bean seedlings. J. M. Poston. bibl il Science 195:301-2 Ja 21 '77
Natural product synthesis and vitamin B_{12}. A. Eschenmoser and C. E. Wintner. bibl il Science 196:1410-20 Je 24 '77

Vitamin C

Battle over vitamin C. J. Mayer. il Fam Health 9:26-8 Ap '77
C riddle: it can't hurt. Sci Digest 81:24-5 Ap '77

Vitamin D

Adequate response of plasma 1,25-dihydroxyvitamin D to parturition in paretic (milk fever) dairy cows. R. L. Horst and others. bibl il Science 196:662-3 My 6 '77
1,25-dihydroxycholecalciferol and parathormone: effects on isolated osteoclast-like and osteoblast-like cells. G. L. Wong and others. bibl il Science 197:663-5 Ag 12 '77
Experimental diabetes reduces circulating 1,25-dihydroxyvitamin D in the rat. L. E. Schneider and others. bibl il Science 196:1452-4 Je 24 '77
25-Hydroxycholecalciferol to 1,25-dihydroxycholecalciferol: conversion impaired by systemic metabolic acidosis. S. W. Lee and others. bibl il Science 195:994-6 Mr 11 '77
Specific high-affinity binding macromolecule for 1,25-dihydroxyvitamin D_3 in fetal bone. B. E. Kream and others. bibl Science 197:1086-8 S 9 '77

Vitamin E

How does vitamin E prevent aging? Sci N 111:341 My 28 '77
Nutritional interrelationships of vitamin E and selenium. G. F. Combs, Jr and M. L. Scott. bibl il BioScience 27:467-73 Jl '77

VITICULTURE
Blue concords are his favorites. A. B. Ferrara. il Org Gard & Farm 24:84-5 D '77
Building a vineyard in Rhode Island wine country; Sakonnet Vineyard. R. Vaughan. il pors Horticulture 55:20-4+, 70-1 S '77
Growing grapes along the Rio Grande. S. Perry. Org Gard & Farm 24:130-2 My '77
If you'd like to make wine, what about a vineyard? il Sunset 159:273-5 O '77
Shaking California's throne. il Time 110:106-7+ N 21 '77
Troubled outlook for chemical farming. M. C. Goldman. il Org Gard & Farm 24:164-6+ F '77

VITTUM, M. T. See Hopp, R. J. jt auth

VIVALDI, Antonio
Four seasons; two recordings. J. R. Oestreich and J. Diether. Am Rec G 40:35-6 Jl '77 *
Various sacred works. P. L. Miller. Am Rec G 40:46+ O '77 *
Vivaldi; current recordings. J. W. Barker. Am Rec G 40:32-3 Ag '77 *

La **VIVANDIERE;** ballet. See Ballet reviews—Single works

VIVANTE, Arturo
Chest; story. New Yorker 53:34-9 Mr 7 '77
Osage orange; story. New Yorker 53:44-7 O 24 '77
Plot. Writer 90:29-32 Ap '77

VIVARIUMS
Nature in a tank; ideas of Susan and Vern French. il McCalls 105:162 O '77

VIVIAN, John
Building a 25-year strawberry bed. il Org Gard & Farm 24:190+ F '77
Joys of cooking with wood; excerpt from Wood heat. il Org Gard & Farm 24:126+ N '77

VIVIAN Beaumont Theater. See Lincoln Center for the Performing Arts, New York—Vivian Beaumont Theater

VIVISECTION
Animal rights: NIH cat sex study brings grief to New York museum. N. Wade; discussion. Science 195:131 Ja 14 '77

VLACH, John
Shotgun houses; with biographical sketch. il Natur Hist 86:4, 50-7 bibl(p 100-1) F '77

VLAD II, Dracul, Prince of Wallachia
Is Dracula really dead? il Time 109:60 My 23 '77
Dracula lives! D. Ansen. il Newsweek 90:74-5+ O 31 '77 *

VLAD II, Tepes. See Vlad II, Dracul, Prince of Wallachia

VLASIC Foods, Inc
Who's got Heinz in a pickle? T. Jaffe. il Forbes 120:63-4 Ag 15 '77

VOCABULARY
Sight words are not going out of style. J. Hood. Educ Digest 42:53-5 Ap '77

VOCABULARY tests
It pays to enrich your word power. P. Funk. See issues of Reader's digest

VOCAL music
See also
Phonograph records—Vocal music

Anecdotes, facetiae, satire, etc.

Short history of deedle. M. Brickman. New Yorker 53:48-9 N 7 '77

VOCAL organs. See Voice

VOCAL training. See Voice culture

VOCATIONAL counseling. See Vocational guidance

VOCATIONAL education
According to Hoyt; interview, ed by S. B. Neill. K. B. Hoyt. il por Am Educ 13:10-13 Mr '77
Art education and career education. F. Bedgone. bibl il Sch Arts 77:42-5 D '77
Career education defined; excerpt from Career education for special populations. K. Hoyt. Am Educ 13:inside cover Mr '77
Career education in the English classroom. R. Caldwell. bibl f il Engl J 66:45-8 N '77
Career education—the California R.O.P.—revisited. V. A. Gallo. bibl Clearing H 51:26-9 S '77
Career investigation and planning in the high school English curriculum. R. E. Roberts. bibl Engl J 66:49-52 N '77
Clearing the air in career education; Houston conference. S. B. Neill. il Am Educ 13:6-9+ Mr '77

VOCATIONAL education—*Continued*
Company helps youngsters launch careers; Rockwell International Corp's Advanced Career Training program. V. Louviere. il Nations Bus 65:60 Je '77
Cutting sex bias out of vocational education. P. Lehmann. Educ Digest 42:33-5 Mr '77
Doctor, lawyer, merchant, chief; career education through art. G. Gale. il Design (US) 78:23 mid-Summ '77
Does occupational education need a different emphasis? J. M. Benjamin. Clearing H 50:401-2 My '77
Facing up to the vo-ed information demand. A. M. Lee. Educ Digest 42:50-3 Ja '77
High school curriculum from a policy point of view. J. T. Gasso. Educ Digest 43:13-16 N '77
How PRYO worked for one student; Sweden. R. E. Belding. il Am Educ 13:12-13 Ag '77
Preparing teenagers for the world of work; Georgia's Career Awareness Program. A. Bledsoe. il Parents Mag 52:23-4 My '77
Rainbow in industrial arts; Occupational Versatility program; Puget Sound Junior High, Seattle. V. Hedrich. Educ Digest 42:53-6 F '77
Short-term training for job skills. Educ Digest 42:56-9 Mr '77
Should we teach about work in the social studies? P. K. Good and others. Educ Digest 42:57-9 My '77
Sweden's vocational strategy. R. Carlson. il Am Educ 13:9-11+ Ag '77
Vocational English. B. G. Rowell. Clearing H 50:241-2 F '77
Vocational oversell. C. R. Duke. Clearing H 50:284 Mr '77
Work, women, and vocational education. C. H. Rieder. il Am Educ 13:27-30 Je '77
Working. M. I. ElLaissi. Engl J 66:65-6 S '77
See also
Apprentices
Business education
Coalition of Publishers for Employment, Inc.
Education, Cooperative
Technical education
United States—Navy—Education

VOCATIONAL education for women
Fitting girls for men's jobs. S. Weiss. il McCalls 104:49 Mr '77

VOCATIONAL Foundation Inc
To be young, black and out of work; excerpt from report. il N Y Times Mag p38-40+ O 23 '77

VOCATIONAL guidance
Career potentials. B. Chamberlain. Am Artist 41:28+ Ag '77
Help for women suddenly on their own; Alliance for Displaced Homemakers. il Changing T 32:45-7 Ja '78
How to get a job; special section. il Esquire 88:51-77+ Jl '77
Sources of job information. B. Chamberlain. Am Artist 41:14+ Jl '77
Stalking the wild job; or, A career library from the ground up; Career Planning Library at the University of Pittsburgh. R. J. Egelston. bibl il Wilson Lib Bull 52:330-5 D '77
When women on their own are thrown onto the job market; work of the Alliance for Displaced Homemakers. il U.S. News 83:55-6 S 26 '77
See also
Occupations
Vocational education
Vocational Foundation Inc

VOCATIONAL literature
Career guides for the arts and humanities; guidebooks produced by the Technical Education Research Center. E. B. Roth. il Am Educ 13:14-15 Je '77

VOCATIONAL rehabilitation
See also
Handicapped—Employment

VOCATIONAL schools. See Vocational-technical schools

VOCATIONAL-technical schools
After high school, what? fraudulent practices of trade schools. W. D. Green. Am Educ 13:19-22 O '77
See also
Illinois Institute of Technology, Chicago

VODKA
Woman's no-nonsense guide to vodka. House B 119:157+ S '77

VODON, Vicki
Locker-room philosopher; interview, ed by J. Kaplan. Seventeen 36:104+ My '77

VOEHRINGER, Arnold
Care and feeding of two-cylinder John Deere tractors. il Org Gard & Farm 24:76-80 Ag '77

VOGEL, Jan
2 simple ideas for recycled decorations. il Ret Liv 17:35-6 D '77

VOGEL, Mike
Creative pendulum of Mike Vogel: graphic artist and entrepreneur. M. C. Nelson. il por Am Artist 41:70-5+ O '77 *

VOGEL, Wolfgang
Fixer. C. R. Whitney. il pors N Y Times Mag p46-50+ Mr 20 '77 *

VOGELSONG, Edward L.
Art of healthy communication; interview. il Fam Health 9:26-8 Jl '77

VOGT, Bill
Carter's water projects: pork barrel sellout? il Outdoor Life 160:34+ N '77
Deer that came in from the cold. il Nat Wildlife 16:50-3 D '77

VOGT, Peter R.
Hot spots; with biographical sketch. il maps Natur Hist 86:2, 36-45 bibl(p 100) Ap '77

VOICE
Acoustics of the singing voice. J. Sundberg. il Sci Am 236:82-4+ bibl(p 150) Mr '77
See also
Speech processing systems

VOICE culture
Most beautiful voice in the world; interview, ed by R. Jacobson. Z. Milanov. il Opera N 41:8+ Ap 9 '77
Schwarzkopf-Legge master classes; singing classes at Juilliard. D. J. Soria. pors Hi Fi 27:MA5-6+ Mr '77
See also
Opera—Instruction and study

VOICE of Ariadne; opera. See Musgrave, T.

VOICE scrambling. See Speech scrambling

VOIGT, Ellen Bryant
Seizure; poem. New Yorker 53:46 Ap 25 '77

VOLAVKA, J. and others
Naloxone in chronic schizophrenia. bibl il Science 196:1227-8 Je 10 '77

VOLCANIC ash, tuff, etc.
Pollen influx and volcanic ash. P. J. Mehringer, Jr and others. bibl il map Science 198:257-61 O 21 '77

VOLCANIC rocks. See Rocks, Igneous

VOLCANOES
Case of earthly indigestion; Japan's Mount Usu. il Time 110:61 Ag 29 '77
Eruptions of the St Augustine volcano: airborne measurements and observations. P. V. Hobbs and others. bibl il Science 195:871-3 Mr 4 '77
Explosive cenozoic volcanism and climatic implications. D. Ninkovich and W. L. Donn; reply. J. P. Kennett and R. C. Thunell. bibl il Science 196:1231-4 Je 10 '77
Hot spots. P. R. Vogt. il maps Natur Hist 86:36-45 bibl(p 100) Ap '77
Pleistocene volcanism and glacial initiation. J. R. Bray. bibl il Science 197:251-4 Jl 15 '77
Unraveling a Mayan mystery. R. J. Trotter. il map Sci N 111:74-5+ Ja 29 '77
Valley of 10,000 wonders. S. K. Hansen. il por Am For 83:26-9 F '77
Volcanic activity and great earthquakes at convergent plate margins. M. J. Carr. bibl il map Science 197:655-7 Ag 12 '77
See also
Hawaii Volcanoes National Park
Kilauea (crater)
Lava
Rainier, Mount
Thera (island)
Volcanic ash, tuff, etc.

VOLES. See Mice

VOLKOVA, Vera
Volkova: pedagogical prima. W. Terry. por Sat R 4:43 Ap 2 '77 *

VOLKSWAGEN (automobile) See Automobiles, Foreign

VOLKSWAGENWERK, ag. See Automobile industry—Germany, West

VOLLARD, Ambroise
Ambroise Vollard—impresario. G. Needham. il por Art N 76:78-80+ S '77 *
Genius disguised as a sloth; survey of work as impresario on view at Museum of Modern Art. R. Hughes. il por Time 109:68-9 Je 20 '77 *
He understood artists. por Horizon 19:27 Jl '77 *
Out of nowhere, he became the top art dealer in Paris. J. Russell. bibl (p 101) il por Smithsonian 8:68-75 Jl '77 *
Put your money where the talent is. B. Rose. il pors Vogue 167:146-7+ Ag '77 *
Vollard: dealer for the demigods; exhibition at the Museum of Modern Art. H. Kramer. il pors N Y Times Mag p28-30+ Je 5 '77 *

VOLLEYBALL
Big Cy wasn't one bit shy; C. Marlowe. J. Jares. por Sports Illus 46:88+ My 23 '77
Sole Pole for the Sol; E. Skorek of the International Volleyball Association. J. Jares. il por Sports Illus 47:44-5 Ag 22 '77

VOLLMER, Arnold H. See Quadri, C. J. Jr. jt auth

VOLLMERHAUSEN, Bob
Indian Peaks: park or playground? il map Nat Parks & Con Mag 51:4-9 My '77

VOLPE, Todd Mitchell. See Bohdan, C. L. jt auth

VOLPONE; drama. See Jonson, B.

VOLTAGE
Average, peak, and arms values. H. French. il Pop Electr 12:68 Jl '77

VOLTAGE regulators
Add voltage regulation to a color photo enlarger. D. W. Schneider. il Pop Electr 12:63-5 N '77
Build a transformerless DC-to-DC voltage doubler. M. J. Buchanan. il Pop Electr 12:55-6 S '77
IC voltage regulators. F. M. Mims. il Pop Electr 12:88-9 O '77
The PUT. J. Darr. il Radio Electr 48:68+ Je '77
Switching regulators reduce power supply cost. D. Raudenbush. il Pop Electr 11:60+ Ap '77

VOLTAGE testers. See Testing instruments

VOLTMETERS
Analog voltmeters (cont) C. Gilmore. il Radio-Electr 48:75-7 F; 69-71+ Mr '77

VOLTOHMMETERS
Equipment reports:
Triplett model 60-NA ruggedized VOM. il Radio-Electr 48:22+ D '77
Triplett model 64 FETVOM. il Radio-Electr 49:30 Ja '78

VOLUNTEER Army. See Military service, Voluntary

VOLUNTEER fire departments. See Fire departments

VOLUNTEER service
Bartering services with your neighbors. Changing T 31:46 N '77
Brazilian students spearhead development; Rondon Project. G. Meek. il Américas 29:6-8 F '77
Dilemmas of national service for youth; with views on Andrew Young's Youth Initiatives Act of 1977. L. H. Martin. Chr Cent 94:228+ Mr 9 '77
Help for people society often ignores. il pors U.S. News 83:46-8 Ag 1 '77
Helping your community as a police volunteer; using retirees. B. O'Neil. il Ret Liv 17:23+ Ag '77
How to get odd jobs done for you—free; Useful Services Exchange; Reston, Va. N. G. Rollins. Good H 184:224 F '77
Jungle mission; DePauw University student-volunteer program. Newsweek 91:66 Ja 9 '78
So long, volunteers. E. Bombeck. Read Digest 110:146 Ap '77
Urban alternative: making do with volunteers; New York City. R. Kraus. il Parks & Rec 12:35-7+ Mr '77
Voluntarism in America: a realistic look ahead; address, May 23, 1977. J. W. Hanley. Vital Speeches 43:634-7 Ag 1 '77
Voluntarism in America; address, April 25, 1977. V. E. Jordan, Jr. Vital Speeches 43:493-5 Je 1 '77
Volunteer helpers of youth groups: take a tax break. Suc Farm 75:K5 Je '77
Whatever happened to lady bountiful? A. Scharffenberger. il Am Home 80:46-7+ Mr '77
When college students offer help to convicts; Vanderbilt Prison Project. il U.S. News 82:49 Ja 31 '77
With the help of a friend; Amicus, Inc's work with prisoners in Minneapolis-St Paul. M. W. Fedo. America 136:463-4 My 21 '77
Year off between high school and college. J. Marks. McCalls 104:68 F '77
See also
Cardinal Ritter Institute, St Louis, Mo.
Hospitals—Volunteer workers
Libraries—Volunteer workers
National Council for Community Services to International Visitors
United States—ACTION

VOLUNTEER system, Military. See Military service, Voluntary

VOLUNTEER tutors. See Tutors and tutoring

VOLUNTEER Urban Consulting Group. See Business consultants

VOLUNTEER women firefighters. See Women firefighters

VOLUNTEER workers. See Volunteer service

VOLUNTEER workers in education
Art appreciation: a practical approach; a volunteer program in Monmouth County, N.J. schools. C. K. Sills. il Sch Arts 76:44+ Mr '77
Charting the grandperson galaxy; Teaching-Learning Communities Project, Ann Arbor, Mich. schools. M. Mehta. Educ Digest 42:22-5 Ja '77
School volunteers needed—want to join up? K. Keating. il Bet Hom & Gard 55:82+ Ap '77

VOLVO (automobile) See Automobiles, Foreign

VOLVO Company. See Automobile industry—Sweden

VOLVO Company-Saab-Scania (firm) merger. See Automobile industry—Acquisitions and mergers

VON BRAUN, Wernher
Von Braun: space pioneering from V-2 warfare to the moon; excerpt from The rockets' red glare. Sci Digest 82:80-1 S '77
about
In memoriam. Space World N-10-166:32-4 O '77
Obituary
Pop Sci 211:79 S '77. H. P. Luckett
Sky & Tel il por 54:193 S '77
Wernher Von Braun: 1912-1977. por Sci N 111: 407 Je 25 '77 •
Will to do it. pors Time 109:71-2 Je 27 '77 •

VON BUCHAU, Stephanie
Bold new face. il Dance Mag 51:38-41 S '77
Sensual stylist. il por Opera N 42:12-16+ S '77
(ed) See Domingo, P. Bel sogno

VONDER HAAR, T. A.
Cures that can kill. Progressive 41:40-3 Ap '77

VON DREELE, W. H.
Anybody got a pin? Diplomatic journey; Going to Jerusalem; poems. Nat R 29:700, 704, 709 Je 24 '77
As the Chinese see us; Post-Easter thoughts; poems. Nat R 29:476, 483 Ap 29 '77
Federal intervention; Modest proposal; If you say so, Mr President; poems. Nat R 29:924, 930, 932 Ag 19 '77
Incident in Stockholm; B-1 doubts; Jimmy sings, O, promise me; poems. Nat R 29:812, 815, 817 Jl 22 '77
Jacob Javits, Mr Republican; Apples of Virginia; Oh dear, oh dear; poems. Nat R 29:1090, 1094, 1096 S 30 '77
Jane's; Jimmy's social security legacy; Yankee doodle; O little town of Bethlehem; poems. Nat R 30:12, 14, 17, 27 Ja 6 '78
Jerry Ford sings Smiles; Suburbs win one; poems. Nat R 29:130, 137 F 4 '77
Jimmy begins the beguine; So long, Korea; Great moments in history; poems. Nat R 29:651, 652, 656 Je 10 '77
Look away, look away; Cask of amontillado; No-growth explained; poems. Nat R 29:863, 868, 871 Ag 5 '77
Minor mores; Vance as tennis ball; Decline and fall; poems. Nat R 29:1030, 1034, 1039 S 16 '77
Old grey mare; Holding back the tide; Rock funk, from Chelsea; poems. Nat R 29:758, 767, 768 Jl 8 '77
Oops; My merry Oldsmobile; We don't spank in NYC; poems. Nat R 29:530, 533, 535 My 13 '77
Our protective FDA; O ye of little faith; Dr Friedman's little lesson; poems. Nat R 29: 370, 374, 375 Ap 1 '77
Paris is worth a mass; Just imagine; poems. Nat R 29:308, 312 Mr 18 '77
Peace, it's wonderful; South Bronx perspective; Inquest in Pretoria; Anyone we know? poems. Nat R 29:1402, 1406, 1412, 1429 D 9 '77
Playing Red light with Warnke; For Cyrus Vance; poems. Nat R 29:245, 255 Mr 4 '77
Poison pen; At them, lads! Is this case analogous? poems. Nat R 29:1277, 1285, 1293 N 11 '77
Quiet arrogance; Now what; Mr. Rabin is confused; poems. Nat R 29:425-6, 428 Ap 15 '77
Sidewalks of New York; Danger: Senators at work; Now voyager; poems. Nat R 29:1158, 1160, 1164 O 14 '77
Strategy for '78; Ian Smith's blacks; Misreading Macbeth; Remembrance of times past; poems. Nat R 29:1470, 1473, 1478, 1487 D 23 '77
Taint; MacArthur; Energizing with Jimmy; poems. Nat R 29:977, 983, 985 S 2 '77
Thou shalt not breed; Canal Zone query; Special, for Mr Carter; poems. Nat R 29:1214, 1217, 1221 O 28 '77
Touring Ethiopia; Disenchanted; Self-denial; poems. Nat R 29:590, 595, 597 My 27 '77
Two cheers for Jimmy; They crossed their hearts; Scrutinizing Howard Baker; Mr Califano explains; poems. Nat R 29:1342, 1344, 1347, 1355 N 25 '77
Watch this one closely; Liddy, too; poems. Nat R 29:193, 197 F 18 '77

VON ECKARDT, Wolf
Architecture. il New Repub 177:31-3 Ag 6; 26-9 Ag 20; 26-8 N 5; 25-6 D 17 '77
This way out—from our mad jumble of signs. il Smithsonian 8:108+ D '77

VON FURSTENBERG, Diane
How to make a million before you're 34; interview, ed by D. Kaye and F. Ruffin. pors Redbook 149:60+ My '77

VO-nguyen-Giap
Famous war general due to take over Vietnamese science. D. Shapley. il Science 198: 173-4 O 14 '77 •

VON HILDEBRAND, Dietrich
Dietrich von Hildebrand, RIP. E. Nielsen. Nat R 29:316-17 Mr 18 '77 •

VON HIPPEL, Frank
Looking back on the Rasmussen report. bibl il Bull Atom Sci 33:42-7 F '77
Protecting the whistle blowers. bibl il Phys Today 30:9+ O '77
—and Williams, R.H.
Toward a solar civilization. bibl il Bull Atom Sci 33:12-15+ O '77
—See Krugmann, H. jt auth

VON HOFFMAN, Nicholas
Don't save the cities: welfare is cheaper. New Repub 176:6+ Mr 12 '77
It isn't cheese. Progressive 41:52 My '77
Let's give it back. Progressive 41:49 N '77
Renaissance. Progressive 41:32 Je '77
What price education? Progressive 41:55 F '77

VON HORVÁTH, Odon. See Horváth, O. von

VON LAZAR, Arpad, and Bode, Ken
Appropriate technology. New Repub 176:11-13 Je 11 '77

VONNEGUT, Kurt, 1922-
Brief encounters on the Inland Waterway. il Motor B & S 140:88-91+ N '77
On reading/writing/freedom; address. Mademoiselle 83:96+ Ag '77

about

Twain and Vonnegut. M. Bobkoff. Engl J 66:55 S '77 *

VON OBENAUER, Heidi
Education briefs. See issues of Dance magazine

VON PUTTKAMER, Jesco
Next 25 years: industrialization of space. bibl il Space World N-10-166:4-13 O '77

VON STADE, Frederica
Opera's exciting new era: Frederica Von Stade's view. il pors U.S. News 83:52 N 7 '77

VON SYDOW, Max. See Sydow, M. von

VOORHOEVE, R. J. H. and others
Perovskite oxides: materials science in catalysis. bibl il Science 195:827-33 Mr 4 '77

VOQUI, Thanh H. See Cheng, T. V. jt auth

VORNADO, Inc-Fed-Mart Corporation merger. See Discount houses (retail trade)—Acquisitions and mergers

VORSTER, Balthazar Johannes
Defiant Vorster; excerpts from interview; ed by R. Watson and P. Younghusband. por Newsweek 90:32 N 7 '77
Sporadic troubles and uprisings but no racial war; interview. il por U.S. News 83:39-40 N 21 '77
White bastion: hanging tough; excerpts from interview, ed by J. Elson and P. Hawthorne. por Time 109:30 Mr 7 '77

about

Avalanche for Vorster. il por Time 110:46 D 12 '77 *
Breaking the ice; W. F. Mondale's meeting in Vienna. S. Fraker and others. pors Newsweek 89:16-17 My 30 '77 *
Color line. B. Pogrund. New Repub 177:15-17 D 17 '77 *
Mondale v. Vorster: tough talk. il pors Time 109:34+ My 30 '77 *
South Africa throws down a gauntlet to the world. il U.S. News 83:37-8 N 7 '77 *
South African muzzle. A. Silk. il Nation 224: 618-21 My 21 '77 *
Time runs out for South Africa. D. Reed. map Read Digest 110:85-90 F '77 *
Vorster calls for elections. il por Time 110:39-40+ O 3 '77 *
Vorster's crocodile. F. Willey and others. il Newsweek 90:37-8 Ag 22 '77 *
What U.S. is up to in Africa; W. F. Mondale's meeting. il pors U.S. News 82:31 My 30 '77 *

VOSS, Gilbert L.
Annobon: forgotten island of the Atlantic; with biographical sketch. il Sea Front 23:101-5, 127 Mr '77

VOS VAN STEENWYK, W. J. Baron de
Western summation of 11th round of MBFR talks; statement, April 15, 1977. Dept State Bull 76:482-4 My 16 '77
Western summation of 12th round of MBFR talks; statement, July 21, 1977. Dept State Bull 77:374-5 S 19 '77

VOTANO, Joseph R. and others
Sickle hemoglobin aggregation: a new class of inhibitors. bibl il Science 196:1216-19 Je 10 '77

VOTERS, Registration of
Diminishing democracy by enlarging it; proposed universal voter registration. New Repub 176:5-6+ Je 18 '77; Reply. M. E. Kinsley. 176:6+ Je 25 '77
Instant registration: results in 5 states. il U.S. News 82:51 My 30 '77
Myth of voter apathy. A. E. Barkan. por Newsweek 89:9 Ja 24 '77
Reform and civic virtue. Chr Cent 94:347 Ap 13 '77
TRB from Washington: get out the vote. New Repub 176:2+ Ap 2 '77

VOTING
Apathetic voter. A. McCarthy. Commonweal 104: 105+ F 18 '77
Helping patients to vote. W. G. Lee. il MH 61:14-16 Summ '77
Meet Mrs America; B. Lowrey as average American voter. J. Miller. por New Repub 176:19-21 Ap 9 '77
On non-voters. E. M. von Kuehnelt-Leddihn. Nat R 29:153 F 4 '77
Yes for permitting weekend voting. il Nations Bus 65:6 Mr '77
See also
Election Day
Presidents—United States—Election
Referendum
Voters, Registration of

VOTIVE statues. See Sculpture, Greek

VOUCHER plan in education
Requiem or rebirth? From voucher to magnet. J. Premazon and P. T. West. Clearing H 51: 38-40 S '77

VOWS
See also
Poverty, Vow of

VOYAGER flights. See Space flight—Voyager flights

VOYAGER project. See Space flight

VOYAGER spacecraft. See Space probes

VOYAGES
China's ancient mariners. S. Steiner. il Natur Hist 86:48-63 bibl(p 110) D '77
Farthest North; voyage of the Reindeer. E. N. Smith. il Yachting 141:68-72 My; 62-5 Je '77
From Eden to India; T. Heyerdahl's latest voyage. il Time 110:116 N 28 '77
Galway Blazer II; voyage around Antarctica. W. B. L. King. il Yachting 141:139-41 Je '77
Inside Cape Horn; excerpts. H. Roth. il por map Motor B & S 139:40-3 Mr; 70-3+ Ap; 68-71+ My; 78-80+ Je; 140:56-7+ Jl; 50-3+ S; 64-7+ O; 86-7+ N; 44-8+ D '77; 141:86-9+ Ja '78
Mighty Magoon rides again; transatlantic crossing. T. West. il por Motor B & S 140:51-3+ Jl '77
North by kicker; passage from Seattle to Ketchikan, Alaska. M. Clevenger. il map Motor B & S 139:64-5+ Mr '77
Ondine vs. Atlantic; attempt to break transatlantic record. R. Humphreys. il Yachting 142: 60-1+ Jl '77
Passage to Hawaii; photographs. A. Brown. Yachting 142:62-5 Ag '77
Revved up to ride on an ocean of trouble; R. Magoon in the Citicorp Trans-Atlantic Challenge. R. Kennedy. il por Sports Illus 46:30-2+ Je 27 '77
St Brendan's fantastic voyage; re-enactment of voyage described in Navigatio Sancti Brendani. G. Schomp. il map Am Hist Illus 12:22-7 Ap '77
Sea and shores as classrooms; sailing on the Aquarius. M. Herron. il pors Smithsonian 8: 99-104 S '77
Strait of Magellan: the ultimate passage. D. Connelly. il Sea Front 23:2-8 Ja '77
Toward Cape Horn; excerpts from Inside Cape Horn. H. Roth. il map Motor B & S 139:40-3 Mr; 70-3+ Ap '77
Voyage of Brendan. T. Severin. il map Nat Geog 152:770-97 D '77
Voyaging with Tristan Jones. T. Jones. il Motor B & S 139:54-5+ F; 62-3+ Mr; 10+ Ap; 94-5+ My '77
Winning the pathless Pacific; first European voyagers. M. Shadbolt. il map Read Digest 111: 98-105 Ag '77
See also
Antarctic exploration
Cruising
Northwest Passage
Polynesia—Discovery and exploration

VOYAGES around the world
Joshua Slocum's magnificent voyage; excerpt from My country. P. Berton. il Read Digest 110:218-20+ F '77
Powering round the globe. C. M. Heintz. il Motor B & S 139:46-9 Mr '77

History

When Argentina conquered California; naval battles fought by Argentine ship on voyage around the world. A. Alonso Piñeiro. il por Américas 29:34-7 Je '77

VOZAR, Linda
Early Bennington potteries. il Ceram Mo 25:54-7 O '77

VREE, Dale
Down the Marxist road with Harvey Cox; excerpt from On synthesizing Marxism and Christianity. Chr Today 21:12-14 Ag 26 '77

VREELAND, Diana
Vanity fair; interview, ed by J. Onassis. il N Y Times Mag p 150-2+ D 11 '77

about

Ruffles and flourishes. S. C. Cowley. il por Newsweek 91:56-7 Ja 2 '78 *

VROMAN, Wayne
Work injuries and earnings of partially disabled men in California. il M Labor R 100:58-60 Ap '77

VUTURO, Robert
Beyond the library tour: those who can, must teach. bibl il Wilson Lib Bull 51:736-40 My '77

VYAS, G. N. and others
Hepatitis B "e" antigen: an apparent association with lactate dehydrogenase isozyme-5. bibl il Science 198:1068-70 D 9 '77

W

WARC. See World Administrative Radio Conference
WCC. See World Council of Churches; World Crafts Council
WHO. See World Health Organization
WHS Distributers (firm) See Book wholesalers—Great Britain
WIC (Women, Infants and Children, Special Supplemental Food Program for) program. See United States—Agriculture, Department of—Food and Nutrition Service
WIFE (Women Involved in Farm Economics) See Agricultural societies
WNET-TV. See Television stations, Educational
WPCF. See Water Pollution Control Federation
W. R. Grace & Company. See Grace, W. R. & Company
W. T. Grant Company. See Grant, W. T, Company
WACHTEL, Stephen S.
H-Y antigen and the genetics of sex determination. bibl Science 198:797-9 N 25 '77

about

Making sure about sex. il por Time 110:57 D 5 '77 *
—See Silvers, W. K. jt auth
WACKERLE, Andrea
Centenarians. il Sat Eve Post 249:68 Mr '77
WADE, Nicholas
Hazards & restraints. Sci Digest 81:25-6 Je '77
Thirty-one favors. New Repub 177:15-17 N 5 '77
WADE, Virginia
Ginny fizz becomes Ginny tonic. C. Kirkpatrick. il por Sports Illus 47:16-17 Jl 11 '77 *
WADERS (boots) See Shoes, boots, rubbers, etc.
WADSWORTH, C. D.
Build this electronic security system. il Radio-Electr 48:36-9 S '77
WADSWORTH, Stephen
Irish Heather. il pors Opera N 42:25-7 D 10 '77
(ed) See Baker, J. Sense and sensibility
(ed) See Ewing, M. Maria Ewing: sharing
(ed) See Farley, C. Real Lulu: Carole Farley
(ed) See Mondschein, P. In touch with their feelings; opera, children and education
WADSWORTH, William H.
Basics for bowhunters. R. Methot. por Outdoor Life 161:22 Ja '78 *
WAFFEN SS troops. See National socialism
WAFFLES. See Pancakes, waffles, etc.
WAGE differentials
How racial bias and social status affect the earnings of young men. G. D. Jud and J. L. Walker. bibl M Labor R 100:44-5 Ap '77
Is your salary up to par? il Changing T 31:24-7 N '77
New wage floor? T. Nicholson and J. B. Copeland. il Newsweek 90:88 S 19 '77
Would the teenwage cut unemployment? il Bus W p 106-8 S 19 '77
Year-round full-time earnings in 1975. A. M. Young. il M Labor R 100:36-41 Je '77
WAGE-price policy
Another weapon against inflation: tax policy. il pors Bus W p94+ O 3 '77
Carter's new option play; tax-based incomes policy. M. Ruby and others. il Newsweek 90:91-2 N 28 '77
Dismal past of guideline policies. il Bus W p85-6+ Ap 4 '77
Let's-talk strategy. il Time 109:48 F 14 '77
See also
United States—Council on Wage and Price Stability

Austria

Incomes policy in Austria under a voluntary partnership. J. Mire. bibl M Labor R 100:13-17 Ag '77

Canada

Controlling inflation in Canada. M. L. Kliman. bibl f Cur Hist 72:166-9 Ap '77
Timetable to end wage-price controls. il Bus W p44 O 31 '77
WAGES
See also
Income
Labor cost
Minimum wage
Profit sharing
Salaries
Tipping
Women—Wages

Cost of living adjustments

Italy's economic crisis: as a first step, modify the inflationary wage index. G. Ackley. Duns R 109:11 F '77
Netherlands: close to a showdown over indexation. Bus W p50 F 7 '77

Statistics

See also
Wage differentials

Taxation

See also
Social security taxes

Germany, West

Labor's new thrust in Germany. Bus W p91+ F 7 '77
Schmidt rides a new crest of confidence. por Bus W p46-7 D 5 '77

Great Britain

Britain: a wage pact at any price. J. E. Pluenneke and J. Pearson. il Bus W p40 My 30 '77
Buying time from the unions; Trades Union Congress vote to limit wage-increase demands. il Time 110:43 S 19 '77
Europe's contentious winter. il Time 109:45 Mr 14 '77
Fragile victory; Trades Union Congress agreement to put off new wage demands. D. Pauly and A. Collings. Newsweek 90:93-4 S 19 '77
Pay, inflation and unemployment; address, September 6, 1977. J. Callaghan. Vital Speeches 44:34-7 N 1 '77
Rising rage of British labor. il Bus W p 109 D 12 '77
Unions break a truce; air-traffic controllers. D. Pauly and M. MacPherson. il Newsweek 90:68+ S 5 '77
Unions scuttle the social contract. il Time 110:24+ Jl 18 '77
Winter of discontent for British workers. il U.S. News 83:49 D 19 '77

Italy

Italy's economic crisis: as a first step, modify the inflationary wage index. G. Ackley. Duns R 109:11 F '77

Netherlands

Netherlands: close to a showdown over indexation. Bus W p50 F 7 '77

United States

Big puzzle: who makes what and why; Time essay. F. Trippett. il Time 109:83-4 Je 13 '77
Despite inflation, your work buys more. il U.S. News 83:44 D 5 '77
Effects of collective bargaining as measured for men in blue-collar jobs. P. J. Andrisani and A. I. Kohen. bibl M Labor R 100:46-9 Ap '77
Employment, hours, and earnings data from establishment surveys. See issues of Monthly labor review
In race against inflation—nip and tuck for many. il U.S. News 83:69 Ag 29 '77
Letting the employees set their own salaries; A. Friedman's policy. V. Louviere. Nations Bus 65:44 F '77
Meany rejects prenotification of wage increases; meeting of Executive Council in Bal Harbour, Fla. L. Bornstein and others. M Labor R 100:84 Ap '77
Private hospitals nearing wage levels in state, local government hospitals. M. Sieling. il M Labor R 100:46-7 My '77
Scheduled wage increases and escalator provisions in 1977. D. LeRoy. bibl f M Labor R 100:20-6 Ja '77
Slowdown in real wages: a postwar perspective. H. M. Douty. bibl il M Labor R 100:7-12 Ag '77
Social contract with labor to limit wage gains would be full of loopholes. A. R. Weber. Duns R 109:9 Ja '77
Wage gains smaller during 1976. J. D. Murphey. bibl il M Labor R 100:3-6 Ap '77
Workers can set their own wages—responsibly. E. E. Lawler. il por Psychol Today 10:109-10+ F '77
Workers on long hours and premium pay, May 1976. S. J. Gallogly. il M Labor R 100:42-5 My '77
See also
Government employees—Salaries, allowances, etc.
Minimum wage—United States
WAGGONER, William G.
How to outwit a drill press. il Pop Sci 210:188+ Ap '77
WAGNER, A. James
Circulation and weather of 1976. maps Weatherwise 30:22-31+ F '77
Record-breaking winter of 1976-77. il maps Weatherwise 30:65-9 Ap '77
WAGNER, Aubrey Joseph
Excerpts from statement on nuclear energy production, January 1977. Cong Digest 56:54+ F '77
WAGNER, Bill
Lo, the poor and sterilized Indian. America 136:75 Ja 29 '77
WAGNER, C. Peter
Intensity of belief: a pragmatic concern for church growth; interview, ed by D. E. Kucharsky. pors Chr Today 21:10-14 Ja 7 '77
WAGNER, Geoffrey
Fund one, fund all. Nat R 29:325 Mr 18 '77

WAGNER, Judith
Prep makes parents more intelligenter. il Am Educ 13:9-12 O '77
WAGNER, Lindsay
Why I chose marriage over living together; interview, ed by S. D. Scott. il por Ladies Home J 94:32+ Ap '77
WAGNER, Madeleine
How not to save a family: a social worker's diary. Ms 6:25-6+ D '77
WAGNER, Richard, 1813-1883
Crux of the Ring; Die Walküre. D. Hamilton. il Opera N 41:8-12 F 19 '77 *
Der fliegende Hollander; Die Walküre; recordings of London and Angel. K. Furie. Hi Fi 27:91-2 Ag '77 *
Flying Dutchman (Der fliegende Holländer) Review
Hi Fi 27:MA28-9 F '77 *
Lohengrin. Reviews
Hi Fi 27:MA23-4 F '77 *
New Repub 176:25-7 Ja 15 '77 *
Die Meistersinger. Review
Hi Fi il 27:MA24-5 F '77 *
Mixed bag: famous Wagner interpreters; 100 years of Bayreuth recordings. C. J. Luten. il Am Rec G 40:10-12+ O '77 *
100 years of Bayreuth; Deutsche Grammophon. C. J. Luten. Am Rec G 40:10-12 N '76 *
Parsifal. Review
Sat R 5:52-3 O 29 '77
Das Rheingold. Review
Hi Fi il 27:MA34-5 My '77 *
Rienzi. Reviews
Hi Fi 27:MA30+ Ag '77 *
New Yorker 52:106-11 F 14 '77 *
Tannhäuser. Reviews
New Yorker 53:77-81 Ja 9 '78 *
Time 111:54 Ja 2 '78 *
Two new Meistersingers. C. J. Luten. il Am Rec G 40:8-9 Mr '77 *
Wagner in English; Valkyrie. D. Arthur. Am Rec G 40:37-8 Mr '77 *
Wagner's masters get their due. D. Hamilton. il Hi Fi 27:89-91 F '77 *
Wagner's Rienzi; performance in San Antonio. Q. Eaton. il Hi Fi 27:MA30+ Ag '77 *
Wagner's Roman colossus. il Hi Fi 27:91-3 Mr '77 *
Wahnfried restored. G. Loney. il Opera N 41: 14-15 F 19 '77 *
Die Walküre. Reviews
Hi Fi il 27:MA27-8 My '77 *
Hi Fi il 27:MA34-5 My '77 *
Opera N 41:16+ F 19 '77 *
WAGNER, Robert Ferdinand, 1944?-
What makes Andy (and Bobby) run? H. Stein. il pors N Y Times Mag p44-7+ N 6 '77 *
WAGNER, Susan
How effective is the National Endowment for the Arts? Pub W 212:45-8 Jl 25 '77
New copyright law primer. Pub W 212:37-42 D 26 '77
News along the Potomac. Pub W 212:280-1 Ag 29; 24 O 10 '77
(ed) See McPherson, W. PW interviews
—See Lottmann, H. R.; Reuter, M. jt auths
WAGNER, Tony
Learning democratically. il Engl J 66:33-7 S '77
WAGNER, Walter
Ardent suitor. J. K. Footlick. il pors Newsweek 90:59 Jl 4 '77 *
WAGNER, Walter F. Jr
Editorial. See issues of Architectural record
WAGONER, Dan
Reviews. D. Hering. Dance Mag 51:26+ Jl '77 *
WAGONER, David
Death of the moon; Thistledown; Gift; Cutting down a tree; Elegy for a minor romantic poet; poems. Poetry 130:155-61 Je '77
Lament for the non-swimmers. Atlantic 239: 69 Je '77
My father's wall; poem. New Yorker 53:97 F 21 '77
Pile-driver; poem. Atlantic 240:74 N '77

about

What we've gathered here against the winter. A. Oberg. Poetry 130:162-7 Je '77 *
WAGONS
Giant wagons take big bites out of bottlenecks. G. Lepper. il Suc Farm 75:34-5 O '77
Gypsy carting in France. L. Dennis and L. Dennis. il Travel 147:58-63 Ap '77
WAHL, Paul
Man-powered aircraft shatters flight records. il Pop Sci 210:16 My '77
On target. See issues of Popular science
WAHLSTROM, Billie J. See Deming, C. J. jt auth
WAHNEFRIED in Bayreuth. See Historic houses, sites, etc.—Germany, West
WAINWRIGHT, Geoffrey
Celtic farmstead in southern Britain; with biographical sketch. il Sci Am 237:15, 156-64+ bibl(p 190) D '77
WAINWRIGHT, Loudon
Faces passed. N Y Times Mag p45+ D 18 '77
WAITE, Ralph
Liveliest theater in town. D. Sullivan. il por Horizon 20:87+ N '77 *
WAITERS and waitresses
Four waitresses: their secret world. D. Gallagher. il Redbook 150:104+ N '77
WAITING. See Time, Use of
WAITING for Godot; drama. See Beckett, S.
WAITING for Uncle Eddie; drama. See Shoemaker, C.
WAITLEY, Douglas
Book contracts: trial and terror. Writers Digest 57:49-50 S '77
WAITS, Tom
Tom Waits: barroom balladeer. pors Time 110:77 N 28 '77 *
WAITZKIN, Howard, and Sharratt, J. A.
Controlling medical expansion. il Society 14: 30-5 Ja '77
WAITZMAN, Norman. See Bollier, D. jt auth
WAKE County, N.C. Public Libraries System. See Libraries—North Carolina
WAKE Forest University, Winston Salem, N.C.
Man of the year at Wake Forest; L. Flynt. Chr Today 21:36 Ap 1 '77
WAKE turbulence. See Atmospheric turbulence
WAKEFULNESS. See Insomnia
WAKEHAM, Duane
Duane Wakeham: sharing a way of seeing; interview, ed by J. McCord. il por Am Artist 41:60-5 N '77
Joe Price: serigraphs in light and tone. il por Am Artist 41:46-51+ O '77
WAKOSHI, Diane
Ring; Tearing up my mother's letters; Hitchhikers; poems. Poetry 130:125-30 Je '77
WALBORN, Nolan R. and Ingerson, T. E.
Structure in the Carina nebula and Eta Carinae. il Sky & Tel 54:22-4 Jl '77
WALCOTT, Derek
Comment. W. Logan. Poetry 130:228-9 Jl '77 *
WALD, Carol
Carol Wald; interview, ed by M. Tinkelman. il Am Artist 41:78-81 Jl '77
WALD, George
Debate by a spirited pair. Sci Digest 81:27-8 Je '77
—and Rayport, Stephen
Vision in annelid worms. bibl il Science 196:1434-9 Je 24 '77
WALDEN, Elizabeth
Marvellous Molly and her Johnson 10 il Yachting 141:80-1 My '77
WALDEN, William
Riposte; poem. New Yorker 53:40 My 23 '77
WALDEN Ponds Wildlife Habitat, Boulder. See Wildlife sanctuaries—Colorado
WALDERS, Joe
CB & sun spots. il Sci Digest 81:24-7 F '77
How the FCC tunes in for CB enforcement. il Pop Sci 210:64-8 Je '77
WALDHEIM, Kurt
Chances for progress on Middle East problem never better; excerpts from press conference, December 8, 1976. por UN Chron 14:88-9 Ja '77
Mr Biko left deep mark on South African scene, says Secretary-General. UN Chron 14:25 O '77
Mr Waldheim opens International Civil Service Commission session. UN Chron 14:40 Mr '77
Mr Waldheim states need for careful preparation for disarmament session. UN Chron 14:20 My '77
Next few weeks crucial for Middle East settlement, says Secretary-General; excerpt from transcript of press conference, September 19, 1977. UN Chron 14:45-7 O '77
S-G confers with President Carter during two-day visit to Washington. il pors UN Chron 14:16-17 Mr '77
Secretary-General addresses women's group on rights; March 8, 1977. il UN Chron 14:51 Ap '77
Secretary-General hopes for progress at disarmament talks. UN Chron 14:19 Mr '77
Secretary-General speaks of Middle East, Uganda, Southern Africa, new United States spirit towards United Nations; excerpts from transcript of news conference, March 1, 1977. UN Chron 14:56-7 Ap '77
Secretary-General's main weapons are reason, persuasion, says reappointed Mr Waldheim; address, December 8, 1976. UN Chron 14:86-7 Ja '77
Stakes high in Southern Africa, Mid-East, Cyprus; dangers of failure ominous—Secretary-General; address. UN Chron 14:5+ Ag '77

about

Assembly appoints Mr Waldheim Secretary-General for second term. UN Chron 14:40 Ja '77 *
S-G sees beginning of work of human rights body as important milestone. UN Chron 14:49 Ap '77 *
Secretary-General addresses OAU summit meeting. UN Chron 14:32 Jl '77 *
Secretary-General back from visits to Vienna and Paris. il UN Chron 14:29 My '77 *
Secretary-General honoured at Kent, Pittsburgh Universities. UN Chron 14:32 Jl '77 *

WALDHEIM, Kurt—about—*Continued*
Secretary-General pays tribute to Secretariat. UN Chron 14:40-1 Ja '77 *
Secretary-General reports to Council on first round of new Cyprus talks. il por UN Chron 14:17-18+ My '77 *
Secretary-General returns from three-week overseas mission. il pors UN Chron 14:10-14 Mr '77 *
Secretary-General visits nine states in Africa, Asia and Europe in July, August. il pors UN Chron 14:21-3 Ag '77 *
Secretary-General visits USSR, Mongolia. il pors UN Chron 14:29-30 O '77 *

WALDMAN, Diane
(ed) See Noland, K. Color, format and abstract art

WALDRON, Charlotte B.
Friends among the nuts. il Org Gard & Farm 24:78-9 S '77
Super strawberries: the organic convincers. il Org Gard & Farm 24:186+ F '77

WALDRON, D'Lynn
Whey's and wherefore's of British aristocratic cheeses. il Holiday 58:38-40+ Je '77

WALES
See also
Cardiff, Wales
Historic houses, sites, etc.—Wales

Nationalism

Kilt bill; defeat of home rule for Wales and Scotland. F. Willey and M. MacPherson. il Newsweek 89:43+ Mr 7 '77
Labor runs afoul of a muddy loch; home rule bill. Time 109:31-2 Mr 7 '77

WALKER, Alice
Advancing Luna—and Ida B. Wells; story. il Ms 6:75-9 Jl '77
Anaïs Nin: 1930-1977. por Ms 5:46 Ap '77
Secrets of the new Cuba. il por Ms 6:71-4+ S '77

WALKER, Charls Edward
Good ol' boy. T. Nicholson and J. Walcott. il por Newsweek 90:83 D 5 '77 *
Reporter at large. E. B. Drew. New Yorker 53:32-6+ Ja 9 '78 *

WALKER, Daniel A.
High-frequency P_n phases observed in the Pacific at great distances. bibl il map Science 197:257-9 Jl 15 '77

WALKER, David
Comment. J. Parini. Poetry 130:293-4 Ag '77 *

WALKER, Diana
Washington scrapbook. il New Repub 177:20-1 Jl 9 '77

WALKER, George D.
Reading poles. il Am For 83:31 Je '77

WALKER, J. Michael, and others
Analog of enkephalin having prolonged opiate-like effects in vivo. bibl il Science 196:85-7 Ap 1 '77

WALKER, James D.
Tracing your own roots—advice from an expert; interview. por U.S. News 82:57 Mr 14 '77

WALKER, James L. See Jud, G. D. jt auth

WALKER, Jeanne Murray
On the language which writes the lecturer; poem. Am Scholar 46:214 Spr '77

WALKER, Jearl
Amateur scientist. See issues of Scientific American, July 1977-

WALKER, Jessie
Share your home for the holidays. House B 119:8+ D '77

WALKER, Kenneth F.
Toward the participatory enterprise: a European trend. bibl f Ann Am Acad 431:1-11 My '77

WALKER, Les
Up a tree; excerpt from Housebuilding for children. il Am Home 80:36-7+ Jl '77

WALKER, Lou Ann
For the kid who has everything. il Esquire 88:68-73 S '77

WALKER, Mary (Richardson)
Pantsuited pioneer of Women's lib, Dr Mary Walker. A. Lockwood. il pors Smithsonian 7:113-14+ Mr '77 *

WALKER, Matthew
Modern wooden boat. il Yachting 141:110+ My '77

WALKER, Sheila S.
What's in a name? il Ebony 32:74-6+ Je '77

WALKER, Ted
Moving; poem. New Yorker 53:46 Ap 18 '77

WALKER, W. Allan, and others
Stimulation by immune complexes of mucus release from goblet cells of the rat small intestine. bibl il Science 197:370-2 Jl 22 '77

WALKER, William N.
America's improving competitiveness promotes export growth. M Labor R 100:47-8 Mr '77

WALKIE-talkies
New band for kiddie-talkies. L. Sands. il Pop Electr 12:46-8 Ag '77

WALKING
Der Volksmarsch ist hier! A. S. Thompson. il Am For 83:36-7 F '77
How to walk happy. Bet Hom & Gard 55:234 S '77
See also
Backpacks and backpacking
Hiking

Anecdotes, facetiae, satire, etc.

Crouch hop and other useful outdoors steps. P. F. McManus. il Field & S 82:58+ D '77

WALKING by animals. See Animal locomotion

WALKING sticks. See Staffs (canes, sticks, etc)

WALKING trails. See Trails

WALKS (paths)
See also
Garden walks

Die **WALKÜRE**; opera. See Wagner, R.

WALL, C. Edward
New look at free magazines. il Am Lib 8:85-9 F '77

WALL, Lillian Allethea (Smith)
My sister, Rosalynn; interview, ed by P. F. Healy. il pors Good H 186:76-7+ Ja '78

WALL climbing. See Stunts

WALL coverings
Double-duty walls: more than just a pretty face. P. Angell. il Pop Mech 147:124-7 Mr '77
8 photo steps to a shingled wall. il Mech Illus 73:116+ D '77
Fresh breeze: new wallcoverings & fabrics that change the pace & pattern of today's rooms. R. Weil. il House B 119:100-5 O '77
How to choose and use wall coverings. P. Angell. il Pop Mech 149:96-8 Ja '78
Institute report: wall coverings—how to choose, how to use. il Good H 184:160 Mr '77
New dimensions for well-known design favorites. il House B 119:144-51 My '77
Walls: new ways with the old stand-bys. Ladies Home J 94:159-60 S '77; Same. Redbook 149:194+ S '77
See also
Wallpaper and wallpapering

WALL decoration. See Mural painting and decoration

WALL desks. See Desks

WALL fastenings. See Fastenings

WALL gardens. See Gardens, Rock

WALL hangings
Hooking, looping and knotting: versatile fiber techniques for rugs and wall hangings; excerpt from Weaving: design and expression. N. Belfer. il Sch Arts 77:20-5 S '77

WALL painting. See Mural painting and decoration

WALL paper. See Wallpaper and wallpapering

WALL shelves. See Shelves

WALL Street journal
Torch passes; new managing editor L. O'Donnell. por Forbes 120:82 D 15 '77

WALLACE, Bruce
Cost of basic research. BioScience 27:83 F '77

WALLACE, Cornelia
Cornelia Wallace; her struggle to save her troubled marriage. M. MacPherson. pors Ladies Home J 94:28+ F '77 *
Messy Wallace divorce. D. Holt and J. B. Cumming. il pors Newsweek 91:23 Ja 9 '78 *

WALLACE, D. H. See Ferrari, T. E. jt auth

WALLACE, Dave
Bracket racing America. il Hot Rod 30:28-32 Ag; 29-32 O; 35-8 N; 32-6 D '77
—See Baskerville, G. jt auth

WALLACE, Dwane L.
Wallace. R. B. Parke. il por Flying 101:257 S '77 *

WALLACE, George Corley
Cornelia Wallace: her struggle to save her troubled marriage. M. MacPherson. pors Ladies Home J 94:28+ F '77 *
Messy Wallace divorce. D. Holt and J. B. Cumming. il pors Newsweek 91:23 Ja 9 '78 *

WALLACE, Irving, and others
Book of lists; excerpt from The book of lists. Ladies Home J 94:169-76 My '77

WALLACE, Les
Charles Lenox Remond: the lost prince of abolitionism. bibl il Negro Hist Bull 40:696-701 My '77

WALLACE, Mike
Mike Wallace's jugular journalism. T. Griffith. por Time 109:69 My 2 '77 *

WALLACE, R. Bruce, and others
Localization of the globin gene in the template active fraction of chromatin of Friend leukemia cells. bibl il Science 198:1166-8 D 16 '77

WALLACE, Richard
Day lily is a delicious ornamental. il Org Gard & Farm 24:95-6 My '77

WALLACE, Robert
More than there is; poem. Commonweal 104:175 Mr 18 '77

WALLACE, Ronald
In the arboretum; poem. Nation 224:93 Ja 22 '77
WALLACE, Ruth
Case of the frustrated corpse; drama. Plays 37:78-80 O '77
WALLACE, Sam P, and Company. See Contractors
WALLACE-CRABBE, Chris
Orpheus; Parthia; poems. Poetry 130:10-11 Ap '77
WALLACH, Amei
Under a western sky. il pors Horizon 20:24-31 D '77
WALLACH, Frances
Programs are for people. Parks & Rec 12:21 Je '77
WALLECHINSKY, David, and others
I've got a little list; excerpt from The book of lists. Read Digest 111:62-4 Ag '77
WALLED gardens. See Gardens
WALLEN, Charles, Jr
Gunning for Brown. Nat R 29:1367 N 25 '77
WALLER, Julian
(ed) See Ramazzini, B. Health issues
—and Whitehead, Lawrence
Health issues (title varies) Craft Horiz 37:56+ Je; 8+ D '77
WALLER, Sam
Sam Waller: eyewitness to history. M. Jones. il pors Ebony 32:79-80+ F '77 *
WALLERSTEIN, Immanuel
South Africa & liberal interventionism. Nation 225:489-92 N 12 '77
WALLETS. See Purses
WALLEYE fishing. See Perch fishing
WALLFISH, Asher
Israel's disillusioned voters. Nation 224:390-3 Ap 2 '77
WALLICH, Henry Christopher
Another weapon against inflation: tax policy. il pors Bus W p94+ O 3 '77 *
WALLIN, Doug
Three critical aspects of underwater photography; with biographical sketch. il Sea Front 23:204-9, 255 Jl '77
WALLIO, Pete
Some thoughts for a new crew. il Yachting 142: 40+ Jl '77
WALLIS, Lamar C.
Branches for the need to know. il por Lib J 102:166-8 Ja 15 '77
WALLPAPER and wallpapering
Landscape wallpaper in the Jeremiah Lee Mansion. C. L. Frangiamore. bibl il Antiques 112: 1174-9 D '77
WALLPAPER collage. See Collage
WALLRAFF, Günter
Great impostor. il pors Time 110:103-4 O 24 '77 *
WALLS, Dwayne
Jesus mania: bigotry in the name of the Lord. il Sat R 4:12-15+ S 17 '77
WALLS, Peter
Enemy also have problems; excerpts from interview, ed by P. Younghusband. por Newsweek 90:37 Jl 11 '77
about
Three soldier peacemakers. pors Time 110:40 N 7 '77 *
WALLS, Willie, Jr
Caught in the lineup. Time 110:44 Jl 18 '77
WALLS
Wall talk. Redbook 148:182+ Ap '77; Same. Ladies Home J 94:176+ Ap '77
See also
Mural painting and decoration
Panel construction
Paneling
Retaining walls
Storage walls
WALLS, Brick
Designing brick masonry walls to avoid structural problems. C. T. Grimm. il Archit Rec 162:124-8 O '77
WALLS, Concrete
Making your own concrete block wall. il Mech Illus 73:118+ My '77
WALLSTROM, Bob
Complete dockside shakedown. il Motor B & S 140:78-9+ S '77
WALLWORTH, John
And the band played on. il Ret Liv 17:46-8 My '77
WAL-Mart Stores, Inc. See Discount houses (retail trade)
WALNUT industry. See Nut industry
WALNUT trees
My black walnut tree. D. Schroeder. il Org Gard & Farm 24:84-6 S '77
See also
Butternut trees
WALROD, Dennis
Stalking the swamp walkers. il Field & S 82: 34-5+ Jl '77
WALRUS Island. See Pribilof Islands
WALRUSES
Gregarious but contentious walrus. F. Bruemmer. il Natur Hist 86:52-61 bibl(p 118) N '77
WALSBY, A. E.
Gas vacuoles of blue-green algae; with biographical sketch. Sci Am 237:20, 90-7 bibl(p 140) Ag '77
WALSH, Arthur C.
Psychochemical treatment counteracts senility. Sci N 111:292 My 7 '77 *
WALSH, Edward R.
Hundred pockets for festivity. il Parks & Rec 12:51-3+ Je '77
Stars in their eyes. por Ret Liv 17:31+ Ag '77
WALSH, James
Biblical vision of justice. il New Cath World 220:145-7 My '77
WALSH, Jim
Favorite pioneer recording artists. See issues of Hobbies
about
Jim Walsh receives new Who's Who honor. Hobbies 82:35 N '77 *
WALSH, John
International trade in electronics: U.S.-Japan competition. bibl il Science 195:1175-9 Mr 18 '77
WALSH, Lawrence
Learning to see things whole. il Sci Digest 81: 51-4 Ap '77
WALSH, Richard A.
Moonies—religious converts or psychic victims? America 136:438-40 My 14 '77
WALSHE, Peter
United States & southern Africa. map Commonweal 104:201-3 Ap 1 '77
WALT Disney Productions. See Disney, Walt, Productions
WALTER, Ingo. See Gladwin, T. N. jt auth
WALTER, Mary Ann. See Reeve, M. R. jt auth
WALTERS, Barbara
Plot to get Barbara Walters; interview, ed by C. Chase. por Ladies Home J 94:84+ O '77
about
Showdown at ABC News. J. Greenfield. il pors N Y Times Mag p32-4+ F 13 '77 *
WALTERS, David M.
Vatican envoy. Chr Today 21:37-8 Jl 29 '77 *
WALTERS, John P.
Spark discharge: application to multielement spectrochemical analysis. bibl il Science 198: 787-97 N 25 '77
WALTERS, Ralph E.
It's tough to fill an FASB vacancy. Bus W p28 Ja 24 '77 *
WALTERS, Terry A.
Build this no-digit digital wall clock. il Radio Electr 48:35-7+ Je '77
WALTHER, Eric G.
Food, energy, and environment triangle. il New Cath World 220:222-5 S '77
WALTON, Bill
Big Bill Walton comes of age. il por Time 109: 50 My 30 '77 *
Walton gang. B. Weber. Sr Schol 110:25 D 1 '77 *
Walton up on high. P. Axthelm. il pors Newsweek 89:75 My 23 '77 *
WALTON, Clem
For whitetails, the sneak play is in. il Outdoor Life 160:65-9 O '77
WALTON, Harold F. See Navratil, J. D. jt auth
WALTON, Nancy Y. See Deutsch, J. A. jt auth
WALTON, Nyle K.
Tequila. il Américas 29:15-18 Ja '77
WALTON, Richard E. See Schlesinger, L. A. jt auth
WALTON, Sam
Day in the life of Sam Walton. H. Seneker. il pors Forbes 120:45-6+ D 1 '77 *
WALTON, Samuel B.
Happiness: who's got it? How you can get it! il Sat Eve Post 249:48-51+ S '77
People like honest sounds. il Sat Eve Post 249: 46-7+ Ap '77
Rebel who became a legend. il pors Sat Eve Post 249:56-7+ D '77
Television's funniest show is on when you're asleep. il Sat Eve Post 249:38-9+ My '77
WALTON, Sir William Turner
Troilus and Cressida. Review
Hi Fi 27:MA38-9 Je '77 *
Troilus and Cressida; EMI recording. C. L. Osborne. Hi Fi 28:106-8 Ja '78 *
WALTRIP, Darrell
If you can't prove it you ain't it. S. Moses. il pors Sports Illus 47:50-2+ O 17 '77 *
WALVIS BAY, Namibia
Security Council urged to take steps to preserve status of Walvis Bay. il UN Chron 14:23-4 O '77
WALZ, Barbra
Here's how they spent the summer; photographs. N Y Times Mag p34-7 S 4 '77
WALZER, Michael
War crimes; excerpt from Just and unjust wars. New Repub 177:17-23 N 5 '77

WALZER, Peter D. and others
Nude mouse: a new experimental model for pneumocystis carinii infection. bibl il Science 197:177-9 Jl 8 '77
WANAGEL, J. See Ruoff, A. L. jt auth
WANDRES, J.
What should you do if you're burgled. il Ret Liv 17:28-30+ Ap '77
WANG, Hwa L. and others
Calling all tempeh lovers. il Org Gard & Farm 24:108+ Je '77
WANG, John B.
Where have all the churches gone? Chr Today 22:12-13 N 18 '77
WANG, Julie C.
Anemia epidemic. Harp Baz 110:91+ Je '77
Breaking out of the pain trap. bibl por Psychol Today 11:78-80+ Jl '77
Cocaine, alcohol & amphetamines: thrillers or killers? Harp Baz 110:86-7+ Je '77
How to prevent accidents. Harp Baz 110:100-1+ Ap '77
Trauma of separation: school, divorce, hospital, death. bibl Harp Baz 110:88+ Jl '77
WANG, Rex Y. and Aghajanian, G. K.
Physiological evidence for habenula as major link between forebrain and mid-brain raphe. bibl il Science 197:89-91 Jl 1 '77
WANG, Tung-hsing
Enforcer from Fragrant Hill. il por Time 110:27 S 5 '77 *
WANKEL engines. See Airplane engines; Automobile engines
WANLASS, Cravens Lamar
Little motor that saves. M. Ruby and M. Kasindorf. por il Newsweek 89:78 My 9 '77 *
WANSHEL, Jeff
Isadora Duncan sleeps with the Russian Navy. Reviews
Dance Mag 51:36-7 My '77 *
New Yorker 52:68-9 F 7 '77 *
Time il 109:57 F 21 '77 *
WANTZ, Sherman P.
Computer stores: a new retailing phenomenon. il Pop Electr 12:70-2 D '77
WAPNER, Raymond M. See Schiller, J. G. jt auth
WAR
Battlefield of the 1990s: it's not sci-fi, it's real. U.S. News 83:48-50 Jl 4 '77
Rumors of war. L. H. Lapham. Harpers 255:8+ S '77
See also
Air warfare
Atomic warfare
Environmental warfare
Indians of North America—Wars
Israel-Arab wars, 1967-
Militarism
Pacifism
Strategy
Vietnames War, 1957-1975
War games
World War, 1914-1918
World War, 1939-1945

Moral aspects

See War and morals
WAR, Ethics of. See War and morals
WAR and emergency powers

United States

Department discusses War Powers Resolution: statement, July 15, 1977. H. J. Hansell. Dept State Bull 77:291-3 Ag 29 '77
WAR and morals
Ethics & armaments. B. Catton. Am Heritage 28:97 Ag '77
War crimes; excerpt from Just and unjust wars. M. Walzer. New Repub 177:17-23 N 5 '77
WAR and peace; opera. See Prokof'ev, S. S.
WAR casualties
See also
Vietnamese War, 1957-1975—Casualties
WAR correspondents
Images of war: Jimmy Hare's photojournalism. E. M. Halliday. il por Am Heritage 28:74-81 Ag '77
See also
Vietnamese War, 1957-1975—War correspondents and photographers
WAR crime trials
Who is in the dock? R. Carroll and T. Nater. il Newsweek 90:43 Jl 11 '77
WAR crimes
See also
War crime trials
WAR criminals. See World War, 1939-1945—War criminals
WAR Department. See United States—War Department
WAR games
Compleat Strategist: the place for war game aficionados. D. Maryles. il Pub W 211:52 Mr 7 '77
See also
Military maneuvers
WAR in art
Guernica: an act of war, a work of art. C. L. Mee, Jr. il por Horizon 19:88-96 My '77
WAR in literature
See also
Vietnamese War, 1957-1975—Fiction
World War, 1914-1918—Fiction
WAR in space. See Space flight—Military use
WAR news
See also
Vietnamese War, 1957-1975—Press reports
Vietnamese War, 1957-1975—War correspondents and photographers
WAR novels. See World War, 1914-1918—Fiction
WAR of 1812. See United States—History—War of 1812
WAR pictures
See also
Israel-Arab War, 1948-1949—Photographs and photography
WAR powers. See War and emergency powers
WAR records. See World War, 1939-1945—Documents, sources, etc.
WARBURG, Sir Siegmund George
S. G. Warburg: the exceptional survivor. por Bus W p62 Mr 14 '77 *
WARBURG, S. G. and Company. See London—Banks
WARD, Alan J.
Mother-to-be's anxiety linked to autism. Sci N 112:374 D 3 '77 *
WARD, Andrew
Classic confrontation. Atlantic 240:97-8 O '77
Filming the unknown. Atlantic 241:90-1 Ja '78
Last mambo. Atlantic 240:98-100 D '77
Lift your feet. Atlantic 239:86-90 F '77
Our misplaced President. il Am Heritage 28:84-5 Je '77
Pencils down. Atlantic 239:77-81 My '77
Rub-out. il Horticulture 55:16-19 Mr '77
Yumbo. Atlantic 239:87-8 My '77
WARD, Barbara M. See Ward, G. W. R. jt auth
WARD, Fred
Working pro looks at Cibachrome. il por Pop Phot 80:112-15+ Ap '77

about

Tariff on truth. M. J. Sobran, Jr. Nat R 29:564-5 My 13 '77 *
WARD, G. M. and others
Beef production options and requirements for fossil fuel. bibl il map Science 198:265-71 O 21 '77
WARD, George
Britain's Ascot of the Left. R. Moss. Nat R 29:1238-40 O 28 '77 *
WARD, Gerald W. R. and Ward, B. M.
Historic houses owned by the Essex Institute in Salem, Massachusetts. bibl il Antiques 112:1130-47 D '77
—See Montgomery, C. F. jt auth
WARD, Hiley H.
Getting the Quakers together. Chr Cent 94:724-6 Ag 17 '77
WARD, James Brent
Workshop: titanium: metal of many colors. il Craft Horiz 37:20-1+ Ag '77
WARD, John
Spare that hardwood! il Design (US) 78:16-18 mid-Summ '77
WARD, John W.
Silicone seals sink in darkroom. il Mod Phot 41:94 Mr '77
WARD, Patricia
Simone Weil: futile heroics. Chr Today 22:26-7 N 4 '77
WARD, Peter A. See Chapman, W. E. jt auth
WARD, Ritchie R.
If you look hard cycles are all over. il por Smithsonian 7:104-10 Mr '77
Just how do cycles affect all of life? il Sci Digest 82:14-16+ Jl '77
WARD, Sheila, and others
(ed) 1977 American artist directory of art schools and workshops. Am Artist 41:D1-40 Mr '77
WARD Foods Inc
Remodeling job shakes Ward Foods. il Bus W p37-8 F 14 '77
Ward Foods' future is unsettled again. Bus W p31-2 Ja 16 '78
WARDAIR Canada. See Airlines—Canada
WARDANA, M. W. C. Dharma-. See Dharma-Wardana, M. W. C.
WARDENBURG, Sylvia
Women who chose the great outdoors; interview, ed by N. H. Clark. por Harp Baz 110:148 Ap '77
WARDENS, Game. See Game wardens
WARDROBES. See Armoires
WARDS. See Guardian and ward
WARD's Natural Science Establishment, Rochester, N.Y.
Ward's a natural science treasure house. W. Trimm. il Conservationist 32:2-7 Jl '77
WAREHOUSES
HUP, MIT share warehousing facilities to reduce costs and improve service. B. McCabe. il Pub W 211:58+ Mr 28 '77

WARFARE. See Military art and science
WARFARIN
Reduced warfarin binding of albumin variants. G. Wilding and others. bibl il Science 195: 991-4 Mr 11 '77
WARHOL, Andy
Andy Warhol sketch of our soup can culture. il pors U.S. News 82:57 Je 27 '77
Beaux arts; exhibition. R. Berenson. Nat R 29:342 Mr 18 '77 *
WARNER, Brian
W. E. Wilson and the Daramona observatory. il Sky & Tel 53:108-10 F '77
WARNER, Denis
Reports & comment: Australia. il Atlantic 240: 26-31 O '77
WARNER, Edwin
Nobel experience. il Horizon 19:46-55 My '77
Suburbia's gift to the cities. il Horizon 20:14-25 S '77
WARNER, Frank
Ma Bell, firebug. Nation 224:684-8 Je 4 '77
WARNER, John William
Rediscovery of America. il por Sat Eve Post 249:12+ Ap '77
about
Elizabeth Taylor talks about her new love, her new life. . ; interview, ed by D. Wigg. E. Taylor. il pors Good H 184:100-3+ F '77 *
Elizabeth Taylor's surprising new life. N. Thimmesch. pors McCalls 104:16+ Jl '77 *
Farmer's wife. S. McElwaine. il pors Ladies Home J 94:70-1+ Ag '77 *
Look at the man Liz found. B. N. MacDougal. il pors Sat Eve Post 249:62-3+ N '77 *
National Velveeta. J. A. Latham. pors Esquire 88:101-4+ N '77 *
WARNER, Ralph, and Ihara, Toni
Lover's guide to living together legally. Ms 6: 54-6+ N '77
WARNER, Rawleigh, 1921-
U.S. energy crisis; address, November 30, 1976. Vital Speeches 43:246-51 F 1 '77
WARNER, Sylvia Townsend
Flora; story. New Yorker 53:38-40 D 19 '77
Qwertyuiop; story. New Yorker 52:27-9 Ja 31 '77
Widow's quilt; story. New Yorker 53:35-8 Je 6 '77
WARNER, William W.
Crabbers, sooks and Jimmies; excerpt from Beautiful swimmers. il Read Digest 111:112-16 O '77
Politics of fish. il Atlantic 240:35-44 Ag '77; Same abr. with title Aboard a fish trawler in the North Atlantic. Read Digest 111:142-7 N '77
Winter comes to the Bay; excerpt from Beautiful swimmers: watermen, crabs and the Chesapeake Bay. il Yachting 141:75-7 F '77
WARNICK, Rodney B. See Heywood, L. A. jt auth
WARNING lights. See Signals and signaling
WARNING systems, Disaster. See Disaster warning systems
WARNKE, Paul Culliton
Progress and problems in arms control negotiations; address, September 19, 1977. Dept State Bull 77:772-7 N 28 '77
Ratification recommended for treaties with U.S.S.R. restricting nuclear testing; statements, July 28, 1977. Dept State Bull 77:310-12 S 5 '77
Real Paul Warnke; excerpts from interview, ed by W. Miale. New Repub 176:22-5 Mr 26 '77
Signal to the Soviets—and to Carter; excerpts from interview. il por Time 109:28 Mr 21 '77
U.S. intent with regard to SALT I interim agreement; statement, September 26, 1977. Dept State Bull 77:642-3 N 7 '77
about
Appointments calendar. F. Getlein. Commonweal 104:133-4 Mr 4 '77 *
Arms and the man. T. Mathews and J. J. Lindsay. por Newsweek 89:29 F 14 '77 *
Carter appointments: fresh moves on sea law, arms control. D. Shapley. Science 195:560-2 F 11 '77 *
Hard-nosed but soft-headed. B. T. Feld. Bull Atom Sci 33:9 Ap '77 *
Hooding the hawks; Senate debate over nomination. Nation 224:354-5 Mr 26 '77 *
Latest round in debate over Russia's aims. il por U.S. News 82:18 F 28 '77 *
Opposition to Warnke mounts in Senate. E. Kozicharow. Aviation W 106:21-2 F 14 '77 *
Proper perch for the dove. por Time 109:23 F 14 '77 *
Senate group questions Warnke closely. E. Kozicharow. Aviation W 106:27 F 28 '77 *
Tale of two confirmations. Nation 224:290-1 Mr 12 '77 *
Warnke in wonderland. Nat R 29:250+ Mr 4 '77 *
Warnke problem. Nation 224:195-6 F 19 '77 *
Warnke's Algerian connection cited. Aviation W 106:22 Mr 14 '77 *
Why not the best? M. Stone. U.S. News 82:88 Mr 21 '77 *

WARRANTY
Guarantees and warranties. Consumer Rep 42: 365-6 D '77
Warning on warranties. il Sr Schol 109:19 Mr 10 '77
WARREN, Barbara Leonard
Of bags and boxes: how to banish the book report form without getting fired. il Engl J 66:70-3 F '77
WARREN, Bruce A.
Deep western boundary current in the eastern Indian Ocean. bibl map Science 196:53-4 Ap 1 '77
WARREN, Charles Hugh
U.S. urges global view of water resource problems; statement at the United Nations Water Conference, March 15, 1977. Dept State Bull 76:437-40 My 2 '77
about
From symbolism to substance. J. B. Craig. Am For 83:23 My '77 *
WARREN, Cora
Three ways to arrange flowers: how to do it with your own plants. il Horticulture 55:70-1 F '77
WARREN, David
10 great shop tricks from a master craftsman. il por Pop Mech 149:90-2 Ja '78
WARREN, Earl
Inside the Supreme Court; excerpt from The memoirs of Earl Warren. il por Atlantic 239: 35-40 Ap '77
about
Burger vs. Warren: whose Court is better? pors U.S. News 82:58 Mr 7 '77 *
WARREN, Elizabeth V.
Books (cont) House B 119:22+ F; 34 Mr; 22+ Je; 24+ Jl; 20 Ag '77
WARREN, F. Eugene
His mind a psalter: the poetry of Charles Reznikoff. Chr Today 22:26-7 D 9 '77
In the rain; poem. Chr Today 21:20 My 6 '77
Philip K. Dick: exile in paradox. Chr Today 21:22-4 My 20 '77
Some good tricks; poem. Chr Today 22:25 D 9 '77
Song into storm; poem. Chr Today 21:14 Je 3 '77
WARREN, Harry
Songsmith nobody knows. E. Calder. il por Am Rec G 40:4-7+ Jl '77 *
WARREN, Joyce
Criticism. Chr Cent 94:41-2 Ja 19 '77
Housekeeping at Mount Vernon. Chr Cent 94: 851-2 S 28 '77
St Mark's, Capitol Hill: patron of the arts. Chr Cent 94:632-3 Jl 6 '77
Tutankhamun adventure. Chr Cent 94:409-10 Ap 27 '77
WARREN, Michael
Catechetical ministry of the Church. il por New Cath World 220:65-8 Mr '77
WARREN, Nigel
Balance of power. il Motor B & S 141:74-6+ Ja '78
Dollar-wise outboard buying; excerpt from Outboard motor handbook. il Motor B & S 139: 96-7+ My '77
Flexible couplings. il Motor B & S 141:43-6 Ja '78
WARREN, Phelps
Glass relating to William III. bibl il Antiques 112:742-9 O '77
WARREN, Robert Penn
Code book lost; Boy wandering in Simms' Valley; poems. Sat R 5:38-9 O 29 '77
First dawn light; poem. New Yorker 53:38 Ap 4 '77
Heart of autumn; Dream; Ah, anima! poems. Atlantic 240:84-6 O '77
Little black heart of the telephone; poem. New Yorker 53:34 My 23 '77
Red-tail hawk and pyre of youth; poem. New Yorker 53:32-3 Jl 18 '77
about
Comment. J. D. McClatchy. Poetry 131:169-75 D '77 *
WARREN, Shirley
Truth about children's lies. Educ Digest 42:51-3 Mr '77
WARREN, Stanley
Claude McKay as an artist. bibl f por Negro Hist Bull 40:685-7 Mr '77
WARREN family
Warren coat-of-arms. H. K. Eilers. il Hobbies 82:146 My '77
WARSAW, Irene
Love story; poem. McCalls 104:82 F '77
WARSAW convention
Treaty prerogatives in debate. Aviation W 107: 29 Ag 1 '77
WARSH, David
Great hamburger paradox. il Forbes 120:166-7 S 15 '77

WARSHIPS
See also
Armored vessels
Monitor (warship)

United States

Cruise of the USS Essex; 32-gun frigate. R. J. Toner. il map Am Hist Illus 11:4-7+ Ja '77

WARSHIPS, Atomic powered
End of the road for big nuclear ships? il U.S. News 82:61 Mr 14 '77

WARSHOFSKY, Fred
Noah, the flood, the facts. map Read Digest 111: 129-34 S '77

WARSHOW, Paul
More is less: comedy and sound. il pors Film Q 31:38-45 Fall '77

WARTS
Warts still defy spung water and more scientific cures. P. Ryan. il Smithsonian 7:164 F '77

WASHBURN, Wilcomb E.
Moral equivalent to football. New Repub 177: 33-6 Jl 23 '77

WASHING apparatus
Power washers speed fall cleanups. S. Renner-Smith. il Pop Sci 211:132 N '77

WASHING machines
Automatic washers & dryers. il Changing T 31: 16-18 Ap '77
How to buy a washer and dryer. Bet Hom & Gard 55:126 N '77
Portable washers and dryers. il Consumer Rep 42:90-6 F '77
Washing machines. il Consumer Rep 42:571-5 O '77

WASHING of clothes. See Laundry

WASHINGTON, Booker Taliaferro
Booker T. Washington: a visit to Florida. R. C. Potter. por Negro Hist Bull 40:744-5 S '77 *

WASHINGTON, George
George Washington's beautiful Nelly; story of the president and his grand-daughter. D. Jackson. il por Am Heritage 28:80-5 F '77 *

Drama

Visitor to Mount Vernon. H. L. Miller. Plays 36:75-82 F '77

Portraits

By George, a Stuart! painting found in New Bedford, Mass. por Time 110:24+ N 28 '77
Engravings of George Washington in the Stanley DeForest Scott collection. S. W. Grote. il Antiques 112:128-33 Jl '77
Washington memorial prints; with editorial comment by W. Garrett. D. T. Deutsch. bibl il por Antiques 111:323, 324-31 F '77

WASHINGTON, James, Jr
James Washington: secrets in stone; interview, ed by R. Hackett. il por Am Artist 41:74-9+ N '77

WASHINGTON, Kenneth R.
Developing self-concepts of urban children. Educ Digest 43:44-6 N '77

WASHINGTON, D.C.
Ferment in Georgetown. W. B. Furlong. il Horizon 19:4-13 Jl '77
Good life in Washington is bad for America; symposium. New Repub 177:5-21+ Jl 9 '77; Discussion. 177:5+ Ag 20 '77
Jimmy Carter's Washington: a city that has come a long way despite problems. il U.S. News 82:31-4 Ja 24 '77
President Carter lights a candle. Sat Eve Post 249:34 Ap '77
See also
Architecture, Domestic—Washington, D.C.
Booksellers and bookselling—Washington, D.C.
Festivals—Washington, D.C.
Music festivals—Washington, D.C.

Art

Washington (title varies) (cont) B. Forgey. il Art N 76:86-7 F; 106+ My; 168 Summ '77
Washington, D.C. J. Shaw-Eagle. il Art N 76:116 S '77

Buildings

Georgetown's nice new neighbor; 1055 Thomas Jefferson Street; with introd by W. Marlin. il Archit Rec 161:95-102 F '77
Pulitzer for Mildred A. Pappas; apartment house newsletter, the Ontario bulletin. N. Ephron. Esquire 87:18+ Mr '77

Churches

To the glory of God; needlework in the Washington National Cathedral. il Good H 185:120-3 D '77

City planning

Washington's plans for the development of Pennsylvania Avenue begin to show signs of real action. W. Hickman. il Archit Rec 162:34 N '77

Crime

Education of John Allen; excerpt from Assault with a deadly weapon: the autobiography of a street criminal, ed by P. Heymann and D. Kelly; with comments by O. Coombs. J. Allen. il Psychol Today 11:96-7+ O '77
TRB from Washington. New Repub 176:4+ Mr 26 '77

Description

Doing the Carter walk. H. Sutton. il map Sat R 4:40+ Ap 30 '77

Economic conditions

Boom town. M. Kondracke. New Repub 177:7-9 Jl 9 '77

Education

Elementary school level sex education. Educ Digest 42:29-32 Ja '77
Growing up white in D.C. schools. R. Jordan. Educ Digest 43:41-3 N '77
Lab classroom: breaking the communication barrier; Horace Mann School. E. Walsh. il Science 196:1425 Je 24 '77
Unique Southwest educational program; Randall Aerospace-Marine Science Program. A. B. Finlayson. il Negro Hist Bull 40:658 Ja '77
Washington's segregated schools. E. Marshall. New Repub 177:15-17 Jl 9 '77
Where officials' kids go to school—few follow Amy's example. il U.S. News 82:34 Ja 24 '76

Galleries and museums

African village on Capitol Hill; Museum of African Art. W. M. Robbins. il Smithsonian 8:55-6 Ag '77
Educational explosion: the Museum of African Art. K. Kuh. il Sat R 4:34-6 My 28 '77
Museum of Modern Art of Latin America. A. J. Lowe. il Américas 29:S1-S12 Mr '77
Report on the National Museum of the Building Arts asks for Federal funds and a home in the Pension Building. il Archit Rec 162:34 D '77
See also
Corcoran Gallery of Art, Washington, D.C.
National Gallery of Art

Historic houses, sites, etc.

See also
White House

Hospitals

Kidney transplant center; Howard University Hospital. M. Burgen. il Ebony 32:59-62+ Ap '77

Hotels, restaurants, etc.

Let's have lunch. R. Shrum. New Repub 177:9-10 Jl 9 '77
Way to escape the Washington stockade. W. Guzzardi, Jr. il Fortune 95:175-6 Ja '77
See also
Night clubs

Housing

District of Columbia/open today; prices of houses in Georgetown. R. Rosenblatt. il New Repub 177:39-40 Jl 9 '77

Monuments, statues, etc.

FDR and the cherry blossoms. il por Horizon 19:56-61 My '77
Missing memorials. New Repub 176:44 Ap 23 '77
See also
Lincoln Memorial

Music

Debuts & reappearances. il Hi Fi 27:MA37 F; MA26 S '77
See also
John F. Kennedy Center for the Performing Arts
National Symphony Orchestra

National Arboretum

Our national bonsai collection. R. Pardo. il Am For 83:14-17+ D '77

Newspapers

See also
Washington post
Washington star-news

Night clubs

See Night clubs

Parks and playgrounds

National Park Service stable by architects Hartman-Cox; in Rock Creek Park. il Archit Rec 161:120-1 F '77

Photographs

Washington scrapbook. D. Walker. il New Repub 177:20-1 Jl 9 '77

Police

Sting's the thing; police-run fencing operations. E. Keerdoja and S. Lesher. Newsweek 89:11 F 28 '77

WASHINGTON, D.C.—*Continued*

Protests, demonstrations, etc.

Greetings for the Shah. il por Time 110:15+ N 28 '77
When Persians collide; Shah's visit. il Newsweek 90:65 N 28 '77

Public buildings

See also
United States—Capitol
United States—State, Department of—Headquarters

Restaurants

See Washington, D.C.—Hotels, restaurants, etc.

Schools

See Washington, D.C.—Education

Social conditions

Carterland's fifth estate. il Time 109:27-8 F 7 '77

Social life and customs

Carter style—beanies, beer and Jesus. S. Quinn. Ms 6:106 Ja '78
How politicians eat reporters for breakfast; G. Sperlin's Washington breakfasts. N. Ephron. Esquire 87:26-7+ Je '77
In or out? social list. Time 110:40 O 24 '77
Rosalynn and Jimmy Carter's Washington; what's in and who's left out. K. Kelley. il por Redbook 149:82+ Je '77
Washington's world of style. T. Bethell. il Harpers 256:66-9+ Ja '78
What the Carters are doing to wipe out divorce in Washington. J. L. Block. il Good H 184:109+ Je '77
What your country can do for you. New Repub 177:5-7 Jl 9 '77

Street traffic

Yellow boots on cars. il U.S. News 82:80 Mr 21 '77

Streets

Washington's plans for the development of Pennsylvania Avenue begin to show signs of real action. W. Hickman. il Archit Rec 162:34 N '77

Subways

Capital underground. il Horizon 20:50 S '77

Terrorism

See Terrorism

Theater

See also
John F. Kennedy Center for the Performing Arts

WASHINGTON (state)
See also
Architecture, Domestic—Washington (state)
Art galleries and museums—Washington (state)
Education—Washington (state)
Environmental policy—Washington (state)
Fishing—Washington (state)
Historic houses, sites, etc.—Washington (state)
Mount Rainier National Park
Natural areas—Washington (state)
Olympic National Park
Rainier, Mount
Recreation areas—Washington (state)
San Juan Islands
Skagit River
Wilderness areas—Washington (state)

Antiquities

Indian Pompeii; Makah village. P. Gwynne and S. Gayle. il Newsweek 90:81-2 S 5 '77

Description and travel

Dixy rocks the Northwest. il pors map Time 110:26-9+ D 12 '77

Politics and government

Surprises from Nation's two women governors. il U.S. News 83:45 O 10 '77

WASHINGTON (state). University, Seattle

School of law

Library

Relating common solutions; two libraries by Mitchell/Giurgola; with introd by C. K. Hoyt. il Archit Rec 162:93-8 Ag '77

WASHINGTON Book Fair. See Book fairs

WASHINGTON Conference on the Limitation of Armaments, 1921. See Disarmament—Conferences

WASHINGTON Heights. See New York (city)

WASHINGTON National Cathedral. See Washington, D.C.—Churches

WASHINGTON post
America's two best newspapers. T. Griffith. il Time 109:70-2 F 7 '77
Editors telling secrets. T. Griffith. il Time 109:80 Mr 14 '77
Managing leaks. L. Kinsolving. Nat R 29:706 Je 24 '77
PW interviews; book editor; ed by S. Wagner. W. McPherson. por Pub W 212:10-11 Ag 8 '77
Press media; address, May 12, 1977. H. Simons. Vital Speeches 43:689-92 S 1 '77
What secrets are sacred? decision to print the King Hussein-CIA story. D. Gelman and others. il por Newsweek 89:40+ Mr 14 '77

WASHINGTON Post Company
American's press: too much power for too few? A. P. Sanoff. il U.S. News 83:27-33 Ag 15 '77
Krusty Kay tightens her grip. por Time 109:70 F 7 '77

WASHINGTON press corps. See Press and politics

WASHINGTON Real Estate Investment Trust. See Real estate investment trusts

WASHINGTON Square, New York City. See New York (city)—Washington Square

WASHINGTON Square; opera. See Pasatieri, T.

WASHINGTON star-news
Star wars; resignation of J. G. Bellows. H. F. Waters and J. B. Copeland. por Newsweek 90:129-30 N 28 '77

WASKOW, Arthur I.
Don't call it treason. Nation 224:178-80 F 12 '77

WASPS
Exotic forest saved by foreign sting. il Sci N 112:69 Jl 30 '77
North American egg parasite successfully controls a different host genus in South America. A. T. Drooz and others. bibl il Science 197:390-1 Jl 22 '77

WASSERMAN, Burton
Exhibitions in sight (cont) il Sch Arts 76:58-61 F; 48-51 Ap; 77:34-7 D '77
Resource materials. See issues of School arts

WASSERMAN, Gary
Promises, payoffs and evasions. il Nation 225:458-61 N 5 '77

WASSERMAN, Harvey
Clamshell Alliance: getting it together. Progressive 41:14-18 S '77
Clamshell reaction. Nation 224:744-9 Je 18 '77
Confrontation at Seabrook. Progressive 41:11-12 Jl '77
Hiroshima remembered. Progressive 41:8 O '77
Industry hides from the sun. il Nation 224:263-6 Mr 5 '77
Resistance nears a critical mass. Nation 225:328-30 O 8 '77
Seabrook stalemate. Progressive 41:41 My '77
Singapore, where 1984 is now. map Progressive 41:34-8 Ap '77

WASSERSTEIN, Wendy
Uncommon women and others. Reviews
Nation 225:667-8 D 17 '77 •
New Yorker 53:115 D 5 '77 •
Time il 110:111 D 5 '77 •

WASSON, Jack
Children of God: disciples of deception; interview, ed by J. M. Hopkins. il por Chr Today 21:18-23 F 18 '77

WASSON, John T. See Bild, R. W. jt auth

WASTE, Disposal of. See Refuse and refuse disposal

WASTE, Industrial. See Trade waste

WASTE, Radioactive. See Radioactive wastes

WASTE, Utilization of. See Refuse, Utilization of

WASTE as fuel. See Refuse as fuel

WASTE disposal in the ocean
Secondary sewage treatment versus ocean outfalls: an assessment. C. B. Officer and J. H. Ryther. bibl il Science 197:1056-60 S 9 '77
Suffocating sea: sludge accumulation in New Jersey Bight. M. Seward. il Oceans 10:60-2 My '77
Water quality: Oceanic Society monitors San Francisco Bay. S. R. Krenzelok. Oceans 10:65 Mr '77

WASTE heat
Fall warm-up: home improvement & decorating guide. B. Niles. il Am Home 80:77+ S '77
Get set for winter. il Changing T 31:6-8 N '77
1977 homeowner's guide to saving energy and money. M. Cubisino. il McCalls 104:121-8 S '77

WASTE heat electric power production. See Electric power production

WASTE in government spending. See United States—Appropriations and expenditures

WASTE products
One company's waste, another's wealth. L. Hastings. il Environment 19:38-40 O '77
See also
Trade waste
Wood waste

WASTE recycling. See Refuse, Utilization of

WASTE treatment plants. See Sewage disposal plants

WASTE water disposal plants. See Sewage disposal plants

WASTE water irrigation. See Sewage irrigation

WASTE water purification. See Sewage purification

WASTE water reclamation. See Water reuse

WATCH industry
Feeling the pulse of the watch market; Time Computer, Inc. Bus W p36+ Ap 25 '77
Great digital watch shake-out. il Bus W p78+ My 2 '77
See also
Bulova Watch Company
Fairchild Camera and Instrument Corporation

Hong Kong

Wong ends his stay at Bulova; returning to Stelux Mfg. Co. il por Bus W p40 N 28 '77

WATCHDOGS
Pet journal. R. Caras. il Ladies Home J 94:36 Ap '77
Watchdog you can live with. M. Rubenstein. il Mech Illus 73:64-5+ O '77

WATCHES
On time. O. R. Hagans. See issues of Hobbies
Watches and clocks. Consumers Res Mag 60:159-61 O '77
See also
Stop watches

WATCHES, Electric
Throw-away digitals you'll want to keep. G. R. Patton. il Pop Mech 147:78-9+ Je '77
Today's digitals. V. E. Smay. il Pop Sci 211:102-3 D '77
Why Gillette stopped its digital watches. Bus W p37-8 Ja 31 '77

Anecdotes, facetiae, satire, etc.

It ticks and it talks—it may be too much; talking wristwatch. P. Ryan. Smithsonian 8:140 D '77

WATER
Extragalactic water hole. il Sky & Tel 54:108 Ag '77
Hydrogen and oxygen from water. E. A. Fletcher and R. L. Moen. bibl il Science 197:1050-6 S 9 '77
See also
Dew
Drinking water
Drops
Irrigation water
Sea water
Waves

Cooling

Rotary water cooler. V. E. Smay. il Pop Sci 211:169 N '77

Electrolysis

See Electrolysis

Microbiology

We found virus in our drinking water; Polio I virus; Fairfax County, Va. J. W. Berry and P. Shaffer. il Am City & County 92:65-6 Je '77
See also
Waterborne infection

Odor removal

See Water purification

Physiological effects

Water: the environment factor. N. Simon. il Vogue 167:167+ Ag '77

Pollution

See Water pollution

Purification

See Water purification

Reuse

See Water reuse

Taste removal

See Water purification

Testing

pHish pfinder? using acidity or alkalinity of water to determine fish populations. J. Scott. il Field & S 82:58+ Jl '77

WATER, Bottled
Bottled water: tastes good but is it really that pure? M. L. Schildkraut. Good H 182:212 S '77
Straight from the source. L. Botto. il N Y Times Mag p68+ Je 26 '77
Taking the cap off bottled water. P. Quimme. il House & Gard 149:106+ Jl '77

Marketing

Perrier in six-packs. il Time 109:69 My 16 '77

WATER, Freezing. See Freezing

WATER, Saline. See Saline water

WATER, Underground
See also
Geysers
Hydrogeology
Wells

Pollution

See Water pollution

WATER-air toilets. See Toilets

WATER bird decoys. See Decoys (hunting)

WATER bird shooting
Amphibious hunter. F. M. Paulson. il Field & S 82:182-3+ O '77
Baiting laws are a mess. J. Phillips. il Outdoor Life 159:63-5+ Je '77
Lead shot; question of waterfowl mortality resulting from lead shot ingestion. Audubon 79:140 Jl '77
Twilight for lead shot? J. Phillips. il Outdoor Life 160:90-1+ Ag '77
Will steel shot work in your gun? J. Carmichel. il Outdoor Life 160:91-2+ Ag '77

WATER bird talk; opera. See Argento, D.

WATER birds
Update: waterfowl; ed by T. Paugh. il Outdoor Life 160:102 O; 58 N; 108 D '77; 161:104 Ja '78
See also
Sea birds
also names of water birds, e.g. Swans

Protection

Just another oil spill; Chesapeake Bay. G. Reiger. Audubon 79:144-8 Ja '77
To save a bird, prevent a spill. Audubon 79:160 Mr '77
See also
Game laws

WATER birds on postage stamps. See Postage stamps

WATER bloom
Allelopathic influence on blue-green bloom sequence in a eutrophic lake. K. I. Keating. bibl il Science 196:885-7 My 20 '77
Toxins from blue-green algae. R. E. Moore. bibl il BioScience 27:797-802 D '77

WATER borne infection. See Waterborne infection

WATER color painting
Frederic Whitaker: Mister watercolor. J. Jennings. il Am Artist 41:68-73+ Ag '77
Watercolor page:
Bonny Lhotka. il por Am Artist 41:76-9+ Ag '77
Charles Schmidt. il por Am Artist 41:62-5+ O '77
Jim Gray. il por Am Artist 41:50-3+ Ap '77
Katharine Steele Renninger. il por Am Artist 41:30-3+ Mr '77
Kenneth Harris. il por Am Artist 41:48-51+ S '77
Mervin Allen Corning. il por Am Artist 41:50-3+ N '77
Sue Wise. il por Am Artist 41:72-5+ F '77
Tony van Hasselt. il por Am Artist 41:48-51+ Je '77
Vincent Ceglia. il por Am Artist 41:48-51+ My '77
W. B. Romeling. W. B. Romeling. il Am Artist 41:52-5+ D '77
Watercolor techniques of J.M.W. Turner. C. E. Luffman. il Am Artist 41:36-9+ Je '77

WATER Conference, United Nations. See United Nations Water Conference

WATER conservation
Gift ideas for the water miser. il Sunset 159:78-9 D '77
How to ration water; Marin County, Calif. M. Friedman. Newsweek 89:73 Mr 21 '77
Marin County: the bucket brigade. J. Boyce. il Time 109:15 F 14 '77
No water or soil leaves these farms. C. E. Sommers. il Suc Farm 75:C40 D '77
PS tests bathroom water-savers. E. Powell. il Pop Sci 211:120-2+ Ag '77
Saving water—before we're down to the last drop. M. R. Skrocki. il McCalls 104:52 S '77
What do you do when you're out of water? Marin County, Calif. J. D. Stroeh. il Am City & County 92:49-50 D '77
See also
Water reuse

WATER consumption
See also
Water meters

WATER cycle. See Hydrologic cycle

WATER distribution
See also
Water towers

WATER drops. See Drops

WATER engine; drama. See Mamet, D.

WATER erosion. See Erosion

WATER filters and filtration. See Filters and filtration

WATER fountains. See Fountains

WATER fowl. See Water birds

WATER fronts
Recall for greenways; excerpt from The public benefits of cleaned water: emerging greenway opportunities. H. Deardorff. il Parks & Rec 12:39a-40a F '77
U.S. journal: New England. C. Trillin. New Yorker 53:101-2+ My 16 '77

WATER games. See Games

WATER gardens
See also
Aquatic plants
Garden pools

WATER heaters
Adventures in alternate energy: O. W. Wood: solar + woodstove heats his water. E. Moran. il Pop Sci 210:48-9 My '77
Dual-use solar wall: pool heat plus handball backboard. D. Houser and R. Stepler. il Pop Sci 210:110-13+ Ap '77
Electricity miser isn't very stingy. il Consumer Rep 42:126 Mr '77
Homebuilt solar hot water heater. il Mech Illus 73:50 Ap '77
How to get hot water from the sun right now. il Pop Mech 148:131-3+ S '77
Now the sun heats our pool. R. J. Pietschmann. il Mech Illus 73:68-9+ Ag '77
Ronald W. Kock: tubular collector in a drain-down system. E. Moran. il Pop Sci 211:52+ D '77
Water heaters. il Consumer Rep 42:298-303 D '77
Water supply. il Consumers Res Mag 60:149-55 O '77
What to expect of solar pool heaters. F. A. Ford. Parks & Rec 12:44-5 My '77

WATER hyacinths
Harvesting a nuisance. J. Queijo. il Environment 19:25-9 Mr '77
Will hyacinths become the first moon flower? il Space World N-2-158:40 F '77

WATER in the body
Bound on "bound water": transverse nuclear magnetic resonance relaxation in barnacle muscle. K. R. Foster and others; discussion. bibl Science 198:1180-2 D 16 '77
See also
Dehydration (physiology)
Drinking (physiology)
Osmoregulation

WATER lilies
August in the garden; plants for a water garden. D. Fell. Horticulture 55:4 Ag '77

WATER meters
Improving water meter efficiency. il Am City & County 92:49-52 Ag '77

Maintenance and repair
Meter tests cut water losses. il Am City & County 92:66 Ja '77
Think twice before repairing water meters. R. L. Williams. Am City & County 92:45-6 F '77

WATER pipes
Tyranny in a glass of water; refusal to use Chesapeake, Va. water supply because of asbestos-cement pipes. C. Cahill. Nation 224:325-6 Mr 19 '77
Well was well, it was the pipes that did it. T. Benfey. Chemistry 50:2 Ap '77

WATER pipes, Plastic
ABCs of plastic pipe. A. S. Jetter. il Mech Illus 73:80+ Ap '77
Flexible tubing gives 50 year design life; polybutylene tubing used by Alameda County water district. il Am City & County 92:65 My '77
Polybutylene pipe. il Yachting 141:95 Ap '77

WATER pitchers. See Pitchers

WATER plants. See Aquatic plants

WATER pollution
Drinkable, but... F. S. Sterrett. bibl il Environment 19:28-36 D '77
Drinking water: getting rid of the carbon tetrachloride. J. L. Marx. Science 196:632-6 My 6 '77
Drinking water: health hazards still not resolved. N. Wade. Science 196:1421-2 Je 24 '77; Discussion. 197:320+ Jl 22 '77
Eight hot issues that affect you now. S. French. il Outdoor Life 159:50+ Ap '77
How much leachate can we afford? question of groundwater pollution at landfill sites. J. J. Reinhardt. il Am City & County 92:48-9 Jl '77
If your drinking water gets tainted, you'll now be told; EPA standards. M. Zeldin. Audubon 79:127 My '77
Water pollution: appearances can be deceiving. J. Raloff. il Sci N 112:428-31 D 24 '77
See also
Eutrophication
Marine pollution
Mercury pollution of rivers, lakes, etc.
Oil pollution of rivers, harbors, etc.
Oil pollution of the sea
Sewage disposal
Steel works—Environmental aspects
Water bloom

Conferences
Land-water symposium asks how to avert a crisis. E. M. Leeper. il BioScience 27:653-4 O '77

Control
Big cleanup; symposium. il Parks & Rec 12:1a-40a F '77
EPA crackdown on water polluters ahead; views of officials. Am City & County 92:8 Ja '77
EPA enforcement push shows little regard for local options. W. L. Forestell. Am City & County 92:88 Ja '77
Pollution can be licked: three areas show how. il U.S. News 82:48-50 F 7 '77
You may qualify for pollution loans from SBA. C. Bickers. Farm J 101:33B Mr '77
See also
Cleaning of lakes, rivers, etc.
Industry and the environment
Sewage purification
Water Pollution Control Federation

Economic aspects
Safe water or jobs? A classic confrontation; Mahoning River Valley and the steel industry. il U.S. News 82:47 F 7 '77

Laws and legislation
But officer, it's just fertilizer! C. Bickers. Farm J 101:Dairy 15 S '77
Diluting water-pollution rules. U.S. News 82:47 Mr 14 '77
Industry cries overkill on clean-water rules. il Bus W p41 O 10 '77
New clean-water law; what it means to you. il U.S. News 83:58 D 5 '77
Push to ease water rules. il Bus W p69+ Mr 21 '77
Washington scene; Breaux amendment to the Federal Water Pollution Control Act. B. Kravetz. Parks & Rec 12:12+ F '77
Water Act revision complete. C. Holden. Science 198:1130 D 16 '77
Water pollution: a case study in the art of compromise. P. Philipps. il Bus W p 134+ D 12 '77
Water pollution control: an overview of the laws. E. C. Beck. il Parks & Rec 12:5a-14a F '77

Measurement
U.S. Canada to study river water quality; Poplar River Basin. Dept State Bull 77:282-3 Ag 29 '77

Physiological effects
Fatal disease; primary amebic meningoencephalitis. S. A. Carter. bibl il Environment 19:16-20 Ap '77

Alaska
Mercury dispersal from lode sources in the Kuskokwim River drainage, Alaska. H. Nelson and others. bibl il map Science 198:820-4 N 25 '77

Great Lakes
Fifth-year review of Great Lakes Water Quality agreement begins. Dept State Bull 76:446 My 2 '77
Stillness (however brief) at Silver Bay; Reserve Mining Company polluting Lake Superior. J. G. Mitchell. il Audubon 79:129-34 S '77

Indiana
Water pollution: the Indiana experiment; phosphate-detergent ban. T. Wyman. Environment 19:2-4 Je '77

Kentucky
Endangered fish of Kentucky streams. B. A. Branson. il Natur Hist 86:64-9 bibl(p 101) F '77

Malaysia
Kuala Juru's struggle for survival. K. S. Jomo. il map Environment 19:41-2 O '77

New Mexico
Killing of a wild river; pollution by Molybdenum Corporation of America, or MolyCorp. D. Kline. Field & S 82:104+ S '77

New York (state)
Champlain: battleground still. P. Brooks. il map Audubon 79:66-77 Ja '77
Hudson: that river's alive. A. J. Hall. il map Nat Geog 153:62-89 Ja '78

Ohio
Infrared photography maps non-point pollution; Toledo. il Am City & County 92:46-7 Ja '77

Vermont
Champlain: battleground still. P. Brooks. il map Audubon 79:66-77 Ja '77

Virginia
Careless Kepone; James River contamination. F. S. Sterrett and C. A. Boss. bibl il map Environment 19:30-6 Mr '77
Chemical plants leave unexpected legacy for two Virginia rivers; mercury pollution. L. J. Carter. map Science 198:1015-20 D 9 '77
It takes a tough man to fowl a tender creek; pollution of Parker Creek by Perdue's Accomac plant in Virginia. G. Reiger. il Audubon 79:142-5 N '77

WATER Pollution Control Federation
EPA: cleanup, not concrete; WPCF conference. Am City & County 92:15 N '77
Jury on land disposal of wastewater still out, Mr Costle; annual conference. S. Baxter. Am City & County 92:28 D '77

WATER pollution control industries. See Pollution control industries

WATER power
See also
Hydroelectric power
Tide power
Wave power

WATER pumps. See Pumps

WATER purification
Centrifuge ends drying bed chores for Pennsylvania water plant; Lancaster. M. B. Freedman. il Am City & County 92:63-4 N '77
Chlorination still the top dog of disinfection. il Am City & County 92:61-4 My '77
End taste and odor complaints with granular activated carbon. C. A. Blanck. il por Am City & County 92:89-90 O '77
Polyelectrolytes: potential chloroform precursors. K. L. E. Kaiser and J. Lawrence. bibl il Science 196:1205-6 Je 10 '77
Polymer cuts cost of Rochester water. D. R. Lawson. il por Am City & County 92:97-8 S '77
Silver shines as pool purifier. il Am City & County 92:18 Ag '77
Sunlight-induced bromate formation in chlorinated seawater. D. L. Macalady and others. bibl il Science 195:1335-7 Mr 25 '77
Will hyacinths become the first moon flower? il Space World N-2-158:40 F '77
See also
Filters and filtration
Space vehicles—Water supply
Water reuse
Water softening
Water treatment plants

WATER purification plants. See Water treatment plants

WATER purifiers, Domestic
Make pure water out of waste; PureCycle computer-controlled system. Am City & County 92:50 S '77

WATER reclamation. See Water reuse

WATER repellents
Home water repellent treatment for fabrics. il Consumers Res Mag 60:34-6 F '77

WATER resources development
Biologists' comments sought on federal water projects. A. J. Grimes. BioScience 27:298-9 Ap '77
Carter's hard line on water projects. il Bus W p25-6 My 2 '77
Carter's water projects: pork barrel sellout? B. Vogt. il Outdoor Life 160:34+ N '77
Hydra lives on. Audubon 79:146 Jl '77
Irrigation, flood control, navigation and user taxes; address, May 6, 1977. J. D. Geary. Vital Speeches 43:536-9 Je 15 '77
Like having your dad die; proposed cancellation of the Central Arizona Project. il Time 109:80 Mr 7 '77
Meanwhile, back on the Hill; controversy surrounding decision to stop funding nineteen water-development projects. S. Fraker and J. J. Lindsay. Newsweek 89:16-17 Mr 28 '77
Pumping billions into the desert: the case against the Central Arizona Project. D. Hanson. il Audubon 79:133-45 My '77; Reply. B. Goldwater. 79:99-100 Jl '77
River basins; question of river basin management. A. W. Smith. Nat Parks & Con Mag 51:2+ My '77
Tougher line coming on water projects. map U.S. News 82:67 My 2 '77
Turning off the water. T. Mathews and M. Lord. il Newsweek 89:26+ Ap 4 '77
Two letters to the Administration; question of river basin management. A. W. Smith. Nat Parks & Con Mag 51:2+ S '77
Water: a billion dollar battleground. il Time 109:16-17+ Ap 4 '77
Water projects dispute: Carter and Congress near a showdown. L. J. Carter. Science 196:1303-5 Je 17 '77
See also
North American Water and Power Alliance
United Nations Water Conference
United States—Water Resources Council
Water supply

WATER reuse
Aquatic farms clean up waste water; water-recycling experiment at Michigan State's Lansing campus. B. Seaquist. il Pop Sci 211:88-9 S '77
Can we use greywater? Org Gard & Farm 24:32-4+ My '77
Gray water put to work in your garden? reusing waste water. il Sunset 158:268-9 My '77
Gray water . . . the hazards and the hope. il Sunset 159:168-9 S '77
Greywater in the garden. R. Wolf. il Org Gard & Farm 24:83-6 Jl '77
No such thing as waste water. . .EPA. il Am City & County 92:25 Ag '77
Wastewater reuse by the truckload; East Bay Municipal Utility District of Oakland. Am City & County 92:40 S '77
Wastewater reuse for potable supplies. W. S. Foster. Am City & County 92:84 Ag '77
Water reclamation—California style; Yuba City plant. il Am City & County 92:78-80 My '77

WATER safety. See Boats and boating—Safety devices and measures

WATER softening
Install your own water softener. R. Day il Pop Sci 211:114-16 D '77
Twin-turbine softener knows when to regenerate. R. Day. il Pop Sci 211:136-7+ O '77

WATER sports. See Aquatic sports

WATER storage
See also
Water towers

WATER supply
Is there an iceberg in your future? K. Frazier. il Sci N 112:298-300 N 5 '77
RCA environmental satellites to play major role in study to predict water supply availability. il Space World N-11-167:34 N '77
Warning: water shortages ahead. il map Time 109:48+ Ap 4 '77
See also
Droughts
Irrigation
Reservoirs
United Nations Water Conference
Water conservation
Water purification
Water reuse
Watersheds

Conferences

Experts ponder icebergs as relief for world water dilemma. C. Holden. il Science 198:274-6 O 21 '77
Icebergs for the desert: cool calculations. il Sci N 112:244 O 15 '77
Towing icebergs. il Time 110:65 O 17 '77

Copper content

Well was well, it was the pipes that did it. T. Benfey. il Chemistry 50:2 Ap '77

Fluoridation

Are we depriving our children of healthy teeth? excerpt from The health robbers, ed by S. Barrett and G. Knight. M. Bernhardt and B. Sprague. il Fam Health 9:30-3 Ap '77
Statistics and the fluoride debate. Sci N 112:262 O 22 '77

Arizona

Like having your dad die; proposed cancellation of the Central Arizona Project. il Time 109:80 Mr 7 '77
Pumping billions into the desert: the case against the Central Arizona Project. D. Hanson. il Audubon 79:133-45 My '77; Reply. B. Goldwater. 79:99-100 Jl '77

California

Auburn Dam: a faulty business. H. Rubin. il Nation 224:563-4 My 7 '77
Blue skies may mean brown links; effect of drought on northern California golf courses. S. Pileggi. il Sports Illus 46:54+ Ap 4 '77
Drought fails to wilt California's harvest. Bus W p40 O 24 '77
Flexible tubing gives 50 year design life; polybutylene tubing used by Alameda County water district. il Am City & County 92:65 My '77
Great California drought; adaptation of address, June 3, 1977. J. H. Lauten. il Am For 83:16-19 O '77
Holy water. J. Didion. Esquire 88:73-4+ D '77
How to ration water; Marin County. M. Friedman. Newsweek 89:73 Mr 21 '77
Marin County: the bucket brigade. J. Boyce. il Time 109:15 F 14 '77
Rationing ends cheap water myth. il Am City & County 92:66-8 My '77
Trickle. M. Mayer. Progressive 41:36 My '77
Tuolumne River: the drought in a microcosm. P. L. Fradkin. map Audubon 79:132-5 Jl '77
Water reclamation—California style; Yuba City plant. il Am City & County 92:78-80 My '77
Waterless West. Time 110:23-4 Ag 15 '77
What do you do when you're out of water? Marin County. J. D. Stroeh. il Am City & County 92:49-50 D '77
Whole old ball game. M. Mayer. Progressive 41:25 S '77
See also
Oakland, Calif.—Water supply
San Francisco—Water supply

Canada

See also
North American Water and Power Alliance

Colorado

Colorado looks west for water. Am City & County 92:37 Ap '77
Fiberglass, stainless steel stop deep well corrosion; Shaw Heights. R. E. Darr. il Am City & County 92:57 Jl '77
See also
Denver—Water supply

England

Water lessons gleaned from England. S. Baxter. Am City & County 92:28 N '77

WATER supply—*Continued*

Louisiana

See also
New Orleans—Water supply

New Jersey

Construction management brings water plant in on time, under budget; Jersey City. J. M. Daly. il Am City & County 92:101-2 O '77

New Mexico

Great Southwest water war. J. Neary. il Sat R 4:18-20+ S 3 '77

New York (state)

Hudson water politics worry county officials. Am City & County 92:9+ My '77

North Carolina

Thirsty developers. Nat Parks & Con Mag 51: 22-3 F '77

Ohio

See also
Cleveland—Water supply

Pennsylvania

Centrifuge ends drying bed chores for Pennsylvania water plant; Lancaster. M. B. Freedman. il Am City & County 92:63-4 N '77

Russia

Russia's ambitious plans to end its water shortage. map U.S. News 83:80 S 12 '77

Saudi Arabia

Iceberg cometh; a possibility of towing icebergs from Antartica to Saudi Arabia. P. Gwynne and others. il Newsweek 90:72 Jl 4 '77
Iceberg express; towing icebergs from Antarctica. il map Sr Schol 110:10-12 D 1 '77
Icebergs for Arabia: the talk heats up. Bus W p21 Jl 4 '77

Southwestern States

Battle over the mighty Colorado. G. Lichtenstein. il map N Y Times Mag p 10-13+ Jl 31 '77; Same abr. Read Digest 111:49-50+ N '77
Desert empire. G. Sibley. map Harpers 255:49-56+ O '77
Troubled waters. P. B. Sears. Natur Hist 86: 112-15 N '77

Tennessee

See also
Memphis, Tenn.—Water supply

Texas

See also
San Antonio, Tex.—Water supply

Underdeveloped areas

See Underdeveloped areas—Water supply

United States

Is U.S. running out of water? il map U.S. News 83:33-5 Jl 18 '77
Water: the next resource crisis? il Nations Bus 65:50-2+ S '77
See also
North American Water and Power Alliance

Virginia

Tyranny in a glass of water; refusal to use Chesapeake water supply. C. Cahill. Nation 224:325-6 Mr 19 '77
We found virus in our drinking water; Polio I virus; Fairfax County. J. W. Berry and P. Shaffer. il Am City & County 92:65-6 Je '77
Well water; illegality of private wells in Chesapeake. C. Cahill. Environment 19:46-8 Je '77

Western States

Drought watch: gloomy to grim. il Time 109:9-10 My 30 '77
Great Western drought of 1977. il map Time 109:76-81 Mr 7 '77
Grim future for the water-short West. il map Bus W p 111-12+ My 23 '77
Long dry winter. S. Fraker and others. il Newsweek 89:22+ Mr 7 '77
Western states adapt to dry-weather siege. Am City & County 92:68 My '77

WATER supply, Rural
UN confronts issue of clean water for human settlements. S. Watt. Archit Rec 161:37 F '77
See also
Cisterns

WATER supply engineering
UN confronts issue of clean water for human settlements. S. Watt. Archit Rec 161:37 F '77
See also
Dams
Water treatment plants

WATER tanks
See also
Water towers

WATER Tower Place. See Chicago—Buildings

WATER towers
Cathodic protection guards Cleveland water system. R. Klimko. il Am City & County 92:54-5 Mr '77

WATER training. See Swimming—Safety devices and measures

WATER transportation, Inland. See Inland water transportation

WATER treatment plants
Construction management brings water plant in on time, under budget; Jersey City, N.J. J. M. Daly. il Am City & County 92:101-2 O '77
Water reclamation—California style; Yuba City plant. il Am City & County 92:78-80 My '77

WATER vapor
Amateur scientist; persistence of water drops on hot surfaces. J. Walker. il Sci Am 237: 126-31 Ag '77
Vapor emission termed greater ozone threat. R. G. O'Lone. il Aviation W 108:38-9 Ja 2 '78

WATER vapor batteries. See Storage batteries

WATER wells. See Wells

WATERBIRD shooting
Winged treasure below the border; waterfowl of northcentral Mexico. J. Samson. il Field & S 82:46-7+ N '77

WATERBORNE infection
Water for the wealthy. J. Stein. il Environment 19:6-14 My '77

WATERCOLOR painting. See Water color painting

WATERFOWL. See Water birds

WATERFOWL shooting. See Water bird shooting

WATERFRONTS. See Water fronts

WATERGATE case
Entertainers. F. Getlein. Commonweal 104:164-6 Mr 18 '77
Facing the music; Nixon interviews. New Repub 176:2+ Je 4 '77
Good soldier Liddy. R. Boeth and E. Clark. il por Newsweek 90:44 S 19 '77
Hunt's tales of Watergate. D. A. Williams and R. Manning. por Newsweek 89:22 Mr 7 '77
Last Nixon show. D. M. Alpern and H. Bruno. il Newsweek 90:34 S 12 '77
Last syllable of recorded time; Nixon interviews. C. L. Westerbeck, Jr. Commonweal 104:339-40 My 27 '77
Letting go of Richard Nixon. R. M. Herhold. Chr Cent 94:582-3 Je 22 '77
Nixon on TV: still more light on Watergate. il por U.S. News 83:81 S 12 '77
Nixon: once more, with feeling. il pors Time 109:21-2+ My 16 '77
Nixon speaks. D. M. Alpern and others. il pors Newsweek 89:25+ My 9 '77
Nixon talks. il pors Time 109:22-4+ My 9 '77
Nixon without Dietrich. F. Getlein. Commonweal 104:324-6 My 27 '77
Nos. 24171-157 and 01489-163(B); jailing of J. Mitchell and H. R. Haldeman. il pors Time 110:11 Jl 4 '77
Notes and comment; Nixon interviews. New Yorker 53:27-8 My 23 '77
Now, another villain; R. Nixon's interviews with David Frost. por Time 110:23 S 12 '77
Of many things. J. O'Hare. America 136:inside cover Je 18 '77
Saturday night live! excerpt from Not above the law. J. Doyle. il pors N Y Times Mag p40+ My 15 '77
Scandal as entertainment; depiction of Watergate case in Washington: behind closed doors. il Time 110:92-3 S 19 '77
Second coming of Leon Jaworski. J. Lelyveld. il por N Y Times Mag p71 Ag 28 '77
Sorry. . .sorry. . .sorry; prisoners' petitions for leniency. il Time 110:19-20 O 17 '77
Still paying the price. Time 109:15 Mr 7 '77
Watching Nixon; symposium. il pors Newsweek 89:28-9+ My 16 '77
Watergate anniversary. E. Keerdoja. il Newsweek 89:10+ Je 20 '77
Where have you gone, Sally Harmony? P. Slansky. Esquire 88:129-32 Jl '77
Why Nixon went on the witness stand. pors U.S. News 82:27-9 My 16 '77
See also
Government investigations—Watergate case

Anecdotes, facetiae, satire, etc.

Don't play it again. R. Lipez. Progressive 41:50 S '77

WATERGATE tapes
Active conspirator; reaction to the Nixon-Frost interview. L. Jaworski. por Newsweek 89:33 My 16 '77
Back with Dick. J. Osborne. New Repub 176: 8-9 My 14 '77
One jump ahead of the sheriff; excerpts from previously unreleased transcripts. T. Mathews and N. Horrock. il Newsweek 89:31 My 9 '77
Those old tapes never fade. Time 109:29 My 16 '77
When the President does it: what the tapes really reveal; opinion of Presidential powers expressed in Nixon-Frost interviews. I. L. Horowitz. Nation 224:751-4 Je 18 '77

WATERGATE trials

Cover-up conspiracy trial

No to Nixon's men; verdict by the Supreme Court on the convictions of John Ehrlichman, H. R. Haldeman and John Mitchell. Time 109:13 Je 6 '77

Supreme embarrassment; news leak describing Supreme Court action on appeals. J. K. Footlick and L. Howard. por Newsweek 89:66 My 9 '77

WATERHOUSE, Alma Jones

Home—how to take it along when you move. House B 119:72+ O '77

WATERING of gardens, lawns, etc.

Can we use greywater? Org Gard & Farm 24:32-4+ My '77

Coping with a water shortage; care of grass in recreation facilities. J. R. Watson. il Parks & Rec 12:54-5+ Jl '77

Drip irrigation and the water thieves; underground pipes for lawns. il Sunset 159:106-7 N '77

Drip irrigation the homemade way. T. Gettings. il Org Gard & Farm 24:56-9 My '77

Gray water put to work in your garden? reusing waste water. il Sunset 158:268-9 My '77

Gray water. . .the hazards and the hope. il Sunset 159:168-9 S '77

Growing annuals with less water. Sunset 158:152 Jl '77

How to water your garden less and enjoy it more; drip irrigation. S. McGilvray. il Horticulture 55:24-7 Je '77

Tree-to-tree canal system saves water and time. il Sunset 158:110 Mr '77

Water in your garden; symposium. il Org Gard & Farm 24:74-92 Jl '77

Water-short gardening; northern California. il Sunset 158:126-9 Ap '77

Watering systems that do it by the drop. J. L. Parker. il Mech Illus 73:113 Jl '77

See also

Garden hose

Sprinklers

WATERING of livestock. See Livestock—Watering

WATERING of plants

Deck garden in water-scarce Marin makes it with gray water. il Sunset 158:256 Ap '77

Greenhouse; system for watering during vacation. J. Kilborn. il Horticulture 55:66-7 Je '77

How to treat thirsty avocados in a water-short year. il Sunset 158:287 Ap '77

What can you do about those thirsty pots? il Sunset 158:96-7 Je '77

WATERLILIES. See Water lilies

WATERLOO, Ia.

Waterloo, Iowa: coming to terms with prosperity. M. King. il Forbes 120:48-52 N 15 '77

WATERMAN, Guy. See Waterman, L. jt auth

WATERMAN, Jill. See Spezzano, C. jt auth

WATERMAN, Laura, and Waterman, Guy

Backpacking with natural foods. il Org Gard & Farm 24:102+ Je '77

WATERMAN, Thomas Talbot

Wild man of Oroville. C. W. Campbell. il por Am Hist Illus 12:18-26+ Je '77 *

WATERMAN Award. See United States—National Science Foundation

WATERMELONS

Grow watermelons in circles. L. Shade. il Org Gard & Farm 24:82-3 Mr '77

WATERPROOF clothing. See Clothing, Waterproof

WATERPROOF fabrics. See Textile fabrics, Water proof

WATERPROOFING

See also

Dampness in buildings

Water repellents

WATERPROOFING paint. See Paint, Protective

WATERS, Frank

Man who killed the deer. H. Welch. Engl J 66:60 Mr '77 *

WATERS, Lyssa

(ed) Why I became a gynecologist. Ms 65:54-5+ F '77

WATERS, Michael

Not just any death; If I die; Preserves; poems. Poetry 130:143-5 Je '77

WATERS, Richard L.

What good is Washington doing libraries? bibl il Am Lib 8:566-8 N '77

WATERSHEDS

On human engineering; Muskingum Watershed Conservancy District in Ohio. L. E. Partain. il Am For 83:32-3+ Je '77

Pollution can be licked: Black Creek. il U.S. News 82:50 F 7 '77

WATERSON, Merlin

Although a rascal, Eli Yale used his means effectively. il por Smithsonian 8:91-7 O '77

WATERWAY cruising. See Cruising

WATERWAYS

See also

Rivers

Europe

See also

Danube River

Europe, Western

See also

Canals—Europe, Western

Russia

See also

Canals—Russia

United States

Bitter battle of the waterways. J. N. Miller. Read Digest 111:83-7 S '77

Selling off the Old South; Tennessee-Tombigbee Waterway project. J. Greene. il map Harpers 254:39-42+ Ap '77

Tenn-Tom and Senator Stennis. W. Rawls, Jr. N Y Times Mag p46 My 8 '77

Tenn-Tom's trials. map Time 109:19 Ap 4 '77

See also

Canals—United States

Cross Florida Barge Canal

Houston Ship Channel

Intracoastal Waterway

Monongahela River

National forests—Waterways

Ohio River

WATERWORKS

See also

American Water Works Association

Dams

WATERWORTH, H. E. See Kaper, J. M. jt auth

WATKINS, Arthur Martin

Add an energy-efficient room at the top. il Pop Sci 210:140+ Mr '77

How you can afford a home of your own. Redbook 150:199+ N '77

WATKINS, Earl, and Burger, John

Make money by computer. il Am City & County 92:57-8 Ap '77

WATKINS, Peter

Peter Watkins's Edvard Munch. J. A. Gomez. bibl f il pors Film Q 30:38-46 Wint '76 *

WATKINS, T. H.

Social history of a singular fruit. il Am Heritage 28:84-7+ Ap '77

WATSON, Barbara M.

Department discusses consular services for Americans abroad; statement, July 14, 1977. il Dept State Bull 77:248-59 Ag 22 '77

Transfer of sanctions treaties with Mexico and Canada; statement, July 13, 1977. Dept State Bull 77:208-10 Ag 15 '77

WATSON, Donald, and Broberg, F. N.

What size solar heating system is economical for a house? excerpt from Designing and building a solar house. il Archit Rec 161:131-4 Mr '77

WATSON, Elkanah

Albany's first city planner. P. Byrne. il por map Conservationist 31:34-7 Ja '77 *

WATSON, Ernest William

Editor remembers; reprint from June 1962 issue; excerpts. por Am Artist 41:35-6 F '77

WATSON, Gayle Hudgens

Détente, then and now. il pors Américas 29:2-7 Ja '77

WATSON, James Dewey

Imaginary monster. por Bull Atom Sci 33:12-13 My '77

In defense of DNA. New Repub 176:11-14 Je 25 '77

WATSON, James R.

Coping with a water shortage. il Parks & Rec 12:54-5+ Jl '77

WATSON, Richard A.

Researcher as spelunker: driven by danger, rewarded by discovery. il Sci Digest 81:48-51 Ap '77

WATSON, Thomas John, 1914-

Pilot in command. il Flying 101:309+ S '77

WATSON, Tom

Augusta's Mr Cool. P. Axthelm. por Newsweek 89:75 Ap 25 '77 *

Braw brawl for Tom and Jack. D. Jenkins. il pors Sports Illus 47:28-30+ Jl 18 '77 *

Choking off criticism with one stroke. S. Pileggi. il por Sports Illus 46:28-30+ Ap 25 '77 *

What a beauty of a Masters. D. Jenkins. il pors Sports Illus 46:24-7+ Ap 18 '77 *

WATT, Charles

Snakebite! What to know—what to do. C. Elliott. il Outdoor Life 160:84-7+ S '77 *

WATT, Douglas

Popular records (cont) New Yorker 53:66-8 Ag 8 '77

WATT, Gordon

Ecologist. Am For 83:36-7 O '77

WATT, Simon

UN confronts issue of clean water for human settlements. Archit Rec 161:37 F '77

WATTENBERG, Ben J.

Likud's victroy. Harpers 255:14-17 Ag '77

Mao's funeral. Harpers 254:31-3 F '77

WATTERS, Jim
(ed) See Nureyev, R. Nureyev as Valentino

WATTMETERS
RF wattmeters and dummy loads. il Radio-Electr 48:58 N '77

WATTS, André
Music, youth, racial equality. pors U.S. News 82:69 Je 6 '77

about

Totally freaked out on music. P. Andrews. il pors Horizon 20:10-16 D '77 *

WATTS, Carol K.
Scenes from a divorce. por Redbook 148:82+ Ap '77

WATTS, H. P.
Hold her at that; story. Yachting 141:188+ Ap '77

WAUKESHA, Wis.

Religious institutions and affairs

See Wisconsin—Religious institutions and affairs

WAVE Hill estate. See Bronx, N.Y.—Historic houses, sites, etc.

WAVE power
Airbags squeeze energy from wave power. D. Scott. il Pop Sci 210:24 Ap '77
Wave power tapped by nodding ducks. D. Scott. il Pop Sci 211:16+ N '77

WAVERLY Consort. See Instrumental ensembles

WAVERTREE (ship) See Sailing vessels

WAVES
Long waves in the eastern equatorial Pacific Ocean: a view from a geostationary satellite. R. Legeckis. bibl il Science 197:1179-81 S 16 '77
Ocean wave patterns under Hurricane Gloria: observation with an airborne synthetic-aperture radar. C. Elachi and others. bibl il Science 198:609-10 N 11 '77
Of rogue waves and little ripples. W. L. Donn. il Motor B & S 139:50-1+ Mr '77
Voices of the surf; excerpt from The outermost house. H. Beston. il Read Digest 111:45-8 D '77

See also

Tidal waves
Wave power

WAX, Judith
Sharing a son with Hare Krishna. il pors N Y Times Mag p40-2+ My 1 '77
You and your marriage. Vogue 167:152+ My '77

WAX, Paul
Sharing a son with Hare Krishna. J. Wax. il pors N Y Times Mag p40-2+ My 1 '77 *

WAX figures
Lewis Sorenson: American doll artist. J. Chiara. il Hobbies 82:38-9 N '77

See also

Waxworks

WAX modeling
Our own wax museum. G. Dostal. il Sch Arts 77:64-5 O '77

WAX museums. See Waxworks

WAXING of skis. See Skis and skiing—Maintenance and repair

WAXMAN, Henry Arnold
Arts bills: pluses and minuses. A. Elsen. il por Art N 76:52-4 O '77 *

WAXWORK. See Wax modeling

WAXWORKS
Wax museums: the Mount Rushmore of pop culture; famous women in wax figures. S. Subtle and R. Reichl. il Ms 6:72-3+ Ja '78

Great Britain

Why Pearson is after Madame Tussaud's. il Bus W p57 D 12 '77

WAY, Kathy Ann
Nampeyo: Hopi potter. il por Ceram Mo 25: 51-3 Mr '77

WAY-out Cinderella; drama. See Cable, H.

WAYNE, Dennis
Dancers before dance. H. Saal. il por Newsweek 90:112 D 12 '77 *
For Dennis Wayne the emphasis is on Dancers. L. Draegin. il pors Dance Mag 51:36-9 N '77 *

WAYNE, John
John Wayne's America; excerpt from America, why I love her. il por Good H 185:138-41+ N '77

WAYS, Max
Hall of Fame for Business Leadership. il Fortune 95:117-23 Ja '77
Myth of the oppresive corporation. Fortune 96:149+ O '77

WAYS and Means Committee. See United States—Congress—House—Ways and Means, Committee on

WAYSIDE Motor Inn; drama. See Gurney, A. R.

WAZIRI, Rafig
Presynaptic electrical coupling in aplysia: effects on postsynaptic chemical transmission. bibl il Science 195:790-2 F 25 '77

WEALES, Gerald
Nine steps to fiscal solvency. N Y Times Mag p 123 Mr 27 '77
Stage (cont) Commonweal 104:20-1, 180-1, 370-1, 431-2 Ja 7, Mr 18, Je 10, Jl 8 '77
Yes, but what was His Holiness wearing? Nation 225:533-5 N 19 '77

WEALTH
Chewing for dollars; Prosperity training. il por Time 110:107 N 28 '77
Redistribution of wealth means bloody politics; Project: Knowledge 2000 conference; excerpts from address. G. A. Almond. por Intellect 105: 205-6 Ja '77
Wealth of the nation. il U.S. News 82:66-7 Mr 21 '77

See also

Income
Leisure class
Rich, The

WEANING of calves. See Calves—Feeding

WEAPONS
Beam weapon hearings due in Congress. Aviation W 106:17-18 My 30 '77
Brown comments on beam weapons. H. Brown. Aviation W 106:12 My 30 '77
Charged debate erupts over Russian beam weapon. N. Wade. Science 196:957-9 My 27 '77
Congress presses strategic changes. C. A. Robinson, Jr. il Aviation W 107:16-20 O 10 '77
General goes zap; question of Gen. G. J. Keegan's comments on Russian weapons. M. Kondracke. New Repub 177:19-22 Jl 2 '77
Great Russian death-beam flap. J. H. Douglas and D. E. Thomsen. il Sci N 111:329+ My 21 '77; Discussion. 112:19 Jl 9 '77
New weapons; technological breakthroughs. Nat R 29:931 Ag 19 '77
Particle beams as ABM weapons: general and physicists differ. N. Wade. por Science 196: 407-8 Ap 22 '77
Soviets push for beam weapon; with editorial comment. C. A. Robinson, Jr. il Aviation W 106:11, 16-23 My 2 '77
Technology revolution in weaponry; cruise missile and neutron bomb. J. H. Douglas. il Sci N 112:60-2+ Jl 23 '77
Updating Willie and Joe. Time 109:26 My 23 '77
Whole new ball game? announcement of Russian particle beam weapon by Aviation week & space technology. Nat R 29:596-7 My 27 '77

See also

Atomic weapons
Firearms
Lasers—Military use
Pistols
Torpedoes

WEAPONS control. See Disarmament

WEAPONS systems
Battlefield of the 1990s: it's not sci-fi it's real. U.S. News 83:48-50 Jl 4 '77
Europeans push new weapons systems. C. A. Robinson, Jr. il Aviation W 106:43-6+ Je 27 '77
Military technology and social structure. M. H. Kaldor. il Bull Atom Sci 33:49-53 Je '77
NATO: nobody wants standardized weapons. il Bus W p 178+ My 16 '77
NATO standardization advances. E. Kozicharow. Aviation W 107:8-10 D 19 '77
Tools of the trade. il Newsweek 89:21 Ap 4 '77
What the deadlock in arms talks is all about. il U.S. News 82:24-5 Ap 11 '77

See also

United States—Armed Forces—Weapons systems
United States—Naval Weapons Center
United States—Navy—Weapons systems

Cost

Acquisition report figures show slight drop in cost. Aviation W 107:15 Ag 29 '77
Arms acquisition reports show $19-billion drop in total costs. Aviation W 107:16-17 N 21 '77
Major weapon system spending detailed. Aviation W 106:22-3 Ja 24 '77
Navy's trident sub: one more massive miscalculation. il U.S. News 83:37 D 12 '77

See also

Airplanes, Military—Cost

Testing

Budget squeeze boosts test, evaluation significance. il Aviation W 106:234-5+ Ja 31 '77

WEAR, Jennifer Harper
Rating the contraceptives. Harp Baz 110:88-9+ Je '77

WEARLY, William Levi
Bureaucratic Babylon; address, September 23, 1977. Vital Speeches 44:44-9 N 1 '77

WEASELS

See also

Fishers (animals)

WEATHER
Circulation and weather of 1976. A. J. Wagner. maps Weatherwise 30:22-31+ F '77
Our changing weather:
Colder winters ahead? G. Alexander. il maps Pop Sci 211:100-3+ O '77
Drought. G. Alexander. il maps Pop Sci 211: 90-4 S '77

WEATHER—*Continued*
Weatherwatch. See issues of Weatherwise
What's happening to our weather? D. Colligan. il Mech Illus 73:132+ My '77
See also
Atmospheric pressure
Cold weather
Droughts
Hot weather
Snow
Storms
Winds
also headings beginning Meteorological, Meteorology

History

100 years ago. Weatherwise 30:46-7 F '77
Unusual weather (cont) il Weatherwise 29:286-7 D '76
Weather of Independence (title varies)
Burgoyne's northern campaign (cont) D. M. Ludlum. maps Weatherwise 29:288-90 D '76
Campaign for Philadelphia: July-November 1977. D. M. Ludlum. il maps Weatherwise 30:114-19 Je '77
Weather 100 years ago; Weather 200 years ago (title varies) (cont) Weatherwise 29:311 D '76

Mental and physiological effects

Air: the environment factor. il Vogue 167:169+ Ag '77
Biometeorology seeks clues to health. R. Wolkomir. il Sci Digest 82:29-32 Ag '77

Research

See Meteorological research

WEATHER, Influence of sun on. See Sun and meteorology
WEATHER and health. See Weather—Mental and physiological effects
WEATHER and plants. See Plants, Effect of climate on
WEATHER bureaus. See Meteorological services
WEATHER control
Modified weather in controversy. Sci Digest 81:84-5 F '77
Nobelist Langmuir's persistence proved cloud-seeding possible despite skeptics. V. Westervelt. Sci Digest 81:23-6 My '77
Stormy weather forecast for those who tinker. M. Davidson. Sci Digest 81:74-5 Je '77
Weather: prediction and control. il map Time 109:55-6 F 21 '77
See also
Rain making

Military use

Weather modification; CIA report. N. Cousins. Sat R 4:4 F 5 '77
WEATHER forecasting
Climate preview (title varies) (cont) maps Weatherwise 29:292-5 D '76
Forecast: unsettled weather ahead. map Time 109:26-7 Ja 31 '77
Forecasting climatic fluctuations: the winter of 1976-77; letter. J. Namias. Science 196:1386-7 Je 24 '77
Much ado about weather. Farm J 101:60 Ag '77
Weather and the futures markets. L. Snyder. il Fortune 95:59-60+ Ap '77
Weather economics. P. A. Samuelson. Newsweek 89:84 F 21 '77
Weather: prediction and control. il map Time 109:55-6 F 21 '77
What's behind this winter. . .and what's ahead. map Sci N 111:100-1 F 12 '77
Why it's so cold. P. Gwynne and others. il maps Newsweek 89:38-9 Ja 31 '77
Winter ahead—not like the last one. map U.S. News 83:40 D 12 '77
See also
United States—National Weather Service
Weather maps
WEATHER maps
Daily weather maps. See issues of Weatherwise
WEATHER modification. See Weather control
WEATHER predictions. See Weather forecasting
WEATHER radar. See Radar meteorology
WEATHER research. See Meteorological research
WEATHER satellites. See Artificial satellites—Meteorological use
WEATHER services. See Meteorological services
WEATHER stripping. See Weatherstripping
WEATHER Underground (organization) See Weathermen (organization)
WEATHER vanes
American metalwork. il Sch Arts 76:39-46 F '77
Collecting weather vanes—an American folk art form. E. V. Warren. il House B 119:14+ My '77
WEATHERFUGS. See Weathermen (organization)

WEATHERLEY, A. H. and Cogger, B. M. G.
Fish culture: problems and prospects. bibl il Science 197:427-30 Jl 29 '77
WEATHERMEN (organization)
Aging radical comes home; M. Rudd. pors Time 110:25 S 26 '77
Infiltrating the underground; FBI capture of Weather Underground members. il Time 111:13 Ja 9 '78
Mark Rudd returns. T. Powers. il Commonweal 104:657-9 O 14 '77
Return of Mark Rudd. R. Boeth and others. il pors Newsweek 90:34 S 26 '77
Undercover man. Newsweek 90:26+ S 5 '77
When G-men break the law; covert operations used against the Weatherfugs. P. Goldman and N. Horrock. il Newsweek 89:28+ My 30 '77
WEATHERSTRIPPING
Weather stripping. il Consumer Rep 42:110-12 F '77
WEATHERVANES. See Weather vanes
WEAVER, James Howard
Larger equation for forestry. por Am For 83:28-9+ N '77
WEAVER, John H. See Rowe, E. M. jt auth
WEAVER, Ken. See Christy, E. J. jt auth
WEAVER, Kenneth F.
Electronic voyage through an invisible world. il Nat Geog 151:274-90 F '77
How soon will we measure in metric? il Nat Geog 152:287-94 Ag '77
Power of letting off steam. il map Nat Geog 152:566-79 O '77
WEAVER, Paul H.
Corporations are defending themselves with the wrong weapon. il Fortune 95:186-7+ Je '77
Do the American people know what they want? Commentary 64:62-7 D '77
Unlocking the gilded cage of regulation. il Fortune 95:178-82+ F '77
WEAVER, Vernon
Pledge from Washington to help small business; interview. pors Nations Bus 65:31-4 Jl '77
about
Big hand for Small Business? por Forbes 120:122 N 1 '77 *
WEAVER ants. See Ants
WEAVING
Adela Akers: the loomed plane; interview, ed by P. Scheinman. A. Akers. il Craft Horiz 37:24-5+ F '77
Looms of Otavalo. J. B. Casagrande. il Natur Hist 86:48-59 O '77
One man's afghan, another man's purl. E. A. Yeager. il pors Ret Liv 17:43 Ap '77
Students write about their artwork; description of Navaho weaving for magazine article. M. Esping. il Sch Arts 76:36-8 F '77
Weaving a swing chair. D. Lynde. il Design (US) 78:20-1 mid-Summ '77
See also
Cane weaving
Indian blankets, rugs, etc (American)
Looms
Rugs and carpets
Tapestry

Exhibitions

Andean warp-patterned weaves. A. P. Rowe. il Craft Horiz 37:38-40 D '77

Study and teaching

Three dimensions in weaving. E. L. Bouchal. il Sch Arts 77:64-5 S '77
Weaving affair. M. Zipadelli and V. Satalino. il pors Sch Arts 76:66-7 Mr '77
WEBB, Aileen Osborn
Our Aileen Osborn Webb. R. Slivka. il por Craft Horiz 37:10-13 Je '77 *
WEBB, Andrea Ivie
Death: the last taboo. Engl J 66:55-6 S '77
WEBB, Del E, Corporation
My way v. their way; F. Sinatra's proxy fight. il por Time 109:65 Ap 11 '77
Sinatra wants more of the Webb action. il Bus W p30-1 Ap 11 '77
WEBB, Jimmy Layne
Jimmy Webb: up and away. J. Maslin. il pors Newsweek 89:93 Je 13 '77 *
WEBB, Marilyn, and Safran, Claire
How far up can a woman grow? il Redbook 149:57-9 My '77
WEBB, Todd
Shows we've seen. H. V. Fondiller. il Pop Phot 81:72+ Jl '77 *
WEBB, Walter Prescott
Walter Prescott Webb. R. A. Trennert. Am West 14:57 Mr '77 *
WEBER, Arnold R.
Economy (cont) por Duns R 109:9 Ja; 110:11 Jl; 9 O '77
High unemployment could have a profound impact on free enterprise. por Duns R 109:11 Ap '77
WEBER, Bruce
Sports. See issues of Senior scholastic including World week

WEBER, Ellen
Incest: sexual abuse begins at home. Ms 5:64-7 Ap '77
WEBER, Karl Maria von
Die drei Pintos; RCA Red Seal recording. J. Noble. Hi Fi 27:110+ Jl '77 *
Making a dent into Weber. P. Althouse. Am Rec G 41:34-5 N '77 *
Weber/Mahler hybrid; Die drei Pintos; Bertini recording. N. F. Karlins. Am Rec G 40:37-9 Jl '77 *
WEBER, Mark
Back to basics: its meaning for school media programs. bibl por SLJ 24:83-5 O '77
WEBER, Melva
Eat and grow beautiful. il Ladies Home J 94:74+ My '77
Health. See issues of Vogue
WEBER-Stephen Products Company. See Barbecue grills—Manufacture
WEBERMAN, Ben
Banks. Forbes 120:110 O 1; 128 N 1; 98 D 1 '77
Bond and capital markets. See issues of Forbes
WEBS, Spider. See Spider webs
WEBSTER, Daniel
(ed) See Wernick, R. Musician of the month: Richard Wernick
WEBSTER, David L.
Obituary
Phys Today por 30:98 My '77. F. Bloch
WEBSTER, George D.
Will federal campaign laws make elections more honest? por Nations Bus 65:61-2+ Ja '77
WEBSTER, James
Bass part in Haydn's early string quartets. bibl il Mus Q 63:390-424 Jl '77
WEBSTER, Robert G. See Kaplan, M. M. jt auth
WEBSTER, Ronald L.
St-st-st-st-st-st-stuttering. M. Pines. il N Y Times Mag p26+ F 13 '77 *
WECHSBERG, Joseph
My favorite European restaurants. il Holiday 58:28-9+ Je '77
News from Vienna. por Opera N 41:32 Mr 12 '77
WECHSLER, Jeffrey
Surrealism's automatic painting lesson. il Art N 76:44-7 Ap '77
WEDDING meals
Personalizing the reception—buffet by bride, groom, friends. il Sunset 158:158-9 Je '77
Wedding party at home; with recipes. M. Eckley. il McCalls 104:134-5+ Je '77
WEDDING photography. See Photography of weddings
WEDDINGS
Weddings: they did it their way; excerpt from The Good housekeeping woman's almanac. Good H 186:165 Ja '78
See also
Marriage customs and rites
Photography of weddings
Wedding meals
WEDEKIND, Frank
Earth spirit; author of the Lulu plays. G. R Marek. il pors Opera N 41:16-17+ Ap 2 '77 *
WEDGEWORTH, Robert
For a big federal fix. J. Berry. Lib J 102:965 My 1 '77 *
State of the Association. il Am Lib 8:380 Jl '77 *
WEDGWOOD, Josiah, and Sons, Ltd. See Potteries
WEDGWOOD pottery. See Pottery, English
WEED, Walker
Wood. il Craft Horiz 37:18-19 Je '77
WEED control
Biological weed control: can the organic grower use it? J. Cox. Org Gard & Farm 24:91-4 My '77
Do more than control weeds. R. Brunoehler. il Suc Farm 75:no3 F36 F '77
EcoFallow: way to grow crop with little rain. R. Alleman. il Suc Farm 75:no3 F50 F '77
How one farmer controls weeds naturally. C. Frye. il Org Gard & Farm 24:87-9 My '77
Natural weed controls that walk, fly and flower. G. Logsdon. Org Gard & Farm 24:80-4 My '77
Now it's biological control of weeds. J. D. Boyd. il Farm J 101:G2-3 Ag '77
See also
Herbicides
Mulching
WEED eaters. See Lawn tools, equipment, and supplies
WEED killers. See Herbicides
WEEDS
Making enemies into friends. R. Rodale. il Org Gard & Farm 24:58-61 F '77
Those wildly successful hateful plants; excerpt. L. J. Crockett. il Sci Digest 82:38-40+ Ag '77
Treasure trove in the weeds. J. Krill. il Org Gard & Farm 24:137-8 Je '77
See also
Amaranths
Aquatic weeds
Cockleburs
Feeds—Weeds

Control

See Weed control

WEEDS in house decoration. See Fruits, vegetables, etc. in decoration
WEEGEE, pseud. See Fellig, A.
WEEKEND activities. See Leisure
WEEKEND houses. See Vacation houses
WEEKEND vacations. See Vacations
WEEKES, Ronald C.
Autographs. Hobbies 82:156 N '77
WEEKLEY, Carolyn J.
Portrait painting in eighteenth-century Annapolis. bibl il Antiques 111:345-53 F '77
WEEKS, Brigitte
Brigitte Weeks on children's books. New Repub 177:26+ D 3 '77
WEEKS, James
Painterly allegories and ceramic parables. T. Albright. il Art N 76:88-9 Ap '77 *
WEEKS, Levi Hinckley
Auburn in Natchez. M. McGehee. bibl il Antiques 111:546-53 Mr '77 *
WEEKS, Lewis E. Jr
Inexpensive evaporator for backyard syrup making. il Org Gard & Farm 24:138-41 F '77
WEEVILS
Head capsule transmission of long-wavelength light in the curculionidae. J. R. Meyer. bibl il Science 196:524-5 Ap 29 '77
Symbiosis runs wild on the backs of high-living weevils. J. L. Gressitt. il Smithsonian 7:135-6+ bibl(p 156) F '77
WEGENER, Judith E. and Haskett, J. A.
Developing a computerized organization file. il Lib J 102:2323-5 N 15 '77
WEI, G. C. T. and Wuensch, B. J.
Comparison of radioactive and stable Tl+ diffusion in potassium chloride: demonstration of a transmutation effect. bibl il Science 197:159-61 Jl 8 '77
Transmutation products may influence radiotracer diffusion rates in an ionic solid. bibl il Science 197:157-9 Jl 8 '77
WEICK, Karl E.
B-school buzzword: creativity. por Bus W p66 Ag 8 '77 *
WEICKER, Lowell Palmer, 1931-
Excerpts from debate on Federal Election Campaign Act Amendments, March 17, 1976. Cong Digest 56:77+ Mr '77
Use tax dollars to elect Congress? interview. pors U.S. News 82:63-4 Ap 25 '77; Same. Current 194:5-7 Jl '77
WEID-NEUWIED, Maximilian Alexander Philipp, Prinz von
Winter at Fort Clark; excerpt from People of the first man, ed by D. Thomas and K. Ronnefeldt. il Am West 14:36-47 Ja '77
WEIDEGER, Paula
Estrogen: the rewards and the risks. McCalls 104:70+ Mr '77
WEIDENBAUM, Murray Lew
Business policy and the public welfare; address, January 14, 1977. Vital Speeches 43:317-20 Mr 1 '77
WEIDHAAS, Peter
How the German book trade is organized. Pub W 212:64-6+ S 12 '77
WEIDLINGER, Paul
Visualizing the effect of earthquakes on the behavior of building structures. il Archit Rec 161:139-42 My '77
WEIDMAN, Gregory R.
Furnishing the museum rooms of the William Paca House. bibl il Antiques 111:165-71 Ja '77
WEIDNER, Bethany
What natural gas shortage? Progressive 41:19-23 Ap '77
WEIGAND, Robert E.
International trade without money. Harvard Bus R 55:28-30+ N '77
WEIGEL, George S. Jr
Hard-noised idealism: a model for disarmament. America 137:186-8 O 1 '77
WEIGER, Ralph James
Midas touch. il por Time 109:43 Mr 14 '77 *
WEIGHING machines
See also
Scales (weighing instruments)
WEIGHT (physiology)
Body weight: reduction by long-term glycerol treatment. D. Wirtshafter and J. D. Davis. bibl il Science 198:1271-4 D 23 '77
In pursuit of hunger: physiological considerations. M. F. Lakat. bibl il Intellect 105:261-2 F '77
Land of the fat. il Time 111:53 Ja 2 '78
Weighing in—how do you figure? L. Beech. Sr Schol 109:18 Ap 21 '77
See also
Diet
Exercise
Obesity

Anecdotes, facetiae, satire, etc.

On my obsession about weight. B.-J. Raphael. Mademoiselle 83:78+ S '77

WEIGHT lifting
Now on the other hand . . .; Record Makers Invitational. S. Pileggi. il Sports Illus 47:16-19 D 12 '77
Pleasure of being the world's strongest woman; J. Todd. S. Pileggi. il pors Sports Illus 47:60-4+ N 14 '77
Power lifters. P. Bonventre and J. Huck. il Newsweek 90:51 S 5 '77
See also
Body building
WEIGHT reducing equipment. See Exercising equipment
WEIGHT reducing preparations
Fenfluramine and fluoxetine spare protein consumption while suppressing caloric intake by rats. J. J. Wurtman and R. J. Wurtman. bibl il Science 198:1178-80 D 16 '77
WEIGHT throwing
See also
Shot putting
WEIGHT Watchers, Inc
New Weight Watchers diet; with recipes. H. LaBarre. Ladies Home J 94:119-26 F '77
WEIGHTS and measures
See also
Cookery—Measurements
Metric system
Scales (measuring instruments)

Anecdotes, facetiae, satire, etc.

Confused by metrics? Try hites and wates. J. P. Matulich. il Sci Digest 81:4+ Je '77
Zern. G. Hill. il Field & S 82:16+ O '77
WEIL, Dorothy
Right to bear arms. il Atlantic 239:64-7 F '77
WEIL, Frank Alan
Begging to disagree. por Forbes 120:152 O 15 '77 *
WEIL, Simone
Life paid up. G. A. White. Commonweal 104:468-70 Jl 22 '77 *
Simone Weil: futile heroics. P. Ward. Chr Today 22:26-7 N 4 '77 *
Simone Weil: waiting for God. L. S. Cunningham. Chr Cent 94:293-4 Mr 30 '77 *
WEILL, Kurt
Real Kurt Weill. A. Porter. il por Hi Fi 27:77-9 My '77 *
Reviews of records. K. H. Kowalke. Mus Q 63:441-6 Jl '77 *
Rise and fall of the city of Mahagonny. Review
Hi Fi 27:MA27+ Ag '77 *
Wealth of Weill. W. Botsford. Am Rec G 40:43-4 My '77 *
WEILL, Michel David-. See David-Weill, M.
WEINBERG, Alvin M.
Is nuclear energy acceptable? bibl Bull Atom Sci 33:54-60 Ap; 4-5 Je '77
We ought to make peace with the breeder reactor; interview. por U.S. News 82:44 Ap 18 '77

about

Nuclear moratorium: study claims that effects would be modest, foresees low growth rate for total energy demand. A. L. Hammond. Science 195:156-7 Ja 14 '77; Discussion. 195:634-6 F 18 '77 *
WEINBERG, Frank
From Wall Street to auto sales—a success story. V. Louviere. il pors Nations Bus 65:76 S '77 *
WEINBERG, Henry
Probation program planning for youthful offenders. il Intellect 106:58-61 Ag '77
WEINBERG, Steven
Future of unified gauge theories; adaptation of address, February 8, 1977. bibl il Phys Today 30:42-3+ Ap '77
WEINER, Janet
Moving without tears. Parents Mag 52:50+ F '77
WEINER, Lois
Unions on the brink. Nation 225:276-7 S 24 '77
WEINGARTEN, Violet
Violet Weingarten. N. Y. Hoffman. por Commonweal 104:533-5 Ag 19 '77 *
WEINGARTNER, Charles
Getting to some basics that the back-to-basics movement doesn't get to. bibl f il Engl J 66:39-44 O '77
Mutterings (cont) Engl J 66:12-14 My '77
WEINGARTNER, Felix
Weingartner, Kleiber, De Sabata: a matter of record. H. Goldsmith. pors Hi Fi 27:94-6 S '77 *
WEINHOLD, Frank
Thermodynamics and geometry. bibl il por Phys Today 29:23-6+ Mr '76; 30:15 Ja '77
WEINSTEIGER, Richard
Work bench made to look good and last. il Org Gard & Farm 24:86-90 Ap '77
—See Smyser, S. jt auth
WEINSTEIN, Allen
Weinstein's controversial Hiss-Chambers probe now scheduled for April release by Knopf; ed by R. Dahlin. Pub W 212:43 D 12 '77
WEINSTEIN, John N. and others
Liposome-cell interaction: transfer and intracellular release of a trapped fluorescent maker. bibl il Science 195:489-92 F 4 '77
WEINSTEIN, Martin Bradley
How to design automotive anti-collision systems. il Radio-Electr 48:44-6 Jl; 52-3+ Ag '77
WEINSTEIN, Robert A.
Cameras at sea. il Am West 14:34-49 My '77
WEINSTOCK, Martin
Screening for cancer. Environment 19:2-4 D '77
WEINTRAUB, Sidney
Another weapon against inflation: tax policy. il pors Bus W p94+ O 3 '77 *
WEIR, Robert M.
Adventures of a haunted whaling man: a diary of 1855-58. il Am Heritage 28:46-65 Ag '77
WEIR, Sandra
Metrics: do the books measure up? il por SL 24:30-1 N '77
WEIS, Franz
Road runners, rattlesnakes and racing. M. Jordan. il pors Car & Dr 22:129-30 Je '77 *
WEISBECKER, Joseph A.
Build the COSMAC Elf: a low cost experimenter's microcomputer (cont) il Pop Electr 11:63-7 Mr; 12:41-6 Jl '77
WEISBERG, D. Kelly
Cinderella children. bibl il por Psychol Today 10:84-6+ Ap '77
WEISBERG, Gabriel P.
Commitment to the past. il Art N 76:150-2 Summ '77
Stamp of Whistler. il Art N 76:66-8+ S '77
WEISBERGER, Bernard A.
Paul Revere. il por Am Heritage 28:24-37 Ap '77
WEISBURGER, Elizabeth K.
Cancer-causing chemicals. bibl il por Chemistry 50:42-8 Ja '77
WEISENBERG, Charles M.
Special report: one for the books: a card trumps the system. Wilson Lib Bull 51:720-1 My '77
WEISER, H. and others
Detection of Lyman α emission from the Saturnian disk and from the ring system. bibl il Science 197:755-7 Ag 19 '77
WEISER, Mort
Everything a traveler should know about passports and visas. il Holiday 58:34-5 Ja '77
WEISER, Paul W.
New life for the Monongahela. il Parks & Rec 12:25a-27a F '77
WEISINGER, Mort
Caution play it safe. il Fam Health 9:44-5+ Je '77
Easiest article to sell. Writer 90:11-14+ S '77
Page nobody reads. Writers Digest 57:19 Mr '77
WEISKOPF, Herman
Baseball. Sports Illus 47:76 S 19 '77
Baseball's week. il Sports Illus 47:100 O 10 '77
Bowling. Sports Illus 46:66 My 9 '77
Football's week. Sports Illus 47:77-8 D 5 '77
Hitters can be ranked. il Sports Illus 47:24-5 Jl 18 '77
Week; baseball. See issues of Sports illustrated published during the baseball season
Week; college basketball. See issues of Sports illustrated published during the basketball season
Week; college football (cont) Sports Illus 47:60+ O 24; 67-8+ O 31; 56+ N 7; 76+ N 14; 59-60+ N 21; 96+ N 28 '77
WEISS, Arnold R.
Those food-related cues magnify your weight problem. Sci Digest 81:33-4 Ap '77
WEISS, David
Life in the Talmud. I. Shenker. il pors N Y Times Mag p44+ S 11 '77 *
WEISS, Jeffrey Friedman-. See Friedman-Weiss, J.
WEISS, John
Scent for a buck. il Outdoor Life 160:70-1+ O '77
War and peace in a bass boat: slob guides, kooky clients. Outdoor Life 160:94+ O '77
Watch the birds catch more fish. il Outdoor Life 159:76-81+ F '77
WEISS, Margaret R.
Camera-eye on Christmas. il Sat R 5:31-2 N 26 '77
Photography (cont) Sat R 4:44-7 F 19; 32-4+ Ap 2; 44-5+ Jl 23; 60-1 Ag 6; 5:40-1 O 15 '77
WEISS, Philip
What do corporations do? New Repub 176:25-6+ My 21 '77
WEISS, R. J. and others
Sulfate aerosol: its geographical extent in the midwestern and southern United States. bibl il Science 195:979-81 Mr 11 '77
WEISS, Theodore
Comment. J. D. McClatchy. Poetry 130:45-7 Ap '77 *
WEISS, W. H.
Your garden: lovely to look at, but is it safe? il Ret Liv 17:19-20 Ag '77
WEISSENBERG, Alexis
Living dangerously. H. Saal. il por Newsweek 90:103+ N 7 '77 *
WEISSER, Susan
How I learned to cope with my difficult baby. il por Redbook 150:42+ N '77
WEISSMAN, Gary
Gary Weissman's catch-22. J. Miller. Progressive 41:10 Ap '77 *

WEISSTEIN, Naomi, and others
Phantom-motion aftereffect. bibl il Science 198: 955-8 D 2 '77

WEISTER, George M.
Oregon yesterdays; with historic photographs. E. W. Buehler. Am West 14:41-53 S '77 *

WEITH, Warren
[Column] (cont) Car & Dr 22:20 Mr; 23:22 Jl; 18 N '77

WEITZ, Paul J.
See also
Space stations—Skylab 2 (1st manned) mission

WEITZMAN, Elliot David
How to get a night's sleep; interview. il por U.S. News 83:62-4 Ag 8 '77

WEIZMAN, Ezer
Why can't Washington listen to us? interview. il por U.S. News 83:60-1 Jl 4 '77

about

Christmas summit. K. Willenson and others. il pors Newsweek 91:12-14 Ja 2 '78 *

WELBORN, Carol B.
Eleventh month; poem. Chr Cent 94:1004 N 2 '77

WELCH, Bruce L.
Nuclear energy on the dole. Nation 224:231-5 F 26 '77

WELCH, Helen
Man who killed the deer; F. Waters' novel. Engl J 66:60 Mr '77

WELCH, James
Comment. R. Holland. Poetry 129:287-8 F '77 *

WELCH, John
John Welch retooled for retirement—literally. J. R. Wolkomir. Ret Liv 17:45+ Ag '77 *

WELCH, Louise E.
Kinds of quiet; poem. Ladies Home J 94:66 F '77

WELCH, Mary Scott
How women just like you are getting better jobs. il Redbook 149:121+ S '77

WELCH, Robert M.
Cleanup of Lake Winona. il map Parks & Rec 12:39-41+ My '77

WELCH, Wayne
Modest proposal. il Forbes 120:37-8 N 15 '77

WELDERS. See Welding—Equipment

WELDING
Laser welding for tricky jobs. S. Renner-Smith. il Pop Sci 210:67 Mr '77

Equipment

Bargain cut-and-weld kit. E. F. Lindsley. il Pop Sci 210:170 Je '77
Hobby welder heats and brazes. E. F. Lindsley. il Pop Sci 210:188 My '77
Little gas-driven arc welder. E. F. Lindsley. il Pop Sci 210:160 Je '77

WELDON, Norman Ross
Take the cash and let the credit go. P. Berman. por Forbes 120:26-7 S 1 '77 *

WELFARE. See Public welfare

WELFARE fraud. See Fraud

WELFARE funds (trade unions) See Trade unions —Benefit funds

WELFARE ISLAND. See Franklin Delano Roosevelt Island

WELFARE work in industry
See also
Company stores

WELK, Lawrence
American spirit—as Lawrence Welk sees it. il pors U.S. News 82:69 Ja 24 '77

WELK, Olen Lee
Driver; interview. New Yorker 52:23-5 Ja 31 '77

WELKER, Marie-Louise
Marseilles-Fos. il map Oceans 10:46-51 Ja '77

WELL drilling. See Oil well drilling

WELLEMEYER, Marilyn
Addicted to perpetual motion. il Fortune 95:55+ Je '77
Bloodless pigeon shoot. il Fortune 95:109+ My '77
Cops for the love of it. il Fortune 95:41+ Ap '77
Middlemen of metal. il Fortune 95:162-7 Mr '77
On your own time. See issues of Fortune
Poetry in motion on the long green. il Fortune 95:67+ F '77
Tuning in on the jazz revival. il Fortune 96: 37-8+ Jl '77

WELLENKAMP, Jeanne
Just plow your problems into the garden. il Org Gard & Farm 25:158 Ja '78

WELLER, L. David, Jr
Recruitment and selection: a devilish process; quiz. Clearing H 50:406-7 My '77

WELLER, Sheila
What some women do for laughs on Saturday night. il Ms 6:46+ O '77
(ed) See Torres, L. Liz Torres: I get my best material from the subways

WELLER method of tornado detection. See Television in meteorology

WELLES, Chris
Index funds. Nation 224:300-4 Mr 12 '77

WELLESLEY, College, Wellesley, Mass.
Mister Nabokov; course taught by V. Nabokov. H. Green. New Yorker 52:32-5 F 14 '77

WELLINGTON, Bill
Ounce of prevention. il Motor B & S 139:74 Mr '77 *

WELLINGTON, James K.
Look at the fundamental school concept; address, November 20, 1976. Vital Speeches 43: 215-20 Ja 15 '77

WELLINGTON, William G. See Rollo, C. D. jt auth

WELLS, Ed, and Hapke, B. W.
Lunar soil; iron and titanium bands in the glass fraction. bibl il Science 195:977-9 Mr 11 '77

WELLS, Elmer E.
Unjustifiable denial of priesthood to black Mormons. bibl il Negro Hist Bull 40:725-7 Jl '77

WELLS, Gloria
18 centerpieces you can make to dress up any table for practically nothing. il Redbook 148: 37-44 Mr '77

WELLS, Melissa F.
U.S. contributions to UNDP and other development funds; statement, November 2, 1977. Dept State Bull 77:872 D 12 '77

WELLS, Selma
Help for people society often ignores. il pors U.S. News 83:46 Ag 1 '77 *

WELLS
Dig yourself a shallow well. J. Martin. Org Gard & Farm 24:81-2 Jl '77
Fiberglass, stainless steel stop deep well corrosion; Shaw Heights, Colo. R. E. Darr. il Am City & County 92:57 Jl '77
New on TV: a look inside your water well. il Farm J 101:C4 S '77
Underground water generates a boom. il Bus W p32-3 Ap 11 '77
See also
Cisterns

WELLSTONE, Paul David
Trouble looming. New Repub 176:14-15 Mr 12 '77

—and Tarbox, Lamont
Confrontation on the prairie. Progressive 41:41-3 D '77

WELSCH, Roger L.
Shelters on the plains; with biographical sketch. il Natur Hist 86:9, 48-53 bibl(p94) My '77

WELSH, A. L. and Hyde, Charlotte
Tahiti. il Trav/Holiday 148:28-32 D '77

WELSH, Frank A. and others
Regions of cerebral ischemia located by pyridine nucleotide fluorescence. bibl il Science 198:951-3 D 2 '77

WELSH National Opera Company. See Opera—Great Britain

WEMBER, Carolyn
Cold comfort; poem. Seventeen 36:151 F '77

WENDEL, Frederick C.
Attitudes of principals toward participatory managerial practices. il Clearing H 50:322-6 Mr '77

WENDEL, William H.
Private & public partnership: the desperate case of Niagara Falls. Harvard Bus R 55:6-8 N '77

WENDERS, Wim
Wenders. S. Kauffman. New Repub 176:26-7 Ja 29 '77 *
Wim Wenders: a worldwide homesickness. M. Covino. il Film Q 31:9-19 Wint '77 *

WENDORFF, Ruth
Separate kitchen pleases us both. il por Ret Liv 17:49-50 Mr '77

WENDY'S International, Inc. See Restaurants—Chain and franchise operations

WENG, Will
Will Weng's farewell puzzle. pors N Y Times Mag p73 F 27 '77

WENGER, Karen
Trials of a letter writer. il por Nation 225:657-9 D 17 '77

WENGERD, Tim
Spotlight on: Tim Wengerd; interview, ed by L. Draegin. il pors Dance Mag 51:55-9 S '77

WENKAM, Robert
Markets & careers; photographic-book producer; interview, ed by H. Chapnick. il por Pop Phot 81:70+ S '77

WENNER, Jann
Rolling stone's new trip. T. Schwartz. il por Newsweek 90:65+ O 3 '77

WENNER, Kate
How they keep them down on The Farm. il N Y Times Mag p74+ My 8 '77

WENNERSTEN, Jack
Working the state house. Nation 225:307-8 O 1 '77

WENNING, Harry
How practical is solar heating? il McCalls 105: 168-73+ O '77 *

WENTZEL, Volkmar
Zulu king weds a Swazi princess. il map Nat Geog 153:46-61 Ja '78

WERBELL, Mitchell Livingston, 3d
Significant little gun. A. St George. il por Esquire 88:69-72+ Ag '77 *

WERBLIN, David A. See Werblin, S.

WERBLIN, Sonny
Miracle in the Meadows. R. Kennedy. il por Sports Illus 47:74-9+ S 12 '77 *

WERKEMA, Gordon R.
Financial crisis that isn't. il por Chr Today 22:22-4 N 4 '77

WERLICH, David P.
Peruvian revolution in crisis. Cur Hist 72:61-4+ F '77

WERNER, Alfred
Always controversial Monsieur Courbet. il por Am Artist 41:58-63+ S '77
Eugene Delacroix: color magician. il por Am Artist 41:38-43+ Ap '77
Marc Chagall at ninety. Progressive 41:35-7 Je '77

WERNER, Ken
Films to give you better snapshots. il Mech Illus 74:62+ Ja '78

WERNER, Laurie
(ed) Can men and women be friends? Answers from famous women and men. Redbook 149:31-2 O '77

WERNER, M. W. and others
Infrared studies of star formation. bibl il Science 197:723-32 Ag 19 '77

WERNICK, Richard
Musician of the month: Richard Wernick; interview, ed by D. Webster. il por Hi Fi 27:MA4-5 Ag '77

WERNICK, Robert
Commoner with lordly air is bringing Versailles back to its days of glory. il por Smithsonian 7:38-47 Mr '77
Risible, visible—who cares as long as it's fun. il pors Smithsonian 7:74-5+ F '77

WERRY, Richard R.
Wide open door to higher education. Intellect 105:251-3 F '77

WERTENBAKER, William
Mining the wealth of the ocean deep. il N Y Times Mag p 14-16+ Jl 17 '77

WERTIME, Theodore A.
What of the world's future? Current 194:49-57 Jl '77

WERTMULLER, Lina
Look, Gideon—: a talk with Lina Wertmüller; ed by G. Bachmann. pors Film Q 30:2-11 Spr '77

about

Lina Wertmüller as political visionary. N. P. Hurley. Chr Cent 94:726-8 Ag 17 '77 *
On Lina Wertmuller. J. Mellen. il por Society 14:82-4 Ja '77 *

WESKER, Arnold
Making the case for Shylock; interview, ed by R. Appignanesi and L. Quart. Nation 225:565-8 N 26 '77

about

Merchant. Reviews
Nation 225:565-8 N 26 '77 *
Nation 225:606 D 3 '77 *
New Yorker 53:81 N 28 '77 *

WESLEY, Richard
Last street play. Reviews
America 136:529 Je 11 '77 *
New Yorker 53:87 My 30 '77 *

WESLEYAN Theological Society. See Religious societies

WESSEL, Morris A.
Bright child, school failure. bibl Parents Mag 53:36+ Ja '78
New mothers want to know; questions and answers. See issues of Parents' magazine & better homemaking

WESSON, Robert G.
Brezhnev's year: politics in the U.S.S.R. Cur Hist 73:109-11+ O '77

WEST, B. C. Jr
N.C. ruling menaces manuscript collections. M. U. Russell. Am Lib 8:471-2 O '77 *

WEST, Carl. See Thomasson, D. jt auth

WEST, Carolyn
Cruising the microcosm of Alaska. il map Yachting 142:65-7 N '77

WEST, Gordon V.
Choosing a depth sounder. il Yachting 142:80-1+ O '77
Coast Guard will monitor CB. Yachting 142:126 D '77
Electronics. See issues of Motor boating & sailing to April 1977
Portable DF. il Yachting 142:68-70+ Jl '77
Single sideband update. Yachting 142:126-7 Ag '77
VHF-FM weather service. il Yachting 142:211-15 S '77

WEST, Jack
Fire. il Motor B & S 139:68-9+ Ap '77
Man & his boat: built to take it. il Motor B & S 139:56-9+ F '77
Omega. il Motor B & S 139:59-61+ Mr '77
Roll aids. il Motor B & S 139:98+ My '77
Transit navigation. il Motor B & S 139:66 My '77

WEST, Jerry
It's a wild West show. C. Kirkpatrick. il Sports Illus 46:14-17 F 14 '77 *
No more tears for Mr Clutch. il por Time 109:63 F 14 '77 *

WEST, Jessamyn
(ed) See Stapleton, R. C. Jimmy Carter's sister: how faith can heal.

WEST, John F.
Edge of Europe; with biographical sketch. il Natur Hist 86:6, 40-7 bibl(p 110) D '77

WEST, Karen
How to get a blue collar. il Ms 5:62-5 My '77

WEST, Kathleen
Something told the wild geese; poem. Am For 83:14 N '77

WEST, Meredith J. See King, A. P. jt auth

WEST, Morris Langlo
How to write a novel. Writer 90:9-11 My '77

WEST, Philip T. See Premazon, J. jt auth

WEST, Rebecca
Inner Queen. il Vogue 167:232-3+ My '77

WEST, Robert V. Jr
Tesoro's $130 million burden. por Bus W p93-4 My 9 '77 *

WEST, Ruth
Name it, she'll make it. il pors Ebony 32:66+ My '77

WEST, Ted
Mighty Magoon rides again. il por Motor B & S 140:51-3+ Jl '77

WEST, Victoria Mary Sackville-. See Sackville-West, V. M.

WEST. See Western States

WEST Bank occupation. See Jordan—Israeli occupation, 1967

WEST BERLIN. See Berlin (West Berlin)

WEST BERLINERS. See Berliners

WEST GROVE, Pa.

Education

See Education—Pennsylvania

WEST in art. See Western States in art

WEST INDIAN poetry

Translations into English

Honey seller; poem; tr by H. A. Norman. P. Barton. Nation 225:700 D 24 '77

WEST INDIES
Rebirth of the Antilles. G. de Zéndegui. il map Américas 29:21-33 Je '77
See also
Antigua (island)
Caribbean Region
Dominican Republic
Grenada
Haiti
Puerto Rico
St Martin (island)
Virgin Islands

Industries

See also
Whaling

WEST INDIES, British
See also
Bequia (island)

WEST INDIES, Netherlands. See Netherlands West Indies

WEST PALM Beach, Fla.
Spiraling arches shape a great space; Temple Beth El in West Palm Beach. il Archit Rec 161:111-14 F '77

WEST POINT Military Academy. See United States Military Academy, West Point

WEST SENECA, N.Y. See Buffalo, N.Y.

WEST Side Tennis Club, Forest Hills. See Sports clubs

WEST VIRGINIA
See also
Agriculture—West Virginia
Education—West Virginia
Fayette County, W.Va.
Housing—West Virginia
New River
Potomac River
Strip mining—West Virginia

Economic conditions

We're not laughing our way to the bank yet; interview. J. D. Rockefeller, 4th. por U.S. News 82:40 My 23 '77

WEST VIRGINIA floods. See Floods—United States

WEST VIRGINIA Heritage Trunk project. See School exhibitions, Traveling

WESTBURY, N.Y.

Recreation

See Recreation—New York (state)

WESTENBERGER, Jane
AFA annual meeting. por Am For 83:20 Jl '77

WESTERBECK, Colin L. Jr
Screen. See issues of Commonweal

WESTERGAARD, John
New era of expansion for small growth companies? interview, ed by A. Hershman. por Duns R 109:117-18+ Ap '77

WESTERLIES. See Winds

WESTERN Air Lines
Blow to Europe's Airbus; effect of Western Air Line's non-purchase decision on Airlines Industries. il Bus W p99 F 14 '77
Western's fleet growth aimed at leisure market. Aviation W 106:28 F 21 '77

WESTERN and country music. See Country music

WESTERN civilization. See Civilization

WESTERN Council of State Librarians. See Libraries—Western States

WESTERN Desert. See Libyan Desert

WESTERN Desert, Egypt. See Sahara Desert

WESTERN Electric Company
Humanizing the workplace: then and now; Hawthorne Studies in personnel management. il Society 15:112-15 N '77
Who won? FCC decision on Western Electric and AT&T. Forbes 119:46 My 1 '77

WESTERN films. See Motion pictures—Westerns

WESTERN Forestry Center, Portland, Ore.
More than a museum. V. H. Black. il Am For 83:12-15 Mr '77

WESTERN Hemisphere
See also
America

WESTERN History Association
Informal chronicle of the Western History Association. R. A. Billington. il Am West 14:30-1+ S '77

WESTERN Home Awards
American Institute of Architects-Sunset magazine Western Home Awards. il Sunset 159:98-113 O '77
Announcing thes 1977 Western Home Awards. il Sunset 158:112-13 F '77

WESTERN legends. See Legends, American

WESTERN red cedar. See Arborvitae

WESTERN Reserve College. See Case Western Reserve University, Cleveland

WESTERN SAHARA
U.S. walks a tightrope in the Sahara. S. W. Sanders. il Bus W p47 Ja 16 '78
See also
Guerrillas—Western Sahara
United Nations—Western Sahara

WESTERN Samoa
See also
United Nations—Western Samoa

WESTERN States
The Coast. J. Didion. See alternate issues of Esquire
East-West. R. Morris. New Repub 177:12-13 D 17 '77
See also
Agriculture—Western States
Art—Western States
Art galleries and museums—Western States
Aviation—Western States
Botany—Western States
Coal mines and mining—Western States
Cowboys
Crime and criminals—Western States
Express highways—Western States
Fishing—Western States
Frontier and pioneer life—United States
Historic houses, sites, etc.—Western States
Hunting—Western States
Libraries—Western States
Music—Western States
Northwestern States
Opera—Western States
Overland journeys to the Pacific
Power resources—Western States
Recreation areas—Western States
Rocky Mountains
Skis and skiing—Western States
Strip mining—Western States
Water supply—Western States
Western History Association
Wilderness areas—Western States
Wildlife conservation—Western States
Wildlife management—Western States

Bibliography

American West review. See issues of American west
Recent Western books. Am West 14:56 Ja; 56 Mr; 58 My; 50 Jl; 56 S '77

Description and travel

[Month] travel in and beyond the West. See issues of Sunset
Riding the U.S./Mexico borderland. W. Oleksy. il map Ret Liv 17:33-6+ Mr '77
Sky hunger. L. McMurtry. il Holiday 58:38-41+ Ap '77
Westward ho! with all the Viorsts in tow. J Viorst. il Redbook 148:57-9 Ap '77
See also
Automobile touring—Western States

Economic conditions

New milestone in the shift to the sunbelt. il Nations Bus 65:69 My '77

History

Cowboy's West: a special issue; symposium. bibl il Am West 14:4-5+ N '77
Eden ravished; the land, pioneer attitudes, and conservation. H. Hague. bibl il Am West 14:30-3+ My '77
See also
Northwestern States—History
Oregon Trail

WESTERN States in art
Frank Schoonover's frontier; excerpt from Frank Schoonover. C. Schoonover. il por Am West 14:38-47 Mr '77
Frederic Remington 1861-1909; reproductions of paintings; with introd by J. J. Dupont. F. Remington. il por Conservationist 31:10-18 Mr '77
He painted the West. J. A. Michener. il Read Digest 110:182-7 My '77
Taos art colony; special issue; with editorial comments. M. C. Nelson. Am Artist 42:6+, 27-63+ Ja '78
See also
Cowboys in art

WESTERN States in literature
Dane Coolidge western writer and photographer. O. Ulph. bibl il por Am West 14:32-5 N '77
See also
Western stories

WESTERN stories
Scorched cowboys: an old Colorado cowhand's tale. H. Beecher. il Am West 14:30-1 N '77

WESTERN Union Corporation
Space-age treadmill. por Forbes 120:59-60 Ag 1 '77

WESTERVELT, Virginia
Nobelist Langmuir's persistence proved cloud-seeding possible despite skeptics. Sci Digest 81:23-6 My '77

WESTGATE, Robert D.
Washington memo. See issues of Retirement living

WESTIN, Alan F.
Patients' rights in medical privacy. Sci N 111:71 Ja 29 '77 *

WESTINGHOUSE Electric Corporation
Gloom on the Monongahela. T. Stevenson. il Sat R 4:6-10+ Ja 22 '77
Issues on trial in the Westinghouse lawsuits; suits charging failure to deliver on uranium supply contracts brought by electric utilities. Bus W p 125-6+ S 26 '77
Opposites: GE grows while Westinghouse shrinks. il Bus W p60-4 Ja 31 '77
Town dilemma; PCB contamination of Bloomington, Ind. sewage. D. Jordan. il map Environment 19:6-15 Mr '77
Uranium pattern Westinghouse buys. Bus W p33 D 26 '77
Uranium thing; utilities suing Westinghouse over uranium contracts. A. J. Mayer and P. L. Abraham. il Newsweek 89:73 F 14 '77
Why is this man smiling? R. Kirby. por Forbes 119:66 My 1 '77

WESTMAN, Walter E.
How much are nature's services worth? bibl Science 197:960-4 S 2 '77

WESTOFF, Charles F.
Trends in American marriage, childbirth, and retirement; excerpts from address. por Intellect 106:93-5 S '77

WESTON, Carol Anne
Is there life after nineteen? il Seventeen 36:134-5+ Mr '77

WESTON, Edward
Strongest way of seeing. il Horizon 20:82-6 N '77 *

WESTON, England
Austen-ized village. M. Green. Atlantic 240:77-81 Jl '77

WESTPHAL, Alice
Ceramics of Ruth Duckworth. il por Craft Horiz 37:48-51 Ag '77

WESTWAY (proposed) See Express highways—New York (state)

WESTWOOD, Norma J.
Woman of Magdala; poem. Chr Cent 94:326 Ap 6 '77

WET flies. See Fishing lures, flies, etc.

WET n' Wild, Orlando, Fla. See Swimming pools

WETERING, Janwillem van de
PW interviews; ed by P. Gardner. por Pub W 212:48-9 S 26 '77

WETHERSFIELD, Conn.
Don't be a slave to your city's computer. il Am City & County 92:69-71 O '77

WETLANDS
Here come the dredgers! Sneak attack on the wetlands; with editorial comment. P. J. Bernstein. il Nation 225:612-18 D 10 '77
Margin of life. R. Allen. il Int Wildlife 7:20-9 Mr '77
Tree nobody liked; red mangrove in Florida Gulf Coast area. R. Gore. il map Nat Geog 151:668-89 My '77
See also
Tidal flats

WETTERAU Inc. See Grocery trade

WETTLAUFER, George, and Wettlaufer, Nancy
Constructing your own slab roller; excerpt from Getting into pots, a basic pottery manual. il Ceram Mo 25:30-2 F '77
Making cranks for production firing. il Ceram Mo 25:64-6 S '77

WETTLAUFER, Nancy. See Wettlaufer, G. jt auth

WETZSTEON, Ross
Woody Allen: schlemiel as sex maniac. il pors Ms 6:14-15 N '77

WEXFORD festival. See Music festivals—Ireland

WEXLER, Mark
Islands in the sun. il Nat Wildlife 16:54-63 D '77
They call it orienteering. il map Nat Wildlife 15:12-16 Je '77
Who can keep up with these kids in the woods? il Nat Wildlife 15:40-3 F '77

about

How Peru saved Paracas. il Int Wildlife 7:24-31 S '77 *

WEXNER, Leslie
Unlimited Limited. il por Forbes 120:77+ N 15 '77 *

WEYERHAEUSER Company
Weyerhaeuser: centralizing research to cut costs and boost productivity. il Bus W p 100-1 Ja 16 '78
Weyerhaeuser gets set for the 21st century. T. Griffith. il Fortune 95:74-9+ Ap '77

WEYMANN, Ray J.
Gone with the wind. D. E. Thomsen. il Sci N 112:106-7 Ag 13 '77 *

WEYMOUTH, Lally
Word from Mamma Buff. il pors Esquire 88: 154-7+ N '77

WEYR, Thomas
Dutton at 125: past, present and future of a noted publisher. il Pub W 212:32-6 N 21 '77
Hungarians have an appetite for reading—and a rich larder to delve into. il Pub W 212:26-8 O 31 '77
(ed) See Ballantine, B. Ballantine Books at quarter century: founders
(ed) See Ballantine, I. Ballantine Books at quarter century: founders
(ed) See Bush, R. Ballantine Books at quarter century: new regime
(tr) See Goeppert K. Frontier: three big publishing houses
(tr) See Martens, A. U. Paperback market: how it differs from America

WHALE models. See Zoological models

WHALE oil. See Oils and fats

WHALEN, George J. See Graf, R. F. jt auth

WHALES
At sea: plesiosaur merely a rotten whale? Sci N 112:68 Jl 30 '77
Gray whale behavior; letter. F. H. Wolfson. Science 195:534 F 11 '77
Hunt for the narwhal: unicorn of the Arctic seas; Inuits of the Canadian Arctic. R. R. Reeves. il Oceans 10:50-7 Jl '77
In pursuit of the narwhal. J. B. Macinnis. il Int Wildlife 7:36-41 My '77
In the company of great whales; humpback whales. J. Hudnall. il Audubon 79:62-73 My '77
International cooperation to protect the whales; UNEP and FAO. S. J. Holt. il Oceans 10:62-4 Jl '77
Issue of survival: bowhead vs. tradition. J. R. Bockstoce. Audubon 79:142-5 S '77
Of men, whales, and Captain Scammon; the gray whale in Baja California lagoons. R. Ellis. il map Nat Parks & Con Mag 51:8-13 O '77
Pseudorca stranding; beaching on the Dry Tortugas. J. W. Porter. il Oceans 10:8-15 Jl '77
Westerlies. G. C. Larson. Flying 100:40+ Ap '77
Whale-watchers; natural history study cruise off Baja California. G. Reiger. il Audubon 79: 74-6+ My '77
Where the whales put on a whale of a show; gray whales in Baja's Magdalena Bay. R. F. Jones. il Sports Illus 46:34-6+ Mr 28 '77
See also
International Whaling Commission
Whaling

Poetry

Whales weep not; excerpt from The complete poems of D. H. Lawrence. D. H. Lawrence. il Oceans 10:21 Jl '77

WHALES, Killer. See Dolphins (mammals)

WHALING
Bowhead whales; ban on Eskimo hunting. Dept State Bull 77:740-1 N 21 '77
Confrontation: Greenpeace Foundation puts itself on the line. E. Perlman. il Oceans 10:58-61 Jl '77
Gray whale protection. R. Storro-Patterson. il Oceans 10:45-9 Jl '77
Issue of survival: bowhead vs. tradition; Eskimo whaling. J. R. Bockstoce. Audubon 79:142-5 S '77
Managing bowhead sperm whale hunts. Sci N 112:406 D 17 '77
Moratorium for the bowhead: Eskimo whaling on ice? J. Walsh. il Science 197:847-50 Ag 26 '77
Saving the bowheads; Eskimo whaling. P. Gwynne and W. J. Cook. il map Newsweek 90:113 N 7 '77
South Georgia island: the great southern fur rush. J. C. Simmons. il Oceans 10:46-51 My '77
To kill a whale. R. McNally. il Oceans 10:62-5 Ja '77
Whale of a problem for the administration; Eskimo hunting of the bowhead whale. J. Walsh. Science 198:384-5 O 28 '77
Whalers of Bequia. E. Kuperschmid. il map Motor B & S 139:40-5 F '77
See also
International Whaling Commission
Scrimshaw

History

Adventures of a haunted whaling man: a diary of 1855-58. R. Weir. il Am Heritage 28:46-65 Ag '77
Charles Scammon: whaler turned naturalist. G. K. Mallory. il Oceans 10:40-4 Jl '77

WHALL, Hugh D.
What makes yard owners cry uncle. il Motor B & S 139:60-1+ F '77

WHARTON, Gary C.
Continuing phenomenon of the religious best seller. Pub W 211:82-3 Mr 14 '77

WHEALON, John Francis, Abp
For you, I am a bishop; with you, I am a Christian. il New Cath World 220:18-19 Ja '77

WHEAT
Bread from scratch; homegrown wheat. H. Rubin. Org Gard & Farm 25:136-9 Ja '78
See also
Flour

Cultivation

Don't wait to fertilize wheat; the time to apply anhydrous. Suc Farm 75:39 D '77
Escape the one-crop trap; spring wheat. G. Lorang. il Farm J 101:K3 Ap '77
Get set for wheat allotments this fall. R. D. Wennblom. il Farm J 101:20A+ Je '77
Wheat costs range from $2.61 to $5.33 per bu. il Farm J 101:16-17 mid-Mr '77

Diseases and pests

New ways to fight wheat diseases. il Farm J 101:A4-5 mid-Mr '77
Wheat diseases: no letup in sight. B. Gergen. il Suc Farm 75:28-9 Ag '77

Harvesting

Gypsies of harvest. N. Proffitt. il Newsweek 90: 65-6 Jl 4 '77
How to get wheat off to plant soybeans earlier. G. Reynolds. il Farm J 101:M4-5 Ja '77
Wheat harvest: family style and corporate. B. Marsik. il Farm J 101:E1-2 N '77

Hybrids

New wheat varieties for eastern belt. Suc Farm 75:A6 My '77
See also
Triticale

Marketing

Wheat grower fears another bad year. C. Bickers. Farm J 101:L4 Ja '77

Prices

All-too-normal granary. il Forbes 120:29-30 Jl 1 '77
Golden glut. T. Nicholson and others. il Newsweek 90:64-5 Jl 4 '77
Here's what's holding wheat prices down. il Suc Farm 75:34 Ag '77
New wheat glut? D. Pauly and others. il Newsweek 89:84 Mr 14 '77
Our big wheat crop—can we sell it? R. D. Wennblom. il Farm J 101:B6-7 Ja '77
Plant not, want not. Newsweek 90:90+ S 12 '77
65% loan rate can help. D. Howe. Farm J 101:9 Mr '77
65% loan rate can hurt wheat. Farm J 101: 44 mid-F '77
Wheat farmers lose out at the White House. Farm J 101:72 O '77
Wheat growers ask for loans at 65%. G. Lorang. Farm J 101:32A Mr '77

Transportation

Wheat women convoy wheat to barge point; protest by WIFE (Women Involved in Farm Economics) Farm J 101:F4 Ag '77

WHEAT surplus. See Surplus products, Agricultural

WHEAT trade
Our big wheat crop—can we sell it? R. D. Wennblom. il Farm J 101:B6-7 Ja '77

WHEATCRAFT, Steven
Finding faint planetary satellites. il Sky & Tel 54:243-5 S '77

WHEATER, Eric L.
Nicaragua. il Travel 148:40-5+ Jl '77

WHEATLEY, Phillis
Poems on various subjects, religious and moral. K. Holder. Engl J 66:68 Mr '77 *

WHEATON College, Wheaton, Ill.
How to beat the beaten path; interview, ed by C. Forbes. C. Kilby. por Chr Today 21:30-2 S 9 '77

WHEDBEE, Lili Tuong-Van
. . .And four to go. il Redbook 148:102-3 F '77

WHEEL balancing. See Automobiles—Wheels

WHEEL bearings, Automobile. See Automobiles—Bearings

WHEELABRATOR-Frye Inc
Annual report for the young tells the business story. il Nations Bus 65:52-3 Jl '77

WHEELBARROWS
Wheelbarrow that costs nothing. A. Stahr. il Mech Illus 73:77 S '77

WHEELER, Candace Thurber
Candace Wheeler, textile designer. W. H. Faude. bibl il por Antiques 112:258-61 Ag '77 *

WHEELER, Elizabeth
(ed) See Place, M. K. Guess who's for the ERA?
(ed) See Solomon, B. Guess who's for the ERA?

WHEELER, Hoyt N. and Kochan, T. A.
Unions and public sector supervisors: the case of fire fighters. bibl f il M Labor R 100:44-8 D '77

WHEELER, Roberta
A little magic. bibl Clearing H 50:345-8 Ap '77

WHEELER, Timothy J.
It happens every spring. Nat R 29:548 My 13 '77

WHEELESS, Leon L. Jr. See Horan, P. K. jt auth

WHEELS
Floating-hub wheel improves ride comfort. D. Scott. il Pop Sci 210:74-5 Ap '77
See also
Automobiles—Wheels

WHEELWRIGHT, Jeff
Furbish lousewort is no joke. New Repub 176: 9-12 My 14 '77

WHELAN, Elizabeth M.
Are you a high cancer risk? Harp Baz 110: 127+ F '77
Baby?...Maybe. il Ms 5:26+ Ap '77
Cancerphobia. Harp Baz 110:95+ Ap '77
Should a career woman have children? Harp Baz 110:101+ F '77
Your health risks at 30. Harp Baz 110:132-3+ O '77
—See Stare, F. J. jt auth
about
Baby talk. B. Carter. il por Newsweek 90:73 Ag 8 '77 *

WHELAN, Joseph P.
Not everyone who says Lord, Lord. . . . il New Cath World 220:16-17 Ja '77

WHELTON, Clark
Instant intimacy. . .and safer than sex. Mademoiselle 83:148+ Je '77
Locker room mystique. il Horizon 21:64-9 Ja '78

WHICH? (periodical) See Periodicals—Great Britain

WHIPPED toppings. See Icings

WHIPPLE, Dan
Losing of the West. Nation 224:717-20 Je 11 '77

WHIRLPOOL baths. See Baths, Whirlpool

WHISKEY
Great scotch. A. Fraser. Mademoiselle 83:73+ S '77
Scotch would like to take you to bed. R. A. De Groot. il Esquire 87:88-90+ F '77
Wonderful offbeat whiskey drinks. H. McNulty. il House & Gard 149:154+ S '77
See also
Liquor industry

WHISTLER, James Abbott McNeill
Stamp of Whistler. G. P. Weisberg. il Art N 76:66-8+ S '77 *

WHISTLES
Clay whistle. R. A. Fromme. il Ceram Mo 25:60-3 Mr; 58-62 Ap '77

WHITAKER, Frederic
Frederic Whitaker: Mister watercolor. J. Jennings. il Am Artist 41:68-73+ Ag '77 *

WHITAKER, Jack
Trenchant words from a talking head. W. Leggett. por Sports Illus 47:55 N 21 '77 *

WHITAKER, Ralph
Storing electricity. il Environment 19:16-20+ Mr '77

WHITAKER, Rogers E. M.
Best of everything. New Yorker 53:29-32 D 19 '77
Coming across; interview. New Yorker 53:26-7 Je 27 '77
Notes and comment. New Yorker 53:27-8 S 19 '77
Old friend. New Yorker 53:28-30 S 26 '77
Wien, Wien. . . New Yorker 53:15-16 Ja 2 '78

WHITAKER, Romulus
—See Whitaker, Z. jt auth
about
They speak for the snakes. S. C. Buch. il pors Int Wildlife 7:16 My '77 *

WHITAKER, Zai
—and Whitaker, Romulus
If they're killers, what good are they? il Int Wildlife 7:12-16 My '77
about
They speak for the snakes. S. C. Buch. il pors Int Wildlife 7:16 My '77 *

WHITBREAD Round-the-World Race. See Yacht racing

WHITBY, James Roy
High finance. Chr Today 21:60-1 Ap 15 '77 *

WHITE, Andrew Dickson
Science versus religion: an old squabble simmers down. M. E. Marty. il Sat R 5:29-32+ D 10 '77 *

WHITE, Bernard J.
Criteria for job satisfaction: is interesting work most important? bibl il M Labor R 100:30-5 My '77

WHITE, Betty
White House years. il por Sat Eve Post 249:16+ Mr '77

WHITE, Bob
Warm-weather companion slides. il Motor B & S 140:102-3 Jl '77

WHITE, Charles Fred
Charles Fred White: a forgotten black poet. R. J. Bresnahan. por Negro Hist Bull 40:659-61 Ja '77 *

WHITE, Charles J. 3d
Teaching kids about law. Todays Educ 66:74-6 Ja '77

WHITE, Dorothy, and White, Harvey
Organizing a club cruise. Yachting 141:85 F '77

WHITE, Edmund
Enigmas and double visions. il pors Horizon 20:48-55 O '77
Miro's latest works. il por Horizon 19:88-96 Jl '77

WHITE, Elwyn Brooks
Compleat New Yorker. M. Muggeridge. il Harpers 254:94+ Mr '77 *
E. B. White on the exercycle. D. Hall. Nat R 29:671-2 Je 10 '77 *

WHITE, Eugene R.
Amdahl's coup stuns the computer industry. por Duns R 109:23-4+ Ap '77 *

WHITE, Harry
Fine art of fleurage. il por Horticulture 55:26-8 O '77

WHITE, Harvey. See White D. jt auth

WHITE, James F.
Our apostasy in worship. Chr Cent 94:842-5 S 28 '77

WHITE, Jean M.
Murder most tidy. il New Repub 177:36-8 Jl 30 '77

WHITE, John
Winter light for greenhouse gardening; excerpt from The solar greenhouse book. il Org Gard & Farm 24:58-9 D '77

WHITE, John W.
TM's claims unsupported in experiments. Sci Digest 82:36-7 Ag '77
What the dying see. Sci Digest 81:71-2 F '77

WHITE, Jonathan W. Jr. See Doner, L. W. jt auth

WHITE, Joyce
Buying and serving jug wines. il Redbook 149: 202+ My '77

WHITE, Katharine Sergeant
Obituary
New Yorker 53:72 Ag 1 '77

WHITE, Mimi. See Nashner, M. jt auth

WHITE, Peter T.
One Canada—or two? il map Nat Geog 151:436-65 Ap '77

WHITE, Phil
All slaves are not created equal! il Mod Phot 41:92-5+ F '77

WHITE, Richard M. See Brodersen, R. W. jt auth

WHITE, Robert H.
Reading skills in the English class. il Clearing H 51:32-5 S '77

WHITE, Robert J.
Medical wonders of Dr Robert White. J. G. Hubbell. il por Read Digest 110:138-42 F '77
New ethical question: head transplants? R. Bahr. il Sci Digest 81:76-8 My '77 *

WHITE, Robert L. and Meindl, J. D.
Impact of integrated electronics in medicine. bibl il Science 195:1119-24 Mr 18 '77

WHITE, Rod L.
Child's play. il por Forbes 119:144 Ap 15 '77 *

WHITE, T. D. and Harris, J. M.
Suid evolution and correlation of African hominid localities. bibl il maps Science 198:13-21 O 7 '77

WHITE, Theodore Harold
Passing on Camelot; excerpt from The book of Merlyn. Harpers 255:49-64 S '77
about
Time Inc.'s internal war over Vietnam; excerpt from The powers that be. D. Halberstam. il Esquire 89:102+ Ja '78 *

WHITE, Walter Francis
NAACP and the Supreme Court: Walter F. White and the defeat of Judge John J. Parker, 1930. D. C. Hine. bibl il por Negro Hist Bull 40:753-7 S '77 *
WHITE-black relations. See Race relations
WHITE collar crimes. See Commercial crimes
WHITE collar workers
White-collar unions and the work humanization movement. E. M. Kassalow. bibl il M Labor R 100:9-13 My '77

Salaries, allowances, etc.

Experienced professionals lead white-collar pay rise. R. Zoltek. il M Labor R 100:48-9 N '77
WHITE Consolidated Industries, Inc
Difference at White Consolidated. il Bus W p 135+ S 26 '77
WHITE flies
Whitefly whammy? control methods. il Sunset 159:78-9 Ag '77
WHITE-haired girl; ballet. See Ballet reviews—Single works
WHITE holes (astronomy) See Astrophysics
WHITE House
Change comes to White House; interview. R. Carter. pors U.S. News 82:31-3 Mr 21 '77
Death of an aged monarch; Dutch elm disease on White House grounds. H. Sidey. il Time 111:13 Ja 16 '78
Family fun in the White House. B. Angelo. il pors Time 110:24-5 Ag 15 '77
Holiday dinners at the White House. H. Haller. il Ladies Home J 94:110-11+ N '77
Home-style Christmas at the White House. il pors U.S. News 83:58-9 D 26 '77
Impressions of power and poetry. il Time 109: 31 Je 20 '77
Inside the White House. Sr Schol 109:14-15 Ja 27 '77
Private life in the White House—behind the scenes with the Carters. il pors U.S. News 82:30-2 F 28 '77
Tennis, folks? White House tennis court. J. Osborne. New Repub 177:11-12 N 26 '77
Tourist view of White House. il U.S. News 83: 59-60 S 19 '77
Why is there no recent women's art in the White House? B. Diamonstein. Art N 76:109-12 D '77
WHITE House Conference on Handicapped Individuals, 1977
Beyond the handicap; preparations by New York educators. J. H. Hoyt. Am Educ 13:25-6 Ap '77
White House Conference hears NRPA position on handicapped. Parks & Rec 12:61 N '77
WHITE House Conference on Library and Information Services (proposed)
Circus of tough balancing acts. J. Berry. Lib J 102:853 Ap 15 '77
White House Conference Advisory Committee. SLJ 23:66+ Mr '77
White House Conference: Advisory Committee named. Lib J 102:529-30 Mr 1 '77
White House Conference planning sessions held. Lib J 102:967-8 My 1 '77
WHITE House Council on International Economic Policy. See United States—Council on International Economic Policy
WHITE House entertaining. See Government entertaining
WHITE House News Photographers competition. See Photography—Competitions
WHITE House Office of Science and Technology Policy. See United States—Science and Technology Policy, Office of
WHITE House photography. See Photography, Journalistic
WHITE House press corps. See Press and politics
WHITE marriage; drama. See Rozewicz, T.
WHITE Motor Corporation
Some speculators like White Motor's looks. J. Madrick. Bus W p150 Mr 21 '77
White Motor sets Freightliner free; termination of marketing agreement. Bus W p30 Mr 7 '77
WHITE Sands National Monument
White Sands of New Mexico. M. Segal. il Travel 148:58-9 O '77
WHITE tailed deer hunting. See Deer hunting
WHITE water boating. See Running rapids
WHITED, Charles
Helen and the dragon. por Read Digest 110: 74-8 F '77
WHITED, Helen Dale
Helen and the dragon. C. Whited. por Read Digest 110:74-8 F '77 *
WHITEFLIES. See White flies
WHITEHEAD, James L.
President goes birding. il pors Conservationist 31:20-3 My '77
WHITEHEAD, Lawrence
(ed) See Ramazzini, B. Health issues
—See Waller, J. jt auth
WHITEHEAD, Ralph, Jr
After Daley, what? Commonweal 104:79-82 F 4 '77
Organization man. Am Scholar 46:351-7 Summ '77
WHITEHEAD, Roy
Bear story. il por Conservationist 32:16-18 S '77
WHITEHURST, James W.
Zoroastrians affirm tradition and change. Chr Cent 94:657-8 Jl 20 '77
WHITESIDE, Thomas
Annals of crime. New Yorker 53:35-8+ Ag 22; 34-6+ Ag 29 '77
Department of amplification. New Yorker 53: 94-6 D 12 '77
Reporter at large. New Yorker 52:36-42+ Ja 24; 53:30-8+ Jl 25 '77
WHITHAM, Thomas G.
Coevolution of foraging in bombus and nectar dispensing in chilopsis: a last dreg theory. bibl il Science 197:593-6 Ag 5 '77
WHITING family
Whiting coat-of-arms. H. K. Eilers. il Hobbies 81:146-7 F '77
WHITLAM, Edward Gough
From Whitlam to Fraser. T. B. Millar. For Affairs 55:854-72 Jl '77 *
WHITLAM, Gough. See Whitlam, E. G.
WHITLEY, Harry
Nettles of noncorformity. J. D. Douglas. Chr Today 21:49-50 Ja 7 '77 *
WHITLOCK, Dave
Versatile flyfisherman. N. Lyons. il pors Outdoor Life 160:74-7+ D '77 *
WHITMAN, Alden
Price of fame. il pors N Y Times Mag p 12-15 My 8 '77
(ed) See Brown, R. L. Growing up a Lindbergh
(ed) See Lindbergh, A. M. Anne Morrow Lindbergh reminisces about life with Lindy
WHITMAN, Ardis
If I should die before I wake. Read Digest 111: 217-20+ D '77
WHITMAN, Charles Joseph
Climbing the tower. H. Crews. Esquire 88:38-9 Ag '77 *
WHITMAN, Ruth
Yellow; poem. New Repub 177:28 S 3 '77
WHITMAN, Walt
Whitman still walks. W. H. Carr. il Conservationist 32:23 Jl '77 *
WHITMORE, Coby
Coby Whitmore. M. Tinkelman. il por Am Artist 41:70-3 Jl '77
WHITNEY, C. A.
Jim; story. New Yorker 53:163-6 N 14 '77
WHITNEY, Craig R.
Fixer. il pors N Y Times Mag p46-50+ Mr 20 '77
WHITNEY, Elinor
The Peterkins visit the bookshop; reprint from November 1924 Horn Book. Horn Bk 53:215-16 Ap '77
WHITNEY, Phyllis A.
Leaving the reader satisfied. Writer 90:13-16+ Ap '77
WHITNEY Biennial. See Art, American—Exhibitions
WHITNEY Museum of American Art, New York
Art. L. Alloway. Nation 224:156 F 5 '77
Marcia's not there to take artistic chances; interview, ed by J. N. Gifford. M. Tucker. il por Ms 5:30+ Ap '77
Whitney Museum. R. Smith. il Art in Am 65:96-9 S '77
WHITNEY Stakes. See Horse racing
WHITSON, Mona M.
Fossil plants you can still grow. il Horticulture 55:22-5 O '77
Moth in the orchid family. Horticulture 55:4 My '77
WHITTAKER, Alfred A.
Saying God loves you to a starving man; interview, ed by D. Kucharsky. pors Chr Today 21:17-21 Ap 1 '77
WHITTAKER, Jim
How to hike straight up. il por Pop Mech 147: 97-9+ Ap '77
WHITTELL, Polly
Wanted. il pors Motor B & S 140:71-2 Ag '77
WHITTEMORE, Reed
Against consensus. Harpers 255:15-17 Jl '77
Newspeak generation. Harpers 254:16+ F '77
WHITTINGHAM, Charles A.
Last meal to look forward to. il Fortune 96:191-2 S '77
Touch of the ocean on the shores of Lake Michigan. il Fortune 95:357-8 My '77
WHITTLESEY, Charles W.
Lost battalion. J. McCarthy. il por Am Heritage 28:86-95 O '77 *
WHITTOW, G. Causey
Hawaiian spinner; with biographical sketch. il Sea Front 23:304-7, 319 S '77
WHOLE grain cookery. See Cookery—Grain
WHOLE grain flour. See Flour
WHOLE wheat bread. See Bread
WHOLESALE price index. See Price indexes

WHOLESALE trade
Finance
Ratios of the wholesalers. il Duns R 110:124-6 O '77
WHOLESALERS, Book. See Book wholesalers
WHOLEY, Jane
Learning Spanish the Fénix way. Clearing H 51:130-5 N '77
WHOOPING cough
Preventive inoculation
Immunization gap. M. Clark. il Newsweek 90: 98 S 19 '77
WHOOPING cranes. See Cranes (birds)
WHORTON, Ty
Shorted out. il Flying 100:32-3 Je '77
WHYTE, William Foote, and Alberti, Giorgio
Industrial community in Peru. Ann Am Acad 431:103-12 My '77
WIBBERLEY, Leonard
Time of the lamb; story. Sat Eve Post 249:58-9 D '77
WICK, Liza
Cleanups and checkups that help you save household energy. House & Gard 149:86+ O '77
WICK, Michael M. and others
L-dopa: selective toxicity for melanoma cells in vitro. bibl il Science 197:468-9 Jl 29 '77
WICKER, Brian
Are nukes cricket? Commonweal 104:708-10 N 11 '77
Ars gratia artis? Commonweal 104:622-4 S 30 '77
Gloomy spring. Commonweal 104:263-4 Ap 29 '77
Pastoral strategy. Commonweal 104:390-1 Je 24 '77
Planning and education. Commonweal 104:134-5 Mr 4 '77
Violence in the streets. Commonweal 104:582-4 S 16 '77
WICKER, Tom
Kennedy without end, amen. il por Esquire 87: 65:9 Je '77
Panama Canal: opposing argument. Current 198: 54-5 D '77
Reforming our election laws. Current 189:3-4 Ja '77
WICKLEIN, John
Must we try for blackout III? il Progressive 41:16-20 N '77
WICKS, Harry
PM workbench. See issues of Popular mechanics
Workshop mini-course. il Pop Mech 148:14 Ag; 132 O; 8 N; 120 D '77; 149:93 Ja '78
WIDE-angle lenses. See Lenses, Photographic
WIDEMAN, Bernard
Getting tough with the press. Progressive 41:47-8 O '77
WIDICK, B. J.
AFL-CIO's growing troubles. Nation 225:168-71 S 3 '77
Big union blues: labor caught in Meany's grip. Nation 226:10-13 Ja 7 '78
Emancipation from Meany. Nation 224:368-72 Mr 26 '77
Labor on labor. Nation 224:675-6 Je 4 '77
No entangling alliances. Nation 225:388 O 22 '77
WIDMAN, F. Lisle
Role of gold in the international monetary system; address, December 3, 1976. Vital Speeches 43:199-201 Ja 15 '77
WIDOW Douglas (literary character) See Women in literature
WIDOWERS
Easing the plight of America's 1.8 million widowers. il U.S. News 83:48+ D 12 '77
Supreme Court strikes down a social security dependency requirement for widowers. Ret Liv 17:13-14 Ap '77
WIDOWS
Adjustment
Widowhood: learning from tragedy. L. Caine. Harp Baz 110:97+ Mr '77
WIECLAW, Wilma
Power in the blood meal. il Org Gard & Farm 24:74-5 O '77
WIEDOEFT, Rudy
More about the Dann Trio and Rudy Wiedoeft. J. Walsh. il pors Hobbies 82:35-6+ Jl; 35-6+ Ag; 35-6+ S '77 *
WIEGAND, G. C.
Thirty years of full employment policies and growing unemployment; address, March 19, 1977. Vital Speeches 43:501-7 Je 1 '77
WIEGAND, Wayne A.
Wayward bookman. bibl il Am Lib 8:134-7, 197-200 Mr-Ap '77
WIEN Air Alaska. See Airlines—Alaska
WIENER, Louise
Can the Commerce Department revolutionize federal policy on the arts? por Am Artist 41: 12 D '77
WIENIEWSKA, Celina
(tr) See Schulz, B. Father's last escape
(tr) See Schulz, B. Loneliness
(tr) See Schulz, B. Sanatorium under the sign of the hour glass
WIERZBICKI, James
AMSA competition—something different. il por Hi Fi 27:MA28-9 O '77
WIESELTIER, Leon
Sherry and skepticism: Oxford days. Am Scholar 46:483-95 Aut '77
WIESENFELD, Zsuzsanna, and others
Licking behavior: evidence of hypoglossal oscillator. bibl il Science 196:1122-4 Je 3 '77
WIESENTHAL, Simon
Wiesenthal's last hunt. il por Time 110:36+ S 26 '77 *
WIFE beating
Battered wives find it hard to get help; study by R. J. Gelles. Psychol Today 11:36+ Je '77
Courts and cops: enemies of battered wives? M. Rockwood. Ms 5:19 Ap '77
How battered women can get help. S. Nelson. Read Digest 110:21-3+ My '77
Killing excuse; wives' murdering husbands because of abuse. il por Time 110:108 N 28 '77
Right not to be beaten; the problem in Appalachia. R. Williams. Psychol Today 11:36 Je '77
Wife abuse. W. C. Nichols. Parents Mag 53:26 Ja '78
Wife beating: a community to the rescue; Philadelphia station KYW-TV. E. J. Pascoe. McCalls 105:81 N '77
Wives, mothers and victims. G. M. Anderson. America 137:46-50 Jl 30 '77
WIGG, David
(ed) See Taylor, E. Elizabeth Taylor talks about her new love, her new life
WIGGINS, Charles E.
Federal payments to crime victims? interview. pors U.S. News 83:55-6 N 28 '77
WIGGINS, Phyllis Wynn
Race still intimidates us. Todays Educ 66:67 N '77
WIGGINTON, Eliot
Earth log: the Foxfire wildfire. P. Hendrickson. il por Audubon 79:108-12 Mr '77 *
WIGHT, Frederick S.
Portrait of a New England town. il Art in Am 65:106-7 My '77
WIGHTMAN, Hazel (Hotchkiss)
Unforgettable Mrs Wightie. H. Wills and D. McDonald. il Read Digest 111:102-5 O '77 *
WIGHTMAN, Marj
Gifted, talented child. Educ Digest 43:51-3 S '77
WIGS
What's what in hair replacement? Bet Hom & Gard 55:69-70 N '77
WIKTOR-JEDRZEJCZAK, Wieslaw, and others
Theta-sensitive cell and erythropoiesis: identification of a defect in W/Wv anemic mice. bibl il Science 196:313-15 Ap 15 '77
WILBER, Bob
Profiles. W. Balliett. por New Yorker 53:45-8+ My 9 '77 *
WILBER, Charles K.
Role of property in an economic system. bibl il New Cath World 220:226-9 S '77
WILBUR, Marion
Herb teas for the whole family. il Org Gard & Farm 24:110+ N '77
My flower garden herbs. il Org Gard & Farm 24:64-8 N '77
WILBUR, Richard
(tr) See Tornai, J. Mr T. S. Eliot cooking pasta
About
Comment. J. D. McClatchy. Poetry 130:44-5 Ap '77 *
WILCOX, Desmond
Englishman's affection for Americans sparks a book and a television series; interview, ed by R. Dahlin. il Pub W 212:55 O 17 '77
WILCOX, Shirley
Five thousand dollar quilt. il Hobbies 81:114-15 F '77
WILCOXEN, Charlotte
Tin-glazed pottery of Puebla, Mexico. bibl il Antiques 111:794-9 Ap '77
WILD Bill. See Hickok, J. B.
WILD and scenic rivers
Preserving our wild and scenic rivers; symposium. il Nat Geog 152:2-59, supp(folded map) Jl '77
WILD animal parks. See Zoological gardens
WILD animal pets. See Pets
WILD animals. See Wildlife
WILD animals in art. See Animals in art
WILD boar hunting
Ugly, pestiferous and prepotent; France. W. Humphrey. il Sports Illus 46:58-62+ F 7 '77
WILD burros. See Burros
WILD Cherry (rock group) See Rock groups
WILD dogs
Dog days on the Plains. G. W. Frame and L. H. Frame. il Int Wildlife 7:48-55 S '77
WILD flower designs. See Design, Decorative—Plant forms

WILD flowers
Roadside beauty. J. Taylor and R. Jenkins. il Conservationist 32:14-21 Jl '77
Wild flowers that will grow in your garden. V. Ferreniea. il Horticulture 55:40-1 My '77
World's greatest wildflower show. E. A. Bauer. il Travel 147:48-53 Mr '77

WILD flowers, Photography of. See Photography of flowers, plants, trees, etc.

WILD geese. See Geese, Wild

WILD horses. See Horses

WILD rivers. See Wild and scenic rivers

WILD sheep. See Mountain sheep

WILD sheep hunting. See Mountain sheep hunting

WILD turkeys. See Turkeys, Wild

WILDE, Margaret D.
Letter from an Argentine prison. Chr Cent 94:901-2 O 12 '77
Living the rest to God. Chr Cent 94:396-7 Ap 27 '77
Paraguayans savor Christian solidarity; visit of Cardinal Paulo Evaristo Arns. Chr Cent 94:302 Mr 30 '77

WILDE, Oscar
Imp of perversity; Salome. G. Schmidgal. il Opera N 41:10-13 F 12 '77 *
Importance of being Earnest. Reviews
New Yorker 53:54 Je 27 '77 *
Time il 109:61 Je 27 '77 *

WILDE, Sim O.
Is compulsory attendance necessary? Educ Digest 42:2-5 Mr '77

WILDENHAIN, Marguerite
Marguerite Wildenhain. R. B. Petterson. il por Ceram Mo 25:21-8 Mr '77 *

WILDER, Robert L.
EEI: a survival tool. il Parks & Rec 12:22-4+ Ag '77

WILDER, Stephen F.
How to drive on ice. . .when it's too slippery to walk. il Pop Mech 148:92-5+ N '77

WILDERNESS areas
Let's save our roadless areas! with editorial comment. D. Sumner. il Liv Wildn 40:3, 25-33 Ja '77
Prescription for a beat-up wilderness. B. Scott. il Nat Wildlife 15:12-16 Ap '77
Problem of the wilderness; reprint from February 1930 issue of Scientific monthly; with introd by G. Marshall. R. Marshall. bibl f il por Liv Wildn 40:28-35 O '76
Whither wilderness? F. Church. il por Am For 83:10-12+ Jl '77
See also
Wild and scenic rivers

History

Friend of the wilderness: John Muir. B. McGinty. il pors map Am Hist Illus 12:4-9+ Jl '77

Alaska

Alaska frontier '77. il Nat Parks & Con Mag 51:28-9 Ap '77
Encounter in the Brooks Range. C. Brown. Liv Wildn 41:23 Jl '77
Guarding the great land: proposals of the Alaska Coalition for protecting a national heritage. il map Liv Wildn 41:20-3+ Jl '77
President's page (cont) C. M. Hunter. Liv Wildn 40:51 Ja '77
Return to the Sheenjek. M. E. Murie. il por map Liv Wildn 41:4-12 Jl '77

California

Hiking to see the golden trout; Golden Trout Wilderness Study Area. Sunset 159:24+ Ag '77
Legacy of Ishi. F. R. Gunsky. il Liv Wildn 40:4-11 Ja '77

Canada

Berger report: northern frontier, northern homeland; excerpt from Northern frontier, northern homeland; with editorial comments. T. R. Berger. il por maps Liv Wildn 41:3, 4-33 Ap '77
See also
Quetico-Superior Region

Colorado

Eagles Nest—classic lesson in wilderness politics. F. Small. Audubon 79:128-31 Jl '77

Minnesota

See also
Quetico-Superior Region

Montana

Is time running out for Taylor-Hilgard? with editorial comment. R. Tawney. il map Liv Wildn 40:3, 34-41 Ja '77

Texas

See also
Big Thicket

Washington (state)

Alpine Lakes Wilderness. il Sunset 158:256 Je '77

Western States

Wild country of the Crow; proposed Absaroka-Beartooth Wilderness Area. G. Wuerthner. il Liv Wildn 41:40-4 Ap '77

WILDERNESS camping. See Camping

WILDERNESS Society
1977: memorable adventures; schedule of trips. Liv Wildn 40:51 O '76

WILDERNESS survival
Arctic almost killed me twice! first man to canoe across the Northwest Passage. T. Dauksza. il map Outdoor Life 159:88-91+ Je '77
Cold-weather survival. J. W. Fears. il Outdoor Life 161:119-20 Ja '78
High adventure: confronting the essentials. R. M. Tapply. il Parks & Rec 12:26-9+ Je '77
If we stay here, we'll die; lost in New Hampshire. F. R. Jones. il Read Digest 110:122-6 Mr '77
If you get lost in the wilderness. J. Lord. il Conservationist 31:35 My '77
Scouts survive island and vice versa. C. Lewis. il Camp Mag 49:6-9 Ja '77
16-day ordeal of John Vihtelic; surviving car crash in Gifford Pinchot National Forest, Ore. E. D'Aulaire and P. O. D'Aulaire. il Read Digest 110:142-6+ Mr '77
Stranded in the merciless sands. F. T. Boylan, Jr. il Read Digest 111:77-81 Ag '77
This accursed land; excerpt from Mawson's will. L. Bickel. il por map Read Digest 111:199-202+ Jl '77
See also
Outward Bound schools

WILDFLOWERS. See Wild flowers

WILDING, George, and others
Reduced warfarin binding of albumin variants. bibl il Science 195:991-4 Mr 11 '77

WILDLIFE
How do they make it through the winter? A. LaBastille. il Nat Wildlife 16:20-5 D '77
Sketch book glimpse at late winter. H. W. Trimm. il Conservationist 31:inside back cover Ja '77
Update: wildlife; ed by T. Paugh. il Outdoor Life 160:104 O; 104 N '77; 161:42 Ja '78
See also
Zoology

Bibliography

Know more, see more. T. Trueblood. il Field & S 82:22+ D '77

Export-import trade

Confessions of an animal trafficker; excerpt from The animal connection. J.-Y. Domalain. il Natur Hist 86:54-67 bibl(p94+) My '77
Smuggling rare animals: latest global racket. il U.S. News 83:50 S 26 '77
See also
Birds—Export-import trade
Convention on International Trade in Endangered Species of Wild Fauna and Flora

WILDLIFE and pesticides. See Pesticides and wildlife

WILDLIFE conservation
Offer too good to refuse; responsibility of the Interior Department for protection of wildlife. N. P. Reed. il Parks & Rec 12:15a-18a F '77
St Hubertus: a conservation legacy. il Int Wildlife 7:42-3 N '77
Wild world must be saved. Philip. il pors Sat Eve Post 249:26-9+ N '77
World of the birdless dog; preserving natural areas and wildlife conservation. B. Tarant. il Field & S 82:156+ S '77
See also
Bird sanctuaries
Birds—Protection
Birds of prey—Protection
Conservation officers
National Wildlife Federation
Pesticides and wildlife
Rare animals
Sea birds—Protection
Water birds—Protection
Wetlands
Wilderness areas
Wildlife management
World Wildlife Fund

International aspects

International cooperation to protect the whales; UNEP and FAO. S. J. Holt. il Oceans 10:62-4 Jl '77

Laws and legislation

Endangered Species Act. K. Shea. bibl il Environment 19:6-15 O '77
Endangered Species Act under fire; a history of wildlife conservation law. M. J. Bean. il Nat Parks & Con Mag 51:16-20 Je '77
See also
Fishery laws and legislation
Marine mammals—Laws and legislation

WILDLIFE conservation—*Continued*

Africa

African wildlife: the end of the game? E. A. Bauer. il Outdoor Life 160:68-73+ D '77
Operation tsetse fly; livestock vs wildlife in United Nations tsetse fly control project. N. Myers. il Int Wildlife 7:33-5 My '77

Alaska

Observations on Alaska. L. S. Clapper and others. il Am For 83:22-3 F '77
Wildlife: the barometer of Alaska. W. E. Towell; reply with rejoinder. J. J. Schnabel. Am For 83:62-3 Mr '77

California, Lower

Of men, whales, and Captain Scammon. R. Ellis. il map Nat Parks & Con Mag 51:8-13 O '77

Kenya

Selling of the zebra. N. Myers. il map Int Wildlife 8:26-31 Ja '78

Namibia

Wildlife in Namibia. P. Younghusband. il Int Wildlife 7:52-63 N '77

Panama

Deliverance! rescue of wildlife trapped by rising waters behind the Bayano Dam. J. Fisher. il Int Wildlife 7:40-7 Jl '77

Peru

How Peru saved Paracas. M. Wexler. il Int Wildlife 7:24-31 S '77

Western States

Uproar over grizzly habitat. G. Laycock. Audubon 79:126 My '77

WILDLIFE conservation associations. See Conservation associations

WILDLIFE conservation officers. See Conservation officers

WILDLIFE in art. See Animals in art

WILDLIFE introduction. See Animal introduction

WILDLIFE management

Fighting the white death; winter feeding. R. Halverston. Outdoor Life 161:69+ Ja '78
Unhuntables are finally getting attention, funds. G. Laycock. Audubon 79:128-32 My '77
We must harvest does or lose our herds. J. O. Cartier. il Outdoor life 160:61-3+ D '77
Wildlife quotas sometimes ignored the real world. L. M. Talbot. il Smithsonian 8:116-18+ My '77

See also

Bird control
United States—Fish and Wildlife Service

Finance

What inflation's doing to hunting, fishing. J. O. Cartier. Outdoor Life 160:66+ S '77

Africa, East

Under the gun; efforts to control elephant populations. N. Myers; discussion. il Int. Wildlife 7:18-19 Mr '77

Alaska

Hunt Alaska now; state laws and wildlife populations. J. Rearden. il Field & S 82:60-1+ Ag '77
In Alaska, another wolf kill up against the wall; with pro and con discussion. L. Morgan; J. Rearden; J. L. Pitts. il Nat Wildlife 15:6-9 Ag '77

See also

Alaska—Fish and Game, Department of

India

Prospects for India's wildlife. Z. Futehally. il Nat Parks & Con Mag 51:17-19 Mr '77

Kenya

Great Kenya wildlife ripoff. J. Samson. il Field & S 82:48-9+ D '77
This is the end of the game; with photographs by P. Beard. B. Rensberger. N Y Times Mag p38-43+ N 6 '77

Minnesota

Big howl in Minnesota; timber wolf controversy. B. Gilbert. il Sports Illus 46:75-7 My 2 '77

New Mexico

Hide-and-seek in New Mexico attempts to capture wild burros at Bandelier National Monument. R. Cantwell. Sports Illus 47:48-9 Ag 1 '77

See also

New Mexico—Game and Fish, Department of

New York (state)

Understanding our bass population. B. D. Shupp. il Conservationist 32:26-9 Jl '77
What is a deer management permit? P. Kelsey. il map Conservationist 32:35-7 N '77

Ohio

Bewildered by a lot of claptrap; vote on banning leghold traps. D. Levin. il Sports Illus 47:70+ N 7 '77
Editorial; voting on controversial trapping law. M. G. Nichols. Field & S 82:6 N '77

Western States

Wild bunch; mustangs. B. Hall. il Nat Wildlife 15:4-11 Ap '77

WILDLIFE on postage stamps. See Postage stamps

WILDLIFE photography. See Photography of animals

WILDLIFE populations

Control

See Wildlife management

WILDLIFE rescue. See Wildlife conservation

WILDLIFE research

See also

Breeding

WILDLIFE sanctuaries

See also

Bird sanctuaries

California

Bird watching near Los Banos. . .here are five places to look. il Sunset 158:59 F '77

Colorado

New wildlife refuge in Boulder; Walden Ponds Wildlife Habitat. il Sunset 159:60 N '77

Michigan

To drill or not to drill; controversy surrounding proposed oil lease of Michigan Audubon Society's Bernard W. Baker Sanctuary. J. G. Mitchell. il Audubon 79:78-85 Ja '77

Nebraska

Sod house frontier; Fort Niobrara National Wildlife Refuge. J. Jordon and C. Jordon. il Travel 148:50-5 Ag '77

Nevada

Refuge ducks are swamped by powerboats, politicians; Ruby Lake National Wildlife Refuge. G. Laycock. Audubon 79:152-3 N '77

New York (state)

Joys of hunting geese; Montezuma National Wildlife Refuge. N. Bryant. il Field & S 82:28-9+ Je '77

South Carolina

Carolina haven for red wolf; introduction in Cape Romain National Wildlife Refuge. P. Laurie. Audubon 79:152 Ja '77
In South Carolina, another transplant runs into trouble; death of transplanted red wolf in Cape Romain National Wildlife Refuge. M. A. T. Neville. il Nat Wildlife 15:10-11 Ag '77

Wisconsin

Uncle Sam says scram! efforts to reduce Canada geese population in Horicon Marsh refuges. B. Gilbert. il maps Audubon 79:42-55 Ja '77

WILDLIFE watching

Get out on a limb! G. Helgeland. il Nat Wildlife 15:34-5 Ag '77

WILE, Raymond R.

At the creation. bibl il por Am Rec G 40:6-10 F '77
(comp) Edison concept. il Am Rec G 41:10-13 D '77
Edison recordings of Serge Rachmaninoff. Am Rec G 40:11-12 F '77

WILENTZ, Joan Steen

Strange world of superpressure. il Pop Sci 210:78-81+ F '77

WILES, Gordon P.

South Africa: are there grounds for hope? Chr Cent 94:400-4 Ap 27 '77

WILES, J. G. See Lewin, A. Y. jt auth

WILES, Jon Whitney

Developmental staging: in pursuit of comprehensive curriculum planning. Clearing H 50:274-7 F '77

WILEY, Bell I.

Admiral Yi and the turtle boats. il por Am Hist Illus 12:44-8 Je '77

WILEY, Harvey Washington

Pizen squad. il pors Chemistry 50:18-21 S '77 •

WILEY, Marcia

Cabin talk. See issues of Yachting

WILEY, Russell

Somewhere over Rainbow Bay. . . il Ret Liv 17:26-8 Ag '77

WILFORD, John Noble

Another small step for man: shuttling into space. il N Y Times Mag p24-5+ Ag 7 '77

WILHELM, John L.

Black holes—the darkest riddle of the universe. il Read Digest 111:68-72 S '77

WILHELM, Ross

Problems with poverty programs. il Intellect 106:7 Jl '77

WILHOIT, Francis M.
Alternatives to political paranoia. il por Intellect 105:289-90 Mr '77
WILKE, Harold H.
Mainstreaming the alienated: the church responds to a new minority. Chr Cent 94:272-5 Mr 23 '77
WILKENS, Lenny
Add super to the Sonics. J. Papanek. il por Sports Illus 48:81-2+ Ja 9 '78 *
WILKES, Donald Fancher
Slow roller. E. Keerdoja. il por Newsweek 90:13+ D 19 '77 *
WILKES, H. Garrison
Breeding crisis for our crops: is the gene pool drying up? map Horticulture 55:52-9 Ap '77
World's crop plant germplasm—an endangered resource. bibl il map Bull Atom Sci 33:8-16 F '77
WILKES-BARRE, Pa.
Coal Street Park by architects Bohlin and Powell. il Archit Rec 161:124-7 F '77
WILKIE, Jane
(ed) What you never knew about your favorite Christmas songs. il Good H 185:92+ D '77
(ed) See Hudson, R. Rock Hudson talks about Rock Hudson—finally!
(ed) See Osmond, M. Marie Osmond: I've got a brother for every mood
(ed) See Rolle, E. Esther Rolle talks about her roots
WILKINS, Barbara
(ed) See Savalas, T. Public believes Kojak
WILKINS, Joan
Guidance centers: where women can find themselves. Good H 184:152+ Je '77
WILKINS, Ronald W. T.
Fluid inclusion assemblages of the stratiform Broken Hill ore deposit, New South Wales, Australia. bibl il Science 198:185-7 O 14 '77
WILKINSON, Bud
Who's number one? il Sat Eve Post 249:64-5+ O '77
WILKINSON, C. F. See Brattsten, L. B. jt auth
WILKINSON, Stephan
Parallax. See issues of Flying, June 1977-
WILKINSON Match, Ltd-Allegheny Ludlum Industries, Inc merger. See Corporations—Acquisitions and mergers—International aspects
WILL
See also
Free will and determinism
WILL of God. See God—Will
WILL the real Abraham Lincoln please stand up: drama. See Grinins, T. A.
WILLAMETTE River
Pollution can be licked. il U.S. News 82:48 F 7 '77
WILLARD, Jess
Destruction of a giant; excerpt from Dempsey. J. Dempsey and B. P. Dempsey. il pors Am Heritage 28:72-83 Ap '77 *
WILLE, Alicia
Lilo Raymond. il Pop Phot 81:92-101+ Jl '77
WILLEMS, Arnold L. See Brown, M. H. jt auth
WILLENS, Harold, and Wyler, L. S.
Setting energy prices. Progressive 41:7 S '77
WILLERMAN, Marvin
Winning isn't everything. bibl Clearing H 50:394-7 My '77
WILLHAM, R. L. See Trenkle, A. jt auth
WILLIAM II, German Emperor
Personal Christianity. il por Sat Eve Post 249:20 Jl '77
WILLIAM III, King of Great Britain
Glass relating to William III. P. Warren. bibl il Antiques 112:742-9 O '77 *
Propaganda in the Revolution of 1688-89. L. G. Schwoerer. bibl f il Am Hist R 82:843-74 O '77 *
WILLIAM H. Jackson Company. See Fireplaces—Marketing
WILLIAM Paca House, Annapolis. See Historic houses, sites, etc.—Maryland
WILLIAMS, Alice S.
Jill Lynne. il por Pop Phot 80:88-91+ Mr '77
WILLIAMS, Andy
Andy and Claudine; interview, ed by B. Messenger. il por Ladies Home J 94:40+ Je '77
WILLIAMS, Art
Infinitive: to witness. D. K. Mano. il Nat R 29:274 Mr 4 '77 *
WILLIAMS, Barbara
Good skate. J. Maynard. il pors N Y Times Mag p70-1 Mr 6 '77
WILLIAMS, Barbara Fischer-. See Fischer-Williams, B.
WILLIAMS, Benjamin
Roots; Black martyr cries; poems. Negro Hist Bull 40:721 Jl '77
WILLIAMS, Betty
Northern Ireland's guerrillas of peace; interview, ed by R. S. Kennedy and P. Klotz-Chamberlin. il por Chr Cent 94:746-51 Ag 31 '77
about
Good news from Norway. pors Chr Cent 94:973 O 26 '77 *
Is peace in Northern Ireland becoming possible at last? pors U.S. News 83:84+ O 24 '77 *
Two Peace Prizes from Oslo. il pors Time 110:54 O 24 '77 *
Two women of Ulster. K. Willenson and A. Collings. il pors Newsweek 90:61 O 24 '77 *
WILLIAMS, Billy Dee
New Clark Gable? interview, ed by M. Mercer. por McCalls 104:120+ F '77
WILLIAMS, C. Herb
Neglected nomad of the saltwater. il Field & S 82:54-6 Jl '77
WILLIAMS, Cecil J.
Space age home. il pors Ebony 32:86-8+ Je '77 *
WILLIAMS, Curtis A. Jr, and Schupf, Nicole
Antigen-antibody reactions in rat brain sites induce transient changes in drinking behavior. bibl il Science 196:328-30 Ap 15 '77
WILLIAMS, Deniece
Free-ee-ee. New Yorker 53:29-30 Ap 4 '77 *
WILLIAMS, Doris Reed. See Evans, W. jt auth
WILLIAMS, Doug
Grambling rifle. P. Bonventre and V. E. Smith. il por Newsweek 90:108 N 21 '77 *
He's already in the big leagues. R. Reid. il por Sports Illus 47:62+ O 31 '77 *
WILLIAMS, Fats
Finally on the side of the law. il pors Ebony 33:74-6+ N '77 *
WILLIAMS, Gerry
Film. D. Hare. Craft Horiz 37:12+ Ap '77 *
WILLIAMS, Gertrude Johnson
Obituary
Ebony por 32:124-5 Jl '77. L. Bennett
WILLIAMS, Gray, Jr
I'm putting my garden to beds. Org Gard & Farm 24:69-73 My '77
WILLIAMS, Gunther Gebel-. See Gebel-Williams, G.
WILLIAMS, Gurney E. 3d
Burn centers: the new miracle workers. il por Fam Health 9:48-52 Jl '77
What to do when a blackout hits. il Pop Mech 148:96-9+ N '77
Your aching back. il Fam Health 9:26-31 Mr '77; Same abr. Sci Digest 81:17-20 Ap; 69-72 My '77
WILLIAMS, Harold Marvin
Chairman Williams digs in at the SEC. il por Bus W p69+ My 30 '77 *
Corporate governance—new heat on outside directors? por Forbes 120:33 O 1 '77 *
Dean as a securities watchdog. por Time 109:61 Ap 11 '77 *
Man for the markets. D. Pauly and others. por Newsweek 89:85-6 Mr 14 '77 *
WILLIAMS, Harrison A. Jr
Excerpt from remarks on amending the Age Discrimination in Employment Act, June 29, 1977. Cong Digest 56:266+ N '77
WILLIAMS, Jay
Letter from England: the magic of the mask. A. Chambers. il Horn Bk 53:92-6 F '77 *
WILLIAMS, Jerry R. See Bechtol, B. E. jt auth
WILLIAMS, Jim
Convertibles: on a new age dawning. il Esquire 87:76-80 Ap '77
WILLIAMS, John
What do you do when you grow up? J. Kaplan. il pors Sports Illus 47:32+ Jl 4 '77 *
WILLIAMS, John A.
Changing times in Plains. Read Digest 111:133-6 Jl '77
WILLIAMS, John G. and Edginton, C. R.
Tuning up for high performance. il Parks & Rec 12:36-40+ O '77
WILLIAMS, John Horter
Best defense . . . il por Forbes 120:146+ N 15 '77 *
WILLIAMS, Marcia
Poor old Harold the henpecked. pors Time 109:43 F 21 '77 *
WILLIAMS, Margot, and Elliott, Paul
Maria Martin: the brush behind Audubon's birds. il Ms 5:14-15+ Ap '77
WILLIAMS, Nina
Streamlined, carefree, timesaving house. il Am Home 80:77-8 O '77
WILLIAMS, Norman
Ancient rites and mysteries; poem. New Yorker 53:218 N 21 '77
WILLIAMS, Oscar R. Jr
Historical impressions of black-Jewish relations prior to World War II. bibl Negro Hist Bull 40:728-31 Jl '77
WILLIAMS, Patrick
Jazz-classical fusion: it's working. G. Lees. il por Hi Fi 27:MA26-7 N '77 *
WILLIAMS, Paul
Severed roots of American Christianity. Nat R 28:840-2; 29:270-1 Ag 6 '76; Mr 4 '77
WILLIAMS, Raymond L.
Think twice before repairing water meters. Am City & County 92:45-6 F '77
WILLIAMS, Richard. See Crandall, R. S. jt auth
WILLIAMS, Richard L.
Justices run nine little law firms at Supreme Court. il Smithsonian 7:84-93 bibl(p 154) F '77

WILLIAMS, Robert
Miranda still stands. C. Panati and L. Howard. por Newsweek 89:80+ Ap 4 '77 *
Through the looking-glass. Nat R 29:428 Ap 15 '77 *
WILLIAMS, Robert H. See Von Hippel, F. jt auth
WILLIAMS, Robert L.
Houses to go—for a song. il House B 119:10+ Ap '77
WILLIAMS, Roger M.
Alimony: the short goodbye. il por Psychol Today 11:70-2+ Jl '77
Are they closing the mental hospitals too soon? bibl il por Psychol Today 10:124-7+ My '77
Clamor over equal rights. il Sat R 4:6-8+ Je 25 '77
Clamor over municipal unions. il Sat R 4:12+ Mr 5 '77
Facelift for Detroit. il Sat R 4:6-8+ My 14 '77
Massing at the grass roots. Sat R 4:14+ Ja 22 '77
New urban pioneers: homesteading in the slums. il Sat R 4:8-14 Jl 23 '77
What Louisville has taught us about busing. il Sat R 4:6-8+ Ap 30 '77
Why children should draw: the surprising link between art and learning. il Sat R 4:10-16 S 3 '77
—See Robitscher, J. jt auth
WILLIAMS, Roger T.
American family: it ain't what it used to be. il MH 60:24-7 Wint '77
WILLIAMS, Stephen F.
Problem of exhaustible resources. il Nat R 29:1352-3+ N 25 '77
WILLIAMS, Ted
I hope Rod Carew hits .400; ed by J. Underwood. il pors Sports Illus 47:20-3 Jl 18 '77
WILLIAMS, Tennessee
Mother yaws; story. Esquire 87:78-80 My '77

about

Tennessee Williams and the Jesuits. G. D. Phillips. America 136:564-5 Je 25 '77 *
Vieux Carré. Reviews
America 136:506 Je 4 '77 *
Nation 224:669 My 28 '77 *
New Yorker 53:83 My 23 '77 *
Time il 109:108 My 23 '77 *
WILLIAMS, W. C.
Ascendancy of the Fonz. bibl Clearing H 50:333-7 Ap '77
WILLIAMS, William Carlos
Through a Spanish looking glass: Williams' poetry in translation. J. Felstiner. Américas 29:5-8 N '77 *
WILLIAMS, Woodbridge
Kenai Fjords: treasure unveiled. il maps Nat Parks & Con Mag 51:4-8 S '77
WILLIAMS Companies
Best defense . . . il por Forbes 120:146+ N 15 '77
WILLIAMSBURG, Va.
Bicentennial hangover. il Time 109:70 Je 13 '77
Modern-day problems threaten a landmark of U.S. history. il U.S. News 83:92-3 O 24 '77
WILLIAMSON, Chilton, Jr
Intelligent co-ed's guide to Tom Wolfe. por Nat R 29:212+ F 18 '77
Treason of the clerisy. Harpers 256:88-90+ Ja '78
WILLIAMSON, Jed. See Eder, S. jt auth
WILLIAMSON, Nancy
College basketball. Sports Illus 46:42+ F 21 '77
Women cash in. il Sports Illus 47:86+ N 28 '77
WILLIAMSON, Patricia Lewis
Saturday School. il Am Educ 13:14-17 Mr '77; Same abr. Educ Digest 43:25-7 S '77
WILLIAMSTOWN Theatre Festival, Mass. See Drama festivals
WILLIE, Charles V.
New face of government. Society 14:14-15 My '77
WILLIG, George
Around City Hall. A. Logan. New Yorker 53:84 Je 27 '77 *
Case closed. New Yorker 53:28-30 Je 13 '77 *
Only way to go is up. S. Moses. il Sports Illus 46:24-6+ Je 6 '77 *
Striving for upward mobility. il pors Time 109:27 Je 6 '77 *
Trade-Center stunts. E. Keerdoja. il pors Newsweek 90:18+ N 7 '77 *
WILLIG, Nancy Tobin
Buffalo (cont) Art N 76:195-6+ N '77
WILLIMON, William H.
Communion as a culinary art. Chr Cent 94:829-30 S 21 '77
Gone with the wind myth. Chr Cent 94:501-2 My 25 '77
Marriage as a subversive activity. il Chr Today 21:15-17 F 18 '77
WILLINGS, John A.
Cross-cultural communication: possibility or pipe-dream? il UNESCO Courier 30:12-16 Ap '77
WILLIS, Willma
Christmas is for children of any age. House B 119:72 N '77
We put the wood place to work. il Ret Liv 17:42-3+ My '77

WILLOW
Coevolution of foraging in bombus and nectar dispensing in chilopsis: a last dreg theory. T. G. Whitham. bibl il Science 197:593-6 Ag 5 '77
WILLS, Bob
Indigenous music. N. Hentoff. Nation 225:30 Jl 2 '77 *
WILLS, Garry
Measuring the impact of erotica. bibl il Psychol Today 11:30-1+ Ag '77
Shirley Verrett gambles on superstardom. il por N Y Times Mag p 15-16+ Ja 30 '77
Under Palladio's spell. Harpers 255:75-7 Ag '77
WILLS, Helen, and MacDonald, David
Unforgettable Mrs Wightie. il Read Digest 111:102-5 O '77
WILLS
Dollars and sense. G. Mahon. Mademoiselle 83:26 D '77
Howard Hughes' messy legacy. il Time 110:78+ O 3 '77
Law and your will; interview. W. C. Clay, Jr. por U.S. News 82:49-50 My 30 '77
Straw man in the Rothko case. J. H. Merryman; discussion. Art N 76:32-3+ Mr '77
Those cases go on and on; H. Hughes' will. Time 109:42+ Je 27 '77
Why you need a will; Before you make a will. H. A. Alpert; L. G. Feld. il Ret Liv 17:26-9 Mr '77
See also
Living wills
Probate law and practice
WILLSON, Don D. See Ellsworth, R. A. jt auth
WILMETH, Don B.
Theatre today. See alternate issues of Intellect
WILMINGTON College, Wilmington, Ohio

Peace Resource Center

What have they done to the rain? work of B. Reynolds. M. Hope. Chr Cent 94:693-5 Ag 3 '77
WILMINGTON Ten case. See Criminal justice, Administration of—North Carolina
WILMINGTON Ten trial. See Trials—North Carolina
WILSON, A. L, family, kidnapping
Night of terror. W. Evans and D. R. Williams. il Good H 185:126-7+ O '77
WILSON, Alexander
Alexander Wilson. D. Maurizi. il pors Conservationist 31:2-7 My '77 *
WILSON, Ann
New nightlife; interview ed by K. Madden. il Vogue 167:259+ N '77
WILSON, Archie L.
Transport efficiency and future economic growth; address, January 12, 1977. Vital Speeches 43:337-9 Mr 15 '77
WILSON, Bates E.
Bates Wilson: wilderness curator. C. H. Smith. por Ret Liv 17:23 Ja '77 *
WILSON, Benjamin J. and others
Perilla ketone: a potent lung toxin from the mint plant, Perilla frutescens britton. bibl il Science 197:573-4 Ag 5 '77
WILSON, Charles
Philippine Church: a letter. America 136:273-4 Mr 26 '77
WILSON, Cynthy
Pieces of me; poem. Ladies Home J 94:104 Ag '77
Your breathing makes no hurricanes; poem. Ladies Home J 94:162 Jl '77
WILSON, David Gordon
Pedaled lawn mower. il Org Gard & Farm 24:87 Je '77
WILSON, David S.
Bad year for paper? Look at some special situations; interview, ed by R. Brady. por Duns R 109:89+ F '77
WILSON, Edmund
View from the sixties: excerpt from New York Jew. A. Kazin. por New Repub 177:33-41 O 15 '77 *
Why is this man scowling? C. Williamson, Jr. Nat R 29:1370-3 N 25 '77 *
WILSON, Edward O.
Are we born to be good? N. Calder. il por Horizon 19:42-9 Mr '77 *
Sociobiology. J. Terrell. Sci Digest 82:58-61 S '77 *
—See Hölldobler, B. K. jt auth
WILSON, Elaine Blume
Are you risking your child's health? il Harp Baz 110:87+ Jl '77
Borderline behavior. Harp Baz 110:228-9+ S '77
Phobias: new freedom from fear. Harp Baz 110:125+ Mr '77
WILSON, Evie. See McCue, M. jt auth
WILSON, George B.
Church and marriage: twin families for growth. America 137:480-3 D 31 '77
WILSON, Hack
Why ain't I in the Hall? with editorial comment. M. Kram. il por Sports Illus 46:4, 88-90+ Ap 11 '77 *

WILSON, Harold
Poor old Harold the henpecked. pors Time 109:43 F 21 '77 *
Was Wilson bugged? Newsweek 90:31 Ag 15 '77 *

WILSON, Helen Van Pelt
How comely the cosmos. il Horticulture 55:28-31 Je '77

WILSON, Howard A.
Growing up with a past. Yale R 66:628-40 Je '77

WILSON, Hugh H.
Obituary
Nation 225:165-6 S 3 '77. C. McWilliams

WILSON, James Q.
Changing criminal sentences. Harpers 255:16-20 N '77
Debate over prisons. il Current 189:26-32 Ja '77

WILSON, John
Lakeside Studio: conserving the printmaking tradition. C. Shapiro and D. Shapiro. il por Art N 76:51-4 Mr '77 *

WILSON, John Anthony Burgess. See Burgess, A. pseud

WILSON, John S. See Heckman, D. jt auth

WILSON, John T. and others
Human globin messenger RNA: importance of cloning for structural analysis. bibl il Science 196:200-2 Ap 8 '77

WILSON, José
Gourmet tips for mail-order menus. il House & Gard 149:149+ S '77

WILSON, Julie
How to protect yourself. Harp Baz 110:93+ Mr '77

WILSON, Kemmons
Place to worship. il por Sat Eve Post 249:37 Ap '77

WILSON, Lanford
Brontosaurus. Review
Nation 225:571 N 26 '77 *

WILSON, Mortimer, Jr
Mortimer Wilson: romantic baroque in the Southwest; interview, ed by B. Cortright. il por Am Artist 41:52-5+ Je '77

WILSON, Paul
Conservative's strategy for conserving money; interview, ed by A. Hershman. il por Duns R 110:105-6+ Jl '77

WILSON, Pete
Pete Wilson of San Diego. C. McWilliams. por Nation 224:305-7 Mr 12 '77 *

WILSON, Peter J.
Problem with simple folk. Natur Hist 86:26-8+ D '77

WILSON, Richard
How to have nuclear power without weapons proliferation. bibl il por Bull Atom Sci 33:39-44 N '77

WILSON, Robert
Adrift among images. F. J. Spieler. il Harpers 254:107+ Mr '77 *
I was sitting on my patio this guy appeared I thought I was hallucinating. Review
New Yorker 53:92 Je 6 '77 *

WILSON, Robert Rathbun
Tevatron. bibl il Phys Today 30:23-7+ O '77

WILSON, Sloan
Education now. Sat R 5:68-9 D 10 '77

WILSON, Thomas F.
Stocks: next year has to be better than 1977; interview. por U.S. News 83:50-2 D 26 '77

WILSON, Tim. See Goodman, M. jt auth

WILSON, Victoria
Somewhere over the rainbow this fall will be books on Oz from Knopf and Random House; interview, ed by R. Dahlin. il Pub W 212:51 Jl 25 '77

WILSON, Wilkie A. and others
Tris buffer attenuates acetylcholine responses in aplysia neurons. bibl il Science 196:440-1 Ap 22 '77
—See Pellmar, T. C. jt auth

WILSON, William. See Jones, J. jt auth

WILSON, William Edward
W. E. Wilson and the Daramona observatory. B. Warner. il Sky & Tel 53:108-10 F '77 *

WILSON, William J. See Fathauer, T. E. jt auth

WILSON, Woodrow
Hazardous course for Carter. H. Sidey. por Time 109:9 Je 27 '77 *
How to think about politicians. W. Karp. il por Horizon 19:14-15 Ja '77 *

WILSON, Zane
Ballet International de Caracas and two of its dancers. N. M. Stoop. il pors Dance Mag 52:51-66 Ja '78 *

WILSON Hicks International Conference on Communication Arts. See Photography—Conferences

WILTON, Shirley M.
Pleasure principle: where is it in kids' art books? il SLJ 23:44-5 F '77

WINCHELL, Verne H.
Denny's takes its menu east. il por Bus W p 110+ S 19 '77 *

WINCHES
Avoiding the reel winch hazard. K. O'Connell. il Motor B & S 141:116-17+ Ja '78
Boat-winch conversion for easier loading. J. W. Rapps. il Pop Sci 210:134 F '77
Winch; pedal unit. D. Branch. il Org Gard & Farm 24:89-91 Je '77

WINCHESTER, Jesse
Exile's return. J. Maslin. il por Newsweek 89:95-6 My 23 '77 *

WINCHESTER Gun Museum, Cody, Wyo. See Museums

WINCHESTER rifles. See Rifles

WIND, Herbert Warren
Sporting scene (cont) il New Yorker 53:58-60+ F 28; 86-104 Mr 28; 108+ My 16; 56-66+ Jl 25; 47-65 Ag 8; 123-6+ O 10 '77

WIND. See Winds

WIND, Solar. See Solar wind

WIND instruments
See also
Horn (musical instrument)
Phonograph records—Wind instruments

WIND power
Community solar and wind energy system. K. H. Hohenemser. Environment 19:3-4 Mr '77
Harnessing the wind: a way of life. il pors Org Gard & Farm 24:36+ O '77
Wind. N. Gluckin. il Sci Digest 82:26-32 O '77
Wind energy from the Yen tornado. J. H. Douglas. il por Sci N 111:31 Ja 8 '77
Wind energy: large and small systems competing. W. D. Metz. il Science 197:971-3 S 2 '77
Wind power for home heating. E. F. Lindsley. il Pop Sci 211:62+ N '77
Wind-power update. K. H. Hohenemser. Environment 19:5+ Ja '77; Reply with rejoinder. D. R. Inglis. 19:43-4 My '77
See also
Windmills

WIND pressure
See also
Anemometers

WIND quintets
Empire Brass Quintet; program at Tully Hall on April 18. Hi Fi 27:MA26 Ag '77

WIND tunnels
NASA reassessing cost, risk of transonic tunnel facility. Aviation W 106:43-4 F 28 '77

WINDBREAKS
Do plants shiver in the north wind? L. Hill. il Org Gard & Farm 24:92-4 O '77
Shelterbelts: farmer's friend or foe? L. Palmer and I. Judd. il Farm J 101:MN1+ mid-F '77

WINDFIELD, Dave
Nobody knows the doubles I've creamed. M. Ludtke. il por Sports Illus 47:44-5 Jl 11 '77 *

WINDHAM, Gordon
Historical tape recordings. L. Dumont. Hobbies 82:58-9+ Jl '77 *

WINDMILLS
Giant eggbeater to harvest the wind. il Mech Illus 73:16 O '77
Stephan Sieradzki: windmill on a boom. E. Moran. il Pop Sci 210:22-3 F '77
Vertical windmill generates kilowatts from monsoons. S. Renner-Smith. il Pop Sci 210:99 Je '77

WINDMULLER, John P.
Establishing international fair labor standards. M Labor R 100:35-6 Mr '77
Industrial democracy and industrial relations. bibl f Ann Am Acad 431:22-31 My '77
(ed) Industrial democracy in international perspective. bibl f Ann Am Acad 431:1-140 My '77

WINDOW boxes. See Flower boxes, planters, etc.

WINDOW cleaners. See Cleaning compositions

WINDOW curtains and draperies. See Curtains and draperies

WINDOW displays. See Show windows

WINDOW locks. See Locks and keys

WINDOW panels, Insulating. See Panel construction

WINDOW screens. See Screens (doors, windows, etc)

WINDOW shades
Measuring for shades and such. Bet Hom & Gard 55:65 Jl '77
These shades roll up from below. il Sunset 158:135 My '77
Window shades. il Good H 184:160+ Je '77

WINDOW shutters. See Shutters

WINDOWS
DIY picture window. R. Stepler. il Pop Sci 211:140-2 S '77
8 ways to give class to your glass. S. Van Zante and others. il Bet Hom & Gard 55:130-5 S '77
Energy outlook for windows. S. Oddo. il House & Gard 149:134-5+ S '77
Five-dollar storm window. R. Weinsteiger. il Org Gard & Farm 24:150+ O '77
Measuring for shades and such. Bet Hom & Gard 55:65 Jl '77
Product reports 78. il Archit Rec 162:61-6 mid-O '77
Quick & easy window channels. J. Capotosto. il Mech Illus 73:108+ My '77

WINDOWS—*Continued*
Remodeling notebook; windows and heat loss. J. H. Ingersoll. House B 119:22 Ag '77
Right way to measure your windows for curtains and draperies. il Good H 185:24 O '77
Solar-ban film and glass keeps your home or RV cool. E. Powell. il Pop Sci 210:144 My '77
What a way to treat a window. il House & Gard 149:136-9 S '77
Window heat loss. A. J. Hand. bibl il Pop Sci 212:97-8+ Ja '78
Windows and doors. M. Cubisino. McCalls 104: 123-4 S '77
Windows: open to ideas. Redbook 148:193+ Ap '77; Same. Ladies Home J 94:186+ Ap '77
Windows with something to hide. N. Mandelbaum. il Ladies Home J 94:92-5 F '77
See also
Glazes and glazing (glass)
Skylights

Maintenance and repair

Anecdotes, facetiae, satire, etc.

How one window became an open & shut case. House B 119:83+ My '77

WINDOWS, Stained glass. See Glass painting and staining

WINDOWS on the World (restaurant) See New York (city)—Hotels, restaurants, etc.

WINDS
Off the garden path: it's an ill wind; lee winds. C. Chandler. Horticulture 55:16+ Ap '77
Sketch book in the wind. W. Trimm. il Conservationist 31:inside back cover Mr '77
Why it's so cold; Arctic westerlies. P. Gwynne and others. il maps Newsweek 89:38-9 Ja 31 '77
Wind caller. B. Nietschmann. il map Natur Hist 86:10-12+ Mr '77
See also
Aviation—Storm hazards
Dust storms
Hurricanes
Monsoons
Mountain waves
Plants, Effect of wind on
Tornadoes
Typhoons

WINDS, Stellar. See Stellar winds

WINDSHEAR monitors. See Aeronautic instruments

WINDSOR Arms Hotel. See Toronto—Hotels, restaurants, etc.

WINDSOR Mill, North Adams, Mass. See Art centers

WINDSURFERS. See Surfboards

WINDSURFING. See Surf riding

WINE
Avanti chianti. F. J. Prial. map N Y Times Mag p 134-5 N 13 '77
Best bottle game. F. J. Prial. N Y Times Mag p 102-4 Ap 24 '77
Beyond Liebfraumilch; white wines from Germany. C. Churchill. Am Home 80:26+ Mr '77
Buying and serving jug wines. J. White. il Redbook 149:202+ My '77
California wines. A. Fraser. il Mademoiselle 83:54+ Ap '77
Case for rosé. L. B. Downs. House B 119:97+ Je '77
Drinkers rejoice: a little wine may kill your virus. T. J. Maugh. Science 196:1074 Je 3 '77
15 (plus) wines ready for all fall parties. House B 119:146-7 N '77
Finger tip guide to white wine. L. B. Downs. House B 119:100-1 Mr '77
For lovers of Europe's wines: a vintage year. il U.S. News 82:73 Mr 21 '77
German wineland tour. N. Karas. il Travel 147: 42-7 My '77
Grapes of autumn. S. Aaron. il Sat R 4:32 Ag 6 '77
Great bargains of Bordeaux. R. Daly. il N Y Times Mag p98-112+ Mr 27 '77
Great wine at soda pop prices; rebottling wine; excerpt from The poorperson's guide to great cheap wines. J. Nelson. il Sat Eve Post 249: 10+ D '77
Have a wine & cheese tasting party. il Good H 184:214 My '77
Independent woman's wine cellar; white wine. E. Greenberg and M. Greenberg. Harp Baz 110:137+ F '77
Insiders' drink. A. Gold and R. Fizdale. il Vogue 167:192-4 Ap '77
Instant expertise. D. Tobias. 80:29 Ap '77
Literary art of wine tasting. F. J. Prial. N Y Times Mag p40-1 S 4 '77
Madeira M'dear. F. J. Prial. il N Y Times Mag p 142-5 D 11 '77
Meal without wine is like a day without sunshine; therapeutic aspects. il Fam Health 9:38-9 Ja '77
Noble rot: a sweet smell of success; botrytised wines. F. J. Prial. N Y Times Mag p30-1 Jl 24 '77
Rare occasion; tasting at the Chateau Lafite-Rothschild. F. J. Prial. il N Y Times Mag p92-3 O 30 '77
Red, light & true. L. B. Downs. House B 119: 159+ My '77
Rioja wines: Spanish gold. C. Churchill. Am Home 80:15+ O '77
Seven great wines; California vintners. B. Ensrud. il Horizon 20:38-46 D '77
Sherry flip. E. Fried. il Sat R 5:28-9 O 29 '77
Simplified art of ordering wine. F. J. Prial. il N Y Times Mag p44-5 Jl 10 '77
Sip of softness; wines and aperitifs. D. Tobias. Am Home 80:32+ S '77
Sweet & low: good dessert wine buys. P. Quimme. House B 119:131+ O '77
Teach yourself wine. F. J. Prial. N Y Times Mag p82+ O 2 '77
To sip beside the sea; muscadet. F. J. Prial. N Y Times Mag p 128-9 O 16 '77
25 perfect picnic wines. P. Quimme. House B 119:81 Ag '77
Understanding sherry. J. Winslow. il Holiday 58:39 S '77
Velvety wines for dessert. B. J. Cutler. por maps House & Gard 150:110+ Ja '78
What's your wine IQ? R. J. Misch. House B 119:84+ N '77
When age counts; Rhône wines. F. J. Prial. il N Y Times Mag p70-1 S 18 '77
Wine: new panacea. M. Blume. Vogue 167:332-3 N '77
Wines, cheeses and fruit. il Ebony 32:114+ F '77
Wines to quench a summer thirst. J. Wilson. il House & Gard 149:102+ Ag '77
Wining alfresco; pick for picnicking; outdoor serving tips. D. Tobias. il Am Home 80:7 Jl '77
Wining with dining; wines for Thanksgiving. A. Fraser. Mademoiselle 83:62+ N '77
Yuletide wines. C. Churchill. il Am Home 80:71-2+ D '77
See also
Champagne
Viticulture

Biblical teaching

Did Jesus drink wine? Time 109:58 Ja 24 '77

Labeling

Rothschild, tapestry, Mouton, and Picasso. S. Drake. il Holiday 58:48-9+ Ja '77
Wine and spirit labels in Harvey's Wine Museum. J. Banister. il Antiques 112:278-81 Ag '77

WINE cellars
Cave at the club; wine cellar at the 21 Club. F. J. Prial. il N Y Times Mag p28-9 D 25 '77
His wine cellar has simple built-in cooling. il Sunset 158:143 Mr '77

WINE cocktails. See Cocktails

WINE festivals. See Festivals

WINE glasses. See Glassware

WINE in religion, folklore, etc.
See also
Wine—Biblical teaching

WINE industry
Building a vineyard in Rhode Island wine country; Sakonnet Vineyard. R. Vaughan. il pors Horticulture 55:20-4+ S '77
California or bust. N. Hazelton. il Nat R 29: 395-6 Ap 1 '77
Grape escape. S. C. Cowley and others. il Newsweek 90:109 O 17 '77
Happy ending in the vineyards; R. D. Strong of Sonoma Vineyards. F. J. Prial. il por N Y Times Mag p61-2 Ag 21 '77
Napa revisited: Freemark Abbey. N. Hazelton. il Nat R 29:275-6 Mr 4 '77
New York state wine; new industry trends. S. Oddo. map House & Gard 149:184+ My '77
Protecting a good name; Walter Taylor of Bully Hill Vineyards vs Taylor Wine Company, New York. il Time 110:89+ O 10 '77
Seven great wines; California vintners. B. Ensrud. il Horizon 20:38-46 D '77
Shaking California's throne. il Time 110:106-7+ N 21 '77
See also
Wineries

France

Rothschild, tapestry, Mouton, and Picasso. S. Drake. il Holiday 58:48-9+ Ja '77
St Emilion: warm, open and easy to like. F. J. Prial. il N Y Times Mag p45-7 Ag 7 '77

WINE museums. See Museums

WINE punch. See Punch (beverage)

WINE racks
Wine rack has sturdy good looks, holds 12 cases. il Sunset 159:104 S '77

WINE-tasting cruises. See Cruising

WINE-tasting parties. See Entertaining

WINEGARDNER, Roy E.
Profits are back, but the thrill is gone. por Forbes 120:56 D 15 '77

WINERIES
Bottling poetry in Napa Valley. J. G. Dunne. Esquire 87:8+ F '77
Champagne touring in Napa. il Sunset 159:58+ O '77
Heart of the Burgundy country. il map Sunset 158:42 Mr '77
New wines of the West; wineries in Oregon and Washington. J. Wilson. map House & Gard 149:170+ Ap '77
New York state wine; new industry trends. S. Oddo. map House & Gard 149:184+ My '77
Sherry sampling in Spain's Jerez. il map Sunset 159:30+ S '77

WINFIELD, Darrell
Marlboro man. M. Smith. il pors Sports Illus 46:58-62+ Ja 17 '77 *

WINFREE, Arthur T.
Phase control of neural pacemakers. bibl il Science 197:761-3 Ag 19 '77 *

WINFREY, Carey
In search of Bella Abzug. il pors N Y Times Mag p 14-16+ Ag 21 '77

WING, Charles G.
Insulating shutters that work. il Org Gard & Farm 24:121-5 N '77

WING shooting. See Game bird shooting

WINGATE, Adina
Copper, Brass, and Bronze. il Craft Horiz 37:16-19 Ag '77

WINGED fruit. See Fruit

WINGERSON, Lois
Eye-safety guide. Harp Baz 110:113+ Ag '77
Psychoactive drugs: do you need them? Harp Baz 110:231+ S '77

WINGS, Airplane. See Airplanes—Wings

WINKLER, Henry
Chicken soup and fear; interview, ed by J. Kirgo. il pors Sat Eve Post 249:58-9+ S '77
Fonzie; interview, ed by E. Kaye. pors Ladies Home J 94:52+ Mr '77
Phasing out the Fonz; interview, ed by E. Miller. il pors Seventeen 36:140-1+ O '77

about

Fooling around with the Fonz. A. L. Ball. il por Redbook 148:107+ Mr '77 *

WINKLER, Karen L.
Sweeping revision of the copyright law. Educ Digest 42:17-19 Ja '77

WINKLER, Win Ann
Terpsichore and Artemis. il Dance Mag 51:77-8 N '77

WINKS, Robin W.
Mysteries. New Repub 176:35-7 Je 11; 177:37-9 S 24; 34-7 N 26 '77

WINN, Dilys
Studies, both frivolous and serious, unravel clues to mysteries in Workman's Murder ink; interview, ed by R. Dahlin. Pub W 212:49 Jl 4 '77

WINN, Marie
Hazards of the plug-in drug; excerpt from The plug-in drug. Parents Mag 52:38+ Je '77
Plug-in drug. Harp Baz 110:90+ Jl '77
Plug-in drug; excerpt. Sat Eve Post 249:40-1+ N '77

about

Forget the message, worry about the medium. R. A. Blake. America 136:276-7 Mr 26 '77 *

WINNIPEG, Manitoba
Going places, finding things in Canada. S. Oddo. il House & Gard 149:74+ Je '77

WINNIPEG Contemporary Dancers. See Dance companies

WINOGRAND, Garry
Medium is the message. D. Davis. il por Newsweek 90:106+ N 7 '77 *
Winogrand's theater of quick takes. T. Papageorge. il N Y Times Mag p57-8+ O 16 '77 *

WINOKUR, Paula
(ed) See Staffel, R. Light of Rudolph Staffel

WINOKUR, Robert
Interview with Robert Winokur; ed by C. Sewalt. il pors Ceram Mo 25:31-5 S '77
(ed) See Staffel, R. Light of Rudolph Staffel

WINONA, Lake (Minnesota)
Cleanup of Lake Winona. R. M. Welch. il map Parks & Rec 12:39-41 My '77

WINPISINGER, William W.
Wimpy takes command. por Time 110:51-2 Jl 11 '77 *
Winpisinger: forging a new left coalition. por Bus W p78-9 F 21 '77 *

WINSLOW, Joyce
Bermuda angle. il Sat Eve Post 249:90-3+ O '77
Love letter to Andalusia. il Holiday 58:36-8+ S '77
Understanding sherry. il Holiday 58:39 S '77
(ed) See Grace Patricia, Princess Grace's Monaco

WINSON, Jonathan, and Abzug, C.
Gating of neuronal transmission in the hippocampus: efficacy of transmission varies with behavioral state. bibl il Science 196:1223-5 Je 10 '77

WINSOR, Jackie
Winsor-built. R. Smith. il Art in Am 65:118-20 Ja '77 *

WINSTON, Harry
Harry Winston: ace of diamonds. J. Stewart-Gordon. il Read Digest 112:183-4+ Ja '78 *

WINSTON, Stephanie
Get smart. J. S. King. Am Home 80:38+ My '77 *

WINSTON-SALEM, N.C.
Culture: a miracle in Carolina. il U.S. News 83:84-5 D 26 '77

Hotels, restaurants, etc

Whiling away the evenings in Winston-Salem. E. Faltermayer. il Fortune 96:157-8 Jl '77

WINSTONATIONALS (drag race) See Drag racing

WINTER, Bernard
Health care: the problem is profits. Progressive 41:16-19 O '77

WINTER, Colin O'Brien, Bp
Namibia: conscience and independence. W. P. Wood. Chr Cent 94:529-31 Je 1 '77 *

WINTER, Kamil
Christianity in Communist Czechoslovakia. Chr Cent 94:919-20 O 12 '77

WINTER, Robert
Second thoughts on the performance of Beethoven's trills. bibl f il Mus Q 63:483-504 O '77

WINTER, Ruth
Arthritis update. Ladies Home J 94:76+ Mr '77

WINTER
Betwixt and between season; excerpt from Tavern lamps are burning. R. F. Hall. il Conservationist 31:48 N '76
Cold; Maine winters. J. N. Cole. il N Y Times Mag p71 Ja 30 '77; Same abr. with title Cold comforts. il Read Digest 112:157-60 Ja '78
How do they make it through the winter? A. LaBastille. il Nat Wildlife 16:20-5 D '77
1976-77 winter in Alaska: unsettled and exceptionally mild. T. F. Fathauer. il maps Weatherwise 30:76-9 Ap '77
Our changing weather. G. Alexander. il maps Pop Sci 211:100-3+ O '77
Sketch book at a touch of winter. H. W. Trimm. il Conservationist 31:Inside back cover N '77
Sketch book glimpse at late winter. H. W. Trimm. il Conservationist 31:Inside back cover Ja '77
Wild winter of 1976-77 in New York State. R. A. Wrightson. il Weatherwise 30:70-5 Ap '77
Wings of winter. H. Borland. Progressive 41:49-50 Mr '77
Winter smells, winter dreams. J. Taylor. il Conservationist 32:48 N '77

See also
Cold weather
Snow
Snowstorms

Anecdotes, facetiae, satire, etc.

Winter—up close and personal. D. Menaker. New Yorker 53:36-8 O 31 '77

WINTER backpacking. See Backpacks and backpacking

WINTER boating. See Boats and boating

WINTER camping. See Camping

WINTER clothing. See Clothing, Cold weather

WINTER conditioning of automobiles. See Automobiles—Maintenance and repair

WINTER driving. See Automobile driving

WINTER fishing. See Fishing, Winter

WINTER flying. See Aviation—Winter flying

WINTER HAVEN, Fla.
Retired mayor sparkplugs sewage treatment change. il Am City & County 92:77 S '77

WINTER hiking. See Hiking

WINTER landscape painting. See Landscape painting

WINTER photography. See Photography—Cold weather conditions

WINTER proofing of houses. See Houses—Maintenance and repair

WINTER resorts
Abominable snow suits; claims for ski injuries. il Time 111:60-1 Ja 16 '78
Lift-line express. C. Breslin. il Esquire 87:90-3 F '77
New peak at Timberline. R. Griffin. il Craft Horiz 37:14-17 O '77
Ski season is off to a snowy start. il Bus W p59 D 12 '77
10 best ski resorts in the world. A. Rand. il Harp Baz 111:8+ D '77

See also
Aspen, Colo.
Squaw Valley, Calif.
Sun Valley, Idaho

WINTER sports

See also
Curling (sports)
Ice boats and ice boating
Skating
Ski racing
Skis and skiing
Snowmobiles and snowmobiling

WINTER survival. See Wilderness survival
WINTER vacations. See Vacations
WINTERACEAE
Compound ovary with open carpels in winteraceae (magnoliales) evolutionary implications. J.-F. Leroy. bibl il Science 196:977-8 My 27 '77
WINTERNATIONALS (drag race) See Drag racing
WINTERS, Anne
Demolition crane; Hall of armor; Still life with pots; Readings in the navigators; poems. Poetry 130:280-4 Ag '77
WINTERS & Company, Inc. See Investment advisers
WINTERTHUR Museum. See Henry Francis du Pont Winterthur Museum
WINTHER, Barbara
Good deeds of Pacca; dramatization of Indian folk tale. Plays 37:14, 56-62 D '77
Ijapa, the tortoise; dramatization of Nigerian tale. Plays 37:57-64 O '77
Wise man of Baghdad; dramatization of Middle Eastern folk tales. Plays 36:44-50 My '77
WINTNER, Claude E. See Eschenmoser, A. jt auth
WINWOOD, Steve
Former Traffic leader travels the solo route. S. Sutherland. por Hi Fi 27:140 S '77 *
WIONCZEK, Miguel S.
Science and technology strategy for the LDC's. Science 196:837 My 20 '77
Some questions for the world jamboree. il Bull Atom Sci 33:29-32 D '77
WIRE
See also
Barbed wire
Electric wire and wiring
WIRE rope. See Rope
WIRE-wrapping tools. See Tools
WIREMAN, Billy O.
1976 declaration of education; address, November 4, 1976. Vital Speeches 43:220-3 Ja 15 '77
WIRETAPPING
Another Panama issue: bugging charges against U.S. U.S. News 83:30 O 10 '77
Bugs in the system; Soviet interception of US phone calls. K. Keegan. New Repub 177:14-15 Ag 6 '77
Business stake in Soviet snooping; phone message interceptions. Bus W p57-8 D 12 '77
Clay feet in Connecticut; case of police chief J. F. Ahern, New Haven. K. McAuliffe. Progressive 41:43-4 N '77
Notes and comment; case of M. Halperin. New Yorker 53:19-21 Ag 22 '77
Telecommunications eavesdropping by NSA on private messages alleged. D. Shapley. Science 197:1061-4 S 9 '77
Vive la Watergaffe! court ruling on French government's wiretapping of Le Canard enchaîné's newspaper offices. Time 109:44 Ja 24 '77
WIRING, Electric. See Electric wire and wiring
WIRSEN, Carl O. See Jannasch, H. W. jt auth
WIRT, Frederick M.
Politics without civics. bibl il Society 14:46-8 My '77
WIRT, Sherwood Eliot
Destination heaven. il Chr Today 21:10-12 Ag 12 '77
WIRTH, Timothy E.
Excerpts from debate on the Federal Elections Campaign Act Amendments, April 1, 1976. Cong Digest 56:86+ Mr '77
WIRTSHAFTER, David, and Davis, J. D.
Body weight: reduction by long-term glycerol treatment. bibl il Science 198:1271-4 D 23 '77
WIRTZ, William Willard
National policy of human resource economics; excerpts from address. por Intellect 106:102 S '77
Spend 2 to 4 billions on a youth-service program; interview. il por U.S. News 82:57-8 F 21 '77
WIRWAHN, Gene
Make motorcyclists wear helmets? interview. il pors U.S. News 83:39-40 Jl '77
WISCONSIN
How absurd federal rules victimize the state. P. J. Lucey. por Nations Bus 65:43-6 My '77
See also
Agriculture—Wisconsin
Camps—Wisconsin
Crime and criminals—Wisconsin
Criminal justice, Administration of—Wisconsin
Dells of the Wisconsin (valley)
Education—Wisconsin
Express highways—Wisconsin
Land—Wisconsin
Libraries—Wisconsin
Opera—Wisconsin
St Croix National Scenic Riverway
Unemployment—Wisconsin
Wildlife sanctuaries—Wisconsin

Description and travel
On the trail of Wisconsin's Ice Age. A. LaBastille. il pors map Nat Geog 152:182-205 Ag '77
Wisconsin: land of the gathering waters. L. Van Goethem. il map Read Digest 111:208-12+ O '77

Religious institutions and affairs
People's parish; Community of the Living Spirit, Waukesha, Wis. M. True. Commonweal 104:496-9 Ag 5 '77; Discussion. 104:610-11+ S 30 '77
WISCONSIN Steel-Envirodyne, Inc merger. See Corporations—Acquisitions and mergers
WISCONSIN. University

Whitewater campus
Mother and daughter back in school; University of Wisconsin-Whitewater's Live In and Learn Program. il Aging 266:6 D '76
WISE, Herbert H. See Friedman-Weiss, J. jt auth
WISE, John
Balloon to cross the ocean in 1859: the Atlantic. D. M. Ludlum. il por Weatherwise 30:154-7 Ag '77 *
WISE, Robert E. Jr
After the strip floods. il Nation 225:18-20 Jl 2 '77
WISE, Sue
Watercolor page; with biographical sketch. il por Am Artist 41:72-5+ F '77
WISE man of Baghdad; drama. See Winther, B.
WISEBERG, Laurie S. and Scoble, H. M.
Human rights as an International League bibl il Society 15:71-5 N '77
WISEMAN, Carter
Racquets reach out. il Horizon 20:82-7 S '77
Recycling the city. il Horizon 21:43-9 Ja '78
WISEMAN, Frederick
Watching Wiseman watch. D. Eames. il por N Y Times Mag p96-102+ O 2 '77 *
WISHART, Lynn
(ed) Reference books of 1976. il por Lib J 102:873-7 Ap 15 '77
WISHART, Ronald S.
Too precious to burn. Conservationist 31:23 N '76
WISSE, Ruth R.
In praise of Chaim Grade. Commentary 63:70-3 Ap '77
—and Cotler, Irwin
Quebec's Jews: caught in the middle. Commentary 64:55-9 S '77
WIT and humor. See Humor
WITCHCRAFT
Art of dreaming; excerpt from The second ring of power. C. Castaneda. il Psychol Today 11:34-6+ D '77
Don Juan's power trip. S. Keen. il por Psychol Today 11:40-2+ D '77
Fertility rites and sorcery in a New Guinea village. G. Gillison. il map Nat Geog 152:124-46 Jl '77
See also
Evil eye
WITCOVER, Jules
Last day of the RFK campaign; interview, ed by L. R. Obst. il por N Y Times Mag p85+ N 13 '77
WITELSON, Sandra F.
Developmental dyslexia: two right hemispheres and none left. bibl Science 195:309-11 Ja 21 '77
about
Dyslexia: a hemispheric explanation. Sci N 111:55 Ja 22 '77 *
WITHERILL, Bob
Your marine operator. Yachting 142:141-2 Jl '77
WITKE, Roxane
Comrade Chiang Ch'ing tells her story; excerpts from Comrade Chiang Ch'ing. il pors Time 109:46-8+ Mr 21 '77
WITKIEWICZ, Stanislaw I.
Crazy locomotive. Review
Nation 224:190 F 12 '77 *
WITNESS bearing (Christianity)
Bearing witness and human rights. J. P. Dobel. Chr Cent 94:751-3 Ag 31 '77
Call the next witness; interviews with celebrities. il Sat Eve Post 249:44+ Ap '77
Infinitive: to witness. D. K. Mano. il Nat R 29:274-5 Mr 4 '77
Should there be a Christian witness to the Jews? I. C. Rottenberg. il Chr Cent 94:352-6 Ap 13 '77; Discussion. 94:631-2 Jl 6 '77
There's a bit of the Pharisee in us all; excerpt from Why not the best? J. Carter. il por Sat Eve Post 249:36+ Ap '77
WITNESS Security Program. See United States—Justice, Department of
WITNESSES
Bystanders' creed: don't meddle in family fights; study by R. Lance Shotland and Margret K. Straw. J. Gaylin. il Psychol Today 10:29-30 F '77
Disappearing witnesses; Justice Department Witness Security Program. il Time 110:41-2 S 12 '77

WITNESSES—*Continued*
Juvenile justice; children on the witness stand at the Al Junior Lewis murder trial in Detroit. D. A. Williams and J. C. Jones. il Newsweek 89:22 Je 27 '77
Mobilizing eyewitnesses to crime: the use of radios and rewards. J. P. Levine. bibl il Intellect 105:254-7 F '77
Perils of doing your duty; testimony of B. Lowe in the Harry Aleman trial. il Time 109:13-14 Je 6 '77
Taking public hearings public; proposed bill to finance participation in hearings at all federal agencies. Bus W p43-4 Mr 7 '77
See also
Crime and criminals—Identification

WITT, Judy
Beyond the cities. il MH 60:4-6 Wint '77

WITT, Steven
Reviews. S. Banes. Dance Mag 51:33-4 Ap '77 *

WITTCOFF, Harold
I have to spend the rest of my life in the future. il por bibl Chemistry 50:8-12 Mr '77

WITTEVEEN, Hendrikus Johannes
Lender of last resort. il por Time 110:52-3 Ag 15 '77 *
Will the IMF let the Saudis buy in? B. Nussbaum. por Bus W p 154 My 16 '77 *

WITTMANN, Otto
Mission of discovery. F. Schulze. il por Art N 76:66-7 Ap '77 *

WITZENBURG, Gary
Designer's designer. il pors Motor T 29:72-4+ Jl '77
Driving impression. il Motor T 29:57-8 S '77
Holley's system. il Motor T 29:73-4+ N '77

WIVES
Can a woman become liberated—and stay married? A. Silberman. Read Digest 111:71-4 Ag '77
Is retirement what your wife makes it? M. G. Stoddard. Ret Liv 17:38 Ap '77
See also
Divorce
Farmers wives
Housewives
Husbands
Marriage
Marriage counseling
Married women
Politicians wives
Presidents—United States—Wives
Public officers—Wives
Separation (law)
Wife beating

Employment

See Married women—Employment

WIXON, Vincent, and Stone, Pat
Getting it out, getting it down: adapting Zoellner's talk-write. bibl f il Engl J 66:70-3 S '77

WIZARD of whiz-bang; drama. See Parsons, N.

WODEHOUSE, Sir Pelham Grenville
Bit of luck for Mabel; story. Sat Eve Post 249:36-7 Mr '77

WODINSKY, Jerome
Hormonal inhibition of feeding and death in octopus: control by optic gland secretion. bibl il Science 198:948-51 D 2 '77
about
Gland dictates death to aging octopus. il Sci N 112:375 D 3 '77 *

WOELFEL, James W.
Listening to B. F. Skinner. Chr Cent 94:1112-16 N 30 '77

WOHL, Lisa Cronin
Equal Credit Opportunity Act: some good news, some not so good. Ms 5:95-7 Mr '77
Mormon connection? The defeat of the ERA in Nevada. Ms 6:68-70+ Jl '77

WOIWODE, Larry
Horses; poem. Atlantic 240:63 N '77
Quail; How it came; Rib; poems; excerpt from Even tide. Harpers 255:80 Ag '77

WOJNILOWER, Albert M.
Bonds: a brighter outlook for longer term investors; interview. por U.S. News 83:52-3 D 26 '77

WOLD, Finn. See Uy, R. jt auth

WOLF, Anton
Madame Jumel. Review
Hi Fi il 27:MA18-19 Ap '77 *

WOLF, Hugo
Songs, vol. 3; Deutsche Grammophon recording. D. Hamilton. Hi Fi 27:103-4+ D '77 *

WOLF, Leonard
Congratulations, you're an epileptic! Psychol Today 11:94+ D '77

WOLF, Markus
Mischa meets his match. il por Time 110:37-8 Jl 25 '77 *

WOLF, Virginia
Cooperative buying—do you save? Camp Mag 49:18-19 Mr '77

WOLF, William B.
International business in Latin America; address, March 1, 1977. Vital Speeches 43:443-7 My 1 '77

WOLF-FERRARI, Ermanno
I quattro rusteghi. Reviews
Hi Fi 27:MA30-2 Jl '77 *
New Yorker 53:106+ Mr 28 '77 *
Il segreto di Susanna. R. V. Lucano. il Am Rec G 40:45-6 My '77 *

WOLF Trap Farm Park for the Performing Arts
Vienna: Busoni's Doktor Faust. R. Jacobson. il Opera N 42:62 O '77
Wolf Trap: Faust & L'Egisto. Hi Fi 27:MA19-20 D '77

WOLFBEIN, Seymour L.
We need a closer tie between education, work; interview. por U.S. News 82:58 F 21 '77

WOLFE, Alan
Carter's Russia watchers. Nation 225:712-15 D 31 '77
Image is substance is image. Nation 224:778-81 Je 25 '77
Obsession with nuclear strategy. Nation 225:265-8 S 24 '77

WOLFE, Bertram David
Obituary
Nat R 29:375 Ap 1 '77. P. P. Witonski

WOLFE, Cary
Dulling the democratic mind. Clearing H 51:4 S '77

WOLFE, Denny T. Jr
Scholar and the pedagogue: different breeds of humanists. Clearing H 50:206-8 Ja '77
Trends, titles, taxonomies—alas! Clearing H 50:236 F '77

WOLFE, Leonhard S. and others
Identification of retinoyl complexes as the autofluorescent component of the neuronal storage material in Batten disease. bibl il Science 195:1360-2; 198:527-8 Mr 25, N 4 '77

WOLFE, Linda
Unfaithful husband. Ladies Home J 94:69+ Ag '77

WOLFE, Sidney M.
Is law on food additives too strict? interview. por U.S. News 82:25-6 My 30 '77

WOLFE, Stephen J. See Bartley, L. W. jt auth

WOLFE, Thomas K.
In our time. il Harpers 255:79 O '77; 256:76 Ja '78
about
Intelligent co-ed's guide to Tom Wolfe. C. Williamson, Jr. por Nat R 29:212+ F 18 '77 *

WOLFE, Tom. See Wolfe, T. K.

WOLFF, Anthony
Of rats and men. N Y Times Mag p88+ My 15 '77
World progress report. See occasional issues of Saturday review

WOLFF, Bob
Here's how to call the shots. W. Leggett. por Sports Illus 46:46 F 28 '77 *

WOLFF, Christian
Lines; Accompaniments. L. Gerber. Am Rec G 40:44 N '76 *

WOLFF, Cynthia Griffin
Woman's place. . .il Sat R 4:8-9 Je 25 '77

WOLFF, Geoffrey
Illuminated history of a model friendship. il Esquire 87:87-9+ My '77
Outdoors. il Esquire 87:48+ Ap '77

WOLFF, Pat
Free-lancing for the religious markets. Writer 90:27-9+ D '77

WOLFF, Ruth
We open in Florence. il por N Y Times Mag p50-2+ D 4 '77

WOLFF, Ursula
Algeria's unearthly cities. il Travel 147:54-9+ F '77

WOLFF, Virginia Euwer
About the gold wire bracelet; story. Seventeen 36:154-5 S '77
Birthday; story. il Ladies Home J 94:66 Ap '77

WOLFGANG, Marvin E.
(ed) Africa in transition. bibl f Ann Am Acad 432:1-119 Jl '77

WOLKOMIR, Richard
Biometeorology seeks clues to health. il Sci Digest 82:29-32 Ag '77

WOLL, Peter. See Jones, R. jt auth

WOLLETT, Bill. See Wollett, M. jt auth

WOLLETT, Mary, and Wollett, Bill
American historical glass. See issues of Hobbies

WOLLHEIM, Donald A.
Science fiction proves to be no fantasy for DAW books, five years old this month; interview, ed by R. Dahlin. il Pub W 211:52 Ap 11 '77

WOLLIN, Lucy
How to make something from nothing. il por Am Lib 8:573 N '77

WOLLNER, Ivan Bodis-. See Bodis-Wollner, I.

WOLMAN, M. Gordon
Interdisciplinary education: a continuing experiment. bibl Science 198:800-4 N 25 '77

WOLMAN, William
Economic diary. See occasional issues of Business week

WOLPER, Roy S.
On writing well. Nation 224:345-6 Mr 19 '77

WOLTERS, Deborah
They do it all for me. Progressive 41:32 Mr '77

WOLTERS, Richard
Pictures. See issues of Writer's digest

WOLVES
Big howl in Minnesota; timber wolf controversy. B. Gilbert. il Sports Illus 46:75-7 My 2 '77
Carolina haven for red wolf; introduction in Cape Romain National Wildlife Refuge. P. Laurie. Audubon 79:152 Ja '77
Courage and the art of wolf maintenance; work of J. Lynch. J. March. il pors Audubon 79:80-2+ N '77
Nobody's neutral about wolves; symposium, ed by B. Vogt. il Nat Wildlife 15:4-13 Ag '77
Where can the wolf survive? L. D. Mech. il map Nat Geog 152:518-37 O '77
Wolf-pack buffer zones as prey reservoirs. L. D. Mech. bibl Science 198:320-1 O 21 '77
Wolf that lost its genes; red wolves. J. H. Shaw and P. A. Jordan. il Natur Hist 86:80-8 bibl(p 111) D '77

Photographs

Wolfpack! attack on moose. J. S. Crawford. il Outdoor Life 159:64-5 Ap '77

WOLYNSKI, Mara
Personal: alone is best. Vogue 167:183-4+ N '77
Thirty: not a dirty word anymore. Vogue 167:150+ O '77

WOMAN. See Women

WOMAN suffrage

United States

Burning question circa 1869: Is there such a thing as sex? Ms 6:21 S '77

WOMEN
Between us. L. Davis. See issues of Vogue
Lost women. See occasional issues of Ms.
Ms. gazette: news from all over; ed by S Braudy and M. Thom. See issues of Ms.
Notes from abroad (cont) Ms 5:112+ Ap; 6:12-15 Ag '77
On being a woman. J. Brothers. See issues of Good housekeeping
To be a woman (cont) Redbook 148:64+ F; 72+ Mr; 82+ Ap; 149:57-64 My '77
Wonderful world of women; excerpt from Good housekeeping woman's almanac. il Good H 185:248-9 O '77
See also
Alcohol and women
Beauty, Personal
Black women
Christmas gifts for women
Education of women
Feminism
Great men and women
Ordination of women
Photography of women
Sex differences
Single women
United Nations Decade for Women
Widows
Wives
Young women

Anatomy and physiology

Are women stronger than men? J. Ullyot. Harp Baz 110:89+ My '77
Top to toe; body proportion. il Mademoiselle 83:144-5 My '77
Why women don't like their bodies; symposium. il Ms 6:47-55+ S '77
See also
Menstruation

Attitudes

Do I want a baby? discussion; comp by C. Dreifus. il McCalls 105:203+ N '77
Experts—and the American woman; special section. il Vogue 167:114-18+ Je '77
See also
Black women—Attitudes

Clothing and dress

See Clothing and dress

Conferences

Abortion, equal rights, and Robert's rules of order; National Women's Conference. J. J. Kilpatrick. Nat R 29:1481-5 D 23 '77
Bella Abzug and the future of American women; National Women's Conference, interview, ed by D. Davis. B. Abzug. por Am Home 80:88-9 N '77
Between the lines; National Women's Conference. S. Chassler. Redbook 150:22 N '77
Can women's lib sell its program? National Women's Conference in Houston. il U.S. News 83:31 D 5 '77
Conference focuses on older women; Maturing Women in America Today, conference held in Dallas. il Aging 275:18-22 S '77
Fearful and the innocent; National Women's Conference and its counterconvention in Houston. M. French. il Horizon 21:30-3 Ja '78
Feminist power: the battle of Houston; Pro-Life, Pro-Family Coalition rally. R. Garlock. il Chr Today 22:38-40 D 30 '77
Fireworks ahead among the majority sex; upcoming Houston conference. J. J. Kilpatrick. Nations Bus 65:13-14 S '77
Houston retrospective; National Women's Conference. A. McCarthy. Commonweal 105:8-12 Ja 6 '78
Memo for the first National Women's Convention: countdown to Houston. L. Van Gelder. il Ms 6:60-2+ N '77
Synthetic oracle. Nat R 29:1407 D 9 '77
That week in Houston; National Women's Conference. A. T. Fleming. il N Y Times Mag p 10-13+ D 25 '77
What American women want; National Women's Conference in Houston. L. K. Howe. McCalls 105:198+ N '77
What next for U.S. women; National Women's Conference 1977. il Time 110:18-22+ D 5 '77
Why women's lib is in trouble. il U.S. News 83:29-32 N 28 '77
With the women at Houston: feminism as national politics. L. Komisar. Nation 225:624-7 D 10 '77
Women at Houston; National Women's Conference. B. Friedan. New Repub 177:15-19 D 10 '77
Women march on Houston. il Time 110:12-14 N 28 '77
Women of Congress speak out; National Women's Conference. il Good H 185:26+ N '77
Women vs. women; state meetings in preparation for Houston conference. S. Fraker and others. il Newsweek 90:34-5+ Jl 25 '77
Women's agenda at Houston. M. Burke. America 137:325-7 N 12 '77
Women's agenda; National Women's Conference in Houston. M. Sheils and others. il Newsweek 90:57+ N 28 '77
Womens' work: making a difference; National Women's Conference. J. C. Lyles. Chr Cent 94:1131-3 D 7 '77

Crime

Increase of female criminals. R. D. Wright and S. E. Wright. Intellect 106:11-12 Jl '77
See also
Girls, Delinquent

Defense

See Self defense for women

Diseases

Facial pain; therapy for women practiced by J. J. Marbach. M. Covell. Vogue 167:34+ Je '77
Your health risks at 30. E. M. Whelan. Harp Baz 110:132-3+ O '77
See also
Anorexia nervosa
Endometriosis
Vaginitis

Economic conditions

Equality begins at home. C. B. Luce. por Sat Eve Post 249:16-17+ O '77
Help wanted: news and cues for working mothers. Parents Mag 52:38-9 Ap '77
Is his money your money too? S. W. Olds. il Redbook 149:120+ S '77
Money: how 35,000 women spend, save and s-t-r-e-t-c-h it; responses to questionnaire. V. Cadden. il McCalls 104:75-80 S '77
Money: the subject harder to talk about than sex. C. Tavris. Ms 6:63-7 N '77
Phallic imperialism: why economic recovery will not work for us. A. Dworkin. Ms 5:101-2+ D '76; Correction 5:14 F '77
Tip sheet on Carter's welfare plan. N. Cornblath-Moshé and C. Burris. Ms 6:55-6+ Ja '78
Why women need insurance, too. R. Provost. Parents Mag 52:20+ Ap '77

Education

See Education of women

Employment

Developing an index to measure female labor force attachment. E. Maret-Havens. bibl il M Labor R 100:35-8 My '77
Dilemma of regulating reproductive risks; safeguarding women's rights and health. Bus W p76-7+ Ag 29 '77
Discrimination and your rights as a woman when you are looking for a job. M. P. Rowe. Parents Mag 52:34+ S '77
Female labor force participation: why projections have been too low. A. M. Sum. bibl il M Labor R 100:18-24 Jl '77
Help for the sexually harassed; the Alliance Against Sexual Coercion. R. Lefkowitz. Ms 6:49 N '77
How women just like you are getting better jobs: battling sex discrimination. M. S. Welch. il Redbook 149:121+ S '77
Labor force participation of married women, March 1976. B. L. Johnson and H. Hayghe. il M Labor R 100:32-6 Je '77
Labor force patterns of divorced and separated women. A. S. Grossman. bibl f il M Labor R 100:48-53 Ja '77

WOMEN—Employment—*Continued*
Occupational health v. civil rights for women. M. Cimons. New Repub 176:24 My 21 '77
Pink-collar workers. G. Steinem. Progressive 41: 54 My '77
Sexual harassment on the job: how to spot it and how to stop it. K. Lindsey. il Ms 6:47-8+ N '77
Shameful sex economics. P. A. Samuelson. Newsweek 90:96 D 12 '77
Sources of growth of the female labor force, 1971-75. R. E. Smith. il M Labor R 100:27-9 Ag '77
To guard or be guarded: discrimination against women as prison guards. M Labor R 100:70-1 O '77
Why help women into careers? address, October 11, 1977. B. A. Stead. Vital Speeches 44:157-60 D 15 '77
Why the Justice Department doesn't want you to know what happened between Otto Passman and Shirley Davis; charge of sex discrimination after dismissal of congressional aide. A. Northrop. il pors Ms 6:57-9 Ja '78
Women and occupational segregation. J. A. Schnepper. il Intellect 105:415-17 Je '77
Women on the job. See issues of McCall's
Women: their impact grows in the job market. il U.S. News 82:58-9 Je 6 '77
Work is not a four-letter word. F. Lear. por Newsweek 90:22-3 O 24 '77
Working woman. L. C. Pogrebin. Ladies Home J 94:46+ Ap; 24+ Je; 39+ Jl; 31-2+ S; 30+ N '77
Workplace hazards: no women need apply. D. McGhee. Progressive 41:20-5 O '77
See also
Black women—Employment
Married women—Employment
Women—Occupations
Women—Wages

Equal rights

Bringing sexual equality to insurance. Bus W p 116 My 23 '77
Equality begins at home. C. B. Luce. por Sat Eve Post 249:16-17+ O '77
Good-news fix. il Ms 6:87-90 Jl '77
Married women get a credit rating; new provisions of Equal Credit Opportunity Act. il Bus W p28-9+ Je 6 '77
Memo for the first National Women's Convention: countdown to Houston. L. Van Gelder. il Ms 6:60-2+ N '77
Ms. gazette: news from all over; ed by S. Braudy and M. Thom. See issues of Ms.
What do women want? address, June 4, 1977. C. Bird. Vital Speeches 43:598-602 Jl 15 '77; Same abr. il Sat Eve Post 249:48-9+ O '77
See also
Civil Rights Act of 1964
National Organization for Women
United Nations—Ad Hoc Group on Equal Rights for Women
United Nations—Commission on the Status of Women
Woman suffrage

Anecdotes, facetiae, satire, etc.

Don't stand for it. B. T. James. Nat R 29:1113 S 30 '77

Equal Rights Amendment (proposed)

See United States—Constitution—Amendments

Health and hygiene

Anemia epidemic; correcting iron deficiency in women by diet. J. C. Wang. Harp Baz 110: 91+ Je '77
Bazaar's action sports health guide; symposium. il Harp Baz 110:84-91+ My '77
Common-sense beauty guide: body. il Harp Baz 110:82-3 Je '77
Deadly new facts about women and smoking. M. L. Schildkraut. Good H 184:217-18 F '77
Health. A. Frank and S. Frank. See issues of Mademoiselle
30 ways to stay looking 30 forever; ideas of experts. il Harp Baz 110:138-41+ O '77
What women don't know about the medicines they take. A. Lake. McCalls 104:117+ Je '77
Woman, wife, mother. M. Newton. See occasional issues of Family health incorporating Today's health
Woman's body, woman's mind. See occasional issues of Ms.
Woman's body: your guide to good health. A. Machiaverna; P. Raber; L. Graeber. Seventeen 36:56-7 Mr '77
See also
Abortion—Psychological aspects
Beauty, Personal
Menopause
Menstruation
Pregnancy
Women—Diseases

Legal status, laws, etc.

Are state laws fair to married women? H. Hyans. McCalls 104:49 Mr '77
Help wanted: news and cues for working mothers. Parents Mag 52:38-9 Ap '77
Keeping women in their place: the male chauvinist Court. C. H. Arber. Nation 225: 654-7 D 17 '77
Legislation to watch—and work for—in the 95th Congress. S. Tenenbaum and J. A. Paulus. Ms 5:99-102 F '77
See also
Divorce
Girls, Delinquent
Woman suffrage
Women—Equal rights

Nutrition

Hungry women in America. L. Schwartz. il Ms 6:60-3+ O '77
Safest diet for every woman on the pill; nutritional side effects. F. J. Stare and E. M. Whelan. Harp Baz 110:120+ Ag '77
Woman doctor's diet; excerpt from A woman doctor's diet for women. B. Edelstein. il Ladies Home J 94:169-76 N '77

Occupations

America's new working woman; interviews. il Harp Baz 110:72-83 Ag '77
Be an apprentice; women and blue-collar jobs. L. Luciano. il Seventeen 36:55 Ap '77
Careers. A. M. Cunningham. Seventeen 36:72 O '77
8 women, 8 very different stories; interviews. ed by C. Calvert. il Mademoiselle 83:204+ Ap '77
Emerging woman. See issues of American home
Finding by niche—at 61. S. Gorsky. McCalls 104:56+ Mr '77
Four waitresses: their secret world. D. Gallagher. il Redbook 150:104+ N '77
How to get a blue collar. K. West. il Ms 5:62-5 My '77
Job strategies; 4 women who knew when to switch. bibl il Mademoiselle 83:150-1+ Mr '77
Jobscope. D. Duke. Mademoiselle 83:197 F; 12+ Ap '77
Mile's Barnard/USC work shops. il Mademoiselle 83:205 Je '77
Where the women workers are: the rise of the pink collar ghetto. G. Steinem. Ms 5:51-2 Mr '77
Work, women, and vocational education. C. H. Rieder. il Am Educ 13:27-30 Je '77
See also
Black women—Occupations
Business and professional women
Cottage industries
Housewives
Policewomen
Secretaries
Stunt women
also Women composers; Women executives and similar headings

Psychology

Bazaar's guide to psychotherapy; symposium. Harp Baz 110:228-33+ S '77
Bazaar's guide to success on the job; symposium. Harp Baz 110:84-9+ Ag '77
Clunks! J. O'Reilly. Ms 6:66-7 Jl '77
Did fear of success fail? L. Shapiro. Ms 6: 19 Jl '77
Does total woman add up? A. T. Fleming. Vogue 167:76 Ag '77
Four successful women talk about what they want—and can't have. M. Thomas and others. pors Redbook 148:92-3+ F '77
Gorging-purging syndrome; bulimarexia. M. Boskind-Lodahl and J. Sirlin. il Psychol Today 10:50-2+ Mr '77
Guidance centers: where women can find themselves. J. Wilkins. Good H 184:152+ Je '77
High cost of living safe; need for women to take risks. C. Calvert. Mademoiselle 83:189+ S '77
Housewife's disease; agoraphobia. B. Delatiner. Good H 184:84+ Je '77
How far up can a woman grow? What psychiatrists are telling women today. M. Webb and C. Safran. il Redbook 149:57-9 My '77
How liberated are you? quiz. J. Muchovej. il Am Home 80:57-8+ Mr '77
On being a woman. J. Brothers. See issues of Good housekeeping
Speaking of love. E. Jong. por Newsweek 89:11 F 21 '77
What do you want to be when your kids grow up? M. S. Miller. il Am Home 80:52-3+ S '77
What single women fear the most. J. Lynch. Harp Baz 110:93+ Mr '77
What to do when you're really depressed. A. Kosner. il McCalls 105:220-1+ N '77
Why a woman can't be a good boss—because no one will let you; group leadership studies by C. Beauvais and Z. Schachtel. Mademoiselle 83:120+ Jl '77
Why some women feel secure—and so many don't. B. G. Harrison. Redbook 148:48+ Mr '77

WOMEN—Psychology—*Continued*
Why women don't like their bodies; symposium. il Ms 6:47-55+ S '77
Women's dreams; ideas of R. Van deCastle. E. Howard. il Ladies Home J 94:50+ Je '77
You ought to be in pictures; rapist-con man O. E. Kendall's use of psychology in impersonation of R. Avedon. R. Rosenblatt. New Repub 177: 45-6 O 1 '77
See also
Abortion—Psychological aspects
Black women—Psychology
Femininity (psychology)

Religious life

Other dimension of your life: faith, values, morals; questionnaire. McCalls 105:27-8 Ja '78

Rights of women

See Women—Equal rights

Social and moral questions

How you think; symposium, ed by K. Lloyd. Vogue 167:128-9+ Je '77
Ladies of easy virtue. M. Springer. il Opera N 42:24+ D 24 '77
See also
Divorce
Misogyny
Prostitution

Volunteer service

See Volunteer service

Wages

Effect on women's earnings of enforcement in Title VII cases. A. H. Beller. bibl il M Labor R 100:56-7 Mr '77
See also
Wage differentials

Canada

See also
Canada—Royal Commission on the Status of Women in Canada

China

Tanka syndrome; effects of nursing babies on one side only; Chinese boat women study. J. Seligmann. il Newsweek 90:52 S 12 '77
Unbound: the women of new China. J. S. Tien. bibl il Intellect 106:37-41 Ag '77

Germany, West

Hit women; killing of J. Ponto. K. Willenson and T. Nater. il pors Newsweek 90:30 Ag 15 '77

Honduras

Honduras: did the Church start something it can't stop? Housewives Clubs. M. Peraza and H. Maurer. il Ms 6:12-15 Ag '77

India

Henna for happiness: India's mehndi art of symbols for all seasons. J. Saksena. il UNESCO Courier 30:18-22 F '77
Purdah in India: life behind the veil. D. W. Jacobson. il por map Nat Geog 152:270-86 Ag '77

Israel

Feminist goes to Israel. L. C. Pogrebin. il Ms 6:69-72+ O '77
Israeli women—more feminine than feminist. Y. Dayan. il por N Y Times Mag p78-80 F 13 '77

Mexico

Women in Mexican society. V. J. Meyer. bibl f Cur Hist 72:120-3+ Mr '77

Peru

History

Liberation à la limeña. V. C. Holmgren. il Américas 29:12-13 Je '77

Russia

Sexual equality and Soviet women. M. P. Sacks. bibl Society 14:48-51 Jl '77

Togo

Madame Mercedes-Benz: merchant of Togo. E. J. Kiers. il Ms 5:112+ Ap '77

United States

Bazaar's guide to women and power; special section. il Harp Baz 111:150-3+ N '77
Experts—and the American woman; special section. il Vogue 167:114-18+ Je '77
Making it happen in [state] F. Ruffin. il Redbook 149:81+ Ag; 82+ S '77
Making it happen in [state] J. L. Carter and F. E. Ruffin. il Redbook 149:70+ O; 150:66+ N; 43+ D '77
12 terrific women; winners of Mademoiselle awards. il Mademoiselle 83:144-7 F '77
Unsung heroine of the year; R. Dabertin. L. Hershey. il por Ladies Home J 94:4 Jl '77
Women in Passage II. il Good H 185:94+ Ag '77
Women of the year 1977. il Ladies Home J 94:75-7 Je '77
Women who rank highest. il U.S. News 82:38 Ap 18 '77
See also
Black women
Minority women
National Organization for Women
Woman suffrage—United States

History

See also
United States—History—Revolution, 1775-1783—Women

WOMEN, Aged. See Aged
WOMEN, Black. See Black women
WOMEN, Famous
Four successful women talk about what they want—and can't have. M. Thomas and others. pors Redbook 148:92-3+ F '77
Six decades of brilliant beauties. il Good H 184: 104-9 Ap '77
See also
Celebrities
WOMEN, Height of. See Stature
WOMEN, Jewish. See Jewish women
WOMEN, Tall. See Stature
WOMEN Against Violence Against Women (organization) See Womens clubs and societies
WOMEN air pilots
They take to the sky; Bessie Coleman Aviators. il Ebony 32:88-90+ My '77
WOMEN alcoholics. See Alcohol and women
WOMEN and alcohol. See Alcohol and women
WOMEN and men
At long last, love; older women with younger men. S. C. Cowley and L. Whitman. il Newsweek 90:80+ O 24 '77
Beyond the male myth; results of questionnaire; excerpt. A. Pietropinto and J. Simenauer. il Ladies Home J 94:126-7+ O '77; Same abr. with title How men really feel about sex and love. Read Digest 112:83-6 Ja '78
Black women/black men: has something gone wrong between them? interviews. A. Poussaint; A. A. Poussaint. il pors Ebony 32:160-2 Ag '77
Can men and women be friends? Answers from famous women and men; ed by L. Werner. il Redbook 149:31-2 O '77
Creative couples. il Am Home 80:34-7+ F '77
Does total woman add up? A. T. Fleming. Vogue 167:76 Ag '77
Flirting. A. Fleming and J. Mariani. il Redbook 148:22+ F '77
Flirting: why, when & how:
Instant intimacy. . .and safer than sex. C. Whelton. Mademoiselle 83:148+ Je '77
Verbal sex—the world's greatest noncontact sport. A. Gross. Mademoiselle 83:149+ Je '77
Gentlemen do prefer blondes. Intellect 106:8-9 Jl '77
How men adjust to a female boss. il Bus W p90+ S 5 '77
How to keep sex from screwing up a friendship; platonic relationships. S. Haller. Mademoiselle 83:118+ D '77
Intelligent woman's guide to sex. J. Coburn. See issues of Mademoiselle, August 1977-
Intelligent woman's guide to sex. K. Durbin. See issues of Mademoiselle to July '77
Keep him happy and you can keep him. L. Robinson. il Ebony 32:52-3+ Ag '77
Liberated love: unmarried, committed & free. G. Chipps. Harp Baz 110:120-1+ My '77
Many ways men pimp their women. N. Hare. il Ebony 33:145-6+ N '77
Marxism: its inadequacy as challenge to man-woman relationships. E. McMillan and E. Wymard. bibl il New Cath World 220:148-51 My '77
Men & women: towards a new eroticism. K. Durbin. Mademoiselle 83:156-7+ N '77
Men confide in wives but wives confide in their friends. Aging 268:17 F '77
Psychiatrist's notebook. T. I. Rubin. Ladies Home J 94:36+ O '77
Sex and tennis: mismatched pair. D. Sheanan. il Am Home 80:27 Ag '77
Sexual courtesy. K. Durbin. Mademoiselle 83: 147+ Mr '77
Southern men, Southern lies. G. Godwin. il Esquire 87:126-9 F '77
Time for working together. il Ebony 32:142-3 Ag '77
What do men really want from women? J. Leonard. Mademoiselle 83:94 Jl '77
What do our masochistic fantasies really mean? excerpt from Going too far: the personal chronicle of a feminist. R. Morgan. Ms 5:66-8+ Je '77
What makes a man a good lover? views of female celebrities, ed by E. Schoen. il Redbook 149:104-5+ Jl '77
When men have women bosses. L. C. Pogrebin. Ladies Home J 94:24+ My '77

WOMEN and men—*Continued*
Women and men; questions and answers. M. Lasswell and N. M. Lobsenz. McCalls 104:86+ Jl; 46+ Ag; 127+ O; 105:50+ N '77; 24+ Ja '78
You & he; symposium. il Mademoiselle 83:164-9+ S '77
Your friends, my friends, our friends. A. Gross. Redbook 149:76+ My '77
See also
Misogyny
Sex differences
Sex role

Anecdotes, facetiae, satire, etc.
Turning on. R. Baker. N Y Times Mag p 10 S 11 '77

WOMEN and outdoor life. See Outdoor life

WOMEN and politics
Meet Mrs America; B. Lowrey as average American voter. J. Miller. por New Repub 176:19-21 Ap 9 '77
Rating Carter; symposium. il por Ms 6:43-60+ Ja '78
See also
National Women's Political Caucus
Women in politics

WOMEN and religion
Brotherly love in today's Church. J. Chittister. il America 136:233-6 Mr 19 '77
Confusion among the faithful. Equal Rights Amendment. M. E. Marty. il Sat R 4:10-11 Je 25 '77
Dominance syndrome. J. M. Luecke. Chr Cent 94:405-7 Ap 27 '77
Lutheran women and creative worship. A. J. Lesher. il Chr Cent 94:697-8+ Ag 3 '77
Religion and an ERA battle in the Rockies; Broomfield, Colo. M. H. Rush. Chr Cent 94:164-5 F 23 '77
Saint and women's lib. J. Deedy. Commonweal 104:418 Jl 8 '77
65,000 women reveal: how religion affects health, happiness, sex and politics. C. Safran. il Redbook 148:126-7+ Ap '77
Women and world religions; conference in Bethesda, Md. R. A. Mitchell. America 136:123-5 F 12 '77
See also
Nuns
Ordination of women
Women—Religious life
Women clergy
Women priests

WOMEN and the church. See Women and religion

WOMEN and the United Nations. See United Nations—Womens participation

WOMEN architects
Architecture; Women in American Architecture: a History and Contemporary Perspective, exhibition. J. H. Kay. Nation 224:474-6 Ap 16 '77
Designing women; Brooklyn Museum exhibition, Women in American Architecture. D. Davis. il Newsweek 89:79-80 Mr 7 '77
Women design space; Brooklyn Museum exhibition, Women in American Architecture. il Ms 5:62-7 Mr '77

WOMEN artists
Art. See occasional issues of Ms.
Art isn't a man's world. W. Rodger. Hobbies 82:148-9 S '77
Canvassing our history; Women Artists: 1550-1950. M. Schapiro. il Ms 6:27-9 Jl '77
Five years of fresh A.I.R. M. Lebov. il Ms 6:22 Ja '78
Gallery (cont) il Ms 5:33-5 F; 43+ My '77
Majority rule; recent exhibitions in Los Angeles. M. Wortz. il Art N 76:92-3 Mr '77
Re-placing women artists in history; Women Artists: 1550-1950, exhibition. J. Butterfield. il Art N 76:40-4 Mr '77
Ruskin refuted; paintings by women artists exhibited at the Brooklyn Museum. R. Berenson. Nat R 29:1378-80 N 25 '77
Toward a complete history of art: Women Artists, 1550-1950. A. Frankenstein. il Art in Am 65:66-9 Mr '77
Why is there no recent women's art in the White House? B. Diamonstein. Art N 76:109-12 D '77
Woman as artist; Brooklyn Museum exhibition of paintings. G. Glueck. N Y Times Mag p48-50+ S 25 '77
Woman's art: it's the only goddam energy around; interview, ed by H. Lyons. M. Schapiro. il por Ms 6:40-3+ D '77
See also
Chicago, J.
Clive, W. J.
Eakins, S. M.
Graves, N.
Martin, M.
Morisot, B.
Phillips, L.
Rockburne, D.
Stettheimer, F.

WOMEN astronauts
Coming soon: women in space. J. Chan. il McCalls 104:56-7 Ap '77

WOMEN athletes
Bazaars top 10 women athletes. il Harp Baz 110:86-7 My '77
Equal play, equal pay; women's sports scholarships. il Newsweek 90:83 S 5 '77
Everyone can do it! marathon runners. J. Kaplan. Seventeen 36:66+ Mr '77
Fruitful past but a shaky future. B. Rhoden. il Ebony 32:60-2+ Ag '77
Jeers for cheerleaders. J. Kaplan. Seventeen 36:42 O '77
New beautiful people; beauty regimen of women athletes. A. Scharffenberger. il Am Home 80:56-8 Je '77
Outdoor look: three leading athletes talk about their beauty problems. il McCalls 104:134-7 Jl '77
Record breaking women. J. H. Douglas and J. A. Miller. il Sci N 112:172-4 S 10 '77
Sports. K. Gilman. See issues of Vogue
Sports. J. Kaplan. See occasional issues of Seventeen
Who's afraid of bulging biceps? A call to arms for women athletes. C. McCall. il Ms 5:26+ My '77
See also
Sports for women
also names of women athletes, e.g. V. Vodon

WOMEN authors
Being a woman. E. Jong. Vogue 167:158+ Mr '77
Does genius have a gender? C. Ozick and J. Burroway. il pors Ms 6:56-7+ D '77
What your favorite authors are working on; comp by A. K. Turner. il Ms 6:58-9+ D '77
Writer's daughter. J. Delton. Seventeen 36:86 Ag '77
See also
O'Connor, F.
Potter, B.
Schreiner, O.
Taylor, M. D.
Weingarten, V.
Women poets

WOMEN automobile racing drivers. See Automobile racing drivers

WOMEN bankers
See also
National Association of Bank Women

WOMEN basketball coaches. See Basketball coaches

WOMEN blue collar workers. See Women—Occupations

WOMEN bums. See Tramps

WOMEN cadets
How women are faring at the Air Academy. G. Lichtenstein. il N Y Times Mag p 104-6+ S 11 '77
Mom, the cadet; Air Force Academy's ruling on pregnancy. il Time 110:14 N 28 '77
So far, so good: a report card on coed military academies. il U.S. News 83:26-9 Jl 11 '77
West Point log: the basic training of Joan Smith. M. Stamell. il pors Ms 6:48-51+ Ag '77
West Point woman; ed by V. Eads. K. Kinzler. il por Seventeen 36:74+ Ap '77
Women warriors. E. Keerdoja. il Newsweek 90:12 S 19 '77

WOMEN chefs. See Cooks

WOMEN clergy
Three young clergywomen: how they're changing their churches. J. T. Freeman. il Redbook 149:24+ Je '77
See also
Ordination of women
Women priests

WOMEN coal miners
Why I decided to go underground. B. Burns. McCalls 104:69+ S '77

WOMEN college presidents
See also
Gray, H. H.

WOMEN college students. See College students, Women

WOMEN college teachers
Court rules against woman biochemist. C. Holden. Science 197:743 Ag 19 '77

WOMEN comedians
What some women do for laughs on Saturday night. S. Weller. il Ms 6:46+ O '77
See also
Tomlin, L.

WOMEN composers
L.A. County Mus: women's works; concerts celebrating women composers. il Hi Fi 27: MA24-5 Je '77
See also
Beach, A. M. C.
Ran, S.
Richter, M.

WOMEN conductors (music)
See also
Boulanger, N.

WOMEN criminals. See Women—Crime

WOMEN editors
Hey, lady, who's in charge here? A. Edwards. por Redbook 148:64+ F '77

WOMEN educators
See also
Women school superintendents and principals

WOMEN entrepreneurs
Alaskan original; school operated by B. Smith. S. Auerbach. pors Am Home 80:41-2 S '77
Businesswomen get a champion at SBA; P. Cloherty. il pors Nation Bus 65:34-6 D '77
How to make a million before you're 34; interviews with six successful business women, ed by D. Kaye and F. Ruffin. pors Redbook 149: 60-1+ My '77
How to start a business of your own. G. Chipps and C. Jessup. bibl Redbook 149:66+ Jl '77
How to start your own business. P. Nelson. McCalls 104:81-2 S '77
Jet-set tycoon; interview, ed by M. Kunz. V. Davis. il pors Am Home 80:24+ Je '77
Making an impression; women in the cosmetics industry. A. Penney. il N Y Times Mag p38-9 Jl 17 '77
Starting a business: women show it's not just a man's world. il U.S. News 83:55-6 Ag 29 '77

WOMEN executives
Employers are insisting on women managers and supervisors. W. Flanagan. Vogue 167:222 Mr '77
Female executives become a target for ads. il Bus W p66 Ag 22 '77
How men adjust to a female boss. il Bus W p90+ S 5 '77
Let's huddle, women; a study by M. Hennig and A. Jardim. Time 109:63 My 2 '77
New breed of studio executives talk about power. Ms 6:53 D '77
Problems of women bosses. M. Burgen. il Ebony 33:94+ N '77
Should you work for a woman? stereotyped female boss. R. Shapiro. Harp Baz 110:85+ Ag '77
They are owners, bosses, workers. M. Bergen. il Ebony 32:122-4+ Ag '77
Two women, three men on a raft. R. Schrank. il Harvard Bus R 55:100-8 My '77
When men have women bosses. L. C. Pogrebin. Ladies Home J 94:24+ My '77
When mothers are also managers. il Bus W p 155-6+ Ap 18 '77
Why corporations are teaching men to think like women. . .and other secret game plans that you may not have been briefed on; excerpt from Games mother never taught you; corporate gamesmanship for women. B. L. Harragan. il Ms 5:62-3+ Je '77
See also
Women entrepreneurs

Clothing and dress

See Clothing and dress

Salaries, pensions, etc.

Double standard for women managers' pay. il Bus W p61+ N 28 '77

Training

See Executives—Training

WOMEN firefighters
Yes, we now have firewomen; volunteers in Rollingwood, Tex. D. Lampe. il House B 119: 12+ Mr '77

WOMEN golfers. See Golfers

WOMEN guides. See Guides

WOMEN hunters
Double on antelope. E. A. Bauer. il Outdoor Life 159:60-3+ F '77
Girl learns to hunt; deer hunting by C. McRae in Nontana. B. McRae. il por Field & S 82: 40-1+ O '77

WOMEN in advertising
Ads insulting women: a long way to go, baby. J. J. Seldin. Nation 224:464-6 Ap 16 '77
Female executives become a target for ads. il Bus W p66 Ag 22 '77
Media mistreatment of women. H. Hyans. McCalls 105:43 Ja '78
No comment. See issues of Ms.
Power of understatement; L. Wyse. il por Harp Baz 111:166+ N '77
Those little eyes so helpless and appealing. R. Rosenblatt. New Repub 176:33 Ap 23 '77

WOMEN in agriculture
See also
Farmers wives

WOMEN in art
Being not doing; sculptures by F. Zuñiga. S. Reich. Art N 76:132+ S '77
Dynamic symmetry of Ruth Egri. C. Collins. il por Am Artist 41:46-51+ D '77
Remember the ladies: women in America, 1750-1815. C. Hunt-Jones. il Antiques 111:762-7 Ap '77
Vive la femme! work of P. P. Rubens. il UNESCO Courier 30:14-15 Je '77

WOMEN in boating
Cabin talk. M. Wiley. See issues of Yachting
Women's opinions sought. Yachting 142:125 Ag '77
See also
Sailboat racing

WOMEN in business. See Business and professional women

WOMEN in drama
Women in modern drama. H. Bock. il Intellect 105:388 My '77

WOMEN in fiction. See Women in literature

WOMEN in fishing. See Fishing

WOMEN in literature
Argument for Milton's Dalila; Samson Agonistes. J. Colony. Yale R 66:562-75 Je '77
Examplar to her sex: Richardson's Clarissa. R. M. Brownstein. Yale R 67:30-47 O '77
Ladies of easy virtue. M. Springer. il Opera N 42:24+ D 24 '77
Not only I the narrator, but I John Cheever; interview, ed by E. Munro. J. Cheever. il pors Ms 5:74-7+ Ap '77
Reviewing the reviewers. L. Ehrenkrantz. Intellect 106:246-8 D '77
Welcome back from the raft, Huck honey! Widow Douglas commentary. K. S. Lynn. Am Scholar 46:338-47 Summ '77
Women's liberature. L. B. Toth. Engl J 66:63-4 S '77
See also
Shakespeare, W.—Characters
Women in drama

WOMEN in medicine
What's ahead for women in medicine. R. S. Yalow. il pors Parents Mag 53:38-9+ Ja '78

WOMEN in motion pictures
Cavani's Night porter: a woman's film? T. De Lauretis. Film Q 30:35-8 Wint '76
Film. See issues of Ms.
Films of Gunvor Nelson. J. M. Gill. bibl il Film Q 30:28-36 Spr '77
Focus: reel women; excerpt from From reverence to rape: the treatment of women in the movies. M. Haskell. il Seventeen 36:52-3 My '77
Helen Van Dongen: an interview; ed by B. Achtenberg. H. Van Dongen. bibl il pors Film Q 30:46-57 Wint '76
Hollywood's new heroines. J. Kroll and others. il pors Newsweek 90:78-82+ O 10 '77
See also
Women in the motion picture industry

Anecdotes, facetiae, satire, etc.

. . .And what are we trying to tell Hollywood? now for the envelopes they didn't open. S. Braudy. il Ms 5:50-2 Ap '77

WOMEN in opera
Fatal women. J. Fludas. il Opera N 41:14-16+ F 12 '77

WOMEN in Passage Program. See Good housekeeping (periodical)

WOMEN in politics
Making it happen in Texas. J. L. Carter and F. E. Ruffin. il Redbook 150:43+ D '77
Two feminists tell how they work; interview, ed by G. Steinem. K. Horbal. pors Ms 6: 52+ Jl '77
See also
Congresswomen
Women in the civil service
Women public officers

History

Moma went to Congress and then to jail; W. M. Huck. D. Dean and M. Dean. il pors Am Hist Illus 12:37-43 N '77

WOMEN in publishing
Kate Murray: pharmacist/magazine publisher; On the line magazine. D. Duke. por Mademoiselle 83:78 O '77
Women in print: an update. K. A. Cassell. il Lib J 102:1352-5 Je 15 '77

WOMEN in religion. See Women and religion

WOMEN in sports. See Women athletes

WOMEN in television
Barbie doll as sex symbol. K. E. Meyer. Sat R 5:45 O 1 '77
Farrah Fawcett-Majors makes me want to scream! M. Rosen. il Redbook 149:102+ S '77
Loving wisdom of TV's Edith Bunker; excerpt from Edith the good. S. Marsh. il Good H 185: 48+ Ag '77
This may be the year to stay tuned. A. Northrop. il Ms 6:44-5+ D '77
Valerie Harper: what Rhoda taught me about marriage & divorce; ed by M. F. Cohen. V. Harper. por Ladies Home J 94:36+ S '77
What some women do for laughs on Saturday night. S. Weller. il Ms 6:46+ O '77
Whatever happened to Mary Richards? B.-J. Raphael. por McCalls 104:20+ S '77
See also
Women in the television industry

WOMEN in the Armed Forces. See Servicewomen

WOMEN in the arts
Applause! Women in the arts. A. L. Ball and F. Ruffin. il Redbook 149:37-44 S '77
Arts explosions; special issue. Ms 6:33-68+ D '77
Creative woman: success requires talent and drive. il Ebony 32:135-8 Ag '77

WOMEN in the Bible
See also
Mary Magdalene, Saint

WOMEN in the civil service
Entry of women into federal job world—at a price. R. K. Baker. il Smithsonian 8:82-4+ Jl '77
WOMEN in the mass media industry
Tell it to Donna Allen; publisher of Media report to women. por K. Barker. Ms 5:20-1 F '77
WOMEN in the motion picture industry
Coming attractions. . .from the folks who are taking over Hollywood. M. Rosen. il Ms 6: 50-3+ D '77
See also
Women motion picture directors
WOMEN in the Navy. See Servicewomen
WOMEN in the phonograph record industry
Pop music:
Olivia: a vinyl victory. L. Borton. il Ms 6:68 D '77
Platter patter: the top 40 music moguls. S. Ditlea. il Ms 6:66-7 D '77
Revolution per minute: woman's labels. B. Pepe. Ms 6:67-8+ D '77
WOMEN in the television industry
Jane Pauley & Sandy Hill: this is your life. A. L. Ball. pors Redbook 150:94+ N '77
News: women want it all; television reporters; interviews. D. English. il Vogue 167:84 Mr '77
Prime time for TV newswomen. il Time 109:85-6 Mr 21 '77
Yes, I can! interview, ed by J. Halloran. R. Merrill. il pors Am Home 80:30-1 Ap '77
WOMEN in the theater
Theater will never be the same. H. Moore. il por Ms 6:36-9+ D '77
WOMEN in trade unions. See Trade unions—Membership
WOMEN judges
See also
Bird, R. E.
WOMEN lawyers
See also
Public prosecutors
WOMEN librarians. See Librarians
WOMEN literary characters. See Women in literature
WOMEN lobbyists. See Lobbyists and lobbying
WOMEN mayors
Lady mayor of Mayersville; U. Blackwell. il pors Ebony 33:53-6+ D '77
WOMEN ministers. See Women clergy
WOMEN motion picture characters. See Women in motion pictures
WOMEN motion picture directors
Varda: watch out. I do not authorize you to use me against other women. . .; interview, ed by J. Thurman. A. Varda. por Ms 6:28 Ja '78
See also
Akerman, C.
Cavani, L.
Moreau, J.
Nelson, G.
Silver, J. M.
Wertmuller, L.
WOMEN museum directors
Where are the women museum directors? T. Trucco. il Art N 76:52-7 F '77
WOMEN museum trustees. See Art galleries and museums—Trustees, boards, committees, etc.
WOMEN museum workers. See Museum workers
WOMEN musicians
Music (cont) il Ms 5:36+ Mr; 6:27-8 N '77
Music: a reflection of jazz women. L. Kuehl. Commonweal 104:625-6 S 30 '77
Notes from the orchestra pit. H. Epstein. Ms 5:106+ Ap '77
See also
Liston, M.
WOMEN newscasters. See Television broadcasting —News
WOMEN novelists. See Women authors
WOMEN opera characters. See Women in opera
WOMEN painters. See Women artists
WOMEN photographers
As the lens turns: women photograph men; excerpt from Women photograph men. M. Haskell. il Ms 6:31-2+ S '77
Family of woman: 5 years in focus; comp by H. Lyons and B. Richer. il Ms 6:56-61 Jl '77
See also
Emmons, C. S.
Käsebier, G. S.
Krementz, J.
MacAdams, C.
Orkin, R.
WOMEN physicians
See also
Walker, M.
WOMEN poets
On the edge of the estate; A. Lorde and R. Stone. S. M. Gilbert. Poetry 129:296-301 F '77
See also
Akhmadulina, B.
Browning, E. B.
Lazarus, E.
Lerman, E.
Monroe, H.
Morgan, R.
Mueller, L.
Oates, J. C.
Stuckey, E.
Swansea, C. W.
Urdang, C.
WOMEN police. See Policewomen
WOMEN priests
Case of women trouble; Episcopal Church. il Time 110:80 O 17 '77
Women of the cloth; Episcopal Church. il Newsweek 90:12+ O 24 '77
See also
Ordination of women
Palmer, A.
WOMEN prison guards. See Prisons—Officials and employees
WOMEN prisoners
What life is like for women in prison. il U.S. News 83:79 N 28 '77
WOMEN public officers
All the President's women; or, What's a nice person like you doing in a job like this? H. D. Schwindt. il Ms 6:50-4+ Ja '78
Attacking the old boy network; appointments of the Carter administration. il Time 109:16-17 Mr 28 '77
Four women who can improve your life; government's new consumer advocates. J. Carper. il Am Home 80:42-3 Ag '77
Slim past, but a strong future. il Ebony 32: 89-92+ Ag '77
Top women bureaucrats talk about jobs, bias and their changing roles. il U.S. News 83:38-40 S 5 '77
Women's advocacy: showdown in Houston. L. Gillan. il Ms 6:19 S '77
See also
Women mayors
WOMEN publishers. See Women in publishing
WOMEN real estate agents. See Real estate agencies and agents
WOMEN recreation workers. See Recreation workers
WOMEN school administrators
No room at the top? il Am Educ 13:20-3+ Je '77
Women and administration: confrontation or accommodation? J. D. Grambs. Educ Digest 42:39-42 Mr '77
WOMEN school superintendents and principals
To the Oakland School District, with Love; Superintendent R. B. Love. C. Pogash. por Ms 5:19 My '77
WOMEN scientists
Still many barriers to women in science. il Sci N 112:279 O 29 '77
Women in science. Sci Am 237:52 Ag '77
Women in science seek equal opportunities. K. E. Hoagland. il BioScience 27:830-1 D '77
Women researchers analyze education, job barriers. N. C. Joyce and P. Q. Hall. Science 198:917-18 D 2 '77
See also
Cudmore, L. L. L.
WOMEN shoppers. See Shopping and shoppers
WOMEN sports journalists. See Sports journalism
WOMEN sportscasters. See Television broadcasting—Sports
WOMEN teachers
See also
Sex discrimination in education
WOMEN television characters. See Women in television
WOMEN trade union officials
She's a fighter on three fronts; A. Wyatt of the Amalgamated Meat Cutters and Butcher Workmen of North America. por Ebony 32:70 Ag '77
WOMEN weight lifters. See Weight lifting
WOMEN writers. See Women authors
WOMEN'S Action Alliance
Equality now! For girls and boys; non-sexist schooling. B. Sprung. il Parents Mag 52:44+ S '77
WOMEN'S City Club of New York
Empty houses; Bronx study. S. T. Atlas. Newsweek 90:100 O 10 '77
WOMENS clubs and societies
Help! how to cope with it all; national and governmental organizations. J. L. Barkas. Redbook 149:81-8 O '77
Honduras: did the Church start something it can't stop? Housewives Clubs. M. Peraza and H. Maurer. il Ms 6:12-15 Ag '77
Jinx Melia: crusader for homemakers; Martha Movement. L. David. il por Good H 184:154+ Je '77
Media mistreatment of women; protest by Women Against Violence Against Women. H. Hyans. McCalls 105:43 Ja '78
Who is Martha and why is she a movement? A. L. Booth. Ms 5:91 My '77
Women's clubs. il Ebony 32:70-3+ Jl '77
See also
National Organization for Women
Outdoor Women (organization)
Women's Action Alliance
Women's City Club of New York
Young Women's Christian Association

WOMENS colleges. See Colleges for women
WOMENS discussion groups. See Discussion groups
WOMENS fishing contests. See Fishing—Competitions
WOMEN'S liberation movement. See Feminism
WOMEN'S Lobby, Inc. See Lobbyists and lobbying
WOMENS organizations. See Womens clubs and societies
WOMENS sports. See Sports for women
WONDER, Stevie
Key of Stevie Wonder. D. J. Evearitt. Chr Today 21:30 F 18 '77 *
Stevie Wonder says it all; Songs in the key of life. il por Hi Fi 27:141-2 F '77 *
WONDERFUL world of Hans Christian Andersen; drama. See Newman, D.
WONDERS of nature. See Natural monuments
WONG, Anthony S. See Crosby, D. G. jt auth
WONG, Chung-po
C.P. Wong makes Bulova tick again. W. Guzzardi, Jr. il por Fortune 95:154-7+ Ap '77 *
Wong ends his stay at Bulova. il por Bus W p40 N 28 '77 *
WONG, Glenda Lyn, and others
1,25-dihydroxycholecalciferol and parathormone: effects on isolated osteoclast-like and osteoblast-like cells. bibl il Science 197:663-5 Ag 12 '77
WONG, Leslie
Roots in China, a first encounter. il por Smithsonian 8:116-20 bibl(p 148) Ap '77
WONG, William S.
Writings on bamboo and wood. bibl il Wilson Lib Bull 51:848-52 Je '77
WONG, Yuk-shan, and others
Cellulases can enhance β glucan synthesis. bibl Science 195:679-81 F 18 '77
WOOD, Abigail
Relating; questions and answers. See issues of Seventeen
WOOD, Arthur MacDougall
Challenges to profit sharing; address, October 20, 1976. Vital Speeches 43:230-3 F 1 '77
WOOD, Enoch
Enoch Wood earthenware found in St Paul's Church, Burslem. P. D. Kingsbury. bibl il Antiques 112:122-7 Jl '77 *
WOOD, Gayle E.
Art in prison. Nation 225:370-2 O 15 '77
WOOD, James H. and others
Primate model for long-term study of intraventricularly or intrathecally administered drugs and intracranial pressure. bibl il Science 195:499-501 F 4 '77
WOOD, Jean M.
Shell game. il Design (US) 78:6-7 Summ '77
WOOD, John
Moose on the loose! il Nat Wildlife 15:4-11 O '77
What is a fisher? il Nat Wildlife 15:18-21 Ap '77
WOOD, Jon
Falling leaves, falling prices. il Sat Eve Post 249:90-2 S '77
WOOD, Joyce L.
Culture and youth. bibl Clearing H 50:240-1 F '77
WOOD, Larry
Farming giant kelp; with biographical sketch. il Sea Front 23:159-66, 191 My '77
Growing crops on sand dunes? il Sea Front 23:228-32 Jl '77
Jetfoil with wings beneath the waves. il Oceans 10:35-7 Mr '77
New mini flattop flies like a plane. il Pop Mech 149:62-3+ Ja '78
WOOD, M. D. and King, N. E.
Relation between earthquakes, weather, and soil tilt. bibl il Science 197:154-6 Jl 8 '77
WOOD, Paul, and Schwartz, Bernard
I mean now: the simplest method of raising kids. pors Psychol Today 11:113-14+ Jl '77
WOOD, Peter
Unloneliness of the long-distance skier. il N Y Times Mag p 19-22+ D 18 '77
White-water high. il N Y Times Mag p66-73 My 22 '77
WOOD, Peter H.
Roots of victory, roots of defeat. New Repub 176:27-8 Mr 12 '77
(ed) See Rossellini, R. I believe in this: a letter from Roberto Rossellini
WOOD, Philip
Throwing a double-walled planter. il por Ceram Mo 25:59-61 My '77
WOOD, Richard E.
English-language shortwave broadcasts; tables (cont) Pop Electr 11:103-6 Mr; 101-4 My; 12:114-17 S; 94-7 N '77
WOOD, Susan
Bazaar: after Calvino; poem. New Yorker 53:193 N 14 '77
WOOD, William
Hi, Mr President. Progressive 41:51 O '77
WOOD, William P.
Murder in Uganda. America 136:216-19 Mr 12 '77
Namibia: conscience and independence. Chr Cent 94:529-31 Je 1 '77
Uganda after Idi Amin. America 137:51-3 Jl 30 '77
WOOD, Willie
Wood can be a putter. B. McDermott. por Sports Illus 47:50-1 Ag 8 '77 *
WOOD
See also
Dry rot
Lumber
Plywood
Shingles

Deterioration

See also
Wood decaying fungi

Staining

See Stains and staining
WOOD and Tower, Inc. See Construction industry—Information services
WOOD as fuel
Back-to-wood boom. il Time 110:103-4 D 5 '77
Energy from wood wastes; excerpt from Energy from solid wastes. P. N. Cheremisinoff and A. C. Morresi. il Environment 19:25-31 My '77
Get more heat by burning wood. il Pop Mech 148:138+ S '77
How to cut, stack and use firewood. il Pop Mech 148:120-3 O '77
Increase your wood power. G. Munson. il Org Gard & Farm 24:95-100 O '77
My flaming affair with firewood. R. Starnes. Outdoor Life 161:12+ Ja '78
Old energy source finds new favor. il U.S. News 83:62 D 5 '77
Other energy crisis: firewood; excerpt from Losing ground: environmental stress and world food prospects. E. P. Eckholm. bibl il Focus 27:9-16 Mr '77; Same abr. with title Poor man's energy crisis. il UNESCO Courier 30:29-31 Jl '77; Same abr. with title Poor man's crisis: firewood. Sci Digest 82:59 O '77
They're cookin' with wood. D. Pauly and R. Manning. il Newsweek 91:53 Ja 2 '78
Wood versus fossil fuel as a source of excess carbon dioxide in the atmosphere: a preliminary report. J. A. S. Adams and others. bibl il Science 196:54-6 Ap 1 '77
WOOD ashes. See Ashes
WOOD ashes as fertilizer. See Fertilizers and manures
WOOD bins. See Woodbins, racks, etc.
WOOD block prints. See Wood engravings
WOOD carving
Art and craft of making decoys. il por Bet Hom & Gard 55:140-1 N '77
Carve your own dream pipe. G. Graves. il Pop Mech 147:255-7 My '77
Decoding the message of African sculpture; mask carvings. O. Balogun. il UNESCO Courier 30:12-15+ My '77
Duck decoys: to carve and collect. il Bet Hom & Gard 55:224 N '77
Expert's secrets for carving lifelike birds. P. Angell. il por Pop Mech 149:94+ Ja '78
Furniture in carved wood in New Mexico il Sunset 158:72+ My '77
Lamu door carving. M. M. Michie. il Design (US) 78:26 mid-Wint '77
Wood masterpieces: China and Japan. J. Brzostoski. il Craft Horiz 37:46-9+ Ap '77
See also
Indians, Wooden
WOOD carving tools. See Tools
WOOD chips. See Wood waste
WOOD construction
Ball residence, Omaha, Nebraska. il Archit Rec 161:90-3 mid-My '77
Three construction projects with wood scraps. E. Levine. il Sch Arts 76:16-17 Je '77
WOOD cutting
How to cut, stack and use firewood. il Pop Mech 148:120-3 O '77
Split wood, not atoms. G. Norman. Esquire 88:40+ D '77
WOOD cutting machines
Car-powered logsplitter. C. Self. il Pop Sci 210:63 Mr '77
Log splitter runs on your car or tractor engine. A. J. Hand. il Pop Sci 211:48 O '77
When an axe is not enough; power splitters. S. Smyser. il Org Gard & Farm 24:132-7 O '77
WOOD decaying fungi
Degradation of wood by fungi; excerpt from Deterioration of materials in a marine environment. J. G. Savory. il Motor B & S 140:47-8 Jl '77
WOOD drying. See Lumber—Drying
WOOD ducks. See Ducks, Wild
WOOD engravings
Printmaking with plywood: a simple and inexpensive method. J. Turner. il Design (US) 79:20 Fall '77

WOOD finishing
How to paint your own woodgrain. il House & Gard 149:104+ Ap '77
Slick finish for teak; oil. R. R. Grams. Motor B & S 140:99 Jl '77
See also
Furniture—Finishing
Stains and staining
Varnish and varnishing
WOOD flooring. See Flooring
WOOD lathes. See Lathes
WOOD Memorial (race) See Horse racing
WOOD poles
Reading poles; utility poles. G. D. Walker. il Am For 83:31 Je '77
WOOD products industry. See Forest products industry
WOOD pulp industry
Brazil
Pulp makers pull back from capital spending. il Bus W p38-9 N 7 '77
WOOD rot fungi. See Wood decaying fungi
WOOD sculpting. See Wood carving
WOOD siding. See Siding (building)
WOOD stove cookery. See Cookery
WOOD stoves. See Camp stoves; Stoves
WOOD waste
Turn problem trees into community assets; grinding into wood chips. il Am City & County 92:45-6 Mr '77
WOOD waste as fuel. See Wood as fuel
WOOD working. See Woodworking
WOODALL, Jerry M. See Tomkiewicz, M. jt auth
WOODARD, George
He really pounds it out. J. Jares. il Sports Illus 47:44+ O 3 '77 *
WOODARD, Samuel L.
Ten ways to help your child succeed. il por Ebony 32:52-4+ O '77
WOODBINS, racks, etc.
Outside firewood rack you can build. R. Weinsteiger. il Org Gard & Farm 24:144-7 O '77
3 firewood projects you can build: toter, weatherproof bin, log box. H. Wicks. il Pop Mech 148: 124-5+ O '77
WOODCARVING. See Wood carving
WOODCHUCK hunting
How we put sport back into chuck hunting. L. Mueller. il Outdoor Life 159:80-1+ Ap '77
1,000-yard chucks. D. Frost. il Outdoor Life 160: 82-3+ Jl '77
WOODCHUCKS
How to raise a woodchuck. F. McNulty. il Audubon 79:50-5 Mr '77
See also
Cookery—Game
WOODCOCK, C. L. F.
Reconstitution of chromatin subunits. bibl il Science 195:1350-2 Mr 25 '77
WOODCOCK, George
Socialist tides in Canada. Progressive 41:25-8 Jl '77
WOODCOCK, Leonard
Excerpt from address on national health insurance, March 1, 1977. Cong Digest 56:216+ Ag '77
Presidential Commission visits Vietnam and Laos to seek information on missing Americans; transcript of news conference, March 23, 1977. Dept State Bull 76:364-6 Ap 18 '77
about
Bridgehead is won in Hanoi. S. Talbott. il por Time 109:17-18 Mr 28 '77 *
WOODCOCK shooting
Woodcock days past, but lovingly remembered. G. Hill. il Field & S 82:48-9+ S '77
WOODCUTTERS. See Lumberjacks
WOODEN boats. See Boats—Materials
WOODEN dolls. See Dolls
WOODEN Indians. See Indians, Wooden
WOODEN poles. See Wood poles
WOODHULL, Victoria (Claflin)
Victorians thought her a downright scandal—as she was. J. Davis. il por Smithsonian 8:131-6+ O '77 *
WOODIWISS, Kathleen
PW interviews; ed by G. Stuttaford. por Pub W 211:6-7 My 30 '77
WOODLAND Park, Springfield Township. See Pennsylvania—Parks and reserves
The **WOODLANDS, Tex.** See New cities and towns—United States
WOODLEY, William Lee, and others
Rainfall results, 1970-1975: Florida Area Cumulus Experiment. bibl il map Science 195:735-42 F 25 '77
WOODLOTS
How to sell stumpage. D. S. Thomas. il Am For 83:36-42 D '77
See also
Forest management
WOODMAN, Jim
Quest in the jungle. J. Underwood. il Sports Illus 48:86-90+ Ja 9 '78 *
WOODPECKERS
Un gran pedazo de carne; search for the rare imperial ivory-billed woodpecker. G. Plimpton. il pors Audubon 79:10-25 N '77
Woodpecker at my window; the pileated woodpecker. M. D. Hodgins. il Am For 83:26-7 D '77
WOODRATS. See Rats
WOODRESS, Frederick A.
Here at the National enquirer. il Writers Digest 57:24-6 Jl '77
WOODROW, Alain
Catholic vote in France. Commonweal 104:261-3 Ap 29 '77
WOODROW Wilson International Center for Scholars
Dialoguing at the Smithsonian; religion and political action. M. E. Marty. Chr Cent 94: 316-17 Ap 6 '77
Wilson Center immerses scholars in think tank. E. P. Morgan. il pors Smithsonian 8:76-83 Ag '77
WOODRUFF, Diana S.
Will you live to be 100? quiz. il Sr Schol 110: 10-11 N 17 '77
WOODRUFF, Judy
Assignment: White House. il pors Redbook 149: 116-17+ Jl '77 *
WOODRUFF, Robert Winship
Hall of Fame for Business Leadership. M. Ways. por Fortune 95:120 Ja '77 *
WOODRUM, Pat
Regional centers—sharing service. il por Lib J 102:165-6 Ja 15 '77
WOODS, Donald
Critic in exile. il por Time 111:31 Ja 16 '78 *
Great escape. S. Strasser and P. Younghusband. il por Newsweek 91:48 Ja 16 '78 *
Silent bystander. W. McWhirter. il por Time 110:38 N 7 '77 *
WOODS, George
Children's book page enhanced in revamped New York times book review; views of editor G. Woods. il por Am Lib 8:269-70 My '77 *
WOODS, John
Comment. J. Parini. Poetry 130:295-6 Ag '77 *
WOODS, Ralph L.
(comp) Deadly conversation. il Esquire 87:108-9 Ap '77
WOODS Hole Oceanographic Institution, Woods Hole, Mass.
Woods Hole mulls Titanic expedition. B. J. Culliton. Science 197:848-9 Ag 26 '77
WOODSON, Carter Godwin
Woodson and the genesis of ASALH. A. Scally. il por Negro Hist Bull 40:653-5 Ja '77 *
WOODSTOCK, N.Y.
New town map. il Archit Rec 161:108-10 F '77
WOODSTOCK Playhouse. See Theater—United States
WOODWARD, Comer Vann
Aging of America. bibl f Am Hist R 82:583-94 Je '77
WOODWARD, J. Arthur, and Goldstein, M. J.
Communication deviance in the families of schizophrenics: a comment on the misuse of analysis of covariance. bibl Science 197:1096-7 S 9 '77
WOODWARD, Joanne
Special kind of love; J. Woodward's work with autistic children. J. Ardmore. il pors Fam Health 9:28-31 F '77 *
WOODWARD, Kenneth L.
How to stop risking your life. il McCalls 105:154+ O '77
WOODWARD, William V.
Smoking in school. Educ Digest 43:56-7 N '77
WOODWARD Stakes. See Horse racing
WOODWELL, George M.
Carbon dioxide question; with biographical sketch. il map Sci Am 238:12, 34-43 Ja '78
WOODWIND instruments
See also
Phonograph records—Woodwind instruments
WOODWORKING
Health issues. J. Waller and L. Whitehead. Craft Horiz 37:8+ D '77
How to work with plywood. A. Lees. il Pop Sci 210:124-6+ Mr '77
10 great shop tricks from a master craftsman. D. Warren. il por Pop Mech 149:90-2 Ja '78
10 shop tricks from a pro; excerpt from The complete book of woodworking. R. Capotosto. il por Pop Mech 148:110-12 Ag '77
Workshop mini-course. il Pop Mech 147:119 Je; 148:14 Ag; 132 O; 8 N; 120 D '77; 149:93 Ja '78
See also
Joints (carpentry)
Turning
Veneers and veneering
Wood carving

WOODWORKING—*Continued*

Projects

Build the ultimate desktop. M. McClintock. il Pop Mech 147:116-18 Ap '77
Here are the 12 winners of the PS/APA. A. Lees. il Pop Sci 211:106-11 Ag '77
Live out and love it! N. Seney and S. Coulter. il Bet Hom & Gard 55:103-13 Je '77
6 wood projects you can build and enjoy this summer. H. Wicks. il Pop Mech 148:96-9 Jl '77
Step-by-step project scrapbook:
Jewelry display rack. il Bet Hom & Gard 55:264 O '77
Kid's folding easel. il Bet Hom & Gard 55:38 Je '77
Kid's furniture. il Bet Hom & Gard 55:54 Jl '77
Toy-box van. il Bet Hom & Gard 55:60 S '77
Wall mounted magazine rack. il Bet Hom & Gard 55:74 O '77
Wordless workshop. R. Doty. See issues of Popular science
See also names of projects, e.g. Chairs

WOODWORKING machinery
Two machines that carve wood. il Mech Illus 73:86+ D '77
See also
Jointers (woodworking machinery)
Routing machines
Sanding machines

WOOL industry
Spanish wool and Dutch rebels: the Middelburg incident of 1574. W. D. Phillips, Jr and C. R. Phillips. bibl f il map Am Hist R 82:312-30 Ap '77

WOOLF, Virginia (Stephen)
Staying in touch. S. Maloff. por Commonweal 104:371-4 Je 10 '77 *
Women are not all alike. A. Kazin. Esquire 88:12+ Jl '77 *

WOOLLEY, Bryan
Hard country friends; story. Redbook 150:68-9 D '77

WOOLLEY, Ellamarie
Obituary
Craft Horiz 37:10+ Ap '77. J. Balmer

WOOLLEY, John T.
Monetary policy instrumentation and the relationship of central banks and governments. bibl f il Ann Am Acad 434:151-73 N '77

WOOLNER, Frank
Camper on the beach. il Field & S 82:46+ My '77

WOOLWICH, John Arthur Thomas Robinson, Bp of. See Robinson, J. A. T.

WOOLWORTH, Frank Winfield
World's tallest building. S. Klaw. il pors Am Heritage 28:86-98 F '77 *

WOOLWORTH, F. W, Company
Woolworth: the last stand of the variety store. il por Bus W p84-5 Ja 9 '78

WOOLWORTH building. See New York (city)—Buildings

WOOSNAM, Phil
Nothing but blue skies does Woosnam see. C. Gammon. il pors Sports Illus 46:38-40+ My 30 '77 *

WOOTEN, James T.
Carter's Georgia guru. il pors N Y Times Mag p 14-18 Mr 20 '77

WOOTERS, J. Dukes, Jr
Cotton's natural comeback. por Forbes 119:80 Ap 1 '77 *

WOOTTERS, John
It all rides on. . .the bullet. il Field & S 82:100+ O '77
Shooting (cont) il Field & S 81:170-2+ Mr; 142-5 Ap; 82:84-6 Jl '77

WORAM, John
If you can't afford more mikes. . .try binaural. il Hi Fi 27:130-2 S '77
1977 Multi-Track Expo. il Hi Fi 27:109 Ag '77
What's out in semipro consoles. il Hi Fi 27:148-9 N '77

WORBY, Mel
Where to go. See issues of Outdoor life

WORD (theology) See Communication (theology)

WORD of God. See Logos (theology)

WORD perception
Visual characteristics of words. P. Dunn-Rankin. il Sci Am 238:122-30 Ja '78

WORD processing equipment
Word processing equipment. il Am City & County 92:55-8 D '77
See also
Addressograph Multigraph Corporation
Computers—Print-out equipment

WORDEN, Willard E.
Shows we've seen. N. Canavor. il Pop Phot 81:138-9 Ag '77 *

WORDINESS. See Verbosity

WORDS
See also
Vocabulary

Psychology

See Language and languages—Psychology

WORDS, Obscene
Let's lower the obscenity level. J. E. Pearce. Read Digest 111:91-2 N '77

WORDSWORTH, William
Poet laureate of nature. P. W. Schmidtchen. il por Hobbies 81:134-6 F '77 *

WORK
Dorothy L. Sayers—for good work, for God's work. C. Forbes. Chr Today 21:16-18 Mr 4 '77
Education, work, and leisure: must they come in that order? F. Best and B. Stern. bibl il M Labor R 100:3-10 Jl '77
Generation that was never going to have to work. M. Jacobson. il Esquire 88:52-4+ Jl '77
Great male cop-out from the work ethic. il Bus W p 156+ N 14 '77
Opting out: the waning of the work ethic. A. Etzioni. Psychol Today 11:18 Jl '77
Recreation renaissance; excerpt from Play behavior. J. Levy. Parks & Rec 12:16-20 D '77
Road less traveled. E. Kohák. il Harpers 225:21-2+ D '77
Work is not a four-letter word. F. Lear. por Newsweek 90:22-3 O 24 '77
See also
Hours of labor
Job satisfaction
Labor and laboring classes
Right to labor

WORK benches
Two new workbenches. S. Bronson. il Pop Sci 210:156 F '77
Underbench tool center. E. E. Allford. il Mech Illus 73:142+ My '77
We try out an uncommon workbench. R. Capotosto. il Mech Illus 74:92-3 Ja '78
Work bench made to look good and last. R. Weinsteiger. il Org Gard & Farm 24:86-90 Ap '77

WORK boats
See also
Tugboats

WORK clothes. See Clothing and dress—Work clothes

WORK ethic. See Work

WORK experience. See Apprentices; Education, Cooperative

WORK Glove Manufacturers Association. See Glove industry

WORK gloves. See Gloves

WORK relief. See Unemployment—Relief measures

WORK rules
Construction works to loosen the rules. il Bus W p32-3 Mr 21 '77

WORK satisfaction. See Job satisfaction

WORK shirts. See Shirts

WORK-study programs. See Education, Cooperative

WORK Wear Corporation. See Clothing industry—United States

WORKBENCHES. See Work benches

WORKERS education. See Labor and laboring classes—Education

WORKHORSES. See Sawhorses

WORKING classes. See Labor and laboring classes

WORKING day. See Hours of labor

WORKING Group on Slavery. See United Nations—Sub-Commission on Prevention of Discrimination and Protection of Minorities

WORKING mothers. See Married women—Employment

WORKING week. See Hours of labor

WORKMENS compensation. See Insurance, Workmens compensation

WORKSHOPS
Home workshops. il Bus W p207-9+ N 14 '77
Machine shop on wheels. il Farm J 101:G1 N '77
Shops engineered for man and machine; farm shops. G. Lepper. il Suc Farm 75:24-7 Ja '77

Equipment

Farm shop that cuts repair bills in half. D. K. O'Brien. il Farm J 101:K4-5 F '77
PM workbench. See issues of Popular mechanics
Treadle power in the workshop. M. Blossom. il Org Gard & Farm 24:83-5 Je '77
See also
Tools

WORKSHOPS, Library. See Library institutes and workshops

WORKSHOPS, Opera. See Opera—Instruction and study

WORKSHOPS, Photographic. See Photography—Study and teaching

WORKTABLES. See Tables

WORLD (newspaper) See Newspapers—South Africa

WORLD, End of the. See End of the world

WORLD Administrative Radio Conference
1979 World Radio Conference; how it will affect you. S. Leinwoll. il Radio-Electr 48:77-80+ My '77
U.S. to oppose broadcast satellite plan. K. Johnsen. Aviation W 106:85-6 Ja 10 '77

WORLD Airways, Inc. See Airlines—Non-scheduled operations
WORLD Alliance of Reformed Churches. See Reformed churches
WORLD Bank. See International Bank for Reconstruction and Development
WORLD Black and African Festival of Arts and Culture. See Festivals—Nigeria
WORLD Community of Islam in the West. See Black Muslims
WORLD Conference for Action Against Apartheid. See Racism—Conferences
WORLD Conference on Faith and Order
Faith and order's semi-centennial. J. R. Nelson. Chr Cent 114:612-13 Jl 6 '77
WORLD Conference to Combat Racism and Racial Discrimination, 1978 (proposed) See Racism—Conferences
WORLD Council of Churches
WCC: supporting a new order. Chr Today 21: 41-2 Ag 26 '77
WORLD Court. See International Court of Justice, The Hague
WORLD Crafts Council
WCC news. See issues of Craft horizons
WORLD cruises. See Voyages around the world
WORLD economics. See Economic conditions; Economic policy
WORLD Expeditionary Association. See Travel clubs
WORLD fairs. See Exhibitions
WORLD Festival of Black Art and Culture. See Festivals—Nigeria
WORLD Food Council. See United Nations World Food Council
WORLD food supply. See Food supply
WORLD Greyhound Classic. See Dog racing
WORLD Health Organization
Brain drain said setting problems for health planners; international migration of physicians. UN Chron 14:33 My '77
Lead and cadmium release; WHO conference on ceramic foodware safety. il Ceram Mo 25:69+ D '77
UN launches cancer survey network. Sci N 111: 326 My 21 '77
WHO announces end to virulent smallpox. Sci N 112:407 D 17 '77
WHO reports on mental health care in South Africa. UN Chron 14:33-4 Ap '77
WORLD Hockey Association-National Hockey League merger. See Hockey, Professional—Acquisitions and mergers
WORLD maps
Map of freedom January 1977. Sr Schol 109:20-1 Ap 7 '77
Map section. Sr Schol 110:23-30 O 20 '77
WORLD military expenditures. See Armed forces—Appropriations and expenditures
WORLD Music Days. See Music festivals
WORLD of Islam Festival. See Festivals—England
WORLD Peace Through Law (organization) See Law societies
WORLD politics
Who started the cold war? with introduction and discussion. C. L. Mee, Jr; W. A. Harriman; E. Abel. il pors Am Heritage 28:8-23 Ag '77
World leaders who'll make news in coming year. il U.S. News 83:44-5 D 26 '77
Worldgram: from the capitals of the world. See issues of U.S. news and world report
See also
Current events
Geopolitics
International relations
United Nations

Bibliography

International affairs (cont) V. S. Kearney. America 136:85-6 Ja 29 '77
World scene (cont) V. S. Kearney. America 136: 426-8 My 7 '77
WORLD Psychiatric Association
Censuring the Soviets. il Time 110:36 S 12 '77
Soviet psychiatric practices criticized. Sci N 112:164-5 S 10 '77
WORLD records
America, the mostest. A. Bernstein. il Am For 83:24-8 Mr '77
See also
Airplane speed records
Automobile speed records
Aviation records
Boat speed records
Sports records
WORLD security. See International security
WORLD Series (baseball) See Baseball, Professional—World Series
WORLD Team Tennis. See Tennis
WORLD temperature changes. See Global temperature changes
WORLD terrorism. See Terrorism—International aspects
WORLD tours
Around the world on a budget. P. L. Pryor. il por Ret Liv 17:26-31 My '77
WORLD trade. See Commerce
WORLD Trade Center. See New York (city)—World Trade Center
WORLD Trade Week. See Special days, weeks, and months
WORLD War, 1914-1918

Aerial operations

Airwar 1914-1918. B. P. Flanagan; E. H. Sims. il Flying 101:75-82 S '77

Campaigns and battles

Lost battalion; 77th Infantry Division in the Argonne. J. McCarthy. il por Am Heritage 28: 86-95 O '77

Fiction

Novels or war novels? M. Taylor. il Commonweal 104:566-71 S 2 '77

Naval operations

Ship that hunted itself; naval battle fought between liners Carmania and Cap Trafalgar. C. Simpson. il pors map Read Digest 111: 188-92+ S '77
WORLD War, 1939-1945

Aerial operations

Airwar 1939-1945. J. Fricker and E. H. Sims. il Flying 101:185-99 S '77
B-17. R. B. Parke. il Flying 100:72-9 Mr '77

Atrocities

See also
Concentration camps
World War, 1939-1945—Jews

Campaigns and battles

Germany

Battle for Germany. Flying 101:195+ S '77

Italy

1943 invasion of Italy. J. L. Stokesbury. il map Am Hist Illus 12:26-37 D '77

Pacific

Battle of the Philippine Sea. M. H. Byrd. il maps Am Hist Illus 12:20-35 Jl '77
War in the Pacific. Flying 101:190-3+ S '77
See also
Pearl Harbor, Attack on, 1941

Diplomatic history

Franklin D. Roosevelt and the coming of war with Germany. B. J. Bernstein. Intellect 105: 360-1 Ap '77

Documents, sources, etc.

Perspectives on the past; Eisenhower's Crusade in Europe. M. Blumenson. il Am Hist Illus 12:48 O '77

Drama

Bridge too far; excerpt from screenplay. W. Goldman. il map Sr Schol 109:21-4 Ap 21 '77

Jews

Challenge of the Holocaust. J. M. Oesterreicher. America 136:525-7 Je 11 '77
Forgetting the Holocaust. C. McConkey. Chr Cent 94:669-70 Jl 20 '77
Heirs of the Holocaust, children of survivors. H. Epstein. il por N Y Times Mag p 12-15+ Je 19 '77; Discussion. p 14+ Jl 24 '77
Hitler and the Holocaust; views of D. Irving. K. L. Woodward and A. Collings. il por Newsweek 90:77 Jl 11 '77
Outwitting the final solution; Jews in Berlin. R. Gay. il Horizon 19:42-7 Ja '77
PW interviews; ed by S. Steinberg. I. Koehn. por Pub W 212:6-7 N 21 '77
Speer: Hitler knew; excerpts from interview, ed by A. Zarca. A. Speer. il por Newsweek 90: 56 S 19 '77

Military currency

Allied Military Currency. G. Rayner. Hobbies 82:131 S '77

Naval operations

Landing ship medium (LSM) H. J. Gorin. il Oceans 10:46-9 Mr '77
Ordeal at Vella Lavella; survivors of sunken U.S.S. Helena; excerpt from Lonely vigil. W Lord. il map Am Heritage 28:30-43 Je '77

Personal narratives

How I defeated the Germans; excerpt from Dear me. P. Ustinov. il Atlantic 240:67-9+ Ag '77

Prisoners and prisons

See also
Concentration camps
Prisoners of war in the United States

Public opinion

Not their finest hour: British aristocrats sympathetic to Hitler. D. Pryce-Jones. il New Repub 176:12-16 My 14 '77

WORLD WAR, 1939-1945—*Continued*

War criminals

Great escape; H. Kappler. K. Willenson and others. il por Newsweek 90:43 Ag 29 '77
Missing cancer patient; H. Kappler. il por Time 110:42-3 Ag 29 '77
Murderous mind; psychological results of tests administered to A. Eichmann. M. Selzer. il por N Y Times Mag p35-7+ N 27 '77
Return of the native; escape of Nazi H. Kappler. F. Getlein. Commonweal 104:580-2 S 16 '77; Discussion. 104:642 O 14 '77
Story behind the book; Wanted! The search for Nazis in America; interview, ed by J. F. Baker. H. Blum. Pub W 211:72 F 7 '77
Wiesenthal's last hunt; search for J. Mengele. il pors Time 110:36+ S 26 '77
See also
War crime trials

Germany

German wartime broadcasts. S. Lipman. Commentary 63:72-5 Mr '77; Discussion. 64:7-8 Jl '77
Inside the götterdämmerung; views of J. Goebbels. il por Time 111:32 Ja 16 '78
Reporter in Germany; the Flakhelfer. D. Lang. New Yorker 53:47-50+ O 3 '77
Springtime with Hitler. il por Newsweek 91:49 Ja 16 '78

Italy

See also
World War, 1939-1945—Campaigns and battles—Italy

Japan

Bombing of Japan. Flying 101:199 S '77
Last sayonara; anniversary services. Time 109:36+ Je 13 '77
Recording that ended World War II; attempt to stop broadcast of recording of Hirohito's surrender speech; with text of speech. F. Bowers. il Hi Fi 27:87-90 O '77
See also
Pearl Harbor, Attack on, 1941

WORLD Wildlife Fund
Seas must live. J. B. Craig. il Am For 83:48-51 Mr '77

WORLDWIDE Church of God
Armstrong's Worldwide Church of God: musical chairs of change. J. M. Hopkins. Chr Today 21:20-3 Ap 1; 22-4 Ap 15 '77
Special report; Ambassador Report. J. M. Hopkins. Chr Today 22:51-2 N 18 '77

WORLEY, James
Living room; poem. Chr Cent 94:1060 N 16 '77

WORMAN, Charles G.
Firearms. See issues of Hobbies

WORMS
Homosexual rape and sexual selection in acanthocephalan worms. L. Abele and S. Gilchrist. bibl Science 197:81-3 Jl 1 '77
See also
Annelids
Earthworms
Nematodes

WORMS, Artificial. See Fishing lures, flies, etc.

WORNALL, John, House. See Kansas City, Mo.—Historic houses, sites, etc.

WORON, Walt
Car care. See issues of Motor trend

WORRY
How you can worry less; excerpt from Your erroneous zones. W. W. Dyer. Read Digest 110:81-4 F '77

WORSHIP
See also
Prayer

WORTH. See Values

WORTHINGTON, Jan
Cancer time bomb: did your mother take DES? Ms 5:16-18 Mr '77

WORTMAN, David
M.F.A. exhibition at Tulane. il Ceram Mo 25:28-9 S '77 *

WORTMAN, Doris Nash
Working the Double-Crostic. N. Ephron. Esquire 87:10+ My '77 *

WORTMAN, Sterling
Food and agriculture; with biographical sketch. il maps Sci Am 235:18, 30-9 bibl(p220) S '76; 236:8+ Ja '77

WORTZ, Melinda Terbeil
Five footnotes to modern art history. il Art N 76:73-5 Ja '77
Los Angeles. See occasional issues of Art news

WOUNDS
Simulated wounds for use in first-aid training. D. Lampe. il Sci Digest 82:76-8 N '77

WOVEN sculpture. See Sculpture

WOYCHUK, Nicholas A.
Shift at the top; Bible Memory Association. E. E. Plowman. Chr Today 22:43 D 30 '77 *

WRANGEL Island
Snow geese are coming! The snow geese are coming! J. H. Phillips. il por Int Wildlife 7:21 N '77

WRAPPING materials
Food wraps. Consumer Rep 42:38-40 D '77

WRAPPING of packages
Apt wraps for food gifts. Bet Hom & Gard 55:60-2 N '77
Bold wrapping paper stamped with fruits and vegetables. il Sunset 159:104 D '77
Colorful cover-ups; dressing your Christmas or Hanukkah presents. il House B 119:120-1 N '77
Gifted wraps. il Redbook 150:130-1 N '77
Japanese gift wraps use flowers, leaves, stems. il Sunset 159:84 Ag '77
Santa on a shoestring. il House & Gard 149:116-19 D '77
Tiny wreath package decorations. il Design (US) 79:8 N '77
Wrapping is the present; Christmas. il House & Gard 149:154-5 N '77
See also
Packaging

WREATHS
See also
Christmas wreaths

WRECKING
See also
Automobiles—Wrecking

WRECKS, Ship. See Shipwrecks

WRENCHES
Tap wrench. R. F. Bessmer. il Pop Mech 149:99 Ja '78
Tool test: impact wrench. H. Wicks. il Pop Mech 148:204 O '77
Torque wrenches. R. Hill. il Pop Sci 212:126+ Ja '78

WRENN, Roger
Eye-catching jewelry. il Design (US) 78:31 mid-Wint '77

WRESTLING
Same state, different champion; NCAA Championships. D. S. Looney. il Sports Illus 46:56+ Mr 28 '77
Suppression of his aggression; L. Kemp, University of Wisconsin wrestler. D. S. Looney. il pors Sports Illus 46:28-31 F 21 '77

WRIGHT, Ben
New reign in Spain. il Sports Illus 47:30-3 Ag 8 '77

WRIGHT, Charles
April; poem. Atlantic 239:45 Ap '77
Clear night; poem. New Yorker 53:123 My 2 '77
Edvard Munch; poem. New Yorker 53:42 Ap 4 '77
Homage to Paul Cézanne; poem. New Yorker 53:36-7 D 19 '77

WRIGHT, Charles (rainmaker)
Rainmakers. J. Schinto. il por Am West 14:28-33 Jl '77 *

WRIGHT, Douglas
Conference focuses on older women. il Aging 275:18-22 S '77

WRIGHT, Frank Lloyd
Eccentric genius of Frank Lloyd Wright. H. S. Conant. bibl il por Intellect 106:164-7 O '77 *
Story behind the book: An autobiography; interview, ed by R. Dahlin. B. Raeburn. Pub W 212:55 Jl 25 '77 *

WRIGHT, Fred W. Jr
Nightmare of Mildred Lee. por Writers Digest 57:38-9 D '77

WRIGHT, G. T.
In Zurich; poem. Esquire 87:36 Ap '77

WRIGHT, Harold
Model railroad sound synthesizer. il Pop Electr 12:80-3 D '77

WRIGHT, Helen M.
Who is your neighbor? New Cath World 220:23 Ja '77

WRIGHT, Jack
Are black youth more romantic about love? il Ebony 32:164-6+ O '77

WRIGHT, James
By the ruins of a gun emplacement; Saint-Benoît-sur-Loire; poem. New Yorker 53:22 Ag 8 '77
With the shell of a hermit crab; poem. New Yorker 53:30 Ag 22 '77

WRIGHT, Jim. See Appelson, H. jt auth

WRIGHT, Joe
Body sounder. il por Ebony 32:166+ S '77 *

WRIGHT, John Winthrop
1400 by 1979. por Forbes 120:53-4 O 15 '77 *

WRIGHT, Karen A.
Do-it-yourself nursery school. il por Redbook 149:38+ Jl '77

WRIGHT, Marshall
Airbags: an insider explains why the DOT should demur. Car & Dr 23:24 S '77

WRIGHT, Richard
Black boy. K. T. Lund. Engl J 66:59-60 Mr '77 *
Richard Wright: his life and writings. J. R. King. bibl il por Negro Hist Bull 40:738-43 S '77 *

WRIGHT, Richard T.
What Christian colleges teach about creation; interview, ed by D. Singer. il Chr Today 21:8-11 Je 17 '77

WRIGHT, Roy Dean, and Wright, S. E.
Increase of female criminals. Intellect 106:11-12 Jl '77

WRIGHT, Russel
Tribute to Russel Wright: pioneering industrial designer, 1903-1976. M. Greif. Craft Horiz 37:44 Ag '77 *

WRIGHT, Russell J.
Restoration of the interior of the William Paca House. il Antiques 111:162-4 Ja '77
Town plan of Annapolis. bibl il maps Antiques 111:148-51 Ja '77

WRIGHT, St Clair
Historic preservation in Annapolis. bibl il Antiques 111:152-7 Ja '77
Paca House garden restored. bibl il Antiques 111:172-3 Ja '77
Saving the William Paca House. il Antiques 111:160-1 Ja '77

WRIGHT, Sharon
Learning to live alone. Am Home 80:26 N '77

WRIGHT, Susan
Recombinant DNA technology: who shall regulate? Bull Atom Sci 33:4-5 O '77

WRIGHT, Susan E. See Wright, R. D. jt auth

WRIGHT brothers
Airborne. J. Gilbert. il Flying 101:66-73+ S '77

WRIGHTSMAN Collection. See Metropolitan Museum of Art, New York

WRIGHTSON, R. A.
Wild winter of 1976-77 in New York State. il Weatherwise 30:70-5 Ap '77

WRIGLEY, Philip Knight, family
Death and taxes. L. Langway and F. Maier. il Newsweek 90:62 Ag 1 '77

WRINKLES. See Skin

WRISTON, Walter Bigelow
Let's create wealth, not allocate shortages; address, May 24, 1977. Vital Speeches 43:653-6 Ag 15 '77

WRISTWATCHES. See Watches

WRITER (periodical)
Survival. L. Conger. Writer 90:11-12 Ap '77

WRITERS. See Authors

WRITERS, Women. See Women authors

WRITERS clubs and societies. See Literary clubs and societies

WRITERS colonies. See Artists and authors colonies

WRITERS conferences. See Authors conferences

WRITING
Handwriting's on the wall. il Seventeen 36:102-3 Jl '77
See also
Calligraphy
Chinese language—Writing

History

From reckoning to writing; work of D. Schmandt-Besserat on the correlation between geometric objects and signs on Sumerian tablets. il Sci Am 237:58 Ag '77
Roots of writing; ancient recording system used in trade; studies of D. Schmandt-Besserat. il por Time 110:76 Ag 1 '77

Materials and instruments

Second whole writer's catalog; authors supplies. il Writers Digest 57:33-40 S '77
Six glorious weeks in Europe—on a buying spree; shopping for writing equipment. P. O'Toole. Vogue 167:254+ Mr '77
See also
Signature writing machines
Tablets (paleography)

Psychological aspects

Variations in writing posture and cerebral organization. J. Levy and M. Reid; discussion. il Science 195:441 F 4 '77

WRITING (authorship) See Authorship; Creative writing

WRITING (composition) See English language—Composition

WRITING for the press. See Journalism—Authorship

WRITING machines, Signature. See Signature writing machines

WRITING of reports. See Report writing

WROUGHT iron
Art in wrought iron: the collection of James C. Sorber, West Chester, Pennsylvania. L. H. Solis-Cohen. il Antiques 111:782-93 Ap '77

WROUGHT iron work. See Ironwork

WUENSCH, B. J. See Wei, G. C .T. jt auth

WUERTHNER, George
Wild country of the Crow. il map Liv Wildn 41:40-4 Ap '77

WUHSIEN, China
Soochow: the Venice of China. F. B. Randall. Art N 76:112+ S '77

WULKE, Joy
Craft on commission. il por Craft Horiz 37:30-1 Ap '77

WUNSCH, Carl
Determining the general circulation of the oceans: a preliminary discussion. bibl il map Science 196:871-5 My 20 '77

WUORINEN, Charles
Recordings and the composer. il Sat R 4:24-5 Jl 23 '77

WURDELMAN, Herbert G.
Make gasoline losses evaporate. il Am City & County 92:39-40 Ja '77

WURF, Jerry
AFSCME. M. Levinson. Nation 225:208-10 S 10 '77 *
Crying Wurf. K. Bode. New Repub 177:14-17 Jl 2 '77 *

WÜRSIG, Bernd, and Würsig, Melany
Photographic determination of group size, composition, and stability of coastal porpoises (tursiops truncatus) bibl il Science 198:755-6 N 18 '77

WÜRSIG, Melany. See Würsig, B. jt auth

WURTMAN, Judith J. and Wurtman, R. J.
Fenfluramine and fluoxetine spare protein consumption while suppressing caloric intake by rats. bibl il Science 198:1178-80 D 16 '77

WURTMAN, Richard J. See Wurtman, J. J. jt auth

WÜRTTEMBERGISCHES Staatstheater. See Opera—Germany, West

WURTZITE
Hexagonal (wurtzite) form of silicon. H. M. Jennings and M. H. Richman; reply. J. S. Kasper and R. H. Wentorf, Jr. il Science 197:599 Ag 5 '77

WUSSLER, Robert J.
Behind the executive shake-up at CBS. il por Bus W p57-8+ O 31 '77 *

WYATT, Addie
She's a fighter on three fronts. por Ebony 32:70 Ag '77 *

WYATT, Jack
29th Transpac. il Yachting 142:222-4 S '77

WYATT, Ray. See Brown, D. G. jt auth

WYCKOFF, Donald L.
Wyckoff resigns to seek new interests. Craft Horiz 37:8 F '77 *

WYCLIFFE Bible Translators, Inc
Beyond Babel; work of Summer Institute of Linguistics Bible translators in Brazil. il Time 111:65 Ja 9 '78
Uncle Cam visits the U.S.S.R. E. E. Plowman. il por Chr Today 22:61-2 D 9 '77
Vanishing breed in Brazil; Summer Institute of Linguistics. Chr Today 22:43-4 D 30 '77

WYE Island
Wye Island. D. J. Preston. il Am For 83:20-2+ N '77

WYETH, Andrew
Wyeth's Siri: order and emotion; excerpt from Two worlds of Andrew Wyeth; with editorial comment. il por Horizon 19:24-9 My '77

about

Andrew Wyeth: oracle of the ordinary. B. Bristow. il Chr Today 21:27-8+ F 4 '77 *
Random thoughts on the most famous painter in America. S. E. Meyer. Am Artist 41:6-7+ F '77 *
Wyeth, the art world and class unconsciousness. C. Ratcliff. il Art in Am 65:15+ Ja '77 *

WYETH, James
From Jamie Wyeth's sketch book; reproduction of drawings. New Repub 176:18-19 Ja 22 '77
To artist Jamie Wyeth, U.S. is moving again. il pors U.S. News 82:90 My 16 '77

WYETH Laboratories. See Drug industry

WYLER, Leopold S. See Willens, H. jt auth

WYMAN, Lance
This way out—from our mad jumble of signs. W. Von Eckardt. il Smithsonian 8:114+ D '77 *

WYMAN, Thomas
Water pollution: the Indiana experiment. Environment 19:2-4 Je '77

WYMARD, Eleanor B.
Academic profile. Commonweal 104:652-7 O 14 '77
—See McMillan, E. jt auth

WYNETTE, Tammy
Country's angels. R. Blount, Jr. il pors Esquire 87:62-7+ Mr '77 *

WYNNE, Edward
Utopianism and education. Educ Digest 42:50-3 My '77

WYNNE, George G.
Regional planning in the Ruhr Valley. il map Parks & Rec 12:21-3 D '77

WYNNE-EDWARDS, Vero Copner
Caring groups and selfish genes. S. J. Gould. Natur Hist 86:20+ D '77 *

WYNTERS, Gail
Maybe this time. M. Pulik. pors Am Home 80:58-9 Ag '77 *

WYOMING
See also
Coal mines and mining—Wyoming
Fishing—Wyoming
Grand Teton National Park
Hunting—Wyoming
Irrigation—Wyoming
Landscape protection—Wyoming
Paleontology—Wyoming
Yellowstone National Park

WYOMING—*Continued*

Politics and government

See also
Politics, Corruption in—Wyoming

WYSE, Lois
Parenting: you learn, too. Vogue 167:243 D '77

about

Great turn-on. por Forbes 120:92 Jl 1 '77 *
Power of understatement. il por Harp Baz 111:166+ N '77 *

WYSER-PRATTE, Guy P.
Killing in Babcock & Wilcox. E. J. Tracy. il pors Fortune 96:266-9 O '77 *

WYSS, Wallace Alfred
Concours: the ultimate car-care contest. il Pop Mech 147:82-4+ Mr '77
Years of the snake. il por Hot Rod 30:31-4+ Je '77

X

X-CHROM lenses. See Lenses

X RAY apparatus and equipment

Manufacture

Xonics' struggle to sharpen its X-rays. il Bus W p80 Ja 24 '77

X RAY astronomy
HEAO raises X-ray source score. Sci N 112:406 D 17 '77
Mission to expand X-ray source study. C. Covault. il Aviation W 106:36-7+ Ap 11 '77
Observatory searches for new X-ray sources. Aviation W 107:22 Ag 29 '77
Some new developments in X-ray astronomy. L. C. Green. il Sky & Tel 53:340-3 My '77
Worldwide burster stakeout. Sky & Tel 54:83 Ag '77
X-ray stars in globular clusters. G. W. Clark. il Sci Am 237:42-55 O '77
X-rays from superclusters of galaxies. il Sky & Tel 54:105 Ag '77

X RAY crystallography. See Crystallography

X RAY microscopes and microscopy
High-resolution soft X-ray microscopy. R. Feder and others. bibl il Science 197:259-60 Jl 15 '77
Into th X-ray microcosm. J. H. Douglas. il Sci N 111:171 Mr 12 '77
Potential operating region for ultrasoft X-ray microscopy of biological materials. D. Sayre and others. bibl il Science 196:1339-40 Je 17 '77

X-22, pseud. See Magriel, P.

XANTHAN gum
Multistranded helix in xanthan polysaccharide. G. Holzwarth and E. B. Prestridge. bibl il Science 197:757-9 Ag 19 '77

XANTHIUM. See Cockleburs

XENIA, Ohio
Good news about disaster; effects of tornado on residents. V. Taylor. bibl il por Psychol Today 11:93-4+ O '77
Xenia sounds off to reduce tornado tragedies; warning system. il Am City & County 92:66 F '77

XENON
Strange xenon, extinct superheavy elements, and the solar neutrino puzzle. O. K. Manuel and D. D. Sabu; R. S. Lewis and others. bibl Science 195:208-10 Ja 14 '77

XENOPUS. See Frogs

XEROX Consultants, Inc. See Xerox Corporation

XEROX Corporation
Big battle in copiers. R. Levy. il Duns R 109:97-9 My '77
Decompression tank for Xerox executives; Xerox Consultants Inc. Bus W p64 My 16 '77
Distance man. il por Forbes 120:192 N 15 '77

XONICS, Inc. See X ray apparatus and equipment—Manufacture

XOX-Nabisco (firm) See Nabisco, Inc

Y

YAF. See Young Americans for Freedom (organization)

YASD. See American Library Association—Young Adult Services Division

YCC. See United States—Youth Conservation Corps

YFC. See Youth for Christ International (organization)

YWCA. See Young Women's Christian Association

YACHT brokers
Broker profile; interviews. Motor B & S 140:108 Jl; 108 Ag; 176 S; 117 N; 117 D '77; 141:237 Ja '78

YACHT building. See Boatbuilding

YACHT club cruises. See Cruising

YACHT clubs
St Francis YC destroyed in fire. J. Carrick. il Yachting 141:166 F '77
World's highest yacht club; Bolivian YC. P. Ellam. il Yachting 141:32 Je '77
See also
New York Yacht Club

YACHT decoration. See Boat decoration

YACHT deliveries. See Boats—Transportation

YACHT Design Institute. See Naval architecture—Study and teaching

YACHT hijacking. See Boat hijacking

YACHT models. See Ship and boat models

YACHT racing
America's Cup. N. King. Nat R 29:1187-8+ O 14 '77
America's Cup news. Yachting 141:190-1 Mr; 201-3 Ap; 204-5 My; 168-9 Je; 142:97 Jl '77
Antigua for action. B. Robinson. il Yachting 142:56-9 Jl '77
Australia sails to the fore; opening trials for America's Cup challengers. C. Phinizy. il Sports Illus 47:48+ Ag 15 '77
Being guided to Newport by a northern star, P. Petterson, designer of Sweden's America's Cup challenger. C. Phinizy. il por Sports Illus 46:38-40+ Mr 7 '77
Bermuda cruising race. T. Gibbs. il Yachting 142:194-5 O '77
Bermuda high: random memories from the first Blue Water Cruising Race, Marion, Mass. to Bermuda. T. Gibbs. Yachting 142:136 S '77
Big STC race week. M. Wiley. il Yachting 142:144-5 Ag '77
British take the Admiral's Cup. H. Somerville. il Yachting 142:52 O '77
Calendar of major sailing events. See issues of Yachting
Captain courageous; T. Turner. P. Bonventre. il por Newsweek 90:77 S 12 '77
Captain outrageous; T. Turner at the America's Cup trials. P. Bonventre and R. Manning. il por Newsweek 90:45-6 Jl 11 '77
Case of the 12.1-meter. . .and other America's Cup fandangos. J. Hammond. Motor B & S 139:79-81 My '77
Coney Island in Newport; commercialization surrounding America's Cup race. il Newsweek 90:72-3 S 5 '77
Courageous wins first Cup trials; America's Cup. J. Rousmaniere. il Yachting 142:50-3+ Ag '77
Courageous won; America's Cup trials. B. Bavier. Yachting 142:54 O '77
Cruising man goes racing. R. M. Dey. il Yachting 141:172+ My '77
Cup afterthoughts. J. Rousmaniere. il Yachting 142:23-5 N '77
Cup of tea for Courageous; America's Cup. C. Phinizy. il Sports Illus 47:26-8+ S 26 '77
Cutting loose in Antigua. J. Hammond. il Motor B & S 140:49-53 Ag '77
Day of reckoning is drawing nigh; America's Cup. C. Phinizy. il Sports Illus 47:24-6+ S 12 '77
Defending the America's Cup; T. Turner. il por Time 110:84-5 S 19 '77
Distance racing. J. Rousmaniere. See issues of Yachting
Eccentric Admiral's Cup. D. Deaver. il Yachting 142:50-2 D '77
European news (title varies) See occasional issues of Yachting
461 you are over! offshore racing. F. Adams. Yachting 141:142-5 Je '77
Getting ready for the big summer; America's Cup preparations. J. Rousmaniere. il Yachting 141:62-71+ F '77
Inherit the winds; America's Cup race. W. J. LaJeunesse. il Sat Eve Post 249:52-3+ S '77
Jack knife tops slow 465-mile race to Newport; Annapolis-Newport Race. C. Van Duyne. Yachting 142:146 Ag '77
Just an inch away from failure; Imp's victory in her division of the SORC. C. Phinizy. il Sports Illus 46:54-5 Mr 7 '77
Mismatch or close miss? America's Cup. B. Bavier. Yachting 142:56 N '77
Month in yachting. See issues of Yachting
Mouth of the South; T. Turner. P. Axthelm. il pors Newsweek 90:74-5+ S 19 '77
Mouth of the South at the helm; T. Turner in America's Cup trials. il por Time 110:44 Ag 8 '77
News from yachting centers. See issues of Yachting
Notes from the classes (cont of) With the racing classes; ed by E. Horan. See issues of Yachting
One on one; America's Cup. R. Vaughan. il pors Motor B & S 140:78-80+ Ag '77
Preparing for Transpac. M. Olson. Yachting 142:36+ Jl '77

YACHT racing—*Continued*
Racing clinic, offshore. See issues of Yachting
Racing, more or less, with the big mast in back; Schooner Cove Schooner Race. T. Gibbs. Yachting 142:158 O '77
Record run on the southern sea; Southern Ocean Racing Conference. C. Phinizy. il Sports Illus 46:22-4+ F 14 '77
Role of the America's Cup Committee. P. Chubb. il Yachting 142:134 Ag '77
Round the World Race gets underway; Whitbread Round-the-World Race. R. Humphreys. il Yachting 142:140 N '77
SORC follow-up. J. Rousmaniere. il Yachting 141:46+ Ap '77
Sailing on a sea of perplexity; America's Cup trials. C. Phinizy. il Sports Illus 47:22-3 Ag 8 '77
Setting sail for the defense; America's Cup trials; with report by N. Williamson. C. Phinizy. il Sports Illus 46:30-5 Je 20 '77
Setting the stage; July Observation Trials. B. Robinson. il Yachting 142:110-11 S '77
Sloops du jour off Newport; America's Cup races. T. Foote. il Time 110:54 O 3 '77
Staging a battle royal on the briny; America's Cup defender trials. C. Phinizy. il por Sports Illus 47:18-20+ Jl 4 '77
Thoughts on the SORC. B. Bavier. Yachting 141:62 Ap '77
Top flight competition; SORC. J. Rousmaniere. il Yachting 141:66-71+ Ap '77
Turner wins Congressional Cup. J. Rousmaniere. il Yachting 141:208 My '77
29th Transpac. J. Wyatt. il Yachting 142:222-4 S '77
23rd challenge; America's Cup; symposium. il Yachting 142:84-119 S '77
Up to the scuppers in cups; Congressional Cup. C. Phinizy. il Sports Illus 46:48+ Mr 28 '77
Why the gap hasn't closed; America's Cup. B. Robinson. il pors Yachting 142:58-60 N '77
See also
Navigation—Competitions
United States Yacht Racing Union

Economic aspects

More than just an entry fee. T. Gibbs. Yachting 142:67 D '77

History

America's Cup history: the 22 challenges since 1870. A. F. Loomis and others. il Yachting 142:148+ S '77
Looking back; nine Cup greats recount their peak memories; America's Cup. il Yachting 142:103-9 S '77
Those glorious J-boats; excerpt from Enterprise to Endeavour: the J-class yachts. I. Dear. il Yachting 142:99-102+ S '77

Photographs

Lady with a camera. D. Beeston. il Yachting 141:76-80 Ap '77
Stingray puts on a show. P. Brown. Yachting 142:70-1 O '77

Rules

Have you read your sailing instructions lately? B. Bentsen. Yachting 141:80-1+ F '77
See also
Yachts—Rating

YACHT racing trophies. See Trophies, Sport

YACHTING (periodical)
Way we were: Yachting through the years. il Yachting 142:50-1 Jl '77

YACHTS

Automobile trailer combination

Trailable sailing yachts. A. J. McMasters. il Mech Illus 73:124-5 F '77

Chartering

See Yachts—Leasing and renting

Design

Being guided to Newport by a northern star, P. Petterson, designer of Sweden's America's Cup challenger. C. Phinizy. il por Sports Illus 46:38-40+ Mr 7 '77
Bruce Farr talks about light displacement and the IOR; interview, ed by M. Pope. B. Farr. il por Yachting 142:72-5 O '77
Designers' forum. See issues of Yachting
Designs; ed by J. Smith. See issues of Yachting
Drawing board. See issues of Motor boating & sailing
How big is 12 meters of boat? T. Bottomley. il Pop Mech 148:76-7+ S '77
Jerry Milgram. J. Rousmaniere. il por Yachting 141:104+ Je '77
Racing clinic, offshore:
Inside Imp. J. Rousmaniere. il Yachting 141:56+ Ap '77
Inside the J-24. J. Rousmaniere. il Yachting 142:72+ S '77
Yachting eyes:
Bertram 58 convertible. J. Smith. il Yachting 142:78-81 Ag '77
Trojan F-44 motor yacht. J. Smith. il Yachting 142:76-9 O '77

Study and teaching

See Naval architecture—Study and teaching

Electronic equipment

See also
Depth indicators
Navigation—Aids and devices
Radio direction finders

Equipment

Twelves' gear. il Yachting 142:118-19 S '77

Exhibitions

See Boats—Exhibitions

Finance

12-meter's budget. J. Rousmaniere. il Yachting 142:203-4 S '77

Interior decoration

See Boat decoration

Leasing and renting

Chartering—how bare is the boat? W. C. Ross. il Yachting 141:170-4 Mr '77
Chartering in Greece. S. Hart. Yachting 141:156-7 Je '77
New area to bareboat opening up the Sardinia-Corsica section of the Med. B. Robinson. il map Yachting 142:68-71 N '77
So you want to be a charter captain . . . D. R. Hart. il Motor B & S 139:23-4+ Ap '77
See also
Fishing boats—Leasing and renting

Maintenance and repair

See also
Boatyards

Materials

See Boats—Materials

Rating

Optimizing ratings. S. Kaufman. il Yachting 142:48+ N '77
PHRF: what it is; how it works; Performance Handicap Racing Fleet System. J. Foyer. il Yachting 141:54+ F '77
Pratt Project update; meeting of the USYRU Handicap Rule Committee. O. C. Torrey, Jr. Yachting 142:30 Jl '77
What is a 12-meter? R. S. Blumenstock. il Yachting 142:144+ S '77

Testing

Performance test:
Fiberform Executive 3300. D. Hart. il Motor B & S 139:36+ My '77
Uniflite 38 convertible. D. Hart. il Motor B & S 140:18-20 D '77

Transportation

See Boats—Transportation

YACHTS and yachting
Boatbuilder and his dream yacht; schooner Island Star. T. Gibbs. il por Yachting 142:74-7 N '77
Cross currents. See issues of Yachting
Cruising yachtsman; ed by T. Gibbs. See issues of Yachting
Dream machine; the Mephistopheles owned by Joel McQuade. B. O'Boyle. il Motor B & S 141:83-5 Ja '78
Editors page. B. Robinson. See issues of Yachting
Fabulous 50's; motor yachts. il Motor B & S 140:56-9+ O '77
From the cockpit. R. N. Bavier. See issues of Yachting
High style in Miami; the Bon Vivant of Beth and Ralph Levitz. L. Bertram. il Motor B & S 140:84 Ag '77
Lessons learned: a practical lifestyle in the Med; trawler yacht Mona Mona. R. Sutton. il Yachting 142:72-6 Ag '77
Man and his boat; C A. Hipkins and his Press On Regardless; lobster yacht. E. Horan. il Yachting 141:92-3 Mr '77
New boats in Yachting. See occasional issues of Yachting
Powerboats for 1978. il Yachting 142:137-8+ O '77
Sailing yacht symposium. A. Adler. il Yachting 141:118+ Ap '77
Serious business of yacht surveying. J. West. il Motor B & S 140:54-6+ S '77
Standing by: handling the twelves' tenders. T. Gibbs. il Yachting 142:96-8 S '77
See also
Cruisers (pleasure boats)
Ice boats and ice boating
Masts and rigging
Navigation
Sailboats
Seamanship
Women in boating
Yacht clubs
Yacht racing

YACHTS and yachting—*Continued*

Bibliography

Book notes and reviews. K. Aamodt. See issues of Yachting

History

Remembrance of things past. B. O'Donovan. il Motor B & S 140:70-2+ Jl '77
Those glorious J-boats; excerpt from Enterprise to Endeavour: the J-class yachts. I. Dear. il Yachting 142:99-102+ S '77

Photographs

Enterprise sailing. J. Rousmaniere. il Yachting 141:147-8 Mr '77

Testing

Performance test:
Willard 40 trawler. D. Hart. il Motor B & S 141:32+ Ja '78

YADDO (artists and authors colony) See Artists and authors colonies

YADIN, Yigael
Israel's Mr Clean. M. Kondracke. New Repub 176:6+ F 26 '77 *
Newest of the Dead Sea Scrolls. il por Time 109: 57-8 Ja 24 '77 *
Yadin jumps in. por Time 110:52 O 31 '77 *

YADLIN, Asher
Israel's troubled choice. A. Deming and M. J. Kubic. il por Newsweek 89:33-4 F 28 '77 *

YAEGER, Judy
Melons ripe for the picking. Org Gard & Farm 24:156-8 My '77

YAGI, N. and others
Return of myosin heads to thick filaments after muscle contraction. bibl il Science 197:685-7 Ag 12 '77

YAHI Indians
Legacy of Ishi. F. R. Gunsky. il Liv Wildn 40:4-11 Ja '77
Wild man of Oroville. C. W. Campbell. il pro Am Hist Illus 12:18-26+ Je '77

YAKIMA, Wash.

Education

See Education—Washington (state)

YAKUTSK, Russia
Five times to Yakutsk. D. Conger. il pors Nat Geog 152:256-69 Ag '77

YAKUZA. See Crime and criminals—Japan

YALE, Elihu
Although a rascal, Eli Yale used his means effectively. M. Waterson. il por Smithsonian 8:91-7 O '77 *

YALE Philharmonia. See Orchestras

YALE Symphony. See Orchestras

YALE University
Bod and man at Yale; charges of sex discrimination for tolerating sexual coercion of female students by male teachers. il Time 110:52-3 Ag 8 '77
Fear and trembling at Yale. G. Graff. Am Scholar 46:467-78 Aut '77
Giving Yale to Connecticut; excerpt from God and man at Yale. W. F. Buckley, Jr. il Harpers 255:43-8+ N '77; Discussion. 256:6 Ja '78
Humanist; A. B. Giamatti appointed president. por Time 111:68 Ja 2 '78
Leap of faith, a leap of action; excerpt from Once to every man. W. S. Coffin. por Chr Cent 94:938-44 O 19 '77
New Haven's presidential search. il Time 110:96+ D 5 '77
Nothing happened; college in the early seventies. F. Iseman. Esquire 88:74-5+ S '77
Once and future King; K. Brewster. M. Sheils and P. Malamud. il por Newsweek 89:63 Ap 18 '77
Renaissance man; A. B. Giamatti. M. Sheils and P. Malamud. por Newsweek 91:45 Ja 2 '78
Women students v. male teachers: sexual harassment at Yale. A. Nelson. Nation 226:7-9 Ja 7 '78
Yale University is preserving its great late-19th-century architecture by remodeling the Old Campus. M. F. Schmertz. il Archit Rec 161:93-100 Mr '77
Yale's blues; nominations for a new president. M. Sheils. il por Newsweek 90:79 D 26 '77

Center for British Art

Anglomania. Nat R 29:786 Jl 8 '77
Lords, ladies and common folk at Yale. A. Frankenstein. il Art N 76:40-3 Summ '77
Man and friend at Yale; Mellon collection of British paintings. il Horizon 19:38 My '77
New stately home. D. Davis. il Newsweek 89: 90-1 Ap 18 '77
There'll always be an England in New Haven. il Horizon 20:60-5 N '77
Yale Center for British Art. V. Scully, Jr. il Archit Rec 161:95-104 Je '77
Yale's shrine to the Age of Reason. il Time 109:63-4 Ap 25 '77

Clubs and societies

Last secrets of Skull and Bones. R. Rosenbaum. il Esquire 88:84-9+ S '77

YALOW, Rosalyn Sussman
Rosalyn Sussman Yalow; interview, ed by G. M. Landau. por Parents Mag 53:38+ Ja '78
What's ahead for women in medicine. il pors Parents Mag 53:38-9+ Ja '78

about

Medicine: hunting hormones. il por Newsweek 90:88 O 24 '77 *
1977 Nobel laureates in science. il pors Chemistry 50:18-20 D '77 *
1977 Nobel Prize in physiology or medicine. J. Meites. il pors Science 198:594-6 N 11 '77 *
Nobel prizes: seven in '77. pors Sci N 112:260-1 O 22 '77 *
Yalow wins half of Nobel prize in medicine. H. R. Leuchtag. por Phys Today 30:78-9 D '77 *

YAMAMOTO, Kenichi
Speed and the single rotor. B. Hartford. il por Pop Mech 147:198 Mr '77 *

YAMASAKI, Minoru
Architect was told world trade so he planned big. R. Lynes. il Smithsonian 8:42-9 Ja '78 *

YAMEY, B. S. See Bauer, P. T. jt auth

YANCEY, Dorothy Cowser
Professor James Emman Kwegyir Aggrey's personality. bibl Negro Hist Bull 40:722-4 Jl '77

YANCEY, Philip
Joni's story. il pors Sat Eve Post 249:75+ S '77
Marriage: minefields on the way to paradise. il Chr Today 21:24-7 F 18 '77

YANG, Shen K. and others
Benzo [α] pyrene diol epoxides: mechanism of enzymatic formation and optically active intermediates. bibl il Science 196:1199-201 Je 10 '77

YANGTAOS
Strange fruits; with recipes. R. Sokolov. il Natur Hist 86:84-7 Mr '77

YANOMAMO Indians. See Indians of South America

YAPLE, Charles H. See Matthews, B. E. jt auth

YAQUI Indians
Passion according to the Yaquis. il UNESCO Courier 30:22-3 Ag '77

YARBROUGH, Donald B.
Sins of Justice Yarbrough. por Time 110:44 Jl 18 '77 *

YARD lighting fixtures. See Lighting fixtures

YARD tools. See Lawn tools, equipment and supplies

YARDLEY, Jonathan
Everybody knew me Al; excerpt from Ring, a biography of Ring Lardner. il Sports Illus 47: 82-6+ Ag 29 '77
Harmony in Great Neck: the friendship of Ring Lardner and F. Scott Fitzgerald; excerpt from Ring: a biography of Ring Lardner. il pors Sat R 4:23-5+ Jl 9 '77

YARDS. See Home grounds

YARHAM, E. R.
New Zealand's king kauri. il Am For 83:16-19+ Ag '77

YARN collage. See Collage

YARN dyeing. See Dyes and dyeing

YARNELL, Jim
Pilot's camera. il Flying 101:170-3 S '77

YASHCHENKO, Vladimir
Just an old-fashioned lad. M. Clark. il por Sports Illus 47:48+ Jl 25 '77 *

YATES, Brock
[Column] See occasional issues of Car and driver
Power play at Parker. il Motor B & S 140:61-3+ Ag '77
30-year heritage of daring. il Sports Illus 47: 33 O 3 '77

YATES, Michael
Trouble with Chavez. por Nation 225:518-20 N 19 '77

YATRON Gus
Excerpts from a statement on federal funds for the financing of election campaigns, February 1977. Cong Digest 56:87+ Mr '77

YAWNING
Ho hum-cholinergic nerves are the culprit. il Sci N 111:359 Je 4 '77

YAZOO CITY, Miss.
Yazoo City; south toward home. W. Morris. il Time 110:13-14 Ag 1 '77

YEAGER, Alice B.
Seckels grow in the Southwest. Org Gard & Farm 24:176-8 Ap '77

YEAGER, Evelyn A.
One man's afghan, another man's purl. il pors Ret Liv 17:43 Ap '77

YEAGER, Robert C.
Doctoring isn't just for doctors. Read Digest 111: 237-8+ D '77
Savagery on the playing fields. il Read Digest 111:23-4+ Jl '77

YEAR round schools. See School year

YEAR Santa forgot Christmas; drama. See Marshall, S. L.

YEATS, Robert S.
High rates of vertical crustal movement near Ventura, California. bibl il map Science 196: 295-8 Ap 15 '77

YEATS, William Butler
Portrait of the artist as an old man. L. Edel. Am Scholar 47:63-8 Wint '77
about
Auden and W.B. Yeats. E. T. Callan. pors Commonweal 104:298-303 My 13 '77 *
YELLEN, Benjamin
Populist Doc. por Forbes 120:190 N 15 '77 *
YELLIG, Jim
Santa Claus is alive and well... J. D. Lewis. il por Ret Liv 17:34+ D '77 *
YELLOW Freight System, Inc. See Trucking
YELLOWHEAD Highway. See Express highways —Canada
YELLOWSTONE National Park
Park Service discloses ripoff operations in land of Old Faithful. Nat Parks & Con Mag 51:26-7 Ag '77
Rocky Mountain high time of your life. V. Landi. il Outdoor Life 159:70-5+ My '77
YEN, J. L. and others
Real-time, very-long-baseline interferometry based on the use of a communications satellite. bibl il Science 198:289-91 O 21 '77
YEN, James T.
Wind energy from the Yen tornado. J. H. Douglas. il por Sci N 111:31 Ja 8 '77 *
YENSER, Stephen
Notebook entry, (Pau, 1971); poem. New Yorker 53:68 Mr 14 '77
YEPSEN, Roger B. Jr
Stocking the cold cellar. il Org Gard & Farm 24:109-10+ S '77
YERGIN, Daniel H.
Answering OPEC. New Repub 176:45-7 Ja 22 '77
Arms zealots. il Harpers 254:64+ Je '77
Europe's nuclear disappointment. New Repub 178:13-16 Ja 7 '78
Politics and Soviet-American trade: the three questions. For Affairs 55:517-38 Ap '77
Soviet trade. New Repub 176:16-17 Je 4 '77
Terrifying prospect: atomic bombs everywhere. il Atlantic 239:46-9+ Ap '77
YES (rock group) See Rock groups
YESBERGER, Jim, and Saffer, M.
Booth design. il Craft Horiz 37:57 Je '77
YESHIVA University, New York
Yeshiva to cut graduate physics and mathematics. B. C. Carr. Phys Today 30:86-7 O '77
YESHIVOT. See Jews—Education
YETI. See Animals, Mythical
YGLESIAS, Jose, and others
Shaggy dog story. il por N Y Times Mag p87 F 20 '77
YI, Sun-shin
Admiral Yi and the turtle boats. B. I. Wiley. il por Am Hist Illus 12:44-8 Je '77 *
YIDDISH literature
In praise of Chaim Grade. R. R. Wisse. Commentary 63:70-3 Ap '77
YIDDISH musicians. See Musicians, Jewish
YIDDISH theater. See Theater—Jews
YIM, John J. and others
Mechanism of suppression in drosophila:control of sepiapterin synthase at the purple locus. bibl il Science 198:1168-70 D 16 '77
YIN, T. C. T. and Mountcastle, V. B.
Visual input to the visuomotor mechanisms of the monkey's parietal lobe. bibl il Science 197:1381-3 S 30 '77
YOES, E. D. Jr
COPS comes to San Antonio. Progressive 41: 33-6 My '77
YOFFE, Emily. See Szulc, T. jt auth
YOGIS
See also
Bhajan
YOGURT
Buy frogurt, or else; H. P. Hood, Inc. il por Forbes 119:56 My 15 '77
Making yogurt the easy way, yogurt makers and recipes. il Good H 185:140+ Jl '77
Marketer who put H. P. Hood on the map; E. Gelsthorpe. il por Duns R 110:30-1 Jl '77
Yogurt. il Consumer Rep 43:7-12 Ja '78
Yogurt & the fountain of youth; filming of Dannon commercial in Soviet Georgia; with recipes. C. Turgeon. il Sat Eve Post 249:18+ O '77
Yogurt—so-so or so good? A. A. Belson. il Vogue 167:140+ Ap '77
See also
Cookery—Yogurt
YOGURT makers. See Kitchen utensils and appliances
YOKOI, Tomoe
Tomoe Yokoi's mezzotints. E. Zeifer. il por Am Artist 41:40-5+ O '77 *
YOKOYAMA, H. and others
Chemical bioinduction of rubber in guayule plant. bibl Science 197:1076-8 S 9 '77
YOKUM, Dan
Another losing year. por Time 110:30 O 24 '77 *
YOON, Sang Cho-chung, and Redler, B. H.
Dibutyryl cyclic AMP mimics ovariectomy: nuclear protein phosphorylation in mammary tumor regression. bibl il Science 197:272-5 Jl 15 '77
YORK, Herbert F.
Eisenhower's other warning: excerpts from address, April 26, 1976. por Phys Today 30:9+ Ja '77
—and Greb, G. A.
Military research and development: a postwar history. bibl il Bull Atom Sci 33:12-22+ Ja '77
Strategic reconnaissance. bibl il Bull Atom Sci 33:33-42 Ap '77
YORUBA (native race) See Africa, West—Native races
YOSEMITE National Park
Fun in the snow near Yosemite's south entrance. il map Sunset 158:46-7 Mr '77
Great Yosemite gold rush. G. Rowell. Audubon 79:135 S '77
What's next for Yosemite? D. Sumner. il Nat Wildlife 15:34-7 O '77
YOSHIMOTO, Yoshio, and others
Human chorionic gonadotropin-like substance in nonendocrine tissues of normal subjects. bibl il Science 197:575-7 Ag 5 '77
YOST, Ed
Longest manned balloon flight. il por Nat Geog 151:208-17 F '77
YOU bet your vocabulary! drama. See Tobias, A.
YOU never can tell; drama. See Shaw, G. B.
YOUMANS, Grant E.
Rural aged. bibl f il Ann Am Acad 429:81-90 Ja '77
YOUNG, A. Thomas. See Martin, J. S. Jr, jt auth
YOUNG, Al
Comment. R. Siegel. Poetry 130:109-10 My '77 *
YOUNG, Andrew J. 1932-
Administration supports increased U.S. contributions to the African Development Fund; statement, April 18, 1977. Dept State Bull 76: 471-2 My 9 '77
Ambassador Young interviewed on Issues and answers; transcript of program, October 30, 1977; ed by B. Clark and others. Dept State Bull 77:791-2+ D 5 '77
Ambassador Young testifies on Rhodesian sanctions bill; statement, February 24, 1977. Dept State Bull 76:271-2 Mr 21 '77
Casual confidence; excerpts from interview, ed by A. Collings. il por Newsweek 90:39 S 12 '77
Challenge to the Economic and Social Council: advancing the quality of life in all its aspects; address, April 19, 1977. Dept State Bull 76: 494-502 My 16 '77
Developments concerning apartheid; World Conference for Action Against Apartheid; statement, August 25, 1977. Dept State Bull 77:446-8 O 3 '77
Framework for a dynamic North-South dialogue; statement, July 8, 1977. Dept State Bull 77: 383-9 S 19 '77
I don't mind being the lightning rod; excerpts from interview, ed by R. Watson and others. il por Newsweek 89:30-1 Mr 28 '77
Initiatives for peace in the Middle East; statement, November 24, 1977. Dept State Bull 77: 884-5 D 19 '77
New unity and a new hope in the Western hemisphere: economic growth with social justice; statement, May 3, 1977. Dept State Bull 76:567-76 My 30 '77
Rhodesia—proposals for a settlement; joint press conference, September 2, 1977. Dept State Bull 77:417-24 O 3 '77
U.N. Security Council condemns South Africa's apartheid policy and imposes a mandatory arms embargo; statements, October 31 and November 4, 1977. Dept State Bull 77:859-65 D 12 '77
U.S. joins U.N. Fund for Agricultural Development; statement, October 4, 1977. Dept State Bull 77:644 N 7 '77
U.S. position on Israeli settlements; statement, October 28, 1977. Dept State Bull 77:821-2 D 5 '77
United States reiterates support for the independence of Namibia and Zimbabwe at Maputo conference; statement, May 19, 1977. Dept State Bull 77:55-8 Jl 11 '77
about
Andrew Young: outspoken ambassador. por Sr Schol 109:6-7 Ap 7 '77
Andy outstrips Fritz; stand on human rights. Nat R 29:654 Je 10 '77 *
Andy Young and the truth. J. L. Jackson. por Newsweek 90:9 Jl 11 '77 *
Andy Young, Andy Young; Playboy interview. P. Goldman and E. Clift. Newsweek 89:34 Je 20 '77 *
Andy Young conundrum. Nat R 29:481 Ap 29 '77 *
Andy Young is at it again. R. Carroll and others. il por Newsweek 89:52 Je 6 '77 *
Anxious for a new start. il por Time 109:43-5 F 21 '77 *

YOUNG, Andrew J. 1932- —about—*Continued*
Are Young's wings being clipped? por U.S. News 82:25 My 2 '77 *
Around City Hall. A. Logan. New Yorker 53: 84-6 Je 27 '77 *
Black man's burden. L. H. Lapham. il Harpers 254:15-16+ Je '77 *
Candor and caution. Chr Cent 94:581-2 Je 22 '77 *
Carter's point man. R. Carroll and others. il por Newsweek 89:39-40 F 14 '77 *
Case is not closed. T. Mathews and others. il por Newsweek 90:51 N 7 '77 *
Corridors of morality. J. Lelyveld. il por N Y Times Mag p 142 O 16 '77 *
Diplomatic dissident. Nation 224:516 Ap 30 '77 *
Do-it-yourself diplomacy. R. Carroll and E. Clift. pors Newsweek 89:36 Mr 21 '77 *
Little less noise, please. Nation 224:738-9 Je 18 '77 *
Muzzle for motor mouth? por Time 109:16 Ap 25 '77 *
New multi-ring spectacle. il por Time 109:29-30 F 14 '77 *
Ordeal of Andy Young. W. F. Buckley, Jr. Nat R 29:740-1 Je 24 '77 *
Our man at the U.N. E. E. Plowman. Chr Today 21:36-8 Ja 7 '77 *
Our new voice at the U.N. J. Lelyveld. il pors N Y Times Mag p 17-19+ F 6 '77 *
Outspoken Andy Young. R. Carroll and E. Clift. il por Newsweek 89:24-6+ Mr 28 '77 *
Peace-plan safari. M. R. Benjamin and others. il pors Newsweek 90:35-6 S 5 '77 *
Plunder on the right. K. Bode. New Repub 177:11-12 N 12 '77 *
Point man, or unguided missile? il por Time 109:27-8 Mr 21 '77 *
United States policy in Africa. R. E. Bissell. bibl f Cur Hist 73:193-5+ D '77 *
Washington notebook. S. Booker. Ebony 32:26 Mr '77 *
Young at heart. J. Pringle. il por Newsweek 89:44 My 30 77 *
Young mission. N. Cousins. Sat R 4:4 Jl 9 '77 *
Young survives another storm; Playboy interview. U.S. News 82:29 Je 20 '77 *

Anecdotes, facetiae, satire, etc.

Amos and Andy Young show. D. K. Mano. Nat R 29:1507-8 D 23 '77

YOUNG, Brigham
Mormons: from persecution to power. R. W. Paul. il Am Heritage 28:74-83 Je '77 *

YOUNG, David Pollock
Names of a hare in English; poem. Poetry 131: 78-87 N '77

YOUNG, Diana, and Simmons, B. J.
We can grow! SLJ 23:44 My '77

YOUNG, Dudley J.
Having cucumber troubles? Try hand pollination. il Org Gard & Farm 24:83-5 F '77

YOUNG, Dwight L.
Historic preservation in Mobile. il Antiques 112: 460-5 S '77

YOUNG, Eugene A.
Interstate land for municipal parks. il Parks & Rec 12:36-8 Ap '77

YOUNG, Gary
Cold did not break; poem. Nation 225:440 O 29 '77
Drought; poem. Nation 225:600 D 3 '77
Winter drought; Winter solstice; poems. Poetry 131:144 D '77

YOUNG, George G.
Universe of stamps. il Sky & Tel 54:366-70 N '77

YOUNG, George M. Jr
Unlikely hero, guaranteed villain. Nat R 29: 554-5 My 13 '77

YOUNG, Gordon
Essence of life: salt. il Nat Geog 152:380-401 S '77

YOUNG, James B. and Landsberg, Lewis
Suppression of sympathetic nervous system during fasting. bibl il Science 196:1473-5 Je 24 '77

YOUNG, Jimmy
I don't really fight to win. P. F. Putnam. il por Sports Illus 47:72+ O 31 '77 *
Jeemy Young! Jeemy Young! Jeemy Young! P. Putnam. il pors Sports Illus 46:22-3 Mr 28 '77 *
Win some, lose some, split the rest. P. Putnam. il pors Sports Illus 47:36-8+ N 14 '77 *

YOUNG, Jordan M.
Brazil: world power 2000? il Intellect 105:406-9 Je '77

YOUNG, Joseph Louis
But will they like it in Chicago? Vasari. il Art N 76:20+ O '77 *

YOUNG, Mahonri Sharp
Detached observer. il Art N 76:114-15 My '77

YOUNG, Marilyn
Critical amnesia. Nation 224:406-8 Ap 2 '77

YOUNG, Patrick
Time. . .and space. . .adding credence to Einstein's work. Sci Digest 82:33-6 Ag '77

YOUNG, Ray
Ever-improving economics of canning. il Org Gard & Farm 24:98-9 Jl '77
Get the most from wood ashes. il Org Gard & Farm 24:160-3 F '77

YOUNG, Rick
Silent night. il Flying 101:23+ Ag '77

YOUNG, Samuel H.
When children have psychic powers; excerpt from Psychic children. il McCalls 104:204-5+ Ap '77

YOUNG, Stuart H.
Breathe easy! il Parents Mag 52:23+ Jl '77

YOUNG, Warren R.
There's a girl on the tracks! il Read Digest 110:91-5 F '77

YOUNG Adult Conservation Corps. See Unemployment—Relief measures

YOUNG Adult Services Division, American Library Association. See American Library Association—Young Adult Services Division

YOUNG adults literature
Adolescent image in American books for children. M. Lystad. Educ Digest 43:50-2 N '77
Identifying high interest/low reading level books. B. S. Bates. bibl il SLJ 24:19-21 N '77
YA literature comes of age. K. L. Donelson. bibl il por Wilson Lib Bull 52:241-7 N '77

Authorship

In their own words; interviews (cont) P. Janeczko. Engl J 66:14-16 Mr; 10-11 S; 20-1 O '77
Nightmare of Mildred Lee. F. W. Wright, Jr. por Writers Digest 57:38-9 D '77
PW interview; ed by J. F. Mercier. P. Zindel. por Pub W 212:6-7 D 5 '77

Bibliography

Adult books for young adults; ed by R. Moorchian. See issues of School library journal
Best books for spring 1977; ed by L. N. Gerhardt and others. il SLJ 23:35-7 My '77
Best books for whom; or, Where have all the grown-ups gone? L. L. Shapiro. Wilson Lib Bull 51:803-4+ Je '77
Best books for YAs. SLJ 23:95 Mr '77; Same. Todays Educ 66:82-4+ S '77
Best books 1977; ed by L. N. Gerhardt and others. il SLJ 24:30-3 D '77
Books for young adults. A. P. Nilsen. il Engl J 66:84-8 S '77
Books for young adults: the 1976 BYA book poll. G. R. Carlsen and others. il Engl J 66: 62-7 Ja '77
Catchers in the rye. C. Michener. il Newsweek 90:85 D 19 '77
Elderly books for youngerly readers (title varies) M. McCue and E. Wilson. See issues of Wilson library bulletin
Outlook tower; adult books of interest to high school readers. M. S. Cosgrave. See issues of Horn book magazine
Paper power (cont) SLJ 23:85-6 Ap; 24:133-4 O '77
Still alive: the best of the best, 1960-1974. Todays Educ 66:97-101 Ja '77

Book reviewers and reviewing

See Book reviewers and reviewing

Study and teaching

Junior novel and the art of literature. R. C. Small, Jr. il Engl J 66:56-9 O '77

YOUNG adults reading
RIF for teenagers. N. L. Marqua. SLJ 23:45 My '77

YOUNG Americans for Freedom (organization)
After the ball was over: decompression, junior division. C. Buckley; discussion. Nat R 29: 141-2+ F 4 '77
Wisdom in New York; ninth national convention. F. R. Dempsey. Nat R 29:1052+ S 16 '77

YOUNG Audiences, Inc
Young Audiences is twenty-five. N. Stevens. il Hi Fi 27:MA12-15 F '77

YOUNG women
Loneliness of a teenage feminist. D. Shaw. il por Ms 6:112-13 N '77
More young women are smoking, and they're smoking more. D. Cohen. Psychol Today 10: 131 Ap '77
See also
Youth

YOUNG Women's Christian Association
Marry-go-round; California YWCA's Responsibility, Experience and Alternatives for Life program for high school students. L. Katz. Seventeen 36:55 Je '77

YOUNGER, Evelle Jansen
Capital punishment; address, July 15, 1977. Vital Speeches 43:682-5 S 1 '77

YOUNGHUSBAND, Peter
Wildlife in Namibia. il Int Wildlife 7:52-63 N '77

YOUNGMAN, Henny
Profiles. A. Hiss. New Yorker 53:46-8+ S 12 '77 *

YOUNGREN, William
Gershwin. New Repub 176:21-4 Ap 23; 27-30 Ap 30; 23-6 My 7; 23-8 My 14 '77
National Public Radio. New Repub 177:25-8 S 10; 23+ S 24 '77

YOUNGSTOWN Sheet & Tube Company
Campbell faces up to hard times. . .again. M. King. il Forbes 120:57-64 N 15 '77
End for Steel City? closing of works. il Time 110:78 O 3 '77
Fear Valley, U.S.A. R. W. Gibbons. Commonweal 104:720-2 N 11 '77
Hard lesson Youngstown taught Lykes. il Bus W p83+ O 3 '77
Huge pink slip for an Ohio city. Bus W p39-40 O 3 '77
Steel blues; closing plant. D. Pauly and J. Lowell. il Newsweek 90:80+ O 3 '77

YOUR arms too short to box with God; musical comedy. See Musical comedy, revue, etc.—Reviews—Single works

YOUR place (periodical)
Bidding for elusive market. il Bus W p72 N 7 '77

YOUTH
Assembly adopts 4 resolutions on youth problems. UN Chron 14:67 Ja '77
Is there life after nineteen? memories of adolescence. C. A. Weston. il Seventeen 36:134-5+ Mr '77
Pleasure and pain of that first crush. A. Bayer. il Seventeen 36:144-5+ My '77
See also
Adolescence
Alcohol and youth
Black youth
Boys
Dating
High school students
Hippies
Libraries—Services to youth
Maturity
Smoking and youth
Students
Television and youth
Young women

Attitudes

Confidence of today's youth; Gallup survey of Dayton, Ohio young adults. Intellect 105:212 Ja '77
European teens: would they like to be Americans? interviews, ed by P. Mann. Seventeen 36:96-7 Jl '77
Hidden revolution. J. L. Stipp. Commonweal 104:427-31 Jl 8 '77
How young America dates. W. B. Furlong. Seventeen 36:226-9+ Ag '77
Kids afraid to grow up. C. Best and W. Best. il Parents Mag 52:58-9+ O '77
Nation's teenagers becoming conservative; Who's who among American high school students survey. Intellect 106:1-2 Jl '77
Teenagers around the world. F. B. Kent. il Sr Schol 109:16-17 Ja 13 '77
What do boys think of independent girls? S. Abrahms. Seventeen 36:51 Jl '77
What kids are saying about their parents. il U.S. News 83:89-90+ N 14 '77

Civil rights

Know your rights. M. Sidell. Seventeen 36:53 O '77

Conduct of life

America's youth: turning back to traditional values. il U.S. News 83:87-8 N 14 '77
There is a moral dimension; pregnant teenagers. E. K. Shriver. Read Digest 111:153-4 N '77
Thirty: not a dirty word anymore. M. Wolynski. Vogue 167:150+ O '77

Anecdotes, facetiae, satire, etc.

Art of being cool. D. Getz. Seventeen 36:70-1+ Ag '77

Crime

Youth crime plague. il Time 110:18-20+ Jl 11 '77; Same abr. with title Kids who kill for kicks. Read Digest 111:108-11 O '77
See also
Juvenile delinquency

Employment

Dilemmas of national service for youth; with views on Andrew Young's Youth Initiatives Act of 1977. L. H. Martin. Chr Cent 94:228+ Mr 9 '77
Keeping ed tech in the picture. L. N. Gerhardt. SLJ 23:7 Ap '77
More summer jobs for youths, but still not enough. il U.S. News 82:47-8 My 2 '77
National youth service; a test program. D. J. Eberly. Current 192:3-12 Ap '77
Students, graduates, and dropouts in the labor market, October 1976. A. M. Young. il M Labor R 100:40-3 Jl '77
What job for you? age eligibility provisions of the Fair Labor Standards Act. il Sr Schol 110:29 S 22 '77
Work in a national park. Nat Parks & Con Mag 51:27-9 N '77
Year off between high school and college. J. Marks. McCalls 104:68 F '77
Youth differential; minimum wage. M. S. Evans. Nat R 29:888 Ag 5 '77
See also
Baby sitters
Black youth—Employment
Student employment

Health and hygiene

Daydream those pounds away; tips for youth on maintaining diets. A. A. Belson. Seventeen 36:234-5+ Ag '77
Nation fails to arouse teenagers against cigarette risks. R. S. Morison. il Intellect 105:298-9 Mr '77

Legal aid

See Legal aid

Nutrition

Truth about teenage food fads. A. M. Marks. il por Parents Mag 52:44-5+ Mr '77

Recreation

See also
Recreation centers

Religious life

Brainwashing & religious freedom. T. Robbins. Nation 224:518 Ap 30 '77
Deprogramming; the cults fight back. Chr Today 21:36-7 Je 17 '77
Eastern cults and western culture: why young Americans are buying Oriental religions; excerpt from Turning East. H. Cox. bibl il por Psychol Today 11:36-40+ Jl 77; Discussion. 11:8+ O '77
Letting go: everybody has the right to be wrong; deprogramming issue. J. C. Lyles. Chr Cent 94:451-3 My 11 '77
Rural church and rural religion: analysis of data from children and youth. H. M. Nelsen and R. H. Potvin. bibl f il Ann Am Acad 429:103-14 Ja '77
Sun Myung Moon and the Unification Church. L. A. Belford. Intellect 105:336-7 Ap '77
Weekend with the Moonies. T. Donohoe. Intellect 105:338-9 Ap '77
See also
Children of God (movement)

Sexual behavior

Adolescents, sex, and education. A. D. Hofmann. Educ Digest 43:24-7 N '77
New sexual revolution. J. Lelyveld. N Y Times Mag p39 Jl 3 '77
Sexual liberation, V.D. and our children. V. Almon. America 137:169-72 S 24 '77

Social and economic status

Ethnic comparison of juvenile offenses and socioeconomic status. G. Calhoun, Jr. bibl il Clearing H 51:58-9 O '77

Suicide

See Suicide

Unemployment

See Unemployment

Volunteer service

See Volunteer service

Europe, Western

European teens: would they like to be Americans? interviews, ed by P. Mann. Seventeen 36:96-7 Jl '77
If you think U.S. has trouble finding jobs for young people. . . il U.S. News 83:101-2 N 28 '77

Great Britain

Pistol-whipped; New Wave rock and British youth. E. Meadows. il Nat R 29:1311-12 N 11 '77

South Africa

Soweto: The Children take charge. W. McWhirter. il map Time 109:28-30 Je 27 '77

Underdeveloped areas

See Underdeveloped areas—Youth

United States

America's youth: angry. . .bored. . .or just confused? G. E. Jones. il U.S. News 83:18-20 Jl 18 '77; Discussion 83:49 Ag 1 '77
Farrah factor; heroes and heroines of American youth. S. Miller. por Ladies Home J 94:34+ Je '77
Nation's youth—impact near its peak. il U.S. News 83:50-1 Ag 15 '77
See also
College students
Dating

YOUTH, Runaway. See Runaways

YOUTH-adult relationship
Our misfit children, young and old; blending the institutionalized aged with the institutionalized young. R. J. Stout. Chr Cent 94:194-6 Mr 2 '77
See also
Generation gap

YOUTH and alcohol. See Alcohol and youth
YOUTH and death
Studying death; Miami Beach Senior High School course. M. Sheils. il Newsweek 89:43 Mr 14 '77
YOUTH and music. See Music and youth
YOUTH and narcotics. See Narcotics and youth
YOUTH and opera. See Music and youth
YOUTH and television. See Television and youth
YOUTH associations
See also
Young Americans for Freedom (organization)
YOUTH centers. See Recreation centers
YOUTH Conservation Corps. See United States—Youth Conservation Corps
YOUTH counseling. See Counseling
YOUTH Employment and Demonstration Projects Act. See Labor laws and legislation—United States
YOUTH for Christ International (organization)
Internationalizing youth for Christ. P. Yancey. Chr Today 21:70-2 S 9 '77
YOUTH market
Resurrecting a ruined company; National Student Marketing Corp. P. Schwab. por Nations Bus 65:102 N '77
YOUTH movement
Reconsiderations: the '60s. M. Cowley. New Repub 177:37-40 Ag 20 '77
United States
See Youth movement
YOUTH orchestras. See Orchestras
YOUTH volunteers. See Volunteer service
YOVEL, Yirmiahu
Why Spinoza was excommunicated. Commentary 64:46-52 N '77
YOW, Debbie
Every Yow has the old know-how. N. Williamson. il pors Sports Illus 46:42+ F 21 '77 *
YOW, Kay
Every Yow has the old know-how. N. Williamson. il pors Sports Illus 46:42+ F 21 '77 *
YOW, Susan
Every Yow has the old know-how. N. Williamson. il pors Sports Illus 46:42+ F 21 '77 *
YU, George T.
China's role in Africa. bibl f Ann Am Acad 432:96-109 Jl '77
YUBA CITY, Calif.
Water supply
See Water supply—California
YUCATAN, Mexico
Antiquities
See also
Chichén Itzá
Description and travel
More winter sun in the Yucatán. T. Cooke. House & Gard 149:114+ N '77
YUCATAN Peninsula
See also
Campeche, Mexico
YUGOSLAVIA
See also
Ballet—Yugoslavia
Industrial relations—Yugoslavia
Montenegro
Political prisoners—Yugoslavia
Seaside resorts—Yugoslavia
Zagreb
Foreign relations
Toast to Tito. T. Szulc. New Repub 177:17-18 S 24 '77
Nationalism
Ethnicity and politics in socialist Yugoslavia. G. K. Bertsch. bibl f il Ann Am Acad 433:88-99 S '77
Politics and government
Ethnicity and politics in socialist Yugoslavia. G. K. Bertsch. bibl f il Ann Am Acad 433:88-99 S '77
YUKON
Berger report: northern frontier, northern homeland; excerpt from Northern frontier, northern homeland; with editorial comments. T. R. Berger. il por maps Liv Wildn 41:3, 4-33 Ap '77
Reporter at large; Alaska. J. McPhee. map New Yorker 53:43-4+ Je 20; 58-80 Je 27; 33-6+ Jl 4; 30-40+ Jl 11 '77
Roughing it in the Yukon. J. Hope. il Int Wildlife 7:20-7 Jl '77
Yukon Territory. R. Chin. il map Travel 148:56-9+ Jl '77
YUKON in literature
Cremation of Sam McGee and The shooting of Dan McGrew: R. Service's ballads. L. Burke. Engl J 66:69-70 Mr '77
YULISH, Charles B.
Nuclear power; address, June 30, 1977. Vital Speeches 43:645-8 Ag 15 '77

YUMA, Ariz.
Sandy streets challenge Yuma sweepers. il Am City & County 92:55 Je '77
YUNICK, Henry. See Yunick, S.
YUNICK, Smokey
Say, Smokey; questions and answers. See issues of Popular science
Smokey's guide to troubleshooting your car. il por Pop Sci 210:121-2+ Je '77
YURICK, Sol
Oliver's story means never having to say you're . . . poor. Ms 5:74-6+ My '77
YURKIEWICZ, Gloria. See Yurkiewicz, W. jt auth
YURKIEWICZ, William, and Yurkiewicz, Gloria
Compost and mulch make peas aplenty. Org Gard & Farm 24:113 Mr '77
YVONNE
Eastwick: five houses; poem. Ms 6:72-3 N '77

Z

Z, Pseud
What Jean Monnet wrought. For Affairs 55:630-5 Ap '77
ZABRISKIE Gallery, Paris. See Photography—Galleries and museums
ZAGANO, Phyllis
Great American writing crisis. Educ Digest 43:56-9 O '77
ZAGORIA, Donald S.
Soviet quandary in Asia. bibl f For Affairs 56:306-23 Ja '78
Why we can't leave Korea. il N Y Times Mag p 17-18+ O 2 '77
ZAGORIA, Sam
Trojan horse at the FEC. New Repub 177:10-11 N 26 '77 *
ZAGREB, Yugoslavia
Zagreb stop-over. H. Koenig and G. Koenig. il Travel 148:32-5+ Jl '77
ZAHABY, Mohammed Hussein
Repentance, retreat and murder. il Time 110:32 Jl 18 '77 *
ZAHEDI, Ardeshir
Our world must not be divided; address, May 7, 1977. Vital Speeches 43:517-20 Je 15 '77
ZAHL, Paul A.
Golden window on the past. il Nat Geog 152:422-35 S '77
ZAHN, Gordon C.
One man's files. America 135:438-42 D 18 '76; Correction. 136:62 Ja 29 '77
ZAHN, Irena von
Multiple view. bibl Art in Am 65:41-3 Ja '77
ZAHN, Joachim
Men behind the 280E. pors Motor T 29:50-1 Ap '77 *
Persuasive man who drives Mercedes. R. Ball. il pors Fortune 96:136-40+ D '77 *
ZAÏRE
See also
Education—Zaïre
Loans, Bank—Zaïre
Military assistance—Zaïre
Military assistance, American—Zaïre
Military assistance, Moroccan—Zaïre
Politics and government
ABC's of fighting in Zaïre. il map U.S. News 82:45-6 Ap 25 '77
Africa isn't Vietnam. New Repub 176:5-6 My 14 '77
Bankers' stakes in Zaire. R. Kramer. map Nation 224:521-4 Ap 30 '77
C'est la guerre. A. De Borchgrave. il Newsweek 89:33+ Ap 25 '77
Cubans, Cubans everywhere. il map Time 109:33-4 Mr 28 '77
Distant war, maybe. Nation 224:484 Ap 23 '77
Mobutu speaks out; excerpts from interview. ed by A. de Borchgrave. S. S. Mobutu. il por Newsweek 89:49-50+ Ap 18 '77
Mobutu's victory. L. Griggs. il por Time 109:43 My 9 '77
Mysterious war in a quagmire. il Time 109:40 Ap 4 '77
New war in Africa? J. Pringle. il map Newsweek 89:37-8 Mr 28 '77
Signs of support. il Time 109:28 Ap 18 '77
Things are looking bad for Mobutu. il por Time 109:38+ Ap 11 '77
Things go better with Coke. A. Deming and others. il Newsweek 89:60+ My 2 '77
Winning a round in a termite war. il Time 109:48-9 My 2 '77
ZAKAS, Spiros
Almost instant furniture. il Time 111:62 Ja 9 '78 *
ZAKEM, Brian
Photographs help patients focus on their problems. Psychol Today 11:22+ S '77

ZAKIN, Richard
Bruno LaVerdiere: clay sculptures. il Ceram Mo 25:26-7 S '77
Oxidation glazes, slips, stains, and bodies for cone 6. il Ceram Mo 25:33-43 Ap '77
ZALEZNIK, Abraham
Managers and leaders: are they different? bibl f Harvard Bus R 55:67-78 My '77
ZAMIATIN, Evgenii Ivanovich
Reconsideration. J. Rubenstein. New Repub 178: 38-40 Ja 7 '78 *
ZAMORA, Alfonso
How to get zapped and still be a champ. P. Putnam. il pors Sports Illus 46:28-9 My 2 '77 *
ZAMORA, Ronald, murder trial. See Trials (murder)
ZAMYATIN, Yevgeny. See Zamiatin, E. I.
ZANAR, Eileen
Reentry ripoff: one housewife's exposé. il Ms 6:83-6+ O '77
ZANN, Leon P.
Symbionts of sea fans & sea whips. il Oceans 10:10-15 Ja '77
ZAPOTEC Indians. See Indians of Mexico
ZAPPA, Paul J.
Puccini on trial. por Opera N 42:28-30 D 17 '77
ZAR und Zimmermann; opera. See Lortzing, A.
ZARATE, Carlos
How to get zapped and still be a champ. P. Putnam. il pors Sports Illus 46:28-9 My 2 '77 *
ZARCA, Albert
(ed) See Speer, A. Speer: Hitler knew
ZARE, Richard N.
Laser separation of isotopes; with biographical sketch. il Sci Am 236:16, 86-7+ F '77
—See Diebold, G. J. jt auth
ZAREM, Bobby
Bobby Zarem, superflack. S. C. Cowley. il pors Newsweek 89:58-9 Ja 31 '77 *
Super flack muscles in. il por Time 109:42-3 Ja 31 '77 *
ZARET, Barry L. See Caride, V. J. jt auth
ZARITSKY, Besse
And I hadn't typed my will; interview, ed by M. Michaels. il por Time 109:19 Mr 21 '77
ZASURSKY, Yassen N. and Kashlev, Y. I.
Mass media and society: Soviet viewpoint. il UNESCO Courier 30:24-7 Ap '77
ZATZ, Martin, and O'Dea, R. F.
Efflux of cyclic nucleotides from rat pineal: release of guanosine 3',5,-monophosphate from sympathetic nerve endings. bibl il Science 197: 174-6 Jl 8 '77
Die ZAUBERFLÖTE; opera. See Mozart, J. C. W. A.
ZAUNER, Phyllis
How to find 277,593 new friends. il por Ret Liv 17:42-3 O '77
ZAUSNER, Eric R.
National energy policy: hard choices can't be avoided. por Duns R 109:97-8+ Je '77
ZAVA, David T. and others
Human breast cancer: biologically active estrogen receptor in the absence of estrogen? bibl il Science 196:663-4 My 6 '77
ZAVITUKHINA, Mariya Pavlovna
Pazyryk. il UNESCO Courier 29:30-3+ D '76
ZAWACKI, Chester S.
Bluefin tuna. il por Conservationist 32:34-6 Jl '77
ZAYRE Corporation
Education of Sumner and Stanley Feldberg. il pors Forbes 119:61-2 My 1 '77
ZEA, Leopoldo
Latin America: the long journey to self-discovery. il UNESCO Courier 30:4-7+ Ag '77
ZEBRAS
Selling of the zebra. N. Myers. il map Int Wildlife 8:26-31 Ja '78
ZEEMAN-effect spectroscopy. See Spectrum analysis
ZEFFIRELLI, Franco
New look at Jesus. H. F. Waters. il Newsweek 89:78-9 Ap 4 '77 *
ZEIEN, Alfred
Payoff in Braun's Americanized style. il Bus W p60+ Ap 18 '77 *
ZEIFER, Ellen
Tomoe Yokoi's mezzotints. il por Am Artist 41:40-5+ O '77
—See Place, J. jt auth
ZEIGER, E. and Hepler, P. K.
Light and stomatal function: blue light stimulates swelling of guard cell protoplasts. bibl il Science 196:887-9 My 20 '77
ZEITLIN, Michelle
Separation; poem. Seventeen 36:38 S '77
ZELDIN, Marvin
If your drinking water gets tainted, you'll now be told. Audubon 79:127 My '77
Mind control, the Edison Electric way. Audubon 79:115-17 Jl '77
ZELENY, Lawrence
Song of hope for the bluebird. il map Nat Geog 151:854-65 Je '77
ZELIG, Eva
Health & beauty. Am Home 80:28+ Je; 30 Jl '77
ZELITCH, Israel. See Oliver, D. J. jt auth
ZELK, Zoltán
Moment; Alone; poems, tr by D. Hoffman. New Repub 176:30 Mr 26 '77
ZELL, Steven P.
Analyzing Puerto Rican migration: problems with the data and the model. bibl il M Labor R 100:29-34 Ag '77
ZELLER, Phillip
Expert's secrets for carving lifelike birds. P. Angell. il por Pop Mech 149:94+ Ja '78 *
ZELLERS, Margaret
Dream isles for night life or quiet beaches; for singles, couples and families. Redbook 149: 196+ O '77
ZELLNER, Ben. See Gradie, J. jt auth
ZELMAN, Benjamin M. See Adler, I. jt auth
ZEMAN, Jack
Past tense. Review
Time 110:96 D 12 '77 *
ZÉNDEGUI, Guillermo de
City planning in the Spanish colonies. il map Américas 29:S1-12 F '77
Hostal Nicolás de Ovando. il Américas 29:21-8 Ag '77
Luminous cosmos of Mario Carreno. il por Américas 29:8-11 My '77
Rebirth of the Antilles. il map Américas 29:21-33 Je '77
Then and now. il Américas 29:9-11 Je '77
ZENDORA, Nancy
Dance impulse. J. Pikula. Dance Mag 51:28-9 Ag '77 *
ZENGEL, Janet E. and Magleby, K. L.
Transmitter release during repetitive stimulation: selective changes produced by Sr^{2+} and Ba^{2+}. bibl il Science 197:67-9 Jl 1 '77
ZENITH Radio Corporation
Troubled Zenith battles stiffer competition. il por Bus W p 128+ O 10 '77
ZERFACE, W. A.
Hire the handicapped librarian! bibl il por Wilson Lib Bull 51:656-60 Ap '77
ZERN, Ed
Exit laughing. See issues of Field & stream
Fishing. See issues of Field & stream, April 1977-
ZERO (airplane) See Aeronautics, Military—History
ZERO-base budgeting. See Budget, Business
ZETETIC (periodical)
Pyrrhonian sledgehammer. N. Wade. Science 197: 646 Ag 12 '77
Schism among psychic-watchers. N. Wade. Science 197:1344 S 30 '77
ZEUTENHORST, Dan
America's teacher of the year. M. S. Miller. por Ladies Home J 94:42+ Ap '77 *
ZEVALLOS, Carlos, and others
San Pablo corn kernel and its friends. bibl il map Science 196:385-9 Ap 22 '77
ZEVIN, Patricia Ernenwein
English studies in the Soviet Union: a specialized language school in Moscow. bibl f Engl J 66:14-16 N '77
ZGUTA, Russell
Witchcraft trials in seventeenth-century Russia. bibl f il Am Hist R 82:1187-207 D '77
ZIA ul-Haq, Mohammed
Zia: so much mistrust; excerpts from interview, ed by E. Behr. il por Newsweek 90:28 Jl 18 '77

about

Evil genius. Time 110:51+ S 19 '77 *
Sir, the troops have come. pors Time 110:29-30 Jl 18 '77 *
ZICH, Arthur
Antic arts (cont) Holiday 58:10+ Je '77
Taiwan; The Philippines. Holiday 58:40-1+ Mr '77
Thinking man's guide to Peking duck. Holiday 58:20 Mr '77
ZIDE, Larry
Will the Elcaset make it? il Hi Fi 27:64-6 F '77
ZIEG, Janine, and others
Recombinational switch for gene expression. bibl il Science 196:170-2 Ap 8 '77
ZIEGLER, John Augustus, 1934-
Hockey 1977-78; interview. il pors Sports Illus 47:36-41 O 17 '77
ZIEGLER, Michael G. See Lake, C. R. jt auth
ZIELENZIGER, David
Collusion at the gas pump. Nation 224:551-4 My 7 '77
Wages of hoodwinking. Nation 225:434-6 O 29 '77
ZIFCACK, Michael G.
Australia/Britain/U.S.A.—a new bookselling era begins. il Pub W 212:40-1 Jl 11 '77
Sale of Rigby's shares heat up debate over foreign ownership. Pub W 212:74-6 S 19 '77
ZIFF Corporation-Rust Craft Greeting Cards, Inc merger. See Corporations—Acquisitions and mergers
ZIMBABWE Development Fund (proposed) See Economic assistance in Rhodesia

ZIMBARDO, Philip G.
How to overcome shyness; excerpt from Shyness: what it is, what to do about it. Ladies Home J 94:62+ My '77
Shyness—the people phobia. Todays Educ 66:47-9 Ja '77
—See Katz, M. jt auth
about
Therapy for the shy. M. Clark and P. S. Greenberg. il por Newsweek 89:72 Je 13 '77 •

ZIMMER, Thomas R.
Men behind the Car of the Year. il pors Motor T 29:38 F '77 •

ZIMMERER, Thomas W.
How to reduce dependence on the boss. Nations Bus 65:55-8 F '77
—and Preston, Paul
Contemporary corporate strategy: a study in change theory. bibl Intellect 105:418-19 Je '77

ZIMMERMAN, D. W. See Melcher, C. L. jt auth

ZIMMERMAN, David R.
Keeping track of hawks. il Audubon 79:2-12 Jl '77
Making contact. il N Y Times Mag p66-7+ F 20 '77
Your family's health. See issues of Ladies' home journal

ZIMMERMAN, John G.
Putting on a hill of a show; photographs. Sports Illus 46:28-32 F 14 '77

ZIMMERMAN, Paul
Making a comeback from nowhere. il pors Sports Illus 47:106-9 D 5 '77

ZIMMERMAN, Thomas F.
Assemblies of God: a leader upheld. E. E. Plowman. Chr Today 21:64-9 S 9 '77 •

ZIMMERMANN, Bernd Alois
Soldiers. Review
Hi Fi il 28:MA35-6 Ja '78 •

ZINC futures. See Commodity exchanges

ZINC in the body
Zinc binding: a difference between human and bovine milk. C. D. Eckhert and others. bibl il Science 195:789-90 F 25 '77

ZINDEL, Paul
Interview with Paul Zindel; ed by P. Janeczko. Engl J 66:20-1 O '77
PW interviews; ed by J. F. Mercier. por Pub W 212:6-7 D 5 '77
about
Ladies at the Alamo. Reviews
New Yorker 53:102 Ap 18 '77 •
Time il 109:31 Ap 18 '77 •

ZIOLKOWSKI, Korczak
Heap big heap. E. M. Halliday. il Am Heritage 28:24-5 Je '77 •
Moving a mountain. D. A. Williams and F. Maier. il por Newsweek 90:28+ Ag 29 '77 •

ZION, Sidney
Troubled world of Mike Burke. il pors N Y Times Mag p30-2+ O 9 '77

ZIONISM
Anti-Zionist resolution. B. Lewis; reply with rejoinder. A. M. Elmessiri. For Affairs 55:641-2 Ap '77
New York and/or Jerusalem. R. Alter. Commentary 64:50-6 Ag '77; Reply. H. Halkin. 64:10+ N '77
Who is Israel? attitudes of American Jews. J. Neusner. il Nat R 29:714-16 Je 24 '77
Zionism and Jewish identity; adaptation of address. J. Katz. Commentary 63:48-52 My '77

ZIPADELLI, Marie, and Satalino, Vicki
Weaving affair. il pors Sch Arts 76:66-7 Mr '77

ZIPPER, Otto
Retrospect. il Motor T 29:93-6+ F '77

ZIRIN, Harold
Sky reporter. Natur Hist 86:100-4 D '77

ZISK, Richie
Old uniforms, new Sox. P. Gammons. il por Sports Illus 46:53-4 My 16 '77 •

ZISKIN, Joel F.
Trek to Nepal's sacred Crystal Mountain. il map Nat Geog 151:500-17 Ap '77

ZITO bakery, New York City. See Bakers and bakeries

ZIZMOR, Jonathan
How to clean & care for your skin; interview. Mademoiselle 83:174-7 Ag '77
—and Foreman, John
Four troublesome nail problems; excerpt from Dr Zizmor's skin care book. il Fam Health 9:36-7 F '77

ZMUDA, Joseph
San Francisco launches world's first water-jet ferry. il Pop Sci 210:102 Ap '77

ZODIAC
Anecdotes, facetiae, satire, etc.
Asian zodiac for librarians. A. Luster. il Am Lib 8:166 Mr '77

ZOELLNER, Robert
Getting it out, getting it down: adapting Zoellner's Talk-write. V. Wixon and P. Stone. bibl f il Engl J 66:70-3 S '77 •

ZOFFANY, Johann
Atrophy through isolation. W. Feaver. Art N 76:102+ Ap '77 •

ZONA pellucida. See Ova

ZONCA, Peter H.
Openness: a formula for communication. Clearing H 50:201-3 Ja '77

ZONIANS. See Americans in the Panama Canal Zone

ZONING law
Arlington Heights case. America 136:90-1 F 5 '77
Common sense on race; Arlington Heights, Ill. zoning refusal case. G. F. Will. Newsweek 89:80 Ja 24 '77
Intent, not impact; Supreme Court decision on Arlington Heights, Ill. zoning law. Time 109:52 Ja 24 '77
Keeping a rein on sex businesses. il Changing T 32:21-3 Ja '78
Right to refuse: rezoning refusal upheld by Supreme Court in Arlington Heights, Ill. case. J. K. Footlick and others. il Newsweek 89:77 Ja 24 '77
Setback in Arlington Heights; Supreme Court ruling on zoning. J. De Muth. America 136:167-8 F 26 '77
Suburban iron curtain; Supreme Court decision on Arlington Heights, Ill. zoning law. Commonweal 104:99-100 F 18 '77
Zoning out low-income families in suburbia; Arlington Heights, Ill. J. S. Fuerst. Chr Cent 94:77-8 F 2 '77

ZOOLOGICAL gardens
America's zingiest zoos. K. Keating. il Bet Hom & Gard 55:137-8 Ag '77
Mobilizing for a barrier-free zoo; Knoxville Zoological Park. il Parks & Rec 12:30+ My '77
New hope for endangered species; Parque Zoológico Nacional, Dominican Republic. J. Duval. il Américas 29:19-23 Ja '77
Safari parks. Audubon 79:150 Ja '77
Smuggling rare animals: latest global racket. il U.S. News 83:50 S 26 '77
See also
National Zoological Park, Washington, D.C.
San Diego, Calif. Zoological Park

Anecdotes, facetiae, satire, etc.
Fabulous zoo. A. H. Leighton. il Américas 29:16-18 F '77

ZOOLOGICAL models
Leviathan model brings us the whale we could never see; work of L. Foster. M. Herron. il pors Smithsonian 8:52-9 bibl(p 114) Ja '78

ZOOLOGICAL research
See also
Fisheries—Research

ZOOLOGY
Zoology (cont) Sci N 111:139, 280, 311, 332; 112:24, 41, 138, 248 F 26, Ap 30, My 14-21, Jl 9-16, Ag 27, O 15 '77
See also
Desert fauna
Natural history
Phenology
Psychology, Comparative
Vivariums
also names of classes, orders, etc. and particular animals, e.g. Rodents

Classification
Telltale wishbone; Archaeopteryx and the question of direct descent of birds from dinosaurs. S. J. Gould. il Natur Hist 86:26+ N '77

Ecology
Critical crossroads; question of critical habitat of endangered species. il map Nat Parks & Con Mag 51:19-22 F '77
Last fight for the grizzly; excerpt from Where the grizzly walks. B. Schneider. il Outdoor Life 161:55-8+ Ja '78
Uproar over grizzly habitat. G. Laycock. Audubon 79:126 My '77
See also
Birds—Ecology
Wildlife management

Africa
African wildlife: the end of the game? E. A. Bauer. il Outdoor Life 160:68-73+ D '77
See also
Elephants
Giraffes
Hyenas
Lions
Wild dogs
Zebras

Alaska
Taming of Alaska. R. Rau; discussion. Nat Wildlife 15:17 Ap '77

Antarctic Regions
Penguins and their neighbors. R. T. Peterson. il map Nat Geog 152:236-55 Ag '77
See also
Penguins
Seals (animals)

ZOOLOGY—*Continued*

Arctic Regions

See also
Caribou
Walruses
Whales

Australia

See also
Kangaroos

Canada

Canadian sketchbook: animals in peril. A. Odum. il Int Wildlife 7:42-3 Mr '77

Costa Rica

See also
Monkeys

Dominican Republic

New hope for endangered species; Parque Zoologico Nacional, Dominican Republic. J. Duval. il Américas 29:19-23 Ja '77

France

Lindberghs liberate monkeys from constraints; Verlhiac Primate Center. R. Chelminski. il pors Smithsonian 7:58-65 bibl(p126) Mr '77

Galápagos Islands

See also
Tortoises

India

If they're killers, what good are they? poisonous snakes. Z. Whitaker and R. Whitaker. il Int Wildlife 7:12-16 My '77
Prospects for India's wildlife. Z. Futehally. il Nat Parks & Con Mag 51:17-19 Mr '77
See also
Leopards

Indonesia

See also
Orangutans

Iran

Fecund mouflon. R. Valdez and L. V. Alamia. il Natur Hist 86:72-7 bibl(p 119) N '77

Israel

Ibex in Israel; Nubian ibex. L. Aronson. il Natur Hist 87:50-5 bibl(p 108) Ja '78

Kalimantan

Hermits of the jungle; with editorial comment. P. S. Rodman. il map Int Wildlife 7:3, 20-5 My '77

Madagascar

See also
Lemurs

Michigan

Geology, vegetation, and vertebrate fauna of Michigan. M. Hensley. bibl map BioScience 27:352-3 My '77

Namibia

Wildlife in Namibia. P. Younghusband. il Int Wildlife 7:52-63 N '77

Russia

Rare look at wildlife in Russia. G. H. Harrison. il por map Int Wildlife 8:4-11 Ja '78

South America

Sticking up for marsupials. S. J. Gould. il Natur Hist 86:22+ O '77

ZOOLOGY, Economic
How much is a pimpleback worth? assigning dollar values to wildlife. Audubon 79:160 My '77
Trapping: new angles on an old controversy. B. Gooch. il Ret Liv 17:41-2 F '77

ZOOLOGY, Marine. See Marine fauna

ZOOM lenses, Photographic. See Lenses, Photographic

ZOOPLANKTON. See Plankton

ZOOS. See Zoological gardens

ZOROASTRIANISM
Zoroastrians affirm tradition and change. J. W. Whitehurst. Chr Cent 94:657-8 Jl 20 '77

ZSCHOCK, Dieter K.
Inequality in Colombia. bibl f il Cur Hist 72: 68-72+ F '77

ZUCCHINI fruitcake. See Cake

ZUCKER, Barbara
Autobiography of visual poems; adaptation of address. il Art N 76:68-73 F '77

ZUCKER, Isabel
Indoor plants. Horticulture 55:2-3+ Je; 2 Jl; 54 Ag; 62-3 S; 53-5 O; 52-3 N; 44+ D '77

ZUCKER, Martin
Great collection of tiny artistry—how it was made. il Smithsonian 8:84-91 My '77

ZUCKER, Seymour
(ed) Economic diary (cont) Bus W p20 Je 13; 14+ Je 27; 14 Jl 25; 14+ Ag 22; 14+ O 3; 28+ N 14; 20+ N 21; 19+ D 5; 14 D 12 '77

ZUCKERMAN, Sam
To own a book. il Am Educ 13:13-16 N '77

ZUCKERMANN, Irma G.
Pathology, adversity, and nursing. bibl Society 14:52-4 Ja '77

ZUERSHER, Dorothy J.
Bringing women into the curriculum. Educ Digest 42:38-40 F '77

ZUKOFSKY, Louis
Comment. B. Howard. Poetry 130:290-2 Ag '77 •

ZULETA, Bernardo
Sixth session of Law of Sea Conference might prove decisive, says Mr. Zuleta; summary of address, March 28, 1977. por UN Chron 14: 37-8+ My '77

ZULUS

Rites and ceremonies

Zulu king weds a Swazi princess. V. Wentzel. il Nat Geog 153:46-61 Ja '78

ZUMBO, Jim
(ed) Catch 'em cold. il Outdoor Life 161:70-3 Ja '78
Monster brown: new record—but will it last? il Outdoor Life 159:68-9+ Je '77

ZUMWALT, Elmo Russell, 1920-
Dangerous delusion. il pors Sat Eve Post 249: 12-14 N '77

ZUÑIGA, Francisco
Being not doing. S. Reich. Art N 76:132+ S '77 •

ZURICH Festival. See Music festivals—Switzerland

ZWASKA, Thomas
How to choose a heat sink. il Pop Electr 11:89 Je '77

ZWEIG, Paul
Master of Ganeshpuri. il Harpers 254:85-8+ My '77

ZWEIG, Phil
Flushing a cooling system. Yachting 141:106 Mr '77

ZWERDLING, Daniel
Chemical catastrophes. Progressive 41:15-19 F '77
Pesticide treadmill. il Nat Parks & Con Mag 51:15-19 S '77

ZWINGER, Ann H.
Eagle's fate and mine are one. il map Audubon 79:50-80+ Jl '77

ZYDECO music. See Music, Popular (songs, etc)

ZYDEK, Fredrick
Last words for Ralph: the oldest goldfish I ever knew; poem. America 137:161 S 24 '77

BOOK REVIEWS

Abbazia, P. Mr Roosevelt's navy: the private war of the U.S. Atlantic fleet, 1939-1942. 1975
Am Hist R 81:1279 D '76. R. W. Leopold
Abbey, E. Monkey wrench gang. 1975
Conservationist 31:33 N '76. A. S. Fick
Liv Wildn 40:40-2 O '76. D. Rawlings
Abel, W. Massenarmut und Hungerkrisen im vorindustriellen Europa: Versuch einer Synopsis. 1974
Am Hist R 82:84-5 F '77. R. Gottfried
Abers, E. S. and Kennel, C. F. Matter in motion: the spirit and evolution of physics. 1977
Phys Today 30:60-1 Jl '77. R. H. March
Abrahamsen, D. Nixon vs. Nixon: an emotional tragedy
Harpers 254:100 Mr '77. M. Malone
Psychol Today 10:68-9 Mr '77. R. S. Liebert
Time 109:29-30 Ap 18 '77
Abramov, S. Z. Perpetual dilemma: Jewish religion in the Jewish state
Commentary 64:84-6 O '77. H. M. Sachar
Abundance effects in classification; proceedings of symposium, Lausanne-Dorigny, Switzerland, 1975; ed. by B. Hauck and P. C. Keenan. 1976
Science 196:777 My 13 '77. E. J. Wampler
Ackerman, B. A. Private property and the Constitution. 1977
Ann Am Acad 433:197-8 S '77. H. N. Carroll
Adamolekun, L. Sékou Touré's Guinea: an experiment in nation building. 1976
Am Hist R 82:407-9 Ap '77. V. Thompson
Adams, A. Listening to Billie
Time 110:67+ D 26 '77. R. Z. Sheppard
Adams, A. B. Sunlight and shadow
Bus W p 14 My 9 '77. S. Atchison
Adams, C. F. Diary of Charles Francis Adams, v5: January 1833-October 1834; v6: November 1834-June 1836; ed. by M. Friedlaender and L. H. Butterfield. 1974
Am Hist R 81:1234-5 D '76. W. T. Doherty
Adams, D. H. and Bell, T. H. Slow viruses
Sci Am 236:140-1 My '77. P. Morrison
Adams, F. C. Economic diplomacy: the export-import bank and American foreign policy 1934-1939. 1976
Ann Am Acad 433:161 S '77. F. Costigliola
Adams, H. H. Harry Hopkins, a biography
Chr Cent 94:1010-11 N 2 '77. H. E. Fey
New Repub 177:29-30+ S 24 '77. F. Freidel
Adams, J. E. Preus of Missouri: and the great Lutheran civil war
America 137:15-16 Jl 2 '77. J. J. Hughes
Adams, J. P. At the heart of the whirlwind
Chr Cent 94:307-8 Mr 30 '77. D. M. Kelley
Adams, M. Single blessedness: observations on the single status in married society. 1976
Ann Am Acad 431:173-4 My '77. R. F. Winch
Intellect 105:447 Je '77. I. R. Hyatt
Adams, M. I. Three authors of alienation: Bombal, Onetti, Carpentier. 1975
Américas 29:26-7 Mr '77. F. Lasarte
Adams, R. Denver. 1977
Art in Am 65:35 N '77. P. Patton
Adams, R. B. Jr. Boston money tree: how the proper men of Boston made, invested and preserved their wealth from colonial days to the space age
Nation 224:661-3 My 28 '77. S. Blumenthal
Adamson, J. B. Epistle of James. 1976
Chr Today 21:29 Je 3 '77. P. Davids
Adler, H. E. Fish behavior: why fishes do what they do. 1975
BioScience 27:212 Mr '77. G. W. Barlow
Adler, M. J. Philosopher at large: an intellectual autobiography
Commonweal 104:661-2 O 14 '7. J. P. Sisk
Sat R 4:25-6 S 3 '77. N. Cousins
Adler, M. J. and Van Doren, C. eds. Great treasury of Western thought: a compendium of important statements on man and his institutions by the great thinkers in Western history
America 137:335 N 12 '77. E. D. Cuffe
Adler, R. Speedboat
Yale R 66:584-91 Je '77. D. Thorburn
Agran, L. Cancer connection: and what we can do about it
Commonweal 104:629-31 S 30 '77. R. Conniff
Nation 225:218-20 S 10 '77. A. L. Huebner
Ahmed, S. Muslim community in Bengal, 1884-1912. 1976
Ann Am Acad 429:153 Ja '77. M. Dembo
Aitken, H. G. J. Syntony and spark: the origins of radio. 1976
Science 196:1083-4 Je 3 '77. R. Belfield
Akin, W. E. Technocracy and the American dream: the technocrat movement, 1900-1941. 1977
Ann Am Acad 434:225-6 N '77. G. M. Haniff
New Repub 177:32-3 S 3 '77. N. Harris
Akrigg, G. P. V. and Akrigg, H. B. British Columbia chronicle, 1778-1846: adventurers by sea and land. 1975
Am Hist R 82:475 Ap '77. G. F. G. Stanley
Albanese, C. L. Sons of the fathers: the civil religion of the American revolution.
Am Hist R 82:1322 D '77. W. S. Hudson
Commonweal 104:627-8 S 30 '77. R. E. Curran
Albertini, R. von. Europäische Kolonialherrschaft, 1880-1940. 1976
Am Hist R 82:1238-9 D '77. D. G. Schilling
Aldridge, A. O. Voltaire and the century of light. 1975
Am Hist R 82:1265 D '77. R. W. Kilcup
Aldwinckle, R. F. More than man: a study in Christology. 1976
Chr Cent 94:1073+ N 16 '77. G. Fackre
Chr Today 21:52-3 S 9 '77. B. Demarest
Aleksandrov, V. A. Sel'skaia obshchina v Rossii (XVII-nachalo XIX v.). 1976
Am Hist R 82:692-3 Je '77. D. Field
Alexander, C. and others. Oregon experiment
Smithsonian 8:106+ Ja '78. B. Clavan
Alexander, C. and others. Pattern language
Smithsonian 8:106+ Ja '78. B. Clavan
Alexander, M. V. C. Charles I's lord treasurer: Sir Richard Weston, earl of Portland (1577-1635). 1975
Am Hist R 82:352-3 Ap '77. R. W. Kenny
Alexander, N. Father of Texas geology: Robert T. Hill. 1976
Am Hist R 82:451 Ap '77. M. M. L. Aldrich
Alford, R. R. Health care politics: ideological and interest group barriers to reform. 1975
Society 14:96 Ja '77. T. R. Marmor
Alfven, H. and Arrhenius, G. Structure and evolutionary history of the solar system. 1975
Phys Today 30:61 Ja '77. I. P. Williams
Allen, D. A. Infrared: the new astronomy
Phys Today 30:53-4 Ap '77. R. Beer
Sky & Tel 53:133-4 F '77. E. P. Ney
Allen, J. Assault with a deadly weapon: the autobiography of a street criminal; ed. by D. H. Kelly and P. Heymann
Harpers 256:87 Ja '78. F. Taliaferro
Nation 226:22-4 Ja 7 '78. A. Lopez
Allen, J. Lord of the dance. 1977
Horn Bk 53:536 O '77. P. Heins
Allen, J. L. Passage through the garden: Lewis and Clark and the image of the American Northwest. 1975
Am Hist R 82:439-40 Ap '77. R. A. Bartlett
Allen, K. S. That Bounty bastard. 1977
Oceans 10:68 N '77. M. Danty
Alley, R. S. Television: ethics for hire? 1977
Intellect 106:171 O '77. R. L. Fischer
Allinson, G. D. Japanese urbanism: industry and politics in Kariya, 1872-1972. 1975
Am Hist R 82:162-3 F '77. B. K. Marshall
Allison, S. Pioneer gentlewoman in British Columbia: the recollections of Susan Allison; ed by M. A. Ormsby. 1976
Am West 14:60 Mr '77. T. C. Hinckley
Allmendinger, D. F. Jr. Paupers and scholars; the transformation of student life in nineteenth-century New England. 1975
Am Hist R 81:1233-4 D '76. M. Lazerson
Alonso, J. M. Althea: the divorce of Adam and Eve
Nation 224:379-80 Mr 26 '77. G. Lyons
Altizer, T. J. J. Self-embodiment of God
Chr Cent 94:986-7 O 26 '77. C. D. Hardwick
Altman, E. and others. Data gathering and instructional manual for performance measures in public libraries. 1976
Lib J 102:1161 My 15 '77. J. R. Freudenthal
Aluko, O. Ghana and Nigeria, 1957-70: a study of inter-African discord. 1976
Am Hist R 82:1034-5 O '77. E. Bustin
Alvarez, E. Travel on southern antebellum railroads, 1828-1860. 1975
Am Hist R 81:1237-8 D '76. M. E. Reed
Aman, J. Les officiers blus dans la marine française au XVIIIe siècle. 1976
Am Hist R 82:366 Ap '77. D. C. Baxter
Amann, P. H. Revolution and mass democracy: the Paris club movement in 1848. 1975
Am Hist R 81:1131 D '76. J. J. Baughman
Ambasz, E. Architecture of Luis Barragan. 1976
Archit Rec 161:45+ Ap '77. C. R. Smith
Ambler, F. Siege of the Villa Lipp
Time 109:97 Je 6 "77. P. Gray
American Bible society. Good news Bible: the Bible in today's English version
America 136:196 Mr 5 '77. M. D. Coogan
American college testing research institute. Schooling and achievement in American society; papers from seminars, 1971-1973; ed. by W. H. Sewell and others. 1976
Science 196:763-5 My 13 '77. B. Heyns

American Geological Institute. Marine sediment transport and environmental management; papers from short course, Key Biscayne, Fla, 1974; ed. by D. J. Stanley and D. J. P. Swift. 1976
Science 196:420-1 Ap 22 '77. R. H. Meade
Amis, K. Alteration
New Repub 176:39-40 My 28 '77. S. Hux
Sat R 4:28-9 F 5 '77. B. Cook
Ammons, A. R. Snow poems
Yale R 67:72, 86-9 O '77. H. Vendler
Amon, A. Orangutan: endangered ape
Sci Am 237:26 D '77. P. Morrison and P. Morrison
Andaya, L. Y. Kingdom of Johor, 1641-1728. 1975
Am Hist R 82:426 Ap '77. H. R. C. Wright
Anderson, A. J. O. and others. eds. and trs. Beyond the Codices: the Nahua view of colonial Mexico. 1976
Am Hist R 82:1103-4 O '77. W. Borah
Anderson, B. Solar energy: fundamentals in building design
Archit Rec 162:43 O '77. G. Allen
Anderson, B. and Riordan, M. Solar home book
Progressive 41:55-6 Ap '77. M. Northcross
Smithsonian 8:130-2 My '77. D. Morris
Anderson, I. H. Jr. Standard-vacuum oil company and United States East Asian policy, 1933-1941
Am Hist R 81:1274 D '76. N. H. Pugach
Anderson, J. R. Language, memory, and thought. 1976
Science 198:922-3 D 2 '77. P. G. Polson
Anderson, R. D. Outcast in their own land: Mexican industrial workers, 1906-1911. 1976
Am Hist R 82:781 Je '77. J. Womack, Jr
Anderson, R. S. Building scientific institutions in India. 1975
Science 195:568-9 F 11 '77. A. M. Moyal
Andors, S. China's industrial revolution: 1949 to the present
Nation 225:24 Jl 2 '77. N. D. Milton and D. Milton
Andreasen, A. R. Disadvantaged consumer. 1975
M Labor R 100:82 Mr '77. R. J. Markin
Andrews, M. L. A. Life that lives on man
Natur Hist 86:88-90 My '77. J. S. Marr
Time 110:65-6 Jl 25 '77. P. Stoler
Angell, R. Five seasons: a baseball companion
Harpers 255:76+ Jl '77. E. Hoagland
Nat R 29:1183 O 14 '77. D. Hall
Newsweek 89:79-80 My 30 '77. J. Kroll
Sat R 4:32+ My 14 '77. P. Andrews
Time 109:95-6 My 16 '77. P. Gray
Anger, K. Hollywood Babylon
New Repub 176:26-9 Ap 2 '77. W. Hughes
Antin, D. Talking at the boundaries
New Repub 176:33-5 Mr 5 '77. M. Perloff
Appel, A. Nabokov's dark cinema. 1974
Film Q 30:38-44 Summ '77. S. Fleischer
Appel, B. Hell's kitchen. 1977
Horn Bk 53:447-8 Ag '77. S. H Holtze
Appelt, H. and others. eds. Die Urkunden der deutschen Könige und Kaiser, v 10, pt 1: die Urkunden Friedrichs 1., 1152-1158. 1975
Am Hist R 82:345 Ap '77. M. B. Dick
Appleman, P. Open doorways
Poetry 130:296-7 Ag '77. J. Parini
Appleton, S. Ladder of the world's joy
Commonweal 104:408-10 Je 24 '77. E. B. Wymard
Appleyard, D. Planning a pluralist city: conflicting realities in Ciudad Guayana. 1976
Ann Am Acad 433:168-9 S '77. I. S. Wiarda
Aptheker, H. ed. Correspondence of W. E. B. DuBois, v 1: Selections, 1877-1934; v2: Selections, 1934-1944. 1973, 1976
Am Hist R 82:444-5 Ap '77. D. L. Lewis
Aquarone, A. and Vernassa, M. eds. Il regime fascista. 1974
Am Hist R 81:1159-60 D '76. E. P. Noether
Ara, A. L'Austria-Ungheria nella politica americana durante la prima guerra mondiale. 1973
Am Hist R 82:200-1 F '77. C. F. Delzell
Aranda, F. Luis Buñuel: a critical biography; tr. by D. Robinson. 1976
Film Q 31:65-7 Fall '77. D. Willis
Arble, M. Long tunnel: a coal miner's journal. 1976
America 136:382 Ap 23 '77. J. De Muth
M Labor R 100:56 Ag '77. R. W. Bednarzik
Nat R 29:672-3 Je 10 '77. D. K. Mano
Nation 225:87-8 Jl 23 '77. D. Lockard
Archdeacon, T. F. New York city, 1664-1710: conquest and change. 1976
Am Hist R 81:1218 D '76. B. Still
Ann Am Acad 429:170-1 Ja '77. L. Billington
Ardoin, J. Callas legacy
New Repub 177:43-4 O 15 '77. P. Robinson
Opera N 42:81 N '77. A. Nino
Argersinger, P. H. Populism and politics: William Alfred Peffer and the People's party. 1974
Am Hist R 82:198-9 F '77. G. Clanton
Arlen, M. View from Highway 1
New Repub 176:34-5 Mr 12 '77. R. Zoglin
Armbruster, F. E. Our children's crippled future: how American education has failed; with P. Bracken
America 137:367-8 N 19 '77. J. W. Donohue
Armerding, C. E. and Gasque, W. W. Dreams, visions and oracles. 1977
Chr Today 21:24 Ag 12 '77. J. V. Dahms
Armes R. Ambiguous image: narrative style in modern European cinema. 1976
Film Q 30:50-2 Summ '77. D. Willis
Armstrong, T. and others. 200 years of American sculpture
Am Artist 41:32+ N '77. A. Werner
Arnold, E. Unretouched woman
Ms 5:86 Je '77. A. Gottlieb
Arrianus, Flavius Arrian, v 1: Anabasis Alexandri, book 1-4; tr. by P. A. Brunt. 1976
Am Hist R 82:1220-3 D '77. J. R. Fears
Arrington, L. J. Building the city of God: community and cooperation among the Mormons. 1976
Am Hist R 82:1071 O '77. M. S. De Pillis
Arrington, L. J. From Quaker to Latter-Day Saint: Bishop Edwin D. Woolley. 1976
Am Hist R 82:1072 O '77. L. Foster
Artaud, A. Selected writings; ed. by S. Sontag
Chr Cent 94:921 O 12 '77. N. Cox
Artibise, A. F. J. Winnipeg: a social history of urban growth, 1874-1914. 1975
Am Hist R 82:219-20 F '77. W. A. McKay
Ashbery, J. Houseboat days
Esquire 89:20+ Ja '78. A. Kazin
Newsweek 90:88+ S 26 '77. W. Clemons
Ashbery, J. Rivers and mountains
Nation 225:182-3+ S 3 '77. C. C. Park
Ashbery, J. Self-portrait in a convex mirror. 1975
Sat R 4:34+ S 17 '77. P. Auster
Ashburner, M. and Novitski, E. eds. Genetics and biology of drosophila, v 1a-c. 1976
BioScience 27:420 Je '77. D. L. Hartl
Science 196:290 Ap 15 '77. A. Chovnick
Ashcraft, N. and Scheflen, A. E. People space: the making and breaking of human boundaries
Psychol Today 10:104+ My '77. J. H. Kay
Ashcroft, N. W. and Mermin, N. D. Solid state physics. 1976
Phys Today 30:61+ Ja '77. S. Smoluchowski
Science 197:753 Ag 19 '77. H. Ehrenreich
Ashkenasi, A. Modern German nationalism. 1976
Ann Am Acad 431:157 My '77. J. S. Wozniak
Ashman, C. Gospel according to Billy; introd. by R. McKuen
Nation 225:696-8 D 24 '77. J. Miles
Asimov, I. Alpha centauri, the nearest star. 1976
Horn Bk 53:195 Ap '77. H. C. Stubbs
Asimov, I. Collapsing universe
Commentary 64:65-6 O '77. J. Marsh
Assante, F. Città e campagne nella Puglia del secolo XIX: l'evoluzione demografica, v4. 1975
Am Hist R 82:384 Ap '77. E. Argento
Association for educational communications and technology. Educational technology: definition and glossary of terms, v 1. 1977
SLJ 24:40 S '77. W. E. Hug
Association of social anthropologists of the commonwealth. Transaction and meaning; papers from conference, Oxford, 1973; ed. by B. Kapferer. 1976
Science 195:772-3 F 25 '77. W. M. O'Barr
Aster, S. Anthony Eden
New Repub 176:59 My 21 '77. P. Terzian
Aster, S. 1939: the making of the second World war. 1973
Am Hist R 81:1101-2 D '76. S. A. Schuker
Athay, R. G. Solar chromosphere and corona: quiet sun. 1976
Sky & Tel 54:136-8 Ag '77. M. R. Kundu
Athearn, R. G. Coloradans. 1976
Am West 14:53 Jl '77. L. L. Meyer
Atkin, E. and Rubin, E. Part-time father
Redbook 149:22+ Jl '77. B. Spock
Atkins, G. P. Latin America in the international political system. 1977
Ann Am Acad 434:206-7 N '77. D. Pierson
Atlas, J. Delmore Schwartz: the life of an American poet
Nation 225:693-4 D 24 '77. E. Wensberg
New Repub 177:30+ D 24 '77. C. Bedient
Newsweek 90:120-1 N 21 '77. W. Clemons
Sat R 5:48+ D 10 '77. W. Arnold
Time 110:82+ D 5 '77. M. Maddocks
Atwater, J. D. Time bomb
Time 110:103-4 O 17 '77. J. Skow
Auchincloss, L. Dark lady
Newsweek 90:72 Ag 1 '77. R. Towers
Time 110:76 Jl 11 '77. R. Z. Sheppard
Auden, W. H. Collected poems; ed by E. Mendelson
Poetry 131:159-64 D '77. D. Lehman
Yale R 66:407-24 Mr '77. H. Vendler
Audus, L. J. ed. Herbicides: physiology, biochemistry, ecology. 2d ed. 2v. 1976
Science 196:419 Ap 22 '77. A. W. Galston
Auerbach, C. Mutation research: problems, results and perspectives. 1976
BioScience 27:362 My '77. B. Wallace
Auerbach, J. S. Unequal justice: lawyers and social change in modern America. 1976
Am Hist R 82:462-3 Ap '77. E. A. Purcell, Jr
Augstein, R. Jesus son of man; tr. by H. Young
America 137:83-4 Ag 13 '77. R. E. Brown
Chr Cent 94:728-30 Ag 17 '77. R. Marius
Chr Today 22:36 N 18 '77. C. C. Anderson
Commonweal 105:22-3 Ja 6 '78. W. P. Loewe
Nat R 29:388 Ap 1 '77. M. B. Martin

Aurigemma, L. Le signe zodiacal du Scorpion dans les traditions accidentales de l'antiquité gréco-latine à la renaissance. 1976
Am Hist R 82:607-8 Je '77. B. P. Copenhaver
Austin, W. H. Relevance of natural science to theology. 1976
Chr Today 21:39 Mr 4 '77. C. B. Kaiser
Auty, P. and Clogg, R. eds. British policy towards wartime resistance in Yugoslavia and Greece. 1975
Am Hist R 82:644 Je '77. H. Cliadakis
Avedon, R. Portraits; with essay by H. Rosenberg. 1976
Art in Am 65:51+ Mr '77. A. Grundberg
Commonweal 104:314-16 My 13 '77. L. Kuehl
Avian physiology; symposium, London, 1973; ed. by M. Peaker. 1975
BioScience 27:213 Mr '77. R. K. Ringer
Avi-Yonah, M. Jews of Palestine: a political history from the Bar Kokhba war to the Arab conquest. 1976
Ann Am Acad 430:187-8 Mr '77. H. Rosenblum
Avi-Yonah, M. ed. World history of the Jewish people, v7: the Herodian period. 1975
Am Hist R 82:705 Je '77. M. Smith
Awerbuch, S. and Wallace, W. A. Policy evaluation for community development: decision tools for local government. 1976
Ann Am Acad 431:174 My '77. I. L. Allen
Axelos, K. Alienation, praxis, and technē in the thought of Karl Marx; tr. by R. Bruzina. 1976
Am Hist R 82:923-4 O '77. D. Gross
Ayling, S. Elder Pitt, Earl of Chatham. 1976
Am Hist R 82:964 O '77. G. B. Cooper
New Repub 176:37-8 Ap 2 '77. P. Terzian

Babcock, R. H. Gompers in Canada: a study in American continentalism before the first world war. 1974
Am Hist R 82:221 F '77. R. C. Brown
Bachrack, S. D. Committee of one million: China lobby politics, 1953-1971. 1976
Am Hist R 82:772-3 Je '77. R. D. Buhite
Ann Am Acad 434:207-9 N '77. P. Van Ness
Bachstein, M. K. Wenzel Jaksch und die sudetendeutsche Sozialdemokratie. 1974
Am Hist R 81:1152 D '76. R. V. Luza
Bader, B. American picturebooks from Noah's ark to The beast within
Commonweal 104:125-6 F 18 '77. G. Weales
Baer, G W. Test case: Italy, Ethiopia, and the League of nations. 1976
Am Hist R 82:1285 D '77. W. C. Askew
Baes, C. F. and Mesmer, R. E. Hydrolysis of cations. 1976
Science 195:1323-4 Mr 25 '77. C. O. Huber
Bagdasarian, N. D. Austro-German rapprochement, 1870-1879: from the Battle of Sedan to the Dual alliance. 1976
Am Hist R 82:673 Je '77. J. Rogainis
Baigell, M. Charles Burchfield
Am Artist 42:20+ Ja '78. A. Werner
Bailey, D. K. and MacDonald, R. eds. Evolution of the crystalline rocks. 1976
Science 196:518 Ap 29 '77. D. S. Barker
Bailey, J. Intent on laughter
America 136:362-3 Ap 16 '77. T. M. Neary
Bailey, T. A. and Dobbs, S. M. Voices of America: the Nation's story in slogans, sayings, and songs. 1976
Am Hist R 82:727 Je '77. M. Plesur
Bailey, T. A. and Ryan, P. B. Lusitania disaster: an episode in modern warfare and diplomacy. 1975
Am Hist R 81:1100 D '76. S. F. Wells, Jr
Bailyn, B. Ordeal of Thomas Hutchinson. 1974
Am Hist R 82:735-6 Je '77. B. W. Sheehan
Bainbridge, B. Quiet life
Ms 6:36-7 Ag '77. N. Rosen
Bairoch, P. Commerce extérieur et développement économique de l'Europe au XIXe siècle. 1976
Am Hist R 82:951-2 O '77. R. Cameron
Baker, J. and Bouillon, J. Josephine
Newsweek 90:106 O 31 '77. M. Jefferson
Bakunin, J. Pierre Leroux and the birth of democratic socialism, 1797-1848. 1976
Am Hist R 82:982 O '77. R. L. Hoffman
Bakunin, M. Confession of Mikhail Bakunin; tr. by R. C. Howes; introd. by L. D. Orton
America 137:85 Ag 13 '77 W. C. Jaskievicz
New Yorker 53:139-41 S 12 '77. G. Steiner
Balawyder, A. Canadian-Soviet relations between the world wars. 1972
Am Hist R 82:220-1 F '77. G. F. G. Stanley
Balderston, M. and Syrett, D. eds. Lost war: letters from British officers during the American revolution; introd. by H. S. Commager. 1975
Am Hist R 81:1227 D '76. M. B. Norton
Baldwin, G. E. and D'Attilio, A. Murex shells of the world: an illustrated guide to the muricidae. 1976
Oceans 10:69 S '77. M. P. Dumont
Baldwin, H. W. Crucial years, 1939-1941: the world at war. 1976
Am Hist R 81:1102 D '76. A. L. Funk
Baldwin, J. Devil finds work
Commonweal 104:404-7 Je 24 '77. W. Sheed
Baltes, H. P. and Hiff, E. R. Spectra of finite systems. 1976
Phys Today 30:55 Ag '77. J. L. Challifour
Bambara, T. C. Sea birds are still alive: collected stories
Ms 6:36+ Jl '77. M. H. Washington
Newsweek 89:76 My 2 '77. M. Jefferson
Bane, M. J. Here to stay: American families in the twentieth century. 1976
Ann Am Acad 434:234-5 N '77. F. G. Caro
Progressive 41:56-8 My '77. P. N. Skerry, Jr
Banham, R. Megastructure: urban futures of the recent past
Archit Rec 162:43-4 O '77. W. Schacht
Banks, L. R. My darling villain. 1977
Horn Bk 53:537 O '77. S. H. Holtze
Banville, J. Doctor Copernicus. 1976
Sky & Tel 54:53-4 Jl '77. P. Rizzo
Barber, R. Strong land and a sturdy. 1976
Horn Bk 53:177 Ap '77. M. M. Burns
Barbera, D. M. Guide to color
Am Artist 41:44-5 F '77. C. Movalli
Barbour, A. J. Painting the seasons in watercolor
Am Artist 41:58-9 F '77. C. Movalli
Barclay, A. Alexander Barclay, mountain man: a narrative of his career, 1810 to 1855; his memorandum diary, 1845 to 1850; ed. by G. P. Hammond. 1976
Am West 14:61 Ja '77. W. Briggs
Barclay, W. Jesus of Nazareth
Chr Cent 94:664-6 Jl 20 '77. G. W. E. Nickelsburg and M. M. Nickelsburg
Barker, E. British policy in south-east Europe in the Second world war. 1976
Am Hist R 82:643-4 Je '77. G. Augustinos
Barker, M. Gladstone and radicalism: the reconstruction of liberal policy, 1885-94. 1975
Am Hist R 82:635-7 Je '77. R. K. Webb
Barker-Benfield, G. J. Horrors of the half-known life: mate attitudes toward women and sexuality in nineteenth-century America. 1976
Am Hist R 82:1328-9 D '77. L. Gordon
Barkin, S. ed. Worker militancy and its consequences, 1965-75: new directions in western industrial relations. 1975
M Labor R 100:83-5 Mr '77. M. Weisz
Bar-Kochva, B. Seleucid army; organization and tactics in the great campaigns. 1976
Am Hist R 82:69-70 F '77. W. McLeod
Barnard, N. and Tamotsu, S. Metallurgical remains of ancient China. 1975
Science 197:753-4 Ag 19 '77. K. C. Chang
Barnes, C. Inside American ballet theatre; with J. Colin
America 137:172-3 S 24 '77. H. J. Bertels
Dance Mag 51:75 N '77. V. Huckenpahler
Barnett, A. D. China policy. 1977
Ann Am Acad 434:209 N '77. A. E. Kane
Cur Hist 73:84-5 S '77
Barnett, L. K. Ignoble savage: American literary racism, 1790-1890. 1976
Ann Am Acad 431:166-7 My '77. R. E. Bieder
Barnett, M. R. Politics of cultural nationalism in South India. 1976
Ann Am Acad 433:169-70 S '77. B. La Brack
Barney, G. O. ed. Unfinished agenda: the citizen's policy guide to environmental issues. 1977
Am For 83:34-6 Ag '77. J. F. Shanklin
Liv Wildn 40:47-8 Ja '77. J. Bishop, Jr
Nat Parks & Con Mag 51:2 Mr '77
Barnum, P. H. ed. Dives and pauper, v 1, pt 1. 1976
Am Hist R 82:619-20 Je '77. W. J. Mulligan
Baron, S. W. Social and religious history of the Jews: late Middle ages and era of European expansion, v 16: Poland-Lithuania, 1500-1650. 2d rev ed. 1976
Am Hist R 81:1166-7 D '76. H. E. Dembrowski
Barondes, S. H. ed. Neuronal recognition. 1976
Science 195:570 F 11 '77. M. Dennis and R. B. Kelly
Barr, A. Black Texans: a history of Negroes in Texas, 1528-1971. 1973
Ann Am Acad 430:205-6 Mr '77. P. W. Brewer
Barr, B. Well church book. 1976
Chr Cent 94:490-1 My 18 '77. F. D. Lueking
Chr Today 21:28 Jl 29 '77. R. Quebedeaux
Barr, C. Ealing studios. 1977
Film Q 30:46-9 Summ '77. D. Willis
Barrett, S. and Knight, G. eds. Health robbers: how to protect your money and your life. 1976
BioScience 27:206 Mr '77. E. M. Whelan and F. J. Stare
Barron, J. and Paul, A. Murder of a gentle land: the untold story of communist genocide in Cambodia. 1977
Nat R 29:1306-7 N 11 '77. J. Greenway
Nation 224:789-94 Je 25 '77. N. Chomsky and E. S. Herman
U.S. News 83:33 Ag 8 '77. J. N. Wallace
Barrows, W. Grassroots politics in an African state: integration and development in Sierra Leone. 1976
Ann Am Acad 430:188-9 Mr '77. S. K. Crosbie

Barry, J. Infamous woman: the life of George Sand
Ms 5:42+ My '77. E. Abeel
Barsam, R. M. In the dark. 1977
Horn Bk 53:325 Je '77. S. H. Holtze
Barth, G. Instant cities: urbanization and the rise of San Francisco and Denver. 1975
Am Hist R 81:1245 D '76. C. Abbott
Barth, J. R. Symbolic imagination: Coleridge and the Romantic tradition
America 137:174+ S 24 '77. J. L. Mahoney
Commonweal 104:351 My 27 '77. A. Taylor
Barth, K. Karl Barth: his life from letters and autobiographical texts; ed. by E. Busch. 1976
Chr Today 22:35-6 O 21 '77. D. G. Bloesch
Barthelme, D. Amateurs
Nation 224:119-20 Ja 29 '77. P. Stevick
New Repub 176:28-9 Mr 19 '77. T. LeClair
Bartley, N. V. and Graham, H. D. Southern politics and the second reconstruction. 1975
Am Hist R 82:217 F '77. J. M. Kousser
Barton, H. A. Count Hans Axel von Fersen: aristocrat in an age of revolution. 1975
Am Hist R 82:121 F '77. C. Gold
Barudio, G. Absolutismus—Zerstörung der "Libertären Verfassung"; Studien zur "Karolinischen Eingewalt" in Schweden zwischen 1680 und 1693. 1976
Am Hist R 82:992-3 O '77. H. P. Liebel
Baryshnikov, M. Baryshnikov at work; ed. by C. E. France. 1976
Am Rec G 41:47-8+ N '77. C. J. Luten
Commonweal 104:539-40 Ag 19 '77. S. Lawson
Barzini, L. O America: when you and I were young. 1977
Horn Bk 53:468 Ag '77. M. S. Cosgrave
Newsweek 89:85-6 Ap 4 '77. P. S. Prescott
Barzun, J. Simple and direct: a rhetoric for writers
Esquire 87:36+ My '77. J. Simon
Baseball encyclopedia
Time 111:77-8 Ja 16 '78. P. Stoler
Baserga, R. Multiplication and division in mammalian cells. 1976
Science 195:973-5 Mr 11 '77. H. Rubin
Bashline, L. J. and Saults, D. eds. America's great outdoors. 1976
Am For 83:39-40 My '77. H. Clepper
Baskin, B. H. and Harris, K. H. eds. Special child in the library. 1976
SLJ 23:44 Ap '77. E .O. Cawthorne
Bass, E. Of separateness and merging
Ms 6:37 N '77. J. Thurman
Bass, L. W. Management by task force. 1975
Ann Am Acad 429:188-91 Ja '77. W. Gomberg
Bate, W. J. Samuel Johnson
New Repub 177:30-2 N 19 '77. N. Nicolson
Newsweek 90:104+ N 28 '77. W. Clemons
Bater, J. H. St Petersburg: industrialization and change. 1976
Am Hist R 82:1025-6 O '77. R. E. Zelnik
Bates, R. H. Rural responses to industrialization: a study of village Zambia. 1976
Ann Am Acad 433:170-1 S '77. R. E. Schecter
Bateson, P. P. G. and Hinde, R. A. eds. Growing points in ethology. 1976
BioScience 27:618 S '77. J. P. Hailman
Bato, J. Sorcerer; ed. by K. F. Donnelly. 1976
Horn Bk 53:165 Ap '77. P. Heins
Battiscombe, G. Shaftesbury: the great reformer 1801-1885. 1975
Chr Today 21:46-8+ My 6 '77. R. V. Pierard
Battista, A. M. Lo spirito liberale e lo spirito religioso: Tocqueville nel dibattito sulla scuola. 1976
Am Hist R 82:334-5 Ap '77. E. T. Gargan
Bauer, A. J. Chilean rural society from the Spanish conquest to 1930. 1975
Am Hist R 82:1108 O '77. B. Loveman
Bauer, C. F. Handbook for storytellers. 1977
SLJ 24:92 O '77. M. B. Iarusso
Bauer, W. China and the search for happiness: recurring themes in four thousand years of Chinese cultural history; tr. by M. Shaw
America 136:509-10 Je 4 '77. J. W. Witek
Baum, G. ed. Journeys
Commonweal 104:186-8 Mr 18 '77. D. Dohen
Baum, G. Religion and alienation
Commonweal 104:186-8 Mr 18 '77. D. Dohen
Baum, R. Prelude to revolution: Mao, the party, and the peasant question, 1962-66. 1975
Am Hist R 81:1203-4 D '76. J. Ch'en
Baum, W. and Weichold, E. Der Krieg der Achsenmächte im Mittelmeer-Raum: die Strategie der Diktatoren. 1973
Am Hist R 82:132 F '77. D. S. Detwiler
Baumann, D. All originality makes a dull church. 1976
Chr Today 21:42+ F 18 '77. W. Brindley
Baumann, M. L. B. Traven: an introduction
New Repub 176:29-31 Ap 2 '77. J. Walt
Time 109:93+ Ap 11 '77. J. Skow
Baumer, F. L. Modern European thought: continuity and change in ideas, 1600-1950
Chr Cent 94:1121 N 30 '77. J. E. Groh
Baumgartner, F. J. Radical reactionaries: the political thought of the French Catholic league. 1975
Am Hist R 82:1263 D '77. R. D. Linder

Baxandall, R. and others. eds. America's working women: a documentary history—1600 to the present
Nation 224:694-6 Je 4 '77. A. Wolfe
Progressive 41:58-9 F '77. A. M. Cunningham
Bayley, C. C. Mercenaries for the Crimea: the German, Swiss, and Italian legions in British service, 1854-1856. 1977
Am Hist R 82:1253-4 D '77. A. N. Gilbert
Bayley, D. H. Forces of order: police behavior in Japan and the United States. 1976
Ann Am Acad 433:185-6 S '77. R. L. Austin
Bayly, C. A. Local roots of Indian politics: Allahabad, 1880-1920. 1975
Am Hist R 82:421-2 Ap '77. B. N. Ramusack
Bazant, J. Los bienes de la Iglesia en México (1856-1875): aspectos económicos y sociales de la revolución liberal. 1971
Am Hist R 82:478 Ap '77. R. J. Knowlton
Be and shell stars; papers from symposium, Bass River, Mass, 1975; ed. by A. Slettebak. 1976
Science 196:777-8 My 13 '77. E. J. Wampler
Beadle, M. Cat: history, biology, and behavior. 1977
Horn Bk 53:560 O '77. M. S. Cosgrave
Newsweek 90:76 Jl 11 '77. M. Jefferson
Beale, H. P. ed. Bibliography of plant viruses and index to research. 1976
BioScience 27:288 Ap '77. K. Maramorosch
Beard, P. H. The end of the game
Sat R 5:43-5 Ja 7 '78
Beattie, A. Chilly scenes of winter
Commentary 63:62-4 F '77
Yale R 66:584-91 Je '77. D. Thorburn
Beattie, A. Distortions
Commentary 63:62-4 F '77
Beatty, D. and Beatty, R. O. Nevada: land of discovery. 1976
Am West 14:55 Jl '77 W. D. Rowley
Beatty, P. Something to shout about. 1976
Horn Bk 53:157 Ap '77. P. Heins
Beauchamp, E. R. American teacher in early Meiji Japan. 1976
Am Hist R 82:417-18 Ap '77. J. F. Howes
Becker, J. Hitler's children: the story of the Baader-Meinhof terrorist gang
Commentary 64:71-2+ N '77. E. M. Breindel
Psychol Today 11:88+ Ag '77. T. Morgan
Time 110:71 Ag 8 '77. D. Tinnin
Beckett, J. C. The Anglo-Irish tradition
America 136:303-4 Ap 2 '77. L. J. McCaffrey
Beckett, S. Ends and odds: eight new dramatic pieces
Nation 224:216-17+ F 19 '77. J. D. O'Hara
New Repub 176:31-2 Mr 5 '77. E. Brater
Sat R 4:20+ Ap 30 '77. P. Auster
Time 109:84+ F 7 '77. P. Gray
Beckett, S. Fizzles
Nation 224:216-17+ F 19 '77. J. D. O'Hara
New Repub 176:31-2 Mr 5 '77. E. Brater
Sat R 4:22-3 Ap 30 '77. P. Auster
Time 109:84+ F 7 '77. P. Gray
Beckett, S. I can't go on, I'll go on: a selection from Samuel Beckett's work; ed. by R. W. Seaver
New Repub 176:31-2 Mr 5 '77. E. Brater
Sat R 4:20+ Ap 30 '77. P. Auster
Bedini, S. A. Thinkers and tinkers. 1975
Am Hist Illus 12:49 Jl '77. H. L. Peterson
Beer, T. Aerospace environment. 1976
Sky & Tel 54:50-2 Jl '77. N. J. MacDonald
Beer, T. Atmospheric waves. 1974
Sea Front 23:60 Ja '77
Beeson, T. Discretion and valour: religious conditions in Russia and Eastern Europe. 1976
Chr Today 22:36-7 N 4 '77. A. H. Winquist
Behlmer, R. and Thomas, T. Hollywood's Hollywood: the movies about the movies
New Repub 176:26-9 Ap 2 '77. W. Hughes
Behn, N. Big stick-up at Brink's
Bus W p 11-12 Je 27 '77. G. L. Williams
Behrman, D. Solar energy: the awakening science. 1976
Sky & Tel 54:133-5 Ag '77. C. A. Federer, Jr
Bell, J. B. Terror out of Zion
New Repub 176:32-5 Je 18 '77. M. Syrkin
Bell, Q. On human finery
Art N 76:104-5 F '77. J. Hobhouse
Bellush, B. Failure of the NRA. 1975
Ann Am Acad 429:191 Ja '77. M. I. Elzy
Belz, H. New birth of freedom: the Republican party and freedmen's rights, 1861 to 1866. 1977
Am Hist R 82:1332 D '77. R. F. Durden
Ben-Sasson, H. H. ed. History of the Jewish people. 1976
Am Hist R 82:1030-1 O '77. J. Neusner
Chr Today 22:40 D 9 '77. D. E. Aune
Ben-Veniste, R. and Frampton, G. Stonewall
New Repub 176:59-60 My 21 '77. P. Terzian
Benade, A. H. Fundamentals of musical acoustics. 1976
Phys Today 30:62-3 Mr '77. J. T. Scott
Benchley, N. Kilroy and the gull; il by J. Schoenherr. 1977
Horn Bk 53:309-10 Je '77. V. Haviland
Benecke, G. Society and politics in Germany, 1500-1750. 1974
Am Hist R 81:1142 D '76. D. S. Detwiler
Benedikt, M. Night cries
Poetry 130:289-90 Ag '77. B. Howard

Benet, M. K. Politics of adoption. 1976
Chr Today 22:43 O 7 '77. R. Case, 2d
Benet, M. K. Writers in love: Katherine Mansfield, George Eliot, Colette, and the men they lived with
Am Scholar 46:399-404 Summ '77. M. Green
Benge, E. J. and others. eds. Elements of modern management. 1976
M Labor R 100:78-9 O '77. T. H. Patten, jr
Bengis, I. I have come here to be alone
Ms 5:38+ F '77. L. S. Schwartz
Bengtsson, H. and Atkinson, G. Orienteering for sport and pleasure
Sci Am 237:40 D '77. P. Morrison and P. Morrison
Benjamin, P. S. Philadelphia Quakers in the industrial age, 1865-1920. 1976
Am Hist R 82:457 Ap '77. P. A. Carter
Ann Am Acad 431:163-4 My '77. R. Detweiler
Benkovitz, M. J. Frederick Rolfe: Baron Corvo
Time 110:71-2 Ag 8 '77. M. Mohs
Bennett, D. TA and the manager. 1976
M Labor R 100:56-7 Jl '77. K. G. Van Auken, jr
Bennett, G. V. Tory crisis in church and state, 1688-1730: the career of Francis Atterbury, Bishop of Rochester. 1975
Am Hist R 82:961-2 O '77. R. E. Boyer
Bennett, J. C. Radical imperative
Commonweal 104:121-2 F 18 '77. R. J. Neuhaus
Bennett, N. Teaching styles and pupil progress
Todays Educ 66:79 N '77. V. A. Sheridan
Benson, E. F. Make way for Lucia
Newsweek 90:73 Jl 4 '77. W. Clemons
Benston, K. W. Baraka: the renegade and the mask
New Repub 176:33-6 Ap 30 '77. A. Rampersad
Bentley, M. Liberal mind, 1914-1929. 1977
Am Hist R 82:1255 D '77. J. A. Thompson
Bequaert, L. H. Single women: alone and together
America 136:56-7 Ja 22 '77. J. L. Lant
Berenbaum, E. Municipal public safety
Am City & County 92:88+ Je '77
Berendzen, R. and others. Man discovers the galaxies. 1976
Phys Today 30:57+ D '77. C. D. Shane
Sci Am 236:140 Ap '77. P. Morrison
Sky & Tel 53:295-6 Ap '77. J. D. Fernie
Berg, S. Grief: poems and versions of poems
Poetry 129:285-7 F '77. R. Holland
Bergamini, J. D. Hundredth year: the United States in 1876
Commonweal 104:25-7 Ja 7 '77. R. V. Remini
Berger, C. Flamenco gitano. 1974
Society 14:85-7 Ja '77. H. S. Becker
Berger, C. Writing of Canadian history: aspects of English-Canadian historical writing, 1900-1970. 1976
Am Hist R 83:1365 D '77. W. H. Heick
Berger, G. M. Parties out of power in Japan, 1931-1941. 1977
Ann Am Acad 434:209-10 N '77. A. Palmer
Berger, P. L. Facing up to modernity; reflections on society, politics, and religion
America 137:363-4 N 19 '77. T. Davis
New Repub 177:33-5 N 5 '77. M. Harrington
Berger, P. L. and Neuhaus, R. J. eds. Against the world for the world: the Hartford appeal and the future of American religion. 1976
Chr Today 21:45-6 My 6 '77. B. Demarest
Intellect 105:283 F '77. L. J. Putnam
Berger, R. Government by judiciary: the transformation of the Fourteenth Amendment
Chr Cent 94:1228-9 D 28 '77. R. W. Lovin
Commentary 64:84+ D '77. E. Abrams
Nat R 29:1320 N 11 '77. W. F. Buckley, jr
Nation 225:628+ D 10 '77. E. R. Larson
Newsweek 90:75 N 14 '77. J. K. Footlick
Berger, T. Little big man. 1964
Nation 225:149-51 Ag 20 '77. F. Turner
Berger, T. Who is Teddy Villanova?
Newsweek 89:85 Ap 4 '77. W. Clemons
Time 109:86 Ap 4 '77. P. Gray
Bergman, I. Four stories
Nation 225:537-8 N 19 '77. H. Kriegel
Bergoffen, W. W. 100 years of federal forestry
Am For 83:54 O '77. J. B. Craig
Bergonzi, B. Gerard Manley Hopkins
America 137:57-8 Jl 30 '77. E. D. Cuffe
New Repub 176:25-6 Je 18 '77. H. Kenner
Berk, S. E. Calvinism versus democracy: Timothy Dwight and the origins of American Evangelical orthodoxy. 1974
Am Hist R 81:1235 D '76. P. C. Nagel
Berkouwer, G. C. Church. 1976
Chr Today 22:46-7 D 9 '77. D. G. Bloesch
Berlanstein, L. R. Barristers of Toulouse in the eighteenth century (1740-1793). 1975
Am Hist R 82:980-1 O '77. R. E. Geisey
Berlin, I. Vico and Herder: two studies in the history of ideas
Yale R 66:XIV+ Je '77
Berns, W. First amendment and the future of American democracy
Commentary 63:79-80+ My '77. W. J. Bennett
Nat R 29:158+ F 4 '77. G. W. Carey
Bernstein, C. and Woodward, B. All the President's men
New Repub 176:35-6 Mr 12 '77. M. da Vinci

Bernstein, M. Nuns
America 136:54-5 Ja 22 '77. J. W. Donohue
Commonweal 104:411-12 Je 24 '77. L. Spear
Berrigan, D. Book of parables
America 137:84-5 Ag 13 '77. T. F. Driver
Berry, A. Iron sun: crossing the universe through black holes
Time 110:70 Ag 15 '77. F. Golden
Berry, M. C. Alaska pipeline: the politics of oil and native land claims. 1975
Am West 14:60 S '77. T. C. Hinckley
Berry, W. Unsettling of America: culture and agriculture
Org Gard & Farm 24:126-33 S '77. G. Logsdon
Berryman, J. Henry's fate and other poems, 1967-72; ed. by J. Haffenden
Nat R 29:834 Jl 22 '77. R. Atwan
Nation 224:630-2 My 21 '77. J. D. O'Hara
New Repub 176:34-5 Je 4 '77. C. Kazin
Time 109:90 Mr 21 '77. P. Gray
Yale R 67:72, 84-6 O '77. H. Vendler
Bersani, L. Future for Astyanax: character and desire in literature
Yale R 66:592-8 Je '77. J. Culler
Berthe, M. Le comté de Bigorre: un milieu rural au bas moyen âge. 1976
Am Hist R 82:342-3 Ap '77. K. Kennelly
Beskrovnyi, L. G. Russkaia armiia i flot v XIX veke: voenno-ekonomicheskii potentsial Rossii. 1973
Am Hist R 82:694 Je '77. J. W. Kipp
Beskrovnyi, L. G. and others, eds. Drevnerusskie kniazhestva X-XIII vv. 1973
Am Hist R 82:691-2 Je '77. G. P. Majeska
Bethancourt, T. E. Dog days of Arthur Cane. 1976
Horn Bk 53:157 Ap '77. P. Heins
Betjeman, J. A nip in the air
Poetry 129:231-2 Ja '77. R. Howard
Bettelheim, B. Uses of enchantment
Todays Educ 66:102 Ja '77. E. Hall
Bettelheim, C. Class struggle in the USSR, v 1: First period: 1917-1923; tr. by B. Pearce. 1976
Am Hist R 82:1296-7 D '77. W. G. Rosenberg
Beyerchen, A. D. Scientists under Hitler
New Yorker 53:196+ D 12 '77. J. Bernstein
Bezzola, G. A. Die Mongolen in Abendländischer Sicht (1220-1270): ein Beitrag zur Frage der Völkerbegegnungen. 1974
Am Hist R 81:1086 D '76. D. Sinor
Bhagwati, J. N. and Srinivasan, T. N. Foreign trade regimes and economic development: India. 1975
Ann Am Acad 432:187-8 Jl '77. J. K. S. Ghandhi
Bhattacharyya, N. N. Ancient Indian rituals and their social contents. 1976
Am Hist R 81:1206 D '76. B. G. Gokhale
Bicha, K. D. Western populism: studies in an ambivalent conservatism. 1976
Am Hist R 82:754-5 Je '77. P. H. Argersinger
Bidart, F. Book of the body
Atlantic 240:102 O '77. D. Hall
Nation 224:763-6 Je 18 '77. J. Atlas
New Repub 177:35-6 O 22 '77. L. Pastan
Yale R 67:72, 78-9 O '77. H. Vendler
Biddle, S. Bolingbroke and Harley. 1974
Am Hist R 81:1105 D '76. I. Kramnick
Biersdorf, J. E. Hunger for experience: vital religious communities in America today
Chr Cent 94:230+ Mr 9 '77. L. E. Schaller
Bilger, H. R. Südafrika in Geschichte und Gegenwart. 1976
Am Hist R 82:408 Ap '77. L. H. Gann
Billias, G. A. Elbridge Gerry: founding father and Republican statesman. 1976
Am Hist R 82:737 Je '77. C. E. Prince
Binion, R. Hitler among the Germans. 1976
Am Hist R 82:1009-10 O '77. G. Cocks
Biochemical aspects of plant-parasite relationships; proceedings of symposium. Hull, England, 1975; ed. by J. Friend and D. R. Threlfall. 1976
Science 197:1071 S 9 '77. D. R. Strong, jr
Biochemical interaction between plants and insects; proceedings of meeting, Tampa, Fla, 1974; ed. by J. W. Wallace and R. L. Mansell. 1976
Science 195:387 Ja 28 '77. L. E. Gilbert
Biochemistry of smooth muscle: proceedings of symposium, Winnipeg, Manitoba, 1975; ed. by N. L. Stephens. 1977
Science 197:858 Ag 26 '77. R. E. Davies
Biological control of water pollution: papers from conference, Philadelphia, 1974; ed. by J. Tourbier and R. W. Pierson. 1976
Science 195:386-7 Ja 28 '77. R. Mitchell
Biological reactive intermediates: proceedings of conference, Turku, Finland, 1975; ed. by D. J. Jollow and others. 1977
Science 198:1029 D 9 '77. M. R. Franklin
Biology and the future of man; proceedings of conference, Sorbonne, 1974; ed. by C. Galperine. 1976
BioScience 27:362 My '77. L. A. Snyder
Biondi, A. and others. Eresia e riforma nell'Italia del cinquecento: miscellanea I. 1974
Am Hist R 82:139-40 F '77. M. P. Gilmore
Biraben, J. N. Les hommes et la peste en France et dans les pays européens et méditerranéens, v 1: La peste dans l'histoire. 1975
Am Hist R 82:73 F '77. V. J. Knapp

Biraben, J. N. Les hommes et la peste en France et dans les pays européens et mediterranéens, v2: Les hommes face à la peste. 1976
Am Hist R 82:936 O '77. V. J. Knapp
Birch, B. C. and Rasmussen, L. L. Bible and ethics in the Christian life
Chr Cent 94:117 F 2 '77. R. H. Boyd
Birmingham, S. Certain people: America's black elite
Sat R 4:40-1 Je 11 '77. L. C. Carter, Jr
Time 109:98 My 16 '77. L. Schreiber
Birnberg, T. B. and Resnick, S. A. Colonial development: an econometric study. 1975
Am Hist R 81:1074-5 D '76. W. W. Rostow
Birren, F. Color perception in art
Am Artist 41:45-6 F '77. C. Movalli
Bishop, E. Geography III. 1976
America 136:552 Je 18 '77. R. F. Mullen
New Repub 176:29-30 F 5 '77. H. Bloom
Newsweek 89:73-73B Ja 31 '77. M. Jefferson
Yale R 66:407-24 Mr '77. H. Vendler
Bishop, Y. M. M, and others. Discrete multivariate analysis. Theory and practice. 1975
Science 196:156-7 Ap 8 '77. I. Olkin
Biswas, A. K. ed. Systems approach to water management. 1976
BioScience 27:688 O '77. D. Scavia
Bitterli, U. Die Wilden und die Zivilisierten: Grundzüge einer Geistes- und Kulturgeschichte der europäisch-überseeischen Begegnung. 1976
Am Hist R 82:347-8 Ap '77. R. G. Cole
Black, D. Behavior of law. 1976
Science 197:149-50 Jl 8 '77. K. F. Koch
Black, E. Southern governors and civil rights. 1976
Ann Am Acad 429:171-2 Ja '77. V. G. Rosenblum
Blackburn, T. C. ed. December's child: a book of Chumash oral narratives. 1975
Am West 14:58 S '77. R. F. Heizer
Blacker, C. and Loewe, M. eds. Ancient cosmologies. 1975
Am Hist R 81:1078 D '76. J. J. Peradotto
Blackey, R. and Paynton, C. Revolution and the revolutionary ideal. 1976
Am Hist R 82:335-6 Ap '77. L. Kaplan
Blackmer, D. L. M. and Tarrow, S. eds. Communism in Italy and France. 1976
Am Hist R 82:955 O '77. M. L. Silsby
Blaich, F. Der Trustkampf (1901-1915): ein Beitrag zum Verhalten der Ministerialbürokratie gegenüber Verbandsinteressen im Wihelminischen Deutschland. 1975
Am Hist R 82:128 F '77. C. Medalen
Blainey, G. Triumph of the nomads: a history of aboriginal Australia. 1976
Am Hist R 82:426-7 Ap '77. S. C. McCulloch
Blair, J. M. Control of oil
Bus W p 14 Mr 21 '77. S. Jackson
Nation 224:246-8 F 26 '77 R. Lekachman
New Repub 177:37-8 Ag 6 '77. M. Harrington
Progressive 41:53-4 Mr '77. J. S. Rosenberg
Blaise, C. and Mukherjee, B. Days and nights in Calcutta
America 136:490 My 28 '77. J. Novak
Newsweek 89:73-4 F 7 '77. M. Jefferson
Blake, P. Form follows fiasco: why modern architecture hasn't worked. 1977
Archit Rec 162:43+ S '77. J. Barnett
Fortune 96:59+ S '77. R. Starr
New Repub 177:43-4 O 1 '77. W. Von Eckardt
Blaker, A. A. Field photography: beginning and advanced techniques. 1976
BioScience 27:484 Jl '77. J. F. Gennaro, Jr
Blanco, R. L. Wellington's surgeon general: Sir James McGrigor. 1974
Am Hist R 82:103-4 F '77. R. J. T. Joy
Blancpain, J.-P. Les Allemands au Chili (1816-1945). 1974
Am Hist R 81:1286-7 D '76. A. J. Bauer
Bland, A. Nureyev image
Commonweal 104:539-40 Ag 19 '77. S. Lawson
Dance Mag 51:27 Ag '77. D. Hering
Blandford, L. Super-wealth
Bus W p 14+ Ap 11 '77. P. B. Finney
Blanshei, S. R. Perugia, 1260-1340: conflict and change in a medieval Italian urban society. 1976
Am Hist R 82:79-80 F '77. R. Schumann
Blasier, C. Hovering giant: U.S. responses to revolutionary change in Latin America. 1976
Am Hist R 82:213 F '77. R. F. Smith
Blasius, D. Bürgerliche Gesellschaft und Kriminalität Zur Sozialgeschichte Preussens im Vormärz. 1976
Am Hist R 82:1274 D '77. C. R. Friedrichs
Blau, J L. Judaism in America: from curiosity to third faith. 1976
Am Hist R 81:1216 D '76. N. W. Cohen
Blaukopf, K. ed. and comp. Mahler—a documentary study; with Z. Roman
Am Rec G 40:57-8 Je '77. J. Diether and N. Karlins
Hi Fi 27:MA38-9 Mr '77. D. Hamilton
Bleikasten, A. Most splendid failure: Faulkner's "The sound and the fury"
Commonweal 104:507-9 Ag 5 '77. P. Samway

Bley, H. Bebel und die Strategie der Kriegsverhütung 1904-1913: eine Studie über Bebels Geheimkontakte mit der britischen Regierung und Edition der Dokumente. 1975
Am Hist R 81:1149 D '76. K. H. Jarausch
Block, F. L. Origins of international economic disorder: a study of United States international monetary policy from World War II to the present. 1977
Am Hist R 82:1352-3 D '77. A. E. Eckes, jr
Nation 224:565-6 My 7 '77. W. A. Williams
Block, S. and Reddaway, P. Psychiatric terror
Nat R 29:1248 O 28 '77. J. A. Rehyansky
New Repub 177:35-6 N 5 '77. H. Fireside
Blocker, J. S. Jr. Retreat from reform: the prohibition movement in the United States, 1890-1913. 1976
Am Hist R 82:1089 O '77. D. J. Pivar
Ann Am Acad 432:170 Jl '77. H. S. Merrill
Bloesch, D. Jesus is victor! Karl Barth's doctrine of salvation. 1976
Chr Today 21:57-8 S 9 '77. E. Lemmon
Blom, J. C. H. De muiterij op de Zeven Provinciën. 1975
Am Hist R 82:377 Ap '77. L. D. Stokes
Bloom, B. S. Human characteristics and school learning
Todays Educ 66:90-1 Mr '77. J. Stallings
Bloom, H. Wallace Stevens: the poems of our climate
America 137:59-60 Jl 30 '77. M. True
New Repub 176:24+ Je 11 '77. K. Burke
New Repub 177:35 D 3 '77. W. H. Pritchard
Poetry 131:165-9 D '77. P. Pettingell
Yale R 67:121-4 O '77. V. Miller
Bloomfield, M. American lawyers in a changing society, 1776-1876. 1976
Am Hist R 82:175-6 F '77. N. Brockman
Blum, H. Wanted! The search for Nazis in America
Newsweek 89:86-7 F 21 '77. M. Jefferson
Blum, J. M. V was for victory: politics and American culture during World war II. 1976
Am Hist R 82:466-7 Ap '77. J. F. Heath
Blumberg, S. A. and Owens, G. Energy and conflict: the life and times of Edward Teller. 1976
Commentary 63:67-70 Ap '77. J. Marsh
Phys Today 30:53-4 F '77. F. Seitz
Blume, F. and others. Protestant church music: a history. 1974
Mus Q 63:114-24 Ja '77. R. F. French
Blumenthal, H. American and French culture, 1800-1900: interchange in art, science, literature, and society. 1975
Am Hist R 81:1233 D '76. H. Peyre
Blumenthal, S. and Yazijian. H. eds. Government by gunplay. 1976
Society 15:126 N '77. D. R. Howard
Blumin, S. M. Urban threshold: growth and change in a nineteenth-century American community. 1976
Am Hist R 82:441-2 Ap '77. D. R. Esslinger
Ann Am Acad 430:206 Mr '77. L. E. Withey
Blundell, T. L. and Johnson, L. N. Protein crystallography. 1976
Science 196:50 Ap 1 '77. H. M. Berman
Bobińska, C. and Pilch, A. eds. Employment-seeking emigrations of the Poles world-wide: XIX and XX C; tr. by D. E. Zukowska. 1975
Am Hist R 81:1168 D '76. C. J. Slovak
Bockelman, W. Gothard: the man and his ministry, an evaluation. 1976
Chr Today 21:28 Je 3 '77. S. E. Smallman
Bockris, J. O. M. Energy: the solar-hydrogen alternative. 1976
Phys Today 30:66-8 Mr '77. A. M. Saperstein
Bockstoce, J. R. Steam whaling in the western Arctic. 1977
Oceans 10:70 Jl '77. R. Storro-Patterson
Bodard, L. French consul
Newsweek 89:83-4 Mr 28 '77. M. Jefferson
Bodde, D. Festivals in classical China: New Year and other annual observances during the Han dynasty, 206 B.C.-A.D. 220. 1975
Am Hist R 82:158-9 F '77. W. Eberhard
Bode, F. A. Protestantism and the new South: North Carolina Baptists and Methodists in political crisis, 1894-1903. 1976
Am Hist R 81:1272 D '76. K. K. Bailey
Bodin, J. Colloquium of the seven about secrets of the sublime; tr. and introd. by M. L. D. Kuntz. 1975
Am Hist R 81:1122 D '76. F. Rosenthal
Boersch-Supan, H. Caspar David Friedrich
Am Artist 41:54-5 F '77. A. Werner
Boffa, G. Storia dell'Unione Sovietica, v 1: Dalla rivoluzione alla seconda guerra mondiale: Lenin e Stalin, 1917-1941. 1976
Am Hist R 82:1026 O '77. R. Stites
Bogan, L. Blue estuaries: poems 1923-1968
Nation 225:182-3+ S 3 '77. C. C. Park
Bogue, A. G. and Taylor, R. eds. University of Wisconsin: one hundred and twenty-five years. 1975
Am Hist R 81:1270 D '76. G. J. Clifford
Böhm, E. Überseehandel und Flottenbau: Hanseatische Kaufmanschaft und deutsche Seerüstung, 1879-1902. 1972
Am Hist R 81:1148-9 D '76. P. J. Kelly

Bohr, A. and Mottelson, B. R. Nuclear structure, v2. 1975
Phys Today 30:59+ Mr '77. G. Breit and G. E. Brown
Boia, L. Evolutia istoriografiei române. 1976
Am Hist R 82:685-6 Je '77. K. Hitchins
Bois, G. Crise du féodalisme: économie rurale et démographie en Normandie orientale du début du 14e siècle au milieu du 16e siècle. 1976
Am Hist R 82:938-9 O '77. T. Evergates
Bokun, B. Man: the fallen ape
Newsweek 91:67 Ja 9 '78. R. Boeth
Boldt, H. Deutsche Staatslehre im Vormarz. 1975
Am Hist R 81:1146 D '76. L. O'Boyle
Bolkhovitinov, N. N. Beginnings of Russian-American relations, 1775-1815; introd. by L. H. Butterfield, tr. by E. Levin. 1975
Am Hist R 82:148-9 F '77. J. T. Alexander
Böll, H. Bread of those early years; tr. by L. Vennewitz
America 136:222-3 Mr 12 '77. D. Coogan
Nation 224:213-14 F 19 '77. S. Maloff
Boltovskoy, E. and Wright, R. Recent foraminifera. 1976
Science 198:924 D 2 '77. A. W. H. Bé
Bombeck, E. Grass is always greener over the septic tank
Ms 5:86-7 Je '77. J. H. Kay
Bond, J. Tex Ritter story
Hi Fi 27:167 O '77. N. Tosches
Bondanella, P. E. Francesco Guicciardini. 1976
Am Hist R 82:139 F '77. R. Starn
Bondy, R. Emissary, a life of Enzo Sereni
New Repub 177:38-9 N 12 '77. M. Syrkin
Bonington, C. Everest the hard way
Bus W p 13-14 My 30 '77. E. Symonds
Bonini, I. V. Le communità di valle in epoca signorile: l'evoluzione della comunita di Valcamonica durante la dominazione viscontea (secc. XIV-XV) 1976
Am Hist R 82:622-3 Je '77. K. Casey
Bonino, J. M. Christians and Marxists: the mutual challenge to revolution. 1976
America 136:132-3 F 12 '77. M. A. Fahey
Chr Today 21:54-5 S 9 '77. J. S. Tinney
Bonnassie, P. La Catalogne du milieu du Xe à la lin du XIe siècle: croissance et mutations d'une société. 2v. 1975, 1976
Am Hist R 82:343 Ap '77. J. N. Hillgarth
Bonwick, C. English radicals and the American revolution. 1977
Am Hist R 82:1245-6 D '77. C. R. Ritcheson
Boorstein, E. Allende's Chile: an inside view
Progressive 41:58-9 O '77. A. Schesch
Booth, A. R. United States experience in South Africa. 1784-1870. 1976
Am Hist R 81:1195 D '76. D. Chanaiwa
Booth, P. Available light
Poetry 130:111-14 My '77. R. Siegel
Borbándi, G. Der Ungarische Populismus. 1976
Am Hist R 82:1019-20 O '77. I. Deák
Bordley, J. 3d and Harvey, A. M. Two centuries of American medicine. 1776-1976. 1976
Am Hist R 82:728-9 Je '77. M. Kaufman
Science 197:750-1 Ag 19 '77. G. G. Reader
Borges, J. L. Book of sand; tr. by N. T. di Giovanni
Sat R 5:30-1 O 15 '77. S. Koch
Time 110:109 N 14 '77. R. Z. Sheppard
Borges, J. L. Gold of the tigers: selected later poems; tr. by A. Reid
Harpers 255:104 N '77. H. Carruth
Bori, P. C. Chiesa primitiva: l'immagine della communità delle origini Atti, 2,42-47; 4,32-37—nella storia della chiesa antica. 1974
Am Hist R 82:340 Ap '77. R. E. A. Palmer
Borisov, Iu. V. and others. eds. Dokumenty vneshnei politiki SSSR, v 18: I ianvaria-31 dekabria 1935 g. 1973
Am Hist R 81:1181-2 D '76. R. M. Slusser
Boros, L. Christian prayer; tr. by D. Smith
America 136:134 F 12 '77. Q. Lauer
Borowski, T. This way for the gas, ladies and gentlemen
Nation 224:505 Ap 23 '77. I. Sanders
Borroff, M. tr. Pearl
Yale R 67:72, 89-90 O '77. H. Vendler
Borsdorf, U. and others. Arbeiterinitiative 1945: antifaschistische Ausschüsse und Reorganisation der Arbeiterbewegund in Deutschland. 1976
Am Hist R 82:1282 D '77. H. Gruber
Boty, G. Gewalt in der Politik: Attentate, Zusammenstösse, Putschversuche, Unruhem in Osterreich 1918 bis 1934. 1976
Am Hist R 82:675-6 Je '77. D. Large
Bouche, D. L'enseignement dans les territoires français de l'Afrique occidentale de 1817 à 1920; mission civilisatrice ou formation d'une élite? 2v. 1975
Am Hist R 81:1191 D '76. R. M. Brace
Boussard, J. Nouvelle histoire de Paris: de la fin du siège de 885-886 à la mort de Philippe Auguste. 1976
Am Hist R 82:938 O '77. G. M. Spiegel
Bowden, C. Killing the hidden waters
Natur Hist 86:112-15 N '77. P. B. Sears
Smithsonian 8:111-13 Ja '78. J. S. Rosenberg
Bower, D. E. Fred Rosenstock: a legend in books and art. 1976
Am West 14:62 My '77. B. Beshoar
Bowers, J. Z and Purcell, E. F. eds. Advances in American medicine: essays at the Bicentennial. 2v. 1976
Science 197:750-1 Ag 19 '77. G. G. Reader
Bowers, W. L. Country life movement in America, 1900-1920. 1974
Am Hist R 81:1269 D '76. R. H. Pells
Bowler, P. J. Fossils and progress: paleontology and the idea of progressive evolution in the nineteenth century. 1976
Science 196:517-18 Ap 29 '77. S. J. Gould
Bowles, S. and Gintis, H. Schooling in capitalist America: educational reform and the contradictions of economic life
Am Scholar 46:254+ Spr '77. D. Ravitch
Bowser, F. P. African slave in colonial Peru, 1524-1650. 1975
Ann Am Acad 432:155-6 Jl '77. F. J. Munch
Boyd, B. M. Mourning the death of magic
Ms 6:39-40+ N '77. C. Betsky
Boyd, E. F. Bloomsbury heritage: their mothers and their aunts
Yale R 66:603-13 Je '77. G. S. Haight
Bozeman, A. ed. Conflict in Africa: concepts and realities. 1976
Ann Am Acad 429:154-6 Ja '77. J. P. Powelson
Bradford, E. Nelson: the essential hero
America 137:366-7 N 19 '77. C. Loughran
Bradley, I. C. Call to seriousness: the evangelical impact on the Victorians. 1976
Am Hist R 82:638-9 Je '77. L. E. Grugel
Chr Today 21:30-1 Jl 29 '77. D. W. Dayton
Brady, I. Wild mouse
Sci Am 237:26 D '77. P. Morrison and P. Morrison
Braestrup, P. Big story: how the American press and television reported and interpreted the crisis of Tet 1968 in Vietnam and Washington. 2v.
Commentary 64:64-8 N '77. P. H. Weaver
Bragg, M. Speak for England: an oral history of England, 1900-1975. 1977
Am Hist R 82:1257 D '77. S. R. Ward
Sat R 4:24+ F 19 '77. C. Sigal
Branca, P. Silent sisterhood: middle class women in the Victorian home. 1975
Am Hist R 82:105 F '77. J. N. Burstyn
Brandes, S. D. American welfare capitalism, 1880-1940. 1976
Am Hist R 81:1261 D '76. M. Heald
Ann Am Acad 433:180-1 S '77. J. R. Conlin
M Labor R 100:67-8 Je '77. T. H. Patten, Jr
Brandon, R. Capitalist romance: Singer and the sewing machine
Bus W p7+ Jl 25 '77. S. Lohr
Newsweek 89:87-8 Je 6 '77. W. Clemons
Brandt, B. Shadow of light; with introd. by C. Connolly and M. Haworth-Booth. 1977
Art in Am 65:39+ N '77. L. Rubinflen
Branscum, R. Saving of P.S; il by G. Rounds. 1977
Horn Bk 53:310 Je '77. S. H. Holtze
Brantlinger, P. Spirit of reform: British literature and politics, 1832-1867
Yale R 67:90-4 O '77. A. D. Culler
Braroe, N. W. Indian and White: self-image and interaction in a Canadian plains community. 1975
Ann Am Acad 431:165-6 My '77. J. R. Conlin
Brathwaite, E. Other exiles
Poetry 130:232-4 Jl '77. J. Silkin
Braudel, F. Afterthoughts on material civilization and capitalism; tr. by P. M. Ranum
New Repub 177:29-30 S 3 '77. D. S. Landes
Braudel, F. and Labrousse, E. eds. Histoire économique et sociale de la France, v3: L'avénement de l'ère industrielle (1789-années 1880). 1976
Am Hist R 82:982-3 O '77. E. B. Ackerman
Braudy, L. World in a frame: what we see in films
Yale R 66:457-62 Mr '77. J. Guicharnaud
Brennan, J. G. Education of a prejudiced man
America 137:446-7 D 17 '77. F. Sweeney
Nation 225:314-16 O 1 '77. E. Wensberg
Brett, M. English church under Henry I. 1975
Am Hist R 82:76 F '77. R. V. Turner
Brewer, J. Party ideology and popular politics at the accession of George III. 1976
Am Hist R 82:356 Ap '77. D. E. Ginter
Brickner, R. P. My second twenty years
New Repub 176:30-2 F 19 '77. L. Kriegel
Bridgers, S. E. Home before dark. 1976
Horn Bk 53:165 Ap '77. S. H. Holtze
Briggs, K. Encyclopedia of fairies
Newsweek 89:85-6 F 21 '77. P. S. Prescott
Time 109:73-4 F 21 '77. P. Gray
Briggs, K. M. Hobberdy Dick. 1977
Horn Bk 53:311 Je '77. P. Heins
Brock, W. R. United States, 1789-1890. 1975
Am Hist R 82:177 F '77. N. C. Burckel
Broda, E. Evolution of bioenergetic processes. 1975
BioScience 27:751 N '77. D. E. Green
Brodeur, P. Zapping of America: microwaves, their deadly risk, and the cover-up
Sat R 5:35-6 Ja 7 '78. R. Claiborne

Brodkey, H. His son, in his arms, in light, aloft
 Atlantic 239:113 Mr '77. B. DeMott
Brodsky, A. T. and others, eds. Stones, bones and skin: ritual and shamanic art
 Sci Am 237:31-2 N '77. P. Morrison
Brody, B. Abortion and the sanctity of human life: a philosophic view. 1975
 Chr Today 21:45-6 Mr 18 '77. R. Case
Brogger, S. Deliver us from love: a radical feminist speaks out
 Ms 5:40-1+ F '77. V. Geng
Brolin, B. C. Failure of modern architecture. 1976
 Archit Rec 161:44+ My '77. R. Miller
 Fortune 96:59+ S '77. R. Starr
Brombert, B. A. Cristina: portraits of a princess
 New Repub 176:26-8 Je 18 '77. G. Brée
 Newsweek 89:78 Je 27 '77. M. Jefferson
 Yale R 67:128-35 O '77. M. Ellmann
Brooks, C. Possibilities of order: Cleanth Brooks and his work; ed. by L. P. Simpson
 Nat R 29:397-8 Ap 1 '77. M. E. Bradford
Brooks, P. Melodramatic imagination: Balzac, Henry James, melodrama and the mode of excess
 Yale R 66:592-8 Je '77. J. Culler
Brooks, P. View from Lincoln hill: man and the land in a New England town. 1976
 Horn Bk 53:341 Je '77. M. S. Cosgrave
Brophy, P. COBOL programming: an introduction for librarians. 1976
 Lib J 102:561 Mr 1 '77. H. Borko
Brotz, H. Politics of South Africa: democracy and racial diversity
 Nat R 29:674-5 Je 10 '77. W. A. Rusher
Brough, J. Food dynasty
 Bus W p 12+ S 5 '77. J. P. Wright
Broumas, O. Beginning with O
 Atlantic 240:102-3 O '77. D. Hall
 Yale R 67:72-3 O '77. H. Vendler
Brower, D. R. Training the nihilists: education and radicalism in tsarist Russia. 1975
 Am Hist R 82:150-1 F '77. P. L. Alston
Brown, A. G. Introduction to subject indexing, a programmed text, v2: UDC and chain procedure in subject cataloging. 1976
 Lib J 102:995 My 1 '77. J. D. Anderson
Brown, D. Hear that lonesome whistle blow
 Newsweek 89:87 My 23 '77. M. Jefferson
Brown, D. Photographs of the American wilderness; pref. by R. Doty; introd. by C. Brown. 1976
 Pop Phot 80:196 My '77. Y. E. Benedek
Brown, E. B. Grains: an illustrated history with recipes
 Sci Am 237:30 D '77. P. Morrison and P. Morrison
Brown, H. Familiar faces, hidden lives: the story of homosexual men in America today
 Commonweal 104:376-8 Je 10 '77. S. C. Charles
Brown, H. O. J. Reconstruction of the Republic. 1977
 Chr Today 21:40-1 S 23 '77. H. B. Gow
Brown, J. M. Gandhi and civil disobedience: the Mahatma in Indian politics, 1928-34. 1977
 Am Hist R 82:1313-14 D '77. D. M. Brown
 New Repub 177:32-5 Jl 9 '77. A. M. Davidon
Brown, J. W. New media in public libraries: a survey of current practices. 1976
 Lib J 102:889 Ap 15 '77. D. Roberts
Brown, K. L. People of Salé: tradition and change in a Moroccan city, 1830-1930. 1976
 Am Hist R 82:1032-3 O '77. A. A. Heggoy
 Ann Am Acad 434:210-12 N '77. P. C. Salzman
Brown, L. Weeds in winter
 Sci Am 236:142 Mr '77. P. Morrison
Brown, L. C. Tunisia of Ahmad Bey, 1837-1855. 1975
 Am Hist R 81:1190 D '76. I. L. Gendzier
Brown, M. Blue jackal. 1977
 Horn Bk 53:304-5 Je '77. S. H. Holtze
Brown, P. L. Megaliths, myths and men
 Am Scholar 46:530-2 Aut '77. O. Gingerich
Brown, R. A. Presidency of John Adams. 1975
 Am Hist R 81:1234 D '76. N. E. Cunningham, Jr
 Ann Am Acad 430:207 Mr '77. P. W. Brewer
Brown, R. C. Robert Laird Borden: a biography, v 1: 1854-1914. 1975
 Am Hist R 82:777-8 Je '77. C. Miller
Brown, R. E. Birth of the Messiah
 Newsweek 90:89+ D 19 '77. K. L. Woodward
Brown, W. A. Prelude to disaster: the American role in Vietnam, 1940-1963. 1975
 Ann Am Acad 432:149-50 Jl '77. T. B. Lam
Brownell, B. A. and Goldfield, D. R. eds. City in southern history: the growth of urban civilization in the South. 1977
 Am Hist R 82:760-1 Je '77. Z. L. Miller
Browning, D. S. Moral context of pastoral care
 Chr Cent 94:1036 N 9 '77. D. B. Watermulder
Browning, R. Duke of Newcastle. 1975
 Am Hist R 82:634 Je '77. J. McKelvey
Bruce-Briggs, B. War against the automobile
 Bus W p 11+ O 31 '77. W. Kroger
 Car & Dr 23:31-3 D '77. P. Bedard

Brunhammer, Y. and others. Art nouveau Belgium France: catalogue of an exhibition organized by the Institute for the arts, Rice university, and the Art institute of Chicago. 1976
 Archit Rec 161:45 Ja '77. M. F. Schmertz
Brush, S. G. Kind of motion we call heat: a history of the kinetic theory of gases in the 19th century. 2v. 1976
 Science 196:783-4 My 13 '77. T. L. Hankins
Bryan, A. Adventures of Aku. 1976
 Horn Bk 53:47 F '77. E. L. Heins
Bryan, H. University libraries in Britain: a new look. 1976
 Lib J 102:561 Mr 1 '77. A. Hamlin
Bryant, K. L. Jr. History of the Atchison, Topeka and Santa Fe railway. 1975
 Am Hist R 81:1237-8 D '76. M. E. Reed
Bryson, B. Gilgamesh: man's first story. 1967
 Horn Bk 53:74-6 F '77
Bryson, R. A. and Murray, T. J. Climates of hunger: mankind and the world's changing weather. 1977
 Weatherwise 30:223 O '77
Bryson, T. A. American diplomatic relations with the Middle East, 1784-1975: a survey. 1977
 Am Hist R 82:1355-6 D '77. A. R. De Luca
Bryson, W. H. Equity side of the exchequer: its jurisdiction, administration, procedures and records. 1975
 Am Hist R 82:91-2 F '77. C. Calton
Buache, F. Cinema of Luis Buñuel; tr. by P. Graham. 1973
 Film Q 31:65-7 Fall '77. D. Willis
Buchanan, D. Treasure of Auchinleck: the story of the Boswell papers. 1974
 Am Hist R 81:1108 D '76. B. M. Duffy
Bucher, B. La sauvage aux seins pendants. 1977
 Am Hist R 82:1233-4 D '77. A. G. Gordon
Buchwald, V. F. Handbook of iron meteorites. 1975
 Sky & Tel 53:296-7 Ap '77. E. L. Fireman
Buck-Morss, S. Origin of negative dialectics: Theodor W. Adorno, Walter Benjamin, and the Frankfurt institute
 New Repub 177:30-2 D 17 '77. C. Maier
Buckle, S. R. T. and Buckle, L. G. Bargaining for justice: case disposition and reform in the criminal courts. 1977
 Ann Am Acad 434:235-6 N '77. W. C. Louthan
Buckley, W. F. Jr. Airborne: a sentimental journey
 Sat Eve Post 249:74-5 Ap '77. D. Brudnoy
Buechner, F. Treasure hunt
 New Repub 177:38-40 S 17 '77. E. Milton
Bühlmann, W. Coming of the third church: an analysis of the present and future of the church
 America 136:487-8 My 28 '77. M. A. Fahey
Bull, H. Anarchical society: a study of order in world politics. 1977
 Ann Am Acad 434:199-200 N '77. J. P. Dunn
Bullard, F. M. Volcanoes of the earth
 Am Scholar 46:524+ Aut '77. K. F. Mather
Bullough, V. L. Sexual variance in society and history. 1976
 Am Hist R 82:921 O '77. M. Goodich
Bunting, E. One more flight. 1976
 Horn Bk 53:158 Ap '77. C. McDonnell
Bunyan, T. Political police in Britain. 1976
 Ann Am Acad 434:218-19 N '77. H. R. Winkler
Burbank, G. When farmers voted red: the gospel of socialism in the Oklahoma countryside, 1910-1924. 1976
 Am Hist R 82:1345-6 D '77. L. Goodwyn
Burbidge, J. Being and will: an essay in philosophical theology
 Commonweal 105:27-8 Ja 6 '78. G. H. Tavard
Burchard, J. Bernini is dead? Architecture and the social purpose
 Commonweal 104:349-50 My 27 '77. E. Cochrane
Burdick, C. B. Japanese siege of Tsingtau: World War I in Asia. 1976
 Am Hist R 82:1051 O '77. R. Dingman
Burg, B. R. Richard Mather of Dorchester. 1976
 Am Hist R 82:1059 O '77. R. Middlekauffe
Burg, D. F. Chicago's white city of 1893. 1976
 Am Hist R 82:194-5 F '77. T. Hines
Burke, E. 3d. Prelude to protectorate in Morocco: precolonial protest and resistance 1860-1912. 1977
 Am Hist R 82:1033-4 O '77. J. J. Cooke
Burke, P. G. Potential scattering in atomic physics. 1977
 Phys Today 30:56-7 D '77. R. St John
Burkholder, J. R. and Redekop, C. eds. Kingdom, cross and community
 Chr Cent 94:571-2 Je 8 '77. W. H. Tiemann
Burkholder, M. A. and Chandler, D. S. From impotence to authority: the Spanish crown and the American audiencias, 1687-1808. 1977
 Am Hist R 82:1373 D '77. L. G. Campbell
Burl, A. Stone circles of the British Isles. 1976
 Am Scholar 46:530-2 Aut '77. O. Gingerich
 Science 197:360-1 Jl 22 '77. B. Wailes
Burnett, J. H. Mycogenetics; an introduction to the general genetics of fungi. 1975
 BioScience 27:54 Ja '77. O. R. Collins

Burney, F. Famous Miss Burney: the diaries and letters of Fanny Burney; ed by B. G. Schrank and D. J. Supino
Ms 5:40+ Ap '77. L. Bernikow
Burns, J. M. Edward Kennedy and the Camelot legacy. 1976
Am Hist R 82:218 F '77. J. F. Heath
Burns, R. Success in America: the yeoman dream and the industrial revolution. 1976
Am Hist R 82:443 Ap '77. R. Weiss
Burr, D. Persecution of Peter Olivi. 1976
Am Hist R 82:1230-1 D '77. D. C. West
Burroughs, J. Great wilderness days in the words of John Burroughs; pref. by S. F. Olson
Conservationist 31:46 Mr '77. A. S. Fick
Burroway, J. Raw silk
Ms 6:34-5 Ag '77. C. E. Rinzler
New Repub 177:36 O 8 '77. W. T. Lhamon, jr
Newsweek 89:88 Ap 4 '77. M. Jefferson
Burrows, W. E. Vigilante! 1976
Am West 14:65 S '77. B. McGinty
Busch, B. C. Mudros to Lausanne: Britain's frontier in west Asia, 1918-1923. 1976
Am Hist R 82:641 Je '77. R. Adelson
Busch, E. Karl Barth: his life from letters and autobiographical texts
Chr Cent 94:488-9 My 18 '77. B. A. Reist
Bush, R. Genesis of Ezra Pound's Cantos
Yale R 66:598-603 Je '77. V. Miller
Bushnell, V. C. ed. History of Antarctic exploration and scientific investigation. Antarctic map folio series, folio 19
Sci Am 237:132 Ag '77. P. Morrison
Busnel, R. G. and Classe, A. Whistled languages
Sci Am 236:141-3 My '77. P. Morrison
Buttinger, J. Vietnam: the unforgettable tragedy
New Repub 176:34 Je 11 '77. M. Peretz
Butzer, K. W. Early hydraulic civilization in Egypt: a study in cultural ecology. 1976
Sci Am 237:151 Jl '77. P. Morrison
Science 196:971-2 My 27 '77. C. E. Stearns
Byars, B. Pinballs. 1977
Horn Bk 53:437 Ag '77. E. L. Heins
Byrnes, R. F. Soviet-American academic exchanges, 1958-1975. 1976
Am Hist R 82:773 Je '77. A. Kassof
Science 195:480-1 F 4 '77. D. Joravsky
Byron, G. G. N. 6th baron. Byron's letters and journals, v6:1818-1819: The flesh is frail; ed by L. A. Marchand
New Repub 176:38-9 My 28 '77. S. Weintraub
Yale R 66:449-52 Mr '77. D. R. Faulkner

Cabanne, P. Pablo Picasso
New Repub 177:32-3 O 22 '77. S. E. Lee
Cady, J. F. History of post-war southeast Asia. 1975
Am Hist R 81:1208-9 D '76. F. N. Trager
Cady, J. F. United States and Burma. 1976
Ann Am Acad 429:156 Ja '77. J. Silverstein
Cahill, S. Earth angels
Commonweal 104:381 Je 10 '77. J. Druska
Caire, G. Freedom of association and economic development. 1977
M Labor R 100:57-8 Ag '77. J. P. Goldberg
Calcium in biological systems; papers from symposium, Surrey, England, 1975. 1976
Science 196:289 Ap 15 '77. M. Bárány
Calder, J. Walking: a guide to beautiful walks and trails in America. 1977
Am For 83:35-6 S '77. M. Bush
Calder, K. J. Britain and the origins of the new Europe, 1914-1918. 1976
Am Hist R 81:1114 D '76. V. S. Mamatey
Calder, N. Key to the universe: a report on the new physics. 1977
Chemistry 50:28 O '77. H. R. Pagels
New Repub 178:33-4 Ja 7 '78. T. Ferris
Caldwell, L. K. and others. Citizens and the environment
Environment 19:4-5 Mr '77. P. DeJoie
Calhoun, J. C. Papers of John C. Calhoun, v8: 1823-1824; ed. by W. E. Hemphill. 1975
Am Hist R 81:1239 D '76. L. E. Tise
Califano, S. Vibrational states. 1976
Phys Today 30:54 Ap '77. J. C. Decius
Callahan, H. Callanan; ed. and introd. by J. Szarkowski. 1976
Art in Am 65:36-7 N '77. S. Rice
Callaway, T. N. Zen way—Jesus way. 1976
Chr Today 21:55-7 S 9 '77. P. Blosser
Calvino, I. Castle of crossed destinies; tr. by W. Weaver
America 136:529-30 Je 11 '77. A. J. Kelly
New Yorker 53:149-50+ Ap 18 '77. J. Updike
Newsweek 89:88 F 14 '77. W. Clemons
Calvino, I. Path to the nest of spiders; tr. by A. Colquhoun
Nation 224:214-16 F 19 '77. T. J. Roberts
Cambridge history of Africa, v3: From c. 1050 to c. 1600; ed. by R. Oliver. 1977
Am Hist R 82:1303-5 D '77. B. G. Martin
Cameron, A. Circus factions: blues and greens at Rome and Byzantium. 1976
Am Hist R 82:1224 D '77. T. E. Gregory
Cammarosano, P. La famiglia de Berardenghi: contributo alla storia della societa senese nei secoli XI-XIII. 1974
Am Hist R 82:621-2 Je '77. D. O. Hughes
Campbell, A. and others. Quality of American life: perceptions, evaluations, and satisfactions. 1976
Society 14:94-5 Ja '77. J. I. deNeufville
Campbell, C. S. Transformation of American foreign relations, 1865-1900. 1976
Am Hist R 82:455 Ap '77. B. Perkins
Campbell, D. M. Authority and the renewal of American theology. 1976
Chr Today 22:36+ N 18 '77. R. K. Johnston
Campbell, F. G. Confrontation in central Europe: Weimar Germany and Czechoslovakia. 1975
Am Hist R 82:145-6 F '77. D. Horna-Perman
Campbell, M. C. Dynamics of change in a slave society: a sociopolitical history of the free coloreds of Jamaica, 1800-1865. 1976
Am Hist R 82:479 Ap '77. F. W. Knight
Campbell, W. D. Brother to a dragonfly
Nation 225:597 D 3 '77. J. Taylor
Sat R 5:44+ D 10 '77. L. L. King
Campion, N. R. Ann the Word: the life of Mother Ann Lee, founder of the Shakers. 1976
Horn Bk 53:67 F '77. V. Haviland
Cannistraro, P. V. La fabbrica del consenso: fascismo e mass media, tr. by G. Ferrara. 1975
Am Hist R 82:388-9 Ap '77. F. Rosengarten
Cannistraro, P. V. and others. eds. Poland and the coming of the Second world war: the diplomatic papers of A. J. Drexel Biddle, Jr., United States ambassador to Poland, 1937-1939. 1976
Am Hist R 82:398 Ap '77. E. D. Wynot, Jr
Canny, N. P. Elizabethan conquest of Ireland: a pattern established, 1565-76. 1976
Am Hist R 82:957-8 O '77. D. B. Quinn
Canovan, M. G. K. Chesterton: radical populist
America 137:248-9 O 15 '77. J. R. Kelly
Nat R 29:1308 N 11 '77. M. J. Sobran, jr
Cappon, L. J. and others. eds. Atlas of early American history: the Revolutionary era, 1760-1790. 1976
Am Hist R 82:432 Ap '77. J. R. Alden
Caputo, P. Rumor of war
Commentary 64:86-8 O '77. W. J. Bennett
Nat R 29:1001-2 S 2 '77. D. K. Mano
Progressive 41:52-3 N '77. M. B. Young
Sat R 4:36-7 Je 11 '77. C. D. B. Bryan
Caraman, P. Lost paradise: the Jesuit reductions of South America
America 136:72 Ja 29 '77. C. J. McNaspy
Commonweal 104:415 Je 24 '77. J. L. McKenzie
Cárcel Ortí, V. Politica eclesial de los gobiernos liberales españoles, (1830-1840). 1975
Am Hist R 81:1135-6 D '76. J. M. Sánchez
Cardinale, H. E. Holy See and the international order. 1976
Am Hist R 82:1213 D '77. H. W. Paul
Carey, S. W. Expanding earth. 1976
Science 196:778 My 13 '77. J. R. Heirtzler
Cargas, H. J. and Wiesel, E. Harry James Cargas in conversation with Elie Wiesel. 1976
Chr Cent 94:594-5 Je 22 '77. L. Kahn
Carpenter, H. Tolkien: a biography
Newsweek 90:74+ Jl 4 '77. R. Towers
Carroll, J. John Carroll papers, v 1: 1755-1791; v2: 1792-1806; v3: 1807-1815; ed. by T. O. Hanley. 1976
Am Hist R 82:736 Je '77. J. T. Ellis
Carroll, L. Lewis Carroll, the wasp in a wig: the suppressed episode of Through the looking glass; introd. by M. Gardner
Time 109:94+ Je 6 '77. S. Kanfer
Carter, E. Writings of Elliot Carter; ed. by E. Stone and K. Stone
Nation 225:630-2 D 10 '77. R. P. Morgan
Carter, E. C. 2d. and others. eds. Enterprise and entrepreneurs in nineteenth- and twentieth-century France. 1976
Am Hist R 82:372 Ap '77. M. S. Smith
Carter, G. and Grant, W. A. Ion implantation of semiconductors. 1976
Phys Today 30:67-8 N '77. J. M. Poate
Carter, G. M. and O'Meara, P. eds. Southern Africa in crisis
Nation 225:632-5 D 10 '77. P. Dreyer
New Repub 177:34-7 S 24 '77. C. A. Crocker
Carter, L. and Spann, G. C. Away from home: letters to my family
Vogue 167:50+ Ag '77. A. Talmey
Carter, P. A. Another part of the twenties
Yale R 66:620-3 Je '77. N. Mills
Carter, S. 3d. Cherokee sunset, a nation betrayed: a narrative of travail and triumph, persecution and exile. 1976
Am West 14:60 Mr '77. T. K. Anderson
Cartier-Bresson, H. About Russia. 1974
Society 14:85-7 Ja '77. H. S. Becker
Cartter, A. M. Ph.D's and the academic labor market. 1976
M Labor R 100:68-9 Je '77. E. Steinberg
Cartwright, J. H. Triumph of Jim Crow: Tennessee race relations in the 1880s. 1976
Ann Am Acad 433:181 S '77. P. H. Howard
Cary, D. S. Hollywood posse
New Repub 176:26-9 Ap 2 '77. W. Hughes

Case, L. M. Edouard Thouvenel et al diplomatie du second empire; tr. by G. De Bertier de Sauvigny
Am Hist R 82:652-3 Je '77. W. F. Spencer
Casey, J. American romance
Nat R 29:950-1 Ag 19 '77. R. Ford
Newsweek 89:99-100 Ap 25 '77. M. Jefferson
Cashman, R. I. Myth of the Lokamanya: Tilak and mass politics in Maharashtra. 1975
Am Hist R 81:1208 D '76. R. P. Tucker
Cassinelli, C. W. Total revolution: a comparative study of Germany under Hitler, the Soviet Union under Stalin, and China under Mao. 1976
Am Hist R 82:337 Ap '77. J. W. Cranston
Catlin, G. Letters and notes on the North American Indians; ed. and introd. by M. M. Mooney. 1976
Am Hist R 81:1243 D '76. W. E. Washburn
Caudill, H. M. Watches of the night
Commonweal 104:414 Je 24 '77. S. Cohen
Progressive 41:56-7 Mr '77. D. J. Cohen
Causley, C. Collected poems 1951-1975
Poetry 129:233-4 Ja '77. R. B. Shaw
Cavallie, J. Från fred till krig: de Finansiella problemen kring krigsutbrottet år 1700. 1975
Am Hist R 62:638 Je '77. H. A. Barton
Caves, R. E. and Uekusa, M. Industrial organization in Japan. 1976
M Labor R 100:58 Jl '77. R. J. Ballon
Cawkwell, T. and Smith, J. M. eds. World encyclopedia of film. 1975
Film Q 30:56-7 Summ '77. L. Artel
Cecil, L. German diplomatic service, 1871-1914. 1976
Am Hist R 82:1002-3 O '77. H. H. Herwig
Cell motility; papers from symposium, Cold Spring Harbor, N.Y, 1976; ed by R. Goldman and others. 3v. 1976
Science 196:773-4 My 13 '77. R. E. Kane
Cell wall biochemistry related to specificity in host-plant pathogen interactions; proceedings of a symposium, Tromsø, Norway, 1976; ed. by S. Solheim and J. Raa. 1977
Science 198:47 O 7 '77. N. T. Keen
Censer, J. R. Prelude to power: the Parisian radical press, 1789-1791. 1976
Am Hist R 82:981 O '77. I. Woloch
Cercignani, C. Theory and application of the Boltzmann equation. 1976
Phys Today 30:66+ Ja '77. R. Aronson
Cerf, B. At Random: the reminiscences of Bennett Cerf; ed. by P. C. Wagner and A. Erskine
Bus W p 19-20 S 12 '77. J. K. Lieberman
Newsweek 90:100+ S 12 '77. R. Sokolov
Sat R 4:26+ S 3 '77. G. Stevens
Time 110:68+ Ag 22 '77. G. Clarke
Chadwick, J. Mycenaean world. 1976
Am Hist R 82:338 Ap '77. E. Vermeule
Sci Am 236:128-30+ F '77. P. Morrison
Chadwick, O. Secularization of the European mind in the nineteenth century. 1976
Am Hist R 81:1098 D '76. J. N. Moody
Chae-Jin, L. Japan faces China: political and economic relations in the Postwar Era. 1976
Ann Am Acad 430:194-5 Mr '77. J. Williams
Chafe, W. H. Women and equality: changing patterns in American culture. 1977
Am Hist R 82:1318-19 D '77. L. W. Banner
Society 14:91 S '77. M. Komarovsky
Yale R 67:150-7 O '77. H. Moglen
Chalfont, A. Montgomery of Alamein. 1976
Am Hist R 82:644-5 Je '77. R. Higham
Chaliand, G. Revolution in the third world: myths and prospects
Nation 225:632-5 D 10 '77. P. Dreyer
Progressive 41:57-8 N '77. G. MacEoin
Chalidze, V. Criminal Russia
New Repub 177:43-4 Ag 6 '77. D. Satter
Chamberlain, N. W. Remaking American values
Bus W p 11 Ja 31 '77. W. R. Dill
Chamberlin, J. E. Harrowing of Eden: white attitudes toward native Americans. 1975
Am Hist R 82:206 F '77. G. B. Nash
Chandler, D. Deep space 3-D: a stereo atlas of the stars
Sci Am 238:30 Ja '78. P. Morrison
Chandler, D. L. Natural superiority of southern politicians: a revisionist history
Nat R 29:784 Jl 8 '77. V. Gold
Chang, K. C. ed. Food in Chinese culture
Natur Hist 86:94-5+ Ag '77. A. Y. Dessaint
Chapman, J. R. ed. Economic independence for women: the foundation for equal rights. 1976
M Labor R 100:66-7 Je '77. M. F. Riche
Charles, A. M. Life of George Herbert
America 137:292 O 29 '77. J. R. Zurek, jr
Charles-Dominique, P. Ecology and behaviour of nocturnal primates: prosimians of equatorial West Africa; tr. by R. D. Martin. 1977
Science 198:923-4 D 2 '77. G. A. Doyle
Chartier, R. and others. L'éducation en France du XVIe au XVIIIe siècle. 1976
Am Hist R 82:648 Je '77. R. L. Kagan
Chase, A. Legacy of Malthus: the social costs of the new scientific racism. 1977
Am Hist R 82:923 O '77. L. J. Friedman
Checkland, S. G. Scottish banking: a history, 1695-1973. 1975
Am Hist R 82:112 F '77. J. P. Judd
Cheek, L. M. Zero-base budgeting comes of age. 1977
Am City & County 92:117 S '77
Cheek, N. H. Jr, and others. Leisure and recreation places. 1976
Parks & Rec 12:31 F '77. R. W. McLellan
Cheever, J. Falconer. 1977
America 136:221-2 Mr 12 '77. J. B. Breslin
Chr Cent 94:633-4 Jl 6 '77. W. A. Kort
Commentary 63:66-9 My '77. J. Romano
Commonweal 104:374-6 Je 10 '77. J. Groth
Harpers 254:88-9 Ap '77. J. Leonard
Nat R 29:833 Jl 22 '77. D. K. Mano
New Repub 176:31 Mr 26 '77. J. McElroy
New Yorker 53:141-2 My 2 '77. S. Lardner
Sat R 4:20-2+ Ap 2 '77. J. Gardner
Society 14:85-7 Jl '77. L. A. Coser
Time 109:79 F 28 '77. R. Z. Sheppard
Chen, C. Sourcebook on health sciences librarianship. 1977
Lib J 102:889 Ap 15 '77. W. K. Beatty
Chen, C. Y. Hsün Yüeh (A.D. 148-209): the life and reflections of an early medieval Confucian. 1975
Am Hist R 82:718-19 Je '77. Y. S. Yu
Chenault, J. Bradley Walker Tomlin. 1975
Art in Am 65:37+ My '77. H. F. Gaugh
Chevalier, R. Roman roads; tr. by N. H. Field
Sci Am 237:52+ S '77. P. Morrison
Chevigny, B. G. Woman and the myth: Margaret Fuller's life and writings
Progressive 41:59-60 My '77. H. N. Meyer
Chiappelli, F. and others. eds. First images of America: the impact of the new world on the old. 2v. 1976
Am Hist Illus 11:50 Ja '77. J. L. Stokesbury
Am Hist R 82:724-6 Je '77. J. J. Lang
Am West 14:60 Ja '77. D. G. Kelley
Chibnall, M. ed. and tr. Ecclesiastical history of Orderic Vitalis, v5; Books IX and X. 1975
Am Hist R 81:1090-1 D '76. C. W. Hollister
Chinese natural history drawings
Natur Hist 86:79-80+ Mr '77. C. Breslin
Chirot, D. Social change in a peripheral society: the creation of a Balkan colony. 1976
Am Hist R 82:1018-19 O '77. L. Olson
Chisman, F. P. Attitude psychology and the study of public opinion. 1977
Ann Am Acad 433:186-7 S '77. P. J. Hannon
Christie, A. Autobiography
Bus W p 13-14 D 5 '77. A. Priest
Time 110:127 N 28 '77. M. Duffy
Chu, M. ed. New China: a Catholic response
America 136:508-9 Je 4 '77. M. Brosseau
Chukovsky, K. Telephone; il. by B. Lent. 1977
Horn Bk 53:651-2 D '77. P. Heins
Chupp, E. L. Gamma-ray astronomy: nuclear transition region. 1976
Science 197:151 Jl 8 '77. R. C. Haymes
Church, R. L. and Sedlak, M. W. Education in the United States: an interpretive history. 1976
Am Hist R 82:170 F '77. M. Lazerson
Clancy, T. H. Introduction to Jesuit life: the constitutions and history through 435 years
America 136:532 Je 11 '77. T. C. Ross
Clapham, C. Liberia and Sierra Leone: an essay in comparative politics. 1976
Am Hist R 82:710-11 Je '77. C. Fyfe
Clark, C. W. Mathematical bioeconomics: the optimal management of renewable resources. 1976
Science 196:1082 Je 3 '77. G. R. Conway
Clark, D. H. and Stephenson, F. R. Historical supernovae
Sci Am 238:28-9 Ja '78. P. Morrison
Clark, E. Eyes, etc: a memoir
Ms 6:38-9 N '77. L. S. Schwartz
Newsweek 90:114+ O 17 '77. W. Clemons
Sat R 5:44 O 29 '77. D. Grumbach
Clark, K. Landscape into art
Am Artist 41:46-7 F '77. C. Movalli
Clark, M. Antonio Gramsci and the revolution that failed
New Repub 177:30-2 D 17 '77. C. Maier
Clark, M. T. Sky is free. 1976
Horn Bk 53:50 F '77. P. Heins
Clark, N. H. Deliver us from evil: an interpretation of American prohibition. 1976
Am Hist R 82:761-2 Je '77. K. A. Kerr
Clark, P. and Slack, P. English towns in transition, 1500-1700. 1976
Am Hist R 82:1243 D '77. W. T. MacCaffrey
Clark, R. L. Jr. ed. Archive-library relations. 1976
Lib J 102:464 F 15 '77. L. Ash
Clark, W. Energy for survival: the alternative to extinction. 1975
BioScience 27:289 Ap '77. V. J. Schaefer
Clarke, A. Selected poems by Austin Clarke, ed. by T. Kinsella
Commonweal 104:92-3 F 3 '77. J. Druska
Clarke, A. M. and Clarke, A. D. B. Early experience: myth and evidence. 1977
Ann Am Acad 434:236-7 N '77. M. Richmond-Abbott

Clarke, C. G. Kingston, Jamaica: urban development and social change, 1692-1962. 1976
Am Hist R 82:227 F '77. E. L. Farley
Ann Am Acad 430:200-1 Mr '77. R. S. Dunn
Claudin, F. Communist movement: from Comintern to Cominform, pt 1: The crisis of the Communist Internationale, tr. by B. Pearce; pt2: The zenith of Stalinism, tr. by F. MacDonagh. 1976
Am Hist R 82:63-4 F '77. A. J. Rieber
Claudin, F. and others. Problemi di storia dell'Internazionale Communista (1919-1939): relazione tenute al Seminario di studi organizzato dalla Fondazione Luigi Einaudi; ed. by A. Agosti. 1974
Am Hist R 82:350-1 Ap '77. J. M. Cammett
Claus, G. and Bolander, K. Ecological sanity
Nat R 29:890+ Ag 5 '77. J. Passmore
Claus, R. and others. Light scattering by phonon-polaritons. 1975
Phys Today 30:58 Jl '77. J. J. Worlock
Clausewitz, C. von. On war; ed. and tr. by M. Howard and P. Paret
New Repub 176:36-7 My 14 '77. E. N. Luttwak
Yale R 66:613-20 Je '77. M. Mandelbaum
Clawson, M. Forests for whom and for what? 1975
Ann Am Acad 431:182 My '77. H. M. Wachtel
Cleary, B. Ramona and her father; il. by A. Tiegreen. 1977
Horn Bk 53:660 D '77. M. M. Burns
Cleaver, D. G. Japanese and Americans: cultural parallels and paradoxes. 1976
Ann Am Acad 429:157 Ja '77. A. Palmer
Cleaver, V. and Cleaver, B. Trial Valley. 1977
Horn Bk 53:319 Je '77. P. Heins
Clecak, P. Crooked paths: reflections on socialism, conservatism, and the welfare state
Commentary 63:94-6 Mr '77. S. Miller
Nation 224:309-11 Mr 12 '77. T. Gitlin
Progressive 41:58-9 My '77. A. Hochschild
Clemens, S. L. Mark Twain speaking; ed. by P. Fatout
New Repub 176:25-6 F 26 '77. J. Ditsky
Cline, R. S. Secrets, spies, and scholars: blueprint of the essential CIA. 1976
Am Hist R 82:1358 D '77. W. L. Langer
Cloudsley-Thompson, J. L. Insects and history. 1976
BioScience 27:562 Ag '77. J. J. McKelvey, jr
Clovio, G. Farnese hours; commentary by W. Smith. 1976
Art N 76:120 My '77. C. E. Gilbert
Clymer, K. J. John Hay: the gentleman as diplomat. 1975
Am Hist R 82:194 F '77. R. W. Leopold
Clynes, M. Sentics: the touch of emotions
Psychol Today 10:98-9 F '77. G. Jonas
CO_2 metabolism and plant productivity; proceedings of symposium, Madison, Wis. 1975; ed by R. H. Burris and C. C. Black. 1976
Science 196:1084 Je 3 '77. G. H. Heichel
Coatsworth, E. Personal geography: almost an autobiography. 1976
Horn Bk 53:326 Je '77. E. L. Heins
Cody, M. L. and Diamond, J. M. eds. Ecology and evolution of communities. 1975
BioScience 27:50 Ja '77. J. R. Krebs
Coerr, E. Sadako and the thousand paper cranes; il. by R. Himler. 1977
Horn Bk 53:438 Ag '77. S. H. Holtze
Coffey, D. J. Dolphins, whales and porpoises: an encyclopedia of sea mammals. 1977
Oceans 10:70-1 Jl '77. J. Dillon
Coffin, W. S. jr. Once to every man: a memoir
Chr Cent 94:1122 N 30 '77. R. J. Neuhaus
Newsweek 90:120+ O 24 '77. R. Boeth
Psychol Today 11:164+ N '77. M. Scarf
Cogley, J. Canterbury tale: experiences and reflections 1916-1976
Chr Cent 94:433-4 My 4 '77. M. K. Stone
Cogliati Arano, L. Medieval health handbook; Tacuinum sanitatis; tr. by O. Ratti and A. Westbrook. 1976
Bioscience 27:186 D '77. R. E. Schultes
Cogniat, R. Pissarro
Am Artist 41:57-8 F '77. A. Werner
Cognition and social behavior; papers from symposium, Pittsburgh, 1975; ed. by J. S. Carroll and J. W. Payne. 1976
Science 196:1309 Je 17 '77. M. Ross
Cohen, M. D. ed. Personal liberty and education. 1976
SLJ 23:122 Mr '77. M. W. Greenberg
Cohn, E. and Millman, S. D. Input-output analysis in public education. 1975
Ann Am Acad 431:182-3 My '77. B. W. Van Der Veur and A. W. Hamood
Cold Spring Harbor Conference on cell proliferation, 3d, 1975. Cell motility, v3; ed. by R. Goldman and others. 3v. 1976
BioScience 27:558+ Ag '77. R. E. Stephens
Cold Spring Harbor symposia on quantitative biology, 1977. Origins of lymphocyte diversity; papers. 1977
Science 198:599 N 11 '77. A. R. Williamson
Cole, B. John Coltrane
Hi Fi 27:137 Je '77. J. S. Wilson
New Repub 176:26-8 F 12 '77. B. Blumenthal
Cole, R. V. Perspective for artists
Am Artist 42:24 Ja '78. C. Movalli
Coleman, K. Colonial Georgia: a history. 1976
Am Hist Illus 11:49-50 F '77. B. I. Wiley
Am Hist R 82:173 F '77. G. C. Rogers, Jr
Coles, J. Archaeology by experiment
Sci Am 237:28-30 O '77. P. Morrison
Coles, R. Children of crisis; v4: Eskimos, Chicanos, Indians; v5: Privileged ones: the well-off and the rich in America
Newsweek 91:75-6 Ja 16 '78. P. S. Prescott
Colette. Blue lantern; tr. by R. Senhouse
New Repub 176:27-9 Je 11 '77. J. C. Oates
Colette. Other one; tr. by R. Senhouse and E. Tait
New Repub 176:27-9 Je 11 '77. J. C. Oates
Colin, P. Neon gobies. 1975
Sea Front 23:379 N '77. R. E. Thresher
Collected paper in avian paleontology honoring the 90th birthday of Alexander Wetmore, ed. by S. L. Olson. 1976
Science 196:288 Ap 15 '77. C. A. Walker
Collias, N. E. and Collias, E. C. eds. External construction by animals
Sci Am 236:136-8 Je '77. P. Morrison
Collins, D. European communities: the social policy of the first phase; v 1. 1976
Am Hist R 82:628-9 Je '77. R. W. Heywood
Collins, G. R. Rebuilding of psychology: an integration of psychology and Christianity
Chr Cent 94:1229-30 D 28 '77. L. R. Rambo
Colp, R. To be an invalid: the illness of Charles Darwin. 1977
Science 196:1431-2 Je 24 '77. W. B. Provine
Commager, H. S. Empire of reason: how Europe imagined and America realized the enlightenment
Nat R 29:1123-4 S 30 '77. F. McDonald
Sat R 4:20-1 My 14 '77. W. W. Wagar
Condit, C. W. Railroad and the city: a technological and urbanistic history of Cincinnati. 1977
Am Hist R 82:1338-9 D '77. A. Fein
Condominas, G. We have eaten the forest; tr. by A. Foulke
Newsweek 90:106+ O 10 '77. M. Jefferson
Condon, R. Abandoned woman
Time 109:73-4 My 30 '77. P. Gray
Confalonieri, A. Banca e industria in Italia, 1894-1906. v 1; Le premesse: dall'abolizione del corso forzoso alla caduta del Credito Mobiliare. 1974
Am Hist R 81:1158 D '76. F. J. Coppa
Confalonieri, A. Banca e industria in Italia, 1894-1906. v2: Il sistema bancario tra due crisi. 1975
Am Hist R 82:385-6 Ap '77. F. J. Coppa
Connelly, T. L. Marble man: Robert E. Lee and his image in American society. 1977
Am Hist R 82:1333 D '77. G. B. Tindall
Connery, J. Abortion: the development of the Roman Catholic perspective
Commonweal 104:604-5 S 16 '77. G. J. McCarron
Connor, S. V. and Skaggs, J. M. Broadcloth and britches: the Santa Fe trade. 1977
Am West 14:54 Jl '77. W. Gard
Conodont paleoecology; proceedings of symposium; Waterloo, Ont, 1975; ed. by C. R. Barnes. 1976
Science 196:1433 Je 24 '77. T. J. M. Schoff
Conrad, S. P. Perish the thought; intellectual women in romantic America, 1830-1860. 1976
Am Hist R 82:1327-8 D '77. C. D. Kinnard
Conrat, M. and Conrat, R. American farm: a photographic history
Sci Am 236:140-1 Je '77. P. Morrison
Conzen, K. N. Immigrant Milwaukee, 1836-1860: accommodation and community in a frontier city. 1976
Am Hist R 82:442 Ap '77. A. T. Brown
Cook, A. Alabama claims: American politics and Anglo-American relations. 1865-1872. 1975
Am Hist R 81:1254 D '76. M. Lester
Cook, B. Dalton Trumbo. 1976
Commonweal 104:636-7 S 30 '77. P. Corwin
Film Q 30:55-6 Summ '77. T. Stempel
Nation 224:566-8+ My 7 '77. M. Rapf
New Repub 176:31-2 Ap 2 '77. F. Levy
Cook, C. Age of alignment: electoral politics in Britain, 1922-1929. 1975
Am Hist R 82:108-9 F '77. V. Bogdanor
Cook, E. M. Jr. Fathers of the towns: leadership and community structure in eighteenth-century New England. 1976
Am Hist R 82:731-2 Je '77. R. D. Brown
Ann Am Acad 430:207-8 Mr '77. L. Becker
Cook, R. Coma
Newsweek 89:102-4 Ap 18 '77. W. Clemons
Cook, S. F. Conflict between the California Indian and white civilization. 1976
Ann Am Acad 431:174-5 My '77. A. H. Derosier, Jr
Cook, S. F. Population of the California Indians, 1760-1970. 1976
Am Hist R 82:1081 O '77. D. H. Ubelaker
Cook, S. F. and Borah, W. Essays in population history: Mexico and the Caribbean, v2. 1974
Am Hist R 82:221-3 F '77. M. J. MacLeod
Cooke, A. Six men
Newsweek 90:107+ S 19 '77. C. Michener
Sat R 5:46-7 O 1 '77. R. Gelatt

Cooke, B. Ministry to word and sacraments: history and theology
America 136:198-9 Mr 5 '77. E. J. Kilmartin
Chr Cent 94:114-15 F 2 '77. J. Raitt
Commonweal 104:475-7 Jl 22 '77. K. G. O'Connell
Cooke, M. G. Romantic will
Yale R 66:449-52 Mr '77. D. R. Faulkner
Cooke, J. R. Free for the taking. 1975
Chr Today 22:37-8 N 4 '77. G. Hawthorne
Coolidge, O. Statesmanship of Abraham Lincoln. 1977
Horn Bk 53:322 Je '77. K. M. Klockner
Cooney, R. and Michalowski, H. eds. Power of the people: active nonviolence in the United States
Commonweal 105:26-7 Ja 6 '78. D. Vellucci
Progressive 41:56-7 O '77. M. True
Cooper, S. Silver on the tree. 1977
Horn Bk 53:660-1 D '77. A. A. Flowers
Coover, R. Public burning
Atlantic 240:98-101 N '77. B. DeMott
Commentary 64:67-9 O '77. P. K. Bell
Nat R 29:1118+ S 30 '77. D. Hall
New Repub 177:37-8 S 17 '77. T. LeClair
Newsweek 90:75-6 Ag 8 '77. W. Clemons
Sat R 4:27-8+ S 17 '77. N. Podhoretz
Time 110:70+ Ag 8 '77. P. Gray
Copeland, L. O. Principles of seed science and technology. 1976
BioScience 27:421 Je '77. S. B. Hendricks
Copeland, P. C. and MacMaster, R. K. Five George Masons: patriots and planters of Virginia and Maryland. 1975
Am Hist R 82:433-4 Ap '77. D. W. Jordan
Copeland, W. R. Uneasy alliance: collaboration between the Finnish opposition and the Russian underground, 1899-1904. 1973
Am Hist R 82:658-9 Je '77. P. K. Hamalainen
Corballis, M. C. and Beale, I. L. Psychology of left and right. 1976
Sci Am 236:142-4 Ap '77. P. Morrison
Science 196:768-9 My 13 '77. C. Trevarthen
Corbett, T. H. Cancer and chemicals
Commonweal 104:629-31 S 30 '77. R. Conniff
Cordasco, F. ed. Bilingual schooling in the United States: a sourcebook for educational personnel. 1976
Ann Am Acad 433:187-8 S '77. F. Shaw
Corea, G. Hidden malpractice
Ms 6:36-7 Ja '78. R. Morgan
Cork, R. Vorticism and abstract art in the first machine age, v1: Origins and development. 1976
Art in Am 65:69 Ja '77. J. Hobhouse
Corlett, W. Dark side of the moon. 1977
Horn Bk 53:668 D '77. C. W. Draper
Corliss, W. R. ed. Handbook of unusual natural phenomena
Smithsonian 8:127-9 S '77. M. Olmert
Cormier, R. I am the cheese
Horn Bk 53:427-8 Ag '77. P. Heins
Corn, A. All roads at once
Poetry 129:226-8 Ja '77. R. Howard
Cornell, J. Great international disaster book
Sci Digest 81:89-90 Ap '77. B. Ford
Cornfield R. and Fallwell, M. Jr. Just country
Hi Fi 27:153 F '77. R. S. Denisoff
Cortot, A. French piano music; tr. by H. Andrews
Am Rec G 41:54-5 N '77. R. Kammerer
Costeloe, M. P. La Primera República Federal de México (1824-1835): un estudio de los partidos políticos en el México independiente. 1975
Am Hist R 82:225 F '77. R. Sinkin
Cotham, P. C. Politics, Americanism, and Christianity. 1976
Chr Today 21:34-8 My 20 '77. S. V. Monsma
Cott, N. Bonds of womanhood, woman's sphere in New England, 1780-1835
Yale R 67:150-7 O '77. H. Moglen
Cottle, T. J. Barred from school: two million children!
America 136:338 Ap 9 '77. J. J. Buckley, Jr
Commonweal 104:252-3 Ap 15 '77. D. Vellucci
Todays Educ 66:94-5 S '77. S. F. Coffey
Cottle, T. J. Busing
America 136:175 F 26 '77. T. Ichniowski
Coughlan, N. Young John Dewey: an essay in American intellectual history. 1975
Am Hist R 82:188 F '77. A. G. Wirth
Council for science and society. Superstar technologies
Bull Atom Sci 33:61-2 My '77. A. Tucker
Courdurié, M. La dette des collectivités publiques de Marseille au XVIIIe siècle: du débat sur le prêt à intérêt au financement par l'emprunt. 1974
Am Hist R 82:368-9 Ap '77. T. F. Sheppard
Coverdale, J. F. Italian intervention in the Spanish civil war. 1975
Ann Am Acad 430:189-90 Mr '77. C. P. Boyd
Cowling, M. Impact of Hitler: British politics and British policy, 1933-1940. 1975
Am Hist R 81:1117-18 D '76. T. E. Hachey
Cox, A. Role of the Supreme court in American government
Nat R 29:1225-8 O 28 '77. P. H. Connolly
Cox, A. M. Dynamics of detente: how to end the arms race. 1976
America 136:400-2 Ap 30 '77. R. L. Walker
Ann Am Acad 431:141-2 My '77. R. R. Pope
Progressive 41:57-8 Mr '77. F. Kaplan
Cox, H. Turning East: the promise and the peril of the new Orientalism
America 137:316-17 N 5 '77. J. A. Saliba
Cox, J. Overkill. 1977
Bull Atom Sci 33:63-4 S '77. S. H. Day, jr
Cox, T. S. Civil-military relations in Sierra Leone: a case study of African soldiers in politics. 1976
Am Hist R 82:155-6 F '77. J. P. Smaldone
Craigie, P. C. Book of Deuteronomy. 1976
Chr Today 21:25-6 Ag 12 '77. R. Youngblood
Creel, H. G. Shen Pu-hai: a Chinese political philosopher of the fourth century B.C. 1975
Am Hist R 82:716-17 Je '77. W. M. Tu
Creeley, R. Selected poems
Atlantic 240:103-4 O '77. D. Hall
Cregier, D. M. Bounder from Wales: Lloyd George's career before the First world war. 1976
Am Hist R 82:362 Ap '77. K. O. Morgan
Cremin, L. A. Traditions of American education. 1976
Am Hist R 82:1320 D '77. S. A. Rippa
Commentary 63:89-91 Je '77. C. E. Finn, Jr.
Todays Educ 66:91+ S '77. J. F. Kett
Crenson, M. A. Federal machine: beginnings of bureaucracy in Jacksonian America. 1975
Am Hist R 81:1240 D '76. T. H. O'Connor
Ann Am Acad 429:172-3 Ja '77. L. H. Croce
Cressman, L. S. Prehistory of the far West: homes of vanished peoples. 1977
Science 198:817-18 N 25 '77. C. I. Busby
Cresswell, H. Game of catch; il by A. Forberg. 1977
Horn Bk 53:312-14 Je '77. P. Heins
Cripps, T. Slow fade to black: the Negro in American film, 1900-1942. 1977
Am Hist R 82:1093-4 O '77. R. Sklar
New Repub 176:33-5 Ap 2 '77. F. Hirsch
Smithsonian 8:139-40+ Ap '77. J. Markus
Crisp, O. Studies in the Russian economy before 1914. 1976
Am Hist R 82:697-8 Je '77. W. M. Pintner
Croce, A. Afterimages
Harpers 256:86 Ja '78. F. Taliaferro
Newsweek 90:101-2+ N 14 '77. J. Kroll
Time 111:71-2 Ja 9 '78. M. Duffy
Crop productivity—research imperatives; report of conference; ed. by A. W. A. Brown and others. 1976
BioScience 27:488 Jl '77. R. S. Loomis
Crosby, A. W. Jr. Epidemic and peace, 1918. 1976
Am Scholar 46:526+ Aut '77. J. Oppenheimer
Ann Am Acad 430:212-13 Mr '77. T. M. Hill
Natur Hist 86:98-9+ Ap '77. G. Majno
Crosby, T. L. Sir Robert Peel's administration, 1841-1846. 1976
Am Hist R 82:357 Ap '77. R. W. Davis
Crosland, M. Women of iron and velvet: French women writers after George Sand
Yale R 66:xxi-xxiii Je '77
Crossan, J. D. Raid on the articulate: comic eschatology in Jesus and Borges
America 136:379-80 Ap 23 '77. J. A. Miles, Jr
Crossick, G. ed. Lower middle class in Britain, 1870-1914. 1977
Am Hist R 82:1252-3 D '77. W. H. Maehl, jr
Crossman, R. Diaries of a cabinet minister, v 1: 1964-1966. 1975
Am Hist R 82:363 Ap '77. D. Rubinstein
New Repub 176:31-2 Je 18 '77. P. McGrath
New Yorker 53:143-6 My 9 '77. N. Bliven
Crossman, R. Myths of cabinet government
New Yorker 53:143-6 My 9 '77. N. Bliven
Crozier, B. Man who lost China; with E. Chou
New Repub 176:72-4 Ja 22 '77. J. Thomson
Cru, J. N. War books: a study in historical criticism, ed. by S. J. Pincetl, jr. 1976
Am Hist R 82:984-5 O '77. F. Field
Crunden, R. M. ed. Superfluous men: conservative critics of American culture, 1900-1945
Commonweal 104:664-6 O 14 '77. D. Aaron
Nation 224:343-5 Mr 19 '77. J. M. Taylor
Csatári, D. Dans la tourmente: les relations hungaro-roumaines de 1940 à 1945; tr. by A. Martel. 1974
Am Hist R 82:1021 O '77. S. D. Kertesz
Cudmore, L. L. L. Center of life: a natural history of the cell
Sci Am 237:32+ D '77. P. Morrison and P. Morrison
Culbert, D. H. News for everyman: radio and foreign affairs in thirties America. 1976
Am Hist R 82:211 F '77. A. A. Offner
Ann Am Acad 429:173 Ja '77. L. D. Hill
Yale R 66:v+ Mr '77
Cullen, M. J. Statistical movement in early Victorian Britain: the foundations of empirical social research. 1975
Am Hist R 82:102-3 F '77. J. Roebuck
Culler, J. Ferdinand de Saussure
Yale R 67:106-15 O '77. L. Nelson, jr

Cullinan, E. Yellow roses
Commonweal 104:540-1 Ag 19 '77. R. Phillips
Culliney, J. L. Forests of the sea: life and death of the continental shelf. 1976
Conservationist 32:43-4 S '77. A. C. Jensen
Oceans 10:69 S '77. N. Rosa
Cullmann, O. Johannine circle
Chr Cent 94:232 Mr 9 '77. H. H. Oliver
Culver, R. D. Life of Christ. 1976
Chr Today 21:29 Jl 8 '77. C. C. Anderson
Culyer, A. J. Need and the National health service: economics and social choice. 1976
Ann Am Acad 434:237-8 N '77. H. E. Frech, 3d
Cummings, B. S. Hew against the grain. 1977
Horn Bk 53:538 O '77. E. L. Heins
Cummins, C. University of South Dakota, 1862-1966. 1975
Am Hist R 82:187-8 F '77. J. F. Hopkins
Cunningham, A. J. ed. Generation of antibody diversity: a new look. 1976
Science 197:450 Jl 29 '77. R. F. Doolittle
Cunningham, I. After ninety. 1977
Art in Am 65:32-3 N '77. C. Ratcliff
Cunningham, J. Come to the edge. 1977
Horn Bk 53:449 Ag '77. E. L. Heins
Cunningham, W. All-American boys
Bus W p 16+ N 14 '77. M. G. Sheldrick
Cupitt, D. Leap of reason
Chr Cent 94:924 O 12 '77. D. W. Ferm
Curio, E. Ethology of predation. 1976
Science 196:157-8 Ap 8 '77. T. W. Schoener
Current, R. N. History of Wisconsin, v2: the Civil war era 1848-1873. 1977
Am Hist R 82:1076-7 O '77. R. H. Jones
Ann Am Acad 433:181-2 S '77. G. Osborn
Currie, H. W. Eugene V. Debs. 1976
Am Hist R 82:758 Je '77. J. H. M. Laslett
Curry, J. L. Poor Tom's ghost. 1977
Horn Bk 53:439 Ag '77. P. Heins
Curtis, J. C. Andrew Jackson and the search for vindication. 1976
Am Hist R 82:743-4 Je '77. C. M. Wiltse
Cushing, D. H. and Walsh, J. J. Ecology of the seas. 1976
Science 198:47 O 7 '77. P. A. Larkin
Cutler, R. G. ed. Cellular aging: concepts and mechanisms. 2v. 1976
Science 198:818-19 N 25 '77. V. J. Cristofalo
Czarnecki, J. Goths in ancient Poland: a study on the historical geography of the Oder-Vistula region during the first two centuries of our era. 1975
Am Hist R 82:72-3 F '77. M. Gimbutas

Daly, J. Cyclic nucleotides in the nervous system. 1977
Science 198:599-60 N 11 '77. J. W. Kebabian
Danielson, M. N. Politics of exclusion. 1976
Ann Am Acad 433:199-200 S '77. M. E. Danzig
Nat R 29:277-8 Mr 4 '77. R. Starr
Society 15:124-5 N '77. D. R. Mandelker
Dankwart, R. A. and Mugno, J. F. OPEC: success and prospects. 1976
Ann Am Acad 430:221 Mr '77. M. A. Holman
Danziger, R. Abd al-Qadir and the Algerians: resistance to the French and internal consolidation. 1977
Am Hist R 82:1306 D '77. K. J. Perkins
Darby, J. Conflict in Northern Ireland: the development of a polarised community. 1976
Ann Am Acad 433:188-9 S '77. A. M. Lee
Dardis, T. Some time in the sun. 1976
Film Q 30:55-6 Summ '77. T. Stempel
Darley, G. Villages of vision. 1976
Am Hist R 82:968-9 O '77. D. J. Olsen
Dart, J. Laughing Savior. 1976
Chr Cent 94:306-7 Mr 30 '77. G. W. E. Nickelsburg
Chr Today 22:36-7 O 21 '77. M. L. Peel
Darton, M. ed. Modern concordance to the New Testament
America 137:251-2 O 15 '77. R. E. Brown
Darwin, C. Charles Darwin's natural selection: being the second part of his big species book written from 1856 to 1858; ed. by R. C. Stauffer. 1975
BioScience 27:361 My '77. L. T. Spencer
Darwin, C. Collected papers; ed by P. H. Barrett. 2v. 1977
Science 196:784-5 My 13 '77. M. T. Ghiselin
Daughen, J. R. and Binzen, P. Cop who would be king: the honorable Frank Rizzo
Nation 225:538-40 N 19 '77. S. D. Solomon
Newsweek 90:96+ N 7 '77. R. Boeth
D'Aulaire, I. and D'Aulaire, E. P. Terrible troll-bird. 1976
Horn Bk 53:69 F '77. S. H. Holtze
David, P. A. and others. Reckoning with slavery: a critical study in the quantitative history of American Negro slavery; introd. by K. M. Stampp. 1976
Am Hist R 82:745-6 Je '77. A. G. Bogue
Davidovich, A. W. Samoderzhavie v epokhu imperializma (klassovaia sushchnost' i evoliutsiia absoliutizma v Rossii). 1975
Am Hist R 82:698-9 Je '77. M. S. Conroy

Davidow, S. Revitalize Hollywood
New Repub 176:26-9 Ap 2 '77. W. Hughes
Davidson, E. H. Gene activity in early development. 2d ed. 1977
Science 197:978-9 S 2 '77. H. Woodland
Davidson, P. O. ed. Behavioral management of anxiety, depression, and pain. 1976
Intellect 105:284 F '77. I. R. Hyatt
Davidson, S. Loose change: three women of the sixties
Commentary 64:70-2 Ag '77. J. L. Crain
Mademoiselle 83:76 O '77. J. Coburn
Newsweek 89:79 My 30 '77. P. S. Prescott
Sat R 4:26-8 My 28 '77. L. Franks
Time 110:77-8 Jl 11 '77. L. Morrow
Davie, D. Ezra Pound
Yale R 66:598-603 Je '77. V. Miller
Davies, D. Centenarians of the Andes. 1975
BioScience 27:54 Ja '77. C. E. Finch
Davies, H. Worship and theology in England: v2: From Andrewes to Baxter and Fox, 1603-1690. 1975
Am Hist R 82:95 F '77. K. W. Shipps
Chr Cent 94:115-17 F 2 '77. H. E. Hogue
Davies, J. G. Christians, politics and violent revolution
America 136:132-3 F 12 '77. M. A. Fahey
Davies, K. and Bloom, E. Painting sharp focus still lifes
Am Artist 41:59+ F '77. C. Movalli
Davies, P. C. W. Space and time in the modern universe. 1977
Phys Today 30:68 N '77. J. D. Nightingale
Davin, D. Woman-work: women and the party in revolutionary China. 1976
Am Hist R 82:1050 O '77. C. Schwarcz
Ann Am Acad 431:148+ My '77. A. D. Ross
Davis, C. D. United States and the second Hague peace conference: American diplomacy and international organization, 1899-1914. 1976
Am Hist R 82:456 Ap '77. R. D. Schulzinger
Ann Am Acad 430:179-80 Mr '77. K. W. Thompson
Davis, C. F. Harvest of a quiet eye: the natural world of John Burroughs; introd. by E. W. Teale. 1976
Pop Phot 81:48+ Jl '77. B. Poli
Davis, G. Childhood and history in America. 1976
Am Hist R 82:1319-20 D '77. R. H. Bremner
Davis, H. E. Fledgling province: social and cultural life in Colonial Georgia, 1733-1776. 1976
Am Hist R 82:733 Je '77. D. T. Morgan
Davis, J. Papers of Jefferson Davis, v2: June 1841-July 1846; ed. by J. T. McIntosh. 1975
Am Hist R 82:1329-30 D '77. D. H. Donald
Davis, M. William Blake: a new kind of man
New Repub 177:34-6 N 19 '77. P. Sherwin
Davis, P. Flag at the pole: three soliloquies; il. by H. Little. 1976
Horn Bk 53:166-7 Ap '77. M. M. Burns
Davis, W. C. Breckinridge: statesman, soldier, symbol. 1974
Am Hist R 81:1252-3 D '76. E. B. Long
Davitz, J. and Davitz, L. Making it from 40 to 50. 1976
Intellect 105:446 Je '77. I. R. Hyatt
Dawidowicz, L. War against the Jews
Commonweal 104:282-3 Ap 29 '77. J. Garvey
Dawisha, A. J. Egypt in the Arab world: the elements of foreign policy. 1976
Ann Am Acad 432:156 Jl '77. W. B. Bishai
Dawkins, R. Selfish gene. 1976
America 136:402 Ap 30 '77. D. J. Sullivan
BioScience 27:692 O '77. C. H. Langley
Natur Hist 86:22+ D '77. S. J. Gould
Psychol Today 10:106+ My '77. L. Tiger
Science 196:757-9 My 13 '77. W. D. Hamilton
Dawley, A. Class and community: the industrial revolution in Lynn. 1976
Am Hist R 82:752-3 Je '77. C. Hoffecker
Ann Am Acad 431:183-4 My '77. A. Theoharis
Day, D. Journey of the wolf
New Repub 176:29-30 Mr 19 '77. T. Luddington
New Yorker 53:110-13 My 30 '77. A. Reid
Dayal, R. Mission for Hammarskjold: the Congo crisis. 1976
Am Hist R 82:711-12 Je '77. A. T. Stephens
Dayton, D. W. Discovering an evangelical heritage. 1976
Chr Today 21:38 Mr 4 '77. E. Jorstad
Deacon, H. J. Where hunters gathered: a study of holocene stone age people in the eastern Cape. 1976
Science 197:359 Jl 22 '77. G. P. Rightmire
Dean, B. China and Great Britain: the diplomacy of commercial relations, 1860-1864. 1974
Am Hist R 82:412 Ap '77. S. W. Barnett
Dean, J. W. Blind ambition: the White House years. 1976
Ann Am Acad 432:170-1 Jl '77. L. S. Wittner
Commentary 63:66-8 F '77. J. Q. Wilson
Dean, W. Rio Claro: a Brazilian plantation system, 1820-1920. 1976
Am Hist R 82:484-5 Ap '77. J. D. Wirth
Ann Am Acad 431:150-1 My '77. P. I. Mandell
DeBakey, M. and Gotto, A. Living heart
Smithsonian 8:126-7 S '77. J. F. Warner

De Blois, L. Policy of the Emperor Gamenus. 1976
Am Hist R 82:614-15 Je '77. M. T. W. Arnheim
Debo, A. Geronimo: the man, his time, his place. 1976
Am Hist Illus 12:47 N '77. D. Brown
Am West 14:64 S '77. O. B. Faulk
Negro Hist Bull 40:735-6 Jl '77. T. D. Perry
De Breffny, B. ed. Irish world: the art and culture of the Irish people
America 137:425-6 D 10 '77. M. Fitzgerald
Debussy, C. Debussy on music; tr. and ed. by R. L. Smith
Hi Fi 27:MA39 S '77. P. J. Smith
Decanio, S. J. Agriculture in the postbellum South: the economics of production and supply. 1975
Am Hist R 82:186 F '77. T. Saloutos
DeConde, A. This affair of Louisiana. 1976
Am Hist Illus 12:47 N '77. G. G. Eggert
Am Hist R 82:1069 O '77. C. L. Egan
Ann Am Acad 431:164-5 My '77. J. B. Sanders
Degas, E. Notebooks of Edgar Degas; ed. by T. Reff
New Repub 177:25-6+ N 12 '77. J. Canaday
Deitchman, S. J. Best-laid schemes: a tale of social research and bureaucracy. 1976
Ann Am Acad 430:213-15 Mr '77. J. J. Palen
Ann Am Acad 433:182-3 S '77. R. T. Shultz
De Jong, G. F. Dutch in America, 1609-1974. 1975
Am Hist R 81:1217-18 D '76. E. Noyes
De Jong, L. Het koninkrijk der Nederlanden in de tweede wereldoorlog; v6, pt1:Juli '42-Mei 43. 1975
Am Hist R 82:120 F '77. W. Warmbrunn
De Jonge, A. Baudelaire: prince of clouds
Time 109:83 F 14 '77. M. Maddocks
Delbanco, N. Possession
New Repub 176:30-2 Mr 19 '77. E. Milton
Deleuze, G. and Guattari, F. Anti-Oedipus: capitalism and schizophrenia
New Repub 177:36-7 D 24 '77. J. Cantor
DeLillo, D. Players
Atlantic 240:94 S '77. A. Heller
Harpers 255:88+ S '77. S. Koch
Nat R 29:1250-1 O 28 '77. Z. Kotker
Nation 225:250-2 S 17 '77. J. D. O'Hara
Newsweek 90:75-6 Ag 29 '77. M. Jefferson
Dell, C. Lincoln and the War Democrats: the grand erosion of conservative tradition. 1975
Am Hist R 81:1251-2 D '76. J. A. Rawley
Del Negro, P. Il mito americano nella Venezia del settecento. 1975
Am Hist R 82:680 Je '77. M. Suozzi
Dempsey, J. Dempsey; with B. P. Dempsey
Newsweek 89:86+ Ap 4 '77. W. Clemons
DeNeir, D. Earthquakes; with introd. by P. L. Ward. 1977
Am For 83:38+ O '77. M. Bush
Denes, M. In necessity and sorrow: life and death in an abortion hospital
Chr Today 21:45-6 Mr 18 '77. R. Case
Commonweal 104:438-9 Jl 8 '77. M. O. Steinfels
New Repub 176:36-7 Ap 30 '77. E. Chesler
Denevan, W. M. ed. Native population of the Americas in 1942. 1976
Am Hist R 82:1370-1 D '77. J. V. Lombardi
Denikin, A. I. Career of a Tsarist officer: memoirs, 1872-1916; tr. by M. Patoski. 1975
Am Hist R 81:1178-9 D '76. G. Brinkley
Denison, E. F. and Chung, W. K. How Japan's economy grew so fast: the sources of postwar expansion. 1976
Ann Am Acad 434:212-13 N '77. J. F. Melby
Dennis, C. Climbing down
Poetry 130:347-8 S '77. D. Allen
Dennis, L. T. Reason for hope. 1976
Chr Today 21:45-7 F 18 '77 M. H. MacDonald
Dennison, G. M. Dorr war: republicanism on trial, 1831-1861. 1976
Am Hist R 81:1241-2 D '76. D. A. Grimsted
Denzler, G. Das Papsttum und der Amtszölibat, v 1: die Zeit bis zur Reformation; v2, von der Reformation bis in die Gegenwart. 1976
Am Hist R 82:945 O '77. E. Peters
Derrida, J. Off grammatology; tr. by G. C. Spivak
New Repub 176:32-4 Ap 16 '77. D. Donoghue
Desmond, A. J. Hot-blooded dinosaurs: a revolution in paleontology. 1976
Horn Bk 53:80 F '77. M. S. Cosgrave
Destler, I. M. and others. Managing an alliance: the politics of U.S.-Japanese relations. 1976
Ann Am Acad 434:212-13 N '77. J. F. Melby
Dethier, V. G. Hungry fly
Sci Am 236:122+ Ja '77. P. Morrison
Deuel, L. Memoirs of Heinrich Schliemann
Harpers 255:70-6 Jl '77. E. Connell
Devanney, J. W. and others. Parable Beach: a primer in coastal zone economics. 1976
Ann Am Acad 434:241-2 N '77. G. S. Goldstein
De Vaucouleurs, G. and others. Second reference catalogue of bright galaxies
Sci Am 236:140+ Ap '77. P. Morrison
Devi, G. and Rau, S. R. Princess remembers: the memoirs of the Maharani of Jaipur
Newsweek 89:79+ Mr 28 '77. P. S. Prescott
Devisse, J. Hincmar: Archevêque de Reims, 845-882 3v. 1975
Am Hist R 82:620-1 Je '77. R. E. Sullivan
Devlin, J. C. and Naismith, G. World of Roger Tory Peterson: an authorized biography. 1977
Bus W p 11-12 D 12 '77. R. Deed
Smithsonian 8:153-4 N '77. E. F. Rivinus
De Vooght, P. L'hérésie de Jean Huss. 1975
Am Hist R 82:1021-2 O '77. H. Kaminsky
De Vries, J. Economy of Europe in an age of crisis, 1600-1750. 1976
Am Hist R 82:623-4 Je '77. J. C. Riley
De Vries, P. Madder music
New Yorker 53:189-90+ N 28 '77. P. Gilliatt
Newsweek 90:16 O 3 '77. R. Boeth
De Zayas, A. M. Nemesis at Potsdam: the Anglo-Americans and the expulsion of the Germans —background, execution, consequences
Nat R 29:838 Jl 22 '77. N. Muhlen
Dick, E. Conquering the great American desert: Nebraska. 1975
Am Hist R 82:450 Ap '77. M. W. M. Hargreaves
Dick, P. K. Maze of death
Chr Today 21:22-4 My 20 '77. E. Warren
Dickinson, P. Walking dead
Newsweek 91:68 Ja 9 '78. P. S. Prescott
Dickinson, P. A. Complete retirement planning book. 1976
Aging 270:43-4 Ap '77. P. Rowe
Dickson, P. Future of the workplace: the coming revolution in jobs. 1975
M Labor R 100:87 Ap '77. L. E. Davis
Dickstein, M. Gates of Eden: American culture in the sixties. 1977
Am Hist R 82:1364 D '77. J. L. Rodnitzky
Atlantic 239:90 Je '77. C. M. Curtis
Commentary 64:73-6 Jl '77. J. Epstein
Commonweal 104:758-9 N 25 '77. W. B. Hixson, jr
Harpers 254:101 Mr '77. M. Malone
Nation 224:501-3 Ap 23 '77. P. Meisel
New Repub 176:52-4 My 21 '77. P. Starr
Newsweek 89:78 Mr 28 '77. W. Clemons
Progressive 41:40 Je '77. W. L. O'Neill
Yale R 66:620-3 Je '77. N. Mills
Dictionary of American history. 7v. rev. ed. 1976
Am Hist R 82:1316-18 D '77. R. H. Ferrell
Didion, J. A book of common prayer
America 137:135-6 S 10 '77. E. W. Shaw
Commentary 64:61-3 Jl '77. J. Romano
Mademoiselle 83:32+ Mr '77. J. Howard
Nat R 29:678 Je 10 '77. B. Stein
New Yorker 53:117-18 Je 20 '77. S. Lardner
Newsweek 89:81 Mr 21 '77. P. S. Prescott
Sat R 4:23-5 Mr 5 '77. F. Raphael
Time 109:87 Mr 28 '77. R. Z. Sheppard
Diest, W. Flottenpolitik und Flottenpropaganda: das Nachrichtenbureau des Reichmarineamtes, 1897-1914. 1976
Am Hist R 82:1004 O '77. A. H. Ganz
Diggins, J. P. Up from communism: conservative odysseys in American intellectual history. 1975
Am Hist R 82:214 F '77. R. Nash
Dillard, A. Holy the firm
America 137:219-20 O 8 '77. R. A. Blake
Dillow, J. C. Solomon on sex
Chr Cent 94:1015 N 2 '77. M. E. Marty
Dimitrov, I. B'lgaro-italianski politicheski otnosheniia, 1922/1943. 1976
Am Hist R 82:1018 O '77. C. A. Moser
Dinerstein, H. S. Making of a missile crisis, October 1962. 1976
Ann Am Acad 429:145-6 Ja '77. H. K. Jacobson
Dineson, I. pseud. Carnival: entertainments and posthumous tales
Nation 225:474-5 N 5 '77. A. Loewinger
New Repub 177:30-2 O 22 '77. R. Brown
New Yorker 53:231-2+ D 5 '77. J. Updike
Sat R 5:54-5 D 10 '77. D. Grumbach
Dingman, R. Power in the Pacific: the origins of naval arms limitation, 1914-1922. 1976
Am Hist R 82:1218 D '77. T. W. Burkman
Dinnerstein, D. Mermaid and the minotaur: sexual arrangements and human malaise
Ms 6:38+ Jl '77. J. Lazarre
Dippie, B. W. Custer's last stand: the anatomy of an American myth. 1976
Am Hist R 82:749-50 Je '77. B. Rosenberg
Am West 14:60 S '77. R. M. Utley
Distin, W. H. and Bishop, R. American clock, a comprehensive pictorial survey, 1723-1900
Antiques 111:1217 Je '77. C. E. Buckley
Ditmanson, H. H. Grace in experience and theology
Chr Cent 94:1008-9 N 2 '77. R. E. Koening
Dixon, B. Magnificent microbes
Am Scholar 46:532-6 Aut '77. P. A. Zahl
Djilas, M. Wartime; tr. by M. B. Petrovich
Commentary 64:75-8 N '77. S. Miller
Nation 225:213-15 S 10 '77. E. Pawel
Newsweek 90:72-3 Jl 25 '77. R. Towers
Dmytryshyn, B. History of Russia. 1977
Am Hist R 82:1290-1 D '77. D. Atkinson
Dobson, C. and Payne, R. Carlos complex
Psychol Today 11:88+ Ag '77. T. Morgan
Dobyns, H. F. Spanish colonial Tucson: a demographic history. 1976
Am Hist R 82:735 Je '77. D. J. Garr
Dobyns, H. F. and Doughty, P. L. Peru: a cultural history. 1976
Am Hist R 82:783 Je '77. F. B. Pike
Cur Hist 72:79 F '77

Dobzhansky, T. and others. Evolution. 1977
Science 197:1272-3 S 23 '77. H. L. Carson
Dodge, E. S. Islands and empires: western impact on the Pacific and East Asia. 1976
Am Hist R 82:925 O '77. J. E. Wills, jr
Ann Am Acad 432:157 Jl '77. M. N. Pearson
Dogan, M. ed. Mandarins of western Europe: the political role of top civil servants. 1975
Ann Am Acad 429:146-7 Ja '77. P. H. Laurent
Doig, D. Mother Teresa: her people and her work
America 136:54-5 Ja 22 '77. J. W. Donohue
Dolan, J. P. Immigrant church: New York's Irish and German Catholics, 1815-1865. 1975
Am Hist R 82:441 Ap '77. H. B. Leonard
Dols, M. W. Black death in the Middle East. 1977
Am Hist R 82:1300 D '77. C. R. Boxer
Donaldson, S. By force of will: the life and art of Ernest Hemingway
New Repub 176:35-6 Je 4 '77. T. Ludington
Donleavy, J. P. Destinies of Darcy Dancer, gentleman
Sat R 5:27 N 12 '77. J. D. Bellamy
Time 110:109+ N 14 '77. P. Gray
Donnelly, J. P. Jean de Brébeuf, 1593-1649. 1976
Am Hist R 82:1101-2 O '77. C. J. Jaenen
Donoghue, D. Sovereign ghost: studies in imagination
New Repub 177:29-31 S 10 '77. K. Burke
Donoso, J. Charleston & other stories; tr. by A. Conrad
Sat R 4:30-1 Jl 9 '77. R. Maurer
Donoso, J. Sacred families; tr. by A. Conrad
Sat R 4:30-1 Jl 9 '77. R. Maurer
Donovan, A. L. Philosophical chemistry in the Scottish enlightenment: the doctrines and discoveries of William Cullen and Joseph Black. 1976
Am Hist R 82:112-13 F '77. S. Mauskopf
Donovan, R. J. Conflict and crisis: the presidency of Harry S. Truman 1945-1948
New Repub 177:39-40 N 26 '77. R. Tugwell
Dorn, E. Collected poems: 1956-1974
Poetry 130:287-8 Ag '77. B. Howard
Dorwart, J. M. Pigtail war; American involvement in the Sino-Japanese war of 1894-1895. 1975
Am Hist R 81:1266 D '76. P. A. Varg
Doty, C. S. From cultural rebellion to counterrevolution: the politics of Maurice Barrès. 1976
Am Hist R 82:372-3 Ap '77. R. Soucy
Dotzenko, G. F. Enku, master carver
Art N 76:66 N '77. R. Castile
Douglas, A. Feminization of American culture
America 137:113-14 Ag 27 '77. R. Senkewicz
Commentary 64:68-71 N '77. S. Schnur
Ms 6:39-40 Ag '77. A. Jones
Nation 225:280-2 S 24 '77. L. Ziff
New Repub 177:31-3 N 12 '77. J. Seelye
Newsweek 89:94 Je 13 '77. M. Jefferson
Time 109:72+ My 30 '77. R. Z. Sheppard
Douglas, E. T. Margaret Sanger: pioneer of the future
Sat Eve Post 249:10-11+ My '77. J. Alexander
Douglas, R. Land, people & politics: a history of the land question in the United Kingdom, 1878-1952. 1976
Ann Am Acad 431:157-8 My '77. J. A. Casada
Downes, E. New York philharmonic guide to the symphony
America 136:402-3 Ap 30 '77. C. McGlinchee
Doyle, J. Not above the law: the battles of Watergate prosecutors Cox and Jaworski; introd. by A. Lewis
Nation 225:121-3 Ag 6 '77. A. Clymer
Newsweek 89:76+ Je 27 '77. J. K. Footlick
Doyle, J. M. and Grimes, G. H. Reference resources: systematic approach. 1976
Lib J 102:343 F 1 '77. J. W. Kraus
Drabble, M. Ice age
Commentary 64:81-3 D '77. P. K. Bell
Harpers 255:87-92 O '77. R. Holmes
Nat R 29:1504 D 23 '77
New Repub 177:28-30 O 22 '77. E. Milton
Newsweek 90:114 O 17 '77. W. Clemons
Newsweek 90:114 O 17 '77. W. Clemons
Progressive 41:55-6 N '77. R. Rubenstein
Sat R 5:39-40 Ja 7 '78. P. Bailey
Time 110:104 O 17 '77. P. Gray
Drake, F. W. China charts the world: Hsü Chi-Yü and his geography of 1848. 1975
Am Hist R 82:411 Ap '77. S. M. Jones
Drake, H. A. In praise of Constantine: a historical study and new translation of Eusebius' Tricennial orations. 1976
Am Hist R 82:931-2 O '77. J. Eadie
Drake, S. ed. Galileo against the philosophers. 1976
Sky & Tel 53:465-8 Je '77. E. Rosen
Drury, R. W. Champion of Merrimack County; il. by F. Wegner. 1976
Horn Bk 53:50-1 F '77. E. L. Heins
Drutman, I. Good company
Am Rec G 40:59-60 My '77. M. Galewski
Dubay, R. W. John Jones Pettus, Mississippi fire-eater: his life and times, 1813-1867. 1975
Am Hist R 82:183 F '77. J. G. Tregle, Jr
Dubinsky, A. M. Far East in the Second World war: an outline history of international relations and national liberation struggle in East and South-East Asia; tr. by V. Epstein. 1972
Am Hist R 82:424-5 Ap '77. Y. Akashi
Dubinsky, D. and Raskin, A. H. David Dubinsky: a life with labor. 1977
M Labor R 100:58 N '77. G. H. Cole
Dubofsky, M. and Van Tine, W. John L. Lewis
Newsweek 90:76 Ag 8 '77. R. Sokolov
DuBois, W. E. B. Correspondence of W.E.B. Du-Bois, v1-2; ed. by H. Aptheker
New Repub 176:28-30 F 19 '77. M. Cooke
Dubos, R. J. Professor, the Institute, and DNA. 1976
Science 195:973 Mr 11 '77. A. W. Ravin
Dubus, A. Separate flights. 1975
Nation 224:248-50 F 26 '77. G. Lyons
Duby, G. and Wallon, A. eds. Histoire de la France rurale, v 1: La formation des campagnes françaises des origines au XIVe siècle; v2: L'âge classique des paysans, 1340-1789; v3: Apogée et crise de la civilisation paysanne, 1789-1914. 1975
Am Hist R 82:115-17 F '77. E. Weber
Ducellier, A. Le drame de Byzance: idéal et échec d'une société chrétienne. 1976
Am Hist R 82:935-6 O '77. T. E. Gregory
Duckham, A. N. and others. eds. Food production and consumption: the efficiency of human food chains and nutrient cycles. 1976
Science 197:1354 S 30 '77. C. P. Timmer
Duff, E. A. and McCamant, J. F. Violence and repression in Latin America: a quantitative and historical analysis. 1976
Am Hist R 82:477 Ap '77. P. H. Smith
Duffy, J. Healers: the rise of the medical establishment. 1976
Am Hist R 82:728 Je '77. J. H. Ellis
Science 196:864 My 20 '77. J. H. Young
Duignan, P. and Gann, L. H. eds. Colonialism in Africa, 1870-1960, v4: The economics of colonialism. 1975
Am Hist R 81:1188-9 D '76. R. F. Betts
Duiker, W. J. Rise of nationalism in Vietnam, 1900-1941. 1976
Am Hist R 82:425 Ap '77. J. P. Harrison
Ann Am Acad 431:151 My '77. J. S. Hoadley
Dulles, A. Resilient Church: the necessity and limits of adaptation
America 137:218-19 O 8 '77. J. Pelikan
Chr Cent 94:1026-9 N 9 '77. L. Gilkey
Dumas, H. Jonoah and the green stone
Commonweal 104:281-5 Ap 29 '77. G. Burnside
Dumbarton Oaks Papers number 29. 1975
Am Hist R 82:615-16 Je '77. D. De F. Abrahamse
Dunaevskii, V. A. Sovetskaia istoriografiia novoi istorii stran Zapada, 1917-1941 gg. 1974
Am Hist R 81:1180 D '76. G. Enteen
Duncan, A. A. M. Scotland: the making of the kingdom. 1975
Am Hist R 81:1119 D '76. R. Frank
Duncan, L. Summer of fear. 1976
Horn Bk 53:167 Ap '77. E. L. Heins
Duncan, S. Jr. and Fiske, D. W. Face-to-face interaction: research, methods, and theory. 1977
Science 198:723 N 18 '77. C. Mayo
Duncan-Jones, R. Economy of the Roman empire: quantitative studies. 1974
Am Hist R 82:612-13 Je '77. W. F. Jashemski
Dunham, V. S. In Stalin's time: middle-class values in Soviet fiction. 1976
Am Hist R 82:1298-9 D '77. E. J. Brown
Ann Am Acad 434:219-220 N '77. S. Letter
Dunkell, S. Sleep positions
Bus W p 12 Mr 28 '77. M. Newman
Dunlop, E. Elizabeth Elizabeth; il by P. Farmer. 1977
Horn Bk 53:314 Je '77. M. M. Burns
Dunlop, I. Van Gogh
Am Artist 41:86+ N '77. A. Werner
Dunlop, J. B. New Russian revolutionaries
America 137:246 O 15 '77. J. Broun
Dunn, J. Distress and comfort
Psychol Today 11:94+ Ag '77. J. Steinberg
Dunn, J. D. G. Jesus and the Spirit: a study of the religious and charismatic experience of Jesus and the first Christians as reflected in the New Testament
Chr Cent 94:281-2 Mr 23 '77. E. G. Homrighausen
Dunne, G. T. Hugo Black and the judicial revolution. 1977
Am Hist R 82:1352 D '77. J. W. Howard, jr
Bus W p 16 My 16 '77. J. K. Lieberman
Commonweal 104:537-9 Ag 19 '77. I. Silver
Sat R 4:25-6 Mr 5 '77. M. Mayer
Dunne, J. G. True confessions
Harpers 255:106-8 N '77. J. Rascoe
Nat R 29:1440-1 D 9 '77. B. Stein
Sat R 5:42-3 O 29 '77. R. M. Strozier
Time 110:121+ N 7 '77. R. Z. Sheppard
Dunson, W. A. ed. Biology of sea snakes. 1975
BioScience 27:813 D '77. H. G. Dowling
Dunstan, B. Learning to paint
Am Artist 41:22+ Jl '77. C. Movalli
Dunstan, B. Paintings in progress
Am Artist 41:30+ Jl '77. C. Movalli
Dupré, C. John Galsworthy: a biography
New Repub 176:24-5 Ap 23 '77. B. Dunlap
Dupré, L. Transcendent selfhood: the loss and rediscovery of the inner life
Chr Cent 94:1070 N 16 '77. P. Green
Commonweal 104:94 F 4 '77. J. R. Kelly

Durán, G. and Durán, M. Autorretratos y espejos. 1977
Américas 29:42-4 Ag '77. P. Vivó
Durant, M. Who named the daisy? Who named the rose?
Horticulture 55:66-9 S '77. A. B. C. Whipple
Durden, R. F. Dukes of Durham, 1865-1929. 1975
Am Hist R 82:457-8 Ap '77. J. A. Pratt
Durfort, C. de. Ourika; tr. by J. Fowles
Nation 225:406-8 O 22 '77. G. Lyons
Durgnat, R. Strange case of Alfred Hitchcock: or, The plain man's Hitchcock. 1974
Film Q 30:57-62 Spr '77. P. Thomas
Durk, D. and Silverman, I. Pleasant avenue connection
New Repub 176:54-5 My 21 '77. D. E. Graham
Durrell, L. Sicilian carousel
Sat R 4:24-5 S 3 '77. P. Fussell
Time 110:71-2+ Ag 29 '77. L. Morrow
Dussel, E. History and the theology of liberation: a Latin American perspective. 1976
Chr Today 22:46+ O 7 '77. J. R. Ross
Dworkin, A. Our blood: prophecies and discourses on sexual politics
Ms 5:45-6 F '77. C. Rosenthal
Dworkin, R. Taking rights seriously
America 136:304-6 Ap 2 '77. J. Lombardi
Commentary 64:75-8 Ag '77. W. J. Bennett
New Repub 176:28-31 Je 25 '77. M. Walzer
Dygert, J. H. Investigative journalist
Bus W p8+ Ja 24 '77. T. Powers
Dyos, H. J. and Wolff, M. eds. Victorian city: images and realities. 2v. 1973
Am Hist R 81:1110 D '76. R. K. Webb

Eames, E. and Goode, J. G. Anthropology of the city—an introduction to urban anthropology. 1977
Am City & County 92:86 Ag '77
Earle, J. R. and others. Spindles and spires: a restudy of religion and social change in Gastonia. 1976
Chr Cent 94:1039-40 N 9 '77. F. B. Edge
Society 14:90-1 Jl '77. W. V. D'Antonio
Eastman, P.F. Advanced first aid for all outdoors: a guide for outdoorsmen, backpackers and all those who venture beyond the range of immediate professional medical assistance. 1976
Am For 83:36 Ap '77. J. Geiger
Eban, A. Abba Eban: an autobiography
Newsweek 91:78+ Ja 16 '78. C. D. May
Sat R 5:56-8 D 10 '77. D. Isaac
Echewa, T. O. Land's lord
Nation 224:440-2 Ap 9 '77. E. Ottenberg
Eckes, A. E. jr. Search for solvency: Bretton Woods and the International monetary system. 1975
Am Hist R 82:1097-8 O '77. G. C. Herring
Eckholm, E. P. Losing ground: environmental stress and world food prospects. 1976
BioScience 27:125 F '77. F. Frazer-Darling
Eden, A. Another world, 1897-1917
New Repub 177:28-30 D 17 '77. L. Bushkoff
Edge, D. O. and Mulkay, M.J. Astronomy transformed: the emergence of radio astronomy in Britain. 1976
Science 196:774-6 My 13 '77. D. J. Kevles
Sky & Tel 53:464-5 Je '77. J. W. Findlay
Edgerton, S. Y. jr. Renaissance discovery of linear perspective
Sci Am 237:146+ Jl '77. P. Morrison
Edwards, D. L. Today's story of Jesus
Chr Cent 94:664-6 Jl 20 '77. G. W. E. Nickelsburg and M. M. Nickelsburg
Edwards, I. E. S. and others. eds. Cambridge ancient history, v 1, pt 2: History of the Middle East and the Aegean Region c. 1380-1000 B.C. 3d ed. 1975
Am Hist R 81:1076-8 D '76. J. Teixidor
Edwards, M. U. Jr. Luther and the false brethren. 1975
Am Hist R 81:1143 D '76. F. J. Wray
Edwards, R. A. Theology of Q: eschatology, prophecy, and wisdom
Chr Cent 94:232-4 Mr 9 '77. M. L. Peel
Eells, G. Ginger, Loretta and Irene who?
Newsweek 89:87 F 21 '77. W. Clemons
Egan, J. Fremont: explorer for a restless nation. 1977
Am West 14:60 My '77. G. R. Stewart
Egret, J. Necker: ministre de Louis XVI, 1776-1790. 1975
Am Hist R 81:1127 D '76. M. J. Sydenham
Ehrlich, P. R. and Feldman, S. S. Race bomb: skin color, prejudice, and intelligence
Progressive 41:42-3 S '77. T. A. Vonder Haar
Ehrlichman, J. Company
Sat R 4:38-9 S 3 '77. K. E. Meyer
Eichenberg, F. Art of the print: masterpieces, history, techniques
Am Artist 41:24-6 O '77. F. Johnson
Eidelberg, P. On the silence of the Declaration of Independence
Nat R 29:673-4 Je 10 '77. M. J. Sobran, Jr
Eidel'man, N. I. Gertsen protiv samoderzhaviia: se kretnaia politicheskaia istoriia Rossii XVIII-XIX vekov i vol'naia pechat'. 1973
Am Hist R 82:150 F '77. A. Gleason
Eikenberg, W. Das Handelshaus der Runtinger zu Regensburg: ein Spiegel süddeutschen Rechts-, Handels-, und Wirtschaftslebens im ausgehenden 14. Jahrhundert. 1976
Am Hist R 82:939-40 O '77. P. W. Strait
Eiseley, L. Another kind of autumn
Harpers 255:104-5 N '77. H. Carruth
Eisenhower, J. N. Special people
Sat Eve Post 249:74+ S '77. F. A. Birmingham
Eisenman, P. and others. Five architects
Harpers 255:77+ Ag '77. N. Silver
Eisenstaedt, A. Eisenstaedt's album: fifty years of friends and acquaintances
Smithsonian 7:143-4 F '77. B. Schiff
Eisner, L. Fritz Lang
New Repub 176:22-3 Ap 9 '77. S. Kauffmann
El-Rayyes, R. and Nahas, D. Guerrillas for Palestine. 1976
Ann Am Acad 432:157-8 Jl '77. H. P. Castleberry
Elazar, D. J. Community and polity: the organizational dynamics of American Jewry
Commentary 63:83-4+ Je '77. J. Weinberg
Elder, J. Bowels of the earth
Sci Am 236:133-4 F '77. P. Morrison
Electrical phenomena at the biological membrane level; proceedings of meeting, Orsay, 1976; ed. by E. Roux. 1977
Science 198:499-500 N 4 '77. J. E. Hall
Electron and photon interactions with atoms; festschrift for Professor Ugo Fano; papers from symposium, Stirling, Scotland, 1974; ed. by H. Kleinpoppen and M. R. C. McDowell. 1976
Science 195:975-6 Mr 11 '77. A. Dalgarno
Eleftheriou, B. E. and Sprott, R. L. eds. Hormonal correlates of behavior. 2v. 1975
BioScience 27:130 F '77. D. D. Thiessen
Elegant, R. S. Dynasty
Nat R 29:1436+ D 9 '77. A. Bakshian, jr
Eliade, M. Occultism, witchcraft, and cultural fashions: essays in comparative religions
Chr Cent 94:155 F 16 '77. P. Green
Elias, J. L. Conscientization and deschooling: Freire's and Illich's proposals for reshaping society
Chr Cent 94:1072-3 N 16 '77. W. Fallaw
Elkind, D. Child development and education
Todays Educ 66:93 S '77. J. B. Raph
Ellenbarg, S. Rousseau's political philosophy: an interpretation from within. 1976
Am Hist R 82:650 Je '77. R Birn
Elliot, E. Let me be a woman. 1976
Chr Today 21:34-5 Ja 7 '77. C. E. Cerling, Jr
Ellis, C. G. Early Caucasian rugs
Antiques 111:572 Mr '77. W. B. Denny
Ellis, J. Eye-deep in hell; trench warfare in World war I
New Repub 177:28-30 D 17 '77. L. Bushkoff
Ellis, J. Social history of the machine gun. 1975
Society 15:116-17 N '77. G. De Gré
Ellis, J. and Moore, R. School for soldiers: West Point and the profession of arms. 1974
Am Hist R 82:462 Ap '77. C. L. Christman
Ellis, R. Book of sharks
Conservationist 32:42 N '77. H. S. Mazet
Ellul, J. Ethics of freedom
Chr Cent 94:490 My 18 '77. V. Eller
Elvin, M. and Skinner, G. W. eds. Chinese city between two worlds. 1974
Am Hist R 82:160-1 F '77. S. C. Lee
Elwood, R. C. Russian social democracy in the underground: a study of the RSDRP in the Ukraine, 1907-1914. 1974
Am Hist R 81:1183-4 D '76. B. D. Weinryb
Ely, J. W. Jr. Crisis of conservative Virginia: the Byrd organization and the politics of massive resistance. 1976
Am Hist R 82:472 Ap '77. R. L. Zangrando
Ely, R. Unto God and Caesar: religious issues in the emerging commonwealth, 1891-1906. 1976
Am Hist R 82:1056 O '77. F. G. Clarke
Emerson, G. Winners and losers: battles, retreats, gains, losses and ruins from a long war
America 136:59 Ja 22 '77. J. B. Breslin
Bus W p 13+ F 7 '77. J. Canan
Commonweal 104:115-18 F 18 '77. S. Maloff
Commonweal 104:147-9 Mr 4 '77. T. Powers
Ms 5:44+ Mr '77. I. Barth
Nat R 29:616-19 My 27 '77. C. Williamson, Jr
Nation 224:406-8 Ap 2 '77. M. Young
New Repub 176:70-2 Ja 22 '77. H. Bigart
Progressive 41:38 Je '77. R. Dudman
Sat R 4:22-3 F 5 '77. C. D. B. Bryan
Time 109:81-2 Ja 24 '77. L. Morrow
Emmanuelli, F.-X. Pouvoir royal et vie régionale en Provence au déclin de la monarchie: psychologie, pratiques administratives, défrancisation de l'Intendance d'Aix, 1745-90, 2v. 1974
Am Hist R 82:368 Ap '77. T. E. Hall
Emmerson, D. K. Indonesia's elite: political culture and cultural politics. 1976
Ann Am Acad 430:190-1 Mr '77. J. M. Van Der Kroef
Engel, L. Critics
Am Rec G 40:62-3 F '77. M. Galekski
Engelman, E. Berggasse 19: Sigmund Freud's home and offices
Sci Am 236:142 Mr '77. P. Morrison

Engler, R. Brotherhood of oil: energy policy and the public interest
Nation 224:536-8 Ap 30 '77. H. S. Kariel
New Repub 177:37-8 Ag 6 '77. M. Harrington
Englund, K. Arbetarförsäkringsfrågen i svensk politik, 1884-1901. 1976
Am Hist R 82:994 O '77. P. V. Thorson
Engstrom, T. W. Making of a Christian leader. 1976
Chr Today 21:36 Ja 21 '77. K. O. Gangel
Entelis, J. P. Pluralism and party transformation in Lebanon: al-Kata'ib, 1936-1970. 1974
Am Hist R 82:1029-30 O '77. W. W. Haddad
Environment and society in transition: world priorities; ed by B. Pregel and others. 1975
BioScience 27:208+ Mr '77. E. M. Mrak
Epp, F. H. Mennonites in Canada, 1786-1920: the history of a separate people. 1974
Am Hist R 81:1282-3 D '76. P. K. Conkin
Epp, F. H. Palestinians: portrait of a people in conflict. 1976
Chr Today 21:28-9 Jl 8 '77. R. Smith
Epps, G. Shad treatment
Nat R 30:37 Ja 6 '78. W. Stillman
Epstein, A. M. Good stones; il. by S. Meddaugh. 1977
Horn Bk 53:439-40 Ag '77. K. Waters
Epstein, E. J. Agency of fear
Commentary 64:78-80 N '77. S. Cropsey
Newsweek 90:113-14 O 17 '77. R. Boeth
Progressive 41:59 D '77. K. McAuliffe
Epstein, J. J. Francis Bacon: a political biography. 1977
Am Hist R 82:1241 D '77. E. R. Foster
Epstein, W. Last chance: nuclear proliferation and arms control. 1976
Ann Am Acad 434:200 N '77. I. Peleg
Intellect 105:366 Ap '77. A. W. Munk
Erdman, P. Crash of '79
Bus W p 10 Mr 7 '77. T. C. O'Donnell
Time 109:64+ Je 13 '77
Erickson, K. T. Everything in its path: destruction of community in the Buffalo Creek flood
Nation 224:277-8 Mr 5 '77. H. M. Caudill
New Repub 176:34-5 Ap 16 '77. T. J. Cottle
Newsweek 89:90-1 Mr 7 '77. M. Jefferson
Progressive 41:40 Jl '77. W. Grant
Psychol Today 10:99-100+ F '77. K. J. Tierney
Sci Am 237:135-6 Ag '77. P. Morrison
Erikson, E. H. Toys and reasons
New Repub 176:30-1 Ap 30 '77. P. M. Spacks
Erikson, T. Reformers: an historical survey of pioneer experiments in the treatment of criminals. 1976
Ann Am Acad 434:238-9 N '77. D. Glaser
Eringen, A. C. and Suhubi, E. S. Elastodynamics. 2v 1974-75
Phys Today 30:65 Ja '77. D. R. Bland
Ernst, B. Magic mirror of M. C. Escher
Sci Am 237:146+ Jl '77. P. Morrison
Esherick, J. W. Reform and revolution in China: the 1911 Revolution in Hunan and Hubei. 1976
Am Hist R 82:1046-8 O '77. M. Gasster
Espinosa, J. M. Inter-American beginnings of US cultural diplomacy, 1936-1948. 1976
Am Hist R 82:1354 D '77. T. L. Karnes
Espy, W. R. Oysterville
Newsweek 89:114-15 My 16 '77. M. Jefferson
Estep, W. R. Anabaptist story. rev ed. 1975
Am Hist R 81:1097 D '76. G. F. Hershberger
Etudes historiques hongroises 1975: publiées à l'occasion du XIVe Congrès international des sciences historiques par la Commission nationale des historiens hongrois. 2v. 1975
Am Hist R 81:1165-6 D '76. R. A. Kann
Evans, J. G. Environment of early man in the British Isles. 1975
Am Hist R 81:1078-9 D '76. R. A. Padgug
Evans, R. I. Konrad Lorenz: the man and his ideas
Psychol Today 11:100+ Jl '77. L. Tiger
Evans, R. J. Feminist movement in Germany, 1894-1933. 1976
Am Hist R 82:1277-8 D '77. C. Messman
Evenhuis, G. What about me? il. by R. Stenberg. 1976
Horn Bk 53:159 Ap '77. M. M. Burns
Evergates, T. Feudal society in the bailliage of Troyes under the counts of Champagne, 1152-1284. 1976
Am Hist R 81:1089-90 D '76. R. Hajdu
Evitts, W. J. Matter of allegiances: Maryland from 1850 to 1861. 1974
Am Hist R 81:1251 D '76. M. C. Kahl
Evolution of brain and behavior in vertebrates; papers from conference, Tallahassee, Fla. 1973; ed by R. B. Masterton and others. 1976
BioScience 27:690 O '77. F. A. Jenkins, jr
Science 196:756-7 My 13 '77. J. H. Kaas
Ewald, U. Estudios sobre hacienda colonial en México: las propiedades rurales del Colegio Espirtu Santo en Puebla; tr. by L. R. Cerna. 1976
Am Hist R 82:779-80 Je '77. W. B. Taylor
Ewen, S. Captains of consciousness: advertising and the social roots of the consumer culture. 1976
Am Hist R 82:1092-3 O '77. O. A. Pease
Ewers, R. O. and Ewers, L. M. Universe to explore. 1976
Sky & Tel 54:417+ N '77. N. P. Edwards
Extreme environments: mechanisms of microbial adaptation; papers from meeting, 1974; ed. by M. R. Heinrich. 1976
BioScience 27:422 Je '77. W. L. Boyd

Fagen, M. D, ed. History of engineering and science in the Bell system, the early years (1875-1925) 1975
Science 196:49-50 Ap 1 '77. K. Birr
Fairbairn, D. Street 8
Newsweek 89:88 F 14 '77. P. S. Prescott
Fairbank, W. America's cultural experiment in China, 1942-1949. 1976
Am Hist R 82:416 Ap '77. P. A. Zimmerman
Ann Am Acad 433:172 S '77. R. P. Gardella
Fairchilds, C. C. Poverty and charity in Aix-en-Provence, 1640-1789. 1976
Am Hist R 81:1123-4 D '76. T. M. Adams
Fajn, M. Journal des hommes libres de tous les pays, 1792-1800. 1975
Am Hist R 82:370 Ap '77. R. Birn
Falcoff, M. and Dolkart, R. H. eds. Prologue to Perón: Argentina in depression and war, 1930-1943. 1976
Am Hist R 81:1286 D '76. R. A. Potash
Falk, S. L. Seventy days to Singapore. 1975
Am Hist R 82:645 Je '77. R. Callahan
Fal'kovich, S. M. Proletariat Rossii i Pol'shi v sovmestnoi revoliutsionnoi bor'be (1907-1912) 1975
Am Hist R 82:403-4 Ap '77. R. D. Lewis
Fallaci, O. Letter to a child never born; tr. by J. Shepley
America 136:279 Mr 26 '77. T. H. Stahel
Falls, J. Boston marathon
Bus W p 14+ Ap 25 '77. D. G. Santry
Time 109:86+ Ap 18 '77. P. Stoler
Farb, P. Humankind
Natur Hist 87:96+ Ja '78. A. Montagu
Farber, L. H. Lying, despair, jealousy, envy, sex, suicide, drugs and the good life
Commonweal 104:188-90 Mr 18 '77. J. B. Elshtain
Farber, N. Six impossible things before breakfast; il. by T. de Paola and others. 1977
Horn Bk 53:307 Je '77. V. Haviland
Farber, S. Revolution and reaction in Cuba, 1933-1960: a political sociology from Machado to Castro. 1976
Am Hist R 82:782 Je '77. R. F. Smith
Farjeon, E. Glass slipper
Horn Bk 53:193-4 Ap '77. S. B. Andrews
Farmer, E. L. Early Ming government: the evolution of dual capitals. 1976
Am Hist R 82:1043-4 O '77. C. O. Hucker
Farrell, J. T. Dunne family
America 136:398-400 Ap 30 '77. D. O'Connell
Farrell, J. T. Literary essays, 1954-1974; ed. by J. A. Robbins
America 136:398-400 Ap 30 '77. D. O'Connell
Farrington, Kip, Jr. Tony the tuna
Field & S 82:182 Je '77. G. L. Sapir
Farwell, B. Great Anglo-Boer war. 1976
Am Hist R 82:106 F '77. C. P. Potholm
Fass, P. S. Damned and the beautiful: American youth in the 1920's. 1977
Am Hist R 82:1346-7 D '77. P. A. Carter
Fast, H. Immigrants
Time 110:120-1+ N 7 '77. R. Z. Sheppard
Fate and effects of petroleum hydrocarbons in marine ecosystems and organisms; proceedings of symposium, Seattle, 1976; ed. by D. A. Wolfe. 1977
Science 198:1030 D 9 '77. P. A. Meyers
Faucci, R. Finanza, amministrazione e pensiero economico: il caso della contabilità di stato da Cavour al fascismo. 1975
Am Hist R 81:1157 D '76. R. Sarti
Faulk, O. B. U.S. camel corps: an army experiment
Am Scholar 46:264-6 Spr '77. P. A. Zahl
Faulkner, D. and Fell, B. Dwellers in the sea. 1976
Oceans 10:69 Ja '77. M. P. Dumont
Faulkner, W. Selected letters of William Faulkner; ed. by J. Blotner
America 136:381 Ap 23 '77. J. W. Crowley
Commonweal 104:507-9 Ag 5 '77. P. Samway
Nat R 29:1373-4 N 25 '77. M. E. Bradford
New Repub 176:30-1 Mr 12 '77. M. Cowley
Newsweek 89:74-5 F 7 '77. W. Clemons
Sat R 4:24+ F 5 '77. J. W. Aldridge
Smithsonian 8:136+ Ap '77. B. Schiff
Fay, P. W. Opium war, 1840-1842: barbarians in the celestial empire in the early part of the nineteenth century and the war by which they forced her gates ajar. 1975
Am Hist R 81:1197 D '76. J. K. Leonard
Fay, S. and Knightley, P. Death of Venice
New Repub 176:34-6 Ja 29 '77. J. M. Edelstein
Feather, L. and Gitler, I. comps. Encyclopedia of jazz in the seventies
Hi Fi 27:148 Mr '77. B. Blumenthal

Feder, E. Heute sprach ich mit. . . : Tagebücher eines Berliner Publizisten, 1926-1932; ed. by C. Lowenthal-Hensel and A. Paucker. 1971
Am Hist R 82:131 F '77. V. L. Lidtke
Feiffer, J. Ackroyd
New Repub 176:33-4 My 14 '77. R. W. Winks
Feinberg, G. What is the world made of?
New Yorker 53:133-4+ S 19 '77. J. Bernstein
Feininger, A. Mountains of the mind: a fantastic journey into reality
Sat R 5:40 O 15 '77. M. Weiss
Feinstein, E. F. Stamford from Puritan to patriot: the shaping of a Connecticut community, 1641-1774. 1976
Am Hist R 82:731 Je '77. C. Collier
Feiveson, H. A. and others. eds. Boundaries of analysis: an inquiry into the Tocks Island Dam controversy. 1976
Ann Am Acad 434:226-7 N '77. C. S. Ascher.
Feldman, I. Leaping clear
Poetry 130:52-3 Ap '77. J. D. McClatchy
Feldstein, M. Sightings. 1977
Art in Am 65:36 N '77. P. Patton
Fellini, F. Fellini on Fellini; tr. by I. Quigley. 1976
Horn Bk 53:80 F '77. M. S. Cosgrave
Fentress, J. C. ed. Simpler networks and behavior. 1976
BioScience 27:486 Jl '77. I. Kupfermann
Ferluga, J. and others. eds. Glossar zur frühmittelalterlichen Geschichte im östlichen Europa; ser A. 1973-1975
Am Hist R 82:81 F '77. L. L. Blodgett
Fernea, E. W. and Bezirgan, B. Q. eds. Middle Eastern Muslim women speak
Ms 6:37 Ja '78. L. Rivlin
Fernie, D. Whisper and the vision. 1976
Sky & Tel 53:379-80 My '77. D. H. DeVorkin
Ferrer Benimeli, J. A. Los archivos secretos vaticanos y la masonería: motivos políticos de una condena pontificia. 1976
Am Hist R 82:950-1 O '77. I. M. Zavala
Ferris, N. B. Desperate diplomacy: William H. Seward's foreign policy, 1861. 1976
Am Hist Illus 12:48 N '77. A. Castel
Am Hist R 82:183 F '77. E. N. Paolino
Ferris, P. Dylan Thomas: a biography
Newsweek 90:93-4+ N 7 '77. M. Jefferson
Time 110:104 O 31 '77. R. Z. Sheppard
Ferris, T. Red limit: the search for the edge of the universe. 1977
Sci Am 237:52 S '77. P. Morrison
Sky & Tel 54:509-12 D '77. J. B. Irwin
Fetter, B. Creation of Elizabethville, 1910-1940. 1976
Am Hist R 82:1034 O '77. E. L. Berger
Feuchtwanger, E. J. Gladstone. 1975
Am Hist R 82:635-7 Je '77. R. K. Webb
Fichtenau, H. Beiträge zur Mediävistik: ausgewählte Aufsätze, v 1: Allgemeine Geschichte. 1975
Am Hist R 82:934 O '77. L. Wallach
Fichter, J. H. Catholic cult of the Paraclete. 1975
Society 14:92-3 Jl '77. C. Nanry
Field, A. Nabokov: his life in part
Nation 225:56-8 Jl 9 '77. J. D. O'Hara
Time 109:97 Je 13 '77. R. Z. Sheppard
Field, D. End of serfdom: nobility and bureaucracy in Russia, 1855-1861. 1976
Am Hist R 82:402 Ap '77. F. A. Miller
Field, F. Three French writers and the Great war: studies in the rise of communism and fascism. 1975
Am Hist R 81:1133 D '76. R. Soucy
Filippini, J.-P. and others, eds. Dossiers sur le commerce français en Méditerranée orientale au XVIIIe siècle. 1976
Am Hist R 82:367 Ap '77. P. W. Bamford
Filler, L. Appointment at Armageddon: muckraking and progressivism in the American tradition. 1976
Am Hist R 82:198 F '77. D. W. Noble
Ann Am Acad 429:174 Ja '77. H. Marks
Fine, J. V. A. Jr. Bosnian Church: a new interpretation: a study of the Bosnian Church and its place in state and society from the 13th to the 15th centuries. 1975
Am Hist R 82:346-7 Ap '77. G. P. Majeska
Finnegan, J. P. Against the specter of a dragon: the campaign for American military preparedness, 1914-1917. 1975
Am Hist R 82:201 F '77. R. Gregory
Finscher, L. Studien zur Geschichte des Streichquartetts, v1. 1974
Mus Q 63:133-43 Ja '77. P. H. Lang
Fischer, A. Sowjetische Deutschlandpolitik im Zweiten Weltkrieg, 1941-1945. 1975
Am Hist R 81:1184 D '76. V. Mastny
Fischer, D. H. Growing old in America
Atlantic 239:98 My '77. M. Spaulding
New Repub 177:32-3 Jl 2 '77. P. Ariès
Fischer-Dieskau, D. Schubert's songs: a biographical study; tr. by K. S. Whitton
Sat R 5:42-3 O 1 '77. I. Kolodin
Time 109:86 Ap 18 '77. W. Bender
Fishbein, H. D. Evolution, development, and children's learning. 1976
Science 196:1310 Je 17 '77. M. Konner
Fisher, L. Presidential spending power. 1975
Am Hist R 82:765 Je '77. H. F. Graff
Fisher, T. Huts, hovels & houses
Sci Am 237:38 D '77. P. Morrison and P. Morrison
Fitz, J. La Pannonie sous Gallian, v 148. 1976
Am Hist R 82:339-40 Ap '77. T. V. Buttrey
Fitzgerald, C. P. Mao Tse-tung and China. 1976
Ann Am Acad 430:191-2 Mr '77. A. L. Hsieh
Fixx, J. F. Complete book of running
America 137:428 D 10 '77. J. P. Parkes
Bus W p 13 Ja 16 '78. A. Swardson
Flack, J. K. Desideratum in Washington: the intellectual community in the capital city, 1870-1900. 1975
Am Hist R 82:453 Ap '77. G. Blodgett
Flamsteed, J. Gresham lectures of John Flamsteed; ed. by E. G. Forbes. 1975
Sky & Tel 54:227-9 S '77. O. Gingerich
Flannery, K. V. ed. Early Mesoamerican village. 1976
Science 195:1319-21 Mr 25 '77. D. W. Lathrap
Fleischner, E. ed. Auschwitz: beginning of a new era? reflections on the holocaust
America 136:525-7 Je 11 '77. J. M. Oesterreicher
Chr Cent 94:595-6 Je 22 '77. J. C. Raines
Fletcher, A. County community in peace and war: Sussex, 1600-1660. 1975
Am Hist R 82:632 Je '77. C. Holmes
Flick, T. M. and others. Guidelines for astronomy courses. 1976
Sky & Tel 54:517 D '77. T. Dickinson
Flink, J. J. Car culture. 1975
Am Hist R 81:1276 D '76. G. S. May
Flood, C. B. Rise and fight again: perilous times along the road to independence
Smithsonian 7:144-5 F '77. E. B. Braly
Florkin, M. Comprehensive biochemistry, v32, pt 4: Early studies on biosynthesis. 1977
Science 198:1028 D 9 '77. R. Olby
Florman, S. C. Existential pleasures of engineering
Archit Rec 162:106-7 mid-Ag '77. H. Berger; A. Tor
Flynn, G. Q. Roosevelt and Romanism: Catholics and American diplomacy, 1937-1945. 1976
Am Hist R 82:467 Ap '77. S. Adler
Fokas, S. G. Hoi Hellenes eis ten potamoploian tov kato Doynabeos; tr. by M. I. Markopouloy. 1975
Am Hist R 82:142 F '77. G. Augustinos
Follman, J. F. Jr. Alcoholics and business: problems, costs, solutions. 1976
M Labor R 100:68-9 Ja '77. L. Perlis
Foner, P. S. History of black Americans: from Africa to the emergence of the cotton kingdom. 1975
Am Hist R 82:180 F '77. W. D. Jordan
Foner, P. S. Labor and the American Revolution. 1977
Am Hist R 82:1064 O '77. C. S. Olton
Ann Am Acad 434:227 N '77. G. B. Engberg
Foner, S. Magnetism: selected topics. 1976
Phys Today 30:58 Je '77. D. C. Mattis
Foot, M. R. D. Resistance: European resistance to Nazism, 1940-45
Newsweek 89:92 Ap 25 '77. P. S. Prescott
Forbath, P. River Congo
Time 110:117+ O 24 '77. P. Stoler
Forbes, D. Hume's philosophical politics. 1975
Am Hist R 81:1106-7 D '76. W. C. Havard
Forche, C. Gathering the tribes
Commonweal 104:762-3 N 25 '77. C. Hahn
Ford, J. M. Which way for Catholic Pentecostals?
America 136:471-2 My 21 '77. B. Nauer
Chr Cent 94:491 My 18 '77. W. E. Mills
Commonweal 104:573-4 S 2 '77. B. Cooke
Ford, R. Piece of my heart
Newsweek 89:89+ F 14 '77. W. Clemons
Ford, T. D. and Cullingford, C. H. D. eds. Science of speleology. 1976
Science 195:776 F 25 '77. B. F. Beck
Ford, W. and Mantle, M. Whitey and Mickey: a joint autobiography of the Yankee years; ed. by J. Durso
New Repub 176:32-3 Je 11 '77. L. D. Rubin, Jr
Sat R 4:33 My 14 '77. R. L. Tobin
Forde-Johnson, J. Hillforts of the Iron Age in England and Wales: a survey of the surface evidence. 1976.
Am Hist R 82:932-3. O '77. D. W. Harding
Fordin, H. Getting to know him
Newsweek 90:122+ N 21 '77. M. Jefferson
Sat R 5:4 D 10 '77. N. Cousins
Foreign relations of the United States, 1948; v 1: pt2: General; the United Nations. 1976
Am Hist R 82:768 Je '77. T. M. Campbell
Foreign relations of the United States, 1948, v5: Near East, south Asia, and Africa, pts 1-2. 1975, 1976
Am Hist R 82:1356-7 D '77. T. G. Patterson
Foreign relations of the United States, 1948, v6: the Far East and Australasia. 1974
Am Hist R 82:770 Je '77. K. R. Young
Foreign relations of the United States, 1949, v 1: National security affairs, foreign economic policy. 1976
Am Hist R 82:770-1 Je '77. J. Gimbel
Foreign relations of the United States, 1950. v2: The United Nations; the Western Hemisphere. 1976
Am Hist R 82:1100 O '77. L. C. Wilson

Forester, T. British Labour party and the working class. 1976
Ann Am Acad 430:192-3 Mr '77. R. G. Cowherd
Forge, A. and Joyes, C. Monet at Giverny
Am Artist 41:16+ S '77. A. Werner
Form, W. H. Blue-collar stratification: autoworkers in four countries. 1976
Ann Am Acad 429:191-2 Ja '77. E. H. Jacobson
M Labor R 100:86 Ap '77. M. Meissner
Form, structure and function in plants; ed. by H. Y. M. Ram and others. 1975
BioScience 27:56 Ja '77. T. A. Steeves
Forman, S. Brazilian peasantry. 1975
Ann Am Acad 430:201-2 Mr '77. T. W. Walker
Fornari, F. Psychoanalysis of war; tr. by A. Pfeifer. 1974
Am Hist R 81:1067-8 D '76. S. E. Cooper
Forrest, A. Society and politics in revolutionary Bordeaux. 1975
Am Hist R 81:1128 D '76. C. Garrett
Forster, E. M. Aspects of the novel
New Repub 177:40-1 Jl 2 '77. H. Wolf
Fossil algae; papers from symposium, Erlangen, West Germany, 1975; ed. by E. Flügel. 1977
Science 197:1072 S 9 '77. S. M. Awramik
Foster, M. H, ed. Tradition and renewal: essays on twentieth-century Latin American literature and culture. 1975
Américas 29:23-4 Ap '77. R. G. Mead, Jr
Foster, R. F. Charles Stewart Parnell: the man and his family. 1976
Am Hist R 82:1262 D '77. E. Larkin
Foster, W. R. Church before the covenants: the Church of Scotland, 1596-1638. 1975
Am Hist R 82:111-12 F '77. R. G. Eaves
Foucault, M. Discipline and punish: the birth of the prison; tr. by A. Sheridan
Newsweek 91:61 Ja 2 '78. W. Clemons
Foucault, M. Surveiller et punir: naissance de la prison. 1976
Am Hist R 82:605-6 Je '77. H. White
Fourquin, G. Lordship and feudalism in the Middle Ages; tr. by I. Sells and A. L. L. Sells. 1976
Am Hist R 82:617 Je '77. E. A. R. Brown
Fowler, W. M. Jr. Rebels under sail: the American navy during the Revolution. 1976
Am Hist R 82:176 F '77. W. J. Morgan
Fowler, W. W. Woman on the American frontier; a valuable and authentic history of the heroism, adventures, privations, captivities, trials, and noble lives and deaths of the pioneer mothers of the Republic. 1974
Am Hist R 82:191 F '77. J. E. Baur
Fowles, J. Daniel Martin
Commentary 64:81-3 D '77. P. K. Bell
Harpers 255:87-92 O '77. R. Holmes
Newsweek 90:110 S 19 '77. R. Boeth
Progressive 41:55-6 N '77. R. Rubenstein
Sat R 5:22-4 O 1 '77. J. Gardner
Time 110:75 S 12 '77. P. Gray
Fox, A. B. Politics of attraction: four middle powers and the United States. 1977
Am Hist R 82:1355 D '77. N. S. Kane
Ann Am Acad 433:162 S '77. G. A. Codding, jr
Fox, H. R. V. Holland House diaries, 1831-1840: the diary of Henry Richard Vassall Fox, Third Lord Holland, ed. by A. D. Kriegel. 1977
Am Hist R 82:965-6 O '77. J. Clive
Fox, P. Widow's children
Nat R 29:217-18 F 18 '77. R. K. Bryant
New Repub 176:27-8 Ja 15 '77. E. Milton
Fox, W. History of the lumber industry in the state of New York
Conservationist 31:43-4 My '77. S. L. Golden
Fox-Genovese, E. Origins of physiocracy: economic revolution and social order in eighteenth-century France. 1976
Am Hist R 82:367 Ap '77. N. S. Hoyt
Fraiberg, L. Insights from the blind: comparative studies of blind and sighted infants
Sci Am 237:32 N '77. P. Morrison
France, C. E. ed. Baryshnikov at work
Dance Mag 51:27 Ag '77. D. Hering
France, R. T. I came to set the earth on fire: a portrayal of Jesus. 1976
Chr Today 21:26 Ag 12 '77. W. A. Elwell
Francis, D. In the frame
Newsweek 89:92-3 Ap 25 '77. W. Clemons
Francis, P. Volcanoes
Sci Digest 81:94 F '77. B. Ford
Francis, R. Collected poems, 1936-1976
Commonweal 104:441-2 Jl 8 '77. M. True
Poetry 131:106-10 N '77. R. B. Shaw
Frank, C. R. jr. Foreign trade and domestic aid. 1977
Ann Am Acad 434:228 N '77. G. K. Bluwey
Frank, J. Dostoevsky: the seeds of revolt, 1821-1849
America 136:111-12 F 5 '77. R. T. Reilly
Commentary 63:90+ Mr '77. M. Friedberg
Commonweal 104:310-11 My 13 '77. J. Meyers
Nat R 29:676+ Je 10 '77. M. S. Ross
New Yorker 53:141-2+ S 12 '77. G. Steiner
Frankel, C. ed. Controversies and decisions: the social sciences and public policy. 1976
Ann Am Acad 429:147-8 Ja '77. D. Martindale
Frankenstein, A. William Sidney Mount
Art N 76:102 F '77. M. S. Young
Frankfort, E. Voice: life at the Village voice
Commonweal 104:444-6 Jl 8 '77. W. O'Rourke
New Repub 176:35-6 Mr 12 '77. M. da Vinci
Franklin, B. Papers of Benjamin Franklin, v 18: January 1 through December 31, 1771; ed. by W. B. Wilcox. 1974
Am Hist R 81:1223-4 D '76. J. A. L. Lemay
Franklin, J. H. Racial equality in America
New Repub 176:82-4 Ja 22 '77. R. Wilkins
Franklin, M. A. Bitterweeds: life with William Faulkner at Rowan Oak
Commonweal 104:507-9 Ag 5 '77. P. Samway
Frantz, J. B. Aspects of the American West: three essays. 1976
Am West 14:56 N '77. R. W. Righter
Fraser, A. Quiet as a nun
America 137:223-4 O 8 '77. D. Coogan
Fraser, D. ed. New poor law in the nineteenth century. 1976
Am Hist R 82:357-8 Ap '77. D. Roberts
Freedman, R. Hanging on: how animals carry their young
Sci Am 237:34+ D '77. P. Morrison and P. Morrison
Freeman, A. M. and others. Economics of environmental policy
Conservationist 31:46 Ja '77. A. Rose
Freeman, R. B. Overeducated American. 1976
America 136:336-8 Ap 9 '77. R. Hassenger
M Labor R 100:55-6 Jl '77. H. Goldstein
Todays Educ 66:80 N '77. W. S. Graybeal
Freidson, E. Doctoring together: a study of professional social control. 1975
Ann Am Acad 429:181 Ja '77. C. Zeleny
Society 14:92-3 Ja '77. R. H. Elling
French, M. Women's room
Harpers 256:84-6 Ja '78. H. Yglesias
Ms 6:30+ Ja '78. S. Sanborn
Newsweek 90:121+ O 24 '77. R. Sokolov
Fried, E. R. and Schultze, C. L. eds. Higher oil prices and the world economy: the adjustment problem. 1975
Ann Am Acad 433:201-2 S '77. R. M. Larsen
Fried, R. M. Men against McCarthy. 1976
Am Hist R 82:215-16 F '77. J. E. Wiltz
Friedlaender, J. S. Patterns of human variation: the demography, genetics, and phenetics of Bougainville Islanders. 1975
Science 196:153-5 Ap 8 '77. M. H. Crawford
Friedlander, L. American monument. 1976
Art in Am 65:51+ Mr '77. A. Grundberg
Friedlander, S. K. Smoke, dust and haze: fundamentals of aerosol behavior. 1977
Phys Today 30:58-9 S '77. W. H. Marlow
Friendly, A. Beaufort of the Admiralty: the life of Sir Francis Beaufort 1774-1857
Bus W p6+ Ag 29 '77. J. Zukosky
Yachting 142:94 D '77. H. Lundbergh
Frisch, M. Sketchbook 1946-1949
New Yorker 53:87-9 Jl 11 '77. V. S. Pritchett
Fritchman, S. H. Heretic: a partisan autobiography
Nation 225:284-5 S 24 '77. C. McWilliams
Fritts, H. C. Tree rings and climate. 1976
Science 197:361-2 Jl 22 '77. T. Webb, 3d
Fritz, P S. English ministers and Jacobitism between the rebellions of 1715 and 1745. 1975
Am Hist R 81:1106 D '76. R. Blackey
Fromm, E. To have or to be? ed. by R. N. Anshen
Nation 224:151-4 F 5 '77. P. Roazen
Psychol Today 10:106-7 F '77. M. B. Smith
Frye, N. Secular scripture: a study of the structure of romance
Yale R 66:xii-xiii Mr '77
Frye, R. N. ed. Cambridge history of Iran, v4: The period from the Arab invasion to the Saljuqs. 1975
Am Hist R 81:1187 D '76. K. Stowasser
Fuchs, E. Looking at maps
Sci Am 237:40 D '77. P. Morrison and P. Morrison
Fuentes, C. Terra nostra; tr. by M. S. Peden
New Repub 176:30-2 Ap 9 '77. G. H. Bell
Fulbert, Abp. Letters and poems of Fulbert of Chartres; ed. and tr. by F. Behrends. 1976
Am Hist R 82:342 Ap '77. E. Peters
Fuller, J. Poems and epistles
Poetry 129:340-7 Mr '77. J. Matthias
Fuller, J. G. We almost lost Detroit
Commonweal 104:59-61 Ja 21 '77. W. J. Lanouette
Fuller, P. Champions
Harpers 254:96-7 My '77. J. Lahr
Fulton, C. and Klein, A. O. Explorations in developmental biology. 1976
BioScience 27:289 Ap '77. R. Hinegardner
Furber, H. Rival empires of trade in the Orient, 1600-1800. 1976
Am Hist R 82:1309 D '77. J. M. Price
Furlong, M. Puritan's progress. 1975
Chr Today 22:38-9 N 4 '77. T. Nettles
Furman, N. S. Walter Prescott Webb: his life and impact. 1976
Am Hist R 82:193-4 F '77. W. R. Jacobs
Furstenberg, F. F. jr. Unplanned parenthood: the social consequences of teenage childbearing. 1976
Ann Am Acad 432:177 Jl '77. M. Levitt
Furth, C. ed. Limits of change: essays on conservative alternatives in Republican China. 1976
Am Hist R 82:1312 D '77. P. West
Fussell, E. Your name is you
Poetry 130:110-11 My '77. R. Siegel

Gablik, S. **Progress in art.** 1977
Art in Am 65:25 S '77. C. Ratcliff
Gadney, R. Constable and his world
Am Artist 41:79-80 Je '77. A. Werner
Gaebelein, F. E. ed. Expositor's Bible commentary, v 10: Romans-Galatians. 1976
Chr Today 21:41-3 Mr 18 '77. W. W. Gasque
Gainer, H. Peptides in neurobiology. 1977
Science 198:1247 D 23 '77. L. Iversen
Gaines, J. R. Wit's end: days and nights of the Algonquin round table
New Repub 177:26-7 D 10 '77. J. S. Allen
Galambos, L. Public image of big business in America, 1880-1940: a quantitative study in social change; with B. B. Spence. 1975
Am Hist R 82:196-7 F '77. A. Raucher
Galbraith, J. K. Age of uncertainty
Bus W p 11+ Ap 4 '77. W. Wolman
Newsweek 89:104+ Ap 18 '77. K. Auchincloss
Sat R 4:43-4 Ap 16 '77. L. Silk
Time 109:85-6 Ap 4 '77. R. Z. Sheppard
Galbraith, J. S. Crown and charter; the early years of the British South Africa company. 1974
Am Hist R 82:105-6 F '77. D. C. Ellinwood, Jr
Gale, W. Compound
Nation 226:22-4 Ja 7 '78. A. Lopez
Gallagher, D. Hannah's daughters: six generations of an American family: 1876-1976
Commonweal 104:628-9 S 30 '77. S. B. Warner, jr
Ms 5:103 Mr '77. L. Dickstein
Gallego, J. A. La política religiosa en España, 1889-1913. 1975
Am Hist R 81:1136 D '76. R. W. Kern
Gallen, J. ed. Christians at prayer
America 137:20 Jl 2 '77. Q. Lauer
Gallo, E. Farmers in revolt: the Revolutions of 1893 in the Province of Santa Fe, Argentina. 1976
Am Hist R 82:1110 O '77. W. J. Fleming
Galsworthy, J. Jocelyn
Nat R 30:38 Ja 6 '78. R. K. Bryant
Galvin, B. No time for good reasons
Poetry 130:167-8 Je '77. E. Butscher
Gambasin, A. Religione e società dalle riforme napoleoniche all'età liberale: clero, sinodi e laicato cattolico in Italia. 1974
Am Hist R 82:384-5 Ap '77. R. Grew
Ganelin, R. Sh. Sovetsko-amerikanskie otnosheniia v kontse 1917—nachale 1918 g. 1975
Am Hist R 82:1297-8 D '77. R. K. Debo
Gantsch, E. and Waddington, C. H. eds. Evolution and consciousness: human systems in transition. 1976
BioScience 27:486+ Jl '77. F. E. Yates
García Cárcel, R. Orígenes de la Inquisición española: el tribunal de Valencia, 1478-1530. 1976
Am Hist R 82:987-8 O '77. P. J. Hauben
García Marquéz, G. Autumn of the patriarch
Chr Cent 94:19 Ja 5 '77. A. P. Klausler
Nat R 29:620+ My 27 '77. R. De Feo
García Marquéz, G. One hundred years of solitude
New Repub 176:35-6 Ap 9 '77. A. Weinblatt
Garden, M. Lyon et les lyonnais au XVIIIe siècle. 1975
Am Hist R 82:368-9 Ap '77. T. F. Sheppard
Gardiner, C. H. Japanese and Peru, 1873-1973. 1975
Am Hist R 82:228-9 F '77. J. E. Worrall
Gardiner, M. Deadly innocents: portraits of children who kill. 1976
Ann Am Acad 429:181-2 Ja '77. J. M. MacDonald
Nat R 29:280-1 Mr 4 '77. J. Kiley
Gardner, J. Life and times of Chaucer
America 136:469-70 My 21 '77. T. A. McVeigh
Newsweek 89:99+ Ap 11 '77. W. Clemons
Sat R 4:46+ Ap 16 '77. A. Quinton
Time 109:96+ My 16 '77. J. Skow
Yale R 67:100-6 O '77. E. T. Donaldson
Gardner, J. October light
Chr Today 21:28 F 18 '77. C. Forbes
Commonweal 104:89 F 4 '77. T. LeClair
New Repub 176:30-2 F 5 '77. J. Hendin
Progressive 41:59-60 F '77. R. Rubenstein
Gardner, J. Poetry of Chaucer
America 136:469-70 My 21 '77. T. A. McVeigh
Newsweek 89:99+ Ap 11 '77. W. Clemons
Yale R 67:100-6 O '77. E. T. Donaldson
Gardner, J. F. Experiment of knowledge
Commonweal 104:249-52 Ap 15 '77. G. W. Shea
Gardner, M. Incredible Dr. Matrix: the world's greatest numerologist
Am Scholar 46:538-43 Aut '77. E. Rothstein
Sci Am 236:145 My '77. P. Morrison
Garliński, J. Fighting Auschwitz: the resistance movement in the concentration camp. 1975
Am Hist R 81:1168-9 D '76. D. S. Wyman
Garner, A. Stone book
Horn Bk 53:479-82 Ag '77. A. Chambers
Garner, P. Emile Gallé
Craft Horiz 37:32-6+ Ag '77. H. Littleton
Garson, B. All the livelong day: the meaning and demeaning of routine work. 1975
M Labor R 100:77 O '77. V. E. Schein
Garvey, C. Play
Psychol Today 11:94+ Ag '77. J. Steinberg
Garvey, J. Saints for confused times
Commonweal 104:446 Jl 8 '77. B. Mutkoski
Gascoigne, B. and Gascoigne, C. Christians
America 137:487 D 31 '77. C. P. Loughran
Gaskell, J. Serpent, the dragon, Atlan, the city, some summer lands
Ms 6:36-8 S '77. A. K. Turner
Gass, W. On being blue: a philosophical inquiry
Nation 224:118-19 Ja 29 '77. P. Stevick
Gasster, M. China's struggle to modernize. 1972
Am Hist R 81:1198-200 D '76. S. M. Jones
Gaunt, D. Utbildning till statens tjänst: en kollektivbiografi av stormaktstidens hovrättsauskultanter. 1975
Am Hist R 82:1271 D '77. G. C. Schoolfield
Gaustad E. S. ed. Rise of Adventism: religion and society in mid-nineteenth-century America. 1975
Am Hist R 81:1248 D '76. C. Wright
Gavin, T. Kingkill
Time 109:85 Je 20 '77. P. Gray
Gavoty, B. Frederic Chopin
Newsweek 90:75-7 S 5 '77. M. Jefferson
Gay, P. Art and act: on causes in history—Manet, Gropius, Mondrian. 1976
Art N 76:52+ N '77. M. L. Gibbs
Am Hist R 82:61 F '77. M. F. Deshmukh
New Yorker 53:121-5 F 21 '77. J. Updike
Gay, P. Freud, Jews and other Germans: master and victims in modernist culture
New Repub 177:40-1 N 26 '77. G. L. Mosse
Gaylin, W. Caring
Commonweal 105:20-2 Ja 6 '78. C. A. Weber
Sat Eve Post 249:78 Mr '77. A. McGlinn
Geanakoplos, D. J. Interaction of the sibling Byzantine and western cultures in the Middle Ages and Italian renaissance. 1976
Am Hist R 82:616-17 Je '77. A. R. Lewis
Gehrels, T. ed. Jupiter: studies of the interior, atmosphere, magnetosphere and satellites. 1976
Science 196:153 Ap 8 '77. J. W. Warwick
Geiss, I. German foreign policy, 1871-1914. 1976
Am Hist R 82:1003-4 O '77. L. Cecil
Gelatt, R. Fabulous phonograph, 1877-1977. 3d ed.
Hi Fi 27:50 S '77. R. Long
Gelpi, D. L. Charism and sacrament: a theology of Christian conversion. 1976
Chr Today 22:45-6 O 7 '77. L. W. Hurtado
General relativity and gravitation; proceedings of conference, Tel-Aviv, 1974; ed. by G. Shaviv and J. Rosen. 1975
Science 195:282 Ja 21 '77. D. M. Eardley
Geophysics of the Pacific Ocean Basin and its margin; papers from symposium, Honolulu, 1974; ed by G. H. Sutton and others. 1976
Science 196:519 Ap 29 '77. P. Lonsdale
George, J. C. Going to the sun
Conservationist 31:42 My '77. M. H. Cahall
George, S. How the other half dies: the real reasons for world hunger
Natur Hist 86:118-21 O '77. D. Morgan
Smithsonian 8:157-9 O '77. M. Yudelman
Georgiev, V. A. Vneshniaia politika Rossii na Blizhnem Vostoke v kontse 30—nachale 40-kh godov XIX v. 1975
Am Hist R 82:694-5 Je '77. E. W. Brooks
Geraldes, A. ed. Effects of interferon on cells, viruses and the immune system. 1975
BioScience 27:817 D '77. J. V. Marcus
Gerber, D. A. Black Ohio and the color line, 1860-1915. 1977
Am Hist R 82:1079-80 O '77. L. H. Fishel, jr
Gérin, W. Elizabeth Gaskell
Yale R 66:432-43 Mr '77. P. M. Spacks
Gerlach, L. R. Prologue to independence: New Jersey in the coming of the American revolution. 1976
Am Hist R 82:430-1 Ap '77. M. M. Klein
Gerlach, R. L. Immigrants in the Ozarks: a study in ethnic geography. 1976
Am Hist R 82:759-60 Je '77. F. C. Luebke
Gerson, L. D. Secret police in Lenin's Russia. 1976
Ann Am Acad 431:158 My '77. F. A. Miller
Gerster, G. Grand design: the earth from above
Sci Am 236:138-40 Je '77. P. Morrison
Gessner, D. Agraverbände in der Weimarer Republik: wirtschaftliche und soziale Voraussetzungen agrarkonservativer Politik vor 1933. 1976
Am Hist R 82:669 Je '77. A. Kovan
Gettleman, S. and Markowitz, J. Courage to divorce
Psychol Today 10:49 Ap '77. E. Dienstag
Giannone, R. Vonnegut: a preface to his novels
America 137:365-6 N 19 '77. B. Mutkoski
Gibbons, B. Wye Island: outsiders, insiders and resistance to change. 1977
Am For 83:20-2+ N '77. D. J. Preston
Bus W p 14+ Je 20 '77. R. Stollman
Smithsonian 8:98-9 Ag '77. D. Sleeper
Gibbs, A. and Harrison, B. Plant virology: the principles. 1976
BioScience 27:422 Je '77. K. Maramorosch
Gibbs, N. H. Grand strategy, v 1: Rearmament policy. 1976
Am Hist R 82:642 Je '77. R. P. Shay, Jr.
Gibert, S. P. Soviet images of America. 1977
Ann Am Acad 434:220-1 N '77. F. B. Marbut

Gibson, J. R. Imperial Russia in frontier America: the changing geography of supply of Russian America, 1784-1867. 1976
Am Hist R 82:178 F '77. C. M. Foust
Gibson, W. M. and Pollard, B. R. Symmetry principles in elementary particle physics. 1976
Phys Today 30:54-5 F '77. A. Zee
Giddens, A. New rules of the sociological method: a positive critique of interpretive sociologies. 1976
Ann Am Acad 432:178 Jl '77. G. H. Conklin
Gifford, T. Man from Lisbon
Bus W p 11 N 7 '77. G. L. Williams
Gilabert, F. M. La abolición de la Inquisición en España. 1975
Am Hist R 82:375 Ap '77. G. M. Addy
Gilbert, A. D. Religion and society in industrial England: church, chapel and social change, 1740-1914. 1976
Am Hist R 82:637-8 Je '77. T. Laqueur
Gilbert, F. ed. Bankiers, Künstler und Gelehrte: unveröffentlichte Briefe der Familie Mendelssohn aus dem 19. Jahrhundert. 1975
Am Hist R 82:662-3 Je '77. W. Weber
Gilbert, M. Winston S. Churchill, v5: 1922-1939, the prophet of truth. 1977
Am Hist R 82:1259 D '77. H. R. Winkler
New Repub 176:58 My 21 '77. P. Terzian
Giles, E. and Friedlaender, J. S. eds. Measures of man: methodologies in biological anthropology. 1976
Science 197:450-1 Jl 29 '77. C. E. Oxnard
Gilkey, L. Reaping the whirlwind: a Christian interpretation of history
America 137:154 S 17 '77. M. O. Boyle
Chr Cent 94:1008 N 2 '77. D. P. McCann
Gill, B. Here at the New Yorker
New Repub 176:35-6 Mr 12 '77. M. da Vinci
Gill, B. Lindbergh alone
New Repub 176:37 Ap 2 '77. P. Terzian
Sat R 4:40-2 Ap 16 '77. A. Whitman
Gillies, O. Who do you think you are?
Nation 224:341-3 Mr 19 '77. P. Green
Gillis, J. R. Development of European society, 1770-1870. 1977
Am Hist R 82:1236-7 D '77. P. N. Stearns
Gilman, A. Later prehistory of Tangier, Morocco. 1975
Science 195:672 F 18 '77. D. Lubell
Gilmore, G. Ages of American law
America 136:532-inside back cover Je 11 '77. J. J. Paris
Gilpin, J. Pleasure and business in western Pennsylvania: the journal of Joshua Gilpin, 1809; ed. by J. E. Walker. 1975
Am Hist R 81:1236 D '76. J. W. Cox
Gimbel, J. Origins of the Marshall plan. 1976
Ann Am Acad 431:142-3 My '77. C. W. Hines
Gimpel, J. Medieval machine: the industrial revolution of the Middle Ages. 1976
Am Hist R 82:933-4 O '77. L. Dresbeck
Ginsberg, A. Beat diary; ed. by A. Knight and K. Knight
New Repub 177:33-5 O 22 '77. R. Kostelanetz
Ginsberg, A. Journals: early fifties, early sixties; ed. by G. Ball
Nation 225:500-1 N 12 '77. R. Elman
New Repub 177:33-5 O 22 '77. R. Kostelanetz
Ginzburg, V. L. Key problems of physics and astrophysics. 1976
Phys Today 30:57 Jl '77. J. L. Greenstein
Giscard d'Estaing, V. Démocratie française
New Repub 176:31-2 Ja 29 '77. P. McCarthy
Gladstone, W. E. Gladstone diaries; v3: 1840-1847, v4: 1848-1854; ed by M. R. D. Foot and H. C. G. Mattrew. 1974, 1975
Am Hist R 82:635-7 Je '77. R. K. Webb
Glanz, R. Jewish woman in America: two female immigrant generations, 1820-1929, v2: The German Jewish woman. 1977
Am Hist R 82:1084-5 O '77. P. E. Hyman
Glaser, E. M. Productivity gains through work-life improvement. 1976
M Labor R 100:64-5 My '77. G. Sherman
Glendinning, V. Elizabeth Bowen
Time 111:76-7 Ja 16 '78. F. Gray
Glock, C. Y. and Bellah, R. N. eds. New religious consciousness. 1976
Chr Cent 94:792+ S 14 '77. W. A. Johnson
Commonweal 104:347-9 My 27 '77. P. R. Messbarger
Society 14:94-5 Jl '77. W. C. Roof
Glynn, S. and Oxborrow, J. Interwar Britain: a social and economic history. 1976
Am Hist R 82:362-3 Ap '77. P. B. Johnson
Gnudi, M. T. ed. and tr. Various and ingenious machines of Agostino Ramelli
Sci Am 236:128 F '77. P. Morrison
Gokhale, N. R. Hailstorms and hailstone growth
Sci Am 237:32 O '77. P. Morrison
Gold, V. PR as in President
Nat R 29:1184-5 O 14 '77. R. Brookhiser
Goldberg, R. L. Systems approach to library program development. 1976
Lib J 102:1257 Je 1 '77. L. Vagianos
Goldblatt, B. Newport Jazz Festival: the illustrated history
Am Rec G 41:51-2 N '77. C. Graham
Goldemberg, I. Fragmented life of Don Jacobo Lerner
Newsweek 89:103 My 9 '77. M. Jefferson
Golden, F. Quasars, pulsars, and black holes. 1976
Sky & Tel 53:130 F '77. M. R. Chartrand, 3d
Goldin, C. D. Urban slavery in the American South, 1820-1860: a quantitative history. 1976
Am Hist R 82:746-7 Je '77. D. R. Goldfield
Ann Am Acad 432:188-9 Jl '77. P. L. Eisenberg
Goldin, M. Why they give: American Jews and their philanthropies
Commentary 64:84+ S '77. M. L. Raphael
Goldman, R. B. Work experiment: six Americans in a Swedish plant. 1976
Society 14:86-7 S '77. W. H. Friedland
Goldsmith, M. and Shaw, E. Europe's giant accelerator: the story of CERN 400 GeV proton synchroton. 1977
Science 197:1175 S 16 '77. A. Roberts
Goldstene, P. N. Collapse of liberal empire: science and revolution in the twentieth century
Nat R 29:501-2 Ap 29 '77. D. Vree
New Repub 178:31-3 Ja 7 '78. A. Tonelson
Gombrich, E. H. Heritage of Apelles
Art N 76:120 O '77. C. E. Gilbert
New Yorker 53:132+ Ap 4 '77. G. Steiner
Gomez, J. Ken Russell: the adaptor as creator
Film Q 31:19-24 Wint '77. M. Dempsey
Gonzalez-Aller, F. Niña Huanca; tr. by M. S. Peden
Time 109:106+ My 23 '77. R. Z. Sheppard
Goodall, D. W. ed. Evolution of desert biota. 1976
BioScience 27:208 Mr '77. R. Dmi'el
Goodell, R. Visible scientists. 1977
Phys Today 30:65-6 N '77. R. W. Nichols
Science 197:977 S 2 '77. G. Basalla
Goodfield, J. Playing God: genetic engineering and the manipulation of life. 1977
Newsweek 90:96+ O 3 '77. P. Gwynne
Psychol Today 11:122+ S '77. R. Restak
Science 198:1144-5 D 16 '77. R. M. May
Goodrum, C. A. Dewey decimated
Am Lib 8:196 Ap '77. A. Plotnik
Goodwin, P. N. and Rao, D. V. Introduction to the physics of nuclear medicine. 1977
Phys Today 30:58+ Je '77. D. R. Shearer
Goodwyn, L. Democratic promise: the Populist movement in America. 1976
Am Hist R 82:753-4 Je '77. R. G. McMath
Intellect 106:88-9 Ag '77. K. D. Bicha
New Repub 176:23-5 F 12 '77. J. Prude
New Yorker 52:114-19 F 7 '77. R. Coles
Progressive 41:56-7 F '77. R. A. Rosenstone
Goody, J. and others. eds. Family and inheritance: rural society in Western Europe, 1200-1800. 1976
Am Hist R 82:943-4 O '77. J. L. Goldsmith.
Gopal, S. Jawaharlal Nehru: a biography, v 1: 1889-1947. 1976
Am Hist R 82:422-3 Ap '77. E. R. Irschick
Gordenker, L. International aid and national decisions: development programs in Malawi, Tanzania, and Zambia. 1976
Ann Am Acad 431:143-4 My '77. D. D. Reynolds
Gordon, B. Political economy in Parliament, 1819-1823. 1977
Am Hist R 82:1247 D '77. R. K. Huch
Gordon, D. J. Literary art and the unconscious
Yale R 66:v+ Je '77
Gordon, L. Woman's body, woman's right: a social history of birth control in America. 1976
Am Hist R 82:1095 O '77 J. S. Lemons
Goslich, S. Die deutsche romantische Oper. 1975
Mus Q 62:603-7 O '76. A. S. Garlington, Jr
Gosling, N. Nadar. 1976
Art in Am 65:39 N '77. B. Lifson
Sat R 4:44-7 F 19 '77. M. R. Weiss
Goubert, P. Clio parmi les hommes: recueil d'articles. 1976
Am Hist R 82:979-80 O '77. W. H. Beik
Gould, C. Paintings of Correggio
Yale R 67:115-21 O '77. E. P. Pillsbury
Gould, S. J. Ever since Darwin
Newsweek 90:104+ N 14 '77. M. Jefferson
Gouldner, A. W. Dialectic of ideology and technology: the origins, grammar, and future of ideology. 1976
Ann Am Acad 433:189-90 S '77. T. J. Knight
Grade, C. Yeshiva; tr. by C. Leviant
Commentary 63:70-3 Ap '77. R. R. Wisse
New Repub 176:24-5 F 26 '77. I. Howe
Graglia, L. A. Disaster by decree: the Supreme court decisions on race and the schools. 1976
Ann Am Acad 430:208-10 Mr '77. J. W. Lamare
Graham, B. How to be born again
Time 110:67-8 Jl 25 '77
Graham, F. Alias program
Bus W p 13+ O 10 '77. J. R. Silkenat
Graham, I. Corpus of Maya hieroglyphic inscriptions, v2 pt 1. 1975
Sci Am 237:46 S '77. P. Morrison
Graham, J. T. Donoso Cortés: utopian romanticist and political realist. 1974
Am Hist R 82:375-6 Ap '77. I. M. Zavala
Gransden, A. Historical writing in England, c. 550 to c. 1307. 1974
Am Hist R 82:75 F '77. B. S. Bachrach

Grant, C. H. Making of modern Belize: politics, society, and British colonialism in Central America. 1976
Am Hist R 82:1105 O '77. W. M. Clegern
Grant, M. Jesus: an historian's review of the gospels
America 137:83 Ag 13 '77. D. J. Harrington
Commonweal 105:22-3 Ja 6 '78. W. P. Loewe
Grant, M. Saint Paul. 1976
Am Hist R 82:71 F '77. J. E. Rexine
Commonweal 104:442-4 Jl 8 '77. J. A. Fitzmyer
Grant, V. Organismic evolution. 1977
Science 197:1272-3 S 23 '77. H. L. Carson
Graves, E. B. ed. Bibliography of English history to 1485. 1975
Am Hist R 82:341 Ap '77. A. Koren
Graves, R. New collected poems
Yale R 67:72, 79-81 O '77. H. Vendler
Gray, D. Women of the West. 1976
Am West 14:53 Jl '77. P. Herr
Gray, J. S. Centennial campaign: the Sioux war of 1876. 1976
Am West 14:59 S '77. J. Burrows
Gray, R. ed. Cambridge history of Africa, v4: from c. 1600 to c. 1790. 1975
Am Hist R 82:709-10 Je '77. R. W. July
Gray, R. Q. Labour aristocracy in Victorian Edinburgh. 1976
Am Hist R 82:360 Ap '77. T. R. Tholfsen
Grayhill, F. C. and Boesen, V. Edward Sheriff Curtis: visions of a vanishing race. 1976
Am West 14:64 My '77. J. C. Ewers
Grechko, A. A. and others. Istoriia vtoroi mirovoi voiny, 1939-1945. v 1-3. 1973, 1974
Am Hist R 81:1182-3 D '76. W. J. Spahr
Grechko, A. A. and others. Istoriia vtoroi mirovoi voiny, 1939-1945. v 4-6 1975, 76
Am Hist R 82:1027 O '77. W. J. Spahr
Greeley, A. M. American Catholic: a social portrait
America 136:338-40 Ap 9 '77. J. A. Coleman
Commonweal 104:541-3 Ag 19 '77. M. A. Neal
Nat R 29:444-5 Ap 15 '77. M. J. Sobran, Jr
Greeley, A. M. Communal Catholic
Commonweal 104:312-14 My 13 '77. J. Cunneen
Greeley, A. M. Neighborhood
Nation 225:729-31 D 31 '77. C. McWilliams
Greeley, R. and Carr, M. H. eds. Geological basis for the exploration of the planets. 1976
Sky & Tel 54:52-3 Jl '77. J. K. Beatty
Green, M. Transatlantic patterns: cultural comparisons of England with America
New Repub 176:33-4 Je 25 '77. J. S. Allen
Green, W. A. British slave emancipation: the sugar colonies and the great experiment, 1830-1865. 1976
Am Hist R 82:480 Ap '77. F. W. Knight
Greenberg, D. Crime and law enforcement in the colony of New York, 1691-1776. 1976
Am Hist R 82:732-3 Je '77. P. U. Bonomi
Greenberg, J. Founder's praise. 1976
Horn Bk 53:341 Je '77. M. S. Cosgrave
Greene, V. For God and country: the rise of Polish and Lithuanian ethnic consciousness in America, 1860-1910. 1975
Am Hist R 81:1259-60 D '76. F. Renkiewicz
Greenhill, B. and others. Archaeology of the boat: a new introductory study; introd. by W. F. Grimes. 1976
Am Hist R 82:606-7 Je '77. L. Casson.
Greenough, W. C. and King, F. P. Pension plans and public policy. 1976
Ann Am Acad 433:204-5 S '77. I. P. Wolf
M Labor R 100:58-9 N '77. W. Bechill
Greenway, J. American tradition: a gallery of rogues
Nat R 29:781 Jl 8 '77. M. J. Sobran
Gregor, A. Past now
Poetry 130:47-9 Ap '77. J. D. McClatchy
Gregory, F. W. Nathan Appleton: merchant and entrepreneur, 1779-1861. 1976
Am Hist R 81:1228-9 D '76. E. J. Perkins
Gregory, K. ed. Your obedient servant: a selection of the most witty, amusing and memorable letters to the Times' of London 1900-1975
New Yorker 52:109-12 Ja 17 '77. M. Panter-Downes
Greig, W. General report on the Gosford estates in County Armagh, 1821; introd. by F. M. L. Thompson and D. Tierney. 1976
Am Hist R 82:975 O '77. L. P. Curtis, jr
Grekulov, E. F. ed. Religüa i tserkov'v istorii rossii (sovetskie istoriki o pravoslavnoi tserkvi v rossii). 1975
Am Hist R 82:691 Je '77. S. A. Zenkovsky
Gribbin, J. Our changing universe
Sky & Tel 53:468-9 Je '77. N. Cohen
Grieb, K. J. Latin American policy of Warren G. Harding. 1976
Am Hist R 82:761 Je '77. D. Healy
Griffin, D. R. God, power, and evil: a process theodicy
Chr Cent 94:961-2 O 19 '77. K. Hamilton
Griffin, D. R. Question of animal awareness: evolutionary continuity of mental experience. 1976
BioScience 27:360-1 My '77. C. G. Beer
Griffin, P. E. Chinese Communist treatment of counterrevolutionaries: 1924-1949
Am Hist R 82:415-16 Ap '77. P. M. Coble, Jr
Grigg, D. B. Agricultural systems of the world: an evolutionary approach. 1974
Am Hist R 81:1069 D '76. G. T. Sharrer
Grigorenko, P. G. Grigorenko papers: writings by General P. G. Grigorenko and documents on his case
America 137:36-7 Jl 16 '77. C. Hughes
Grimes, O. F. Jr. Housing for low-income urban families: economics and policy in the developing world. 1976
Ann Am Acad 430:222-3 Mr '77. W. F. Smith
M Labor R 100:58-9 Ag '77. W. H. Leahy
Grimm, J., and Grimm, W. Sleeping beauty; il. by T. S. Hyman. 1977
Horn Bk 53:659 D '77. M. M. Burns
Grindle, M. S. Bureaucrats, politicians, and peasants in Mexico: a case study in public policy. 1977
Am Hist R 82:1375 D '77. H. G. Campbell
Gripe, M. Green coat; tr. by S. La Farge. 1977
Horn Bk 53:539 O '77. P. Heins
Gripe, M. In the time of the bells; il. by H. Gripe. 1976
Horn Bk 53:51 F '77. S. H. Holtze
Grivet, P. Microwave circuits and amplifiers: the physics of transmission lines at high and very high frequencies, v2. 1976
Phys Today 30:68 Mr '77. F. E. Borgnis
Gröbli, F. Ambassador Du Luc und der Trücklibund von 1715: französische Diplomatie und eidgenössisches Gleichgewicht in den letzten Jahren Ludwigs XIV. 2v. 1975
Am Hist R 82:677 Je '77. W. Roosen
Grolle, C. G. Complete guide to electrical and electronic repairs. 1976
Consumers Res Mag 60:20 S '77
Gross, B. and Gross, R. eds. Children's rights movement: overcoming the oppression of young people
America 137:198+ O 1 '77. G. M. Anderson
Psychol Today 10:110+ My '77. J. K. Footlick
Gross, J.-P. Saint-Just, sa politique et ses missions. 1976
Am Hist R 82:369-70 Ap '77. M. Kennedy
Grossman, A. And the dew lay all night upon my branch
Poetry 130:50-2 Ap '77. J. D. McClatchy
Grossman, L. Democratic Party and the Negro: northern and national politics, 1868-92. 1976
Am Hist R 82:443 Ap '77. M. L. Benedict
Grossmann, W. Johann Christian Edelmann: from orthodoxy to Enlightenment. 1976
Am Hist R 82:1273-4 D '77. R L. Harrison, jr
Grosul, G. S. Dunaiskie kniazhestva v politike Rossii, 1774-1806. 1975
Am Hist R 82:1293-4 D '77. O. Subtelny
Growing points in ethology; proceedings of conference, Cambridge, 1975; ed. by P. P. Bateson and R. A. Hinde. 1976
Science 195:671-2 F 18 '77. H. S. Hoffman
Gruber, C. S. Mars and Minerva: World War I and the uses of the higher learning in America. 1976
Am Hist R 82:202 F '77. S. Herman
Grugel, L. E. George Jacob Holyoake: a study in the evolution of a Victorian radical. 1976
Am Hist R 82:358 Ap '77. W. L. Arnstein
Grun, P. Cytoplasmic genetics and evolution. 1976
BioScience 27:360 My '77. K. P. Van Winkle-Swift
Gudeman, S. Relationships, residence and the individual: a rural Panamanian community. 1976
Ann Am Acad 432:178-9 Jl '77. S. Leacock
Guest, I. Divine Virginia: a biography of Virginia Zucchi. 1976
Dance Mag 51:74 N '77. S. J. Cohen
Guest, J. Ordinary people
Yale R 66:584-91 Je '77. D. Thorburn
Guiliano, E. ed. Lewis Carroll observed: a collection of unpublished photographs, drawings, poetry and new essays. 1976
Commonweal 104:439-41 Jl 8 '77. R. Phillips
Horn Bk 53:462 Ag '77. M. C. Livingston
Guillemin, J. Urban renegades: the cultural strategy of American Indians. 1975
Ann Am Acad 431:165-6 My '77. J. R. Conlin
Guillermaz, J. Chinese Communist Party in power, 1949-1976; tr. by A. Destenay
America 136:509-10 Je 4 '77. J. W. Witek
Nation 225:22 Jl 2 '77. N. D. Milton and D. Milton
Guinness, A. E. ed. Joy of nature, how to observe and appreciate the great outdoors. 1977
Am For 83:45-6 D '77. J. P. Jackson
Guinness, O. In two minds. 1976
Chr Today 22:33-4 D 30 '77. J. M. Houston
Güiraldes, R. Don Segundo Sombra
Americas 29:2-5 Ap '77. E. A. Echevarría
Guralnik, S. M. Science and the ante-bellum American college. 1975
Am Hist R 82:742-3 Je '77. A. H. Dupree
Gurley, J. G. China's economy and the Maoist strategy
Nation 225:23 Jl 2 '77. N. D. Milton and D. Milton

Gurnham, R. History of the trade union movement in the hosiery and knitwear industry, 1776-1976. 1976
Am Hist R 82:359 Ap '77. R. A. Church
Gurr, T. R. Rogues, rebels, and reformers: a political history of urban crime and conflict. 1976
Ann Am Acad 432:179-80 Jl '77. J. C. Snell
Gurr, T. R. and others. Politics of crime and conflict: a comparative history of four cities. 1977
Am Hist R 82:1216-17 D '77. E. Monkkonen
Ann Am Acad 434:201-2 N '77. D. LeFave
Gusev, K. V. Partiia eserov: ot melkoburzhuaznogo revoliutsionarizma k kontrrevoliutsii. 1975
Am Hist R 82:703 Je '77. M. Melançon
Gustavson, C. G. Mansion of history. 1976
Am Hist R 82:331-2 Ap '77. L. J. Goldstein
Gutman, H. G. Black family in slavery and freedom, 1750-1925. 1976
Am Hist R 82:744-5 Je '77. D. B. Davis
Am Scholar 46:384+ Summ '77. J. D. Anderson
America 136:340-1 Ap 9 '77. H. X. Connolly
Commonweal 104:666-7 O 14 '77. C. P. Ripley
Gutman, H. G. Work, culture, and society in industrializing America: essays in American working-class and social history. 1976
Am Hist R 82:195-6 F '77. D. Brody
Gutteridge, D. Jr. Defense rests its case. 1975
Chr Today 21:27 Jl 8 '77. R. Cleath
Gutteridge, R. German evangelical church and the Jews, 1879-1950. 1976
Am Hist R 82:1000-1 O '77. D. R. Borg

Haak, B. Rembrandt drawings
Am Artist 41:26+ Je '77. A. Werner
Habachi, L. Obelisks of Egypt: skyscrapers of the past
Sci Am 237:36 D '77. P. Morrison and P. Morrison
Hacker, F. J. Crusaders, criminals, crazies: terror and terrorism in our time
New Repub 176:27-30 My 14 '77. M. Syrkin
Sat R 4:30-1 F 5 '77. J. Schreiber
Hacker, M. Separations
Poetry 129:292-3 F '77. R. Holland
Hacker, P. M. S. and Raz, J. eds. Law, morality and society: essays in honour of H. L. A. Hart
America 137:488 D 31 '77. T. M. Gannon
Haferkorn, F. Soziale Vorstellungen Heinrich von Sybels. 1976
Am Hist R 82:999 O '77. C. E. McCelland
Haffenden, P. S. New England and the English nation, 1689-1713. 1974
Am Hist R 82:170-1 F '77. S. S. Webb
Hagan, W. T. United States—Comanche relations: the reservation years. 1976
Am West 14:55 Jl '77. C. Miner
Hagel, J. 3d. Alternative energy strategies: constraints and opportunities. 1976
Ann Am Acad 433:202-3 S '77. S. P. Gupta and M. C. Gupta
Hahn, E. Mabel: a biography of Mabel Dodge Luhan
Newsweek 89:103+ My 9 '77. M. Jefferson
Haines, G. K. What makes a lemon sour? il. by J. McCaffery. 1977
Horn Bk 53:467 Ag '77. H. Stubbs
Hair, W. I. Carnival of fury: Robert Charles and the New Orleans race riot of 1900. 1976
Am Hist R 82:460-1 Ap '77. R. V. Haynes
Haites, E. F. and others. Western river transportation: the era of early internal development, 1810-1860. 1975
Am Hist R 81:1237 D '76. J. H. Krenkel
Ann Am Acad 429:193 Ja '77. J. P. Maddex, Jr.
Halbach, A. J. Die Südafrikanischen Bantu-Homelands: Konzeption, Struktur, Entwicklungsperspektiven. 1976
Am Hist R 82:1040 O '77. L. H. Gann
Hale, J. R. ed. Renaissance Venice. repr. 1976
Am Hist R 82:140-1 F '77. E. Muir
Halebsky, S. Mass society and political conflict: toward a reconstruction theory. 1976
Ann Am Acad 433:164-5 S '77. H. G. Reid
Hales, E. E. Y. Chariot of fire
Time 109:91-2 Mr 7 '77. M. Mohs
Haley, A. Roots: the saga of an American family
America 136:341-2 Ap 9 '77. C. Holt
Chr Today 21:19-22 My 6 '77
Horn Bk 53:342 Je '77. M. S. Cosgrave
Ms 5:45 F '77. L. Clifton
Nat R 29:278-9 Mr 4 '77. A. Crawford
New Yorker 52:112+ F 14 '77. J. Anderson
Yale R 67:144-6 O '77. M. G. Cooke
Halkin, H. Letters to an American Jewish friend: a Zionist's polemic
Commentary 64:50-6 Ag '77. R. Alter
Hall, A. S. Point of entry: a study of client reception in the social services. 1974
Ann Am Acad 430:216 Mr '77. H. L. Witmer
Hall, D. G. E. Henry Burney: a political biography. 1974
Am Hist R 82:166-7 F '77. B. B. Kling
Hall, E. Possible impossibilities: a look at parapsychology. 1977
Horn Bk 53:458 Ag '77. S. H. Holtze

Halle, L. J. Out of chaos. 1977
Am Hist R 82:1209-10 D '77. S. Bailey
Progressive 41:57-8 O '77. W. Grant
Haller, J. S. jr. and Haller, R. M. Physician and sexuality in Victorian America. 1974
Am Hist R 82:1328-9 D '77. L. Gordon
Hallett, R. Africa since 1875: a modern history. 1974
Am Hist R 81:1189-90 D '76. P. Duignan
Halliday, J. Political history of Japanese capitalism. 1975
Am Hist R 82:722 Je '77. W. B. Hauser
Hallman, W. E. ed. So there's a community college in your town: a guide for local church ministry with the nearby community college
Chr Cent 94:459-60 My 11 '77. M. A. Marty
Halperin-Donghi, T. Politics, economics and society in Argentina in the revolutionary period; tr. by R. Southern. 1975
Am Hist R 82:230 F '77. R. A. Potash
Halsey, R. S. Classical music recordings: for home and library. 1976
Lib J 102:1357 Je 15 '77. P. L. Miller
Hamblin, D. J. That was the life. 1977
Pop Phot 81:146+ O '77. J. G. Morris
Hamburger, J. Macaulay and the Whig tradition. 1976
Am Hist R 82:965 O '77. D. D. Goldstein
Hamby, A. L. Imperial years: the United States since 1939. 1976
Am Hist R 82:468 Ap '77. D. R. McCoy
Hamermesh, D. S. Jobless pay and the economy. 1977
M Labor R 100:60 N '77. P. S. Barth
Hamermesh, D. S. Labor in the public and nonprofit sectors. 1975
M Labor R 100:66 Ja '77. D. Bellante
Hamilton, A. Papers of Alexander Hamilton, v24: November 1799-June 1800; ed. by H. C. Syrett. 1976
Am Hist R 82:1325-6 D '77. R. M. Bell
Hamilton, M. W. Sir William Johnson: colonial American, 1715-1763. 1976
Am Hist R 82:432 Ap '77. J. H. O'Donnell, 3d
Hamilton, V. Arilla sun down
Chr Today 21:26 Ap 15 '77. B. M. Greene
Hamm, M. F. ed. City in Russian history. 1976
Am Hist R 81:1173-4 D '76. J. P. McKay
Hammerstein, N. Jus und Historie: ein Beitrag zur Geschichte des historischen Denkens an deutschen Universitaten im späten 17. und im 18. Jahrhundert. 1972
Am Hist R 81:1144-5 D '76. H. P. Liebel
Hammond, J. John Hammond on record; with I. Townsend
Newsweek 90:93 N 7 '77. H. Saal
Hammond, T. T. ed. Anatomy of Communist takeovers. 1975
Am Hist R 82:64-5 F '77. R. V. Burks
Hamscher, A. N. Parlement of Paris after the Fronde, 1653-1673. 1976
Am Hist R 82:977-8 O '77. S. Kettering
Handke, P. Moment of true feeling; tr. by R. Manheim
Nat R 29:1303-4+ N 11 '77. R. De Feo
New Yorker 53:136+ S 26 '77. J. Updike
Sat R 4:22-4 Je 25 '77. S. Kauffmann
Handy, R. T. History of the churches in the United States and Canada
America 136:530-1 Je 11 '77. P. E. Czuchlewski
Chr Cent 94:700 Ag 3 '77. T. Sinclair-Faulkner
Commonweal 104:763-4 N 25 '77. H. W. Bowden
Hanley, J. Dream journey
Nat R 29:341-2 Mr 18 '77. R. De Feo
Hanrahan, J. D. and Gruenstein, P. Lost frontier: the marketing of Alaska
Nation 226:21-2 Ja 7 '78. W. R. Hunt
Hansen, J. P. and McDonald I. R. Theory of simple liquids. 1976
Phys Today 30:71-2 My '77. D. Henderson
Science 197:150-1 Jl 8 '77. B. J. Alder
Hanson, E. D. Origin and early evolution of animals. 1977
Science 198:1146 D 16 '77. A. J. Kohn
Harcourt, P. Six European directors: essays on the meaning of film style. 1974
Film Q 30:49-50 Summ '77. D. Willis
Hard, M. E. Mushroom, edible and otherwise
Horticulture 55:55 Ag '77. W. Tiffney
Hardesty, D. L. Ecological anthropology. 1977
BioScience 27:813 D '77. A. P. Vayda
Hardie, F. Abyssinian crisis. 1974
Am Hist R 81:1194 D '76. A. Iadarola
Hardy, T. Portable Thomas Hardy; with introd. by J. Moynahan
New Repub 177:40-1 O 1 '77. H. C. Webster
Harkabi, Y. Arab strategies and Israel's response
Commentary 64:70+ O '77. E. Grossman
Harkness, G. and Kraft, C. F. Biblical backgrounds of the Middle East conflict
Chr Cent 94:492 My 18 '77. S. J. Cohen
Harlow, L. F. Without fear or favor. 1976
Am City & County 92:78 Ap '77
Harnack, C. Under my wings everything prospers
Newsweek 89:78-9 Je 27 '77. R. Towers
Harnad, S. and others, eds. Lateralization in the nervous system. 1977
BioScience 27:690 O '77. D. Friedman

Harper, C. Introduction to mathematical physics. 1976
Phys Today 30:56 Ap '77. R. D. Young
Harrington, M. Vast majority: a journey to the world's poor
New Repub 178:34-6 Ja 7 '78. S. Kaplan
Harris, A. S. and Nochlin, L. Women artists, 1550-1950. 1977
Am Hist R 82:1215-16 D '77. R. M. Isherwood
Nation 224:285-6 Mr 5 '77. L. Alloway
Yale R 67:x-xi+ O '77
Harris, B. Lover
Ms 5:42 Ap '77. J. Larkin
Harris, C. H. 3d. Mexican family empire: the Latifundio of the Sanchez Navarros, 1765-1867. 1975
Am Hist R 82:224 F '77. A. T. Bryan
Americas 29:24-5 Ap '77. T. G. Powell
Harris, F. R. Potomac fever
New Repub 176:60 My 21 '77. P. Terzian
Progressive 41:39-40 Jl '77. L. Whitten
Harris, M. Cannibals and kings
Newsweek 90:126+ N 21 '77. R. Boeth
Psychol Today 11:130+ O '77. J. Pfeiffer
Harris, R. ed. Political economy of Africa. 1975
Ann Am Acad 429:154-6 Ja '77. J. P. Powelson
Harrison, D. jr. Who pays for clean air: the cost and benefit distribution of federal automobile emission standards. 1975
Ann Am Acad 434:241-2 N '77. G. S. Goldstein
Harrison, G. H. Roger Tory Peterson's dozen birding hot spots; introd by R. T. Peterson. 1976
Am For 83:30+ F '77. M. Bush
Smithsonian 8:153-4 N '77. E. F. Rivinus
Harrison, J. P. Long march to power: a history of the Chinese Communist party, 1921-72. 1972
Am Hist R 81:1200-1 D '76. L. Dittmer
Harrison, K. Framework of Anglo-Saxon history to A.D. 900. 1976
Am Hist R 81:1087-8 D '76. R. Frank
Harrison, W. Africana
Atlantic 239:90 Je '77. E. S. Duvall
Harriss, G. L. King, Parliament, and public finance in medieval England to 1369. 1975
Am Hist R 82:77 F '77. C. R. Young
Hart, D. Thou swell, thou witty
Am Rec G 40:63 D '76. J. Holden
Hart, R. A. Eccentric tradition: American diplomacy in the Far East. 1976
Am Hist R 82:772 Je '77. M. H. Hunt
Hart, R. I. G. in Peking: letters of Robert Hart, Chinese maritime customs, 1868-1907; ed. by J. Fairbank and others. 2v. 1976
Am Hist R 82:159-60 F '77. E. G. Beal, Jr
Hartle, D. L. Our uncertain heritage: genetics and human diversity. 1977
BioScience 27:812 D '77. J. Herrmann
Hartman, M. S. Victorian murderesses: a true history of thirteen respectable French and English women accused of unspeakable crimes. 1977
Am Hist R 82:1237 D '77. K. E. McCrone
Bus W p 14 Ap 18 '77. D. B. Moskowitz
Ms 5:40 Ap '77. A. Jones
New Repub 176:32-3 My 14 '77. J. M. White
Time 109:80+ F 28 '77. P. Blake
Hartt, J. N. Theological method and imagination
Chr Cent 94:1169 D 14 '77. J. P. Crossley, jr
Harvey, J. Black prince and his age. 1976
Am Hist R 82:341 Ap '77. M. Aitschul
Harvey, J. H. and others, eds. New directions in attribution research, v 1. 1976
Science 196:765-6 My 13 '77. M. R. Lepper
Hassler, J. Four miles to Pinecone. 1977
Horn Bk 53:531-2 O '77. A. A. Flowers
Hastings, A. African Christianity
Commonweal 105:26 Ja 6 '78. E. Hillman
Hastings, A. Faces of God: reflections on Church and society
Commonweal 104:574 S 2 '77. D. Dohen
Hatje, A. K. Befolkningsfrågan och välfärden: debatten om familjepolitik och nativitetsökning under 1930-och 1940-talen. 1974
Am Hist R 82:122 F '77. S. Koblik
Hattaway, H. General Stephen D. Lee. 1976
Am Hist R 82:184 F '77. H. B. Hammett
Hatzfeldt, P. G. von. Botschafter Paul Graf von Hatzfeldt: nachgelassene papiere, 1838, 1901; ed. by G. Ebel and M. Behnen. 1976
Am Hist R 82:1001-2 O '77. J. S. Mortimer
Haugaard, E. C. Messenger for Parliament. 1976
Horn Bk 53:55-6 F '77. E. L. Heins
Haupts, L. Deutsche Friedenspolitik, 1918-1919: eine Alternative zur Machtpolitik des Ersten Weltkrieges. 1976
Am Hist R 82:666 Je '77. W. Jannen, Jr
Hawkins, D. Science and ethics of equality
Sci Am 238:28 Ja '78. P. Morrison
Hayden, D. Seven American utopias: the architecture of communitarian socialism, 1790-1975. 1976
Am Hist R 82:1086-7 O '77. H. R. Grant
Hayden, R. Angle of ascent
Poetry 130:226-8 Jl '77. W. Logan
Hayden, S. Voyage
Time 109:82-3 Ja 24 '77. J. Skow
Hayes, B. Midnight express; with W. Hoffer
Newsweek 89:89-90 Mr 7 '77. P. S. Prescott
Haynes, R. V. Night of violence: the Houston riot of 1917. 1976
Am Hist R 82:461 Ap '77. M. E. Fletcher
Hayward, B. Haywire
Harpers 254:77-80 Je '77. A. Sarris
Newsweek 89:76-7 Mr 14 '77. P. S. Prescott
Time 109:91 Mr 28 '77. G. Clarke
Hazen, B. A. Soviet propaganda: a case study of the Middle East conflict. 1976
Ann Am Acad 431:144-5 My '77. D. D. Barry
Hazo, S. Inscripts
Poetry 129:290-2 F '77. R. Holland
Heacox, C. E. Education of an outdoorsman
Conservationist 32:44-5 S '77. A. Woldt
Headley, O. Queen Charlotte. 1976
Am Hist R 82:99 F '77. E. A. Reitan
Healy, D. Gunboat diplomacy in the Wilson era: the U.S. navy in Haiti, 1915-1916. 1976
Am Hist R 81:1266-7 D '76. L. D. Langley
Heaney, S. North
Poetry 129:236-9 Ja '77. R. B. Shaw
Hebblethwaite, P. Runaway church
Commonweal 104:90-2 F 4 '77. J. Garvey
Hebly, J. H. Protestants in Russia. 1976
Chr Today 22:36-7 N 4 '77. A. H. Winquist
Hecht, A. Millions of strange shadows
Nation 225:188-90 S 3 '77. S. Madoff
Poetry 131:103-6 N '77. R. Howard
Hechterm, M. Internal colonialism: the Celtic fringe in British national development. 1975
Ann Am Acad 429:162-3 Ja '77. A. M. Lee
Heckscher, A. and Robinson, P. Open spaces: the life of American cities. 1977
Am City & County 92:65 Jl '77
New Repub 176:51 My 21 '77. W. Von Eckardt
Heeney, B. Different kind of gentleman: parish clergy as professional men in early and mid-Victorian England. 1976
Am Hist R 82:1248 D '77. A. Engel
Heick, W. H. ed. History and myth: Arthur Lower and the making of Canadian nationalism. 1975
Am Hist R 82:218-19 F '77. L. S. Fallis
Heidenheimer, A. J. and others. Comparative public policy: the politics of social choice in Europe and America. 1975
Ann Am Acad 430:193-4 Mr '77. E. S. Einhorn
Heider, K. G. Ethnographic film. 1976
Film Q 31:52-3 Wint '77. B. Nichols
Heighton, E. J. and Cunningham, D. R. Advertising in the broadcasting media. 1976
Intellect 105:285 F '77. R. L. Fischer
Heilman, S. C. Synagogue life: a study in symbolic interaction. 1976
Ann Am Acad 431:175-6 My '77. S. J. Fox
Commentary 63:92-4 Je '77. D. Singer
Heinonen, O. P. and others. Birth defects and drugs in pregnancy. 1977
Science 198:1246 D 23 '77. I. Leck
Heintz, K. M. Retirement communities: for adults only. 1976
Aging 270:44-5 Ap '77
Heinze, R. W. Proclamations of the Tudor kings. 1976
Am Hist R 82:629-31 Je '77. S. E. Lehmberg
Helldorfer, M. ed. Sexuality: a seminar on sexuality and brotherhood
America 137:176 S 24 '77. T. E. Clarke
Heller, N. and Williams, J. Regionalists
Am Artist 41:16+ Je '77. C. Movalli
Heller, R. and Willatt, N. Can you trust your banks?
Bus W p 12+ N 21 '77. T. C. O'Donnell
Heller, W. W. Economy: old myths and new realities. 1976
America 136:115-16 F 5 '77. J. J. Piderit
Commonweal 104:56-9 Ja 21 '77. M. Harrington
Intellect 105:366-7 Ap '77. J. M. Rock
Hellman, L. Scoundrel time; introd by G. Wills
Esquire 88:28+ Ag '77. A. Kazin
Helmer, J. Deadly simple mechanics of society. 1976
Society 14:82-3 My '77. J. L. Stanley
Helmreich, W. B. Wake up, wake up, to do the work of the creator
Commentary 64:72-4 Ag '77. J. H. Lehmann
Hemingway, M. W. How it was
America 136:55-6 Ja 22 '77. B. Reynolds
Hemmings, F. W. Life and times of Emile Zola
New Repub 177:41-3 O 15 '77. G. Brée
Henderson, D. Season of birds
Conservationist 31:42 My '77. W. R. Nelson
Henderson, W. O. Rise of German industrial power, 1834-1914. 1976
Am Hist R 82:124-5 F '77. R. Cameron
Henneman, J. B. Royal taxation in fourteenth-century France: the captivity and ransom of John II, 1356-1370. 1976
Am Hist R 82:1229-30 D '77. F. J. Pegues
Hennig, M. and Jardim, A. Managerial woman. 1977
M Labor R 100:74 D '77. C. Egan
Ms 5:26-7+ Je '77. E. Bernay
Henry, A. F. Nuclear-reactor analysis. 1975
Phys Today 30:53+ Je '77. E. Melkonian
Henry, B. British botanical and horticultural literature before 1800. 3v. 1975
BioScience 27:752-3 N '77. F. G. Meyer.
Henry, C. F. H. God, revelation and authority, v 1, 2. 1976
Chr Today 21:42 Ap 1 '77. R. H. Nash

Henry, C. F. H. God, revelation and authority, v 1: God who speaks and shows: preliminary considerations. 1976
Chr Cent 94:515 My 25 '77. R. R. Caemmerer
Henry, C. F. H. God, revelation and authority, v2: God who speaks and shows: fifteen theses, pt 1. 1976
Chr Cent 94:515 My 25 '77. R. R. Caemmerer
Hentoff, N. Does anybody give a damn? Nat Hentoff on education
Commonweal 104:247-9 Ap 15 '77. R. Kuczkowski
Todays Educ 66:79 N '77. J. Norman
Hentschel, V. Die deutschen Freihändler und der volkswirtschaftliche Kongress, 1858 bis 1885. 1975
Am Hist R 82:997-8 O '77. W. O. Shanahan
Hepburn, H. R. ed. Insect integument. 1976
Science 195:280-1 Ja 21 '77. J. Lai-Fook
Heppenheimer, T. A. Colonies in space. 1977
Chemistry 50:27 N '77. A. M. Russell
Herberg, W. Faith enacted as history: essays in biblical history
Chr Cent 94:826 S 21 '77. W. R. Comstock
Herndon. B. Mary Pickford and Douglas Fairbanks
Newsweek 90:110+ N 28 '77. J. Baker
Herr, M. Dispatches
Atlantic 241:92 Ja '78. B. DeMott
Commonweal 104:788-80 D 9 '77. T. Powers
Harpers 225:108-9 D '77. M. Malone
Sat R 5:36-8 Ja 7 '78. W. Plummer
Time 110:119 N 7 '77. P. Gray
Herrin, L. Rio Loja ringmaster
New Repub 176:31-2 Je 11 '77. B. Yogoda
Hersey, J. Walnut door
Nat R 29:951-2 Ag 19 '77. W. Plummer
Hershkowitz, L. Tweed's New York: another look. 1977
Am Hist Illus 12:49 D '77. M. Klein
Am Hist R 82:1085 O '77. J. Mushkat
Ann Am Acad 434:228-9 N '77. F. Shaw
Commentary 63:83-6 Mr '77. S. Weaver
Herwig, H. H. Politics of frustration: the United States in German naval planning, 1889-1941. 1976
Am Hist R 82:1005 O '77. K. W. Bird
Hess, J. L. and Hess, K Taste of America
Am Scholar 46:404-8 Summ '77. R. Gay
Hess, S. Organizing the presidency. 1976
Ann Am Acad 432:150-1 Jl '77. C. Grafton
New Repub 176:26-8 F 26 '77. R. G. Tugwell
Hesse, H. and Mann, T. Hesse/Mann letters; ed. by A. Carlsson and V. Michels; tr. by R. Mannheim
Nation 225:309-11 O 1 '77. L. Kriegel
Nation 225:343-6 O 8 '77. L. Kriegel
Hewes, J. E. jr. From Root to McNamara: army organization and administration, 1900-1963. 1976
Am Hist R 82:1092 O '77. D. C. James
Ann Am Acad 434:229-30 N '77. O. W. Eads, jr
Hey, J. S. Radio universe. 1975
Sky & Tel 54:135 Ag '77. G. L. Verschuur
Heyck, T. W. Dimensions of British radicalism: the case of Ireland, 1874-95. 1974
Am Hist R 82:970 O '77. M. R. Temmel
Hick, J. Death and eternal life
America 136:251-2 Mr 19 '77 P. J. Rossi
Hick, J. ed. Myth of God incarnate
America 137:270-1 O 22 '77. J. J. O'Donnell
Chr Cent 94:740-2 Ag 31 '77. T. Beeson
Chr Cent 94:1146-7 D 7 '77. M. L. Peel
Chr Today 21:30+ S 23 '77
Chr Today 22:34-5 N 4 '77. J. R. W. Stott
Hickman, H. ed. Ritual in a new day: an invitation
Chr Cent 94:384-6 Ap 20 '77. J. C. Lyles
Higgins, G. V. Dreamland
Newsweek 90:71-2 Ag 22 '77. M. Stevens
Higgs, R. Competition and coercion: blacks in the American economy, 1865-1914. 1977
Am Hist R 82:1340-1 D '77. J. D. Reid, jr
Higham, C. Adventures of Conan Doyle: the life of the creator of Sherlock Holmes
Yale R 66:432-43 Mr '77. P. M. Spacks
Higham, J. Send these to me: Jews and other immigrants in urban America. 1975
Am Hist R 82:755-6 Je '77. R. J. Vecoli
Higham, R. ed. Intervention or abstention: the dilemma of American foreign policy. 1975
Am Hist R 81:1265 D '76. J. D. Doenecke
Highet, G. Immortal profession: the joys of teaching and learning
Am Scholar 46:258+ Spr '77. W. J. Dannhauser
Highwater, J. Song from the earth: American Indian painting. 1976
Am West 14:58 Mr '77. J. C. Ewers
Higman, B. W. Slave population and economy in Jamaica, 1807-1834. 1976
Am Hist R 82:1104-5 O '77. W. A. Green
Hildebrand, G. C. and Porter, G. Cambodia: starvation and revolution. 1976
Nation 224:789-94 Je 25 '77. N. Chomsky and E. S. Herman
Hill, A. Closed world of love
America 137:311-12 N 5 '77. J. W. Donohue
Hill, B. W. Growth of parliamentary parties, 1689-1742. 1976
Am Hist R 82:962-3 O '77. H. Horwitz
Hill, C. Milton and the English revolution
New Repub 178:30-1 Ja 7 '78. D. Bush
Hill, D. Joseph Smith: the first Mormon
Chr Cent 94:921-2 O 12 '77. L. Foster
New Repub 176:29-31 My 7 '77. J. Seelye
Hill, D. O. and Adamson, R. Early Victorian album: the photographic masterpieces (1843-1847) of David Octavius Hill and Robert Adamson; ed by C. Ford
Smithsonian 8:127-8+ My '77. M. A. Tighe
Hill, E. Greener earth; introd by S. Adams. 1977
Am For 83:34+ N '77. M. Bush
Hill, F. Victorian Lincoln. 1975
Am Hist R 82:639-40 Je '77. L. G. Bailey
Hill, J. D. Civil war sketchbook of Charles Ellery Stedman
New Repub 176:28-9 Je 4 '77. T. Rosengarten
Hill, R. W. Comparative physiology of animals: an environmental approach. 1976
BioScience 27:558 Ag '77. F. L. Strand
Hillaby, J. Journey through love. 1977
Horn Bk 53:468-9 Ag '77. M. S. Cosgrave
Hillgarth, J. N. Spanish kingdoms, 1250-1516, v 1: 1250-1410; precarious balance. 1976
Am Hist R 82:344 Ap '77. R. I. Burns
Himmelberg, R. F. Origins of the National recovery administration: business, government, and the Trade association issue, 1921-1933. 1976
Am Hist R 82:208 F '77. R. D. Cuff
Hindle, B. ed. America's wooden age: aspects of its early technology. 1975
Am Hist R 81:1213 D '76. H. I. Sharlin
Hindley, G. Saladin. 1976
Am Hist R 82:706 Je '77. R. S. Humphreys
Hine, L. W. America & Lewis Hine: photographs 1904-1940; with essay by A. Trachtenberg. 1977
Art in Am 65:39+ N '77. L. Rubinflen
New Repub 177:29-31 O 29 '77. I. Howe
Yale R 66:xviii-xxi Je '77
Hine, L. W. Men at work: photographic studies of modern men and machines
Sci Am 237:36+ D '77. P. Morrison and P. Morrison
Hingley, R. New life of Anton Chekhov
New Repub 176:26-7 Ap 23 '77. J. Beatty
Yale R 66:432-43 Mr '77. P. M. Spacks
Hirsch, F. Social limits to growth: a Twentieth century fund study
Am Scholar 46:230+ Spr '77. M. Mayer
America 136:308 Ap 2 '77. P. D. McNelis
Chr Cent 94:813-15 S 21 '77. J. Bakunin
Progressive 41:42-3 Jl '77. V. Lebow
Hirschman, A. O. Passions and the interests
New Repub 177:33-4 S 24 '77. R. Lekachman
Hirst, S. Life in a narrow place: the Havasupai of the Grand Canyon. 1976
Am West 14:62 S '77. D. G. Pike
Hiss, T. Laughing last: Alger Hiss.
Nat R 29:443-4 Ap 15 '77. W. A. Rusher
Nation 224:405-6 Ap 2 '77. M. Meeropol and R. Meeropol
History of furniture; introd. by F. Watson
Art N 76:106 F '77. C. F. Montgomery
Hitchman, J. Such a strange lady: a biography of Dorothy L. Sayers. 1975
Chr Today 21:38 Mr 4 '77. C. Forbes
Ho, P.-T. Cradle of the East: an inquiry into the indigenous origins of techniques and ideas of neolithic and early historic China, 5000-1000 B.C. 1976
Am Hist R 82:716 Je '77. L. J. Bilsky
Hoak, D. E. King's council in the reign of Edward VI. 1976
Am Hist R 82:352 Ap '77. M. Levine
Hobhouse, J. Everybody who was anybody: a biography of Gertrude Stein
Art N 76:128-9 Mr '77. A. Frankenstein
Hochman, S. Endangered species
Ms 6:39-40+ N '77. C. Betsky
Hockings, P. ed. Principles of visual anthropology. 1975
Film Q 31:51-2 Wint '77. B. Nichols
Hodas, D. Business career of Moses Taylor: merchant, finance capitalist, and industrialist. 1976
Am Hist R 82:1073 O '77. G. Browne
Hodder, I. and Orton, C. Spatial analysis in archaeology. 1976
Science 196:972-3 My 27 '77. G. L. Cowgill
Hodges, C. W. Namesake
Horn Bk 53:477-8 Ag '77. S. Long
Hodges, D. C. Argentina, 1943-1976: the national revolution and resistance. 1976
Am Hist R 82:1111-12 O '77. P. B. Goodwin, jr
Hodgson, G. America in our time
America 136:359-60 Ap 16 '77. F. K. Kelly
Commentary 63:72-4 F '77. E. Abrams
Commonweal 104:758-9 N 25 '77. W. B. Hixson, jr
New Repub 176:52-4 My 21 '77. P. Starr
Progressive 41:57-8 F '77. G. Burnside
Hodgson, M. Quintet: five American dance companies
America 137:172-3 S 24 '77. H. J. Bertels
Hodgson, P. C. New birth of freedom: a theology of bondage and liberation
Chr Cent 94:543 Je 1 '77. F. Herzog
Hoexter, C. K. From Canton to California: the epic of Chinese immigration. 1976
Horn Bk 53:178 Ap '77. A.-L. Louie

Hoffman, A. Property of
Horn Bk 53:561 O '77. M. S. Cosgrave
Newsweek 89:87+ My 23 '77. M. Jefferson
Hoffman, B. R. Luther and the mystics. 1976
Chr Today 21:30 Jl 29 '77. D. G. Bloesch
Hoffman, H. H. Descriptive cataloging in a new light: polemical chapters for librarians. 1976
Lib J 102:692 Mr 15 '77. R. J. Hyman
Hoffmann, P. History of the German resistance, 1933-1945
Newsweek 89:92 Ap 25 '77. P. S. Prescott
Hofsten, E. and Lundström, H. Swedish population history: main trends from 1750 to 1970. 1976
Am Hist R 82:1271-2 D '77. L. K. Berkner
Hogan, M. J. Informal entente: the private structure of cooperation in Anglo-American economic diplomacy, 1918-1928. 1977
Ann Am Acad 434:230-1 N '77. R. A. Karlsrud
Hoke, J. Discovering the world of the three-toed sloth
Sci Am 237:26+ D '77. P. Morrison and P. Morrison
Hokkanen, K. Krieg und Frieden in der politischen Tagesliteratur Deutschlands zwischen Baseler und Lunéviller Frieden (1795-1801). 1975
Am Hist R 82:996-7 O '77. O. Connelly and P. Becker
Holderness, B. A. Pre-industrial England: economy and society, 1500-1750. 1976
Am Hist R 82:1242-3 D '77. E. L. Jones
Holl, A. Death and the devil
Chr Cent 94:514 My 25 '77. P. B. Mather
Holland, C. Two ravens. 1977
Horn Bk 53:469 Ag '77. M. S. Cosgrave
Holland, I. Alan and the animal kingdom. 1977
Horn Bk 53:314-15 Je '77. A. A. Flowers
Holland, J. American journey: a Theology for the Americas working paper
Commonweal 104:598-600 S 16 '77. D. O'Brien
Hollander, J. Reflections on espionage
Poetry 130:41-4 Ap '77. J. D. McClatchy
Holmer, P. L. C. S. Lewis: the shape of his faith and thought. 1976
Chr Cent 94:260 Mr 16 '77. B. F. Wade
Chr Today 21:37 Ja 21 '77. C. Forbes
Commonweal 104:93-4 F 4 '77. M. Zeik
Holmes, G. Good Parliament. 1975
Am Hist R 82:77 F '77. T. Callahan, Jr
Holmes, U. T. 3d. Ministry and imagination
Chr Cent 94:458 My 11 '77. L. Mudge
Commonweal 104:475-7 Jl 22 '77. K. G. O'Connell
Holtzman, E. Lysosomes: a survey. 1976
BioScience 27:288 Ap '77. P. J. Edelson
Holzman, R. S. Adapt or perish: the life of General Roger A. Pryor, C.S.A. 1976
Am Hist R 82:184 F '77. L. J. Graybar
Hook, J. Baroque age in England. 1976
Am Hist R 82:355 Ap '77. H. J. Jensen
Hoopes, J. Van Wyck Brooks: in search of American culture. 1977
Am Hist R 82:1347-8 D '77. A. F. Wertheim
Nation 225:471-4 N 5 '77. J. Lears
Hoover, D. W. Red and the black. 1976
Am Hist R 82:726 Je '77. T. F. Gossett
Hoover, H. M. Delikon. 1977
Horn Bk 53:449-50 Ag '77. A. A. Flowers
Hoover, J. P. Sucre, soldado y revolucionario; tr. by F. Rivera. 1975
Am Hist R 82:480-1 Ap '77. T. Blossom
Hope, J. Yukon
Smithsonian 8:143-4 Ap '77. D. Lancashire
Hopfinger, A. J. Intermolecular interactions and biomolecular organization. 1977
BioScience 27:818 D '77. D.Cowburn
Phys Today 30:59 S '77. E. Pollard
Hoppe, A. Tiddling tennis theorem
Sports Illus 47:8 Ag 8 '77. J. D. Reed
Hopper, R. J. Early Greeks. 1977
Am Hist R 82:926 O '77. C. G. Thomas
Horan, J. D. Authentic wild West: the gunfighters. 1976
Am West 14:62 Ja '77. K. L. Steckmesser
Horgan, P. Thin mountain air
Newsweek 90:96+ S 12 '77. R. Boeth
Horn, M. World encyclopedia of the comics
Commonweal 104:378-80 Je 10 '77. B. Hogarth
Horowitz, D. L. Courts and social policy
America 136:452 My 14 '77. J. J. Paris
Horowitz, H. L. Culture and the city: cultural philanthropy in Chicago from the 1880s to 1917. 1976
Am Hist R 82:1088 O '77. L. B. Miller
Horowitz, I. L. Ideology and utopia in the United States, 1956-1976. 1977
America 136:359-60 Ap 16 '77. F. K. Kelly
Ann Am Acad 432:171-2 Jl '77. H. B. Gow
Horvat, B. Yugoslav economic system: the first labor-managed economy in the making. 1976
Ann Am Acad 433:198 S '77. N. J. J. Farley
Horwitz, J. They went thataway. 1976
Am West 14:58 N '77. E. Maves
Horwitz, M. J. Transformation of American law, 1780-1860. 1977
Am Hist R 82:1067 O '77. K. Newmyer
New Repub 176:34-5 Mr 26 '77. P. H. Schuck
Hoshizaki, B. J. Fern growers manual
Horticulture 55:13-15 Mr '77. M. J. Balick

Howard, M. ed. Theory and practice of war. 1975
Am Hist R 81:1067 D '76. S. J. Stearns
Howard, R. Fellow feelings
Poetry 130:36-40 Ap '77. R. K. Martin
Howe, D. W. ed. Victorian America. 1976
Am Hist R 82:748-9 Je '77. T. Bender
Howe, I. World of our fathers: the journey of the East European Jews to America and the life they found and made. 1976
Am Hist R 82:189 F '77. E. Alexander
Howe, I. and Greenberg, E. eds. Ashes out of hope: fiction by Soviet-Yiddish writers
New Repub 178:37-8 Ja 7 '78. R. Berman
Howe, L. K. Pink collar workers: inside the world of women's work
Nation 224:694-6 Je 4 '77. A. Wolfe
Newsweek 89:82 Mr 21 '77. M. Jefferson
Howson, Colin, ed. Method and appraisal in the physical sciences: the critical background to modern science, 1800-1905. 1976
Science 196:517 Ap 29 '77. L. Laudan
Hoyle, F. On Stonehenge
Am Scholar 46:530-2 Aut '77. O. Gingerich
Hoyle, F. Ten faces of the universe. 1977
Sky & Tel 54:135-6 Ag '77. M. H. Liller
Space World N-8-164:32-4 Ag '77
Hözle, E. Die Selbstentmachtung Europas: das Experiment des Eriedens vor und in Ersten Welkrieg. 1975
Am Hist R 82:626-7 Je '77. S. Wank
Huan T'an. Hsin-Lun (new treatise) and other writings by Huan T'an (43 B.C.-28 A.D.) tr. by T. Pokora. 1975
Am Hist R 81:1196 D '76. C.-Y. Chen
Hubbell, J. G. POW: a definitive history of the American prisoner-of-war experience in Vietnam, 1964-1973
Nat R 29:837-8 Jl 22 '77. R. W. Merry
Huck, C. S. Children's literature in the elementary school. 1976
SLJ 24:33 N '77. R. Gordon
Huddle, N. and others. Island of dreams. 1975
Bull Atom Sci 33:63-4 Ja '77. F. von Hippel
Hudnut, R. K. Church growth is not the point. 1975
Chr Today 21:33 Ja 7 '77. H. A. Snyder
Hudson, C. Southeastern Indians. 1976
Am Hist R 82:1057-8 O '77. F. Jennings
Hudson, W. D. Wittgenstein and religious belief. 1975
Chr Today 21:41-3 Mr 4 '77. J. D. Spiceland
Huemer, P. Sektionschef Robert Hecht und die Zerstörung der Demokratie in Osterreich: eine historischpolitische Studie. 1975
Am Hist R 82:676 Je '77. R. J. Rath
Huffaker, C. B. and Messenger, P. S. eds. Theory and practice of biological control. 1976
BioScience 27:685 O '77. E. R. Mitchell
Science 198:1029 D 9 '77. M. J. Way
Huggett, F. E. Land question and European society. 1975
Am Hist R 82:81-3 F '77. A. Plakans
Huggins, N. I. Black odyssey
New Repub 177:32-3 N 5 '77. T. Rosengarten
Huggins, N. I. ed. Voices from the Harlem Renaissance. 1976
Am Hist Illus 11:49-50 Ja '77. C. F. Cooney
Hughes, J. D. Ecology in ancient civilizations. 1975
Am Hist R 81:1078-9 D '76. R. A. Padgug
Hughes, P. E. Interpreting prophecy. 1976
Chr Today 21:40-2 Ap 15 '77. W. W. Gasque
Hughes, T. and Costello, J. Battle of the Atlantic
Bus W p6+ Ja 9 '78. P. Stillwell
Hughes, T. P. Plasmas and laser light. 1975
Phys Today 30:54-6 Ap '77. J. E. Bayfield
Hulliger, F. Structural chemistry of layer-type phases. 1977
Science 198:1030 D 9 '77. F. Disalvo
Humfrey, M. Sea shells of the West Indies: a guide to the marine molluscs of the Caribbean. 1975
Sea Front 23:378 N '77
Humphrey, D. C. From King's college to Columbia, 1746-1800. 1976
Am Hist R 82:172-3 F '77. F. Rudolph
Humphrey, W. Farther off from heaven
America 137:203-4 O 1 '77. T. I. Ichniowski
Hundley, N. Jr. ed. Chicano; introd. by M. Meier and F. Rivera. 1975
Am Hist R 81:1269 D '76. G. L. Seligmann, Jr
Hunsaker, D. ed. Biology of marsupials. 1977
Science 198:1147 D 16 '77. R. M. F. S. Sadleir
Hunsinger, G. ed. and tr. Karl Barth and radical politics. 1976
Chr Cent 94:489-90 My 18 '77. J. D. Godsey
Chr Today 21:33 Ag 26 '77. J. Buckley
Hunt, I. William
Horn Bk 53:540 O '77. M. M. Burns
Hunt, J C. People's party in Württemberg and southern Germany, 1890-1914: the possibilities of democratic politics. 1975
Am Hist R 81:1153 D '76. J. J. Cahill
Hunt, P. Gift of the unicorn. 1965
Nation 224:345-6 Mr 19 '77. R. S. Wolper
Hunt, W. R. North of 53°: the wild days of the Alaska-Yukon mining frontier, 1870-1914. 1974
Am Hist R 81:1249-50 D '76. S. Haycox
Hunter, M. Wicked one. 1977
Horn Bk 53:442 Ag '77. A. A. Flowers

Hunter, S. and Jacobus, J. Modern art
America 137:173-4 S 24 '77. R. Berenson
Hurezeanu, D. ed. Nouvelles études d'histoire: publiées à l'occasion du XIVᵉ Congrès des sciences historiques: San Francisco, 1975. 1975
Am Hist R 81:1164 D '76. F. Kellogg
Hurley, A. C. Electron correlation in small molecules
Phys Today 30:55-6 S '77. N. Y. Ohrn
Hurley, A. C. Introduction to the electron theory of small molecules. 1977
Phys Today 30:55-6 S '77. N. Y. Ohrn
Hus, A. Les siècles d'or de l'histoire étrusque (675-475 avant J.-C.). 1976
Am Hist R 82:68-9 F '77. J. J. Reich
Hutchins, R.E. Trails to nature's mysteries: the life of a working naturalist. 1977
Horn Bk 53:558 O '77. S. Gagné
Hutchinson, W. R. Modernist impulse in American Protestantism. 1976
Am Hist R 82:199 F '77. D. W. Howe
Chr Cent 94:544 Je 1 '77. L. J. Averill
Huxtable, A. L. Kicked a building lately?
America 136:361 Ap 16 '77. R. Berenson
Commonweal 104:601-3 S 16 '77. W. Andrews
Hyam, R. Britain's imperial century, 1815-1914: a study of empire and expansion. 1976
Am Hist R 82:361-2 Ap '77. H. R. Winkler
Hyatt, I. T. jr. Our ordered lives confess: three nineteenth-century American missionaries in East Shantung. 1976
Am Hist R 82:1046 O '77. G. K. Harrington
Hyman, H. M. Union and confidence: the 1860s. 1976
Am Hist R 82:1076 O '77. F. L. Klement
Hyman, S. Marriner S. Eccles: private entrepreneur and public servant. 1976
Am Hist R 82:1348-9 D '77. E. W. Hawley
Duns R 109:114+ Je '77. L. Smith
Hymer, S. H. International operations of national firms: a study of direct foreign investment. 1976
Ann Am Acad 430:223-4 Mr '77. M. Wilkins
Hynes, S. Auden generation: literature and politics in England in the 1930's
America 137:249-51 O 15 '77. A. Fremantle
Commentary 64:78-9+ S '77. R. Berman
New Repub 176:27-9 Ap 16 '77. C. Sykes

Illich, I. Medical nemesis: the expropriation of health. 1976
Bull Atom Sci 33:62-3 F '77. R. J. Haggerty
Society 14:88-90 Ja '77. B. Barber
Illick, J. E. Colonial Pennsylvania: a history. 1976
Am Hist Illus 12:50 Je '77. F. S. Klein
Imhof, A. E. Aspekte der Bevölkerungsentwicklung in den nordischen Ländern, 1720-1750. 1976
Am Hist R 82:992 O '77. H. Moller
Infield, G. B. Leni Riefenstahl: the fallen film goddess. 1976
America 136:112-13 F 5 '77. R. A. Blake
Film Q 31:61-2 Wint '77. J. Bergstrom
Influenza: virus, vaccines, and strategy; proceedings of meeting, Rougemont, 1976; ed. by P. Selby. 1976
Science 197:43 Jl 1 '77. R. W. Schlesinger
Information broker/free-lance librarian—new careers—new library services workshop, Syracuse, N.Y. Proceedings; ed. by B. B. Minor. 1976
Lib J 102:1356 Je 15 '77. F. M. Blake
Ingham, K. Kingdom of Toro in Uganda. 1975
Am Hist R 81:1193-4 D '76. G. N. Uzoigwe
Insect development; papers from symposium, London, 1975; ed. by P. A. Lawrence. 1976
Science 196:772-3 My 13 '77. S. J. Counce
Institute for the Study of Educational Policy. Equal educational opportunity for blacks in U.S. higher education: an assessment
Todays Educ 66:103-4 Ja '77. M. M. Fisher
In 't Veld, N. K. C. A. ed. De SS en Nederland: documenten uit SS archieven, 1935-1945; v 1: Inleiding/Documenten, 1935-1942; v2: Documenten, 1943-1945. 1976
Am Hist R 82:657 Je '77. E. L. Presseisen
International Biological Programme 2: Crop genetic resources for today and tomorrow; ed. by O. H. Frankel and J. G. Hawkes. 1975
BioScience 27:125 F '77 F. T Ledig
International Biological Programme 5: Small mammals; ed. by F. B. Golley and others. 1975
BioScience 27:128 F '77. D. J. Shure
International Biological Programme 7: Symbiotic nitrogen fixation in plants; ed. by P. S. Nutman. 1976
BioScience 27:132 F '77. C. C. Delwiche
International Biological Programme 9; Studies in biological control; ed. by V. L. Delucchi. 1976
BioScience 27:286 Ap '77. D. H. Janzen
International Biological Programme 10: Marine mussels; ed. by B. L. Bayne. 1976
Science 195:281-2 Ja 21 '77. M. J. Greenberg
International conference on aquaculture nutrition, 1975. Proceedings; ed. by K. S. Price and others. 1976
BioScience 27:688 O '77. R. C. May
International conference on environment and society in transition, 2d, New York, 1975
BioScience 27:208+ Mr '77. E. M. Mrak
International conference on the physics of electronic and atomic collisions, Seattle, 1975. Physics of electronic and atomic collisions; papers, ed. by J. S. Risley and R. Geballe. 1976
Science 195:975-6 Mr 11 '77. A. Dalgarno
International estuarine research conference, 2d, Myrtle Beach, S.C. 1973. Estuarine research; papers; ed. by L. E. Cronin. 2v. 1975
BioScience 27:52 Ja '77. R. M. Darnell
International estuarine research conference, 3d, Galveston, Tex. 1975. Estuarine processes; papers; ed. by M. Wiley. 2v. 1976-7
Science 198:724-5 N 18 '77. S. M. Adams
International federation of library associations. Reading in a changing world: papers presented at the 38th session of the IFLA general council, Budapest, 1972; ed. by F. E. Mohrhardt. 1976
Lib J 102:2221 N 1 '77. E. Jussim
International Josquin Festival conference, New York City, June, 1971. Josquin Des Pres; proceedings; ed. by E. E. Lowinsky; with B. J. Blackburn. 1976
Hi Fi 27:MA37-8 N '77. S. T. Sommer
Mus Q 63:549-55 O '77. A. Newcomb
International spore symposium. 2d. Provo, Utah. 1975. Fungal spore; papers; ed. by D. J. Weber and W. M. Hess. 1976
BioScience 27:56 Ja '77 V. W. Cochrane
International symposium on structure and conformation of nucleic acids and protein-nucleic acid interactions; proceedings; ed by M. Sundarlingam and S. T. Rao. 1975
Science 195:170 Ja 14 '77. P. R. Schimmel
Iredell, J. Papers of James Iredell, v 1: 1767-1777; v2: 1778-1783. 1976
Am Hist R 82:1061-2 O '77. P. D. Chase
Irving, D. Hitler's war. 1977
Am Hist R 82:1281 D '77. D. E. Showalter
Ann Am Acad 434:221-2 N '77. A. L. Weeks
Commentary 64:76+ S '77. L. Bushkoff
Nat R 29:946-8+ Ag 19 '77
New Repub 177:28-30 Jl 9 '77. G. A. Craig
New Yorker 53:82-6 Ag 29 '77. N. Bliven
Newsweek 90:77 Jl 11 '77. K. L. Woodward and A. Collings
Irving, D. Trail of the fox
New Repub 177:41-2 N 26 '77. S. Chapman
Newsweek 90:105-6 O 31 '77. R. Boeth
Sat R 5:28 N 12 '77. G. H. Reeves
Irwin G. Seventh earl: a dramatized biography. 1976
Chr Today 21:46-8+ My 6 '77. R. V. Pierard
Isaacman, A. F. Tradition of resistance in Mozambique: the Zambesi Valley, 1850-1921; with B. Isaacman. 1977
Am Hist R 82:713-14 Je '77. D. Chanaiwa
Ann Am Acad 434:213-14 N '77. R. Sigwalt
Isherwood, C. Christopher and his kind, 1929-1939
Yale R 67:128-35 O '77. M. Ellmann
Isichel, E. History of the Igbo people. 1976
Am Hist R 81:1190-1 D '76. F. K. Ekechi
Izenberg, G. N. Existentialist critique of Freud: the crisis of autonomy. 1976
Am Hist R 82:625-6 Je '77. M. Poster
Izenour, G. C. Theater design. 1977
Intellect 106:254-5 D '77. D. B. Wilmeth
New Repub 177:26-8 Ag 6 '77. S. Kauffmann

Jackman, S. W. Nicholas Cardinal Wiseman
America 137:291-2 O 29 '77. T. P. Hill
Jackson, A. Place called home: a history of low-cost housing in Manhattan. 1976
Am Hist R 82:1085-6 O '77. R. Lubove
Ann Am Acad 432:172-3 Jl '77. S. J. LaGumina
Jackson, J. D. Classical electrodynamics. 2d ed. 1975
Phys Today 30:61-2 Jl '77. R. K. P. Zia
Jackson, S. L. and others, eds. Century of service: librarianship in the United States and Canada. 1976
Lib J 102:2016 O 1 '77. J. Emmons
Jacob, M. C. Newtonians and the English revolution, 1689-1720. 1976
Am Hist R 82:353-5 Ap '77. R. S. Westfall
Jacobson, C. Wilderness canoeing and camping
Hi Fi 27:MA39 Jl '77. P. J. Smith
Jacobson, B. and Webster, J. G. Medicine and clinical engineering. 1977
Phys Today 30:56-7 Ag '77. J. Hale
Jacobson, C. Wilderness canoeing and camping
Conservationist 32:43 S '77. R. M. Kuhfahl
Jacoby, N. H. and others. Bribery and extortion in world business
Fortune 96:49+ D '77. P. P. Gabriel
Jacoby, R. Social amnesia: a critique of conformist psychology from Adler to Laing. 1975
Society 14:90 My '77. J. H. Rubin
Jaenen, C. J. Friend and foe: aspects of French-Amerindian cultural contact in the sixteenth and seventeenth centuries. 1976
Am Hist R 82:474 Ap '77. E. P. Patterson
Ann Am Acad 431:166-7 My '77. R. E. Bieder

Jaenen, C. J. Role of the church in New France. 1976
Am Hist R 82:1366 D '77. C. E. O'Neill
Jain, J. P. After Mao what? 1976
Ann Am Acad 431:152 My '77. J. D. Jordan
James, S. V. Colonial Rhode Island: a history. 1975
Am Hist R 81:1215 D '76. P. J. Coleman
Janis, E. P. and MacNeil, W. eds. Photography in the humanities
Art N 76:60+ N '77. G. Thornton
Janis, I. L. and Mann, L. Decision making: a psychological analysis of conflict, choice, and commitment. 1977
Science 197:1355-6 S 30 '77. J. Brehm
Jarry, A. Supermale; tr. by R. Gladstone and B. Wright
New Yorker 53:179-80+ O 10 '77. J. Updike
Jäschke, K.-U. Burgenbau und Landesverteidigung um 900: Überlegungen zu Beispielen aus Deutschland, Frankreich und England. 1975
Am Hist R 81:1091-2 D '76. L. G. Duggan
Jay, J. John Jay: the making of a revolutionary, v 1: unpublished papers, 1745-1780; ed. by R. B. Morris. 1975
Am Hist R 81:1224 D '76. R. Walsh
Jaynes, J. Origin of consciousness in the breakdown of the bicameral mind. 1977
Ann Am Acad 434:239 N '77. S. R. Waxman
Atlantic 239:90-1 My '77. B. DeMott
Jeanneney, J.-N. François de Wendel en republique: l'argent et le pouvoir, 1914-1940. 1976
Am Hist R 82:655 Je '77. G. Silvestri
Jeeves, M. A. Psychology and Christianity: the view both ways. 1976
Chr Cent 94:1229-30 D 28 '77. L. R. Rambo
Chr Today 22:35 N 18 '77. K. E. Farnsworth
Jefferson, T. Papers of Thomas Jefferson, v 19: 24 January to 31 March 1791; ed. by J. P. Boyd. 1974
Am Hist R 81:1226-7 D '76. M. R. Zahniser
Jellison, C. A. Tomatoes were cheaper: tales from the thirties. 1977
Am Hist R 82:1347 D '77. G. Wolfskill
Jellison, R. M. ed. Society, freedom, and conscience: the American revolution in Virginia, Massachusetts, and New York. 1976
Am Hist R 82:432-3 Ap '77. L. R. Gerlach
Jencks, C. Inequality: a reassessment of the effect of family and schooling in America, 1972
Ann Am Acad 434:101-13 N '77. L. B. Joseph
Jenkins, H. Valley renewed. 1977
Am For 89:9 Mr '77. J. B. Craig
Am For 89:32-3+ Je '77. L. E. Partain
Jennings, E. Growing-points
Poetry 129:347-50 Mr '77. J. Matthias
Jennings, F. Invasion of America: Indians, colonialism, and the cant of conquest. 1975
Am Hist R 82:168-9 F '77. J. P. Ronda
Jensen, M. ed. Documentary history of the ratification of the Constitution; v 1: Constitutional documents and records, 1776-1781; v2: Ratification of the Constitution by the states: Pennsylvania. 1976
Am Hist R 82:740 Je '77. J. A. Monroe
Jervis, R. Perception and misperception in international politics. 1976
Ann Am Acad 432:151-2 Jl '77. W. S. Thompson
Jewell, D. Duke: a portrait of Duke Ellington
Hi Fi 27:167 O '77. J. S. Wilson
Jewett, R. and Lawrence, J. S. American monomyth. 1977
Ann Am Acad 434:239-41 N '77. T. J. Knight
Jewsbury, G. F. Russian annexation of Bessarabia, 1774-1828: a study of imperial expansion. 1976
Am Hist R 82:393 Ap '77. B. Jelavich
Jhabvala, R. P. How I became a holy mother and other stories
America 136:279-80 Mr 26 '77. A. J. Kelly
Jick, L. A. Americanization of the synagogue, 1820-1870. 1976
Am Hist R 82:189 F '77. L. Dinnerstein
Johansons, A. Latvijas kultùras vèsture, 1710-1800. 1975
Am Hist R 82:1023 O '77. E. Anderson
John, E. A. H. Storms brewed in other men's worlds: the confrontation of Indians, Spanish, and French in the Southwest, 1540-1795. 1975
Am Hist R 81:1220 D '76. S. V. Connor
John, L. ed. Cosmology now. 1976
Sky & Tel 54:131-2 Ag '77. J. D. Fernie
Johnson, E. Charles Dickens: his tragedy and triumph
Harpers 225:107-8 D '77. M. Malone
Time 110:98+ D 19 '77. P. Gray
Johnson, E. D. and Harris, M. H. History of libraries in the western world. 3d ed. 1976
Lib J 102:464 F 15 '77. J. W. Kraus
Johnson, E. H. Modern art and the object. 1976
Art in Am 65:35 My '77. S. Gablik
Johnson, F. ed. Start early for an early start: you and the young child. 1976
SLJ 23:40 My '77. B. M. Cheatham
Johnson, H. World atlas of wine: a complete guide to the wines & spirits of the world
Sci Am 238:31 Ja '78. P. Morrison
Johnson, H. B. Order upon the land: the U.S. rectangular land survey and the upper Mississippi country. 1976
Am Hist R 82:451 Ap '77. T. G. Manning
Johnson, H. C. Frederick the Great and his officials. 1975
Am Hist R 81:1145-6 D '76. J. G. Gagliardo
Johnson, J. T. Ideology, reason, and the limitation of war: religious and secular concepts, 1200-1740. 1975
Am Hist R 82:88-9 F '77. P. Paret
Johnson, P. Enemies of society
Harpers 255:92 S '77. M. Malone
Nation 225:252-4 S 17 '77. J. Taylor
Johnson, P. History of Christianity. 1976
Am Hist R 82:332-3 Ap '77. J. E. Groh
America 136:197-8 Mr 5 '77. C. P. Loughran
Nat R 29:446+ Ap 15 '77. A. Bakshian, Jr
Johnson, R. A. ed. Psychohistory and religion: the case of Young man Luther
Chr Cent 94:1170+ D 14 '77. E. J. Curtin, jr
Chr Today 22:50 O 7 '77. L. Rambo
Johnson, R. S. Messiaen. 1975
Mus Q 62:607-12 O '76. R. P. Morgan
Johnson, S. Roman forts of the Saxon shore. 1976
Am Hist R 82:613-14 Je '77. J. W. Eadie
Johnstone, J. W. C. and others. News people: a sociological portrait of American journalists and their work. 1976
Ann Am Acad 432:173-4 Jl '77. J. B. Manheim
Jonas, G. Stuttering: the disorder of many theories
Esquire 88:8+ O '77
Jonasson, G. Per Edvin Sköld, 1946-1951; with L. Sköld. 1976
Am Hist R 82:378-9 Ap '77. A. W. Andersen
Jones, A. H. Bronze Age civilization: the Philistines and the Danites. 1975
Am Hist R 82:67-8 F '77. G. K. Sams
Jones, C. and Way, O. R. British children's authors: interviews at home. 1976
Horn Bk 53:463 Ag '77. V. Haviland
Jones, D. Chartism and the Chartists. 1975
Am Hist R 82:101 F '77. E. J. Evans
Jones, D. C. Court-martial of George Armstrong Custer. 1976
Am West 14:58 Mr '77. R. M. Utley
Jones, D. W. Cart and cwidder. 1977
Horn Bk 53:443 Ag '77. E. L. Heins
Jones, D. W. Dogsbody. 1977
Horn Bk 53:319 Je '77. P. Heins
Jones, E. E. Strategies for new churches
Chr Cent 94:230+ Mr 9 '77. L. E. Schaller
Jones, F. C. Changing mood in America
New Repub 177:31-2 N 5 '77. L. A. Daniels
Jones, G. D, ed. Anthropology and history in Yucatan. 1977
Science 198:45-6 O 7 '77. G. H. Gossen
Jones, J. F. and Herrick, J. M. Citizens in service: volunteers in social welfare during the depression, 1929-1941. 1976
Am Hist R 82:464-5 Ap '77. N. P. Weiss
Jones, K. W. Arya Dharm: Hindu consciousness in 19th century Punjab. 1976
Ann Am Acad 433:172-4 S '77. P. Spear
Jones, P. d'A. Since Columbus: poverty and pluralism in the history of the Americas. 1976
Ann Am Acad 430:202-3 Mr '77. W. Petersen
Jones, R. L'idéologie de l'Action Catholique, 1917-1939. 1974
Am Hist R 82:220 F '77. J. Hellman
Jones-Lee, M. W. Value of life: an economic analysis. 1976
Intellect 106:171-2 O '77. A. M. Freeman, 3d
Jong, E. How to save your own life
Esquire 88:22+ Jl '77. J. Simon
Nat R 29:498 Ap 29 '77. D. K. Mano
Newsweek 89:82-3 Mr 28 '77. J. Maslin
Time 109:74+ Mr 14 '77. L. Morrow
Jordan, D. A. Northern expedition: China's national revolution of 1926-1928. 1976
Am Hist R 82:719-20 Je '77. J. E. Sheridan
Josephson, E. F. SKP och Komintern, 1921-1924; motsättingarna inom Sveriges kommunistiska parti och dess relationer till den kommunistiska Internationalen. 1976
Am Hist R 82:1272 D '77. A. T. Anderson
Josephson, H. James T. Shotwell and the rise of internationalism in America. 1975
Am Hist R 82:210 F '77. B. W. Cook
Josquin Des Prés. Missa Pange lingua; ed by T. Warburton. 1977
Mus Q 63:436-40 Jl '77. S. Boorman
Josselin, R. Diary of Ralph Josselin, 1616-1683; ed. by A. MacFarlane. 1976
Am Hist R 82:959-60 O '77. M. Lee, jr
Jouanna, A. L'idée de race en France au XVIème siècle et au début du XVIIème siècle (1498-1614) 3v. 1976
Am Hist R 82:647-8 Je '77. M. C. Horowitz
Jowett, G. Film: the democratic art. 1976
Am Hist R 82:466 Ap '77. T. Cripps
Jowitt, D. Dance beat: selected views and reviews, 1967-1976
Ms 6:38-40 S '77. L. Shapiro
New Repub 177:44-5 O 15 '77. R. Copeland
Newsweek 90:101-2+ N 14 '77. J. Kroll
Judt, T. La reconstruction du parti socialiste, 1921-1926. 1976
Am Hist R 82:373-4 Ap '77. S. P. Kramer

Juhnke, J. C. People of two kingdoms: the political acculturation of the Kansas Mennonites. 1975
Am Hist R 81:1282-3 D '76. P. K. Conkin
Jullian, P. Montmartre
Am Artist 41:35+ N '77. A. Werner
July, R. W. Precolonial Africa: an economic and social history. 1975
Am Hist R 82:154-5 F '77. S. Feierman
Junker, D. Der unteilbare Weltmarkt: das ökonomische Interesse in der Aussenpolitik der USA 1933-1941. 1975
Am Hist R 81:1153 D '76. J. J. Cahill
Jupiter: studies of the interior, atmosphere, magnetosphere and satellites; ed. by T. Gehrels and M. S. Matthews. 1976
Sky & Tel 54:416 N '77. W. A. Baum
Juvenile hormones; proceedings of conference, Lake Geneva, Wis, 1975; ed. by L. I. Gilbert. 1976
BioScience 27:564 Ag '77. J. D. O'Connor
Juzbašić, D. Izgradnja željeznica u Bosni i Hercegovini u svjetlu austrougarske politike od okupacije do kraja Kállayeve ere. 1974
Am Hist R 82:1014-15 O '77. R. Donia

Kahl, J. A. Modernization, exploitation and dependency in Latin America: Germani, Gonzalez Casanova, and Cardoso. 1976
Américas 29:26 Mr '77. C. Guillén
Kalb, M. and Koppel, T. In the national interest
Time 110:99 D 19 '77. L. Morrow
Kalivoda, R. Revolution und ideologie: der Hussitismus; tr. by H. Thorwart and M. Gletter. 1976
Am Hist R 82:623 Je '77. J. Klassen
Kallner, R. Herzl und Rathenau: Wege jüdischer Existenz an der Wende des 20. Jahrhunderts. 1976
Am Hist R 82:1001 O '77. D. G. Sanford
Kalsbeek, L. Contours of a Christian philosophy: an introduction to Herman Dooyeweerd's thought. 1975
Chr Today 21:44 F 4 '77. R. Countess
Kamiński, F. Religione e chiesa in Polonia, 1945-1975: saggio storico-instituzionale. 1976
Am Hist R 82:689-90 Je '77. R. Camp
Kammen, M. Colonial New York. 1975
Am Hist Illus 12:49 Jl '77. A. Keller
Kammler, H. Die Feudalmonarchien: politische und wirtschaftlichsoziale Eaktoren ihrer Entwicklung und Funktionsweise. 1974
Am Hist R 82:74 F '77. B. Lyon
Kandal, E. R. Cellular basis of behavior: an introduction to behavioral neurobiology. 1976
Science 198:815-16 N 25 '77. C. F. Stevens
Kann, R. A. Erzherzog Franz Ferdinand Studien. 1976
Am Hist R 82:136 F '77. P. W. Schroeder
Kanter, R. M. Men and women of the corporation. 1977
Science 198:920-2 D 2 '77. A. Levine
Kaplan, G. H. and others. Almanac for computers
Sci Am 236:130-1 Ja '77. P. Morrison
Kaplan, L. Politics and religion during the English Revolution: the Scots and the Long Parliament, 1643-1645. 1976
Am Hist R 82:959 O '77. P. Christianson
Kaplan, S. L. Bread, politics and political economy in the reign of Louis XV. 2v. 1976
Am Hist R 82:1263-4 D '77. R. Forster
Kaplan, T. Anarchists of Andalusia, 1868-1903. 1977
Am Hist R 82:1268 D '77. C. P. Boyd
New Repub 176:32-3 Ap 30 '77. J. Womeck, Jr
Kapp, Y. Eleanor Marx. 2v
Nation 225:725-7 D 31 '77. J. S. Allen
Newsweek 91:62 Ja 2 '78. M. Jefferson
Karageorghis, V. View from the bronze age: Mycenaean and Phoenician discoveries at Kition. 1976
Am Hist R 82:611-12 Je '77. M. M. Eisman
Kardanov, E. Iz istorii otnoshenii mezhdu adygskimi narodami i Rossiei v XVI veke (1550-1580). 1972
Am Hist R 81:1171-2 D '76. D. C. Matuszewski
Karl, B. D. Charles E. Merriam and the study of politics. 1974
Am Hist R 82:1096 O '77. R. Lowitt
Karlinsky, S. Sexual labyrinth of Nikolai Gogol
New Yorker 53:99-102 F 28 '77. G. Steiner
Karp, L. Genetic engineering: threat or promise?
Nat R 29:346 Mr 18 '77. M. S. Evans
Karp, L. E. Genetic engineering: threat or promise?
Psychol Today 10:112+ Ap '77. T. M. Powledge
Kasper, W. Jesus the Christ
America 136:249-51 Mr 19 '77. L. J. O'Donovan
Kaspi, A. La France et le concours américain, février 1917-novembre 1918. 3v. 1975
Am Hist R 81:1131-2 D '76. J. C. Cairns
Kater, M. H. Studentenschaft und Rechtsradikalismus in Deutschland, 1918-1933: eine sozialgeschichtliche Studie zur Bildungskrise in der Weimarer Republik. 1975
Am Hist R 81:1150 D '76. M. Steinberg
Kates, G. N. Years that were fat: the last of old China. 1976
Ann Am Acad 433:174 S '77. C. L. Beahan
Katz, B. ed. Library lit. 7—the best of 1976. 1977
Lib J 102:2143 O 15 '77. S. Rothstein
Katz, M. B. People of Hamilton, Canada West: family and class in a mid-nineteenth-century city. 1975
Am Hist R 82:475-6 Ap '77. G. A. Stelter
Ann Am Acad 432:180-2 Jl '77. P. George
Katzenbach, M. The grab
Newsweek 91:68 Ja 9 '78. M. Jefferson
Katzenstein, P. J. Disjoined partners: Austria and Germany since 1815. 1976
Am Hist R 82:134 F '77. A. D. Low
Kauffman, E. G. and Hazel, J. E. eds. Concepts and methods of biostratigraphy. 1977
Science 198:285-6 O 21 '77. W. C. Sweet
Kauffman, J. H. and Harder, L. Anabaptists four centuries later: a profile of five Mennonite and Brethren in Christ denominations. 1975
Am Hist R 81:1097 D '76. G. F. Hershberger
Kaufman, M. American medical education: the formative years, 1765-1910. 1976
Am Hist R 82:729 Je '77. J. F. Kett
Kaufmann, W. Future of the humanities
Commonweal 104:247-9 Ap 15 '77. R. Kuczkowski
Kaufmann, W. Religions in four dimensions: existential and aesthetic, historical and comparative. 1976
Chr Today 22:32 D 30 '77. R. F. Young
Kaufmann, W. J. 3d. Cosmic frontiers of general relativity 1977
Phys Today 30:54-5 Ag '77. W. Rindler
Sky & Tel 54:413-16 N '77. B. J. Carr
Kaufmann, W. J. 3d. Astronomy: the structure of the universe. 1977
Sky & Tel 53:299+ Ap '77. T. Page
Kay, K and Peary, G. eds. Women and the cinema: a critical anthology. 1977
Film Q 31:53-5 Wint '77. S. Flitterman
Kealey, G. S. and Warrian, P. eds. Essays in Canadian working class history. 1976
Am Hist R 82:776-7 Je '77. A. R. McCormack
Keating, T. and others. Fake's progress
Art N 76:120+ O '77. J. E. Patterson
New Repub 177:41-3 O 1 '77. D. Hofstadter
Kedar, B. Z. Merchants in crisis: Genoese and Venetian men of affairs and the fourteenth-century depression. 1976
Am Hist R 82:941-2 O '77. J. C. Davis
Kedourie, E. In the Anglo-Arab labyrinth: the McMahan-Husayn correspondence and its interpretations, 1914-1939. 1976
Am Hist R 82:109 F '77. P. Jabber
Keegan, J. Face of battle
America 136:134-5 F 12 '77. J. B. Breslin
Commonweal 104:566-71 S 2 '77. M. Taylor
Yale R 66:424-32 Mr '77. F. A. Pottle
Keenan, P. C. and McNeil, R. C. Atlas of spectra of the cooler stars. 1976
Sky & Tel 54:419-21 N '77. D. Overbye
Kees, W. Collected poems of Weldon Kees; ed. by D. Justice
Poetry 130:285-7 Ag '77. B. Howard
Keith, H. H. and Hayes, R. A. eds. Perspectives on armed politics in Brazil. 1976
Am Hist R 82:784-5 Je '77. F. D. Mccann
Keith, R. G. Conquest and agrarian change: the emergence of the hacienda system on the Peruvian coast. 1976
Am Hist R 82:1107 O '77. J. Lockhart
Ann Am Acad 431:184-5 My '77. G. Dalton
Kelber, W. ed. Passion in Mark
Chr Cent 94:337-8 Ap 6 '77. P. J. Achtemeier
Kellenbenz, H. Rise of the European economy: an economic history of continental Europe from the fifteenth to the eighteenth century; rev. and ed. by G. Benecke. 1976
Am Hist R 82:83 F '77. C. R. Phillips
Keller, M. Affairs of state: public life in late nineteenth century America. 1977
Am Hist R 82:1083-4 O '77. G. W. McFarland
Ann Am Acad 432:174 Jl '77. R. C. Esbenshade
Kelley, D. M. Why churches should not pay taxes
America 137:196-7 O 1 '77. P. J. Weber
Chr Cent 94:663 Jl 20 '77. F. V. Mills
Kelsey, D. H. Uses of Scripture in recent theology
Chr Cent 94:43-4 Ja 19 '77. E. Farley
Kelsey, M. T. Other side of silence: a guide to Christian meditation
America 136:133 F 12 '77 T. E. Clarke
Kendall, A. Tender tyrant: Nadia Boulanger, a life devoted to music
Hi Fi 27:MA36-7 S '77. C. Brook
Keneally, T. Season in purgatory
America 136:492 My 28 '77. P. H. Connolly
New Yorker 53:132-4 My 23 '77. G. Steiner
Newsweek 89:72-3 F 7 '77. M. Jefferson
Keniston, K. and Carnegie council on children. All our children: the American family under pressure
America 137:456-9 D 24 '77. J. W. Donohue
Kennan, G. F. Cloud of danger: current realities of American foreign policy
Commentary 64:30-5 N '77. E. N. Luttwak
New Repub 177:38-40 Ag 6 '77. B. Ulam
New Yorker 53:70-3 Ag 8 '77. R. Rovere
Kennedy, E. Time for being human
America 137:467-8 D 24 '77. E. McMahon

Kennedy, P. M. Rise and fall of British naval mastery. 1976
Am Hist R 82:356 Ap '77. C. J. Bartlett
Oceans 10:68 Mr '77. M. A. Jackson
Kennedy, R. Come again in the spring; il. by M. Sewall. 1976
Horn Bk 53:154 Ap '77. S. H. Holtze
Kennedy, R. Porcelain man; il. by M. Sewell. 1976
Horn Bk 53:39 F '77. E. L. Heins
Kentner, L. Piano
Am Rec G 40:61 Mr '77. E. Richmond
Kephart, H. Our southern highlanders; a narrative of adventure in the southern Appalachians and a study of life among the mountaineers; introd by G. Ellison. 1976
Am For 83:38-9 My '77. M. Bush
Kernek, S. J. Distractions of peace during war: the Lloyd George government's reactions to Woodrow Wilson, December, 1916-November, 1918. 1975
Am Hist R 81:1114-15 D '76. A. Marrin
Kernochan, S. Dry hustle
Ms 5:80-2 Je '77. S. Weller
Kerr, G. H. Formosa: licensed revolution and the home rule movement, 1895-1945. 1974
Am Hist R 81:1210 D '76. W.-H. Hsu
Kerr, M. E. I'll love you when you're more like me. 1977
Horn Bk 53:668-9 D '77. P. Heins
Kersey, H. A. Jr. Pelts, plumes, and hides: white traders among the Seminole Indians, 1870-1930. 1976
Am Hist R 81:1263 D '76. M. Zanger
Kershaw, G. E. Gentlemen of large property & judicious men; the Kennebeck proprietors, 1749-1775. 1975
Am Hist R 81:1221 D '76. B. H. Newcomb
Kessell, J. L. Friars, soldiers, and reformers: Hispanic Arizona and the Sonora mission frontier 1767-1856. 1976
Am West 14:64 My '77. O. B. Faulk
Kessler, J. Polarized electrons. 1976
Phys Today 30:61 Jl '77. C. L. Foiles
Kessler, L. D. K'ang-hsi and the consolidation of Ch'ing rule, 1661-1684. 1976
Am Hist R 82:1044-5 O '77. S. Wu
Kett, J. F. Rites of passage: adolescence in America, 1790 to the present
America 137:456-9 D 24 '77. J. W. Donohue
Kevles, B. A. Watching the wild apes. 1976
Horn Bk 53:338-9 Je '77. S. Gagné
Keyes, C. F. Golden Peninsula: culture and adaptation in mainland Southeast Asia. 1977
Ann Am Acad 434:214-15 N '77. M. D. Zamora
Keyes, R. Is there life after high school?
America 136:107-9 F 5 '77. J. W. Donohue
Khatibi, A. and Sijelmassi, M. Splendour of Islamic calligraphy
America 136:511-12 Je 4 '77. P. J. Awn
Khrenov, I. A. and others, eds. Dokumenty i materialy po istorii sovetsko-pol'skikh otnoshenii, v9: Ianvar' 1946 g.-dekabr' 1949 g. 1976
Am Hist R 82:1299 D '77. R. F. Staar
Kidder Smith, G. E. and Davidson, M. B. Architecture in America. 2v.
Commonweal 104:601-3 S 16 '77. W. Andrews
Kieckhefer, R. European witch trials: their foundations in popular and learned culture, 1300-1500. 1976
Ann Am Acad 429:182-3 Ja '77. R. W. England, Jr.
Kiel, H. Looking at pictures with Bernard Berenson
Am Artist 41:47+ F '77. A. Werner
Kienast, W. Deutschland und Frankreich in der Kaiserzeit (900-1270): Weltkaiser und Einzelkönige. 1974-75
Am Hist R 81:1086 D '76. F. J. Pegues
Kieswetter, J. K. Etienne-Denis Pasquier: the last chancellor of France. 1977
Am Hist R 82:1266 D '77. D. H. Pinkney
Kiley, J. C. Self-rescue; introd. by W. F. Buckley
Nat R 29:1441-2 D 9 '77. M. J. Sobran, jr
Kilgore, J. Being a man in a woman's world. 1976
Chr Today 21:44+ F 4 '77. E. Mathiasen
Kilmer, A. D. and others. Sounds from silence: recent discoveries in ancient Near Eastern music
Sci Am 237:28+ O '77. P. Morrison
Kilpatrick, J. J. Foxe's union and other stretchers, tall tales, and discursive reminiscences of happy years in Scrabble, Virginia
Nat R 29:1182 O 14 '77. L. D. Rubin, jr
Kimberlin, R. H. ed. Slow virus diseases of animals and man
Sci Am 236:140-1 My '77. P. Morrison
Kimmich, C. M. Germany and the League of Nations. 1976
Am Hist R 82:1006 O '77. M. M. Lee
King, E. A. Space geology. 1976
Sky & Tel 54:54-5 Jl '77. P. D. Lowman, Jr
King, R. C. ed. Handbook of genetics. 5v. 1974-6
BioScience 27:484 Jl '77. D. L. Hartl
Kingman, L. Break a leg, Betsy Maybe! 1976
Horn Bk 53:56-7 F '77. E. L. Heins
Kingsbury, J. D. Matthew: structure, Christology, kingdom
Chr Cent 94:336-7 Ap 6 '77. M. L. Peel
Kingston, M. H. Woman warrior: memoirs of a girlhood among ghosts. 1976
America 136:176 F 26 '77. J. B. Breslin
Horn Bk 53:198 Ap '77. M. S. Cosgrave
Kinnard, D. War managers
Sat R 5:38-9 Ja 7 '78. W. Goodman
Kinross, L. Ottoman centuries
New Repub 176:31-2 My 7 '77. R. W. Howe
Kira, A. Bathroom. new ed. 1976
Archit Rec 161:45+ F '77. K. Bloomer
Király, B. K. Ferenc Deák. 1975
Am Hist R 81:1164-5 D '76. G. Barany
Kirby, D. G. ed. and tr. Finland and Russia, 1808-1920: from autonomy to independence. 1975
Am Hist R 82:379 Ap '77. P. K. Hamalainen
Kirby, E. S. Russian studies of China: progress and problems of Soviet sinology. 1976
Am Hist R 81:1185 D '76. R. C. Thornton
Kirby-Smith, H. T. United States observatories: a directory and travel guide
Sci Am 236:142 Ap '77. P. Morrison
Kirchner, W. Studies in Russian-American commerce, 1820-1860. 1975
Am Hist R 82:148-9 F '77. J. T. Alexander
Kirkpatrick, J. New presidential elite: men and women in national politics. 1976
Ann Am Acad 432:152-3 Jl '77. P. Lenchner
Society 15:118-20 N '77. E. C. Ladd, jr
Kisch, B. Scales and weights: a historical outline. repr. 1975
Phys Today 30:68 Ja '77. H. C. Wolfe
Kissinger, H. A. American foreign policy
New Yorker 53:70-3 Ag 8 '77. R. Rovere
Kister, K. F. ed. Encyclopedia buying guide. 1976
Consumers Res Mag 60:31 Jl '77
Kistiakowsky, G. B. Scientist at the White House: the private diary of President Eisenhower's special assistant for science and technology; introd. by C. S. Maier. 1976
Am Hist R 82:1100-1 O '77. G. W. Reichard
Bull Atom Sci 33:62-4 Ap '77. D. F. Hornig
New Repub 176:66-8+ Ja 22 '77. J. B. Wiesner
Science 195:168-9 Ja 14 '77. H. Scoville, Jr
Kiyosaki, W. S. North Korea's foreign relations: the politics of accommodation, 1945-1975. 1976
Ann Am Acad 431:152-3 My '77. C. S. Lee
Klagsbrun, F. Too young to die: youth and suicide. 1976
Horn Bk 53:183 Ap '77. M. Dickens
Klaits, J. Printed propaganda under Louis XIV: absolute monarchy and public opinion. 1977
Am Hist R 82:978-9 O '77. A. L. Moote
Klein, H. ed. First World War in fiction
Commonweal 104:566-71 S 2 '77. M. Taylor
Klein, R. S. Portrait of an early American family: the Shippens of Pennsylvania across five generations. 1975
Am Hist R 81:1229 D '76. T. Wendel
Kling, B. B. Partner in empire: Dwarkanath Tagore and the age of enterprise in Eastern India. 1977
Ann Am Acad 433:175 S '77. H. Spodek
Klingenstein, G. Der Aufstieg des Hauses Kaunitz: Studien zur Herkunft und Bildung des Staatskanzlers Wenzel Anton. 1975
Am Hist R 82:135 F '77. W. J. McGill
Klingman, P. D. Josiah Walls: Florida's black congressman of reconstruction. 1976
Am Hist R 82:446-7 Ap '77. C. Vincent
Kluger, R. Members of the tribe
Newsweek 90:112+ S 19 '77. J. N. Baker
Sat R 5:34 O 15 '77. L. Caplan
Knapp, V. J. Europe in the era of social transformation: 1700-present. 1976
Am Hist R 82:82-3 F '77. A. Plakans
Knightley, P. First casualty—from the Crimea to Vietnam: the war correspondent as hero, propagandist, and myth maker. 1975
Am Hist R 81:1074 D '76. S. E. Cooper
Knittl, Z. Optics of thin films. 1976
Phys Today 30:59-60 F '77. P. H. Berning
Knoke, D. Change and continuity in American politics. 1976
Ann Am Acad 432:153 Jl '77. G. Baroni and F. Rotondaro
Knoll, P. W. Rise of the Polish monarchy: Piast Poland in east central Europe, 1320-1370. 1972
Am Hist R 81:1094 D '76. I. Boba
Knowles, D. Bare ruined choirs: the dissolution of the English monasteries. 1976
Am Hist R 82:93 F '77. B. D. Hill
Knox, R. Experiments in astronomy for amateurs
Sky & Tel 54:225-7 S '77. G. Lovi
Koblik, S. ed. Sweden's development from poverty to affluence, 1750-1970; tr. by J. Johnson. 1975
Am Hist R 81:1139 D '76. H. A. Barton
Koch, K. Duplications
America 136:551-2 Je 18 '77. P. LaSalle
New Repub 177:35-6 O 22 '77. L. Pastan
Koch, K. I never told anybody: teaching poetry writing in a nursing home
America 136:551-2 Je 18 '77. P. LaSalle
Commonweal 104:247-9 Ap 15 '77. R. Kuczkowski
Koegler, H. Concise Oxford dictionary of ballet. 1977
Dance Mag 51:26 Ag '77. D. Vaughan

Koehler, S. ed. Its's your environment: things to think about—things to do; il. by S. H. Bingham. 1976
Horn Bk 53:324-5 Je '77. K. M. Klockner
Koehn, I. Mischling, second degree: my childhood in Nazi Germany. 1977
Horn Bk 53:671-2 D '77. E. L. Heins
Kohl, H. On teaching
Todays Educ 66:91 Mr '77. J. M. Gray
Kohn, R. H. Eagle and sword: the Federalists and the creation of the military establishment in America, 1783-1802. 1975
Am Hist Illus 11:49 F '77. M. Blumenson
Kohout, P. White book
Nation 225:282-4 S 24 '77. E. Brater
Kolker, V. M. and Levit, I. Z. Vneshniaia politika Rumynii i rumyno-sovetskie otnosheniia (Sentiabr' 1939-iiun' 1941). 1971
Am Hist R 81:1164 D '76. S. Fischer-Galati
Kolko, G. Main currents in modern American history. 1976
Am Hist R 82:427-8 Ap '77. J. Braeman
America 136:360-1 Ap 16 '77. R. M. Senkewicz
Ann Am Acad 432:175 Jl '77. D. B. Schewe
Commonweal 104:218-19 Ap 1 '77. M. Kammen
Progressive 41:56-8 Ap '77. R. Stone
Kolodny, A. Lay of the land: metaphor as experience and history in American life and letters
Am Scholar 46:399-404 Summ '77. M. Green
Komendant, A. E. 18 years with architect Louis I. Kahn
Archit Rec 162:106-7 mid-Ag '77. H. Berger; A. Tor
Komjathy, A. T. Crises of France's East Central European diplomacy, 1933-1938. 1976
Am Hist R 82:985 O '77. P. S. Wandycz
Konecky, E. Allegra Maud Goldman
Ms 5:37+ Ap '77. A. K. Shulman
Konrád, G. City builder; tr. by I. Sanders
Nation 224:504 Ap 23 '77. I. Sanders
Time 110:128 N 28 '77. P. Gray
Koop, C. E. Right to live: the right to die. 1976
Chr Today 21:45-6 Mr 18 '77. R. Case
Kopelev, L. To be preserved forever; ed. and tr. by A. Austin
America 137:36-7 Jl 16 '77. C. Hughes
New Repub 177:40-1 N 12 '77. A. Astrachan
Korb, L. J. Joint chiefs of staff: the first twenty-five years. 1976
Ann Am Acad 431:167-8 My '77. T. H. Williams
Korbel, J. Twentieth-century Czechoslovakia: the meanings of its history. 1977
Am Hist R 82:1287-8 D '77. V. S. Mamatey
New Repub 176:33 Je 11 '77. M. Peretz
Korda, M. Power! How to get it, how to use it. 1975
Society 15:127-8 N '77. M. Rejai
Korda, M. Success!
Psychol Today 11:162+ N '77. C. Welles
Kornblum, W. Blue-collar community. 1974
Society 14:88-90 S '77. P. M. Hall
Kornweibel, T. Jr. No crystal stair: black life and the Messenger, 1917-1928. 1976
Am Hist R 82:204 F '77. L. Finkle
Kors, A. C. D'Holbach's coterie: an enlightenment in Paris. 1976
Am Hist R 82:649-50 Je '77. I. F. Knight
Korshin, P. J. ed. Widening circle: essays on the circulation of literature in eighteenth-century Europe. 1976
Am Hist R 82:948-9 O '77. F. A. Kafker
Kosinski, J. Blind date
Newsweek 90:121-2 N 21 '77. R. Sokolov
Time 110:104+ O 31 '77. P. Gray
Kosnick, A. and others. Human sexuality: new directions in American Catholic thought
America 137:14-15 Jl 2 '77. J. Gaffney
Commonweal 104:505-7 Ag 5 '77. R. McInerny
Kostas, S. ed. Architect: chapters in the history of the profession. 1976
Am Hist R 82:924-5 O '77. R. Wiedenhoeft
Kotker, Z. Certain man
Chr Cent 94:364 Ap 13 '77. D. Hornbeck
Commonweal 104:287 Ap 29 '77. J. Druska
Nat R 29:164-5 F 4 '77. D. K. Mano
New Repub 176:24-5 F 19 '77. R. Brown
Kotlowitz, R. Boardwalk
Commentary 64:63-5 Jl '77. D. Merkin
New Repub 176:31-2 Ja 15 '77. S. Maloff
Kotz, N. and Kotz, M. L. Passion for equality: George Wiley and the movement
Nation 225:341-3 O 8 '77. J. Beatty
New Repub 177:30-1 N 5 '77. D. P. Moynihan
Kotzwinkle, W. Fata morgana
Sat R 4:23-4 Ap 30 '77. H. Alpert
Kowet, D. Rich who own sports
Bus W p14-15 My 2 '77. G. L. Williams
Kozik, Z. Partie i stronnictwa polityczne w krakowskiem, 1945-1947. 1974
Am Hist R 82:688-9 Je '77. T. Swietochowski
Kraay, C. M. Archaic and classical Greek coins. 1976
Am Hist R 82:926-7 O '77. R. R. Holloway
Krajewski, W. Correspondence principle and growth of science
Sci Am 237:32+ N '77. P. Morrison
Krammer, A. Forgotten friendship: Israel and the Soviet bloc, 1947-53. 1974
Am Hist R 81:1188 D '76. I. T. Naamani
Kramnick, I. Rage of Edmund Burke: portrait of an ambivalent conservative
Nat R 29:1122-3 S 30 '77. M. J. Sobran jr.
New Repub 177:32-4 N 19 '77. G. Himmelfarb
Kranz, H. Participatory bureaucracy: women and minorities in a more representative public service. 1976
M Labor R 100:57 Jl '77. R. A. Hamilton
Kranzler, D. Japanese, Nazis and Jews: the Jewish refugee community of Shanghai, 1938-1945. 1976
Am Hist R 82:714-15 Je '77. L. S. Forman
Krasuski, J. Stosunki polsko-niemieckie, 1919-1932. 1975
Am Hist R 82:397-8 Ap '77. A. M. Cienciala
Kraus, J. Big ear. 1976
Phys Today 30:56 Ap '77. B. F. Burke
Sky & Tel 53:130-1 F '77. W. T. Sullivan, 3d
Kraybill, D. B. Our star-spangled faith. 1976
Chr Today 21:34-8 My 20 '77. S. V. Monsma
Kren, G. M. and Rappoport, L. H. eds. Varieties of psychohistory. 1976
Am Hist R 82:62-3 F '77. R. L. Schoenwald
Kreuger, M. Show boat
Newsweek 90:122+ N 21 '77. M. Jefferson
Krieger, L. Essay on the theory of enlightened despotism. 1975
Am Hist R 81:1072-3 D '76. H. C. Payne
Kroeber, A. L. Yurok myths. 1976
Am West 14:58 S '77. R. F. Heizer
Kroeker, M. E. Great Plains command: William B. Hazen in frontier West. 1976
Am West 14:57 N '77. R. I. Nichols
Krutilla, J. V. and Fisher, A. C. Economics of natural environments: studies in the valuation of commodity and amenity resources. 1975
Liv Wildn 40:36-8 O '76. A. Scott
Kübler-Ross, E. On death and dying
Commonweal 104:471-3 Jl 22 '77. J. Garvey
Kucerová, K. Chorváti a Srbi v strednej Eurôpe: k etnickým, hospodárskym a sociálnym otázkam v 16-17 storocí. 1976
Am Hist R 82:1286 D '77. T. M. Barker
Kuczynski, P. P. Peruvian democracy under economic stress: an account of the Belaúnde administration, 1963-1968. 1977
Am Hist R 82:1376 D '77. P. F. Klarén
Kuffler, S. W. and Nicholls, J. G. From neuron to brain; a cellular approach to the function of the nervous system. 1976
BioScience 27:358 My '77. W. G. Van Der Kloot
Science 198:815-16 N 25 '77. C. F. Stevens
Kuhn, R. Demon of noontide: ennui in western literature
Yale R 66:453-7 Mr '77. L. Nelson, Jr
Kuhne, G. W. Dynamics of personal follow-up. 1976
Chr Today 21:34-5 Ja 21 '77. R. A. Case, 2d
Kulczykowski, M. Chlopskie tkactwo bawelniane w ośrodku andrychowskim w XIX wieku. 1976
Am Hist R 82:1022-3 O '77. R. D. Lewis
Küng, H. On being a Christian. 1976
Chr Cent 94:202-4 Mr 2 '77. D. Tracy
Chr Today 21:50-1 My 6 '77. D. G. Bloesch
Commonweal 104:407-8 Je 24 '77. J. Pelikan
Kunze, R. Wonderful years; tr. by J. Neugroschel
New Yorker 53:141-4 S 26 '77. J. Updike
Newsweek 89:103 My 9 '77. P. S. Prescott
Kurelek, W. Northern nativity. 1976
Horn Bk 53:151-2 Ap '77. M. M. Burns
Kushner, H. I. Conflict on the Northwest coast: American-Russian rivalry in the Pacific Northwest, 1790-1867. 1975
Am Hist R 81:1231 D '76. D. F. Long
Kusmer, K. L. Ghetto takes shape: black Cleveland, 1870-1930. 1976
Am Hist R 82:190 F '77. H. P. Chudacoff
Küther, C. Räuber und Gauner in Deutschland: das organisierte Bandenwesen im 18. und frühen 19. Jahrhundert. 1976
Am Hist R 82:661-2 Je '77. M. W. Gray
Kuznetsov, S. I. Microflora of lakes and its geochemical activity. 1975
BioScience 27:285 Ap '77. J. T. Staley
Kvetko, M. and Ličko, M. J. eds. Zbornik úvah a osobných spomienok o slovenskom národnom povstaní. 1976
Am Hist R 82:687 Je '77. Y. Jelinek
Kyselka, W. and Lanterman, R. North star to southern cross. 1976
Sci Am 236:130 Ja '77. P. Morrison
Sky & Tel 53:212-13 Mr '77. C. A. Federer, Jr.

LaBastille, A. Woodswoman. 1976
Conservationist 31:44 Ja '77. K. M. Beil
Liv Wildn 40:38-40 O '76. P. H. Oehser
Lacan, J. Ecrits: a selection; tr. by A. Sheridan
New Repub 177:34-5 N 12 '77. S. Schneiderman
Lacey, R. Majesty: Elizabeth II and the House of Windsor
Nat R 29:730+ Je 24 '77. W. Murchison
New Repub 176:26-8 F 19 '77. J. L. Lant
Newsweek 89:88 Mr 7 '77. W. Clemons
Sat R 4:20-2 Mr 5 '77. E. Lucie-Smith
Time 109:87+ Mr 7 '77. M. Maddocks
Lacina, V. Krize Československého zemědělství, 1928-1934. 1974
Am Hist R 82:144-5 F '77. Z. Pryor

Ladner, J. A. Mixed families: adoption across racial boundaries
Smithsonian 8:128+ D '77. S. L. Butler
La Haye, T. and La Haye, B. Act of marriage. 1976
Chr Today 21:41 Mr 18 '77. C. E. Cerling, Jr
Laing, L. Archaeology of late Celtic Britain and Ireland c. 400-1200 AD. 1975
Am Hist R 81:1087 D '76. B. S. Bachrach
Laird, C. Chemenuevis. 1976
Am West 14:54 N '77. V. Leon
Lakatos, I. Proofs and refutations: the logic of mathematical discovery. 1976
Science 196:782-3 My 13 '77. P. Kitcher
Lamarsh, J. R. Introduction to nuclear engineering. 1975
Phys Today 30:53 Je '77. E. Melkonian
Lambert, J. H. Cosmological letters on the arrangement of the world-edifice; tr. by S. L. Jaki. 1976
Phys Today 30:61 F '77 R. C. Hart
Sky & Tel 53:380-2 My '77. J. A. Henderson
Lamphear, J. Traditional history of the Jie of Uganda. 1976
Am Hist R 82:1035-6 O '77. D. W. Cohen
Lamson, P. Roger Baldwin: founder of the American civil liberties union; a portrait
Chr Cent 94:179-80 F 23 '77. H. F. Fey
Progressive 41:58-9 D '77. H. Bresler
Landis, B. I. Value judgments in arbitration: a case study of Saul Wallan. 1977
M Labor R 100:76 D '77. R. R. France
Lane, H. Wild boy of Aveyron
Sci Am 236:124-6 Ja '77. P. Morrison
Lang, J. Conquest and commerce: Spain and England in the Americas. 1975
Am Hist R 81:1219 D '76. J. T. Juricer
Lange, O. L. and others, eds. Water and plant life: problems and modern approaches. 1976
BioScience 27:751 N '77. T. T. Kozlowski
Langewiesche, D. Liberalismus und Demokratie in Württemberg zwischen Revolution und Reichsgründung. 1974
Am Hist R 81:1147 D '76. J. F. Harris
Langford, P. Eighteenth century, 1688-1815. 1976.
Am Hist R 82:963-4 O '77. I. K. Steele
Langlois, C. Un diocèse breton au début du XIXe siècle: le diocèse de Vannes au XIXe siècle, 1800-1830. 1974
Am Hist R 82:370-1 Ap '77. G. D. Balsama
Langone, J. Bombed, buzzed, smashed or . . . sober: a book about alcohol. 1976
Horn Bk 53:62 F '77. M. M. Burns
Langridge, D. W. Classification and indexing in the humanities. 1976
Lib J 102:692 Mr 15 '77. J. M. Perreault
Langton, J. Paper chains. 1977
Horn Bk 53:450 Ag '77. V. Haviland
Lanham, R. A. Motives of eloquence: literary rhetoric in the Renaissance
Yale R 66:462-7 Mr '77. M. Rose
Lansdowne, J. T. Birds of the West coast
Sci Am 236:144 Mr '77. P. Morrison
Lapiner, A. Pre-Columbian art of South America. 1976
Américas 29:44-6 O '77. L. Patten
Lappe, F. M. and others. Food first: beyond the myth of scarcity
Progressive 41:53-5 D '77. M. Hertsgaard
Laqueur, T. W. Religion and respectability: Sunday schools and working class culture, 1780-1850. 1976
Am Hist R 82:1250-1 D '77. R. K. Webb
Laqueur, W. Guerrilla; a historical and critical study. 1976
Commentary 63:81-2 Je '77. S. Cropsey
New Repub 176:32-5 Je 18 '77. M. Syrkin
Laqueur, W. History of Zionism. 1976
Am Hist R 82:65-6 F '77. S. M. Poppel
Laqueur, W. Terrorism
Bus W il p 17+ O 17 '77. H. Arneson
Laran, M. and Saussay, J. eds. La Russie ancienne, IXe-XVIIe siècles. 1975
Am Hist R 82:147 F '77. L. Langer
Large, B. Martinû
Am Rec G 41:58-9 D '77. R. F. Kennedy
Larkin, E. Roman Catholic church and the creation of the modern Irish state, 1878-1886. 1975
Am Hist R 82:113-14 F '77. D. H. Akenson
Larkin, J. Housework
Ms 5:46-7+ F '77. A. Rich
Larkin, P. Girl in winter
Commonweal 104:632+ S 30 '77. J. Heidenry
Larsen, K. Forsvar og Folkeforbund: en studie i venstres og det konservative folkepartis forsvarspolitiske meningsdannelse, 1918-1922. 1976
Am Hist R 82:121 F '77. W. D. Andersen
Lash, J. P. Roosevelt and Churchill, 1939-1941: the partnership that saved the West. 1976
Am Hist R 82:1098-9 O '77. W. F. Kimball
Ann Am Acad 432:164-5 Jl '77. F. Bealey
Nat R 29:160-2 F 4 '77. H. V. Jaffa
New Repub 176:76-8 Ja 22 '77. F. Freidel
Lasker, J. Merry ever after: the story of two medieval weddings. 1976
Horn Bk 53:40 F '77. P. Heins
Laskin, A. I. and Lechevalier, H. A. eds. Handbook of microbiology. 4v. 1973
BioScience 27:481-2 Jl '77. G. Stotzky
Laskin, A. I. and Lechevalier, H. A. eds. Handbook of microbiology. condensed ed. 1974
BioScience 27:481-2 Jl '77. G. Stotzky
Lasky, M. J. Utopia and revolution: on the origins of a metaphor, or some illustrations of the problem of political temperament and intellectual climate and how ideas, ideals, and ideologies have been historically related. 1976
Am Hist R 82:1208 D '77. W. W. Wagar
America 137:154-6 S 17 '77. P. H. Connolly
Commentary 63:74-6 My '77. P. Hollander
Nat R 29:780-1 Jl 8 '77. J. Burnham
New Repub 177:36-7 D 3 '77. J. Kirkpatrick
Lasky, V. It didn't start with Watergate
Commentary 64:78-80 O '77. M. F. Plattner
Nat R 29:537-8 My 13 '77
Nat R 29:893-4 Ag 5 '77. W. A. Rusher
Time 110:20+ S 12 '77
Latham, S. Leathercraft
Field & S 82:156 N '77
Latsis, S. ed. Method and appraisal in economics. 1976
Intellect 105:368+ Ap '77. R. M. Larsen
Lauren, P. G. Diplomats and bureaucrats: the first institutional responses to twentieth-century diplomacy in France and Germany. 1976
Am Hist R 82:351 Ap '77. L. L. Farrar, Jr
Laux, J. M. In first gear: the French automobile industry to 1914. 1976
Am Hist R 82:984 O '77. H. D. Peiter
Lavender, D. California: a Bicentennial history. 1976
Am West 14:52 Jl '77. P. Kollings
Lavender, D. David Lavender's Colorado. 1976
Am West 14:54 N '77. J. K. Folsom
Lavin, M. Shrine and other stories
America 137:426-8 D 10 '77. M. Donnarumma
Lawson, E. L. and Yamamori, T. Church growth: everybody's business. 1976
Chr Today 21:32 Ja 7 '77. R. A. Bodey
Lawson, S. F. Black ballots: voting rights in the South, 1944-1969. 1976
Am Hist R 82:1101 O '77. I. A. Newby
Ann Am Acad 434:231-2 N '77. J. J. McCorry
Lazell, J. D. This broken archipelago: Cape Cod and the islands, amphibians and reptiles
Sci Am 237:26 D '77. P. Morrison and P. Morrison
Leakey, R. E. and Lewin, R. Origins: what new discoveries reveal about the emergence of our species and its possible future
Psychol Today 11:134+ O '77. J. Pfeiffer
Sat R 5:24+ N 12 '77. A. Montagu
Lebergott, S. American economy: income, wealth, and want. 1976
M Labor R 100:85-6 Mr '77. P. Gottschalk
Le Bihan, A. Francs-maçons et ateliers parisiens de la Grande Loge de France au XVIIIe siècle (1760-1795). 1973
Am Hist R 81:1126 D '76. J. R. Censer
Lebow, R. N. White Britain and black Ireland: the influence of stereotypes on colonial policy. 1976
Am Hist R 82:364-5 Ap '77. R. E. Burns
Le Carré, J. pseud. Honourable schoolboy
America 137:221-3 O 8 '77. T. Davis
Bus W p 11+ O 3 '77. D. D. McCrary
Newsweek 90:84+ S 26 '77. D. Ansen
Time 110:58-60+ O 3 '77. S. Kanfer
Lecha-Marzo, F. de M. La Cuestión religiosa en las cortes constituyentes de la II república española. 1975
Am Hist R 81:1135-6 D '76. J. M. Sánchez
Leckie, J. and others. Other homes and garbage
Smithsonian 8:130-2 My '77. D. Morris
Le Corbeiller, C. China trade porcelain: patterns of exchange; foreword by J. G. Phillips
Antiques 111:1041-2 My '77. H. A. C. Forbes
Lecourt, D. Marxism and epistemology: Bachelard, Canguilhem, Foucault; tr. by B. Brewster. 1975
Am Hist R 81:1073-4 D '76. N. Levine
Ledbetter, R. History of the Malthusian League, 1877-1927. 1976
Am Hist R 82:640 Je '77. P. Branca
Ledeen, M. A. First Duce: D'Annunzio at Fiume. 1977
Am Hist R 82:1284-5 D '77. A. De Grand
Commentary 64:93-5 D '77. J. Shattan
New Repub 177:30-2 D 17 '77. C. Maier
Lee, A. J. Origins of the popular press in England, 1855-1914. 1976
Ann Am Acad 433:190 S '77. F. B. Wickwire
Lee, C.-J. Japan faces China: political and economic relations in the postwar era. 1976
Am Hist R 82:715 Je '77. A. W. Burks
Lee, K. Ten thousand goddam cattle: a history of the American cowboy in song, story and verse. 1976
Am West 14:63 S '77. J. I. White
Lee, L. Appreciation of stained glass
Craft Horiz 37:10 O '77. R. Kehlmann
Lee, L. One by one
Newsweek 90:100+ D 5 '77. W. Clemons
Lee, L. Walking through the fire
America 137:311-12 N 5 '77. J. W. Donohue
Lee, L. and others. Stained glass
Craft Horiz 37:18-19 F '77. R. Kehlmann

Lee, R. B. and DeVore, I. eds. Kalahari hunter-gatherers; studies of the !Kung San and their neighbors. 1976
Sci Am 236:146 Ap '77. P. Morrison
Science 196:761-3 My 13 '77. B. J. Williams
Leff, G. Dissolution of the medieval outlook: an essay on intellectual and spiritual change in the fourteenth century. 1976
Am Hist R 82:1227 D '77. M. L. Colish
Leff, G. William of Ockham: the metamorphosis of scholastic discourse. 1975
Am Hist R 82:618-19 Je '77. R. Mather
Le Guin, U. K. ed. Nebula award stories eleven
America 136:381-2 Ap 23 '77. W. E. McNelly
Le Guin, U. K. Orsinian tales. 1976
Horn Bk 53:198-9 Ap '77. M. S. Cosgrave
Le Guin, U. K. Very far away from anywhere else. 1976
Horn Bk 53:57 F '77. E. L. Heins
Leibenstein, H. Beyond economic man: a new foundation for microeconomics. 1976
M Labor R 100:87-8 Ap '77. R. S. Higgins
Leigh, M. Mobilizing consent: public opinion and American foreign policy, 1937-1947. 1976
Am Hist R 82:763-4 Je '77. G. Q. Flynn
Ann Am Acad 432:153-4 Jl '77. D. G. Bishop
Lekachman, R. Economists at bay: why the experts will never solve your problems. 1976
M Labor R 100:90-1 F '77. L. Teper
Society 14:93-4 My '77. M. Perlman
Lekai, L. J. Cistercians: ideals and reality
America 137:364-5 N 19 '77. D. Wechter
Lemps, C. H. de Géographie du commerce de Bordeaux à la fin du règne de Louis XIV. 1975
Am Hist R 82:365-6 Ap '77. R. W. Unger
Lens, S. Day before doomsday. An anatomy of the nuclear arms race. 1977
Bull Atom Sci 33:63-4 S '77. S. H. Day, jr
Progressive 41:39 Ag '77. J. M. Swomley, jr
Lentricchia, F. Robert Frost: modern poetics and the landscapes of self
Yale R 67:vi+ O '77
Leong, Sow-theng. Sino-Soviet diplomatic relations, 1917-1926. 1976
Ann Am Acad 433:165-6 S '77. J. Silverstein
Le Patourel, J. Norman empire. 1976
Am Hist R 82:1229 D '77. C. W. Hollister
Lerman, E. Come the sweet by and by
Poetry 130:348-50 S '77. D. Allen
Lerner, G. Female experience: an American documentary
Ms 5:41-2 My '77. E. Merriam
Le Roy Ladurie, E. Montaillou, village occitan de 1294 à 1324. 1975
Am Hist R 81:1090 D '76. C. T. Wood
Leruez, J. Economic planning and politics in Britain. 1975
Ann Am Acad 432:165-6 Jl '77. S. P. Koff
Lesberg, S. Violence in our time
Commonweal 105:26 Ja 6 '78. D. Vellucci
Lesley, C. Remembered laughter
New Yorker 52:89-90+ Ja 2 '77. K. Tynan
Leslie, A. Clare Sheridan
Smithsonian 8:126+ D '77. J. Sakol
Lester, J. Man for Arkansas: Sid McMath and the southern reform tradition. 1976
Am Hist R 82:1351-2 D '77. V. V. Hamilton
Lester, R. I. Confederate finance and purchasing in Great Britain. 1975
Am Hist R 81:1254 D '76. M. Lester
Leuthold, W. African ungulates: a comparative review of their ethology and behaviorial ecology. 1977
Science 198:723-4 N 18 '77. S. M. Green
Levenson, S. Maud Gonne
Ms 6:38-40 O '77. E. Simpson
Leventhal, H. In the shadow of the Enlightenment: occultism and Renaissance science in eighteenth-century America. 1976
Am Hist R 82:431 Ap '77. C. Hansen
Levering, R. B. American opinion and the Russian alliance, 1939-1945. 1976
Am Hist R 82:764 Je '77. M. Small
Levin, B. Forespoken. 1976
Horn Bk 53:58 F '77. A. A. Flowers
Levine, D. A. Internal combustion: the races in Detroit, 1915-1926. 1976
Am Hist R 82:461-2 Ap '77. K. L. Kusmer
Ann Am Acad 431:168-9 My '77. E. L. Thornbrough
Levine, J. A. 'Who will raise the children? New options for fathers (and mothers)
Ms 5:48-9+ Mr '77. B. Garson
Levine, L. W. Black culture and black consciousness: Afro-American folk thought from slavery to freedom
Nation 224:311-13 Mr 12 '77. J. H. Bryant
Smithsonian 8:153-5 O '77. L. Brooks
Levine, P. Names of the lost
Poetry 130:298-300 Ag '77. J. Parini
Levison, H. W. Artists pigments: lightfastness tests and ratings
Am Artist 41:33-5 Jl '77. C. Movalli
Levitan, S. A. and Alderman, K. C. Child care & ABC's too. 1975
M Labor R 100:67-8 Ja '77. J. R. Lyle
Levitan, S. A. and Taggart, R. Promise of greatness. 1976
Ann Am Acad 429:183-4 Ja '77. A. A. Aichinger
Levitin, S. Beyond another door. 1977
Horn Bk 53:315 Je '77. S. H. Holtze
Levy, J. Memoir of an art gallery. 1977
Art in Am 65:35+ My '77. H. Herrera
New Yorker 53:84-6 Jl 4 '77. H. Rosenberg
Levy, R. S. Downfall of the anti-Semitic political parties in imperial Germany. 1975
Am Hist R 82:127 F '77. M. A. Meyer
Lewin, B. Gene expression, v3: Plasmids and phages. 1977
BioScience 27:819 D '77. A. Campbell
Lewin, R. A. ed. Genetics of algae. 1976
Science 195:281 Ja 21 '77 R. Sager
Lewinski, J. and Clark, B. Colour in focus. 1976
Pop Phot 81:84 S '77. I. J. Neubart
Lewis, B. ed. Islam and the Arab world: faith, people, culture
Commentary 63:86-8 Ap '77. W. M. Brinner
Lewis, C. E. and others. Right to health: the problems of access to primary medical care. 1976
Ann Am Acad 432:182-3 Jl '77. C. S. Bourgeois
Lewis, C. M. Prologue to the Chinese revolution: the transformation of ideas and institutions in Hunan Province, 1891-1907. 1976
Am Hist R 82:1311-12 D '77. H. M. Metzgar
Ann Am Acad 433:175-6 S '77. E. L. Farmer
Lewis, C. S. Dark tower and other stories
New Repub 176:29-30 Ap 16 '77. U. K. Le Guin
Lewis, C. S. Joyful Christian
America 137:486-7 D 31 '77. J. B. Breslin
Lewis, D. L. Public image of Henry Ford: an American folk hero and his company. 1976
Am Hist Illus 12:50 My '77. M. Klein
Lewis, G. Testing Christianity's truth claims: approaches to Christian apologetics. 1976
Chr Today 21:46-7 Ap 1 '77. J. Warwick
Lewis, O. and others. Four men: living the revolution: an oral history of contemporary Cuba
America 137:114 Ag 27 '77. J. A. Saliba
Nat R 29:895-6 Ag 5 '77. J. Greenway
Nation 224:759+ Je 18 '77. J. Yglesias
Lewis, O. and others. Four women living the revolution: an oral history of contemporary Cuba
America 137:246-8 O 15 '77. J. Saliba
Leyda, J. Dianying: an account of films and the film audience in China. 1972
Am Hist R 82:417 Ap '77. R. Witke
Leymarie, J. Picasso: artist of the century
America 137:244-5 O 15 '77. D. Leder
Leys, S. pseud. Chinese shadows
Nat R 29:1244-5 O 28 '77. F. B. Randall
Nation 225:21 Jl 2 '77. N. D. Milton and D. Milton
New Repub 177:40-2 Ag 6 '77. B. I. Schwartz
New Yorker 53:177-82 O 24 '77. J. Updike
Newsweek 90:93 S 12 '77. R. Watson
Lhotsky, A. Aus dem Nachlass; ed. by H. Wagner and H. Koller. 1976
Am Hist R 82:80 F '77. H. Gross
Li, D. J. tr. Civilization of China: from the formative period to the coming of the West. 1975
Am Hist R 82:157-8 F '77. C. Leban
Li, L. Japanese army in North China, 1937-1941: problems of political and economic control. 1975
Am Hist R 82:418 Ap '77. W. Whitson
Ann Am Acad 430:195-6 Mr '77. W. H. Elsbree
La libération de la France: actes du Colloque International tenu à Paris du 28 au 31 octobre 1974. 1976
Am Hist R 82:986-7 O '77. S. P. Kramer
Liddell, R. Cavafy: a biography
New Repub 177:36-7 O 22 '77. B. D. Schwartz
New Yorker 53:63-8 Ag 1 '77. H. Moss
Yale R 67:128-35 O '77. M. Ellmann
Lidz, T. Person—his and her development throughout the life cycle. 1976
MH 61:24 Spr '77. M. P. Unterberg
Lieberman, P. On the origins of language. 1975
Science 195:774-5 F 25 '77. M. F. Gibbons, Jr
Liebert, R. J. Disintegration and political action: the changing functions of city government in America. 1976
Ann Am Acad 431:169 My '77. N. Wikstrom
Liehm, M. and Liehm, A. J. Most important art: east European film after 1945. 1977
Am Hist R 82:1290 D '77. D. Kiziria-Smith
New Repub 177:34-6 S 3 '77. J. Simon
Life of Cola di Rienzo, tr. by J. Wright. 1975
Am Hist R 82:346 Ap '77. R. C. Cusimano
Lifton, R. J. Life of the self: toward a new psychology
Commonweal 104:188-90 Mr 18 '77. J. B. Elshtain
Lind, L. R. Studies in pre-Vesalian anatomy: biography, translations, documents. 1975
Am Hist R 82:382-3 Ap '77. G. B. Risse
Lindberg, D. C. Theories of vision from Al-Kindi to Kepler. 1976
Am Hist R 82:334 Ap '77. B. Eastwood
Lindblom, C. E. Politics and markets: the world's political economic systems
Bus W p 17+ D 26 '77. R. G. Magnuson
New Repub 177:32-4 D 17 '77. R. Lekachman
Linden, E. Alms race: the impact of American voluntary aid abroad. 1976
Ann Am Acad 430:180-1 Mr '77. J. M. Hunter

Linden, G. M. Politics principle: Congressional voting on the Civil War amendments and pro-Negro measures, 1838-69. 1976
Am Hist R 82:1077-8 O '77. L. P. Curry
Lindquist, E. Bethany in Kansas: the history of a college. 1975
Am Hist R 82:187-8 F '77. J. F. Hopkins
Lindsey, H. Terminal generation; with C. C. Carlson. 1976
Chr Today 21:40-2 Ap 15 '77. W. W. Gasque
Lintz, J. jr, and Simonett, D. S. eds. Remote sensing of environment. 1976
BioScience 27:752 N '77. C. E. Olson, jr
Phys Today 30:56 Ag '77. F. C. Billingsley
Sci Am 236:138-40 Je '77. P. Morrison
Lionni, L. Parallel botany
Time 110:102 O 31 '77. P. Stoler
Lippman, W. Public persons; ed by G. A. Harrison
New Repub 176:28-9 Mr 12 '77. J. Reston
Lipset, S. M. and Riesman, D. Education and politics at Harvard. 1975
Am Hist R 81:1277-8 D '76. S. Diamond
Lipsky, Yu. N. ed. Atlas obratnoi storony luny, pt3. 1975
Sky & Tel 53:214-15 Mr '77. L. G. Jacchia
Lipton, L. Super 8 book
Mod Phot 41:70 Ag '77. T. Galluzzo
Lipton, M. Why poor people stay poor: urban bias in world development. 1977
Ann Am Acad 433:200-1 S '77. J. E. Dizard
Lipton, M. and Firn, J. Erosion of a relationship: India and Britain since 1960. 1976
Ann Am Acad 429:157-8 Ja '77. P. Lyon
Liss, P. K. Mexico under Spain, 1521-1556: society and the origins of nationality. 1975
Am Hist R 82:1373-4 D '77. R. E. Quirk
List, A. Jr. and List, I. Wall in the forest: the woodlands of North America. 1977
Am For 83:28+ D '77. M. Bush
Horn Bk 53:559 O '77. S. Gagné
Sci Am 237:34 D '77. P. Morrison and P. Morrison
Litteljohn, B. and Drew, W. Superior: the haunted shore. 1975
Liv Wildn 41:34-6 Ap '77. K. Denis
Littell, F. H. Macmillan atlas history of Christianity
America 136:97-8 Mr 5 '77. C. P. Loughran
Little, B. Sir Christopher Wren: a historical biography. 1975
Am Hist R 82:98 F '77. S. J. Greenblatt
Liu, A. P. L. Political culture & group conflict in Communist China. 1976
Ann Am Acad 430:196-7 Mr '77. G. P. Jan
Liu, W. C. and Lo, Y. I. eds. Sunflower splendor: three thousand years of Chinese poetry
America 136:110-11 F 5 '77 J. F. Cotter
Liublinskaia, A. D. and others, eds. Problemy paleografii i kodikologii v SSSR. 1974
Am Hist R 82:1291-2 D '77. D. C. Waugh
Lively, P. Stitch in time. 1976
Horn Bk 53:52-3 F '77. V. Haviland
Lloyd, A. War in the trenches
New Repub 177:28-30 D 17 '77. L. Bushkoff
Lloyd, F. E. Carnivorous plants
Sci Am 236:143-4 My '77. P. Morrison
Lloyd, T. H. English wool trade in the Middle Ages. 1977
Am Hist R 82:1228 D '77. M. Mate
Lo, H.-M. ed. Correspondence of G. E. Morrison, v 1: 1895-1912. 1976
Am Hist R 82:413 Ap '77. H. Z. Schiffrin
Loades, D. M. Politics and the Nation, 1450-1660: obedience, resistance, and public order. 1975
Am Hist R 82:91 F '77. R. M. Warnicke
Lobby, D. Demystification of Yap: dialectics of culture on a Micronesian island. 1976
Science 195:1321-2 Mr 25 '77. J. L. Fischer
Locke, J. Correspondence of John Locke, v 1, 2; ed. by E. S. De Beer. 1976
Am Hist R 82:960 O '77. E. J. Hundert
Lockhart, J. and Otte, E. trs. and eds. Letters and people of the Spanish Indies: sixteenth century. 1976
Am Hist R 81:1284 D '76. J. L. Phelan
Américas 29:25-6 F '77 F. P. Hebblethwaite
Lockwood, C. Manhattan moves uptown
Sat R 4:21-2 F 19 '77. R. Gelatt
Lockwood, S. C. Augustine Heard and company, 1858-1862: American merchants in China. 1971
Am Hist R 82:412 Ap '77. S. W. Barnett
Loeb, A. L. Space structures: their harmony and counterpoint. 1976
Phys Today 30:56-7 F '77. S. C. Abrahams
Loebl, E. My mind on trial
America 137:36-7 Jl 16 '77. C. Hughes
Commentary 63:84-6 Ap '77. S. Cropsey
New Repub 176:32-4 Mr 26 '77. A. Brumberg
Loehlin, J. C. and Nichols, R. C. Heredity, environment, and personality: a study of 850 sets of twins. 1976
Science 195:869-70 Mr 4 '77. I. I. Gottesman and H. H. Goldsmith
Loewe, M. Crisis and conflict in Han China, 104 BC to AD 9. 1975
Am Hist R 82:717-18 Je '77. Y. S. Yu
Loewenberg, R. J. Equality on the Oregon frontier; Jason Lee and the Methodist mission, 1834-43. 1976
Am Hist R 82:742 Je '77. J. F. Cocks

Lohse, E. New Testament environment. 1976
Chr Today 21:48-9 F 4 '77. D. E. Aune
Lomask, M. Minor miracle; an informal history of the National science foundation. 1976
Science 196:750-2 My 13 '77. S. A. Lakoff
Lombardi, J. V. People and places in Colonial Venezuela. 1976
Am Hist R 82:782-3 Je '77. W. Borah
Longacre, E. G. Mounted raids of the Civil war. 1975
Am Hist R 81:1252 D '76. A. R. Sunseri
Longacre, R. E. Anatomy of speech motions
Chr Today 21:40+ My 6 '77. C. F. H. Henry
Longeon, C. Une province française à la Renaissance: la vie intellectuelle en Forez au XVIe siècle. 1975
Am Hist R 82:976-7 O '77. E. Schalk
Loos, A. Cast of thousands
New Repub 176:32-3 Ap 2 '77. J. Bachrach
López, A. Revolt of the Comuñeros, 1721-1735: a study in the colonial history of Paraguay. 1976
Am Hist R 82:1110 O '77. J. S. Saeger
Lopez, C.-A. and Herbert, E. W. Private Franklin: the man and his family. 1975
Am Hist R 81:1223 D '76. C. B. Currey
Lopez, R. S. Commercial revolution of the Middle Ages, 950-1350. 1976
Am Hist R 81:1083-4 D '76. D. Nicholas
Lord, D. C. John F. Kennedy: the politics of confrontation and conciliation. 1977
Am Hist R 82:1364-5 D '77. B. Miroff
Lord, W. Lonely vigil: coastwatchers of the Solomons
Nat R 29:1249-50 O 28 '77. P. L. Buckley
Time 110:72+ Ag 1 '77. R. Z. Sheppard
Lorde, A. Coal
Commonweal 104:762-3 N 25 '77. C. Hahn
Lorde, A. New York head shop and museum
Poetry 129:296-301 F '77. S. M Gilbert
Lorenz, K. Behind the mirror
Psychol Today 11:100+ Jl '77 L. Tiger
Lortie, D. C. Schoolteacher
Commonweal 104:249-52 Ap 15 '77. G. W. Shea
Losick, R. and Chamberlin, M. eds. RNA polymerase. 1976
Science 197:247-8 Jl 15 '77. J. E. Dahlberg
Loughmiller, C. and Loughmiller, L. eds. and comps. Big Thicket legacy
Smithsonian 8:116+ Je '77. E. B. Braly
Louis Philippe, King of the French. Memoirs: 1773-1793; tr. by J. Hardman
New Yorker 53:82-5 Ja 9 '78. N. Bliven
Loveman, B. Struggle in the country: politics and rural labor in Chile, 1919-1973. 1976
Ann Am Acad 434:242 N '77. I. Roxborough
Lovering, R. B. American opinion and the Russian alliance, 1939-1945. 1976
Ann Am Acad 432:166-7 Jl '77. D. T. Cattell
Lovett, R. W. ed. Documents from the Harvard university archives, 1638-1750, pt4: Documents, 1638-1722; pt5: Documents, 1722-1750. 1975
Am Hist R 82:171-2 F '77. R. Middlekauff
Lovins, A. B. Soft energy paths: toward a durable peace
Nation 225:501+ N 12 '77. F. D. Baldwin
Lovoll, O. S. Folk epic: the Bygdelag in America. 1975
Am Hist R 81:1264 D '76. C. H. Chrislock
Low, D. A. and Smith, A. eds. History of East Africa, v3. 1976
Am Hist R 82:1308-9 D '77. R. G. Gregory
Lowe, D. Lost Chicago. 1975
Am Scholar 46:506-13 Aut '77. M. E. Prior
Lowell, R. Day by day
Esquire 89:20+ Ja '78. A. Kazin
Newsweek 90:77 S 5 '77. J. Kroll
Sat R 5:26-8 O 1 '77. L. Simpson
Time 110:70-1 Ag 29 '77. P. Gray
Lowell, R. Selected poems. 1976
Horn Bk 53:199 Ap '77. M. S. Cosgrave
Yale R 66:407-24 Mr '77. H. Vendler
Lowenkoph, M. Politics in Liberia: the conservative road to development. 1976
Ann Am Acad 431:153 My '77. T. H. Etzold
Lowenthal, A. F. ed. Peruvian experiment. 1976
Ann Am Acad 432:158-9 Jl '77. F. D. Miller
Lowrance, W. W. Of acceptable risk: science and the determination of safety. 1976
BioScience 27:130 F '77. J. C. Flato
Lowry, B. Come back, Lolly Ray
Newsweek 89:87 F 14 '77. M. Jefferson
Lowry, L. Summer to die; il. by J. Oliver. 1977
Horn Bk 53:451 Ag '77. M. M. Burns
Luard, E. Types of international society. 1976
Ann Am Acad 431:145 My '77. N. D. Palmer
Lubell, C. ed. Textile collections of the world, v 1: United States and Canada; v2: United Kingdom and Ireland
Craft Horiz 37:19 F '77. M. Sonday
Lubrano, L. L. Soviet sociology of science. 1976
Science 197:856 Ag 26 '77. Y. M. Rabkin
Lucas, R. R. Valley of discord: church and society along the Connecticut river, 1636-1725. 1976
Am Hist R 82:730-1 Je '77. A. T. Vaughan
Lucie-Smith, E. Joan of Arc
Harpers 255:92-3 O '77. F. Taliaferro
Lukacs, J. Last European war: September 1939/December 1941. 1976
Am Hist R 81:1102-3 D '76. G. Wright

Lukas, M. and Lukas, E. Teilhard: the man, the priest, the scientist
America 136:470-1 My 21 '77. T. M. King
Commonweal 104:509 Ag 5 '77. J. P. Appleyard
Nat R 29:1309+ N 11 '77. F. Clinton
Lumley, E. K. Forgotten mandate: a British district officer in Tanganyika. 1976
Ann Am Acad 431:153-4 My '77. J. Vansina
Lunacharsky, A. On literature and art. rev ed. 1973
Art in Am 65:27 Jl '77. D. Davis
Lunde, K. Isabel Bishop
Am Artist 41:50+ F '77. A. Werner
Lunt, J. John Burgoyne of Saratoga. 1975
Am Hist R 81:1228 D '76. H. F. Rankin
Luntinen, P. Baltic question, 1903-1908. 1975
Am Hist R 82:399-400 Ap '77. E. Anderson
Lupo, A. Liberty's chosen home: the politics of violence in Boston
Nation 224:661-3 My 28 '77. S. Blumenthal
Time 109:93-4+ Mr 21 '77. E. Magnuson
Luraghi, R. Gli Stati Uniti. 1974
Am Hist R 82:168 F '77. E. M. Thomas
Luria, A. R. Cognitive development: its cultural and social foundations; tr. by M. Lopez-Morillas and L. Solotaroff. 1976
Science 196:767 My 13 '77. S. H. White
Luttwak, E. N. Grand strategy of the Roman Empire: from the first century A.D. to the third. 1977
Am Hist R 82:930-1 O '77. R. MacMullen
Ann Am Acad 434:222-3 N '77. A. M. Ward
Commentary 64:73-6 S '77. B. Brodie
New Repub 176:55-7 My 21 '77. Z. Yavetz
Luža, R. Austro-German relations in the Anschluss era. 1975
Am Hist R 82:380-1 Ap '77. K. V. Klemperer
Lykes, R. W. Higher education and the United States Office of education (1867-1953). 1975
Am Hist R 82:203 F '77. W. Rudy
Lyman, H. H. Reading and the adult new reader. 1977
Lib J 102:2143 O 15 '77. G. R. Shields
Lynch, J. H. Simoniacal entry into religious life from 1000 to 1260: a social, economic and legal study. 1976
Am Hist R 82:934-5 O '77. L. K. Little
Lynch, K. Managing the sense of a region. 1976
Ann Am Acad 433:191 S '77. O. D. Windsor
Yale R 67:147-9 O '77. M. Lustig
Lyon, D. Christians and sociology. 1976
Chr Today 22:43-5 O 7 '77. D. E. Carlson and D. Ward
Lyons, C. H. To wash an Aethiop white: British ideas about black African educability, 1530-1960. 1975
Am Hist R 82:92 F '77. W. H. Pease
Lyons, F. S. L. Charles Stewart Parnell
America 137:366 N 19 '77. L. Dugan
Lyons, M. France under the directory. 1975
Am Hist R 81:1128-9 D '76. J. R. Censer

MRNA: the relation of structure to function; papers from symposium, Gatlinburg, Tenn, 1976; ed. by W. E. Cohn and E. Volkin. 1976
Science 196:644 My 6 '77. J. F. Scott
Maag R. C. and others, eds. Observe and understand the sun. 1977
Sky & Tel 54:221 S '77. J. M. Pasachoff
Maamägi, V. and others. eds. Eesti NSV ajalugu, v3: 1917. aasta märtsist kuni 50-ndate aastate alguseni. 1971
Am Hist R 82:146-7 F '77. T. Raun
Mabro, R. and Radwan, S. Industrialization of Egypt, 1939-1973: policy and performance. 1976
Am Hist R 82:707 Je '77. R. L. Tignor
McAleer, J. Rex Stout: a biography
Sat R 5:4 D 10 '77. N. Cousins
McAllister, L. G. and Tucker, W. E. Journey to faith: a history of the Christian church (Disciples of Christ) 1975
Am Hist R 81:1236 D '76. J. Findlay
Macaulay, D. Castle
Sci Am 237:38-9 D '77. P. Morrison and P. Morrison
Macaulay, D. Underground. 1976
Horn Bk 53:63 F '77. M. M. Burns
Macaulay, T. B. Letters of Thomas Babington Macaulay, v3: January 1834-August 1841; v4: September 1841-December 1848; ed. by T. Pinney
New Repub 177:31-3 S 10 '77. J. Clive
McBride, T. M. Domestic revolution: the modernisation of household service in England and France, 1820-1920. 1976
Am Hist R 82:625 Je '77. J. W. Scott
McCabe, C. J. and others. Golden door: artist immigrants of America, 1876-1976
Am Artist 41:22-3+ Je '77. A. Werner
McCaffrey, A. Dragonsinger. 1977
Horn Bk 53:320 Je '77. M. M. Burns
MacCaffrey, I. C. Spenser's allegory: the anatomy of imagination
Yale R 67:124-8 O '77. A. B. Giamatti
MacCannell, D. Tourist: a new theory of the leisure class. 1976
Ann Am Acad 429:184-6 Ja '77. I. R. Stuart

McCarthy, A. Circles: a Washington story
America 137:132 S 10 '77. P. McMurray
Commonweal 104:759-60 N 25 '77. B. Mutkoski
Time 110:77 Jl 11 '77. E. Magnuson
McCarthy, C. Pleasures of the game
Sports Illus 47:10 O 10 '77. J. Yardley
McCartney, E. J. Optics of the atmosphere: scattering by molecules and particles. 1976
Phys Today 30:76-7 My '77. F. F. Hall, Jr
Science 196:1084-5 Je 3 '77. J. N. Howard
McClintick, D. Stealing from the rich: the Home-Stake oil swindle
Esquire 88:102+ D '77. J. K. Galbraith
McClung, R. M. Lost wild worlds: the story of extinct and vanishing wildlife of the Eastern hemisphere. 1976
Horn Bk 53:339 Je '77. S. Gagné
Smithsonian 7:145-6+ F '77. C. Ogburn
Maccoby, M. Gamesman: the new corporate leaders. 1977
America 136:510-11 Je 4 '77. R. Hassenger
Atlantic 239:89-91 Ap '77. R. Todd
Bus W p 11 F 14 '77. A. Priest
Commentary 63:94-6 Je '77. S. Rothman
Sat R 4:38-9 Ja 22 '77. P. Roazen
Science 198:920-2 D 2 '77. A. Levine
McConnell, F. D. Spoken seen. 1975
Film Q 30:38-44 Summ '77. S. Fleischer
McCord, P. J. ed. Pope for all Christians
Commonweal 104:280-1 Ap 29 '77. J. L. McKenzie
McCormmach, R. ed. Historical studies in the physical sciences, v4. 1975
Am Hist R 82:66 F '77. A. L. Norberg
McCormmach, R. ed. Historical studies in the physical sciences, v7. 1976
Am Hist R 82:922 O '77. J. Z. Fullmer
McCreary, A. Corrymeela: hill of harmony in Northern Ireland
America 136:489 My 28 '77. J. Joyce
Commonweal 104:410 Je 24 '77. D. Bowman
McCullough, C. Thorn birds
America 136:468-9 My 21 '77. J. B. Breslin
Commonweal 104:473-5 Jl 22 '77. S. Kroll
Harpers 255:78-9 Jl '77. C. Nicol
Newsweek 89:93+ Ap 25 '77. W. Clemons
Time 109:85 My 9 '77. P. Gray
McCullough, D. Path between the seas: the creation of the Panama Canal, 1870-1914
Atlantic 240:85-7 Jl '77. J. Kaplan
Newsweek 89:96 Je 13 '77. W. Clemons
Sat R 4:38-9 Je 11 '77. A. Riding
Smithsonian 8:94-5 Ag '77. J. Barbato
Macdonald, C. Transplants
Poetry 129:289-90 F '77. R. Holland
MacDonald, W. L. Pantheon: design, meaning, and progeny
Sci Am 236:148 Mr '77. P. Morrison
McDonnell, K. Charismatic renewal and the churches
Commonweal 104:573-4 S 2 '77. B. Cooke
MacDougall, M. We almost made it
New Repub 176:34-6 My 7 '77. K. Bode
McElroy, J. Plus
New Repub 176:28-9 Mr 19 '77. T. LeClair
McFadden, C. Serial: a year in the life of Marin County
Commentary 64:76-8 O '77. D. Merkin
Ms 6:44-5 N '77. S. Weller
Sat R 4:49 S 3 '77. T. H. Middleton
McFarland, G. W. Mugwumps, morals and politics, 1884-1920. 1975
Am Hist R 82:459 Ap '77. J. M. Dobson
McFarland, K. D. Harry H. Woodring: a political biography of FDR's controversial Secretary of war. 1975
Am Hist R 82:468-9 Ap '77. G. E. Wheeler
Macfarlane, A. Psychology of childbirth
Psychol Today 11:94+ Ag '77. J. Steinberg
McGee, J. S. Godly man in Stuart England: Anglicans, puritans, and the two tables, 1620-1670. 1976
Am Hist R 82:631-2 Je '77. T. Liu
Ann Am Acad 434:223 N '77. J. L. Haines
McGovern, J. R. Yankee family. 1975
Am Hist R 81:1230 D '76. F. McDonald
McGraw, E. J. Really weird summer. 1977
Horn Bk 53:532-3 O '77. E. L. Heins
Machaliński, Z. Gospodarcza myśl morska II rzeczypospolitej (1919-1939). 1975
Am Hist R 82:397 Ap '77. S. M. Horak
Machlup, F. ed. Essays on Hayek
Nat R 29:502 Ap 29 '77. W. A. Wallis
Machlup, F. History of thought on economic integration. 1977
Ann Am Acad 434:242-3 N '77. C. E. Staley
Machovec, M. Marxist looks at Jesus. 1976
Chr Cent 94:596-7 Je 22 '77. F. S. Fiorenza
Chr Today 21:54-5 S 9 '77. J. S. Tinney
McHugh, H. Dangers
Ms 6:36 N '77. J. Thurman
McHugh, J. T. ed. Death, dying and the law. 1976
Chr Today 21:30+ Ag 26 '77. R. A. Case, 2d
McIlvanney, W. Laidlaw
Time 109:68-9 Je 27 '77. P. Gray
McInerny, R. Gate of heaven
Commonweal 104:184-6 Mr 18 '77. D. O'Connell
McInerny, R. Rogerson at bay
Commonweal 104:184-6 Mr 18 '77. D. O'Connell

Mack, J. E. Prince of our disorder: the life of T. E. Lawrence. 1976
Commentary 64:51-6 Jl '77. E. Kedourie
Commonweal 104:470-3 Jl 22 '77. J. B. Elshtain
Progressive 41:41-2 Jl '77. T. J. Spinner, Jr
Mackay, A. L. comp. Scientific quotations: the harvest of a quiet eye; ed. by M. Ebison
Sci Am 237:137-8 Ag '77. P. Morrison
McKay, D. H. Housing and race in industrial society. 1977
Ann Am Acad 434:243-5 N '77. W. F. Smith
McKay, J. P. Tramways and trolleys: the rise of urban mass transport in Europe. 1976
Am Hist R 82:349-50 Ap '77. C. L. Gilb
McKee, A. Death raft
Psychol Today 10:92-3 Mr '77. M. Johnston
MacKenzie, N. and MacKenzie, J. Fabians
Nation 224:663-4 My 28 '77. A. Fremantle
New Repub 176:35-7 Mr 5 '77. S. Weintraub
Sat R 4:26-7 Ap 2 '77. W. Arnold
McKeown, T. Modern rise of population. 1976
Science 197:652-3 Ag 12 '77. E. Van De Walle
Mackie, E. W. Science and society in prehistoric Britain
Am Scholar 46:530-2 Aut '77. O. Gingerich
McLaren, A. Mammalian chimeras. 1976
Sci Am 237:57+ S '77. P. Morrison
Science 195:1323 Mr 25 '77. W. K. Whitten
MacLeish, A. New and collected poems, 1917-1976
Poetry 130:102-7 My '77. R. Siegel
McLellan, D. S. Dean Acheson: the State department years. 1976
Am Hist R 82:771-2 Je '77. A. Deconde
America 136:58-9 Ja 22 '77. F. X. Winters
McLellan, V. and Avery, P. Voices of guns
Progressive 41:41 Ag '77. C. Fager
McMillan, P. J. Marina and Lee
Newsweek 90:105 O 31 '77. R. Sokolov
Time 110:106+ N 14 '77. P. Blake
MacMullen, R. Roman government's response to crisis, A.D. 235-337. 1976
Am Hist R 82:614 Je '77. S. I. Oost
McNeal, R. H. ed. Resolutions and decisions of the Communist party of the Soviet Union, v 1: The Russian Social Democratic Labour party, 1898-October 1917, ed. by R. C. Elwood; v2: The early Soviet period: 1917-1929, ed. by R. Gregor; v3: The Stalin years: 1929-1953, ed. by R. H. McNeal; v4: The Khrushchev years, 1953-1964, ed. by G. Hodnett. 1974
Am Hist R 81:1178 D '76. R. P. Browder
McNeill, J. J. Church and the homosexual
Chr Cent 94:155-6 F 16 '77. H. W. Stroup, Jr
Commonweal 104:376-8 Je 10 '77. S. C. Charles
McNeill, W. H. Plagues and peoples. 1976
Am Hist R 82:604-5 Je '77. N. J. G. Pounds
Am Scholar 46:526+ Aut '77. J. Oppenheimer
Bus W p 17-18 Ag 15 '77. J. Kapstein
Natur Hist 86:95-6+ Ap '77. G. Majno
Macneish, R. S. and others. Prehistory of the Tehuacán Valley, v5: Excavations and reconnaissance. 1975
Am Hist R 82:223 F '77. C. Gabel
McPhee, J. Coming into the country
Atlantic 241:91-2 Ja '78. B. DeMott
Bus W p 11 D 19 '77. S. G. Michaud
Nation 226:21-2 Ja 7 '78. W. R. Hunt
New Repub 178:36-7 Ja 7 '78. C. Murphy
Time 110:78+ D 5 '77. P. Gray
McPhee, J. John McPhee reader; ed. by W. L. Howarth
America 136:115 F 5 '77. T. Ichniowski
Sat R 4:36-7 Ja 22 '77. A. Wolff
McPherson, J. A. Elbow room
Newsweek 90:116 O 17 '77. M. Jefferson
McPherson, J. M. Abolitionist legacy: from Reconstruction to the NAACP. 1976
Am Hist R 81:1256-7 D '76. G. M. Fredrickson
McQuarrie, D. A. Statistical mechanics. 1976
Phys Today 30:58-9 F '77. C. E. Reid
MacQuitty, W. Island of Isis: Philae, temple of the Nile
Sci Am 237:151 Jl '77. P. Morrison
Macrae, D. jr. Social function of social science. 1976
Ann Am Acad 433:191-3 S '77. D. Silverman
Madariaga, S. de. Morning without noon: memoirs
New Repub 176:34 Ap 9 '77. N. Sacks
Maddow, B. Faces, a narrative history of the portrait in photography. 1977
Art in Am 65:37+ N '77. S. Schwartz
Madison, J. Papers of James Madison, v9: 9 April 1786-24 May 1787, with supplement 1781-1784; ed. by W. M. E. Rachal. 1975
Am Hist R 81:1226 D '76. J. A. Schutz
Madsen, A. Hearts and minds: the common journey of Simone de Beauvoir and Jean-Paul Sartre
Progressive 41:55-6 D '77. H. McDonald
Maegaard, J. Studien zur Entwicklung des dodekaphonen Satzes bei Arnold Schönberg, v1: Chronologischer Teil; v2: Analyticher Teil; v3: Notenbeilage. 1972
Mus Q 63:273-82 Ap '77. G. Perle
Maeroff, G. I. and Buder, L. New York times guide to suburban public schools: Long Island, Westchester and Rockland, Connecticut, New Jersey
Todays Educ 66:102 Ja '77. S. Villano

Magnou Nortier, E. La société laïque et l'église dans la province ecclésiastique de Narbonne (zone cispyrénéenne) de la fin du VIIIe à la fin du XIe siècle. 1974
Am Hist R 82:937-8 O '77. K. G. Madison
Mahan, A. T. Letters and papers of Alfred Thayer Mahan, 3v. ed. by R. Seager, 2d and D. D. Maguire, 1976
Am Hist R 82:454 Ap '77. P. Karsten
Mahapatra, J. Father's house
Poetry 130:350-2 S '77. D. Allen
Mahapatra, J. Rain of rites
Poetry 130:350-2 S '77. D. Allen
Mailer, N. Genius and lust: a journey through the major writings of Henry Miller
Nation 224:117-18 Ja 29 '77. W. Curnow
Maimann, H. Politik im Wartesaal: österreichische Exilpolitik in Grossbritannien, 1938-1945. 1975
Am Hist R 82:137 F '77. J. Haag
Majno, G. Healing hand: man and wound in the ancient world. 1975
Am Hist R 82:66-7 F '77. J. Scarborough
Conservationist 31:45-6 Mr '77. R. A. Morse
Malalgoda, K. Buddhism in Sinhalese society, 1750-1900: a study of religious revival and change. 1976
Am Hist R 82:423-4 Ap '77. M. Adas
Ann Am Acad 432:159-60 Jl '77. D. E. Smith
Malettke, K. Opposition und Konspiration unter Ludwig XIV: Studien zu Kritik und Widerstand gegen System und Politik des französischen Königs während der ersten Hälfte seiner persönlichen Regierung. 1976
Am Hist R 82:979 O '77. L. Rothkrug
Malloy, J. M. ed. Authoritarianism and corporatism in Latin America. 1977
Am Hist R 82:1102-3 O '77. R. H. Chilcote
Maloney, E. A. History of Buckingham County. 1976
Negro Hist Bull 40:736 Jl '77. A. Scally
Malraux, A. Lazarus
Commonweal 104:821-2 D 23 '77. W. Weathers
Malraux, A. Picasso's mask
New Yorker 52:79-81 Ja 31 '77. V. S. Pritchett
Maltby, A. ed. Classification in the 1970s: a second look. 1976
Lib J 102:2017 O 1 '77. J. D. Anderson
Mamalakis, M. J. Growth and structure of the Chilean economy: from independence to Allende. 1976
Ann Am Acad 432:189-90 Jl '77. J. R. Behrman
Mamdani, M. Politics and class formation in Uganda. 1976
Am Hist R 82:714 Je '77. M. C. Young
Manchester, W. Controversy: and other essays in journalism 1950-1975
Nat R 29:162+ F 4 '77. W. Murchison
Mancuso, T. F. Help for the working wounded 1976
M Labor R 100:63-4 My '77. H. C. Morton
Mandel, N. J. Arabs and Zionism before World War I. 1977
Am Hist R 82:1031-2 O '77. B. C. Busch
Mandelbaum, M. Anatomy of historical knowledge. 1977
Am Hist R 82:1209 D '77. R. Stromberg
Mandell, M. Being safe. 1972
Consumers Res Mag 60:29 F '77
Mandelstam, O. Selected essays; tr. by S. Monas
New Yorker 53:152-4+ S 12 '77. G. Steiner
Mander, A. V. Blood ties: a woman's history; with S. F. Hofbauer
Ms 5:108-9 My '77. L. S. Schwartz
Manglapus, R. S. Japan in Southeast Asia: collision course. 1976
Ann Am Acad 431:155-6 My '77. P. W. Van Der Veur
Manglapus, R. S. Philippines: the silenced democracy. 1976
Ann Am Acad 429:158-9 Ja '77. L. M. Purnell
Mann, B. Die Württemberger und die deutsche Nationalversammlung, 1848-49. 1975
Am Hist R 82:662 Je '77. F. Eyck
Mann, H. Der Untertan
Nation 225:346-8 O 8 '77. M. Kowal
Mann, T. and Kahler, E. Exceptional friendship: the correspondence of Thomas Mann and Erich Kahler; tr. by R. Winston and C. Winston
Nation 225:309-11 O 1 '77. L. Kriegel
Nation 225:343-6 O 8 '77. L. Kriegel
Mann, T. and Kerényi, K. Mythology and humanism: the correspondence of Thomas Mann and K. Kerényi; tr. by A. Gelley
Nation 225:309-11 O 1 '77. L. Kriegel
Nation 225:343-6 O 8 '77. L. Kriegel
Mann, W. Operas of Mozart
Hi Fi 28:MA37 Ja '78. P. J. Smith
Manniche, L. tr. and il. How Djadja-em-ankh saved the day: a tale from ancient Egypt. 1977
Horn Bk 53:301 Je '77. P. Heins
Manning, B. English people and the English revolution. 1640-1649. 1976
Am Hist R 82:96 F '77. C. Holmes
Manton, J. Mary Carpenter and the children of the streets. 1976
Am Hist R 82:358-9 Ap '77. M. Vicinus
Manvell, R. and Fraenkel, H. Hundred days to Hitler. 1974
Am Hist R 81:1100-1 D '76. D. B. Stenzel

March, N. H. and Tosi, M. P. Atomic dynamic in liquids. 1977
Phys Today 30:69+ O '77. K. E. Gubbins
Science 197:150-1 Jl 8 '77. B. J. Alder
Marchalonis, J. J. ed. Comparative immunology. 1976
BioScience 27:620 S '77. R. T. Kubo
Marcus, G. J. Heart of oak: a survey of British sea power in the Georgian era. 1975
Am Hist R 82:99-100 F '77. R. A. Courtemanche
Marcus, H. G. Life and times Menelik II: Ethiopia, 1844-1913. 1975
Am Hist R 82:1305-6 D '77. R. L. Hess
Marcus, J. R. Early American Jewry: the Jews of New York, New England and Canada, 1649-1794, v 1. 1975
Am Hist R 81:1216-17 D '76. L. A. Jick
Marder, A. Operation Menace: the Dakar expedition and the Dudley North affair. 1976
Am Hist R 82:110-11 F '77. D. Stafford
Mare, Lusco-Indicum: études et documents sur l'histoire de l'Océan Indien et des pays riverains à l'époque e la domination portugaise, v 1. 1971
Am Hist R 81:1137-8 D '76. A. L. Udovitch
Margaria, R. Biomechanics and energetics of muscular exercise. 1976
Sci Am 236:147-8 Mr '77. P. Morrison
Science 196:50-1 Ap 1 '77. R. E. Davies
Markova, Z. B'lgarskoto ts'rkovno-natsionalno dvizhenie do Krimskata voina. 1976
Am Hist R 82:1017 O '77. J. D. Bell
Markovitch, T. J. Histoire des industries françaises: les industries lainieres de Colbert à la revolution. 1976
Am Hist R 82:649 Je '77. J. J. Hurt
Marks, G. and Beatty, W. K. Epidemic. 1976
Am Hist R 82:604-5 Je '77. N. J. G. Pounds
Marks, S. Illusion of peace: international relations in Europe, 1918-1933. 1976
Am Hist R 82:1239 D '77. W. E. Scott
Markus, R. A. Christianity in the Roman world. 1974
Am Hist R 82:1223 D '77. J. S. Preus
Marlow, H. C. and Davis, H. M. American search for woman. 1976
Am Hist R 82:473 Ap '77. M. C. Davis
Marquand, D. Ramsay MacDonald. 1977
Am Hist R 82:1256-7 D '77. S. Koss
New Repub 177:29-32 O 8 '77. M. Muggeridge
Márquez, G. G. Autumn of the patriarch: tr. by G. Rabassa
Am Scholar 46:266-9 Spr '77. M. Kaplan
Marrin, A. Nicholas Murray Butler. 1976
Am Hist R 82:204 F '77. B. G. Rader
Mars, F. Witness in Philadelphia
Nation 225:597-8 D 3 '77. J. Taylor
Marsh, N. Last ditch
Newsweek 89:91 Je 20 '77. M. Jefferson
Marsh, R. M. and Mannari, H. Modernization and the Japanese factory. 1976
Ann Am Acad 429:159-61 Ja '77. C. Hoffman
Marshall, G. C. Memoirs of my services in the World War, 1917-1918; introd by J. L. Collins, jr. 1976
Am Hist Illus 12:47-8 N '77. F. C. Pogue
Marshall, I. H. Origins of New Testament Christology. 1976
Chr Today 21:42-3 S 23 '77. L. W. Hurtado
Marshall, J. Papers of John Marshall, v 1: Correspondence and papers, November 10, 1775-June 23, 1788; account book, September 1783-June 1788; ed. by H. A. Johnson. 1974
Am Hist R 81:1225 D '76. M. Bloomfield
Marshall, P. J. East Indian fortunes: the British in Bengal in the eighteenth century. 1976
Am Hist R 82:1245 D '77. E. B. Jones
Martin, A. James J. Hill and the opening of the Northwest. 1976
Am Hist R 82:751 Je '77. S. Salsbury
Am West 14:62 My '77. C. Miner
Fortune 95:63+ Ja '77. G. Burck
Martin, D. Battered wives. 1976
Society 14:92-3 S '77. B. Star
Martin, G. Madam secretary: Frances Perkins. 1976
Am Hist R 82:209 F '77. B. Bellush
Martin, J. B. Adlai Stevenson and the world: the life of Adlai E. Stevenson. 1977
Newsweek 90:117+ O 24 '77. W. Clemons
Martin, J. B. Adlai Stevenson of Illinois: the life of Adlai E. Stevenson. 1976
Am Hist R 82:471 Ap '77. R. A. Lee
Martin, M. L. Kimbangu: an African prophet and his church. 1976
Chr Today 22:42 O 7 '77. I. Hexham
Martin, T. Race first: the ideological and organizational struggles of Marcus Garvey and the Universal negro improvement association. 1976
Am Hist R 82:205-6 F '77. A. Meier
Ann Am Acad 429:174-5 Ja '77. R. W. Logan
Martínez, C. P. S. Repercusiones de Pavón en Mendoza a través del periodismo (1861-1863). 1973
Am Hist R 82:483-4 Ap '77. J. T. Criscenti
Marty, M. E. Nation of behavers. 1976
Ann Am Acad 431:176-7 My '77. D. Schnall
Chr Cent 94:68 Ja 26 '77. D. M. Kelley
Commonweal 104:347-9 My 27 '77. P. R. Messbarger
Martz, J. D. and Baloyra, E. A. Electoral mobilization and public opinion: the Venezuelan campaign of 1973. 1976
Ann Am Acad 433:176-7 S '77. R. H. Chilcote
Marwil, J. Trails of counsel: Francis Bacon in 1621. 1976
Am Hist R 82:97 F '77. R. Howell, Jr.
Marx, W. Acts of God, acts of man
Conservationist 32:43 S '77. A. S. Fick
Smithsonian 8:96-7 Jl '77. J. S. Rosenberg
Masada, Y. Analysis of essential oils by gas chromatography and mass spectrometry
Sci Am 236:134-5 F '77. P. Morrison
Maselli, D. Tra risveglio e millennio: storia delle chiese cristiane dei fratelli, 1836-1886. 1974
Am Hist R 81:1156-7 D '76. R. M. Bell
Mason, L. and Ludman, J. eds. Print collector's quarterly: an anthology of essays on eminent printmakers of the world. 10v
Am Artist 41:22-3 O '77. D. Preiss
Mason, T. W. Sozialpolitik im Dritten Reich: Arbeiterklasse und Volksgemeinschaft. 1977
Am Hist R 82:1008-9 O '77. W. Jannen, jr
Masselos, J. C. Towards nationalism: group affiliations and the politics of public associations in nineteenth-century western India. 1974
Am Hist R 82:163-4 F '77. T. R. Metcalf
Masterson, J. R. Psychotherapy of the borderline adult. 1976
MH 61:23 Spr '77. D. I. Carson
Masterton, R. B. and others, eds. Evolution, brain, and behavior: persistent problems. 1976
BioScience 27:690 O '77. F. A. Jenkins, jr
Science 196:756-7 My 13 '77. J. H. Kaas
Mathews, V. H. Libraries for today and tomorrow: how do we pay for them? Who uses them? Who staffs them? What are their services? introd. by A. B. Martin. 1976
Lib J 102:561 Mr 1 '77. L. Estabrook
Mathieu, J. P. Optics. 1975
Phys Today 30:56 D '77. S. S. Ballard and A. J. Adams
Mathieu, L. Gustave Moreau
Art N 76:64 N '77. A. Frankenstein
Matile, P. Lytic compartment of plant cells. 1975
BioScience 27:54 Ja '77. R. A. Leigh
Matson, P. H. Place in the country: A narrative on the imperfect art of homesteading and the value of ignorance
Nat R 29:1004 S 2 '77. N. Muhlen
Matsunaga, S. M. and Ping, C. Rulemakers of the house. 1976
Ann Am Acad 431:169-70 My '77. M. F. Rice
Matthew, D. Medieval European community. 1977
Am Hist R 82:1225-6 D '77. E. Peters
Matthias, J. Turns
Poetry 129:234-5 Ja '77. R B. Shaw
Mattingly, P. H. Classless profession
Commonweal 104:249-52 Ap 15 '77. G. W. Shea
Mattson, R. Regeneration
Sci Am 237:60+ S '77. P. Morrison
Matzkin, M. A. Super 8 film makers handbook
Mod Phot 41:70-1 Ag '77. T. Galluzzo
Maurstad, B. L. ed. Library and the contemporary arts. 1977
Lib J 102:2143 O 15 '77. J. Sabine
Mauskopf, S. H. Crystals and compounds: molecular structure and composition in nineteenth-century French science. 1976
Am Hist R 82:983-4 O '77. L. P. Williams
Maxa, R. Dare to be great
Bus W p 14 F 21 '77. D. Dunn
Maximov, V. E. ed. Kontinent
Nat R 29:396-7 Ap 1 '77. R. Brookhiser
Maxwell, W. Over by the river and other stories
New Repub 177:28-9 S 10 '77. J. C. Oates
May, E. R. Making of the Monroe doctrine. 1975
Am Hist R 81:1238-9 D '76. L. S. Kaplan
Ann Am Acad 432:175-6 Jl '77. R. Schlatter
May, G. S. Most unique machine: the Michigan origins of the American automobile industry. 1975
Am Hist R 82:200 F '77. J. J. Flink
May, H. F. Enlightenment in America. 1976
Am Hist R 82:722-3 Je '77. J. Appleby
America 136:342-3 Ap 9 '77. J. L. Connelly
May, H. S. Tragedy of Erasmus: a psychohistoric approach. 1975
Am Hist R 82:376-7 Ap '77. W. K. Ferguson
May, R. M. ed. Theoretical ecology: principles and applications. 1976
Science 196:51 Ap 1 '77. J. Roughgarden
Mayr, E. Evolution and the diversity of life: selected essays. 1976
Science 195:867 Mr 4 '77. P. H. Raven
Mazer, N. F. Dear Bill, remember me? and other stories. 1976
Horn Bk 53:58-9 F '77. A. A. Flowers
Mazer, N. F. and Mazer, H. Solid gold kid. 1977
Horn Bk 53:451-2 Ag '77. E. L. Heins
Mazlish, B. Revolutionary ascetic: evolution of a political type. 1976
Am Hist R 82:336-7 Ap '77. P. Loewenberg
Commonweal 104:470-3 Jl 22 '77. J. B. Elshtain

Meaburn, J. Detection and spectrometry of faint light. 1976
Phys Today 30:58+ Jl '77. D. C. O'Shea
Meaning in anthropology; papers from conference, Santa Fe, N.M. 1974; ed. by K. H. Basso and H. A. Selby. 1976
Science 195:279-80 Ja 21 '77. M. J. Swartz
Mechanic, D. ed. Growth of bureaucratic medicine: an inquiry into the dynamics of patient behavior and the organization of medical care. 1976
Ann Am Acad 432:182-3 Jl '77. C. S. Bourgeois
Society 14:88-90 Ja '77. B. Barber
Mechanisms of mineralization in the invertebrates and plants; papers from symposium, Georgetown, S.C. 1974; ed. by N. Watabe and K. M. Wilbur. 1976
BioScience 27:818 D '77. H. D. Isenberg
Science 196:1311 Je 17 '77. K. M. Towe
Medicine in seventeenth century England: a symposium held at UCLA in honor of C. D. O'Malley; ed. by A. G. Debus. 1974
Am Hist R 82:95-6 F '77. J. Duffy
Medieval learning and literature: essays presented to Richard William Hunt; ed. by J. J. G. Alexander and M. T. Gibson. 1976
Am Hist R 82:73-4 F '77. R. W. Pfaff
Medlin, V. D. and Parsons, S. L. eds. Nabokov and the Russian provisional government, 1917; introd. by R. P Browder. 1976
Am Hist R 81:1177-8 D '76. W. G. Rosenberg
Medved, M. and Wallechinsky, D. What really happened to the class of '65?
America 136:107-9 F 5 '77. J. W. Donohue
Commonweal 104:54-6 Ja 21 '77. E. McConville
Medvedev, R. A. ed. Samizdat register
Nation 225:727-9 D 31 '77. A. J. Rieber
New Repub 177:40-1 N 12 '77. A. Astrachan
Sat R 4:37-8 S 17 '77. S. Jacoby
Medvedev, R. A. and Medvedev, Z. A. Khrushchev: the years in power; tr. by A. R. Durkin. 1976
Am Hist R 82:1028 O '77. A. Dallin
Commentary 63:74-6 F '77. J. Rubenstein
Mee, C. L. Jr. Visit to Haldeman and other states of mind
Time 109:99-100 Je 13 '77. L. Morrow
Mehring, M. High resolution NMR spectroscopy in solids. 1976
Phys Today 30:67+ O '77. A. N. Garroway
Mehta, V. Mahatma Gandhi and his apostles
America 136:570-1 Je 25 '77. J. Novak
Commonweal 104:600-1 S 16 '77. M. Zeik
Nation 225:26-8 Jl 2 '77. L. A. Gordon
New Repub 177:32-5 Jl 9 '77. A. M. Davidon
Sat R 14:34-5 Ja 22 '77. B. Cook
Meier, B. Die Tonarten der klassischen Vokalpolyphonie nach den Quellen dargestellt. 1974
Mus Q 62:591-7 O '76. P. Bergquist
Meier, R. Richard Meier, architect; introd. by K. Frampton
Archit Rec 161:45 Je '77. J. Barnett
Meilrach, D. Z. Creating small wood objects, as functional sculpture. 1976
Am For 83:36-7 Je '77. M. Bush
Meinel, A. B. and Meinel, M. P. Applied solar energy: an introduction. 1976
Phys Today 30:66 Ja '77. P. E. Glaser
Meislin, J. ed. Rehabilitation medicine and psychiatry. 1976
MH 60:30-1 Wint '77. H. C. Modlin
Meisner, M. and Murphey, R. eds. Mozartian historian: essays on the works of Joseph R. Levenson. 1976
Am Hist R 82:157 F '77. A. Feuerwerker
Meister, D. and Loftis, A. Long time coming: the struggle to unionize America's farm workers
America 137:38-9 Jl 16 '77. G. Higgins
Nation 224:693-4 Je 4 '77. C. Biffle
Meland, B. E. Fallible forms and symbols: discourses on method in a theology of culture
Chr Cent 94:1042-3 N 9 '77. S. Cain
Melham, T. John Muir's wild America. 1976
Pop Phot 81:74+ Jl '77. B. Poli
Mellaart, J. Neolithic of the Near East. 1976
Am Hist R 81:1185-6 D '76. P. E. L. Smith
Mellen, J. Waves at Genji's door: Japan through its cinema. 1976
Film Q 31:55-8 Wint '77. S. Thornton
Meller, H. E. Leisure and the changing city, 1870-1914. 1976
Am Hist R 82:969 O '77. L. L. Shiman
Mellor, J. W. New economics of growth: a strategy for India and the developing world. 1976
Ann Am Acad 430:224-5 Mr '77 J. Das Gupta
Mellor, R. Thea Romī: the worship of the goddess Roma in the Greek world. 1975
Am Hist R 82:339 Ap '77. J. R. Fears
Melnikas, A. Corpus of the miniatures in the manuscripts of Decretum Gratiani. 3v
Art N 76:103-4 F '77. C. E. Gilbert
Meltzer, M. Taking root: Jewish immigrants in America. 1976
Horn Bk 53:65 F '77. A. A. Flowers
Meltzer, M. Violins and shovels: the WPA arts projects. 1976
Horn Bk 53:178-9 Ap '77. E. L. Heins

Mencken, H. L. New Mencken letters; ed. by C. Bode
Am Scholar 46:411-13 Summ '77. W. Haley
America 136:571-2 Je 25 '77. T. Ichniowski
New Repub 176:31-2 Mr 12 '77. M. S. Ross
Sat R 4:34 F 5 '77. R. F. Moss
Mendelowitz, D. M. Guide to drawing
Am Artist 41:35+ Jl '77. C. Movalli
Mendershausen, H. Coping with the oil crisis: French and German experiences. 1976
Ann Am Acad 433:201-2 S '77. R. M. Larsen
Menendez, A. J. Religion at the polls
Chr Cent 94:1040-2 N 9 '77. C. E. Brewster
Mentally retarded and society; proceedings of conference, Niles, Mich. 1974; ed. by M. J. Begab and S. A. Richardson. 1975
Science 196:1192-4 Je 10 '77. E. Zigler
Menuhin, Y. Unfinished journey
Hi Fi 27:MA37-8 S '77. S. Fleming
New Repub 176:34-5 My 14 '77. L. Botstein
Sat R 4:54-5 Ap 16 '77. R. Gelatt
Menuhin, Y. and Primrose, W. Yehudi Menuhin music guides
Am Rec 40:61-2 F '77. E. Belov
Mercier, V. Beckett/Beckett
Commonweal 104:605-6 S 16 '77. P. Corwin
Nation 225:215-16 S 10 '77. E. Brater
Sat R 4:22 Ap 30 '77. P. Auster
Meredith, D. L. Search at Loch Ness. 1977
BioScience 27:817 D '77. J. R. Greenwell
Merkl, P. H. Political violence under the Swastika: 581 early Nazis. 1975
Am Hist R 82:669-71 Je '77. R. A. Pois
Merrill, B. Jr. Jefferson's nephews: a frontier tragedy. 1976
Am Hist R 82:741 Je '77. F. M. Brodie
Am West 14:61 Mr '77. J. A. Herndon
New Repub 176:32-4 Mr 12 '77. T. Rosengarten
Merrill, J. Divine comedies: poems
Nation 224:181-3 F 12 '77. C. C. Park
Merrill, R. Between acts: an irreverent look at opera and other madness; with R. Saffron
Am Rec G 40:58-9 Mr '77. M. Galewski
Merwin, W. S. Houses and travellers
New Repub 177:35-6 O 22 '77. L. Pastan
Methods of experimental physics, v 12B and v 12C; ed. by M. L. Meeks. 1976
Sky & Tel 53:385-8 My '77. E. B. Fomalont
Metlitzki, D. Matter of Araby in medieval England. 1977
Am Hist R 82:1227-8 D '77. D. W. Robertson, jr
Metzger, T. A. Escape from predicament: Neo-Confucianism and China's evolving political culture. 1977
Am Hist R 82:1310 D '77. J. D. Langlois, jr
Meyer, H. Der Zweite Kappeler Krieg: die Krise der schweizerischen Reformation. 1976
Am Hist R 82:1283 D '77. J. W. Zophy
Meyer, J. A. Cristero rebellion: the Mexican people between church and state, 1926-1929; tr. by R. Southern. 1976
Am Hist R 82:1374-5 D '77. K. M. Schmitt
Meyer, S. ed. Forty watercolorists and how they work
Am Artist 41:25+ S '77. C. Movalli
Michals, D. Real dreams: photo stories. 1976
Art in Am 65:32-3 N '77. C. Ratcliff
Pop Phot 81:142 S '77. Y. Kalmus
Michel, B. Banques et banquiers en autriche au debut du 20e siècle. 1976
Am Hist R 82:674-5 Je '77. L. Schofer
Michelson, W. Environmental choice, human behavior, and residential satisfaction. 1977
Science 197:1354-5 S 30 '77. M. J. Munson
Michener, J. Sports in America
Commonweal 104:118-21 F 18 '77. M. Naison
Mickey, P. A. and Wilson, R. L. What new creation? the agony of church restructure
Chr Cent 94:411-12 Ap 27 '77. J. L. Weidman
Microtubules and microtubule inhibitors; proceedings of symposium, Beerse, Belgium. 1975; ed. by M. Borgers and M. de Brabander. 1975
Science 196:421-2 Ap 22 '77. J. B. Olmsted
Middelhoek, S. and others. Physics of computer memory devices. 1976
Phys Today 30:64+ Mr '77. E. L. Boyd
Miers, S. Britain and the ending of slave trade. 1975
Am Hist R 81:1109 D '76. R. A. Austen
Migdalski, E. C. and Fichter, G. S. Fresh and saltwater fishes of the world. 1976
Oceans 10:70 My '77. J. E. McCosker
Miles, B. All it takes is practice. 1976
Horn Bk 53:54 F '77. S. H. Holtze
Millard, C. W. Sculpture of Edgar Degas. 1976
Art in Am 65:25+ S '77. A. Elsen
Miller, A. C. Photographs of a frontier: the photography of Peter Britt
Pop Phot 80:188 My '77. N. Canavor
Miller, A. S. Modern corporate state: private governments and the American Constitution. 1976
Ann Am Acad 432:190-2 Jl '77. H. L. Johnson
Progressive 41:53-5 Ap '77. D. D. Martin
Miller, C. and Swift, K. Words and women: new language in new times
Ms 6:42 O '77. J. Shapiro
Miller, D. T. and Nowak, M. Fifties: the way we really were
Commonweal 104:822-4 D 23 '77. R. E. Long

Miller, H. Revolutionary college: American Presbyterian higher education, 1707-1837. 1976
Am Hist R 82:1062-3 O '77. D. C. Humphrey
Miller, H. H. George Mason: gentleman revolutionary. 1975
Am Hist R 82:433-4 Ap '77. D. W. Jordan
Miller, J. C. Kings and kinsmen: early Mbundu states in Angola. 1976
Am Hist R 81:1195 D '76. P. M. Martin
Miller, K. Cockburn's millennium. 1976
Am Hist R 82:1260-1 D '77. M. W. McCahill
Miller, M. A. Kropotkin. 1976
Am Hist R 81:1176 D '76. P. Avrich
Miller, O. W. Frontier in Alaska and the Matanuska colony. 1975
Am Hist R 81:1249-50 D '76. S. Haycox
Miller, R. G. Philadelphia—the Federalist city: a study of urban politics. 1789-1801. 1976
Am Hist R 82:437-8 Ap '77. P. Goodman
Miller, V. I. Soldatskie komitety russkoi armii v 1917 g. (vozniknovenie i nachal'nyi period deiatel hosti). 1974
Am Hist R 82:702-3 Je '77. A. Wildman
Miller, W. H. ed. Dynamics of molecular collisions, 2v 1976
Science 198:601 N 11 '77. J. C. Light
Miller, W. R. Cops and bobbies: police authority in New York and London, 1830-1870. 1977
Am Hist R 82:1217-18 D '77. E. J. Watts
Millett, R. Guardians of the dynasty
America 136:571 Je 25 '77. J. R. Brockman
Millhauser, S. Portrait of a romantic
Nation 225:250-2 S 17 '77. J. D. O'Hara
Millman, L. Our like will not be there again: notes from the west of Ireland
Newsweek 89:86-7 Je 6 '77. W. Clemons
Milsom, S. F. C. Legal framework of English feudalism: the Maitland lectures given in 1972. 1976
Am Hist R 82:619 Je '77. S. S. Walker
Mims, W. B. Linear electric field effect in paramagnetic resonance. 1976
Phys Today 30:69 O '77. C. P. Poole, jr
Miner, H. C. Corporation and the Indian: tribal sovereignty and industrial civilization in Indian territory, 1865-1907. 1976
Am Hist R 82:192 F '77. W. G. Robbins
Am West 14:61 S '77. R. N. Ellis
Mingay, G. E. Gentry: the rise and fall of a ruling class. 1976
Am Hist R 82:963 O '77. E. A. Wasson
Minge, W. A. Acoma: Pueblo in the sky. 1976
Am Hist R 82:207 F '77. S. L. Tyler
Mintz, M. and Cohen, J. S. Power, inc
New Repub 176:79-80 Ja 22 '77. L. J. Paper
Minus, P. M. jr. Catholic rediscovery of Protestantism
Commonweal 104:631-2 S 30 '77. K. McDonnell
Miroff, B. Pragmatic illusions: the presidential politics of John F. Kennedy. 1976
Am Hist R 82:775-6 Je '77. C. M. Brauer
Mirsky, J. Sir Aurel Stein: archaeological explorer
Am Scholar 47:134-7 Wint '77. P. Fussell
Harpers 255:70-6 Jl '77. E. Connell
Mirsky, M. J. My search for the Messiah
Commonweal 104:637-8 S 30 '77. A. A. Cohen
Mische, G. and Mische, P. Toward a human world order; beyond the national security straitjacket. 1977
Ann Am Acad 434:202-3 N '77. C. Chatfield
Misgeld, K. Die "Internationale Gruppe demokratischer Sozialisten" in Stockholm, 1942-1945; zur sozialistischen Friedensdiskussion während des Zweiten Weltkrieges. 1976
Am Hist R 82:954-5 O '77. D. K. Buse
Misner, P. Papacy and development: Newman and the primacy of the Pope. 1976
Am Hist R 82:639 Je '77. H. A. Macdougall
Mitchell, D. Gustav Mahler: the *Wunderhorn* years (chronicles and commentaries). 1976
Mus Q 63:128-33 Ja '77. Z. Roman
Mitchell, R. H. Thought control in prewar Japan. 1976
Am Hist R 82:721 Je '77. G. M. Berger
Ann Am Acad 432:160-1 Jl '77. G. O. Totten, 3d
Mitchell, S. W. Madeira party
N Y Times Mag p 142-5 D 11 '77. F. J. Prial
Mitford, J. Fine old conflict
Nat R 29:1120-1 S 30 '77. S. Rodman
New Repub 177:32-4 O 8 '77. P. Johnson
Newsweek 90:71+ Ag 29 '77. R. Towers
Progressive 41:53-5 N '77. A. M. Davidon
Time 110:64 S 5 '77. M. Maddocks
Mockler, A. Francis of Assisi (the wandering years)
Commonweal 104:253-5 Ap 15 '77. B. Mutkoski
Modras, R. Paul Tillich's theology of the church: a Catholic appraisal
America 136:247-9 Mr 19 '77. M. A. Fahey
Molecular anthropology: genes and proteins in the evolutionary ascent of the primates; papers from symposium, Burg Wartenstein, Austria, 1975; ed. by M. Goodman and others. 1976
Science 198:286-7 O 21 '77. R. J. Britten
Moliter, J. W. Architectural photography. 1976
Archit Rec 161:44 My '77. J. M. Davern
Mollenkott, V. R. Women, men and the Bible
Chr Cent 94:700-1 Ag 3 '77. J. F. Jansen
Sat Eve Post 249:74 Ap '77. L. Hudson
Molloy, A. Wampum. 1977
Horn Bk 53:323 Je '77. K. M. Klockner
Moltmann, J. Church in the power of the Spirit: a contribution to Messianic ecclesiology
America 137:53-5 Jl 30 '77. J. J. O'Donnell
Molz, R. K. Federal policy and library support. 1976
Lib J 102:889 Ap 15 '77. A. Ladenson
Momaday, N. S. Names: a memoir
Am West 14:49 Jl '77. J. Burrows
Harpers 254:94-5 F '77. E. Abbey
Momigliano, A. Alien wisdom: the limits of Hellenization. 1976
Am Hist R 81:1079 D '76. C. G. Starr
Momigliano, A. Essays in ancient and modern historiography
Yale R 67:135-9 O '77. D. Kagan
Mommsen H. and others, eds. Industrielles System und politische Entwicklung in der Weimarer Republik: Verhandlungen des Internationalen Symposiums in Bochum vom 12.-17. Juni 1973. 1974
Am Hist R 81:1149-50 D '76. H. W. Gatzke
Monaco, J. How to read a film. 1977
Film Q 31:60-1 Wint '77. B. Kawin
Monaco, P. Cinema and society: France and Germany during the twenties. 1976
Am Hist R 82:90-1 F '77. T. L. Sakmyster
Film Q 30:53-5 Summ '77. P. Thomas
Monkkonen, E. H. Dangerous class: crime and poverty in Columbus, Ohio, 1860-1885. 1975
Am Hist R 81:1257-8 D '76. L. J. Iorizzo
Monnet, Jean. Memoirs. 1976
For Affairs 55:630-5 Ap '77. Z, pseud
Monod, H. Mémoires du Landamman Monod pour servir à l'histoire de la Suisse en 1815; ed by J.-C. Biaudet and M.-C. Jequier. 3v. 1975
Am Hist R 82:678 Je '77. H. F. Young
Monsagrati, G. Federalismo e unità nell'azione di Enrico Cernuschi (1848-1851). 1976
Am Hist R 82:385 Ap '77. K. J. Kirkland
Montale, E. Poet in our time; tr. by A. Hamilton
New Repub 176:35-6 F 5 '77. W. S. Di Piero
Monter, E. W. Witchcraft in France and Switzerland: the borderlands during the Reformation. 1976
Ann Am Acad 429:182-3 Ja '77. R. W. England, Jr.
Montesinos Malo, A. El peso de la nube parda. 1974
Américas 29:25-6 Ap '77. M. Gowland de Gallo
Montgomery, J. W. Shaping of America. 1976
Chr Today 21:34-8 My 20 '77. S. V. Monsma
Moody, R. A. Life after life
Commonweal 104:473 Jl 22 '77. J. Garvey
Nat R 29:1004-5 S 2 '77. J. A. Rehyansky
Moody, T. W. and others, eds. New history of Ireland, v3: Early modern period, 1534-1691. 1976
Am Hist R 82:364 Ap '77. K. S. Bottigheimer
Moon: a new appraisal from space missions and laboratory analyses; papers from meeting, London, 1975. 1977
Science 198:286 O 21 '77. G. W. Wetherill
Mooney, C. F. Religion and the American dream: the search for freedom under God
America 137:487-8 D 31 '77. S. J. Weber
Moore, C. and Allen, G. Dimensions: space, shape & scale in architecture. 1976
Archit Rec 162:37 Jl '77. R. Gindroz and D. Lewis
Moore, D. L. Late Lord Byron: posthumous dramas
New Repub 176:38-9 My 28 '77. S. Weintraub
Moore, H. ed. New women's theatre: ten plays by contemporary American women
Ms 6:37-8 Ag '77. L. Stone
Moore, J. and Fraser, J. Campaign for president: the managers look at '76
New Repub 177:34-5 D 17 '77. K. Bode
Moore, J. N. Matter of records: Fred Gaisberg and the golden era of the gramophone
Hi Fi 27:50+ S '77. R. Long
Moore, J. P. Revolt in Louisiana: the Spanish occupation. 1766-1770. 1976
Am Hist R 82:734 Je '77. J. Sosin
Moore, L. Echoes of American ballet; ed. and introd. by I. Guest. 1976
Dance Mag 51:74 N '77. S. J. Cohen
Moore, W. H. Kefauver committee and the politics of crime, 1950-1952. 1974
Am Hist R 82:471-2 Ap '77. R. Griffith
Ann Am Acad 431:170-2 My '77. J. P. Conrad
Morante, E. History: a novel; tr. by W. Weaver
Commentary 64:60-2 Ag '77. J. Romano
Commonweal 104:536-7 Ag 19 '77. I. Sanders
Esquire 87:42+ Je '77. A. Kazin
Horizon 19:39 My '77
Newsweek 89:76+ My 2 '77. P. S. Prescott
Sat R 4:24-5 Ap 2 '77. D. Grumbach
Time 109:85 My 2 '77. P. Gray
Moravcsik, M. J. Science development: the building of science in less developed countries. 1975
Phys Today 30:56+ S '77. M. Schoijet
Mordden, E. Better foot forward: the history of American musical theater
Am Rec G 40:59-61 N '76. M. Galewski
Moreau, G. Restless journey of James Agee; tr. by M. Kleiger and M. Schiff.
New Repub 176:30-1 Ap 16 '77. T. S. Matthews
Smithsonian 8:114+ Je '77. C. McCarthy

Moreno Fraginals, M. Sugarmill: the socioeconomic complex of sugar in Cuba. 1976
Am Hist R 82:781-2 Je '77. B. J. Calder
Morgan, D. W. Socialist left and the German revolution: a history of the German Independent social democratic party, 1917-1922. 1975
Am Hist R 82:666-7 Je '77. W. Struve
Morgan, E. Falling apart: the rise and fall of urban civilization
America 137:39-40 Jl 16 '77. T. J. Hann
Morgan, F. Poems of the two worlds
America 136:550 Je 18 '77. J. F. Cotter
Morgan, J. P. House of lords and the Labour government, 1964-1970. 1975
Am Hist R 82:111 F '77. A. F. Havighurst
Morgan, R. Lady of the beasts
Ms 5:47-8 Mr '77. H. Cooper
Poetry 130:301-3 Ag '77. J. Parini
Morison, S. E. Sailor historian: the best of Samuel Eliot Morison; ed. by E. M. Beck
America 137:447-8 D 17 '77. D. Coogan
Smithsonian 8:131-2 D '77. J. F. Warner
Morley, H. Blessing outside us
Harpers 255:103-4 N '77. H. Carruth
Morphology and biology of reptiles; papers from symposium, London, 1975; ed by A. d' A. Bellairs and C. B. Cox. 1976
Science 196:866 My 20 '77. D. B. Wake
Morrill, J. S. Revolt of the provinces: conservatives and radicals in the English civil war, 1630-1650. 1976
Am Hist R 82:353 Ap '77. P. Zagorin
Morris, D. Manwatching: a field guide to human behavior
Time 111:78+ Ja 16 '78. J. Leo
Morris, H. On guilt and innocence
New Repub 176:28-30 Ja 15 '77. N. S. Care
Morris, J. N. Life beside this one
Poetry 129:235-6 Ja '77. R. B. Shaw
Morris, L. I believe in revelation. 1976
Chr Today 21:24-5 Ag 12 '77. G. W. Knight
Morris, M. B. Excursion into creative sociology. 1977
Ann Am Acad 433:193-4 S '7. W. M. Dobriner
Morris, R. Papers of Robert Morris, 1781-1784, v2: August-September 1781; ed. by E. J. Ferguson. 1975
Am Hist R 81:1225-6 D '76. B. M. Wilkenfeld
Morris, R. Uncertain greatness: Henry Kissinger and American foreign policy
Nation 225:376-7 O 15 '77. A. Beam
Newsweek 90:86+ S 26 '77. C. D. May
Morris, R. J. Cholera 1823: the social response to an epidemic. 1976
Am Hist R 82:1248 D '77. C. E. Rosenberg
Morrison, S. R. Chemical physics of surfaces. 1977
Science 197:1356 S 30 '77. M. A. Ratner
Morrison, T. Song of Solomon
Nation 225:536 N 19 '77. E. Frederick
New Yorker 53:217-18+ N 7 '77. S. Lardner
Newsweek 90:93 S 12 '77. M. Jefferson
Time 110:76+ S 12 '77. A. Wigan
Morse, E. L. Foreign policy and interdependence in Gaullist France. 1973
Ann Am Acad 431:159-60 My '77. J. Colton
Morse, J. M. Prejudice and literature
America 136:307 Ap 2 '77. D. Kirby
Morse, P. M. In at the beginnings: a physicist's life. 1977
Bull Atom Sci 33:46-7 N '77. J. Wilson
Phys Today 30:51-3 Ag '77. H. Feshbach
Science 196:776 My 13 '77. R. D. Richtmyer
Morsey, K. T. E. Lawrence und der arabische Aufstand 1916/18. 1976
Am Hist R 82:1302 D '77. R. Olson
Moscow, A. Rockefeller inheritance
Bus W p 14+ O 24 '77. W. G. Shepherd, jr
Moses, J. A. Politics of illusion: the Fischer controversy in German historiography. 1975
Am Hist R 82:129-30 F '77. J. Remak
Mosley, L. Lindbergh: a biography. 1976
Am Hist Illus 11:49 Ja '77. A. Keller
Am Hist R 82:470-1 Ap '77. B. L. Larson
Mosley, N. Julian Grenfell: his life and the times of his death, 1888-1915. 1976
Am Hist R 82:640-1 Je '77. S. Hynes
New Yorker 53:118-22 Je 13 '77. M. Panter-Downes
Moss, B. H. Origins of the French labor movement, 1830-1914: the socialism of skilled workers. 1976
Am Hist R 82:371-2 Ap '77. C. H. Johnson
Moss, N. Pleasures of deception
Bus W p 11-12 Jl 11 '77. W. G. Shepherd, Jr
Mostow, G. D. ed. Mathematical models for cell rearrangement. 1975
BioScience 27:816 D '77. R. J. Good
Motherwell, R. Robert Motherwell; text by H. H. Arnason
Art N 76:128-9 D '77. S. Hunter
Motz, L. On the path of Venus. 1976
Sky & Tel 54:319+ O '77. P. V. Rizzo
Moureaux, P. Les préoccupations statistiques du gouvernement des Pays-Bas autrichiens et la dénombrement des industries dressé en 1764. 1971
Am Hist R 82:376 Ap '77. F. F. Mendels
Mousnier, R. Recherches sur la strafication sociale à Paris aux XVIIe et XVIIIe siècles l'echantillon de 1634, 1635. 1976
Am Hist R 82:648-9 Je '77. C. C. Lougee
Mouw, R. J. Politics and the Biblical drama. 1976
Chr Cent 94:791 S 14 '77. T. Thompson
Chr Today 21:34-8 My 20 '77. S. V. Monsma
Movius, H. L. Jr. Excavation of the Abri Pataud. 1975
Science 196:969-70 My 27 '77. P. A. Mellars
Moynihan, M. New world primates: adaptive radiation and the evolution of social behavior, languages, and intelligence
Sci Am 237:152 Jl '77. P. Morrison
Moys, E. M. ed. Manual of law librarianship: the use and organization of legal literature. 1976
Lib J 102:343 F 1 '77. D. Henke
Mueller, J. Films on ballet and modern dance: notes and a directory
Sat R 5:44-5 O 15 '77. W. Terry
Mueller, L. Private life
Poetry 130:346-7 S '77. D. Allen
Muir, E. Autobiography
New Repub 176:39-41 Je 18 '77. R. B. Shaw
Muir, E. Collected poems
New Repub 176:39-41 Je 18 '77. R. B. Shaw
Muir, W. K. Jr. Police: streetcorner politicians
New Repub 176:35-7 Mr 26 '77. J. Lardner
New Yorker 53:188-90+ O 17 '77. R. Coles
Muirden, J. Astronomy with binoculars. 1976
Sky & Tel 53:384-5 My '77. E. G. Oravec
Muirden, J. Beginner's guide to astronomical telescope making. 1975
Sky & Tel 53:469-71 Je '77. R. E. Cox
Mukařovsky, J. Word and verbal art; selected essays; tr. and ed. by J. Burbank and P. Steiner
Yale R 67:106-15 O '77. L. Nelson, jr
Müllen, K. and Pregosin, P. S. Fourier transform NMR techniques: a practical approach. 1977
Phys Today 30:57-8 Ag '77. J. W. Cooper
Müller, D. H. Idealismus und Revolution: zur Opposition der Jungen gegen den sozialdemokratischen Parteivorstand, 1890 bis 1894. 1975
Am Hist R 82:126-7 F '77. R. F. Wheeler
Munro, J. F. Africa and the international economy, 1800-1960. 1976
Am Hist R 82:1032 O '77. P. Manning
Munro-Smith, R. Merchant ship types
Sci Am 236:126-8 Ja '77. P. Morrison
Muraskin, W. A. Middle-class blacks in a white society: Prince Hall freemasonry in America. 1975
Am Hist R 81:1230-1 D '76. E. L. Thornbrough
Murdoch, I. Henry and Cato
New Repub 176:25-6 F 19 '77. B. Allen
Murphey, R. Outsiders: the Western experience in India and China. 1977
Ann Am Acad 434:215-16 N '77. H. Furber
Murphree, J. T. When God says you're OK. 1976
Chr Today 21:33-4 Ja 7 '77. C. Dickson
Murray, K. M. E. Caught in the web of words: James A. H. Murray and the Oxford English dictionary
New Repub 177:33-4 N 12 '77. J. M. Edelstein
New Yorker 53:221-2+ N 21 '77. G. Steiner
Sat R 5:30 N 12 '77. D. Grumbach
Time 110:67 D 26 '77. L. Morrow
Murray, R. K. 103rd ballot: Democrats and the disaster in Madison square garden. 1976
Am Hist R 82:202-3 F '77. B. Noggle
Musgrove, M. Ashanti to Zulu: African traditions; il. by L. Dillon and D. Dillon. 1976
Horn Bk 53:179 Ap '77. P. Heins
Musical instruments of the world: an illustrated encyclopedia; ed by the Diagram Group
Am Rec G 40:59 N '76. J. Holden
Mutch, T. A. and others. Geology of Mars. 1977
Science 197:554 Ag 5 '77. W. K. Hartmann
Muzzarelli, R. A. A. Chitin. 1977
Science 198:392-3 O 28 '77. M. Locke
Myers, C. A. Prophet's army: Trotskyists in America, 1928-1914. 1977
Am Hist R 82:1350 D '77. D. H. Bennett
Myrdal, A. Game of disarmament: how the United States and Russia run the arms race
America 136:400-2 Ap 30 '77. R. L. Walker
Horizon 19:90-2 Mr '77. C. L. Mee, Jr
Progressive 41:55-6 My '77. R. A. Falk
Sci Am 236:139 My '77. P. Morrison

Nabokov, V. Real life of Sebastian Knight
Nation 225:56-8 Jl 9 '77. J. D. O'Hara
Nader, R. and others. Taming the giant corporation. 1976
Ann Am Acad 432:190-2 Jl '77. H. L. Johnson
Progressive 41:53-5 Ap '77. D. D. Martin
Naipaul, V. S. India: a wounded civilization
America 136:570-1 Je 25 '77. J. Novak
Nation 225:26-8 Jl 2 '77. L. A. Gordon
New Repub 177:30-2 Jl 9 '77. P. L. Berger
Newsweek 89:84+ Je 6 '77. M. Jefferson
Time 109:86+ Je 20 '77. W. E. Smith
Najarian, H. H. Sex lives of animals without backbones. 1976
Oceans 10:70 My '77. J. Dillon

Nakamura, H. Parallel developments: a comparative history of ideas. 1975
Chr Today 21:47-8 F 4 '77. R. Brow
Nardi, P. Mariano Sozzini: giureconsulto senese del quattrocento. 1974
Am Hist R 82:139-40 F '77. M. P. Gilmore
Narkiewicz, O. A. Green flag: Polish populist politics, 1867-1970. 1976
Am Hist R 82:396-7 Ap '77. W. W. Soroka
Narlikar, J. Structure of the universe. 1977
Phys Today 30:68-70 N '77. D. N. Schramm
Nasatir, A. P. Borderland in retreat: from Spanish Louisiana to the far Southwest. 1976
Am Hist R 82:439 Ap '77. D. J. Weber
Am West 14:54 Jl '77. J. L. Kessell
Nash, G. H. Conservative intellectual movement in America since 1945. 1976
Am Hist R 82:215 F '77. A. Guttmann
Nash, M. Provoked wife: the life and times of Susannah Cibber
Atlantic 239:92-3 Je '77. P. Davison
Nathan, A. J. Peking politics, 1918-1923: factionalism and the failure of constitutionalism. 1976
Am Hist R 82:161 F '77. F. G. Chan
Nathan, L. Returning your call
Poetry 130:225-6 Jl '77. W. Logan
Nation of nations: the people who came to America as seen through objects and documents exhibited at the Smithsonian Institution; ed. by P. C. Marzio. 1976
Horn Bk 53:199-200 Ap '77. M. S. Cosgrave
National aeronautics and space administration. Possible relationships between solar activity and meteorological phenomena: proceedings of symposium, Greenbelt, Md, 1973; ed. by W. R. Bandeen and S. P. Maran. 1975
Science 195:670-1 F 18 '77. J. A. Eddy
National commission on library and information science. National inventory of library needs, 1975. 1977
Am Lib 8:491-2 O '77. E. Castagna
Nato advanced study institute, Oslo, 1973. Evolution and morphology of the trilobita, trilobitoidea and merostomata; proceedings; ed. by A. Martinsson. 1975
Science 197:653-4 Ag 12 '77. M. E. Taylor
Nato advanced study institute, Oxford, England, 1974. Metabolic compartmentation and neurotransmissions; proceedings; ed by S. Berl and others. 1975
Science 197:152 Jl 8 '77. I. Diamond
Nechkina, M. V. Vasilii Osipovich Kliuchevskii: istoriia zhizni i tvorchestva. 1974
Am Hist R 82:697 Je '77. T. P. Dilkes
Needham, J. Science and civilisation in China, v5: Chemistry and chemical technology, pt 2: Spagyrical discovery and invention: magistries of gold and immortality; with Lu Gwei-Djen. 1974
Am Hist R 82:1041-3 O '77. N. Sivin
Needham, J. Science and civilisation in China, v5: Chemistry and chemical technology; pt3, Spagyrical discovery and invention: historical survey, from cinnabar elixirs to synthetic insulin; with Ho Ping-Yü and Lu Gwei-Djen.
Am Hist R 82:409-10 Ap '77. E. Samuel
Science 196:155-6 Ap 8 '77. P. M. Rattansi
Needleman, J. and Lewis, D. eds. On the way to self-knowledge
America 136:488-9 My 28 '77. A. Fremantle
Nehring, K. Matthias Corvinus, Kaiser Friedrich III, und das Reich: zum hunyadisch-habsburgischen Gegensatz im Donauraum. 1975
Am Hist R 82:394 Ap '77. L. S. Domonkos
Neidle, C. S. America's immigrant women. 1976
Am Hist R 82:756-7 Je '77. A. K. Harris
Neil, J. M. Toward a national taste: America's quest for aesthetic independence. 1975
Am Hist R 81:1232 D '76. D. T. Miller
Neisser, U. Cognition and reality: principles and implications of cognitive psychology. 1976
Science 198:816-17 N 25 '77. D. E. Rumelhart
Nelkin, D. Science textbook controversies and the politics of equal time. 1977
Science 196:752-4 My 13 '77. J. Guthrie
Nelli, H. S. Business of crime: Italians and syndicate crime in the United States. 1976
Ann Am Acad 431:170-2 My '77. J. P. Conrad
Intellect 105:445-6 Je '77. T. M. Pitkin
Nelson, D. Managers and workers: origins of the new factory system in the United States, 1880-1920. 1975
Am Hist R 81:1261-2 D '76. P. Uselding
M Labor R 100:67-8 Je '77. T. H. Patten, Jr
Nelson, D. S. ed. Immunobiology of the macrophage. 1976
Science 195:387 Ja 28 '77. B. A. Askonas
Nelson, D. W. Heart mountain: the history of an American concentration camp. 1976
Am Hist R 82:469-70 Ap '77. J. Modell
Nelson, J. Captive voices: the report of the Commission of inquiry into high school journalism. 1974
Ann Am Acad 430:216-17 Mr '77. T. Levy
Nelson, P. D. General Horatio Gates: a biography. 1976
Am Hist Illus 12:50 O '77. J. L. Stokesbury
Ann Am Acad 429:175-6 Ja '77. R. A. Brown
Nelson, R. R. Moon and the ghetto: an essay on public policy analysis. 1977
Intellect 106:87-8 Ag '77. W. Stevenson
Nelson, W. H. and Prittie, T. Economic war against the Jews
New Repub 177:46 N 26 '77. M. Peretz
Neruda, P. Memoirs; tr. by H. St Martin
America 137:116 Ag 27 '77. C. Inda
Commentary 63:84-6 My '77. M. Falcoff
Horizon 19:94-5 Ja '77. C. L. Mee, Jr.
Nat R 29:340-1 Mr 18 '77. S. Rodman
Progressive 41:58 Ap '77. M. True
Sat R 4:18-20 F 19 '77. R. Maurer
Yale R 67:128-35 O '77. M. Ellmann
Nesbitt, M. B. Labor relations in the Federal government service. 1976
Ann Am Acad 434:232-3 N '77. D. Fellman
Neuhaus, R. J. Time toward home: the American experiment as revelation. 1975
Chr Today 21:43-5 Mr 18 '77. M. J. Van Eldern
Neural principles in vision; papers from symposium, Munich, 1975; ed. by F. Zettler and R. Weiler. 1976
Science 197:43-4 Jl 1 '77. P. Witkovsky
Nevelson, L. Dawns + dusks: Louise Nevelson; with D. MacKown
America 137:35-6 Jl 16 '77. D. Leder
Art in Am 65:53+ Mr '77. R. Smith
Neville, A. C. Animal asymmetry
Sci Am 236:142 Ap '77. P. Morrison
New Columbia encyclopedia. 1975
Consumers Res Mag 60:13 F '77. W. T. Johnston
New frontiers in astronomy: readings from Scientific American; introd. by O. Gingerich
Space World N-8-164:34 Ag '77
Newby, P. H. Kith
Newsweek 90:76 Ag 15 '77. M. Jefferson
Newell, R. C. ed. Adaptation to environment: essays on the physiology of marine animals. 1976
Science 196:644 My 6 '77. J. E. Bardach
Newfield, J. and DuBrul, P. Abuse of power: the permanent government and the fall of New York
New Repub 176:23-4 Je 11 '77. R. Lekachman
Newman, G. Comparative deviance: perception and law in six cultures. 1976
Ann Am Acad 432:183-4 Jl '77. A. L. Wood
Newman, J. H. Letters and diaries of John Henry Newman, v31; ed. by C. S. Dessain and T. Gornall
America 137:184-6 O 1 '77. V. F. Blehl
Newman, R. Night spell; il. by P. Burchard. 1977
Horn Bk 53:443 Ag '77. P. Heins
Newman, S. March 1939: the British guarantee to Poland, a study in the continuity of British foreign policy. 1976
Am Hist R 82:642-3 Je '77. D. Lammers
Newmark, G. This school belongs to you and me
Todays Educ 66:94 S '77. J. R. Watson
Newton, H. White women. 1976
Art in Am 65:51+ Mr '77. A. Grundberg
Newton, I. Mathematical papers, v7; ed by D. T. Whiteside. 1976
Science 196:864-5 My 20 '77. M. S. Mahoney
Nibbelink, D. D. Picturing people. 1976
Pop Phot 80:131+ My '77. I. J. Neubart
Nicholas, H. G. United States and Britain. 1975
Am Hist R 81:1222 D '76. A. K. Henrikson
Nichols, R. Song of the pearl. 1976
Horn Bk 53:59 F '77. P. Heins
Nicholson, B. and Wright, C. Georges de La Tour
Am Artist 41:55-6 F '77. A. Werner
Nicholson, W. Clever Bill. 1977
Horn Bk 53:694-6 D '77. S. G. Lanes
Nicolson, N. Mary Curzon
Newsweek 91:67-8 Ja 9 '78. W. Clemons
Nida, E. A. ed. Book of a thousand tongues. 2d ed
Sci Am 237:46+ S '77. P. Morrison
Nida, E. A. Good news for everyone: how to use the Good News Bible. 1977
Chr Today 22:39-40 N 4 '77. H. Boonstra
Nie, N. H. and others. Changing American voter. 1976
Am Hist R 82:762-3 Je '77. E. C. Ladd, Jr.
Ann Am Acad 429:176-7 Ja '77. R. J. Huckshorn
Nies, J. Seven women: portraits from the American radical tradition. 1977
Horn Bk 53:544-5 O '77. M. M. Burns
Nilles, J. M. and others. Telecommunications-transportation tradeoff: options for tomorrow
Fortune 95:81-2 F '77
Nin, A. Delta of Venus: erotica
New Repub 177:35-6 Ag 20 '77. A. Crutcher
Nipperdey, T. Gesellschaft, Kultur, Theorie: gesammelte Aufsätze zur neueren Geschichte. 1976
Am Hist R 82:665 Je '77. H. M. Ermarth
Nipperdey, T. Reformation, Revolution, Utopie: Studien zum 16. Jahrhundert. 1975
Am Hist R 81:1096-7 D '76. D. E. Thomas, Jr
Nisbet, R. Sociology as an art form
America 136:256-7 Mr 19 '77. J. R. Kelly
Nat R 29:216-17 F 18 '77. K. O'Lessker
Nisbett, A. Konrad Lorenz: a biography
Natur Hist 86:78-82+ Je '77. G. E. Allen
Psychol Today 11:100+ Jl '77. L. Tiger

Nish, C. Francois-Étienne Cugnet, 1719-1751: entrepreneur et entreprises en Nouvelle-France. 1976
Am Hist R 82:1366-7 D '77. G. F. G. Stanley
Nishihara, M. Japanese and Sukarno's Indonesia: Tokyo-Jakarta relations, 1951-1966. 1976
Ann Am Acad 431:155-6 My '77. P. W. Van Der Veur
Niven, D. Bring on the empty horses
Sat Eve Post 249:78-9+ Mr '77. D. Brudnoy
Noble, D. F. America by design: science, technology, and the rise of corporate capitalism. 1977
New Repub 177:32-3 S 3 '77. N. Harris
Progressive 41:38-9 Ag '77. J. Buell
Science 198:722-3 N 18 '77. W. D. Lewis
Noble, M. and Graham, B. You can grow camellias
Horticulture 55:6+ N '77. W. Ackerman
Noel, R. S. Mythology of Middle-earth. 1977
Horn Bk 53:469-70 Ag '77. M. S. Cosgrave
Nolan, J. Why I live in the forest
Poetry 130:169 Je '77. E. Butscher
Nomikos, E. V. and North, R. C. International crisis: the outbreak of World War I. 1976
Am Hist R 82:626 Je '77. P. G. Halpern
Ann Am Acad 433:166 S '77
Noren, C. H. Camera of my family. 1976
Commonweal 104:628-9 S 30 '77. S. B. Warner, jr
Pop Phot 80:131 My '77. Y. E. Benedek
Smithsonian 8:132-3 My '77. M. Kernan
Norman, E. R. Church and society in England, 1770-1970: a historical study. 1976
Am Hist R 82:966-7 O '77. P. Marsh
Norris, F. Pit
New Repub 177:37-9 N 19 '77. J. Solkoff
Norton, A. Red hart magic; il. by D. Diamond. 1976
Horn Bk 53:160 Ap '77. M. M. Burns
Notestein, L. L. Wooster of the Middle West, v2: 1911-1944
Am Hist R 81:1270 D '76. G. J. Clifford
Nourse, A. E. Vitamins
Sci Am 237:32 D '77. P. Morrison and P. Morrison
Novak, M. Joy of sports
Chr Cent 94:433 My 4 '77. R. J. Bueter
Commonweal 104:118-21 F 18 '77. M. Naison
Novick, S. Electric war: the fight over nuclear power
Nation 224:245-6 F 26 '77. H. Wasserman
Novotny, A. Alice's world, the life and photography of an American original: Alice Austen 1866-1952
Ms 6:44 O '77. N. K. Robinson
Nuclear energy policy study group. Nuclear power: issues and choices. 1977
Bull Atom Sci 33:58-63 Je '77. J. P. Holdren
Numbers, R. L. Creation by natural law: Laplace's nebular hypothesis in American thought. 1977
Am Hist R 82:1335 D '77. H. Winnik
Science 197:977 S 2 '77. R. C. Tobey
Numbers, R. L. Prophetess of health: a study of Ellen G. White. 1976
Am Hist R 82:464 Ap '77. J. H. Young
Nuñez Muñoz, M. F. La iglesia y la restauración, 1875-1881. 1976
Am Hist R 82:989-90 O '77. N. A. Rosenblatt
Nunn, F. M. Military in Chilean history: essays on civil-military relations, 1810-1973. 1976
Am Hist R 82:784 Je '77. R. Oppenheimer
Nussbaum, A. and Phillips, R. A. Contemporary optics for scientists and engineers. 1976
Phys Today 30:74-6 My '77. C. P. Frahm
Nye, R. A. Origins of crowd psychology: Gustave LeBon and the crisis of mass democracy in the Third republic. 1975
Am Hist R 81:1131 D '76. J. J. Baughman

Oakeshott, M. On human conduct. 1975
Ann Am Acad 430:181-2 Mr '77. R. L. Hunt
Oaks, D. H. and Hill, M. S. Carthage conspiracy: the trial of the accused assassins of Joseph Smith. 1975
Am Hist R 81:1248 D '76. M. Feldberg
Oates, J. C. Childwold
New Repub 176:36-7 My 28 '77. I. H. Chayes
Oates, J. C. Fabulous beasts
Poetry 130:107-9 My '77. R. Siegel
Oates, J. C. Night-side
New Repub 177:44-5 N 26 '77. N. Delbanco
Oates, S. B. With malice toward none: the life of Abraham Lincoln. 1977
Am Hist Illus 12:49 Ag '77. C. F. Cooney
Am Hist R 82:1074-5 O '77. R. N. Current
O'Bannon, G. W. Turkoman carpet
Antiques 111:572+ Mr '77. R. E. Tschebull
Obelkevich, J. Religion and rural society: South Lindsey, 1825-1875. 1976
Am Hist R 82:967-8 O '77. J. F. C. Harrison
Oboler, E. M. Ideas and the university library: essays of an unorthodox academic librarian. 1977
Lib J 102:2221 N 1 '77. G. R. Lyle

O'Brien, E. I hardly knew you
Newsweek 91:62+ Ja 2 '78. P. S. Prescott
O'Brien, F. Flann O'Brien reader, ed. by S. Jones
Time 111:70-1 Ja 9 '78. P. Gray
O'Brien, F. Stories and plays
America 136:530 Je 11 '77. M. Fitzgerald
O Broin, L. Revolutionary underground: the story of the Irish Republican Brotherhood, 1858-1924. 1976
Am Hist R 82:975-6 O '77. L. J. McCaffrey
O'Connell, M. R. Counter reformation, 1559-1610. 1974
Am Hist R 82:86-8 F '77. E. Cochrane
O'Dell, S. Carlota. 1977
Horn Bk 53:670 D '77. M. M. Burns
O'Dell, S. 290. 1976
Horn Bk 53:160-1 Ap '77. V. Haviland
Oden, T. C. Should treatment be terminated. 1976
Chr Today 21:30+ Ag 26 '77. R. A. Case, 2d
O'Fahey, R. S. and Spaulding, J. L. Kingdoms of the Sudan. 1975
Am Hist R 81:1192 D '76. P. Mellini
Ogburn, C. Adventure of birds; il. by M. Kalmenoff. 1976
Horn Bk 53:82-3 F '77. M. S. Cosgrave
Ogburn, C. Railroads, the great American adventure. 1977
Am For 83:36-8 Jl '77. M. Bush
Ogburn, C. Southern Appalachians, a wilderness quest. 1975
Am For 83:38-9 My '77. M. Bush
Ogilvy, J. A. Many dimensional man: decentralizing self, society, and the sacred
Atlantic 240:102-3 N '77. B. DeMott
Ohanian, H. C. Gravitation and spacetime. 1976
Phys Today 30:59 Ja '77. W. Rindler
O'Keeffe, G. Georgia O'Keeffe. 1976
Am Artist 41:89+ Jl '77. A. Werner
America 137:35-6 Jl 16 '77. D. Leder
Art in Am 65:53+ Mr '77. R. Smith
Art N 76:102-3 F '77. M. S. Young
Sat R 4:44-6 Ja 22 '77. K. Kuh
O'Keefe, J. A. Tektites and their origin. 1976
Sky & Tel 54:315-18 O '77. U. B. Marvin
O'Leary, M. K. and Coplin, W. D. Quantitative techniques in foreign policy analysis and forecasting. 1975
Ann Am Acad 432:154-5 Jl '77. R. Roett
Oliver, A. Auguste Edouart's silhouettes of eminent Americans, 1839-1844; introd. by A. H. Mayor
Antiques 112:980 N '77. K. Schmiegel
Olmstead, A. L. New York City mutual savings banks, 1819-1861. 1976
Am Hist R 82:743 Je '77. H. Cohen
Olmsted, F. L. Papers of Frederick Law Olmsted. v 1. Formative years, 1822-1852; ed. by C. C. McLaughlin
Smithsonian 8:118+ Je '77. W. Morgan
Olsen, D. J. Growth of Victorian London. 1976
Am Hist R 82:968 O '77. M. Wolff
Sat R 4:21-2 F 19 '77. R. Gelatt
Olson, M. C. Unacceptable risk: the nuclear power controversy
Commonweal 104:59-61 Ja 21 '77. W. J. Lanouette
Nation 224:245-6 F 26 '77. H. Wasserman
Olson, R. W. Siege of Mosul and Ottoman-Persian relations, 1718-1743: a study of rebellion in the capital and war in the provinces of the Ottoman empire. 1975
Am Hist R 81:1186 D '76. C. E. Farah
Olson, S. F. Reflections from the North Country. 1976
Liv Wildn 40:48-9 Ja '77. C. McCarthy
Omran, A. R. and Standley, C. C. eds. Family formation patterns and health: an international collaborative study in India, Iran, Lebanon, Philippines, and Turkey. 1976
Science 197:1273-4 S 23 '77. T. K. Burch
O'Neal, H. Vision shared: a classic portrait of America and its people, 1935-1943. 1976
Am West 14:62 S '77. S. Crouch
O'Neil, W. M. Time and the calendars
Sci Am 236:128+ Ja '77. P. Morrison
Ong, W. J. Interfaces of the word
America 137:287-8 O 29 '77. J. M. Phelan
Oppler, A. C. Legal reform in occupied Japan. 1976
Ann Am Acad 429:161 Ja '77. A. E. Kane
Oraison, M. Homosexual question; tr. by J. Z. Flinn
America 136:549-50 Je 18 '77. J. J. McNeill
Ord-Hume, A. W. J. G. Perpetual motion: the history of an obsession
Sci Am 237:30+ N '77. P. Morrison
Ordish, G. Year of the butterfly. 1975
BioScience 27:212 Mr '77. L. P. Brower
Organ, T. W. Western approaches to Eastern philosophy
Chr Cent 94:156 F 16 '77. R. Kysar
Ornstein, R. E. Mind field
New Repub 176:35-6 Ap 16 '77. R. D. Rosen
Orr, J. M. Libraries as communication systems. 1977
Lib J 102:1469 Jl '77. E. Jussim
Orr, L. Jules Michelet: nature, history, and language. 1976
Am Hist R 82:651-2 Je '77. C. Rearick

Orton, J. Complete plays
Nation 225:116-18 Ag 6 '77. G. Weales
Osgood, W. and Hurley, L. Snowshoe book
Conservationist 31:33 N '76. J. W. Kelly
Osthaus, C. R. Freedmen, philanthropy, and fraud: a history of the Freedman's savings bank. 1976
Am Hist R 82:445-6 Ap '77. W. S. McFeely
O'Toole, J. Energy and social change. 1976
Ann Am Acad 433:202-3 S '77. S. P. Gupta and M. C. Gupta
Otten, J. and Shelley, F. D. When your parents grow old
Psychol Today 11:108-9+ Je '77. P. Koenig
Otto, V. Staatsverständnis des parlamentarischen Rates: ein Beitrag zur Entstehungsgeschichte des Grundgesetzes für die Bundesrepublik Deutschland. 1971
Am Hist R 82:133 F '77. C. G. Anthon
Ouellet, F. Le Bas-Canada, 1791-1840: changements structuraux et crise. 1976
Am Hist R 82:1367-8 D '77. T. J. A. Le Goff
Ousby, I. Bloodhounds of heaven: the detective in English fiction from Godwin to Doyle
New Yorker 53:141-2+ Ap 25 '77. G. Steiner
Yale R 66:444-8 Mr '77. M. Byrd
Ousmane, S. Xala; tr. by C. Wake
Nation 224:440-2 Ap 9 '77. E. Ottenberg
New Yorker 53:141-2+ My 16 '77. J. Updike
Ovendale, R. Appeasement and the English speaking world: Britain, the United States, the dominions, and the policy of appeasement, 1937-1939. 1975
Am Hist R 81:1117-18 D '76. T. E. Hachey
Overmyer, D. L. Folk Buddhist religion: dissenting sects in late traditional China. 1976
Am Hist R 82:1045 O '77. J. A. Berling
Owen, H. and Schultze, C. L. eds. Setting national priorities
Commonweal 104:56-9 Ja 21 '77. M. Harrington
Owens, B. Working (I do it for the money)
Newsweek 90:75 O 10 '77. D. Davis
Özbudun, E. Social change and political participation in Turkey. 1977
Ann Am Acad 433:177-8 S '77. W. Spencer

Pace, D. K. Christian's guide to effective jail and prison ministries. 1976
Chr Today 22:34 O 21 '77. J. de Vries
Pack, R. Keeping watch
Poetry 130:343-4 S '77. D. Allen
Packard, V. People shapers
Bus W p 14+ N 28 '77. O. Port
Chr Cent 94:1096 N 23 '77. T. L. Benson
New Repub 177:31-2 D 10 '77. R. Hassenger
Psychol Today 11:122+ S '77. R. Restak
Page, T. and Page, L. W. eds. Space science and astronomy: escape from earth. 1976
Sky & Tel 53:297-8 Ap '77. R. Hillenbrand
Painter, G. D. William Caxton
New Repub 177:37-8 Jl 2 '77. J. M. Edelstein
Painter, N. I. Exodusters
New Repub 176:21-2 F 12 '77. T. Rosengarten
Palais, J. B. Politics and policy in traditional Korea. 1975
Am Hist R 81:1205 D '76. A. W. Burks
Palmer, C. A. Slaves of the white god: blacks in Mexico, 1570-1650. 1976
Am Hist R 82:477-8 Ap '77. H. S. Klein
Palmer, R. and Parsons, N. eds. Roots of rural poverty in central and southern Africa
Nation 225:632-5 D 10 '77. P. Dreyer
Palmer, R. S. ed. Handbook of North American birds, v2-3 Waterfowl. 1976
Conservationist 31:45 Mr '77. R. G. Wolk
Smithsonian 7:148+ F '77. S. D. Ripley
Palmquist, P. E. Fine California views: the photographs of A. W. Ericson
Pop Phot 80:188+ My '77. N. Canavor
Palmquist, P. E. With nature's children
Ms 5:86 Je '77. A. M. Cunningham
Pop Phot 80:188 My '77. N. Canavor
Panitch, L. Social democracy and industrial militancy: the Labor party, the trade unions and incomes policy, 1945-1974. 1976
Ann Am Acad 430:225-6 Mr '77. M. E. Murphy
Pannenberg, W. Theology and the philosophy of science; tr. by F. McDonagh
America 136:569 Je 25 '77. B. McDermott
Chr Cent 94:1037+ N 9 '77. T. Peters
Papanikolas, H. Z. ed. Peoples of Utah. 1976
Am West 14:59 Mr '77. G. O. Larson
Parenti, M. Democracy for the few
New Repub 177:35 D 24 '77. M. J. Ulmer
Paret, P. Clausewitz and the state. 1976
Am Hist R 82:89-90 F '77. F. B. M. Hollyday
New Repub 176:36-7 My 14 '77. E. N. Luttwak
Yale R 66:613-20 Je '77. M. Mandelbaum
Park, E. Nanette
Bus W p 13 My 23 '77. R. Cochran
Parker, D. B. Crime by computer
Sci Am 237:26+ O '77. P. Morrison
Parker, R. A. C. Coke of Norfolk: a financial and agricultural study, 1707-1842. 1975
Am Hist R 81:1105 D '76. D. Spring
Parker, S. Sociology of leisure. 1976
Ann Am Acad 429:185-6 Ja '77. I. R. Stuart
Parker, W. N. and Jones, E. L. eds. European peasants and their markets: essays in agrarian economic history. 1976
Am Hist R 82:83-4 F '77. K. F. Drew
Parkinson, C. N. Gunpowder treason and plot
Smithsonian 8:98-9 Jl '77. R. Beeston
Parkman, A. David Jayne Hill and the problem of world peace. 1975
Am Hist R 81:1265-6 D '76. R. Stone
Parks, J. H. Joseph E. Brown of Georgia. 1977
Am Hist R 82:1334 D '77. J. T. Moore
Parks, P. World you never see: underwater life
Sci Am 236:144 Mr '77. P. Morrison
Parman, D. L. Navajos and the New deal. 1976
Am Hist R 82:206-7 F '77. L. C. Kelly
Parrish, R. Growing up in Hollywood
New Repub 176:26-9 Ap 2 '77. W. Hughes
Parrott, J. E. and Stuckes, A. D. Thermal conductivity of solids. 1975
Phys Today 30:60 F '77. P. G. Klemens
Parry, A. Terrorism: from Robespierre to Arafat. 1976
Ann Am Acad 434:203-4 N '77. R. Shultz
New Repub 176:27-30 My 14 '77. M. Syrkin
Sat Eve Post 249:78-9+ My '77. D. Brudnov
Sat R 4:30-1 F 5 '77. J. Schreiber
Parry, N. and Parry, J. Rise of the medical profession. 1976
Ann Am Acad 431:177-8 My '77. A. B. Davis
Parsons, W. B. Engineers and engineering in the Renaissance. 1976
Am Hist R 82:678-9 Je '77. B. Hansen
Partridge, E. Dictionary of catch phrases
Esquire 88:46+ N '77. J. Simon
Pascal, F. Hangin' out with Cici. 1977
Horn Bk 53:541 O '77. A. A. Flowers
Pasquill, F. Atmospheric diffusion. 2d ed. 1974
Phys Today 30:55+ Je '77. P. Michael
Passachoff, J. M. Contemporary astronomy. 1977
Sky & Tel 54:132-3 Ag '77. D. A. Pierce
Pastor, P. Hungary between Wilson and Lenin: the Hungarian Revolution of 1918-1919 and the big three. 1976
Am Hist R 82:1020 O '77. E. S. Balogh
Patinkin, D. Keynes' monetary thought: a study of its development. 1976
Intellect 105:446-7 Je '77. J. M. Rock
Patterson, D. S. Toward a warless world: the travail of the American peace movement, 1887-1914. 1976
Am Hist R 82:758-9 Je '77. R. Marchand
Patterson, J. T. ed. Paths to the present: interpretive essays on American history since 1930. 1975
Am Hist R 81:1273 D '76. R. T. Ruetten
Patterson, K. D. Northern Gabon coast to 1875. 1975
Am Hist R 81:1192 D '76. S. H. Broadhead
Patterson, O. Ethnic chauvinism: the reactionary impulse
Nation 225:729-31 D 31 '77. C. McWilliams
Patterson, W. C. Nuclear power
Commonweal 104:59-61 Ja 21 '77. W. J. Lanouette
Pauck, M. and Pauck, W. Paul Tillich: his life and thought; v 1: Life. 1976
Chr Cent 94:388-9 Ap 20 '77. R. M. Brown
Chr Today 22:45-6 D 9 '77. L. Rambo
Pavese, C. Hard labor: poems by Cesare Pavese; tr. by W. Arrowsmith
New Repub 176:30-1 My 14 '77. M. Bell
Pawson, M. and Buisseret, D. Port Royal, Jamaica. 1975
Am Hist R 82:227 F '77. E. L. Farley
Paxton, J. Developing common market: the structure of the E.E.C. in theory and in practice, 1957-1976. 1976
Ann Am Acad 432:167-8 Jl '77. J. R. Silkenat
Payne, B. I. Life in a wooden o
New Repub 176:50 My 21 '77. O. B. Hardison, Jr
Payne, H. C. Philosophes and the people. 1976
Ann Am Acad 430:217-18 Mr '77. G. Williamson, Jr
Pearce, J. C. Magical child: rediscovering nature's plan for our children
Psychol Today 11:102+ Je '77. E. White
Pearson, M. N. Merchants and rulers in Gujarat: the response to the Portuguese in the sixteenth century. 1976
Am Hist R 81:1206 D '76. C. R. Boxer
Peck, R. Are you in the house alone? 1976
Horn Bk 53:60 F '77. P. Heins
Péladeau, M. B. Chansonetta: the life and photographs of Chansonetta Stanley Emmons, 1858-1937; introd. by B. Abbott. 1977
Art in Am 65:34-5 N '77. R. H. Cohen
Pelé. My life and the beautiful game: the autobiography of Pelé; with R. L. Fish. 1977
Américas 29:46-7 O '77. B. Clarke
Pélissier, R. Les bibliothèques en Chine pendant la première moitié du XXe siècle. 1971
Am Hist R 81:1198 D '76. M. Donovan
Pelling, H. Winston Churchill
Progressive 41:60-1 F '77. A. Burnham
Pelotte, D. E. John Courtney Murray: theologian in conflict; foreword by M. Marty
Commonweal 104:150-2 Mr 4 '77. P. Scharper

Pemberton, J. E. Politics and public libraries in England and Wales 1850-1970. 1977
Lib J 102:2141 O 15 '77. H. Lancour
Peña, J. E. de la. With Santa Anna in Texas: a personal narrative of the Revolution; tr. and ed. by C. Perry. 1975
Am Hist R 81:1247 D '76. S. V. Connor
Pendry, J. B. Low energy electron diffraction: the theory and its application to determination of surface structure. 1974
Phys Today 30:57-8 F '77. G. P. Alldredge
Penner, J. Going blind
Newsweek 89:102-4 Ap 18 '77. W. Clemons
Penner, S. S. and Iceman, L. Energy, v2: Non-nuclear energy technologies. 1975
Phys Today 30:66-8 Mr '77. A. M. Saperstein
Percival, J. Roman villa: an historical introduction. 1977
Am Hist R 82:929 O '77. L. Richardson, jr
Percy, W. Lancelot. 1977
America 136:220-1 Mr 12 '77. E. D. Cuffe
Atlantic 239:113-15 Mr '77. R. Todd
Chr Cent 94:634-6 Jl 6 '77. R. Wood
Harpers 254:86-8 Ap '77. A. Dubus
Nat R 29:562-4 My 13 '77. R. Ford
Nation 224:533+ Ap 30 '77. E. Chesnick
New Repub 176:32-4 F 5 '77. J. C. Oates
New Yorker 53:141-4 My 2 '77. S. Lardner
Newsweek 89:73 F 28 '77. P. Prescott
Progressive 41:40-1 Je '77. J. Egerton
Sat R 4:28-9 Mr 19 '77. B. Cook
Society 14:85-7 Jl '77. L. A. Coser
Time 109:86-7 Mr 7 '77. P. Gray
Pereira, J. Hindu theology: a reader
America 136:199-201 Mr 5 '77. J. Moffitt
Pérez, L. A. Jr. Army politics in Cuba, 1898-1958. 1976
Ann Am Acad 431:156 My '77. S. K. Purcell
Perkins, D. History of modern poetry: from the 1890s to the high modernist mode
Am Scholar 46:396-9 Summ '77. P. Shaw
Commonweal 104:441-2 Jl 8 '77. M. True
Nation 224:183-5 F 12 '77. O. Seavey
Perkins, D. H. ed. China's modern economy in historical perspective. 1975
Am Hist R 82:414 Ap '77. Y. Tzong-Shian
Perlmutter, A. Military and politics in modern times
Progressive 41:43-4 S '77. Tran-van-Dinh
Perloff, M. Frank O'Hara: poet among painters
Nation 225:694-6 D 24 '77. J. D. O'Hara
New Repub 177:35-7 S 10 '77. J. Atlas
Perry, M. Silence to the drums: a survey of the literature of the Harlem Renaissance. 1976
Negro Hist Bull 40:714 My '77. W. Hackett
Personnel evaluation institute, Charleston, Ill, October 24-26, 1975. Proceedings; ed. by F. M. Pollard. 1976
Lib J 102:2327 N 15 '77. J. D. Veenstra
Perspectives and irony in American slavery; ed. by H. P. Owens. 1976
Am Hist R 82:1330 D '77. A. J. Lane
Pescatello, A. M. Power and pawn: the female in Iberian families, societies, and cultures. 1976
Am Hist R 82:944 O '77. C. E. Lida
Petersen, K. and Wilson J. J. Women artists: recognition and reappraisal from the early middle ages to the twentieth century
Ms 5:84+ Je '77. A. M. Cunningham
Peterson, M. D. Adams and Jefferson: a revolutionary dialogue
Nat R 29:344 Mr 18 '77. F. McDonald
Peterson, P. E. School politics Chicago style. 1976
Ann Am Acad 431:178-9 My '77. J. A. Sigler
Peterson, S. Living tradition of Maria Martinez
Craft Horiz 37:10+ D '77. R. Coe
Petras, J. and Morley, M. United States and Chile: imperialism and the overthrow of the Allende government. 1975
Am Hist R 82:481-2 Ap '77. J. Rybácker-Mlýnková
Pétrement, S. Simone Weil: a life; tr. by R. Rosenthal. 1977
America 136:278 Mr 26 '77. W. Russell
Chr Cent 94:336 Ap 6 '77. M. M. Shideler
Commentary 63:76+ Je '77. E. Grossman
Commonweal 104:468-70 Jl 22 '77. G. A. White
Ms 6:40+ S '77. N. Rosen
Nation 224:664-6 My 28 '77
Psychol Today 10:110+ Ap '77 D. Mapel
Sat R 4:22-4 F 19 '77. B. Cook
Petrovich, M. B. History of modern Serbia, 1804-1918. 1976
Am Hist R 82:1014 O '77. P. Auty
Petulla, J. M. American environmental history: the exploitation and conservation of natural resources. 1977
Am West 14:63 S '77. P. N. Carroll
Pevsner, N. History of building types
Art N 76:184 Summ '77. G. Weisberg
Peyrefitte, A. Chinese; tr. by G. Webb
Sat R 4:20-1 Je 25 '77. J. A. Cohen
Peyser, J. Boulez: composer, conductor, enigma
Am Rec G 40:7 Ag '77. B. Pernick
Hi Fi 27:MA39-40 Mr '77. P. J. Smith
Pfeiffer, J. E. Emergence of society: a prehistory of the establishment. 1977
Science 198:183-4 O 14 '77. C. L. Redman
Pfeiffer, R. History of classical scholarship from 1300-1850. 1976
Am Hist R 82:610 Je '77. D. Sullivan
Pfister, C. Agrarkonjunktur und Witterungsverlauf im westlichen schweizer Mittelland zur Zeit der Okonomischen Patrioten, 1755-1797: ein Beitrag zur Umwelt- und Wirtschaftsgeschichte des 18. Jahrhunderts. 1975
Am Hist R 82:138 F '77. J. G. Gagliardo
Phelan, J. Howard Hughes: the hidden years
Sat Eve Post 249:80-1 N '77. D. Brudnoy
Phelan, J. M. Mediaworld: programming the public
America 137:196 O 1 '77. K. N. L. Cissna
Phillips, D. A. Night watch: 25 years of peculiar service
Bus W p 11 Mr 14 '77. B. Agnew
Nat R 29:499 Ap 29 '77. E. H. Hunt
Phillips, G. A. General strike: the politics of industrial conflict. 1976
Am Hist R 82:973 O '77. J. H. M. Laslett
Phillips, J. Will to survive
Smithsonian 8:122-4 S '77. D. Lancashire
Vogue 167:241 My '77
Phinney, E. ed. Librarian and the patient: an introduction to library services for patients in health care institutions. 1977
Lib J 102:1737 S 1 '77. M. M. Kinney
Phipson, J. Cats. 1976
Horn Bk 53:54 F '77. P. Heins
Photochemical and photobiological reviews; ed. by K. C. Smith. VI. 1976
BioScience 27:214 Mr '77. B. A. Zilinskas
Physics in industry; proceedings of conference, Dublin, 1976; ed. by E. O'Mongain and C. P. O'Toole. 1976
Phys Today 30:71 O '77. F. E. Jamerson
Physics of Ap-stars; proceedings of colloquium, Vienna, 1975; ed. by W. W. Weiss and others. 1976
Science 196:777 My 13 '77. E. J. Wampler
Picon, G. Surrealists and surrealism 1919-1939; tr. by J. Emmons
Art N 76:48+ N '77. B. M-P. Leefmans
Piepkorn, A. C. Profiles in belief, v 1
Chr Cent 94:762 Ag 31 '77. J. H. Leith
Pike, D. W. Les français et la guerre d'Espagne, 1936-1939. 1975
Am Hist R 81:1133-4 D '76. I. M. Wall
Pike, F. B. and Stritch, T. eds. New corporatism: social-political structures in the Iberian world. 1974
Am Hist R 82:231-2 F '77. J. F. Petras
Pileggi, N. Blye, private eye
Time 109:88+ Mr 28 '77. M. Duffy
Pillorget, R. Les mouvements insurrectionnels de Provence entre 1596 et 1715. 1975
Am Hist R 81:1122-3 D '76. S. Kettering
Pimlott, D. and others. Oil under the ice: offshore drilling in the Canadian Arctic. 1976
Liv Wildn 40:44-7 Ja '77. J. P. Milton
Pinchin, J. L. Alexandria still: Forster, Durrell, and Cavafy
New Repub 177:36-7 O 22 '77. B. D. Schwartz
Pini, A. I. La popolazione di Imola e del suo territorio nel XIII e XIV secolo. 1976
Am Hist R 82:940-1 O '77. S. R. Blanshei
Pinkney, A. Red, black, and green: black nationalism in the United States. 1976
Am Hist R 81:1268 D '76. W. M. Tuttle, Jr
Pinkowski, E. Pills, pen & politics: the story of General Leon Jastremski, 1843-1907. 1974
Am Hist R 81:1260 D '76. E. F. Haas
Pinkwater, D. M. Hoboken chicken emergency. 1977
Horn Bk 53:316 Je '77. V. Haviland
Pinsky, R. Sadness and happiness
Poetry 129:228-9 Ja '77. R. Howard
Pinsky, R. Situation of poetry: contemporary poetry and its traditions
America 136:490+ My 28 '77. P. Zagano
Nation 225:186-8 S 3 '77. H. Vendler
Pinter, H. A la recherche du temps perdu: the Proust screenplay
New Repub 177:22-3 D 24 '77. S. Kauffmann
Pippidi, D. M. Scythica Minora: recherches sur les colonies grecques du littoral roumain de la Mer Noire. 1975
Am Hist R 81:1080-1 D '76. C. D. Hamilton
Pirie, V. Triple crown
Commonweal 104:280-1 Ap 29 '77. J. L. McKenzie
Pitkin, T. M. Keepers of the gate: a history of Ellis Island. 1975
Am Hist R 81:1267 D '76. R. Ernst
Pitkin, T. M. and Cordasco, F. Black hand: a chapter in ethnic crime. 1977
Intellect 106:254 D '77. D. N. Alloway
Pitt-Rivers, J. Fate of Shechem, or the politics of sex: essays in the anthropology of the Mediterranean
Yale R 67:139-44 O '77. A. Welsh
Piven, F. F. and Cloward, R. A. Poor people's movements
Nation 225:341-3 O 8 '77. J. Beatty
New Repub 178:34-6 Ja 7 '78. S. Kaplan
Pizer, V. Ink, Ark, and all that: how American places got their names; il. by T. Huffman. 1976
Horn Bk 53:66 F '77. M. M. Burns

Planchart, A. E. Repertory of tropes at Winchester. 1977
Mus Q 63:556-61 O '77. E. H. Roesner
Planetary satellites; papers from colloquium, Ithaca, N.Y, 1974; ed. by J. A. Burns, 1977
Science 198:1147-8 D 16 '77. W. M. Kaula
Plaschka, R. G. and others. Innere Front: Militärassistenz, Widerstand und Umsturz in der Donaumonarchie, 1918, v 1: Zwischen Streik und Meuterei; v2: Umsturz. 1974
Am Hist R 81:1163 D '76. A. D. Low
Plasma physics: nonlinear theory and experiments; proceedings of symposium, Lerum, Sweden, 1976; ed by H. Wilhelmsson. 1977
Science 197:248 Jl 15 '77. H. Lashinsky
Platter, F. Tagebuch (lebensbeschreibung), 1536-1567; ed. by V. Lötscher. 1976
Am Hist R 82:676-7 Je '77. E. W. Monter
Plessen, M. L. Die Wirksamkeit des Vereins für Socialpolitik von 1872-1890: Studien zum Kathederund Staatssozialismus. 1975
Am Hist R 82:663-4 Je '77. C. Landauer
Plimpton, G. One more July
Bus W p 11 Ag 22 '77. M. Newman
Plimpton, G. Shadow box
Time 110:99-100+ D 19 '77. J. Skow
Plimpton, G. ed. Writers at work: the Paris review interviews; introd. by W. Sheed. 4th series
Commentary 63:76-8 F '77. J. Wilson
New Repub 176:32-3 Ja 29 '77. J. Atlas
Plumly, S. Out-of-the-body travel
Nation 225:182-3+ S 3 '77. C. C. Park
Pogrebin, B. B. and Arnold, S. eds. Basic labor relations. 1976
M Labor R 100:60-1 N '77. T. Bornstein
Pohl, H. Studien zur Wirtschaftsgeschichte Lateinamerikas. 1976
Am Hist R 82:1372 D '77. W. Schiff
Poirier, R. Robert Frost: the work of knowing
Sat R 5:51-3 D 10 '77. K. Pollitt
Pois, R. A. Bourgeois democrats of Weimar Germany. 1976
Am Hist R 82:1007 O '77. E. L. Evans
Polette, N. E is for everybody. 1976
SLJ 23:122 Mr '77. P. J. Yuill
Polk, J. K. Correspondence of James K. Polk, v3: 1835-1836; ed. by H. Weaver and K. L. Hall. 1975
Am Hist R 81:1247 D '76. M. G. Baxter
Pollack, H. Jewish folkways in Germanic lands (1648-1806) studies in aspects of daily life. 1971
Am Hist R 82:1273 D '77. S. Milton
Pollock, B. Playing for change. 1977
Horn Bk 53:320-1 Je '77. S. H. Holtze
Pombeni, P. Le Cronache Sociali di Dossetti, 1947-1951: geografia di un movimento di opinione. 1976
Am Hist R 82:389-90 Ap '77. P. V. Cannistraro
Ponchaud, F. Cambodge année zéro. 1977
Nation 224:789-94 Je 25 '77. N. Chomsky and E. S. Herman
Ponicsan, D. Tom Mix died for your sins. 1975
Am West 14:59 Ja '77. J. K. Folsom
Poole, J. Touch and go. 1976
Horn Bk 53:60 F '77. M. M. Burns
Pope-Hennessy, J. Fra Angelico
Am Artist 41:56-7 F '77. R. Werner
Porges, I. Edgar Rice Burroughs: the man who created Tarzan
Commonweal 104:182-4 Mr 18 '77. B. Hogarth
Porter, B. Lion's share: a short history of British imperialism, 1850-1970. 1976
Am Hist R 82:361-2 Ap '77. H. R. Winkler
Porter, K. A. Never-ending wrong
Commentary 64:95-6 D '77. R. Starr
Commonweal 104:571-2 S 2 '77. J. Deedy
Porter, P. Living in a calm country
Poetry 129:350-3 Mr '77. J. Matthias
Porter, R. W. Versatile satellite
Sci Am 237:40+ D '77. P. Morrison and P. Morrison
Portes, A. and Walton, J. Urban Latin America: the political condition from above and below. 1976
Ann Am Acad 430:203-4 Mr '77. D. Hindley
Posner, R. A. Antitrust law: an economic perspective. 1976
Ann Am Acad 433:203-4 S '77. R. H. Wolf
Post, J. D. Last great subsistence crisis in the western world. 1977
Am Hist R 82:1211 D '77. W. H. McNeill
Sci Am 237:148+ Jl '77. P. Morrison
Post, R. C. Physics, patents, and politics: a biography of Charles Grafton Page. 1976
Am Hist R 82:1336 D '77. S. G. Kohlstedt
Smithsonian 8:126-7 My '77. D. F. Dickinson
Postal, B. and Koppman, L. American Jewish landmarks: a travel guide and history, v 1: Northeast
Smithsonian 7:121-3 Mr '77. R. Rinehart
Poste, G. and Nicolson, G. L. Cell surface in animal embryogenesis and development. 1976
Science 198:500 N 4 '77. R. Marchase
Poster, M. Existential Marxism in postwar France: from Sartre to Althusser. 1976
Am Hist R 81:1134-5 D '76. D. Pace
Potamkin, H. A. Compound cinema: selected film writings of Harry Alan Potamkin; ed. by L. Jacobs. 1977
Film Q 30:52-3 Summ '77. J. Leyda
Potter, D. M. Freedom and its limitations in American life; ed. by D. E. Fehrenbacher. 1976
Am Hist R 82:1315-16 D '77. J. Higham
Yale R 66:580 Je '77. E. S. Morgan
Potter, D. M. Impending crisis, 1848-1861; ed. by D. E. Fehrenbacher. 1976
Am Hist R 82:182 F '77. H. Hamilton
Potter, E. B. Nimitz. 1976
Am Hist Illus 12:49 D '77. R. Maddox
Am Hist R 82:766 Je '77. C. G. Reynolds
Poulantzas, N. Classes in contemporary capitalism; tr. by D. Fernbach. 1975
Am Hist R 81:1073-4 D '76. N. Levine
Society 14:84-8 My '77. W. L. McBride
Poulantzas, N. Fascism and dictatorship: the Third international and the problem of fascism; tr. by J. White. 1974
Society 14:84-8 My '77. W. L. McBride
Poulantzas, N. Political power and social classes; tr. by T. O'Hagan and others. 1975
Society 14:84-8 My '77. W. L. McBride
Pound, E. Collected early poems of Ezra Pound; ed. by M. J. King
Yale R 66:598-603 Je '77. V. Miller
Powell, A. Infants of the spring
New Repub 176:29-31 Je 11 '77. C. D. Benson
Newsweek 90:107+ S 19 '77. C. Michener
Powers, E. Journal of Madame Royale. 1976
Horn Bk 53:173-4 Ap '77. P. Heins
Powers, R. Newscasters
Progressive 41:40 Ag '77. A. Hochschild
Pratt, C. Critical phase in Tanzania, 1945-1968: Nyerere and the emergence of a socialist strategy. 1976
Am Hist R 82:1037-8 O '77. J. G. Liebenow
Pratt, H. J. Gray lobby. 1976
Ann Am Acad 433:204-5 S '77. I. P. Wolf
Premack, D. Intelligence in ape and man. 1976
Science 196:755-6 My 13 '77. N. K. Humphrey
Preminger, O. Preminger: an autobiography
New Repub 176:35-7 Ap 2 '77. S. Lawson
Sat Eve Post 249:75 O '77. D. Brudnoy
Prescott, D. M. Reproduction of eukaryotic cells. 1976
Science 196:866-7 My 20 '77. W. Plaut
Preston, P. ed. Spain in crisis: the evolution and decline of the Franco regime. 1976
Am Hist R 82:119 F '77. V. R. Pilapil
Price, D. C. Russia and the roots of the Chinese revolution, 1896-1911. 1974
Am Hist R 82:413-14 Ap '77. T. Ganschow
Price, D. D. Science since Babylon. 1975
Intellect 105:285-6 F '77. J. A. Goldman
Price, R. Economic modernisation of France. 1975
Am Hist R 81:1125 D '76. M. S. Smith
Price, R. ed. Revolution and reaction: 1848 and the second French republic. 1976
Am Hist R 81:1130 D '76. D. H. Pinkney
Price, R. K. With Nixon
Commonweal 105:25-6 Ja 6 '78. R. L. King
Nat R 29:1257 O 28 '77. W. F. Buckley, jr
New Repub 177:8-9+ O 8 '77. J. Osborne
Newsweek 90:104 N 28 '77. R. Boeth
Price, R. M. Society and bureaucracy in contemporary Ghana. 1975
Ann Am Acad 429:161-2 Ja '77. C. Baxter
Primack, J. and von Hippel, F. Advice and dissent: scientists in the political arena. 1974
Org Gard & Farm 24:54 F '77. W. Graham
Pritchett, V. S. Gentle barbarian: the life and work of Turgenev
America 137:16-17 Jl 2 '77. R. T. Reilly
New Repub 176:26-7 Ap 23 '77. J. Beatty
Newsweek 89:113+ My 16 '77. P. S. Prescott
Sat R 4:22+ My 14 '77. H. Muchnic
Time 109:103+ My 23 '77. S. Kanfer
Problems in vertebrate evolution; papers from symposium, London, 1976; ed. by S. M. Andrews and others. 1977
Science 198:499 N 4 '77. R. Estes
Protheroe, W. M. and others. Astronomy. 1976
Sky & Tel 54:222-3+ S '77. K. Janes
Pryce-Jones, D. Unity Mitford: an inquiry into her life and the frivolity of evil
Commentary 64:76-80 Jl '77. H. Maccoby
New Repub 177:33-5 Ag 20 '77. P. Stansky
Newsweek 89:80 My 30 '77. W. Clemons
Psyllas, G. Apomnēmoneumata tou biou mou; ed. by E. G. Prevelakis. 1974
Am Hist R 81:1161-2 D '76. J. A. Petropulos
Pudney, J. Lewis Carroll and his world. 1976
Commonweal 104:439-41 Jl 8 '77. R. Phillips
Horn Bk 53:200 Ap '77. M. S. Cosgrave
Pugsley, A. ed. Works of Isambard Kingdom Brunel: an engineering appreciation
Sci Am 236:144-6 Ap '77. P. Morrison
Puhle, H-J. Politische Agrarbewegungen in kapitalistischen Industriegesellschaften: Deutschland, USA und Frankreich im 20. Jahrhundert. 1975
Am Hist R 81:1070 D '76. K. D. Barkin
Puig, M. Buenos Aires affair; tr. by S. J. Levine
Commonweal 104:412-14 Je 24 '77. R. Christ

Pullapilly, C. K. Caesar Baronius: counter-reformation historian. 1975
Am Hist R 82:88 F '77. R. Bireley
Pullman, B. ed. Quantum mechanics of molecular conformations. 1976
Science 197:1072-3 S 9 '77. J. J. Kaufman
Purcell, S. K. Mexican profit-sharing decision: politics in an authoritarian regime. 1975
Ann Am Acad 429:193-5 Ja '77. L. V. Padgett
Purdy, S. B. Hole in the fabric: science, contemporary literature and Henry James
America 137:18-19 Jl 2 '77. D. Kirby
Purifoy, L. M. Harry Truman's China policy: McCarthyism and the diplomacy of hysteria, 1947-1951. 1976
Am Hist R 82:1358-9 D '77. L. S. Wittner

Quazza, G. Resistenza e storia d'Italia: problemi e ipotesi di ricerca. 1976
Am Hist R 82:683 Je '77. A. De Grand
Queneau, R. Sunday of life; tr. by B. Wright
New Yorker 53:179-80+ O 10 '77. J. Updike
Quennell, P. Marble foot, an autobiography, 1905-1938
Nat R 29:1121 S 30 '77. A. Bakshian, jr
New Repub 176:28-9 My 7 '77. P. Stansky
Quinlan, J. and Quinlan, J. Karen Ann: the Quinlans tell their story; with P. Battelle
America 137:317-18 N 5 '77. J. J. Fitzpatrick
Quiroga, H. Decapitated chicken and other stories; tr. by M. S. Peden
Commonweal 104:285-6 Ap 29 '77. R. De Feo

Raab, L. Collector of cold weather
Poetry 130:49-50 Ap '77. J. D. McClatchy
Yale R 66:407-24 Mr '77. H. Vendler
Raaflaub, K. Dignitatis contentio: Studien zur Motivation und politischen Taktik im Bürgerkrieg zwischen Caesar und Pompeius. 1974
Am Hist R 81:1082 D '76. D. K. Clift
Rabb, T. K. Struggle for stability in early modern Europe. 1975
Am Hist R 82:81-3 F '77. A. Plakans
Rabinowitch, A. Bolsheviks come to power: the revolution of 1917 in Petrograd. 1976
Am Hist R 82:701-2 Je '77. R. G. Suny
New Repub 176:35-6 Je 18 '77. R. A. Rosenstone
Rabinowitz, D. New lives: survivors of the Holocaust living in America
America 136:489-90 My 28 '77. J. Riemer
Commonweal 104:282-3 Ap 29 '77. J. Garvey
Rabkin, E. S. Fantastic in literature
Yale R 66:444-8 Mr '77. M. Byrd
Radkey, O. H. Unknown civil war in Soviet Russia: a study of the green movement in the Tambov region, 1920-1921. 1976
Am Hist R 82:703-4 Je '77. P. Kenez
Radwin, G. E. and D'Attilio, A. Murex shells of the world: an illustrated guide to the muricidae. 1976
BioScience 27:564 Ag '77. W. K. Emerson
Radzinowicz, L. and King, J. Growth of crime
Nat R 29:1375 N 25 '77. E. Van Den Haag
Ragsdale, K. B. Quicksilver: Terlingua and the Chisoso mining company. 1976
Am Hist R 82:1095-6 O '77. J. B. Allen
Rahner, K. Meditations on the sacraments
America 137:86 Ag 13 '77. R. M. Liddy
Rahner, K. Theological investigations, v 14: Ecclesiology, questions in the church, the church in the world; tr. by D. Bourke
America 136:246-7 Mr 19 '77. A. Dulles
Raina, P. Stosunki polsko-niemieckie, 1937-1939: prawdziwy charakter polityki zagranicznej Josefa Becka. 1975
Am Hist R 82:688 Je '77. W. Jedrzejewicz
Raines, H. My soul is rested: movement days in the deep South remembered
Nation 225:598+ D 3 '77. A. Lopez
Ramelli, A. Various and ingenious machines of Agostino Ramelli (1588); tr. by M. T. Gnudi. 1976
Am Hist R 82:679 Je '77. R. Hall
Rampersad, A. Art and imagination of W.E.B. DuBois
New Repub 176:28-30 F 19 '77. M. Cooke
Rand McNally atlas of the oceans
Time 111:76 Ja 2 '78. P. Stoler
Randall, W. S. and Solomon, S. D. Building 6. 1977
Environment 19:45 Ag '77. J. McCaull
Rank and file: Civil war essays in honor of Bell Irvin Wiley; ed. by J. I. Roberston, jr, and R. M. McMurry. 1976
Am Hist R 82:1331-2 D '77. C. S. Campbell
Ranucci, E. R. and Rollins, W. E. Curiosities of the cube
Sci Am 237:42 D '77. P. Morrison and P. Morrison
Rapp, R. T. Industry and economic decline in seventeenth-century Venice. 1976
Am Hist R 82:140-1 F '77. E. Muir
Rather, D. and Hershkowitz, M. Camera never blinks
Progressive 41:40 Ag '77. A. Hochschild
Raven, P. H. and Raven, T. E. Genus epilobium (onagraceae) in Australasia. 1976
Science 197:45 Jl 1 '77. S. Carlquist
Ray, M. Beyond the desert gate. 1977
Horn Bk 53:670 D '77. A. A. Flowers
Ray, S. F. Lens in action. 1976
Sky & Tel 54:229 S '77. R. E. Cox
Raymond, R. L. Justification of knowledge. 1976
Chr Today 22:34 N 18 '77. R. H. Countess
Raynor, H. Music and society since 1815
Commentary 64:80+ O '77. E. Rothstein
Read, P. P. Polonaise
Commonweal 104:311-12 My 13 '77. G. Reedy
Read, W. H. America's mass media merchants. 1977
Ann Am Acad 433:205-6 S '77. C. S. Greenwald
Reader, J. and Croze, H. Pyramids of life; illuminations of nature's fearful symmetry
Sci Am 237:34 D '77. P. Morrison and P. Morrison
Smithsonian 8:157-9 N '77. G. E. Watson
Reardon, B. Liberalism and tradition: aspects of Catholic thought in nineteenth-century France. 1975
Am Hist R 81:1129-30 D '76. J. N. Moody
Reck, D. Music of the whole earth. 1977
Horn Bk 53:470 Ag '77. M. S. Cosgrave
Reed, M. C. Investment in railways in Britain, 1820-1844: a study in the development of the capital market. 1975
Am Hist R 82:102 F '77. D. N. McCloskey
Reed, W. John Clymer
Am Artist 41:27-9 My '77. C. Movalli
Reeves, R. Convention
Chr Cent 94:267-8 Mr 23 '77. J. W. Wall
Commentary 64:70+ S '77. N. W. Polsby
New Repub 176:34-6 My 7 '77. K. Bode
Newsweek 89:88-9 Mr 7 '77. P. S. Prescott
Sat R 4:35-6 Mr 19 '77. R. Lekachman
Reff, T. Degas: the artist's mind. 1976
Art in Am 65:37 My '77. A. C. Birnholz
Art N 76:30 Ja '77. G. P. Weisberg
New Repub 177:25-6+ N 12 '77. J. Canaday
Reff, T. Manet: Olympia
Art N 76:30 Ja '77. G. P. Weisberg
Reflections on biochemistry: in honour of Severo Ochoa; papers from symposium, Barcelona and Madrid, 1975; ed by A. Ronberg and others. 1976
Science 196:769-71 My 13 '77. J. T. Edsall
Regehr, T. D. Canadian northern railway: pioneer road of the northern prairies, 1895-1918. 1976
Am Hist R 82:1368-9 D '77. D. McCalla
Reich, C. Sorcerer of Bolinas reef
Am Scholar 46:393-6 Summ '77. W. Nichols
New Repub 176:32-3 F 19 '77. C. Tucker
Yale R 66:432-43 Mr '77. P. M. Spacks
Reichert, W. O. Partisans of freedom: a study in American anarchism. 1976
Am Hist R 82:452-3 Ap '77. L. Perry
Reid, B. L. Lives of Roger Casement
Progressive 41:41-2 Jl '77. T. J. Spinner, Jr
Yale R 66:432-43 Mr '77. P. M. Spacks
Reid, C. Courant in Göttingen and New York; the story of an improbable mathematician. 1976
Science 195:775 F 25 '77. J. L. Heilbron
Reid, J. P. Better kind of hatchet: law, trade, and diplomacy in the Cherokee nation during the early years of European contact. 1976
Am Hist R 82:429 Ap '77. B. Graymont
Reill, P. H. German enlightenment and the rise of historicism. 1975
Am Hist R 82:125-6 F '77. C. E. McClelland
Reischauer, E. O. Japanese
Commentary 64:87-8 S '77. C. Horner
Nat R 29:1247 O 28 '77. W. A. Rusher
New Repub 177:42-3 Ag 6 '77. R. A. Rosenstone
Reisler, M. By the sweat of their brow: Mexican immigrant labor in the United States, 1900-1940. 1976
Am Hist R 82:757-8 Je '77. A. Hoffman
Am West 14:57 N '77. G. Stanley
Reisman, D. A. Adam Smith's sociological economics. 1976
Ann Am Acad 429:195 Ja '77. K. De Schweinitz, Jr.
Les relations franco-belges de 1830 à 1934. 1975
Am Hist R 81:1129 D '76. P.-H. Laurent
Remini, R. V. Revolutionary age of Andrew Jackson. 1976
Am Hist R 82:178-9 F '77. F. N. Stites
Rensberger, B. Cult of the wild
Newsweek 90:70 Ag 22 '77. P. Gwynne
Reuther, V. G. Brothers Reuther and the story of the UAW: a memoir. 1976
Am Hist R 82:208-9 F '77. M. Dubofsky
Ann Am Acad 429:196 Ja '77. H. M. Teaf, Jr
M Labor R 100:61-2 My '77. J. Stieber
Revel, J.-F. Totalitarian temptation; tr. by D. Hapgood
Commentary 64:79-80 Ag '77. S. Haseler
Esquire 88:42+ N '77. A. Kazin
Nat R 29:999-1001 S 2 '77. C. Williamson, Jr
Nation 225:252-4 S 17 '77. J. Taylor
Time 110:90+ Jl 18 '77. E. Warner

Rezneck, S. Unrecognized patriots: the Jews in the American revolution. 1975
Am Hist R 81:1216-17 D '76. L. A. Jick
Rhoads, E. J. M. China's republican revolution: the case of Kwangtung, 1895-1913. 1975
Am Hist R 81:1198-200 D '76. S. M. Jones
Rhodes, A. Propaganda: the art of persuasion, World war II; ed. by V. Margolin
America 136:112-13 F 5 '77. R. A. Blake
Commonweal 104:572-3 S 2 '77. G. C. Zahn
Rhys, J. Sleep it off, lady
Commonweal 104:632+ S 30 '77. J. Heidenry
Riasanovsky, N. V. Parting of ways: government and the educated public in Russia, 1801-1855. 1977
Am Hist R 82:1024-5 O '77. W. B. Lincoln
Ricasoli, B. Carteggi di Bettino Ricasoli, v26: I gennaio 1870-31 dicembre 1872; ed. by S. Camerani. 1974
Am Hist R 82:1011-12 O '77. E. P. Noether
Rice, C. D. Rise and fall of black slavery. 1975
Am Hist R 82:180 F '77. W. D. Jordan
Rich, A. Of woman born: motherhood as experience and institution
America 136:172-3 F 26 '77. E. McPherson
Rich, J. W. Declaring war in the Roman Republic in the period of transmarine expansion. 1976
Am Hist R 82:930 O '77. J. E. Phillips
Richard, A. Into the road. 1976
Horn Bk 53:167-8 Ap '77. E. L. Heins
Richard, S. ed. Great musicals of the American theatre. 2v.
Am Rec G 40:59-61 Mr '77. M. Galewski
Richardson, D. Pilgrimage
New Repub 176:33-4 F 19 '77. G. G. Fromm
Richardson, D. K. Cost of environmental protection. 1976
Am City & County 92:80+ Mr '77
Richardson, J. Local historian's encyclopedia. 1975
Am Hist R 82:956-7 O '77. F. A. Youngs, jr
Richey, R. ed. Denominationalism
Chr Cent 94:957-8 O 19 '77. J. H. Smylie
Richmond, J. Discover Toronto
Smithsonian 8:98 Jl '77. D. Landcashire
Rickover, H. G. How the battleship Maine was destroyed. 1976
Am Hist R 82:454-5 Ap '77. R. E. Johnson
Ridpath, I. ed. Illustrated encyclopedia of astronomy and space. 1976
Sky & Tel 53:213-14 Mr '77. P. Rizzo
Righini Bonelli, M. L. and Shea, W. R. eds Reason, experiment, and mysticism in the scientific revolution. 1975
Am Hist R 81:1096 D '76. A. E. Shapiro
Ringelblum, E. Polish-Jewish relations during the Second World war; ed. by J. Kermish and S. Krakowski; tr. by D. Allon and others. 1976
Am Hist R 82:399 Ap '77. E. D. Wynot, Jr
Ringer, R. J. Looking out for #1
Newsweek 90:78 Jl 25 '77. H. F. Waters
Ringertz, N. R. and Savage, R. E. Cell hybrids. 1976
BioScience 27:622 S '77. C. W. Anderson
Science 198:1248 D 23 '77. T. B. Shows
Ripley, C. P. Slaves and freedmen in Civil War Louisiana. 1976
Am Hist R 82:747-8 Je '77. L. S. Gerteis
Ripley, S. D. Rails of the world
Natur Hist 86:106-8 D '77. R. Arbib
Sat R 5:43 N 26 '77. D. Grumbach
Ritsos, Y. Fourth dimension: selected poems of Yannis Ritsos; tr. by R. Dalven
Harpers 255:104 N '77. H. Carruth
Nation 224:347 Mr 19 '77. S. Hazo
Ritter, E. Das Deutsche Austland-Institut in Stuttgart, 1917-1945; ein Beispiel deutscher Volkstrumsarbeit zwischen den Weltkriegen. 1976
Am Hist R 82:1006-7 O '77. J. W. Baird
Roazen, P. Erik H. Erikson: the power and limits of a vision
Chr Cent 94:858-9 S 28 '77. L. Rambo
New Repub 176:30-1 Ap 30 '77. P. M. Spacks
Robards, A. W. ed. Dynamic aspects of plant ultrastructure. 1974
BioScience 27:210 Mr '77. W. M. Laetsch
Robb, P. G. Government of India and reform: policies towards politics and the Constitution, 1916-1921. 1976
Am Hist R 82:1053 O '77. B. C. Busch
Robbins, K. Abolition of war: the "peace movement" in Britain, 1914-1919. 1976
Am Hist R 82:972-3 O '77. T. C. Kennedy
Robert, M. From Oedipus to Moses: Freud's Jewish identity
New Repub 176:30-1 Ja 15 '77. J. Stampfer
Roberts, J. Revolution and improvement: the western world, 1775-1847. 1976
Ann Am Acad 429:163-4 Ja '77. E. T. Gargan
Roberts, M. Fans!
Commonweal 104:118-21 F 18 '77. M. Naison
Roberts, W. D. Don't hurt Laurie! il. by R. Sanderson. 1977
Horn Bk 53:444 Ag '77. S. H. Holtze
Robertson, D. B. Theory of party competition. 1976
Ann Am Acad 429:148-9 Ja '77. T. P. Wolfe
Robinson, A. H. and Petchenik, B. B. Nature of maps: essays toward understanding maps and mapping
Am Scholar 46:262+ Spr '77. B. Hayes
Sci Am 236:144+ Mr '77. P. Morrison
Robinson, E. J. Seascape painter's problem book
Am Artist 41:21-2 Jl '77. C. Movalli
Robinson, G. O. Forest service: a study in public land management. 1975
Am Hist R 81:1271 D '76. V. Wiser
Robinson, J. A. T. Redating the New Testament. 1976
Chr Cent 94:410 Ap 27 '77. J. D. Kingsbury
Chr Today 21:43-5 Ap 15 '77. D. E. Aune
Robinson, T. C. L. ed. Future of science. 1977
Phys Today 30:65-6 N '77. R. W. Nichols
Robock, S. H. Brazil: a study in development progress. 1975
Américas 29:24-5 Ja '77. F. Meissner
Rochester, S. I. American liberal disillusionment: in the wake of World War I. 1977
Ann Am Acad 434:233 N '77. J. T. Kirby
Rochester, S. I. Takeoff at mid-century: federal civil aviation policy in the Eisenhower years, 1953-1961. 1976
Am Hist R 82:1362 D '77. L. H. Brune
Rock, D. Politics in Argentina 1890-1930: the rise and fall of radicalism. 1975
Am Hist R 81:1285-6 D '76. C. Solberg
Rock, R. ed. Argentina in the twentieth century. 1975
Am Hist R 82:1111 O '77. T. F. McGann
Rockefeller Foundation. Future for insecticides; proceedings of conference, Bellagio, Italy, 1974; ed. by R. L. Metcalf and J. J. McKelvey. 1976
Science 195:169-70 Ja 14 '77. H. Oberlander
Rockwood, J. To spoil the sun. 1976
Horn Bk 53:168 Ap '77. V. Haviland
Rodewald, C. Money in the age of Tiberius. 1976
Am Hist R 82:70-1 F '77. R. L. Hohlfelder
Rodgers, H. I. Search for security: a study in Baltic diplomacy, 1920-1934. 1975
Am Hist R 81:1170 D '76. D. M. Crowe, Jr
Rodriguez Monegal, E. ed. Borzoi anthology of Latin American literature; with T. Colchie
New Repub 176:29-30 Ap 9 '77. J. S. Brushwood
Rodríguez O, J. E. Emergence of Spanish America: Vicente Rocafuerte and Spanish Americanism, 1808-1832. 1975
Am Hist R 82:224-5 F '77. C. A. Hale
Roelker, J. R. Mathu of Kenya: a political study. 1976
Am Hist R 82:1038-9 O '77. J. Spencer
Roessingh, H. K. Inlandse tabak: expansie en contractie van een handelsgewas in de 17e en 18e eeuw in Nederland. 1976
Am Hist R 82:1269-70 D '77. J. De Vries
Rogers, M. Biohazard. 1977
Psychol Today 11:122+ S '77. R. Restak
Science 198:1144-5 D 16 '77. R. M. May
Smithsonian 8:109-11 Ja '78. J. Stein
Rogers, W. E. Program facilities: planning for needs
Camp Mag 49:42-3 Ja '77. J. H. Salomon
Roman, P. Some modern mathematics for physicists and other outsiders. 2v. 1975
Phys Today 30:72+ My '77. A. Lenard
Romero Maura, J. La rosa de fuego—republicanos y anarquistas: la política de los obreros barceloneses entre el desastre colonial y la semana trágica, 1899-1909. 1975
Am Hist R 81:1137 D '76. J. C. Ullman
Roobol, W. H. Tsereteli—a democrat in the Russian revolution: a political biography; tr. by P. Hyams and L. Richards. 1976
Am Hist R 82:1295-6 D '77. R. G. Suny
Roonwal, M. L. and Mohnot, S. M. Primates of South Asia: ecology, sociobiology, and behavior. 1977
Science 198:724 N 18 '77. J. G. Fleagle
Roosen, W. J. Age of Louis XIV: the rise of modern diplomacy. 1976
Am Hist R 82:624 Je '77. J. T. O'Connor
Root, W. and Rochemont, R. de. Eating in America: a history
Am Scholar 46:404-8 Summ '77. R. Gay
Rose, H. and Rose, S. eds. Political economy of science: ideology of/in the natural sciences. 1977
Science 197:246-7 Jl 15 '77. D. Joravsky
Rose, H. and Rose, S. eds. Radicalisation of science ideology of/in the natural sciences. 1977
Science 197:246-7 Jl 15 '77. D. Joravsky
Rose, W. L. ed. Documentary history of slavery in North America. 1976
Am Hist R 81:1212 D '76. S. Stuckey
Rosen, C. Arnold Schoenberg. 1975
Mus Q 63:124-28 Ja '77. J. Sachs
Rosen, E. A. Hoover, Roosevelt, and the brains trust: from depression to New Deal
New Repub 177:32-3 S 24 '77. J. A. Garraty
Rosenberg, N. Perspectives on technology. 1976
Ann Am Acad 432:192-3 Jl '77. C. Goldin
Rosenfeld, A. Plot to destroy Israel: the road to Armageddon. 1977
Ann Am Acad 434:216 N '77. H. N. Howard

Rosenfeld, A. Prolongevity
America 136:173-5 F 26 '77. D. Christiansen
Sci Digest 81:93-4 F '77. B. Ford
Rosenfeld, A. Second genesis: the coming control of life
Nat R 29:346 Mr 18 '77. M. S. Evans
Rosenfeld, S. S. Time of their dying
Psychol Today 11:108-9+ Je '77. P. Koenig
Rosenthal, N. George Rickey
Smithsonian 8:154-6 N '77. C. J. McCabe
Rosett, A. and Cresey, D. R. Justice by consent. 1976
Ann Am Acad 429:149 Ja '77. J. F. Henderson
Rositzke, H. CIA's secret operations
Nat R 29:782+ Jl 8 '77. H. Hunt
Ross, B. and Ross, C. Modern and classic wood-burning stoves, and the grass roots energy revival. 1976
Am For 83:46-7 Mr '77. M. Bush
Ross, C. Sunlight convergence solar burn. 1976
Sky & Tel 54:318-19 O '77. J. White
Rossabi, M. China and inner Asia: from 1368 to the present day. 1975
Am Hist R 82:410 Ap '77. F. Michael
Rossi, I. ed. Unconscious in culture: the structuralism of Claude Lévi-Strauss in perspective. 1974
Ann Am Acad 431:179-80 My '77. S. Vatuk
Rossi, P. H. and Lyall, K. C. Reforming public welfare: a critique of the negative income tax experiment. 1976
Ann Am Acad 431:185-6 My '77. P. Kantor
Rossie, J. G. Politics of command in the American revolution. 1975
Am Hist R 81:1227-8 D '76. N. Callahan
Rossiter, F. R. Charles Ives and his America. 1975
Mus Q 62:597-603 O '76. S. Blum
Rossiter, M. W. Emergence of agricultural science: Justus Liebig and the Americans, 1840-1880. 1975
Am Hist R 81:1244 D '76. E. E. Lampard
Rossmoore, H. W. Microbes, our unseen friends
Sci Am 237:32 D '77. P. Morrison and P. Morrison
Rossner, J. Attachments
Ms 6:36-7 O '77. A. K. Turner
Sat R 5:30 O 1 '77. D. Grumbach
Rostagni, C. M. ed. Il carteggio Antonelli-Barili, 1859-1861. 1973
Am Hist R 81:1157-8 D '76. E. Carrillo
Rotblat, J. ed. Nuclear reactors: to breed or not to breed. 1977
Bull Atom Sci 33:63-4 Je '77. H. A. Feiveson
Roth, G. D. Joseph Von Fraunhofer. 1976
Sky & Tel 54:49-50 Jl '77. E. E. Both
Roth, P. Professor of desire
Atlantic 240:101-2 N '77. B. DeMott
Commentary 64:60-3 N '77. P. K. Bell
Nat R 29:1302-3 N 11 '77. H. Kenner
Nation 225:373-6 O 15 '77. P. M. Spacks
Newsweek 90:83+ S 26 '77. R. Boeth
Sat R 5:24+ O 1 '77. R. Feld
Time 110:78 S 26 '77. P. Gray
Rothenberg, G. E. Army of Francis Joseph. 1976
Am Hist R 82:136 F '77. W. A. Jenks
Rothwell, H. ed. English historical documents, v3: 1189-1327. 1975
Am Hist R 82:75-6 F '77. J. S. Beckerman
Rothwell, N. V. Human genetics. 1977
BioScience 27:812 D '77. J. Herrmann
Rounds, G. Mr. Yowder and the steamboat. 1977
Horn Bk 53:308-9 Je '77. S. H. Holtze
Rovere, R. H. Arrivals and departures: a journalists' memoirs
New Repub 176:74+ Ja 22 '77. H. Salisbury
Rowe, H. E. Save America! 1976
Chr Today 21:34-8 My 20 '77. S. V. Monsma
Rowe, J. Hard-rock men: Cornish immigrants and the North American mining frontier. 1974
Am Hist R 81:1246 D '76. M. Walsh
Rowse, A. L. Homosexuals in history: a study of ambivalence in society, literature and the arts. 1977
Am Hist R 82:1212 D '77. A. N. Gilbert
Chr Cent 94:1077 N 16 '77. W. Muehl
Roxborough, I. and others. Chile: the state and revolution. 1977
Am Hist R 82:1108-9 O '77. P. W. Drake
Roy, P. Theory of lepton-hadron processes at high energies: partons, scale invariance, and light-cone physics. 1975
Phys Today 30:55-6 F '77. L. Litt
Royal entomological society. Insect development; papers from symposium; ed. by P. A. Lawrence. 1976
BioScience 27:753 N '77. A. G. Richards
Rozman, G. Urban networks in Russia, 1750-1800, and premodern periodization. 1976
Am Hist R 81:1173-4 D '76. J. P. McKay
Rubin, B. Media, politics and democracy
Nation 225:439-42 O 29 '77. H. I. Schiller
Rubin, L. B. Worlds of pain: life in the working-class family. 1976
Ms 6:43-4 N '77. B. Garson
Progressive 41:56-8 My '77. P. N. Skerry, Jr
Society 14:82-3 S '77. G. Handel
Rubin, R. L. Party dynamics: the Democratic coalition and the politics of change. 1976
Ann Am Acad 429:177-8 Ja '77. J. Petrocik
Rubin, V. A. Individual and state in ancient China: essays on four Chinese philosophers; tr. by S .I. Levine. 1976
Am Hist R 82:409 Ap '77. J .S. Major
Rubinstein, A. Z. ed. Soviet and Chinese influence in the third world. 1976
Ann Am Acad 430:182-3 Mr '77. I. Peleg
Rubinstein, H. L. Captain Luckless: James, first duke of Hamilton, 1606-1649. 1976
Am Hist R 82:97 F '77. R. Howell, Jr
Ruddick, S. and Daniels, P. eds. Working it out: 23 women writers, artists, scientists, and scholars talk about their lives and work
Ms 5:82+ Je '77 V. Gornick
New Repub 176:31-3 Je 25 '77. P. Filene
Newsweek 90:74-5 Jl 25 '77. R. Sokolov
Progressive 41:56-7 D '77. W. Schwartz
Rudman, M. K. Children's literature: an issues approach
Horn Bk 53:18-19 F '77. E. L. Heins
Horn Bk 53:502-3 O '77. E. L. Heins
Rudofsky, B. Prodigious builders
Bus W p 10 S 26 '77. F. Levy
Rudolph, R. L. Banking and industrialization in Austria-Hungary: the role of banks in the industrialization of the Czech crownlands, 1873-1914. 1976
Am Hist R 82:674 Je '77. D. F. Good
Ruhe, B. Many happy returns: the art and sport of boomeranging
Sci Am 237:40 D '77. P. Morrison and P. Morrison
Ruiz, R. E. Labor and the ambivalent revolutionaries: Mexico, 1911-1923. 1975
Ann Am Acad 429:193-5 Ja '77. L. V. Padgett
Rukeyser, M. Gates
Nation 224:348 Mr 19 '77. L. Wagner
Ruland, R. America in modern European literature: from image to metaphor. 1976
Am Hist R 82:61-2 F '77. K. M. Roemer
Rumbaugh, D. M. ed. Language learning by a chimpanzee: the LANA project. 1977
Science 196:755-6 My 13 '77. N. K. Humphrey
Runblom, H. and Norman, H. eds. From Sweden to America: a history of the migration. 1976
Am Hist R 82:377-8 Ap '77. E. Lindquist
Rusco, E. R. Good time coming? black Nevadans in the nineteenth century. 1976
Am Hist R 81:1246 D '76. E. L. Thornbrough
Ann Am Acad 433:183-4 S '77. L. Billington
Rushmer, R. F. Humanizing health care: alternative futures for medicine. 1975
Ann Am Acad 430:218-19 Mr '77. H. A. Weeks
Russell, C. A. Voices of American fundamentalism: seven biographical studies. 1976
Am Hist R 82:1094 O '77. E. Jorstad
Chr Today 21:26 Jl 8 '77. E. Jorstad
Russell, F. President makers. 1976
Ann Am Acad 430:210 Mr '77. M. L. Fausold
Russell, H. S. Long, deep furrow
Smithsonian 8:142-3 Ap '77. H. Mitchell
Russell, R. and Chase, C. Life is a banquet
America 137:271-2 O 22 '77. M. Donnarumma
Newsweek 90:113 O 17 '77. R. Sokolov
Russell, W. R. and Dewar, A. J. Explaining the brain. Opus 72. 1975
BioScience 27:52 Ja '77. W. R. Klemm
Russett, C. E. Darwin in America: the intellectual response, 1865-1912. 1976
Ann Am Acad 430:210-11 Mr '77. G. Osborn
Ryan, C. Longest day
Am Hist Illus 12:50 My '77. M. Blumenson
Ryan, R. A. Keats: the religious sense
Yale R 66:449-52 Mr '77. D. R. Faulkner
Ryde, N. Atoms and molecules in electric fields. 1976
Science 196:867 My 20 '77. W. Happer
Ryder, A. Kingdom of Naples under Alfonso the Magnanimous: the making of a modern state. 1976
Am Hist R 82:942 O '77. H. Nader
Ryrie, C. C. Living end. 1976
Chr Today 21:40-2 Ap 15 '77. W. W. Gasque
Rystad, G. Ambiguous imperialism: American foreign policy and domestic politics at the turn of the century. 1975
Am Hist R 82:1342-3 D '77. R. L. Beisner

SIF cells; papers from meeting, Bethesda, Md, 1975; ed. by O. Eränkö. 1976
Science 198:818 N 25 '77. D. M. McDonald
Sabbag, R. Snowblind
Nat R 29:1180+ O 14 '77. D. K. Mano
Sablinsky, W. Road to bloody Sunday: Father Gapon and the St Petersburg massacre of 1905. 1976
Am Hist R 82:699-700 Je '77. D. W. Treadgold
Sachar, H. M. History of Israel: from the rise of Zionism to our time. 1976
Am Hist R 82:707-8 Je '77. R. Patai
Chr Cent 94:663 Jl 20 '77. S. Cain
Commentary 63:68-72 F '77. J. Shattan
Sachs, M. December tale. 1976
Horn Bk 53:162 Ap '77. M. M. Burns
Sachse, W L. Lord Somers: a political portrait. 1975
Am Hist R 81:1104 D '76. D. G. Greene

Sacks, M. P. Women's work in Soviet Russia: continuity in the midst of change. 1976
Society 14:84-5 S '77. J. Bernard
Safford, F. Ideal of the practical: Colombia's struggle to form a technical elite. 1976
Am Hist R 82:229 F '77. W. P. McGreevey
Ann Am Acad 430:204+ Mr '77. D. L. Huddle and A. Gomez-Rivas
Safire, W. Full disclosure
America 137:132 S 10 '77. P. McMurray
Bus W p6-7 Jl 4 '77. R. E. Farrell
New Repub 177:35-6 Jl 9 '77. S. Hess
Newsweek 89:91 Je 20 '77. R. Sokolov
Sat Eve Post 249:80+ N '77. J. Alexander
Sat R 4:28+ Jl 9 '77. J. A. Lukas
Safrai, S. and others. eds. Compendia rerum iudaicarum ad Novum Testamentum: the Jewish people in the first century, sec 1, v2. 1977
Chr Today 22:32-3 O 21 '77. D. E. Aune
Safrai, S. and Stern, M. eds. Jewish people in the first century
Chr Cent 94:1070+ N 16 '77. D. M. Hay
Sagan, C. Dragons of Eden: speculations on the evolution of human intelligence
America 137319-20 N 5 '77. C. Reingold
Atlantic 240:91 Ag '77. R. Manning
Commentary 64:66-70 Ag '77. R. J. Herrenstein
New Yorker 53:87-90 Ag 22 '77. J. Updike
Newsweek 89:79-80 Je 27 '77. R. Sokolov
Sahlins, M. Culture and practical reason. 1976
Ann Am Acad 433:194-5 S '77. R. A. Hahn
Science 197:553 Ag 5 '77. M. J. Swartz
Sahlins, M. Use and abuse of biology; an anthropological critique of sociobiology. 1976
Science 195:773-4 F 25 '77. G. G. Simpson
St John, D. Hush
Poetry 130:344-6 S '77. D. Allen
St John, S. Life in the forests of the Far East; introd. by T. Harrisson. 2v. 1974
Am Hist R 81:1210-11 D '76. C. A Lockard
Salert, B. Revolutions and revolutionaries: four theories. 1976
Am Hist R 82:335 Ap '77. T. R. Gurr
Salmon, J. H. M. Society in crisis: France in the sixteenth century. 1976
Am Hist R 81:1121 D '76. R. F. Kierstead
Sampson, A. Arms bazaar: from Lebanon to Lockheed
Atlantic 240:94-5 S '77. S. Reiner
Bus W p8 Ag 8 '77. J. Canan
Nat R 29:1442-3 D 9 '77. M. Copeland
New Repub 177:36-7 N 19 '77. D. R. Katz
Newsweek 90:75-6 Jl 11 '77. W. Clemons
Progressive 41:41-2 S '77. F. Kaplan
Sat R 4:36-8 Jl 23 '77. S. Karnow
Samuels, C. T. Mastering the film and other essays
New Repub 177:32-5 D 24 '77. S. Lawson
Samuels, P. and Samuels, H. Illustrated biographical encyclopedia of artists of the American West
Am Artist 41:10 Mr '77
Sanchez, P. A. Properties and management of soils in the tropics. 1976
BioScience 27:686 O '77. D. N. Munns
Sánchez-Albornoz, N. Population of Latin America: a history; tr. by W. A. R. Richardson. 1974
Am Hist R 82:221-3 F '77. M. J. MacLeod
Sandage, A. Hubble atlas of galaxies
Sci Am 236:141-2 Ap '77. P. Morrison
Sandage, A. and others, eds. Galaxies and the universe. 1976
Science 195:481-2 F 4 '77. I. R. King
Sanders, J. W. Education of an urban minority: Catholics in Chicago, 1833-1965. 1977
Am Hist R 82:1087 O '77. J. M. Allswang
America 136:322-4 Ap 9 '77. J. W. Donohue
Commonweal 104:662-4 O 14 '77. R. Whitehead, jr
Sanders, L. Second deadly sin
Time 110:73 Ag 29 '77. J. Skow
Sandiford, K. A. P. Great Britain and the Schleswig-Holstein question, 1848-64: a study in diplomacy, politics, and public opinion. 1975
Am Hist R 81:1111 D '76. O. Anderson
Sandmel, S. ed. Tomorrow's American
Chr Cent 94:1009-10 N 2 '77. L. S. Cunningham
Sandmel, S. and others, eds. New English Bible with the apocrypha: Oxford study edition
Chr Cent 94:572-3 Je 8 '77. K. H. Richards
Sando, J. S. Pueblo Indians. 1976
Am West 14:64 S '77. M. Gormly
Sanford, D. Me & Ralph: is Nader safe for America?
Nat R 29:279-80 Mr 4 '77. P. Minot
Santschi, C. Les évêques de Lausanne et leurs historiens des origines au XVIIIe siècle: érudition et societé. 1975
Am Hist R 82:365 Ap '77. R. M. Kingdon
Sapir, B. ed. Lavrov: years of emigration: letters and documents, v 1: Lavrov and Lopatin; v2: From "Vpered!" to the group of the old Narodovol'tsy. 1974
Am Hist R 82:402-3 Ap '77. A. Gleason
Sargent, T. D. Legion of night: the underwing moths. 1976
Science 196:288-9 Ap 15 '77. J. A. Powell
Sarraute, N. Fools say; tr. by M. Jolas
Sat R 4:28 Ap 2 '77. S. Koch
Sartori, G. Parties and party systems: a framework for analysis. vol. 1. 1976
Ann Am Acad 431:146 My '77. R. J. Sickels
Sartre, J. P. Life/situations: essays written and spoken
America 137:17 Jl 2 '77. R. E. Lauder
Saunders, D. S. Insect clocks. 1976
BioScience 27:560 Ag '77. J. D. Palmer
Sauvy, A. Livres saisis à Paris entre 1678 et 1701. 1972
Am Hist R 81:1124 D '76. R. Birn
Savage, W. S. Blacks in the West. 1977
Am Hist R 82:1078-9 O '77. L. B. De Graaf
Am West 14:52 Jl '77. T. Kornweibel, Jr
Saxton, A. Indispensable enemy: labor and the anti-Chinese movement in California. 1975
Am Hist R 81:1267-8 D '76. D. A. Williams
Sayles, J. Union dues
Nation 225:408-9 O 22 '77. E. McConville
New Repub 177:40-1 S 17 '77. B. Allen
Newsweek 90:72+ Ag 1 '77. M. Jefferson
Scamozzi, O. B. Le fabbriche e i disegni di Andrea Palladio
Harpers 255:75-7 Ag '77. G. Wills
Scarlatti, A. Operas of Alessandro Scarlatti; ed by D. J. Grout and others. 1974
Mus Q 63:268-72 Ap '77. S. Hansell
Schachter, O. Sharing the world's resources. 1977
Ann Am Acad 434:204-5 N '77. M. O. Clement
Nat R 29:620 My 27 '77. E. Van Den Haag
Schaeffer, F. A. How should we then live?
Nat R 29:345 Mr 18 '77. D. K. Mano
Schaeffer, P. J. L'Alsace et l'Allemagne de 1945 à 1949. 1976
Am Hist R 82:987 O '77. A. F. Peterson
Schafer, R. M. Tuning of the world
Hi Fi 27:MA38 N '77. P. J. Smith
Newsweek 90:74 Jl 25 '77. M. Jefferson
Sci Am 238:29-30 Ja '78. P. Morrison
Schafer, W. J. and Riedel, J. Art of ragtime: form and meaning of an original black American art; with M. Polad and R. Thompson
Am Rec G 40:61-2 N '76. R. Kammerer
Schaffer, R. Mothering
Psychol Today 11:94+ Ag '77. J. Steinberg
Schandler, H. Y. Unmaking of a president: Lyndon Johnson and Vietnam
America 137:88 Ag 13 '77. F. K. Kelly
Commentary 64:87-8+ D '77. N. W. Polsby
New Repub 176:30-1 Je 18 '77. M. S. Ross
Schapiro, M. Romanesque art, v 1
Art N 76:46+ N '77. W. Cahn
Schapsmeier, E. L. and Schapsmeier, F. H. Ezra Taft Benson and the politics of agriculture: the Eisenhower years, 1953-1961. 1975
Am Hist R 81:1281 D '76. I. May, Jr
Schaumburg, F. D. Judgment reserved: a landmark environmental case. 1976
Environment 19:45-7 Ag '77. O. Fanning
Scheffer, V. B. Natural history of marine mammals
Sci Am 237:31-2 O '77. P. Morrison
Schell, O. In the People's Republic: an American's firsthand view of living and working in China
Nation 224:598-600 My 14 '77. J. M. Taylor
New Repub 177:40-2 Ag 6 '77. B. I. Schwartz
Newsweek 89:110+ My 16 '77. W. Clemons
Sat R 4:20-1 Je 25 '77. J. A. Cohen
Schellhase, K. C. Tacitus in Renaissance political thought. 1976
Am Hist R 82:946 O '77. G. Griffiths
Schieder, T. ed. Staatsgründungen und Nationalitätsprinzip; with P. Alter. 1974
Am Hist R 81:1071 D '76. H. C. Meyer
Schiffer, H. and others. Chinese export porcelain: standard patterns and forms, 1780 to 1880
Antiques 111:1041-2 My '77. H. A. C. Forbes
Schlebecker, J. T. Whereby we thrive: a history of American farming, 1607-1972. 1975
Am Hist R 82:169-70 F '77. S. B. Hilliard
Sci Am 236:140-1 Je '77. P. Morrison
Schlumbohm, J. Freiheit: die Anfänge der bürgerlichen Emanzipationsbewegung in Deutschland im Spiegel ihres Leitwortes (ca. 1760-ca. 1880). 1975
Am Hist R 82:661 Je '77. J. J. Sheehan
Schmertz, R. Picture book of songs & ballads; arr. by L. B. Thomssen; ed. by J. Davidson. 1976
Archit Rec 161:45 Je '77. J. M. Davern
Schmid, A. P. Churchills privater Krieg: Intervention und Konterrevolution im russischen Bürgerkrieg, November 1918-März 1920. 1974
Am Hist R 82:107-8 F '77. I. Avakumovic
Schmidgall, G. Literature as opera
New Repub 177:27-9 D 10 '77. P. Robinson
Schmidt, M. My brother Gloucester
Poetry 130:237-9 Jl '77. J. Silkin
Schmidt, S. O. Stanovlenie rossiiskogo samoderzhavstva: issledovanie sotsial'no-politicheskoi istorii vremeni Ivana Groznogo. 1973
Am Hist R 81:1170-1 D '76. E. L. Keenan
Schneidau, H. N. Sacred discontent: the Bible and western tradition. 1977
Am Hist R 82:1212-13 D '77. J. Mbiti

Schneider, S. H. Genesis strategy: climate and global survival; with L. E. Mesirow. 1976
BioScience 27:128 F '77. J. E. Oliver
Conservationist 31:45 Ja '77. S. L. Golden
Environment 19:44-5 Ag '77. D. L. Sills
Schneider, W. Food, foreign policy and raw material cartels. 1976
Ann Am Acad 430:183-4 Mr '77. W. R. Kintner
Schneiderman, J. Sergei Zubatov and revolutionary Marxism: the struggle for the working class in tsarist Russia. 1976
Am Hist R 82:152 F '77. A. Ascher
Schnell, D. E. Carnivorous plants of the United States and Canada
Sci Am 236:143-5 My '77. P. Morrison
Schob, D. E. Hired hands and plowboys: farm labor in the Midwest, 1815-60. 1975
Am Hist R 81:1238 D '76. G. Clanton
Schofer, L. Formation of a modern labor force: Upper Silesia, 1865-1914. 1975
Ann Am Acad 429:164-6 Ja '77. T. J. Rice
Scholem, G. On Jews and Judaism in crisis: selected essays; ed. by W. J. Dannhauser
Commentary 63:78+ Mr '77. C. Raphael
Schor, J. Henry Highland Garnet: a voice of black radicalism in the nineteenth century. 1977
Am Hist R 82:1341 D '77. H. A. Reed
Schorer, M. Pieces of life
New Repub 177:42-3 N 26 '77. Z. Kotker
Schorr, D. L. Clearing the air
Newsweek 90:90+ O 31 '77. H. F. Waters and N. Stadtman
Schram, M. Running for president
New Repub 176:34-6 My 7 '77. K. Bode
Schran, P. Guerrilla economy: the development of the Shensi-Kansu-Ninghsia border region, 1937-1945. 1976
Ann Am Acad 433:178 S '77. J. D. Jordan
Schrank, J. Snap, crackle and popular taste: the illusion of free choice in America
Nation 225:439-42 O 29 '77. H. I. Schiller
Schuker, S. A. End of French predominance in Europe: the financial crisis of 1924 and the adoption of the Dawes plan. 1976
Am Hist R 82:654-5 Je '77. M. Trachtenberg
New Repub 177:30-2 S 3 '77. J. Joll
Schulz, B. Street of crocodiles; tr. by C. Wieniewska
Nation 224:376-8 Mr 26 '77. J. Rostropowicz
Schulz, G. Aufstieg des Nationalsozialismus: Krise und Revolution in Deutschland. 1975
Am Hist R 82:380 Ap '77. D. Orlow
Schumacher, E. F. Guide for the perplexed. 1977
Org Gard & Farm 24:52+ O '77. J. Cox
Schumacher, E. F. Small is beautiful: economics as if people mattered. 1973
Am Scholar 46:230+ Spr '77. M. Mayer
Chr Cent 94:325-8 Ap 6 '77. C. Fager
Schumacher, E. J. Politics, bureaucracy, and rural development in Senegal. 1975
Ann Am Acad 430:197-8 Mr '77. S. T. Barnes
Schumann, P. Die deutschen Historikertage von 1893 bis 1937: die Geschichte einer fachhistorischen Institution im Spiegel der Presse. 1975
Am Hist R 82:664-5 Je '77. G. D. Stark
Schustereit, H. Linksliberalismus und Sozialdemokratie in der Weimarer Republik: eine vergleichende Betrachtung der Politik von DDP und SPD, 1919-1930. 1975
Am Hist R 82:130 F '77. R. F. Wheeler
Schuursma, R. L. Het onaannemelijk tractaat: het verdrag met Belgie van 3 april 1925 in de Nederlandse publieke opinie. 1975
Am Hist R 82:656-7 Je '77. G. D. Homan
Schwartz, C. Cole Porter, a biography
Time 110:64-5 Jl 25 '77. G. Clarke
Schwartz, M. Radical protest and social structure: the Southern Farmers' Alliance and cotton tenancy, 1880-1890. 1976
Am Hist R 82:1082-3 O '77. J. M. Wiener
Schwarz, K. Die Lage der Handwerksgesellen in Bremen während des 18. Jahrhunderts. 1975
Am Hist R 82:123-4 F '77. F. B. Tipton, Jr
Sciascia, L. One way or another
New Repub 177:41-2 S 17 '77. J. Ahern
Scitovsky, T. Joyless economy. 1976
M Labor R 100:62-3 My '77. K. E. Boulding
Scobie, J. R. Buenos Aires: plaza to suburb, 1870-1910. 1974
Am Hist R 82:1377 D '77. M. Falcoff
Scortia, T. N. and Robinson, F. M. Prometheus crisis
Commonweal 104:59-61 Ja 21 '77. W. J. Lanouette
Scott, F. D. Scandinavia. rev ed. 1975
Am Hist R 81:1139 D '76. H. A. Barton
Scott, J. C. Moral economy of the peasant: rebellion and subsistence in southeast Asia. 1976
Ann Am Acad 432:161-2 Jl '77. R. L. Beals
Scott, J. D. Return of the buffalo; il. by O. Sweet. 1976
Horn Bk 53:170 Ap '77. E. L. Heins
Scott, N. A. Poetry of civic virtue: Eliot, Malrauz, Auden
Chr Cent 94:543-4 Je 1 '77. C. Walsh
Scott, O. J. James I. 1976
Chr Today 21:26-7 Ag 12 '77. R. J. Rushdoony
Scott, O. J. Voice of virtue. 1974
Chr Today 21:26-7 Ag 12 '77. R. J. Rushdoony
Scott, P. Staying on
Newsweek 90:76+ Ag 8 '77. R. Towers
Time 110:89 Jl 18 '77. P. Gray
Scott, V. Poems for a friend in late winter
Ms 6:37-8 N '77. J. Thurman
Scully, J. Disfarmer: the Heber Springs portraits 1939-1946. 1976
Art in Am 65:34-5 N '77. R. H. Cohen
Scupham, P. Prehistories
Poetry 130:234-7 Jl '77. J. Silkin
Seagrass ecosystems; papers from workshop, Leiden, Netherlands, 1973; ed. by C. P. McRoy and C. Helfferich. 1977
Science 197:1071-2 S 9 '77. W. E. Odum
Sealey, R. History of the Greek city states, ca. 700-338 B.C. 1977
Am Hist R 82:927-8 O '77. W. R. Connor
Searle, G. R. Eugenics and politics in Britain, 1900-1914. 1976
Science 198:498 N 4 '77. R. S. Cowan
Sears, H. D. Sex radicals: free love in high Victorian America
Newsweek 90:71 Ag 1 '77. R. Sokolov
Seelye, J. Prophetic waters: the river in early American life and literature
America 137:201-3 O 1 '77. H. J. Cloke
Nation 224:727-9 Je 11 '77. O. Seavey
Segal, E. W. Love story
Ms 5:74-6+ My '77. S. Yurick
Segal, E. W. Oliver's story
Ms 5:74-6+ My '77. S. Yurick
New Repub 176:39-41 Mr 26 '77. R. Rosenblatt
Segal, G. George Segal; text by J. van der Marck. 1975
Art N 76:136 S '77. A. Elsen
Segal, L. Lucinella
Nation 224:122-4 Ja 29 '77. M. Washburn
Segovia, A. Segovia: an autobiography of the years 1893-1920; tr. by W. F. O'Brien
Hi Fi 27:MA40 My '77
Segrè, C. G. Fourth shore: the Italian colonization of Libya. 1975
Am Hist R 81:1160-1 D '76. R. L. Hess
Seidman, R. J. One smart Indian
New Repub 177:37-9 O 8 '77. W. Rundall, jr
Seifert, H. Power for the church. 1976
Chr Today 21:28 Jl 29 '77. R. Quebedeaux
Seitter, W. C. Atlas for objective prism spectra, v2. 1975
Sky & Tel 54:419-21 N '77. D. Overbye
Seldes, G. Even the gods can't change history: the facts speak for themselves
Nation 224:280-1 Mr 5 '77. S. Blumenthal
Selén, K. Genevestä Tukholmaan: Suomen Turvallisuuspolitiikan painopisteen siirtyminen Kansainliitosta pohjoismaiseen yhteistyöhön, 1931-1936. 1974
Am Hist R 81:1141 D '76. P. K. Hamalainen
Selinger, B. Chemistry in the market place. 1975
Consumers Res Mag 60:26 My '77
Sellassie, H. Autobiography of Emperor Haile Sellassie I: my life and Ethiopia's progress, 1892-1937; tr. and anno. by E. Ullendorff. 1976
Am Hist R 82:156-7 F '77. B. Harris, Jr
Sellers, C. Patience Wright: American artist and spy in George III's London
Yale R 67:128-35 O '77. M. Ellmann
Selzer, R. Mortal lessons: notes on the art of surgery
Newsweek il 89:72 Ja 24 '77. P. S. Prescott
Time 109:82 Ja 24 '77. P. Stoler
Semmel, B. Methodist revolution. 1973
Am Hist R 81:1107 D '76. R. J. Helmstadter
Senn, M. J. E. ed. Speaking out for America's children
America 137:198+ O 1 '77. G. M. Anderson
Sennett, R. Fall of public man. 1977
Am Hist R 82:1214-15 D '77. G. Barth
Atlantic 239:94-6 F '77. R. Todd
Chr Cent 94:824+ S 21 '77. L. G. Tait
Commentary 63:81-4 Ap '77. S. Miller
Nat R 29:675-6 Je 10 '77. S. S. McDonald
Nation 225:118-21 Ag 6 '77. M. Berman
Newsweek 89:71 F 7 '77. K. L. Woodward
Sergean, R. Librarianship and information work: job characteristics and staffing needs. 1976
Lib J 102:2327 N 15 '77. B. R. Wilkinson
Seton, E. T. Worlds of Ernest Thompson Seton; ed. by J. G. Samson. 1976
Am West 14:64 S '77. T. H. Hunt
Seton-Watson, R. W. R. W. Seton-Watson and the Yugoslavs: correspondence, 1906-1941; ed. by H. Seton-Watson and others. 1976
Am Hist R 82:1015-16 O '77. B. E. Bigelow
Seung, T. K. Cultural thematics: the formation of the Faustian ethos. 1976
Am Hist R 82:1231 D '77. D. J. Wilcox
Sevareid, E. Not so wild a dream
Commonweal 104:94 F 4 '77. R. A. Schroth
Sevost'ianov, G. N. and others. Materialy pervogo simpoziuma sovetskikh istorikov-amerikanistov (30 noiabria-3 dekabria 1971 g.) 2v. 1973
Am Hist R 81:1258-9 D '76. H. Rogger
Sewell, A. Black beauty
Horn Bk 53:356-60 Je '77. A. Chambers
Sewell, J. P. UNESCO and world politics: engaging in international relations. 1975
Am Hist R 81:1076 D '76. A. M. Winkler

Sewell, R. H. Ballots for freedom: antislavery politics in the United States, 1837-1860. 1976
Am Hist R 82:181-2 F '77. M. L. Dillon
Sexton, A. Anne Sexton: a self-portrait in letters; ed. by L. G. Sexton and L. Ames
Harpers 255:105 N '77. H. Carruth
Sat R 5:40+ O 29 '77. K. Pollitt
Time 110:124+ N 28 '77. R. Z. Sheppard
Seybold, J. W. Fundamentals of modern composition
Pub W 211:68 Je 6 '77. P. D. Doebler
Shaban, M. A. Islamic history: a new interpretation, v2: A.D. 750-1055. 1976
Am Hist R 82:405-6 Ap '77. M. R. Waldman
Shadowitz A. and Walsh, P. Dark side of knowledge
Sci Digest 81:88-9 Mr '77. B. Ford
Shaffer, A. H. Politics of history: writing the history of the American revolution, 1783-1815. 1975
Am Hist R 81:1222 D '76. G. A. Billias
Shana, R. Nepali politics: retrospect and prospect. 1975
Ann Am Acad 430:198-9 Mr '77. J. G. Gunnell
Shands, W. E. and Healy, R. G. Lands nobody wanted
Am For 83:9 Jl '77. J. B. Craig
Nat Parks & Con Mag 51:20 D '77. L. S. Minckler
Shapiro, T. Painters and politics: the European avant-garde and society, 1900-1925. 1976
Am Hist R 82:627-8 Je '77. B. I. Lewis
Shapiro, Y. Formative years of the Israeli Labour party: the organization of power, 1919-1930. 1976
Am Hist R 82:406-7 Ap '77. B. Wasserstein
Sharot, S. Judaism: a sociology. 1976
Am Hist R 82:333 Ap '77. P. C. Albert
Sharp, T. Wartime alliance and the zonal division of Germany. 1975
Ann Am Acad 429:166-7 Ja '77. W. B. Bellis
Sharp, W. F. Slavery on the Spanish frontier: the Colombian Chocó, 1680-1810. 1976
Am Hist R 82:1106-7 O '77. M. P. Brungardt
Shaughnessy, M. P. Errors and expectations: a guide for the teacher of basic writing
Atlantic 240:95 S '77. C. M. Curtis
Shaw, D. Fourier transform N.M.R. spectroscopy. 1976
Phys Today 30:57-8 Ag '77. J. W. Cooper
Shaw, R. Dagger John: the unquiet life and times of Archbishop John Hughes of New York
America 137:220-1 O 8 '77. J. Hennesey
Shaw, S. History of the Ottoman Empire and modern Turkey, v 1: Empire of the Gazis: the rise and decline of the Ottoman Empire, 1280-1808. 1976
Am Hist R 82:1029 O '77. R. A. Abou-el-Haj
Shea, J. Hour of the unexpected
America 137:86+ Ag 13 '77. P. T. Rohrbach
Shebl, J. In this wild water: the suppressed poems of Robinson Jeffers
Nat R 29:1060-1 S 16 '77. H. Kenner
Shedd, C. Exciting church. 3v. 1975
Chr Today 21:42+ F 18 '77. W. Brindley
Sheed, W. Transatlantic blues
Newsweek 91:76+ Ja 16 '78. W. Clemons
Time 111:75-6 Ja 2 '78. R. Z. Sheppard
Sheehan, P. W, and Perry, C. W. Methodologies of hypnosis: a critical appraisal of contemporary paradigms of hypnosis. 1976
Science 198:600-1 N 11 '77. F. J. Evans
Sheehy, G. Passages
Sat Eve Post 249:78 My '77. A. McGlinn
Shelley, M. Annotated Frankenstein
New Repub 177:29-31 D 10 '77. R. J. Myers
Shelton, B. K. Reformers in search of yesterday: Buffalo in the 1890s. 1976
Am Hist R 82:753 Je '77. J. B. Crooks
Sheng, Y. Sun Yat-sen university in Moscow and the Chinese revolution: a personal account. 1971
Am Hist R 81:1201-3 D '76. L. Dittmer
Shenkin, B. N. Health care for migrant workers: policies and politics. 1975
Ann Am Acad 430:218-19 Mr '77. H. A. Weeks
Sheridan, J. E. China in disintegration: the republican era in Chinese history, 1912-1949. 1975
Am Hist R 82:415 Ap '77. F. G. Chan
Sherman, G. W. Pessimism of Thomas Hardy: a social study
New Repub 177:40-1 O 1 '77. H. C. Webster
Sherman, J. Soaring
Dance Mag 51:26 Ag '77. L. Draegin
Sherwin, K. To fly like a bird: the story of man-powered aircraft
Sci Am 237:152-3 Jl '77. P. Morrison
Sherwin, M. J. World destroyed: the atomic bomb and the grand alliance. 1975
Am Hist R 81:1075-6 D '76. J. A. Huston
Shideler, J. H. ed. Agriculture in the development of the Far West. 1975
Am Hist R 81:1243-4 D '76. C. C. Spence
Shimmon, R. ed. Reader in library management. 1976
Lib J 102:692 Mr 15 '77. L. Vagianos
Shimoda, K. ed. High-resolution laser spectroscopy. 1976
Science 196:973 My 27 '77. W. M. Fairbank, Jr
Shipman, H. L. Black holes, quasars, and the universe. 1976
Sky & Tel 53:211 Mr '77. J. B. Irwin
Shipton, C. K. Sibley's Harvard graduates, v 17: Biographical sketches of those who attended Harvard college in the classes, 1768-1771. 1975
Am Hist R 81:1220-1 D '76. T. R. Crane
Shirendev, B. and Sanjdorj, M. eds. History of the Mongolian people's republic, v3: The contemporary period; tr. and anno. by W. A. Brown and U. Onon. 1976
Am Hist R 82:162 F '77. L. Moses
Shirer, W. L. Twentieth century journey: a memoir of a life and the times, v 1:1904-30
New Repub 176:25-6 F 12 '77. D. L. Eder
Shklar, J. H. Freedom and independence: a study of the political ideas of Hegel's Phenomenology of mind. 1976
Am Hist R 81:1098-9 D '76. F. Nauen
Shogan, R. Promises to keep
Nat R 30:13 Ja 6 '78. Cato (pseud)
Shorey, H. H. Animal communication by pheromones. 1976
Science 195:569-70 F 11 '77. E. O. Wilson
Shorrock, W. I. French imperialism in the Middle East: the failure of French policy in Syria and Lebanon, 1900-1914. 1976
Am Hist R 82:653-4 Je '77. W. W. Haddad
Ann Am Acad 434:217 N '77. G. L. Fowler
Short, N. and others. Mission to earth: Landsat views the world. 1977
Space World N-5-161:33-4 My '77
Shoup, L. and Minter, W. Imperial brain trust: the Council on foreign relations and United States foreign policy. 1977
Ann Am Acad 434:205 N '77. R. D. Schulzinger
Shover, J. L. First majority—last minority: the transforming of rural life in America. 1976
Am Hist R 82:1082 O '77. E. L. Schapsmeier
Showalter, D. E. Railroads and rifles: soldiers, technology, and the unification of Germany. 1975
Am Hist R 81:1148 D '76. R. W. Lougee
Showalter, E. Literature of their own: British women novelists from Brontë to Lessing
Ms 6:45+ N '77. G. W. Sweeney
Yale R 67:150-7 O '77. H. Moglen
Shy, J. People numerous and armed: reflections on the military struggle for American independence. 1976
Am Hist R 82:436 Ap '77. H. F. Rankin
Sibley, C. Small blessings
America 137:368 N 19 '77. M. Mitarotondo
Sider, R. J. Rich Christians in an age of hunger: a biblical study
Chr Today 22:46+ D 30 '77. G. I. Mavrodes
Sidorov, A. L. Ekonomicheskoe polozhenie Rossii v gody pervoi mirovoi voiny. 1973
Am Hist R 82:153 F '77. M. F. Hamm
Siegel, M. B. Watching the dance go by
Ms 6:38-40 S '77. L. Shapiro
Newsweek 90:101-2+ N 14 '77. J. Kroll
Sieveking, G. de G. and others, eds. Problems in economic and social archaeology. 1976
Science 198:183 O 14 '77. R. J. Carpenter
Šik, O. Das kommunistische Machtsystem. 1976
Am Hist R 82:684-5 Je '77. I. Volgyes
Sik, O. Third way: Marxist-Leninist theory and modern industrial society; tr. by M. Sling. 1976
Society 15:121-3 N '77. S. Rousseas
Silk, L. Economists
Nat R 29:445-6 Ap 15 '77. M. S. Ross
New Repub 176:78-9 Ja 22 '77. M. J. Ulmer
Silk, L. and Vogel, D. Ethics and profits: the crisis of confidence in American business. 1976
Ann Am Acad 432:193-4 Jl '77. A. Q. J. Shaikh
New Repub 176:78 Ja 22 '77. M. J. Ulmer
Progressive 41:53-5 Ap '77. D. D. Martin
Silko, L. M. Ceremony
Harpers 254:80-2 Je '77. H. Carruth
Newsweek 90:73-4 Jl 4 '77. M. Jefferson
Sillitoe, A. Widower's son
New Repub 177:34-5 S 10 '77. E. J. Kenney, Jr
Newsweek 90:72+ Ag 15 '77. R. Sokolov
Sat R 4:38-40 Jl 23 '77. M. Wood
Time 110:70-1 Ag 22 '77. P. Gray
Sills, B. Bubbles: a self-portrait
Opera N 41:5 Mr 5 '77. R. Jacobson
Silver, A. Samurai film. 1977
Film Q 31:58-60 Wint '77. S. Thornton
Silverman, M. Drugging of the Americas: how multinational drug companies say one thing about their products to physicians in the United States, and another thing to physicians in Latin America. 1976
Ann Am Acad 433:195-6 S '77. T. F. Garrity
Silverstone, B. and Hyman, H. K. You and your aging parent. 1975
Aging 272:34 Je '77
Psychol Today 11:108-9+ Je '77. P. Koenig
Simckes, S. Comatose kids
Yale R 66:584-91 Je '77. D. Thorburn
Simic, C. Charon's cosmology
Yale R 67:72, 74-6 O '77. H. Vendler
Simmerman, M. H, and Milburn, J. A. eds. Transport in plants I; phloem transport. 1975
BioScience 27:288 Ap '77. J. E. Hendrix
Simmons, R. C. American colonies: from settlement to independence. 1976
Am Hist R 82:1058-9 O '77. R. E. Brown

Simon, L. Biography of Alice B. Toklas
Esquire 88:33-4+ D '77. A. Kazin
New Repub 177:36-7 Ag 20 '77. D. Sutherland
Simons, H. Simons' list book
Smithsonian 8:97-8 Jl '77. R. L. Williams
Simpson, A. W. B. History of the common law of contract: the rise of the action of assumpsit. 1975
Am Hist R 82:78 F '77. D. W. Sutherland
Simpson, D. Dark companions: the African contribution to the European exploration of East Africa. 1975
Am Hist R 82:156 F '77. M. Ylvisaker
Simpson, G. G. Penguins: past and present, here and there. 1976
Oceans 10:70 S '77. N. Rosa
Simpson, J. American family: a history in photographs. 1976
Pop Phot 81:146 O '77. Y. E. Benedek
Simpson, M. A. and Lloyd, T. H. eds. Middle class housing in Britain. 1977
Am Hist R 82:1250 D '77. R. V. Steffel
Sinclair, A. Jack: a biography of Jack London
New Repub 177:34-6 O 8 '77. R. Whittemore
Sinclair, A. R. E. African buffalo. a study of resource limitation of populations. 1977
Science 197:857-8 Ag 26 '77. J. F. Eisenberg
Sinclair, K. Walter Nash. 1976
Am Hist R 82:1315 D '77. S. C. McCulloch
Singer, I. B. Naftali the storyteller and his horse, Sus and other stories; il. by M. Zemach. 1976
Horn Bk 53:162-3 Ap '77. V. Haviland
Singer, J. Androgyny: toward a new theory of sexuality
Psychol Today 10:96+ Mr '77. J. Wren-Lewis
Singhal, R. P. How to save your life and home from natural disasters. 1977
Weatherwise 30:175 Ag '77
Singleton, F. Twentieth-century Yugoslavia. 1976
Am Hist R 82:393 Ap '77. J. Rothschild
Siskind, A. Places: Aaron Siskind photographs
New Repub 177:33-5 O 29 '77. W. Drenttel
Sisson, R. A. Will in love. 1977
Horn Bk 53:321 Je '77. E. L. Heins
Sivan, E. Communisme et nationalisme en Algérie, 1920-1962. 1976
Am Hist R 82:1307 D '77. A. A. Heggoy
Sive, H. R. Music's Connecticut Yankee: an introduction to the life and music of Charles Ives. 1977
Horn Bk 53:323-4 Je '77. E. L. Heins
Skehan, E. M. Rocky Marciano
Commonweal 104:760-2 N 25 '77. W. Arnold
Skeist, I. ed. Handbook of adhesives
Sci Am 237:37-8 N '77. P. Morrison
Skilling, H. G. Czechoslovakia's interrupted revolution. 1976
Ann Am Acad 431:160 My '77. E. Davidson
Sklar, R. Movie-made America: a cultural history of American movies. 1975
Am Hist R 81:1275-6 D '76. M. R. Greco
Skrynnikov, R. G. Ivan Groznyi. 1975
Am Hist R 81:1170 D '76. A. Kleimola
Sky, A. and Stone, M. Unbuilt America: forgotten architecture in the United States from Thomas Jefferson to the space age; introd by G. R. Collins. 1976
Archit Rec 161:43+ F '77. M. Filler
Art N 76:112 Ap '77. M. Hoelterhoff
N Y Times Mag p44-5+ Ja 30 '77. A. L. Huxtable
Nation 224:409-10 Ap 2 '77. J. H. Kay
Smithsonian 7:120-1 Mr '77. W. Morgan
Slater, P. Footholds: understanding the shifting sexual and family tensions in our culture; ed. by W. S. Palmer
Nation 224:154-6 F 5 '77. E. Z. Friedenberg
Slaven, A. Development of the west of Scotland: 1750-1960. 1975
Am Hist R 82:363-4 Ap '77. A. W. Coats
Slavin, N. When two or more are gathered together. 1976
Art in Am 65:51+ Mr '77. A. Grundberg
Slavitt, D. Vital signs: new and selected poems
Poetry 129:294-5 F '77. R. Holland
Slow virus infections of the central nervous system; proceedings of workshop, Würzburg, Germany, 1975; ed. by V. ter Meulen and M. Katz. 1977
Science 198:48 O 7 '77. W. J. Hadlow
Smail, T.A. Reflected glory. 1976
Chr Today 21:44-5 Ap 1 '77. C. B. Murphey
Smart, W. M. Textbook on spherical astronomy. 1977
Sky & Tel 54:323-4 O '77. J. Ashbrook
Smedley, A. Portraits of Chinese women in revolution; ed. by J. MacKinnon and S. Mackinnon
Nation 225:24-6 Jl 2 '77. J. Milton
Smelser, M. Life that Ruth built: a biography. 1975
Am Hist R 81:1276-7 D '76. E. C. Murdock
Smelser, R. M. Sudeten problem, 1933-1938: Volkstumspolitik and the formulation of Nazi foreign policy. 1975
Am Hist R 81:1152 D '76. R. V. Luza
Smith, A. Inquiry into the nature and causes of the wealth of nations; ed. by E. Cannan. 1977
Intellect 106:89 Ag '77. R. M. Larsen
Smith, B. F. Reaching judgment at Nuremberg. 1977
Am Hist R 82:1281-2 D '77. B. S. Viault
Smith, C. Carlos: portrait of a terrorist
Commentary 64:71-2+ N '77. E. M. Breindel
Psychol Today 11:88+ Ag '77. T. Morgan
Smith, C. F. Vladiovostok under red and white rule: revolution and counterrevolution in the Russian Far East, 1920-1922. 1976
Am Hist R 81:1179-80 D '76. N. H. Gaworek
Smith, D. Cumberland station
Commonweal 105:23-5 Ja 6 '78. J. Druska
Yale R 66:407-24 Mr '77. H. Vendler
Smith, D. M. Mussolini's Roman Empire. 1976
Am Hist R 82:388 Ap '77. B. F. Brown
Ann Am Acad 429:167-8 Ja '77. C. F. Delzell
Smith, E. A. Whig principles and party politics: Earl Fitzwilliam and the Whig party, 1748-1833. 1975
Am Hist R 82:100 F '77. R. A. Kelch
Smith, F. G. Pulsars. 1977
Phys Today 30:55-6 D '77. S. P. Maran
Smith, G. Windsinger. 1976
Am West 14:58 N '77. S. Mikesell
Smith, G. E. K. Pictorial history of architecture in America. 2v
Antiques 112:978+ N '77. J. Farber
Smith, J. ed. Psychiatry and the humanities, v 1
Am Scholar 47:140-4 Wint '77. J. Brent
Smith, J. H. Death of classical paganism
America 137:136 S 10 '77. R. E. Carter
New Yorker 53:208-10+ N 14 '77. G. Steiner
Smith, M. C. Nightwing
Newsweek 90:100+ D 5 '77. W. Clemons
Smith, M. J. jr. World war II at sea: a bibliography of sources in English. 3v 1976
Am Hist R 82:1218-19 D '77. S. Sandler
Smith, M. R. Harpers Ferry Armory and the new technology: the challenge of change. 1977
Science 196:1432 Je 24 '77. E. S. Ferguson
Smith, P. Jefferson: a revealing biography
Yale R 66:432-43 Mr '77. P. M. Spacks
Smith, P. C. F. Fired by Manley Zeal
Smithsonian 8:155-7 O '77. J. F. Warner
Smith, R. E. F. Peasant farming in Muscovy. 1977
Am Hist R 82:1292-3 D '77. J. Blum
Smyth, H. M. Secrets of the fascist era: how Uncle Sam obtained some of the top-level documents of Mussolini's period. 1975
Am Hist R 82:211 F '77. A. Cassels
Snell, J. L. and Schmitt, H. A. Democratic movement in Germany, 1789-1914. 1976
Am Hist R 82:995-6 O '77. T. S. Hamerow
Snepp, F. Decent interval
Newsweek 90:71 N 28 '77. T. Mathews
Snetsinger, R. Diary of a mad planner
Nation 224:408-9 Ap 2 '77. J. H. Kay
Snyder, L. L. Varieties of nationalism: a comparative study. 1976
Am Hist R 81:1099 D '76. A. D. Low
Snyder, N. and others. Photography catalog
Pop Phot 80:22+ F '77. J. Deschin
Sobolev, G. L. Revoliutsionnoe soznanie rabochikh i soldat Petrograda v 1917: period dvoevlastiia. 1973
Am Hist R 81:1176-7 D '76. A. Rabinowitch
Soboul, A. Problèmes paysans de la révolution (1789-1848) études d'histoire révolutionnaire. 1976
Am Hist R 82:1235-6 D '77. J. B. Cameron, jr
Social anthropology and medicine; papers from conference, Canterbury, England, 1972. 1976
Science 197:1174-5 S 16 '77. D. Landy
Société de Chimie Physique. Lasers in physical chemistry and biophysics; proceedings of meeting, Thiais, France, 1975; ed. by J. Joussot-Dubien. 1975
Science 195:481 F 4 '77. A. Lewis
Soil conditioners: proceedings of symposium, Las Vegas, 1973. 1975
BioScience 27:213 Mr '77. L. H. Stolzy
Sokolov, S. School for fools; tr. by C. Proffer
Commentary 64:68-9 S '77. J. Rubenstein
Solberg, C. Oil power: the rise and imminent fall of an American empire
Chr Cent 94:384 Ap 20 '77. R. L. Means
Solé, J. L'amour en occident à l'époque moderne. 1976
Am Hist R 82:349 Ap '77. V. L. Bullough
Solomon, B. B. Black empowerment: social work in oppressed communities. 1976
Ann Am Acad 433:196-7 S '77. A. Dobelstein
Solov'eva, A. M. Zheleznodorozhnyi transport Rossii vo vtoroi polovine XIX v. 1975
Am Hist R 82:149 F '77. R. M. Haywood
Solzhenitsyn, A. Prussian nights: a poem; tr. by R. Conquest
America 137:245-6 O 15 '77. J. F. Cotter
Time 110:63-4 Jl 25 '77. P. Blake
Sonneman, E. Real time, 1968-1974. 1976
Art in Am 65:32-3 N '77. C. Ratcliff
Sonnino, S. Carteggio 1914-1922, v 1: 1914-1916; v2: 1916-1922; ed. by P. Pastorelli. 1974, 1975
Am Hist R 82:387 Ap '77. R. Albrecht-Carrié
Sontag, F. Sun Myung Moon and the Unification Church
Chr Cent 94:922 O 12 '77. J. H. Gill

Sontag, S. On photography. 1977
Art in Am 65:31-2 N '77. S. Schwartz
Newsweek 90:98+ D 5 '77. D. Davis
Sat R 5:46-8 D 10 '77. E. Grossman
Time 110:66-7 D 26 '77. R. Hughes
Sorauf, F. J. Wall of separation: the constitutional politics of church and state. 1976
Am Hist R 81:1281-2 D '76. L. P. Beth
Chr Cent 94:260 Mr 16 '77. J. M. Swomley, Jr
Chr Today 21:26 Jl 8 '77. D. Kelley
Sosna, M. In search of the silent South: southern liberals and the race issue
Nation 225:598 D 3 '77. J. Taylor
Sources, effects & sinks of hydrocarbons in the aquatic environment; proceedings of symposium, Washington, D.C. 1976. 1976
BioScience 27:692 O '77. R. W. Traxler
South American handbook
New Yorker 53:80-2 Jl 25 '77. A. Reid
Southern, T. and Rivers, L. Donkey and the darling. 1977
Art N 76:108 Ap '77. S. Boorsch
Soyer, R. Diary of an artist
Art N 76:128 D '77. J. Shaw-Eagle
Spanier, D. Total poker
Bus W p 11-12 Je 6 '77. J. Hoerr
Spark, M. Takeover
Commonweal 104:25 Ja 7 '77. I. Malin
Speaight, R. Shakespeare: the man and his achievement
New Repub 176:48-9 My 21 '77. S. Schoenbaum
Spence, C. C. Territorial politics and government in Montana, 1864-89. 1976
Am Hist R 82:191 F '77. M. G. Burlingame
Spence, E. Devil hole. 1977
Horn Bk 53:444 Ag '77. E. L. Heins
Spence, M. L. and Jackson, D. eds. Expeditions of John Charles Fremont, v2: The bear flag revolt and the court-martial; v2 supp: Proceedings of the court-martial. 1973
Am Hist R 82:179 F '77. J. Caughey
Spiegel, A. Fiction and the camera eye: visual consciousness in film and the modern novel. 1976
Film Q 30:44-6 Summ '77. B. Kawin
Spier, P. Noah's ark
Sci Am 237:36 D '77. P. Morrison and P. Morrison
Spoto, D. Art of Alfred Hitchcock: fifty years of his motion pictures. 1976
Film Q 30:57-62 Spr '77. P. Thomas
Spradley, J. P. and Mann, B. J. Cocktail waitress: woman's work in a man's world
Ms 5:106+ My '77. F. Whyatt
Spriano, P. Occupation of the factories: Italy 1920; tr. by G. A. Williams
New Repub 177:30-2 D 17 '77. C. Maier
Spurr, S. H. American forest policy in development. 1976
Am For 83:12-13+ Ag '77. W. Koehler
Staar, R. F. ed. Yearbook on international Communist affairs, 1976. 1976
Am Hist R 82:338 Ap '77. R. T. Fisher, Jr
Stäblein, B. Schriftbild der einstimmingen Musik. 1975
Mus Q 63:283-6 Ap '77. R. Steiner
Stacey, F. British government, 1966-1975: the years of reform. 1975
Ann Am Acad 432:165-6 Jl '77. S. P. Koff
Stachura, P. D. Nazi youth in the Weimar Republic; introd. by P. H. Merkl. 1976
Am Hist R 82:1007-8 O '77. L. D. Walker
Stainback, B. Very different love story: Burt and Linda Pugach's account of their triumph over tragedy
Ms 5:34+ Ap '77. B. G. Harrison
Stallibrass, A. Self-respecting child
Ms 6:42+ O '77. J. Holt
Stanford, J. L. Tornado: accounts of tornadoes in Iowa. 1977
Weatherwise 30:134-5 Je '77
Stanley, D. T. Prisoners among us: the problem of parole. 1976
Ann Am Acad 432:184-5 Jl '77. N. Johnston
Stannard, D. E. Puritan way of death: a study in religion, culture, and social change
New Repub 177:32-4 D 10 '77. H. McDonald
Stanton, W. Great United States exploring expedition of 1838-1842. 1975
Am Hist R 81:1242 D '76. D. F. Long
Stark, J. P. Solid state diffusion. 1976
Phys Today 30:53-4 Ag '77. S. J. Rothman
Starrels, J. M. and Mallinckrodt, A. M. Politics in the German Democratic Republic. 1975
Ann Am Acad 429:168 Ja '77. P. H. Merkl
Stearns, P. N. Old age in European society: the case of France. 1976
Am Hist R 82:1266-7 D '77. P. O'Brien
Stebbins, T. E. Jr. American master drawings and watercolors
Am Artist 41:22+ Ag '77. A. Werner
Antiques 112:758+ O '77. C. E. Buckley
Steele, C. Major libraries of the world: a selective guide. 1977
Lib J 102:1584 Ag '77. A. Hamlin
Steele, M. Q. True men. 1976
Horn Bk 53:55 F '77. P. Heins
Steele, W. O. Man with the silver eyes
Chr Today 21:26 Ap 15 '77. B. M. Greene
Steen, H. K. U.S. forest service: a history. 1976
Am For 83:15-16 F '77. S. H. Spurr
Am Hist R 82:750 Je '77. D. Strong
Am West 14:63 My '77. W. T. Jackson
Steere, W. C. Biological abstracts/BIOSIS: the first fifty years, the evolution of a major science information service. 1976
BioScience 27:750 N '77. O. E. Reynolds
Stefansson, T. Golden future. 1977
Horn Bk 53:317 Je '77. V. Haviland
Steffens, H. J. Development of Newtonian optics in England. 1977
Am Hist R 82:1244 D '77. R. E. Schofield
Steffens, L. Shame of the cities
New Repub 177:37-9 Jl 9 '77. R. Stinson
Steig, W. Amazing bone. 1976
Horn Bk 53:153 Ap '77. V. Haviland
Stein, B. Work and welfare in Britain and USA. 1976
M Labor R 100:92-3 F '77. R. S. Smith
Stein, B. and Stein, H. On the brink
Fortune 96:71-2 Ag '77. J. Davenport
Nat R 29:1002+ S 2 '77. J. R. Coyne, Jr
Stein, R. G. Architecture and energy. 1977
Science 198:391-2 O 28 '77. D. Watson
Stein, Z. Famine and human development: the Dutch hunger winter of 1944/45
Sci Am 237:148+ Jl '77. P. Morrison
Steinbeck, J. Acts of King Arthur and his noble knights; ed. by C. Horton
New Repub 176:34-5 F 5 '77. M. C. Williams
Steinbruner, J. D. Cybernetic theory of decision: new dimensions of political analysis. 1974
Ann Am Acad 429:149-52 Ja '77. R. J. Art
Steiner, G. Y. and Milius, P. H. Children's cause. 1976
M Labor R 100:75 D '77. K. C. Alderman
Steiner, J. M. Power politics and social change in National Socialist Germany: a process of escalation into mass destruction. 1976
Ann Am Acad 429:168-9 Ja '77. R. M. Hunt
Steiner, S. Vanishing white man. 1976
Am West 14:59 Mr '77. D. Lavender
Steinhoff, J. Wohin treibt die NATO? Probleme der Verteidigung Westeuropas. 1976
Ann Am Acad 432:168 Jl '77. J. D. Elliott
Steitz, W. Die Entstehung der Köln-Mindener Eisenbahngesellschaft: ein Beitrag zur Frühgeschichte der deutschen Eisenbahnen und des preussischen Aktienwesens. 1974
Am Hist R 81:1147 D '76. D. E. Showalter
Stelmach, G. E. ed. Motor control. 1976
Science 195:482 F 4 '77. E. V. Evarts
Steneck, N. H. Science and creation in the Middle ages: Henry of Langenstein (d.1397) on Genesis. 1976
Am Hist R 82:78-9 F '77. B. Hansen
Stepan, N. Beginnings of Brazilian science: Oswaldo Cruz, medical research and policy, 1890-1920. 1976
Am Hist R 82:485 Ap '77. C. O'Neil
Stephan, J. J. Kuril Islands: Russo-Japanese frontier in the Pacific. 1975
Am Hist R 82:404-5 Ap '77. M. B. Jansen
Stephens, J. Loners, losers, and lovers: elderly tenants in a slum hotel. 1976
Ann Am Acad 430:219-20 Mr '77 P. T. McFarlane
Stephens, W. B. Sources for English local history. 1973
Am Hist R 82:956-7 O '77. F. A. Youngs, jr
Stephenson, J. Women in Nazi society. 1976
Am Hist R 81:1154-5 D '76. R. Bridenthal
Stern, F. Gold and iron: Bismarck, Bleichröder, and the building of the German empire. 1977
Am Hist R 82:1275 D '77. K. J. Bade
Am Scholar 47:126+ Wint '77. J. P. Stern
Commentary 63:72+ My '77. E. N. Luttwak
New Repub 176:28-9 F 26 '77. W. Laqueur
Stern, H. P. Birds, beasts, blossoms, and bugs: the nature of Japan
Horticulture 55:14-15 Ap '77. A. Eliot
Stern, J. F. and Hendry, E. R. Swimming pools & the law. 1977
Am City & County 92:118 S '77
Stern, L. Wrong horse
Time 111:72 Ja 9 '78. S. Talbott
Stern, R. Natural shocks
Newsweek 91:61-2 Ja 2 '78. P. S. Prescott
Stevens, H. Souvenirs and prophecies: the young Wallace Stevens
Am Scholar 46:408-11 Summ '77. J. Atlas
America 137:59-60 Jl 30 '77. M. True
Nation 224:472 Ap 16 '77. J. D. McClatchy
New Repub 176:57-8 My 21 '77. J. H. Miller
Yale R 66:581-4 Je '77. H. Bloom
Stevens, R. W. Vain hopes, grim realities: the economic consequences of the Vietnam war. 1976
Ann Am Acad 430:184-5 Mr '77. W. E. Spellman
Environment 19:39-41 Ap '77. J. McCaull
Stevenson, A. Papers of Adlai Stevenson, v5: Visit to Asia, the Middle East, and Europe, March-August 1953; ed. by W. Johnson. 1975
Am Hist R 82:216-17 F '77. H. G. Nicholas
Stevenson, E. Park maker: a life of Frederick Law Olmsted. 1977
Am For 83:32+ Ag '77. M. Bush
Sat R 4:26-7+ My 14 '77. J. H. Kay

Stevenson, J. and Quinault, R. eds. Popular protest and public order: six studies in British history, 1790-1920. 1975
Am Hist R 82:101 F '77. E. J. Evans
Stewart, A. C. Silas and Con. 1977
Horn Bk 53:666 D '77. M. M. Burns
Stierlin, H. Adolf Hitler: a family perspective. 1976
Am Hist R 82:1279-80 D '77. R. G. L. Waite
Stillman, W. J. Articles and despatches from Crete, ed. with an introd. by G. G. Arnakis. 1976
Am Hist R 82:391 Ap '77. G. J. Marcopoulos
Stillwell, R. ed. Princeton encyclopedia of classical sites
Am Hist R 82:611 Je '77. J. R. Fears
Chr Cent 94:1147-8 D 7 '77. E. Krentz
Stivers, R. Hair of the dog: Irish drinking and American stereotype. 1976
Am Hist R 82:1339-40 D '77. E. Dwyer
Society 14:88-9 Jl '77. A. M. Greeley
Stockfisch, J. A. Plowshares into swords; managing the American defense establishment. 1973
Am Hist R 81:1279-80 D '76. E. C. Hanson
Stockholm international peace research institute. Armaments and disarmament in the nuclear age: a handbook. 1976
Bull Atom Sci 33:63-4 O '77. A. Steiner
Stoianovich, T. French historical method: the Annales paradigm. 1976
Am Hist R 82:331 Ap '77. A. Kuzminski
Ann Am Acad 432:169 Jl '77. R. Wohl
Stoicescu, N. Vlad Tepes
Am Hist R 82:1286-7 D '77. R. R. Florescu
Stokes, T. Boning the dreamer
Poetry 129:229-31 Ja '77. R. Howard
Stolz, U. Ferris wheel. 1977
Horn Bk 53:317-18 Je '77. E. L. Heins
Stone, C. N. Economic growth and neighborhood discontent. 1976
Ann Am Acad 429:186-7 Ja '77. J. E. Hughes
Stone, D. Polish politics and national reform, 1775-1788. 1976
Am Hist R 82:1288-9 D '77. W. W. Soroka
Stone, J. Mystery of B. Traven
New Repub 176:29-31 Ap 2 '77. J. Walt
Time 109:93+ Ap 11 '77. J. Skow
Stone, M. When God was a woman. 1976
Horn Bk 53:342-3 Je '77. M. S. Cosgrave
Stone, R. Cheap
Poetry 129:296-301 F '77. S. M. Gilbert
Stone, R. Reynolds Stone engravings; with introd. by the artist and appreciation by K. Clark
Pub W 213:52 Ja 2 '78. C. B. Grannis
Stonehouse, B. and Gilmore, D. eds. Biology of marsupials. 1977
Science 198:1147 D 16 '77. R. M. F. S. Sadleir
Stoner, C. and Parke, J. A. All God's children: the cult experience—salvation or slavery
America 137:38 Jl 16 '77. R. A. Walsh
Storey, D. Saville
Newsweek 89:94+ Je 13 '77. P. S. Prescott
Sat R 4:38-40 Jl 23 '77. M. Wood
Storey, M. Heartland, a natural history of Onondaga County
Conservationist 32:43 N '77. P. Kelsey
Storoni Mazzolani, L. Empire without end; tr. by J. McConnell and M. Pei. 1976
Am Hist R 82:612 Je '77. H. W. Benario
Stover, J. F. History of the Illinois central railroad. 1975
Am Hist R 82:1337-8 D '77. J. F. Doster
Strait, P. Cologne in the twelfth century. 1974
Am Hist R 81:1091-2 D '76. L. G. Duggan
Stranger, J. Fox at drummers' darkness; il. by W. Geldart. 1977
Horn Bk 53:534-5 O '77. E. L. Heins
Strangwayes-Booth, J. Cricket in the thorn tree: Helen Suzman and the Progressive party
Commonweal 104:574-5 S 2 '77. S. Cohen
Strasburger, E. Strasburger's textbook of botany; ed by D. von Denffer; tr by P. Bell and D. Coomber. 1976
BioScience 27:286 Ap '77. D. D. Ritchie
Strausfeld, N. J. Atlas of an insect brain. 1976
BioScience 27:562 Ag '77. J. Grossfield
Strauss, A. L. Images of the American city. 1976
Ann Am Acad 430:220 Mr '77. J. van Til
Strauss, R. and Zweig, S. Confidential matter: the letters of Richard Strauss and Stefan Zweig, 1931-1935; tr. by M. Knight; foreword by E. E. Lowinski
New Repub 177:36-8 N 12 '77. G. L. Mosse
Strick, A. Injustice for all
Nation 225:153-5 Ag 20 '77. D. Rudovsky
New Repub 176:37-8 Mr 26 '77. S. B. Kanner
Stringfellow, W. Conscience and obedience: the politics of Romans 13 and Revelation 13 in the light of the Second coming
Chr Cent 94:987-8 O 26 '77. F. Sherman
Stringfellow, W. and Towne, A. Death and life of Bishop Pike. 1976
Chr Today 21:38-9 My 20 '77. J. W. Montgomery
Commonweal 104:53-4 Ja 21 '77. C. Davis
Stroman, D. F. Medical establishment and social responsibility. 1976
Ann Am Acad 430:220-1 Mr '77. J. W. Weiss

Structure and evolution of close binary systems; proceedings of symposium, Cambridge, England, 1975; ed. by P. Eggleston and others. 1976
Science 197:449-50 Jl 29 '77. R. P. Kraft
Structure sociale et developpement culturel des villes sud-Est européenes et adriatiques aux XVIIIe siècles. 1975
Am Hist R 82:390-1 Ap '77. S. M. Stuard
Strumpel, B. ed. Economic means for human needs: social indicators of well-being and discontent. 1976
M Labor R 100:91-2 F '77. K. C. Land
Stuard, S. M. ed. Women in medieval society. 1976
Am Hist R 81:1084 D '76. C. J. Blaisdell
Stuart-Harris, C. H. and Schild, G. C. Influenza: the viruses and the disease. 1976
Science 197:43 Jl 1 '77. R. W. Schlesinger
Studdert-Kennedy, G. Evidence and explanation in social science. 1975
Ann Am Acad 431:180-1 My '77. W. J. Williams
Stueart, R. D. and Eastlick, J. T. Library management. 1977
Lib J 102:995 My 1 '77. D: Sinclair
Sturges, P. P. Endless chain of nature: experiment at Hubbard Brook. 1976
Am For 83:35-6 Ap '77. M. Bush
Sturmberger, H. Adam Graf Herberstorff: Herrschaft und Freiheit im konfessionellen Zeitalter. 1976
Am Hist R 82:1010-11 O '77. R. Bireley
Sturtevant, D. R. Popular uprisings in the Philippines, 1840-1940. 1976
Am Hist R 82:164 F '77. G. K. Goodman
Ann Am Acad 432:162 Jl '77. B. Fegan
Subcellular mechanisms in reproductive neuroendocrinology; papers from symposium, Jamaica Plain, Mass, 1975, ed. by J. Naftolin and others. 1976
Science 196:1194 Je 10 '77. D. Pearson
Sugar, P. F. Southeastern Europe under Ottoman rule, 1354-1804: A history of East Central Europe, v4. 1977
Ann Am Acad 434:223-4 N '77. J. S. Roucek
Suh, D. S. and Lee, C. J. eds. Political leadership in Korea. 1976
Am Hist R 82:419-20 Ap '77. B. H. Hazard
Summerfield, H. That myriad-minded man: a biography of George William Russell, A.E. 1867-1935. 1976
Am Hist R 82:114-15 F '77. H. Mulvey
Suntharalingam, R. Politics and nationalist awakening in south India, 1852-1891. 1974
Am Hist R 81:1207 D '76. K. W. Jones
Supplement to the Oxford English dictionary; v2: H-N; ed. by R. W. Burchfield. 1976
Yale R 67:94-9 O '77. F. C. Robinson
Supree, B. and Ross, A. Bear's heart: scenes from the life of a Cheyenne artist of one hundred years ago with pictures by himself. 1977
Horn Bk 53:545 O '77. E. L. Heins
Surface membrane receptors; proceedings of symposium; ed by R. A. Bradshaw and others. 1976
BioScience 27:422 Je '77. R. A. Capaldi
Suslov, I. Here's to your health, Comrade Shifrin! tr. by M. Bronstein
Commentary 64:67-8 S '77. J. Rubenstein
Susman, G. I. Autonomy at work: a sociotechnical analysis of participative management. 1976
Society 14:86-7 S '77. W. H. Friedland
Sutcliff, R. Blood feud. 1977
Horn Bk 53:541 O '77. V. Haviland
Sutherland, J. A. Victorian novelists and publishers
Am Scholar 47:118+ Wint '77. E. Moers
Sutherland, N. Children in English-Canadian society: framing the twentieth-century consensus. 1976
Am Hist R 82:1369 D '77. R. M. Mennel
Sutherland, Z. and Arbuthnot, M. H. Children and books. 1977
SLJ 24:33 N '77. R. Gordon
Sutton, D. How to throw a curveball
Sci Am 237:39-40 D '77. P. Morrison and P. Morrison
Suzuki, D. T. and Griffiths, A. J. F. Introduction to genetic analysis. 1976
BioScience 27:686 O '77. B. H. Judd
Svestka, Z. Solar flares. 1976
Phys Today 30:72 O '77. E. N. Parker
Sky & Tel 53:132-3 F '77. R. E. Loughhead
Swanberg, W. A. Norman Thomas: the last idealist. 1976
Am Hist R 82:1097 O '77. B. M. Stave
Chr Cent 94:180-1 F 23 '77. M. Frakes
Commentary 63:78-80 F '77. R. Starr
Nation 224:86-7 Ja 22 '77. R. J. Walton
Sweets, J. F. Politics of resistance in France, 1940-1944: a history of the Mouvements unis de la résistance. 1976
Am Hist R 82:985-6 O '77. A. L. Funk
Swierenga, R. P. Acres for cents: delinquent tax auctions in frontier Iowa. 1976
Am Hist R 82:440-1 Ap '77. P. W. Gates
Synan, V. Aspects of Pentecostal-Charismatic origins. 1975
Chr Today 21:44-5 F 18 '77. J. S. Tinney

Sywottek, J. Mobilmachung für den totalen Krieg: die propagandistische Vorbereitung der deutschen Bevölkerung auf den zweiten Weltkrieg. 1976
Am Hist R 82:131-2 F '77. J. W. Baird
Szasz, T. Schizophrenia: the sacred symbol of psychiatry
Nation 224:149-51 F 5 '77. R. Jacoby
Szawloski, R. System of the International Organizations of the Communist countries. 1976
Ann Am Acad 433:167-8 S '77. J. F. Copper

Talese, G. Kingdom and the power
New Repub 176:35-6 Mr 12 '77. M. da Vinci
Tambiah, S. J. World conqueror and world renouncer: a study of Buddhism and polity in Thailand against a historical background. 1976
Am Hist R 82:425-6 Ap '77. C. M. Wilson
Tannenbaum, E. R. 1900: the generation before the Great war. 1976
Am Hist R 82:1238 D '77. E. Weber
Tapley, L. Ski touring in New England and New York
Conservationist 32:42-3 N '77. A. Coggeshall
Tapper, T. Political education and stability: elite responses to political conflict. 1976
Ann Am Acad 430:185-6 Mr '77. P. L. Rosen
Tar, Z. Frankfurt school: the critical theories of Max Horkheimer and Theodor W. Adorno
New Repub 177:30-2 D 17 '77. C. Maier
Tate, J. Viper jazz
Poetry 130:221-3 Jl '77. W. Logan
Yale R 66:407-24 Mr '77. H. Vendler
Tauber, P. Last best hope
America 137:272 O 22 '77. N. Yanes-Hoffman
Newsweek 90:75 S 5 '77. R. Sokolov
Tavard, G. H. Way of love
America 136:380-1 Ap 23 '77. J. Gaffney
Taylor, A. H. Travail and triumph: black life and culture in the South since the Civil war. 1977
Am Hist R 82:1362-3 D '77. L. W. Levine
Ann Am Acad 433:184 S '77. S. F. Lawson
Taylor, H. Underwater with Nikonos & Nikon systems. 1977
Oceans 10:71 Jl '77. M. P. Dumont
Taylor, J. C. America as art
Commonweal 104:502-4 Ag 5 '77. D. O'Brien
Taylor, J. G. Louisiana reconstructed, 1863-1877. 1975
Am Hist R 81:1255 D '76. E. A. Davis
Taylor, L. and Warren, D. B. Texas furniture, the cabinetmakers and their work, 1840-1880; foreword by I. Hogg
Antiques 111:571 Mr '77. J. J. Poesch
Taylor, L. J. comp. Librarian's handbook. 1976
Lib J 102:1584 Ag '77. S. Goldstein
Taylor, M. J. ed. Foundations for Christian education in an era of change. 1976
Chr Today 21:33 Ag 26 '77. K. O. Gangel
Taylor, P. In the Miro District and other stories
Commonweal 104:540-1 Ag 19 '77. R. Phillips
New Repub 176:33-4 My 7 '77. S. Goodwin
Taylor, S. W. Kingdom or nothing: the life of John Taylor, militant Mormon. 1976
Am West 14:62 Ja '77. W. P. McKinnon
Taylor, T. Odyssey of Ben O'Neal; il by R. Cuffari. 1977
Horn Bk 53:318 Je '77. A. A. Flowers
Teal, M. Bird of passage; il. by T. Lewin. 1977
Horn Bk 53:445 Ag '77. B. Robinson
Tedrow, J. C. F. Soils of the polar landscapes. 1977
Science 196:779-80 My 13 '77. P. Colinvaux
Temin, P. Did monetary forces cause the Great Depression? 1976
M Labor R 100:69-70 Ja '77 G. J. Viksnins
Terkel, S. Talking to myself: a memoir of my times
Nation 224:696 Je 4 '77. R. J. Walton
Newsweek 89:102 Ap 18 '77. M. Jefferson
Progressive 41:39-40 Je '77. G. Burnside
Psychol Today 10:109 Ap '77. T. Kidder
Sat R 4:18-20 Ap 30 '77. R. Lekachman
Time 109:85 Ap 18 '77. P. Gray
Terzioski, R. Denatsionalizatorskata dejnost na burgarskite kulturno-porosvetni institutsii vo Makedonija (Skopska i Bitolska okupatsiona oblast), 1941-1944. 1974
Am Hist R 82:1016-17 O '77. P. Shashko
Theodorescu, R. Bizant, Balcani, occident la începuturile culturii medievale Românesti (secolele X-XIV). 1974
Am Hist R 81:1162-3 D '76. K. Hitchins
Theroux, P. Consul's file
Harpers 255:90+ S '77. M. Malone
Nat R 30:44+ Ja 6 '78. R. Cumare
New Repub 177:33-4 S 10 '77. N. Delbanco
Newsweek 90:72 Ag 15 '77. R. Towers
Sat R 4:30-2 S 3 '77. J. Yardley
Time 110:66-7 S 5 '77. R. Z. Sheppard
Thielicke, H. Evangelical faith
Chr Today 21:26-8 Je 3 '77. R. Johnston
Thimm, A. L. Business ideologies in the reform-progressive era, 1880-1914. 1976
Am Hist R 82:458-9 Ap '77. W. Graebner
Thiry, J. Les années de jeunesse de Napoléon Bonaparte, 1769-1796. 1975
Am Hist R 82:117 F '77. J. M. P. McErlean
Tholfsen, T. R. Working class radicalism in mid-Victorian England. 1977
Am Hist R 82:1251-2 D '77. F. M. Leventhal
Thomas, D. and Davenport, J. Death of the King's canary
New Repub 177:42-3 S 17 '77. L. J. Davis
Thomas, D. and Ronnefeldt, K. eds. People of the first man: life among the Plains Indians in their final days of glory. 1976
Am West 14:57 My '77. W. G. Bell
Natur Hist 86:94-9 F '77. A. M. Josephy, Jr
Thomas, D. L. Lords of the land
Bus W p 10+ F 28 '77. J. Zukosky
Thomas, G. S. Perennial garden plants. 1976
Sunset 158:152 F '77
Thomas, J. N. Institute of Pacific relations: Asian scholars and American politics. 1974
Am Hist R 82:212 F '77. B. R. Babu
Thomas, L. H. Renaissance of Canadian history: a biography of A. L. Burt. 1975
Am Hist R 82:218-19 F '77. L. S. Fallis
Thomas, P. D. G. British politics and the stamp act crisis: the first phase of the American revolution, 1763-1767. 1975
Ann Am Acad 430:211 Mr '77. W. T. Generous, Jr
Thomas, R. S. Laboratories of the spirit
Poetry 130:230-2 Jl '77. J. Silkin
Thomas, W. S. Fort Davis and the Texas frontier: paintings by Captain Arthur T. Lee, Eighth U.S. Infantry. 1976
Am West 14:60 Ja '77. W. G. Bell
Thompson, B. Black walnut for profit: a guide to risks and rewards
Am For 83:42 F '77. R. Pardo
Thompson, D. F. John Stuart Mill and representative government. 1976
Am Hist R 82:637 Je '77. L. B. Zimmer
Thompson, E. P. William Morris, romantic to revolutionary
Nation 225:53-5 Jl 9 '77. M. Peckham
New Repub 176:29-31 Je 4 '77. R. Bienvenu
Sat R 4:29-30 Je 25 '77. W. Arnold
Time 109:67-8 Je 27 '77. R. Hughes
Thompson, E. V. Chase the wind
Sat R 4:38-40 Jl 23 '77. M. Wood
Thompson, G. Army and the Navajo: the Bosque Redondo reservation experiment, 1863-1868. 1976
Am Hist R 82:448 Ap '77. M. E. Kroeker
Thompson, G. Lupe
Newsweek 90:73-4 Jl 25 '77. R. Sokolov
Thompson, G. Planning & design of library buildings. 2d rev ed. 1977
Lib J 102:2413 D 1 '77. J. Orne
Thompson, G. H. Arkansas and reconstruction: the influence of geography, economics, and personality. 1976
Am Hist R 82:446 Ap '77. J. G. Taylor
Ann Am Acad 432:176-7 Jl '77. G. E. Bayliss
Thompson, I. A. A. War and government in Habsburg Spain, 1560-1620. 1976
Am Hist R 82:988 O '77. P. Stewart
Thompson, J. A. Deuteronomy. 1974
Chr Today 21:25-6 Ag 12 '77. R. Youngblood
Thompson, L. and Winnick, R. H. Robert Frost: the later years, 1938-1963
Chr Cent 94:338-9 Ap 6 '77. A. P. Klausler
Commentary 63:86-90 Mr '77. E. Hirsch
Commonweal 104:215-18 Ap 1 '77. S. Maloff
Nat R 29:836-7 Jl 22 '77. H. Kenny
New Repub 176:37-40 Mr 5 '77 C. Bedient
New Yorker 53:137-9 Ap 11 '77. N. Bliven
Thompson, P. Edwardians: the remaking of British society. 1975
Am Hist R 81:1113 D '76. R. G. Hebert
Thompson, S. O. American book design and William Morris
Pub W 212:68 N 7 '77. P. D. Doebler
Thomson, B. P. Spain: forgotten ally of the American revolution. 1976
Ann Am Acad 430:212 Mr '77. A. E. Van Dusen
Thomson, D. America in the dark: Hollywood and the gift of unreality
New Repub 177:45-7 O 15 '77. S. Lawson
Thornhill, W. ed. Modernization of British government. 1975
Am Hist R 81:1119 D '76. V. Bogdanor
Thrupp, S. L. Society and history: essays; ed. by R. Grew and N. H. Steneck. 1977
Am Hist R 82:1226 D '77. J. A. Raftis
Tice, G. Artie Van Blarcum, an extended portrait
Mod Phot 41:8+ Jl '77. J. Scully
Tichy, W. Poisons: antidotes & anecdotes
Sci Am 237:30+ D '77. P. Morrison and P. Morrison
Tiffou, E. Essai sur la pensée morale de Salluste à la lumière de ses prologues. 1975
Am Hist R 82:70 F '77. H. W. Benario
Tignor, R. L. Colonial transformation of Kenya: Kamba, Kikuyu, and Maasai from 1900 to 1939. 1976
Ann Am Acad 430:199-200 Mr '77. K. D. D. Henderson
Tihany, L. C. History of Middle Europe from the earliest times to the age of the World Wars. 1976
Am Hist R 82:1013-14 O '77. L. P. Meriage
Tillich, P. Socialist decision; tr. by F. Sherman
Chr Cent 94:923 O 12 '77. M. H. MacDonald

Tillin, A. M. and Quinly, W. J. eds. Standards for cataloging nonprint materials: an interpretation and practical application. 4th ed. 1976
SLJ 23:46 F '77
Tilman, H. W. Triumph and tribulation
Yachting 141:96 Je '77. T. Gibbs
Tilton, T. A. Nazism, neo-nazism, and the peasantry. 1975
Am Hist R 81:1153-4 D '76. K. A. Schleunes
Tindall, G. B. Ethnic southerners. 1976
Am Hist R 82:759 Je '77. B. Clayton
New Repub 176:80-2 Ja 22 '77. L. D. Rubin, Jr
Tinker, H. Separate and unequal: India and the Indians in the British Commonwealth, 1920-1950. 1976
Am Hist R 82:423 Ap '77. F. F. Conlon
Ann Am Acad 432:162-3 Jl '77. R. P. Tucker
Tipton, F. B. Jr. Regional variations in the economic development of Germany during the nineteenth century. 1976
Am Hist R 82:997 O '77. U. Heyn
Ann Am Acad 431:160-1 My '77. L. L. Farrar, Jr
Tits-Dieuaide, M.-J. La formation des prix céréaliers en Brabant et en Flandre au XVe siècle. 1975
Am Hist R 82:120 F '77. J. L. Goldsmith
Toaff, A. Gli Ebrei a Perugia. 1975
Am Hist R 82:382 Ap '77. D. B. Ruderman
Tobey, J. L. History of ideas: a bibliographical introduction, v2: Medieval and early modern Europe. 1977
Am Hist R 82:921-2 O '77. D. R. Kelley
Tobin, G. M. Making of a history: Walter Prescott Webb and the Great Plains. 1976
Am Hist R 82:452 Ap '77. E. R. Bingham
Todd, M. Northern barbarians, 100 B.C.-A.D. 300. 1976
Am Hist R 81:1083 D '76. P. Mackendrick
Todorov, T. Poetics of prose
America 137:290 O 29 '77. D. Kirby
Toland, J. Adolf Hitler. 1976
Am Hist R 82:1280 D '77. G. L. Weinberg
America 136:253-6 Mr 19 '77. G. C. Zahn
Nat R 29:500-1 Ap 29 '77. A. L. Miller
Nation 224:87-9 Ja 22 '77. W. S. Allen
Progressive 41:60-1 F '77. A. Burnham
Tolbert, N. E. and Osmond, C. B. eds. Photorespiration in marine plants. 1976
Science 196:645 My 6 '77. R. K. Trench
Tolf, R. W. Russian Rockefellers: the saga of the Nobel family and the Russian oil industry. 1976
Am Hist R 82:696 Je '77. J. Long
Nat R 29:389-90 Ap 1 '77. J. Burnham
Tolkien, J. R. R. Father Christmas letters; ed by B. Tolkien. 1976
Horn Bk 53:551-2 O '77. A. A. Flowers
Tolkien, J. R. R. Silmarillion; ed. by C. Tolkien
America 137:315-16 N 5 '77. D. Coogan
Chr Today 22:30-1 O 7 '77. C. Forbes
Harpers 255:95-6+ N '77. C. Nicol
Nat R 29:1439-40 D 9 '77. R. Brookhiser
New Repub 177:38-40 O 1 '77. L. J. Davis
Newsweek 90:114+ O 24 '77. M. Jefferson
Tomašević, N. Magic world of Ivan Generalić; tr. by J. Shepley
Am Artist 41:14-16 Je '77. A. Werner
Tomasi, S. M. Piety and power: the role of the Italian parishes in the New York metropolitan area, 1880-1930. 1975
Am Hist R 81:1262 D '76. J. W. Pratt
Tomkins, C. Scene: reports on post-modern art. 1976
Art in Am 65:69 Ja '77. D. Bourdon
Toniolo, E. and Hill, R. eds. Opening of the Nile basin: writings by members of the Catholic mission to Central Africa on the geography and ethnography of the Sudan, 1842-1881. 1975
Am Hist R 82:155 F '77. J. W. Frost
Torrance, T. F. Space, time and resurrection. 1976
Chr Today 22:40+ D 9 '77. R. S. Anderson
Toscano, M. Alto Adige—South Tyrol: Italy's frontier with the German world; ed. by G. A. Carbone. 1976
Am Hist R 82:386 Ap '77. C. F. Delzell
Tourtellot, A. B. Benjamin Franklin: the shaping of genius: the Boston years. 1977
Am Hist R 82:1060-1 O '77. W. S. Hanna
Tower, D. B. ed. Nervous system. 3v. 1976
Science 196:419-20 Ap 22 '77. J. G. Hildebrand
Towns, E. Getting a church started. 1975
Chr Today 21:42+ F 18 '77. W. Brindley
Townsend, J. R. Top of the world; il. by J. Wallner. 1977
Horn Bk 53:446 Ag '77. V. Haviland
Townsend, J. R. Visitors. 1977
Horn Bk 53:671 D '77. E. L. Heins
Toynbee, A. Mankind and mother earth: a narrative history of the world. 1976
Am Hist R 82:60 F '77. W. H. McNeill
Trager, P. Photographs of architecture. 1977
Art in Am 65:35 N '77. C. Robinson
Trani, E. P. and Wilson, D. L. Presidency of Warren G. Harding. 1977
Am Hist R 82:1344 D '77. R. K. Murray
Transport and transfer processes in plants; proceedings of symposium, Canberra, Australia, 1975; ed by I. J. Wardlaw and J. B. Passioura. 1976
BioScience 27:421 Je '77. P. J. Kramer
Travis, S. Jesus hope. 1976
Chr Today 21:40-2 Ap 15 '77. W. W. Gasque
Tree physiology and yield improvement; papers from meeting, Edinburgh, 1975; ed by M. G. R. Cannell and F. T. Last. 1976
Science 196:865-6 My 20 '77. M. H. Zimmermann
Trefousse, H. L. Impeachment of a president: Andrew Johnson, the blacks, and reconstruction. 1975
Am Hist R 82:185 F '77. J. L. Wakelyn
Treitschke, H. von. History of Germany in the nineteenth century: selections from the translation of Eden and Cedar Paul; ed. and introd. by G. A. Craig. 1975
Am Hist R 82:125-6 F '77. C. E. McClelland
Trevor-Roper, H. Hermit of Peking: the hidden life of Sir Edmund Backhouse
Bus W p 10-11+ Je 13 '77. H. Menzies
Commonweal 104:634-6 S 30 '77. P. Terzian
New Repub 176:31-2 Je 4 '77. H. Fairlie
Newsweek 89:100+ Ap 18 '77. P. S. Prescott
Time 109:85+ My 9 '77. S. Schoffman
Trevor-Roper, H. Princes and artists: patronage and ideology at four Habsburg courts, 1517-1633
Art N 76:62+ N '77. M. S. Young
Tribe, L. H. and others, eds. When values conflict: essays on environmental analysis, discourse and decision. 1976
Bull Atom Sci 33:71-2 Mr '77. R. S. Berry
Triggle, D. J. and Triggle, C. R. Chemical pharmacology of the synapse. 1976
Science 197:1175-6 S 16 '77. R. E. Zigmond
Trilling, D. We must march my darlings: a critical decade
America 137:133-4 S 10 '77. G. Reedy
Commentary 64:66+ Jl '77. H. Kramer
Nat R 29:832-3 Jl 22 '77. M. J. Sobran, Jr
Nation 224:757-9 Je 18 '77. R. Radosh
New Repub 177:31-3 Ag 20 '77. I. Howe
Sat R 4:22-4 My 28 '77. B. Cook
Time 109:99 Je 13 '77. P. Blake
Trilling, L. Liberal imagination
New Repub 176:30-2 Ap 23 '77. Q. Anderson
Trilling, L. Middle of the journey
New Repub 176:29-30 Ap 23 '77. T. Samet
Trocme, E. Formation of the gospel according to Mark
Chr Cent 94:280-1 Mr 23 '77. M. L. Peel
Troeltsch, P. Ernst Troeltsch and the future of theology; ed by J. P. Clayton
Chr Cent 94:234 Mr 9 '77. R. H. King
Troitskii, S. M. Russkii absoliutizm i dvorianstvo v XVIII v.: formirovanie biurokratii. 1974
Am Hist R 81:1172-3 D '76. R. D. Givens
Trolander, J. A. Settlement houses and the Great Depression. 1975
Am Hist R 81:1273-4 D '76. D. J. Rothman
Trotter, A. Britain and East Asia, 1933-1937. 1975
Am Hist R 82:110 F '77. R. J. Gowen
Trucchi, L. Francis Bacon
Am Artist 41:94-6 Jl '77. A. Werner
Trudgill, E. Madonnas and Magdalens: the origins and development of Victorian sexual attitudes. 1976
Am Hist R 82:104-5 F '77. K. E. McCrone
Tsytovich, V. N. Theory of turbulent plasma; tr. by D. L. Burdick. 1977
Science 197:361 Jl 22 '77. J. E. Walsh
Tu, W. M. Neo-Confucian thought in action: Wang Yang-ming's youth (1472-1509). 1976
Am Hist R 82:1044 O '77. J. F. Handlin
Tucker, N. ed. Suitable for children? Controversies in children's literature. 1976
Horn Bk 53:67-8 F '77. V. Haviland
Tucker, R. W. Inequality of nations
Commentary 64:74-5 Ag '77. M. Ledeen
Fortune 95:139+ My '77. P. Berger
Nat R 29:343-4 Mr 18 '77. K. O'Lessker
Tudge, C. Famine business
Sat R 5:31-2 O 15 '77. S. A. Tomkievicz
Tugwell, R. G. Compromising of the Constitution: early departures. 1976
Ann Am Acad 431:172-3 My '77. J. M. Sosin
Turner, G. L. ed. Patronage of science in the nineteenth century. 1976
Science 195:568 F 11 '77. R. Kargon
Turow, S. One L: an inside account of life in the first year at Harvard law school
Newsweek 90:76 O 17 '77. J. K. Footlick
Tuska, J. Filming of the West. 1976
Am West 14:59 Ja '77. J. K. Folsom
Tyler, A. Earthly possessions
Ms 6:35-6 Ag '77. K. Bouton
New Repub 176:35-6 My 28 '77. N. Delbanco
New Yorker 53:130+ Je 6 '77. J. Updike
Newsweek 89:75 My 2 '77. M. Jefferson
Tyler, G. ed. Mexican-American tomorrow: educational and economic perspectives. 1976
Intellect 105:367-8 Ap '77. F. Cordasco
Tyrrell, R. E. Jr. ed. Future that doesn't work: social democracy's failures in Britain
Commentary 64:82-4 S '77. M. Novak
Nat R 29:727-30 Je 24 '77
New Repub 176:31-2 Je 18 '77. P. McGrath
Sat Eve Post 249:74 O '77. J. Burkhart

Uhalley, S. Jr. Mao Tse-Tung, a critical biography. 1975
Am Hist R 81:1203-4 D '76. J. Ch'en
Uhlman, F. Reunion
New Yorker 53:85-9 Ag 15 '77. G. Steiner
Uhnak, D. Investigation
Newsweek 90:70-1 Ag 22 '77. M. Jefferson
Ulam, A. B. In the name of the people: prophets and conspirators in prerevolutionary Russia. 1977
Ann Am Acad 434:224-5 N '77. J. W. Long
New Repub 176:26-8 Je 4 '77. B. DeMott
Newsweek 89:100+ Ap 11 '77. M. Jefferson
Ulam, S. M. Adventures of a mathematician
Am Scholar 46:538-43 Aut '77. E. Rothstein
Sci Am 236:136 Je '77. P. Morrison
Ulanov, A. and Ulanov, B. Religion and the unconscious
Chr Cent 94:204-5 Mr 2 '77. L. R. Rambo
Ullmann, H. P. Der Bund der Industriellen: Organisation, Einfluss and Politik kleinund mittelbetrieblicher Industrieller im deutschen Kaiserreich, 1895-1914. 1976
Am Hist R 82:1276 D '77. C. Medalen
Ullmann, L. Changing
Harpers 254:100-1 Mr '77. M. Malone
Ms 5:41-2+ Mr '77. J. Lazarre
New Repub 176:32-3 Ap 2 '77. J. Bachrach
Sat Eve Post 249:72-3 S '77. D. Brudnoy
Ullmann, W. Law and politics in the Middle ages: an introduction to the sources of medieval political ideas. 1975
Am Hist R 81:1085 D '76. J. Sutherland
Ulmschneider, H. Götz von Berlichingen: ein adeliges Leben der deutschen Renaissance. 1974
Am Hist R 82:123 F '77. L. W. Spitz
Unger, A. L. Totalitarian party: party and people in Nazi Germany and Soviet Russia. 1974
Am Hist R 81:1100-1 D '76. D. B. Stenzel
Ungerer, G. Spaniard in Elizabethan England: the correspondence of Antonio Pérez's exile, v 1. 1975
Am Hist R 81:1135 D '76. J. Hitchcock
United States. Department of State. Foreign relations of the United States, 1949, v 1: Far East and Australasia, pt 1. 1975
Am Hist R 82:1359-60 D '77. K. R. Young
United States. Department of State. Foreign relations of the United States, 1950, v6: East Asia and the Pacific. 1976
Am Hist R 82:1359-60 D '77. K. R. Young
United States. Department of State. Foreign relations of the United States, 1950, v7: Korea. 1976
Am Hist R 82:1360-1 D '77. T. Higgins
Updike, J. Marry me: a romance
Commonweal 104:89-90 F 4 '77. T. LeClair
Yale R 66:584-91 Je '77. D. Thorburn
Urdang, C. Picnic in the cemetery
Poetry 130:223-5 Jl '77. W. Logan
Ustinov, P. Dear me
Sat R 4:33 S 3 '77. W. Cole
Uvarov, B. Grasshoppers and locusts, v2: Behavior, ecology, biogeography, population dynamics. 1977
Science 198:1247-8 D 23 '77. M. J. D. White

Valenzuela, A. Political brokers in Chile: local government in a centralized polity. 1977
Ann Am Acad 434:217-18 N '77. R. H. Dix
Valley of Mexico; studies in pre-Hispanic ecology and society; papers from seminar, Santa Fe, N.M, 1972; ed. by E. R. Wolf. 1976
Science 196:759-61 My 13 '77. K. V. Flannery
VanBuren, P. M. Burden of freedom: Americans and the God of Israel
Chr Cent 94:307 Mr 30 '77. F. Sherman
Van den Ende, H. Sexual interactions in plants: the role of specific substances in sexual reproduction. 1976
Science 197:151-2 Jl 8 '77. G. Van den Ende and H. G. Linskens
Van Der Wal, S. L. ed. Officiële bescheiden betreffende de Nederlands-Indonesische betrekkingen, 1945-1950, v4: 31 maart-16 juli 1946; v5: 16 juli-28 okt. 1946. 1974
Am Hist R 82:164-5 F '77. G. D. Homan
Van Deventer, D. E. Emergence of provincial New Hampshire, 1623-1741. 1976
Am Hist R 82:429 Ap '77. F. J. Bremer
Vann, J. A. Swabian Kreis: institutional growth in the Holy Roman Empire, 1648-1715. 1975
Am Hist R 82:348-9 Ap '77. S. W. Rowan
Van Nostrand's scientific encyclopedia
Consumers Res Mag 60:41 Mr '77
Van Zandt, R. P. Astronomy for the amateur. 3d ed. v 1: Planetary astronomy. 1977
Sky & Tel 54:518 D '77. C. A. Federer, jr
Van Zwanenberg, R. M. A. and King, A. Economic history of Kenya and Uganda, 1800-1970. 1975
Am Hist R 81:1193 D '76. R. D. Wolff
Varona, A. J. Francisco Bilbao, revolucionario de América: vida y pensamiento, estudio de sus ensayos y trabajos periodísticos. 1973
Am Hist R 82:231 F '77. V. C. Peloso
Vasilevskaia, I. I. Kolonial'naia politika Iaponii v Koree nakanune anneksii (1904-1910 gg.) 1975
Am Hist R 82:720-1 Je '77. H. R. Spendelow
Vatter, H. G. Drive to industrial maturity: the U.S. economy, 1860-1914. 1976
Am Hist R 82:456-7 Ap '77. W. D. Lewis
Vaughan, D. Frederick Ashton and his ballets
Dance Mag 51:75-6 N '77. J. Anderson
Vawter, B. On Genesis: a new reading
America 137:466 D 24 '77. J. S. Kselman
Veatch, R. Canada and the League of Nations. 1975
Am Hist R 81:1283-4 D '76. G. G. Stanley
Ann Am Acad 431:146-7 My '77. C. R. Davy
Veatch, R. M. Death, dying, and the biological revolution. 1976
Chr Cent 94:337 Ap 6 '77. J. G. Blankinship
Chr Today 21:30+ Ag 26 '77. R. A. Case, 2d
Vecchi, O. L'Amfiparnaso; tr. and ed. by C. Adkins. 1977
Mus Q 63:434-6 Jl '77. S. T. Sommer
Ventura, P. Magic well. 1976
Horn Bk 53:42 F '77. E. L. Heins
Ventura, P. and Ventura, M. Painter's trick. 1977
Horn Bk 53:526 O '77. C. W. Draper
Venturi, F. Settecento riformatore; v2: La chiesa e la repubblica dentro i loro limiti, 1758-1774. 1976
Am Hist R 82:681-2 Je '77. C. M. Lovett
Vercoutter, J. and others. Image of the black in Western art, v1: From the Pharaohs to the fall of the Roman Empire
Sat R 4:24-5 Ap 30 '77. J. D. Cooney
Vernberg, F. J. Physiological responses of marine biota to pollutants. 1977
BioScience 27:750 N '77. J. S. Corbin
Vernberg, F. J. and Vernberg, W. B. Pollution and physiology of marine organisms. 1974
Sea Front 23:187 My '77. J. E. Randall
Vernon, R. Storm over the multinationals: the real issues. 1977
Ann Am Acad 434:245 N '77. R. C. McKibbin
Vicker, R. This hungry world. 1975
M Labor R 100:78 O '77. M. G. Blase
Vidal, G. 1876: a novel. 1976
Commonweal 104:25-7 Ja 7 '77. R. V. Remini
Vidal, G. Matters of fact and of fiction: essays 1973-76
Commentary 63:72-5 Je '77. J. Epstein
Esquire 88:22-4 Ag '77. J. Simon
Harpers 254:97-8 My '77. E. White
Newsweek 89:102 My 9 '77. W. Clemons
Vigezzi, B. Giolitti e Turati: un incontro mancato. 2v. 1976
Am Hist R 82:1283-4 D '77. S. Saladino
Villani, S. Isotope separation
Sci Am 237:136-7 Ag '77. P. Morrison
Villena, G. L. Los ministros de la audiencia de Lima en el reinado de los Borbones (1700-1821): esquema de un estudio sobre un núcleo dirigente. 1974
Am Hist R 82:481 Ap '77. M. A. Burkholder
Viñas Martin, A. El oro español en la guerra civil. 1976
Am Hist R 82:990-1 O '77. R. H. Whealey
Viola, H. J. Indian legacy of Charles Bird King. 1976
Am West 14:57 My '77. W. G. Bell
Vital, D. Origins of Zionism. 1975
Ann Am Acad 429:169-70 Ja '77. H. Rosenblum
Vlastos, G. Plato's universe
Sci Am 237:132-5 Ag '77. P. Morrison
Vliet, R. G. Solitudes
Commonweal 104:824-5 D 23 '77. W. S. Di Piero
Voight, M. J. and Harris, M. H. eds. Advances in librarianship; v7. 1977
Lib J 102:1469 Jl '77. G. Lyle
Voigt, E. B. Claiming kin
Nation 225:123 Ag 6 '77. E. Hirsch
Yale R 66:407-24 Mr '77. H. Vendler
Voinovich, V. Ivankiad; tr. by D. Lapeza
Nat R 29:1374 N 25 '77. D. K. Mano
New Repub 177:40-1 N 12 '77. A. Astrachan
Newsweek 90:71+ Ag 1 '77. R. Towers
Sat R 4:37-8 S 17 '77. S. Jacoby
Voinovich, V. Life and extraordinary adventures of private Ivan Chonkin; tr by R. Lourie. 1977
Commentary 64:68 S '77. J. Rubenstein
Horn Bk 53:343 Je '77. M. S. Cosgrave
Nat R 29:679 Je 10 '77. V. Gold
Nation 224:281-3 Mr 5 '77. P. Dreyer
Newsweek 89:87 F 14 '77. P. S. Prescott
Von Hirsch, A. Doing justice: the choice of punishments, report of the Committee for the study of incarceration
America 137:6-9 Jl 2 '77. K. Menninger
Von Pezold, J. D. Reval, 1670-1687: Rat, Gilden und schwedische Stadtherrschaft. 1975
Am Hist R 82:690 Je '77. E. Anderson
Voss, G. L. Seashore life of Florida and the Caribbean. 1976
Oceans 10:69-70 S '77. J. Dillon
Vovelle, M. Piété baroque et déchristianisation en Provence au XVIIIe siècle: les attitudes devant la mort d'après les clauses des testaments. 1973
Am Hist R 81:1125 D '76. W. H. Williams

Vovelle, M. Religion et révolution: la déchristianisation de l'an II. 1976
Am Hist R 82:650-1 Je '77. T. Tackett
Vree, D. On synthesizing Marxism and Christianity. 1976
America 136:451 My 14 '77. A. C. Varga
Chr Cent 94:763-4 Ag 31 '77. R. Quebedeaux
Chr Today 21:28-9 Ag 12 '77. C. F. H. Henry
Vucinich, A. Social thought in tsarist Russia: the quest for a general science of society, 1861-1917. 1976
Am Hist R 81:1174-5 D '76. G. L. Yaney
Ann Am Acad 431:161-2 My '77. I. Spector
Vylder, S. de. Allende's Chile: the political economy of the rise and fall of the Unidad Popular. 1976
Ann Am Acad 433:171-2 S '77. D. M. Billikopf

Wade, N. Ultimate experiment: man-made evolution. 1977
Bus W p 18+ S 19 '77. S. G. Michaud
Newsweek 90:96+ O 3 '77. P. Gwynne
Science 198:1144-5 D 16 '77. R. M. May
Smithsonian 8:109-11 Ja '78. J. Stein
Wagner, C. P. Your church can grow. 1976
Chr Cent 94:230+ Mr 9 '77. L. E. Schaller
Chr Today 21:32 Ja 7 '77. R. A. Bodey
Wagner, F. Isaac Newton im Zwielicht zwischen Mythos und Forschung: Studien zur Epoche der Aufklärung. 1976
Am Hist R 82:1234 D '77. M. C. Jacob
Wagner, G. End of education
Nat R 29:390-1 Ap 1 '77. J. Hart
Wagner, J. V. ed. Der Parlamentarische Rat, 1948-1949: Akten und Protokolle; v 1: Vorgeschitchte. 1975
Am Hist R 82:672 Je '77. F. E. Hirsch
Wagner, R. Richard Wagner: das braune Buch; ed by J. Bergfeld. 1975
Mus Q 63:264-8 Ap '77. R. Koprowski
Wagoner, D. Collected poems 1956-1976
Poetry 130:162-7 Je '77. A. Oberg
Wahl, J. and Wahl, S. I can count the petals of a flower
Sci Am 237:42 D '77. P. Morrison and P. Morrison
Wainwright, S. A. and others. Mechanical design in organisms
Sci Am 236:132-3 F '77. P. Morrison
Waite, R. G. L. Psychopathic god: Adolf Hitler
Commentary 64:76+ S '77. L. Bushkoff
New Repub 177:28-30 Jl 9 '77. G. A. Craig
New Yorker 53:82-6 Ag 29 '77. N. Bliven
Wakefield, D. All her children
Commonweal 104:122-5 F 18 '77. E. Larsen
Wakefield, D. Home free
Commonweal 104:822-4 D 23 '77. R. E. Long
New Repub 176:32-3 Mr 19 '77. J. Klinkowitz
Wakeman, F. Jr. Fall of imperial China. 1975
Am Hist R 81:1197-8 D '76. D. J. Li
Wakeman, F. Jr. and Grant, C. eds. Conflict and control in late imperial China. 1976
Am Hist R 82:159 F '77. H. Pei
Wakoski, D. Waiting for the king of Spain
Nation 224:348 Mr 19 '77. L. Wagner
Walcott, D. Sea Grapes
Nation 224:185-6 F 12 '77. R. Pevear
Poetry 130:228-9 Jl '77. W. Logan
Waldman, D. Joseph Cornell
America 137:422 D 10 '77. D. Leder
Walicki, A. Slavophile controversy: history of a conservative utopia in nineteenth-century Russian thought; tr. by H. Andrews-Rusiecka. 1975
Am Hist R 82:151 F '77. A. Gleason
Walkenstein, E. Don't shrink to fit! A confrontation with dehumanization in psychiatry and psychology
Commonweal 105:20-2 Ja 6 '78. C. A. Weber
Psychol Today 10:93-4+ Mr '77. P. Roazen
Walker, A. Meridian
Commonweal 104:285-5 Ap 29 '77. G. Burnside
Walker, B. J. and Blake, I. F. Computer security and protection structures
Sci Am 237:26+ O '77. P. Morrison
Walker, D. Moving out
Poetry 130:293-4 Ag '77. J. Parini
Walker, E. Nine years with the Spokane Indians: the diary, 1838-1848, of Elkanah Walker; ed by C. M. Drury. 1976
Am West 14:58 Ja '77. L. Waldron
Walker, H. T. and Montgomery, P. K. Teaching media skills: an instructional program for elementary and middle school students. 1977
SLJ 24:36 D '77. N. Storck
Walker, J. S. Henry A. Wallace and American foreign policy. 1976
Am Hist R 82:767 Je '77. N. D. Markowitz
Walker, J. W. St G. Black Loyalists: the search for a promised land in Nova Scotia and Sierra Leone, 1783-1870. 1976
Am Hist R 82:1066-7 O '77. L. Spitzer
Wall, B. H. and Gibb, G. S. Teagle of Jersey standard. 1974
Am Hist R 81:1275 D '76. F. J. Munch
Wallace, W. Foreign policy process in Britain. 1976
Ann Am Acad 431:147-8 My '77. E. Waldman
Wallechinsky, D. and others. Book of lists
Time 109:87 My 2 '77. P. Gray
Wallis, J. Agenda for biblical people. 1976
Chr Today 21:29 Jl 29 '77. R. K. Johnston
Wallis, W. A. Overgoverned society. 1976
Ann Am Acad 430:186+ Mr '77. H. F. Alderfer
Walsh, J. J. ed. 1977 guide to microforms in print: incorporating International microforms in print. 1977
Lib J 102:2141 O 15 '77. A. Tannenbaum
Walsh, M. R. Doctors wanted: no women need apply
Smithsonian 8:95-8 Ag '77. P. Brooks
Walter, I. International economics of pollution. 1976
Ann Am Acad 430:226-7 Mr '77. W. W. Ross
Walter, M. R. ed. Stromatolites. 1976
Science 196:780-2 My 13 '77. R. N. Ginsburg
Walters, R. G. Antislavery appeal: American abolitionism after 1830. 1977
Am Hist R 82:1073-4 O '77. W. H. Pease
Walworth, A. America's moment; 1918, American diplomacy at the end of World war I. 1977
Am Hist R 82:1091 O '77. L. E. Gelfand
Ann Am Acad 433:166-7 S '77. E. A. Stettner
Progressive 41:42 Je '77. B. Solomon
Wampler, J. All their own: people and the places they build
Archit Rec 162:41 N '77. R. Campbell
Nation 224:408 Ap 2 '77. J. H. Kay
Sci Am 236:136-8 Je '77. P. Morrison
Wandruszka, A. and Urbanitsch, P. eds. Die Habsburgermonarchie, 1848-1918, v2: Verwaltung und Rechtswesen. 1975
Am Hist R 82:135 F '77. J. Held
Ward, B. Home of man. 1976
Ann Am Acad 429:152 Ja '77. H. N. Howard
Bull Atom Sci 33:62-4 My '77. R. L. Meier
Chr Cent 94:68-9 Ja 26 '77. N. Lederer
Ward, H. ed. New library buildings: 1976 issue, years 1973-1974. 1976
Lib J 102:1161 My 15 '77. J. Orne
Ward, J. M. Colonial self-government: the British experience, 1759-1856. 1976
Am Hist R 82:633 Je '77. R. W. Winks
Warncke, R. Planning library workshops and institutes. 1976
Lib J 102:182 Ja 15 '77. D. Perlov
Warner, L. Astronomy for the southern hemisphere. 1975
Sky & Tel 53:382-4 My '77. M. D. Overbeek
Warner, L. S. From slave to abolitionist; il. by T. Feelings. 1976
Horn Bk 53:174 Ap '77. M. M. Burns
Warner, M. Alone of all her sex: the myth and cult of the Virgin Mary
Commonweal 104:23-5 Ja 7 '77. G. A. Lindbeck
Warner, M. In a dark wood
Chr Cent 94:1098+ N 23 '77. R. Kaftan
Warner, S. T. Kingdoms of elfin
Time 109:73-4 F 21 '77. P. Gray
Warner, W. W. Beautiful swimmers
Smithsonian 8:6 Ag '77. S. D. Ripley
Warren, E. Memoirs of Earl Warren
Commonweal 104:537-9 Ag 19 '77. I. Silver
Nat R 29:1245-7 O 28 '77. I. Younger
Sat R 4:26-7 Jl 9 '77. A. Barth
Warren, R. P. Place to come to
America 136:448 My 14 '77. T. H. Stahel
Atlantic 239:96 My '77. P. Davison
Newsweek 89:81-2 Mr 21 '77. M. Jefferson
Sat R 4:30+ Mr 19 '77. R. Howard
Time 109:74 Mr 14 '77. R. Z. Sheppard
Warren, R. P. Selected poems, 1923-1975
America 136:447-8 My 14 '77. J. F. Cotter
Commentary 63:76-7 Ap '77. J. Romano
Poetry 131:169-75 D '77. J. D. McClatchy
Yale R 67:72, 81-4 O '77. H. Vendler
Warwick, P. French popular front: a legislative analysis. 1977
Am Hist R 82:1267-8 D '77. J. F. Sweets
Washington, B. T. Papers, v5 1899-1900; ed. by L. R. Harlan and R. W. Smock. 1976
Am Hist R 82:1342 D '77. J. Stein
Washington, G. Diaries of George Washington, v 1: 1748-65; v2: 1766-70; ed. by D. Jackson and D. Twohig. 1976
Am Hist R 82:1060 O '77. G. M. Curtis, 3d
Wasserman, G. Politics of decolonialization: Kenya Europeans and the land issue: 1960-1965. 1976
Am Hist R 82:1039 O '77. M. P. K. Sorrenson
Watkins, T. H. Mirror of the dream: an illustrated history of San Francisco. 1976
Am West 14:61 Mr '77. B. McGinty
Watson, D. Designing and building a solar house: your place in the sun
Archit Rec 162:43 O '77. G. Allen
Watson, G. E. Birds of the Antarctic and sub-Antarctic
Smithsonian 8:124-6 S '77. L. J. Halle
Watson, W. E. Cell biology of brain. 1976
BioScience 27:358 My '77. W. G. Van Der Kloot
Watts, R. O. and McGee, I. J. Liquid state chemical physics. 1976
Phys Today 30:71-2 My '77. D. Henderson

Waugh, E. Diaries of Evelyn Waugh; ed. by M. Davie
America 137:424-5 D 10 '77. P. Matthews
Newsweek 90:102+ O 31 '77. W. Clemons
Sat R 5:26 N 12 '77. M. Green
Time 110:102-3 O 17 '77. R. Z. Sheppard
Weatherby, M. J. Squaring off: Mailer vs. Baldwin
New Repub 176:36-7 Je 18 '77. A. Gordon
Webb, B. Our partnership; ed. by B. Drake and M. I. Cole. 1975
Am Hist R 81:1115-16 D '76. F. M. Schweitzer
Webb, R. E. Accident hazards of nuclear power plants. 1976
Phys Today 30:63-4 Mr '77. H. W. Lewis
Webb, S. and Webb, B. Constitution for the socialist commonwealth of Great Britain; introd. by S.H. Beer. 1975
Am Hist R 81:1115-16 D '76. F. M. Schweitzer
Webb, S. and Webb, B. Methods of social study; introd. by T. H. Marshall. 1975
Am Hist R 81:1115-16 D '76. F. M. Schweitzer
Weber, A. R. In pursuit of price stability: the wage-price freeze of 1971. 1973
Ann Am Acad 431:186-7 My '77. J. Horvath
Weber, E. Peasants into Frenchmen: the modernization of rural France, 1870-1914. 1976
Am Hist R 82:653 Je '77. J. A. Silver
Ann Am Acad 431:162-3 My '77. M. M. Farrar
Weber, J. A. Grow or die?
Nat R 29:890+ Ag 5 '77. J. Passmore
Weber, L. J. Who shall live? 1976
Chr Today 21:30+ Ag 26 '77. R. A. Case, 2d
Webster, C. Great instauration: science, medicine and reform, 1626-1660. 1975
Am Hist R 82:353-5 Ap '77. R. S. Westfall
Science 195:385-6 Ja 28 '77. R. G. Frank, Jr
Webster, R. A. Industrial imperialism in Italy, 1908-1915. 1975
Am Hist R 82:141-2 F '77. A. Patrucco
Wedge, E. F. ed. Nefertiti graffiti
Art N 76:21+ Summ '77. Vasari
Weeks, G. C. Oscar Carleton McCulloch, 1843-1891: preacher and practitioner of applied Christianity. 1976
Am Hist R 82:752 Je '77. J. H. Dorn
Weglyn, M. Years of infamy: the untold story of America's concentration camps; introd. by J. A. Michener. 1976
Am Hist R 82:765-6 Je '77. A. A. Hansen
Wehmeyer, L. B. School librarian as educator. 1976
SLJ 23:44 Ap '77. E. McCorkle
Weil, S. Simone Weil reader; ed. by G. A. Panichas
America 137:152+ S 17 '77. J. R. Kelly
Ms 6:40+ S '77. N. Rosen
New Repub 177:33-7 Jl 2 '77. J. C. Oates
Weinberg, M. Chance to learn: a history of race and education in the United States
Progressive 41:55-6 O '77. J. Egerton
Weinberg, S. First three minutes: a modern view of the origin of the universe. 1977
Commentary 64:65 O '77. J. Marsh
New Repub 178:33-4 Ja 7 '78. T. Ferris
New Yorker 53:133-4+ S 19 '77. J. Bernstein
Sci Am 237:52 S '77. P. Morrison
Science 197:752 Ag 19 '77. D. W. Sciama
Sky & Tel 54:512-13+ D '77. D. Overbye
Weiner, M. A. Taster's guide to beer
Commonweal 104:605 S 16 '77. R. A. Schroth
Weingarten, V. Half a marriage
Commonweal 104:533-5 Ag 19 '77. N. Y. Hoffman
Weinreb, L. L. Denial of justice: criminal process in the United States
Nation 225:153-5 Ag 20 '77. D. Rudovsky
Weinstein, F. B. Indonesian foreign policy and the dilemma of dependence—from Sukarno to Soharto. 1976
Ann Am Acad 432:163-4 Jl '77. J. F. Melby
Weinstein, R. A. and Booth, L. Collection, use, and care of historical photographs
Pop Phot 81:146-7 Ag '77. K. Poli
Weisberg, J. S. Meteorology: the earth and its weather. 1976
Sky & Tel 53:298-9 Ap '77. C. A. Federer
Weisbord, V. B. Radical life
Progressive 41:53-5 N '77. A. M. Davidon
Weiss, R. S. Marital separation
Psychol Today 10:50 Ap '77. E. Dienstag
Weiss, T. Fireweeds
Poetry 130:45-7 Ap '77. J. D. McClatchy
Yale R 66:407-24 Mr '77. H. Vendler
Weisser, H. British working-class movements and Europe, 1815-48. 1976
Am Hist R 82:360 Ap '77. J. Roebuck
Ann Am Acad 429:164-6 Ja '77. T. J. Rice
Weisser, M. R. Peasants of the Montes: the roots of rural rebellion in Spain. 1977
Am Hist R 82:989 O '77. W. J. Callahan
Weizenbaum, J. Computer power and human reason: from judgment to calculation. 1976
Phys Today 30:68+ Ja '77. J. McCarthy
Welch, J. Riding the earthboy 40
Poetry 129:287-8 F '77. R. Holland
Welch, T. F. Toshakan: libraries in Japanese society. 1976
Lib J 102:1161 My 15 '77. R. L. Gitler
Weldon, F. Words of advice
Newsweek 90:73-4+ Ag 15 '77. M. Jefferson
Time 110:71+ Ag 22 '77. J. Skow
Wells, F. J. Long-run availability of phosphorus
Sci Am 236:131 Ja '77. P. Morrison
Wells, R. V. Population of the British colonies in America before 1776: a survey of census data. 1975
Am Hist R 82:428 Ap '77. J. J. Waters
Wende, P. Radikalismus im Vormärz: Untersuchungen zur politischen Theorie der frühen deutschen Demokratie. 1975
Am Hist R 82:379-80 Ap '77. T. S. Hamerow
Wendorf, F. and Schild, R. Prehistory of the Nile Valley. 1976
Science 196:971-2 My 27 '77. C. E. Stearns
Wertheim, A. F. New York little renaissance: iconoclasm, modernism, and nationalism in American culture 1908-1917. 1976
Am Hist R 82:465-6 Ap '77. M. W. Brown
Wertheimer, B. M. We were there: the story of working women in America
Ms 6:44+ O '77. E. Sweet
New Repub 176:31-3 Je 25 '77. P. Filene
Weslager, C. A. Stamp Act Congress. 1976
Am Hist R 82:1063 O '77. R. A. Ryerson
Wesson, R. G. Why Marxism?
Nat R 29:282-3 Mr 4 '77. T. Molnar
West, D. C. ed. Joachim of Fiore in Christian thought: essays on the influence of the Calabrian prophet. 2v. 1975
Am Hist R 81:1092-3 D '76. E. K. Burger
West, P. Yenching university and Sino-Western relations, 1916-1952. 1976
Am Hist R 82:1049-50 O '77. L. E. Eastman
West, R. Rebecca West: a celebration; introd. by S. Hynes
Am Scholar 47:131-4 Wint '77. W. Haley
Nat R 30:35-7 Ja 6 '78. N. King
Nation 225:442-3 O 29 '77. A. Fremantle
New Repub 176:28-30 Je 18 '77. H. Mitgang
New Yorker 53:152-4+ O 3 '77. M. Panter-Downes
Sat R 5:24-6 O 15 '77. M. Green
Westby, D. L. Clouded vision: the student movement in the United States in the 1960s. 1976
Society 14:96 Jl '77. R. S. Denisoff
Westergaard, J. and Resler, H. Class in a capitalist society: a study of contemporary Britain. 1976
Ann Am Acad 432:185-6 Jl '77. S. Leventman
Westerhoff, J. H. Tomorrow's church. 1976
Chr Today 21:28 Jl 29 '77. R. Quebedeaux
Westernhagen, K. von. Forging of the Ring: Richard Wagner's composition sketches for Der Ring des Nibelungen; tr. by A. Whittall and M. Whittall
Hi Fi 27:MA39-40 My '77
Westing, A. H. Ecological consequences of the second Indochina War
Horticulture 55:12-13 Mr '77. A. W. Galston
Weston, E. Edward Weston nudes: sixty photographs; text by C. Wilson. 1977
Art in Am 65:39+ N '77. L. Rubinflien
New Repub 177:31-3 O 29 '77. J. Canaday
Wetering, J. van de. Japanese corpse
Time 110:67 S 5 '77. M. Duffy
Wetmore, R. Y. First on the land: the North Carolina Indians. 1975
Am Hist R 81:1263 D '76. W. S. Powell
Weymouth, L. America in 1876: the way we were
Commonweal 104:25-7 Ja 7 '77. R. V. Remini
Whaley, W. G. Golgi apparatus. 1975
BioScience 27:132 F '77. M. Locke
Wheeler, R. F. USPD und Internationale: sozialistischer Internationalismus in der Zeit der Revolution; tr. by A. Blansdorf. 1975
Am Hist R 82:666-7 Je '77. W. Struve
Wheeler-Bennett, J. Friends, enemies and sovereigns
New Repub 176:59 My 21 '77. P. Terzian
Whelan, E. Baby? . . .Maybe: a guide to making the most fateful decision of your life
Newsweek 90:73 Ag 8 '77. B. Carter
Wheller, G. C. and Wheller, J. Ant larvae: review and synthesis. 1976
Science 195:975 Mr 11 '77. E. O. Wilson
Whitaker, A. P. United States and the Southern cone: Argentina, Chile, and Uruguay. 1976
Am Hist R 82:1109 O '77. J. R. Scobie
Whitaker, C. H. ed. Bertram Grosvenor Goodhue —architect and master of many arts; introd. by P. Goldberger. 1925. repr. 1976
Archit Rec 162:41+ Ag '77. R. B. Oliver
Whitcombe, E. Agrarian conditions in Northern India, v 1: The United Provinces under British rule, 1860-1900. 1972
Am Hist R 82:1052 O '77. T. Raychaudhuri
White, D. S. Splintered party: national liberalism in Hessen and the Reich, 1867-1918. 1976
Am Hist R 82:664 Je '77. J. F. Flynn
White, E. B. Essays of E. B. White
Commonweal 104:765 N 25 '77. J. Deedy
White, E. B. Letters of E. B. White; ed. by D. L. Guth. 1976
Am Scholar 46:237-8+ Spr '77. S. Brown
Harpers 254:94+ Mr '77. M. Muggeridge
Horn Bk 53:201 Ap '77. M. S. Cosgrave
Nat R 29:671-2 Je 10 '77. D. Hall
New Repub 176:23-4 F 26 '77. R. H. Rovere
Sat Eve Post 249:72 S '77 A. McGlinn

White, K. D. Farm equipment of the Roman world. 1975
Am Hist R 81:1081-2 D '76. J. W. Eadie
White, L. J. eds. Chronicle of a congressional journey: the Doolittle committee in the Southwest, 1865. 1975
Am Hist R 81:1255 D '76. B. A. Storey
White, P. Fringe of leaves
Chr Cent 94:410-11 Ap 27 '77. L. Dickerson
Harpers 254:92-3 F '77. E. Connell
New Yorker 53:131-2 My 23 '77. G. Steiner
Newsweek il por 89:71-2 Ja 24 '77. P. S. Prescott
White, R. C. Jr. and Hopkins, C. H. Social gospel: religion and reform in changing America
Commonweal 104:603-4 S 16 '77. P. D. Finks
White, T. H. Book of Merlyn; prologue by S. T. Warner
America 137:224 O 8 '77. J. Mullin
Atlantic 240:96 S '77. M. Spaulding
Whitecotton, J. W. Zapotecs: princes, priests, and peasants. 1977
Am Hist R 82:1371-2 D '77. D. Butterworth
Whiteman, M. Gentlemen in crisis: the first century of the Union league of Philadelphia, 1862-1962. 1975
Am Hist R 81:1258 D '76. R. J. Connors
Whiteside, A. G. Socialism of fools: Georg Ritter von Schönerer and Austrian pan-Germanism. 1975
Am Hist R 82:136-7 F '77. W. A. Jenks
Whitford, F. Japanese prints and western painters
Am Artist 41:26+ O '77. F. Johnson
Whitney, E. M. comp. and ed. Black Hawk war, 1831-1832, v2: Letters and papers. 1975
Am Hist R 81:1241 D '76. M. Schmitt
Whitney, F. C. Mass media and mass communications in society. 1975
Intellect 105:283-4 F '77. R. L. Fischer
Whittemore, E. Sinai tapestry
Nation 225:216-18 S 10 '77. A. Heilbut
Wicklund, R. A. and Brehm, J. W. Perspectives on cognitive dissonance. 1976
Science 195:1322-3 Mr 25 '77. M. E. Shaw
Widmer, E. Russian ecclesiastical mission in Peking during the eighteenth century. 1976
Am Hist R 82:410-11 Ap '77. P. S. Ropp
Wieczynski, J. L. Russian frontier: the impact of borderlands upon the course of early Russian history. 1976
Am Hist R 82:692 Je '77. C. J. Halperin
Wiersbe, W. Walking with the giants: a minister's guide to good reading and great preaching. 1976
Chr Today 21:41-2 S 23 '77. R. G. Clouse
Wiesel, E. Messengers of God: biblical portraits and legends
Commonweal 104:220-1 Ap 1 '77. J. Reimer
Wiesenthal, S. Sunflower
Chr Cent 94:544 Je 1 '77. B. C. Lane
Commonweal 104:282-3 Ap 29 '77. J. Garvey
Wiesflecker, H. Kaiser Maximilian I.: das Reich, Osterreich und Europa an der Wende zur Neuzeit; v2: Reichsreform und Kaiserpolitik, 1493-1500: Entmachtung des Konigs im Reich und in Europa. 1975
Am Hist R 82:659-60 Je '77. J. A. Mears
Wiesmann, S. ed. Gustav Mamer in Vienna; tr by A. Shelley
Am Rec G 40:57-8 Je '77. J. Diether and N. Karlins
Hi Fi 27:MA38-9 Mr '77. D. Hamilton
Wilbur, C. M. Sun Yat-sen: frustrated patriot. 1976
Am Hist R 82:1048-9 O '77. K. R. Chong
America 136:304 Ap 2 '77. W. J. Richardson
Ann Am Acad 433:179 S '77. P. A. Cohen
Wilbur, R. Mind-reader
Poetry 130:44-5 Ap '77. J. D. McClatchy
Wilbur, R. Responses: prose pieces, 1953-1976
America 136:362 Ap 16 '77. J. T. Edelman
Nation 225:469-71 N 5 '77. C. C. Park
Wilcox, R. K. Shroud
America 137:449 D 17 '77. C. J. McNaspy
Wilczynski, J. Multinationals and East-West relations: towards transideological collaboration. 1976
Ann Am Acad 432:186 Jl '77. R. E. Kanet
Wilde, M. C. and Borsten, O. Loving gentleman
Commonweal 104:507-9 Ag 5 '77. P. Samway
Newsweek 89:74-5 F 7 '77. W. Clemons
Wilder, A. N. Theopoetic: theology and the religious imagination
Chr Cent 94:363-4 Ap 13 '77. W. A. Kort
Wildermuth, K. and Tang, Y. C. Unified theory of the nucleus. 1977
Phys Today 30:62-3 Jl '77. E. Sheldon
Wiles, M. What is theology?
America 136:258+ Mr 19 '77. J. B. Breslin
Wilke, E. T. P. W. Political decadence in imperial Germany: personnel-political aspects of the German government crisis, 1894-97. 1976
Am Hist R 82:1276-7 D '77. L. Cecil
Wilkinson, B. Ludell and Willie. 1977
Horn Bk 53:452 Ag '77. V. Haviland
Wilkinson, D. Revolutionary civil war: the elements of victory and defeat. 1975
Am Hist R 82:64 F '77. C. E. Black
Ann Am Acad 429:153 Ja '77. J. S. Roucek
Wilks, I. Asante in the nineteenth century: the structure and evolution of a political order. 1975
Am Hist R 82:1036-7 O '77. E. Reynolds
Willan, T. S. Inland trade: studies in English internal trade in the sixteenth and seventeenth centuries. 1976
Am Hist R 82:958-9 O '77. F. T. Melton
Willard, B. Miller's boy; il. by G. Floyd. 1976
Horn Bk 53:164 Ap '77. E. L. Heins
Williams, C. K. With ignorance
Nation 224:763-6 Je 18 '77. J. Atlas
Williams, E. Harriet Monroe and the poetry renaissance: the first ten years of Poetry, 1912-22
Poetry 131:39-51 O '77. J. Parisi
Yale R 66:x+ eJ '77
Williams, H. L. No room for doubt. 1976
Chr Today 21:27 Jl 8 '77. R. Cleath
Williams, J. G. Simulation activities in library, communication, and information science; with E. Pope. 1976
Lib J 102:182 Ja 15 '77. E. Jussim
Williams, L. E. Southeast Asia: a history. 1976
Am Hist R 82:1055 O '77. D. J. Steinberg
Williams, R. L. Manners and murders in the world of Louis Napoleon. 1976
Am Hist R 82:118-19 F '77. B. F. Martin, Jr
Williams, T. Androgyne, mon amour
New Repub 176:32-4 Je 4 '77. G. Weales
Williams, T. Tennessee Williams' letters to Donald Windham, 1940-65; ed. by D. Windham. 1977
Atlantic 240:90 S '77. B. DeMott
Time 109:94 F 7 '77. G. Clarke
Williams, T. Tsuga's children
Time 109:88 My 9 '77. R. Z. Sheppard
Williams, W. A. America confronts a revolutionary world: 1776-1976. 1976
Am Hist R 82:724 Je '77. T. C. Kennedy
America 136:57-8 Ja 22 '77. R. M. Senkewicz
Williams, W. H. America's first hospital: the Pennsylvania hospital, 1751-1841. 1976
Am Hist R 82:438 Ap '77. R. L. Numbers
Wilmerding, J. American art
Am Artist 41:52+ F '77. A. Werner
Antiques 112:524 S '77. J. D. Prown
Wilson, D. Long march, 1935: the epic of Chinese communism's survival. 1972
Am Hist R 81:1200-1 D '76. L. Dittmer
Wilson, D. W. Governor Charles Robinson of Kansas. 1975
Am Hist R 81:1256 D '76. G. Clanton
Wilson, E. Letters on literature and politics: 1912-1972; ed. by E. Wilson; with introd. by D. Aaron and foreword by L. Edel
America 137:448 D 17 '77. M. Wimsatt
Nat R 29:1370-3 N 25 '77. C. Williamson, jr
Nation 225:437-9 O 29 '77. L. Kriegel
New Repub 177:47-8 O 15 '77. R. Rosenblatt
New Yorker 53:59-62 Ja 2 '78. V. S. Pritchett
Newsweek 90:95-6 O 3 '77. W. Clemons
Sat R 5:36-9 O 29 '77. M. Cowley
Wilson, E. Margaret Fuller: bluestocking, romantic, revolutionary. 1977
Horn Bk 53:460 Ag '77. E. L. Heins
Wilson, E. G. Loyal blacks. 1976
Am Hist R 82:1066-7 O '77. L. Spitzer
Wilson, E. R. Uphill for peace: Quaker impact on Congress. 1975
Am Hist R 81:1280 D '76. P. A. Carter
Wilson, H. Governance of Britain. 1976
Am Hist R 82:1260 D '77. P. Stansky
Nat R 29:894-5 Ag 5 '77. C. Welch
New Repub 176:33-4 Ja 29 '77. R. W. Howe
Wilson, P. Community elite and the public library: the uses of information in leadership. 1977
Lib J 102:1584 Ag '77. N. Lushington
Wilson, W. Papers of Woodrow Wilson, v 16: 1905-1907; v 17: 1907-1908; v 18: 1908-1909; v 19: 1909-1910; v20: 1910; ed. by A. S. Link and others. 1973-5
Am Hist R 82:1089-91 O '77. H. Hawkins
Wilson, W. Papers of Woodrow Wilson, v21: 1910; ed. by A. S. Link and others. 1976
Ann Am Acad 429:178-9 Ja '77. L. Filler
Wilson, W. Papers of Woodrow Wilson, v21: 1910; v22: 1910-1911; ed. by A. S. Link and others. 1976, 1977
Am Hist R 82:1343-4 D '77. S. W. Livermore
Wilson, W. A. Folklore and nationalism in modern Finland. 1976
Am Hist R 82:994-5 O '77. M. Rintala
Windom, H. L. and Duce, R. A. Marine pollutant transfer. 1976
Science 198:392 O 28 '77. R. J. Livingston
Winge, S. Die Wirtschaftliche Aufbau-Vereiningung (WAV), 1945-53: Entwicklung und Politik einer undoktrinären politischen Partei in der Bundesrepublik in der ersten Nachkriegszeit. 1976
Am Hist R 82:672-3 Je '77. D. Prowe
Winks, R. W. American's guide to Britain
Smithsonian 8:152-3 O '77. B. Schiff
Winn, M. Plug-in drug: television, children, and the family
Am Scholar 47:137-40 Wint '77. J. Amberg
America 136:276-7 Mr 26 '77. R. A. Blake
Sat R 4:27-8 Mr 5 '77. B. Cook
Todays Educ 66:82 N '77. B. Z. Friedlander

Winsor, M. P. Starfish, jellyfish, and the order of life: issues in nineteenth-century science. 1976
Science 195:868 Mr 4 '77. F. Farley
Winter, D. Help yourself to a job: a guide for retirees. 1976
Aging 270:42 Ap '77
Winters, N. Girl on the coca-cola tray
Ms 5:44 Ap '77. S. Weller
Winters, S. B. and others. Intellectual and social developments in the Habsburg empire from Maria Theresa to World war I. 1975
Am Hist R 82:143 F '77. S. B. Kimball
Wirz, A. Von Sklavenhandel zum kolonialen Handel: Wirtschaftsräume und Wirtschaftsformen in Kamerun vor 1914. 1972
Am Hist R 82:712 Je '77. R. Raphael
Wise, D. American police state: the government against the people. 1976
Commonweal 104:382 Je 10 '77. S. Cohen
Intellect 106:87 Ag '77. A. G. Theoharis
New Repub 176:38-9 Mr 26 '77. M. Skube
Wise, W. Massacre at Mountain Meadows: an American legend and a monumental crime. 1976
Am Hist R 82:1072 O '77. C. S. Peterson
Am West 14:60 S '77. B. Procter
Wistrich, R. S. Revolutionary Jews from Marx to Trotsky. 1976
Am Hist R 82:337 Ap '77. D. G. Sanford
Commentary 63:78-81 Ap '77. H. MacCoby
Witcover, J. Marathon: the pursuit of the presidency, 1972-1976
Atlantic 240:90+ S '77. R. Manning
Commentary 64:70+ S '77. N. W. Polsby
New Repub 177:34-5 D 17 '77. K. Bode
Newsweek 90:88-9 Jl 18 '77. J. Doyle
Progressive 41:40-1 S '77. F. Mankiewicz
Witke, R. Comrade Chiang Ch'ing. 1977
Cur Hist 73:84 S '77
Nat R 29:619 My 27 '77. F. B. Randall
Nation 225:21-2 Jl 2 '77. N. D. Milton and D. Milton
New Repub 176:23-8 Je 25 '77. S. Leys
Newsweek 89:75 My 2 '77. W. Clemons
Sat R 4:20-1 Je 25 '77. J. A. Cohen
Witney, K. P. Jutish forest: a study of the Weald of Kent from 450 to 1380 A.D. 1976
Am Hist R 82:936-7 O '77. N. J. G. Pounds
Witte, P. W. On common ground: Protestant and Catholic evangelicals. 1975
Chr Today 22:48-50 O 7 '77. W. W. Wells
Wittgenstein, L. Wittgenstein's lectures on the foundations of mathematics; Cambridge 1939; ed. by C. Diamond
Am Scholar 46:538-43 Aut '77. E. Rothstein
Wodehouse, P. G. Uncollected Wodehouse; ed by D. A. Jasen
Nat R 29:732-3 Je 24 '77. L. Bridges
Wogaman, J. P. Christian method of moral judgment
America 136:548 Je 18 '77. J. Gaffney
Wolf, M. and Witke, R. eds. Women in Chinese society. 1975
Am Hist R 82:719 Je '77. C. L. P. Tao
Wolf, S. G. Urban village: population, community, and family structure in Germantown, Pennsylvania, 1683-1800. 1977
Am Hist R 82:1321 D '77. M. Zuckerman
Wolfe, T. Mauve gloves & madmen, clutter & vine: and other stories, sketches and essays
America 136:113+ F 5 '77. G. Reedy
Commentary 63:76+ My '77. D. Rabinowitz
Nat R 29:212+ F 18 '77. C. Williamson, Jr
Nation 224:278-80 Mr 5 '77. J. Beatty
Wolff, C. G. Feast of words: the triumph of Edith Wharton
America 136:450 My 14 '77. J. W. Crowley
Ms 6:80 N '77. A. Jones
Wolitzer, H. In the flesh
Ms 6:40+ O '77. M. Saxton
New Yorker 53:68-70 D 26 '77. L. Harris
Newsweek 90:110+ S 19 '77. R. Sokolov
Sat R 5:30-1 O 1 '77. D. Grumbach
Wollenberg, C. M. All deliberate speed: segregation and exclusion in California schools, 1855-1975. 1977
Ann Am Acad 433:185 S '77. D. G. Farrelly
Wolpert, S. New history of India. 1977
Am Hist R 82:1313 D '77. J. R. McLane
Wolters, R. New negro on campus: black college rebellions of the 1920s. 1975
Am Hist R 82:205 F '77. J. Boskin
Wolterstorff, N. Reason within the bounds of religion. 1976
Chr Today 21:32+ Ja 21 '77. G. I. Mavrodes
Wong, J. T. Kinetics of enzyme mechanisms. 1975
BioScience 27:214 Mr '77. A. T. Phillips
Wood, J. E. Jr. ed. Baptists and the American experience
Chr Cent 94:492-4 My 18 '77. L. L. Greenfield
Woodall, R. and Watkins, T. H. Taken by the wind: vanishing architecture of the West. 1977
Art in Am 65:35 N '77. C. Robinson
Woods, J. Striking the earth
Poetry 130:295-6 Ag '77. J. Parini
Woods, R. Another kind of love: homosexuality and spirituality
America 136:549-50 Je 18 '77. J. J. McNeill
Woodward, R. L. Jr. Central America: a nation divided. 1976
Am Hist R 82:226 F '77. F. D. Parker
Woolf, V. Diary of Virginia Woolf, v 1: 1915-1919; ed. by A. O. Bell.
Ms 6:34-6 Ja '78. E. Hawkes
Woolf, V. Letters of Virginia Woolf, v 1: 1888-1912; ed. by N. Nicolson and J. Trautmann
New Yorker 53:90-6 Jl 18 '77. W. Maxwell
Woolf, V. Letters of Virginia Woolf, v2: 1912-1922; ed. by N. Nicolson and J. Trautmann
Commonweal 104:371-4 Je 10 '77. S. Maloff
New Repub 176:27-9 Ap 23 '77. R. Brown
New Yorker 53:90-6 Jl 18 '77. W. Maxwell
Newsweek por 89:71 Ja 24 '77. M. Jefferson
Progressive 41:60 My '77. E. Pendleton
Yale R 66:603-13 Je '77. G. S. Haight
Woolf, V. Moments of being: unpublished autobiographical writings of Virginia Woolf; ed by J. Schulkind
America 136:449-50 My 14 '77. D. Menagh
Esquire 88:12+ Jl '77. A. Kazin
Nat R 29:785 Jl 8 '77. V. Miller
New Repub 176:27-9 Ap 23 '77. R. Brown
New Yorker 53:115-17 Mr 7 '77. W. Maxwell
Newsweek por 89:71 Ja 24 '77. M. Jefferson
Yale R 66:603-13 Je '77. G. S. Haight
Woolf, V. Pargiters; ed. by M. A. Leaska
Ms 6:34-6 Ja '78. E. Hawkes
Wootton, R. J. Biology of the sticklebacks. 1976
Science 197:451 Jl 29 '77. M. A. Bell
Woram, J. M. Recording studio handbook
Hi Fi 27:152-3 F '77. F. Miller
Worley, R. Gathering of strangers: understanding the life of your church
Chr Cent 94:1011-12 N 2 '77. B. A. Blumer
Wortman, R. S. Development of a Russian legal consciousness. 1976
Am Hist R 82:695-6 Je '77. N. V. Riasanovsky
Wray, J. L. Calcareous algae. 1977
Science 197:44 Jl 1 '77. W. H. Adey
Wrenn, T. P. and Mulloy, E. D. America's forgotten architecture
Smithsonian 7:120-1 Mr '77. W. Morgan
Wriggins, S. H. White monkey king: a Chinese fable; il. by R. Solbert. 1977
Horn Bk 53:529-30 O '77. P. Heins
Wright, E. ed. Red, white and true blue: the Loyalists in the Revolution. 1976
Am Hist R 82:1065-6 O '77. C. Berkin
Wright, E. R. ed. Korean policies in transition. 1975
Am Hist R 82:418-19 Ap '77. A. C. Nahm
Wright, H. C. Oral antecedents of Greek librarianship. 1977
Lib J 102:2016 O 1 '77. M. H. Harris
Wright, J. L. Jr. Britain and the American frontier, 1783-1815. 1976
Am Hist R 81:1231 D '76. C. B. Cone
Wright, J. L. Jr. Florida in the American revolution. 1975
Am Hist R 82:739-40 Je '77. J. D. L. Holmes
Wright, R. American hunger
Newsweek 89:81 My 30 '77. M. Jefferson
Time 109:74 My 30 '77. E. Warner
Wright, S. Evolution and the genetics of populations, v3: Experimental results and evolutionary deductions. 1977
Science 196:1191-2 Je 10 '77. F. J. Ayala
Wrigley, C. J. David Lloyd George and the British Labour movement: peace and war. 1976
Am Hist R 82:106-7 F '77. F. M. Leventhal
Wu, T. W. Sian incident: a pivotal point in modern Chinese history. 1976
Am Hist R 82:1049 O '77. E. Lubot
Wu, Y.-L. Strategic land ridge: Peking's relations with Thailand, Malaysia, Singapore, and Indonesia. 1975
Am Hist R 81:1204 D '76. P. Van Ness
Wurtman, R. J. and Wurtman, J. J. eds. Nutrition and the brain. 2v. 1977
Science 198:287-8 O 21 '77. J. Dobbing
Wuthnow, R. Consciousness reformation. 1976
Ann Am Acad 432:186-7 Jl '77. D. Rudy
Wynn, N. A. Afro-American and the Second World war. 1976
Am Hist R 82:469 Ap '77. R. Polenberg
Wynne-Edwards, V. C. Animal dispersion in relation to social behavior. 1962
Natur Hist 86:20+ D '77. S. J. Gould

Yamamori, T. and Lawson, E. L. Introducing church growth. 1975
Chr Today 21:32 Ja 7 '77. R. A. Bodey
Yardley, J. Ring: a biography of Ring Lardner
America 137:288+ O 29 '77. J. J. McAleer
Atlantic 240:95-6 S '77. C. M. Curtis
Bus W p6-7 Ag 1 '77. E. Chigounis
Newsweek 90:71 Ag 22 '77. R. Sokolov
Time 110:69 Ag 15 '77. S. Kanfer
Yates, G. G. What women want: the ideas of the Movement. 1975
Ann Am Acad 429:187-8 Ja '77. G. H. Huganir
Yep, L. Child of the owl. 1977
Horn Bk 53:447 Ag '77. V. Haviland
Yepson, R. B. Jr. ed. Organic plant protection
Conservationist 31:34 N '76. J. A. Taylor

Yerby, R. Up, up and away. 1976
Chr Today 21:40-2 Ap 15 '77. W. W. Gasque
Yergin, D. Shattered peace: the origins of the cold war and the national security state. 1977
Bull Atom Sci 33:58-60 D '77. M. D. Feld
Bus W p8-9 Jl 18 '77. W. H. McNeill
Commentary 64:64+ Ag '77. E. N. Luttwak
Fortune 96:81+ N '77. H. E. Meyer
Nation 225:55-6 Jl 9 '77. B. Kuklick
New Repub 177:30-2 Jl 2 '77. H. E. Salisbury
Newsweek 90:89+ Jl 18 '77. C. D. May
Progressive 41:54-5 O '77. B. J. Bernstein
Yevtushenko, Y. From desire to desire
America 137:245-6 O 15 '77. J. F. Cotter
Yoder, H. S. Generation of basaltic magma. 1976
Science 197:554-5 Ag 5 '77. I. D. MacGregor
Yonge, C. M. and Thompson, T. E. Living marine molluscs. 1976
BioScience 27:818 D '77. W. K. Emerson
York, H. F. Advisors: Oppenheimer, Teller, and the superbomb. 1976
Am Hist R 82:211-12 F '77. R. G. Hewlett
Am Scholar 46:536-8 Aut '77. J. Bernstein
Young, A. Geography of the near past
Poetry 130:109-10 My '77. R. Siegel
Young, A. F. ed. American revolution: explorations in the history of American radicalism. 1976
Am Hist R 82:737-9 Je '77. J. Lemisch
Progressive 41:54-5 Mr '77. M. True
Young, T. D. Gentleman in a dustcoat; a biography of John Crowe Ransom
New Repub 176:2-3 F 12 '77. L. D. Rubin, Jr
Yu, A. C. ed. and tr. Journey to the West, v 1
Chr Cent 94:958+ O 19 '77. D. L. Overmyer
Yu, F. T. S. Optics and information theory. 1976
Phys Today 30:57-8 Je '77. J. P. Gordon
Yzermans, V. A. People I love
Commonweal 104:380-1 Je 10 '77. J. B. Sheerin

Zakythinos, D. A. Le despotat grec de Morée, v 1: Histoire politique; v2: Vie et institutions; ed. by C Maltézou. 1975
Am Hist R 81:1093 D '76. G. P. Majeska
Zaleznik, A. and Kets DeVries, M. F. R. Power and the corporate mind. 1975
Ann Am Acad 429:188-91 Ja '77. W. Gomberg
Zaliński, H. Kszalt polityczny Polsky w ideologii Towarzystwa demokratycznego Polskiego (1832-1846) 1976
Am Hist R 82:1289 D '77. C. Morley
Zamyatin, Y. We
New Repub 178:38-40 Ja 7 '78. J. Rubenstein
Zayas, A. M. de. Nemesis at Potsdam: the Anglo-Americans and the expulsion of the Germans, background, consequences, execution. 1977
Ann Am Acad 433:163-4 S '77. T. Ropp
Zeman, Z. Masaryks: the making of Czechoslovakia. 1976
Am Hist R 82:143-4 F '77. V. S. Mamatey
Zhuikov, G. S. Peterburgskie marksisty i gruppa Osvobozhdenie truda. 1975
Am Hist R 81:1175 D '76. N. Naimark
Ziedonis, A. Jr and others. eds. Baltic history. 1974
Am Hist R 81:1169 D '76. I. E. Eichhorn
Ziegler, P. Melbourne: a biography of William Lamb 2nd viscount Melbourne. 1976
Am Hist R 82:634-5 Je '77. A. D. Kriegel
Ziemke, E. F. U.S. army in the occupation of Germany, 1944-1946. 1975
Am Hist R 82:470 Ap '77. H. L. Coles
Ziman, J. Force of knowledge. 1976
Intellect 106:255-6 D '77. J. A. Goldman
Ziolkowski, T. Disenchanted images: a literary iconology
America 137:18 Jl 2 '77. P. Heinegg
Yale R 67:106-15 O '77. L. Nelson, jr
Zuckerman, H. Scientific elite: Nobel laureates in the United States. 1977
Science 196:754-5 My 13 '77. J. L. Heilbron
Zuidema, G. D. ed. Johns Hopkins atlas of human functional anatomy. 1977
BioScience 27:560 Ag '77. R. C. Crafts
Zukofsky, L. A 22 & 23
Poetry 130:290-2 Ag '77. B. Howard
Zumwalt, E. R. Jr. On watch: a memoir. 1976
Am Hist R 82:473-4 Ap '77. G. E. Wheeler
Ann Am Acad 429:179-80 Ja '77. P. Conway
Zunino, P. G. La questione cattolica nella sinistra italiana (1919-1939). 1975
Am Hist R 81:1159 D '76. E. Carrillo
Zysman, J. Political strategies for industrial order: state, market, and industry in France. 1977
Ann Am Acad 434:245-6 N '77. R. P. Claude

NOTES

NOTES

NOTES

NOTES

NOTES

NOTES

NOTES

NOTES

NOTES

NOTES